Best Books
for Children

Recent Titles in the
Children's and Young Adult Literature Reference Series

Catherine Barr, Series Editor

Best Books for Boys: A Resource for Educators
Matthew D. Zbaracki

Beyond Picture Books: Subject Access to Best Books for Beginning Readers
Barbara Barstow, Judith Riggle, and Leslie Molnar

A to Zoo: Subject Access to Children's Picture Books. Supplement
to the 7th Edition
Carolyn W. Lima and Rebecca L. Thomas

Gentle Reads: Great Books to Warm Hearts and Lift Spirits, Grades 5–9
Deanna J. McDaniel

Best New Media, K–12: A Guide to Movies, Subscription Web Sites, and Educational
Software and Games
Catherine Barr

Historical Fiction for Young Readers (Grades 4–8): An Introduction
John T. Gillespie

Twice Upon a Time: A Guide to Fractured, Altered, and Retold Folk and Fairy Tales
Catharine Bomhold and Terri E. Elder

Popular Series Fiction for K–6 Readers: A Reading and Selection Guide. 2nd Edition
Rebecca L. Thomas and Catherine Barr

Popular Series Fiction for Middle School and Teen Readers: A Reading and Selection
Guide. 2nd Edition
Rebecca L. Thomas and Catherine Barr

Best Books for High School Readers, Grades 9–12. 2nd Edition
Catherine Barr and John T. Gillespie

Best Books for Middle School and Junior High Readers, Grades 6–9. 2nd Edition
Catherine Barr and John T. Gillespie

Green Reads: Best Environmental Resources for Youth, K–12
Lindsey Patrick Wesson

Best Books for Children

PRESCHOOL THROUGH GRADE 6
9th Edition

Catherine Barr and John T. Gillespie

Children's and Young Adult Literature Reference
Catherine Barr, Series Editor

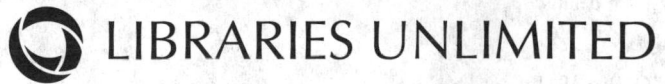

LIBRARIES UNLIMITED

AN IMPRINT OF ABC-CLIO, LLC
Santa Barbara, California • Denver, Colorado • Oxford, England

Copyright © 2010 by Catherine Barr and John T. Gillespie

Library of Congress Cataloging-in-Publication Data

Barr, Catherine, 1951–
  Best books for children : preschool through grade 6 / Catherine Barr and
John T. Gillespie. — 9th ed.
     p. cm. — (Children's and young adult literature reference series)
  Includes bibliographical references and index.
  ISBN 978-1-59158-575-6 (hardcover : acid-free paper) 1. Children—Books
and reading—United States. 2. Children's literature—Bibliography.
3. Best books—United States. I. Gillespie, John Thomas, 1928- II. Title.
  Z1037.G48 2010
  011.62—dc22   2009049873

ISBN: 978-1-59158-575-6

14 13 12 11 10 1 2 3 4 5

This book is also available on the World Wide Web as an eBook.
Visit www.abc-clio.com for details.

ABC-CLIO, LLC
130 Cremona Drive, P.O. Box 1911
Santa Barbara, California 93116-1911

Contents

History and Geography

Social Institutions and Issues

Personal Development

Physical and Applied Sciences

Recreation

Major Subjects Arranged Alphabetically

Preface

This is the ninth edition of *Best Books for Children*. The primary aim of this work, as with the earlier editions, is to provide a list of books recommended to satisfy both a child's recreational reading needs and the demands of a typical school curriculum. These recommendations are gathered from a number of sources, which are discussed on the following pages. For greatest depth, coverage has been limited to the age group from preschool children through readers in grade 6. Books that could be used with advanced sixth graders but are best suited to readers in grades 6 through 9 are listed in the companion volume *Best Books for Middle School and Junior High Readers* (2nd ed., Libraries Unlimited, 2009). It is suggested that this title be used to enrich collections for gifted fifth- and sixth-grade readers. A third volume, *Best Books for Senior High Readers* (2nd ed., Libraries Unlimited, 2009), covers grades 9 through 12.

Of the 26,XXX titles in this ninth edition of *Best Books for Children*, 26,475 are individually numbered entries. The remaining 1,XXX titles — those cited within the annotations — are additional recommended titles by the main entry author. More than one third of the 25,XXX numbered entries are new to this edition.

In most cases, at least two recommendations were required from the sources consulted for a title to be considered for listing. However, a single recommendation could also make a title a candidate for inclusion. This was particularly true of nonfiction books in a series. The reviewing policies of many journals do not allow for the inclusion of all titles in a series. Some give little or no coverage to series books, while others review only representative titles or list titles without reviews. Where only a single recommendation was available, the reviewing history of the series was taken into consideration and books in the series were often examined and evaluated by the editor from copies supplied by the publisher. In these cases, such criteria as availability, currency, accuracy, usefulness, and relevance were applied.

Several sources were used to compile this annotated bibliography. At the outset, there was a thorough perusal and evaluation of the entries in the eighth (2006) edition of *Best Books for Children* and its supplement. All out-of-print titles were dropped, as well as those that were considered no longer timely or suitable.

The other sources consulted were numerous and varied. The major tools were current reviewing periodicals, principally *Booklist*, *Bulletin of the Center for Children's Books*, *Horn Book*, *Library Media Connection,* and *School Library Journal.*

It is hoped that this bibliography will be used in four different ways: (1) as a tool to evaluate the adequacy of existing collections; (2) as a book selection instrument for beginning and expanding collections; (3) as an aid for giving reading guidance to children; and (4) as a base for the preparation of bibliographies and reading lists. To increase the book's usefulness, particularly in the two latter areas, the chosen titles are arranged under broad interest areas or, as in the case of nonfiction works, by curriculum-oriented subjects rather than by the Dewey Decimal Classification System.

For example, a book on religious practices in colonial America might be cataloged under religion, but in this book it would be included with other books on "United States — Colonial Period." In this way, analogous titles that otherwise would be in separate sections are brought together and can be seen in relation to other books on the same broad topic.

In general, the titles that appear in the section Books for Younger Readers are those usually read to children or used in assisted-reading situations. The one exception in this section is the listing of "Books for Beginning Readers." This area contains books of fiction easy enough to be read by beginning readers; nonfiction beginning readers are integrated into the appropriate subject areas with mention in the annotation that the work is suitable for beginning readers. Interactive books, such as books containing tabs, pop-ups, or flaps, are integrated into appropriate sections but their annotations mention the nature of their format.

The "Imaginative Stories" section in the Picture Books area is divided into two categories: Fantasies and Imaginary Animals. The first contains both books that depict humans, usually children, in fanciful, unrealistic situations (many bordering on the supernatural) and books that include (as characters) such mythical creatures as dragons and unicorns. The Imaginary Animals category includes stories about anthropomorphized animals that engage in human activities (such as pigs going to school) and display human motivations and behavior.

Simple chapter books and similar nonfiction titles that bridge the reading abilities and interests of children in the upper primary grades and early middle grades are integrated into the appropriate sections for older readers and their annotations indicate that they are easily read.

In the Fiction for Older Readers areas, only general anthologies of short stories are included under "Short Stories and Anthologies." Collections of short stories on a single topic, such as sports stories, are found under that specific topic. In the fiction section labeled "Ethnic Groups," only those novels in which ethnicity is the central theme are included. Other novels that simply include members of minority groups are integrated into other more appropriate topical areas. Similarly, in the nonfiction Biography section under "African Americans," "Hispanic Americans," and "Native Americans," only those individuals who have been associated primarily with race-related activities are included. For example, a biography of Martin Luther King, Jr., would be found under "African Americans" but a life story of athlete Wilma Rudolph would be under sports biographies. Also in the nonfiction area, general books of science projects and experiments are found under "General Science — Experiments and Projects," but books of activities relating to a specific area of science are included in that area.

Some types of books have been omitted from this bibliography. These include reference books such as dictionaries and encyclopedias, professional books (for example, other bibliographies), and such mass-market series as the Nancy Drew and Hardy Boys books.

A listing of "Major Subjects Arranged Alphabetically" provides both the range of entry numbers and page numbers for the largest subject areas covered in the volume. Other features also continued are the International Standard Book Number (ISBN) for both hardcover and paperback editions, nonfiction series titles, and Dewey Decimal numbers for nonfiction titles. Also included are review citations for all books published and reviewed from 1985 through July 2005. These review citations provide sources from which to obtain more detailed information about each of the books listed:

Booklist (BL)
Bulletin of the Center for Children's Books (BCCB)
Horn Book (HB)
Horn Book Guide (HBG)
Library Media Connection (LMC)
School Library Journal (SLJ)

The citing of only one review does not necessarily mean that the book received only a single recommendation; it might also have been listed in one or more of the other sources consulted. Books without review citations or Dewey numbers are pre-1985 imprints and reprints of older recommended books recently brought back into print (the original publication date is indicated within the annotation if it was readily available).

An asterisk following a review citation denotes an outstanding recommendation from that source.

Entry Information

Titles in the main section of the book are assigned an entry number. Entries contain the following information where applicable: (1) author or editor; (2) title; (3) suitable grade levels; (4) adapter or translator; (5) indication of illustrations or illustrator's name (usually only for picture books); (6) series title; (7) date of publication; (8) publisher and price of hardbound edition (LB=library binding); (9) ISBN of hardbound edition; (10) paperback (paper) publisher (if no publisher is listed, it is the same as the hardbound edition) and price; (11) ISBN of paperback edition; (12) number of pages; (13) annotation; (14) review citations; (15) Dewey Decimal number; (16) for an increasing number of entries, indication that an audio version is available.

Indexes

Best Books for Children includes three indexes: author/illustrator, book title, and subject/grade level. Authors and illustrators are listed alphabetically by last name, followed by book titles and entry numbers; fiction titles are indicated by (F). The Title Index includes both main entry titles and internal titles cited within the annotation, all with entry numbers and (F) notations.

The Subject/Grade Level Index includes thousands of subject headings. Within each subject, entries are listed according to grade-level suitabilities. For example, under the subject Humorous Stories there may be numerous entry numbers given first for Primary (P) readers; then for the Primary-Intermediate (PI) group; for the Intermediate (I) group; for the Intermediate-Junior High (IJ) readers; and finally for all readers, covering grades from preschool through grade 8 (All). This will enable the professional to select the most appropriate titles for use. Biographical entries are listed in this index by the last name of the subject of the biography. The following codes are used to give approximate grade level:

P (Primary) preschool through grade 3
PI (Primary-Intermediate) grades 2 through 4
I (Intermediate) grades 4 through 6
IJ (Intermediate-Junior High) grades 5 through 8 (or in a few cases some higher grades)
All (All readers) preschool through grade 8 (or higher)

Specific, more exact grade-level suitabilities are given (parenthetically) for each book in its main text entry. To facilitate quick reference, all listings in all indexes refer the user to entry number, not page number.

Many people were involved in the preparation of this bibliography. We are especially grateful to Barbara Ittner of Libraries Unlimited for her encouragement and support, and to Christine McNaull and Julie Miller, who make production of this large book possible.

Catherine Barr
John Gillespie

Literature

Books for Younger Readers

Alphabet, Concept, and Counting Books

Alphabet Books

1 *ABC USA* (K–2). Illus. by Martin Jarrie. 2005, Sterling $14.95 (978-1-4027-1619-5). 32pp. A strikingly illustrated celebration of American culture and history, from alligator to Zydeco. (Rev: BL 2/15/05; SLJ 5/05) [421.1]

2 Agee, Jon. *Z Goes Home* (1–3). Illus. by author. 2003, Hyperion $16.95 (978-0-7868-1987-4). Offering much for both the visually and verbally inclined, this offbeat alphabet book follows the letter Z home after a day's work on the zoo sign. (Rev: HB 11/03; HBG 4/04; SLJ 9/03)

3 Alda, Arlene. *Arlene Alda's ABC* (PS–K). Illus. 1993, Tricycle $12.95 (978-1-883672-01-0). 32pp. Objects turn into letters in this unusual alphabet book. (Rev: BL 1/1/94)

4 Allen, Susan, and Jane Lindaman. *Read Anything Good Lately?* (K–2). Illus. by Vicky Enright. 2003, Millbrook LB $22.90 (978-0-7613-2322-8). 32pp. From "an atlas at the airport to "the zodiac at the zoo," this alphabet book suggests places and ways to read. (Rev: BL 5/15/03; HBG 10/03; SLJ 7/03) [028]

5 Allen, Susan, and Jane Lindaman. *Written Anything Good Lately?* (1–4). Illus. by Vicky Enright. 2006, Millbrook LB $15.95 (978-0-7613-2426-3). 32pp. This attractive alphabet book introduces different types of writing — an autobiography, a brilliant book report, detailed directions, Valentine's verses, and so forth. (Rev: HBG 10/06; LMC 11/06; SLJ 4/06) [808]

6 Anno, Mitsumasa. *Anno's Alphabet: An Adventure in Imagination* (PS–2). Illus. by author. 1992, HarperCollins paper $24.99 (978-0-06-443315-0). 64pp. A most unusual and distinctive alphabet book that shows the letters as pieces of rough-grained wood and, on the opposite pages, objects beginning with that letter. An excellent introduction to art as well.

7 Ashman, Linda. *M Is for Mischief: An A to Z of Naughty Children* (K–2). Illus. by Nancy Carpenter. 2008, Dutton $16.99 (978-0-525-47564-4). 48pp. From Angry Abby to Zany Zelda this is an entertaining catalog of bad behavior. (Rev: BCCB 7–8/08; BL 8/08; LMC 11/08)

8 Aylesworth, Jim. *Little Bitty Mousie* (PS–2). Illus. by Michael Hague. 2007, Walker $16.95 (978-0-8027-9637-0). 32pp. A little mouse explores the house she lives in, finding everything from an Apple to a cat Z'ing. (Rev: BL 10/15/07; SLJ 10/07)

9 Aylesworth, Jim. *Naughty Little Monkeys* (PS–1). Illus. by Henry Cole. 2003, Dutton $16.99 (978-0-525-46940-7). When the (human) parents go out for the evening, their 26 little monkeys run riot — Andy making paper planes, Brooke bouncing, Carla eating cake, and so forth. (Rev: BL 9/1/03; HBG 4/04; SLJ 8/03)

10 Aylesworth, Jim. *Old Black Fly* (PS–2). Illus. by Stephen Gammell. 1992, Holt $16.95 (978-0-8050-1401-3). 32pp. A fun alphabet book that describes the 26 awful things Old Black Fly did one day. (Rev: BCCB 7–8/92; BL 2/15/92*; HB 5/92; SLJ 4/92*)

11 Azarian, Mary. *A Gardener's Alphabet* (K–2). Illus. by author. 2000, Houghton $17.00 (978-0-618-03380-5). Stunning black woodcuts hand-tinted with watercolors are featured in this handsome alphabet book that uses words associated with gardens and gardening. (Rev: BCCB 9/00; BL 4/15/00; HBG 10/00; SLJ 6/00)

12 Bar-El, Dan. *Alphabetter* (PS–1). Illus. by Graham Ross. 2006, Orca $17.95 (978-1-55143-439-1). The alphabet and the 26 children taking part in an activity are out of synch; the child holding A needs an item held by B and so forth; a humorous and interesting approach. (Rev: SLJ 12/06)

13 Bataille, Marion. *ABC3D* (1–4). Illus. by author. 2008, Roaring Brook $19.95 (978-1-59643-425-7).

32pp. A three-dimensional alphabet book full of surprises and delights. (Rev: BLO 12/16/08)

14 Beaton, Clare. *Zoe and Her Zebra* (PS). Illus. 1999, Barefoot Books $14.95 (978-1-902283-75-3). 32pp. A clever alphabet book in which children named for each letter of the alphabet (e.g., Alice, Ben) are chased by animals similarly arranged (e.g., alligator, bear). (Rev: BL 10/15/99; SLJ 12/99)

15 Beccia, Carlyn. *Who Put the B in Ballyhoo?* (2–4). Illus. 2007, Houghton $16.00 (978-0-618-71718-7). 32pp. From A for awesome to Z for zippy, this is an alphabetical tour of circus acts of the past. (Rev: BL 4/1/07)

16 Berg, Cami. *D Is for Dolphin* (PS–3). Illus. by Janet Biondi. 1991, Windom $18.95 (978-1-879244-01-6). 56pp. In this alphabet book, every letter stands for a word associated with dolphins. (Rev: BCCB 6/91; BL 9/15/91; SLJ 7/91)

17 Blackstone, Stella. *Alligator Alphabet* (PS). Illus. by Stephanie Bauer. 2005, Barefoot Books $16.99 (978-1-84148-494-5). A bright A to Z of animal parent-and-baby pairs. (Rev: SLJ 1/06)

18 Bond, Michael. *Paddington Bear and the Busy Bee Carnival* (PS–1). Illus. by R. W. Alley. 1998, HarperCollins $13.95 (978-0-06-027765-9). 40pp. A pleasant picture book in which Paddington Bear enters a contest by listing all the things he sees that begin with the letter *B*. (Rev: BL 5/15/98; HBG 10/98; SLJ 8/98)

19 Bonder, Dianna. *Accidental Alphabet* (K–2). Illus. by author. 2003, Whitecap $16.95 (978-1-55285-394-8). A bouncy rhyming text accompanies detailed illustrations. (Rev: SLJ 5/03)

20 Boynton, Sandra. *A Is for Angry: An Animal and Adjective Alphabet* (PS–K). Illus. 1987, Workman paper $6.95 (978-0-89480-507-3). 48pp. Adjectives are the focus of this alphabet book.

21 Bruel, Nick. *Bad Kitty* (K–2). 2005, Roaring Brook $15.95 (978-1-59643-069-3). 40pp. In this cleverly conceived alphabet book, a cat misbehaves wildly when she discovers that the only foods in the house are unappealing vegetables ranging from asparagus to zucchini. (Rev: BL 12/15/05; SLJ 10/05)

22 Bruel, Nick. *Poor Puppy* (PS–2). Illus. by author. 2007, Roaring Brook $16.95 (978-1-59643-270-3). 40pp. Counting and alphabet are combined when Kitty won't play with Puppy and Puppy must amuse himself. (Rev: BL 9/1/07; SLJ 1/08)

23 Bullard, Lisa. *Not Enough Beds!* (PS–K). Illus. by Joni Oeltjenbruns. 1999, Lerner $15.95 (978-1-57505-356-1). 32pp. In this alphabet book, family members must find unusual sleeping arrangements when they all arrive for Christmas. (Rev: BL 9/15/99; HBG 3/00; SLJ 10/99)

24 Bunting, Eve. *Girls A to Z* (K–3). Illus. by Suzanne Bloom. 2002, Boyds Mills $15.95 (978-1-56397-147-1). 32pp. An alphabet book filled with girls pretending to be grown-ups with interesting jobs (such as astronauts and gondoliers). (Rev: BL 9/15/02; HBG 3/03; SLJ 10/02)

25 Butler, Dori. *F Is for Firefighting* (PS–1). Illus. by Joan C. Waites. 2007, Pelican $15.95 (978-1-58980-420-3). This alphabet book introduces firefighting tools and vehicles in an entertaining format. (Rev: SLJ 6/07)

26 Buzzeo, Toni. *"R" Is for Research* (2–4). Illus. by Nicole Wong. 2008, Upstart $17.95 (978-1-60213-030-2). Students researching cats learn how to use the resources of the library as the humorous tabby called Cal D. Cat comments on their progress. (Rev: LMC 11/08*; SLJ 9/08) [027.62]

27 *C Is for Caboose: Riding the Rails from A to Z* (PS–1). Illus. 2007, Chronicle $14.95 (978-0-8118-5643-0). 32pp. A simple alphabet book that offers lots of railroad lore and an attractive vintage look. (Rev: BL 4/15/07) [385]

28 Cahoon, Heather. *Word Play ABC* (1–3). Illus. by author. 1999, Walker LB $16.85 (978-0-8027-8684-5). 32pp. Each letter of the alphabet is accompanied by a pun or play on words; for example, for C, there is a picture of a crocodile in a pot and the word *crock-pot*. (Rev: BCCB 7–8/99; BL 7/99; HBG 10/99; SLJ 4/99)

29 Capucilli, Alyssa Satin. *Mrs. McTats and Her Houseful of Cats* (PS–1). Illus. by Joan Rankin. 2001, Simon & Schuster $16.00 (978-0-689-83185-0). 32pp. Mrs. McTats adds alphabetically named stray cats (and one dog) to her household in this nicely illustrated and humorous book that teaches numbers as well. (Rev: BL 9/1/01; HBG 10/01; SLJ 8/01)

30 Carlson, Nancy. *ABC I Like Me!* (PS–1). Illus. 1997, Viking $16.99 (978-0-670-87458-3). 32pp. A little pig and his friends take a trip through the alphabet. (Rev: BL 4/1/97; SLJ 6/97)

31 Castella, Krystina, and Brian Boyl. *Discovering Nature's Alphabet* (2–10). Photos by authors. 2006, Heyday $15.95 (978-1-59714-021-8). Photographs of letters of the alphabet formed by nature will fascinate children and adults. (Rev: SLJ 5/06)

32 Catalanotto, Peter. *Matthew A.B.C.* (PS–2). Illus. 2002, Simon & Schuster $14.95 (978-0-689-84582-6). 32pp. There is a Matthew for every letter of the alphabet in Mrs. Tuttle's class, and each boy has a special characteristic to match his letter. (Rev: BL 7/02; HB 7/02; HBG 10/02; SLJ 6/02)

33 Chaplin, Susan Gibbons. *I Can Sign My ABCs* (K–3). Illus. by Laura McCaul. 1986, Gallaudet Univ. $12.50 (978-0-930323-19-6). 56pp. The ABCs of sign language, with color illustrations. (Rev: BL 2/15/87)

34 Cheney, Lynne. *America: A Patriotic Primer* (2–4). 2002, Simon & Schuster $16.95 (978-0-689-85192-6). 40pp. The wife of the former vice president presents an alphabet book for older children that outlines the virtues of America's democracy. (Rev: BCCB 3/02; BL 6/1–15/02; HBG 3/03; SLJ 7/02) [973]

35 Chesworth, Michael. *Alphaboat* (2–4). Illus. 2002, Farrar $16.00 (978-0-374-30244-3). 32pp. Spirited rhyming wordplay and cartoon illustrations take the crew of the Alphaboat on a lively journey in search of lost treasure. (Rev: BL 10/15/02; HBG 10/03; SLJ 9/02)

36 Chin-Lee, Cynthia. *A Is for Asia* (K–4). Illus. by Yumi Heo. 1997, Orchard LB $16.99 (978-0-531-33011-1). 32pp. A variety of topics, from geography to holidays, are covered in this unique alphabet book. (Rev: BCCB 5/97; BL 3/1/97; SLJ 4/97)

37 Chin-Lee, Cynthia, and Terri de la Pena. *A Is for the Americas* (2–4). Illus. by Enrique O. Sánchez. 1999, Orchard LB $16.99 (978-0-531-33194-1). 32pp. An alphabet book for older children that uses geographical and historical names — most of them associated with Hispanic and Native American culture. (Rev: BL 9/1/99; HBG 3/00; SLJ 10/99) [970]

38 Chung, Hyechong. *K Is for Korea* (K–3). Illus. by Prodeepta Das. 2008, Frances Lincoln $16.95 (978-1-84507-789-1). 32pp. An alphabetical introduction to Korea and its culture. (Rev: BL 12/1/08; SLJ 12/08) [951.905]

39 Cleary, Brian P. *Peanut Butter and Jellyfishes: A Very Silly Alphabet Book* (PS–2). Illus. by Betsy E. Snyder. 2007, Millbrook LB $15.95 (978-0-8225-6188-0). Children will enjoy searching for letters of the alphabet hidden in this book of alphabetical nonsense verse. (Rev: SLJ 5/07)

40 Cline-Ransome, Lesa. *Quilt Alphabet* (PS–1). Illus. by James Ransome. 2001, Holiday House $17.95 (978-0-8234-1453-6). 32pp. In this alphabet picture book, the letters are incorporated into quilt squares and accompanied by riddles. (Rev: BL 9/1/01; HBG 3/02; SLJ 11/01) [811]

41 Compestine, Ying Chang. *D Is for Dragon Dance* (K–1). Illus. by YongSheng Xuan. 2006, Holiday $17.95 (978-0-8234-1887-9). 32pp. Bright illustrations are the highlight of this alphabet book about the Chinese New Year. (Rev: BL 2/1/06; SLJ 3/06) [394.261]

42 Cronin, Doreen. *Click, Clack, Quackity-Quack: An Alphabetical Adventure* (PS). Illus. by Betsy Lewin. 2005, Simon & Schuster $12.95 (978-0-689-87715-5). 24pp. Set in a barnyard and featuring the cows that type (from *Click, Clack, Moo*), this appealing alphabet book follows preparations for a picnic. (Rev: BL 9/15/05; SLJ 11/05*)

43 Crowther, Robert. *My Pop-up Surprise ABC* (PS–K). Illus. by author. 1997, Orchard $16.95 (978-0-531-30038-1). A simple alphabet book that uses large, easily manipulated flaps and pull tabs. (Rev: SLJ 8/97)

44 Darling, Kathy. *ABC Cats* (K–3). Illus. by Tara Darling. 1998, Walker LB $16.85 (978-0-8027-8667-8). 32pp. Full-color photos of cats illustrate this charming alphabet book. (Rev: BL 11/1/98; HBG 10/99; SLJ 11/98)

45 Delessert, Etienne. *A Was an Apple Pie: An English Nursery Rhyme* (PS–2). Illus. 2005, Creative Editions $18.95 (978-1-56846-196-0). 32pp. Colorful modern art graces this alphabet book based on a 17th-century nursery rhyme. (Rev: BL 1/1–15/06; SLJ 1/06) [428.1]

46 Demarest, Chris L. *Alpha Bravo Charlie: The Military Alphabet* (K–3). Illus. 2005, Simon & Schuster $16.95 (978-0-689-86928-0). 40pp. From Alpha to Zulu, this large-format book introduces the military alphabet and corresponding U.S. Navy sig-nal flags with many full-color illustrations of military scenes. (Rev: BL 5/15/05) [355]

47 Demarest, Chris L. *Firefighters A to Z* (PS–K). Illus. 2000, Simon & Schuster $16.95 (978-0-689-83798-2). 40pp. Beginning with "A is for Alarm," this is a large-format alphabet book showing fire fighters, their equipment, and their activities. (Rev: BL 7/00; HB 7/00; HBG 3/01; SLJ 12/00)

48 DiTerlizzi, Tony. *G Is for One Gzonk! An Alpha-Number-Bet Book* (K–3). Illus. by author. 2006, Simon & Schuster $16.95 (978-0-689-85290-9). This clever tribute to Dr. Seuss and Edward Lear takes readers on a chaotic romp through a poetic alphabet full of fantastic beings and unruly numbers. (Rev: SLJ 10/06)

49 Dog Artlist Collection. *The Dog from Arf! Arf! to Zzzzzz* (PS–2). 2004, HarperCollins LB $16.89 (978-0-06-059858-7). "Fetch" and "Good dog" are just two of the dog-related entries in this alphabet book full of puppies. (Rev: SLJ 7/04)

50 Doran, Ella, et al. *A Is for Artist: An Alphabet* (PS–2). Illus. 2005, Abrams $19.95 (978-1-85437-556-8). 56pp. This striking alphabet book introduces young readers to art in a wide array of forms, ranging from a simple black-and-white photograph to the multicolored paint spatters of an abstract painting. (Rev: BL 11/1/05)

51 Downie, Mary Alice. *A Pioneer ABC* (K–2). Illus. by Mary Jane Gerber. 2005, Tundra $15.95 (978-0-88776-688-6). This attractive alphabet book shows young readers what life was like for Loyalists who migrated to Canada after the American Revolution. (Rev: SLJ 11/05)

52 Dugan, Joanne. *ABC NYC: A Book About Seeing New York City* (K–3). Photos by author. 2005, Abrams $14.95 (978-0-8109-5854-8). An urban ABC that introduces New York's sites, shapes, and sounds. (Rev: SLJ 6/05)

53 Edwards, Richard. *Amazing Animal Alphabet* (PS–1). Illus. 1999, Orchard $14.95 (978-0-531-30123-4). Arranged in alphabetical order, different animals are found hiding under flaps in this interactive book. (Rev: BL 12/15/99; SLJ 6/99)

54 Edwards, Wallace. *Alphabeasts* (PS–K). Illus. 2002, Kids Can $15.95 (978-1-55337-386-5). 32pp. Rhyming couplets caption lavish, full-page illustrations of animals from alligator to zebra. (Rev: BL 11/1/02; HBG 3/03; SLJ 12/02)

55 Ehlert, Lois. *Eating the Alphabet: Fruits and Vegetables from A to Z* (PS–1). Illus. by author. 1989, Harcourt $16.00 (978-0-15-224435-4); paper $5.95 (978-0-15-201036-2). 32pp. An eye-catching alphabet book. (Rev: BL 3/15/89; HB 5/89; SLJ 6/89)

56 Elya, Susan Middleton. *F Is for Fiesta* (K–2). Illus. by G. Brian Karas. 2006, Putnam $12.99 (978-0-399-24225-0). 32pp. This small, bright alphabet book presents Spanish words relating to celebrations within a mainly English text. (Rev: BL 2/1/06; SLJ 2/06)

57 Elya, Susan Middleton, and Merry Banks. *N Is for Navidad* (PS–2). Illus. by Joe Cepeda. 2007, Chronicle $14.95 (978-0-8118-5205-0). 32pp. Readers follow a Mexican family through their Christmas celebration in this rhyming alphabet book that introduces many Spanish words. (Rev: BCCB 1/08; BL 11/1/07; HB 11/07; LMC 5/08)

58 Ernst, Lisa Campbell. *The Turn-Around, Upside-Down Alphabet Book* (PS–2). Illus. by author. 2004, Simon & Schuster $15.95 (978-0-689-86585-5). Each letter becomes three different objects as the book is turned; for example, the A is also a beak, an ice cream cone, and the point of a star. (Rev: HB 7/04; LMC 1/05; SLJ 8/04) [428.1]

59 Farrell, John. *Stargazer's Alphabet: Night-Sky Wonders from A to Z* (3–5). 2007, Boyds Mills $16.95 (978-1-59078-466-2). 32pp. Photographs of heavenly bodies accompany rhyming text describing astronomical wonders from A to Z. Based on a song from the author's CD *Oh, Yeah!* (Rev: SLJ 5/07)

60 Faulkenberry, Lauren. *What Do Animals Do on the Weekend? Adventures from A to Z* (K–3). Illus. by author. 2002, Novello Festival $17.95 (978-0-9708972-4-4). An alliterative approach to animal activities, where kangaroos kayak and penguins picnic, that also conveys factual information. (Rev: SLJ 10/02)

61 Fisher, Valorie. *Ellsworth's Extraordinary Electric Ears and Other Amazing Alphabet Anecdotes* (PS–2). 2003, Simon & Schuster $16.95 (978-0-689-85030-1). This fun-packed alphabet book introduces readers to 26 wildly diverse scenes and stories. (Rev: HBG 10/03; SLJ 7/03)

62 Fleming, Denise. *Alphabet Under Construction* (PS–2). Illus. 2002, Holt $16.95 (978-0-8050-6848-1). 32pp. An industrious mouse assembles an alphabet using actions that start with each letter. (Rev: BCCB 10/02; BL 8/02; HB 9/02; HBG 3/03; SLJ 9/02)

63 Floca, Brian. *The Racecar Alphabet* (PS–2). Illus. by author. 2003, Simon & Schuster $15.95 (978-0-689-85091-2). Sports cars, stock cars, Formula 1 — they're all included in this attractive, alliterative alphabet book. (Rev: HB 11/03; HBG 4/04; SLJ 11/03)

64 Frampton, David. *My Beastie Book of ABC: Rhymes and Woodcuts* (PS–3). Illus. by author. 2002, HarperCollins LB $15.89 (978-0-06-028824-2). Animals from A to Z are introduced with a letter, rhyme, and illustration. (Rev: BCCB 9/02; HBG 10/02; SLJ 5/02)

65 Geisert, Arthur. *Pigs from A to Z* (1–4). Illus. by author. 1986, Houghton $18.00 (978-0-395-38509-8). 64pp. Complicated etchings hide letters, and it will take somewhat older-than-usual alphabet book readers to figure them out. (Rev: BL 11/15/86; HB 1/87; SLJ 12/86)

66 Gelber, Lisa, and Jody Roberts. *P Is for Peanut: A Photographic ABC* (4–6). 2007, Getty $9.95 (978-0-89236-878-5). A selection of black-and-white photographs from the J. Paul Getty Museum is presented in an imaginative alphabetical format. For lovers of photography as well as for children. (Rev: SLJ 5/07)

67 Girnis, Meg. *A B C for You and Me* (PS–2). Illus. by Shirley Leamon Green. 2000, Whitman $16.99 (978-0-8075-0101-6). 32pp. Using photographs of children with Down syndrome, this alphabet book celebrates the beauty of all kinds of children. (Rev: BL 7/00; HB 5/00; HBG 10/00; SLJ 4/00)

68 Grassby, Donna. *A Seaside Alphabet* (1–3). Illus. by Susan Tooke. 2000, Tundra $19.95 (978-0-88776-516-2). Picture puzzles and nautical scenes featuring the seaside introduce the alphabet. (Rev: HBG 10/00; SLJ 6/00)

69 Gritz, Ona. *Tangerines and Tea: My Grandparents and Me* (PS–K). Illus. by Yumi Heo. 2005, Abrams $15.95 (978-0-8109-5871-5). 32pp. An alliterative alphabet book featuring two preschoolers visiting their grandparents' farm. (Rev: BL 5/15/05)

70 Grobler, Piet. *Little Bird's ABC* (PS). Illus. 2005, Front St. $8.95 (978-1-932425-52-9). 32pp. A small, square beautifully illustrated alphabet of birds making often humorous sounds. (Rev: BL 11/15/05; SLJ 12/05) [411]

71 Grossman, Bill. *My Little Sister Hugged an Ape* (K–3). Illus. by Kevin Hawkes. 2004, Knopf LB $18.99 (978-0-517-80018-8). A little girl hugs a variety of unlikely animals from apes to zebras. (Rev: HB 11/04; SLJ 11/04)

72 Haas, Jessie. *Appaloosa Zebra: A Horse Lover's Alphabet* (PS–3). Illus. by Margot Apple. 2002, HarperCollins LB $15.89 (978-0-688-17881-9). 40pp. This informative alphabet book for girls who love horses features a different breed for almost every letter. (Rev: BL 1/1–15/02; HBG 10/02; SLJ 2/02)

73 Hague, Kathleen. *Alphabears: An ABC Book* (PS–K). Illus. by Michael Hague. 1984, Holt paper $5.95 (978-0-8050-1637-6). 32pp. Twenty-six lovable bears are introduced, one for each letter.

74 Hanson, Anders. *Nan and Nick* (PS–1). Series: First Sounds. 2005, ABDO LB $19.93 (978-1-59679-176-3). 23pp. An alphabet book, part of a series, featuring photographs of items that begin with the letter N, followed by simple rebus sentences using the words. (Rev: SLJ 7/05) [428.1]

75 Harrison, Ted. *A Northern Alphabet: A Is for Arctic* (K–2). Illus. by author. 1989, Tundra paper $7.95 (978-0-88776-233-8). 32pp. Scenes, people, and objects associated with the far north are used in this alphabet book. A reissue.

76 Herzog, Brad. *A Is for Amazing Moments: A Sports Alphabet* (2–4). Illus. by Melanie Rose. 2009, Sleeping Bear $17.95 (978-1-58536-360-5). 40pp. Four-line rhymed verses, each accompanied by a lively oil painting and brief information, range from Amazin' Mets to a clock approaching Zero. (Rev: BLO 1/13/09) [796]

77 Herzog, Brad. *H Is for Home Run: A Baseball Alphabet* (1–4). Illus. by Melanie Rose. 2004, Sleeping Bear $16.95 (978-1-58536-219-6). An alphabet book full of alliteration and baseball lore. (Rev: SLJ 8/04) [796.357]

78 Hoban, Tana. *26 Letters and 99 Cents* (PS–1). Illus. by author. 1987, Greenwillow $17.89 (978-0-688-06362-7). 32pp. An ABC and counting book

combined by turning the book upside down. (Rev: BCCB 4/87; BL 3/1/87; SLJ 4/87)

79 Hobbie, Holly. *Toot and Puddle: Puddle's ABC* (PS–1). Illus. 2000, Little, Brown $14.95 (978-0-316-36593-2). 48pp. To teach Otto the turtle the alphabet, little pig Puddle paints 26 clever pictures that illustrate the letters. (Rev: BCCB 12/00; BL 9/15/00; HBG 3/01; SLJ 11/00)

80 Hopkins, Lee Bennett. *Alphathoughts: Alphabet Poems* (2–6). Illus. by Marla Baggetta. 2003, Boyds Mills $15.95 (978-1-56397-979-8). An alphabet book that can be used on several levels with brief verses that describe the chosen words. (Rev: BL 4/1/03; HBG 10/03; SLJ 3/03)

81 Howell, Theresa. *A Is for Airplane / A es para Avión* (PS–2). Illus. by David Brooks. 2003, Rising Moon $6.95 (978-0-87358-831-7). A bilingual alphabet book with bright illustrations. (Rev: SLJ 3/03)

82 Howell, Will C. *Zoo Flakes ABC* (PS–2). Illus. 2002, Walker LB $16.85 (978-0-8027-8827-6). 32pp. Clever cut-paper snowflakes depict the alphabet in animal forms — O is for Octopus, for example — and children will enjoy finding the elusive animals hidden in each flake. Also includes directions on making snowflake cutouts. (Rev: BL 12/1/02; HBG 3/03; SLJ 3/03) [736]

83 Hughes, Shirley. *Alfie's ABC* (PS–1). Illus. 1998, Lothrop $16.00 (978-0-688-16126-2). 32pp. An alphabet book that uses children's favorite things (e.g., "S is for seaside, swimming, and sand castles") to introduce each letter. (Rev: BL 8/98*; HBG 3/99; SLJ 9/98)

84 Inkpen, Mick. *Kipper's A to Z: An Alphabet Adventure* (PS–2). Illus. 2001, Harcourt $16.95 (978-0-15-202594-6). 56pp. Arnold the pig and Kipper the dog find animals, sounds, and actions that run from A to Z. (Rev: BL 5/15/01; HBG 10/01; SLJ 6/01*)

85 Jackson, Woody. *A Cow's Alfalfa-Bet* (PS–1). Illus. by author. 2003, Houghton $15.00 (978-0-618-16599-5). Striking watercolors of New England countryside illustrate an interesting choice of alphabet words. (Rev: HBG 4/04; SLJ 9/03) [428.1]

86 Jernigan, Gisela. *Agave Blooms Just Once* (2–4). Illus. by E. Wesley Jernigan. 1989, Harbinger paper $10.95 (978-0-943173-44-3). An alphabet book introducing the flora and fauna of the Sonoran Desert in rhyming verse. (Rev: BL 3/1/90)

87 Jirankova-Limbrick, Martina. *The Artful Alphabet* (PS–2). Illus. 2003, Candlewick $16.99 (978-0-7636-2187-2). 72pp. This highly visual alphabet book offers lots of interest for young eyes. (Rev: BL 2/1/04; HBG 4/04; SLJ 1/04) [428.1]

88 Jocelyn, Marthe. *ABC x 3: English, Español, Français* (PS–K). Illus. by Tom Slaughter. 2005, Tundra $12.95 (978-0-88776-707-4). 32pp. This multilingual alphabet book gives words in English, French, and Spanish, often underlining their similarity. (Rev: BL 12/15/05; SLJ 10/05) [411]

89 Johnson, Jean. *Firefighters A to Z* (PS–1). Illus. 1985, Walker LB $11.85 (978-0-8027-6590-1). 39pp. An alphabet book organized around the work-ings of a fire-fighting unit. Others in this series are: *Librarians A to Z* (1989); *Police Officers A to Z* (1986); *Postal Workers A to Z* (1987); *Teachers A to Z* (1987). (Rev: BL 3/1/86)

90 Johnson, Odette, and Bruce Johnson. *Apples, Alligators and Also Alphabets* (PS–K). Illus. 1992, Stoddart paper $3.95 (978-0-19-540906-2). 32pp. An inventive alphabet book with whimsical words and actions. (Rev: BL 4/15/91; SLJ 6/91)

91 Johnston, Tony. *P Is for Piñata: A Mexico Alphabet* (K–4). Illus. by John Parra. 2008, Sleeping Bear $17.95 (978-1-58536-144-1). 40pp. A colorful alphabet-book introduction to Mexico with rhymed lines for younger readers and detailed sidebars for older readers. (Rev: BL 12/15/08; SLJ 1/09)

92 Joyce, Susan. *ABC Animal Riddles* (K–3). Illus. by Doug DuBosque. 1998, Peel $13.95 (978-0-939217-51-9). 32pp. For each letter of the alphabet, there is a mystery animal whose identity can be determined from an accompanying rhyming riddle. (Rev: BL 7/99; HBG 10/99; SLJ 4/99) [818]

93 Joyce, Susan. *ABC Nature Riddles* (K–3). Illus. by Doug DuBosque. Series: ABC Riddles. 2000, Peel $13.95 (978-0-939217-53-3). An appealing book with an imaginative rhyming text and color drawings that presents a nature riddle for each letter of the alphabet. (Rev: HBG 3/01; SLJ 10/00)

94 Joyce, Susan. *Alphabet Riddles* (K–3). Illus. by Doug DuBosque. 1998, Peel $13.95 (978-0-939217-50-2). A rhyming riddle book with clues that include the first and last letters and characteristics of the answer. (Rev: BL 7/98; HBG 10/98; SLJ 6/98)

95 Kalman, Bobbie. *Christmas Long Ago from A to Z* (K–2). Series: AlphaBasiCs. 1999, Crabtree LB $25.27 (978-0-86505-385-4); paper $7.95 (978-0-86505-415-8). 31pp. An alphabet book that uses the symbols and activities associated with Christmas as a source for the letters. (Rev: SLJ 10/99)

96 Kalman, Maira. *What Pete Ate from A to Z* (1–3). Illus. 2001, Penguin $16.99 (978-0-399-23362-3). 40pp. Pete the dog eats everything in sight — all the way through the alphabet. (Rev: BL 9/1/01; HB 1/02; HBG 3/02; SLJ 9/01*)

97 Kirk, David. *Miss Spider's ABC* (PS–3). Illus. 1998, Scholastic $16.95 (978-0-590-28279-6). 32pp. An ABC book in which a number of creatures, mainly bugs, prepare a surprise party for Miss Spider. (Rev: BL 12/1/98; HBG 3/99; SLJ 12/98)

98 Kontis, Alethea. *Alpha Oops! The Day Z Went First* (K–2). Illus. by Bob Kolar. 2006, Candlewick $15.99 (978-0-7636-2728-7). 56pp. Z is tired of being last in the alphabet, and other letters also decide they want better. (Rev: BL 9/1/06; SLJ 9/06)

99 Korman, Susan. *P Is for Philadelphia* (1–5). Illus. 2005, Temple Univ. $16.95 (978-1-59213-107-5). An alphabetical tour of a city full of diversity, with text on the left and illustrations by local schoolchildren on the right. (Rev: SLJ 6/05)

100 Krull, Kathleen. *M Is for Music* (PS–3). Illus. by Stacy Innerst. 2003, Harcourt $16.00 (978-0-15-201438-4). From anthem/accordion to zydeco/zither/zippy, Krull and Innerst provide a lively introduction to musical concepts. (Rev: HBG 4/04; SLJ 9/03)

101 Layne, Steven L. *Thomas's Sheep and the Great Geography Test* (1–3). Illus. by Perry Board. 1998, Pelican $15.95 (978-1-56554-274-7). In this alphabet book, Thomas sends four imaginary sheep on a worldwide trip, which involves a variety of activities such as acting in Australia and kayaking in Kenya. (Rev: HBG 10/98; SLJ 9/98)

102 Layne, Steven L., and Deborah Dover Layne. *T Is for Teachers: A School Alphabet* (K–4). Illus. by Doris Ettlinger. 2005, Sleeping Bear $16.95 (978-1-58536-159-5). An informative, rhyming alphabet book celebrating the joys of school. (Rev: SLJ 8/05)

103 Lear, Edward. *An Edward Lear Alphabet* (1–2). Illus. by Vladimir Radunsky. 1999, HarperCollins LB $14.89 (978-0-06-028114-4). 32pp. Introduces the nonsense alphabet of Edward Lear accompanied by droll illustrations. (Rev: BL 4/1/99; HBG 10/99; SLJ 6/99) [821]

104 Lear, Edward, and Suse MacDonald. *A Was Once an Apple Pie* (PS–K). Illus. 2005, Scholastic $12.99 (978-0-439-66056-3). 32pp. Lear's nonsense alphabet is only slightly altered in this version with bright, folksy artwork. (Rev: BL 8/05; SLJ 8/05*) [821]

105 Leopold, Niki Clark. *K Is for Kitten* (PS–2). Illus. by Susan Jeffers. 2002, Penguin $15.99 (978-0-399-23563-4). 32pp. An alphabet book about a girl and her kitten, with lovely artwork. (Rev: BL 9/15/02; HBG 3/03; SLJ 9/02) [811.6]

106 Leuck, Laura. *Jeepers Creepers: A Monstrous ABC* (PS–K). Illus. by David Parkins. 2003, Chronicle $15.95 (978-0-8118-3509-1). Twenty-six goofy monsters go through the typical daily routine of preschoolers. (Rev: BCCB 9/03; HBG 4/04; SLJ 12/03)

107 Lobel, Anita. *Animal Antics: A to Z* (PS). Illus. 2005, Greenwillow LB $16.89 (978-0-06-051815-8). 32pp. Striking circus-themed illustrations spotlight animals from "adoring alligators" to "zany zebras." (Rev: BL 11/1/05; SLJ 9/05) [791.3]

108 Lobel, Anita. *Away from Home* (PS–3). Illus. 1994, Greenwillow $15.89 (978-0-688-10355-2). 32pp. Each letter of the alphabet depicts a boy in a different place, e.g., Adam arrives in Amsterdam. (Rev: BCCB 9/94; BL 8/94; SLJ 10/94)

109 Lobel, Arnold. *On Market Street* (PS–1). Illus. by Anita Lobel. 1981, Greenwillow $17.89 (978-0-688-84309-0); Morrow paper $6.99 (978-0-688-08745-6). 40pp. A merry alphabet book with objects from apples to zippers.

110 MacDonald, Suse. *Alphabatics* (PS–1). Illus. by author. 1986, Macmillan $17.95 (978-0-02-761520-3). 64pp. An alphabet book that forms a letter into part of the picture illustrating the sound of the letter, such as "m" as part of a mustache. (Rev: BL 12/15/86; SLJ 12/86)

111 MacDonald, Suse. *Alphabet Animals: A Slide-and-Peek Adventure* (PS–K). Illus. by author. 2008, Simon & Schuster $12.99 (978-1-4169-5045-5). Animals in the shape of letters give clues and pull-out panels reveal the animal itself and its name. (Rev: SLJ 12/08)

112 McDonnell, Flora. *Flora McDonnell's ABC* (PS–K). Illus. 1997, Candlewick $16.99 (978-0-7636-0118-8). 32pp. A witty, delightful introduction to the alphabet using animals and fish engaging in zany activities. (Rev: BCCB 7–8/97; BL 4/15/97)

113 McLeod, Bob. *Superhero ABC* (K–3). Illus. 2006, HarperCollins $17.99 (978-0-06-074514-1). 40pp. From Astro-Man ("Astro-Man Is Always Alert for an Alien Attack") to the Zinger, this alphabet book leaps off the pages. (Rev: BCCB 2/06; BL 1/1–15/06*; HB 3/06; HBG 10/06; SLJ 2/06*)

114 McLimans, David. *Gone Wild: An Endangered Animal Alphabet* (3–6). Illus. by author. 2006, Walker $16.95 (978-0-8027-9563-2). This strikingly illustrated alphabet book introduces a different endangered animal for each letter from A to Z. Caldecott Honor Book, 2007. (Rev: SLJ 11/06)

115 Madden, Caolan. *Let's Have Fun with Alphabet Riddles* (K–2). Series: Let's Find Out. 2007, Children's Pr. LB $18.00 (978-0-531-14868-6). These clever riddles, one for each letter of the alphabet, will build the skills of young children, who will find that the letters are formed from the answers. (Rev: SLJ 7/07)

116 Marino, Gianna. *Zoopa: An Animal Alphabet* (PS–2). Illus. by author. 2005, Chronicle $14.95 (978-0-8118-4789-6). This clever, colorful title introduces a menagerie of animals, from ant to zebra. (Rev: SLJ 10/05)

117 Martin, Bill, Jr., and John Archambault. *Chicka Chicka Boom Boom* (PS–2). Illus. by Lois Ehlert. 1989, Simon & Schuster $15.00 (978-0-671-67949-1). 32pp. The letters of the alphabet enjoy a series of adventures. (Rev: BL 10/15/89*; HB 1/90*; SLJ 11/89)

118 Martin, Mary Jane. *From Anne to Zach* (PS–K). Illus. by Michael Grejniec. 1996, Boyds Mills $16.95 (978-1-56397-573-8). This ABC book introduces the alphabet by using a lot of first names, both common and obscure. (Rev: SLJ 12/96)

119 Maurer, Donna. *Annie, Bea, and Chi Chi Dolores: A School Day Alphabet* (PS–4). Illus. by Denys Cazet. 1993, Orchard LB $16.99 (978-0-531-08617-9). A day in a kindergarten supplies the letters to introduce an alphabet. (Rev: BL 2/13/93; HB 7/93; SLJ 5/93)

120 Melmed, Laura K. *New York, New York! The Big Apple from A to Z* (PS–2). Illus. by Frane Lessac. 2005, HarperCollins LB $17.89 (978-0-06-054876-6). From American Museum of Natural History to Bronx Zoo, this is a lively alphabetical guide to New York, full of factoids and interesting features, plus a useful map. (Rev: SLJ 6/05)

121 Merriam, Eve. *Where Is Everybody? An Animal Alphabet* (PS–3). Illus. by Diane deGroat. 1992, Simon & Schuster paper $14.95 (978-0-671-64964-7). 40pp. An alphabet book with many, many details in each picture. (Rev: BL 6/15/89; HB 7/89)

122 Micklethwait, Lucy, ed. *I Spy: An Alphabet in Art* (K–2). Illus. 1992, Greenwillow $19.99 (978-0-688-11679-8). 64pp. Young readers are asked to find objects in full-page reproductions of paintings. (Rev: BCCB 2/93; BL 11/1/92; HB 1/93; SLJ 10/92)

123 Milich, Zoran. *The City ABC Book* (PS–2). Illus. 2001, Kids Can $15.95 (978-1-55074-942-7). 32pp. A Canadian photojournalist cleverly uses pictures of city structures to introduce the letters of the alphabet. (Rev: BCCB 3/01; BL 4/15/01; HB 7/01; HBG 10/01; SLJ 6/01)

124 Miller, Jane. *Farm Alphabet Book* (PS–K). Illus. 1987, Scholastic paper $3.50 (978-0-590-31991-1). 32pp. Photographs of farm life make an unusual ABC book.

125 Miranda, Anne. *Alphabet Fiesta: An English/Spanish Alphabet Story* (PS–2). Illus. 2001, Turtle $18.95 (978-1-890515-29-4); paper $12.95 (978-1-890515-30-0). 54pp. The letters of the alphabet are introduced using Spanish and English words in this story of a zebra's birthday party. (Rev: BL 9/15/01; HBG 3/02; SLJ 1/02)

126 Moncure, Jane Belk. *My "a" Sound Box* (K–1). Illus. by Colin King. Series: New Sound Box Library. 2000, Child's World LB $22.79 (978-1-56766-767-7). 30pp. Many words beginning with the letter "a" are found and put in the "a" sound box. Others in this series are *My "c" Sound Box,"* and *My "d" Sound Box* (both 2000). (Rev: SLJ 3/01)

127 Mora, Pat. ¡*Marimba! Animales from A to Z* (PS–1). Illus. by Doug Cushman. 2006, Clarion $16.00 (978-0-618-19453-7). 32pp. A happy A to Z of animals frolic down the street in English and Spanish. (Rev: SLJ 11/06)

128 Morales, Yuri. *Just in Case* (K–3). Illus. by author. 2008, Roaring Brook $16.95 (978-1-59643-329-8). 32pp. Part trickster story, part ghost story, and part Mexican American alphabet book, this follows a well-dressed skeleton who collects presents from A to Z for Grandma Beetle's birthday party. (Rev: BCCB 12/08; BL 9/15/08; HB 1/09; LMC 5/09; SLJ 9/08)

129 Most, Bernard. *A B C T-Rex* (PS–K). Illus. 2000, Harcourt $13.00 (978-0-15-202007-1). 32pp. A comical ABC book in which a suburban dinosaur eats his way through the alphabet. (Rev: BL 4/1/00; HBG 10/00; SLJ 4/00)

130 Murphy, Liz. *ABC Doctor* (PS–K). Illus. 2007, Blue Apple $15.95 (978-1-59354-593-2). 36pp. Introduces the ABCs of a visit to the doctor's office, with reassuring explanations. (Rev: BL 4/1/07)

131 *Museum ABC: The Metropolitan Museum of Art* (K–3). Illus. 2002, Little, Brown $16.95 (978-0-316-07170-3). 60pp. The artwork is stunning in this simple alphabet book from the Metropolitan Museum of Art. (Rev: BL 11/15/02; HBG 3/03; SLJ 9/02) [708.147]

132 *My Big Alphabet Book* (PS–K). Series: Big Tab Board Books. 1999, DK $9.99 (978-0-7894-4681-7). An oversized board book that uses photos, drawings, and tabs to introduce the letters of the alphabet. (Rev: SLJ 2/00)

133 Napier, Matt. *Z Is for Zamboni: A Hockey Alphabet* (K–4). Illus. by Melanie Rose. 2002, Sleeping Bear $19.95 (978-1-58536-065-9). Historical highlights and facts about the game are presented in a simple Λ to Z using Canadian spellings. (Rev: SLJ 4/03)

134 Nickle, John. *Alphabet Explosion! Search and Count from Alien to Zebra* (PS–2). Illus. by author. 2006, Random $16.95 (978-0-375-83598-8). 40pp. A hunt-and-seek game in which young readers search for animals and objects whose names begin with each letter of the alphabet. (Rev: BL 10/1/06; SLJ 9/06) [428.1]

135 O'Keefe, Susan Heyboer. *Hungry Monster ABC* (K–2). Illus. by Lynn Munsinger. 2007, Little, Brown $12.99 (978-0-316-15574-8). Ten monsters (from *One Hungry Monster*) create chaos at school in this rhyming alphabet book that includes alphabet flash cards. (Rev: SLJ 6/07)

136 Pallotta, Jerry. *The Construction Alphabet Book* (PS–2). Illus. by Rob Bolster. 2006, Charlesbridge $16.95 (978-1-57091-437-9); paper $7.95 (978-1-57091-438-6). 32pp. From aerial lift to zipper, this volume offers arresting illustrations plus pertinent facts. (Rev: BL 7/06; SLJ 8/06) [624]

137 Pallotta, Jerry. *The Frog Alphabet Book . . . and Other Awesome Amphibians* (PS–1). Illus. by Ralph Masiello. 1990, Charlesbridge $16.95 (978-0-88106-463-6); paper $6.95 (978-0-88106-462-9). 32pp. This alphabet book introduces amphibians and gives salient facts about different varieties. (Rev: BL 9/1/90)

138 Pallotta, Jerry. *The Skull Alphabet Book* (2–5). Illus. by Ralph Masiello. 2002, Charlesbridge $16.95 (978-0-88106-914-3); paper $7.95 (978-0-88106-915-0). 32pp. This unusual and challenging book features paintings of animal skulls from anteater to zebra, giving subtle verbal and visual clues to the identity of each animal. (Rev: BL 9/1/02; HBG 3/03; SLJ 7/02) [573.7]

139 Paul, Ann W. *Eight Hands Round: A Patchwork Alphabet* (1–4). Illus. by Jeanette Winter. 1991, HarperCollins LB $15.89 (978-0-06-024704-1). 32pp. An alphabet book that shows how the art of patchwork grew and why. (Rev: BCCB 7–8/91; BL 6/1/91; SLJ 7/91)

140 Pearson, Debora. *Alphabeep: A Zipping, Zooming ABC* (PS–K). Illus. by Edward Miller. 2003, Holiday House $17.95 (978-0-8234-1722-3). From "ambulance" to "zamboni," this is a celebration of moving vehicles and road signs. (Rev: HBG 4/04; SLJ 9/03)

141 Pelletier, David. *The Graphic Alphabet* (PS–2). Illus. 1996, Orchard $17.99 (978-0-531-36001-9). 32pp. Letters of the alphabet are pictured in various imaginative positions. (Rev: BCCB 12/96; BL 11/1/96; HB 11/96; SLJ 11/96)

142 Pinto, Sara. *The Alphabet Room* (PS). Illus. 2003, Bloomsbury $16.95 (978-1-58234-841-4). 56pp. Flaps lift to reveal a room that gradually fills up with all the items mentioned — apples, bowl, cat, and so forth. (Rev: BL 2/1/04*) [428.1]

143 Plant, Andrew. *Could a Tyrannosaurus Play Table Tennis?* (K–4). Illus. by author. 2006, Kane paper $8.95 (978-1-929132-97-3). Combines the merits of an alphabet book and a guide to dinosaurs, introducing a prehistoric reptile for every letter from A to Z and profiling each featured dinosaur by era, size, diet, and habitat, along with a lighthearted illustration. (Rev: SLJ 8/06)

144 Pratt, Kristin J. *A Swim Through the Sea* (PS–3). Illus. by author. 1994, Dawn $16.95 (978-1-883220-03-7); paper $7.95 (978-1-883220-04-4). An alphabet book in which Seamore the seahorse introduces a number of creatures from the deep. (Rev: SLJ 8/94)

145 Pratt, Kristin J. *A Walk in the Rainforest* (2–4). Illus. by author. 1992, Dawn $16.95 (978-1-878265-99-9); paper $7.95 (978-1-878265-53-1). 33pp. In this book written and illustrated by a high school student, plants and animals found in the rain forest are used to introduce the alphabet. (Rev: SLJ 7/92)

146 Raczka, Bob. *3-D ABC: A Sculptural Alphabet* (PS–2). Illus. Series: Bob Raczka's Art Adventures. 2006, Lerner LB $23.93 (978-0-7613-9456-3). 32pp. This cleverly crafted alphabet book introduces a wide array of 20th-century sculptures. (Rev: BL 11/1/06; SLJ 11/06*) [730]

147 Rash, Andy. *Agent A to Agent Z* (PS–2). Illus. 2004, Scholastic $16.95 (978-0-439-36882-7). 40pp. From A to Z, spies undertake often-ridiculous missions and end up in bizarre situations; an imaginatively illustrated, hard-boiled offering. (Rev: BL 1/1–15/04; HB 3/04; SLJ 2/04)

148 Rey, H. A. *Curious George Learns the Alphabet* (K–2). Illus. by author. 1963, Houghton $16.00 (978-0-395-16031-2); paper $6.95 (978-0-395-13718-5). 72pp. George makes learning the alphabet a wonderful and amusing game.

149 Rose, Deborah L. *Into the A, B, Sea* (PS–3). Illus. by Steve Jenkins. 2000, Scholastic $16.99 (978-0-439-09696-6). 40pp. From anemones to zooplankton, this alphabet book cleverly explores all sorts of sea life. (Rev: BCCB 12/00; BL 9/15/00; HBG 10/01; SLJ 10/00) [591.77]

150 Rosenberg, Liz. *A Big and a Little Alphabet* (PS–1). Illus. by Vera Rosenberry. 1997, Orchard LB $16.99 (978-0-531-33050-0). 32pp. An ABC book that uses big and small animals to show the differences between upper and lowercase. (Rev: BL 11/1/97; HBG 3/98; SLJ 10/97)

151 Rumford, James. *There's a Monster in the Alphabet* (1–4). Illus. 2002, Houghton $16.00 (978-0-618-22140-0). 40pp. An imaginative and complex alphabet book that looks at the origins of the letters, incorporating mythology and the Phoenician alphabet, with attractive Grecian-style illustrations. (Rev: BL 12/1/02; SLJ 10/02) [398.2]

152 Salzmann, Mary Elizabeth. *Ann and Alan* (PS–1). Series: First Sounds. 2005, ABDO LB $19.93 (978-1-59679-126-8). 23pp. An alphabet book, part of a series, featuring photographs of items that begin with the letter A, followed by simple rebus sentences using the words. Also use *Deb and Dan* (2005). (Rev: SLJ 7/05)

153 Schafer, Kevin. *Penguins ABC* (PS–K). Photos by author. 2002, NorthWord $14.95 (978-1-55971-

831-8). An alphabet book that will please penguin lovers. (Rev: SLJ 1/03)

154 Schnur, Steven. *Spring: An Alphabet Acrostic* (2–5). Illus. by Leslie Evans. 1999, Clarion $16.00 (978-0-395-82269-2). 32pp. An alphabet book of poems about spring in which the first letter of each line of the poem combines in acrostic fashion to spell the name of the object described. Also in this series are books on the other three seasons. (Rev: BL 4/1/99; HBG 10/99; SLJ 4/99) [793.73]

155 Scillian, Devin. *P Is for Passport: A World Alphabet* (2–5). Illus. 2003, Sleeping Bear $19.95 (978-1-58536-157-1). Two dozen artists illustrated this alphabetical look at travel and at things that are part of the lives of people everywhere — B is for Bread, for example, and M is for music. (Rev: HBG 4/04; SLJ 3/04) [910]

156 Seeger, Laura Vaccaro. *Walter Was Worried* (PS–2). 2005, Roaring Brook $15.95 (978-1-59643-066-2). The weather provokes different reactions in children whose names start with each letter of the alphabet. (Rev: SLJ 8/05)

157 Seeley, Laura L. *The Book of Shadowboxes: A Story of the ABC's* (PS–3). Illus. 1990, Peachtree $17.95 (978-0-934601-65-8). Using objects in shadowboxes as illustrations, the letters of the alphabet are introduced. (Rev: SLJ 4/91)

158 Seuss, Dr. *Dr. Seuss' ABC* (K–2). Illus. by author. 1963, Random $11.99 (978-0-394-90030-8). 72pp. A master author creates a strikingly popular alphabet book.

159 Shapiro, Zachary. *We're All in the Same Boat* (K–3). Illus. by Jack E. Davis. 2009, Putnam $16.99 (978-0-399-24393-6). 32pp. When Noah is fed up with the alphabetical miseries of the animals on the ark — complaining camels, grumpy giraffes — he reminds them that they're all in the same situation and the alphabet turns to enthusiastic elephants, foxes telling fables . . . . (Rev: BL 1/1–15/09; SLJ 1/09)

160 Shindler, Ramon, and Wojciech Graniczewski. *Found Alphabet* (1–3). Illus. 2005, Houghton $16.00 (978-0-618-44232-4). 32pp. Brief verses and appealing photographs show found objects from airplane to zebra. (Rev: BL 6/1–15/05; SLJ 7/05)

161 Shoulders, Michael. *The ABC Book of American Homes* (1–3). Illus. by Sarah S. Brannen. 2008, Charlesbridge $17.95 (978-1-57091-565-9); paper $7.95 (978-1-57091-566-6). 32pp. An alphabetical look at American dwellings — from apartment to pueblo to White House to yurt. (Rev: BL 8/08; LMC 11/08) [728.0973]

162 Shulman, Mark. *A Is for Zebra* (1–3). Illus. by Tamara Petrosino. 2006, Sterling $14.95 (978-1-4027-3494-6). 32pp. With colorful cartoons, this funny variation on the traditional alphabet book turns the spotlight on the final letter of each word, as in the title example. (Rev: BL 3/15/06) [428.1]

163 Shulman, Mark. *AA Is for Aardvark: Double the Letters, Double the Fun* (PS–3). Illus. by Tamara Petrosino. 2005, Sterling LB $14.95 (978-1-4027-2871-6). Letters appearing twice in a row are the focus of this inventive and effective alphabet book. (Rev: SLJ 2/06)

164 Sierra, Judy. *The Sleepy Little Alphabet: A Bedtime Story from Alphabet Town* (PS–1). Illus. by Melissa Sweet. 2009, Knopf $16.99 (978-0-375-84002-9). 40pp. Uppercase parents and lowercase children humorously struggle through familiar bedtime routines in a book filled with amusing, detailed illustrations and rhyming text. (Rev: BL 7/09; SLJ 6/09)

165 Sierra, Judy. *There's a Zoo in Room 22* (PS–2). Illus. by Barney Saltzberg. 2000, Harcourt $16.00 (978-0-15-202033-0). 40pp. Miss Darling introduces an animal alphabet to her students including such pets as Claude the Cat, Katy Katydid, and Vincent Vulture. (Rev: BCCB 10/00; BL 8/00; HBG 3/01; SLJ 10/00)

166 Sloat, Teri. *Patty's Pumpkin Patch* (PS–2). Illus. 1999, Penguin $15.99 (978-0-399-23010-3). 32pp. From seed to pumpkin stand, this alphabet book presents the stages in the growth of a pumpkin and discusses all the creatures that visit the plant while it is growing. (Rev: BCCB 10/99; BL 9/1/99; HBG 3/00; SLJ 10/99)

167 Smith, Marie, and Roland Smith. *Z Is for Zookeeper: A Zoo Alphabet* (K–4). Illus. by Henry Cole. 2005, Sleeping Bear $16.95 (978-1-58536-158-8). "Animals," "brooms," and "quarantine" are only three of the letters in this text that also includes additional information for the curious reader. (Rev: SLJ 9/05)

168 Sobel, Jane. *Shiver Me Letters: A Pirate ABC* (PS–2). Illus. by Henry Cole. 2006, Harcourt $16.00 (978-0-15-216732-5). 32pp. Animal buccaneers may have to walk the plank if they don't manage to track down every letter from A to Z. (Rev: BL 6/1–15/06; SLJ 6/06)

169 Sobel, June. *B Is for Bulldozer: A Construction ABC* (PS–K). Illus. by Melissa Iwai. 2003, Harcourt $16.00 (978-0-15-202250-1). This appealing alphabet book focuses on the construction of a roller coaster, introducing a new tool, material, or piece of construction equipment for each letter of the alphabet. (Rev: HBG 10/03; SLJ 7/03)

170 Spirin, Gennady. *A Apple Pie* (PS–2). Illus. 2005, Philomel $16.99 (978-0-399-23981-6). 32pp. This whimsical alphabet book full of lovely, detailed watercolor paintings revives a 17th-century nursery rhyme and introduces verbs for the letters from A to Z. (Rev: BL 11/1/05; SLJ 9/05)

171 Stewig, John W. *The Animals Watched: An Alphabet Book* (K–2). Illus. by Rosanne Litzinger. 2007, Holiday $16.95 (978-0-8234-1906-7). 32pp. Animal pairs from aardvarks to zebras (and including urodeles and other unfamiliar animals) give their viewpoints on the voyage aboard Noah's ark. (Rev: BL 11/1/07; SLJ 9/07)

172 *T Is for Tugboat: Navigating the Seas from A to Z* (PS–2). Illus. 2008, Chronicle $15.99 (978-0-8118-6094-9). 32pp. With an attractive mix of vintage and contemporary images, this alphabet book covers all things nautical, starting with "Anchor," "Ahoy!," and "Aground." (Rev: BL 5/1/08; SLJ 7/08) [623.8]

173 *The Timbertoes ABC Alphabet Book* (PS–1). Illus. 1997, Boyds Mills $7.95 (978-1-56397-604-9). 32pp. The Timbertoes, a family of wooden figures, introduce the letters of the alphabet. (Rev: BL 3/1/97; SLJ 7/97)

174 Tobias, Tobi, ed. *A World of Words: An ABC of Quotations* (PS–3). Illus. by Peter Malone. 1998, Lothrop LB $15.89 (978-0-688-12130-3). 40pp. Poems and brief quotations are arranged alphabetically under such subjects as Animal, Book, Yard, and Zoo. (Rev: BL 10/1/98; HBG 3/99; SLJ 9/98) [811]

175 Ulmer, Wendy. *A Isn't for Fox: An Isn't Alphabet* (PS–K). Illus. by Laura Knorr. 2008, Sleeping Bear $16.95 (978-1-58536-319-3). 32pp. Rhyming couplets tell what a letter does not stand for before offering a word that does start with it. (Rev: BL 4/15/08; LMC 10/08; SLJ 7/08)

176 Vidrine, Beverly Barras. *Thanksgiving Day Alphabet* (1–3). Illus. by Alison Davis Lyne. 2006, Pelican paper $7.95 (978-1-58980-338-1). This colorful Thanksgiving alphabet book introduces people, places, and things related to the holiday's history. (Rev: SLJ 11/06) [394.2649]

177 Wallace, Nancy Elizabeth. *Alphabet House* (PS–2). Illus. 2005, Marshall Cavendish $16.95 (978-0-7614-5192-1). 32pp. Inside Alphabet House, which is home to a rabbit family, young readers will find multiple examples of words that begin with each letter of the alphabet. (Rev: BL 11/1/05; SLJ 10/05)

178 Wells, Rosemary. *Max's ABC* (PS–K). 2006, Viking $15.99 (978-0-670-06074-0). 32pp. Brief episodes featuring rabbit siblings Max and Ruby introduce every letter from A to Z. (Rev: BL 6/1–15/06; SLJ 5/06)

179 Wilbur, Helen L. *M Is for Meow* (3–6). Illus. by Robert Papp. 2007, Sleeping Bear $17.95 (978-1-58536-304-9). Realistic illustrations accompany facts about all sorts of cats in this installment in this alphabet series. (Rev: SLJ 5/07)

180 Winter, Jeanette. *Calavera Abecedario: A Day of the Dead Alphabet Book* (K–3). Illus. 2004, Harcourt $16.00 (978-0-15-205110-5). 48pp. With a story about preparing for Mexico's Dia de los Muertos as a backdrop, Winter presents an alphabet celebrating the skeletons that mark the holiday. (Rev: BL 11/1/04; SLJ 5/05) [394.266]

181 Wisnewski, Andrea. *A Cottage Garden Alphabet* (2–4). Illus. 2003, Godine $18.95 (978-1-56792-229-5). 64pp. Beautiful cut-paper illustrations of a garden's bounty accompany each letter of the alphabet. (Rev: BL 2/15/03; HBG 10/03; SLJ 5/03) [635]

182 Wojtowycz, David. *Animal ABC* (K–1). Illus. by author. 2000, David & Charles $14.95 (978-1-86233-107-5). A host of animals from an athletic aardvark to a zig-zag zebra introduce the alphabet. (Rev: SLJ 9/00)

183 Wood, Audrey. *Alphabet Adventure* (PS–2). Illus. by Bruce Wood. 2001, Scholastic $16.95 (978-0-439-08069-9). 40pp. The 26 letters are on their way to teach a child the alphabet when they encounter some difficulties in this inventive book illustrated with glowing, computer-generated graphics. (Rev: BL 9/1/01; HBG 3/02; SLJ 9/01)

184 Wood, Audrey. *Alphabet Mystery* (PS–2). Illus. by Bruce Wood. 2003, Scholastic $16.99 (978-0-439-44337-1). When Little x disappears, the other 25 letters of the alphabet launch a search. (Rev: BL 12/1/03; HBG 4/04; SLJ 11/03)

185 Wood, Audrey. *Alphabet Rescue* (PS–2). Illus. by Bruce Wood. 2006, Scholastic $15.99 (978-0-439-85316-3). 40pp. Readers join the lowercase letters of the alphabet as they repair an old fire truck and come to the rescue of other letters that need help. (Rev: BL 11/15/06; SLJ 10/06)

186 Yorinks, Arthur. *The Alphabet Atlas* (1–4). Illus. by Adrienne Yorinks and Jeanyee Wong. 1999, Winslow $19.95 (978-0-89081-714-8). This alphabet book features countries of the world and, on each page, an illustration using different textiles in the shape of the country. (Rev: SLJ 7/99)

187 Ziefert, Harriet. *ABC Dentist* (K–3). Illus. by Liz Murphy. 2008, Blue Apple $15.95 (978-1-934706-31-2). 36pp. An alphabetical reassurance that a visit to the dentist is not going to be a horrible experience. (Rev: BL 11/15/08; SLJ 11/08) [617.6]

Concept Books

GENERAL

188 Aber, Linda Williams. *Grandma's Button Box* (K–1). Illus. by Page Eastburn O'Rourke. 2002, Kane paper $4.95 (978-1-57565-110-1). 32pp. When a young girl drops her grandmother's button box, she and her cousins try different ways of sorting them out in this simple concept book. (Rev: BL 4/15/02)

189 Abramson, Beverley. *Off We Go!* (PS). Photos by author. 2006, Tundra $15.95 (978-0-88776-728-9). Multicultural children enjoy a multitude of energetic activities in this book of few words. (Rev: HBG 10/06; SLJ 6/06)

190 Alda, Arlene. *Hello, Good-bye* (PS–K). Illus. by author. 2009, Tundra $16.95 (978-0-88776-900-9). 32pp. A great conversation starter, this concept book features eye-catching color photographs that demonstrate opposites such as "straight" and "slanted" and "old" and "new." (Rev: BL 1/1–15/09; SLJ 5/09)

191 Alda, Arlene. *Here a Face, There a Face* (PS–3). Illus. 2008, Tundra $14.95 (978-0-88776-845-3). 24pp. Here Alda looks at the "faces" we see in all sorts of objects. (Rev: BL 2/15/08; SLJ 6/08)

192 Aliki. *Feelings* (K–2). Illus. 1984, Greenwillow $16.89 (978-0-688-03832-8); Morrow paper $6.99 (978-0-688-06518-8). 32pp. An introduction to various emotions.

193 Asim, Jabari. *Whose Knees Are These?* (PS). Illus. by LeUyen Pham. 2006, Little, Brown $6.99 (978-0-316-73576-6). A happy brown-skinned baby rejoices in bending knees in this simple board book with simple rhymes and lively illustrations. Also use *Whose Toes Are Those?* (2006). (Rev: SLJ 6/06)

194 Baker, Alan. *Little Rabbits' First Time Book* (PS–K). Illus. 1999, Kingfisher $10.95 (978-0-7534-5220-2). 16pp. The activities of three bunnies throughout a day illustrate the passage of hours, which can be traced by using the movable hands on a clock. (Rev: BL 12/1/99; SLJ 2/00)

195 Baker, Keith. *Just How Long Can a Long String Be?* (PS–2). Illus. by author. 2009, Scholastic $16.99 (978-0-545-08661-5). 32pp. Ant and Bird consider the various uses of string (for a banjo, a balloon, a yoyo, a fishing line, and so forth) and the lengths needed. (Rev: BL 4/15/09; HB 7/09; SLJ 5/09)

196 Barraclough, Sue. *Fast and Slow* (PS–K). Illus. Series: How Do Things Move? 2006, Raintree LB $14.95 (978-1-4109-2261-8). 24pp. The concept of speed is illustrated in spreads depicting two objects moving at different paces. (Rev: BL 4/1/06) [531]

197 Bauer, Marion Dane. *One Brown Bunny* (PS–K). Illus. by Ivan Bates. 2009, Scholastic $14.99 (978-0-439-68010-3). 32pp. This double-duty concept book does colors and numbers from 1 through 10. (Rev: BL 12/1/08; SLJ 4/09)

198 Bauer, Marion Dane. *Toes, Ears, and Nose!* (PS). Illus. by Karen Katz. 2003, Simon & Schuster $5.99 (978-0-689-84712-7). In this colorful lift-the-flap title, preschoolers are introduced to various parts of the human body. (Rev: SLJ 6/03)

199 Beaton, Clare. *Daisy Gets Dressed* (PS–K). Illus. 2005, Barefoot Books $15.99 (978-1-84148-197-5). 24pp. A seek-and-find book that requires the reader to identify among many patterns the right pieces of clothing to complete Daisy's outfit. (Rev: BL 5/1/05)

200 Beaton, Clare. *How Big Is a Pig?* (PS–K). Illus. 2000, Barefoot Books $14.99 (978-1-84148-077-0). 32pp. Double-page spreads are used in this amusing book that illustrates opposites in animals — fast and slow dogs and quiet and jumpy frogs. (Rev: BL 10/1/00; HBG 3/01; SLJ 12/00)

201 Beeke, Tiphanie. *Roar Like a Lion! A First Book About Sounds* (PS). Illus. 2001, Sterling $7.95 (978-1-86233-143-3). 16pp. This fun-filled book about a mouse trying to find friends will have preschoolers making all kinds of jungle noises. (Rev: BL 3/1/02)

202 Behrens, Janice. *Let's Find Rain Forest Animals: Up, Down, Around* (PS–1). Illus. Series: Let's Find Out. 2007, Scholastic LB $18.00 (978-0-531-14874-7). 32pp. Readers guess which rain forest animals are shown in cropped photographs and in the process learn "position" words; factual information is appended. (Rev: BL 4/1/07) [591.734]

203 Bender, and Bender. *Ribbit! Flip and See Who Froggy Can Be* (K–3). Illus. by authors. 2007, HarperCollins $16.99 (978-0-06-113820-1). Flip pages divided into three horizontal sections allow children to "dress" Froggy in different zany outfits. (Rev: SLJ 8/07)

204 Berenstain, Stan, and Jan Berenstain. *Inside, Outside, Upside Down* (PS–1). Illus. by authors. 1968, Random LB $11.99 (978-0-394-91142-7). A bear has a brief trip that explains various concepts.

205 Bernhard, Durga. *Earth, Sky, Wet, Dry: A Book of Nature Opposites* (PS–2). Illus. 2000, Orchard LB $17.99 (978-0-531-33213-9). 40pp. Opposites are introduced using scenes from nature that demonstrate, for example, the difference between light and dark. (Rev: BL 2/1/00; HBG 10/00; SLJ 3/00)

206 Bernhard, Durga. *To and Fro, Fast and Slow* (PS–2). Illus. 2001, Walker LB $16.85 (978-0-8027-8783-5). 32pp. This clever, well-illustrated concept book uses a girl's visits to her mother's country home and her father's city apartment to show opposites. (Rev: BL 11/1/01; HBG 3/02; SLJ 9/01)

207 Blackstone, Stella. *Baby High, Baby Low* (PS). Illus. by Denise Fraifield and Fernando Azevedo. 1998, Holiday House $14.95 (978-0-8234-1345-4). 32pp. The author introduces the concept of opposites — such as high and low — using illustrations of activities involving babies of many races and their parents. (Rev: BL 12/1/98; HBG 3/99; SLJ 10/98)

208 Blackstone, Stella. *You and Me* (PS–1). Illus. by Giovanni Manna. 2000, Barefoot Books $15.99 (978-1-84148-263-7). 32pp. The author explores the concept of opposites using a boy and a girl on double-page spreads engaging in different activities. (Rev: BL 12/1/00; HBG 3/01; SLJ 12/00)

209 Boutignon, Beatrice. *Not All Animals Are Blue* (PS–K). Illus. by author. 2009, Kane $15.95 (978-1-933605-96-8). 48pp. Which sentences describe which animals? Each spread offers five animals and five questions. (Rev: BL 3/15/09; HB 5/09; SLJ 5/09)

210 Brown, Lisa. *How to Be* (PS–2). 2006, HarperCollins $16.99 (978-0-06-054635-9). 32pp. A little brother and sister have lots of fun imitating different animals. (Rev: BL 7/06; SLJ 6/06)

211 Brown, Margaret Wise. *Bumble Bugs and Elephants: A Big and Little Book* (PS). Illus. by Clement Hurd. 2006, HarperCollins $14.99 (978-0-06-074512-7). With its appealing blend of colorful artwork and rhythmic text, this picture book originally published in 1938 provides simple examples of opposite sizes in the animal world. (Rev: SLJ 3/06)

212 Bullard, Lisa. *Long and Short: An Animal Opposites Book* (K–2). Series: A+ Books: Animal Opposites. 2005, Capstone LB $23.93 (978-0-7368-4275-4). 32pp. Animal pairings — a python and a bat, for example — introduce the concept of opposites. Also use *Loud and Quiet* (2005). (Rev: SLJ 1/06) [590]

213 Butler, John. *Can You Growl Like a Bear?* (PS–K). Illus. by author. 2007, Peachtree $15.95 (978-1-56145-396-2). 32pp. From the click of a dolphin to the howl of a wolf, this "sound-along" picture book highlights 10 animals, ending with a suggestion of the sound of sleep. (Rev: BL 9/1/07; SLJ 9/07)

214 Butler, John. *If You See a Kitten* (PS). Illus. by author. 2003, Peachtree $13.95 (978-1-56145-108-1). Cuddly kittens, pudgy pigs, and slithery snakes are among the animals introduced with suggested one-word responses — "Ahhh!" or "Yikes," for example. (Rev: BL 3/03; HBG 10/03; SLJ 5/03)

215 Carle, Eric. *From Head to Toe* (PS). Illus. 1997, HarperCollins LB $17.89 (978-0-06-023516-1). 32pp. Children make the same movements as animals in this concept book illustrated with lively collages. (Rev: BCCB 6/97; BL 4/15/97; SLJ 4/97) [613.7]

216 Carle, Eric. *My Very First Book of Words* (PS–1). Illus. by author. 1985, HarperCollins $2.95 (978-0-690-57368-8). 10pp. A nicely illustrated beginning word book, printed on heavy stock cards.

217 Carrier, Lark. *Do Not Touch* (1–3). Illus. by author. 1991, Picture Book paper $15.95 (978-0-88708-061-6). 28pp. A picture book with the concept of words within words. (Rev: BL 4/1/89)

218 Carter, David A. *More Bugs in Boxes* (PS–3). Illus. 1990, Simon & Schuster $13.95 (978-0-671-69577-4). A board book that explores the world of shapes and colors. (Rev: SLJ 8/90)

219 Cendrars, Blaise. *Shadow* (K–3). Trans. and illus. by Marcia Brown. 1982, Macmillan $17.00 (978-0-684-17226-2). 40pp. This Caldecott winner (1983) explores the mysterious world of shadows.

220 Charles, N. N. *What Am I? Looking Through Shapes at Apples and Grapes* (PS–K). Illus. by Leo Dillon and Diane Dillon. 1994, Scholastic $16.95 (978-0-590-47891-5). 36pp. Geometric shapes are used creatively to illustrate a number of clever riddles in this interactive book. (Rev: BL 11/15/94; SLJ 1/95)

221 Chesanow, Neil. *Where Do I Live?* (K–3). Illus. by Ann Iosa. 1995, Barron's paper $7.99 (978-0-8120-9241-7). 48pp. The concept of belonging is explored, from a room of one's own to being a part of the solar system. (Rev: BL 2/1/96) [910]

222 Clark, Emma Chichester. *Mimi's Book of Opposites* (PS). Illus. by author. Series: A Mimi Book. 2003, Charlesbridge $9.95 (978-1-57091-574-1). In this appealing concept book, Mimi the monkey and her little brother explore the world of opposites. (Rev: HBG 4/04; SLJ 11/03)

223 Crews, Nina. *A High, Low, Near, Far, Loud, Quiet Story* (PS). Illus. 1999, Greenwillow LB $15.89 (978-0-688-16795-0). 24pp. The activities of a sister and younger brother are used to introduce a number of opposites. (Rev: BL 9/15/99; HBG 3/00; SLJ 12/99)

224 Crowther, Robert. *Opposites* (PS–1). Illus. 2005, Candlewick $12.99 (978-0-7636-2783-6). 16pp. Bright collage artwork and clever, sturdy pull-tab and lift-the-flap features illustrate opposites — happy and sad, full and empty, and so forth. (Rev: BL 9/1/05; SLJ 9/05) [428.1]

225 Cumpiano, Ina. *Quinito, Day and Night / Quinito, día y noche* (PS–K). Illus. by José Ramírez. 2008, Children's Pr. $16.95 (978-0-89239-226-1). 32pp. A bright, bilingual look at opposites, presented by the little boy last seen in *Quinito's Neighborhood* (2005). (Rev: BL 7/08; SLJ 9/08)

226 Davis, Nancy. *A Garden of Opposites* (PS–K). Illus. by author. 2009, Random $10.99 (978-0-375-85666-2). 26pp. This concept book uses a farm garden to show eight sets of opposites. (Rev: BLO 5/15/09; SLJ 4/09)

227 Emberley, Rebecca. *My Opposites / Mis Opuestos* (PS). 2000, Little, Brown $5.95 (978-0-316-23345-3). 20pp. A concept board book that introduces opposites in English and Spanish. (Rev: BCCB 12/00*; HBG 3/01; SLJ 9/00)

228 Falconer, Ian. *Olivia's Opposites* (PS). Illus. 2002, Simon & Schuster $6.99 (978-0-689-85088-2). 12pp. A simple board book featuring Olivia the pig that demonstrates the concept of opposites. (Rev: BL 7/02; HBG 10/02; SLJ 6/02)

229 Falwell, Cathryn. *Word Wizard* (K–3). Illus. 1998, Clarion $16.00 (978-0-395-85580-5). 32pp. In this picture book, Anna discovers the world of anagrams while eating a bowl of alphabet cereal, then she embarks on a series of adventures in which, for example, she turns an ocean into a canoe. (Rev: BL 5/15/98; HBG 10/98)

230 Fleming, Denise. *The Everything Book* (PS). Illus. 2000, Holt $18.95 (978-0-8050-6292-2). 64pp. This book offers all sorts of information on topics ranging from the seasons and days of the week to parts of the body plus poems, songs, and games. (Rev: BCCB 10/00; BL 7/00; HBG 3/01; SLJ 10/00)

231 Ford, Miela. *What Color Was the Sky Today?* (PS–1). Illus. by Sally Noll. 1997, Greenwillow LB $14.93 (978-0-688-14559-0). 24pp. Using fewer than 100 words, this book introduces the concepts of colors, counting, time, and the weather. (Rev: BL 5/1/97; SLJ 3/97)

232 Freymann, Saxton, and Joost Elffers. *Food for Thought: The Complete Book of Concepts for Growing Minds* (PS). Illus. 2005, Scholastic $14.95 (978-0-439-11018-1). 64pp. Colors, letters, numbers, opposites, and shapes are all introduced using the authors' signature fruits and vegetables. (Rev: BL 1/1–15/05; SLJ 3/05)

233 Friday, Mary Ellen. *It's a Bad Day* (PS–K). Illus. by Glin Dibley. 2006, Rising Moon $15.95 (978-0-87358-904-8). Discouraging events that can turn a good day into a bad day are put into perspective in this simple and charming book. (Rev: SLJ 5/07)

234 Gabriel, Nat. *Sam's Sneaker Squares* (1–2). Illus. by Ron Fritz. 2002, Kane paper $4.95 (978-1-57565-114-9). 32pp. In this concept book, Sam learns about measurements to determine the cost of mowing lawns. (Rev: BL 4/15/02)

235 Gibbons, Gail. *Playgrounds* (PS–1). Illus. by author. 1985, Holiday House LB $16.95 (978-0-8234-0553-4). 32pp. A concept book that shows young readers playground scenes that are familiar. (Rev: BCCB 6/85; BL 5/15/85; SLJ 5/85)

236 Gordon, Sharon. *Dirty Clean* (PS–2). Series: Bookworms: Just the Opposite. 2003, Benchmark LB $21.36 (978-0-7614-1569-5). 23pp. A primer in the contrast between things that are dirty and things that are clean and how they might get that way. (Rev: HBG 4/04; SLJ 3/04)

237 Gordon, Sharon. *Fast Slow* (PS–2). Series: Bookworms: Just the Opposite. 2003, Benchmark LB $21.36 (978-0-7614-1570-1). 23pp. The contrast between fast and slow is explored through various means of transportation, from rollerskates to cars. (Rev: HBG 4/04; SLJ 3/04)

238 Got, Yves. *Sweet Dreams, Sam* (PS). Illus. 2000, Chronicle $8.95 (978-0-8118-2985-4). This interactive book uses different textures to explore the sense of touch, such as simulating the crinkly skin of an elephant. (Rev: BL 12/1/00)

239 Gravett, Emily. *Orange Pear Apple Bear* (PS–1). Illus. by author. 2007, Simon & Schuster $12.99 (978-1-4169-3999-3). A brown bear stars in this book about shapes, colors, and sequence. (Rev: SLJ 4/07*)

240 Grejniec, Michael. *Good Morning, Good Night* (PS). Illus. 1997, North-South paper $6.95 (978-1-55858-704-5). 28pp. A concept book with basic vocabulary that demonstrates opposites. (Rev: BL 3/15/93; SLJ 8/93)

241 Harper, Charise Mericle. *Amy and Ivan* (PS). Illus. by author. 2006, Tricycle $12.95 (978-1-58246-134-2). 24pp. Amy is planning a surprise party for her friend Ivan in this bright, square, lift-the-flap book with numbers and colors for children to name. (Rev: BL 5/15/06; SLJ 9/06)

242 Harper, Dan. *Telling Time with Big Mama Cat* (PS–2). Illus. by Barry Moser and Cara Moser. 1998, Harcourt $15.00 (978-0-15-201738-5). 28pp. Using a foldout clock with movable hands, young readers can trace the daily activities of Big Mama Cat while they learn to tell time. (Rev: BCCB 11/98; BL 8/98*; HBG 3/99; SLJ 12/98)

243 Harper, Jamie. *Splish Splash, Baby Bundt* (PS). Illus. by author. 2007, Candlewick $6.99 (978-0-7636-3240-3). A board book recipe for a successful bathtime — 1 sticky Baby Bundt, 1 family of rubber ducks . . . (Rev: SLJ 1/08)

244 Harris, Pamela. *Hot, Cold, Shy, Bold* (PS–K). Illus. 1998, Kids Can $10.95 (978-1-55074-153-7). 32pp. A successful book of opposites that uses a rhyming text and color photos. (Rev: BL 3/15/98; HBG 10/98) [428.1]

245 Harris, Trudy. *Pattern Fish* (PS–1). Illus. by Anne Canevari Green. 2000, Millbrook LB $22.60 (978-0-7613-1712-8). This attractive concept book explores the world of patterns. (Rev: BCCB 9/00; HBG 10/01; SLJ 12/00)

246 Hartman, Gail. *As the Crow Flies: A First Book of Maps* (PS–1). Illus. by Harvey Stevenson. 1993, Aladdin paper $5.99 (978-0-689-71762-8). 32pp. The concept of maps is introduced by using the environments of different animals. (Rev: BL 3/1/91; HB 5/91; SLJ 3/91)

247 Herman, Gail. *Bad Luck Brad* (1–2). Illus. by Stephanie Roth. Series: Math Matters. 2002, Kane paper $4.95 (978-1-57565-112-5). 32pp. The concept of probability is explored when a series of misfortunes occur to Brad on a single day. (Rev: BL 5/1/02)

248 Hicks, Barbara Jean. *I Like Black and White* (PS). Illus. by Lila Prap. 2006, ME Media $9.95 (978-1-58925-057-4). 24pp. Simple black-and-white art (with color accents) and brief, rhyming text depict animals, patterns, and shapes. (Rev: BL 5/15/06)

249 Hills, Tad. *What's Up, Duck?* (PS). Illus. by author. Series: Duck and Goose. 2008, Random $6.99 (978-0-375-84738-7). 22pp. Duck, Goose, and Thistle illustrate nine opposites — loud and quiet, front and back, and so forth — in this board book. (Rev: BL 4/1/08) [428.1]

250 Hindley, Judy. *Ten Bright Eyes* (PS–1). Illus. by Alison Bartlett. 1998, Peachtree $14.95 (978-1-56145-173-9). As a mother bird roams the countryside looking for food for her young, the reader is introduced to numbers, shapes, and patterns as well as some related activities. (Rev: HBG 10/98; SLJ 11/98)

251 Hoban, Tana. *Black on White* (PS). Illus. 1993, Greenwillow $6.99 (978-0-688-11918-8). The photographs show black objects on a white background. A companion book is *White on Black* (1993). (Rev: HB 7/93; SLJ 8/93)

252 Hoban, Tana. *What Is That?* (PS). Illus. 1994, Greenwillow paper $6.99 (978-0-688-12920-0). 12pp. Using silhouettes, a number of common animals are pictured in this board book. Also use *Who Are They?* (1994). (Rev: BL 12/1/94; HB 11/94; SLJ 11/94)

253 Holland, Gini. *Light and Heavy* (K–1). Series: I Know Opposites. 2007, Gareth Stevens LB $17.27 (978-0-8368-8295-7); paper $4.50 (978-0-8368-8300-8). 16pp. Bright photographs and simple text illustrate such opposites as a light toy truck and a heavy fire truck. Also use *Soft and Hard* and *Alive and Not Alive* (both 2007). (Rev: SLJ 12/07) [530.8]

254 Horowitz, Dave. *Twenty-six Princesses* (PS–2). Illus. by author. 2008, Putnam $15.99 (978-0-399-24607-4). 32pp. From Alice to Zaire, 26 royal young ladies — presented in portraits and rhyming couplets that capture their nature — set off to meet the prince (er, frog). (Rev: BCCB 6/08; LMC 11/08; SLJ 4/08)

255 Hudson, Cheryl W. *Hands Can* (PS). Photos by John-Francis Bourke. 2003, Candlewick $14.99 (978-0-7636-1667-0). Bright colors and eye-catching photos draw readers into this display of movements and expressions made with hands. (Rev: BL 10/1/03; HBG 4/04; SLJ 12/03)

256 Hutchins, Hazel. *A Second Is a Hiccup: A Child's Book of Time* (PS–2). Illus. by Kady M. Denton. 2007, Scholastic $16.99 (978-0-439-83106-2). Children will recognize the many examples given here for seconds, minutes, and hours and what can be accomplished within their parameters. (Rev: BL 1/1–15/07; SLJ 3/07*)

257 Jocelyn, Marthe. *A Day with Nellie* (PS). Illus. by author. 2002, Tundra $15.95 (978-0-88776-600-8). 24pp. Numbers, colors, the alphabet, and other concepts are introduced as readers follow preschooler Nellie through the activities of her ordinary day. (Rev: BL 12/1/02; HBG 3/03; SLJ 1/03)

258 Jocelyn, Marthe. *Same Same* (PS–K). Illus. by Tom Slaughter. 2009, Tundra $15.95 (978-0-88776-885-9). 24pp. Bright illustrations depict sets of three objects that are alike — "round things," for exam-ple, and "things that make music." (Rev: BCCB 2/09; BL 3/1/09; SLJ 3/09)

259 Jolivet, Joëlle. *Almost Everything* (PS–2). Illus. 2005, Roaring Brook $19.95 (978-1-59643-090-7). 40pp. This large-format collection of images, a follow-up to *Zoo-ology* (2003), is organized into 13 categories, including tools, the human body, historical costumes, and trees and flowers. (Rev: BL 11/1/05; SLJ 11/05) [423]

260 Kassirer, Sue. *What's Next, Nina?* (1–3). Illus. by Page Eastburn O'Rourke. Series: Math Matters. 2001, Kane paper $4.95 (978-1-57565-106-4). 32pp. Nina must reconstruct a broken necklace of beads in this story that subtly but effectively introduces the concept of patterns. (Rev: SLJ 2/02)

261 Katz, Karen. *Ten Tiny Tickles* (PS). Illus. 2005, Simon & Schuster $14.95 (978-0-689-85976-2). 32pp. A simple book that celebrates the various parts of a baby and offers counting opportunities as well. (Rev: BL 7/05; SLJ 7/05)

262 Krauss, Ruth. *A Hole Is to Dig* (PS). Illus. by Maurice Sendak. 1952, HarperCollins $16.95 (978-0-06-023405-8); paper $6.95 (978-0-06-443205-4). 48pp. Child-perceived definitions, such as "the world is so you have something to stand on," complemented by whimsical drawings.

263 Kroll, Steven. *That Makes Me Mad!* (PS–1). Illus. by Christine Davenier. 2002, North-South LB $16.50 (978-1-58717-184-0). A newly illustrated edition of the 1976 story about Nina and everything that makes her mad. (Rev: HBG 3/03; SLJ 8/02)

264 Laden, Nina. *Grow Up!* (PS). Illus. 2003, Chronicle $6.95 (978-0-8118-3761-3). 26pp. A well-illustrated, rhyming board book about growing up in which a kitten becomes a cat, a puppy becomes a dog, a seedling become a tree, and so forth. (Rev: BL 5/15/03)

265 Lewis, J. Patrick. *Big Is Big (and Little, Little): A Book of Contrasts* (PS–1). Illus. by Bob Barner. 2007, Holiday House $16.95 (978-0-8234-1909-8). Big, sad, fat, dark, and hot animals meet their opposites in this delightfully illustrated book. (Rev: SLJ 5/07)

266 Lewison, Wendy Cheyette. *Two Is for Twins* (PS). Illus. by Hiroe Nakata. 2006, Viking $16.99 (978-0-670-06128-0). 40pp. This bright picture book celebrates things that come in pairs, especially twins. (Rev: BL 5/15/06; SLJ 4/06)

267 Lunn, Carolyn. *A Whisper Is Quiet* (1–2). Illus. by Clovis Martin. 1989, Children's Book Pr. paper $4.95 (978-0-516-42087-5). 32pp. A concept book introduces opposites. (Rev: BL 3/1/89)

268 Maccarone, Grace. *Monster Math School Time* (K–2). Illus. by Margaret A. Hartelius. Series: Hello Math Reader. 1997, Scholastic $3.99 (978-0-590-30859-5). A beginning reader that teaches how to tell time through the antics of 12 monsters and their daily activities. (Rev: SLJ 1/98)

269 Marks, Jennifer L. *Sorting by Size* (K–3). Series: Sorting. 2006, Capstone LB $23.93 (978-0-7368-6740-5). 32pp. Simple text and everyday examples show how to sort by size; also use *Sorting Money* and *Sorting Toys* (both 2006). (Rev: SLJ 4/07)

270 Marzollo, Jean. *I Spy School Days: A Book of Picture Riddles* (PS–2). Illus. by Walter Wick. Series: I Spy. 1995, Scholastic $13.99 (978-0-590-48135-9). 38pp. Riddles and puzzles using photographs are featured, each related to school activities. (Rev: BL 12/1/95; SLJ 10/95)

271 Medina, Sarah. *Jealous* (PS–K). Illus. by Jo Brooker. Series: Feelings. 2007, Heinemann LB $21.36 (978-1-4034-9294-4); paper $5.99 (978-1-4034-9301-9). 24pp. Jealousy is an unpleasant but common feeling, and this book conveys this emotion though simple text and illustrations. (Rev: SLJ 8/07)

272 Medina, Sarah. *Proud* (PS–K). Illus. by Jo Brooker. Series: Feelings. 2007, Heinemann LB $21.36 (978-1-4034-9296-8); paper $5.99 (978-1-4034-9303-3). 24pp. It feels good to be proud of a job well done, and this book conveys that emotion though simple text and illustrations. (Rev: SLJ 8/07)

273 Miura, Taro. *Tools* (PS–K). Illus. 2006, Chronicle $15.95 (978-0-8118-5519-8). 40pp. This attractive introduction to a wide array of tools offers children the chance to guess which occupations they are used in. (Rev: BL 11/1/06; SLJ 10/06) [621.9]

274 Morris, Ann. *Play* (PS–3). Illus. 1998, Lothrop $15.00 (978-0-688-14551-4). 32pp. A concept book that shows children from different countries engaged in various play activities common to their cultures. (Rev: BL 5/15/98) [790.1]

275 Murphy, Chuck. *Slide 'n Seek: Opposites* (PS–K). Illus. Series: Slide 'n Seek. 2001, Simon & Schuster $5.99 (978-0-689-84476-8). 12pp. Pull-tabs are used effectively to illustrate opposites in this small board book. (Rev: BL 12/15/01) [513]

276 Murphy, Mary. *If . . .* (PS–K). Illus. by author. 2000, Houghton paper $4.95 (978-0-618-03399-7). In this flap book, a little penguin demonstrates cause and effect (e.g., if you plant a seed/a tree can grow). The concept of choice is explored in the companion volume *You Choose* (2000). (Rev: SLJ 6/00)

277 Murphy, Stuart J. *Game Time!* (2–3). Illus. by Cynthia Jabar. 2000, HarperCollins LB $15.89 (978-0-06-028025-3); paper $5.99 (978-0-06-446732-2). 33pp. The concept of measuring time — including weeks, days, hours, and seconds — is explored in this exciting tale of the Huskies, a girls' soccer team, and their big game. (Rev: HBG 3/01; SLJ 1/01)

278 Murphy, Stuart J. *The Greatest Gymnast of All* (PS–K). Illus. by Cynthia Jabar. Series: MathStart. 1998, HarperCollins LB $15.89 (978-0-06-027609-6); paper $5.99 (978-0-06-446718-6). 40pp. Using Zoe's gymnastics routine as a framework, the rhyming text introduces opposites, such as inside and outside, on and off, and high and low. (Rev: BL 12/1/98; HBG 3/99; SLJ 12/98) [516]

279 Murphy, Stuart J. *It's About Time!* (PS–2). Illus. Series: MathStart. 2005, HarperCollins $16.99 (978-0-06-055768-3); paper $5.99 (978-0-06-055769-0). 40pp. Introduces time-telling by linking everyday activities to the time of day; both analog and digital clocks are featured. (Rev: BL 3/1/05) [529]

280 Murphy, Stuart J. *Rabbit's Pajama Party* (PS–K). Illus. by Frank Remkiewicz. Series: MathStart. 1999, HarperCollins LB $15.89 (978-0-06-027617-1); paper $5.99 (978-0-06-446722-3). 40pp. Rabbit and friends enjoy a number of events in this concept book, which explains terms in sequencing such as *about, then,* and *when.* (Rev: BL 12/1/99; HBG 3/00; SLJ 9/99) [515]

281 Nilsen, Anna. *My Best Friends* (PS–K). Illus. by Emma Dodd. 2003, Gingham Dog $15.95 (978-0-7696-3159-2). Brightly colored cartoon characters illustrate the importance — and challenges — of friendship. (Rev: HBG 4/04; SLJ 1/04)

282 Olson, Nathan. *Animal Patterns* (1–2). Series: Finding Patterns. 2006, Capstone LB $23.93 (978-0-7368-6728-3). 32pp. Patterns that appear on animals (or that are made by them) are featured in large color photographs on well-designed pages. Also use *City Patterns, Food Patterns,* and *People Patterns.* (Rev: SLJ 5/07)

283 Parr, Todd. *The Daddy Book* (PS–K). Illus. 2002, Little, Brown $14.95 (978-0-316-60799-5). 32pp. A bright, simple book that points out the differences, and the similarities, between fathers. Also use the companion volume *The Mommy Book* (2002). (Rev: BL 3/15/02; HBG 10/02; SLJ 5/02)

284 Patilla, Peter. *Patterns* (2–4). Illus. Series: Math Links. 1999, Heinemann LB $21.36 (978-1-57572-967-1). 32pp. Different patterns are introduced in this concept book that uses double-page spreads and is arranged by order of difficulty. (Rev: BL 2/1/00; SLJ 12/99) [510]

285 Patricelli, Leslie. *Baby Happy Baby Sad* (PS). Illus. by author. Series: Leslie Patricelli board books. 2008, Candlewick $6.99 (978-0-7636-3245-8). 24pp. Happiness (holding a balloon) and sadness (seeing ice cream hit the ground) are concepts easily understood from these pages. (Rev: BCCB 4/08; SLJ 4/08)

286 Patricelli, Leslie. *No No Yes Yes* (PS). Illus. by author. Series: Leslie Patricelli board books. 2008, Candlewick $6.99 (978-0-7636-3244-1). 24pp. Patricelli illustrates opposites while showing a toddler behaving appropriately and inappropriately in a variety of everyday situations. (Rev: BCCB 4/08; SLJ 4/08) [428.1]

287 Payne, Nina. *Four in All* (PS–3). Illus. by Adam Payne. 2001, Front St $15.95 (978-1-886910-16-4). 32pp. A girl takes an imaginary journey in this richly illustrated, captivating verse for younger readers that uses four-word lines to present items that come in fours (such as north, east, south, and west) and is wonderfully illustrated by the author's son. (Rev: BCCB 12/01; BL 1/1–15/02; HBG 3/02; SLJ 12/01*)

288 Pearson, Susan. *Hooray for Feet!* (PS–1). Illus. by Roxanna Baer-Block. 2005, Blue Apple $12.95 (978-1-59354-093-7). In rhyming text, this appealing picture book celebrates feet and the many wonders they can perform. (Rev: SLJ 11/05)

289 Penner, Lucille R. *Where's That Bone?* (PS–2). Illus. by Lynn Adams. Series: Math Matters. 2000, Kane paper $4.95 (978-1-57565-097-5). 32pp. A dog forgets where he has buried his bones so Jill draws him a map in this concept book about distance and maps. (Rev: SLJ 2/01)

290 Penner, Lucille R. *X Marks the Spot!* (1–2). Illus. by Jerry Smath. 2002, Kane paper $4.95 (978-1-57565-111-8). 32pp. Brothers Leo and Jake learn to read charts to find treasures in their new hometown in this clever concept book. (Rev: BL 4/15/02)

291 Petelinsek, Kathleen, and E. Russell Primm. *Opposites / Los contrarios* (K–2). Illus. by Nichole Day Diggins. Series: Talking Hands. 2006, The Child's World LB $21.36 (978-1-59296-454-3). 24pp. Students demonstrate simple words using American Sign Language; the text is in both English and Spanish. (Rev: SLJ 6/06) [419]

292 Pinto, Sara. *Apples and Oranges: Going Bananas with Pairs* (PS–2). Illus. by author. 2008, Bloomsbury Children's $16.95 (978-1-59990-103-9). 32pp. A humorous introduction to "compare and contrast" thinking that could lead to interesting out-of-the-box discussions. (Rev: BL 1/1–15/08; LMC 1/08; SLJ 1/08)

293 Raschka, Chris. *Five for a Little One* (PS–K). Illus. by author. 2006, Simon & Schuster $16.95 (978-0-689-84599-4). 48pp. A thoughtful young bunny shares the glories of the five senses in this picture book with unusual, eye-catching illustrations. (Rev: BL 6/1–15/06; SLJ 7/06)

294 Redding, Suc. *Up Above and Down Below* (PS). Illus. by author. 2006, Chronicle $14.95 (978-0-8118-4876-3). 32pp. Worlds above and below — hikers and cavers, golfers and gophers, cruise passengers and crew, for example — are contrasted in this imaginative book for preschoolers. (Rev: BL 5/15/06; SLJ 7/06)

295 Reidy, Hannah. *All Sorts of Clothes* (PS). Illus. by Emma Dodd. Series: All Sorts of Things. 2005, Picture Window LB $25.26 (978-1-4048-1063-1). 24pp. This toddler-friendly book helps little ones identify different articles of clothing. (Rev: BL 4/1/05)

296 Reidy, Hannah. *All Sorts of Noises* (PS). Illus. by Emma Dodd. Series: All Sorts of Things. 2005, Picture Window LB $25.26 (978-1-4048-1064-8). 24pp. Introduces noises of all kinds, from birds chirping to alarm clocks and street sounds. (Rev: SLJ 6/05)

297 Rosenthal, Amy Krouse. *Duck! Rabbit!* (PS–1). Illus. by Tom Lichtenheld. 2009, Chronicle $16.99 (978-0-8118-6865-5). 40pp. Is it a duck or a rabbit? A visual debate full of fun and color. (Rev: BL 4/1/09; HB 5/09; LMC 8/09; SLJ 5/09)

298 Rotner, Shelley. *Lots of Feelings* (PS–1). Photos by author. 2003, Millbrook LB $21.90 (978-0-7613-2896-4). 24pp. Close-up photographs show children displaying a variety of emotions. (Rev: HBG 4/04; SLJ 4/04)

299 Rotner, Shelley. *Parts* (PS–1). Illus. 2001, Walker LB $17.85 (978-0-8027-8754-5). 32pp. Close-up shots of parts of everyday objects are accompanied by rhymes that give additional clues to the whole object that is revealed on the next page. (Rev: BCCB 6/01; BL 6/1–15/01; HBG 10/01; SLJ 5/01)

300 Rubin, Susan G. *Matisse: Dance for Joy* (PS–K). Illus. by author. 2008, Chronicle $6.99 (978-0-8118-6288-2). 24pp. A board-book introduction to the work of Matisse, using the artist's cutout collages and rhythmic text. (Rev: BLO 6/17/08) [709.2]

301 Savadier, Elivia. *Will Sheila Share?* (PS–K). Illus. by author. 2008, Roaring Brook $12.95 (978-1-59643-289-5). 24pp. Sheila finds sharing very difficult until her grandmother shows her sharing will make her happy. (Rev: SLJ 4/08)

302 Schaefer, Lola M. *What's Up, What's Down?* (PS–2). Illus. by Barbara Bash. 2002, HarperCollins $17.99 (978-0-06-029757-2). 32pp. A fascinating and innovative approach that involves turning the book sideways and following arrows up and down to see the world from the point of view of various plants and animals. (Rev: BL 12/1/02; HBG 3/03; SLJ 1/03) [500]

303 Schwartz, David M. *If You Hopped Like a Frog* (K–4). Illus. by James Warhola. 1999, Scholastic $16.95 (978-0-590-09857-1). 32pp. This picture book discusses the concepts of ratio and proportion, using animal facts to explore topics such as relative strength. (Rev: BCCB 12/99; BL 11/15/99; HBG 3/00; SLJ 11/99) [513.2]

304 Seeger, Laura Vaccaro. *Black? White! Day? Night!* (PS–2). Illus. 2006, Roaring Brook $16.95 (978-1-59643-185-0). 24pp. A creative introduction to opposites using full-page flaps, cutouts, and bright colors. (Rev: BCCB 11/06; BL 11/1/06; HBG 4/07; SLJ 11/06*) [428.1]

305 Seeger, Laura Vaccaro. *First the Egg* (PS–K). Illus. by author. 2007, Roaring Brook $14.95 (978-1-59643-272-7). 32pp. Die-cut pages and cleverly layered images integrated with spare text present examples of development in nature (from egg to chicken, tadpole to frog) and in the making of a story (word, story, paint, picture). Caldecott Honor Book, 2008. (Rev: BL 2/1/08; HB 11/07; LMC 1/08; SLJ 11/07) [571.8] ∩

306 Sendak, Maurice. *The Nutshell Library* (PS–3). Illus. by author. 1962, HarperCollins $16.95 (978-0-06-025500-8). Miniature volumes include an alphabet book, *Alligators All Around,* and a counting book, *One Was Johnny* (both 1962).

307 Silvano, Wendi. *What Does the Wind Say?* (PS–K). Illus. by Joan M. Delehanty. 2006, North-Word $15.95 (978-1-55971-954-4). A gentle book with watercolor illustrations and rhyming text that poses questions about various parts of nature — "What do the stars do?" "What does the moon play?" (Rev: SLJ 11/06)

308 Simon, Francesca. *Calling All Toddlers* (PS–K). Illus. by Susan Winter. 1999, Orchard $15.95 (978-0-531-30120-3). 33pp. In 16 verses, children are introduced to colors, shapes, movement, humor, and play. (Rev: BCCB 2/99; BL 4/15/99; HBG 10/99; SLJ 6/99)

309 Siomades, Lorianne. *Kangaroo and Cricket* (PS–1). Illus. by author. 1999, Boyds Mills $12.95 (978-1-56397-780-0). Two different animals on every page reveal how they are similar; for example, both dogs and squirrels bury things. (Rev: HBG 3/00; SLJ 12/99)

310 Slate, Joseph. *Miss Bindergarten Celebrates the 100th Day of Kindergarten* (PS–1). Illus. by Ashley Wolff. 1998, Dutton $16.99 (978-0-525-46000-8). 32pp. Superteacher Miss Bindergarten asks her students to bring 100 things to class to celebrate the 100th day of kindergarten in this combination alphabet and counting book. (Rev: BL 10/15/98; HBG 3/99; SLJ 9/98)

311 Sper, Emily. *The Kids' Fun Book of Jewish Time* (1–4). Illus. by author. 2006, Jewish Lights $16.99 (978-1-58023-311-8). Lift-the-flap and pull-the-tab features add interest to this introduction to the Jewish calendar. (Rev: SLJ 11/06) [296.4]

312 Spicer, Maggee, and Richard Thompson. *We'll All Go Flying* (PS–K). Illus. by Kim LaFave. 2002, Fitzhenry & Whiteside $16.95 (978-1-55041-698-5). Colors, shapes, sounds, and animals are all presented from the platform of a hot-air balloon in this counting book with movable flaps. (Rev: SLJ 12/02)

313 Spurr, Elizabeth. *Farm Life* (PS–1). Illus. by Steve Björkman. 2003, Holiday House $16.95 (978-0-8234-1777-3). 32pp. Basic colors and numbers 1 to 10 are taught by exploring the buildings on a farm. (Rev: BL 3/15/03; HBG 10/03; SLJ 6/03)

314 Stinson, Kathy. *A Pocket Can Have a Treasure in It* (PS–K). Illus. by Deirdre Betteridge. 2008, Annick LB $18.95 (978-1-55451-126-6); paper $6.95 (978-1-55451-125-9). 32pp. A friendly concept book — with a new sibling twist — about things found inside other things. (Rev: BCCB 9/08; SLJ 9/08)

315 Swinburne, Stephen. *What's Opposite?* (PS–1). Illus. 2000, Boyds Mills $16.95 (978-1-56397-881-4). 32pp. Using handsome photographs, this book explores the world of common opposites. (Rev: BL 9/1/00; HBG 3/01; SLJ 10/00)

316 Szekeres, Cyndy. *I Love My Busy Book* (PS–1). Illus. 1997, Scholastic $12.95 (978-0-590-69195-6). 48pp. Concepts including colors, manners, and parts of the body are introduced in double-page spreads. (Rev: BCCB 3/97; BL 2/1/97; SLJ 4/97)

317 Thomas, Shelley Moore. *Somewhere Today: A Book of Peace* (PS–3). Illus. by Eric Futran. 1998, Whitman $15.95 (978-0-8075-7545-1). 24pp. A book in which children and their activities illustrate the concepts of peaceful living, sharing, helping, and joining together. (Rev: BL 4/1/98; HBG 10/98; SLJ 8/98)

318 Timmers, Leo. *Who Is Driving?* (PS–K). Illus. 2007, Bloomsbury $12.95 (978-1-59990-021-6). 32pp. Readers must guess which animal is driving each of seven vehicles in this interesting picture puzzle with clue-laden illustrations. (Rev: BL 12/15/06)

319 Tomczyk, Mary. *Shapes, Sizes and More Surprises!* (PS–1). Illus. by Loretta Braren. Series: Little Hands Early Learning Books. 1996, Williamson paper $12.95 (978-0-913589-95-3). 141pp. An activity book for youngsters filled with stories, puzzles, counting exercises, and games. (Rev: SLJ 10/96)

320 Van Fleet, Matthew. *One Yellow Lion* (PS). Illus. by author. 1992, Dial $10.99 (978-0-8037-1099-3). This book, with foldout pages and plenty of drawings of animals, presents the concepts of color and counting. (Rev: SLJ 9/92)

321 Whitman, Candace. *Lines That Wiggle* (PS–1). Illus. by Steve Wilson. 2009, Blue Apple $14.99 (978-1-934706-54-1). 36pp. Concept book explores in rhyme a deceptively simple line. (Rev: BL 6/1–15/09)

322 Wilson-Max, Ken. *Wake Up, Sleep Tight* (PS–K). Illus. 1998, Scholastic $11.95 (978-0-590-76779-8). 16pp. Two simple board books in one — one about morning activities and the other about going to bed — are unified by a cutout clock with movable hands. Readers can change the clock to the hours mentioned in each rhyme. (Rev: BL 11/1/98)

323 Wormell, Christopher. *Teeth, Tales and Tentacles: An Animal Counting Book* (PS–3). 2004, Running Pr. $18.95 (978-0-7624-2100-8). 64pp. This clever animal-themed counting book operates on several levels, serving as an introduction to numbers for preschoolers, an overview of 20 different animal species from around the world, and a collection of fascinating facts and figures about those animals and their behavior. (Rev: BL 10/1/04*)

324 Yoon, Salina. *Opposnakes: A Lift-the-Flap Book About Opposites* (PS–K). Illus. by author. 2009, Simon & Schuster $9.99 (978-1-4169-7875-6). 16pp. Simple text, funny illustrations, and a deft structure work together to teach about opposites. (Rev: SLJ 6/09)

COLORS

325 Barry, Frances. *Duckie's Rainbow* (PS). Illus. by author. 2004, Candlewick $7.99 (978-0-7636-2066-0). Duckie passes many vivid colors as she hurries home in this fan-shaped board book with collage art. (Rev: SLJ 7/04) [813.6]

326 *Big Yellow Trucks and Diggers: Colors* (PS). 2003, Chronicle $6.95 (978-0-8118-4030-9). Colors are introduced through eye-catching photographs of appealing machines. (Rev: SLJ 1/04) [624]

327 Carle, Eric. *Hello, Red Fox* (K–3). Illus. 1998, Simon & Schuster $16.00 (978-0-689-81775-5). 32pp. The author invites readers to experience a simple story by employing the phenomenon whereby staring at a color and then at a blank white page reveals a complementary color as if by magic. (Rev: BCCB 7–8/98; BL 4/1/98; HBG 10/98; SLJ 7/98)

328 Catalanotto, Peter. *Kitten Red, Yellow, Blue* (PS–K). Illus. 2005, Simon & Schuster $15.95 (978-0-689-86562-6). 32pp. Both colors and professions are introduced in this clever story that involves color-coding a batch of kittens according to their owners. (Rev: BL 2/15/05; SLJ 3/05)

329 *Color* (K–3). Photos and illus. by Ella Doran, et al. 2006, Abrams $19.95 (978-1-85437-697-8). Primary colors, complementary colors, hue, tint, and many other concepts about color are all covered here, in a fittingly colorful package with some movable features. (Rev: SLJ 6/07)

330 Ehlert, Lois. *Color Farm* (PS–K). Illus. 1990, HarperCollins LB $17.89 (978-0-397-32441-5). 40pp. Various animals are pictured by using a number of different shapes and colors. (Rev: BL 11/15/90; HB 1/91; SLJ 11/90)

331 Ehlert, Lois. *Color Zoo* (PS–2). Illus. by author. 1989, HarperCollins LB $17.89 (978-0-397-32260-2). 32pp. How basic shapes can be combined to make familiar objects. (Rev: BL 5/15/89; SLJ 4/89)

332 Emberley, Rebecca. *My Colors / Mis Colores* (PS). 2000, Little, Brown $5.95 (978-0-316-23347-7). 20pp. A board book in English and Spanish introduces the basic colors. (Rev: BCCB 12/00*; HBG 3/01; SLJ 9/00)

333 Fontes, Justine. *Black Meets White* (PS–2). Illus. by Geoff Waring. 2005, Candlewick $12.99 (978-0-7636-1933-6). Cutouts and lift-the-flap features highlight this tale of two colors, which cleverly introduces various patterns. (Rev: SLJ 11/05)

334 Fox, Christyan, and Diane Fox. *What Color Is That, PiggyWiggy?* (PS–K). Illus. 2001, Handprint $5.95 (978-1-929766-17-8). 20pp. In this book about colors, PiggyWiggy dons articles of clothing of different hues until he becomes a perfect circus clown. (Rev: BL 4/1/01; SLJ 8/01)

335 Goldsen, Louise. *Colors* (K–2). Illus. by P. M. Valet and Sylvaine Perols. 1991, Scholastic paper $12.95 (978-0-590-45236-6). Through the use of clear acetate sheets, various colors are introduced and identified. (Rev: SLJ 5/92) [535.5]

336 Gunzi, Christiane. *My Very First Look at Colors* (PS–K). Illus. by Steve Gorton. Series: My Very First Look. 2001, Two-Can $8.95 (978-1-58728-236-2); paper $5.95 (978-1-58728-276-8). 24pp. A concept book that uses photographs of everyday objects to teach preschoolers about colors. (Rev: BL 2/15/02; HBG 10/02; SLJ 2/02) [535.6]

337 Harrison, Carlos. *Ruben's Rainbow / El Arco Iris de Ruben* (K–2). Illus. by Grizelle Paz. 2001, Globo Libros $15.95 (978-0-9706953-0-7). Ruben tumbles from a world of black and white into a world full of color in this bilingual text accompanied by a CD. (Rev: SLJ 1/02)

338 Hoban, Tana. *Colors Everywhere* (PS–K). Illus. 1995, Greenwillow $17.89 (978-0-688-12763-3). 32pp. A wordless picture book that identifies the colors found in each of the photographs used. (Rev: BCCB 3/95; BL 5/1/95; HB 7/95; SLJ 7/95)

339 Hoban, Tana. *Is It Red? Is It Yellow? Is It Blue?* (PS). Illus. 1978, Morrow paper $6.99 (978-0-688-07034-2). 32pp. Without words, this picture book explains the concept of color.

340 Hoban, Tana. *Red, Blue, Yellow Shoe* (PS). Illus. by author. 1986, Greenwillow paper $6.99 (978-0-688-06563-8). 12pp. A very simple introduction to color in a board book. (Rev: BCCB 1/87; BL 10/15/86; HB 11/86)

341 Holm, Sharon L. *Zoe's Hats: A Book of Colors and Patterns* (PS–1). Illus. 2003, Boyds Mills $13.95 (978-1-59078-042-8). 32pp. Zoe has fun trying on all manner of hats in this simple book for the very young. (Rev: BL 2/1/03; HBG 10/03; SLJ 2/03)

342 Horacek, Petr. *Strawberries Are Red* (PS). Illus. by author. 2001, Candlewick $4.99 (978-0-7636-1461-4). Fruit and colors are introduced on brightly illustrated double-page spreads. Also use *What Is Black and White?* (2001). (Rev: SLJ 8/01)

343 Jonas, Ann. *Color Dance* (PS–K). Illus. 1989, Greenwillow $17.89 (978-0-688-05991-0). 32pp. Dancers wave colored scarves and introduce various colors. (Rev: BL 8/89; SLJ 12/89)

344 Lionni, Leo. *Little Blue and Little Yellow* (PS–1). Illus. by author. 1959, Astor-Honor $14.95 (978-0-8392-3018-2). All the characters are blobs of color; an ingenious story intended to give the young child an awareness of color.

345 MacDonald, Suse. *Shape by Shape* (PS–2). Illus. by author. 2009, Simon & Schuster $14.99 (978-1-4169-7147-4). 24pp. Progressive, bright die-cut shapes finally reveal a whole dinosaur on a fold-out spread. (Rev: BL 5/1/09; SLJ 6/09)

346 MacKinnon, Debbie. *Eye Spy Colors* (PS–K). Illus. by Anthea Sieveking. 1998, Charlesbridge $8.95 (978-0-88106-334-9). 24pp. Colors are introduced through a series of double-page spreads and peepholes. (Rev: BL 1/1–15/99; HBG 3/99)

347 Martin, Bill, Jr. *Brown Bear, Brown Bear, What Do You See?* (PS–1). Illus. by Eric Carle. 1992, Holt $15.95 (978-0-8050-1744-1). 32pp. This brightly illustrated easy-reader book first appeared in 1967 and is a fine introduction to colors. (Rev: BL 3/1/92; SLJ 5/92)

348 Micklethwait, Lucy. *I Spy Colors in Art* (K–3). Illus. 2007, Greenwillow $19.99 (978-0-06-134837-2). 40pp. Images by artists including Magritte and Picasso invite children to look closely at colors. (Rev: BL 9/15/07; SLJ 9/07) [752]

349 Milich, Zoran. *City Colors* (PS–1). Photos by author. 2004, Kids Can $14.95 (978-1-55337-542-5). Starting with basic colors (a red bus, a blue wall), the author works through a city's spectrum (from a green swing to a pink conduit) in this attractive concept book. (Rev: SLJ 5/04) [535.6]

350 Miller, Margaret. *I Love Colors* (PS–1). Illus. Series: Look Baby! 1999, Simon & Schuster $4.99 (978-0-689-82356-5). 14pp. In this board book about colors, babies are shown wearing different-colored headgear. (Rev: BL 8/99; SLJ 8/99)

351 Mockford, Caroline. *Cleo's Color Book* (PS). Illus. by author. 2006, Barefoot Books $15.99 (978-1-905236-30-5). 32pp. The orange cat featured in *Cleo's Alphabet Book* and *Cleo's Counting Book* (both 2003) observes the colors around her in this beginning concept book. (Rev: BL 5/15/06; SLJ 4/06)

352 Otoshi, Kathryn. *One* (PS–K). Illus. by author. 2008, KO Kids $16.95 (978-0-9723946-4-2). The color Red is a successful bully until One turns up and challenges Red's ascendance; in turn the other colors become numbers too — Yellow is two, Green is three — and support the bullied, quiet Blue. (Rev: BL 11/15/08*; LMC 3/08*; SLJ 12/08)

353 Park, Linda Sue. *What Does Bunny See? A Book of Colors and Flowers* (PS). Illus. by Maggie Smith. 2005, Clarion $15.00 (978-0-618-23485-1). 32pp.

Poppies, violets, primroses, and lilies are among the flowers Bunny sees in a colorful garden in this rhyming presentation of blossoms and their colors. (Rev: BL 3/1/05; SLJ 6/05)

354 Robertson, Patrisha. *Cirque du Soleil: Parade of Colors* (K–4). Photos by Cirque du Soleil. 2003, Abrams $15.95 (978-0-8109-4515-9). 32pp. In this lushly illustrated concept book, young readers are introduced to colors in a parade of performers from the famed Cirque du Soleil. (Rev: HBG 4/04; SLJ 1/04)

355 Rodrigue, George. *Why Is Blue Dog Blue?* (PS–3). Illus. 2002, Stewart, Tabori & Chang $16.95 (978-1-58479-162-1). 40pp. The artist explains why he paints his dog different colors depending on the situation. (Rev: BL 6/1–15/02; HBG 10/02)

356 Rowe, Jeannette. *YoYo's Colors* (PS). Illus. by author. Series: YoYo. 2002, Tiger Tales $3.95 (978-1-58925-682-8). YoYo the yellow dog introduces preschoolers to other vividly colored creatures in this board book. Also use *YoYo's Numbers* and *YoYo's Toys* (both 2002). (Rev: SLJ 6/03)

357 Seeger, Laura Vaccaro. *Lemons Are Not Red* (PS–2). Illus. 2004, Roaring Brook $14.95 (978-1-59643-008-2). 32pp. Various objects introduce colors in this attractive small book that ends with a bedtime message. (Rev: BL 1/1–15/05)

358 Shahan, Sherry. *Spicy Hot Colors / Colores Picantes* (PS–1). Illus. by Paula Barragán. 2004, August House $16.95 (978-0-87483-741-4). 24pp. Spicy-hot art and rhythmic descriptions introduce colors in both English and Spanish. (Rev: BL 9/15/04; SLJ 11/04) [535.6]

359 Shannon, George. *White Is for Blueberry* (PS–K). Illus. by Laura Dronzek. 2005, Greenwillow LB $17.89 (978-0-06-029276-8). 40pp. Plants and animals are linked to unexpected colors (for instance, crows are pink . . . when newly hatched from their eggs) in this lushly illustrated book. (Rev: BL 3/15/05; SLJ 5/05)

360 Siomades, Lorianne. *My Box of Color* (PS–1). Illus. by author. 1998, Boyds Mills $12.95 (978-1-56397-711-4). This book helps children explore their perceptions of color by presenting common objects in unusual colors and asking, for instance, whether a blue sun would be just as warm. (Rev: HBG 3/99; SLJ 11/98)

361 Swinburne, Stephen. *What Color Is Nature?* (PS–K). Illus. 2002, Boyds Mills $15.95 (978-1-56397-967-5); paper $9.95 (978-1-59078-008-4). 32pp. Using bright photographs of children, animals, and plants, different colors are introduced. (Rev: BL 6/1–15/02; HBG 10/02)

362 Tafuri, Nancy. *Blue Goose* (PS–K). Illus. by author. 2008, Simon & Schuster $15.99 (978-1-4169-2834-8). 32pp. Blue Goose, Red Hen, Yellow Chick, and White Duck decide to add color to their stark surroundings, first working alone and then blending their colors to create purple doors, orange shutters, and even green grass. (Rev: BCCB 2/08; BL 11/15/07; SLJ 1/08)

363 Thompson, Richard, and Maggee Spicer. *We'll All Go Sailing* (PS–1). Illus. by Kim La Fave. 2001, Fitzhenry & Whiteside $16.95 (978-1-55041-662-6). 48pp. A concept book that introduces colors along with a variety of sea creatures. (Rev: BL 5/15/01; SLJ 7/01) [591.77]

364 Thong, Roseanne. *Red Is a Dragon: A Book of Colors* (PS–2). Illus. by Grace Lin. 2001, Chronicle $18.95 (978-0-8118-3177-2). 180pp. This concept book, a companion to *A Book of Shapes* (2000), is illustrated with Chinese American images. (Rev: BL 11/15/01; HBG 3/02; SLJ 1/02)

365 Wood, Audrey. *The Deep Blue Sea: A Book of Colors* (PS). Illus. by Bruce Wood. 2005, Scholastic $15.99 (978-0-439-75382-1). 40pp. Bright tropical artwork introduces basic colors. (Rev: BL 7/05; SLJ 8/05)

PERCEPTION

366 Ashbe, Jeanne. *What's Inside* (PS). Illus. by author. Series: Curious Nell. 2000, Kane $9.95 (978-0-916291-97-6). This flap book explores the inside of things, such as a suitcase and a TV set — and examines three different stages of an unborn baby's development. (Rev: BCCB 6/00; HB 5/00; HBG 10/00; SLJ 5/00)

367 Burns, Kate. *Jump Like a Frog!* (PS–K). Illus. 1999, David & Charles $6.95 (978-1-899607-35-8). 12pp. Five picture puzzles are found in this flap book, which asks young readers to find hidden animals. Also use *Snap like a Crocodile*. (Rev: BL 9/15/99; SLJ 10/99)

368 Carrier, Lark. *There Was a Hill* . . . (PS–1). Illus. by author. 1991, Picture Book paper $15.95 (978-0-907234-70-8). 40pp. An attractive picture book with a guessing game woven into the irresistible pages. (Rev: BL 9/15/85; SLJ 10/85)

369 Carter, David A. *One Red Dot* (K–2). Illus. by author. 2005, Simon & Schuster $19.95 (978-0-689-87769-8). This attractive pop-up book challenges readers to find the single red dot that is hidden somewhere in each of its 10 paper sculptures. (Rev: SLJ 11/05)

370 Ciboul, Adele. *The Five Senses* (PS–K). Trans. by Anthea Bell. Illus. by Clementine Colliner. Series: Explore Your World. 2006, Firefly $15.95 (978-1-55407-007-7). 28pp. An appealing, interactive introduction to the senses, with lots of pullouts, flaps, pictures, and photos. (Rev: BL 10/15/06) [612.8]

371 Hoban, Tana. *Is It Rough? Is It Smooth? Is It Shiny?* (PS). Illus. by author. 1984, Greenwillow $17.99 (978-0-688-03823-6). 32pp. Textures are explored in a series of photographs.

372 Kuskin, Karla. *Green as a Bean* (PS–2). Illus. by Melissa Iwai. 2007, HarperCollins $17.99 (978-0-06-075332-0). Thought-provoking "what if" questions challenge young readers to consider what they might be if they were different colors, textures, shapes, sounds, or sizes; previously published as *Square as a House*. (Rev: BL 11/1/06; SLJ 2/07)

373 Maclay, Elise. *The Forest Has Eyes* (PS–2). Illus. by Bev Doolittle. 1998, Greenwich Workshop

$16.95 (978-0-86713-055-3). 32pp. Each of these nature paintings has a subject camouflaged within it (e.g., a snow pattern on a mountain is actually an eagle). (Rev: BL 10/15/98; SLJ 11/98) [970]

374 McMillan, Bruce. *Mouse View: What the Class Pet Saw* (PS–3). Illus. 1993, Holiday House LB $16.95 (978-0-8234-1008-8). 32pp. Familiar classroom sights are shown from a mouse's point of view. (Rev: BL 3/15/93*; SLJ 4/93)

375 Robert, Francois, and Jean Robert. *Find a Face* (PS–2). 2004, Chronicle $15.95 (978-0-8118-4338-6). Faces are everywhere in this inventive collection of photographs of objects ranging from light switches to shoe heels. (Rev: SLJ 8/04) [779]

376 Shaw, Charles. *It Looked Like Spilt Milk* (K–2). Illus. by author. 1947, HarperCollins LB $17.89 (978-0-06-025565-7); paper $6.99 (978-0-06-443159-0). 30pp. White material appears on each page, but its identity is not revealed until the end. Originally published in 1947.

SIZE AND SHAPE

377 Aber, Linda Williams. *Carrie Measures Up* (K–2). Illus. by Joy Allen. Series: Math Matters. 2001, Kane paper $4.95 (978-1-57565-100-2). 32pp. Carrie gets totally carried away measuring things around the house. (Rev: SLJ 6/01)

378 Adler, David A. *Shape Up! Fun with Triangles and Other Polygons* (2–5). Illus. by Nancy Tobin. 1998, Holiday House $16.95 (978-0-8234-1346-1). An introduction to shapes and angles, using household items such as pretzels, bread, and pencil and paper. (Rev: BCCB 9/98; HBG 10/98; SLJ 9/98)

379 Blackstone, Stella. *Ship Shapes* (PS). Illus. by Siobhan Bell. 2006, Barefoot Books $15.99 (978-1-905236-34-3). Two children and a dog set sail on a raft and encounter a variety of different shapes. (Rev: SLJ 8/06)

380 Carter, David. *Whoo? Whoo?* (PS–1). Illus. by author. 2007, Simon & Schuster $12.99 (978-1-4169-3816-3). Stylized animals made from shapes are hiding here, and young readers will build visualization skills trying to see them. (Rev: SLJ 8/07)

381 Dotlich, Rebecca. *What Is Round?* (PS). Illus. by Maria Ferrari. Series: Harper Growing Tree. 1999, HarperCollins $9.95 (978-0-694-01208-4). 24pp. The concept of roundness is explored in this picture book, which shows many objects that are round and others that are not. (Rev: BL 7/99; HBG 10/99; SLJ 4/99)

382 Dotlich, Rebecca. *What Is Square?* (PS). Photos by Maria Ferrari. Series: Harper Growing Tree. 1999, HarperCollins $9.95 (978-0-694-01207-7). All kinds of square objects are presented in this interactive concept book. (Rev: HBG 10/99; SLJ 8/99)

383 Emberley, Rebecca. *My Shapes / Mis Formas* (PS). 2000, Little, Brown $5.95 (978-0-316-23355-2). 20pp. Different shapes are introduced in English and Spanish in this board book. (Rev: BCCB 12/00*; HBG 3/01; SLJ 9/00)

384 Ernst, Lisa Campbell. *Round Like a Ball* (PS–2). Illus. by author. 2008, Blue Apple $15.95 (978-1-934706-01-5). 36pp. What is this round thing shaped like a ball? A family follows bold visual cues. (Rev: BL 4/1/08; LMC 10/08)

385 Falwell, Cathryn. *Shape Space* (PS–2). Illus. 1992, Houghton $17.82 (978-0-395-61305-4). 32pp. A cut-paper girl plays and builds with colorful cut-paper shapes. (Rev: BL 10/15/92; HB 1/93; SLJ 10/92)

386 Florian, Douglas. *A Pig Is Big* (PS–K). Illus. 2000, Greenwillow $17.99 (978-0-688-17125-4). 24pp. Using animals as subjects, this book explores the concept of comparative size. (Rev: BCCB 12/00*; BL 9/15/00; HB 11/00; HBG 3/01; SLJ 10/00)

387 Fox, Christyan, and Diane Fox. *What Shape Is That, PiggyWiggy?* (PS). Illus. by authors. 2002, Handprint $5.95 (978-1-929766-44-4). Shapes including squares, circles, arches, triangles, and diamonds are demonstrated as a pig and his teddy bear build a house in this board book. (Rev: SLJ 6/02)

388 Gordon, Sharon. *Big Small* (PS–2). Series: Bookworms: Just the Opposite. 2003, Benchmark LB $21.36 (978-0-7614-1568-8). 23pp. A young girl's various possessions are bigger than her little brother's in this exploration of the concept of size. (Rev: HBG 4/04; SLJ 3/04) [155.7]

389 Greene, Rhonda Gowler. *When a Line Bends . . . A Shape Begins* (PS–2). Illus. by James Kaczman. 1997, Houghton $16.00 (978-0-395-78606-2). In this concept book, 10 different shapes — including a circle, square, triangle, diamond, and heart — are introduced. (Rev: HBG 3/98; SLJ 10/97)

390 Gunzi, Christiane. *My Very First Look at Shapes* (PS–K). Illus. by Steve Gorton. Series: My Very First Look. 2001, Two-Can $8.95 (978-1-58728-238-6); paper $5.95 (978-1-58728-278-2). 24pp. Shapes are introduced using colorful photographs of easily recognized objects. Also use *My Very First Look at Sizes* (2001). (Rev: BL 2/15/02; HBG 10/02; SLJ 2/02) [516]

391 Hammersmith, Craig. *Patterns* (K–2). Series: Spyglass Books. 2003, Compass Point LB $19.93 (978-0-7565-0452-6). 24pp. Ideal for beginning readers, this brightly illustrated concept book shows how diverse arrangements of colors and shapes form recognizable patterns. (Rev: SLJ 10/03) [152.14]

392 Henkes, Kevin. *Circle Dogs* (PS–K). Illus. by Dan Yaccarino. 1998, Greenwillow LB $14.89 (978-0-688-15447-9). 32pp. Everyday circular shapes are explored in this picture book about a toddler and his two pet "circle" dachshunds. (Rev: BCCB 11/98; BL 9/15/98; HBG 3/99; SLJ 9/98)

393 Hoban, Tana. *Cubes, Cones, Cylinders, and Spheres* (PS–K). Illus. 2000, Greenwillow LB $18.89 (978-0-688-15326-7). 24pp. Delightful pictures introduce different shapes in everyday objects. (Rev: BCCB 12/00; BL 10/15/00; HBG 3/01; SLJ 10/00) [513]

394 Hoban, Tana. *Is It Larger? Is It Smaller?* (PS–1). Illus. by author. 1997, Morrow paper $6.99 (978-0-688-15287-1). 32pp. Effective photographs and design illustrate the concepts of large and small, without words. (Rev: BCCB 4/85; BL 3/15/85; SLJ 4/85)

395 Hoban, Tana. *Shapes, Shapes, Shapes* (PS–1). Illus. by author. 1986, Greenwillow $17.89 (978-0-688-05833-3). 32pp. Eleven shapes are sought in the color photos. (Rev: BCCB 4/86; BL 3/1/86; HB 5/86)

396 Hoban, Tana. *So Many Circles, So Many Squares* (PS–1). Illus. 1998, Greenwillow $16.99 (978-0-688-15165-2). 32pp. In this wordless concept book, the author explores different things that are round or square. (Rev: BL 3/1/98; HB 7/98; HBG 10/98; SLJ 3/98) [516]

397 Hutchins, Pat. *Shrinking Mouse* (PS–K). Illus. 1997, Greenwillow $15.89 (978-0-688-13962-9). 32pp. A clever exploration of space and perspective using woodland animals and birds. (Rev: BL 2/15/97; SLJ 4/97*)

398 Jenkins, Steve. *Big and Little* (PS–2). Illus. 1996, Houghton $16.00 (978-0-395-72664-8). 32pp. The concept of size is explored in this book that contrasts various animals. (Rev: BL 10/1/96; SLJ 10/96*)

399 Kalan, Robert. *Blue Sea* (K–3). Illus. by Donald Crews. 1979, Morrow paper $6.99 (978-0-688-11509-8). 24pp. Big fish and little fish in the sea convey the idea of size.

400 MacDonald, Suse. *Sea Shapes* (PS–K). Illus. 1994, Harcourt $13.95 (978-0-15-200027-1); paper $6.00 (978-0-15-201700-2). 32pp. Sea creatures and attractive collages are used to introduce a number of shapes. (Rev: BL 9/1/94; HB 11/94; SLJ 11/94)

401 MacKinnon, Debbie. *Eye Spy Shapes: A Peephole Book* (PS). Photos by Anthea Sieveking. 2000, Charlesbridge $6.95 (978-0-88106-135-2). In this interactive book, various shapes are introduced through a peephole guessing game. (Rev: HBG 10/01; SLJ 9/00)

402 Micklethwait, Lucy. *I Spy: Shapes in Art* (PS–2). 2004, Greenwillow $19.99 (978-0-06-073193-9). 40pp. A variety of shapes can be identified in beautiful reproductions of well-known works of art. (Rev: BL 8/04; SLJ 9/04) [701]

403 Montague-Smith, Ann. *First Shape Book* (PS–1). Illus. by Mandy Stanley. 2002, Kingfisher $12.95 (978-0-7534-5433-6). 47pp. Cartoon illustrations and a series of questions and games introduce shapes, mirror images, pairs, and size in a way that encourages identification, matching, and counting. (Rev: SLJ 7/02)

404 Murphy, Chuck. *Slide 'n Seek: Shapes* (PS–K). Illus. Series: Slide 'n Seek. 2001, Simon & Schuster $5.99 (978-0-689-84477-5). 12pp. This small board book introduces shapes using pull-tabs and clear, bright illustrations. (Rev: BL 12/15/01) [513]

405 Murphy, Stuart J. *The Best Bug Parade* (PS–1). Illus. by Holly Keller. Series: MathStart. 1996, HarperCollins LB $15.89 (978-0-06-025872-6); paper $5.99 (978-0-06-446700-1). 33pp. A parade of bugs is used to introduce the concept of size. Also use *Circus Shapes*, which introduces circles, squares, triangles, and so forth, and *Captain Invinci-ble and the Space Shapes*, which looks at 3-dimensional shapes. (Rev: BCCB 5/96; SLJ 6/96)

406 Murphy, Stuart J. *Let's Fly a Kite* (PS–3). Illus. by Brian Floca. 2000, HarperCollins LB $15.89 (978-0-06-028035-2); paper $5.99 (978-0-06-446737-7). 40pp. Geometry and symmetry in everyday life are the concepts explored in this picture book about two quarreling siblings. (Rev: BL 9/15/00; HBG 3/01; SLJ 11/00)

407 *Museum Shapes* (PS–2). Illus. 2005, Little, Brown $16.99 (978-0-316-05698-4). 48pp. Using artifacts from the collections of New York's Metropolitan Museum of Art, this concept book introduces readers to 10 geometric forms, including the square, circle, rectangle, triangle, crescent, heart, star, and diamond. (Rev: BL 10/1/05; SLJ 12/05) [516]

408 Myller, Rolf. *How Big Is a Foot?* (K–2). Illus. by author. 1991, Dell paper $3.99 (978-0-440-40495-8). The problem of relative sizes, humorously and imaginatively described.

409 Neuschwander, Cindy. *Pastry School in Paris: An Adventure in Capacity* (PS–3). Illus. by Bryan Langdo. 2009, Holt $16.95 (978-0-8050-8314-9). 32pp. Twins Bibi and Matt attend classes at a small Parisian cooking school and learn about measurements. (Rev: BL 6/1–15/09)

410 Olson, Nathan. *Spheres* (K–2). Illus. Series: 3-D Shapes. 2007, Capstone LB $23.93 (978-1-4296-0052-1). 32pp. Using child-friendly examples (bubbles, oranges, snowballs), this book introduces the nature of a sphere and includes well-known examples of spheres plus a craft project. Also use *Pyramids* and *Cylinders* (both 2007). (Rev: SLJ 2/08) [516]

411 Patilla, Peter. *Measuring* (2–4). Illus. Series: Math Links. 1999, Heinemann LB $21.36 (978-1-57572-965-7). 32pp. A clear, attractive presentation of concepts involved in measuring that uses a series of double-page spreads. (Rev: BL 2/1/00) [530.8]

412 Pollack, Pam, and Meg Belviso. *Chickens on the Move* (1–2). Illus. by Lynn Adams. 2002, Kane paper $4.95 (978-1-57565-113-2). 32pp. In this witty concept book, three children use 24 feet of fencing to create coops of different shapes to house their grandfather's three chickens. (Rev: BL 4/15/02)

413 Rau, Dana Meachen. *Rectangles* (PS–2). Illus. Series: Bookworms: The Shape of the World. 2006, Marshall Cavendish $22.79 (978-0-7614-2282-2). 23pp. A bright, small-format introduction to rectangles with minimal text. (Rev: BL 10/15/06; SLJ 1/07) [516]

414 Rau, Dana Meachen. *A Star in My Orange: Looking for Nature's Shapes* (PS–2). Illus. 2002, Millbrook LB $22.90 (978-0-7613-2414-0). 32pp. Through colorful photographs and simple text, this book explores shapes such as stars and spirals as they occur in nature. (Rev: BL 2/1/02; HBG 10/02; SLJ 5/02) [516]

415 Salzmann, Mary Elizabeth. *Circles* (PS–1). Series: What Shape Is It? 2000, ABDO LB $19.93 (978-1-57765-163-5). 24pp. A slim book that introduces circles and various objects that are circular in shape. Also use *Rectangles*, *Stars*, *Triangles* (all 2000). (Rev: HBG 10/00; SLJ 7/00)

416 Schlein, Miriam. *Round and Square* (PS–2). Illus. by Linda Bronson. 1999, Mondo $15.95 (978-1-57255-719-2). 32pp. With a rhyming text, this colorful picture book introduces the concepts of round and square. (Rev: BL 1/1–15/00)

417 Scott, Janine. *The Shape of Things* (K–2). Illus. Series: Spyglass Books. 2003, Compass Point LB $19.93 (978-0-7565-0453-3). 24pp. This photo-filled concept book introduces young readers to a wide array of different shapes, including circles, boxes, and stars. (Rev: SLJ 10/03) [516]

418 Scott, Janine. *Take a Guess: A Look at Estimation* (K–2). Illus. Series: Spyglass Books. 2003, Compass Point LB $19.93 (978-0-7565-0446-5). 24pp. This photo-filled volume introduces the concept of estimation and making approximations. (Rev: SLJ 12/03) [519.5]

419 Swinburne, Stephen. *Lots and Lots of Zebra Stripes: Patterns in Nature* (PS–2). Illus. 1998, Boyds Mills $16.95 (978-1-56397-707-7). 32pp. Using wonderful photos, this book explores repeating patterns of lines and shapes and shows how they can be found in a number of objects great and small. (Rev: BL 9/15/98; HBG 3/99; SLJ 12/98) [778.9]

420 Thong, Roseanne. *Round Is a Mooncake* (PS–1). Illus. by Grace Lin. 2000, Chronicle $13.95 (978-0-8118-2676-1). 40pp. An Asian American girl looks at shapes she sees in her neighborhood in this book that explores circles, squares, and rectangles. (Rev: BL 12/1/00; HBG 3/01; SLJ 8/00)

421 Walsh, Ellen S. *Mouse Shapes* (PS–K). Illus. by author. 2007, Harcourt $16.00 (978-0-15-206091-6). 40pp. Three mice use colorful, assorted shapes to frighten away a pesky cat. (Rev: BL 7/07; HB 7/07; SLJ 7/07)

422 Wells, Robert E. *Is a Blue Whale the Biggest Thing There Is?* (PS–3). Illus. 1993, Whitman LB $16.99 (978-0-8075-3655-1); paper $6.95 (978-0-8075-3656-8). 32pp. The concept of size is explored, first by comparing an elephant to the huge blue whale and ending with our galaxy being compared to the universe. (Rev: BCCB 11/93; BL 12/15/93; SLJ 1/94)

423 Wells, Robert E. *What's Smaller Than a Pygmy Shrew?* (1–4). Illus. 1995, Whitman LB $16.99 (978-0-8075-8837-6); paper $6.95 (978-0-8075-8838-3). 32pp. The concept of smallness is explored using examples from nature. (Rev: BL 8/95; SLJ 5/95)

424 Wilson, Zachary. *A Circle in the Sky* (K–2). Illus. by JoAnn Aldinolfi. 2006, Children's Pr. LB $19.50 (978-0-531-12570-0). 32pp. A small girl's imaginative ideas serve as a framework for introducing four basic shapes. (Rev: BL 11/15/06)

Counting and Number Books

425 Adler, David A. *How Tall How Short How Far Away* (K–3). Illus. by Nancy Tobin. 1999, Holiday House $16.95 (978-0-8234-1375-1). Methods of measurement such as length, height, and distance are introduced in this attractive concept book. (Rev: BCCB 9/99; BL 4/1/99; HB 3/99; HBG 10/99; SLJ 4/99) [530.8]

426 Alda, Arlene. *Arlene Alda's 1 2 3* (PS–2). Illus. 1998, Tricycle $12.95 (978-1-883672-71-3). 24pp. Photographs of shapes that look like numbers, such as a 3 found in the curl of a banana peel, illustrate the numbers 1 to 10 and back again. (Rev: BL 11/1/98; HB 11/98; HBG 3/99; SLJ 12/98)

427 Anderson, Lena. *Tea for Ten* (PS). Trans. from Swedish by Elisabeth Kallick Dyssegaard. Illus. by author. 2000, R&S $14.00 (91-29-64557-3). This rhyming counting book features a number of delightful animals including Hedgehog, Duck, Teddy, Frog, Pig, and Elephant. (Rev: HBG 10/00; SLJ 5/00)

428 Andreasen, Dan. *The Baker's Dozen: A Counting Book* (PS). Illus. by author. 2007, Holt $16.95 (978-0-8050-7809-1). 32pp. Numbers of tasty treats are created by a lively baker in this well-illustrated counting book. (Rev: BL 7/07; SLJ 9/07)

429 Anno, Mitsumasa. *Anno's Counting Book: An Adventure in Imagination* (PS–K). Illus. by author. 1977, HarperCollins LB $17.89 (978-0-690-01288-0); paper $6.99 (978-0-06-443123-1). 32pp. An appealing book on numbers in which the same landscapes are used throughout; houses, birds, trees, and people are added as the seasons progress.

430 Appelt, Kathi. *Bat Jamboree* (PS–2). Illus. by Melissa Sweet. 1996, Morrow $15.89 (978-0-688-13883-7). A delightful counting book that focuses on the annual Bat Jamboree staged by some enterprising bats. (Rev: SLJ 9/96)

431 Appelt, Kathi. *Bats on Parade* (K–3). Illus. by Melissa Sweet. 1999, Morrow LB $15.89 (978-0-688-15666-4). 32pp. Basic multiplication is introduced in this story about a bat parade told with rhymes and peppy illustrations. (Rev: BL 4/1/99; HBG 10/99; SLJ 6/99)

432 Bailey, Linda. *Goodnight, Sweet Pig* (PS–2). Illus. by Josee Masse. 2007, Kids Can LB $16.95 (978-1-55337-844-0). Poor pig is trying to sleep, but her bed is crowded by noisy pigs arriving one after the other. (Rev: SLJ 6/07)

433 Baker, Keith. *Big Fat Hen* (PS–1). Illus. 1994, Harcourt $15.00 (978-0-15-292869-8). 32pp. A counting book that uses the rhyme "One, two, buckle my shoe" as a basis. (Rev: BL 4/1/94; SLJ 4/94)

434 Baker, Keith. *Quack and Count* (PS–1). Illus. 1999, Harcourt $14.00 (978-0-15-292858-2). 24pp. This book shows how to have fun with the number seven while counting ducks in various combinations to reach that number. (Rev: BL 10/15/99; HBG 3/00; SLJ 11/99)

435 Bang, Molly. *Ten, Nine, Eight* (PS–1). Illus. by author. 1983, Greenwillow $17.89 (978-0-688-00907-6); Morrow paper $6.99 (978-0-688-10480-1). 24pp. A counting-down book (from 10 to 1) involving an African American child going to bed. (Rev: BL 11/15/98)

436 Barry, Frances. *Duckie's Ducklings: A One-to-Ten Counting Book* (PS). Illus. 2005, Candlewick

$7.99 (978-0-7636-2514-6). 32pp. As Mother Duckie searches desperately for her 10 ducklings, one by one, members of her brood line up directly behind her. (Rev: BL 2/15/05)

437 Bates, Ivan. *Five Little Ducks* (PS). Illus. 2006, Scholastic $12.99 (978-0-439-74693-9). 24pp. Based on the classic children's song, this counting book follows a mother duck as she tries to round up her wandering ducklings. (Rev: BL 1/1–15/06; SLJ 2/06)

438 Beaton, Clare. *One Moose, Twenty Mice* (PS–1). Illus. 1999, Barefoot Books $14.95 (978-1-902283-37-1). 32pp. A counting book containing different animals from 1 to 20, but posing the question "Where's the cat?" (Rev: BCCB 7–8/99; BL 5/15/99; SLJ 6/99)

439 Berkes, Marianne. *Over in the Arctic: Where the Cold Winds Blow* (PS–1). Illus. by Jill Dubin. 2008, Dawn $16.95 (978-1-58469-109-9); paper $8.95 (978-1-58469-110-5). 32pp. This rhyming counting book based on "Over in the Meadow" showcases Arctic animals and their babies. (Rev: SLJ 9/08)

440 Berkes, Marianne. *Over in the Jungle: A Rainforest Rhyme* (PS–3). Illus. by Jeanette Canyon. 2007, Dawn $16.95 (978-1-58469-091-7); paper $8.95 (978-1-58469-092-4). Animals and plants of the rain forest fashioned from clay are featured in this fact-filled counting book. (Rev: SLJ 5/07)

441 Berry, Lynne. *Duck Dunks* (PS–K). Illus. by Hiroe Nakata. 2008, Holt $16.95 (978-0-8050-8128-2). 32pp. Five little ducks have fun at the seaside in this appealing companion to the counting book *Duck Skates* (2005). (Rev: BLO 7/29/08; SLJ 6/08)

442 Berry, Lynne. *Duck Skates* (PS–K). Illus. by Hiroe Nakata. 2005, Holt $15.95 (978-0-8050-7219-8). 32pp. Simple math concepts and numbers from 1 to 10 are integrated into this appealing picture-book story of five ducks enjoying a snowy day. (Rev: BL 10/1/05; SLJ 11/05)

443 Blackstone, Stella. *Cleo's Counting Book* (PS). Illus. by Caroline Mockford. 2003, Barefoot Books $15.99 (978-1-84148-207-1). Cleo the cat counts what she sees in the great outdoors. (Rev: HBG 10/03; SLJ 9/03)

444 Blackstone, Stella. *Counting Cockatoos* (PS–K). Illus. by Stephanie Bauer. 2006, Barefoot Books $16.99 (978-1-905236-31-2). Beautifully painted birds and other animals frolic on the pages of this book that counts from 1 to 12. (Rev: SLJ 5/06)

445 Boueri, Marijean. *Lebanon 1-2-3* (PS–2). Illus. by Mona Trad Dabaji. 2005, Publishing Works $16.95 (978-1-933002-03-3). 32pp. Set in Lebanon, this brightly illustrated, trilingual (Arabic, English, and French) counting book introduces the numbers from 1 to 10. (Rev: BL 11/1/05; SLJ 11/05) [513.2]

446 Bowen, Betsy. *Gathering: A Northwoods Counting Book* (K–4). Illus. by author. 1999, Houghton $16.00 (978-0-395-98133-7); paper $6.95 (978-0-395-98134-4). This counting book shows preparations taken in the North for a long, hard winter, starting in the spring with planting a garden. (Rev: HBG 3/00; SLJ 9/99)

447 Brooks, Alan. *Frogs Jump: A Counting Book* (PS–1). Illus. by Steven Kellogg. 1996, Scholastic $15.95 (978-0-590-45528-2). 48pp. Madcap animals introduce basic numbers through unusual activities. (Rev: BL 10/15/96; SLJ 10/96)

448 Burns, Marilyn. *How Many Feet? How Many Tails? A Book of Math Riddles* (1–2). Illus. by Lynn Adams. 1996, Scholastic paper $3.99 (978-0-590-67360-0). 32pp. During a walk with Grandpa, a child learns about numbers in this easy-to-read book. (Rev: BL 2/1/97)

449 Burton, Katherine. *One Gray Mouse* (PS). Illus. by Kim Fernandes. 1997, Kids Can $12.95 (978-1-55074-225-1). 24pp. Different numbers of animals are presented in this pleasant picture book that teaches the concepts of counting and colors. (Rev: BL 11/15/97; SLJ 12/97) [513.2]

450 Butler, John. *Ten in the Den* (PS–1). Illus. by author. 2005, Peachtree $15.95 (978-1-56145-344-3). Taking a cue from the rhyme "Ten in the Bed," 10 cuddly animals roll one by one down a hill and settle in for a nap. (Rev: SLJ 9/05)

451 Byrd, Lee Merrill. *Lover Boy / Juanito el cariñoso: A Bilingual Counting Book* (PS–2). Trans. by David Dorado Romo. Illus. by Francisco Delgado. 2006, Cinco Puntos $15.95 (978-0-938317-38-8). A little boy enjoys giving kisses to everyone he sees (whether they enjoy it or not) in this book that counts kisses in English and Spanish. (Rev: SLJ 6/06)

452 Cabrera, Jane. *Over in the Meadow* (PS). Illus. 2000, Holiday House $16.95 (978-0-8234-1490-1). 32pp. Readers learn numbers while naming animals and copying their actions in this fresh new treatment of the traditional counting song. (Rev: BCCB 5/00; BL 2/1/00; HBG 10/00; SLJ 4/00) [513.2]

453 Carle, Eric. *Roosters Off to See the World* (PS–K). Illus. by author. 1991, Picture Book $16.95 (978-0-88708-042-5). 28pp. In this counting book originally published in 1972, a rooster gathers together a group of animals to explore the world. Addition and subtraction are also introduced.

454 Catalanotto, Peter. *Daisy 1, 2, 3* (PS–1). Illus. by author. 2003, Simon & Schuster $15.95 (978-0-689-85457-6). Mrs. Tuttle, who has 20 Dalmatians — all called Daisy — in her obedience class, comes up with an ingenious way to tell them apart. (Rev: BL 11/1/03; HBG 4/04; SLJ 12/03)

455 Cato, Sheila. *Addition* (1–4). Illus. by Sami Sweeten. Series: A Question of Math Book. 1999, Carolrhoda LB $25.26 (978-1-57505-320-2). 32pp. Using cartoon characters and one addition problem per double-page spread, this book demonstrates the basic processes of addition. Also use *Subtraction* and *Counting and Numbers* (both 1999). (Rev: HBG 3/00; SLJ 11/99)

456 Cato, Sheila. *Division* (1–4). Illus. by Sami Sweeten. Series: A Question of Math Book. 1999, Carolrhoda LB $25.26 (978-1-57505-319-6). 32pp. Using a series of problems followed by clear answers and explanations, the principles of division are covered. Also use *Multiplication* (1999). (Rev: HBG 3/00; SLJ 11/99)

457 Cave, Kathryn. *One Child, One Seed: A South African Counting Book* (K–2). Photos by Gisele Wulfson. 2003, Holt $16.95 (978-0-8050-7204-4). 32pp. Cave interweaves basic counting skills with information about life in rural Natal in this innovative book that features beautiful photographs. (Rev: BL 5/1/03; HBG 10/03; SLJ 8/03) [513.2]

458 Chaconas, Dori. *One Little Mouse* (PS–K). Illus. by LeUyen Pham. 2002, Viking $15.99 (978-0-670-88947-1). 32pp. A little mouse searching for a new house visits other animals' homes before deciding that his own is best of all, in a rhyming text that teaches children to count up to 10 and back down again. (Rev: BL 9/1/02; HBG 10/02; SLJ 8/02)

459 Chae, In Seon. *How Do You Count a Dozen Ducklings?* (PS–1). Illus. by Seung Ha Rew. 2006, Albert Whitman $16.95 (978-0-8075-1718-5). 32pp. A mother duck uses various math strategies to keep track of her newly hatched ducklings. (Rev: BL 9/15/06; SLJ 9/06)

460 Chandra, Deborah. *Miss Mabel's Table* (PS–2). Illus. by Max Grover. 1994, Harcourt $14.95 (978-0-15-276712-9). 32pp. A counting book about Miss Mabel, her restaurant, and the food she serves. (Rev: BCCB 4/94; BL 3/15/94; SLJ 6/94)

461 Cheng, Andrea. *Grandfather Counts* (PS–3). Illus. by Ange Zhang. 2000, Lee & Low $15.95 (978-1-58430-010-6). 32pp. In this unusual counting book, Helen, a little Chinese-American girl, and her grandfather count the cars on a passing train in both English and Chinese. (Rev: BL 12/15/00; HBG 3/01; SLJ 11/00)

462 Chorao, Kay. *Number One Number Fun* (PS–1). Illus. 1995, Holiday House LB $15.95 (978-0-8234-1142-9). 32pp. Simple arithmetic is highlighted through a series of clever rhymes involving addition and subtraction. (Rev: BCCB 2/95; BL 2/15/95; SLJ 3/95)

463 Christelow, Eileen. *Five Little Monkeys Go Shopping* (PS–2). Illus. by author. 2007, Clarion $16.00 (978-0-618-82161-7). 32pp. Will Mom bring the right number of monkeys home from the back-to-school sale? (Rev: SLJ 10/07)

464 Christelow, Eileen, retel. *Five Little Monkeys Jumping on the Bed* (PS–K). Illus. by Eileen Christelow. 1989, Ticknor $15.00 (978-0-89919-769-2); paper $5.95 (978-0-395-55701-3). An exuberant rendition of the favorite nursery rhyme. (Rev: BL 6/1/89)

465 Christelow, Eileen. *Five Little Monkeys Sitting in a Tree* (PS–K). Illus. 1991, Houghton $16.00 (978-0-395-54434-1). 32pp. The numbers 1 through 5 are taught through the antics of five little monkeys. A sequel is: *Don't Wake Up Mama!* (1992). (Rev: BL 5/15/91; SLJ 8/91)

466 Clark, Emma Chichester. *Mimi's Book of Counting* (PS). Illus. by author. Series: A Mimi Book. 2003, Charlesbridge $9.95 (978-1-57091-573-4). In this appealing counting book, Mimi the monkey and her visiting grandmother find everyday household items that they count from 1 to 10. (Rev: HBG 4/04; SLJ 11/03)

467 Clements, Andrew. *A Million Dots*. 48th ed. (K–3). Illus. by Mike Reed. 2006, Simon & Schuster $16.95 (978-0-689-85824-6). 48pp. The million dots on these pages will give young readers a feeling for the magnitude of the number, enhanced by the numerical facts/trivia scattered through the book. (Rev: BL 6/1–15/06; SLJ 7/06) [513.2]

468 Coats, Lucy. *Down in the Daisies: A Baby Animal Counting Book* (PS–1). Illus. by Emily Bolam. 2003, Orion $16.95 (978-1-85881-513-8). This beautifully illustrated counting book spotlights baby animals and their mothers in all kinds of weather. (Rev: SLJ 10/03)

469 Cohn, Scotti. *One Wolf Howls* (PS–2). Illus. by Susan Detwiler. 2009, Sylvan Dell $16.95 (978-1-934359-92-1); paper $8.95 (978-1-60718-037-1). 32pp. This rhyming picture book combines counting — by month and number of wolves — up to 12 with basic information about wolves' lives, behavior, and endangered status. (Rev: BL 4/1/09; SLJ 6/09) [599.773]

470 Coleman, Michael. *One, Two, Three, Oops!* (PS–K). Illus. by Gwyneth Williamson. 1999, Little Tiger $14.95 (978-1-888444-45-2). 32pp. When Mr. Rabbit begins to count his children, he has to work out which ones have been counted and which haven't. (Rev: BL 1/1–15/99; HBG 10/99; SLJ 3/99)

471 Cotten, Cynthia. *At the Edge of the Woods: A Counting Book* (PS–2). Illus. by Reg Cartwright. 2002, Holt $16.95 (978-0-8050-6354-7). 32pp. Gentle verse and bright, primitive paintings are used in this incremental tale of a forest day, in which 1 chipmunk, 2 young deer, and then more and more animals appear. (Rev: BL 12/1/02; HBG 3/03; SLJ 6/03)

472 Crews, Donald. *Ten Black Dots* (PS–K). Illus. by author. 1986, Greenwillow $17.89 (978-0-688-06068-8). 32pp. Dots form an integral part of this counting book, originally published in 1968, such as "five dots make buttons on a coat." (Rev: BL 3/1/86; SLJ 5/86)

473 Cronin, Doreen. *Click, Clack, Splish, Splash: A Counting Adventure* (PS). Illus. by Betsy Lewin. 2006, Simon & Schuster $12.95 (978-0-689-87716-2). 24pp. A cumulative counting book about farm animals sneaking off for a secret fishing trip. (Rev: BL 1/1–15/06; SLJ 1/06)

474 *Curious George Learns to Count from 1 to 100* (PS–2). Illus. by Anna Grossnickle Hines. 2005, Houghton $16.00 (978-0-618-47602-2). 64pp. As part of his town's centennial celebration, the inquisitive little monkey learns how to count to 100. (Rev: BL 9/15/05; SLJ 10/05)

475 Cuyler, Margery. *100th Day Worries* (K–2). Illus. by Arthur Howard. 2000, Simon & Schuster $16.00 (978-0-689-82979-6). 32pp. In this counting book, 1st-grader Jessica is asked to bring 100 objects to celebrate the 100th day of school. (Rev: BCCB 2/00; BL 11/1/99; HBG 10/00; SLJ 1/00)

476 Dahl, Michael. *Eggs and Legs: Counting by Twos* (PS–2). Illus. by Todd Ouren. Series: Know Your Numbers. 2005, Picture Window LB $25.26

(978-1-4048-0945-1). 24pp. Counting by twos to 20 is the focus of a lively story with bright cartoons and numerals hidden within the text and illustrations. Also use *Pie for Piglets: Counting by Twos* (2005). (Rev: SLJ 6/05)

477 Dahl, Michael. *One Big Building: A Counting Book About Construction* (PS–K). Illus. by Todd Ouren. Series: Know Your Numbers. 2004, Picture Window LB $25.26 (978-1-4048-0580-4). 24pp. "Fun Facts" about construction are included along with numbers from 1 to 12 — "one big plan" and "twelve stories tall." Also use *From the Garden: A Counting Book About Growing Food* (2004). (Rev: BL 4/1/04; SLJ 6/04) [513.2]

478 Dahl, Michael. *Pie for Piglets: Counting by Twos* (PS–K). Illus. Series: Know Your Numbers. 2005, Picture Window LB $25.26 (978-1-4048-0943-7). 24pp. An entertaining introduction to counting by 2, with numbers hidden within the text and illustrations. Other titles in this series include *Hands Down: Counting by Fives* and *Lots of Ladybugs! Counting by Fives* (2005). (Rev: SLJ 6/05)

479 Delessert, Etienne. *Hungry for Numbers* (PS–2). Illus. by author. 2006, Creative Editions $18.95 (978-1-56846-198-4). 32pp. Ten hungry creatures eat delicious fruit — from 1 banana to 10 blueberries. (Rev: SLJ 11/06)

480 Demarest, Chris L. *Smokejumpers One to Ten* (PS–1). Illus. 2002, Simon & Schuster $17.00 (978-0-689-84120-0). 32pp. A counting book featuring courageous and hardworking parachuting fire fighters. (Rev: BCCB 7–8/02; BL 7/02; HBG 10/02; SLJ 7/02) [634.9]

481 Denise, Anika. *Pigs Love Potatoes* (PS–K). Illus. by Christopher Denise. 2007, Philomel $15.99 (978-0-399-24036-2). 40pp. Mama enlists the help of her family of pigs to wash, peel and cook potatoes in this charming counting book. (Rev: BCCB 9/07; BL 6/1–15/07; SLJ 7/07)

482 De Regniers, Beatrice S. *So Many Cats!* (PS–1). Illus. by Ellen Weiss. 1985, Houghton paper $6.95 (978-0-89919-700-5). 32pp. One by one, new cats arrive at the narrator's house, until there are 12. (Rev: BL 1/1/86; HB 11/85; SLJ 1/86)

483 deRubertis, Barbara. *A Collection for Kate* (1–2). Illus. by Gioia Fiammenghi. Series: Math Matters. 1999, Kane paper $4.95 (978-1-57565-089-0). 32pp. In this easy reader, Kate adds up her classmates' collections for a "collection week" at school and discovers that, when she combines her own small collections, she isn't far behind them after all. (Rev: BL 12/1/99; SLJ 1/00)

484 deRubertis, Barbara. *Count on Pablo* (1–2). Illus. by Rebecca Thornburgh. Series: Math Matters. 1999, Kane paper $4.95 (978-1-57565-090-6). 32pp. In this easy reader, a boy helps his grandmother gather, count, group, and package vegetables for market. (Rev: BL 12/1/99; SLJ 1/00)

485 deRubertis, Barbara. *Lulu's Lemonade* (1–3). Illus. by Paige Billin-Frye. Series: Math Matters. 2000, Kane paper $4.95 (978-1-57565-093-7). 32pp. In this easy-reader, Mattie and Martin learn measurements like teaspoons, cups, pints, etc., as they prepare a gallon of lemonade. (Rev: SLJ 6/00)

486 Donaldson, Julia. *One Ted Falls Out of Bed* (PS–2). Illus. by Anna Currey. 2006, Holt $15.95 (978-0-8050-7787-2). 32pp. An impressive assortment of toys and three mice come to the aid of a teddy bear that's fallen out of his owner's bed, giving the reader the opportunity to count up to 10 and down again. (Rev: BL 6/1–15/06; SLJ 6/06)

487 Durango, Julia. *Cha-Cha-Chimps* (PS–K). Illus. by Eleanor Taylor. 2006, Simon & Schuster $15.95 (978-0-689-86456-8). 32pp. Ten little chimps go to Mambo Jamba's for a lively dance session in this rhythmic counting book. (Rev: BL 1/1–15/06; SLJ 2/06)

488 Edwards, Pamela Duncan. *Roar! A Noisy Counting Book* (PS–2). Illus. by Henry Cole. 2000, HarperCollins LB $15.89 (978-0-06-028385-8). 32pp. A boisterous counting book involving animals, a jungle habitat, and lots of lions roaring. (Rev: BL 8/00; HBG 10/00; SLJ 6/00)

489 Ehlert, Lois. *Fish Eyes: A Book You Can Count On* (PS–K). Illus. 1990, Harcourt $14.95 (978-0-15-228050-5). 32pp. Compelling color and design introduce this counting book. (Rev: BL 3/1/90*; SLJ 5/90)

490 Ehrhardt, Karen. *This Jazz Man* (PS–2). Illus. by R. G. Roth. 2006, Harcourt $16.00 (978-0-15-205307-9). 32pp. The well-known song "This Old Man" is presented here with a lively jazz theme, featuring different jazz musicians as children rhyme and count to nine. (Rev: BL 11/15/06; SLJ 12/06)

491 Elliott, David. *One Little Chicken: A Counting Book* (PS–K). Illus. by Ethan Long. 2007, Holiday $16.95 (978-0-8234-1983-8). 24pp. Bouncy rhyming text and expressive illustrations show chickens flapping their wings to different dance styles: "Three chickens practice their ballet. Four chickens swing the night away." (Rev: BL 11/15/07; SLJ 12/07)

492 Emberley, Rebecca. *My Numbers / Mis Numeros* (PS). 2000, Little, Brown $5.95 (978-0-316-23350-7). 20pp. This counting board book introduces the numbers in both English and Spanish. (Rev: BCCB 12/00*; HBG 3/01; SLJ 9/00)

493 Evans, Lezlie. *Can You Count Ten Toes? Count to 10 in 10 Different Languages* (PS–3). Illus. by Denis Roche. 1999, Houghton $16.00 (978-0-395-90499-2). 32pp. Using double-page spreads, children from several countries count different objects from 1 to 10 in their native language. (Rev: BL 3/15/99; HBG 10/99; SLJ 6/99) [513.2]

494 Ewing, Susan. *Ten Rowdy Ravens* (PS–6). Illus. by Evon Zerbetz. 2005, Alaska Northwest $15.95 (978-0-88240-606-0); paper $8.95 (978-0-88240-610-7). The mischievous nature of ravens is highlighted in this entertaining counting book. (Rev: SLJ 1/06)

495 Falconer, Ian. *Olivia Counts* (PS). Illus. 2002, Simon & Schuster $6.99 (978-0-689-85087-5). 12pp. A simple board book featuring Olivia the pig with 1 beach ball, 2 bows, and so forth up to 10. (Rev: BCCB 6/02; BL 7/02; HBG 10/02; SLJ 6/02)

496 Falwell, Cathryn. *Feast for 10* (PS–K). Illus. 1993, Houghton $16.00 (978-0-395-62037-3). 32pp. Using the common experience of shopping and preparing dinner, this book, which features an African American family, teaches youngsters the numbers from 1 to 10. (Rev: BCCB 6/93; BL 6/1–15/93; SLJ 6/93)

497 Falwell, Cathryn. *Turtle Splash! Countdown at the Pond* (PS–K). Illus. 2001, Greenwillow LB $17.89 (978-0-06-029463-2). 32pp. A rhythmic countdown to bedtime as one turtle after another — for a total of 10 — splashes into a lake as evening comes closer and animals arrive at the water's edge. (Rev: BL 8/01; HBG 3/02; SLJ 9/01*)

498 Fleming, Denise. *Count!* (PS–K). Illus. by author. 1992, Holt $16.95 (978-0-8050-1595-9). Brightly colored animals and birds are used to introduce basic numbers. (Rev: SLJ 3/92)

499 Franco, Betsy. *Birdsongs* (PS–2). Illus. by Steve Jenkins. 2007, Simon & Schuster $16.99 (978-0-689-87777-3). 32pp. Nature lesson and counting book are combined in this beautifully illustrated collection of avian collages. (Rev: BL 1/1–15/07; SLJ 1/07)

500 French, Vivian. *One Ballerina Two* (PS–K). Illus. by Jan Ormerod. 1991, Lothrop $13.95 (978-0-688-10333-0). 32pp. The focus is on ballet in this simple counting book. (Rev: BCCB 12/91; BL 12/1/91; SLJ 12/91)

501 Friedman, Aileen. *The King's Commissioners* (K–2). Illus. by Susan Guevara. 1995, Scholastic $14.95 (978-0-590-48989-8). 40pp. In this sophisticated counting book, a king decides to take an inventory of his employees. (Rev: BCCB 2/95; BL 2/15/95; SLJ 3/95)

502 Fromental, Jean-Luc, and Joëlle Jolivet. *365 Penguins* (PS–2). Illus. 2006, Abrams $17.95 (978-0-8109-4460-2). 32pp. A family's problems — and mathematical calculations — multiply when an additional penguin arrives every day for a year; a lively, oversize picture book. (Rev: BL 1/1–15/07; SLJ 12/06)

503 Fuller, Jill. *Springtime Addition* (PS–K). Series: Rookie Read-about Math. 2004, Children's Pr. LB $20.50 (978-0-516-24422-8). 31pp. A simple, colorful, and interesting introduction to addition featuring outdoor attractions. Also use *Toy Box Subtraction* and *A Garden Full of Sizes* (both 2004). (Rev: SLJ 3/05) [513.2]

504 Garland, Michael. *How Many Mice?* (PS–2). Illus. by author. 2007, Dutton $15.99 (978-0-525-47833-1). 32pp. Prompted by questions in the text, children will count and seek hidden clues in this appealing story about mice dodging a fox, an owl, and other dangers as they carry food back to their home. (Rev: BL 6/1–15/07; SLJ 6/07)

505 Gayzagian, Doris K. *One White Wishing Stone: A Beach Day Counting Book* (PS). Illus. by Kristina Swarner. 2006, National Geographic $16.95 (978-0-7922-5110-1). In this gentle counting book, a little girl spending a day at the beach with her mother counts off the wondrous treasures she discovers for her sandcastle. (Rev: SLJ 11/06)

506 Gershator, Phillis. *Zoo Day ¡Olé! A Counting Book* (PS–1). Illus. by Santiago Cohen. 2009, Marshall Cavendish $17.99 (978 0 7614 5462 5). 32pp. Combining counting, Spanish words, and animals, this is an enjoyable trip to the zoo. (Rev: BL 5/1/09; SLJ 4/09) [513.2]

507 Giganti, Paul. *Each Orange Had Eight Slices* (PS–3). Illus. by Donald Crews. 1992, Greenwillow $17.89 (978-0-688-10429-0). This well-designed book challenges young readers to think analytically about what it portrays. (Rev: BCCB 4/92; BL 3/15/92; SLJ 3/92) [513.5]

508 Giganti, Paul. *How Many Blue Birds Flew Away? A Counting Book with a Difference* (PS–K). Illus. by Donald Crews. 2005, Greenwillow LB $16.89 (978-0-06-000763-8). 32pp. Attractive colorful illustrations pose addition and subtraction puzzles. (Rev: BL 10/15/05; SLJ 9/05)

509 Giganti, Paul. *How Many Snails?* (PS–K). Illus. by Donald Crews. 1988, Greenwillow $15.89 (978-0-688-06370-2). 24pp. A counting book that focuses on visual discrimination as well as numbers. (Rev: BL 8/88; SLJ 3/89)

510 Gillham, Bill. *How Many Sharks in the Bath?* (PS). Illus. by Christyan Fox. 2005, Frances Lincoln $14.95 (978-1-84507-288-9). The zany animal antics in this colorful counting book give readers an opportunity to practice numbers from 0 to 10. (Rev: SLJ 1/06)

511 Ginkel, Anne. *I've Got an Elephant* (PS–2). Illus. by Janie Bynum. 2006, Peachtree $16.95 (978-1-56145-373-3). 32pp. A little girl's elephant gets lonely when she goes to school and invites an elephant friend over, and then another, and then another — until this rhyming counting book reaches 10. (Rev: BL 9/15/06; SLJ 9/06)

512 Giogas, Valarie. *In My Backyard* (PS–3). Illus. by Katherine Zecca. 2007, Sylvan Dell $15.95 (978-0-9777423-1-8); paper $8.95 (978-1-9343591-7-4). 32pp. As well as counting to 10, readers become familiar with the names of 10 animals and learn facts about them and about how to deal with injured animals. (Rev: LMC 11/07; SLJ 11/07) [591.5]

513 Girnis, Meg. *1, 2, 3 for You and Me* (PS–1). Photos by Shirley Leamon Green. 2001, Whitman LB $16.99 (978-0-8075-6107-2). Smiling children with Down's syndrome are shown holding toys and everyday objects in this simple counting book. (Rev: HBG 10/01; SLJ 7/01)

514 Grossman, Virginia. *Ten Little Rabbits* (PS–1). Illus. by Sylvia Long. 1991, Chronicle $13.95 (978-0-87701-552-9). 32pp. This counting book of rabbits dressed as Indians introduces the cultures of various American tribes. (Rev: BL 4/1/91; SLJ 6/91)

515 Gunzi, Christiane. *My Very First Look at Numbers* (PS–K). Illus. by Steve Gorton. Series: My Very First Look. 2001, Two-Can $8.95 (978-1-58728-237-9); paper $5.95 (978-1-58728-277-5). 24pp. Photographs of everyday objects are used to teach preschoolers about numbers. (Rev: BL 2/15/02; HBG 10/02; SLJ 2/02) [513.2]

516 Gustafson, Scott. *Scott Gustafson's Animal Orchestra: A Counting Book* (K–3). Illus. 1995, Greenwich Workshop $14.95 (978-0-86713-030-0). 32pp. An assembly of animals in tuxedo splendor. (Rev: BL 1/15/89; SLJ 2/89)

517 Guy, Ginger F. *¡Fiesta!* (PS–2). Illus. by Rene King Moreno. 1996, Greenwillow $16.99 (978-0-688-14331-2). Numbers are introduced in English and Spanish in this book about collecting articles to celebrate a Mexican fiesta. (Rev: SLJ 9/96)

518 Hague, Kathleen. *Ten Little Bears* (PS–K). Illus. by Michael Hague. 1999, Morrow LB $15.89 (978-0-688-16732-5). 24pp. In this counting book, 10 little bears go out to play, but one by one they become separated. (Rev: BL 5/15/99; HBG 10/99)

519 Halls, Kelly M. *I Bought a Baby Chicken* (PS–1). Illus. by Karen Stormer Brooks. 2000, Boyds Mills $14.95 (978-1-56397-800-5). 32pp. In this comical counting book, a young girl and her family go out to buy some baby chickens. (Rev: BL 4/1/00; HBG 10/00; SLJ 7/00)

520 Harris, Trudy. *Jenny Found a Penny* (K–3). Illus. by John Hovell. Series: Math Is Fun! 2007, Millbrook LB $23.93 (978-0-8225-6725-7). 32pp. Jenny's story of earning, saving, and spending is interwoven with a lesson on counting money. (Rev: SLJ 10/07)

521 Harris, Trudy. *100 Days of School* (PS–K). Illus. by Beth Griffis Johnson. 1999, Millbrook LB $22.90 (978-0-7613-1271-0). 32pp. Various combinations of familiar objects are used to reach the number 100 in this innovative counting book. (Rev: BL 11/15/99; HBG 3/00; SLJ 11/99)

522 Harris, Trudy. *20 Hungry Piggies: A Number Book* (PS–2). Illus. by Andrew N. Harris. 2007, Millbrook LB $15.95 (978-0-8225-6370-9). Twenty little piggies unwittingly foil the plans of a hungry wolf in this funny take on the original toe-counting nursery game. (Rev: SLJ 5/07)

523 Harshman, Marc. *Only One* (PS–3). Illus. by Barbara Garrison. 1993, Dutton $15.99 (978-0-525-65116-1). 32pp. This counting book shows that a collective noun consists of several parts, for example, nine players make a baseball team. (Rev: BL 5/15/93)

524 Helakoski, Leslie. *The Smushy Bus* (K–2). Illus. by Sal Murdocca. 2002, Millbrook LB $22.90 (978-0-7613-1398-4). 32pp. Mr. Mathers, the clever bus driver, manages to fit 76 kids into a bus with four seats in this adventure combined with an early introduction to mathematical concepts. (Rev: BL 10/15/02; HBG 3/03; SLJ 11/02)

525 Helman, Andrea. *1, 2, 3 Moose: A Pacific Northwest Counting Book* (PS–2). Illus. by Art Wolfe. 1996, Sasquatch $15.95 (978-1-57061-078-3). 32pp. A 1-to-20 counting book that employs the flora and fauna of the Pacific Northwest. (Rev: BL 11/1/96; SLJ 1/97) [428.1]

526 Hoban, Tana. *Count and See* (PS–K). Illus. 1972, Macmillan LB $17.00 (978-0-02-744800-9). 40pp. Beginning with numbers 1 to 15, then going to 100; clear photographs of familiar objects are easily recognized and fun to count.

527 Hoban, Tana. *Let's Count* (PS–1). Illus. 1999, Greenwillow $16.99 (978-0-688-16008-1). 40pp. Amazing photos are used in this counting book to highlight objects from 1 to 15, then by tens to 50, and finally to 100. (Rev: BL 9/15/99; HBG 3/00; SLJ 9/99) [513.2]

528 Holland, Cheri. *Maccabee Jamboree: A Hanukkah Countdown* (PS). Illus. by Rosalyn Schanzer. 1998, Kar-Ben paper $4.95 (978-1-58013-019-6). Eight Maccabees play different Hanukkah games as one by one they disappear in this counting book. (Rev: SLJ 10/98)

529 Holub, Joan. *Apple Countdown* (PS–2). Illus. by Jan Smith. 2009, Albert Whitman $16.99 (978-0-8075-0398-0). 32pp. This easy reading counting book rhymes its way across the pages. (Rev: SLJ 6/09)

530 Hughes, Shirley. *Alfie's 1-2-3* (PS). Illus. 2000, Lothrop $15.95 (978-0-688-17705-8). 32pp. Playful activities of a preschooler's day form the framework of this simple counting book. (Rev: BL 4/15/00; HBG 10/00; SLJ 5/00)

531 Hulme, Joy N. *Sea Squares* (K–3). Illus. by Carol Schwartz. 1993, Hyperion paper $5.95 (978-1-56282-520-1). 32pp. Children can visualize multiplication in this picture book with an underwater theme. (Rev: BL 12/1/91; SLJ 1/92) [513.5]

532 Hutchins, Pat. *One Hunter* (PS–2). Illus. by author. 1982, Morrow paper $6.99 (978-0-688-06522-5). 24pp. A counting book with a hunter and hidden African animals.

533 Hutchins, Pat. *Ten Red Apples* (PS–2). Illus. 2000, Greenwillow $17.99 (978-0-688-16797-4). 32pp. A charming counting book about a farmer and his apple crop. (Rev: BL 5/1/00; HBG 10/00; SLJ 5/00)

534 Jay, Alison. *1 2 3: A Child's First Counting Book* (K–2). Illus. by author. 2007, Dutton $15.99 (978-0-525-47836-2). 40pp. A little girl falls asleep with a book of fairy tales open in her hands and dreams she appears in 10 fairy-tale scenes in this picture book with beautiful illustrations. (Rev: BL 9/15/07; SLJ 9/07)

535 Jennings, Linda. *Nine Naughty Kittens* (PS–1). Illus. by Caroline Jayne Church. 1999, Little Tiger $14.95 (978-1-888444-62-9). A flap book that is also a counting book about kittens. (Rev: BCCB 1/00; HBG 3/00; SLJ 2/00)

536 Jocelyn, Marthe. *One Some Many* (PS–K). Illus. by Tom Slaughter. 2004, Tundra $11.95 (978-0-88776-675-6). A counting book in rhyme that creatively introduces the differences between "many," "few," "some," "none," and "more." (Rev: SLJ 6/04)

537 Katz, Karen. *Mommy Hugs* (PS). Illus. 2006, Simon & Schuster $12.95 (978-0-689-87772-8). 32pp. This appealing counting book deals in the hugs that a baby gets throughout the day. (Rev: BL 2/15/06; SLJ 4/06)

538 Katz, Karen. *Ten Tiny Babies* (PS). Illus. by author. 2008, Simon & Schuster $14.99 (978-1-4169-3546-9). 32pp. This rhythmic and colorful counting book follows 10 babies through simple activities, ending with a bath and bedtime. (Rev: BL 7/08; SLJ 9/08)

539 Keller, Laurie. *Grandpa Gazillion's Number Yard* (PS–K). Illus. 2005, Holt $16.95 (978-0-8050-6282-3). 32pp. Junkyard owner Grandpa Gazillion sees numbers in very different ways, introducing his concepts for using 1 through 20. (Rev: BL 11/15/05; SLJ 11/05)

540 Kellogg, Steven. *Give the Dog a Bone* (K–3). Illus. 2000, North-South LB $15.88 (978-1-58717-002-7). 40pp. A riotous counting book that involves a grand total of 250 dogs (and 1 chicken). (Rev: BL 12/1/00; HBG 3/01; SLJ 11/00)

541 Kelly, Mij. *One More Sheep* (PS–2). Illus. by Russell Ayto. 2006, Peachtree $16.95 (978-1-56145-378-8). 30pp. Sam always falls asleep when he tries to count his herd of 10 sheep, and one night when a wolf (dressed in sheep's clothing) tries to sneak in, the sheep must work hard to keep Sam awake so he can count to 11. (Rev: BL 11/15/06; SLJ 10/06)

542 Kimmelman, Leslie. *How Do I Love You?* (PS–1). Illus. by Lisa McCue. 2005, HarperCollins $14.99 (978-0-06-001200-7). In this counting-book celebration of parental love, an adult crocodile lists 20 reasons why it loves its child. (Rev: SLJ 2/06)

543 Kitamura, Satoshi. *When Sheep Cannot Sleep: The Counting Book* (PS–1). Illus. by author. 1986, Farrar paper $5.95 (978-0-374-48359-3). 32pp. Woolly the sheep can't sleep so he takes a walk — chasing 1 butterfly, watching 2 ladybugs, and so on. (Rev: BL 10/1/86; HB 11/86; SLJ 12/86)

544 Koller, Jackie F. *Seven Spunky Monkeys* (K–2). Illus. by Lynn Munsinger. 2005, Harcourt $16.00 (978-0-15-202519-9). Over a week, a group of seven monkeys dwindles down to none as each in turn falls in love and runs off to get married; an entertaining companion to *One Monkey Too Many* (1999). (Rev: SLJ 9/05)

545 Koontz, Robin. *Up All Night Counting: A Pop-up Book* (PS–K). Illus. by author. 2006, Simon & Schuster $10.95 (978-1-4169-0706-0). This colorful 1-to-10 counting book with pop-ups and flaps features nighttime creatures such as bats, owls, flying squirrels, raccoons, crickets, and foxes. (Rev: SLJ 8/06)

546 Kroll, Virginia. *Equal Shmequal* (K–3). Illus. by Philomena O'Neill. 2005, Charlesbridge paper $6.95 (978-1-57091-892-6). 32pp. The animals want to play tug-of-war like the children in the playground but have trouble working out how to divide into equal teams. (Rev: SLJ 9/05)

547 Kusugak, Michael A. *My Arctic 1, 2, 3* (K–3). Illus. by Vladyana Krykorka. 1996, Annick $16.95 (978-1-55037-505-3); paper $6.95 (978-1-55037-504-6). Using Arctic animals as a focus, this counting book presents the numbers 1 through 10, 20, 100, and a million in both English and the Inuit language. (Rev: SLJ 5/97)

548 Law, Diane. *Come Out and Play* (PS). 2006, North-South $9.95 (978-0-7358-2060-9). 24pp. A counting book that incorporates multiculturalism through language (each number is shown in English,

Spanish, German, French, and Chinese) and through the characters (the children are of different ethnicities and live in different settings). (Rev: BL 5/1/06; SLJ 7/06)

549 Lee, Huy Voun. *1, 2, 3, Go!* (PS–1). Illus. 2001, Holt $16.00 (978-0-8050-6205-2). 32pp. This introduction to Chinese numbers gives the Chinese characters for 1 to 10 and for the words used to illustrate each number. (Rev: BL 2/1/01; HBG 10/01) [495.1]

550 Leedy, Loreen. *Fraction Action* (K–2). Illus. 1994, Holiday House LB $17.95 (978-0-8234-1109-2). 32pp. How to divide various objects and the meaning of fractions are explored in this simple, colorful arithmetic book. (Rev: BCCB 3/94; BL 3/15/94) [513.2]

551 Leedy, Loreen. *Missing Math: A Number Mystery* (K–2). Illus. by author. 2008, Marshall Cavendish $16.99 (978-0-7614-5385-7). 32pp. Ack! How does a town cope when it's deprived of all its numbers? (Rev: BL 4/1/08; LMC 8/08; SLJ 6/08)

552 Leedy, Loreen. *Subtraction Action* (1–3). Illus. 2000, Holiday House $17.95 (978-0-8234-1454-3). 32pp. In seven short chapters, Miss Prime and her class learn how to do subtraction. (Rev: BL 9/15/00; HBG 3/01; SLJ 9/00)

553 Le Sieg, Theo. *Wacky Wednesday* (PS–1). Illus. by George Booth. 1974, Random $11.99 (978-0-394-92912-5). 48pp. In this counting book, every page has a number of things out of place.

554 Lessac, Frane. *Island Counting 123* (PS–K). Illus. 2005, Candlewick $12.99 (978-0-7636-1960-2). 24pp. Set in the Caribbean, this counting book features warm island scenes. (Rev: BL 5/15/05)

555 Lesser, Carolyn. *Spots: Counting Creatures from Sky to Sea* (PS–1). Illus. by Laura Regan. 1999, Harcourt $16.00 (978-0-15-200666-2). 32pp. Spotted creatures such as jaguars, butterflies, and squids are used to introduce numbers from 1 to 10. (Rev: BCCB 5/99; BL 3/15/99; HBG 10/99; SLJ 4/99) [513.2]

556 Ljungkvist, Laura. *Follow the Line* (K–2). Illus. by author. 2006, Viking $16.99 (978-0-670-06049-8). The line leads through all sorts of settings, encouraging children to count objects ranging from fire hydrants to babies sleeping in a village. (Rev: SLJ 5/06)

557 Lodge, Bernard. *How Scary!* (PS–K). Illus. 2001, Houghton $15.00 (978-0-618-11547-1). 32pp. One growling giant, 2 dreadful dragons, and so on up to 10 rattling robots all add up to a satisfying Halloween counting book. (Rev: BL 9/1/01; HBG 3/02; SLJ 9/01)

558 Long, Lynette. *Dealing with Addition* (1–3). 1998, Charlesbridge LB $15.95 (978-0-88106-269-4); paper $6.95 (978-0-88106-270-0). Playing cards are used to teach addition in this entertaining book. (Rev: HBG 10/98; SLJ 9/98)

559 Maccarone, Grace. *Monster Math Picnic* (1). Illus. by Margaret A. Hartelius. Series: Hello Math Reader. 1998, Scholastic paper $3.99 (978-0-590-37127-8). 24pp. Using 10 monsters as subjects, this simple math book explores the various combinations of numbers that add up to 10. (Rev: BL 5/1/98; SLJ 7/98)

560 Maccarone, Grace. *Monster Money* (PS–1). Illus. by Margaret A. Hartelius. Series: Hello Reader! 1998, Scholastic paper $3.99 (978-0-590-12007-4). In this math concept book, several monsters learn how to count money when they go to a pet store to a buy a pet. (Rev: SLJ 2/99)

561 MacDonald, Suse. *Fish, Swish! Splash, Dash! Counting Round and Round* (PS–2). Illus. by author. 2007, Simon & Schuster $8.99 (978-1-4169-3605-3). Young children will enjoy counting 10 colorful fish, then turning the book and counting back down to 1. Die-cut pages contribute to the entertaining design. (Rev: SLJ 6/07)

562 McFarland, Lyn Rossiter. *Mouse Went Out to Get a Snack* (PS–1). Illus. by Jim McFarland. 2005, Farrar $16.00 (978-0-374-37672-7). One piece of cheese, 2 plump plums — these are just the first of the luxury items the mouse hopes to get back to his hole. (Rev: LMC 8/05*; SLJ 3/05)

563 McGrath, Barbara Barbieri. *The Baseball Counting Book* (PS–1). Illus. by Brian Shaw. 1999, Charlesbridge $15.95 (978-0-88106-332-5); paper $6.95 (978-0-88106-333-2). 32pp. Two Little League teams compete while the reader learns numbers from zero to 20. (Rev: BL 2/15/99; HBG 10/99; SLJ 3/99) [513.2]

564 McGrath, Barbara Barbieri. *The Cheerios Counting Book* (PS). Illus. by Rob Bolster and Frank Mazzola. 1998, Scholastic $10.95 (978-0-590-00321-6). 32pp. Using round cereal bits as objects to count, this book explains the numbers 1 to 10 and then groups of 10 up to 100. (Rev: BL 10/1/98; HBG 3/99; SLJ 9/98)

565 McMillan, Bruce. *Jelly Beans for Sale* (PS–2). Illus. 1996, Scholastic $15.95 (978-0-590-86584-5). 32pp. Counting and basic math concepts are illustrated in this book about selling candies. (Rev: BCCB 10/96; BL 9/1/96; SLJ 10/96) [332.4]

566 McMillan, Bruce. *One, Two, One Pair!* (PS) Illus. 1996, Scholastic paper $4.99 (978-0-590-46082-8). 32pp. The concept of pairs is explored with sharp color images. (Rev: BCCB 2/91; BL 1/15/91; SLJ 2/91) [515.5]

567 Mannis, Celeste Davidson. *One Leaf Rides the Wind: Counting in a Japanese Garden* (PS–2). Illus. by Susan Kathleen Hartung. 2002, Viking $15.99 (978-0-670-03525-0). A Japanese girl counts the plants and objects in a traditional garden in this elegant book that also introduces haiku and the tea ceremony. (Rev: HBG 3/03; SLJ 10/02)

568 Mariconda, Barbara. *Sort It Out!* (PS–2). Illus. by Sherry Rogers. 2008, Sylvan Dell $16.95 (978-1-934359-11-2); paper $8.95 (978-1-934359-32-7). 32pp. Packrat enjoys sorting his belongings in a variety of ways in this rhyming introduction to basic set theory. (Rev: SLJ 9/08)

569 Markle, Sandra. *How Many Baby Pandas?* (K–3). Illus. 2009, Walker $15.99 (978-0-8027-9783-4). 24pp. Readers can count pandas as they learn about young pandas' diet, physical character-

istics, and behavior. (Rev: BCCB 5/09; BL 4/1/09; SLJ 4/09) [599.789]

570 Marzollo, Jean. *Ten Cats Have Hats: A Counting Book* (PS–K). Illus. by David McPhail. 1994, Scholastic $6.95 (978-0-590-20656-3). A counting book that uses intriguing pictures containing unusual details to present numbers 1 to 10. (Rev: SLJ 11/94)

571 Marzollo, Jean. *Ten Little Christmas Presents* (PS–K). Illus. by author. 2008, Scholastic paper $9.99 (978-0-545-02791-5). 32pp. Ten small animals gather to see what's inside the 10 Christmas presents labeled with their names and their pictures in this counting book that has a matching game at the end. (Rev: BL 9/1/08)

572 Melville, Kirsty. *Splash! A Penguin Counting Book* (PS–1). Illus. by Jonathan Chester. 2001, Tricycle paper $6.95 (978-1-58246-042-0). 32pp. A slight story teaches counting from 1 to 10 using charming penguins. (Rev: BL 1/1–15/01)

573 Merriam, Eve. *Ten Rosy Roses* (PS–1). Illus. by Julia Gorton. 1999, HarperCollins LB $14.89 (978-0-06-027888-5). 32pp. In this counting rhyme from 10 down to 1, children pick roses to make a bouquet for their teacher. (Rev: BCCB 4/99; BL 6/1–15/99; HBG 10/99; SLJ 6/99)

574 Michelson, Richard. *Ten Times Better* (PS–1). Illus. by Leonard Baskin. 2000, Marshall Cavendish $17.95 (978-0-7614-5070-2). 40pp. In this counting book, various animals brag about the number of appendages they have; for example, the squid is proud of his 10 tentacles. (Rev: BCCB 1/01; BL 10/1/00; HBG 3/01; SLJ 10/00)

575 Milich, Zoran. *City 123* (PS–K). Illus. 2005, Kids Can $15.95 (978-1-55337-540-1). 32pp. City scenes — 2 yellow cabs, 7 tall buildings — show numbers from 1 to 10. (Rev: BL 5/15/05; SLJ 5/05) [513.2]

576 Miller, Jane. *Farm Counting Book* (PS–1). Illus. by author. 1992, Simon & Schuster LB $5.95 (978-0-671-66552-4). 24pp. A counting book using photographs of farm animals.

577 Min, Laura. *Mrs. Sato's Hens* (1–2). Illus. by Benrei Huang. 1994, Scott Foresman $6.50 (978-0-673-36193-6). 8pp. In an easy-to-read counting book, every morning Mrs. Sato counts the eggs that her hens are laying. (Rev: BL 1/1/95)

578 Miranda, Anne. *Vroom, Chugga, Vroom-Vroom* (PS–1). Illus. by David Murphy. 1998, Turtle $15.95 (978-1-890515-07-2). 30pp. A number book in which race cars numbered 1 to 20 battle it out on the action-filled racetrack. (Rev: BL 5/1/98; HBG 10/98; SLJ 7/98)

579 Modesitt, Jeanne. *Oh, What a Beautiful Day! A Counting Book* (PS). Illus. by Robin Spowart. 2009, Boyds Mills $16.95 (978-1-56397-409-0). 24pp. A young girl enjoys a beautiful day as she counts the animals around her and plays with them. (Rev: BL 3/1/09; SLJ 6/09)

580 Modesitt, Jeanne. *One, Two, Three Valentine's Day* (PS–1). Illus. by Robin Spowart. 2002, Boyds Mills $15.95 (978-1-56397-868-5). 32pp. A counting book in which Mr. Mouse takes valentine gifts to his friends, to 1 frog, 2 pigs, and so forth up to his 10 little sons. (Rev: BL 1/1–15/03; HBG 3/03; SLJ 1/03)

581 Mora, Pat. *Uno, Dos, Tres: One, Two, Three* (PS–2). Illus. by Barbara Lavallee. 1996, Clarion $15.00 (978-0-395-67294-5). 43pp. The numbers 1 to 10 are introduced in English and Spanish. (Rev: BL 6/1–15/96; HB 5/96; SLJ 4/96)

582 Morales, Yuri. *Just a Minute: A Trickster Tale and Counting Book* (PS–2). Illus. by author. 2003, Chronicle $15.95 (978-0-8118-3758-3). This satisfying book combines counting — in both English and Spanish — and Spanish culture with Grandma's success in sending death away for another year. (Rev: BL 12/1/03*; HBG 4/04; SLJ 12/03) [398.2]

583 *Mother Goose: Numbers on the Loose* (PS–2). Illus. by Leo Dillon. 2007, Harcourt $17.00 (978-0-15-205676-6). 56pp. The artwork has a high 'diction' that will keep the adults engaged in this traditional learn to count rhyming book. Twenty-four rhythmic counting rhymes caper across pages illustrated with lively characters. (Rev: BCCB 11/07; BL 9/1/07; HB 11/07; LMC 1/08; SLJ 10/07) [398.8]

584 Mullins, Patricia. *One Horse Waiting for Me* (PS–1). Illus. 1998, Simon & Schuster paper $16.00 (978-0-689-81381-8). 32pp. All kinds of horses, even those from fantasies, appear in this handsome counting book. (Rev: BCCB 3/98; BL 3/1/98*; HBG 10/98; SLJ 5/98)

585 Murphy, Stuart J. *Jack the Builder* (PS). Illus. by Michael Rex. Series: MathStart. 2006, HarperCollins paper $5.99 (978-0-06-055775-1). 40pp. As Jack keeps adding more blocks, he can make more and more sophisticated constructions. Also use *A Fair Bear Share* (1998), which introduces groups of 10; *The Penny Pot* (1998), about counting coins; *Henry the Fourth* (1999), which introduces ordinal numbers; *Double the Ducks* (2003), *Leaping Lizards* (2005), which teaches counting by multiples of 5 and 10. (Rev: BL 1/1–15/06) [513.2]

586 Nagel, Karen. *The Lunch Line* (2–4). Illus. by Jerry Zimmerman. 1996, Scholastic $3.99 (978-0-590-60246-4). 32pp. Kim has lost her lunch and must buy one in this simple book on calculation. (Rev: BL 2/1/97)

587 Napoli, Donna Jo, and Richard Tchen. *Corkscrew Counts: A Story About Multiplication* (K–3). Illus. by Anna Currey. 2008, Holt $16.95 (978-0-8050-7664-6). 32pp. This story follows 12 children and a parrot who go to Corkscrew the pig's birthday party and play a variety of games that require teams of different numbers. (Rev: BLO 8/28/08)

588 Ochiltree, Dianne. *Cats Add Up! Math Activities by Marilyn Burns* (1–2). Illus. by Marcy Dunn-Ramsey. 1998, Scholastic paper $3.99 (978-0-590-12005-0). 40pp. In this easy-to-read counting book, a little girl starts with 1 cat and soon has 10. (Rev: BL 3/15/99)

589 Ochs, Carol P. *When I'm Alone* (PS–3). Illus. by Vicki Jo Redenbaugh. 1993, Carolrhoda LB $14.95 (978-0-87614-752-8). 32pp. In this counting book, various animals upset a girl's attempts to keep her part of the house tidy. (Rev: BL 2/1/93; SLJ 6/93)

590 O'Keefe, Susan Heyboer. *One Hungry Monster: A Counting Book in Rhyme* (PS–K). Illus. by Lynn Munsinger. 2001, Little, Brown $5.95 (978-0-316-60804-6). 16pp. A little boy tries to keep 10 hungry monsters out of trouble. (Rev: BL 3/1/01)

591 Olson, K. C. *Construction Countdown* (PS–1). Illus. by David Gordon. 2004, Holt $14.95 (978-0-8050-6920-4). 32pp. Rhyming text and colorful illustrations of big construction trucks appear on double-page spreads, counting down from 10. (Rev: BL 5/15/04; SLJ 7/04) [629.22]

592 *1 to 10 and Back Again: A Getty Museum Counting Book* (K–2). Photos by Jack Ross. Illus. by Nancy Ogami. 1999, Getty Museum $16.95 (978-0-89236-525-8). This counting book, which features French phrases, cleverly uses the numbers 1 to 10 as the furniture and items found in the Getty Museum are counted. (Rev: HBG 3/00; SLJ 7/99)

593 *One, Two, Skip a Few! First Number Rhymes* (PS–1). Illus. by Roberta Arenson. 1998, Barefoot Books $15.95 (978-1-901223-99-6). 32pp. Using different folk rhymes — like "one potato, two potato" — this energetic book covers numbers, counting, subtraction, and even some multiplication. (Rev: BL 12/1/98; SLJ 9/98) [398.8]

594 Packard, Edward. *Big Numbers* (1–4). Illus. by Sal Murdocca. 2000, Millbrook LB $22.90 (978-0-7613-1570-4). 32pp. This oversize book also deals with oversize numbers from 1 to 10 to 100, 1,000, and then on to a million, billion, trillion, etc. (Rev: BCCB 3/00; BL 3/15/00; HBG 10/00; SLJ 4/00)

595 Pallotta, Jerry. *Ocean Counting: Odd Numbers* (PS–2). Illus. by Shennen Bersani. 2005, Charlesbridge $16.95 (978-0-88106-151-2); paper $6.95 (978-0-88106-150-5). 32pp. Facts about marine animals are interwoven into this lively counting book that concentrates on odd numbers. (Rev: BL 2/1/05; SLJ 3/05) [513.2]

596 Pallotta, Jerry. *Underwater Counting: Even Numbers* (1–3). Illus. by David Biedrzycki. 2001, Charlesbridge $16.95 (978-0-88106-952-5); paper $6.95 (978-0-88106-800-9). 32pp. A variety of underwater creatures are introduced in this counting book that gives even numbers from zero to 50. (Rev: BL 3/1/01; HBG 10/01)

597 Parenteau, Shirley. *One Frog Sang* (K–2). Illus. by Cynthia Jabar. 2006, Candlewick $15.99 (978-0-7636-2394-4). From 1 to 10, and down again, groups of frogs enjoy a spring evening. (Rev: SLJ 4/07)

598 Parker, Kim. *Counting in the Garden* (PS). Illus. 2005, Scholastic $16.95 (978-0-439-69452-0). 32pp. Colorful garden scenes shelter animals in groups from 1 to 10. (Rev: BL 6/1–15/05; SLJ 4/05)

599 Paul, Ann Whitford. *Count on Culebra: Go from 1 to 10 in Spanish* (PS–1). Illus. by Ethan Long. 2008, Holiday $16.95 (978-0-8234-2124-4). 32pp. This zany counting book follows Iguana as she goes in search of a cure for her stubbed toe, introducing Spanish words and counting concepts. (Rev: BL 2/15/08; SLJ 7/08)

600 Peek, Merle. *Roll Over! A Counting Song* (PS). Illus. by author. 1991, Houghton paper $6.99 (978-

0-395-58105-6). 32pp. A counting book from 10 to 1 about animals in a bed.

601 Penner, Lucille R. *Lights Out!* (1–3). Illus. by Jerry Smath. Series: Math Matters. 2000, Kane paper $4.95 (978-1-57565-092-0). 32pp. The concept of subtraction is explored in this story about a girl who watches as the 32 lights outside her apartment go out. (Rev: SLJ 6/00)

602 Perl, Erica S. *Ninety-Three in My Family* (K–3). Illus. by Mike Lester. 2006, Abrams $15.95 (978-0-8109-5760-2). In a funny story full of counting opportunities, a young boy identifies the members of his extended family that includes his parents, two sisters, and a mind-boggling assortment of pets and other creatures, including a pygmy hippo. (Rev: SLJ 10/06)

603 Pinczes, Elinor J. *Inchworm and a Half* (PS–3). Illus. by Randall Enos. 2001, Houghton $15.00 (978-0-395-82849-6). 32pp. The concept of fractions is explored in this amusing book about different-sized inchworms and the objects they measure. (Rev: BCCB 3/01; BL 3/15/01; HBG 10/01)

604 Pinczes, Elinor J. *One Hundred Hungry Ants* (K–3). Illus. by Bonnie Mackain. 1993, Houghton $16.00 (978-0-395-63116-4). 32pp. Ants group and regroup on their march to a picnic site. (Rev: BL 3/1/93; SLJ 8/93)

605 Pinczes, Elinor J. *A Remainder of One* (PS–2). Illus. by Bonnie Mackain. 1995, Houghton $16.00 (978-0-395-69455-8). 32pp. An arithmetic book that uses a parade of beetles before the queen as a focal point. (Rev: BL 3/1/95*; SLJ 5/95)

606 Raffi. *Five Little Ducks* (PS–1). Illus. by Jose Aruego and Ariane Dewey. 1988, Crown paper $5.99 (978-0-517-58360-9). 32pp. Mother Duck and her ducklings waddle "over the hills and far away" in this addition to the Songs to Read series. (Rev: BL 6/1/89; HB 5/89)

607 Rathmann, Peggy. *10 Minutes till Bedtime* (K–2). Illus. 1998, Penguin $17.99 (978-0-399-23103-2). 46pp. A very active counting book involving a 10-minute countdown to bed for a little boy and 10 mischievous hamsters numbered 1 through 10. (Rev: BCCB 12/98; BL 10/15/98; HB 9/98; HBG 3/99; SLJ 9/98)

608 Reidy, Hannah. *All Sorts of Numbers* (PS). Illus. by Emma Dodd. Series: All Sorts of Things. 2005, Picture Window LB $25.26 (978-1-4048-1062-4). 24pp. A bright introduction to numbers from 1 to 5. (Rev: SLJ 6/05)

609 Reiser, Lynn. *Hardworking Puppies* (PS–2). 2006, Harcourt $16.00 (978-0-15-205404-5). 40pp. In this attractive countdown tale, 10 bored puppies — one by one — are assigned professional tasks such as guide dog, sled dog, therapy dog. (Rev: BL 6/1–15/06; SLJ 4/06)

610 Rocklin, Joanne. *The Case of the Shrunken Allowance* (1–3). Illus. by Cornelius Van Wright and Ying-Hwa Hu. Series: Hello Reader! 1999, Scholastic paper $3.99 (978-0-590-12006-7). The concept of money denominations and making change are introduced in a light plot about P. B.'s shrinking savings. (Rev: SLJ 3/99)

611 Rocklin, Joanne. *One Hungry Cat* (1–2). Illus. by Rowan Barnes-Murphy. Series: Hello Math Reader. 1997, Scholastic paper $3.99 (978-0-590-93972-0). A slapstick easy reader that introduces simple arithmetic by using cookies that a hungry cat enjoys eating. (Rev: BL 5/1/97; SLJ 7/97)

612 Root, Phyllis. *One Duck Stuck* (PS–1). Illus. by Jane Chapman. 1998, Candlewick $15.99 (978-0-7636-0334-2). 40pp. In this counting book that uses alliterative rhymes, different animals try to free a duck that gets stuck in the muck. (Rev: BL 4/1/98; HBG 10/98; SLJ 6/98)

613 Rose, Deborah L. *One Nighttime Sea* (PS–2). Illus. by Steve Jenkins. 2003, Scholastic $16.95 (978-0-439-33906-3). 40pp. This counting book uses rhyming text to introduce young readers to numbers from 1 to 10 as well as common marine animals. (Rev: HBG 4/04; SLJ 9/03) [513.2]

614 Rose, Deborah L. *The Twelve Days of Kindergarten: A Counting Book* (PS–1). Illus. by Carey Armstrong-Ellis. 2003, Abrams $14.95 (978-0-8109-4512-8). The wonders of kindergarten are introduced along with numbers from 1 alphabet to 12 eggs. (Rev: HBG 4/04; SLJ 8/03) [372.21]

615 Rose, Deborah L. *The Twelve Days of Springtime: A School Counting Book* (PS–1). Illus. by Carey Armstrong-Ellis. 2009, Abrams $15.95 (978-0-8109-8330-4). 32pp. Spring is the focus of this entertaining counting book featuring a rambunctious kindergarten class. (Rev: SLJ 4/09)

616 Rose, Deborah L. *The Twelve Days of Winter: A School Counting Book* (K–3). Illus. by Carey Armstrong-Ellis. 2006, Abrams $14.95 (978-0-8109-5472-4). The melody of "The Twelve Days of Christmas" provides the framework for this cumulative counting verse that celebrates the joys of winter. (Rev: SLJ 10/06)

617 Roth, Susan L. *Night-Time Numbers: A Scary Counting Book* (PS–1). Illus. by author. Series: A Barefoot Beginner Book. 1999, Barefoot Books $15.95 (978-1-84148-001-5). Monsters and an angel are used to introduce the numbers 1 to 10 in his book illustrated with collages. (Rev: SLJ 10/99)

618 Sayre, April P., and Jeff Sayre. *One Is a Snail, Ten Is a Crab: A Counting by Feet Book* (PS–2). Illus. by Randy Cecil. 2003, Candlewick $15.99 (978-0-7636-1406-5). Readers count up to 10 and then in multiples of 10 to 100, using animal feet as units. (Rev: HBG 10/03; SLJ 7/03) [513.2]

619 Schafer, Kevin. *Penguins 123* (PS–K). Photos by author. 2002, NorthWord $14.95 (978-1-55971-830-1). A counting book that will grab the attention of penguin lovers. (Rev: SLJ 1/03)

620 Schlein, Miriam. *More Than One* (PS–3). Illus. by Donald Crews. 1996, Greenwillow $15.89 (978-0-688-14103-5). 24pp. Using the concept of "one" as a framework, other numbers and groups of numbers are introduced. (Rev: BCCB 1/97; BL 11/1/96; SLJ 12/96) [513]

621 Schulman, Janet. *10 Trick-or-Treaters: A Halloween Counting Book* (PS–K). Illus. by Linda Davick. 2005, Knopf $9.95 (978-0-375-83225-3). Ten little trick-or-treaters head out into the night, but one by one are scared off by various Halloween creatures. (Rev: SLJ 8/05)

622 Seeger, Laura Vaccaro. *One Boy* (PS–3). Illus. by author. 2008, Roaring Brook $14.95 (978-1-59643-274-1). 32pp. Part counting book, part eye-catching picture book, and part clever die-cut exploration of words within words. (Rev: BL 10/15/08*; HB 11/08; LMC 1/09; SLJ 10/08)

623 Shahan, Sherry. *Cool Cats Counting* (K–3). Illus. by Paula Barragán. 2005, August House $16.95 (978-0-87483-757-5). Lively illustrations and rhythmic text introduce numbers from 1 to 10, with a translation of the key words into Spanish. (Rev: SLJ 10/05)

624 Shea, Pegi Deitz, and Cynthia Weill. *Ten Mice for Tet* (PS–2). Illus. by To Ngoc Trang and Pham Vi t Dinh. 2003, Chronicle $15.95 (978-0-8118-3496-4). This handsome counting book introduces numbers 1 through 10 plus the traditions of the Vietnamese New Year. (Rev: HBG 4/04; SLJ 12/03) [394.2]

625 Simon, Charnan. *One Happy Classroom* (1–2). Illus. by Rebecca M. Thornburgh. 1997, Children's Book Pr. LB $19.50 (978-0-516-20318-8). 32pp. An easy-to-read counting book that takes place in a classroom and involves counting from 1 to 10 and back. (Rev: BL 5/1/97)

626 Singer, Marilyn. *City Lullaby* (PS–2). Illus. by Carll Cneut. 2007, Clarion $16.00 (978-0-618-60703-7). 32pp. In this counting book set in the city, a baby sleeps happily through the blare of 10 horns and the roar of 2 motorbikes but is woken by the sound of 1 bird. (Rev: BL 10/15/07; HB 1/08; SLJ 10/07)

627 Singer, Marilyn. *Quiet Night* (PS–K). Illus. by John Manders. 2002, Clarion $15.00 (978-0-618-12044-4). 32pp. A riotous romp of a counting book in which the quiet of night turns into a symphony of animal noises. (Rev: BCCB 6/02; BL 3/15/02; HBG 10/02; SLJ 3/02)

628 Siy, Alexandra. *One Tractor: A Counting Book* (PS). Illus. by Jacqueline Rogers. 2008, Holiday $16.95 (978-0-8234-1923-4). 32pp. A little boy's dreams are populated with 1 tractor, 2 airplanes, 3 floating boats, and so on, and he helps with the action at every point. (Rev: BL 3/1/08; SLJ 2/08)

629 Skinner, Daphne. *All Aboard!* (1–3). Illus. by Jerry Smath. Series: Math Matters. 2007, Kane paper $4.95 (978-1-57565-239-9). 32pp. Two children and their grandmother must stick to a schedule as they travel to a wedding. Readers will be challenged by the math problems about time that are integrated into the story. (Rev: SLJ 6/07)

630 Slater, Teddy. *Stay in Line* (1–2). Illus. 1996, Scholastic paper $3.99 (978-0-590-22713-1). 32pp. Children on a field trip learn various numerical ways of lining up. (Rev: BL 8/96)

631 Slaughter, Tom. *1 2 3* (PS–K). Illus. by author. 2003, Tundra $11.95 (978-0-88776-664-0). A cleverly designed counting book that introduces the numbers 1 through 10. (Rev: SLJ 11/03) [513.2]

632 Smith, Danna. *Two at the Zoo: A Counting Book* (PS–K). Illus. by Valeria Petrone. 2009, Harcourt $16.00 (978-0-547-04982-3). 32pp. Clear rhyming text and colorful illustrations lead the reader through the zoo counting from 1 to 10 with a little boy and his grandfather. (Rev: SLJ 2/09)

633 Smith, Maggie. *Counting Our Way to Maine* (PS–2). Illus. 1995, Orchard LB $16.99 (978-0-531-08734-3). 32pp. Numbers from 1 to 20 are introduced by using a family's summer trip to Maine. (Rev: BCCB 3/95; BL 4/1/95; SLJ 5/95*)

634 Smith, Maggie. *One Naked Baby: Counting to Ten and Back Again* (PS). Illus. by author. 2007, Knopf $15.99 (978-0-375-83329-8). A simple, colorful counting book in which a harried mother tries to cope with her lively toddler at bath time. (Rev: SLJ 1/07)

635 Spowart, Robin. *Ten Little Bunnies* (PS). Illus. by author. 2001, Scholastic $7.95 (978-0-439-20863-5). A gentle counting book that can double as a bedtime story. (Rev: HBG 10/01; SLJ 8/01)

636 Stiegemeyer, Julie. *Gobble Gobble! Crash!* (PS–2). Illus. by Valeri Gorbachev. 2008, Dutton $16.99 (978-0-525-47959-8). 32pp. A flock of wild turkeys wake up a drowsy barnyard in this rhyming counting book with watercolor illustrations. (Rev: BLO 8/28/08; SLJ 8/08)

637 Swinburne, Stephen. *Water for One, Water for Everyone: A Counting Book of African Animals* (PS–2). Illus. by Melinda Levine. 1998, Millbrook LB $22.90 (978-0-7613-0269-8); paper $6.95 (978-0-7613-0347-3). Animals, from 1 tortoise to 10 elephants, come to an African watering hole in this simple counting book, which also gives the numbers in Swahili. (Rev: HBG 10/98; SLJ 6/98)

638 Swinburne, Stephen. *What's a Pair? What's a Dozen?* (PS–1). Illus. 2000, Boyds Mills $15.95 (978-1-56397-827-2). 32pp. This advanced mathematical concept book introduces words and phrases such as even and odd, first and second, uni- and bi-, and baker's dozen. (Rev: BL 3/15/00; HBG 10/00; SLJ 4/00) [510]

639 Szekeres, Cyndy. *I Can Count 100 Bunnies: And So Can You!* (PS–1). Illus. 1999, Scholastic $12.95 (978-0-590-38361-5). 48pp. Wilbur counts 99 bunnies who come to welcome number 100 — Wilbur's new baby sister. (Rev: BL 1/1–15/99; HBG 10/99; SLJ 2/99)

640 Szekeres, Cyndy. *Learn to Count, Funny Bunnies* (PS). Illus. by author. 2000, Scholastic $6.99 (978-0-439-14994-5). In this board book, youngsters will learn to count to 10 as the relatives of Wilbur Bunny arrive for his birthday party. (Rev: HBG 4/04; SLJ 5/00)

641 Tafuri, Nancy. *The Big Storm: A Very Soggy Counting Book* (PS–K). Illus. by author. 2009, Simon & Schuster $15.99 (978-1-4169-6795-8). 32pp. Readers count from 1 to 10 as they watch animals seeking shelter from a storm. (Rev: BLO 5/27/09)

642 Tang, Greg. *Math Fables* (PS–1). Illus. by Heather Cahoon. 2004, Scholastic $16.95 (978-0-439-45399-8). 40pp. Groupings of numbers are shown through rhyming stories with colorful art. (Rev: BL 2/1/04; SLJ 3/04) [513.2]

643 Thompson, Lauren. *How Many Cats?* (K–2). Illus. by Robin Eley. 2009, Hyperion $15.99 (978-1-4231-0801-6). 32pp. Count to 20 with this houseful of energetic and mischievous cats. (Rev: BL 4/1/09; LMC 5/09; SLJ 5/09)

644 Thornhill, Jan, adapt. *Over in the Meadow* (PS–2). Illus. by Jan Thornhill. 2004, Maple Tree $16.95 (978-1-897066-08-9). Unusual illustrations add to the charm of this inventive rendition of a traditional counting song. (Rev: SLJ 1/05)

645 Tildes, Phyllis L. *Counting on Calico* (PS–K). Illus. 1995, Charlesbridge paper $6.95 (978-0-88106-862-7). 32pp. The features of a calico cat are used to introduce basic numbers, ending with 20 wet paw prints. (Rev: BL 6/1–15/95)

646 *The Timbertoes 123 Counting Book* (PS–1). Illus. 1997, Boyds Mills $7.95 (978-1-56397-627-8). 32pp. Basic numbers are introduced by the Timbertoes, a family of wooden figures, when they visit an apple orchard. (Rev: BL 3/1/97; SLJ 7/97)

647 *Toddler Two* (PS). Illus. by Winnie Cheon. 2000, Lee & Low $6.95 (978-1-58430-015-1). The concept of two is explored in this interactive board book with flaps and pop-ups. (Rev: SLJ 1/01)

648 Toft, Kim Michelle, and Allan Sheather. *One Less Fish* (K–3). Illus. 1998, Charlesbridge $15.95 (978-0-88106-322-6); paper $6.95 (978-0-88106-323-3). 32pp. Counting down from 12 to 1, this book shows the perils fish face, including such threats as offshore oil drilling. (Rev: BL 7/98; HBG 10/98) [513.2]

649 Trinca, Rod, and Kerry Argent. *One Woolly Wombat* (PS–2). Illus. by Kerry Argent. 1985, Kane paper $7.95 (978-0-916291-10-5). 32pp. A charming 1-to-14 counting book featuring Australian animals. (Rev: BL 7/85; HB 7/85; SLJ 9/85)

650 *Trucks and Diggers One to Ten: Counting* (PS). 2003, Chronicle $6.95 (978-0-8118-4029-3). Numbers are introduced through eye-catching photographs of appealing machines. (Rev: SLJ 1/04)

651 Wadsworth, Olive A. *Over in the Meadow: A Counting Rhyme* (PS–1). Illus. by Anna Vojtech. 2002, North-South $15.95 (978-0-7358-1596-4). 32pp. This classic nursery counting rhyme is given a fresh look with double-page spreads and stunning watercolors. (Rev: BL 4/15/02; HBG 10/02; SLJ 4/02)

652 Wallace, Nancy Elizabeth. *Count Down to Clean Up!* (PS–2). Illus. 2001, Houghton $14.00 (978-0-618-10130-6). 32pp. Ten bunnies take a trip to the park, gathering supplies as they go, in this counting book with cut-paper artwork. (Rev: BL 9/15/01; HBG 3/02; SLJ 10/01)

653 Walsh, Ellen S. *Mouse Count* (PS–K). Illus. 1991, Harcourt $13.00 (978-0-15-256023-2). 32pp. In this counting book, 10 little mice fall asleep unaware that a hungry snake is nearby. (Rev: BL 2/15/91; HB 5/91; SLJ 5/91)

654 Walton, Rick. *One More Bunny: Adding from One to Ten* (PS–1). Illus. by Paige Miglio. 2000, Lothrop LB $15.89 (978-0-688-16848-3). 24pp. Readers participate in this counting book as they are asked to find bunnies in illustrations and add them up. (Rev: BL 4/15/00; HBG 10/00; SLJ 7/00)

655 Watson, Amy, et al. *The Folk Art Counting Book* (PS–2). Illus. 1992, Abrams $12.95 (978-0-8109-3306-4). 40pp. Collections from the Rockefeller Folk Art Center in Williamsburg, Virginia, invite the younger reader to count to 20. (Rev: BL 6/15/92; SLJ 8/92) [745]

656 Wells, Robert. *Can You Count to a Googol?* (PS–1). Illus. 2000, Whitman $16.99 (978-0-8075-1060-5); paper $6.95 (978-0-8075-1061-2). 32pp. This counting book starts with 1 and moves to 10, 100, 1,000 until reaching a googol, the number 1 followed by 100 zeros. (Rev: BL 3/1/00; HBG 10/00; SLJ 5/00)

657 Williams, Rozanne Lanczak. *Adding* (PS–1). Illus. Series: I Can Do Math. 2004, Gareth Stevens LB $22.00 (978-0-8368-4108-4). 24pp. A question-and-answer format and abundant photographs introduce addition. Also use *Subtracting*, *Crayola Counting*, and *Learning About Coins* (all 2004).

658 Williams, Rozanne Lanczak. *The Coin Counting Book* (PS–3). Illus. 2001, Charlesbridge $16.95 (978-0-88106-325-7); paper $6.95 (978-0-88106-326-4). 32pp. This counting book uses coins to show how five pennies make a nickel and so on until the reader discovers the various combinations that make a dollar. (Rev: BL 3/1/01; HBG 10/01)

659 Wilson, Karma. *A Frog in the Bog* (PS–2). Illus. by Joan Rankin. 2003, Simon & Schuster $16.95 (978-0-689-84081-4). A humorous counting book in which a hungry frog consumes progressively larger swamp snacks, including "one tick," "two fleas," "three flies," and "four slugs." (Rev: BL 11/1/03; HBG 4/04; SLJ 12/03)

660 Winter, Jeanette. *Josefina* (PS–3). Illus. 1996, Harcourt $15.00 (978-0-15-201091-1). 36pp. An original counting book that features the Mexican woman Josefina and her amazing collection of clay figures. (Rev: BCCB 10/96; BL 10/15/96*; SLJ 10/96)

661 Wojtowycz, David. *Animal Antics from 1 to 10* (PS). Illus. 2000, Holiday House $16.95 (978-0-8234-1552-6). 26pp. When readers visit Hotel 1 2 3, they are introduced to the numbers 1 to 10 and some very unusual beasts like 2 tangoing toucans. (Rev: BL 10/15/00; HBG 3/01; SLJ 10/00)

662 Yektai, Niki. *Bears at the Beach: Counting 10 to 20* (PS–1). Illus. 1996, Millbrook LB $21.90 (978-0-7613-0047-2). 32pp. A wordless counting book that covers numbers from 10 to 20. (Rev: BL 7/96; SLJ 6/96)

663 Zabar, Abbie. *55 Friends* (PS–3). Illus. by author. 1994, Hyperion $13.95 (978-0-7868-0021-6). In a fanciful text, animals from 1 to 10 are introduced and then combined in various ways to reach 55. (Rev: SLJ 11/94)

664 Ziefert, Harriet. *A Dozen Ducklings Lost and Found* (K–2). Illus. by Donald Dreifuss. 2003, Houghton $15.00 (978-0-618-14175-3). 32pp. While proudly parading her dozen ducklings through the barnyard, Mother Duck loses some in newly dug postholes. (Rev: BL 3/15/03; HBG 10/03; SLJ 3/03)

665 Ziefert, Harriet. *Knick-Knack Paddywhack* (PS–K). Illus. by Emily Bolam. 2005, Sterling $5.95 (978-1-4027-2292-9). A boy, a dog, some bones, and an old man figure in this appealing counting-oriented version of the familiar song. (Rev: SLJ 10/05)

Bedtime Books and Nursery Rhymes

Bedtime Books

666 Adler, David A. *It's Time to Sleep, It's Time to Dream* (PS–K). Illus. by Kay Chorao. 2009, Holiday $16.95 (978-0-8234-1924-1). 32pp. Poetic text and illustrations evoke the four seasons in this gentle bedtime book. (Rev: BL 3/1/09; SLJ 4/09)

667 Alborough, Jez. *Yes* (PS). Illus. 2006, Candlewick $15.99 (978-0-7636-3183-3). 40pp. Bobo, the chimp seen in *Hug* (2000) is back and this time he's excited about having a bath but definitely not ready to go to bed. (Rev: BL 11/15/06; SLJ 10/06)

668 *All the Pretty Little Horses: A Traditional Lullaby* (PS–K). Illus. by Linda Saport. 1999, Clarion $15.00 (978-0-395-93097-7). 32pp. In this version of the classic lullaby, pictures from a bygone era depict an African American woman rocking her baby on a porch in the rural South. (Rev: BL 11/1/99; HBG 3/00; SLJ 12/99) [782.4]

669 Appelt, Kathi. *I See the Moon* (PS–K). Illus. by Debra R. Jenkins. 1997, Eerdmans $15.00 (978-0-8028-5118-5). 24pp. A bedtime book about a little girl all alone on the sea in a tiny boat. (Rev: BCCB 5/97; BL 3/15/97)

670 Apperley, Dawn. *Good Night, Sleep Tight, Little Bunnies* (PS). Illus. by author. 2002, Scholastic $9.95 (978-0-439-22525-0). A rhyming refrain and cartoon images depict young animals settling down for the night. (Rev: HBG 10/02; SLJ 5/02)

671 Arnold, Tedd. *Five Ugly Monsters* (PS–K). Illus. 1995, Scholastic $6.95 (978-0-590-22226-6). 24pp. Several groups of monsters interrupt a little boy's plans to go to sleep. (Rev: BCCB 10/95; BL 11/15/95; SLJ 12/95)

672 Arro, Lena. *Good Night, Animals* (PS–1). Trans. by Joan Sandin. Illus. by Catarina Kruusval. 2002, Farrar $15.00 (91-29-65654-0). 28pp. A cumulative bedtime story in which two children who decide to camp out soon find their tent packed with animals. (Rev: BCCB 12/02; BL 12/15/02; HBG 3/03; SLJ 2/03)

673 Ashman, Linda. *Starry Safari* (PS–K). Illus. by Jeff Mack. 2005, Harcourt $16.00 (978-0-15-204766-5). 40pp. A little girl with a vivid imagination turns bedtime into an exciting safari. (Rev: BL 8/05; SLJ 7/05)

674 Averbeck, Jim. *In a Blue Room* (PS–1). Illus. by Tricia Tusa. 2008, Harcourt $16.00 (978-0-15-205992-7). 32pp. Alice wants to sleep in a blue room and despite her mother's efforts to lull her to sleep it is only when the moon bathes the room in a blue light that Alice is ready to dream. (Rev: BCCB 5/08; BL 4/1/08; SLJ 6/08) ⌒

675 Banks, Kate. *And If the Moon Could Talk* (PS–2). Illus. by Georg Hallensleben. 1998, Farrar $15.00 (978-0-374-30299-3). 32pp. At bedtime, a little girl's actions are duplicated in the outside world by a number of different animals. (Rev: BCCB 4/98; BL 2/15/98; HB 3/98*; HBG 10/98; SLJ 2/98*)

676 Banks, Kate. *Close Your Eyes* (PS). Illus. by Georg Hallensleben. 2002, Farrar $16.00 (978-0-374-31382-1). 40pp. A thoroughly enjoyable, dreamily illustrated story about a little tiger who doesn't want to fall asleep, and his mother's patient reassurances. (Rev: BL 10/15/02; HB 9/02; HBG 3/03; SLJ 7/02)

677 Banks, Kate. *The Night Worker* (PS–2). Illus. by Georg Hallensleben. 2000, Farrar $16.00 (978-0-374-35520-3). 40pp. Alex follows his Papa, a construction worker on the night shift, and helps him all night long until morning when he comes home to bed. (Rev: BCCB 7–8/00; BL 8/00*; HBG 3/01; SLJ 8/00)

678 Barger, Jan. *Bedtime, Nelly* (PS–K). Illus. by author. 2004, Charlesbridge $14.95 (978-1-58089-094-6). Nelly postpones sleep with a litany of good nights. (Rev: SLJ 8/04)

679 Beaton, Clare. *Mrs. Moon: Lullabies for Bedtime* (PS–1). Illus. by author. 2003, Barefoot Books $19.99 (978-1-84148-176-0). 48pp. This collection of lullabies and bedtime poetry includes many old favorites and is accompanied by a musical CD. (Rev: HBG 4/04; SLJ 1/04) [782.4]

680 Beaumont, Karen. *Baby Danced the Polka* (PS). Illus. by Jennifer Plecas. 2004, Dial $12.99 (978-0-8037-2587-4). Baby prefers dancing to sleeping in this lively bedtime book with flaps hiding stuffed animal dancing partners. (Rev: BL 2/15/04; HB 5/04; SLJ 6/04)

681 Beck, Andrea. *Elliot's Noisy Night* (PS–1). Illus. 2002, Kids Can $12.95 (978-1-55337-011-6). 32pp. Elliot the toy moose infects his friends with his fears about the noises at night and they all end up sleeping in Elliot's room. (Rev: BL 1/1–15/03; HBG 3/03)

682 Beck, Ian. *Home Before Dark* (PS–K). Illus. 2001, Scholastic $15.95 (978-0-439-17522-7). 32pp. A stuffed bear falls out of Lily's stroller in a park, but manages to find his way back home just in time to accompany Lily to bed. (Rev: BL 3/1/01; HBG 10/01; SLJ 3/01)

683 Blomgren, Jennifer. *Where Do I Sleep? A Pacific Northwest Lullaby* (PS–2). Illus. by Andrea Gabriel. 2001, Sasquatch $15.95 (978-1-57061-258-9). 32pp. A peaceful bedtime book featuring animals native to the Pacific Northwest bedding down for the night. (Rev: BL 11/1/01; HBG 3/02; SLJ 11/01)

684 Boelts, Maribeth. *Looking for Sleepy* (PS). Illus. by Bernadette Pons. 2004, Whitman LB $14.95 (978-0-8075-0447-5). A bedtime picture book starring Little Bear and his patient father. (Rev: SLJ 4/04)

685 Bogan, Paulette. *Goodnight Lulu* (PS–2). Illus. by author. 2003, Bloomsbury $15.95 (978-1-58234-803-2). A mother hen reassures her chick that she will protect her from any potential dangers in this delightful bedtime book. (Rev: HBG 10/03; SLJ 7/03)

686 Bradman, Tony. *Daddy's Lullaby* (PS). Illus. by Jason Cockcroft. 2002, Simon & Schuster $16.95 (978-0-689-84295-5). 32pp. Late at night, a father tries to soothe his baby to sleep by quietly making his way around the house with the child in his arms. (Rev: BL 4/15/02; HBG 10/02; SLJ 5/02)

687 Branford, Henrietta. *Little Pig Figwort Can't Get to Sleep* (PS–K). Illus. by Claudio Munoz. 2002, Clarion $14.00 (978-0-618-15968-0). 32pp. When Little Pig Figwort can't sleep he sets out to find other creatures that have the same problem. (Rev: BCCB 5/02; BL 6/1–15/02; HBG 10/02; SLJ 7/02)

688 Brian, Janeen. *Where Does Thursday Go?* (PS–K). Illus. by Stephen M. King. 2002, Clarion $14.00 (978-0-618-21264-4). 32pp. A little bear and his friend search for Thursday, wondering where the day goes when nighttime comes, in this attractive book that makes a great bedtime story. (Rev: BL 3/1/02; HBG 10/02; SLJ 4/02)

689 Bright, Paul. *Under the Bed* (PS). Illus. by Ben Cort. 2004, Good Bks. $16.00 (978-1-56148-436-2). A boy is afraid of creatures under his bed, and it turns out they are also afraid of him in this book with amusing illustrations. (Rev: SLJ 8/04)

690 Brisson, Pat. *Star Blanket* (PS–1). Illus. by Erica Magnus. 2003, Boyds Mills $15.95 (978-1-56397-889-0). Laura's father tells her the familiar story of the time-worn, star-studded blanket on her bed. (Rev: HBG 4/04; SLJ 12/03)

691 Brown, Marc. *Arthur's Really Helpful Bedtime Book* (PS–2). Adapted by Stephen Krensky. Illus. by author. 1998, Random LB $15.99 (978-0-679-88468-2). 44pp. The characters from the Arthur books are featured in these retellings of ten classic stories including "The Princess and the Pea," "The Three Little Pigs," and "The Frog Prince." (Rev: SLJ 3/99)

692 Brown, Margaret Wise. *Goodnight Moon* (PS). Illus. by Clement Hurd. 1947, HarperCollins LB $16.89 (978-0-06-020706-9); paper $6.99 (978-0-06-443017-3). 32pp. A soothing go-to-sleep story. A pop-up book version is *The Goodnight Moon Room: A Pop-Up Book* (1985).

693 Brown, Margaret Wise. *Sheep Don't Count Sheep* (PS). Illus. by Benrei Huang. 2003, Simon & Schuster $14.95 (978-0-689-83346-5). 32pp. A little lamb can't get to sleep because there's too much going on in the field, so his mother tells him to count butterflies. (Rev: BL 1/1–15/03; HBG 10/03; SLJ 3/03)

694 Bunting, Eve. *No Nap* (PS–1). Illus. by Susan Meddaugh. 1989, Houghton $16.00 (978-0-89919-813-2). 28pp. Whenever bedtime is suggested, Susie says, "No nap." (Rev: BCCB 10/89; BL 9/15/89; HB 1/90; SLJ 10/89)

695 Butler, John. *Hush, Little Ones* (PS). Illus. 2002, Peachtree $15.95 (978-1-56145-269-9). 32pp. A very visual bedtime book full of sleeping animals — birds in nests, monkeys up trees, a penguin between his father's feet. (Rev: BL 11/15/02; HBG 3/03; SLJ 10/02)

696 Cabrera, Jane. *Ten in the Bed* (PS). Illus. 2006, Holiday $16.95 (978-0-8234-2027-8). 32pp. In a good-night countdown, 10 stuffed animals with different occupations strut their stuff. (Rev: BL 10/1/06; SLJ 9/06)

697 Capucilli, Alyssa Satin. *Little Spotted Cat* (PS–K). Illus. by Dan Andreasen. 2005, Dial $14.99 (978-0-8037-2692-5). 32pp. A traditional story book about a kitten who gets into all sorts of trouble when his mother tells him that it's nap time. (Rev: BL 3/15/05; SLJ 6/05)

698 Carlstrom, Nancy White. *Swim the Silver Sea, Joshie Otter* (PS–K). Illus. by Ken Kuroi. 1997, Penguin paper $7.99 (978-0-698-11447-0). 40pp. At bedtime, a baby otter swims back to his mother and the love she gives him. (Rev: BL 4/1/93; SLJ 5/93)

699 Cazet, Denys. *Night Lights: 24 Poems to Sleep On* (PS–2). Illus. by author. 1997, Orchard LB $16.99 (978-0-531-33010-4). There are 24 bedtime rhymes in this nighttime collection; some are lullabies, others are amusing poems about animals at night. (Rev: SLJ 5/97)

700 Charlip, Remy. *Baby Hearts and Baby Flowers* (PS–K). Illus. by author. 2001, Greenwillow LB $15.89 (978-0-06-029592-9). Babies, puppies, and kittens are found "everywhere" in this gentle bedtime book. (Rev: HBG 10/02; SLJ 1/02)

701 Charlip, Remy. *Sleepytime Rhyme* (PS). Illus. 1999, Greenwillow $17.99 (978-0-688-16271-9). 24pp. In this bedtime book, a mother plays with her child while listing the body parts she loves. (Rev: BCCB 10/99; BL 11/15/99; HBG 3/00; SLJ 9/99)

702 Child, Lauren. *I Am Not Sleepy and I Will Not Go to Bed* (PS–3). Illus. Series: Charlie and Lola. 2001, Candlewick $16.99 (978-0-7636-1570-3). 32pp. Charlie tries to get his imaginative little sister to go to bed. (Rev: BL 8/01; HBG 3/02; SLJ 9/01)

703 Cohen, Caron Lee. *Martin and the Giant Lion* (PS–K). Illus. by Elizabeth Sayles. 2002, Clarion $15.00 (978-0-618-04908-0). 32pp. After he is tucked into bed, Martin travels via his purple truck to a land where he plays with a family of lions. (Rev: BL 4/15/02; HBG 10/02; SLJ 7/02)

704 Cooper, Elisha. *Bear Dreams* (PS). 2006, Greenwillow $16.99 (978-0-06-087428-5). 40pp. It's almost time to hibernate, but Bear, a cub, has places to go and things to do, until finally he tires himself out. (Rev: BL 10/1/06; SLJ 9/06)

705 Cowell, Cressida. *What Shall We Do with the Boo-Hoo Baby?* (PS–1). Illus. by Ingrid Godon. 2000, Scholastic $15.95 (978-0-439-15311-9). 32pp. Animals try different tactics to hush a crying baby and become so tired that they nap, which causes the baby to smile. (Rev: BCCB 2/01; BL 1/1–15/01; HBG 3/01; SLJ 3/01)

706 Crum, Shutta. *All on a Sleepy Night* (K–2). Illus. by Sylvie Daigneault. 2002, Stoddart $15.95 (978-

0-7737-3315-2). 24pp. The sounds of his grandparents' house lull a young boy to sleep in this rhyming picture book. (Rev: BL 9/15/02; HBG 3/03; SLJ 5/02)

707 Daddo, Andrew. *Goodnight, Me* (PS). Illus. by Emma Quay. 2007, Bloomsbury $11.95 (978-1-59990-153-4). 32pp. At the end of a busy day, a baby orangutan says good night to every part of his body from his toes to his nose. (Rev: SLJ 12/07)

708 Davies, Jacqueline. *The Night Is Singing* (PS–K). Illus. by Krysten Brooker. 2006, Dial $16.99 (978-0-8037-3004-5). 40pp. The sounds of the night lull a little girl to sleep in this rhyming, soothing picture book. (Rev: BL 5/15/06; SLJ 6/06)

709 Deniers, Dominique. *Every Single Night* (PS–K). Trans. by Sarah Quinn. Illus. by Nicolas Debon. 2006, Groundwood $17.95 (978-0-88899-699-2). 32pp. Little Simon simply can't fall asleep until his father completes their nighttime ritual full of images of a wonderful world full of nature. (Rev: BL 3/15/06; SLJ 5/06)

710 deVries, Maggie. *How Sleep Found Tabitha* (PS–K). Illus. by Sheena Lott. 2002, Orca $16.95 (978-1-55143-193-2). 32pp. Pastel watercolor illustrations provide an excellent backdrop for this story of a sleepless child. (Rev: BL 8/02; HBG 10/02; SLJ 8/02)

711 Dodds, Dayle Ann. *The Prince Won't Go to Bed!* (PS–K). Illus. by Krysten Brooker. 2007, Farrar $16.00 (978-0-374-36108-2). 32pp. The whole royal household struggles to get the teeny-tiny Prince to go to bed until his sister gives him a good night kiss. (Rev: BL 10/1/07; HB 1/08; SLJ 12/07)

712 Dragonwagon, Crescent. *Is This a Sack of Potatoes?* (PS–1). Illus. by Catherine Stock. 2002, Marshall Cavendish $15.95 (978-0-7614-5089-4). 32pp. Charlie hides under the covers at bedtime in this lift-the-flap book with charming watercolor illustrations. (Rev: BL 12/15/02; HBG 3/03; SLJ 11/02)

713 Dunbar, Joyce. *Tell Me Something Happy Before I Go to Sleep* (PS). Illus. by Debi Gliori. 1998, Harcourt $16.00 (978-0-15-201795-8). A young bunny has trouble getting to sleep until she begins thinking of all the nice things that will happen to her the next day. (Rev: HBG 3/99; SLJ 11/98)

714 Dyer, Jane. *Animal Crackers: A Delectable Collection of Pictures, Poems, and Lullabies for the Very Young* (PS). Illus. 1996, Little, Brown $17.95 (978-0-316-19766-3). 64pp. An immensely appealing collection of lullabies, poems, and nursery rhymes accompanied by muted illustrations. (Rev: BCCB 3/96; BL 4/15/96; SLJ 5/96)

715 Eduar, Gilles. *Dream Journey* (PS–K). Illus. by author. 1999, Orchard $15.95 (978-0-531-30202-6). While a little boy sleeps on his back, a camel travels through oceans, jungles, mountains, cities, and storms. (Rev: HBG 3/00; SLJ 12/99)

716 Ehrlich, Fred. *Does a Baboon Sleep in a Bed?* (PS). Illus. by Emily Bolam. Series: Early Experiences. 2006, Blue Apple $13.50 (978-1-59354-142-2); paper $5.95 (978-1-59354-143-9). 32pp. Where do animals sleep? Not in beds, as people do, informs this bedtime book, which offers factual

information about the sleeping habits of six different kinds of animals. (Rev: BL 5/15/06) [649]

717 Emberley, Ed. *Go Away, Big Green Monster!* (PS–1). Illus. 1993, Little, Brown $15.95 (978-0-316-23653-9). 32pp. This toy book deals with a child's nighttime fears in a lighthearted way that will be both a joy and a comfort to young people. (Rev: BCCB 3/93; BL 4/15/93*; HB 7/93)

718 Engel, Diana. *Circle Song* (PS–1). Illus. 1999, Marshall Cavendish $15.95 (978-0-7614-5040-5). 32pp. A brief bedtime rhyme that evokes circles, including the moon. (Rev: BL 4/1/99; HBG 10/99; SLJ 6/99)

719 Faulkner, Keith. *The Scared Little Bear: A Not-Too-Scary Pop-up Book* (PS–2). Illus. by Jonathan Lambert. 2000, Scholastic $9.95 (978-0-531-30267-5). A pop-up book in which a young bear discovers that the scary sounds he hears in the night are only his father snoring. (Rev: SLJ 2/01)

720 Fernandes, Eugenie. *Baby Dreams* (PS). Illus. by author. 1999, Stoddart $13.95 (978-0-7737-3139-4). An imaginative view of the images a sleeping baby might experience — being in a land of sleeping infants or being cradled on a rabbit's back. (Rev: SLJ 1/00)

721 Ferreri, Della Ross. *How Will I Ever Sleep in This Bed?* (PS). Illus. by Capucine Mazille. 2005, Sterling LB $12.95 (978-1-4027-1492-4). Unable to adjust to his new, larger bed, a young boy fills it up with his stuffed toys, leaving no room for himself. (Rev: SLJ 1/06)

722 Fore, S. J. *Tiger Can't Sleep* (PS–1). Illus. by R. W. Alley. 2006, Viking $15.99 (978-0-670-06078-8). 32pp. An imaginative little boy tries to get the noisy tiger in his closet to quiet down so he can get some sleep. (Rev: BL 12/15/05; SLJ 2/06)

723 Fox, Mem. *A Bedtime Story* (PS–2). Illus. by Elivia Savadier. 1996, Mondo $13.95 (978-1-57255-136-7). Polly and Bed Rabbit look forward to a bedtime story from their parents. (Rev: SLJ 12/96)

724 Fox, Mem. *Sleepy Bears* (PS–2). Illus. by Kerry Argent. 1999, Harcourt $16.00 (978-0-15-202016-3). 32pp. Mama Bear sings a different lullaby to each of her six cubs as they settle in for a winter's sleep. (Rev: BL 11/15/99; HBG 3/00; SLJ 10/99)

725 Fox, Mem. *Time for Bed* (PS). Illus. by Jane Dyer. 1993, Harcourt $16.00 (978-0-15-288183-2). 32pp. Various animals put their babies to sleep in this quiet bedtime book. (Rev: BCCB 10/93; BL 10/1/93; SLJ 10/93)

726 Fox, Mem. *Where the Giant Sleeps* (PS–2). Illus. by Vladimir Radunsky. 2007, Harcourt $16.00 (978-0-15-205785-5). 32pp. The slumbering places of giants, wizards, and other fairy tale characters are revealed in two-page spreads mimicking the view through a spyglass. (Rev: BL 11/15/07; LMC 1/08; SLJ 11/07)

727 Frampton, David. *The Whole Night Through: A Lullaby* (PS–1). Illus. 2001, HarperCollins LB $15.89 (978-0-06-028826-6). 32pp. A boisterous little leopard is determined to stay awake. (Rev: BL 5/15/01; HBG 10/01; SLJ 6/01*)

728 Freedman, Claire. *Good Night, Sleep Tight* (PS–K). Illus. by Rory Tyger. 2003, Abrams $14.95 (978-0-8109-4513-5). In this heartwarming bedtime story, Grandma Bear gets little Archie to sleep when she tells him stories about putting his mother to bed. (Rev: BL 12/15/03; HBG 4/04; SLJ 12/03)

729 Freedman, Claire. *Night-Night, Emily!* (PS). Illus. by Jane Massey. 2003, Tiger Tales $15.95 (978-1-58925-032-1). In this gentle bedtime story, little Emily is distressed when she can't find Mr. Teddy, her favorite stuffed animal; she tries substituting other stuffed toys, but she's unable to fall asleep until she discovers Mr. Teddy hidden beneath a pillow. (Rev: SLJ 1/04)

730 Freedman, Claire. *Snuggle Up, Sleepy Ones* (PS–1). Illus. by Tina Macnaughton. 2005, Good Bks. $16.00 (978-1-56148-475-1). A sleepytime book with cuddly animals settling in for the night. (Rev: SLJ 7/05)

731 Gabriel, Andrea. *My Favorite Bear* (PS–1). Illus. 2003, Charlesbridge $15.95 (978-1-58089-038-0). 32pp. To get her little bear to sleep, a mother bear sings a song about different kinds of bears. (Rev: BL 2/15/03; HBG 10/03; SLJ 2/03)

732 Garelick, May. *Look at the Moon* (K–3). Illus. by Barbara Garrison. 1996, Mondo $14.95 (978-1-57255-142-8). 30pp. A young girl wonders if animals experience the same thrill of seeing moonlight as she does. (Rev: BL 11/15/96; SLJ 1/97)

733 Gay, Michel. *Zee Is Not Scared* (PS–2). Trans. from French by Marie Mianowski. Illus. by author. 2004, Clarion $15.00 (978-0-618-43931-7). 29pp. A little zebra can't settle down to sleep in this translation of a French story, and decides to dress up as a ghost and scare his parents. (Rev: SLJ 4/04)

734 George, Lindsay Barrett. *My Bunny and Me* (PS–2). Illus. 2001, Greenwillow LB $15.89 (978-0-688-16075-3). 32pp. A boy draws a bunny that comes to life and the two play together until the boy goes to bed and the bunny hops off into a field. (Rev: BL 1/1–15/01; HBG 10/01)

735 Gerber, Carole. *Firefly Night* (PS–3). Illus. by Marty Husted. 2000, Charlesbridge $16.95 (978-1-58089-051-9); paper $6.95 (978-1-58089-066-3). 32pp. Based on some lines from Longfellow's *Hiawatha*, this is the gentle story of a young Chippewa girl who is guided home at night by a firefly. (Rev: BL 11/1/00; HBG 3/01; SLJ 1/01)

736 Gerber, Carole. *Hush! A Gaelic Lullaby* (PS–2). Illus. by Marty Husted. 1997, Whispering Coyote $16.95 (978-1-879085-57-2). In this lullaby, an Irish family puts baby to bed while taking precautions against a storm that is approaching their farm. (Rev: HB 1, 3, 5/97; HBG 3/98; SLJ 1/98)

737 Gerstein, Mordicai. *Bedtime, Everybody!* (PS–2). Illus. 1996, Hyperion LB $13.49 (978-0-7868-2138-9). 32pp. Daisy has difficulty getting her many stuffed animals to go to bed. (Rev: BL 6/1–15/96; SLJ 6/96)

738 Glass, Beth Raisner, and Susan Lubner. *Noises at Night* (PS–1). Illus. by Bruce Whatley. 2005, Abrams $15.95 (978-0-8109-5750-3). In this unusual bedtime story told in rhyming couplets, the mys-

terious sounds of nighttime inspire a young boy to dream of grand adventures with his teddy bear. (Rev: SLJ 10/05)

739 Gliori, Debi. *Polar Bolero: A Bedtime Dance* (PS–2). Illus. 2001, Harcourt $16.00 (978-0-15-202436-9). 32pp. When it's too hot to sleep, a young polar bear heads to the place where they dance the Polar Bolero. (Rev: BL 5/1/01; HBG 10/01; SLJ 6/01)

740 Goodman, Joan E. *Bernard's Nap* (PS–1). Illus. by Dominic Catalano. 1999, Boyds Mills $14.95 (978-1-56397-728-2). 32pp. While trying to get Bernard, a baby elephant, to take his nap, the rest of his family nod off, but not Bernard — until he eventually gives in. (Rev: BL 3/15/99; HBG 10/99; SLJ 4/99)

741 Greenberg, David T. *Enchanted Lions* (PS–2). Illus. by Kristina Swarner. 2009, Dutton $16.99 (978-0-525-47938-3). 32pp. A young girl sets off for a nighttime adventure on the back of an enchanted lion. (Rev: BL 5/15/09; SLJ 6/09)

742 Greenstein, Elaine. *Dreaming: A Countdown to Sleep* (PS–1). Illus. 2000, Scholastic $15.95 (978-0-439-06302-9). 32pp. With a text that involves counting down from 10 to 1, this picture book evokes a dreamy atmosphere before sleep comes. (Rev: BCCB 5/00; BL 2/1/00; HBG 3/01; SLJ 6/00)

743 Griffin, Sandra U. *Earth Circles* (PS–3). Illus. by author. 1989, Walker LB $13.85 (978-0-8027-6845-2). The circle of life from birth to death, including the need to sleep at the end of each day, is introduced as it appears in nature. (Rev: SLJ 11/89)

744 Guy, Ginger F. *Go Back to Bed!* (K–2). Illus. by James Bernardin. 2006, Carolrhoda $15.95 (978-1-57505-750-7). Edwin comes up with lots of excuses not to go to sleep and imagines exciting things happening downstairs. (Rev: SLJ 6/06)

745 Hague, Kathleen. *Good Night, Fairies* (PS–3). Illus. by Michael Hague. 2002, North-South $15.95 (978-1-58717-134-5). 40pp. This magical bedtime book has a mother explaining to her child all the jobs performed by fairies. (Rev: BL 3/15/02; HBG 10/02)

746 Harley, Bill. *Nothing Happened* (K–2). Illus. by Ann Miya. 1995, Tricycle $14.95 (978-1-883672-09-6). 32pp. Jack is determined to stay awake so he can share in all the exciting things he believes happen to his family when he is asleep. (Rev: BL 4/15/95; SLJ 6/95)

747 Harris, Peter. *The Night Pirates* (PS–K). Illus. by Deborah Allwright. 2006, Scholastic $17.99 (978-0-439-79959-1). 32pp. A boy named Tom joins a band of tough girl pirates in this rhyming bedtime story full of humor. (Rev: BL 2/1/06; SLJ 3/06)

748 Harris, Robie H. *Maybe a Bear Ate It!* (PS–2). Illus. by Michael Emberley. 2008, Scholastic $15.99 (978-0-439-92961-5). 40pp. As a small animal gets ready for bed, he realizes that his favorite book is missing and imagines many improbable reasons for its disappearance. (Rev: BL 12/15/07; LMC 1/08; SLJ 1/08)

749 Harrison, Troon. *The Dream Collector* (PS–3). Illus. by Alan Daniel and Lea Daniel. 1999, Kids

Can $15.95 (978-1-55074-437-8). 32pp. When the dream collector can't collect all the creatures left over from people's dreams because of a broken truck, little Zachary gives him a hand. (Rev: BL 3/1/99; HBG 10/99; SLJ 7/99)

750 Harshman, Marc. *All the Way to Morning* (PS–3). Illus. by Felipe Davalos. 1999, Marshall Cavendish $15.95 (978-0-7614-5042-9). 32pp. On a camping trip, a father tells his son what children in other countries such as Israel, Japan, and Kenya hear as they go to sleep at night. (Rev: BL 9/15/99; HBG 3/00; SLJ 11/99)

751 Henry, Rohan. *Good Night, Baby Ruby* (PS). Illus. by author. 2009, Abrams $14.95 (978-0-8109-8323-6). 32pp. Toddler Ruby is much too active to go to bed, and evades her mother at every turn. (Rev: SLJ 3/09)

752 Hest, Amy. *Kiss Good Night* (PS–1). Illus. by Anita Jeram. 2001, Candlewick $15.99 (978-0-7636-0780-7). 32pp. Sam, a little bear, cannot fall asleep without his mother's goodnight kiss. (Rev: BL 10/1/01; HBG 3/02; SLJ 11/01*)

753 Hindley, Judy. *Sleepy Places* (PS–K). Illus. by Tor Freeman. 2006, Candlewick $15.99 (978-0-7636-2983-0). 32pp. This colorful bedtime book examines the various places where animals sleep. (Rev: BL 4/15/06; SLJ 5/06)

754 Hines, Anna Grossnickle. *My Own Big Bed* (PS–K). Illus. by Mary Watson. 1998, Greenwillow $16.99 (978-0-688-15599-5). 24pp. At bedtime, a young girl enjoys her new, roomy bed, where Mommy and Daddy can sit next to her. (Rev: BL 10/15/98; HBG 3/99; SLJ 4/99)

755 Ho, Minfong. *Hush! A Thai Lullaby* (PS–3). Illus. by Holly Meade. 1996, Orchard LB $16.99 (978-0-531-08850-0). 32pp. In this lullaby, a mother quiets the animals, one by one, so that her baby can sleep. (Rev: BCCB 4/96; BL 4/15/96; HB 11/96; SLJ 3/96)

756 Hoellwarth, Cathryn C. *The Underbed* (PS–K). Illus. by Sibyl G. Grieg. 1990, Good Bks. $12.95 (978-0-934672-79-5). 24pp. Mother helps Tucker get rid of the monster he believes is under the bed. (Rev: BL 3/1/91; SLJ 7/91)

757 Holub, Joan. *Bed, Bats, and Beyond* (2–3). Illus. by Mernie Gallagher-Cole. 2008, Darby Creek $14.95 (978-1-58196-077-8). 64pp. Its morning and time for bed but young bat Fink can't get to sleep, so the whole bat family pitches in with stories. (Rev: SLJ 12/08)

758 Imai, Ayano. *The 108th Sheep* (PS–K). Illus. by author. 2007, ME Media $15.95 (978-1-58925-063-5). 32pp. An oversize bedtime/counting book in which sleepless young Emma decides to count sheep. (Rev: BL 6/1–15/07; SLJ 5/07)

759 Inches, Alison. *The Stuffed Animals Get Ready for Bed* (PS–K). Illus. by Bryan Langdo. 2006, Harcourt $16.00 (978-0-15-216466-9). 32pp. It's bedtime, but the stuffed animals aren't sleepy yet and it's up to their young owner to get them settled down. (Rev: BL 8/06; SLJ 9/06)

760 Ives, Penny. *Rabbit Pie* (PS). Illus. 2006, Viking $15.99 (978-0-670-05951-5). 32pp. A mother rabbit follows nightly rituals as she readies her six little bunnies for sleep. (Rev: BL 1/1–15/06; SLJ 5/06)

761 James, Betsy. *The Dream Stair* (K–3). Illus. by Richard J. Watson. 1990, HarperCollins $13.95 (978-0-06-022787-6). 32pp. After Grandmother tucks her into bed, a little girl dreams of wandering "past clouds, past angels." (Rev: BL 3/1/90; SLJ 7/90)

762 Jennings, Sharon. *No Monsters Here* (PS–K). Illus. by Ruth Ohi. 2004, Fitzhenry & Whiteside $14.95 (978-1-55041-787-6). 24pp. A young boy reassures his fearful father, checking there are no monsters under his father's bed before he settles down for the night. (Rev: BL 9/1/04; SLJ 10/04)

763 Joosse, Barbara M. *In the Night Garden* (PS–K). Illus. by Elizabeth Sayles. 2008, Holt $16.95 (978-0-8050-6671-5). Bedtime slips into surreal dream time for three little girls who imagine themselves impressive animals. (Rev: SLJ 12/08)

764 Joosse, Barbara M. *Roawr!* (PS–K). Illus. by Jan Jutte. 2009, Philomel $16.99 (978-0-399-24777-4). 40pp. An exciting bedtime story featuring a boy who must first trap a bear. (Rev: BL 12/1/08; SLJ 3/09)

765 Jordan, Sandra. *Down on Casey's Farm* (PS–K). Illus. by author. 1996, Orchard LB $16.99 (978-0-531-08853-1). A bedtime book that introduces a number of farm animals through the fantasies of a young boy. (Rev: SLJ 10/96)

766 Kanevsky, Polly. *Sleepy Boy* (K–2). Illus. by Stephanie Anderson. 2006, Simon & Schuster $15.95 (978-0-689-86735-4). 32pp. A small boy remembers the lion cub he saw at the zoo as he cuddles with his daddy in this charming bedtime book. (Rev: BL 4/15/06; SLJ 5/06)

767 Katz, Karen. *Counting Kisses* (PS). Illus. 2001, Simon & Schuster $14.00 (978-0-689-83470-7). 32pp. Every family member showers a baby with kisses until the young child peacefully drops off to sleep. (Rev: BCCB 2/01; BL 2/1/01; HBG 10/01; SLJ 2/01)

768 Katz, Karen. *Princess Baby, Night-Night* (PS–K). Illus. by author. 2009, Random $14.99 (978-0-375-84462-1). 32pp. Princess Baby is not tired and to prove it she falls asleep on the floor. (Rev: BL 12/1/08; SLJ 1/09)

769 Kavanagh, Peter. *I Love My Mama* (PS–1). Illus. by Jane Chapman. 2003, Simon & Schuster $12.95 (978-0-689-85691-4). A mother elephant and her baby spend their day traversing the beautiful African landscape before settling down to sleep in the grass. (Rev: HBG 10/03; SLJ 4/03)

770 Kiesler, Kate, ed. *Fishing for a Dream: Ocean Lullabies and Night Dreams* (PS–2). Illus. 1999, Clarion $16.00 (978-0-395-94149-2). 32pp. A collection of lullabies that focus on the nighttime sea and the images it evokes. (Rev: BL 12/15/99; HBG 3/00; SLJ 12/99) [782.4215]

771 Koller, Jackie F. *No Such Thing* (K–3). Illus. by Betsy Lewin. 1997, Boyds Mills $15.95 (978-1-56397-490-8). 32pp. A monster and her son under the bed are undergoing the same comforting bedtime rituals as a real mother and son. (Rev: BCCB 3/97; BL 4/1/97; SLJ 6/97)

772 Kono, Erin Eitter. *Hula Lullaby* (PS–2). Illus. 2005, Little, Brown $15.99 (978-0-316-73591-9). 32pp. In her mother's lap, a Hawaiian girl listens to descriptions of the warm world around her until she falls asleep. (Rev: BL 5/1/05)

773 Levine, Joan. *Topsy-Turvy Bedtime* (K–3). Illus. by Tony Auth. 2008, Candlewick $14.99 (978-0-7636-3008-9). 32pp. Arathusela must put her parents to bed and they prove very difficult, wanting to watch TV, asking for another drink . . . (Rev: BCCB 5/08; BL 6/1–15/08)

774 Lewis, Kim. *Good Night, Harry* (PS–K). Illus. by author. 2004, Candlewick $15.99 (978-0-7636-2206-0). Harry the elephant can't sleep, so Lulu and Ted — also soft toy animals — sit up with him until he drifts off. (Rev: SLJ 4/04)

775 Lewis, Paeony. *No More Yawning!* (PS–1). Illus. by Brita Granström. 2008, Scholastic $16.99 (978-0-545-02957-5). 32pp. Seems like Florence and her toy monkey Arnold need a hundred things before they can go to sleep; includes endnotes with tips on falling asleep. (Rev: BL 1/1–15/08; SLJ 4/08)

776 Lindbergh, Reeve. *Our Nest* (PS–1). Illus. by Jill McElmurry. 2004, Candlewick $15.99 (978-0-7636-1286-3). 32pp. The comforts of all sorts of nests — from birds in trees to fish in water and boats in harbors — are celebrated in this gentle book. (Rev: BL 4/15/04*; SLJ 5/04)

777 Lindgren, Astrid. *I Don't Want to Go to Bed* (PS–1). Trans. by Barbara Lucas. Illus. by Ilon Wikland. 1988, Farrar $12.95 (91-29-59066-3). 32pp. Five-year-old Larry won't go to bed until Aunt Lottie gives him a pair of magic glasses. (Rev: BL 12/1/88; SLJ 4/89)

778 Loh, Morag. *Tucking Mommy In* (PS–1). Illus. by Donna Rawlins. 1988, Orchard paper $5.95 (978-0-531-07025-3). 40pp. Mommy falls asleep and the children tuck her in. (Rev: BCCB 9/88; BL 10/1/88; SLJ 10/88)

779 London, Jonathan. *Froggy Goes to Bed* (PS–K). Illus. by Frank Remkiewicz. 2000, Viking $15.99 (978-0-670-88860-3). 32pp. The nighttime rituals become so prolonged that Froggy's mother falls asleep before he does. (Rev: BL 3/1/00; HBG 10/00; SLJ 6/00)

780 Long, Sylvia. *Hush Little Baby* (PS–1). Illus. 1997, Chronicle $12.95 (978-0-8118-1416-4). 32pp. This song, a tender lullaby, focuses on the relationship between a mother and her baby bunny. (Rev: BL 6/1–15/97)

781 Lyon, George E. *Sleepsong* (PS–K). Illus. by Peter Catalanotto. 2009, Atheneum $16.99 (978-0-689-86973-0). 40pp. A little girl's parents get her ready for bed. (Rev: BL 12/1/08; SLJ 1/09)

782 McBratney, Sam. *You're All My Favorites* (PS–K). Illus. by Anita Jeram. 2004, Candlewick $15.99 (978-0-7636-2442-2). Three little bears worry that they are not good enough until they are reassured by their parents. (Rev: HB 9/04; SLJ 11/04)

783 McCain, Becky Ray. *Grandmother's Dreamcatcher* (K–2). Illus. by Stacey Schuett. 1998, Whitman $15.95 (978-0-8075-3031-3). 32pp. A young Chippewa boy goes to live with his grandmother, who cures him of having bad dreams by placing a dreamcatcher above his bed. (Rev: BL 10/1/98; HBG 3/99; SLJ 12/98)

784 McCullough, Sharon Pierce. *Bunbun at Bedtime* (PS). Illus. 2001, Barefoot Books $14.99 (978-1-84148-438-9). 24pp. Bunbun dallies while his brother and sister get ready for bed until a scary noise prompts a burst of activity. (Rev: BL 10/1/01; HBG 3/02; SLJ 11/01)

785 MacDonald, Margaret Read. *The Squeaky Door* (PS–2). Illus. by Mary Newell Depalma. 2006, HarperCollins $15.99 (978-0-06-028373-5). 40pp. A funny retelling of the story of a boy who can't sleep because he's scared of his squeaking door, with eye-catching typography and bright cartoon illustrations. (Rev: BL 12/1/05; SLJ 1/06)

786 MacDonald, Margaret Read. *Tuck-Me-In Tales: Bedtime Stories from Around the World* (PS–1). Illus. by Yvonne Davis. 1996, August House $19.95 (978-0-87483-461-1). 64pp. Five traditional bedtime stories from around the world are lavishly illustrated. (Rev: BL 10/1/96; SLJ 11/96) [398.2]

787 McDonald, Megan. *My House Has Stars* (PS–3). Illus. by Peter Catalanotto. 1996, Orchard LB $17.99 (978-0-531-08879-1). 32pp. Eight children from around the world tell about their homes in the evening and at night. (Rev: BCCB 11/96; BL 11/1/96; SLJ 10/96)

788 MacLachlan, Patricia. *Who Loves Me?* (PS). Illus. by Amanda Sheperd. 2005, HarperCollins LB $15.89 (978-0-06-027977-6). 40pp. A little girl and her cat check off all the people who love her. (Rev: BL 6/1–15/05; SLJ 5/05)

789 McMullan, Kate. *If You Were My Bunny* (PS–K). Illus. by David McPhail. 1996, Scholastic $7.95 (978-0-590-52749-1). 32pp. A bedtime book with lullabies sung by different loving animal mothers to their attentive offspring. (Rev: BL 5/1/96; HB 7/96)

790 Mallat, Kathy. *Seven Stars More!* (PS). Illus. by author. 1998, Walker $14.95 (978-0-8027-8675-3). A counting book that is also a bedtime book about a little girl who counts objects to put herself to sleep. (Rev: HBG 3/99; SLJ 11/98)

791 Marlow, Layn. *Hurry Up and Slow Down* (PS–2). Illus. by author. 2009, Holiday $16.95 (978-0-8234-2178-7). 32pp. Hare and Tortoise are good friends who find their differences are easily conquered. (Rev: BL 2/1/09; SLJ 2/09)

792 Melling, David. *Good Knight Sleep Tight* (PS–2). Illus. 2006, Barron's $14.99 (978-0-7641-5878-0). 32pp. The baby princess cannot sleep because the cat has destroyed her pillow, so an intrepid young knight is sent in search of suitably fluffy material. (Rev: BL 2/1/06; SLJ 3/06)

793 Melmed, Laura K. *Jumbo's Lullaby* (PS). Illus. by Henri Sorensen. 1999, Lothrop LB $15.89 (978-0-688-16996-1). 24pp. Mama Elephant tries to get her young child to sleep by describing how other animals go to bed. (Rev: BL 10/1/99; HBG 3/00; SLJ 9/99)

794 Millen, C. M. *Blue Bowl Down: An Appalachian Rhyme* (PS–1). Illus. by Holly Meade. 2004, Candlewick $16.99 (978-0-7636-1817-9). 32pp. Appealing cut-paper art and a lullaby rhyme depict an Appalachian mother and her toddler son step by step as they prepare bread dough for baking early the next morning. (Rev: BL 5/1/04; SLJ 9/04)

795 Morales, Yuri. *Little Night* (PS–2). Illus. 2007, Roaring Brook $16.95 (978-1-59643-088-4). 32pp. Although she doesn't want to go to bed, Little Night has a bath in falling stars and a nightdress crocheted from clouds. (Rev: BL 2/1/07)

796 Morgan, Mary. *Sleep Tight, Little Mouse* (PS). Illus. by author. 2003, Knopf LB $14.99 (978-0-375-92308-1). 32pp. As he gets ready for bed, Little Mouse considers other options — such as a bird's nest or kangaroo's pouch — but decides that the best sleeping place is his own. (Rev: BL 5/15/03; HBG 10/03; SLJ 8/03)

797 Mortensen, Denise Dowling. *Good Night Engines* (PS). Illus. by Melissa Iwai. 2003, Clarion $15.00 (978-0-618-13537-0). 32pp. At bedtime, a variety of forms of transport come to a halt and settle down for the night. (Rev: BL 12/15/03; HBG 4/04; SLJ 12/03)

798 Murray, Dennis. *The Stars Are Waiting* (PS–K). Illus. by Jacqueline Rogers. 1998, Marshall Cavendish $15.95 (978-0-7614-5024-5). 32pp. In this bedtime book, nighttime beckons all the animals of the forest to go to sleep and finally does the same to three young children in a neighboring farmhouse. (Rev: BL 8/98; HBG 10/98; SLJ 6/98)

799 Myers, Tim. *Dark Sparkle Tea: And Other Bedtime Poems* (2–4). Illus. by Kelley Cunningham. 2006, Boyds Mills $16.95 (978-1-59078-288-0). 32pp. Rhythmic poems featuring funny, lively wordplay describe bouncy bedtimes. (Rev: BL 3/15/06; SLJ 6/06) [811]

800 Nakamura, Katherine Riley. *Song of Night: It's Time to Go to Bed* (PS). Illus. by Linnea Riley. 2002, Scholastic $15.95 (978-0-439-26678-9). 40pp. Animal parents help their beloved children get ready for bed in this charming bedtime book. (Rev: BL 2/1/02; HBG 10/02; SLJ 5/02)

801 Neubecker, Robert. *Beasty Bath* (PS–1). Illus. by author. 2005, Scholastic $14.99 (978-0-439-64000-8). As she has a bath and gets ready for bed, a little girl imagines herself as many beasts and monsters. (Rev: SLJ 1/06)

802 Newman, Leslea. *Daddy's Song* (PS–1). Illus. by Karen Ritz. 2007, Holt $16.95 (978-0-8050-6975-4). A father sings an imaginative, loving song to his daughter as he puts her to bed. Bright, beautiful illustrations bring the song to life. (Rev: SLJ 6/07)

803 Noll, Amanda. *I Need My Monster* (K–2). Illus. by Howard McWilliam. 2009, Flashlight $16.95 (978-0-9799746-2-5). 32pp. Ethan can't sleep when his under-the-bed monster Gabe goes fishing, so he interviews a series of replacement monsters. (Rev: BL 3/15/09; LMC 8/09; SLJ 4/09)

804 Numeroff, Laura. *When Sheep Sleep* (PS–K). Illus. by David McPhail. 2006, Abrams $15.95 (978-0-8109-5469-4). 32pp. A little girl, struggling to fall asleep, decides to try counting sheep but is disheartened to find that all the sheep are already asleep. (Rev: BL 9/1/06; SLJ 10/06)

805 Ongman, Gudrun. *The Sleep Ponies* (PS–1). Illus. 2000, MindCastle $16.95 (978-0-9677204-0-1). 32pp. Dreaming children are able to ride sleep ponies and travel through wonderful landscapes in this soothing picture book. (Rev: BL 12/15/00)

806 Oppenheim, Joanne. *The Prince's Bedtime* (PS–1). Illus. by Miriam Latimer. 2006, Barefoot Books $16.99 (978-1-84148-597-3). The prince refuses to go to sleep despite many inducements until a wise woman arrives with bedtime stories. (Rev: SLJ 12/06)

807 Osofsky, Audrey. *Dreamcatcher* (PS–3). Illus. by Ed Young. 1992, Orchard LB $16.99 (978-0-531-08588-2). 32pp. An Ojibwa baby watches everyday events in his family's life and later sleeps peacefully. (Rev: BCCB 7–8/92; BL 2/15/92; SLJ 4/92)

808 Owens, Mary Beth. *Panda Whispers* (PS–2). Illus. by author. 2007, Dutton $16.99 (978-0-525-47171-4). After a succession of animals wish their babies happy dreams, a father does the same to his human child. (Rev: SLJ 4/07)

809 Pank, Rachel. *Sonia and Barnie and the Noise in the Night* (PS–K). Illus. 1991, Scholastic paper $13.95 (978-0-590-44657-0). 32pp. Her cowardly cat may hide up in a tree, but brave and bossy Sonia takes on the "monster" who frightened them. (Rev: BL 6/1/91; SLJ 12/91)

810 Paul, Ann Whitford. *If Animals Kissed Goodnight* (PS–2). Illus. by David Walker. 2008, Farrar $16.95 (978-0-374-38051-9). 40pp. A mother and her child preparing for bed discuss how various animals behave at nighttime. (Rev: BL 6/1–15/08; SLJ 6/08)

811 Peck, Jan. *Way Up High in a Tall Green Tree* (PS–1). Illus. by Valeria Petrone. 2005, Simon & Schuster $15.95 (978-1-4169-0071-9). A girl says good-night to all sorts of jungle animals, then settles down to sleep in her bed full of similar rainforest toys. (Rev: SLJ 9/05)

812 Perl, Erica S. *Chicken Bedtime Is Really Early* (PS). Illus. by George Bates. 2005, Abrams $14.95 (978-0-8109-4926-3). 32pp. Baby farm animals — chicks, calves, bunnies, hamsters — turn in early to get some rest before the rooster crows in this bedtime picture book. (Rev: BL 3/15/05; SLJ 4/05)

813 Peters, Lisa Westberg. *Sleepyhead Bear* (PS). Illus. by Ian Schoenherr. 2006, Greenwillow $16.99 (978-0-06-059675-0). 32pp. Little Bear, glad to find some friendly butterflies after being bothered by pesky bugs, settles down for a good night's sleep in this simple bedtime book. (Rev: BL 5/15/06; SLJ 5/06)

814 Pfister, Marcus. *Bertie at Bedtime* (PS–1). Illus. by author. 2008, North-South $16.95 (978-0-7358-2194-1). 32pp. A young hippo called Bertie resists bedtime until his father is totally worn out. (Rev: BL 4/15/08; SLJ 5/08)

815 Philip, Neil, ed. *Weave Little Stars into My Sleep: Native American Lullabies* (2–4). Illus. by Edward S. Curtis. 2001, Clarion $16.00 (978-0-618-08856-0). 48pp. Fifteen Native American lullabies are accompanied by sepia-toned illustrations and background information. (Rev: BL 10/15/01; HBG 3/02; SLJ 11/01) [782.4215]

816 Pitcher, Caroline. *The Winter Dragon* (K–2). Illus. by Sophy Williams. 2004, Lincoln $15.95 (978-1-84507-322-0). 36pp. Young Rory's dragon warms the winter nights, leaving the boy with memories of comfort and companionship when spring arrives. (Rev: BL 10/15/04; SLJ 1/05)

817 Puttock, Simon. *Earth to Stella!* (PS–2). Illus. by Philip Hopman. 2006, Clarion $16.00 (978-0-618-58535-9). 32pp. As she brushes her teeth and gets ready for bed, young Stella alternates between her fantasy of outer space and the reality of her attentive father. (Rev: SLJ 3/06)

818 Radzinski, Kandy. *Where to Sleep* (PS–K). Illus. by author. 2009, Sleeping Bear $15.95 (978-1-58536-436-7). 32pp. A kitten finds a comfy spot at the feet of its "best friend" in this nap/bedtime book set on a farm. (Rev: BL 4/1/09; SLJ 5/09)

819 Raschka, Chris. *Can't Sleep* (PS–1). Illus. 1995, Orchard LB $15.99 (978-0-531-08779-4). 32pp. A young dog with insomnia takes comfort in having the moon watch over him until he goes to sleep. (Rev: BCCB 10/95; BL 9/15/95; SLJ 9/95*)

820 Raya-Norman, Faye. *Wolf Songs* (PS–2). Illus. by Richard Ziehler-Martin. 1999, Portunus $15.95 (978-1-886440-04-3). In this bedtime fantasy, young Matthew is led on a night walk by a silver wolf and is accompanied by a full moon, northern lights, and stars. (Rev: SLJ 2/00)

821 Rex, Michael. *You Can Do Anything, Daddy!* (PS–K). Illus. 2007, Putnam $14.99 (978-0-399-24298-4). 32pp. When a little boy at bedtime asks his tie-wearing dad if he'd save him if pirates took him, the action morphs into an adventurous rescue full of pirates, snakes, robots, and more, with the son proffering apple juice and bandages at its end; detail-filled illustrations emulate comics. (Rev: BL 1/1–15/07)

822 Robbins, Maria Polushkin. *Mother, Mother, I Want Another* (PS–2). Illus. by Jon Goodell. 2005, Knopf LB $16.99 (978-0-375-92588-7). 32pp. A newly illustrated edition of the bedtime story in which Mrs. Mouse misinterprets her son's request. (Rev: BL 2/15/05; SLJ 3/05)

823 Rock, Lois. *I Wish Tonight* (PS–2). Illus. by Anne Wilson. 2000, Good Bks. $16.00 (978-1-56148-315-0). In bed at night, a young boy wishes on a star and travels into a world of make-believe. (Rev: SLJ 12/00)

824 Rockhill, Dennis. *Ocean Whisper / Susurro del oceano* (PS–2). Trans. by Eida de la Vega. Illus. by author. 2005, Raven Tree $16.95 (978-0-9741992-4-5). 32pp. A bilingual poem introduces a wordless picture book in which a boy's whale poster and goldfish morph into a dreamlike undersea world. (Rev: SLJ 2/06)

825 Rockwell, Anne. *Here Comes the Night* (PS–K). Illus. by author. 2006, Holt $16.95 (978-0-8050-7663-9). A little boy's mommy helps him get ready for bed and drift off to dreamland. (Rev: SLJ 6/06)

826 Roep, Nanda. *Kisses* (PS). Illus. by Marijke Ten Cate. 2002, Front St. $15.95 (978-1-886910-85-0). Goodnight kisses are the focus of this richly illustrated, gentle story. (Rev: HBG 3/03; SLJ 1/03)

827 Rosenthal, Amy Krouse. *Little Hoot* (PS–2). Illus. by Jen Corace. 2008, Chronicle $12.99 (978-0-8118-6023-9). 36pp. Little Hoot's mean parents make him stay up late playing, when he'd rather be asleep like all his friends. (Rev: BCCB 3/08; SLJ 4/08)

828 Roth, Carol. *Little Bunny's Sleepless Night* (PS–K). Illus. by Valeri Gorbachev. 1999, North-South LB $15.88 (978-0-7358-1070-9). 32pp. Little Bunny is lonely at night, so he tries sleeping with other animals. Each proves unsatisfactory (e.g., Bear snores), and so he returns home happily to his own bed. (Rev: BL 6/1–15/99; HBG 10/99; SLJ 7/99)

829 Russo, Marisabina. *The Bunnies Are Not in Their Beds* (K–2). Illus. by author. 2006, Random $15.99 (978-0-375-83961-0). Three bunny siblings are too full of energy to go to sleep despite their parents' frequent admonitions. (Rev: BL 2/1/07; SLJ 12/06)

830 Rydell, Katy. *Wind Says Good Night* (PS–1). Illus. by David Jorgensen. 1994, Houghton $16.00 (978-0-395-60474-8). 42pp. This cumulative bedtime story tells how all the animals and birds cooperate so a little girl can go to sleep. (Rev: BCCB 5/94; BL 4/1/94; SLJ 4/94*)

831 Saltzberg, Barney. *Cornelius P. Mud, Are You Ready for Bed?* (PS). Illus. 2005, Candlewick $15.99 (978-0-7636-2399-9). 32pp. Asked many pre-bed questions ("Have you used the bathroom?"), Cornelius the pig blithely lies "yes" but the illustrations tell the truth. (Rev: BL 5/1/05; SLJ 3/05)

832 Sanroman, Susana. *Señora Regañona* (PS–3). Illus. by Domi. 1998, Douglas & McIntyre $14.95 (978-0-88899-320-5). 32pp. A child conquers her fear of the dark, which she calls "Señora Regañona," when she flies into the sky one night and makes a friend of the Señora. (Rev: BL 8/98; HBG 10/98; SLJ 9/98)

833 Sayles, Elizabeth. *The Goldfish Yawned* (PS–1). Illus. by author. 2005, Holt $16.95 (978-0-8050-7624-0). A sleepy young child sets sail on a magical boat trip. (Rev: SLJ 1/06)

834 Schotter, Roni. *Bunny's Night Out* (PS–1). Illus. by Margot Apple. 1989, Little, Brown $13.95 (978-0-316-77465-9). A bunny sneaks out at night and experiences adventures before coming home to his welcome bed. (Rev: SLJ 7/89)

835 Schroeder, Lisa. *Baby Can't Sleep* (PS). Illus. by Viviana Garofoli. 2005, Sterling LB $12.95 (978-1-4027-2171-7). Counting sheep doesn't always put babies to sleep! (Rev: SLJ 1/06)

836 Scotton, Rob. *Russell the Sheep* (PS–1). Illus. by author. 2005, HarperCollins LB $18.89 (978-0-06-059849-5). Russell the sheep just can't sleep; he tries counting feet — and then stars — and then sheep . . . (Rev: SLJ 4/05)

837 Shea, Bob. *Dinosaur vs. Bedtime* (PS–K). Illus. by author. 2008, Hyperion $15.99 (978-1-4231-1335-5). 40pp. A plucky little dinosaur conquers most challenges of the day but finds bedtime the hardest of all. (Rev: BCCB 10/08; HB 9/08; SLJ 11/08)

838 Shulevitz, Uri. *So Sleepy Story* (PS). Illus. by author. 2006, Farrar $16.00 (978-0-374-37031-2). 32pp. A magical dance in the middle of the night enlivens a small boy's room. (Rev: BCCB 10/06; BL 7/06; HB 1/07; HBG 4/07; SLJ 8/06*)

839 Siegen-Smith, Nikki, comp. *A Pocketful of Stars: Poems About the Night* (K–3). Illus. by Emma Shaw-Smith. 1999, Barefoot Books $16.95 (978-1-902283-84-5). 40pp. An anthology of 21 short poems about the night and sleep by such poets as Walter de la Mare, Ogden Nash, and Ann Bonner. (Rev: SLJ 1/00) [811]

840 Smee, Nicola. *No Bed Without Ted* (PS–1). Illus. by author. 2005, Bloomsbury $14.95 (978-1-58234-963-3). A girl heading for bed can't find her favorite teddy bear without her mother's help in this lift-the-flap book. (Rev: SLJ 7/05)

841 Sobel, June. *The Goodnight Train* (PS–K). Illus. by Laura Huliska-Beith. 2006, Harcourt $16.00 (978-0-15-205436-6). The Goodnight Train picks up a cast of colorful characters as it counts down the time until lights-out. (Rev: SLJ 10/06)

842 Spetter, Jung-Hee. *Lily and Trooper's Spring* (PS). Illus. 1999, Front St. $8.95 (978-1-886910-36-2). 32pp. Lily and her dog, Trooper, have a series of misadventures while attempting a quiet picnic in the country, and both of them need baths before bedtime. (Rev: BL 5/1/99; SLJ 7/99)

843 Spetter, Jung-Hee. *Lily and Trooper's Summer* (PS–K). Illus. 1999, Front St. $8.95 (978-1-886910-37-9). 32pp. Lily and her dog, Trooper, spend a wonderful day outdoors and then are so tired that they fall asleep on top of the covers. (Rev: BL 5/15/99; SLJ 7/99)

844 Spinelli, Eileen. *Naptime, Laptime* (PS). Illus. by Melissa Sweet. 1995, Scholastic $6.95 (978-0-590-48510-4). 24pp. A child wonders where various animals sleep and then decides it's best on grandmother's lap. (Rev: BCCB 2/96; BL 12/1/95; SLJ 2/96)

845 Spinelli, Eileen. *When Papa Comes Home Tonight* (PS). Illus. by David McPhail. 2009, Simon & Schuster $16.99 (978-1-4169-1028-2). 32pp. A young boy describes the things that he and Papa do at the close of day. (Rev: BL 4/1/09; SLJ 4/09)

846 Sproule, Gail. *Singing the Dark* (PS–2). Illus. by Sheena Lott. 2001, Fitzhenry & Whiteside $16.95 (978-1-55041-648-0). 40pp. Every night, Kaylie's mother sings a song "calling darkness" to greet the night, and Kaylie chimes in. (Rev: BL 12/15/01)

847 Steinbrenner, Jessica. *My Sleepy Room* (PS). Illus. by Elizabeth Wolf. 2004, Handprint $15.95 (978-1-59354-007-4). Bess's "sleepy room" is a

comforting place where she reads, plays with toys, and sometimes sleeps. (Rev: SLJ 7/04)

848 Stevenson, James. *What's Under My Bed?* (1–3). Illus. by author. 1983, Greenwillow LB $15.89 (978-0-688-02327-0); Morrow paper $4.95 (978-0-688-09350-1). 32pp. A grandfather helps reduce his grandchildren's fears. A sequel is: *Worse Than Willy!* (1984).

849 Tafuri, Nancy. *I Love You, Little One* (PS–1). Illus. 1998, Scholastic $15.95 (978-0-590-92159-6). 32pp. In this bedtime story, different animal mothers try to tell their children how much they love them. (Rev: BL 2/1/98; HBG 10/98; SLJ 3/98)

850 Thompson, Lauren. *Little Quack's Bedtime* (PS–K). Illus. by Derek Anderson. 2005, Simon & Schuster $14.95 (978-0-689-86894-8). Mama Duck succeeds in getting four of her ducklings off to sleep, but Little Quack needs special attention. (Rev: SLJ 2/05)

851 Trapani, Iza. *Shoo Fly!* (PS–1). Illus. by author. 2000, Charlesbridge LB $15.95 (978-1-58089-052-6). This adaptation of a perky song concerns a little mouse and pesky fly and how they are both tucked in at night. (Rev: SLJ 1/01)

852 Wahl, Jan. *Elf Night* (1–3). Illus. by Peter Weevers. 2002, Carolrhoda $15.25 (978-1-57505-512-1). 32pp. A young boy spends a magical time with the fairy folk until he goes back to his bed. (Rev: BL 5/1/02; HBG 10/02; SLJ 5/02)

853 Wallace, Nancy E. *Rabbit's Bedtime* (PS). Illus. by author. 1999, Houghton $9.95 (978-0-395-98266-2). Before a youngster goes to sleep, he and his mother recall all the loving things they did together during the day. (Rev: HBG 3/00; SLJ 11/99)

854 Watts, Frances. *Kisses for Daddy* (PS). Illus. by David Legge. 2008, Trafalgar $15.95 (978-1-921272-43-1). 24pp. Father Bear succeeds in persuading a cranky young bear to go to bed as he shows all the ways baby animals kiss their dads. Children's Book Council of Australia Honour Book, 2006. (Rev: BL 6/1–15/08)

855 Weeks, Sarah. *Counting Ovejas* (2–4). Illus. by David Diaz. 2006, Simon & Schuster $16.95 (978-0-689-86750-7). 40pp. A young insomniac learns to count sheep in English and Spanish. (Rev: BL 6/1–15/06; SLJ 6/06)

856 Welch, Willy. *Grumpy Bunnies* (PS–1). Illus. by Tammie Lyon. 2000, Charlesbridge $16.95 (978-1-58089-053-3); paper $6.95 (978-1-58089-060-1). 32pp. The day improves as it goes along for three little rabbits who go to bed looking forward to tomorrow. (Rev: HBG 10/00; SLJ 5/00)

857 Wells, Rosemary. *Goodnight Max* (PS). Illus. by author. 2000, Viking $11.99 (978-0-670-88707-1). In this board book that contains touch-and-feel surprises Max the rabbit has to change his pajamas three times before he can get to sleep. (Rev: BL 6/1–15/03; HBG 10/03; SLJ 4/00)

858 Whybrow, Ian. *The Noisy Way to Bed* (PS–1). Illus. by Tiphanie Beeke. 2004, Scholastic $16.95 (978-0-439-55689-7). A little boy collects a parade of noisy farm animals on his way to bed. (Rev: SLJ 3/04)

859 Wild, Margaret. *Nighty Night!* (PS–1). Illus. by Kerry Argent. 2001, Peachtree $15.95 (978-1-56145-246-0). 32pp. Simple, rhythmic text and rich, humorous illustrations describe animal babies resisting their parents' efforts to put them to bed. (Rev: BCCB 9/01; BL 9/1/01; HBG 3/02; SLJ 9/01)

860 Wiles, Deborah. *One Wide Sky: A Bedtime Lullaby* (PS–K). Illus. by Tim Bowers. 2003, Harcourt $16.00 (978-0-15-202334-8). In this appealing bedtime and counting story, three children and two young squirrels enjoy the delights of the leafy backyard. (Rev: HBG 10/03; SLJ 6/03)

861 Wilson, Karma. *Sleepyhead* (PS). Illus. by John Segal. 2006, Simon & Schuster $15.95 (978-1-4169-1241-5). 32pp. A kitten tries to get her teddy bear ready to go to bed but he keeps putting it off with pleas for more hugs, kisses, books, drinks, and so forth. (Rev: BL 11/15/06; SLJ 10/06)

862 Wing, Natasha. *Go to Bed, Monster!* (PS). Illus. by Sylvie Kantorovitz. 2007, Harcourt $16.00 (978-0-15-205775-6). 40pp. A little girl who is not ready for bed draws herself a playmate monster, but after they play she is tired and must stay awake drawing pictures of things that will satisfy the monster and eventually get him to sleep. (Rev: BL 11/1/07; SLJ 10/07)

863 Winthrop, Elizabeth. *Asleep in a Heap* (PS–1). Illus. by Mary Morgan. 1993, Holiday House LB $15.95 (978-0-8234-0992-1). 32pp. Julia is much too busy to go to bed, but her antics send the rest of the family to sleep. (Rev: BL 11/15/93; SLJ 1/94)

864 Winthrop, Elizabeth. *Maggie and the Monster* (PS–K). Illus. by Tomie dePaola. 1987, Holiday House LB $16.95 (978-0-8234-0639-5); paper $5.95 (978-0-8234-0698-2). 32pp. Every single night a small girl monster comes into Maggie's room. (Rev: BL 4/1/87; SLJ 5/87)

865 Wright, Michael. *Jake Stays Awake* (PS–2). Illus by author. 2007, Feiwel & Friends $16.95 (978-0-312-36797-8). 32pp. When Jake insists on sleeping with Mom and Dad, they counteroffer with alternative sleeping places for all three that Jake considers unsuitable. (Rev: BL 9/1/07; SLJ 9/07)

866 Yolen, Jane. *How Do Dinosaurs Say Goodnight?* (PS–1). Illus. by Mark Teague. 2000, Scholastic $16.99 (978-0-590-31681-1). 40pp. A bedtime book that features all sorts of baby dinosaurs behaving like human children at bedtime. (Rev: BCCB 6/00; BL 4/1/00*; HBG 10/00; SLJ 6/00)

867 Yolen, Jane. *Sleep, Black Bear, Sleep* (K–2). Illus. by Brooke Dyer. 2007, HarperCollins $15.99 (978-0-06-081560-8). 32pp. A lulling rhyme and snuggly illustrations of animals in their various beds grace this bedtime book. (Rev: BL 11/15/06; SLJ 2/07)

868 Ziefert, Harriet. *Clara Ann Cookie, Go to Bed!* (PS–3). Illus. by Emily Bolam. 2000, Houghton $15.00 (978-0-395-97381-3). 32pp. Clara Ann, who has been resisting her mother's efforts to put her to bed, gets the same treatment when her teddy bear refuses to accompany her when she finally gives in. (Rev: BL 9/1/00; HBG 3/01; SLJ 10/00)

869 Ziefert, Harriet. *Mommy, I Want to Sleep in Your Bed!* (PS). Illus. by Elliot Kreloff. 2005, Blue Apple $15.95 (978-1-59354-103-3). 40pp. Charlie the puppy begs to sleep with his parents but finally is happily tucked in after a story. (Rev: BL 12/15/05; SLJ 11/05)

Nursery Rhymes

870 Ada, Alma Flor, and F. Isabel Campoy, sels. *Pio Peep! Traditional Spanish Nursery Rhymes* (PS–2). 2003, HarperCollins LB $16.89 (978-0-688-16020-3). 64pp. English-language adaptations retain the rhythm and poetry of these Spanish rhymes. (Rev: HBG 10/03; SLJ 7/03) [398.8]

871 Aylesworth, Jim. *The Completed Hickory Dickory Dock* (PS–K). Illus. by Eileen Christelow, 1994, Aladdin paper $5.99 (978-0-689-71862-5). 32pp. The "whole" story of what happened when the clock struck. (Rev: BL 10/1/90; SLJ 2/91) [811]

872 Beaton, Clare, comp. *Mother Goose Remembers* (PS). Illus. by Clare Beaton. 2000, Barefoot Books $18.99 (978-1-84148-073-2). 64pp. A highly appealing collection of 46 Mother Goose rhymes with pictures made of felt and other fabrics. (Rev: HBG 3/01; SLJ 9/00)

873 Beaton, Clare. *Playtime Rhymes for Little People* (PS–K). Illus. 2001, Barefoot Books $18.99 (978-1-84148-425-9). 64pp. Forty familiar children's rhymes are accompanied by embroidered collages. (Rev: BCCB 12/01; BL 10/15/01; HBG 3/02; SLJ 11/01) [398.8]

874 Beil, Karen M. *A Cake All for Me!* (PS–2). Illus. by Paul Meisel. 1998, Holiday House $16.95 (978-0-8234-1368-3). Using a nursery rhyme format, this is the story of Piggy who makes a cake and shares it with others. (Rev: HBG 3/99; SLJ 9/98)

875 Bornstein, Harry, and Karen L. Saulnier. *Nursery Rhymes from Mother Goose Told in Signed English* (K–2). Illus. by Patricia Peters and Linda C. Tom, 1993, Gallaudet Univ. $14.95 (978-0-930323-99-8). 41pp. Fourteen rhymes with signing symbols for the deaf. (Rev: SLJ 6/93) [398.8]

876 Boyle, Alison. *Twinkle, Twinkle, Little Star* (PS). Illus. 2000, David & Charles $10.95 (978-1-86233-111-2). In this interactive book using the familiar rhyme, a little star enters a house looking for a bear. (Rev: BL 12/1/00)

877 Cabrera, Jane. *Old Mother Hubbard* (PS). Illus. 2001, Holiday House $15.95 (978-0-8234-1659-2). 32pp. Old Mother Hubbard's dog is up to some new tricks in this colorful and imaginative rendition of the familiar nursery rhyme. (Rev: BCCB 11/01; BL 9/1/01; HBG 3/02; SLJ 1/02) [821.7]

878 Catalano, Dominic. *Hush! A Fantasy in Verse* (PS). Illus. by author. 2003, Gingham Dog $14.95 (978-1-57768-679-8). In this charming variation on the traditional nursery song/rhyme "Hush Little Baby," a father tries to comfort his young daughter after she wakes up from a bad dream. (Rev: HBG 4/04; SLJ 1/04)

879 Chapman, Jane. *Sing a Song of Sixpence: A Pocketful of Nursery Rhymes and Tales* (PS). 2004, Candlewick $15.99 (978-0-7636-2545-0). 64pp. Striking acrylic artwork highlights this collection of familiar nursery rhymes and three fairy tales ("Goldilocks," "The Three Little Pigs," and "The Little Red Hen"). (Rev: BL 9/1/04; SLJ 10/04) [398.8]

880 Conway, David. *The Great Nursery Rhyme Disaster* (PS–2). Illus. by Melanie Williamson. 2009, Tiger Tales $15.95 (978-1-58925-080-2). 32pp. Little Miss Muffet looks for adventure in other nursery rhymes such as "Jack and Jill" and "Hey Diddle, Diddle" only to realize, after many exciting and colorful moments, that her own rhyme is where she belongs. (Rev: LMC 10/09; SLJ 5/09)

881 Crews, Nina. *The Neighborhood Mother Goose* (PS–2). Photos by author. 2004, Greenwillow LB $18.89 (978-0-06-051574-4). 63pp. "Mother" in this case is a real goose in a city park, and the illustrations portray urban youngsters and scenery. (Rev: HB 5/04; SLJ 1/04) [398.8]

882 Edwards, Pamela Duncan, retel. *Miss Polly Has a Dolly* (PS–1). Illus. by Elicia Castaldi. 2003, Penguin $15.99 (978-0-399-23857-4). A rhyming rope-jumping chant is expanded and set to music, with finger-play motions provided. (Rev: HBG 4/04; SLJ 11/03)

883 Edwards, Pamela Duncan. *The Neat Line: Scribbling Through Mother Goose* (PS–2). Illus. by Diana Cain Bluthenthal. 2005, HarperCollins LB $17.89 (978-0-06-623971-2). 32pp. A baby scribble grows up to be a Neat Line and works its way into a book of nursery rhymes to help the familiar characters out of their predicaments. (Rev: BL 3/15/05; SLJ 5/05)

884 Engelbreit, Mary. *Mary Engelbreit's Mother Goose: One Hundred Best-Loved Verses* (PS–1). 2005, HarperCollins $19.99 (978-0-06-008171-3). 128pp. Popular illustrator Engelbreit offers her artistic interpretation of 100 well-known and less-familiar nursery rhymes. (Rev: SLJ 3/06) [398.8]

885 Fitzgerald, Joanne. *Yum! Yum!* (PS–K). Illus. by author. 2008, Fitzhenry & Whiteside $18.95 (978-1-55041-888-0). 32pp. Nursery rhymes featuring food are illustrated with charming watercolor illustrations. (Rev: BL 12/1/07; SLJ 12/07) [398.8]

886 French, Vivian. *The Daddy Goose Treasury* (PS–K). Illus. by AnnaLaura Cantone, et al. 2006, Scholastic $18.99 (978-0-439-79608-8). 93pp. Daddy Goose, a relative of Mother Goose, provides the back stories for nursery rhymes such as "Little Miss Muffet" and "Old King Cole." (Rev: SLJ 9/06) [398.8]

887 Fyleman, Rose. *Mary Middling and Other Silly Folk: Nursery Rhymes and Nonsense Poems* (PS). Illus. by Katja Bandlow. 2004, Clarion $16.00 (978-0-618-38141-8). 28pp. Catchy rhymes first published in 1931 are revived in picture-book form with suitably silly illustrations. (Rev: BL 11/15/04; SLJ 9/04) [821]

888 Galdone, Paul. *Three Little Kittens* (2–4). Illus. by author. 1986, Houghton $16.00 (978-0-89919-

426-4); paper $5.95 (978-0-89919-796-8). 32pp. A lively reworking of the old nursery rhyme. (Rev: BL 10/1/86; SLJ 12/86) [398.8]

889 Green, Alison. *Mother Goose's Storytime Nursery Rhymes* (PS–1). Illus. by Axel Scheffler. 2007, Scholastic $19.99 (978-0-439-90306-6). 128pp. Mother Goose is an actual goose in this collection, telling her little ones rhyming stories that a heron writes down. Young listeners will enjoy the appealing illustrations. (Rev: SLJ 8/07)

890 Grey, Mini. *The Adventures of the Dish and the Spoon* (K–3). 2006, Knopf $16.95 (978-0-375-83691-6). 32pp. This tale fleshes out the adventures of the Dish that ran away with the Spoon, a romance that goes bad when the two rob a bank to continue financing their high life. (Rev: BL 6/1–15/06; SLJ 4/06)

891 Hale, Sarah Josepha. *Mary Had a Little Lamb* (PS–1). Illus. by Salley Mavor. 1995, Orchard LB $16.99 (978-0-531-08725-1). 32pp. An effective version of the famous rhyme using collages for illustrations. (Rev: BCCB 5/95; BL 5/15/95; HB 3/95, 7/95, 11/95; SLJ 6/95*) [811]

892 Hallworth, Grace, ed. *Down by the River: Afro-Caribbean Rhymes, Games, and Songs for Children* (PS–1). Illus. by Caroline Binch. 1996, Scholastic $16.95 (978-0-590-69320-2). 40pp. More than 20 playground rhymes from the Caribbean are included in this joyful book illustrated with watercolors. (Rev: BCCB 1/97; BL 10/15/96; SLJ 12/96) [811]

893 Harper, Charise Mericle. *There Was a Bold Lady Who Wanted a Star* (PS–2). Illus. 2002, Little, Brown $15.95 (978-0-316-14673-9). 32pp. "The Little Old Lady Who Swallowed a Fly" is traded in for a modern lady who tries various modes of transport in her efforts to catch a star. (Rev: BCCB 11/02; BL 11/15/02; HBG 3/03; SLJ 9/02) [782]

894 Hayes, Sarah. *This Is the Bear* (PS). Illus. by Helen Craig. 1993, HarperCollins LB $11.89 (978-0-397-32171-1); Candlewick paper $2.50 (978-0-06-443103-3). 32pp. Written in "House That Jack Built" style, the story of the bear named Fred who is taken to the local dump and awaits rescue. A reissue. A sequel is *This Is the Bear and the Picnic Lunch* (1989). (Rev: BL 4/1/86; SLJ 9/86) [398.8]

895 *Hickory, Dickory, Dock: And Other Favorite Nursery Rhymes* (PS). Illus. by Sanja Rescek. 2006, Tiger Tales $7.95 (978-1-58925-786-3). A gentle board-book collection of classic nursery rhymes illustrated with cartoon art. Also use *Twinkle, Twinkle, Little Star: And Other Favorite Bedtime Rhymes* (2006). (Rev: SLJ 4/06) [398.8]

896 Hines, Anna Grossnickle. *1, 2, Buckle My Shoe* (PS–K). Illus. by author. 2008, Harcourt $16.00 (978-0-15-206305-4). 32pp. Patchwork illustrations adorn this version of the popular counting nursery rhyme. (Rev: BL 5/15/08; SLJ 5/08)

897 Hoberman, Mary Ann. *Bill Grogan's Goat* (PS–3). Illus. by Nadine Bernard Westcott. 2002, Little, Brown $14.95 (978-0-316-36232-0). 32pp. The classic nonsense rhyme about Bill Grogan and the goat that is always in trouble is retold with clever illustrations. (Rev: BL 4/15/02; HBG 10/02; SLJ 4/02)

898 Hoberman, Mary Ann. *You Read to Me, I'll Read to You: Very Short Mother Goose Tales to Read Together* (1–4). Illus. by Michael Emberley. 2005, Little, Brown $16.99 (978-0-316-14431-5). 32pp. Variations on familiar Mother Goose rhymes, meant to be read aloud by two readers. (Rev: SLJ 9/05) [398.2]

899 Horowitz, Dave. *Humpty Dumpty Climbs Again* (PS–K). Illus. by author. 2008, Putnam $16.99 (978-0-399-24773-6). 32pp. Humpty Dumpty is roused from his post-traumatic depression by the news that one of the king's horses is in trouble. (Rev: BL 12/15/08; HB 1/09; LMC 1/09; SLJ 10/08)

900 *The House That Jack Built* (K–2). Illus. by Diana Mayo. 2001, Barefoot Books $15.99 (978-1-84148-251-4). Double-page illustrations in bold colors bring new life to the classic rhyme. (Rev: BL 10/15/01; HBG 3/02; SLJ 1/02) [398.8]

901 Hysom, Dennis. *Wooleycat's Musical Theater* (PS–1). Illus. by Christine Walker. Series: Wooleycat's Favorite Nursery Rhymes. 2003, Tortuga $18.95 (978-1-889910-25-3). 32pp. Ten nursery rhymes are retold with new twists (the cow that jumped over the moon becomes an astronaut, for instance) and set to music on an accompanying CD. (Rev: SLJ 4/04) [398.8]

902 *If You Love a Nursery Rhyme* (PS–K). Illus. by Susanna Lockheart. 2009, Barron's $18.99 (978-0-7641-6186-). 24pp. A large-format collection of 12 nursery rhymes, several with gatefold pages that offer a choice of illustrations. (Rev: BL 4/15/09) [398.8]

903 Kadair, Deborah Ousley. *There Was an Ol' Cajun* (K–3). Illus. by author. 2002, Pelican $15.95 (978-1-56554-917-3). Instead of a fly, the ol' Cajun swallows all manner of swamp life before coming across an alligator. (Rev: HBG 10/02; SLJ 12/02) [398.8]

904 Linch, Tanya. *Three Little Kittens* (PS–K). Illus. by author. 2001, Gullane $12.95 (978-1-86233-204-1). The kittens' mittens are lost and dirtied, then found and washed, all with mother's forgiveness. (Rev: SLJ 1/02) [398.2]

905 McMullan, Kate. *Baby Goose* (PS). Illus. by Pascal LeMaitre. 2004, Hyperion $15.99 (978-0-7868-0430-6). 34pp. Traditional nursery rhymes follow the hands around the clock and feature child-friendly adaptations and illustrations. (Rev: BL 11/15/04; SLJ 11/04) [398.8]

906 Marshall, James. *James Marshall's Mother Goose* (PS–1). Illus. by author. 1979, Farrar paper $6.95 (978-0-374-43723-7). 40pp. An ebullient, breezy treatment of traditional material. [398.8]

907 Martin, Bill. *"Fire! Fire!" Said Mrs. McGuire* (PS–1). Illus. by Vladimir Radunsky. 2006, Harcourt $16.00 (978-0-15-205725-1). 32pp. A group of mice sound the alarm when they think they see a fire through a keyhole in this rhyming picture book; a final cutout reveals candles on the cat's birthday cake. (Rev: BL 5/1/06; SLJ 6/06) [811]

908 Montgomery, Michael G., and Wayne Montgomery. *Over the Candlestick: Classic Nursery Rhymes and the Real Stories Behind Them* (PS). Illus. by Michael G. Montgomery. 2002, Peachtree $16.95 (978-1-56145-259-0). 32pp. A large-format collection of classic nursery rhymes and a bit of the history behind them, with full-page illustrations. (Rev: BL 3/15/02; HBG 10/02; SLJ 6/02) [398.8]

909 Moses, Will. *Will Moses Mother Goose* (PS–1). Illus. by author. 2003, Philomel $17.99 (978-0-399-23744-7). 61pp. A whimsically illustrated collection of nursery rhymes and riddles, some well known and others less familiar. (Rev: HBG 4/04; SLJ 9/03) [398.8]

910 Mother Goose. *Mother Goose: A Canadian Sampler* (PS–1). 1996, Groundwood $18.95 (978-0-88899-213-0). 63pp. Using illustrations from 29 of Canada's prominent picture book illustrators, this is a fine edition of Mother Goose rhymes. (Rev: SLJ 5/96)

911 Mother Goose. *Mother Goose: A Collection of Classic Nursery Rhymes* (PS–K). Illus. by Michael Hague. 1984, Holt $18.95 (978-0-8050-0214-0). 80pp. Forty-five nursery rhymes delicately illustrated. [398.8]

912 Mother Goose. *Real Mother Goose* (PS–3). Illus. by Blanche Fisher Wright. 1991, Checkerboard $12.95 (978-1-56288-041-5). 128pp. A reprint of the golden anniversary edition with introduction by May Hill Arbuthnot. [398.8]

913 Mother Goose. *The Real Mother Goose Clock Book* (PS–1). Illus. by Blanche Fisher Wright. 1991, Checkerboard $6.95 (978-1-56288-095-8). 22pp. Time-related rhymes and a clock with movable hands help children associate the clock with daily routines. [398.8]

914 Mother Goose. *Tomie dePaola's Mother Goose* (PS–1). Illus. by Tomie dePaola. 1985, Penguin $25.99 (978-0-399-21258-1). 127pp. Large format and lavish illustrations accompany these old favorites. (Rev: BCCB 11/85; BL 9/1/85; HB 1/86) [398.8]

915 *My First Nursery Rhymes* (PS). Illus. by Bruce Whatley. Series: Growing Tree. 1999, HarperCollins $10.99 (978-0-694-01205-3). 24pp. A joyous collection of ten favorite rhymes, including "Little Bo-Peep" and "Humpty Dumpty." (Rev: BL 2/1/99; HBG 10/99; SLJ 4/99) [398.8]

916 Opie, Iona, ed. *Here Comes Mother Goose* (PS). Illus. by Rosemary Wells. 1999, Candlewick $21.99 (978-0-7636-0683-1). 107pp. More than 50 well-known nursery rhymes are given fresh interpretations through clever new illustrations. (Rev: BCCB 12/99; BL 10/1/99*; HB 11/99; HBG 3/00; SLJ 10/99) [398.8]

917 Opie, Iona, ed. *Mother Goose's Little Treasures* (PS–K). Illus. by Rosemary Wells. 2007, Candlewick $17.99 (978-0-7636-3655-5). 56pp. Twenty-two little-known rhymes are collected here. (Rev: BL 9/1/07; SLJ 9/07) [398.8]

918 Opie, Iona, ed. *My Very First Mother Goose* (PS). Illus. by Rosemary Wells. 1996, Candlewick $21.99 (978-1-56402-620-0). 108pp. A basic collection of 60 standard rhymes illustrated with imagination and charm. (Rev: BCCB 12/96; BL 9/1/96; HB 11/96; SLJ 10/96*) [398.8]

919 Oxenbury, Helen. *The Helen Oxenbury Nursery Collection* (PS–1). Illus. 2004, Knopf LB $21.99 (978-0-375-92992-2). 96pp. This charming collection of poems, rhymes, and stories is drawn from previous books that are now out of print. (Rev: BL 12/1/04) [398.8]

920 Pearson, Tracey Campbell. *Little Miss Muffet* (PS). Illus. by author. 2005, Farrar $5.95 (978-0-374-30862-9). This adaptation of the popular nursery rhyme shows a young girl acting out the story line, spider and all. (Rev: SLJ 10/05) [398.8]

921 Petersham, Maud, and Miska Petersham. *The Rooster Crows: A Book of American Rhymes and Jingles* (K–2). Illus. by authors. 1969, Macmillan LB $17.00 (978-0-02-773100-2). 64pp. Rope skipping, counting, and other game rhymes form the bulk of this jaunty collection. A reissue of the 1946 Caldecott Medal winner. [398.8]

922 Pierce, Terry, ed. *Counting Your Way: Number Nursery Rhymes* (PS–K). Illus. by Andrea Petrlik Huseinovic. 2007, Picture Window $25.26 (978-1-4048-2346-4). 32pp. Twenty familiar rhymes featuring numbers are highlighted on attractively illustrated pages. (Rev: BL 4/1/07) [398.8]

923 Prelutsky, Jack. *Beneath a Blue Umbrella* (PS–2). Illus. by Garth Williams. 1990, Greenwillow $18.99 (978-0-688-06429-7). 64pp. A miscellany of 28 gaily illustrated rhymes by Mother Goose; good read-aloud material. (Rev: BCCB 3/90; HB 3/90; SLJ 6/90) [398.8]

924 Ross, Tony. *Three Little Kittens and Other Favorite Nursery Rhymes* (PS). Illus. by author. 2009, Holt $16.95 (978-0-8050-8885-4). 96pp. A grandfather reading to his grandaughter is the framing concept that opens and closes this large-format collection of 49 Mother Goose rhymes, each featuring its own watercolor illustration. (Rev: BCCB 7–8/09; BL 2/1/09; SLJ 4/09) [398.8]

925 Sabuda, Robert. *Movable Mother Goose* (PS–1). 1999, Simon & Schuster $19.95 (978-0-689-81192-0). Pop-ups and flaps are used to illustrate this collection of favorite Mother Goose rhymes. (Rev: BL 12/15/99; HBG 3/00; SLJ 2/00)

926 Sayre, April P. *Trout, Trout, Trout! A Fish Chant* (PS–2). Illus. by Trip Park. 2004, NorthWord $15.95 (978-1-55971-889-9). Bright cartoon illustrations complement this bouncy fish-related chant. (Rev: SLJ 7/04) [597.17]

927 Scanlon, Elizabeth Garton. *A Sock Is a Pocket for Your Toes: A Pocket Book* (PS–2). Illus. by Robin P. Glasser. 2004, HarperCollins $15.99 (978-0-06-029526-4). 32pp. This delightful rhyme book takes a broad brush to the concept of pockets — picturing a cave as a pocket for bears and ears as pockets for whispers. (Rev: BL 2/15/04; SLJ 2/04) [811]

928 Sewall, Marcia. *Animal Song* (PS–K). Illus. by author. 1988, Little, Brown $14.95 (978-0-316-78191-6). 128pp. An old chanting rhyme using animal names. (Rev: BL 3/15/88; SLJ 6–7/88) [398.8]

929 Sierra, Judy. *Monster Goose* (K–3). Illus. by Jack E. Davis. 2001, Harcourt $16.00 (978-0-15-202034-7). 56pp. Gruesome, gross, and goofy versions of familiar Mother Goose rhymes. (Rev: BCCB 12/01; BL 9/15/01; HBG 3/02; SLJ 9/01) [811]

930 Sierra, Judy. *Schoolyard Rhymes* (K–3). Illus. by Melissa Sweet. 2005, Knopf $15.95 (978-0-375-82516-3). 40pp. This collection of schoolyard rhymes includes such favorites as "Liar, Liar, Pants on Fire" and "Lady with the Alligator Purse." (Rev: BL 8/05; SLJ 10/05) [398.8]

931 Siomades, Lorianne. *Three Little Kittens* (PS–1). Illus. 2000, Boyds Mills $12.95 (978-1-56397-845-6). 32pp. The classic nursery rhyme is given a bright, mischievous treatment that involves both the kittens and some thieving mice. (Rev: BL 2/15/00; HBG 10/00; SLJ 4/00)

932 Spicer, Maggee, and Richard Thompson. *When They Are Up . . .* (PS–3). Illus. by Kirsti Anne Wakelin. 2004, Fitzhenry & Whiteside $14.95 (978-1-55041-707-4). This imaginative twist on the nursery song about the Duke of York's 10,000 men has them involved in such things as capturing armadillos and knitting socks; music and lyrics are appended. (Rev: SLJ 5/04) [811]

933 Stevens, Janet, and Susan Stevens Crummel. *And the Dish Ran Away with the Spoon* (K–3). Illus. 2001, Harcourt $17.00 (978-0-15-202298-3). 48pp. Familiar nursery rhymes are reworked with droll results. (Rev: BL 4/1/01*; HB 7/01; HBG 10/01; SLJ 5/01)

934 Still, James. *An Appalachian Mother Goose* (K–3). Illus. by Paul Johnson. 1998, Univ. Pr. of Kentucky $27.50 (978-0-8131-2070-6). 64pp. Familiar nursery rhymes are given an Appalachian flavor in these short poems by Kentucky's former poet laureate. (Rev: BL 3/1/99) [398.8]

935 *Sylvia Long's Mother Goose* (PS–K). Illus. by Sylvia Long. 1999, Chronicle $19.95 (978-0-8118-2088-2). 109pp. Animals, reptiles, and insects replace humans in the delightful illustrations featured in this Mother Goose anthology. (Rev: BCCB 12/99; BL 11/15/99; HBG 3/00; SLJ 12/99*) [398.8]

936 Taback, Simms. *This Is the House That Jack Built* (PS–2). Illus. 2002, Penguin $15.99 (978-0-399-23488-0). 32pp. An inventive, spirited take on the traditional nursery rhyme that focuses on the house and its contents. (Rev: BCCB 10/02; BL 10/1/02*; HB 11/02; HBG 3/03; SLJ 9/02*) [398.8]

937 *Teddy Bear, Teddy Bear: A Traditional Rhyme* (PS). Illus. by Timothy Bush. 2005, HarperCollins $14.99 (978-0-06-057835-0). A new take on the familiar rhyme, with hand motions for children to perform along with the chant. (Rev: SLJ 7/05) [398.8]

938 Trapani, Iza. *Here We Go 'Round the Mulberry Bush* (PS–1). Illus. by author. 2006, Charlesbridge paper $6.95 (978-1-58091-699-8). Animals feast on a vegetable garden in this take on the familiar nursery rhyme. (Rev: SLJ 7/06) [398.8]

939 Trapani, Iza, retel. *Mary Had a Little Lamb* (PS–1). Illus. by Iza Trapani. 1998, Whispering Coyote $16.95 (978-1-58089-009-0). An expanded version of the nursery rhyme in which the little lamb has misadventures in a farmyard. (Rev: HBG 3/99; SLJ 11/98)

940 Unobagha, Uzo. *Off to the Sweet Shores of Africa* (PS). Illus. by Julia Cairns. 2000, Chronicle $16.95 (978-0-8118-2378-4). 56pp. Playful verses about African subjects are contained in this collection that seems inspired by Mother Goose. (Rev: BL 11/1/00; HBG 3/01; SLJ 10/00) [811]

941 Ward, Jennifer, and T. J. Marsh. *Somewhere in the Ocean* (PS–1). Illus. by Kenneth J. Spengler. 2000, Northland $15.95 (978-0-87358-748-8). 32pp. The nursery rhyme "Over in the Meadow" is changed so the setting is now the ocean and the animals are all sea creatures. (Rev: BL 4/1/00; HBG 10/00; SLJ 7/00)

942 Wells, Rosemary. *The Bear Went Over the Mountain* (PS). Illus. Series: Bunny Reads Back. 1998, Scholastic $5.99 (978-0-590-02910-0). 16pp. A board book that presents the familiar nursery rhyme with pictures showing a little bear leaving his mother, going over the mountain, and returning with a gift of flowers for her. (Rev: BL 12/15/98; HBG 3/99; SLJ 2/99)

943 Wells, Rosemary. *The Itsy-Bitsy Spider* (PS). Illus. Series: Bunny Reads Back. 1998, Scholastic $5.99 (978-0-590-02911-7). 16pp. The familiar nursery rhyme about a tiny spider climbing a waterspout is presented in a clever format in this board book. (Rev: BL 12/15/98; HBG 3/99; SLJ 2/99)

944 Yolen, Jane, ed. *The Lap-Time Song and Play Book* (PS). Illus. by Margot Tomes. 1989, Harcourt $15.95 (978-0-15-243588-2). 32pp. A collection of 16 nursery games and songs with a history for each and simple piano arrangements. (Rev: BL 10/1/89; HB 11/89; SLJ 10/89) [782.42]

945 Yolen, Jane, ed. *This Little Piggy* (PS). Illus. by Will Hillenbrand. 2006, Candlewick $19.99 (978-0-7636-1348-8). 80pp. A large-format anthology of rhymes, songs, lap games, and finger plays of various kinds, with annotations, pig-filled illustrations, musical notations, and an accompanying CD. (Rev: BL 1/1–15/06*; SLJ 2/06*) [398.8]

946 Zelinsky, Paul. *Knick-Knack Paddywhack! A Moving Parts Book* (PS–3). Illus. 2002, Dutton $18.99 (978-0-525-46908-7). 8pp. This miracle of pull-tabs and flaps is a delicious combination of familiar, bouncy rhyme and counting song full of comedy and small details. (Rev: BCCB 2/03; BL 11/1/02; HB 1/03; HBG 3/03; SLJ 12/02) [782.42164]

947 Zemach, Margot. *Some from the Moon, Some from the Sun: Poems and Songs for Everyone* (K–3). Illus. 2001, Farrar $17.00 (978-0-374-39960-3). 48pp. A collection of traditional children's poems and rhymes illustrated by Caldecott Medal winner Margot Zemach. (Rev: BL 10/1/01; HB 9/01*; HBG 3/02; SLJ 8/01*) [398.8]

Stories Without Words

948 Andreasen, Dan. *The Treasure Bath* (PS). Illus. by author. 2009, Holt $16.99 (978-0-8050-8686-7). 40pp. An imaginative boy bakes with his mother and then takes a bath in this wordless picture book. (Rev: BL 6/1–15/09)

949 Aruego, Jose. *Look What I Can Do!* (K–2). Illus. by author. 1971, Macmillan paper $5.99 (978-0-689-71205-0). 32pp. An almost wordless picture book about the antics that result when one caribou challenges another.

950 Bang, Molly. *The Grey Lady and the Strawberry Snatcher* (PS–1). Illus. by author. 1984, Macmillan $16.00 (978-0-02-708140-4). 48pp. The snatcher tries to get the strawberries from the Grey Lady.

951 Banyai, Istvan. *Zoom* (1–3). Illus. 1995, Viking $16.99 (978-0-670-85804-0). 64pp. A clever picture book that begins with small objects and zooms to larger perspectives. (Rev: BCCB 2/95; BL 2/1/95; SLJ 3/95)

952 Briggs, Raymond. *The Snowman* (K–3). Illus. by author. 1978, Random $17.00 (978-0-394-83973-8); paper $7.99 (978-0-394-88466-0). 32pp. A small boy has adventures with the snowman he has made.

953 Carle, Eric. *Do You Want to Be My Friend?* (PS–K). Illus. by author. 1971, HarperCollins LB $18.89 (978-0-690-01137-1); paper $6.99 (978-0-06-443127-9). 32pp. The end of an animal's tail appears on each page, and the child must guess the animal before turning the page to see the rest of it.

954 Crews, Donald. *Truck* (1–3). Illus. by author. 1980, Greenwillow $17.89 (978-0-688-84244-4); Morrow paper $6.99 (978-0-688-10481-8). 32pp. This picture book traces a truck trip from loading dock to its San Francisco destination.

955 Day, Alexandra. *Carl's Masquerade* (PS–1). Illus. 1992, Farrar $12.95 (978-0-374-31094-3). 32pp. Carl, the rottweiler baby-sitter, takes his young charge and follows its parents to a masquerade ball. (Rev: BCCB 12/92; BL 2/1/93; SLJ 11/92)

956 dePaola, Tomie. *The Hunter and the Animals: A Wordless Picture Book* (K–3). Illus. by author. 1981, Holiday House LB $17.95 (978-0-8234-0397-4); paper $6.95 (978-0-8234-0428-5). 32pp. A hunter lost in the forest is helped by the animals.

957 Faller, Regis. *Polo: The Runaway Book* (PS–2). Illus. by author. 2006, Roaring Brook $16.95 (978-1-59643-189-8). 80pp. In this almost-wordless picture-book adventure, Polo the dog chases an alien that has run off with his new book. (Rev: BL 12/1/06; SLJ 1/07*)

958 Faller, Regis. *Polo and Lily* (PS–2). Illus. by author. 2009, Roaring Brook $9.95 (978-1-59643-496-7). 32pp. A wordless picture book in which Polo, a floppy-eared puppy who lives happily in a large tree, makes friends with a rabbit named Lily. (Rev: LMC 8/09; SLJ 7/09)

959 Geisert, Arthur. *Hogwash* (K–3). Illus. by author. 2008, Houghton $16.00 (978-0-618-77332-9). 32pp. Mama pigs put their piglets through an intricate cleaning process in this wordless book with detailed illustrations. (Rev: BL 1/1–15/08)

960 Goodale, Rebecca. *Island Dog* (PS–1). Illus. by author. 1999, Two Dog $17.95 (978-1-891090-03-5). In this wordless picture book, a dog spends a playful day on an island in Maine. (Rev: SLJ 1/00)

961 Kamm, Katja. *Invisible / Visible* (PS–2). Illus. by author. 2006, North-South $12.95 (978-0-7358-2052-4). A wordless picture book in which elements appear and disappear depending on colors and other visual tricks. (Rev: SLJ 7/06)

962 Khing, T. T. *Where Is the Cake Now?* (PS–K). Illus. by author. 2009, Abrams $12.95 (978-0-8109-8926-9). 32pp. Picnicking animals are dismayed when they discover their dessert is missing yet again and begin pointing fingers at each other in this entertaining, wordless adventure. (Rev: BLO 6/16/09; HB 7/09; SLJ 6/09)

963 King, Stephen Michael. *Leaf* (PS–1). Illus. by author. 2009, Roaring Brook $14.95 (978-1-59643-503-2). 64pp. An appealing, wordless book in which a bird drops a seed on a little boy's long-haired, messy head and the boy and his dog carefully nurture the seed's growth. (Rev: BCCB 6/09; LMC 10/09; SLJ 4/09)

964 Lee, Suzy. *Wave* (K–3). Illus. by author. 2008, Chronicle $15.99 (978-0-8118-5924-0). 40pp. A little girl learns to dance with the sea during a day at the beach in this wordless picture book. (Rev: SLJ 5/08)

965 Lehman, Barbara. *Museum Trip* (PS–2). Illus. 2006, Houghton $15.00 (978-0-618-58125-2). 40pp. A boy on a visit to an art museum suddenly finds himself inside a series of artistic mazes; a wordless book with clever illustrations. (Rev: BL 4/15/06*; HB 5/06; HBG 10/06; LMC 1/07; SLJ 5/06)

966 Lehman, Barbara. *The Red Book* (PS–2). Illus. by author. 2004, Houghton $12.95 (978-0-618-42858-8). 32pp. A story without words in which a red book connects children across the world. Caldecott Honor Book. (Rev: BL 10/1/04*; HB 9/04; SLJ 11/04*)

967 Lehman, Barbara. *Trainstop* (PS–2). Illus. by author. 2008, Houghton $16.00 (978-0-618-75640-7). 32pp. A girl on a train ride daydreams of rescuing an aviator in a world of little people in this story told entirely in pictures. (Rev: BL 1/1–15/08; SLJ 7/08)

968 McCully, Emily Arnold. *Picnic* (PS–2). Illus. by author. 1984, HarperCollins LB $16.89 (978-0-06-024100-1). 32pp. An eventful picnic for the mouse family.

969 McCully, Emily Arnold. *School* (PS–1). Illus. by author. 1987, HarperCollins LB $15.89 (978-0-06-024133-9); paper $5.95 (978-0-06-443233-7). 32pp. The littlest mouse decides to follow her siblings to school to see what it's like. (Rev: BL 9/1/87; SLJ 10/87)

970 Martin, Rafe. *Will's Mammoth* (K–2). Illus. by Stephen Gammell. 1989, Penguin $17.99 (978-0-399-21627-5). 32pp. A boy named Will travels back in time to when mammoths and saber-toothed tigers roamed the earth. (Rev: BCCB 11/89; BL 9/15/89; HB 3/90*; SLJ 10/89*)

971 Newgarden, Mark. *Bow-Wow Bugs a Bug* (1–3). Illus. by Megan Montague Cash. 2007, Harcourt $12.95 (978-0-15-205813-5). This wordless picture book is designed like a giant comic strip that follows the adventures of a dog and a bug. (Rev: HB 7/07; SLJ 7/07)

972 Nyeu, Tao. *Wonder Bear* (PS–1). Illus. by author. 2008, Dial $17.99 (978-0-8037-3328-2). 48pp. Two children grow a giant white bear with a magic hat that produces all kinds of wonders. (Rev: BL 9/15/08; SLJ 9/08)

973 Rogers, Gregory. *Midsummer Knight* (K–2). 2007, Roaring Brook $16.95 (978-1-59643-183-6). 32pp. A wordless story in which an Elizabethan bear enters a world reminiscent of Shakespeare's *A Midsummer Night's Dream* and finds himself embroiled in royal intrigue. (Rev: BL 4/1/07)

974 Schories, Pat. *Breakfast for Jack* (PS–2). Illus. by author. 2004, Front St. $13.95 (978-1-932425-16-1). Jack the dog is very worried when his family leaves in the morning without giving him breakfast in this wordless book. Also use *Jack and the Missing Piece* (2004). (Rev: HB 1/05; SLJ 11/04)

975 Schories, Pat. *Jack and the Night Visitors* (PS–K). Illus. 2006, Front St. $13.95 (978-1-932425-33-8). 32pp. Jack the dog and his young master entertain aliens in this wordless but very expressive picture book, the third in a series. (Rev: BL 4/15/06; SLJ 6/06)

976 Schories, Pat. *Jack Wants a Snack* (PS–2). Illus. by author. 2008, Front St. $13.95 (978-1-59078-546-1). 32pp. A bright dog named Jack disrupts a little girl's tea party in this lively, wordless picture book. (Rev: HB 9/08; SLJ 9/08)

977 Sís, Peter. *Dinosaur!* (PS–K). Illus. 2000, Greenwillow $16.99 (978-0-688-17049-3). 24pp. In this wordless book, the bath a boy takes with his toy dinosaur is suddenly transformed into a prehistoric scene where many dinosaurs are roaming in their native habitat. (Rev: BCCB 6/00; BL 3/15/00; HB 7/00; HBG 10/00; SLJ 6/00)

978 Tafuri, Nancy. *Junglewalk* (PS–K). Illus. by author. 1988, Greenwillow LB $15.93 (978-0-688-07183-7). 32pp. A bedtime story sends a young boy off to dreamland and adventures with a majestic tiger. (Rev: BL 3/1/88; HB 3/88)

979 Van Allsburg, Chris. *The Mysteries of Harris Burdick* (1–8). Illus. by author. 1984, Houghton $18.95 (978-0-395-35393-6). 32pp. A group of pictures are presented and youngsters are asked to supply the stories.

980 van Ommen, Sylvia. *The Surprise* (PS–1). Illus. by author. 2007, Front St. $15.95 (978-1-932425-85-7). 32pp. This wordless book presents many mysteries in its story about a sheep who dyes her wool red and then shears it off. What is she doing? (Rev: BL 5/15/07; SLJ 5/07)

981 Varon, Sara. *Chicken and Cat* (PS–2). Illus. 2006, Scholastic $16.99 (978-0-439-63406-9). 20pp. Cat comes to visit Chicken in New York City but is not impressed with urban life, and the two decide to plant a garden; a wordless story that manages to cover a number of themes. (Rev: BL 2/1/06; SLJ 5/06*)

982 Vincent, Gabrielle. *A Day, a Dog* (PS–4). Illus. 2000, Front St. $16.95 (978-1-886910-51-5). 72pp. A wordless book that tells the story of a dog that is dumped by its owners and how it learns to survive. (Rev: BCCB 4/00; BL 7/00; HB 5/00; HBG 10/00; SLJ 6/00)

983 Weitzman, Jacqueline Preiss. *You Can't Take a Balloon into the Metropolitan Museum* (K–3). Illus. by Robin P. Glasser. 1998, Dial $18.99 (978-0-8037-2301-6). 35pp. In this wordless picture book, a guard tends a balloon for a girl who is visiting the Metropolitan Museum of Art. When it gets loose, he chases it around Central Park and into the Plaza Hotel. (Rev: BL 11/15/98*; HB 11/98; HBG 3/99; SLJ 12/98)

984 Weitzman, Jacqueline Preiss. *You Can't Take a Balloon into the Museum of Fine Arts* (K–3). 2002, Dial $18.99 (978-0-8037-2570-6). 40pp. In this wordless book, a runaway balloon causes mishaps as it floats around the city of Boston. (Rev: BL 6/1–15/02*; HBG 10/02; SLJ 8/02)

985 Wiesner, David. *Free Fall* (PS–K). Illus. by author. 1988, Lothrop LB $17.89 (978-0-688-05584-4); paper $6.99 (978-0-688-10990-5). 32pp. An atlas falls from a boy's lap as he sleeps and opens his imagination to exotic places. (Rev: BCCB 5/88; BL 6/1/88; SLJ 6–7/88)

Picture Books

Imaginative Stories

FANTASIES

986 Ada, Alma Flor. *With Love, Little Red Hen* (K–3). Illus. by Leslie Tryon. 2001, Simon & Schuster $16.00 (978-0-689-82581-1). 40pp. Little Red Hen writes to Hetty Henny about moving to the Hidden Forest, where her neighbors are other characters from children's stories. Third in a series including *Dear Peter Rabbit* (1994) and *Yours Truly, Goldilocks* (1998). (Rev: BL 9/15/01; HB 1/02; HBG 3/02; SLJ 10/01)

987 Agee, Jon. *The Incredible Painting of Felix Clousseau* (PS–3). Illus. by author. 1988, Farrar paper $4.95 (978-0-374-43582-0). 32pp. A very laid-back artist is oblivious to the havoc his paintings cause. (Rev: BCCB 11/88; BL 11/1/88; HB 1/89)

988 Ahlberg, Allan. *The Pencil* (K–2). Illus. by Bruce Ingman. 2008, Candlewick $16.99 (978-0-7636-3894-8). 48pp. It's amazing how much trouble a lonely pencil can get into when it starts to draw things — and then to try to erase them. (Rev: BCCB 9/08; HB 1/09; 11/08; SLJ 9/08)

989 Ahlberg, Allan. *Shopping Expedition* (PS–1). Illus. by André Amstutz. 2005, Candlewick $16.99 (978-0-7636-2586-3). 32pp. A fanciful little girl describes how a shopping expedition goes dramatically awry in this story involving blizzards, floods, and jungles. (Rev: BL 5/1/05)

990 Almond, David. *Kate, the Cat and the Moon* (PS–2). Illus. by Steve Lambert. 2005, Doubleday $15.95 (978-0-385-74691-5). 32pp. On a night with a full moon, Kate is transformed into a cat and joins her own pet on a journey through magical scenes under the stars; includes a fold-out. (Rev: BCCB 10/05; BL 7/05; HBG 4/06; LMC 1/06; SLJ 9/05)

991 Anderson, Bob. *Obo* (K–3). Illus. by author. 1999, Hampton Roads $16.95 (978-1-57174-123-3). 45pp. A young monkey who is enchanted with the song of a pretty little bird sets out to find the bird's home, which is known as Paradise. (Rev: SLJ 8/99)

992 Andreae, Giles. *Captain Flinn and the Pirate Dinosaurs* (1–3). Illus. by Russell Ayto. 2005, Simon & Schuster $15.95 (978-1-4169-0713-8). 32pp. A schoolboy finds a pirate crying in his classroom's supply closet and volunteers to help the hapless buccaneer regain control of his ship, which has been stolen by dinosaurs. (Rev: BCCB 12/05; BL 12/1/05; HBG 4/06; SLJ 12/05)

993 Andres, Kristina. *Good Little Wolf* (PS–K). Illus. by author. 2008, North-South $12.95 (978-0-7358-2210-8). 32pp. A toy wolf emphasizes all the characteristics that make him a good wolf in this picture book with tiny, fine illustrations. (Rev: BL 12/1/08; SLJ 12/08)

994 Argueta, Manlio. *Magic Dogs of the Volcanoes: Los Perros Mágicos de los Volcanoes* (K–3). Illus. by Elly Simmons. 1990, Children's Book Pr. $14.95 (978-0-89239-064-9). 30pp. From El Salvador, this dual-language book tells the story of the magical dogs that live at the foot of volcanoes. (Rev: SLJ 2/91)

995 Armstrong, Jennifer. *The Snowball* (K–1). Illus. by Jean Pidgeon. 1996, Random paper $3.99 (978-0-679-86444-8). 32pp. A snowball gathers up children as it rolls down a hill. (Rev: BL 2/1/97)

996 Arnold, Caroline. *The Terrible Hodag and the Animal Catchers* (1–3). Illus. by John Sandford. 2006, Front St $15.95 (978-1-59078-166-1). 32pp. Olee Swenson and his lumberjack friends help to protect the Hodag, a blueberry-eating monster, from capture. (Rev: BL 4/1/06; HBG 10/06; LMC 1/07; SLJ 3/06)

997 Arrou-Vignod, Jean-Philippe. *Rita and Whatsit* (PS–2). Illus. by Olivier Tallec. 2009, Chronicle $14.99 (978-0-8118-6550-0). 32pp. A talking dog soothes a very grumpy girl. (Rev: BL 6/1–15/09)

998 Ashman, Linda. *Rub-a-Dub Sub* (K–2). Illus. by Jeff Mack. 2003, Harcourt $16.00 (978-0-15-202658-5). Rhyming text complemented by vivid artwork follows a little boy on an underwater fantasy in a bright orange submarine. (Rev: HBG 10/03; SLJ 7/03)

999 Auch, Mary Jane. *The Easter Egg Farm* (PS–2). Illus. 1992, Holiday House LB $17.95 (978-0-8234-0917-4). 32pp. Humor and chaos infect a chicken ranch where the owner wears dangling earrings and trendy clothes and Pauline the hen lays "ugly" eggs. (Rev: BL 3/1/92*; SLJ 4/92)

1000 Auch, Mary Jane. *Monster Brother* (PS–2). Illus. 1994, Holiday House LB $15.95 (978-0-8234-1095-8). 32pp. Rodney is visited by a monster every night, but his brother, Sidney, has a unique solution. (Rev: BCCB 11/94; BL 11/15/94; SLJ 11/94)

1001 Avi. *Things That Sometimes Happen: Very Short Stories for Little Listeners* (PS). Illus. by Marjorie Priceman. 2002, Simon & Schuster $16.95 (978-0-689-83914-6). 40pp. Lively new illustrations enhance this collection of nine varied stories originally published in 1970. (Rev: BL 10/1/02; HBG 10/03; SLJ 11/02)

1002 Aylesworth, Jim. *The Full Belly Bowl* (K–3). Illus. by Wendy A. Halperin. 1999, Simon & Schuster $16.00 (978-0-689-81033-6). 40pp. In this handsomely illustrated tale, an old man who is always hungry is given a magical food bowl by a tiny creature he has saved from being eaten by a fox. (Rev: BCCB 12/99; BL 11/1/99*; HBG 3/00; SLJ 10/99)

1003 Aylesworth, Jim. *The Tale of Tricky Fox* (PS–2). Illus. by Barbara McClintock. 2001, Scholastic $16.95 (978-0-439-09543-3). 32pp. Tricky Fox, who thinks he has caught a pig for dinner, is outwitted by an old woman who puts a ferocious bulldog in the fox's sack instead. (Rev: BCCB 3/01; BL 2/1/01; HB 3/01*; HBG 10/01; SLJ 3/01)

1004 Babin, Claire. *Gus Is a Tree* (K–3). Illus. by Olivier Tallec. 2008, Enchanted Lion $14.95 (978-1-59270-078-3). Gus drowses in the schoolyard and dreams he is a big tree feeling wind, night, and rain. (Rev: SLJ 12/08)

1005 Baca, Ana. *Benito's Sopaipillas / La sopaipillas de Benito* (2–4). Trans. from Spanish by Carolina Villarroel. Illus. by Anthony Accardo. 2007, Arte Publico $15.95 (978-1-55885-370-6). Cristina's aunt tells her the story of her great-grandfather Benito and how he made it rain by making sopaipillas, a kind of fried pastry. In English and Spanish. (Rev: SLJ 7/07)

1006 Baicker, Karen. *Pea Pod Babies* (PS). Illus. by Sam Williams. 2003, Handprint $15.95 (978-1-59354-003-6). In this appealing rhyming story, three babies growing up in a pea pod resent their similarity and go their own ways. (Rev: BL 11/15/03; HBG 4/04; SLJ 12/03)

1007 Bailey, Debbie. *Let's Pretend* (PS). Photos by Susan Huszar. Series: Talk-About-Books. 1999, Annick $5.95 (978-1-55037-558-9). In the color photos in this board book, children play by taking the roles of parents, doctors, cooks, monsters, firemen, and princesses. (Rev: SLJ 9/99)

1008 Baker, Jeannie. *Where the Forest Meets the Sea* (K–4). Illus. by author. 1988, Greenwillow $16.89 (978-0-688-06364-1). 32pp. A young boy travels through a reef and arrives in the rain forest in Australia and pretends he has gone back in time. (Rev: BCCB 5/88; BL 6/15/88; SLJ 7/88)

1009 Baker, Keith. *The Magic Fan* (PS–2). Illus. 1989, Harcourt $14.95 (978-0-15-250750-3). 32pp. Village people don't like Yoshi's magic bridge until it saves them from a tidal wave. (Rev: BCCB 2/90; BL 11/1/89; HB 1/90; SLJ 10/89*)

1010 Baker, Lisa. *Harold and the Purple Crayon: Dinosaur Days* (PS–1). Illus. Series: Harold and the Purple Crayon. 2002, HarperCollins $14.99 (978-0-06-000541-2). 40pp. Harold uses his crayon to journey to a jungle and play with dinosaurs. (Rev: BL 2/15/03; HBG 3/03; SLJ 1/03)

1011 Balian, Lorna. *Humbug Witch* (1–3). Illus. by author. 1992, Humbug LB $14.95 (978-1-881772-24-8). 32pp. A little witch doesn't seem to get the hang of witchcraft.

1012 Balian, Lorna. *Leprechauns Never Lie* (K–3). Illus. by author. 1994, Humbug LB $14.95 (978-1-881772-07-1). 32pp. Lazy Ninny Nanny is outwitted by a clever leprechaun.

1013 Balian, Lorna. *Wilbur's Space Machine* (PS–1). Illus. 1990, Holiday House LB $19.95 (978-0-8234-0836-8). 32pp. Violet and Wilbur build a space machine to escape the world's pollution and an unwelcome guest, Googie. (Rev: BL 10/15/90; SLJ 2/91)

1014 Balouch, Kristen. *Mystery Bottle* (K–3). Illus. 2006, Hyperion $15.99 (978-0-7868-0999-8). 32pp. A mysterious bottle whisks a 7-year-old boy on a fantastical journey to Iran and a meeting with his grandfather. (Rev: BL 2/1/06)

1015 Bang, Molly. *Delphine* (PS–1). Illus. by author. 1988, Morrow $12.95 (978-0-688-05636-0). 32pp. Delphine takes a wild ride down the mountain to the post office where Gram's gift awaits her. (Rev: BCCB 10/88; HB 9/88; SLJ 9/88)

1016 Bang, Molly. *The Paper Crane* (PS–1). 1985, Greenwillow paper $6.99 (978-0-688-07333-6). 32pp. A paper crane left by a thankful stranger leads to good fortune for a restaurant owner down on his luck. (Rev: BCCB 3/86; BL 1/15/86; HB 1/86)

1017 Banks, Kate. *Max's Dragon* (PS–2). Illus. by Boris Kulikov. 2008, Farrar $16.95 (978-0-374-39921-4). 32pp. Max's interest in wordplay draws his croquet-playing brothers in when his supposed dragon in the clouds is closely followed by a thunderstorm. (Rev: BL 3/1/08; HB 3/08; SLJ 2/08)

1018 Barrett, Judith. *Cloudy with a Chance of Meatballs* (K–3). Illus. by Ron Barrett. 1978, Macmillan $16.00 (978-0-689-30647-1); paper $5.99 (978-0-689-70749-0). 32pp. In the land of ChewandSwallow, food falls from the skies.

1019 Barrett, Judith. *Pickles to Pittsburgh: The Sequel to Cloudy with a Chance of Meatballs* (K–2). Illus. by Ron Barrett. 1997, Simon & Schuster $16.00 (978-0-689-80104-4). The people of the town of Chewandswallow take all their excess food and distribute it around the world — for example, eggplants to Ecuador and pickles to Pittsburgh. (Rev: HBG 3/98; SLJ 11/97)

1020 Bartels, Alice L. *The Grandmother Doll* (PS–2). Illus. by Dusan Petricic. 2001, Annick LB $17.95 (978-1-55037-667-8); paper $6.95 (978-1-55037-666-1). Grandmother, mother, and Katy find ways to communicate their needs across the generations in this fantasy story. (Rev: HBG 10/01; SLJ 8/01)

1021 Barwin, Gary. *The Magic Mustache* (K–3). Illus. by Stephane Jorisch. 1999, Annick LB $17.95

(978-1-55037-607-4); paper $6.95 (978-1-55037-606-7). In this fantasy, a nose who lives with his parents, two eyes, goes to market to trade a pair of eyeglasses for food. (Rev: SLJ 3/00)

1022 Base, Graeme. *The Sign of the Seahorse: A Tale of Greed and High Adventure in Two Acts* (1–3). Illus. 1992, Abrams $19.95 (978-0-8109-3825-0). 48pp. A fable about undersea life that brings a lesson about the dangers of pollution. (Rev: BL 11/15/92; SLJ 11/92)

1023 Bateman, Teresa. *Fiona's Luck* (K–5). Illus. by Kelly Murphy. 2007, Charlesbridge $15.95 (978-1-57091-651-9). A leprechaun king gets upset with humans' profligate use of luck and steals the luck away, leaving an unhappy population and a girl called Fiona who is determined to get it back; set against the backdrop of the potato famine. (Rev: SLJ 4/07) ☊

1024 Bateman, Teresa. *Harp O' Gold* (PS–2). Illus. by Jill Weber. 2001, Holiday House $16.95 (978-0-8234-1523-6). 32pp. When Irish minstrel Tom trades his old harp for a new bright gold one owned by a leprechaun, he knows he has made a good exchange but still longs for his old harp. (Rev: BL 3/1/01; HBG 10/01)

1025 Bateman, Teresa. *Keeper of Soles* (K–2). Illus. by Yayo. 2006, Holiday $16.95 (978-0-8234-1734-6). 32pp. Colin the cobbler outsmarts the Grim Reaper, persuading him he needs "soles" not "souls" and offering him progressively more impressive footwear. (Rev: BL 3/1/06; SLJ 4/06)

1026 Bateman, Teresa. *Leprechaun Gold* (PS–K). Illus. by Rosanne Litzinger. 1998, Holiday House $16.95 (978-0-8234-1344-7). 32pp. After Donald O'Dell refuses a gift of gold for saving a leprechaun's life, the little one devises a scheme to reward him. (Rev: BL 8/98; HB 7/98; HBG 10/98; SLJ 6/98)

1027 Bateman, Teresa. *The Merbaby* (1–3). Illus. by Patience Brewster. 2001, Holiday House $16.95 (978-0-8234-1531-1). 32pp. A fisherman catches a merbaby and is rewarded when he returns it to the sea. (Rev: BCCB 9/01; BL 9/15/01; HBG 3/02; SLJ 1/02)

1028 Bauer, Marion Dane. *If Frogs Made Weather* (PS–2). Illus. by Dorothy Donohue. 2005, Holiday House $16.95 (978-0-8234-1622-6). A boy speculates about how the weather would be if the animals had their way. (Rev: SLJ 5/05)

1029 Bauer, Marion Dane. *If You Had a Nose Like an Elephant's Trunk* (PS–3). Illus. by Susan Winter. 2001, Holiday House $16.95 (978-0-8234-1589-2). 32pp. A girl playfully imagines what she could do if she had the features or attributes of different animals. (Rev: BL 9/15/01; HBG 3/02; SLJ 9/01)

1030 Baum, L. Frank. *The Wizard of Oz* (K–3). Illus. by Lisbeth Zwerger. 1996, North-South $19.95 (978-1-55858-638-3). 103pp. A Viennese artist reworks this classic tale with unusual, refreshing illustrations and an abridged text. (Rev: BL 10/15/96; SLJ 11/96*)

1031 Baumgart, Klaus. *Laura's Secret* (PS–2). Trans. from German by Judy Waite. Illus. by author. 2003,

Tiger Tales $16.95 (978-1-58925-031-4). Laura makes a wish on her secret star and soon the kite she and her younger brother Tommy made is flying high. (Rev: SLJ 1/04)

1032 Baynton, Martin. *Jane and the Dragon* (K–3). Illus. by author. 2007, Candlewick paper $4.99 (978-0-7636-3570-1). In her zeal to become a knight despite those who say all knights are men, Jane sets out to rescue the prince from a dragon, becomes a great friend of the dragon, and goes on to become a real knight; a tie-in to an animated TV series. (Rev: SLJ 4/07)

1033 Beaty, Andrea. *When Giants Come To Play* (PS–2). Illus. by Kevin Hawkes. 2006, Abrams $16.95 (978-0-8109-5759-6). 32pp. Young Anna whiles away an idyllic summer afternoon in the company of two very large playmates. (Rev: BL 9/15/06; SLJ 10/06)

1034 Beck, Andrea. *Elliot Digs for Treasure* (PS–2). Illus. 2001, Kids Can $12.95 (978-1-55074-806-2). 32pp. When stuffed toy Elliot Moose and his friends decide to dig for buried treasure they get stuck in the hole, and only persistence and cooperation can get them out. (Rev: BL 11/1/01; HBG 3/02; SLJ 11/01)

1035 Beck, Andrea. *Elliot's Bath* (PS–1). Illus. 2001, Kids Can $12.95 (978-1-55074-802-4). 32pp. Elliot, a toy mouse, and Socks, a rag monkey, are looking forward to performing in the evening's talent show, but when they fall into a bathroom sink they become so soggy they are afraid they won't be able to perform. (Rev: BL 3/15/01; HBG 10/01)

1036 Beck, Andrea. *Elliot's Emergency* (PS–2). Illus. 1998, Kids Can $12.95 (978-1-55074-441-5). 32pp. Elliot Moose, a stuffed toy, panics when he snags his fur on a nail. His friend Beaverton sews him up good as new. (Rev: BL 11/15/98; HBG 3/99; SLJ 12/98)

1037 Beck, Ian. *Emily and the Golden Acorn* (K–2). Illus. 1992, Simon & Schuster paper $14.00 (978-0-671-75979-7). Emily's favorite oak tree is transformed into a sailing ship. (Rev: SLJ 11/92)

1038 Beck, Ian. *Teddy's Snowy Day* (PS–K). Illus. 2002, Scholastic $15.95 (978-0-439-17520-3). 32pp. The simple story of a teddy bear who gets left out in the snow, has a wonderful time at first, and happily finds a ride home when he tires. (Rev: BL 10/1/02; HBG 3/03; SLJ 10/02)

1039 Bee, William. *Beware of the Frog* (1–4). Illus. by author. 2008, Candlewick $15.99 (978-0-7636-3920-4). A frog protects old Mrs. Collywobbles, gobbling up those who threaten her — Greedy Goblin, Smelly Troll, and Giant Hungry Ogre. (Rev: LMC 1/09; SLJ 7/08)

1040 Beeke, Jemma, and Tiphanie Beeke. *The Brand New Creature* (PS–2). 1998, Sterling $14.95 (978-1-899607-66-2). 32pp. When a young girl sets out to find a crocodile, she realizes that she doesn't know what a crocodile looks like, so she must ask the identity of a number of animals she meets. (Rev: BL 1/1–15/99; SLJ 6/99)

1041 Bell, Cece. *Sock Monkey Boogie-Woogie: A Friend Is Made* (PS–2). Illus. 2004, Candlewick

$14.99 (978-0-7636-2392-0). 32pp. Sock Monkey creates the dance partner of his dreams — out of argyle socks — in this energetic romp about a Big Celebrity Dance. (Rev: BL 1/1–15/05; SLJ 1/05)

1042 Bell, Cece. *Sock Monkey Goes to Hollywood: A Star Is Bathed* (PS–K). Illus. by author. 2003, Candlewick $13.99 (978-0-7636-1962-6). When Sock Monkey is nominated for an Oswald Award as Best Supporting Toy in a motion picture, he faces the challenge of getting clean enough to attend. (Rev: HBG 4/04; SLJ 12/03)

1043 Bell, Cece. *Sock Monkey Rides Again* (PS–2). Illus. by author. 2007, Candlewick $13.99 (978-0-7636-3089-8). Cast in a starring role as a singing cowboy, Sock Monkey seems poised to make it big, but his future begins to look a little shaky when he can't bring himself to kiss the leading lady. (Rev: SLJ 1/07)

1044 *Benjamin's First Book* (PS). Illus. 1997, Sterling $5.95 (978-0-8069-0389-7). 26pp. A board book that features photos of a delightful teddy bear named Benjamin. Also use *Benjamin's Toys* and *Shopping with Benjamin* (both 1997). (Rev: BL 2/1/98)

1045 Berger, Lou. *The Elephant Wish* (PS–3). Illus. by Ana Juan. 2008, Random $16.99 (978-0-375-83962-7). 48pp. Eliza gets her birthday wish and sets off on an elephant-borne adventure only to find an elderly neighbor has followed her. (Rev: BL 12/1/08; SLJ 9/08)

1046 Bergman, Mara. *Snip Snap! What's That?* (PS–2). Illus. by Nick Maland. 2005, Greenwillow $16.99 (978-0-06-077754-8). 32pp. When an alligator creeps into their apartment, three children frighten him back into a manhole in this picture book with a refrain made for shouting. (Rev: BL 3/1/05; SLJ 6/05)

1047 Berkeley, Jon. *Chopsticks* (2–4). Illus. 2005, Random $16.95 (978-0-375-83309-0). 32pp. When the moon is full over Hong Kong, Chopsticks the mouse and a wooden dragon he helped to free take off on wonderful adventures. (Rev: BL 12/1/05; SLJ 12/05)

1048 Berkeley, Laura. *The Seeds of Peace* (K–3). Illus. by Alison Dexter. 1999, Barefoot Books LB $15.95 (978-1-84148-007-7). An old hermit tries to show an unhappy, wealthy merchant how he can plant the seeds of peace within himself. (Rev: SLJ 1/00)

1049 Berkeley, Laura. *The Spirit of the Maasai Man* (K–3). Illus. 2000, Barefoot Books $16.95 (978-1-902283-74-6). 32pp. When animals in a zoo hear the song of the Maasai Man they remember their natural homes. (Rev: BL 3/15/00; SLJ 7/00)

1050 Bernasconi, Pablo. *The Wizard, the Ugly, and the Book of Shame* (1–4). Illus. by author. 2005, Bloomsbury $16.95 (978-0-7475-8399-8). While the wizard is away, his assistant sets off a disastrous chain of events when he tries to cast a spell on his own. (Rev: SLJ 1/06)

1051 Bernheimer, Kate. *The Girl in the Castle Inside the Museum* (PS–1). Illus. by Nicoletta Ceccoli. 2008, Random $16.99 (978-0-375-83606-0). 32pp.

A lonely little girl who lives in a tiny castle inside a snow globe, inside a museum, tries to think of a way to find some friends. (Rev: BCCB 2/08; BL 6/1–15/08; LMC 3/08; SLJ 2/08)

1052 Bertrand, Lynne. *Granite Baby* (K–2). Illus. by Kevin Hawkes. 2005, Farrar $16.00 (978-0-374-32761-3). 40pp. A tall tale set in New Hampshire about five giant sisters who learn to care for a tiny baby one of them carves from granite. (Rev: BL 4/1/05; SLJ 4/05)

1053 Birchmore, Daniel A. *The White Curtain* (PS–2). Illus. by Gail Lucas. 1997, Cucumber Island Storytellers $15.95 (978-1-887813-09-9). Gusts of wind blow a white curtain outdoors, where it can enjoy exploring the world. (Rev: SLJ 2/98)

1054 Blackstone, Stella. *An Island in the Sun* (K–3). Illus. by Nicoletta Ceccoli. 2002, Barefoot Books $15.99 (978-1-84148-193-7). 24pp. A boy in a small sailboat visits an island where he plays with a polka-dot dog before taking him home at night. (Rev: BL 5/1/02; HBG 10/02; SLJ 7/02)

1055 Blaikie, Lynn. *Beyond the Northern Lights* (PS–2). Illus. 2006, Fitzhenry & Whiteside $16.95 (978-1-55005-123-0). 32pp. A young girl imagines wonderful flights with a raven to the seas and skies of the north of the world. (Rev: BL 1/1–15/07; SLJ 3/07)

1056 Bloom, Becky. *Mice Make Trouble* (K–2). Illus. by Pascal Biet. 2000, Orchard LB $16.99 (978-0-531-33253-5). 32pp. When he uses his sister's magical pencils, everything that Henry draws comes to life, including six mischievous mice. (Rev: BL 4/1/00; HBG 10/00; SLJ 3/00)

1057 Bloom, Suzanne. *Piggy Monday: A Tale About Manners* (PS–1). Illus. 2001, Whitman $16.99 (978-0-8075-6529-2). 40pp. Mrs. Hubbub's class has turned into pigs and it's up to the Pig Lady to transform them back into children by teaching them some manners. (Rev: BL 8/01; HBG 3/02; SLJ 1/02)

1058 Bluitgen, Kare. *A Boot Fell from Heaven* (PS–2). Illus. by Chiara Carrer. 2003, Kane $15.95 (978-1-929132-45-4). When God travels to Earth to retrieve a boot He's dropped, He gets little help from the planet's inhabitants until he comes across a little boy. (Rev: BL 5/15/03; SLJ 6/03)

1059 Boesky, Amy. *Planet Was* (K–3). Illus. by Nadine Bernard Westcott. 1990, Little, Brown $14.95 (978-0-316-10084-7). 32pp. Young Prince Hierre introduces change into the life of Planet Was. (Rev: BL 12/1/90; SLJ 1/91)

1060 Bond, Rebecca. *The Great Doughnut Parade* (PS–K). Illus. by author. 2007, Houghton $17.00 (978-0-618-77705-1). 40pp. A small boy with a doughnut tied to his belt attracts a parade of human and animal followers. (Rev: BL 10/1/07; SLJ 9/07)

1061 Bowen, Anne. *I Know an Old Teacher* (K–3). Illus. by Stephen Gammell. 2008, Carolrhoda $16.95 (978-0-8225-7984-7). 32pp. As her students watch in horror, their teacher eats the class pets she has taken home for the weekend; told in a traditional cumulative pattern. (Rev: BCCB 9/08; BL 8/08; LMC 3/09; SLJ 9/08)

1062 Bowen, Anne. *Tooth Fairy's First Night* (K–2). Illus. by Jon Berkeley. 2005, Carolrhoda $15.95 (978-1-57505-753-8). A young tooth fairy finds her first assignment more taxing than she expected. (Rev: SLJ 6/05)

1063 Bradman, Tony. *Midnight in Memphis* (1–2). Illus. by Martin Chatterton. Series: Blue Bananas. 2001, Crabtree LB $22.60 (978-0-7787-0848-3); paper $4.95 (978-0-7787-0894-0). 48pp. After a UFO damages their pyramid in Egypt, Mommy Mummy and her mummy family hire some ladies to repair it in this humorous fantasy. (Rev: BL 5/1/02; SLJ 8/02)

1064 Bradman, Tony. *Red Riding Hood Takes Charge* (2–5). Illus. by Sarah Warburton. Series: After Happily Ever After. 2009, Stone Arch $17.99 (978-1-4342-1308-2). 56pp. After her bad experience with the wolf, Little Red's grandmother is lonely and her granddaughter searches for ways to cheer her up. (Rev: BLO 3/19/09; SLJ 6/09)

1065 Breathed, Berkeley. *Edwurd Fudwupper Fibbed Big: Explained by Fannie Fudwupper* (K–3). Illus. by author. 2000, Little, Brown $15.95 (978-0-316-10675-7). A boy's constant fibbing gets him into serious trouble particularly when it causes the arrival of an angry monster from space. (Rev: HBG 3/01; SLJ 11/00)

1066 Breathed, Berkeley. *Mars Needs Moms!* (PS–2). Illus. 2007, Philomel $16.99 (978-0-399-24736-). 48pp. After Milo's mom is abducted by Martians, he learns to appreciate all the things mothers do in this hilarious and brightly illustrated book. (Rev: BCCB 4/07; BL 5/1/07; SLJ 5/07)

1067 Brett, Jan. *Trouble with Trolls* (PS–3). Illus. 1992, Penguin $16.99 (978-0-399-22336-5). 32pp. In this Scandinavian-type tale, Treva has trouble with trolls when they try to steal her dog Tuffi. (Rev: BCCB 12/92; BL 9/1/92*; SLJ 9/92)

1068 Briant, Ed. *Don't Look Now* (K–2). Illus. by author. 2009, Roaring Brook $16.95 (978-1-59643-345-8). 32pp. This graphic novel fantasy of few words features two brothers who learn to work together. (Rev: HB 5/09; SLJ 6/09)

1069 Briggs, Raymond. *Jim and the Beanstalk* (PS–2). Illus. by author. 1997, Penguin paper $5.99 (978-0-698-11577-4). 40pp. A humorous, fast-moving sequel to the well-known tale.

1070 Briggs, Raymond. *The Puddleman* (K–2). Illus. 2006, Trafalgar paper $7.99 (978-0-09-945642-1). 32pp. Out for a walk with his grandfather, a young boy is disappointed by the lack of puddles until he runs into the Puddleman, who has some on his back. (Rev: BL 11/1/06)

1071 Brisson, Pat. *Tap-Dance Fever* (PS–2). Illus. by Nancy Cote. 2005, Boyds Mills $15.95 (978-1-59078-290-3). 32pp. Annabelle Applegate's nonstop tap dancing annoys her neighbors — until the day her tapping charms the rattlesnakes. (Rev: BL 3/1/05; SLJ 3/05)

1072 Brooks, Nigel, and Abigail Horner. *Country Mouse Cottage: How We Lived a Hundred Years Ago* (PS–2). Illus. 2000, Walker $15.95 (978-0-8027-8752-1). 32pp. In England circa 1900, Edward Country Mouse takes the reader on a tour of his rural house including the kitchen, laundry room, bed, bathroom, and even the schoolroom. (Rev: BCCB 12/00; BL 3/1/01; HBG 3/01; SLJ 12/00)

1073 Brown, Calef. *Tippintown: A Guided Tour* (PS–2). Illus. by author. 2003, Houghton $16.00 (978-0-618-14972-8). This rollicking, brightly illustrated story, told in rhyme, transports young readers to the magical world of Tippintown, where the guide has an elephant's trunk and the gargoyles play games. (Rev: HBG 10/03; SLJ 5/03)

1074 Brown, Jeff. *Flat Stanley* (K–3). Illus. by Scott Nash. 2006, HarperCollins $16.99 (978-0-06-112904-9). Flattened to a thickness of half an inch, Stanley Lambchop discovers that his new shape has some decided advantages in this new version of the book published in 1964. (Rev: SLJ 12/06)

1075 Brown, Jeff. *Invisible Stanley* (2–3). Illus. by Steve Björkman. 1996, HarperCollins paper $4.25 (978-0-06-442029-7). 81pp. When Stanley suddenly becomes invisible, he performs many humanitarian acts, including foiling a bank robbery. (Rev: SLJ 12/96)

1076 Brown, Kerry Hannula. *Tupag the Dreamer* (PS–3). Illus. by Linda Saport. 2001, Marshall Cavendish $15.95 (978-0-7614-5076-4). Banished from his long-ago village at a time when all was dark and cold, lazy Tupag meets Raven the creator and is accorded his one wish, for a season of light. (Rev: HBG 10/01; SLJ 5/01)

1077 Brown, Marc. *Witches Four* (PS–1). Illus. by author. 1980, Parents LB $5.95 (978-0-8193-1014-9). 48pp. Four witches lose their magic hats, which are found by four homeless cats.

1078 Brown, Margaret Wise. *The Fierce Yellow Pumpkin* (PS–1). Illus. by Richard Egielski. 2003, HarperCollins LB $16.89 (978-0-06-024481-1). A tiny pumpkin yearns to grow up to be fierce, like the scarecrow, and eventually gets his wish. (Rev: HBG 4/04; SLJ 8/03)

1079 Browne, Anthony. *My Dad* (PS–3). Illus. 2001, Farrar $16.00 (978-0-374-35101-4). 32pp. A little boy imagines all the things his dad could do if he wanted — walk on a tightrope or sing in the opera, for example. (Rev: BL 3/1/01; HBG 10/01)

1080 Brownlow, Mike. *Mickey Moonbeam* (PS–2). Illus. by author. 2006, Bloomsbury $16.95 (978-1-58234-704-2). Mickey Moonbeam receives a distress call from his pen pal Quiggle and rushes in his spaceship to the rescue, only to discover that Quiggle is gigantic! (Rev: SLJ 11/06)

1081 Brumbeau, Jeff. *The Quiltmaker's Journey* (K–3). Illus. by Gail de Marken. 2005, Scholastic $17.95 (978-0-439-51219-0). 56pp. Readers find out what prompted a young girl to become the Quiltmaker in this prequel to *The Quiltmaker's Gift* (1999); with bright quilt-themed illustrations. (Rev: BL 3/1/05; SLJ 4/05)

1082 Bryan, Sean. *A Boy and His Bunny* (PS–1). Illus. by Tom Murphy. 2005, Arcade $14.95 (978-1-55970-725-1). A boy wakes up with a bunny on his head but allays his mother's concerns with the reassurance that this will in no way limit his activities. (Rev: SLJ 6/05)

1083 Buehner, Caralyn. *Snowmen at Night* (PS). Illus. by Mark Buehner. 2002, Penguin $15.99 (978-0-8037-2550-8). 32pp. Captivating illustrations and breezy text put snowmen into action (sledding, playing baseball, and drinking iced cocoa), revealing why snowmen look so tuckered out in the mornings. (Rev: BL 10/15/02; HBG 3/03; SLJ 10/02)

1084 Buffett, Jimmy, and Savannah Buffett. *The Jolly Mon* (2–5). Illus. by Lambert Davis. 1988, Harcourt $16.00 (978-0-15-240530-4). 32pp. The story of Jolly Mon in the Caribbean whose musical voice gains him a magical guitar. (Rev: BCCB 6/88; BL 4/1/88; SLJ 7/88)

1085 Buffett, Jimmy, and Savannah Buffett. *Trouble Dolls* (K–3). Illus. by Lambert Davis. 1991, Harcourt $16.00 (978-0-15-290790-7). 32pp. Four tiny dolls come alive to help a young girl search for her missing father. (Rev: BL 3/15/91; SLJ 6/91)

1086 Bunting, Eve. *Ducky* (PS–2). Illus. by David Wisniewski. 1997, Clarion $15.00 (978-0-395-75185-5). 32pp. A yellow plastic duck has many adventures when he is washed overboard from an ocean liner. (Rev: BL 8/97; HB 11/97; HBG 3/98; SLJ 9/97)

1087 Bunting, Eve. *My Robot* (K–2). Illus. by Dagmar Fehlau. Series: Green Light Reader. 2006, Harcourt $12.95 (978-0-15-205593-6). 24pp. In this beginning reader with brief sentences and a repetitive refrain, a young African American boy describes the attributes of Cecil, the robot who is his best friend. (Rev: BL 3/15/06; SLJ 6/06)

1088 Bunting, Eve. *Night of the Gargoyles* (PS–3). Illus. by David Wiesner. 1994, Clarion $16.00 (978-0-395-66553-4). 28pp. A horror story in which gargoyles come alive at night. (Rev: BCCB 11/94; BL 10/1/94; SLJ 10/94*)

1089 Bunting, Eve. *Riding the Tiger* (2–4). Illus. by David Frampton. 2001, Clarion $16.00 (978-0-395-79731-0). 32pp. In this picture-book fantasy about the abuse of power, a young boy realizes how frightening he can become when he rides through town on the back of a ferocious tiger. (Rev: BL 3/1/01*; HBG 10/01; SLJ 3/01)

1090 Bunting, Eve. *That's What Leprechauns Do* (PS–2). Illus. by Emily Arnold McCully. 2006, Clarion $16.00 (978-0-618-35410-8). 32pp. The job of three leprechauns is to place the pot of gold at the end of rainbows, but mischief often diverts them, and nobody ever finds the gold anyway. (Rev: BL 1/1–15/06; SLJ 2/06)

1091 Burningham, John. *The Magic Bed* (PS). Illus. by author. 2003, Knopf LB $18.99 (978-0-375-92423-1). Georgie chooses an antique bed to replace his crib and soon finds his nights are full of magical adventures. (Rev: HBG 4/04; SLJ 10/03)

1092 Burningham, John. *Mr. Grumpy's Outing* (PS–K). Illus. 2001, Holt $6.95 (978-0-8050-6629-6). 20pp. A board-book version of the tale of Mr. Grumpy and the animals he takes for a trip down the river. (Rev: BL 4/1/01; HBG 3/02)

1093 Burns, Marilyn. *The Greedy Triangle* (K–3). Illus. by Gordon Silveria. 1995, Scholastic $16.95 (978-0-590-48991-1). 40pp. A little triangle is tired of his shape and becomes a quadrilateral. (Rev: BCCB 3/95; BL 2/1/95; SLJ 3/95)

1094 Bursik, Rose. *Amelia's Fantastic Flight* (PS–3). Illus. 1994, Holt paper $6.95 (978-0-8050-3386-1). 32pp. Amelia flies from country to country in the plane she has built, returning home in time for dinner. (Rev: BL 3/1/92)

1095 Butterworth, Nick. *The Rescue Party* (PS–1). Illus. by author. 1993, Little, Brown $14.95 (978-0-316-11923-8). A park keeper enjoys playing with his animal buddies until a young rabbit falls down a well. (Rev: SLJ 2/94)

1096 Carle, Eric. *Draw Me a Star* (PS–2). Illus. 1992, Penguin $16.99 (978-0-399-21877-4). 36pp. The story of creation is told through the artist's drawings of various objects. (Rev: BCCB 12/92; BL 9/15/92; SLJ 10/92)

1097 Carle, Eric. *Little Cloud* (PS–K). Illus. 1996, Penguin $16.99 (978-0-399-23034-9). 32pp. A little cloud transforms itself into a variety of shapes and finally produces rain. (Rev: BL 4/1/96; HB 5/96; SLJ 5/96)

1098 Carle, Eric. *Papa, Please Get the Moon for Me* (PS–K). Illus. by author. 1986, Picture Book $19.00 (978-0-88708-026-5). 32pp. A little girl's father gets a high ladder to climb to the moon, but has to admit it's too large to bring home. (Rev: BL 6/1/86; SLJ 8/86)

1099 Carle, Eric. *10 Little Rubber Ducks* (PS–1). Illus. 2005, HarperCollins LB $20.89 (978-0-06-074076-4). 36pp. Ten rubber ducks fall off a ship and float off in different directions; the tenth is adopted by a mother duck despite the fact that it can only squeak, not quack. (Rev: BL 5/1/05; SLJ 1/05)

1100 Carlstrom, Nancy White. *The Way to Wyatt's House* (PS–K). Illus. by Mary Morgan. 2000, Walker LB $16.85 (978-0-8027-8742-2). 32pp. Two quiet children have a loud and lovely time visiting with friend Wyatt and all the animals on his farm. (Rev: BL 9/1/00; HBG 3/01; SLJ 10/00)

1101 Carmack, Lisa Jobe. *Philippe in Monet's Garden* (PS–1). Illus. by Lisa Canney Chesaux. 1998, Museum of Fine Arts, Boston $10.95 (978-0-87846-456-2). 24pp. A frog escapes to Monet's Giverny garden where he gives the artist some tips and inspiration. (Rev: BL 1/1–15/99; HBG 3/99)

1102 Carr, Jan. *Big Truck and Little Truck* (PS–3). Illus. by Ivan Bates. 2000, Scholastic $15.95 (978-0-439-07177-2). 32pp. On Farley's farm, Little Truck remembers everything Big Truck has taught him and is able to save himself after sliding into a ditch. (Rev: BL 11/15/00; HBG 3/01; SLJ 11/00)

1103 Carr, Jan. *Greedy Apostrophe: A Cautionary Tale* (1–3). Illus. by Ethan Long. 2007, Holiday House $16.95 (978-0-8234-2006-3). Greedy Apostrophe keeps showing up where he shouldn't in this amusing story about a commonly misused punctuation mark. (Rev: SLJ 7/07)

1104 Carrick, Carol. *Patrick's Dinosaurs on the Internet* (1–2). Illus. by David Milgrim. 1999, Clarion $16.00 (978-0-395-50949-4). 32pp. A dinosaur appears on young Patrick's computer screen and then whisks the boy off to a distant planet where the dinosaurs now live. (Rev: BL 12/1/99; HBG 3/00; SLJ 9/99)

1105 Carroll, Lewis. *Alice's Adventures in Wonderland* (K–6). Illus. by Robert Sabuda. 2003, Simon & Schuster $24.95 (978-0-689-84743-1). 12pp. Dazzling — but perhaps delicate — pop-ups adorn this faithful adaptation of Lewis Carroll's classic story. (Rev: BL 3/15/04; HB 11/03; HBG 4/04; SLJ 11/03)

1106 Carter, Anne. *From Poppa* (K–3). Illus. by Kasia Charko. 2001, Lobster $16.95 (978-1-894222-02-0). 32pp. A girl and her grandfather make an enchanted duck decoy. (Rev: BL 10/1/01)

1107 Carter, Anne. *Tall in the Saddle* (K–2). Illus. by David McPhail. 1999, Orca $8.95 (978-1-55143-154-3). 32pp. As a boy walks down a modern city street, everything becomes transformed into a scene from the Wild West. (Rev: BL 9/1/99; HBG 3/00; SLJ 9/99)

1108 Cepeda, Joe. *The Swing* (PS–3). Illus. by author. 2006, Scholastic $15.99 (978-0-439-14260-1). Embarrassed by her family, which is constantly losing things, Josey retreats to her swing and discovers that the old oak tree magically contains all the lost items. (Rev: SLJ 10/06)

1109 Chambers, Catherine. *The Elephants' Ears* (PS–1). Illus. by Caroline Mockford. 2000, Barefoot Books $15.95 (978-1-84148-052-7). 32pp. A story about brother and sister elephants that explains why the ears of the elephants are different in India and in Africa. (Rev: BL 4/1/00; SLJ 4/00)

1110 Chang, Grace. *Jin Jin the Dragon* (1–3). Illus. by Chong Chang. 2008, Enchanted Lion $16.95 (978-1-59270-102-5). 45pp. Jin Jin, a golden dragon, meets many animals on his quest to find his true identity in this well-written book that features Chinese watercolors and information on dragons' importance in China. (Rev: LMC 11/08; SLJ 7/08)

1111 Charles, Veronika M. *Stretch, Swallow and Stare* (K–4). Illus. by author. 1999, Stoddart $16.95 (978-0-7737-3098-4). A young boy finds his sister with the help of three female companions, each of whom possesses an unusual power. (Rev: SLJ 1/00)

1112 Charlip, Remy, and Burton Supree. *Mother Mother I Feel Sick Send for the Doctor Quick Quick Quick* (PS–K). Illus. 2001, Tricycle $16.95 (978-1-58246-043-7). 48pp. A boy who complains of being sick is operated on and objects including a teapot and a bicycle are removed from his stomach. (Rev: BL 3/1/01; HBG 10/01)

1113 Child, Lauren. *Who's Afraid of the Big Bad Book?* (K–3). Illus. by author. 2003, Hyperion $16.99 (978-0-7868-0926-4). While reading his favorite book of fairy tales, young Herb falls asleep and awakes to find himself in the middle of a fairy tale world in which the characters scold him for treating their book badly. (Rev: BCCB 1/04; BL 1/1–15/04; HBG 4/04; SLJ 12/03)

1114 Chrismer, Melanie. *Phoebe Clappsaddle and the Tumbleweed Gang* (K–3). Illus. by Virginia M. Roeder. 2002, Pelican $15.95 (978-1-56554-966-1). Talented young Phoebe gets the best of a gang of mean cowpokes in this tall tale set in the Old West. (Rev: HBG 3/03; SLJ 1/03)

1115 Christiana, David. *The First Snow* (PS–3). Illus. 1996, Scholastic $15.95 (978-0-590-22855-8). 32pp. Aunt Arctica persuades Mother Nature to let Winter come into her kingdom. (Rev: BL 2/1/97; SLJ 2/97)

1116 Chwast, Seymour. *Harry, I Need You!* (1–3). Illus. by author. 2002, Houghton $15.00 (978-0-618-17917-6). Harry is an imaginative child who conjures up all sorts of scenarios when his mother calls for him. (Rev: SLJ 9/02)

1117 Cibula, Matt. *What's Up With You, Taquandra Fu?* (K–2). Illus. by Brian Strassburg. 1997, Zino $16.95 (978-1-55933-212-5). Taquandra Fu is an oddball, but when she tries to become conventional she prefers her old, erratic self. (Rev: SLJ 4/98)

1118 Clark, Emma Chichester. *Catch That Hat!* (K–2). Illus. 1990, Little, Brown $12.95 (978-0-316-14496-4). 28pp. A rhymed story about the adventures of a runaway hat. (Rev: BL 5/15/90*; SLJ 8/90)

1119 Clark, Emma Chichester. *Eliza and the Moonchild* (PS–1). Illus. by author. 2008, Trafalgar $16.95 (978-1-84270-577-3). 32pp. An alien called Moonchild is surprised to find the Earth dark when he arrives, but a young girl assures him that with the rise of the sun the colors he has admired will return. (Rev: BLO 7/31/08; SLJ 6/08)

1120 Clerk, Jessica. *The Wriggly, Wriggly Baby* (PS). Illus. by Laura Rankin. 2002, Scholastic $16.95 (978-0-590-96067-0). 32pp. A squirmy baby slithers through a number of fantastic adventures in this rollicking tale. (Rev: BL 10/1/02; HBG 3/03; SLJ 9/02)

1121 Clibbon, Meg. *Imagine You're a Mermaid!* (K–4). Illus. by Lucy Clibbon. Series: Imagine This! 2003, Annick $19.95 (978-1-55037-791-0); paper $7.95 (978-1-55037-790-3). A pun-filled book all about mermaids and what they're really like. (Rev: SLJ 3/04)

1122 Coffelt, Nancy. *Dogs in Space* (PS–2). Illus. 1993, Harcourt $14.95 (978-0-15-200440-8). 32pp. High-flying dogs visit one planet after another. (Rev: BL 2/15/93; SLJ 4/93)

1123 Coffelt, Nancy. *Tom's Fish* (PS–2). Illus. 1994, Harcourt $13.95 (978-0-15-200587-0). 32pp. Tom can't understand why his pet goldfish, Jessie, swims upside down. (Rev: BL 3/15/94; HB 9/93; SLJ 5/94)

1124 Cole, Babette. *Princess Smartypants Rules* (1–3). Illus. Series: Princess Smartypants. 2005, Penguin $15.99 (978-0-399-24349-3). 32pp. A superbaby turns Princess Smartypants' world upside-down in this zany tale that includes dragons, an evil count, and a prince. (Rev: BL 3/1/05; SLJ 3/05)

1125 Cole, Brock. *Good Enough to Eat* (PS–3). Illus. by author. 2007, Farrar $16.00 (978-0-374-32737-8). 32pp. Frightened villagers offer a helpless girl with no name to a giant ogre, but the girl gets the best of them all with a little magic. (Rev: BCCB 11/07; BL 10/1/07; HB 9/07; SLJ 1/08)

1126 Cole, Brock. *Larky Mavis* (PS–3). Illus. 2001, Farrar $16.00 (978-0-374-34365-1). 32pp. Eccentric Larky Mavis finds a baby inside a peanut, which she calls Heart's Delight and cares for despite universal disdain. (Rev: BCCB 9/01; BL 7/01; HB 9/01*; HBG 3/02; SLJ 8/01)

1127 Cole, Joanna. *Golly Gump Swallowed a Fly* (PS–3). Illus. by Bari Weissman. 1982, Parents $5.95 (978-0-8193-1069-9). 48pp. A new version of "The Old Woman Who Swallowed a Fly" story.

1128 Compton, Kenn, and Joanne Compton. *Granny Greenteeth and the Noise in the Night* (PS–2). Illus. by Kenn Compton. 1993, Holiday House LB $14.95 (978-0-8234-1051-4). In this humorous cumulative tale, Granny Greenteeth tries to get help to discover what is making the noise that comes from under her bed. (Rev: SLJ 3/94)

1129 Conrad, Pam. *The Tub People* (PS–2). Illus. by Richard Egielski. 1989, HarperCollins $15.95 (978-0-06-021340-4); paper $6.99 (978-0-06-443306-8). 32pp. In this fantasy, wooden figures who enjoy playing in the tub are swept down the drain. (Rev: BCCB 11/89; BL 8/89; HB 11/89*; SLJ 12/89)

1130 Coplestone, Lis. *Noah's Bed* (PS–2). Illus. by Jim Coplestone. 2004, Frances Lincoln $14.95 (978-1-84507-002-1). Frightened by the torrential rainstorm, various animals sneak one by one into bed with Noah, Mrs. Noah, and grandson Eber. (Rev: SLJ 6/04)

1131 Corey, Shana. *First Graders from Mars: Episode 4 — Tera, Star Student* (K–2). Illus. by Mark Teague. 2003, Scholastic $15.95 (978-0-439-26634-5). 29pp. Purple-haired Tera discovers bossiness is unwelcome in her 1st-grade Martian classroom. (Rev: HBG 4/04; SLJ 8/03)

1132 Corey, Shana. *First Graders from Mars: Episode 3 — Nergal and the Great Space Race* (1–3). Illus. by Mark Teague. 2002, Scholastic paper $4.50 (978-0-439-42443-1). 32pp. It's Health Week on Mars, and Nergal isn't looking forward to the space race. (Rev: SLJ 1/03)

1133 Coristine, Philip. *Serena and the Wild Doll* (K–3). Illus. by Julia Gukova. 2000, Annick LB $19.95 (978-1-55037-649-4); paper $6.95 (978-1-55037-648-7). 32pp. Serena, a proper doll who lives in an attic, is joined by a wild doll in a tattered dress and a fox, and the three venture out to see the city. (Rev: BL 2/15/01; HBG 3/01; SLJ 11/00)

1134 Cosentino, Ralph. *Batman: The Story of the Dark Knight* (1–3). Illus. by author. 2008, Viking $15.99 (978-0-670-06255-3). 40pp. A well-designed picture-book/comic-book introduction to the superhero's life, told in simple first-person text. (Rev: BL 7/08; SLJ 9/08) [741.5]

1135 Cotten, Cynthia. *Snow Ponies* (K–3). Illus. by Jason Cockcroft. 2001, Holt $15.95 (978-0-8050-6063-8). Snow ponies released by Old Man Winter turn the world white everywhere they roam. (Rev: HBG 3/02; SLJ 12/01)

1136 Cowen-Fletcher, Jane. *Nell's Elf* (K–2). Illus. by author. 2006, Candlewick $14.99 (978-0-7636-

2391-3). A little girl bored on a rainy day cheers up when the elf she draws comes alive and shows her how to enjoy life. (Rev: SLJ 4/06)

1137 Cowley, Joy. *Chicken Feathers* (3–5). Illus. by David Elliot. 2008, Philomel $15.99 (978-0-399-24791-0). 160pp. While Josh's mother is in hospital awaiting the arrival of a new baby, Josh is also preoccupied with his talking pet hen, Semolina, who alerts him to a fox plot. (Rev: BL 5/15/08; HB 5/08; LMC 8/08; SLJ 4/08)

1138 Cowley, Joy. *Mrs. Wishy-Washy's Farm* (PS–1). Illus. by Elizabeth Fuller. 2003, Philomel $15.99 (978-0-399-23872-7). Obsessed with cleanliness, Mrs. Wishy-Washy decides it's time to scrub all the animals on the farm; to escape their date with the tub, her cow, duck, and pig run off, only to find themselves in loads of trouble and longing to be reunited with their master. (Rev: HBG 10/03; SLJ 7/03)

1139 Cowley, Joy. *Singing Down the Rain* (K–2). Illus. by Jan S. Gilchrist. 1997, HarperCollins LB $14.89 (978-0-06-027603-4). 32pp. Fantasy and reality blend in this story about a young girl, a drought, and a young woman who is a "rain singer." (Rev: BL 11/15/97; SLJ 10/97)

1140 Crew, Gary. *Pig on the Titanic: A True Story* (K–2). Illus. by Bruce Whatley. 2005, HarperCollins LB $18.89 (978-0-06-052306-0). 32pp. A music-box pig named Maxixe describes the sinking of the *Titanic* and how his music keeps up the spirits of the children in his lifeboat in this compelling story based on reality. (Rev: BL 6/1–15/05; SLJ 5/05)

1141 Crummel, Susan Stevens. *All in One Hour* (PS–1). Illus. by Dorothy Donohue. 2003, Marshall Cavendish $16.95 (978-0-7614-5129-7). 32pp. Paper-cut collage illustrations tell a "This Is the House That Jack Built" type story featuring a mouse, a cat, a dog, a dogcatcher, a robber, and a police officer. (Rev: BL 3/15/03; HBG 10/03; SLJ 5/03)

1142 Cullen, Lynn. *Little Scraggly Hair: A Dog on Noah's Ark* (PS–3). Illus. by Jacqueline Rogers. 2003, Holiday House $16.95 (978-0-8234-1772-8). With an Appalachian flair, this tells the story of Noah's ark and as a bonus explains why dogs have wet noses. (Rev: BCCB 2/04; BL 11/1/03; HBG 4/04; SLJ 12/03)

1143 Cuyler, Margery. *Monster Mess!* (PS). Illus. by S. D. Schindler. 2008, Simon & Schuster $14.99 (978-0-689-86405-6). 40pp. A tired monster feels he has to clean up a little boy's bedroom before he can go to sleep. (Rev: BL 6/1–15/08; SLJ 7/08)

1144 Czernecki, Stefan. *Lilliput 5357* (PS–2). Illus. by author. 2006, Simply Read $16.95 (978-1-894965-32-3). Driven from his playground by a bunch of bullies, Lilliput 5357, a diminutive robot, searches desperately for somewhere new to play. (Rev: SLJ 4/06)

1145 Czernecki, Stefan. *Zorah's Magic Carpet* (K–3). Illus. by author. 1996, Hyperion LB $15.49 (978-0-7868-2066-5). In this tale set in Morocco, a young woman weaves a magic carpet that takes her to exotic places that she later weaves into other carpets. (Rev: HB 7/96; SLJ 4/96)

1146 Daniels, Teri. *G-Rex* (K–2). Illus. by Tracey Campbell Pearson. 2000, Orchard LB $17.99 (978-0-531-33243-6). A boy turns himself into a dinosaur so he can get more attention at home. (Rev: HBG 3/01; SLJ 10/00)

1147 Davies, Jacqueline. *The House Takes a Vacation* (1–3). Illus. by Lee White. 2007, Marshall Cavendish $16.99 (978-0-7614-5331-4). Readers who enjoy puns will appreciate this story about a house that decides it deserves a vacation as much as its residents do. (Rev: SLJ 5/07)

1148 Davol, Marguerite W. *How Snake Got His Hiss* (PS–3). Illus. by Mercedes McDonald. 1996, Orchard LB $15.99 (978-0-531-08768-8). 32pp. Not only does this tale tell how a snake got its hiss but also how the hyena got its spots and the lion its mane. (Rev: BCCB 4/96; BL 4/15/96; SLJ 3/96)

1149 Davol, Marguerite W. *The Loudest, Fastest, Best Drummer in Kansas* (PS–2). Illus. by Cat B. Smith. 2000, Orchard LB $16.99 (978-0-531-33191-0). 32pp. In this tall tale, Maggie proves that the loud noises she makes on her drums can have beneficial results. (Rev: BL 3/15/00; HBG 10/00; SLJ 5/00)

1150 Davol, Marguerite W. *The Paper Dragon* (PS–3). Illus. by Robert Sabuda. 1997, Simon & Schuster $18.00 (978-0-689-31992-1). 60pp. This story set in China tells how Mi Fei accomplishes his task of putting a destructive dragon to sleep. (Rev: BL 10/15/97*; HBG 3/98; SLJ 11/97)

1151 Day, Jan. *Kissimmee Pete, Cracker Cow Hunter: A Tall Tale* (2–4). Illus. by Janeen Mason. 2005, Pelican $15.95 (978-1-58980-325-1). Kissimmee Pete, a cowboy on Florida's frontier, is involved in a ever-escalating series of adventures that add to the string of adjectives describing his prowess. (Rev: SLJ 12/05)

1152 Day, Lucille Lang. *Chain Letter* (1–3). Illus. by Doug Dworkin. 2005, Heyday $14.95 (978-1-59714-011-9). An outrageous chain letter makes its way around the globe in this tongue-in-cheek tale. (Rev: SLJ 9/05)

1153 Deacon, Alexis. *Beegu* (K–2). Illus. by author. 2003, Farrar $16.00 (978-0-374-30667-0). Stranded on Earth after her spaceship crashes, Beegu, an appealing yellow alien, finds acceptance from small earthlings but is driven away at every turn by adults. (Rev: HBG 4/04; SLJ 11/03)

1154 Deeble, Jason. *Sir Ryan's Quest* (K–3). Illus. by author. 2009, Roaring Brook $16.95 (978-1-59643-330-4). 32pp. With saucepan-helmet on head, little Sir Ryan sets out on a knightly household adventure. (Rev: BL 4/1/09; SLJ 4/09)

1155 Deedy, Carmen A. *The Library Dragon* (K–2). Illus. by Michael P. White. 1994, Peachtree $16.95 (978-1-56145-091-6). The new librarian is a real fire-breathing dragon who in time learns to trust children with her books. (Rev: BCCB 2/95; SLJ 12/94)

1156 DeFelice, Cynthia. *One Potato, Two Potato* (1–3). 2006, Farrar $16.00 (978-0-374-35640-8).

32pp. A poor elderly Irish couple used to sharing their one chair, their one coat, are down to their last potato when they discover a magic pot in this appealing adaptation of a Chinese folk tale. (Rev: BL 9/1/06; SLJ 8/06)

1157 Dematons, Charlotte. *Let's Go* (K–3). Illus. 2001, Front St. $15.95 (978-1-886910-65-2). 32pp. A young boy's trip to the corner store turns into a magical adventure. (Rev: BL 5/15/01; HBG 10/01; SLJ 10/01)

1158 Dematons, Charlotte. *Looking for Cinderella* (PS–3). Illus. 1996, Front St. $15.95 (978-1-886910-13-3). 32pp. In an old windmill, Hilda encounters many fairy tale characters, including Hansel and Gretel and Tom Thumb. (Rev: BCCB 10/96; BL 9/15/96; SLJ 1/97)

1159 Demi. *The Boy Who Painted Dragons* (K–2). Illus. by author. 2007, Simon & Schuster $21.99 (978-1-4169-2469-2). 52pp. A boy named Ping paints dragons everywhere, but is secretly afraid of them and is forced to face his fears. (Rev: BL 9/15/07; LMC 11/07; SLJ 9/07)

1160 Demi. *Liang and the Magic Paintbrush* (2–4). Illus. by author. 1980, Holt paper $5.95 (978-0-8050-0801-2). 32pp. A boy in old China finds that everything he dreams comes to life.

1161 de Monfreid, Dorothée. *Dark Night* (PS–K). Illus. by author. 2009, Random $14.99 (978-0-375-85687-7). 40pp. Scared by the animals in the forest, little Felix ends up in a rabbit's home and there finds a devil's mask with which he manages to escape — but then there are a lot of frightened beasts to reassure. (Rev: BL 7/09)

1162 dePaola, Tomie. *Angels, Angels Everywhere* (PS). Illus. by author. 2005, Putnam $14.99 (978-0-399-24370-7). DePaola presents angels who provide guidance for children in almost every aspect of daily life — including "the wake up angel," "the popcorn angel," and "the babysitting angel." (Rev: SLJ 10/05)

1163 dePaola, Tomie. *Big Anthony: His Story* (PS–3). Illus. 1998, Penguin $16.99 (978-0-399-23189-6). 32pp. Klutzy Big Anthony goes out on his own to earn his fortune and finds himself at the door of the Italian witch Strega Nona. (Rev: BL 11/15/98; HBG 3/99; SLJ 11/98)

1164 dePaola, Tomie. *Bill and Pete* (K–2). Illus. by author. 1996, Penguin paper $6.99 (978-0-698-11400-5). 32pp. Pete is a toothbrush (alias a bird) who helps young Bill in a series of world misadventures.

1165 dePaola, Tomie. *Jamie O'Rourke and the Pooka* (PS–3). Illus. 2000, Penguin $16.99 (978-0-399-23467-5). 32pp. A humorous original folktale about the laziest man in Ireland and the strange donkey-like beast, the pooka, that helps clean his house. (Rev: BL 1/1–15/00; HBG 10/00; SLJ 3/00)

1166 dePaola, Tomie. *Sing, Pierrot, Sing: A Picture Book in Mime* (PS–2). Illus. by author. 1983, Harcourt paper $3.95 (978-0-15-274989-7). 32pp. A group of children comfort Pierrot at his loss of Columbine.

1167 dePaola, Tomie. *Strega Nona Meets Her Match* (K–2). Illus. 1993, Penguin $17.99 (978-0-399-22421-8). 34pp. Strega Amelia comes to town and takes away business from the town's other witch, Strega Nona. (Rev: BCCB 12/93; BL 11/1/93; HB 11/93)

1168 dePaola, Tomie. *Strega Nona Takes a Vacation* (K–3). Illus. 2000, Penguin $16.99 (978-0-399-23562-7). 32pp. While Strega Nona is away on vacation, Big Anthony uses too many bath crystals and creates enough soapsuds to flow into town. (Rev: BL 10/15/00; HBG 3/01; SLJ 10/00)

1169 Desimini, Lisa. *Moon Soup* (PS–3). Illus. 1993, Hyperion LB $15.49 (978-1-56282-464-8). 32pp. An unusual man concocts a brew he calls moon soup and flies to the moon to eat it. (Rev: BL 11/1/93; SLJ 1/94)

1170 Desimini, Lisa. *Sun and Moon: A Giant Love Story* (PS–3). Illus. 1999, Scholastic $16.95 (978-0-590-18720-6). 40pp. An enchanting fable about the growing love between a girl and a boy whose heads are literally in the clouds. (Rev: BCCB 1/99; BL 1/1–15/99; HBG 10/99; SLJ 3/99)

1171 de Varennes, Monique. *The Jewel Box Ballerinas* (PS–2). Illus. by Ana Juan. 2007, Random $16.99 (978-0-375-83605-3). 40pp. A lonely rich lady loves her two little jewel box ballerinas so much that they — and she — come to life. (Rev: BL 2/1/08; HB 11/07; SLJ 11/07)

1172 Devlin, Wende, and Harry Devlin. *Old Black Witch!* (K–3). Illus. by Harry Devlin. 1992, Macmillan $13.95 (978-0-02-729185-8). 32pp. When Nicky and his mother buy an old house, they find a witch living in the chimney. (Rev: BL 11/15/92)

1173 Dillon, Jana. *Lucky O'Leprechaun Comes to America* (PS–1). Illus. by author. 2000, Pelican $15.95 (978-1-56554-816-9). A fantasy in which Lucky O'Leprechaun gets caught in the luggage of three Irish immigrant girls and is forced to travel with them to America. (Rev: HBG 10/01; SLJ 1/01)

1174 Ditchfield, Christin. *Cowlick!* (PS–K). Illus. by Rosalind Beardshaw. 2007, Random $14.99 (978-0-375-83540-7). 40pp. Interpreting its title literally, this rhyming romp depicts a cow depositing drooly kisses upon slumbering children's heads, with predictable results next morning. (Rev: BL 1/1–15/07; SLJ 1/07)

1175 DiTerlizzi, Tony. *Jimmy Zangwow's Out-of-This-World Moon Pie Adventure* (K–2). Illus. by author. 2000, Simon & Schuster $16.00 (978-0-689-82215-5). When Jimmy's mother refuses to give him a Moon Pie, the young boy travels to the moon to get his own. (Rev: BCCB 5/00; HBG 10/00; SLJ 4/00)

1176 DiTerlizzi, Tony. *Ted* (PS–1). Illus. by author. 2001, Simon & Schuster $16.00 (978-0-689-83235-2). A young boy succeeds in getting his father's attention through a lively imaginary friend. (Rev: BCCB 2/01; HBG 10/01; SLJ 4/01)

1177 Docherty, Thomas. *Little Boat* (PS–K). Illus. by author. 2009, Candlewick $15.99 (978-0-7636-4428-4). 40pp. A courageous little tugboat sets out into the vast and dangerous sea to find its companions. (Rev: BL 5/15/09; SLJ 8/09)

1178 Doherty, Berlie. *Jinnie Ghost* (2–4). Illus. by Jane Ray. 2005, Frances Lincoln $16.95 (978-1-84507-292-6). 44pp. Jinnie Ghost visits sleeping children throughout the night, leaving each one with a different dream. (Rev: BL 10/15/05; SLJ 2/06)

1179 Dollinger, Renate. *The Rabbi Who Flew: A Grandma Hanne Sheyne Story* (K–3). Illus. 2000, Booksmythe $18.00 (978-0-945585-20-6). 48pp. When a rabbi gains the power to fly, his friends realize that he has holes in his shoes and devise a plan to mend them. (Rev: BL 2/1/01)

1180 Donaldson, Julia. *Charlie Cook's Favorite Book* (PS–2). Illus. by Axel Scheffler. 2006, Dial $16.99 (978-0-8037-3142-4). 32pp. Charlie is led through 10 different fairy tales by the books' characters themselves in this amusing circular take on some familiar stories. (Rev: BL 5/1/06; SLJ 7/06)

1181 Donaldson, Julia. *Room on the Broom* (K–3). Illus. by Axel Scheffler. 2001, Dial $16.99 (978-0-8037-2657-4). 32pp. A witch's animal friends cleverly save her from a dragon in this rhyming tale featuring entertaining illustrations. (Rev: BCCB 9/01; BL 9/1/01; HBG 3/02; SLJ 9/01)

1182 Donnelly, Liza. *Dinosaur Beach* (PS–2). Illus. by author. 1991, Scholastic paper $2.50 (978-0-685-43744-5). A boy and his dog spend a lovely day playing with the dinosaurs at a beach. (Rev: SLJ 7/89)

1183 Donnelly, Liza. *Dinosaur Garden* (PS–3). Illus. 1991, Scholastic paper $3.25 (978-0-590-43172-9). 32pp. Rex's seedlings sprout into a tropical jungle that is soon home to plant-eating dinosaurs. (Rev: BL 4/15/90; SLJ 3/90)

1184 Donohue, Moira Rose. *Alfie the Apostrophe* (1–3). Illus. by JoAnn Adinolfi. 2006, Albert Whitman $16.95 (978-0-8075-0255-6). 32pp. A lively tale about a little apostrophe who makes his mark trying out for a school talent show directed by Mr. Asterisk. (Rev: BL 8/06; SLJ 8/06)

1185 Donohue, Moira Rose. *Penny and the Punctuation Bee* (1–3). Illus. by Jenny Law. 2008, Albert Whitman $16.95 (978-0-8075-6477-6). 32pp. A humorous look at punctuation, in which Penny, a period, and Quentin, a question mark, prepare for a contest against an irritating exclamation mark. (Rev: BL 7/08; LMC 8/08; SLJ 5/08)

1186 Dorros, Arthur. *Abuela* (K–2). Illus. by Elisa Kleven. 1991, Dutton $16.99 (978-0-525-44750-4). 40pp. Rosalba and her grandmother fly over New York City in her imagination. (Rev: BCCB 9/92; BL 10/15/91*; HB 11/91*; SLJ 10/91)

1187 Doucet, Sharon Arms. *Alligator Sue* (K–2). Illus. by Anne Wilsdorf. 2003, Farrar $17.00 (978-0-374-30218-4). When a hurricane sweeps Sue away from her houseboat home in a Louisiana swamp, she finds herself adopted by a very large family of alligators. (Rev: HBG 4/04; SLJ 9/03)

1188 Doyle, Malachy. *The Dancing Tiger* (K–2). Illus. by Steve Johnson and Lou Fancher. 2005, Viking $15.99 (978-0-670-06020-7). A girl and a tiger dance together by the full moon in this nicely illustrated story with poetic text. (Rev: SLJ 7/05)

1189 Doyle, Malachy. *Hungry! Hungry! Hungry!* (K–3). Illus. by Paul Hess. 2001, Peachtree $15.95 (978-1-56145-241-5). A young boy asks a "ghastly goblin" many questions about his size and other scary features. (Rev: BCCB 4/01; HBG 10/01; SLJ 7/01)

1190 Drawson, Blair. *Flying Dimitri* (K–3). Illus. 1997, Orchard $14.95 (978-0-531-30037-4). 40pp. A fantasy in which a young boy flies to Mars to save a princess but is happy to get home, where his father tucks him into bed. (Rev: BL 12/15/97; HBG 3/98; SLJ 4/98)

1191 Drawson, Blair. *Mary Margaret's Tree* (K–3). Illus. 1996, Orchard LB $16.99 (978-0-531-08871-5). 32pp. In this fantasy, Mary Margaret views the change of seasons from atop a tree that she has planted. (Rev: BL 10/1/96; SLJ 10/96)

1192 Drescher, Henrik. *Simon's Book* (PS–1). Illus. by author. 1983, Lothrop paper $6.95 (978-0-688-10484-9). 32pp. A frightening monster chases Simon through the pages of his drawing pad.

1193 Dunbar, Joyce. *Magic Lemonade* (1–2). Illus. by Jan McCafferty. Series: Blue Bananas. 2001, Crabtree LB $12.95 (978-0-613-52875-7); paper $4.46 (978-0-7497-4645-2). 48pp. Bossy Zoe proves to be a difficult but imaginative playmate in this amusing fantasy. (Rev: BL 5/1/02)

1194 Dunbar, Polly. *Hello Tilly* (PS). Illus. by author. Series: Tilly and Friends. 2008, Candlewick $12.99 (978-0-7636-4109-2). 32pp. For toddlers, this is a pleasing book about Tilly, who lives with five animal friends in a little yellow house and enjoy simple pleasures. (Rev: SLJ 6/09)

1195 Dunbar, Polly. *Penguin* (PS). Illus. by author. 2007, Candlewick $15.99 (978-0-7636-3404-9). 40pp. Ben goes to great lengths trying to get his new pet penguin to talk, but the mute penguin finds a way to communicate after saving Ben from the jaws of a lion. (Rev: BL 6/1–15/07; SLJ 7/07)

1196 Duquennoy, Jacques. *The Ghosts' Trip to Loch Ness* (PS–2). Illus. by author. 1996, Harcourt $11.00 (978-0-15-201440-7). A quartet of ghosts travels to Scotland for a glimpse of the Loch Ness monster in this amusing fantasy. (Rev: BCCB 10/96; SLJ 10/96)

1197 Dyer, Sarah. *Five Little Fiends* (K–3). Illus. 2002, Bloomsbury $15.95 (978-1-58234-751-6). 32pp. In this unusual picture book, the little fiends of the title emerge from statues to steal parts of the environment, until they realize the error of their ways. (Rev: BL 9/1/02; SLJ 9/02)

1198 Eaton, Deborah, and Susan Halter. *No One Told the Aardvark* (PS–2). Illus. by Jim Spence. 1997, Charlesbridge paper $6.95 (978-0-88106-871-9). In this humorous story, a young boy thinks of all the advantages there would be if he were different animals. (Rev: SLJ 6/97)

1199 Edwards, Pamela Duncan. *The Leprechaun's Gold* (PS–2). Illus. by Henry Cole. 2004, Harper-Collins LB $16.89 (978-0-06-623975-0). 32pp. Young Tom's determination to become the finest

harpist in Ireland is foiled by leprechauns. (Rev: BL 1/1–15/04; SLJ 2/04)

1200 Edwards, Pamela Duncan. *The Old House* (PS–1). Illus. by Henry Cole. 2007, Dutton $16.99 (978-0-525-47796-9). 32pp. A lonely old house becomes a happy home when a family fixes it up and moves in. (Rev: BL 10/1/07; LMC 1/08; SLJ 11/07)

1201 Eeckhout, Emmanuelle. *There's No Such Thing as Ghosts!* (PS–1). Illus. by author. 2008, Kane $13.95 (978-1-933605-91-3). 32pp. Readers get lots of laughs as a little boy hunting ghosts explores a haunted house, butterfly net in hand, but fails to see any of the many phantoms hovering there. (Rev: HB 1/09; SLJ 11/08)

1202 Egielski, Richard. *Buz* (PS–2). Illus. 1995, HarperCollins LB $15.89 (978-0-06-023567-3). 32pp. A bug that is eaten accidently by a boy finally finds an escape route via the boy's ear. (Rev: BCCB 10/95; BL 8/95; SLJ 9/95)

1203 Einhorn, Edward. *A Very Improbable Story* (1–3). Illus. by Adam Gustavson. 2008, Charlesbridge $16.95 (978-1-57091-871-1); paper $7.95 (978-1-57091-872-8). 32pp. What are the chances you'll wake up with a talking cat named Odds on your head? This feline will not go away until Ethan wins a game of probability. (Rev: BL 2/1/08; LMC 10/08; SLJ 2/08)

1204 Eitzen, Ruth. *Tara's Flight* (K–2). Illus. by Allan Eitzen. 2008, Boyds Mills $16.95 (978-1-59078-563-8). 32pp. The story of Noah's ark is retold through the eyes of Noah's grandson, Aram, whose pet dove serves as a useful messenger. (Rev: BL 2/15/08; SLJ 3/08)

1205 Ellery, Amanda. *If I Had a Dragon* (PS–2). Illus. by Tom Ellery. 2006, Simon & Schuster $14.95 (978-1-4169-0924-8). 40pp. A boy imagines what would happen if his baby brother were a dragon, and decides he likes having a human sibling better. (Rev: BL 7/06; SLJ 7/06)

1206 Ellery, Amanda. *If I Were a Jungle Animal* (PS–1). Illus. by Tom Ellery. 2009, Simon & Schuster $15.99 (978-1-4169-3778-4). 40pp. Bored in the outfield, Morton imagines himself as a variety of animals until his teammates interrupt him. (Rev: LMC 8/09; SLJ 4/09)

1207 Elliott, George. *The Boy Who Loved Bananas* (PS–2). Illus. by Andrej Krystoforski. 2005, Kids Can $15.95 (978-1-55337-744-3). After watching the monkeys at the zoo, Matthew vows only to eat bananas, which is fine until he morphs into a monkey himself. (Rev: SLJ 6/05)

1208 Elya, Susan Middleton. *Fairy Trails: A Story Told in English and Spanish* (PS). Illus. by Mercedes McDonald. 2005, Bloomsbury $16.95 (978-1-58234-927-5). 32pp. On their way to their aunt's house, Miguel and Maria meet a variety of fairy-tale characters — Aladdin, Cinderella, and so forth — in a rhyming text sprinkled with Spanish words and names. (Rev: BL 5/15/05)

1209 Esterl, Arnica. *Okino and the Whales* (K–3). Illus. by Marek Zawadzki. 1995, Harcourt $16.00 (978-0-15-200377-7). 32pp. A mother tells her son the story of how his great-great-grandmother rescued her daughter from the underwater kingdom of Iwa. (Rev: BL 10/15/95; SLJ 1/96)

1210 Fancher, Lou, adapt. *The Velveteen Rabbit* (PS–2). Illus. by Steve Johnson and Lou Fancher. 2002, Simon & Schuster $16.95 (978-0-689-84134-7). With appealing illustrations and very readable text, Fancher retells the story of a stuffed rabbit that becomes real. (Rev: HBG 3/03; SLJ 12/02)

1211 Federspiel, Jürg. *Alligator Mike* (1–3). Illus. by Petra Rappo. 2007, North-South $15.95 (978-0-7358-2124-8). Mike discovers that New York City is full of unhappy alligators that want to go home to Florida and decides to do what he can to help. (Rev: SLJ 4/07)

1212 Feiffer, Jules. *The House Across the Street* (PS–2). Illus. 2002, Hyperion $15.95 (978-0-7868-0910-3). 32pp. Cartoon-style illustrations show the house across the street, where a boy's imaginary self doesn't have to obey his parents and can do whatever he wants — like eating with his elbows on the table and even putting a swimming pool in the bedroom. (Rev: BCCB 1/03; BL 12/1/02; HBG 3/03; SLJ 2/03)

1213 Fenton, Joe. *What's Under the Bed?* (K–2). Illus. by author. 2008, Simon & Schuster $15.99 (978-1-4169-4943-5). 32pp. Fred finally realizes that the monster under the bed is his teddy bear, but uncomfortable questions remain. (Rev: SLJ 9/08)

1214 Fernandes, Eugenie. *Sleepy Little Mouse* (PS–K). Illus. by Kim Fernandes. 2000, Kids Can $12.95 (978-1-55074-701-0). 24pp. When Little Mouse cries at nap time, she produces so many tears that her bed floats down a river and into the sea where she is found by sea creatures. (Rev: BL 10/1/00; HBG 3/01)

1215 Flaherty, A. W. *The Luck of the Loch Ness Monster: A Tale of Picky Eating* (K–3). Illus. by Scott Magoon. 2007, Houghton $16.00 (978-0-618-55644-1). 40pp. A young girl's refusal to eat oatmeal on an ocean trip to Scotland, and a sea worm's hunger, apparently gave birth to a legend. (Rev: BL 10/1/07; SLJ 9/07)

1216 Fleischman, Paul. *Sidewalk Circus* (K–3). Illus. by Kevin Hawkes. 2004, Candlewick $15.99 (978-0-7636-1107-1). 32pp. Triggered by posters advertising an upcoming circus, a young girl's imagination transforms the events of everyday life into a dizzying series of colorful circus performances. (Rev: BL 4/15/04*; HB 5/04; SLJ 7/04)

1217 Fleischman, Paul. *Weslandia* (K–3). Illus. by Kevin Hawkes. 1999, Candlewick $15.99 (978-0-7636-0006-8). 40pp. In this offbeat fantasy, unconventional Wesley cultivates magical seeds that serve as the basis of a new civilization. (Rev: BCCB 7–8/99; BL 7/99*; HB 3/99; HBG 10/99; SLJ 6/99)

1218 Fletcher, Ralph. *The Sandman* (PS–K). Illus. by Richard Cowdry. 2008, Holt $16.95 (978-0-8050-7726-1). 32pp. A miniature man named Tor discovers the secret of sleep and in his mouse-drawn carriage travels far and wide helping insomniac children. (Rev: BL 7/08; SLJ 5/08)

1219 Florczak, Robert. *Yikes!!!* (PS). Illus. by author. 2003, Scholastic $15.95 (978-0-590-05043-2). A young child encounters some fearsome creatures on an imaginary journey and utters suitable cries of dismay. (Rev: BL 11/15/03; HBG 4/04; SLJ 12/03)

1220 Floyd, Madeleine. *Cold Paws, Warm Heart* (PS). Illus. 2005, Candlewick $15.99 (978-0-7636-2761-4). 32pp. A little girl named Hannah seeks to warm up a lonely polar bear named Cold Paws. (Rev: BL 12/1/05; SLJ 7/06)

1221 Foley, Greg. *Willoughby and the Lion* (PS–2). Illus. by author. 2009, HarperCollins $17.99 (978-0-06-154750-8). 40pp. A beautiful golden lion grants young Willoughby 10 wishes but warns that unless the boy chooses the most wonderful thing of all, the lion will remain trapped on his rock in the backyard forever; counting opportunities arise as Willoughby struggles to find the perfect wish. (Rev: BL 1/1–15/09; SLJ 2/09)

1222 Foreman, Michael. *Jack's Fantastic Voyage* (K–3). Illus. 1992, Harcourt $14.95 (978-0-15-239496-7). 32pp. Jack doubts that his grandfather really had the adventures he claims until one night the two experience together an equally amazing voyage. (Rev: BL 11/15/92; SLJ 11/92)

1223 Fowles, Shelley. *Climbing Rosa* (PS–2). Illus. 2006, Frances Lincoln $15.95 (978-1-84507-079-3). 32pp. Brightly colored artwork enlivens this tale of Rosa, a poor young woman who climbs a towering tree to win the hand of a prince. (Rev: BL 4/1/06; SLJ 5/06)

1224 Fox, Mem. *The Magic Hat* (PS–1). Illus. by Tricia Tusa. 2002, Harcourt $16.00 (978-0-15-201025-6). 32pp. A magic hat transforms the people on whose heads it lands into a variety of different animals in this charming fantasy. (Rev: BCCB 7–8/02; BL 4/15/02; HBG 10/02; SLJ 4/02)

1225 Fox, Mem. *The Straight Line Wonder* (K–4). Illus. by Marc Rosenthal. 1997, Mondo $14.95 (978-1-57255-206-7). 24pp. Three straight lines are dear friends until one of them wants to change its shape. (Rev: BL 10/15/97; HBG 3/98; SLJ 1/98)

1226 Franson, Scott E. *Un-Brella* (PS–3). Illus. by author. 2007, Roaring Brook $15.95 (978-1-59643-179-9). A little girl enjoys a day at the beach although it's snowing out and conversely a day in the snow during a hot summer, all with the help of her "un-brella." (Rev: SLJ 4/07)

1227 Frascino, Edward. *Nanny Noony and the Magic Spell* (PS–3). Illus. by author. 1988, Pippin $15.95 (978-0-945912-00-2). 32pp. How the spell on the farm is undone. (Rev: BL 11/15/88; SLJ 1/89)

1228 Fraser, Mary Ann. *I. Q. Gets Fit* (PS–2). Illus. 2007, Walker $15.95 (978-0-8027-9558-8). 32pp. The Student Fitness Challenge inspires class mouse I.Q. to begin an exercise program and start watching what he eats and drinks. (Rev: BL 5/1/07; SLJ 6/07)

1229 Frazier, Craig. *Stanley Goes Fishing* (PS–1). Illus. by author. Series: Stanley. 2006, Chronicle $15.95 (978-0-8118-5244-9). Stanley, having no luck fishing in a stream, tries in the sky instead and there they are! (Rev: SLJ 6/06)

1230 Frazier, Craig. *Stanley Goes for a Drive* (PS–3). Illus. by author. 2004, Chronicle $15.95 (978-0-8118-4429-1). Out for a drive in his pickup on a hot summer day, Stanley milks a spotted cow, tosses the milk to the sky, and enjoys the resulting clouds and rain; the simple text is enhanced by wonderful illustrations. (Rev: SLJ 9/04)

1231 Freedman, Deborah. *Scribble* (K–2). Illus. by author. 2007, Knopf $15.99 (978-0-375-83966-5). Lucie's scribbles on her big sister's drawing create a story about a scribbled cat and a princess that live happily every after. (Rev: SLJ 6/07)

1232 Freeman, Don. *A Rainbow of My Own* (K–3). Illus. by author. 1966, Puffin paper $5.99 (978-0-14-050328-9). 32pp. A boy's search for a rainbow ends in his own home.

1233 Freymann, Saxton, and Joost Elffers. *Gus and Button* (PS–3). 2001, Scholastic $15.95 (978-0-439-11015-0). 32pp. This tale about a bland-colored mushroom boy and his mushroom dog on a quest to find a colorful place that contrasts with their life is artfully illustrated with computer-enhanced photographs of vegetables. (Rev: BL 11/15/01; HBG 3/02; SLJ 12/01)

1234 Gackenbach, Dick. *Barker's Crime* (PS–2). Illus. 1996, Harcourt $15.00 (978-0-15-200628-0). 32pp. Greedy Mr. Gobble takes Barker the dog to court for inhaling the aroma of the miser's meals. (Rev: BL 3/1/96; SLJ 7/96)

1235 Gackenbach, Dick. *Harry and the Terrible Whatzit* (PS–2). Illus. by author. 1979, Houghton $16.00 (978-0-395-28795-8); paper $7.95 (978-0-89919-223-9). 32pp. Harry follows his mother into the dark cellar to confront the terrible two-headed Whatzit.

1236 Gaiman, Neil. *Crazy Hair* (PS–3). Illus. by Dave McKean. 2009, HarperCollins $18.99 (978-0-06-057908-1). 32pp. This is a surreal story about a man who claims his madcap tresses are home to a wide variety of residents. (Rev: BL 3/15/09; SLJ 6/09)

1237 Galdone, Paul. *The Magic Porridge Pot* (K–3). Illus. by author. 1976, Houghton $16.00 (978-0-395-28805-4). 32pp. The familiar tale of the magic pot that produces porridge but runs amuck when the words that stop it are forgotten.

1238 Gall, Chris. *Dear Fish* (1–4). Illus. by author. 2006, Little, Brown $16.99 (978-0-316-05847-6). All sorts of fish venture onto land to visit Peter after he sends them an invitation in the form of a message in a bottle. (Rev: SLJ 5/06)

1239 Gall, Chris. *There's Nothing to Do on Mars* (K–3). Illus. by author. 2008, Little, Brown $16.99 (978-0-316-16684-3). Poor Davey, living on Mars proves boring until he and his robotic dog unexpectedly unleash a torrent of water resulting in a huge population increase and his father's decision to move on to Saturn. (Rev: SLJ 2/08)

1240 Garland, Michael. *Miss Smith Reads Again!* (K–3). Illus. by author. Series: Miss Smith. 2006, Dutton $15.99 (978-0-525-47722-8). This follow-up to *Miss Smith's Incredible Storybook* finds Miss Smith's class transported to the age of the dinosaurs when she reads from Arthur Conan Doyle's *The Lost World*. (Rev: SLJ 7/06)

1241 Gay, Marie-Louise. *On My Island* (PS–1). Illus. 2001, Groundwood $16.95 (978-0-88899-396-0). 32pp. In this fantasy set on an island, a young boy who shares his home with a variety of animals claims nothing ever happens, but the opposite is true. (Rev: BL 3/15/01)

1242 Gebhard, Wilfried. *What Eddie Can Do* (PS–1). Illus. 2004, Kane $15.95 (978-1-929132-60-7). 32pp. Eddie doesn't have time to learn to tie his shoelaces as he's too busy enjoying his elaborate imaginary adventures; shoelace tying instructions included. (Rev: BL 3/1/04; SLJ 7/04)

1243 Gershator, David, and Phillis Gershator. *Palampam Day* (PS–2). Illus. by Enrique O. Sánchez. 1997, Marshall Cavendish $15.95 (978-0-7614-5002-3). 32pp. Set in the West Indies, this story tells about a boy who is suddenly having conversations with all sorts of objects, like a coconut, a dog, and a bowl of bananas. (Rev: BL 8/97; HBG 3/98; SLJ 9/97)

1244 Gerstein, Mordicai. *A Book* (K–3). Illus. by author. 2009, Roaring Brook $16.95 (978-1-59643-251-2). 48pp. A little girl whose family lives in a book wanders through a variety of stories — fairy tales, mysteries, adventures, and so forth — searching for a story of her own. (Rev: BCCB 7–8/09; BL 3/15/09; HB 5/09; LMC 8/09; SLJ 5/09)

1245 Gerstein, Mordicai. *Carolinda Clatter!* (PS–2). Illus. 2005, Roaring Brook $16.95 (978-1-59643-063-1). 40pp. When Carolinda Clatter is born, her penchant for noise threatens the whole town of Pupickton, which is perched atop a sleeping giant's stomach. (Rev: BL 6/1–15/05)

1246 Gerstein, Mordicai. *Minifred Goes to School* (PS–3). Illus. by author. 2009, HarperCollins $17.99 (978-0-06-075889-9). 32pp. Minifred the kitten grows into a cat who goes to school with the human children and learns well but shows a total disregard for rules. (Rev: BCCB 9/09; BL 4/1/09; SLJ 6/09)

1247 Gilliland, Judith Heide. *Not in the House, Newton!* (PS–3). Illus. by Elizabeth Sayles. 1995, Clarion $16.00 (978-0-395-61195-1). 32pp. When Newton draws objects using his magical red crayon, they jump off the pages. (Rev: BL 12/15/95; SLJ 1/96)

1248 Gillmor, Don. *Yuck, a Love Story* (K–4). Illus. by Marie-Louise Gay. 2000, Stoddart $14.95 (978-0-7737-3218-6). Austin Grouper develops a crush on the girl next door and, to prove his love, lassos the moon as a gift. (Rev: SLJ 11/00)

1249 Gilman, Phoebe. *The Gypsy Princess* (PS–3). Illus. 1997, Scholastic $15.95 (978-0-590-86543-2). 32pp. Cinnamon tires of being a princess and longs for the gypsy life. (Rev: BCCB 3/97; BL 2/1/97; SLJ 3/97)

1250 Glassman, Peter. *My Working Mom* (K–3). Illus. by Tedd Arnold. 1994, Morrow $15.89 (978-0-688-12260-7). This working mom is different from others because she is a practicing witch. (Rev: BCCB 5/94; SLJ 8/94)

1251 Gliori, Debi. *The Trouble with Dragons* (K–4). Illus. by author. 2008, Walker $16.99 (978-0-8027-9789-6). 32pp. Dragons threaten the environment by overpopulation, cutting down trees, building expansively, generating garbage, and blowing hot air until the other animals convince them of the errors of their ways and they start to conserve, reduce, reuse, and recycle. (Rev: LMC 3/09; SLJ 11/08)

1252 Goldberg, Myla. *Catching the Moon* (PS–2). Illus. by Chris Sheban. 2007, Scholastic $16.99 (978-0-439-57686-4). The moon assists an old fisherwoman by helping her keep the tides away from her house and dock. The moon's light is beautifully depicted in the illustrations. (Rev: SLJ 6/07)

1253 Gollub, Matthew. *Ten Oni Drummers* (K–4). Illus. by Kazuko Stone. 2000, Lee & Low $15.95 (978-1-58430-011-3). Ten Japanese oni, or goblins, come to a boy's house and scare away his spooky dreams in this fantasy that also introduces Japanese numbers from 1 to 10. (Rev: HBG 3/01; SLJ 1/01)

1254 Gordon, David. *Smitten* (PS–2). Illus. by author. 2007, Simon & Schuster $15.99 (978-1-4169-2440-1). A single pink mitten and a lonely blue sock team up to look for their other halves but discover that all they need is each other. (Rev: BCCB 12/07; SLJ 2/08)

1255 Gralley, Jean. *The Moon Came Down on Milk St* (PS–1). Illus. by author. 2004, Holt $16.95 (978-0-8050-7266-2). A variety of community workers rush to help when the moon falls out of the sky and breaks into pieces. (Rev: SLJ 11/04)

1256 Grambling, Lois G. *Abigail Muchmore: An Original Tale* (K–3). Illus. by Susan Havice. 2003, Marshall Cavendish $16.95 (978-0-7614-5116-7). Fed up with the constant buffeting of her property by Mr. West Wind, Abigail Muchmore comes up with a clever scheme to bring him around to her way of thinking. (Rev: BL 5/15/03; HBG 10/03; SLJ 5/03)

1257 Grambling, Lois G. *Can I Bring My Pterodactyl to School, Ms. Johnson?* (PS–K). Illus. by Judy Love. 2006, Charlesbridge $16.95 (978-1-58089-044-1); paper $6.95 (978-1-58089-141-7). 32pp. A boy tries to convince his teacher to let him bring a pterodactyl to school. (Rev: BL 12/15/05; SLJ 3/06)

1258 Grambling, Lois G. *This Whole Tooth Fairy Thing's Nothing But a Big Rip-off!* (K–2). Illus. by Thomas Payne. 2002, Marshall Cavendish $15.95 (978-0-7614-5104-4). Little Hippo and the Tooth Fairy come to an agreement when she arrives late for the appropriate exchange. (Rev: HBG 10/02; SLJ 7/02)

1259 Grambling, Lois G. *The Witch Who Wanted to Be a Princess* (K–2). Illus. by Judy Love. 2002, Charlesbridge LB $15.95 (978-1-58089-062-5). Young witch Bella longs to be a princess, but witches are now endangered and are forbidden from transforming themselves. (Rev: HBG 3/03; SLJ 8/02)

1260 Grandits, John. *The Travel Game* (K–2). Illus. by R. W. Alley. 2009, Clarion $16.00 (978-0-618-56420-0). 32pp. Rather than take a nap, Tad plays the travel game with his grandmother, and this time they choose Hong Kong and take an imaginary trip there. (Rev: BLO 6/23/09; SLJ 7/09)

1261 Graves, Keith. *Frank Was a Monster Who Wanted to Dance* (PS–2). Illus. 1999, Chronicle $12.95 (978-0-8118-2169-8). 26pp. Frank, a monster, dances so strenuously at a theater that his head becomes undone and he loses his brains. (Rev: BCCB 6/99; BL 7/99; HBG 3/00; SLJ 7/99)

1262 Graves, Keith. *Three Nasty Gnarlies* (K–3). Illus. by author. 2003, Scholastic $16.95 (978-0-439-24090-1). Although inspired by a beautiful butterfly to improve their appearance, three nasty gnarlies — Grubby Gurgle, Stanky Stoo, and Ooga-Mooga — have little success. (Rev: BCCB 1/04; BL 11/15/03; HBG 4/04; SLJ 12/03)

1263 Gravett, Emily. *Monkey and Me* (PS–K). Illus. by author. 2008, Simon & Schuster $15.99 (978-1-4169-5457-6). 32pp. A little girl plays with her stuffed monkey and imagine them meeting a series of wild animals. (Rev: BL 2/1/08; HB 5/08; LMC 3/08; SLJ 4/08)

1264 Gray, Libba M. *Is There Room on the Feather Bed?* (PS–1). Illus. by Nadine Bernard Westcott. 1997, Orchard $16.95 (978-0-531-30013-8). 32pp. On a rainy night, animals ask to be allowed to share the comfortable feather bed of a farm couple. (Rev: BL 3/1/97; SLJ 4/97)

1265 Greban, Tanguy. *Sarah So Small* (PS). Illus. by Quentin Greban. 2004, Milk & Cookies $16.95 (978-0-689-03594-4). 32pp. Three-year-old Sarah shrinks rapidly after swallowing a magic pearl that her father stole from a visiting witch named Hazel. (Rev: BL 1/1–15/05; SLJ 10/04)

1266 Grey, Mini. *Ginger Bear* (PS–K). Illus. by author. 2007, Knopf $15.99 (978-0-375-84253-5). 32pp. A gingerbread bear comes to life and bakes some other animals so he can have friends. (Rev: BCCB 9/07; BL 7/07; HB 7/07; SLJ 6/07)

1267 Grey, Mini. *Traction Man Is Here!* (PS–2). Illus. 2005, Knopf LB $17.99 (978-0-375-93191-8). 32pp. A little boy's action figure sets off on adventures all around the house as the boy uses household objects for imaginative play. (Rev: BL 3/1/05; SLJ 6/05)

1268 Grey, Mini. *Traction Man Meets Turbodog* (PS–2). Illus. by author. 2008, Knopf $16.99 (978-0-375-85583-2). 32pp. The robotic Turbodog turns out to be no replacement for Traction Man's sidekick Scrubbing Brush in this humorous and satisfying sequel to *Traction Man Is Here!* (2005). (Rev: BL 9/1/08; HB 1/09; SLJ 8/08)

1269 Grindley, Sally. *Mucky Duck* (PS). Illus. by Neal Layton. 2003, Bloomsbury $13.95 (978-1-58234-821-6). Oliver Dunkley enjoys spending time with Mucky Duck, who lives in a pond behind Oliver's house and who seems to create mess wherever she goes. (Rev: HBG 10/03; SLJ 7/03)

1270 Grindley, Sally. *Polar Skater* (PS–2). Illus. by Heli Hieta. 2004, Lobster $15.95 (978-1-894222-88-4). A little girl gains confidence on her ice skates and she leaves her father to skim through a fanciful polarscape full of arctic animals. (Rev: SLJ 1/05)

1271 Grobler, Piet. *Hey, Frog!* (PS–K). Illus. 2002, Front St. $15.95 (978-1-886910-84-3). 32pp. Humorous illustrations and fast-reading text tell the story of a greedy frog who drinks all the water on the African savannah, leaving the other thirsty animals to plot their revenge, including the tickly eels. (Rev: BL 1/1–15/03; HB 1/03; HBG 3/03; SLJ 1/03)

1272 Gruelle, Johnny. *Raggedy Ann Stories* (PS–3). Illus. 1993, Macmillan LB $16.00 (978-0-02-737585-5). 96pp. This story features the lovable rag doll. A reissue. Also use: *Raggedy Andy Stories* (1993).

1273 Guthrie, Donna. *The Witch Who Lives Down the Hall* (PS–2). Illus. by Amy Schwartz. 1985, Harcourt $12.95 (978-0-15-298610-0). 32pp. A young boy thinks his new high-rise neighbor is a witch, and proves it when the two of them fly above the city on her magic carpet. (Rev: BCCB 1/86; BL 9/15/85; SLJ 10/85)

1274 Gutierrez, Akemi. *The Pirate and Other Adventures of Sam and Alice* (K–2). Illus. by author. Series: Sam and Alice. 2007, Houghton $17.00 (978-0-618-73737-6). Three Sam and Alice stories appear in this book: "Space Patrol," "The Genius Crocodile," and "The Pirate," all full of adventure and unlikely events. (Rev: SLJ 6/07)

1275 Gutiérrez, Elisa. *Picturescape* (PS–2). Illus. by author. 2005, Simply Read $16.95 (978-1-894965-24-8). A boy's trip to an art museum turns into a magical excursion as each colorful painting transports him to a thrilling new location; a beautifully illustrated wordless book. (Rev: SLJ 2/06)

1276 Haas, Irene. *Bess and Bella* (PS–K). Illus. 2006, Simon & Schuster $14.95 (978-1-4169-0013-9). 32pp. A bird called Bella drops in with a suitcase of goodies cheers Bess's lonely winter. (Rev: BL 12/15/05*; HBG 10/06; SLJ 2/06)

1277 Haas, Irene. *A Summertime Song* (PS–3). Illus. 1997, Simon & Schuster paper $16.00 (978-0-689-50549-2). 32pp. A frog presents a little girl with a magic paper hat that shrinks her so she is able to attend a birthday party with little animals like a mouse and an inchworm. (Rev: BL 5/15/97; HB 5/97; SLJ 6/97)

1278 Hächler, Bruno. *What Does My Teddy Bear Do All Night?* (PS–K). Trans. from German by Charise Myngher. Illus. by Birte Müller. 2005, Minedition $14.99 (978-0-698-40029-0). A young girl and her teddy bear play together long after the child's bedtime, and even after the child finally falls asleep her faithful stuffed animal keeps watch over her. (Rev: SLJ 12/05)

1279 Hakala, Marjorie Rose. *Mermaid Dance* (PS–2). Illus. by Mark Jones. 2009, Blue Apple $16.99 (978-1-934706-47-3). 40pp. Mermaids have a party on the first night of summer. (Rev: SLJ 6/09)

1280 Hale, Nathan. *The Devil You Know* (K–4). Illus. by author. 2005, Walker $16.95 (978-0-8027-8981-5). The Fells get more than they bargained for when they invite Ms. Phisto into their home to get rid of their resident devil. (Rev: SLJ 8/05)

1281 Hale, Nathan. *Yellowbelly and Plum Go to School* (PS–1). Illus. by author. 2007, Putnam $16.99 (978-0-399-24624-1). Yellowbelly takes his teddy bear, Plum, to the first day of school and together they learn some new games to play. (Rev: SLJ 8/07)

1282 Harris, Peter. *Ordinary Audrey* (PS–2). Illus. by David Runert. 2001, ME Media $14.95 (978-1-58925-014-7). 32pp. When 5-year-old Deadwood Deb, a dangerous cowgirl, isn't around to defend her town against invading outlaws, her timid twin sister Audrey must take her place in this tale set in the Wild West. (Rev: BCCB 2/02; BL 2/15/02)

1283 Harrison, Carlos. *Ruben's Jungle / La selva de Ruben* (PS–2). Illus. by Grizelle Paz. 2003, Globo Libros $16.95 (978-0-9706953-1-4). Ruben visits the jungle in this appealing bilingual story, packaged with an audio CD. (Rev: SLJ 7/03)

1284 Harrison, David L. *The Animals' Song* (PS–K). Illus. by Chris L. Demarest. 1997, Boyds Mills $14.95 (978-1-56397-144-0). 32pp. When a little girl and boy play their flute and drum, all the animals join in. (Rev: BCCB 6/97; BL 4/1/97; SLJ 3/97)

1285 Hazen, Barbara S. *Who Is Your Favorite Monster, Mama?* (PS–2). Illus. by Maryann Kovalski. 2006, Hyperion $15.99 (978-0-7868-1810-5). 32pp. Mama Monster reassures little Harry when he feels slighted by the attention she gives to his siblings. (Rev: BL 7/06; SLJ 4/06)

1286 Heap, Sue. *Danny's Drawing Book* (PS–1). Illus. by author. 2008, Candlewick $9.99 (978-0-7636-3654-8). 32pp. Danny and his friend Ettie use his sketchbook to create an illustrated story about the animals at the zoo. (Rev: BL 5/15/08; SLJ 3/08)

1287 Heidbreder, Robert. *I Wished for a Unicorn* (PS–3). Illus. by Kady M. Denton. 2000, Kids Can $14.95 (978-1-55074-543-6). 32pp. A young girl's dog is transformed into a unicorn and together they travel into a magic land. (Rev: BCCB 5/00; BL 4/15/00; HBG 10/00; SLJ 8/00)

1288 Heidbreder, Robert. *Lickety-Split* (PS–2). Illus. by Dusan Petricic. 2007, Kids Can $15.95 (978-1-55337-710-8). 32pp. A boy's imaginary adventures are described in inventive wordplay. (Rev: SLJ 10/07)

1289 Heidbreder, Robert. *A Sea-Wishing Day* (PS–2). Illus. by Kady M. Denton. 2007, Kids Can $15.95 (978-1-55337-707-8). 32pp. A little boy's imagination carries him and his dog, Skipper, on an exciting high-seas adventure. (Rev: BL 3/15/07)

1290 Heine, Theresa. *Star Seeker: A Journey to Outer Space* (2–4). Illus. by Victor Tavares. 2006, Barefoot Books $16.99 (978-1-905236-36-7). 32pp. Strong illustrations of the planets and other bodies enhance the rhyming text in this fantasy of travel into space aboard a series of unlikely conveyances — including armchairs, hobby horses, and paper airplanes. (Rev: BL 4/15/06; SLJ 3/07)

1291 Heller, Linda. *Today Is the Birthday of the World* (PS–K). Illus. by Alison Jay. 2009, Dutton $16.99 (978-0-525-47905-5). 32pp. On the world's birthday, God celebrates animals' attributes. (Rev: BL 5/1/09; SLJ 6/09)

1292 Henkes, Kevin. *Oh!* (PS). Illus. by Laura Dronzek. 1999, Greenwillow LB $14.89 (978-0-688-17054-7). 24pp. A delightful picture book that depicts how children and a variety of animals react to a fresh fall of snow. (Rev: BCCB 10/99; BL 10/1/99*; HBG 3/00; SLJ 10/99)

1293 Hennessy, B. G. *Claire and the Unicorn Happy Ever After* (K–3). Illus. by Susan Mitchell. 2006, Simon & Schuster $12.95 (978-1-4169-0815-9). Claire and her toy unicorn journey to a land full of literary characters and ask what it takes to make someone happy ever after. (Rev: SLJ 2/06)

1294 Herrera, Juan Felipe. *Super Cilantro Girl / La Supernina del Cilantro* (K–3). Illus. by Honorio Robledo Tapia. 2003, Children's Book Pr. $16.95 (978-0-89239-187-5). 30pp. Transformed into a giant green superheroine, 8-year-old Esmeralda Sinfronteras uses her newfound powers to rescue her mother, who can't return to the United States without a green card. (Rev: HBG 4/04; SLJ 12/03)

1295 Hicks, Barbara Jean. *Jitterbug Jam: A Monster Tale* (1–3). Illus. by Alexis Deacon. 2005, Farrar $16.00 (978-0-374-33685-1). 40pp. A monster is frightened by the little boy under his bed in this picture book with amusing artwork. (Rev: BL 3/1/05)

1296 High, Linda Oatman. *Cool Bopper's Choppers* (K 3). Illus. by John O'Brien. 2007, Boyds Mills $16.95 (978-1-59078-379-5). When Cool Bopper's dentures fly out of his mouth and end up down the drain, the sax player heads to the beach, where he spies them blowing a tune on a seashell. (Rev: SLJ 5/07)

1297 Highet, Alistair. *The Yellow Train* (K–3). Illus. by François Roca. 2000, Creative $17.95 (978-1-56846-128-1). 40pp. Theo and Grandpa travel back in time and embark on a magical journey through unspoiled landscapes as they ride the Yellow Train with Grandpa at the controls. (Rev: BL 12/15/00; HBG 3/01; SLJ 12/00)

1298 Hoberman, Mary Ann. *Miss Mary Mack* (PS). Illus. by Nadine Bernard Westcott. 2001, Little, Brown $5.95 (978-0-316-36642-7). 24pp. This bouncy board book presents a clapping rhyme that features Miss Mary Mack and her pet elephant. (Rev: BL 2/15/01; HBG 3/02)

1299 Hogg, Gary. *Beautiful Buehla and the Zany Zoo Makeover* (PS–1). Illus. by Victoria Chess. 2006, HarperCollins $15.99 (978-0-06-009420-1). 32pp. It's picture day at the zoo, and Beautiful Buehla gives the reluctant animals quite extreme makeovers. (Rev: BL 5/1/06; SLJ 5/06)

1300 Holwitz, Peter. *Stick Kid* (PS–2). Illus. by author. 2003, Philomel $13.99 (978-0-399-24163-5). A stick figure child comes to life and grows up in this imaginative story with rhyming text. (Rev: SLJ 4/04)

1301 Horn, Emily. *Excuse Me . . . Are You a Witch?* (PS–3). Illus. by Pawel Pawlak. 2003, Charlesbridge LB $15.95 (978-1-58089-093-9). Having read that witches favor black cats as companions, Herbert the black kitten searches long and hard for a witch but

is about to give up when a class of aspiring witches adopts him. (Rev: HBG 4/04; SLJ 8/03)

1302 Hubbard, Patricia. *My Crayons Talk* (PS–1). Illus. by G. Brian Karas. 1996, Holt $15.95 (978-0-8050-3529-2). 32pp. Crayons in a box unite to produce a series of colorful pictures. (Rev: BCCB 5/96; BL 4/1/96; SLJ 5/96)

1303 Hughes, Shirley. *Stories by Firelight* (K–3). Illus. 1993, Lothrop $16.00 (978-0-688-04568-5). 64pp. This collection of stories, many of which are fantasies, explore wintry themes and are linked by poems. (Rev: BL 12/1/93; SLJ 1/94)

1304 Hughes, Ted. *How the Whale Became and Other Stories* (PS–3). Illus. by Jackie Morris. 2000, Orchard $25.00 (978-0-531-30303-0). 96pp. From the great English poet, this is a collection of creation fables explaining how individual creatures, such as the whale, owl, and cat, came to be. (Rev: BCCB 12/00; BL 12/1/00*; HBG 10/01; SLJ 11/00)

1305 Hughes, Vi. *Aziz the Storyteller* (K–3). Illus. by Stefan Czernecki. 2002, Crocodile $15.95 (978-1-56656-456-4). Aziz, a lover of storytelling, trades the family's donkey for a special carpet, which proves worthwhile despite his father's ire. (Rev: HBG 10/02; SLJ 11/02)

1306 Huntington, Amy. *One Monday* (PS–1). Illus. 2001, Scholastic $16.95 (978-0-439-29304-4). 32pp. A blustery wind blows through Annabelle's farm, causing mayhem for the animals who live there. (Rev: BL 2/1/02; HBG 3/02; SLJ 12/01)

1307 Hutchins, Hazel. *It's Raining, Yancy and Bear* (PS). Illus. by Ruth Ohi. 1998, Annick $15.95 (978-1-55037-529-9); paper $5.95 (978-1-55037-528-2). Yancy, a young boy, and his stuffed friend, Bear, change places, visit a museum with Grandfather, and later plant a garden. (Rev: SLJ 1/99)

1308 Hutchins, Pat. *The Very Worst Monster* (K–2). Illus. by author. 1985, Greenwillow $16.89 (978-0-688-04011-6); paper $7.99 (978-0-688-07816-4). 32pp. A monster family has a new addition, and Hazel is not happy with her baby brother. (Rev: BCCB 4/85; HB 5/87; SLJ 5/85)

1309 Ichikawa, Satomi. *Come Fly with Me* (PS–1). Illus. by author. 2008, Philomel $15.99 (978-0-399-24679-1). 40pp. Cosmos, a wooden toy plane, and Woggy, a black-and-white stuffed dog, escape their limited environment and fly out of the toy box to explore the rooftops of Paris. (Rev: BL 2/1/08; SLJ 4/08)

1310 Ichikawa, Satomi. *La La Rose* (PS). Illus. 2004, Penguin $15.99 (978-0-399-24029-4). 40pp. Atmospheric illustrations draw readers into the adventures of a pink stuffed rabbit who is separated from her young owner in Paris's Luxembourg Gardens. (Rev: BL 1/1–15/04; SLJ 2/04)

1311 Inkpen, Mick. *Nothing* (PS–K). Illus. 1998, Orchard $14.95 (978-0-531-30076-3). 32pp. A stuffed toy that is left behind when a family moves finds a new home with the help of a cat. (Rev: BCCB 3/98; BL 3/15/98; HBG 10/98; SLJ 6/98)

1312 Inns, Christopher. *Help!* (PS–K). Illus. by author. 2004, Frances Lincoln $14.95 (978-1-84507-004-5). The blue rabbit Dr. Hopper and brown dog Nurse Barker from *Next! Please* go on emergency calls to help other toy animals. (Rev: SLJ 6/04)

1313 Ishinabe, Fusako. *Spring Snowman* (PS–1). Illus. 1991, Garrett LB $14.60 (978-0-944483-83-1). 32pp. Animals in the forest find that when spring comes their snowman disappears. (Rev: BL 5/1/91)

1314 Issacs, Anne. *Pancakes for Supper!* (PS–2). Illus. by Mark Teague. 2006, Scholastic $15.99 (978-0-439-64483-9). 40pp. Alone in the wilderness after falling from her parents' wagon, young Toby uses her wits — and most of her clothes — to bargain her way back to civilization in this entertaining tall tale with arresting illustrations. (Rev: BCCB 11/06; BL 10/15/06; HB 11/06; HBG 4/07; LMC 3/07; SLJ 10/06*)

1315 Janisch, Heinz, and Silke Leffler. *"I Have a Little Problem," Said the Bear* (PS–2). Illus. by Silke Leffler. 2009, North-South $16.95 (978-0-7358-2235-1). 32pp. Bear has a problem but everybody's got more advice to offer than time to listen. (Rev: BL 12/15/08; LMC 10/09; SLJ 3/09)

1316 Jarman, Julia. *Class Three at Sea* (PS). Illus. by Lynne Chapman. 2008, Carolrhoda $16.95 (978-0-8225-7617-4). 32pp. A class field trip turns into adventure in this pirate fantasy. (Rev: SLJ 9/08)

1317 Jeffers, Oliver. *The Incredible Book Eating Boy* (PS–3). Illus. by author. 2007, Philomel $16.99 (978-0-399-24749-1). Facts and stories get all jumbled up in Henry when he eats too many books, so he decides it would be smarter to read them instead. Varied typefaces and collages make the illustrations appealing. (Rev: SLJ 6/07)

1318 Jeffers, Oliver. *The Way Back Home* (PS–1). Illus. by author. 2008, Philomel $16.99 (978-0-399-25074-3). 32pp. A little boy flies an airplane to the moon, where he runs out of gas; luckily a young Martian also arrives there by spacecraft and after initial uncertainty the two become friends and help each other out of their predicaments. (Rev: BL 4/15/08; LMC 5/08; SLJ 4/08)

1319 Jeffers, Susan. *My Pony* (K–3). Illus by author. 2003, Hyperion $15.99 (978-0-7868-1995-9). A young girl who cannot have the horse she wants draws pictures of one, and it carries her on fantastic adventures. (Rev: HBG 4/04; SLJ 11/03)

1320 Jennings, Sharon. *The Happily Ever Afternoon* (PS–K). Illus. by Ron Lightburn. 2006, Annick LB $19.95 (978-1-55037-945-7); paper $7.95 (978-1-55037-944-0). 24pp. As his parents prepare for his birthday party, an imaginative little boy battles dragons — the family cat and dog — to get to the treasure, a kitchen full of birthday treats. (Rev: BL 8/06)

1321 Johnson, Paul B. *Bearhide and Crow* (K–3). Illus. 2000, Holiday House $16.95 (978-0-8234-1470-3). 32pp. When Amos, a happy-go-lucky farmer, gets cheated by shifty Sam, Crow helps him get even. (Rev: BCCB 5/00; BL 4/1/00; HBG 10/00; SLJ 5/00)

1322 Johnson, Paul B. *The Cow Who Wouldn't Come Down* (K–2). Illus. 1993, Orchard LB $15.99 (978-0-531-08631-5). 32pp. Miss Rosemary has prob-

lems getting her cow back to earth once it learns how to fly. (Rev: BCCB 7–8/93; BL 2/1/93; HB 5/93; SLJ 5/93*)

1323 Jonas, Ann. *The Trek* (PS–1). Illus. by author. 1985, Morrow paper $6.99 (978-0-688-08742-5). 32pp. A young girl imagines she is trekking through a dangerous jungle on her way to school. (Rev: BCCB 3/86; BL 11/15/85; SLJ 10/85)

1324 Jorg, Sabine. *Mina and the Bear* (1–4). Trans. by Charise Neugebauer. Illus. by Alexander Reichstein. 1999, North-South LB $15.88 (978-0-7858-1037-7). Mina's health is endangered because of her intense longing for a teddy bear, so after a bear story from the doctor, she becomes a bear. (Rev: BL 4/1/99)

1325 Joslin, Mary. *The Shore Beyond* (K–3). Illus. by Alison Jay. 2000, Good Bks. $16.00 (978-1-56148-316-7). 28pp. In this parable about the journey through life, two girls weave willows into boats so they can explore the world beyond their homes. (Rev: BL 12/1/00; SLJ 2/01)

1326 Joslin, Mary. *The Tale of the Heaven Tree* (K–3). Illus. by Meilo So. 1999, Eerdmans $16.00 (978-0-8028-5190-1). In this story, a small child hears a voice from the Maker to help save Earth by planting trees. (Rev: BL 10/1/99; HBG 3/00; SLJ 3/00)

1327 Joyce, William. *Sleepy Time Olie* (PS–K). Illus. 2001, HarperCollins LB $15.89 (978-0-06-029614-8). 48pp. This brightly colored, rollicking picture book about space-kid Olie (first seen in *Rolie Polie Olie* [1999] and *Snowie Rolie* [2000]) finds him building a laugh-ray to fix his grandfather's broken smile. (Rev: BL 11/15/01; HBG 3/02; SLJ 10/01)

1328 Jukes, Mavis. *You're a Bear* (PS–2). Illus. by Steve Johnson and Lou Fancher. 2003, Knopf LB $18.99 (978-0-375-90267-3). A young girl dons a furry hooded jacket and pretends to be a bear. (Rev: BL 12/1/03; HBG 4/04; SLJ 12/03)

1329 Kain, Karen. *The Nutcracker* (1–3). Illus. by Rajka Kupesic. 2005, Tundra $18.95 (978-0-88776-696-1). 32pp. In this handsome adaptation of "The Nutcracker" based on a National Ballet of Canada production, Marie and her brother Misha watch the toys battle and visit the Sugar Plum Fairy's palace. (Rev: BL 11/1/05; SLJ 10/05) [792.8]

1330 Kane, Tracy. *Fairy Houses* (K–3). Illus. by author. 2001, Great White Dog Picture Co. $15.95 (978-0-9708104-5-8). Kristen builds a fairy house that attracts many animals but will fairies ever come? (Rev: SLJ 1/02)

1331 Kann, Victoria, and Elizabeth Kann. *Pinkalicious* (K–2). 2006, HarperCollins $17.99 (978-0-06-077639-8). 40pp. Despite warnings from her parents, a little girl gobbles up so many pink cupcakes that she turns pink herself. (Rev: BL 6/1–15/06; SLJ 8/06)

1332 Karim, Roberta. *This Is a Hospital, Not a Zoo!* (K–3). Illus. by Sue Truesdell. 1998, Clarion $15.00 (978-0-395-72070-7). 48pp. When nurses and doctors want to poke or prod young Filbert MacFee, he simply turns himself into a wild animal like a penguin or giraffe. (Rev: BL 3/1/98)

1333 Karlin, Nurit. *The Tooth Witch* (PS–K). Illus. by author. 1985, HarperCollins LB $13.89 (978-0-397-32120-9). 32pp. The story of Abra Cadabra and how she becomes the first Tooth Fairy. (Rev: BCCB 10/85; BL 6/15/85; SLJ 9/86)

1334 Karlins, Mark. *Starring Lorenzo, and Einstein Too* (K–2). Illus. by Sandy Nichols. 2009, Dial $16.99 (978-0-8037-3220-9). 32pp. Little Lorenzo, budding scientist and reluctant member of his family's vaudeville act, takes off with Albert Einstein to explore the universe but finds himself homesick. (Rev: BL 4/1/09; LMC 8/09; SLJ 4/09)

1335 Kastner, Jill. *Princess Dinosaur* (PS–K). Illus. 2001, Greenwillow LB $15.89 (978-0-688-17046-2). 32pp. An action-filled picture book about the adventures of Princess Dinosaur and her friends Cowboy Tex, a toy, and Bettina, a doll. (Rev: BCCB 5/01; BL 4/15/01; HBG 10/01; SLJ 5/01)

1336 Keats, Ezra Jack. *Regards to the Man in the Moon* (PS–1). Illus. by author. 1987, Macmillan paper $5.99 (978-0-689-71160-2). 32pp. Lewis and his friend visit outer space via their imaginations. Originally published in 1981.

1337 Keens-Douglas, Richardo. *The Miss Meow Pageant* (K–3). Illus. by Marie Lafrance. 1998, Annick LB $16.95 (978-1-55037-537-4); paper $6.95 (978-1-55037-536-7). Henrietta, a teacher, adopts a stray cat she names Sparrow and decides to enter her pet in "The Miss Meow Pageant." (Rev: SLJ 1/99)

1338 Keller, Laurie. *The Scrambled States of America* (K–3). Illus. 1998, Holt $16.95 (978-0-8050-5802-4). In this lighthearted introduction to the 50 states, Kansas and Nebraska decide to have a party where the states exchange places, but complications occur when, for example, Minnesota gets a sunburn while Florida is freezing. (Rev: BCCB 10/98; BL 1/1–15/99; HBG 3/99; SLJ 11/98)

1339 Keller, Laurie. *The Scrambled States of America Talent Show* (K–3). Illus. by author. 2008, Holt $16.95 (978-0-8050-7997-5). 40pp. The states have a wild time at their talent show, providing additional facts in this companion to *The Scrambled States of America* (1998). (Rev: BL 8/08; SLJ 8/08)

1340 Kelley, Marty. *Fall Is Not Easy* (PS–K). Illus. 1998, Zino $12.95 (978-1-55933-234-7). 32pp. In the fall of the year, a tree tries out new colors and designs for its leaves, including red-and-white stripes, polka dots, and rainbow faces. (Rev: BL 1/1–15/99)

1341 Kellogg, Steven. *The Missing Mitten Mystery* (PS–1). Illus. 2000, Dial $16.99 (978-0-8037-2566-9). 32pp. In this reworking of the 1974 title, a little girl sets off with her dog Oscar to find a lost mitten and discovers it is acting as the heart of a snowman. (Rev: BL 10/15/00*; HBG 3/01)

1342 Kellogg, Steven. *Ralph's Secret Weapon* (PS–3). Illus. by author. 1983, Dial paper $3.95 (978-0-8037-0307-0). 32pp. Ralph's bassoon playing is so bad, his aunt thinks it will charm a bothersome sea monster.

1343 Kennedy, Kim. *Pirate Pete* (K–3). Illus. by Doug Kennedy. 2002, Abrams $15.95 (978-0-8109-4356-8). 32pp. Pete and his parrot share a series of swashbuckling adventures after he steals a treasure map from a queen. (Rev: BL 6/1–15/02; HBG 10/02)

1344 Kennedy, Kim. *Pirate Peter's Giant Adventure* (PS–2). Illus. by Doug Kennedy. 2006, Abrams $15.95 (978-0-8109-5965-1). 32pp. Pirate Pete and his trusty parrot sidekick brave the perils of Thunder Island to rescue the Sea-Fairy Sapphire and return it to the sea; a sequel to *Pirate Pete* (2002). (Rev: BL 6/1–15/06)

1345 Kennedy, Kim. *Pirate Pete's Talk Like a Pirate* (K–2). Illus. by Doug Kennedy. 2007, Abrams $15.95 (978-0-8109-9348-8). 40pp. This third book in the series features Pirate Pete and his parrot searching for a crew on Rascal Island. (Rev: BL 12/1/07; SLJ 4/08)

1346 Ketteman, Helen. *Bubba, The Cowboy Prince: A Fractured Texas Tale* (K–3). Illus. by James Warhola. 1997, Scholastic $16.95 (978-0-590-25506-6). 32pp. A Western version of the Cinderella story in which a cow is the fairy godmother. (Rev: BL 12/1/97; HBG 3/98)

1347 Ketteman, Helen. *Heat Wave* (K–3). Illus. by Scott Goto. 1998, Walker LB $16.85 (978-0-8027-8645-6). 32pp. In this hilarious fantasy, a heat wave gets stuck on a rural weather vane causing a great upheaval for plants and animals. (Rev: BL 2/1/98; HBG 10/98; SLJ 3/98)

1348 Ketteman, Helen. *Luck with Potatoes* (1–3). Illus. by Brian Floca. 1995, Orchard LB $15.99 (978-0-531-08773-2). 32pp. A tall tale about a farmer who finds his lost cows in the giant potatoes he has been growing. (Rev: BL 10/1/95; SLJ 10/95)

1349 Khalsa, Dayal Kaur. *Green Cat* (PS–K). Illus. 2002, Tundra $14.95 (978-0-88776-586-5). 24pp. This posthumous offering tells the tale of a brother and sister who bicker over the space in their room, until a big green cat shows them just how crowded the room can get. (Rev: BL 3/15/02; HBG 10/02; SLJ 5/02)

1350 Kimmel, Elizabeth C. *My Penguin Osbert in Love* (PS–2). Illus. by H. B. Lewis. 2009, Candlewick $16.99 (978-0-7636-3032-4). 48pp. Joe takes his penguin Osbert to the South Pole to see the southern lights and Osbert falls for the lovely Aurora; a nicely illustrated sequel to *My Penguin Osbert* (2004). (Rev: BL 2/1/09; SLJ 5/09)

1351 Kimmel, Eric A. *A Cloak for the Moon* (PS–3). Illus. by Katya Krenina. 2001, Holiday House $16.95 (978-0-8234-1493-2). 32pp. A tailor heads for China in search of material for a cloak for the moon, and earns a luminous thread as a reward for a good deed. (Rev: BCCB 4/01; BL 7/01; HBG 10/01; SLJ 5/01)

1352 Kimmel, Eric A. *The Erie Canal Pirates* (K–3). Illus. by Andrew Glass. 2002, Holiday House $16.95 (978-0-8234-1657-8). 32pp. A humorous tale about a captain battling pirates on the Erie Canal, using the traditional folk song as a base. (Rev: BCCB 11/02; BL 10/15/02; HBG 3/03; SLJ 11/02)

1353 Kimmel, Eric A. *Grizz!* (PS–3). Illus. by Andrew Glass. 2000, Farrar $17.00 (978-0-374-36824-1). 288pp. Cowboy Lucky Doolin makes a pact with the devil that he will gain great wealth if he doesn't bathe, shave, or change his clothes for seven years. (Rev: BL 5/1/00; HBG 9/00; SLJ 3/00)

1354 Kimmel, Eric A. *Pumpkinhead* (1–3). Illus. by Steve Haskamp. 2001, Winslow $15.95 (978-1-890817-33-6). Pumpkinhead sets off on a quest to find out if everyone in the world has a pumpkin head, only to be turned off course by a pair of pesky squirrels. (Rev: HBG 3/02; SLJ 9/01)

1355 Kimmel, Eric A. *Robin Hook, Pirate Hunter!* (PS–3). Illus. by Michael Dooling. 2001, Scholastic $15.95 (978-0-590-68199-5). 32pp. A teenage super-hero dressed like Robin Hood thwarts pirates with the help of other children and some animals. (Rev: BL 1/1–15/01; HBG 10/01; SLJ 3/01)

1356 Kimmel, Eric A. *The Tale of Ali Baba and the Forty Thieves: A Story from the Arabian Nights* (1–3). Illus. by Will Hillenbrand. 1996, Holiday House LB $15.95 (978-0-8234-1258-7). 30pp. Ali Baba and the story of his amazing treasure trove are covered in colorful prose. (Rev: BCCB 2/97; BL 12/1/96; SLJ 12/96)

1357 Kinsey-Warnock, Natalie. *The Fiddler of the Northern Lights* (K–3). Illus. by Leslie Bowman. 1996, Dutton $16.99 (978-0-525-65215-1). 32pp. A fantasy set in the far North about a fiddler whose music makes the northern lights dance. (Rev: BL 11/15/96; SLJ 11/96)

1358 Kinsey-Warnock, Natalie. *On a Starry Night* (PS–1). Illus. by David McPhail. 1994, Orchard LB $16.99 (978-0-531-08670-4). 32pp. When her father throws her into the air, a young girl visits the stars before returning to his arms. (Rev: BL 2/1/94; HB 7/94; SLJ 5/94)

1359 Kipling, Rudyard. *Rikki-Tikki-Tavi* (1–3). Illus. by Lambert Davis. 1992, Harcourt $18.00 (978-0-15-267015-3). 44pp. A mongoose overcomes snakes that live in the garden of an English family in India. (Rev: BL 9/15/92)

1360 Kirk, Daniel. *Library Mouse: A Friend's Tale* (K–3). Illus. by author. 2009, Abrams $15.95 (978-0-8109-8927-6). 32pp. Sam, library mouse and author/illustrator, gains a young friend and collaborator. (Rev: BL 5/15/09; SLJ 4/09)

1361 Kirkpatrick, Karey. *Disney's James and the Giant Peach* (K–3). Illus. by Lane Smith. 1996, Disney LB $16.89 (978-0-7868-5039-6). 48pp. A simplified retelling of Roald Dahl's work, aimed at the primary grades. (Rev: BCCB 6/96; BL 5/1/96)

1362 Kleven, Elisa. *The Paper Princess* (K–2). Illus. 1994, Dutton $16.99 (978-0-525-45231-7). 32pp. A paper princess created by a little girl flies over the city and learns about life. (Rev: BL 7/94; SLJ 6/94*)

1363 Kleven, Elisa. *The Paper Princess Finds Her Way* (PS–1). Illus. by author. 2003, Dutton $16.99 (978-0-525-46911-7). Ignored by the now-grown girl who made her, a paper princess flies off in search of new adventures. (Rev: HBG 4/04; SLJ 10/03)

1364 Kleven, Elisa. *The Paper Princess Flies Again: (With Her Dog!)* (K–2). Illus. 2005, Tricycle $15.95 (978-1-58246-146-5). 32pp. The Paper Princess (a paper doll) and her faithful canine companion embark on an adventure-filled search for a gift to give to Lucy, their owner. (Rev: BL 12/1/05; SLJ 12/05)

1365 Knapman, Timothy. *Mungo and the Spiders from Space* (K–3). Illus. by Adam Stower. 2009, Dial $16.99 (978-0-8037-3277-3). 32pp. When Mungo finds that the last page of his superhero book is missing, his mother suggests that he make up the rest. (Rev: BL 2/1/09; SLJ 4/09)

1366 Knutson, Kimberley. *Jungle Jamboree* (PS–1). Illus. 1998, Marshall Cavendish $15.95 (978-0-7614-5032-0). 32pp. In this rainy day fantasy, a group of children who are confined to the house have an imaginary jungle adventure. (Rev: BL 9/1/98; HBG 3/99; SLJ 11/98)

1367 Kohara, Kazuno. *Ghosts in the House!* (PS–1). Illus. by author. 2008, Roaring Brook $12.95 (978-1-59643-427-1). 32pp. Undeterred by the fact that she and her cat have moved into a haunted house, the young witch catches the ghosts, tosses them in the washer, and makes some lovely linens. (Rev: BL 9/1/08; HB 1/09)

1368 Komaiko, Leah. *My Perfect Neighborhood* (K–2). Illus. by Barbara Westman. 1990, HarperCollins $13.95 (978-0-06-023287-0). 32pp. In jiving rhymes, a young girl surveys her most unusual neighborhood. (Rev: BL 3/1/90; SLJ 8/90)

1369 Krauss, Ruth. *The Carrot Seed* (K–1). Illus. by Crockett Johnson. 1945, HarperCollins LB $17.89 (978-0-06-023351-8); paper $6.99 (978-0-06-443210-8). 24pp. A young boy is convinced that the seeds he plants will grow, in spite of his family's doubts.

1370 Krensky, Stephen. *Too Many Leprechauns: Or How That Pot o' Gold Got to the End of the Rainbow* (K–4). Illus. by Dan Andreasen. 2007, Simon & Schuster $12.99 (978-0-689-85112-4). A horde of leprechauns descends on the quiet Irish town of Dingle, and Finn O'Finnegan decides to find a way to get them to leave. (Rev: BL 2/15/07; SLJ 2/07)

1371 Kroll, Steven. *The Candy Witch* (PS–1). Illus. by Marylin Hafner. 1979, Scholastic paper $2.50 (978-0-590-44509-2). 32pp. A family of witches perform good work except for the youngest, who undoes their work.

1372 Krulik, Nancy. *Anyone But Me* (2–4). Illus. by John and Wendy. Series: Katie Kazoo, Switcheroo. 2002, Grosset paper $3.99 (978-0-448-42653-2). 80pp. Katie, who can change at will, becomes a hamster and transforms a bully who is scared of hamsters into a nice person. In *Out to Lunch* (2002), she becomes a cafeteria worker and improves the food. (Rev: SLJ 5/02)

1373 Kvasnosky, Laura McGee. *Really Truly Bingo* (PS–1). Illus. by author. 2008, Candlewick $15.99 (978-0-7636-3210-6). 32pp. Bea's imaginary dog named Bingo gets her into lots of trouble as they play together in the garden. (Rev: BCCB 6/08; BL 4/15/08; HB 5/08; SLJ 7/08)

1374 Landalf, Helen. *The Secret Night World of Cats* (PS–1). Illus. by Mark Rimland. 1998, Smith & Kraus $16.95 (978-1-57525-117-2). 32pp. When Amanda's cat goes missing one night, the little girl ventures into a forest where she encounters many cats and is finally reunited with her own beloved pet. (Rev: BL 9/15/98; HBG 3/99; SLJ 9/98)

1375 Landry, Leo. *The Snow Ghosts* (PS–2). Illus. by author. 2003, Houghton $9.95 (978-0-618-19655-5). Playful snow ghosts live in the far, far north. (Rev: BCCB 11/03; HBG 4/04; SLJ 11/03)

1376 Landry, Leo. *Space Boy* (PS–1). Illus. by author. 2007, Houghton $16.00 (978-0-618-60568-2). 32pp. It's too noisy to go to sleep, so young Nicholas takes off for the moon instead, where he enjoys a picnic before returning home to a peaceful house. (Rev: BL 10/15/07; HB 9/07; SLJ 10/07)

1377 Langley, Jonathan. *Missing!* (PS–K). Illus. 2000, Marshall Cavendish $15.95 (978-0-7614-5078-8). 32pp. Lupin the cat, not realizing that it is school vacation, sets off to meet preschooler Daisy and is disturbed when the child doesn't appear. (Rev: BCCB 11/00; BL 9/1/00; HBG 3/01; SLJ 9/00)

1378 Larson, Kirby. *The Magic Kerchief* (PS–3). Illus. by Rosanne Litzinger. 2000, Holiday House $15.95 (978-0-8234-1473-4). 32pp. Griselda, an old grump whose bluntness alienates everyone, dons a magic kerchief that allows her only to say nice things. (Rev: BL 8/00; HB 9/00; HBG 3/01; SLJ 10/00)

1379 Lasky, Kathryn. *The Gates of the Wind* (PS–3). Illus. by Janet Stevens. 1995, Harcourt $15.00 (978-0-15-204264-6). Even though she is living a comfortable life, Gamma Lee decides one day to set out with her donkey to explore the Gates of the Wind. (Rev: SLJ 10/95)

1380 Laube, Sigrid. *The Flower Ball* (K–3). Trans. from German by Philip Boehm. Illus. by Silke Leffler. 2006, Pumpkin House $15.95 (978-0-9646010-2-4). When a carrot and a cauliflower attend the Flower Ball, the flowers realize that vegetables aren't so bad after all. (Rev: SLJ 7/06)

1381 Lawler, Janet. *If Kisses Were Colors* (PS–1). Illus. by Alison Jay. 2003, Dial $15.99 (978-0-8037-2617-8). 32pp. A fanciful series of characterizations of kisses — as colors, pebbles, comets, flowers, and more — are accompanied by appealing illustrations. (Rev: BL 3/1/03; HBG 10/03; SLJ 3/03)

1382 Lawson, Janet. *Audrey and Barbara* (K–2). Illus. 2002, Simon & Schuster $13.95 (978-0-689-83896-5). 32pp. A little girl and her reluctant cat take a pretend voyage to India in a bathtub. (Rev: BL 9/15/02; HB 5/02; HBG 10/02; SLJ 7/02)

1383 Lazo, Caroline. *Someday When My Cat Can Talk* (K–2). Illus. by Krysten Brooker. 2008, Random $16.99 (978-0-375-83754-8). 32pp. A little girl imagines all the fun her cat could have on a trip to Europe. (Rev: BL 3/15/08; SLJ 3/08)

1384 Lechner, John. *The Clever Stick* (K–2). Illus. by author. 2009, Candlewick $14.99 (978-0-7636-

3950-1). 40pp. A clever stick figures out how to communicate. (Rev: BLO 5/15/09; SLJ 7/09)

1385 Lechner, John. *Sticky Burr: Adventures in Burrwood Forest* (K–3). Illus. by author. 2007, Candlewick $15.99 (978-0-7636-3054-6). 48pp. This fast-paced, graphic-novel-style book chronicles the adventures of a tiny forest burr who is bullied by the other burrs but eventually gets to show his real mettle. (Rev: BL 7/07; SLJ 7/07)

1386 Lee, Suzy. *The Zoo* (2–5). Illus. by author. 2007, Kane $15.95 (978-1-933605-28-9). The animals sneak out of their cages for a special play time with a little girl during her family's visit to the zoo. (Rev: SLJ 6/07)

1387 Leedahl, Shelley A. *The Bone Talker* (PS–2). Illus. by Bill Slavin. 2000, Red Deer $15.95 (978-0-88995-214-0). 32pp. To help cheer up elderly Grandmother Bones, a little girl gets her to begin making a quilt that later becomes a patchwork of fields across the Great Plains. (Rev: BL 4/15/00)

1388 Leedy, Loreen. *Follow the Money!* (1–3). Illus. 2002, Holiday House $17.95 (978-0-8234-1587-8). 32pp. George, a newly minted quarter, has a busy day from delivery at the bank through many adventures to his eventual return to the bank. (Rev: BCCB 4/02; BL 4/15/02*; HBG 10/02; SLJ 5/02)

1389 Leedy, Loreen. *How Humans Make Friends* (1–4). Illus. 1996, Holiday House $15.95 (978-0-8234-1223-5). 32pp. Zork, an extraterrestrial, learns about human behavior, the nature of friendship, and the importance of sharing. (Rev: BL 4/1/96; SLJ 7/96)

1390 Leedy, Loreen. *The Potato Party and Other Troll Tales* (PS–2). Illus. by author. 1989, Holiday House LB $14.95 (978-0-8234-0761-3). 32pp. A delightful collection of seven original stories about trolls. (Rev: SLJ 12/89)

1391 Le Guin, Ursula K. *A Ride on the Red Mare's Back* (PS–2). Illus. by Julie Downing. 1992, Orchard LB $17.99 (978-0-531-08591-2). 48pp. This original fairy tale tells how a girl rescues her brother from the trolls. (Rev: BCCB 10/92; BL 6/15/92; HB 3/93; SLJ 9/92*)

1392 Lehman, Barbara. *Rainstorm* (PS–2). Illus. 2007, Houghton $16.00 (978-0-618-75639-1). 32pp. On a rainy, shut-in day, a boy finds a chest and a key that lead him down a ladder, up some stairs and onto a sunny island with playmates at the ready; sophisticated, boldly lined art captures the recurrent adventures in this wordless fantasy. (Rev: BL 1/1–15/07)

1393 Le Néouanic, Lionel. *Little Smudge* (PS–1). Illus. by author. 2006, Boxer Bks. LB $14.95 (978-1-905417-22-3). The artwork stands out in this story of a little black smudge searching for acceptance by other shapes. (Rev: SLJ 1/07)

1394 Leonard, Marie. *Tibili: The Little Boy Who Didn't Want to Go to School* (K–3). Illus. by Andree Prigent. 2002, Kane $15.95 (978-1-929132-20-1). 36pp. An African child is reluctant to start school but, when the animals show him how important reading is, he changes his mind. (Rev: BL 6/1–15/02; HBG 10/02; SLJ 4/02)

1395 Lerner, Harriet, and Susan Goldhor. *Franny B. Kranny, There's a Bird in Your Hair!* (PS–3). Illus. by Helen Oxenbury. 2001, HarperCollins LB $15.89 (978-0-06-029503-5). 40pp. A bird settles in Franny's hair when her overabundant locks are put up for a special occasion, and she refuses to dislodge it. (Rev: BCCB 9/01; BL 6/1–15/01; HB 7/01; HBG 10/01; SLJ 6/01)

1396 Leslie, Amanda. *Who's That Scratching at My Door? A Peekaboo Riddle Book* (PS–K). Illus. by author. 2001, Handprint $12.95 (978-1-929766-19-2). A young boy is looking for a friend, but the animals that keep showing up at the door (actually, under the flap) are never quite right until a puppy turns up. (Rev: HBG 10/01; SLJ 7/01)

1397 Lester, Helen. *Princess Penelope's Parrot* (PS–1). Illus. by Lynn Munsinger. 1996, Houghton $15.00 (978-0-395-78320-7). 32pp. A browbeaten parrot gets revenge on a bossy princess. (Rev: BCCB 1/97; BL 9/1/96; HB 1–12/96; SLJ 10/96)

1398 Lester, Helen. *The Wizard, the Fairy and the Magic Chicken* (K–2). Illus. by Lynn Munsinger. 1983, Houghton paper $6.95 (978-0-395-47945-2). 32pp. Three friends are in competition with their magic tricks.

1399 Lester, Julius. *The Hungry Ghosts* (K–1). Illus. by Geraldo Valério. 2009, Dial $16.99 (978-0-8037-2513-3). 40pp. Young Malcolm, who lives beside a graveyard, realizes that three ghosts are only making eerie noises because they're hungry. But what do ghosts eat? (Rev: BL 5/15/09; SLJ 8/09)

1400 Lester, Julius. *Shining* (K–3). Illus. by John Clapp. 2003, Harcourt $17.00 (978-0-15-200773-7). Shunned by her fellow villagers because she refuses to speak, Shining eventually finds her voice and becomes the leader of her people. (Rev: BCCB 12/03; HBG 4/04; SLJ 11/03)

1401 Leuck, Laura. *My Monster Mama Loves Me So* (PS). Illus. by Mark Buehner. 1999, Lothrop LB $15.93 (978-0-688-16867-4). A slight, humorous tale in which a little monster tells the ways his mother loves him — like attending his beastball games. (Rev: HBG 3/00; SLJ 1/00)

1402 Levert, Mireille. *An Island in the Soup* (PS). Illus. 2001, Groundwood $15.95 (978-0-88899-403-5). 32pp. Victor of the Noodle experiences great danger while traveling through his soup. (Rev: BL 7/01; HBG 10/01; SLJ 6/01)

1403 Levine, Gail C. *Betsy Who Cried Wolf!* (PS–2). Illus. by Scott Nash. 2002, HarperCollins LB $16.89 (978-0-06-028764-1). 40pp. A wolf tries to outwit the new shepherd, 8-year-old Betsy, but she manages to make him an ally. (Rev: BCCB 10/02; BL 7/02; HBG 10/02; SLJ 6/02)

1404 Lewis, Kim. *Hooray for Harry* (PS–2). 2006, Candlewick $15.99 (978-0-7636-2962-5). 32pp. Accompanied by his friends Lulu the lamb and Ted the teddy bear, Harry the stuffed elephant goes in search of his missing blanket. (Rev: BL 6/1–15/06; SLJ 4/06)

1405 Lewis, Paul Owen. *The Jupiter Stone* (PS–3). Illus. by author. 2003, Tricycle $15.95 (978-1-58246-107-6). When a boy discovers a strange rock of extraterrestrial origin that has laid undiscovered on the Earth's surface for millions of years, he enlists the help of NASA to see that the stone is returned to the vastness of outer space. (Rev: SLJ 9/03)

1406 Lia, Simone. *Billy Bean's Dream* (PS–3). Illus. by author. 2000, David & Charles $15.95 (978-1-86233-260-7). Billy, a jelly bean, longs to travel into space and nearly gets his wish in this zany tale with bold illustrations. (Rev: SLJ 4/01)

1407 Light, Steve. *The Shoemaker Extraordinaire* (PS–1). Illus. 2003, Abrams $14.95 (978-0-8109-4236-3). 32pp. The tale of Hans Crispin, who makes magical shoes for a giant named Barefootus. (Rev: BL 3/15/03; HBG 4/04; SLJ 7/03)

1408 Lillegard, Dee. *Tiger, Tiger* (PS–2). Illus. by Susan Guevara. 2002, Penguin $16.99 (978-0-399-22633-5). 32pp. Dramatic illustrations add to this exciting story, in which lonely Pocu finds a magic feather in the hot jungle and uses it and his imagination to create a tiger — a very hungry tiger. (Rev: BL 1/1–15/03; HBG 3/03; SLJ 12/02)

1409 Lindenbaum, Pija. *Bridget and the Gray Wolves* (PS–2). Illus. 2001, Farrar $14.00 (91-29-65395-9). 24pp. Timid little Bridget always expects the worst, but when she becomes surrounded by wolves she surprisingly becomes leader of the pack in this humorous reversal full of funny lupines. (Rev: BCCB 9/01; BL 12/15/01; HBG 3/02; SLJ 11/01)

1410 Lindenbaum, Pija. *Bridget and the Moose Brothers* (PS–1). Trans. from Swedish by Kjersti Board. Illus. by author. 2004, R&S $16.00 (91-29-66046-7). Bridget wants a baby brother or sister, but what she gets instead is a trio of uncouth moose. (Rev: SLJ 5/04)

1411 Lindenbaum, Pija. *Bridget and the Muttonheads* (PS–2). Trans. by Kjersti Board. Illus. 2002, Farrar $16.00 (91-29-65650-8). 28pp. Little Bridget, on vacation with her parents and bored by the pool, wanders off to find an adventure of her own in this imaginative tale. (Rev: BL 8/02; HB 11/02; HBG 3/03; SLJ 1/03)

1412 Lindgren, Astrid. *Mirabelle* (PS–2). Trans. from Swedish by Elisabeth Kallick Dyssegaard. Illus. by Pija Lindenbaum. 2003, R&S $15.00 (91-29-65821-7). Translated into English, this charming Swedish tale tells how 8-year-old Britta plants a seed given to her by a stranger and is pleasantly surprised when the seed sprouts into a doll like the one she has long been wanting. (Rev: BL 5/15/03; HBG 10/03; SLJ 8/03) [839.7]

1413 Lindgren, Astrid. *Most Beloved Sister* (2–4). Trans. by Elisabeth Kallick Dyssegaard. Illus. by Hans Arnold. 2002, Farrar $15.00 (91-29-65502-1). 28pp. When her baby brother is born, Barbara's imaginary twin sister, Lalla-Lee, comes to her rescue and the two have a day of magical adventures together in this vividly illustrated story that was originally published a half-century ago. (Rev: BL 7/02; HBG 10/02; SLJ 8/02)

1414 Lloyd-Jones, Sally. *Old MacNoah Had an Ark* (K–2). Illus. by Jill Newton. 2008, HarperBlessings

$16.99 (978-0-06-055717-1). 32pp. Lloyd-Jones uses "Old MacDonald Had a Farm" as a base for a rollicking view of the animals aboard Noah's ark. (Rev: BL 6/1–15/08; SLJ 4/08)

1415 Loki. *Jake Greenthumb* (PS–2). Illus. by Jason Gaillard. 2002, Mondo $15.95 (978-1-59034-186-5). 32pp. Jake's thumb is so green that the plants he is looking after threaten to take over his room. (Rev: HBG 10/02; SLJ 9/02)

1416 Long, Melinda. *How I Became a Pirate* (PS–3). Illus. by David Shannon. 2003, Harcourt $16.00 (978-0-15-201848-1). The charms of a life aboard a pirate ship wane as Jeremy Jacob realizes he misses bedtime stories and goodnight kisses. (Rev: HBG 4/04; SLJ 9/03)

1417 López, Brigitta Garcia. *Dreamflight* (K–2). Trans. by Marianne Martens. Illus. 2005, North-South $16.95 (978-0-7358-2024-1). 40pp. Young Max awakens one night to discover his rather plump guardian angel driving around his bedroom in a racing car. (Rev: BL 12/15/05)

1418 Lowell, Susan. *The Bootmaker and the Elves* (K–4). Illus. by Tom Curry. 1997, Orchard LB $16.99 (978-0-531-33044-9). 32pp. The old folktale is given a new setting, the Old West, and a new subject, cowboy boots. (Rev: BL 9/15/97; HB 11/97; HBG 3/98; SLJ 11/97)

1419 Lucas, David. *Nutmeg* (1–3). 2006, Knopf $16.95 (978-0-375-83519-3). 32pp. Pigtailed Nutmeg is tired of the same old fare for breakfast, lunch, and dinner, but things get a little crazy after she receives a magic spoon. (Rev: BL 8/06; SLJ 8/06)

1420 Lucas, David. *Whale* (PS–1). Illus. by author. 2007, Knopf $16.99 (978-0-375-84338-9). 32pp. When a tsunami leaves a beached whale in its wake, Joe and his grandma consult the mystical powers of nature to solve the problem. (Rev: BCCB 9/07; BL 6/1–15/07; LMC 8/07; SLJ 6/07)

1421 Luján, Jorge. *Sky Blue Accident / Accidente celeste* (K–1). Trans. from Spanish by Elisa Amado. Illus. by Piet Grobler. 2007, Groundwood $16.95 (978-0-88899-805-7). This story in English and Spanish has a boy accidentally breaking off a bit of the sky when he falls off his bike. (Rev: SLJ 7/07)

1422 Lund, Deb. *Monsters on Machines* (PS–1). Illus. by Robert Neubecker. 2008, Harcourt $16.00 (978-0-15-205365-9). 40pp. Bright, lively illustrations add to the appeal of this story about young monsters using construction machines to build a haunted house. (Rev: SLJ 9/08)

1423 Lyon, George E. *My Friend, the Starfinder* (K–2). Illus. by Stephen Gammell. 2008, Atheneum $16.99 (978-1-4169-2738-9). 40pp. A little girl listens to her neighbor tell the fairytale like story of how as a boy he met a star and found himself at the end of a rainbow. (Rev: BCCB 3/08; BL 1/1–15/08; HB 3/08; LMC 3/08*; SLJ 3/08) ∩

1424 Lyons, Dana. *The Tree* (PS–2). Illus. by David Danioth. 2002, Illumination Arts $16.95 (978-0-9701907-1-0). An 800-year-old Douglas fir describes its life in simple verse and worries that its future is threatened. (Rev: SLJ 10/02)

1425 McAllister, Angela. *Mama and Little Joe* (PS). Illus. by Terry Milne. 2007, Simon & Schuster $15.99 (978-1-4169-1631-4). 32pp. Timeworn and tattered, stuffed kangaroos Mama and Little Joe get the cold shoulder from the newer, brighter stuffed toys at their new home, but when Little Joe is accidentally discarded the newer toys rise to the occasion and offer to help find him. (Rev: BL 4/1/07)

1426 McCaughrean, Geraldine. *Blue Moon Mountain* (1–3). Illus. by Nicki Palin. 2007, Simply Read $16.95 (978-1-894965-56-9). 32pp. Joy follows a moonlit path to Blue Mountain, the magical home of the fantastical creatures of myth, legend, and literature. (Rev: BL 3/15/07; SLJ 4/1/07)

1427 McClintock, Barbara. *Dahlia* (PS–2). Illus. 2002, Farrar $16.00 (978-0-374-31678-5). 32pp. When Charlotte is given a frilly doll named Dahlia, she includes her in her tomboy adventures in this picture book set in the Victorian age. (Rev: BCCB 10/02; BL 9/1/02; HB 9/02*; HBG 3/03; SLJ 11/02*)

1428 McDaniels, Preston. *A Perfect Snowman* (PS–1). Illus. by author. 2007, Simon & Schuster $15.99 (978-1-4169-1026-8). 40pp. Built by a wealthy boy, every element of the snowman seems perfect, but the real value comes when the snowman shares what he has with those around him. (Rev: BL 12/1/07; SLJ 10/07)

1429 McDonald, Megan. *Ant and Honey Bee: What a Pair!* (PS–2). Illus. by G. Brian Karas. 2005, Candlewick $13.99 (978-0-7636-1265-8). 32pp. Ant and Honey Bee set off happily for the costume party, but rain ruins their efforts and they must improvise hastily. (Rev: BL 2/15/05; SLJ 4/05)

1430 McDonald, Megan. *It's Picture Day Today!* (PS–K). Illus. by Katherine Tillotson. 2009, Atheneum $16.99 (978-1-4169-2434-0). 32pp. A class made up of art materials — squiggles, sequins, pom-poms, buttons, glue, and so forth — is very excited on Picture Day. (Rev: BL 5/1/09; HB 7/09; SLJ 6/09)

1431 McDonald, Megan. *When the Library Lights Go Out* (PS–2). Illus. by Katherine Tillotson. 2005, Simon & Schuster $16.95 (978-0-689-86170-3). 40pp. After the library has closed for the night, storytime puppets Rabbit and Lion launch a search for their friend Hermit Crab. (Rev: BL 11/1/05; SLJ 11/05)

1432 MacDonald, Ross. *Bad Baby* (K–2). Illus. 2005, Roaring Brook $16.95 (978-1-59643-064-8). 32pp. Superhero Jack, first seen in *Another Perfect Day* (2002), begins to rethink his wish for a little sister when the reality turns out to be far different than he had imagined. (Rev: BCCB 11/05; BL 10/1/05*; HB 9/05; HBG 4/06; SLJ 9/05)

1433 McElmurry, Jill. *Mad About Plaid* (K–2). Illus. 2000, HarperCollins LB $14.89 (978-0-688-16952-7). 32pp. Madison Pratt finds a magical plaid purse that turns everything the same plaid pattern. (Rev: BL 4/1/00; HBG 10/00; SLJ 5/00)

1434 MacGill-Callahan, Sheila. *The Last Snake in Ireland: A Story About St. Patrick* (PS–2). Illus. by Will Hillenbrand. 1999, Holiday House $16.95

(978-0-8234-1425-3). 32pp. The last snake in Ireland eludes St. Patrick and finds himself a resident of Loch Ness. (Rev: BCCB 3/99; BL 3/15/99; HBG 10/99; SLJ 3/99)

1435 McKissack, Patricia C. *Where Crocodiles Have Wings* (K–2). Illus. by Bob Barner. 2005, Holiday $16.95 (978-0-8234-1748-3). 32pp. A rhyming fantasy set in a land where "surprises grow on trees" full of happy animals engaging in unusual activities. (Rev: BL 9/15/05; SLJ 10/05)

1436 McKissack, Patricia C., and Onawumi Jean Moss. *Precious and the Boo Hag* (K–2). Illus. by Krysten Brooker. 2005, Simon & Schuster $16.95 (978-0-689-85194-0). 40pp. Precious, stuck home alone with a stomachache when her mother and brother must leave, resists multiple attempts by the Boo Hag to gain entry to the house. (Rev: BL 2/1/05; SLJ 3/05)

1437 McMillan, Bruce. *Ghost Doll* (K–1). Illus. by author. 1997, Apple Island paper $10.00 (978-0-934313-01-8). 32pp. Chrissy changes a ghost doll into the real thing.

1438 McMillan, Bruce. *The Remarkable Riderless Runaway Tricycle* (K–3). Illus. by author. 1985, Apple Island paper $10.00 (978-0-934313-00-1). 48pp. A tricycle, unwilling to be consigned to the dump, sets out on its own trip. This reissued picture book was first published in 1978 and contains black-and-white photographs.

1439 McMullan, Kate. *I Stink!* (PS–3). Illus. by James McMullan. 2002, HarperCollins LB $17.89 (978-0-06-029849-4). 40pp. In this boldly illustrated picture book, a garbage truck describes its activities during its nightly rounds. (Rev: BCCB 6/02; BL 6/1–15/02; HB 5/02*; HBG 10/02; SLJ 5/02)

1440 McNaughton, Janet. *Brave Jack and the Unicorn* (K–3). Illus. by Susan Tooke. 2005, Tundra $15.95 (978-0-88776-677-0). 32pp. Drawing on traditional Newfoundland tales, this is the story of Jack, who is sent off in search of his older brothers and succeeds in finding them — as well as a wife — with the help of plants and animals that reward him with magical gifts. (Rev: BL 6/1–15/05)

1441 McNeil, Florence, and David McPhail. *Sail Away* (PS–2). Illus. by David McPhail. 2000, Orca $15.95 (978-1-55143-147-5). 32pp. Nautical terms are explained in this picture book about a boy dressed as a pirate who, with his animal friends, sails a pirate ship. (Rev: BCCB 10/00; BL 10/1/00; HBG 3/01; SLJ 12/00)

1442 McPhail, David. *Boy on the Brink* (PS–2). Illus. by author. 2006, Holt $15.95 (978-0-8050-7618-9). 32pp. In his dreams, a boy reviews and expands dramatically on the day's events. (Rev: BL 5/15/06; SLJ 5/06)

1443 McPhail, David. *Edward and the Pirates* (PS–3). Illus. 1997, Little, Brown $15.95 (978-0-316-56344-4). 32pp. The pirates that Edward is reading about come alive and kidnap him. (Rev: BCCB 7–8/97; BL 4/15/97; SLJ 5/97)

1444 McPhail, David. *Edward in the Jungle* (PS–3). Illus. 2002, Little, Brown $15.95 (978-0-316-56391-8). 32pp. While reading about Tarzan, Edward is transported to Africa where he is saved from a menacing crocodile by the Lord of the Jungle. (Rev: BCCB 4/02; BL 4/1/02; HBG 10/02; SLJ 3/02)

1445 McPhail, David. *The Party* (PS–1). Illus. 1990, Little, Brown $14.95 (978-0-316-56330-7). 32pp. A little boy and his stuffed toys have a party after Dad falls asleep. (Rev: BL 10/1/90; SLJ 11/90)

1446 MacRae, Tom. *The Opposite* (1–3). Illus. by Elena Odriozola. 2006, Peachtree $15.95 (978-1-56145-371-9). After the Opposite, a strange-looking creature, appears in his bedroom one morning, Nate finds that everything he does turns out the opposite of what he intended. (Rev: SLJ 10/06)

1447 Madden, Don. *The Wartville Wizard* (K–3). Illus. by author. 1986, Macmillan paper $5.99 (978-0-689-71667-6). 32pp. An old man who picks up litter is given the "power over trash" by Mother Nature in this tale about littering. (Rev: BL 11/1/86; SLJ 1/87)

1448 Madinaveitia, Horacio. *Sir Robert's Little Outing* (K–3). Illus. 1992, Wonder Well LB $13.95 (978-1-879567-01-6); paper $7.95 (978-1-879567-00-9). 30pp. An oafish knight, Sir Robert, sets out on a quest to win the fair Princess Dorothea. (Rev: BL 1/1/93)

1449 Mahy, Margaret. *Bubble Trouble* (PS–1). Illus. by Polly Dunbar. 2009, Clarion $16.00 (978-0-547-07421-4). 32pp. It takes a human ladder, a slingshot, and a good catch to save a baby who is floating away in a bubble. (Rev: BL 4/15/09; HB 5/09; SLJ 5/09)

1450 Mahy, Margaret. *Simply Delicious!* (K–3). Illus. by Jonathan Allen. 1999, Orchard $15.95 (978-0-531-30181-4). 32pp. As Mr. Minky bicycles home with a super ice-cream cone for his son, he attracts a number of jungle beasts who follow him for a taste. (Rev: BL 9/1/99; HB 9/99; HBG 3/00; SLJ 9/99)

1451 Maloney, Peter, and Felicia Zekauskas. *The Magic Hockey Stick* (K–3). Illus. 1999, Dial $16.99 (978-0-8037-2476-1). 40pp. When her mother buys Wayne Gretzky's hockey stick at an auction, a young hockey player notices that, although her game improves by using the magic stick, Gretzky's declines. (Rev: BL 12/1/99; HBG 10/00; SLJ 10/99)

1452 Marciano, John Bemelmans. *There's a Dolphin in the Grand Canal* (K–2). Illus. 2005, Viking $15.99 (978-0-670-05987-4). 40pp. Bored despite the fact that he lives in Venice, Luca gets a thrilling ride over the city on the back of a dolphin. (Rev: BL 6/1–15/05)

1453 Marin, Cheech. *Cheech and the Spooky Ghost Bus* (K–2). Illus. by Orlando L. Ramirez. 2009, HarperCollins $17.99 (978-0-06-113211-7). 32pp. The school bus stops by the graveyard and it's pretty spooky from then on. (Rev: BL 6/1–15/09; SLJ 6/09)

1454 Masini, Beatrice. *A Brave Little Princess* (K–3). Illus. by Octavia Monaco. 2000, Barefoot Books $16.99 (978-1-84148-267-5). 32pp. A tiny princess doesn't look her age so she goes out into the world to prove that she is stronger and braver than she looks. (Rev: BL 10/1/00; HBG 3/01; SLJ 2/01)

1455 Mayer, Mercer. *The Bravest Knight* (PS–2). Illus. 2007, Dial $16.99 (978-0-8037-3206-3). 32pp. A young boy dreams of living in the olden days, in a world of knights, castles, dragons, and — um — scary trolls — in this newly illustrated update of Mayer's *Terrible Troll* (1968). (Rev: BL 5/1/07; SLJ 6/07)

1456 Mayer, Mercer. *Shibumi and the Kitemaker* (2–4). Illus. 1999, Marshall Cavendish $18.95 (978-0-7614-5054-2). 48pp. An original folktale about an emperor's daughter who is shocked at the peasants' living conditions in her father's kingdom and wants him to do something about it. (Rev: BL 10/15/99; HBG 10/00; SLJ 9/99)

1457 Mayhew, James. *Katie and the Mona Lisa* (K–3). Illus. 1999, Orchard $15.95 (978-0-531-30177-7). 32pp. In the company of Mona Lisa, Katie enters several famous Renaissance paintings to regain Mona Lisa's famous smile. (Rev: BCCB 9/99; BL 9/1/99; HBG 3/00; SLJ 12/99)

1458 Mayhew, James. *Katie and the Sunflowers* (K–3). Illus. 2001, Scholastic $16.95 (978-0-531-30325-2). 32pp. Katie's museum escapades continue with a romp through Van Gogh, Gauguin, and Cezanne canvases that involves sunflowers, still lifes, and a chase through a cafe. (Rev: BL 6/1–15/01; HBG 10/01; SLJ 7/01)

1459 Mayhew, James. *The Knight Who Took All Day* (K–2). Illus. by author. 2005, Scholastic $15.99 (978-0-439-74829-2). Determined to impress a princess by vanquishing a dragon, a self-centered knight has so much trouble finding one that the princess tames the beast herself. (Rev: SLJ 10/05)

1460 Meadows, Michelle. *Pilot Pups* (PS–K). Illus. by Dan Andreasen. 2008, Simon & Schuster $15.99 (978-1-4169-2484-5). 32pp. Toy dogs take to the air to rescue a toy train that has been abandoned outside. (Rev: BL 7/08; SLJ 4/08)

1461 Meddaugh, Susan. *Cinderella's Rat* (K–2). Illus. 1997, Houghton $16.00 (978-0-395-86833-1). 32pp. An amusing picture book that tells what happened to the rat that was turned into Cinderella's coachman. (Rev: BL 10/1/97; HB 9/97; HBG 3/98; SLJ 10/97*)

1462 Meddaugh, Susan. *Harry on the Rocks* (PS–2). Illus. 2003, Houghton $15.00 (978-0-618-27603-5). 32pp. Stranded on an island, Harry befriends its only other inhabitant, a dragon. (Rev: BL 2/15/03; HBG 10/03; SLJ 5/03)

1463 Meddaugh, Susan. *The Witch's Walking Stick* (PS–2). Illus. 2005, Houghton $16.00 (978-0-618-52948-3). 32pp. Bullied by her older brother and sister, Margaret runs away and happens upon a magic stick (acquiring a new canine friend in the process); she then uses the stick to cast suitably awful spells on her evil siblings. (Rev: BL 7/05; SLJ 9/05)

1464 Medearis, Angela Shelf. *The Ghost of Sifty Sifty Sam* (K–3). Illus. by Jacqueline Rogers. 1997, Scholastic $14.95 (978-0-590-48290-5). 32pp. A chef named Dan uses his cooking to tame a ghost

whose wailings have made a house unfit for living. (Rev: BL 12/1/97; HBG 3/98; SLJ 11/97)

1465 Melling, David. *The Kiss That Missed* (PS–2). Illus. by author. 2002, Barron's $14.95 (978-0-7641-5451-5). A royal kiss goes astray and must be retrieved from a spooky forest full of dangers. (Rev: HBG 3/03; SLJ 12/02)

1466 Meyer, Eleanor Walsh. *The Keeper of Ugly Sounds* (PS–2). Illus. by Vlad Guzner. 1998, Winslow $16.95 (978-1-890817-02-2). 32pp. A young boy is responsible for stuffing bad noises caused by unpleasant acts into bags and sending them out to sea — a chore that he comes to find disagreeable. (Rev: BL 12/1/98; SLJ 1/99)

1467 Milgrim, David. *Another Day in the Milky Way* (PS–1). Illus. by author. 2007, Putnam $15.99 (978-0-399-24548-0). Upset when he wakes up on the wrong planet, young Monty looks desperately for someone who can help him get back to Earth and then remembers he's been in this situation before. (Rev: BL 2/15/07; SLJ 2/07)

1468 Milord, Susan. *The Ghost on the Hearth* (PS–2). Illus. by Lydia Dabcovich. 2003, Vermont Folklife Center $15.95 (978-0-916718-18-3). 32pp. A well-illustrated ghost story set in early 19th-century Quebec, in which a young girl returns from the dead to the house in which she worked. (Rev: BL 2/1/04; HBG 4/04; SLJ 12/03)

1469 Milord, Susan. *Pebble: A Story About Belonging* (PS–2). Illus. by author. 2007, HarperCollins $15.99 (978-0-06-085807-0). 32pp. On a rocky coastline a small round pebble longs to become something special and its dream comes true when a young boy visits the beach with his family and selects the pebble as a keepsake. (Rev: BL 11/15/07; SLJ 2/08)

1470 Min, Willemien. *Peter's Patchwork Dream* (PS–K). Illus. 1999, Barefoot Books $15.95 (978-1-902283-45-6). 26pp. Peter, who is sick in bed, enters the world of his patchwork quilt and is soon traveling through fields, orchards, and across the sea. (Rev: BL 5/1/99; SLJ 6/99)

1471 Mitchell, Adrian. *Nobody Rides the Unicorn* (1–4). Illus. by Stephen Lambert. 2000, Scholastic $16.95 (978-0-439-11204-8). 32pp. An evil king tricks a young girl into capturing the unicorn, but when she realizes what has happened she is able to free him. (Rev: BCCB 2/00; BL 4/15/00; HBG 10/00; SLJ 1/01)

1472 Morgan, Mary. *Dragon Pizzeria* (PS–3). Illus. by author. 2008, Knopf $16.99 (978-0-375-82309-1). 40pp. A pizzeria run by dragons in fairy-tale land allows readers many chances for guessing. Who would have ordered a topic of magic beans? Porridge? (Rev: SLJ 4/08)

1473 Morrissey, Dean, and Stephen Krensky. *The Crimson Comet* (PS–2). Illus. by Dean Morrissey. 2006, HarperCollins LB $17.89 (978-0-06-008070-9). Nora becomes alarmed when the light of the moon suddenly blinks out, so she and her brother Jack board a rocket and head off to see if they can offer assistance to the Man-in-the-Moon. (Rev: SLJ 12/06)

1474 Morrow, Tara Jaye. *Just Mommy and Me* (PS). Illus. by Katy Bratun. 2004, HarperCollins LB $13.89 (978-0-06-000725-6). Told in rhyme, with an imaginative graphic layout, this is the story of a little boy who thinks about what fun it would be if he and his mother were monkeys. (Rev: SLJ 4/04)

1475 Moser, Lisa. *The Monster in the Backpack* (1–2). Illus. by Noah Z. Jones. 2006, Candlewick $14.99 (978-0-7636-2390-6). 40pp. Initially startled to discover a monster in her backpack, Annie soon develops a warm spot in her heart for the strange and mischievous yet endearing creature. (Rev: SLJ 8/06)

1476 Munsch, Robert. *Mud Puddle* (PS–2). Illus. by Sami Suomalainen. 1996, Annick LB $16.95 (978-1-55037-469-8); paper $5.95 (978-1-55037-468-1). 32pp. Jule Ann is attacked by a mud puddle every time she leaves her house. (Rev: BL 4/1/96)

1477 Murphy, Stuart J. *A Pair of Socks* (PS–1). Illus. by Lois Ehlert. 1996, HarperCollins LB $15.89 (978-0-06-025880-1). 40pp. A sock sets out to find its lost mate. (Rev: BL 10/1/96; SLJ 12/96)

1478 Muth, Jon J. *The Three Questions: Based on a Story by Leo Tolstoy* (PS–3). Illus. 2002, Scholastic $17.99 (978-0-439-19996-4). 32pp. A conversation-starter about a boy who finds the answers to his philosophical questions in an act of kindness. (Rev: BL 3/15/02; HBG 10/02; SLJ 6/02)

1479 Muth, Jon J. *Zen Ties* (K–3). Illus. by author. 2008, Scholastic $17.99 (978-0-439-63425-0). 40pp. Stillwater the giant panda, in the company of his nephew Koo, persuades his three young friends to befriend a cranky elderly neighbor. (Rev: BL 2/15/08; SLJ 4/08)

1480 Namioka, Lensey. *The Hungriest Boy in the World* (K–3). Illus. by Aki Sogabe. 2001, Holiday House $16.95 (978-0-8234-1542-7). 32pp. A little Japanese boy swallows a hunger monster that causes the boy to eat everything in sight. (Rev: BL 4/1/01; HB 5/01; HBG 10/01; SLJ 4/01)

1481 Napoli, Donna Jo. *Albert* (K–2). Illus. by Jim LaMarche. 2001, Harcourt $16.00 (978-0-15-201572-5). 32pp. When Albert, a reclusive man, sticks a hand out of his apartment window, two cardinals build a nest in it and Albert must stay in this position until the birds' eggs hatch. (Rev: BL 3/1/01; HBG 10/01)

1482 Nara, Yoshitomo. *The Lonesome Puppy* (PS). Illus. by author. 2008, Chronicle $17.99 (978-0-8118-5640-9). 40pp. A puppy so large he spans the Pacific Ocean is lonely until a little girl climbs high enough to recognize him for what he is. (Rev: BL 6/1–15/08; SLJ 7/08)

1483 Nash, Scott. *Tuff Fluff: The Case of Duckie's Missing Brain* (1–3). Illus. 2004, Candlewick $16.99 (978-0-7636-1882-7). 32pp. Tuff Fluff, a stuffed toy rabbit detective, takes on a tough assignment when he agrees to look into the mysterious disappearance of Duckie's brain. (Rev: BL 5/1/04; SLJ 7/04)

1484 Neubecker, Robert. *Courage of the Blue Boy* (PS–K). Illus. 2006, Tricycle $15.95 (978-1-58246-182-3). 32pp. A blue boy and his blue cow search for lands with other colors and eventually find a multicolor city that has no blue; it's up to the boy to add this. (Rev: BL 11/1/06; SLJ 11/06)

1485 Newman, Leslea. *Cats, Cats, Cats!* (PS–2). Illus. by Erika Oller. 2001, Simon & Schuster $16.00 (978-0-689-83077-8). 32pp. When Mrs. Brown goes to bed at night, her 60 cats knit, eat, read, write, perform, and party. (Rev: BCCB 3/01; BL 2/15/01; HBG 10/01; SLJ 3/01)

1486 Nez, John. *One Smart Cookie* (PS–2). 2006, Albert Whitman $16.99 (978-0-8075-6099-0). 32pp. Cookie the dog comes to school and outshines Duffy and Nash in reading and writing ability. (Rev: BL 9/15/06; SLJ 10/06)

1487 Nickle, John. *The Ant Bully* (PS–1). Illus. 1999, Scholastic $16.99 (978-0-590-39591-5). 32pp. Lucas terrorizes the ants in his backyard until they shrink him and put him on trial. (Rev: BCCB 2/99; BL 2/1/99; HB 1/99; HBG 10/99; SLJ 3/99)

1488 Nickle, John. *TV Rex* (K–3). Illus. 2001, Scholastic $15.95 (978-0-439-12043-2). 40pp. Rex crawls inside the TV set to fix it and soon finds he has become part of a series of different programs including a wrestling show and a soap opera. (Rev: BCCB 3/01; BL 1/1–15/01; HBG 10/01)

1489 Nielsen-Fernlund, Susin. *Hank and Fergus* (PS–2). 2003, Orca $16.95 (978-1-55143-245-8). Hank, always conscious of his birthmark, conjures up an imaginary dog called Fergus, who keeps him company until he finds a real friend. (Rev: HBG 4/04; SLJ 2/04)

1490 Niemann, Christoph. *The Police Cloud* (PS–2). Illus. 2007, Random $15.99 (978-0-375-83963-). 32pp. A little white cloud dreams of being a police officer but discovers fire fighting may be better suited to his skills. (Rev: BL 5/1/07; HB 3/07; SLJ 6/07)

1491 Nightingale, Sandy. *Cider Apples* (K–3). Illus. 1996, Harcourt $15.00 (978-0-15-201244-1). 32pp. Fairies help a young girl and her grandmother save an ailing apple tree. (Rev: BL 9/1/96; SLJ 11/96)

1492 Nimmo, Jenny. *Pig on a Swing* (PS). Illus. by Caroline Uff. 2003, Hodder $16.95 (978-0-340-85241-5). Bored at the playground, a little boy conjures up a menagerie of creatures to keep him company. (Rev: SLJ 1/04)

1493 Nishimura, Kae. *I Am Dodo: Not a True Story* (PS–3). Illus. by author. 2005, Clarion $15.00 (978-0-618-33614-2). 32pp. A lone surviving dodo living in New York City is eager to elude capture. (Rev: SLJ 9/05)

1494 Nolen, Jerdine. *Big Jabe* (1–4). Illus. by Kadir Nelson. 2000, Lothrop LB $16.89 (978-0-688-13663-5). 32pp. An original tall tale about a man of unusual strength who could lead slaves to freedom. (Rev: BCCB 9/00; BL 4/1/00; HB 7/00; HBG 10/00; SLJ 6/00)

1495 Nolen, Jerdine. *Harvey Potter's Balloon Farm* (K–3). Illus. by Mark Buehner. 1994, Morrow $16.99 (978-0-688-07887-4). 32pp. In this tall tale, a little girl learns all the secrets of trade when she visits Harvey's balloon farm and discovers how they are grown. (Rev: BL 4/15/94; HB 7/94; SLJ 5/94)

1496 Nolen, Jerdine. *Hewitt Anderson's Great Big Life* (K–3). Illus. by Kadir Nelson. 2005, Simon & Schuster $16.95 (978-0-689-86866-5). Born into a family of giants, little Hewitt fails to develop properly, but despite his diminutive size he constantly proves his worth. (Rev: BL 3/1/04; SLJ 5/05)

1497 Nolen, Jerdine. *Raising Dragons* (PS–2). Illus. by Elise Primavera. 1998, Harcourt $16.00 (978-0-15-201288-5). 32pp. An African American child raises a dragon named Hank on her parents' farm and teaches him to perform useful chores. Eventually, though, she must take him to a land where he will be with his own kind. (Rev: BCCB 6/98; BL 4/1/98; HB 3/98; HBG 10/98; SLJ 4/98)

1498 Nolen, Jerdine. *Thunder Rose* (K–3). Illus. by Kadir Nelson. 2003, Harcourt $16.00 (978-0-15-216472-0). Born during a fierce thunderstorm, Thunder Rose is an African American child of extraordinary talent and magical ability in this vividly illustrated story set in the West. (Rev: HBG 4/04; SLJ 9/03)

1499 Norac, Carl. *Monster, Don't Eat Me!* (1–3). Trans. from Dutch by Elisa Amado. Illus. by Carll Cneut. 2007, Groundwood $18.95 (978-0-88899-800-2). Poor Alex, a little well-dressed piglet, is nearly eaten by a monster but saved when the monster's mother stops her son from snacking. (Rev: SLJ 8/07)

1500 Norling, Beth. *The Stone Baby* (K–2). Illus. by author. 2003, Lothian $18.95 (978-0-7344-0353-7). A little girl protects a stone baby through a series of adventures, including encounters with wild animals and pirates. (Rev: SLJ 5/04)

1501 Novak, Matt. *No Zombies Allowed* (K–2). Illus. by author. 2002, Simon & Schuster $16.95 (978-0-689-84130-9). Witch Wizzle and Witch Woddle are busy crossing names off their monster party guest list because of bad behavior the year before. (Rev: BCCB 9/02; HB 9/02; HBG 3/03; SLJ 8/02)

1502 Noyes, Deborah. *It's Vladimir!* (K–3). Illus. by Christopher Mills. 2001, Marshall Cavendish $15.95 (978-0-7614-5071-9). 32pp. A young vampire is impatient to learn how to turn into a bat. (Rev: BL 10/15/01; HBG 3/02; SLJ 10/01)

1503 O'Brien, John. *Poof!* (PS–2). Illus. by author. 1999, Boyds Mills $16.95 (978-1-56397-815-9). A sleepy wizard and his wife avoid daily chores by waving their magic wands; "Poof!" they solve each problem. (Rev: HBG 3/00; SLJ 11/99)

1504 O'Connor, George. *Sally and the Something* (PS–2). 2006, Roaring Brook $16.95 (978-1-59643-141-6). 32pp. Bored young Sally sets off for the pond where she befriends a strange-looking creature and they try to find activities they both enjoy. (Rev: BL 6/1–15/06; SLJ 3/06)

1505 Oliviero, Jamie. *Som See and the Magic Elephant* (1–3). Illus. by Jo'Anne Kelly. 1995, Hyperion $14.95 (978-0-7868-0025-4). 32pp. Before Som See's great aunt dies, she wants to touch a white elephant. With the help of magical powers, Som See

is eventually able to grant her wish. (Rev: BL 5/1/95; SLJ 5/95)

1506 Olson, Mary W. *An Alligator Ate My Brother* (PS–2). Illus. by Tammie Lyon. 2000, Boyds Mills $15.95 (978-1-56397-803-6). 32pp. Paul can't convince his parents that an alligator has just eaten baby brother Jimmy. (Rev: BCCB 12/00; BL 12/1/00; HBG 3/01; SLJ 11/00)

1507 O'Malley, Kevin, and Patrick O'Brien. *Captain Raptor and the Space Pirates* (1–3). Illus. by Patrick O'Brien. 2007, Walker $16.95 (978-0-8027-9571-7). 32pp. Captain Raptor's mission is to save his home planet from raiding space pirates in this new graphic novel adventure that will appeal to reluctant readers. (Rev: BL 9/1/07; SLJ 9/07)

1508 Oram, Hiawyn. *Rubbaduck and Ruby Roo* (PS–1). Illus. by David Lucas. 2005, Boyds Mills $15.95 (978-1-59078-356-6). 32pp. Rubbaduck is angry when rag doll Ruby Roo eats up everything in his kitchen and trades away his coat, but all ends well when Ruby's magic turns to gold. (Rev: BL 3/1/05; SLJ 3/05)

1509 Ormondroyd, Edward. *Theodore: The Adventures of a Smudgy Bear* (PS–1). Illus. by Juli Kangas. 2009, Dial $16.99 (978-0-8037-3163-9). 32pp. A well-loved teddy bear has to find a way back home when he is unexpectedly laundered and becomes unrecognizable to Lucy; a new edition of a story first published in 1966, with bright illustrations. (Rev: BLO 6/23/09; SLJ 7/09)

1510 Palatini, Margie. *Piggie Pie!* (K–3). Illus. by Howard Fine. 1995, Clarion $16.00 (978-0-395-71691-5). 32pp. Gritch the Witch is off to Old MacDonald's farm in search of eight plump pigs for her favorite pie. (Rev: BL 9/1/95*; SLJ 11/95*)

1511 Palatini, Margie. *Zak's Lunch* (K–3). Illus. by Howard Fine. 1998, Clarion $16.00 (978-0-395-81674-5). 32pp. When faced with a simple ham-and-cheese sandwich for lunch, Zak dreams of owning his own restaurant, where he will have delicious, forbidden foods every day. (Rev: HBG 10/98; SLJ 6/98)

1512 Palazzo, Tony. *Magic Crayon* (PS–2). Illus. by author. 1967, Lion LB $12.95 (978-0-87460-089-6). Imaginative fun for very young readers.

1513 Papineau, Lucie. *Gontrand and the Crescent Moon* (K–4). Trans. from French by David Homel. Illus. by Alain Reno. 1999, Dominique & Friends paper $8.95 (978-1-894363-15-0). Set in prehistoric times, this is the story of how the moon was formed in order to guide a group of lost children home. (Rev: SLJ 2/00)

1514 Paquette, Ammi-Joan. *The Tiptoe Guide to Tracking Fairies* (PS–2). Illus. by Christa Unzner. 2009, Tanglewood $15.95 (978-1-933718-20-0). 32pp. All you need to know about the places where fairies like to hide. (Rev: BL 5/1/09; SLJ 9/09)

1515 Paraskevas, Betty. *The Tangerine Bear* (PS–2). Illus. by Michael Paraskevas. 1997, HarperCollins LB $14.89 (978-0-06-205147-9). 32pp. Toy Tangerine Bear wants to become part of a family, but nobody wants him because his smile was sewn on upside down. (Rev: BL 11/1/97)

1516 Park, Barbara. *Ma! There's Nothing to Do Here!* (PS–K). Illus. by Viviana Garofoli. 2007, Random $15.99 (978-0-375-83852-1). 32pp. A baby waiting to be born humorously complains about being bored. (Rev: BL 12/15/07; SLJ 3/08)

1517 Parnall, Peter. *Spaces* (1–3). Illus. 1993, Millbrook LB $22.90 (978-1-56294-336-3). 32pp. A fantastic view of what unusual creatures and thoughts can fill all sorts of spaces. (Rev: BL 12/1/93; SLJ 12/93)

1518 Passen, Lisa. *The Incredible Shrinking Teacher* (K–3). 2002, Holt $15.95 (978-0-8050-6452-0). 32pp. Strict teacher Irma Birnbaum gets her just desserts when she faces a series of indignities after being shrunk. (Rev: BL 6/1–15/02; HBG 10/02; SLJ 5/02)

1519 Paterson, Katherine. *Celia and the Sweet, Sweet Water* (1–4). Illus. by Vladimir Vagin. 1998, Clarion $15.00 (978-0-395-91324-6). 32pp. On a quest to get some sweet water to help cure her mother's ills, Celia and her talking dog set out to find the village her mother comes from. (Rev: BL 9/1/98; HBG 3/99; SLJ 9/98)

1520 Paterson, Katherine. *The King's Equal* (2–5). Illus. by Vladimir Vagin. 1992, HarperCollins LB $18.89 (978-0-06-022497-4). 64pp. An arrogant king learns humility when the bride he wants does not want him. (Rev: BCCB 1/93; BL 7/92; SLJ 9/92*)

1521 Pawagi, Manjusha. *The Girl Who Hated Books* (K–3). Illus. by Leanne Franson. 1999, Beyond Words $14.95 (978-1-896764-11-5). 24pp. When nonreader Meena accidentally frees a lot of book characters, such as Humpty Dumpty and Ali Baba, from the pages of their books, she has to read the whole family library to find where they belong. (Rev: BL 11/1/99; SLJ 6/99)

1522 Peck, Jan. *Way Far Away on a Wild Safari* (PS–K). Illus. by Valeria Petrone. 2006, Simon & Schuster $15.95 (978-1-4169-0072-6). A little boy's safari through the African savannah turns out to be a date with Grandma's animal cookies. (Rev: SLJ 6/06)

1523 Peet, Bill. *Big Bad Bruce* (K–3). Illus. by author. 1982, Houghton $17.00 (978-0-395-25150-8); paper $8.95 (978-0-395-32922-1). Bruce encounters a witch and is shrunk to the size of a chipmunk.

1524 Peet, Bill. *The Caboose Who Got Loose* (K–3). Illus. by author. 1980, Houghton $17.00 (978-0-395-14805-1); paper $8.95 (978-0-395-28715-6). 48pp. When Katy Caboose is jarred loose from the rest of the train, she gets her wish to be a "cabin in the trees," free from noise and smoke.

1525 Peet, Bill. *Jennifer and Josephine* (1–3). Illus. by author. 1980, Houghton paper $8.95 (978-0-395-29608-0). Jennifer, an old touring car, and her friend Josephine the cat, are driven through several adventures by a reckless driver.

1526 Pelletier, Andrew. *Sixteen Miles to Spring* (K–3). Illus. by Katya Krenina. 2002, Whitman $16.95 (978-0-8075-7388-4). 32pp. A fanciful explanation of spring in which two friends travel from south to north each year, starting at Christmas and spreading seeds as they go. (Rev: BCCB 4/02; BL 5/1/02; HBG 10/02; SLJ 6/02)

1527 Pendziwol, Jean, and Martine Gourbault. *No Dragons for Tea: Fire Safety for Kids (and Dragons)* (PS–1). Illus. 1999, Kids Can $14.95 (978-1-55074-569-6). 32pp. A young girl's pet dragon sneezes, and her experiences with the ensuing blaze teach fire safety to readers. (Rev: BCCB 4/99; BL 2/1/99; HBG 10/99; SLJ 4/99)

1528 Perret, Delphine. *The Big Bad Wolf and Me* (1–3). Illus. 2006, Sterling $9.95 (978-1-4027-3725-1). 64pp. With his confidence almost gone, Big Bad Wolf is not very scary at all, so Boy takes pity and tries to help poor animal to recoup. (Rev: BL 11/1/06)

1529 Perry, Sarah. *If . . .* (K–4). Illus. 1995, Getty Museum $16.95 (978-0-89236-321-6). 46pp. Using a number of unconventional statements beginning with "if," this imaginative book presents a series of eyecatching, ingenious pictures to illustrate each phrase. (Rev: BCCB 1/96; BL 10/15/95*; HBG 9/99; SLJ 2/96)

1530 Persun, Morgan Reed. *No Pets Allowed* (PS–2). Illus. by Timothy Banks. 1998, Journey Bks. paper $5.49 (978-1-57924-077-6). 30pp. Every time Percy speaks the name of an animal, that creature appears, until his apartment is jammed. (Rev: SLJ 2/99)

1531 Petrie, Kathye Fetsko. *Flying Jack* (K–3). Illus. by Paula J. Mahoney. 2003, Boyds Mills $15.95 (978-1-56397-971-2). This heartwarming tale recounts the story of Jack, who has dreamed of flying since he was a small boy. (Rev: HBG 4/04; SLJ 10/03)

1532 Pickering, Jimmy. *Skelly the Skeleton Girl* (PS–3). Illus. by author. 2007, Simon & Schuster $12.99 (978-1-4169-1192-0). A slightly spooky little girl goes looking for the owner of a lost bone in this Halloween-y story. (Rev: SLJ 8/07)

1533 Pilkey, Dav. *Ricky Ricotta's Giant Robot* (2–4). Illus. by Martin Ontiveros. 2000, Scholastic $16.95 (978-0-590-30719-2). 111pp. Ricky Ricotta, a tiny mouse, is a victim of bullying until he becomes friends with a large robot who protects him. (Rev: BCCB 5/00; HBG 10/00; SLJ 4/00)

1534 Pilkey, Dav. *Ricky Ricotta's Giant Robot vs. the Mutant Mosquitoes from Mercury* (1–3). Illus. by Martin Ontiveros. 2000, Scholastic paper $4.99 (978-0-590-30722-2). 127pp. Ricky the mouse and his robot friend fight extraterrestrial insects and an evil robot. (Rev: SLJ 10/00)

1535 Pilkey, Dav. *Ricky Ricotta's Mighty Robot vs. the Stupid Stinkbugs from Saturn* (2–4). Illus. by Martin Ontiveros. 2003, Scholastic $16.99 (978-0-439-37644-0); paper $4.99 (978-0-439-37645-7). 125pp. After the evil Sergeant Stinkbug kidnaps his cousin Lucy, Ricky Ricotta, stalwart mouse, and his trusty robot friend come to the rescue. (Rev: HBG 4/04; SLJ 1/04)

1536 Pilkey, Dav. *When Cats Dream* (PS–3). Illus. 1992, Orchard LB $16.99 (978-0-531-08597-4). 32pp. Cats' dreams are more fun and more colorful than their reality. (Rev: BCCB 9/92; BL 8/92; HB 3/93; SLJ 9/92*)

1537 Pinkney, Andrea D. *Peggony-Po: A Whale of a Tale* (K–2). Illus. by Brian Pinkney. 2006, Hyperion $16.99 (978-0-7868-1958-4). 32pp. Peggony-Po, a young boy carved from a piece of driftwood by a peg-legged African American sailor, tries to retrieve the leg of his creator from the whale that ate it in this action-packed tall tale. (Rev: BL 4/1/06; SLJ 6/06*)

1538 Pinkwater, Daniel. *Bear's Picture* (K–3). Illus. by D. B. Johnson. 2008, Houghton $16.00 (978-0-618-75923-1). 32pp. A standoff between an artistic bear and a couple of opinionated gentlemen demonstrates the importance of creativity and belief in oneself; a newly illustrated edition of a 1972 title. (Rev: BCCB 5/08; BL 2/1/08; SLJ 4/08)

1539 Plourde, Lynn. *Dino Pets* (PS–1). Illus. by Gideon Kendall. 2007, Dutton $15.99 (978-0-525-47778-5). A little boy's efforts to find the perfect dinosaur pet result in a houseful of dinos. Facts about dinosaurs accompany the humorous story. (Rev: SLJ 6/07)

1540 Plourde, Lynn. *Spring's Sprung* (PS–1). Illus. by Greg Couch. 2002, Simon & Schuster $16.00 (978-0-689-84229-0). March, April, and May are querulous siblings who test Mother Earth's patience in this ode to spring. (Rev: HBG 10/02; SLJ 3/02)

1541 Polacco, Patricia. *Appelemando's Dreams* (PS–2). Illus. 1991, Penguin $17.99 (978-0-399-21800-2). 32pp. Appelemando teaches the townspeople that they should never question the importance of dreams. (Rev: BL 10/15/91; SLJ 9/91)

1542 Polacco, Patricia. *Emma Kate* (PS–2). Illus. 2005, Philomel $16.99 (978-0-399-24452-0). 32pp. A little girl and her elephant best friend do everything together — even having their tonsils out at the same time — and it may take readers some time to work out that it is the girl who is imaginary, not the elephant. (Rev: BL 9/15/05; SLJ 11/05)

1543 Polacco, Patricia. *Rechenka's Eggs* (K–2). Illus. by author. 1988, Penguin $16.99 (978-0-399-21501-8). 32pp. Old Babushka saves a wild goose, and when her decorated eggs are broken, the goose repays her kindness by laying her own decorated eggs. (Rev: BCCB 6/88; BL 4/1/88; SLJ 5/88)

1544 Polacco, Patricia. *Something About Hensley's* (PS–4). Illus. by author. 2006, Philomel $16.99 (978-0-399-24538-1). Newly relocated to the town, a family in dire straits finds its every wish magically fulfilled in Hensley's general store. (Rev: SLJ 8/06)

1545 Portis, Antoinette. *Not a Stick* (PS–K). Illus. by author. 2008, HarperCollins $12.99 (978-0-06-112325-2). 32pp. An imaginative little pig demonstrates the many things a stick can be other than a stick (a sword, a fishing rod, and so forth). (Rev: BL 2/15/08; HB 3/08; SLJ 1/08)

1546 Prelutsky, Jack. *The Wizard* (K–2). Illus. by Brandon Dorman. 2007, Greenwillow $16.99 (978-0-06-124076-8). 32pp. A wicked suburban wizard ponders evil deeds and casts spells in this richly illustrated book. (Rev: BL 9/1/07; SLJ 7/07)

1547 Proimos, James. *Patricia von Pleasantsquirrel* (K–2). Illus. by author. 2009, Dial $15.99 (978-0-8037-3066-3). 56pp. Patricia von Pleasantsquirrel has delusions of grandeur and leaves home in search of suitably royal treatment; this tongue-in-cheek story will be enjoyed by fans of *Where the Wild Things Are.* (Rev: HB 3/09; SLJ 2/09)

1548 Pulver, Robin. *Silent Letters Loud and Clear* (K–3). Illus. by Lynn Rowe Reed. 2008, Holiday $16.95 (978-0-8234-2127-5). 32pp. The silent letters (in knee, wrong, and so forth) take offense when the students in Mr. Wright's class deride them, and they decide to fight back. (Rev: BLO 8/28/08; HB 5/08; SLJ 6/08)

1549 Puttock, Simon. *Yours Truly, Louisa* (PS–2). Illus. by Jo Kiddie. 2009, HarperCollins $17.99 (978-0-06-136634-5). 32pp. This barn yarn follows a fastidious pig in her quest for cleanliness from farm to city and back to farm again. (Rev: BLO 2/9/09; SLJ 2/09)

1550 Pyle, Howard. *Bearskin* (1–4). Illus. by Trina S. Hyman. 1997, Morrow $15.89 (978-0-688-09838-4). 48pp. An abandoned youngster is cared for by a bear and grows up to be a dragon-slaying hero. (Rev: BL 11/1/97*; HB 9/97; HBG 3/98; SLJ 8/97*)

1551 Rasmussen, Halfdan. *The Ladder* (K–3). Trans. by Marilyn Nelson. Illus. by Pierre Pratt. 2006, Candlewick $17.99 (978-0-7636-2282-4). 62pp. A ladder sets off to view more of the world and encounters many people who wish to climb it. (Rev: BL 6/1–15/06)

1552 Rassmus, Jens. *Farmer Enno and His Cow* (1–5). Trans. by Dominic Barth. Illus. by author. 1998, Orchard $14.95 (978-0-531-30081-7). Farmer Enno denies his obsessive dream to buy a ship and become a sailor until his wise cow gives him some sound advice. (Rev: HBG 10/98; SLJ 4/98)

1553 Ratnett, Michael. *Monster Train* (K–3). Illus. by June Goulding. 2000, Orchard $15.95 (978-0-531-30293-4). This interactive book uses pop-ups and other devices to illustrate a ride on a monster train with passengers like Frankenstein. (Rev: BL 12/1/00)

1554 Rawson, Katherine. *If You Were a Parrot* (K–2). Illus. by Sherry Rogers. 2006, Sylvan Dell $15.95 (978-0-9764943-9-3). Illustrations of children with parrot features — beaks, feet, voice, and feathers — show the power of imagination and inform about parrots' physical and behavioral characteristics. (Rev: SLJ 12/06)

1555 Ray, Jane. *The Apple-Pip Princess* (PS–2). Illus. by author. 2008, Candlewick $16.99 (978-0-7636-3747-7). 32pp. Planting a tiny apple seed from a box of her dead mother's treasures, Serenity transforms her dustbowl kingdom into a lush paradise. (Rev: BL 3/15/08; SLJ 4/08)

1556 Ray, Jane. *Can You Catch a Mermaid?* (PS–2). Illus. by author. 2008, Orchard $12.95 (978-1-84616-269-5). 32pp. Lonely Eliza is happy to become friends with mermaid Freya, but does she have the strength to help her friend return to her own home? (Rev: BL 1/1–15/09)

1557 Ray, Mary L. *All Aboard!* (PS–2). Illus. by Amiko Hirao. 2002, Little, Brown $14.95 (978-0-316-73507-0). 32pp. The rabbit named Mr. Barnes, who appears to be traveling alone, belongs in fact to the little girl on the same train. (Rev: BL 11/1/02; HBG 3/03; SLJ 10/02)

1558 Rayner, Catherine. *Sylvia and Bird* (PS–2). Illus. by author. 2009, Good Bks. $16.95 (978-1-56148-661-8). 32pp. A lonely dragon called Sylvia befriends a little yellow bird. (Rev: BL 5/1/09)

1559 Reed, Neil. *The Midnight Unicorn* (K–2). Illus. by author. 2006, Sterling LB $14.95 (978-1-4027-3218-8). Millie and her dog Casper go on a wonderful journey when the statue of a unicorn springs to life. (Rev: SLJ 1/07)

1560 Rex, Michael. *My Freight Train* (PS–K). Illus. 2002, Holt $15.95 (978-0-8050-6682-1). 32pp. A little boy segues from playing with his toy train to a day as engineer of a real freight train, and explains every detail of the train and his duties. (Rev: BL 11/15/02; HBG 3/03; SLJ 11/02)

1561 Reynolds, Adrian. *Pete and Polo's Farmyard Adventure* (PS–K). Illus. 2002, Scholastic $16.95 (978-0-439-30913-4). 32pp. A boy named Pete and his toy polar bear search for missing ducks after they discover the pond has dried up. (Rev: BL 8/02; HBG 10/02; SLJ 7/02)

1562 Reynolds, Peter H. *The North Star* (K–3). Illus. by author. 2009, Candlewick $16.99 (978-0-7636-3677-7). 64pp. A bright star guides a little boy as he travels through the world. (Rev: BL 6/1–15/09; SLJ 5/09)

1563 Reynolds, Peter H. *So Few of Me* (K–3). Illus. by author. 2006, Candlewick $14.00 (978-0-7636-2623-5). Young Leo feels so overburdened that he wishes there were more of him to handle all his tasks, but when his wish is granted — many times over — he soon finds himself longing for the good old days. (Rev: SLJ 12/06)

1564 Richardson, Judith B. *Old Winter* (PS–1). Illus. by R. W. Alley. 1996, Orchard LB $16.99 (978-0-531-08883-8). 32pp. Old Winter is so angry at people criticizing his season that he decides to remain in the North although spring is scheduled to arrive. (Rev: BCCB 12/96; BL 10/1/96; SLJ 12/96)

1565 Ringgold, Faith. *Tar Beach* (PS–2). Illus. 1991, Crown LB $18.99 (978-0-517-58031-8). 32pp. A little girl on the rooftop of her apartment building dreams of soaring over New York City. (Rev: BCCB 3/91; BL 1/1/91; HB 5/91*; SLJ 2/91*)

1566 Roberts, Bethany. *Monster Manners* (PS–2). Illus. by Andrew Glass. 1996, Clarion $15.00 (978-0-395-69850-1). 32pp. A rhyming book that explains basic manners with brilliantly colored illustrations and the antics of three often misbehaving monsters. (Rev: SLJ 4/96)

1567 Roberts, David, and Corina Fletcher. *Ghoul School* (K–4). Illus. 2000, Abrams $17.95 (978-0-8109-4140-3). A pop-up book about a school run by Ms. Vampira where strange things take place, like eating worms for lunch. (Rev: BL 12/1/00)

1568 Robertson, M. P. *The Dragon Snatcher* (PS–2). Illus. 2005, Dial $16.99 (978-0-8037-3103-5). 32pp. George and his dragon sidekick work to foil an evil wizard who's determined to rid the world of dragons; the third installment in a series that began with *The Egg* (2001) and *The Great Dragon Rescue* (2004). (Rev: BL 12/1/05; SLJ 10/05)

1569 Robinson, Fiona. *The Useful Moose: A Truthful, Moose-full Tale* (K–2). Illus. by author. 2004, Abrams $14.95 (978-0-8109-4925-6). Always fond of moose, Molly's affection deepens when a trio visits her apartment and helps her with household chores. (Rev: SLJ 1/05)

1570 Robinson, Sue. *Bear in the Barnyard* (PS–2). Illus. by Tony Morris. 2004, Good Bks. $16.00 (978-1-56148-430-0). A teddy bear thinks he's ready for farm life but gets some surprises. (Rev: SLJ 9/04)

1571 Robinson, Tim. *Tobias, the Quig and the Rumplenut Tree* (PS–4). Illus. by author. 2000, Winslow $16.95 (978-1-890817-20-6). In this fantasy, Tobias must free the quig, an unusual bird, so the bird can spread seeds of the rumplenut tree. (Rev: HBG 10/00; SLJ 10/00)

1572 Robledo, Honorio. *Nico Visits the Moon* (PS–2). Illus. 2001, Cinco Puntos $15.95 (978-0-938317-57-9). 32pp. Baby Nico floats to the moon when he grabs a bunch of balloons intended to hang things out of his reach. (Rev: BL 11/1/01; HBG 3/02; SLJ 12/01)

1573 Robles, Anthony D. *Lakas and the Manilatown Fish / Si Lakas at ang Isdang Manilatown* (K–3). Trans. by Eloisa D. de Jesus and Magdalena de Guzman. Illus. by Carl Angel. 2003, Children's Book Pr. $16.95 (978-0-89239-182-0). 32pp. In this whimsical bilingual (English and Tagalog) story, a young Filipino boy and his father race through the streets of San Francisco in pursuit of a fish that can talk, jump, and play. (Rev: HB 5/03; HBG 10/03; SLJ 10/03)

1574 Rocco, John. *Moonpowder* (PS–1). Illus. by author. 2008, Hyperion $15.99 (978-1-4231-0011-9). 48pp. Eli prides himself on his ability to fix things but suffers from continuing bad dreams until Mr. Moon asks his help repairing the Moonpowder Factory; rich, inventive illustrations add to the story's appeal. (Rev: BL 6/1–15/08; LMC 3/08; SLJ 4/08)

1575 Rohmann, Eric. *Clara and Asha* (PS–2). Illus. 2005, Roaring Brook $16.95 (978-1-59643-031-0). 40pp. This story of a little girl's friendship with an imaginary giant fish named Asha features arresting illustrations. (Rev: BL 7/05; SLJ 8/05)

1576 Root, Phyllis. *Aunt Nancy and Old Man Trouble* (K–2). Illus. by David Parkins. 1996, Candlewick $16.99 (978-1-56402-374-2). 32pp. Aunt Nancy outwits Old Man Trouble by posing a question he can't answer. (Rev: BCCB 3/96; BL 5/1/96; HB 9/96; SLJ 5/96)

1577 Root, Phyllis. *Big Momma Makes the World* (PS–2). Illus. by Helen Oxenbury. 2003, Candlewick $16.99 (978-0-7636-1132-3). 48pp. Glowing illustrations depict the take-charge Big Momma, baby on hip, as she creates the world and admires her work, though she does have to keep an eye on the humans to make sure they "straighten up." (Rev: BCCB 2/03; BL 1/1–15/03*; HB 3/03*; HBG 10/03; SLJ 3/03)

1578 Root, Phyllis. *Grandmother Winter* (PS–2). Illus. by Beth Krommes. 1999, Houghton $16.00 (978-0-395-88399-0). 32pp. When Grandmother Winter shakes out her quilt and causes a snowfall, all nature responds to the coming of winter. (Rev: BCCB 10/99; BL 11/15/99; HB 9/99; HBG 3/00; SLJ 9/99)

1579 Root, Phyllis. *Lucia and the Light* (K–3). Illus. by Mary GrandPré. 2006, Candlewick $16.99 (978-0-7636-2296-1). 32pp. Brave Lucia battles frightening trolls in order to rescue the sun and bring back the daylight that has disappeared from her northern winter. (Rev: BL 12/1/06*; SLJ 12/06)

1580 Rosenthal, Amy Krouse. *Spoon* (PS–1). Illus. by Scott Magoon. 2009, Hyperion $15.99 (978-1-4231-0685-2). 40pp. A spoon called Spoon has self-esteem problems in this humorous insider's look at cutlery. (Rev: BL 12/1/08; SLJ 6/09)

1581 Roth, Susan L. *Grandpa Blows His Penny Whistle Until the Angels Sing* (PS–3). Illus. 2001, Barefoot Books $16.99 (978-1-84148-247-7). 40pp. Using his penny whistle, Grandpa calls on angels to awaken Little Boy James, his grandson, who has fallen from a church roof. (Rev: BL 4/1/01; HBG 10/01; SLJ 5/01*)

1582 Rozen, Anna. *The Merchant of Noises* (K–5). Trans. from French by Carl W. Scarbrough. Illus. by François Avril. 2006, Godine $18.95 (978-1-56792-321-6). Mr. Bing sells strange devices to make odd sounds that children will enjoy hearing and making themselves. (Rev: SLJ 6/07)

1583 Rumford, James. *The Nine Animals and the Well* (1–3). Illus. 2003, Houghton $16.00 (978-0-618-30915-3). 32pp. Nine animals bear birthday gifts for the raja (three almond cakes, four sugar cones), each worried that his gift is not good enough, in this combination of charming text and counting book. (Rev: BL 7/03; HB 5/03; HBG 10/03; SLJ 6/03)

1584 Rusch, Elizabeth. *A Day with No Crayons* (PS–2). Illus. by Chad Cameron. 2007, Rising Moon $15.95 (978-0-87358-910-9). 32pp. When Liza runs out of paper and expands onto the wall, her crayons are confiscated and the world loses its bright colors. (Rev: SLJ 4/08)

1585 Ryan, Pam Muñoz. *Mice and Beans* (PS–2). Illus. by Joe Cepeda. 2001, Scholastic $16.95 (978-0-439-18303-1). 32pp. Readers get a mouse's perspective in this story of mice helping Rosa Maria prepare for her grandchild's birthday celebration that interweaves Spanish expressions. (Rev: BCCB 10/01; BL 9/15/01; HBG 3/02; SLJ 10/01)

1586 Ryder, Joanne. *Rainbow Wings* (K–4). Illus. by Victor Lee. 2000, HarperCollins LB $15.89 (978-0-688-14129-5). 40pp. This fantasy in which children get wings to fly also presents the different kinds of wings found in nature such as those of an owl and a monarch butterfly. (Rev: BL 5/1/00; HBG 10/00; SLJ 5/00)

1587 Ryder, Joanne. *The Snail's Spell* (K–2). Illus. by Lynne Cherry. 1992, Puffin paper $5.99 (978-0-14-050891-8). 32pp. A little boy knows how a snail feels when he shrinks to that size. Originally published in 1982.

1588 Rylant, Cynthia. *Dog Heaven* (PS–1). Illus. 1995, Scholastic $16.95 (978-0-590-41701-3). 32pp. In dog heaven, dogs run and play and wait for their absent friends. (Rev: BCCB 10/95; BL 8/95; HBG 4/04; SLJ 10/95)

1589 Rylant, Cynthia. *The Great Gracie Chase: Stop That Dog!* (PS–1). Illus. by Mark Teague. 2001, Scholastic $15.95 (978-0-590-10041-0). 40pp. Gracie Rose decides to break the rules and take a walk by herself, causing a frantic neighborhood search when she seems to be lost. (Rev: BCCB 3/01; BL 2/15/01; HBG 10/01)

1590 Rylant, Cynthia. *Scarecrow* (K–3). Illus. by Lauren Stringer. 1998, Harcourt $16.00 (978-0-15-201084-3). 40pp. A gentle scarecrow tells about his contented life, how he appreciates nature, and of his many animal friends. (Rev: BCCB 6/98; BL 4/1/98; HBG 10/98; SLJ 4/98)

1591 Rymond, Lynda Gene. *Oscar and the Mooncats* (PS–2). Illus. by Nicoletta Ceccoli. 2007, Houghton $16.00 (978-0-618-56316-6). 40pp. Oscar the cat loves to jump and one night leaps all the way to the moon where he meets some mooncats but chooses to return to his boy. (Rev: BL 10/15/07; SLJ 1/08)

1592 Sabuda, Robert. *The Blizzard's Robe* (K–3). Illus. 1999, Simon & Schuster $16.00 (978-0-689-31988-4). 32pp. In return for the kindness of the people, the monster Blizzard gives them the Northern Lights to illuminate the winter darkness. (Rev: BL 11/15/99; HBG 3/00; SLJ 10/99)

1593 Sabuda, Robert. *Peter Pan: A Classic Collectible Pop-Up* (1–4). Illus. by author. 2008, Simon & Schuster $29.99 (978-0-689-85364-7). 14pp. Striking pop-ups are combined with inset envelopes that retell the original story. (Rev: BLO 12/16/08)

1594 Sage, Angie. *Molly and the Birthday Party* (PS–1). Illus. by author. 2001, Peachtree $9.95 (978-1-56145-248-4). Fuzzy, green Molly goes to Olly's birthday party but is reluctant to hand over his present. She also appears in *Molly at the Dentist* (2001). (Rev: HBG 3/02; SLJ 11/01)

1595 Saltzberg, Barney. *This Is a Great Place for a Hot Dog Stand* (1–3). Illus. 1995, Hyperion LB $15.49 (978-0-7868-2057-3). 32pp. The hot dog stand that the monster Izzy operates is threatened by the construction of a super shopping mall. (Rev: BL 4/15/95; SLJ 5/95)

1596 Santoro, Scott. *Farm-Fresh Cats* (PS–2). Illus. by author. 2006, HarperCollins LB $16.89 (978-0-06-078179-8). Life gets confusing for farmer Ray and his wife Norma when green cats mysteriously turn up in the field where they planted cabbages. (Rev: SLJ 8/06)

1597 Sasso, Sandy Eisenberg. *God Said Amen* (1–3). Illus. by Avi Katz. 2000, Jewish Lights $16.95 (978-1-58023-080-3). Two children are able to settle the differences between their two kingdoms so that each kingdom can profit from the strengths of the other. (Rev: SLJ 3/01)

1598 Satrapi, Marjane. *Monsters Are Afraid of the Moon* (PS). Illus. by author. 2006, Bloomsbury

$15.95 (978-1-58234-744-8). Marie cuts the moon out of the sky and puts it in her bedroom to keep monsters at bay, but this causes widespread unrest among the cat population and the cat king must step in to resolve the situation. (Rev: SLJ 10/06)

1599 Say, Allen. *River Dream* (1–3). Illus. by author. 1988, Houghton $16.00 (978-0-395-48294-0); paper $6.95 (978-0-395-65749-2). 32pp. In a dream, Mark learns you don't need to kill fish to enjoy fishing. (Rev: HB 11/88)

1600 Schaap, Martine. *Mop to the Rescue* (PS–K). Illus. by Alex de Wolf. Series: Mop and Family. 1999, Front St. $15.95 (978-0-8126-0167-1). 40pp. Seven short stories for the very young about a lovable sheepdog named Mop. (Rev: BL 5/1/99; HBG 10/99; SLJ 11/99)

1601 Schaap, Martine. *Mop's Backyard Concert* (PS–1). Illus. by Alex de Wolf. Series: Mop and Family. 2000, McGraw-Hill $12.95 (978-1-57768-892-1). 30pp. Twins Julie and Justin lose their dog Mop in a park only to find him singing in a six-piece band. Also enjoy *Mop's Treasure Hunt*. (Rev: BCCB 1/01; HBG 3/01; SLJ 3/01)

1602 Schachner, Judith Byron. *Yo, Vikings!* (K–3). Illus. 2002, Dutton $16.99 (978-0-525-46889-9). 32pp. In this fantasy, a girl imagines that she is a Viking and when a Viking ship arrives for her, she takes several of her friends on a high adventure. (Rev: BL 6/1–15/02; HBG 10/02; SLJ 8/02)

1603 Schaefer, Lola M. *Frankie Stein* (PS–1). Illus. by Kevan Atteberry. 2007, Marshall Cavendish $14.99 (978-0-7614-5358-1). 32pp. Frankie is born cute and there's little mom and dad can do to make him scary until he figures it out for himself. (Rev: BL 9/15/07; SLJ 9/07)

1604 Schanzer, Rosalyn. *Davy Crockett Saves the World* (K–3). Illus. 2001, HarperCollins LB $17.89 (978-0-688-16992-3). 32pp. Davy Crockett is called upon to battle Halley's Comet in this tall tale rich with colorful illustrations. (Rev: BCCB 2/02; BL 11/15/01; HBG 10/02; SLJ 8/01)

1605 Scheer, Julian. *By the Light of the Captured Moon* (PS–3). Illus. by Ronald Himler. 2001, Holiday House $16.95 (978-0-8234-1624-0). 32pp. Billy captures the moon but soon finds he can't hide it and must let it go again. (Rev: BL 5/1/01; HBG 10/01; SLJ 3/01)

1606 Schertle, Alice. *Little Blue Truck* (1–3). Illus. by Jill McElmurry. 2008, Harcourt $16.00 (978-0-15-205661-2). 32pp. Animals rush to the rescue when a friendly little blue pickup truck gets into trouble, whereas an uppity big dump truck finds itself without support but does learn a valuable lesson. (Rev: BL 4/1/08; HB 5/08; SLJ 7/08)

1607 Schertle, Alice. *Little Blue Truck Leads the Way* (PS). Illus. by Jill McElmurry. 2009, Harcourt $16.00 (978-0-15-206389-4). 40pp. A little blue truck ventures into the city and is uncomfortable until the mayor selects it for a special role in this book whose varying views and bright colors invite preschoolers into a bustling city filled with all kinds of vehicles. (Rev: BL 7/09; SLJ 10/09)

1608 Schneider, Christine. *I'm Bored!* (K–2). Illus. by Hervé Pinel. 2006, Clarion $15.00 (978-0-618-65760-5). 36pp. Charlie is amazed to find that his toys are just as bored as he is and together they stage an elaborate imaginary battle. (Rev: SLJ 4/06)

1609 Schneider, Howie. *Chewy Louie* (PS–1). Illus. 2000, Rising Moon $15.95 (978-0-87358-765-5). 32pp. Louie can't stop chewing things, but when he starts on the family car and the house, his family must act to stop him. (Rev: BL 8/00; HBG 10/00; SLJ 11/00)

1610 Schnitzlein, Danny. *The Monster Who Ate My Peas* (1–4). Illus. by Matt Faulkner. 2001, Peachtree $15.95 (978-1-56145-216-3). A demanding monster asks for a boy's prize possessions in return for eating his peas. (Rev: HBG 3/02; SLJ 1/02)

1611 Schubert, Ingrid, and Dieter Schubert. *Abracadabra* (PS–1). Illus. 1997, Front St. $15.95 (978-1-886910-17-1). 32pp. Macrobius the Magician delights in causing confusion by having animals exchange body parts. (Rev: BL 7/97)

1612 Schubert, Ingrid, and Dieter Schubert. *There's a Crocodile Under My Bed!* (PS–1). Illus. by authors. 2005, Front St. $15.95 (978-1-932425-48-2). Little Peggy overcomes her fears and befriends the crocodile beneath her bed. (Rev: SLJ 12/05)

1613 Schulman, Janet, ed. *The 20th Century Children's Book Treasury: Celebrated Picture Books and Stories to Read Aloud* (PS–3). Illus. 1998, Knopf $40.00 (978-0-679-88647-1). 308pp. This anthology (a good introduction to children's literature for parents) condenses in size and shape 44 important picture books by such artists as Maurice Sendak, Wanda Gág, and Shirley Hughes. (Rev: BL 10/15/98; HB 11/98; HBG 3/99; SLJ 12/98)

1614 Schwab, Eva. *Robert and the Robot* (PS–K). Illus. 2001, Front St. $15.95 (978-1-886910-59-1). 32pp. An alien robot helps Robert clean up his room as a thank you for providing him with batteries. (Rev: BL 7/01; HBG 10/01; SLJ 5/01)

1615 Schwartz, Amy, and Leonard Marcus. *Oscar: The Big Adventure of a Little Sock Monkey* (K–3). Illus. by Amy Schwartz. 2006, HarperCollins $16.99 (978-0-06-072622-5). 32pp. Oscar the sock monkey braves the wilds of New York City to get to his owner, Susie, when she forgets to take an important item to school. (Rev: BL 5/15/06; SLJ 6/06)

1616 Schwartz, Roslyn. *The Mole Sisters and the Piece of Moss* (PS–K). Illus. by author. Series: The Mole Sisters. 1999, Annick LB $14.95 (978-1-55037-583-1); paper $4.95 (978-1-55037-582-4). The mole sisters find an unhappy piece of moss and take it on an adventure. Also use *The Mole Sisters and the Rainy Day* (1999). (Rev: SLJ 2/00)

1617 Schwarz, Viviane. *Timothy and the Strong Pajamas* (PS–2). Illus. by author. 2008, Scholastic $16.99 (978-0-545-03329-9). 40pp. A little lemur named Timothy Smallbeast dons reconditioned pajamas and gains super abilities — until the pajamas rip, his amazing powers evaporate, and he needs help to rescue his toy monkey. (Rev: BCCB 3/08; BL 2/1/08; HB 5/08; LMC 3/08; SLJ 3/08)

1618 Scieszka, Jon. *The Good, the Bad and the Goofy* (2–5). Illus. by Lane Smith. 1992, Viking $15.99 (978-0-670-84380-0). 70pp. There are many near escapes when Joe, Fred, and Sam are taken back in time to 1868 and the days of the Chisholm Trail. (Rev: SLJ 7/92)

1619 Scieszka, Jon. *Smash! Crash!* (PS–K). Illus. by David Gordon. 2008, Simon & Schuster $16.99 (978-1-4169-4133-0). 42pp. Jack Truck and Dump Truck Dan are having fun smashing and crashing when who should turn up but Wrecking Crane Rosie, who actually needs their help to demolish a building. (Rev: BCCB 3/08; BL 11/15/07; SLJ 1/08)

1620 Scruggs, Afi-Odelia. *Jump Rope Magic* (PS–4). Illus. by David Diaz. 2000, Scholastic $16.95 (978-0-590-69327-1). 40pp. This picture book incorporates a number of jump rope rhymes into the story of friends who love skipping rope in spite of a neighbor who hates to hear the noise. (Rev: BCCB 6/00; BL 2/1/00; HBG 10/00; SLJ 4/00)

1621 Seibold, J. Otto. *The Fuchsia Is Now* (PS–K). Illus. by author. 2006, Scholastic $16.99 (978-0-439-63559-2). A little girl named Fuchsia has her wishes granted by a fairy when she adorns a favorite hat with a flower. (Rev: SLJ 5/06)

1622 Selick, Henry. *Moongirl* (K–2). Illus. by Peter Chan. 2006, Candlewick $22.99 (978-0-7636-3068-3). 48pp. Out for a night of fishing with his squirrel friend, Leon finds himself pulled into a magical adventure on the moon; based on the animated short by the same name, this edition includes a DVD. (Rev: BL 11/1/06; SLJ 12/06)

1623 Sendak, Maurice. *Maurice Sendak's Really Rosie* (1–4). Illus. by author. 1975, HarperCollins paper $13.95 (978-0-06-443138-5). 48pp. A book based on the TV presentation, including seven songs used in the program.

1624 Sendak, Maurice. *Outside Over There* (PS–3). Illus. by author. 1981, HarperCollins paper $9.95 (978-0-06-443185-9). 40pp. Goblins steal Ira's baby sister and leave another made of ice.

1625 Sendak, Maurice. *Where the Wild Things Are* (K–3). Illus. by author. 1988, HarperCollins LB $18.89 (978-0-06-025493-3); paper $8.95 (978-0-06-443178-1). 48pp. The few moments' wild reverie of a small unruly boy who has been sent supperless to his room. Caldecott Medal winner, 1964.

1626 Seuss, Dr. *And to Think That I Saw It on Mulberry Street* (K–3). Illus. by author. 1989, Random LB $15.99 (978-0-394-94494-4). 32pp. A rhyme about what Marco saw on Mulberry Street.

1627 Seuss, Dr. *Bartholomew and the Oobleck* (K–2). Illus. by author. 1949, Random LB $12.99 (978-0-394-90075-9). What happens when sticky green stuff begins falling instead of snow? Also use: *McElligot's Pool* (1947).

1628 Seuss, Dr. *The Butter Battle Book* (K–2). Illus. by author. 1984, Random LB $14.99 (978-0-394-96580-2). 48pp. A warning about the nuclear arms race in words and pictures.

1629 Seuss, Dr. *The 500 Hats of Bartholomew Cubbins* (K–2). Illus. by author. 1989, Random $15.99 (978-0-394-94484-5). 48pp. What happened when Bartholomew couldn't take his hat off before the king.

1630 Seuss, Dr. *On Beyond Zebra!* (K–2). Illus. by author. 1955, Random LB $16.99 (978-0-394-90084-1). A nonsense alphabet that begins after Z.

1631 Sharratt, Nick. *The Foggy Foggy Forest* (PS–1). Illus. by author. 2008, Candlewick $12.99 (978-0-7636-3921-1). 32pp. This quirky picture book's effect builds with each turn of a translucent page — what is in this foggy, foggy forest? A fairy queen on a trampoline, Red Riding Hood selling ice cream, Cinderella and Snow White playing with water pistols . . . (Rev: BL 12/1/08)

1632 Shaw-MacKinnon, Margaret. *Tiktala* (1–3). Illus. by Laszlo Gal. 1996, Holiday House $15.95 (978-0-8234-1221-1). 32pp. In this fantasy, an Inuit girl gains sufficient knowledge and wisdom to become a soapstone carver. (Rev: BL 7/96; HB 7/96; SLJ 5/96)

1633 Shea, Bob. *Big Plans* (K–3). Illus. by Lane Smith. 2008, Hyperion $17.99 (978-1-4231-1100-9). 48pp. A little boy in an empty classroom dreams about impressing the world with his big plans. (Rev: BL 2/15/08; LMC 1/08; SLJ 6/08)

1634 Shea, Pegi Deitz. *The Boy and the Spell* (K–3). Illus. by Serena Riglietti. Series: Musical Stories. 2007, Pumpkin House $16.95 (978-0-964601-04-8). 32pp. When Thomas has a tantrum in his bedroom, his various possessions rebel and set out to teach him a lesson; based on the story line of the opera *L'Enfant et les Sortilèges* with music by Maurice Ravel and libretto by Colette. (Rev: BL 4/1/07)

1635 Shields, Carol Diggory. *Colors* (1–3). Illus. by Svjetlan Junakovic. Series: Animagicals. 2000, Handprint $9.95 (978-1-929766-04-8). 24pp. Poems, riddles, illustrations, and flaps are used imaginatively to present colors. Also use in a similar format: *Music* (2000). (Rev: BL 1/1–15/01; HBG 3/01; SLJ 12/00)

1636 Shields, Carol Diggory. *Food Fight!* (PS–2). Illus. by Doreen Gay-Kassel. 2002, Handprint $15.95 (978-1-929766-29-1). Pun-filled fun for the contents of the kitchen while the humans are asleep. (Rev: HBG 3/03; SLJ 10/02)

1637 Shields, Carol Diggory. *On the Go* (PS–2). Illus. by Svjetlan Junakovic. Series: Animagicals. 2001, Handprint $9.95 (978-1-929766-14-7). This tall, narrow book uses rhyming riddles, illustrations, and flaps to tickle young imaginations about animal movements. Also use *Patterns* (2001). (Rev: HBG 10/01; SLJ 8/01)

1638 Shields, Gillian. *The Perfect Bear* (PS–1). Illus. by Gary Blythe. 2008, Simon & Schuster $16.99 (978-1-4169-5363-0). 26pp. A white teddy bear who is proud of his looks is upset when his young owner gets him dirty, but when he becomes lost, he realizes how much he misses her. (Rev: SLJ 4/08)

1639 Shields, Gillian. *Tom's Tree* (PS–2). Illus. by Gemma Raynor. 2009, Good Bks. $16.95 (978-1-56148-663-2). 32pp. As a boy, Tom plants a tree and dreams about its exotic future, but the tree grows slowly and Tom moves away; when he returns with his own son, he is pleased that the boy experiences the same dreams. (Rev: BL 5/1/09; SLJ 6/09)

1640 Shulevitz, Uri. *When I Wore My Sailor Suit* (K–3). Illus. by author. 2009, Farrar $16.95 (978-0-374-34749-9). 32pp. A boy's imagination sets sail on a neighbor's model ship. (Rev: BL 6/1–15/09; SLJ 8/09)

1641 Siddals, Mary M. *I'll Play With You* (PS–1). Illus. by David Wisniewski. 2000, Clarion $14.00 (978-0-395-90373-5). 28pp. Children invite various aspects of the natural world like the sun and clouds to come and play with them. (Rev: BCCB 12/00; BL 10/1/00; HBG 3/01; SLJ 11/00)

1642 Silverman, Erica. *Big Pumpkin* (PS–1). Illus. by S. D. Schindler. 1992, Macmillan $16.00 (978-0-02-782683-8). 32pp. A witch gets help from several friends, including a ghost, a vampire, and a bat, to pick a huge pumpkin in her garden. (Rev: BL 9/1/92; HB 3/93; SLJ 9/92)

1643 Sís, Peter. *Ballerina!* (PS–K). Illus. 2001, Greenwillow $17.99 (978-0-688-17944-1). 24pp. In this fantasy, little Terry acts out her dreams of being the "best ballerina of all." (Rev: BCCB 5/01; BL 4/1/01; HBG 10/01; SLJ 4/01)

1644 Sís, Peter. *Fire Truck* (PS–K). Illus. 1998, Greenwillow $16.99 (978-0-688-15878-1). 24pp. A young boy becomes so obsessed with fire trucks that he becomes one. Only the lure of pancakes can bring him back to his little-boy body. (Rev: BCCB 1/99; BL 9/15/98; HB 9/98; HBG 3/99; SLJ 9/98)

1645 Sís, Peter. *Madlenka* (PS–3). Illus. 2000, Farrar $17.00 (978-0-374-39969-6). 48pp. When Madlenka finds she has a loose tooth, she wanders through her culturally diverse neighborhood telling everyone about her condition in this, at times surreal, picture book. (Rev: BCCB 10/00; BL 9/1/00; HB 9/00; HBG 3/01; SLJ 10/00)

1646 Sís, Peter. *Madlenka's Dog* (PS–2). Illus. 2002, Farrar $17.00 (978-0-374-34699-7). 40pp. A flap book in which many of Madlenka's friends imagine what her invisible dog looks like. (Rev: BCCB 6/02; BL 4/1/02*; HB 3/02*; HBG 10/02; SLJ 4/02*)

1647 Slater, Dashka. *Firefighters in the Dark* (PS–1). Illus. by Nicoletta Ceccoli. 2006, Houghton $16.00 (978-0-618-55459-1). With sirens sounding in the distance, a young girl imagines the rescues that are under way — saving princesses, rescuing boys who have bounced into space . . . (Rev: SLJ 10/06)

1648 Smith, Lane. *Pinocchio the Boy; or, Incognito in Collidi* (K–3). Illus. 2002, Viking $16.99 (978-0-670-03585-4). 48pp. What happens after Pinocchio is turned into a real boy is the subject of this inventive picture book. (Rev: BL 8/02; HB 9/02; HBG 3/03; SLJ 9/02*)

1649 Smith, Linda. *Mrs. Biddlebox* (PS–2). Illus. by Marla Frazee. 2002, HarperCollins LB $17.89 (978-0-06-029782-4). 32pp. Mrs. Biddlebox is having a bad day and decides to cook it away, making a cake of the various components — gloom, fog, sky, and so on — and eating the result before happily greeting the night. (Rev: BCCB 1/03; BL 11/15/02; HB 11/02; HBG 3/03; SLJ 10/02)

1650 Smith, Stu. *Goldilocks and the Three Martians* (PS–2). Illus. by Michael Garland. 2004, Dutton $15.99 (978-0-525-46972-8). In search of a planet that's just right, Goldilocks investigates a house on Mars. (Rev: SLJ 8/04)

1651 Sorel, Edward. *Johnny on the Spot* (K–4). Illus. 1998, Simon & Schuster $16.00 (978-0-689-81293-4). 32pp. When Johnny's ancient radio starts receiving tomorrow's news, he becomes an overnight sensation. (Rev: BL 8/98; HBG 3/99; SLJ 11/98)

1652 Spalding, Andrea. *It's Raining, It's Pouring* (PS–3). Illus. by Leslie Elizabeth Watts. 2001, Orca $15.95 (978-1-55143-186-4). 32pp. A little girl sets out into the clouds on a thundery day to find the old man mentioned in the song and he rewards her kindness by stopping the storm. (Rev: BL 10/1/01; HBG 10/02; SLJ 9/01)

1653 Spalding, Andrea. *Sarah May and the New Red Dress* (K–3). Illus. by Janet Wilson. 1999, Orca $14.95 (978-1-55143-117-8). A little girl wants a red dress and with the help of the West Wind, she gets her wish. (Rev: BL 2/1/99; HBG 10/99; SLJ 6/99)

1654 Spangler, Brie. *The Grumpy Dump Truck* (PS–2). Illus. by author. 2009, Knopf $15.99 (978-0-375-85839-0). 40pp. Bertand the dump trunk is cranky and clanky until he meets a porcupine construction worker. (Rev: BL 6/1–15/09; SLJ 6/09)

1655 Speck, Katie. *Maybelle in the Soup* (1–3). Illus. by Paul Ratz de Tagyos. 2007, Holt $15.95 (978-0-8050-8092-6). 58pp. Maybelle the cockroach decides to sample some soup from the Peabodys' table and her appearance sets off a chaotic melee that ends with surprisingly happy results for herself and her friend Henry the flea. (Rev: BL 11/15/07; HB 11/07; SLJ 12/07)

1656 Sperring, Mark. *Find-a-Saurus* (PS–1). Illus. by Alexandra Steele-Morgan. 2003, Scholastic $15.95 (978-0-439-53162-7). Despite his mother's insistence that all dinosaurs are extinct, Marty is convinced that the creatures are just good at hiding, so he sets off to find one. (Rev: HBG 4/04; SLJ 1/04)

1657 Sperring, Mark. *Mermaid Dreams* (PS–K). Illus. by Pope Twins. 2006, Scholastic $16.99 (978-0-439-79610-1). As her mother gets her ready for bed, young Meriam recounts the undersea adventures of her day. (Rev: SLJ 8/06)

1658 Sperring, Mark. *Wanda's First Day* (K–2). Illus. by Kate Pope. 2004, Scholastic $15.95 (978-0-439-62773-3). 32pp. On her first day in a new school, Wanda, a youthful witch, finds herself the only pupil of her kind in a classroom full of fairies. (Rev: BL 8/04; SLJ 7/04)

1659 Spinelli, Eileen. *Sophie's Masterpiece: A Spider's Tale* (PS–2). Illus. by Jane Dyer. 2001, Simon & Schuster $16.00 (978-0-689-80112-9). 32pp. As her last project, an unappreciated spider named Sophie weaves a beautiful baby blanket for a pregnant woman. (Rev: BL 4/15/01*; HB 7/01; HBG 10/01; SLJ 5/01)

1660 Steig, William. *Caleb and Kate* (PS–3). Illus. by author. 1977, Farrar paper $5.95 (978-0-374-

41038-4). 32pp. Because he constantly quarrels with his wife, Caleb is transformed into a dog by a witch.

1661 Steig, William. *Wizzil* (K–4). Illus. by Quentin Blake. 2000, Farrar $16.00 (978-0-374-38466-1). 32pp. A rollicking story about Wizzil the witch and her revenge for almost being killed by farmer DeWitt Frimp. (Rev: BCCB 10/00; BL 10/1/00*; HB 7/00; HBG 3/01; SLJ 8/00)

1662 Stein, David Ezra. *Monster Hug!* (PS–K). Illus. by author. 2007, Putnam $15.99 (978-0-399-24637-1). 32pp. A boisterous romp in which two large monsters have great fun playing together before morphing into human children. (Rev: BL 10/15/07; SLJ 9/07)

1663 Stein, Mathilde. *Mine!* (PS–2). Illus. by Mies van Hout. 2007, Boyds Mills $16.95 (978-1-59078-506-5). A greedy ghost finally learns to share when he is befriended by Charlotte, the little girl whose house he is "haunting." (Rev: SLJ 8/07)

1664 Stewart, Joel. *Dexter Bexley and the Big Blue Beastie* (PS–2). Illus. 2007, Holiday $16.95 (978-0-8234-2068-1). 32pp. Dexter Bexley runs into a voracious Big Blue Beastie who threatens to eat the boy, but Dexter resourcefully comes up with one idea after another to keep the creature otherwise occupied. (Rev: BL 4/1/07)

1665 Stewart, Sarah. *The Money Tree* (PS). Illus. by David Small. 1991, Farrar $16.00 (978-0-374-35014-7). 32pp. Miss McGillicuddy's pleasant life is interrupted when a strange tree begins blooming with paper money. (Rev: BCCB 12/91*; BL 10/15/91; HB 1/92; SLJ 1/92)

1666 Stewig, John W. *Clever Gretchen* (K–3). Illus. by Patricia Wittmann. 2000, Marshall Cavendish $15.95 (978-0-7614-5066-5). 32pp. In order to win the bride of his choice, young Hans must promise to obey a goat-footed man after a period of seven years. (Rev: BL 9/15/00; HBG 3/01; SLJ 10/00)

1667 Stockton, Frank R. *The Bee-Man of Orn* (1–3). Illus. by P. J. Lynch. 2004, Candlewick $17.99 (978-0-7636-2239-8). 48pp. The century-old children's fantasy about an old beekeeper who seeks his true origins is newly illustrated in a large-format picture book. (Rev: BL 2/15/04*; SLJ 3/04)

1668 Stone, Phoebe. *When the Wind Bears Go Dancing* (PS–1). Illus. 1997, Little, Brown $15.95 (978-0-316-81701-1). 32pp. While the wind makes noises outside, a little girl dreams of dancing with five white bears in the midnight sky. (Rev: BL 1/1–15/98; HBG 3/98; SLJ 1/98)

1669 Strom, Maria Diaz. *Rainbow Joe and Me* (1–3). Illus. 1999, Lee & Low $15.95 (978-1-880000-93-9). 32pp. In this picture book, using African American characters, a blind musician shows painter Eloise how he creates colors through his music. (Rev: BL 11/15/99; HBG 3/00; SLJ 11/99)

1670 Sturges, Philemon. *Crocky Dilly* (1–4). Illus. by Paige Miglio. 1998, Museum of Fine Arts, Boston $14.95 (978-0-87846-458-6). 32pp. This story tells how, in ancient Egypt, the crocodile became known as the Queen of the Nile. (Rev: BL 4/1/99; SLJ 5/99)

1671 Sturgis, Alexander. *Dan's Angel: A Detective's Guide to the Language of Paintings* (PS–3). Illus. by Lauren Child. 2003, Kane $16.95 (978-1-929132-47-8). Young Dan likes mysteries and is pleased when Fra Angelico's Angel Gabriel steps out of "The Annunciation" and helps him to find the stories hidden within the famous paintings. (Rev: HBG 4/04; SLJ 11/03)

1672 Suen, Anastasia. *Raise the Roof!* (PS–1). Illus. by Elwood H. Smith. 2003, Viking $15.99 (978-0-670-89282-2). 32pp. A house is constructed despite a dog's "help" in this picture book with cartoon-like, stylized illustrations. (Rev: BCCB 2/03; BL 2/15/03; HB 3/03; HBG 10/03; SLJ 2/03)

1673 Sussman, Michael. *Otto Grows Down* (PS–1). Illus. by Scott Magoon. 2009, Sterling $14.95 (978-1-4027-4703-8). 36pp. On his 6th birthday, Otto wishes his baby sister had never been born and the clock starts moving backward, taking Otto along with it. (Rev: BL 4/15/09; LMC 10/09; SLJ 4/09)

1674 Tauss, Marc. *Superhero* (PS–2). Illus. 2005, Scholastic $16.99 (978-0-439-62734-4). 40pp. Maleek, an African American boy with a secret identity, springs into action when his city's parks and playgrounds start mysteriously disappearing. (Rev: BL 8/05; SLJ 12/05)

1675 Tazewell, Charles. *The Littlest Angel* (PS–3). Illus. by Paul Micich. 1991, Ideals $16.95 (978-0-8249-8516-5). 32pp. A young angel in heaven keeps getting into trouble because there is nothing to do. (Rev: BL 9/15/91; SLJ 10/98)

1676 Teague, Mark. *The Secret Shortcut* (PS–3). Illus. 1996, Scholastic $14.95 (978-0-590-67714-1). 32pp. Pirates, space aliens, and a plague of frogs are only three of the obstacles that prevent Wendell and Floyd from getting to school on time. (Rev: BL 9/15/96; SLJ 11/96)

1677 Tellis, Annabel. *If My Dad Were a Dog* (PS–2). Photos by Tracy Morgan. Illus. by author. 2007, Scholastic $16.99 (978-0-439-91387-4). A child imagines what a day would be like if Daddy were a dog. Photographs enhanced with cartoon drawings add to the zaniness. (Rev: SLJ 5/07)

1678 Thayer, Jane. *Gus Loves His Happy Home* (PS–2). Illus. by Seymour Fleishman. 1989, Shoe String LB $17.50 (978-0-208-02249-3). With time on his hands, Gus the Friendly Ghost goes for a ride on the tail of a kite. (Rev: BL 2/15/90; SLJ 2/90)

1679 Thomas, Peggy. *Joshua the Giant Frog* (K–3). Illus. by Cat B. Smith. 2005, Pelican $15.95 (978-1-58980-267-4). A huge green frog turns out to be very useful in this tall tale set on the Erie Canal, as he pulls barges and deepens the canal. (Rev: SLJ 4/05)

1680 Thomas, Shelley Moore. *A Cold Winter's Good Knight* (PS–2). Illus. by Jennifer Plecas. 2008, Dutton $15.99 (978-0-525-47964-2). 32pp. The three little dragons who have previously appeared in an easy-reader series attend a fancy ball and learn about manners in this picture book. (Rev: BL 2/1/09; HB 1/09; SLJ 12/08)

1681 Thomas, Shelley Moore. *Take Care, Good Knight* (PS–2). Illus. by Paul Meisel. 2006, Dutton

$15.99 (978-0-525-47695-5). 32pp. When a wizard leaves three little dragons in charge of his cats while he's away, disaster threatens until the Good Knight shows up to set things right; a large-format picture-book featuring the characters from the Easy Readers series. (Rev: BL 9/15/06)

1682 Thompson, Richard. *The Follower* (PS–3). Illus. by Martin Springett. 2000, Fitzhenry & Whiteside $15.95 (978-1-55041-532-2). 32pp. A picture-book poem about a witch who is being followed by a creature that the reader can detect hidden in the illustrations. (Rev: BL 12/15/00; SLJ 12/00)

1683 Tibo, Gilles. *Simon and the Snowflakes* (PS–1). Illus. 1991, Tundra paper $4.95 (978-0-88776-274-1). 24pp. Young Simon likes to count snowflakes as they come down. (Rev: BL 12/15/88; SLJ 4/89)

1684 Tillman, Nancy. *On the Night You Were Born* (PS). Illus. by author. 2006, Feiwel & Friends $16.95 (978-0-312-34606-5). 32pp. The wind, rain, moon, and a variety of creatures big and small welcome the wondrous arrival of a baby, and celebrate its uniqueness. (Rev: BL 12/1/06)

1685 Timmers, Leo. *Happy with Me* (K–2). Illus. 2002, Tallfellow/Smallfellow $16.95 (978-1-931290-08-1). 32pp. After considering the ups and downs of being different animals, a little boy decides he's happy being himself in this colorful picture book. (Rev: BL 7/02)

1686 Tompert, Ann. *Grandfather Tang's Story* (K–3). Illus. by Robert Andrew Parker. 1990, Crown LB $17.99 (978-0-517-57272-6). 32pp. As a Chinese grandfather tells his granddaughter a tale about two foxes, he arranges Chinese puzzles to form the animals' shapes. (Rev: BCCB 4/90; BL 4/15/90; SLJ 5/90)

1687 Tripp, Paul. *Tubby the Tuba* (K–3). Illus. by Henry Cole. 2006, Dutton $16.99 (978-0-525-47717-4). 32pp. With a little help from a friendly frog, Tubby the tuba shows the orchestra that he can play melodies just as well as any other instrument; packaged with a CD, this is a story that first appeared in a film in 1947. (Rev: BL 12/1/06; SLJ 11/06) ☊

1688 Tzannes, Robin. *Professor Puffendorf's Secret Potions* (K–4). Illus. by Korky Paul. 1992, Checkerboard $16.95 (978-1-56288-267-9). 36pp. A scientist's secret potions are used in her absence by her lazy assistant, Slag. (Rev: BL 2/1/93)

1689 Ungerer, Tomi. *Tortoni Tremolo: The Cursed Musician* (K–3). Illus. 1998, Roberts Rinehart $16.95 (978-1-57098-226-2). 32pp. A fantasy about a musician whose musical notes turn into edible nuggets. (Rev: BL 1/1–15/99; HBG 10/99)

1690 Uribe, Veronica. *Buzz, Buzz, Buzz* (PS–1). Trans. by Veronica Uribe and Elisa Amado. Illus. by Gloria Calderon. 2001, Douglas & McIntyre $15.95 (978-0-88899-430-1). 32pp. A brother and sister disturbed by an annoying mosquito seek help from the animals in the jungle. (Rev: BL 7/01; HBG 10/01; SLJ 8/01)

1691 Van Allsburg, Chris. *Bad Day at Riverbend* (K–3). Illus. 1995, Houghton $19.95 (978-0-395-67347-8). 32pp. This book, set in the Old West, is about a strange light that freezes everything that it touches. (Rev: BCCB 9/95; BL 10/15/95; SLJ 10/95)

1692 Van Allsburg, Chris. *Ben's Dream* (2–4). Illus. by author. 1982, Houghton $16.95 (978-0-395-32084-6). 32pp. Ben dreams that he is in a flood and passing the great landmarks of the world.

1693 Van Allsburg, Chris. *Jumanji* (1–4). Illus. by author. 1981, Houghton $18.95 (978-0-395-30448-8). A board game that two children play brings out a jungle world. Caldecott Medal winner, 1982.

1694 Van Allsburg, Chris. *Just a Dream* (K–3). Illus. 1990, Houghton $18.95 (978-0-395-53308-6). 48pp. Walter, who doesn't recycle his trash, takes a trip into the future and finds the situation bleak. (Rev: BCCB 11/90; BL 10/15/90; HB 1/91; SLJ 12/90)

1695 Van Allsburg, Chris. *The Stranger* (K–2). Illus. by author. 1986, Houghton $18.95 (978-0-395-42331-8). 32pp. Farmer Bailey hits a man with his car and brings him home. Autumn is unaccountably delayed until the strange man departs. (Rev: BL 10/1/86; HB 11/86; SLJ 11/86)

1696 Van Allsburg, Chris. *The Widow's Broom* (K–2). Illus. 1992, Houghton $18.95 (978-0-395-64051-7). 32pp. In this tale of good and evil, a witch's broom falls from the sky with the witch still on it. (Rev: BCCB 10/92*; BL 9/15/92*; HB 1/93; SLJ 11/92*)

1697 Van Allsburg, Chris. *The Wretched Stone* (K–3). Illus. 1991, Houghton $18.95 (978-0-395-53307-9). 32pp. A magical stone that some sailors find turns them into monkeys. (Rev: BCCB 11/91; BL 10/1/91; HB 1/92*; SLJ 11/91)

1698 Van Allsburg, Chris. *Zathura: A Space Adventure* (K–3). Illus. 2002, Houghton $18.00 (978-0-618-25396-8). 32pp. Twenty years after the publication of *Jumanji*, this sequel rockets Danny and Walter Budwing off to an exciting adventure on the planet Zathura. (Rev: BL 11/15/02; HB 11/02; HBG 3/03; SLJ 11/02)

1699 Van Camp, Richard. *A Man Called Raven* (K–3). Illus. by George Littlechild. 1997, Children's Book Pr. $15.95 (978-0-89239-144-8). A man appears to two boys who have injured a raven and tells them the story of the terrible consequences that befell a man who did the same thing. (Rev: SLJ 6/97)

1700 Vande Velde, Vivian. *Troll Teacher* (PS–3). Illus. by Mary Jane Auch. 2000, Holiday House $16.95 (978-0-8234-1503-8). 32pp. Elizabeth and her classmates can't convince anyone that their new teacher, Miss Turtledove, is really a mean old troll. (Rev: BL 11/15/00; HBG 3/01; SLJ 10/00)

1701 Van Dusen, Chris. *Down to the Sea with Mr. Magee* (K–4). Illus. 2000, Chronicle $13.95 (978-0-8118-2499-6). 32pp. Mr. Magee and his little dog, Dee, are shipwrecked by a playful whale and find themselves on top of a huge spruce tree. (Rev: BCCB 5/00; BL 6/1–15/00; HBG 10/00; SLJ 5/00)

1702 Van Dusen, Chris. *If I Built a Car* (K–2). Illus. 2005, Dutton $15.99 (978-0-525-47400-5). 32pp. Wonderful parodies of 1950s concepts of the future illustrate a boy's over-the-top plans to redesign the boring family car. (Rev: BL 5/15/05)

1703 Vaughan, Richard Lee. *Eagle Boy: A Pacific Northwest Native Tale* (PS–3). Illus. by Lee Christiansen. 2000, Sasquatch $16.95 (978-1-57061-171-1). 32pp. When Eagle Boy is left behind by his people, the eagles with whom he has shared his fishing catch bring him food. (Rev: BL 1/1–15/01; HBG 10/01; SLJ 12/00)

1704 Vigna, Judith. *Boot Weather* (PS–K). Illus. by author. 1989, Whitman LB $14.95 (978-0-8075-0837-4). 32pp. Kim puts on her boots to play in the snow and imagines all sorts of exciting adventures. (Rev: BCCB 2/89; BL 3/1/89; SLJ 5/89)

1705 Vivian, Bart. *Imagine* (1–3). Illus. 1998, Beyond Words $14.95 (978-1-885223-72-2). 32pp. This book invites daydreamers to think about what everyday objects could become and what the future might bring — with a little imagination. (Rev: BL 10/1/98; HBG 3/99; SLJ 12/98)

1706 Voake, Steve. *Daisy Dawson Is on Her Way!* (2–4). Illus. by Jessica Meserve. 2008, Candlewick $14.99 (978-0-7636-3740-8). 112pp. On her way to school, trying not to be late as usual, Daisy Dawson meets a butterfly that bestows on her the ability to communicate with animals — and many adventures ensue. (Rev: BCCB 6/08; BL 5/1/08; LMC 10/08; SLJ 4/08)

1707 von Olfers, Sibylle. *Mother Earth and Her Children* (PS–1). Trans. by Jack Zipes. Illus. by Sieglinde Schoen Smith. 2007, Breckling $17.95 (978-1-933308-18-0). 32pp. A translation of a German story about Mother Earth's children who sleep underground during the winter and emerge in the spring; illustrated with sections of a quilt that appears in full at the end. (Rev: BLO 1/15/08; SLJ 2/08)

1708 Vulliamy, Clara. *Small* (PS–K). Illus. 2002, Clarion $15.00 (978-0-618-19459-9). 32pp. When Tom has an overnight visit with his grandmother, he forgets his stuffed mouse, Small, but Small manages to make his way to Granny's. (Rev: BCCB 4/02; BL 4/15/02; HBG 10/02; SLJ 4/02)

1709 Waldman, Neil. *The Starry Night* (PS–2). Illus. 1999, Boyds Mills $16.95 (978-1-56397-736-7). 32pp. Bernard takes an artist named Vincent around New York City to find a suitable scene to paint, and in turn, Vincent takes Bernard to the Museum of Modern Art and shows him *Starry Night* before disappearing. Could it have been Vincent van Gogh? (Rev: BCCB 1/00; BL 11/1/99; HBG 3/00; SLJ 10/99)

1710 Wallace, Ian. *The Sleeping Porch* (K–2). Illus. by author. 2008, Groundwood $18.95 (978-0-88899-826-2). 32pp. A boy and a cat have wonderful adventures in this sleep fantasy with stunning artwork. (Rev: LMC 3/09; SLJ 9/08)

1711 Walter, Mildred P. *Brother to the Wind* (K–2). Illus. by Leo Dillon and Diane Dillon. 1985, Lothrop LB $15.89 (978-0-688-03812-0). 32pp. A folklike tale set in Africa about a boy who wants to fly. (Rev: BCCB 3/85; HB 7/85; SLJ 5/85)

1712 Walton, Rick. *Noah's Square Dance* (PS–3). Illus. by Thor Wickstrom. 1995, Lothrop $16.00 (978-0-688-11186-1). 32pp. Noah acts as caller during a square dance involving the animals on his ark. (Rev: BL 9/1/95; SLJ 10/95)

1713 Ward, Nick. *Farmer George and the Hungry Guests* (PS–K). Illus. 2001, Pavilion $14.95 (978-1-86205-436-3). 32pp. Farmer George investigates his missing breakfast ingredients and finds that four hungry foxes have helped themselves. (Rev: BL 4/15/01)

1714 Warnes, Tim. *Happy Birthday, Dotty!* (PS–1). Illus. by author. 2003, Tiger Tales $15.95 (978-1-58925-026-0). Dotty the dog is having a birthday, but her friends are nowhere to be found; after noticing a trail of arrows, she follows them to one gift after another and, finally, to a gathering of friends all ready to celebrate with her. (Rev: SLJ 4/03)

1715 Wayland, April Halprin. *To Rabbittown* (PS–1). Illus. by Robin Spowart. 1989, Scholastic paper $3.95 (978-0-590-44777-5). 32pp. A poem about a girl and her pet rabbit and their journey. (Rev: BL 2/1/89; SLJ 4/89)

1716 Weilerstein, Sadie R. *K'tonton's Sukkot Adventure* (PS–3). Illus. by Joe Boddy. 1993, Jewish Publication Soc. $9.95 (978-0-8276-0502-2). A tiny boy disobeys his father and attends Sukkot services in the synagogue by hiding in a small box. (Rev: SLJ 3/94)

1717 Welling, Peter J. *Andrew McGroundhog and His Shady Shadow* (1–3). Illus. by author. 2001, Pelican $15.95 (978-1-56554-711-7). Andrew McGroundhog's shadow is cold and wants Andrew to hibernate for the winter. (Rev: HBG 10/01; SLJ 8/01)

1718 Wells, Philip. *Daddy Island* (PS–K). Illus. by Niki Daly. 2001, Barefoot Books $15.99 (978-1-84148-197-5). 24pp. A boy imagines himself as all kinds of things — a crab, a wild storm, a rock — as he completes the mundane task of getting ready for bed. (Rev: BL 11/15/01; HBG 3/02; SLJ 12/01)

1719 Westcott, Nadine Bernard. *The Giant Vegetable Garden* (PS–K). Illus. by author. 1981, Little, Brown $14.95 (978-0-316-93129-8); paper $4.95 (978-0-316-93130-4). 32pp. A mayor gets his town's residents to grow large vegetables.

1720 Whatley, Bruce. *Clinton Gregory's Secret* (K–2). Illus. by author. 2008, Abrams $15.95 (978-0-8109-9364-8). 32pp. Clinton Gregory has wonderful, adventurous dreams every night. (Rev: BL 3/1/08; LMC 3/08; SLJ 5/08)

1721 Whelan, Gloria. *The Miracle of Saint Nicholas* (PS–3). Illus. by Judith G. Brown. 1997, Ignatius $14.95 (978-1-883937-18-8). 32pp. After the end of Communism, a young Russian boy who vows to clean up his local church is helped by a miracle. (Rev: BL 11/1/97; HBG 3/98)

1722 White, Amanda. *Sand Sister* (PS–1). Illus. by Yuri Morales. 2004, Barefoot Books $16.99 (978-1-84148-617-8). 32pp. A lonely little girl draws a figure in the sand that promptly comes to life only to disappear after a happy day together, but the girl's sadness is alleviated by the news that she will soon have a sibling of her own. (Rev: BL 3/15/04; SLJ 10/04)

1723 Whybrow, Ian. *Sammy and the Dinosaurs* (PS–2). Illus. by Adrian Reynolds. 1999, Orchard $15.95 (978-0-531-30207-1). A charming fantasy about a young boy's attachment to his toy dinosaurs and how he accidentally lost and recovered them. (Rev: BCCB 9/99; HB 9/99; HBG 3/00; SLJ 9/99)

1724 Whybrow, Ian. *Sammy and the Robots* (PS–1). Illus. by Adrian Reynolds. 2001, Scholastic $15.95 (978-0-531-30327-6). Sammy's robot is off being mended and when Sammy's grandmother must go into the hospital, Sammy realizes she needs a robot to look after her. (Rev: HBG 10/01; SLJ 7/01)

1725 Wiesner, David. *June 29, 1999* (PS–3). Illus. 1992, Houghton $16.00 (978-0-395-59762-0). 32pp. Holly sends small growing vegetables into space in balloons and reaps a fantastic harvest. (Rev: BCCB 11/92; BL 10/15/92; HB 1/93*; SLJ 11/92*)

1726 Wiesner, David. *Sector 7* (K–4). Illus. 1999, Clarion $16.00 (978-0-395-74656-1). 48pp. In an almost wordless fantasy, a young boy who enjoys drawing is taken to a cloud terminal where clouds are hoping they will be made into new exciting shapes. Caldecott Honor Book, 2000. (Rev: BCCB 1/00*; BL 9/15/99; HB 9/99; HBG 3/00; SLJ 9/99)

1727 Wiesner, David, and Kim Kahng. *The Loathsome Dragon* (PS–2). Illus. by David Wiesner. 2005, Clarion $16.00 (978-0-618-54359-5). 32pp. A revised edition of the fairy tale about a beautiful princess who is turned into a dragon by her jealous stepmother, the queen, and must await the return of her wandering brother to free her from the evil spell. (Rev: BL 2/15/05; SLJ 4/05) [398.2]

1728 Wild, Margaret. *Midnight Babies* (PS–K). Illus. by Ann James. 2001, Clarion $15.00 (978-0-618-10412-3). 32pp. At night, Baby Brenda slips past sleeping Mom and Dad and heads for the Midnight Cafe where the dancing is about to begin. (Rev: BL 2/15/01*; HBG 10/01)

1729 Wild, Margaret. *The Pocket Dogs* (PS–K). Illus. by Stephen M. King. 2001, Scholastic $15.95 (978-0-439-23973-8). 32pp. Little dogs Biff and Buff are carried around in the pockets of their master's coat, but Biff slips through a hole in his pocket and finds he is lost in a huge grocery store. (Rev: BCCB 3/01; BL 2/1/01*; HBG 10/01)

1730 Willard, Nancy. *The Sorcerer's Apprentice* (1–4). Illus. by Leo Dillon and Diane Dillon. 1993, Scholastic $16.95 (978-0-590-47329-3). 32pp. Sylvia, the sorcerer's apprentice, is overcome when she is directed to make clothes for the many creatures found in the magician's house. (Rev: BCCB 1/94; BL 11/1/93; SLJ 1/94)

1731 Williams, Arlene. *Dragon Soup* (K–3). Illus. by Sally J. Smith. 1996, H. J. Kramer $15.95 (978-0-915811-63-2). 32pp. Tonlu visits the Cloud Dragons to get help in avoiding an arranged marriage. (Rev: BL 7/96; SLJ 6/96)

1732 Williams, Arlene. *Tiny Tortilla* (PS). Illus. by G. Brian Karas. 2005, Dutton $15.99 (978-0-525-47382-4). 32pp. Hungry Juan Carlos discovers that his tiny piece of tortilla has magical properties. (Rev: BL 7/05; SLJ 8/05)

1733 Williams, C. K. *How the Nobble Was Finally Found* (K–2). Illus. by Stephen Gammell. 2009, Harcourt $17.00 (978-0-15-205460-1). 40pp. In which a winged, long-eared creature who spends a lot of time in the space between Wednesday and Thursday, and with no experience with humans, ventures into the real world and finds friends. (Rev: BL 6/1–15/09; SLJ 9/09)

1734 Williams, Linda. *The Little Old Lady Who Was Not Afraid of Anything* (PS–1). Illus. by Megan Lloyd. 1986, HarperCollins LB $17.89 (978-0-690-04586-4); paper $6.99 (978-0-06-443183-5). 32pp. The scary tale of a little old woman who comes upon two big shoes in the forest going clomp clomp all by themselves. (Rev: BCCB 10/86; BL 10/1/86; SLJ 1/87)

1735 Willis, Jeanne. *The Boy Who Thought He Was a Teddy Bear* (PS–2). Illus. by Susan Varley. 2002, Peachtree $15.95 (978-1-56145-270-5). Three bears bring up a little boy as if he were their own. (Rev: HBG 3/03; SLJ 12/02)

1736 Willis, Jeanne. *Do Little Mermaids Wet Their Beds?* (PS–1). Illus. by Penelope Jossen. 2001, Whitman $15.95 (978-0-8075-1668-3). 32pp. With a little help from a mermaid, 4-year-old Cecelia stops wetting her bed. (Rev: BL 6/1–15/01; HBG 3/02; SLJ 5/01)

1737 Wilson, Sarah. *George Hogglesberry: Grade School Alien* (K–2). Illus. by Chad Cameron. 2002, Tricycle $14.95 (978-1-58246-063-5). 38pp. George comes from planet Frollop II, and he just can't seem to get things right in 2nd grade. (Rev: HBG 3/03; SLJ 12/02)

1738 Winch, John. *The Old Man Who Loved to Sing* (PS–3). Illus. 1996, Scholastic paper $4.99 (978-0-590-22641-7). 40pp. The animals in the valley are unhappy when their neighbor, an old man, stops serenading them. (Rev: BL 4/15/96; HB 7/96; SLJ 4/96)

1739 Winch, John. *The Old Woman Who Loved to Read* (PS–1). Illus. 1997, Holiday House $16.95 (978-0-8234-1281-5); paper $6.95 (978-0-8234-1348-5). 32pp. An old woman buys a farmhouse in which to retire and read, but she finds unexpected chores awaiting her. (Rev: BL 3/1/97; SLJ 5/97)

1740 Winnick, Karen B. *Barn Sneeze* (PS–1). Illus. 2002, Boyds Mills $15.95 (978-1-56397-948-4). 32pp. The animals in Sue's barn are sneezing, so Sue brings them some tea — and sneezes too. (Rev: BL 5/15/02; HBG 10/02; SLJ 6/02)

1741 Winthrop, Elizabeth. *A Very Noisy Girl* (PS–K). Illus. by Ellen Weiss. 1991, Holiday House LB $14.95 (978-0-8234-0858-0). When Elizabeth's mother asks her to be quiet, Elizabeth responds by turning herself into a dog. (Rev: SLJ 5/91)

1742 Wisniewski, David. *Tough Cookie* (K–3). Illus. 1999, Lothrop $17.99 (978-0-688-15337-3). 32pp. A parody on hard-boiled detective novels, this story involves Tough Cookie, his former girlfriend, Pecan Sandy, and Cookie's old partner, Chips, who has been badly hurt by Fingers. (Rev: BL 11/1/99; HBG 3/00; SLJ 9/99)

1743 Wolff, Ferida. *Seven Loaves of Bread* (K–4). Illus. by Katie Keller. 1993, Morrow LB $15.93 (978-0-688-11112-0). 32pp. Rose does a poor job when she takes over the bread-baking chores that Milly has to abandon because of illness. (Rev: BL 9/15/93; SLJ 11/93*)

1744 Wolff, Patricia R. *The Toll-Bridge Troll* (PS–2). Illus. by Kimberly B. Root. 1995, Harcourt $15.00 (978-0-15-277665-7). 24pp. Trigg outwits a troll who demands a toll for crossing the bridge that leads to Trigg's school. (Rev: BL 4/15/95; HB 9/95; SLJ 6/95)

1745 Wood, Audrey. *The Bunyans* (K–3). Illus. by David Shannon. 1996, Scholastic $15.95 (978-0-590-48089-5). 32pp. Meet the rest of the Bunyan family, including two gigantic children. (Rev: BCCB 1/97; BL 9/15/96; SLJ 12/96*)

1746 Wood, Audrey. *Elbert's Bad Word* (PS–1). Illus. by author. 1988, Harcourt $15.00 (978-0-15-225320-2). 32pp. A bad word flies into Elbert's mouth, which gets him in trouble, so he goes to the local wizard for help. (Rev: BL 10/1/88; HB 1/89; SLJ 10/88)

1747 Wood, Audrey. *The Rude Giants* (PS–3). Illus. 1993, Harcourt $13.95 (978-0-15-269412-8). 32pp. Clever Gerda convinces two dirty, ugly, rude giants to clean up the castle before they eat everybody. (Rev: BCCB 6/93; BL 3/1/93*; SLJ 5/93)

1748 Wood, Audrey, and Mark Teague. *The Flying Dragon Room* (PS–3). Illus. 1996, Scholastic $15.95 (978-0-590-48193-9). 32pp. With a set of tools he has been given, young Patrick creates a fantastic home, complete with a friendly dinosaur. (Rev: BL 4/1/96*; SLJ 3/96)

1749 Wood, Audrey, and Don Wood. *Piggies* (PS–K). Illus. by Don Wood. 1991, Harcourt $16.00 (978-0-15-256341-7). 32pp. Fingers can become piggies in this imaginative book with elaborate artwork. (Rev: BCCB 4/91*; BL 3/1/91*; SLJ 5/91*)

1750 Wood, David. *Under the Bed!* (PS–K). Illus. by Richard Fowler. 2006, Barron's $9.99 (978-0-7641-5926-8). A huge pop-up monster, revealed on the final page of the book, is under Dad's bed. (Rev: SLJ 7/06)

1751 Wood, Nancy. *Mr. and Mrs. God in the Creation Kitchen* (K–2). Illus. by Timothy Basil Bring. 2006, Candlewick $16.99 (978-0-7636-1258-0). 32pp. In this amusing twist on the creation story, Mr. and Mrs. God work feverishly in their heavenly kitchen to whip up the Earth and the creatures that will populate it. (Rev: BCCB 5/06; BL 4/15/06*; HBG 10/06; LMC 10/06; SLJ 6/06)

1752 Woodruff, Elvira. *The Wing Shop* (PS–2). Illus. by Stephen Gammell. 1991, Holiday House LB $17.95 (978-0-8234-0825-2). 32pp. In an effort to get back to the street where he once lived, Matthew tries to fly with a variety of wings. (Rev: BCCB 6/91; BL 3/15/91; HB 5/91; SLJ 11/91)

1753 Wormell, Christopher. *The Big Ugly Monster and the Little Stone Rabbit* (PS–2). Illus. by author. 2004, Knopf LB $17.99 (978-0-375-92891-8).

When a very ugly and lonely monster dies, the place where he lived bursts into bloom. (Rev: BCCB 9/04; SLJ 9/04)

1754 Wormell, Christopher. *The Sea Monster* (K–3). Illus. by author. 2005, Jonathan Cape $16.99 (978-0-224-07025-6). When a little boy is pulled out to sea by the strong currents, a kindly sea monster comes to his rescue. (Rev: SLJ 3/06)

1755 Yaccarino, Dan. *The Birthday Fish* (PS–K). Illus. 2005, Holt $16.95 (978-0-8050-7493-2). 32pp. Although she was about to throw away the goldfish she received for her birthday instead of the hoped-for pony, Cynthia decides to keep it when it speaks to her. (Rev: BL 5/15/05)

1756 Yaccarino, Dan. *The Lima Bean Monster* (K–3). Illus. by Adam McCauley. 2001, Walker LB $16.85 (978-0-8027-8777-4). 32pp. Sammy buries unwanted lima beans in a vacant lot, with monstrous results. (Rev: BL 9/1/01; HBG 3/02; SLJ 9/01)

1757 Yaccarino, Dan. *Zoom! Zoom! Zoom! I'm Off to the Moon* (PS–K). Illus. 1997, Scholastic $15.95 (978-0-590-95610-9). 32pp. A little boy boards his red rocket for a trip to the moon and back. (Rev: BL 11/15/97; HB 9/97; HBG 3/98; SLJ 12/97)

1758 Yang, James. *Joey and Jet in Space* (PS–2). Illus. by author. Series: Joey and Jet. 2006, Simon & Schuster $15.95 (978-0-689-86927-3). When Joey's dog Jet disappears, Joey searches everywhere — even outer space. (Rev: SLJ 6/06)

1759 Yep, Laurence. *The City of Dragons* (K–3). Illus. by Jean Tseng and Mou-Sien Tseng. 1995, Scholastic $14.95 (978-0-590-47865-6). 32pp. A boy's very sad face moves dragons to shed tears of pearls. (Rev: BL 11/15/95; SLJ 11/95)

1760 Yoo, Taeeun. *The Little Red Fish* (PS–2). 2007, Dial $15.99 (978-0-8037-3145-5). 40pp. On a trip to a library with his grandfather, young boy falls into a fantasy world when he awakes to find his pet fish is missing; a beautiful and unusual book, much of it wordless. (Rev: BL 4/15/07)

1761 Yorinks, Arthur. *Homework* (K–2). Illus. by Richard Egielski. 2009, Walker $16.99 (978-0-8027-9585-4). 32pp. Tony's homework has not been done yet again, so his pencils, pens, ruler, and so on decide to do it for him. (Rev: BL 5/1/09; HB 7/09; SLJ 7/09)

1762 Yorinks, Arthur. *Louis the Fish* (PS–2). Illus. by Richard Egielski. 1980, Farrar paper $5.95 (978-0-374-44598-0). 32pp. The story of an unhappy man who is turned into a fish.

1763 Yorinks, Arthur. *Mommy?* (1–3). Illus. by Maurice Sendak. 2006, Scholastic $24.95 (978-0-439-88050-3). 12pp. In this lively, almost wordless pop-up book, a pajama-clad boy encounters all sorts of monsters as he wanders through creepy surroundings in search of his mother. (Rev: BL 8/06)

1764 Yorinks, Arthur. *The Witch's Child* (1–3). Illus. by Jos A. Smith. 2007, Abrams paper $16.95 (978-0-8109-9349-5). 34pp. A cruel and powerful witch named Rosina longs for a daughter in this dark tale with a happy ending. (Rev: LMC 1/08; SLJ 10/07)

1765 Ziefert, Harriet. *Mighty Max* (PS). Illus. by Elliot Kreloff. 2008, Blue Apple $15.95 (978-1-

934706-36-7). 40pp. In his role as Mighty Max, the little superhero saves the day over and over again — rebuilding a sand castle, rescuing lunch from gulls. (Rev: BL 12/1/08; SLJ 2/09)

1766 Zimmerman, Andrea, and David Clemesha. *Digger Man* (PS–K). Illus. by authors. 2003, Holt $15.95 (978-0-8050-6628-9). A little boy fantasizes about using his big yellow digger to create a park where he and his younger brother can play. (Rev: BL 9/1/03; HBG 4/04; SLJ 12/03)

IMAGINARY ANIMALS

1767 Adams, Jean Ekman. *Clarence Goes Out West and Meets a Purple Horse* (K–2). Illus. 2000, Rising Moon $15.95 (978-0-87358-753-2). 32pp. Smoky, a purple horse, introduces a tenderfoot piglet named Clarence to all the fun of line dancing, card playing, and other cowboy pleasures. (Rev: BL 4/1/00; HBG 10/00; SLJ 6/00)

1768 Agee, Jon. *Milo's Hat Trick* (PS–2). Illus. 2001, Hyperion $15.95 (978-0-7868-0902-8). 32pp. Milo isn't much of a magician until he meets a bear who knows hat tricks. (Rev: BL 7/01; HB 5/01*; HBG 10/01; SLJ 5/01*)

1769 Alborough, Jez. *Some Dogs Do* (PS–2). Illus. by author. 2003, Candlewick $15.99 (978-0-7636-2201-5). In this whimsical tale told in rhyming verse, a puppy named Sid takes flight on his way to school one day. (Rev: HBG 4/04; SLJ 12/03)

1770 Alborough, Jez. *Super Duck* (PS–1). Illus. by author. 2009, Kane $15.95 (978-1-933605-89-0). 32pp. A book called *Super Duck* inspires Duck to adopt the guise of superhero in this sixth adventure. Earlier installments in the series include *Duck in the Truck* (2000), *Fix-It Duck* (2002), *Duck's Key, Where Can It Be?* (2005), and *Hit the Ball Duck* (2006). (Rev: BL 5/1/09; SLJ 3/09)

1771 Alborough, Jez. *Tall* (PS). Illus. by author. 2005, Candlewick $15.99 (978-0-7636-2784-3). The other animals try to help Bobo (the chimpanzee of 2000's *Hug*) to feel tall, but in the end he is glad to be little enough to be cuddled by his mama. (Rev: BL 9/1/05; SLJ 9/05)

1772 Alexander, Sue. *There's More . . . Much More* (PS–1). Illus. by Patience Brewster. 1987, Harcourt $12.95 (978-0-15-200605-1). 32pp. A squirrel helps a little girl to fill a flower basket and understand the beauties of the forest. (Rev: BL 11/15/87; SLJ 12/87)

1773 Allard, Harry. *Starlight Goes to Town* (K–2). Illus. by George Booth. 2008, Farrar $16.95 (978-0-374-37187-6). 32pp. When Ethel AKA Starlight, a little Tennessee chicken, dreams of a glamorous life, a fairy godmother appears right on cue and Starlight begins laying eggs filled with dreams come true; ink-and-watercolor artwork. (Rev: BL 9/15/08; SLJ 9/08)

1774 Allen, Jonathan. *I'm Not Cute!* (PS–K). Illus. 2006, Hyperion $14.99 (978-0-7868-3720-5). 32pp. Baby Owl rejects all compliments, asserting that he is really "a huge, sleek hunting machine," until his mother agrees that he's not cute and realizes that it's definitely time for bed. (Rev: BCCB 6/06; BL 4/15/06; HBG 10/06; SLJ 3/06)

1775 Allen, Jonathan. *"I'm Not Scared!"* (PS). Illus. 2007, Hyperion $14.99 (978-0-7868-3722-9). 32pp. Baby Owl knows that owls stay up all night and is indignant at the idea that he might be scared of the dark. (Rev: BL 5/1/07; SLJ 7/07)

1776 Alter, Anna. *Abigail Spells* (K–2). Illus. by author. 2009, Knopf $16.99 (978-0-375-85617-4). 40pp. George the bear helps Abigail practice for a spelling bee and cheers her up when she flubs the world "elephant." (Rev: BL 3/15/09; SLJ 6/09)

1777 Alter, Anna. *Estelle and Lucy* (PS–K). Illus. 2001, Greenwillow LB $14.89 (978-0-688-17883-3). 24pp. Estelle, a kitten, shows her younger sister, Lucy, a mouse, all the things that older children can do that younger ones are forbidden to do. (Rev: BL 4/1/01*; HBG 10/01; SLJ 7/01)

1778 Alter, Anna. *Francine's Day* (PS–K). Illus. by author. 2003, Greenwillow LB $16.89 (978-0-06-623937-8). Francine the fox is a reluctant student and would rather stay in bed than get up and get ready, but she dutifully goes about her daily schedule, finding moments of enjoyment in spite of herself. (Rev: HBG 4/04; SLJ 9/03)

1779 Anaya, Rudolfo. *Roadrunner's Dance* (K–3). 2000, Hyperion $15.99 (978-0-7868-0254-8). 32pp. The bully Snake is defeated when Desert Woman creates Roadrunner, who is able to get the best of Snake through his unique dance. (Rev: BCCB 12/00; BL 12/15/00; HBG 3/01; SLJ 9/00)

1780 Anderson, Derek. *Romeo and Lou Blast Off* (PS–1). Illus. by author. 2007, Simon & Schuster $15.99 (978-1-4169-3784-5). 32pp. Romeo (a penguin) and Lou (a polar bear) become two innocents abroad when their homemade snow rocket ship blasts off and lands in a city, which they misconstrue for another planet. (Rev: BL 11/1/07; SLJ 1/08)

1781 Anderson, Peggy Perry. *Joe on the Go* (PS–1). Illus. 2007, Houghton $16.00 (978-0-618-77331-2). 32pp. Little Joe the frog has a hard time getting anyone to play with him at the family reunion until Grandma arrives. (Rev: BL 3/15/07; HBG 10/07)

1782 Anderson, Peggy Perry. *Let's Clean Up!* (PS–2). Illus. 2002, Houghton $15.00 (978-0-618-19602-9). 32pp. Rhyming text tells the story of little frog Joe, who can't resist messing up the room his mother just cleaned. (Rev: BL 3/1/02; HBG 10/02; SLJ 4/02)

1783 Andreae, Giles. *Cock-a-doodle-doo! Barnyard Hullabaloo* (PS). Illus. by David Wotjowycz. 2000, Little Tiger $14.95 (978-1-888444-75-9). 32pp. Singsong verses describe the activities of some farmyard animals and the sounds they make. (Rev: BL 3/15/00; HBG 10/00; SLJ 5/00)

1784 Andreae, Giles. *Heaven Is Having You* (PS). Illus. by Vanessa Cabban. 2002, Tiger Tales $15.95 (978-1-58925-016-1). Grandma Bear sees heaven all around her, especially when Little Bear is with her. (Rev: SLJ 7/02)

1785 Andreae, Giles. *Love Is a Handful of Honey* (PS–1). Illus. by Vanessa Cabban. 1999, Little Tiger

$14.95 (978-1-888444-58-2). 32pp. The daily activities of a little bear, depicted in gentle watercolors, express the joy of childhood and the wonder of love. (Rev: BL 12/1/99; HBG 3/00; SLJ 11/99)

1786 Anholt, Catherine, and Laurence Anholt. *Happy Birthday Chimp and Zee* (PS). Illus. by authors. 2006, Frances Lincoln $15.95 (978-1-84507-507-1). For Chimp and Zee, monkey twins, the highlight of their birthday is a party thrown by their friends, a party they almost miss when they become lost in a swamp. (Rev: SLJ 4/06)

1787 Appelt, Kathi. *Oh, My Baby, Little One* (PS–K). Illus. by Jane Dyer. 2000, Harcourt $16.00 (978-0-15-200041-7). 32pp. When baby bird goes off to school, Mama misses her and begins to worry about her well-being. (Rev: BL 3/1/00; HBG 10/00; SLJ 4/00)

1788 Apperley, Dawn. *Don't Wake the Baby* (PS–2). Illus. by author. 2001, Bloomsbury $16.95 (978-0-7475-5003-7). A young squirrel tries unsuccessfully to keep quiet so as not to disturb her sleeping sibling. (Rev: SLJ 12/01)

1789 Apperley, Dawn. *Hello Little Chicks* (PS). Illus. by author. 2000, David & Charles $3.95 (978-1-86233-181-5). This board book uses rhymes and watercolor paintings to describe the activities of little chicks. Also use: *Hello Little Ducks, Hello Little Lamb*, and *Hello Little Piglet* (all 2000). (Rev: SLJ 2/01)

1790 Archer, Dosh, and Mike Archer. *Looking After Little Ellie* (PS–K). Illus. 2005, Bloomsbury $15.95 (978-1-58234-971-8). 32pp. Six mice agree to babysit a baby elephant and find this more challenging than they had expected, especially when it comes to diaper changing. (Rev: BL 2/15/05; SLJ 4/05)

1791 Armstrong, Alan. *Whittington* (5–8). Illus. by S. D. Schindler. 2005, Random LB $16.99 (978-0-375-92864-2). 208pp. Happy to have found a place to live, Whittington the cat regales the other barnyard animals with tales of his famous forebears. Newbery Honor Book, 2006. (Rev: BL 5/15/05; SLJ 8/05*)

1792 Arno, Iris Hiskey. *The Secret of the First One Up* (K–2). Illus. by Renee Graef. 2003, NorthWord $15.95 (978-1-55971-867-7). Young groundhog Lila is the first in her family to awaken after a long winter's sleep and learns about the importance of her shadow. (Rev: SLJ 12/03)

1793 Arnold, Katya. *Duck, Duck, Goose?* (PS–1). Illus. 1997, Holiday House $16.95 (978-0-8234-1296-9). 32pp. Goose tries in vain to improve her appearance by swapping body parts with other animals. (Rev: BL 7/97; HB 9/97; SLJ 9/97)

1794 Arnold, Katya, retel. *Me Too! Two Small Stories About Small Animals* (PS). Illus. by Katya Arnold. 2000, Holiday House $15.95 (978-0-8234-1483-3). Two gentle animal stories that are translations from the work of Vladimir Suteev. (Rev: HB 3/00; HBG 10/00; SLJ 3/00)

1795 Arnold, Katya. *Meow!* (PS–K). Illus. 1998, Holiday House $16.95 (978-0-8234-1361-4). 32pp. While searching for the animal who says "meow," a puppy encounters a number of different animals, each of whom produces its own distinctive sound.

(Rev: BCCB 7–8/98; BL 4/15/98; HBG 10/98; SLJ 5/98)

1796 Arnold, Marsha Diane. *Prancing, Dancing Lily* (PS–2). Illus. by John Manders. 2004, Dial $16.99 (978-0-8037-2823-3). Lily the cow may soon be the leader of her herd, but first she sets off on a long journey to gain experience; cartoon illustrations add to the fun. (Rev: SLJ 3/04)

1797 Arnold, Marsha Diane, and Vernise Elaine Pelzel. *Hugs on the Wind* (PS–K). Illus. by Elsa Warnick. 2006, Abrams $15.95 (978-0-8109-5968-2). A gentle story of Little Cottontail, who misses his grandfather and decides to send him hugs and kisses via the wind. (Rev: HBG 10/06; SLJ 3/06)

1798 Arnold, Tedd. *Green Wilma, Frog in Space* (PS–2). Illus. by author. 2009, Dial $16.99 (978-0-8037-2698-7). 32pp. Wilma the frog is mistaken for an alien child and takes an unscheduled trip into space. (Rev: BL 5/1/09; SLJ 6/09)

1799 Aroner, Miriam. *Clink, Clank, Clunk!* (PS). Illus. by Dominic Catalano. 2006, Boyds Mills $15.95 (978-1-59078-270-5). Rabbit's car is on its last legs, but he manages to drive his animal friends to town one last time before junking the vehicle and buying a shiny red auto to replace it. (Rev: HBG 10/06; SLJ 4/06)

1800 Arrhenius, Peter. *The Penguin Quartet* (K–3). Illus. by Ingela Peterson. 1998, Carolrhoda $15.95 (978-1-57505-252-6). Four dapper penguins — soon to be dads — find it boring waiting for their eggs to hatch, so they pack them up and go to New York where they become the popular Penguin Quartet. (Rev: HBG 3/99; SLJ 11/98)

1801 Asch, Frank. *Baby Bird's First Nest* (PS–2). Illus. by author. 1999, Harcourt $14.00 (978-0-15-201726-2). When Baby Bird falls out of her nest, Little Frog helps her back after a series of adventures. (Rev: HBG 10/99; SLJ 6/99)

1802 Asch, Frank. *Just Like Daddy* (PS–1). Illus. by author. 1984, Simon & Schuster paper $5.99 (978-0-671-66457-2). 32pp. Fatherhood is explained by a bear and his dad in this warm, humorous book. Another Bear story is: *Milk and Cookies* (Parents Magazine Pr. 1982).

1803 Asch, Frank. *Moondance* (PS–K). Illus. 1993, Scholastic $12.95 (978-0-590-45487-2). 32pp. Bear wants to dance with the moon, but doesn't feel worthy of the honor. (Rev: BL 2/15/93; SLJ 6/93)

1804 Asch, Frank. *Mr. Maxwell's Mouse* (2–4). Illus. by Devin Asch. 2004, Kids Can $15.95 (978-1-55337-486-2). 32pp. To celebrate a promotion, Mr. Maxwell, a well-dressed and self-important cat, visits his favorite restaurant and unwisely orders raw mouse. (Rev: BL 10/1/04; SLJ 9/04*)

1805 Asch, Frank. *Sand Cake* (K–2). Illus. by author. 1979, Parents LB $5.95 (978-0-8193-0986-0). 48pp. On the beach, Papa Bear makes a sand cake.

1806 Asch, Frank, and Vladimir Vagin. *Dear Brother* (K–3). Illus. 1992, Scholastic $13.95 (978-0-590-43107-1). 32pp. Two mouse brothers read letters from two ancestors that prove how important a brother can be. (Rev: BCCB 2/92; BL 6/15/92; SLJ 4/92)

1807 Asch, Frank, and Vladimir Vagin. *Insects from Outer Space* (PS–2). Illus. by Vladimir Vagin. 1995, Scholastic $14.95 (978-0-590-45489-6). 32pp. Insects from outer space and their earthling counterparts enjoy each other at the Bug Ball. (Rev: BL 2/1/95; SLJ 4/95)

1808 Asher, Sandy. *Here Comes Gosling!* (PS–2). Illus. by Keith Graves. 2009, Philomel $16.99 (978-0-399-25085-9). 32pp. Eye-catching illustrations and believable toddler behavior entertain in this tale of friends Froggie and Rabbit who wait expectantly for the arrival of the baby gosling. (Rev: BLO 6/16/09; SLJ 6/09)

1809 Asher, Sandy. *What a Party!* (PS–1). Illus. by Keith Graves. 2007, Philomel $15.99 (978-0-399-24496-4). Excited about the birthday party for his grandfather, Froggie doesn't want all the fun to end. (Rev: BL 2/1/07; SLJ 2/07)

1810 Ashman, Linda. *Can You Make a Piggy Giggle?* (PS–K). Illus. by Henry Cole. 2002, Dutton $12.99 (978-0-525-46881-3). 32pp. While trying in vain to make a pig laugh, a boy draws giggles from other farm animals in this funny picture book with cartoon-style illustrations. (Rev: BCCB 4/02; BL 7/02; HBG 10/02; SLJ 6/02)

1811 Asquith, Ros. *Mrs Pig's Night Out* (PS–2). Illus. by Selina Young. 2003, Hodder $17.95 (978-0-340-81707-0). Mrs. Pig's youngsters take full advantage of Mom's night out despite Mr. Pig's presence. (Rev: BL 5/15/03; SLJ 8/03)

1812 Auch, Mary Jane. *Bantam of the Opera* (K–3). Illus. 1997, Holiday House LB $16.95 (978-0-8234-1312-6). 32pp. Luigi, a bantam rooster with a huge voice, gets his chance at the Cosmopolitan Opera Company. (Rev: BL 10/1/97; HBG 3/98; SLJ 10/97*)

1813 Auch, Mary Jane. *Bird Dogs Can't Fly* (PS–1). Illus. 1993, Holiday House LB $15.95 (978-0-8234-1050-7). 32pp. Blue, a bird dog, nurses an injured goose back to health. (Rev: BL 10/15/93; SLJ 12/93)

1814 Auch, Mary Jane. *Eggs Mark the Spot* (PS–3). Illus. 1996, Holiday House $16.95 (978-0-8234-1242-6). 32pp. A hen copies onto her eggs some portraits painted by famous artists. (Rev: BL 3/15/96; SLJ 5/96)

1815 Auch, Mary Jane. *Hen Lake* (PS–3). Illus. 1995, Holiday House LB $16.95 (978-0-8234-1188-7). 32pp. The hen Poulette stages her own ballet and also gets the best of snooty Mr. Peacock. (Rev: BL 8/95; SLJ 10/95)

1816 Auch, Mary Jane. *Peeping Beauty* (PS–3). Illus. 1993, Holiday House LB $16.95 (978-0-8234-1001-9). 32pp. Poulette the hen decides she wants to be a ballerina. (Rev: BL 3/1/93; SLJ 4/93*)

1817 Auch, Mary Jane. *Poultrygeist* (PS–1). Illus. by Mary Jane Auch and Herm Auch. 2003, Holiday House $17.95 (978-0-8234-1756-8). Upset by the noise made by rowdy roosters Rudy and Ralph, Clarissa the cow and Sophie the pig dress up as a spooky "poultrygeist." (Rev: HBG 4/04; SLJ 9/03)

1818 Auch, Mary Jane. *Souperchicken* (K–2). Illus. by Herm Auch. 2003, Holiday House $16.95 (978-0-8234-1704-9). 32pp. Talented hen Henrietta saves her aunts from the "Souper Soup Co." truck on their way to what they think is a free vacation, but is in fact the soup pot. (Rev: BL 3/15/03; HBG 10/03; SLJ 5/03)

1819 Avi. *A Beginning, a Muddle, and an End: The Right Way to Write Writing* (1–3). Illus. by Tricia Tusa. 2008, Harcourt $14.95 (978-0-15-205555-4). 176pp. Full of fun and wordplay, this sequel to *The End of the Beginning: Being the Adventures of a Small Snail (and an Even Smaller Ant)* (2004), follows Avon the Snail and Edward the Ant in their writing efforts. (Rev: BCCB 5/08; BL 7/08; LMC 11/08)

1820 Axelrod, Amy. *Pigs in the Pantry: Fun with Math and Cooking* (PS–2). Illus. by Sharon McGinley-Nally. 1997, Simon & Schuster $14.00 (978-0-689-80665-0). 40pp. The story of Mr. Pig's disastrous cooking spree, with some added math facts about measuring ingredients. (Rev: BCCB 5/97; BL 3/1/97; SLJ 4/97)

1821 Axelrod, Amy. *Pigs on a Blanket* (K–3). Illus. by Sharon McGinley-Nally. 1996, Simon & Schuster paper $14.00 (978-0-689-80505-9). 32pp. Unforeseen problems cause delays for a pig family that wants to spend a day at the beach. (Rev: BL 5/15/96; SLJ 6/96)

1822 Axelrod, Amy. *Pigs Will Be Pigs* (K–3). Illus. by Sharon McGinley-Nally. 1994, Four Winds paper $14.00 (978-0-02-765415-8). 40pp. To finance a dinner out, the pig family engages in a money hunt around the house. (Rev: BCCB 2/94; BL 2/15/94; SLJ 5/94*)

1823 Aylesworth, Jim. *Aunt Pitty Patty's Piggy* (PS–K). Illus. by Barbara McClintock. 1999, Scholastic $15.95 (978-0-590-89987-1). 32pp. A delightful cumulative tale involving Aunt Pitty Patty's efforts to get her pig home and the many animals she asks for help. (Rev: BCCB 12/99; BL 9/15/99*; HB 9/99; HBG 3/00; SLJ 10/99)

1824 Badescu, Ramona. *Big Rabbit's Bad Mood* (PS–1). Illus. by Delphine Durand. 2009, Chronicle $16.99 (978-0-8118-6666-8). 32pp. Big Rabbit's mood is so horrible that it becomes an actual ugly thing that won't go away until his friends and his mother show up, surprising Big Rabbit with cake and presents for his birthday. (Rev: BL 7/09; SLJ 6/09)

1825 Baek, Matthew J. *Panda and Polar Bear* (PS–K). Illus. by author. 2009, Dial $16.99 (978-0-8037-3359-6). 32pp. A panda bear and a polar bear meet accidentally, become friends, and explore their differences. (Rev: BL 7/09; SLJ 7/09)

1826 Baguley, Elizabeth. *A Long Way from Home* (PS–2). Illus. by Jane Chapman. 2008, Tiger Tales $15.95 (978-1-58925-074-1). Noah, the smallest bunny in his burrow, has a yen for wide open spaces and hitches a ride to the frozen north; although he loves the snowy terrain for a while he soon becomes cold and lonely. (Rev: SLJ 12/08)

1827 Baicker-McKee, Carol. *Mimi* (PS–K). Illus. by author. 2008, Bloomsbury $15.95 (978-1-59990-065-0). 32pp. Readers follow Mimi, a little pig, as she navigates through the events of a busy day without her pet roly-poly bug, Frank. (Rev: BLO 12/30/08; SLJ 8/08)

1828 Bailey, Linda. *The Farm Team* (PS–2). Illus. by Bill Slavin. 2006, Kids Can $16.95 (978-1-55337-850-1). 32pp. The animals from Farmer Stolski's farm compete valiantly in a championship hockey game against their archrivals, the Bush League Bandits, a team made up of creatures from the wild. (Rev: BL 10/1/06; SLJ 11/06)

1829 Baker, Alan. *Little Rabbits' First Farm Book* (PS). Illus. 2001, Kingfisher $11.95 (978-0-7534-5352-0). 29pp. Four rabbits complete chores on a farm, introducing children to facts about various animals through illustrations, informational sidebars, and games at the end of the book. (Rev: BL 11/15/01; HBG 10/02; SLJ 2/02)

1830 Baker, Barbara. *One Saturday Evening* (1–3). Illus. by Kate Duke. 2007, Dutton $13.99 (978-0-525-47103-5). 48pp. In this easy-to-read chapter book, Mama and Papa Bear at last have some peace and quiet after enduring the happy chaos of putting their four bear cubs to bed; a sequel to 1994's *One Saturday Morning*. (Rev: BCCB 10/07; BL 7/07; SLJ 8/07)

1831 Baker, Keith. *Who Is the Beast?* (K–2). Illus. 1990, Harcourt $14.95 (978-0-15-296057-5). 32pp. A tiger tries to make the other jungle animals less afraid of him. (Rev: BL 9/1/90; HB 11/90; SLJ 11/90)

1832 Bancroft, Catherine, and Hannah C. Gruenberg. *Felix's Hat* (K–3). Illus. by Hannah C. Gruenberg. 1993, Macmillan LB $14.95 (978-0-02-708325-5). 32pp. Felix Frog cannot be consoled when he loses his favorite possession, an orange hat. (Rev: BL 3/15/93; SLJ 7/93)

1833 Bang, Molly. *Goose* (PS–3). Illus. 1996, Scholastic $10.95 (978-0-590-89005-2). 40pp. After hatching from her egg, Duckling finds a surrogate family with a group of woodchucks. (Rev: BCCB 12/96; BL 9/15/96*; HB 11/96; SLJ 11/96*)

1834 Bardhan-Quallen, Sudipta. *Tightrope Poppy the High-Wire Pig* (PS–2). Illus. by Sarah Dillard. 2006, Sterling LB $14.95 (978-1-4027-2411-4). When the circus holds auditions, Poppy the pig decides to realize her dream of becoming a tightrope walker. (Rev: SLJ 3/06)

1835 Barnes, Laura T. *Ernest and Elston* (PS–2). Illus. by Carol A. Camburn. 2005, Barnesyard $15.95 (978-0-9674681-6-7). Elston the rooster worries that his crowing disturbs the other farm animals, and Ernest, a miniature donkey endowed with sympathy and understanding, tries to reassure him that he's perfect. (Rev: SLJ 10/05)

1836 Barnes, Laura T. *Ernest and the Big Itch* (K–3). Illus. by Carol A. Camburn. 2002, Barnesyard $15.95 (978-0-9674681-2-9). 32pp. Two birds help Ernest, a donkey, find a new place to scratch his itch. (Rev: BL 5/15/02; SLJ 9/02)

1837 Barnes, Laura T. *Teeny Tiny Ernest* (PS–K). Illus. by Carol A. Camburn. 2000, Barnesyard $15.95 (978-0-9674681-1-2). 32pp. Ernest, a miniature donkey, tries different methods to look taller

but the other animals tell him that they never noticed that he was small because beauty comes from within. (Rev: BL 11/15/00; SLJ 3/01)

1838 Barringer, William. *Gregory and Alexander* (K–1). Illus. by Kim LaFave. 2003, Orca $15.95 (978-1-55143-252-6). An unlikely friendship between a mouse named Gregory and a caterpillar named Al is the focus of this gentle story. (Rev: HBG 10/03; SLJ 9/03)

1839 Base, Graeme. *Jungle Drums* (PS–2). Illus. 2004, Abrams $18.95 (978-0-8109-5044-3). 40pp. A diminutive warthog named Ngiri Mdogo makes his mark when he acquires magical drums in this brightly illustrated, oversize book. (Rev: BL 9/1/04; SLJ 10/04)

1840 Bass, Jules. *Herb, the Vegetarian Dragon* (K–3). Illus. by Debbie Harter. 1999, Barefoot Books LB $15.95 (978-1-902283-36-4). Herb, a gentle vegetarian dragon, is wrongfully accused of people-eating and escapes death only with the help of a brave girl. (Rev: SLJ 7/99)

1841 Bassede, Francine. *A Day with the Bellyflops* (PS–2). Illus. by author. 2000, Orchard LB $15.99 (978-0-531-33242-9). Constant interruptions by her three piglets prevent Mrs. Bellyflop from getting her work done. (Rev: HBG 10/00; SLJ 3/00)

1842 Bateman, Teresa. *Fluffy: The Scourge of the Sea* (PS–2). Illus. by Michael Chesworth. 2005, Charlesbridge $14.95 (978-1-58089-099-1). 32pp. Despite his dandified appearance, poodle Fluffy wins his captors' respect when seized by a pack of canine pirates. (Rev: BL 1/1–15/05; SLJ 3/05)

1843 Bateman, Teresa. *The Frog with the Big Mouth* (K–2). Illus. by Will Terry. 2008, Albert Whitman $16.99 (978-0-8075-2621-7). 32pp. A reprise of the story of a big-mouthed South American rain forest frog who brags about his fly-catching skills. (Rev: SLJ 9/08)

1844 Bateman, Teresa. *Hunting the Daddyosaurus* (PS–K). Illus. by Benrei Huang. 2002, Whitman $15.95 (978-0-8075-1433-7). 32pp. A brother and sister dinosaur parade around the house looking for their father and finally find him in his easy chair. (Rev: BL 5/1/02; HBG 10/02; SLJ 3/02)

1845 Bauer, Marion Dane. *Frog's Best Friend* (1–2). Illus. by Diane D. Hearn. 2002, Holiday House $14.95 (978-0-8234-1501-4). 32pp. Frog wants Turtle to be his exclusive best friend but Turtle also wants to be friends with Squirrel, Bird, and Otter. (Rev: BL 5/1/02; HBG 10/02; SLJ 6/02)

1846 Baum, Louis. *The Mouse Who Braved Bedtime* (PS). Illus. by Sue Hellard. 2006, Bloomsbury $16.95 (978-1-58234-691-5). Troubled by a persistent nightmare, Milo the mouse seeks advice from family members but in the end must find the courage to confront his fears. (Rev: SLJ 10/06)

1847 Baumgart, Klaus. *Where Are You, Little Green Dragon?* (PS–2). Illus. by author. 1993, Hyperion $12.95 (978-1-56282-344-3); paper $4.95 (978-0-7868-1073-4). 32pp. The Little Green Dragon with his friendly fly share many adventures. (Rev: SLJ 8/93)

1848 Bearn, Emily. *Tumtum and Nutmeg: Adventures Beyond Nutmouse Hall* (2–4). Illus. by Nick Price. 2009, Little, Brown $16.99 (978-0-316-02703-8). 512pp. Three adventures involve Tumtum and Nutmeg, a married pair of mice who try to look after the human children who share their house. (Rev: BL 4/15/09; SLJ 5/09)

1849 Beaton, Clare. *How Loud Is a Lion?* (PS). Illus. 2002, Barefoot Books $14.99 (978-1-84148-896-7). 24pp. Elegant, stylish animals are introduced in this book for toddlers that asks, "How loud is a lion?" (Rev: BL 4/1/02; HBG 10/02; SLJ 6/02)

1850 Beaty, Andrea. *Doctor Ted* (K–2). Illus. by Pascal LeMaitre. 2008, Simon & Schuster $14.99 (978-1-4169-2820-1). 32pp. After bumping his knee, a little bear called Ted decides to become a doctor, but his professional skills do not meet with immediate appreciation. (Rev: BCCB 4/08; BL 6/1–15/08; HB 5/08; SLJ 4/08)

1851 Beaumont, Karen. *Duck, Duck, Goose! (A Coyote's on the Loose!)* (PS–1). Illus. by Jose Aruego and Ariane Dewey. 2004, HarperCollins $17.99 (978-0-06-050802-9). 32pp. Fear of a coyote in their midst (in fact, a dirty bunny) spreads through the farmyard animals like wildfire. (Rev: BL 3/1/04; SLJ 2/04)

1852 Beaumont, Karen. *Move Over, Rover!* (PS–K). Illus. by Jane Dyer. 2006, Harcourt $16.00 (978-0-15-201979-2). 40pp. Rover the dog offers shelter in his doghouse during a rainstorm and it gets very crowded until Skunk arrives. (Rev: BL 9/1/06; SLJ 9/06)

1853 Beaumont, Karen. *Who Ate All the Cookie Dough?* (PS–1). Illus. by Eugene Yelchin. 2008, Holt (978-0-8050-8267-8). Who did eat that dough? A variety of animals tell Kanga they did not do it and in the end a lift-up flap reveals the culprit — Kanga's own little joey. (Rev: SLJ 7/08)

1854 Bechtold, Lisze. *Edna's Tale* (PS–2). Illus. 2001, Houghton $15.00 (978-0-618-09164-5). 32pp. Edna's tail is her pride and joy and the cat is mortified when she arrives at a party covered in foliage. (Rev: BL 5/1/01; HBG 10/01; SLJ 6/01)

1855 Bechtold, Lisze. *Sally and the Purple Socks* (PS–2). Illus. by author. 2008, Philomel $15.99 (978-0-399-24734-7). 40pp. Sally the duck gets some new purple socks that grow and grow — becoming first a scarf and cap, then curtains, then a blanket, then a tent — until a rain shower returns them to foot-size. (Rev: BL 6/1–15/08; SLJ 6/08)

1856 Becker, Bonny. *A Visitor for Bear* (PS–2). Illus. by Kady M. Denton. 2008, Candlewick $16.99 (978-0-7636-2807-9). 56pp. Bear doesn't want any visitors but after a persistent mouse wears down his resistance, Bear discovers the pleasures of having company. (Rev: BL 2/15/08; HB 3/08; SLJ 2/08)

1857 Bedford, David. *Big Bears Can!* (K–2). Illus. by Gaby Hansen. 2001, Tiger Tales $14.95 (978-1-58925-006-2). Big Bear has to babysit his little brother but can't resist his sibling's taunts, with messy results. (Rev: SLJ 8/01)

1858 Bedford, David. *The Copy Crocs* (PS–2). Illus. by Emily Bolam. 2004, Peachtree $15.95 (978-1-56145-304-7). Crocodile's friends follow him everywhere he goes and copy whatever he does. (Rev: SLJ 3/04)

1859 Bedford, David. *Little Bear's Big Sweater* (PS–1). Illus. by Caroline Pedler. 2009, Good Bks. $16.95 (978-1-56148-656-4). 32pp. Big Bear passes his favorite sweater down to his younger brother and is initially annoyed when Little Bear gets it dirty. (Rev: BL 4/15/09; SLJ 5/09)

1860 Bedford, David. *Little Otter's Big Journey* (K–2). Illus. by Susan Winter. 2006, Good Bks. $16.00 (978-1-56148-548-2). Left on his own when his mother goes in search of food, Little Otter enjoys himself at first but soon begins to miss her and asks other animals to help him find her. (Rev: SLJ 12/06)

1861 Bedford, David. *Mole's in Love* (PS–2). Illus. by Rosalind Beardshaw. 2009, Tiger Tales $15.95 (978-1-58925-084-0); paper $6.95 (978-1-58925-417-6). 32pp. Spring brings hopes of romance but Mole's poor eyesight hampers his early efforts. (Rev: SLJ 3/09)

1862 Bedford, David. *Shaggy Dog and the Terrible Itch* (PS–2). Illus. by Gwyneth Williamson. 2001, Barron's $12.95 (978-0-7641-5391-4). Poor Shaggy Dog can't reach his back and needs scratching help from friends, and, it turns out, a good bath. (Rev: HBG 3/02; SLJ 1/02)

1863 Bedford, David. *Touch the Sky, My Little Bear* (PS–K). Illus. by Jane Chapman. 2001, Handprint $15.95 (978-1-929766-20-8). 32pp. A little polar bear wonders what it would be like to be big like his mother. (Rev: BL 4/15/01; HBG 10/01; SLJ 5/01)

1864 Beiser, Tim. *Bradley McGogg: The Very Fine Frog* (PS–K). Illus. by Rachel Berman. 2009, Tundra $17.95 (978-0-88776-864-4). 24pp. A hungry frog sets out to visit his neighbors only to find that they eat the most disgusting things! (Rev: SLJ 3/09)

1865 Bell, Cece. *Bee-Wigged* (K–2). Illus. by author. 2008, Candlewick $16.99 (978-0-7636-3614-2). 40pp. Jerry the bee's very large size has prejudiced others against him, but when he dons a wig (actually a guinea pig) he is suddenly accepted. (Rev: SLJ 3/09)

1866 Bell, Cece. *Itty Bitty* (PS–1). Illus. by author. 2009, Candlewick $9.99 (978-0-7636-3616-6). 32pp. Itty Bitty, a very small dog, works hard to make his home in a huge bone, and despite his size, confidently travels into the city to find just the right items to decorate and cozily furnish his space. (Rev: BL 7/09)

1867 Benjamin, A. H. *It Could Have Been Worse* (PS–K). Illus. by Tim Warnes. 1998, Little Tiger $14.95 (978-1-888444-26-1). 28pp. After suffering a series of accidents, Mouse thinks he is having an unlucky day, but each misadventure has actually saved him from his natural enemies. (Rev: BL 5/15/98; HBG 10/98)

1868 Berenstein, Stan, and Jan Berenstain. *The Berenstain Bears in the Dark* (PS–2). Illus. by authors. 1982, Random paper $3.25 (978-0-394-85443-4). 32pp. Brother and Sister Bear in one of a very large series of books.

1869 Berger, Barbara Helen. *Thunder Bunny* (PS–1). Illus. by author. 2007, Philomel $16.99 (978-0-399-22035-7). By being brave during a storm, a bunny learns to love being blue even though her brothers and sisters are ordinary brown. (Rev: SLJ 7/07)

1870 Berger, Joe. *Bridget Fidget and the Most Perfect Pet* (PS–2). Illus. by author. 2009, Dial $16.99 (978-0-8037-3405-0). 32pp. Bridget Fidget is sure that the box they just delivered must contain her unicorn. (Rev: BL 6/1–15/09; SLJ 6/09)

1871 Berger, Samantha. *Martha Doesn't Say Sorry!* (PS–3). Illus. by Bruce Whatley. 2009, Little, Brown $15.99 (978-0-316-06682-2). 40pp. For this little otter, sorry is the hardest word to say. (Rev: BCCB 7–8/09; SLJ 6/09)

1872 Bergman, Tamar. *Where Is?* (PS–1). Illus. by Rutu Modan. 2002, Houghton $15.00 (978-0-618-09539-1). 24pp. A young kitten who is left with his grandparents spends the day wondering where his mother has gone. (Rev: BL 12/15/02; HBG 3/03; SLJ 9/02)

1873 Bergren, Lisa Tawn. *God Found Us You* (PS–1). Illus. by Laura J. Bryant. 2009, Harper-Collins $10.99 (978-0-06-113176-9). 40pp. A mother fox and her adopted son talk about the day he came home and why he couldn't stay with his birth mother. (Rev: BL 5/1/09; SLJ 4/09)

1874 Berkes, Marianne. *Marsh Music* (K–3). Illus. by Robert Noreika. 2000, Millbrook LB $14.95 (978-0-7613-1850-7). 32pp. From dawn to dusk, the world is alive with the sound of frogs making music in this amusing book about marsh life, nature, and song. (Rev: BL 12/1/00; HBG 3/01; SLJ 12/00)

1875 Berkner, Laurie. *Victor Vito and Freddie Vasco: Two Polar Bears on a Mission to Save the Klondike Cafe!* (PS–2). Illus. by Henry Cole. 2004, Scholastic $16.95 (978-0-439-42914-6). A pair of polar bears from Alaska travel around the United States looking for new dishes to serve at their Klondike Cafe. (Rev: SLJ 3/04)

1876 Berliner, Franz. *Wildebeest* (PS–1). Illus. by Lilian Brogger. 1991, Ideals $13.95 (978-0-8249-8488-5). 32pp. When a wildebeest changes his nature, he gets a new name — gnu. (Rev: BL 1/15/92)

1877 Bernstein, Dan. *The Tortoise and the Hare Race Again* (PS–2). Illus. by Andrew Glass. 2006, Holiday House $16.95 (978-0-8234-1867-1). Neither tortoise nor hare is truly pleased by the outcome of their first race, so they schedule a rematch. (Rev: SLJ 4/06)

1878 Berry, Lynne. *Duck Tents* (PS–K). Illus. by Nakata Hiroe. 2009, Holt $16.95 (978-0-8050-8696-6). 32pp. Five little ducks set off on a backyard camping adventure, have fun toasting marshmallows, and worry about the sounds of the night in this charming story that includes counting guidance. (Rev: BCCB 9/09; BL 4/1/09; SLJ 4/09)

1879 Billingsley, Franny. *Big Bad Bunny* (PS–2). Illus. by G. Brian Karas. 2008, Atheneum $16.99 (978-1-4169-0601-8). 40pp. Mama Mouse tucks in her brood while a fearsome bunny is on the loose; the nature of this scary personage (actually a baby mouse in a bunny suit) is revealed at the end. (Rev: BL 3/15/08; HB 3/08; SLJ 4/08)

1880 Billout, Guy. *The Frog Who Wanted to See the Sea* (K–2). Illus. by author. 2007, Creative Editions LB $17.95 (978-1-56846-188-5). 32pp. The illustrations shine in this story about a frog who leaves her pond for an adventurous trip to the sea. (Rev: BL 11/15/07)

1881 Bingham, Mindy. *Minou* (1–3). Illus. by Itoko Maeno. 1987, Advocacy $14.95 (978-0-911655-36-0). 64pp. When Minou loses her home in Paris, a smart cat named Celeste grooms her to become a mouser at Notre Dame. (Rev: BL 9/1/87; SLJ 6–7/87)

1882 Birchall, Mark. *Rabbit's Wooly Sweater* (PS–K). Illus. by author. 2001, Carolrhoda LB $15.95 (978-1-57505-465-0). When little Rabbit's new sweater is washed, it shrinks to become the perfect size for Mr. Cuddles, the stuffed toy that is Rabbit's best friend. (Rev: HBG 10/01; SLJ 3/01)

1883 Birney, Betty. *Surprises According to Humphrey* (2–4). 2008, Putnam $14.99 (978-0-399-24730-9). 192pp. Humphrey, the classroom hamster, faces new pleasures and challenges — a hamster ball, a janitor replaced by an alien (?), and a teacher considering retirement. (Rev: BL 2/1/08; SLJ 2/08)

1884 Bishop, Gavin. *Stay Awake, Bear!* (PS–1). Illus. by author. 2000, Orchard LB $16.99 (978-0-531-33249-8). Old Bear and his neighbor decide that hibernation is a waste of time and so decide to stay awake all winter. (Rev: HBG 10/00; SLJ 3/00)

1885 Björkman, Steve. *Supersnouts!* (PS–1). Illus. 2004, Holiday House $16.95 (978-0-8234-1810-7). 32pp. A young pig named Hamlet gets a chance to join the Superhero Pig Patrol in this pun- and action-packed story. (Rev: BL 4/1/04; SLJ 5/04)

1886 Blackaby, Susan. *Rembrandt's Hat* (PS–3). 2002, Houghton $15.00 (978-0-618-11452-8). Rembrandt the bear has lost his hat and tries many inventive substitutes before finding one that suits him. (Rev: BCCB 5/02; BL 4/15/02; HBG 10/02; SLJ 7/02)

1887 Blackstone, Stella. *Bear at Work* (PS–K). Illus. by Debbie Harter. Series: Bear. 2008, Barefoot Books paper $6.99 (978-1-84686-110-9). 32pp. Bear is a mail carrier in this book and readers follow his journey through the town, delivering letters and packages to a variety of destinations. Also use *Bear on a Bike* and *Bear's Busy Family* (both 1999), *Bear About Town* (2000), and *Bear at Home* and *Bear in Sunshine* (both 2001). (Rev: BL 5/15/08; SLJ 6/08)

1888 Blackstone, Stella. *Bear's Busy Family* (PS–1). Illus. by Debbie Harter. Series: Bear. 1999, Barefoot Books $13.95 (978-1-902283-90-6). 32pp. This book about members of a young bear's family can be used to introduce the names and relationships in an extended family. (Rev: BL 9/15/99; SLJ 8/99)

1889 Blackstone, Stella. *Cleo in the Snow* (PS). Illus. by Caroline Mockford. 2002, Barefoot Books $14.99 (978-1-84148-951-3). A kitten sensibly decides that a warm spot in front of the fire is more fun than sledding. (Rev: HBG 3/03; SLJ 11/02)

1890 Blackstone, Stella. *Cleo on the Move* (K–2). Illus. by Caroline Mockford. Series: Cleo the Cat. 2002, Barefoot Books $14.99 (978-1-84148-898-1). Cleo the cat and Caspar the dog are moving to a new house. (Rev: HBG 3/03; SLJ 10/02)

1891 Blackstone, Stella. *There's a Cow in the Cabbage Patch* (PS–1). Illus. by Clare Beaton. 2001, Barefoot Books $14.99 (978-1-84148-333-7). 32pp. All the farm animals seem to be in the wrong places until the sound of the dinner bell straightens them out. (Rev: BCCB 4/01; BL 4/15/01; HBG 10/01; SLJ 5/01)

1892 Blackwood, Mary. *Derek the Knitting Dinosaur* (PS–2). Illus. by Kerry Argent. 1990, Carolrhoda LB $15.95 (978-0-87614-400-8); paper $5.95 (978-0-87614-540-1). 32pp. This dinosaur prefers to knit woolly socks and sweaters rather than terrorize the neighborhood like his uncivilized siblings. (Rev: BL 7/90; SLJ 7/90)

1893 Blathwayt, Benedict. *Dinosaur Chase!* (PS–1). Illus. by author. 2006, Hutchinson $16.99 (978-0-09-189293-7). Fin the dinosaur is having a good time with his friends when a group of bullies tries to break up their fun; detailed illustrations enhance the story. (Rev: SLJ 9/06)

1894 Blight, Peter. *The Lonely Giraffe* (PS). Illus. by Michael Terry. 2005, Bloomsbury $16.99 (978-0-7475-6894-0). The story of a previously ignored giraffe who uses his long neck to help others and make new friends. (Rev: SLJ 7/05)

1895 Blood, Charles L., and Martin Link. *The Goat in the Rug* (K–2). Illus. by Nancy W. Parker. 1990, Simon & Schuster paper $5.99 (978-0-689-71418-4). 40pp. How a Navajo rug is made, from the goat Geraldine's point of view.

1896 Bloom, Suzanne. *A Mighty Fine Time Machine* (PS–1). Illus. by author. 2009, Boyds Mills $16.95 (978-1-59078-527-0). 24pp. Samantha, an anteater, helps her aardvark friend Grant and armadillo friend Antoine but they cannot make their newly acquired time machine work, so Samantha turns it into a bookmobile. (Rev: BL 5/1/09; SLJ 3/09)

1897 Bloom, Suzanne. *A Splendid Friend, Indeed* (PS–2). Illus. 2005, Boyds Mills $15.95 (978-1-59078-286-6). 32pp. Goose is talkative and outgoing, while Bear is quiet and introverted, but somehow the two manage to strike up a lasting friendship. (Rev: BL 2/15/05; SLJ 5/05)

1898 Bloom, Suzanne. *Treasure* (PS–2). Illus. by author. 2007, Boyds Mills $15.95 (978-1-59078-457-0). Goose mistakes Bear's tic-tac-toe game for a treasure map and insists that they immediately start digging; the treasure they find is an enjoyable day together. (Rev: LMC 1/08; SLJ 2/08)

1899 Bodnar, Judit Z. *Tale of a Tail* (PS–2). Illus. by John Sandford. 1998, Lothrop LB $15.89 (978-0-688-12175-4). 48pp. When Bear asks to share Fox's catch of fresh fish, Fox suggests he catch his own by hanging his tail in the water as bait. The water freezes, encasing Bear's tail in ice, but Bear thinks of an ingenious solution. (Rev: BCCB 11/98; BL 10/1/98*; HBG 3/99; SLJ 11/98)

1900 Boelts, Maribeth. *Big Daddy, Frog Wrestler* (PS–2). Illus. by Benrei Huang. 2000, Whitman $14.95 (978-0-8075-0717-9). 32pp. Curtis, a frog, is proud that Big Daddy is a championship wrestler, but when his father leaves to fight in a big tournament his son's pride turns to loneliness. (Rev: BL 3/1/00; HBG 10/00; SLJ 3/00)

1901 Boelts, Maribeth. *Dry Days, Wet Nights* (PS–K). Illus. by Kathy Parkinson. 1994, Whitman LB $14.95 (978-0-8075-1723-9); paper $5.95 (978-0-8075-1724-6). 32pp. Little Bunny, who is out of diapers during the day, is upset when he wets the bed at night. (Rev: BCCB 4/94; BL 5/1/94; SLJ 4/94)

1902 Boelts, Maribeth. *You're a Brother, Little Bunny!* (PS–K). Illus. by Kathy Parkinson. 2001, Whitman $16.99 (978-0-8075-9446-9). 32pp. Little Bunny's parents help him to adjust when the arrival of his baby brother doesn't quite meet his expectations. (Rev: BL 12/1/01; HBG 3/02; SLJ 1/02)

1903 Bogan, Paulette. *Lulu the Big Little Chick* (PS–K). Illus. by author. 2009, Bloomsbury $16.99 (978-1-59990-343-9). 24pp. Lulu resents being small and tries to assert her independence. (Rev: BL 5/1/09)

1904 Bond, Felicia. *Tumble Bumble* (PS–K). Illus. 1996, Front St. $13.95 (978-1-886910-15-7). 32pp. A simple rhyme about the adventures of a bug that goes for a walk. (Rev: BL 11/15/96; SLJ 10/96)

1905 Bond, Michael. *Paddington Bear* (PS–2). Illus. by R. W. Alley. 1998, HarperCollins $15.99 (978-0-06-027854-0). 32pp. A simple version of the first Paddington story in which the bear meets the Brown family in Paddington Station. (Rev: BL 1/1–15/99; HBG 3/99)

1906 Bond, Michael. *Paddington Bear in the Garden* (PS–2). Illus. by R. W. Alley. 2002, HarperCollins $16.99 (978-0-06-029696-4). 32pp. When Paddington finds that a pile of concrete has been placed on his garden plot, he decides to create a rock garden. (Rev: BL 4/15/02; HBG 10/02)

1907 Bond, Michael. *Paddington Here and Now* (3–5). Illus. by R. W. Alley. 2008, HarperCollins $15.99 (978-0-06-147364-7). 176pp. Fifty years from his first appearance, Paddington retains his charm as he has new adventures in contemporary London. (Rev: BL 5/15/08; HB 9/08; SLJ 8/08)

1908 Bonnett-Rampersaud, Louise. *Bubble and Squeak* (PS–1). Illus. by Susan Banta. 2006, Marshall Cavendish $14.99 (978-0-7614-5310-9). Older mouse sister Bubble is definitely not afraid of monsters but asks her mother what she would do if her younger sibling was afraid in the night. (Rev: SLJ 10/06)

1909 Bonning, Tony. *Another Fine Mess* (PS–2). Illus. by Sally Hobson. 1998, Little Tiger $14.95 (978-1-888444-43-8). 32pp. Fox unloads a mess of trash into Badger's living room, but it eventually ends up back at Fox's front door. (Rev: BL 11/15/98; HBG 3/99; SLJ 2/99)

1910 Borden, Louise. *Off to First Grade* (PS–1). Illus. by Joan Rankin. 2008, Simon & Schuster $16.99 (978-0-689-87395-9). 40pp. In this cheerful first-day-of-school story told in verse, a diverse array of animal characters ride the bus, get their pictures taken, and express their concerns and hopes for the coming year in 1st grade. (Rev: BCCB 7–8/08; BL 8/08; SLJ 8/08)

1911 Bornstein, Ruth. *Little Gorilla* (PS). Illus. by author. 1986, Houghton $15.00 (978-0-395-28773-6); paper $5.95 (978-0-89919-421-9). 32pp. Even though Little Gorilla grows into a big gorilla, everyone still loves him.

1912 Bosschaert, Greet. *Teenie Bird and How She Learned to Fly* (PS–1). Illus. 2001, Abrams $12.95 (978-0-8109-3586-0). 32pp. Teenie Bird is afraid of flying but keeps trying until she is a success. (Rev: BL 3/1/01; HBG 10/01; SLJ 3/01)

1913 Bourgeois, Paulette. *Franklin and the Thunderstorm* (PS–K). Illus. by Brenda Clark. 1998, Kids Can $10.95 (978-1-55074-403-3). Unlike his animal friends, Franklin the turtle is afraid of thunderstorms until the wise old owl tells him what causes them. Other recommended titles in this popular series include *Franklin's Bad Day*(1997), *Franklin's Class Trip* (1999), and *Franklin Goes to the Hospital* (2000). Also available is *Franklin's Friendship Treasury* (2000), an anthology of four previously published stories including *Franklin Has a Sleepover* (1996), *Franklin's Bad Day* (1996) and *Franklin's Secret Club* (1998). (Rev: HBG 10/98; SLJ 7/98)

1914 Bradley, Kimberly Brubaker. *Ballerino Nate* (PS–K). Illus. by R. W. Alley. 2006, Dial $16.99 (978-0-8037-2954-4). 32pp. Nate the puppy's desire to become a ballet dancer is diminished when his older brother insists that only girls can be ballerinas. (Rev: BL 2/1/06; SLJ 3/06)

1915 Bradman, Tony. *A Goodnight Kind of Feeling* (PS–1). Illus. by Clive Scruton. 1998, Holiday House $15.95 (978-0-8234-1351-5). 32pp. A young cat spends a wonderful day walking in the park, going on an amusement park ride, and having a bath. (Rev: BL 6/1–15/98; HBG 10/98; SLJ 6/98)

1916 Brandenberg, Franz. *Nice New Neighbors* (K–2). Illus. by Aliki. 1990, Scholastic paper $2.75 (978-0-590-44117-9). 56pp. A family of mouse children generously include their neighbors, who formerly spurned them, when they decide to give a play — The Three Blind Mice.

1917 Braun, Sebastien. *I Love My Daddy* (PS). Illus. by author. 2004, HarperCollins $12.99 (978-0-06-054311-2). The story of Baby Bear's day and all the things he does with his father. (Rev: SLJ 4/04)

1918 Breen, Steve. *Stick* (PS–K). Illus. 2007, Dial $16.99 (978-0-8037-3124-0). 32pp. Brave little frog Stick is transported off for a great adventure when he tries to catch a dragonfly; the colorful and varied illustrations add to the humor and tension. (Rev: BL 3/15/07)

1919 Brennan-Nelson, Denise. *Grady the Goose* (PS–3). Illus. by Michael Glenn Monroe. 2006, Sleeping Bear $16.95 (978-1-58536-282-0). Young goose Grady, who is prone to wandering, is left behind when her family flies south and faces many dangers before a farmer comes to her aid. (Rev: SLJ 1/07)

1920 Brett, Jan. *Armadillo Rodeo* (PS–2). Illus. 1995, Penguin $16.99 (978-0-399-22803-2). 32pp. Nearsighted Bo, an armadillo, has fun when he wanders onto the Curly H Ranch. (Rev: BCCB 10/95; BL 9/15/95; SLJ 10/95)

1921 Brett, Jan. *Berlioz Bear* (K–3). Illus. 1991, Penguin $16.99 (978-0-399-22248-1). 32pp. Berlioz, a bear, is mystified by a strange buzz coming from his bass fiddle. (Rev: BL 9/15/91; HB 11/91; SLJ 10/91*)

1922 Brett, Jan. *Comet's Nine Lives* (PS–3). Illus. 1996, Penguin $16.99 (978-0-399-22931-2). 30pp. Comet, a white cat, has many adventures on Nantucket Island until finding a permanent home in a lighthouse. (Rev: BL 10/15/96; SLJ 12/96)

1923 Brett, Jan. *Fritz and the Beautiful Horses* (K–3). Illus. by author. 1987, Houghton $16.00 (978-0-395-30850-9); paper $6.99 (978-0-395-45356-8). 32pp. Pony Fritz is ostracized by the other horses and leads a lonely life.

1924 Brett, Jan. *The Hat* (PS–3). Illus. 1997, Penguin $16.99 (978-0-399-23101-8). 32pp. When a red wool stocking is blown onto the head of Hedgie the hedgehog, he maintains that it is his new hat. (Rev: BL 9/1/97*; HBG 3/98; SLJ 9/97)

1925 Brett, Jan. *Hedgie Blasts Off!* (PS–2). 2006, Putnam $16.99 (978-0-399-24621-0). 32pp. Hedgie's dream of becoming an astronaut comes true when the diminutive hedgehog is dispatched to the planet Mikkop on a mission to repair a malfunctioning volcano. (Rev: BL 8/06; SLJ 9/06)

1926 Brett, Jan. *Hedgie's Surprise* (PS–1). Illus. 2000, Penguin $16.99 (978-0-399-23477-4). 32pp. Henny wants to have family but a hungry troll named Tomten keeps stealing her eggs until she gets help from Hedgie the hedgehog. (Rev: BCCB 10/00; BL 9/1/00; HBG 3/01; SLJ 9/00)

1927 Brett, Jan. *Honey . . . Honey . . . Lion!* (PS–2). Illus. 2005, Putnam $16.99 (978-0-399-24463-6). 32pp. A honeyguide bird takes revenge on a greedy honey badger and leads him through a variety of obstacles that end at the feet of a lion. (Rev: BL 9/1/05; SLJ 9/05)

1928 Brett, Jan. *Town Mouse, Country Mouse* (PS–3). Illus. 1994, Penguin LB $16.99 (978-0-399-22622-9). 32pp. A town cat and a country owl, both of whom enjoy mice for dinner, decide to change places. (Rev: BL 9/1/94; SLJ 9/94)

1929 Brewster, Patience. *Rabbit Inn* (PS–K). Illus. 1991, Little, Brown $14.95 (978-0-316-10747-1). Two rabbits run an inn and their guests help to spruce up the place. (Rev: SLJ 7/91)

1930 Bridwell, Norman. *Clifford's Good Deeds* (PS–1). Illus. by author. 1985, Scholastic paper $3.99 (978-0-590-44292-3). 32pp. Clifford is a large shaggy dog whose efforts to be helpful result in comic mishaps. Also use: *Clifford Takes a Trip* (1985); *Clifford's Tricks* (1986); *Clifford the Big Red Dog* (1988); *Clifford the Small Red Puppy* (1990); *Clifford at the Circus* (1985); *Clifford Goes to Hollywood* (1986).

1931 Brimner, Larry Dane. *Cat on Wheels* (PS–3). Illus. by Mary Peterson. 2000, Boyds Mills $15.95 (978-1-56397-747-3). 32pp. A cat imagines what it would be like to travel through town on an orange skateboard with bright blue wheels. (Rev: BL 12/1/00; HBG 3/01; SLJ 11/00)

1932 Brock, Betty. *No Flying in the House* (2–4). Illus. by Wallace Tripp. 1970, HarperCollins paper $5.99 (978-0-06-440130-2). A small dog seeks shelter for herself and her human friends.

1933 Brodzinsky, Anne Braff. *The Mulberry Bird: An Adoption Story*. Rev. ed. (K–4). Illus. by Diane Stanley. 1996, Perspectives $16.00 (978-0-944034-15-9). 47pp. The process of adoption is the subject of this book about a little bird whose mother can't care for him and so she allows another bird couple to take her place. (Rev: SLJ 11/96)

1934 Brooks, Erik. *The Practically Perfect Pajamas* (1–3). Illus. 2000, Winslow $16.95 (978-1-890817-22-0). 32pp. Percy the polar bear is made fun of by his peers because of his red, star-studded pajamas, but he is cold and miserable without them. (Rev: BL 5/15/00; HBG 10/00; SLJ 5/00)

1935 Brooks, Erik. *Slow Days, Fast Friends* (PS–2). Illus. by author. 2005, Albert Whitman $16.95 (978-0-8075-7437-9). Forced by injury to move at a very slow pace, Howard the cheetah befriends Quince the sloth and learns to appreciate the joys of nature. (Rev: SLJ 1/06)

1936 Brown, Jo. *Hoppity Skip Little Chick* (PS). Illus. by author. 2005, Tiger Tales $15.95 (978-1-58925-045-1). Little Chick has fun with the other animals on the farm, but he is thrilled to discover that he has some siblings of his own. (Rev: BL 3/1/04; SLJ 5/05)

1937 Brown, Jo. *Where's My Mommy?* (PS–K). Illus. by author. 2002, Tiger Tales $14.95 (978-1-58925-019-2). A crocodile baby seeking its mother is humorously persuaded that it's not a monkey, an elephant, a donkey, a tiger, or a zebra. (Rev: SLJ 7/02)

1938 Brown, Ken. *Nellie's Knot* (PS–K). Illus. 1993, Macmillan LB $13.95 (978-0-02-714930-2). 32pp. In order not to forget something, a young elephant ties a knot in her trunk, but then she can't remember why. (Rev: BL 4/15/93)

1939 Brown, Ken. *The Scarecrow's Hat* (PS–1). Illus. 2001, Peachtree $15.95 (978-1-56145-240-8). 32pp. Through a series of barters and exchanges a resourceful chicken finally gets what she wants, the scarecrow's hat. (Rev: BL 3/15/01; HBG 10/01)

1940 Brown, Ken. *What's the Time, Grandma Wolf?* (PS–2). Illus. 2001, Peachtree $15.95 (978-1-56145-250-7). 32pp. All the animals in the woods are wary of Grandma Wolf, but curiosity keeps pulling them closer in this suspenseful story that turns out well in the end. (Rev: BL 7/01; HBG 3/02; SLJ 9/01)

1941 Brown, Marc. *Arthur, It's Only Rock 'n' Roll* (1–3). Illus. 2002, Little, Brown $15.95 (978-0-316-11854-5). 32pp. Arthur the aardvark's friend Francine starts a band, U Stink, that is invited to play with the successful Backstreet Boys. Also use *Arthur's Tractor: A Fairy Tale with Mechanical Parts* (2003). (Rev: BL 11/1/02; HBG 3/03; SLJ 12/02)

1942 Brown, Marc. *Arthur Lost and Found* (PS–K). Illus. 1998, Little, Brown $15.95 (978-0-316-10912-3). 32pp. In a balanced tale of fun and caution, Arthur and his pal Buster get lost on the wrong side of town. Also included in this series are *Arthur and the Crunch Cereal Contest* and *Arthur's Mystery Envelope* (both 1998). (Rev: BL 12/1/98; HBG 3/99; SLJ 1/99)

1943 Brown, Marc. *Arthur Writes a Story* (PS–3). Illus. 1996, Little, Brown $15.95 (978-0-316-10916-1). 32pp. Arthur's classmates embellish the simple story of how he got his puppy. Also use *Arthur's New Puppy* (1993), *Arthur's Chicken Pox* (1994), and *Arthur's Computer Disaster* (1997). (Rev: BL 9/15/96; SLJ 9/96)

1944 Brown, Marc. *Arthur's Family Treasury* (PS–1). Illus. 2000, Little, Brown $18.95 (978-0-316-12147-7). 96pp. Three previously published books about Arthur the aardvark (*Arthur's Birthday*, *Arthur's Family Vacation*, and *Arthur's Baby*) are included in this entertaining anthology. (Rev: BL 6/1–15/00; HBG 10/00)

1945 Brown, Marc. *Arthur's Teacher Moves In* (PS–1). Illus. 2000, Little, Brown $15.95 (978-0-316-11979-5). 32pp. When Arthur invites his teacher to stay at his home until his roof is repaired, the aardvark is labeled teacher's pet by the other students. (Rev: BL 11/1/00; HBG 3/01; SLJ 1/01)

1946 Brown, Marc. *Arthur's Underwear* (PS–1). Illus. 1999, Little, Brown $15.95 (978-0-316-11012-9). 32pp. Arthur experiences the ultimate embarrassment when his pants rip and reveal his underwear. (Rev: BL 1/1–15/00; HBG 3/00)

1947 Brown, Marc. *D.W.'s Guide to Perfect Manners* (PS–2). Illus. by author. 2006, Little, Brown $15.99 (978-0-316-12106-4). Arthur the aardvark challenges little sister D.W. to be the model of good behavior for a full 24 hours. (Rev: SLJ 8/06)

1948 Brown, Marc. *D.W.'s Library Card* (PS–2). Illus. by author. 2001, Little, Brown $14.95 (978-0-316-11013-6). Arthur the aardvark teaches little sister D.W. how to look after — and enjoy — library books. (Rev: HBG 3/02; SLJ 12/01)

1949 Brown, Marc. *D.W.'s Lost Blankie* (PS). Illus. 1998, Little, Brown $13.95 (978-0-316-10914-7). 24pp. Arthur's little sister, D.W., is inconsolable when she loses her beloved blankie. Luckily, Mom knows where to find it. (Rev: BL 5/15/98; HBG 10/98; SLJ 5/98)

1950 Brown, Marc, and Laurie Krasny Brown. *The Bionic Bunny Show* (2–3). Illus. by Marc Brown. 1984, Little, Brown $14.95 (978-0-316-11120-1). 32pp. An ordinary rabbit becomes a super TV star thanks to makeup magic.

1951 Brown, Margaret Wise. *The Runaway Bunny* (PS–K). Illus. by Clement Hurd. 1972, HarperCollins LB $16.89 (978-0-06-020766-3); paper $6.99 (978-0-06-443018-0). 40pp. With nine colorful illustrations, this new edition of an old favorite is a charming story of mother bunny's love for her restless youngster, who keeps trying to escape but is always found.

1952 Brown, Margaret Wise. *Sailor Boy Jig* (PS–K). Illus. by Dan Andreasen. 2002, Simon & Schuster $16.00 (978-0-689-83348-9). 32pp. A sailor puppy dances the jig, catches his supper, and gets ready for bed in this previously unpublished rhyme. (Rev: BL 3/15/02; HBG 10/02; SLJ 6/02)

1953 Brown, Ruth. *The Old Tree* (PS–2). Illus. by author. 2007, Candlewick $16.99 (978-0-7636-3461-2). 32pp. The animal residents of an old tree band together to protect it from destruction. (Rev: BL 10/1/07; SLJ 11/07)

1954 Browne, Anthony. *Little Beauty* (PS–3). Illus. by author. 2008, Candlewick $16.99 (978-0-7636-3959-4). 32pp. A lonely gorilla who knows sign language and a little cat become devoted companions in this twist on Beauty and the Beast. (Rev: BL 10/1/08; LMC 3/09; SLJ 11/08)

1955 Browne, Anthony. *Piggybook* (K–2). Illus. by author. 1990, Knopf paper $7.99 (978-0-679-80837-4). 32pp. Mrs. Piggot walks out when her family turns into real pigs and takes her for granted. (Rev: BCCB 10/86; BL 10/1/86; SLJ 10/86)

1956 Bruce, Lisa. *Fran's Friend* (PS–2). Illus. by Rosalind Beardshaw. 2003, Bloomsbury $15.95 (978-1-58234-777-6). 32pp. Fred the dog tries unsuccessfully to help Fran with her craft project. (Rev: BL 3/1/03; HBG 10/03; SLJ 5/03)

1957 Bruchac, Joseph. *Turtle's Race with Beaver: A Traditional Seneca Story* (1–3). Illus. by Jose Aruego and Ariane Dewey. 2003, Penguin $15.99 (978-0-8037-2852-3). 32pp. Turtle and Beaver compete for ownership of a pond in this variant on a Seneca Indian tale that resembles Aesop's story of the tortoise and the hare. (Rev: BL 9/15/03; HBG 4/04; SLJ 10/03)

1958 Brun-Cosme, Nadine. *Big Wolf and Little Wolf* (PS–1). Illus. by Olivier Tallec. 2009, Enchanted Lion $16.95 (978-1-59270-084-4). 32pp. Little Wolf spends time with Big Wolf and then leaves. (Rev: BL 6/1–15/09)

1959 Bruss, Deborah. *Book! Book! Book!* (PS–K). Illus. by Tiphanie Beeke. 2001, Scholastic $16.95 (978-0-439-13525-2). 40pp. A crew of bored animals head to the library and try to make the librarian understand. (Rev: BCCB 2/01; BL 5/15/01; HBG 10/01; SLJ 5/01)

1960 Buckingham, Matt. *Bright Stanley* (PS–K). Illus. by author. 2006, Tiger Tales $15.95 (978-1-58925-059-8). Hurrying to catch up with the other fish in his school, Stanley encounters a number of fascinating underwater characters; gold-foil scales adorn Stanley and his school. (Rev: SLJ 1/07)

1961 Buehner, Caralyn. *Superdog: The Heart of a Hero* (PS–1). Illus. by Mark Buehner. 2004, HarperCollins $16.99 (978-0-06-623620-9). 32pp. Dexter, a determined dachshund, is successful in his bid to become a superhero and even manages to rescue his former nemesis, Cleevis the tomcat. (Rev: BL 4/1/04; SLJ 2/04)

1962 Bunting, Eve. *Hurry! Hurry!* (PS–K). Illus. by Jeff Mack. 2007, Harcourt $16.00 (978-0-15-

205410-6). 40pp. All the animals of the farmyard gather to greet a new chick into the world. (Rev: BL 2/1/07)

1963 Bunting, Eve. *Little Bear's Little Boat* (PS). Illus. by Nancy Carpenter. 2003, Clarion $12.00 (978-0-395-97462-9). 32pp. Little Bear is devoted to his boat, but when he grows too big for it he happily turns it over to a smaller bear. (Rev: HBG 10/03; SLJ 8/03)

1964 Bunting, Eve. *Mouse Island* (K–2). Illus. by Dominic Catalano. 2008, Boyds Mills $15.95 (978-1-59078-447-1). 32pp. Lonely Mouse lives by himself on an island until he rescues a creature — a cat! — from a sinking ship. (Rev: BL 3/15/08; SLJ 4/08)

1965 Bunting, Eve. *The Wedding* (K–2). Illus. by Iza Trapani. 2003, Charlesbridge LB $15.95 (978-1-58089-040-3). Miss Brindle Cow gives many animals a ride to a wedding, and surprises them on arrival with the announcement that she is the bride. (Rev: HBG 4/04; SLJ 8/03)

1966 Burg, Sarah Emmanuelle. *One More Egg* (PS–1). Illus. by author. 2006, North-South $15.95 (978-0-7358-2001-2). In search of an egg, a rabbit and a chicken tour the farm meeting its residents; point readers to the endpapers to get the full story. (Rev: SLJ 2/06)

1967 Burningham, John. *It's a Secret!* (PS–1). Illus. by author. 2009, Candlewick $16.99 (978-0-7636-4275-4). 56pp. Where do cats go at night? Out cat dancing. (Rev: BCCB 9/09; BL 6/1–15/09; SLJ 6/09)

1968 Bush, John. *The Fish Who Could Wish* (PS–2). Illus. by Korky Paul. 1991, Kane paper $7.95 (978-0-916291-48-8). The adventures of a fish whose wishes always come true. (Rev: SLJ 8/91)

1969 Butler, John. *Ten in the Meadow* (PS). Illus. by author. 2006, Peachtree $15.95 (978-1-56145-372-6). Bear and nine of his animal friends play a game of hide-and-seek. (Rev: SLJ 9/06)

1970 Butler, M. Christina. *One Winter's Day* (PS–1). Illus. by Tina Macnaughton. 2006, Good Bks. $16.00 (978-1-56148-532-1). After his flimsy hut blows away during a snowstorm, Little Hedgehog travels to shelter in his friend Badger's house and along the way generously gives his warm clothes to other shivering animals. (Rev: SLJ 11/06)

1971 Butler, M. Christina. *Snow Friends* (PS). Illus. by Tina Macnaughton. 2005, Good Bks. $16.00 (978-1-56148-485-0). After Little Bear and his animal friends make a snowman, they decide to make a smaller snowman to keep the first one company; pages have a "sparkling glitter" finish. (Rev: SLJ 11/05)

1972 Buzzeo, Toni. *Dawdle Duckling* (PS–2). Illus. by Margaret Spengler. 2003, Dial $15.99 (978-0-8037-2731-1). A daydreaming duckling tries the patience of his mother in this appealing picture book with lyric text and rich artwork. (Rev: BL 5/15/03; HBG 10/03; SLJ 4/03)

1973 Buzzeo, Toni. *Ready or Not, Dawdle Duckling* (PS–2). Illus. by Margaret Spengler. Series: Dawdle Duckling. 2005, Dial $15.99 (978-0-8037-2959-9). 32pp. Dawdle, a slightly eccentric duckling, doesn't quite get the point of hide-and-seek. (Rev: BL 3/1/05; SLJ 3/05)

1974 Bynum, Janie. *Kiki's Blankie* (PS–K). Illus. by author. 2009, Sterling $14.95 (978-1-4027-5910-9). 32pp. Kiki, a little monkey, finds her missing blankie but it's in a tree above a crocodile. Will Kiki find a way to get it back? (Rev: BL 5/15/09; SLJ 6/09)

1975 Bynum, Janie. *Nutmeg and Barley* (K–2). 2006, Candlewick $15.99 (978-0-7636-2382-1). 32pp. Nutmeg the squirrel and Barley the mouse have little in common, but their friendship transcends their differences. (Rev: BL 2/1/06; SLJ 1/06)

1976 Cabrera, Jane. *Dog's Day* (PS–K). Illus. 2000, Orchard $12.95 (978-0-531-30262-0). 32pp. Dog has a fine day swinging on the trees with Monkey and playing games with other animal friends but best of all is having fun with his dad. (Rev: BL 2/1/00; HBG 10/00; SLJ 3/00)

1977 Cabrera, Jane. *The Lonesome Polar Bear* (PS–2). Illus. by author. 2003, Random $13.95 (978-0-375-82410-4). A polar bear cub searches desperately for a friend; a friendly snow cloud tries to help by providing lots of snow creatures for the cub to enjoy, but these quickly melt away. (Rev: HBG 4/04; SLJ 1/04)

1978 Calhoun, Mary. *Cross-Country Cat* (K–2). Illus. by Erick Ingraham. 1979, Morrow paper $6.99 (978-0-688-06519-5). 40pp. A Siamese cat named Henry sets out on a cross-country skiing adventure.

1979 Calhoun, Mary. *Hot-Air Henry* (PS–4). Illus. by Erick Ingraham. 1981, Morrow paper $6.99 (978-0-688-04068-0). 40pp. Siamese cat Henry sneaks into the basket of a hot-air balloon.

1980 Callahan, Sean. *The Bear Hug* (PS–K). Illus. by Laura J. Bryant. 2006, Albert Whitman $15.95 (978-0-8075-0596-0). Cubby's grandfather teaches him bear behavior, including how to hug. (Rev: SLJ 3/06)

1981 Calmenson, Stephanie. *Jazzmatazz!* (PS–1). Illus. by Bruce Degen. 2008, HarperCollins $16.99 (978-0-06-077289-5). 32pp. A little mouse gets a whole neighborhood involved in his jazzy improvisations. (Rev: BL 1/1–15/08; SLJ 3/08)

1982 Cannon, Janell. *Crickwing* (1–4). Illus. 2000, Harcourt $16.00 (978-0-15-201790-3). 48pp. Crickwing, a starving cockroach-artist, joins forces with some plucky leafcutter ants to rout a group of voracious army ants in this gripping story set in a rain forest. (Rev: BL 10/15/00*; HBG 3/01; SLJ 11/00)

1983 Cannon, Janell. *Stellaluna* (PS–3). Illus. 1993, Harcourt $16.00 (978-0-15-280217-2). 48pp. Stellaluna, a fruit bat, is separated from her mother and raised by birds. (Rev: BL 4/1/93; SLJ 6/93)

1984 Cannon, Janell. *Verdi* (K–3). Illus. 1997, Harcourt $16.00 (978-0-15-201028-7). 48pp. A baby python named Verdi has fun and adventures when he travels alone in the rain forest. (Rev: BCCB 6/97; BL 4/15/97; SLJ 5/97)

1985 Caple, Kathy. *Duck and Company* (1–3). Illus. by author. 2007, Holiday House paper $4.95 (978-0-8234-2125-1). 32pp. A series of shoppers put bookstore owners Duck and Rat through a variety of challenges in this funny volume that will appeal to reluctant readers. (Rev: BCCB 10/07; LMC 3/08; SLJ 10/07)

1986 Capucilli, Alyssa Satin. *Katy Duck* (PS). Illus. by Henry Cole. 2007, Simon & Schuster $7.99 (978-1-4169-1901-8). Katy Duck loves to dance at home but is a little unsure of ballet class until she sees what fun it can be. (Rev: SLJ 7/07)

1987 Capucilli, Alyssa Satin. *Katy Duck Is a Caterpillar* (PS–2). Illus. by Henry Cole. 2009, Simon & Schuster $14.99 (978-1-4169-6061-4). 32pp. Katy Duck is devastated when she is given the role of a caterpillar in the spring dance recital. (Rev: BL 12/1/08; SLJ 2/09)

1988 Carle, Eric. *The Grouchy Ladybug* (PS–K). Illus. by author. 1977, HarperCollins $15.00 (978-0-690-01391-7). 48pp. A grouchy ladybug, who is looking for a fight, challenges every insect and animal she meets regardless of size. Brilliantly illustrated in collage, the pages vary in size with the size of the animal.

1989 Carle, Eric. *The Mixed-Up Chameleon* (PS–2). Illus. by author. 1984, HarperCollins LB $18.89 (978-0-690-04397-6); paper $6.99 (978-0-06-443162-0). 32pp. A new edition of the story of a chameleon who finally decides to be himself.

1990 Carle, Eric. *"Slowly, Slowly, Slowly," Said the Sloth* (K–3). Illus. by author. 2002, Philomel $16.99 (978-0-399-23954-0). A sloth explains to a variety of jungle animals the reasons why he likes to take things easy in this beautifully illustrated book. (Rev: HBG 3/03; SLJ 9/02)

1991 Carle, Eric. *The Very Busy Spider* (PS–K). Illus. by author. 1989, Penguin $21.99 (978-0-399-21166-9). 32pp. A spider spins its web in this striking picture book. Also use the story of a crab that outgrows his shell in: *A House for Hermit Crab* (1991, Picture Book). (Rev: BCCB 5/85; BL 6/1/85; SLJ 5/85)

1992 Carle, Eric. *The Very Clumsy Click Beetle* (PS–1). Illus. 1999, Penguin $21.99 (978-0-399-23201-5). 32pp. A click beetle learns to use its life-saving device of clicking to turn over when it is on its back, but only in the nick of time. (Rev: BL 10/1/99; HBG 3/00; SLJ 11/99)

1993 Carle, Eric. *The Very Hungry Caterpillar* (PS–2). Illus. by author. 1981, Penguin $21.99 (978-0-399-20853-9). 32pp. A caterpillar eats a great deal and then spins its cocoon.

1994 Carle, Eric. *The Very Lonely Firefly* (PS–1). Illus. 1995, Penguin $22.99 (978-0-399-22774-5). 32pp. A little firefly searches for some of his own kind but is confused by such lights as candles and fireworks. (Rev: BCCB 7–8/95; BL 5/15/95; HB 9/95; SLJ 8/95)

1995 Carle, Eric. *The Very Quiet Cricket* (PS–1). Illus. 1990, Penguin $22.99 (978-0-399-21885-9). 48pp. A newly hatched cricket has a problem getting his wings to chirp. (Rev: BCCB 11/90; BL 10/1/90; HB 1/91; SLJ 12/90)

1996 Carle, Eric, and Kazuo Iwamura. *Where Are You Going? To See My Friend!* (K–2). Illus. 2003, Scholastic $19.95 (978-0-439-41659-7). 40pp. A dog asks various animals to come and meet his friend in this charming and inventive bilingual English-Japanese picture book. (Rev: BL 1/1–15/03; HB 5/03; HBG 10/03; SLJ 3/03)

1997 Carlson, Nancy. *First Grade, Here I Come!* (PS–1). 2006, Viking $15.99 (978-0-670-06127-3). 32pp. Henry the mouse reviews his experiences on the first day in 1st grade and realizes he quite enjoyed it after all. (Rev: BL 8/06; SLJ 7/06)

1998 Carlson, Nancy. *Harriet and the Garden* (PS–1). Illus. by author. 1982, Carolrhoda LB $15.95 (978-0-87614-184-7). 32pp. Harriet, a childlike dog, has several simple adventures. Others in the series are: *Harriet and the Roller Coaster; Harriet and Walt; Harriet's Recital* (all 1982).

1999 Carlson, Nancy. *Harriet and the Roller Coaster* (PS–2). Illus. 2003, Carolrhoda $15.95 (978-1-57505-053-9). 32pp. A 20th-anniversary edition of the classic story about Harriet's courage and George's unexpected lack of it. (Rev: BL 1/1–15/04; HBG 4/04)

2000 Carlson, Nancy. *Henry's Amazing Imagination* (PS–1). Illus. by author. 2008, Viking $15.99 (978-0-670-06296-6). 32pp. Henry the mouse's stories at show-and-tell are so imaginative that his classmates accuse him of fibbing, so his teacher asks him to write his stories down instead. (Rev: BL 6/1–15/08; LMC 11/08; SLJ 8/08)

2001 Carlson, Nancy. *How About a Hug?* (PS–K). Illus. 2001, Viking $15.99 (978-0-670-03506-9). 32pp. A pig family awards hugs in a variety of circumstances. (Rev: BL 7/01; HBG 3/02; SLJ 12/01)

2002 Carlson, Nancy. *I Like Me!* (PS–K). Illus. by author. 1988, Puffin paper $6.99 (978-0-14-050819-2). 32pp. An exuberant book that teaches how to appreciate oneself. (Rev: BL 6/15/88; SLJ 9/88)

2003 Carlson, Nancy. *Look Out, Kindergarten, Here I Come! / ¡Preparate Kindergarten! Alla voy!* (PS–3). Trans. by Teresa Mlawer. Illus. 2004, Viking $15.99 (978-0-670-03673-8). 32pp. A bilingual story about Henry the mouse's ambivalence toward his first day of kindergarten. (Rev: BL 3/1/04; SLJ 9/04)

2004 Carlson, Nancy. *Loudmouth George and the Cornet* (PS–2). Illus. by author. 1983, Carolrhoda LB $15.95 (978-0-87614-214-1). 32pp. George, a rabbit, gets dismissed from the school band. Others in the series are: *Loudmouth George and the Big Race; Loudmouth George and the Fishing Trip; Loudmouth George and the New Neighbors; Loudmouth George and the Sixth-Grade Bully* (all 1983).

2005 Carlson, Nancy. *Loudmouth George Earns His Allowance* (PS–2). Illus. 2007, Carolrhoda $15.95 (978-0-8225-6560-4). 32pp. George the rabbit ends up doing more work after his brothers "help" him with his chores in this brightly illustrated book. (Rev: BL 5/1/07)

2006 Carlson, Nancy. *Smile a Lot!* (PS–2). Illus. 2002, Carolrhoda $15.95 (978-0-87614-869-3). 32pp. A happy frog greets the challenges of daily life — going to the dentist, spelling tests — with a big smile and a happy attitude. (Rev: BL 9/15/02; HBG 3/03; SLJ 10/02)

2007 Carlson, Nancy. *Think Big!* (PS–2). Illus. by author. 2005, Carolrhoda $15.95 (978-1-57505-622-7). A very small frog learns to love his size after some encouragement from his mother. (Rev: SLJ 9/05)

2008 Carman, Patrick. *Saving Mister Nibbles!* (1–3). Illus. by Jim Madsen. 2008, Scholastic $12.99 (978-0-545-01930-9). 74pp. Eliot the squirrel and his friends are horrified to see a stuffed squirrel being presented as a birthday gift and determine to rescue it from a life in captivity. (Rev: BL 6/1–15/08; LMC 3/08) ∩

2009 Carr, Jan. *Swine Divine* (PS–1). Illus. by Robert Bender. 1999, Holiday House $15.95 (978-0-8234-1434-5). 32pp. Rosie the pig is honored to be photographed in a bonnet and tutu by Mr. Porkpie, but she would rather be on the farm rolling in the mud and eating her swill. (Rev: BL 3/1/99; HBG 10/99; SLJ 6/99)

2010 Carrick, Carol. *What Happened to Patrick's Dinosaurs?* (K–2). Illus. by Donald Carrick. 1988, Houghton $16.00 (978-0-89919-406-6); paper $5.95 (978-0-89919-797-5). Patrick explains to his young brother his theory of how dinosaurs disappeared: they left by spaceship. (Rev: HB 8–9/86; SLJ 5/86)

2011 Casad, Mary Brooke. *Bluebonnet at the Marshall Train Depot* (2–4). Illus. by Benjamin Vincent. 1999, Pelican $15.95 (978-1-56554-311-9). Bluebonnet, an armadillo, visits a museum that was once a train depot and learns something about Texas's railroad history. (Rev: SLJ 3/00)

2012 Casanova, Mary. *One-Dog Canoe* (PS–1). Illus. by Ard Hoyt. 2003, Farrar $16.50 (978-0-374-35638-5). 32pp. A girl and her dog are crowded out when other animals decide to pile into their canoe. (Rev: BL 2/15/03; HBG 10/03; SLJ 3/03)

2013 Cassels, Jean. *Br'er Rabbit Captured! A Dr. David Harleyson Adventure* (1–4). Illus. by author. 2007, Walker $17.95 (978-0-8027-9556-4). 32pp. Famous pig painter David Harleyson heads south to depict Br'er Rabbit — but first he and his nephew John D. have to find the bunny; told in nuanced southern rhythm. (Rev: SLJ 10/07)

2014 Catalano, Dominic. *Mr. Basset Plays* (K–3). Illus. 2003, Boyds Mills $15.95 (978-1-59078-007-7). 32pp. Reginald E. Basset, a hound of means, realizes that money isn't everything. (Rev: BL 3/1/03; HBG 10/03; SLJ 3/03)

2015 Catalanotto, Peter. *Dylan's Day Out* (PS–2). Illus. 1989, Watts LB $16.99 (978-0-531-08429-8). 32pp. Dylan, a bored dalmatian, escapes for a day of freedom. (Rev: BL 10/1/89; SLJ 11/89)

2016 Catchpool, Michael. *Where There's a Bear, There's Trouble!* (PS–2). Illus. by Vanessa Cabban. 2002, ME Media $14.95 (978-1-58925-002-4). 32pp. Geese and mice follow a bouncy bear in search of honey and all goes well until they arrive at a hive full of threatening bees. (Rev: BL 12/1/02)

2017 Cauley, Lorinda Bryan. *The Trouble with Tyrannosaurus Rex* (PS–2). Illus. by author. 1988, Harcourt paper $7.00 (978-0-15-290881-2). 32pp. The story of how Duckbill and Ankylosaurus scare away Tyrannosaurus Rex, the terror of the forest. (Rev: BL 4/1/88; SLJ 9/88)

2018 Caumartin, Francois. *Now You See Them, Now You Don't* (PS–2). Trans. from French by David Homel. Illus. by author. 1996, Firefly paper $4.95 (978-1-55209-007-7). 20pp. Whimsical illustrations show animals trying to disguise themselves in different ways to fool Simon the hunter. (Rev: SLJ 1/97)

2019 Cave, Kathryn. *Henry's Song* (PS–K). Illus. by Sue Hendra. 2000, Eerdmans $16.00 (978-0-8028-5198-7). 26pp. When the other animals objects to the quality of Henry's singing voice, the Maker encourages them to sing together in harmony. (Rev: BL 4/15/00; HBG 10/00; SLJ 9/00)

2020 Cazet, Denys. *A Fish in His Pocket* (PS–2). Illus. by author. 1987, Orchard paper $5.95 (978-0-531-07021-5). 32pp. Russell the bear causes the death of a fish — accidentally — in this story of who is responsible when an accident ends in death. (Rev: BL 8/87; SLJ 12/87)

2021 Cazet, Denys. *Will You Read to Me?* (PS–2). Illus. 2007, Atheneum $16.99 (978-1-4169-0935-4). 32pp. Hamlet's fellow pigs refuse to listen to his stories or read to him, so he goes to the pond and there finds an appreciative audience. (Rev: BL 5/1/07; SLJ 7/07)

2022 Cecil, Randy. *Duck* (PS–1). Illus. by author. 2008, Candlewick $15.99 (978-0-7636-3072-0). 40pp. A wooden carousel duck nurses a real duckling until he grows old enough to fly, which is a challenge for them both; but Duck's rewards come when a fully grown Duckling returns and takes Duck up into the air. (Rev: BL 2/1/08; LMC 3/08; SLJ 3/08)

2023 Chaconas, Dori. *Coriander the Contrary Hen* (PS–1). Illus. by Marsha Carrington. 2007, Carolrhoda LB $15.95 (978-1-57505-749-1). Coriander never does as she's told, and young listeners will revel in her obstinateness. (Rev: SLJ 6/07)

2024 Chaconas, Dori. *Mousie Love* (K–2). Illus. by Josee Masse. 2009, Bloomsbury $16.99 (978-1-59990-111-4). 32pp. A charming tale of old-fashioned romance between mice Tully and Frill. (Rev: BL 5/1/09)

2025 Charles, Faustin, and Michael Terry. *The Selfish Crocodile* (PS–2). Illus. 1999, Little Tiger $14.95 (978-1-888444-56-8). 32pp. A selfish crocodile won't allow any animals in his river until a little mouse helps him and he realizes the value of friendship. (Rev: BL 6/1–15/99)

2026 Chataway, Carol. *The Perfect Pet* (PS–2). Illus. by Greg Holfeld. 2002, Kids Can $14.95 (978-1-55337-178-6). Pigs Hamlet, Pygmalion, and Podge are seeking the perfect pet, and find one through a process of elimination. (Rev: HBG 10/02; SLJ 7/02)

2027 Chen, Chih-Yuan. *Artie and Julie* (PS–2). Illus. by author. 2008, Heryin $17.95 (978-0-9787550-3-4). 48pp. A young lion and young rabbit form an unexpected friendship when they both take shelter from a storm in the same dark cave; the split-page format allows the reader to follow the lion's story or the rabbit's story or to read them together as an integrated whole. (Rev: BLO 9/2/08; SLJ 9/08)

2028 Chen, Chih-Yuan. *The Featherless Chicken* (K–3). Illus. by author. 2006, Heryin $16.95 (978-0-9762056-9-2). A featherless young chicken agonizes about his looks and his rejection by his peers. (Rev: SLJ 10/06)

2029 Chen, Chih-Yuan. *Guji Guji* (PS–3). Illus. by author. 2004, Kane $15.95 (978-1-929132-67-6). Guji Guji, a crocodile raised by a duck, faces difficult decisions when he grows to maturity. (Rev: SLJ 11/04)

2030 Cherry, Lynne. *The Armadillo from Amarillo* (K–3). Illus. 1994, Harcourt $16.00 (978-0-15-200359-3). 32pp. Sasparillo the armadillo wanders the earth and travels on a space shuttle to find out where he fits into the grand scheme of things. (Rev: BL 3/1/94; SLJ 4/94)

2031 Cherry, Lynne. *How Groundhog's Garden Grew* (PS–3). Illus. 2003, Scholastic $16.99 (978-0-439-32371-0). 40pp. Squirrel shows Groundhog how to plant a garden, with delicious results come harvest time. (Rev: BL 2/1/03; HBG 10/03; SLJ 2/03)

2032 Chorao, Kay. *The Cats Kids* (PS–K). Illus. 1998, Holiday House $16.95 (978-0-8234-1405-5). 48pp. Three simple tales about three sibling kittens present experiences typical of brothers and sisters everywhere. (Rev: BL 11/1/98; HBG 3/99; SLJ 11/98)

2033 Chorao, Kay. *Pig and Crow* (PS–2). Illus. 2000, Holt $16.95 (978-0-8050-5863-5). 32pp. Pig gets help for his loneliness from Crow, who tries several ways to rid Pig of the blues. (Rev: BL 7/00*; HB 5/00; HBG 10/00; SLJ 6/00)

2034 Christelow, Eileen. *Five Little Monkeys Wash the Car* (PS–1). Illus. 2000, Clarion $15.00 (978-0-395-92566-9). 33pp. Mama, a monkey, gets help from her five little monkeys when she decides to sell the rickety old family car. (Rev: BL 5/1/00; HBG 10/00; SLJ 5/00)

2035 Christelow, Eileen. *Five Little Monkeys with Nothing to Do* (PS–1). Illus. 1996, Clarion $16.00 (978-0-395-75830-4). 36pp. Five little monkeys prepare for their Grandma Bessie's visit. (Rev: BCCB 12/96; BL 9/1/96; SLJ 11/96)

2036 Christelow, Eileen. *The Great Pig Escape* (PS–1). Illus. 1994, Clarion $15.00 (978-0-395-66973-0). 32pp. On their way to be sold at market, some pigs escape and disguise themselves as humans. (Rev: BL 9/15/94; SLJ 11/94)

2037 Christelow, Eileen. *The Great Pig Search* (K–3). Illus. 2001, Clarion $15.00 (978-0-618-04910-3). 32pp. Farmer Bert and his wife Ethel travel to Florida to search in vain for their runaway pigs, who evade them by donning hilarious disguises. (Rev: BL 9/1/01; HB 3/02; HBG 10/02; SLJ 9/01*)

2038 Christelow, Eileen. *Jerome Camps Out* (PS–3). Illus. 1998, Clarion $16.00 (978-0-395-75831-1). 32pp. On a camping trip, alligator Jerome gets even with the camp bully, Buster, who has put Jerome's clothes in a tree. (Rev: BL 4/15/98; HBG 10/98; SLJ 6/98)

2039 Christelow, Eileen. *The Robbery at the Diamond Dog Diner* (PS–1). Illus. by author. 1988, Houghton paper $6.95 (978-0-89919-722-7). 32pp. Some zany goings-on at the Diamond Dog Diner when Glenda Feathers announces that jewel thieves are in town. (Rev: BCCB 10/86; BL 11/1/86; SLJ 2/86)

2040 Church, Caroline Jayne. *Digby Takes Charge* (PS–1). Illus. by author. 2007, Simon & Schuster $14.99 (978-1-4169-3441-7). 32pp. Digby the sheepdog learns that his stubborn sheep will only respond to his requests when he uses the word "please." (Rev: BL 6/1–15/07; SLJ 8/07)

2041 Church, Caroline Jayne. *One Smart Goose* (PS–2). Illus. 2005, Scholastic $16.95 (978-0-439-68765-2). 32pp. A clever goose uses camouflage to hide from a fox, earning the respect of his fellow geese. (Rev: BL 3/1/05; SLJ 5/05)

2042 Church, Caroline Jayne. *Ping Pong Pig* (PS–1). Illus. by author. 2008, Holiday House $16.95 (978-0-8234-2176-3). 32pp. Ping Pong, a little pig, disrupts the farmyard with his efforts to fly, so the other animals band together and get him a trampoline. (Rev: SLJ 9/08)

2043 Churchill, Vicki. *Sometimes I Like to Curl Up in a Ball* (PS). Illus. by Charles Fuge. 2001, Sterling $12.95 (978-1-86233-253-9). Wombat is a lively preschooler who tackles all kinds of activities with gusto. (Rev: SLJ 1/02)

2044 Clement, Gary. *The Great Poochini* (PS–2). Illus. by author. 1999, Groundwood $15.95 (978-0-88899-331-1). By day he is Jack, an ordinary dog, but at night he becomes the Great Poochini, the famous canine opera singer whose important role is *Dog Giovanni*. (Rev: SLJ 12/99*)

2045 Clements, Andrew. *Big Al and Shrimpy* (PS–2). Illus. by Yoshi. 2002, Simon & Schuster $16.95 (978-0-689-84247-4). Little Shrimpy gets the chance to reward Big Al's kindness by helping him get his fin free. (Rev: HBG 3/03; SLJ 11/02)

2046 Clements, Andrew. *Circus Family Dog* (PS–2). Illus. by Sue Truesdell. 2000, Clarion $16.00 (978-0-395-78648-2). 32pp. When a new, active dog joins the circus, old Grumps must learn a new trick to keep up. (Rev: BCCB 7–8/00; BL 6/1–15/00; HBG 10/00; SLJ 8/00)

2047 Coffey, Maria. *A Cat in a Kayak* (K–2). Illus. by Eugenie Fernandes. 1998, Annick LB $16.95 (978-1-55037-509-1); paper $6.95 (978-1-55037-508-4). Cat Teelo leaves his house in an effort to escape the noisy animals his young master brings there, but he finds that in the long run home is best. (Rev: SLJ 7/98)

2048 Cole, Babette. *Hurrah for Ethelyn* (K–3). Illus. 1991, Little, Brown $14.95 (978-0-316-15189-4). 32pp. A rat named Ethelyn bests the school bully, Tina Toerat. (Rev: BL 9/1/91; SLJ 3/92)

2049 Cole, Babette. *Lady Lupin's Book of Etiquette* (PS–3). Illus. by author. 2002, Peachtree $14.95 (978-1-56145-257-6). Lady Lupin sets about teaching her puppies proper behavior (don't bark with your mouth full, and so forth). (Rev: HBG 10/02; SLJ 7/02)

2050 Cooper, Helen. *Delicious!* (PS–1). Illus. by author. 2007, Farrar $16.00 (978-0-374-31756-0). 32pp. What can you do with a picky eater when Duck's favorite pumpkin soup is out of season? Cat and Squirrel must use their imaginations in this third book in the series that began with *Pumpkin Soup* (1999). (Rev: BL 9/1/07; SLJ 9/07)

2051 Cooper, Helen. *A Pipkin of Pepper* (PS–2). Illus. 2005, Farrar $16.00 (978-0-374-35953-9). 32pp. Duck gets lost when he accompanies friends Cat and Squirrel to the city to buy salt for the soup in this companion to *Pumpkin Soup* (1997). (Rev: BL 8/05; SLJ 9/05)

2052 Coulman, Valerie. *Sink or Swim* (K–2). Illus. by Roge Girard. 2003, Lobster $15.95 (978-1-894222-54-9). Another adventure for Ralph the cow — this time, with help from his friends, he learns to swim. (Rev: SLJ 5/04)

2053 Cousins, Lucy. *Maisy, Charley, and the Wobbly Tooth* (PS–1). Series: Maisy. 2006, Candlewick $12.99 (978-0-7636-2904-5). 32pp. Supportive mouse Maisy accompanies her crocodile friend Charlie to the dentist, where he learns about brushing his teeth. (Rev: BL 5/1/06)

2054 Cousins, Lucy. *Maisy Goes Swimming* (PS). Illus. 1990, Little, Brown $13.95 (978-0-316-15834-3). Maisy, a mouse, goes to a swimming pool in this book that contains many flaps and tabs. Also use: *Maisy Goes to Bed* (1990). (Rev: BCCB 10/90*; SLJ 9/90)

2055 Cousins, Lucy. *Maisy Goes to the Library* (PS–K). Illus. 2005, Candlewick $12.99 (978-0-7636-2669-3). 32pp. In this colorfully illustrated picture book, Maisy the mouse goes to the library in search of a book about fish and a peaceful setting in which to read it. (Rev: BL 8/05; SLJ 8/05)

2056 Cousins, Lucy. *Where Are Maisy's Friends?* (PS). Illus. by author. 2000, Candlewick $4.99 (978-0-7636-1119-4). A flap board book in which the reader is asked to play hide-and-seek with Maisy, a mouse, and her friends by lifting the flaps. Also use: *Where Does Maisy Live?* (2000). (Rev: SLJ 12/00)

2057 Cowan, Charlotte. *Katie Caught a Cold* (PS–2). Illus. by Katy Bratun. Series: Dr. Hippo. 2008, Hippocratic $17.95 (978-0-9753516-3-5). A bear called Katie has a bad cold and can't go ice skating so Dr. Hippo is consulted; *Peeper Has a Fever* and *Sadie's Sore Throat* also describe common childhood problems and their treatment. (Rev: SLJ 7/08)

2058 Cowley, Joy. *The Mouse Bride* (PS–1). Illus. by David Christiana. 1995, Scholastic $13.95 (978-0-590-47503-7). 32pp. A tiny mouse sets out to find a husband and after many rejections finds the mouse of her dreams. (Rev: BCCB 11/95; BL 1/1–15/96; SLJ 11/95)

2059 Cowley, Joy. *Snake and Lizard* (K–4). Illus. by Gavin Bishop. 2008, Kane $14.95 (978-1-933605-83-8). 85pp. In 15 short, funny episodes Snake and Lizard enjoy their unlikely friendship and resolve each and every conflict. (Rev: HB 11/08; LMC 3/08; SLJ 12/08*)

2060 Cresp, Gael. *The Tale of Gilbert Alexander Pig* (PS–2). Illus. 2000, Barefoot Books $15.95 (978-1-84148-215-6). 32pp. A clever little pig who realizes that the wolf could be a serious threat reaches an agreement with him so they can help each other. (Rev: BL 3/15/00; SLJ 8/00)

2061 Crimi, Carolyn. *Henry and the Buccaneer Bunnies* (PS–2). Illus. by John Manders. 2005, Candlewick $15.99 (978-0-7636-2449-1). 40pp. More interested in books than buccaneering, Henry the bunny endures the taunts of his shipmates but saves the day with his book smarts when their pirate ship is wrecked on a desert island. (Rev: BL 12/1/05; SLJ 11/05)

2062 Crimi, Carolyn. *Tessa's Tip-Tapping Toes* (PS–2). Illus. by Marsha Carrington. 2002, Scholastic $16.95 (978-0-439-31768-9). 32pp. A dancing mouse and a singing cat decide they can no longer stifle their talents, and soon have the whole household joining in. (Rev: BL 3/1/02; HBG 10/02)

2063 Cronin, Doreen. *Click, Clack, Moo: Cows That Type* (PS–3). Illus. by Betsy Lewin. 2000, Simon & Schuster $15.00 (978-0-689-83213-0). 32pp. In this humorous tale, barnyard animals go on strike for better working conditions including electric blankets for cold nights. Caldecott Honor Book, 2001. (Rev: BCCB 9/00; BL 4/1/00; HB 3/00; HBG 10/00)

2064 Cronin, Doreen. *Dooby Dooby Moo* (PS–3). Illus. by Betsy Lewin. 2006, Simon & Schuster $16.95 (978-0-689-84507-9). 40pp. In this lively farmyard tale, Farmer Brown's animals compete in a local talent show in hopes of winning the first prize — a trampoline. (Rev: BL 8/06; SLJ 8/06)

2065 Cronin, Doreen. *Duck for President* (K–3). Illus. by Betsy Lewin. 2004, Simon & Schuster $15.95 (978-0-689-86377-6). Bored with his life, Duck arranges and wins an election to replace Farmer Brown as head of the farm and then winds up running the country; voting problems and Duck's campaign techniques add to the fun for adults. (Rev: SLJ 3/04)

2066 Cronin, Doreen. *Giggle, Giggle, Quack* (PS–1). Illus. by Betsy Lewin. 2002, Simon & Schuster $15.00 (978-0-689-84506-2). 32pp. A hilarious cartoon story about novice Bob and his attempts to care for some farm animals in spite of the intervention of bossy Duck. (Rev: BCCB 6/02; BL 4/15/02; HB 5/02; HBG 10/02; SLJ 6/02)

2067 Cronin, Doreen. *Stretch* (PS–1). Illus. by Scott Menchin. 2009, Atheneum $15.99 (978-1-4169-5341-8). 40pp. Stretch is a lively dog who leads a yoga class and clearly demonstrates many ways of stretching. (Rev: BL 5/15/09; SLJ 8/09)

2068 Cronin, Doreen. *Thump, Quack, Moo: A Whacky Adventure* (PS–2). Illus. by Betsy Lewin. 2008, Atheneum $16.99 (978-1-4169-1630-7). 42pp. The ever-inventive Duck has his own ideas about the design of Farmer Brown's contribution to the annual Corn Maze Festival. (Rev: BL 7/08; SLJ 8/08)

2069 Crow, Kristyn. *Cool Daddy Rat* (K–2). Illus. by Mike Lester. 2008, Putnam $16.99 (978-0-399-24375-2). 32pp. Bass player Cool Daddy Rat, with his stowaway son Ace, head for Manhattan night life in this lively, jazzy romp. (Rev: LMC 11/08; SLJ 4/08)

2070 Crummel, Susan Stevens. *Ten-Gallon Bart* (K–2). Illus. by Dorothy Donohue. 2006, Marshall Cavendish $16.95 (978-0-7614-5246-1). 32pp. Ten-Gallon Bart, the canine sheriff of Dog City, is convinced to put his retirement plans on hold when he hears that Billy the Kid, an outlaw goat, is headed for town; colorful language and humorous collage illustrations capture the feel of the Old West. (Rev: BL 4/1/06; SLJ 4/06)

2071 Crummel, Susan Stevens. *Ten-Gallon Bart and the Wild West Show* (K–2). Illus. by Dorothy Donohue. 2008, Marshall Cavendish $16.99 (978-0-7614-5391-8). 40pp. Bart, the former sheriff of Dog City first seen in *Ten-Gallon Bart* (2006) enters a bull-riding competition that poses interesting challenges. (Rev: BL 4/1/08; SLJ 5/08)

2072 Crunk, Tony. *Grandpa's Overalls* (PS–1). Illus. by Scott Nash. 2001, Scholastic $15.95 (978-0-531-30321-4). 32pp. When Grandpa's overalls run away, he is left unable to work; but then Grandma's nightie takes off too, and the whole neighborhood (all dogs) gives chase. (Rev: BCCB 5/01; BL 8/01; HBG 10/01; SLJ 7/01)

2073 *Curious George and the Puppies* (PS–K). Illus. 1998, Houghton $12.95 (978-0-395-91217-1); paper $3.95 (978-0-395-91215-7). 24pp. This is one of a new series of eight books about the mischievous monkey. Other titles include *Curious George Goes to a Movie, Curious George Makes Pancakes,* and *Curious George's Dream.* (Rev: BL 11/15/98; HBG 3/99)

2074 Currey, Anna. *Tickling Tigers* (PS–K). Illus. 1996, Barron's $12.95 (978-0-8120-6594-7); paper $5.95 (978-0-8120-9594-4). 32pp. Hannibal, a little mouse, narrowly escapes capture by several tigers whom he has enraged. (Rev: BL 10/15/96)

2075 Curtiss, A. B. *In the Company of Bears* (K–2). Illus. by Barbara Stone. 1994, Oldcastle LB $18.95 (978-0-932529-72-5). Humorous illustrations depict polar bears engaging in many human activities. (Rev: SLJ 9/94)

2076 Cushman, Doug. *Mystery at the Club Sandwich* (1–4). Illus. by author. 2004, Clarion $15.00 (978-0-618-41969-2). 30pp. In this entertaining hard-boiled detective story, elephant sleuth Nick Trunk — who works for peanuts — investigates the disappearance of Maggie Trouble's lucky marbles. (Rev: SLJ 1/05)

2077 Cusimano, Maryann K. *You Are My I Love You* (PS–2). Illus. by Satomi Ichikawa. 2001, Penguin $16.99 (978-0-399-23392-0). 32pp. Rhyming text and warm illustrations celebrate the relationship between mother and baby teddy bears during a day's activities. (Rev: BL 5/1/01; HBG 10/01; SLJ 5/01)

2078 Cutler, Jane. *Rose and Riley* (K–2). Illus. by Thomas F. Yezerski. 2005, Farrar $15.00 (978-0-374-36340-6). 48pp. Little vole Rose tends to expect the worst in all situations, but her friend

Riley the groundhog is always there to allay her concerns. (Rev: BCCB 3/05; SLJ 3/05)

2079 Cuyler, Margery. *Groundhog Stays Up Late* (PS–2). Illus. by Jean Cassels. 2005, Walker $16.95 (978-0-8027-8939-6). 32pp. Awake during a cold and lonely winter, Groundhog tricks his sensible, hibernating friends into waking up early only to have them plot an effective revenge. (Rev: BL 12/1/05; SLJ 12/05)

2080 Dahl, Roald. *The Enormous Crocodile* (K–3). Illus. by Quentin Blake. 1978, Puffin paper $5.99 (978-0-14-036556-6). 48pp. Animals band together to save a group of children from becoming a crocodile's lunch.

2081 Daly, Niki. *Welcome to Zanzibar Road* (PS–3). 2006, Clarion $16.00 (978-0-618-64926-6). 32pp. A gentle story about the animals living in the busy community of Zanzibar Road, including Mama Jumbo, who adopts chicken Little Chiko. (Rev: BL 5/1/06; SLJ 7/06) 🎧

2082 D'Amico, Carmela. *Ella Sets the Stage* (PS–1). Illus. by Steve D'Amico. 2006, Scholastic $16.99 (978-0-439-83152-9). 48pp. Ella the elephant is initially afraid of the forthcoming talent show, but discovers that she has a distinct gift for organization and planning. (Rev: BL 10/15/06; SLJ 10/06)

2083 D'Amico, Carmela. *Ella Takes the Cake* (PS–K). Illus. by Steven D'Amico. 2005, Scholastic $16.99 (978-0-439-62794-8). 48pp. Ella the elephant wants to help out in her mother's bakery and finally proves she can be useful when she successfully delivers a cake to a customer. (Rev: BL 8/05; SLJ 9/05)

2084 D'Amico, Carmela, and Steve D'Amico. *Ella Sets Sail* (PS–1). Illus. by Carmela D'Amico. 2008, Scholastic $16.99 (978-0-439-83155-0). 48pp. When Ella the elephant goes off to sea to retrieve her lucky red hat, she finds herself very lucky to find her way safely home again. (Rev: BL 8/08; SLJ 7/08)

2085 Dans, Peter E. *Perry's Baltimore Adventure: A Bird's-Eye View of Charm City* (K–3). Illus. by Kim Harrell. 2003, Tidewater $11.95 (978-0-87033-540-2). This beautifully illustrated tale of a peregrine falcon family also introduces readers to Baltimore's major attractions. (Rev: SLJ 8/03)

2086 Darbyshire, Kristen. *Put It On the List!* (PS–K). Illus. by author. 2009, Dutton $16.99 (978-0-525-47906-2). 32pp. A family of chickens learns to keep a shopping list after getting tired of running out of essential items like syrup and toilet paper. (Rev: BL 2/1/09; SLJ 2/09)

2087 Daugherty, James. *Andy and the Lion* (1–4). Illus. by author. 1938, Puffin paper $5.99 (978-0-14-050277-0). 80pp. A popular, modern version of the story of Androcles and the lion.

2088 Davenier, Christine. *Leon and Albertine* (PS–1). Illus. 1998, Orchard $15.95 (978-0-531-30072-5). 32pp. Leo, a pig, is attracted to Albertine, a chicken who is decidedly not interested. (Rev: BCCB 3/98; BL 2/1/98; HBG 10/98; SLJ 3/98*)

2089 Davis, Katie. *Party Animals* (PS–2). Illus. by author. 2002, Harcourt $15.00 (978-0-15-216675-

5). A tiny blue ant feels left out of preparations for a festive party. (Rev: HBG 3/03; SLJ 12/02)

2090 Davis, Katie. *Who Hops?* (PS–1). Illus. 1998, Harcourt $13.00 (978-0-15-201839-9). 36pp. A nonsense book in which a variety of animals perform impossible feats, such as cows hopping like frogs. (Rev: BL 9/15/98; HBG 3/99; SLJ 9/98)

2091 Davol, Marguerite W. *Batwings and the Curtain of Night* (PS–4). Illus. by Mary GrandPré. 1997, Orchard $15.95 (978-0-531-30005-3). 32pp. In order to get more light, some nocturnal animals decide to pull back the curtain of night in this creation story. (Rev: BCCB 4/97; BL 4/15/97; SLJ 4/97)

2092 Day, Alexandra. *Carl Goes to Daycare* (PS–2). Illus. 1993, Farrar $12.95 (978-0-374-31093-6). 32pp. In an emergency, Carl the rottweiler has to take care of youngsters at a day care center. (Rev: BCCB 11/93; BL 12/15/93; SLJ 12/93)

2093 Day, Alexandra. *Carl's Afternoon in the Park* (2–6). Illus. 1991, Farrar $12.95 (978-0-374-31109-4). 32pp. Carl, a rottweiler, is placed in charge of a puppy and a toddler while Mom goes for tea with a friend in the park. (Rev: BCCB 11/91; BL 10/15/91; SLJ 11/91)

2094 Day, Alexandra. *Carl's Christmas* (PS–K). Illus. 1990, Farrar $12.95 (978-0-374-31114-8). 32pp. On Christmas Eve, Carl, a big black dog, takes the baby he is caring for out to greet the world. (Rev: BCCB 10/90; BL 11/1/90)

2095 Day, Alexandra. *Follow Carl!* (PS–2). Illus. 1998, Farrar $12.95 (978-0-374-34380-4). 32pp. Carl, the enterprising rottweiler, and a group of children play follow-the-leader. The children soon find themselves rolling in the grass, fetching sticks, and chasing a squirrel. (Rev: BL 8/98; HBG 3/99)

2096 Day, David. *King of the Woods* (K–2). Illus. by Ken Brown. 1993, Four Winds LB $13.95 (978-0-02-726361-9). A little wren defeats all the stronger animals in the forest and claims as her own the golden apple she has found. (Rev: SLJ 3/94)

2097 Deacon, Alexis. *Slow Loris* (PS–2). Illus. 2002, Kane $15.95 (978-0-916291-27-3). 32pp. During the day Loris the lion is lethargic, but at night he leads a secret life. (Rev: BCCB 5/02; BL 6/1–15/02)

2098 De Beer, Hans. *Little Polar Bear and the Big Balloon* (K–2). Trans. from German by Rosemary Lanning. Illus. by author. 2002, North-South LB $16.50 (978-0-7358-1533-9). Little polar bear Lars and a puffin friend take a trip in a brightly colored hot-air balloon. (Rev: HBG 3/03; SLJ 11/02)

2099 De Beer, Hans. *Little Polar Bear Finds a Friend* (PS–2). 1990, North-South $13.95 (978-1-55858-092-3). 32pp. A clever walrus is able to help Lars, a polar bear, escape captors. (Rev: BL 11/15/90; SLJ 2/91)

2100 De Brunhoff, Jean. *The Story of Babar, the Little Elephant* (PS). Illus. by author. 1937, Random LB $5.99 (978-0-394-90575-4). A time-tested reading favorite about the little French elephant. (Rev: HBG 3/03)

2101 De Brunhoff, Laurent. *Babar and the Succotash Bird* (PS–1). Illus. 2000, Abrams $16.95 (978-0-

8109-5700-8). 32pp. Alexander, Babar the elephant's son, encounters a magical bird that squawks "Succotash" and gives him the power of flight. (Rev: BL 12/1/00; HBG 3/01; SLJ 12/00)

2102 De Brunhoff, Laurent. *Babar's Museum of Art* (K–3). Illus. by author. 2003, Abrams $16.95 (978-0-8109-4597-5). 44pp. Babar and Celeste set up an art museum in Celesteville's abandoned train station and fill it with works of art from their personal collection — which boasts pachyderm versions of many classics. (Rev: HBG 4/04; SLJ 11/03)

2103 De Brunhoff, Laurent. *Babar's World Tour* (PS–2). Illus. Series: Babar. 2005, Abrams $16.95 (978-0-8109-5780-0). 48pp. Babar and Celeste take their children on a round-the-world tour in this large-format picture book. (Rev: BL 10/1/05; SLJ 1/06)

2104 Degen, Bruce. *Daddy Is a Doodlebug* (PS–1). Illus. 2000, HarperCollins LB $15.89 (978-0-06-028416-9). 40pp. A little bug and his dad spend a fine day together. (Rev: BL 6/1–15/00; HBG 10/00; SLJ 4/00)

2105 deGroat, Diane. *Brand-New Pencils, Brand-New Books* (PS–2). Illus. Series: Gilbert. 2005, HarperCollins $15.99 (978-0-06-072613-3). 32pp. Gilbert's excitement about starting 1st grade is mixed with fears; but at the end of the day he recognizes that it wasn't all bad. (Rev: BL 8/05; SLJ 9/05)

2106 deGroat, Diane. *Good Night, Sleep Tight, Don't Let the Bedbugs Bite!* (PS–K). Illus. Series: Gilbert. 2002, North-South LB $15.88 (978-1-58717-129-1). 32pp. Gilbert's spooky first night at camp reveals that other campers are just as fearful as he. (Rev: BL 7/02; HB 7/02; HBG 10/02; SLJ 8/02)

2107 deGroat, Diane. *No More Pencils, No More Books, No More Teacher's Dirty Looks!* (K–2). Series: Gilbert. 2006, HarperCollins $15.99 (978-0-06-079114-8). 32pp. As the end-of-school awards ceremony nears, Gilbert the possum worries there will be no prize for him. (Rev: BL 6/1–15/06; SLJ 6/06)

2108 Delaney, Michael. *Birdbrain Amos, Mr. Fun* (2–3). Illus. by author. Series: Amos. 2006, Philomel $15.99 (978-0-399-24278-6). 160pp. Amos the hippo, determined to show Amoeba, the tick bird who lives on his head, that he's fun takes her — and her relatives and, more importantly, her imaginary friend — on a trip to the Serengeti. (Rev: SLJ 7/06)

2109 Delessert, Etienne. *Alert!* (1–3). Illus. by author. 2007, Houghton $17.00 (978-0-618-73474-0). 31pp. A solitary mole called Tobias loves his pebble collection and is distraught when he hears from a so-called friend that there are robbers about. (Rev: SLJ 4/07)

2110 Demarest, Chris L. *Honk!* (PS–1). Illus. by author. 1998, Boyds Mills $11.95 (978-1-56397-221-8). Using flaps, different animals and the sounds they make are revealed in this story about a lost duck. (Rev: HBG 3/99; SLJ 10/98)

2111 Denim, Sue. *The Dumb Bunnies* (K–2). Illus. by Dav Pilkey. 1994, Scholastic $13.95 (978-0-590-47708-6). 32pp. The story of the three dumb bunnies and their hectic misadventures. (Rev: BL 1/15/94; SLJ 3/94)

2112 Denim, Sue. *The Dumb Bunnies Go to the Zoo* (1–3). Illus. by Dav Pilkey. 1997, Scholastic $13.95 (978-0-590-84735-3). 32pp. The three Dumb Bunnies go to the zoo, where they create havoc. (Rev: BL 4/1/97; SLJ 3/97)

2113 Denim, Sue. *Make Way for Dumb Bunnies* (1–3). Illus. by Dav Pilkey. 1996, Scholastic $12.95 (978-0-590-58286-5). 32pp. A slapstick tale about the misadventures of an unthinking rabbit family. (Rev: BL 2/1/96; SLJ 3/96)

2114 Denslow, Sharon P. *Big Wolf and Little Wolf* (PS–K). Illus. by Cathie Felstead. 2000, Greenwillow $17.99 (978-0-688-16174-3). 32pp. Little Wolf is frightened by strange noises coming from the bushes and discovers it is his mother playing a trick on him. (Rev: BCCB 7–8/00; BL 5/1/00; HBG 10/00; SLJ 5/00)

2115 Depalma, Mary Newell. *The Strange Egg* (PS–2). Illus. by author. 2001, Houghton $15.00 (978-0-618-09507-0). A monkey has to explain to a small bird that it is sitting on an orange. (Rev: HBG 10/01; SLJ 5/01)

2116 dePaola, Tomie. *Bill and Pete Go Down the Nile* (K–3). Illus. by author. 1987, Penguin $16.99 (978-0-399-21395-3); paper $6.99 (978-0-698-11401-2). 32pp. A crocodile and a bird in a delightful romp down the Nile. (Rev: BL 5/1/87; SLJ 9/87)

2117 dePaola, Tomie. *Four Friends in Autumn* (PS–2). Illus. by author. 2004, Simon & Schuster $14.95 (978-0-689-85980-9). In this tale adapted from *Four Stories for Four Seasons* (1980), four friends — Missy Cat, Mistress Pig, Master Dog, and Mister Frog — gather for dinner at Mistress Pig's house. (Rev: SLJ 11/04)

2118 dePaola, Tomie. *The Knight and the Dragon* (1–3). Illus. by author. 1998, Penguin $17.99 (978-0-399-20707-5); paper $5.99 (978-0-698-11623-8). An inexperienced knight and an inexperienced dragon prepare themselves to do battle.

2119 dePaola, Tomie. *Little Grunt and the Big Egg: A Prehistoric Fairy Tale* (PS–2). Illus. by author. 2006, Putnam $16.99 (978-0-399-24529-9). 32pp. A new edition of the story about the prehistoric boy who adopts a dinosaur called George. (Rev: BL 5/15/06)

2120 dePaola, Tomie. *Meet the Barkers: Morgan and Moffat Go to School* (PS–1). Illus. 2001, Penguin $13.99 (978-0-399-23708-9). 32pp. Terrier siblings Morgie and Moffie have always been different — Moffie is smart, Morgie gregarious — and these characteristics hold true when they start school. (Rev: BL 6/1–15/01; HBG 3/02; SLJ 8/01)

2121 dePaola, Tomie. *A New Barker in the House* (PS–2). Illus. Series: The Barkers. 2002, Penguin $13.99 (978-0-399-23865-9). 32pp. When the Barker family adopts Spanish-speaking Marcos, twins Morgie and Moffie try hard to make him feel comfortable in this book full of Spanish words and charming art. (Rev: BL 7/02; HBG 10/02; SLJ 6/02)

2122 dePaola, Tomie. *T-Rex Is Missing!* (1–2). Illus. by author. 2002, Grosset paper $3.99 (978-0-448-

42870-3). 32pp. The disappearance of a toy dinosaur causes a major falling out between two animal friends. (Rev: HBG 10/03; SLJ 2/03)

2123 dePaola, Tomie. *Trouble in the Barkers' Class* (K–2). Illus. by author. 2003, Penguin $14.99 (978-0-399-24164-2). Moffie and Morgie Barker, twin terriers, are disappointed when the newcomer to their class, Carole Anne, turns out to be an ill-tempered bully. (Rev: HBG 4/04; SLJ 10/03)

2124 Desimini, Lisa. *Dot the Fire Dog* (PS–3). Illus. 2001, Scholastic $16.95 (978-0-439-23322-4). 40pp. Dot the Dalmatian rescues a kitten while helping her fire fighter owners put out a fire. (Rev: BL 10/1/01; HB 11/01; HBG 3/02; SLJ 12/01)

2125 De Vries, Anke. *My Elephant Can Do Almost Anything* (PS–1). Illus. by Ilja Walraven. 1996, Front St. $14.95 (978-1-886910-06-5). A boy's imaginary playmate, an elephant, is upset when the boy goes to school. (Rev: BCCB 6/96; HB 7/96; SLJ 6/96)

2126 De Vries, Anke. *Piggy's Birthday Dream* (PS). Illus. by Jung-Hee Spetter. 1997, Front St. $14.95 (978-1-886910-21-8). 32pp. Piggy is so shy that she doesn't tell any of the barnyard animals it's her birthday, but they plan their own surprise for her. (Rev: BL 11/15/97; HBG 3/98; SLJ 11/97)

2127 Dewan, Ted. *Bing: Get Dressed* (PS). Illus. by author. Series: Bing Bunny. 2004, Random $5.95 (978-0-385-75020-2). Bing gets dressed with supervision and advice from Flop in this bright, small-format book. Also use *Bing: Paint Day* (2004). (Rev: BL 2/15/04; SLJ 7/04)

2128 Dewan, Ted. *Bing: Go Picnic* (PS). Illus. 2005, Random $5.99 (978-0-375-75056-4). 24pp. Bing the bunny and stuffed animal Flop plan a picnic outdoors but are rained out and must set up indoors instead. Also use *Make Music* (2005). (Rev: BL 5/1/05)

2129 Dewdney, Anna. *Llama Llama Misses Mama* (PS–K). Illus. by author. Series: Llama Llama. 2009, Viking $16.99 (978-0-670-06198-3). 40pp. Little Llama Llama approaches the start of school with some trepidation but finds it's not as bad as he feared. (Rev: SLJ 6/09)

2130 Dewdney, Anna. *Nobunny's Perfect* (PS–1). Illus. by author. 2008, Viking $12.99 (978-0-670-06288-1). 32pp. Young rabbits exhibit amazingly childlike bad behaviors. (Rev: BL 1/1–15/08; SLJ 8/08)

2131 DiCamillo, Kate. *Mercy Watson Goes for a Ride* (PS–2). Illus. by Chris Van Dusen. Series: Mercy Watson. 2006, Candlewick $12.99 (978-0-7636-2332-6). 80pp. Plump pig Mercy gives Mr. Watson an unexpectedly exciting ride in his pink Cadillac. (Rev: BL 5/1/06; SLJ 6/06)

2132 DiCamillo, Kate. *Mercy Watson Thinks Like a Pig* (PS–2). Illus. by Chris Van Dusen. 2008, Candlewick $12.99 (978-0-7636-3265-6). 80pp. The animal control officer is called when Mercy the pig eats the Lincoln sisters' petunias. Can Mercy elude capture? (Rev: BL 6/1–15/08; SLJ 8/08)

2133 Dickson, Louise. *The Vanishing Cat* (PS–2). Illus. by Pat Cupples. 2001, Kids Can $14.95 (978-

1-55337-026-0); paper $6.95 (978-1-55074-836-9). 39pp. Detective dogs Lu and Clancy suspect that a cruise ship magician, a cat, is up to no good. (Rev: HBG 3/02; SLJ 12/01)

2134 Dillard, Sarah. *Perfectly Arugula* (PS–K). Illus. by author. 2009, Sterling $14.95 (978-1-4027-5954-3). 36pp. Arugula is a hedgehog with a passion for tidiness and order, which doesn't exactly fit with her party plans. (Rev: BLO 3/24/09)

2135 Dodd, Emma. *Dog's Noisy Day: A Story to Read Aloud* (PS–K). Illus. 2003, Dutton $14.99 (978-0-525-47015-1). 32pp. Dog tries to imitate the sounds he hears around the farm, from a rooster's crow to a bee's buzz. (Rev: BL 2/15/03; HBG 10/03; SLJ 3/03)

2136 Dodd, Emma. *Just Like You* (PS). Illus. by author. Series: Templar Bks. 2008, Dutton $10.99 (978-0-525-47933-8). 24pp. A baby bear enumerates why he loves big bear. (Rev: SLJ 4/08)

2137 Dodd, Emma. *No Matter What* (PS). Illus. by author. 2008, Dutton $10.99 (978-0-525-47932-1). 24pp. A simple story about a mother elephant and her love for her child. (Rev: BL 4/1/08; SLJ 2/08)

2138 Donaldson, Julia. *The Fish Who Cried Wolf* (PS–K). Illus. by Axel Scheffler. 2008, Scholastic $15.99 (978-0-439-92825-0). 40pp. Tiddler, a little fish given to elaborate excuses, finds his tall tales useful when he winds up far from home. (Rev: BCCB 6/08; BL 8/08; LMC 10/08; SLJ 6/08)

2139 Donaldson, Julia. *The Snail and the Whale* (PS–3). Illus. by Axel Scheffler. 2004, Dial $17.99 (978-0-8037-2922-3). A tiny snail, anxious to see the world, attaches itself to a humpback whale, and the two enjoy rhythmic, rhyming travels. (Rev: SLJ 2/04)

2140 Donaldson, Julia. *Where's My Mom?* (PS–1). Illus. by Axel Scheffler. 2008, Dial $16.99 (978-0-8037-3228-5). 32pp. A butterfly tries to help a lost monkey find his mother but misunderstandings about the mother's anatomy abound. (Rev: SLJ 5/08)

2141 Donnio, Sylviane. *I'd Really Like to Eat a Child* (PS–K). Trans. from French by Leslie Martin. Illus. by Dorothée de Monfreid. 2007, Random $14.99 (978-0-375-83761-6). A small crocodile tired of the food his mother offers says he would prefer to eat a child and sets off to do so. (Rev: SLJ 4/07)

2142 Donohue, Dorothy. *Veggie Soup* (PS–3). Illus. 2000, Winslow $16.95 (978-1-890817-21-3). 40pp. When Miss Bun, a rabbit, decides to create her own veggie soup, each of her friends brings a different ingredient. (Rev: BL 11/15/00; HBG 3/01; SLJ 10/00)

2143 Doray, Malika. *One More Wednesday* (PS–3). Trans. by Suzanne Freeman. Illus. 2001, Greenwillow LB $15.89 (978-0-06-029590-5). 48pp. A young animal misses his grandmother when she dies but comes to realize that his memories of their good times bring comfort. (Rev: BL 6/1–15/01; HBG 10/01; SLJ 7/01)

2144 Dorros, Arthur. *City Chicken* (PS–2). Illus. by Henry Cole. 2003, HarperCollins LB $16.89 (978-

0-06-028483-1). 40pp. Adventurous city chicken Henrietta takes a trip to the country, encounters an industrial egg farm, and gladly returns to her quiet city life. (Rev: BCCB 2/03; BL 3/15/03; HB 3/03; HBG 10/03; SLJ 2/03)

2145 Dotlich, Rebecca Kai. *Grandpa Loves* (PS–K). Illus. by Kathryn Brown. 2005, HarperCollins LB $16.89 (978-0-06-029406-9). 32pp. A young pig describes all the things her grandfather loves — billiards, backpacking, flipping pancakes, and so forth. (Rev: BL 6/1–15/05; SLJ 5/05)

2146 Dotlich, Rebecca Kai. *Mama Loves* (PS–1). Illus. by Kathryn Brown. 2004, HarperCollins $14.99 (978-0-06-029407-6). 32pp. A tally of all the things that Mama Pig loves to do with her baby daughter. (Rev: BL 3/1/04)

2147 Downey, Lynn. *Matilda's Humdinger* (1–3). Illus. by Tim Bowers. 2006, Knopf $15.95 (978-0-375-82403-6). Matilda the cat is a terrible waitress but a great storyteller. (Rev: SLJ 10/06)

2148 Downey, Lynn. *The Tattletale* (PS–K). Illus. by Pam Paparone. 2006, Holt $16.95 (978-0-8050-7152-8). 32pp. Humorous art adds to the fun in this story about two pig brothers that carries a message about telling tales and bullying. (Rev: BL 11/1/06; SLJ 11/06)

2149 Downing, Julie. *No Hugs Till Saturday* (PS–1). Illus. by author. 2008, Clarion $16.00 (978-0-618-91078-6). 32pp. A little dragon named Felix clearly demonstrates his displeasure when his mother punishes him for misbehavior but comes to realize he is also depriving himself. (Rev: BL 7/08; SLJ 7/08)

2150 Doyle, Malachy. *Big Pig* (PS–2). Illus. by John Bendall-Brunello. 2006, Simon & Schuster $19.95 (978-0-689-87484-0); paper $9.99 (978-0-689-87485-7). Pig has grown too big to keep in the house, so John Henry must take the ample porker to the local pig farm, but when John Henry has a mishap on the way home, Pig comes to the rescue. (Rev: SLJ 11/06)

2151 Drachman, Eric. *Bad Rats* (PS–2). Illus. by James Muscarello. 2008, Kidwick $18.95 (978-0-9703809-4-4). 40pp. Five little rats who love art and music are told that this is bad behavior and sent to Professor Perimeter for reeducation; luckily the professor recognizes their creativity and in fact learns instead from them. Comes with a CD of the story. (Rev: BL 6/1–15/08; SLJ 5/08)

2152 Dubanevich, Arlene. *Pig William* (PS–1). Illus. by author. 1985, Simon & Schuster LB $14.95 (978-0-02-733200-1). 32pp. Pig William is such a dawdler that his brothers leave without him for a picnic. (Rev: BCCB 12/85; BL 1/15/86)

2153 Dubosarsky, Ursula. *The Terrible Plop* (PS–K). Illus. by Andrew Joyner. 2009, Farrar $15.95 (978-0-374-37428-0). 40pp. Falling apples cause concern to lounging animals in this entertaining picture book full of rhyme and repetition. (Rev: BL 7/09)

2154 Duffield, Katy S. *Farmer McPeepers and His Missing Milk Cows* (K–3). Illus. by Steve Gray. 2003, Rising Moon $15.95 (978-0-87358-825-6). When Farmer McPeepers's dairy cows steal his eyeglasses, he looks for them all day while his cows

have a great day off; the illustrations provide the fun. (Rev: HBG 4/04; SLJ 10/03)

2155 Duke, Kate. *The Tale of Pip and Squeak* (PS–2). Illus. by author. 2007, Dutton $16.99 (978-0-525-47777-8). Two little mice — Pip, who likes to paint, and Squeak, who likes to sing — realize that their talents are best used together to throw a party for their friends. (Rev: SLJ 5/07)

2156 Dunbar, Joyce. *A Chick Called Saturday* (PS–1). Illus. by Brita Granström. 2003, Eerdmans $16.00 (978-0-8028-5260-1). Saturday, an inquisitive chick, is disappointed in life until he discovers that he's got a real talent for crowing. (Rev: HBG 4/04; SLJ 8/03)

2157 Dunbar, Joyce. *Eggday* (PS–K). Illus. by Jane Cabrera. 1999, Holiday House $15.95 (978-0-8234-1510-6). 32pp. Dora the Duck declares that tomorrow is Eggday and that each animal, including the horse and pig, should bring their eggs. (Rev: BL 4/1/99; HB 5/99; HBG 10/99; SLJ 7/99)

2158 Dunbar, Joyce. *Oddly* (K–2). Illus. by Patrick Benson. 2009, Candlewick $16.99 (978-0-7636-4274-7). 40pp. Strange creatures form a bond with a little boy on the beach. (Rev: BL 6/1–15/09; SLJ 7/09)

2159 Dunbar, Joyce. *Tell Me What It's Like to Be Big* (K–3). Illus. by Debi Gliori. 2001, Harcourt $16.00 (978-0-15-202564-9). 32pp. Detailed, vivid images illustrate the story of Willa the rabbit, who is frustrated because she is too little to reach the food on the table. (Rev: BL 12/15/01; HBG 3/02; SLJ 9/01)

2160 Dunbar, Joyce. *Where's My Sock?* (PS–2). Illus. by Sanja Rescek. 2006, Scholastic $15.99 (978-0-439-74831-5). 32pp. Pippin the mouse can't find his yellow sock and enlists the help of Tog the cat; they find socks all over the house and match them all up (in a very colorful fold-out) only to discover the missing sock where they least expected. (Rev: BL 1/1–15/06; SLJ 2/06)

2161 Dunrea, Olivier. *Gossie and Gertie* (PS). Illus. 2002, Houghton $9.95 (978-0-618-17676-2). 32pp. A little gosling named Gossie learns a lesson in individuality when her best friend Gertie no longer wants to do everything she does. Also use *Gossie* (2002). (Rev: BL 8/02; HB 1/03*; HBG 3/03; SLJ 9/02*)

2162 Dunrea, Olivier. *Ollie* (PS–1). Illus. by author. 2003, Houghton $9.95 (978-0-618-33928-0). Goslings Gossie and Gertie grow impatient waiting for their sibling Ollie to hatch from his egg. (Rev: HBG 4/04; SLJ 7/03)

2163 Dunrea, Olivier. *Ollie the Stomper* (PS). Illus. by author. 2003, Houghton $9.95 (978-0-618-33930-3). Ollie, the contrary gosling who refused to emerge from his egg in *Ollie* (2003), first decides he wants boots and then that he needs a swim instead. (Rev: HBG 4/04; SLJ 7/03)

2164 Durango, Julia. *Pest Fest* (PS–2). Illus. by Kurt Cyrus. 2007, Simon & Schuster $16.99 (978-0-689-85569-6). Who will win the title Best Pest of the Year at the Pest Fest talent show? Readers will enjoy the rhyming text that extols the virtues of many insects and the beautiful illustrations that accompany it. (Rev: LMC 10/07; SLJ 7/07)

2165 Eduar, Gilles. *Jooka Saves the Day* (PS–2). Trans. by Dominic Barth. Illus. 1997, Orchard $15.95 (978-0-531-30036-7). 40pp. Jooka tries to be like all the crocodiles in the rain forest, but it is impossible because he is really a dragon. (Rev: BL 12/1/97; HB 9/97; HBG 3/98; SLJ 9/97)

2166 Edvall, Lilian. *The Rabbit Who Couldn't Find His Daddy* (PS–2). Trans. from Swedish by Elisahctli Kallick Dyssegaard. Illus. by Sara Gimbergsson. 2006, Farrar $16.00 (91-29-66429-2). Rabbit wakes up in the middle of the night and can't find Daddy, so he and his little sister set off to find him and get locked out of the house. (Rev: SLJ 4/06)

2167 Edvall, Lilian. *The Rabbit Who Didn't Want to Go to Sleep* (PS). Trans. from Swedish by Elisabeth Kallick Dyssegaard. Illus. by Sara Gimbergsson. 2004, R&S $15.00 (91-29-66001-7). The little rabbit just doesn't want to go to sleep . . . there are still cars to race. (Rev: SLJ 6/04)

2168 Edwards, Pamela Duncan. *Livingstone Mouse* (PS–2). Illus. by Henry Cole. 1996, HarperCollins LB $15.89 (978-0-06-025870-2). 32pp. A mouse decides that China would be a nice place for him to build his nest. (Rev: BL 10/1/96; SLJ 9/96)

2169 Edwards, Pamela Duncan. *McGillycuddy Could!* (PS). Illus. by Sue Porter. 2005, HarperCollins LB $15.89 (978-0-06-029002-3). Kangaroo McGillycuddy's ability to hop, jump, bounce, and kick fails to impress the other animals at the farm. (Rev: BCCB 2/05; HB 3/05; SLJ 3/05)

2170 Edwards, Pamela Duncan. *The Mixed-Up Rooster* (PS). Illus. by Megan Lloyd. 2006, HarperCollins $15.99 (978-0-06-028999-7). 32pp. A rooster who prefers to stay up at night finds a new position on the farm in this entertaining story. (Rev: BL 7/06; SLJ 8/06)

2171 Edwards, Pamela Duncan. *Ms. Bitsy Bat's Kindergarten* (PS–K). Illus. by Henry Cole. 2005, Hyperion $15.99 (978-0-7868-0669-0). 32pp. The second day of kindergarten proves stressful when the students learn that Mr. Fox won't be back. (Rev: BL 8/05; SLJ 8/05)

2172 Edwards, Wallace. *The Extinct Files: My Science Project* (K–3). Illus. by author. 2006, Kids Can $17.95 (978-1-55337-971-3). Wally's science project reveals a great deal about contemporary dinosaurs' physical characteristics, habitat, diet, communication, and defenses — much of it unexpected. (Rev: SLJ 11/06)

2173 Egan, Tim. *Burnt Toast on Davenport Street* (K–2). Illus. 1997, Houghton $16.00 (978-0-395-79618-4). 32pp. A fly — who has granted Arthur, a dog, three wishes — gets the wishes mixed up in this hilarious fantasy. (Rev: BL 4/15/97; SLJ 5/97*)

2174 Egan, Tim. *Dodsworth in Paris* (K–3). Illus. by author. 2008, Houghton $15.00 (978-0-618-98062-8). 48pp. A mouse named Dodsworth and a wacky duck are off to Paris where the duck tries hard, really, not to get into trouble. (Rev: BL 9/1/08; HB 1/09)

2175 Egan, Tim. *A Mile from Ellington Station* (K–3). Illus. 2001, Houghton $15.00 (978-0-618-00393-8). 32pp. Preston, a bear who is a checkers champion, is beaten by a multitalented dog from France named Marley, so Preston claims Marley is a sorcerer. (Rev: BL 4/15/01; HBG 10/01; SLJ 5/01)

2176 Egan, Tim. *Roasted Peanuts* (1–3). Illus. 2006, Houghton $16.00 (978-0-618-33718-7). 32pp. Sam the horse and Jackson the cat are best friends who love baseball but although Jackson is a great pitcher only Sam is talented enough to make the team; Jackson gets a job selling peanuts, however, and his throwing skills have results. (Rev: BL 4/15/06; SLJ 5/06)

2177 Egan, Tim. *Serious Farm* (K–3). Illus. by author. 2003, Houghton $15.00 (978-0-618-22694-8). Farmer Fred takes life too seriously and his livestock decides to get him to lighten up. (Rev: HB 9/03; HBG 4/04; SLJ 10/03)

2178 Ehlert, Lois. *Boo to You!* (PS–1). Illus. by author. 2009, Simon & Schuster $17.99 (978-1-4169-8625-6). 42pp. The mice hold a harvest party despite the presence of a scary cat. (Rev: BL 5/15/09; SLJ 8/09)

2179 Ehlert, Lois. *Mole's Hill* (PS–2). Illus. 1994, Harcourt $15.00 (978-0-15-255116-2). 32pp. Fox demands that Mole move from her hill, but she is able to outwit him and remain. (Rev: BCCB 4/94; BL 3/15/94; HB 7/94; SLJ 5/94)

2180 Ehlert, Lois. *Nuts to You!* (PS–2). Illus. 1993, Harcourt $16.00 (978-0-15-257647-9). A rural squirrel shows how he gathers food in the big city. (Rev: BL 3/1/93; HB 3/93; SLJ 4/93)

2181 Ehlert, Lois. *Top Cat* (PS–1). Illus. 1998, Harcourt $16.00 (978-0-15-201739-2). 40pp. Top Cat resents the arrival of a new striped kitten in his household, but soon they become friends. (Rev: BL 8/98; HBG 3/99; SLJ 9/98)

2182 Ehrlich, Amy. *Baby Dragon* (PS–1). Illus. by Will Hillenbrand. 2008, Candlewick $16.99 (978-0-7636-2840-6). 32pp. Sad Baby Dragon takes a risk when he is left alone overnight, but he outwits the treacherous Crocodile and is relieved when his mother returns on schedule the next morning. (Rev: LMC 1/09; SLJ 9/08)

2183 *THE ELEPHANT'S BALL* (2–5). Illus. by Pauline Baynes. 2007, Eerdmans $17.00 (978-0-8028-5316-5). An old poem is enlivened with beautiful art depicting all sorts of animals at a ball. (Rev: SLJ 5/07)

2184 Elliott, Laura Malone. *Hunter and Stripe and the Soccer Showdown* (PS–2). Illus. by Lynn Munsinger. 2005, HarperCollins $15.99 (978-0-06-052759-4). 32pp. The friendship between raccoons Hunter and Stripe is tested when they end up on rival soccer teams. (Rev: BL 9/1/05; SLJ 9/05)

2185 Elliott, Laura Malone. *Hunter's Best Friend at School* (PS–1). Illus. by Lynn Munsinger. 2002, HarperCollins LB $17.89 (978-0-06-000231-2). 32pp. Hunter's mother offers guidance when Hunter explains that he doesn't really enjoy being naughty but wants to stay friends with mischievous fellow raccoon Stripes. (Rev: BCCB 10/02; BL 10/1/02; HBG 3/03; SLJ 9/02)

2186 Ellwand, David, and Ruth Ellwand. *Midas Mouse* (PS–2). Photos by David Ellwand. 2000, Lothrop $14.95 (978-0-688-16745-5). 32pp. Midas Mouse gets his wish and everything he touches turns to gold, but he realizes he has problems when his cheese is inedible. (Rev: BL 10/1/00; HBG 3/01; SLJ 11/00)

2187 Elwell, Peter. *Adios Oscar! A Butterfly Fable* (K–2). Illus. by author. 2009, Scholastic $16.99 (978-0-545-07159-8). 32pp. When a caterpillar becomes a gray moth rather than a monarch butterfly, he is disappointed, but with support, he still follows his dream of being with the monarchs in Mexico. (Rev: LMC 10/09; SLJ 5/09)

2188 Elya, Susan Middleton. *Eight Animals Bake a Cake* (2–4). Illus. by Lee Chapman. 2002, Penguin $15.99 (978-0-399-23468-2). 32pp. Too many animals almost spoil the cake in this appealing picture book that introduces Spanish words and includes a recipe for pineapple upside-down cake. (Rev: BL 7/02; HBG 3/03; SLJ 8/02)

2189 Elya, Susan Middleton. *Eight Animals on the Town* (1–3). Illus. by Lee Chapman. 2000, Penguin $15.99 (978-0-399-23437-8). 32pp. English and Spanish words are mixed in this delightful story about eight animals who head into town for dinner. (Rev: BCCB 1/01; BL 12/1/00; HBG 3/01; SLJ 9/00)

2190 Emmett, Jonathan. *Bringing Down the Moon* (PS–2). Illus. by Vanessa Cabban. 2001, Candlewick $15.99 (978-0-7636-1577-2). 24pp. Little Mole tries to capture the moon from the sky. (Rev: BL 2/1/02; HBG 3/02; SLJ 1/02)

2191 Emmett, Jonathan. *Diamond in the Snow* (PS–2). Illus. by Vanessa Cabban. 2007, Candlewick $15.99 (978-0-7636-3117-8). A young mole emerges from his hole to see his first snow, and decides that an icicle is a diamond. (Rev: SLJ 4/07)

2192 Emmett, Jonathan. *Dinosaurs After Dark* (PS). Illus. by Curtis Jobling. 2002, HarperCollins $14.99 (978-0-00-198375-5). Little Bobby investigates a strange noise one night and comes across a herd of lively dinosaurs. (Rev: BCCB 3/02; SLJ 6/02)

2193 Emmett, Jonathan. *I Love You Always and Forever* (PS–K). Illus. by Daniel Howarth. 2007, Scholastic $14.99 (978-0-439-91654-7). Father mouse Longtail and daughter Littletail spend an enjoyable day together that ends with reassurances of love; wonderful illustrations blend with the gentle text. (Rev: SLJ 4/07)

2194 Emmett, Jonathan. *No Place Like Home* (PS–1). Illus. by Vanessa Cabban. 2005, Candlewick $15.99 (978-0-7636-2554-2). Mole's friends all recommend new homes for him, but each has disadvantages, so Mole decides to return underground. (Rev: SLJ 3/05)

2195 Emmett, Jonathan. *This Way, Ruby!* (PS). Illus. by Rebecca Harry. 2007, Scholastic $16.99 (978-0-439-87992-7). Ruby the duckling moves more slowly than her siblings but her powers of observation

are keen, which proves a godsend when there is an unexpected storm. (Rev: BL 12/15/06; SLJ 2/07)

2196 Eriksson, Eva. *A Crash Course for Molly* (PS–2). Trans. by Elisabeth Kallick Dyssegaard. Illus. Series: Molly. 2005, Farrar $16.00 (91-29-66156-0). 32pp. It's mishap after mishap when Molly the pig practices riding her bike at the park. (Rev: BL 4/1/05; SLJ 6/05)

2197 Erlbruch, Wolf. *The Miracle of the Bears* (K–2). Trans. from German by Michael Reynolds. Illus. by author. 2006, Europa paper $14.95 (978-1-933372-21-1). A young bear tackles — in an appropriately vague way — the perennial question of where babies come from; funny with a touch of romance. (Rev: SLJ 11/06)

2198 Ernst, Lisa Campbell. *Sylvia Jean, Drama Queen* (PS–2). Illus. 2005, Dutton $16.99 (978-0-525-46962-9). 40pp. When a town-wide costume party is announced, everyone assumes that Sylvia Jean, a fashion-conscious piglet, will take home the grand prize for best costume. (Rev: BL 9/15/05; SLJ 9/05)

2199 Esbaum, Jill. *Stanza* (PS–2). Illus. by Jack E. Davis. 2009, Harcourt $16.00 (978-0-15-205998-9). 32pp. Stanza, a fearsome dog with the heart of a poet, persuades his two brothers to tap their creative juices and stop terrorizing the neighborhood. (Rev: BL 5/1/09; SLJ 5/09)

2200 Evans, Cambria. *Martha Moth Makes Socks* (PS–2). Illus. by author. 2006, Houghton $16.00 (978-0-618-55745-5). In preparation for her birthday celebration with friends Flit and Flora, Martha Moth samples some of the delectable clothing items she plans to serve at the party, but she overdoes it, leaving little to share with her guests. (Rev: BL 5/1/06; SLJ 4/06)

2201 Evans, Lezlie. *The Bunnies' Trip* (PS–K). Illus. by Kay Chorao. 2008, Hyperion $16.99 (978-0-7868-1898-3). 32pp. Eight little bunnies struggle to pack for a journey. (Rev: BL 4/1/08)

2202 Ezra, Mark. *The Frightened Little Owl* (PS–K). Illus. by Gavin Rowe. 1997, Interlink $14.95 (978-1-56656-264-5). 32pp. Fearful Little Owl takes her first flight in order to find her mother and discovers that she likes it. (Rev: BL 6/1–15/97; SLJ 7/97)

2203 Ezra, Mark. *The Hungry Otter* (PS–2). Illus. by Gavin Rowe. 1996, Crocodile $14.95 (978-1-56656-216-4). When Little Otter saves a crow from a fox, the crow, in turn, helps the otter by breaking holes in the ice so that the animal can fish. (Rev: SLJ 4/97)

2204 Falconer, Ian. *Olivia* (PS–K). Illus. 2000, Simon & Schuster $16.00 (978-0-689-82953-6). 40pp. An outstanding picture book about Olivia, a delightful little pig, who is a bundle of energy and talent. Caldecott Honor Book 2001. (Rev: BCCB 11/00*; BL 8/00*; HBG 3/01; SLJ 9/00)

2205 Falconer, Ian. *Olivia . . . and the Missing Toy* (PS–1). Illus. by author. 2003, Simon & Schuster $16.95 (978-0-689-85291-6). When her favorite stuffed animal mysteriously disappears, Olivia the pig turns sleuth in this story with witty illustrations. (Rev: BL 9/1/03*; HBG 4/04; SLJ 10/03)

2206 Falconer, Ian. *Olivia Forms a Band* (PS–1). Illus. by author. 2006, Simon & Schuster $17.95 (978-1-4169-2454-8). 50pp. Disconsolate when she learns that there will be no band performing at the fireworks exhibition, Olivia the energetic pig comes up with a plan to supply the music all by herself. (Rev: BL 6/1–15/06; SLJ 6/06*)

2207 Falconer, Ian. *Olivia Saves the Circus* (PS–1). Illus. 2001, Simon & Schuster $16.00 (978-0-689-82954-3). 32pp. Olivia, the little pig full of talented energy, describes how she took over each and every role when the circus was hit by a rash of earaches. (Rev: BCCB 11/01; BL 8/01; HB 11/01; HBG 3/02; SLJ 10/01)

2208 Faller, Regis. *The Adventures of Polo* (PS–2). Illus. 2006, Roaring Brook $16.95 (978-1-59643-160-7). 80pp. In this wordless graphic novel, Polo the dog sets off in a tiny boat on a series of magical adventures. (Rev: BL 3/15/06; SLJ 6/06*)

2209 Farooqi, Musharraf Ali. *The Cobbler's Holiday or Why Ants Don't Wear Shoes* (K–3). Illus. by Eugene Yelchin. 2008, Roaring Brook $16.95 (978-1-59643-234-5). 32pp. Snappily dressed ants discard their flashy shoes and discover they can dance just fine without them. (Rev: LMC 1/09; SLJ 9/08)

2210 Faulkner, Keith. *The Wide-Mouthed Frog* (PS–1). Illus. by Jonathan Lambert. 1996, Dial $13.99 (978-0-8037-1875-3). 14pp. An interactive book that pictures a variety of animals and their eating habits. (Rev: BL 2/1/96; SLJ 4/96)

2211 Fearnley, Jan. *Martha in the Middle* (PS). Illus. by author. 2008, Candlewick $15.99 (978-0-7636-3800-9). 40pp. Tired of feeling neglected as the middle child, Martha the mouse decides to run away but at the end of the garden meets a clever frog who explains that being in the middle can be special. (Rev: BL 6/1–15/08; SLJ 7/08)

2212 Feiffer, Jules. *Bark, George* (PS–3). Illus. 1999, HarperCollins LB $18.89 (978-0-06-205186-8). 32pp. When puppy George is asked to bark by his mother, he manages to produce a range of animal sounds including a "meow" and a "moo," but never an "arf." (Rev: BCCB 11/99; BL 8/99*; HBG 3/00; SLJ 9/99)

2213 Fernandes, Eugenie. *Busy Little Mouse* (PS–K). Illus. by Kim Fernandes. 2002, Kids Can $12.95 (978-1-55074-776-8). 24pp. Joyful, three-dimensional art is used to illustrate this lighthearted tale of various farm animals who play together. (Rev: BL 4/15/02)

2214 Ferri, Giuliano. *Little Tad Grows Up* (PS–1). Illus. by author. 2007, Minedition $16.99 (978-0-698-40060-3). Tad is not looking forward to changing from tadpole to frog but soon discovers that legs can come in handy. (Rev: SLJ 7/07)

2215 Finn, Isobel. *The Very Lazy Ladybug* (PS–1). Illus. by Jack Tickle. 2001, Tiger Tales $15.95 (978-1-58925-007-9). This ladybug is so lazy that she can't be bothered to fly and hops rides with a variety of animals instead, until she is finally forced to take to the air. (Rev: BCCB 5/01; SLJ 7/01)

2216 Flack, Marjorie. *Ask Mr. Bear* (PS–1). Illus. by author. 1968, Macmillan $14.00 (978-0-02-735390-7); paper $5.99 (978-0-02-043090-2). 32pp. To find a present for his mother's birthday, Danny asks a variety of animals for suggestions, with little success until he meets Mr. Bear.

2217 Fleming, Candace. *Gator Gumbo* (K–3). Illus. by Sally Anne Lambert. 2004, Farrar $16.00 (978-0-374-38050-2). 32pp. Aging Monsieur Gator, taunted by his animal neighbors in the swamp, turns the table on them when he decides to cook up a pot of gumbo "just like Maman used to make." (Rev: BL 4/1/04; HB 3/04; SLJ 2/04)

2218 Fleming, Denise. *The Cow Who Clucked* (PS–2). 2006, Holt $16.95 (978-0-8050-7265-5). 40pp. Cow awakens to find that she is clucking like a chicken and sets out to track down her missing "moo." (Rev: BL 9/1/06; SLJ 8/06*)

2219 Fleming, Denise. *Lunch* (PS–K). Illus. 1992, Holt $16.95 (978-0-8050-1636-9). 30pp. A mouse samples all the goodies on a banquet table and gets fatter and fatter. (Rev: BCCB 12/92; BL 11/1/92; HB 1/93; SLJ 12/92*)

2220 Fleming, Denise. *Mama Cat Has Three Kittens* (PS–K). Illus. 1998, Holt $15.95 (978-0-8050-5745-4). 32pp. Two of Mama Cat's kittens are well behaved, but the third, Boris, just loves to nap. (Rev: BCCB 12/98; BL 11/15/98; HBG 3/99; SLJ 11/98)

2221 Fleming, Denise. *Time to Sleep* (PS–1). Illus. 1997, Holt $16.95 (978-0-8050-3762-3). 32pp. In this cumulative tale, Bear passes along the information that winter is on the way. (Rev: BL 10/1/97; HBG 3/98; SLJ 11/97)

2222 Foley, Greg. *Good Luck Bear* (PS). Illus. by author. 2009, Viking $15.99 (978-0-670-06258-4). 32pp. Bear searches for a four-leaf clover and the promised luck it will bring despite the discouraging attitude of many of his animal friends. (Rev: BL 11/15/08; SLJ 3/09)

2223 Foley, Greg. *Thank You Bear* (PS–K). Illus. 2007, Viking $15.99 (978-0-670-06165-5). 32pp. Bear is quite pleased with his latest find — a tiny, empty box — and is disappointed by his friends' reactions until he shows it to Mouse, who promptly curls up in it. (Rev: BL 4/15/07; SLJ 3/07*)

2224 Fontenot, Mary Alice. *Clovis Crawfish and Echo Gecko* (PS–2). Illus. by Julie Dupré Buckner. 2003, Pelican $15.95 (978-1-56554-708-7). In bayou country, Lizette Lizard introduces Clovis Crawfish and his friends to Echo Gecko, a shy little lizard who would like to learn French; a Cajun glossary is appended. (Rev: HBG 10/03; SLJ 5/03)

2225 Fontes, Justine Korman. *Signs of Spring* (K–2). Illus. by Rob Hefferan. 2002, Mondo $14.95 (978-1-59034-189-6). 24pp. On their way to school, Lucy, a mouse, and Zack, a chipmunk, gather signs of spring for show-and-tell. (Rev: BL 6/1–15/02; HBG 10/02; SLJ 8/02)

2226 Ford, Bernette. *No More Bottles for Bunny!* (PS). Illus. by Sam Williams. 2007, Boxer Bks. LB $12.95 (978-1-905417-34-6). Children reluctant to make the switch from the bottle to the cup will find encouragement in this story, about a bunny who decides to put aside his bottle to join in a tea party. (Rev: SLJ 5/07)

2227 Ford, Bernette. *No More Pacifier for Piggy!* (PS). Illus. by Sam Williams. 2008, Sterling $12.95 (978-1-905417-89-6). 26pp. An appealing young pig learns to get along without his pacifier through a game of peekaboo. (Rev: BLO 7/29/08; SLJ 8/08)

2228 Foreman, Michael. *The Littlest Dinosaur* (PS–K). Illus. by author. 2008, Walker $16.95 (978-0-8027-9759-9). 32pp. The littlest dinosaur may be small but he's sensitive and brave, and his actions — and friendship with a lonely tall dinosaur — rescue the rest of his larger family. (Rev: BL 5/15/08; LMC 8/08; SLJ 5/08)

2229 Foreman, Michael. *The Littlest Dinosaur's Big Adventure* (PS–K). Illus. by author. 2009, Walker $16.99 (978-0-8027-9545-8). 32pp. The Littlest Dinosaur, a triceratops, is in the scary woods when he meets a young pterodactyl who is also nervous and discovers that he has some courage after all. (Rev: BL 5/1/09; SLJ 5/09)

2230 Fox, Christyan, and Diane Fox. *Astronaut PiggyWiggy* (PS). Illus. by authors. 2002, Handprint $9.95 (978-1-929766-41-3). The ever-imaginative PiggyWiggy looks through his telescope and pictures himself blasting off and visiting distant places in this book with fold-out flaps. For other career options, consider *Goodnight PiggyWiggy* (2000), *Bathtime PiggyWiggy* and *Fire Fighter PiggyWiggy* (2001), and *Pirate PiggyWiggy* (2003). (Rev: HBG 10/02; SLJ 7/02)

2231 Fox, Diane, and Christyan Fox. *Tyson the Terrible* (PS–2). Illus. by authors. 2007, Bloomsbury $12.95 (978-1-58234-734-9). Far less formidable than the reputation that precedes him, Tyson the little Tyrannosaurus rex turns out to be just a lonely dinosaur looking for some friends. (Rev: SLJ 2/07)

2232 Fox, Mem. *Hattie and the Fox* (PS–K). Illus. by Patricia Mullins. 1987, Macmillan $16.00 (978-0-02-735470-6); paper $5.99 (978-0-689-71611-9). 32pp. A cumulative tale about a big black hen who spies a fox in the farmyard. (Rev: BL 3/15/87; HB 5/87; SLJ 5/87)

2233 Fox, Mem. *Hunwick's Egg* (PS–2). Illus. by Pamela Lofts. 2005, Harcourt $16.00 (978-0-15-216318-1). 32pp. A kindly bandicoot adopts and cares for an egg that is actually a stone in this strikingly illustrated book that shows the plants and animals of Australia's desert habitat. (Rev: BL 2/15/05; SLJ 3/05)

2234 Fox, Mem. *Koala Lou* (PS–2). Illus. by Pamela Lofts. 1989, Harcourt $15.00 (978-0-15-200502-3). 32pp. A young koala named Koala Lou finds that her mother is too busy with her younger children to shower the same affection on her as before. (Rev: BL 11/15/89; HB 11/89; SLJ 1/90)

2235 Fox, Mem. *Possum Magic* (K–2). Illus. by Julie Vivas. 1990, Harcourt $15.00 (978-0-15-200572-6); paper $6.00 (978-0-15-263224-3). 32pp. Grandmother Opossum makes Hush invisible, and then forgets how she did it in this tale from Down Under. (Rev: BL 12/1/87; SLJ 12/87)

2236 Fox, Mem. *Where Is the Green Sheep?* (PS–1). Illus. by Judy Horacek. 2004, Harcourt $15.00 (978-0-15-204907-2). A beginning reader in rhyme featuring sheep in all kinds of activities, with the added fillip of a search for the green sheep. (Rev: HB 5/04; SLJ 4/04)

2237 Frascino, Edward. *Nanny Noony and the Dust Queen* (PS–3). Illus. 1990, Pippin LB $15.95 (978-0-945912-09-5). 32pp. Nanny Noony must grapple with a powerful sorceress, the Dust Queen. (Rev: BL 6/15/90; SLJ 9/90)

2238 Fraser, Mary Ann. *I.Q., It's Time* (PS–K). Illus. by author. 2005, Walker $15.95 (978-0-8027-8978-5). Adorable mouse I.Q. (last seen in 2003's *I.Q. Goes to the Library*) is back in the classroom, helping the children tell time as they get ready for Parents' Night. (Rev: SLJ 8/05)

2239 Freedman, Claire. *Follow That Bear If You Dare!* (PS–2). Illus. by Alison Edgson. 2008, Good Bks. $16.00 (978-1-56148-588-8). 28pp. Hare is very interested in bears and asks his rabbit friend Rumbly to accompany him on a bear hunt, following the advice in *The Best Book of Bear Hunting*; it's only after an encounter with a bear cub — and when they turn to the last page of the book — that the two adventurers realize that bears eat rabbits. (Rev: BL 6/1–15/08; SLJ 8/08)

2240 Freedman, Claire. *Where's Your Smile, Crocodile?* (PS–K). Illus. by Sean Julian. 2001, Peachtree $16.95 (978-1-56145-251-4). Kyle the crocodile can't seem to smile, no matter how hard others try to amuse him, until he comes across a sad little lion and tries in turn to cheer him up. (Rev: HBG 3/02; SLJ 11/01)

2241 Freeman, Don. *Bearymore* (K–3). Illus. by author. 1979, Puffin paper $6.99 (978-0-14-050279-4). 40pp. A circus bear must build a new act, but he hibernates instead.

2242 Freeman, Don. *Corduroy* (PS–1). Illus. by author. 1968, Puffin paper $6.99 (978-0-14-050173-5). 32pp. The amusing story of a toy bear whose one missing button from his green corduroy overalls almost costs him the opportunity of belonging to someone. A sequel is: *A Pocket for Corduroy* (1978).

2243 Freeman, Don. *Dandelion* (K–2). Illus. by author. 1964, Puffin paper $5.99 (978-0-14-050218-3). 48pp. A vain lion goes to a barber shop before a party and makes himself unrecognizable to his friends.

2244 Freeman, Don. *Earl the Squirrel* (PS–K). Illus. 2005, Viking $15.99 (978-0-670-06019-1). 48pp. Earl the squirrel must learn to find acorns on his own in this funny, action-packed posthumous story by the author of *Corduroy*. (Rev: BL 9/15/05; SLJ 10/05)

2245 Freeman, Don. *Gregory's Shadow* (PS–1). Illus. 2000, Viking $15.99 (978-0-670-89328-7). 32pp. Gregory Groundhog doesn't want to be separated from his shadow nor does he want six more weeks of winter — what a dilemma! (Rev: BL 1/1–15/01; HBG 3/01; SLJ 2/01)

110

2246 Freeman, Don. *Manuelo the Playing Mantis* (K–2). Illus. 2004, Viking $15.99 (978-0-670-03684-4). 32pp. Manuelo the praying mantis longs to make music but is frustrated in his efforts until a clever spider helps him construct a cello. (Rev: BL 4/15/04; SLJ 4/04)

2247 French, Jackie. *Diary of a Wombat* (K–2). Illus. by Bruce Whatley. 2003, Clarion $14.00 (978-0-618-38136-4). A wombat relates her daily life in her diary; most entries deal with eating and sleeping until some friendly humans arrive. (Rev: HBG 4/04; SLJ 8/03)

2248 French, Jackie. *Josephine Wants to Dance* (K–2). Illus. by Bruce Whatley. 2007, Abrams $15.95 (978-0-8109-9431-7). 32pp. Josephine the kangaroo, who loves to dance, gets the chance she's dreamed of when the prima ballerina twists her ankle. (Rev: BL 11/1/07; SLJ 11/07)

2249 French, Jackie. *Too Many Pears!* (PS–1). Illus. by Bruce Whatley. 2003, Star Bright $16.95 (978-1-932065-47-3). Pamela the cow develops a real love for pears in this humorously illustrated picture book. (Rev: HBG 4/04; SLJ 11/03)

2250 Friedman, Jim. *The Mysterious Misadventures of Foy Rin Jin: A Decidedly Dysfunctional Dragon* (K–3). Illus. by Patti Stren. 1999, HarperCollins LB $15.89 (978-0-06-028551-7). Because he breathes water instead of fire, an unhappy dragon leaves his conventional colleagues and finds happiness with humans. (Rev: HBG 3/00; SLJ 1/00)

2251 Friend, Catherine. *The Perfect Nest* (K–2). Illus. by John Manders. 2007, Candlewick $16.99 (978-0-7636-2430-9). Jack the cat has a longing for a lovely omelet and builds a perfect nest, which succeeds in drawing a chicken, a duck, and a goose, but sadly Jack's plan just won't work. (Rev: SLJ 3/07*)

2252 Fries, Claudia. *A Pig Is Moving In!* (PS–2). Illus. 2000, Orchard LB $16.99 (978-0-531-33307-5). 32pp. A fox, a hen, and a hare are mistaken when they jump to the conclusion that, because their new neighbor is a pig, he will be dirty and messy. (Rev: BL 12/15/00; HBG 3/01; SLJ 9/00)

2253 Froehlich, Margaret W. *That Kookoory!* (1–3). Illus. by Marla Frazee. 1995, Harcourt $15.00 (978-0-15-277650-3). 40pp. This picture book tells of the confrontation between a prideful rooster and his arch enemy the weasel. (Rev: BCCB 5/95; BL 4/15/95; HB 7/95; SLJ 5/95)

2254 Fuge, Charles. *My Dad!* (PS–K). Illus. by author. 2003, Sterling $12.95 (978-1-4027-0707-0). A little bear scares away his playmates, one by one, by boasting about his father's fearsomeness, then finds himself all alone in the forest. (Rev: HBG 4/04; SLJ 4/04)

2255 Fuge, Charles. *Swim, Little Wombat, Swim!* (PS–K). Illus. by author. 2005, Sterling LB $12.95 (978-1-4027-2375-9). Little Wombat meets a platypus and learns how to swim as well as not to make snap judgements. (Rev: SLJ 11/05)

2256 Futterer, Kurt. *Emile* (PS–2). Trans. by Bronwen Gray Specht and Ingrid MacGillis. Illus. by Ralf Futterer. 2004, MacAdam $17.95 (978-1-931561-95-2). 32pp. Emile, a white cat who lives in a pristine home, finds himself covered in color after a visit to van Gogh's studio and his new appearance inspires his owners to adopt a brighter life. (Rev: BL 1/1–15/05)

2257 Galloway, Ruth. *Clumsy Crab* (PS–K). Illus. by author. 2005, Tiger Tales $15.95 (978-1-58925-050-5). Nipper the crab is not fond of his clumsy claws until he realizes they will allow him to save Octopus when he is entangled in seaweed. (Rev: SLJ 2/06)

2258 Galloway, Ruth. *Fidgety Fish* (PS–3). Illus. by author. 2001, Tiger Tales $14.95 (978-1-58925-012-3). A rambunctious little fish is sent out to swim until he's tired, and ignores warnings to stay away from Big Fish. (Rev: SLJ 2/02)

2259 Gantos, Jack. *The Nine Lives of Rotten Ralph* (K–3). Illus. by Nicole Rubel. 2009, Houghton $16.00 (978-0-618-80046-9). 32pp. According to the vet, Ralph has used eight of his nine lives; can Sarah get the disobedient cat to change his ways? (Rev: BL 4/1/09; HB 5/09; SLJ 4/09)

2260 Gantos, Jack. *Rotten Ralph* (K–3). Illus. by Nicole Rubel. 1976, Houghton $16.00 (978-0-395-24276-6); paper $7.95 (978-0-395-29202-0). 48pp. Ralph is truly a nasty cat — mean and disruptive — until he is reformed under unusual circumstances. Sequels include *Worse Than Rotten, Ralph* (1982), *Back to School for Rotten Ralph* (1998), and *Wedding Bells for Rotten Ralph* (1999).

2261 Garland, Michael. *Hooray José!* (K–3). Illus. by author. 2007, Marshall Cavendish $14.99 (978-0-7614-5345-1). José make the winning shot in a basketball game against the Rats, proving to his teammates that even little mice deserve a chance to play. (Rev: SLJ 5/07)

2262 Garland, Michael. *Last Night at the Zoo* (K–3). Illus. 2001, Boyds Mills $15.95 (978-1-56397-759-6). 32pp. The animals at the zoo are bored, so they break out and head for a night at Club Boogie. (Rev: BL 7/01; HBG 3/02; SLJ 5/01)

2263 Gavril, David. *Penelope Nuthatch and the Big Surprise* (PS–2). Illus. 2006, Abrams $14.95 (978-0-8109-5762-6). 32pp. Penelope Nuthatch thinks her friend Luther is taking her to the ballet and spends time and money preening and primping; so she is very disappointed to find that her "unforgettable surprise" is a trip to a water park, and it takes a while for her to recover and join in. (Rev: BL 1/1–15/06; SLJ 2/06)

2264 Gay, Marie-Louise. *Caramba* (K–3). Illus. 2005, Groundwood $16.95 (978-0-88899-667-1). 40pp. Caramba the cat is sad that he cannot to fly like the other cats, but then he finds out that unlike them he is able to swim! (Rev: BL 10/1/05; SLJ 11/05)

2265 Geisert, Arthur. *The Giant Ball of String* (K–3). Illus. 2002, Houghton $16.00 (978-0-618-13221-8). 32pp. The children (piglets, actually) of Rumpus Ridge, Wisconsin, devise a clever scheme to reclaim their town's giant ball of string, which a nearby town has taken captive. (Rev: BL 9/15/02; HBG 3/03; SLJ 9/02)

2266 Geisert, Arthur. *Lights Out* (K–3). Illus. 2005, Houghton $16.00 (978-0-618-47892-7). 32pp. In this compelling, nearly wordless picture book, an ingenious little pig who's afraid of the dark figures out an elaborate contraption that will turn off his bedroom light after he's already fallen asleep. (Rev: BCCB 10/05; BL 11/1/05*; HB 11/05; HBG 4/06; SLJ 12/05)

2267 Geisert, Arthur. *Mystery* (2–4). Illus. by author. 2003, Houghton $16.00 (978-0-618-27293-8). 32pp. The illustrations are the focus of this story about a little pig who investigates the theft of paintings from the art museum. (Rev: HBG 4/04; SLJ 10/03)

2268 Geisert, Arthur. *Oops* (K–3). 2006, Houghton $16.00 (978-0-618-60904-8). 32pp. Just a little spilled milk sets off a chain of events that destroys a pig family's house in this wordless story. (Rev: BL 9/1/06; SLJ 10/06)

2269 George, Lindsay Barrett. *Alfred Digs* (PS–2). Illus. by author. 2008, Greenwillow $16.99 (978-0-06-078760-8). 40pp. Alfred the aardvark has a pet ant called Itty Bitty who heads off to the zoo one day; Alfred sets off in pursuit and encounters many letters of the alphabet on the way (the action takes place within a dictionary). (Rev: BL 4/1/08; SLJ 6/08)

2270 George, Lindsay Barrett. *The Secret* (PS–2). Illus. by author. 2005, HarperCollins LB $16.89 (978-0-06-029600-1). 32pp. Mr. Snail whispers his secret to a mouse, who whispers it to a beetle, who passes it on to a turtle, and so forth until the secret ("I love you") finally makes it to Miss Snail. (Rev: BL 3/1/04; SLJ 5/05)

2271 Gerritsen, Paula. *Nuts* (PS–2). Illus. 2006, Front St. $15.95 (978-1-932425-66-6). 32pp. With an autumn chill in the air, Mouse travels to the nut tree to gather food for the coming winter but discovers that all the nuts have blown away. (Rev: BL 3/1/06; SLJ 3/06)

2272 Gershator, David, and Phillis Gershator. *Moon Rooster* (K–3). Illus. by Megan Halsey. 2001, Marshall Cavendish $15.95 (978-0-7614-5092-4). A young rooster persists in crowing at the moon despite human annoyance. (Rev: HBG 3/02; SLJ 12/01)

2273 Gerstein, Mordicai, and Susan Y. Harris. *Daisy's Garden* (PS–3). Illus. 1995, Hyperion LB $15.49 (978-0-7868-2080-1). 32pp. A year in the life of a garden tended by rabbits, mice, groundhogs, goats, and other animals. (Rev: BL 7/95; SLJ 4/95)

2274 Gibbs, Lynne. *Schooltime for Sammy* (PS–K). Illus. by Melanie Mitchell. Series: Growing Pains. 2003, Gingham Dog $12.95 (978-1-57768-482-4); paper $4.95 (978-1-57768-931-7). Sammy the chimp prefers to play in the treetops of his jungle home until he hears about all the fun he missed at school. (Rev: HBG 4/04; SLJ 1/04)

2275 Giffard, Hannah. *Pablo Goes Hunting* (1–3). Illus. 2005, Frances Lincoln $15.95 (978-1-84507-284-1). 32pp. Pablo the fox kit and his siblings Poppy and Pumpkin encounter numerous obstacles in their search for food; a spin-off from a cartoon series. (Rev: BL 9/1/05)

2276 Ginsburg, Mirra. *Across the Stream* (PS–2). Illus. by Nancy Tafuri. 1982, Greenwillow $17.89 (978-0-688-01206-9); Morrow paper $6.99 (978-0-688-10477-1). 24pp. Mother hen saves her three chicks from the fox.

2277 Ginsburg, Mirra, trans. *The Chick and the Duckling* (PS–K). Adapted from the Russian by V. Suteyev. Illus. by Jose Aruego and Ariane Dewey. 1988, Simon & Schuster paper $4.95 (978-0-689-71226-5). 32pp. A duck and a chick who hatch at the same time become constant companions.

2278 Giovanni, Nikki. *The Grasshopper's Song: An Aesop's Fable Revisited* (3–6). Illus. by Chris Raschka. 2008, Candlewick $16.99 (978-0-7636-3021-8). 56pp. In this retelling set in a courtroom, a grasshopper sues the ants when he is denied his share of the harvest, claiming that it was his music that enabled them to work efficiently. (Rev: BL 5/15/08; LMC 10/08*; SLJ 6/08)

2279 Glenn, Sharlee. *Just What Mama Needs* (PS–2). Illus. by Amiko Hirao. 2008, Harcourt $16.00 (978-0-15-205759-6). 32pp. Abby is an inventive young dog who takes on a different role — a pirate on Monday, a detective on Tuesday — every day except Sunday, when she is just herself but continues to help her mother with chores. (Rev: BL 4/15/08; SLJ 5/08)

2280 Gliori, Debi. *Flora's Blanket* (PS). Illus. 2001, Scholastic $15.95 (978-0-531-30305-4). 32pp. Flora, a young bunny, cannot sleep because her favorite blanket has disappeared. (Rev: BL 5/15/01; HBG 10/01; SLJ 7/01*)

2281 Gliori, Debi. *Mr. Bear Says, Are You There, Baby Bear? A Lift-the-Flap Book* (PS). Illus. by author. 1999, Orchard $9.95 (978-0-531-30182-1). Movable flaps are used in this story about Papa Bear's search for his missing child. (Rev: SLJ 1/00)

2282 Gliori, Debi. *Mr. Bear to the Rescue* (PS–1). Illus. 2000, Orchard $15.95 (978-0-531-30276-7). 32pp. When bunny Flora is missing, Mr. Bear loads his tools into his carriage and sets off to help. (Rev: BL 11/15/00; HBG 10/01; SLJ 11/00)

2283 Gliori, Debi. *No Matter What* (PS–K). Illus. 1999, Harcourt $16.00 (978-0-15-202061-3). 32pp. Small, a young fox, tests the love that Large feels for him through a series of questions to determine the extent of this love. (Rev: BL 11/15/99; HBG 3/00; SLJ 11/99)

2284 Gliori, Debi. *Where Did That Baby Come From?* (PS–2). Illus. 2005, Harcourt $16.00 (978-0-15-205373-4). 32pp. A tiger cub wonders where his new sibling came from — a store? outer space? the zoo? — but happily accepts his presence in the end. (Rev: BL 3/1/05; SLJ 4/05)

2285 Godwin, Laura. *The Best Fall of All* (K–1). Illus. by Jane Chapman. 2002, Simon & Schuster $14.95 (978-0-689-84713-4). 32pp. Honey the cat and Happy the dog learn to have fun in the fallen leaves. (Rev: BL 12/1/02; HBG 3/03; SLJ 10/02)

2286 Goldsmith, Howard. *Sleepy Little Owl* (PS–1). Illus. by Denny Bond. 1997, McGraw-Hill $12.95 (978-0-07-024543-3). 30pp. Through a series of daytime adventures, a young owl realizes that he is a nocturnal creature. (Rev: SLJ 2/98)

2287 Gollub, Matthew. *Gobble, Quack, Moon* (PS–2). Illus. by Judy Love. 2002, Tortuga $18.95 (978-1-889910-20-8). 32pp. Katie the cow and her barnyard friends hop on a rocket ship and spend a happy time on the moon. (Rev: BL 6/1–15/02)

2288 Gollub, Matthew. *The Jazz Fly* (PS–2). Illus. by Karen Hanke. 2000, Tortuga $17.95 (978-1-889910-17-8). 32pp. A bouncy book with an accompanying CD about a hip fly, his jazz talk, and his job in a club as a drummer. (Rev: BL 8/00; SLJ 8/00)

2289 Goodman, Joan Elizabeth. *Bernard Goes to School* (PS–K). Illus. by Dominic Catalano. 2001, Boyds Mills $15.95 (978-1-56397-958-3). 32pp. Although he feels shy at first, Bernard the elephant eventually is able to say goodbye to his parents on his first day of preschool. (Rev: BCCB 9/01; BL 10/1/01; HBG 3/02; SLJ 8/01)

2290 Goodman, Joan Elizabeth. *Bernard Wants a Baby* (PS–K). Illus. by Dominic Catalano. 2004, Boyds Mills $15.95 (978-1-59078-088-6). Although he has expressed a wish for siblings, young elephant Bernard is uncertain when triplets arrive. (Rev: SLJ 7/04)

2291 Goodrich, Carter. *The Hermit Crab* (K–2). Illus. by author. 2009, Simon & Schuster $16.99 (978-1-4169-3892-7). 40pp. A timid hermit crab inadvertently saves the day in this well-illustrated underwater story. (Rev: SLJ 6/09)

2292 Goppel, Christine. *Anna Aphid* (PS–3). Illus. by author. 2005, North-South $16.95 (978-0-7358-2007-4). Anna Aphid enjoys an exciting tour of the world, which readers can see is simply a plant sitting on a windowsill. (Rev: SLJ 3/06)

2293 Gorbachev, Valeri. *Big Little Elephant* (K–2). Illus. 2005, Harcourt $16.00 (978-0-15-205195-2). 32pp. Little Elephant finds his size can be a real obstacle when it comes to playing with his new-found friends. (Rev: BL 10/1/05; SLJ 9/05)

2294 Gorbachev, Valeri. *The Big Trip* (PS–2). Illus. 2004, Penguin $15.99 (978-0-399-23965-6). 32pp. Goat throws a wet blanket on his friend Pig's vacation plans when he questions the safety of every possible form of transportation. (Rev: BL 5/1/04; SLJ 3/04)

2295 Gorbachev, Valeri. *Dragon Is Coming!* (PS–2). Illus. by author. 2009, Harcourt $16.00 (978-0-15-205196-9). 44pp. Misunderstanding and panic ensue when the animals think a storm cloud is a dragon, but all is well once the storm is over and they realize what has happened. (Rev: BL 7/09; SLJ 5/09)

2296 Gorbachev, Valeri. *Heron and Turtle* (PS–2). Illus. by author. 2006, Philomel $15.99 (978-0-399-24321-9). Heron and Turtle are close friends despite their difference in size. (Rev: SLJ 11/06)

2297 Gorbachev, Valeri. *Molly Who Flew Away* (PS–1). Illus. by author. 2009, Philomel $16.99 (978-0-399-25211-2). 32pp. Molly the mouse enjoys a day at the country fair with her friends — until she buys too many balloons and is wafted aloft. (Rev: BL 5/15/09; SLJ 6/09)

2298 Gorbachev, Valeri. *That's What Friends Are For* (PS–1). Illus. 2005, Philomel $15.99 (978-0-399-23966-3). 32pp. When Goat sees Pig crying, he imagines all kinds of disasters that might explain the situation. (Rev: BL 5/15/05)

2299 Gorbachev, Valeri. *Whose Hat Is It?* (PS–K). Illus. by author. 2004, HarperCollins LB $15.89 (978-0-06-053435-6). A turtle patiently seeks the owner of a pink hat found swept away by the wind. (Rev: SLJ 7/04)

2300 Gore, Leonid. *Mommy, Where Are You?* (PS–K). Illus. by author. 2009, Atheneum $16.99 (978-1-4169-5505-4). 32pp. A little mouse named Ozzy looks everywhere for his mother. (Rev: BCCB 4/09; BL 5/1/09; SLJ 5/09)

2301 Goss, Linda. *The Frog Who Wanted to Be a Singer* (K–3). Illus. by Cynthia Jabar. 1996, Orchard LB $16.99 (978-0-531-08745-9). 40pp. Scorned by both frogs and birds because he wants to sing, a young frog astounds everyone with his talent. (Rev: BCCB 4/96; BL 4/15/96*; SLJ 5/96)

2302 Graham, Margaret B. *Be Nice to Spiders* (PS–2). Illus. by author. 1967, HarperCollins LB $17.89 (978-0-06-022073-0). 32pp. Helen, Billy's pet spider, makes all the animals at the zoo happy when she spins webs and catches flies for them.

2303 Gralley, Jean. *Very Boring Alligator* (PS). Illus. 2001, Holt $15.95 (978-0-8050-6328-8). 32pp. A boring alligator just won't go away — until a little girl makes up her mind to get rid of him. (Rev: BL 9/15/01; HBG 3/02; SLJ 10/01)

2304 Grant, Nicola. *Don't Be So Nosy, Posy!* (PS–1). Illus. by Tim Warnes. 2004, Tiger Tales $15.95 (978-1-58925-036-9). Piglet Posy is insatiably curious and pokes her nose into everybody's business; eventually this annoying trait pays off. (Rev: SLJ 4/04)

2305 Gravett, Emily. *The Odd Egg* (PS–2). Illus. by author. 2009, Simon & Schuster $15.99 (978-1-4169-6872-6). 32pp. Duck is happy to find an egg to sit on, even though it's a suspicious-looking green-spotted giant of an egg that draws general derision. What will pop out? (Rev: BCCB 1/09; BL 1/1–15/09; HB 1/09; LMC 5/09; SLJ 1/09)

2306 Gravett, Emily. *Wolves* (PS–2). Illus. by author. 2006, Simon & Schuster $15.95 (978-1-4169-1491-4). 40pp. A rabbit is so engrossed in reading the book about wolves that he borrowed from the library that he doesn't realize he's face to face with a real live wolf. (Rev: BL 12/1/06; SLJ 8/06*)

2307 Gray, Kes. *Cluck O'clock* (PS–3). Illus. by Mary McQuillan. 2004, Holiday House $16.95 (978-0-8234-1809-1). 32pp. Time plays an important role in this chicken-themed story that counts off the hours from first light — four "o'cluck" — until midnight. (Rev: BL 4/1/04; SLJ 3/04)

2308 Gray, Kes. *The Get Well Soon Book* (PS–1). Illus. by Mary McQuillan. 2000, Millbrook LB $22.90 (978-0-7613-1922-1). 32pp. An entertaining picture book that tells how different animals can have accidents and illnesses — Cynthia centipede sprains 98 ankles playing field hockey and Danny the Dalmatian breaks out in stripes. (Rev: BL 12/15/00; HBG 3/01; SLJ 2/01)

2309 Gray, Kes. *Our Twitchy* (PS–1). Illus. by Mary McQuillan. 2003, Holt $15.95 (978-0-8050-7454-3). When Twitchy the rabbit wonders why his parents don't look like him, his adoptive mother and father — a cow and horse — explain that they love him just the way he is. (Rev: HBG 4/04; SLJ 12/03)

2310 Gray, Libba M. *Small Green Snake* (PS–1). Illus. by Holly Meade. 1994, Orchard LB $15.99 (978-0-531-08694-0). 32pp. A disobedient garter snake wanders away from home and finds himself a prisoner in a jelly jar. (Rev: BL 9/15/94*; SLJ 9/94)

2311 Greene, Rhonda Gowler. *Firebears: The Rescue Team* (PS–2). Illus. by Dan Andreasen. 2005, Holt $15.95 (978-0-8050-7010-1). 32pp. The bears of Fire Station Number Eight have a busy day responding to calls ranging from a kitten stuck in a tree to a blazing store. (Rev: BL 6/1–15/05)

2312 Greene, Stephanie. *Not Just Another Moose* (K–3). Illus. by Andrea Wallace. 2000, Marshall Cavendish $15.95 (978-0-7614-5061-0). A year in the life of Hildy, a pig, and Moose, who worries his antlers won't grow back in the spring. (Rev: HBG 10/00; SLJ 5/00)

2313 Greene, Stephanie. *Pig Pickin'* (1–3). Illus. by Joe Mathieu. Series: Moose and Hildy. 2006, Marshall Cavendish $14.99 (978-0-7614-5324-6). 56pp. Hildy the pig asks Moose to join her on a trip down south to a pig pickin', an event she mistakenly believes is a porcine beauty contest. (Rev: SLJ 10/06)

2314 Gretz, Susanna. *Riley and Rose in the Picture* (K–3). Illus. 2005, Candlewick $16.99 (978-0-7636-2681-5). 32pp. Riley the dog and Rose the cat, natural antagonists, try to get along by drawing pictures inside on a rainy day. (Rev: BL 8/05; SLJ 9/05)

2315 Guarino, Deborah. *Is Your Mama a Llama?* (PS–K). Illus. by Steven Kellogg. 1989, Scholastic $14.95 (978-0-590-41387-9). 32pp. A pleasing study of who belongs to whom, as a koala and her baby clutch each other or an opossum ambles off with babies aboard her back. (Rev: BCCB 11/89; BL 10/1/89; SLJ 10/89)

2316 Guest, Elissa Haden. *Harriet's Had Enough* (PS–2). Illus. by Paul Meisel. 2009, Candlewick $15.99 (978-0-7636-3454-4). 32pp. Harriet, a little raccoon, has an argument with her mother about picking up her toys and decides to run away from home. (Rev: BL 4/1/09; SLJ 4/09)

2317 Gugler, Laurel Dee. *There's a Billy Goat in the Garden* (PS–1). Illus. by Clare Beaton. 2003, Barefoot Books $14.99 (978-1-84148-089-3). 32pp. A tiny bee chases a billy goat from the garden after the dog, pig, donkey, cow, and horse are unsuccessful. (Rev: BL 3/15/03; HBG 10/03; SLJ 4/03)

2318 Gusti. *Half of an Elephant* (K–3). Illus. by author. 2006, Kane $15.95 (978-1-933605-09-8). A wacky, inventively illustrated tale of a world split in two, as the front half of an odd-looking elephant desperately tries to find its back half. (Rev: SLJ 9/06)

2319 Gutman, Anne. *Gaspard and Lisa at the Museum* (PS–1). Illus. by Georg Hallensleben. 2001, Knopf $9.95 (978-0-375-81117-3). 32pp. Young animals Gaspard and Lisa have an adventure during their class trip to the Museum of Natural History. Also use *Gaspard in the Hospital* (2001). (Rev: BL 11/15/01; HBG 3/02; SLJ 11/01)

2320 Gutman, Anne. *Gaspard at the Seashore* (PS). Illus. by Georg Hallensleben. 2002, Knopf $9.95 (978-0-375-81118-0). 32pp. Little Gaspard dreams of daring water sports at the seashore, but is afraid because he can't swim. (Rev: BL 8/02; HBG 10/02; SLJ 5/02)

2321 Gutman, Anne. *Lisa in New York* (PS). Illus. by Georg Hallensleben. 2002, Knopf $9.95 (978-0-375-81119-7). 32pp. Lisa gets lost while visiting her uncle, who lives in New York City. (Rev: BL 8/02; HBG 10/02; SLJ 5/02)

2322 Gutman, Anne, and Georg Hallensleben. *Lisa's Airplane Trip* (PS–1). Illus. 2001, Knopf $9.95 (978-0-375-81114-2). 32pp. Lisa, a small white rabbit, enjoys the thrill of traveling alone on an airplane for the first time, particularly when she in taken into the cockpit. (Rev: BL 2/1/01; HB 5/01; HBG 10/01)

2323 Hadithi, Mwenye. *Hot Hippo* (PS–3). Illus. by Adrienne Kennaway. 1986, Little, Brown LB $14.95 (978-0-316-33722-9). A folktale-like story of Hot Hippo, who longed to live in the water, and the god of everything, who wanted him to live on land. (Rev: BL 12/1/86; HB 1/87; SLJ 2/87)

2324 Hafner, Marylin. *Molly and Emmett's Surprise Garden* (K–2). Illus. by author. 2001, McGraw-Hill $12.95 (978-1-57768-895-2). 30pp. When Molly and Emmett the cat are planting a garden, Emmett opens all the packets at the same time and the seeds get all mixed up. (Rev: HBG 10/01; SLJ 8/01)

2325 Hager, Sarah. *Dancing Matilda* (PS–2). Illus. by Kelly Murphy. 2005, HarperCollins $15.99 (978-0-06-051452-5). A little kangaroo named Matilda dances her way through the pages of this book with rhyming text and lovely illustrations. (Rev: SLJ 8/05)

2326 Hall, Algy Craig. *Fine as We Are* (PS). Illus. by author. 2008, Boxer Bks. $14.95 (978-1-905417-72-8). 32pp. Happy as an only child, Little Frog suddenly finds himself overrun with noisy little siblings who follow him everywhere. (Rev: LMC 8/08; SLJ 4/08)

2327 Hall, Martin. *Charlie and Tess* (PS–2). Illus. by Catherine Walters. 1996, Little Tiger $14.95 (978-1-888444-06-3). 28pp. An orphaned lamb that has been raised by a farmer's family later saves his flock on a snowy night. (Rev: BL 4/15/97; SLJ 3/97)

2328 Hall, Nancy Christen. *Mouse at Night* (PS–K). Illus. by Buket Erdogan. 2000, Orchard $14.95 (978-0-531-30260-6). 32pp. At night in Miss Bumbly's house, a mouse emerges from its hole and engages in all sorts of activities, including preparing breakfast for Miss Bumbly. (Rev: BL 5/1/00; HBG 10/00; SLJ 4/00)

2329 Hample, Stoo. *I Will Kiss You: Lots and Lots and Lots!* (PS). 2005, Candlewick $15.99 (978-0-

7636-2787-4). 32pp. A mother bunny enumerates the many opportunities each day offers for planting a kiss on her toddler. (Rev: BL 2/1/06; SLJ 5/06)

2330 Harley, Bill. *Sitting Down to Eat* (K–3). Illus. by Kitty Harvill. 1996, August House $15.95 (978-0-87483-460-4). In this cumulative tale, a boy invites so many animals into his house that it explodes. (Rev: SLJ 1/97)

2331 Harper, Anita. *It's Not Fair!* (PS–K). Illus. by Mary McQuillan. 2007, Holiday $16.95 (978-0-8234-2094-0). 32pp. A young cat is jealous that her new baby brother gets all the attention, but the roles are later reversed when the baby grows older and is frustrated that he can't do all the fun things his big sister can do; originally published in 1986, this edition features new illustrations. (Rev: BL 7/07; SLJ 10/07)

2332 Harper, Charise Mericle. *When Randolph Turned Rotten* (PS–2). Illus. by author. 2007, Knopf $16.99 (978-0-375-84071-5). 40pp. Jealous of Ivy the goose's invitation to an all-girls party, friend Randolph the beaver loads her down with "essential" items, which — it turns out — save the day. (Rev: BL 11/15/07; HB 1/08; LMC 1/08; SLJ 12/07*)

2333 Harper, Jamie. *Miss Mingo and the First Day of School* (K–3). Illus. by author. 2006, Candlewick $15.99 (978-0-7636-2410-1). On the first day of school, Miss Mingo the flamingo and her animal students discuss the characteristics that make them special and different. (Rev: SLJ 8/06)

2334 Harris, Lee. *Never Let Your Cat Make Lunch for You* (K–2). Illus. by Debbie Tilley. 1999, Tricycle $12.95 (978-1-883672-80-5). 24pp. Although at times the images produced are somewhat gross (e.g., mouse sandwiches), this is a humorous tale of why cats can't prepare proper meals for humans. (Rev: BL 10/15/99; HBG 3/00; SLJ 12/99)

2335 Harrison, David L. *Farmer's Dog Goes to the Forest: Rhymes for Two Voices* (K–3). Illus. by Arden Johnson-Petrov. 2005, Boyds Mills $15.95 (978-1-59078-242-2). 32pp. A farmer's dog exchanges simple rhyming questions and answers with the animals in this sequel to *Farmer's Garden* (2005). (Rev: BL 9/1/05; SLJ 9/05)

2336 Harrison, David L. *A Farmer's Garden: Rhymes for Two Voices* (PS–1). Illus. by Arden Johnson-Petrov. 2000, Boyds Mills $15.95 (978-1-56397-776-3). 32pp. A farmer's dog asks various animals and plants what they like best about the farmer's garden and what they do there. (Rev: BL 9/1/00; HBG 10/01; SLJ 11/00)

2337 Harrison, Joanna. *Dear Bear* (PS–2). Illus. 1994, Carolrhoda LB $15.95 (978-0-87614-839-6). 32pp. Katie is afraid of the bear that lives under the stairs and writes him a letter about her fear. (Rev: BCCB 1/95; BL 1/1/95; SLJ 2/95*)

2338 Harter, Debbie. *The Animal Boogie* (PS–2). Illus. by author. 2000, Barefoot Books $14.99 (978-1-84148-094-7). A rhythmic text adds to the fun of seeing various animals boogie-ing to lively music. (Rev: HBG 10/01; SLJ 12/00)

2339 Harvey, Damian. *Just the Thing!* (PS). Illus. by Lynne Chapman. 2005, Gingham Dog $15.95 (978-0-7696-4300-7). Big Gorilla, irritated by a pesky itch on his back, travels far and wide in search of relief but finally finds a cure back home. (Rev: SLJ 1/06)

2340 Haseley, Dennis. *A Story for Bear* (K–3). Illus. by Jim LaMarche. 2002, Harcourt $16.00 (978-0-15-200239-8). 32pp. Although he doesn't understand the words she is saying, a young bear responds to the stories a woman reads to him. (Rev: BL 5/1/02; HBG 10/02; SLJ 3/02)

2341 Hassett, John, and Ann Hassett. *Charles of the Wild* (PS–K). Illus. 1997, Houghton $16.00 (978-0-395-78575-1). 32pp. A timid little dog has some tame encounters that he interprets as exciting adventures. (Rev: BL 4/1/97; SLJ 5/97)

2342 Hayes, Karel. *The Winter Visitors* (PS–3). Illus. by author. 2007, Down East $15.95 (978-0-89272-750-6). 32pp. No sooner does a family pack up and leave its summer home in the woods than a family of bears moves in in this story of few words. (Rev: SLJ 11/07)

2343 Hayward, Linda. *The King's Chorus* (PS–2). Illus. by Jennifer P. Goldfinger. 2006, Clarion $16.00 (978-0-618-51618-6). 32pp. Kadoodle the rooster keeps the whole barnyard awake with his constant crowing until Honketta the goose comes up with a solution. (Rev: BL 2/15/07)

2344 Hazen, Lynne. *The Amazing Trail of Seymour Snail* (1–3). Illus. by Doug Cushman. 2009, Holt $16.95 (978-0-8050-8698-0). 64pp. Seymour Snail gets a job in an art gallery and his own work finally receives recognition. (Rev: BL 3/1/09)

2345 Heal, Gillian. *Grandpa Bear's Fantastic Scarf* (K–3). Illus. 1997, Beyond Words $14.95 (978-1-885223-41-8). 30pp. A young bear learns about life's meaning through studying the colors in his grandpa's scarf, a visual record of his life. (Rev: BL 4/1/97; SLJ 7/97)

2346 Heide, Florence Parry. *The One and Only Marigold* (PS–3). Illus. by Jill McElmurry. 2009, Random $16.99 (978-0-375-84031-9). 40pp. Four linked stories follow the deepening friendship of Marigold, a contrary 2nd-grade monkey, and her hippo friend, Maxine, whose only desire is to fit in. (Rev: BCCB 1/09; BL 2/1/09; LMC 5/09; SLJ 2/09)

2347 Heide, Florence Parry, and Sylvia Van Clief. *That's What Friends Are For* (PS–2). Illus. by Holly Meade. 2003, Candlewick $15.99 (978-0-7636-1397-6). 40pp. Poor Theodore the elephant has hurt his leg and gets totally useless advice from most of the animals in the forest. (Rev: BL 3/15/03; HBG 10/03; SLJ 5/03)

2348 Heinz, Brian. *Red Fox at McCloskey's Farm* (K–4). Illus. by Chris Sheban. 2006, Creative Editions $17.95 (978-1-56846-195-3). 30pp. In this action-packed rhyming tale, Farmer McCloskey and his hound dog foil Fox's plan to raid the hen house. (Rev: SLJ 11/06)

2349 Helakoski, Leslie. *Big Chickens Fly the Coop* (PS–2). Illus. by Henry Cole. 2008, Dutton $15.99 (978-0-525-47915-4). 32pp. Four adventurous chickens set off into the wide world to find the farmhouse, but they mistake many other buildings for this structure, which turns out to be right next to the coop. (Rev: BL 1/1–15/08; SLJ 6/08)

2350 Helakoski, Leslie. *Woolbur* (PS–1). Illus. by Lee Harper. 2008, HarperCollins $16.99 (978-0-06-084726-5). 32pp. Woolbur the sheep is a nonconformist who would rather run with the dogs than hang with the flock. (Rev: BL 1/1–15/08; SLJ 1/08) ∩

2351 Heller, Nicholas. *Elwood and the Witch* (PS–1). Illus. by Joseph A. Smith. 2000, Greenwillow LB $15.89 (978-0-688-16946-6). 32pp. Elwood the pig gets on a witch's broom by mistake and doesn't know how to land it. (Rev: BL 8/00; HBG 3/01; SLJ 9/00)

2352 Helmer, Diana Star. *The Cat Who Came for Tacos* (PS–2). 2003, Whitman LB $16.99 (978-0-8075-5106-6). Flynn the cat is invited into the home of Senor Tom and Senora Rosa where he enjoys a meal of tuna tacos and learns some valuable lessons about table manners. (Rev: HBG 4/04; SLJ 9/03)

2353 Henkes, Kevin. *Chrysanthemum* (PS–1). Illus. 1991, Greenwillow $17.89 (978-0-688-09700-4). 32pp. Other mouse children make fun of Chrysanthemum's name until her music teacher helps out. (Rev: BCCB 10/92; BL 8/91; HB 9/91*; SLJ 9/91*)

2354 Henkes, Kevin. *Julius, the Baby of the World* (PS–3). Illus. 1990, Greenwillow $17.89 (978-0-688-08944-3). 32pp. Lilly, a girl mouse, has a fit of jealousy when her baby brother gets all the attention in the family. (Rev: BCCB 11/90; BL 11/1/90; HB 1/91*; SLJ 10/90*)

2355 Henkes, Kevin. *Julius's Candy Corn* (PS). Illus. by author. 2003, Greenwillow $6.99 (978-0-06-053789-0). Julius the mouse has been forbidden to touch the 10 cupcakes, so he decides to count the candy corns on their tops instead, and it's easier to count in your mouth . . . . (Rev: HBG 4/04; SLJ 8/03)

2356 Henkes, Kevin. *Kitten's First Full Moon* (PS). Illus. by author. 2004, Greenwillow LB $16.89 (978-0-06-058829-8). A kitten mistakes the moon for a bowl of milk and is determined to lap it up. Caldecott Medal winner, 2005. (Rev: BL 2/15/04*; HB 5/04; SLJ 4/04)

2357 Henkes, Kevin. *Owen* (PS). Illus. 1993, Greenwillow $17.89 (978-0-688-11450-3). 24pp. Owen, a mouse, loves his fuzzy yellow blanket more than anything. (Rev: BL 8/93*)

2358 Henkes, Kevin. *Owen's Marshmallow Chick* (PS). Illus. 2002, Greenwillow $6.99 (978-0-06-001012-6). 24pp. Little Owen the mouse loves all the candy in his Easter basket, most especially the marshmallow chick. (Rev: BCCB 2/02; BL 1/1–15/02; HBG 10/02; SLJ 2/02)

2359 Henkes, Kevin. *Sheila Rae, the Brave* (PS–1). Illus. by author. 1987, Greenwillow $17.89 (978-0-688-07156-1). 32pp. Sheila Rae, a mouse, fears nothing until she takes the wrong way home. (Rev: BL 9/1/87; SLJ 9/87)

2360 Henkes, Kevin. *Sheila Rae's Peppermint Stick* (PS). 2001, HarperCollins $6.99 (978-0-06-029451-9). 24pp. Mouse Sheila Rae is tormenting her sister with tricky challenges when she falls and breaks the prized peppermint stick in half, prompting her to share it forthwith. (Rev: HB 9/01*; HBG 3/02; SLJ 12/01*)

2361 Henkes, Kevin. *A Weekend with Wendell* (PS–1). Illus. by author. 1986, Morrow paper $6.99 (978-0-688-14024-3). 32pp. Wendell makes his weekend stay seem like a year to Sophie Mouse, until they have a meeting of the minds. (Rev: BCCB 10/86; BL 9/1/86; SLJ 10/86)

2362 Henkes, Kevin. *Wemberly Worried* (PS–1). Illus. 2000, Greenwillow $17.99 (978-0-688-17027-1). 32pp. Wemberly, a little mouse girl, is a real worrywart until she makes a new friend at school who makes the world look less scary. (Rev: BCCB 9/00; BL 8/00; HB 9/00; HBG 3/01; SLJ 8/00)

2363 Henkes, Kevin. *Wemberly's Ice-Cream Star* (PS). Illus. by author. 2003, Greenwillow $6.99 (978-0-06-050405-2). Wemberly the mouse finds a solution to her ice cream conundrum: if she gets two bowls and waits until it melts, it won't drip and she can share with her stuffed rabbit. (Rev: HBG 10/03; SLJ 5/03)

2364 Hest, Amy. *Guess Who, Baby Duck!* (PS–K). Illus. by Jill Barton. 2004, Candlewick $14.99 (978-0-7636-1981-7). When Baby Duck has a cold, her grandfather brings an album of pictures to cheer her up. (Rev: SLJ 5/04)

2365 Hest, Amy. *Little Chick* (PS–K). Illus. by Anita Jeram. 2009, Candlewick $17.99 (978-0-7636-2890-1). 56pp. Three short stories present Little Chick tackling different situations: waiting impatiently for a carrot to grow, learning to fly a kite, and trying to catch a star. (Rev: BL 4/15/09; SLJ 5/09)

2366 Hest, Amy. *You Can Do It, Sam* (PS–K). Illus. by Anita Jeram. 2003, Candlewick $15.99 (978-0-7636-1934-3). Sam the bear and his mother bake cakes for their neighbors, and Sam makes the deliveries all by himself. (Rev: HBG 4/04; SLJ 10/03)

2367 Hill, Ros. *Shamoo: A Whale of a Cow* (PS–2). Illus. by author. 2005, Milk & Cookies $15.95 (978-0-689-04634-6). After running away from the farm, a water-loving cow named Shamoo heads for the ocean where he befriends a humpback whale and learns the ways of the sea but finds he's longing for home. (Rev: SLJ 11/05)

2368 Hill, Susanna Leonard. *Punxsutawney Phyllis* (K–3). Illus. by Jeffrey Ebbeler. 2005, Holiday $17.95 (978-0-8234-1872-5). 32pp. Punxsutawney Phyllis, a groundhog, hopes to take over the weather forecasting duties long performed by her Uncle Phil. (Rev: BL 12/1/05; SLJ 10/05)

2369 Hillenbrand, Jane. *What a Treasure!* (PS–K). Illus. by Will Hillenbrand. 2006, Holiday House $16.95 (978-0-8234-1896-1). When Mole gets a new shovel he begins to dig for treasure; he finds lots of things for his friends (twigs, shells, nuts) but the best treasure is his own — a new mole friend. (Rev: SLJ 4/06)

2370 Hillenbrand, Will. *Down by the Station* (PS–2). Illus. 1999, Harcourt $15.00 (978-0-15-201804-7). 40pp. Inspired by the song "Down by the Station," this joyful picture book depicts a train that is taking baby animals to a children's zoo. (Rev: BL 10/15/99; HB 11/99; HBG 3/00; SLJ 10/99)

2371 Hillenbrand, Will. *Louie!* (K–3). Illus. by author. 2009, Philomel $16.99 (978-0-399-24707-1). 32pp. Louie the pig's artistic talents are generally ignored until he is sent to work in a hotel, and there his illustrations — of a girl with appendicitis who lives in a convent school where the students walk in lines of two — are appreciated; based loosely on the life of Ludwig Bemelmans. (Rev: BCCB 6/09; BL 3/15/09; LMC 8/09; SLJ 3/09)

2372 Hillenbrand, Will. *My Book Box* (PS–K). Illus. by author. 2006, Harcourt $16.00 (978-0-15-202029-3). A diminutive elephant finds a cardboard box and considers all the things that he might be able to do with it before finally deciding to make it into a book box. (Rev: SLJ 10/06)

2373 Hillerman, Tony. *Buster Mesquite's Cowboy Band* (PS–2). Illus. by Ernest Franklin. 2001, Buffalo Medicine $19.95 (978-0-914001-11-9). 32pp. The artwork is the highlight of this story about a burro who loses his job and starts a band with other musically inclined animals. (Rev: BL 11/1/01)

2374 Hills, Tad. *Duck and Goose: How Are You Feeling?* (PS). Illus. by author. 2009, Schwartz & Wade $6.99 (978-0-375-84629-8). 22pp. Duck and Goose display a variety of emotions as they face a storm and try to build structures in this appealing board book. (Rev: BLO 1/13/09; SLJ 3/09)

2375 Hills, Tad. *Duck, Duck, Goose* (PS–1). Illus. by author. 2006, Random $14.95 (978-0-375-83611-4). A foolish duck and a goose squabble over a spotted ball they think is an egg, but finally realize their mistake and become friends. (Rev: BL 3/1/07; SLJ 1/06)

2376 Himmelman, John. *Tudley Didn't Know* (PS–2). Illus. by author. 2006, Sylvan Dell $15.95 (978-0-9764943-6-2). 32pp. Because he doesn't know he can't, Tudley the turtle is ready to try anything — flying, singing, hopping, and so forth. (Rev: BL 5/15/06; SLJ 8/06)

2377 Hindley, Judy. *Do Like a Duck Does!* (PS–K). Illus. by Ivan Bates. 2002, Candlewick $14.99 (978-0-7636-1668-7). 40pp. A mama duck out-foxes a fox in this charming, brightly illustrated picture book. (Rev: BCCB 4/02; BL 3/1/02; HBG 10/02)

2378 Hissey, Jane. *Little Bear Lost* (PS–K). Illus. 1994, Sandvick paper $9.99 (978-1-881445-44-9). 32pp. Just when the picnic is about to begin, Little Bear is missing. (Rev: BL 11/1/89)

2379 Hobbie, Holly. *Toot and Puddle: I'll Be Home for Christmas* (PS–2). Illus. by author. 2001, Little, Brown $15.95 (978-0-316-36623-6). While Puddle the pig has been eagerly preparing for Toot's return from a trip to Scotland, Toot is spared from a disappointing delay when a sleigh mysteriously picks him up and wafts him home to a happy reunion. (Rev: HBG 3/02; SLJ 10/01)

2380 Hobbie, Holly. *Toot and Puddle: Top of the World* (PS–2). Illus. 2002, Little, Brown $15.95 (978-0-316-36513-0). 32pp. Toot and Puddle, the friendly pigs, visit France and Nepal before decid-

ing that home beckons. Also use *Toot and Puddle: Charming Opal* (2003). (Rev: BL 10/1/02; HBG 3/03)

2381 Hobbie, Holly. *Toot and Puddle: Wish You Were Here* (PS–3). Illus. by author. 2005, Little, Brown $16.99 (978-0-316-36602-1). Stung by a bee while off on an exotic trip, Toot the pig turns violet and must be nursed back to health by his friends Puddle and Opal. (Rev: SLJ 10/05)

2382 Hobbie, Holly. *Toot and Puddle: You Are My Sunshine* (PS–2). Illus. by author. 1999, Little, Brown $14.95 (978-0-316-36562-8). In this story about friendship, two little piglets, Tulip and Puddle, try to cheer up their friend Toot, who is feeling blue. (Rev: BCCB 9/99; HBG 3/00; SLJ 8/99)

2383 Hobbs, Will. *Howling Hill* (K–3). Illus. by Jill Kastner. 1998, Morrow LB $15.89 (978-0-688-15430-1). 40pp. Hanni, a wolf cub, gets lost and must rely on a bear to help her home in this survival story. Hanni also learns how to howl like the rest of her family. (Rev: BL 9/1/98; HBG 3/99; SLJ 10/98)

2384 Hockinson, Liz. *Marcello the Movie Mouse* (1–3). Illus. by Kathryn Otoshi. 2006, KO Kids $16.95 (978-0-9723946-2-8). Marcello Mousetriani, a tiny mouse who lives in a movie theater, works feverishly to realize his dream of making a film of his own. (Rev: SLJ 9/06)

2385 Holabird, Katharine. *Angelina at the Palace* (K–2). Illus. by Helen Craig. Series: Angelina Ballerina. 2005, Viking $13.99 (978-0-670-06048-1). When her dance teacher falls ill, Angelina the mouse must teach a special dance to three of Mouseland's princesses. (Rev: SLJ 10/05)

2386 Holt, Kimberly Willis. *Skinny Brown Dog* (PS–2). Illus. by Donald Saaf. 2007, Holt $16.95 (978-0-8050-7587-8). 40pp. A stray dog finally succeeds in persuading Benny, a polar bear who owns a bakery, to give him a home. (Rev: BL 7/07; LMC 11/07; SLJ 6/07)

2387 Honigsberg, Peter Jan. *Armful of Memories* (K–2). Illus. by Tony Morse. 2002, RDR $17.95 (978-1-57143-089-2). 32pp. Newbery Mole sells all of his deceased grandparents' possessions in order to get rich, but soon realizes his memories are worth more than money. (Rev: BL 1/1–15/02; HBG 10/02)

2388 Hooper, Meredith. *Dogs' Night* (K–4). Illus. by Allan Curless and Mark Burgess. 2000, Millbrook LB $22.90 (978-0-7613-1824-8). 32pp. The dogs in the National Gallery in London leave their paintings once a year for a party, but on this occasion they get mixed up and enter the wrong paintings in this hilarious picture book. (Rev: BL 3/15/00; HBG 10/00; SLJ 7/00)

2389 Hoopes, Lyn Littlefield. *My Own Home* (PS–2). Illus. by Ruth Richardson. 1991, HarperCollins $13.95 (978-0-06-022570-4). A lost little owl is looking for his home. (Rev: SLJ 6/91)

2390 Horacek, Petr. *Look Out, Suzy Goose* (PS–1). Illus. by author. 2008, Candlewick $14.99 (978-0-7636-3803-0). 32pp. Tired of the noise made by her fellow geese, Suzy (of *Silly Suzy Goose* [2006]) wanders into the woods by herself; it is her own loud honking that brings rescue from the predators on her track. (Rev: BL 8/08; SLJ 7/08)

2391 Horacek, Petr. *Silly Suzy Goose* (PS–1). Illus. 2006, Candlewick $14.99 (978-0-7636-3040-9). 32pp. Suzy Goose longs to be different and imagines herself as all kinds of other animals, but a frightening encounter with a lion convinces her that there is safety in numbers; exuberant art enhances the fun. (Rev: BL 2/15/06*; HBG 10/06; SLJ 4/06)

2392 Horning, Sandra. *The Giant Hug* (PS–2). Illus. by Valeri Gorbachev. 2005, Knopf LB $17.99 (978-0-375-92477-4). 40pp. Owen the pig sends his grandmother a giant hug that must be passed from person to person by mail workers across the country. (Rev: BL 1/1–15/05; SLJ 2/05)

2393 Horse, Harry. *Little Rabbit Lost* (PS–2). Illus. 2002, Peachtree $15.95 (978-1-56145-273-6). 32pp. Detailed watercolors set the scene as Little Rabbit's birthday trip to RabbitWorld is almost ruined when he gets lost. (Rev: BL 12/1/02; HBG 3/03; SLJ 10/02)

2394 Horse, Harry. *Little Rabbit Runaway* (PS–K). Illus. 2005, Peachtree $15.95 (978-1-56145-343-6). 32pp. Upset when his parents scold him, Little Rabbit runs away from home, but it's not long before he wishes he could return. (Rev: BL 10/1/05; SLJ 9/05)

2395 Howe, James. *Horace and Morris But Mostly Dolores* (PS–2). Illus. by Amy Walrod. 1999, Simon & Schuster $16.00 (978-0-689-31874-0). 32pp. Three mice — two boys and a girl — decide to join unisex clubs, but in time they leave them for a day of exploring together. (Rev: BCCB 3/99; BL 2/15/99*; HBG 10/99; SLJ 3/99)

2396 Howe, James. *I Wish I Were a Butterfly* (PS–2). Illus. by Ed Young. 1987, Harcourt $17.00 (978-0-15-200470-5). 28pp. Cricket thinks he's ugly; then a butterfly hears his music and wishes he were a cricket. (Rev: BL 11/1/87; SLJ 11/87)

2397 Howe, James. *Rabbit-cadabra!* (2–4). Illus. by Jeff Mack. Series: Bunnicula and Friends. 2006, Simon & Schuster $14.95 (978-0-689-85727-0). 42pp. An easy chapter book about Chester, Howie, and Harold's plan to outsmart a magician who's bringing his vampire-bunny act to Toby's school. (Rev: SLJ 6/06)

2398 Hubery, Julia. *A Friend for All Seasons* (PS–2). Illus. by Mei Matsuoka. 2007, Atheneum $15.99 (978-1-4169-2685-6). 32pp. The arrival of fall and preparations for their winter sleep makes Robbie Raccoon wonder if Father Oak is sad that his leaves are falling off. (Rev: BL 7/07; SLJ 8/07)

2399 Hubery, Julia. *A Friend Like You* (K–2). Illus. by Caroline Pedler. 2009, Good Bks. $16.95 (978-1-56148-660-1). 32pp. A monkey and a panda share a nature adventure. (Rev: SLJ 6/09)

2400 Hume, Lachie. *Clancy the Courageous Cow* (PS–2). Illus. 2007, Greenwillow $16.99 (978-0-06-117249-6). 32pp. An outcast among his fellow Belted Galloway cattle because he has no belt, Clancy is in despair until he uses his unique appearance to infiltrate the neighboring Hereford herd, with which the Belted Galloways have long been feuding. (Rev: BL 3/15/07; SLJ 3/07)

2401 Huneck, Stephen. *Sally Goes to the Farm* (PS–2). Illus. 2002, Abrams $17.95 (978-0-8109-4498-5). 40pp. Sally the dog visits a farm and has a wonderful time with Molly and other animal friends in this picture book with simple text and large, bold pictures that add to the story. (Rev: BL 7/02; HBG 10/02; SLJ 7/02)

2402 Hunter, Jana Novotny. *I Can Do It!* (PS). Illus. by Lucy Richards. 2006, Frances Lincoln $15.95 (978-1-84507-127-1). Little Guinea Pig has a satisfying day at preschool, finding perfect activities to match his moods. (Rev: SLJ 8/06)

2403 Hurd, Thacher. *Art Dog* (PS–3). Illus. 1996, HarperCollins LB $15.89 (978-0-06-024425-5). 32pp. Arthur, a canine museum guard with artistic abilities, solves the mystery of the missing painting, the *Mona Woofa*. (Rev: BCCB 2/96; BL 1/1–15/96; SLJ 2/96)

2404 Hurd, Thacher. *Mama Don't Allow: Starring Miles and the Swamp Band* (PS–1). Illus. by author. 1984, HarperCollins LB $16.89 (978-0-06-022690-9); paper $6.99 (978-0-06-443078-4). 40pp. The Swamp Band finds that the only audience that likes them is the alligator.

2405 Hurd, Thacher. *Mystery on the Docks* (1–3). Illus. by author. 1983, HarperCollins paper $6.99 (978-0-06-443058-6). 32pp. Ralph, an opera lover, rescues his favorite singer from rat-kidnappers.

2406 Hutchins, Pat. *Good-Night, Owl!* (PS–K). Illus. by author. 1972, Macmillan LB $16.00 (978-0-02-745900-5). 32pp. Owl is kept awake by animal noises as various animals perch on a branch of his tree; but when darkness falls, owl has his turn and wakes everyone with his screeches.

2407 Hutchins, Pat. *Little Pink Pig* (PS–1). Illus. 1994, Greenwillow $15.95 (978-0-688-12014-6). 32pp. Little Pig fails to heed his mother's call for bedtime because he is busy chasing a butterfly. (Rev: BL 4/1/94; HB 5/94; SLJ 5/94)

2408 Hutchins, Pat. *Rosie's Walk* (K–2). Illus. by author. 1968, Macmillan LB $16.00 (978-0-02-745850-3); paper $5.99 (978-0-02-043750-5). 32pp. Rosie the hen miraculously escapes capture by a fox.

2409 Hutchins, Pat. *What Game Shall We Play?* (PS–K). Illus. 1995, Morrow paper $6.99 (978-0-688-13573-7). 24pp. Duck and Frog ask several of their animal friends what game they should play. (Rev: BCCB 10/90; BL 10/15/90; HB 11/90; SLJ 9/90*)

2410 Inkpen, Mick. *The Great Pet Sale* (PS–1). Illus. 1999, Orchard $14.95 (978-0-531-30130-2). 16pp. At a pet store sale, a rat, priced at only one cent, hopes that a young boy will choose him. (Rev: BL 4/15/99; HBG 10/99; SLJ 7/99)

2411 Inkpen, Mick. *Kipper* (PS–K). Illus. 1992, Talman $15.95 (978-1-85430-333-2). 32pp. When Kipper the dog cleans his basket and gets rid of his toys, he finds it is impossible to be as comfortable as he was before. (Rev: BL 4/1/92; SLJ 5/92)

2412 Irbinskas, Heather. *How Jackrabbit Got His Very Long Ears* (K–3). Illus. by Kenneth J. Spengler. 1994, Northland LB $15.95 (978-0-87358-566-

8). 32pp. When Jackrabbit fails to follow the instructions of the Great Spirit, he is given big ears so that he can hear better. (Rev: BL 6/1–15/94)

2413 Ives, Penny. *Celestine, Drama Queen* (PS–K). Illus. by author. 2009, Scholastic $16.99 (978-0-545-08149-8). 32pp. Convinced of her future as a star, young duck Celestine is distressed when she suffers from stage fright. (Rev: BL 2/1/09; SLJ 2/09)

2414 Iwamura, Kazuo. *Hooray for Spring!* (PS–K). Illus. by author. 2009, North-South $15.95 (978-0-7358-2228-3). 32pp. Three young squirrels — Mick, Mack, and Molly — try to feed a hungry baby bird and are surprised that it chooses to eat a worm. (Rev: BL 4/15/09; SLJ 6/09)

2415 Jackson, Chris. *The Gaggle Sisters River Tour* (PS–2). Illus. 2002, Lobster $16.95 (978-1-894222-58-7). 32pp. Sadie the duck is the star of the show on the river, until her hat is ruined and sister Dorothy, the behind-the-scenes toiler, saves the day. (Rev: BL 12/15/02; SLJ 1/03)

2416 Jackson, Chris. *The Gaggle Sisters Sing Again* (K–2). Illus. by author. 2003, Lobster $15.95 (978-1-894222-56-3). The singing geese of *The Gaggle Sisters River Tour* (2002) are seen in four humorous vignettes with watercolor cartoon illustrations. (Rev: SLJ 12/03)

2417 James, Simon. *Little One Step* (PS–2). Illus. 2003, Candlewick $15.99 (978-0-7636-2070-7). 32pp. When the youngest duck gets tired, his siblings encourage him to persevere. (Rev: BL 3/15/03; HBG 10/03; SLJ 4/03)

2418 Jeffers, Oliver. *The Great Paper Caper* (PS–K). Illus. by author. 2009, Philomel $17.99 (978-0-399-25097-2). 40pp. Forest animals investigate why branches and trees are disappearing and find a bear who has been using them to make paper airplanes for a contest. (Rev: BL 12/15/08; LMC 5/09; SLJ 1/09)

2419 Jenkins, Emily. *Love You When You Whine* (PS). Illus. by Sergio Ruzzier. 2006, Farrar $15.00 (978-0-374-34652-2). A mother cat loves her little daughter no matter what mischief she does — from whining and painting the walls to having a terrible tantrum. (Rev: SLJ 10/06)

2420 Jennings, Linda. *Scramcat* (PS–2). Illus. by Rhian N. James. 1994, Crocodile $13.95 (978-1-56656-137-2). A stray cat that is shunned by everyone suddenly becomes popular when it foils a robbery. (Rev: SLJ 11/94)

2421 Jennings, Sharon. *Priscilla and Rosy* (PS–2). Illus. by Linda Hendry. 2001, Fitzhenry & Whiteside $15.95 (978-1-55041-676-3). 32pp. Detailed illustrations complement this story of two rat best friends, in which Priscilla deals with competing invitations and finally recognizes that friendship is most important. (Rev: BL 12/15/01; SLJ 1/02)

2422 Jennings, Sharon. *Priscilla's Paw de Deux* (K–3). Illus. by Linda Hendry. 2002, Fitzhenry & Whiteside $15.95 (978-1-55041-718-0). 36pp. Priscilla the rat sneaks into a dance studio after hours to practice ballet, only to meet up with a menacing cat. (Rev: BL 12/15/02; SLJ 2/03)

2423 Jeram, Anita. *Bill's Belly Button* (PS–1). Illus. 1991, Little, Brown $14.95 (978-0-316-46114-6). 32pp. Bill, an elephant, becomes alarmed when he discovers he does not have a belly button. (Rev: BL 9/15/91; SLJ 10/91)

2424 Jeschke, Susan. *Perfect the Pig* (K–2). Illus. by author. 1981, Scholastic paper $6.95 (978-0-8050-4704-2). 40pp. The adventures of a winged pig named Perfect.

2425 Johansen, Hanna. *The Duck and the Owl* (1–3). Illus. by Kathi Bhend. 2005, Godine $17.95 (978-1-56792-285-1). 72pp. A duck and an owl dance around the idea of friendship but find their different behaviors and characteristics difficult to overcome. (Rev: BL 1/1–15/06; SLJ 2/06)

2426 Johansen, Hanna. *Henrietta and the Golden Eggs* (1–3). Trans. by John S. Barrett. Illus. by Kathi Bhend. 2002, Godine $16.95 (978-1-56792-210-3). 64pp. The story of Henrietta, a chicken with dreams of freedom, is told with intricate pen-and-ink drawings. (Rev: BL 3/15/03; HBG 10/03)

2427 Johansen, K. V. *Pippin Takes a Bath* (PS–1). Illus. by Bernice Lum. 1999, Kids Can $12.95 (978-1-55074-627-3). 32pp. Pippin the dog refuses to take a bath until he has an encounter with a skunk. (Rev: BL 11/15/99; HBG 3/00; SLJ 11/99)

2428 Johnson, D. B. *Four Legs Bad, Two Legs Good!* (K–3). Illus. by author. 2007, Houghton $16.00 (978-0-618-80909-7). 32pp. Orvie the pig wears the bossy boots in this barnyard family until Duck rebels. (Rev: BCCB 12/07; BL 10/1/07; LMC 1/08; SLJ 11/07)

2429 Johnson, D. B. *Henry Builds a Cabin* (PS–3). Illus. 2002, Houghton $15.00 (978-0-618-13201-0). 32pp. A sensible bear called Henry convinces his friends that a Thoreau-style cabin, and the great outdoors, is all that he needs to be happy. (Rev: BCCB 5/02; BL 3/15/02*; HB 7/02; HBG 10/02; SLJ 3/02)

2430 Johnson, D. B. *Henry Climbs a Mountain* (K–3). Illus. by author. 2003, Houghton $15.00 (978-0-618-26902-0). In this third picture book based on the life of Thoreau, Henry the bear is jailed for nonpayment of taxes and escapes into the scenery he has drawn on the wall, joining a stranger who is traveling north to freedom. (Rev: BL 10/1/03*; HBG 4/04; SLJ 9/03)

2431 Johnson, D. B. *Henry Hikes to Fitchburg* (PS–3). Illus. 2000, Houghton $16.00 (978-0-395-96867-3). 32pp. Henry the bear decides to take a nature walk to Fitchburg while his friend will ride the train in this amusing take-off on Thoreau's attitudes and his New England circle. (Rev: BCCB 7–8/00; BL 4/15/00*; HB 5/00; HBG 10/00; SLJ 6/00)

2432 Johnson, Gillian. *My Sister Gracie* (PS–3). Illus. by author. 2000, Tundra $16.95 (978-0-88776-514-8). Fabio, a dog, wants a thoroughbred brother to play with but his family adopts a female mutt from the pound. (Rev: HBG 3/01; SLJ 12/00)

2433 Johnson, Jane. *Are You Ready for Bed?* (PS–K). Illus. by Gaby Hansen. 2002, Tiger Tales $14.95 (978-1-58925-017-8). Just as exhausted Mrs. Rabbit gets one child off to sleep, another wakes up. (Rev: SLJ 12/02)

2434 Johnson, Paul B. *The Goose Who Went Off in a Huff* (PS–1). Illus. 2001, Scholastic $15.95 (978-0-531-30317-7). 40pp. Magnolia the goose starts acting oddly when she is overwhelmed by a maternal urge. (Rev: BL 5/15/01; HBG 10/01; SLJ 7/01)

2435 Johnson, Paul B. *The Pig Who Ran a Red Light* (PS–2). Illus. 1999, Orchard LB $16.99 (978-0-531-33136-1). 32pp. Gertrude the cow, who is being mimicked by George the pig, solves the problem by acting like a pig. (Rev: BL 5/1/99; HBG 10/99; SLJ 3/99)

2436 Johnston, Tony. *The Chizzywink and the Alamagoozlum* (PS–3). Illus. by Robert Bender. 1998, Holiday House $16.95 (978-0-8234-1359-1). 32pp. A humorous tale about several animals trying to prevent a giant mosquito (or chizzywink) from entering their house and eating their maple syrup (the alamagoozlum). (Rev: BL 6/1–15/98; HBG 10/98; SLJ 6/98)

2437 Johnston, Tony. *The Iguana Brothers: A Tale of Two Lizards* (PS–2). Illus. by Mark Teague. 1995, Scholastic $15.95 (978-0-590-47468-9). 32pp. Dom and Tom, iguana brothers, have many differences but remain best friends. (Rev: BCCB 7–8/95; BL 1/15/95*; SLJ 4/95)

2438 Joyce, William. *Bently and Egg* (PS–3). Illus. 1992, HarperCollins $17.95 (978-0-06-020385-6); paper $7.99 (978-0-06-443352-5). Bently, a frog, is asked to egg-sit for his friend the duck. (Rev: BCCB 3/92; BL 1/1/92; HB 3/92; SLJ 4/92*)

2439 Joyce, William. *The Leaf Men and the Brave Good Bugs* (PS–3). Illus. 1996, HarperCollins LB $16.89 (978-0-06-027238-8). 40pp. The good bugs in a garden join to help restore an old woman's sickly rosebush. (Rev: BL 10/1/96; SLJ 10/96)

2440 Kaczman, James. *A Bird and His Worm* (PS–2). Illus. 2002, Houghton $15.00 (978-0-618-09460-8). 32pp. A bird and his friend, a worm, learn a lesson about strangers in their travels south. (Rev: BCCB 12/02; BL 9/15/02; HBG 3/03; SLJ 9/02)

2441 Kalan, Robert. *Moving Day* (PS–1). Illus. by Yossi Abolafia. 1996, Greenwillow $17.89 (978-0-688-13949-0). 32pp. A hermit crab sets out to find a new home. (Rev: BL 6/1–15/96; SLJ 7/96)

2442 Kalman, Maira. *Ooh-La-La (Max in Love)* (PS–4). Illus. 1991, Viking $17.99 (978-0-670-84163-9). 32pp. Max the dog falls for Crepes Suzette, a dalmatian, in fascinating Paris. (Rev: BL 10/15/91; SLJ 11/91)

2443 Kasza, Keiko. *Badger's Fancy Meal* (PS–2). Illus. 2007, Putnam $16.99 (978-0-399-24603-6). 32pp. This creatively designed volume features Badger's unsuccessful attempts to capture a mole, a rat, and a rabbit — who ironically end up in his den and eat up his stores of food. (Rev: BL 5/1/07; HB 5/07; SLJ 7/07)

2444 Kasza, Keiko. *Don't Laugh, Joe!* (PS–1). Illus. 1997, Penguin $17.99 (978-0-399-23036-3). 32pp. A young opossum has an unusual problem: He can't stop giggling while playing dead. (Rev: BL 8/97; SLJ 6/97)

2445 Kasza, Keiko. *The Mightiest* (1–3). Illus. 2001, Penguin $16.99 (978-0-399-23586-3). 32pp. Lion, Bear, and Elephant argue about who among them is the mightiest, but they are all outdone by an old woman. (Rev: BL 9/1/01; HBG 3/02; SLJ 11/01)

2446 Kasza, Keiko. *A Mother for Choco* (PS–1). Illus. 1992, Penguin LB $15.99 (978-0-399-21841-5). 32pp. A little bird sets out to find his mother and is adopted by a kindly bear. (Rev: BCCB 4/92; BL 3/15/92; HB 5/92; SLJ 4/92*)

2447 Kasza, Keiko. *My Lucky Day* (K–2). Illus. by author. 2003, Penguin $15.99 (978-0-399-23874-1). A hungry fox can't believe his luck when a piglet comes knocking, but the little pig has many sensible suggestions and in the end the fox is too tired to eat. (Rev: HB 9/03; HBG 4/04; SLJ 9/03)

2448 Katz, Avner. *Tortoise Solves a Problem* (K–3). Illus. 1993, HarperCollins LB $12.89 (978-0-06-020799-1). 32pp. While searching for a new house, the tortoise invents the tortoise shell. (Rev: BL 1/15/93)

2449 Kaufmann, Nancy. *Bye, Bye!* (PS). Illus. by Jung-Hee Spetter. 2003, Front St. $14.95 (978-1-886910-95-9). On the first day of school, Daddy stays with his piglet son until the teacher makes him leave. (Rev: HBG 4/04; SLJ 10/03)

2450 Keller, Holly. *Geraldine and Mrs. Duffy* (PS–K). Illus. 2000, Greenwillow LB $15.89 (978-0-688-16888-9). 32pp. It takes some doing but new babysitter Mrs. Duffy gradually wins over hostile Geraldine, a little pig, and her brother Willy. (Rev: BL 10/1/00; HBG 3/01; SLJ 8/00)

2451 Keller, Holly. *Geraldine's Blanket* (PS–2). Illus. by author. 1988, Morrow paper $6.99 (978-0-688-07810-2). 32pp. A little pig named Geraldine becomes extremely attached to a blanket her aunt gave her.

2452 Keller, Holly. *Help! A Story of Friendship* (PS–K). Illus. by author. 2007, Greenwillow $16.99 (978-0-06-123913-7). 32pp. After hearing a rumor that his best friend Snake is dangerous, Mouse falls into a deep hole only to discover that Snake is the only one who can rescue him. (Rev: BL 9/1/07; HB 1/08; SLJ 9/07)

2453 Keller, Holly. *Nosy Rosie* (PS). 2006, Greenwillow $16.99 (978-0-06-078758-5). 32pp. Nosy Rosie's super-sensitive fox nose comes in handy one day when a baby is lost in the woods. (Rev: BL 7/06; SLJ 9/06*)

2454 Keller, Holly. *Pearl's New Skates* (PS–2). Illus. 2005, Greenwillow LB $17.89 (978-0-06-056281-6). 24pp. Pearl the rabbit is delighted with her new ice skates but finds them surprisingly difficult to use. (Rev: BL 1/1–15/05; SLJ 2/05)

2455 Keller, Holly. *Sophie's Window* (PS–2). Illus. 2005, Greenwillow $15.99 (978-0-06-056282-3). 32pp. When Caruso, a little pigeon who is afraid to fly, is blown out of his family home, he is rescued by a nice dog called Sophie. (Rev: BL 9/15/05; SLJ 8/05)

2456 Keller, Laurie. *Do Unto Otters: A Book About Manners* (K–3). Illus. by author. 2007, Holt $16.95 (978-0-8050-7996-8). 32pp. When an otter family moves in next door, Mr. Rabbit is unsure how to behave and reflects on how he himself would like to be treated, providing a useful and amusing primer on good manners. (Rev: BL 10/15/07; LMC 1/08; SLJ 9/07) ⌒

2457 Kelley, Ellen A. *Buckamoo Girls* (2–4). Illus. by Tom Curry. 2006, Abrams $15.95 (978-0-8109-5471-7). Cows Susanna and Joanna imagine themselves as the Buckamoo Girls, two adventurous cowgirls having a rollicking good time in the Wild, Wild West. (Rev: SLJ 1/07)

2458 Kelley, Ellen A. *My Life as a Chicken* (PS–2). Illus. by Michael Slack. 2007, Harcourt $16.00 (978-0-15-205306-2). 40pp. In this action-packed picture-book story told in rhyming text, chicken Pauline Poulet is constantly on the move, bouncing from one near-tragedy to the next in an adventure that includes pirates, a typhoon, and a balloon ride. (Rev: BL 4/1/07)

2459 Kelley, True. *Blabber Mouse* (1–3). Illus. 2001, Dutton $15.99 (978-0-525-46742-7). 32pp. Blabber Mouse's classmates finally are forced to devise a solution to stop his chatter when he reminds teacher that she forgot to assign homework. (Rev: BL 12/1/01; HBG 3/02; SLJ 10/01)

2460 Kelley, True. *The Blabber Report* (1–3). Illus. by author. 2007, Dutton $15.99 (978-0-525-47809-6). 32pp. Young Blabber Mouse, first seen in the eponymous 2001 title, here learns — with the help of his friends — about preparing classroom presentations. (Rev: BL 9/1/07; SLJ 7/07)

2461 Kellogg, Steven, retel. *Chicken Little* (1–3). Illus. by Steven Kellogg. 1985, Morrow paper $6.99 (978-0-688-07045-8). 32pp. A wacky version of the old favorite. (Rev: BCCB 11/85; BL 9/1/85; SLJ 10/85)

2462 Kellogg, Steven. *The Mysterious Tadpole: 25th Anniversary Edition* (PS–2). Illus. 2002, Dial $16.99 (978-0-8037-2788-5). 36pp. This anniversary edition brings a slightly longer text and new illustrations to the story of the tadpole that won't stop growing. (Rev: BL 11/1/02; HBG 3/03)

2463 Kelly, John, and Cathy Tincknell. *Scoop! An Exclusive by Monty Molenski* (1–5). Illus. by authors. 2007, Candlewick $15.99 (978-0-7636-3059-1). Monty the mole takes his camera and reporter's notebook on his search for news, but fails to see the outrageous events going on right in front of him. (Rev: SLJ 5/07)

2464 Kempter, Christa. *Dear Little Lamb* (PS–2). Trans. from German by Michelle Maczka. Illus. by Frauke Weldin. 2006, North-South $16.95 (978-0-7358-2086-9). A clever wolf strikes up a pen-pal relationship with a young lamb, hoping eventually for a tasty meal, but the lamb's smart mother sees the danger and scuppers the wolf's plot. (Rev: SLJ 10/06)

2465 Kempter, Christa. *Wally and Mae* (PS–2). Illus. by Frauke Weldin. 2008, North-South $16.95 (978-0-7358-2208-5). 32pp. Two unlikely friends — a bunny and a bear — figure out how to work with, through, and around each other's quirky habits. (Rev: SLJ 9/08)

2466 Kennedy, Kim. *Hee-Haw-Dini and the Great Zambini* (K–3). Illus. by Doug Kennedy. 2009, Abrams $15.95 (978-0-8109-7025-0). 32pp. A donkey named Hee-Haw and a mouse named Chester persist in their dream of becoming magicians — and a lucky find helps them along the way. (Rev: BL 4/1/09; SLJ 4/09)

2467 Kent, Jack. *Joey* (PS–2). Illus. by author. 1987, Simon & Schuster $11.95 (978-0-671-66459-6). 32pp. Joey, a young kangaroo, is not allowed out of his mother's pouch, so he invites his friends in.

2468 Kern, Noris. *I Love You with All My Heart* (PS–K). Illus. 1998, Chronicle $14.95 (978-0-8118-2031-8). 32pp. Several Arctic animals tell a polar bear cub how their mothers love them. (Rev: BL 4/15/98; HBG 10/98; SLJ 8/98)

2469 Ketteman, Helen. *Armadillo Tattletale* (K–3). Illus. by Keith Graves. 2000, Scholastic $16.99 (978-0-590-99723-2). 32pp. In this original folktale, Armadillo's ears are cut down to a proper size to stop him from hearing — and passing on — gossip. (Rev: BCCB 11/00; BL 12/15/00; HBG 3/01; SLJ 9/00)

2470 Kettner, Christine. *An Ordinary Cat* (PS–K). Illus. 1991, HarperCollins LB $13.89 (978-0-06-023173-6). 32pp. Inwardly, William is not the ordinary cat that everyone sees. (Rev: BL 1/1/91; SLJ 12/91)

2471 Kilaka, John. *Fresh Fish: A Tale from Tanzania* (K–3). Illus. by author. 2005, Groundwood $16.95 (978-0-88899-656-5). 28pp. Despite Sokwe Chimpanzee's generosity, Dog steals fish from him and is put on trial by the other animals; he is sentenced, makes his penance, and all is forgiven. (Rev: BCCB 6/05; SLJ 6/05)

2472 Kim, Byung-Gyu, and K. T. Hao. *The 100th Customer* (PS–2). Illus. by Giuliano Ferri. 2005, Purple Bear $15.95 (978-1-933327-03-7). 32pp. In this heartwarming tale about the power of generosity, Ben Bear and Chris Croc, co-owners of a pizza restaurant arrange to help a hungry boy and his grandmother. (Rev: BL 11/1/05; SLJ 1/06)

2473 Kindermans, Martine. *You and Me* (PS). Trans. by Sasha Quinton. Illus. by author. 2006, Philomel $15.99 (978-0-399-24471-1). A mother goose expresses her love for her gosling in this gentle book with lovely watercolor art. (Rev: SLJ 1/06)

2474 Kinerk, Robert. *Clorinda* (PS–2). Illus. by Steven Kellogg. 2003, Simon & Schuster $15.95 (978-0-689-86449-0). After a very brief stint as a performer, Clorinda the cow heads back to the farm and there shares her knowledge of ballet. (Rev: BL 11/1/03; HBG 4/04; SLJ 11/03)

2475 King, Bob. *Sitting on the Farm* (PS–1). Illus. by Bill Slavin. 1992, Scholastic paper $7.99 (978-0-590-73979-5). 32pp. In successive verses of a silly song, a young girl calls on animals to remove a bug from her knee. (Rev: BL 2/1/92; SLJ 8/92)

2476 Kirk, Daniel. *Library Mouse* (K–3). Illus. by author. 2007, Abrams $32.00 (978-0-8109-9346-4). 32pp. Sam the mouse lives in the library and one night places his own book on the shelves for the children to read. (Rev: BL 9/1/07; SLJ 10/07)

2477 Kirk, David. *Little Miss Spider* (PS–1). Illus. 1999, Scholastic $12.95 (978-0-439-08389-8). 32pp. After hatching, Little Miss Spider sets out to find her mother and is helped by a kindly green beetle named Betty; introduces a new smaller format. Also use *Little Miss Spider at Sunny Patch School* (2000). (Rev: BL 12/1/99; HBG 3/00; SLJ 11/99)

2478 Kirk, David. *Miss Spider's Wedding* (K–4). Illus. 1995, Scholastic $16.95 (978-0-590-56866-1). 40pp. Miss Spider finds she is very wrong when she thinks handsome Spiderus Reeves is "Mr. Right." A sequel to *Miss Spider's Tea Party* (1993) and followed by *Miss Spider's New Car* (1997). (Rev: BL 10/1/95; SLJ 10/95)

2479 Kirwan, Wednesday. *Nobody Notices Minerva* (PS–2). Illus. by author. 2007, Sterling $14.95 (978-1-4027-4728-1). 32pp. A Boston terrier called Minerva behaves very badly in an effort to get a little attention. (Rev: BL 10/15/07) ⌒

2480 Kleven, Elisa. *Sun Bread* (PS–1). Illus. 2001, Dutton $16.99 (978-0-525-46674-1). 32pp. Longing for sun, the baker makes a sun-shaped loaf so enticing that the animals cheer up and sun breaks through the clouds. (Rev: BL 5/1/01; HBG 10/01; SLJ 6/01)

2481 Kleven, Elisa. *The Wishing Ball* (PS–K). Illus. 2006, Farrar $16.00 (978-0-374-38449-4). 32pp. Convinced that a rubber ball will bring her luck, Nellie, a stray cat, follows the bouncing ball and succeeds in finds a happy new life. (Rev: BL 2/1/06; SLJ 2/06)

2482 Klise, Kate. *Little Rabbit and the Night Mare* (K–2). Illus. by M. Sarah Klise. 2008, Harcourt $16.00 (978-0-15-205717-6). 32pp. Plucky Little Rabbit conquers his Night Mare and even uses it as the subject of his dreaded class report. (Rev: BLO 6/17/08; SLJ 8/08)

2483 Klise, Kate. *Why Do You Cry? Not a Sob Story* (PS–2). Illus. by M. Sarah Klise. 2006, Holt $16.95 (978-0-8050-7319-5). 32pp. Little Rabbit finds out that crying's OK when others reveal what makes them cry. (Rev: BL 5/1/06; SLJ 7/06)

2484 Knister. *A Promise Is a Promise* (PS–1). Trans. from German by Kathryn Bishop. Illus. by Eve Tharlet. 2006, Minedition $16.99 (978-0-698-40040-5). Bruno the marmot befriends a bright yellow dandelion and, when she has gone to seed, honors her wish that he blow her seeds away, although this worries him greatly. (Rev: SLJ 8/06)

2485 Knowles, Sheena. *Edwina the Emu* (PS–1). Illus. by Rod Clement. 1997, HarperCollins paper $6.99 (978-0-06-443483-6). At the zoo, Edwina the emu leaves her husband to tend their eggs while she goes out looking for a job. (Rev: SLJ 9/97)

2486 Knudsen, Michelle. *Library Lion* (PS–2). Illus. by Kevin Hawkes. 2006, Candlewick $15.99 (978-0-7636-2262-6). 48pp. Miss Merriweather, the head librarian, is very particular about the library's rules, but she's not sure what to do when a lion pays a visit. (Rev: BL 8/06; SLJ 8/06*)

2487 Koehler, Phoebe. *Making Room* (PS–1). Illus. 1993, Macmillan LB $14.95 (978-0-02-750875-8). 48pp. A large dog makes room in his household for a woman, a baby, and a cat. (Rev: BL 3/15/93; SLJ 8/93)

2488 Kolar, Bob. *Big Kicks* (PS–3). Illus. by author. 2008, Candlewick $16.99 (978-0-7636-3390-5). 40pp. Biggie Bear is a quiet stamp collector who succeeds in the most unexpected way when he reluctantly agrees to help the local soccer team. (Rev: BL 9/1/08; SLJ 9/08)

2489 Kolar, Bob. *Racer Dogs* (PS–2). Illus. 2003, Dutton $16.99 (978-0-525-45939-2). 32pp. Dogs zoom racecars around a track and end up in a jumbled pileup in this funny picture book. (Rev: BL 2/1/03; HBG 10/03; SLJ 3/03)

2490 Koller, Jackie F. *Baby for Sale* (PS–2). Illus. by Janet Pedersen. 2002, Marshall Cavendish $16.95 (978-0-7614-5106-8). 32pp. Rabbit Peter, fed up with his baby sister, tries to sell her to the neighbors but finally decides to keep her when he realizes that he loves her. (Rev: BL 9/1/02; HBG 3/03; SLJ 9/02)

2491 Komoda, Beverly. *The Too Hot Day* (PS–K). Illus. 1991, HarperCollins LB $14.89 (978-0-06-021612-2). 32pp. Mama and her bunny family try to escape the heat through a variety of activities. (Rev: BL 5/15/91; SLJ 8/91)

2492 Komoda, Beverly. *The Winter Day* (PS–1). Illus. 1991, HarperCollins $13.95 (978-0-06-023301-3). 32pp. The Hopper children, a group of rabbits, are enjoying the snow until a bully named Spike spoils their fun. (Rev: BL 12/1/91; SLJ 1/92)

2493 Kopelke, Lisa. *Excuse Me!* (K–2). Illus. 2003, Simon & Schuster $15.95 (978-0-689-85111-7). 32pp. Frog, a notorious burper, discovers (after living among other belchers) that it's better to be polite. (Rev: BL 2/15/03; HBG 10/03; SLJ 4/03)

2494 Kopelke, Lisa. *Tissue, Please!* (PS–1). Illus. by author. 2004, Simon & Schuster $15.95 (978-0-689-86248-9). Frog has a very runny nose and discovers that tissues do serve a purpose. (Rev: SLJ 11/04)

2495 Kovalski, Maryann. *Brenda and Edward* (PS–2). Illus. 1997, Kids Can $14.95 (978-0-919964-77-8). 32pp. Two dogs who adore each other are separated until, years later, a series of coincidences brings them back together. (Rev: BL 10/15/97; SLJ 9/97)

2496 Kovalski, Maryann. *Omar on Ice* (PS–2). Illus. 1999, Fitzhenry & Whiteside $12.95 (978-1-55041-507-0). 32pp. Omar, a young bear, learns he can produce beautiful pictures on the ice when he whirls and swirls while skating. (Rev: BL 10/15/99)

2497 Kovalski, Maryann. *Queen Nadine* (K–2). Illus. by author. 1998, Orca $14.95 (978-1-55143-093-5). When a farmer sells his cows to raise corn, he decides to keep Nadine, the dreamy loner of his herd. (Rev: HBG 3/99; SLJ 12/98)

2498 Kranendonk, Anke. *Just a Minute* (PS–K). Illus. by Jung-Hee Spetter. 1998, Front St. $14.95 (978-1-886910-29-4). 32pp. Every time Piggy wants attention, mama says "Just a minute," little knowing what mischief her son is up to in the meantime. (Rev: BL 4/15/98; HBG 10/98; SLJ 7/98)

2499 Kraus, Robert. *Big Squeak, Little Squeak* (PS–1). Illus. by Kevin O'Malley. 1996, Orchard LB $16.99 (978-0-531-08774-9). 32pp. Two little mice outwit Mr. Kit Kat, the owner of the local cheese store, who is intent on capturing them. (Rev: BL 10/15/96; SLJ 10/96)

2500 Kraus, Robert. *Herman the Helper* (PS–K). Illus. by Jose Aruego and Ariane Dewey. 1987, Simon & Schuster paper $6.99 (978-0-671-66270-7). Herman, a green octopus, helps his many friends with his many arms. A reissued title, as are: *Another Mouse to Feed* and *Milton the Early Riser* (both 1987).

2501 Kraus, Robert. *Leo the Late Bloomer* (PS–K). Illus. by Jose Aruego. 1971, HarperCollins LB $17.89 (978-0-87807-043-5). 32pp. Leo, a lion, is just a late bloomer, as Mother tells Father, but Father is worried. Finally Leo blooms — he can read, write, and eat neatly. A beguiling, humorous story.

2502 Kraus, Robert. *Mouse in Love* (PS–2). Illus. by Jose Aruego and Ariane Dewey. 2000, Orchard LB $16.99 (978-0-531-33297-9). 32pp. Mouse searches high and low for the mouse of his dreams and finds that she lives next door. (Rev: BCCB 11/00; BL 9/15/00; HBG 3/01; SLJ 8/00)

2503 Kraus, Robert. *Whose Mouse Are You?* (PS–1). Illus. by Jose Aruego. 1970, Macmillan paper $5.99 (978-0-689-71142-8). 32pp. A young mouse is asked eight questions by his family — which should delight young children who are asked similar questions by their families.

2504 Kressley, Carson. *You're Different and That's Super* (PS–1). Illus. by Jared Lee. 2005, Simon & Schuster $12.95 (978-1-4169-0070-2). 64pp. Trumpet is different from all the other foals — he has a horn — and he suffers prejudice until his uniqueness comes in handy when fire strikes the farm. (Rev: SLJ 5/06)

2505 Krishnaswami, Uma. *Remembering Grandpa* (K–3). Illus. by Layne Johnson. 2007, Boyds Mills $16.95 (978-1-59078-424-2). A little rabbit tries to ease her grandmother's grief over her husband's death. (Rev: SLJ 4/07)

2506 Kroll, Steven. *Jungle Bullies* (PS–1). Illus. by Vincent Nguyen. 2006, Marshall Cavendish $16.99 (978-0-7614-5297-3). Mama Monkey teaches the bullying bigger animals a lesson about sharing. (Rev: SLJ 11/06)

2507 Kroll, Virginia. *On the Way to Kindergarten* (PS–2). Illus. by Elisabeth Schlossberg. 2006, Putnam $15.99 (978-0-399-24168-0). 32pp. As Bear gets ready to go to kindergarten, rhyming couplets celebrate the many milestones in his first five years of development. (Rev: BL 2/15/06; SLJ 3/06)

2508 Kroll, Virginia. *Really Rabbits* (PS–2). Illus. by Philomena O'Neill. 2006, Charlesbridge $16.95 (978-1-57091-897-1); paper $6.95 (978-1-57091-898-8). 32pp. Pet rabbits Tulip and Snuggle mystify their human owners when they help out around the house during the night in hopes of getting more attention during the day. (Rev: BL 7/06; SLJ 8/06)

2509 Kromhout, Rindert. *Little Donkey and the Baby-Sitter* (PS–K). Trans. by Marianne Martens. Illus. by Annemarie van Haeringen. 2006, North-South $15.95 (978-0-7358-2057-9). A little donkey

causes all sorts of trouble for his hen baby-sitter in this gentle and amusing book. (Rev: SLJ 7/06)

2510 Krosoczka, Jarrett J. *Punk Farm* (PS–2). Illus. 2005, Knopf LB $17.99 (978-0-375-92429-3). 40pp. When the farmer's away, the animals play a rock version of "Old MacDonald Had a Farm." (Rev: BL 5/1/05)

2511 Krosoczka, Jarrett J. *Punk Farm on Tour* (PS–2). Illus. by author. 2007, Knopf $15.99 (978-0-375-83343-4). 40pp. The barnyard animals take their rock band on the road with their new hit: "The wheels on the van go round and round." (Rev: SLJ 10/07)

2512 Krupinski, Loretta. *Pirate Treasure* (PS–2). Illus. 2006, Dutton $15.99 (978-0-525-47579-8). 40pp. When a storm drives their pirate ship upriver, Captain Oliver and First Mate Rosie, both mice, decide to trade their buccaneering ways for life as farmers. (Rev: BL 2/15/06; SLJ 3/06)

2513 Kudrna, C. Imbior. *To Bathe a Boa* (PS). Illus. by author. 1986, Carolrhoda LB $15.95 (978-0-87614-306-3); paper $5.95 (978-0-87614-490-9). A little boy hunts high and low for his boa, who doesn't want a bath. (Rev: BL 1/1/87; SLJ 2/87)

2514 Kulka, Joe. *Wolf's Coming!* (PS). Illus. 2007, Carolrhoda $15.95 (978-1-57505-930-3). 32pp. Word spreads among the woodland animals that the wolf is coming and they all scurry inside, but only to give him a pleasant surprise on his birthday. (Rev: BL 4/15/07)

2515 Kurtz, Rob. *Seamus McNamus: The Goat Who Would Be King* (PS–2). Illus. by Mike Lester. 2009, IDW $16.99 (978-1-60010-337-7). 40pp. When things on the farm get tough, a plucky young goat sets out to find work. (Rev: BL 6/1–15/09)

2516 Kvasnosky, Laura McGee. *Frank and Izzy Set Sail* (PS–1). Illus. 2004, Candlewick $15.99 (978-0-7636-2146-9). 32pp. Frank, a reclusive bear, and Izzy, an adventurous rabbit, manage to have a great time on a overnight jaunt to Crescent Island despite their differences in temperament. (Rev: BL 5/15/04; SLJ 6/04)

2517 Kvasnosky, Laura McGee. *See You Later, Alligator* (PS–K). Illus. 1995, Harcourt $10.00 (978-0-15-200301-2). 24pp. Popular sayings are used to describe a little alligator's day at school. (Rev: BL 9/15/95; SLJ 11/95)

2518 Laden, Nina. *Roberto: The Insect Architect* (2–4). Illus. 2000, Chronicle $15.95 (978-0-8118-2465-1). 40pp. A termite named Roberto achieves his dream of being an architect by planning and building a shelter for homeless bugs. (Rev: BCCB 12/00; BL 11/15/00; HBG 3/01)

2519 Laden, Nina. *When Pigasso Met Mootisse* (K–2). Illus. 1998, Chronicle $15.95 (978-0-8118-1121-7). 40pp. Two painters, Pigasso, a pig, and Mootisse, a bull, become rivals in the art world in this takeoff on the Picasso-Matisse feud. (Rev: BL 11/1/98; HBG 3/99; SLJ 11/98)

2520 Laguna, Sofie. *Too Loud Lily* (PS–1). Illus. by Kerry Argent. 2004, Scholastic $14.95 (978-0-439-57913-1). 32pp. A little hippopotamus who just can't help being loud finds that her booming voice is a hit with the school's new drama teacher. (Rev: BL 2/15/04; SLJ 3/04)

2521 Lakin, Patricia. *Camping Day!* (PS–2). Illus. by Scott Nash. 2009, Dial $16.99 (978-0-8037-3309-1). 40pp. The crocodile friends seen in *Snow Day* (2002) go on an exciting camping trip that turns sour when spooky nighttime sounds and shadows send them scrambling home to finish the trip in the safe familiarity of their own backyards. (Rev: BLO 6/16/09; SLJ 6/09)

2522 Lakin, Patricia. *Clarence the Copy Cat* (PS–2). Illus. by John Manders. 2002, Doubleday LB $17.99 (978-0-385-90854-2). 32pp. Clarence the cat is a pacifist and won't catch mice, which makes it difficult for him to find a home until he discovers the library, but even there a mouse finally turns up and causes much hilarity. (Rev: BL 11/1/02; HBG 3/03; SLJ 10/02)

2523 Lakin, Patricia. *Snow Day!* (PS–1). Illus. by Scott Nash. 2002, Dial $15.99 (978-0-8037-2642-0). 32pp. There's a twist to this story of four crocodiles playing in the snow — they're all school principals. (Rev: BL 11/15/02; HBG 3/03; SLJ 11/02)

2524 Lamb, Albert. *Sam's Winter Hat* (PS). Illus. by David McPhail. 2006, Scholastic $6.99 (978-0-439-79304-9). 32pp. Sam Bear is very forgetful and needs the help of his family and friends to find all of his misplaced items, including the blue winter hat his Grandma made. (Rev: BL 12/1/06; SLJ 10/06)

2525 Landa, Norbert. *Little Bear and the Wishing Tree* (PS–K). Illus. by Simon Mendez. 2007, Good Bks. $16.95 (978-1-56148-566-6). In Bertie Bear's special tree he learns a lesson about sharing even when he doesn't feel like it. (Rev: SLJ 8/07)

2526 Landolf, Diane Wright. *Hog and Dog* (PS–K). Illus. by Jennifer Beck Harris. Series: Step into Reading. 2005, Random LB $11.99 (978-0-375-93165-9); paper $3.99 (978-0-375-83165-2). 32pp. Hog and Dog are good friends despite the occasional disagreement in this fast-paced book for beginning readers. (Rev: BL 10/15/05)

2527 Landry, Leo. *Fat Bat and Swoop* (1–3). Illus. by author. 2005, Holt $15.95 (978-0-8050-7003-3). 64pp. Full of mischief, Fat Bat and Swoop the owl scare Emily the cow only to find themselves scared by Emily in return. (Rev: SLJ 12/05)

2528 Landstrom, Lena. *Boo and Baa Have Company* (PS–2). Trans. by Joan Sandin. Illus. by Olof Landstrom. 2006, Farrar $15.00 (91-29-66546-9). 40pp. Comical mishaps ensue when sheep Boo and Baa attempt to rescue a cat stuck in a tree and to do some vacuuming. (Rev: BL 8/06; HB 9/06; HBG 4/07; SLJ 9/06)

2529 Landstrom, Lena. *Four Hens and a Rooster* (PS–2). Trans. by Joan Sandin. Illus. by Olof Landstrom. 2005, Farrar $16.00 (91-29-66336-9). 28pp. Tired of being pushed around by a bullying rooster, four hens take a class in self-esteem. (Rev: BL 10/1/05; SLJ 12/05)

2530 Landstrom, Lena. *A Hippo's Tale* (PS–2). Illus. 2007, Farrar $15.00 (91-29-66603-1). 32pp. In this gentle story, Mrs. Hippopotamus discovers a clever solution to deal with the intruders on her private beach. (Rev: BL 5/1/07; SLJ 7/07)

2531 Landstrom, Olof, and Lena Landstrom. *Boo and Baa at Sea* (PS). Illus. 1997, Farrar $7.95 (91-29-63921-2). 26pp. In this simple reading book, Boo and Baa get stuck when they take out a rowboat. Also use *Boo and Baa on a Cleaning Spree* (1997). (Rev: BL 7/97; SLJ 7/97)

2532 Landstrom, Olof, and Lena Landstrom. *Boo and Baa in a Party Mood* (PS). Trans. by Joan Sandin. Illus. 1996, Farrar paper $7.95 (91-29-63918-2). 22pp. In this simple picture book, two young sheep, Boo and Baa, prepare for a friend's birthday party. Also use *Boo and Baa in Windy Weather* (1996). (Rev: BL 11/1/96)

2533 Landstrom, Olof, and Lena Landstrom. *Boo and Baa in the Woods* (PS–K). Illus. 2000, Farrar $7.95 (91-29-64754-1). 28pp. Boo and Baa, two sheep, are disappointed when they can't find berries to pick, but some ants accidentally show them a spot where berries are abundant. Also use *Boo and Baa Get Wet* (2000). (Rev: BL 11/15/00; HBG 3/01; SLJ 9/00)

2534 Langreuter, Jutta. *Little Bear Brushes His Teeth* (PS–K). Illus. by Vera Sobat. 1997, Millbrook LB $21.40 (978-0-7613-0190-5); paper $7.95 (978-0-7613-0230-8). 32pp. Little Bear pretends he is a soldier fighting bacteria when he brushes his teeth. Also use *Little Bear Goes to Kindergarten* (1997). (Rev: BL 2/1/97; SLJ 7/97)

2535 Lansky, Vicki. *It's Not Your Fault, KoKo Bear: A Read-Together Book for Parents and Young Children During Divorce* (PS–2). Illus. by Jane Prince. 1998, Book Peddlers paper $5.99 (978-0-916773-47-2). When KoKo Bear's parents divorce, the cub goes through the emotions associated with it: anger, guilt, confusion, and sadness. (Rev: HBG 10/98; SLJ 6/98)

2536 Larios, Julie Hofstrand. *On the Stairs* (PS–1). Illus. by Mary Hofstrand Cornish. 1999, Front St. $15.95 (978-1-886910-34-8). 32pp. Using rhyming verse, this book portrays two mice and the fun they have naming each of the 12 steps on their stairs. (Rev: BL 12/15/99; HBG 3/00; SLJ 12/99)

2537 Lasky, Kathryn. *Poodle and Hound* (1–3). Illus. by Mitch Vane. 2009, Charlesbridge $12.95 (978-1-58089-322-0). 48pp. In the three stories in this book, Poodle and Hound discover that even though they often are annoyed by each other, their differences can be interesting and helpful. (Rev: BL 7/09; SLJ 7/09)

2538 Lasky, Kathryn. *Tumble Bunnies* (K–2). Illus. by Marylin Hafner. 2005, Candlewick $15.99 (978-0-7636-2265-7). Clyde, a bunny who never seems to get picked for the team, is pleased to discover the pleasure of individual events such as trampoline. (Rev: SLJ 4/05)

2539 Lass, Bonnie, and Philemon Sturges. *Who Took the Cookies from the Cookie Jar?* (PS–K). Illus. by Ashley Wolff. 2000, Little, Brown $14.95 (978-0-316-82016-5). 32pp. A little skunk, dressed as a cowboy, becomes a detective and inquires of various animals who stole the cookies from the cookie jar. (Rev: BCCB 12/00; BL 10/15/00; HBG 3/01; SLJ 10/00)

2540 Lawrence, John. *This Little Chick* (PS–K). Illus. 2002, Candlewick $15.99 (978-0-7636-1716-5). 32pp. A little chick learns the many languages of the barnyard as he visits his animal friends. (Rev: BCCB 4/02; BL 2/1/02; HBG 10/02; SLJ 3/02*)

2541 Layne, Steven L. *Love the Baby* (PS–K). Illus. by Ard Hoyt. 2007, Pelican $15.95 (978-1-58980-392-3). 32pp. A young rabbit has trouble adjusting to the arrival of his new sibling. (Rev: BL 4/1/07)

2542 Layton, Neal. *Hot Hot Hot* (K–3). Illus. by author. 2004, Candlewick $15.99 (978-0-7636-2148-3). A lighthearted story about a pair of woolly mammoths, Oscar and Arabella, and how they try to keep cool when summer suddenly comes in the middle of the Ice Age. (Rev: HB 7/04; SLJ 6/04)

2543 Layton, Neal. *The Mammoth Academy* (2–4). 2008, Holt $16.95 (978-0-8050-8708-6). 160pp. Woolly mammoth Oscar isn't happy about starting school but soon finds a friend in Fox in this funny, fast-paced book set in the Ice Age. (Rev: BLO 9/2/08)

2544 Leaf, Munro. *The Story of Ferdinand* (K–4). Illus. by Robert Lawson. 1936, Puffin paper $7.99 (978-0-14-050234-3). 72pp. The classic story of the bull who wants only to sit and smell flowers.

2545 Lebrun, Claude. *Little Brown Bear Does Not Want to Eat* (PS). Illus. by Daniele Bour. Series: Little Brown Bear Books. 1996, Children's Book Pr. LB $12.00 (978-0-531-07823-5); paper $3.50 (978-0-531-17823-2). A simple book about a childhood problem and its solution. Also use *Little Brown Bear Is Growing Up* and *Little Brown Bear Wants to Be Read To* (both 1996). (Rev: SLJ 9/96)

2546 Lee, Ho Baek. *While We Were Out* (PS–1). Illus. by author. 2003, Kane $15.95 (978-1-929132-44-7). An adventurous white rabbit finds herself home alone and decides to try some of the luxuries of human life. (Rev: BL 4/15/03*; HB 7/03; HBG 10/03; SLJ 6/03)

2547 Leedy, Loreen. *The Furry News: How to Make a Newspaper* (1–4). Illus. 1990, Holiday House LB $17.95 (978-0-8234-0793-4). 32pp. Big Bear becomes disgusted with his local newspaper and decides to publish his own. (Rev: BCCB 5/90; BL 5/1/90)

2548 Leedy, Loreen. *The Great Trash Bash* (K–2). Illus. 1991, Holiday House LB $17.95 (978-0-8234-0869-6). Mayor Hippo discovers that his town has too much trash. (Rev: SLJ 5/91)

2549 Leedy, Loreen. *The Monster Money Book* (2–4). Illus. 1992, Holiday House LB $17.95 (978-0-8234-0922-8). 32pp. Sarah joins a monster club and learns about various denominations of money. (Rev: BCCB 3/92; BL 3/15/92; SLJ 6/92)

2550 Leedy, Loreen. *Pingo the Plaid Panda* (PS–K). Illus. by author. 1989, Holiday House LB $13.95 (978-0-8234-0727-9). 32pp. A panda whose fur is plaid feels he is not liked because he is different. (Rev: SLJ 7/89)

2551 Lerman, Rory S. *Charlie's Checklist* (PS–2). Illus. by Alison Bartlett. 1997, Orchard paper $14.95 (978-0-531-30001-5). 32pp. When Charlie the puppy places a want ad to find a new home in the city, his young country master is forlorn at the thought of him leaving. (Rev: BCCB 6/97; BL 6/1–15/97; SLJ 5/97)

2552 Leslie, Amanda. *Are Chickens Stripy? A Lift-the-Flap Book* (PS). Illus. by author. 2000, Handprint $4.95 (978-1-929766-09-3). A flap book that describes the behavior of various animals in an amusing way. Also use *Do Crocodiles Moo?* (2000). (Rev: SLJ 12/00)

2553 Lester, Helen. *Batter Up Wombat* (PS–K). Illus. by Lynn Munsinger. 2006, Houghton $16.00 (978-0-618-73784-0). 32pp. Wordplay abounds in this story of an Australian wombat whose efforts to play ball are unusual, but whose skill at digging tunnels is much appreciated when the National Wildlife League game is interrupted by a tornado. (Rev: BL 9/15/06; SLJ 10/06)

2554 Lester, Helen. *Hooway for Wodney Wat* (PS–2). Illus. by Lynn Munsinger. 1999, Houghton $16.00 (978-0-395-92392-4). 32pp. A humorous story about Wodney Wat and his problems pronouncing the letter r. (Rev: BL 5/1/99; HB 7/99; HBG 10/99; SLJ 5/99)

2555 Lester, Helen. *Me First* (PS–3). Illus. by Lynn Munsinger. 1992, Houghton $16.00 (978-0-395-58706-5). 32pp. Pinkerton the pig is so pushy that he will do anything to be first. (Rev: BL 10/1/92; HB 11/92; SLJ 10/92*)

2556 Lester, Helen. *A Porcupine Named Fluffy* (PS–K). Illus. by Lynn Munsinger. 1986, Houghton $16.00 (978-0-395-36895-4); paper $6.95 (978-0-395-52018-5). Fluffy's ridiculous name leads to a friendship with a rhino, with another ridiculous name — Hippo. (Rev: BL 4/15/86; SLJ 8/86)

2557 Lester, Helen. *Score One for the Sloths!* (PS–3). Illus. by Lynn Munsinger. 2001, Houghton $16.00 (978-0-618-10857-2). 32pp. A school full of sleepy sloths faces closure for its low test scores and it's up to a new student called Sparky to save the day. (Rev: BL 8/01; HB 9/01; HBG 3/02; SLJ 10/01)

2558 Lester, Helen. *The Sheep in Wolf's Clothing* (PS–2). Illus. by Lynn Munsinger. 2007, Houghton $16.00 (978-0-618-86844-5). 32pp. The sheepish tale of young and insecure Ewetopia whose skill at dressing up saves the day as well as the flock. (Rev: BCCB 10/07; BL 10/1/07; SLJ 9/07)

2559 Lester, Helen. *Something Might Happen* (PS). Illus. by Lynn Munsinger. 2003, Houghton $16.00 (978-0-618-25406-4). 32pp. Afraid of almost everything, Twitchly Fidget the lemur hides in his lonely hut until his Aunt Bridget dispels his fears and reveals a new way to live. (Rev: HBG 4/04; SLJ 9/03)

2560 Lesynski, Loris. *Night School* (1–3). Illus. 2001, Annick LB $18.95 (978-1-55037-585-5); paper $5.95 (978-1-55037-584-8). 32pp. Being a night owl, Eddie likes the idea of Night School until he realizes that many of the students are not like him. (Rev: BL 6/1–15/01; HBG 10/01)

2561 Levy, Janice. *Gonzalo Grabs the Good Life* (K–2). Illus. by Bill Slavin. 2009, Eerdmans $17.50 (978-0-8028-5328-8). 32pp. Gonzalo the rooster wins the lottery and promptly leaves his farm job and heads for the high life in this humorous book full of wordplay. (Rev: BL 3/1/09; SLJ 3/09)

2562 Lewis, Gill. *The Most Precious Thing* (PS). Illus. by Louise Ho. 2006, Good Bks. $16.00 (978-1-56148-534-5). Little Bear and her mother stroll through the woods identifying precious things — the daughter being the most precious of all. (Rev: SLJ 12/06)

2563 Lewis, Kevin. *Dinosaur Dinosaur* (PS–2). Illus. by Daniel Kirk. 2006, Scholastic $15.99 (978-0-439-60371-3). 32pp. A dinosaur kid has a typical dinosaur (human) day in rhyming text and humorous art full of details like "The Dinosaur Times" newspaper, Dino Puffs cereal, and a "trilobite farm." (Rev: BL 2/1/06; SLJ 3/06)

2564 Lewis, Kevin. *My Truck Is Stuck!* (PS–K). Illus. by Daniel Kirk. 2002, Hyperion $14.99 (978-0-7868-0534-1). 40pp. When their dump truck gets stuck, the two dogs hauling a load of bones seek help, in this amusing, brightly illustrated book with a teasing subplot and some basic counting reminders. (Rev: BL 11/1/02; HBG 3/03; SLJ 10/02)

2565 Lewis, Kim. *Seymour and Henry* (PS). Illus. by author. 2009, Candlewick $15.99 (978-0-7636-4243-3). 32pp. Soft pastel illustrations enhance this gentle tale of two ducklings who disobediently run off and hide, become cold, wet, and scared, and return to their mother who lovingly tucks them into bed. (Rev: BLO 6/19/09; SLJ 5/09)

2566 Lewis, Paeony. *I'll Always Love You* (PS). Illus. by Penny Ives. 2002, Tiger Tales paper $5.95 (978-1-58925-360-5). Alex Bear's mother is disappointed when he behaves badly but always forgives him and says she'll love him. (Rev: SLJ 8/02)

2567 Lewis, Rob. *Brothers and Sisters* (PS–1). Illus. by author. 2005, Hodder $16.99 (978-0-340-86600-9). The good and the bad side of having siblings are presented in the two halves of this book about young rabbits. (Rev: SLJ 4/05)

2568 Lewison, Wendy C. *Shy Vi* (PS–K). Illus. by Stephen J. Smith. 1993, Simon & Schuster paper $14.00 (978-0-671-76968-0). 28pp. A little mouse named Violet is so shy that she can't speak above a whisper. (Rev: BL 5/1/93; SLJ 7/93)

2569 Leznoff, Glenda. *Pigmalion* (K–2). Illus. by Rachel Berman. 2002, Tradewind $15.95 (978-1-896580-20-3). Little pig Juliet is a skilled singer, actor, and dancer but so shy that she must rehearse in private when she's chosen for the part of Eliza Piglittle. (Rev: SLJ 8/02)

2570 Lies, Brian. *Bats at the Beach* (K–2). 2006, Houghton $16.00 (978-0-618-55744-8). 32pp. A family of bats spends a pleasant night at the beach, using "moon-tan lotion" and eating "bug-mallows." (Rev: BL 8/06; SLJ 6/06)

2571 Lin, Grace. *Olvina Flies* (PS–1). Illus. 2003, Holt $15.95 (978-0-8050-6711-8). 32pp. Olvina, a hen, is reluctant to take her first airplane ride but finds a friend in a fellow traveler, a penguin. (Rev: BL 2/1/03; HB 5/03; HBG 10/03; SLJ 4/03)

2572 Lincoln, Hazel. *Little Elephant's Trunk* (PS–K). Illus. by author. 2006, Albert Whitman $15.95 (978-0-8075-4591-1). A baby elephant unsure what to do with his trunk watches his elders and experiments. (Rev: SLJ 10/06)

2573 Lindgren, Barbro. *Benny's Had Enough!* (PS–K). Trans. by Elisabeth Kallick Dyssegaard. Illus. by Olof Landstrom. 1999, Farrar $14.00 (91-29-64563-8). 28pp. A little piglet runs away but finds that life outside his comfortable home is difficult. (Rev: BL 10/15/99; HB 11/99; HBG 3/00; SLJ 12/99)

2574 Lindgren, Barbro. *Oink, Oink Benny* (PS). Trans. by Elisabeth Kallick Dyssegaard. Illus. by Olof Landstrom. 2008, Farrar $16.00 (91-29-66855-7). 28pp. Benny and Binky, young pig brothers, head for the mudhole despite their mother's admonitions. (Rev: BCCB 5/08; BL 4/1/08; HB 5/08; SLJ 5/08)

2575 Lionni, Leo. *Alexander and the Wind-Up Mouse* (K–2). Illus. by author. 1969, Pantheon paper $5.99 (978-0-394-82911-1). 32pp. Alexander, a real mouse, envies Willy, a toy, windup mouse, who is loved and cuddled.

2576 Lionni, Leo. *The Biggest House in the World* (PS–2). Illus. by author. 1968, Knopf paper $5.99 (978-0-394-82740-7). 32pp. A young snail, desiring a larger shell, receives fatherly advice and decides that small accommodations are an asset in regaining his mobility.

2577 Lionni, Leo. *Fish Is Fish* (K–2). Illus. by author. 1970, Knopf paper $5.99 (978-0-394-82799-5). 32pp. A fable about a fish who learns from a frog how to be happy just being himself.

2578 Lionni, Leo. *Frederick* (PS–2). Illus. by author. 1967, Knopf LB $18.99 (978-0-394-91040-6); paper $5.99 (978-0-394-82614-1). 40pp. A field mouse appears to be ignoring the coming of winter, but actually he is not.

2579 Lionni, Leo. *The Greentail Mouse* (PS–2). Illus. 2003, Knopf $15.95 (978-0-375-82399-2). 32pp. A reissue of a 1973 picture book that tells the story of field mice who must learn to trust each other again. (Rev: BL 1/1–15/03; HBG 10/03)

2580 Lionni, Leo. *Inch by Inch* (PS–2). Illus. by author. 1962, Astor-Honor $15.95 (978-0-8392-3010-6). When the birds demand that he measure the length of a nightingale's song, this clever, captive inchworm inches his way to freedom.

2581 Lionni, Leo. *Matthew's Dream* (K–3). Illus. 1995, Random paper $5.99 (978-0-679-87318-1). With his imagination, Matthew, a little mouse, can turn his dismal home into something stunning. (Rev: BCCB 3/91; BL 1/1/91; SLJ 4/91*)

2582 Lionni, Leo. *Swimmy* (PS–1). Illus. by author. 1963, Knopf paper $5.99 (978-0-394-82620-2). 40pp. A remarkable little fish instructs the rest of his school in the art of protection — swim in the formation of a gigantic fish! Beautiful, full-color illustrations.

2583 Lithgow, John. *Mahalia Mouse Goes to College* (PS–2). Illus. by Igor Oleynikov. 2007, Simon & Schuster $17.99 (978-1-4169-2715-0). 40pp. Mahalia Mouse crashes a Harvard science class, befriends a professor, and earns her degree in this charming story that was part of Lithgow's commencement address at Harvard in 2005; with CD. (Rev: BL 6/1–15/07; SLJ 5/07)

2584 Lithgow, John. *Marsupial Sue* (K–3). Illus. by Jack E. Davis. 2001, Simon & Schuster $17.95 (978-0-689-84394-5). Sue the kangaroo is unhappy with her fate and wishes she were another kind of animal. (Rev: HBG 3/02; SLJ 11/01)

2585 Lithgow, John. *Micawber* (PS–2). Illus. by C. F. Payne. 2002, Simon & Schuster LB $17.95 (978-0-689-83341-0). An art-loving squirrel spends a summer in the country mastering brushes and colors, and returns triumphantly to New York to open a gallery above the Central Park carousel in this book/CD combination. (Rev: HBG 3/03; SLJ 9/02)

2586 Livingston, Irene. *Finklehopper Frog Cheers* (PS–1). Illus. by Brian Lies. 2005, Tricycle $14.95 (978-1-58246-138-0). Finklehopper Frog and his rabbit friend Ruby both have fears about attending the town picnic. (Rev: BL 3/1/04; SLJ 5/05)

2587 Lloyd, Sam. *Mr. Pusskins: A Love Story* (PS–2). Illus. by author. 2006, Simon & Schuster $14.95 (978-1-4169-2517-0). 32pp. Tired of the smothering love of his young owner, Mr. Pusskins the cat sets off to see what life is like outside his narrowly defined world, but he soon longs for the comforts of home. (Rev: BL 11/1/06; HBG 4/07; SLJ 1/07)

2588 Lloyd, Sam. *Mr. Pusskins and Little Whiskers* (PS–1). Illus. by author. 2008, Atheneum $15.99 (978-1-4169-5796-6). 32pp. Mr. Pusskins's contented new life is threatened when Emily brings a rambunctious kitten home. (Rev: BLO 7/29/08; SLJ 5/08)

2589 Lobel, Arnold. *Fables* (2–4). Illus. by author. 1980, HarperCollins LB $17.89 (978-0-06-023974-9); paper $6.99 (978-0-06-443046-3). 48pp. An Americanized Aesop with excellent illustrations. Caldecott Medal winner, 1981.

2590 Lobel, Gill. *Too Small for Honey Cake* (PS–2). Illus. by Sebastien Braun. 2006, Harcourt $16.00 (978-0-15-206097-8). 32pp. Little Fox is sad when he thinks the new baby has taken his place in Daddy Fox's heart. (Rev: BL 9/1/06; SLJ 10/06)

2591 Lobel, Gillian. *Little Honey Bear and the Smiley Moon* (PS–2). Illus. by Tim Warnes. 2006, Good Bks. $16.00 (978-1-56148-533-8). Little Honey Bear, Lily Long Ears, and Teeny Tiny Mouse hope to visit the moon but become lost in the dark woods and are eventually rescued by Mommy Bear. (Rev: SLJ 11/06)

2592 London, Jonathan. *Froggy Plays Soccer* (PS–1). Illus. by Frank Remkiewicz. 1999, Viking $15.99 (978-0-670-88257-1). 32pp. Froggy is a failure during the soccer game to win the City Cup until he gets a reminder from Dad and kicks the winning goal. Also use *Let's Go, Froggy!* (1994), *Froggy Goes to School* (1996), *Froggy's First Kiss* (1998),

Froggy Eats Out (2001), *Froggy Plays in the Band* and *Froggy Goes to the Doctor* (2002), *Froggy's Day with Dad* (2004), and *Froggy Plays T-Ball* (2007). (Rev: BL 3/1/99; HBG 10/99; SLJ 3/99)

2593 Loomis, Christine. *Hattie Hippo* (PS). Illus. by Robert Neubecker. 2006, Scholastic $16.99 (978-0-439-54340-8). 32pp. Four episodes follow Hattie the young hippo through a series of minor mishaps. (Rev: BL 8/06; SLJ 8/06)

2594 Lorenz, Lee. *A Weekend in the City* (PS–2). Illus. 1991, Pippin $15.95 (978-0-945912-15-6). 32pp. Pig and Duck search for some common ground with friend Moose when they propose a visit to the city for his birthday. (Rev: BCCB 11/91; BL 1/1/92; SLJ 12/91)

2595 Low, Joseph. *Mice Twice* (K–3). Illus. by author. 1986, Macmillan paper $5.99 (978-0-689-71060-5). 32pp. Cat invites Mouse to dinner but Mouse brings along Dog. Reissue of 1980 publication.

2596 Lowell, Susan. *The Three Little Javelinas* (PS–3). Illus. by Jim Harris. 1992, Northland LB $15.95 (978-0-87358-542-2). 32pp. This Americanized version of the "Three Little Pigs" features a coyote instead of the wolf. (Rev: BL 1/1/93)

2597 Lucas, David. *Peanut* (PS–2). Illus. by author. 2008, Candlewick $15.99 (978-0-7636-3925-9). 32pp. A tiny monkey is filled with fear — he is afraid of wild animals, rain, the setting sun — until a beetle causes him to fall and he recognizes his own abilities. (Rev: SLJ 3/09)

2598 Lund, Deb. *All Aboard the Dinotrain* (K–2). Illus. by Howard Fine. 2006, Harcourt $16.00 (978-0-15-205237-9). 40pp. In this spirited sequel to *Dinosailors* (2003), a band of adventurous dinosaurs goes for a memorable ride on a runaway train. (Rev: BL 4/1/06; SLJ 5/06)

2599 Lund, Deb. *Dinosailors* (K–2). Illus. by Howard Fine. 2003, Harcourt $16.00 (978-0-15-204609-5). 40pp. Six dinosaurs set out to sea with humorous results told in rhyming verse. (Rev: BL 9/1/03; HBG 4/04; SLJ 9/03)

2600 McAllister, Angela. *Barkus, Sly and the Golden Egg* (K–2). Illus. by Sally Anne Lambert. 2002, Bloomsbury $15.95 (978-1-58234-764-6). Three crafty chickens plan a clever escape from two dastardly foxes and alert the townspeople to the foxes' thieving ways. (Rev: SLJ 9/02)

2601 McAllister, Angela. *Brave Bitsy and the Bear* (PS–3). Illus. by Tiphanie Beeke. 2006, Clarion $16.00 (978-0-618-63994-6). 29pp. Grateful for the help of a big bear who helped her to get back home when she was lost in the woods, Bitsy the toy bunny finds a way to repay his kindness. (Rev: SLJ 10/06)

2602 McAllister, Angela. *Take a Kiss to School* (PS). Illus. by Sue Hellard. 2006, Bloomsbury $15.95 (978-1-58234-702-8). 32pp. Digby the mole's mother gives him a reassuring collection of kisses to build up his courage for his second day at school. (Rev: BL 8/06; SLJ 7/06)

2603 Macaulay, David. *Why the Chicken Crossed the Road* (K–3). Illus. by author. 1987, Houghton $16.00 (978-0-395-44241-8). 32pp. Readers will enjoy the humor of this chain reaction set off when one chicken crosses the road. (Rev: BCCB 11/87; BL 10/15/87; SLJ 12/87)

2604 McBratney, Sam. *Yes We Can!* (PS–K). Illus. by Charles Fuge. 2007, HarperCollins $16.99 (978-0-06-121515-5). Little Roo, Quacker Duck, and Country Mouse find out that it's no fun when friends tease one another and learn to encourage one another instead. (Rev: SLJ 7/07)

2605 McCarty, Peter. *Little Bunny on the Move* (PS–K). Illus. 1999, Holt $15.95 (978-0-8050-4620-5). 32pp. A snow white bunny sets out on a long journey to find a home. (Rev: BCCB 11/99; BL 12/15/99; HBG 3/00; SLJ 12/99*)

2606 McCarty, Peter. *T Is for Terrible* (PS–K). Illus. by author. 2004, Holt $15.95 (978-0-8050-7404-8). A Tyrannosaurus with low self-esteem decides that his behavior just comes naturally. (Rev: SLJ 8/04)

2607 McCaughrean, Geraldine. *Unicorns! Unicorns!* (K–2). Illus. by Sophie Windham. 1997, Holiday House LB $15.95 (978-0-8234-1319-5). 32pp. Because they are busy helping other animals, two unicorns fail to get on Noah's ark. (Rev: BL 11/15/97; HBG 3/98; SLJ 10/97)

2608 McClements, George. *Dinosaur Woods* (PS–1). Illus. by author. 2009, Simon & Schuster $16.99 (978-1-4169-8626-3). 40pp. Threatened by destruction of their habitat, a group of canny (and endangered) animals create a fierce dinosaur to scare off the demolition team. (Rev: BL 5/1/09; LMC 10/09; SLJ 6/09)

2609 McClements, George. *Ridin' Dinos with Buck Bronco* (1–3). Illus. by author. 2007, Harcourt $16.00 (978-0-15-205989-7). 32pp. All you need to know about riding and caring for dinosaurs of various kinds. (Rev: BL 10/15/07; SLJ 9/07)

2610 McCullough, Sharon Pierce. *Bunbun at the Fair* (PS). Illus. by author. 2002, Barefoot Books $14.99 (978-1-84148-900-1). Bunbun, a mischievous little rabbit, goes missing at the fair and his siblings search for him. (Rev: HBG 3/03; SLJ 12/02)

2611 McCully, Emily Arnold. *Monk Camps Out* (PS–1). Illus. 2000, Scholastic $15.95 (978-0-439-09976-9). 32pp. Mouse parents help their son Monk to set up his tent in the backyard and then wait up during the night wondering if their son will become frightened and lonely and want to come back in. (Rev: BL 5/15/00; HB 3/00; HBG 10/00; SLJ 4/00)

2612 McCully, Emily Arnold. *School* (PS–K). Illus. 2005, HarperCollins $15.99 (978-0-06-623856-2). 32pp. Bitty the mouse follows her older siblings to school and has a happy time in this new version of the 1987 wordless classic that features brief text and a larger format. (Rev: BL 8/05; SLJ 9/05)

2613 McCully, Emily Arnold. *Speak Up, Blanche!* (K–3). Illus. 1991, HarperCollins LB $14.89 (978-0-06-024228-2). 32pp. The sheep Eva drops granddaughter Blanche off to apprentice at the theatrical bears theater. (Rev: BL 9/1/91*; SLJ 9/91)

2614 MacDonald, Alan. *Beware of the Bears!* (K–3). Illus. by Gwyneth Williamson. 1998, Little Tiger $14.95 (978-1-888444-28-5). 32pp. After Goldilocks

makes a mess of the bears' house, they get even by making a mess in a house they mistakenly believe to be hers. (Rev: BL 5/15/98; HBG 10/98)

2615 MacDonald, Amy. *The Spider Who Created the World* (PS–3). Illus. by G. Brian Karas. 1996, Orchard LB $16.99 (978-0-531-08855-5). 32pp. To find a place to lay her egg, Nobb the spider creates the earth with fire and water in this original creation story. (Rev: BCCB 5/96; BL 4/15/96; HB 9/96; SLJ 3/96)

2616 MacDonald, Margaret Read. *Bat's Big Game* (K–3). Illus. by Eugenia Nobati. 2008, Albert Whitman $16.95 (978-0-8075-0587-8). 32pp. In this retelling of a traditional tale, Bat is determined he wants to be on the winning team in the Animals versus Birds soccer game, but is soon rejected for poor sportsmanship. (Rev: BL 6/1–15/08; LMC 8/08; SLJ 6/08)

2617 MacDonald, Margaret Read. *Pickin' Peas* (PS–3). Illus. by Pat Cummings. 1998, HarperCollins LB $15.89 (978-0-06-027970-7). 32pp. Little Girl uses various tactics to prevent Mr. Rabbit from picking the peas in her garden. (Rev: BL 7/98; HBG 10/98; SLJ 10/98)

2618 McDonald, Megan. *Hen Hears Gossip* (PS–2). Illus. by Joung Un Kim. 2008, Greenwillow $16.99 (978-0-06-113876-8). 32pp. Hen's gossip is passed around the farm until the facts are totally unrecognizable. (Rev: BL 7/08; SLJ 4/08)

2619 MacDonald, Suse. *Elephants on Board* (PS–1). Illus. 1999, Harcourt $15.00 (978-0-15-200951-9). 32pp. When their truck breaks down, 10 elephants try to commandeer another vehicle, with humorous results. (Rev: BL 3/15/99; HBG 10/99; SLJ 6/99)

2620 McDonnell, Patrick. *The Gift of Nothing* (1–4). Illus. by author. 2005, Little, Brown $14.99 (978-0-316-11488-2). Mooch the cat puzzles over an appropriate gift for Earl, a dog who has everything in this book featuring the characters from the "Mutts" comic strip. (Rev: SLJ 1/06)

2621 McDonnell, Patrick. *Just Like Heaven* (K–3). Illus. by author. 2006, Little, Brown $14.99 (978-0-316-11493-6). In this sequel to *The Gift of Nothing*, Mooch the cat awakens from a nap to find himself surrounded by fog and, hearing children laughing and smelling perfume, assumes he's in heaven. (Rev: SLJ 11/06)

2622 McElligott, Matthew. *Bean Thirteen* (K–3). Illus. by author. 2007, Putnam $15.99 (978-0-399-24535-0). How to evenly share thirteen beans? This is the challenge that bugs Flora and Ralph face, and what gets them thinking about division. A wonderful introduction to division for young learners. (Rev: SLJ 6/07)

2623 McElligott, Matthew. *The Lion's Share* (1–3). Illus. by author. 2009, Walker $16.99 (978-0-8027-9768-1). 32pp. A sensitive ant turns the tables on impolite and greedy animals who have been invited to the king of the jungle's annual party; the story offers opportunities to practice division and multiplication. (Rev: BL 1/1–15/09; SLJ 2/09)

2624 McEvoy, Anne. *Betsy B. Little* (PS–1). Illus. by Jacqueline Rogers. 2009, HarperCollins $17.99

(978-0-06-059337-7). 32pp. Betsy, a cheerful giraffe, is exceedingly tall and unsuited to her dream of being a ballerina but she eventually learns to deal with her height in a highly satisfying way. (Rev: BL 1/1–15/09; SLJ 1/09)

2625 McGuire, Leslie. *Brush Your Teeth, Please* (PS–K). Illus. by Jean Pidgeon. Series: Joshua Morris Books. 1993, Reader's Digest $10.99 (978-0-89577-474-3). A pop-up book with movable "toothbrushes" in an animal story designed to get kids to brush their teeth. (Rev: SLJ 9/93)

2626 McKee, David. *Elmer and the Kangaroo* (PS–K). Illus. 2000, HarperCollins $15.99 (978-0-688-17951-9). 32pp. Elmer, a patchwork elephant, helps a kangaroo newly arrived in the forest to gain confidence about his jumping ability. (Rev: BL 5/15/00; HBG 10/00; SLJ 5/00)

2627 McKee, David. *Elmer and the Lost Teddy Bear* (PS–K). Illus. 1999, Lothrop $15.99 (978-0-688-16912-1). 32pp. Elmer, the patchwork elephant, helps Baby Elephant who is sad because he has lost his teddy bear. (Rev: BL 6/1–15/99; HBG 10/99; SLJ 7/99)

2628 McKee, David. *Elmer in the Snow* (PS–1). Illus. by author. 1995, Lothrop $15.99 (978-0-688-14596-5). In this picture book, a patchwork elephant takes some other elephants to snow-covered mountains so they will appreciate the meaning of cold. (Rev: SLJ 12/95)

2629 McKee, David. *I Can Too!* (PS). Illus. by author. 1997, Lothrop $15.95 (978-0-688-15547-6). In this pop-up book, an elephant takes a walk in the jungle and confronts a variety of animals with different talents. (Rev: HBG 3/98; SLJ 1/98)

2630 McKee, David. *Zebra's Hiccups* (PS–3). Illus. 1993, Simon & Schuster paper $14.00 (978-0-671-79440-8). Zebra begins to hiccup so violently that he begins to lose his stripes. (Rev: SLJ 6/93)

2631 McLellan, Stephanie Simpson. *The Chicken Cat* (PS–1). Illus. by Sean Cassidy. 2000, Fitzhenry & Whiteside $14.95 (978-1-55041-531-5). 40pp. Merlin, a kitten, learns to fly and takes his friend Guinevere, a hen, for a ride. (Rev: BL 7/00; SLJ 12/00)

2632 McLeod, Emilie W. *The Bear's Bicycle* (PS–2). Illus. by David McPhail. 1986, Little, Brown paper $5.95 (978-0-316-56206-5). 32pp. A small boy and his teddy bear have an exciting bicycle ride as he gives the bear safety lessons. When the bear, grown to grizzly bear proportions, does not follow the safety rules, it suffers the consequences.

2633 McMillan, Bruce. *The Problem with Chickens* (PS–2). Illus. by Gunnella. 2005, Houghton $16.00 (978-0-618-58581-6). 32pp. The chickens bought by the women of an Icelandic village begin to act more like their owners than like birds. (Rev: BL 9/15/05; SLJ 9/05*)

2634 McMullan, Kate. *Pearl and Wagner: Three Secrets* (K–2). Illus. by R. W. Alley. 2004, Dial $15.99 (978-0-8037-2574-4). 48pp. Pearl the rabbit and Wagner the mouse share secrets during trips to an ice cream factory and a birthday party at an amusement park. (Rev: BL 5/15/04; SLJ 5/04)

2635 McNulty, Faith. *The Elephant Who Couldn't Forget* (1–3). Illus. by Marc Simont. 1980, HarperCollins $11.95 (978-0-06-024145-2). 64pp. A moral lesson about an elephant who was unable to forgive and forget. Reissue of 1980 publication.

2636 McPhail, David. *The Bear's Toothache* (PS–K). Illus. by author. 1972, Little, Brown paper $5.95 (978-0-316-56325-3). 32pp. A very funny story of a little boy's attempt to help extract a bear's tooth and rid him of his toothache.

2637 McPhail, David. *Big Brown Bear Goes to Town* (PS–1). Illus. by author. 2006, Harcourt $16.00 (978-0-15-205317-8). 40pp. Big Brown Bear has an idea to protect his friend Rat's car from the elements, so together the two go into town to get the necessary materials. (Rev: BL 6/1–15/06; SLJ 5/06)

2638 McPhail, David. *Big Brown Bear's Up and Down Day* (PS). Illus. by author. 2003, Harcourt $16.00 (978-0-15-216407-2). Big Brown Bear is not at all happy when Rat tries to trick him out of his slipper, but in time the two become friends who share. (Rev: BCCB 10/03; BL 11/03; HBG 4/04; SLJ 11/03)

2639 McPhail, David. *The Blue Door: A Fox and Rabbit Story* (K–2). Illus. by John O'Connor. 2001, Fitzhenry & Whiteside $15.95 (978-1-55041-647-3). Fox and Rabbit set off to visit Fox's storytelling uncle in the city, but all they know about his whereabouts is that he has a blue door. (Rev: SLJ 2/02)

2640 McPhail, David. *Budgie and Boo* (PS–K). Illus. by author. 2009, Abrams $15.95 (978-0-8109-8324-3). 32pp. A bunny called Boo and a bear named Budgie grow a friendship and a garden in three brief chapters. (Rev: BL 4/1/09; SLJ 3/09)

2641 McPhail, David. *Drawing Lessons from a Bear* (PS–2). Illus. 2000, Little, Brown $14.95 (978-0-316-56345-1). 32pp. An old bear reminisces about his life as a cub and how he decided to devote his life to drawing and teaching others the love of drawing. (Rev: BCCB 3/00; BL 2/15/00; HBG 10/00; SLJ 5/00)

2642 McPhail, David. *Emma in Charge* (PS–K). Illus. by author. 2005, Dutton $12.99 (978-0-525-47411-1). The young bear has a busy day shepherding her toys through school — math, spelling, music, recess — followed by a checkup and a trip to the "zoo." (Rev: BL 5/1/04; SLJ 6/05)

2643 McPhail, David. *Lost!* (PS–K). Illus. 1990, Little, Brown $14.95 (978-0-316-56329-1). 32pp. A young boy tries to help a bear get home from the big city. (Rev: BL 4/1/90; HB 5/90; SLJ 6/90)

2644 McPhail, David. *Mole Music* (PS–3). Illus. 1999, Holt $15.95 (978-0-8050-2819-5). 32pp. Mole, who lives underground, attracts a large aboveground audience when he becomes a superb violinist. (Rev: BCCB 5/99; BL 2/15/99; HBG 10/99; SLJ 4/99)

2645 McPhail, David. *Sylvie and True* (PS–2). Illus. by author. 2007, Farrar $15.00 (978-0-374-37364-1). 32pp. The four brief chapters in this book feature the friendship of Sylvie, a rabbit, and True, a water snake. (Rev: BL 12/1/07; SLJ 12/07)

2646 Mahoney, Daniel J. *The Saturday Escape* (K–2). Illus. 2002, Clarion $14.00 (978-0-618-13326-0). 32pp. Three friends shirk their chores in order to make it to library story time. (Rev: BL 3/15/02; HB 5/02; HBG 10/02; SLJ 3/02)

2647 Mallat, Kathy. *Brave Bear* (PS–K). Illus. 1999, Walker $15.95 (978-0-8027-8704-0). 24pp. A bear cub helps a baby bluebird that has fallen from its nest, by climbing the tree to put the bird back in its home. (Rev: BL 12/1/99; HB 9/99; HBG 3/00; SLJ 9/99)

2648 Mallat, Kathy. *Just Ducky* (PS). Illus. 2002, Walker LB $16.85 (978-0-8027-8825-2). 24pp. Ducky has no luck convincing Frog, Mouse, or Bee to play with him, so he plays with his own reflection in a pond in this colorful picture book. (Rev: BL 9/1/02; HBG 3/03; SLJ 11/02)

2649 Mammano, Julie. *Rhinos Who Play Soccer* (PS–3). Illus. 2001, Chronicle $12.95 (978-0-8118-2779-9). 32pp. Soccer fans will welcome this jargon-filled story of Rhinos versus All-Stars. (Rev: BL 7/01; HBG 10/01; SLJ 7/01)

2650 Mammano, Julie. *Rhinos Who Skateboard* (K–4). Illus. by author. 1999, Chronicle $12.95 (978-0-8118-2356-2). A batch of happy rhinos enjoy skateboarding as they fly through the air and invent a whole new vocabulary. (Rev: SLJ 8/99)

2651 Mangan, Anne. *The Smallest Bear* (PS–K). Illus. by Joanne Moss. 1998, Crocodile $14.95 (978-1-56656-266-9). A small bear finds a hive filled with honey, and his paws are just tiny enough to fit inside. (Rev: HBG 10/98; SLJ 7/98)

2652 Markel, Michelle. *Tyrannosaurus Math* (1–3). Illus. by Doug Cushman. 2009, Tricycle $15.99 (978-1-58246-282-0). 32pp. A young math-loving T. Rex drives his family crazy with his constant calculating until one day he uses his math abilities to save his sister. (Rev: BL 7/09)

2653 Marshall, James. *George and Martha* (PS–1). Illus. by author. 1972, Houghton $16.00 (978-0-395-16619-2); paper $6.95 (978-0-395-19972-5). 48pp. The friendship of two hippos leads to some very humorous situations. Also use the sequels: *George and Martha Encore* (1973); *George and Martha Rise and Shine* (1977); *George and Martha One Fine Day* (1982); *George and Martha Back in Town* (1984); *George and Martha Tons of Fun* (1986).

2654 Marshall, James. *George and Martha Round and Round* (K–2). Illus. by author. 1988, Houghton $16.00 (978-0-395-46763-3); paper $6.95 (978-0-395-58410-1). 48pp. Five stories about hippos George and Martha. (Rev: BCCB 9/88; BL 9/15/88; SLJ 9/88)

2655 Martin, Bill, Jr. *A Beasty Story* (PS–3). Illus. by Steven Kellogg. 1999, Harcourt $17.00 (978-0-15-201683-8). 40pp. Four mice explore a dark, dark house to find the beast they know lives inside. (Rev: BL 9/15/99; HBG 3/00; SLJ 9/99)

2656 Martin, Bill, Jr. *Chicken Chuck* (PS–2). Illus. by Steven Salerno. 2000, Winslow $16.95 (978-1-890817-31-2). When Chicken Chuck eats a blue seed, a blue feather sprouts from his forehead and he becomes the hit of the barnyard. (Rev: HBG 10/00; SLJ 6/00)

2657 Martin, Bill, Jr., and John Archambault. *Barn Dance!* (PS–2). Illus. by Ted Rand. 1986, Holt $16.95 (978-0-8050-0089-4); paper $6.95 (978-0-8050-0799-2). 32pp. The animals are holding a lively barn dance on a full-moon night. (Rev: BL 1/15/87; SLJ 2/87)

2658 Martin, Bill, Jr., and Michael Sampson. *Kitty Cat, Kitty Cat, Are You Waking Up?* (PS–1). Illus. by Laura J. Bryant. 2008, Marshall Cavendish $14.99 (978-0-7614-5438-0). 24pp. A mother cat struggles to get her young kitten up and off to school in this humorous rhyming narrative enhanced by lively watercolors. (Rev: BL 7/08; SLJ 9/08)

2659 Martin, Bill, Jr., and Michael Sampson. *The Little Squeegy Bug* (K–2). Illus. by Patrick Corrigan. 2001, Winslow $16.95 (978-1-890817-90-9). 32pp. A little bug becomes a firefly with help and persistence. (Rev: BCCB 1/02; BL 9/1/01; HBG 10/02; SLJ 9/01)

2660 Martin, David. *All for Pie, Pie for All* (PS–2). Illus. by Valeri Gorbachev. 2006, Candlewick $15.99 (978-0-7636-2393-7). 32pp. After the cat family enjoys an apple pie cooked by Grandma Cat, the remaining piece is carted away by Grandma Mouse, who sees that her whole family is fed, leaving a tiny piece that provides a satisfying meal for a family of ants. (Rev: BL 9/15/06)

2661 Martin, David. *Piggy and Dad Go Fishing* (PS–2). Illus. by Frank Remkiewicz. 2005, Candlewick $14.99 (978-0-7636-2506-1). Piggy is a sensitive soul and can't bring himself to put a worm on a hook or keep a fish once he has caught it. (Rev: SLJ 5/05)

2662 Massie, Elizabeth, and Barbara Spilman Lawson. *Jambo, Watoto! Hello, Children!* (K–2). Illus. by Marsha Heatwole. 1998, Creative Arts $15.95 (978-0-9642712-3-4). Four young cheetahs remember their mother's advice and, when she goes out hunting, they stay put in their hiding place in spite of being tempted to come out by other animals. (Rev: SLJ 1/99)

2663 Masurel, Claire. *Domino* (PS–1). Illus. by David Walker. 2007, Candlewick $8.99 (978-0-7636-2862-8). Little Domino can go where the big dogs can't, a skill that comes in handy when a ball rolls under a fence. A cheerful tale for very young children. (Rev: SLJ 5/07)

2664 Matsuoka, Mei. *Footprints in the Snow* (PS–3). Illus. by author. 2008, Holt $16.95 (978-0-8050-8792-5). 32pp. Tired of the bad rap, Wolf begins to write a story about a nice wolf, which in turn frames a secondary story whose twists surprise even Wolf. (Rev: BL 9/15/08; LMC 1/09)

2665 Maybarduk, Linda. *James the Dancing Dog* (PS–3). Illus. by Gillian Johnson. 2004, Tundra $15.95 (978-0-88776-619-0). 24pp. The whimsical tale of a beagle that longs to dance and eventually enjoys a moment of balletic glory. (Rev: BL 11/15/04)

2666 Meade, Holly. *John Willy and Freddy McGee* (PS–1). Illus. 1998, Marshall Cavendish $15.95

(978-0-7614-5033-7). 32pp. John Willy and Freddy McGee, two guinea pigs, escape from their cage and have fun in the pockets of a pool table until the balls begin dropping on them. (Rev: BCCB 1/99; BL 9/1/98; HB 1/99; HBG 3/99; SLJ 9/98)

2667 Meddaugh, Susan. *Tree of Birds* (PS–1). Illus. 1990, Houghton $16.00 (978-0-395-53147-1). 32pp. When Harry nurses Sally, an injured bird, back to health, her friends arrive to make sure Harry doesn't keep her as a pet. (Rev: BCCB 3/90; BL 4/1/90; HB 9/90; SLJ 4/90)

2668 Meeuwissen, Tony. *Remarkable Animals: 1,000 Amazing Amalgamations* (PS–1). Illus. 1998, Orchard $15.95 (978-0-531-30066-4). Ten animals, including an alligator and rhinoceros, are divided into three sections, and flipping through the pages creates strange new animals. (Rev: BCCB 5/98; BL 1/1–15/99; HB 7/98; HBG 10/98; SLJ 4/98)

2669 Mercer, Peggy. *Ten Cows to Texas* (K–2). Illus. by Bill Crews. 2005, Handprint $16.95 (978-1-59354-116-3). 40pp. With dreams of stardom dancing in their heads, Mimi the cow and nine of her bovine sisters embark on a road trip from Lonesome Cow, Georgia, to an audition in El Paso, Texas. (Rev: BL 12/1/05; SLJ 11/05)

2670 Miller, Edna. *Mousekin's Family* (1–3). Illus. by author. 1972, Prentice Hall LB $9.95 (978-0-13-604462-8). 32pp. Complications occur when a little white-footed mouse mistakenly believes she has found a relative. Other titles in the series are: *Mousekin's Close Call* (1980); *Mousekin's Fables* (1982).

2671 Miller, Pat. *Substitute Groundhog* (K–3). Illus. by Kathi Ember. 2006, Albert Whitman $16.99 (978-0-8075-7643-4). Sidelined by the flu just before his big weather-predicting day, Groundhog auditions other animals to replace him. (Rev: SLJ 12/06)

2672 Miller, Ruth. *The Bear on the Bed* (PS–2). Illus. by Bill Slavin. 2002, Kids Can $15.95 (978-1-55337-036-9). A boisterous bear takes over a little girl's cabin at camp, with consequences sure to please children if not adults. (Rev: HBG 10/02; SLJ 7/02)

2673 Mitton, Tony. *Dinosaurumpus!* (PS). Illus. by Guy Parker-Rees. 2003, Scholastic $15.95 (978-0-439-39514-4). 32pp. Party with the dinosaurs in this joyous, energetic picture book with vivid, comical illustrations showing the dancing dinos in all their scaly glory. (Rev: BL 1/1–15/03; HBG 10/03; SLJ 3/03)

2674 Mitton, Tony. *Down by the Cool of the Pool* (PS–2). Illus. by Guy Parker-Rees. 2002, Scholastic $16.99 (978-0-439-30915-8). A group of animals dance and leap around the pool until they all fall in — and continue to party in the water. (Rev: HBG 10/02; SLJ 7/02)

2675 Mitton, Tony. *Farmer Joe and the Music Show* (PS–1). Illus. by Guy Parker-Rees. 2009, Scholastic $16.99 (978-0-545-12493-5). 32pp. Poor Old Joe suddenly realizes that music will bring his farm back to life, and soon the animals and even the plants are happy again. (Rev: BL 4/15/09; SLJ 9/09)

2676 Mitton, Tony. *The Tale of Tales* (PS–2). Illus. by Peter Bailey. 2004, Random $15.95 (978-0-385-75016-5). 112pp. A group of animals making their way to Volcano Valley to hear "the tale of tales" recount their own favorite stories as they travel. (Rev: BL 4/15/04; SLJ 4/04)

2677 Mitton, Tony. *A Very Curious Bear* (PS–1). Illus. by Paul Howard. 2009, Random $16.99 (978-0-375-85083-7). 32pp. A little bear is full of questions — "Why does the sun come and light up the day?" — that are asked and answered in rhyme. (Rev: BL 4/1/09; SLJ 5/09)

2678 Moncomble, Gérard. *Pippin* (PS–2). Trans. by Alexandra Simon. Illus. by Xavière Devos. 2006, North-South $15.95 (978-0-7358-2062-3). Pippin the kitten is normal in most respects but he cannot purr. (Rev: SLJ 4/06)

2679 Monroe, Chris. *Monkey with a Tool Belt* (K–3). Illus. by author. 2008, Carolrhoda LB $16.95 (978-0-8225-7631-0). A mechanically minded monkey named Chico Bon Bon puts his tool belt to good effect when he is captured by an organ grinder. (Rev: BCCB 6/08; SLJ 2/08)

2680 Monroe, Chris. *Monkey with a Tool Belt and the Noisy Problem* (PS–2). Illus. by author. 2009, Carolrhoda $16.95 (978-0-8225-9247-1). 32pp. Using the tools in his trusty belt, Chico the monkey rescues an elephant named Clark from the laundry chute; detailed illustrations add to the appeal. (Rev: BCCB 7–8/09; BL 4/1/09; SLJ 3/09)

2681 Moodie, Fiona. *Noko and the Night Monster* (PS–K). Illus. 2001, Marshall Cavendish $15.95 (978-0-7614-5093-1). 32pp. The friends of Takadu the aardvark band together to rid him of his fear of the Night Monster in this nicely illustrated, appealing story. (Rev: BL 12/1/01; HBG 3/02; SLJ 12/01)

2682 Moon, Nicola. *Alligator Tails and Crocodile Cakes* (1–3). Illus. by Andy Ellis. Series: I Am Reading. 2005, Kingfisher paper $3.95 (978-0-7534-5853-2). 48pp. Two short stories for beginning readers star Alligator and Crocodile, who play a game of hide-and-seek (difficult with those long revealing tails!) and bake a cake. (Rev: BL 12/1/05; SLJ 9/05)

2683 Moon, Nicola. *Mouse Tells the Time* (K–1). Illus. by Anthony Morris. 2003, Pavilion $16.95 (978-1-84365-000-3). Mouse searches for a more efficient way to mark the passage of time in this nicely illustrated book that includes a foldout page showing four clocks that indicate key hours of the day. (Rev: SLJ 6/03)

2684 Mora, Pat. *Delicious Hullabaloo: Pachanga deliciosa* (PS–1). Illus. by Francisco Mora. 1999, Arte Publico $14.95 (978-1-55885-246-4). 32pp. In this bilingual book, lizards, armadillos, and other exotic animals enjoy dancing at a desert dinner party. (Rev: BL 5/1/99; HBG 3/99; SLJ 3/99)

2685 Morgan, Michaela. *Brave, Brave Mouse* (PS–K). Illus. by Michelle Cartlidge. 2004, Whitman $15.95 (978-0-8075-0869-5). 32pp. Little Mouse fights his many fears by silently repeating rhymes that reinforce his inner strength. (Rev: BL 1/1–15/05; SLJ 11/04)

2686 Morgan, Michaela. *Bunny Wishes* (K–2). Illus. by Caroline Jayne Church. 2007, Scholastic $16.99 (978-0-439-91812-1). 32pp. The wind carries Teeny and Tino's wish lists into the hands of the baby mice who play with the words until a new message is revealed in this sequel to *Dear Bunny* (2006). (Rev: BL 11/1/07)

2687 Morgan, Michaela. *Dear Bunny* (K–2). Illus. by Caroline Jayne Church. 2006, Scholastic $15.99 (978-0-439-74833-9). 32pp. Tino and Teeny, two shy but lovestruck bunnies, leave each other love notes that are shredded by a family of mice building a nest; all ends well when the mice realize what they have done and make amends. (Rev: BL 2/1/06; SLJ 1/06)

2688 Morgan, Michaela. *Helpful Betty Solves a Mystery* (PS–2). Illus. by Moira Kemp. Series: On My Own. 1994, Carolrhoda LB $18.60 (978-0-87614-832-7). While traveling through the jungle helping friends, Betty, a hippo, solves the mystery of a missing egg. Also use *Helpful Betty to the Rescue* (1994). (Rev: BCCB 9/94; SLJ 10/94)

2689 Morozumi, Atsuko. *Mommy Is That You?* (PS–K). Illus. by author. 2008, Mathew Price $14.95 (978-1-935021-04-9). 32pp. A gentle story of newly hatched little ducklings seeking their home and their mother. (Rev: SLJ 2/09)

2690 Morrow, Barbara Olenyik. *Mr. Mosquito Put on His Tuxedo* (K–2). Illus. by Ponder Goembel. 2009, Holiday $16.95 (978-0-8234-2072-8). 32pp. The exquisitely dressed Mr. Mosquito saves the day at the insect-only royal ball and is dubbed the "Royal Pest" in this nicely illustrated tale. (Rev: BL 1/1–15/09; HB 5/09; SLJ 2/09)

2691 Morton, Jane, and Ted Dreier. *Moozie's Kind Adventure* (K–2). Illus. by Jane Royse. Series: Moozie Adventures. 1999, Best Friends $14.95 (978-0-9662268-1-2). Moozie, a gentle cow, saves some ducklings who are endangered by a herd of stampeding cows. (Rev: SLJ 1/00)

2692 Morton-Shaw, Christine, and Greg Shaw. *Wake Up, Sleepy Bear!* (PS–K). Illus. by John Butler. 2006, Viking $12.99 (978-0-670-06175-4). In this gentle tale told in rhyming verse, young woodland animals awaken from sleep and are urged to assemble to welcome a newborn fawn. (Rev: SLJ 11/06)

2693 Moss, Miriam. *A Babysitter for Billy Bear* (PS–1). Illus. by Anna Currey. 2008, Dial $16.99 (978-0-8037-3269-8). 32pp. Billy Bear and his toy rabbit experience their first evening with a babysitter. (Rev: BL 7/08; SLJ 6/08)

2694 Moss, Miriam. *Bare Bear* (PS–2). Illus. by Mary McQuillan. 2005, Holiday House $16.95 (978-0-8234-1934-0). 32pp. Busby the bear finds himself bare after the wind blows his clothes off a clothesline; during his search to find the garments he meets some oddly dressed animals and an ogre. (Rev: BL 3/15/05; SLJ 3/05)

2695 Moss, Miriam. *Don't Forget I Love You* (PS–2). Illus. by Anna Currey. 2004, Dial $15.99 (978-0-8037-2920-9). 32pp. A mother bear and her son have a difficult morning when they get off to a late start. (Rev: BL 1/1–15/04; SLJ 2/04)

2696 Moss, Miriam. *I'll Be Your Friend, Smudge!* (PS–2). Illus. by Lynne Chapman. 2002, Gullane $12.95 (978-1-86233-207-2). Young mouse Smudge is crying because she has no friends when Hare turns up and befriends her. Also use *Smudge's Grumpy Day*, *It's My Turn, Smudge!*, and *A New House for Smudge* (all 2002). (Rev: SLJ 8/02)

2697 Moss, Miriam. *The Snow Bear* (PS–1). Illus. by Maggie Kneen. 2001, Dutton $15.99 (978-0-525-46658-1). Winter scenes and spare, poetic text depict a polar bear cub who gets help from other animals in his search for his mother. (Rev: HBG 3/02; SLJ 10/01)

2698 Most, Bernard. *Cock-A-Doodle-Moo!* (PS–1). Illus. 1996, Harcourt paper $13.00 (978-0-15-201252-6). 32pp. When a rooster develops a voice problem, a cow tries to help out. (Rev: BL 9/1/96; SLJ 12/96)

2699 Most, Bernard. *The Cow That Went Oink* (PS–1). Illus. 1990, Harcourt $13.00 (978-0-15-220195-1). A cow and a pig are ridiculed because they aren't the same as other farm animals. (Rev: HB 7/90; SLJ 12/90)

2700 Most, Bernard. *If the Dinosaurs Came Back* (1–3). Illus. by author. 1978, Harcourt $16.00 (978-0-15-238020-5); paper $6.00 (978-0-15-238021-2). 32pp. All the things that might happen if dinosaurs came back to the world.

2701 Moyer, Marshall M. *Rollo Bones, Canine Hypnotist* (K–4). Illus. 1998, Tricycle $14.95 (978-1-883672-65-2). 32pp. Rollo Bones, an amazing dog who can hypnotize people, realizes that he must hypnotize his master to keep him in line. (Rev: BL 6/1–15/98; HBG 10/98; SLJ 7/98)

2702 Mozelle, Shirley. *The Pig Is in the Pantry, the Cat Is on the Shelf* (PS–1). Illus. by Jennifer Plecas. 2000, Clarion $15.00 (978-0-395-78627-7). 32pp. When farmer McDuffel goes to town leaving the farmhouse door open, the animals take over, singing, cooking, taking baths, and making a big mess. (Rev: BL 8/00; HBG 10/00; SLJ 5/00)

2703 Mraz, David. *Little Goose* (K–1). Illus. by Margot Apple. 2009, Tricycle $15.99 (978-1-58246-190-8). 32pp. Little Goose wonders why he's so fond of round things and consults other animals. (Rev: BL 4/15/09; SLJ 4/09)

2704 Muller, Robin. *Hickory, Dickory, Dock* (K–2). Illus. by Suzanne Duranceau. 1994, Scholastic $15.95 (978-0-590-47278-4). 32pp. A cat throws a party with unexpected guests in this book with a rhyme for each hour of the day. (Rev: BL 5/1/94; SLJ 5/94)

2705 Müller, Birte. *I Can Dress Myself!* (PS–K). Trans. by Marianne Martens. Illus. by author. 2007, North-South $16.95 (978-0-7358-2128-6). 32pp. Mother tries to be patient as Daisy, a young rabbit, insists on getting herself dressed. (Rev: BL 5/15/07; SLJ 6/07)

2706 Muntean, Michaela. *Do Not Open This Book!* (K–3). Illus. by Pascal LeMaitre. 2006, Scholastic $15.99 (978-0-439-66037-2). 32pp. The action here centers on a cranky pink pig/would-be author who objects to those who are trying to read his work in progress; the simple process of turning the pages draws the reader into the story. (Rev: BL 3/15/06)

2707 Murphy, Jill. *Mr. Large in Charge* (PS–2). Illus. by author, 2007, Candlewick $16.99 (978-0-7636-3504-6); paper $6.99 (978-0-7636-2739-3). 40pp. Chaos ensues when Mr. Large, patriarch of an elephant family, takes over child rearing and household chores while his sick wife rests in bed. (Rev: BL 6/1–15/07)

2708 Murphy, Mary. *I Am an Artist* (PS). Illus. by author. 2000, Houghton $4.95 (978-0-618-03401-7). In this appealing board book, a little penguin plays at being a nurse, cowboy, and model. The same penguin is featured in *I Make A Cake* (2000). (Rev: SLJ 6/00)

2709 Murphy, Mary. *I Like It When* . . . (PS). Illus. 1997, Harcourt $10.95 (978-0-15-200039-4). 32pp. A small penguin tells her mother of her favorite things that they do together. (Rev: BL 4/1/97; SLJ 5/97)

2710 Murray, Marjorie Dennis. *Don't Wake up the Bear!* (PS–2). Illus. by Patricia Wittmann. 2003, Marshall Cavendish $14.95 (978-0-7614-5107-5). A number of woodland creatures find refuge from the icy blasts of winter in the cozy cave of a hibernating bear. (Rev: HBG 4/04; SLJ 11/03)

2711 Murray, Marjorie Dennis. *Hippo Goes Bananas!* (PS–1). Illus. by Kevin O'Malley. 2006, Marshall Cavendish $14.95 (978-0-7614-5224-9). Hippo has a toothache, and his strange behavior unnerves the other animals in this cumulative tale. (Rev: SLJ 5/06)

2712 Muth, Jon J. *Zen Shorts* (K–3). Illus. 2005, Scholastic $17.99 (978-0-439-33911-7). 40pp. A beautifully illustrated introduction to Zen thinking through Stillwater the panda, who tells three children meaningful stories that make them see the world and each other in new ways. Caldecott Honor Book, 2006. (Rev: BL 3/1/05; SLJ 2/05)

2713 Myers, Walter Dean. *The Blues of Flats Brown* (K–3). Illus. by Nina Laden. 2000, Holiday House $16.95 (978-0-8234-1480-2). 32pp. Two junkyard dogs, the musical Flats Brown and his friend Caleb, escape their mean owner — who wants to make them fighting dogs — by means of Flats' great blues playing. (Rev: BCCB 2/00; BL 3/1/00*; HBG 10/00; SLJ 3/00)

2714 Napoli, Donna Jo, and Eva Furrow. *Bobby the Bold* (PS–2). Illus. by Ard Hoyt. 2006, Dial $16.99 (978-0-8037-2990-2). 32pp. Ignored by the chimps with which he's quartered at the zoo, Bobby the bonobo escapes to visit a hair salon for a makeover that he hopes will help him to fit in; cartoon-style art animates this lesson about being different. (Rev: BL 4/1/06; SLJ 6/06)

2715 Neugebauer, Charise. *The Real Winner* (K–2). Illus. by Barbara Nascimbeni. 2000, North-South LB $15.88 (978-0-7358-1253-6). An overly competitive raccoon named Rocky learns how to relax and love life by following the example of a kind young hippo. (Rev: HBG 10/00; SLJ 7/00)

2716 Newman, Jeff. *Reginald* (PS–3). Illus. by author. 2003, Doubleday LB $17.99 (978-0-385-90862-7). Despite the animosity of his animal neighbors, Reginald the bull loves his life in the Amazon rain forest. (Rev: HBG 4/04; SLJ 12/03)

2717 Newman, Leslea. *Where Is Bear?* (PS). Illus. by Valeri Gorbachev. 2004, Harcourt $16.00 (978-0-15-204936-2). Bear disappears during a forest animals' game of hide-and-seek. (Rev: SLJ 11/04)

2718 Nishimura, Kae. *Bunny Lune* (K–2). Illus. by author. 2007, Clarion $15.00 (978-0-618-71606-7). 32pp. After learning about a Japanese lunar celebration, Bunny Lune becomes preoccupied with the moon and comes up with harebrained schemes to raise money for his own lunar voyage. (Rev: BL 5/15/07; SLJ 8/07)

2719 Nitto, Tomio. *The Red Rock: A Graphic Fable* (K–2). 2006, Groundwood $15.95 (978-0-88899-669-5). 32pp. To save his beloved valley from destruction by developers, Old Beaver and his animal friends mount a campaign to block the project. (Rev: BL 4/15/06; LMC 11/06)

2720 Noguès, Jean-Come. *House for a Mouse* (PS–2). Trans. by J. Alison James. Illus. by Anne Velghe. 2005, North-South $15.95 (978-0-7358-2017-3). While searching for a home of her own, Little Mouse encounters an artist and agrees to pose as his model. (Rev: SLJ 11/05)

2721 Nolan, Janet. *A Father's Day Thank You* (PS–K). Illus. by Kathi Ember. 2007, Albert Whitman $16.99 (978-0-8075-2291-2). 32pp. For Father's Day, Harvey the bear cub decides to do a drawing of all the things his dad has done for him. (Rev: BL 4/1/07)

2722 Nolan, Lucy. *A Fairy in a Dairy* (PS–2). Illus. by Laura J. Bryant. 2003, Marshall Cavendish $16.95 (978-0-7614-5130-3). Decked out in a pink tutu, Pixie the cow brings dairy magic to the town of Buttermilk Hollow, which finds itself in dire financial straits. (Rev: HBG 4/04; SLJ 11/03)

2723 Norac, Carl. *I Love You So Much* (PS–1). Illus. by Claude K. Dubois. 1998, Doubleday $9.95 (978-0-385-32512-7). Lola the hamster is looking for the proper occasion to tell her famiy that she loves them. (Rev: HBG 10/98; SLJ 2/98)

2724 Nordholm, Gayle. *The Rainbow Tiger* (PS–1). Illus. by Jennifer Frohwerk. 2002, Hara $16.95 (978-1-883697-52-5). 40pp. After his wish is granted, a tiger regrets that he asked to exchange his stripes for the colors of a peacock. (Rev: BL 5/1/02)

2725 Novak, Matt. *Mouse TV* (PS–3). Illus. 1994, Orchard LB $17.99 (978-0-531-08706-0). 32pp. When their TV breaks down, a mouse family, all of whom are TV addicts, must find new ways to amuse themselves. (Rev: BCCB 10/94; BL 9/1/94; SLJ 10/94*)

2726 Numeroff, Laura. *If You Give a Moose a Muffin* (PS–2). Illus. by Felicia Bond. Series: If You Give a . . . 1991, HarperCollins LB $17.89 (978-0-06-024406-4). 32pp. This circular tale begins with a moose being lured to a boy's house to receive a muffin. (Rev: BCCB 9/91; BL 7/91; SLJ 12/91*)

2727 Numeroff, Laura. *If You Give a Mouse a Cookie* (PS–K). Illus. by Felicia Bond. Series: If You Give a . . . 1985, HarperCollins LB $17.89 (978-0-

06-024587-0). 32pp. A little mouse asks for a variety of things until the floor is a clutter of goods. This is followed by *If You Take a Mouse to the Movies* (2000) and *If You Take a Mouse to School* (2002). (Rev: BCCB 7–8/85; BL 6/1/85; HBG 10/01; SLJ 5/85)

2728 Numeroff, Laura. *If You Give a Pig a Pancake* (PS–1). Illus. by Felicia Bond. Series: If You Give a . . . . 1998, HarperCollins LB $16.89 (978-0-06-026687-5). 32pp. Giving a pig a pancake leads from one consequence to another until we get back to a new plate of pancakes. A sequel is *If You Give a Pig a Party* (2000), in which the enthusiastic protagonist wants a better and better party. (Rev: BCCB 6/98; BL 5/15/98; HBG 10/98; SLJ 7/98)

2729 Numeroff, Laura. *What Mommies Do Best / What Daddies Do Best* (PS–1). Illus. by Lynn Munsinger. 1998, Simon & Schuster $13.00 (978-0-689-80577-6). 40pp. In these two stories the reader discovers that both parents do all of the activities pictured — making snowmen, reading stories, watching the sunset -- equally well. (Rev: BL 4/1/98; HBG 3/99; SLJ 4/98)

2730 Numeroff, Laura, and Nate Evans. *The Jellybeans and the Big Dance* (PS–2). Illus. by Lynn Munsinger. 2008, Abrams $15.95 (978-0-8109-9352-5). 32pp. Emily the dog loves to dance but her animal friends in her class are less enthusiastic (Bitsy wants to paint, Anna to read, and Nicole to play soccer) until Emily shows them how they can each use their interests to create a special routine. (Rev: BL 4/15/08; SLJ 6/08)

2731 Nunez, Marisa. *Camilla the Zebra* (PS). Trans. from Spanish by Susana Lopez Rubio. Series: Books for Dreaming. 2003, Kalandraka $14.95 (84-95730-39-1). Camilla the zebra is heartbroken when a gust of wind blows away seven of her stripes but pleased when her friends offer inventive replacements. (Rev: SLJ 11/03)

2732 Oates, Joyce Carol. *Come Meet Muffin!* (PS–2). Illus. by Mark Graham. 1998, Ecco $18.00 (978-0-88001-556-1). 32pp. Muffin, a wise young cat, guides two lost fawns back to their mother but has problems finding his way back home. (Rev: BL 8/98; HBG 3/99; SLJ 1/99)

2733 Oates, Joyce Carol. *Where Is Little Reynard?* (1–3). Illus. by Mark Graham. 2003, HarperCollins LB $16.89 (978-0-06-029583-7). Little Reynard is the runt of the litter of kittens and his diminutive size has made him shy and withdrawn, but all that changes for the better after a confidence-boosting frolic with some friendly young foxes. (Rev: HBG 4/04; SLJ 9/03)

2734 Odanaka, Barbara. *A Crazy Day at the Critter Café* (K–2). Illus. by Lee White. 2009, Simon & Schuster $16.99 (978-1-4169-3914-6). 32pp. A quiet day at the Critter Café is interrupted when a busload of rude and hungry animals arrives. (Rev: BL 5/1/09; SLJ 6/09)

2735 Odanaka, Barbara. *Smash! Mash! Crash! There Goes the Trash!* (PS–2). Illus. by Will Hillenbrand. 2006, Simon & Schuster $15.95 (978-0-689-85160-5). 32pp. From their bedroom, two little pigs watch a pair of garbage trucks making their early morning rounds, picking up everything from old furniture to stinky diapers; rhyming text and expressive illustrations add to the fun. (Rev: BL 12/1/06; SLJ 11/06)

2736 Oh, Jiwon. *Mr. Monkey's Classroom* (K–2). Illus. 2005, HarperCollins LB $15.89 (978-0-06-055722-5). 32pp. On his first day at school, Mouse becomes jealous when his friend Cat — one year older — rushes off to join old friends; a sequel to *Cat and Mouse: A Delicious Tale* (2003). (Rev: BL 8/05)

2737 Ohi, Ruth. *Clara and the Bossy* (PS–2). Illus. 2006, Firefly LB $19.95 (978-1-55037-943-3); paper $5.95 (978-1-55037-942-6). 32pp. Clara the guinea pig learns some important lessons about being true to herself when a bossy new friend's demands become too much. (Rev: BL 8/06)

2738 Ohi, Ruth. *A Trip with Grandma* (PS–1). Illus. by author. 2007, Annick LB $19.95 (978-1-55451-072-6); paper $5.95 (978-1-55451-071-9). 32pp. Frightened at first by the prospect of being separated from his parents, young gerbil Sprout comes to enjoy a road trip with his sister and Grandma. (Rev: BL 5/15/07)

2739 O'Keefe, Susan Heyboer. *Baby Day* (PS). Illus. by Robin Spowart. 2006, Boyds Mills $15.95 (978-1-59078-981-0). 32pp. A day in the life of a baby bear looked after by loving parents. (Rev: BL 3/1/06)

2740 O'Keefe, Susan Heyboer. *Love Me, Love You* (PS). Illus. by Robin Spowart. 2001, Boyds Mills $15.95 (978-1-56397-837-1). 32pp. A simple but beautifully rendered story about a mother rabbit and baby engaged in everyday activities. (Rev: BL 4/15/01; HBG 10/01; SLJ 4/01)

2741 O'Malley, Kevin. *Bud* (K–3). Illus. 2000, Walker LB $16.85 (978-0-8027-8719-4). 32pp. When a storm ruins the garden of young Bud, a rhino, his grandfather helps him set things straight. (Rev: BCCB 6/00; BL 4/1/00; HBG 10/00; SLJ 6/00)

2742 O'Malley, Kevin. *Leo Cockroach . . . Toy Tester* (PS–2). Illus. 1999, Walker LB $16.85 (978-0-8027-8690-6). 32pp. Leo Cockroach feels he is unappreciated as a prize toy tester, so he decides to move on. (Rev: BCCB 6/99; BL 4/15/99; HBG 10/99; SLJ 4/99)

2743 Oram, Hiawyn. *Badger's Bad Mood* (PS–3). Illus. by Susan Varley. 1998, Scholastic $15.95 (978-0-590-18920-0). 32pp. In order to get Badger out of his blue funk, his animal friends arrange an awards ceremony to honor him for being a true friend. (Rev: BCCB 5/98; BL 5/15/98; HBG 10/98; SLJ 8/98)

2744 Oram, Hiawyn. *The Wrong Overcoat* (PS–1). Illus. by Mark Birchall. 2000, Carolrhoda $15.95 (978-1-57505-453-7). 32pp. In spite of compliments about the new coat his mother bought him, little Chimp dislikes it and takes it back to the store for a replacement. (Rev: BL 7/00; HBG 10/00; SLJ 6/00)

2745 Ormerod, Jan. *If You're Happy and You Know It!* (PS). Illus. by Lindsey Gardiner. 2003, Star Bright $15.95 (978-1-932065-07-7); paper $5.95

(978-1-932065-10-7). 32pp. Animals demonstrate ways to show happiness in this update of the classic song. (Rev: BL 3/15/03; HBG 10/03; SLJ 5/03)

2746 Ormerod, Jan. *When an Elephant Comes to School* (PS–2). Illus. 2005, Scholastic $16.95 (978-0-439-73967-2). 32pp. An elephant's first day at school is made easier by thoughtful actions on the part of other students. (Rev: BL 6/1–15/05)

2747 Ormondroyd, Edward. *Broderick* (PS–3). Illus. by John Larrecq. 1969, Houghton LB $4.77 (978-0-686-86580-3). 40pp. Broderick, a mouse, loves to chew books, but one night he stops chewing and reads one. The book is on surfing, and it changes his life!

2748 Palatini, Margie. *Bad Boys* (K–2). Illus. by Henry Cole. 2003, HarperCollins LB $16.89 (978-0-06-000103-2). Willy and Wally Wolf, on the run from the Three Little Pigs and Little Red Riding Hood, dress up in sheep's clothing in the hope of fooling Trudie Ewe and Meryl Sheep. (Rev: BCCB 11/03; BL 11/15/03; HBG 4/04; LMC 3/04; SLJ 11/03)

2749 Palatini, Margie. *Bad Boys Get Cookie!* (K–3). Illus. by Henry Cole. 2006, HarperCollins $17.99 (978-0-06-074436-6). Wolves Willy and Wally — last seen in *Bad Boys* (2003) — pass themselves off as detectives and set go off in pursuit of a cookie that's run away from the bakery. (Rev: SLJ 10/06)

2750 Palatini, Margie. *Bad Boys Get Henpecked!* (K–2). Illus. by Henry Cole. 2009, HarperCollins $17.99 (978-0-06-074433-5). 32pp. Hapless bad boys Willy and Wally Wolf nurture dreams of a chicken dinner and disguise themselves as handymen, offering to clean out the coop. (Rev: BL 7/09; SLJ 5/09)

2751 Palatini, Margie. *Boo-Hoo Moo* (K–2). Illus. by Keith Graves. 2009, HarperCollins $17.99 (978-0-06-114375-5). 32pp. Whimsical, colorful illustrations and clever text tell a funny tale of farm animal friends who hold singing auditions for a chorus to accompany sad Hilda Mae Heifer's despondent mooing. (Rev: SLJ 2/09)

2752 Palatini, Margie. *Earthquack!* (PS–1). Illus. by Barry Moser. 2002, Simon & Schuster $15.95 (978-0-689-84280-1). 32pp. The barnyard becomes alarmed, Henny-Penny-style, when the animals feel what they think is an earthquake in this rhyming tale. (Rev: BCCB 7–8/02; BL 7/02; HBG 10/02; SLJ 6/02)

2753 Palatini, Margie. *Gorgonzola: A Very Stinkysaurus* (PS–2). Illus. by Tim Bowers. 2007, HarperCollins $16.99 (978-0-06-073897-6). 32pp. A stinky dinosaur with a sad history learns about soap, toothpaste, and mouthwash in this funny take on cleanliness. (Rev: SLJ 5/08)

2754 Palatini, Margie. *Lousy Rotten Stinkin' Grapes* (PS–2). Illus. by Barry Moser. 2009, Simon & Schuster $15.99 (978-0-689-80246-1). 32pp. Fox's rigid plans for reaching the grapes on a high vine are rejected by all the animals whose aid he enlists. (Rev: BL 6/1–15/09; LMC 10/09; SLJ 7/09)

2755 Palatini, Margie. *No Biting, Louise* (PS–K). Illus. by Matthew Reinhart. 2007, HarperCollins $16.99 (978-0-06-052627-6). 32pp. Young alligator Louise struggles to rid herself of her nasty habit of biting, and when she overcomes the problem, it changes to burping. (Rev: BL 11/1/07; SLJ 9/07)

2756 Palatini, Margie. *Oink?* (PS–2). Illus. by Henry Cole. 2006, Simon & Schuster $15.95 (978-0-689-86258-8). 40pp. Two pigs — Thomas and Joseph — successfully resist the other farm animals' pressure to get in shape. (Rev: BL 3/15/06; SLJ 3/06)

2757 Palatini, Margie. *Shelly* (PS–2). Illus. by Guy Francis. 2006, Dutton $15.99 (978-0-525-47565-1). 32pp. Reluctant duckling Shelly remains in his shell while his three slightly older siblings are already developing their own personalities. (Rev: BL 2/1/06; SLJ 2/06)

2758 Palatini, Margie. *Stinky Smelly Feet: A Love Story* (PS–3). Illus. by Ethan Long. 2004, Dutton $15.99 (978-0-525-47201-8). Love between ducks Douglas and Dolores prevails despite Douglas's extremely smelly feet. (Rev: BCCB 6/04; SLJ 6/04)

2759 Parker, Marjorie Blain. *Mama's Little Duckling* (PS). Illus. by Mike Wohnoutka. 2008, Dutton $15.99 (978-0-525-47950-5). A little duck named Dandelion seeks independence but is only allowed to go off by himself after he has warned his mother of impending danger. (Rev: SLJ 2/08)

2760 Parr, Todd. *Otto Goes to Bed* (PS–K). Illus. by author. 2003, Little, Brown $9.95 (978-0-316-73873-6). The title character, a yellow dog with one red ear and one blue ear, does everything he can to put off going to bed, but his attitude changes when he discovers how much fun he can have in his dreams. (Rev: HBG 10/03; SLJ 7/03)

2761 Parr, Todd. *Otto Goes to School* (PS). Illus. 2005, Little, Brown $9.99 (978-0-316-83533-6). 24pp. Otto, the colorful dog with many human characteristics, heads off for his first day at school. (Rev: BL 8/05; SLJ 9/05)

2762 Parr, Todd. *Otto Goes to the Beach* (PS–K). Illus. by author. 2003, Little, Brown $9.95 (978-0-316-73870-5). Otto, a most unusually colored dog, goes to the beach in search of friends and after rejections by an ill-tempered crab and a surfing cat finally finds a kindred spirit in a purple poodle with a pink coiffure. (Rev: HBG 10/03; SLJ 7/03)

2763 Partis, Joanne. *Stripe* (PS–1). Illus. 2000, Lerner $14.95 (978-1-57505-450-6). 32pp. Stripe, a curious little tiger, disobeys his parents and wanders alone into the jungle with near-disastrous results. (Rev: BL 4/15/00; HBG 10/00; SLJ 7/00)

2764 Partis, Joanne. *Stripe's Naughty Sister* (PS). Illus. by author. 2002, Carolrhoda LB $15.95 (978-0-87614-466-4). The tiger cub's baby sister spoils his games with his friends and exhausts him into the bargain. (Rev: HBG 10/02; SLJ 4/02)

2765 Paul, Ann Whitford. *Fiesta Fiasco* (PS–2). Illus. by Ethan Long. 2007, Holiday $16.95 (978-0-8234-2037-7). 32pp. Some basic Spanish vocabulary words are incorporated into this charming book about animal friends learning about gift-giving; colorful gouache-pencil illustrations add to the book's appeal. (Rev: BCCB 7–8/07; BL 5/15/07; SLJ 5/07)

2766 Paul, Ann Whitford. *Little Monkey Says Good Night* (PS–K). Illus. by David Walker. 2003, Farrar $16.00 (978-0-374-34609-6). 32pp. Before going to bed, Little Monkey goes into the circus tent to say goodnight to all the performers. (Rev: BL 3/15/03; HBG 10/03; SLJ 7/03)

2767 Payne, Emmy. *Katy No-Pocket* (PS–1). Illus. by H. A. Rey. 1973, Houghton $17.00 (978-0-395-17104-2); paper $6.95 (978-0-395-13717-8). 32pp. Until Katy finds an apron with pockets, she is very sad, for she has no way to carry her baby.

2768 Payne, Tony, and Jan Payne. *The Hippo-Not-Amus* (K–2). Illus. by Guy Parker-Rees. 2004, Scholastic $16.95 (978-0-439-56418-2). Portly is a disaffected hippo and he explores a variety of other physical possibilities. (Rev: SLJ 9/04)

2769 Pearson, Susan. *Slugs in Love* (K–2). Illus. by Kevin O'Malley. 2006, Marshall Cavendish $16.99 (978-0-7614-5311-6). Marylou, a shy garden slug, writes love poems in slime to a slug named Herbie, but his replies keep going astray and she doesn't know how he feels about her until they finally meet at a tomato. (Rev: SLJ 3/07*)

2770 Pearson, Tracey Campbell. *Bob* (PS–K). Illus. 2002, Farrar $16.00 (978-0-374-39957-3). 32pp. Bob the rooster's wide-ranging animal vocabulary — he can meow, moo, and ribbet with the best of them — succeeds in scaring off a fox. (Rev: BL 11/15/02; HBG 3/03; SLJ 8/02)

2771 Pearson, Tracey Campbell. *Myrtle* (PS). Illus. 2004, Farrar $15.00 (978-0-374-35157-1). 32pp. Cowed by the mean new neighbor, Myrtle the mouse gains courage when her aunt returns from safari and tells her about confronting lions. (Rev: BL 1/1–15/04; SLJ 5/04)

2772 Peet, Bill. *Cock-a-Doodle Dudley* (PS–3). Illus. 1990, Houghton $17.00 (978-0-395-55331-2). 48pp. Dudley takes credit for making the sun rise. (Rev: BCCB 10/90; BL 9/15/90; HB 11/90; SLJ 11/90)

2773 Peet, Bill. *Cowardly Clyde* (K–2). Illus. by author. 1984, Houghton paper $8.95 (978-0-395-36171-9). 48pp. A horse named Clyde quivers in fear at the thought of fighting a dragon with his master, Sir Galavant. Other titles by this author and publisher are: *Ant and the Elephant* (1980); *The Luckiest One of All* (1985); *No Such Things* (1985); *Pamela Camel* (1986); *Farewell to Shady Glade* (1991).

2774 Peet, Bill. *Eli* (1–3). Illus. by author. 1984, Houghton paper $8.95 (978-0-395-36611-0). 48pp. An old lion is saved from hunters by playing dead. Others by Bill Peet and published by Houghton are: *Hubert's Hair-Raising Adventure* (1959); *Ella* (1964); *Chester the Worldly Pig* (1978); *Kermit the Hermit* (1980); *Cyrus the Unsinkable Sea Serpent* (1982).

2775 Peet, Bill. *The Gnats of Knotty Pine* (K–3). Illus. by author. 1984, Houghton $16.00 (978-0-395-21405-3); paper $7.95 (978-0-395-36612-7). The tiny gnats help save the animals of Knotty Pine at hunting time.

2776 Peet, Bill. *Whingdingdilly* (2–4). Illus. by author. 1977, Houghton $17.00 (978-0-395-24729-7); paper $9.95 (978-0-395-31381-7). Scamp, tired of leading a dog's life, is transformed by a witch. Some others by this author and publisher are: *The Spooky Tail of Prewitt Peacock* (1973); *Merle the High Flying Squirrel* (1974); *Fly, Homer, Fly* (1979); *Randy's Dandy Lions* (1979); *Huge Harold* (1982); *How Droofus the Dragon Lost His Head* (1983); *The Pinkish, Purplish, Bluish Egg* (1984).

2777 Peet, Bill. *Zella, Zack, and Zodiac* (PS–1). Illus. 1986, Houghton $16.00 (978-0-395-41069-1); paper $7.95 (978-0-395-52207-3). 32pp. The tale of Zack, an ostrich adopted by Zella the zebra, and Zella's colt Zodiac, whom Zack saves. (Rev: BCCB 6/86; BL 3/16/86; SLJ 5/86)

2778 Peguero, Leone. *Lionel and Amelia* (PS–1). Illus. by Adrian Peguero and Gerard Peguero. 1996, Mondo paper $4.95 (978-1-57255-197-8). 30pp. The mice, who want to be friends, copy each other's ways but decide it's best to be natural. (Rev: BL 1/1–15/97)

2779 Pennypacker, Sara. *Pierre in Love* (PS–2). Illus. by Petra Mathers. 2007, Scholastic $16.99 (978-0-439-51740-9). 40pp. Pierre the mouse/ fisherman is smitten with Catherine the rabbit/ballet teacher but has trouble plucking up courage to declare his love. (Rev: BL 12/15/06; SLJ 3/07)

2780 Perry, Phyllis J. *The Secret of the Silver Key* (2–4). Illus. by Ron Lipking. Series: Fribble Mouse Library Mystery. 2003, Upstart paper $16.95 (978-1-932146-03-5). 90pp. Fribble uses the library to help solve the mystery of an old chest his grandparents have given him. (Rev: SLJ 3/04)

2781 Petz, Moritz. *Wish You Were Here* (PS–2). Illus. by Quentin Greban. 2005, North-South $15.95 (978-0-7358-2005-0). 32pp. Separated for five long days, friends Hedgehog and Mouse exchange letters and eagerly anticipate their reunion. (Rev: BL 10/1/05; SLJ 12/05)

2782 Pfanner, Louise. *Little Lucie's Diary* (PS). Illus. by author. 2008, Trafalgar $12.95 (978-1-877003-68-4). 32pp. Little Lucie and Pip, mouse friends, have simple adventures together in this book that is made up partly of diary entries. (Rev: BL 6/1–15/08)

2783 Pfister, Marcus. *Bertie: Just Like Daddy* (PS–1). Illus. by author. 2009, North-South $16.95 (978-0-7358-2224-5). 32pp. A little hippo called Bertie wants to do everything just like Dad. (Rev: BLO 1/21/09; SLJ 3/09)

2784 Pfister, Marcus. *Henri, Egg Artiste* (K–3). Trans. by J. Alison James. Illus. by author. 2007, North-South $15.95 (978-0-7358-2130-9). 32pp. Henri, a rabbit, creates Easter eggs painted in the style of famous works of art, including Egyptian art, Monet, and van Gogh. (Rev: BL 12/15/07; SLJ 3/08)

2785 Pfister, Marcus. *Holey Moley* (K–2). Trans. by J. Alison James. 2006, North-South $16.95 (978-0-7358-2064-7). Two brothers who happen to be moles learn that it's better to work together than to argue. (Rev: SLJ 6/06)

2786 Pfister, Marcus. *Rainbow Fish and the Big Blue Whale* (PS–K). Trans. by J. Alison James. Illus.

1998, North-South LB $18.88 (978-0-7358-1010-5). 32pp. Rainbow Fish and his friends are afraid that a whale who arrives in their area will eat all the krill and then eat them. Earlier books in the series include *The Rainbow Fish* (1992) and *Rainbow Fish to the Rescue!* (1995). (Rev: BL 9/15/98; HBG 3/99; SLJ 9/98)

2787 Pichon, Liz. *The Three Horrid Little Pigs* (PS–2). Illus. by author. 2008, Tiger Tales $15.95 (978-1-58925-077-2). 32pp. This happily fractured tale tells the story of three horrid little pigs and the sincerely kind wolf who teaches them how to build homes of their own. (Rev: BLO 9/17/08; LMC 1/09)

2788 Pichon, Liz. *The Very Ugly Bug* (PS–2). Illus. by author. 2005, Tiger Tales $15.95 (978-1-58925-048-2). The very ugly bug is afraid that she doesn't have her friends' ability to fly, or to hide, or to disguise herself in order to avoid being eaten. (Rev: BCCB 5/05; SLJ 5/05)

2789 Piepmeier, Charlotte. *Lucy's Journey to the Wild West: A True Story* (1–3). Illus. by Sally Blakemore. 2002, Azro $19.95 (978-1-929115-07-5). 40pp. Lucy the Labrador relates the new sights as her owners move to New Mexico from North Carolina in this story that comes with a map of the trip. (Rev: BL 2/15/03; SLJ 6/03)

2790 Piers, Helen. *Who's in My Bed?* (PS). Illus. by Dave Saunders. 1999, Marshall Cavendish $15.95 (978-0-7614-5046-7). 21pp. Farm animals displace one another when taking over sleeping places in this picture book that uses flaps to tell its story. (Rev: BCCB 7–8/99; BL 4/15/99; HB 5/99; HBG 10/99; SLJ 7/99)

2791 Pilkey, Dav. *Dog Breath: The Horrible Trouble with Hally Tosis* (PS–2). Illus. 1994, Scholastic $16.99 (978-0-590-47466-5). 32pp. Hally Tosis, a dog with terrible breath, uses his affliction to capture two burglars. (Rev: BL 9/15/94; HB 11/94; SLJ 1/95)

2792 Pilkey, Dav. *The Moonglow Roll-o-Rama* (PS–3). Illus. 1995, Orchard LB $16.99 (978-0-531-08726-8). 32pp. Some animals steal off at night to a magical roller skating rink, which is why they sleep during the day. (Rev: BCCB 3/95; BL 2/1/95; SLJ 3/95)

2793 Pinkwater, Daniel. *Bad Bears and a Bunny: An Irving and Muktuk Story* (K–2). Illus. by Jill Pinkwater. 2005, Houghton $16.00 (978-0-618-33926-6). 32pp. Irving and Muktuk, the two naughty polar bears who live in a New Jersey zoo, come up against one tough rabbit. (Rev: BL 2/15/05; SLJ 3/05)

2794 Pinkwater, Daniel. *Bad Bears in the Big City: An Irving and Muktuk Story* (K–3). Illus. by Jill Pinkwater. 2004, Houghton $16.00 (978-0-618-25208-4). 32pp. In a sequel to *Two Bad Bears* (2001), the unrepentant duo, now confined to their quarters at a New Jersey zoo, break out and embark on a muffin hunt. (Rev: BL 3/1/04; SLJ 4/04)

2795 Pinkwater, Daniel. *Irving and Muktuk: Two Bad Bears* (PS–3). Illus. by Jill Pinkwater. 2001, Houghton $15.00 (978-0-618-09334-2). 32pp. Two polar bears plot to steal the main attraction from a town's blueberry muffin festival. (Rev: BL 9/15/01; HBG 3/02; SLJ 9/01)

2796 Pochocki, Ethel. *The Blessing of the Beasts* (K–3). Illus. by Barry Moser. 2007, Paraclete $18.95 (978-1-55725-502-0). 32pp. Francesca, a cockroach, and Martin, a skunk, make their way to St. John the Divine in New York City for the annual blessing of the animals. (Rev: BL 10/1/07)

2797 Polisar, Barry L. *The Trouble with Ben* (PS–3). Illus. by David Clark. 1992, Rainbow $14.95 (978-0-938663-13-3). 32pp. A young bear annoys his human classmates by indulging in bearlike activities. (Rev: BL 6/1/92; SLJ 7/92)

2798 Portis, Antoinette. *A Penguin Story* (PS–2). Illus. by author. 2009, HarperCollins $17.99 (978-0-06-145688-6). 40pp. Edna, a little penguin, sets off to find something more colorful than black and white and blue. (Rev: BL 11/15/08; HB 3/09; SLJ 1/09)

2799 Posthuma, Sieb. *Benny* (PS–1). Illus. 2003, Kane $15.95 (978-1-929132-43-0). 32pp. A dog's sniffing ability is impaired when he comes down with a cold. (Rev: BCCB 3/03; BL 2/15/03; HB 7/03; HBG 10/03; SLJ 8/03)

2800 Potter, Beatrix. *The Complete Adventures of Peter Rabbit* (K–3). Illus. by author. 1982, Puffin paper $8.99 (978-0-14-050444-6). 96pp. An omnibus of the Peter Rabbit stories.

2801 Potter, Beatrix. *The Tales of Peter Rabbit and Benjamin Bunny* (1–2). Adapted by Sindy McKay. Illus. by author. Series: We Both Read. 1998, Treasure Bay $7.99 (978-1-891327-01-8). Two texts, one for parents and the other for children, face each other in this version that uses the original illustrations. (Rev: SLJ 3/99)

2802 Prater, John. *On Top of the World* (PS). Illus. 1998, Mondo $15.95 (978-1-57255-649-2). Four stuffed animals sneak out one night for some fun on a playground slide. (Rev: BL 2/1/99; HBG 3/99)

2803 Price, Mathew. *Don't Worry, Alfie* (PS). Illus. by Emma Chichester Clark. 1999, Orchard $9.95 (978-0-531-30127-2). In this tab book, a mother assures her bear-cub son, Alfie, that she will protect him. Also use *Where's Alfie?* (1999). (Rev: SLJ 7/99)

2804 Price, Mathew. *Patch Finds a Friend* (PS–K). Illus. by Emma Chichester Clark. 2000, Orchard $5.95 (978-0-531-30264-4). A tab book in which Patch, a little spotted puppy, makes friends with a small, gray cat. Also use *Patch and the Rabbits* (2000). (Rev: SLJ 5/00)

2805 Prince, Joshua. *I Saw an Ant in a Parking Lot* (PS–2). Illus. by Macky Pamintuan. 2007, Sterling $14.95 (978-1-4027-3823-4). 24pp. As a parking lot attendant watches in horror, a minivan and a meandering ant seem certain to cross paths with disastrous results; the comical art adds to the general silliness. (Rev: BL 4/1/07)

2806 Pritchett, Dylan. *The First Music* (K–3). Illus. by Erin Bennett Banks. 2006, August House $16.95 (978-0-87483-776-6). 32pp. All the animals of the jungle, each with their own sound, join together to create music in this rhythmic cumulative African tale. (Rev: BL 11/15/06; SLJ 1/07)

2807 Pryor, Bonnie. *The Porcupine Mouse* (PS–2). Illus. by Maryjane Begin. 1988, Morrow $15.89 (978-0-688-07154-7). 32pp. Louie and Dan don't heed Mama Mouse's warnings when they go off to find a home of their own. (Rev: BL 3/1/88; SLJ 9/88)

2808 Puttock, Simon. *Goat and Donkey in Strawberry Sunglasses* (PS–1). Illus. by Russell Julian. 2007, Good Bks. $16.00 (978-1-56148-572-7). 28pp. Goat can't read Donkey's shopping list, so he buys all the wrong things at the market in this whimsical, brightly illustrated picture book. Also use *Goat and Donkey in the Great Outdoors* (2007), in which they end up camping in the backyard. (Rev: BL 5/15/07; SLJ 6/07)

2809 Puttock, Simon. *Miss Fox* (PS–1). Illus. by Holly Swain. 2007, Frances Lincoln $15.95 (978-1-84507-475-3). 32pp. Even though the other animal children like the substitute teacher, Lily Lamb is rightly suspicious of Miss Fox's motives. (Rev: BCCB 1/08; BL 11/1/07)

2810 Quackenbush, Robert. *Henry's Awful Mistake* (PS–2). Illus. by author. 1981, Parents LB $5.95 (978-0-8193-1040-8). 48pp. Henry, a duck, tries to rid his horse of an ant. A sequel is: *Henry's Important Date* (1982).

2811 Quackenbush, Robert. *Lost in the Amazon: A Miss Mallard Mystery* (2–4). Illus. 1990, Pippin LB $15.95 (978-0-945912-11-8). Miss Mallard, the detective duck, is off on another case, this one in Brazil. (Rev: SLJ 1/91)

2812 Rand, Gloria. *Willie Takes a Hike* (1–3). Illus. by Ted Rand. 1996, Harcourt $15.00 (978-0-15-200272-5). 32pp. In spite of his elaborate preparations, Willie the mouse gets lost on a hiking trip. (Rev: BL 4/1/96; SLJ 6/96)

2813 Raschka, Chris. *Arlene Sardine* (K–2). Illus. by author. 1998, Orchard LB $16.99 (978-0-531-33111-8). The whimsical story of Arlene's two-year life, from her birth in a fjord to her final resting place in a can. (Rev: BCCB 9/98; HBG 3/99; SLJ 9/98)

2814 Raschka, Chris. *The Blushful Hippopotamus* (PS–K). Illus. by author. 1996, Orchard LB $15.99 (978-0-531-08882-1). Young Roosevelt Hippopotamus can't control his blushing and is ridiculed by his sister. (Rev: HB 9/96; SLJ 9/96)

2815 Rathmann, Peggy. *Good Night, Gorilla* (PS–1). Illus. 1994, Penguin $14.99 (978-0-399-22445-4). 40pp. After the zookeeper says good night to his animals, a playful gorilla lets them out of their cages. (Rev: BCCB 5/94; BL 7/94; HB 7/94; SLJ 7/94)

2816 Rawlinson, Julia. *Fletcher and the Falling Leaves* (PS–2). Illus. by Tiphanie Beeke. 2006, Greenwillow $16.99 (978-0-06-113401-2). 32pp. When his favorite tree begins to lose its leaves, Fletcher the fox becomes convinced that the tree is sick. (Rev: BL 8/06; SLJ 8/06*)

2817 Rawlinson, Julia. *Mule School* (PS–2). Illus. by Lynne Chapman. 2008, Good Bks. $16.95 (978-1-56148-597-0). 32pp. Stomper the mule doesn't toe the line at Mule School, but his contrariness proves an advantage when a dam bursts and floods the valley. (Rev: BLO 7/30/08; SLJ 8/08)

2818 Rayner, Catherine. *Augustus and His Smile* (PS–2). Illus. by author. 2006, Good Bks. $16.00 (978-1-56148-510-9). Augustus the tiger travels the world looking for his lost smile only to find it while looking into a puddle. (Rev: SLJ 8/06)

2819 Reibstein, Mark. *Wabi Sabi* (K–3). Illus. by Ed Young. 2008, Little, Brown $16.99 (978-0-316-11825-5). 40pp. Wabi Sabi, a Japanese cat, sets out to discover what her name means and learns about the link between beauty and simplicity; this handsome book is illustrated with arresting collages. (Rev: BL 9/1/08; HB 1/09; SLJ 9/08) ◖

2820 Reich, Janet. *Gus and the Green Thing* (PS–2). Illus. by author. 1993, Walker LB $9.85 (978-0-8027-8253-3). A dog named Gus follows a leaf from the bleak city into the countryside and finds a new green world. (Rev: SLJ 10/93)

2821 Reid, Barbara. *The Subway Mouse* (PS–2). Illus. 2005, Scholastic $15.95 (978-0-439-72827-0). 40pp. Nib the mouse, who has lived his entire life in a busy subway station, sets out to find what lies beyond the confines of his subterranean world; clever 3-D photo-collages bring the story to life. (Rev: BL 9/1/05*; HBG 10/05; LMC 10/05; SLJ 8/05)

2822 Reiser, Lynn. *Little Clam* (PS–1). Illus. 1998, Greenwillow LB $14.89 (978-0-688-15909-2). 32pp. Little Clam shows that he can protect himself when he is attacked first by a seagull, then a sea star, and finally a conch. (Rev: BL 8/98; HB 9/98; HBG 3/99; SLJ 11/98)

2823 Reiser, Lynn. *Play Ball with Me!* (PS–1). Illus. by author. 2006, Knopf $9.95 (978-0-375-83244-4). Readers guess which game — basketball, soccer, baseball, or football — a kitten will play next as they turn the pages of this sturdy book with creative die-cut pages. (Rev: SLJ 8/06)

2824 Rex, Michael. *Dunk Skunk* (PS–K). Illus. by author. 2005, Penguin $10.99 (978-0-399-24281-6). Athletic animals with rhyming names — Goal Mole, Hurdle Turtle — are shown in action. (Rev: SLJ 4/05)

2825 Rey, H. A. *Curious George* (K–4). Illus. by author. 1941, Houghton $16.00 (978-0-395-15993-4); paper $6.95 (978-0-395-15023-8). 56pp. A small monkey finds himself in difficulties due to his mischievous curiosity. Also use by the same author: *Curious George Takes a Job* (1947); *Curious George Rides a Bike* (1952); *Curious George Gets a Medal* (1957).

2826 Rey, H. A., and Margaret Rey. *Whiteblack the Penguin Sees the World* (PS–2). Illus. 2000, Houghton $16.00 (978-0-618-07389-4). 32pp. A well-crafted plot about a penguin who leaves Penguinland for a series of adventures that include hatching two ostrich eggs. (Rev: BL 11/1/00; HBG 3/01; SLJ 11/00)

2827 Rey, Margaret. *Curious George Flies a Kite* (K–2). Illus. by H. A. Rey. 1973, Houghton $16.00

(978-0-395-16965-0); paper $6.95 (978-0-395-25937-5). 80pp. More predicaments are encountered by this fun-loving monkey. Also use by the same author: *Curious George Goes to the Hospital* (1973).

2828 Reynolds, Aaron. *Chicks and Salsa* (K–2). Illus. by Paulette Bogan. 2005, Bloomsbury $15.95 (978-1-58234-972-5). A rooster with gourmet aspirations inspires Farmer Nuthatcher's other animals to add some zest and imagination to their eating habits. (Rev: SLJ 11/05)

2829 Richardson, John. *Grunt* (PS–K). Illus. by author. 2002, Clarion $15.00 (978-0-618-15974-1). The runt of the litter of piglets, Wee-skin-and-bones, runs away from the scorn of his siblings and meets a kindly boar who's into positive thinking. (Rev: BCCB 6/02; HBG 10/02; SLJ 5/02)

2830 Riddell, Chris. *Platypus and the Birthday Party* (PS). Illus. by author. 2003, Harcourt $16.00 (978-0-15-204753-5). Platypus, with the help of his friend Echidna, throws a birthday party for Bruce, his favorite stuffed animal. (Rev: HBG 4/04; SLJ 12/03)

2831 Riley, Linnea. *Mouse Mess* (PS–2). Illus. 1997, Scholastic $16.95 (978-0-590-10048-9). 32pp. While the human family is asleep upstairs, a messy mouse is creating havoc downstairs in a search for food. (Rev: BL 10/1/97; HBG 3/98; SLJ 11/97*)

2832 Rinck, Maranke. *I Feel a Foot!* (PS–2). Illus. by Martijn van der Linden. 2008, Boyds Mills $16.95 (978-1-59078-638-3). 32pp. In this reimagining of "The Blind Men and the Elephant," Turtle, Bat, Octopus, Bird, and Goat — awakened in the dark in their hammock — feel around to see what disturbed them and each find something different. (Rev: BLO 9/2/08; SLJ 9/08)

2833 Ritchie, Alison. *Me and My Dad!* (PS–1). Illus. by Alison Edgson. 2007, Good Bks. $16.95 (978-1-56148-565-9). 28pp. This beautifully illustrated book chronicles a happy day a bear cub spends with his loving father. (Rev: BL 5/1/07; SLJ 8/07)

2834 Ritchie, Alison. *What Bear Likes Best!* (PS–K). Illus. by Dubravka Kolanovic. 2005, Good Bks. $16.00 (978-1-56148-473-7). Sometimes, Bear is just too big and gets in everyone's way, but his friends love him anyway. (Rev: SLJ 8/05)

2835 Rix, Jamie. *Giddy Goat* (PS–2). Illus. by Lynne Chapman. 2003, Gingham Dog $14.95 (978-0-7696-3161-5). The inspiring story of Giddy, a mountain goat who shuns the heights favored by his family until the plight of a lamb lost in the mountains helps him conquer his fears. (Rev: HBG 4/04; SLJ 12/03)

2836 Robberecht, Thierry. *Sam Is Not a Loser* (PS–1). Illus. by Philippe Goossens. 2008, Clarion $12.00 (978-0-618-99210-2). 32pp. Young wolf Sam only likes to play if he's winning and backs out of a soccer game because he thinks his team will lose. (Rev: BL 4/1/08; SLJ 5/08)

2837 Robberecht, Thierry. *Sam's New Friend* (PS–K). Illus. by Philippe Goossens. 2008, Clarion $12.00 (978-0-618-91448-7). 32pp. Tough guy Sam the dog doesn't think boys play with girls until

Sam's mother brings home a sad little white kitten named Ellie. (Rev: BL 2/15/08; SLJ 2/08)

2838 Roberts, Bethany. *Double Trouble Groundhog Day* (PS–2). Illus. by Lorinda Bryan Cauley. 2008, Holt $16.95 (978-0-8050-8280-7). 40pp. Groundhog twins Gregory and Greta must decide which of them will assume their grandfather's duties as weather forecaster; when February 2 rolls around Gregory finds he needs his sister's support. (Rev: BLO 7/30/08)

2839 Rocco, John. *Wolf! Wolf!* (K–3). Illus. by author. 2007, Hyperion $15.99 (978-1-4231-0012-6). The Aesop fable about a boy who cries wolf is reconfigured in an Asian setting with humorous twists. (Rev: SLJ 2/07)

2840 Rockwell, Anne. *Brendan and Belinda and the Slam Dunk!* (PS–1). Illus. by Paul Meisel. 2007, HarperCollins $15.99 (978-0-06-028443-5). 40pp. Young pigs Brendan and Belinda's lives are so entwined with basketball that they can't even find time to play in the snow. (Rev: BL 7/07; SLJ 12/07)

2841 Rockwell, Anne. *Chip and the Karate Kick* (K–2). Illus. by Paul Meisel. 2004, HarperCollins LB $15.89 (978-0-06-028446-6). 40pp. Chip the rabbit is so eager to earn a belt in karate that he almost loses sight of the martial art's true spirit. (Rev: BL 5/1/04; SLJ 6/04)

2842 Rockwell, Norman. *Willie Was Different* (1–3). Illus. by author. 1994, Berkshire House $16.95 (978-0-936399-61-4). After achieving world renown as a composer, Willie the wood thrush decides it is best to return to his forest home. (Rev: SLJ 12/94)

2843 Roddie, Shen. *You're Too Small!* (PS–2). Illus. by Steve Lavis. 2004, Tiger Tales $15.95 (978-1-58925-038-3); paper $6.95 (978-1-58925-385-8). A little mouse finds that his small size can be a big advantage. (Rev: SLJ 6/04)

2844 Rodman, Mary Ann. *Surprise Soup* (PS–1). Illus. by G. Brian Karas. 2009, Viking $15.99 (978-0-670-06274-4). 32pp. Kevie the bear's culinary efforts come under some criticism as he, his older brother, and father make soup while they're waiting for the new baby to arrive. (Rev: BCCB 6/09; BL 3/15/09; SLJ 3/09)

2845 Rodriguez, Edel. *Sergio Makes a Splash!* (PS–1). Illus. by author. 2008, Little, Brown $15.99 (978-0-316-06616-7). 32pp. Even equipped with life preserver, floaties, and snorkel, a young penguin named Sergio is reluctant to get in the water. (Rev: BL 5/15/08; SLJ 4/08)

2846 Rodriguez, Edel. *Sergio Saves the Game* (PS–2). Illus. by author. 2009, Little, Brown $15.99 (978-0-316-06617-4). 40pp. Sergio the penguin finally finds his place in the game of soccer after trying and failing several times. (Rev: BLO 6/16/09; HB 7/09; SLJ 7/09)

2847 Rohmann, Eric. *A Kitten Tale* (PS). Illus. by author. 2008, Knopf $15.99 (978-0-517-70915-3). 32pp. Four kittens contemplate the coming of winter with mixed expectations — three fear the cold, while the fourth "can't wait" for the snow — and when the snow arrives the brave one persuades his mates to play in it. (Rev: BCCB 1/08; BL 11/1/07; LMC 1/08; SLJ 2/08)

2848 Rohmann, Eric. *My Friend Rabbit* (PS–3). Illus. by author. 2007, Square Fish paper $6.99 (978-0-312-36752-7). 32pp. A paperback edition of the funny 2002 book about a mouse who plays with his friend Rabbit despite Rabbit's tendency to attract trouble. Caldecott Medal, 2003. (Rev: BL 3/02; SLJ 5/02)

2849 Root, Phyllis. *Oliver Finds His Way* (PS–2). Illus. by Christopher Denise. 2002, Candlewick $14.99 (978-0-7636-1383-9). 40pp. Oliver, a little bear, chases a leaf until he gets lost but soon figures out how to return to Mama and Papa in this autumn picture book. (Rev: BCCB 12/02; BL 9/15/02; HB 1/03; HBG 3/03; SLJ 10/02)

2850 Root, Phyllis. *Toot Toot Zoom!* (PS–K). Illus. by Matthew Cordell. 2009, Candlewick $15.99 (978-0-7636-3452-0). 40pp. Pierre the fox hopes to make friends on the other side of the mountain, but instead he ends up finding several friends along the way. (Rev: BCCB 6/09; SLJ 5/09)

2851 Rosen, Michael. *Bear's Day Out* (PS–2). Illus. by Adrian Reynolds. 2007, Bloomsbury $16.95 (978-1-59990-007-0). 32pp. A large and chatty bear travels from the seaside to the city only to find it's too noisy there. (Rev: BL 9/1/07; SLJ 10/07)

2852 Rosenthal, Amy Krouse. *Little Oink* (PS–2). Illus. by Jen Corace. 2009, Chronicle $14.99 (978-0-8118-6655-2). 36pp. To his parents' despair, Little Oink likes to be clean and tidy. (Rev: BCCB 6/09; BLO 5/15/09)

2853 Rosoff, Meg. *Meet Wild Boars* (PS–2). Illus. by Sophie Blackall. 2005, Holt $15.95 (978-0-8050-7488-8). 32pp. Wild boars Morris, Boris, Horace, and Doris make for very impolite house guests in this outrageously funny picture book. (Rev: BL 3/15/05)

2854 Ross, Tony. *Centipede's 100 Shoes* (PS–1). Illus. by author. 2003, Holt $15.95 (978-0-8050-7298-3). Young readers will find some valuable math lessons in this charming tale of a young centipede who decides he needs some shoes to protect his many feet; his mother buys 50 pairs, only to discover that there are 58 shoes left over after the little creature has been fully shod. (Rev: HBG 10/03; SLJ 6/03)

2855 Ross, Tony. *Silly Silly* (PS–K). Illus. by author. 1999, Andersen $19.95 (978-0-86264-740-7). A silly book about two silly characters, a mouse and a goose, who agree to a contest to see who can tell the silliest story. (Rev: SLJ 2/00)

2856 Rotenberg, Lisa. *Rodeo Pup* (PS–2). Illus. 1998, Firefly LB $14.95 (978-1-55209-245-3). 32pp. Told by his young owner, this is the story of Rodeo Pup, a feisty dalmatian who becomes so famous he eventually has his own Web site. (Rev: BL 9/15/98; SLJ 11/98)

2857 Roth, Susan L. *Great Big Guinea Pigs* (K–2). Illus. 2006, Bloomsbury $17.95 (978-1-58234-724-0). 32pp. To help her son fall asleep, a mother guinea pig tells him a tale about their oversized prehistoric ancestors; this is fiction served full of facts.

(Rev: BL 10/15/06; HBG 4/07; LMC 3/07; SLJ 11/06)

2858 Roth, Susan L. *It's Still a Dog's New York: A Book of Healing* (K–3). Illus. by author. 2001, National Geographic $12.00 (978-0-7922-7050-8). In this sequel to *It's a Dog's New York* (2001), New York dogs Pepper and Rover discuss their feelings about September 11, 2001. (Rev: HBG 10/02; SLJ 6/02)

2859 Rowe, Jeannette. *YoYo Goes Next Door* (PS–1). Illus. by author. 2003, Tiger Tales paper $5.95 (978-1-58925-368-1). In this delightful lift-the-flap picture book, YoYo the yellow dog visits the homes of several neighborhood friends, enjoying a special adventure at each stop. (Rev: SLJ 8/03)

2860 Rowe, Jeannette. *YoYo Goes to the Park* (PS–1). Illus. by author. 2003, Tiger Tales paper $5.95 (978-1-58925-369-8). In this colorfully illustrated lift-the-flap book, YoYo, a yellow dog with one red ear and one blue ear, visits the park and has fun feeding the ducks, riding his scooter, playing on the slide and swings, and flying a kite. (Rev: SLJ 8/03)

2861 Rowe, John A. *I Want a Hug* (PS–K). Illus. by author. 2007, Penguin $16.99 (978-0-698-40064-1). 32pp. Little Elvis is a hedgehog and seeks hugs despite his prickliness. (Rev: BL 9/15/07)

2862 Rowinski, Kate. *Ellie Bear and the Fly-Away Fly* (PS–2). Illus. by Dawn Peterson. 1993, Down East $14.95 (978-0-89272-335-5). On a fishing trip with her uncle, L. L. Bear, Ellie Bear catches a trout but decides to spare its life. (Rev: SLJ 4/94)

2863 Rubel, Nicole. *Ham and Pickles: First Day of School* (K–2). 2006, Harcourt $16.00 (978-0-15-205039-9). 32pp. Pickles the guinea pig is worried about her first day of school and her older brother Ham is definitely not helping. (Rev: BL 8/06; SLJ 7/06)

2864 Rubin, Vicky. *The Three Swingin' Pigs* (1–4). Illus. by Rhode Montijo. 2007, Holt $16.95 (978-0-8050-7335-5). The three little pigs are now a jazz trio whose music is appreciated by even the big bad wolf in this take on the fairy tale. (Rev: SLJ 6/07)

2865 Rudolph, Marguerita. *Grey Neck* (PS–3). Illus. by Leslie Shuman Kranz. 1988, Stemmer $13.95 (978-0-88045-068-3). 32pp. Grey Neck can't leave for the yearly journey south because of a broken wing. (Rev: BL 6/1/88; SLJ 9/88)

2866 Ruelle, Karen Gray. *Dear Tooth Fairy* (K–2). Illus. by author. Series: A Harry and Emily Adventure. 2006, Holiday House $14.95 (978-0-8234-1929-6). 32pp. Emily, a kitten, is thrilled when her loose tooth finally comes out and she receives a visit from the Tooth Fairy. (Rev: BL 3/1/06; SLJ 5/06)

2867 Ruelle, Karen Gray. *Mother's Day Mess* (1–2). Illus. 2003, Holiday House $14.95 (978-0-8234-1773-5); paper $4.95 (978-0-8234-1781-0). 32pp. Kittens Harry and Emily make great plans for Mother's Day, but somehow they don't quite succeed. (Rev: BL 3/1/03; HBG 10/03; SLJ 3/03)

2868 Rumford, James. *Calabash Cat and His Amazing Journey* (K–3). Illus. by author. 2003, Houghton

$16.00 (978-0-618-22423-4). Calabash Cat, searching for the point where the world ends, travels farther and farther afield with different animals serving as his guide for each leg of the journey. (Rev: HB 11/03; HBG 4/04; SLJ 9/03)

2869 Rush, Christopher. *Venus Peter Saves the Whale* (1–3). Illus. by Mairi Hedderwick. 1992, Pelican $15.95 (978-0-88289-928-2). 26pp. On an isolated Scottish island, seagulls want a young boy to save a stranded whale. (Rev: BL 6/1/92)

2870 Russell, Natalie. *Moon Rabbit* (PS–1). Illus. by author. 2009, Viking $16.99 (978-0-670-01170-4). 32pp. In a big city a lonely little rabbit finds a kindred spirit in the park. (Rev: BL 4/15/09; SLJ 6/09)

2871 Ryan, Pam Muñoz. *Nacho and Lolita* (1–3). Illus. by Claudia Rueda. 2005, Scholastic $16.99 (978-0-439-26968-1). 40pp. This charming story, inspired by a Mexican folk tale, features a rare and beautiful pitacohi bird that falls in love with a swallow and uses his colorful feathers to guide her home to San Juan Capistrano after her annual migration. (Rev: BL 10/1/05; SLJ 10/05)

2872 Ryder, Joanne. *Bear of My Heart* (PS). Illus. by Margie Moore. 2006, Simon & Schuster $12.95 (978-0-689-85947-2). A mother bear expresses her love for her cub in tender words and lovely illustrations. (Rev: SLJ 2/07)

2873 Ryder, Joanne. *Dance by the Light of the Moon* (PS–2). Illus. by Guy Francis. 2007, Hyperion $15.99 (978-0-7868-1820-4). 40pp. Weaving in the chorus from the song "Buffalo Gals," this upbeat rhyming tale centers on a moonlit barn dance attended by gussied-up animals. (Rev: BL 1/1–15/07; SLJ 1/07)

2874 Rylant, Cynthia. *The Octopus* (2–4). Illus. by Preston McDaniels. 2005, Simon & Schuster $14.95 (978-0-689-86246-5). 64pp. The Lighthouse Family, consisting of Pandora the mother cat, Sebold the father dog, and two mice children, forges a friendship with Cleo, a shy octopus. (Rev: BL 10/1/05)

2875 Rylant, Cynthia. *Poppleton Has Fun* (PS–1). Illus. by Mark Teague. 2000, Scholastic $15.95 (978-0-590-84839-8). 56pp. This book in the Poppleton Pig series contains three short stories about sharing. (Rev: BL 11/15/00; HBG 3/01; SLJ 12/00)

2876 Sacre, Antonio. *The Barking Mouse* (PS–1). Illus. by Alfredo Aguirre. 2003, Whitman LB $16.99 (978-0-8075-0571-7). A mouse mother impresses her family with her barking abilities when a cat threatens them in this attractively illustrated retelling of a Cuban tale. (Rev: HBG 10/03; SLJ 6/03)

2877 Sadler, Marilyn. *Money, Money, Honey Bunny!* (PS–K). Illus. by Roger Bollen. Series: Bright and Early Books. 2006, Random $8.99 (978-0-375-83370-0). 39pp. This appealing beginning reader describes in rhyming text the uncommonly generous ways of Honey Bunny, who shops for gifts for her friends. (Rev: BL 11/15/05; SLJ 2/06)

2878 Sakai, Komako. *The Snow Day* (PS–K). Illus. by author. 2009, Scholastic $16.99 (978-0-545-01321-5). 40pp. A 5-year-old bunny who lives in a high-rise apartment wakes up one morning to dis-cover a magically transformed world, one that offers both inconvenience and delights. (Rev: BCCB 2/09; BL 1/1–15/09; SLJ 12/08)

2879 Saller, Carol. *Pug, Slug, and Doug the Thug* (K–2). Illus. by Vicki Jo Redenbaugh. 1994, Carolrhoda LB $14.95 (978-0-87614-803-7). 32pp. In this Western tale, a young boy captures three outlaws when he accidentally starts a chain of events that prove to be their downfall. (Rev: BL 4/1/94)

2880 Salley, Coleen. *Epossumondas* (PS–3). Illus. by Janet Stevens. 2002, Harcourt $16.00 (978-0-15-216748-6). 40pp. A bumbling little possum can't seem to get anything right in this uproarious adaptation of a classic Louisiana tale. (Rev: BCCB 10/02; BL 8/02; HB 11/02; HBG 3/03; SLJ 9/02*)

2881 Salley, Coleen. *Epossumondas Saves the Day* (K–3). Illus. by Janet Stevens. 2006, Harcourt $16.00 (978-0-15-205701-5). It's his birthday and Mama is baking biscuits for Epossumondas the possum when she realizes she needs sody sallyratus; several guests head out to the store but fail to return, so the birthday boy goes to investigate. (Rev: SLJ 12/06*)

2882 Saltzberg, Barney. *Cornelius P. Mud, Are You Ready for Baby?* (PS–K). Illus. by author. 2009, Candlewick $15.99 (978-0-7636-3596-1). 32pp. Cornelius the pig greets his new baby brother with a distinct lack of enthusiasm and asks if the baby can be returned. (Rev: BL 3/1/09; SLJ 2/09)

2883 Saltzberg, Barney. *Crazy Hair Day* (K–3). Illus. by author. 2003, Candlewick $15.99 (978-0-7636-1954-1). Stanley the hamster, who sports spikily colorful hair, is mortified to learn that it's School Picture Day, not Crazy Hair Day. (Rev: HBG 4/04; SLJ 12/03)

2884 Saltzberg, Barney. *Stanley and the Class Pet* (PS–2). Illus. by author. 2008, Candlewick $15.99 (978-0-7636-3595-4). 32pp. Stanley the hamster is allowed to take the class bird home for the weekend but is persuaded by his friend Larry to let Figgy out of his cage. (Rev: BL 8/08; SLJ 7/08)

2885 Saltzberg, Barney. *Star of the Week* (K–2). Illus. 2006, Candlewick $15.99 (978-0-7636-2914-4). 32pp. Stanley the hamster's turn as Star of the Week at school does not start off well. (Rev: BL 2/1/06; SLJ 2/06)

2886 Sampson, Michael, and Mary Beth Sampson. *Star of the Circus* (PS–K). Illus. 1997, Holt $14.95 (978-0-8050-4284-9). 32pp. Each of a group of egocentric animals thinks that he or she is the star of the circus. (Rev: BL 4/1/97; SLJ 3/97)

2887 Santore, Charles. *Three Hungry Pigs and the Wolf Who Came to Dinner* (K–2). Illus. 2005, Random $16.95 (978-0-375-82646-7). 32pp. Banished after she samples the white truffles she's supposed to be hunting, Bianca and her piglets find an unlikely ally in a wolf. (Rev: BL 11/15/05)

2888 Sardegna, Jill. *The Roly-Poly Spider* (PS–K). Illus. by Tedd Arnold. 1994, Scholastic $13.95 (978-0-590-47119-0). 32pp. A fat spider uses age-old devices like flattery to lure insect meals into its web. (Rev: BL 11/15/94; SLJ 1/95)

2889 Sattler, Jennifer. *Sylvie* (PS–2). Illus. by author. 2009, Random $15.99 (978-0-375-85708-9). 40pp. A young flamingo who wonders why she is always in the pink, tries out other colors. (Rev: BCCB 7–8/09; BL 6/1–15/09; SLJ 4/09)

2890 Scamell, Ragnhild. *Three Bags Full* (K–1). Illus. by Sally Hobson. 1993, Orchard $14.95 (978-0-531-05486-4). 26pp. Millie the sheep gives so much of her wool to her friends that she begins to feel the cold. (Rev: BL 7/93)

2891 Schachner, Judith Byron. *The Grannyman* (PS–3). Illus. 1999, Dutton $15.99 (978-0-525-46122-7). 32pp. In this fantasy an old cat fondly remembers all his activities as a youngster including stalking wildebeest and playing Bach. (Rev: BCCB 1/00; BL 3/15/00; HBG 3/00; SLJ 11/99)

2892 Schachner, Judy. *Skippyjon Jones and the Big Bones* (K–3). Illus. by author. Series: Skippyjon Jones. 2007, Dutton $16.99 (978-0-525-47884-3). 32pp. Skippyjon, the Siamese kitten who thinks he's a dog, goes dinosaur hunting in the persona of Skippito Friskito. (Rev: SLJ 12/07) 🎧

2893 Schachner, Judy. *Skippyjon Jones in Mummy Trouble* (K–3). Illus. by author. 2006, Dutton $16.99 (978-0-525-47754-9). Skippyjon, the adventurous Siamese kitten who thinks he is a chihuahua, takes a trip to ancient Egypt. (Rev: SLJ 11/06)

2894 Schlein, Miriam. *Little Raccoon's Big Question* (PS–1). Illus. by Ian Schoenherr. 2004, HarperCollins $15.99 (978-0-06-052116-5). 32pp. A gentle story with evocative illustrations in which a playful Little Raccoon asks his mother when she loves him most. (Rev: BL 4/15/04; SLJ 3/04)

2895 Schneider, Josh. *You'll Be Sorry* (PS–K). Illus. by author. 2007, Clarion $15.00 (978-0-618-81932-4). 32pp. Samantha the mouse ignores her parents' warning not to hit her brother and finds she really is sorry. (Rev: BL 9/15/07; SLJ 2/08)

2896 Schoenherr, Ian. *Pip and Squeak* (PS–1). Illus. by author. 2007, HarperCollins $16.99 (978-0-06-087253-3). Pip and Squeak, mice on the way to rabbit Gus's birthday party, realize they have forgotten the present (a lump of cheese) and must find a substitute; the illustrations offer interesting perspectives. (Rev: BL 1/1/07; SLJ 1/07)

2897 Schoenherr, Ian. *Read It, Don't Eat It!* (PS–1). Illus. by author. 2009, HarperCollins $17.99 (978-0-06-172455-8). 32pp. Featuring animals demonstrating various behaviors, this is book of easy rules for enjoying books and the library. (Rev: BL 4/1/09; SLJ 4/09)

2898 Schubert, Dieter, and Ingrid Schubert. *Ophelia* (PS–K). Illus. by Ingrid Schubert. 2009, Boyds Mills $16.95 (978-1-59078-659-8). 24pp. As Ophelia the hippo rushes to help her friend Kevin the alligator, who has butterflies in his stomach, she explains to other animals what's happening and each misinterprets what she says. (Rev: BL 3/15/09; LMC 8/09; SLJ 3/09)

2899 Schubert, Ingrid, and Dieter Schubert. *Bear's Egg* (PS–2). Illus. 1999, Front St. $15.95 (978-1-886910-46-1). 32pp. When Bear becomes the owner of some untended goose eggs, he faces such problems as hatching the eggs and teaching the young goslings how to survive. (Rev: BL 10/1/99; HBG 3/00; SLJ 11/99)

2900 Schubert, Ingrid, and Dieter Schubert. *Beaver's Lodge* (PS). Illus. 2001, Front St. $15.95 (978-1-886910-68-3). 32pp. While Beaver is ill, Bear and Hedgehog build him a house but forget to give it a door. (Rev: BL 7/01; HBG 10/01; SLJ 5/01)

2901 Schubert, Ingrid, and Dieter Schubert. *There's a Hole in My Bucket* (PS–2). Illus. 1998, Front St. $15.95 (978-1-886910-28-7). 32pp. Bear and his friend Hedgehog try to repair a hole in a bucket so that Bear can water his flowers. Fortunately the rain comes and solves their problems. (Rev: BL 5/15/98; HBG 10/98; SLJ 7/98)

2902 Schubert, Ingrid, and Dieter Schubert. *There's Always Room for One More* (PS–1). Illus. by authors. 2002, Front St. $15.95 (978-1-886910-77-5). A butterfly adds the final ounce that tips over the raft bearing Beaver, Badger, Bear, Hedgehog, Mole, and Hare. (Rev: HBG 10/02; SLJ 4/02)

2903 Schuurmans, Hilde. *Sidney Won't Swim* (PS–K). Illus. by author. 2001, Charlesbridge LB $15.95 (978-0-570-91476-1). A young dog doesn't want to take swimming lessons until his friends show him how much fun it can be. (Rev: SLJ 2/01)

2904 Schwartz, Amy. *Tiny and Hercules* (PS–2). Illus. by author. 2009, Roaring Brook $16.95 (978-1-59643-253-6). 32pp. Tiny, the elephant, and Hercules, the mouse, are just another odd couple headed for happiness. (Rev: BL 6/1–15/09; HB 5/09; SLJ 5/09)

2905 Schwartz, Corey Rosen, and Tali Klein. *Hop! Plop!* (PS–2). Illus. by Olivier Dunrea. 2006, Walker $15.95 (978-0-8027-8056-0). 32pp. Elephant and Mouse are friends, but they find it difficult to play together. (Rev: BL 4/15/06; SLJ 5/06)

2906 Schwartz, Henry. *How I Captured a Dinosaur* (PS–K). Illus. by Amy Schwartz. 1989, Orchard paper $6.95 (978-0-531-07028-4). 32pp. Liz discovers a dinosaur on a camping trip and takes him home. (Rev: BCCB 2/89; BL 2/1/89; SLJ 4/89)

2907 Schwartz, Roslyn. *The Mole Sisters and the Blue Egg* (PS–K). Illus. 2001, Annick LB $14.95 (978-1-55037-705-7); paper $4.95 (978-1-55037-704-0). 32pp. The energetic Mole sisters aren't sure what they're seeking, but they have a great time on their quest and discover their quarry is a beautiful blue eggshell that makes a perfect swing. Also use *The Mole Sisters and the Moonlit Night* (2001). (Rev: BL 12/15/01)

2908 Schwartz, Roslyn. *The Mole Sisters and the Busy Bees* (PS). 2000, Annick $4.95 (978-1-55037-663-0); paper $4.95 (978-1-55037-662-3). 32pp. A small book in which two mole sisters watch bees as they go about their work. Also use *The Mole Sisters and the Wavy Wheat* (2000). (Rev: SLJ 11/00)

2909 Schwartz, Roslyn. *The Mole Sisters and the Cool Breeze* (PS–K). Illus. 2002, Annick LB $14.95 (978-1-55037-771-2); paper $4.95 (978-1-55037-770-5). 32pp. The engaging Mole sisters use leaves as fans on a hot day with amusing consequences in this small book. Also use *The Mole Sisters and the*

Question (2002). (Rev: BL 1/1–15/03; HBG 3/03; SLJ 1/03)

2910 Schwartz, Roslyn. *Tales from Parc la Fontaine* (K–1). Illus. by author. Series: Parc la Fontaine. 2006, Firefly $19.95 (978-1-55451-044-3); paper $7.95 (978-1-55451-043-6). 48pp. Three short stories present the lives and aspirations of three thoughtful creatures — a pet bird trying to "act wild," a lonely snail called Fiona, and a bug called Angela who has only one day of life. (Rev: BL 11/1/06; SLJ 1/07)

2911 Scotton, Rob. *Russell and the Lost Treasure* (PS–2). 2006, HarperCollins $15.99 (978-0-06-059851-8). 32pp. Armed with the Super-Duper Treasure Seeker, Russell the sheep sets off to track down the lost treasure of Frogsbottom and at first believes he has only found junk; a sequel to *Russell the Sheep* (2005). (Rev: BL 6/1–15/06; SLJ 5/06)

2912 Scotton, Rob. *Splat the Cat* (PS–1). Illus. by author. 2008, HarperCollins $16.99 (978-0-06-083154-7). 40pp. Splat the cat does not want to go to school and takes along his pet mouse Seymour, only to learn that cats are supposed to chase mice; detailed illustrations add to the humor of this simple story. (Rev: BL 7/08; SLJ 7/08)

2913 Sebastian, John. *J.B.'s Harmonica* (K–3). Illus. by Garth Williams. 1993, Harcourt $13.95 (978-0-15-240091-0). 32pp. A young bear is so bad at playing the harmonica that the neighbors complain. (Rev: BL 3/15/93; SLJ 4/93)

2914 Segal, John. *Alistair and Kip's Great Adventure!* (PS–2). Illus. by author. 2008, Simon & Schuster $15.99 (978-1-4169-0280-5). 32pp. An orange cat named Alexander and a shy beagle called Kip set off on a hair-raising nautical adventure. (Rev: SLJ 5/08)

2915 Segal, John. *Carrot Soup* (PS–2). Illus. 2006, Simon & Schuster $12.95 (978-0-689-87702-5). 32pp. Rabbit loves carrots and looks after his garden carefully, so he is very upset when all his carrots disappear, but his unhappiness evaporates when he gets home and finds all his friends there with bowls of soup. (Rev: BL 2/15/06; SLJ 5/06)

2916 Segal, John. *Far Far Away!* (PS–1). Illus. by author. 2009, Philomel $16.99 (978-0-399-25007-1). 32pp. When Piggie says he's leaving, Mother Pig does everything she can to help him. (Rev: BL 6/1–15/09)

2917 Selkowe, Valrie M. *Happy Birthday to Me!* (PS–K). Illus. by John Sandford. 2001, HarperCollins LB $15.89 (978-0-688-16680-9). 32pp. A young rabbit finds a key that leads him to a roomful of characters who sing his favorite song. (Rev: BL 8/01; HBG 10/01; SLJ 6/01)

2918 Senderak, Carol Hunt. *Mommy in My Pocket* (PS–1). Illus. by Hiroe Nakata. 2006, Hyperion $12.99 (978-0-7868-5596-4). A young rabbit nervous about her first day at school wishes she could shrink her mother and take her along. (Rev: SLJ 3/06)

2919 Serfozo, Mary. *Whooo's There?* (PS–2). Illus. by Jeffrey Scherer. 2007, Random $9.99 (978-0-375-84050-0). An owl notes fellow animals that are

out at night in this rhyming book about nocturnal activity. (Rev: SLJ 8/07)

2920 Serwacki. *Doorknob the Rabbit and the Carnival of Bugs* (PS–2). Illus. by author. 2005, Tricycle $14.95 (978-1-58246-143-4). Doorknob foolishly opens the door without checking who's there and in come 6,000 bugs; Doorknob's efforts to get rid of them include mice, who move in too, followed by cats, who also show no signs of leaving. (Rev: SLJ 5/05)

2921 Seuss, Dr. *Horton Hears a Who!* (K–3). Illus. by author. 1954, Random LB $16.99 (978-0-394-90078-0). The children's favorite elephant discovers a whole town of creatures so small that they live on a speck of dust. Other titles by Dr. Seuss: *Horton Hatches the Egg* (1940); *If I Ran the Zoo* (1950); *If I Ran the Circus* (1956); *Yertle the Turtle and Other Stories* (1958).

2922 Shah, Idries. *The Silly Chicken* (K–3). Illus. by Jeff Jackson. 2000, Hoopoe $17.00 (978-1-883536-19-0). 32pp. An amusing story about a chicken who convinces the inhabitants of a town that the earth is going to swallow them up. (Rev: BL 12/15/00; SLJ 3/01)

2923 Shannon, David. *Duck on a Bike* (PS–1). Illus. 2002, Scholastic $16.99 (978-0-439-05023-4). 40pp. A funny tale about a duck who dares to ride a bike, and the reactions of his farm-animal friends. (Rev: BCCB 3/02; BL 2/15/02; HB 3/02; HBG 10/02; SLJ 3/02*)

2924 Shannon, George. *Lizard's Guest* (K–2). Illus. by Jose Aruego and Ariane Dewey. 2003, Greenwillow LB $16.89 (978-0-06-009084-5). When Lizard accidentally stomps on Skunk's toes while singing and dancing, the barely-injured Skunk plays on the tiny reptile's conscience, winning from Lizard a promise to wait on Skunk hand and foot until his injuries heal. (Rev: HBG 10/03; SLJ 6/03)

2925 Shannon, George. *Lizard's Home* (K–2). Illus. by Jose Aruego and Ariane Dewey. 1999, Greenwillow LB $15.89 (978-0-688-16003-6). 32pp. Lizard devises a plan to win back his favorite resting place — a rock that has been taken over by Snake. (Rev: BL 10/1/99; HBG 3/00; SLJ 9/99)

2926 Shannon, George. *The Secret Chicken Club* (PS–2). Illus. by Deborah Zemke. 2005, Handprint $15.95 (978-1-59354-118-7). 40pp. Three humorous episodes set in the farmyard of *Wise Acres* (2004) feature Debbie the cow who wants to be part of the Secret Chicken Club and an ambitious rooster. (Rev: BL 12/15/05; SLJ 1/06)

2927 Shannon, George. *Tippy-Toe Chick, Go!* (PS–K). Illus. by Laura Dronzek. 2003, HarperCollins LB $17.89 (978-0-06-029824-1). 32pp. Little Chick is a dreamer, but she saves the day when a dog threatens Mother Hen and her brood. (Rev: BCCB 3/03; BL 1/1–15/03; HB 1/03*; HBG 10/03; SLJ 2/03)

2928 Shannon, George. *Wise Acres* (K–2). Illus. by Deborah Zemke. 2004, Handprint $15.95 (978-1-59354-041-8). The animals on Wise Acres farm are presented in three stories — of a lost tambourine, a lonely ram, and an aging turkey worried about his wrinkles. (Rev: SLJ 7/04)

2929 Shannon, Margaret. *Gullible's Troubles* (PS–3). Illus. 1998, Houghton $15.00 (978-0-395-83933-1). 32pp. A humorous story about an innocent little guinea pig named Gullible who is tricked and teased but wins out in the end. (Rev: BCCB 7–8/98; BL 4/1/98; HB 7/98; HBG 10/98; SLJ 5/98)

2930 Sharkey, Niamh. *The Ravenous Beast* (PS–2). Illus. by author. 2003, Candlewick $16.99 (978-0-7636-2182-7). In this fantastical but reassuringly upbeat tale, the Ravenous Beast, a dinosaur-like creature, takes on all challengers to the title of "hungriest animal of all." (Rev: HBG 4/04; SLJ 12/03)

2931 Sharmat, Marjorie W. *I'm Terrific* (PS–1). Illus. by Kay Chorao. 1977, Holiday House LB $15.95 (978-0-8234-0282-3); paper $6.95 (978-0-8234-0955-6). 32pp. An amusing story of a bear cub who thinks he is marvelous and insists on telling everyone so.

2932 Sharmat, Marjorie W. *Tiffany Dino Works Out* (PS–3). Illus. by Nate Evans. 1995, Simon & Schuster paper $15.00 (978-0-689-80309-3). 32pp. Tiffany Dino becomes upset with her weight and decides to do something about it. (Rev: BL 11/15/95; SLJ 12/95)

2933 Sharmat, Mitchell. *Gregory, the Terrible Eater* (PS–3). Illus. by Jose Aruego and Ariane Dewey. 1980, Macmillan $16.00 (978-0-02-782250-2); Scholastic paper $4.99 (978-0-590-43350-1). 32pp. Gregory, a young goat, prefers a diet of fruit and vegetables to paper, shoes, and clothing.

2934 Shaw, Hannah. *Sneaky Weasel* (K–3). Illus. by author. 2009, Knopf $15.99 (978-0-375-85625-9). 32pp. When nobody comes to his party, Weasel, both sneaky and a bully, must reconsider the way he treats others; the funny text is extended by detailed illustrations of Weasel's misdeeds. (Rev: BL 4/15/09; SLJ 6/09)

2935 Shaw, Nancy. *Sheep Blast Off!* (PS–1). Illus. by Margot Apple. 2008, Houghton $15.00 (978-0-618-13168-6). 32pp. The sheep we know from books including *Sheep in a Jeep* (1986) find a spaceship and decide to explore. (Rev: BL 8/08; SLJ 4/08)

2936 Shaw, Nancy. *Sheep Take a Hike* (PS–1). Illus. by Margot Apple. 1994, Houghton $15.00 (978-0-395-68394-1). 32pp. When they get lost in the woods, a flock of sheep find their way home because of bits of wool left on bushes. (Rev: BL 9/15/94; HB 11/94; SLJ 9/94*)

2937 Shea, Bob. *New Socks* (PS–2). Illus. by author. 2007, Little, Brown $12.99 (978-0-316-01357-4). A self-confident little chicken flaunts his spiffy new orange socks, which will give him great prestige — even gaining recognition from the president. (Rev: SLJ 4/07)

2938 Sherry, Kevin. *I'm the Biggest Thing in the Ocean* (PS). Illus. by author. 2007, Dial $16.99 (978-0-8037-3192-9). A giant squid insists that he is bigger than anything else in the ocean, even when he's swallowed by a whale. Bathtub stickers are included. (Rev: SLJ 5/07)

2939 Shields, Carol Diggory. *The Bugliest Bug* (PS–2). Illus. by Scott Nash. 2002, Candlewick $15.99 (978-0-7636-0784-5). On her way to the Bugliest Bug Contest, Damselfly Dilly recognizes that the judges are really spiders in disguise. (Rev: HBG 10/02; SLJ 5/02)

2940 Shields, Carol Diggory. *Wombat Walkabout* (PS–2). Illus. by Sophie Blackall. 2009, Dutton $16.99 (978-0-525-47865-2). 32pp. Set in the Australian outback, this rhyming story involves six little wombats who are being trailed by a hungry dingo but are smart enough to outwit him. (Rev: BL 1/1–15/09; HB 3/09; LMC 5/09; SLJ 2/09)

2941 Shore, Diane Z., and Jessica Alexander. *Look Both Ways: A Cautionary Tale* (PS–2). Illus. by Teri Weidner. 2005, Bloomsbury $15.95 (978-1-58234-968-8). Little Filbert the squirrel learns to be careful crossing the street after a close call. (Rev: SLJ 7/05)

2942 Shulman, Lisa. *Over in the Meadow at the Big Ballet* (PS–K). Illus. by Sarah Massini. 2007, Putnam $16.99 (978-0-399-24289-2). All the animals in the meadow, under the guidance of a swan and a cat, put on a beautiful ballet performance in this rhyming story. (Rev: SLJ 5/07)

2943 Sidjanski, Brigitte. *Little Chicken and Little Duck* (PS–2). Trans. from German by Kathryn Bishop. Illus. by Sarah Emmanuelle Burg. 2007, Minedition $16.99 (978-0-698-40055-9). Can Little Chicken and Little Duck be friends, even when their mothers disapprove? It turns out that the answer is yes when the mothers discover their children aren't so different after all. (Rev: SLJ 6/07)

2944 Sierra, Judy. *Counting Crocodiles* (PS–1). Illus. by Will Hillenbrand. 1997, Harcourt $16.00 (978-0-15-200192-6). 40pp. A hungry monkey wants bananas from a neighboring island, but she is afraid that crocodiles will catch her if she tries to swim. (Rev: BL 9/1/97; HBG 3/98; SLJ 10/97)

2945 Sierra, Judy. *Good Night Dinosaurs* (PS–1). Illus. by Victoria Chess. 1996, Clarion $15.00 (978-0-395-65016-5). 32pp. Stylized drawings of dinosaurs portray them in humorous day-to-day activities, such as snoozing in the mud and sucking on baby bottles. (Rev: BCCB 3/96; BL 1/1–15/96; HB 7/96; SLJ 4/96)

2946 Sierra, Judy. *Preschool to the Rescue* (PS–K). Illus. by Will Hillenbrand. 2001, Harcourt $15.00 (978-0-15-202035-4). 32pp. A group of animal preschoolers come to the rescue of a pizza van and other vehicles that are stuck in a huge mud puddle. (Rev: BCCB 4/01; BL 4/15/01; HB 5/01; HBG 10/01; SLJ 5/01)

2947 Siminovich, Lorena. *Alex and Lulu: Two of a Kind* (PS–1). Illus. by author. 2009, Candlewick $14.99 (978-0-7636-4423-9). 32pp. A young girl cat named Lulu and a boy dog called Alex consider their differences but decide that they don't matter. (Rev: BL 5/1/09; SLJ 5/09)

2948 Simmonds, Posy. *Baker Cat* (PS–2). Illus. 2006, Red Fox paper $8.99 (978-0-09-945596-7). 32pp. The baker's cat is so overworked that the mice take pity on him, but this entente cordiale may have its limits. (Rev: BL 3/1/06)

2949 Simmons, Jane. *Come Along, Daisy!* (PS). Illus. 1998, Little, Brown $12.95 (978-0-316-79790-0). 32pp. Daisy, a duckling, becomes distracted by the pond life around her, gets lost, and decides not to stray again after her mother finds her. (Rev: BCCB 9/98; BL 6/1–15/98*; HBG 10/98; SLJ 8/98)

2950 Simmons, Jane. *Daisy Says "Here We Go 'Round the Mulberry Bush"* (PS). Illus. by author. 2002, Little, Brown $7.95 (978-0-316-79811-2). Duckling Daisy enjoys dancing along to the song until it's time for bed in this board book. Also use *Daisy Says "If You're Happy and You Know It"* (2002). (Rev: SLJ 8/02)

2951 Simmons, Jane. *Together* (PS–K). Illus. by author. 2007, Knopf $15.99 (978-0-375-84339-6). 32pp. Even though they are friends, dogs Mousse and Nut have a disagreement and must learn to accept each other's differences. (Rev: BL 7/07; SLJ 8/07)

2952 Simmons, Steven J. *Percy to the Rescue* (PS–3). Illus. by Kim Howard. 1998, Charlesbridge $15.95 (978-0-88106-390-5). 32pp. Percy, a blue pigeon who visits the tourist sites in London daily, helps rescue two boys who are trapped on an island in a park lake. (Rev: BL 8/98; HBG 3/99)

2953 Simon, Francesca. *Hugo and the Bully Frogs* (PS–1). Illus. by Caroline Jayne Church. 1999, David & Charles $14.95 (978-1-86233-093-1). Poor Hugo, a little frog, is intimidated by three big bullies in his pond until he gets help from a duck. (Rev: SLJ 3/00)

2954 Simon, Francesca. *Where Are You?* (PS). Illus. by David Melling. 1998, Peachtree $12.95 (978-1-56145-179-1). 32pp. Harry, a little dog, follows his interest in food while in a supermarket. When he becomes separated from Grandpa, though, he experiences the fear of being lost. (Rev: BL 12/1/98; HBG 3/99; SLJ 5/99)

2955 Simont, Marc. *The Goose That Almost Got Cooked* (K–2). Illus. 1997, Scholastic $15.95 (978-0-590-69075-1). 40pp. A Canada goose is happy to leave the flock and join some white geese on a farm until she realizes that in this situation she might become somebody's dinner. (Rev: BL 11/1/97; HBG 3/98; SLJ 8/97*)

2956 Sklansky, Amy E. *The Duck Who Played the Kazoo* (PS–K). Illus. by Tiphanie Beeke. 2008, Clarion $15.00 (978-0-618-42854-0). 32pp. A duck's talent with the kazoo helps him make friends when a hurricane sweeps him from his home lake. (Rev: BCCB 2/08; BL 1/1–15/08; SLJ 2/08)

2957 Slate, Joseph. *Miss Bindergarten Plans a Circus with Kindergarten* (PS–2). Illus. by Ashley Wolff. 2002, Dutton $16.99 (978-0-525-46884-4). Miss Bindergarten and her alphabetical charges each have a role to play in the circus. (Rev: HBG 3/03; SLJ 12/02)

2958 Slate, Joseph. *Story Time for Little Porcupine* (PS–3). Illus. by Jacqueline Rogers. 2000, Marshall Cavendish $15.95 (978-0-7614-5073-3). 32pp. At bedtime Papa and Little Porcupine trade stories similar to folktales, like Papa's story on how a trickster moon got the best of Big Porcupine. (Rev: BL 10/15/00; HBG 3/01; SLJ 10/00)

2959 Smallman, Steve. *The Lamb Who Came for Dinner* (PS–K). Illus. by Joelle Dreidemy. 2007, Tiger Tales $15.95 (978-1-58925-506-3). 32pp. A little lamb knocks on an old wolf's door just in time for dinner, but the lamb's sweet nature saves it from the cooking pot. (Rev: SLJ 10/07)

2960 Smallman, Steve. *The Very Greedy Bee* (PS–K). Illus. by Jack Tickle. 2007, Tiger Tales $15.95 (978-1-58925-065-9). A greedy bee learns to share when he is too full of honey to move and kindhearted insects help him home. (Rev: SLJ 5/07)

2961 Smee, Nicola. *Clip-Clop* (PS–K). Illus. by author. 2006, Boxer Bks. $18.95 (978-1-905417-09-4). Mr. Horse takes his animal friends on a rollicking ride that ends with a fall into a haystack. (Rev: SLJ 6/06*)

2962 Smith, Mary Ann, and Katie Smith Milway. *Cappuccina Goes to Town* (PS–2). Illus. by Eugenie Fernandes. 2002, Kids Can $15.95 (978-1-55074-807-9). Cappuccina goes shopping, and all the shopkeepers seem oblivious to the fact that she's a cow. (Rev: HBG 10/02; SLJ 8/02)

2963 Sneed, Brad. *Deputy Harvey and the Ant Cow Caper* (K–3). Illus. by author. 2005, Dial $16.99 (978-0-8037-3023-6). Deputy Harvey of Ant Hill vows to track down the culprits responsible for rustling half of the community's herd of ant cows. (Rev: SLJ 11/05)

2964 Snow, Alan. *The Truth About Cats* (K–4). Illus. 1996, Little, Brown $14.95 (978-0-316-80282-6). 32pp. With great daring, this book reveals that cats are really aliens from the Planet Nip. A companion to *How Dogs Really Work!* (1993). (Rev: BL 4/15/96; SLJ 3/96)

2965 Soto, Gary. *Chato Goes Cruisin'* (PS–2). Illus. by Susan Guevara. 2005, Penguin $16.99 (978-0-399-23974-8). 32pp. Disappointed to find themselves on a dog-only cruise, Chato and Novio Boy, cool cats from LA, nonetheless set off in search of help when the dogs all fall ill. (Rev: BL 5/1/05; SLJ 6/05)

2966 Soto, Gary. *Chato's Kitchen* (PS–3). Illus. by Susan Guevara. 1995, Penguin $16.99 (978-0-399-22658-8). 32pp. In his Los Angeles barrio home, the cat Chato extends an invitation to some mice to come to dinner. (Rev: BL 3/1/95; HB 9/95; SLJ 7/95*)

2967 Spanyol, Jessica. *Little Neighbors on Sunnyside Street* (PS). Illus. by author. 2007, Candlewick $16.99 (978-0-7636-2986-1). 64pp. Sunnyside Street is a busy place, with animal neighbors enjoying all kinds of activities, attending a party, and heading for bed. (Rev: BL 7/07)

2968 Spelman, Cornelia Maude. *When I Care About Others* (K–2). Illus. by Kathy Parkinson. Series: The Way I Feel. 2002, Whitman LB $15.99 (978-0-8075-8889-5). 24pp. Readers are encouraged to be kind to others through the simple story of a little bear shown treating others as he likes to be treated. (Rev: BL 7/02; HBG 10/02; SLJ 7/02)

2969 Spelman, Cornelia Maude. *When I Feel Angry* (PS–1). Illus. by Nancy Cote. 2000, Whitman $15.99 (978-0-8075-8888-8). 32pp. A young bunny finds that he can deal in a number of ways with the anger he sometimes feels: by resting, crying, exercising, or asking for help. (Rev: BL 3/15/00; HBG 10/00; SLJ 4/00)

2970 Spelman, Cornelia Maude. *When I Feel Sad* (PS–2). Illus. by Kathy Parkinson. Series: The Way I Feel. 2002, Whitman LB $15.99 (978-0-8075-8891-8). A guinea pig describes what makes her feel sad. (Rev: HBG 3/03; SLJ 1/03)

2971 Spelman, Cornelia Maude. *When I Feel Scared* (PS–K). Illus. by Kathy Parkinson. Series: The Way I Feel. 2002, Whitman LB $15.99 (978-0-8075-8890-1). 24pp. A little bear talks about his fears, how some fears help him survive, and how others are unnecessary. (Rev: BL 4/15/02; HBG 10/02; SLJ 7/02)

2972 Spinelli, Eileen. *Bath Time* (PS). Illus. by Janet Pedersen. 2003, Marshall Cavendish $14.95 (978-0-7614-5117-4). 32pp. A little penguin has lots of fun preparing for and then having his bath. (Rev: BL 3/15/03; HBG 10/03; SLJ 6/03)

2973 Spinelli, Eileen. *Callie Cat, Ice Skater* (PS–2). Illus. by Anne Kennedy. 2007, Albert Whitman $16.95 (978-0-8075-1042-1). 32pp. Callie is a little cat who loves ice skating and agrees to enter a competition even though she is happiest when skating purely for pleasure. (Rev: BCCB 12/08; BL 10/15/07; SLJ 12/07)

2974 Spinelli, Eileen. *Peace Week in Miss Fox's Class* (PS–2). Illus. by Anne Kennedy. 2009, Albert Whitman $16.99 (978-0-8075-6379-3). 32pp. Peace Week — no quarrels, be nice to others — proves challenging but possible for Miss Fox's animal class. (Rev: BL 4/15/09; LMC 10/09; SLJ 5/09)

2975 Spinelli, Eileen. *Princess Pig* (PS–2). Illus. by Tim Bowers. 2009, Knopf $16.99 (978-0-375-84571-0). 40pp. When the wind bestows a princess's scarf on a young pig, she decides she is indeed royal. (Rev: BL 5/1/09; SLJ 6/09)

2976 Spinelli, Eileen. *Something to Tell the Grandcows* (PS–2). Illus. by Bill Slavin. 2004, Eerdmans $16.00 (978-0-8028-5236-6). 32pp. Hoping to have a story to impress her grandcows, Emmadine the cow signs up to join Byrd's 1933 expedition to the South Pole. (Rev: BL 4/1/04; SLJ 3/04)

2977 Spinelli, Eileen. *Three Pebbles and a Song* (PS–2). Illus. by S. D. Schindler. 2003, Dial $16.99 (978-0-8037-2528-7). Moses, a young mouse, is distracted by the world around him and fails to collect the supplies his family needs, but Mama, Papa, and sister Missy have taken care of this and he is able to entertain them with his own discoveries. (Rev: HBG 4/04; SLJ 9/03)

2978 Spurling, Margaret. *Bilby Moon* (PS–2). Illus. by Danny Snell. 2001, Kane $14.95 (978-1-929132-06-5). 32pp. Bilby wonders where the moon has gone and is eventually reassured that it will come back. (Rev: BL 5/1/01; HBG 10/01)

2979 Stadler, Alexander. *Beverly Billingsly Borrows a Book* (PS–2). Illus. 2002, Harcourt $16.00 (978-0-15-202510-6). 32pp. Beverly is thrilled to have her own library card, until she hears some scary rumors about what happens to children with overdue books. (Rev: BL 3/15/02; HBG 3/03; SLJ 4/02)

2980 Stadler, Alexander. *Beverly Billingsly Takes a Bow* (K–2). Illus. by author. 2003, Harcourt $16.00 (978-0-15-216816-2). A last-minute case of the jitters keeps Beverly from winning one of the lead roles in the school play, but on opening night she comes to the rescue when the star performer suffers from her own stage fright. (Rev: HBG 10/03; SLJ 4/03)

2981 Stadler, Alexander. *Beverly Billingsly Takes the Cake* (PS–2). Illus. 2005, Harcourt $16.00 (978-0-15-205357-4). 32pp. When Beverly's attempts to make a perfect cake are foiled, her mother helps her come up with a solution. (Rev: BL 4/1/05; SLJ 4/05)

2982 Steffensmeier, Alexander. *Millie Waits for the Mail* (K–2). Illus. by author. 2007, Walker $16.95 (978-0-8027-9662-2). Millie the cow loves to get mail — so much so that in her enthusiasm she crushes the mailman's bike. Funny illustrations add to the story. (Rev: SLJ 8/07)

2983 Steig, William. *Doctor De Soto* (K–3). Illus. by author. 1982, Farrar $16.00 (978-0-374-31803-1). A mouse dentist outwits a fox.

2984 Steig, William. *Farmer Palmer's Wagon Ride* (K–2). Illus. by author. 1992, Farrar paper $4.95 (978-0-374-42268-4). Farmer Palmer, a pig, and the hired hand, a donkey, have a disastrous ride home from the market in this engaging nonsensical bit of fun.

2985 Steig, William. *Gorky Rises* (1–3). Illus. by author. 1986, Farrar paper $4.95 (978-0-374-42784-9). 32pp. A frog named Gorky concocts a formula that sends him on a magical journey.

2986 Steig, William. *Solomon the Rusty Nail* (K–2). Illus. by author. 1985, Farrar paper $6.95 (978-0-374-46903-0). 32pp. A rabbit's ability to change himself into a rusty nail whenever he wishes leads him to some interesting adventures and keeps him away from the prowling cat. (Rev: BCCB 3/86; BL 1/1/86; SLJ 2/86)

2987 Steig, William. *Sylvester and the Magic Pebble* (K–3). Illus. by author. 1988, Simon & Schuster paper $5.99 (978-0-671-66269-1). 32pp. A donkey who collects pebbles finds a red stone that will grant wishes — and off Sylvester goes on a series of adventures. Caldecott Medal winner, 1970.

2988 Steinberg, Laya. *Thesaurus Rex* (PS–3). Illus. by Debbie Harter. 2003, Barefoot Books $15.99 (978-1-84148-042-8). Readers follow Thesaurus Rex, a little turquoise-colored dinosaur, through a typical, vocabulary-expanding day of junior dino antics. (Rev: HBG 4/04; LMC 1/04; SLJ 12/03)

2989 Stephens, Helen. *Ahoyty-Toyty* (K–2). Illus. by author. 2004, Random LB $16.99 (978-0-385-75040-0). Two dogs learn about social classes while on a cruise. (Rev: SLJ 6/04)

2990 Stevens, Janet, and Susan Stevens Crummel. *Cook-a-Doodle-Doo!* (PS–3). Illus. 1999, Harcourt $17.00 (978-0-15-201924-2). 48pp. A group of farm animals are happy to help Big Brown Rooster prepare strawberry shortcake in this delightful farce. (Rev: BCCB 7–8/99; BL 4/15/99*; HB 5/99; HBG 10/99; SLJ 4/99)

2991 Stevens, Janet, and Susan Stevens Crummel. *Jackalope* (K–3). Illus. by Janet Stevens. 2003, Harcourt $17.00 (978-0-15-216736-3). 56pp. A wild and wacky multilayered story of a jackrabbit who wants to be scary and his fairy godrabbit's humorous efforts to oblige. (Rev: BL 3/15/03; HBG 10/03; SLJ 7/03)

2992 Stevenson, James. *Flying Feet* (1–3). Illus. 2004, Greenwillow $15.99 (978-0-06-051975-9). 48pp. The animal residents of Mud Flat become dance crazy when a team of (larcenous) traveling tap dancers comes to town. (Rev: BL 2/1/04; SLJ 3/04)

2993 Stevenson, James. *Heat Wave at Mud Flat* (K–2). Illus. 1997, Greenwillow $14.89 (978-0-688-14206-3). 32pp. During a very hot, dry period, a rainmaker visits Mud Flat and the animal inhabitants react in different ways. (Rev: BL 5/15/97; HB 7/97; SLJ 5/97*)

2994 Stevenson, James. *The Most Amazing Dinosaur* (PS–3). Illus. 2000, Greenwillow LB $15.89 (978-0-688-16433-1). 32pp. When Wilfred, a rat, takes refuge from a snowstorm in a natural history museum, he is given a tour by other resident creatures. (Rev: BL 7/00; HBG 10/00; SLJ 6/00)

2995 Stevenson, James. *Mud Flat Spring* (PS–2). Illus. 1999, Greenwillow LB $14.89 (978-0-688-15773-9). 40pp. In nine short stories, the various animals of Mud Flat greet the spring. (Rev: BL 5/1/99; HBG 10/99; SLJ 3/99)

2996 Stewart, Amber. *I'm Big Enough* (PS–K). Illus. by Layn Marlow. 2007, Scholastic $12.99 (978-0-439-90666-1). Bean hides her beloved Blankie for safekeeping, then forgets where she left it and realizes she can do without it. (Rev: SLJ 5/07)

2997 Stewart, Amber. *No Babysitters Allowed* (PS–1). Illus. by Laura Rankin. 2008, Bloomsbury $16.99 (978-1-59990-154-1). 32pp. Just the thought of an evening with a new babysitter gives Hopscotch the bunny a tummy ache. (Rev: SLJ 11/08)

2998 Stewart, Amber. *Rabbit Ears* (PS–2). Illus. by Laura Rankin. 2006, Bloomsbury $16.95 (978-1-58234-959-6). 32pp. Hopscotch will do almost anything to avoid having his ears washed and it comes as a revelation when he sees his older cousin Bobtail washing his own. (Rev: BL 2/1/06; SLJ 4/06)

2999 Stewart, Paul. *A Little Bit of Winter* (PS–K). Illus. by Chris Riddell. 1999, HarperCollins $14.95 (978-0-06-028278-3). 24pp. Before Hedgehog hibernates, he asks Rabbit to save him a bit of winter, and Rabbit obliges by saving a snowball. (Rev: BL 3/1/99; HBG 10/99; SLJ 3/99)

3000 Stewart, Paul. *Rabbit's Wish* (PS–1). Illus. by Chris Riddell. 2001, HarperCollins $12.95 (978-0-06-029518-9). 32pp. Rabbit and Hedgehog get a chance to play together — a rare event, since Hedgehog sleeps during the day. (Rev: BL 10/15/01; HBG 10/01; SLJ 7/01)

3001 Stickland, Paul. *Dinosaur Stomp: A Monster Pop-Up* (PS–K). Illus. 1996, Dutton $16.99 (978-0-525-45591-2). This pop-up book involves dancing dinosaurs. (Rev: BL 12/15/96; SLJ 2/97)

3002 Stiegemeyer, Julie. *Cheep! Cheep!* (PS–K). Illus. by Carol Baicker-McKee. 2006, Bloomsbury $9.95 (978-1-58234-682-3). A simple story for very young children about three chicks who fall asleep while watching over an egg. (Rev: SLJ 3/06)

3003 Stock, Catherine. *A Porc in New York* (PS–2). Illus. 2007, Holiday $16.95 (978-0-8234-1994-4). 32pp. Having already been introduced to the delights of Paris in *A Spree in Paree* (2004), French farmer Monmouton's farm animals decide it's time to see New York City and see such wonders as "Blooming Dells." (Rev: BL 3/15/07; HBG 10/07)

3004 Stock, Catherine. *A Spree in Paree* (PS–2). Illus. 2004, Holiday House $16.95 (978-0-8234-1720-9). 32pp. Monsieur Monmouton is persuaded to take his farm animals to Paris, where they act like crass tourists and generally have a great time throwing their weight around. (Rev: BL 3/15/04; SLJ 5/04)

3005 Stoeke, Janet Morgan. *Minerva Louise and the Red Truck* (PS–1). Illus. 2002, Dutton $14.99 (978-0-525-46909-4). 32pp. The silly hen Minerva Louise gets taken for a ride in the farm truck and, as usual, misinterprets everything she sees. (Rev: BL 12/1/02; HB 11/02; HBG 3/03; SLJ 9/02)

3006 Sturges, Philemon. *This Little Pirate* (PS–K). Illus. by Amy Walrod. 2005, Dutton $16.99 (978-0-525-46440-2). 40pp. Colorful illustrations and humorous text follow two bands of pig pirates fighting over a box until they become so tired they declare a truce and settle down to enjoy its contents. (Rev: BL 6/1–15/05)

3007 Suteyev, V. *Mushroom in the Rain* (K–2). Trans. by Mirra Ginsburg. Illus. by Jose Aruego and Ariane Dewey. 1987, Macmillan paper $5.99 (978-0-689-71441-2). 32pp. An ant huddled under a mushroom in the rain makes room for a variety of animals. A reissued 1974 book.

3008 Sutton, Jane. *The Trouble with Cauliflower* (PS–2). Illus. by Jim Harris. 2006, Dial $16.99 (978-0-8037-2707-6). 32pp. Mortimer the koala is sure cauliflower brings bad luck, but he eats a bowl or two to please his friend Sadie. (Rev: BL 2/15/06; SLJ 3/06)

3009 Swallow, Pamela C. *Groundhog Gets a Say* (K–2). Illus. by Denise Brunkus. 2005, Putnam $15.99 (978-0-399-23876-5). 40pp. A proud groundhog expound on the attributes of his species in this humorous text with excellent illustrations. (Rev: BL 12/15/05; SLJ 1/06)

3010 Sykes, Julie. *Dora's Eggs* (PS). Illus. by Jane Chapman. 1997, Little Tiger $14.95 (978-1-888444-09-4). Dora the hen is disappointed when none of the animals pay attention to her first eggs; but when they hatch, it is a different matter. (Rev: HBG 3/98; SLJ 12/97)

3011 Sykes, Julie. *I Don't Want to Take a Bath* (PS–1). Illus. by Tim Warnes. 1997, Little Tiger $14.95 (978-1-888444-20-9). 32pp. Little Tiger avoids taking a bath by running into the jungle to play with friends. (Rev: BL 12/1/97; HBG 3/98)

3012 Sykes, Julie. *Little Tiger's Big Surprise!* (PS–K). Illus. by Tim Warnes. 1999, Little Tiger $14.95 (978-1-888444-52-0). Little Tiger runs away when he is told he will soon have a little brother or sister but, when he returns, he is delighted with the new baby. (Rev: HBG 3/00; SLJ 2/00)

3013 Sykes, Julie. *Smudge* (PS–K). Illus. by Jane Chapman. 1998, Little Tiger $14.95 (978-1-888444-44-5). 32pp. When Smudge, a dog, and his friends are caught in a rainstorm, they try to get into a house for shelter, but their attempts fail — until Smudge gets a winning idea. (Rev: BL 10/15/98; HBG 3/99; SLJ 10/98)

3014 Sykes, Julie. *Wait for Me, Little Tiger!* (PS–1). Illus. by Tim Warnes. 2001, Tiger Tales $14.95 (978-1-58925-009-3). Little Tiger reluctantly takes his annoying little sister out to play, and of course she disappears. (Rev: SLJ 7/01)

3015 Tafuri, Nancy. *The Busy Little Squirrel* (PS–K). Illus. by author. 2007, Simon & Schuster $15.99 (978-0-689-87341-6). 32pp. Attractive illustrations abound in this autumn-themed story about a busy squirrel preparing for the winter in spite of his friends' offers of fun. (Rev: BL 6/1–15/07; SLJ 11/07)

3016 Tafuri, Nancy. *Goodnight, My Duckling* (PS). Illus. 2005, Scholastic $16.95 (978-0-439-39881-7). 32pp. A turtle comes to the rescue of a straggler duckling. (Rev: BL 1/1–15/05; SLJ 4/05)

3017 Tafuri, Nancy. *Have You Seen My Duckling?* (PS–2). Illus. by author. 1984, Greenwillow $17.89 (978-0-688-02798-8); Morrow paper $6.99 (978-0-688-10994-3). 24pp. Mother Duck asks a number of animals if they have seen her missing duckling.

3018 Tafuri, Nancy. *Where Did Bunny Go?* (PS). 2001, Scholastic $15.95 (978-0-439-16959-2). 32pp. Bunny disappears during a game of hide-and-seek and his friends worry that he is angry until he returns to reassure them of his friendship in this gentle story. (Rev: BL 12/1/01; HBG 3/02; SLJ 12/01)

3019 Tafuri, Nancy. *You Are Special, Little One* (PS–1). Illus. by author. 2003, Scholastic $16.95 (978-0-439-39879-4). Six different animal babies ask their parents about the qualities that make them special. (Rev: HBG 4/04; SLJ 10/03)

3020 Takao, Yuko. *A Winter Concert* (K–2). Illus. by author. 1997, Millbrook LB $18.40 (978-0-7613-0301-5). As a mouse listens to a concert, his black-and-white world slowly becomes one of color. (Rev: HBG 3/98; SLJ 1/98)

3021 Talley, Linda. *Thank You, Meiling* (K–3). Illus. by Itoko Maeno. 1999, MarshMedia $16.95 (978-1-55942-118-8). 30pp. A young duck learns about courtesy and Chinese traditions as she accompanies a boy on his preparations for the Chinese Moon Festival celebration. (Rev: SLJ 3/00)

3022 Tankard, Jeremy. *Boo Hoo Bird* (K–3). Illus. by author. 2009, Scholastic $14.99 (978-0-545-06570-2). 32pp. When Boo Hoo Bird gets a boo-boo, all

the other animals try to offer consolation. (Rev: BL 4/1/09; HB 5/09; SLJ 4/09)

3023 Tankard, Jeremy. *Grumpy Bird* (PS–K). Illus. by author. 2007, Scholastic $12.99 (978-0-439-85147-3). Too grumpy to fly, Bird decides to take a walk through the forest and is joined by one animal after another until the walk has turned into a game and brightened Bird's mood remarkably. (Rev: SLJ 2/07)

3024 Tashiro, Chisato. *Five Nice Mice* (PS–2). Trans. by Sayako Uchida. Illus. by author. 2007, Penguin $16.99 (978-0-698-40058-0). 32pp. Gorgeous watercolor and pastel illustrations bring to life this story of five mice who, after being rejected by the frogs' orchestra, decide to form their own musical ensemble. (Rev: BL 5/15/07; SLJ 6/07)

3025 Taylor, Eleanor. *Beep, Beep, Let's Go!* (PS). Illus. 2005, Bloomsbury $15.95 (978-1-58234-973-2). 32pp. Various animals use various forms of transport to get to the beach, where they have a wonderful time. (Rev: BL 5/1/05)

3026 Taylor, Eleanor. *My Friend the Monster* (PS–K). Illus. by author. 2008, Bloomsbury $16.95 (978-1-59990-232-6). 32pp. When his family moves to a new house, a lonely little fox befriends the giant monster he finds hiding beneath his bed. (Rev: BL 9/1/08; SLJ 9/08)

3027 Taylor, Thomas. *The Loudest Roar* (PS–3). Illus. by author. 2003, Scholastic $15.95 (978-0-439-50130-9). The animals of the jungle decide to teach a noisy young tiger a lesson. (Rev: HBG 10/03; SLJ 3/03)

3028 Teague, Mark. *Funny Farm* (PS–K). Illus. by author. 2009, Scholastic $16.99 (978-0-439-91499-4). 32pp. Edward, a big city dog, gets a dose of country living when he visits the farm. (Rev: BL 11/15/08; SLJ 4/09)

3029 Teague, Mark. *Pigsty* (PS–3). Illus. 1994, Scholastic $15.95 (978-0-590-45915-0). 32pp. Even messy Wendell, a pig, resents his friends creating chaos in his room. (Rev: BL 9/15/94; SLJ 10/94*)

3030 Teckentrup, Britta. *Big Smelly Bear* (PS). Illus. by author. 2007, Boxer Bks. $12.95 (978-1-905417-37-3). Big Smelly Bear makes a friend after he finally takes a bath in this cheery book about the value of cleanliness. (Rev: SLJ 6/07)

3031 Tekavec, Heather. *Storm Is Coming!* (PS–1). Illus. by Margaret Spengler. 2002, Dial $16.99 (978-0-8037-2626-0). 32pp. A group of frightened animals bunch together in the barn, anticipating the arrival of Storm and comforted by the fact that the howling wind, flashing light, and rain will scare him away. (Rev: BL 3/1/02; HBG 10/02; SLJ 3/02)

3032 Tekavec, Heather. *What's That Awful Smell?* (PS–2). Illus. by Margaret Spengler. 2004, Dial $15.99 (978-0-8037-2660-4). A bad smell in the barn has the animals searching for its source, which turns out not to be the piglet they first suspect. (Rev: HB 7/04; SLJ 4/04)

3033 Testa, Fulvio. *Time to Get Out* (PS–K). Illus. by author. 1993, Tambourine LB $13.93 (978-0-688-12908-8). A cumulative story about a boy and several animals that join forces to track down a loud noise they hear on a tropical island. (Rev: SLJ 10/93)

3034 Theobald, Joseph. *Marvin Wanted More!* (PS–3). Illus. by author. 2003, Bloomsbury $16.95 (978-0-7475-5631-2). Marvin is a sheep with an uncontrollable appetite, and the consequences just grow and grow. (Rev: SLJ 9/03)

3035 Thompson, Lauren. *Little Quack's New Friend* (PS–K). Illus. by Derek Anderson. 2006, Simon & Schuster $14.95 (978-0-689-86893-1). Little Quack the duck meets Little Ribbit the frog, and together the new friends enjoy a fun-filled day at the pond. (Rev: SLJ 2/06)

3036 Thompson, Lauren. *Mouse's First Day of School* (PS). Illus. by Buket Erdogan. 2003, Simon & Schuster $12.95 (978-0-689-84727-1). Mouse finds many items of interest when he finds his way into the classroom in this small book with large, bold type. (Rev: BL 7/03; HBG 4/04; SLJ 9/03)

3037 Thompson, Lauren. *Mouse's First Fall* (PS). Illus. by Buket Erdogan. 2006, Simon & Schuster $12.95 (978-0-689-85837-6). 32pp. In this picture-book celebration of fall, Mouse and his sister Minka frolic among the brightly colored leaves. Also use *Mouse's First Summer* (2004) and *Mouse's First Spring* and *Mouse's First Snow* (both 2005). (Rev: BL 9/15/06; SLJ 10/06)

3038 Thompson, Lauren. *Wee Little Chick* (PS–1). Illus. by John Butler. 2008, Simon & Schuster $14.99 (978-1-4169-3468-4). 32pp. She may be small but the wee little chick has big ambitions. (Rev: BL 5/15/08; SLJ 1/08)

3039 Thoms, Susan Collins. *Cesar Takes a Break* (1–3). Illus. by Rogé. 2008, Sterling $14.95 (978-1-4027-3653-7). 32pp. It's spring break and the children are all gone, but Cesar the 2nd-grade class iguana finds there's lots of fun things to do around school. (Rev: BL 5/1/08; SLJ 6/08)

3040 Thomson, Pat. *Drat That Fat Cat* (PS–1). Illus. by Ailie Busby. 2003, Scholastic $15.95 (978-0-439-47195-4). In this bright and bouncy cumulative tale, a very fat cat grows even fatter as, one by one, he consumes virtually everything he encounters. (Rev: BCCB 1/04; BL 1/1–15/04; HB 1/04; HBG 4/04; SLJ 12/03)

3041 Tomlinson, Jill. *The Cat Who Wanted to Go Home* (PS–2). Illus. by Paul Howard. 2006, Egmont $17.99 (978-1-4052-0600-6). A French cat named Suzy, looking for a comfortable place for a nap, climbs unsuspecting into the basket of a hot-air balloon and awakes to find herself on the way to England. (Rev: SLJ 1/07)

3042 Tompert, Ann. *Just a Little Bit* (PS–K). Illus. by Lynn Munsinger. 1993, Houghton $17.00 (978-0-395-51527-3). 32pp. In this cumulative tale, several animals try to help Mouse balance the scales when he tries to seesaw with Elephant. (Rev: BL 11/1/93; HB 9/93; SLJ 12/93)

3043 Tompert, Ann. *Nothing Sticks Like a Shadow* (PS–3). Illus. by Lynn Munsinger. 1988, Houghton paper $7.95 (978-0-395-47950-6). 32pp. Rabbit tries to get rid of his shadow.

3044 Trewin, Trudie. *I Lost My Kisses* (PS–K). Illus. by Nick Bland. 2008, Scholastic $14.99 (978-0-545-05557-4). 32pp. An Australian cow in polka-dot tights searches high and low for her lost kisses. (Rev: BL 3/15/08; SLJ 4/08)

3045 Trivizas, Eugene. *The Three Little Wolves and the Big Bad Pig* (K–4). Illus. by Helen Oxenbury. 1993, Macmillan $17.00 (978-0-689-50569-0). 32pp. In this role-reversal story, three wolves are menaced by a big, bad pig who knocks their house down with a sledgehammer when huffing and puffing won't do the trick. (Rev: BCCB 9/93; BL 9/1/93; SLJ 12/93*)

3046 Turnbull, Ann. *Too Tired* (K–2). Illus. by Emma Chichester Clark. 1994, Harcourt $13.95 (978-0-15-200549-8). 32pp. There is a crisis on the ark when Noah discovers that the sloths are too tired to board. (Rev: BL 3/15/94; SLJ 4/94)

3047 Tyson, Leigh Ann. *An Interview with Harry the Tarantula* (PS–3). Illus. by Henrik Drescher. 2003, National Geographic $15.95 (978-0-7922-5122-4). A spoof talk-show in which Harry Spyder reveals to Katy Did some of the details of a frightening experience with a human, conveying factual information on tarantulas in the process. (Rev: HBG 4/04; SLJ 12/03)

3048 Ungerer, Tomi. *Crictor* (PS–2). Illus. by author. 1958, HarperCollins paper $6.99 (978-0-06-443044-9). 32pp. A boa constrictor becomes the hero of a small French town after he captures a burglar.

3049 Urbanovic, Jackie. *Duck at the Door* (PS–2). 2007, HarperCollins $17.99 (978-0-06-121438-7). 32pp. Max the duck, left behind when his flock flies south, takes refuge in a house already full of pets and makes a bit of a nuisance of himself. (Rev: BL 4/1/07; SLJ 3/07)

3050 Urbanovic, Jackie. *Duck Soup* (PS–2). Illus. by author. 2008, HarperCollins $16.99 (978-0-06-121441-7). 32pp. There's a feather in the soup! Could Duck have fallen in? In a chaotic panic his friends attempt to save him. (Rev: BCCB 2/08; BL 1/1–15/08; SLJ 1/08)

3051 Usui, Kanako. *The Fantastic Mr. Wani* (PS–1). Illus. by author. 2006, Tiger Tales $15.95 (978-1-58925-054-3). In a rush to get to a party, Mr. Wani the crocodile gets help from a series of kindly creatures. (Rev: SLJ 4/06)

3052 Vail, Rachel. *Over the Moon* (K–2). Illus. by Scott Nash. 1998, Orchard $15.95 (978-0-531-30068-8). 32pp. A creative monkey director is adapting the rhyme "Hey Diddle Diddle" for the stage but has problems getting the cow to jump over the moon. (Rev: BL 9/15/98; HBG 3/99; SLJ 9/98)

3053 Valckx, Catharina. *Lizette's Green Sock* (PS–K). Illus. 2005, Clarion $15.00 (978-0-618-45298-9). 32pp. A little bird is thrilled to find a single green sock, and sports it on her foot before moving it to her head. (Rev: BL 5/1/05; SLJ 5/05)

3054 Van Allsburg, Chris. *Two Bad Ants* (1–4). Illus. by author. 1988, Houghton $18.95 (978-0-395-48668-9). 32pp. The story of two adventuresome ants. (Rev: BCCB 12/88; BL 10/1/88; SLJ 11/88)

3055 van Genechten, Guido. *Ricky* (PS–2). Illus. by author. 2008, Clavis $16.95 (978-1-60537-009-5). 30pp. Ricky the rabbit takes a lot of teasing on account of his floppy ear. (Rev: BLO 1/13/09)

3056 Van Leeuwen, Jean. *Chicken Soup* (PS–1). Illus. by David Gavril. 2009, Abrams $16.95 (978-0-8109-8326-7). 32pp. When they hear the big soup pot is out in the farm kitchen, all the chickens rush to hide — except for Little Chickie, who has a cold. (Rev: BL 5/1/09; SLJ 4/09)

3057 van Lieshout, Maria. *Peep! A Little Book About Taking a Leap* (PS–K). Illus. by author. Series: A Little Book. 2009, Feiwel & Friends $12.99 (978-0-312-36915-6). 48pp. On a walk with his family a little yellow chick called Peep is scared to jump off a high curb. (Rev: BL 5/1/09; SLJ 3/09)

3058 Van Straaten, Harmen. *Duck's Tale* (K–2). Trans. from Dutch by Marianne Martens. Illus. by author. 2007, North-South $16.95 (978-0-7358-2133-0). Duck can't write and Toad can't read, but they can pretend, so Toad "reads" a story that Duck has "written" to a group of their animal friends. (Rev: SLJ 5/07)

3059 Van Straaten, Harmen. *For Me?* (PS–3). Trans. by MaryChris Bradley. Illus. by author. 2007, North-South $16.95 (978-0-7358-2163-7). 32pp. Seeking to make new friends, a newcomer sends Duck and each of his neighbors an anonymous red rose. (Rev: BL 2/15/08; SLJ 1/08)

3060 Varley, Susan. *Badger's Parting Gifts* (1–4). Illus. by author. 1984, Morrow paper $7.99 (978-0-688-11518-0). 32pp. After initial grief, the animals retain happy memories of their dead friend, Badger. (Rev: SLJ 1/00)

3061 Vaughan, Marcia. *Kissing Coyotes* (K–4). Illus. by Kenneth J. Spengler. 2002, Rising Moon $15.95 (978-0-87358-814-0). Jack Rabbit's boasting is out of hand and his animal friends require that he follow through on his claims. (Rev: SLJ 2/03)

3062 Vere, Ed. *The Getaway* (K–2). Illus. by author. 2007, Simon & Schuster $16.99 (978-1-4169-4789-9). 32pp. In this adventure, a mouse cheese thief named Fingers McGraw asks readers to be on the lookout for an elephant, Detective Jumbo Wayne, Jr., who chases him through street scenes illustrated with bright mixed-media. (Rev: BCCB 9/07; BL 11/15/07; SLJ 1/08)

3063 Vischer, Phil. *Sidney and Norman: A Tale of Two Pigs* (K–3). Illus. by Justin Gerard. 2006, Thomas Nelson $15.99 (978-1-4003-0834-7). 32pp. In this fable-like tale of two very different pigs who are invited to visit God, young readers learn some valuable lessons about the pitfalls of judging others. (Rev: BL 10/1/06)

3064 Von Buhler, Cynthia. *But Who Will Bell the Cats?* (K–2). Illus. by author. 2009, Houghton $16.00 (978-0-618-99718-3). 32pp. With detailed, creepy illustrations, this is an ingenious followup to Aesop's tale in which a clever mouse prevails against terrible odds to attain his goal in a battle against the cats. (Rev: BL 7/09; HB 8–10/09; SLJ 9/09)

3065 Vrombaut, An. *Clarabella's Teeth* (PS). Illus. by author. 2003, Clarion $15.00 (978-0-618-33379-0). Clarabella the crocodile misses out on all the fun with her friends because she's busy brushing her teeth. (Rev: HBG 10/03; SLJ 4/03)

3066 Waber, Bernard. *An Anteater Named Arthur* (PS–2). Illus. by author. 1967, Houghton paper $6.95 (978-0-395-25936-8). 48pp. A mother anteater despairs of her son Arthur, who has problems very much like those of a young boy.

3067 Waber, Bernard. *Bearsie Bear and the Surprise Sleepover Party* (PS–K). Illus. 1997, Houghton $16.00 (978-0-395-86450-0). 40pp. A number of animals are given shelter for the night; but when the porcupine tries to bed down, everybody leaves. (Rev: BL 10/1/97; HB 9/97; HBG 3/98; SLJ 10/97)

3068 Waber, Bernard. *The House on East 88th Street* (K–2). Illus. by author. 1973, Houghton $16.00 (978-0-395-18157-7); paper $6.95 (978-0-395-19970-1). 48pp. The adventures of a pet crocodile (Lyle) who lives with a family in a New York City brownstone. Other books about Lyle include *Lyle, Lyle, Crocodile* (1965), *Lyle and the Birthday Party* (1966), *Lyle Finds His Mother* (1974), *Lovable Lyle* (1977), and *Funny, Funny Lyle* (1987).

3069 Waber, Bernard. *Ira Says Goodbye* (K–2). Illus. 1988, Houghton $16.00 (978-0-395-48315-2); paper $6.99 (978-0-395-58413-2). 40pp. Ira is sad because his best friend is moving away. (Rev: BCCB 10/88; BL 9/1/88; SLJ 9/88)

3070 Waber, Bernard. *Lyle at the Office* (PS–3). Illus. 1994, Houghton $16.00 (978-0-395-70563-6). 46pp. Lyle becomes very popular when he spends a day helping out in Mr. Primm's office. (Rev: BL 6/1–15/94; SLJ 9/94*)

3071 Waber, Bernard. *The Mouse That Snored* (PS–3). Illus. 2000, Houghton $15.00 (978-0-395-97518-3). 32pp. A mouse who has a terrible snore moves into a house where everyone hates noise so much they won't even eat celery. (Rev: BL 8/00; HB 11/00; HBG 3/01; SLJ 10/00)

3072 Waber, Bernard. *The Snake: A Very Long Love Story* (PS). Illus. by author. 1978, Houghton LB $7.95 (978-0-685-02310-5). A long trip brings the snake back home again.

3073 Waddell, Martin. *Bee Frog* (PS). Illus. by Barbara Firth. 2007, Candlewick $14.99 (978-0-7636-3310-3). Little Bee Frog wants to be a scary dragon, but no one in her family will play along until she hops off to a little pond for a while. (Rev: SLJ 5/07)

3074 Waddell, Martin. *Harriet and the Crocodiles* (1–3). Illus. by Mark Burgess. 1984, Little, Brown $11.95 (978-0-316-91622-6). Harriet loses her pet crocodile and sets out to find him.

3075 Waddell, Martin. *Mimi and the Dream House* (PS–2). Illus. by Leo Hartas. 1998, Candlewick paper $3.99 (978-0-7636-0387-8). A little mouse named Mimi constructs the house of her dreams. (Rev: BL 4/15/98; SLJ 7/98)

3076 Waddell, Martin. *Owl Babies* (PS–1). Illus. by Patrick Benson. 1992, Candlewick $15.99 (978-1-56402-101-4). 32pp. Three small owls, left alone by their mother, wonder if she is coming back. (Rev: BL 12/1/92; HB 3/93; SLJ 12/92)

3077 Waddell, Martin. *Sleep Tight, Little Bear* (PS–K). Illus. by Barbara Firth. Series: Little Bear. 2005, Candlewick $15.99 (978-0-7636-2439-2). 32pp. Little Bear finds a small cave and makes it his own special place; when he gets permission to spend the night there alone, however, he finds himself thinking of home. (Rev: BL 1/1–15/06; SLJ 12/05)

3078 Waechter, Philip. *Me!* (PS–K). Trans. by Christopher Franceschelli. Illus. 2005, Handprint $9.95 (978-1-59354-087-6). 64pp. Minimal text and simple illustrations tell the story of a bear whose self-confidence is all bravado. (Rev: BL 7/05; SLJ 7/05)

3079 Wagner, Karen. *Bravo, Mildred and Ed!* (PS–3). Illus. by Janet Pedersen. 2000, Walker $16.95 (978-0-8027-8734-7); paper $17.85 (978-0-8027-8735-4). Although mice Mildred and Ed enjoy doing things together, they also learn to be independent in this charming tale. (Rev: HBG 3/01; SLJ 9/00)

3080 Wahl, Jan. *Rabbits on Mars* (PS–3). Illus. by Kimberly Schamber. 2003, Lerner $15.25 (978-1-57505-511-4). 32pp. Three rabbits who are tired of dodging traffic and dogs set off for Mars, which they imagine to be full of carrots. (Rev: BL 3/15/03; HBG 10/03; SLJ 7/03)

3081 Wahl, Jan. *Three Pandas* (PS–1). Illus. by Naava. 2000, Boyds Mills $15.95 (978-1-56397-749-7). 32pp. Three little pandas have a series of misadventures when they explore beyond their bamboo forest; so they decide to head back home. (Rev: BL 2/15/00; HBG 10/00; SLJ 5/00)

3082 Wallace, Nancy E. *Apples, Apples, Apples* (K–2). Illus. 2000, Winslow $15.95 (978-1-890817-19-0). 40pp. When a rabbit family goes to an orchard to pick apples, they learn a lot about the fruit, the varieties, and how they grow. (Rev: BL 10/15/00; HBG 3/01; SLJ 9/00)

3083 Wallace, Nancy E. *A Taste of Honey* (PS–2). Illus. 2000, Winslow $15.95 (978-1-890817-51-0). 32pp. Little bear Lily asks Poppy where honey comes from, and his answers trace the story of honey from the jar back to the bees. (Rev: BL 2/15/01; HBG 10/01)

3084 Wallace, Nancy Elizabeth. *Baby Day!* (PS). Illus. 2003, Houghton $9.95 (978-0-618-27576-2). 32pp. A baby rabbit and mother spend a happy day together in this board book with cut-paper illustrations. (Rev: BL 2/15/03; HBG 10/03; SLJ 3/03)

3085 Wallace, Nancy Elizabeth. *The Kindness Quilt* (PS–2). 2006, Marshall Cavendish paper $16.99 (978-0-7614-5313-0). 48pp. After hearing the Aesop's fable about the lion and the mouse, Minna the bunny and her classmates are inspired to show kindness to others and to make a giant kindness quilt. (Rev: BL 10/1/06; SLJ 11/06)

3086 Wallace, Nancy Elizabeth. *Pumpkin Day!* (PS–2). Illus. 2002, Marshall Cavendish $16.95 (978-0-7614-5128-0). 32pp. A rabbit family visits a pumpkin farm to learn how they grow, before picking some for carving and eating. (Rev: BCCB 10/02; BL 8/02; HBG 3/03; SLJ 11/02)

3087 Wallace, Nancy Elizabeth. *Seeds! Seeds! Seeds!* (K–3). Illus. 2004, Marshall Cavendish $16.95 (978-0-7614-5159-4). 40pp. A package from Grandpa gets Buddy Bear involved in a variety of activities involving seeds. (Rev: BL 4/15/04; SLJ 6/04)

3088 Wallace, Nancy Elizabeth. *Shells! Shells! Shells!* (PS–2). Illus. by author. 2007, Marshall Cavendish $16.99 (978-0-7614-5332-1). 32pp. Buddy the bear learns all about shells during a walk along the beach with his mother; back matter includes facts and an activity. (Rev: BL 5/15/07; SLJ 5/07)

3089 Walsh, Ellen S. *Dot and Jabber and the Big Bug Mystery* (PS–1). Illus. by author. 2003, Harcourt $15.00 (978-0-15-216518-5). Dot and Jabber, mouse detectives, use their sleuthing skills to find out why the insects they've been watching all seem to be disappearing. (Rev: HBG 4/04; SLJ 11/03)

3090 Walsh, Ellen S. *For Pete's Sake* (PS–1). Illus. 1998, Harcourt $15.00 (978-0-15-200324-1). Pete is an alligator who thinks he is a flamingo just like all his feathered friends — until he accidentally meets some other alligators. (Rev: BL 10/15/98; HB 11/98; HBG 3/99; SLJ 11/98)

3091 Walsh, Ellen S. *Hop Jump* (PS–1). Illus. 1993, Harcourt $13.95 (978-0-15-292871-1). 32pp. Most of the other frogs enjoy hopping, but Betsy prefers to dance. (Rev: BL 11/1/93; HB 11/93; SLJ 10/93)

3092 Walsh, Ellen S. *Mouse Paint* (PS–K). Illus. 1989, Harcourt $14.00 (978-0-15-256025-6). 32pp. Three mice paint themselves as camouflage and find they like their new look. (Rev: BL 5/15/89; HB 7/89; SLJ 9/89)

3093 Walsh, Ellen S. *Samantha* (PS–1). Illus. 1996, Harcourt $14.00 (978-0-15-252264-3). 32pp. Samantha, a mouse, doesn't want to become too dependent on the protection that her fairy godmother gives her. (Rev: BCCB 6/96; BL 2/15/96; SLJ 5/96)

3094 Walton, Rick. *Bertie Was a Watchdog* (PS–1). Illus. by Arthur Robins. 2002, Candlewick $10.99 (978-0-7636-1385-3). Bertie the dog doesn't look fierce, but he's smart. (Rev: HBG 10/02; SLJ 8/02)

3095 Walton, Rick. *Bunny School: A Learning Fun-for-All* (PS–K). Illus. by Paige Miglio. 2005, HarperCollins $16.99 (978-0-06-057508-3). 32pp. At Cottontail School, the bunnies enjoy their first day; rhyming verses and detailed illustrations depict typical experiences. (Rev: BL 8/05; SLJ 9/05)

3096 Walton, Rick. *Once There Was a Bull . . . (frog)* (K–3). Illus. by Greg Hally. 1995, Gibbs Smith $15.95 (978-0-87905-652-0). 32pp. This clever story about a bullfrog searching for his lost hop uses the splitting of compound words to create different perceptions. (Rev: BL 12/15/95)

3097 Walton, Rick. *What Do We Do with the Baby?* (PS–K). Illus. by Paige Miglio. 2008, HarperCollins $16.99 (978-0-06-008419-6). 32pp. A rabbit family takes care of its new baby bunny; the illustrations add to the gentle fun. (Rev: BL 2/15/08; SLJ 3/08)

3098 Ward, Helen. *The Rooster and the Fox: A Tale from Chaucer* (K–3). Illus. 2003, Millbrook LB $24.90 (978-0-7613-2920-6). 40pp. "The Nun's Priest's Tale" about the proud rooster and the wily fox is adapted here in an effective tale using elegant, readable text and realistic watercolor art that makes the various animals come to life. (Rev: BCCB 2/03; BL 1/1–15/03; HBG 10/03; SLJ 10/04)

3099 Ward, Nick. *Come On, Baby Duck!* (PS–1). Illus. by author. 2004, Good Bks. $16.00 (978-1-56148-447-8). A baby duck is too scared to swim until his teddy falls in. (Rev: SLJ 11/04)

3100 Wardlaw, Lee. *The Chair Where Bear Sits* (PS–K). Illus. by Russell Benfanti. 2001, Winslow $14.95 (978-1-890817-85-5). 56pp. Eye-catching illustrations tell the cumulative tale, in the vein of "The House That Jack Built," of a baby bear who delights in the commotion caused by spilled juice. (Rev: BL 11/15/01; SLJ 2/02)

3101 Waring, Richard. *Hungry Hen* (PS). Illus. by Caroline Jayne Church. 2002, HarperCollins $16.99 (978-0-06-623880-7). 32pp. A greedy fox waits for a hen to grow fatter, but gets a surprise when he finally tries to eat her in this suspenseful and beautiful presentation. (Rev: BCCB 3/02; BL 1/1–15/02; HBG 10/02; SLJ 1/02*)

3102 Warnes, Tim. *Chalk and Cheese* (K–2). Illus. by author. 2008, Simon & Schuster $16.99 (978-1-4169-1378-8). 32pp. Cheese, an English country mouse, visits his pen pal Chalk, a dog, and together they form an unusual friendship as they enjoy the energy and sights of New York City. (Rev: BCCB 12/08; BL 9/15/08; LMC 1/09)

3103 Waterton, Betty. *A Salmon for Simon* (K–3). Illus. by Ann Blades. 1991, Salem paper $14.95 (978-0-88899-107-2). 32pp. A small Canadian Indian has a great adventure with a live salmon.

3104 Watson, Richard J. *The Magic Rabbit* (PS–1). Illus. 2005, Scholastic $16.99 (978-0-590-47964-6). 40pp. A white rabbit pops out of a hat and discovers that he's got some pretty amazing magical abilities, but somehow all this isn't much fun without a friend to share it. (Rev: BL 1/1–15/05; SLJ 4/05)

3105 Watt, Melanie. *Augustine* (PS–2). 2006, Kids Can $16.95 (978-1-55337-885-3). 32pp. Augustine the penguin is nervous about the family's move to the North Pole, but her artistic talent means she makes friends quickly; this is an interesting introduction to famous paintings. (Rev: BL 11/15/06; SLJ 11/06)

3106 Watt, Melanie. *Chester's Back!* (K–2). Illus. by author. 2008, Kids Can $18.95 (978-1-55453-287-2). 32pp. The calico cat first seen in *Chester* (2007) tussles with the author for control of a fairy tale. (Rev: BCCB 12/08; SLJ 9/08)

3107 Watt, Melanie. *Leon the Chameleon* (PS–K). Illus. 2001, Kids Can $14.95 (978-1-55074-867-3). 32pp. Leon's color changes clash with the background, leaving him embarrassed and lonely. (Rev: BL 4/1/01; HBG 3/02; SLJ 4/01)

3108 Watt, Melanie. *Scaredy Squirrel* (1–3). 2006, Kids Can $14.95 (978-1-55337-959-1). 40pp. Imagining all the dangers around him, Scaredy Squirrel doesn't dare venture from his tree — until the day he discovers he can fly. (Rev: BL 5/1/06; SLJ 6/06)

3109 Watt, Melanie. *Scaredy Squirrel at the Beach* (1–3). Illus. by author. 2008, Kids Can $15.95 (978-1-55453-225-4). 32pp. Scaredy Squirrel is so frightened by the idea of being at the beach that he decides to create his own seaside at the base of his favorite tree, but what he really needs is a seashell. What to do? (Rev: BL 6/1–15/08; SLJ 5/08)

3110 Watt, Melanie. *Scaredy Squirrel Makes a Friend* (PS–3). Illus. by author. 2007, Kids Can $14.95 (978-1-55453-181-3). A timid squirrel discovers that finding good friends may mean putting aside his fears. (Rev: SLJ 5/07)

3111 Watts, Leslie Elizabeth. *The Baabaasheep Quartet* (PS–2). Illus. 2005, Fitzhenry & Whiteside $16.95 (978-1-55041-890-3). 32pp. Four sheep have difficulty adjusting to life in the city but are optimistic when they see a singing contest they mistakenly believe is for sheep only. (Rev: BL 12/15/05; SLJ 2/06)

3112 Weaver, Tess. *Opera Cat* (2–4). Illus. by Andrea Wesson. 2002, Clarion $15.00 (978-0-618-09635-0). 32pp. Alma the cat rescues her mistress, the opera diva Madame SoSo, by singing the solos when Madame SoSo comes down with laryngitis in this humorous book with lovely illustrations. (Rev: BL 10/1/02; SLJ 12/02)

3113 Webster, Christine. *Otter Everywhere* (PS–1). Illus. by Tim Nihoff. 2007, Candlewick $15.99 (978-0-7636-2921-2); paper $5.99 (978-0-7636-2922-9). 40pp. Beginning readers will enjoy these simple stories about a friendly little otter. (Rev: SLJ 8/07)

3114 Weeks, Sarah. *Bunny Fun* (PS–K). Illus. by Sam Williams. 2008, Harcourt $14.00 (978-0-15-205838-8). 40pp. On a rainy day, young rabbit and his mouse friend enjoy a pillow fight and a game of dress-up. (Rev: BL 2/15/08; SLJ 12/07)

3115 Weeks, Sarah. *Catfish Kate and the Sweet Swamp Band* (PS–2). Illus. by Elwood H. Smith. 2009, Atheneum $16.99 (978-1-4169-4026-5). 32pp. The all-girl Sweet Swamp Band has a fine time playing jazzy music but the Skunktail Boys prefer to read and find the noise annoying; can a compromise be reached? (Rev: BL 5/15/09; LMC 10/09; SLJ 5/09)

3116 Weeks, Sarah. *I'm a Pig* (PS–2). Illus. by Holly Berry. 2005, HarperCollins LB $16.89 (978-0-06-074344-4). Appealing illustrations accompany a pig's expressions of happiness with her life and herself. (Rev: SLJ 5/05)

3117 Weeks, Sarah. *Overboard!* (PS). Illus. by Sam Williams. 2006, Harcourt $14.00 (978-0-15-205046-7). 40pp. Rhythmic text and colorful artwork celebrate a toddler's fascination with tossing objects of every kind "overboard." (Rev: BL 2/15/06; SLJ 4/06)

3118 Weeks, Sarah. *Two Eggs, Please* (PS–1). Illus. by Betsy Lewin. 2003, Simon & Schuster $15.95 (978-0-689-83196-6). Differing tastes are clearly — and amusingly — shown as an assortment of animal customers order eggs prepared in various ways. (Rev: HB 9/03; HBG 4/04; SLJ 6/04)

3119 Weigelt, Udo. *Super Guinea Pig to the Rescue* (K–3). Illus. by Nina Spranger. 2007, Walker $16.95 (978-0-8027-9705-6). 32pp. A little guinea pig hopes to impress his fellow pets by donning the role of his TV hero Super Guinea Pig. (Rev: BCCB 1/08; BL 10/1/07; SLJ 10/07)

3120 Weiss, Leatie. *My Teacher Sleeps in School* (K–2). Illus. by Ellen Weiss. 1985, Puffin paper $5.99 (978-0-14-050559-7). 32pp. Because their teacher is always there, two elephant children believe their teacher lives in school.

3121 Wells, Rosemary. *Carry Me!* (PS). Illus. 2006, Hyperion $15.99 (978-0-7868-0396-5). 32pp. An alert baby bunny with an attentive mother and father enjoys asking its parents to carry, sing, talk, tell stories . . . (Rev: BCCB 2/06; BL 11/1/05; HBG 10/06; SLJ 1/06)

3122 Wells, Rosemary. *Felix and the Worrier* (PS–2). Illus. by author. 2003, Candlewick $12.99 (978-0-7636-1405-8). Felix the guinea pig starts to fret about all sorts of things when a strange yellow creature called the Worrier begins bothering him. (Rev: HBG 4/04; SLJ 10/03)

3123 Wells, Rosemary. *Max Cleans Up* (PS–3). Illus. 2000, Viking $15.99 (978-0-670-89218-1). 32pp. Max's idea of cleaning up his room is to stuff everything into the front pocket of his overalls in this story about a delightful rabbit. (Rev: BL 2/1/01; HBG 10/01; SLJ 12/00)

3124 Wells, Rosemary. *Max's Bunny Business* (PS–1). Illus. by author. 2008, Viking $15.99 (978-0-670-01105-6). 32pp. Little rabbit Ruby and her friend Louise set up a lemonade stand to earn money to buy matching rings, but Ruby's brother Max foils their plan. (Rev: BL 3/1/08; HB 5/08; SLJ 6/08)

3125 Wells, Rosemary. *Only You* (PS–K). Illus. by author. 2003, Viking $14.99 (978-0-670-03634-9). A baby bear tells his mother how important she is to him. (Rev: HBG 10/03; SLJ 5/03)

3126 Wells, Rosemary. *Otto Runs for President* (K–2). Illus. by author. 2008, Scholastic $15.99 (978-0-545-03722-8). 32pp. Will popular poodle Tiffany or athletic bulldog Charlie walk off with the election for president at Barkadelphia School? Or does Otto, a thoughtful mutt, stand a chance? (Rev: BL 7/08; SLJ 8/08)

3127 Wells, Rosemary. *Read to Your Bunny* (PS). Illus. by author. 1998, Scholastic $7.95 (978-0-590-30284-5). Using a cast of bunnies, the author shows that reading can be fun anywhere. (Rev: BL 5/1/98; HBG 10/98; SLJ 3/98)

3128 Wells, Rosemary. *Ruby's Beauty Shop* (PS–K). Illus. 2002, Viking $16.99 (978-0-670-03553-3). 32pp. Max the bunny gets a beauty makeover from his big sister Ruby and her friend Louise — and then Max does his own. (Rev: BCCB 11/02; BL 8/02; HBG 3/03; SLJ 10/02)

3129 Wells, Rosemary. *Yoko Writes Her Name* (PS–2). Illus. by author. 2008, Hyperion $15.99 (978-0-7868-0371-2). 32pp. Yoko's Japanese letters initially cause her distress in kindergarten, but she eventually learns her ABCs and her classmates come to recognize some Japanese. (Rev: BL 7/08; SLJ 8/08)

3130 Weninger, Brigitte. *A Ball for All* (PS–1). Trans. from German by Kathryn Bishop. Illus. by Eve Tharlet. 2006, Minedition $16.99 (978-0-698-40049-8). Max Mouse and his animal friends enjoy playing a game of ball until Rico Raccoon, the local bully, shows up and steals the ball; the following day Max urges his friends to invite Rico to join them and they all have fun together. (Rev: SLJ 11/06)

3131 Weninger, Brigitte. *Bye-Bye Binky* (PS). Trans. from German by Kathryn Bishop. Illus. by Yusuke Yonezu. 2007, Minedition $15.99 (978-0-698-40048-1). Nora (a kitten) and her animal friends play with her pacifier in various ways before she happily sends it off into the sky on a balloon. This story will encourage children reluctant to part with their binkies. (Rev: SLJ 5/07)

3132 Weninger, Brigitte. *Davy, Soccer Star!* (1–3). Illus. by Eve Tharlet. 2008, North-South $16.95 (978-0-7358-2196-5). 32pp. Davy and his Wild Rabbits hop to the task of getting into shape for the big match with the Bad Badgers. (Rev: BLO 8/28/08)

3133 Weninger, Brigitte. *Stay in Bed, Davy* (PS–1). Trans. by Marianne Martens. Illus. by Eve Tharlet. 2006, North-South $15.95 (978-0-7358-2048-7). Davy the rabbit is sick and his mother has told him to stay in bed, but his friend Eddie and cousin Kiki still find ways to have fun. (Rev: SLJ 3/06)

3134 Weston, Carrie. *If a Chicken Stayed for Supper* (PS–3). Illus. by Sophie Fatus. 2007, Holiday $16.95 (978-0-8234-2067-4). 32pp. Five little foxes disobediently leave their den while their mother is out hunting for a chicken; when they become lost, a chicken volunteers to guide them home, posing a dilemma for mother. (Rev: BL 3/15/07)

3135 Weston, Carrie. *The New Bear at School* (PS–2). Illus. by Tim Warnes. 2008, Scholastic $12.99 (978-0-545-05783-7). 32pp. A class full of cuddly little animals are surprised to find their new classmate is not a dear little teddy bear but a "hairy, scary grizzly bear." (Rev: BL 8/08; LMC 10/08; SLJ 7/08)

3136 Wheeler, Lisa. *Castaway Cats* (K–2). Illus. by Ponder Goembel. 2006, Simon & Schuster $16.95 (978-0-689-86232-8). 32pp. Stranded on a desert island, 15 independently minded cats decide to build a boat, and although they don't succeed in this they do set aside their differences and eventually decide to stay on the island. (Rev: BL 8/06; SLJ 6/06*)

3137 Wheeler, Lisa. *Dino-Hockey* (PS–2). Illus. by Barry Gott. 2007, Carolrhoda $16.95 (978-0-8225-6191-0). 32pp. It's Meat-Eaters versus Veggiesaurs in this fast and furious hockey game full of fun and facts. (Rev: BL 9/1/07; LMC 1/08; SLJ 12/07)

3138 Wheeler, Lisa. *Hokey Pokey: Another Prickly Love Story* (PS–1). Illus. by Janie Bynum. 2006, Little, Brown $15.99 (978-0-316-00090-1). Eager to please his girlfriend, Barb the hedgehog, Cushion the porcupine tries to learn how to dance, but his attempts all end in failure until Barb offers to provide the lessons; a sequel to *Porcupining: A Prickly Love Story* (2003). (Rev: SLJ 1/06)

3139 Wheeler, Lisa. *Old Cricket* (PS–2). Illus. by Ponder Goembel. 2003, Simon & Schuster $16.95 (978-0-689-84510-9). Old Cricket pleads a string of ailments to avoid having to get to work, but an encounter with a hungry crow finally sets him straight. (Rev: BL 5/15/03; HBG 10/03; SLJ 5/03)

3140 Wheeler, Lisa. *One Dark Night* (PS–K). Illus. by Ivan Bates. 2003, Harcourt $16.00 (978-0-15-202318-8). In this mildly spooky adventure tale with a twist at the end, told in rhyme, Mouse and Mole confront the menaces of the night as they traverse the forest and swamp. (Rev: HBG 10/03; SLJ 6/03)

3141 Wheeler, Lisa. *Porcupining: A Prickly Love Story* (PS–1). Illus. by Janie Bynum. 2003, Little, Brown $14.95 (978-0-316-98912-1). A lonely porcupine tries unsuccessfully to woo a succession of animals before finding the right one. (Rev: HBG 10/03; SLJ 1/03)

3142 Wheeler, Lisa. *Sailor Moo: Cow at Sea* (1–3). Illus. by Ponder Goembel. 2002, Simon & Schuster $16.95 (978-0-689-84219-1). 32pp. A rhyming, humorous picture book about a young cow who longs to have a life at sea and ends up on a cattle barge turned pirate ship. (Rev: BL 5/1/02; HBG 3/03; SLJ 8/02)

3143 Whippo, Walt. *Little White Duck* (PS–3). Illus. by Joan Paley. 2000, Little, Brown $13.95 (978-0-316-03227-8). 32pp. The old song about Little White Duck and other animals enjoying a pond is given a fresh treatment with vibrant collage illustrations. (Rev: BCCB 5/00; BL 2/1/00; HBG 10/00; SLJ 4/00)

3144 White, Kathryn. *When They Fight* (PS–K). Illus. by Cliff Wright. 2000, Winslow $14.95 (978-1-890817-46-6). 32pp. A young badger is terrorized and runs away when his parents quarrel. (Rev: BL 4/15/00; HBG 3/01; SLJ 6/00)

3145 Whybrow, Ian. *Bella Gets Her Skates On* (PS–K). Illus. by Rosie Reeve. 2007, Abrams $15.95 (978-0-8109-9416-4). 32pp. Bella Rabbit worries when she faces a new task but with the loving support of Daddy Rabbit, she finds her confidence. (Rev: BL 12/1/07; SLJ 11/07)

3146 Whybrow, Ian. *Harry and the Dinosaurs Say "Raahh!"* (PS–1). Illus. by Adrian Reynolds. 2004, Random $14.95 (978-0-375-82542-2). A new adventure for Harry and his magical dinosaurs, this one involving a trip to the dentist with a tyrannosaurus for company. (Rev: HB 5/04; SLJ 3/04)

3147 Whybrow, Ian. *Little Wolf's Book of Badness* (2–4). Illus. by Tony Ross. 1999, Carolrhoda LB $14.95 (978-1-57505-410-0). 132pp. In this hilarious story, Little Wolf is too well behaved so he is sent to Cunning College to learn how to be bad. (Rev: HBG 3/00; SLJ 11/99)

3148 Whybrow, Ian. *Parcel for Stanley* (PS–2). Illus. by Sally Hobson. 1998, Levinson $14.95 (978-1-899607-53-2). A simple story in which a rabbit, who has a sorry reputation, shines after he learns a few magic tricks. (Rev: SLJ 3/99)

3149 Wickstrom, Lois. *Oliver: A Story About Adoption* (PS–3). Illus. by Priscilla Marden. 1991, Our Child Pr. $14.95 (978-0-9611872-5-5). When lizard Oliver receives a reprimand from his adoptive father, he thinks his real parents would behave differently. (Rev: SLJ 2/92)

3150 Wiesner, David. *Tuesday* (PS–2). Illus. 1991, Houghton $17.00 (978-0-395-55113-4). 32pp. Frogs have a wonderful time on Tuesday. Will the pigs have as great a time one week later? Caldecott Medal winner, 1992. (Rev: BCCB 5/91; BL 5/1/91; SLJ 5/91*)

3151 Wild, Margaret. *Kiss Kiss!* (PS–2). Illus. by Bridget Strevens-Marzo. 2004, Simon & Schuster $12.95 (978-0-689-86279-3). A baby hippo sets off on his morning stroll through the jungle without first kissing his mother. (Rev: BL 1/1–15/04; SLJ 1/04)

3152 Wild, Margaret. *Piglet and Mama* (PS–K). Illus. by Stephen Michael King. 2005, Abrams $14.95 (978-0-8109-5869-2). 32pp. Poor piglet searches all over the farm for his mama, leading to a joyous reunion. (Rev: BL 3/1/05; SLJ 6/05)

3153 Wild, Margaret. *Piglet and Papa* (PS–K). Illus. by Stephen Michael King. 2007, Abrams $14.95 (978-0-8109-1476-6). 32pp. Piglet worries that her papa has stopped loving her, and she finds comfort and reassurance in this tender story. (Rev: BL 5/1/07; SLJ 7/07)

3154 Wild, Margaret. *Tom Goes to Kindergarten* (PS–1). Illus. by David Legge. 2000, Whitman $15.95 (978-0-8075-8012-7). 32pp. Mr. and Mrs. Panda overstay their welcome when they accompany their son Tom on his first day in school. (Rev: BL 5/1/00; HBG 10/00; SLJ 4/00)

3155 Wilhelm, Hans. *Hello Sun!* (PS–2). Illus. by author. 2003, Carolrhoda LB $15.25 (978-1-57505-348-6). Quentin, a hedgehog, is a mostly nocturnal creature, so he is completely enchanted when he first sees the rays of the sun; he decides to build a tree house so he will have the best possible view of the sun and, despite some teasing from a fox, gets the job done in record time. (Rev: HBG 4/04; SLJ 1/04)

3156 Wilhelm, Hans. *More Bunny Trouble* (PS–1). Illus. by author. 1989, Scholastic paper $4.99 (978-0-590-41590-3). 32pp. Ralph is tapped to baby-sit his bunny sister, but he lets her get out of sight and lost. (Rev: BL 3/1/89; SLJ 5/89)

3157 Wilhelm, Hans. *The Royal Raven* (PS–3). Illus. 1996, Scholastic $15.95 (978-0-590-54337-8). 32pp. A raven named Crawford tries to become special by changing his appearance. (Rev: BL 3/15/96; SLJ 7/96)

3158 Wilhelm, Hans. *Tyrone the Horrible* (PS–2). Illus. by author. 1988, Scholastic paper $4.99 (978-0-590-41472-2). 32pp. Tyrone the terrible bully dinosaur is making Boland's prehistoric life a misery. (Rev: BL 9/1/88; SLJ 12/88)

3159 Willans, Tom. *Wait! I Want to Tell You a Story* (K–4). Illus. by author. 2005, Simon & Schuster

$15.95 (978-0-689-87166-5). Using a traditional delaying tactic, a series of animals about to be eaten cry "Wait! I want to tell you a story." (Rev: BCCB 3/05; HB 5/05; SLJ 5/05)

3160 Willems, Mo. *Don't Let the Pigeon Stay Up Late!* (PS). Illus. 2006, Hyperion $12.99 (978-0-7868-3746-5). 32pp. The irrepressible pigeon of *Don't Let the Pigeon Drive the Bus!* is not tired and has no intention of going to bed. (Rev: BL 2/15/06; SLJ 4/06*)

3161 Willems, Mo. *I Love My New Toy!* (K–2). Illus. by author. Series: Elephant and Piggie. 2008, Hyperion $8.99 (978-1-4231-0961-7). 64pp. A "mishap" with a new toy threatens the friendship between Elephant and Piggie. Also use *I Will Surprise My Friend!* (2008). (Rev: BL 7/08)

3162 Willems, Mo. *My Friend Is Sad* (PS–1). Illus. Series: Elephant and Piggie. 2007, Hyperion $8.99 (978-1-4231-0297-7). 64pp. Gerald the elephant is sad and Piggie, dressing in costumes, does his best to cheer him up but fails because Gerald does not recognize his best friend, and believes Piggie is missing all the fun. (Rev: BCCB 7–8/07; BL 4/1/07; HB 5/07)

3163 Williams, Barbara. *Albert's Gift for Grandmother* (K–2). Illus. by Doug Cushman. 2006, Candlewick $15.99 (978-0-7636-2097-4). 32pp. Downcast because he doesn't have a gift for his grandmother's birthday, Albert the turtle, first seen in *Albert's Impossible Toothache* (2003), finally comes up with an idea that he thinks will please her. (Rev: BL 11/1/06; SLJ 12/06)

3164 Williams, Garth. *Benjamin's Treasure* (PS–1). Illus. by Rosemary Wells and Garth Williams. 2001, HarperCollins LB $15.89 (978-0-06-028741-2). 32pp. When Benjamin, a rabbit, is shipwrecked on a deserted island, he finds a treasure chest but realizes his greatest treasure is his wife back home. (Rev: BL 2/15/01; HBG 10/01)

3165 Willis, Jeanne. *Cottonball Colin* (PS–2). Illus. by Tony Ross. 2008, Eerdmans $16.00 (978-0-8028-5331-8). 26pp. The smallest mouse in the family, who has been overprotected by his mother, gets more adventure than he bargains for after he has been wrapped in cotton wool for safety. (Rev: BCCB 3/08; LMC 11/08; SLJ 4/08)

3166 Willis, Jeanne. *Gorilla! Gorilla!* (PS–2). Illus. by Tony Ross. 2006, Simon & Schuster $15.95 (978-1-4169-1490-7). A mouse who has lost her baby is chased around the world by a fierce gorilla — who is only trying to help. (Rev: SLJ 7/06)

3167 Willis, Jeanne. *Misery Moo* (PS–2). Illus. by Tony Ross. 2005, Holt $16.95 (978-0-8050-7672-1). Misery Moo won't be cheered despite a little lamb's best efforts, so he gives up and goes off in a state of depression of his own. (Rev: BL 5/15/04; SLJ 6/05)

3168 Willis, Jeanne. *Mommy Do You Love Me?* (PS). Illus. by Jan Fearnley. 2008, Candlewick $15.99 (978-0-7636-3470-4). 32pp. Little Chick tests his mother's love with a series of challenges only to keep getting the same results. (Rev: BL 3/15/08; SLJ 4/08)

3169 Willis, Jeanne. *Never Too Little to Love* (PS–K). Illus. by Jan Fearnley. 2004, Candlewick $10.99 (978-0-7636-2267-1). 32pp. Too-Little, a tiny mouse, climbs on successively higher objects in an attempt to reach his lady love in this well-designed, tall book. (Rev: BL 2/1/05)

3170 Willis, Jeanne. *Tadpole's Promise* (K–4). Illus. by Tony Ross. 2005, Simon & Schuster $15.95 (978-0-689-86524-4). A caterpillar and a tadpole declare undying love and promise that neither of them will ever change. (Rev: BCCB 7–8/05; SLJ 5/05)

3171 Willner-Pardo, Gina. *Spider Storch, Rotten Runner* (2–3). Illus. by Nick Sharratt. 2001, Whitman LB $11.95 (978-0-8075-7594-9). 83pp. In this beginning chapter book, Spider dreads the Third-Grade Olympics because he can't run fast and must take part in the relay race. (Rev: HBG 3/02; SLJ 12/01)

3172 Wilson, Karma. *Animal Strike at the Zoo. It's True* (PS–3). Illus. by Margaret Spengler. 2006, HarperCollins $16.99 (978-0-06-057502-1). A sad little girl reminds the animals at the zoo that their job really is important. (Rev: SLJ 6/06)

3173 Wilson, Karma. *Bear Feels Scared* (PS–1). Illus. by Jane Chapman. 2008, Simon & Schuster $16.99 (978-0-689-85986-1). 40pp. Lost in a storm in the forest, a frightened Bear frets about the strange noises while back home his worried friends send out a rescue party. (Rev: BLO 9/2/08; SLJ 9/08) ∩

3174 Wilson, Karma. *Bear Snores On* (PS–1). Illus. by Jane Chapman. 2002, Simon & Schuster $16.00 (978-0-689-83187-4). 40pp. On a cold winter night, animals gather in a sleeping bear's cave to share food and warmth in this charming story told in rhyme. (Rev: BL 1/1–15/02; HBG 10/02; SLJ 1/02*)

3175 Wilson, Karma. *Bear Wants More* (PS–2). Illus. by Jane Chapman. 2003, Simon & Schuster $16.95 (978-0-689-84509-3). When spring comes, Bear wakes up and is extremely hungry. (Rev: BCCB 3/03; BL 4/15/03; HBG 10/03; SLJ 2/03)

3176 Wilson, Karma. *Bear's New Friend* (PS–2). Illus. by Jane Chapman. Series: Bear. 2006, Simon & Schuster $16.95 (978-0-689-85984-7). Who could Bear's new friend be? Readers will enjoy the clues that lead to the discovery of an owl in a tree. (Rev: SLJ 7/06)

3177 Wilson, Karma. *Hilda Must Be Dancing* (PS–2). Illus. by Suzanne Watts. 2004, Simon & Schuster $15.95 (978-0-689-84788-2). Hilda the hippo shakes the ground when she dances through the jungle, disturbing her neighbors. (Rev: SLJ 3/04)

3178 Wilson, Karma. *Mortimer's First Garden* (PS–2). Illus. by Dan Andreasen. 2009, Simon & Schuster $16.99 (978-1-4169-4203-0). 32pp. Mortimer the mouse plants a sunflower seed and, with some help from God, reaps a bountiful harvest. (Rev: BCCB 3/09; BL 2/1/09; SLJ 3/09)

3179 Wilson, Karma. *Sakes Alive! A Cattle Drive* (K–3). Illus. by Karla Firehammer. 2005, Little,

Brown $15.99 (978-0-316-98841-4). 32pp. Cows Molly and Mabel steal the farmer's truck and take off on an exciting "cattle drive." (Rev: BL 5/1/05)

3180 Winget, Susan. *Tucker's Four-Carrot School Day* (PS–1). Illus. 2005, HarperCollins $12.99 (978-0-06-054642-7). 40pp. A kindly teacher and a photo of his family help Tucker Rabbit to survive his first day at school. (Rev: BL 8/05; SLJ 9/05)

3181 Winthrop, Elizabeth. *Bear and Roly-Poly* (K–3). Illus. by Patience Brewster. 1996, Holiday House $15.95 (978-0-8234-1197-9). 32pp. Nora brings Bear a baby sister in the form of Roly-Poly panda. (Rev: BL 3/1/96; SLJ 5/96)

3182 Wise, William. *Christopher Mouse: The Tale of a Small Traveler* (3–5). Illus. by Patrick Benson. 2004, Bloomsbury $15.95 (978-1-58234-878-0). 152pp. Christopher Mouse, who learned his mother's lessons well, relates with humor and intelligence the ups and downs of his varied life. (Rev: BL 4/1/04*; SLJ 6/04)

3183 Wise, William. *Zany Zoo* (K–2). Illus. by Lynn Munsinger. 2006, Houghton $16.00 (978-0-618-18891-8). 32pp. Wacky animals and even wackier wordplay are presented in this appealing blend of rhyming verse and colorful artwork. (Rev: BL 4/15/06; SLJ 8/06)

3184 Wishinsky, Frieda. *Give Maggie a Chance* (K–2). Illus. by Dean Griffiths. 2002, Fitzhenry & Whiteside $15.95 (978-1-55041-682-4). 32pp. Maggie is an imaginative little cat who is terrified of public speaking and resents Kimberly's self-confidence in front of the class. (Rev: SLJ 12/02)

3185 Wisniewski, David. *Sumo Mouse* (PS–3). Illus. 2002, Chronicle $16.95 (978-0-8118-3492-6). 32pp. Giant slapstick superhero Sumo Mouse comes to the rescue of kidnapped Tokyo mice in a complex plot that combines lots of action, comedy, and drama. (Rev: BCCB 1/03; BL 1/1–15/03; HBG 3/03; SLJ 12/02)

3186 Wollman, Jessica. *Andrew's Bright Blue T-Shirt* (PS–2). Illus. by Ana L. Escriva. 2002, Doubleday $14.95 (978-0-385-74616-8). 32pp. A young fox named Andrew dreams of playing soccer and wears his brother's hand-me-down soccer T-shirt every day, until he tragically grows out of it — and his brother says he's now old enough to play. (Rev: BL 10/1/02; HBG 3/03; SLJ 10/02)

3187 Wood, A. J. *The Little Penguin* (PS–2). Illus. by Stephanie Boey. 2002, Dutton $15.99 (978-0-525-47023-6). 32pp. A visually appealing, tender book about a young, fuzzy penguin who longs for his father's refined look. (Rev: BL 10/15/02; HBG 3/03; SLJ 12/02)

3188 Wood, Audrey. *Jubal's Wish* (PS–3). Illus. by Don Wood. 2000, Scholastic $17.99 (978-0-439-16964-6). 32pp. Jubal wants his friends to join him on a picnic but they are too busy to attend in this story about friendship. (Rev: BL 12/1/00; HBG 3/01; SLJ 10/00)

3189 Wood, Audrey. *Little Penguin's Tale* (PS–2). Illus. 1989, Harcourt $13.95 (978-0-15-246475-2). 32pp. Little Penguin's escapades result in his being swallowed by a whale. (Rev: BL 11/15/89)

3190 Wood, Audrey. *Silly Sally* (PS). Illus. 1992, Harcourt $16.00 (978-0-15-274428-1). 32pp. This delightful nonsense book tells of Silly Sally and her trip into town walking backwards and upside down. (Rev: BCCB 6/92; BL 3/15/92*; SLJ 4/92)

3191 Wood, Douglas. *What Dads Can't Do* (PS–2). Illus. by Doug Cushman. 2000, Simon & Schuster $14.00 (978-0-689-82620-7). An amusing picture book in which a baby dinosaur lists all the things that regular people can do but dads can't, like crossing the street without holding hands or reading a book by themselves. (Rev: HBG 10/00; SLJ 5/00)

3192 Wood, Douglas. *What Grandmas Can't Do* (PS–K). Illus. by Doug Cushman. 2005, Simon & Schuster $14.95 (978-0-689-84647-2). A follow-up to *What Moms Can't Do* (2001) and *What Dads Can't Do* (2000), this loving picture book features a dinosaur grandma who can't hug without a kiss, but is capable of plenty of other things. (Rev: SLJ 7/05)

3193 Wood, Douglas. *What Moms Can't Do* (PS). Illus. by Doug Cushman. 2001, Simon & Schuster $14.00 (978-0-689-83358-8). A young dinosaur helps his mother with all her chores but there is one thing he can't duplicate and that is her love for him. (Rev: HBG 10/01; SLJ 3/01)

3194 Wood, Douglas. *What Teachers Can't Do* (PS–2). Illus. by Doug Cushman. 2002, Simon & Schuster $14.95 (978-0-689-84644-1). 32pp. A young dinosaur looks at all the silly and odd things teachers can't do — be late for school, add 2 + 2, for example. (Rev: BL 8/02; HBG 3/03; SLJ 10/02)

3195 Wood, Jakki. *Never Say Boo to a Goose!* (PS). Illus. by Clare Beaton. 2002, Barefoot Books $14.99 (978-1-84148-255-2). 24pp. Tiger the kitten ignores his mother's warning and sets off to find out what happens when he says "boo!" to a goose, if only he can find one. (Rev: BL 12/1/02; HBG 3/03; SLJ 11/02)

3196 Woods, Noah. *Tom Cat* (PS–2). Illus. by author. 2004, Random LB $16.99 (978-0-375-92497-2). Tom Cat has identity problems until he learns how to "meow." (Rev: SLJ 8/04)

3197 Woodworth, Viki. *Daisy the Dancing Cow* (PS–3). Illus. by author. 2003, Boyds Mills $15.95 (978-1-59078-059-6). Daisy, last seen in *Daisy the Firecow* (2001), is relegated to a backstage job at the theater until a dancer is injured. (Rev: HBG 4/04; SLJ 10/03)

3198 Woodworth, Viki. *Daisy the Firecow* (PS–1). Illus. 2001, Boyds Mills $15.95 (978-1-56397-934-7). 32pp. Daisy the cow is bored on the farm and becomes a fire station's mascot. (Rev: BL 7/01; HBG 10/01)

3199 Wormell, Christopher. *Henry and the Fox* (K–2). Illus. by author. 2008, Trafalgar $19.95 (978-0-224-07044-7). 32pp. Henry the cowardly cockerell's plan to show himself in a brave light takes an unexpected turn and, to his surprise, convinces the other animals of his courage. (Rev: BLO 5/30/08; SLJ 2/08)

3200 Wormell, Mary. *Hilda Hen's Scary Night* (PS–K). Illus. 1996, Harcourt $14.00 (978-0-15-200990-8). 32pp. In the morning, Hilda Hen sets out to find the creatures that had frightened her the night before. (Rev: BL 9/15/96; SLJ 10/96)

3201 Wormell, Mary. *Hilda Hen's Search* (PS–1). Illus. 1994, Harcourt $13.95 (978-0-15-200069-1). 32pp. Hilda Hen wanders the barnyard looking for a suitable place to lay her eggs. (Rev: BL 12/1/94; SLJ 11/94)

3202 Wright, Johanna. *The Secret Circus* (PS–K). Illus. by author. 2009, Roaring Brook $16.95 (978-1-59643-403-5). 32pp. A mouse family travels to see a tiny circus in Paris that is known only to mice. (Rev: BL 4/15/09; SLJ 4/09)

3203 Wu, Liz. *Rosa Farm* (2–4). Illus. by Matt Phelan. 2006, Knopf $15.95 (978-0-375-83681-7). 134pp. Gallileon, a young rooster, is nervous about filling in for his father, but welcoming the rising sun turns out to be only the beginning of a difficult day. (Rev: SLJ 1/07)

3204 Yaccarino, Dan. *Unlovable* (PS–1). Illus. by author. 2002, Holt $15.95 (978-0-8050-6321-9). 32pp. A puppy who is teased unmercifully about his funny looks befriends a dog he can't see — and who can't see him — on the other side of the fence. (Rev: BL 11/15/01; HBG 10/02; SLJ 1/02)

3205 Yates, Louise. *A Small Surprise* (PS–K). Illus. by author. 2009, Knopf $16.99 (978-0-375-85698-3). 40pp. Little rabbit would like to do more grown up things but all he can manage is a few disappearing tricks. (Rev: BL 6/1–15/09; SLJ 5/09)

3206 Yee, Brenda Shannon. *Hide and Seek* (PS–K). Illus. by Debbie Tilley. 2001, Scholastic $15.95 (978-0-531-30302-3). 32pp. A mouse finds he enjoys playing hide-and-seek with the woman of the house. (Rev: BL 5/15/01; HBG 10/01; SLJ 7/01)

3207 Yee, Patrick. *Winter Rabbit* (PS). Illus. by author. 1994, Viking $13.99 (978-0-670-85353-3). A bear and a squirrel build a huge snow bunny before they begin their winter sleep. (Rev: SLJ 7/94)

3208 Yee, Wong H. *Abracadabra!* (K–3). Illus. by author. 2007, Houghton $15.00 (978-0-618-75926-2). 48pp. In this sequel to *Upstairs Mouse, Downstairs Mole*, Minkus the Magnificent's performance disappoints magic-fan Mole who then questions magic's existence, but Mouse soon convinces Mole that magic is all around them — in tadpoles turning into frogs, in the full moon, in fireflies, and so forth. (Rev: BL 11/1/07; HB 11/07; SLJ 12/07)

3209 Yee, Wong H. *Fireman Small: Fire Down Below!* (K–2). Illus. by author. 2001, Houghton $15.00 (978-0-618-00707-3). Children will learn safety tips while reading this charming story of a very small fireman who rescues the occupants of a hotel. (Rev: HB 11/01; HBG 3/02; SLJ 10/01)

3210 Yee, Wong H. *Here Come Trainmice!* (PS). 2000, Houghton $4.95 (978-0-395-98401-7). 14pp. This board book describes the different cars of a train, all of which are populated by expressive mice, and all the parts of a train ride. A companion volume about trucks is *Hooray for Truckmice!* (2000). (Rev: SLJ 11/00)

3211 Yee, Wong H. *Upstairs Mouse, Downstairs Mole* (1–3). Illus. 2005, Houghton $15.00 (978-0-618-47313-7). 48pp. Mole and Mouse, who live in the same oak tree, overcome their differences and forge a strong friendship. (Rev: BL 11/1/05; SLJ 10/05)

3212 Yolen, Jane. *Baby Bear's Chairs* (PS). Illus. by Melissa Sweet. 2005, Harcourt $16.00 (978-0-15-205114-3). 40pp. A tiny bear realizes that no chair can match the comfort of sitting in his father's lap. (Rev: BL 12/1/05)

3213 Yolen, Jane. *Dimity Duck* (PS). Illus. by Sebastien Braun. 2006, Philomel $15.99 (978-0-399-24632-6). 32pp. Appealing art and rhyming verse follow Dimity Duck through a satisfying day, including playtime with her friend Frumity Frog then happily climbing into her nest for bedtime. (Rev: BL 6/1–15/06; SLJ 6/06)

3214 Yolen, Jane. *How Do Dinosaurs Get Well Soon?* (PS–1). Illus. by Mark Teague. 2003, Scholastic $16.99 (978-0-439-24100-7). 40pp. Humorous, full-color illustrations are coupled with rhyming text to show giant young dinosaurs who must learn how to behave while ill (taking medicine, resting, and so forth). Also use *How Do Dinosaurs Eat Their Food?* (2005) and *How Do Dinosaurs Go to School?* (2007). (Rev: BL 1/1–15/03*; HB 3/03; HBG 10/03; SLJ 2/03)

3215 Yolen, Jane. *Off We Go!* (PS–K). Illus. by Laurel Molk. 2000, Little, Brown $12.95 (978-0-316-90228-1). 32pp. A bouncy picture book about several animals, all of whom are on their way to visit their grandmothers. (Rev: BCCB 3/00; BL 3/15/00; HBG 10/00; SLJ 5/00)

3216 Yorinks, Arthur. *Hey, Al* (2–4). Illus. 1986, Farrar $17.00 (978-0-374-33060-6); paper $5.95 (978-0-374-42985-0). 32pp. Eddie the dog wants to change his life, but when a bird takes him and Al the janitor to a bird-inhabited island, Eddie isn't quite so sure. Caldecott Medal winner, 1987. (Rev: BL 1/1/87; SLJ 3/87)

3217 Young, Selina. *Big Dog and Little Dog Go Sailing* (1–2). Series: Blue Bananas. 2001, Crabtree $22.60 (978-0-7787-0845-2); paper $4.95 (978-0-7787-0891-9). 48pp. When they go boating, two individualistic dogs experience some amazing adventures including an encounter with a whale. (Rev: BL 5/1/02)

3218 Zalben, Jane Breskin. *Don't Go!* (PS–K). Illus. 2001, Clarion $16.00 (978-0-618-07250-7). 32pp. A gentle story of a young elephant who is comforted to have his stuffed toy with him on his first day of preschool. (Rev: BL 8/01; HBG 3/02; SLJ 9/01)

3219 Zalben, Jane Breskin. *Pearl Plants a Tree* (PS–2). Illus. 1995, Simon & Schuster paper $14.00 (978-0-689-80034-4). 32pp. A little lamb learns from her grandfather and plants an apple seed that later sprouts. (Rev: BL 11/15/95; SLJ 1/96)

3220 Zane, Alexander. *The Wheels on the Race Car* (PS–K). Illus. by James Warhola. 2005, Scholastic LB $14.95 (978-0-439-59080-8). In an exciting, action-packed combination of bright illustrations and compelling verse, rambunctious animals pilot racecars around a track, stopping for fill-ups and tune-ups. (Rev: BL 2/1/05; LMC 8/05; SLJ 3/05)

3221 Ziefert, Harriet. *Buzzy Had a Little Lamb* (PS). Illus. 2005, Blue Apple $9.95 (978-1-59354-068-5). 32pp. Buzzy the donkey can't bear the thought of being separated from his beloved stuffed lamb, but he must learn to adjust when it's time to begin school. (Rev: BL 7/05; SLJ 8/05)

3222 Ziefert, Harriet. *Egad Alligator!* (PS–3). Illus. by Todd McKie. 2002, Houghton $16.00 (978-0-618-14171-5). 40pp. Little Gator doesn't understand why people are afraid of him until he experiences fear himself when he sits on a python. (Rev: BCCB 9/02; BL 4/15/02; HBG 10/02; SLJ 4/02)

3223 Zolotow, Charlotte. *Mr. Rabbit and the Lovely Present* (PS–3). Illus. by Maurice Sendak. 1977, HarperCollins paper $6.95 (978-0-06-443020-3). 32pp. A little girl meets Mr. Rabbit, and together they find the perfect birthday gift for her mother.

Realistic Stories

ADVENTURE STORIES

3224 Agee, Jon. *Terrific* (K–2). Illus. 2005, Hyperion $15.95 (978-0-7868-5184-3). 32pp. Stranded on a desert island when his cruise ship sinks, Eugene Mudge — who views life through the lens of his pessimism — begins to change his negative attitude when a talking parrot takes him under his wing. (Rev: BL 10/15/05; HB 11/05; LMC 1/06; SLJ 9/05)

3225 Ahlberg, Allan. *It Was a Dark and Stormy Night* (K–3). Illus. by Janet Ahlberg. 1994, Viking $13.99 (978-0-670-85159-1). 32pp. A young captive of robbers escapes in the confusion caused by their acting out a story that he has told them. (Rev: BCCB 7–8/94; BL 5/1/94)

3226 Arnold, Marsha Diane. *The Bravest of Us All* (PS–3). Illus. by Brad Sneed. 2000, Dial $16.99 (978-0-8037-2409-9). 32pp. When a tornado comes, young Ruby Jane helps her older sister to take shelter. (Rev: BCCB 6/00; BL 5/1/00; HBG 10/00; SLJ 5/00)

3227 Axtell, David. *We're Going on a Lion Hunt* (PS–1). Illus. 2000, Holt $15.95 (978-0-8050-6159-8). 32pp. In this variation on the familiar chant, two African girls go out on a lion hunt. (Rev: BCCB 5/00; BL 2/15/00; HBG 10/00; SLJ 5/00)

3228 Bailey, Linda. *When Addie Was Scared* (1–3). Illus. by Wendy Bailey. 1999, Kids Can $14.95 (978-1-55074-431-6). 32pp. Though Addie is a fearful, timid child, she summons up great courage to frighten off a hawk when it attacks her grandmother's chickens. (Rev: BL 11/15/99; HBG 3/00; SLJ 11/99)

3229 Beard, Darleen Bailey. *Twister* (PS–3). Illus. by Nancy Carpenter. 1999, Farrar $16.00 (978-0-374-37977-3). 32pp. While two children hide in a cellar near their trailer home during a tornado, their mother ventures out to help an elderly neighbor. (Rev: BL 2/1/99; HBG 10/99; SLJ 3/99)

3230 Becker, Shari. *Maxwell's Mountain* (2–4). Illus. by Nicole Wong. 2006, Charlesbridge $15.95 (978-1-58089-047-2). 32pp. Maxwell is a serious but adventurous little boy and he prepares carefully for his climb up the mountain in the playground near his new house. (Rev: BL 2/1/06; SLJ 2/06)

3231 Blake, Robert J. *Swift* (K–3). Illus. by author. 2007, Philomel $16.99 (978-0-399-23383-8). 48pp. After a grizzly attacks his father, Johnnie and his dog Swift set out across the Alaskan wilderness to get help. (Rev: BL 9/15/07; HB 9/07; SLJ 9/07)

3232 Burningham, John. *Mr. Gumpy's Motor Car* (K–3). Illus. by author. 1976, HarperCollins LB $18.89 (978-0-690-00799-2). 48pp. Mr. Gumpy takes his daughter and an assortment of animals for a ride in the country in his old-fashioned touring car. Companion to: *Mr. Gumpy's Outing* (Holt 1995).

3233 Buzzeo, Toni. *Adventure Annie Goes to Work* (PS). Illus. by Amy Wummer. 2009, Dial $16.99 (978-0-8037-3233-9). 32pp. Annie (aka Adventure Girl) turns a trip to Mommy's office into an opportunity to show her skills. (Rev: BL 2/1/09; SLJ 1/09)

3234 Caines, Jeannette. *Just Us Women* (PS–2). Illus. by Pat Cummings. 1984, HarperCollins paper $6.99 (978-0-06-443056-2). 32pp. A little African American girl is looking forward to a car ride she is going to take with her aunt.

3235 Caple, Kathy. *Hillary to the Rescue* (PS–3). Illus. 2000, Carolrhoda $15.95 (978-1-57505-420-9). 32pp. Hillary overdresses for her drama club winter outing but finds that these clothes are useful when she has to seek help after the group's bus breaks down. (Rev: BL 11/15/00; HBG 3/01; SLJ 12/00)

3236 Carrick, Carol. *Left Behind* (PS–2). Illus. by Donald Carrick. 1988, Houghton $16.60 (978-0-89919-535-3). 32pp. On a class visit to the city aquarium, Christopher gets left behind at the subway stop. (Rev: BCCB 9/88; BL 9/15/88; HB 9/88)

3237 Carter, Anne Laurel. *Under a Prairie Sky* (PS–3). Illus. by Alan Daniel and Lea Daniel. 2002, Orca $16.95 (978-1-55143-226-7). 32pp. A Canadian boy gets a taste of being a Mountie when he rescues his younger brother from a coming storm. (Rev: BL 5/15/02; HBG 10/02; SLJ 6/02)

3238 Cowley, Joy. *The Video Shop Sparrow* (2–4). Illus. by Gavin Bishop. 1999, Boyds Mills $15.95 (978-1-56397-826-5). 32pp. Two youngsters, noticing that a sparrow is trapped in a store that will be closed for two weeks, try to get help in rescuing the bird. (Rev: BL 12/1/99; HBG 3/00; SLJ 12/99)

3239 Crews, Donald. *Sail Away* (PS–3). Illus. 1995, Greenwillow LB $15.93 (978-0-688-11054-3). 32pp. A family weathers a storm in their sailboat. (Rev: BCCB 4/95; BL 4/1/95; HB 9/95; SLJ 5/95*)

3240 Cummings, Pat. *Harvey Moon, Museum Boy* (K–2). Illus. by author. 2008, HarperCollins $16.99 (978-0-688-17889-5). 32pp. Harvey Moon's class trip to the museum becomes an adventure when his pet lizard, Zippy, escapes and Harvey spends an exciting night in the museum complete with encounters with mummies and dinosaurs. (Rev: BL 12/1/07; SLJ 3/08)

3241 Demas, Corinne. *Hurricane!* (K–3). Illus. by Lenice Strohmeier. 2000, Marshall Cavendish

$15.95 (978-0-7614-5052-8). 32pp. Inspired by Hurricane Bob of 1991, this picture book tells how a little girl and her family prepare for, experience, and survive a hurricane on Cape Cod. (Rev: BL 3/1/00; HBG 10/00; SLJ 4/00)

3242 Di Fiori, Larry. *Jackie and the Shadow Snatcher* (K–2). Illus. 2006, Knopf $15.95 (978-0-375-87515-1). 32pp. With the help of his dog Baxter and elderly friend Mr. Socrates, young Jackie hopes to recover his shadow from the villainous Shadow Snatcher in this picture-book-sized graphic novel set in the first half of the 20th century with detailed black-and-white illustrations. (Rev: BL 4/15/06; SLJ 7/06)

3243 Doyen, Denise. *Once Upon a Twice* (PS–1). Illus. by Barry Moser. 2009, Random $16.99 (978-0-375-85612-9). 32pp. Young Jam disregards the adults' warnings and ventures at night into the swamp where many perils await in this slightly scary book filled with rich nonsensical language. (Rev: BL 7/09)

3244 Elya, Susan Middleton. *Say Hola to Spanish at the Circus* (PS–4). Illus. by Loretta Lopez. Series: Say Hola to Spanish. 2000, Lee & Low $15.95 (978-1-880000-92-2). 32pp. Using English and about 70 Spanish words, this brightly illustrated book combines the two languages in an introduction to the fun and excitement of the circus. (Rev: BL 7/00; HBG 10/00; SLJ 7/00)

3245 Enderle, Judith R., and Stephanie G. Tessler. *Nell Nugget and the Cow Caper* (K–2). Illus. by Paul Yalowitz. 1996, Simon & Schuster paper $15.00 (978-0-689-80502-8). In this humorous Western tale, Nell Nugget sets out to find the culprit who has rustled her favorite cow, Goldie. (Rev: BCCB 5/96; HB 9/96; SLJ 7/96)

3246 English, Karen. *Big Wind Coming!* (PS–2). Illus. by Cedric Lucas. 1996, Whitman LB $14.95 (978-0-8075-0726-1). 32pp. A severe windstorm and its effects on an African American family as seen through the eye of the young daughter. (Rev: BCCB 1/97; BL 10/15/96; SLJ 11/96)

3247 Fagan, Cary. *Thing-Thing* (K–2). Illus. by Nicolas Debon. 2008, Tundra $18.95 (978-0-88776-839-2). 32pp. A rejected little stuffed creature's long fall ends happily; illustrations full of scary perspectives add to this lighthearted tale. (Rev: HB 9/08; SLJ 9/08)

3248 Fleming, Candace. *Sunny Boy! The Life and Times of a Tortoise* (K–2). Illus. by Anne Wilsdorf. 2005, Farrar $16.00 (978-0-374-37297-2). 40pp. In this fact-based picture book, Sunny Boy, a 100-year-old tortoise, tells about the many adventures in his life, including a trip over Niagara Falls in a barrel with his daredevil owner. (Rev: BL 8/05; SLJ 8/05)

3249 Fox, Mem. *Tough Boris* (PS–3). Illus. by Kathryn Brown. 1994, Harcourt $16.00 (978-0-15-289612-6). 32pp. Boris is a rough and tough pirate, but when his parrot dies, he cries. (Rev: BL 3/1/94; HB 5/94; SLJ 5/94)

3250 Funke, Cornelia. *Pirate Girl* (K–2). Illus. by Kerstin Meyer. 2005, Scholastic $15.99 (978-0-439-

71672-7). 32pp. A band of pirates meet their match when they kidnap young Molly. (Rev: BL 6/1–15/05)

3251 Gershator, Phillis. *Tiny and Bigman* (K–3). Illus. by Lynne W. Cravath. 1999, Marshall Cavendish $15.95 (978-0-7614-5044-3). 32pp. On their Caribbean island, Miss Tiny, who is married to Mr. Bigman, vows that, in spite of an oncoming hurricane, she will remain home to have her baby. (Rev: BCCB 12/99; BL 10/15/99; HBG 3/00; SLJ 11/99)

3252 Graham, Georgia. *The Strongest Man This Side of Cremona* (PS–3). Illus. 1998, Northern Lights $15.95 (978-0-88995-182-2). 32pp. Young Matthew and his dad seek shelter when a tornado approaches their farm on the Canadian prairie. (Rev: BL 2/1/99; SLJ 5/99)

3253 Haynes, Max. *Dinosaur Island* (PS–2). Illus. 1991, Lothrop $13.95 (978-0-688-10329-3). 32pp. Maddy and Bing travel in a land where dinosaurs are hidden in the pictures. (Rev: BL 10/1/91; SLJ 1/92)

3254 Huggins, Peter. *Trosclair and the Alligator* (PS–2). Illus. by Lindsey Gardiner. 2006, Star Bright $15.95 (978-1-932065-98-5). 32pp. Trosclair ignores his father's advice and goes searching for turtle eggs in a Louisiana swamp that's dominated by a rogue alligator known as Gargantua. (Rev: BL 4/15/06; SLJ 3/06)

3255 Jam, Teddy. *The Fishing Summer* (K–3). Illus. by Ange Zhang. 1997, Douglas & McIntyre $12.95 (978-0-88899-285-7). 32pp. A boy stows away on his uncle's fishing boat and works hard to learn the family trade. (Rev: BL 9/15/97; SLJ 2/98)

3256 Jane, Pamela. *The Big Monkey Mix-up* (1–4). Illus. by Cathy Bobak. 1997, Avon paper $3.99 (978-0-380-78951-1). 65pp. A simple mystery that revolves around a missing monkey and Benjamin's desire to lose at least one of his baby teeth. (Rev: SLJ 1/98)

3257 Jardine, Alan. *Sloop John B: A Pirate's Tale* (PS–1). Illus. by Jimmy Pickering. 2005, Milk & Cookies $17.95 (978-0-689-03596-8). A boy and his grandfather fight off pirates aboard the *John B* in this beautifully illustrated book inspired by the traditional folk song; comes with a music CD. (Rev: SLJ 7/05)

3258 Jezek, Alisandra. *Miloli's Orchids* (K–3). Illus. by Yoshi Miyake. 1991, Raintree LB $22.83 (978-0-8172-2784-5). 31pp. Written by a youngster, this story set in Hawaii tells of a young girl's attempts to save orchids from a volcano. (Rev: SLJ 6/91)

3259 Johnson, Scott. *I Can't Wait Until I'm Old Enough to Hunt with Dad* (1–3). Illus. by Karen Johnson. 1995, Deer Pond $14.95 (978-1-887251-56-3). 32pp. A young boy accompanies his father on a bow-and-arrow deer hunt. (Rev: BL 2/1/96)

3260 Keats, Ezra Jack. *Maggie and the Pirate* (1–3). Illus. by author. 1987, Scholastic paper $5.99 (978-0-590-44852-9). 32pp. Maggie tries to find the kidnapper of her pet cricket. A reissue of the 1979 edition.

3261 Kimmel, Eric A. *Four Dollars and Fifty Cents* (2–4). Illus. by Glen Rounds. 1990, Holiday House LB $16.95 (978-0-8234-0817-7). 32pp. To get out of paying a bad debt, cowboy Shorty Long pretends to be dead. (Rev: BL 9/15/90; HB 1/91*; SLJ 11/90)

3262 Look, Lenore. *Ruby Lu, Brave and True* (1–3). Illus. by Anne Wilsdorf. 2004, Simon & Schuster $15.95 (978-0-689-84907-7). 112pp. Ruby, a Chinese American 8-year-old, deals with family, school, and cultural problems in this appealing book with a glossary of terms. (Rev: BL 1/1–15/04; SLJ 2/04)

3263 Lumry, Amanda, and Laura Hurwitz. *Amazon River Rescue* (K–4). Illus. by Sarah McIntyre. Series: Adventures of Riley. 2004, Eaglemont Pr. $15.95 (978-0-9662257-9-2). Riley and Alice come across animals including a jaguar when they get lost in the Amazon; lots of sidebars supply factual information. (Rev: SLJ 11/04)

3264 McCarthy, Meghan. *Steal Back the Mona Lisa!* (K–2). Illus. by author. 2006, Harcourt $16.00 (978-0-15-205368-0). Jack sets out to track down the "crooked crooks" who stole da Vinci's painting from the Louvre; full of humor and melodrama, and with a note that describes a time it really was stolen. (Rev: SLJ 10/06)

3265 Maguire, Gregory. *Crabby Cratchitt* (PS–3). Illus. by Andrew Glass. 2000, Clarion $15.00 (978-0-395-60485-4). 32pp. Crabby Cratchitt, who can't stand the clucking of her hen, decides to solve the problem by having a chicken dinner, until she sees the hen's nest filled with eggs. (Rev: BL 9/1/00; HBG 3/01; SLJ 8/00)

3266 Martin, Bill, Jr., and John Archambault. *The Ghost-Eye Tree* (K–3). Illus. by Ted Rand. 1985, Holt $16.95 (978-0-8050-0208-9); paper $6.95 (978-0-8050-0947-7). 32pp. A brother and sister are sent to fetch a pail of milk on a spooky night past the Ghost-Eye Tree. (Rev: BL 12/15/85; HB 1/86; SLJ 2/86)

3267 Martin, Bill, Jr., and John Archambault. *White Dynamite and Curly Kidd* (1–3). Illus. by Ted Rand. 1986, Holt paper $6.95 (978-0-8050-1018-3). 48pp. A nervous fan carries on a conversation with a bull rider who is about to break out of the chute on White Dynamite. (Rev: BL 7/86; SLJ 4/86)

3268 Mauner, Claudia, and Elisa Smalley. *Zoe Sophia in New York: The Mystery of the Pink Phoenix Papers* (1–3). 2006, Chronicle $14.95 (978-0-8118-4877-0). 32pp. Zoe Sophia's Great-Aunt Dorothy comes to New York for a visit, during which they see many sites and search for a missing diary; a sequel to *Zoe Sophia's Scrapbook* (2003). (Rev: BL 6/1–15/06; SLJ 4/06)

3269 Mayhew, James. *Miranda the Explorer: A Magical Round-the-World Adventure* (1–3). Illus. by author. 2003, Orion $16.95 (978-1-84255-000-7). Another adventure for the plucky Miranda of *Miranda the Castaway*, this time involving a perilous round-the-world trip by hot-air balloon, sprinkled with foreign words and images. (Rev: BL 1/1–15/04; SLJ 6/04)

3270 Mitton, Tony. *Once Upon a Tide* (PS–K). Illus. by Selina Young. 2006, Random $16.95 (978-0-385-75100-1). Two small children have an adventurous and imaginative day at the beach searching for buried treasure. (Rev: SLJ 5/06)

3271 Patneaude, David. *A Piece of the Sky* (5–8). 2007, Albert Whitman $15.95 (978-0-8075-6536-0). 178pp. In Oregon to help his grandfather settle into an assisted-living residence, 14-year-old Russell and his new friend Phoebe, pursued by a sinister character, set off on an unexpectedly dangerous meteorite search. (Rev: SLJ 5/07)

3272 Rosen, Michael J. *We're Going on a Bear Hunt* (PS–2). Illus. by Helen Oxenbury. 1989, Macmillan $17.00 (978-0-689-50476-1). 40pp. The storytelling favorite is re-created with expansive pictures that capture the enthusiasm of the story. (Rev: BCCB 9/89; BL 8/89*; HB 11/89*; SLJ 8/89*)

3273 Rylant, Cynthia. *Tulip Sees America* (PS–3). Illus. by Lisa Desimini. 1998, Scholastic $15.95 (978-0-590-84744-5). 32pp. A young man and his dog travel across the United States and find a place by the sea in Oregon where they want to stay. (Rev: BL 3/15/98; HBG 10/98; SLJ 4/98)

3274 San Souci, Daniel. *The Amazing Ghost Detectives* (1–4). Illus. by author. Series: Clubhouse Books. 2006, Tricycle $15.95 (978-1-58246-165-6). Danny and the rest of the gang return to find someone has been in their clubhouse but the lock is untouched; could it be a ghost? (Rev: SLJ 4/07)

3275 Sauer, Tammi. *Cowboy Camp* (PS–2). Illus. by Mike Reed. 2005, Sterling $14.95 (978-1-4027-2224-0). 32pp. Avery seems an unlikely candidate for Cowboy Camp, but he eventually proves his worth when he foils an evil scheme by Black Bart. (Rev: BL 2/15/06; SLJ 3/06)

3276 Seymour, Tres. *We Played Marbles* (K–3). Illus. by Dan Andreasen. 1998, Orchard LB $16.99 (978-0-531-33074-6). 32pp. The Civil War battle that took place at Fort Craig, Kentucky, unfolds as two boys play an innocent game on its site. (Rev: BL 2/15/98; HBG 10/98; SLJ 3/98)

3277 Steig, William. *Brave Irene* (K–2). Illus. by author. 1986, Farrar $17.00 (978-0-374-30947-3). 32pp. The incredible adventures of Irene, who sets out in a snowstorm to deliver the duchess's new dress for the ball. (Rev: BCCB 12/86; BL 11/1/86; HB 11/86)

3278 Stevenson, James. *"Could Be Worse!"* (K–3). Illus. by author. 1977, Morrow paper $6.99 (978-0-688-07035-9). 32pp. Grandpa's response to minor catastrophes is always the same.

3279 Stutson, Caroline. *Cowpokes* (PS–2). Illus. by Daniel San Souci. 1999, Lothrop $16.99 (978-0-688-13973-5). 24pp. Takes the reader through an action-packed day spent by high-spirited cartoon cowboys riding, roping, eating, making mistakes, and bedding down at night. (Rev: BL 9/15/99; HBG 3/00; SLJ 9/99)

3280 Sullivan, Silky. *Grandpa Was a Cowboy* (K–3). Illus. by Bert Dodson. 1996, Orchard LB $16.99 (978-0-531-08861-6). 32pp. A young orphan is intrigued by the tales his grandfather spins about his career as a cowboy. (Rev: BL 4/1/96; SLJ 4/96)

3281 Swanson, Diane. *The Balloon Sailors* (2–4). Illus. by Krystyna Lipka-Sztarballo. 2003, Annick

LB $15.95 (978-1-55037-809-2). A family in a kingdom divided by a guarded stone wall decides to fly over it in a hot-air balloon; a postscript likens the situation to Berlin after World War II. (Rev: SLJ 3/04)

3282 Trueman, Terry. *Hurricane* (5–7). 2008, HarperCollins $15.99 (978-0-06-000018-9). 144pp. José is 13 when Hurricane Mitch hits his village in Honduras and he must deal with the death and destruction left behind. (Rev: BL 12/1/07; SLJ 3/08)

3283 Van Allsburg, Chris. *The Garden of Abdul Gasazi* (K–3). Illus. by author. 1979, Houghton $18.95 (978-0-395-27804-8). 32pp. Young Alan wanders into the garden of a retired magician with unexpected results.

3284 Wallace, Ian. *A Winter's Tale* (K–3). Illus. 1997, Douglas & McIntyre $15.95 (978-0-88899-286-4). 32pp. A gentle outdoor adventure in which Abigail is taken camping by her father and brother to celebrate her ninth birthday. (Rev: BL 10/15/97; SLJ 12/97)

3285 Ward, Helen. *The Boat* (1–3). Illus. by Ian Andrew. 2005, Simply Read $16.95 (978-1-894965-18-7). 32pp. When flooding threatens an old man and his menagerie of animals, it is a young boy who tries to save them all. (Rev: BL 6/1–15/05)

3286 Ward, Lynd. *The Biggest Bear* (K–3). Illus. by author. 1952, Houghton $16.00 (978-0-395-14806-8); paper $6.95 (978-0-395-15024-5). 88pp. Johnny wanted a bearskin on his barn so he went looking for the biggest bear. Caldecott Medal winner, 1953.

3287 Wheeler, Lisa. *Seadogs: An Epic Ocean Operetta* (PS–2). Illus. by Mark Siegel. 2004, Simon & Schuster $16.95 (978-0-689-85689-1). 40pp. In Victorian times, a little girl dog enjoys going to an operetta about and starring seagoing dogs in this comic-book-style story for the youngest readers. (Rev: BL 2/1/04; HB 3/04; SLJ 3/04)

3288 Wiesner, David. *Hurricane* (1–3). Illus. 1990, Houghton $16.00 (978-0-395-54382-5). 32pp. Two boys take refuge in their hideout in a tree during a hurricane watch. (Rev: BCCB 11/90; BL 12/15/90; HB 1/91; SLJ 10/90*)

3289 Williams, Vera B. *Three Days on a River in a Red Canoe* (K–3). Illus. by author. 1981, Greenwillow $16.89 (978-0-688-84307-6); Morrow paper $6.99 (978-0-688-04072-7). 32pp. A little girl describes a canoe trip with her cousins and their mother.

3290 Zagwyn, Deborah Turney. *The Sea House* (K–3). Illus. 2002, Tricycle $15.95 (978-1-58246-030-7). 32pp. Clee and her brother have an adventure on their uncle's boat. (Rev: BL 4/1/02; HBG 10/02; SLJ 6/02)

COMMUNITY AND EVERYDAY LIFE

3291 Adorjan, Carol. *I Can! Can You?* (PS–K). Illus. by Miriam Nerlove. 1990, Whitman LB $15.99 (978-0-8075-3491-5). 24pp. A little girl tells about the skills she has mastered. (Rev: BL 12/15/90; SLJ 2/91)

3292 Agassi, Martine. *Hands Are Not for Hitting* (PS–1). Illus. by Marieka Heinlen. 2000, Free Spirit paper $11.95 (978-1-57542-077-6). 35pp. This book preaches the lesson that there are better things for hands to do than hurting other people. (Rev: SLJ 2/01)

3293 Ajmera, Maya. *Global Babies* (PS). Illus. 2007, Charlesbridge $6.95 (978-1-58089-174-5). 18pp. Many ethnic groups are represented in this book consisting of close-up photographs of babies' faces. (Rev: BL 7/07)

3294 Albee, Sarah. *Clever Trevor* (1–3). Illus. by Paige Billin-Frye. Series: Science Solves It! 2003, Kane paper $4.99 (978-1-57565-123-1). 32pp. When a gang of bullies invades the playground, clever Trevor uses scientific principles to outsmart them. (Rev: SLJ 6/03)

3295 Alberto, Daisy. *No Rules for Rex!* (1–3). Illus. by Jerry Smath. Series: Social Studies Connects. 2005, Kane paper $4.99 (978-1-57565-146-0). 32pp. Rex learns about the importance of following rules in this book designed to support social studies curricula. (Rev: SLJ 9/05)

3296 Aliki. *Hello! Good-bye!* (PS–2). Illus. 1996, Greenwillow $14.89 (978-0-688-14334-3). 32pp. The many ways of saying "hello" and "good-bye" around the world. (Rev: BCCB 12/96; BL 7/96; SLJ 9/96)

3297 Aliki. *Quiet in the Garden* (PS–K). Illus. by author. 2009, Greenwillow $17.99 (978-0-06-155207-6). 32pp. A little boy quietly watches the animals in his garden, imagining their conversations. (Rev: BCCB 3/09; BL 11/15/08; SLJ 2/09)

3298 Allen, Kathryn Madeline. *This Little Piggy's Book of Manners* (PS–1). Illus. by Nancy Wolff. 2003, Holt $15.95 (978-0-8050-6769-9). Bright illustrations demonstrate both good and bad behavior on the part of a number of little piggies. (Rev: HBG 4/04; SLJ 11/03)

3299 Allen, Kit. *Slide, Already!* (PS–2). Illus. 2005, Houghton $12.00 (978-0-618-49643-3). 32pp. A simple story about the fears and joys involved in a boy's first experience on a slide. (Rev: BL 6/1–15/05)

3300 Amado, Elisa. *Tricycle* (PS–2). Illus. by Alfonso Ruano. 2007, Groundwood $17.95 (978-0-88899-614-5). 32pp. When Margarita, a child of privilege in Guatemala, sees her friend Rosario steal her bicycle, she says nothing, keenly aware of the poverty in which her friend lives. (Rev: BL 4/1/07; SLJ 6/07)

3301 Anderson, Sara. *A Day at the Market* (PS–2). Illus. by author. 2006, Handprint $14.95 (978-1-59354-149-1). The sights and sounds of Seattle's Pike Place Market are depicted in rhyme and artistic collages in this large-format board book. (Rev: SLJ 5/06)

3302 Antoine, Héloïse. *Curious Kids Go to Preschool: Another Big Book of Words* (PS). Illus. by Ingrid Godon. 1996, Peachtree $13.95 (978-1-56145-129-6). An introduction to preschool experiences through defining such words as *school bus, backpack,* and *lunch box.* (Rev: SLJ 11/96)

3303 Appelt, Kathi. *The Best Kind of Gift* (K–2). Illus. by Paul B. Johnson. 2003, HarperCollins LB $17.89 (978-0-688-15393-9). In this heartwarming tale of Appalachia, Jory Timmons find that he has gifts to offer despite his small size. (Rev: HBG 10/03; SLJ 6/03)

3304 Appelt, Kathi. *Watermelon Day* (PS–3). Illus. by Dale Gottlieb. 1996, Holt $15.95 (978-0-8050-2304-6). Young Jesse grows impatient waiting for her watermelon to grow sufficiently so that it can be eaten when her pappy declares it is a watermelon day. (Rev: BCCB 1/96; SLJ 6/96)

3305 Armstrong-Ellis, Carey. *Prudy's Problem and How She Solved It* (K–2). Illus. 2002, Abrams $14.95 (978-0-8109-0569-6). 32pp. Unconventional Prudy collects everything until her room is so full that a single gum wrapper causes it to explode. (Rev: BL 12/15/02; HBG 3/03; SLJ 10/02)

3306 Arnold, Tedd. *Even More Parts: Idioms from Head to Toe* (1–3). Illus. by author. 2004, Dial $16.99 (978-0-8037-2938-4). In this entertaining sequel to *Parts* (1997) and *More Parts* (2001), the boy given to literal interpretations of idioms — "I lost my head" — is ready to go to school. (Rev: SLJ 1/05)

3307 Arnold, Tedd. *More Parts* (1–4). Illus. by author. 2001, Dial $16.99 (978-0-8037-1417-5). A young boy is terrified by phrases that seem to threaten survival such as "laugh your head off" and "give him a hand." (Rev: BCCB 9/01; HBG 3/02; SLJ 9/01)

3308 Atkins, Jeannine. *Get Set! Swim!* (K–3). Illus. by Hector Viveros Lee. 1998, Lee & Low $15.95 (978-1-880000-66-3). 32pp. Jessenia's mother and brother attend her swim meet, and swimming reminds Jessenia of her mother's home in Puerto Rico. (Rev: BL 5/15/98; HBG 10/98; SLJ 5/98)

3309 Ayres, Katherine. *Matthew's Truck* (PS). Illus. by Hideko Takahashi. 2005, Candlewick $8.99 (978-0-7636-2269-5). 24pp. A toddler-friendly board book about a little boy imagining himself the driver of his toy dump truck. (Rev: BL 3/1/05)

3310 Baer, Edith. *This Is the Way We Eat Our Lunch: A Book About Children Around the World* (PS–3). Illus. by Steve Björkman. 1995, Scholastic $14.95 (978-0-590-46887-9). 32pp. A visit to lunchtime in nine states, two Canadian provinces, and 11 other countries, with accompanying recipes and food facts. (Rev: BCCB 9/95; BL 9/15/95; SLJ 9/95)

3311 Baer, Gene. *Thump, Thump, Rat-a-Tat-Tat* (PS–K). Illus. by Lois Ehlert. 1991, HarperCollins paper $5.99 (978-0-06-443265-8). 32pp. Re-creates the sights and sounds of a marching band. (Rev: BCCB 2/90; BL 11/1/89*; HB 9/89*; SLJ 1/90)

3312 Baguley, Elizabeth. *Meggie Moon* (PS–2). Illus. by Gregoire Mabire. 2005, Good Bks $16.00 (978-1-56148-474-4). Digger and Tiger spurn Meggie Moon's overtures because she's a girl, but they change their tune when she constructs a snappy-looking race car from scraps and refuse. (Rev: SLJ 10/05)

3313 Baicker, Karen. *Tumble Me Tumbily* (PS). Illus. by Sam Williams. 2002, Handprint $15.95 (978-1-929766-61-1). 36pp. Three rhymes — two bouncy ones for waking up and eating, and a quieter one for bedtime — are decorated by illustrations that introduce a vast cast of characters. (Rev: BL 11/1/02; HBG 3/03; SLJ 4/03)

3314 Baicker, Karen. *You Can Do It Too!* (PS). Illus. by Ken Wilson-Max. 2005, Handprint $13.95 (978-1-59354-080-7). 24pp. A girl encourages her little brother to do as she is doing. (Rev: BL 6/1–15/05)

3315 Bailey, Linda. *The Best Figure Skater in the Whole Wide World* (PS–2). Illus. by Alan Daniel and Lea Daniel. 2001, Kids Can $15.95 (978-1-55074-879-6). Lizzy dreams of becoming a world-class figure skater, but has to accept being cast as a tree. (Rev: HBG 3/02; SLJ 12/01)

3316 Baker, Jeannie. *Home* (K–3). Illus. 2004, Greenwillow $16.99 (978-0-06-623935-4). 32pp. Without a single word, Baker tells a compelling story of the value of conservation and environmental action. (Rev: BL 3/15/04*; HB 3/04; SLJ 3/04)

3317 Baker, Jeannie. *Window* (2–4). Illus. 1991, Greenwillow $17.89 (978-0-688-08918-4). 24pp. The changes from a rural to an urban setting are traced in the changes seen through a window. (Rev: BCCB 3/91; BL 4/15/91; HB 5/91; SLJ 3/91*)

3318 Bang, Molly. *Yellow Ball* (PS–1). Illus. 1991, Morrow LB $15.89 (978-0-688-06315-3). 24pp. The yellow ball over the sea on the jacket becomes the focus of a game of catch. (Rev: BCCB 4/91; BL 3/1/91*; SLJ 5/91)

3319 Banks, Kate. *The Great Blue House* (PS–2). Illus. by Georg Hallensleben. 2005, Farrar $16.00 (978-0-374-32769-9). 40pp. A vacation house sits quiet and empty during the winter — or is it? Inviting illustrations show animal movements and house noises. (Rev: BL 6/1–15/05)

3320 Barber, Barbara E. *Allie's Basketball Dream* (PS–3). Illus. by Darryl Ligasan. 1996, Lee & Low $15.95 (978-1-880000-38-0). 32pp. When she receives her first basketball, Allie perseveres until she is able to shoot a basket. (Rev: BCCB 2/97; BL 1/1–15/97; SLJ 11/96)

3321 Barber, Barbara E. *Saturday at The New You* (PS–3). Illus. by Anna Rich. 1994, Lee & Low $14.95 (978-1-880000-06-9). 32pp. Shauna, an African American girl, has fun on Saturdays helping at her mother's beauty shop. (Rev: BCCB 12/94; BL 12/1/94; SLJ 1/95)

3322 Barron, Rex. *Showdown at the Food Pyramid* (PS–2). Illus. by author. 2004, Penguin $16.99 (978-0-399-23715-7). The foods of the pyramid battle over their positions until chaos ensues and a new, sensible structure is needed. (Rev: SLJ 7/04)

3323 Barton, Byron. *Building a House* (PS–2). Illus. by author. 1981, Greenwillow LB $17.89 (978-0-688-84291-8); Morrow paper $6.99 (978-0-688-09356-3). 32pp. The stages of building a house are simply presented.

3324 Bateson-Hill, Margaret. *Shota and the Star Quilt* (PS–3). Illus. by Christine Fowler. 1998, Zero to Ten $14.95 (978-1-84089-021-1). 32pp. Shota, a Lakota girl, and her friend Esther persuade their landlord not to tear down their apartment building, by showing him a star quilt that celebrates their apartment home. (Rev: BL 2/1/99; HBG 3/99)

3325 Bean, Jonathan. *At Night* (PS–K). Illus. by author. 2007, Farrar $15.00 (978-0-374-30446-1). 32pp. Shadows and light expressed in this book's watercolor illustrations complement the gentle text about a young girl seeking the peace and open air of her rooftop at night. (Rev: BCCB 10/07; BL 7/07; HB 1/09; SLJ 9/07)

3326 Beaumont, Karen. *I Like Myself!* (PS–1). Illus. by David Catrow. 2004, Harcourt $16.00 (978-0-15-202013-2). Bright illustrations enliven the humorous verse about a girl who likes herself both inside and out. (Rev: BCCB 7–8/04; SLJ 7/04)

3327 Bechdolt, Jack. *Little Boy with a Big Horn* (K–3). Illus. by Dan Yaccarino. 2008, Random $14.99 (978-0-375-83903-0). 32pp. Since Ollie only knows one song to play on the tuba and the townspeople are tired of it, Ollie practices in a rowboat where he is able to warn approaching ships of the nearby rocks. (Rev: BL 12/1/07; SLJ 3/08)

3328 Bergstein, Rita M. *Your Own Big Bed* (PS). Illus. by Susan Kathleen Hartung. 2008, Viking $15.99 (978-0-670-06079-5). 36pp. Bergstein compares the transition from crib to real bed with natural changes that young animals experience. (Rev: BL 7/08; SLJ 7/08)

3329 Berner, Rotraut Susanne. *In the Town All Year 'Round* (PS–2). Illus. by author. 2008, Chronicle $16.99 (978-0-8118-6474-9). 72pp. An intriguing look at how the activities of people in a town change with the seasons. (Rev: BL 11/15/08; SLJ 12/08)

3330 Bernhard, Durga. *In the Fiddle Is a Song: A Lift-the-Flap Book of Hidden Potential* (PS–1). 2006, Chronicle $10.95 (978-0-8118-4951-7). 24pp. Flaps reveal the potential within objects — the huge oak tree within a single acorn, the loaf of bread within a sheaf of wheat. (Rev: BL 6/1–15/06; SLJ 6/06)

3331 Bertram, Debbie, and Susan Bloom. *The Best Book to Read* (K–2). Illus. by Michael Garland. 2008, Random $14.99 (978-0-375-84702-8). 32pp. On a trip to the library, a young boy learns that there are lots of kinds of books, something for everyone. (Rev: BL 4/15/08; LMC 8/08; SLJ 6/08)

3332 Bertram, Debbie, and Susan Bloom. *The Best Time to Read* (K–2). Illus. by Michael Bloom. 2005, Random LB $16.99 (978-0-375-93025-6). 32pp. The whole family — even the dog — seems to have better things to do than listen to a little boy read. (Rev: BL 5/15/05)

3333 Best, Cari. *Red Light, Green Light, Mama and Me* (PS–2). Illus. by Niki Daly. 1995, Orchard LB $16.99 (978-0-531-08752-7). 32pp. Lizzie spends an exciting day with her mother, who is a children's librarian in a big downtown library. (Rev: BCCB 9/95; BL 9/1/95; SLJ 10/95)

3334 Best, Cari. *Sally Jean, the Bicycle Queen* (K–2). Illus. by Christine Davenier. 2006, Farrar $16.00 (978-0-374-36386-4). Sally Jean comes up with her own solution when her parents can't afford to buy her a new bike. (Rev: BL 5/1/06; SLJ 5/06*)

3335 Birdseye, Tom. *Airmail to the Moon* (K–2). Illus. by Stephen Gammell. 1988, Holiday House LB $16.95 (978-0-8234-0683-8); paper $6.95 (978-0-8234-0754-5). 32pp. Motor-mouth Ora Mae vows to "send to the moon" the one who stole her tooth. (Rev: BL 3/15/88; HB 5/88; SLJ 5/88)

3336 Blackstone, Stella. *Baby Rock, Baby Roll* (PS–1). Illus. by Denise and Fernando. 1997, Holiday House LB $13.95 (978-0-8234-1311-9). 32pp. Three children from different races bounce through a day's activities. (Rev: BL 9/1/97; HBG 3/98; SLJ 10/97)

3337 Blackstone, Stella. *Making Minestrone* (K–3). Illus. by Nan Brooks. 2000, Barefoot Books $15.99 (978-1-84148-211-8). 32pp. A group of multiethnic kids get together under the supervision of a lonely boy to make a fine batch of minestrone soup. (Rev: BL 10/1/00; HBG 3/01; SLJ 10/00)

3338 Boelts, Maribeth. *Those Shoes* (K–3). Illus. by Noah Z. Jones. 2007, Candlewick $15.99 (978-0-7636-2499-6). 40pp. African American Jeremy longs for the cool high-top sneakers that many of the kids are wearing, but with the help of his grandmother, learns the meaning of "wants," "needs" and compassion, and finally enjoys the new boots he needed to wear in the snow. (Rev: BCCB 12/07; BL 11/1/07; HB 11/07; LMC 1/08; SLJ 12/07)

3339 Bogart, Jo Ellen. *Jeremiah Learns to Read* (K–3). Illus. by Laura Fernandez. 1999, Orchard $15.95 (978-0-531-30190-6). 32pp. An elderly farmer named Jeremiah is taught to read by the local teacher and children in a one-room school, and in exchange he shares with them some of his animal lore. (Rev: BL 9/15/99; HBG 3/00; SLJ 10/99)

3340 Borden, Louise. *The Lost-and-Found Tooth* (K–2). Illus. by Adam Gustavson. 2008, Simon & Schuster $16.99 (978-1-4169-1814-1). 40pp. Mr. Reilly uses the losing of teeth as the basis for learning a number of skills, and 2nd-grader Lucy longs to be able to add her name to the roster. (Rev: BL 7/08; SLJ 8/08)

3341 Boswell, Addie. *The Rain Stomper* (PS). Illus. by Eric Velasquez. 2008, Marshall Cavendish $16.99 (978-0-7614-5393-2). 32pp. When a heavy storm rains on Jazmin's parade, the little African American girl tries to chase the rain away. (Rev: BL 9/1/08; SLJ 9/08)

3342 Bourgeois, Paulette. *Big Sarah's Little Boots* (PS–1). Illus. by Brenda Clark. 1992, Scholastic paper $4.95 (978-0-590-42623-7). 32pp. Preschooler Sarah can't understand why her favorite yellow boots have shrunk. (Rev: BL 1/1/90; SLJ 11/89)

3343 Boynton, Sandra. *Hey! Wake Up!* (PS). Illus. by author. 2000, Workman $6.95 (978-0-7611-1976-0). A board book about morning activities like yawning, stretching, breakfast, and getting dressed. Also use *Pajama Time!* (2000). (Rev: SLJ 2/01)

3344 Brandenberg, Alexa. *I Am Me!* (PS). Illus. by author. 1996, Harcourt $12.00 (978-0-15-200974-8). After toddlers mention a number of careers they are interested in, they engage in activities related to each. (Rev: SLJ 12/96)

3345 Bregoli, Jane. *The Goat Lady* (2–4). Illus. by author. 2004, Tilbury House $16.95 (978-0-88448-260-4). Wonderful paintings enhance this story of an elderly French Canadian woman who was not accepted by the people of her Massachusetts town because she raised goats and failed to fit in. (Rev: SLJ 3/05) [759.13]

3346 Brenner, Barbara. *Good Morning, Garden* (K–3). Illus. by Denise Ortakales. 2004, NorthWord $15.95 (978-1-55971-888-2). Attractive illustrations show a young girl greeting the flowers, plants, insects, and animals in her garden. (Rev: SLJ 6/04)

3347 Brisson, Pat. *Melissa Parkington's Beautiful, Beautiful Hair* (K–2). Illus. by Suzanne Bloom. 2006, Boyds Mills $15.95 (978-1-59078-409-9). 40pp. Admired for the color and luster of her long, black hair, Melissa Parkington longs to be recognized for something more significant and finds a way to do something for others with her hair. (Rev: SLJ 11/06)

3348 Brisson, Pat. *The Summer My Father Was Ten* (PS–3). Illus. by Andrea Shine. 1998, Boyds Mills $15.95 (978-1-56397-435-9). A father tells his daughter while they plant a garden together of the guilt he felt when, as a child, he vandalized a neighbor's garden. (Rev: BCCB 5/98; BL 2/1/98*; HBG 10/98; SLJ 4/98)

3349 Brooks, Erik. *Octavius Bloom and the House of Doom* (1–3). Illus. by author. 2003, Whitman LB $16.99 (978-0-8075-5820-1). In this detective story told in rhyming verse, Octavius Bloom, new boy in town, decides to investigate mysterious Priscilla O'Moore's ramshackle shed. (Rev: HBG 10/03; SLJ 6/03)

3350 Brown, Marc, and Stephen Krensky. *Dinosaurs, Beware! A Safety Guide* (PS–2). Illus. by authors. 1984, Little, Brown paper $7.95 (978-0-316-11219-2). 32pp. Sixty safety tips are illustrated with drawings of dinosaurs.

3351 Brown, Margaret Wise. *Another Important Book* (PS–1). Illus. by Chris Raschka. 1999, HarperCollins LB $16.89 (978-0-06-026283-9). 32pp. In a series of rhymes, this book identifies important achievements and developments in the first six years of a child's life. (Rev: BCCB 1/00; BL 10/15/99; HB 9/99; HBG 3/00; SLJ 9/99)

3352 Brown, Margaret Wise. *A Child's Good Morning Book* (PS). Illus. by Karen Katz. 2009, HarperCollins $17.99 (978-0-06-128864-7). 32pp. A new edition of the classic picture-book story about a new day dawning for plants, animals, and children. (Rev: BL 11/15/08; SLJ 1/09)

3353 Brown, Margaret Wise. *Red Light, Green Light* (PS–K). Illus. by Leonard Weisgard. 1994, Scholastic paper $4.95 (978-0-590-44559-7). 40pp. This introduction to traffic signs was first published in 1944.

3354 Brown, Peter. *The Curious Garden* (PS–2). Illus. by author. 2009, Little, Brown $16.99 (978-0-316-01547-9). 40pp. A little boy named Liam decides to look after a few sad plants alongside a train track in a gray and gloomy city and his efforts result in a citywide renaissance. (Rev: BL 5/15/09; SLJ 4/09)

3355 Bunting, Eve. *Peepers* (K–3). Illus. by James Ransome. 2001, Harcourt $16.00 (978-0-15-260297-

0). 32pp. Two brothers come to appreciate the beauty of the fall colors so admired by the tourists, or "Leaf Peepers," who visit their New England town. (Rev: BL 9/1/01; HBG 3/02; SLJ 10/01)

3356 Bunting, Eve. *Smoky Night* (K–3). Illus. by David Diaz. 1994, Harcourt $16.00 (978-0-15-269954-3). 32pp. Two families, one Korean American and the other African American, reach out to one another during the terrible Los Angeles riots. Caldecott Medal winner, 1995. (Rev: BCCB 3/94; BL 3/1/94; HB 5/94; SLJ 5/94*)

3357 Burleigh, Robert. *Clang! Clang! Beep! Beep! Listen to the City* (PS–1). Illus. by Beppe Giacobbe. 2009, Simon & Schuster $14.99 (978-1-4169-4052-4). 32pp. A day in the sounds of the city — from garbage can bang to the last slamming door. (Rev: BL 6/1–15/09; SLJ 5/09)

3358 Burleigh, Robert. *I Love Going Through This Book* (PS–K). Illus. by Dan Yaccarino. 2001, HarperCollins $15.99 (978-0-06-028805-1). 32pp. This boisterous excursion through a book, courtesy of a young boy and animal friends, introduces young readers to the parts of a book and the fun of reading. (Rev: BCCB 6/01; BL 6/1–15/01; HBG 10/01; SLJ 6/01)

3359 Burningham, John. *Edwardo: The Horriblest Boy in the Whole Wide World* (PS–3). Illus. by author. 2007, Knopf $16.99 (978-0-375-84053-1). The power of positive reinforcement is emphasized in this story of Edwardo, whose behavior becomes worse and worse the more he is criticized but improves dramatically when he is praised. (Rev: BL 1/1–15/07; SLJ 2/07*)

3360 Burton, Virginia Lee. *The Little House* (1–3). Illus. by author. 1978, Houghton $16.00 (978-0-395-18156-0); paper $7.99 (978-0-395-25938-2). Story of a little house in the country that over the years witnesses change and progress. Caldecott Medal winner, 1943. (Rev: HBG 10/03)

3361 Butler, Dori. *The Truth About Truman School* (5–8). 2008, Albert Whitman $15.95 (978-0-8075-8095-0). 170pp. Zebby and Amr start an alternative, online school newspaper and soon learn that not all postings are fit to print in this story told from many characters' points of view. (Rev: BL 3/15/08; SLJ 5/08)

3362 Caines, Jeannette. *I Need a Lunch Box* (PS–K). Illus. by Pat Cummings. 1988, HarperCollins paper $6.99 (978-0-06-443341-9). 32pp. Mama says no to a lunch box for a little boy who hasn't yet started school. (Rev: BL 9/15/88; SLJ 12/88)

3363 Capucilli, Alyssa Satin. *The Potty Book for Boys* (PS). 2000, Barron's $5.95 (978-0-7641-5232-0). 32pp. The male narrator explains how he receives his own potty, how he sits on it, and how he is rewarded if successful. The same story from a girl's point of view is in *The Potty Book for Girls* (2000). (Rev: SLJ 9/00)

3364 Caraballo, Samuel. *Estrellita en la Ciudad Grande / Estrellita in the Big City* (K–3). Illus. by Pablo Torrecilla. 2008, Piñata $15.95 (978-1-55885-498-7). 32pp. Estrellita is an immigrant in New York City and her growing understanding of the

English language and her new home is shown through her many conversations with her grandmother in Puerto Rico. (Rev: SLJ 2/09)

3365 Carlson, Nancy. *Get Up and Go!* (PS–K). Illus. 2006, Viking $15.99 (978-0-670-05981-2). 32pp. Carlson emphasizes the importance of exercise and examines its many benefits. (Rev: BL 12/1/05; SLJ 2/06)

3366 Carlson, Nancy. *I Don't Like to Read!* (K–2). Illus. by author. 2007, Viking $15.99 (978-0-670-06191-4). 32pp. Frustrated by the difficulty of learning to read, Henry the mouse tries to mask his feelings by saying that reading is "boring" and "dumb." (Rev: BL 7/07; LMC 11/07; SLJ 7/07)

3367 Carlson, Nancy. *There's a Big, Beautiful World Out There!* (K–2). Illus. 2002, Viking $15.99 (978-0-670-03580-9). 32pp. Written just after September 11, 2001, this book uses cheery illustrations and a chatty approach to potential terrors to reassure children that anxieties are normal and the world is still a good place. (Rev: BL 10/1/02; HBG 3/03; SLJ 11/02)

3368 Carlstrom, Nancy White. *The Snow Speaks* (PS–2). Illus. by Jane Dyer. 1992, Little, Brown $15.95 (978-0-316-12861-2). 32pp. Children enjoy the various aspects of a snowstorm in the country from the first flakes to the coming of the snowplows. (Rev: BL 9/15/92)

3369 Carluccio, Maria. *The Sounds Around Town* (PS). Illus. by author. 2008, Barefoot Books $16.99 (978-1-905236-28-2). 24pp. A look at the sounds of a toddler's day — birds, cars, kittens, bathwater, and so forth. (Rev: BL 5/15/08; SLJ 7/08)

3370 Carney, Margaret. *At Grandpa's Sugar Bush* (PS–3). Illus. by Janet Wilson. 1998, Kids Can $16.95 (978-1-55074-341-8). 32pp. During his spring vacation, a young boy visits his grandparents on their Ontario farm and assists them in making maple syrup. (Rev: BL 4/1/98; HBG 10/98; SLJ 4/98)

3371 Carter, Anne Laurel. *My Home Bay* (PS). Illus. by Alan Daniel and Lea Daniel. Series: Northern Lights Books for Children. 2004, Red Deer $17.95 (978-0-88995-284-3). When her family moves clear across Canada from Vancouver to Nova Scotia, young Gwyn is initially disdainful of her new surroundings. (Rev: BL 2/1/04; SLJ 8/04)

3372 Caseley, Judith. *On the Town: A Community Adventure* (K–3). Illus. 2002, HarperCollins LB $17.89 (978-0-06-029585-1). 32pp. For a school assignment, Charlie and his mother visit people and places in the neighborhood but, afterward, Charlie realizes that home is best. (Rev: BL 4/15/02; HBG 10/02; SLJ 5/02)

3373 Catalanotto, Peter. *Emily's Art* (K–3). Illus. 2001, Simon & Schuster $16.00 (978-0-689-83831-6). 32pp. Emily is so disappointed when her picture doesn't win the art contest that she says she'll never paint again. (Rev: BCCB 9/01; BL 7/01; HBG 10/01; SLJ 6/01*)

3374 Charlip, Remy, and Lillian Moore. *Hooray for Me!* (PS–2). Illus. by Vera B. Williams. 1996, Tricycle $14.95 (978-1-883672-43-0). 36pp. A new edition of an old favorite that explores a child's relationships. (Rev: BL 11/15/96)

3375 Chessa, Francesca. *Holly's Red Boots* (PS–2). Illus. by author. 2008, Holiday $16.95 (978-0-8234-2158-9). 32pp. Holly's search for her red boots takes so long that by the time she finds them, the snow has melted, but now she can go out and puddle jump with Mom. (Rev: BL 9/1/08; SLJ 9/08)

3376 Chinn, Karen. *Sam and the Lucky Money* (PS–2). Illus. by Cornelius Van Wright and Ying-Hwa Hu. 1995, Lee & Low $15.95 (978-1-880000-13-7). Sam decides that the money he has received at Chinese New Year would be best used by giving it to a poor stranger. (Rev: SLJ 12/95)

3377 Chocolate, Deborah N. *El Barrio* (K–3). Illus. by David Diaz. 2009, Holt $16.95 (978-0-8050-7457-4). 32pp. A Latino boy describes his electric city neighborhood and the events that take place there; includes a glossary of Spanish words. (Rev: BLO 2/9/09; SLJ 3/09)

3378 Choung, Euh-hee. *Minji's Salon* (PS). Illus. by author. 2008, Kane $15.95 (978-1-933605-67-8). 36pp. Minji goes to work on her dog's hair while her mother is at the beauty salon, trying out many styles and techniques (including an ice cream rinse); double-page spreads show the parallel primping. (Rev: BL 7/08; SLJ 8/08)

3379 Clary, Margie Willis. *A Sweet, Sweet Basket* (K–4). Illus. by Dennis L. Brown. 1995, Sandlapper $15.95 (978-0-87844-127-3). 40pp. An older woman explains to her granddaughter how baskets are woven from the sweetgrass that grows in South Carolina. (Rev: BL 9/1/95)

3380 Clements, Andrew. *Workshop* (PS–1). Illus. by David Wisniewski. 1999, Clarion $16.00 (978-0-395-85579-9). As a young apprentice becomes involved in the creation of a carousel, all of the tools of the woodworker are introduced. (Rev: BCCB 7–8/99; BL 4/15/99*; HBG 10/99; SLJ 5/99) [621.9]

3381 Cocca-Leffler, Maryann. *Bus Route to Boston* (PS–2). Illus. 2000, Boyds Mills $15.95 (978-1-56397-723-7). 32pp. The author-illustrator recalls the thrill of living outside Boston and taking trips by bus into the big city to shop and see the sights. (Rev: BL 2/1/00; HBG 10/00; SLJ 4/00)

3382 Cohn, Diana. *¡Sí, Se Puede! / Yes, We Can! Janitor Strike in L.A.* (PS–3). Illus. by Francisco Delgado. 2002, Cinco Puntos $15.95 (978-0-938317-66-1). 32pp. Mexican American boy Carlitos supports his janitor mother in seeking to start a union, in this bilingual picture book based on a Los Angeles strike in 2000. (Rev: BL 10/1/02; HBG 3/03; SLJ 11/02*)

3383 Cole, Henry. *Jack's Garden* (PS–4). Illus. 1995, Greenwillow $17.99 (978-0-688-13501-0). 24pp. In this cumulative tale, the plants and insects found in Jack's garden are introduced. (Rev: BCCB 5/95; BL 4/1/95; HB 5/95; SLJ 5/95)

3384 Cole, Joanna. *My Big Boy Potty Book* (PS). Illus. by Maxie Chambliss. 2000, HarperCollins $6.99 (978-0-688-17042-4). 32pp. In this reassuring picture book, Michael is told that he will succeed in potty training because practice makes perfect. The female counterpart is *My Big Girl Potty Book* (2000). (Rev: BL 2/1/01; HBG 3/01; SLJ 11/00)

3385 Cole, Joanna. *My Friend the Doctor* (PS–K). Illus. by Maxie Chambliss. 2005, HarperCollins $6.99 (978-0-06-050500-4). 32pp. Cartoon illustrations and brief text depict a little girl's visit to the doctor for a checkup that includes getting a shot. (Rev: BL 7/05; SLJ 9/05)

3386 Coleman, Evelyn. *To Be a Drum* (K–3). Illus. by Aminah Robinson. 1998, Whitman LB $16.95 (978-0-8075-8006-6). 32pp. Daddy Wes tells two children about the history of African Americans and their struggles as revealed in the rhythm of drumbeats. (Rev: BL 2/15/98; HBG 10/98; SLJ 5/98)

3387 Collier, Bryan. *Uptown* (PS–3). Illus. 2000, Holt $15.95 (978-0-8050-5721-8). 32pp. A young boy points out the sights and delights of Harlem — shopping on 125th Street and going to a jazz club. (Rev: BCCB 11/00; BL 6/1–15/00; HBG 10/00; SLJ 7/00)

3388 Cooper, Elisha. *Beach* (K–2). 2006, Scholastic $16.99 (978-0-439-68785-0). 40pp. Double-page watercolor spreads and a simple text celebrate the joys of a day at the beach. (Rev: BL 6/1–15/06; SLJ 7/06)

3389 Cooper, Elisha. *A Good Night Walk* (PS). 2005, Scholastic $16.99 (978-0-439-68783-6). 40pp. This gentle picture book captures the ebb and flow of neighborhood life as a parent and child take an evening stroll. (Rev: BCCB 10/05; BL 11/1/05*; HB 11/05; HBG 4/06; SLJ 9/05)

3390 Copeland, Cynthia L. *What Are You Waiting For?* (K–1). Illus. by Mike Gordon. Series: Silly Millies. 2003, Millbrook LB $17.90 (978-0-7613-2804-9). 31pp. As a young boy surveys the site for a new playground, he approaches construction workers as they arrive and urges them to get busy. (Rev: HBG 10/03; SLJ 6/03)

3391 Cotten, Cynthia. *Rain Play* (PS–2). Illus. by Javaka Steptoe. 2008, Holt $16.95 (978-0-8050-6795-8). 32pp. Cotton highlights the pleasures and dangers of a thunderstorm in this simple story of a rainy day. (Rev: BL 2/15/08; SLJ 6/08)

3392 Coulman, Valerie. *I Am a Ballerina* (PS–1). Illus. by Sandra Lamb. 2004, Lobster $15.95 (978-1-894222-91-4). 32pp. The engaging tale of aspiring ballerina Molly. (Rev: BL 2/1/05; SLJ 3/05)

3393 Cousins, Lucy. *Maisy's Amazing Big Book of Words* (PS). Illus. by author. 2007, Candlewick $14.99 (978-0-7636-0794-4). 32pp. This oversized volume with a colorful, lift-the-flap format introduces words relating to everyday categories such as transport, food, and clothes. (Rev: BL 6/1–15/07; SLJ 8/07)

3394 Cowell, Cress. *That Rabbit Belongs to Emily Brown* (PS–K). Illus. by Neal Layton. 2007, Hyperion $16.99 (978-1-4231-0645-6). 40pp. Young Emily loves her tattered old stuffed rabbit named Stanley, with whom she has many adventures, and refuses to give him up even when offered much newer toys. (Rev: BL 4/1/07)

3395 Cox, Judy. *Now We Can Have a Wedding!* (PS–2). Illus. by DyAnne Disalvo-Ryan. 1998, Holiday House LB $15.95 (978-0-8234-1342-3). 32pp. The narrator goes from apartment to apartment in her building and sees that everyone is making a different national dish to bring to her sister's wedding. (Rev: BL 2/15/98; HBG 10/98; SLJ 3/98)

3396 Crews, Donald. *Night at the Fair* (K–2). Illus. 1998, Greenwillow $14.89 (978-0-688-11484-8). 24pp. Game booths, food concessions, and the Ferris wheel are only three of the attractions at a country fair that are highlighted in this engaging book. (Rev: BCCB 6/98; BL 3/1/98; HB 5/98; HBG 10/98; SLJ 4/98)

3397 Crews, Donald. *Shortcut* (PS–3). Illus. 1992, Greenwillow $17.89 (978-0-688-06437-2). 32pp. Seven children follow a railroad track back home as the train gets closer and closer. (Rev: BCCB 10/92*; BL 10/15/92*; HB 1/93*; SLJ 11/92)

3398 Crews, Nina. *Below* (PS–K). Illus. 2006, Holt $16.95 (978-0-8050-7728-5). 32pp. Striking photographs tell the story of Jack's efforts to rescue Guy, his action figure, when Guy falls through a hole in the stairs. (Rev: BL 3/1/06; SLJ 3/06)

3399 Crews, Nina. *One Hot Summer Day* (PS–K). Illus. 1995, Greenwillow $14.89 (978-0-688-13394-8). 24pp. Using collages, the author illustrates the many activities associated with a hot summer's day. (Rev: BCCB 6/95; BL 6/1–15/95; HB 7/95; SLJ 6/95)

3400 Crews, Nina. *Snowball* (PS–1). Illus. 1997, Greenwillow $14.89 (978-0-688-14929-1). 24pp. This is the story of an African American child in a city and how she gets her wish for snow. (Rev: BL 12/1/97; HBG 3/98; SLJ 9/97)

3401 Crum, Shutta. *Thunder-Boomer* (PS–2). Illus. by Carol Thompson. 2009, Clarion $16.00 (978-0-618-61865-1). 32pp. Vibrant illustrations add atmosphere as a welcome summer thunderstorm hits a farm and brings a new kitten to live with the family. (Rev: BL 7/09; SLJ 6/09)

3402 Cummins, Julie. *Country Kid, City Kid* (K–2). Illus. by Ted Rand. 2002, Holt $16.95 (978-0-8050-6467-4). Ben's life on the farm and Jody's life in the city are contrasted on facing pages. (Rev: HBG 3/03; SLJ 11/02)

3403 Cupiano, Ina. *Quinito's Neighborhood / El vecindario de Quinito* (PS–2). Illus. by José Ramírez. 2005, Children's Book Pr. $16.95 (978-0-89239-209-4). 24pp. Readers meet Quinito's neighbors and find out what they all do in warm illustrations and bilingual text. (Rev: BL 12/1/05; SLJ 10/05*)

3404 Curtis, Carolyn. *I Took the Moon for a Walk* (PS–2). Illus. by Alison Jay. 2004, Barefoot Books $16.99 (978-1-84148-611-6). 32pp. A young boy enjoys a nighttime stroll around his neighborhood with the moon as his companion; antique-looking panoramic illustrations add to the dreamlike text. (Rev: BL 4/1/04; SLJ 6/04)

3405 Curtis, Jamie Lee. *I'm Gonna Like Me: Letting Off a Little Self-Esteem* (1–3). Illus. by Laura Cornell. 2002, HarperCollins LB $17.89 (978-0-06-

028762-7). 32pp. Humorous, detailed illustrations and rhyming text show a boy and girl taking turns liking themselves. (Rev: BL 10/1/02; HBG 3/03; SLJ 10/02)

3406 Curtis, Jamie Lee. *Is There Really a Human Race?* (K–2). Illus. by Laura Cornell. 2006, HarperCollins $16.99 (978-0-06-075346-7). 40pp. When did this race start? Where is it going? Is it important to win? A mother thoughtfully helps her son unravel these difficult questions. (Rev: BL 9/15/06; SLJ 8/06*)

3407 Cutler, Jane. *Common Sense and Fowls* (3–5). Illus. by Lynne Barasch. 2005, Farrar $16.00 (978-0-374-32262-5). 136pp. In this sequel to *Family Dinner* (1995), Rachel and Brian try to alleviate a dispute and improve communication by offering Mrs. Krnc styrofoam vowels and Mr. Gioai styrofoam consonants. (Rev: SLJ 3/05)

3408 Cuyler, Margery. *From Here to There* (PS–3). Illus. by Yu Cha Pak. 1999, Holt $16.95 (978-0-8050-3191-1). 32pp. A little girl describes where she lives in an ever-widening address — from town to county to state and so on. (Rev: BL 6/1–15/99; HBG 10/99; SLJ 5/99)

3409 Cuyler, Margery. *Please Play Safe! Penguin's Guide to Playground Safety* (PS). 2006, Scholastic $15.99 (978-0-439-52832-0). 32pp. Penguin and his friend cleverly demonstrate the do's and don'ts of playground behavior. (Rev: BL 8/06; SLJ 8/06)

3410 Danis, Naomi. *Walk with Me* (PS). Illus. by Jacqueline Rogers. Series: Story Corner. 1995, Scholastic $6.95 (978-0-590-45855-9). A mother and her preschool daughter combine a pleasant outdoor walk with some nature study. (Rev: SLJ 8/95)

3411 Danneberg, Julie. *First Day Jitters* (K–4). Illus. by Judy Love. 2000, Charlesbridge $16.95 (978-1-58089-054-0). 32pp. A little girl imagines all the terrible things that could happen to her on her first day of school, but is pleasantly surprised with the real thing. (Rev: BL 3/15/00; HBG 10/00; SLJ 5/00)

3412 Dean, Carol Shorey. *The Live Bale of Hay: A Real Maine Adventure* (1–3). Illus. by Sandra Dunn. 2005, Down East $15.95 (978-0-89272-674-5). A bear that looks like a bale of hay is scared away by their dog's barking and two girls get safely home in this gentle adventure. (Rev: SLJ 8/05)

3413 De La Hoya, Oscar. *Super Oscar* (PS–2). Trans. by Andrea Montejo. Illus. by Lisa Kopelke. 2006, Simon & Schuster $15.95 (978-1-4169-0611-7). Oscar turns into Super Oscar to help his parents get ready for a picnic in this bilingual (Spanish and English) story. (Rev: SLJ 6/06)

3414 Delton, Judy. *My Mom Made Me Go to Camp* (1–3). Illus. by Lisa McCue. 1993, Dell paper $2.99 (978-0-440-40838-3). 32pp. Archie, who does not want to attend summer camp, gradually changes his mind. (Rev: BL 1/1/91; SLJ 2/91)

3415 Depalma, Mary Newell. *The Nutcracker Doll* (1–3). Illus. by author. 2007, Scholastic $16.99 (978-0-439-80242-0). 32pp. DePalma, mother of a dancer, takes readers on a tour of the ballet world as young Kepley is cast in a tiny part in a *Nutcracker*

production. (Rev: BCCB 12/07; BL 11/1/07; HB 11/07)

3416 Derby, Sally. *My Steps* (PS–1). Illus. by Adjoa J. Burrowes. 1996, Lee & Low $15.95 (978-1-880000-40-3). 32pp. An African American city child tells what a wonderful playground her front steps can be. (Rev: BL 10/15/96; SLJ 10/96)

3417 Devine, Monica. *Carry Me, Mama* (PS–1). Illus. by Pauline Paquin. 2002, Stoddart $15.95 (978-0-7737-3317-6). A beautifully illustrated story of a mother gently persuading her child to walk further and further. (Rev: HB 5/02; HBG 10/02; SLJ 7/02)

3418 Disalvo-Ryan, DyAnne. *Grandpa's Corner Store* (K–3). Illus. 2000, HarperCollins LB $15.89 (978-0-688-16717-2). 40pp. When Grandpa decides to sell his grocery store, Lucy devises a plan to get him to change his mind. (Rev: BL 5/1/00; HBG 10/00; SLJ 7/00)

3419 Disalvo-Ryan, DyAnne. *Spaghetti Park* (K–2). Illus. 2002, Holiday House $16.95 (978-0-8234-1682-0). 32pp. A haven for down-and-outs is transformed into a popular neighborhood park with a lively bocce court. (Rev: BL 11/15/02; HBG 3/03; SLJ 1/03)

3420 *Do Skyscrapers Touch the Sky? First Questions and Answers About the City* (PS–K). Illus. 1994, Time-Life $14.95 (978-0-7835-0886-3). 48pp. Obvious questions about city life — like "What's under the street?" — are answered in well-illustrated double-page spreads. (Rev: BL 2/1/95) [307.76]

3421 Doherty, Berlie. *Coconut Comes to School* (PS–2). Illus. by Ivan Bates. 2003, HarperCollins $17.95 (978-0-00-710433-8). The simple story of Coconut the donkey and how she rescues the teacher who had previously failed to appreciate her. (Rev: SLJ 9/03)

3422 Dooley, Norah. *Everybody Bakes Bread* (K–3). Illus. by Peter J. Thornton. 1996, Carolrhoda LB $15.95 (978-0-87614-864-8). 40pp. On an errand for her mother, Carrie sees her neighbors bake a variety of breads in this sequel to *Everybody Cooks Rice* (1991). (Rev: BL 3/1/96; SLJ 4/96)

3423 Dorros, Alex, and Arthur Dorros. *Numero Uno* (K–3). Illus. by Susan Guevara. 2007, Abrams $16.95 (978-0-8109-5764-0). 32pp. Mexican villagers tire of the argument between two men, one strong and the other smart, over who is most valuable to the community; with the help of a local boy, both men come to see the pointlessness of their conflict. (Rev: BL 5/15/07; HB 7/07; SLJ 8/07)

3424 Doughty, Rebecca. *Lost and Found* (K–2). Illus. 2005, Putnam $12.99 (978-0-399-24177-2). 32pp. Always in a rush, young Lucy is forever losing things; after looking under her bed, she resolves to take more time in the future. (Rev: BL 8/05)

3425 Doughty, Rebecca. *Oh No! Time To Go! A Book of Goodbyes* (PS–2). Illus. by author. 2009, Random $15.99 (978-0-375-84981-7). 40pp. How many ways are there to say goodbye? A young boy reviews many choices and describes the worst of his goodbye experiences. (Rev: BL 3/1/09; SLJ 4/09)

3426 Drescher, Henrik. *McFig and McFly: A Tale of Jealousy, Revenge, and Death (with a Happy Ending)* (K–3). Illus. by author. 2008, Candlewick $17.99 (978-0-7636-3386-8). 40pp. Neighbors McFig and McFly are so focused on their efforts to outbuild each other that they fail to notice that their children Anton and Rosie have fallen in love. (Rev: BL 6/1–15/08; LMC 10/08; SLJ 5/08)

3427 Driscoll, Laura. *The Blast Off Kid* (1–2). Illus. by Rebecca Thornburgh. Series: Math Matters. 2003, Kane paper $4.99 (978-1-57565-130-9). 32pp. Jim hopes to collect 10,000 Blast Off Bar wrappers so he can win a trip to space camp, and it is his skill in grouping them that makes it possible to keep track. (Rev: SLJ 1/04)

3428 Drummond, Allan. *Tin Lizzie* (PS–3). Illus. by author. 2008, Farrar $16.95 (978-0-374-32000-3). 32pp. Eliza and her siblings go for a ride in Grandpa's restored Model T and look with dismay at all the changes cars have made to the landscape and atmosphere in the years since the old car was built. (Rev: BL 7/08; SLJ 7/08)

3429 Duncan, Debbie. *When Molly Was in the Hospital: A Book for Brothers and Sisters of Hospitalized Children* (PS–2). Illus. by Nina Ollikainen. Series: MiniMed. 1994, Rayve $12.95 (978-1-877810-44-2). The experiences of a young girl whose younger sister faces major surgery and the many conflicting emotions she feels. (Rev: SLJ 3/95)

3430 Dunn, Todd. *We Go Together!* (PS–K). Illus. by Miki Sakamoto. 2007, Sterling $12.95 (978-1-4027-3260-7). 24pp. A rhyming text describes familiar items that go together like "leaves and fall" and "horse and wagon." (Rev: BL 12/1/07; SLJ 12/07)

3431 Edwards, Pamela Duncan. *Jack and Jill's Treehouse* (K–3). Illus. by Henry Cole. 2008, HarperCollins $16.99 (978-0-06-009077-7). 24pp. In this cumulative tale with a familiar ring Jack and Jill build a tree house and their work is duplicated by a pair of robins constructing their own nest. (Rev: BL 5/15/08; SLJ 5/08)

3432 Edwards, Richard. *Fly with the Birds: A Word and Rhyme Book* (PS–K). Illus. by Satoshi Kitamura. 1996, Orchard $12.95 (978-0-531-09491-4). In this flap book, a child narrates her day, from waking up to bedtime and dreamland. (Rev: SLJ 3/96)

3433 Edwardson, Debby Dahl. *Whale Snow* (PS–2). Illus. by Annie Patterson. 2003, Charlesbridge $15.95 (978-1-57091-393-8). Amiqaqq, a young Inupiat boy, attends the first whaling feast of the winter season and learns about the important role the whale plays in Inupiat culture and the welfare of his small Alaskan village. (Rev: BL 8/03; HBG 4/04; LMC 1/04; SLJ 12/03)

3434 Ehlert, Lois. *Circus* (PS–2). Illus. 1992, HarperCollins $16.99 (978-0-06-020252-1). 40pp. The razzle-dazzle of the circus is translated into the relative quiet of the picture-book experience. (Rev: BL 1/1/92; HB 3/92; SLJ 4/92) [791.3]

3435 Ehlert, Lois. *Growing Vegetable Soup* (PS–K). Illus. by author. 1987, Harcourt $15.00 (978-0-15-232575-6); paper $6.00 (978-0-15-232580-0). 40pp. Father and child plant seeds and sprouts "to grow vegetable soup." Also use: *Planting a Rainbow* (1988). (Rev: BL 3/1/87; SLJ 3/87)

3436 Ehlert, Lois. *Leaf Man* (PS–2). Illus. 2005, Harcourt $16.00 (978-0-15-205304-8). 40pp. An imaginative story about autumn leaves. (Rev: BL 6/1–15/05)

3437 Ehlert, Lois. *Market Day: A Story Told with Folk Art* (PS–2). Illus. 2000, Harcourt $16.00 (978-0-15-202158-0). 36pp. This picture book depicts a day when the farmers load their trucks with goods and go to the market to buy and sell, and work and play. (Rev: BCCB 7–8/00; BL 5/15/00; HBG 10/00; SLJ 7/00)

3438 Ehrlich, Fred. *Does a Panda Go to School?* (PS–K). Illus. by Emily Bolam. Series: Early Experiences. 2003, Handprint $10.95 (978-1-59354-017-3). Bright illustrations fill this small-format, question-and-answer explanation of some of the differences between animals and children. Also use the similarly humorous *Does a Yak Get a Haircut?* (Rev: SLJ 2/04) [372.21]

3439 Ellis, Sarah. *Next Stop!* (PS–K). Illus. by Ruth Ohi. 2000, Fitzhenry & Whiteside $13.95 (978-1-55041-539-1). 32pp. Little Claire helps the bus driver by calling out the names of the streets and the special attractions found at each stop. (Rev: BL 12/1/00; SLJ 1/01)

3440 Elya, Susan Middleton. *Bebé Goes Shopping* (K–2). Illus. by Steven Salerno. 2006, Harcourt $16.00 (978-0-15-205426-7). 40pp. A child's visit to the supermarket with his mother introduces a number of Spanish vocabulary words in the rhyming text, which is enhanced by retro-style illustrations. (Rev: BCCB 6/06; BL 2/15/06*; HBG 10/06; SLJ 5/06)

3441 Elya, Susan Middleton. *Bebé Goes to the Beach* (PS–2). Illus. by Steven Salerno. 2008, Harcourt $16.00 (978-0-15-206000-8). 40pp. Bebé and his mother spend a day doing lots of activities at the beach in this rhyming bilingual sequel to *Bebé Goes Shopping* (2006). (Rev: BCCB 7–8/08; BL 5/15/08; SLJ 5/08)

3442 Elya, Susan Middleton. *Oh No, Gotta Go #2* (PS–K). Illus. by Lynne Avril. 2007, Putnam $15.99 (978-0-399-24308-0). A little girl at a picnic realizes that she needs to use the potty in this companion to *Oh No, Gotta Go*. Many Spanish words are incorporated into the rhyming text. (Rev: BCCB 7–8/07; SLJ 7/07)

3443 Elya, Susan Middleton. *Tooth on the Loose* (PS–1). Illus. by Jenny Mattheson. 2008, Putnam $16.99 (978-0-399-24459-9). 32pp. Will a little girl's tooth fall out in time for her to buy a gift for her father's birthday? Told in English and Spanish, this is a charming rhyming story with glossary, pronunciation guide, and evocative illustrations. (Rev: BL 7/08; SLJ 8/08)

3444 Ericsson, Jennifer A. *A Piece of Chalk* (PS–1). Illus. by Michelle Shapiro. 2007, Roaring Brook $16.95 (978-1-59643-057-0). 32pp. A cheerful story about a little girl with a brand new box of chalk and a long driveway. (Rev: BL 9/1/07; SLJ 10/07)

3445 Erlbruch, Wolf. *The Big Question* (K–3). 2005, Europa paper $14.95 (978-1-933372-03-7). 52pp. A variety of answers to life's biggest question — why am I here? — can be found in the pages of this tall, creative book that won the 2004 Ragazzi Award at the Bologna Book Fair. (Rev: BL 1/1–15/06)

3446 Esbensen, Barbara J. *Jumping Day* (PS–1). Illus. by Maryann Cocca-Leffler. 1999, Boyds Mills $9.95 (978-1-56397-709-1). 24pp. A delightful look at a girl at play as she skips her way to school. (Rev: HBG 10/99; SLJ 4/99)

3447 Evans, Lezlie. *Sometimes I Feel Like a Storm Cloud* (PS–1). Illus. by Marsha Carrington. 1999, Mondo $15.95 (978-1-57255-621-8). 32pp. A girl's moods are expressed in a series of similes that capture her feelings. (Rev: BL 12/15/99)

3448 Fair, Sylvia. *The Bedspread* (K–2). Illus. by author. 1982, Morrow $16.95 (978-0-688-00877-2). 32pp. Two old ladies decide to embroider their bedspreads.

3449 Falwell, Cathryn. *Mystery Vine: A Pumpkin Surprise* (PS–2). Illus. by author. 2009, Harper-Collins $16.99 (978-0-06-177198-9). 32pp. Activities and recipes are included in this cheerful rhyming story about a brother and sister planting, tending, and harvesting a pumpkin vine. (Rev: BLO 6/19/09)

3450 Farrell, John. *It's Just a Game* (K–3). Illus. by John E. Cymerman. 1999, Boyds Mills $15.95 (978-1-56397-785-5). 32pp. Even though they lose every game but one, and in spite of parents who are overcompetitive, a group of kids enjoy playing on their soccer team. (Rev: BL 12/1/99; HBG 3/00; SLJ 11/99)

3451 Field, Rachel. *General Store* (PS–1). Illus. by Nancy W. Parker. 1988, Little, Brown $15.95 (978-0-316-28163-8). 24pp. A poem that extols the charms of the old-fashioned store. Another version has illustrations by Giles Laroche (1988, Little, Brown). (Rev: BCCB 5/88; BL 3/1/88; HB 5/88)

3452 Fitz-Gibbon, Sally. *On Uncle John's Farm* (1–3). Illus. by Brian Deines. 2005, Fitzhenry & Whiteside $15.95 (978-1-55041-691-6); paper $8.95 (978-1-55041-886-6). A gentle story of a little girl's busy day on the farm. (Rev: BL 3/1/04; SLJ 5/05)

3453 Fitz-Gibbon, Sally. *Two Shoes, Blue Shoes, New Shoes!* (PS–1). Illus. by Farida Zaman. 2002, Fitzhenry & Whiteside $14.95 (978-1-55041-729-6). 32pp. This colorfully illustrated picture book focuses on a child's joy and excitement about a new pair of shoes. (Rev: SLJ 4/03)

3454 Fitzgerald, Joanne. *This Is Me and Where I Am* (PS–2). Illus. 2004, Fitzhenry & Whiteside $14.95 (978-1-55041-819-4). 32pp. A young child gradually focuses in on his small point in the universe and then expands his view again. (Rev: BL 10/1/04; SLJ 11/04)

3455 Fitzpatrick, Marie-Louise. *There* (PS–2). Illus. by author. 2009, Roaring Brook $17.95 (978-1-59643-087-7). 32pp. A little girl reflects on eternal questions including "When will I get There?" and "Will it take long to get There"? (Rev: BLO 5/27/09; SLJ 5/09)

3456 Fleischman, Sid. *The Scarebird* (PS–2). Illus. by Peter Sís. 1988, Greenwillow $15.89 (978-0-688-07318-3). 32pp. An old farmer named Lonesome John puts up a headless scarecrow to scare the birds, but then decides to give the scarecrow a head. (Rev: BCCB 9/88; BL 9/15/88; SLJ 9/88)

3457 Fleming, Candace. *Imogene's Last Stand* (1–3). Illus. by Nancy Carpenter. 2009, Random $16.99 (978-0-375-83607-7). 40pp. A determined activist, young Imogene cleverly fights for the preservation of the Liddleville Historical Society. (Rev: BCCB 11/09; BL 7/09; HB 11/09; LMC 11/09; SLJ 10/09)

3458 Fleming, Denise. *Where Once There Was a Wood* (PS–2). Illus. 1996, Holt $16.95 (978-0-8050-3761-6). 32pp. A piece of land is described as it was before a housing development changed it. (Rev: BCCB 3/96; BL 5/1/96; SLJ 6/96)

3459 Fletcher, Ralph. *The Circus Surprise* (PS–2). Illus. by Vladimir Vagin. 2001, Clarion $15.00 (978-0-395-98029-3). 32pp. Despite all his training, Nick panics when he gets lost at the circus. (Rev: HBG 10/01; SLJ 6/01)

3460 Ford, Bernette. *No More Diapers for Ducky!* (PS). Illus. by Sam Williams. 2006, Sterling $12.95 (978-1-905417-08-7). 32pp. A fluffy duckling makes the transition from wearing diapers to using the potty. (Rev: BL 6/1–15/06; SLJ 8/06)

3461 Ford, Christine. *Snow!* (PS). Illus. by Candace Whitman. Series: Growing Tree. 1999, Harper-Collins $9.95 (978-0-694-01199-5). 24pp. For the very young, this is a rhyming story about a brother and sister who spend a snowy day outdoors with their dad and pet dog. (Rev: BL 1/1–15/00; HBG 3/00; SLJ 12/99)

3462 Ford, Miela. *My Day in the Garden* (PS–3). Illus. by Anita Lobel. 1999, Greenwillow LB $15.89 (978-0-688-15542-1). 24pp. Little girls at home on a rainy day use their imaginations and the costumes they find to create an indoor garden. (Rev: BCCB 3/99; BL 5/1/99; HBG 10/99; SLJ 5/99)

3463 Fox, Mem. *Hello Baby!* (PS). Illus. by Steve Jenkins. 2009, Simon & Schuster $16.99 (978-1-4169-8513-6). 32pp. Rhyming questions and eye-catching art ask young readers to consider just who they are, comparing themselves with a variety of animals. (Rev: BCCB 9/09; BL 5/15/09; SLJ 4/09)

3464 Fox, Paula. *Traces* (2–3). Illus. by Karla Kuskin. 2008, Front St. $16.95 (978-1-932425-43-7). 32pp. An interesting meditation on the traces that things leave behind — ripples in the water, a jet trail, a turtle's tracks in the sand. (Rev: BL 3/1/08; SLJ 4/08)

3465 Freeman, Mylo. *Potty!* (PS). Illus. by author. 2002, Tricycle $13.95 (978-1-58246-070-3). All the animals of the jungle try out a potty, but it's a small child's bottom that fits it properly. (Rev: HBG 10/02; SLJ 4/02)

3466 Friedman, Laurie. *A Style All Her Own* (PS–1). Illus. by Sharon Watts. 2004, Carolrhoda $15.95 (978-1-57505-599-2). Isabelle Ashley Parker McBride likes to dress in her own style, even when she's asked to be a flower girl, but her aunt manages to negotiate a compromise. (Rev: SLJ 4/05)

3467 Fucile, Tony. *Let's Do Nothing!* (1–3). Illus. by author. 2009, Candlewick $16.99 (978-0-7636-3440-7). 40pp. Sal and Frankie try very hard to do nothing after exhausting themselves doing everything else in this lively, vividly illustrated book. (Rev: BL 7/09; SLJ 7/09)

3468 Gardella, Tricia. *Blackberry Booties* (PS–2). Illus. by Glo Coalson. 2000, Orchard LB $16.99 (978-0-531-33184-2). 32pp. Mikki Jo works hard picking blackberries and then uses bartering techniques to get a pair of booties made for her newborn cousin. (Rev: BCCB 4/00; BL 3/15/00; HBG 10/00; SLJ 5/00)

3469 Garland, Sarah. *Ellie's Breakfast* (PS). Illus. by author. 2001, Red Fox paper $8.95 (978-0-09-969261-4). Father and Ellie do their morning chores — feeding the animals and collecting the eggs. (Rev: SLJ 3/02)

3470 Garland, Sherry. *The Summer Sands* (PS–1). Illus. by Robert J. Lee. 1995, Harcourt $15.00 (978-0-15-282492-1). 32pp. Children and their parents use their old Christmas trees to act as a windbreak to form new sand dunes. (Rev: BL 4/15/95; SLJ 6/95)

3471 Gary, Meredith. *Sometimes You Get What You Want* (PS–2). Illus. by Lisa Brown. 2008, HarperCollins $16.99 (978-0-06-114015-0). 32pp. A brother and sister acknowledge the times during the day when they do and don't get what they want. (Rev: BL 5/15/08; HB 5/08; SLJ 4/08)

3472 Gauch, Patricia Lee. *Tanya and the Red Shoes* (PS–2). Illus. by Satomi Ichikawa. 2002, Penguin $16.99 (978-0-399-23314-2). 40pp. Young ballet dancer Tanya finds out that graduating to toe shoes isn't everything she thought it would be. (Rev: BL 3/1/02; HB 5/02; HBG 10/02; SLJ 3/02)

3473 Gay, Marie-Louise. *When Stella Was Very, Very Small* (PS–K). Illus. by author. Series: Stella. 2009, Groundwood $16.95 (978-0-88899-906-1). 32pp. Stella's fans will enjoy getting to see her as a baby and growing through various stages, and appreciate her ever-plucky attitude toward the world around her. (Rev: BL 7/09)

3474 George, Kristine O'Connell. *Book!* (PS). Illus. by Maggie Smith. 2001, Clarion $9.95 (978-0-395-98287-7). 32pp. A toddler finds great joy in his first picture book in this engaging package of friendly text and lively illustrations. (Rev: BL 12/1/01; HBG 3/02; SLJ 10/01) [811]

3475 Gerber, Carole. *Blizzard* (PS–K). Illus. by Marty Husted. 2001, Charlesbridge $15.95 (978-1-58089-064-9). 32pp. A boy describes in verse the delight of being cozy and warm inside while a winter storm rages outside. (Rev: BL 9/15/01; HBG 3/02; SLJ 10/01)

3476 Gershator, Phillis. *Listen, Listen* (PS–2). Illus. by Alison Jay. 2007, Barefoot Books $16.99 (978-1-84686-084-3). 32pp. A tour of the sounds of the changing seasons in a country town. (Rev: BL 11/15/07; LMC 3/08; SLJ 11/07)

3477 Gershator, Phillis, and David Gershator. *Summer Is Summer* (PS–K). Illus. by Sophie Blackall. 2006, Holt $16.95 (978-0-8050-7444-4). 32pp. In this gentle picture book, two girls — one African American, the other white — and their brothers make the most of summer, finding countless ways to have fun. (Rev: BL 4/15/06; SLJ 6/06*)

3478 Gerstein, Mordicai. *Leaving the Nest* (PS–2). Illus. by author. 2007, Farrar $16.00 (978-0-374-34369-9). In a single backyard youngsters — a kitten, a blue jay, a squirrel, and a girl — experiment with new skills under the watchful eyes of their mothers. (Rev: BL 3/1/07; SLJ 4/07)

3479 Gibbons, Gail. *Fire! Fire!* (PS–2). Illus. by author. 1984, HarperCollins $16.89 (978-0-690-04416-4); paper $6.99 (978-0-06-446058-3). 40pp. The various ways a fire is fought.

3480 Gibbons, Gail. *How a House Is Built* (PS–K). Illus. 1990, Holiday House LB $16.95 (978-0-8234-0841-2). 32pp. A good introduction to the construction of a wood frame house. (Rev: BL 10/15/90; SLJ 10/90) [690]

3481 Glaser, Linda. *Our Big Home: An Earth Poem* (2–3). Illus. by Elisa Kleven. 2000, Millbrook LB $21.90 (978-0-7613-1650-3). 32pp. Some of the common joys of life — such as water, dirt, sun, moon, wind, sky, dark, and the fact one is alive — are celebrated with outstanding illustrations. (Rev: BL 5/15/00; HBG 10/00; SLJ 4/00)

3482 Godwin, Laura. *The Flower Girl* (PS–3). Illus. by John Wallace. 2000, Hyperion $12.99 (978-0-7868-0408-5). A description of a wedding from the flower girl's point of view. (Rev: SLJ 2/01)

3483 Godwin, Laura. *The Ring Bearer* (K–2). Illus. by John Wallace. 2006, Hyperion $12.99 (978-0-7868-5510-0). In this colorful picture book, rhymed couplets outline the responsibilities of the ring bearer during a wedding ceremony; a companion to *The Flower Girl* (2000). (Rev: SLJ 2/06)

3484 Godwin, Laura. *This Is the Firefighter* (PS–K). Illus. by Julian Hector. 2009, Hyperion $15.99 (978-1-4231-0800-9). 32pp. Rhyming couplets and bright illustrations show how fire fighters respond to a call for help. (Rev: BL 3/15/09; HB 3/09; SLJ 3/09)

3485 Gold, August. *Thank You, God, for Everything* (PS–2). Illus. by Wendy A. Halperin. 2009, Putnam $16.99 (978-0-399-24049-2). 32pp. Young Daisy appreciates and is grateful for all the things in her world. (Rev: BL 12/15/08; SLJ 1/09)

3486 Gold, August. *Where Does God Live?* (PS–1). Illus. by Matthew J. Perlman. 2001, SkyLight Paths paper $8.99 (978-1-893361-39-3). 32pp. With help from her parents, a little girl who wonders where God lives begins to see evidence of him all around her. (Rev: BL 10/1/01)

3487 Gomi, Taro. *Everyone Poops* (PS). Trans. by Amanda M. Stinchecum. Illus. Series: Can You Believe It! 1993, Kane $12.95 (978-0-916291-45-7). 28pp. This book shows that all animals poop and that this is a natural part of life. (Rev: BCCB 4/93; BL 5/15/93) [612]

3488 Gomi, Taro. *My Friends / Mis amigos* (PS–1). Illus. by author. 2006, Chronicle LB $14.50 (978-0-8118-4849-7); paper $6.95 (978-0-8118-5204-3). Animals, friends, family, and teachers all have something to teach a little girl in this bilingual book. (Rev: SLJ 6/06)

3489 González, Ada Acosta. *Mayte and the Bogeyman / Mayte y el Cuco* (2–4). Illus. by Christina Rodriguez. 2006, Piñata $15.95 (978-1-55885-442-0). Presented in both Spanish and English, this is an entertaining and colorfully illustrated story about Mayte and Pepito's assumption that Don Aparicio the ice cream man has evil intentions. (Rev: SLJ 6/06)

3490 Good, Merle, and Dan Boltz. *Dan's Pants: The Adventures of Dan, the Fabric Man* (K–3). Illus. by Cheryl Benner. 2000, Good Bks. $16.00 (978-1-56148-307-5). Dan and his wife Fran sell fabrics, and over the years Fran sews many patches from different bolts of cloth to mend Dan's pants. (Rev: SLJ 12/00)

3491 Grahn, Geoffrey. *What's Going on in There?* (K–3). Illus. by author. 2005, Scholastic $14.95 (978-0-439-57495-2). Readers must take time to examine each spread and identify what is really taking place in Grahnville (the pizza cook is really assembling a dinosaur, for example). (Rev: SLJ 3/05)

3492 Grambling, Lois G. *My Mom Is a Firefighter* (K–2). Illus. by Jane Manning. 2007, HarperCollins $16.99 (978-0-06-058640-9). 32pp. A young boy with a firefighter mom describes the duties of a firefighter and station-house life. (Rev: BL 10/1/07; SLJ 10/07)

3493 Grant, Brianna K. *We Are Girls Who Love to Run / Somos chicas y a nosotras nos encanta correr* (K–3). Trans. by Ana C. Venegas. Illus. by Nicholas A. Wright. 2008, Balanced Steps $17.99 (978-0-9798511-1-7). 32pp. In English and Spanish, this is a celebration of being a girl and enjoying running. (Rev: BL 6/1–15/08)

3494 Gray, Libba M. *When Uncle Took the Fiddle* (PS–2). Illus. by Lloyd Bloom. 1999, Orchard $15.95 (978-0-531-30137-1). 32pp. Although it's bedtime, an Appalachian family and their neighbors come to life when Uncle picks up his fiddle and starts to play. (Rev: BCCB 11/99; BL 9/15/99; HBG 3/00; SLJ 11/99)

3495 Gray, Nigel. *My Dog, My Cat, My Mama, and Me!* (PS). Illus. by Bob Graham. 2007, Candlewick LB $8.99 (978-0-7636-3639-5). 24pp. A lift-the-flap book that allows the reader to view the arrival of new puppies, new kittens, and finally new babies. (Rev: BL 12/15/07; SLJ 1/08)

3496 Gray, Rita. *Easy Street* (PS–1). Illus. by Mary Bono. 2006, Dutton $15.99 (978-0-525-47657-3). Rhyming text and colorful illustrations depict the building of an asphalt street. (Rev: SLJ 6/06)

3497 Gray, Rita. *Nonna's Porch* (PS–2). Illus. by Terry Widener. 2004, Hyperion $15.99 (978-0-7868-1613-2). On her porch, Nonna knits a blanket that depicts the summer scene. (Rev: SLJ 11/04)

3498 Greenberg, Melanie Hope. *Mermaids on Parade* (K–2). Illus. by author. 2008, Putnam $16.99 (978-0-399-24708-8). 32pp. This happy story about a young girl taking part in the Coney Island Mermaid Parade paints a bright picture of the beginning of summer. (Rev: BL 6/1–15/08; LMC 11/08; SLJ 7/08)

3499 Greenfield, Eloise. *Big Friend, Little Friend* (PS). Illus. by Jan S. Gilchrist. 1991, Writers & Readers $4.95 (978-0-86316-204-6). 12pp. This is one of a series of board books about the everyday activities of some African American children. Also use: *Daddy and I; I Make Music;* and *My Doll, Keshia* (all 1991). (Rev: BL 12/15/91; SLJ 12/91)

3500 Gregory, Nan. *Amber Waiting* (PS–1). Illus. by Kady M. Denton. 2003, Red Deer $17.95 (978-0-88995-258-4). When Dad is late — as always — picking Amber up from kindergarten, the little girl imagines ways to get even. (Rev: BL 5/15/03*; SLJ 7/03)

3501 Griffin, Kitty, and Kathy Combs. *Cowboy Sam and Those Confounded Secrets* (PS–2). Illus. by Mike Wohnoutka. 2001, Clarion $16.00 (978-0-618-08854-6). 32pp. Sam keeps the town's secrets under his 10-gallon hat, but it eventually becomes full. (Rev: HBG 3/02; SLJ 12/01)

3502 Grimes, Nikki. *Come Sunday* (PS–3). Illus. by Michael Bryant. 1996, Eerdmans $16.00 (978-0-8028-5108-6); paper $8.00 (978-0-8028-5134-5). 32pp. Young Latasha finds that going to church on Sunday is an exciting adventure. (Rev: BCCB 3/97; BL 6/1–15/96*; SLJ 6/97)

3503 Gundersheimer, Karen. *Find Cat, Wear Hat* (PS). Illus. 1995, Scholastic $5.95 (978-0-590-48061-1). 24pp. A beginner's book in which each page explains in two words the accompanying picture. Similar in scope is the author's *Splish Splash, Bang Crash* (1995). (Rev: BL 1/15/95; SLJ 9/95)

3504 Hamilton, Kersten. *Firefighters to the Rescue!* (PS–2). Illus. by Rich Davis. 2005, Viking $15.99 (978-0-670-03503-8). 32pp. Fire fighters rush to a house fire in this story that also shows their routine and the fire station. (Rev: BL 5/15/05)

3505 Hamm, Diane J. *Laney's Lost Momma* (PS–1). Illus. by Sally G. Ward. 1991, Whitman LB $16.99 (978-0-8075-4340-5). 32pp. Mother and daughter are reunited after Laney loses her mother in a department store. (Rev: BL 1/1/92; SLJ 12/91)

3506 Hannigan, Katherine. *Emmaline and the Bunny* (1–3). Illus. by author. 2009, Greenwillow $17.99 (978-0-06-162654-8). 112pp. Tidiness is the rule in Neatasapin but when shunned young Emmaline seeks friendship with a wild bunny, things begin changing for the better; inventive wordplay adds to the fun. (Rev: BL 1/1–15/09; HB 3/09; SLJ 3/09)

3507 Harper, Jessica. *Nora's Room* (PS–1). Illus. by Lindsay Harper duPont. 2001, HarperCollins LB $15.89 (978-0-06-029137-2). 32pp. Everyone in the family wonders what's making the incredible noise coming from Nora's room. (Rev: BL 7/01; HBG 10/01; SLJ 7/01)

3508 Hartland, Jessie. *Night Shift* (K–2). Illus. by author. 2007, Bloomsbury $16.95 (978-1-59990-025-4). 32pp. Fourteen wee-hour occupations are highlighted, one per double-page spread, providing a new look at all the work that gets done while most people sleep. (Rev: BCCB 11/07; BL 11/15/07; HB 1/08; LMC 11/07; SLJ 12/07)

3509 Hautzig, David. *At the Supermarket* (PS–2). Illus. 1994, Orchard LB $17.99 (978-0-531-08682-7). 32pp. An hour-by-hour account that describes in pictures and text what happens during a single day in a modern supermarket. (Rev: BL 3/15/94; SLJ 5/94) [381]

3510 Havill, Juanita. *Jamaica's Find* (PS–1). Illus. by Anne S. O'Brien. 1986, Houghton $16.00 (978-0-395-39376-5); paper $6.95 (978-0-395-45357-5). 32pp. Jamaica finds a stuffed dog, which she brings home, but her parents make her return to the park where she found it, and where she also finds its true owner. Also use: *Jamaica Tag-Along* (1989). (Rev: BCCB 5/86; BL 4/1/86; SLJ 8/86)

3511 Hayes, Joe. *A Spoon for Every Bite* (PS–3). Illus. by Rebecca Leer. 1996, Orchard LB $16.99 (978-0-531-08799-2). 32pp. A poor couple fools a rich neighbor into spending his fortune for spoons. (Rev: BCCB 4/96; BL 3/15/96; SLJ 4/96)

3512 Hayes, Sarah. *Eat Up, Gemma* (PS–1). Illus. by Jan Ormerod. 1988, Lothrop $16.00 (978-0-688-08149-2). 32pp. Gemma is at the stage where food is mostly a toy. (Rev: BCCB 9/88; BL 9/1/88; HB 11/88)

3513 Heide, Florence Parry. *Some Things Are Scary* (PS–1). Illus. by Jules Feiffer. 2000, Candlewick $15.99 (978-0-07-361222-5). 40pp. This is a book about everyday things that young children might find scary — being hugged by a huge adult or finding out that your best friend's best friend isn't you. (Rev: BL 10/15/00*; SLJ 1/01*)

3514 Heide, Iris van der. *The Red Chalk* (PS–2). Illus. by Marije Tolman. 2006, Front St. $19.95 (978-1-932425-79-6). 32pp. Bored with her red chalk, Sara swaps it with Tim for his marbles, but the marbles soon lose their allure and she continues to trade until she finds something that suits her — red chalk. (Rev: BL 9/1/06; SLJ 1/07)

3515 Helldorfer, M. C. *Got to Dance* (PS). Illus. by Hiroe Nakata. 2004, Doubleday LB $17.99 (978-0-385-90865-8). A young girl with a lot of energy loves to dance in this story set in a city in the heat of summer. (Rev: SLJ 8/04)

3516 Henkes, Kevin. *Good-bye, Curtis* (PS–K). Illus. by Marisabina Russo. 1995, Greenwillow $17.89 (978-0-688-12828-9). 24pp. After 42 years of service, mailcarrier Curtis makes his last rounds. (Rev: BL 10/15/95; HB 11/95; SLJ 10/95)

3517 Hennessy, B. G. *Because of You* (PS–2). Illus. by Hiroe Nakata. 2005, Candlewick $15.99 (978-0-7636-1926-8). 24pp. A picture book focusing on what children can do to serve others and to make the world a better place. (Rev: BL 3/1/05)

3518 Heo, Yumi. *One Afternoon* (PS–1). Illus. 1994, Orchard $15.95 (978-0-531-06845-8). 32pp. A mother and her son discover on a big-city walk that everything from a jackhammer to a cash register makes its own distinctive sound. (Rev: BL 8/94; HB 11/94; SLJ 11/94)

3519 Herrera, Juan Felipe. *Grandma and Me at the Flea / Los Meros Meros Remateros* (2–4). Illus. by Anita De Lucio-Brock. 2002, Children's Book Pr. $15.95 (978-0-89239-171-4). 32pp. A bilingual story about a boy named Juanito who helps his grandmother at a California flea market. (Rev: BL 4/1/02; HBG 10/02)

3520 Hershenhorn, Esther. *Chicken Soup by Heart* (K–3). Illus. by Rosanne Litzinger. 2002, Simon & Schuster $16.95 (978-0-689-82665-8). 32pp. Rudie and his mother make chicken soup with some special additives for Mrs. Gittel, Rudie's elderly neighbor and babysitter. (Rev: BCCB 1/03; BL 9/1/02; HBG 3/03; SLJ 11/02)

3521 Hesse, Karen. *Come On, Rain!* (K–2). Illus. by Jon J. Muth. 1999, Scholastic $17.99 (978-0-590-33125-8). 32pp. A delightful book about a group of children who enjoy a cloudburst during a sweltering day in the big city. (Rev: BCCB 4/99; BL 2/1/99; HB 7/99; HBG 10/99; SLJ 3/99)

3522 Hest, Amy. *The Purple Coat* (K–2). Illus. by Amy Schwartz. 1992, Macmillan paper $5.99 (978-0-689-71634-8). 32pp. This year Gabrielle wants a purple coat instead of the navy blue coat she always wears, and Grandpa the tailor comes up with an ingenious solution. (Rev: BL 9/1/86; HB 1/87; SLJ 11/86)

3523 High, Linda O. *Barn Savers* (PS–3). Illus. by Ted Lewin. 1999, Boyds Mills $15.95 (978-1-56397-403-8). 32pp. A boy and his father dismantle a barn to save it from bulldozers and salvage its parts for new uses. (Rev: BL 11/1/99*; HBG 3/00; SLJ 11/99)

3524 High, Linda O. *Beekeepers* (K–2). Illus. by Doug Chayka. 1998, Boyds Mills $15.95 (978-1-56397-486-1). 32pp. A little girl, under the guidance of her grandfather, engages in the many activities involved in bee-keeping, including gathering the honey. (Rev: BCCB 4/98; BL 5/15/98; HBG 3/99; SLJ 6/98)

3525 Hill, Frances. *The Bug Cemetery* (PS–1). Illus. by Vera Rosenberry. 2002, Holt $16.95 (978-0-8050-6370-7). A bug-cemetery-lemonade-stand-business turns serious when Billy's cat dies. (Rev: HBG 10/02; SLJ 4/02)

3526 Hindley, Judy. *Baby Talk* (PS). Illus. by Brita Granström. 2006, Candlewick $15.99 (978-0-7636-2971-7). 32pp. A day in the life of a toddler is chronicled in rhyming verse and appealing illustrations. (Rev: BL 2/15/06; SLJ 3/06)

3527 Hines, Anna Grossnickle. *What Can You Do in the Snow?* (PS). Illus. by Thea Kliros. 1999, Greenwillow $5.95 (978-0-688-16078-4). This small board book filled with watercolor paintings shows multicultural children building snowmen and engaging in other winter activities. Also use *What Can You Do in the Wind?* (1999). (Rev: HBG 10/99; SLJ 6/99)

3528 Hines, Anna Grossnickle. *What Can You Do in the Sun?* (PS). Illus. by Thea Kliros. 1999, Greenwillow $6.95 (978-0-688-16080-7). 20pp. Several experiences that are associated with being in the sun are joyfully presented in this board book. A companion book is *What Can You Do in the Wind?* (Rev: BL 6/1–15/99; HBG 10/99; SLJ 6/99)

3529 Hoban, Julia. *Amy Loves the Rain* (PS–K). Illus. by Lillian Hoban. 1989, HarperCollins $9.95

(978-0-06-022357-1). 24pp. Amy sits in her car seat as they go to pick up Daddy in the rain. Also use: *Amy Loves the Sun* (1988). (Rev: BL 4/15/89; HB 7/89)

3530 Hoban, Julia. *Amy Loves the Snow* (PS). Illus. by Lillian Hoban. 1989, HarperCollins $9.95 (978-0-06-022361-8). 24pp. A simple text that dramatizes the fun youngsters have in the snow. (Rev: BL 10/1/89; SLJ 10/89)

3531 Hoberman, Mary Ann. *All Kinds of Families!* (K–3). Illus. by Marc Boutavant. 2009, Little, Brown $16.99 (978-0-316-14633-3). 40pp. In rhyming text, Hoberman looks at all the kinds of families there are — from human families to socks in the drawer. (Rev: BLO 5/15/09; SLJ 8/09)

3532 Hoppe, Paul. *Hat* (PS–1). Illus. by author. 2009, Bloomsbury $14.99 (978-1-59990-247-0). 32pp. Henry finds a hat and wonders at its amazing attributes but worries that its owner might want it back. (Rev: BL 3/1/09; SLJ 4/09)

3533 Hoppey, Tim. *Tito, the Firefighter / Tito, el bombero* (1–3). Trans. by Eida de la Vega. Illus. by Kimberly Hoffman. 2005, Raven Tree $16.95 (978-0-9724973-3-6). 32pp. In this English/Spanish picture book with appealing illustrations, 8-year-old Tito's ability to speak both languages helps neighborhood firemen and paves the way for a ride on the fire truck. (Rev: SLJ 10/05)

3534 Houghton, Eric. *The Crooked Apple Tree* (PS–2). Illus. by Caroline Gold. 1999, Barefoot Books LB $15.95 (978-1-902283-59-3). A year in the life of a young brother and sister as they play imaginative games around an old apple tree as the seasons change. (Rev: SLJ 7/99)

3535 Hubbell, Patricia. *Black All Around!* (PS–2). Illus. by Don Tate. 2003, Lee & Low $16.95 (978-1-58430-048-9). 32pp. An African American girl looks around to discover that the world is full of lovely things that are black, such as a lake at night and her Momma's cheek. (Rev: BL 2/15/03; HBG 10/03; SLJ 5/03)

3536 Hudson, Cheryl W., and Bernette G. Ford. *Bright Eyes, Brown Skin* (PS). Illus. by George Ford. 1990, Just Us Bks. $12.95 (978-0-940975-10-1). 24pp. This book features four African American children on a typical day in preschool. (Rev: BL 12/1/90*; SLJ 1/91)

3537 Hughes, Shirley. *Alfie and the Big Boys* (PS–1). Illus. by author. 2008, Random $17.95 (978-0-370-32884-3). 32pp. Preschooler Alfie admires the popular Ian from afar until the day comes when he can help the older boy. (Rev: BL 9/15/08)

3538 Hughes, Shirley. *Two Shoes, New Shoes* (PS). Illus. by author. 1986, Lothrop paper $4.95 (978-0-688-04207-3). 24pp. A rhyming board book about clothes. (Rev: BL 12/15/86; HB 1/87; SLJ 12/86)

3539 Humphries, Tudor. *Hiding* (PS–K). Illus. 1997, Orchard $14.95 (978-0-531-30056-5). 32pp. After she has been scolded by her mother, a little girl goes into hiding until she becomes lonely. (Rev: BL 12/1/97; HBG 3/98; SLJ 3/98)

3540 Hurd, Thacher. *Zoom City* (PS). Illus. by author. 1998, HarperCollins $6.99 (978-0-694-01057-8). A board book that contains bright, action-filled illustrations of cars zooming around. (Rev: HBG 10/98; SLJ 6/98)

3541 Hutchins, Pat. *Bumpety Bump* (PS–K). Illus. 2006, Greenwillow $15.99 (978-0-06-055999-1). 32pp. A young boy and his grandfather harvest fruits and vegetables from the garden watched by a little red hen that later provides them with an egg; cross-sections show the plants above and below ground. (Rev: BL 2/1/06; SLJ 4/06)

3542 Hutchins, Pat. *The Doorbell Rang* (K–2). Illus. by author. 1986, Greenwillow $17.89 (978-0-688-05252-2); Morrow paper $6.99 (978-0-688-09234-4). 24pp. Every time the doorbell rings, it means more of Ma's cookies are eaten, which leaves less for Victoria and Sam — until Grandma arrives with a package. (Rev: BCCB 3/86; BL 6/15/86; SLJ 4/86)

3543 Intrater, Roberta G. *Smile!* (PS). Photos by Roberta Grobel Intrater. Series: Babyfaces. 1997, Scholastic $4.95 (978-0-590-05899-5). In this board book, a toddler responds to a photographer's requests. Also use *Peek-a-Boo!* (1997). (Rev: SLJ 2/98)

3544 Ireland, Karin. *Don't Take Your Snake for a Stroll* (K–2). Illus. by David Catrow. 2003, Harcourt $16.00 (978-0-15-202361-4). In rhyming verse and colorful artwork, a young boy is warned about the consequences of taking unusual pets on a variety of different outings. (Rev: BL 5/15/03; HBG 10/03; SLJ 10/03)

3545 Isaacs, Gwynne L. *While You Are Asleep* (PS–2). Illus. by Cathi Hepworth. 1991, Walker LB $13.85 (978-0-8027-6986-2). 32pp. This picture book describes the intersecting lives of several people who work at night. (Rev: BL 9/1/91; SLJ 8/91)

3546 Isadora, Rachel. *Peekaboo Bedtime* (PS). Illus. by author. 2008, Putnam $16.99 (978-0-399-24384-4). 32pp. The African American toddler seen in *Peekaboo Morning* (2002) is now playing peekaboo before going to bed. (Rev: BCCB 9/08; BL 6/1–15/08; SLJ 6/08)

3547 Isadora, Rachel. *Peekaboo Morning* (PS–K). Illus. 2002, Penguin $15.99 (978-0-399-23602-0). 32pp. An African American toddler plays peekaboo with friends, relatives, and family pets in this delightful book for preschoolers. (Rev: BCCB 7–8/02; BL 3/1/02; HBG 10/02; SLJ 7/02)

3548 Isadora, Rachel. *Uh-Oh!* (PS). Illus. by author. 2008, Harcourt $16.00 (978-0-15-205765-7). 32pp. "Uh oh!" is this African American toddler's response to the many small mishaps of a day. (Rev: BL 2/15/08; HB 5/08; SLJ 7/08)

3549 Isadora, Rachel. *Yo, Jo!* (PS–K). Illus. 2007, Harcourt $16.00 (978-0-15-205783-1). 40pp. Young Jomar is a street-savvy kind with vocabulary to match in this evocative book. (Rev: BL 2/1/07)

3550 Jabar, Cynthia. *Bored Blue? Think What You Can Do!* (PS–1). Illus. 1991, Little, Brown $14.95 (978-0-316-43458-4). 32pp. This book suggests all sorts of activities for bored kids, some of them in the world of fantasy, in rhyming text. (Rev: BL 4/1/91; SLJ 6/91)

3551 Jacobs, Paul Dubois, and Jennifer Swender. *My Subway Ride* (K–3). Illus. by Selina Alko. 2004, Gibbs Smith $15.95 (978-1-58685-357-0). New York City's subway comes alive in the rhythmic text and bright illustrations that depict landmark sites. (Rev: SLJ 9/04)

3552 Jakob, Donna. *Tiny Toes* (PS–1). Illus. by Mireille Levert. 1995, Hyperion LB $14.49 (978-0-7868-2009-2). 32pp. Toes engage in a variety of activities, including dancing. (Rev: BL 4/1/95; SLJ 6/95)

3553 Jarman, Julia. *Big Red Tub* (PS–K). Illus. by Adrian Reynolds. 2004, Scholastic $14.95 (978-0-439-67232-0). 32pp. This bath-time book full of color and adventure features little Stan and Stella plus a cast of non-human characters. (Rev: BL 1/1–15/05)

3554 Jenkins, Emily. *What Happens on Wednesdays* (PS–1). Illus. by Lauren Castillo. 2007, Farrar $16.00 (978-0-374-38303-9). 40pp. A young child catalogs the events of a typical Wednesday — getting up, her father taking her to school, her mother picking her up after lunch, and so forth. (Rev: BCCB 11/07; BL 10/15/07; SLJ 8/07)

3555 Jenness, Aylette. *Come Home with Me: A Multicultural Treasure Hunt* (1–4). Photos by Max Belcher. Illus. by Laura DeSantis. Series: Kids Bridge. 1993, New Pr. $16.95 (978-1-56584-064-5). 48pp. A treasure hunt that introduces four cultural groups represented in various neighborhoods in Boston. (Rev: SLJ 4/94)

3556 Jennings, Sharon. *Into My Mother's Arms* (PS–K). Illus. by Ruth Ohi. 2000, Fitzhenry & Whiteside $14.95 (978-1-55041-533-9). 32pp. A mother and her daughter spend a busy day, starting with breakfast, continuing with activities like going shopping, and finally coming home to bed. (Rev: BL 5/15/00; SLJ 7/00)

3557 Jesset, Aurore. *Loopy* (PS–2). Illus. by Barbara Korthues. 2008, North-South $16.95 (978-0-7358-2175-0). 32pp. After leaving a favorite toy at the doctor's office, a child imagines all sorts of terrible fates that may befall it. (Rev: BL 6/1–15/08; SLJ 7/08)

3558 Johnson, Angela. *Lily Brown's Paintings* (K–2). Illus. by E. B. Lewis. 2007, Scholastic LB $16.99 (978-0-439-78225-8). Young Lily Brown's paintbrush takes her from everyday scenes into a world of imagination. (Rev: BL 2/1/07; SLJ 2/07)

3559 Johnson, Angela. *Rain Feet* (PS). Illus. by Rhonda Mitchell. 1994, Orchard $5.99 (978-0-531-06849-6). 12pp. A little African American boy enjoys splashing through puddles in this board book. Also use *Mama Birds, Baby Birds* (1994). (Rev: BL 12/1/94; HB 9/94; SLJ 1/95)

3560 Johnson, Angela. *Shoes Like Miss Alice's* (PS–K). Illus. by Ken Page. 1995, Orchard LB $16.99 (978-0-531-08664-3). 32pp. Sally resents her baby-sitter Miss Alice until she sees her wide assortment of shoes. (Rev: BL 3/15/95; SLJ 7/95)

3561 Johnson, Angela. *Violet's Music* (PS–2). Illus. 2004, Dial $16.99 (978-0-8037-2740-3). 32pp. Violet has always loved music and is thrilled when she finally meets some kindred spirits. (Rev: BL 3/15/04; SLJ 2/04)

3562 Johnson, D. B. *Eddie's Kingdom* (PS–2). Illus. 2005, Houghton $16.00 (978-0-618-56299-2). 32pp. Through his art, young Eddie resolves the complaints of his neighbors and brings peace to their apartment building. (Rev: BL 10/15/05; SLJ 11/05)

3563 Johnson, David. *Snow Sounds: An Onomatopoeic Story* (PS–2). Illus. 2006, Houghton $16.00 (978-0-618-47310-6). 32pp. Illustrations and onomatopoeias tell the story of a young boy's snowy morning. (Rev: BL 9/1/06; SLJ 10/06)

3564 Johnson, Paul B. *Farmers' Market* (PS–2). 1997, Orchard LB $16.99 (978-0-531-33014-2). 32pp. On Saturdays during the summer, Laura and her family sell their produce at the Farmers' Market in Lexington, Kentucky. (Rev: BCCB 4/97; BL 3/15/97; SLJ 6/97)

3565 Johnston, Tony. *The Quilt Story* (PS–2). Illus. by Tomie dePaola. 1996, Penguin paper $5.99 (978-0-698-11368-8). 32pp. The star of this book is the quilt, which gives fun, warmth, and comfort to two generations. (Rev: BCCB 7–8/85; BL 8/85; SLJ 9/85)

3566 Jones, Sylvie. *Who's in the Tub?* (PS–K). Illus. by Pascale Constantin. 2007, Blue Apple $15.95 (978-1-59354-612-0). 38pp. With the help of a variety of animals, Willy emerges squeaky clean in this tightly rhymed bathtub saga. (Rev: SLJ 10/07)

3567 Joosse, Barbara M. *Love Is a Good Thing to Feel* (PS–2). Illus. by Jennifer Plecas. 2008, Philomel $12.99 (978-0-399-25168-9). 32pp. A little girl with a stuffed bunny friend bounces through this book discussing the many ways to show and enjoy love. (Rev: BL 1/1–15/09; SLJ 12/08)

3568 Joosse, Barbara M. *Please Is a Good Word to Say* (PS–2). Illus. by Jennifer Plecas. 2007, Philomel $12.99 (978-0-399-24217-5). 32pp. Amusing illustrations and text enliven this manners handbook that presents illustrative anecdotes. (Rev: BL 6/1–15/07; SLJ 7/07)

3569 Jordan, June. *Kimako's Story* (K–3). Illus. by Kay Burford. 1991, Houghton paper $3.95 (978-0-395-60338-3). 42pp. Seven-year-old Kimako explores her neighborhood.

3570 Karns, Marie. *The Incredible Peepers of Penelope Budd* (PS–K). Illus. by Amy Wummer. 2005, Gibbs Smith $15.95 (978-1-58685-405-8). With one blue eye and one brown eye, young Penelope Budd sees the world around her in a different light. (Rev: SLJ 1/06)

3571 Katz, Karen. *Can You Say Peace?* (PS). Illus. by author. 2006, Holt $15.95 (978-0-8050-7893-0). 32pp. Drawings of children from around the world are featured along with collages representing their country of origin and the word for "peace" in their native language. (Rev: BL 5/15/06; SLJ 9/06)

3572 Katz, Karen. *The Colors of Us* (PS–1). Illus. 1999, Holt $15.95 (978-0-8050-5864-2). 32pp. Lena discovers that her friends and neighbors are all delicious shades of brown like the foods she enjoys, including peanut butter and chocolate cupcakes.

(Rev: BCCB 12/99; BL 9/15/99; HBG 3/00; SLJ 9/99)

3573 Katz, Karen. *A Potty for Me! A Lift-the-Flap Instruction Manual* (PS). Illus. by author. 2005, Simon & Schuster $7.99 (978-0-689-87423-9). A child learns to use the potty in this encouraging book with entertaining flaps to lift. (Rev: SLJ 8/05)

3574 Katz, Karen. *Twelve Hats for Lena: A Book of Months* (PS–3). Illus. by author. 2002, Simon & Schuster $16.95 (978-0-689-84873-5). Lena creates hats that are suitable for each month of the year, and hat-making directions are included. (Rev: HBG 3/03; SLJ 10/02)

3575 Kerley, Barbara. *One World, One Day* (PS–3). Illus. 2009, National Geographic $17.95 (978-1-4263-0460-6). 48pp. Clear color photographs show how children around the world live their lives — from what they eat for breakfast to where they go to school, the games they play, and so forth. (Rev: BL 5/15/09; SLJ 6/09) [305.23409]

3576 Kesselman, Wendy. *Sand in My Shoes* (PS–3). Illus. by Ronald Himler. 1995, Hyperion LB $15.49 (978-0-7868-2045-0). 32pp. At the end of summer, a little girl says good-bye to the beach she loves but still retains little remembrances like sand in her shoes. (Rev: BL 6/1–15/95; SLJ 7/95)

3577 Klinting, Lars. *What Do You Want?* (PS). Illus. 2006, Groundwood $15.95 (978-0-88899-636-7). 36pp. This import from Sweden with charming, simple illustrations explores the desires of various animate and inanimate objects, including a bird, bee, chair, chicken, and pillow. (Rev: BL 3/1/06; SLJ 4/06)

3578 Knutson, Kimberley. *Beach Babble* (PS–K). Illus. 1998, Marshall Cavendish $15.95 (978-0-7614-5026-9). 32pp. The sounds of a day at the beach are re-created in this picture book illustrated with collage artwork. (Rev: BL 6/1–15/98; HBG 10/98; SLJ 7/98)

3579 Koller, Jackie F. *Bouncing on the Bed* (PS). Illus. by Anna Grossnickle Hines. 1999, Orchard LB $16.99 (978-0-531-33138-5). 32pp. A description by a toddler of all the fun things in a typical day, such as bouncing on the bed, sliding down the stairs, and snuggling down at bedtime. (Rev: BL 2/1/99; HBG 10/99; SLJ 4/99)

3580 Konnecke, Ole. *Anthony and the Girls* (PS–2). Trans. by Nancy Seitz. 2006, Farrar $15.00 (978-0-374-30376-1). 32pp. Little Anthony's attempts to win the attention of two girls in a nearby sandbox all fail until he bursts into tears, bringing them running to his side. (Rev: BL 6/1–15/06; SLJ 2/06)

3581 Koski, Mary. *Impatient Pamela Calls 9-1-1* (PS–K). Illus. by Dan Brown. 1998, Trellis LB $15.95 (978-0-9663281-9-6). 32pp. Impatient Pamela learns a number of skills and puts them to use calling 911 when her neighbor Martin begins choking. (Rev: BL 12/1/98)

3582 Krasilovsky, Phyllis. *The Very Little Boy* (PS–1). Illus. by Karen Gundersheimer. 1992, Scholastic paper $4.95 (978-0-590-44762-1). In this book that describes development, a young boy grows physically and is able to accomplish more skills. (Rev: SLJ 12/92)

3583 Krauss, Ruth. *The Growing Story* (PS–K). Illus. by Helen Osenbury. 2007, HarperCollins $16.99 (978-0-06-024716-4). 40pp. In this new edition of Krauss's classic story published in 1947, a young boy observes growth everywhere around him and wonders if he is growing too. (Rev: BL 4/1/07; SLJ 7/1/07)

3584 Krebs, Laurie. *The Beeman* (PS–2). Illus. by Valeria Cis. 2008, Barefoot Books $16.99 (978-1-84686-146-8). 40pp. This new edition of the book in which a beekeeper shows his granddaughter around his hives and explains how honey is made features new illustrations and appended information. (Rev: BL 4/15/08; SLJ 6/08)

3585 Kroll, Virginia. *Boy, You're Amazing!* (1–3). Illus. by Sachiko Yoshikawa. 2004, Whitman $15.95 (978-0-8075-0868-8). 32pp. In this appealing companion to *Girl, You're Amazing*, Kroll celebrates in rhyming text the unique character traits and abilities of boys. (Rev: BL 4/15/04; SLJ 5/04)

3586 Kroll, Virginia. *Cristina Keeps a Promise* (1–3). Illus. by Enrique O. Sánchez. Series: The Way I Act. 2006, Albert Whitman $15.99 (978-0-8075-1350-7). Cristina gives up a chance to meet her favorite author so she can keep a promise and attend her brother's Special Olympics track meet. (Rev: SLJ 1/07)

3587 Kroll, Virginia. *Everybody Has a Teddy* (PS–K). Illus. by Sophie Allsopp. 2007, Sterling $12.95 (978-1-4027-3580-6). 32pp. A little boy describes his classmates' teddy bears in detail and then his own — not a teddy bear but a toy monkey called Muh. (Rev: BL 3/15/07)

3588 Kroll, Virginia. *Girl, You're Amazing!* (K–3). Illus. by Melisande Potter. 2001, Whitman $15.95 (978-0-8075-2930-0). 32pp. This picture book is a pep talk that tells girls they can do anything they want and be anyone they wish. (Rev: BL 4/1/01; HBG 10/01; SLJ 4/01)

3589 Kroll, Virginia. *Good Neighbor Nicholas* (1–3). Illus. by Nancy Cote. Series: The Way I Act. 2006, Albert Whitman $15.99 (978-0-8075-2998-0). Nicholas clashes with his cranky, older neighbor on a number of occasions until he begins to understand some of the reasons the older man is so unhappy. (Rev: SLJ 1/07)

3590 Kroll, Virginia. *Jason Takes Responsibility* (1–3). Illus. by Nancy Cote. Series: The Way I Act. 2005, Albert Whitman $15.99 (978-0-8075-2537-1). Jason loses one of the invitations to his grandmother's birthday party on his way to the post office, but he does his best to make things right on the day. (Rev: SLJ 1/06)

3591 Kroll, Virginia. *Makayla Cares About Others* (PS–1). Illus. by Nancy Cote. 2007, Albert Whitman $15.99 (978-0-8075-4945-2). 32pp. Young Makayla overcomes her fear of bugs to help her neighbor Mrs. MacFee dig a memory garden for her cat. (Rev: BL 4/1/07)

3592 Kruusval, Catarina. *Franny's Friends* (PS–K). Trans. by Joan Sandin. Illus. by author. 2008, Farrar

$16.00 (978-91-296-6836-0). 32pp. Franny and her friends — seven stuffed animals — set off on a picnic outing but Little Heddy Hedgehog and Itty Bitty Kitty go missing when they fall into a hole. (Rev: BL 6/1–15/08; SLJ 5/08)

3593 Kulling, Monica, and Nan Walker. *The Messiest Room on the Planet* (1–4). Illus. by Jerry Smath. 2009, Kane paper $5.95 (978-1-57565-282-5). 32pp. Lucas enters his friend Jon's room in a Messiest Room on the Planet contest in this story that includes explanations of concepts such as "before," "during," and "after." (Rev: BLO 2/9/09; SLJ 8/09)

3594 Kunhardt, Edith. *I'm Going to Be a Police Officer* (PS–2). Illus. 1995, Scholastic paper $3.25 (978-0-590-25485-4). 32pp. An average day in a small-town police officer's day as seen through the eyes of his two children, who spend time with him at the police station. (Rev: BL 1/1–15/96)

3595 Kuskin, Karla. *The Philharmonic Gets Dressed* (1–4). Illus. by Marc Simont. 1982, HarperCollins $16.99 (978-0-06-023622-9); paper $6.99 (978-0-06-443124-8). 48pp. One hundred and five musicians are across town getting ready for a big concert.

3596 Lachtman, Ofelia Dumas. *Pepita Packs Up / Pepita empaca* (PS–2). Trans. by Gabriela Baeza Ventura. Illus. by Alex Pardo DeLange. 2005, Piñata $15.95 (978-1-55885-431-4). In this appealing bilingual picture book, a little girl faces moving day with mixed emotions — sadness at leaving her old friends and neighbors behind but anticipation about what awaits at her new home. (Rev: SLJ 2/06)

3597 Laden, Nina. *Ready, Set, Go!* (PS). Illus. by author. 2000, Chronicle $6.95 (978-0-8118-2601-3). An interactive book in which cut-out circles reveal activities that are viewed completely when the page is turned. (Rev: SLJ 9/00)

3598 Larios, Julie. *Have You Ever Done That?* (PS–3). Illus. by Anne Hunter. 2001, Front St. $15.95 (978-1-886910-49-2). Rhythmic questions stir a child's imagination and reveal his dreamlike views of the world around him. (Rev: HBG 3/02; SLJ 12/01)

3599 Larsen, Kirsten. *Tara Pays Up!* (1–3). Illus. by Paige Billin-Frye. 2006, Kane $4.99 (978-1-57565-187-3). 32pp. Tara learns that the taxes she has to pay in the store go toward many of the services she enjoys. (Rev: BL 8/06)

3600 Lawrence, Mary. *What's That Sound?* (1–3). Illus. by Lynn Adams. Series: Science Solves It! 2002, Kane paper $4.99 (978-1-57565-118-7). 32pp. Tim's older sister Amy shrugs off every spooky sound he hears, and scientific sidebars explain how each one was made. (Rev: SLJ 10/02)

3601 Leghorn, Lindsay. *Proud of Our Feelings* (PS–2). Illus. by author. 1995, Magination $11.95 (978-0-945354-68-0). A little girl demonstrates the various emotions that her friends feel, like friendliness, sadness, happiness, silliness, and anger. (Rev: SLJ 4/96)

3602 Levert, Mireille. *Lucy's Secret* (PS–1). Illus. 2004, Douglas & McIntyre $16.95 (978-0-88899-566-7). 32pp. Lucy is eager for her seeds to grow into plants, but Anna Zinnia explains the need for patience. (Rev: BL 3/15/04; SLJ 4/04)

3603 Levy, Constance. *The Story of Red Rubber Ball* (PS–K). Illus. by Hiroe Nakata. 2004, Harcourt $16.00 (978-0-15-216589-5). A simple, rhythmic story about a ball left in a park and the various animals that take a look at it. (Rev: SLJ 7/04)

3604 Lewis, Kim. *The Shepherd Boy* (PS–2). Illus. 1990, Macmillan LB $13.95 (978-0-02-758581-0). 32pp. A young boy who longs to be a shepherd like his father practices on a toy lamb. (Rev: BL 12/1/90; SLJ 12/90)

3605 Lewis, Paeony. *No More Cookies!* (PS–K). Illus. by Brita Granström. 2005, Scholastic $16.95 (978-0-439-68332-6). 32pp. Florence is very inventive in her efforts to get at the cookie jar. (Rev: BL 5/1/05; SLJ 5/05)

3606 Lin, Grace. *Dim Sum for Everyone* (PS–K). Illus. 2001, Knopf $14.95 (978-0-375-81082-4). 32pp. Text and appealing illustrations show an Asian family enjoying a meal at a dim sum restaurant in Chinatown. (Rev: BL 6/1–15/01; HBG 3/02; SLJ 7/01)

3607 Lin, Grace. *Fortune Cookie Fortunes* (K–2). Illus. 2004, Knopf $15.95 (978-0-375-81521-8). 32pp. The fortune cookies that follow a meal are the focus of this story featuring the family from *Dim Sum for Everyone* (2001). (Rev: BL 2/15/04; SLJ 6/04)

3608 Lomas Garza, Carmen. *In My Family / En Mi Familia* (1–4). Illus. 1996, Children's Book Pr. $15.95 (978-0-89239-138-7). 32pp. In 13 paintings labeled bilingually, the artist portrays his childhood in Kingsville, Texas. (Rev: BL 11/1/96; HB 11/96)

3609 Loomis, Christine. *In the Diner* (PS–1). Illus. by Nancy Poydar. 1994, Scholastic $14.95 (978-0-590-46716-2). 32pp. Lots of action words in short sentences are used to describe the hustle and bustle of a diner. (Rev: BL 4/15/94; SLJ 5/94)

3610 Loomis, Christine. *Rush Hour* (PS–2). Illus. by Mari Takabayashi. 1996, Houghton $16.95 (978-0-395-69129-8). 32pp. Catchy rhymes and lively illustrations show what working parents do after they leave home in the morning. (Rev: BL 7/96; SLJ 9/96)

3611 Lord, Janet. *Albert the Fix-It Man* (PS–2). Illus. by Julie Paschkis. 2008, Peachtree $15.95 (978-1-56145-433-4). 32pp. When Albert the "Fix-It Man" gets ill, the neighbors join together to offer support. (Rev: BL 3/15/08; HB 5/08; SLJ 4/08)

3612 Ludy, Mark. *The Grump* (2–4). Illus. by author. 2000, Green Pastures $16.95 (978-0-9664276-1-5). Lydia, a little deaf girl, is able to reform the village grump through small acts of kindness. (Rev: SLJ 2/01)

3613 Lukasewich, Lori. *The Night Fire* (PS–1). Illus. by author. 2001, Stoddart $15.95 (978-0-7737-3296-4). Rhyming couplets and bright illustrations follow fire fighters through a nighttime blaze. (Rev: SLJ 1/02)

3614 Lunn, Janet. *Come to the Fair* (K–2). Illus. by Gilles Pelletier. 1997, Tundra $15.95 (978-0-88776-409-7). The Martin family prepares for a visit to the county fair and spends an enjoyable day there. (Rev: HBG 3/98; SLJ 2/98)

3615 Lyon, George E. *Come a Tide* (PS–2). Illus. by Stephen Gammell. 1990, Orchard LB $16.99 (978-0-531-08454-0). 32pp. Grandma knows the tide will rise after a four-day deluge. (Rev: BL 2/1/90*; HB 3/90; SLJ 6/90*)

3616 Lyon, George E. *Weaving the Rainbow* (K–2). Illus. by Stephanie Anderson. 2004, Simon & Schuster $15.95 (978-0-689-85169-8). 40pp. A well-illustrated, step-by-step picture-book story of an artist who raises sheep, shears the wool, processes it, and finally produces a woven work of art. (Rev: BL 2/15/04; SLJ 2/04)

3617 Lyon, George E. *Who Came Down That Road?* (K–3). Illus. by Peter Catalanotto. 1992, Orchard paper $5.95 (978-0-531-07073-4). 32pp. The story of a road through history. (Rev: BL 9/1/92; SLJ 10/92)

3618 Lyons, Kelly Starling. *One Million Men and Me* (PS–2). Illus. by Peter Ambush. 2007, Just Us Bks. $16.95 (978-1-933491-07-3). 32pp. The 1995 Million Man March in Washington, D.C., is described from the perspective of a little girl attending with her father. (Rev: BL 10/15/07; SLJ 11/07)

3619 McAllister, Angela. *Be Good, Gordon* (PS–2). Illus. by Tim Archbold. 2002, Bloomsbury paper $8.95 (978-0-7475-5580-3). Young Gordon is taken aback when his new babysitter wants to do all the things he's forbidden to enjoy. (Rev: SLJ 1/03)

3620 Macaulay, David. *Shortcut* (K–4). Illus. 1995, Houghton $15.95 (978-0-395-52436-7). 64pp. The lives of six people cross in a series of different stories. The author also uses this method of overlapping storytelling in *Black and White* (1990). (Rev: BCCB 9/95; BL 10/15/95; HB 3/95; SLJ 9/95*)

3621 McCarty, Peter. *Baby Steps* (PS–K). Illus. 2000, Holt $16.00 (978-0-8050-5953-3). 32pp. Using clear pencil illustrations, this book traces the growth of baby Suki from one day old to her first steps at one year old. (Rev: BCCB 10/00; BL 10/1/00; HBG 3/01; SLJ 10/00)

3622 McDonald, Megan. *The Potato Man* (K–3). Illus. by Ted Lewin. 1991, Orchard LB $16.99 (978-0-531-08514-1). 32pp. Grampa recalls the time when his neighborhood was regularly visited by peddlers, including the potato man. (Rev: BCCB 2/91; BL 1/15/91*; HB 5/91)

3623 McDonnell, Patrick. *Art* (PS–K). Illus. 2006, Little, Brown $14.99 (978-0-316-11491-2). 40pp. In this imaginative picture book, an aspiring young artist named Art celebrates art in all its varied forms. (Rev: BL 4/1/06; SLJ 4/06)

3624 McGhee, Alison. *Bye-bye, Crib* (PS–K). Illus. by Ross MacDonald. 2008, Simon & Schuster $16.99 (978-1-4169-1621-5). 32pp. With the help of his blanket, pillow, and stuffed animal Baby Kitty, a little boy summons the courage to move into a big, real bed. (Rev: BCCB 6/08; BL 4/15/08; SLJ 2/08)

3625 McGrath, Bob. *Uh Oh! Gotta Go! Potty Tales from Toddlers* (PS). Illus. by Shelley Dieterichs. 1996, Barron's $5.95 (978-0-8120-6564-0). About 20 children describe different potty experiences in

this unusual book that will help in toilet training. (Rev: SLJ 1/97) [613]

3626 McGregor, Merideth. *Cowgirl* (PS–1). Illus. 1992, Walker LB $15.85 (978-0-8027-8171-0). 32pp. Simple, direct text describes the routines of life on a present-day ranch. (Rev: BCCB 2/93; BL 10/1/92; SLJ 12/92) [636.2]

3627 McKee, David. *The Conquerors* (K–3). Illus. by author. 2004, Handprint $16.95 (978-1-59354-078-4). The ruler of a large country conquers neighboring nations "so they can be like us" but fails to recognize that the culture sometimes flows in the other direction. (Rev: BCCB 1/05; HB 1/05; SLJ 2/05)

3628 MacKinnon, Debbie. *My Day* (PS–K). Illus. by Anthea Sieveking. 1999, Little, Brown $7.95 (978-0-316-64898-1). Everyday activities of children are pictured in this interactive book that uses tabs to show action. (Rev: BL 12/15/99)

3629 MacLean, Kole. *Even Firefighters Hug Their Moms* (PS–K). Illus. by Mike Reed. 2002, Dutton $16.99 (978-0-525-46996-4). 32pp. A young boy is so immersed in his elaborate role-playing (as fire fighter, police officer, doctor) that he's too busy to give his mother the requested hug. (Rev: BL 11/15/02; HBG 3/03; SLJ 10/02)

3630 MacLennan, Cathy. *Chicky Chicky Chook Chook* (PS–1). Illus. by author. 2007, Boxer Bks. LB $12.95 (978-1-905417-40-7). An onomatopoeic story full of animal sounds and creative rhymes, featuring a group of animals as the weather changes from warm sun to rain. (Rev: SLJ 4/07*)

3631 McMenemy, Sarah. *Jack's New Boat* (PS–K). Illus. 2005, Candlewick $15.99 (978-0-7636-2477-4). 32pp. With bright collage-and-gouache illustrations, this is the story of young Jack's new toy boat, which is lost almost as soon as he gets it but luckily is later found. (Rev: BL 5/1/05)

3632 McNamara, Margaret. *Earth Day* (PS–1). Illus. by Mike Gordon. Series: Robin Hill School Ready-to-Read. 2008, Aladdin LB $13.89 (978-1-4169-5536-8); paper $3.99 (978-1-4169-5535-1). 32pp. Emma decides to start her environmental efforts slowly — brushing without the water running, recycling, and so forth. (Rev: BLO 4/14/09)

3633 McNaughton, Colin. *Potty Poo-Poo Wee-Wee!* (PS). Illus. 2005, Candlewick $9.99 (978-0-7636-2781-2). 40pp. Littlesaurus, a young dinosaur, is having problems with toilet training and further confounds matters with his potty mouth. (Rev: BL 8/05; SLJ 8/05)

3634 McPhail, David. *Farm Morning* (PS–K). Illus. by author. 1985, Harcourt $15.95 (978-0-15-227299-9). 32pp. A little girl and her father do early-morning farm chores. (Rev: BCCB 12/85; BL 11/15/85; HB 11/85)

3635 McPhail, David. *NO!* (K–3). Illus. by author. 2009, Roaring Brook $16.95 (978-1-59643-288-8). 48pp. A little boy living in a war zone sets off to mail a letter to the president in this compelling, almost wordless story. (Rev: BL 3/15/09; SLJ 5/09)

3636 McPhail, David. *The Teddy Bear* (PS–2). Illus. 2002, Holt $15.95 (978-0-8050-6414-8). 32pp. A young boy generously gives his teddy bear to a homeless man who has become attached to it. (Rev: BL 5/1/02*; HBG 10/02; SLJ 6/02)

3637 McQuinn, Anna. *Lola at the Library* (PS). Illus. by Rosalind Beardshaw. 2006, Charlesbridge paper $6.95 (978-1-58089-142-4). A trip to the library with her mother is a treat for little Lola. (Rev: SLJ 7/06)

3638 Maestro, Betsy. *Taxi: A Book of City Words* (PS–1). Illus. by Giulio Maestro. 1989, Houghton paper $6.95 (978-0-395-54811-0). A taxi picks up and drops off people over the city and introduces new words. (Rev: BL 4/15/89; SLJ 4/89)

3639 Mahy, Margaret. *Down the Dragon's Tongue* (PS–3). Illus. by Patricia MacCarthy. 2000, Orchard $15.95 (978-0-531-30272-9). 32pp. When Mr. Prospero, a very proper gentleman, takes his twin children to a playground, he falls in love with riding the slide known as the Dragon's Tongue. (Rev: BL 7/00; HBG 3/01; SLJ 12/00)

3640 Maisner, Heather. *Time to See the Doctor* (PS). Illus. by Kristina Stephenson. Series: First Time Stories. 2004, Kingfisher paper $5.95 (978-0-7534-5737-5). 24pp. Although he has a fever and sore ears, Ben won't let the doctor near him until his older sister shows that it's OK. (Rev: BL 1/1–15/05)

3641 Manushkin, Fran. *Let's Go Riding in Our Strollers* (2–4). Illus. by Benrei Huang. 1993, Hyperion LB $14.49 (978-1-56282-391-7). 32pp. In a big city, two children enjoy all the excitement of being taken out for a ride by their mothers in their strollers. (Rev: BL 6/1–15/93)

3642 Martin, Bill, Jr., and John Archambault. *Here Are My Hands* (PS). Illus. by Ted Rand. 1987, Holt $15.95 (978-0-8050-0328-4). 32pp. Children indicate body parts, such as a boy pointing to a bandaged knee, which is for "falling down." (Rev: BL 7/87; SLJ 6–7/87)

3643 Martin, Bill, Jr., and John Archambault. *Listen to the Rain* (PS–2). Illus. by James Endicott. 1988, Holt $15.95 (978-0-8050-0682-7). 32pp. A rhyming story about rain with double-page watercolors. (Rev: SLJ 10/88)

3644 Martin, Bill, Jr., and John Archambault. *Up and Down on the Merry-Go-Round* (PS–1). Illus. by Ted Rand. 1988, Holt paper $4.95 (978-0-8050-1638-3). 32pp. A full-color merry-go-round whirls its delighted passengers in rhyming cadence. (Rev: BL 6/15/88; HB 7/88)

3645 Martin, David. *We've All Got Bellybuttons!* (PS–K). Illus. by Randy Cecil. 2005, Candlewick $15.99 (978-0-7636-1775-2). Cartoon animals explore their bodies and ask the reader to mimic their movements (clapping, closing eyes, opening mouths, and so forth). (Rev: BCCB 2/05; SLJ 2/05)

3646 Martin, Jacqueline B. *On Sand Island* (PS–2). Illus. by David A. Johnson. 2003, Houghton $16.00 (978-0-618-23151-5). Carl, who lives on an island in Lake Superior, dreams of having a boat and, with the help of the community, he succeeds in building one. (Rev: BCCB 10/03; BL 8/03; HBG 4/04; LMC 3/04; SLJ 11/03)

3647 Mathers, Petra. *Lottie's New Beach Towel* (PS–2). Illus. 1998, Simon & Schuster $15.00 (978-0-689-81606-2). 32pp. Lottie shows her ingenuity when she puts her new beach towel to a variety of uses, including making an improvised sail and shaping it into a veil for a bride. (Rev: BL 6/1–15/98; HB 5/98; HBG 10/98; SLJ 6/98)

3648 May, Eleanor. *Who Needs It?* (K–3). Illus. by Blanche Sims. Series: Social Studies Connects. 2009, Kane paper $5.95 (978-1-57565-281-8). 32pp. Gus and Mickey have very different ideas about what to take on a camping trip in this funny story that includes sidebars about basic human needs. (Rev: BL 3/1/09)

3649 Medearis, Angela Shelf. *Dancing with the Indians* (K–3). Illus. by Samuel Byrd. 1991, Holiday House LB $16.95 (978-0-8234-0893-1). 32pp. A young African American girl and her family attend a powwow of the Oklahoma Seminoles. (Rev: BCCB 11/91; BL 12/1/91; SLJ 1/92)

3650 Medearis, Angela Shelf. *Poppa's New Pants* (K–3). Illus. by John Ward. 1995, Holiday House LB $15.95 (978-0-8234-1155-9). 32pp. Shortening father's new pants to fit him causes a minor family crisis. (Rev: BCCB 7–8/95; BL 6/1–15/95; SLJ 6/95)

3651 Menchin, Scott. *Taking a Bath with the Dog and Other Things That Make Me Happy* (PS–K). Illus. by author. 2007, Candlewick $15.99 (978-0-7636-2919-9). Sweet Pea surveys her friends and neighbors (some human, some animal) to find out what makes them happy and also figures out what she most enjoys. (Rev: SLJ 7/07)

3652 Merz, Jennifer. *Playground Day!* (PS–1). Illus. by author. 2007, Clarion $16.00 (978-0-618-81696-5). 32pp. A little girl enjoys an afternoon at the playground imagining herself a variety of different animals. (Rev: BL 10/1/07; SLJ 10/07)

3653 Meyerhoff, Jenny. *Third Grade Baby* (2–4). Illus. by Jill Weber. 2008, Farrar $15.00 (978-0-374-37482-2). 112pp. When Polly starts 3rd grade she is the only child who hasn't lost a tooth; is she too old for the tooth fairy? (Rev: BCCB 11/08; BL 12/1/08; SLJ 11/08)

3654 Meyers, Susan. *Everywhere Babies* (PS). Illus. by Marla Frazee. 2001, Harcourt $16.00 (978-0-15-202226-6). 32pp. A charming representation of the first year of a baby's life with a rhyming text and watercolors showing babies being fed and playing games like peek-a-boo. (Rev: BL 3/1/01; HB 5/01*; HBG 10/01)

3655 Meyers, Susan. *This Is the Way a Baby Rides* (PS–2). Illus. by Hiroe Nakata. 2005, Abrams $15.95 (978-0-8109-5763-3). 40pp. A lively toddler has fun at a picnic and his many movements are mimicked by animal babies on parallel spreads. (Rev: BL 10/1/05; SLJ 12/05)

3656 Mikkelsen, Jon. *Kids Against Hunger* (1–3). Illus. by Nathan Lueth. 2008, Stone Arch LB $15.95 (978-1-4342-0790-6). 40pp. This illustrated easy chapter book follows three boys who volunteer for a nonprofit organization feeding the needy. (Rev: BLO 12/4/08; SLJ 2/09)

3657 Milgrim, David. *Amelia Makes a Movie* (K–2). Illus. by author. 2008, Putnam $16.99 (978-0-399-24670-8). 32pp. Amelia and her little brother join forces to make a movie, which is shown in comic-strip panels; technical details will attract young readers. (Rev: BL 2/1/08; SLJ 4/08)

3658 Milgrim, David. *Time to Get Up, Time to Go* (PS–K). Illus. by author. 2006, Clarion $15.00 (978-0-618-51998-9). 32pp. A very busy young boy looks after himself and his stuffed doll during an activity-filled day; the minimal text and eye-focusing illustrations work well together. (Rev: SLJ 4/06)

3659 Miller, Pat. *We're Going on a Book Hunt* (PS–2). Illus. by Nadine Bernard Westcott. 2008, Upstart $17.95 (978-1-60213-007-4). 32pp. A lively introduction to the library featuring a bear cub class, adapted from *We're Going on a Bear Hunt*. (Rev: BL 7/08; LMC 11/08)

3660 Miranda, Anne. *Baby-Sit* (PS). Illus. by Dorothy Stott. 1990, Little, Brown $9.95 (978-0-316-57454-9). The activities of two children and their baby-sitter are portrayed. (Rev: SLJ 10/90)

3661 Miranda, Anne. *To Market, To Market* (K–2). Illus. by Janet Stevens. 1997, Harcourt $16.00 (978-0-15-200035-6). 36pp. A wildly funny picture book about market day misunderstandings. (Rev: BL 11/1/97; HB 11/97; HBG 3/98; SLJ 1/98)

3662 Mitchell, Lori. *Different Just Like Me* (K–3). Illus. 1999, Charlesbridge LB $15.95 (978-0-88106-975-4). 32pp. April's experiences during the week, when she meets new people, help her appreciate her much-anticipated weekend visit with her Grammie. (Rev: BL 3/1/99; HBG 10/99; SLJ 3/99)

3663 Mizzoni, Chris. *Clancy with the Puck* (PS–2). Illus. by author. 2007, Raincoast $16.95 (978-1-55192-804-3). 32pp. Told in rhyming couplets, this is the story of a gifted yet arrogant hockey star who helps move the Hogtown Maple Buds to the Stanley Cup finals only to fall short when he gets a chance at the winning goal. (Rev: BL 11/1/07; LMC 1/08; SLJ 1/08)

3664 Mora, Pat. *Maria Paints the Hills* (K–3). Illus. by Maria Hesch. 2002, Museum of New Mexico paper $9.95 (978-0-89013-410-8). 32pp. A simple story and stunning folk-art illustrations capture the life of a little girl in New Mexico. (Rev: BL 12/15/02; HBG 3/03)

3665 Morris, Ann. *Hats, Hats, Hats* (PS–1). Illus. by Ken Heyman. 1989, Morrow paper $6.99 (978-0-688-12274-4). 32pp. A full-color display of varieties of hats. Also use: *Bread, Bread, Bread* (1989). (Rev: BL 4/15/89; SLJ 5/89)

3666 Morris, Ann. *Houses and Homes* (PS–1). Illus. 1992, Lothrop LB $16.89 (978-0-688-10169-5). 32pp. A fascinating look at how houses are built around the world. (Rev: BCCB 12/92; BL 10/1/92)

3667 Morris, Carla. *The Boy Who Was Raised by Librarians* (K–2). Illus. by Brad Sneed. 2007, Peachtree $16.95 (978-1-56145-391-7). 32pp. Melvin spends so much time at the library that the librarians become like family. (Rev: BL 5/1/07; LMC 10/07; SLJ 6/07)

3668 Mortensen, Denise Dowling. *Ohio Thunder* (PS–3). Illus. by Kate Kiesler. 2006, Clarion $16.00 (978-0-618-59542-6). 32pp. Rhyming verse and dramatic artwork describe a summer thunderstorm above the fields of an Ohio farm. (Rev: BL 4/15/06; SLJ 5/06)

3669 Morton, Christine. *Picnic Farm* (PS–K). Illus. by Sarah Barringer. 1998, Holiday House LB $15.95 (978-0-8234-1332-4). After touring a farm, a little girl and boy have a picnic using some of its produce, like eggs, bread, butter, and fruit. (Rev: HBG 10/98; SLJ 3/98)

3670 Mould, Wendy. *Ants in My Pants* (PS–K). Illus. 2001, Clarion $15.00 (978-0-618-09640-4). 32pp. Jacob wants to play with his trains and comes up with inventive ways to delay getting dressed to go shopping. (Rev: BL 8/01; HBG 3/02; SLJ 9/01)

3671 Muirhead, Margaret. *Mabel, One and Only* (PS–1). Illus. by Lynne Avril. 2009, Dial $16.99 (978-0-8037-3198-1). 32pp. When their adult friends are all too busy to play, Mabel and her dog Jack turn a box into a spaceship; when the adults turn up she generously invites them into her game. (Rev: BLO 2/2/09; SLJ 4/09)

3672 Munro, Roxie. *Circus* (PS–1). Illus. by author. 2006, Chronicle $15.95 (978-0-8118-5209-8). This colorful lift-the-flap book captures all the excitement of the circus and incorporates simple seek-and-find features in every elaborate spread. (Rev: SLJ 12/06)

3673 Munsch, Robert. *Ribbon Rescue* (PS–1). Illus. by Eugenie Fernandes. 1999, Scholastic $11.95 (978-0-590-89012-0). 32pp. A Mohawk girl named Jillian is so helpful to all the members of a wedding party that they make her the flower girl. (Rev: BL 7/99; HBG 10/99; SLJ 6/99)

3674 Nash, Margaret. *Secret in the Mist* (PS–2). Illus. by Stephen Lambert. 1999, Sterling $14.95 (978-1-899607-98-3). 32pp. A young boy secretly plants a seed and watches it grow both day and night. Finally, his secret is revealed when a beautiful sunflower appears. (Rev: BL 6/1–15/99; SLJ 9/99)

3675 Nikola-Lisa, W. *America: My Land, Your Land, Our Land* (K–3). Illus. 1997, Lee & Low $15.95 (978-1-880000-37-3). 32pp. A handsome picture book that shows many of the contrasts that are present in the United States. (Rev: BL 9/1/97; SLJ 7/97)

3676 Nikola-Lisa, W. *Summer Sun Risin'* (PS–1). Illus. by Don Tate. 2002, Lee & Low $16.95 (978-1-58430-034-2). A gentle story of a young African American boy's busy day on the farm — looking after the animals, plowing, picnicking, fishing, and bedtime stories. (Rev: HBG 10/02; SLJ 5/02)

3677 Noble, Sheilagh. *More!* (PS). Illus. 2000, Zero to Ten $9.95 (978-1-84089-127-0). 24pp. A sweet story about a mother and a daughter enjoying a walk in the park. (Rev: BL 1/1–15/01)

3678 Noonan, Julia. *Bath Day* (PS). Illus. by author. Series: Puppy and Me. 2000, Scholastic $6.99 (978-0-439-11492-9). A slight story about a little girl who plays in her wading pool with her dog. Also use *Breakfast Time* (2000). (Rev: HBG 10/00; SLJ 8/00)

3679 Novak, Matt. *Flip Flop Bop* (PS–1). Illus. by author. 2005, Roaring Brook $15.95 (978-1-59643-049-5). Summertime means flip-flop time for the dancing children in this happy picture book. (Rev: SLJ 7/05)

3680 Nunes, Susan. *The Last Dragon* (PS–3). Illus. by Chris K. Soentpiet. 1995, Clarion $16.00 (978-0-395-67020-0). 32pp. A Chinese American boy named Peter gets everyone in Chinatown to help him repair a 10-man dragon he has purchased. (Rev: BL 5/1/95; SLJ 5/95)

3681 Nye, Naomi Shihab. *Baby Radar* (PS). Illus. by Nancy Carpenter. 2003, Greenwillow LB $16.89 (978-0-688-15949-8). The world is seen from the low-down viewpoint of a toddler in a stroller on a fine fall day. (Rev: HBG 4/04; SLJ 9/03)

3682 O'Book, Irene. *Maybe My Baby* (PS). Photos by Paula Hible. 1998, HarperCollins $6.99 (978-0-694-00872-8). A simple board book in which babies wear a series of job-related hats to help toddlers identify different careers. (Rev: SLJ 6/98)

3683 O'Connor, Jane. *Fancy Nancy's Favorite Fancy Words: From Accessories to Zany* (K–2). Illus. by Robin P. Glasser. 2008, HarperCollins $12.99 (978-0-06-154923-6). 32pp. Fancy Nancy introduces some fancy words in this alphabetical guide to her style and ambitions. (Rev: BL 8/08)

3684 Ohi, Ruth. *Pants Off First!* (PS). Illus. Series: Early Bird Boardbook. 2001, Fitzhenry & Whiteside $6.95 (978-1-55041-667-1). 16pp. As a little boy undresses, he puts his clothes on his pets in this humorous story that ends with a twist. (Rev: BL 7/01)

3685 Olsen, Sylvia. *Yetsa's Sweater* (PS–3). Illus. by Joan Larson. 2006, Sono Nis $17.95 (978-1-55039-155-8). Yetsa and her grandmother clean, card, and spin fleece into wool in this story featuring Cowichan traditions in British Columbia. (Rev: SLJ 5/07)

3686 O'Neill, Alexis. *Estela's Swap* (K–3). Illus. by Enrique O. Sánchez. 2002, Lee & Low $16.95 (978-1-58430-044-1). 32pp. Colorful illustrations accompany this story of Estela, a Hispanic girl who wants to sell a music box to earn money for dance lessons. (Rev: BL 12/15/02; HBG 3/03; SLJ 10/02)

3687 Osborne, Mary Pope. *Rocking Horse Christmas* (PS–3). Illus. by Ned Bittinger. 1997, Scholastic $16.95 (978-0-590-92955-4). 32pp. A young boy has many adventures on his favorite toy, a wooden rocking horse, but in time he outgrows it. (Rev: BL 10/1/97; HBG 3/98; SLJ 10/97)

3688 Oxenbury, Helen. *Pig Tale* (K–2). Illus. 2005, Simon & Schuster $16.95 (978-1-4169-0277-5). 32pp. Two pigs, Briggs and his wife Bertha, are thrilled when they become rich but soon find that money isn't everything after all. (Rev: BL 5/15/05)

3689 Oxenbury, Helen. *Tom and Pippo Go Shopping* (PS). Illus. by author. 1989, Macmillan paper $5.95 (978-0-689-71278-4). 14pp. The toddler and his toy monkey on a new adventure. Also use: *Tom and Pippo in the Garden; Tom and Pippo See the Moon;*

Tom and Pippo's Day (all 1989). (Rev: BL 3/15/89; HB 5/89)

3690 Pallotta, Jerry. *Going Lobstering* (PS–2). Illus. by Rob Bolster. 1990, Charlesbridge $16.95 (978-0-88106-475-9); paper $7.95 (978-0-88106-474-2). 32pp. A boy and his sister spend a fascinating day on a lobster boat. (Rev: BL 12/1/90)

3691 Parr, Todd. *The Feel Good Book* (PS–2). Illus. by author. 2002, Little, Brown $14.95 (978-0-316-07206-9). A list of things that make you feel good is illustrated with lively art. (Rev: HBG 3/03; SLJ 10/02)

3692 Parr, Todd. *It's Okay to Be Different* (PS–2). Illus. by author. 2001, Little, Brown $14.95 (978-0-316-66603-9). Readers learn that it's OK to be adopted, to wear glasses, to have an unusual nose, to lose a race — and to have a pet worm. (Rev: HBG 3/02; SLJ 10/01)

3693 Parr, Todd. *Reading Makes You Feel Good* (PS–K). Illus. 2005, Little, Brown $15.99 (978-0-316-16004-9). 32pp. This brightly colored picture book examines the many benefits of reading and the many places you can read, alone or with others. (Rev: BL 12/1/05; SLJ 9/05)

3694 Patricelli, Leslie. *Binky* (PS). Illus. by author. 2005, Candlewick $6.99 (978-0-7636-2364-7). A board book about losing a beloved pacifier. Also use *Blankie* (2005). (Rev: SLJ 7/05)

3695 Patricelli, Leslie. *Blankie* (PS). 2005, Candlewick $6.99 (978-0-7636-2363-0). 24pp. A toddler-friendly board book about a child and a much-loved blanket. (Rev: BL 4/1/05)

3696 Paul, Alison. *The Crow (A Not So Scary Story)* (PS–2). Illus. by author. 2007, Houghton $16.00 (978-0-618-66380-4). 40pp. A young boy conjures up all kinds of scary scenarios after peaking at a crow outside the window. (Rev: BL 10/1/07; SLJ 11/07)

3697 Paul, Ann Whitford. *Word Builder* (K–3). Illus. by Kurt Cyrus. 2009, Simon & Schuster $16.99 (978-1-4169-3981-8). 32pp. This clever extended metaphor follows a boy in a hard hat as he works step-by-step from letter to word to sentence to paragraph to chapter until finally he has a full book. (Rev: BL 1/1–15/09; SLJ 1/09)

3698 Pearson, Debora. *Sophie's Wheels* (PS). Illus. by Nora Hilb. 2006, Annick LB $18.95 (978-1-55451-038-2); paper $6.95 (978-1-55451-037-5). Sophie, the sister of Leo in *Leo's Tree* (2004), appreciates the importance of wheels in her life — on strollers, on supermarket carts, on tricycles and bicycles. (Rev: BL 12/1/06; SLJ 3/07)

3699 Perez, Amada Irma. *My Very Own Room / Mi propio cuartito* (1–3). Illus. by Maya Christina Gonzalez. 2000, Children's Book Pr. $15.95 (978-0-89239-164-6). 32pp. A bilingual story about a young Mexican American girl who is looking for a little privacy in her crowded home. (Rev: BCCB 11/00; BL 7/00; HB 11/00; HBG 3/01; SLJ 8/00)

3700 Phillips, Christopher. *Ceci Ann's Day of Why* (PS–K). Illus. by Shino Arihara. 2006, Tricycle $14.95 (978-1-58246-171-7). 32pp. Vivid illustrations are paired with questions about everything in a little girl's life. (Rev: BL 1/1–15/07)

3701 Pilkey, Dav. *The Paperboy* (PS–1). Illus. 1996, Orchard LB $15.99 (978-0-531-08856-2). 32pp. This book reflects the thoughts of a young boy when he makes early-morning rounds on his paper route with his dog. (Rev: BCCB 3/96; BL 3/1/96*; HB 7/96; SLJ 3/96*)

3702 Pilutti, Deb. *The City Kid and the Suburb Kid* (PS–3). Illus. by Linda Bleck. 2008, Sterling LB $14.95 (978-1-4027-4002-2). 38pp. Which is better — city or suburb? This "flip the book over" volume allows readers to experience urban Jack's visit to the 'burbs and his cousin Adam's time in the city. (Rev: SLJ 5/08)

3703 Pinkney, Sandra L. *Read and Rise* (K–3). Photos by Myles C. Pinkney. Illus. 2006, Scholastic $15.99 (978-0-439-30929-5). 40pp. Part of the National Urban League's Read and Rise literacy campaign, this blend of verse and color photography emphasizes the importance of reading. (Rev: BL 2/1/06; SLJ 1/06)

3704 Pinkney, Sandra L. *Shades of Black: A Celebration of Our Children* (PS–2). Illus. by Myles C. Pinkney. 2000, Scholastic $17.99 (978-0-439-14892-4). 40pp. This book of beautiful photographs shows children whose skin is of various shades of black and whose eyes and hair also show a diversity. (Rev: BCCB 1/01; BL 11/1/00; HBG 3/01; SLJ 12/00)

3705 Piumini, Roberto. *Doctor Me Di Cin* (2–4). Illus. by Piet Grobler. 2001, Front St. $15.95 (978-1-886910-67-6). A crafty Chinese doctor eventually succeeds in luring a pallid prince outside to get some fresh air. (Rev: HBG 3/02; SLJ 10/01)

3706 Pocock, Rita. *Annabelle and the Big Slide* (PS). Illus. 1989, Harcourt $10.95 (978-0-15-200407-1). 32pp. Annabelle summons up her courage to climb the ladder and zoom down the playground slide. (Rev: BL 1/1/90; IIB 11/89; SLJ 12/89)

3707 Polacco, Patricia. *Aunt Chip and the Great Triple Creek Dam Affair* (K–3). Illus. 1996, Penguin $16.99 (978-0-399-22943-5). 32pp. Because of television, a whole town forgets how to read until Aunt Chip, the town librarian, intervenes. (Rev: BCCB 6/96; BL 4/15/96; SLJ 5/96*)

3708 Pollak, Barbara. *Our Community Garden* (PS–3). Illus. by author. 2004, Beyond Words $15.95 (978-1-58270-109-7). A group of children tend the vegetables in their plots and enjoy a feast at harvest time. (Rev: SLJ 11/04)

3709 Portis, Antoinette. *Not a Box* (PS–K). Illus. by author. 2007, HarperCollins $12.99 (978-0-06-112322-1). 32pp. With a little imagination, a box is not just a box. (Rev: BL 12/1/06; SLJ 1/07)

3710 Preller, James. *Mighty Casey* (PS–3). Illus. by Matthew Cordell. 2009, Feiwel & Friends $16.95 (978-0-312-36764-0). 32pp. The Delmar Dogs, never a great team, are having a bad day (bees, scraped knees, and needs to pee add to their woes) until Casey Jenkins — one of the poorest players — comes up to bat and saves the day. (Rev: BL 4/1/09; SLJ 3/09)

3711 Prosek, James. *A Good Day's Fishing* (2–4). Illus. 2004, Simon & Schuster $15.95 (978-0-689-85327-2). 40pp. A child sorts through his fishing tackle, describing the value of various pieces of equipment and what they can catch. (Rev: BL 2/15/04; SLJ 5/04)

3712 Purmell, Ann. *Apple Cider Making Days* (PS–2). Illus. by Joanne Friar. 2002, Millbrook LB $14.95 (978-0-7613-2364-8). 32pp. Making cider is a family activity in this colorful book with detailed illustrations of the process. (Rev: BL 12/1/02; HBG 3/03; SLJ 1/03)

3713 Purmell, Ann. *Maple Syrup Season* (1–4). Illus. by Jill Weber. 2008, Holiday $16.95 (978-0-8234-1891-6). 32pp. A fictional family works together to make maple syrup; includes informative endmatter. (Rev: BL 3/15/08; SLJ 3/08)

3714 Quinsey, Mary Beth. *Why Does That Man Have Such a Big Nose?* (PS–1). Illus. by Wilson Chan. 1986, Parenting LB $16.95 (978-0-943990-25-5); paper $6.95 (978-0-943990-24-8). 32pp. Explaining some of the physical differences among people and how or why they happen. (Rev: BL 1/1/87; SLJ 12/86)

3715 Raczka, Bob. *Summer Wonders* (PS–3). Illus. by Judy Stead. 2009, Albert Whitman $16.99 (978-0-8075-7653-3). 32pp. Minimal rhyming text and colorful illustrations celebrate summer. (Rev: SLJ 6/09)

3716 Ransom, Candice F. *The Big Green Pocketbook* (PS–1). Illus. by Felicia Bond. 1993, HarperCollins LB $16.89 (978-0-06-020849-3). 32pp. At every stop during a day of errands with her mother, a little girl is given something for her empty pocketbook. (Rev: BL 7/93; SLJ 7/93)

3717 Raschka, Chris. *New York Is English, Chattanooga Is Creek* (1–3). Illus. 2005, Simon & Schuster $16.95 (978-0-689-84600-7). 40pp. New York City hosts a party for other American cities, each of which arrives in a costume inspired by its name's origins. (Rev: BL 10/1/05; SLJ 10/05)

3718 Rau, Dana Meachen. *Ways to Go* (K–1). Illus. by Jane Conteh-Morgan. 2001, Compass Point LB $14.95 (978-0-7565-0071-9). 24pp. Minimal text and appealing illustrations portray a choice of modes of transport. (Rev: SLJ 10/01) [388]

3719 Ray, Mary L. *Christmas Farm* (K–2). Illus. by Barry Root. 2008, Harcourt $17.00 (978-0-15-216290-0). 32pp. Five-year-old Parker helps his neighbor plant 744 Christmas trees and in the years that follow, both the trees and the boy grow. (Rev: BCCB 12/08; BL 9/15/08; HB 11/08; LMC 11/08)

3720 Ray, Mary L. *Red Rubber Boot Day* (PS). Illus. by Lauren Stringer. 2000, Harcourt $16.00 (978-0-15-213756-4). 32pp. Told from a child's point of view, this book gives details on the indoor and outdoor activities that are possible on a rainy day. (Rev: BL 3/15/00; HBG 10/00; SLJ 4/00)

3721 Reed, Lynn Rowe. *Big City Song* (PS). 2006, Holiday $16.95 (978-0-8234-1988-3). 32pp. Bright illustration and simple rhythms celebrate the sights and sounds of urban life. (Rev: BL 9/15/06)

3722 Reichert, Amy. *While Mama Had a Quick Little Chat* (K–3). Illus. by Alexandra Boiger. 2005, Simon & Schuster $15.95 (978-0-689-85170-4). 40pp. Rose's mother is on the phone for ages, and Rose, who is supposed to be getting ready for bed, is unable to stop hordes of visitors from taking over their home. (Rev: BL 6/1–15/05)

3723 Reynolds, Aaron. *Metal Man* (K–3). Illus. by Paul Hoppe. 2008, Charlesbridge $15.95 (978-1-58089-150-9). 32pp. A man who makes sculptures from scrap metal helps young Devon, an African American boy, to create his own work. (Rev: BCCB 7–8/08; BLO 9/2/08; SLJ 7/08)

3724 Rice, David L. *Because Brian Hugged His Mother* (PS–3). Illus. by K. Dyble Thompson. 1999, Dawn $16.95 (978-1-883220-90-7); paper $7.95 (978-1-883220-89-1). 32pp. The hug that Brian gives his mother produces a string of kindnesses throughout the community. (Rev: BL 8/99; HBG 10/99)

3725 Richmond, Marianne. *Hooray for You! A Celebration of "You-ness"* (PS–2). Illus. by author. 2001, Waldman $15.95 (978-0-931674-44-0). Differences in cultures, characteristics, and goals are all shown to be of value. (Rev: HBG 3/02; SLJ 1/02)

3726 Robberecht, Thierry. *Sarah's Little Ghosts* (PS–2). Illus. by Philippe Goossens. 2007, Houghton $16.00 (978-0-618-89210-5). 32pp. When Sarah lies about breaking her mother's necklace, little ghosts start to plague her. (Rev: SLJ 11/07)

3727 Roddie, Shen. *Toes Are to Tickle* (PS). Illus. by Kady M. Denton. 1997, Tricycle $13.95 (978-1-883672-49-2). 24pp. A playful picture book that gives pleasant definitions to common articles, like "A tree is to hide behind." (Rev: BL 6/1–15/97; SLJ 9/97)

3728 Rogers, Paul. *Tiny* (K–3). Illus. by Korky Paul. 2002, Kane paper $7.95 (978-1-929132-26-3). A twist on the house, street, town, country, continent progression that moves out from a flea to a star. (Rev: SLJ 8/02)

3729 Rollings, Susan. *New Shoes, Red Shoes* (PS–K). Illus. 2000, Orchard $15.95 (978-0-531-30268-2). 32pp. Bouncy rhymes are used in this slight story about the fun of going to pick out a new pair of shoes. (Rev: BL 2/1/00; HBG 10/00; SLJ 5/00)

3730 Roop, Peter, and Connie Roop. *A City Album* (2–3). Illus. Series: Long Ago and Today. 1998, Heinemann LB $19.92 (978-1-57572-600-7). 24pp. Using old and new photographs, this work compares city life today, when people ride subway trains, buses, cars, and bicycles, with city life a century ago, when people walked or rode horses. (Rev: BL 12/15/98) [307.76]

3731 Roop, Peter, and Connie Roop. *A School Album* (2–3). Illus. 1998, Heinemann LB $19.92 (978-1-57572-603-8). 24pp. Using double-page spreads and historic and modern photos, schools of 100 years ago are compared to schools today. (Rev: BL 12/15/98) [372.97]

3732 Roosa, Karen. *Beach Day* (PS–K). Illus. by Maggie Smith. 2001, Clarion $16.00 (978-0-618-02923-5). 32pp. Lively art and detailed illustrations depict a day at the beach for a group of multicultural children. (Rev: BL 5/1/01; HBG 10/01; SLJ 4/01)

3733 Rose, Emma. *Ballet Magic: A Pop-up Book* (PS–1). Illus. by Jan Palmer. 1996, Scholastic $12.95 (978-0-590-26242-2). 12pp. Various ballet positions and movements are shown in this pop-up book. (Rev: BL 12/15/96)

3734 Rosenberry, Vera. *Run, Jump, Whiz, Splash* (PS–2). Illus. by author. 1999, Holiday House $15.95 (978-0-8234-1378-2). A simple but lyrical account of the activities of two children throughout the seasons of a year. (Rev: HBG 3/00; SLJ 9/99)

3735 Rosenberry, Vera. *Vera Goes to the Dentist* (PS–3). Illus. 2002, Holt $16.95 (978-0-8050-6668-5). 32pp. Vera is so frightened by her first trip to the dentist that she runs out of the office, but she is finally caught and becomes calm enough to finish the examination. (Rev: BL 4/1/02; HBG 10/02; SLJ 5/02)

3736 Rosenberry, Vera. *Vera Rides a Bike* (K–2). Illus. 2004, Holt $16.95 (978-0-8050-7125-2). 32pp. Vera makes the daunting transition from a tricycle to a two-wheeler. (Rev: BL 5/15/04; HB 5/04; SLJ 7/04)

3737 Rosenthal, Amy Krouse. *Little Pea* (PS–2). Illus. by Jen Corace. 2005, Chronicle $12.95 (978-0-8118-4658-5). Little Pea is a happy child until it comes to meals, when he struggles through the candy courses waiting with anticipation for the dessert of spinach. (Rev: BL 3/1/04; SLJ 5/05)

3738 Rosenthal, Amy Krouse. *One of Those Days* (K–3). Illus. by Rebecca Doughty. 2006, Putnam $13.99 (978-0-399-24365-3). 32pp. This whimsical picture book imagines dozens of ways in which a child's day can take a turn for the worse but holds out hope that things will turn around tomorrow. (Rev: BL 6/1–15/06; SLJ 5/06)

3739 Rosenthal, Amy Krouse. *Yes Day!* (PS–1). Illus. by Tom Lichtenheld. 2009, HarperCollins $14.99 (978-0-06-115259-7). 40pp. Once a year on Yes Day a young child gets to do everything he wants. (Rev: BL 4/1/09; SLJ 5/09)

3740 Ross, Michael Elsohn. *Play with Me* (PS–1). Illus. by Julie Downing. 2009, Tricycle $12.99 (978-1-58246-255-4). 32pp. Animals and people at play with their babies. (Rev: SLJ 6/09)

3741 Roth, Julie Jersild. *Knitting Nell* (2–4). Illus. by author. 2006, Houghton $16.00 (978-0-618-54033-4). Nell, a quiet girl, finds added confidence when her knitting talent is recognized at the county fair. (Rev: SLJ 7/06)

3742 Rotner, Shelley, and Sheila Kelly. *Feeling Thankful* (PS–2). Illus. 2000, Millbrook LB $20.90 (978-0-7613-1918-4). 24pp. This simple photo-essay enumerates the many things, such as a family or a pet, for which children can be thankful. (Rev: BL 12/1/00; HBG 3/01; SLJ 12/00) [179]

3743 Rotner, Shelley, and Ken Kreisler. *Citybook* (PS–K). Illus. by Shelley Rotner. 1994, Orchard LB $16.99 (978-0-531-08687-2). 32pp. Ken explains why he loves visiting the city in this picture book filled with color photos of big-city life and sights. (Rev: BL 2/15/94; HB 5/94; SLJ 3/94)

3744 Rounds, Glen. *Cowboys* (PS–1). Illus. 1991, Holiday House LB $16.95 (978-0-8234-0867-2). 32pp. A day in the life of a cowboy is described in sparse text and shown in complementary illustrations. (Rev: BCCB 4/91; BL 6/1/91; SLJ 5/91)

3745 Russell, Joan Plummer. *Aero and Officer Mike: Police Partners* (2–4). Illus. by Kris Turner Sinnenberg. 2001, Boyds Mills $17.95 (978-1-56397-931-6). 32pp. Aero is Officer Mike's police dog, and the two of them are shown working together in this book of photographs and text. (Rev: BL 9/15/01; HBG 3/02; SLJ 12/01) [363.2]

3746 Ruurs, Margriet. *When We Go Camping* (PS–3). Illus. by Andrew Kiss. 2001, Tundra $14.95 (978-0-88776-476-9). 32pp. The joys of camping are brought to life in this detailed, realistically illustrated story of siblings on a camping trip with their parents. (Rev: BL 12/15/01; HBG 10/01; SLJ 7/01)

3747 Ryder, Joanne. *Won't You Be My Hugaroo?* (PS–K). Illus. by Melissa Sweet. 2006, Harcourt $16.00 (978-0-15-205778-7). 40pp. Hugs of all kinds — from the job-well-done hug to a parent's loving bedtime hug — are shown with happy animal characters. (Rev: BL 3/1/06)

3748 Rylant, Cynthia. *All in a Day* (PS–1). Illus. by Nikki McClure. 2009, Abrams $17.95 (978-0-8109-8321-2). 32pp. What might happen in a day? This is an old-fashioned, poetic look at the various ways to enjoy a new day. (Rev: BL 4/1/09; SLJ 5/09)

3749 Rylant, Cynthia. *Appalachia: The Voices of Sleeping Birds* (PS–3). Illus. by Barry Moser. 1991, Harcourt $17.00 (978-0-15-201605-0). 32pp. A loving book in simple text and art about remembering Appalachia. (Rev: BCCB 6/91; BL 2/1/91*; HB 9/91*; SLJ 4/91*) [974]

3750 Rylant, Cynthia. *Let's Go Home: The Wonderful Things About a House* (PS–3). Illus. by Wendy A. Halperin. 2002, Simon & Schuster $16.00 (978-0-689-82326-8). 32pp. A delightful look at different types of houses and their interiors. (Rev: BL 4/15/02*; HBG 10/02; SLJ 6/02) [392.3]

3751 Rylant, Cynthia. *Mr. Griggs' Work* (PS–2). Illus. by Julie Downing. 1989, Orchard paper $6.95 (978-0-531-07037-6). 32pp. Mr. Griggs, who works at the post office, loves his job. (Rev: BCCB 2/89; BL 2/1/89; HB 3/89)

3752 Sabuda, Robert. *Cookie Count: A Tasty Pop-Up* (PS–1). Illus. 1997, Simon & Schuster $19.95 (978-0-689-81191-3). 12pp. Pop-ups involving food are featured in this book, including an amazing gingerbread house. (Rev: BL 12/15/97; HBG 10/98)

3753 Sakai, Komako. *Emily's Balloon* (PS). Illus. by author. 2006, Chronicle $14.95 (978-0-8118-5219-7). A young girl is saddened when her helium-filled balloon is blown high into the branches of a tree in her backyard. (Rev: SLJ 4/06)

3754 Salat, Cristina. *Peanut's Emergency* (K–2). Illus. by Tammie Lyon. 2002, Charlesbridge $16.95 (978-1-57091-440-9); paper $6.95 (978-1-57091-441-6). 32pp. Peanut seeks help when her mother is late picking her up from school in this story about what to do in an "emergency." (Rev: BL 9/15/02; HBG 3/03)

3755 Sayre, April P. *It's My City! A Singing Map* (PS–1). Illus. by Denis Roche. 2001, Greenwillow LB $15.89 (978-0-688-16916-9). A little girl doesn't need directions because she has made up her own onomatopoeic song that describes the route. (Rev: HB 11/01; HBG 3/02; SLJ 10/01)

3756 Scanlon, Liz Garton. *All the World* (PS–1). Illus. by Marla Frazee. 2009, Simon & Schuster $17.99 (978-1-4169-8580-8). 40pp. Rhyme, rhythm, and expressive illustrations relate the mundane aspects of life to the larger surrounding world in a book good for reading aloud. (Rev: BCCB 10/09; BL 7/09; HB 9/09; LMC 10/09; SLJ 8/09)

3757 Schaefer, Carole Lexa. *The Bora-Bora Dress* (PS–3). Illus. by Catherine Stock. 2005, Candlewick $16.99 (978-0-7636-1234-4). 32pp. Lindsay is upset when she's told she must wear a dress for a party at her aunt's house, but a brightly colored island frock soon catches her eye. (Rev: BL 8/05*)

3758 Schaefer, Carole Lexa. *Someone Says* (PS–K). Illus. by Pierr Morgan. 2003, Viking $15.99 (978-0-670-03664-6). A group of young schoolchildren enjoy themselves with creative play. (Rev: HBG 4/04; SLJ 11/03)

3759 Schaefer, Lola M. *Toolbox Twins* (PS). Illus. by Melissa Iwai. 2006, Holt $16.95 (978-0-8050-7733-9). 32pp. Young Vincent and his dad, each with his own toolbox, work on chores around the house. (Rev: BL 9/15/06; SLJ 10/06)

3760 Schertle, Alice. *All You Need for a Snowman* (PS–K). Illus. by Barbara Lavallee. 2002, Harcourt $16.00 (978-0-15-200789-8). 32pp. As the text describes the essentials for making a successful snowman, a group of children are shown building two gigantic examples. (Rev: BCCB 1/03; BL 11/15/02; HB 11/02; HBG 3/03; SLJ 12/02)

3761 Schick, Eleanor. *I Am: I Am a Dancer* (PS–1). Illus. by author. 2002, Marshall Cavendish $15.95 (978-0-7614-5097-9). A girl in a leotard imitates animals, clouds, and a dreamer. (Rev: HBG 10/02; SLJ 1/03)

3762 Schotter, Roni. *Dreamland* (K–2). Illus. by Kevin Hawkes. 1996, Orchard LB $16.99 (978-0-531-08858-6). 40pp. Theo's fanciful drawings of strange inventions become real when his uncle creates an amusement park. (Rev: BL 4/1/96; SLJ 4/96*)

3763 Schotter, Roni. *Nothing Ever Happens on 90th Street* (PS–2). Illus. by Krysten Brooker. 1997, Orchard LB $17.99 (978-0-531-08886-9). 32pp. Eva's writing assignment changes how her neighborhood acts and interacts. (Rev: BL 3/1/97; SLJ 3/97*)

3764 Schrock, Jan West. *Give a Goat* (1–3). Illus. by Aileen Darragh. 2008, Tilbury House $16.95 (978-0-88448-301-4). 32pp. Inspired by a story of giving, a 5th-grade class sets about earning enough money to make their own contribution; the work of Heifer International is the focus of this book. (Rev: BL 6/1–15/08; LMC 1/09)

3765 Schubert, Leda. *Here Comes Darrell* (PS–2). Illus. by Mary Azarian. 2005, Houghton $16.00 (978-0-618-41605-9). 32pp. Darrell the handyman spends so much time helping out his neighbors that he overlooks some important chores around home, but when a storm takes the roof off Darrell's barn his neighbors show their appreciation for all he's done. (Rev: BL 10/1/05; SLJ 11/05)

3766 Schwartz, Amy. *A Glorious Day* (PS). Illus. by author. 2004, Simon & Schuster $16.95 (978-0-689-84802-5). Readers watch the various residents of a city apartment building going about their daily life. (Rev: HB 5/04; SLJ 4/04)

3767 Schwartz, Amy. *What James Likes Best* (PS). Illus. 2003, Simon & Schuster $16.95 (978-0-689-84059-3). 32pp. This oversize book contains four stories about preschooler James, who likes expeditions. (Rev: BCCB 3/03; BL 3/1/03*; HB 5/03; HBG 10/03; SLJ 3/03)

3768 Schwartz, Ellen. *Abby's Birds* (PS–3). Illus. by Sima Elizabeth Shefrin. 2007, Tradewind $16.95 (978-1-896580-86-9). 32pp. Abby learns to fold paper cranes from her elderly Japanese neighbor, Mrs. Naka, and then fills a winter tree with numerous paper cranes to welcome Mrs. Naka home after a hospital stay. (Rev: BL 12/1/07; LMC 3/08)

3769 Scott, Ann H. *Brave as a Mountain Lion* (K–3). Illus. by Glo Coalson. 1996, Clarion $16.00 (978-0-395-66760-6). 32pp. Spider, a Shoshone boy, gets help from his family to conquer his fears, but it is from watching a real spider that he gets real help. (Rev: BCCB 2/96; BL 3/15/96; SLJ 4/96)

3770 Scrimger, Richard. *Princess Bun Bun* (PS–K). Illus. by Gillian Johnson. 2002, Tundra $12.95 (978-0-88776-543-8). Winifred and her family are off to visit Uncle Dave in the Castle Apartments, a name that conjures moats and monsters until Uncle Dave sets them right. (Rev: HBG 10/02; SLJ 7/02)

3771 Sears, William, et al. *You Can Go to the Potty* (PS). Illus. by Renée Andriani. 2002, Little, Brown $12.95 (978-0-316-78888-5). 32pp. This introduction to toilet training is designed for adults to read with children, combining text for the young with sidebars for the adults. (Rev: BL 11/15/02; HBG 3/03; SLJ 11/02)

3772 Seskin, Steve, and Allen Shamblin. *A Chance to Shine* (PS–2). Illus. by R. Gregory Christie. 2006, Tricycle $16.95 (978-1-58246-167-0). 32pp. This attractive picture-book version of a 1991 song tells how an African American father's act of kindness helps his son to look beyond color and social status in judging others. (Rev: BL 4/15/06)

3773 Seuss, Dr. *Oh, the Places You'll Go!* (PS–3). Illus. 1990, Random LB $17.99 (978-0-679-90527-1). This book of advice for youngsters tells them that in spite of problems, they can succeed. (Rev: BL 1/1/90*; SLJ 3/90)

3774 Seymour, Tres. *The Smash-up Crash-up Derby* (K–2). Illus. by S. D. Schindler. 1995, Orchard LB $16.99 (978-0-531-08731-2). 32pp. A boy and members of his family enjoy the fall fair, particularly the demolition derby. (Rev: BCCB 3/95; BL 2/1/95; SLJ 3/95)

3775 Shannon, Terry Miller, and Timothy Warner. *Tub Toys* (PS–1). Illus. by Lee Calderon. 2002, Tricycle $14.95 (978-1-58246-066-6). A little boy gets ready for bath time by collecting all his toys. (Rev: HBG 3/03; SLJ 2/03)

3776 Sharratt, Nick, and Stephen Tucker. *The Time It Took Tom* (PS–2). Illus. by Nick Sharratt. 2000, Little Tiger $14.95 (978-1-888444-63-6). It takes three weeks to restore the living room to normal after Tom goes wild with a can of red paint. (Rev: HBG 10/00; SLJ 3/00)

3777 Shelby, Anne. *Homeplace* (PS–2). Illus. by Wendy A. Halperin. 1995, Orchard LB $17.99 (978-0-531-08732-9). 32pp. A grandmother tells her grandchild about the history of her family and the old homestead. (Rev: BCCB 5/95; BL 2/15/95; SLJ 4/95*)

3778 Shelby, Anne. *The Someday House* (PS–2). Illus. by Rosanne Litzinger. 1996, Orchard LB $16.99 (978-0-531-08860-9). 32pp. Three children imagine living in a variety of different houses and settings. (Rev: BL 3/1/96; SLJ 4/96)

3779 Shulevitz, Uri. *Snow* (PS). Illus. 1998, Farrar $16.00 (978-0-374-37092-3). 32pp. A young child is able to see the beauty in a single snowflake whereas the more sophisticated adults cannot. (Rev: BCCB 1/99; BL 10/15/98*; HB 1/99; HBG 3/99; SLJ 12/98)

3780 Shulman, Lisa. *The Moon Might Be Milk* (PS–2). Illus. by Will Hillenbrand. 2007, Dutton $16.99 (978-0-525-47647-4). 32pp. Rosie asks a number of animals what the moon is made of and they all have different ideas — the cat says milk, the hen says an egg, the dog says butter — and then Rosie's grandmother combines all these ingredients to make moon-shaped sugar cookies; includes a recipe. (Rev: BL 2/15/07*)

3781 Siddals, Mary M. *Millions of Snowflakes* (PS). Illus. by Elizabeth Sayles. 1998, Clarion $13.00 (978-0-395-71531-4). 25pp. Using cool pastel drawings and a spare, rhyming text, this playful story describes all the things one can do in the snow, such as making angels and catching snowflakes. (Rev: BL 11/1/98; HBG 3/99; SLJ 9/98)

3782 Sierra, Judy. *Ballyhoo Bay* (PS–2). Illus. by Derek Anderson. 2009, Simon & Schuster $16.99 (978-1-4169-5888-8). 40pp. When art teacher Mirra Bella learns that a new development threatens Ballyhoo Beach, she organizes a protest and an alternate plan. (Rev: BLO 6/17/09; LMC 8/09; SLJ 2/09)

3783 Sierra, Judy. *Born to Read* (PS–2). Illus. by Marc Brown. 2008, Knopf $16.99 (978-0-375-84687-8). 40pp. A little boy named Sam's inordinate love of reading makes this a good choice for literacy units. (Rev: BL 8/08; LMC 3/09)

3784 Simon, Charnan. *A Greedy Little Pig* (1–3). Illus. by Marcy Ramsey. Series: Magic Door to Learning. 2006, The Child's World LB $21.36 (978-1-59296-622-6). 24pp. A lovable but greedy pig learns a valuable lesson; a section on trying new foods follows the story. Also use *Big Bad Buzz, Jeremy Jones, Clumsy Guy,* and *Messy Molly* (all 2006). (Rev: SLJ 4/07)

3785 Singer, Marilyn. *Block Party Today!* (K–2). Illus. by Stephanie Roth. 2004, Knopf LB $18.99

(978-0-375-92216-9). 32pp. After a jump rope dispute, the lure of the block party in her Brooklyn neighborhood prompts Lola to make up with her friends. (Rev: BL 5/15/04; SLJ 5/04)

3786 Singer, Marilyn. *Fred's Bed* (PS). Illus. by JoAnn Adinolfi. 2001, HarperCollins $9.95 (978-0-694-01451-4). Fred wants a new bed and his teasing mother offers him all kinds of choices — an eagle's nest, a rabbit hole, and so forth. (Rev: HBG 10/01; SLJ 12/01)

3787 Singer, Marilyn. *Shoe Bop!* (PS–2). Illus. by Hiroe Nakata. 2008, Dutton $15.99 (978-0-525-47939-0). 32pp. What does a young girl do when her favorite sneakers die? A series of rhyming couplets explores the possibilities. (Rev: BL 9/1/08; SLJ 7/08)

3788 Siomades, Lorianne. *A Place to Bloom* (PS). Illus. by author. 1997, Boyds Mills $9.95 (978-1-56397-656-8). A collection of random thoughts about attitudes, likes, dislikes, and emotions, all expressed in catchy rhymes. (Rev: HBG 3/98; SLJ 9/97)

3789 Skultety, Nancy. *From Here to Here* (PS–K). Illus. by Tammie Lyon. 2005, Boyds Mills $15.95 (978-1-59078-092-3). 32pp. Farmer Dibble asks for a new road and he gets just that, with its construction and all the equipment involved well documented. (Rev: BL 5/15/05; SLJ 5/05)

3790 Slingsby, Janet. *Hetty's 100 Hats* (PS–2). Illus. by Emma Dodd. 2005, Good Bks. $16.00 (978-1-56148-456-0). With some help, Hetty puts together a collection of 100 hats of all types in this book that is perfect for 100th-day-of-school celebrations. (Rev: SLJ 8/05)

3791 Smith, Cynthia Leitich. *Jingle Dancer* (PS–2). Illus. by Cornelius Van Wright and Ying-Hwa Hu. 2000, Morrow LB $17.89 (978-0-688-16242-9). 32pp. Jenna, a Native American girl, gathers metal jingles to sew onto her dress so she can make pleasant sounds when she dances in the next powwow. (Rev: BCCB 7–8/00; BL 5/15/00; HBG 10/00; SLJ 7/00)

3792 Smith, Dana Kessimakis. *A Brave Spaceboy* (PS–2). Illus. by Laura Freeman. 2005, Hyperion $15.99 (978-0-7868-0933-2). On moving day, a boy and his younger sibling invest an empty box with spaceship powers and imagine themselves exploring the stars. (Rev: BL 3/1/04; HB 3/04; SLJ 5/05)

3793 Smith, Lois T. *Carrie and Carl Play* (PS). Illus. by author. 2007, Candlewick paper $5.99 (978-0-7636-1690-8). Young children will enjoy lifting flaps to discover what Carrie and Carl are up to next during a fun day of play. (Rev: SLJ 7/07)

3794 Soto, Gary. *Facts of Life* (5–8). 2008, Harcourt $16.00 (978-0-15-206181-4). 192pp. Soto offers 10 new stories about important events in the lives of Latino tweens and teens living in California. (Rev: BL 3/1/08; SLJ 7/08)

3795 Spetter, Jung-Hee. *Lily and Trooper's Fall* (PS–K). Illus. 1999, Front St. $8.95 (978-1-886910-38-6). 32pp. Lily and her fun-loving dog Trooper enjoy such fall activities as jumping in a pile of leaves. Also use *Lily and Trooper's Winter* (1999). (Rev: BL 12/1/99; HBG 3/00; SLJ 10/99)

3796 Spier, Peter. *People* (2–4). Illus. by author. 1980, Doubleday $16.95 (978-0-385-13181-0); paper $12.95 (978-0-385-24469-5). 48pp. A view of people's varying life-styles and ways of life.

3797 Spinelli, Eileen. *The Best Time of Day* (PS–2). Illus. by Bryan Langdo. 2005, Harcourt $16.00 (978-0-15-205051-1). 32pp. In rhyming text, farm residents — both human and animal — muse about their favorites time of day. (Rev: BL 10/15/05; SLJ 1/06)

3798 Spinelli, Eileen. *A Safe Place Called Home* (K–2). Illus. by Christy Hale. 2001, Marshall Cavendish $15.95 (978-0-7614-5085-6). 32pp. A boy is glad to know that home is at the end of a scary walk during which dogs bark and a bully looks threatening. (Rev: BCCB 9/01; BL 10/1/01; HBG 3/02; SLJ 2/02)

3799 Spinelli, Eileen. *Someday* (PS–2). Illus. by Rosie Winstead. 2007, Dial $16.99 (978-0-8037-2941-4). 32pp. A young girl imagines herself accomplishing amazing feats in the future, even while she is enjoying her daily life. (Rev: BCCB 9/07; BL 6/1–15/07; SLJ 5/07)

3800 Stainton, Sue. *The Chocolate Cat* (PS–1). Illus. by Anne Mortimer. 2007, HarperCollins $16.99 (978-0-06-057245-7). 32pp. A cranky chocolate maker and his lazy cat live a dull existence until the confectioner decides to make a batch of scrumptious chocolate mice, inspiring a frenzy of chocolate creativity that cheers up the whole town. (Rev: BL 11/1/07; SLJ 1/08)

3801 Stevens, Jan R. *Carlos Digs to China / Carlos Excava Hasta la China* (K–2). Trans. by Mario Lamo-Jimenez. Illus. by Jeanne Arnold. 2001, Rising Moon LB $15.95 (978-0-87358-764-8). A bilingual story in which Carlos decides to dig to China so that he can taste all that wonderful food. (Rev: HBG 10/01; SLJ 6/01)

3802 Stevens, Janet, and Susan Stevens Crummel. *Plaidypus Lost* (PS–1). Illus. by Janet Stevens. 2004, Holiday House $16.95 (978-0-8234-1561-8). 40pp. A little girl keeps finding and losing the platypus the Grandma made from an old plaid shirt. (Rev: BL 3/15/04; SLJ 5/04)

3803 Stevenson, James. *Popcorn* (2–5). Illus. 1998, Greenwillow $16.99 (978-0-688-15261-1). 64pp. Daily life in a small seaside town is captured in a series of quiet, moving poems illustrated with exquisite watercolors. (Rev: BCCB 4/98; BL 5/1/98*; HB 5/98; HBG 10/98; SLJ 5/98)

3804 Stewart, Sarah. *The Library* (K–3). Illus. by David Small. 1995, Farrar $16.00 (978-0-374-34388-0). 32pp. The life story of a woman who loved reading books so much that eventually a library was named after her. (Rev: BCCB 5/95; BL 3/15/95; HB 7/95; SLJ 9/95)

3805 Stock, Catherine. *Island Summer* (K–2). Illus. 1999, Lothrop $16.00 (978-0-688-12780-0). 32pp. After a cold winter, an island springs back to life when the summer residents arrive, only to become quiet again when they leave in the fall. (Rev: BL 10/15/99; HBG 3/00; SLJ 9/99)

3806 Strickland, Michael R. *Haircuts at Sleepy Sam's* (PS–2). Illus. by Keaf Holliday. 1998, Boyds Mills $15.95 (978-1-56397-562-2). Although two African American brothers have a note from their mother for the barber telling him how to cut their hair, the barber, Sam, gives them the cut they want. (Rev: BL 10/15/98; HBG 3/99; SLJ 11/98)

3807 Sturges, Philemon. *I Love Tools!* (PS–1). Illus. by Shari Halpern. 2006, HarperCollins LB $14.89 (978-0-06-009288-7). Various tools are introduced as a family works to build a birdhouse. (Rev: SLJ 6/06)

3808 Swanson, Susan Marie. *The House in the Night* (PS–K). Illus. by Beth Krommes. 2008, Houghton $16.00 (978-0-618-86244-3). 40pp. A beautifully illustrated cumulative tale celebrating night and a reassuring sense of order. Caldecott Medal, 2009. (Rev: BL 4/15/08; SLJ 4/08)

3809 Tafolla, Carmen. *What Can You Do with a Paleta?* (PS–3). Illus. by Magaly Morales. 2009, Tricycle $14.99 (978-1-58246-221-9). 32pp. On a warm night in the barrio, the bell of the paleta wagon signals the welcome popsicle treat; bright illustrations add to the appeal. (Rev: BL 5/15/09)

3810 Takabayashi, Mari. *I Live in Brooklyn* (1–2). Illus. 2004, Houghton $16.00 (978-0-618-30899-6). 32pp. Michelle, 6, lives in Brooklyn and describes the routines of her life there. (Rev: BL 2/15/04; HB 7/04; SLJ 4/04)

3811 Tarpley, Natasha A. *Bippity Bop Barbershop* (PS–1). Illus. by E. B. Lewis. 2002, Little, Brown $15.95 (978-0-316-52284-7). 32pp. Miles accompanies his father to the local barbershop for his first haircut. (Rev: BCCB 3/02; BL 2/15/02; HBG 10/02; SLJ 2/02)

3812 Tarpley, Natasha A. *I Love My Hair!* (PS–1). Illus. by E. B. Lewis. 1998, Little, Brown $15.95 (978-0-316-52275-5). 32pp. A young African American girl has fun creating different styles with her hair. (Rev: BCCB 4/98; BL 2/15/98; HBG 10/98; SLJ 2/98)

3813 Terasaki, Todd. *Ghosts for Breakfast* (2–4). Illus. by Shelly Shinjo. 2002, Lee & Low $16.95 (978-1-58430-046-5). 32pp. The Troublesome Trio informs Farmer Tanaka that there are ghosts in his field, so the farmer investigates, only to find that the ghosts are daikon radishes hanging to dry. (Rev: BL 1/1–15/03; HBG 3/03; SLJ 10/02)

3814 Terry, Sonya. *"L" Is for Library* (1–3). Illus. by Nicole Wong. 2006, Upstart $16.95 (978-1-932146-44-8). A cat conducts a tour of the library, introducing print and nonprint resources for every letter from A to Z. (Rev: SLJ 8/06)

3815 Thomas, Peggy. *Snow Dance* (K–2). Illus. by Paul Facklam. 2008, Pelican $15.95 (978-1-58980-478-4). 32pp. Will a good snow dance produce the snow day that Ruthie is longing for? (Rev: BL 4/1/08; SLJ 8/08)

3816 Thompson, Carol. *Baby Days* (PS). Illus. 1991, Macmillan $15.95 (978-0-02-789235-2). 48pp. Illustrates a number of activities that toddlers can engage in from waking to bedtime. (Rev: BL 12/1/91; SLJ 1/92)

3817 Thong, Roseanne. *Gai See: What You Can See in Chinatown* (1–3). Illus. by Yangsook Choi. 2007, Abrams $16.95 (978-0-8109-9337-2). 40pp. Readers get a rhyming tour of a typical Chinatown *gai see* or street market. (Rev: BL 9/1/07; SLJ 11/07)

3818 Tildes, Phyllis L. *Billy's Big-Boy Bed* (PS). Illus. by author. 2002, Charlesbridge LB $15.95 (978-1-57091-475-1). Billy gets a new, big bed but prefers to remain in his crib for the time being. (Rev: HBG 10/02; SLJ 3/02)

3819 Torrey, Richard. *Almost* (PS–K). Illus. by author. 2009, HarperCollins $17.99 (978-0-06-156166-5). 40pp. Jack, nearly 6 years old, can almost do everything but it's the "almost" that frustrates him. (Rev: BL 4/1/09; SLJ 4/09)

3820 Train, Mary. *Time for the Fair* (K–2). Illus. by Karel Hayes. 2005, Down East $15.95 (978-0-89272-694-3). Grace learns a little about the rhythms of the seasons as she anxiously awaits the arrival of the annual farmer's fair. (Rev: SLJ 12/05)

3821 Tresselt, Alvin. *White Snow Bright Snow* (K–3). Illus. by Roger Duvoisin. 1988, Lothrop LB $17.89 (978-0-688-51161-6); Morrow paper $6.99 (978-0-688-08294-9). Small-town snowfall is chronicled in this reissued Caldecott Medal winner of 1948.

3822 Turner, Nancy Byrd. *When Young Melissa Sweeps* (PS–3). Illus. by Debrah Santini. 1998, Peachtree $15.95 (978-1-56145-157-9). 30pp. First published in 1927, this poem captures a young girl's joy and enthusiasm as she dances with her broom while cleaning the house. (Rev: BL 5/1/98; HBG 10/98)

3823 Tusa, Tricia. *Bunnies in My Head* (PS–2). Illus. 1998, Univ. of Texas. M. D. Anderson Cancer Center $20.00 (978-0-9664551-8-2). 32pp. Using a brief story line, this book reproduces the artwork created by children at the Anderson Cancer Center in Houston, Texas. (Rev: BL 2/1/99; SLJ 2/99)

3824 Tutu, Archbishop Desmond, and Douglas Carlton Abrams. *God's Dream* (PS–K). Illus. by LeUyen Pham. 2008, Candlewick $16.99 (978-0-7636-3388-2). 40pp. This picture book shows a group of multicultural toddlers learning about empathy and sharing. (Rev: BL 8/08)

3825 Upjohn, Rebecca. *Lily and the Paper Man* (PS–2). Illus. by Renné Benoit. 2007, Second Story $14.95 (978-1-897187-19-7). 24pp. Although Lily has avoided the homeless man in her neighborhood, when the weather turns cold, she demonstrates true compassion by collecting warm clothing for him. (Rev: BL 12/1/07; LMC 3/08)

3826 Van Der Heide, Iris. *A Strange Day* (K–2). Illus. by Marijke ten Cate. 2007, Boyds Mills $16.95 (978-1-932425-94-9). Jack unwittingly helps his neighbors while wandering through town on a windy day in this story set in the Netherlands. (Rev: SLJ 5/07)

3827 Van Wert, Faye. *Empty Pockets* (PS–1). Illus. by author. 2000, Greene Bark $16.95 (978-1-880851-61-6). When Stevie's mother discovers a frog in his dresser drawer, she puts a stop to his hobby of bringing home everything he finds. (Rev: SLJ 3/01)

3828 Villaseñor, Victor. *The Stranger and the Red Rooster / El forastero y el gallo rojo* (2–4). Trans. by Gabriela Baeza Ventura. Illus. by José Jara. 2006, Piñata $15.95 (978-1-55885-420-8). Presented in both English and Spanish, this is the story of how a frightening man with a scar is welcomed into his new community once he has a rooster in his arms. (Rev: SLJ 6/06)

3829 Viorst, Judith. *Just in Case* (K–2). Illus. by Diana Cain Bluthenthal. 2006, Simon & Schuster $15.95 (978-0-689-87164-1). 40pp. Charlie likes to be prepared for any eventuality, but when his friends throw him a birthday party he discovers that surprises can be fun. (Rev: BL 12/1/05; SLJ 1/06)

3830 Walker, Nan. *The Midnight Kid* (1–3). Illus. by Barry Gott. Series: Science Solves It! 2007, Kane paper $4.99 (978-1-57565-238-2). 32pp. Peter performs a mini experiment — trying not to sleep for three nights — and discovers that sleep is important to his health. Facts about sleep are presented in sidebars. (Rev: SLJ 5/07)

3831 Walton, Rick. *A Very Hairy Scary Story* (K–3). Illus. by David Clark. 2004, Penguin $15.99 (978-0-399-23858-1). On her way home later than promised, a girl sees lots of scary things in the night. (Rev: SLJ 8/04)

3832 Weatherford, Carole Boston. *Jazz Baby* (PS). Illus. by Laura Freeman. 2002, Lee & Low $11.95 (978-1-58430-039-7). A crew of ethnically diverse youngsters dances to the beat of a lively rhyme and jazz instruments. (Rev: HBG 10/02; SLJ 6/02)

3833 Weaver, Tess. *Frederick Finch, Loudmouth* (PS–2). Illus. by Debbie Tilley. 2008, Clarion $16.00 (978-0-618-45239-2). 32pp. After many failures, Frederick's loud voice finally helps him to win a competition at the state fair. (Rev: BL 6/1–15/08; SLJ 6/08)

3834 Weeks, Sarah. *If I Were a Lion* (PS–1). Illus. by Heather Solomon. 2004, Simon & Schuster $15.95 (978-0-689-84836-0). 40pp. A little girl who has been criticized for her "wild" behavior goes on the defensive and imagines what truly wild behavior would involve. (Rev: BL 3/15/04; SLJ 4/04)

3835 Weidt, Maryann N. *Daddy Played Music for the Cows* (PS–3). Illus. by Henri Sorensen. 1995, Lothrop LB $14.93 (978-0-688-10058-2). 32pp. Life on a farm is recorded in this story of a girl who grows from baby to school age in this environment. (Rev: BL 10/1/95; SLJ 10/95)

3836 Wellington, Monica. *Ana cultiva manzanas / Apple Farmer Annie* (PS–2). Illus. by author. 2004, Dutton LB $10.99 (978-0-525-47252-0). The Spanish translation appears in large type above the smaller-type English original about a happy apple farmer. (Rev: BL 9/04; SLJ 9/04)

3837 Wellington, Monica. *Mr. Cookie Baker* (PS–K). 2006, Dutton $15.99 (978-0-525-47763-1). 32pp. A new edition of the colorful picture book following Mr. Baker through his day, from mixing the dough

through enjoying the last of the cookies. (Rev: BL 10/1/06)

3838 Wellington, Monica. *Pizza at Sally's* (PS–K). 2006, Dutton $14.99 (978-0-525-47715-0). 32pp. This brightly illustrated picture book follows Sally the pizzeria owner as she goes through all the steps of making a pizza; a recipe is appended. (Rev: BL 8/06; SLJ 6/06)

3839 Wellington, Monica. *Truck Driver Tom* (PS–2). Illus. by author. 2007, Dutton $15.99 (978-0-525-47831-7). 32pp. Tom picks up produce on a farm and delivers it in the city before spending the night in his cab; the bright detailed illustrations invite close examination. (Rev: BL 11/1/07; SLJ 11/07)

3840 Wells, Rosemary. *Bingo* (PS). Illus. by author. Series: Bunny Reads Back. 1999, Scholastic $5.99 (978-0-590-02913-1). A variation on this familiar song makes Bingo a female in this enchanting board book. (Rev: SLJ 7/99)

3841 Whiting, Sue. *The Firefighters* (PS–2). Illus. by Donna Rawlins. 2008, Candlewick $15.99 (978-0-7636-4019-4). 32pp. Miss Iverson's class has a great time playing fire fighters and afterward gets a surprise tour of a real fire engine with real firemen. (Rev: BL 9/1/08)

3842 Wickstrom, Sylvie. *I Love You, Mister Bear* (PS–1). Illus. by author. 2004, HarperCollins LB $15.89 (978-0-06-029332-1). Young Sosha rescues a dilapidated stuffed bear from a yard sale and takes it home for some special care and love. (Rev: BL 1/1–15/04; SLJ 1/04)

3843 Wilcox, Brad. *Hip, Hip, Hooray for Annie McRae!* (PS–1). Illus. by Julie Hansen Olson. 2001, Gibbs Smith $15.95 (978-1-58685-058-6). Annie McRae has a healthy self-confidence and when her parents and teachers forget to praise her one day, she simply does it herself. (Rev: HBG 3/02; SLJ 10/01)

3844 Willems, Mo. *Time to Pee!* (PS). Illus. by author. 2003, Hyperion $12.99 (978-0-7868-1868-6). This useful guide to toilet training is enlivened by illustrations of tiny mice carrying signs with helpful advice and words of reassurance. (Rev: HBG 4/04; SLJ 12/03) [649]

3845 Williams, Carol Ann. *Booming Bella* (K–3). Illus. by Tatjana Mai-Wyss. 2008, Putnam $16.99 (978-0-399-24277-9). 32pp. Bella's loud comments on everything around her are criticized during a trip to the art museum, but her big voice proves useful when she realizes she's on the wrong bus. (Rev: BL 6/1–15/08; LMC 10/08; SLJ 7/08)

3846 Williams, Sue. *I Went Walking* (PS–K). Illus. by Julie Vivas. 1990, Harcourt $13.95 (978-0-15-200471-2). 32pp. This book involves guessing the identity of animals hidden in pictures during a boy's afternoon walk. (Rev: BCCB 12/92; BL 9/1/90*; HB 11/90; SLJ 10/90*)

3847 Williams, Vera B. *Cherries and Cherry Pits* (K–3). Illus. by author. 1986, Morrow paper $6.99 (978-0-688-10478-8). 40pp. Three tales and pictures from young Bidemmi, a black girl, about giving, loving, and making art. (Rev: BL 10/15/86; HB 9/86; SLJ 10/86)

3848 Wilson, Karma. *How to Bake an American Pie* (PS–2). Illus. by Raúl Colón. 2007, Simon & Schuster $16.99 (978-0-689-86506-0). 40pp. A cat and a dog whip up a recipe consisting of such ingredients as purple mountain majesty, liberty, courage, and fruited plains. (Rev: BL 4/1/07)

3849 Wilson, Sarah. *Hocus Focus* (2–3). Illus. by Amy Wummer. Series: Science Solves It! 2004, Kane paper $4.99 (978-1-57565-136-1). 32pp. Jack and Gina, one near-sighted and the other far-sighted, decide to work together rather than wear glasses and suffer taunts; an eye chart and scientific information are appended. (Rev: BL 3/15/04; SLJ 6/04)

3850 Winthrop, Elizabeth. *Shoes* (PS–K). Illus. by William Joyce. 1986, HarperCollins paper $6.99 (978-0-06-443171-2). 32pp. Rhyming verse about shoes and feet. (Rev: BL 10/1/86; HB 1/87; SLJ 12/86)

3851 Wishinsky, Frieda. *Nothing Scares Us* (PS–2). Illus. by Neal Layton. 2000, Carolrhoda LB $15.95 (978-1-57505-490-2). Two dear friends who think they are fearless discover that each has a secret, hidden fear. (Rev: BCCB 10/00; HBG 3/01; SLJ 11/00)

3852 Wolfe, Frances. *One Wish* (PS–1). 2004, Tundra $15.95 (978-0-88776-662-6). 32pp. A young girl dreams of having a cottage by the sea in this gentle story with detailed oil paintings. (Rev: BL 6/1–15/04; SLJ 6/04)

3853 Wolfe, Frances. *Where I Live* (PS–1). Illus. 2001, Tundra $14.95 (978-0-88776-529-2). 32pp. A little girl describes where she lives (the seaside) and her activities there. (Rev: BCCB 5/01; BL 5/1/01; HBG 10/01; SLJ 4/01)

3854 Wolff, Nancy. *Tallulah in the Kitchen* (K–2). Illus. 2005, Holt $16.95 (978-0-8050-7463-5). 32pp. Tallulah, a cat, and her sidekicks crocodile Freddie and pig Roxie whip up some pancakes and impart information about cooking in general. (Rev: BL 6/1–15/05)

3855 Wong, Janet S. *The Dumpster Diver* (1–3). Illus. by David Roberts. 2007, Candlewick $16.99 (978-0-7636-2380-7). 32pp. The children of an apartment complex enjoy helping Steve the electrician dive for buried treasure in the dumpster in the back alley; the group then creates new and inventive objects from the retrieved "junk." (Rev: BL 2/15/07*)

3856 Wood, Audrey. *The Napping House Wakes Up* (PS–2). Illus. by Don Wood. 1994, Harcourt $17.95 (978-0-15-200890-1). 20pp. All sorts of actions take place in this interactive version of the popular picture book. (Rev: BL 11/15/94; SLJ 11/94)

3857 Wood, Douglas. *Nothing to Do* (PS–2). Illus. by Wendy A. Halperin. 2006, Dutton $16.99 (978-0-525-47656-6). 32pp. Nothing to do? Try reading a book, sailing a toy boat, walking through the woods, or any of the other low-tech activities that children may find unexpectedly satisfying. (Rev: BL 5/1/06; SLJ 5/06)

3858 Wood, Douglas. *A Quiet Place* (K–3). Illus. by Dan Andreasen. 2002, Simon & Schuster $16.95 (978-0-689-81511-9). 32pp. A boy searches for a secluded place to be alone with his thoughts, far from the noise and bustle of the city. (Rev: BL 2/15/02; HBG 10/02; SLJ 7/02)

3859 Wood, Douglas. *The Secret of Saying Thanks* (PS–2). Illus. by Greg Shed. 2005, Simon & Schuster $16.95 (978-0-689-85410-1). 32pp. This beautifully illustrated picture book underlines the importance of showing gratitude for the wonders around us. (Rev: BL 10/15/05; SLJ 10/05)

3860 Woodruff, Elvira. *Can You Guess Where We're Going?* (PS–3). Illus. by Cynthia Fisher. 1998, Holiday House $15.95 (978-0-8234-1387-4). Gramps gives clues to his grandson as to their destination — a place filled with excitement, adventure, and entertainment — which turns out to be the local library. (Rev: HBG 3/99; SLJ 1/99)

3861 Wyeth, Sharon D. *Something Beautiful* (PS–3). Illus. by Chris K. Soentpiet. 1998, Doubleday $16.95 (978-0-385-32239-3). 32pp. In spite of the squalor and poverty around her, a small African American girl is able to find some things of beauty in her neighborhood. (Rev: BCCB 12/98; BL 9/15/98; HBG 3/99; SLJ 12/98)

3862 Yashima, Taro. *Umbrella* (PS–1). Illus. by author. 1958, Puffin paper $6.99 (978-0-14-050240-4). 32pp. A 3-year-old Japanese American girl, born in New York City, longs for a rainy day so she can use her new blue umbrella and red rubber boots.

3863 Yee, Wong H. *Fireman Small* (PS–K). Illus. 1994, Houghton $16.00 (978-0-395-68987-5). 28pp. Every time Fireman Small tries to sleep, he must respond to another emergency. (Rev: BL 2/1/95; SLJ 12/94)

3864 Yee, Wong H. *Tracks in the Snow* (PS). Illus. by author. 2003, Holt $15.95 (978-0-8050-6771-2). A simple story, told in rhyming text, about a young girl who traces tracks in the snow to see who made them and finally realizes she made them herself the day before. (Rev: BL 12/1/03; HB 11/03; HBG 4/04; SLJ 12/03)

3865 Yee, Wong H. *Who Likes Rain?* (PS–1). Illus. by author. 2007, Holt $14.95 (978-0-8050-7734-6). 32pp. A little girl heads outdoors on a rainy day and discovers that many plants and animals really like rain — but not all. (Rev: BL 3/1/07*)

3866 Yim, Natasha. *Otto's Rainy Day* (PS). Illus. by Pamela R. Levy. 2000, Charlesbridge LB $15.95 (978-1-57091-400-3). 32pp. While Mom is trying to get work done on her home computer, little Otto craves attention and is constantly getting into trouble. (Rev: BL 6/1–15/00; HBG 10/01; SLJ 8/00)

3867 Yolen, Jane. *Mama's Kiss* (PS–1). Illus. by Daniel Baxter. 2008, Chronicle $14.99 (978-0-8118-6683-5). 32pp. One of Mama's thrown kisses misses its mark and travels hither and thither before ending up where it was intended. (Rev: BL 12/15/08; SLJ 2/09)

3868 Young, Amy. *Belinda Begins Ballet* (PS–2). Illus. by author. 2008, Viking $15.99 (978-0-670-06244-7). 32pp. When an insensitive school talent show director casts Belinda as a clown because of her huge feet, Belinda stays true to her love of ballet and enchants her audience with a surprise performance. (Rev: BL 11/1/07; SLJ 4/08)

3869 Young, Amy. *Belinda in Paris* (PS–2). Illus. 2005, Viking $15.99 (978-0-670-03693-6). 32pp. Belinda, the big-footed ballerina, arrives in Paris for a big performance only to discover that her specially made pointe shoes are on their way to Pago Pago. (Rev: BL 1/1–15/05; SLJ 4/05)

3870 Young, Amy. *Belinda the Ballerina* (PS–2). Illus. 2003, Viking $15.99 (978-0-670-03549-6). 32pp. Belinda is rejected by ballet judges because of her huge feet, and she sadly abandons dance until a band arrives at Fred's Fine Food and her feet can't resist. (Rev: BL 3/1/03; HBG 10/03; SLJ 3/03)

3871 Ziefert, Harriet. *Circus Parade* (PS–2). Illus. by Tanya Roitman. 2005, Blue Apple $15.95 (978-1-59354-088-3). A parade of circus characters, ranging from majorettes and clowns to elephants and horses, march through a colorful town to a lively rhyming chant. (Rev: SLJ 10/05)

3872 Ziefert, Harriet. *My Forever Dress* (K–2). Illus. by Liz Murphy. 2009, Blue Apple $16.99 (978-1-934706-45-9). 40pp. As a girl grows, her grandmother recycles her favorite dress into something that will fit. (Rev: BLO 5/27/09; SLJ 6/09)

3873 Zimmerman, Andrea. *Fire Engine Man* (PS–K). Illus. by David Clemesha. 2007, Holt $15.95 (978-0-8050-7905-0). 32pp. A boy affectionately includes his little brother in his dreams of someday becoming a firefighter. (Rev: BL 5/1/07; SLJ 7/07)

3874 Zolotow, Charlotte. *I Like to Be Little* (K–3). Illus. by Erik Blegvad. 1987, HarperCollins paper $6.99 (978-0-06-443248-1). 32pp. The advantages of being small are explored in this 1966 picture book originally titled *I Want to Be Little*.

FAMILY STORIES

3875 Abdullah, Patricia. *Saving Daddy* (K–2). Illus. by Alexandra Cabri. 2007, Eeci $17.95 (978-1-933193-16-8). 32pp. Daddy's kidneys fail but his life is saved after son James sends out a computer plea for help; the elderly donor, Amina, a white woman, is embraced by James's African American family. (Rev: BL 2/1/07)

3876 Ackerman, Karen. *Song and Dance Man* (K–3). Illus. by Stephen Gammell. 1988, Knopf LB $16.99 (978-0-394-99330-0); paper $6.99 (978-0-679-81995-0). 32pp. Up in the attic, Grandpa shows three children what it's like to be a song-and-dance man. Caldecott Medal winner, 1989. (Rev: BCCB 11/88; BL 10/1/88; HB 11/88)

3877 Ada, Alma Flor. *I Love Saturdays y Domingos* (PS–3). Illus. by Elivia Savadier. 2002, Simon & Schuster $16.95 (978-0-689-31819-1). 32pp. A little girl visits Grandma and Grandpa on Saturday and Abuelito and Abuelita on Sunday in this multicultural story that incorporates Spanish words and phrases. (Rev: BL 2/1/02; HBG 10/02; SLJ 1/02)

3878 Adams, Diane. *I Can Do It Myself!* (PS–K). Illus. by Nancy Hayashi. 2009, Peachtree $15.95 (978-1-56145-471-6). 32pp. Emily Pearl takes pride in her ability (sort of) to look after herself until bedtime comes and her independence evaporates. (Rev: BL 3/15/09; SLJ 4/09)

3879 Adler, David A. *It's a Baby, Andy Russell* (3–5). Illus. by Leanne Franson. 2005, Harcourt $14.00 (978-0-15-216742-4). 128pp. Andy and his sister Rachel are glad that the new baby is arriving but worried about coexisting with Aunt Janet while their mother is in hospital. (Rev: BL 5/15/05; SLJ 3/05)

3880 Adler, Victoria. *All of Baby, Nose to Toes* (PS). Illus. by Hiroe Nakata. 2009, Dial $14.99 (978-0-8037-3217-9). 32pp. From head to toe this cheerful volume celebrates all things baby. (Rev: BL 5/15/09; SLJ 7/09)

3881 Adoff, Arnold. *Black Is Brown Is Tan* (K–3). Illus. by Emily Arnold McCully. 1973, HarperCollins $15.95 (978-0-06-020083-1). 32pp. A story in rhyme, which needs to be read aloud for greater understanding, depicts the warmth and companionship of an interracial family.

3882 Alexander, Martha. *Where Does the Sky End, Grandpa?* (PS). Illus. by author. 1992, Harcourt $12.95 (978-0-15-295603-5). In this gentle story, a young girl walks through the pastures with her grandfather. (Rev: SLJ 7/92)

3883 Alexander, Sue. *One More Time, Mama* (PS–2). Illus. by David Soman. 1999, Marshall Cavendish $15.95 (978-0-7614-5051-1). 32pp. A mother tells her daughter of the long wait she had through three seasons — spring, summer, and fall — until the little girl was born. (Rev: BL 11/15/99; HBG 3/00; SLJ 11/99)

3884 Aliki. *The Two of Them* (K–4). Illus. by author. 1987, Morrow paper $6.99 (978-0-688-07337-4). 32pp. A moving story of a tender relationship between a child and her grandfather.

3885 Aliki, *Welcome, Little Baby* (PS–K). Illus. by author. 1987, Greenwillow $16.99 (978-0-688-06810-3). 24pp. Addressed to the newborn child and celebrating the innocence of the infant. (Rev: BL 3/1/87; SLJ 6–7/87)

3886 Allen, Janet. *Best Little Wingman* (K–3). Illus. by Jim Postier. 2005, Boyds Mills $15.95 (978-1-59078-197-5). Janny is happy to help her father plowing the roads in rural Maine. (Rev: SLJ 3/05)

3887 Altman, Alexandra Jessup. *Waiting for Benjamin: A Story About Autism* (1–4). Illus. by Susan Keeter. 2008, Albert Whitman $15.95 (978-0-8075-7364-8). 32pp. Alexander has trouble accepting the extra attention paid to his younger brother Benjamin, who is autistic. (Rev: BL 7/08; LMC 8/08; SLJ 7/08)

3888 Altman, Linda J. *Singing with Momma Lou* (2–5). Illus. by Larry Johnson. 2002, Lee & Low $16.95 (978-1-58430-040-3). 32pp. Tamika uses photograph albums to help her grandmother, who suffers from Alzheimer's disease, remember some of her past. (Rev: BL 5/15/02; HBG 10/02; SLJ 6/02)

3889 Amado, Elisa. *Cousins* (1–4). Illus. by Luis Garay. 2004, Groundwood $16.95 (978-0-88899-459-2). The narrator is a little girl who has difficulty living in two cultures — her extended family is of different ethnic backgrounds. (Rev: SLJ 5/04) [813]

3890 Andreae, Giles. *There's a House Inside My Mommy* (PS–1). Illus. by Vanessa Cabban. 2002, Whitman $15.95 (978-0-8075-7853-7). 32pp. Rhythmic text and simple, affectionate illustrations show a young boy's impressions of the baby growing inside his mother. (Rev: BL 11/1/02; HBG 3/03; SLJ 11/02)

3891 Anholt, Catherine, and Laurence Anholt. *Big Book of Little Children* (PS–K). Illus. by authors. 2003, Candlewick $15.99 (978-0-7636-2210-7). 79pp. Spreads bearing bright watercolor-and-ink illustrations include words, phrases, or rhymes about little children and their feelings and activities. (Rev: HBG 4/04; SLJ 1/04)

3892 Anholt, Laurence. *Seven for a Secret* (1–3). Illus. by Jim Coplestone. 2006, Frances Lincoln $15.95 (978-1-84507-300-8). 32pp. A dying man leaves a treasure for his granddaughter, whose family has been enduring a financial crisis. (Rev: BL 5/1/06; SLJ 6/06)

3893 *Are We There Yet?* (K–2). Illus. by Dale Gottlieb. Series: I'm Going to Read! 2005, Sterling $11.95 (978-1-4027-2714-6); paper $3.95 (978-1-4027-2713-9). 32pp. This beginning reader portrays a girl and her younger brother pestering their father as he drives them to the toy store. (Rev: BL 10/15/05)

3894 Argueta, Jorge. *Xochitl and the Flowers / Xochitl, la nina de las flores* (K–3). Illus. by Carl Angel. 2003, Children's Book Pr. $16.95 (978-0-89239-181-3). 31pp. Newly arrived in San Francisco from their native El Salvador, Xochitl Flores and her family have problems adapting to their new home but find joy in the flowers they grow and sell. (Rev: BL 12/1/03; HBG 4/04; SLJ 12/03)

3895 Armas, Teresa. *Remembering Grandma / Recordando a Abuela* (1–3). Trans. by Gabriela Baeza Ventura. Illus. by Pauline Rodriguez Howard. 2003, Piñata $14.95 (978-1-55885-344-7). Lorena brings comfort to her grandfather when they share her dead grandmother's prized belongings in this appealing bilingual story. (Rev: BL 5/15/03; SLJ 7/03)

3896 Ashman, Linda. *Mama's Day* (PS). Illus. by Jan Ormerod. 2006, Simon & Schuster $15.95 (978-0-689-83475-2). 32pp. The bond between mothers and their babies is celebrated in a charming blend of verse and ink-and-gouache illustrations. (Rev: BL 3/15/06; SLJ 5/06)

3897 Ashman, Linda. *When I Was King* (PS–1). Illus. by David McPhail. 2008, HarperCollins $16.99 (978-0-06-029051-1). 32pp. A boy used to being the only child in the house — the king — expresses his discontent directly to his new baby brother. (Rev: BL 10/1/08; SLJ 10/08)

3898 Asim, Jabari. *Daddy Goes to Work* (PS–2). Illus. by Aaron Boyd. 2006, Little, Brown $15.99 (978-0-316-73575-9). 32pp. The story of a young African American girl's day at work with her father is told in rhyming couplets. (Rev: BL 2/1/06; SLJ 6/06)

3899 Aska, Warabe. *Tapicero Tap Tap* (PS–2). Illus. 2006, Tundra $16.95 (978-0-88776-760-9). 24pp. A Spanish furniture maker Tapicero Tap Tap tells his grandson how he put aside his boyhood dreams of travel to care for his family after his father was killed. (Rev: BL 3/1/06)

3900 Asquith, Ros. *My Do It!* (PS). Illus. by Sam Williams. 2000, DK paper $5.95 (978-0-7894-5648-9). An enjoyable flap book in which a little boy insists that he do a lot of chores that his mother would ordinarily do. (Rev: SLJ 10/00)

3901 Aston, Dianna. *Mama Outside, Mama Inside* (PS–K). Illus. by Susan Gaber. 2006, Holt $15.95 (978-0-8050-7716-2). 32pp. This appealing picture book explores the parallels between two expectant mothers — one a bird and the other a human. (Rev: BL 2/15/06; SLJ 3/06)

3902 Austin, Heather. *Visiting Aunt Sylvia's: A Maine Adventure* (K–2). Illus. by author. 2002, Down East $15.95 (978-0-89272-523-6). A young narrator looks back at happy times at Aunt Sylvia's cabin in rural Maine — stacking wood, skiing, roasting marshmallows, swimming in the summer, and other seasonal memories. (Rev: HBG 10/03; SLJ 2/03)

3903 Baca, Ana. *Chiles for Benito / Chiles para Benito* (K–3). Trans. by Jose Juan Colin. Illus. by Anthony Accardo. 2003, Piñata $15.95 (978-1-55885-389-8). In New Mexico, Cristina hears stories about her ancestor's magic seeds as she and her grandmother string red chiles to dry. (Rev: BL 12/15/03; SLJ 12/03)

3904 Ballard, Robin. *I Used to Be the Baby* (PS–K). Illus. 2002, HarperCollins LB $15.89 (978-0-06-029587-5). 24pp. A little boy helps take care of his toddler brother but still expects to spend time on his mother's lap. (Rev: BL 5/1/02; HBG 10/02; SLJ 5/02)

3905 Bang, Molly. *In My Heart* (PS–2). Illus. 2006, Little, Brown $15.99 (978-0-316-79617-0). 32pp. A mother emphasizes to her child that she is always in her heart, throughout the day. (Rev: BL 1/1–15/06; SLJ 1/06)

3906 Banks, Kate. *Max's Words* (K–3). Illus. by Boris Kulikov. 2006, Farrar $16.00 (978-0-374-39949-8). 32pp. When Max's older brothers refuse to share their stamp and coin collections with him, the young boy starts a very special collection of his own. (Rev: BL 9/1/06; SLJ 9/06*)

3907 Banks, Kate. *That's Papa's Way* (PS–1). Illus. by Lauren Castillo. 2009, Farrar $16.95 (978-0-374-37445-7). 40pp. A simple, gentle story about a little girl and her father who enjoy a quiet day fishing together even though they tackle the worms differently; soothing pastel illustrations add atmosphere. (Rev: BL 2/1/09; SLJ 5/09)

3908 Barbour, Karen. *Little Nino's Pizzeria* (PS–2). Illus. by author. 1990, Harcourt paper $6.00 (978-0-15-246321-2). 32pp. When his father's business turns big, Tony is only in the way. (Rev: BL 9/15/87; SLJ 11/87)

3909 Barclay, Jane. *Going on a Journey to the Sea* (PS–1). Illus. by Doris Barrette. 2002, Lobster $16.95 (978-1-894222-34-1). 32pp. A boy and his sister spend a pleasant day at the beach in this rhyming picture book. (Rev: BL 5/15/02; SLJ 8/02)

3910 Barnwell, Ysaye M. *No Mirrors in My Nana's House* (PS–3). Illus. by Synthia Saint James. 1998, Harcourt $18.00 (978-0-15-201825-2). 32pp. The idea that people can find beauty in humble surroundings and can rise above a demeaning environment is presented in this picture book about an African American family. (Rev: BL 9/15/98; HBG 3/99; SLJ 10/98)

3911 Barrett, John M. *Daniel Discovers Daniel* (2–3). Illus. by Joe Servello. 1980, Human Sciences $16.95 (978-0-87705-423-8). 32pp. Daniel tries to satisfy his father's need for a sports-minded son.

3912 Baryshnikov, Mikhail. *Because* . . . (K–3). Illus. by Vladimir Radunsky. 2007, Simon & Schuster $16.99 (978-0-689-87582-3). A story by the famous ballet dancer about a grandmother who can't keep herself from dancing. (Rev: SLJ 5/07)

3913 Battle-Lavert, Gwendolyn. *The Music in Derrick's Heart* (PS–3). Illus. by Colin Bootman. 2000, Holiday House $16.95 (978-0-8234-1353-9). 32pp. The power of music is explored in this gentle story about a young African American boy who is learning to play the harmonica by taking lessons from his uncle Booker T. (Rev: BCCB 3/00; BL 2/15/00*; HBG 10/00; SLJ 3/00)

3914 Bea, Holly. *Bless Your Heart* (PS–K). Illus. by Kim Howard. 2001, H. J. Kramer $15.00 (978-0-915811-94-6). 32pp. A mother offers many blessings to her children as they enjoy a colorful day by the sea. (Rev: BL 10/1/01; HBG 3/02)

3915 Bee, William. *Whatever* (K–2). Illus. by author. 2005, Candlewick $12.99 (978-0-7636-2886-4). Billy is supremely indifferent to his father's amazing efforts to amuse him, always saying "whatever." (Rev: SLJ 1/06)

3916 Benjamin, Floella. *My Two Grannies* (PS–1). Illus. by Margaret Chamberlain. 2008, Frances Lincoln $16.95 (978-1-84507-643-6). Granny Vero was born in Trinidad and Granny Rose in Yorkshire, and their differences really show when they both come to look after Alvina when her parents are away. (Rev: SLJ 12/08)

3917 Bergström, Gunilla. *Very Tricky, Alfie Atkins,* (PS–K). Trans. from Swedish by Elisabeth Kallick Dyssegaard. Illus. by author. 2005, Farrar $15.00 (91-29-66152-8). 27pp. Alfie is allowed to play with his father's tools but only gets his father's attention when he needs the forbidden saw; a charming story first published in Sweden in the 1970s. (Rev: SLJ 9/05)

3918 Berry, Matt. *Up on Daddy's Shoulders* (PS). Illus. by Lucy Corvino. 2006, Scholastic paper $6.99 (978-0-439-67045-6). 32pp. This picture book beautifully captures a young boy's joy and feelings of invincibility as he rides tall on his father's shoulders. (Rev: BL 9/1/06; SLJ 6/06)

3919 Bertram, Debbie. *The Best Place to Read* (PS–1). Illus. by Michael Garland. 2003, Random $14.95 (978-0-375-82293-3). 32pp. The poor protagonist searches for a good spot to settle down and read his new book, and eventually finds the perfect

place with his mother. (Rev: BL 1/1–15/03; HBG 10/03; SLJ 5/03)

3920 Bertrand, Diane Gonzales. *The Empanadas That Abuela Made / Las empanadas que hacia la abuela* (K–2). Trans. by Gabriela Baeza Ventura. Illus. by Alex Pardo DeLange. 2003, Piñata $15.95 (978-1-55885-388-1). Presented in the form of a cumulative rhyme, this bilingual tale suitable for beginning and ESL readers follows Abuela step-by-step as she prepares her popular pumpkin empanadas. (Rev: SLJ 12/03)

3921 Bertrand, Diane Gonzales. *Family, Familia* (1–4). Trans. by Julia Mercedes Castilla. Illus. by Pauline Rodriguez Howard. 1999, Piñata $14.95 (978-1-55885-269-3). A bilingual book in which Daniel Gonzalez enjoys a Tex-Mex feast when he goes to a family reunion in San Antonio. (Rev: HBG 3/00; SLJ 9/99)

3922 Bertrand, Diane Gonzales. *Sip, Slurp, Soup, Soup / Caldo, Caldo, Caldo* (K–3). Illus. by Alex P. DeLange. 1997, Piñata $14.95 (978-1-55885-183-2). A simple bilingual book about a family making soup. (Rev: HBG 3/98; SLJ 8/97)

3923 Best, Cari. *Are You Going to Be Good?* (PS–2). Illus. by G. Brian Karas. 2005, Farrar $16.00 (978-0-374-30394-5). 32pp. With illustrations that show a child's perspective this is the story of Robert's first grown-up party and the number of "don'ts" he has to remember. (Rev: BL 9/1/05; SLJ 9/05)

3924 Best, Cari. *What's So Bad About Being an Only Child?* (PS–1). Illus. by Sophie Blackall. 2007, Farrar $16.00 (978-0-374-39943-6). 32pp. Rosemary, an only child, attempts to resolve the frustrations that come with being the sole focus of her parents' attention. (Rev: BL 9/1/07; SLJ 11/07)

3925 Binch, Caroline. *The Princess and the Castle* (PS–K). Illus. 2006, Red Fox paper $8.99 (978-0-09-943236-4). 32pp. Her father died at sea when she was young, so Genevieve is wary of the sea and initially cool to the fisherman her mother brings into their life. (Rev: BL 12/15/05; SLJ 2/06)

3926 Birdseye, Tom. *A Regular Flood of Mishap* (PS–3). Illus. by Megan Lloyd. 1994, Holiday House LB $16.95 (978-0-8234-1070-5). 32pp. In spite of accidentally causing a number of disasters, Ima Bean finds she is still wanted by her family. (Rev: BL 3/15/94; SLJ 3/94)

3927 Birdseye, Tom. *Waiting for Baby* (PS–K). Illus. by Loreen Leedy. 1991, Holiday House LB $14.95 (978-0-8234-0892-4). 32pp. A young boy eagerly awaits an arrival in the family and later is happy with his baby brother. (Rev: BL 1/1/91; SLJ 11/91)

3928 Biro, Maureen Boyd. *Walking with Maga* (PS–3). Illus. by Joyce Wheeler. 2001, All About Kids $16.95 (978-0-9700863-4-1). 32pp. A young girl accompanies her beloved grandmother Maga on walks, finding joy in what they see and the people they meet. (Rev: BL 12/15/01; HBG 3/03; SLJ 7/02)

3929 Bogart, Jo Ellen. *Gifts* (PS–2). Illus. by Barbara Reid. 1996, Scholastic $15.95 (978-0-590-55260-8). 44pp. A joyful picture book in which a grandmother presents her granddaughter with a variety of imaginative gifts. (Rev: BL 2/1/96; SLJ 3/96*)

3930 Bond, Rebecca. *Just Like a Baby* (PS–2). Illus. 1999, Little, Brown $14.95 (978-0-316-10416-6). 32pp. Everyone in the family contributes to preparing a cradle for the new baby, and the baby responds by sleeping happily in it. (Rev: BCCB 9/99; BL 9/15/99; HBG 3/00; SLJ 9/99)

3931 Bootman, Colin. *Fish for the Grand Lady* (PS–2). 2006, Holiday $16.95 (978-0-8234-1898-5). 32pp. The natural beauty and lilting speech of Trinidad are showcased in this gentle tale of two brothers who set out to catch some fish for their grandmother to cook. (Rev: BL 10/15/06; SLJ 10/06)

3932 Bosak, Susan V. *Something to Remember Me By* (PS–3). Illus. by Laurie McGaw. 1997, Communication Project $15.95 (978-1-896232-01-0). 32pp. This touching story about the loving relationship between a girl and her grandmother that lasts until the girl is grown and the old lady dies. (Rev: BL 11/1/97; SLJ 12/97)

3933 Bouchard, David. *Nokum Is My Teacher* (K–3). Illus. by Allen Sapp. 2007, Fitzhenry & Whiteside $21.95 (978-0-88995-367-3). 32pp. A young Cree boy's grandmother helps him to understand why he has to go to school with white people; the text is in both Cree and English. (Rev: BL 4/15/07)

3934 Bourgeois, Paulette. *Oma's Quilt* (PS–3). Illus. by Stephane Jorisch. 2001, Kids Can $15.95 (978-1-55074-777-5). 32pp. Grumpy Oma hates her new life in a nursing home, so granddaughter Emily and her mother decide to make her a special quilt. (Rev: BCCB 12/01; BL 12/15/01; HBG 3/02; SLJ 11/01)

3935 Bowen, Anne. *How Did You Grow So Big, So Soon?* (PS–2). Illus. by Marni Backer. 2003, Carolrhoda LB $15.95 (978-0-87614-024-6). A little boy and his mother, on the eve of his starting school, talk about his life so far. (Rev: HBG 4/04; SLJ 3/04)

3936 Boyd, Lizi. *I Love Mommy* (PS). Illus. by author. 2004, Candlewick $8.99 (978-0-7636-2216-9). A frog mother and child spend a happy day together in this simple, attractive book. Also use *I Love Daddy* (2004), about a similarly happy day. (Rev: SLJ 6/04)

3937 Boyden, Linda. *The Blue Roses* (K–3). Illus. by Amy Córdova. 2002, Lee & Low $16.95 (978-1-58430-037-3). 32pp. When her beloved grandfather dies, Rosalie remembers the lessons he taught her in the garden. (Rev: BCCB 9/02; BL 5/15/02; HBG 10/02; SLJ 6/02)

3938 Brannen, Sarah S. *Uncle Bobby's Wedding* (PS–2). Illus. by author. 2008, Putnam $15.99 (978-0-399-24712-5). 32pp. Little guinea pig Chloe is worried that her favorite uncle won't have time for her when he marries his boyfriend, Jamie. (Rev: BL 1/1–15/08; SLJ 4/08)

3939 Braun, Sebastien. *I Love My Mommy* (PS). Illus. by author. 2004, HarperCollins $15.99 (978-0-06-054310-5). An oversized format, large print, and bright colors enhance this look at relationships between mothers and children, using animals as the storytellers. (Rev: SLJ 4/04)

3940 Briant, Ed. *A Day at the Beach* (PS–1). Illus. by author. 2005, HarperCollins LB $17.89 (978-0-06-079982-3). A panda family planning a day at the beach has to go home to pick up forgotten items so many times that before they know it, the entire day is gone. (Rev: SLJ 6/06)

3941 Bridges, Margaret Park. *Am I Big or Little?* (PS–2). Illus. by Tracy Dockray. 2000, North-South LB $14.88 (978-1-58717-020-1). 32pp. A loving relationship between mother and child is shown as they discuss the ways in which the girl is big and the ways in which she is little. (Rev: BL 10/1/00; HBG 3/01; SLJ 9/00)

3942 Bridges, Margaret Park. *If I Were Your Mother* (PS–K). Illus. by Kady M. Denton. 1999, Morrow $15.95 (978-0-688-15190-4). 32pp. While talking with her mother, a little girl imagines that their roles are reversed. (Rev: BL 8/99; HBG 10/99; SLJ 5/99)

3943 Bringsvaerd, Tor Age. *When Two Get Up* (PS–K). Illus. by Tina Soli. 2009, MacKenzie Smiles $14.95 (978-0-9815761-4-5). 36pp. A toddler and her father go through regular morning activities all the while pretending to be all manner of stuffed and real animals and objects. (Rev: BLO 1/14/09)

3944 Brisson, Pat. *Hobbledy-Clop* (PS–K). Illus. by Maxie Chambliss. 2003, Boyds Mills $15.95 (978-1-56397-888-3). In the repetitive style of an old Irish folktale, this is the story of Brendan O'Doyle's visit to his grandmother, accompanied by a growing troop of animals. (Rev: HBG 10/03; SLJ 2/03)

3945 Brown, Alan. *Nikki and the Rocking Horse* (PS–2). Illus. by Peter Utton. 1999, HarperCollins paper $9.95 (978-0-00-664517-7). Nikki's mother can't afford the rocking horse her daughter wants, so she makes one in a woodworking class. (Rev: SLJ 2/00)

3946 Brown, Marc. *D.W., Go to Your Room!* (PS–K). Illus. 1999, Little, Brown $13.95 (978-0-316-10905-5). 32pp. D.W. is sent to her room for grabbing a toy from her baby sister, but soon after, she is won over by her young sister's smile. (Rev: BL 6/1–15/99; HBG 10/99; SLJ 7/99)

3947 Browne, Anthony. *My Mom* (PS–2). Illus. 2005, Farrar $16.00 (978-0-374-35098-7). 32pp. The mom in this book with clever illustrations is sometimes frazzled, sometimes dazzling, but always her child's hero. (Rev: BL 3/1/05; SLJ 6/05)

3948 Bunting, Eve. *A Day's Work* (K–3). Illus. by Ronald Himler. 1994, Clarion $16.00 (978-0-395-67321-8). 32pp. A young Mexican American boy must act as guardian and interpreter for his grandfather, newly arrived from Mexico and looking for work. (Rev: BCCB 10/94; BL 11/1/94; SLJ 1/95)

3949 Bunting, Eve. *Flower Garden* (PS–1). Illus. by Kathryn Hewitt. 1994, Harcourt $16.00 (978-0-15-228776-4). 32pp. A girl and her father create a window box of flowers as a birthday present for her mother. (Rev: BL 2/15/94*; HB 5/94; SLJ 4/94*)

3950 Bunting, Eve. *Jin Woo* (PS–3). Illus. by Chris K. Soentpiet. 2001, Clarion $16.00 (978-0-395-93872-0). 32pp. David is uncertain about his new little brother who is arriving from Korea, but the child, Jin Woo, soon wins his heart. (Rev: BL 3/15/01; HBG 10/01)

3951 Bunting, Eve. *The Memory String* (K–3). Illus. by Ted Rand. 2000, Clarion $16.00 (978-0-395-86146-2). 32pp. Laura begins to accept her stepmother, Jane, after Jane helps Laura search for lost buttons from her collection, each of which is associated with a member of her family. (Rev: BL 8/00; HBG 3/01; SLJ 8/00)

3952 Bunting, Eve. *My Big Boy Bed* (PS). Illus. by Maggie Smith. 2003, Clarion $15.00 (978-0-618-17742-4). 32pp. A 3-year-old boy celebrates his graduation from crib to "big boy bed" and thinks of all the new possibilities it opens to him. (Rev: HBG 4/04; SLJ 11/03)

3953 Bunting, Eve. *My Mom's Wedding* (K–3). Illus. by Lisa Papp. 2006, Sleeping Bear $16.95 (978-1-58536-288-2). Pinky's mom is getting remarried and Pinky has mixed feelings about the wedding and her new stepfather. (Rev: SLJ 3/07)

3954 Bunting, Eve. *My Red Balloon* (PS). Illus. by Kay Life. 2005, Boyds Mills $15.95 (978-1-59078-263-7). 32pp. With a "Welcome Home" balloon clutched in his tiny hand, a little boy waits on the dock for his father to return from months at sea aboard an aircraft carrier. (Rev: BL 7/05; SLJ 9/05)

3955 Bunting, Eve. *A Picnic in October* (K–3). Illus. by Nancy Carpenter. 1999, Harcourt $16.00 (978-0-15-201656-2). 32pp. As usual, Grandma has her birthday party on Ellis Island, so she can relive her arrival in America many years before. (Rev: BL 10/15/99; HBG 3/00; SLJ 10/99)

3956 Bunting, Eve. *Sunshine Home* (K–3). Illus. by Diane deGroat. 1994, Clarion $16.00 (978-0-395-63309-0). 32pp. Timmie is unhappy when he visits his grandmother in her nursing home for the first time. (Rev: BCCB 4/94; BL 3/15/94; SLJ 4/94)

3957 Bunting, Eve. *The Wall* (K–2). Illus. by Ronald Himler. 1990, Houghton $16.00 (978-0-395-51588-4). 32pp. A picture book on the subject of the Vietnam Veterans War Memorial. (Rev: BCCB 7–8/92; BL 4/1/90*; HB 7/90; SLJ 5/90*)

3958 Bunting, Eve. *The Wednesday Surprise* (PS–2). Illus. by Donald Carrick. 1989, Houghton $16.00 (978-0-89919-721-0); paper $5.95 (978-0-395-54776-2). 32pp. Anna is proudest of Grandma's surprise — Grandma has learned to read, and Anna has taught her. (Rev: BCCB 3/89; BL 3/1/89; SLJ 6/89)

3959 Burrowes, Adjoa J. *Grandma's Purple Flowers* (PS–3). Illus. 2000, Lee & Low $15.95 (978-1-880000-73-1). 32pp. A young African American girl grieves after her beloved grandmother's death but gains acceptance when, in the spring, her grandmother's flowers bloom. (Rev: BL 11/1/00; HBG 3/01; SLJ 12/00)

3960 Busse, Sarah Martin, and Jacqueline B. Martin. *Banjo Granny* (PS). Illus. by Barry Root. 2006, Houghton $16.00 (978-0-618-33603-6). 32pp. A rhythmic tall tale in which a banjo-toting bluegrass-loving grandmother travels far and wide to pay a visit to her newborn grandchild. (Rev: BL 11/1/06; SLJ 12/06*)

3961 Buzzeo, Toni. *The Sea Chest* (2–4). Illus. by Mary GrandPré. 2002, Dial $16.99 (978-0-8037-2703-8). 32pp. An elderly aunt tells her niece, who is eagerly awaiting an adopted sister, about the girl her family found in a sea chest and adopted many years ago. (Rev: BL 9/15/02; HBG 3/03; SLJ 8/02)

3962 Cabrera, Jane. *Mommy, Carry Me Please!* (PS–1). Illus. by author. 2006, Holiday House $16.95 (978-0-8234-1935-7). Shows the many different and special ways in which animal and human mothers carry their babies. (Rev: SLJ 2/06)

3963 Campbell, Louisa. *Phoebe's Fabulous Father* (K–2). Illus. by Bridget S. Taylor. 1996, Harcourt $14.00 (978-0-15-200996-0). Phoebe has always respected her cello-playing father; but when she finds out how much of his music he has sacrificed for his family, she grows to love him more. (Rev: BCCB 11/96; SLJ 12/96)

3964 Campos, Tito. *Muffler Man / El Hombre Mofle* (K–3). Illus. by Lamberto Alvarez and Beto Alvarez. 2001, Arte Publico $14.95 (978-1-55885-318-8). 32pp. Young Mexican Chuy Garcia and his mother are finally able to follow Chuy's father to the United States, where Chuy persuades his father to indulge his artistic abilities. (Rev: BL 12/15/01; SLJ 1/02)

3965 Capucilli, Alyssa Satin. *My Dad and Me* (PS–K). Illus. by Susan Mitchell. 2009, Simon & Schuster $7.99 (978-1-4169-5828-4). 16pp. A revised edition of *Only My Dad and Me* (2003), this features new illustrations and a modified, multicultural text about a father and child enjoying outdoor activities; a companion volume is *My Mom and Me* (2009). (Rev: BLO 3/24/09)

3966 Carlson, Nancy. *My Family Is Forever* (PS–1). Illus. 2004, Viking $15.99 (978-0-670-03650-9). 32pp. A young Asian girl muses about families and considers the characteristics she shares with her adoptive Caucasian parents: "I'm a good cook like my dad, and a wonderful dancer like my mom." (Rev: BL 4/1/04; SLJ 3/04)

3967 Carlstrom, Nancy White. *Before You Were Born* (PS–2). Illus. by Linda Saport. 2002, Eerdmans $17.00 (978-0-8028-5185-7). 32pp. This exceptional story inspired by Psalm 139 celebrates the bond between parents and children. (Rev: BL 2/1/02; HBG 10/02; SLJ 6/02)

3968 Carney, Margaret. *The Biggest Fish in the Lake* (K–3). Illus. by Janet Wilson. 2001, Kids Can $15.95 (978-1-55074-720-1). 32pp. A young girl describes her happy experiences fishing with her grandfather. (Rev: BL 7/01; HBG 10/01; SLJ 7/01)

3969 Carter, Donna Renee. *Music in the Family* (K–2). Illus. by Cortrell J. Harris. 1995, Lindsey $15.95 (978-1-885242-01-3). 30pp. Oliver is crushed when the family tells him that he doesn't play his saxophone well enough to join them in an international music competition. (Rev: SLJ 2/96)

3970 Caseley, Judith. *In Style with Grandma Antoinette* (K–2). Illus. by author. 2005, Tanglewood $15.95 (978-0-9749303-4-3). Little Rosie is at first hesitant to spend the day at the hair salon where her grandmother works, but once there she pitches in to help and has a wonderful time. (Rev: SLJ 1/06)

3971 Catalanotto, Peter. *The Painter* (PS–2). Illus. by author. Series: Richard Jackson Books. 1995, Orchard LB $16.99 (978-0-531-08765-7). A joyous picture book that celebrates a loving relationship between a girl and her artist-father. (Rev: SLJ 9/95*)

3972 Cates, Karin. *The Secret Remedy Book: A Story of Comfort and Love* (PS–2). Illus. by Wendy A. Halperin. 2003, Scholastic $16.95 (978-0-439-35226-0). 32pp. Auntie Zep produces the perfect remedy for Lolly's homesickness. (Rev: HBG 4/04; SLJ 8/03)

3973 Cazet, Denys. *Dancing* (PS–1). Illus. 1995, Orchard LB $16.99 (978-0-531-08766-4). 32pp. The crying of his baby brother drives Alex out of the house onto the porch, where he is comforted by his father. (Rev: BL 9/15/95; SLJ 9/95)

3974 Chaconas, Dori. *Dancing with Katya* (K–3). Illus. by Constance R. Bergum. 2006, Peachtree $16.95 (978-1-56145-376-4). 32pp. When Katya, who has dreamed of being a ballerina, is stricken by polio and forced to wear heavy braces, her older sister Anna tries to keep her from surrendering to despair; set in the early 20th century. (Rev: BL 9/1/06; SLJ 9/06)

3975 Chall, Marsha Wilson. *Sugarbush Spring* (PS–1). Illus. by Jim Daly. 2000, Lothrop LB $16.89 (978-0-688-14908-6). A little girl in Minnesota tells about the annual collection of sap from the family sugar bush and how the sap is turned into syrup. (Rev: BL 1/1–15/04; HBG 10/00; SLJ 3/00)

3976 Charlip, Remy. *A Perfect Day* (PS–1). 2007, Greenwillow $16.99 (978-0-06-051972-8). 40pp. A gentle story about all the things a boy and his father can enjoy in a day. (Rev: BL 5/1/07; SLJ 5/07*)

3977 Cheng, Andrea. *Goldfish and Chrysanthemums* (PS–2). Illus. by Michelle Chang. 2003, Lee & Low $16.95 (978-1-58430-057-1). To cheer up her Chinese-born grandmother, Nancy builds a fishpond and borders it with chrysanthemums, just like Ni Ni had as a child. (Rev: HBG 10/03; SLJ 6/03)

3978 Cheng, Andrea. *The Lemon Sisters* (PS–2). Illus. by Tatjana Mai-Wyss. 2006, Putnam $16.99 (978-0-399-24023-2). 32pp. The sight of three young sisters playing together in the snow gladdens the heart of an elderly woman who recalls fun with her own sisters who have long since moved away. (Rev: BL 12/15/05; SLJ 1/06)

3979 Cheng, Andrea. *When the Bees Fly Home* (PS–2). Illus. by Joline McFadden. 2002, Tilbury House $16.95 (978-0-88448-238-3). 32pp. A boy who lacks self-confidence finds he has an unsuspected talent as he works to help his bee-keeping family in this novel that includes plenty of bee facts and lovely watercolors. (Rev: BL 7/02; HBG 3/03)

3980 Chessa, Francesca. *The Mysterious Package* (PS–1). Illus. by author. 2007, Bloomsbury $16.95 (978-1-59990-028-5). 32pp. The arrival of a large box sets twins Charlie and Frances fighting over what it is, who it's for, etc.; however, it turns out the package was delivered in error and sibling rivalry

dissipates when the real, much smaller package arrives, allowing the twins to accomplish something together. (Rev: BL 7/07; SLJ 7/07)

3981 Choi, Sook N. *Halmoni and the Picnic* (K–3). Illus. by Karen M. Dugan. 1993, Houghton $16.00 (978-0-395-61626-0). 24pp. A grandmother newly arrived from Korea has difficulty adjusting to New York City. (Rev: BL 8/93)

3982 Clements, Andrew. *Because Your Daddy Loves You* (PS–K). Illus. by R. W. Alley. 2005, Clarion $16.00 (978-0-618-00361-7). 32pp. A daddy is shown helping a child in many ways in this picture book that celebrates the everyday things fathers do. (Rev: BL 3/1/05)

3983 Coffelt, Nancy. *Fred Stays with Me!* (PS–K). Illus. by Tricia Tusa. 2007, Little, Brown $16.99 (978-0-316-88269-9). 32pp. A little girl copes with her parents' divorce by clinging tenaciously to her dog Fred, who, despite his sometimes unfortunate behavior, is a source of comfort. (Rev: BCCB 9/07; BL 5/1/07; HB 1/09; SLJ 6/07)

3984 Cohen, Barbara. *Molly's Pilgrim.* Rev. ed. (1–4). Illus. by Daniel Duffy. 1998, Lothrop $17.99 (978-0-688-16279-5); paper $3.99 (978-0-688-16280-1). 32pp. The mother of a Russian immigrant girl makes her child a pilgrim doll modeled on herself, a modern-day pilgrim. (Rev: BL 11/15/98; HBG 3/99)

3985 Cohen, Caron Lee. *Everything Is Different at Nonna's House* (PS). Illus. by Hiroe Nakata. 2003, Clarion $16.00 (978-0-618-07335-1). 32pp. A little city boy delights in his grandparents' farm far from the hustle-bustle of his urban home. (Rev: HBG 10/03; SLJ 7/03)

3986 Cohen, Deborah Bodin. *Papa Jethro: A Story of Moses' Interfaith Family* (PS–1). Illus. by Jane Dippold. 2007, Kar-Ben $17.95 (978-1-58013-250-3); paper $7.95 (978-1-58013-252-7). 32pp. Rachel, who is Jewish, wonders why her grandfather goes to church and he tells her the biblical story of Jethro and his grandson Gershom and how they loved each other despite their different religions. (Rev: BL 10/1/07; SLJ 10/07)

3987 Cohen, Miriam. *My Big Brother* (PS–2). Illus. by Ronald Himler. 2004, Star Bright $15.95 (978-1-59572-007-8). 40pp. When the older brother he idolizes joins the army, a young African American boy assumes the "big brother" role for his younger sibling. (Rev: BL 1/1–15/05)

3988 Colato Laínez, René. *Playing Lotería / El juego de la lotería* (1–3). Illus. by Jill Arena. 2005, Luna Rising $15.95 (978-0-87358-881-2). In this engaging bilingual picture book, a young boy visits his grandmother in Mexico and agrees to teach her some English words if she will tutor him in Spanish. (Rev: SLJ 10/05)

3989 Cole, Brock. *Fair Monaco* (K–3). Illus. by author. 2004, Front St. $16.95 (978-1-932425-07-9). An anxiety-ridden grandmother struggles to look after her three girl grandchildren and the power of the girls' dreams makes their lives brighter. (Rev: SLJ 1/05)

3990 Cole, Joanna. *I'm a Big Brother* (PS–1). Illus. by Maxie Chambliss. 1997, Morrow $6.99 (978-0-688-14507-1). 32pp. Babies and their activities and needs are introduced in terms a big brother can understand. A companion volume that covers the same material is *I'm a Big Sister* (1997). (Rev: BL 3/1/97; SLJ 4/97)

3991 Collins, Suzanne. *When Charlie McButton Lost Power* (K–3). Illus. by Mike Lester. 2005, Putnam $15.99 (978-0-399-24000-3). Charlie surprises himself by having fun playing with his little sister when a power outage puts a stop to his electronic fun. (Rev: SLJ 7/05)

3992 Conway, David. *The Most Important Gift of All* (PS–K). Illus. by Karen Littlewood. 2006, School Specialty $15.95 (978-0-7696-4618-3). 32pp. Excited about the birth of her brother, a young Kenyan girl wanders in search of love, a gift she wants to give to her new sibling; the story is told in a traditional folktale style with large, warm illustrations. (Rev: BL 4/1/06; SLJ 5/06)

3993 Cook, Stephen. *Day Out with Daddy* (PS–1). Illus. by author. 2006, Walker $16.95 (978-0-8027-8059-1). A mischievous boy tells his own version of his special day with his father; the illustrations show something closer to the truth. (Rev: SLJ 5/06)

3994 Cooke, Trish. *Full, Full, Full, of Love* (PS–1). Illus. by Paul Howard. 2003, Candlewick $15.99 (978-0-7636-1851-3). 32pp. A young boy enjoys a family dinner at his grandmother's house in this happy, cozy picture book. (Rev: BCCB 3/03; BL 2/15/03; HBG 10/03; SLJ 2/03)

3995 Cooney, Barbara. *Island Boy* (2–4). Illus. by author. 1988, Puffin paper $6.99 (978-0-14-050756-0). 40pp. The life of Matthias Tibbetts of Tibbetts Island, Maine, who sails the world and returns home to raise his own family. (Rev: BCCB 10/88; BL 10/1/88; SLJ 10/88)

3996 Cooper, Melrose. *Gettin' Through Thursday* (1–3). Illus. by Nneka Bennett. 1998, Lee & Low $15.95 (978-1-880000-67-0). In this sweet story of a single-parent African American family, Mama is proud that her 3rd-grade son makes the honor roll, but the family is too poor to have a celebration. (Rev: HBG 10/99; SLJ 1/99)

3997 Corey, Dorothy. *Will There Be a Lap for Me?* (PS–1). Illus. by Nancy Poydar. 1992, Whitman LB $15.99 (978-0-8075-9109-3). 24pp. When her mother's lap becomes smaller because she is expecting a baby, Lyle misses her favorite place to sit and be loved. (Rev: BL 3/1/92; SLJ 6/92)

3998 Coste, Marion. *Finding Joy* (PS–2). Illus. by Yong Chen. 2006, Boyds Mills $16.95 (978-1-59078-192-0). 32pp. This story opens with Chinese parents sadly leaving their baby girl and closes with the same girl, renamed Joy, at home with her new American parents. (Rev: BL 1/1–15/07; SLJ 11/06)

3999 Cowell, Cressida. *Don't Do That, Kitty Kilroy!* (PS–K). Illus. by author. 2000, Orchard $15.95 (978-0-531-30209-5). Kitty's mother agrees to let her rambunctious daughter do her own thing for a day, with predictable results. (Rev: HBG 10/00; SLJ 3/00)

4000 Cowen-Fletcher, Jane. *Mama Zooms* (PS–1). Illus. 1994, Scholastic $19.95 (978-0-590-72848-5); paper $4.99 (978-0-590-45775-0). 32pp. Mama's "zooming machine" turns out to be her wheelchair. (Rev: BL 4/15/93; SLJ 5/93)

4001 Cox, Judy. *My Family Plays Music* (PS–1). Illus. by Elbrite Brown. 2003, Holiday House $16.95 (978-0-8234-1591-5). A young girl from a multiracial musical family introduces each person and the instrument and kind of music played. (Rev: HBG 4/04; SLJ 10/03)

4002 Coyle, Carmela LaVigna. *Do Princesses Really Kiss Frogs?* (PS–3). Illus. by Mike Gordon and Carl Gordon. 2005, Rising Moon $15.95 (978-0-87358-880-5). While on a walk with her father and the family dog, a little girl peppers her dad with questions. (Rev: SLJ 11/05)

4003 Coyle, Carmela LaVigna. *Do Princesses Wear Hiking Boots?* (PS–1). Illus. by Mike Gordon. 2003, Rising Moon $15.95 (978-0-87358-828-7). In this charming tale, presented in rhyming text, a little girl asks her mother what princesses are like and discovers, to her surprise, that they're not all that different from her. (Rev: SLJ 8/03)

4004 Crews, Donald. *Bigmama's* (PS–2). Illus. 1991, Greenwillow $17.89 (978-0-688-09951-0). 32pp. A family's annual summer trip to grandparents' house in the country is a celebration of childhood memories. (Rev: BCCB 11/91*; BL 11/15/91*; HB 9/91; SLJ 10/91) [921]

4005 Crowe, Carole. *Turtle Girl* (K–2). Illus. by Jim Postier. 2008, Boyds Mills $16.95 (978-1-59078-262-0). 32pp. Magdalena's efforts to help the sea turtles that arrive on their island make her feel connected to the beloved grandmother who recently died. (Rev: BL 2/15/08; LMC 3/08; SLJ 4/08)

4006 Cruise, Robin. *Little Mamá Forgets* (PS–2). Illus. by Stacey Dressen-McQueen. 2006, Farrar $16.00 (978-0-374-34613-3). 40pp. Lucy's Mexican American grandmother is losing her memory and Lucy must remind her how to do simple things, but the older woman still manages to remember some of the important things in life. (Rev: BL 1/1–15/06; HBG 10/06; LMC 1/07; SLJ 8/06)

4007 Crum, Shutta. *My Mountain Song* (K–3). Illus. by Ted Rand. 2004, Clarion $16.00 (978-0-618-15970-3). 32pp. Brenda Gail collects favorite memories to make her very own song in this story set in her great-grandparents' home in the Kentucky highlands. (Rev: BL 5/1/04; SLJ 6/04)

4008 Cummings, Pat. *Angel Baby* (PS–2). Illus. 2000, Lothrop LB $15.89 (978-0-688-14822-5). 24pp. Amanda Lynn, who has to take care of her baby brother, knows he isn't the angel baby everyone thinks he is. (Rev: BCCB 7–8/00; BL 6/1–15/00; HBG 10/00; SLJ 6/00)

4009 Cunha, Francisco. *My Very Own Lighthouse* (PS–2). Illus. 2006, Winged Chariot $16.95 (978-1-905341-01-6). 32pp. Worried about her fisherman father out at sea, a young girl builds a lighthouse in her window to help guide her father home. (Rev: BL 11/15/06)

4010 Curtis, Marci. *Big Brother, Little Brother* (K–3). Illus. 2004, Dial $12.99 (978-0-8037-2870-7). 40pp. As this photoessay shows, brothers comes in all shapes, sizes, colors, and temperaments. (Rev: BL 5/15/04; SLJ 7/04)

4011 Czech, Jan M. *The Coffee Can Kid* (PS–2). Illus. by Maurie J. Manning. 2002, Child Welfare League of America paper $9.95 (978-0-87868-821-0). 24pp. Six-year-old Annie asks her father to retell the story of her birth in Asia and her adoption. (Rev: BL 7/02; SLJ 7/02)

4012 D'Antonio, Nancy. *Our Baby from China: An Adoption Story* (PS–2). Illus. 1997, Whitman LB $15.99 (978-0-8075-6162-1). 24pp. The story of a couple's journey to China, where they adopt a little girl, and their trip home with the baby. (Rev: BL 3/1/97; SLJ 6/97)

4013 D'Arc, Karen Scourby. *"My Grandmother Is a Singing Yaya"* (PS–2). Illus. by Diane Palmisciano. 2001, Scholastic $15.95 (978-0-439-29309-9). 32pp. A little girl is afraid she will be embarrassed at a Grandparents' Day picnic by her grandmother, who is given to bursting into song at odd moments. (Rev: BL 1/1–15/02; HBG 3/02; SLJ 11/01)

4014 Davol, Marguerite W. *Black, White, Just Right!* (PS–1). Illus. by Irene Trivas. 1993, Whitman LB $16.99 (978-0-8075-0785-8). 32pp. A child with mixed-race parentage enjoys the many differences she sees in her parents, not only their color. (Rev: BL 11/1/93)

4015 Deedy, Carmen A. *Agatha's Feather Bed: Not Just Another Wild Goose Story* (PS–2). Illus. by Laura L. Seeley. 1991, Peachtree $15.95 (978-1-56145-008-4). 32pp. Agatha is ashamed when she learns that six geese are featherless so she could have a featherbed. (Rev: BL 6/1/91; SLJ 9/91)

4016 Demas, Corinne. *Nina's Waltz* (K–3). Illus. by Deborah Lanino. 2000, Orchard LB $17.99 (978-0-531-33281-8). When wasp stings prevent Nina's father from playing the fiddle in a competition, she steps in to take his place. (Rev: HBG 3/01; SLJ 11/00)

4017 dePaola, Tomie. *The Baby Sister* (PS–1). Illus. 1996, Penguin $17.99 (978-0-399-22908-4). 32pp. When Tommy's mother has a baby, his grandmother comes to stay. (Rev: BL 3/15/96; HB 5/96; SLJ 5/96)

4018 dePaola, Tomie. *Tom* (K–2). Illus. 1993, Penguin LB $16.99 (978-0-399-22417-1). 32pp. A picture book about the special relationship between the author/artist and his grandfather. (Rev: BCCB 5/93; BL 1/15/93*; HB 7/93*; SLJ 4/93)

4019 dePaola, Tomie. *Watch Out for the Chicken Feet in Your Soup* (K–2). Illus. by author. 1974, Simon & Schuster $12.95 (978-0-685-35587-9); paper $5.95 (978-0-685-35588-6). 32pp. Joey is a little embarrassed to take his friend Eugene to his old-fashioned Italian grandmother's for a visit, but in spite of her strange foreign ways, both boys pronounce the visit a great success.

4020 Derby, Sally. *No Mush Today* (PS). Illus. by Nicole Tadgell. 2008, Lee & Low $16.95 (978-1-60060-238-2). 32pp. Fed up with daily routine and her wailing baby brother, Nonie, a young African American girl, seeks refuge with her grandmother, but by the end of the day recognizes that maybe home is best. (Rev: BL 9/1/08; SLJ 9/08)

4021 Dodd, Anne W. *The Story of the Sea Glass* (K–2). Illus. by Mary Beth Owens. 1999, Down East $15.95 (978-0-89272-416-1). 32pp. A young girl and her grandmother revisit the seaside house where Nana used to live, and this visit inspires memories of past events. (Rev: BL 2/1/00; HBG 3/00; SLJ 3/00)

4022 Dorros, Arthur. *Papa and Me* (PS–K). Illus. by Rudy Gutierrez. 2008, HarperCollins $16.99 (978-0-06-058156-5). 32pp. A warm story of a Latino boy and his father as they spend an enjoyable day together; with glowing illustrations and Spanish words. (Rev: BL 3/15/08; SLJ 5/08)

4023 Downes, Belinda. *Baby Days: A Quilt of Rhymes and Pictures* (PS–K). Illus. 2006, Candlewick $14.99 (978-0-7636-2786-7). 32pp. Embroidered into the pages of this picture book, each of which resembles a quilt square, are snippets of poetry and song; game pieces; images of objects children love; and pictures of children at play. (Rev: BL 2/1/06)

4024 Doyle, Roddy. *Her Mother's Face* (K–3). Illus. by Freya Blackwood. 2008, Scholastic $16.99 (978-0-439-81501-7). 32pp. Set in Dublin, this sensitive story tells of Siobhan's longing to fill the painful emptiness left by her mother's death. (Rev: BL 9/15/08; LMC 1/09)

4025 Driscoll, Laura. *Super Specs* (K–2). Illus. by Barry Gott. 2005, Kane paper $4.95 (978-1-57565-145-3). 32pp. Molly, fed up with her younger brother's teasing about her new glasses, uses her math skills to convince her sibling that the glasses give her special powers. (Rev: BL 8/05)

4026 Duble, Kathleen Benner. *Pilot Mom* (PS–3). Illus. by Alan Marks. 2003, Charlesbridge LB $15.95 (978-1-57091-555-0). Jenny's mother, an Air Force pilot, is due to leave on a mission to Europe and the two make preparations for her departure. (Rev: HBG 4/04; SLJ 1/04)

4027 Duke, Shirley Smith. *No Bows!* (PS). Illus. by Jenny Mattheson. 2006, Peachtree $15.95 (978-1-56145-356-6). 32pp. A strong-minded little girl makes her preferences quite clear throughout the day. (Rev: BL 7/06; SLJ 4/06)

4028 Dunbar, James. *When I Was Young: One Family Remembers 300 Years of History* (PS–2). Illus. by Martin Remphry. 1999, Carolrhoda LB $15.95 (978-1-57505-359-2). Josh hears about his family and traces its history back to the 1600s with glimpses of 7-year-old children through the ages. (Rev: HBG 3/00; SLJ 9/99)

4029 Duncan, Alice Faye. *Honey Baby Sugar Child* (PS). Illus. by Susan Keeter. 2005, Simon & Schuster $15.95 (978-0-689-84678-6). 32pp. An African American mother expresses love for her toddler in reassuring colloquial text accompanied by warm illustrations. (Rev: BL 2/1/05; SLJ 3/05)

4030 Dupasquier, Philippe. *A Sunday with Grandpa* (PS–2). Illus. by author. 1999, Andersen $19.95

(978-0-86264-791-9). A sunny picture book from England about a young girl who visits her loving grandfather in the countryside. (Rev: SLJ 7/99)

4031 Dwyer, Mindy. *Quilt of Dreams* (1–3). Illus. 2000, Graphic Arts Center $15.95 (978-0-88240-522-3); paper $8.95 (978-0-88240-521-6). 32pp. Katy wants to finish the quilt that her grandmother began before her death. (Rev: BL 3/15/01; HBG 10/01; SLJ 1/01)

4032 Ellis, Sarah. *Big Ben* (PS–1). Illus. by Kim LaFave. 2001, Fitzhenry & Whiteside $15.95 (978-1-55041-679-4). 32pp. Preschooler Ben feels left out when he doesn't get a report card like his older siblings, until they create one especially for him. (Rev: BL 1/1–15/02; HB 3/02; HBG 10/02; SLJ 2/02)

4033 Elya, Susan Middleton. *Adiós, Tricycle* (PS–K). Illus. by Elisabeth Schlossberg. 2009, Putnam $16.99 (978-0-399-24522-0). 32pp. A young pig catalogs the items in his family's yard sale; Spanish words with glossary. (Rev: BL 6/1–15/09)

4034 Elya, Susan Middleton. *Oh No, Gotta Go!* (PS–1). Illus. by G. Brian Karas. 2003, Penguin $15.99 (978-0-399-23493-4). A young girl's outing turns into a frantic search for a bathroom in this amusing book that introduces several Spanish words and phrases into the poetic text. (Rev: HBG 10/03; SLJ 7/03)

4035 Enderle, Judith, and Stephanie Jacob Gordon. *Smile, Principessa!* (PS–1). Illus. by Serena Curmi. 2007, Simon & Schuster $16.99 (978-1-4169-1004-6). 40pp. "Dethroned" siblings will relate to Principessa, who feels insecure as her new baby brother is lavished with attention. (Rev: BL 6/1–15/07; SLJ 7/07)

4036 England, Kathryn. *Grandfather's Wrinkles* (PS–2). Illus. by Richard McFarland. 2007, Flashlight $15.95 (978-0-9729225-9-3). Grandfather explains how he got his wrinkles, formed on happy occasions on which he smiled. (Rev: LMC 1/08; SLJ 2/08)

4037 English, Karen. *Speak English for Us, Marisol!* (PS–3). Illus. by Enrique O. Sánchez. 2000, Whitman $16.99 (978-0-8075-7554-3). 32pp. Marisol, a young Latin American girl, often acts as a translator to help various members of her family. (Rev: BL 9/15/00; HBG 3/01; SLJ 9/00)

4038 Eschbacher, Roger. *Road Trip* (K–3). Illus. by Thor Wickstrom. 2006, Dial $16.99 (978-0-8037-2927-8). 40pp. A rhyming story about a family's road trip and all its boredom, anticipation, excitement, and surprises. (Rev: BL 5/15/06; SLJ 7/06)

4039 Evans, Lezlie. *If I Were the Wind* (PS–1). Illus. by Victoria Lisi. 1997, Ideals $14.95 (978-1-57102-096-3). 32pp. A mother says that even if she is changed by enchantment into other objects she will still protect and love her young daughter. (Rev: BL 8/97; SLJ 6/97)

4040 Fazio, Brenda Lena. *Grandfather's Story* (PS–3). Illus. 1996, Sasquatch $15.95 (978-1-57061-028-8). 32pp. In a Japanese setting, this story tells how a grandfather teaches his young grandson about life. (Rev: BL 11/15/96; SLJ 3/97)

4041 Feiffer, Jules. *The Daddy Mountain* (PS–1). Illus. 2004, Hyperion $15.95 (978-0-7868-0912-7). 32pp. Feiffer charts the progress of a little girl as she climbs her dad as though he were a jungle gym. (Rev: BL 5/1/04; HB 5/04; SLJ 6/04)

4042 Feiffer, Kate. *My Mom Is Trying to Ruin My Life* (1–3). Illus. by Diane Goode. 2009, Simon & Schuster $16.99 (978-1-4169-4100-2). 32pp. Young Emma is embarrassed by her parents and dreams of having them thrown in jail, but finally recognizes that they can actually be useful to have around. (Rev: BL 3/15/09; SLJ 5/09)

4043 Finkelstein, Ruth. *Big Like Me! A New Baby Story* (PS–K). Illus. by Esther Touson. 2001, Hachai $10.95 (978-1-929628-04-9). 32pp. Benny has just learned some basic skills from his older brother when a new baby joins his Orthodox Jewish family. (Rev: BL 8/01; HBG 3/02; SLJ 1/02)

4044 Fisher, Iris L. *Katie-Bo: An Adoption Story* (PS–3). Illus. by Miriam Schaer. 1988, Adama $12.95 (978-0-915361-91-5). The story of Katie-Bo, who is coming from Korea to join her new family, told through the eyes of a young boy. (Rev: BL 5/15/88; SLJ 8/88)

4045 Fisher, Valorie. *My Big Brother* (PS–K). Illus. 2002, Simon & Schuster $14.95 (978-0-689-84327-3). 40pp. The amazing feats of one big brother, from the point of view of his baby sibling. (Rev: BCCB 7–8/02; BL 9/15/02; HBG 3/03; SLJ 7/02)

4046 Fisher, Valorie. *My Big Sister* (PS–1). Photos by author. 2003, Simon & Schuster $14.95 (978-0-689-85479-8). A baby's comical view of his big sister is enhanced by the effective photographs. (Rev: HBG 4/04; SLJ 11/03)

4047 Fitzpatrick, Marie-Louise. *Silly Mommy, Silly Daddy* (PS–1). Illus. by author. 2006, Frances Lincoln $15.95 (978-1-84507-547-7). Young Beth is downcast and all attempts to cheer her up prove unsuccessful until her sister appears starts making faces. (Rev: SLJ 9/06)

4048 Fleischman, Paul. *The Birthday Tree* (K–3). Illus. by Barry Root. 2008, Candlewick $16.99 (978-0-7636-2604-4). 32pp. A tree that mirrors the well-being of their fourth child brings worry and comfort to parents whose three older sons died at sea; a reissue of a 1979 publication, with new illustrations. (Rev: BL 1/1–15/08; SLJ 2/08)

4049 Fleischman, Paul. *Lost! A Story in String* (1–4). Illus. by C. B. Mordan. 2000, Holt $15.95 (978-0-8050-5583-2). 30pp. When the electricity goes off during a storm, Grandmother entertains her little granddaughter with an adventure story. (Rev: BCCB 10/00; BL 7/00; HBG 10/00; SLJ 6/00)

4050 Fletcher, Ralph. *Grandpa Never Lies* (PS–2). Illus. by Harvey Stevenson. 2000, Clarion $16.00 (978-0-395-79770-9). 32pp. A little girl has a special relationship with her grandparents and when her grandmother dies, the little girl and Grandpa mourn together. (Rev: BL 12/15/00; HBG 3/01; SLJ 11/00)

4051 Fournier Le Ray, Anne-Laure. *Grandparents!* (PS–K). Illus. by Roser Capdevila. 2003, Kane $10.95 (978-1-929132-46-1). A gentle look at grandparents and the ways in which they differ and are the same. (Rev: SLJ 6/03)

4052 Fox, Mem. *Ten Little Fingers and Ten Little Toes* (PS–K). Illus. by Helen Oxenbury. 2008, Harcourt $16.00 (978-0-15-206057-2). 32pp. This appealing picture book features groups of multicultural babies in their different environments. (Rev: BL 11/15/08; HB 1/09; SLJ 12/08)

4053 Fox, Mem. *Whoever You Are* (K–3). Illus. by Leslie Staub. 1997, Harcourt $16.00 (978-0-15-200787-4). 32pp. A reassuring book for children that tells them that regardless of their situations, there are toher like them all over the world. (Rev: BL 10/1/97; HBG 3/98; SLJ 10/97)

4054 French, Vivian. *Oliver's Fruit Salad* (PS–2). Illus. by Alison Bartlett. 1998, Orchard $14.95 (978-0-531-30087-9). 32pp. Oliver remembers how he helped his grandfather pick fruit in his garden, and this helps him enjoy the fruit salad he prepares with his mother and grandparents. (Rev: BCCB 10/98; BL 10/15/98; HBG 3/99; SLJ 9/98)

4055 French, Vivian, and Alex Ayliffe. *Not Again, Anna!* (PS). Illus. 1998, Sterling $14.95 (978-1-899607-96-9). 24pp. In this book with foldout pages, Little Anna learns to care for her stuffed bunny in the same way her mother cares for her. (Rev: BL 1/1–15/99; SLJ 3/99)

4056 Friedman, Darlene. *Star of the Week: A Story of Love, Adoption, and Brownies with Sprinkles* (PS–3). Illus. by Roger Roth. 2009, HarperCollins $17.99 (978-0-06-114136-2). 32pp. Six-year-old Cassidy-Li uses photographs and her own drawings to tell the story of her adoption from China. (Rev: BL 4/1/09; SLJ 6/09)

4057 Friedman, Ina R. *How My Parents Learned to Eat* (2–4). Illus. by Allen Say. 1987, Houghton $16.00 (978-0-395-35379-0); paper $6.99 (978-0-395-44235-7). 32pp. John, an American, and Aiko, a Japanese girl, learn each other's eating habits.

4058 Fruisen, Catherine Myler. *My Mother's Pearls* (PS–3). Illus. 2000, Cedco $12.95 (978-0-7683-2177-7). 32pp. A little girl tells about the six generations of women in her family who have worn the family heirloom string of pearls. (Rev: BL 8/00; HBG 3/01)

4059 Funke, Cornelia. *The Wildest Brother* (PS–2). Trans. by Chantal Wright. Illus. by Kerstin Meyer. 2006, Scholastic $16.99 (978-0-439-82862-8). 32pp. Imaginative young Ben is a brave boy during the day, protecting his sister from dragons and other imaginary creatures, but he still needs her reassurance at night. (Rev: BL 7/06; SLJ 6/06)

4060 Gadot, A. S. *The First Gift* (K–2). Illus. by Marie Lafrance. 2006, Lerner $15.95 (978-1-58013-146-9); paper $6.95 (978-1-58013-149-0). 24pp. This appealing picture book provides an introduction to the origins of names and also takes a brief look at the diversity of first names found in different parts of the globe; includes information on Jewish naming customs. (Rev: BL 10/1/06)

4061 Galindo, Mary Sue. *Icy Watermelon / Sandia fria* (PS–3). Illus. by Pauline Rodriguez Howard. 2000, Arte Publico $14.95 (978-1-55885-306-5).

32pp. In this bilingual English and Spanish book, three Latino children share stories and jokes with their parents and grandparents on a porch where they are eating watermelon. (Rev: BL 12/15/00; SLJ 1/01)

4062 Garden, Nancy. *Molly's Family* (PS–2). Illus. by Sharon Wooding. 2004, Farrar $16.00 (978-0-374-35002-4). 32pp. Although hurt by a classmate's remark about the makeup of her family — "no one has two mommies" — Molly comes to see that families come in all sorts of packages. (Rev: BL 4/15/04; HB 7/04; SLJ 5/04)

4063 Garrett, Ann. *Keeper of the Swamp* (2–4). Illus. by Karen Chandler. 1999, Turtle $16.95 (978-1-890515-12-6). A poignant story about a young boy who makes a special trip with his dying grandfather to a swamp to feed an alligator that the grandfather had saved from poachers. (Rev: HBG 3/00; SLJ 7/99)

4064 Gay, Marie-Louise. *What Are You Doing, Sam?* (PS). Series: Stella and Sam. 2006, Groundwood $14.95 (978-0-88899-734-0). 32pp. Red-headed big sister Stella keeps a close eye on her younger brother Sam as he tries to teach new tricks to Fred the dog. Earlier books in the series include *Stella, Star of the Sea* (1999), *Stella, Queen of the Snow* (2000), *Stella, Fairy of the Forest* (2002), *Good Morning, Sam* and *Good Night, Sam* (2003), and *Stella, Princess of the Sky* (2004). (Rev: BL 9/1/06; SLJ 9/06)

4065 George, Kristine O'Connell. *Up!* (PS). Illus. by Niroe Nakata. 2005, Clarion $15.00 (978-0-618-06489-2). 32pp. A little girl and her daddy enjoy a day at the park in this rhyming picture book. (Rev: BL 3/1/05; SLJ 3/05)

4066 Gerdner, Linda, and Sarah Langford. *Grandfather's Story Cloth: Yawg Daim Paj Ntaub Dab Neeg* (K–3). Illus. by Stuart Loughridge. 2008, Shen's $16.95 (978-1-885008-34-3). 32pp. Chersheng's grandfather has Alzheimer's but he can still remember the past as he "reads" the story cloth of how the family fled from soldiers; English and Hmong appear side by side. (Rev: BL 9/1/08; SLJ 9/08)

4067 Gewing, Lisa. *Mama, Daddy, Baby and Me* (PS). Illus. by Donna Larimer. 1989, Spirit $14.95 (978-0-944296-04-2). 32pp. In simple rhymes, a youngster responds to a new baby in the house. (Rev: BL 12/1/89; SLJ 12/89)

4068 Gilchrist, Jan Spivey. *Indigo and Moonlight Gold* (K–3). Illus. 1993, Black Butterfly $13.95 (978-0-86316-210-7). 32pp. A tender moment between a mother and child is described in moving prose and beautiful oil paintings. (Rev: BCCB 2/94; BL 3/1/94; SLJ 5/94)

4069 Gillard, Denise. *Music from the Sky* (PS–1). Illus. by Stephen Taylor. 2001, Douglas & McIntyre $15.95 (978-0-88899-311-3). 32pp. A music-loving young African American girl spends time with her grandpa, who makes her a flute so she can make her own music. (Rev: BL 2/15/01; HBG 10/01)

4070 Gilles, Almira Astudillo. *Willie Wins* (PS–3). Illus. by Carl Angel. 2001, Lee & Low $16.00 (978-1-58430-023-6). 32pp. Willie isn't much interested in his father's stories of his youth in the Philippines, but when he needs a money bank for a school project, the coconut alkansiya his father gives him has a surprise in it. (Rev: BL 5/1/01; HBG 10/01; SLJ 6/01)

4071 Gilmore, Rachna. *A Gift for Gita* (2–3). Illus. by Alice Priestley. 2002, Tilbury House paper $7.95 (978-0-88448-239-0). 24pp. When Gita's father is offered a job back in their native India, the immigrant family must make a choice. (Rev: BL 9/15/02)

4072 Gilmore, Rachna. *Making Grizzle Grow* (K–3). Illus. by Leslie Elizabeth Watts. 2008, Fitzhenry & Whiteside $16.95 (978-1-55041-885-9). 32pp. After her father says he can't come out and play with her, a very angry Emily builds a very scary snow dinosaur that threatens to eat her father up. (Rev: BL 1/1–15/08; SLJ 3/08)

4073 Godfrey, Jan. *Sam's New Baby* (PS–1). Illus. by Jane Coulson. 1998, Abingdon $2.99 (978-0-687-09570-4). 24pp. Sam discovers that everyone's fingerprints are different. After his baby sister is born, he examines her fingers through a magnifying glass and realizes that she, too, is a unique being. (Rev: BL 9/15/98)

4074 Gold, August. *Does God Hear My Prayer?* (PS–1). Photos by Diane Hardy Waller. 2005, Sky-Light Paths paper $8.99 (978-1-59473-102-0). A child learns what prayer is — and what it isn't — in this gentle book with rhyming text. (Rev: SLJ 7/05)

4075 Good, Merle. *Reuben and the Blizzard* (K–3). Illus. by P. Buckley Moss. 1995, Good Bks. $14.95 (978-1-56148-184-2). 32pp. Young Reuben and his Amish family weather a blizzard and help a neighbor get to the hospital. (Rev: BL 1/1–15/96; SLJ 4/96)

4076 Good, Merle. *Reuben and the Quilt* (PS–3). Illus. by P. Buckley Moss. 1999, Good Bks. $16.00 (978-1-56148-234-4). 32pp. To help with a neighbor's medical bills, an Amish family sews a quilt, but when it is stolen before the auction, they create an unusual plan for its recovery. (Rev: BL 6/1–15/99; SLJ 6/99)

4077 Goode, Diane. *The Most Perfect Spot* (PS–2). 2006, HarperCollins $16.99 (978-0-06-072697-3). 32pp. Jack and his Mama try to enjoy a picnic at the park and end up wet, muddy — and the new owners of a stray puppy. (Rev: BL 5/1/06; SLJ 5/06*)

4078 Gore, Leonid. *When I Grow Up* (PS). Illus. by author. 2009, Scholastic $16.99 (978-0-545-08597-7). 32pp. A little boy wonders what he will be when he grows up and considers many options (a raindrop becoming a river, a caterpillar becoming a butterfly) before deciding that he'll be like his father. (Rev: BL 4/15/09; SLJ 6/09)

4079 Gove, Doris. *My Mother Talks to Trees* (K–3). Illus. by Marilynn H. Mallory. 1999, Peachtree $15.95 (978-1-56145-166-1). 32pp. At first, a little girl finds walking with her mother an embarrassing experience because her mother talks to the trees, but eventually the girl changes her mind and begins talking to a sapling in her yard. (Rev: BL 5/1/99; HBG 10/99; SLJ 7/99)

4080 Graham, Bob. *Spirit of Hope* (PS–3). Illus. 1996, Mondo $14.95 (978-1-57255-202-9). 30pp. The Fairweathers face a crisis when they are told to vacate their home. (Rev: BL 12/1/96; SLJ 3/97)

4081 Grambling, Lois G. *Daddy Will Be There* (PS–K). Illus. by Walter Gaffney-Kessell. 1998, Greenwillow $15.99 (978-0-688-14983-3). 24pp. Even though a little girl engages in many different activities, like playing with her friends, she is happy with the assurance that sooner or later she will be reunited with her father. (Rev: BL 5/15/98; HBG 10/98; SLJ 6/98)

4082 Grambling, Lois G. *Grandma Tells a Story* (PS–1). Illus. by Fred Willingham. 2001, Charlesbridge LB $15.95 (978-1-58089-057-1). Two grandparents are overjoyed to learn that a longed-for grandchild is on its way in this gentle story with bright illustrations. (Rev: HBG 10/01; SLJ 7/01)

4083 Gray, Libba M. *My Mama Had a Dancing Heart* (PS–3). Illus. by Raúl Colón. 1995, Orchard LB $16.99 (978-0-531-08770-1). 32pp. Evocative pictures are used to illustrate a series of imaginative experiences shared by a mother and daughter in each of the seasons. (Rev: BL 9/15/95*; SLJ 9/95*)

4084 Greenfield, Eloise. *First Pink Light* (PS–1). Illus. by Jan S. Gilchrist. 1991, Writers & Readers $13.95 (978-0-86316-207-7). A young African American boy waits in a rocking chair to greet his father, who has been away for a year. (Rev: BL 12/15/91; SLJ 1/92)

4085 Greenfield, Eloise. *Grandpa's Face* (K–3). Illus. by Floyd Cooper. 1988, Philomel $16.99 (978-0-399-21525-4); Penguin paper $6.99 (978-0-698-11381-7). 32pp. Tamika worries about her grandfather's reactions. (Rev: BL 11/15/88; HB 3/89; SLJ 11/88)

4086 Greenfield, Eloise. *She Come Bringing Me That Little Baby Girl* (K–2). Illus. by John Steptoe. 1990, HarperCollins paper $6.99 (978-0-06-443296-2). 32pp. Kevin resents all the attention the new baby is getting; most of all he resents the fact that she is a girl.

4087 Grimes, Nikki. *Welcome, Precious* (PS–2). Illus. by Bryan Collier. 2006, Scholastic $16.99 (978-0-439-55702-3). 32pp. A young African American family welcomes a new baby to the many wonders of the world. (Rev: BL 9/1/06; SLJ 11/06)

4088 Grossmann-Hensel, Katharina. *Papa Is a Pirate* (K–2). Illus. by author. 2009, North-South $16.95 (978-0-7358-2237-5). 32pp. Here is a fun twist on the pirate story that has a gentle father telling his doubtful son that he is in fact a dashing pirate, not an office worker. (Rev: SLJ 5/09)

4089 Gurley, Nan. *Twice Yours: A Parable of God's Gift* (K–3). Illus. by Bill Farnsworth. 2002, Zondervan $14.99 (978-0-310-70194-1). 40pp. A grandfather tells his grandson a story relating to the words of the apostle Peter. (Rev: BL 2/1/02)

4090 Guthrie, Donna. *Grandpa Doesn't Know It's Me: A Family Adjusts to Alzheimer's Disease* (K–3). Illus. by Katy K. Arnsteen. 1986, Human Sciences paper $10.95 (978-0-89885-308-7). The story of Lizzie, who adores her grandfather, and the tragedy of her grandfather's Alzheimer's disease. (Rev: BCCB 7–8/86; BL 8/86)

4091 Guy, Ginger F. *My Grandma / Mi abuelita* (PS–1). Illus. by Vivi Escriva. 2007, HarperCollins $15.99 (978-0-06-079098-1). 24pp. A father, son, and daughter fly from their city to Grandmother's tropical home in this engagingly illustrated bilingual story. (Rev: BL 1/1–15/07)

4092 Hanrahan, Brendan. *My Sisters Love My Clothes* (PS–2). Illus. by Lise Stork. 1992, Perry Heights Pr. $12.95 (978-0-9630181-0-6). 32pp. Young Louie has a smart wardrobe, but his sisters keep borrowing his clothes. (Rev: BCCB 4/92; BL 9/1/92)

4093 Hanson, Warren. *Grandpa Has a Great Big Face* (PS–K). Illus. by Mark Elliott. 2006, Harper-Collins LB $17.89 (978-0-06-078776-9). A child's grandfather seems larger than life — big enough to hold a city in his hands or bridge a river with his foot. (Rev: SLJ 5/06)

4094 Harper, Jessica. *I Like Where I Am* (PS–2). Illus. by G. Brian Karas. 2004, Penguin $15.99 (978-0-399-23479-8). 32pp. A little boy faces the trauma of moving in this playfully illustrated book with a happy ending. (Rev: BL 2/15/04; SLJ 3/04)

4095 Harper, Jessica. *Lizzy's Do's and Don'ts* (1–3). Illus. by Lindsay Harper duPont. 2002, Harper-Collins LB $15.89 (978-0-06-623861-6). 40pp. Cartoon art helps to convey the messages of this book, in which a mother and daughter realize they say "don't" to each other far too often. (Rev: BL 3/15/02; HBG 10/02; SLJ 7/02)

4096 Harper, Jessica. *Uh-oh, Cleo* (K–3). Illus. by Jon Berkeley. 2008, Putnam $14.99 (978-0-399-24671-5). 64pp. This appealing chapter book features 8-year-old Cleo, one of six children in a warm family, who has a stitches party after getting hit in the head. (Rev: BL 4/1/08; LMC 3/08; SLJ 8/08)

4097 Harper, Jessica. *Uh-oh, Cleo: Underpants on My Head* (K–3). Illus. by Jon Berkeley. 2009, Putnam $14.99 (978-0-399-24672-2). 64pp. Eight-year-old Cleo Small and her family get caught in a freak summer snowstorm at the top of Mount Baldy. (Rev: BL 2/1/09; SLJ 3/09)

4098 Harrington, Janice N. *Roberto Walks Home* (K–2). Illus. by Jody Wheeler. 2008, Viking $15.99 (978-0-670-06316-1). 40pp. Forced to walk home alone after his brother forgets to pick him up from school, an angry Roberto falls asleep and dreams a sweet revenge. (Rev: BL 11/15/08; SLJ 12/08)

4099 Harris, Robie H. *The Day Leo Said I Hate You!* (K–3). Illus. by Molly Bang. 2008, Little, Brown $16.99 (978-0-316-06580-1). 40pp. Leo and his mother allow their mutual frustration to escalate until Leo blurts out the dreaded words. (Rev: BL 9/1/08; SLJ 8/08)

4100 Harris, Robie H. *Don't Forget to Come Back!* (PS–2). Illus. by Harry Bliss. 2004, Candlewick $15.99 (978-0-7636-1782-0). 40pp. A little girl strongly protests her parents' departure for the evening but ends up having a delightful time with the baby-sitter; a newly illustrated version of a 1978 title. (Rev: BL 3/1/04; HB 3/04; SLJ 3/04)

4101 Harshman, Marc. *Roads* (PS–2). 2002, Marshall Cavendish $16.95 (978-0-7614-5112-9). 32pp. A thoughtful picture book about traveling from a child's perspective. (Rev: BL 10/15/02; HBG 3/03; SLJ 9/02)

4102 Haseley, Dennis. *The Skywriter* (PS–2). Illus. by Dennis Nolan. 2008, Roaring Brook $16.95 (978-1-59643-252-9). 32pp. A boy named Charles recognizes the joy he derived from his now-abandoned toys and decides to save them for a new younger brother. (Rev: BLO 7/29/08; LMC 1/09; SLJ 10/08)

4103 Haskins, Francine. *I Remember "121"* (PS–3). Illus. 1991, Children's Book Pr. $14.95 (978-0-89239-100-4). 32pp. This is an autobiographical sketch of the artist growing up in an African American neighborhood in Washington, D.C. (Rev: BL 12/15/91; SLJ 3/92) [973]

4104 Haughton, Emma. *Rainy Day* (PS–1). Illus. by Angelo Rinaldi. 2000, Lerner $6.95 (978-1-57505-452-0). A boy and his father spend a day together and must find a way to work around the rain. (Rev: BL 3/1/03; HBG 9/00; SLJ 8/00)

4105 Havill, Juanita. *Treasure Map* (PS–2). Illus. by Elivia Savadier. 1992, Houghton $16.00 (978-0-395-57817-9). 32pp. Alicia hears the story of how her great-grandmother left Mexico and came to the United States. (Rev: BL 3/1/92; SLJ 6/92)

4106 Hawxhurst, Joan C. *Bubbe and Gram: My Two Grandmothers* (PS–3). Illus. by Jane K. Bynum. 1996, Dovetail $12.95 (978-0-9651284-2-1). 32pp. From his two grandmothers — one Jewish, the other Christian — a young girl learns about and accepts two ways of worship. (Rev: BL 1/1–15/97)

4107 Haynes, Max. *Grandma's Gone to Live in the Stars* (PS–2). Illus. 2000, Whitman $15.95 (978-0-8075-3026-9). 32pp. In this simple luminous book about death, Grandma, who is dying, hovers over the things and people she loves, including her sleeping family, to say goodbye. (Rev: BL 12/1/00*; HBG 3/01; SLJ 12/00)

4108 Hazen, Barbara S. *If It Weren't for Benjamin (I'd Always Get to Lick the Icing Spoon)* (PS–2). Illus. by Laura Hartman. 1979, Human Sciences paper $10.95 (978-0-89885-172-4). 32pp. A younger sibling recounts the reasons for his sense of injustice.

4109 Hector, Julian. *The Little Matador* (PS–2). Illus. by author. 2008, Hyperion $15.99 (978-1-4231-0779-8). 40pp. A little boy just wants to draw but his parents want him to follow family tradition and fight bulls, and amazingly the Little Matador manages to combine the two. (Rev: BL 5/15/08; LMC 1/09)

4110 Henderickson, Karen. *Baby and I Can Play and Fun with Toddlers* (PS–K). Illus. by Marina Megale. 1990, Parenting LB $17.95 (978-0-943990-57-6); paper $7.95 (978-0-943990-56-9). 56pp. This book tells preschoolers how to play safely with young babies. (Rev: BL 9/1/90) [649.64]

4111 Henderson, Kathy. *And the Good Brown Earth* (PS). Illus. by author. 2004, Candlewick $15.99 (978-0-7636-2301-2). A well-illustrated story about

Joe and his grandmother enjoying all four seasons in the garden. (Rev: SLJ 4/04)

4112 Henderson, Kathy. *Look at You!* (PS). 2007, Candlewick $15.99 (978-0-7636-2745-4). 40pp. Diverse babies and toddlers explore the world, eat, play, crawl, and clap in soft, oversize watercolors. (Rev: BL 2/15/07*)

4113 Henkes, Kevin. *Shhhh* (PS–1). Illus. 1989, Greenwillow $17.89 (978-0-688-07986-4). 24pp. A little girl wakes up the whole household with her horn. (Rev: BL 8/89; SLJ 1/90)

4114 Henson, Heather. *Grumpy Grandpa* (K–2). Illus. by Ross MacDonald. 2009, Atheneum $16.99 (978-1-4169-0811-1). 40pp. Grandpa is a grouch until he and his grandson go fishing. (Rev: BL 5/15/09; HB 9/09; SLJ 7/09)

4115 Heo, Yumi. *Father's Rubber Shoes* (PS–3). Illus. 1995, Orchard LB $16.99 (978-0-531-08723-7). 32pp. Yungsu's father tells his lonely son why the family has moved to the United States. (Rev: BL 9/15/95; HB 11/95; SLJ 11/95)

4116 Heo, Yumi. *One Sunday Morning* (PS–1). Illus. 1999, Orchard LB $16.99 (978-0-531-33156-9). 32pp. Minho dreams that he and his father spend a day in the park experiencing its sights and sounds. (Rev: BCCB 5/99; BL 4/1/99; HB 3/99; HBG 10/99; SLJ 4/99)

4117 Heo, Yumi. *Ten Days and Nine Nights* (PS–2). Illus. by author. 2009, Random $16.99 (978-0-375-84718-9). 40pp. A little girl marks off the days on her calendar in anticipation of the upcoming arrival of her new adopted sister from Korea. (Rev: BL 4/1/09; HB 5/09; SLJ 5/09)

4118 Herman, Charlotte. *The Memory Cupboard: A Thanksgiving Story* (PS–2). Illus. by Ben F. Stahl. 2003, Whitman LB $16.95 (978-0-8075-5055-7). Katie is upset when she breaks her grandmother's gravy boat, but Grandma shows her that memories are more important than possessions. (Rev: BL 9/1/03; HBG 4/04; SLJ 11/03)

4119 Hesse, Karen. *Poppy's Chair* (K–3). Illus. by Kay Life. 1993, Macmillan LB $14.95 (978-0-02-743705-8). 32pp. Leah learns from her grandmother how to accept her grandfather's death. (Rev: BL 3/15/93; SLJ 7/93)

4120 Hesse, Karen. *Spuds* (PS–2). Illus. by Wendy Watson. 2008, Scholastic $16.99 (978-0-439-87993-4). 32pp. A warm free-verse story about three hungry children who set out to gather potatoes left after the harvest but instead come home with stones. (Rev: BCCB 12/08; BL 9/15/08; LMC 1/09; SLJ 9/08)

4121 High, Linda Oatman. *Winter Shoes for Shadow Horse* (PS–3). Illus. by Ted Lewin. 2001, Boyds Mills $15.95 (978-1-56397-472-4). 32pp. A boy shoes a horse for the very first time under the watchful eye of his blacksmith father. (Rev: BL 9/1/01; HBG 3/02; SLJ 10/01)

4122 Hines, Anna Grossnickle. *Daddy Makes the Best Spaghetti* (PS–K). Illus. by author. 1986, Houghton paper $5.95 (978-0-89919-794-4). The story of the warm relationship between a father and

son as they spend time together doing things at home. (Rev: BL 3/1/86; HB 9/86; SLJ 5/86)

4123 Hines, Anna Grossnickle. *My Grandma Is Coming to Town* (PS–K). Illus. by Melissa Sweet. 2003, Candlewick $13.99 (978-0-7636-1237-5). 24pp. When grandma visits Albert for the first time since he was a baby, he is shy and hides while grandma waits patiently. (Rev: BL 3/15/03; HBG 10/03; SLJ 7/03)

4124 Hoberman, Mary Ann. *I'm Going to Grandma's* (PS–K). Illus. by Tiphanie Beeke. 2007, Harcourt $16.00 (978-0-15-216592-5). 32pp. A gentle story about a child's nervousness the first time she spends the night with Grandma and Grandpa. (Rev: BL 4/1/07)

4125 Hoestlandt, Jo. *Gran, You've Got Mail!* (3–6). Illus. by Aurelie Abolivier. 2008, Delacorte $14.99 (978-0-385-73565-0). 128pp. Annabelle and her great-grandmother form a friendship through writing letters. (Rev: BL 11/15/08; LMC 11/09; SLJ 9/08)

4126 Holman, Sandy Lynne. *Grandpa, Is Everything Black Bad?* (PS–3). Illus. by Lela Kometiani. 1998, Culture C.O.-O.P. $18.95 (978-0-9644655-0-3). 32pp. A child named Montsho thinks that black is often associated with things that are bad, but his beloved grandfather assures him that black is beautiful. (Rev: BL 1/1–15/99; SLJ 12/98)

4127 Holmberg, Bo R. *A Day with Dad* (K–3). Illus. by Eva Eriksson. 2008, Candlewick $15.99 (978-0-7636-3221-2). 32pp. Young Tim spends a happy day with his visiting father. (Rev: BL 4/15/08; HB 5/08; SLJ 8/08)

4128 Holt, Kimberly Willis. *Waiting for Gregory* (PS–2). Illus. by Gabi Swiatkowska. 2006, Holt $16.95 (978-0-8050-7388-1). 32pp. Young Iris eagerly awaits the birth of her new cousin, a boy to be named Gregory. (Rev: BL 2/1/06; SLJ 3/06)

4129 Hooks, Bell. *Homemade Love* (PS). Illus. by Shane W. Evans. 2002, Hyperion $16.99 (978-0-7868-0643-0). 32pp. An African American girl revels in the love of her supportive parents in this brightly illustrated book. (Rev: BCCB 2/03; BL 2/1/03; HBG 3/03; SLJ 12/02)

4130 Horse, Harry. *Little Rabbit's New Baby* (PS–1). Illus. by author. 2008, Peachtree $15.95 (978-1-56145-431-0). 32pp. Little Rabbit struggles with his new role as a big brother. (Rev: SLJ 4/08)

4131 Howard, Elizabeth F. *Flower Girl Butterflies* (PS–2). Illus. by Christiane Kromer. 2004, Greenwillow $15.99 (978-0-688-17809-3). 32pp. Sarah is scared of being a flower girl until she actually starts down the aisle. (Rev: BL 3/1/04; SLJ 4/04)

4132 Howard, Elizabeth F. *What's in Aunt Mary's Room?* (PS–2). Illus. by Cedric Lucas. 1996, Clarion $16.00 (978-0-395-69845-7). 32pp. Aunt Flossie explains the importance in the life of this African American family of the book stored in Aunt Mary's room, the family Bible. A sequel to *Aunt Flossie's Hats (and Crab Cakes Later)* (1991). (Rev: BL 2/15/96; SLJ 5/96)

4133 Howard, Elizabeth F. *When Will Sarah Come?* (PS–K). Illus. by Nina Crews. 1999, Greenwillow

LB $15.89 (978-0-688-16181-1). 24pp. On Sarah's first day at school, younger brother Jonathan waits impatiently for her return. (Rev: BCCB 10/99; BL 10/15/99; HBG 3/00; SLJ 9/99)

4134 Hughes, Shirley. *The Big Alfie and Annie Rose Storybook* (2–3). Illus. by author. 1989, Lothrop $18.00 (978-0-688-07672-6). 64pp. Stories, poems, and eye-catching artwork featuring Alfie and his little sister. (Rev: BCCB 4/89; BL 3/15/89; HB 5/89)

4135 Hughes, Shirley. *The Big Alfie Out of Doors Storybook* (PS–2). Illus. 1992, Lothrop $17.00 (978-0-688-11428-2). 64pp. Four-year-old Alfie has four happy experiences with different members of his family. (Rev: BCCB 10/92*; BL 10/15/92; HB 1/93; SLJ 10/92)

4136 Hundal, Nancy. *Camping* (PS–3). Illus. by Brian Deines. 2002, Fitzhenry & Whiteside $16.95 (978-1-55041-668-8). 32pp. Luminous illustrations form the backdrop for a young girl's discovery that camping in the wilderness has its delights after all. (Rev: BL 12/1/02; SLJ 11/02)

4137 Hunter, Jana Novotny. *When Daddy's Truck Picks Me Up* (PS–1). Illus. by Carol Thompson. 2006, Albert Whitman $15.95 (978-0-8075-8914-4). A little boy at preschool can't concentrate for anticipating the moment when his dad will pick him up in his big tanker truck. (Rev: SLJ 10/06)

4138 Hutchins, Hazel. *I'd Know You Anywhere* (PS). Illus. by Ruth Ohi. 2002, Annick LB $19.95 (978-1-55037-747-7); paper $7.95 (978-1-55037-746-0). 24pp. A father reassures his son that he'd know him no matter how he was disguised in this book for very young readers. (Rev: BL 12/15/02; HBG 3/03; SLJ 4/03)

4139 Hutchins, Pat. *Titch* (K–3). Illus. by author. 1971, Macmillan paper $5.99 (978-0-689-71688-1). 32pp. Titch, the youngest in the family, enjoys a moment of triumph. A sequel is: *You'll Soon Grow into Them, Titch* (1983, Greenwillow).

4140 Igus, Toyomi. *Two Mrs. Gibsons* (K–3). Illus. by Daryl Wells. 1996, Children's Book Pr. $14.95 (978-0-89239-135-6). 32pp. The two Mrs. Gibsons in a young girl's life are her mother and her grandmother. (Rev: BCCB 5/96; BL 5/15/96; SLJ 10/96)

4141 Igus, Toyomi. *When I Was Little* (K–3). Illus. by Higgins Bond. 1992, Just Us Bks. $14.95 (978-0-940975-32-3). 32pp. Noel finds it hard to believe there was no television and other things he takes for granted when his African American grandfather was growing up. (Rev: BL 3/1/93)

4142 Jabar, Cynthia. *Wow! It Sure Is Good to Be You!* (PS–2). Illus. by author. 2006, Houghton $9.95 (978-0-618-58132-0). Phone calls and letters help a little girl realize that even if the people you love are far away, they can still be with you. (Rev: SLJ 6/06)

4143 Jacobs, Julie. *My Heart Is a Magic House* (PS–K). Illus. by Bernadette Pons. 2007, Albert Whitman $16.99 (978-0-8075-5335-0). A young squirrel called Stephanie worries about being supplanted by the new sibling that's on the way, but her mother reassures her that she will simply add another room to her heart. (Rev: SLJ 4/07)

4144 Jacobs, Kate. *A Sister's Wish* (K–2). Illus. by Nancy Carpenter. 1996, Hyperion LB $15.49 (978-0-7868-2112-9). A little girl longs to have a sister of her own but later realizes that being a good sister to her brothers is nice, too. (Rev: SLJ 7/96)

4145 Jagtenberg, Yvonne. *Jack's Kite* (K–2). Illus. by author. 2004, Roaring Brook LB $22.90 (978-0-7613-2904-6). Jack has a kite but he is waiting — and waiting — for his father to come and show him how to fly it. (Rev: HB 1/05; SLJ 2/05)

4146 Jarrett, Clare. *Jamie* (PS–2). Illus. by author. 2002, HarperCollins $13.95 (978-0-00-198414-1). Jamie and his grandfather care for a needy bird in this quiet tale. (Rev: SLJ 9/02)

4147 Jeffs, Stephanie. *Jenny: Coming to Terms with the Death of a Sibling* (K–4). Illus. by Jacqui Thomas. 2006, Abingdon $14.00 (978-0-687-49709-6). 29pp. Jenny must cope with her sister's illness and death and asks Jesus to take care of her in heaven. (Rev: SLJ 3/07)

4148 Jenkins, Emily. *Daffodil* (PS–2). Illus. by Tomek Bogacki. 2004, Farrar $16.00 (978-0-374-31676-1). 32pp. Rose, Violet, and Daffodil are triplets, and their mother likes to dress them in clothes that match their names until Daffodil rebels and the trio finally get to choose their own clothes. (Rev: BL 3/15/04; HB 5/04; SLJ 5/04)

4149 Jenkins, Emily. *Daffodil, Crocodile* (PS–2). Illus. by Tomek Bogacki. 2007, Farrar $16.00 (978-0-374-39944-3). 32pp. Tired of being lumped into a category with her sisters, Daffodil dons a handmade crocodile head and enjoys a day of wild individuality and self-expression; a sequel to *Daffodil* (2004). (Rev: BCCB 6/07; BL 5/15/07; HB 5/07; SLJ 7/07)

4150 Jenkins, Emily. *Five Creatures* (PS–K). Illus. by Tomek Bogacki. 2001, Farrar $16.00 (978-0-374-32341-7). 32pp. Child-like drawings are used in this book that describes the everyday activities of a family and their two cats in an entertaining format that is also an exercise in reasoning. (Rev: BCCB 2/01; BL 3/15/01*; HB 3/01*; HBG 10/01)

4151 Jennings, Sharon. *The Bye-Bye Pie* (1–3). Illus. by Ruth Ohi. 1999, Fitzhenry & Whiteside $12.95 (978-1-55041-405-9). 32pp. Chocolate pies are on the menu as two brothers, Alfie and Joey, make preparations for a surprise party for Grandma. (Rev: BL 11/15/99)

4152 Jocelyn, Marthe. *Mayfly* (PS–2). 2004, Tundra $14.95 (978-0-88776-676-3). 32pp. Three young siblings' happy summer at a rustic lakeside cabin are captured in paper-and-fabric collages. (Rev: BL 8/04; SLJ 5/04)

4153 Johnson, Angela. *The Aunt in Our House* (PS–3). Illus. by David Soman. 1996, Orchard LB $16.99 (978-0-531-08852-4). 32pp. An aunt brings new life and interesting talents during a visit to her brother's biracial family. (Rev: BL 3/1/96; SLJ 4/96)

4154 Johnson, Angela. *Do Like Kyla* (PS–1). Illus. by James Ransome. 1990, Orchard $15.95 (978-0-531-05852-7); paper $6.95 (978-0-531-07040-6). 32pp. The younger of two sisters imitates the older sibling all day long. (Rev: BL 2/15/90; SLJ 4/90)

4155 Johnson, Angela. *One of Three* (PS–K). Illus. by David Soman. 1991, Orchard paper $6.99 (978-0-531-07061-1). 32pp. A young African American girl remembers the good times growing up with two older sisters. (Rev: BL 7/91; SLJ 10/91)

4156 Johnson, Angela. *The Wedding* (K–2). Illus. by David Soman. 1999, Orchard LB $17.99 (978-0-531-33139-2). Through the eyes of young Daisy, the reader experiences all the excitement of the preparations for her sister's wedding. (Rev: BCCB 3/99; HBG 10/99; SLJ 3/99)

4157 Johnson, Angela. *When I Am Old with You* (PS–2). Illus. by David Soman. 1990, Orchard LB $16.99 (978-0-531-08484-7); paper $6.95 (978-0-531-07035-2). 32pp. A young African American boy daydreams of all the things he and his grandfather can do when the youngster grows older. (Rev: BL 9/1/90; SLJ 9/90*)

4158 Johnson, Dolores. *Grandma's Hands* (1–3). Illus. by author. 1998, Marshall Cavendish $15.95 (978-0-7614-5025-2). Initially unhappy at having to live with his grandmother on her farm, a young African American boy grows to love her and her home. (Rev: HBG 10/98; SLJ 5/98)

4159 Johnson, Lindan Lee. *The Dream Jar* (PS–2). Illus. by Serena Curmi. 2005, Houghton $16.00 (978-0-618-17698-4). 32pp. With the help of her older sister, a young girl learns the secret of transforming nightmares into pleasant dreams. (Rev: BL 12/1/05; SLJ 12/05)

4160 Johnston, Tony. *Uncle Rain Cloud* (PS–3). Illus. by Fabricio Vandenbroeck. 2001, Charlesbridge $15.95 (978-0-88106-371-4). 32pp. A touching picture about Carlos' cranky Uncle Tomas who becomes animated and happy only when telling stories about his homeland, Mexico, and its culture. (Rev: BL 2/15/01*; HBG 10/01)

4161 Jolin, Dominique. *It's Not Fair!* (PS–3). Illus. by author. 1996, Crossing Pr. $14.95 (978-0-89594-780-2). A patient father listens as his daughter complains that her friends have more than she does and then reminds her that she has him. (Rev: SLJ 8/96)

4162 Joosse, Barbara M. *Grandma Calls Me Beautiful* (PS–2). Illus. by Barbara Lavallee. 2008, Chronicle $16.99 (978-0-8118-5815-1). 32pp. A Hawaiian grandmother tells her granddaughter how much she is loved; a glossary defines Hawaiian words and the illustrations evoke island life. (Rev: BL 6/1–15/08; SLJ 6/08)

4163 Joosse, Barbara M. *I Love You the Purplest* (PS–1). Illus. by Mary Whyte. 1996, Chronicle $15.95 (978-0-8118-0718-0). 32pp. Two young brothers compete for the attention of their mother, who demonstrates that she loves them equally. (Rev: BL 10/15/96; SLJ 5/97)

4164 Joosse, Barbara M. *Mama, Do You Love Me?* (PS–2). Illus. by Barbara Lavallee. 1991, Chronicle $14.95 (978-0-87701-759-2). An Eskimo girl asks her mother if she will still be loved even when she is naughty. (Rev: BCCB 12/91; HB 11/91; SLJ 11/91)

4165 Joosse, Barbara M. *Nikolai, the Only Bear* (PS–K). Illus. by Renata Liwska. 2005, Philomel $16.99 (978-0-399-23884-0). A misfit bear who has lived in a Russian orphanage for several years is finally adopted by an American couple who are bear-friendly. (Rev: SLJ 4/05)

4166 Joosse, Barbara M. *Papa, Do You Love Me?* (PS–2). Illus. by Barbara Lavallee. 2005, Chronicle $15.95 (978-0-8118-4265-5). 32pp. A Maasai father happily repeats expressions of unconditional love for his son. (Rev: BL 7/05; SLJ 8/05)

4167 Joslin, Mary. *The Goodbye Boat* (PS–2). Illus. by Claire St Louis Little. 1999, Eerdmans $16.00 (978-0-8028-5186-4). 28pp. As a metaphor for death, a grandmother leaves her family behind and goes on a long sea journey. (Rev: BL 5/1/99; HBG 10/99; SLJ 6/99)

4168 Jukes, Mavis. *Like Jake and Me* (2–3). Illus. by Lloyd Bloom. 1987, Knopf paper $7.99 (978-0-394-89263-4). 32pp. Alex and his stepfather explore the meaning of fear.

4169 Juster, Norton. *The Hello, Goodbye Window* (PS–2). Illus. by Chris Raschka. 2005, Hyperion $15.95 (978-0-7868-0914-1). 32pp. A little girl enjoys visiting Nanna and Poppy's house and looking out their special window. Caldecott Medal, 2006. (Rev: BL 3/15/05; SLJ 3/05)

4170 Kallok, Emma. *Gem* (K–3). Illus. by Joel Bower. 2001, Tricycle $14.95 (978-1-58246-027-7). 32pp. A saxophone-playing neighbor welcomes a new baby into the world with her own special song. (Rev: BL 6/1–15/01; HBG 3/02; SLJ 4/01)

4171 Kaplan, John. *Mom and Me* (PS–1). Illus. 1996, Scholastic $10.95 (978-0-590-47294-4). 32pp. In photographs and text, three children talk about their mothers and what these maternal bonds mean to them. (Rev: BL 3/1/96; SLJ 4/96) [306]

4172 Katz, Karen. *Over the Moon: An Adoption Tale* (PS–1). Illus. 1997, Holt $16.95 (978-0-8050-5013-4). 32pp. A husband and wife prepare for the baby they are going to adopt. (Rev: BL 9/1/97; HBG 3/98; SLJ 9/97)

4173 Katz, Karen. *Princess Baby* (PS–1). Illus. by author. 2008, Random $14.99 (978-0-375-84119-4). 32pp. A little girl prefers to be addressed with her proper title, not silly names like "Buttercup" and "Cupcake." (Rev: BL 1/1–15/08; SLJ 3/08)

4174 Keller, Holly. *Miranda's Beach Day* (PS–K). Illus. by author. 2009, HarperCollins $17.99 (978-0-06-158298-1). 32pp. Miranda and her Mom spend a happy day at the beach in this simple, reassuring story. (Rev: BL 4/1/09; SLJ 4/09)

4175 Kennedy, Frances. *The Just-Right, Perfect Present* (K–3). Illus. by Sheila Aldridge. 2007, Tricycle $14.95 (978-1-58246-199-1). 32pp. After Donna's nasty cousin steals her choice of poem to read at their grandparents' anniversary celebration, Donna's family pitches in so she can learn another poem, which turns out to be even better. (Rev: BL 7/07; LMC 11/07; SLJ 11/07)

4176 Knister. *Sophie's Dance* (K–3). Illus. by Mandy Schlunt. 2007, Penguin $16.99 (978-0-698-40056-6). 32pp. Sophie and her grandma dance the night away in this enjoyable, carefree book. (Rev: BL 6/1–15/07)

4177 Knowlton, Laurie Lazzaro. *A Young Man's Dance* (K–3). Illus. by Layne Johnson. 2006, Boyds Mills $15.95 (978-1-59078-259-0). Now that his beloved grandmother has been institutionalized with Alzheimer's disease, her young grandson is reluctant to visit her, but he discovers that although the old woman no longer remembers much about her earlier life she still loves to dance. (Rev: SLJ 4/06)

4178 Komaiko, Leah. *Just My Dad and Me* (K–3). Illus. by Jeffrey Greene. Series: Laura Geringer Books. 1995, HarperCollins LB $15.89 (978-0-06-024574-0). A young girl's dream of spending a day alone with her father is dashed when a carload of relatives arrives. (Rev: SLJ 7/95*)

4179 Kosofsky, Chaim. *Much, Much Better* (PS–3). Illus. by Jessica Schiffman. 2006, Hachai $14.95 (978-1-929628-22-3). The prophet Elijah, who disguises himself as a poor traveler, visits a generous couple and tells them they will be blessed with a baby. (Rev: SLJ 3/07)

4180 Koutsky, Jan Dale. *My Grandma, My Pen Pal* (2–4). Illus. 2002, Boyds Mills $15.95 (978-1-56397-118-1). 24pp. The story of a granddaughter's relationship with her grandmother, in the form of a treasured scrapbook. (Rev: BL 5/15/02; HBG 10/02; SLJ 6/02)

4181 Kovalski, Maryann. *Take Me Out to the Ball Game* (PS–2). 2004, Fitzhenry & Whiteside $15.95 (978-1-55041-897-2). 32pp. The familiar lyrics to "Take Me Out ot the Ball Game" form the framework for this picture-book story of two young sisters' exciting excursion to Yankee Stadium with their grandmother. (Rev: BL 8/04; SLJ 10/04)

4182 Kraus, Robert. *Little Louie the Baby Bloomer* (PS–2). Illus. by Jose Aruego. 1998, HarperCollins LB $15.89 (978-0-06-026294-5). 32pp. Leo is worried about his younger brother, who can't do anything right. (Rev: BL 3/15/98; HBG 10/98; SLJ 7/98)

4183 Krauss, Ruth. *You're Just What I Need* (PS). Illus. by Julia Noonan. 1998, HarperCollins $15.95 (978-0-06-027514-3). 32pp. A sentimental picture book in which a mother wonders what the strange bundle could be under the blankets in her bed, knowing, of course, that it is her young child playing a game of hide-and-seek. (Rev: BL 7/98; HBG 10/98; SLJ 7/98)

4184 Krishnaswami, Uma. *Bringing Asha Home* (1–3). Illus. by Jamel Akib. 2006, Lee & Low $16.95 (978-1-58430-259-9). 32pp. Arun, a young Indian American boy, eagerly awaits the arrival of a new sister, who is being adopted from his father's native country of India. (Rev: BL 10/15/06; SLJ 11/06)

4185 Kroll, Virginia. *She Is Born: A Celebration of Daughters* (K–3). Illus. by John Rowe. 2000, Beyond Words $15.95 (978-1-885223-94-4). 32pp. This happy book introduces a baby girl into the world with examples of how she will be lovingly treated. (Rev: BL 7/00; HBG 10/00; SLJ 8/00)

4186 Krosoczka, Jarrett J. *Giddy Up, Cowgirl* (PS–K). Illus. 2006, Viking $15.99 (978-0-670-06050-4). 40pp. Lively illustrations add to the humor of this story about a little girl who is determined to help her mother and the often less-than-helpful results. (Rev: BL 1/1–15/06; SLJ 2/06)

4187 Kurtz, Jane. *Faraway Home* (PS–3). Illus. by E. B. Lewis. 2000, Harcourt $16.00 (978-0-15-200036-3). 32pp. In this moving family story, a young African American girl has to adjust to the fact that her father must return home to Ethiopia to care for his sick mother. (Rev: BCCB 5/00; BL 2/15/00*; HBG 10/00; SLJ 4/00)

4188 Kurtz, Jane. *In the Small, Small Night* (PS–2). Illus. by Rachel Isadora. 2005, Greenwillow LB $17.89 (978-0-06-623813-5). 32pp. Abena tells her little brother, Kofi, stories from Ghana, their homeland, to help him fall asleep and to calm his fears about adjusting to their new country. (Rev: BL 3/15/05; SLJ 2/05)

4189 Kuskin, Karla. *I Am Me* (PS–2). Illus. by Dyanna Wolcott. 2000, Simon & Schuster $14.00 (978-0-689-81473-0). 32pp. Although a young girl realizes that she resembles other members of her family (she has her mother's green eyes, for example), she is, nevertheless, a distinct individual. (Rev: BL 6/1–15/00; HBG 10/00; SLJ 7/00)

4190 Lakin, Patricia. *Dad and Me in the Morning* (K–3). Illus. by Robert G. Steele. 1994, Whitman LB $16.99 (978-0-8075-1419-1). 32pp. A deaf boy and his father communicate their feelings to each other as they watch a sunrise. (Rev: BL 4/1/94; SLJ 6/94)

4191 LaMarche, Jim. *Up* (PS–3). 2006, Chronicle $16.95 (978-0-8118-4445-1). 32pp. A magical tale about a boy who discovers he has a special power (levitation) and uses it to prove to his father and older brother that he's big and can be a fisherman too. (Rev: BL 11/15/06)

4192 Laminack, Lester L. *Saturdays and Teacakes* (PS–2). Illus. by Chris Soentpiet. 2004, Peachtree $16.95 (978-1-56145-303-0). 32pp. In this nostalgic tale set in 1960s Alabama, a boy rides his bicycle to his grandmother's house, where he mows the lawn and enjoys her teacakes. (Rev: BL 4/1/04; SLJ 4/04)

4193 Laminack, Lester L. *The Sunsets of Miss Olivia Wiggins* (K–4). Illus. by Constance R. Bergum. 1998, Peachtree $15.95 (978-1-56145-139-5). 32pp. Although it appears that Miss Olivia Wiggins, an Alzheimer's disease sufferer, does recognize her daughter and great-grandson when they visit her at a nursing home, inwardly she is recalling pleasant times from the past. (Rev: BL 5/1/98; HBG 10/98; SLJ 7/98)

4194 Landolf, Diane Wright. *What a Good Big Brother!* (PS–K). Illus. by Steve Johnson. 2009, Random $16.99 (978-0-375-84258-0). 40pp. There's a new little sister in the house and only helpful Cameron has the magic to soothe the crying baby. (Rev: BL 2/1/09; SLJ 2/09)

4195 Langley, Karen. *Shine* (K–2). Illus. by Jonathan Langley. 2002, Marshall Cavendish $15.95 (978-0-7614-5127-3). Jimmy worries that his busy father won't come to see him as the star of Bethlehem. (Rev: HBG 3/03; SLJ 1/03)

4196 Larsen, Andrew. *The Imaginary Garden* (PS–1). Illus. by Irene Luxbacher. 2009, Kids Can $16.95 (978-1-55453-279-7). 32pp. Theodora's grandfather has moved to an apartment and no longer has a garden, so he and Theo decide to create an imaginary one, starting with a stone wall painted on a large canvas. (Rev: BL 3/15/09; SLJ 3/09)

4197 Lasky, Kathryn. *Before I Was Your Mother* (PS–2). Illus. by LeUyen Pham. 2003, Harcourt $16.00 (978-0-15-201464-3). 40pp. Ruby's mother tells Ruby tales about her own childhood and her friends and activities. (Rev: BL 3/15/03; HBG 10/03; SLJ 5/03)

4198 Lawler, Janet. *A Father's Song* (PS). Illus. by Lucy Corvino. 2006, Sterling $12.95 (978-1-4027-2501-2). 24pp. In rhyming verse, a father expresses love for his son as the two spend a day together in the park. (Rev: BL 3/1/06; SLJ 3/06)

4199 Lears, Laurie. *Becky the Brave: A Story About Epilepsy* (PS–3). Illus. by Gail Piazza. 2002, Whitman LB $16.99 (978-0-8075-0601-1). Sarah admires her older sister Becky's confidence and composure, but Becky has not been brave enough to tell her classmates about her epilepsy. (Rev: HBG 10/02; SLJ 5/02)

4200 Lears, Laurie. *Megan's Birthday Tree: A Story About Open Adoption* (K–3). Illus. by Bill Farnsworth. 2005, Whitman $15.95 (978-0-8075-5036-6). 32pp. Megan worries that she will be forgotten when her birth mother, Kendra, moves to a new house, but she is reassured that they will still see one another. (Rev: BL 3/1/05; SLJ 6/05)

4201 LeBox, Annette. *Wild Bog Tea* (K–3). Illus. by Harvey Chan. 2001, Groundwood $16.95 (978-0-88899-406-6). 32pp. A man's gentle remembrances of childhood with his grandfather include walks through the bogs and marshes of Labrador. (Rev: BL 12/15/01; HBG 3/02; SLJ 9/01)

4202 Lee, Spike, and Tonya Lewis Lee. *Please, Baby, Please* (K–2). Illus. by Kadir Nelson. 2002, Simon & Schuster $16.95 (978-0-689-83233-8). 32pp. An appealing picture book by movie director Spike Lee and his producer wife that shows a mother continually pleading with her toddler to behave, until at bedtime it's the little one who begs for a goodnight kiss. (Rev: BCCB 2/03; BL 12/1/02; HBG 3/03; SLJ 12/02)

4203 Leedy, Loreen. *Who's Who in My Family?* (PS–1). Illus. 1995, Holiday House LB $16.95 (978-0-8234-1151-1). 32pp. Family relationships and the words used to describe them are the subject of this book on all kinds of families. (Rev: BCCB 3/95; BL 3/1/95; SLJ 4/95)

4204 Leighton, Audrey O. *A Window of Time* (K–3). Illus. by Rhonda Kyrias. 1995, NADIA $15.95 (978-0-9636335-1-4). 32pp. Shawn is troubled by his grandfather's frequent loss of memory and mental confusion. (Rev: BL 2/1/96)

4205 Leijten, Aileen. *Hugging Hour!* (PS–2). Illus. by author. 2009, Philomel $15.99 (978-0-399-24680-7). 32pp. Drew (or "Drool") is nervous about spending the night at Grandma's house for the first time. (Rev: BCCB 1/09; BL 2/1/09)

4206 Lester, J. D. *Mommy Calls Me Monkeypants* (PS–K). Illus. by Hiroe Nakata. 2009, Robin Corey $7.99 (978-0-375-84502-4). 26pp. A lighthearted board-book exploration of affectionate nicknames. (Rev: BLO 4/24/09; SLJ 3/09)

4207 Leuck, Laura. *I Love My Pirate Papa* (PS–2). Illus. by Kyle M. Stone. 2007, Harcourt $16.00 (978-0-15-205664-3). 32pp. A little boy tells of his life aboard ship with his pirate father. (Rev: BL 9/15/07; SLJ 9/07)

4208 Levine, Abby. *Daddies Give You Horsey Rides* (PS–1). Illus. by John Bendall-Brunello. 2004, Whitman $16.95 (978-0-8075-1429-0). 32pp. Animal fathers display the varied ways in which they add value to their children's lives in this simple book with a lively rhyme and humorous illustrations. (Rev: BL 3/15/04; SLJ 5/04)

4209 Levy, Janice. *Abuelito Eats with His Fingers* (1–3). Illus. by Layne Johnson. 1999, Eakin $14.95 (978-1-57168-177-5). Tina is ashamed of her crude, peasantlike grandfather, but one day she discovers they share a love of art. (Rev: HBG 3/00; SLJ 9/99)

4210 Lewis, Cynthia C. *Dilly's Big Sister Diary* (2–4). Illus. by author. 1998, Millbrook LB $19.90 (978-0-7613-0414-2). Eight-year-old Dilly is given a diary by her parents to chronicle the development of her new younger brother, Matthew. (Rev: HBG 3/99; SLJ 2/99)

4211 Lewis, Rob. *Hide-and-Seek with Grandpa* (1–3). Illus. by author. 1997, Mondo paper $4.50 (978-1-57255-226-5). 48pp. Young Finley is always surprised at his Grandpa Bear's vim and vigor. Also use *Grandpa Comes to Stay* (1997). (Rev: SLJ 8/97)

4212 Lichtenheld, Tom. *What's with This Room?* (PS–3). Illus. by author. 2005, Little, Brown $15.99 (978-0-316-59286-4). A little boy assures his parents that everything in his extremely messy room serves an important educational purpose. (Rev: SLJ 11/05)

4213 Lin, Grace. *Kite Flying* (K–3). 2002, Knopf $14.95 (978-0-375-81520-1). 32pp. A Chinese girl describes the family ritual of making and flying kites. (Rev: BL 6/1–15/02; HBG 10/02; SLJ 7/02)

4214 Lin, Grace. *The Ugly Vegetables* (K–2). Illus. 1999, Charlesbridge LB $16.95 (978-0-88106-336-3). 32pp. A Chinese American girl is disappointed in the dullness of her family garden compared with the lovely flowers she sees in other gardens — until harvest time when her mother makes a delicious soup from all the unusual Chinese vegetables. (Rev: BL 9/15/99; HB 9/99; HBG 3/00; SLJ 9/99)

4215 Lindahl, Inger. *Bertil and the Bathroom Elephants* (PS–K). Trans. from Swedish by Elisabeth Kallick Dyssegaard. Illus. by Eva Lindstrom. 2003, R&S $15.00 (91-29-65944-2). Three-year-old Bertil starts to believe that his invented elephants really do exist under the bathtub and refuses to use the bathroom at all. (Rev: HB 9/03; HBG 4/04; SLJ 12/03)

4216 Lindbergh, Reeve. *My Hippie Grandmother* (PS–2). Illus. by Abby Carter. 2003, Candlewick $15.99 (978-0-7636-0671-8). 24pp. A little girl talks about her grandmother, who went to Woodstock and has a flower power poster. (Rev: BL 3/1/03; HBG 10/03; SLJ 4/03)

4217 Lindbergh, Reeve. *My Little Grandmother Often Forgets* (PS–2). Illus. by Kathryn Brown. 2007, Candlewick $16.99 (978-0-7636-1989-3). 32pp. A little boy describes his grandmother's forgetfulness with love and understanding. (Rev: BL 4/15/07)

4218 Lloyd, Jennifer. *Looking for Loons* (PS–2). Illus. by Kirsti Anne Wakelin. 2007, Simply Read $16.95 (978-1-894965-54-5). 32pp. A family gathers one by one on the front porch to watch for the loons arriving on the lake. (Rev: BL 2/15/08; SLJ 1/08)

4219 Lloyd-Jones, Sally. *How to Be a Baby — By Me, the Big Sister* (K–3). Illus. by Sue Heap. 2007, Random $15.99 (978-0-375-83843-9). An older sister lists the many, many things that babies can't do before realizing that there are a few benefits to babies as well. (Rev: BCCB 4/07; BL 11/15/06*; HB 1/07; HBG 10/07; SLJ 2/07)

4220 Lo, Ginnie. *Mahjong All Day Long* (PS–2). Illus. by Beth Lo. 2005, Walker LB $17.85 (978-0-8027-8942-6). 32pp. The game of mahjong is important in a Chinese family's rituals and enjoyment of life. (Rev: BL 2/15/05; SLJ 5/05)

4221 Lobel, Anita. *Potatoes, Potatoes* (K–3). Illus. 2004, Greenwillow LB $16.89 (978-0-06-051818-9). 40pp. A new edition of a 1967 picture book about two brothers whose mother teaches them to make peace. (Rev: BL 1/1–15/04)

4222 Lohans, Alison. *Waiting for the Sun* (K–2). Illus. by Marilyn Mets and Peter Ledwon. 2002, Red Deer $16.95 (978-0-88995-240-9). After a lot of anticipation, Mollie is disappointed at first by the sight of her new baby brother. (Rev: SLJ 7/02)

4223 Long, Earlene. *Gone Fishing* (PS–2). Illus. by Richard Brown. 1987, Houghton paper $5.95 (978-0-395-44236-4). 32pp. A loving story of a boy's fishing trip with his father.

4224 Look, Lenore. *Alvin Ho: Allergic to Camping, Hiking, and Other Natural Disasters* (2–4). Illus. by LeUyen Pham. 2009, Random $15.99 (978-0-375-85705-8). 176pp. Anxious 2nd-grader Alvin Ho is back in another comical, sensitive story centered around his worries over surviving a planned camping trip with his father. (Rev: BCCB 9/09; BLO 6/16/09; HB 8–9/09; SLJ 7/09) ∩

4225 Look, Lenore. *Love as Strong as Ginger* (K–4). Illus. by Stephen T. Johnson. 1999, Simon & Schuster $15.00 (978-0-689-81248-4). 40pp. A young Chinese American girl goes to visit a cannery in the Seattle area where her grandmother, a recent immigrant, has to work backbreaking hours to earn a living. (Rev: BL 10/15/99*; HB 5/99; HBG 10/99; SLJ 7/99)

4226 Look, Lenore. *Uncle Peter's Amazing Chinese Wedding* (K–2). Illus. by Yumi Heo. 2006, Simon & Schuster $16.95 (978-0-689-84458-4). 40pp. As her Chinese American family prepares for Peter's wedding, Jenny worries she will lose her special relationship with her uncle. (Rev: BCCB 1/06; BL 12/15/05*; HBG 10/06; LMC 8/06; SLJ 1/06)

4227 Lord, Janet. *Here Comes Grandma!* (PS–K). Illus. by Julie Paschkis. 2005, Holt $12.95 (978-0-8050-7666-0). 32pp. A grandmother goes to great lengths to visit her beloved grandchild. (Rev: BL 10/1/05; SLJ 9/05)

4228 Louie, Therese On. *Raymond's Perfect Present* (K–2). Illus. by Suling Wang. 2002, Lee & Low $16.95 (978-1-58430-055-7). 32pp. A tender story about a boy who can't afford flowers for his sick mother, but instead plants seeds. (Rev: BL 10/15/02; HBG 3/03; SLJ 11/02)

4229 Luthardt, Kevin. *Flying* (PS–1). Illus. by author. 2009, Peachtree $15.95 (978-1-56145-430-3). 32pp. "Why can't I fly?" asks a little African American boy, and he and his father set off on an imaginative trip. (Rev: BL 3/15/09; SLJ 4/09)

4230 Lyon, George E. *Five Live Bongos* (PS–1). Illus. by Jacqueline Rogers. 1994, Scholastic $15.95 (978-0-590-46654-7). 40pp. Five brothers and sisters make so much noise indoors that they are banished to the garage. (Rev: BL 10/15/94; SLJ 10/94)

4231 Lyon, George E. *No Dessert Forever!* (PS–K). Illus. by Peter Catalanotto. 2006, Simon & Schuster $16.95 (978-1-4169-0385-7). 40pp. A young girl vents her frustrations with life through discussions with her doll; the brief text is amplified by the realistic, warm watercolors. (Rev: BL 11/1/06; SLJ 12/06)

4232 McCaughrean, Geraldine. *My Grandmother's Clock* (K–3). Illus. by Stephen Lambert. 2002, Clarion $15.00 (978-0-618-21695-6). 32pp. A grandmother explains to her young granddaughter how she tells time: by relying on life's rhythms, rather than on clocks. (Rev: BL 9/15/02; HB 1/03; HBG 3/03; SLJ 9/02)

4233 McCloskey, Robert. *One Morning in Maine* (1–3). Illus. by author. 1952, Puffin paper $6.99 (978-0-14-050174-2). An exciting day, the loss of Sal's first tooth, is realistically recaptured by this fine storyteller and in the large, extraordinary blue-pencil drawings of Penobscot Bay. Also use: *Blueberries for Sal* (1948).

4234 McConnell, Sarah. *Don't Mention Pirates* (PS–2). Illus. by author. 2006, Barron's $14.99 (978-0-7641-5945-9). Although the Silver family has renounced its pirate past, it quickly reconsiders matters after young Scarlet discovers some buried gold. (Rev: SLJ 8/06)

4235 McCormack, Caren McNelly. *The Fiesta Dress: A Quinceañera Tale* (K–2). Illus. by Martha Aviles. 2009, Marshall Cavendish $17.99 (978-0-7614-5467-0). 40pp. Little Lolo, used to being the center of attention, is feeling neglected on her older sister's 15th birthday, but when her dog steals Eva's white sash it's Lolo who is suddenly in the forefront. (Rev: BCCB 5/09; BLO 3/5/09; SLJ 3/09)

4236 McCormick, Wendy. *The Night You Were Born* (PS–2). Illus. by Sophy Williams. 2000, Peachtree $15.95 (978-1-56145-225-5). 32pp. While waiting for news of the arrival of a sibling, Jamie listens to a story about the night he was born. (Rev: BL 1/1–15/01; HBG 3/01; SLJ 12/00)

4237 McDonald, Rae A. *A Fishing Surprise* (PS–2). Illus. by Kathleen Kemly. 2007, NorthWord $16.95 (978-1-55971-977-3). 32pp. A quiet summer day of fishing unexpectedly ends with an apple pie. (Rev: SLJ 10/07)

4238 McElroy, Lisa. *Love, Lizzie: Letters to a Military Mom* (1–3). Illus. by Diane Paterson. 2005, Albert Whitman $16.99 (978-0-8075-4777-9). 32pp. In letters to her mom, a soldier serving overseas, young Lizzie describes her life — the good things and the bad — and includes maps that show details of key events. (Rev: BL 9/1/05; SLJ 10/05)

4239 McFarlane, Sheryl. *Waiting for the Whales* (PS–3). Illus. by Ron Lightburn. 1991, Orca paper $7.95 (978-0-920501-96-2). 32pp. On his lonely island an old man and his granddaughter await the sighting of the summer whales. (Rev: BL 5/15/93; SLJ 6/93)

4240 McGhee, Alison. *Little Boy* (PS–K). Illus. by Peter H. Reynolds. 2008, Atheneum $15.99 (978-1-4169-5872-7). 40pp. "Your yellow cup . . . your big cardboard box" and "a puddle to jump/sand to dump" — these are a few of the things a father appreciates in his son's life in this poetic reflection illustrated with images of a lively child. (Rev: BL 6/1–15/08; LMC 5/08; SLJ 6/08)

4241 MacK, Todd. *Princess Penelope Takes Charge!* (PS–2). Illus. by Julia Gran. 2006, Scholastic $16.99 (978-0-439-67380-8). Penelope wanted a baby sister and is not very excited when Dexter arrives instead, until she decides to welcome him into her personal kingdom. (Rev: SLJ 6/06)

4242 McKenna, Sharon. *Good Morning, Sunshine: A Grandpa Story* (PS–1). 2007, Red Cygnet $17.95 (978-1-60108-003-5). 32pp. Grandpa's happy morning routine brightens his granddaughter's mood in this brightly illustrated picture book. (Rev: BL 5/1/07)

4243 MacLachlan, Patricia. *Through Grandpa's Eyes* (1–3). Illus. by Deborah Kogan Ray. 1980, HarperCollins LB $16.89 (978-0-06-024043-1); paper $6.99 (978-0-06-443041-8). 48pp. John's blind grandfather shares with him the special way he sees and moves in the world.

4244 McMillan, Bruce. *Step by Step* (PS). Illus. by author. 1990, Apple Island LB $15.00 (978-0-688-07234-6). 28pp. Photos trace Evan from four months until he becomes a fast walker at 14 months. (Rev: BL 9/1/87; HB 11/87; SLJ 9/87)

4245 Mahoney, Daniel J. *A Really Good Snowman* (K–3). Illus. by author. 2005, Clarion $15.00 (978-0-618-47554-4). 32pp. Happy to be free of his little sister Nancy for a while, Jack enters a snowman-building contest with two of his friends, but he quickly abandons this to come to her aid when older boys harass her. (Rev: SLJ 11/05)

4246 Mahy, Margaret. *A Busy Day for a Good Grandmother* (PS–3). Illus. by Margaret Chamberlain. 1993, Macmillan $14.95 (978-0-689-50595-9). 32pp. Mrs. Oberon is an unconventional grandmother who rides skateboards and fights vultures and alligators. (Rev: BL 10/15/93; SLJ 9/93)

4247 Makhijani, Pooja. *Mama's Saris* (PS–2). Illus. by Elena Gomez. 2007, Little, Brown $16.99 (978-0-316-01105-1). 32pp. A young Indian American girl admires her mother's saris and wants to wear one herself. (Rev: BL 4/15/07)

4248 Maloney, Peter, and Felicia Zekauskas. *His Mother's Nose* (K–3). Illus. 2001, Dial $15.99 (978-0-8037-2545-4). 40pp. Percival learns that he is special even if many of his traits and features were inherited from family members. (Rev: BL 9/1/01; HBG 3/02; SLJ 10/01)

4249 Manning, Mick, and Brita Granström. *Supermom* (PS–K). Illus. 2001, Whitman $16.99 (978-0-8075-7666-3). 32pp. Using both humans and animals as subjects, this book explores the many tasks that mothers perform. (Rev: BL 3/15/01; HBG 10/01)

4250 Manushkin, Fran. *How Mama Brought the Spring* (K–3). Illus. by Holly Berry. 2008, Dutton $16.99 (978-0-525-42027-9). 32pp. Mom gets a winter-weary Rosie out of her bed with the story of how the little girl's Russian Grandma brought spring to Mintz; includes a blintz recipe. (Rev: BCCB 2/08; BL 1/1–15/08; LMC 3/08; SLJ 1/08)

4251 Many, Paul. *Dad's Bald Head* (PS–2). Illus. by Kevin O'Malley. 2007, Walker $15.95 (978-0-8027-9579-3). Pete is a bit taken aback when his dad shaves his head (although Dad was already nearly bald) but slowly gets used to the new look. (Rev: SLJ 6/07)

4252 Manzano, Sonia. *A Box Full of Kittens* (PS–2). Illus. by Matt Phelan. 2007, Atheneum $16.99 (978-0-689-83089-1). 40pp. Young Ruthie, aspiring superhero, feels confident of her ability to look after her pregnant aunt, but a box of kittens distract her attention. (Rev: BL 5/1/07; SLJ 8/07)

4253 Mario, Heidi Stetson. *I'd Rather Have an Iguana* (PS–1). Illus. 1999, Charlesbridge $14.95 (978-0-88106-357-8). 32pp. Big sister doesn't want to have a baby brother, but one day when they are alone, she changes her mind. (Rev: BL 1/1–15/99; HBG 10/99; SLJ 4/99)

4254 Martin, Jacqueline B. *The Water Gift and the Pig of the Pig* (K–2). Illus. by Linda S. Wingerter. 2003, Houghton $15.00 (978-0-618-07436-5). When the pig that is an important part of their family history disappears, Isabel discovers that — like her grandfather — she has the ability to locate precious things. (Rev: HB 5/03; HBG 10/03; SLJ 6/03)

4255 Maslac, Evelyn Hughes. *Finding a Job for Daddy* (PS–3). Illus. by Kay Life. 1996, Whitman LB $14.95 (978-0-8075-2437-4). 32pp. Laura tries to cheer up her father, who is out of work. (Rev: BL 4/1/96)

4256 Matze, Claire Sidhom. *The Stars in My Geddoh's Sky* (PS–3). Illus. by Bill Farnsworth. 1999, Whitman $14.95 (978-0-8075-5332-9). An Arab grandfather (geddoh) from Palestine comes to the U.S. to visit the family of his grandson, Alex. (Rev: BL 5/15/99; HBG 10/99; SLJ 5/99)

4257 Mauner, Claudia, and Elisa Smalley. *Zoe Sophia's Scrapbook: An Adventure in Venice* (1–4). Illus. by Claudia Mauner. 2003, Chronicle $14.95

(978-0-8118-3606-7). Nine-year-old Zoe Sophia, accompanied by her dachshund Mickey, explores the wonders of Venice during a visit to her Great-Aunt Dorothy in this picture book for older readers using a diary format. (Rev: BL 5/15/03; HBG 10/03; SLJ 8/03)

4258 May, Kathy L. *Molasses Man* (PS–3). Illus. by Felicia Marshall. 2000, Holiday House $16.95 (978-0-8234-1438-3). 32pp. Seen through the eyes of a young African American boy, this is the story of how his family makes molasses under the supervision of Grandpa, the Molasses Man. (Rev: BL 10/1/00; HBG 3/01; SLJ 10/00)

4259 Mazer, Norma Fox. *Has Anyone Seen My Emily Greene?* (PS–1). Illus. by Christine Davenier. 2007, Candlewick $15.99 (978-0-7636-1384-6). 32pp. Little Emily Greene makes her dad play a boisterous game of hide-and-seek before she'll eat lunch. (Rev: BL 5/1/07; SLJ 6/07)

4260 Melmed, Laura K. *A Hug Goes Around* (PS–k). Illus. by Betsy Lewin. 2002, HarperCollins LB $15.89 (978-0-688-14681-8). 32pp. In spite of minor disasters, a family muddles through because they can comfort each other with hugs. (Rev: BL 6/1–15/02)

4261 Meltzer, Amy. *A Mezuzah on the Door* (K–2). Illus. by Janice Fried. 2007, Kar-Ben $17.95 (978-1-58013-249-7); paper $7.95 (978-1-58013-251-0). 32pp. Noah is having trouble adjusting to his new home in the suburbs, but he feels much better after they celebrate Hanukkat Habayit and he and his old friends touch the mezuzah. (Rev: BL 11/1/07; SLJ 10/07)

4262 Mennen, Ingrid. *One Round Moon and a Star for Me* (PS–1). Illus. by Niki Daly. 1994, Orchard LB $16.99 (978-0-531-08654-4). 32pp. In this tale that takes place in Lesotho, a young boy needs reassurance when a new baby arrives in the family. (Rev: BCCB 4/94; BL 2/15/94; SLJ 9/94)

4263 Mercier, Deirdre McLaughlin. *Yesterday We Had a Hurricane / Ayer tuvimos un huracán* (PS–2). Illus. by author. 2006, Bumble Bee $17.95 (978-0-9754342-9-1). In this reassuring bilingual picture book, a mother comforts a child during and after a frightening storm. (Rev: SLJ 10/06)

4264 Meserve, Jessica. *Can Anybody Hear Me?* (1–3). Illus. by author. 2008, Clarion $16.00 (978-0-547-02834-7). 32pp. Jack is too quiet to get much attention in his rambunctious family and nobody pays attention to him when he says he's going up the mountain; only when he becomes lost and calls for help does his family finally hear him. (Rev: SLJ 11/08)

4265 Meserve, Jessica. *Small Sister* (PS–2). Illus. by author. 2007, Clarion $16.00 (978-0-618-77658-0). A little sister seems a little bigger when she rescues her big sister's pet parrot. (Rev: SLJ 6/07)

4266 Michaels, William. *Clare and Her Shadow* (PS–1). Illus. by author. 1991, Shoe String LB $17.50 (978-0-208-02301-8). While on a walk with her grandmother, Clare discovers her shadow. (Rev: SLJ 2/92)

4267 Michelson, Richard. *Oh No, Not Ghosts!* (1–3). Illus. by Adam McCauley. 2006, Harcourt $16.00 (978-0-15-205186-0). 44pp. As a boy and his little sister try to settle down to sleep, the brother teasingly escalates all the horrors they might face — ghosts, demons, goblins, giants, and skeletons. (Rev: SLJ 8/06)

4268 Michelson, Richard. *Too Young for Yiddish* (K–4). Illus. by Neil Waldman. 2002, Charlesbridge $15.95 (978-0-88106-118-5). 32pp. A young boy wants his grandfather to teach him the Yiddish language in this poignant tale that is part history, part family story. (Rev: BL 3/1/02; HBG 10/02; SLJ 3/02)

4269 Miller, Margaret. *Baby Faces* (PS). Illus. 1998, Simon & Schuster $4.99 (978-0-689-81911-7). 14pp. A board book in which babies' faces are used to illustrate different moods and attitudes. (Rev: BL 7/98; HBG 10/98; SLJ 7/98)

4270 Miller, Margaret. *What's on My Head?* (PS). Illus. 1998, Simon & Schuster $4.99 (978-0-689-81912-4). 14pp. In this board book, babies wear such unusual headgear as a firefighter's hat, bean-bag animals, and a rubber duck. (Rev: BL 7/98; HBG 10/98; SLJ 7/98)

4271 Miller, William. *Zora Hurston and the Chinaberry Tree* (PS–3). Illus. by Cornelius Van Wright and Ying-Hwa Hu. 1994, Lee & Low $15.95 (978-1-880000-14-4); paper $6.99 (978-1-880000-33-5). 32pp. A picture book that explores the trauma experienced by the author Zora Hurston when her beloved mother died when the girl was only nine. (Rev: BL 10/15/94; SLJ 12/94) [813]

4272 Mills, Claudia. *The Totally Made-up Civil War Diary of Amanda MacLeish* (3–5). 2008, Farrar $16.00 (978-0-374-37696-3). 208pp. Amanda's fictional Civil War diary, a history project, begins to resemble her home life as her parents separate and she and her best friend grow apart. (Rev: BL 1/1–15/08; SLJ 5/08)

4273 Milord, Susan. *Love That Baby!* (PS). Illus. 2005, Houghton $7.95 (978-0-618-56323-4). 16pp. This delightful lift-the-flap book celebrates the interaction between babies and their parents. (Rev: BL 10/1/05; SLJ 11/05)

4274 Mitchell, Rhonda. *The Talking Cloth* (PS–2). Illus. 1997, Orchard LB $16.99 (978-0-531-33004-3). 32pp. When Amber drapes her aunt's cloth from Ghana around herself, she pretends she is an Ashanti princess. (Rev: BCCB 6/97; BL 2/15/97; SLJ 7/97)

4275 Monk, Isabell. *Blackberry Stew* (PS–2). Illus. by Janice L. Porter. 2005, Carolrhoda $15.95 (978-1-57505-605-0). 32pp. Hope learns that she can keep her grandfather alive in her memory in this story of a warm African American family. (Rev: BL 2/1/05; SLJ 6/05)

4276 Monk, Isabell. *Family* (PS–2). Illus. by Janice L. Porter. 2001, Carolrhoda $15.95 (978-1-57505-485-8). 32pp. Celebrates the fun and food of an African American family reunion (complete with recipes). (Rev: BL 2/15/01; HBG 10/01)

4277 Monk, Isabell. *Hope* (K–3). Illus. by Janice L. Porter. 1999, Carolrhoda LB $15.95 (978-1-57505-230-4). Hope's great aunt Poogee tells the little girl that she should be proud of her biracial background and that her white father and African American mother represent two important cultures. (Rev: HBG 10/99; SLJ 6/99)

4278 Montanari, Eva. *Tiff, Taff, and Lulu* (K–2). Illus. by author. 2004, Houghton $16.00 (978-0-618-40238-0). Three monster sisters put aside their differences when their mother is injured in an accident. (Rev: SLJ 9/04)

4279 Moore-Mallinos, Jennifer. *Mom Has Cancer!* (K–2). Illus. by Marta Fàbrega. 2008, Barron's paper $6.99 (978-0-7641-4074-7). 32pp. Here is a straightforward and comforting look at a little boy's struggles to cope when his mother is sick. (Rev: SLJ 5/09)

4280 Mora, Pat. *Let's Eat! / ¡A Comer!* (PS–2). Illus. by Maribel Suárez. Series: My Family / Mi familia. 2008, HarperCollins $12.99 (978-0-06-085038-8). 24pp. In English and Spanish, a family gathers to enjoy a meal together. (Rev: BL 4/1/08; SLJ 4/08)

4281 Mora, Pat. *Pablo's Tree* (PS–3). Illus. by Cecily Lang. 1994, Macmillan paper $16.00 (978-0-02-767401-9). 32pp. Ever since his daughter adopted young Pablo, grandfather decorates a tree on the anniversary of the boy's arrival. (Rev: BCCB 9/94; BL 11/1/94; HB 11/94)

4282 Morrison, Toni, and Slade Morrison. *Peeny Butter Fudge* (K–1). Illus. by Joe Cepeda. 2009, Simon & Schuster $16.99 (978-1-4169-8332-3). 32pp. Three happy children spend the day with their grandmother who disregards their mother's strict list and instead provides many fun activities culminating in the making of fudge, which softens the mother's attitude when the smell reminds her of long ago. (Rev: BL 7/09; SLJ 9/09)

4283 Moser, Lisa. *Watermelon Wishes* (K–2). Illus. by Stacey Schuett. 2006, Clarion $16.00 (978-0-618-56433-0). 32pp. In this appealing story, a young boy and his grandfather spend the summer tending a watermelon patch they planted together, and the boy hopes to harvest one very special melon that will grant him a wish: to spend another summer of fun with his granddad. (Rev: SLJ 12/06)

4284 Napoli, Donna Jo. *The Wishing Club: A Story About Fractions* (1–3). Illus. by Anna Currey. 2007, Holt $16.95 (978-0-8050-7665-3). 32pp. Wishing upon a star, four siblings use fractions to work out how to get the pet they want. (Rev: BL 6/1–15/07; LMC 1/08; SLJ 9/07)

4285 Nevius, Carol. *Building with Dad* (PS–2). Illus. by Bill Thomson. 2006, Marshall Cavendish $16.99 (978-0-7614-5312-3). 32pp. Eye-catching vertical spreads illustrate this story about a young boy who accompanies his contractor dad to the construction site of a new school. (Rev: BL 9/1/06; SLJ 10/06)

4286 Newman, Leslea. *Felicia's Favorite Story* (PS–1). Illus. by Adriana Romo. 2003, Two Lives paper $9.95 (978-0-9674468-5-1). 24pp. Felicia, who was born in Guatemala, loves to hear her adop-

tive parents — two women — tell her how she came to be a member of their family. (Rev: SLJ 10/03)

4287 Newman, Marjorie. *Just Like Me* (PS). Illus. by Ken Wilson-Max. 2006, Walker $15.95 (978-0-8027-8080-5). Tom resents his new baby brother because the infant is suddenly the center of attention, but when his parents explain that the baby will grow up just as he has, the older boy accepts his role as big brother. (Rev: SLJ 4/06)

4288 Nielsen-Fernlund, Susin. *Mormor Moves In* (PS–1). 2004, Orca $16.95 (978-1-55143-291-5). Astrid has a hard time adapting to the arrival of her bereaved Swedish grandmother. (Rev: SLJ 11/04)

4289 Nolen, Jerdine. *Pitching In for Eubie* (PS–2). Illus. by E. B. Lewis. 2007, HarperCollins $16.99 (978-0-688-14917-8). 32pp. Lily's older sister Eubie gets a scholarship to college, and Lily tries to find a way to contribute to her room and board like everyone else in the family; set in rural America, this is a warm family story. (Rev: BCCB 1/08; BL 10/15/07; SLJ 12/07)

4290 Norac, Carl. *My Daddy Is a Giant* (PS). Illus. by Ingrid Godon. 2005, Clarion $16.00 (978-0-618-44399-4). 32pp. Eye-catching illustrations draw readers into this simple story of a boy who idolizes his father. (Rev: BL 6/1–15/05; SLJ 5/05)

4291 North, Sherry. *Because You Are My Baby* (PS). Illus. by Marcellus Hall. 2008, Abrams $15.95 (978-0-8109-9482-9). 32pp. In rhythmic rhyming text, a mother describes the ways she would love her baby if she were a skywriter, a chef, a mountaineer, and so forth. (Rev: BL 4/1/08)

4292 Numeroff, Laura. *What Grandmas Do Best / What Grandpas Do Best* (PS–K). Illus. by Lynn Munsinger. 2000, Simon & Schuster $14.00 (978-0-689-80552-3). 40pp. This is an upside-down book that if read one way shows children happy with their grandmothers and, when turned over, shows similar scenes with grandfathers. (Rev: BL 11/15/00; HBG 3/01; SLJ 10/00)

4293 O'Callahan, Jay. *Orange Cheeks* (PS–2). Illus. by Patricia Raine. 1993, Peachtree $15.95 (978-1-56145-073-2). 40pp. A young boy tries not to create trouble when he visits his grandmother. (Rev: BL 7/93)

4294 O'Connor, Jane. *Ready, Set, Skip!* (PS–1). Illus. by Ann James. 2007, Viking $15.99 (978-0-670-06216-4). 36pp. With help from her mother, a young girl finally learns how to skip. (Rev: BL 7/07; HB 5/07; SLJ 7/07)

4295 O'Connor, Jane. *The Snow Globe Family* (PS–2). Illus. by S. D. Schindler. 2006, Putnam $16.99 (978-0-399-24242-7). 40pp. Two families — a large one living in a house and a tiny one living on the mantelpiece within a snow globe — enjoy a winter storm. (Rev: BL 10/1/06; SLJ 12/06)

4296 O'Connor, Joe. *Where Did Daddy's Hair Go?* (PS–2). Illus. by Henry Payne. 2006, Random $14.95 (978-0-375-83571-1). Daddy has "lost" his hair. Where did it go? Did it hurt? Does it matter? (Rev: SLJ 4/06)

4297 O'Hair, Margaret. *Star Baby* (PS). Illus. by Erin Eitter Kono. 2005, Clarion $16.00 (978-0-618-

30668-8). 32pp. This gentle picture book chronicles in rhythmic rhyming text and soft acrylic artwork a day in the life of a mother and child. (Rev: BL 10/15/05; SLJ 10/05)

4298 O'Hair, Margaret. *Twin to Twin* (PS). Illus. by Thierry Courtin. 2003, Simon & Schuster $15.95 (978-0-689-84494-2). Toddler twins — brother and sister — are shown going about their daily lives in a friendly text and lively illustrations. (Rev: BL 6/1–15/03; HBG 10/03; SLJ 5/03)

4299 Ohi, Ruth. *And You Can Come Too* (PS–2). Illus. 2005, Annick $19.95 (978-1-55037-905-1); paper $5.95 (978-1-55037-904-4). 32pp. After her father scolds her for squabbling with her little sister, Sara decides to run away from home but allows her younger sibling to come along, and Dad even helps with building a tent in the backyard. (Rev: BL 10/1/05)

4300 Ohi, Ruth. *Me and My Brother* (PS–1). Illus. by author. 2007, Annick LB $19.95 (978-1-55451-092-4); paper $5.95 (978-1-55451-091-7). 24pp. Warm and realistic, this rhyming book captures the ups and downs of life with a little brother. (Rev: BL 11/1/07)

4301 Ohi, Ruth. *Me and My Sister* (PS–K). Illus. by author. 2005, Annick LB $19.95 (978-1-55037-893-1); paper $5.95 (978-1-55037-892-4). In simple rhyming text, a girl describes the events — good and bad — of a day with her toddler sister. (Rev: BL 7/05; SLJ 10/05)

4302 Okimoto, Jean D., and Elaine M. Aoki. *The White Swan Express: A Story About Adoption* (K–3). Illus. by Meilo So. 2002, Clarion $16.00 (978-0-618-16453-0). 32pp. This story alternates between adoptive parents in North America and the children awaiting adoption in China, with information on the legalities of adopting children and on China's policies on childbirth. (Rev: BL 11/1/02; HBG 3/03; SLJ 2/03)

4303 O'Leary, Sara. *When You Were Small* (1–3). Illus. by Julie Morstad. 2006, Simply Read $16.95 (978-1-894965-36-1). 32pp. When Henry was small, he was *really* small, according to his father, who tells tales of Henry once fitting in his shirt pocket in this imaginatively illustrated book. (Rev: BL 5/1/06; SLJ 10/06)

4304 Ormerod, Jan. *Ballet Sisters: The Duckling and the Swan* (PS–2). Illus. by author. 2007, Scholastic paper $5.99 (978-0-439-82281-7). 32pp. For beginning readers, this is the story of a graceful older sister who takes ballet lessons and an awkward younger sister who wants to dance. (Rev: BL 12/1/06; SLJ 1/07)

4305 Ormerod, Jan. *Molly and Her Dad* (PS–2). Illus. by Carol Thompson. 2008, Roaring Brook $17.95 (978-1-59643-285-7). 32pp. Molly doesn't know much about her dad and loves to imagine what he's like; then he finally arrives and although he's not quite what she expected they get along just fine. (Rev: BCCB 9/08; BL 1/1–15/09; LMC 1/09; SLJ 9/08)

4306 Ormerod, Jan. *Who's Whose?* (K–3). Illus. 1998, Lothrop LB $15.89 (978-0-688-14679-5).

32pp. A delightful, breezy account of the members of three families, their activities, and how they help one another. (Rev: BL 3/15/98; HBG 10/98; SLJ 4/98)

4307 Orona-Ramirez, Kristy. *Kiki's Journey* (K–2). Illus. by Jonathan Warm Day. 2006, Children's Book Pr. $16.95 (978-0-89239-214-8). 32pp. A young Native American girl who was born on a reservation but has grown up in Los Angeles travels back to the Taos Pueblo where she learns some important lessons about her heritage. (Rev: BL 9/1/06; SLJ 10/06)

4308 Ostrow, Vivian. *My Brother Is from Outer Space: The Book of Proof* (K–3). Illus. by Eric Brace. 1996, Whitman LB $14.95 (978-0-8075-5325-1). 32pp. Alex is convinced that his young brother is really an alien from outer space. (Rev: BCCB 5/96; BL 4/1/96; SLJ 6/96)

4309 Pak, Soyung. *Dear Juno* (PS–2). Illus. by Susan Kathleen Hartung. 1999, Viking $17.99 (978-0-670-88252-6). 32pp. Although he can't read Korean, Juno is able to piece together clues about the contents of the letter he has received from his grandmother in Seoul. (Rev: BCCB 1/00; BL 11/15/99; HBG 3/00; SLJ 12/99)

4310 Paradis, Susan. *My Daddy* (PS–1). Illus. 1998, Front St. $15.95 (978-1-886910-30-0). 32pp. A wonderful picture book about a boy's admiration for his father, who can perform such wonders as riding a two-wheeled bike and finding his way home from work alone. (Rev: BL 7/98*; HBG 10/98; SLJ 1/99)

4311 Paradis, Susan. *My Mommy* (PS–1). Illus. 2002, Front St. $15.95 (978-1-886910-73-7). 32pp. Radiant, cheery illustrations that feature sly peeks at wild animals accompany a little girl's simple list of the reasons she loves her mother. (Rev: BL 1/1–15/03; HBG 3/03; SLJ 1/03)

4312 Paradis, Susan. *Snow Princess* (PS–2). Illus. 2005, Front St. $16.95 (978-1-932425-31-4). 32pp. Waiting for her father's return from work on a snowy day, a little girl lets her imagination run wild. (Rev: BL 11/1/05; SLJ 1/06)

4313 Park, Frances, and Ginger Park. *The Have a Good Day Cafe* (1–3). Illus. by Katherine Potter. 2005, Lee & Low $16.95 (978-1-58430-171-4). 32pp. Concerned about his grandmother's homesickness for her native Korea, young Mike suggests her ethnic foods might revive business at their food cart. (Rev: BL 9/1/05; SLJ 8/05)

4314 Parr, Todd. *The Family Book* (PS–2). Illus. by author. 2003, Little, Brown $15.95 (978-0-316-73896-5). Families of all kinds are celebrated in bright, humorous illustrations. (Rev: HBG 4/04; SLJ 12/03)

4315 Parr, Todd. *The Grandma Book* (1–4). Illus. by author. 2006, Little, Brown $9.99 (978-0-316-05802-5). A simple celebration of all kinds of grandmothers and the different ways they show love to their grandchildren. Also use *The Grandpa Book* (2006). (Rev: SLJ 4/06)

4316 Parr, Todd. *We Belong Together: A Book About Adoption and Families* (PS–K). Illus. by author. 2007, Little, Brown $15.99 (978-0-316-01668-1).

32pp. With humor and warmth, Parr looks at the many ways in which families come together. (Rev: BL 7/07; SLJ 10/07)

4317 Partridge, Elizabeth. *Whistling* (PS–2). Illus. by Anna Grossnickle Hines. 2003, Greenwillow LB $16.89 (978-0-06-050236-2). A beautifully illustrated portrait of the close relationship between a father and son as they enjoy a camping trip. (Rev: HBG 10/03; SLJ 4/03)

4318 Patrick, Denise Lewis. *Ma Dear's Old Green House* (PS–2). Illus. by Sonia Lynn Sadler. 2004, Just Us Bks. $16.95 (978-0-940975-55-2). 32pp. A young African American girl recalls the joys of a summer spent at her grandmother's house in the South. (Rev: BL 2/1/05; SLJ 1/05)

4319 Patrick, Denise Lewis. *Red Dancing Shoes* (PS–2). Illus. by James Ransome. 1993, Morrow $15.89 (978-0-688-10393-4). Grandma gives her young granddaughter a new pair of dancing shoes. (Rev: BL 3/1/93; SLJ 3/93)

4320 Patrick, Jean L. S. *If I Had a Snowplow* (PS–1). Illus. by Karen M. Dugan. 2001, Boyds Mills $14.95 (978-1-56397-746-6). A loving boy tells his mother what he would do for her if he had various objects (a truck, a tractor, a bulldozer). (Rev: HBG 3/02; SLJ 12/01)

4321 Pearson, Debora. *Leo's Tree* (PS–K). Illus. by Nora Hilb. 2004, Annick LB $19.95 (978-1-55037-845-0); paper $5.95 (978-1-55037-844-3). Leo and the linden tree planted when he was a baby grow together; when sister Sophie arrives, another sapling is added. (Rev: SLJ 6/04)

4322 Pellegrini, Nina. *Families Are Different* (PS–3). Illus. 1991, Holiday House LB $16.95 (978-0-8234-0887-0). 32pp. Two adopted Korean girls gradually adjust to their new American family. (Rev: BL 12/15/91; SLJ 10/91)

4323 Pelley, Kathleen T. *Inventor McGregor* (PS). Illus. by Michael Chesworth. 2006, Farrar $16.00 (978-0-374-33606-6). 32pp. Prolific inventor Hector McGregor is moved to a new office in the city but finds that without his family and his country home, his muse has deserted him. (Rev: BL 2/15/06; SLJ 4/06)

4324 Pelton, Mindy L. *When Dad's at Sea* (PS–1). Illus. by Robert G. Steele. 2004, Whitman $16.99 (978-0-8075-6339-7). 32pp. Emily learns to deal with feelings of loss and fear during the six months her father is deployed at sea as a Navy pilot. (Rev: BL 3/15/04; SLJ 7/04)

4325 Perez, Amada Irma. *Nana's Big Surprise / Nana, Que Sorpresa!* (1–3). Illus. by Maya Christina Gonzalez. 2007, Children's Book Pr. $16.95 (978-0-89239-190-5). 24pp. In this brightly illustrated bilingual picture book, Amada and her siblings hope a gift of some baby chicks will lift the spirits of their visiting grandmother who's still grieving the death of her husband. (Rev: BL 3/15/07)

4326 Perkins, Lynne Rae. *The Broken Cat* (PS–2). Illus. 2002, Greenwillow LB $16.89 (978-0-06-029264-5). 32pp. While Frank waits with his injured cat at the vet's office, his mother, aunt, and

grandmother distract him with a story about the time his mother broke her arm. (Rev: BL 3/15/02; HB 5/02*; HBG 10/02; SLJ 6/02)

4327 Perkins, Lynne Rae. *Pictures from Our Vacation* (K–2). Illus. 2007, Greenwillow $16.99 (978-0-06-085097-5). 40pp. The daughter narrates this story, documented with photographs and maps, of a family's vacation and its mixture of boredom and welcome surprises. (Rev: BCCB 7–8/07; BL 5/1/07; HB 1/08; SLJ 6/07)

4328 Perl, Erica S. *Chicken Butt!* (PS–K). Illus. by Henry Cole. 2009, Abrams $12.95 (978-0-8109-8325-0). 32pp. A small boy tests his father's endurance with constant questions along the lines of "You know why?" "Chicken thigh!" (Rev: BL 4/15/09; SLJ 4/09)

4329 Perry, Elizabeth. *Think Cool Thoughts* (PS–2). Illus. by Linda Bronson. 2005, Clarion $16.00 (978-0-618-23493-6). 32pp. Angel, her mother, and her aunt flee the heat downstairs to spend a lovely summer night watching the stars from the roof of their apartment building. (Rev: BL 7/05; SLJ 8/05)

4330 Pham, LeUyen. *Big Sister, Little Sister* (PS–2). Illus. 2005, Hyperion $15.99 (978-0-7868-5182-9). 40pp. The tensions between younger and older sisters are captured in simple text and lively illustrations. (Rev: BL 6/1–15/05)

4331 Piven, Hanoch. *My Dog Is as Smelly as Dirty Socks: And Other Funny Family Portraits* (K–3). Illus. 2007, Random $15.99 (978-0-375-84052-4). 40pp. A child describes family members in similes that are shown in portraits — Dad is "jumpy as a spring" and so forth. (Rev: BL 5/1/07; SLJ 6/07*)

4332 Piven, Hanoch. *The Scary Show of Mo and Jo* (PS–2). Illus. by author. 2005, Running Pr. $18.95 (978-0-7624-2097-1). Two siblings try to outdo one another with creative disguises that are artfully conceived in Piven's collages. (Rev: SLJ 11/05)

4333 Plourde, Lynn. *Dad, Aren't You Glad?* (PS–2). Illus. by Amy Wummer. 2005, Dutton $12.99 (978-0-525-47362-6). A little boy tries to give his father a treat by taking over his chores, with predictable consequences. (Rev: SLJ 3/05)

4334 Plourde, Lynn. *Thank You, Grandpa* (K–3). Illus. by Jason Cockcroft. 2003, Dutton $15.99 (978-0-525-46992-6). 32pp. When a girl's grandfather dies, she uses what she learned on their nature walks together to say good-bye. (Rev: BL 2/15/03; HBG 10/03; SLJ 4/03)

4335 Polacco, Patricia. *In Our Mothers' House* (1–4). Illus. by author. 2009, Philomel $17.99 (978-0-399-25076-7). 48pp. An African American narrator, one of three adopted multicultural siblings, recalls the happy childhood they had with their mothers Marmee and Meema. (Rev: BL 5/1/09; LMC 10/09; SLJ 5/09)

4336 Polacco, Patricia. *My Ol' Man* (1–3). Illus. 1995, Penguin $16.99 (978-0-399-22822-3). 32pp. Two youngsters enjoy the stories that their traveling-salesman father tells when he comes home. (Rev: BL 4/1/95; SLJ 5/95)

4337 Polacco, Patricia. *My Rotten Redheaded Older Brother* (K–3). Illus. 1994, Simon & Schuster

$16.00 (978-0-671-72751-2). 30pp. A young girl engages in a fierce rivalry with her brother in spite of an underlying love. (Rev: BL 9/15/94; SLJ 10/94*)

4338 Polacco, Patricia. *Rotten Richie and the Ultimate Dare* (1–3). 2006, Philomel $16.99 (978-0-399-24531-2). 48pp. Tired of her brother Richie's teasing about her ballet classes, Trish challenges her obnoxious sibling to show what he can do on the dance floor; a companion to *My Rotten Redheaded Older Brother* (1999). (Rev: BL 4/15/06; SLJ 5/06)

4339 Polacco, Patricia. *Thunder Cake* (PS–3). Illus. 1990, Penguin $16.99 (978-0-399-22231-3). 32pp. A grandmother helps her young granddaughter conquer her fears of electrical storms by eating Thunder Cake. (Rev: BCCB 3/90; BL 2/15/90*; HB 3/90; SLJ 3/90*)

4340 Polacco, Patricia. *When Lightning Comes in a Jar* (2–4). Illus. 2002, Penguin $16.99 (978-0-399-23164-3). 40pp. An autobiographical remembrance of fun, games, and traditions at family reunions. (Rev: BL 8/02; HBG 10/02; SLJ 6/02)

4341 Pomerantz, Charlotte. *The Chalk Doll* (PS–1). Illus. by Frane Lessac. 1989, HarperCollins paper $6.99 (978-0-06-443333-4). 32pp. Rose is sick, and Mother tells her stories of her Jamaican girlhood. (Rev: BL 5/15/89; HB 7/89)

4342 Porter-Gaylord, Laurel. *I Love My Daddy Because . . .* (PS–K). Illus. by Ashley Wolff. 1991, Dutton $7.99 (978-0-525-44624-8). 24pp. Reasons for loving one's father are illustrated through both human and animal examples. A companion volume is *I Love My Mommy Because . . .* (Rev: BCCB 2/91; BL 4/15/91; SLJ 1/92)

4343 Pow, Tom. *Tell Me One Thing, Dad* (PS–1). Illus. by Ian Andrew. 2004, Candlewick $15.99 (978-0-7636-2474-3). 32pp. To postpone the moment when her bedroom light will be turned off for the night, young Molly asks her father about a variety of real and imaginary creatures. (Rev: BL 4/1/04*; SLJ 6/04)

4344 Prigger, Mary Skillings. *Aunt Minnie and the Twister* (PS–2). Illus. by Betsy Lewin. 2002, Clarion $15.00 (978-0-618-11136-7). 32pp. Aunt Minnie and her nine nieces and nephews run to the root cellar to escape a twister that turns their house completely around. (Rev: BL 2/15/02; HB 5/02; HBG 10/02; SLJ 4/02)

4345 Prigger, Mary Skillings. *Aunt Minnie McGranahan* (PS–2). Illus. by Betsy Lewin. 1999, Clarion $15.00 (978-0-395-82270-8). 32pp. Minnie McGranahan accepts nine orphaned nieces and nephews into her household, and although she regulates their schedules, there is always time for fun. (Rev: BCCB 5/99; BL 5/1/99; HBG 10/99; SLJ 5/99)

4346 Pringle, Laurence. *Bear Hug* (K–3). Illus. by Kate S. Palmer. 2003, Boyds Mills $15.95 (978-1-56397-876-0). Jesse and Becky go camping with Dad and really hope to see a bear. (Rev: HBG 10/03; SLJ 2/03)

4347 Pullen, Zachary. *Friday My Radio Flyer Flew* (PS–2). Illus. by author. 2008, Simon & Schuster $16.99 (978-1-4169-3983-2). 32pp. A little boy and his father enjoy restoring an old Radio Flyer and envisaging what it might be able to do. (Rev: SLJ 5/08)

4348 Purmwell, Ann. *Christmas Tree Farm* (PS–2). Illus. by Jill Weber. 2006, Holiday $16.95 (978-0-8234-1886-2). 32pp. A warm story about a Christmas tree farm, the excitement during the winter holidays, and the work that continues all year round. (Rev: BL 9/1/06; SLJ 10/06)

4349 Quigley, Mary. *Granddad's Fishing Buddy* (PS–2). Illus. by Stephane Jorisch. 2007, Dial $16.99 (978-0-8037-2942-1). 32pp. Charmingly written and illustrated, this story about a young girl who goes fishing with her grandfather highlights the simple joy of spending quality time with older family members. (Rev: BL 5/15/07; SLJ 6/07)

4350 Rahaman, Vashanti. *Read for Me, Mama* (PS–1). Illus. 1997, Boyds Mills $15.95 (978-1-56397-313-0). 32pp. An African American boy hopes that his mother, a hotel maid, will have time to read a story to him. (Rev: BCCB 3/97; BL 2/15/97; SLJ 4/97)

4351 Rand, Gloria. *The Cabin Key* (K–3). Illus. by Ted Rand. 1994, Harcourt $15.00 (978-0-15-213884-4). 32pp. A young girl tells about the wonderful things she loves about the family's log cabin in the mountains. (Rev: BCCB 10/94; BL 11/1/94; SLJ 11/94)

4352 Rau, Dana Meachen. *Yahoo for You* (K–1). Illus. by Cary Pilo. 2002, Compass Point LB $18.60 (978-0-7365-0177-4). 32pp. Grandma likes to engage in all sorts of activities with her cute granddaughter but draws the line at going on a roller coaster. (Rev: BL 5/1/02)

4353 Raven, Margot Theis. *Circle Unbroken* (PS–3). Illus. by E. B. Lewis. 2004, Farrar $16.00 (978-0-374-31289-3). A grandmother teaches her granddaughter how to make Gullah baskets and tells her about her African heritage. (Rev: BL 5/15/04; SLJ 4/04)

4354 Regan, Dian C. *Daddies* (PS). Illus. by Mary Morgan. 1996, Scholastic $5.95 (978-0-590-47973-8). 32pp. Children engage in a variety of activities with their fathers. (Rev: BL 6/1–15/96; SLJ 7/96)

4355 Reid, Margarette S. *The Button Box* (K–3). Illus. by Sarah Chamberlain. 1990, Dutton $16.99 (978-0-525-44590-6). 24pp. A boy imagines interesting stories behind the different buttons in his grandmother's button box. (Rev: BCCB 3/90; BL 4/15/90; SLJ 9/90)

4356 Reiser, Lynn. *My Baby and Me* (PS). Illus. by Penny Gentieu. 2008, Knopf $16.99 (978-0-375-85205-3). 32pp. Toddlers are shown interacting with their younger siblings in large-format pages with photographs and simple text. (Rev: BL 5/15/08; SLJ 8/08)

4357 Reiser, Lynn. *You and Me, Baby* (PS–1). Photos by Penny Gentieu. 2006, Knopf $15.95 (978-0-375-83401-1). Simple text accompanies a collection of appealing photographs of babies from diverse backgrounds and their parents. (Rev: SLJ 10/06)

4358 Reynolds, Peter. *Ish* (PS–2). Illus. 2004, Candlewick $14.00 (978-0-7636-2344-9). 32pp. Ramon is an aspiring young artist who nearly quits when his older brother belittles his work; fortunately, his little sister has better taste. (Rev: BL 11/1/04; SLJ 1/05*)

4359 Reynolds, Peter. *My Very Big Little World* (PS–K). Illus. 2006, Simon & Schuster $15.95 (978-0-689-87621-9). 40pp. SugarLoaf, a captivating middle child, introduces young readers to the important people and places in her life. (Rev: BL 4/15/06; SLJ 1/06)

4360 Reynolds, Peter H. *The Best Kid in the World* (PS–2). Illus. by author. 2006, Simon & Schuster $15.95 (978-0-689-87624-0). Jealous that her older brother once received a "Best Kid in the World" award, SugarLoaf sets out to do a number of good deeds, but things don't go exactly as she planned. (Rev: SLJ 8/06)

4361 Ries, Lori. *Fix It, Sam* (PS–K). Illus. by Sue Ramá. 2007, Charlesbridge $15.95 (978-1-57091-598-7); paper $6.95 (978-1-57091-722-6). 32pp. Little Petey relies on big brother Sam for lots of help, but discovers that he can fix things, too; bright mixed media art extends the text. (Rev: BL 1/1–15/07; SLJ 2/07)

4362 Ries, Lori. *Punk Wig* (K–3). Illus. by Erin Eitter Kono. 2008, Boyds Mills $16.95 (978-1-59078-486-0). 32pp. A little boy describes how his mother's cancer has affected his life. (Rev: BL 3/1/08; SLJ 4/08)

4363 Ries, Lori. *Super Sam!* (PS–1). 2004, Charlesbridge $14.95 (978-1-58089-041-0). When he dons a blankie cape, Sam becomes a superhero and his toddler brother Petey is full of awe. (Rev: SLJ 9/04)

4364 Robberecht, Thierry. *Back into Mommy's Tummy* (PS–K). Illus. by Philippe Goossens. 2005, Clarion $15.00 (978-0-618-58106-1). 32pp. A 5-year-old girl whose mother is pregnant says she wants to go back into Mommy's tummy, where the center of attention is. (Rev: BL 12/1/05; SLJ 2/06)

4365 Rockwell, Anne. *Father's Day* (PS–2). Illus. by Lizzy Rockwell. 2005, HarperCollins LB $15.89 (978-0-06-051378-8). 40pp. A class of children write books about their fathers, showing the wide diversity of family situations. (Rev: BL 5/15/05; SLJ 5/05)

4366 Rodman, Mary Ann. *A Tree for Emmy* (PS–2). Illus. by Tatjana Mai-Wyss. 2009, Peachtree $15.95 (978-1-56145-475-4). 32pp. Eager to have a tree like her grandmother's mimosa for her birthday, Emmy is initially distressed to learn it will take years for a sapling to bear flowers. (Rev: BL 5/15/09; SLJ 3/09)

4367 Root, Phyllis. *The Name Quilt* (PS–1). Illus. by Margot Apple. 2003, Farrar $16.00 (978-0-374-35484-8). 32pp. When Sadie stays at Grandma's, she sleeps under a patchwork quilt embroidered with names and listens to Grandma's stories about these relatives. (Rev: BL 3/15/03; HBG 10/03; SLJ 5/03)

4368 Rosen, Michael J. *A Drive in the Country* (K–3). Illus. by Marc Burckhardt. 2007, Candlewick $16.99 (978-0-7636-2140-7). 32pp. A family of five, plus one dog, takes a gentle Sunday drive in

the country and finds lots to enjoy. (Rev: BL 9/15/07; SLJ 11/07)

4369 Rosenbaum, Andria Warmflash. *A Grandma Like Yours / A Grandpa Like Yours* (PS–1). Illus. by Barb Björnson. 2006, Lerner LB $16.95 (978-1-58013-167-4); paper $6.95 (978-1-58013-168-1). One side of this flipbook extols the virtues of Jewish grandmas (in the guise of friendly animals), and the other, Jewish grandpas. (Rev: SLJ 5/06)

4370 Rosenberg, Liz. *The Silence in the Mountains* (1–3). Illus. by Chris K. Soentpiet. 1999, Orchard LB $16.99 (978-0-531-33084-5). 32pp. Iskander and his family must leave their war-torn country and find peace in America. (Rev: BL 2/1/99; HBG 10/99; SLJ 7/99)

4371 Rosenberg, Liz. *This Is the Wind* (PS–2). Illus. by Renee Reichert. 2008, Roaring Brook $16.95 (978-1-59643-268-0). 32pp. Imitating the structure of "This Is the House that Jack Built," this is the story of a child's birth on a windy night on a farm. (Rev: BLO 1/13/09; SLJ 10/08)

4372 Rosenberry, Vera. *The Growing-Up Tree* (K–1). Illus. by author. 2003, Holiday House $16.95 (978-0-8234-1718-6). An apple tree planted when he was a baby plays an important role throughout Alfred's life. (Rev: BL 1/1–15/04; HBG 4/04; SLJ 10/03)

4373 Rouss, Sylvia. *My Baby Brother* (K–2). Illus. by Liz Goulet Dubois. 2002, Jonathan David $14.95 (978-0-8246-0445-5). 24pp. Sarah, a young Jewish girl, initially resists the description of her new baby brother as a "miracle." (Rev: BL 10/1/02)

4374 Russo, Marisabina. *The Big Brown Box* (PS–1). Illus. 2000, Greenwillow $17.99 (978-0-688-17096-7). 32pp. Sam uses a big brown box to imagine all sorts of objects and when his younger brother gets a smaller brown box the two pretend the boxes are space ships. (Rev: BL 5/1/00; HBG 10/00; SLJ 5/00)

4375 Russo, Marisabina. *Come Back, Hannah!* (PS). Illus. 2001, HarperCollins LB $15.89 (978-0-688-17384-5). 32pp. Hannah is an excellent crawler and exhausts her mother as she scoots around the house getting into everything. (Rev: BL 8/01; HBG 10/01; SLJ 7/01)

4376 Russo, Marisabina. *The Trouble with Baby* (PS–1). Illus. by author. 2003, Greenwillow LB $16.89 (978-0-06-008925-2). Siblings Hannah and Sam have always had a good time playing together, but when Hannah gets a new doll named Baby, Sam gets jealous and refuses to play; eventually Hannah comes up with a solution that brings sister and brother together again. (Rev: HBG 10/03; SLJ 6/03)

4377 Ryder, Jeanne. *My Mother's Voice* (K–2). Illus. by Peter Catalanotto. 2006, HarperCollins $15.99 (978-0-06-029509-7). 32pp. This gentle picture book celebrates the role of a mother's voice in a loving relationship with her daughter. (Rev: BL 4/15/06; SLJ 4/06)

4378 Saenz, Benjamin Alire. *A Gift from PapaDiego* (K–4). Illus. by Geronimo Garcia. 1998, Cinco Puntos paper $10.95 (978-0-938317-33-3). 40pp. Little Diego wants a Superman suit so he can fly to Mexico to visit with his beloved grandfather. When that fails, his disappointment is lessened by the news that his grandfather is coming to visit. (Rev: BL 5/1/98; HB 7/98)

4379 Saenz, Benjamin Alire. *A Perfect Season for Dreaming / Un tiempo perfecto para soñar* (K–3). Illus. by Esau Andrade Valencia. 2008, Cinco Puntos $17.95 (978-1-933693-01-9). 40pp. At the age of 78, Octavio Rivera is experiencing wonderful dreams, which he shares with his 6-year-old granddaughter; readers learn to count to 10 in both Spanish and English with this bilingual book. (Rev: HB 1/09; SLJ 4/09)

4380 St. Anthony, Jane. *Grace Above All* (5–7). 2007, Farrar $16.00 (978-0-374-39940-5). 176pp. In this gentle story set in the 1960s, 13-year-old Grace expects to have a boring summer watching over her siblings but a neighboring boy and Great Aunt Hilda provide unexpected interest. (Rev: BL 5/15/07; SLJ 7/07)

4381 Salonen, Roxane Beauclair. *First Salmon* (K–3). Illus. by Jim Fowler. 2005, Boyds Mills $15.95 (978-1-59078-171-5). 32pp. Charlie, a young Native American boy still grieving over the death of his beloved Uncle Joe, finds it hard to get excited about the annual First Salmon celebration. (Rev: BL 10/15/05; SLJ 11/05)

4382 Samuels, Barbara. *Happy Valentines Day, Dolores* (K–2). Illus. 2006, Farrar $16.00 (978-0-374-32844-3). 32pp. Despite her promise to quit snooping in her older sister's room, Dolores simply can't resist trying on a necklace she finds in a valentine box, with disastrous consequences; the detailed cartoon illustrations add to the fun. (Rev: BL 11/15/05*; HBG 10/06; SLJ 1/06*)

4383 Sandburg, Carl. *The Huckabuck Family and How They Raised Popcorn in Nebraska and Quit and Came Back* (K–3). Illus. by David Small. 1999, Farrar $16.00 (978-0-374-33511-3). 40pp. This story, part of the author's *Rootabaga Stories,* tells of the Huckabuck family, their trials and tribulations, travels, and eventual return to their farm. (Rev: BCCB 9/99; BL 9/15/99; HB 9/99; HBG 3/00; SLJ 8/99)

4384 Sanders-Wells, Linda. *Maggie's Monkeys* (K–2). Illus. by Abby Carter. 2009, Candlewick $16.99 (978-0-7636-3326-4). 32pp. Maggie's big brother will not pretend that there are pink monkeys living in their refrigerator until the day his friends tease Maggie and, out of love, he defends Maggie and her monkeys. (Rev: BCCB 6/09; SLJ 5/09)

4385 Sasso, Sandy Eisenberg. *For Heaven's Sake* (K–3). Illus. by Kathryn Kunz Finney. 1999, Jewish Lights $16.95 (978-1-58023-054-4). 32pp. Young Isaiah wonders where heaven is and discovers, through his wise grandmother, that it is all around you. (Rev: BL 10/1/99; SLJ 1/00)

4386 Savadier, Elivia. *Time to Get Dressed!* (PS). Illus. 2006, Roaring Brook $14.95 (978-1-59643-161-4). 32pp. Simple text and charming pictures depict Dad's patience as he struggles to get his toddler dressed for day care. (Rev: BL 4/1/06; SLJ 3/06)

4387 Say, Allen. *Grandfather's Journey* (PS–3). Illus. by author. 1993, Houghton $16.95 (978-0-395-57035-7). 32pp. An autobiographical story that chronicles the passages of generations of the author's family as they moved between Japan and the United States. Winner of the 1994 Caldecott Medal. (Rev: BL 7/93*; SLJ 9/98)

4388 Say, Allen. *The Lost Lake* (2–4). Illus. 1989, Houghton $16.00 (978-0-395-50933-3). 32pp. Realizing that he is not paying sufficient attention to his son, Dad takes him on a camping trip. (Rev: BCCB 1/90; BL 10/1/89; HB 1/90; SLJ 12/89*)

4389 Schertle, Alice. *Down the Road* (PS–3). Illus. by E. B. Lewis. 1995, Harcourt $16.00 (978-0-15-276622-1). 40pp. Hetty accidentally breaks the eggs that she has been carefully carrying from the store for her family's breakfast. (Rev: BCCB 12/95; BL 9/15/95*; SLJ 4/96)

4390 Schindel, John. *Dear Daddy* (K–3). Illus. by Dorothy Donohue. 1995, Whitman LB $15.99 (978-0-8075-1531-0). 32pp. Jesse longs to see his dad, who lives miles away. Finally, in a telephone conversation, they plan for a summer visit. (Rev: BL 5/1/95; SLJ 5/95)

4391 Schlein, Miriam. *The Story About Me* (PS–1). Illus. by Kristina Stephenson. 2004, Whitman $16.99 (978-0-8075-7631-1). 32pp. A grandmother tells her granddaughter about all the anticipation and happiness that preceded the little girl's birth. (Rev: BL 5/1/04; SLJ 5/04)

4392 Schlessinger, Laura C., and Martha L. Lambert. *Why Do You Love Me?* (PS–1). Illus. by Paul Meisel. 1999, HarperCollins $15.95 (978-0-06-027866-3). 40pp. A reassuring story in which a mother tells her young son that in spite of his mischievous behavior she still loves him. (Rev: HBG 10/99; SLJ 4/99)

4393 Schotter, Roni. *The House of Joyful Living* (PS–2). Illus. by Terry Widener. 2008, Farrar $16.95 (978-0-374-33429-1). 32pp. A young girl loves the diverse community in her New York tenement building and the parties they have on the roof; but the forthcoming new baby makes her worry that this world will change. (Rev: BCCB 1/09; BL 11/15/08; SLJ 11/08)

4394 Schotter, Roni. *Mama, I'll Give You the World* (1–3). Illus. by S. Saelig Gallagher. 2006, Random $16.95 (978-0-375-83612-1). 40pp. To repay her mother for all her loving kindness, young Maria plans a very special birthday surprise. (Rev: BL 8/06; SLJ 9/1/06*)

4395 Schwartz, Amy. *A Teeny Tiny Baby* (PS–1). Illus. 1994, Orchard LB $17.99 (978-0-531-08668-1). 32pp. A teeny tiny baby tells about all the things he likes and dislikes about his status. (Rev: BCCB 9/94; BL 7/94*; SLJ 9/94*)

4396 Schwartz, Joanne. *Our Corner Grocery Store* (PS–2). Illus. by Laura Beingessner. 2009, Tundra $19.95 (978-0-88776-868-2). 32pp. Anna Maria gets to play store for real on Saturday at her grandparents' grocery store. (Rev: BCCB 6/09; BL 5/15/09; SLJ 5/09)

4397 Scrimger, Richard. *Eugene's Story* (PS–1). Illus. by Gillian Johnson. 2003, Tundra $15.95 (978-0-88776-544-5). Eugene triumphs over his bossy big sister in this imaginative tale. (Rev: HBG 4/04; SLJ 3/04)

4398 Selway, Martina. *Don't Forget to Write* (PS–2). Illus. 1992, Ideals $12.95 (978-0-8249-8543-1). 28pp. On a visit to Grandad's farm, Rosie writes letters daily to her mother. (Rev: BL 6/1/92; SLJ 8/92)

4399 Shahan, Sherry. *That's Not How You Play Soccer, Daddy!* (K–2). Illus. by Tatjana Mai-Wyss. 2007, Peachtree $15.95 (978-1-56145-416-7). 32pp. Young Mikey takes soccer very seriously while Dad is happy just to play for fun. (Rev: BL 9/1/07; SLJ 10/07)

4400 Shannon, David. *No, David!* (PS–K). Illus. 1998, Scholastic $16.99 (978-0-590-93002-4). 32pp. It seems that everything young David does is met with a "No!" from his mother, but in spite of her criticism, he knows she loves him. (Rev: BCCB 9/98; BL 9/1/98; HBG 3/99; SLJ 8/98)

4401 Shannon, David. *Oh, David! A Diaper David Book* (PS). Illus. by author. 2005, Scholastic $6.99 (978-0-439-68881-9). In a board book prequel to the preschool David, we see the toddler unrolling toilet paper, refusing food, and filling his diaper, before a last cuddle with his long-suffering mother. Also use *Oops! A Diaper David Book* (2005). (Rev: BCCB 3/05; SLJ 3/05)

4402 Shapiro, Jody Fickes. *Up, Up, Up! It's Apple-Picking Time* (K–3). Illus. by Kitty Harvill. 2003, Holiday House $16.95 (978-0-8234-1610-3). Author Jody Fickes Shapiro beautifully evokes all the color and wonder of autumn and harvest in this story of a family's visit to the apple farm of Grandma and Grandpa. (Rev: HBG 4/04; SLJ 9/03)

4403 Sherkin-Langer, Ferne. *When Mommy Is Sick* (PS–2). Illus. by Kay Life. 1995, Whitman $12.95 (978-1-80758-894-6). 32pp. A first-person narrative about the emptiness a young girl feels when her mother is hospitalized. (Rev: BL 3/15/95; SLJ 5/95)

4404 Shipton, Jonathan. *Baby Baby Blah Blah Blah!* (PS–2). Illus. by Francesca Chessa. 2009, Holiday $16.95 (978-0-8234-2213-5). 32pp. When Emily hears there's a new baby coming, she works her way through a list of pros and cons until she gets to the heart of the matter: what about me? (Rev: BCCB 4/09; BLO 2/9/09; SLJ 3/09)

4405 Shough, Carol Gandee. *All the Mamas: A True Love Story for Mothers and Daughters of All Ages* (K–2). Illus. 1998, Summerhouse $16.95 (978-1-887714-29-7). 32pp. The never-ending cycle of mother love is traced in one family as a contemporary mother holds and kisses her baby, just as her mother did to her and just as preceding generations of mothers held and kissed their babies. (Rev: BL 8/98; SLJ 9/98)

4406 Shough, Carol Gandee. *All the Papas: A True Love Story for Fathers and Their Children* (K–4). Illus. by author. 1999, Summerhouse $16.95 (978-1-887714-36-5). 32pp. Based on the author's family history, this book pictures eight generations of fathers and their loving relationships with their families. (Rev: SLJ 7/99)

4407 Showers, Paul. *The Listening Walk* (K–2). Illus. by Aliki. 1991, HarperCollins LB $15.89 (978-0-06-021638-2). A boy and his father listen to the sounds around them as they walk. (Rev: SLJ 7/91)

4408 Shulevitz, Uri. *The Treasure* (K–2). Illus. by author. 1979, Farrar $16.00 (978-0-374-37740-3); paper $5.95 (978-0-374-47955-8). 32pp. A man discovers that the most valuable things in life are usually found at home.

4409 Singer, Marilyn. *Didi and Daddy on the Promenade* (PS–K). Illus. by Marie-Louise Gay. 2001, Clarion $14.00 (978-0-618-04640-9). 32pp. Didi and her father love to walk and play on Sunday mornings on the Brooklyn Heights Promenade that overlooks the Manhattan skyline. (Rev: BCCB 4/01; BL 4/1/01; HBG 10/01; SLJ 5/01)

4410 Singer, Marilyn. *The One and Only Me* (PS–K). Illus. by Nicole Rubel. 2000, HarperCollins $9.95 (978-0-694-01279-4). A little girl explains how she is like various members of her extended family in this charming family story illustrated with brightly colored cartoons. (Rev: HBG 10/00; SLJ 7/00)

4411 Skeers, Linda. *The Impossible Patriotism Project* (1–3). Illus. by Ard Hoyt. 2007, Dial $16.99 (978-0-8037-3138-7). 32pp. In this touching yet humorous book, a boy discovers the true nature of patriotism as he honors his father, who is serving overseas in the military, as part of a school project. (Rev: BL 5/1/07; SLJ 8/07)

4412 Slier, Deborah. *Hello Baby* (PS). Illus. 1988, Checkerboard $2.95 (978-1-56288-087-3). 12pp. A board book that shows basic actions, such as sitting and crying, for the toddler. Also use: *Baby's Words; Busy Baby* (both 1988). (Rev: BCCB 7–8/88; BL 7/88)

4413 Smalls, Irene. *Kevin and His Dad* (PS–1). Illus. by Michael Hays. 1999, Little, Brown $15.95 (978-0-316-79899-0). 32pp. An African American boy and his dad spend a day together — first helping around the house, then playing baseball, and going to a movie. (Rev: BCCB 5/99; BL 2/15/99; HBG 10/99; SLJ 5/99)

4414 Smalls, Irene. *My Nana and Me* (PS–K). Illus. by Cathy Ann Johnson. 2005, Little, Brown $15.99 (978-0-316-16821-2). 32pp. An African American preschooler tells about a very special day spent with her grandmother. (Rev: BL 11/1/05; SLJ 10/05)

4415 Smith, Patricia. *Janna and the Kings* (PS–2). Illus. by Aaron Boyd. 2003, Lee & Low $16.95 (978-1-58430-088-5). Janna, a young African American girl, hesitantly returns to the barbershop her grandfather loved before he died. (Rev: BL 11/15/03; HBG 4/04; SLJ 11/03)

4416 Smith, Will. *Just the Two of Us* (PS–1). Illus. by Kadir Nelson. 2001, Scholastic $16.95 (978-0-439-08792-6). 32pp. Smith uses his song "Just the Two of Us" as the foundation for this celebration of a father's love for his son. (Rev: BL 7/01; HBG 10/01; SLJ 6/01)

4417 Smothers, Ethel Footman. *Auntee Edna* (K–3). Illus. by Wil Clay. 2001, Eerdmans $16.00 (978-0-

8028-5154-3). Tokee doesn't look forward to staying the night with elderly Auntee Edna but has a wonderful time. (Rev: HBG 10/01; SLJ 8/01)

4418 Smythe, Anne. *Islands* (K–2). Illus. by Laszlo Gal. 1996, Douglas & McIntyre $14.95 (978-0-88899-238-3). 32pp. A mother and a daughter skate across a frozen lake to three small islands and examine wildlife in this quiet picture book. (Rev: BL 12/1/96)

4419 Soman, David, and Jacky Davis. *Ladybug Girl* (PS–2). Illus. by David Soman. 2008, Dial $16.99 (978-0-8037-3195-0). 32pp. Lulu, wearing red-and-black polka-dot wings, is on her own for the morning and must make up her own diversions. (Rev: BL 4/1/08; SLJ 3/08)

4420 Soto, Gary. *If the Shoe Fits* (PS–3). Illus. by Terry Widener. 2002, Penguin $16.99 (978-0-399-23420-0). 32pp. Rigo, who is sick of wearing hand-me-downs, gets a new pair of loafers for his ninth birthday. (Rev: BCCB 3/02; BL 1/1–15/02; HB 7/02; HBG 10/02; SLJ 1/02)

4421 Spalding, Andrea. *Bottled Sunshine* (1–3). Illus. by Ruth Ohi. 2005, Fitzhenry & Whiteside $16.95 (978-1-55041-703-6). A young boy's memories of his last visit with his grandmother provide comfort after her death; the illustrations complement the gentle story. (Rev: SLJ 10/05)

4422 Spalding, Andrea. *The Most Beautiful Kite in the World* (PS–2). Illus. by Leslie Watts. 2003, Fitzhenry & Whiteside $15.95 (978-1-55041-716-6). Jenny is disappointed when her father gives her a homemade kite, but she forgets her pique as she learns to add enhancements. (Rev: SLJ 8/03)

4423 Spinelli, Eileen. *When Mama Comes Home Tonight* (PS–1). Illus. by Jane Dyer. 1998, Simon & Schuster $14.00 (978-0-689-81065-7). 32pp. A touching picture book that describes the activities that a mother and child engage in when the two are reunited after Mother gets home from work. (Rev: BL 7/98*; HBG 3/99; SLJ 11/98)

4424 Spinelli, Eileen. *When You Are Happy* (PS–2). Illus. by Geraldo Valério. 2006, Simon & Schuster $16.95 (978-0-689-86251-9). 40pp. Members of a family reassure a little girl that they love her. (Rev: BL 3/1/06; SLJ 3/06)

4425 Spiro, Ruth. *Lester Fizz, Bubble-Gum Artist* (2–4). Illus. by Thor Wickstrom. 2008, Dutton $16.99 (978-0-525-47861-4). 32pp. Lester, an untalented individual in a family full of artists, finally finds inspiration in a mouthful of gum; a funny story full of wordplay. (Rev: BLO 10/7/08; SLJ 10/08)

4426 Springer, Susan Woodward. *Seldovia Sam and the Very Large Clam* (2–4). Illus. by Amy Meissner. Series: Seldovia Sam. 2003, Alaska Northwest paper $6.95 (978-0-88240-570-4). 64pp. Another adventure for Sam and his dog in Alaska, this time involving a perilous search for a giant clam. (Rev: SLJ 4/04)

4427 Stanton, Karen. *Papi's Gift* (PS–2). Illus. by Rene King Moreno. 2007, Boyds Mills $16.95 (978-1-59078-422-8). 32pp. Graciela desperately misses her father, who has left their village in Mexico to pick fruit in California; she treasures their weekly phone calls and prays for his return. (Rev: BL 4/15/07)

4428 Steptoe, John. *Baby Says* (PS). Illus. by author. 1988, Lothrop LB $17.89 (978-0-688-07424-1). 32pp. An almost wordless picture book catching the exchange between a baby and a big brother. (Rev: BL 4/1/88; HB 7/88; SLJ 3/88)

4429 Steptoe, John. *Stevie* (PS–2). Illus. by author. 1969, HarperCollins paper $6.99 (978-0-06-443122-4). 32pp. A small African American boy eloquently expresses his resentment at having to share his possessions and mother with a temporary younger boarder who becomes "kinda like a little brother"; illustrated in bold line and color.

4430 Stevenson, Harvey. *Grandpa's House* (PS–1). Illus. by author. 1994, Hyperion LB $15.49 (978-1-56282-589-8). A simple text is used with effective pictures to convey the fine time young Woody has during a visit with his grandfather. (Rev: SLJ 6/94)

4431 Stewart, Sarah. *The Friend* (1–3). Illus. by David Small. 2004, Farrar $16.00 (978-0-374-32463-6). Belle, daughter of wealthy and distant parents, and Bea, African American housekeeper, spend much of their time together at the family's house on the beach. (Rev: BL 8/04; SLJ 8/04)

4432 Stilz, Carol C. *Grandma Buffalo, May and Me* (K–3). Illus. by Constance R. Bergum. 1995, Sasquatch $14.95 (978-1-57061-015-8). 32pp. Poppy visits parts of Montana where her great-grandmother once lived and does the same things her ancestor did, like plant an apple tree and feed the buffalo. (Rev: BL 10/1/95; SLJ 12/95)

4433 Stoeke, Janet Morgan. *Waiting for May* (K–3). Illus. by author. 2005, Dutton $16.99 (978-0-525-47098-4). A family adopting a girl from China waits impatiently for the journey there to begin. (Rev: SLJ 6/05)

4434 Struve-Bodeen, Stephanie. *The Best Worst Brother* (K–4). Illus. by Charlotte Fremaux. 2005, Woodbine $15.95 (978-1-890627-68-3). Emma discovers that it will take hard work to teach Isaac, her little brother who has Down's syndrome, to use sign language in this sequel to *We'll Paint the Octopus Red* (1998). (Rev: SLJ 9/05)

4435 Sturges, Philemon. *How Do You Make a Baby Smile?* (PS–1). Illus. by Bridget Strevens-Marzo. 2007, HarperCollins $16.99 (978-0-06-076072-4). 24pp. This story uses animals and rhyming text to show young children different ways to make babies smile. (Rev: BL 7/07; SLJ 7/07)

4436 Stuve-Bodeen, Stephanie. *We'll Paint the Octopus Red* (PS–2). Illus. by Pam DeVito. 1998, Woodbine $15.95 (978-1-890627-06-5). 28pp. A young girl thinks of all the things that she and her new baby brother can do together. When she is told that he has Down syndrome, she maintains that they still will do those things, though now each activity might take a little longer. (Rev: BL 9/15/98; HBG 3/99; SLJ 12/98)

4437 Sugarman, Brynn Olenberg. *Rebecca's Journey Home* (PS–2). Illus. by Michelle Shapiro. 2006, Lerner $17.95 (978-1-58013-157-5). 32pp. This tender story of a Jewish American family adopting a Vietnamese baby girl also provides insight into both cultures. (Rev: BL 1/1–15/07; SLJ 11/06)

4438 Sullivan, Sarah. *Dear Baby: Letters from Your Big Brother* (PS–K). Illus. by Paul Meisel. 2005, Candlewick $14.99 (978-0-7636-2126-1). 40pp. During the first year of his baby sister's life, her big brother records his thoughts about her development and his growing love for her. (Rev: BL 9/15/05; SLJ 9/05)

4439 Taylor, Ann. *Baby Dance* (PS). Illus. by Marjorie van Heerden. Series: Harper Growing Tree. 1999, HarperCollins $6.99 (978-0-694-01206-0). In this board book, an African American dad and his baby daughter play to a series of catchy rhymes. (Rev: BCCB 5/99; SLJ 3/99)

4440 Tessler, Manya. *Yuki's Ride Home* (K–3). Illus. by author. 2008, Bloomsbury $16.95 (978-1-59990-023-0). 32pp. After spending the day with her grandmother, a Japanese girl faces a bicycle ride in the dark. (Rev: BL 4/1/08; LMC 3/08; SLJ 2/08)

4441 Thiel, Annie. *Chloe's New Baby Brother* (1–4). Illus. by William M. Edwards and Karen Marjoribanks. 2006, Playdate Kids $14.95 (978-1-933721-01-9). Only child Chloe learns that the arrival of a new sibling will not affect her parents' love for her. (Rev: SLJ 9/06)

4442 Thomas, Eliza. *The Red Blanket* (PS–2). Illus. by Joe Cepeda. 2004, Scholastic $15.95 (978-0-439-32253-9). 32pp. This endearing tale of a young woman's journey to China to adopt a child is based on events from the author's life. (Rev: BL 5/15/04; SLJ 7/04)

4443 Thomas, Elizabeth. *Green Beans* (PS–2). Illus. by Vicki Jo Redenbaugh. 1992, Carolrhoda LB $15.95 (978-0-87614-708-5). 32pp. Gramma, who is trying too hard to make her green beans grow, lets granddaughter Dorothea take over. (Rev: BCCB 2/93; BL 9/15/92; SLJ 1/93)

4444 Thomas, Naturi. *Uh-oh! It's Mama's Birthday!* (PS–3). Illus. by Keinyo White. 1997, Whitman LB $13.95 (978-0-8075-8268-8). 24pp. An African American boy gives his mother what she really wants on her birthday: a big hug. (Rev: BL 2/15/97; HB 3/97; SLJ 5/97)

4445 Thomas, Patricia. *Red Sled* (PS–2). Illus. by Chris L. Demarest. 2008, Boyds Mills $16.95 (978-1-59078-559-1). 32pp. A father and son go sledding at night in this simple story told in rhyming pairs of words. (Rev: BL 9/1/08; HB 9/08; SLJ 8/08)

4446 Thong, Roseanne. *Tummy Girl* (PS–K). Illus. by Sam Williams. 2007, Holt $15.95 (978-0-8050-7609-7). 32pp. Rhyming text and a photo-album format celebrate a baby growing into a toddler and then into a schoolgirl. (Rev: BL 4/1/07)

4447 Tiffault, Benette W. *A Quilt for Elizabeth* (1–4). Illus. by Mary McConnell. 1992, Centering paper $8.95 (978-1-56123-034-1). After Elizabeth accepts her father's death, she and her grandmother begin a quilt using patches of his clothing. (Rev: SLJ 8/92)

4448 Tompert, Ann. *Will You Come Back for Me?* (PS). Illus. by Robin Kramer. 1988, Whitman LB $14.95 (978-0-8075-9112-3); paper $6.95 (978-0-8075-9113-0). 32pp. Her mother must go to work and the little girl must go to day care, but she worries that her mother won't come back for her. (Rev: BCCB 12/88; BL 11/1/88; SLJ 1/89)

4449 Toten, Teresa. *Bright Red Kisses* (PS–K). Illus. by Deirdre Betteridge. 2005, Annick LB $19.95 (978-1-55037-909-9); paper $7.95 (978-1-55037-908-2). 32pp. A young girl helps her mother prepare for an evening out, from running the bath to choosing the best lipstick, which will kiss her when her mother returns. (Rev: BL 1/1–15/06)

4450 Tunnell, Michael O. *Mailing May* (K–3). Illus. by Ted Rand. 1997, Morrow LB $15.89 (978-0-688-12879-1). 32pp. Unable to afford a rail ticket, May's father sends her parcel post to visit her grandmother. (Rev: BL 8/97; HB 9/97; HBG 3/98; SLJ 9/97)

4451 Turner-Denstaedt, Melanie. *The Hat That Wore Clara B.* (K–3). Illus. by Frank Morrison. 2009, Farrar $16.95 (978-0-374-32794-1). 32pp. Even though she has been told not to touch the impressive hat that her grandmother wears to a special Sunday service, Clara secretly attempts to try it on, accidentally crushes it, and is generously forgiven. (Rev: BCCB 7–8/09; SLJ 5/09)

4452 Urdahl, Catherine. *Emma's Question* (PS–K). Illus. by Janine Dawson. 2009, Charlesbridge $16.95 (978-1-58089-145-5); paper $7.95 (978-1-58089-146-2). 32pp. Emma's grandmother is in the hospital, and Emma has lots of questions, including "Are you going to die?" (Rev: BCCB 2/09; BL 2/1/09; SLJ 5/09)

4453 Vamos, Samantha R. *Before You Were Here, Mi Amor* (PS–2). Illus. by Santiago Cohen. 2009, Viking $15.99 (978-0-670-06301-7). 32pp. In English interlaced with Spanish words, a mother tells her unborn child how the happy family is preparing for the little one's arrival. (Rev: BCCB 4/09; BL 2/15/09; SLJ 3/09)

4454 Van den Abeele, Veronique. *Still My Grandma* (K–2). Illus. by Claude K. Dubois. 2007, Eerdmans $16.00 (978-0-8028-5323-3). 28pp. Camille watches her grandma sink into Alzheimer's disease and tries to help and show her love when she can. (Rev: BL 10/15/07; SLJ 10/07)

4455 Van Leeuwen, Jean. *Benny and Beautiful Baby Delilah* (PS–K). Illus. by LeUyen Pham. 2006, Dial $16.99 (978-0-8037-2891-2). 32pp. Bennie finds his "beautiful" baby sister very trying until he succeeds in making her smile; excellent artwork adds to the heartwarming story. (Rev: BL 2/1/06; SLJ 3/06*)

4456 Velasquez, Eric. *Grandma's Records* (K–3). Illus. 2001, Walker LB $17.85 (978-0-8027-8761-3). 32pp. A young boy enjoys summers full of Latin music with his grandmother in Spanish Harlem in this novel based on the author's own memories. (Rev: BL 5/15/01; HBG 10/01; SLJ 9/01)

4457 Vestergaard, Hope. *Driving Daddy* (PS–1). Illus. by Thierry Courtin. 2003, Dutton $6.99 (978-0-525-47032-8). 24pp. A small-format book in which a little boy gets to ride on his father's shoulders. (Rev: BL 3/1/03; HBG 10/03; SLJ 3/03)

4458 Vigil-Pinon, Evangelina. *Marina's Muumuu / El Muumuu de Marina* (2–5). Illus. by Pablo Torrecilla. 2001, Arte Publico $14.95 (978-1-55885-350-8). 32pp. A bilingual story about a girl named Marina who dreams of wearing a colorful, tropical muumuu like those from her grandmother's home. (Rev: BL 1/1–15/02; SLJ 1/02)

4459 Viorst, Judith. *Alexander and the Terrible, Horrible, No Good, Very Bad Day* (K–3). Illus. by Ray Cruz. 1972, Macmillan LB $14.00 (978-0-689-30072-1); paper $4.99 (978-0-689-71173-2). Alexander wakes up to a bad day and things get progressively worse as the hours wear on, until he thinks he may escape it all and go to Australia.

4460 Viorst, Judith. *Alexander, Who's Not (Do You Hear Me? I Mean It!) Going to Move* (PS–3). Illus. by Robin P. Glasser. 1995, Simon & Schuster LB $15.00 (978-0-689-31958-7). 42pp. Alexander of bad-day fame, faces another crisis when he adamantly refuses to move to the family's new home. (Rev: BCCB 11/95; BL 8/95*; SLJ 10/95*)

4461 Viorst, Judith. *I'll Fix Anthony* (PS–3). Illus. by Arnold Lobel. 1969, Macmillan paper $4.99 (978-0-689-71202-9). 32pp. A young boy has a field day planning revenge on an older brother.

4462 Viorst, Judith. *Nobody Here but Me* (PS–2). Illus. by Christine Davenier. 2008, Farrar $16.95 (978-0-374-35540-1). 40pp. It's almost dinnertime and everybody in the house is busy as a little boy wanders around trying to get their attention in this cheerful look at how families operate. (Rev: BL 9/15/08; SLJ 8/08)

4463 Voake, Charlotte. *Hello Twins* (PS). Illus. by author. 2006, Candlewick $15.99 (978-0-7636-3003-4). 32pp. Little Charlotte and Simon may be twins, but they are different and they like it that way. (Rev: BL 5/15/06; SLJ 7/06)

4464 Waboose, Jan B. *Firedancers* (1–4). Illus. by C. J. Taylor. 2000, Stoddart $14.95 (978-0-7737-3138-7). 32pp. A young Ojibwa girl visits Smooth Rock Island at night and joins her grandmother as a Firedancer. (Rev: BL 7/00)

4465 Wahl, Jan. *Mabel Ran Away with the Toys* (PS–2). Illus. by Liza Woodruff. 2000, Charlesbridge $16.95 (978-1-58089-059-5); paper $6.95 (978-1-58089-067-0). Little Mabel has problems adjusting when a new baby disrupts her schedule. (Rev: HBG 3/01; SLJ 9/00)

4466 Waldherr, Kris. *Harvest* (PS–1). Illus. 2001, Walker LB $16.85 (978-0-8027-8793-4). 32pp. A girl and her mother harvest and prepare fruits and vegetables from the garden in order to prepare for winter in this simple yet memorable autumn story. (Rev: BL 11/15/01; HBG 3/02; SLJ 11/01)

4467 Walvoord, Linda. *Razzamadaddy* (PS–1). Illus. by Sachiko Yoshikawa. 2004, Marshall Cavendish $14.95 (978-0-7614-5158-7). A father and son enjoy a day at the beach, depicted in rhyming text and vivid illustrations. (Rev: SLJ 7/04)

4468 Wangerin, Walter. *I Am My Grandpa's Enkelin* (1–3). Illus. by Don Tate. 2007, Paraclete $18.95 (978-1-55725-468-9). 32pp. A young girl describes her German immigrant grandfather's farm and the lessons he has taught her in this fictional memoir that extends into the girl's adult years. (Rev: BL 2/15/08; SLJ 6/08)

4469 Weston, Tamson. *Hey, Pancakes!* (PS–1). Illus. by Stephen Gammell. 2003, Harcourt $17.00 (978-0-15-216502-4). Rhyming verse and mixed-media artwork portray three siblings energetically cooking up a sloppy batch of pancakes. (Rev: HBG 4/04; SLJ 9/03)

4470 Wheeler, Lisa. *Jazz Baby* (PS–1). Illus. by R. Gregory Christie. 2007, Harcourt $16.00 (978-0-15-202522-9). 40pp. A bouncing African American baby enjoys music along with the rest of the family in this rhythmic volume with vibrant illustrations. (Rev: BCCB 12/07; BL 10/15/07; HB 1/08; SLJ 1/08)

4471 Whelan, Gloria. *Jam and Jelly by Holly and Nelly* (K–2). Illus. by Gijsbert van Frankenhuyzen. 2002, Sleeping Bear $17.95 (978-1-58536-109-0). 48pp. A captivating story of a mother's determination to buy her daughter a coat so she can go to school in the cold. (Rev: BL 12/15/02; SLJ 1/03)

4472 Whybrow, Ian. *A Baby for Grace* (PS–1). Illus. by Christian Birmingham. 1998, Kingfisher $14.95 (978-0-7534-5142-7). 32pp. Everything that a young girl tries to do to be helpful around the house, including holding the new baby, is greeted with the same response, "No, Grace." (Rev: BL 10/1/98; HBG 3/99; SLJ 1/99)

4473 Wigersma, Tanneke. *Baby Brother* (PS–1). Illus. by Nynke Mare Talsma. 2005, Front St $16.95 (978-1-932425-55-0). In a letter to her grandmother, little Mia focuses on her cat's delivery of five kittens, only mentioning the birth of her baby brother at the end; illustrations fill in the gaps. (Rev: SLJ 11/05)

4474 Wild, Margaret. *Our Granny* (PS–1). Illus. by Julie Vivas. 1994, Ticknor $17.00 (978-0-395-67023-1). 32pp. All kinds of grandmothers from the glamorous and kinky to cuddly and plain are celebrated in this lively picture book. (Rev: BCCB 5/94; BL 1/15/94*; HB 5/94; SLJ 4/94*)

4475 Willhoite, Michael. *Daddy's Roommate* (PS–2). Illus. 1990, Alyson paper $10.95 (978-1-55583-118-9). 32pp. After his parents' divorce, a young boy finds that his father has a male partner and on weekends the boy enjoys visiting the two of them. (Rev: BCCB 2/91; BL 3/1/91; SLJ 4/91)

4476 Williams, Karen Lynn. *Circles of Hope* (PS–K). Illus. by Linda Saport. 2005, Eerdmans $16.00 (978-0-8028-5276-2). 32pp. In Haiti, a boy called Facile struggles to grow a tree as a gift for his new baby sister, finally building a protective circle of stones. (Rev: BL 5/15/05; SLJ 4/05)

4477 Williams, Linda E. *The Best Winds* (K–3). Illus. by Eujin Kim Neilan. 2006, Boyds Mills $16.95 (978-1-59078-274-3). 32pp. Jinho ignores his grandfather's stories of ancient Korean traditions as the two work to create a kite, but when the young boy carelessly damages the kite he learns to appreciate his cultural heritage. (Rev: BL 4/1/06; SLJ 3/06)

4478 Williams, Vera B. *A Chair for Always* (PS–2). Illus. by author. 2009, HarperCollins $16.99 (978-0-

06-172279-0). 40pp. The rose-covered chair first featured in *A Chair for My Mother* (1982) plays an important role in this fourth book, in which Rosa is anticipating a new cousin and there is tension about the dilapidated state of the beloved chair. (Rev: BL 5/15/09; SLJ 5/09) 🎧

4479 Williams, Vera B. *A Chair for My Mother* (PS–2). Illus. by author. 1982, Greenwillow $17.89 (978-0-688-00915-1). 32pp. After fire destroys their home, Rose and her mother and grandmother save to buy a nice new chair. Two sequels are: *Something Special for Me* (1983); *Music, Music for Everyone* (1984).

4480 Williams, Vera B. *Lucky Song* (PS–K). Illus. 1997, Greenwillow $14.89 (978-0-688-14460-9). 24pp. Evie is a lucky girl because all of her wants and needs are satisfied by her loving family. (Rev: BL 10/1/97*; HB 9/97; HBG 3/98; SLJ 8/97*)

4481 Wilson, Karma. *Mama Always Comes Home* (PS). Illus. by Brooke Dyer. 2005, HarperCollins LB $16.89 (978-0-06-057506-9). A mother tells her child that she will always come home, using animal stories as reassuring examples. (Rev: SLJ 5/05)

4482 Wilson, Sarah. *Friends and Pals and Brothers, Too* (PS–1). Illus. by Leo Landry. 2008, Holt $16.95 (978-0-8050-7643-1). 32pp. Two young brothers play together throughout the year in this engaging picture book. (Rev: BL 5/15/08; SLJ 5/08)

4483 Winch, John. *Keeping Up with Grandma* (PS–3). Illus. 2000, Holiday House $16.95 (978-0-8234-1563-2). 32pp. Grandma wants to start mountain climbing, whitewater canoeing, and hot-air ballooning but she and Grandpa later decide that their usual quiet life is better. (Rev: BL 11/15/00; HBG 3/01; SLJ 11/00)

4484 Wing, Natasha L. *Jalapeno Bagels* (PS–2). Illus. by Robert Casilla. 1996, Simon & Schuster $15.00 (978-0-689-80530-1). 32pp. Pablo, who comes from a racially mixed family, finds his life is enriched by both cultures. (Rev: BL 6/1–15/96; SLJ 7/96)

4485 Winthrop, Elizabeth. *I'm the Boss!* (PS–1). Illus. by Mary Morgan. 1994, Holiday House LB $15.95 (978-0-8234-1113-9). 32pp. Julia is tired of being bossed around and wants her chance to be a dictator. (Rev: BL 5/1/94; SLJ 7/94)

4486 Winthrop, Elizabeth. *Promises* (1–3). Illus. by Betsy Lewin. 2000, Clarion $16.00 (978-0-395-82272-2). 32pp. Sarah's mother is very ill with cancer and the young girl misses the good times they had before she became sick. (Rev: BL 6/1–15/00; HBG 10/00; SLJ 6/00)

4487 Winthrop, Elizabeth. *Squashed in the Middle* (K–3). Illus. by Pat Cummings. 2005, Holt $16.95 (978-0-8050-6497-1). 32pp. Middle child Daisy gets her family's attention when she goes to a friend's house all on her own. (Rev: BL 4/1/05; SLJ 6/05)

4488 Wolff, Ashley. *Me Baby, You Baby* (PS). Illus. by author. 2004, Dutton $14.99 (978-0-525-46952-0). This book follows two toddlers (a white girl and a black boy) and their mothers through a busy day,

including a visit to the zoo. (Rev: BL 3/1/04*; HB 3/04; SLJ 3/04)

4489 Wong, Janet S. *Homegrown House* (K–3). Illus. by E. B. Lewis. 2009, Simon & Schuster $16.99 (978-0-689-84718-9). 40pp. A little girl reluctantly prepares for yet another move to yet another house. (Rev: BL 6/1–15/09; SLJ 7/09)

4490 Wood, Douglas. *Grandad's Prayers of the Earth* (K–3). Illus. by P. J. Lynch. 1999, Candlewick $16.99 (978-0-7636-0660-2). 32pp. A boy and his grandfather talk about prayer, and after the old man's death, the boy remembers his gentle ways and his loving faith. (Rev: BL 12/1/99; HBG 3/00; SLJ 1/00)

4491 Woodson, Jacqueline. *Visiting Day* (K–2). Illus. by James Ransome. 2002, Scholastic $15.95 (978-0-590-40005-3). 32pp. This is a gentle family story of a little African American girl's visit to her father in prison. (Rev: BCCB 12/02; BL 11/1/02; HB 11/02; HBG 3/03; SLJ 9/02)

4492 Woodtor, Dee Parmer. *Big Meeting* (K–3). Illus. by Dolores Johnson. 1996, Simon & Schuster $16.00 (978-0-689-31993-8). 32pp. A celebration of a down-home family reunion is chronicled in this joyous book. (Rev: BL 9/1/96; SLJ 9/96)

4493 Wyse, Lois, and Molly Rose Goldman. *How to Take Your Grandmother to the Museum* (1–3). Illus. by Marie-Louise Gay. 1998, Workman $12.95 (978-0-7611-0990-7). 48pp. When a young boy discovers that his grandmother has never been to New York City's American Museum of Natural History, he takes her on his own special guided tour. (Rev: BL 1/1–15/99; HBG 3/99; SLJ 12/98)

4494 Yaccarino, Dan. *Every Friday* (PS–K). Illus. 2007, Holt $16.95 (978-0-8050-7724-7). 32pp. A father and son enjoy their weekly Friday breakfast together. (Rev: BL 2/1/07)

4495 Yektai, Niki. *Triplets* (PS–2). Illus. 1998, Millbrook LB $21.40 (978-0-7613-0351-0). 32pp. This lively picture book explores the rivalry among three siblings and its humorous consequences. (Rev: BL 5/15/98; HBG 10/98; SLJ 8/98)

4496 Yolen, Jane. *Soft House* (PS–K). Illus. by Wendy A. Halperin. 2005, Candlewick $15.99 (978-0-7636-1697-7). 32pp. To fight boredom on a rainy day, a girl and her younger brother use household items to build a cozy fort. (Rev: BL 11/1/05)

4497 Young, Ed. *My Mei Mei* (PS–2). Illus. 2006, Philomel $16.99 (978-0-399-24339-4). 32pp. A moving story about Antonia — who herself was adopted from China — and her difficult adjustment to life with her newly adopted infant sister, also from China. (Rev: BL 1/1–15/06; SLJ 2/06*)

4498 Zagwyn, Deborah Turney. *Apple Batter* (K–3). Illus. 1999, Tricycle $14.95 (978-1-883672-92-8). 32pp. Loretta plants and cares for three apple trees while her young son develops an interest in baseball in this picture book that ends with both interests converging. (Rev: BL 1/1–15/00; HBG 3/00; SLJ 12/99)

4499 Zalben, Jane Breskin. *Baby Babka, the Gorgeous Genius* (K–4). Illus. by Victoria Chess. 2004, Clarion $15.00 (978-0-618-23489-9). 38pp. Beryl is disappointed when the new baby is another boy, but Uncle Morty has a solution. (Rev: SLJ 11/04)

4500 Zamorano, Ana. *Let's Eat!* (PS–2). Illus. by Julie Vivas. 1997, Scholastic $15.95 (978-0-590-13444-6). 32pp. A loving Spanish family enjoys Mama's food even more when she returns home from the hospital with baby Rosa. (Rev: BCCB 4/97; BL 5/15/97; SLJ 4/97*)

4501 Zemach, Margot. *Eating up Gladys* (PS–2). Illus. by Kaethe Zemach. 2005, Scholastic $16.99 (978-0-439-66490-5). 32pp. When Gladys, their bossy older sister, pushes them just a little too far, younger siblings Rose and Hilda plot a spectacular revenge. (Rev: BL 9/1/05; SLJ 9/05)

4502 Ziefert, Harriet. *Bigger than Daddy* (PS). Illus. by Elliot Kreloff. 2006, Blue Apple $15.95 (978-1-59354-147-7). 36pp. On a trip to the park, Edward wants to switch roles with his daddy and do grown-up things. (Rev: BL 5/1/06; SLJ 8/06)

4503 Ziefert, Harriet. *Clara Ann Cookie* (PS–1). Illus. by Emily Bolam. 1999, Houghton $15.00 (978-0-395-92324-5). 32pp. After waking, Clara Ann is in a terrible mood until Mom makes a game of getting dressed and preparing to face the world. (Rev: BL 3/1/99; HBG 10/99; SLJ 4/99)

4504 Ziefert, Harriet. *Grandma, It's for You!* (PS–1). Illus. by Lauren Browne. 2006, Blue Apple $15.95 (978-1-59354-109-5). Little Lulu fashions a very special hat to give to her grandmother. (Rev: SLJ 8/06)

4505 Ziefert, Harriet. *My Friend Grandpa* (K–3). Illus. by Robert Wurzburg. 2004, Blue Apple $15.95 (978-1-59354-063-0). A celebration of the close relationship Emma shares with her grandfather and the happy times they spend in the country. (Rev: SLJ 11/04)

4506 Ziefert, Harriet. *A New Coat for Anna* (K–3). Illus. by Anita Lobel. 1986, Knopf paper $6.99 (978-0-394-89861-2). 40pp. It's been a long time since Anna has had a new coat, and her mother vows to get one for her in this story of post-World War II Europe. (Rev: BCCB 3/87; BL 12/15/86; SLJ 12/86)

4507 Ziefert, Harriet. *31 Uses for a Mom* (PS–K). Illus. by Rebecca Doughty. 2003, Penguin $12.99 (978-0-399-23862-8). 32pp. Moms turn out to be fairly useful things in this list that covers a wide range of attributes. (Rev: BL 1/1–15/03; HBG 10/03; SLJ 3/03)

4508 Ziefert, Harriet. *Waiting for Baby* (PS–K). Illus. by Emily Bolam. 1998, Holt $13.95 (978-0-8050-5929-8). After weeks of suspense, Max gets so tired of waiting for his brother to be born that he goes out to play and then, of course, the blessed event occurs. (Rev: BL 12/15/98; HBG 3/99; SLJ 5/99)

4509 Zisk, Mary. *The Best Single Mom in the World: How I Was Adopted* (PS–K). Illus. by author. 2001, Whitman LB $16.99 (978-0-8075-0666-0). A little girl and her mother tell the tale of her adoption across the sea. (Rev: HBG 3/02; SLJ 1/02)

4510 Zolotow, Charlotte. *A Father Like That* (K–3). Illus. by LeUyen Pham. 2007, HarperCollins $16.99 (978-0-06-027864-9). 40pp. First published in 1971 and now updated with new illustrations, this is the story of a young African American boy who imagines the father who left before he was born. (Rev: BL 5/15/07; SLJ 7/07)

4511 Zolotow, Charlotte. *If It Weren't for You* (PS–2). Illus. by G. Brian Karas. 2006, HarperCollins $15.99 (978-0-06-027875-5). As big sister fantasizes about what life would be like without her younger sibling, her younger sister behaves with such uncharacteristic kindness that the older girl decides she'd just as soon keep her around. (Rev: SLJ 10/06)

4512 Zolotow, Charlotte. *The Quarreling Book* (K–2). Illus. by Arnold Lobel. 1963, HarperCollins paper $6.99 (978-0-06-443034-0). 32pp. Father's failure to kiss mother one morning triggers a series of quarrels, but the pet dog sets things right. Also use: *The Hating Book* (1969).

4513 Zolotow, Charlotte. *William's Doll* (PS–3). Illus. by William Pene du Bois. 1972, HarperCollins paper $6.99 (978-0-06-443067-8). 32pp. William wanted a doll, much to his father's dismay; but when Grandma comes to visit she presents William with a doll, saying that now he will have an opportunity to practice being a good father.

4514 Zuckerman, Linda. *I Will Hold You 'til You Sleep* (PS). Illus. by Jon J. Muth. 2006, Scholastic $16.99 (978-0-439-43420-1). With poetic text and gentle illustrations, this book celebrates parents' love for a child throughout the years. (Rev: SLJ 10/06)

4515 Zweibel, Alan. *Our Tree Named Steve* (1–3). Illus. by David Catrow. 2005, Penguin $15.99 (978-0-399-23722-5). A sad story about a beloved tree knocked down by a storm. (Rev: BL 2/1/04; SLJ 4/05)

FRIENDSHIP STORIES

4516 Aliki. *We Are Best Friends* (K–3). Illus. by author. 1982, Morrow paper $6.99 (978-0-688-07037-3). 32pp. Robert is at a loss when his best friend moves away.

4517 Appelt, Kathi. *Bubba and Beau, Best Friends* (PS–K). Illus. by Arthur Howard. 2002, Harcourt $16.00 (978-0-15-202060-6). 32pp. Bubba, a little boy, and Beau, his puppy, are unhappy when the smelly blanket they love is washed and now smells of soap. (Rev: BCCB 4/02; BL 4/1/02; HBG 10/02; SLJ 7/02)

4518 Atwood, Margaret. *Up in the Tree* (PS–2). Illus. 2006, Groundwood $14.95 (978-0-88899-729-6). 32pp. In this engaging two-color picture book first published in 1976, the Canadian author tells the story of two boys who make their home in a tree. (Rev: BL 4/1/06)

4519 Baker, Roberta. *Olive's First Sleepover* (1–3). Illus. by Debbie Tilley. 2007, Little, Brown $16.99 (978-0-316-73418-9). 32pp. Olive's first sleepover at her friend Lizard's house is full of fun and, when the lights go out, spooky sounds. (Rev: BL 7/07; SLJ 7/07)

4520 Barrows, Annie. *Bound to Be Bad* (1–3). Illus. by Sophie Blackall. 2008, Chronicle $14.99 (978-0-

8118-6265-3). 124pp. Ivy learns about St. Francis and resolves to reform herself as well as Bean and the bully Matt. (Rev: BL 2/1/09; HB 3/09) ⌒

4521 Beaumont, Karen. *Being Friends* (PS–2). Illus. by Joy Allen. 2002, Dial $16.99 (978-0-8037-2529-4). 32pp. Two girls, best friends despite their different personalities, have fun together in this rhyming picture book. (Rev: BL 9/15/02; HBG 10/02; SLJ 7/02)

4522 Blabey, Aaron. *Pearl Barley and Charlie Parsley* (K–1). Illus. by author. 2008, Front St. $16.95 (978-1-59078-596-6). 32pp. Pearl and Charlie are best friends even though they are different in every way. (Rev: BCCB 11/08; SLJ 9/08)

4523 Blake, Quentin. *Fantastic Daisy Artichoke* (PS–1). Illus. by author. 2001, Red Fox paper $11.00 (978-0-09-940006-6). Rhythmic text and bright, lively drawings tell the story of the fun two children had when they met their friend Daisy. (Rev: SLJ 10/01)

4524 Bley, Anette. *A Friend* (PS–1). Illus. by author. 2009, Kane $14.95 (978-1-935279-00-6). 36pp. Diverse scenarios demonstrate the value of friendship. (Rev: BL 3/1/09)

4525 Bluthenthal, Diana Cain. *Matilda the Moocher* (PS–2). Illus. 1997, Orchard LB $16.99 (978-0-531-33003-6). 32pp. Libby gets tired of her friend Matilda's constant borrowing of her possessions and money. (Rev: BL 3/15/97; SLJ 5/97)

4526 Bottner, Barbara. *Rosa's Room* (PS–1). Illus. by Beth Spiegel. 2004, Peachtree $15.95 (978-1-56145-302-3). 32pp. Rosa's room in her new house seems strangely empty until she finds a friend to share it. (Rev: BL 4/1/04; SLJ 5/04)

4527 Brown, Laurie Krasny. *How to Be a Friend: A Guide to Making Friends and Keeping Them* (K–3). Illus. by Marc Brown. 1998, Little, Brown $14.95 (978-0-316-10913-0). 32pp. Using humanlike dinosaurs as subjects, this practical guide shows how to make friends and keep their friendship. (Rev: BL 10/15/98; HB 11/98; HBG 3/99; SLJ 9/98)

4528 Bunge, Daniela. *Cherry Time* (K–2). Trans. from German by Kathryn Bishop. Illus. by author. 2007, Minedition $16.99 (978-0-698-40057-3). A boy overcomes his shyness with the help of his dog in this story translated from the German. (Rev: SLJ 7/07)

4529 Carmi, Giora. *A Circle of Friends* (K–2). Illus. by author. 2003, Star Bright $15.95 (978-1-932065-00-8). In this heartwarming, wordless picture book, a young boy unknowingly sets in motion a circle of kindness when he shares his muffin with a homeless man he finds sleeping on a park bench. (Rev: HBG 4/04; SLJ 1/04)

4530 Carr, Jan. *Frozen Noses* (PS–K). Illus. by Dorothy Donohue. 1999, Holiday House $16.95 (978-0-8234-1462-8). 32pp. Collage illustrations and an interesting text are used to describe three friends having fun outdoors on a cold winter's day. (Rev: BL 9/15/99; HBG 3/00; SLJ 9/99)

4531 Chodos-Irvine, Margaret. *Best Best Friends* (PS–K). Illus. by author. 2006, Harcourt $16.00 (978-0-15-205694-0). 40pp. In this charming story

for the very young, preschool jealousy briefly interrupts Clare and Mary's best-friendship. (Rev: BCCB 9/06; BL 5/1/06; HB 5/06; HBG 10/06; SLJ 6/06)

4532 Davies, Sally J. K. *When William Went Away* (K–3). Illus. 1999, Carolrhoda $15.95 (978-1-57505-303-5). 32pp. When Matthew's best friend William moves away, the boy is lost until Mary moves in next door, and William finds out that girls can also be friends. (Rev: BL 8/99; HBG 3/00; SLJ 7/99)

4533 Edwards, Nancy. *Glenna's Seeds* (K–2). Illus. by Sarah K. Hoctor. 2001, Child & Family $9.95 (978-0-87868-788-6). Glenna gives away a packet of marigold seeds and thereby starts off a chain of kind events that involves all the people on the block. (Rev: SLJ 4/01)

4534 English, Karen. *Nikki and Deja* (1–3). Illus. by Laura Freeman. 2008, Clarion $15.00 (978-0-618-75238-6). 80pp. Two African American 3rd-grade girls struggle to keep their friendship afloat when a new girl moves into the neighborhood. (Rev: BL 2/1/08; SLJ 6/08)

4535 Failing, Barbara Larmon. *Lasso Lou and Cowboy McCoy* (PS–2). Illus. by Tedd Arnold. 2003, Dial $16.99 (978-0-8037-2578-2). McCoy's 10-gallon hat is not enough to turn him into a cowboy, but Lasso Lou is patient and helps him to learn the ropes. (Rev: HBG 4/04; SLJ 10/03)

4536 Feldman, Eve B. *Billy and Milly, Short and Silly* (PS–2). Illus. by Tuesday Mourning. 2009, Putnam $16.99 (978-0-399-24651-7). 32pp. A collection of 13 tightly rhymed little stories (mostly four words long) about a little girl and boy, with satisfying visual interplays. (Rev: HB 9/09; SLJ 7/09*)

4537 Foley, Greg. *Don't Worry Bear* (PS). Illus. by author. 2008, Viking $19.99 (978-0-670-06245-4). 40pp. A soothing story about Bear's emotional changes as his friend Caterpillar goes through a big change. (Rev: BL 1/1–15/08; SLJ 2/08)

4538 Foreman, Jack. *Say Hello* (PS–1). Illus. by Michael Foreman. 2008, Candlewick $15.99 (978-0-7636-3657-9). 32pp. A lonely dog gets to play with a group of children and then invites a lonely boy to join them too. (Rev: BL 8/08*; SLJ 7/08)

4539 Fox, Mem. *Wilfrid Gordon McDonald Partridge* (K–2). Illus. by Julie Vivas. 1989, Kane $14.95 (978-0-916291-04-4); paper $7.95 (978-0-916291-26-6). 32pp. The heartwarming story of the boy with four names who collects memorabilia in a box to take to his friend with four names in a nursing home because he has heard she is losing her memory. (Rev: BL 2/15/86; HB 1/86; SLJ 2/86)

4540 Gleeson, Libby. *Half a World Away* (K–2). Illus. by Freya Blackwood. 2007, Scholastic $15.99 (978-0-439-88977-3). Best friends Louie and Amy are devastated when Amy moves from Australia to New York City, but they find a way to communicate nonetheless. (Rev: BL 3/1/07*; SLJ 2/07)

4541 Greenfield, Eloise. *The Friendly Four* (PS–2). Illus. by Jan Spivey Gilchrist. 2006, HarperCollins $16.99 (978-0-06-000759-1). 48pp. Drum has been dreading a dull summer and is happily surprised when three other African American children move into the neighborhood and they all become friends; an upbeat story told in a series of free-verse poems. (Rev: BL 4/15/06; SLJ 8/06)

4542 Grimes, Nikki. *Danitra Brown, Class Clown* (K–3). Illus. by E. B. Lewis. 2005, HarperCollins $16.99 (978-0-688-17290-9). 32pp. Zuri worries about her ailing mother and about the new school year in this latest story — presented in simple rhyming verses with expressive watercolors — about her close friendship with Danitra Brown. (Rev: BL 8/05; SLJ 9/05*)

4543 Havill, Juanita. *Brianna, Jamaica, and the Dance of Spring* (PS–3). Illus. by Anne S. O'Brien. 2002, Houghton $16.00 (978-0-618-07700-7). 32pp. Asian American Brianna longs to play the role of butterfly in the dance recital. (Rev: BL 3/15/02; HBG 10/02; SLJ 4/02)

4544 Havill, Juanita. *Jamaica and Brianna* (PS–1). Illus. by Anne S. O'Brien. 1993, Houghton $16.00 (978-0-395-64489-8). 32pp. Jamaica is upset when her friend, Brianna, makes fun of her hand-me-down boots. (Rev: BCCB 11/93; BL 10/15/93; HB 11/93; SLJ 10/93)

4545 Henkes, Kevin. *Chester's Way* (PS–2). Illus. by author. 1988, Greenwillow $17.89 (978-0-688-07608-5). 32pp. Chester and Wilson are best friends and will have nothing to do with new girl Lilly, until she bails them out of trouble. (Rev: BL 9/1/88; HB 9/88; SLJ 9/88)

4546 Horvath, David. *Bossy Bear* (PS–1). Illus. by author. 2007, Hyperion $12.99 (978-1-4231-0336-3). A bossy bear learns that being bossy is no way to make friends. Contemporary, anime-like illustrations add to the appeal. (Rev: SLJ 6/07)

4547 Hughes, Susan. *Earth to Audrey* (1–3). Illus. by Stéphanie Poulin. 2005, Kids Can $16.95 (978-1-55337-843-3). Audrey, a summer visitor to Ray's town, is so different that at first he thinks she's an alien, and as time goes by she teaches him a new way of looking at the world. (Rev: SLJ 1/06)

4548 Jahn-Clough, Lisa. *Alicia's Best Friends* (PS–1). Illus. 2003, Houghton $15.00 (978-0-618-23951-1). 32pp. Alicia must find a solution when her four close friends insist she choose one as her best friend. (Rev: BL 3/15/03; HBG 10/03; SLJ 3/03)

4549 Jahn-Clough, Lisa. *Little Dog* (PS–2). Illus. 2006, Houghton $16.00 (978-0-618-57405-6). 32pp. An artist named Rosa and a hungry Little Dog used to living on the streets find happiness and friendship in the countryside. (Rev: BL 4/15/06; SLJ 5/06)

4550 Jahn-Clough, Lisa. *My Friend and I* (PS). Illus. 1999, Houghton $15.00 (978-0-395-93545-3). 32pp. A little girl and her friend quarrel after one of their toys breaks, but soon they make up. (Rev: BL 4/15/99; HBG 10/99; SLJ 5/99)

4551 Jahn-Clough, Lisa. *Simon and Molly Plus Hester* (PS–K). Illus. 2001, Houghton $15.00 (978-0-618-08220-9). 32pp. The relationship between two best friends changes when a third playmate joins them. (Rev: BL 9/1/01; HBG 3/02; SLJ 9/01)

4552 Jam, Teddy. *The Stoneboat* (1–3). Illus. by Ange Zhang. 1999, Douglas & McIntyre $15.95 (978-0-88899-368-7). 32pp. In this Canadian story, a boy and his older brother save the life of their cranky neighbor and gradually break down the barriers of race and prejudice that separate them. (Rev: BCCB 12/99; BL 1/1–15/00; HBG 10/00; SLJ 1/00)

4553 Jeffers, Dawn. *Vegetable Dreams / Huerto soñado* (K–2). Trans. by Eida de la Vega. Illus. by Claude Schneider. 2006, Raven Tree $16.95 (978-0-9741992-9-0). 32pp. A little girl plants a vegetable garden with the help of a kind, elderly neighbor and together they watch it grow; in Spanish and English. (Rev: SLJ 6/06)

4554 Jeffers, Oliver. *Lost and Found* (PS–K). Illus. 2006, Philomel $15.99 (978-0-399-24503-9). 32pp. Finding a penguin on his doorstep, a little boy decides to take him home to the South Pole; it is only when he has put the penguin ashore that he realizes that all the bird wanted was a friend. (Rev: BL 12/15/05; SLJ 1/06)

4555 Jones, Rebecca C. *Matthew and Tilly* (PS–2). Illus. by Beth Peck. 1995, Puffin paper $6.99 (978-0-14-055640-7). 32pp. Matthew, a white boy, and Tilly, a black girl, resume their close friendship after an argument. (Rev: BL 1/15/91; SLJ 3/91)

4556 Keats, Ezra Jack. *Goggles!* (K–3). Illus. by author. 1987, Macmillan paper $4.95 (978-0-689-71157-2). 40pp. Dachshund Willie outmaneuvers some neighborhood bullies trying to confiscate the motorcycle goggles found by Peter. Bold collage paintings perfectly capture inner-city neighborhood scenes.

4557 Keats, Ezra Jack. *Whistle for Willie* (PS–1). Illus. by author. 1964, Puffin paper $6.99 (978-0-14-050202-2). After many false starts, Peter at last learns to whistle.

4558 King, Stephen M. *Henry and Amy (Right-Way-Round and Upside Down)* (PS–1). Illus. 1999, Walker LB $16.85 (978-0-8027-8687-6). 32pp. Henry, who can't get anything right, meets Amy, who never makes mistakes, and they become friends. (Rev: BL 6/1–15/99; HBG 10/99; SLJ 6/99)

4559 Kline, Suzy. *Horrible Harry and the Ant Invasion* (2–4). Illus. by Frank Remkiewicz. 1989, Viking $14.99 (978-0-670-82469-4). 64pp. Horrible Harry becomes class monitor for the ant farm. (Rev: BL 12/1/89; SLJ 3/90)

4560 Kroll, Virginia. *Forgiving a Friend* (PS–K). Illus. by Paige Billin-Frye. Series: The Way I Act. 2005, Albert Whitman $15.95 (978-1-80750-618-6). 32pp. Seth, furious with Jacob for damaging his toy truck, refuses to accept his friend's apology, but soon learns an important lesson about forgiveness when he accidentally breaks a lamp himself. (Rev: BL 10/1/05)

4561 Kroll, Virginia. *Pink Paper Swans* (K–4). Illus. by Nancy L. Clouse. 1994, Eerdmans $15.00 (978-0-8028-5081-2). 32pp. In this account of how Janetta Jackson began helping Mrs. Tsujimoto, an origami expert, there are instructions for making a pink swan. (Rev: BCCB 10/94; BL 7/94; SLJ 8/94)

4562 Krosoczka, Jarrett J. *My Buddy, Slug* (PS–2). Illus. by author. 2006, Knopf $15.95 (978-0-375-83342-7). Alex upsets his friend the slug and must make an apology. (Rev: SLJ 9/06)

4563 Lachtman, Ofelia Dumas. *Tina and the Scarecrow Skins / Tina y las Pieles de Espantapajaros* (2–5). 2002, Arte Publico $14.95 (978-1-55885-373-7). 32pp. A story, told in both English and Spanish, of Tina and her friend Little Bell, who dresses oddly and makes up strange words, but ends up saving the day (and the tamales). (Rev: BL 2/15/03; SLJ 3/03)

4564 Lester, Alison. *Tessa Snaps Snakes* (K–2). Illus. by author. 1991, Houghton paper $13.95 (978-0-685-52551-7). In double-page spreads, seven little children reveal their secrets and pet dislikes. (Rev: HB 11/91; SLJ 12/91)

4565 Lindenbaum, Pija. *Mini Mia and Her Darling Uncle* (K–2). Trans. from Swedish by Elisabeth Kallick Dyssegaard. Illus. by author. 2007, Farrar $16.00 (978-91-29-66734-9). 40pp. Little Mia struggles with having to share her beloved uncle with his friend Fergus until Fergus plays soccer with her. (Rev: SLJ 12/07)

4566 Lonborg, Rosemary. *Helpin' Bugs* (PS–2). Illus. by Diane R. Houghton. 1995, Little Friend $14.95 (978-0-9641285-2-1). 32pp. Lonely Hanna finds happiness helping her neighbor Douglas create a bug village. (Rev: BL 1/1–15/96; SLJ 2/96)

4567 Lyon, George E. *Together* (PS–2). Illus. by Vera Rosenberry. 1989, Orchard $15.95 (978-0-531-05831-2); paper $6.95 (978-0-531-07047-5). 32pp. Short poems explore the meaning of togetherness and friendship. (Rev: BL 9/15/89; HB 11/89; SLJ 9/89) [811]

4568 McCormick, Wendy. *Daniel and His Walking Stick* (PS–2). Illus. by Constance R. Bergum. 2005, Peachtree $15.95 (978-1-56145-330-6). On a trip to the country, Jesse meets a friend of her dead grandfather and the two become good friends, taking daily walks and talking about nature. (Rev: BL 3/1/04; HB 7/04; SLJ 5/05)

4569 Marx, Patricia. *Dot in Larryland: The Big Little Book of an Odd-Sized Friendship* (PS–3). Illus. by Roz Chast. 2009, Bloomsbury $16.99 (978-1-59990-181-7). 40pp. An unexpected friendship forms between minuscule Dot and extra-large Larry. (Rev: BCCB 1/09; BL 11/15/08; LMC 5/09; SLJ 2/09)

4570 Michelin, Linda. *Zuzu's Wishing Cake* (PS). Illus. by D. B. Johnson. 2006, Houghton $16.00 (978-0-618-64640-1). 32pp. Zuzu loves to make things and uses all her creative energies in an effort to make the new boy next door smile. (Rev: BL 10/1/06; SLJ 10/06)

4571 Michelson, Richard. *Across the Alley* (1–3). 2006, Putnam $16.99 (978-0-399-23970-0). 32pp. Abe, a young Jewish boy, and Willie, his African American neighbor across the alley, nurture their friendship and their dreams, and discover unsuspected talents for baseball and the violin. (Rev: BL 9/1/06; SLJ 10/06)

4572 Munson, Derek. *Enemy Pie* (K–3). Illus. by Tara Calahan King. 2000, Chronicle $14.95 (978-0-8118-2778-2). A young boy is nice to a boy he doesn't like and ends up having a good time. (Rev: BCCB 1/01; HBG 3/01; SLJ 12/00)

4573 Negron, Ray. *The Greatest Story Never Told: The Babe and Jackie* (K–3). Illus. by Laura Seeley. 2008, HarperCollins $17.99 (978-0-06-147161-2). 40pp. A batboy takes two hospitalized boys on a journey to meet baseball greats Babe Ruth and Jackie Robinson and helps them understand that people of different races can get along just fine. (Rev: BL 9/1/08)

4574 Noyes, Deborah. *Prudence and Moxie: A Tale of Mismatched Friends* (K–3). Illus. by AnnaLaura Cantone. 2009, Houghton $16.00 (978-0-618-41607-3). 32pp. Prudence and Moxie, both aptly named, maintain a close friendship despite their differences and help each other conquer their fears. (Rev: BL 4/15/09; SLJ 4/09)

4575 Okimoto, Jean D. *Dear Ichiro* (K–2). Illus. by Doug Keith. 2002, Kumagai $16.95 (978-1-57061-373-9). 32pp. Grampa's comments about the end of hostile feelings between Americans and Japanese make Henry reconsider his recent rupture with his friend Oliver. (Rev: BL 11/15/02; HBG 3/03; SLJ 3/03)

4576 Perkins, Lynne Rae. *The Cardboard Piano* (PS–K). Illus. by author. 2008, Greenwillow $17.99 (978-0-06-154265-7). 32pp. Despite their different ethnic backgrounds, Debbie and Tina enjoy their friendship until piano lessons get in the way. (Rev: BCCB 11/08; BL 1/1–15/09; HB 1/09; SLJ 11/08)

4577 Polacco, Patricia. *The Bee Tree* (K–3). Illus. 1993, Penguin $16.99 (978-0-399-21965-8). 32pp. After gathering honey from the bee tree with his granddaughter, Grampa explains that sweet things also can be found in books. (Rev: BL 3/1/93; HB 5/93; SLJ 6/93*)

4578 Polacco, Patricia. *Mrs. Katz and Tush* (K–4). Illus. 1992, Bantam $15.00 (978-0-553-08122-0). 32pp. A lonely Jewish widow is befriended by an African American boy who brings her a kitten to love. (Rev: BCCB 7–8/92; BL 4/15/92; HB 11/92; SLJ 7/92)

4579 Rand, Gloria. *A Pen Pal for Max* (K–3). Illus. by Ted Rand. 2005, Holt $16.95 (978-0-8050-7586-1). 32pp. Maximiliano, who lives on a Chilean fruit farm, slips a note into a box of grapes bound for the United States and is delighted when he gets a letter from 10-year-old Maggie; their friendship grows and Maggie's school helps when Max's is hit by an earthquake. (Rev: BL 10/15/05; SLJ 10/05)

4580 Raschka, Chris. *Yo! Yes?* (K–4). Illus. 1993, Orchard LB $16.99 (978-0-531-08619-3). 32pp. This picture book consists of a conversation between two boys, one white, one African American. (Rev: BCCB 4/93; BL 3/15/93; HB 5/93; SLJ 5/93*)

4581 Redbank, Tennant. *Which Way, Wendy?* (1–3). Illus. by Rebecca Thornburgh. Series: Social Studies Connects. 2005, Kane paper $4.99 (978-1-57565-147-7). 32pp. New girl Wendy makes some friends by reading and returning a map they lost; ends with a page on how to read maps. (Rev: BL 3/1/05)

4582 Reiser, Lynn. *My Way / A mi manera: A Margaret and Margarita Story / Un cuento de Margarita y Margaret* (PS–K). Illus. 2007, Greenwillow $15.99 (978-0-06-084101-0). 32pp. This bilingual picture book focuses on a friendship: although each friend has her own style, each learns from the other; refreshingly, Reiser emphasizes commonalities rather than differences. (Rev: BL 1/1–15/07)

4583 Reynolds, Marilynn. *A Present for Mrs. Kazinski* (PS–3). Illus. by Lynn Smith-Ary. 2001, Orca $15.95 (978-1-55143-196-3). 32pp. Frank is thrilled that Mrs. Kazinski likes the gift he chooses for her 80th birthday. (Rev: BL 10/15/01; HBG 3/02)

4584 Robbins, Jacqui. *The New Girl . . . and Me* (PS–2). Illus. by Matt Phelan. 2006, Simon & Schuster $16.95 (978-0-689-86468-1). 32pp. Shy Mia hangs back at first but mention of a pet iguana gives her the courage to approach new girl Shakeeta and the two become friends. (Rev: BCCB 9/06; BL 7/06*; SLJ 7/06)

4585 Rodman, Mary Ann. *My Best Friend* (PS–2). Illus. by E. B. Lewis. 2005, Viking $15.99 (978-0-670-05989-8). 32pp. Lily, 6, is crushed when Tamika, one of the girls she sees each week at the pool, doesn't want to be best friends. (Rev: BL 3/15/05; SLJ 5/05)

4586 Rosenbluth, Roz. *Getting to Know Ruben Plotnick* (K–3). Illus. by Maurie J. Manning. 2005, Flashlight $15.95 (978-0-9729225-5-5). David worries what will happen when his new friend Ruben — the most popular boy in class — meets David's grandmother, whose dementia has made her behavior erratic. (Rev: SLJ 11/05)

4587 Ryan, Pam Muñoz. *A Box of Friends* (K–2). Illus. by Mary Whyte. 2003, Gingham Dog $14.95 (978-1-57768-420-6). Annie's grandmother helps her put together a box of memories, to cheer her after a move to a new house. (Rev: HBG 10/03; SLJ 9/03)

4588 San Souci, Daniel. *The Mighty Pigeon Club* (K–2). Illus. by author. Series: Clubhouse Books. 2007, Tricycle $15.95 (978-1-58246-213-4). 32pp. Taking in a flock of pigeons proves much more problematic than the children in this clubhouse expected. (Rev: BL 9/1/07; LMC 3/08)

4589 Schotter, Roni. *Captain Snap and the Children of Vinegar Lane* (K–3). Illus. by Marcia Sewall. 1989, Orchard paper $5.95 (978-0-531-07038-3). 32pp. A bitter old man frightens the children away with his snapping fingers, until one day they discover he is ill. (Rev: BL 5/1/89; SLJ 5/89)

4590 Schubert, Ingrid, and Dieter Schubert. *Wild Will* (K–2). Illus. 1994, Carolrhoda LB $14.95 (978-0-87614-816-7). 32pp. Gradually, young Frank breaks down the hostility that a retired pirate feels toward people. (Rev: BL 9/15/94; SLJ 8/94)

4591 Scieszka, Jon. *Cowboy and Octopus* (PS–2). Illus. by Lane Smith. 2007, Viking $16.99 (978-0-670-91058-8). 40pp. Cowboy and Octopus enjoy an unlikely friendship and some perfectly silly adventures. (Rev: BCCB 9/07; BL 7/07; HB 9/07; LMC 11/07; SLJ 9/07)

4592 Shriver, Maria. *What's Wrong with Timmy?* (K–3). Illus. by Sandra Spieled. 2001, Little, Brown $14.95 (978-0-316-23337-8). 48pp. Eight-year-old Kate makes friends with Timmy, a boy who is mentally retarded, and wonders what it feels like to be Timmy. (Rev: BL 10/1/01; HBG 3/02; SLJ 1/02)

4593 Slaughter, Hope. *A Cozy Place* (PS–K). Illus. by Susan Torrence. 1991, Red Hen LB $15.95 (978-0-931093-13-5). 32pp. Two girls discover that it is each other's presence that makes a place cozy. (Rev: BL 6/1/91)

4594 Snihura, Ulana. *I Miss Franklin P. Shuckles* (K–3). Illus. by Leanne Franson. 1998, Annick LB $15.95 (978-1-55037-517-6); paper $5.95 (978-1-55037-516-9). When school starts, Molly decides to drop Franklin as a friend, but when she does she realizes how much she misses him. (Rev: SLJ 6/98)

4595 Starkman, Neal. *The Riddle* (K–2). Illus. by Ellen Sasaki. 1990, Comprehensive Health paper $10.00 (978-0-935529-13-5). 50pp. When a class assignment matches them together, Maria and a shy boy named Pete become friends. (Rev: BL 9/1/90)

4596 Steptoe, John. *Creativity* (PS–3). Illus. by E. B. Lewis. 1997, Clarion $17.00 (978-0-395-68706-2). 32pp. An African American boy wonders why a new class member who is as dark-skinned as himself can only speak Spanish. (Rev: BL 2/15/97; SLJ 4/97)

4597 Stone, Phoebe. *Go Away, Shelley Boo!* (1–3). Illus. by author. 1999, Little, Brown $15.95 (978-0-316-81677-9). A young girl imagines that her new neighbor next door is a real hellion, but she turns out to be a great friend. (Rev: HBG 3/00; SLJ 11/99)

4598 Stroud, Bettye. *Down Home at Miss Dessa's* (PS–3). Illus. by Felicia Marshall. 1996, Lee & Low $14.95 (978-1-880000-39-7). 32pp. When Miss Dessa is injured, neighborhood children help her in this story of African Americans in the South. (Rev: BCCB 12/96; BL 12/15/96; SLJ 1/97)

4599 Teevin, Toni. *What to Do? What to Do?* (PS–2). Illus. by Janet Pedersen. 2006, Clarion $16.00 (978-0-618-44632-2). 32pp. When too many birds begin clamoring for lonely Sophie's home-baked bread, she consults a fortune teller and makes new friends. (Rev: BL 5/1/06; SLJ 7/06)

4600 Viorst, Judith. *Rosie and Michael* (1–3). Illus. by Lorna Tomei. 1974, Macmillan $15.00 (978-0-689-30439-2); paper $4.99 (978-0-689-71272-2). 40pp. In spite of the many tricks they play on one another, Rosie and Michael are still friends.

4601 Von Konigslow, Andrea Wayne. *Bing and Chutney* (PS–K). Illus. by author. 1999, Annick LB $16.95 (978-1-55037-609-8); paper $5.95 (978-1-55037-608-1). Two female friends separate to seek their own fortunes and, after each is successful, they are reunited. (Rev: SLJ 1/00)

4602 Wallace, Nancy E. *Paperwhite* (PS–1). Illus. 2000, Houghton $15.00 (978-0-618-04283-8). 32pp. In spite of their age differences, Lucy and neighbor Miss Mamie enjoy each other's company and engage in such activities as planting narcissus bulbs for the spring. (Rev: BCCB 11/00; BL 11/15/00; HBG 3/01; SLJ 10/00)

4603 Whitcomb, Mary E. *Odd Velvet* (K–3). Illus. by Tara Calahan King. 1998, Chronicle $13.95 (978-0-8118-2004-2). 32pp. Because she dresses and behaves differently than other children in her school, Velvet is ignored by them, but gradually they change their ways. (Rev: BCCB 1/99; BL 11/1/98; HBG 3/99; SLJ 1/99)

4604 Wiles, Deborah. *Freedom Summer* (K–3). Illus. by Jerome Lagarrigue. 2001, Simon & Schuster $16.00 (978-0-689-83016-7). 32pp. Set in the South during desegregation, this is the story of the friendship between John Henry Waddell, an African American boy, and the narrator, who is white. (Rev: BCCB 2/01; BL 2/15/01; HB 5/01; HBG 10/01; SLJ 2/01)

4605 Woloson, Eliza. *My Friend Isabelle* (PS–1). Illus. by Bryan Gough. 2003, Woodbine House $14.95 (978-1-890627-50-8). Charlie describes his friendship with Isabelle, a girl with Down syndrome, emphasizing that the differences between them (he's tall, she's short; he's fast, she's slow) help to make their relationship even more rewarding. (Rev: HBG 4/04; SLJ 12/03)

4606 Woodson, Jacqueline. *The Other Side* (K–3). Illus. by E. B. Lewis. 2001, Penguin $16.99 (978-0-399-23116-2). 32pp. The story of a white girl and a black girl who form a friendship despite the barrier between their houses. (Rev: BCCB 2/01; BL 2/15/01*; HBG 10/01; SLJ 1/01)

4607 Yee, Brenda Shannon. *Sand Castle* (PS–2). Illus. by Thea Kliros. 1999, Greenwillow $16.99 (978-0-688-16194-1). As Jen builds a sandcastle, other children come to help and add distinctive parts in this story about cooperation and friendship. (Rev: HB 7/99; HBG 10/99; SLJ 6/99)

4608 Zolotow, Charlotte. *I Know a Lady* (PS–2). Illus. by James Stevenson. 1984, Morrow paper $6.99 (978-0-688-11519-7). 24pp. Sally loves a kind old lady who lives in the neighborhood.

HUMOROUS STORIES

4609 Ackerman, Karen. *Bean's Big Day* (K–4). Illus. by Paul Mombourquette. 2004, Kids Can $15.95 (978-1-55337-444-2). Someone in the small early-20th-century town of Bean, Pennsylvania, is going to be chosen to be in a movie in this story told by an 8-year-old narrator called Cricket. (Rev: SLJ 5/04)

4610 Addy, Sharon Hart. *When Wishes Were Horses* (PS–3). Illus. by Brad Sneed. 2002, Houghton $15.00 (978-0-618-13166-2). 32pp. Zeb's wishes for horses spiral out of control as each wish is granted, causing great crowding and confusion in an Old West town. (Rev: BL 12/1/02; SLJ 11/02)

4611 Agee, Jon. *The Retired Kid* (K–3). Illus. by author. 2008, Hyperion $16.99 (978-1-4231-0314-1). 32pp. At the age of 8, Brian decides he's had enough of school, music lessons, babysitting, and so forth, and takes off to Florida and the Happy Sunset Retirement Community. (Rev: BCCB 7–8/08; BL 4/15/08; LMC 5/08; SLJ 6/08)

4612 Ahlberg, Allan. *The Runaway Dinner* (PS–3). Illus. by Bruce Ingman. 2006, Candlewick $15.99 (978-0-7636-3142-0). A sausage called Melvin decides he does not want to be eaten by young Banjo Cannon and takes flight, setting the stage for a frantic chase as the boy, his parents, the rest of the meal, kitchen furniture, and cutlery follow in pursuit. (Rev: BCCB 11/06; HBG 4/07; SLJ 12/06)

4613 Ahrens, Robin Isabel. *Dee and Bee* (PS–1). Illus. by Amanda Haley. 2000, Winslow $14.95 (978-1-890817-26-8). 32pp. Identical twin sisters often switch identities to fool their friends and family and, sometimes, even the reader. (Rev: BL 4/15/00)

4614 Allard, Harry. *The Stupids Have a Ball* (K–3). Illus. by James Marshall. 1984, Houghton paper $6.95 (978-0-395-36169-6). The whole Stupid family decides to celebrate when the children bring home terrible report cards from school. Two others in the series: *The Stupids Step Out* (1974); *The Stupids Die* (1981).

4615 Allard, Harry. *The Stupids Take Off* (K–3). Illus. by James Marshall. 1989, Houghton $17.00 (978-0-395-50068-2). 32pp. The irresistible noodleheads set off on a fourth adventure, this time to avoid a visit from Uncle Carbuncle. (Rev: BCCB 10/89; BL 10/1/89; SLJ 10/89)

4616 Amato, Mary. *The Chicken of the Family* (PS–1). Illus. by Delphine Durand. 2008, Putnam $16.99 (978-0-399-24196-3). 32pp. A zany story in which Henrietta's older sisters manage to convince her that she is not a child but a chicken. (Rev: BCCB 3/08; BL 2/1/08; SLJ 3/08)

4617 Anderson, Derek. *Gladys Goes Out to Lunch* (PS–2). Illus. by author. 2005, Simon & Schuster $15.95 (978-0-689-85688-4). Gladys the gorilla leaves the zoo in search of the source of a delicious smell, and tests various food (pizza, ice cream) before finding a cart selling banana bread. (Rev: SLJ 8/05)

4618 Anderson, Laurie Halse. *The Hair of Zoe Fleefenbacher Goes to School* (K–2). Illus. by Ard Hoyt. 2009, Simon & Schuster $16.99 (978-0-689-85809-3). 32pp. Zoe's hair is both talented and determined (it learned to open the cookie jar at the age of 2, after all) but the 1st-grade teacher's strict rules pose a real problem. (Rev: BL 4/15/09; LMC 10/09)

4619 Anderson, Peggy Perry. *Chuck's Band* (PS–1). Illus. by author. 2008, Houghton $16.00 (978-0-618-96506-9). 32pp. When farmer Chuck buys himself a banjo and a mandolin for his goat, all the other animals want in on the fun except for Fat Cat Pat, who has special demands. (Rev: BL 2/15/08; HB 5/08; SLJ 3/08)

4620 Anderson, Peggy Perry. *Chuck's Truck* (PS–2). Illus. by author. 2006, Houghton $16.00 (978-0-618-66836-6). 32pp. A rhyming story about a farmer whose truck is overfull of friendly animals, with lively illustrations. (Rev: HB 5/06; HBG 10/06; SLJ 5/06)

4621 Andreae, Giles. *Pants* (PS–2). Illus. by Nick Sharratt. 2003, Random $12.95 (978-0-385-75014-

1). Cartoon-style illustrations highlight a rambunctious look at undergarments of all patterns and sizes. (Rev: HBG 4/04; SLJ 11/03)

4622 Appelt, Kathi. *Bubba and Beau Meet the Relatives* (PS–2). Illus. by Arthur Howard. 2004, Harcourt $16.00 (978-0-15-216630-4). 32pp. Newly clean, Baby Bubba and Beau the dog greet the arriving relatives before heading straight back to the mudhole, this time with baby Arlene in tow. (Rev: BL 3/15/04; HB 7/04; SLJ 5/04)

4623 Armstrong, Jennifer. *Once Upon a Banana* (PS–2). Illus. by David Small. 2006, Simon & Schuster $16.95 (978-0-689-84251-1). 48pp. A hilarious chain of accidents results when a monkey carelessly discards a banana peel on a busy sidewalk; rhyming street signs serve as captions for this wordless story. (Rev: BCCB 12/06; BL 11/1/06; HB 1/07; HBG 4/07; LMC 1/07; SLJ 12/06*)

4624 Arnold, Marsha Diane. *Roar of a Snore* (PS). Illus. by Pierre Pratt. 2006, Dial $16.99 (978-0-8037-2936-0). Jack is being kept awake by a loud snoring sound, so he awakens the rest of his family, along with the dog and farm animals, and together they try to find out who's responsible. (Rev: HBG 4/0; SLJ 8/06*)

4625 Arnold, Tedd. *The Twin Princes* (K–3). Illus. by author. 2007, Dial $16.99 (978-0-8037-2696-3). 32pp. Twin chicken princes — one good, one bad — compete to inherit the kingdom in this pun-filled story. (Rev: BL 3/1/07*)

4626 Asch, Frank. *Monsieur Saguette and His Baguette* (PS–1). Illus. by author. 2004, Kids Can $14.95 (978-1-55337-461-9). A loaf of French bread assists in all sorts of adventures in this humorous Parisian romp. (Rev: SLJ 6/04)

4627 Ashman, Linda. *To the Beach!* (PS). Illus. by Nadine Bernard Wescott. 2005, Harcourt $16.00 (978-0-15-216490-4). 32pp. So many things are forgotten that the anticipated day at the beach ends up being a day in the backyard. (Rev: BL 5/1/05; SLJ 6/05)

4628 Atwood, Margaret. *Bashful Bob and Doleful Dorinda* (K–3). Illus. by Dusan Petricic. 2006, Bloomsbury Children's $17.95 (978-1-59990-004-9). 32pp. Alliteration and clever use of color enhance this Cinderella-like story of two hard-done-by children who wind up heroes. (Rev: BL 11/1/06)

4629 Auch, Mary Jane. *The Princess and the Pizza* (K–2). Illus. by Mary Jane Auch and Herm Auch. 2002, Holiday House $16.95 (978-0-8234-1683-7). In a fractured fairy tale, Paulina easily wins the contest for the prince's hand, but prefers instead to open a Pizza Palace. (Rev: BCCB 3/02; HBG 10/02; SLJ 5/02)

4630 Bachelet, Gilles. *My Cat, the Silliest Cat in the World* (PS–2). 2006, Abrams $16.95 (978-0-8109-4913-3). 32pp. A funny story of a "cat" that's not a cat at all but an elephant with a decidedly feline demeanor. (Rev: BL 6/1–15/06; SLJ 4/06)

4631 Bachelet, Gilles. *When the Silliest Cat Was Small* (PS–2). Illus. by author. Series: My Cat, the Silliest Cat in the World. 2007, Abrams $16.95 (978-0-8109-9415-7). 32pp. This is the story of the "kittenhood" of the cat that is really an elephant. (Rev: BL 10/15/07; SLJ 12/07)

4632 Baehr, Patricia. *Mouse in the House* (PS–1). Illus. by Laura Lydecker. 1994, Holiday House LB $15.95 (978-0-8234-1102-3). When a mouse moves into Mrs. Teapot's house, she tries a number of unsuccessful ploys to get rid of it. (Rev: SLJ 9/94)

4633 Baker, Keith. *Hide and Snake* (PS–K). Illus. 1991, Harcourt $15.00 (978-0-15-233986-9). 32pp. A snake hides in each of the double-page spreads depicting everyday life. (Rev: BL 11/15/91; SLJ 12/91*)

4634 Barrett, Judi. *Never Take a Shark to the Dentist and Other Things Not to Do* (PS–2). Illus. by John Nickle. 2008, Atheneum $16.99 (978-1-4169-0724-4). 34pp. Advice such as "Never hold hands with a lobster" is paired with full-page illustrations showing the reasons underlying the tip. (Rev: BL 4/1/08; LMC 8/08; SLJ 5/08)

4635 Barrett, Judith. *Animals Should Definitely Not Wear Clothing* (PS–1). Illus. by Ron Barrett. 1970, Macmillan $13.95 (978-0-689-20592-7); paper $5.99 (978-0-689-70807-7). 32pp. Humorous idea expressed in brief text and comic drawings. A sequel is: *Animals Should Definitely Not Act Like People* (Simon & Schuster 1988).

4636 Bartram, Simon. *Bob's Best-Ever Friend* (PS–3). Illus. by author. 2009, Candlewick $16.99 (978-0-7636-4425-3). 32pp. Astronaut Bob is back and focused on looking for a pet to be his best friend while all sorts of crazy things (shown in the illustrations) happen around him. (Rev: BL 7/09; SLJ 5/09)

4637 Becker, Suzy. *Manny's Cows: The Niagara Falls Tale* (PS–2). 2006, HarperCollins $15.99 (978-0-06-054152-1). 40pp. Disaster strikes when Manny, a farm boy who tends a herd of 500 cows, takes them with him on a vacation trip to Niagara Falls. (Rev: BL 6/1–15/06; SLJ 6/06)

4638 Berry, Lynne. *The Curious Demise of a Contrary Cat* (K–2). Illus. by Luke LaMarca. 2006, Simon & Schuster $12.95 (978-1-4169-0211-9). 40pp. Repetition and predictability are hallmarks of this wacky story about Cat's refusal to pitch in and help Witch with her party. (Rev: BL 11/1/06; SLJ 8/06)

4639 Best, Cari. *Montezuma's Revenge* (PS–2). Illus. by Diane Palmisciano. 1999, Orchard LB $16.99 (978-0-531-33198-9). 32pp. To show his owner's family his worth, the dog Montezuma switches places with Wild Bill, a dog from the wrong side of the tracks. (Rev: BL 11/15/99; HBG 3/00; SLJ 11/99)

4640 Best, Cari. *When Catherine the Great and I Were Eight!* (PS–2). Illus. by Giselle Potter. 2003, Farrar $16.00 (978-0-374-39954-2). One thing after another goes wrong when 8-year-old Sara and her Russian grandmother set off for the beach in this sequel to *Three Cheers for Catherine the Great* (1999). (Rev: HB 9/03; HBG 4/04; SLJ 9/03)

4641 Birdseye, Tom, and Debbie H. Birdseye. *She'll Be Comin' Round the Mountain* (K–3). Illus. by Andrew Glass. 1994, Holiday House LB $15.95

(978-0-8234-1032-3). 32pp. A variation on the old song that tells about a group of mountain folk who are awaiting Tootie's comin' round the mountain for a visit. (Rev: BL 7/94; SLJ 9/94)

4642 Bishop, Claire Huchet. *Five Chinese Brothers* (1–3). Illus. by Kurt Wiese. 1988, Penguin paper $5.99 (978-0-698-11357-2). 64pp. Physically identical in every way, each of the five Chinese brothers has one distinguishing trait that saves the lives of all of them.

4643 Blake, Quentin. *Mrs. Armitage: Queen of the Road* (PS–2). Illus. by author. 2003, Peachtree $15.95 (978-1-56145-287-3). The adventurous Mrs. Armitage and her dog set off in an old jalopy and take it in their stride when it starts losing parts and winds up a mere skeleton of a car. (Rev: HBG 4/04; SLJ 10/03)

4644 Blankenship, Lee Ann. *Mr. Tuggle's Troubles* (K–3). Illus. by Karen Dugan. 2005, Boyds Mills $15.95 (978-1-59078-196-8). Mr. Tuggle has trouble looking after his clothes and looks stranger and stranger as he devises various replacements. (Rev: SLJ 10/05)

4645 Bloch, Serge. *Butterflies in My Stomach and Other School Hazards* (PS–2). Illus. by author. 2008, Sterling $12.95 (978-1-4027-4158-6). 32pp. A little boy's first day of school is made more confusing by the profusion of new, incomprehensible phrases in this funny look at the use of language. (Rev: BL 8/08; LMC 3/09; SLJ 9/08)

4646 Bloom, Suzanne. *The Bus for Us* (PS–K). Illus. 2001, Boyds Mills $13.95 (978-1-56397-932-3). 32pp. A humorous story that describes children waiting to be picked up on the first day of school. (Rev: BL 3/15/01*; HBG 10/01)

4647 Bluemle, Elizabeth. *My Father the Dog* (PS–2). Illus. by Randy Cecil. 2006, Candlewick $15.99 (978-0-7636-2222-0). 32pp. A girl (convincingly) equates her father's habits with those of her pet dog in this entertaining picture book. (Rev: BL 5/15/06; SLJ 7/06)

4648 Bock, Lee. *Oh, Crumps! / Ay, caramba!* (PS–2). Trans. by Eida de la Vega. Illus. by Morgan Midgett. 2003, Raven Tree LB $16.95 (978-0-9720192-4-8). 32pp. A humorous tale, in both English and Spanish, about an exhausted farmer trying to keep up with his never-ending tasks and "repair the cow, climb the fence, milk the hay, and mow the silo." (Rev: HBG 10/03; SLJ 7/03)

4649 Bourgeois, Paulette. *Too Many Chickens!* (PS–3). Illus. by Bill Slavin. 1990, General Dist. Services paper $4.95 (978-1-55074-067-7). 32pp. A gift of chicken eggs to a class of elementary school children brings unexpected results. (Rev: BL 8/91; SLJ 6/91)

4650 Bowen, Anne. *What Do Teachers Do (After YOU Leave School?)* (K–3). Illus. by Barry Gott. 2006, Carolrhoda LB $15.95 (978-1-57505-922-8). Visions of teachers gone wild — dancing in the gym, roller-skating down the corridors, writing on the walls — may convince young children that teachers don't really live in the school. (Rev: SLJ 11/06)

4651 Bradman, Tony. *Michael* (PS–3). Illus. by Tony Ross. 1998, Trafalgar paper $9.95 (978-0-86264-759-9). 32pp. Brainy Michael won't pay attention in class; he just wants to learn about spacecraft. (Rev: BL 1/15/91; SLJ 3/91)

4652 Bright, Paul. *I'm Not Going Out There!* (K–2). Illus. by Ben Cort. 2006, Good Bks. $16.00 (978-1-56148-535-2). A little boy hides beneath his bed and refuses to come out, but he makes it clear that it's not the fearsome creatures in his bedroom that are keeping him there but rather his annoying sister. (Rev: SLJ 11/06)

4653 Broach, Elise. *Cousin John Is Coming!* (K–3). Illus. by Nate Lilly. 2006, Dial $16.99 (978-0-8037-3013-7). Ben and his cat recall the various horrors of Cousin John's last visit while Ben's mother rhapsodizes about John's forthcoming arrival; cartoon illustrations provide much of the humor. (Rev: SLJ 7/06)

4654 Broach, Elise. *When Dinosaurs Came with Everything* (PS–1). Illus. by David Small. 2007, Atheneum $16.99 (978-0-689-86922-8). 40pp. Want a dinosaur? They're available — free — at every store in this funny book. (Rev: BCCB 10/07; BL 9/15/07; HB 1/08; LMC 11/07; SLJ 9/07)

4655 Broadley, Leo. *Pedro the Brave* (PS–2). Illus. by Holly Swain. 2002, ME Media $14.95 (978-1-58925-024-6). 32pp. Clever Pedro outwits the wolf that plans to eat him and his animal friends by feeding the wolf Pedro's special (fiery) hot sauce. (Rev: BCCB 2/03; BL 12/1/02; SLJ 4/03)

4656 Brown, Margaret Wise. *The Dirty Little Boy* (K–2). Illus. by Steven Salerno. 2001, Winslow $16.95 (978-1-890817-52-7). First published in 1939 under a different title, this is the story of a little boy who tries to get clean by imitating animals' baths. (Rev: HBG 10/01; SLJ 5/01)

4657 Brown, Peter. *Chowder* (PS–2). 2006, Little, Brown $15.99 (978-0-316-01180-8). 32pp. Chowder is a bulldog with unusual talents and has little in common with the other dogs in his neighborhood, but he finally finds friends when a petting zoo opens nearby. (Rev: BL 9/1/06; HBG 4/07; LMC 3/07; SLJ 9/06)

4658 Brown, Peter. *Flight of the Dodo* (K–2). Illus. by author. 2005, Little, Brown $15.99 (978-0-316-11038-9). Penguin and a handful of other flightless birds join forces to invent a flying machine; both text and illustrations are full of fun. (Rev: SLJ 12/05)

4659 Brown, Ruth. *The Big Sneeze* (PS–K). Illus. by author. 1997, Morrow paper $4.95 (978-0-688-15282-6). 32pp. A fly lands on a farmer's nose; he sneezes, and havoc breaks out in the barnyard. (Rev: BCCB 2/86; BL 9/15/85; SLJ 10/85)

4660 Bruel, Nick. *Who Is Melvin Bubble?* (K–4). Illus. by author. 2006, Roaring Brook $16.95 (978-1-59643-116-4). This humorous profile of Melvin Bubble contains sometimes contradictory views of Melvin from his parents, dog, teddy bear, Santa Claus, and even a monster that lives in Melvin's closet. (Rev: SLJ 8/06)

4661 Bryan, Sean. *A Girl and Her Gator* (K–2). Illus. by Tom Murphy. 2006, Arcade $14.99 (978-1-55970-798-5). A silly story about Claire, who is unsettled at first when she discovers an alligator on her head, but, assured that the gator should cause no change in her activities, the young girl blithely carries on with her everyday routine. (Rev: SLJ 8/06)

4662 Buehner, Caralyn. *The Queen of Style* (K–3). Illus. by Mark Buehner. 2008, Dial $16.99 (978-0-8037-2878-3). 40pp. A charming tale about a quirky queen who enrolls in beauty school and practices on her subjects and their sheep. (Rev: SLJ 9/08)

4663 Bunting, Eve. *My Backpack* (PS–K). Illus. 1997, Boyds Mills $16.95 (978-1-56397-433-5). 32pp. A young boy thinks he is doing everyone a favor when he gathers a lot of objects around the house and stores them in his backpack for safekeeping. (Rev: BL 5/1/97; SLJ 4/98)

4664 Butler, Dorothy. *Another Happy Tale* (PS–2). Illus. by John Hurford. 1992, Crocodile $12.95 (978-0-940793-88-0). Mabel and Ned are so ill prepared to bring up their baby girl that they accidentally sell her as part of a litter of pigs. (Rev: SLJ 4/92)

4665 Byars, Betsy. *The Golly Sisters Go West* (1–3). Illus. by Sue Truesdell. 1986, HarperCollins LB $16.89 (978-0-06-020884-4); paper $3.99 (978-0-06-444132-2). 64pp. In six stories, two adventurous women take on frontier life and the Wild West. (Rev: BCCB 11/86)

4666 Carrick, Carol. *Big Old Bones: A Dinosaur Tale* (PS–3). Illus. by Donald Carrick. 1992, Houghton paper $7.95 (978-0-395-61582-9). 32pp. Professor Potts finds a bunch of old bones to take back East to assemble. (Rev: BL 3/1/89; HB 5/89; SLJ 5/89)

4667 Carrier, Lisa, and Lenore Hart. *T. Rex at Swan Lake* (PS–1). Illus. by Chris Demarest. 2004, Dutton $16.99 (978-0-525-47177-6). A dinosaur skeleton tired of being on display in a museum decides to try her hand at ballet. (Rev: BL 8/04; SLJ 8/04)

4668 Chaconas, Dori. *Virginnie's Hat* (K–2). Illus. by Holly Meade. 2007, Candlewick $16.99 (978-0-7636-2397-5). 32pp. Intent on retrieving her hat from a tall tree in the bayou, Virginnie seems unaware that animals are showing a great deal of interest in her toes. (Rev: BL 6/1–15/07; SLJ 5/07)

4669 Charlip, Remy. *Little Old Big Beard and Big Young Little Beard* (PS). Illus. by Tamara Rettenmund and Tamara Rettenmund. 2003, Marshall Cavendish $16.95 (978-0-7614-5142-6). Two bearded cowboys embark on a search for their missing cow, but they are so inept that the cow has to find them. (Rev: HBG 4/04; SLJ 10/03)

4670 Charlip, Remy. *Why I Will Never Ever Ever Ever Have Enough Time to Read This Book* (K–3). Illus. by Jon J. Muth. 2000, Tricycle $14.95 (978-1-58246-018-5). 40pp. A humorous book about a little girl who has so many things to do, like homework and calling friends, that she will never to able to finish the big book that is always at her side. (Rev: BL 1/1–15/01; HBG 3/01; SLJ 9/00)

4671 Chartrand, Lili. *Taming Horrible Harry* (K–3). Trans. from French by Susan Ouriou. Illus. by Rogé. 2006, Tundra $16.95 (978-0-88776-772-2). What the monster called Harry enjoys most is scaring children — until he learns to read and discovers the joy of books; offbeat illustrations add to the appeal. (Rev: SLJ 7/06)

4672 Child, Lauren. *But Excuse Me That Is My Book* (PS–2). Illus. Series: Charlie and Lola. 2006, Dial $16.99 (978-0-8037-3096-0). 32pp. Colorful collage-style art portrays the story of little Lola, who is deeply disappointed when she discovers that the book she absolutely loves best has been checked out of the library by somebody else; eventually her big — and very patient — brother Charlie helps her find a substitute. (Rev: BL 4/1/06; SLJ 4/06*)

4673 Child, Lauren. *Clarice Bean, That's Me* (PS–2). Illus. by author. 1999, Candlewick $16.99 (978-0-7636-0961-0). 32pp. Clarice Bean's house is so crowded that she hopes she will be sent to her room as a punishment so she can be alone for a while. Also use *Clarice Bean, Guess Who's Babysitting?* (2001) and *What Planet Are You From, Clarice Bean?* (2002). (Rev: HBG 3/00; SLJ 12/99)

4674 Child, Lauren. *I Want a Pet* (PS–1). Illus. 1999, Tricycle $13.95 (978-1-883672-82-9). 24pp. A hilarious story about a family that cannot agree on the perfect pet. (Rev: BL 4/15/99; HB 5/99; HBG 10/99; SLJ 5/99)

4675 Child, Lauren. *I Will Never Not Ever Eat a Tomato* (PS–2). Illus. by author. Series: Charlie and Lola. 2000, Candlewick $15.99 (978-0-7636-1188-0). Charlie gets his fussy little sister to eat by calling the food by exotic names. (Rev: HBG 3/01; SLJ 11/00)

4676 Child, Lauren. *Say Cheese!* (K–3). Illus. by author. Series: Charlie and Lola. 2007, Dial $16.99 (978-0-8037-3095-3). 32pp. Despite warnings to keep tidy for her school photograph, Lola manages to get herself messed up; luckily big brother Charlie knows how to save the day. (Rev: BL 11/1/07; SLJ 9/07)

4677 Child, Lauren. *Snow Is My Favorite and My Best* (PS–K). Series: Charlie and Lola. 2006, Dial $16.99 (978-0-8037-3174-5). 32pp. Charlie's little sister Lola is so enthusiastic about snow that she's devastated when it melts, and Charlie has to persuade her that snow every day would be boring and inconvenient. (Rev: BCCB 12/06; BL 9/15/06; HBG 4/07; SLJ 11/06)

4678 Chodos-Irvine, Margaret. *Ella Sarah Gets Dressed* (PS). Illus. by author. 2003, Harcourt $16.00 (978-0-15-216413-3). Toddler Ella Sarah will not accept the fashion advice of her family, preferring to dress herself in vivid attire for her tea party. Caldecott Honor Book, 2004. (Rev: BL 6/1–15/03*; HBG 10/03; SLJ 7/03)

4679 Christelow, Eileen. *The Five-Dog Night* (PS–3). Illus. 1993, Clarion $16.00 (978-0-395-62399-2). 36pp. On cold nights, cranky old Ezra finds an unusual use for his five pet dogs. (Rev: BL 9/15/93; SLJ 10/93)

4680 Christelow, Eileen. *Letters from a Desperate Dog* (PS–2). 2006, Clarion $16.00 (978-0-618-51003-0). 32pp. Emma the dog feels badly treated by her owner George and seeks the advice of a canine columnist in the *Weekly Bone*. (Rev: BL 10/1/06; SLJ 11/06)

4681 Cibula, Matt. *The Contrary Kid* (2–4). Illus. by Brian Strassburg. 1995, Zino $16.95 (978-1-55933-177-7). 32pp. Cartoons and rhymes are used to tell about the antics of a kooky kid who revels in being different. (Rev: BL 1/1–15/96; SLJ 7/96)

4682 Clarke, Gus. *Nothing But Trouble* (PS–2). Illus. by author. 1998, Andersen paper $9.95 (978-0-86264-841-1). Maisie's day begins with her baby brother rudely wakening her, and her mother spilling cereal on her head — then things go from bad to worse. (Rev: SLJ 3/99)

4683 Clement, Rod. *Grandpa's Teeth* (PS–3). Illus. 1998, HarperCollins $16.99 (978-0-06-027671-3). 32pp. When Grandpa's false teeth are stolen, a nationwide search is begun. (Rev: BL 2/15/98; HBG 10/98; SLJ 3/98*)

4684 Clements, Andrew. *Double Trouble in Walla Walla* (1–3). Illus. by Sal Murdocca. 1997, Millbrook LB $21.90 (978-0-7613-0306-0). A girl is sent to the principal's office when she can't stop speaking in hyphenated words, like mish-mash. (Rev: HBG 3/98; SLJ 1/98)

4685 Clifford, Rowan. *Rodeo Ron and His Milkshake Cows* (K–2). Illus. 2005, Knopf LB $17.99 (978-0-375-93195-6). 32pp. When Rodeo Ron rides into the town of Cavity with his four cows of different hues, the soda bar owners challenge him to a shake-off — milkshakes vs. soft drinks — with the children as judges. (Rev: BL 6/1–15/05; SLJ 6/05)

4686 Colandro, Lucille. *There Was a Cold Lady Who Swallowed Some Snow!* (PS–2). Illus. by Jared Lee. 2003, Scholastic paper $5.95 (978-0-439-47109-1). 32pp. This twist on the familiar story has the old lady devouring everything a strange combination of items, but when everything comes back out, there's the makings of a snowman. (Rev: BL 2/1/04)

4687 Cole, Brock. *Buttons* (K–3). Illus. 2000, Farrar $16.00 (978-0-374-31001-1). 32pp. When their father bursts his buttons, three daughters set out separately to bring him new ones, in this charming, humorous tale. (Rev: BCCB 3/00; BL 2/15/00*; HB 3/00; HBG 10/00; SLJ 4/00)

4688 Collins, Ross. *Dear Vampa* (K–2). Illus. by author. 2009, HarperCollins $16.99 (978-0-06-135534-9). 32pp. The Pires, a four-vampire family, are displeased when the sun-loving, boisterously cheerful Wolfsons move in next door in this funny story that ends with a twist (the Wolfsons are in fact werewolves). (Rev: BL 6/1–15/09)

4689 Copp, Jim. *Jim Copp, Will You Tell Me a Story? Three Uncommon Clever Tales* (K–2). Illus. by Lindsay duPont. 2008, Harcourt $17.95 (978-0-15-206331-3). 56pp. Three humorous short stories by Jim Copp are illustrated in the book and performed by the late Copp on the accompanying CD. (Rev: BL 12/1/08; SLJ 11/08)

4690 Cordsen, Carol Foskett. *Market Day* (PS–1). Illus. by Douglas B. Jones. 2008, Dutton $16.99 (978-0-525-47883-6). 32pp. It is definitely not a good idea for the Benson family to leave for the market without feeding the cow! (Rev: BCCB 9/08; BL 5/15/08; LMC 8/08; SLJ 6/08)

4691 Cote, Genevieve. *What Elephant?* (K–3). Illus. by author. 2006, Kids Can $16.95 (978-1-55337-875-4). When his neighbors express skepticism, George decides that perhaps he was mistaken when he saw an elephant in his house. (Rev: SLJ 12/06)

4692 Crandall, Court. *Hugville* (PS–1). Illus. by Joe Murray. 2005, Random $13.95 (978-0-375-82418-0). The mayor of Hugville proudly conducts a tour of his town, pointing out all the different types of hugs that are practiced there. (Rev: SLJ 1/06)

4693 Crimi, Carolyn. *The Louds Move In!* (K–2). Illus. by Regan Dunnick. 2006, Marshall Cavendish $14.95 (978-0-7614-5221-8). Although the neighbors have been annoyed by the noise created by the Loud family, they become worried when the din suddenly subsides. (Rev: SLJ 5/06)

4694 Cronin, Doreen. *Bounce* (PS). Illus. by Scott Menchin. 2007, Simon & Schuster $14.00 (978-1-4169-1627-7). 40pp. In this appealing sequel to *Wiggle* (2005), simple, rhyming text and colorful artwork combine to capture the essence of bouncing. (Rev: BL 3/15/07)

4695 Cronin, Doreen. *Diary of a Fly* (PS–2). Illus. by Harry Bliss. 2007, HarperCollins $15.99 (978-0-06-000156-8). 40pp. Fly shares her worries about her first day of school and interacts with characters from *Diary of a Worm* (2003) and *Diary of a Spider* (2005) in this humorous book with lots of gross aspects. (Rev: BL 11/1/07; HB 1/08; SLJ 10/07)

4696 Cronin, Doreen. *Diary of a Spider* (PS–3). Illus. by Harry Bliss. 2005, HarperCollins $15.99 (978-0-06-000153-7). A young spider's diary reveals typical concerns — molting, reassuring unhappy friends, worries about strange food, relations with flies, and vacuum drills. (Rev: SLJ 8/05)

4697 Cronin, Doreen. *Diary of a Worm* (PS–1). Illus. by Harry Bliss. 2003, HarperCollins LB $17.89 (978-0-06-000151-3). Presented in the form of a diary, this amusing title features a young earthworm who muses about the pros and cons of life as a worm. (Rev: BL 10/1/03; HB 11/03; HBG 4/04; SLJ 10/03)

4698 Cronin, Doreen. *Wiggle* (PS–K). Illus. by Scott Menchin. 2005, Simon & Schuster $12.95 (978-0-689-86375-2). 40pp. A playful dog urges children to wiggle their way through the day. (Rev: BL 5/1/05; SLJ 6/05)

4699 Crunk, Tony. *Railroad John and the Red Rock Run* (1–3). Illus. by Michael Austin. 2006, Peachtree $16.95 (978-1-56145-363-4). 32pp. Train engineer John overcomes some daunting challenges to deliver passenger Lonesome Bob to his wedding on time; illustrations reminiscent of daguerreotypes complement this tall tale. (Rev: BL 4/1/06; SLJ 5/06)

4700 Cutbill, Andy. *The Cow That Laid an Egg* (PS–2). Illus. by Russell Ayto. 2008, HarperCollins $16.99 (978-0-06-137295-7). 32pp. With the help of some friendly chickens, an ordinary cow named Marjorie lays an extraordinary egg that soon hatches into chicken who says "moo." (Rev: BL 2/15/08; SLJ 2/08)

4701 Cuyler, Margery. *Skeleton Hiccups* (2–4). Illus. by S. D. Schindler. 2002, Simon & Schuster $14.95 (978-0-689-84770-7). 32pp. A skeleton tries to rid himself of a bad case of hiccups and is finally scared out of them by looking in the mirror. (Rev: BCCB 9/02; BL 9/15/02; HB 9/02; HBG 3/03; SLJ 10/02)

4702 Cuyler, Margery. *That's Good! That's Bad!* (PS–K). Illus. by David Catrow. 1993, Holt paper $6.95 (978-0-8050-2954-3). 32pp. A boy's red balloon whisks him aloft for a series of adventures. (Rev: BCCB 12/91; BL 12/1/91; SLJ 11/91)

4703 Cuyler, Margery. *That's Good! That's Bad! In the Grand Canyon* (K–3). Illus. by David Catrow. 2002, Holt $16.95 (978-0-8050-5975-5). 32pp. A boy visiting the Grand Canyon has some "BAD" (but funny) close calls before he catches up with his grandmother. (Rev: BL 5/15/02; HBG 10/02; SLJ 6/02)

4704 Davidson, Ellen Dee. *Princess Justina Albertina: A Cautionary Tale* (PS–1). Illus. by Michael Chesworth. 2007, Charlesbridge $15.95 (978-1-57091-652-6). The willful Princess Justina Albertina wants a pet — a perfect pet — and is satisfied with none until her faithful nanny brings her a gryphon; and then the trouble begins. (Rev: SLJ 3/07)

4705 DeFelice, Cynthia. *Old Granny and the Bean Thief* (K–2). Illus. by Cat B. Smith. 2003, Farrar $16.00 (978-0-374-35614-9). When a thief steals some of Old Granny's beans and the sheriff is out of town, she enlists the help of a motley crew, including an alligator and a cactus. (Rev: HB 9/03; HBG 4/04; SLJ 9/03)

4706 DeFelice, Cynthia. *Willy's Silly Grandma* (K–3). Illus. by Shelley Jackson. 1997, Orchard LB $16.99 (978-0-531-33012-8). Willy's Grandma spouts a lot of silly superstitions, but she is right in telling Willy not to go by the Old Swamp at night. (Rev: BCCB 6/97; HB 5/97; SLJ 4/97*)

4707 Delton, Judy. *Blue Skies, French Fries* (2–3). Illus. by Alan Tiegreen. 1988, Dell paper $3.99 (978-0-440-40064-6). 80pp. The Pee Wee scouts earn badges. Also use: *Lucky Dog Days; Peanut Butter Pilgrims; Camp Ghost-Away* (all 1988). (Rev: BL 2/15/89)

4708 dePaola, Tomie. *Pancakes for Breakfast* (PS–2). Illus. by author. 1978, Harcourt $14.95 (978-0-15-259455-8); paper $5.00 (978-0-15-670768-8). 32pp. The trials and travails of a country woman who decides to make some pancakes.

4709 Derby, Sally. *King Kenrick's Splinter* (K–3). Illus. by Leonid Gore. 1994, Walker LB $15.85 (978-0-8027-8323-3). 32pp. King Kenrick is afraid to have a splinter removed from his big toe. (Rev: BL 11/1/94; SLJ 1/95)

4710 Derby, Sally. *Whoosh Went the Wind!* (K–3). Illus. by Vincent Nguyen. 2006, Marshall Cavendish $16.99 (978-0-7614-5309-3). 32pp. In this live-ly picture book, an imaginative little boy explains to his skeptical teacher how the wind made him late for school. (Rev: BL 10/15/06; SLJ 10/06)

4711 De Regniers, Beatrice S. *May I Bring a Friend?* (PS–2). Illus. by Beni Montresor. 1971, Macmillan LB $16.95 (978-0-689-20615-3); paper $5.99 (978-0-689-71353-8). 48pp. The king and queen invite a small boy to tea, and each time he goes, he takes a friend — a seal, a hippopotamus, and several lions. Caldecott Medal winner, 1965.

4712 Dodds, Dayle Ann. *Sing, Sophie!* (PS–1). Illus. by Rosanne Litzinger. 1997, Candlewick $15.99 (978-0-7836-0131-1). 32pp. Everyone ignores Sophie's singing talent except her baby brother, who prefers it to the sound of thunder. (Rev: BL 5/15/97; SLJ 6/97)

4713 Dodds, Dayle Ann. *Where's Pup?* (PS–K). Illus. by Pierre Pratt. 2003, Dial $12.99 (978-0-8037-2744-1). A clown makes the rounds of his fellow circus performers in a frantic search for his missing puppy; a final fold-out page reveals the pup's location atop a pyramid of acrobats. (Rev: HB 3/03*; HBG 10/03; SLJ 7/03)

4714 Downey, Lynn. *Sing, Henrietta! Sing!* (PS–3). Illus. by Tony Sansevero. 1997, Ideals $14.95 (978-1-57102-103-8). George loves his dear friend Henrietta, but he finds her singing earsplitting. (Rev: SLJ 7/97)

4715 Dragonwagon, Crescent. *The Bat in the Dining Room* (1–4). Illus. by S. D. Schindler. 1997, Marshall Cavendish $15.95 (978-0-7614-5007-8). 32pp. When a bat causes havoc after flying into the crowded dining room, Melissa gently coaxes the creature out. (Rev: BL 10/1/97; HBG 3/98; SLJ 9/97)

4716 Dunbar, Polly. *Where's Tumpty?* (PS–K). Illus. by author. Series: Tilly and Friends. 2009, Candlewick $12.99 (978-0-7636-4273-0). 32pp. A very funny story about a large blue elephant's efforts to disappear. (Rev: BL 3/1/09; SLJ 5/09)

4717 Durant, Alan. *Burger Boy* (PS–2). Illus. by Mei Matsuoka. 2006, Clarion $16.00 (978-0-618-71466-7). 32pp. Benny's mother warns him that if he eats nothing but burgers he'll turn into one and that's just what happens in this hilarious picture book. (Rev: BL 11/15/06; SLJ 10/06)

4718 Dyer, Heather. *Tina and the Penguin* (K–2). Illus. by Mireille Levert. 2002, Kids Can $14.95 (978-1-55074-947-2). 32pp. Tina fails in her elaborate efforts to keep her penguin secret in this humorous story with funny illustrations. (Rev: BL 1/1–15/03; HBG 3/03; SLJ 11/02)

4719 Eaton, Maxwell, III. *Best Buds* (1–3). Illus. by Maxwell Eaton. 2006, Knopf $12.99 (978-0-375-83803-3). Max (who looks a lot like Charlie Brown) and his best friend Pinky the pig have adventures together on Saturdays, until the week when Pinky disappears; bright cartoon pictures add to the humor. (Rev: SLJ 2/07)

4720 Eaton, Maxwell, III. *The Mystery* (K–2). Illus. by Eaton. Series: The Adventures of Max and Pinky. 2008, Knopf $12.99 (978-0-375-83807-1). Max and Pinky together painted the barn red, so who has since been repainting it? A funny story with elaborate devices to catch the perp. (Rev: SLJ 12/08)

4721 Egan, Tim. *The Trial of Cardigan Jones* (K–3). Illus. by author. 2004, Houghton $16.00 (978-0-618-40237-3). Although he only sniffed the pie, Cardigan, a moose who is clumsy with his antlers, is put on trial for theft. (Rev: BCCB 10/04; SLJ 9/04)

4722 Elliott, David. *Hazel Nutt, Mad Scientist* (K–2). Illus. by True Kelley. 2003, Holiday House $16.95 (978-0-8234-1711-7). Mad scientist Hazel Nutt wins over frightened villagers with the strange creatures she creates in her lab — singer Dracula-la-la and piano-monster combo Frankensteinway. (Rev: HBG 4/04; SLJ 3/04)

4723 Ellis, Sarah. *The Queen's Feet* (K–2). Illus. by Dusan Petricic. 2006, Red Deer $17.95 (978-0-88995-320-8). 32pp. Queen Daisy's unruly feet finally get totally out of line and she has to rein them in this humorous story full of wordplay. (Rev: BL 5/1/06; SLJ 4/06)

4724 Elya, Susan Middleton. *Cowboy Jose* (K–1). Illus. by Tim Raglin. 2005, Penguin $15.99 (978-0-399-23570-2). 32pp. In bouncy rhyming English and Spanish, a poor Mexican cowboy seeks the money to impress Rosita but in the end decides to spend it on his faithful horse. (Rev: BL 2/1/05; SLJ 4/05)

4725 Emmett, Jonathan. *Someone Bigger* (PS–1). Illus. by Adrian Reynolds. 2004, Clarion $16.00 (978-0-618-44397-0). 32pp. Dad says Sam is too little to handle the kite, it needs someone bigger; and of course so it proves as a whole string of people and animals are pulled into the air until Sam acts to save the day. (Rev: BL 3/1/04; SLJ 5/04)

4726 English, Karen. *Just Right Stew* (PS–1). Illus. by Anna Rich. 1998, Boyds Mills $15.95 (978-1-56397-487-8). Friends and relatives offer advice concerning ingredients as Victoria's mother and aunt try to prepare oxtail soup. (Rev: BL 2/15/98; HBG 10/98; SLJ 3/98)

4727 Ernst, Lisa Campbell. *Stella Louella's Runaway Book* (PS–2). Illus. 1998, Simon & Schuster $16.00 (978-0-689-81883-7). 40pp. Stella Louella traces the whereabouts of her lost library book by questioning various townspeople who have read it and passed it along. (Rev: BCCB 12/98; BL 8/98; HBG 3/99; SLJ 9/98)

4728 Esbaum, Jill. *Estelle Takes a Bath* (PS–2). Illus. by Mary Newell Depalma. 2006, Holt $16.95 (978-0-8050-7741-4). 32pp. Estelle's comfortable bath is rudely interrupted by a little field mouse. (Rev: BL 1/1–15/07; SLJ 11/06)

4729 Esbaum, Jill. *Stink Soup* (1–4). Illus. by Roger Roth. 2004, Farrar $16.00 (978-0-374-37252-1). While on vacation at grandmother's farm, Willie keeps misbehaving (and letting older sister Annabelle take the blame) — until he encounters a skunk. (Rev: SLJ 3/04)

4730 Espinosa, Laura. *Otis and Rae and the Grumbling Splunk* (PS–3). Illus. by Leo Espinosa. 2008, Houghton $12.95 (978-0-618-98206-6). 32pp. Adventurous Rae goes to sleep and careful Otis

attempts to brave the dark night in this story featuring a Grumbling Splunk. (Rev: HB 5/08; SLJ 5/08)

4731 Everitt, Betsy. *Mean Soup* (PS–1). Illus. 1992, Harcourt $16.00 (978-0-15-253146-1). 32pp. Horace gets rid of his nasty thoughts and feelings by throwing them into a pot and making mean soup. (Rev: BL 3/15/92*; SLJ 7/92)

4732 Fallon, Jimmy. *Snowball Fight!* (PS–1). Illus. by Adam Stower. 2005, Dutton $15.99 (978-0-525-47456-2). A boy and his younger sister enjoy a snow day off school in this book with action-packed cartoon illustrations. (Rev: SLJ 11/05)

4733 Fearnley, Jan. *The Search for the Perfect Child* (PS–K). Illus. by author. 2006, Candlewick $15.99 (978-0-7636-3231-1). 40pp. The coolest dog in the world is searching for a perfect child and has a number of criteria laid out. (Rev: BL 12/1/06; SLJ 11/06)

4734 Feiffer, Jules. *By the Side of the Road* (2–4). 2002, Hyperion $15.95 (978-0-7868-0908-0). 64pp. A boy becomes so fed up with being bossed around by his dad that he decides to set out on his own. (Rev: BCCB 9/02; BL 6/1–15/02*; HBG 10/02; SLJ 5/02)

4735 Feiffer, Kate. *Double Pink* (K–3). Illus. by Bruce Ingman. 2005, Simon & Schuster $15.95 (978-0-689-87190-0). Young Madison's single-minded love for the color pink gets out of control. (Rev: SLJ 11/05)

4736 Feiffer, Kate. *Henry, the Dog with No Tail* (K–2). Illus. by Jules Feiffer. 2007, Simon & Schuster $16.99 (978-1-4169-1614-7). 32pp. Sad, tailless Henry visits a tailor to have one made and goes to Battery Park for a device that will make it wag, but after the tail wags out of control he decides to do without, retaining only a "tale" to tell. (Rev: BL 11/1/07; SLJ 10/07)

4737 Feiffer, Kate. *President Pennybaker* (PS–1). Illus. by Diane Goode. 2008, Simon & Schuster $16.99 (978-1-4169-1354-2). 32pp. Life just isn't fair, so Luke runs for president — with his dog as running mate — and discovers that even being the boss doesn't mean he will get enough time for TV. (Rev: BL 8/08; LMC 10/08; SLJ 8/08)

4738 Fisher, Doris, and Dani Sneed. *One Odd Day* (K–2). Illus. by Karen Lee. 2006, Sylvan Dell $15.95 (978-0-9768823-3-6). In this humorous story told in rhyming text, a young boy awakens one day to discover that everything around him is truly odd: his dog has five legs and his shirt has three sleeves. (Rev: SLJ 12/06)

4739 Fleming, Candace. *Muncha! Muncha! Muncha!* (PS–2). Illus. by G. Brian Karas. 2002, Simon & Schuster $16.00 (978-0-689-83152-2). 32pp. Mr. McGreely goes to great lengths to defend his vegetable garden from a group of clever rabbits in this hilarious story. (Rev: BCCB 3/02; BL 1/1–15/02; HBG 10/02; SLJ 2/02*)

4740 Fleming, Candace. *Tippy-Tippy-Tippy, Hide!* (PS–K). Illus. by G. Brian Karas. 2007, Simon & Schuster $16.99 (978-0-689-87479-6). 40pp. In this sequel to *Muncha! Muncha! Muncha!* (2002), Mr. McGreely is determined to keep the rabbits out of his cozy house and barricades it so thoroughly that he can't get out when spring finally arrives. (Rev: BL 12/15/06; SLJ 1/07)

4741 Foreman, Mark. *Granpa Jack's Tattoo Tales* (1–3). Illus. by author. 2007, Farrar $16.00 (978-0-374-32768-2). 40pp. Chloe can always count on Granpa Jack for a tall tale about one of his many elaborate tattoos. (Rev: BL 1/1–15/08; SLJ 12/07)

4742 Fox, Mem. *Guess What?* (PS–2). Illus. by Vivienne Goodman. 1990, Harcourt $15.00 (978-0-15-200452-1). 32pp. Through a series of questions, a strange lady, who is a witch, is introduced. (Rev: BL 9/1/90; HB 11/91; SLJ 11/90)

4743 Fox, Mem. *A Particular Cow* (PS–2). Illus. by Terry Denton. 2006, Harcourt $16.00 (978-0-15-200250-3). Out for her Saturday walk, a cow collides with a clothesline, ends up with a pair of bloomers on her head, and slapstick mayhem follows. (Rev: SLJ 9/06)

4744 Fox, Mem. *Shoes from Grandpa* (PS–K). Illus. by Patricia Mullins. 1992, Orchard paper $6.95 (978-0-531-07031-4). 32pp. A cumulative story about buying clothes for a growing Jessie. (Rev: BL 2/15/90; HB 3/90; SLJ 4/90*)

4745 Frazee, Marla. *A Couple of Boys Have the Best Week Ever* (K–3). Illus. by author. 2008, Harcourt $16.00 (978-0-15-206020-6). 40pp. Best friends James and Eamon attend nature camp each day but the enthusiastic reports they give to Eamon's grandparents differ quite a lot from reality; the illustrations add to the fun. Caldecott Honor Book, 2009. (Rev: BL 3/1/08; HB 3/08; SLJ 3/08*)

4746 Frazee, Marla. *Walk On! A Guide for Babies of All Ages* (PS–K). Illus. 2006, Harcourt $16.00 (978-0-15-205573-8). 40pp. A humorous how-to guide for babies who are just learning to walk. (Rev: BL 4/1/06; SLJ 4/06*)

4747 Freedman, Michelle. *The Ravioli Kid: An Original Spaghetti Western* (K–3). Illus. by Jason Abbott. 2005, Gibbs Smith $15.95 (978-1-58685-438-6). In this rollicking, pun-filled western tale, 7-year-old Stellina Pomodoro faces off against Angel Hair and the Anti-Pasta Gang. (Rev: SLJ 4/06)

4748 Freeman, Don. *Mop Top* (K–2). Illus. by author. 1978, Puffin paper $6.99 (978-0-14-050326-5). 48pp. Moppy changes his mind about a haircut after being mistaken for a floor mop by a nearsighted shopper.

4749 French, Jackie. *Pete the Sheep-Sheep* (PS–1). Illus. by Bruce Whatley. 2005, Clarion $14.00 (978-0-618-56862-8). 32pp. Shaun, a newly arrived sheep shearer at Shaggy Gully, shows the old timers that he can easily outperform them and their sheepdogs with the help of Pete, his "sheep-sheep." (Rev: BL 1/1–15/06; SLJ 11/05)

4750 French, Vivian. *Oliver's Milk Shake* (PS–1). Illus. by Alison Bartlett. 2001, Scholastic $15.95 (978-0-531-30304-7). 32pp. Oliver's aunt sees the picky eater drinking orange soda for breakfast and puts Oliver through a busy day of pro-milk orientation before he explains her mistake. (Rev: BL 8/01; HBG 10/01; SLJ 6/01)

4751 French, Vivian. *Oliver's Vegetables* (PS–2). Illus. by Alison Bartlett. 1995, Orchard $14.95 (978-0-531-09462-4). 32pp. Longing for some French fries, Oliver promises to eat anything he finds in his Grandpa's vegetable garden, hoping to find potatoes. (Rev: BL 9/15/95; SLJ 10/95)

4752 French, Vivian, and Alex Ayliffe. *Let's Go, Anna!* (PS). 2000, David & Charles $14.95 (978-1-86233-074-0). 32pp. A flap book that relates Anna's hilarious misadventures during a shopping trip and at the same time gives youngsters a chance to count to five and learn the concept of size. (Rev: BL 1/1–15/01; SLJ 3/01)

4753 Frienz, D. J. *Where Will Nana Go Next? An Illustrated Tour of 19 Places to Go and Things to Do Across America and the World* (PS–1). Illus. by Sean Garber. 1999, Howling at the Moon $15.95 (978-0-9654333-0-3). Feisty Nana and her dog Spike visit some of America's tourist sights, in this book illustrated with bright, humorous cartoons. (Rev: SLJ 8/99)

4754 Funke, Cornelia. *Princess Pigsty* (K–2). Trans. from German by Chantal Wright. Illus. by Kerstin Meyer. 2007, Scholastic $16.99 (978-0-439-88554-6). Princess Isabella is bored with her privileged life and longs to be normal; when she throws her crown away and refuses to cooperate, her father punishes her with work that she thoroughly enjoys. (Rev: SLJ 4/07)

4755 Geist, Ken. *The Three Little Fish and the Big Bad Shark* (PS–1). Illus. by Julia Gorton. 2007, Scholastic $6.99 (978-0-439-71962-9). This spoof of the three little pigs story takes place in the ocean, with fish instead of pigs and the role of the big bad wolf played by a shark. (Rev: LMC 10/07; SLJ 6/07)

4756 Gemignani, Tony. *Tony and the Pizza Champions* (PS–3). Illus. by Matthew Trueman. 2009, Chronicle $16.99 (978-0-8118-6162-5). 44pp. Full of energy and puns, this is the story — based on fact — of an American pizza making team competing in the World Pizza Championship in Italy; includes recipes. (Rev: SLJ 6/09)

4757 Geringer, Laura. *A Three Hat Day* (PS–1). Illus. by Arnold Lobel. 1985, HarperCollins paper $6.99 (978-0-06-443157-6). 32pp. R. R. Pottle the Third is a gentleman who loves hats in this tale of loneliness and finding someone who cares. (Rev: BCCB 1/86; BL 9/15/85; HB 11/85)

4758 Gibbons, Faye. *The Day the Picture Man Came* (K–2). Illus. by Sherry Meidell. 2003, Boyds Mills $16.95 (978-1-56397-161-7). 32pp. The members of the Howard family prepare to have their picture taken by a traveling photographer in this funny story set in the Georgia mountains. (Rev: BL 2/15/03; HBG 10/03; SLJ 3/03)

4759 Gibbons, Faye. *Emma Jo's Song* (K–3). Illus. by Sherry Meidell. 2001, Boyds Mills $15.95 (978-1-56397-935-4). 32pp. Emma Jo is the hit of the family reunion when she sings a duet with a howling dog. (Rev: BL 4/1/01; HBG 10/01; SLJ 5/01)

4760 Gibbons, Faye. *Mama and Me and the Model T* (PS–3). Illus. by Ted Rand. 1999, Morrow LB

$15.89 (978-0-688-15299-4). 40pp. In this delightful sequel to *Mountain Wedding,* Mama shows that it's not just the menfolk who can drive the new Model T around the farm. (Rev: BL 11/15/99; HBG 3/00; SLJ 11/99)

4761 Gibbons, Faye. *Mountain Wedding* (K–4). Illus. by Ted Rand. 1996, Morrow $16.89 (978-0-688-11349-0). 40pp. A series of humorous mishaps delay the wedding of widow Searcy and widower Long. (Rev: BCCB 9/96; BL 4/1/96; HB 5/96; SLJ 4/96)

4762 Gifford, Peggy. *Moxy Maxwell Does Not Love Stuart Little* (2–4). Illus. 2007, Random $12.99 (978-0-375-83915-3). 112pp. A fast-paced, funny tale about a girl who will do just about anything except finish reading her assigned summer book: *Stuart Little.* (Rev: BCCB 7–8/07; BL 7/07; HB 9/07; SLJ 7/07)

4763 Gill-Brown, Vanessa. *Rufferella* (K–3). Illus. by Mandy Stanley. 2001, Scholastic $12.95 (978-0-439-25617-9). 32pp. Diamante transforms her dog into Rufferella, who reaches great heights as a singer until meeting her downfall, a plateful of sausages. (Rev: BL 8/01; HBG 10/01; SLJ 8/01)

4764 Golembe, Carla. *Dog Magic* (PS–2). Illus. 1997, Houghton $16.00 (978-0-395-81662-2). 32pp. Molly Gail thinks that the new slippers she received for her birthday have magically cured her fear of dogs. (Rev: BL 11/1/97; HBG 3/98; SLJ 9/97)

4765 Goodhart, Pippa. *Arthur's Tractor: A Fairy Tale with Mechanical Parts* (PS–2). Illus. by Colin Paine. 2003, Bloomsbury $15.95 (978-1-58234-847-6). 32pp. While Arthur is busy working on his tractor, he stumbles into a funny fairy tale. (Rev: BL 2/15/03; HBG 10/03; SLJ 3/03)

4766 Gosney, Joy. *Naughty Parents* (PS). Illus. by author. 2000, Millbrook LB $21.90 (978-0-7613-1823-1). In this humorous tale of role reversal, a little girl must take care of her parents when they spend an afternoon in the park, including finding them at the "Missing Parents Booth." (Rev: HBG 10/00; SLJ 5/00)

4767 Gottlieb, Dale. *Where Jamaica Go?* (PS–1). Illus. 1996, Orchard LB $15.99 (978-0-531-08875-3). 32pp. In Afro-Caribbean jargon, Jamaica travels downtown, to the beach, and on a trip in her father's van. (Rev: BL 10/1/96; SLJ 11/96)

4768 Graham, Bob. *Dimity Dumpty* (PS–2). Illus. by author. 2007, Candlewick $15.99 (978-0-7636-3078-2). 40pp. Dimity is Humpty Dumpty's diffident little sister who conquers her timidity when her brother needs help. (Rev: BL 12/1/06)

4769 Graves, Keith. *Loretta: Ace Pinky Scout* (1–2). Illus. 2002, Scholastic $16.95 (978-0-439-36831-5). 40pp. Loretta discovers that not everyone can be perfect when she fails to earn her marshmallow toasting badge in this bright and silly spoof about scouting. (Rev: BL 10/15/02; HBG 3/03; SLJ 12/02)

4770 Graves, Keith. *The Unexpectedly Bad Hair of Barcelona Smith* (K–3). Illus. by author. 2006, Philomel $16.99 (978-0-399-24273-1). Barcelona sees dangers all around him and takes all precau-

tions until the day his hair takes over. (Rev: SLJ 6/06)

4771 Gray, Kes. *006 and a Half* (K–2). Illus. by Nick Sharratt. 2007, Abrams $10.95 (978-0-8109-1719-4). 32pp. Daisy goes undercover as a secret agent but is frustrated when no one seems to be able to decipher her secret coded language. (Rev: BL 4/1/07)

4772 Greenberg, David. *Crocs!* (K–2). Illus. by Lynn Munsinger. 2008, Little, Brown $15.99 (978-0-316-07306-6). 32pp. A little boy leaves the city to get away from the roaches, pigeons, and other critters only to find himself on an island overrun with crocodiles. (Rev: BL 4/15/08; LMC 1/09; SLJ 4/08)

4773 Greene, Carol. *The Golden Locket* (K–3). Illus. by Marcia Sewall. 1992, Harcourt $13.95 (978-0-15-231220-6); paper $5.00 (978-0-15-201008-9). 32pp. Miss Teaberry's generosity leads to amusing complications in this picture book. (Rev: BCCB 7–8/92; BL 4/1/92; HB 5/92; SLJ 5/92)

4774 Grey, Mini. *Egg Drop* (PS–1). Illus. by author. 2009, Knopf $16.99 (978-0-375-84260-3). 32pp. *Egg Drop* is a darkly humorous tale of an egg who wants to fly and learns the consequences of not waiting to hatch. (Rev: BL 7/09; SLJ 6/09)

4775 Griffin, Kitty, and Kathy Combs. *The Foot-Stomping Adventures of Clementine Sweet* (K–2). Illus. by Mike Wohnoutka. 2004, Clarion $15.00 (978-0-618-24746-2). 32pp. The feisty Clementine Sweet makes her presence felt in her Texas town. (Rev: BL 3/1/04; SLJ 3/04)

4776 Grossman, Bill. *Timothy Tunny Swallowed a Bunny* (PS–2). Illus. by Kevin Hawkes. 2001, HarperCollins $14.95 (978-0-06-028010-9). 32pp. Eighteen nonsense poems explore comic situations, such as the boy who grew a new nose every year. (Rev: BCCB 2/01; BL 2/15/01; HB 3/01*; HBG 10/01; SLJ 3/01)

4777 Halperin, Wendy A. *When Chickens Grow Teeth* (K–3). Illus. 1996, Orchard LB $16.99 (978-0-531-08876-0). 32pp. Confined to bed because of an accident, Toine makes himself useful by hatching some chicken eggs. (Rev: BL 10/15/96; SLJ 9/96)

4778 Hamilton, Arlene. *Only a Cow* (PS–2). Illus. by Dean Griffiths. 2006, Fitzhenry & Whiteside $16.95 (978-1-55041-871-2). 32pp. A boisterous cow called Lucille longs to run, and gets her chance when she finds herself in a horse race at the county fair. (Rev: BL 1/1–15/07)

4779 Harley, Bill. *Dirty Joe, the Pirate: A True Story* (PS–2). Illus. by Jack E. Davis. 2008, HarperCollins $16.99 (978-0-06-623780-0). 32pp. Dirty Joe and his crew happily sail the seas searching for dirty socks until they come up against Stinky Annie and her impressive loot of underwear; in the ensuing melee it turns out that Joe and Annie are siblings! (Rev: SLJ 5/08)

4780 Harrington, Janice N. *The Chicken-Chasing Queen of Lamar County* (PS–2). 2007, Farrar $16.00 (978-0-374-31251-0). 32pp. A young African American girl who enjoys chasing chickens decides to forgo the fun when she finds her main target tending to a flock of new chicks. (Rev: BL 2/1/07)

4781 Harris, Peter. *Perfect Prudence* (1–3). Illus. by Deborah Allwright. 2003, Gingham Dog $15.95 (978-1-57768-437-4). So perfect is Prudence that she ends up with not only every role in the school play but all the backstage jobs as well; in the end, however, it becomes clear, despite Prudence's valiant efforts, that it's too big a job for just one person. (Rev: HBG 10/03; SLJ 8/03)

4782 Harrison, Joanna. *Grizzly Dad* (PS–1). Illus. by author. 2009, Random $16.99 (978-0-385-75173-5). 32pp. It takes a day of play to retrieve the real Dad from the grizzly bear that woke up that morning. (Rev: BL 5/15/09; SLJ 8/09)

4783 Hartman, Bob. *The Wolf Who Cried Boy* (PS–2). Illus. by Tim Raglin. 2002, Penguin $16.99 (978-0-399-23578-8). 32pp. The cautionary tale is turned inside-out in this humorous story in which a wolf spots a pack of boy scouts. (Rev: BCCB 7–8/02; BL 7/02; HB 5/02; HBG 10/02; SLJ 6/02)

4784 Hartry, Nancy. *Jocelyn and the Ballerina* (PS–3). Illus. by Linda Hendry. 2000, Fitzhenry & Whiteside $14.95 (978-1-55041-649-7). 32pp. Jocelyn is so attached to her tutu that she puts it on under the beautiful pink dress she has to wear to a wedding. (Rev: BL 12/15/00; SLJ 1/01)

4785 Harvey, Matt. *Shopping with Dad* (PS–3). Illus. by Miriam Latimer. 2008, Barefoot Books $16.99 (978-1-84686-172-7). 32pp. A little girl's sneeze in the grocery store causes a series of unhappy events in this funny story. (Rev: SLJ 9/08)

4786 Haseley, Dennis. *The Invisible Moose* (PS–2). Illus. by Steven Kellogg. 2006, Dial $16.99 (978-0-8037-2892-9). 40pp. A shy Canadian moose in love with a lovely girl moose who is captured by a trapper uses an invisibility potion to follow her to New York City; a funny story of magic, romance, and adventure. (Rev: BL 2/1/06; SLJ 3/06)

4787 Hassett, Ann. *Mouse in the House* (PS–2). Illus. by John Hassett. 2004, Houghton $15.00 (978-0-618-35317-0). 32pp. Nana Quimby's discovery of a mouse in the house leads to even greater headaches as family members introduce one animal after another to rid the dwelling of an unwelcome guest. (Rev: BL 4/15/04*; HB 5/04; SLJ 3/04)

4788 Hassett, John, and Ann Hassett. *Cat Up a Tree* (PS–2). Illus. 1998, Houghton $16.00 (978-0-395-88415-7). 32pp. As the number of cats increases in a tree outside her house, Nana Quimby tries several sources for help, starting with the firehouse and the police station and ending with the post office and the library, but finally she has do something about it herself. (Rev: BCCB 11/98; BL 10/15/98*; HBG 3/99; SLJ 10/98)

4789 Havill, Juanita. *Just Like a Baby* (PS–2). Illus. by Christine Davenier. 2009, Chronicle $15.99 (978-0-8118-5026-1). 32pp. It's hard to think about what you'll be when you grow up when you're still in your crib. (Rev: SLJ 6/09)

4790 Hawkes, Kevin. *The Wicked Big Toddlah* (PS–1). Illus. 2007, Knopf $16.99 (978-0-375-82427-2). 40pp. A baby of gargantuan proportions

is born in Maine, posing daunting challenges for the normal-sized people who must care for him. (Rev: BL 4/15/07)

4791 Hayes, Joe. *The Gum-Chewing Rattler* (K–3). Illus. by Antonio Castro L. 2006, Cinco Puntos $16.95 (978-0-938317-99-9). In this amusing tall tale, inspired by the author's childhood in small-town Arizona, a young boy is saved from the bite of a rattlesnake by a wad of bubble gum. (Rev: SLJ 1/07)

4792 Heide, Florence Parry. *A Promise Is a Promise* (K–2). Illus. by Tony Auth. 2007, Candlewick $15.99 (978-0-7636-2285-5). George's parents promised he could have a pet — so why do they keep objecting to the creatures he brings home? (Rev: SLJ 6/07)

4793 Helakoski, Leslie. *Big Chickens* (PS–4). Illus. by Henry Cole. 2006, Dutton $15.99 (978-0-525-47575-0). 32pp. When a wolf is spotted in the barnyard, four hens run for their lives but find they gain courage when it's really needed. (Rev: BL 2/1/06; SLJ 2/06)

4794 Henkes, Kevin. *Lilly's Big Day* (PS–K). Illus. 2006, Greenwillow $16.99 (978-0-06-074236-2). 40pp. Lilly is beside herself with excitement at the thought of being flower girl at her teacher's wedding, but there's a slight problem — he hasn't asked her. (Rev: BL 3/1/06*; SLJ 4/06*)

4795 Hicks, Barbara Jean. *The Secret Life of Walter Kitty* (PS–2). Illus. by Dan Santat. 2007, Knopf $16.99 (978-0-375-83196-6). Poor Walter Kitty dreams of being a superhero cat; his owner does not see this potential and insists on cuddling Walter and calling him "Snookums." (Rev: BCCB 6/07; SLJ 7/07)

4796 Hill, Susanna Leonard. *No Sword Fighting in the House* (1–3). Illus. by True Kelley. 2007, Holiday $14.95 (978-0-8234-1916-6). 32pp. Readers will enjoy this funny story about two brothers who decide to "joust" atop two cows and end up ruining their mother's prized daffodils. (Rev: BL 5/1/07; HB 5/07; SLJ 8/07)

4797 Himmelman, John. *Chickens to the Rescue* (PS–2). Illus. 2006, Holt $16.95 (978-0-8050-7951-7). 32pp. Farmer Greenstalk's chickens come to the rescue of farm residents — both human and animal — in this entertaining romp. (Rev: BL 11/1/06; SLJ 10/06*)

4798 Hoberman, Mary Ann. *The Seven Silly Eaters* (PS–3). Illus. by Marla Frazee. 1997, Harcourt $16.00 (978-0-15-200096-7). 40pp. A humorous picture book about Mrs. Peters and her brood of picky eaters. (Rev: BCCB 5/97; BL 3/1/97; HB 5/97; SLJ 3/97)

4799 Hogg, Gary. *Look What the Cat Dragged In!* (K–3). Illus. by Mike Wohnoutka. 2005, Dutton $15.99 (978-0-525-46984-1). 32pp. When the slothful Lazybones family begins to talk of replacing their faithful cat with a dog, the hardworking feline plots revenge. (Rev: BL 11/1/05; SLJ 2/06)

4800 Hooper, Meredith. *Celebrity Cat* (K–3). Illus. by Bee Willey. 2006, Frances Lincoln $15.95 (978-1-84507-290-2). 36pp. Felissima, a cat with a passion for art, creates her own renditions of famous paintings to include cats in each one. (Rev: BL 11/15/06; SLJ 12/06)

4801 Hopkins, Jackie Mims. *The Gold Miner's Daughter: A Melodramatic Fairy Tale* (K–2). Illus. by Jon Goodell. 2006, Peachtree $15.95 (978-1-56145-362-7). 32pp. In this modern-day fable presented in the form of a stage production, Gracie Pearl encounters a series of classic fairy tale characters as she struggles to find a way to save her home and mine from an evil banker. (Rev: BL 2/15/06; SLJ 4/06)

4802 Horowitz, Dave. *Five Little Gefiltes* (PS–2). Illus. by author. 2007, Putnam $12.99 (978-0-399-24608-1). In this Yiddish-flavored takeoff on "Five Little Ducklings," five young gefilte fish swim off on their own and explore the delights of New York City in the early 20th century. (Rev: SLJ 2/07)

4803 Horse, Harry. *The Last Polar Bears* (1–4). Illus. by author. 2007, Peachtree $12.95 (978-1-56145-379-5). 104pp. Through letters from Grandfather to his grandchild, readers learn about his expedition — with his faithful dog Roo, who seems unsuited to this task — to see the last polar bears before they become extinct. (Rev: LMC 1/08; SLJ 12/07)

4804 Horton, Joan. *Math Attack* (1–3). Illus. by Krysten Brooker. 2009, Farrar $16.95 (978-0-374-34861-8). 40pp. This entertaining picture book in rhyme tells what happens when a little girl is asked to answer one more math question than she can handle. (Rev: BL 1/1–15/09; SLJ 3/09)

4805 Howard, Arthur. *Serious Trouble* (PS–2). Illus. by author. 2003, Harcourt $16.00 (978-0-15-202664-6). Despite his serious parents, Prince Ernest is determined to become a jester, and he shows some talent at this when he coaxes a laugh from a three-headed dragon and thereby saves the kingdom. (Rev: HB 11/03; HBG 4/04; SLJ 11/03)

4806 Howe, James. *Horace and Morris Say Cheese (Which Makes Dolores Sneeze!)* (K–2). Illus. by Amy Walrod. 2009, Simon & Schuster $16.99 (978-0-689-83940-5). 32pp. Dolores suddenly becomes allergic to cheese but can she give it up? (Rev: BL 8/09; HB 7/09; SLJ 7/09)

4807 Hubbell, Patricia. *Pots and Pans* (PS). Illus. by Diane deGroat. 1998, HarperCollins $10.99 (978-0-694-01072-1). Baby clears out the kitchen cupboards, producing chaos and a mad clattering as the child bangs away at the pots and pans. (Rev: BCCB 9/98; BL 8/98; HBG 10/98; SLJ 6/98)

4808 Hughes, Ted. *My Brother Bert* (PS–1). Illus. by Tracey Campbell Pearson. 2009, Farrar $16.95 (978-0-374-39982-5). 40pp. Bert's little sister finds more than she expected when she invades her brother's room in this poem with riotous illustrations of a menagerie running wild. (Rev: BL 2/1/09; HB 5/09; SLJ 5/09)

4809 Hurd, Thacher. *Bad Frogs* (PS–2). Illus. by author. 2009, Candlewick $15.99 (978-0-7636-3253-3). 40pp. These misbehaving frogs — all 170 of them — get up to constant mischief in this brightly illustrated book. (Rev: BCCB 4/09; SLJ 6/09)

4810 Hutchins, Pat. *Don't Forget the Bacon!* (K–3). Illus. by author. 1976, Morrow paper $6.99 (978-0-688-08743-2). 32pp. A young boy mixes up the shopping list on a trip to the grocery store.

4811 Inkpen, Mick. *Billy's Beetle* (PS–2). Illus. 1992, Harcourt $13.95 (978-0-15-200427-9). 32pp. Even with the help of a trained dog, Billy is not able to find his lost beetle. (Rev: BL 4/15/92; SLJ 8/92)

4812 Isaacs, Anne. *Swamp Angel* (K–4). Illus. by Paul Zelinsky. 1994, Dutton $17.99 (978-0-525-45271-3). 40pp. Angelica Longrider is a true tall-tale heroine because, among her many accomplishments, she is able to lasso a tornado. (Rev: BCCB 11/94; BL 10/15/94*; SLJ 12/94*)

4813 Jackson, Alison. *The Ballad of Valentine* (K–3). Illus. by Tricia Tusa. 2002, Dutton $16.99 (978-0-525-46720-5). 32pp. This parody of "My Darling, Clementine" stars a comic Valentine performing everyday tasks in her cabin while an admirer tries and fails to send her expressions of love. (Rev: BCCB 1/03; BL 11/15/02; SLJ 12/02)

4814 Jackson, Alison. *Thea's Tree* (1–3). Illus. by Janet Pedersen. 2008, Dutton $16.99 (978-0-525-47443-2). 32pp. When the seed Thea planted for her science project sprouts a vine bearing a golden egg, a singing harp, gold coins, and other marvels, Thea consults experts from scientists to bankers; the illustrations add to the zany humor. (Rev: BL 7/08; LMC 10/08; SLJ 4/08)

4815 Jackson, Ellen. *Scatterbrain Sam* (K–3). Illus. by Matt Faulkner. 2001, Charlesbridge $15.95 (978-0-88106-394-3). 32pp. In this tall-tale adaptation of a Welsh story, Scatterbrain Sam seeks a cure for his brain and in the process finds true love. (Rev: BL 8/01; HBG 3/02; SLJ 7/01)

4816 Jam, Teddy. *The Charlotte Stories* (1–3). Illus. by Harvey Chan. 1996, Groundwood $14.95 (978-0-88899-210-9). 48pp. Charlotte is a candid 7-year-old who can't avoid trouble because of her open, honest nature. (Rev: SLJ 12/96)

4817 James, Simon. *Baby Brains and RoboMom* (PS–2). Illus. by author. 2008, Candlewick $15.99 (978-0-7636-3463-6). 32pp. The talented young Baby Brains invents a robot to help his mother with her chores, but RoboMom soon takes on too much. (Rev: BL 4/1/08; SLJ 5/08)

4818 James, Simon. *Baby Brains Superstar* (PS). Illus. 2005, Candlewick $15.99 (978-0-7636-2894-9). 32pp. In this appealing sequel to *Baby Brains* (2004), young Baby, a musical prodigy because Mom wore earphones on her belly, decides to pursue a career in rock 'n' roll, performing before a massive audience. (Rev: BL 9/15/05; SLJ 11/05)

4819 Jarka, Jeff. *Love That Puppy! The Story of a Boy Who Wanted to Be a Dog* (PS–1). Illus. by author. 2009, Holt $12.95 (978-0-8050-8741-3). 32pp. A pleasantly silly story that will give readers something to chew on. (Rev: SLJ 6/09)

4820 Jinkins, Jim. *Shrinky Pinky!* (1–3). Illus. Series: Pinky Dinky Doo. 2005, Random $12.95 (978-0-375-83234-5). 48pp. Pinky tells her younger brother a tall tale about how she dealt with a bully named Lane Puppytray. (Rev: BL 12/1/05)

4821 Johnson, Arden. *The Lost Tooth Club* (K–2). Illus. by author. 1998, Tricycle $13.95 (978-1-883672-55-3). Olivia tries various methods to lose her loose front tooth, so she can join the exclusive Lost Tooth Club. (Rev: HBG 10/98; SLJ 6/98)

4822 Johnson, Paul B. *Mr. Persnickety and Cat Lady* (K–2). Illus. by Paul Johnson. 2000, Orchard LB $16.99 (978-0-531-33283-2). A humorous story about Mr. Persnickety who tries to get rid of his neighbor's 37 cats until his house is infested with mice. (Rev: BCCB 7–8/00; HBG 3/01; SLJ 11/00)

4823 Johnson, Paul B. *On Top of Spaghetti* (PS–2). Illus. 2006, Scholastic $15.99 (978-0-439-74944-2). 32pp. The lyrics of Tom Glazer's song about spaghetti provide the framework for this tale of a runaway meatball. (Rev: BL 4/15/06; SLJ 5/06)

4824 Jonas, Ann. *Round Trip* (PS–4). Illus. by author. 1983, Morrow paper $6.99 (978-0-688-09986-2). 32pp. A book to read forward, backward, and then upside down.

4825 Jonas, Ann. *Watch William Walk* (PS–K). Illus. 1997, Greenwillow $14.89 (978-0-688-14175-2). 24pp. An alphabet adventure in which the entire story is told with words that begin with *w*. (Rev: BL 4/1/97; HB 7/97; SLJ 4/97)

4826 Joyce, William. *A Day with Wilbur Robinson* (PS–2). 2006, HarperCollins $16.99 (978-0-06-089098-8). 40pp. A young friend visits Wilbur Robinson at home, meets his extraordinary family, and gets swept up in some unforgettable adventures in this wacky romp, an expanded version of the 1990 title. (Rev: BL 8/06)

4827 Kanninen, Barbara. *A Story with Pictures* (K–3). Illus. by Lynn Rowe Reed. 2007, Holiday House $16.95 (978-0-8234-2049-0). 32pp. A young author engages in a humorous battle with her illustrator for control of her story, teaching readers much about the structure of books in the process. (Rev: LMC 1/08; SLJ 10/07)

4828 Katz, Alan. *Don't Say That Word!* (PS–1). Illus. by David Catrow. 2007, Simon & Schuster $16.99 (978-0-689-86971-6). 40pp. Michael almost says seven bad words as he tells his mom about his school day in this hilariously picture book. (Rev: BCCB 9/07; BL 7/07; LMC 10/07; SLJ 7/07)

4829 Keane, Dave. *Bobby Bramble Loses His Brain* (1–3). Illus. by David Clark. 2009, Clarion $16.00 (978-0-547-05644-9). 32pp. When Bobby falls and knocks the top off his head, his brain takes off, prompting a frantic chase. (Rev: BCCB 6/09; BL 4/15/09; SLJ 6/09)

4830 Kelley, Marty. *The Rules* (K–3). Illus. by author. 2000, Zino $12.95 (978-1-55933-284-2). Though the text offers many important dos and don'ts, the pictures show children humorously breaking each of the rules. (Rev: BL 9/15/03; HBG 4/04; SLJ 12/00)

4831 Kelly, Mij. *Where's My Darling Daughter?* (PS). Illus. by Katharine McEwen. 2006, Good Bks. $16.00 (978-1-56148-537-6). Certain that he has misplaced his baby daughter (who is on her father's back the whole time), Poppa Bombola sets off on a frantic search. (Rev: SLJ 12/06)

4832 Ketteman, Helen. *Shoeshine Whittaker* (1–3). Illus. by Scott Goto. 1999, Walker LB $16.85 (978-0-8027-8715-6). 32pp. In Mudville, Shoeshine guarantees how long his shine will last — and lives to regret it. (Rev: BL 10/15/99; HBG 3/00; SLJ 10/99)

4833 Kimmel, Eric A. *The Great Texas Hamster Drive* (PS–2). Illus. by Bruce Whatley. 2007, Marshall Cavendish $16.99 (978-0-7614-5357-4). 40pp. Legendary cowboy Pecos Bill orders a pair of pet hamsters for his daughter without sufficient forethought and ends up herding their offspring clear up to Chicago. (Rev: BL 10/1/07; LMC 1/08; SLJ 10/07)

4834 Kimmel, Eric A. *I Took My Frog to the Library* (PS–K). Illus. by Blanche Sims. 1992, Puffin paper $5.99 (978-0-14-050916-8). 32pp. A number of different animals create havoc when they visit the library. (Rev: BL 2/15/90; SLJ 3/90)

4835 Kimmel, Eric A. *Little Britches and the Rattlers* (K–2). Illus. by Vincent Nguyen. 2008, Marshall Cavendish $16.99 (978-0-7614-5432-8). 32pp. Little Britches must negotiate with seven threatening rattlesnakes on her way to the rodeo in this humorous repetitive story. (Rev: BL 9/15/08; LMC 3/09; SLJ 9/08)

4836 Kirsch, Vincent X. *Natalie and Naughtily* (K–3). Illus. by author. 2008, Bloomsbury $16.99 (978-1-59990-269-2). 32pp. Twins Natalie and Naughtily, who live above a department store, disobey the rules and decide to go and "help" the customers. (Rev: LMC 3/09; SLJ 11/08)

4837 Kiser, Kevin. *Buzzy Widget* (1–4). Illus. by John O'Brien. 1999, Marshall Cavendish $15.95 (978-0-7614-5057-3). Buzzy, a compulsive inventor, creates mechanical helpmates including CHEF, MAID, and WIFE. (Rev: HBG 3/00; SLJ 10/99)

4838 Kloske, Geoffrey. *Once Upon a Time, the End (Asleep in 60 Seconds)* (K–3). Illus. by Barry Blitt. 2005, Simon & Schuster $15.95 (978-0-689-86619-7). 40pp. An exhausted father tells his insatiable child hilariously abbreviated versions of fairy tales and nursery rhymes. (Rev: BCCB 12/05; BL 11/15/05*; HBG 4/06; SLJ 10/05)

4839 Koller, Jackie F. *Horace the Horrible: A Knight Meets His Match* (PS–3). Illus. by Jackie Urbanovic. 2003, Marshall Cavendish $16.95 (978-0-7614-5150-1). The humorous tale of Horace's knightly efforts to entertain his unhappy niece, the Princess Minuette. (Rev: BCCB 12/03; HBG 4/04; SLJ 11/03)

4840 Koller, Jackie F. *Peter Spit a Seed at Sue* (PS–3). Illus. by John Manders. 2008, Viking $15.99 (978-0-670-06309-3). 32pp. Four friends turn a dull summer day into a watermelon-seed-spitting adventure that infects the whole town. (Rev: LMC 11/08*; SLJ 9/08)

4841 Kopelke, Lisa. *The Younger Brother's Survival Guide: By Matt* (PS–3). Illus. by author. 2006, Simon & Schuster $15.95 (978-0-689-86249-6). Matt offers helpful and humorous advice on how to survive life with an older sibling. (Rev: SLJ 3/06)

4842 Kraft, Jim. *The No-Good Do-Good Pirates* (PS–2). Illus. by Lynne Avril. 2008, Albert Whitman $16.99 (978-0-8075-5695-5). 32pp. A thoroughly silly story in which four young pirates wreak havoc as they try to figure out how to do a good deed; cartoon illustrations add to the fun. (Rev: BCCB 11/08; SLJ 9/08)

4843 Krensky, Stephen. *Big Bad Wolves at School* (PS–2). Illus. by Brad Sneed. 2007, Simon & Schuster $15.99 (978-0-689-83799-9). 32pp. Rufus, a happy-go-lucky young wolf, finds classes at the Big Bad Wolf Academy a little too challenging for his tastes; energetic illustrations add to the hilarity. (Rev: BL 4/1/07)

4844 Krosoczka, Jarrett J. *Baghead* (PS–2). Illus. 2002, Knopf $15.95 (978-0-375-81566-9). 40pp. Confounding the skeptics, Josh succeeds in spending a day with a paper bag over his head, but his reason for doing so remains hidden until the end. (Rev: BL 11/15/02; HBG 3/03; SLJ 10/02)

4845 Laden, Nina. *Peek-a-Who?* (PS). Illus. by author. 2000, Chronicle $6.95 (978-0-8118-2602-0). A board book that uses die-cut windows so the reader can play a game of peek-a-boo. (Rev: SLJ 7/00)

4846 Lasky, Kathryn. *Two Bad Pilgrims* (2–4). Illus. by John Manders. 2009, Viking $16.99 (978-0-670-06168-6). 40pp. Fact and fiction are interwoven in this graphic-novel-style account of the Billington family (known for "generally poor behavior" aboard the *Mayflower*) in which sons Johnny and Francis get a chance to correct the record. (Rev: BL 7/09)

4847 Lattimore, Deborah N. *The Lady with the Ship on Her Head* (PS–2). Illus. 1990, Harcourt $14.95 (978-0-15-243525-7). 32pp. In 18th-century France, Madame Pompenstance is unaware that a ship has landed on her hair. (Rev: BL 3/15/90; SLJ 6/90)

4848 Lawston, Lisa. *A Pair of Red Sneakers* (PS–2). Illus. by B. B. Sams. 1998, Orchard LB $16.99 (978-0-531-33104-0). 32pp. Miles imagines all the wonderful things he could do with a new pair of red sneakers, only to discover the store is out of them. (Rev: BL 10/1/98; HBG 3/99; SLJ 9/98)

4849 Lendler, Ian. *An Undone Fairy Tale* (K–3). Illus. by Whitney Martin. 2005, Simon & Schuster $15.95 (978-0-689-86677-7). 32pp. A fairy tale involving a princess locked in a tower spins out of control when the illustrator and narrator can't keep up. (Rev: BL 1/1–15/06; SLJ 12/05)

4850 Lerman, Josh. *How to Raise Mom and Dad: (Instructions from Someone Who Figured It Out)* (K–3). Illus. by Greg Clarke. 2009, Dutton $16.99 (978-0-525-47870-6). 32pp. An older sister instructs her younger brother in the art of dealing with parents. (Rev: BCCB 4/09; BL 3/1/09; SLJ 2/09)

4851 Lester, Helen. *It Wasn't My Fault* (PS–1). Illus. by Lynn Munsinger. 1985, Houghton $17.00 (978-0-395-35629-6). 32pp. Nerdy Murdley Gurdson tries to discover why an ostrich laid an egg on his head. (Rev: BCCB 6/85; BL 3/1/85; SLJ 5/85)

4852 Lester, Helen. *Tacky Goes to Camp* (PS–2). Illus. by Lynn Munsinger. 2009, Houghton $16.00 (978-0-618-98812-9). 32pp. Tacky the penguin saves the day when a bear threatens Camp Whoopihaha. Earlier books featuring Tacky include *Tacky the Penguin* (1988), *Three Cheers for Tacky* (1994),

Tacky in Trouble (1998), *Tacky and the Emperor* (2000), *Tackylocks and the Three Bears* (2002), and *Tacky and the Winter Games* (2005). (Rev: BL 4/1/09; HB 5/09; SLJ 4/09)

4853 Levine, Martha Peaslee. *Stop That Nose!* (PS–1). Illus. by Lee White. 2006, Marshall Cavendish $14.95 (978-0-7614-5280-5). Dad's nose flies off in a sneezing fit and young David chases valiantly after it as it continues to sneeze, ejecting all sorts of things en route. (Rev: SLJ 4/06)

4854 Levitin, Sonia. *A Single Speckled Egg* (K–3). Illus. by John Larrecq. 1976, Houghton $6.95 (978-0-87466-074-6). 40pp. Three foolish farmers are outwitted by their wives in this ridiculous tale told in the folk tradition.

4855 Lillegard, Dee. *Balloons Balloons Balloons* (PS–1). Illus. by Bernadette Pons. 2007, Dutton $16.99 (978-0-525-45940-8). Children and adult react in different ways when a town is inundated with colorful balloons. (Rev: SLJ 2/07)

4856 Lithgow, John. *Marsupial Sue Presents "The Runaway Pancake"* (K–2). Illus. by Jack Davis. 2005, Simon & Schuster $17.95 (978-0-689-87847-3). 40pp. Marsupial Sue the kangaroo — here cast in the role of Auntie May — and her friends are staging their version of "The Gingerbread Man"; Lithgow reads the story on an accompanying CD. (Rev: BL 11/1/05; SLJ 10/05) ∩

4857 Lithgow, John. *The Remarkable Farkle McBride* (K–2). Illus. by C. F. Payne. 2000, Simon & Schuster $16.00 (978-0-689-83340-3). Farkle McBride tires of each musical instrument he tries until he realizes he was born to become a conductor. (Rev: BCCB 6/00; HBG 3/01; SLJ 9/00)

4858 Lloyd, Sam. *Chief Rhino to the Rescue* (PS–1). Illus. by author. 2009, Holt $14.99 (978-0-8050-8821-2). 32pp. Fire Chief Rhino rushes to put out a fire only to discover it's the 100 candles on Great-Granny Wrinkles' birthday cake; detailed illustrations add to the fun. (Rev: BL 7/09; SLJ 9/09)

4859 Lloyd-Jones, Sally. *How to Get Married . . . by Me, the Bride* (K–2). Illus. by Sue Heap. 2009, Random $16.99 (978-0-375-84118-7). 40pp. An entertaining primer for little bridal wannabes, with advice on such topics as picking a spouse and then good places to wed (a castle, a playroom . . .). (Rev: BCCB 6/09; BLO 5/27/09; SLJ 4/09)

4860 Lobel, Arnold. *Ming Lo Moves the Mountain* (PS–3). Illus. by author. 1982, Morrow paper $6.99 (978-0-688-10995-0). 32pp. A humorous tale about a man's attempt to move a mountain away from his house.

4861 London, Sara. *Firehorse Max* (PS–1). Illus. 1997, HarperCollins LB $14.89 (978-0-06-205095-3). 32pp. Grandpa Lev's new horse, a former horse at the firehouse, has a behavioral problem when fire bells ring. (Rev: BL 10/1/97; SLJ 10/97)

4862 Long, Kathy. *The Runaway Shopping Cart* (PS–2). Illus. by Susan Estelle Kwas. 2007, Dutton $16.99 (978-0-525-47187-5). When the shopping cart Kaleb's sitting in gets loose and starts rolling through town it attracts a train of followers, Gingerbread Man-style. (Rev: SLJ 4/07)

4863 Lorbiecki, Marybeth. *Paul Bunyan's Sweetheart* (1–3). Illus. by Renee Graef. 2007, Sleeping Bear $16.95 (978-1-58536-289-9). 32pp. Paul Bunyan pursues his dream girl Lucette, who is as big a hero as Bunyan (literally), and must pass her love test in this story written in true tall-tale style. (Rev: BL 11/15/07; SLJ 9/07)

4864 Lord, John Vernon. *The Giant Jam Sandwich* (PS–2). Illus. by author. 1987, Houghton $17.00 (978-0-395-16033-6); paper $6.95 (978-0-395-44237-1). A rhymed verse about the citizens of Itching Down who make a giant jam sandwich to attract wasps.

4865 Low, Alice. *Aunt Lucy Went to Buy a Hat* (PS–1). Illus. by Laura Huliska-Beith. 2004, HarperCollins $15.99 (978-0-06-008971-9). 32pp. An imaginative and well-illustrated story told in rhyme about forgetful Aunt Lucy's search for a hat. (Rev: BL 2/1/04; SLJ 3/04)

4866 Lubner, Susan. *Ruthie Bon Bair, Do Not Go to Bed with Wringing Wet Hair!* (PS–3). Illus. by Bruce Whatley. 2006, Abrams $15.95 (978-0-8109-5470-0). Little Ruthie refuses to follow her mother's advice and ends up with all kinds of horrid hair problems. (Rev: SLJ 11/06)

4867 Lucas, David. *Halibut Jackson* (PS–1). Illus. 2004, Knopf $16.95 (978-0-375-82690-0). 32pp. Shy Halibut aims to be invisible and wears clothes intended to blend in to his surroundings, but he misinterprets a royal invitation and attracts a lot of attention. (Rev: BL 2/1/04; SLJ 3/04)

4868 McClements, George. *Baron von Baddie and the Ice Ray Incident* (K–2). Illus. by author. 2008, Harcourt $16.00 (978-0-15-206138-8). 40pp. Being bad is just no fun if you don't have good guys to go up against. (Rev: BCCB 9/09; BL 11/15/08; LMC 3/09; SLJ 9/08)

4869 McClements, George. *Night of the Veggie Monster* (PS–3). Illus. by author. 2008, Bloomsbury $14.95 (978-1-59990-061-2). Ack! A pea on the plate! This is a funny story about a critical moment. (Rev: BCCB 1/08; HB 3/08; LMC 3/08; SLJ 2/08)

4870 McCloskey, Robert. *Burt Dow, Deep-Water Man* (K–3). Illus. by author. 1963, Puffin paper $6.99 (978-0-14-050978-6). 64pp. The humorous tale of an old Maine fisherman who caught a whale by the tail and then used a multicolored Band-Aid to cover the hole.

4871 McCloskey, Robert. *Lentil* (K–3). Illus. by author. 1940, Puffin paper $6.99 (978-0-14-050287-9). 64pp. Tale of a boy who can't carry a tune, yet learns to play the harmonica.

4872 MacDonald, Alan. *Trolls, Go Home!* (2–4). Illus. by Mark Beech. Series: Troll Trouble. 2007, Bloomsbury $14.95 (978-1-59990-077-3); paper $5.95 (978-1-59990-078-0). 128pp. When the Trolls move in next door, the Priddles are initially very uncomfortable. (Rev: BCCB 9/07; BL 5/1/07; SLJ 10/07)

4873 McDonald, Megan. *Beetle McGrady Eats Bugs!* (PS–2). Illus. by Jane Manning. 2005, HarperCollins LB $17.89 (978-0-06-001355-4). Beetle is an adventurous soul and for Fun with Food Week declares that she will eat an ant. (Rev: BL 3/1/04; SLJ 5/05)

4874 McElligott, Matthew. *Backbeard and the Birthday Suit: The Hairiest Pirate Who Ever Lived* (K–2). Illus. 2006, Walker $16.95 (978-0-8027-8065-2). 32pp. Blackbeard the pirate trades his dilapidated buccaneering duds for a stylish new outfit much to the surprise of his crew. (Rev: BL 4/15/06; SLJ 4/06)

4875 McElmurry, Jill. *I'm Not a Baby!* (PS–2). 2006, Random $16.95 (978-0-375-83614-5). 32pp. Leo Leotardi, the youngest member of his family, has difficulty convincing family members that he's no longer a baby; Victorian-era illustrations of Leo bursting out of his baby clothes add to the fun. (Rev: BL 6/1–15/06; HBG 4/07; SLJ 7/06*)

4876 McEvoy, Greg. *The Ice Cream King* (K–3). Illus. by author. 1998, Stoddart $13.95 (978-0-7737-3069-4). After graduating from King School, Lionel finds there are few openings, so he compromises and becomes an ice-cream seller known as "The Ice Cream King." (Rev: SLJ 12/98)

4877 McGee, Marni. *Winston the Book Wolf* (PS–2). Illus. by Ian Beck. 2006, Walker $16.95 (978-0-8027-9569-4). 32pp. In this amusing send-up of the Little Red Riding Hood story, the wolf has an appetite for books, behavior that infuriates the librarian, but he's shown the error of his ways and taught to read — and not eat — the books by a little girl named Rosie who just happens to be wearing a red hood. (Rev: SLJ 12/06)

4878 McKy, Katie. *Pumpkin Town! (Or, Nothing Is Better and Worse Than Pumpkins)* (K–3). Illus. by Pablo Bernasconi. 2006, Houghton $16.00 (978-0-618-60569-9). José and his brothers don't know quite what to do when the pumpkin seeds they discarded at the end of the last growing season take root and threaten to overrun the town. (Rev: SLJ 11/06)

4879 McMullan, Kate. *I'm Bad!* (PS–1). Illus. by Jim McMullan. 2008, HarperCollins $16.99 (978-0-06-122971-8). 40pp. A hungry tyrannosaurus boasts about his size and badness but fails to find anything to eat in this funny book that ends with a foldout of his much huger mother. (Rev: BL 4/1/08; HB 5/08; SLJ 5/08)

4880 McNaughton, Colin. *Captain Abdul's Little Treasure* (K–3). Series: Captain Abdul. 2006, Candlewick $14.99 (978-0-7636-3045-4). 48pp. The treasure on Captain Abdul's ship is a baby, and his pirate baby-sitters love playing with him despite their gruff appearances. (Rev: BL 5/1/06)

4881 McNaughton, Colin. *We're Off to Look for Aliens* (PS–3). Illus. by author. 2008, Candlewick $15.99 (978-0-7636-3636-4). 40pp. A pleasing story within a story with a surprise ending, this title features humorous rhyming text and illustrations. (Rev: LMC 11/08; SLJ 9/08)

4882 Madison, Alan. *The Littlest Grape Stomper* (K–2). Illus. by Giselle Potter. 2007, Random $16.99 (978-0-375-83675-6). This whimsical tall tale describes the story behind the Grape Lakes, in which a boy called Sixto Poblano — disinclined to use the six toes he has on each foot to stomp grapes — squishes a huge vatful and then spills it out, creating a massive flood. (Rev: SLJ 4/07)

4883 Madison, Alan. *Pecorino Plays Ball* (K–2). Illus. by AnnaLaura Cantone. 2006, Simon & Schuster $15.95 (978-0-689-86522-0). 40pp. Although he's never caught or pitched a baseball before, young Pecorino Sasquatch looks forward to his first Little League game. (Rev: BL 2/1/06; SLJ 3/06)

4884 Madison, Alan. *Pecorino's First Concert* (K–2). Illus. by AnnaLaura Cantone. 2005, Simon & Schuster $15.95 (978-0-689-85952-6). Pecorino goes to the orchestra and gets trapped in a tuba in this amusing tale. (Rev: SLJ 8/05)

4885 Mahy, Margaret. *Down the Back of the Chair* (PS–2). Illus. by Polly Dunbar. 2006, Clarion $16.00 (978-0-618-69395-5). 32pp. A family in search of lost car keys discovers lots more under the chair cushions (including a diamond ring, a ski, and a lion) in this rhyming jaunt. (Rev: BL 5/1/06; SLJ 6/06)

4886 Mangas, Brian. *Follow That Puppy!* (PS–2). Illus. by R. W. Alley. 1991, Simon & Schuster paper $12.95 (978-0-671-70780-4). When Puppy escapes his elderly owner while out for a walk, an exciting chase occurs. (Rev: SLJ 11/91)

4887 Manning, Maurie J. *The Aunts Go Marching* (PS–1). Illus. 2003, Boyds Mills $15.95 (978-1-59078-026-8). 32pp. Aunts (rather than the usual ants) march to town in this version of the familiar children's song. (Rev: BL 2/1/03; HB 5/03; HBG 10/03; SLJ 4/03)

4888 Manushkin, Fran. *The Shivers in the Fridge* (PS–1). Illus. by Paul Zelinsky. 2006, Dutton $16.99 (978-0-525-46943-8). 40pp. Readers may take some time to work out that the very cold characters In this fanciful picture book are actually members of a family of refrigerator magnets. (Rev: BCCB 10/06; BL 10/15/06; HB 11/06; HBG 4/07; SLJ 10/06)

4889 Martchenko, Michael. *Ma, I'm a Farmer* (1–3). Illus. by author. 2003, Annick paper $5.95 (978-1-55037-696-8). Computer geek-turned-farmer, Fred soon discovers that rural life is not quite as stress-relieving as he had hoped, so he decides to apply his technological know-how to agrarian problems, with hilarious consequences. (Rev: SLJ 1/04)

4890 Martin, Bill, Jr. *The Maestro Plays* (PS–K). Illus. by Vladimir Radunsky. 1994, Holt $15.95 (978-0-8050-1746-5). 38pp. A circus setting is used to show all the different instruments the maestro plays. (Rev: BCCB 12/94; BL 11/1/94; SLJ 11/94*)

4891 Martin, Bill, Jr., and Michael Sampson. *Little Granny Quarterback* (K–3). Illus. by Michael Chesworth. 2001, Boyds Mills $15.95 (978-1-56397-930-9). A zany story in which Granny Whiteoak, a star football player in her day, saves her team from defeat. (Rev: HBG 3/02; SLJ 12/01)

4892 Marzollo, Jean. *I Spy Funhouse: A Book of Picture Riddles* (PS–3). Photos by Walter Wick. 1993, Scholastic $13.99 (978-0-590-46293-8). 40pp. This entertaining book consists of a series of picture puz-

zles involving an amusement park fun house and of a series of rhyming word clues. (Rev: BL 5/15/93; SLJ 4/93) [793]

4893 Mazer, Anne. *The No-Nothings and Their Baby* (PS–3). Illus. by Ross Collins. 2000, Scholastic $15.95 (978-0-590-68049-3). 40pp. Three goofy stories about Mr. and Mrs. No-Nothing and their misguided efforts to bring up a baby. (Rev: BL 1/1–15/01; HBG 3/01; SLJ 11/00)

4894 Meddaugh, Susan. *Martha Blah Blah* (PS–2). Illus. 1996, Houghton $16.00 (978-0-395-79755-6). 32pp. Martha the dog, who talks after eating alphabet soup, finds her vocabulary constricted when the soup company reduces the letters in each can. Other installments in this series are *Martha Calling* (1994), *Martha Walks the Dog* (1998), *Martha and Skits* (2000), and *Perfectly Martha* (2004). (Rev: BCCB 12/96; BL 9/15/96; HB 11/96; SLJ 11/96*)

4895 Meddaugh, Susan. *Martha Speaks* (PS–3). Illus. 1992, Houghton $16.99 (978-0-395-63313-7). 32pp. Helen feeds her dog alphabet soup, and suddenly Martha can talk! (Rev: BCCB 11/92*; BL 9/1/92*; HB 1/93*; SLJ 12/92)

4896 Melling, David. *The Scallywags* (PS–2). Illus. 2007, Barron's $14.99 (978-0-7641-5991-6). 32pp. The wolf family known as the Scallywags decide to reform their behavior after the other animals totally reject them, but they go much too far in the other direction. (Rev: BL 2/1/07)

4897 Mickelson, Scott. *Artichoke Boy* (PS–2). Illus. by author. 2009, Boyds Mills $16.95 (978-1-59078-605-5). 32pp. A boy with an unusual affection for artichokes sees them everywhere; mixed-media collages and cartoon illustrations extend the lighthearted rhymes. (Rev: BL 2/1/09; SLJ 3/09)

4898 Mora, Pat. *Doña Flor: A Tall Tale About a Giant Woman with a Great Big Heart* (PS–2). Illus. by Raúl Colón. 2005, Knopf $15.95 (978-0-375-82337-4). 40pp. When the cries of a fearsome beast frighten her fellow villagers, Doña Flor, a woman of monumental stature, sets off to find out what's causing the animal's distress only to discover the perpetrator is much less threatening than expected. (Rev: BL 12/1/05; SLJ 10/05)

4899 Morgan, Christopher. *Pirates Eat Porridge* (1–3). Illus. by Neil Curtis. 2007, Roaring Brook $12.95 (978-1-59643-304-5). 80pp. After a wayward treasure map blows into Billy and Heidi's treehouse, its demanding pirate owner comes to claim it and the treehouse is transformed into a ship, whisking them off to an island where the children learn pirate ways. (Rev: BL 11/15/07; SLJ 3/08)

4900 Most, Bernard. *Whatever Happened to the Dinosaurs?* (1–3). Illus. by author. 1984, Harcourt paper $4.95 (978-0-15-295296-9). 32pp. Fantastic explanations to the title question.

4901 Munsch, Robert. *Alligator Baby* (PS–2). Illus. by Michael Martchenko. 1997, Scholastic $10.95 (978-0-590-21101-7). 29pp. An amusing story about overwrought parents who bring different baby animals home from the zoo, thinking each is their child. (Rev: HBG 3/98; SLJ 11/97)

4902 Munsch, Robert. *Get Out of Bed!* (PS–2). Illus. by Alan Daniel and Lea Daniel. 1998, Scholastic $10.95 (978-0-590-76977-8). 32pp. Because she has watched television all night, Amy can't get out of bed in the morning, so her family takes her to school in her bed, with humorous results. (Rev: BL 9/15/98; HBG 3/99; SLJ 9/98)

4903 Munsch, Robert. *Munschworks: The First Munsch Collection* (PS–3). Illus. by Michael Martchenko. 1998, Annick $19.95 (978-1-55037-523-7). 128pp. This omnibus volume includes five of Robert Munsch's popular picture books, including *The Paper Bag Princess, David's Father,* and *Thomas' Snowsuit.* (Rev: BL 1/1–15/99)

4904 Munsch, Robert. *Munschworks 2: The Second Munsch Treasury* (PS–2). Illus. by Michael Martchenko and Helene Desputeaux. 1999, Annick $19.95 (978-1-55037-553-4). 136pp. This anthology contains five of Robert Munsch's picture books including *Purple, Green and Yellow*, *Pigs*, and *Something Good*. (Rev: BL 1/1–15/00; HBG 3/00)

4905 Munsch, Robert. *Stephanie's Ponytail* (1–3). Illus. by Michael Martchenko. 1996, Firefly $16.95 (978-1-55037-485-8); paper $5.95 (978-1-55037-484-1). Stephanie is annoyed when every one of her style changes is copied by class members and her teacher. (Rev: SLJ 11/96)

4906 Munsch, Robert, and Michael Kusugak. *Munschworks 3: The Third Munsch Treasury* (PS–2). Illus. by Vladyana Krykorka and Michael Martchenko. 2000, Annick $19.95 (978-1-55037-633-3). 144pp. A large book that is a compilation of five of Munsch's previously published picture books including *Stephanie's Ponytail* (1986), *Angela's Airplane* (1988), and *A Promise Is a Promise* (1988). (Rev: BL 2/1/01; HBG 10/01) [813]

4907 Myers, Lynne B., and Christopher Myers. *Turnip Soup* (PS–2). Illus. by Katie Keller. 1994, Hyperion LB $14.49 (978-1-56282-446-4). 32pp. George is afraid that there is a Komodo dragon in his basement, and he is right. (Rev: BL 11/15/94; SLJ 2/95)

4908 Nedwidek, John. *Ducks Don't Wear Socks* (K–3). Illus. by Lee White. 2008, Viking $15.99 (978-0-670-06136-5). 32pp. A serious-minded little girl learns to laugh through her relationship with a nattily dressed duck. (Rev: BL 6/1–15/08; SLJ 5/08)

4909 Newman, Jeff. *Hippo! No, Rhino* (K–2). Illus. by author. 2006, Little, Brown $15.99 (978-0-316-15573-1). A rhino at the zoo is mistakenly labeled a hippo in this almost-wordless tale. (Rev: SLJ 7/06)

4910 Nikola-Lisa, W. *Can You Top That?* (K–3). Illus. by Hector Viveros Lee. 2000, Lee & Low $15.95 (978-1-880000-99-1). 32pp. A group of children try to outdo each other by naming the strange animals they have at home, but a young African American tops them all by claiming he can produce an elephant — and he can, a little stuffed one. (Rev: BL 9/15/00; HBG 10/01; SLJ 12/00)

4911 Noble, Trinka Hakes. *Jimmy's Boa and the Bungee Jump Slam Dunk* (K–3). Illus. by Steven Kellogg. 2003, Dial $16.99 (978-0-8037-2600-0). Jimmy and his pet boa constrictor create havoc

when they visit the school gym, where dance lessons are taking place. (Rev: HBG 4/04; SLJ 9/03)

4912 Noble, Trinka Hakes. *Meanwhile, Back at the Ranch* (PS–1). Illus. by Tony Ross. 1987, Puffin paper $6.99 (978-0-14-054564-7). 32pp. A humorous Western adventure concerning Rancher Hicks and his drive into Sleepy Gulch for some excitement. (Rev: BL 4/1/87; SLJ 5/87)

4913 Nolan, Lucy. *The Lizard Man of Crabtree County* (K–3). Illus. by Jill Kastner. 1999, Marshall Cavendish $15.95 (978-0-7614-5049-8). 32pp. A young boy, who dresses up as a bush, causes a commotion when he is mistaken for the Lizard Man. (Rev: BCCB 10/99; BL 11/15/99; HBG 3/00; SLJ 10/99)

4914 Nolen, Jerdine. *Plantzilla* (1–3). Illus. by David Catrow. 2002, Harcourt $16.00 (978-0-15-202412-3). 32pp. Third-grader Mortimer takes charge of the classroom plant, nicknamed Plantzilla, for the summer, and peculiar things begin to happen. (Rev: BCCB 11/02; BL 10/15/02; HBG 3/03; SLJ 9/02)

4915 Nolen, Jerdine. *Plantzilla Goes to Camp* (1–3). Illus. by David Catrow. 2006, Simon & Schuster $16.95 (978-0-689-86803-0). 32pp. Mortimer's pet plant is not allowed at his summer camp but manages to sneak in anyway and save him from a bully; a sequel to *Plantzilla* (2002). (Rev: BL 4/15/06; SLJ 3/06)

4916 Novak, Matt. *The Pillow War* (PS–2). Illus. 1998, Orchard LB $16.99 (978-0-531-33048-7). 32pp. Millie and Fred have a pillow fight over who will sleep with Sam the dog, but Sam has other plans. (Rev: BL 2/15/98; HBG 10/98; SLJ 3/98)

4917 Novak, Matt. *Too Many Bunnies* (PS–K). Illus. by author. 2005, Roaring Brook $7.95 (978-1-59643-038-9). Enhanced by a die-cut format, this is the story of five overcrowded bunnies who spy an invitingly empty hole across the field and one by one hop over there only to find they are no better off. (Rev: BCCB 2/05; HB 3/05; SLJ 6/05)

4918 O'Connor, George. *Uncle Bigfoot* (K–2). Illus. by author. 2008, Roaring Brook $15.95 (978-1-59643-271-0). 32pp. When the gigantic and hairy Uncle Bernie comes to stay, a young boy learns that people are not all the same. (Rev: BL 5/1/08; LMC 11/08; SLJ 6/08)

4919 O'Connor, Jane. *Bonjour Butterfly* (PS). Illus. by Robin P. Glasser. Series: Fancy Nancy. 2008, HarperCollins $16.99 (978-0-06-123588-7). 32pp. The little glamor queen is displeased when she has to miss her friend's butterfly party and go to her grandparents' anniversary party. (Rev: BL 3/15/08; SLJ 5/08)

4920 O'Connor, Jane. *Fancy Nancy* (PS–2). Illus. by Robin P. Glasser. 2006, HarperCollins $17.99 (978-0-06-054209-2). 32pp. Nancy, a fashion-obsessed young girl, is determined to give the rest of her family a badly needed makeover. (Rev: BL 1/1–15/06; SLJ 2/06)

4921 Offill, Jenny. *17 Things I'm Not Allowed to Do Anymore* (PS–K). Illus. by Nancy Carpenter. 2006, Schwartz & Wade $15.99 (978-0-375-83596-4). 32pp. The mischievous narrator of this appealing picture book recounts some of the things she's been forbidden to do — stapling her brother's hair to the pillow, freezing flies in ice cubes, and so forth. (Rev: BL 11/1/06; SLJ 11/06*)

4922 Oller, Erika. *The Cabbage Soup Solution* (PS–2). Illus. 2004, Dutton $15.99 (978-0-525-47005-2). 32pp. Old Elsie's cats solve the mystery of who has been tampering with the cabbage crop — rabbits. (Rev: BL 2/15/04; SLJ 2/04)

4923 Olson, David J. *The Thunderstruck Stork* (PS–2). Illus. by Lynn Munsinger. 2007, Albert Whitman $15.95 (978-0-8075-7910-7). 32pp. After Webster the stork collides with a hot-air balloon, families start receiving unlikely babies (sparrows get a piglet, for example) but everyone adapts happily. (Rev: BL 10/15/07; LMC 1/08; SLJ 9/07)

4924 O'Malley, Kevin. *Gimme Cracked Corn and I Will Share* (K–2). Illus. by author. 2007, Walker $16.95 (978-0-8027-9684-4). 32pp. Corny jokes and wordplays add to the humor of this story of a chicken searching for food. (Rev: BL 12/1/07; HB 1/08; LMC 1/08; SLJ 8/07)

4925 Oppel, Kenneth. *The King's Taster* (K–3). Illus. by Lou Fancher. 2009, HarperCollins $17.99 (978-0-06-075372-6). 32pp. In this story about picky eating, a dog called Max is the king's food taster and is puzzled by the new monarch's fussiness. (Rev: BL 3/15/09; HB 7/09; SLJ 6/09)

4926 Oppenheim, Shulamith Levey. *What Is the Full Moon Full Of?* (PS–2). Illus. by Cyd Moore. 1997, Boyds Mills $14.95 (978-1-56397-479-3). 32pp. Every one of the animals has a different answer when Jonas asks what the moon is full of. (Rev: BL 12/1/97; HBG 3/98; SLJ 12/97)

4927 Orlean, Susan. *Lazy Little Loafers* (K–2). Illus. by G. Brian Karas. 2008, Abrams $16.95 (978-0-8109-7027-4). 32pp. An older sister has a critical point of view regarding the value of babies. (Rev: BL 9/1/08)

4928 Palatini, Margie. *Bedhead* (K–3). Illus. by Jack E. Davis. 2000, Simon & Schuster $16.00 (978-0-689-82397-8). No one can tame Oliver's wild hair and so he must wear his trusty blue baseball hat to school. (Rev: BCCB 10/00; HBG 3/01; SLJ 7/00)

4929 Palatini, Margie. *The Cheese* (K–3). Illus. by Steve Johnson. 2007, HarperCollins $16.99 (978-0-06-052630-6). 32pp. This wonderfully silly book turns "The Farmer in the Dell" on its head, telling the story of the song's characters as they puzzle over why "the cheese stands alone." (Rev: BCCB 9/07; BL 5/15/07; SLJ 6/07)

4930 Palatini, Margie. *The Perfect Pet* (PS–2). Illus. by Bruce Whatley. 2003, HarperCollins LB $16.89 (978-0-06-000109-4). When Elizabeth's parents reject every suggestion for a new pet, the young girl adopts a tiny bug that she names Doug. (Rev: BL 7/03; HBG 10/03; SLJ 5/03)

4931 Palatini, Margie. *Three French Hens* (PS–2). Illus. by Richard Egielski. 2005, Hyperion $15.99 (978-0-7868-5167-6). 40pp. Three French hens — Collette, Poulette, and Fifi — sent as a gift to M. Philippe Renard end up instead in the clutches of Phil Fox, who welcomes the trio as potential food

but is soon transformed by their kind attentions. (Rev: BCCB 11/05; BL 11/1/05; HB 11/05; HBG 4/06; LMC 11/05; SLJ 10/05*)

4932 Palatini, Margie. *The Three Silly Billies* (PS–2). Illus. by Barry Moser. 2005, Simon & Schuster $15.95 (978-0-689-85862-8). 32pp. A troll stops characters from different fairy tales from crossing his bridge in this rollicking takeoff on the Billy Goats Gruff story. (Rev: BL 3/1/05)

4933 Parkinson, Curtis. *Emily's Eighteen Aunts* (PS–2). Illus. by Andrea Wayne von Konigslow. 2003, Fitzhenry & Whiteside $15.95 (978-0-7737-3336-7). 32pp. Feeling neglected with a new baby in the house, Emily advertises for an aunt and ends up with 18. (Rev: BL 2/15/03; SLJ 4/03)

4934 Parnell, Robyn. *My Closet Threw a Party* (PS–2). Illus. by Jimmy Pickering. 2005, Sterling $14.95 (978-1-4027-1298-2). A little girl finds an inventive way of explaining the total mess in her closet. (Rev: BL 5/1/04; SLJ 6/05)

4935 Parpan, Justin. *Gwango's Lonesome Trail* (1–5). Illus. by author. 2006, Red Cygnet $17.95 (978-1-60108-004-2). Gwango, a lonely dinosaur, wanders the contemporary Southwest in search of a friend; handsome paintings show the landscape and the humorous text has a retro feel. (Rev: SLJ 12/06)

4936 Patschke, Steve. *The Spooky Book* (K–3). Illus. by Matt McElligott. 1999, Walker LB $16.85 (978-0-8027-8693-7). 32pp. Two children, in separate houses, don't realize that they are reading scary books about each other and their spooky homes. (Rev: BCCB 9/99; BL 10/15/99; HBG 3/00; SLJ 11/99)

4937 Pinkwater, Daniel. *Bad Bear Detectives: An Irving and Muktuk Story* (PS–2). Illus. by Jill Pinkwater. Series: Irving and Muktuk. 2006, Houghton $16.00 (978-0-618-43125-0). 32pp. Who stole the muffins? Two falsely accused polar bears set out to find the real suspects. (Rev: BL 7/06; SLJ 8/06)

4938 Pinkwater, Daniel. *Bad Bears Go Visiting* (K–3). Illus. by Jill Pinkwater. 2007, Houghton $16.00 (978-0-618-43126-7). 32pp. Naughty polar bears Irving and Muktuk break out of the zoo and pay an unexpected and rowdy visit to the Beachball family. (Rev: BL 4/1/07)

4939 Pinkwater, Daniel. *The Big Orange Splot* (K–2). Illus. by author. 1992, Scholastic paper $4.99 (978-0-590-44510-8). 32pp. A cumulative story about the effects of dropping a can of orange paint on the roof of Mr. Plumbean's house.

4940 Pinkwater, Daniel. *Rainy Morning* (PS–2). Illus. by Jill Pinkwater. 1999, Simon & Schuster $16.00 (978-0-689-81143-2). 32pp. During a rainstorm, Mr. and Mrs. Submarine open their kitchen to all sorts of creatures, and soon it is filled with everything from a wildebeest to Ludwig van Beethoven and the U.S. Marine Band. (Rev: BCCB 3/99; BL 3/1/99; HBG 10/99; SLJ 3/99)

4941 Pinkwater, Daniel. *Sleepover Larry* (PS–2). Illus. by Jill Pinkwater. 2007, Marshall Cavendish $16.99 (978-0-7614-5314-7). 32pp. Larry the polar bear has a sleepover and his friends enjoy dancing, a movie, pizza, and other delicacies. Earlier books about Larry include *Bongo Larry* (1998), *Ice Cream Larry* (1999), and *Dancing Larry* (2006). (Rev: SLJ 11/07)

4942 Plourde, Lynn. *Grandpappy Snippy Snappies* (PS–K). Illus. by Christopher Santoro. 2009, HarperCollins $17.99 (978-0-06-028050-5). 32pp. Grandpappy's cure-all snappy suspenders fail to work when Grandmammy is hauled off by crows in this lively story full of wordplay. (Rev: BL 4/15/09; SLJ 5/09)

4943 Plourde, Lynn. *A Mountain of Mittens* (PS–1). Illus. by Mitch Vane. 2007, Charlesbridge $15.95 (978-1-57091-585-7). 32pp. A humorous tale about a mountainous lost-and-found box full of mittens and a townful of frustrated parents. (Rev: BL 6/1–15/07; SLJ 10/07)

4944 Polacco, Patricia. *Ginger and Petunia* (K–3). Illus. by author. 2007, Philomel $16.99 (978-0-399-24539-8). 40pp. Petunia's sitter is a no-show and the pampered pet pig is left to her own devices, with comical results. (Rev: BL 5/1/07; SLJ 6/07)

4945 Polacco, Patricia. *The Graves Family* (K–3). Illus. by author. 2003, Philomel $16.99 (978-0-399-24034-8). The townspeople steer a wide berth around the spooky Graves family's blood-red house until a decorating guru gives the Graves' home his stamp of approval. (Rev: HBG 4/04; SLJ 9/03)

4946 Polacco, Patricia. *In Enzo's Splendid Gardens* (1–4). Illus. 1997, Penguin $16.99 (978-0-399-23107-0). 32pp. A cumulative tale of chaos in an outdoor Italian restaurant begun by an innocent bee. (Rev: BL 8/97; SLJ 5/97)

4947 Polhemus, Coleman. *The Crocodile Blues* (PS–2). Illus. by author. 2007, Candlewick $16.99 (978-0-7636-3543-5). 48pp. A nearly wordless tale in which a man and his pet cockatoo discover, much to their dismay, the true nature of the egg they bring home from the store. (Rev: SLJ 11/07)

4948 Polisar, Barry L. *Don't Do That! A Child's Guide to Bad Manners, Ridiculous Rules, and Inadequate Etiquette*. Rev. ed. (K–4). Illus. by David Clark. 1995, Rainbow $14.95 (978-0-938663-20-1). An irreverent book of manners that, for example, tells how to pick one's nose properly in public. (Rev: SLJ 8/95)

4949 Porte, Barbara Ann. *Chickens! Chickens!* (PS–2). Illus. by Greg Henry. 1995, Orchard LB $15.99 (978-0-531-08727-5). 32pp. A humorous tale of a man who achieves fame through his many paintings of chickens. (Rev: BCCB 4/95; BL 2/1/95; HB 3/95; SLJ 4/95)

4950 Powell, Anna. *Don't Say That, Willy Nilly!* (K–2). Illus. by David Roberts. 2005, Good Bks. $16.00 (978-1-56148-488-1). Willy Nilly has an amazing knack for saying the wrong thing at the wrong time. (Rev: SLJ 10/05)

4951 Poydar, Nancy. *Mailbox Magic* (PS–2). Illus. 2000, Holiday House $15.95 (978-0-8234-1525-0). 32pp. Will, who longs to get mail, collects box tops to send away for a cereal bowl. (Rev: BL 6/1–15/00; HBG 10/01; SLJ 9/00)

4952 Priest, Robert. *The Old Pirate of Central Park* (PS–2). Illus. 1999, Houghton $16.00 (978-0-395-90505-0). 32pp. Old Pirate launches a replica of his ship, the *Laughing Dog,* in Central Park's sailboat pond, only to find that a retired queen wants to do the same with her ocean liner, the S.S. *Uppity Princess.* (Rev: BCCB 9/99; BL 4/1/99; HBG 10/99; SLJ 6/99)

4953 Pulver, Robin. *Axle Annie* (PS–3). Illus. by Tedd Arnold. 1999, Dial $15.99 (978-0-8037-2096-1). 32pp. Shifty Rhodes and friends conspire to get extra ice and snow on a steep hill so that the school bus, driven by Axle Annie, will not be able to make it and there will be, at long last, a snow day in Burskyville. (Rev: BL 2/15/00; HBG 3/00; SLJ 10/99)

4954 Radunsky, Vladimir, and Eugenia Radunsky. *Yucka Drucka Droni* (1–3). Illus. 1998, Scholastic $15.95 (978-0-590-09837-3). 40pp. A European tale that is a tongue twister about three brothers who marry three sisters and have children with strange names. (Rev: BCCB 7–8/98; BL 2/1/98; HBG 10/98; SLJ 3/98*)

4955 Ransom, Jeanie Franz. *Grandma U* (K–2). Illus. by Lucy Corvino. 2002, Peachtree $15.95 (978-1-56145-214-9). Molly McCool goes to Grandma University to prepare for an impending arrival in this entertaining tale. (Rev: HBG 3/03; SLJ 12/02)

4956 Ransom, Jeanie Franz. *What Do Parents Do? (When You're Not Home)* (PS–2). Illus. by Cyd Moore. 2007, Peachtree $16.95 (978-1-56145-409-9). 32pp. Apparently parents get up to all sorts of things in their children's absence — jumping on the bed, dressing up the dog . . . (Rev: BL 4/1/07)

4957 Ransom, Jeanie Franz. *What Really Happened to Humpty?* (1–4). Illus. by Stephen Axelsen. 2009, Charlesbridge $15.95 (978-1-58089-109-7). 32pp. Humpty's brother Joe, a tough detective, investigates who pushed Humpty in this funny mystery set in Mother Gooseland. (Rev: BL 5/1/09; SLJ 5/09)

4958 Rash, Andy. *Are You a Horse?* (PS–2). Illus. by author. 2009, Scholastic $16.99 (978-0-439-72417-3). 32pp. Aspiring cowboy Roy has got himself a hat and he's got himself a saddle but he hasn't got a clue as to what he's supposed to put it on. (Rev: BL 1/1–15/09; SLJ 2/09)

4959 Rathmann, Peggy. *The Day the Babies Crawled Away* (K–2). Illus. by author. 2003, Penguin $17.99 (978-0-399-23196-4). A picture book with effective oversize illustrations and a simple story about a toddler who comes to the rescue after babies crawl away from their preoccupied parents. (Rev: BCCB 12/03; BL 9/15/03; HB 9/03; HBG 4/04; LMC 3/04; SLJ 11/03)

4960 Reed, Lynn Rowe. *Please Don't Upset P.U. Zorilla* (PS–1). Illus. by author. 2006, Knopf $15.95 (978-0-375-83654-1). P.U. Zorilla, a skunk, finds it hard to hold down a job until his stinky spray succeeds in foiling a robbery and Mayor Tootlebee offers him a job as police chief. (Rev: SLJ 10/06)

4961 Reiss, Mike. *The Great Show-and-Tell Disaster* (1–4). Illus. by Mike Cressy. 2001, Price Stern

Sloan $13.99 (978-0-8431-7680-3). All kinds of words are turned into anagrams with unfortunate consequences in this humorous, oversized book. (Rev: HBG 3/02; SLJ 1/02)

4962 Rex, Adam. *Pssst!* (K–3). Illus. by author. 2007, Harcourt $16.00 (978-0-15-205817-3). 40pp. Animals at the zoo burden a young girl with a lot of seemingly wacky requests in this funny book with unusual artwork. (Rev: BCCB 10/07; HB 1/08; SLJ 10/07)

4963 Reynolds, Aaron. *Buffalo Wings* (K–3). Illus. by Paulette Bogan. 2007, Bloomsbury $16.95 (978-1-59990-062-9). 32pp. In preparation for the big game on TV, a misguided rooster sets off in search of something called Buffalo Wings. (Rev: LMC 11/07; SLJ 12/07)

4964 Robart, Rose. *The Cake That Mack Ate* (PS–K). Illus. by Maryann Kovalski. 1991, Little, Brown paper $5.95 (978-0-316-74891-9). A cumulative tale featuring a festive party table. (Rev: BL 3/1/87; SLJ 6–7/87)

4965 Robertson, M. P. *Hieronymus Betts and His Unusual Pets* (PS–1). Illus. by author. 2005, Frances Lincoln $15.95 (978-1-84507-289-6). Hieronymus Betts introduces his menagerie of unusually awful pets, but he asserts that there's one thing that's even worse — a little brother! (Rev: SLJ 2/06)

4966 Robinson, Fay. *Faucet Fish* (PS–2). Illus. by Wayne Anderson. 2005, Dutton $15.99 (978-0-525-47166-0). 32pp. Elizabeth can't seem to get her parents' attention, even when all types of fish begin to come out of the bathroom faucet. (Rev: BL 8/05; SLJ 8/05)

4967 Root, Phyllis. *Paula Bunyan* (K–2). Illus. by Kevin O'Malley. 2009, Farrar $16.95 (978-0-374-35759-7). 32pp. Paul Bunyan's younger sister Paula, who is "as tall as a pine tree and as strong as a dozen moose," finds her size a great inconvenience and spends her time in the North Woods rescuing forests. (Rev: BCCB 6/09; BL 3/1/09; SLJ 3/09)

4968 Rosenthal, Betsy R. *It's Not Worth Making a Tzimmes Over!* (PS–2). Illus. by Ruth Rivers. 2006, Albert Whitman $16.99 (978-0-8075-3677-3). 32pp. This humorous picture book chronicles a cooking experiment gone wrong and introduces young readers to an unflappable grandmother and a handful of Yiddish terms. (Rev: BL 3/15/06; SLJ 5/06)

4969 Rosenthal, Marc. *Phooey!* (PS–K). Illus. by author. 2007, HarperCollins $16.99 (978-0-06-075248-4). 40pp. A boy unwittingly sets off a chain of wildly funny events after he declares in a fit of boredom that "nothing ever happens around here." (Rev: BCCB 9/07; BL 7/07; HB 9/07; SLJ 9/07)

4970 Rosoff, Meg. *Jumpy Jack and Googily* (PS–1). Illus. by Sophie Blackall. 2008, Holt $16.95 (978-0-8050-8066-7). 32pp. A snail called Jumpy Jack, who is afraid of monsters, relies on his friend Googily (who is actually a monster) to check behind trees and under tables. (Rev: BL 3/15/08; LMC 11/08*; SLJ 5/08)

4971 Ross, Tony. *I Want My Tooth* (K–2). Illus. by author. 2005, Kane paper $4.95 (978-1-929132-85-0). When the Little Princess loses one of her teeth, she orders everyone in the castle to search for it. (Rev: SLJ 10/05)

4972 Rumford, James. *Don't Touch My Hat* (K–2). Illus. 2007, Knopf $16.99 (978-0-375-83782-1). 40pp. Sheriff John relies on his lucky 10-gallon hat until the night he rushes off to catch some bad men wearing his wife's fancy plumed chapeau. (Rev: BL 12/15/06; SLJ 1/07)

4973 Ruurs, Margriet. *Wake Up, Henry Rooster!* (PS–2). Illus. by Sean Cassidy. 2006, Fitzhenry & Whiteside $16.95 (978-1-55041-952-8). 32pp. Henry the rooster is no early bird and the farm life gets out of whack as he sleeps off his late nights. (Rev: BL 5/15/06; SLJ 7/06)

4974 Ryan-Lush, Geraldine. *Hairs on Bears* (K–3). Illus. by Normand Cousineau. 1994, Annick LB $14.95 (978-1-55037-351-6); paper $4.95 (978-1-55037-352-3). A humorous picture book about the problems caused when the family pooch begins to shed his hair. (Rev: SLJ 12/94)

4975 Rylant, Cynthia. *Alligator Boy* (PS–2). Illus. by Diane Goode. 2007, Harcourt $16.00 (978-0-15-206092-3). 32pp. A boy decides to wear an alligator costume and delights in being different in this well-illustrated, rhyming tale. (Rev: BL 5/15/07; LMC 8/07; SLJ 6/07)

4976 Salerno, Steven. *Harry Hungry!* (PS). Illus. by author. 2009, Houghton $16.00 (978-0-15-206257-6). 40pp. Harry the toddler eats his way through all the alphabet cookies, the mailbox, a mountain, and even a piece of the sky in this brightly illustrated tribute to the intensity of a child's hunger. (Rev: BCCB 3/09; BLO 1/14/09; HB 3/09; SLJ 2/09)

4977 Saltzberg, Barney. *Where, Oh, Where Is My Underwear? A Pop-Up Book* (PS–K). Illus. 1994, Hyperion $9.95 (978-1-56282-694-9). 12pp. A search for underwear leads to great fun pulling tabs and lifting flaps in this interactive book. (Rev: BL 11/15/94)

4978 Samuels, Barbara. *Dolores Meets Her Match* (1–3). Illus. by author. Series: Dolores and Duncan. 2007, Farrar $16.00 (978-0-374-31758-4). 32pp. Dolores is confident of her cat Duncan's unique abilities until new girl Hillary arrives with the remarkable Harold. (Rev: BL 2/15/08; HB 11/07; SLJ 11/07)

4979 SanAngelo, Ryan. *Spaghetti Eddie* (PS–2). Illus. by Jackie Urbanovic. 2002, Boyds Mills $15.95 (978-1-56397-974-3). 32pp. Eddie uses his favorite food — spaghetti — to help a neighbor with broken shoelaces, to fashion a fishing net, and even to stop a robbery. (Rev: BL 8/02; HBG 3/03; SLJ 9/02)

4980 Sayre, April P. *Noodle Man: The Pasta Superhero* (K–3). Illus. by Stephen Costanza. 2002, Scholastic $16.95 (978-0-439-29307-5). 40pp. Al Dente saves his family's business when the pasta machine he invents helps him perform heroic feats all over town in this pun-filled tale. (Rev: BL 2/15/02; HBG 10/02; SLJ 3/02)

4981 Scamell, Ragnhild. *Ouch!* (PS–1). Illus. by Michael Terry. 2006, Good Bks. $16.00 (978-1-56148-511-6). Poor Hedgehog has an apple stuck in her spines and all her friends' efforts to help her backfire until she comes across Goat. (Rev: SLJ 7/06)

4982 Scheer, Julian. *Rain Makes Applesauce* (K–2). Illus. by Marvin Bileck. 1964, Holiday House $16.95 (978-0-8234-0091-1). 36pp. A series of silly statements nonsensically presented and accompanied by humorous detailed pictures.

4983 Schertle, Alice. *The Adventures of Old Bo Bear* (PS–2). Illus. by David Parkins. 2006, Chronicle $16.95 (978-0-8118-3476-6). 28pp. After his favorite teddy bear loses an ear in a much-needed washing, his owner takes him off for some energetic play that involves quite a lot of dirt plus some potential explanations for the missing appendage. (Rev: BL 2/1/06; SLJ 2/06)

4984 Schneider, Christine M. *Picky Mrs. Pickle* (K–2). Illus. by author. 1999, Walker LB $16.85 (978-0-8027-8703-3). Mrs. Pickle has a pickle fetish and her stubborn niece tries to introduce her to other tastes. (Rev: HBG 3/00; SLJ 9/99)

4985 Schnetzler, Pattie. *Widdermaker* (K–4). Illus. by Rick Sealock. 2002, Carolrhoda LB $15.95 (978-0-87614-647-7). On their way to capture a pesky longhorn called the Widdermaker, Cowpoke Pete and his steed Desert Rose create the Painted Desert and Monument Valley in this zany tall tale. (Rev: HBG 3/03; SLJ 11/02)

4986 Schotter, Roni. *The Boy Who Loved Words* (2–4). Illus. by Giselle Potter. 2006, Random $16.95 (978-0-375-83601-5). 40pp. A boy called Selig loves words, and after collecting many on scraps of paper — and suffering the scorn of his classmates — he decides to distribute them around. (Rev: BL 2/1/06*; SLJ 4/06*)

4987 Schwarz, Viviane. *Shark and Lobster's Amazing Undersea Adventure* (PS–2). 2006, Candlewick $15.99 (978-0-7636-2910-6). 40pp. Shark and Lobster convince their undersea friends to build a fortress to protect themselves against tigers, then realize the folly of their phobia. (Rev: BL 7/06)

4988 Scieszka, Jon. *Baloney (Henry P.)* (1–4). Illus. by Lane Smith. 2001, Viking $16.99 (978-0-670-89248-8). 32pp. A small green alien comes up with a humdinger of an excuse for being late to school in this story full of humor. (Rev: BCCB 5/01; BL 5/15/01*; HB 5/01; HBG 10/01; SLJ 5/01)

4989 Scieszka, Jon. *The Stinky Cheese Man: And Other Fairly Stupid Tales* (2–6). Illus. by Lane Smith. 1992, Viking $17.99 (978-0-670-84487-6). 56pp. Lots of fun with fractured fairy tales. (Rev: BCCB 10/92*; BL 9/1/92; HB 11/92*; HBG 10/02; SLJ 9/92*)

4990 Scillian, Devin. *Brewster the Rooster* (K–3). Illus. by Lee White. 2007, Sleeping Bear $16.95 (978-1-58536-311-7). 32pp. A nearsighted rooster crows at inappropriate times of day until little Julie suggests that he needs glasses. (Rev: BL 7/07; SLJ 8/07)

4991 Sendak, Maurice. *Chicken Soup with Rice: A Book of Months* (K–3). Illus. by author. 1962, HarperCollins LB $16.89 (978-0-06-025535-0). 48pp. A rhyming story that takes one through each of the months with the always suitable chicken soup with rice.

4992 Seuss, Dr., and Jack Prelutsky. *Hooray for Diffendoofer Day!* (K–4). Illus. by Lane Smith. 1998, Knopf LB $18.99 (978-0-679-99008-6). 56pp. With this story about an unusual teacher named Miss Bonkers, Prelutsky and Smith complete the sketches Dr. Seuss left when he died in 1991. (Rev: BCCB 6/98; BL 5/1/98; HBG 10/98; SLJ 6/98)

4993 Seymour, Tres. *I Love My Buzzard* (K–3). Illus. by S. D. Schindler. 1994, Orchard LB $16.99 (978-0-531-08669-8). 32pp. Mom gives up and decides to leave when her young son's menagerie grows and grows. (Rev: BL 1/15/94; SLJ 4/94)

4994 Seymour, Tres. *Too Quiet for These Old Bones* (PS–1). Illus. by Paul Johnson. 1997, Orchard LB $16.99 (978-0-531-33052-4). 32pp. To their surprise, four children discover that Granny doesn't really want the quiet they expect and instead would like to make a racket. (Rev: BL 11/15/97; HBG 3/98; SLJ 10/97)

4995 Shannon, David. *David Gets in Trouble* (PS–1). Illus. 2002, Scholastic $16.99 (978-0-439-05022-7). 32pp. David of *No, David* (1998) and *David Goes to School* (1999) denies any responsibility for the trouble he causes — until bedtime, when he finally apologizes to Mom. (Rev: BL 9/15/02; HB 1/03; HBG 3/03; SLJ 9/02*)

4996 Shannon, David. *The Rain Came Down* (PS–2). Illus. 2000, Scholastic $16.99 (978-0-439-05021-0). 32pp. Rain creates chaos in a big city as every living thing reacts in surprise. (Rev: BCCB 12/00; BL 10/15/00; HB 9/00; HBG 3/01; SLJ 10/00)

4997 Sharmat, Marjorie W. *Gila Monsters Meet You at the Airport* (PS–2). Illus. by Byron Barton. 1980, Macmillan paper $4.95 (978-0-689-71383-5). 32pp. A young boy imagines all sorts of horrible things about his move from New York City.

4998 Shulman, Mark. *Mom and Dad Are Palindromes* (1–4). Illus. by Adam McCauley. 2006, Chronicle $15.95 (978-0-8118-4328-7). Once Bob finds out what palindromes are, he sees them everywhere — more than 100 in all. (Rev: SLJ 6/06)

4999 Sierra, Judy. *Mind Your Manners, B. B. Wolf* (PS–2). Illus. by J. Otto Seibold. 2007, Knopf $16.99 (978-0-375-83532-2). 40pp. A seriously fractured fairy tale about the big bad wolf learning manners so that he can attend the library tea. (Rev: BL 9/1/07; HB 7/07; LMC 11/07; SLJ 8/07)

5000 Sierra, Judy. *The Secret Science Project That Almost Ate the School* (1–3). Illus. by Stephen Gammell. 2006, Simon & Schuster $16.95 (978-1-4169-1175-3). A young girl orders a science fair project by mail, but neglects to read the directions on its package carefully. (Rev: SLJ 11/06)

5001 Sierra, Judy. *Thelonius Monster's Sky-High Fly Pie: A Revolting Rhyme* (PS–2). Illus. by Edward Koren. 2006, Knopf $16.95 (978-0-375-83218-5). 40pp. Thelonius invites friends to enjoy a pie of flies, but the fly takes off before he can enjoy it in this funny rhyming story illustrated in cartoonist Koren's signature style. (Rev: BL 5/1/06; SLJ 5/06*)

5002 Simms, Laura. *Rotten Teeth* (K–3). Illus. by David Catrow. 1998, Houghton $16.00 (978-0-395-82850-2). 32pp. Melissa has many things she could bring to school for show-and-tell, such as the alligator that lives in her family's doghouse. But her final choice is so disgusting that she will be remembered forever in the school's history. (Rev: BCCB 12/98; BL 9/1/98; HBG 3/99; SLJ 9/98)

5003 Slater, Dashka. *Baby Shoes* (PS). Illus. by Hiroe Nakata. 2006, Bloomsbury $15.95 (978-1-58234-684-7). 32pp. Baby's new white shoes are soon covered in multicolor stains as he and his mother take a walk. (Rev: BL 5/1/06; HBG 10/06; SLJ 5/06)

5004 Sloat, Teri. *The Thing That Bothered Farmer Brown* (PS–1). Illus. by Nadine Bernard Westcott. 1995, Orchard LB $16.99 (978-0-531-08733-6). 32pp. A pesky mosquito keeps Farmer Brown and all the farm animals awake. (Rev: BL 2/1/95; SLJ 3/95)

5005 Sloat, Teri. *This Is the House That Was Tidy and Neat* (PS–1). Illus. by R. W. Alley. 2005, Holt $16.95 (978-0-8050-6921-1). 32pp. A father arrives home to find his house in havoc, and it all started with a cookie. (Rev: BL 5/1/05)

5006 Slobodkina, Esphyr. *Caps for Sale* (K–3). Illus. by author. 1947, HarperCollins LB $17.89 (978-0-06-025778-1); paper $6.99 (978-0-06-443143-9). 48pp. When some monkeys engage in a bit of monkey business, the cap peddler must use his imagination to retrieve his wares.

5007 Slonim, David. *He Came with the Couch* (K–3). Illus. by author. 2005, Chronicle $15.95 (978-0-8118-4430-7). A wacky story about a family buys that buys a sofa that's the home of a funny-looking creature suffering from "upholsterosis." (Rev: SLJ 11/05)

5008 Smith, Lane. *Madam President* (K–2). Illus. by author. 2008, Hyperion $16.99 (978-1-4231-0846-7). 40pp. A little girl fantasizes about her duties as president — giving orders (for waffles), negotiating treaties (between a cat and dog), appointing a cabinet made up of toys, and generally behaving in exemplary fashion. (Rev: BCCB 7–8/08; BL 5/1/08; LMC 3/08; SLJ 7/08) 🎧

5009 Smith, Stu. *The Bubble Gum Kid* (K–2). Illus. by Julia Woolf. 2006, Running Pr. $15.95 (978-0-7624-2046-9). Billy Bob Glum asks his sister to teach him how to blow a bubble so he can impress an annoying bully named Double Chin Dan; a fast-paced story told in rhyming text. (Rev: SLJ 12/06)

5010 Snicket, Lemony. *The Lump of Coal* (1–3). Illus. by Brett Helquist. 2008, HarperCollins $12.99 (978-0-06-157428-3). 40pp. A tuxedo-wearing lump of coal with an artistic bent sets off in search of a purpose in life in this small volume. (Rev: BL 9/15/08; HB 11/08)

5011 Spinelli, Eileen. *Silly Tilly* (PS–2). Illus. by David Slonim. 2009, Marshall Cavendish $16.99 (978-0-7614-5525-7). 32pp. Tilly is a very silly goose indeed, but when the other animals on the farm ask her to behave, they find they miss her antics. (Rev: BL 3/15/09; SLJ 3/09)

5012 Stadler, John. *The Cats of Mrs. Calamari* (PS–2). Illus. 1997, Orchard $15.95 (978-0-531-30020-6). 32pp. When Mrs. Calamari discovers that her new landlord hates cats, she must think of unusual ways to save her large brood. (Rev: BL 3/1/97*; SLJ 5/97)

5013 Stanley, Diane. *Raising Sweetness* (PS–3). Illus. by G. Brian Karas. 1999, Penguin $16.99 (978-0-399-23225-1). 32pp. The kindly sheriff of Possum Trot adopts Sweetness and seven other orphans, and to show her appreciation, Sweetness arranges a reunion between the sheriff and his girlfriend. (Rev: BCCB 2/99; BL 2/15/99; HB 3/99; HBG 10/99; SLJ 1/99*)

5014 Stanley, Diane. *Saving Sweetness* (PS–3). Illus. by G. Brian Karas. 1996, Penguin $16.99 (978-0-399-22645-8). 32pp. After she runs away from an orphanage, Sweetness must save the sheriff who has been trying to catch her. (Rev: BCCB 11/96; BL 1/1–15/97*; HB 9/96; SLJ 11/96*)

5015 Steig, Jeanne. *Fleas!* (PS–2). Illus. by Britt Spencer. 2008, Philomel $16.99 (978-0-399-24756-9). 32pp. A cumulative/circular tale in which a dog gives a farmer fleas and the farmer swaps the fleas for a young lady's troublesomely talkative uncle and the trades continue until we're back with the fleas. (Rev: BL 5/15/08; SLJ 5/08)

5016 Steig, William. *The Amazing Bone* (K–2). Illus. by author. 1983, Farrar $17.00 (978-0-374-30248-1). 32pp. A bone that talks saves a piglet from being eaten by a fox in this nonsensical and witty story.

5017 Steig, William. *Pete's a Pizza* (PS–K). Illus. 1998, HarperCollins $16.99 (978-0-06-205157-8). 32pp. Pete is in a terrible mood until his parents pretend he is a pizza and begin kneading him, tossing him in the air, and sprinkling him with flour. (Rev: BL 10/1/98*; HB 9/98; HBG 3/99; SLJ 11/98)

5018 Stevens, Jan R. *Carlos and the Skunk: Carlos y el Zorrillo* (1–4). Illus. by Jeanne Arnold. 1997, Northland LB $15.95 (978-0-87358-591-0). 32pp. A bilingual book in which Carlos tangles with a skunk. (Rev: BL 5/15/97; HBG 3/98)

5019 Stevens, Janet, and Susan Stevens Crummel. *Help Me, Mr. Mutt!* (1–3). Illus. by Janet Stevens. 2008, Harcourt $17.00 (978-0-15-204628-6). 56pp. Text and art work in tandem to extend the jokes as Mr. Mutt writes an advice column for hapless dogs. (Rev: BL 3/15/08; LMC 11/08; SLJ 5/08)

5020 Stevenson, James. *Yard Sale* (2–4). Illus. 1996, Greenwillow $14.89 (978-0-688-14127-1). 32pp. All of the creatures of Mud Flat participate in an unusual yard sale. (Rev: BL 3/15/96; HB 7/96; SLJ 7/96*)

5021 Stuart, Chad. *The Ballymara Flood* (PS–3). Illus. by George Booth. 1996, Harcourt $15.00 (978-0-15-205698-8). 40pp. A boy's innocent bath time ritual ends in a flood. (Rev: BL 4/1/96; SLJ 6/96)

5022 Sydor, Colleen. *Camilla Chameleon* (K–2). Illus. by Pascale Constantin. 2005, Kids Can $16.95 (978-1-55337-482-4). A zany story about Camilla, whose ability to blend in with her surroundings stems from her mother's craving for cream-of-chameleon soup when she was pregnant; then her mother gets pregnant again and develops a taste for cream of pterodactyl soup . . . (Rev: SLJ 6/06)

5023 Tafuri, Nancy. *This Is the Farmer* (PS). Illus. 1994, Morrow $17.99 (978-0-688-09468-3). 24pp. A series of amusing cause-and-effect situations begin when a farmer gives a good-morning kiss to his wife. (Rev: BL 5/15/94; HB 9/94; SLJ 5/94)

5024 Taylor, Alastair. *Mr. Blewitt's Nose* (K–2). Illus. by author. 2005, Houghton $16.00 (978-0-618-42353-8). Primrose and her amazingly smelly dog search for the owner of a lost nose in this amusing book. (Rev: SLJ 7/05)

5025 Taylor, Sean. *When a Monster Is Born* (PS–K). Illus. by Nick Sharratt. 2007, Roaring Brook $16.95 (978-1-59643-254-3). 32pp. A humorous look at the various opportunities awaiting a young monster and the life choices that must be made. (Rev: BCCB 10/07; BL 6/1–15/07; HB 7/07; SLJ 6/07)

5026 Teague, Mark. *Baby Tamer* (PS–3). Illus. 1997, Scholastic $15.95 (978-0-590-67712-7). 32pp. Amanda, the new baby-sitter, proves unflappable when tested by the Eggmont children. (Rev: BL 8/97; HBG 3/98; SLJ 10/97)

5027 Teague, Mark. *Dear Mrs. LaRue: Letters from Obedience School* (K–3). Illus. 2002, Scholastic $16.99 (978-0-439-20663-1). 32pp. Poor Ike LaRue sends pitiful letters home to his owner, complaining about the conditions at doggy school, but the pictures belie his words. (Rev: BL 11/1/02; HBG 3/03; SLJ 9/02)

5028 Teague, Mark. *LaRue for Mayor: Letters from the Campaign* (K–3). Illus. by author. 2008, Scholastic $16.99 (978-0-439-78315-6). 32pp. As in earlier books featuring LaRue the dog, this title uses correspondence and contrasting illustrations to present different perspectives on LaRue's campaign for mayor. (Rev: BL 12/15/07; SLJ 3/08)

5029 Thomas, Jan. *Rhyming Dust Bunnies* (PS–2). Illus. by author. 2009, Simon & Schuster $12.99 (978-1-4169-7976-0). 40pp. Happy, oblivious dust bunnies Ed, Ned, and Ted rhyme constantly, correct nervous Bob for not rhyming, and ignore his warnings in this funny book. (Rev: BCCB 1/09; SLJ 2/09)

5030 Thompson, Kay. *Eloise Takes a Bawth* (PS–3). Illus. by Hilary Knight. 2002, Simon & Schuster $17.95 (978-0-689-84288-7). 80pp. The effervescent Eloise ignores Nanny's warnings about her "bawth" and the resulting flood succeeds in making more realistic the Venetian Masked Ball taking place below. (Rev: BL 12/1/02; HB 1/03; HBG 3/03; SLJ 12/02)

5031 Tobin, Jim. *Sue MacDonald Had a Book* (PS–1). Illus. by Dave Coverly. 2009, Holt $16.95 (978-0-8050-8766-6). 40pp. In this amusing take on the familiar "Old MacDonald Had a Farm," Sue MacDonald must find the vowels *AEIOU* that have escaped from her book. (Rev: BL 7/09; SLJ 6/09)

5032 Urbanovic, Jackie. *Duck and Cover* (PS–2). Illus. by author. 2009, HarperCollins $17.99 (978-0-06-121444-8). 40pp. Irene is surprised when an alligator asks for shelter at her house full of homeless animals. (Rev: BL 11/15/08; SLJ 2/09)

5033 Van Allsburg, Chris. *Probuditi!* (PS–2). 2006, Houghton $18.95 (978-0-618-75502-8). 32pp. Inspired by the performance of a professional magician, young Calvin hypnotizes his sister and then panics when he can't remember the magic word that will undo the spell; eye-catching sepia illustrations full of humor add to the nostalgic atmosphere. (Rev: BL 11/1/06; SLJ 12/06*)

5034 Van Laan, Nancy. *Nit-Pickin'* (PS–K). Illus. by George Booth. 2008, Atheneum $15.99 (978-0-689-83898-9). 32pp. A little girl copes with lice in this boisterous romp in verse and cartoon illustrations. (Rev: BL 7/08; SLJ 7/08)

5035 Van Lieshout, Elle, and Erik van Os. *Lovey and Dovey* (K–3). Illus. by Mies van Hout. 2009, Boyds Mills $16.95 (978-1-59078-660-4). 32pp. Lovey and Dovey, a couple thrown in jail for stealing a pair of socks, find ways to embellish their cell until they are genuinely upset to be released. (Rev: LMC 8/09; SLJ 4/09)

5036 Varela, Barry. *Gizmo* (K–2). Illus. by Ed Briant. 2007, Roaring Brook $16.95 (978-1-59643-115-7). 32pp. A zany tale of a professor who invents a perpetual motion machine, the "Gizmo," which becomes a point of controversy in his city. (Rev: BL 5/1/07; LMC 10/07; SLJ 5/07)

5037 Waechter, Phillip. *Rosie and the Nightmares* (K–2). Illus. 2005, Handprint $15.95 (978-1-59354-115-6). 32pp. Tormented by monster-filled nightmares, Rosie the bunny seeks help from a dream specialist and visits a Tunnel of Fear. (Rev: BL 12/1/05; SLJ 11/05)

5038 Walker, Sally M. *The Vowel Family: A Tale of Lost Letters* (1–3). Illus. by Kevin Luthardt. 2008, Carolrhoda $16.95 (978-0-8225-7982-3). 32pp. Pm and Sm marry and with the arrival of children come some helpful vowels (Alan, Ellen, Iris, Otto, and Ursula) in this smart and funny play on language and vowels. (Rev: BL 3/15/08; SLJ 2/08)

5039 Walsh, Melanie. *Do Pigs Have Stripes?* (PS–1). Illus. 1996, Houghton $15.00 (978-0-395-73976-1). 40pp. Nonsensical questions about animals (like the title) produce equally entertaining answers. (Rev: BL 3/1/96; HB 5/96; SLJ 4/96)

5040 Walter, Virginia. *"Hi, Pizza Man!"* (PS–2). Illus. by Ponder Goembel. 1995, Orchard LB $16.99 (978-0-531-08735-0). 32pp. Vivian wonders what sort of messenger will deliver the pizza that she and her mother have ordered. (Rev: BL 1/15/95; HB 3/95; SLJ 3/95)

5041 Walton, Rick. *Suddenly, Alligator! An Adverbial Tale* (1–4). Illus. by Jim Bradshaw. 2004, Gibbs Smith $15.95 (978-1-58685-313-6). Full of adverbs, this is the story of a boy whose well-worn socks are so aromatic they cause an alligator to pass out. (Rev: SLJ 11/04)

5042 Warburton, Tom. *1000 Times No* (PS–1). Illus. by author. 2009, HarperCollins $17.99 (978-0-06-154263-3). 32pp. Noah does not, absolutely not, want to do what his mother says and finds many ways of saying so. (Rev: BL 3/15/09; SLJ 4/09)

5043 Waterton, Betty. *A Bumblebee Sweater* (K–2). Illus. by Kim LaFave. 2007, Fitzhenry & Whiteside $16.95 (978-1-55455-028-9). 32pp. The sweater that Nellie's grandmother knits for Nellie to wear to her spring concert shrinks with many washings to the point that only the dog can wear it. (Rev: BL 10/15/07; SLJ 11/07)

5044 Weeks, Sarah. *Mrs. McNosh Hangs Up Her Wash* (PS–K). Illus. by Nadine Bernard Westcott. 1998, HarperCollins $14.99 (978-0-694-01076-9). 24pp. On wash day, Mrs. McNosh gets carried away and begins hanging out such items as the newspaper, the dog, and the phone to dry. (Rev: BCCB 5/98; BL 4/15/98; HBG 10/98; SLJ 7/98)

5045 Weeks, Sarah. *Oh My Gosh, Mrs McNosh!* (PS–1). Illus. by Nadine Bernard Westcott. 2002, HarperCollins LB $15.89 (978-0-06-008858-3). 32pp. Mrs. McNosh suffers a series of misadventures when her dog George breaks free from his leash and she chases him through town. (Rev: BCCB 5/02; BL 5/1/02; HBG 10/02; SLJ 6/02)

5046 Weis, Carol. *When the Cows Got Loose* (PS–2). Illus. by Ard Hoyt. 2006, Simon & Schuster $16.95 (978-0-689-85166-7). 40pp. While Ida Mae is daydreaming about how to get famous, the cows she's been watching wander off, and now she must get busy to round them back up; the illustrations of eccentric cows match the droll tone of the story. (Rev: BL 6/1–15/06; SLJ 8/06)

5047 Westcott, Nadine Bernard. *Peanut Butter and Jelly: A Play Rhyme* (PS–K). Illus. by author. 1987, Puffin paper $6.99 (978-0-14-054852-5). 32pp. A play rhyme describes the making of this food that is a children's favorite. (Rev: BL 10/1/87; SLJ 9/87)

5048 Whatley, Bruce, and Rosie Smith. *Captain Pajamas* (PS–2). Illus. by Bruce Whatley. 2000, HarperCollins LB $15.89 (978-0-06-026614-1). 32pp. Late one night Brian believes that aliens have landed, but the sounds he hears are only his dog trying to get into the fridge. (Rev: BCCB 9/00; BL 5/15/00; HBG 10/00; SLJ 6/00)

5049 Wheeler, Lisa. *Bubble Gum, Bubble Gum* (PS–1). Illus. by Laura Huliska-Beith. 2004, Little, Brown $15.95 (978-0-316-98894-0). 32pp. In bouncy rhyming verse and bold illustrations, a number of different animals become snared by a big gob of bubble gum in the middle of the road. (Rev: BL 5/15/04; SLJ 5/04)

5050 White, Linda. *Too Many Pumpkins* (PS–2). Illus. by Megan Lloyd. 1996, Holiday House LB $17.95 (978-0-8234-1245-7). 28pp. Rebecca Estelle, who hates pumpkins, finds she has a bumper crop in her garden. (Rev: BCCB 12/96; BL 9/15/96; SLJ 11/96)

5051 Whybrow, Ian. *Badness for Beginners: A Little Wolf and Smellybreff Adventure* (K–3). Illus. by Tony Ross. Series: Little Wolf and Smellybreff. 2005, Carolrhoda LB $16.95 (978-1-57505-861-0).

Little Wolf's efforts to be bad fail to impress the rest of his family. (Rev: SLJ 9/05)

5052 Willems, Mo. *Don't Let the Pigeon Drive the Bus!* (PS). Illus. by author. 2003, Hyperion $12.99 (978-0-7868-1988-1). A pigeon with ambitions, right now to drive the school bus, is shown in attitudes that preschoolers will instantly recognize. Caldecott Honor Book, 2004. (Rev: BL 9/1/03*; HB 7/03; HBG 10/03; SLJ 5/03)

5053 Willems, Mo. *I Am Invited to a Party!* (K–2). Illus. by author. Series: Elephant and Piggie. 2007, Hyperion $8.99 (978-1-4231-0687-6). 64pp. Piggie asks her elephant friend Gerald to help her get ready for her first party. (Rev: BCCB 11/07; HB 1/08; SLJ 10/07)

5054 Willems, Mo. *Knuffle Bunny: A Cautionary Tale* (PS–K). Illus. by author. 2004, Hyperion $15.99 (978-0-7868-1870-9). 40pp. Trixie leaves her beloved stuffed animal at the laundromat in this hilarious tale about the difficulties of communicating. Caldecott Honor Book. (Rev: BL 9/15/04*; HB 9/04; SLJ 10/04*)

5055 Willems, Mo. *Knuffle Bunny Too: A Case of Mistaken Identity* (PS–K). Illus. by author. 2007, Hyperion $16.99 (978-1-4231-0299-1). 48pp. Double trouble begins when lookalike toy bunnies return home from school with the wrong preschool "mommies." Caldecott Honor Book, 2008. (Rev: BCCB 11/07; BL 9/1/07; HB 11/07; SLJ 8/07)

5056 Willems, Mo. *Leonardo, the Terrible Monster* (PS–K). Illus. 2005, Hyperion $15.99 (978-0-7868-5294-9). 48pp. Leonardo's failure to frighten anyone leads him to formulate a plan to "scare the tuna salad" out of young Sam. (Rev: BL 7/05; SLJ 8/05*) ∩

5057 Willems, Mo. *Naked Mole Rat Gets Dressed* (PS–2). Illus. by author. 2009, Disney $16.99 (978-1-4231-1437-6). 40pp. Wilbur is an unusual naked mole rat — he likes to wear clothes, and fancy clothes at that. Will his colony accept this behavior? (Rev: BCCB 2/09; BL 11/15/08; LMC 5/09; SLJ 2/09)

5058 Willems, Mo. *The Pigeon Has Feelings, Too!* (PS). Illus. by author. 2005, Hyperion $6.99 (978-0-7868-3650-5). The pigeon of *Don't Let the Pigeon Drive the Bus* (2003) is back in this board book, making all sorts of faces to reveal his emotions. (Rev: SLJ 8/05)

5059 Willems, Mo. *The Pigeon Wants a Puppy!* (PS). Illus. by author. 2008, Hyperion $14.99 (978-1-4231-0960-0). 32pp. Pigeon wants a puppy and he wants it now, but when a (huge) puppy does arrive he rapidly changes his mind. (Rev: BL 5/1/08; HB 7/08; SLJ 6/08)

5060 Willems, Mo. *There Is a Bird on Your Head!* (K–2). Illus. by author. Series: Elephant and Piggie. 2007, Hyperion $8.99 (978-1-4231-0686-9). 64pp. What could be more entertaining than a bird on your head? Try a whole nest. Gerald the elephant and Piggie figure it out together. (Rev: HB 1/08; SLJ 10/07)

5061 Willems, Mo. *Today I Will Fly!* (PS–1). Illus. by author. Series: Elephant and Piggie. 2007, Hyperion $8.99 (978-1-4231-0295-3). 64pp. Piggie's announcement that he plans to fly is met with skepticism by his pal, Gerald the elephant. (Rev: BCCB 7–8/07; BL 4/1/07; HB 5/07)

5062 Williams, Vera B. *"More More More," Said the Baby: 3 Love Stories* (PS). Illus. 1990, Greenwillow $17.89 (978-0-688-09174-3). 32pp. All the ways that parents and grandparents play with youngsters are portrayed in this humorous picture book. (Rev: BCCB 10/90; BL 10/1/90; HB 11/90; SLJ 10/90*)

5063 Willis, Jeanne. *I Want to Be a Cowgirl* (PS–2). Illus. by Tony Ross. 2002, Holt $14.95 (978-0-8050-6997-6). 24pp. A city girl dreams of forsaking her dolls and tea parties for life as a cowgirl. (Rev: BL 3/15/02; HBG 10/02; SLJ 7/02)

5064 Wilson, Karma. *Moose Tracks!* (PS–2). Illus. by Jack E. Davis. 2006, Simon & Schuster $16.95 (978-0-689-83437-0). 32pp. A thoroughly silly story narrated by the owner of a very untidy house who can identify the sources of much of the mess, but not the culprit who left moose tracks all over the place. (Rev: BL 2/15/06; SLJ 4/06)

5065 Winthrop, Elizabeth. *The Biggest Parade* (K–3). Illus. by Mark Ulriksen. 2006, Holt $16.95 (978-0-8050-7685-1). Chairman of the town's 250th birthday parade, Harvey wants to include everyone, even his basset hound Fred; Fred refuses but, in the end, it seems that Fred has identified the place he is needed most — as a spectator. (Rev: SLJ 10/06)

5066 Winthrop, Elizabeth. *Dancing Granny* (PS–2). Illus. by Salvatore Murdocca. 2003, Marshall Cavendish $16.95 (978-0-7614-5141-9). Granny has a grand time at the party at the zoo, dancing with many animals, including a fetching bear. (Rev: HBG 4/04; SLJ 10/03)

5067 Wood, Audrey. *King Bidgood's in the Bathtub* (PS–2). Illus. by Don Wood. 1985, Harcourt $16.00 (978-0-15-242730-6). 32pp. No one can get the king out of his bathtub, until the young page thinks of pulling the plug. (Rev: BCCB 1/86; BL 10/1/85; SLJ 11/85)

5068 Wood, Audrey. *The Napping House* (PS–2). Illus. by Don Wood. 1984, Harcourt $16.00 (978-0-15-256708-8). 32pp. A cumulative story about all the members of a household taking a nap except for a flea.

5069 Wright, Michael. *Jake Starts School* (1–3). Illus. by author. 2008, Feiwel & Friends $16.95 (978-0-312-36798-5). 32pp. Jake's first day at school is so scary that his parents stay with him. (Rev: BL 5/15/08; LMC 8/08; SLJ 8/08)

5070 Young, Amy. *Belinda and the Glass Slipper* (PS–2). 2006, Viking $15.99 (978-0-670-06082-5). 32pp. In this sequel to *Belinda the Ballerina*, Belinda faces competition from a formidable — and underhanded — rival. (Rev: BL 10/1/06; SLJ 10/06)

5071 Zemach, Kaethe. *Just Enough and Not Too Much* (PS–2). Illus. by author. 2003, Scholastic $16.95 (978-0-439-37724-9). Simon the Fiddler has acquired too much stuff, so he throws a party and requires the guests to take a chair, hat, and toy home with them. (Rev: HBG 4/04; SLJ 10/03)

5072 Ziefert, Harriet. *There Was a Little Girl, She Had a Little Curl* (PS). Illus. by Elliot Kreloff. 2006, Blue Apple $9.95 (978-1-59354-161-3). Preschooler Isabel decides to cut her own hair. (Rev: SLJ 10/06)

5073 Zimelman, Nathan. *How the Second Grade Got $8,205.50 to Visit the Statue of Liberty* (K–3). Illus. by Bill Slavin. 1992, Whitman LB $16.99 (978-0-8075-3431-1). 32pp. Second-graders try to raise money for a field trip, with humorous results. (Rev: BL 9/15/92)

NATURE AND SCIENCE

5074 Allan, Nicholas. *Where Willy Went: The Big Story of a Little Sperm!* (PS–1). Illus. 2005, Knopf LB $17.99 (978-0-375-93030-0). 32pp. An unusual and appealing overview of the human reproductive process, in which Willy, a sperm who has spent his life polishing his swimming skills, triumphs over his competitors and fertilizes the egg. (Rev: BL 2/1/05; SLJ 3/05)

5075 Anderson, David A. *The Rebellion of Humans: An African Spiritual Journey* (K–4). Illus. by Claude Joachim. 1994, Sights $18.95 (978-0-9629978-6-0). 32pp. This ecological tale tells about an African tribe that forgets the lessons of the past and creates a wasteland by destroying the forests. A sequel to *The Origin of Life on Earth* (1992). (Rev: BL 10/1/94)

5076 Asch, Frank. *The Earth and I* (PS–2). Illus. 1994, Harcourt $15.00 (978-0-15-200443-9). 32pp. A young boy shares many thoughts and activities with his friend the earth. (Rev: BL 1/15/95; HBG 4/04; SLJ 10/94)

5077 Asch, Frank. *Like a Windy Day* (K–2). Illus. by Frank Asch and Devin Asch. 2002, Harcourt $15.00 (978-0-15-216376-1). 32pp. A little girl thinks about all the neat things the wind can do and imagines herself playing with the personified wind that floats overhead. (Rev: BL 10/1/02; HBG 3/03; SLJ 10/02)

5078 Asch, Frank. *The Sun Is My Favorite Star* (PS–1). Illus. 2000, Harcourt $15.00 (978-0-15-202127-6). 32pp. A little girl sings the praises of the sun and the light that it gives her. (Rev: BL 11/1/00; HBG 3/01; SLJ 10/00)

5079 Aston, Dianna. *An Orange in January* (PS–1). Illus. by Julie Maren. 2007, Dial $16.99 (978-0-8037-3146-2). 32pp. Readers follow the life of an orange from its original blossom through harvest and packing until it finally ends up being shared among a little boy's friends. (Rev: BL 10/15/07; LMC 11/07; SLJ 11/07)

5080 Atwell, Debby. *River* (K–3). Illus. 1999, Houghton $16.00 (978-0-395-93546-0). 32pp. This book describes the changes that occur to an American river over time, and the reader gets an antipollution lesson along the way. (Rev: BL 11/1/99; HBG 3/00; SLJ 11/99)

5081 Ayres, Katherine. *Up, Down, and Around* (PS–1). Illus. by Nadine Bernard Westcott. 2007, Candlewick $16.99 (978-0-7636-2378-4). 32pp. This lively picture book captures the excitement of gardening as two young children help a man plant vegetables, some of which grow up while others grow down. (Rev: BL 3/15/07)

5082 Baillie, Marilyn. *Nose to Toes* (PS–1). Illus. by Marisol Sarrazin. 2001, Boyds Mills $15.95 (978-1-56397-319-2). Bright, clean illustrations and simple text show children exploring their similarities to different animals. (Rev: HBG 3/02; SLJ 10/01)

5083 Baines, Becky. *The Bones You Own: A Book About the Human Body* (K–2). Illus. 2009, National Geographic $14.95 (978-1-4263-0410-1). 30pp. A meaty introduction with a lighthearted approach. (Rev: SLJ 6/09)

5084 Baker, Sanna Anderson. *Mississippi Going North* (K–3). Illus. by Bill Farnsworth. 1996, Whitman LB $15.95 (978-0-8075-5164-6). A picture book about a family that explores the northern part of the Mississippi River by canoe and sees many animals and birds. (Rev: SLJ 10/96)

5085 Bang, Molly. *Common Ground: The Water, Earth, and Air We Share* (PS–3). Illus. 1997, Scholastic $14.95 (978-0-590-10056-4). 32pp. A parable in which villagers misuse their grazing areas points out the modern environmental problem of wasting the earth's resources. (Rev: BL 10/1/97*; HB 11/97; HBG 3/98; SLJ 10/97)

5086 Banks, Kate. *Gift from the Sea* (PS–3). Illus. by Georg Hallensleben. 2001, Farrar $16.00 (978-0-374-32566-4). 40pp. This book traces the past of an ancient rock that a boy finds on the beach. (Rev: BL 4/15/01; HB 5/01; HBG 10/01; SLJ 6/01)

5087 Barner, Bob. *Dinosaurs Roar, Butterflies Soar!* (1–3). Illus. by author. 2009, Chronicle $16.99 (978-0-8118-5663-8). 32pp. A fascinating look at the relationship between dinosaurs and butterflies. (Rev: SLJ 6/09)

5088 Base, Graeme. *Uno's Garden* (2–4). Illus. 2006, Abrams $19.95 (978-0-8109-5473-1). 40pp. Uno builds a home in a beautiful forest, surrounded by Moopaloops, Lumpybums, and Frinklepods, but the colorful setting attracts more and more people until the plants and animals are almost all gone; the attractive illustrations offer opportunities for counting and finding items. (Rev: BL 11/15/06)

5089 Baskwill, Jane. *Somewhere* (PS–1). Illus. by Trish Hill. 1996, Mondo $13.95 (978-1-57255-131-2). A simple rhyme and drawings of simple outdoor scenes are used to introduce the beauty and variety of nature. (Rev: HBG 4/04; SLJ 5/96)

5090 Below, Halina. *Chestnut Dreams* (PS–1). Illus. by author. 2000, Fitzhenry & Whiteside $14.95 (978-1-55041-545-2). 40pp. The life cycle of a horse chestnut tree is explored in this picture book that shows a girl and her grandmother enjoying and observing the tree through several seasons. (Rev: SLJ 1/01)

5091 Berger, Carin. *OK Go* (PS–K). Illus. by author. 2009, HarperCollins $17.99 (978-0-06-157666-9). 32pp. Go green message delivered in recycled material collage. (Rev: BL 6/1–15/09; SLJ 4/09)

5092 Borden, Louise. *Caps, Hats, Socks, and Mittens: A Book About the Four Seasons* (PS–K). Illus. by Lillian Hoban. 1989, Scholastic paper $5.99 (978-0-590-44872-7). Children are introduced to the uniqueness of each season. (Rev: BL 2/15/89; SLJ 4/89)

5093 Brinckloe, Julie. *Fireflies!* (PS–1). Illus. by author. 1986, Simon & Schuster paper $4.99 (978-0-689-71055-1). 32pp. A boy catches fireflies one evening, but when their light grows dim, he releases them. (Rev: BL 5/1/85; HB 9/85; SLJ 4/85)

5094 Brown, Margaret Wise. *Wait Till the Moon Is Full* (PS–1). Illus. by Garth Williams. 1948, HarperCollins paper $6.99 (978-0-06-443222-1). 32pp. The fears of night are dispelled in this tender story about raccoons.

5095 Buchanan, Ken. *This House Is Made of Mud* (PS–1). Illus. by Libba Tracy. 1994, Northland LB $14.95 (978-0-87358-593-4); paper $6.95 (978-0-87358-580-4). 32pp. A child describes his adobe house in the Sonoran Desert and the plants and animal life around it. (Rev: BL 9/15/91)

5096 Buell, Janet. *Sail Away, Little Boat* (PS–3). Illus. by Jui Ishida. 2006, Carolrhoda LB $15.95 (978-1-57505-821-4). From its launching in a brook by a young girl and boy, a plucky toy sailboat heads ever downriver — past fish, deer, and other animals — until it reaches a seashore and is quickly adopted by other children. (Rev: SLJ 4/06)

5097 Bunting, Eve. *Anna's Table* (K–2). Illus. by Taia Morley. 2003, NorthWord $15.95 (978-1-55971-841-7). 32pp. Anna collects treasures that she finds — such as mouse bones, dead butterflies — and keeps them on her nature table. (Rev: BL 3/15/03; SLJ 10/03)

5098 Bunting, Eve. *Butterfly House* (K–2). Illus. by Greg Shed. 1999, Scholastic $17.99 (978-0-590-84884-8). 32pp. A young girl and her grandfather rescue a caterpillar and observe it change into a butterfly. (Rev: BL 6/1–15/99; HBG 10/99; SLJ 4/99)

5099 Bunting, Eve. *Secret Place* (K–3). Illus. by Ted Rand. 1996, Clarion $16.00 (978-0-395-64367-9). 32pp. A young boy finds a place in the city where wildlife still exists. (Rev: BL 9/1/96; SLJ 9/96)

5100 Bunting, Eve. *Someday a Tree* (PS–3). Illus. by Ronald Himler. 1993, Houghton $16.00 (978-0-395-61309-2). 32pp. In spite of attention from friends, a sick tree continues to die. (Rev: BL 3/1/93; SLJ 5/93)

5101 Bunting, Eve. *Sunflower House* (PS–2). Illus. by Kathryn Hewitt. 1996, Harcourt $15.00 (978-0-15-200483-5). 32pp. A boy plants some sunflower seeds and witnesses the dramatic miracle of plant growth. (Rev: BL 4/1/96; SLJ 5/96)

5102 Cannon, Annie. *The Bat in the Boot* (PS–2). Illus. 1996, Orchard LB $16.99 (978-0-531-08795-4). 32pp. Two children nurture a baby bat until its mother comes to rescue it. (Rev: BL 4/1/96; SLJ 6/96)

5103 Carle, Eric. *The Tiny Seed* (K–2). Illus. by author. 1991, Picture Book $16.00 (978-0-88708-015-9). 32pp. A tiny seed travels by the wind, survives all sorts of perils, and grows into a flower. A reissue.

5104 Carlstrom, Nancy White. *What Does the Sky Say?* (K–2). Illus. by Tim Ladwig. 2001, Eerdmans

$17.00 (978-0-8028-5208-3). 32pp. A poetic celebration of the sky and all its changing features. (Rev: BCCB 7–8/01; BL 7/01; HBG 10/01; SLJ 12/01)

5105 Carr, Jan. *Dappled Apples* (PS–1). Illus. by Dorothy Donohue. 2001, Holiday House $15.95 (978-0-8234-1583-0). 32pp. Cut-paper collages and rhyming text celebrate autumn as three children and a dog enjoy themselves. (Rev: BL 10/1/01; HBG 3/02; SLJ 9/01)

5106 Carr, Jan. *Splish, Splash, Spring* (PS–1). Illus. by Dorothy Donohue. 2001, Holiday House $16.95 (978-0-8234-1578-6). 32pp. It is spring and young playmates and a dog enjoy all its pleasures — playing in the rain, digging for worms, and flying kites. (Rev: BL 4/1/01; HBG 10/01; SLJ 5/01)

5107 Cash, Megan Montague. *What Makes the Seasons?* (PS–2). Illus. by author. 2003, Viking $15.99 (978-0-670-03598-4). A young African American girl and her cat experience the charms of each of the four seasons. (Rev: HBG 4/04; SLJ 10/03)

5108 Cherry, Lynne. *The Great Kapok Tree: A Tale of the Amazon Rain Forest* (K–3). Illus. 1990, Harcourt $16.00 (978-0-15-200520-7). 32pp. A carefully researched picture book of the Amazon rain forest. (Rev: BL 3/15/90; HB 5/90; SLJ 5/90)

5109 Chin, Jason. *Redwoods* (PS–3). Illus. by author. 2009, Roaring Brook $16.95 (978-1-59643-430-1). 40pp. A little boy finds a book about redwood trees on a subway platform and his train ride is transformed into a journey of discovery. (Rev: BL 4/1/09; HB 5/09; SLJ 5/09)

5110 Christian, Peggy. *If You Find a Rock* (1–3). Illus. by Barbara Hirsch Lember. 2000, Harcourt $16.00 (978-0-15-239339-7). 32pp. This book illustrated with photographs tells of the varieties and purposes of rocks, such as rocks for skipping across ponds or for hiding little creatures. (Rev: BCCB 7–8/00; BL 4/1/00; HBG 10/00; SLJ 4/00)

5111 Clark, Joan. *Snow* (PS–K). Illus. by Kady M. Denton. 2006, Groundwood $16.95 (978-0-88899-712-8). After a solid month of snow the landscape around Sammy's house is deeply covered, so the young boy climbs to his rooftop to survey the scene and imagine what is going on beneath the blanket of snow. (Rev: SLJ 9/06)

5112 Cole, Henry. *I Took a Walk* (PS–K). Illus. 1998, Greenwillow $16.99 (978-0-688-15115-7). 28pp. A boy narrates his walk through woods and a meadow, by a stream and a pond, as he observes an assortment of animals, plants, and insects. (Rev: BCCB 3/98; BL 5/1/98; HB 5/98; HBG 10/98; SLJ 5/98)

5113 Cole, Henry. *On Meadowview Street* (K–2). Illus. by author. 2007, Greenwillow $16.99 (978-0-06-056481-0). 32pp. A young girl moves with her family to the suburbs and creates a small patch of wilderness within the confines of their otherwise sterile development. (Rev: BL 6/1–15/07; SLJ 9/07)

5114 Cole, Henry. *On the Way to the Beach* (PS–3). Illus. by author. 2003, Greenwillow $16.99 (978-0-688-17515-3). On the fold-out illustrations, readers look for a variety of plant and animal life — a snowy egret, a terrapin, a prickly pear — as they follow a young girl on a walk to the beach. (Rev: BL 5/15//3; HBG 10/03; SLJ 5/03)

5115 Condra, Estelle. *See the Ocean* (K–2). Illus. by Linda Crockett-Blassingame. 1994, Ideals $14.95 (978-1-57102-005-5). 32pp. A blind girl, using her inner feelings, is the first to detect the ocean. (Rev: BL 10/15/94; SLJ 10/94)

5116 Crumpacker, Bunny. *Alexander's Pretending Day* (PS–K). Illus. by Dan Andreasen. 2005, Dutton $15.99 (978-0-525-46936-0). 32pp. Alexander plays "what if" and his mother always responds with a reassuring answer. (Rev: BL 2/15/05; SLJ 4/05)

5117 Cyrus, Kurt. *Tadpole Rex* (PS–2). Illus. by author. 2008, Harcourt $16.00 (978-0-15-205990-3). 40pp. An effective rhyming tale about an ancient polliwog evolving into a frog is followed by an endnote on the history of frogs, frog fossils, and current threats to their survival. (Rev: BL 8/08; LMC 11/08; SLJ 6/08)

5118 Deady, Kathleen W. *All Year Long* (PS–2). Illus. by Linda Bronson. 2004, Carolrhoda $15.95 (978-1-57505-537-4). 32pp. A young girl explains how changes in her family's activities signal the arrival of a new season. (Rev: BL 4/15/04; SLJ 4/04)

5119 Demunn, Michael. *The Earth Is Good: A Chant in Praise of Nature* (PS–1). Illus. by Jim McMullan. 1999, Scholastic $15.95 (978-0-590-35010-5). Accompanied by her puppy, a little girl explores the earth, including mountains, fields, an ocean, and forests. (Rev: HBG 10/99; SLJ 8/99)

5120 Depalma, Mary Newell. *The Grand Old Tree* (PS–1). Illus. 2005, Scholastic $16.99 (978-0-439-62334-6). 32pp. The life and death of a grand tree is celebrated in an appealing blend of simple text and art. (Rev: BL 11/15/05; SLJ 12/05)

5121 dePaola, Tomie. *Charlie Needs a Cloak* (PS–1). Illus. by author. 1982, Simon & Schuster paper $5.95 (978-0-671-66467-1). The facts about cloth making are humorously presented in this story of Charlie, a shepherd.

5122 dePaola, Tomie. *The Cloud Book* (K–3). Illus. by author. 1975, Holiday House LB $16.95 (978-0-8234-0259-5); paper $6.95 (978-0-8234-0531-2). 32pp. The 10 most common clouds, along with related myths and sayings.

5123 dePaola, Tomie. *The Quicksand Book* (1–3). Illus. by author. 1977, Holiday House LB $16.95 (978-0-8234-0291-5); paper $6.95 (978-0-8234-0532-9). 32pp. Science is both informative and entertaining in this story of Jungle Girl, who falls into a patch of quicksand.

5124 Desimini, Lisa, et al. *All Year Round* (PS–1). Illus. 1997, Scholastic $15.95 (978-0-590-36097-5). 32pp. Four artists have contributed their illustrations and short poems to this book about the seasons. (Rev: BL 12/15/97; HBG 3/98)

5125 Dorros, Arthur. *Feel the Wind* (PS–2). Illus. by author. 1989, HarperCollins LB $15.89 (978-0-690-04741-7); paper $5.99 (978-0-06-445095-9). 32pp. Defining what causes the wind to blow. (Rev: BL 4/1/89; SLJ 6/89)

5126 Dunn, Judy. *The Little Rabbit* (K–2). Illus. by Phoebe Dunn. 1980, Random paper $3.25 (978-0-394-84377-3). 32pp. A real rabbit family is introduced in photographs.

5127 Dunn, Phoebe. *Farm Animals* (PS). Illus. by author. 1984, Random $3.99 (978-0-394-86254-5). 28pp. An introduction to more than 15 farm animals.

5128 Dussling, Jennifer. *Picky Peggy* (1–3). Illus. by Lynn Adams. Series: Science Solves It! 2004, Kane paper $4.99 (978-1-57565-138-5). 32pp. Peggy is a picky eater, but — with the help of her pet duckling — she learns the importance of a balanced diet; solid scientific information is woven into the story. (Rev: BL 2/15/04; SLJ 6/04)

5129 Dussling, Jennifer. *Rainbow Mystery* (1–3). Illus. by Barry Gott. Series: Science Solves It! 2002, Kane paper $4.99 (978-1-57565-119-4). 32pp. Annie and Mike solve a mystery (rainbows on a wall) by discovering a science concept (prisms). (Rev: BL 9/15/02)

5130 Easwaran, Eknath. *The Monkey and the Mango: Stories of My Granny* (K–2). Illus. by Ilka Jerabek. 1996, Nilgiri Pr. $14.95 (978-0-915132-82-9). 29pp. In the southern Indian state of Kerala, a grandmother tells her grandson a number of stories that tell about the wonders of nature, creation, and humankind's relation to all creatures. (Rev: HBG 4/04; SLJ 8/96)

5131 Ehlert, Lois. *Feathers for Lunch* (PS–2). Illus. 1990, Harcourt $16.00 (978-0-15-230550-5). 32pp. A wide variety of American birds are introduced by way of a cat's stalking activities. (Rev: BCCB 1/91; BL 9/1/90; HB 11/90*; HBG 4/04; SLJ 12/90)

5132 Ehlert, Lois. *In My World* (PS–1). Illus. 2002, Harcourt $15.00 (978-0-15-216269-6). 40pp. Die-cut shapes are used to present various flora and fauna and other phenomena of nature in this impressive picture book. (Rev: BL 5/1/02*; HB 7/02; HBG 10/02; SLJ 5/02)

5133 Ehlert, Lois. *Pie in the Sky* (PS–2). Illus. 2004, Harcourt $16.00 (978-0-15-216584-0). 40pp. A well-designed and well-illustrated book about a "pie tree" that supplies cherries for the birds and animals as well as fruit for pie; a recipe is included. (Rev: BL 2/15/04; HB 7/04; SLJ 4/04)

5134 Ehlert, Lois. *Red Leaf, Yellow Leaf* (PS–2). Illus. 1991, Harcourt $16.00 (978-0-15-266197-7). 32pp. A child tells of buying, planting, and caring for a sugar maple tree. (Rev: BCCB 10/91; BL 10/1/91*; HB 11/91*; SLJ 11/91)

5135 Elliott, David. *Evangeline Mudd and the Golden-Haired Apes of the Ikkinasti Jungle* (2–4). Illus. by Andrea Wesson. 2004, Candlewick $15.99 (978-0-7636-1876-6). 196pp. Eight-year-old heroine Evangeline finds herself deeply involved in foiling a plot to destroy the rain forest. (Rev: SLJ 3/04)

5136 Erdrich, Lise. *Bears Make Rock Soup and Other Stories* (2–4). Illus. by Lisa Fifield. 2002, Children's Book Pr. $16.95 (978-0-89239-172-1). 32pp. A collection of short stories and art depicting the Native American connection to animals and the earth. (Rev: BCCB 1/03; BL 8/02; HBG 3/03; SLJ 9/02)

5137 Ernst, Lisa Campbell. *Wake Up, It's Spring!* (PS–K). Illus. 2004, HarperCollins LB $17.89 (978-0-06-008986-3). 32pp. The arrival of a warm spring sun is celebrated as plants, animals, and people bask in its rays. (Rev: BL 1/1–15/04; SLJ 2/04)

5138 Fife, Dale H. *Empty Lot* (K–3). Illus. by Jim Arnosky. 1996, Sierra Club paper $6.95 (978-0-87156-859-5). Harry realizes that his empty country lot is actually alive with all kinds of wildlife. (Rev: SLJ 8/91)

5139 Fisher, Aileen. *The Story Goes On* (PS–3). Illus. by Mique Moriuchi. 2005, Roaring Brook $16.95 (978-1-59643-037-2). A circular nature tale in which a seed sprouts and grows, a bug finds it appetizing, a frog eats the bug, and so forth through the shooting of a hawk to the final enrichment of the soil. (Rev: HB 9/96; SLJ 6/05)

5140 Fisher, Leonard Everett. *Sky, Sea, the Jetty, and Me* (1–3). Illus. 2001, Marshall Cavendish $15.95 (978-0-7614-5082-5). 32pp. A young narrator at the seashore experiences the excitement and violence of a sudden storm. (Rev: BL 3/15/01; HBG 10/01)

5141 Fleming, Denise. *The First Day of Winter* (PS–K). Illus. 2005, Holt $15.95 (978-0-8050-7384-3). 32pp. A snowman receives a nice selection of presents in this twist on "The Twelve Days of Christmas." (Rev: BL 12/15/05; SLJ 12/05)

5142 Fleming, Denise. *In the Small, Small Pond* (PS–K). Illus. 1993, Holt $16.95 (978-0-8050-2264-3); paper $6.95 (978-0-8050-5983-0). 30pp. In a series of collages, a frog views a year of changing seasons in a small pond. (Rev: BL 9/1/93; HB 9/93; SLJ 9/93*)

5143 Fletcher, Ralph. *Twilight Comes Twice* (K–2). Illus. by Kate Kiesler. 1997, Clarion $16.00 (978-0-395-84826-5). 32pp. In radiant illustrations, the author describes two times of day: the evening at twilight and dawn, when twilight colors are again present. (Rev: BL 10/15/97; HBG 3/98; SLJ 10/97)

5144 Fletcher, Ralph J. *Hello, Harvest Moon* (K–3). Illus. by Kate Kiesler. 2004, Houghton $16.00 (978-0-618-16451-6). 32pp. The glow of the harvest moon shines over the peaceful neighborhood in this gentle book. (Rev: BL 9/1/03; HBG 4/04; SLJ 9/03)

5145 Ford, Bernette. *First Snow* (PS). Illus. by Sebastien Braun. 2005, Holiday $16.95 (978-0-8234-1937-1). 32pp. A bunny and his siblings enjoy exploring their first snowfall under the light of the moon. (Rev: BL 11/1/05*; HBG 4/06; SLJ 9/05*)

5146 Franco, Betsy. *Bees, Snails, and Peacock Tails: Patterns and Shapes . . . Naturally* (PS–2). Illus. by Steve Jenkins. 2008, Simon & Schuster $16.99 (978-1-4169-0386-4). 40pp. Poems and collages explore patterns and shapes in nature, with an appendix of scientific facts. (Rev: BL 9/1/08; SLJ 9/08) [811]

5147 Franco, Betsy. *Pond Circle* (PS–1). Illus. by Stefano Vitale. 2009, Simon & Schuster $16.99 (978-1-4169-4021-0). 32pp. Introduction to woodland ecology using a "House that Jack Built" formula. (Rev: BL 6/1–15/09; HB 7/09; SLJ 5/09)

5148 Frasier, Debra. *On the Day You Were Born* (K–2). Illus. 1991, Harcourt $16.00 (978-0-15-257995-1). 32pp. The wonders of nature and the interdependence of all living things are celebrated in this book that introduces science in a personalized way. (Rev: BL 6/15/91; SLJ 6/91*)

5149 Frasier, Debra. *Out of the Ocean* (PS–3). Illus. 1998, Harcourt $16.00 (978-0-15-258849-6). 40pp. A mother and her child explore the many gifts that the ocean can give, such as a seashell or pelican feathers. (Rev: BL 4/15/98; HBG 10/98; SLJ 8/98)

5150 Freedman, Claire. *One Magical Day* (PS–K). Illus. by Tina Macnaughton. 2007, Good Bks. $16.95 (978-1-56148-567-3). A nicely illustrated, simple account of a beautiful day among the flora and fauna of the country. (Rev: SLJ 8/07)

5151 Gackenbach, Dick. *Mighty Tree* (PS). Illus. 1992, Harcourt $13.95 (978-0-15-200519-1). 32pp. This large picture book presents the uses and wonder of trees. (Rev: BL 4/1/92; SLJ 6/92) [582.16]

5152 George, Jean Craighead. *Luck* (PS–2). Illus. by Wendell Minor. 2006, HarperCollins $16.99 (978-0-06-008201-7). 32pp. Luck is a sandhill crane whose rescue from a plastic six-pack holder, growth, and migration are presented in beautiful artwork and prose in this compelling picture book. (Rev: BL 5/1/06; SLJ 6/06)

5153 George, Kristine O'Connell. *Hummingbird Nest: A Journal of Poems* (K–4). Illus. by Barry Moser. 2004, Harcourt $16.00 (978-0-15-202325-6). 48pp. George conveys the magic of watching a hummingbird raise a family in these short poems partnered by watercolors. (Rev: BL 2/1/04*; SLJ 4/04)

5154 George, Lindsay Barrett. *In the Snow: Who's Been Here?* (PS–1). Illus. 1995, Greenwillow $16.89 (978-0-688-12321-5). 40pp. On their way to go sledding, two children discover clues showing that various animals are present in this nature book that supplies interesting explanations. (Rev: BL 12/1/95; SLJ 12/95)

5155 George, William T. *Box Turtle at Long Pond* (2–3). Illus. by Lindsay B. George. 1989, Greenwillow LB $15.89 (978-0-688-08185-0). 24pp. Box Turtle ambles out from a rotting log on Long Pond at the beginning of the day. (Rev: BL 9/1/89; SLJ 10/89*)

5156 Gibbons, Gail. *The Reasons for Seasons* (K–3). Illus. 1995, Holiday House LB $16.95 (978-0-8234-1174-0). 32pp. The seasons, their causes, and the changes they produce are introduced. (Rev: BL 4/1/95; SLJ 5/95) [525]

5157 Gibbons, Gail. *The Seasons of Arnold's Apple Tree* (PS–1). Illus. by author. 1984, Harcourt $15.00 (978-0-15-271246-4); paper $6.00 (978-0-15-271245-7). 32pp. Arnold's apple tree is useful in all seasons.

5158 Gibbons, Gail. *The Vegetables We Eat* (K–3). Illus. by author. 2007, Holiday $16.95 (978-0-8234-2001-8). 32pp. A wide-ranging introduction to vegetables and their nutritional benefits. (Rev: BL 9/1/07; SLJ 7/07) [635]

5159 Glaser, Linda. *It's Spring* (PS–1). Illus. by Susan Swan. Series: Celebrate the Seasons. 2002, Millbrook LB $21.90 (978-0-7613-1760-9). 32pp. A boy enjoys a spring day and muses on the changing seasons. Also use *It's Fall* (2001), *It's Winter* (2002), and *It's Summer!* (2003). (Rev: BL 5/15/02; HBG 10/02; SLJ 3/02)

5160 Godkin, Celia. *When the Giant Stirred: Legend of a Volcanic Island* (K–3). Illus. 2002, Fitzhenry & Whiteside $18.95 (978-1-55041-683-1). 40pp. A handsomely illustrated story of a people who must leave a lush island when its volcano erupts, with a clear description of the natural cycle of renewal. (Rev: BL 11/1/02; SLJ 12/02)

5161 Godkin, Celia. *Wolf Island* (1–3). Illus. by author. 2007, Fitzhenry & Whiteside $17.95 (978-1-55455-007-4); paper $9.95 (978-1-55455-008-1). 32pp. When a wolf family leaves an island, this sets in motion a chain of events that changes the whole ecology; previously published in 1993, this new edition has more visual appeal. (Rev: BL 2/15/07; SLJ 4/07)

5162 Gomi, Taro. *Spring Is Here / Llegó la primavera* (PS). Illus. by author. 2006, Chronicle $14.50 (978-0-8118-4759-9); paper $6.95 (978-0-8118-4760-5). The changing seasons are artfully illustrated using a calf as the background in this book with text in both English and Spanish. (Rev: SLJ 6/06*)

5163 Griessman, Annette. *Like a Hundred Drums* (PS–K). Illus. by Julie Monks. 2006, Houghton $15.00 (978-0-618-55878-0). 32pp. A summer thunderstorm interrupts a day on a farm in this simple picture book with folk-art illustrations. (Rev: BL 5/1/06; SLJ 6/06)

5164 Haas, Jessie. *Sugaring* (PS–2). Illus. by Joseph A. Smith. 1996, Greenwillow $17.99 (978-0-688-14200-1). 24pp. The stages of making maple sugar and syrup are examined when Nora decides to help her grandfather in this late winter ritual. A sequel to *Mowing* (1994) and *No Foal Yet* (1995). (Rev: BL 11/15/96; SLJ 10/96)

5165 Hader, Berta, and Elmer Hader. *The Big Snow* (PS–3). Illus. by authors. 1972, Macmillan LB $17.00 (978-0-02-737910-5); paper $6.95 (978-0-689-71757-4). 48pp. How all the little animals of a country hillside survive a heavy winter storm. Caldecott Medal winner, 1949.

5166 Hall, Zoe. *The Apple Pie Tree* (PS–2). Illus. by Shari Halpern. 1996, Scholastic $16.95 (978-0-590-62382-7). 32pp. The changes that occur to an apple tree during one year are described by two sisters. (Rev: BCCB 12/96; BL 10/1/96; SLJ 12/96)

5167 Hall, Zoe. *The Surprise Garden* (PS–1). Illus. by Shari Halpern. 1998, Scholastic $15.95 (978-0-590-10075-5). 32pp. A charming book in which children plant seeds and tend their gardens until the plants grow into marvelous vegetables. (Rev: BCCB 3/98; BL 1/1–15/98; HBG 10/98; SLJ 3/98)

5168 Haskins, Lori. *Butterfly Fever* (1–3). Illus. by Jerry Smath. Series: Science Solves It! 2004, Kane paper $4.99 (978-1-57565-134-7). 32pp. Fourth-grader Ellie discovers that her new town is a destination for migrating monarch butterflies, and with her classmates she learns all about them. (Rev: BL 2/15/04; SLJ 6/04)

5169 Hayward, Linda. *Monster Bug* (1–2). Illus. by Diane Palmisciano. Series: Science Solves It! 2004, Kane paper $4.99 (978-1-57565-135-4). 32pp. Scared the day before by the image of a monster bug, Kyle realizes the nature of shadows and plots revenge with an even more frightening sight. (Rev: SLJ 6/04)

5170 Henkes, Kevin. *So Happy!* (1–3). Illus. by Anita Lobel. 2005, Greenwillow LB $16.89 (978-0-06-056484-1). 32pp. Everything changes for a bored little boy in the Southwest when the rain comes. (Rev: BL 2/1/05; SLJ 3/05)

5171 Hoberman, Mary Ann. *Right Outside My Window* (K–2). Illus. by Nicholas Wilton. 2002, Mondo $15.95 (978-1-59034-194-0). 24pp. Simple two-line rhymes describe the beautiful changing views through the four seasons. (Rev: BL 8/02; HBG 10/02; SLJ 11/02)

5172 Hoberman, Mary Ann. *Whose Garden Is It?* (PS–1). Illus. by Jane Dyer. 2004, Harcourt $16.00 (978-0-15-202631-8). 40pp. The gardener, the plants, the creatures of the garden, and the sun and the rain all come forward to claim credit to the title question as elderly Mrs. McGee and a young child stroll admiringly through it. (Rev: BL 4/15/04; SLJ 5/04)

5173 Horacek, Petr. *Butterfly Butterfly: A Book of Colors* (PS–K). Illus. 2007, Candlewick $12.99 (978-0-7636-3343-1). 16pp. While waiting for a beautifully butterfly to reappear, a little girl enjoys other insects in this rewarding picture book with die-cut holes and a final pop-up of the returning butterfly. (Rev: BL 4/15/07)

5174 *How Big Is the Ocean? First Questions and Answers About the Beach* (PS–3). Illus. Series: First Questions and Answers. 1994, Time-Life $14.95 (978-0-7835-0897-9). 48pp. Basic questions about the ocean — such as "Why is it blue?" — are answered in this picture book. (Rev: BL 3/1/95; HBG 4/04; SLJ 1/04) [508]

5175 Howell, Will C. *I Call It Sky* (K–3). Illus. by John Ward. 1999, Walker LB $16.85 (978-0-8027-8678-4). Concepts of weather are explored as children play through snow, rain, fog, and other weather phenomena. (Rev: BL 5/1/99; HBG 10/99; SLJ 6/99)

5176 Hubbell, Patricia. *Hurray for Spring!* (PS–K). Illus. by Taia Morley. 2005, North Word $15.95 (978-1-55971-913-1). 32pp. A little boy describes the many joys of spring in accessible first-person rhyming text. (Rev: BL 5/15/05; SLJ 4/05)

5177 Hughes, Shirley. *Out and About* (PS–1). Illus. 1988, Lothrop $16.00 (978-0-688-07690-0). 48pp. A colorful journey through the seasons in a picture book of poems. (Rev: BCCB 6/88; BL 3/15/88; SLJ 5/88)

5178 Jackson, Ellen. *Brown Cow, Green Grass, Yellow Mellow Sun* (K–2). Illus. by Victoria Raymond. 1995, Hyperion LB $14.89 (978-0-7867-2006-4). 32pp. The process of getting milk from a cow and turning it into butter is the subject of this picture

book illustrated with photos of objects made from modeling clay. (Rev: BL 6/1–15/95; SLJ 5/95)

5179 Jackson, Ellen. *Earth Mother* (PS–2). Illus. by Leo Dillon and Diane Dillon. 2005, Walker $16.95 (978-0-8027-8992-1). 32pp. Earth Mother is presented with conflicting requests from Man, Frog, and Mosquito and declares that all is well; excellent illustrations add to the serenity with beautiful scenery. (Rev: BL 8/05*; SLJ 9/05)

5180 Jarrett, Clare. *Arabella Miller's Tiny Caterpillar* (PS–2). Illus. by author. 2008, Candlewick $16.99 (978-0-7636-3660-9). 32pp. This rhymed story about a little girl who finds a tiny striped caterpillar and cares for it until it becomes a butterfly. (Rev: BL 3/1/08; SLJ 4/08)

5181 Johnston, Tony. *The Whole Green World* (PS–1). Illus. by Elisa Kleven. 2005, Farrar $15.00 (978-0-374-38400-5). A little girl and her dog plant seeds and enjoy the results in this rhyming verse presented within detailed circular illustrations. (Rev: SLJ 4/05)

5182 Jones, Betty, comp. *A Child's Seasonal Treasury* (PS–2). Illus. by Betty Jones. 1997, Tricycle $24.95 (978-1-883672-30-0). 136pp. For each of the seasons, a collection of poems, songs, fingerplays, and activities. (Rev: SLJ 10/97)

5183 Karas, G. Brian. *Atlantic* (PS–3). Illus. 2002, Penguin $15.99 (978-0-399-23632-7). 32pp. In this first-person narrative, the Atlantic Ocean tells what and where it is, how people view it, and how it is affected by the moon and sun. (Rev: BCCB 4/02; BL 4/15/02*; HBG 10/02; SLJ 6/02)

5184 Keats, Ezra Jack. *The Snowy Day* (PS–1). Illus. by author. 1962, Puffin paper $6.99 (978-0-14-050182-7). 40pp. A young African American boy's delight during his first snowfall. Caldecott Medal winner, 1963.

5185 Killion, Bette. *The Same Wind* (2–5). Illus. by Barbara B. Falk. 1992, HarperCollins LB $14.89 (978-0-06-021051-9). 32pp. The many kinds of winds and their uses are explored in this picture book. (Rev: BL 1/1/93)

5186 Knudsen, Michelle. *Bugged!* (1–3). Illus. by Blanche Sims. Series: Science Solves It. 2008, Kane paper $5.95 (978-1-57565-259-7). 32pp. Mosquitoes seem to be very attracted to Riley and he is determined to find out why in this readable title that lots of bug facts with a scientific approach to research and problem solving. (Rev: BL 2/1/08; SLJ 7/08)

5187 Knudsen, Michelle. *A Moldy Mystery* (1–3). Illus. by Barry Gott. Series: Science Solves It! 2006, Kane paper $4.99 (978-1-57565-167-5). 32pp. Jeff throws out some moldy food containers only to discover that they were part of his older brother's science project and he must work out how to replace them; lots of facts appear in "Did you know?" boxes. (Rev: BL 4/15/06)

5188 Kroll, Virginia. *The Seasons and Someone* (K–3). Illus. by Tatsuro Kiuchi. 1994, Harcourt $15.00 (978-0-15-271233-4). 32pp. In this exquisite picture book, a little Eskimo girl watches the changes of seasons from her Northern home. (Rev: BL 12/1/94; SLJ 1/95*)

5189 Kurtz, Jane, and Christopher Kurtz. *Water Hole Waiting* (PS–3). Illus. by Lee Christiansen. 2002, HarperCollins LB $18.89 (978-0-06-029851-7). 32pp. A picture book about animals taking turns drinking at an African water hole. (Rev: BCCB 6/02; BL 5/15/02; HBG 10/02; SLJ 5/02*)

5190 Lakin, Patricia. *Hurricane!* (1–3). Illus. by Vanessa Lubach. 2000, Millbrook LB $21.90 (978-0-7613-1616-9). 32pp. A girl and her father make preparations to withstand Hurricane Bob and after the storm has passed survey the damage. (Rev: BL 10/15/00; HBG 3/01; SLJ 1/01)

5191 Leedy, Loreen. *Blast Off to Earth! A Look at Geography* (PS–3). Illus. 1992, Holiday House LB $17.95 (978-0-8234-0973-0). 32pp. An alien teacher and his students take a class trip to Earth. (Rev: BL 11/1/92; SLJ 1/93) [910]

5192 Levine, Evan. *Not the Piano, Mrs. Medley!* (PS–2). Illus. by S. D. Schindler. 1991, Watts LB $16.99 (978-0-531-08556-1). 32pp. Mrs. Medley, Max, and Word the dog pack just about everything — except bathing suits — to go to the beach. (Rev: BL 7/91*; HB 9/91; SLJ 11/91*)

5193 Lewis, J. Patrick. *Earth and Me: Our Family Tree* (K–4). Illus. by Christopher Canyon. Series: A Sharing Nature with Children Book. 2002, Dawn $16.95 (978-1-58469-031-3); paper $7.95 (978-1-58469-030-6). Rich artwork and lyric text introduce animals of all kinds — and one boy — appreciating the beauty and bounty of their environment. (Rev: HBG 10/02; SLJ 4/02)

5194 Locker, Thomas. *Walking with Henry: Based on the Life and Works of Henry David Thoreau* (2–4). Illus. 2002, Fulcrum $17.95 (978-1-55591-355-7). 32pp. A fictionalized account of Henry David Thoreau as he hikes through the wilderness, describing his beliefs about man's relationship with nature. (Rev: BL 12/1/02; HBG 3/03; SLJ 1/03) [818]

5195 London, Jonathan. *Dream Weaver* (PS–2). Illus. by Rocco Baviera. 1998, Harcourt $17.00 (978-0-15-200944-1). 32pp. A boy watches a spider on its web and later dreams of weaving his own web to catch falling stars. (Rev: BL 4/1/98; HBG 10/98; SLJ 7/98)

5196 London, Jonathan. *Park Beat: Rhymin' Through the Seasons* (PS–3). Illus. by Woodleigh Hubbard. 2001, HarperCollins LB $15.89 (978-0-688-13995-7). Snappy verses and detailed illustrations with changing perspectives describe how a park changes with the seasons. (Rev: HBG 10/01; SLJ 5/01)

5197 Luke, Melinda. *Green Dog* (1–3). Illus. by Jane Manning. Series: Science Solves It! 2002, Kane paper $4.99 (978-1-57565-115-6). 32pp. Teddy investigates the cause of murky water in the goldfish bowl and discovers algae. (Rev: BL 9/15/02)

5198 Maass, Robert. *When Autumn Comes* (PS–2). Illus. 1990, Holt paper $6.95 (978-0-8050-2349-7). 32pp. What people do as autumn progresses, with large, handsome photos. (Rev: BL 10/1/90; SLJ 9/90) [508]

5199 Maass, Robert. *When Summer Comes* (K–2). Illus. 1993, Holt paper $5.95 (978-0-8050-4706-6). 30pp. In this tribute to the joys of summer, many of the activities associated with this season are pictured in photographs. (Rev: BL 6/1–15/93; SLJ 6/93) [508]

5200 McCloskey, Robert. *Time of Wonder* (1–4). Illus. by author. 1957, Puffin paper $6.99 (978-0-14-050201-5). 64pp. Full-color watercolors illustrate this poetic text describing a summer on the Maine coast and the hurricane that hits it. Caldecott Medal winner, 1958.

5201 McCue, Lisa. *Quiet Bunny* (PS–1). Illus. by author. 2009, Sterling LB $14.95 (978-1-4027-5719-8). 32pp. A bunny in search of his "voice" drives this lovely story. (Rev: SLJ 6/09)

5202 McCurdy, Michael. *Hannah's Farm: The Seasons on an Early American Homestead* (1–3). Illus. by author. 1988, Holiday House LB $12.95 (978-0-8234-0700-2). 32pp. The seasons are presented on this 19th-century farm in Massachusetts. (Rev: BL 11/15/88; SLJ 2/89)

5203 McGinty, Alice B. *Thank You, World* (PS–1). Illus. by Wendy A. Halperin. 2007, Dial $16.99 (978-0-8037-2705-2). 32pp. Children from eight different nations around the world are shown appreciating all kinds of things — trees, grass, breezes, and so forth. (Rev: BL 10/15/07; SLJ 12/07)

5204 Maestro, Betsy. *Snow Day* (PS–2). Illus. by Giulio Maestro. 1992, Scholastic paper $4.95 (978-0-590-46083-5). 32pp. While families stay home because of the heavy snow, snow removal crews are doing their job. (Rev: BCCB 10/89; BL 11/1/89; SLJ 1/90) [628]

5205 Major, Beverly. *Over Back* (1–3). Illus. by Thomas B. Allen. 1993, HarperCollins LB $14.89 (978-0-06-020287-3). A young African American girl takes the reader on a nature tour behind her house. (Rev: BL 2/1/93; SLJ 3/93)

5206 Michels, Tilde. *What a Beautiful Day!* (PS–2). Illus. by Thomas Muller. 1992, Carolrhoda LB $19.95 (978-0-87614-739-9). 32pp. On a beautiful summer morning, young Peter enjoys nature as he walks in the woods. (Rev: BL 1/15/93; SLJ 4/93)

5207 Milton, Joyce. *Honeybees* (1–3). Illus. by Pete Mueller. Series: All Aboard Science Reader. 2003, Grosset paper $3.99 (978-0-448-42846-8). 48pp. An accessible introduction to honeybees for beginning readers, including information on how their community works and where honey comes from. (Rev: BL 5/15/03; HBG 10/03) [595.79]

5208 Mitton, Tony. *Rainforest Romp* (PS–1). Illus. by Ant Parker. Series: Amazing Animals. 2009, Kingfisher $9.99 (978-0-7534-6298-0). 24pp. Rabbit, Mouse and Bird study a variety of animals in the rain forest; rhyming text highlights various characteristics. (Rev: BL 4/1/09) [578.734]

5209 Mockford, Caroline. *What's This?* (PS–1). Illus. 2000, Barefoot Books $15.95 (978-1-84148-018-3). 32pp. This simple picture book describes the cultivation and growth of a sunflower seed and plant by a little girl and brown bird. (Rev: BL 5/1/00; SLJ 8/00) [631.5]

5210 Mora, Pat. *Listen to the Desert / Oye al Desierto* (PS–2). Illus. by Francisco Mora. 1994, Clarion $16.00 (978-0-395-67292-1). Using double-page spreads, this book in English and Spanish introduces the animals and sounds found in a Southwestern desert. (Rev: HBG 4/04; SLJ 10/94) [574.5]

5211 Nidey, Kelli. *When Autumn Falls* (PS–1). Illus. by Susan Swan. 2004, Whitman LB $16.99 (978-0-8075-0490-1). Falling leaves, apples, and temperatures are just some of the features of autumn highlighted. (Rev: SLJ 9/04)

5212 O'Malley, Kevin. *Straight to the Pole* (PS–3). Illus. by author. 2003, Walker LB $16.85 (978-0-8027-8868-9). A little boy struggles melodramatically through a snowstorm, and just when all hope seems to be lost, two sled-riding friends appear to tell him that school's been canceled for the day. (Rev: HBG 4/04; SLJ 11/03)

5213 Pallotta, Jerry. *Dory Story* (PS–4). Illus. by David Biedrzycki. 2000, Charlesbridge $15.95 (978-0-88106-075-1). 32pp. An ocean food chain from krill-eating plankton to huge orcas eating tuna is explored in this story of a boy's imaginary dory trip into the depths. (Rev: BL 2/1/00*; HBG 10/00; SLJ 3/00)

5214 Paterson, Diane. *Hurricane Wolf* (K–3). Illus. 2006, Albert Whitman $16.99 (978-0-8075-3438-0). 32pp. Together with his parents, young Noah prepares for the arrival of Hurricane Anna and then assesses the damage after the storm has passed. (Rev: BL 3/1/06; SLJ 3/06)

5215 Peet, Bill. *The Wump World* (1–3). Illus. by author. 1981, Houghton $17.00 (978-0-395-19841-4); paper $8.95 (978-0-395-31129-5). An animal parable in which pollution and the waste of natural resources are the main themes.

5216 Perkins, Lynne Rae. *Snow Music* (PS–2). Illus. by author. 2003, Greenwillow LB $16.89 (978-0-06-623958-3). A simple, musical story of a boy searching for his runaway dog in the snow, showing the tracks of deer, rabbits, squirrels. (Rev: BCCB 12/03; BL 9/1/03; HB 11/03; HBG 4/04; LMC 3/04; SLJ 11/03)

5217 Peters, Lisa Westberg. *The Sun, the Wind, and the Rain* (K–3). Illus. by Ted Rand. 1988, Holt paper $6.95 (978-0-8050-1481-5). 48pp. The creation and evolution of mountains using the analogy of a little girl at the beach. (Rev: BL 10/15/88; HB 11/88; HBG 4/04; SLJ 10/88)

5218 Petit, Genevieve. *The Seventh Walnut* (K–3). Illus. by Joelle Boucher. 1992, Wellington $13.95 (978-0-922984-10-7). 32pp. The story of how a walnut, dropped on the ground, grows into a tree; translated from the French. (Rev: BCCB 10/92; BL 12/1/92) [574]

5219 Pettenati, Jeanne K. *Galileo's Journal: 1609–1610* (1–3). Illus. by Paolo Rui. 2006, Charlesbridge $16.95 (978-1-57091-879-7); paper $6.95 (978-1-57091-880-3). 32pp. Galileo records in a fictional journal the events of eight key months in his life, a period during which he developed a telescope and made discoveries about the solar system. (Rev: BL 8/06)

5220 Powell, Consie. *The First Day of Winter* (1–3). Illus. 2005, Albert Whitman $16.99 (978-0-8075-2450-3). 32pp. In rhyming text that follows the pattern of "The 12 Days of Christmas," this counting picture book celebrates various aspects of the winter season. (Rev: BL 1/1–15/06; SLJ 1/06)

5221 Prelutsky, Jack. *It's Snowing! It's Snowing!* (1–4). Illus. by Jeanne Titherington. 1984, Greenwillow $18.89 (978-0-688-01513-8). 48pp. A few story poems on the experiences and joys of winter. (Rev: BL 1/1–15/04; SLJ 1/04)

5222 Raczka, Bob. *Snowy, Blowy Winter* (PS–1). Illus. by Judy Stead. 2008, Albert Whitman $16.99 (978-0-8075-7526-0). 32pp. Simple spare rhymes and color cartoon illustrations feature multicultural families enjoying all the best of the season. (Rev: BLO 10/7/08; SLJ 12/08)

5223 Ravishankar, Anushka. *Tiger on a Tree* (PS–2). Illus. by Pulak Biswas. 2004, Farrar $15.00 (978-0-374-37555-3). In this impressively illustrated chanting tale from India, villagers capture a tiger and then wonder what they should do with it — in the end, they let it go. (Rev: HB 5/04; SLJ 3/04)

5224 Rawlinson, Julia. *Fletcher and the Springtime Blossoms* (PS–2). Illus. by Tiphanie Beeke. 2009, Greenwillow $17.99 (978-0-06-168855-3). 32pp. Fletcher, a little fox, believes winter has returned when he mistakes blossoms for snowflakes. (Rev: BL 12/1/08; SLJ 4/09)

5225 Riha, Susanne. *Animals and the Seasons: The Cycle of Nature* (1–3). Trans. from German by Annette Betz. Illus. by author. 2000, Blackbirch $22.45 (978-1-56711-429-4). 30pp. This book of stunning illustrations and text takes the reader through the four seasons and depicts the flora and fauna of each. (Rev: HBG 10/00; SLJ 9/00)

5226 Rockwell, Anne. *The Storm* (K–3). Illus. by Robert Sauber. 1994, Hyperion LB $16.49 (978-0-7868-2013-9). The morning after a violent storm hits their coastal home, a young girl and her mother walk the beach and view all the accumulated debris. (Rev: SLJ 11/94)

5227 Root, Phyllis. *If You Want to See a Caribou* (PS–2). Illus. by Jim Meyer. 2004, Houghton $16.00 (978-0-618-39314-5). 32pp. Set on a wooded island in Lake Superior, this gentle book celebrates the caribou in poetry and woodblock images. (Rev: BL 4/15/04; SLJ 4/04)

5228 Rosenberry, Vera. *Who Is in the Garden?* (PS–2). Illus. 2001, Holiday House $16.95 (978-0-8234-1529-8). 32pp. A little boy tours a garden and finds such wonders as wrens in a birch tree, a snake in a grape vine, and a turtle under the rhubarb. (Rev: BL 3/1/01; HBG 10/01) [577.5]

5229 Rotner, Shelley. *Senses at the Seashore* (PS–1). Illus. 2006, Millbrook LB $22.60 (978-0-7613-2897-1). 32pp. This colorful book shows how children can use their five senses to experience all the joys of a day at the beach. (Rev: BL 4/15/06; SLJ 10/06)

5230 Rotner, Shelley, and Steve Calcagnino. *The Body Book* (PS–K). Illus. 2000, Orchard LB $16.99 (978-0-531-33256-6). 32pp. As well as pointing out the different parts of the body, this picture book shows that people are basically the same even though they come in different sizes, shapes, and colors. (Rev: BL 3/1/00; HBG 10/00; SLJ 5/00) [611]

5231 Rucki, Ani. *When the Earth Wakes* (PS–1). Illus. 1998, Scholastic $15.95 (978-0-590-05951-0). 32pp. The text describes the changes that occur in the spring, and the pictures show a bear cub and its mother waking up and entering the world again. (Rev: BL 3/1/98; HBG 10/98; SLJ 3/98)

5232 Ryan, Pam Muñoz. *Hello Ocean* (PS–2). Illus. by Mark Astrella. 2001, Charlesbridge $16.95 (978-0-88106-987-7); paper $6.95 (978-0-88106-988-4). 32pp. A young girl who is visiting an ocean beach describes how this experience affects her senses. (Rev: BL 3/1/01*; HBG 10/01)

5233 Ryder, Joanne. *Each Living Thing* (PS–3). Illus. by Ashley Wolff. 2000, Harcourt $16.00 (978-0-15-201898-6). 32pp. In a gentle, rhyming text, the author cautions readers to respect and protect all living things. (Rev: BL 4/15/00; HBG 10/00; SLJ 4/00)

5234 Ryder, Joanne. *The Waterfall's Gift* (1–3). Illus. by Richard J. Watson. 2001, Sierra Club $15.95 (978-0-87156-579-2). A young girl visits a waterfall in the woods and marvels at the beauties of nature. (Rev: HBG 3/02; SLJ 8/01)

5235 Rylant, Cynthia. *In November* (PS–2). Illus. by Jill Kastner. 2000, Harcourt $16.00 (978-0-15-201076-8). 32pp. Lovely oil paintings and poetic language are used to evoke November atmosphere and activities, including a Thanksgiving feast and the coming of winter. (Rev: BL 9/1/00*; HBG 3/01; SLJ 9/00)

5236 Rylant, Cynthia. *This Year's Garden* (PS–K). Illus. by Mary Szilagyi. 1984, Macmillan paper $4.95 (978-0-689-71122-0). 32pp. A year in the garden in drawings and gentle text.

5237 Sabuda, Robert. *Winter's Tale* (K–3). Illus. Series: Classic Collectible Pop-Up. 2005, Simon & Schuster $26.95 (978-0-689-85363-0). 12pp. Spectacular pop-ups celebrate the winter landscape and wildlife. (Rev: BL 9/1/05; SLJ 9/05)

5238 St. Pierre, Stephanie. *What the Sea Saw* (PS–3). Illus. by Beverly Doyle. 2006, Peachtree $16.95 (978-1-56145-359-7). Beautiful paintings accompany simple rhyming text about all there is to see at the seaside. (Rev: SLJ 6/06)

5239 Schaefer, Lola M. *An Island Grows* (PS–2). Illus. by Cathie Felstead. 2006, Greenwillow $16.99 (978-0-06-623930-9). 40pp. The birth of an island (through a volcanic eruption) and its development and habitation by plants, animals, and people are told in simple rhyme; good both for fiction browsers and for science classes. (Rev: BL 7/06; SLJ 7/06)

5240 Schnur, Steven. *Spring Thaw* (K–3). Illus. by Stacey Schuett. 2000, Viking $15.99 (978-0-670-87961-8). 32pp. A poetic picture book that depicts signs of spring in a rural setting. (Rev: BL 3/1/00; HBG 10/00; SLJ 2/00)

5241 Schwartz, Amy. *A Beautiful Girl* (PS). 2006, Roaring Brook $16.95 (978-1-59643-165-2). 32pp. On her way to the market Jenna meets four friendly animals, each of which remarks on one of her physical characteristics. (Rev: BL 8/06; SLJ 8/06)

5242 Seuss, Dr. *The Lorax* (K–3). Illus. by author. 1971, Random LB $16.99 (978-0-394-92337-6). 64pp. The Lorax, a little brown creature, has tried in vain to ward off pollution and ecological blight, but Onceler, who wanted the trees for his business, would not heed the warning.

5243 Shea, Pegi Deitz. *New Moon* (PS–1). Illus. by Cathryn Falwell. 1996, Boyds Mills $14.95 (978-1-56397-410-6). 24pp. Vinnie and her big brother explore the various phases of the moon. (Rev: BL 1/1–15/97; SLJ 10/96)

5244 Shelby, Anne. *The Man Who Lived in a Hollow Tree* (K–3). Illus. by Cor Hazelaar. 2009, Atheneum $17.99 (978-0-689-86169-7). 40pp. A carpenter plants two trees for every tree he cuts down. (Rev: BCCB 4/09; BL 6/1–15/09; LMC 8/09; SLJ 2/09)

5245 Shetterly, Susan Hand. *Shelterwood* (K–3). Illus. by Rebecca Haley McCall. 1999, Tilbury House $16.95 (978-0-88448-210-9). 40pp. Set in Maine, this picture book shows the lessons a girl learned from her grandfather about nature and how to preserve the earth's riches. (Rev: BL 3/1/00; SLJ 3/00)

5246 Sidjanski, Brigitte. *The River* (PS–2). Illus. by Bernadette Watts. 2008, Penguin $16.99 (978-0-698-40077-1). 32pp. A river's journey to the sea is recorded through the experiences of five little pine cones that fall into a passing brook and join the current. (Rev: BL 2/15/08; LMC 3/08; SLJ 4/08)

5247 Stringer, Lauren. *Winter Is the Warmest Season* (PS–2). Illus. 2006, Harcourt $16.00 (978-0-15-204967-6). 40pp. A young boy lists the many reasons he feels that winter — not summer — is the warmest season of the year. (Rev: BL 9/1/06; HBG 4/07; SLJ 11/06)

5248 Stynes, Barbara W. *Walking with Mama* (PS–K). Illus. 1997, Dawn $14.95 (978-1-883220-56-3); paper $6.95 (978-1-883220-57-0). 24pp. A nature walk through the forest with his mother is described by a toddler. (Rev: BL 9/15/97)

5249 Swanson, Susan Marie. *To Be Like the Sun* (PS–1). Illus. by Margaret Chudos-Irvine. 2008, Harcourt $16.00 (978-0-15-205796-1). 40pp. A young girl plants a sunflower seed and watches it grow into a tall golden bloom. (Rev: BL 4/15/08; LMC 11/08; SLJ 4/08)

5250 Tamar, Erika. *The Garden of Happiness* (PS–3). Illus. by Barbara Lambase. 1996, Harcourt $16.00 (978-0-15-230582-6). 40pp. Marisol's seed, planted in a New York City cracked sidewalk, grows into a huge sunflower. (Rev: BL 7/96*; SLJ 5/96)

5251 Taylor, Joanne. *Full Moon Rising* (1–3). Illus. by Susan Tooke. 2002, Tundra $16.95 (978-0-88776-548-3). An attractive, poetic introduction to the full moons of the year. (Rev: HBG 3/03; SLJ 12/02) [523.3]

5252 Taylor, Theodore. *Hello, Arctic!* (PS–2). Illus. by Margaret Chodos-Irvine. 2002, Harcourt $16.00 (978-0-15-201577-0). 40pp. A simple text and dramatic illustrations show the changing Arctic seasons and the animals and plants found there. (Rev: BL 10/1/02; HBG 3/03; SLJ 11/02)

5253 Titherington, Jeanne. *Pumpkin Pumpkin* (PS–1). Illus. by author. 1986, Greenwillow $17.89 (978-0-688-05696-4); Morrow paper $6.99 (978-0-688-09930-5). 24pp. A simple, rhythmic picture book about the facts of plant life. (Rev: BCCB 3/86; BL 3/15/86; SLJ 4/86)

5254 Tresselt, Alvin. *Hide and Seek Fog* (K–2). Illus. by Roger Duvoisin. 1965, Lothrop LB $18.89 (978-0-688-51169-2); Morrow paper $7.99 (978-0-688-07813-3). 32pp. Pastel watercolors quietly reflect obscure seashore scenes as the mysterious, deepening fog rolls in from the sea.

5255 Udry, Janice May. *A Tree Is Nice* (PS). Illus. by Marc Simont. 1957, HarperCollins LB $18.89 (978-0-06-026156-6); paper $6.99 (978-0-06-443147-7). 32pp. The many delights to be had in, with, or under a tree: picking apples, raking leaves, swinging, or just sitting in the shade. Caldecott Medal winner, 1957.

5256 Waboose, Jan B. *Morning on the Lake* (K–3). Illus. by Karen Reczuch. 1998, Kids Can $15.95 (978-1-55074-373-9). 32pp. Three stories about an Ojibwa grandfather and his young grandson, their walks in a forest, and the mystical bond they feel with nature. (Rev: BL 3/15/98; HBG 10/98; SLJ 5/98)

5257 Walker, Rob D. *Once upon a Cloud* (K–3). Illus. by Matt Mahurin. 2005, Scholastic $16.95 (978-0-439-68879-6). 40pp. The author explores all the possibilities of what clouds might be, from cotton candy to puffs of pipe smoke, in lighthearted rhyme with imaginative illustrations. (Rev: BL 3/1/05; SLJ 3/05)

5258 Wallace, Nancy Elizabeth. *Leaves! Leaves! Leaves!* (PS–2). Illus. by author. 2003, Marshall Cavendish $16.95 (978-0-7614-5140-2). Buddy Bear and his mother observe the dramatic changes in leaves and trees over the course of the seasons. (Rev: HBG 4/04; SLJ 9/03)

5259 Waring, Geoff. *Oscar and the Frog: A Book About Growing* (PS–2). Illus. by author. Series: Start with Science. 2007, Candlewick $11.99 (978-0-7636-3558-9). 32pp. Oscar, a kitten, asks questions about growth and development that are answered by a knowledgeable frog. (Rev: BL 12/15/07; SLJ 2/08)

5260 Wellington, Monica. *Zinnia's Flower Garden* (K–2). Illus. by author. 2005, Dutton $14.99 (978-0-525-47368-8). An informative tour of gardens and gardening, in the company of Zinnia and her animal friends. (Rev: SLJ 2/05)

5261 Wiesner, David. *Flotsam* (PS–2). Illus. 2006, Clarion $17.00 (978-0-618-19457-5). 40pp. On a visit to the seaside a young boy finds an old-fashioned camera containing a film full of amazing images among the flotsam tossed on the beach in this inventive wordless book. Caldecott Medal, 2007. (Rev: BCCB 9/06; BL 8/06; HB 9/06; HBG 4/07; LMC 1/07; SLJ 9/06*)

5262 Yerxa, Leo. *Last Leaf First Snowflake to Fall* (K–3). Illus. 1994, Orchard LB $17.99 (978-0-531-08674-2). 32pp. Two Indians explore the countryside and canoe across a pond in this picture book that explores the coming of winter. (Rev: BL 10/1/94; SLJ 12/94)

5263 Yorinks, Arthur. *Happy Bees!* (PS–1). Illus. by Carey Armstrong-Ellis. 2005, Abrams $15.95 (978-0-8109-5866-1). A buzzing group of happy bees enjoy themselves while causing havoc among humans and animals. (Rev: SLJ 4/05)

OTHER TIMES, OTHER PLACES

5264 Adams, Jeanie. *Going for Oysters* (K–3). Illus. by author. 1993, Whitman LB $15.95 (978-0-8075-2978-2). A picture book that uses a simple story to introduce Australian aboriginal life by depicting life in a native outback community. (Rev: SLJ 1/94)

5265 Addy, Sharon Hart. *Lucky Jake* (PS–2). Illus. by Wade Zahares. 2007, Houghton $17.00 (978-0-618-47286-4). 40pp. Jake's dad is prospecting for gold, barely scratching out a living, but Jake knows how to take the little they have and use it to make them a better life. (Rev: BL 4/15/07)

5266 Adler, David A. *The Babe and I* (PS–2). Illus. by Terry Widener. 1999, Harcourt $16.00 (978-0-15-201378-3). 32pp. During the Great Depression, the young narrator sells newspapers on the street, and one day Babe Ruth buys a paper from him. (Rev: BCCB 6/99; BL 3/15/99*; HB 3/99; HBG 10/99; SLJ 5/99)

5267 Alakija, Polly. *Catch That Goat!* (PS–2). Illus. by author. 2002, Barefoot Books $16.99 (978-1-84148-908-7). Young Ayoka's goat runs amok in the market in this beautifully illustrated story set in Nigeria. (Rev: HBG 3/03; SLJ 12/02)

5268 Alalou, Elizabeth, and Ali Alalou. *The Butter Man* (K–3). Illus. by Julie Klear Essakalli. 2008, Charlesbridge $14.95 (978-1-58089-127-1). 32pp. As her father cooks couscous in his special pot, he tells Nora about his childhood in Morocco and the famine that hit the Atlas mountains. (Rev: BCCB 4/08; BL 1/1–15/08; HB 5/08; LMC 10/08; SLJ 2/08)

5269 Alda, Arlene. *Morning Glory Monday* (PS–2). Illus. by Maryann Kovalski. 2003, Tundra $17.95 (978-0-88776-620-6). To lift the spirits of her mother, who is homesick for Italy, a young girl plants morning glory seeds in the window boxes of her family's early-20th-century New York City tenement, and the vines spread to brighten the whole community. (Rev: BL 1/1–15/04; HBG 4/04; SLJ 11/03)

5270 Aliki. *Marianthe's Story: Painted Words / Spoken Memories* (K–3). Illus. by author. 1998, Greenwillow LB $17.89 (978-0-688-15662-6). In this book combining two stories, the first tells how Mari, a young immigrant girl, expresses herself in her paintings; in the second, Mari relates life in her native land. (Rev: BCCB 1/99; HB 9/98; HBG 3/99; SLJ 10/98)

5271 Alrawi, Karim. *The Girl Who Lost Her Smile* (1–4). Illus. by Stefan Czernecki. 2000, Winslow $16.95 (978-1-890817-17-6). 40pp. A Middle Eastern tale about a young girl who has lost her smile and is told she will only get it back when a great artist paints a picture she likes. (Rev: BL 11/1/00; HBG 3/01; SLJ 12/00)

5272 Alvarez, Julia. *A Gift of Gracias* (1–3). Illus. by Beatriz Vidal. 2005, Knopf $15.95 (978-0-375-82425-8). 40pp. The patron saint of the Dominican Republic — Nuestra Señora de la Altagracia — features in this story of a family facing a devastating crop failure. (Rev: BL 9/15/05; HBG 4/06; LMC 1/06; SLJ 11/05)

5273 Anaya, Rudolfo. *The First Tortilla: A Bilingual Story* (2–4). Trans. by Enrique R. Lamadrid into Spanish. Illus. by Amy Córdova. 2007, Univ. of New Mexico $16.95 (978-0-8263-4214-0). A traditional Mexican story about a town saved from starvation by the gift of corn from a mountain spirit. In both English and Spanish. (Rev: SLJ 7/07)

5274 Anholt, Laurence. *Camille and the Sunflowers: A Story About Vincent van Gogh* (PS–3). Illus. 1994, Barron's $14.95 (978-0-8120-6409-4). 32pp. Young Camille befriends the artist van Gogh when he comes to paint in his village in the Netherlands. (Rev: BL 12/1/94; SLJ 2/95)

5275 Anholt, Laurence. *The Magical Garden of Claude Monet* (PS–3). Illus. 2003, Barren's $14.95 (978-0-7641-5574-1). 32pp. Julie and her dog spend a day with Impressionist painter Claude Monet in this fictionalized look at the artist's later work, with illustrations echoing Monet's style. (Rev: BL 2/15/04; HBG 4/04; SLJ 5/04)

5276 Applegate, Katherine. *The Buffalo Storm* (PS–2). Illus. by Jan Ormerod. 2007, Clarion $16.00 (978-0-618-53597-2). 32pp. As her family travels on a wagon train to a new home in Oregon, Hallie misses her grandmother, whose past words of encouragement not only help Hallie face her fear of storms but also experience the adventures of the journey west. (Rev: BL 12/1/07; HB 1/08; LMC 11/07; SLJ 10/07)

5277 Arnold, Marsha Diane. *The Pumpkin Runner* (K–3). Illus. by Brad Sneed. 1998, Dial $16.99 (978-0-8037-2124-1). 32pp. Based on a true story, this picture book tells of a 61-year-old Australian farmer who eats pumpkins for energy and wins a footrace against younger, better-trained opponents. (Rev: BCCB 11/98; BL 11/1/98; HBG 3/99; SLJ 12/98)

5278 Arrigan, Mary. *Mario's Angels: A Story About the Artist Giotto* (K–3). Illus. by Gillian McClure. 2006, Frances Lincoln $15.95 (978-1-84507-404-3). 32pp. In this appealing picture-book blend of fact and fiction, young Mario suggests that Italian Renaissance artist Giotto include some angels in the fresco that he's painting and offers to pose. (Rev: BL 11/1/06; SLJ 12/06)

5279 Ashman, Linda. *Come to the Castle!* (1–3). Illus. by S. D. Schindler. 2009, Roaring Brook $16.95 (978-1-59643-155-3). 40pp. A story about the Earl of Daftwood throwing a feast and tournament serves as the framework for a rhyming overview of life in a medieval castle with detailed illustrations. (Rev: BCCB 5/09; BL 3/15/09; HB 5/09; LMC 8/09; SLJ 5/09)

5280 Avi. *Finding Providence: The Story of Roger Williams* (2–3). Illus. by James Watling. 1997, HarperCollins LB $15.89 (978-0-06-025294-6). 48pp. An easy-to-read book that tells, through the eyes of Roger Williams's daughter, the story of Williams's Boston trial and escape to the wilderness. (Rev: BCCB 3/97; BL 2/1/97; HB 5/97; SLJ 3/97)

5281 Baasansuren, Bolormaa, and Helen Mixter. *My Little Round House* (K–4). Illus. by Bolormaa Baasansuren. 2009, Groundwood $18.95 (978-0-88899-934-4). 32pp. A Mongolian child called Jilu describes the first year of his life and the activities of his nomad family. (Rev: BL 5/1/09; SLJ 4/09)

5282 Bania, Michael. *Kumak's House: A Tale of the Far North* (PS–2). Illus. 2002, Alaska Northwest $15.95 (978-0-88240-540-7); paper $8.95 (978-0-88240-541-4). 32pp. In this story packed with details about Arctic life, Kumak finds his house really feels quite large when all the animals he has taken in finally leave. (Rev: BL 9/1/02; HBG 10/02; SLJ 1/03)

5283 Banim, Lisa. *American Dreams* (2–3). Illus. Series: Stories of the States. 1993, Silver Moon LB $14.95 (978-1-881889-34-2). 80pp. In this story set in California, the friendship between Jeannie and Amy, a Japanese American girl, is shattered when World War II breaks out. (Rev: SLJ 12/93)

5284 Barren, T. A. *High as a Hawk: A Brave Girl's Historic Climb* (1–4). Illus. by Ted Lewin. 2004, Penguin $17.99 (978-0-399-23704-1). 32pp. In 1905, an 8-year-old girl climbs more than 14,000 feet to the top of Longs Peak in Colorado; panoramic illustrations enhance this story based on truth. (Rev: BL 3/1/04; SLJ 5/04)

5285 Barron, T. A. *The Day the Stones Walked: A Tale of Easter Island* (2–4). Illus. by William Low. 2007, Philomel $16.99 (978-0-399-24263-2). A story about the mysterious Easter Island sculptures coming to the aid of a little boy whose father helped to carve them. (Rev: SLJ 7/07)

5286 Bartone, Elisa. *Peppe the Lamplighter* (2–4). Illus. by Ted Lewin. 1993, Morrow paper $6.99 (978-0-688-15469-1). 32pp. The story of an immigrant Italian boy who is a lamplighter in turn-of-the-century New York City. (Rev: BCCB 5/93; BL 4/15/93; SLJ 7/93)

5287 Bauld, Jane Scoggins. *Journey of the Third Seed* (K–2). Illus. by Cynthia G. Darr. 2001, Eakin $16.95 (978-1-57168-428-8); paper $9.95 (978-1-57168-429-5). Three lotus seeds lost at sea a thousand years ago resurface, and the third seed journeys to America where lotus blossoms from the plant now flourish. (Rev: HBG 10/01; SLJ 7/01)

5288 Baylor, Byrd. *One Small Blue Bead* (1–4). Illus. by Ronald Himler. 1992, Macmillan $16.00 (978-0-684-19334-2). 32pp. A story of an early tribe of cave dwellers in the American Southwest. First published in 1965. (Rev: BL 3/1/92; SLJ 4/92)

5289 Bell, Lili. *The Sea Maidens of Japan* (K–4). Illus. by Erin M. Brammer. 1997, Ideals $14.95 (978-1-57102-095-6). 32pp. A Japanese girl who is afraid of diving is expected to become an ama — a woman who dives to the ocean floor to harvest seafood. (Rev: BCCB 5/97; BL 6/1–15/97; SLJ 6/97)

5290 Bemelmans, Ludwig, and John Bemelmans Marciano. *Madeline in America and Other Holiday Tales* (PS–3). Illus. 1999, Scholastic $19.95 (978-0-590-03910-9). This Madeline tale was completed by the author's grandson. The book also contains a few other short stories, including one about Christmas. (Rev: BL 11/15/99; HBG 10/00; SLJ 2/00)

5291 Benchley, Nathaniel. *Sam the Minuteman* (2–4). Illus. by Arnold Lobel. 1969, HarperCollins LB $16.89 (978-0-06-020480-8); paper $3.99 (978-0-06-444107-0). 64pp. An easy-to-read book that gives information on the way of life at the beginning of the Revolution.

5292 Beskow, Elsa. *Pelle's New Suit* (PS–3). Illus. by author. 1989, Gryphon $15.95 (978-0-86315-092-0). 16pp. A Swedish story of the steps in getting a new suit for a small boy, from shearing the lamb to tailoring.

5293 Bildner, Phil. *Shoeless Joe and Black Betsy* (2–4). Illus. by C. F. Payne. 2002, Simon & Schuster $17.00 (978-0-689-82913-0). 40pp. Mixed-media illustrations complement this tale about Shoeless Joe Jackson and Ol' Charlie, the man who fashioned the bat known as Black Betsy. (Rev: BL 2/15/02; HBG 10/02; SLJ 4/02)

5294 Bildner, Phil. *The Shot Heard 'Round the World* (2–4). Illus. by C. F. Payne. 2005, Simon & Schuster $16.95 (978-0-689-86273-1). 32pp. The story of the fateful (for baseball fans) summer of 1951, when the Giants beat the Brooklyn Dodgers in a playoff, accompanied by nostalgic artwork. (Rev: BL 3/1/05; SLJ 5/05) [796.357]

5295 Birtha, Becky. *Grandmama's Pride* (K–3). Illus. by Colin Bootman. 2005, Albert Whitman $16.95 (978-0-8075-3028-3). 32pp. In 1956, African American Sarah Marie, with her sister and grandmother, travels by bus to the South and learns about segregation. (Rev: BL 11/1/05; SLJ 11/05)

5296 Blos, Joan W. *The Heroine of the Titanic: A Tale Both True and Otherwise of the Life of Molly Brown* (1–4). Illus. by Tennessee Dixon. 1991, Morrow $16.99 (978-0-688-07546-0). 40pp. A picture-book biography of the boisterous survivor of the Titanic who later became a Colorado legend. (Rev: BCCB 9/91; BL 8/91; SLJ 9/91)

5297 Booth, David. *The Dust Bowl* (K–4). Illus. by Karen Reczuch. 1997, Kids Can $16.95 (978-1-55074-295-4). 32pp. A story about a poor Canadian farm family living in a Western dust bowl during the 1930s. (Rev: BL 9/1/97; SLJ 12/97)

5298 Brace, Steve. *From Beans to Batteries* (PS–2). Illus. by Annie Kubler. Series: One World. 1999, Child's Play paper $6.99 (978-0-85953-799-5). Village life in Peru is depicted in this tale about a boy who walks to a market to trade beans for batteries to use in his radio. (Rev: SLJ 6/99)

5299 Bradby, Marie. *Momma, Where Are You From?* (PS–3). Illus. by Chris K. Soentpiet. 2000, Orchard LB $17.99 (978-0-531-33105-7). 32pp. At her daughter's request, an African American woman

describes her life in the rural South during segregation. (Rev: BCCB 3/00; BL 2/15/00; HBG 10/00; SLJ 4/00)

5300 Bradby, Marie. *More Than Anything Else* (K–3). Illus. by Chris K. Soentpiet. 1996, Orchard LB $16.99 (978-0-531-08764-0). 32pp. A fictionalized account of the childhood of Booker T. Washington, told in a picture book format. (Rev: BL 7/95; SLJ 11/95*)

5301 Breen, Steve. *Violet the Pilot* (1–3). Illus. by author. 2008, Dial $16.99 (978-0-8037-3125-7). 32pp. Violet, a mechanical wizard almost since birth, at the age of 8 enters an air show with a plane she's built herself but stops in mid-competition to save Boy Scouts in trouble. (Rev: BL 1/1–15/08; SLJ 2/08)

5302 Brett, Jan. *Daisy Comes Home* (K–3). Illus. 2002, Penguin $16.99 (978-0-399-23618-1). 32pp. Detailed artwork complements this tale, set in China, of a put-upon chicken named Daisy who is washed down the river, and the resolute young owner who rescues her. (Rev: BCCB 3/02; BL 3/15/02*; HBG 10/02; SLJ 3/02)

5303 Bridges, Shirin Yim. *Ruby's Wish* (K–2). Illus. by Sophie Blackall. 2002, Chronicle $15.95 (978-0-8118-3490-2). 32pp. Ruby is an intelligent girl from a wealthy Chinese family who aspires to go to university at a time when few girls were educated, and to her surprise gets her wish. (Rev: BCCB 10/02; BL 11/15/02; HBG 3/03; SLJ 2/03)

5304 Bridges, Shirin Yim. *The Umbrella Queen* (K–3). Illus. by Taeeun Yoo. 2008, Greenwillow $16.99 (978-0-06-075040-4). 40pp. In a village in Thailand Noot is now old enough to contribute to her family's umbrella business, but finds the traditional flower and butterfly designs boring and her own elephant paintings finally gain recognition — from the king himself! (Rev: BL 7/08; SLJ 6/08)

5305 Bryant, Jen. *Call Me Marianne* (K–3). Illus. by David A. Johnson. 2006, Eerdmans $16.00 (978-0-8028-5242-7). 32pp. In 1940s Brooklyn, young Jonathan encounters poet Marianne Moore at the zoo and the two discuss poetry and the work of poets; a biography of Moore is appended. (Rev: BL 2/15/06; SLJ 3/06)

5306 Buchmann, Stephen, and Diana Cohn. *The Bee Tree* (2–6). Illus. by Paul Mirocha. 2007, Cinco Puntos $17.95 (978-0-938317-98-2). Nizam is thrilled to be part of the annual honey hunt in this story based on traditional practices in Malaysia. Facts on honey collection in Malaysia follow the story. (Rev: LMC 11/07; SLJ 7/07)

5307 Bunting, Eve. *Gleam and Glow* (1–4). Illus. by Peter Sylvada. 2001, Harcourt $16.00 (978-0-15-202596-0). 32pp. A Bosnian mother and children flee their home leaving two precious golden fish in the pond and later return from a refugee camp to find their home ruined but the pond full of golden fish. (Rev: BCCB 12/01; BL 12/15/01; HBG 3/02; SLJ 9/01)

5308 Bunting, Eve. *Going Home* (K–3). Illus. by David Diaz. 1996, HarperCollins LB $15.89 (978-0-06-026297-6). 32pp. Carlos and his family leave their adopted home in California to visit their original home in Mexico. (Rev: BCCB 12/96; BL 10/1/96; SLJ 9/96)

5309 Bunting, Eve. *I Have an Olive Tree* (PS–3). Illus. by Karen Barbour. 1999, HarperCollins LB $15.89 (978-0-06-027574-7). Sophia, a Greek American girl, and her mother go to Greece to revisit their family home and the olive tree that Sophia's grandfather planted before he died. (Rev: BCCB 5/99; BL 5/15/99; HB 7/99; HBG 10/99; SLJ 5/99)

5310 Bunting, Eve. *Pop's Bridge* (K–3). Illus. by C. F. Payne. 2006, Harcourt $17.00 (978-0-15-204773-3). 32pp. Robert and Charlie are proud of their fathers, who are working on the construction of San Francisco's Golden Gate Bridge, but Robert secretly thinks his father's role as a "skywalker" is more important. (Rev: BL 4/15/06; SLJ 6/06)

5311 Bunting, Eve. *So Far from the Sea* (K–4). Illus. by Chris K. Soentpiet. 1998, Clarion $16.00 (978-0-395-72095-0). 32pp. A young Japanese-American girl and her family visit the former internment camp of Manzanar and recall the family's hardships and experiences during their imprisonment from 1942 to the end of World War II. (Rev: BCCB 7–8/98; BL 5/1/98; HB 5/98; HBG 10/98; SLJ 6/98)

5312 Bynum, Eboni, and Roland Jackson. *Jamari's Drum* (K–4). 2004, Groundwood $16.95 (978-0-88899-531-5). Jamari has always loved the sound of the great village drum, but when he takes over its drumming he neglects his duty and disaster nearly ensues. (Rev: HB 1/05; SLJ 11/04)

5313 Campbell, Bebe Moore. *Stompin' at the Savoy* (2–4). Illus. by Richard Yarde. 2006, Philomel $16.99 (978-0-399-24197-0). 40pp. Young Mindy reconsiders her decision to skip an upcoming jazz dance recital after she is magically transported to 1920s Harlem and a night at the Savoy Ballroom. (Rev: BL 8/06; SLJ 3/07)

5314 Capatti, Bérénice. *Klimt and His Cat* (1–3). Illus. by Octavia Monaco. 2005, Eerdmans $18.00 (978-0-8028-5282-3). 40pp. Klimt's cat, Katze, describes his interesting life with the artist in this book full of beautiful illustrations. (Rev: BL 2/1/05)

5315 Carbone, Elisa. *Night Running: How James Escaped with the Help of His Faithful Dog* (2–4). Illus. by E. B. Lewis. 2008, Knopf $16.99 (978-0-375-82247-6). 32pp. Based on fact, this is the remarkable story of a slave boy and his dog who together succeed in escaping to freedom. (Rev: BL 2/1/08; HB 3/08; LMC 1/08; SLJ 1/08)

5316 Castaldo, Nancy F. *Pizza for the Queen* (PS–2). Illus. by Melisande Potter. 2005, Holiday $16.95 (978-0-8234-1865-7). 32pp. This captivating, fact-based tale tells how a Neapolitan pizza maker came up with the recipe for Pizza Margherita — a pie fit for a queen. (Rev: BL 11/15/05; SLJ 9/05)

5317 Castaneda, Omar S. *Abuela's Weave* (K–3). Illus. by Enrique O. Sánchez. 1993, Lee & Low $15.95 (978-1-880000-00-7). 32pp. In Guatemala, a young girl and her grandmother take their handicrafts to sell at a fiesta. (Rev: BL 8/93; SLJ 7/93)

5318 Celenza, Anna Harwell. *Bach's Goldberg Variations* (K–3). Illus. by JoAnn E. Kitchel. 2005, Charlesbridge $19.95 (978-1-57091-510-9). 32pp. This story of the Bach variations that helped a young man win a job as harpsichordist to a count includes a CD of the music. (Rev: BL 5/15/05)

5319 Celenza, Anna Harwell. *The Heroic Symphony* (K–4). Illus. by JoAnn E. Kitchel. 2004, Charlesbridge $19.95 (978-1-57091-509-3). Watercolor illustrations enliven this detailed story of Beethoven's "Eroica" symphony and how he struggled to complete it despite his increasing deafness. (Rev: SLJ 3/04)

5320 Chaconas, Dori. *Pennies in a Jar* (K–2). Illus. by Ted Lewin. 2007, Peachtree $16.95 (978-1-56145-422-8). 32pp. A boy whose father has left to fight in World War II wrestles with his fear of horses as he looks for a gift to send his father. (Rev: BL 10/1/07; SLJ 10/07)

5321 Chall, Marsha Wilson. *Prairie Train* (K–3). Illus. by John Thompson. 2003, HarperCollins LB $16.89 (978-0-688-13434-1). A young girl details her first train trip — a visit to Grandma in St. Paul, Minnesota — and the passing scenery of the early 20th century. (Rev: HBG 4/04; LMC 3/04; SLJ 12/03)

5322 Chamberlin, Mary, and Rich Chamberlin. *Mama Panya's Pancakes: A Village Tale from Kenya* (K–3). Illus. by Julia Cairns. 2005, Barefoot Books $16.99 (978-1-84148-139-5). Mama Panya is worried she won't have enough pancakes for all the people her son Adika has invited, but all the guests bring their own contributions and there is plenty to go round in this story set in Kenya. (Rev: BL 3/1/04; SLJ 5/05)

5323 Chapman, Nancy Kapp. *Tripper's Travels: An International Scrapbook* (K–3). Illus. by Lee Chapman. 2005, Marshall Cavendish $16.95 (978-0-7614-5240-9). Tripper the dog's round-the-world travels are preserved in a scrapbook with maps and factual information. (Rev: SLJ 12/05)

5324 Charles, Veronika M. *The Birdman* (K–3). Illus. by Annouchka Gravel Galouchko. 2006, Tundra $17.95 (978-0-88776-740-1). 32pp. Deeply shaken by the unexpected death of his wife and children, Nobi the tailor eases his grief by buying caged birds and setting them free; set in Calcutta, this is based on a true story. (Rev: BL 10/1/06; SLJ 12/06)

5325 Chen, Chih-Yuan. *On My Way to Buy Eggs* (PS). Illus. by author. 2003, Kane $15.95 (978-1-929132-49-2). In this import from Taiwan, a little girl on her way to buy eggs finds delights and adventure all around her. (Rev: HBG 4/04; SLJ 10/03)

5326 Cheripko, Jan. *Brother Bartholomew and the Apple Grove* (1–3). Illus. by Kestutis Kasparavicius. 2004, Boyds Mills $15.95 (978-1-59078-096-1). 32pp. Brother Stephen believes he can do a better job of looking after the orchard than old Brother Bartholomew, but he soon learns the dangers of pride. (Rev: BL 3/1/04; SLJ 4/04)

5327 Choi, Yangsook. *Peach Heaven* (K–2). Illus. 2005, Farrar $16.00 (978-0-374-35761-0). 32pp. A Korean girl and her grandmother rejoice when peaches from a mountaintop orchard rain down on their house during a storm. (Rev: BL 3/15/05)

5328 Claverie, Jean. *Little Lou* (2–3). Illus. 1990, Creative Ed. $22.60 (978-0-88682-329-0). 48pp. Little Lou describes how he was introduced to blues music when he was a child in the thirties. (Rev: BL 4/15/91)

5329 Cohen, Deborah Bodin. *Nachshon, Who Was Afraid to Swim: A Passover Story* (K–3). Illus. by Jago. 2009, Lerner $17.95 (978-0-8225-8764-4); paper $8.95 (978-0-8225-8765-1). 32pp. This picture book takes a biblical reference and expands it into a character study of a brave young boy, Nachson, who faces his fear of water by being the first to take the plunge into the sea during the Israelite's exodus from Egypt. (Rev: BLO 2/9/09; SLJ 3/09)

5330 Collier, Mary Jo, and Peter Collier. *The King's Giraffe* (1–3). Illus. by Stéphane Poulin. 1996, Simon & Schuster $16.00 (978-0-689-80679-7). 40pp. In 1826, the pasha of Egypt sent the King of France an unusual gift: a giraffe. (Rev: BCCB 3/96; BL 6/1–15/96; SLJ 3/96)

5331 Compestine, Ying Chang. *The Story of Chopsticks* (K–3). Illus. by YongSheng Xuan. 2001, Holiday House $16.95 (978-0-8234-1526-7). 32pp. An inventive tale of the origin of chopsticks that includes a lesson in table manners and a simple recipe. (Rev: BL 1/1–15/02; HBG 10/02; SLJ 12/01)

5332 Compestine, Ying Chang. *The Story of Kites* (K–3). Illus. by YongSheng Xuan. 2003, Holiday House $16.95 (978-0-8234-1715-5). Those irrepressible Kang brothers try a variety of methods of scaring the birds away from the rice fields before succeeding by inventing kites. (Rev: BL 4/15/03; HBG 10/03; SLJ 5/03)

5333 Compestine, Ying Chang. *The Story of Noodles* (1–3). Illus. by YongSheng Xuan. 2002, Holiday House $16.95 (978-0-8234-1600-4). 32pp. The inventive Kang brothers of *The Story of Chopsticks* return to help their mother in the emperor's cooking contest. (Rev: BCCB 2/03; BL 11/1/02; HBG 3/03; SLJ 11/02)

5334 Compestine, Ying Chang. *The Story of Paper* (K–3). Illus. by YongSheng Xuan. 2003, Holiday House $16.95 (978-0-8234-1705-6). Disciplined for inattentiveness in class, the resourceful Kang brothers search for a way to redeem themselves and end up inventing paper. (Rev: BL 12/15/03; HBG 4/04; SLJ 11/03)

5335 Connor, Leslie. *Miss Bridie Chose a Shovel* (1–4). Illus. by Mary Azarian. 2004, Houghton $16.00 (978-0-618-30564-3). 32pp. Miss Birdie makes a wise decision when she chooses a shovel rather than a keepsake to take from Ireland to her new life in America in 1856. (Rev: BL 3/1/04*; SLJ 5/04)

5336 Conway, David. *Lila and the Secret of Rain* (PS–2). Illus. by Jude Daly. 2008, Frances Lincoln $16.95 (978-1-84507-407-4). 32pp. A Kenyan girl succeeds in bringing much-needed rain to her parched village in this beautifully illustrated picture book. (Rev: BL 7/08; SLJ 7/08)

5337 Coombs, Kate. *The Secret-Keeper* (1–4). Illus. by Heather Solomon. 2006, Simon & Schuster $16.95 (978-0-689-83963-4). Keeping the secrets of everyone in the village weighs so heavily on Kalli that she becomes ill, only to recover when she hears some happy news. (Rev: SLJ 7/06)

5338 Cooper, Floyd. *Willie and the All-Stars* (1–3). Illus. by author. 2008, Philomel $16.99 (978-0-399-23340-1). 32pp. In 1942 10-year-old Willie learns that there really may be a future for black baseball players in this appealing book with sepia illustrations. (Rev: BL 9/1/08)

5339 Cordsen, Carol Foskett. *The Milkman* (PS–2). Illus. by Douglas B. Jones. 2005, Dutton $15.99 (978-0-525-47208-7). 32pp. In a former, easier time, Mr. Plimpton delivers milk and eggs and a great deal more — gifts, cards, and lost puppies, for example. (Rev: BL 5/1/05)

5340 Corey, Shana. *Players in Pigtails* (PS–3). Illus. by Rebecca Gibbon. 2003, Scholastic $16.95 (978-0-439-18305-5). Corey tells the story of a fictional character named Katie Casey who helps start the All-American Girls Professional Baseball League during World War II. (Rev: BL 3/1/04; HBG 10/03; SLJ 4/03)

5341 Corey, Shana. *You Forgot Your Skirt, Amelia Bloomer!* (1–3). Illus. by Chesley McLaren. 2000, Scholastic $18.99 (978-0-439-07819-1). The story of Amelia Bloomer, how she founded a newspaper, worked for women's rights, and started a dress craze. (Rev: BCCB 2/00; BL 2/1/00*; HBG 10/00; SLJ 3/00)

5342 Cotten, Cynthia. *Abbie in Stitches* (K–3). Illus. by Beth Peck. 2006, Farrar $16.00 (978-0-374-30004-3). 32pp. In 19th-century New York State, Abbie resists pressure to do needlework, much preferring to read. (Rev: BL 9/1/06; SLJ 9/06)

5343 Cowcher, Helen. *Whistling Thorn* (PS–3). Illus. 1993, Scholastic $14.95 (978-0-590-47299-9). 40pp. A nonfiction account of why the thorn trees of Africa's grasslands whistle when the wind blows through them. (Rev: BL 10/15/93; SLJ 10/93) [583]

5344 Crisp, Marty. *Titanicat* (K–3). Illus. by Robert Papp. 2008, Sleeping Bear $17.95 (978-1-58536-355-1). 32pp. Based on a true story, this picture book tells the tale of a ship's boy who literally misses the boat when he attempts to return a kitten to its mother. (Rev: BL 8/08; LMC 3/09; SLJ 7/08)

5345 Cullen, Lynn. *Moi and Marie Antoinette* (1–3). Illus. by Amy Young. 2006, Bloomsbury $16.95 (978-1-58234-958-9). 32pp. Marie Antoinette's dog Sebastien chronicles his mistress's life from the age of 13 to becoming queen of France. (Rev: BL 11/1/06)

5346 Cunnane, Kelly. *For You Are a Kenyan Child* (PS–K). Illus. by Ana Juan. 2006, Simon & Schuster $16.95 (978-0-689-86194-9). 40pp. A young Kenyan boy is forgiven for his inattention to his cattle in this gentle story that conveys lots of information about rural Africa. (Rev: BL 2/1/06; SLJ 1/06*)

5347 Cutler, Jane. *Guttersnipe* (K–3). Illus. by Emily Arnold McCully. 2009, Farrar $16.95 (978-0-374-32813-9). 32pp. Set in the early 20th century in a

Canadian city, this story follows Ben, a 10-year-old Jewish boy who tries to help his immigrant family to make ends meet after the death of his father. (Rev: BL 1/1–15/09)

5348 Daly, Niki. *Happy Birthday, Jamela* (PS–K). Series: Jamela. 2006, Farrar $16.00 (978-0-374-32842-9). 32pp. Jamela's mother makes her buy boring, sensible shoes to go with her birthday dress, so Jamela brightens them up with beads in this fourth book about the young South African girl. (Rev: BL 8/06; SLJ 8/06)

5349 Danneberg, Julie. *Cowboy Slim* (PS–2). Illus. by Margot Apple. 2006, Charlesbridge $15.95 (978-1-58089-045-8). 32pp. Slim, a newcomer to the WJ Ranch, wants nothing more than to be a cowboy, but at first his love for poetry seems to get in the way of his dream. (Rev: BL 2/15/06; SLJ 2/06)

5350 Day, Marie. *Quennu and the Cave Bear* (K–3). Illus. by author. 1999, Owl $17.95 (978-1-895688-86-3); paper $6.95 (978-1-895688-87-0). 32pp. A young girl conquers her fear of cave bears and paints one on the wall during a prehistoric ceremony; includes accurate information about cave art. (Rev: HBG 10/99; SLJ 5/99)

5351 Delgado, María Isabel. *Chave's Memories / Los Recuerdos de Chave* (PS–3). Illus. by Yvonne Symank. 1996, Piñata $14.95 (978-1-55885-084-2). A bilingual picture book in which a woman recalls her trips as a child from Brownsville, Texas, to her grandparents' ranch in northern Mexico. (Rev: SLJ 12/96)

5352 Demas, Corinne. *The Boy Who Was Generous with Salt* (K–3). Illus. by Michael Hays. 2002, Marshall Cavendish $15.95 (978-0-7614-5099-3). As cook aboard a fishing vessel in 1850, Ned plots to get home in time for his ninth birthday. (Rev: HBG 10/02; SLJ 5/02)

5353 Demi. *The Greatest Power* (K–3). Illus. 2004, Simon & Schuster $19.95 (978-0-689-84503-1). 40pp. Ping, introduced in *The Empty Pot* (1990), invites all the children in his empire to consider what might be the greatest power in the world, with interesting results. (Rev: BL 2/1/04; SLJ 3/04)

5354 Demi. *The Magic Pillow* (K–3). Illus. by author. 2008, Simon & Schuster $19.99 (978-1-4169-2470-8). 40pp. A magic pillow cures a poor Chinese boy named Ping of his dreams of wealth and fame; traditional illustrations add atmosphere. (Rev: BL 7/08; HB 7/08; LMC 8/08; SLJ 7/08)

5355 dePaola, Tomie. *Pascual and the Kitchen Angels* (PS–2). Illus. 2004, Penguin $16.99 (978-0-399-24214-4). 32pp. The patron saint of cooks is introduced in a charming story of a boy who communes with the animals and requires the help of angels when asked to make a meal. (Rev: BL 1/1–15/04; SLJ 2/04)

5356 dePaola, Tomie. *The Song of Francis* (PS–1). Illus. by author. 2009, Putnam $16.99 (978-0-399-25210-5). 32pp. This simple volume distills the essence of St. Francis and his joyful appreciation for and love of nature as he sings about Brother Sun and Sister Moon. (Rev: BL 1/1–15/09; SLJ 1/09)

5357 Diakité, Penda. *I Lost My Tooth in Africa* (PS–2). Illus. by Baba Wague Diakité. 2006, Scholastic $16.99 (978-0-439-66226-0). 32pp. While visiting her extended family in the West African nation of Mali, a young girl loses her tooth and is treated to a visit from the African Tooth Fairy. (Rev: BL 2/1/06; SLJ 1/06)

5358 Dorros, Arthur. *Julio's Magic* (K–2). Illus. by Ann Grifalconi. 2005, HarperCollins LB $17.89 (978-0-06-029005-4). 32pp. Julio, a young Mexican wood-carver, helps his elderly teacher, Iluminado, to create the winning entry for the annual wood-carving contest. (Rev: BL 1/1–15/05; SLJ 1/05)

5359 Edwards, David. *The Pen That Pa Built* (K–2). Illus. by Ashley Wolff. 2007, Tricycle $14.95 (978-1-58246-153-3). 32pp. Set in the 19th century, this title uses rhyming text and textured illustrations to present the processes of shearing sheep, carding and spinning, dyeing, and so forth, ending with a snuggly blanket. (Rev: BL 11/15/07; LMC 1/08; SLJ 10/07)

5360 Edwards, Pamela Duncan. *Barefoot: Escape on the Underground Railroad* (K–4). Illus. by Henry Cole. 1997, HarperCollins LB $15.89 (978-0-06-027138-1). 32pp. The birds and other animals in a forest seem to work together to help an escaped slave. (Rev: BL 2/15/97; SLJ 2/97*)

5361 Elvgren, Jennifer Riesmeyer. *Josias, Hold the Book* (1–3). Illus. by Nicole Tadgell. 2006, Boyds Mills $15.95 (978-1-59078-318-4). 32pp. Living in rural Haiti, Josias must work in the garden instead of going to school until he realizes that book-learning could improve their crops. (Rev: BL 2/15/06; SLJ 3/06)

5362 Ernst, Lisa Campbell. *Sam Johnson and the Blue Ribbon Quilt* (K–3). Illus. by author. 1983, Lothrop LB $17.89 (978-0-688-01517-6); Morrow paper $6.99 (978-0-688-11505-0). 32pp. The men and the women vie for honors in the quilting contest.

5363 Esbaum, Jill. *Ste-e-e-e-eamboat A-comin'!* (K–4). Illus. by Adam Rex. 2005, Farrar $16.00 (978-0-374-37236-1). 40pp. The excitement of the arrival of the packet *S. L. Clemens* at sleepy towns on the Mississippi in 1867 is portrayed in rhyming verse and beautiful realistic illustrations. (Rev: SLJ 3/05)

5364 Esbaum, Jill. *To the Big Top* (K–2). Illus. by David Gordon. 2008, Farrar $16.95 (978-0-374-39934-4). 32pp. In the early 20th century the circus is coming to Willow Grove and Benny and Sam are thrilled to help with setting up the Big Top. (Rev: BL 4/15/08; SLJ 8/08)

5365 Evans, Freddi Williams. *Hush Harbor: Praying in Secret* (K–3). Illus. by Erin Bennett Banks. 2008, Carolrhoda $16.95 (978-0-8225-7965-6). 32pp. Slaves praying at night in their secret "hush harbor" are warned that patrols are on the lookout and quickly return home; an author's note provides history and insight, and evocative paintings add atmosphere. (Rev: BL 10/1/08; SLJ 11/08)

5366 Faulkner, Matt. *The Pirate Meets the Queen* (K–3). Illus. 2005, Philomel $15.99 (978-0-399-

24038-6). 32pp. Granny O'Malley, the 16th-century Irish pirate, tells her life story and describes her showdown with Queen Elizabeth I over the capture of Granny's son Toby. (Rev: BL 5/15/05; SLJ 6/05)

5367 Faulkner, Matt. *A Taste of Colored Water* (1–3). Illus. by author. 2008, Simon & Schuster $16.99 (978-1-4169-1629-1). 48pp. A segregation story told through the eyes of a white girl, Lulu, who with her cousin Jelly comes face to face with racism in a southern city in the 1960s. (Rev: BL 2/1/08; SLJ 2/08)

5368 Feder, Paula K. *The Feather-Bed Journey* (K–3). Illus. by Stacey Schuett. 1995, Whitman LB $15.95 (978-0-8075-2330-8). 32pp. Grandma tells her grandchildren how her favorite feather pillow was once part of a large feather bed that kept her warm in a Jewish ghetto during World War II. (Rev: BCCB 12/95; BL 10/15/95; SLJ 11/95)

5369 Feeney, Stephanie. *A Is for Aloha* (PS–K). Photos by Jeff Reese. 1985, Univ. of Hawaii $13.95 (978-0-8248-0722-1). A simple introduction to Hawaii and its many cultures.

5370 Fern, Tracey E. *Buffalo Music* (PS–2). Illus. by Lauren Castillo. 2008, Clarion $16.00 (978-0-618-72341-6). 32pp. The story of the near-extinction of the buffalo is told from the point of view of Molly, a woman who in the late 1800s raises two orphan calves; based on the real life of Mary Ann Goodnight. (Rev: BL 4/15/08; SLJ 6/08)

5371 Fern, Tracey E. *Pippo the Fool* (1–3). Illus. by Pau Estrada. 2009, Charlesbridge $15.95 (978-1-57091-655-7). 48pp. A fictionalized account of the life and work of Filippo Brunelleschi, a characterful goldsmith who unexpectedly (in the opinion of others) won the competition to design and build the dome of the Cathedral of Florence. (Rev: BL 1/1–15/09; SLJ 6/09)

5372 Fine, Edith Hope, and Judith Pinkerton. *Armando and the Blue Tarp School* (K–2). Illus. by Hernan Sosa. 2007, Lee & Low $16.95 (978-1-58430-278-0). 48pp. Armando, who lives in Tijuana and helps his father sifting through trash at the dump, gets a chance to attend a school set up on a blue tarp on the ground. (Rev: BL 11/15/07; LMC 1/08; SLJ 10/07)

5373 Fleming, Candace. *Boxes for Katje* (K–3). Illus. by Stacey Dressen-McQueen. 2003, Farrar $16.00 (978-0-374-30922-0). Based on actual events, this is a heartwarming story of an Indiana town's efforts to help Dutch people suffering from severe postwar shortages in 1945. (Rev: HB 9/03; HBG 4/04; SLJ 9/03)

5374 Fletcher, Susan. *Dadblamed Union Army Cow* (K–3). Illus. by Kimberly B. Root. 2007, Candlewick $16.99 (978-0-7636-2263-3). 32pp. The story of a cow that accompanies a Union soldier into battle during the Civil War. (Rev: BL 7/07; LMC 11/07; SLJ 8/07)

5375 Foreman, Michael. *Mia's Story: A Sketchbook of Hopes and Dreams* (1–3). 2006, Candlewick $15.99 (978-0-7636-3063-8). 32pp. Mia, a young resident of a poverty-stricken Chilean village, beautifies her community with the pretty flowers she finds while searching for a missing puppy. (Rev: BL 8/06; SLJ 8/06)

5376 Francis, David "Panama", and Bob Reiser. *David Gets His Drum* (K–2). Illus. by Eric Velasquez. 2002, Marshall Cavendish $16.95 (978-0-7614-5088-7). 32pp. African American jazz musician "Panama" Francis loved music from a young age and here tells the sad story of his first drum. (Rev: BL 11/15/02; HBG 3/03; SLJ 10/02)

5377 Francis, Pauline. *Sam Stars at Shakespeare's Globe* (2–4). Illus. by Jane Tattersfield. 2006, Frances Lincoln $15.95 (978-1-84507-406-7). 32pp. A picture-book account of a boy named Sam who acts in the Globe Theatre and aspires to the role of Juliet. (Rev: BL 11/1/06; SLJ 12/06)

5378 Friedman, Robin. *The Silent Witness: A True Story of The Civil War* (K–3). Illus. by Claire A. Nivola. 2005, Houghton $16.00 (978-0-618-44230-0). A touching story about the young owner of a rag doll that was present at the surrender of the Confederacy in 1865; the girl never saw it after that day but it is now on display in Appomattox. (Rev: BCCB 6/05; HB 5/05; SLJ 6/05)

5379 Fuchs, Bernie. *Ride Like the Wind: A Tale of the Pony Express* (K–4). Illus. by author. 2004, Scholastic $16.95 (978-0-439-26645-1). 32pp. The fictional adventures of young Pony Express rider Johnny Free and his pony JennySoo are augmented by historical material. (Rev: SLJ 3/04)

5380 Funke, Cornelia. *The Princess Knight* (PS–2). Trans. by Anthea Bell. Illus. by Kerstin Meyer. 2004, Scholastic $15.95 (978-0-439-53630-1). 32pp. Princess Violetta can joust, ride, and use a sword as well as her older brothers, so when her father wants to give her away as a tournament prize on her 16th birthday, she dons a disguise and takes part in the contest herself. (Rev: BL 2/1/04*; SLJ 3/04)

5381 Garaway, Margaret K. *Ashkii and His Grandfather* (K–3). Illus. by Harry Warren. 1995, Old Hogan $14.95 (978-0-9638851-7-3); paper $8.95 (978-0-9638851-6-6). 33pp. A young Navajo boy helps his grandfather at summer sheep camp. (Rev: BL 3/1/90)

5382 Garay, Luis. *The Kite* (K–2). Illus. 2002, Tundra $14.95 (978-0-88776-503-2). 32pp. Francisco, a Latin American boy who must help support his family after his father's death, dreams of having a kite. (Rev: BL 8/02; HBG 10/02; SLJ 12/02)

5383 Garay, Luis. *Pedrito's Day* (K–3). Illus. 1997, Orchard $14.95 (978-0-531-09522-5). 32pp. Pedrito, a Mexican boy, is heartbroken when he loses the money he had saved to buy a bicycle. (Rev: BL 3/1/97; SLJ 4/97)

5384 Garcia, Cristina. *The Dog Who Loved the Moon* (K–3). Illus. by Sebastia Serra. 2008, Atheneum $15.99 (978-1-4169-1836-3). 32pp. With rich illustrations and rhythmic text, this is an enjoyable story about a Cuban girl named Pilar who loves to dance and her dog, Paco, who won't join her because he's obsessed with the moon. (Rev: BL 4/15/08; SLJ 4/08)

5385 Garland, Sherry. *The Buffalo Soldier* (K–3). Illus. by Ronald Himler. 2006, Pelican $15.95 (978-1-58980-391-6). 32pp. This overview of the "buffalo soldiers" — members of the all-African American cavalry regiments that served after the Civil War — is told from the viewpoint of a fictional recruit who is a former slave; includes eye-catching illustrations and a historical note. (Rev: BL 11/1/06; SLJ 12/06)

5386 Geeslin, Campbell. *Elena's Serenade* (1–3). Illus. by Ana Juan. 2004, Simon & Schuster $16.95 (978-0-689-84908-4). 40pp. Elena proves her father wrong and succeeds in blowing magnificent pieces of glass in this story set in Mexico. (Rev: BL 3/1/04; SLJ 3/04)

5387 George, Jean Craighead. *Nutik, the Wolf Pup* (PS–3). Illus. by Ted Rand. 2001, HarperCollins LB $17.89 (978-0-06-028165-6). 40pp. Amaroq nurses a wolf pup back to health and then must give him up and return him to the pack. (Rev: BL 2/1/01; HBG 10/01; SLJ 3/01)

5388 Germein, Katrina. *Big Rain Coming* (PS–2). Illus. by Bronwyn Bancroft. 2000, Clarion $16.00 (978-0-618-08344-2). 32pp. In the Australian Outback where it gets very hot, every living creature is waiting for the rain that Old Joseph claims is on its way. (Rev: BL 8/00; HBG 3/01; SLJ 9/00)

5389 Gershator, Phillis. *Sky Sweeper* (K–3). Illus. by Holly Meade. 2007, Farrar $16.00 (978-0-374-37007-7). 40pp. This is the beautifully illustrated, challenging story of Takeboki, who as a boy takes a job tending the gardens at a Zen temple, work he enjoys despite its simplicity. (Rev: BL 3/15/07)

5390 Gerstein, Mordicai. *The Mountains of Tibet* (K–3). Illus. by author. 1989, HarperCollins paper $6.99 (978-0-06-443211-5). 32pp. A woodcutter spends his life in a Tibetan valley in this story of reincarnation. (Rev: BL 11/15/87; HB 11/87; SLJ 11/87)

5391 Gibfried, Diane. *Brother Juniper* (K–2). Illus. by Meilo So. 2006, Clarion $16.00 (978-0-618-54361-8). Brother Juniper, a follower of Father Francis of Assisi, is so generous that he gives away the monks' church, bit by bit, to the poor; for this he is condemned by his brothers but commended by the saint. (Rev: SLJ 5/06)

5392 Glass, Andrew. *Bewildered for Three Days: As to Why Daniel Boone Never Wore His Coonskin Cap* (2–3). Illus. 2000, Holiday House $16.95 (978-0-8234-1446-8). 32pp. After several hair-raising adventures including spending a night in a hollow log with a mother raccoon, Daniel Boone swears off wearing his coonskin cap forever. (Rev: BCCB 11/00; BL 9/1/00; HBG 10/01; SLJ 10/00)

5393 Goble, Paul. *Death of the Iron Horse* (K–2). Illus. by author. 1993, Simon & Schuster paper $5.99 (978-0-689-71686-7). 32pp. Rail sabotage from the Indian point of view, set in 1867. (Rev: BCCB 4/87; BL 4/1/87; HB 5/87)

5394 Gonzalez, Lucia. *The Storyteller's Candle / La velita de los cuentos* (K–3). Illus. by Lulu Delacre. 2008, Children's Book Pr. $16.95 (978-0-89239-222-3). 32pp. Set in the winter of 1929, this large bilingual picture book tells the story of how New York City's first Puerto Rican librarian, Pura Belpre, influenced the lives of two little Latino girls who very much wanted something to read. (Rev: BL 3/15/08; LMC 11/08; SLJ 4/08)

5395 Gourley, Robbin. *Bring Me Some Apples and I'll Make You a Pie: A Story About Edna Lewis* (K–3). Illus. by author. 2009, Clarion $16.00 (978-0-618-15836-2). 48pp. Recipes and rhymes add atmosphere to this story based on the life of the granddaughter of an emancipated slave who became a famous chef. (Rev: BCCB 1/09; BL 2/1/09; SLJ 2/09) [921]

5396 Graham, Christine. *When Pioneer Wagons Rumbled West* (PS–2). Illus. by Sherry Meidell. 1998, Deseret $14.95 (978-1-57345-272-4). 26pp. This picture book illustrates the hardships faced by Mormon families and the importance of prayer in their lives as they journeyed to settle land for their new home in Utah. (Rev: BL 9/15/98; SLJ 12/98)

5397 Green, Norma B. *The Hole in the Dike* (K–2). Illus. by Eric Carle. 1975, Scholastic paper $4.95 (978-0-590-46146-7). 32pp. Brilliant illustrations accompany this simple retelling of the Mary Mapes Dodge story of the boy who put his finger in the dike and saved his Dutch town.

5398 Grifalconi, Ann. *Ain't Nobody a Stranger to Me* (PS–3). Illus. by Jerry Pinkney. 2007, Hyperion $16.99 (978-0-7868-1857-0). 32pp. Based on a true story, this book features a grandfather telling his granddaughter how he escaped slavery with the help of courageous strangers on the Underground Railroad. (Rev: BL 5/1/07; SLJ 5/07)

5399 Haddon, Mark. *Footprints on the Moon* (K–3). Illus. by Christian Birmingham. 2009, Candlewick $16.99 (978-0-7636-4440-6). 32pp. A little boy (based on the author) gazes at the moon and dreams about the astronauts landing there. (Rev: LMC 10/09; SLJ 6/09)

5400 Hall, Bruce Edward. *Henry and the Kite Dragon* (PS–2). Illus. by William Low. 2004, Penguin $15.99 (978-0-399-23727-0). 40pp. A cultural clash in 1920s New York City pits kite-flying 8-year-old Henry and his friends from Chinatown against pet pigeon-owning children from nearby Little Italy. (Rev: BL 5/15/04; SLJ 8/04)

5401 Hall, Donald. *Ox-Cart Man* (K–3). Illus. by Barbara Cooney. 1979, Puffin paper $6.99 (978-0-14-050441-5). 40pp. The cycle of production and sale of goods in 19th-century New England is pictured in human terms. Caldecott Medal winner, 1980.

5402 Hanson, Regina. *A Season for Mangoes* (PS–2). Illus. by Eric Velasquez. 2005, Clarion $15.00 (978-0-618-15972-7). 32pp. Sareen, a young Jamaican girl, struggles to find the confidence to address the mourners at her beloved grandmother's wake, or "sit-up." (Rev: BL 2/1/05; SLJ 5/05)

5403 Harper, Jo, and Josephine Harper. *Prairie Dog Pioneers* (PS–3). Illus. by Craig Spearing. 1998, Turtle $16.95 (978-1-890515-10-2). 48pp. This historical adventure story tells of the experiences of Mae Dean and her family as they travel by covered wagon to their new home in the Texas panhandle. (Rev: BL 9/15/98; HBG 3/99; SLJ 10/98)

5404 Hartfield, Claire. *Me and Uncle Romie: A Story Inspired by the Life and Art of Romare Bearden* (K–3). Illus. by Jerome Lagarrigue. 2002, Dial $16.99 (978-0-8037-2520-1). 40pp. James enjoys spending time with his uncle, the Harlem Renaissance artist Romare Bearden, in this picture book with reproductions of the artist's work. (Rev: BL 2/15/03; HBG 3/03; SLJ 12/02)

5405 Haseley, Dennis. *Twenty Heartbeats* (2–4). Illus. by Ed Young. 2008, Roaring Brook $16.95 (978-1-59643-238-3). 32pp. A treat for art lovers, this is the story, set in earlier times, of a man who seeks a portrait of his beloved horse. (Rev: BCCB 4/08; BL 5/1/08; LMC 5/08; SLJ 4/08)

5406 Hayes, Joe. *A Spoon for Every Bite / Una cuchara para cada bocado* (1–4). Illus. by Rebecca Leer. 2005, Cinco Puntos paper $8.95 (978-0-938317-93-7). A bilingual version of the story in which a poor couple fools a rich neighbor into spending his fortune on spoons. (Rev: SLJ 10/05)

5407 Heide, Florence Parry, and Judith Heide Gilliland. *Sami and the Time of the Troubles* (1–4). Illus. by Ted Lewin. 1992, Houghton $16.00 (978-0-395-55964-2). 40pp. This compelling picture book shows a modern Beirut family caught up in the horrors of war. (Rev: BL 4/1/92*; HB 7/92; SLJ 5/92*)

5408 Heller, Linda. *The Castle on Hester Street* (K–3). Illus. by Boris Kulikov. 2007, Simon & Schuster $15.99 (978-0-689-87434-5). 40pp. With corrections from Grandma, Grandpa tells an elaborate story of their immigration to America to escape the persecution of Jews in Russia. (Rev: BL 12/15/07; SLJ 10/07)

5409 Henson, Heather. *Angel Coming* (PS–2). Illus. by Susan Gaber. 2005, Simon & Schuster $15.95 (978-0-689-85531-3). 40pp. A child living in the Appalachian Mountainous in the early 20th century anxiously awaits the arrival of a member of the Frontier Nursing Service — known by locals as "angels on horseback" — who will help the child's mother through childbirth. (Rev: BL 7/05*; SLJ 7/05)

5410 Henson, Heather. *That Book Woman* (2–4). Illus. by David Small. 2008, Atheneum $16.99 (978-1-4169-0812-8). 40pp. Young Cal's desire to read is sparked and later fulfilled when a traveling librarian journeys up to his remote mountain home in this book set in the 1930s. (Rev: BCCB 10/08; BL 9/15/08; HB 11/08; LMC 1/09)

5411 Herbauts, Anne. *Prince Silencio* (1–3). Trans. from French by Zoe Bedrick. 2006, Enchanted Lion $14.95 (978-1-59270-055-4). Prince Silencio ("Silence") teaches his noisy subjects the value of occasional quiet times in this story translated from the French. (Rev: SLJ 6/06)

5412 Hershenhorn, Esther. *Fancy That* (K–3). Illus. by Megan Lloyd. 2003, Holiday House $16.95 (978-0-8234-1605-9). In the 1840s, a young orphan named Pip travels the countryside trying to earn money as a portrait painter, but his realistic style

fails to please his customers. (Rev: BL 9/15/03; HBG 4/04; SLJ 11/03)

5413 High, Linda Oatman. *Tenth Avenue Cowboy* (K–2). Illus. by Bill Farnsworth. 2008, Eerdmans $17.00 (978-0-8028-5330-1). 32pp. A lonely boy named Ben moves from a ranch to crowded New York City in the early 1900s but still makes his cowboy dreams come true — alongside the city's railroad tracks. (Rev: BLO 8/28/08; SLJ 9/08)

5414 Hoberman, Mary Ann. *Mrs. O'Leary's Cow* (K–2). Illus. by Jenny Mattheson. 2007, Little, Brown $16.99 (978-0-316-14840-5). 32pp. With new verses added to the classic song and a transition to a rural environment, this is the humorous story of firefighters' efforts to save the barn after the cow kicks over the lantern. (Rev: BL 4/1/07)

5415 Hoffman, Mary. *Boundless Grace* (PS–3). Illus. by Caroline Binch. 1995, Dial $16.99 (978-0-8037-1715-2). 32pp. Grace's father sends airplane tickets for her to visit him in Gambia and meet his new family. (Rev: BCCB 6/95; BL 4/15/95; HB 7/95; SLJ 5/95*)

5416 Hoffman, Mary. *The Color of Home* (PS–3). Illus. by Karin Littlewood. 2002, Penguin $17.99 (978-0-8037-2841-7). 32pp. A young Somalian boy who has emigrated to America to escape civil war has trouble adjusting to his new life until he is able to paint pictures of his fears and hopes. (Rev: BCCB 10/02; BL 10/15/02; HBG 3/03; SLJ 9/02)

5417 Hofmeyr, Dianne. *The Faraway Island* (PS–3). Illus. by Jude Daly. 2008, Frances Lincoln $16.95 (978-1-84507-644-3). 32pp. This simple story about an unhappy man who chooses to live on a barren island and ends up transforming it into a beautiful haven is based on the experiences of Fernando Lopez, who transformed St. Helena. (Rev: BLO 3/5/09; SLJ 3/09)

5418 Homan, Lynn M., and Thomas Reilly. *The Tuskegee Airmen Story* (K–3). Illus. by Rosalie M. Shepherd. 2002, Pelican $15.95 (978-1-58980-005-2). 32pp. A grandfather tells of his days as a Tuskegee Airman during World War II. (Rev: BL 2/15/03; HBG 3/03)

5419 Hong, Lily T. *The Empress and the Silkworm* (PS–3). Illus. 1995, Whitman LB $16.95 (978-0-8075-2009-3). 32pp. A Chinese empress uses the silk threads she finds when she discovers the cocoons of silkworms to make a robe for the emperor. (Rev: BCCB 12/95; BL 9/15/95; SLJ 11/95)

5420 Hopkinson, Deborah. *Abe Lincoln Crosses a Creek: A Tall, Thin Tale (Introducing His Forgotten Frontier Friend)* (PS–3). Illus. by John Hendrix. 2008, Random $16.99 (978-0-375-83768-5). 40pp. In 1816 7-year-old Abe falls into Knob Creek and is rescued by his friend Austin; commentary by both author and illustrator add to the story. (Rev: BCCB 10/08; BL 9/15/08; HB 9/08; LMC 11/08; SLJ 9/08)

5421 Hopkinson, Deborah. *Saving Strawberry Farm* (PS–2). Illus. by Rachel Isadora. 2005, Greenwillow LB $18.89 (978-0-688-17401-9). 32pp. During the Depression, young Davy plays a key role in helping Miss Elsie to save her strawberry farm. (Rev: BL 5/1/05)

5422 Hopkinson, Deborah. *Under the Quilt of Night* (K–2). Illus. by James Ransome. 2002, Simon & Schuster $16.00 (978-0-689-82227-8). 40pp. A young slave girl describes her dangerous escape through the Underground Railroad. (Rev: BCCB 2/02; BL 2/15/02; HB 7/02; HBG 10/02; SLJ 1/02*)

5423 Howard, Ellen. *The Log Cabin Church* (K–3). Illus. by Ronald Himler. 2002, Holiday House $16.95 (978-0-8234-1740-7). 32pp. Elvirey initially questions her Michigan frontier community's desire to build a church in this sequel to *The Log Cabin Quilt* (1996) and *The Log Cabin Christmas* (2000). (Rev: BL 10/1/02; HBG 3/03; SLJ 10/02)

5424 Howard, Ellen. *The Log Cabin Quilt* (K–3). Illus. by Ronald Himler. 1996, Holiday House LB $16.95 (978-0-8234-1247-1). 28pp. Quilting scraps help chink the holes in a log cabin in this story of Western pioneers. (Rev: BCCB 10/96; BL 12/15/96; SLJ 10/96)

5425 Hubbard, Crystal. *Catching the Moon* (PS–2). Illus. by Randy DuBurke. 2005, Lee & Low $16.95 (978-1-58430-243-8). 32pp. In the 1920s, a young African American girl is determined to become a professional baseball player; based on the life of Toni Stone (1921–1996). (Rev: BL 9/1/05; SLJ 11/05)

5426 Hughes, Monica. *A Handful of Seeds* (K–3). Illus. by Luis Garay. 1996, Orchard $15.95 (978-0-531-09498-3). 32pp. When Concepcion moves from the country to the city, she brings some seeds with her to start a garden in the barrio. (Rev: BCCB 6/96; BL 4/1/96; SLJ 3/96)

5427 Hurst, Carol Otis. *Rocks in His Head* (K–3). Illus. by James Stevenson. 2001, Greenwillow LB $17.89 (978-0-06-029404-5). 32pp. A man pursues his interest in rock collecting from childhood through raising a family in the Depression until he succeeds in turning a hobby into a career. (Rev: BCCB 12/01; BL 6/1–15/01; HB 7/01; HBG 10/01; SLJ 6/01)

5428 Hurst, Carol Otis. *Terrible Storm* (K–2). Illus. by S. D. Schindler. 2007, Greenwillow $16.99 (978-0-06-009001-2). 32pp. Two grandfathers separately share their memories of the blizzard that hit New England in 1888. (Rev: BL 11/15/06; SLJ 1/07)

5429 Ichikawa, Satomi. *My Father's Shop* (K–2). Illus. 2006, Kane $15.95 (978-1-929132-99-7). 32pp. Mustafa, son of a Moroccan rug seller, doesn't enjoy learning foreign words from his father but in a romp through the local marketplace he attracts the attention of many tourists and brings them back to the rug shop. (Rev: BL 2/15/06)

5430 Iijima, Geneva Cobb. *The Way We Do It in Japan* (K–3). Illus. by Paige Billin-Frye. 2002, Whitman $16.99 (978-0-8075-7822-3). 32pp. When Gregory's family moves to Japan, he learns about the differences between Japanese and American culture. (Rev: BCCB 3/02; BL 5/15/02; HBG 10/02; SLJ 4/02)

5431 Isadora, Rachel. *Bring on That Beat* (PS–2). Illus. by author. 2002, Penguin $16.99 (978-0-399-23232-9). 32pp. In this rhyming, rhythmic ode to jazz set in 1930s Harlem, a band plays on a street corner and a crowd gathers to listen. (Rev: BCCB 1/02; BL 2/15/02; HBG 10/02; SLJ 1/02)

5432 Jacobson, Rick. *The Master's Apprentice* (2–4). Illus. by Laura Fernandez. 2008, Tundra $18.95 (978-0-88776-783-8). 32pp. Marco, young apprentice to the artist Michelangelo and victim of a treacherous older apprentice, appears doomed to disappoint either his father or his master in this intense story about character. (Rev: BL 3/15/08; SLJ 5/08)

5433 Johnson, Angela. *I Dream of Trains* (PS–2). Illus. by Loren Long. 2003, Simon & Schuster $16.95 (978-0-689-82609-2). A young African American boy working in the cotton fields of the Mississippi Delta dreams of riding away to a better life on a locomotive driven by the legendary Casey Jones. (Rev: HBG 4/04; SLJ 10/03)

5434 Johnson, Angela. *Just Like Josh Gibson* (PS–2). Illus. by Beth Peck. 2004, Simon & Schuster $15.95 (978-0-689-82628-3). 32pp. Negro Leagues legend Josh Gibson is a source of inspiration in this story about an African American girl who finds success at baseball in the 1940s. (Rev: BL 2/15/04; SLJ 3/04)

5435 Johnson, Angela. *The Rolling Store* (K–3). Illus. by Peter Catalanotto. 1997, Orchard LB $16.99 (978-0-531-33015-9). 32pp. A young African American girl tells her friend about the traveling store in a truck that used to visit their community during her grandfather's childhood. (Rev: BCCB 5/97; BL 2/15/97; SLJ 4/97)

5436 Johnson, Angela. *A Sweet Smell of Roses* (K–2). Illus. by Eric Velasquez. 2005, Simon & Schuster $16.95 (978-0-689-83252-9). 32pp. Two African American sisters sneak out of their house to hear a speech by Martin Luther King Jr. (Rev: BL 2/1/05; SLJ 3/05)

5437 Johnson, Angela. *Wind Flyers* (1–3). Illus. by Loren Long. 2007, Simon & Schuster $16.99 (978-0-689-84879-7). 32pp. A young African American boy proudly describes his great-great-uncle's prowess as a flyer and one of the Tuskegee Airmen. (Rev: BL 12/1/06; SLJ 1/07)

5438 Jungman, Ann. *The Most Magnificent Mosque* (1–4). Illus. by Shelley Fowles. 2004, Frances Lincoln $15.95 (978-1-84507-012-0). A beautiful mosque in Cordoba, Spain, is saved from destruction through the combined support of three friends — a Christian, a Jew, and a Muslim — who played in its gardens when they were young. (Rev: SLJ 9/04)

5439 Kajikawa, Kimiko. *Tsunami!* (PS–3). Illus. by Ed Young. 2009, Philomel $16.99 (978-0-399-25006-4). 32pp. An old Japanese man sets his prized rice fields on fire in an attempt to save the villagers from a killer wave. (Rev: BL 11/15/08; SLJ 1/09)

5440 Karim, Roberta. *Kindle Me a Riddle* (K–2). Illus. by Bethanne Andersen. 1999, Greenwillow LB $16.89 (978-0-688-16204-7). 40pp. In frontier America, a family traces the origins of their simple pioneer home and its contents, such as the candles that were once beeswax. (Rev: BL 9/1/99; HBG 3/00; SLJ 1/00)

5441 Kay, Verla. *Covered Wagons, Bumpy Trails* (PS–3). Illus. by S. D. Schindler. 2000, Penguin $16.99 (978-0-399-22928-2). A rhyming tale with excellent paintings that depicts the hardships and triumphs of a pioneer family and their journey to California. (Rev: HB 1/01; HBG 3/01; SLJ 11/00)

5442 Kay, Verla. *Gold Fever* (K–3). Illus. by S. D. Schindler. 1999, Penguin $15.99 (978-0-399-23027-1). 32pp. A young man encounters many obstacles while traveling to the California Gold Rush but, when he doesn't find gold, must go home disappointed. (Rev: BL 1/1–15/99; HB 3/99; HBG 10/99; SLJ 3/99)

5443 Kay, Verla. *Tattered Sails* (K–3). Illus. by Dan Andreasen. 2001, Penguin $15.99 (978-0-399-23345-6). 32pp. A description of the difficult voyage of three Pilgrim children and their parents on their way to America in search of a better life. (Rev: BL 10/15/01; HBG 3/02; SLJ 9/01)

5444 Kellerhals-Stewart, Heather. *Brave Highland Heart* (PS–1). Illus. by Werner Zimmerman. 1999, Stoddart $15.95 (978-0-7737-3099-1). 32pp. A little Scottish girl fears she will be denied permission to go the ceilidh, a traditional Scottish party that will be held in the family barn, but her father allows her to stay up and enjoy the fun and dancing. (Rev: BL 8/99; SLJ 6/99)

5445 Kessler, Cristina. *The Best Beekeeper of Lalibela: A Tale from Africa* (PS–2). Illus. by Leonard Jenkins. 2006, Holiday $16.95 (978-0-8234-1858-9). 32pp. Almaz, a young Ethiopian girl, is determined to prove the men wrong and succeed at keeping bees and producing honey. (Rev: BL 8/06; SLJ 8/06)

5446 Ketcham, Sallie. *Bach's Big Adventure* (PS–3). Illus. by Timothy Bush. 1999, Orchard LB $17.99 (978-0-531-33140-8). 32pp. Ten-year-old Bach journeys to Hamburg to hear the man who is supposedly the greatest organist in the world. (Rev: BCCB 5/99; BL 4/1/99; HBG 10/99; SLJ 6/99)

5447 Khan, Rukhsana. *The Roses in My Carpets* (1–4). Illus. by Ronald Himler. 1998, Holiday House $15.95 (978-0-8234-1399-7). 32pp. A young Afghan boy who lives in a refugee camp dreams of freedom and a place without bombs or warfare as he learns to weave carpets. (Rev: BL 11/15/98; HBG 3/99; SLJ 11/98)

5448 Khan, Rukhsana. *Silly Chicken* (PS–2). Illus. by Yunmee Kyong. 2005, Viking $15.99 (978-0-670-05912-6). 32pp. A young Pakistani girl named Rani is jealous of her mother's affection for the family chicken. (Rev: BL 1/1–15/05; SLJ 4/05)

5449 Kimmel, Eric A. *Stormy's Hat: Just Right for a Railroad Man* (PS–2). Illus. by Andrea U'Ren. 2008, Farrar $16.95 (978-0-374-37262-0). 32pp. In the early 1900s, railroad engineer Stormy's long-term search for a suitable hat drives his wife Ida to design one herself, which leads to a successful international business; this story is based on fact, and the hats are still worn today. (Rev: BL 1/1–15/08; SLJ 5/08)

5450 Kimmelman, Leslie. *Everybody Bonjours!* (PS–2). Illus. by Sarah McMenemy. 2008, Knopf $16.99 (978-0-375-84443-0). 40pp. A little girl and her family take a guided tour of Paris in clever rhyme and watercolor art. (Rev: BL 8/08; SLJ 4/08)

5451 Kinsey-Warnock, Natalie. *From Dawn till Dusk* (K–3). Illus. by Mary Azarian. 2002, Houghton $16.00 (978-0-618-18655-6). 40pp. The author describes her childhood on a Vermont farm, contrasting the hard work with the resulting benefits as she details the different activities throughout the year. (Rev: BL 11/15/02; HBG 3/03; SLJ 10/02)

5452 Kinsey-Warnock, Natalie. *Nora's Ark* (K–3). Illus. by Emily Arnold McCully. 2005, HarperCollins LB $17.89 (978-0-06-029517-2). 32pp. The house that Grandpa is building up on the hill proves useful after all when the storms come in this story based on flooding in Vermont in 1927. (Rev: BL 5/15/05)

5453 Kirk, Connie Ann. *Sky Dancers* (1–3). Illus. by Christy Hale. 2004, Lee & Low $16.95 (978-1-58430-162-2). 32pp. John Cloud, a young Mohawk boy, is overwhelmed by New York City and by the skill and daring of his steelworker father, laboring far above the ground on the Empire State Building. (Rev: BL 11/15/04; SLJ 1/05)

5454 Kitamura, Satoshi. *Stone Age Boy* (1–4). Illus. by author. 2007, Candlewick $15.99 (978-0-7636-3474-2). 37pp. Suddenly transported to the Stone Age, a boy meets a girl named Om and learns all about life there, including tools, cave paintings, hunting, and cooking. (Rev: HB 1/08; LMC 3/08; SLJ 1/08)

5455 Krebs, Laurie. *We're Riding on a Caravan: An Adventure on the Silk Road* (1–3). Illus. by Helen Cann. 2005, Barefoot Books $16.99 (978-1-84148-343-6). 32pp. This richly illustrated picture book follows a family of silk traders as they travel China's Silk Road. (Rev: BL 11/1/05; SLJ 1/06)

5456 Krensky, Stephen. *Dangerous Crossing: The Revolutionary Voyage of John and John Quincy Adams* (2–4). Illus. by Greg Harlin. 2005, Dutton $16.99 (978-0-525-46966-7). 32pp. This book based on diary accounts and including powerful watercolor paintings brings to life the perilous 1778 voyage of young John Quincy and his father aboard the *Boston*. (Rev: BL 3/1/05; SLJ 2/05)

5457 Krensky, Stephen. *Sisters of Scituate Light* (1–3). Illus. by Stacey Schuett. 2008, Dutton $16.99 (978-0-525-47792-1). 32pp. During the war of 1812 teenage sisters Rebecca and Abbie, alone at the lighthouse their father runs, succeed in scaring off British soldiers who are coming ashore; this exciting tale is based on a true story. (Rev: BL 4/15/08; LMC 10/08; SLJ 6/08)

5458 Krishnaswami, Uma. *Chachaji's Cup* (K–3). Illus. by Soumya Sitaraman. 2003, Children's Book Pr. $16.95 (978-0-89239-178-3). 32pp. Neel, an Indian boy living in the United States, listens to his great-uncle Chachaji's Hindu legends and his stories of the hardships and dangers he faced as a child refugee during the partition of India and Pakistan in 1947. (Rev: BL 3/15/03; HBG 10/03; SLJ 6/03)

5459 Krishnaswami, Uma. *Monsoon* (PS–2). Illus. by Jamel Akib. 2003, Farrar $16.00 (978-0-374-35015-

4). A young girl in India and her family await the arrival of the monsoon rains in this attractive picture book full of Indian culture, with informative back matter. (Rev: BCCB 1/04; BL 9/1/03; HBG 4/04; LMC 3/04; SLJ 12/03)

5460 Kroeger, Mary Kay, and Louise Borden. *Paperboy* (K–4). Illus. by Ted Lewin. 1996, Clarion $17.00 (978-0-395-64482-9). 32pp. In 1927 Cincinnati, a young paperboy has trouble selling his newspapers when boxing champ Jack Dempsey loses the prizefight. (Rev: BCCB 3/96; BL 3/15/96; HB 9/96; SLJ 8/96*)

5461 Kroll, Virginia. *Especially Heroes* (3–5). Illus. by Tim Ladwig. 2003, Eerdmans $16.00 (978-0-8028-5221-2). 32pp. The narrator remembers an incident in 1962, when her father reacted to an attack on a black woman in their neighborhood. (Rev: BL 2/1/03; HBG 10/03; SLJ 4/03)

5462 Kroll, Virginia. *Sweet Magnolia* (1–3). Illus. by Laura Jacques. 1995, Charlesbridge paper $6.95 (978-0-88106-414-8). When Denise visits her grandmother, a naturalist, in Louisiana, she learns about the flora and fauna of the swamps and tastes Cajun food. (Rev: SLJ 2/96)

5463 Krull, Kathleen, and Paul Brewer. *Fartiste* (K–3). Illus. by Boris Kulikov. 2008, Simon & Schuster $16.99 (978-1-4169-2828-7). 40pp. Joseph Pujol was a real "fartiste" who in Paris circa 1900 blew the audiences away with his gassy abilities. (Rev: BCCB 6/08; BL 8/08; HB 9/08; LMC 10/08; SLJ 7/08)

5464 Kushner, Tony. *Brundibar* (1–4). Illus. by Maurice Sendak. 2003, Hyperion $19.95 (978-0-7868-0904-2). 56pp. This poignant story, based on a Czech opera originally performed by children at a concentration camp, tells how two children, Pepecik and Anniku, struggle to get milk for their sick mother. (Rev: BL 11/15/03; HBG 4/04; SLJ 12/03)

5465 Kusugak, Michael A. *Arctic Stories* (2–4). Illus. by Vladyana Krykorka. 1998, Annick $18.95 (978-1-55037-452-0); paper $6.95 (978-1-55037-453-7). 40pp. Three stories about an Inuit girl growing up in a village around northern Hudson Bay are simply told with full-page watercolors. (Rev: BL 11/1/98; SLJ 3/99)

5466 Kyuchukov, Hristo. *My Name Was Hussein* (1–3). Illus. by Allan Eitzen. 2004, Boyds Mills $15.95 (978-1-56397-964-4). 32pp. Based on the author's childhood experiences, this sobering tale looks at persecution of a Roma group in Bulgaria. (Rev: BL 4/15/04; SLJ 4/04)

5467 Lachenmeyer, Nathaniel. *The Origami Master* (PS–2). Illus. by Aki Sogabe. 2008, Albert Whitman $16.99 (978-0-8075-6134-8). 32pp. A Japanese origami master learns important lessons from a little bird; includes directions for folding an origami bird. (Rev: BL 10/1/08; SLJ 10/08)

5468 Lamorisse, Albert. *The Red Balloon* (1–3). Illus. by author. 1967, Doubleday $16.95 (978-0-385-00343-8); paper $10.95 (978-0-385-14297-7). 45pp. Pascal possesses a magic balloon that leads him on a tour of Paris, and he must defend the balloon from a gang of boys bent on bursting it.

5469 Lanteigne, Helen. *The Seven Chairs* (K–3). Illus. by Maryann Kovalski. 1998, Orchard $14.95 (978-0-531-30110-4). 32pp. A picture book that traces the history of seven chairs that were carved by a woodworker in England several centuries ago. (Rev: BL 9/1/98; HBG 3/99; SLJ 11/98)

5470 Lawlor, Laurie. *Old Crump: The True Story of a Trip West* (1–3). Illus. by John Winch. 2002, Holiday House $16.95 (978-0-8234-1608-0). 32pp. The members of a wagon train and their ox, Old Crump, find themselves lost in Death Valley in 1850. (Rev: BL 3/15/02; HBG 10/02; SLJ 6/02)

5471 Lawson, Julie. *Arizona Charlie and the Klondike Kid* (K–3). Illus. by Kasia Charko. 2003, Orca $15.95 (978-1-55143-250-2). Young Ben, an aspiring Gold Rush entertainer, finds the stage more alarming than he expected but shows his mettle when he encounters a thief. (Rev: HBG 10/03; SLJ 9/03)

5472 Lawson, Julie. *Emma and the Silk Train* (1–5). Illus. by Paul Mombourquette. 1998, Kids Can $15.95 (978-1-55074-388-3). 32pp. When a train carrying bales of silk is derailed, Emma joins the search for the lost silk, finds a bale, and gets stuck on a small island. Based on the true story of a "silker" derailment in 1927. (Rev: BL 11/1/98; HBG 3/99; SLJ 10/98)

5473 Lawson, Julie. *The Klondike Cat* (1–3). Illus. by Paul Mombourquette. 2002, Kids Can $15.95 (978-1-55337-013-0). 32pp. Noah doesn't get in trouble for bringing his cat on the journey to the Klondike in 1896 because it turns out that mousers are in great demand. (Rev: BL 11/15/02; HBG 3/03; SLJ 1/03)

5474 Lee, Huy Voun. *In the Leaves* (K–3). Illus. 2005, Holt $16.95 (978-0-8050-6764-4). 32pp. On a trip to a farm, Xiao Ming is eager to introduce his friends to the 10 Chinese characters he has learned, and to explain their relationship to the surrounding world; includes effective illustrations and a pronunciation guide. (Rev: BL 8/05; SLJ 8/05)

5475 Lee-Tai, Amy. *A Place Where Sunflowers Grow / Sabaku Ni Saita Himawari* (1–3). Illus. by Felicia Hoshino. 2006, Children's Book Pr. $16.95 (978-0-89239-215-5). 32pp. In English and Japanese, this is a gentle story of the Japanese internment in World War II, featuring a young Japanese American girl who tries to adjust by painting pictures. (Rev: BL 8/06)

5476 Lendroth, Susan. *Ocean Wide, Ocean Deep* (PS–2). Illus. by Raul Allen. 2008, Tricycle $15.99 (978-1-58246-232-5). 32pp. Set in 19th-century New England, this title follows a young girl as she yearns in rhymed couplets for the return of her sailor father. (Rev: BLO 12/11/08; SLJ 10/08)

5477 Leonetti, Mike. *Swinging for the Fences: Hank Aaron and Me* (2–4). Illus. by David Kim. 2008, Chronicle $15.99 (978-0-8118-5662-1). 32pp. Little Leaguer Mark, whose batting leaves something to be desired, is a big fan of Hank Aaron and Aaron's advice helps him to improve his game. (Rev: BL 5/15/08; SLJ 5/08)

5478 Le Tord, Bijou. *A Bird or Two: A Story About Henri Matisse* (K–3). Illus. 1999, Eerdmans $18.00 (978-0-8028-5184-0). 32pp. Using Matisse-like paintings, this picture book tells about the artist and the south of France that he loved. (Rev: BL 11/15/99; HBG 3/00; SLJ 2/00)

5479 Levine, Ellen. *Henry's Freedom Box* (1–3). Illus. by Kadir Nelson. 2007, Scholastic $16.99 (978-0-439-77733-9). 40pp. A fictionalized account of the dangerous and exciting story of a young slave who escaped to freedom in a packing crate, traveling by train and by steamboat until he arrived in Philadelphia. Caldecott Honor Book, 2008. (Rev: BL 2/1/07)

5480 Levine, Ellen. *The Tree That Would Not Die* (1–4). Illus. by Ted Rand. 1995, Scholastic $14.95 (978-0-590-43724-0). 32pp. The story of the 400-year-old Treaty Oak in Texas and the important historical events that it witnessed. (Rev: BCCB 10/95; BL 11/1/95*; SLJ 12/95) [813]

5481 Levitin, Sonia. *Boom Town* (PS–3). Illus. by Cat B. Smith. 1998, Orchard LB $17.99 (978-0-531-33043-2). 40pp. In Gold Rush California, Amanda gets rich making wonderful gooseberry pies. A companion to *Nine for California* (1996). (Rev: BCCB 5/98; BL 2/15/98; HB 3/98; HBG 10/98; SLJ 3/98)

5482 Levitin, Sonia. *Junk Man's Daughter* (PS–3). Illus. by Guy Porfirio. Series: Tales of Young America. 2007, Sleeping Bear $17.95 (978-1-58536-315-5). 40pp. When Papa cannot find work in America, Hanna and her brothers help earn money for the family by collecting junk to sell. (Rev: BL 12/1/07; SLJ 4/08)

5483 Lewin, Hugh. *Jafta* (K–3). Illus. by Lisa Kopper. 1983, Lerner paper $4.95 (978-0-87614-494-7). 24pp. There are six volumes in this set that are about a black South African child and his father. Others are: *Jafta's Father* (1983); *Jafta's Mother* (1983); *Jafta: The Journey* (1984); *Jafta: The Town* (1984); *Jafta and the Wedding* (1988).

5484 Lewis, Alan K. *I Grew Up on a Farm* (1–4). Illus. by Bob Fletcher. 2005, Moo Pr. LB $19.95 (978-0-9766805-2-9). 32pp. Simple text and black-and-white family photographs describe growing up on a farm during the 1950s. (Rev: SLJ 2/06)

5485 Lewis, Rose. *I Love You Like Crazy Cakes* (PS–3). Illus. by Jane Dyer. 2000, Little, Brown $14.95 (978-0-316-52538-1). 32pp. The author, an American, presents a fictional account of her trip to China to adopt a baby girl. (Rev: BL 9/1/00; HBG 10/01; SLJ 10/00)

5486 Lindgren, Astrid. *The Tomten* (PS–2). Illus. by Harald Wiberg. 1997, Penguin paper $6.99 (978-0-698-11591-0). 32pp. The friendly troll speaks in Tomten language only animals and children understand. By the same author, illustrator, and publisher: *The Tomten and the Fox* (1989).

5487 Lindsey, Kathleen D. *Sweet Potato Pie* (1–3). Illus. by Charlotte Riley-Webb. 2003, Lee & Low $16.95 (978-1-58430-061-8). When foreclosure threatens the farm, Sadie, an 8-year-old African American girl, pitches in with the rest of her family to sell sweet potato pies. (Rev: BL 9/15/03; HBG 4/04; SLJ 12/03)

5488 Lipp, Frederick. *The Caged Birds of Phnom Penh* (PS–3). Illus. by Ronald Himler. 2001, Holiday House $16.95 (978-0-8234-1534-2). 32pp. Ary, an 8-year-old girl living in Cambodia, tests the proverb that says "letting a caged bird go free makes wishes come true." (Rev: BCCB 4/01; BL 4/1/01; HBG 3/02; SLJ 5/01)

5489 Lipp, Frederick. *Running Shoes* (K–2). Illus. by Jason Gaillard. 2008, Charlesbridge $16.95 (978-1-58089-175-2); paper $7.95 (978-1-58089-176-9). 32pp. After she gets a pair of shoes, Sophy, a Cambodian girl, runs 5 miles each way to get to the school where she is the only girl. (Rev: BL 1/1–15/08; LMC 10/08; SLJ 2/08)

5490 Littlesugar, Amy. *Freedom School, Yes!* (PS–3). Illus. by Floyd Cooper. 2001, Penguin $16.99 (978-0-399-23006-6). 40pp. Based on fact, this is the story of volunteers who came South during the civil rights struggle in 1964 and set up "freedom schools." (Rev: BCCB 2/01; BL 2/15/01; HBG 10/01; SLJ 1/01)

5491 Lofthouse, Liz. *Ziba Came on a Boat* (1–3). Illus. by Robert Ingpen. 2007, Kane $15.95 (978-1-933605-52-4). 32pp. Lofthouse, who has worked with Afghan refugees, tells a simple story of a little girl named Ziba who hopes for a safer life as she travels by sea on a small fishing boat; beautiful illustrations add to the impact. (Rev: BL 11/1/07; LMC 1/08; SLJ 10/07)

5492 London, Jonathan. *Hurricane!* (K–3). Illus. by Henri Sorensen. 1998, Lothrop $17.99 (978-0-688-12977-4). 32pp. Two boys experience the fierceness of a hurricane when it strikes their Puerto Rico home. (Rev: BL 8/98; HBG 3/99; SLJ 1/99)

5493 Lorbiecki, Marybeth. *Jackie's Bat* (1–3). Illus. by Brian Pinkney. 2006, Simon & Schuster $15.95 (978-0-689-84102-6). 40pp. A young batboy named Joey reveals his prejudice when Jackie Robinson joins the Brooklyn Dodgers and his subsequent growing admiration for the player. (Rev: BL 2/1/06; SLJ 1/06)

5494 Lord, Michelle. *Little Sap and Monsieur Rodin* (2–4). Illus. by Felicia Hoshino. 2006, Lee & Low $16.95 (978-1-58430-248-3). 32pp. Little Sap, a dancer from Cambodia, is flattered to be noticed by the artist Auguste Rodin in this story based on actual events and illustrated with lovely mixed-media paintings. (Rev: BL 5/1/06)

5495 Lowell, Susan. *The Elephant Quilt! Stitch by Stitch to California* (K–3). Illus. by Stacey Dressen-McQueen. 2008, Farrar $16.95 (978-0-374-38223-0). 40pp. With her grandmother, Lily Rose stitches a quilt of her family's journey west by covered wagon in 1859. (Rev: BCCB 5/08; BL 4/15/08; SLJ 7/08)

5496 Lubner, Susan. *A Horse's Tale: A Colonial Williamsburg Adventure* (PS–1). Illus. by Margie Moore. 2008, Abrams $16.95 (978-0-8109-9490-4). 32pp. In colonial Williamsburg Lancer, Garrick the Gardener's horse, is feeling blue and many of the citizens (animals dressed as humans) have opinions on what ails him; the consensus is that he's lonely and needs a friend. Images introduce the town, and the various jobs are explained. (Rev: BL 5/1/08; SLJ 6/08)

5497 Lunge-Larsen, Lise. *Noah's Mittens: The Story of Felt* (K–3). Illus. by Matthew Trueman. 2006, Houghton $16.00 (978-0-618-32950-2). 32pp. In this whimsical picture-book tale, Noah finds a use for the sheep's wool after it becomes thickly matted during the lengthy journey of the ark. (Rev: BL 10/15/06; SLJ 12/06)

5498 Lyon, George E. *Dreamplace* (K–4). Illus. by Peter Catalanotto. 1993, Orchard $15.95 (978-0-531-05466-6); paper $6.95 (978-0-531-07101-4). 32pp. A poetic text about a girl who sees the 800-year-old site of the Anasazi and dreams of when the tribe lived there long ago. (Rev: BCCB 3/93; BL 3/15/93*; HB 3/93; SLJ 3/93*)

5499 McAlister, Caroline. *Holy Molé!* (K–2). Illus. by Stefan Czernecki. 2007, August House $16.95 (978-0-87483-775-9). The author spins a tale about the creation of the first molé in a serendipitous accident in a Mexican monastery's kitchen. (Rev: SLJ 8/07)

5500 McBrier, Page. *Beatrice's Goat* (K–3). Illus. by Lori Lohstoeter. 2001, Simon & Schuster $16.00 (978-0-689-82460-9). 40pp. Beatrice longs to attend school in her Ugandan village, and when her family gets a goat from an aid organization, it provides enough income to send her there. (Rev: BCCB 2/01; BL 2/15/01; HBG 10/01; SLJ 2/01)

5501 McCaughrean, Geraldine. *The Jesse Tree* (2–4). Illus. by Bee Willey. 2005, Eerdmans $20.00 (978-0-8028-5288-5). 96pp. A curious young boy pesters a crotchety old woodcarver into telling him Bible stories about the Old Testament characters who are the spiritual ancestors of Jesus Christ. (Rev: BL 10/1/05; SLJ 1/06)

5502 McClintock, Barbara. *Adele and Simon* (K–3). Illus. 2006, Farrar $16.00 (978-0-374-38044-1). 40pp. As Adele escorts her little brother home from school through the streets of 1900s Paris, the boy manages to lose something at every stop along the way; endpaper maps add to this view of the City of Light. (Rev: BL 6/1–15/06; HB 9/06; HBG 4/07; LMC 3/07; SLJ 8/06)

5503 McCully, Emily Arnold. *Beautiful Warrior: The Legend of the Nun's Kung Fu* (K–4). Illus. 1998, Scholastic $19.99 (978-0-590-37487-3). 40pp. In this beautiful picture book, two women learn kung fu and use it in different ways in 17th-century China. (Rev: BCCB 3/98; BL 2/1/98; SLJ 2/98*)

5504 McCully, Emily Arnold. *The Escape of Oney Judge: Martha Washington's Slave Finds Freedom* (2–4). Illus. by author. 2007, Farrar $16.00 (978-0-374-32225-0). In this fictionalized account of the escape of one of Martha Washington's slaves, Oney Judge travels with the Washingtons to Philadelphia where she meets free blacks and begins to appreciate the concept of freedom. (Rev: BCCB 6/07; BL 11/15/06; SLJ 2/07)

5505 McCully, Emily Arnold. *Mirette and Bellini Cross Niagara Falls* (PS–3). Illus. 2000, Penguin $15.99 (978-0-399-23348-7). 32pp. A thrilling adventure story in which young Mirette and her guardian, the high-wire-artist, Bellini, come to the States for the ultimate stunt, crossing Niagara Falls on a wire. (Rev: BCCB 1/01; BL 11/15/00; HBG 10/01; SLJ 11/00)

5506 McCully, Emily Arnold. *Mirette on the High Wire* (PS–2). Illus. 1992, Penguin $16.99 (978-0-399-22130-9). 32pp. Set in Paris 100 years ago, this is the story of how a young girl helps a high-wire performer regain his courage. Caldecott Medal winner, 1993. (Rev: BCCB 10/92*; BL 11/15/92; SLJ 10/92)

5507 McDonald, Megan. *Saving the Liberty Bell* (K–3). Illus. by Marsha Carrington. 2005, Simon & Schuster $16.95 (978-0-689-85167-4). 32pp. In this exciting, fact-based story from the American Revolution, 11-year-old John Jacob Mickley tells how he helped to hide the Liberty Bell from British troops. (Rev: BL 7/05; SLJ 7/05)

5508 MacDonald, Suse. *Nanta's Lion: A Search and Find Adventure* (PS–1). Illus. 1995, Morrow $15.00 (978-0-688-13125-8). 24pp. An interactive book about an African girl who sets out to find the lion that has been stealing cattle from her village. (Rev: BL 4/15/95; SLJ 5/95)

5509 MacKall, Dandi Daley. *A Girl Named Dan* (1–3). Illus. by Renee Graef. 2008, Sleeping Bear $16.95 (978-1-58536-351-3). 32pp. In 1961 Dandi is excluded from baseball simply because she's a girl. (Rev: BLO 7/30/08; LMC 10/08; SLJ 6/08)

5510 McKay, Lawrence, Jr. *Caravan* (1–4). Illus. by Darryl Ligasan. 1995, Lee & Low $14.95 (978-1-880000-23-6). A boy tells about going on his first caravan through the mountains in Afghanistan to trade his family's furs for grain. (Rev: SLJ 12/95)

5511 McKissack, Patricia C. *Goin' Someplace Special* (K–3). Illus. by Jerry Pinkney. 2001, Simon & Schuster $16.00 (978-0-689-81885-1). 40pp. Young Tricia Ann sets off on her first journey by herself and must navigate the South of the 1950s, working out where an African American is allowed to go. (Rev: BCCB 9/01; BL 8/01; HB 11/01; HBG 3/02; SLJ 9/01)

5512 McKissack, Patricia C. *Ma Dear's Aprons* (PS–3). Illus. by Floyd Cooper. 1997, Simon & Schuster $16.00 (978-0-689-81051-0). 32pp. During the early 1900s in Alabama, Ma Dear must support her family by doing domestic work. (Rev: BCCB 6/97; BL 2/15/97; HB 5/97; SLJ 6/97)

5513 MacLachlan, Patricia. *Three Names* (K–3). Illus. by Alexander Pertzoff. 1991, HarperCollins LB $16.89 (978-0-06-024036-3). 32pp. A boy repeats the stories that his great-grandfather told him of growing up in pioneer days. (Rev: BCCB 1/92; BL 8/91; HB 9/91; SLJ 7/91)

5514 McMillan, Bruce. *How the Ladies Stopped the Wind* (K–2). Illus. by Guennella. 2007, Houghton $16.00 (978-0-618-77330-5). 32pp. In windy Iceland, determined women plant trees as a windbreak and try to discourage the sheep from eating them.

(Rev: BCCB 10/07; BL 10/1/07; HB 1/08; SLJ 12/07)

5515 McNulty, Faith. *If You Decide to Go to the Moon* (K–3). Illus. by Steven Kellogg. 2005, Scholastic $16.99 (978-0-590-48359-9). 48pp. McNulty describes how it will feel to travel to the moon in this mock guide for prospective travelers. (Rev: BCCB 11/05; BL 11/1/05; HB 9/05; HBG 4/06; LMC 1/06; SLJ 10/05*)

5516 Madrigal, Antonio H. *Erandi's Braids* (PS–3). Illus. by Tomie dePaola. 1999, Penguin $16.99 (978-0-399-23212-1). 32pp. Erandi, a young member of a poor 1950s Mexican family, reluctantly decides to sell her beautiful hair to help her family. (Rev: BL 1/1–15/99*; HBG 10/99; SLJ 2/99)

5517 Manson, Ainslie. *A Dog Came, Too: A True Story* (1–3). Illus. by Ann Blades. 1993, Macmillan $13.95 (978-0-689-50567-6). 32pp. In a fictionalized format, this is the story of the dog that accompanied explorer Alexander Mackenzie across Canada to the Pacific Ocean. (Rev: BCCB 3/93; BL 5/1/93; SLJ 2/04) [917.1]

5518 Manson, Ainslie. *Just Like New* (1–4). Illus. by Karen Reczuch. 1996, Douglas & McIntyre $14.95 (978-0-88899-228-4). 32pp. During World War II, a Canadian girl sends her favorite doll to a deprived English youngster at Christmas. (Rev: BCCB 1/97; BL 11/15/96; SLJ 12/96)

5519 Marceau, Fani. *Panorama: A Foldout Book* (1–3). Illus. by Joëlle Jolivet. 2009, Abrams $19.95 (978-0-8109-8332-8). 32pp. An oversize tour of locations around the world with poetic descriptions and dramatic panoramic woodcut illustrations that fold out. (Rev: BL 3/1/09; HB 7/09)

5520 Marciano, John Bemelmans. *Madeline and the Cats of Rome* (PS–1). Illus. by author. 2008, Viking $17.99 (978-0-670-06297-3). 48pp. Sightseeing in Rome, Miss Clavel and the "twelve little girls in two straight lines" have their camera stolen and Madeline and her dog, Genevieve, give chase. (Rev: BL 9/1/08)

5521 Medearis, Angela Shelf. *Rum-a-Tum-Tum* (PS–3). Illus. by James Ransome. 1997, Holiday House LB $16.95 (978-0-8234-1143-6). 32pp. All the color, excitement, and sound of a market in the French Quarter of New Orleans at the turn of the century are captured in this picture book. (Rev: BCCB 7–8/97; BL 5/1/97; SLJ 7/97)

5522 Meunier, Brian. *Bravo, Tavo!* (K–3). Illus. by Perky Edgerton. 2007, Dutton $16.99 (978-0-525-47478-4). 32pp. A Mexican boy who loves basketball learns about sacrifice and community spirit in this well-written story. (Rev: BL 5/15/07; SLJ 8/07)

5523 Michelson, Richard. *Happy Feet: The Savoy Ballroom Lindy Hoppers and Me* (K–3). Illus. by E. B. Lewis. 2005, Harcourt $16.00 (978-0-15-205057-3). 32pp. A young African American boy hears the story of the opening of Harlem's Savoy Ballroom on the night he himself was born; this story beautifully evokes the mood of the 1920s. (Rev: BL 11/1/05; SLJ 11/05)

5524 Miller, William. *The Bus Ride* (PS–1). Illus. by John Ward. 1998, Lee & Low $15.95 (978-1-880000-60-1). 32pp. Set in the segregated South during the 1950s, this picture book tells of the consequences faced by a young girl when she dares to sit in the front of a bus. (Rev: BL 8/98; HBG 3/99; SLJ 10/98)

5525 Miller, William. *The Piano* (K–3). Illus. by Susan Keeter. 2000, Lee & Low $15.95 (978-1-880000-98-4). 32pp. In the segregated South in the early 1900s, music-loving Tia is taught to play the piano by the elderly woman for whom she cleans house. (Rev: BCCB 10/00; BL 7/00; HBG 10/00; SLJ 7/00)

5526 Miller, William. *Rent Party Jazz* (1–4). Illus. by Charlotte Riley-Webb. 2001, Lee & Low $16.95 (978-1-58430-025-0). 32pp. A young African American boy named Sonny and an old jazz musician named Smilin' Jack throw a rent party to help Sonny's mother in 1930s New Orleans. (Rev: BL 11/15/01; HBG 3/02; SLJ 11/01)

5527 Miller, William. *Richard Wright and the Library Card* (K–4). Illus. by R. Gregory Christie. 1997, Lee & Low $16.95 (978-1-880000-57-1). 32pp. In this story based on fact, African American Richard Wright, growing up in the segregated South, borrows books from the all-white library by pretending he is taking them to his white boss. (Rev: BCCB 3/98; BL 12/1/97; HBG 3/98; SLJ 2/98)

5528 Mollel, Tololwa M. *My Rows and Piles of Coins* (PS–3). Illus. by E. B. Lewis. 1999, Clarion $16.00 (978-0-395-75186-2). 32pp. Saruni, a Tanzanian boy, scrimps and saves to buy a bicycle, so he can help his mother with her chores. (Rev: BCCB 10/99; BL 8/99; HBG 3/00; SLJ 8/99)

5529 Montes, Marisa. *Juan Bobo Goes to Work* (PS–3). Illus. by Joe Cepeda. 2000, HarperCollins LB $17.89 (978-0-688-16234-4). 32pp. A charming story — set in Puerto Rico and using many Spanish words and phrases — about Juan Bobo who makes a rich girl laugh and is rewarded with a ham every Sunday. (Rev: BL 2/1/01; HBG 3/01; SLJ 10/00)

5530 Mora, Pat. *The Song of Francis and the Animals* (K–3). Illus. by David Frampton. 2005, Eerdmans $16.00 (978-0-8028-5253-3). 32pp. This poetic narrative celebrates the close bonds between Saint Francis and the animals he encountered throughout his life. (Rev: BL 10/15/05; SLJ 10/05)

5531 Morrow, Barbara Olenyik. *A Good Night for Freedom* (K–4). Illus. by Leonard Jenkins. 2004, Holiday House $16.95 (978-0-8234-1709-4). 32pp. In 1839, young Hallie helps two runaway slave girls despite her father's warnings not to do so. (Rev: BL 3/1/04; SLJ 2/04)

5532 Myers, Tim. *Basho and the Fox* (K–3). Illus. by Oki S. Han. 2000, Marshall Cavendish $15.95 (978-0-7614-5068-9). 32pp. Basho, Japan's famous haiku poet, meets a fox who promises not to eat the poet's cherries if he can produce a poem that the fox thinks is worthy. (Rev: BL 9/15/00; HB 9/00; HBG 3/01; SLJ 10/00)

5533 Naden, Corinne J., and Rose Blue. *Ron's Big Mission* (K–2). Illus. by Don Tate. 2009, Dutton $16.99 (978-0-525-47849-2). 32pp. Nine-year-old Ron McNair, who would later become an astronaut and die in the 1986 *Challenger* explosion, challenges his local library's refusal to give him a library card because he is African American. (Rev: BL 2/1/09; SLJ 2/09)

5534 Namioka, Lensey. *The Laziest Boy in the World* (K–3). Illus. by YongSheng Xuan. 1998, Holiday House $16.95 (978-0-8234-1330-0). 32pp. A humorous story about a Chinese boy who is so lazy he washes alternate sides of his face each day, and the thief who makes him change his ways. (Rev: BL 11/1/98; HBG 3/99; SLJ 10/98)

5535 Napoli, Donna Jo, and Elena Furrow. *Ready to Dream* (K–3). Illus. by Bronwyn Bancroft. 2009, Bloomsbury $16.99 (978-1-59990-049-0). 32pp. Ally, a young artist visiting Australia, meets an Aboriginal woman who mentors the young girl's artistic spirit. (Rev: BL 12/15/08; SLJ 2/09)

5536 Nelson, S. D. *The Star People: A Lakota Story* (PS–2). Illus. by author. 2003, Abrams $14.95 (978-0-8109-4584-5). When two Lakota siblings, Sister Girl and Young Wolf, wander far from home and encounter a multitude of dangers, they are guided to safety by the Star People, the spirits of the Old Ones. (Rev: HBG 4/04; SLJ 9/03)

5537 Nelson, Vaunda Micheaux. *Almost to Freedom* (1–3). Illus. by Colin Bootman. Series: Carolrhoda Picture Books. 2003, Carolrhoda $15.95 (978-1-57505-342-4). 40pp. This moving story, narrated by the rag doll of a slave child, describes how the child, Lindy, and her family escape to freedom on the Underground Railroad. (Rev: BL 9/15/03; HBG 4/04; SLJ 12/03)

5538 Nez, John Abbott. *Cromwell Dixon's Sky-Cycle* (K–3). Illus. by author. 2009, Putnam $16.99 (978-0-399-25041-5). 32pp. An intriguing fictionalized story set in the early years of the 20th century and describing 14-year-old Cromwell Dixon's determination to pedal into the sky; a one-page biography adds details. (Rev: BL 8/09; LMC 10/09; SLJ 7/09)

5539 Nikola-Lisa, W. *Magic in the Margins: A Medieval Tale of Bookmaking* (K–3). Illus. by Bonnie Christensen. 2007, Houghton $17.00 (978-0-618-49642-6). 32pp. Working as an apprentice in a medieval monastery's scriptorium, Simon, a young orphan, dreams of illuminating manuscripts. (Rev: BL 4/1/07)

5540 Nobisso, Josephine. *The Weight of a Mass: A Tale of Faith* (K–3). Illus. by Katalin Szegedi. 2002, Gingerbread House $17.95 (978-0-940112-09-4); paper $9.95 (978-0-940112-10-0). In a land where most people have abandoned their faith, an old woman reveals the power of the Mass. (Rev: HBG 3/03; SLJ 1/03)

5541 Noguchi, Rick, and Deneen Jenks. *Flowers from Mariko* (K–3). Illus. by Michelle Reiko Kumata. 2001, Lee & Low $16.95 (978-1-58430-032-8). 32pp. When Mariko's Japanese American family is released from an internment camp after World War II, they must work to rebuild the life they lost. (Rev: BL 11/1/01; HBG 3/02; SLJ 11/01)

5542 Noyes, Deborah. *Hana in the Time of the Tulips* (K–3). Illus. by Bagram Ibatoulline. 2004, Candlewick $16.99 (978-0-7636-1875-9). 40pp. When

her father is swept up in the tulip mania gripping 17th-century Holland, young Hana seeks to regain his attention; the illustrations evoke paintings by Rembrandt. (Rev: BL 11/1/04; SLJ 10/04)

5543 Olaleye, Isaac. *Lake of the Big Snake: An African Rain Forest Adventure* (K–3). Illus. by Claudia Shepard. 1998, Boyds Mills $15.95 (978-1-56397-096-2). In this story set in an African rain forest, two boys disobey their mothers, wander away from home, and encounter a giant snake. (Rev: BL 10/15/98; HBG 3/99; SLJ 11/98)

5544 Olofsson, Helena. *The Little Jester* (K–3). Illus. 2002, R&S $16.00 (91-29-65499-8). 28pp. French monks reluctantly open the doors of the monastery to a jester, who then performs a miracle. (Rev: BL 3/15/02; HBG 10/02; SLJ 5/02)

5545 O'Neal, Deborah, and Angela Westengard. *The Trouble with Henry: A Tale of Walden Pond* (PS–2). Illus. by S. D. Schindler. 2005, Candlewick $16.99 (978-0-7636-1828-5). 40pp. A fictional account of Thoreau's efforts to keep Walden Pond free of industry; a note adds biographical information. (Rev: BL 10/15/05; SLJ 10/05)

5546 Oppenheim, Shulamith Levey. *Ali and the Magic Stew* (PS–3). Illus. by Winslow Pels. 2002, Boyds Mills $15.95 (978-1-56397-869-2). 32pp. In this Persian tale, a proud, spoiled merchant's son learns humility when he must beg for coins to save his father's life. (Rev: BCCB 5/02; BL 4/15/02; HBG 10/02; SLJ 4/02)

5547 Oppenheim, Shulamith Levey. *Yanni Rubbish* (K–3). Illus. by Doug Chayka. 1999, Boyds Mills $15.95 (978-1-56397-668-1). 28pp. Yanni, a young Greek trash collector, is embarrassed when his friends make fun of him and his dusty wagon, until he and his mother paint and decorate his cart so it becomes the pride of the town. (Rev: BL 3/1/99; HBG 10/99; SLJ 8/99)

5548 Ormerod, Jan. *Lizzie Nonsense: A Story of Pioneer Days* (PS–2). Illus. 2005, Clarion $15.00 (978-0-618-57493-3). 32pp. The power of imagination is shown in this beautifully illustrated story of Lizzie and her mother, pioneers living alone on Australia's frontier while Papa goes away to work. (Rev: BL 9/15/05; SLJ 9/05)

5549 Orr, Katherine. *My Grandpa and the Sea* (K–3). Illus. 1990, Carolrhoda LB $19.95 (978-0-87614-409-1). 32pp. When Grandpa loses his fishing business to modern-day fishermen, he finds a new way of earning a living. (Rev: BCCB 11/90; BL 10/1/90)

5550 Pace, Lorenzo. *Jalani and the Lock* (PS–K). Illus. 2001, Rosen $23.95 (978-0-8239-9700-8). 32pp. A young African boy named Jalani, who spends years as a slave, passes the lock from his chains on to his grandchildren. (Rev: BL 2/15/01)

5551 Panahi, H. L. *Bebop Express* (K–2). Illus. by Steve Johnson. 2005, HarperCollins LB $16.89 (978-0-06-057191-7). 32pp. Rhythm and atmosphere make this a jazzy train trip from New York to New Orleans. (Rev: BL 6/1–15/05)

5552 Park, Frances, and Ginger Park. *Good-Bye, 382 Shin-Dang Dong* (1–3). Illus. by Yangsook Choi.

2002, National Geographic $16.95 (978-0-7922-7985-3). Jangmi is sad to leave Korea and her friends and move to Massachusetts. (Rev: HBG 3/03; SLJ 10/02)

5553 Park, Frances, and Ginger Park. *The Royal Bee* (K–3). Illus. by Christopher Zhong-Yuan Zhang. 2000, Boyds Mills $16.95 (978-1-56397-614-8). A simple tale about a poor Korean boy growing up in the late 19th century and his efforts to get an education so he can lift himself and his mother out of poverty. (Rev: HBG 10/00; SLJ 4/00)

5554 Park, Frances, and Ginger Park. *Where on Earth Is My Bagel?* (K–3). Illus. by Grace Lin. 2001, Lee & Low $16.00 (978-1-58430-033-5). A Korean boy hungry for a bagel sends a message to New York by pigeon but only receives a recipe in return, which his local baker is happy to make in this book full of bagel shapes. (Rev: HBG 3/02; SLJ 9/01)

5555 Park, Linda Sue. *Bee-bim Bop!* (PS–2). Illus. by Ho Baek Lee. 2005, Clarion $15.00 (978-0-618-26511-4). 32pp. A hungry Korean girl helps her mother shop for ingredients and then prepare a favorite meal; the recipe is included. (Rev: BL 10/15/05; SLJ 9/05)

5556 Park, Linda Sue. *The Firekeeper's Son* (K–3). Illus. by Julie Downing. 2004, Clarion $16.00 (978-0-618-13337-6). 40pp. In the early 19th-century Korea, a young boy must take his father's place and light the bonfire that is part of the signal system; beautiful watercolor illustrations complement the picture-book story. (Rev: BL 2/1/04; SLJ 5/04)

5557 Patz, Nancy. *Who Was the Woman Who Wore the Hat?* (3–6). Illus. 2003, Dutton $14.99 (978-0-525-46999-5). 48pp. The hat, part of the exhibit in the Jewish Historical Museum in Amsterdam, inspires the author to reflect on what the woman who wore it was like. (Rev: BL 2/15/03; HBG 10/03; SLJ 3/03)

5558 Pendziwol, Jean E. *Marja's Skis* (1–3). Illus. by Jirina Marton. 2007, Groundwood $17.95 (978-0-88899-674-9). 32pp. After the death of her father, Marja, a young Finnish immigrant, feels overwhelmed by the difficulties her family faces in the 19th-century Canadian logging town where they live, yet she finds the courage to rescue a man who is in danger. (Rev: BL 12/1/07; SLJ 10/07)

5559 Pendziwol, Jean E. *The Red Sash* (1–3). Illus. by Nicolas Debon. 2005, Groundwood $16.95 (978-0-88899-589-6). 40pp. A young mixed-race boy, son of a voyageur — fur traders who wore red sashes, describes life in and around Lake Huron in the early 19th century. (Rev: BL 12/1/05; SLJ 1/06)

5560 Pennypacker, Sara. *Sparrow Girl* (K–3). Illus. by Yoko Tanaka. 2009, Hyperion $16.99 (978-1-4231-1187-0). 40pp. A little girl called Ming-Li rebels against Chairman Mao's misguided war on sparrows in 1958. (Rev: BCCB 2/09; BL 1/1–15/09; LMC 5/09; SLJ 3/09)

5561 Perkins, Mitali. *Rickshaw Girl* (2–5). Illus. by Jamie Hogan. 2007, Charlesbridge $13.95 (978-1-58089-308-4). 91pp. Naima is a talented painter of the traditional alpana patterns but she longs to do more to help her poor Bangladeshi family, even driving her father's rickshaw, an occupation forbidden to girls. (Rev: BCCB 5/07; BL 11/1/06; HB 5/6–07; LMC 5/07; SLJ 4/07)

5562 Phillipps, J. C. *Wink: The Ninja Who Wanted to Be Noticed* (PS–2). Illus. by author. 2009, Viking $15.99 (978-0-670-01092-9). 32pp. Wink's love of self-expression makes him unsuited to a career as a ninja, but he finds a way to use his training in a circus. (Rev: BCCB 6/09; BL 1/1–15/09; SLJ 2/09)

5563 Pilegard, Virginia Walton. *The Warlord's Alarm: A Mathematical Adventure* (K–3). Illus. by Nicolas Debon. 2006, Pelican $15.95 (978-1-58980-378-7). 32pp. In ancient China, Chuan invents a method of measuring time so that he can awaken his master in the middle of the night; a note explains how water clocks work. (Rev: BL 11/1/06; SLJ 11/06)

5564 Pilegard, Virginia Walton. *The Warlord's Beads* (K–3). Illus. by Nicolas Debon. 2001, Pelican $15.95 (978-1-56554-863-3). 32pp. In this story set in China, a boy invents a primitive abacus to help his father keep track of the warlord's riches. (Rev: BL 2/1/02; HBG 3/02; SLJ 2/02)

5565 Pilegard, Virginia Walton. *The Warlord's Fish* (PS–2). Illus. by Nicolas Debon. 2002, Pelican $15.95 (978-1-56554-964-7). 32pp. A tale set in ancient China that explores the history of the compass. (Rev: BL 2/1/03; HBG 3/03; SLJ 2/03)

5566 Pilegard, Virginia Walton. *The Warlord's Messengers* (K–2). Illus. by Nicolas Debon. 2005, Pelican $15.95 (978-1-58980-271-1). 32pp. Friends Chuan and Jing Jing use their math skills and ingenuity to come up with a plan to satisfy a Chinese emperor's wishes. (Rev: BL 11/15/05; SLJ 12/05)

5567 Pilegard, Virginia Walton. *The Warlord's Puzzle* (K–3). Illus. by Nicolas Debon. 2000, Pelican $15.95 (978-1-56554-495-6). 32pp. A handsome tile given to a Chinese warlord is broken into various geometric shapes and only a simple peasant can solve the puzzle and put it together again. (Rev: BL 4/1/00; HBG 10/00; SLJ 6/00)

5568 Polacco, Patricia. *Babushka Baba Yaga* (PS–3). Illus. 1993, Penguin $16.99 (978-0-399-22531-4). 32pp. In this reversal of the traditional Russian folklore, the witch Baba Yaga is really a kindly grandmother named Babushka. (Rev: BL 8/93)

5569 Polacco, Patricia. *The Butterfly* (K–4). Illus. 2000, Penguin $16.99 (978-0-399-23170-4). 32pp. Based on a true story, this picture book tells of a little girl growing up in France during World War II who becomes aware that her family is hiding a Jewish family in the cellar. (Rev: BCCB 6/00; BL 4/1/00; HBG 10/00; SLJ 5/00)

5570 Porte, Barbara Ann. *Ma Jiang and the Orange Ants* (K–3). Illus. by Annie Cannon. 2000, Orchard LB $17.99 (978-0-531-33241-2). 32pp. Ma Jiang devises an unusual way to catch carnivorous "orange" ants to sell to fruit growers for pest control. (Rev: BL 10/15/00; HBG 3/01; SLJ 12/00)

5571 Preus, Margi. *The Peace Bell* (1–3). Illus. by Hideko Takahashi. 2008, Holt $16.95 (978-0-8050-7800-8). 32pp. In this fictional memoir based on real events, a Japanese grandmother tells the story of Japanese village life before, during, and after World War II and of "the peace bell" recovered by American sailors. (Rev: BLO 8/28/08; LMC 3/09)

5572 Prince, April Jones. *Twenty-One Elephants and Still Standing* (1–3). Illus. by François Roca. 2005, Houghton $16.00 (978-0-618-44887-6). 32pp. Was this new wonder, the Brooklyn Bridge, safe? P. T. Barnum and his 21 elephants crossed in 1884. (Rev: BL 10/15/05; SLJ 11/05*)

5573 Pryor, Bonnie. *The House on Maple Street* (PS–1). Illus. by Beth Peck. 1987, Morrow paper $6.99 (978-0-688-12031-3). 32pp. Chris and Jenny find a small china cup and begin a kind of history exploration from the house on Maple Street. (Rev: BL 4/1/87; SLJ 5/87)

5574 Pushker, Gloria Teles. *Toby Belfer Visits Ellis Island* (PS–1). Illus. by Judith Hierstein. Series: Toby Belfer. 2003, Pelican $15.95 (978-1-58980-117-2). 32pp. Toby learns about her Jewish heritage from her great-grandmother, and then visits the museum on Ellis Island. (Rev: BL 1/1–15/04; HBG 4/04)

5575 Rabin, Staton. *Casey Over There* (K–3). Illus. by Greg Shed. 1994, Harcourt $14.95 (978-0-15-253186-7). 32pp. In this picture book, Aubrey's brother is fighting in the trenches, while he is growing up in Brooklyn during World War I. (Rev: BL 3/15/94; SLJ 5/94)

5576 Ransom, Candice F. *The Promise Quilt* (K–3). Illus. by Ellen Beier. 1999, Walker LB $16.85 (978-0-8027-8695-1). 32pp. In this picture book set in the South during the Civil War, Addie loses her father when he joins General Lee and his fight for "the cause." (Rev: BL 11/1/99; HBG 3/00; SLJ 11/99)

5577 Ransom, Candice F. *Rescue on the Outer Banks* (1–3). Illus. by Karen Ritz. 2002, Carolrhoda LB $23.93 (978-0-87614-460-2); paper $5.95 (978-0-87614-815-0). 48pp. A 10-year-old boy narrates the true story of an 1896 sea rescue by an African American lifeboat crew, a feat that was officially recognized 100 years later. (Rev: HBG 10/02; SLJ 4/02)

5578 Rao, Sandhya. *My Mother's Sari* (PS–K). Illus. by Nina Sabnani. 2006, North-South $14.95 (978-0-7358-2101-9). 28pp. A little Indian girl shows the many uses for her mother's sari; the endpapers show how a sari is wrapped. (Rev: BL 8/06)

5579 Rappaport, Doreen, and Lyndall Callan. *Dirt on Their Skirts: The Story of the Young Women Who Won the World Championship* (PS–3). Illus. by E. B. Lewis. 2000, Dial $16.99 (978-0-8037-2042-8). 40pp. A fictionalized account of the 1946 championship game of the All-American Girls Professional Baseball League. (Rev: BCCB 2/00; BL 1/1–15/00; HBG 10/00; SLJ 3/00)

5580 Ravishankar, Anushka. *To Market! To Market* (PS–2). Illus. by Emanuele Scanziani. 2007, Tara $16.95 (978-8-1862-1199-1). 32pp. In India a girl visits a lively indoor market and looks at all the things she could buy with her few coins; the unusual format allows for illustrations showing a wide expanse. (Rev: BL 7/07)

5581 Ray, Mary L. *Basket Moon* (K–3). Illus. by Barbara Cooney. 1999, Little, Brown $15.95 (978-0-316-73521-6). 32pp. A 19th-century boy is embarrassed when townspeople call him and his father, a basket weaver, "hillbillies," but gradually he is able to reaffirm the love he feels for his dad. (Rev: BCCB 9/99; BL 6/1–15/99; HB 11/99; HBG 3/00; SLJ 9/99)

5582 Reddix, Valerie. *Dragon Kite of the Autumn Moon* (K–3). Illus. by Jean Tseng. 1992, Lothrop LB $13.93 (978-0-688-11031-4). 32pp. When Grandfather becomes sick, Tad-Tin must fly his kite alone in this tale set in Formosa. (Rev: BL 5/15/92; SLJ 8/92)

5583 Reed, Jennifer B. *The Falling Flowers* (K–3). Illus. by Dick Cole. 2005, Shen's $16.95 (978-1-885008-28-2). Mayumie and her grandmother enjoy viewing Tokyo's cherry blossoms in this book illustrated with beautiful watercolors. (Rev: SLJ 6/06)

5584 Reiser, Lynn. *Tortillas and Lullabies: Tortillas y cancioncitas* (PS–3). Illus. by Corazones Valientes. 1998, Greenwillow $16.99 (978-0-688-14628-3). 40pp. Three generations of Latin American women are depicted in this bilingual story of how love and gifts have been exchanged in a family through the years. (Rev: BL 4/1/98; HB 5/98; SLJ 4/98)

5585 Reynolds, Marilynn. *The Name of the Child* (1–3). Illus. by Don Kilby. 2002, Orca $16.95 (978-1-55143-221-2). 32pp. Nervous young Lloyd is sent to the country during the 1918 flu epidemic for his safety, but ends up having to take charge in the midst of a storm. (Rev: BL 1/1–15/03; HBG 3/03; SLJ 1/03)

5586 Richardson, Jean. *The Courage Seed* (2–3). Illus. by Pat Finney. 1993, Eakin $14.95 (978-0-89015-902-6). 71pp. When her parents are killed, a young Navajo girl is fearful that she will lose her tribal ways when she goes to live with an aunt in Houston. (Rev: SLJ 2/94)

5587 Ringgold, Faith. *Cassie's Word Quilt* (K–3). Illus. 2002, Knopf $13.95 (978-0-375-81200-2). 32pp. This simple wordbook uses a quilt pattern of pictures to introduce the daily life of Cassie, a little girl living in New York City in 1939. (Rev: BL 3/1/02; HBG 10/02; SLJ 2/02)

5588 Rodanas, Kristina. *The Blind Hunter* (K–2). Illus. by author. 2003, Marshall Cavendish $16.95 (978-0-7614-5132-7). Blind Chirobo accompanies Muteye on a hunting trip and proves that there is much that he can "see" with his other senses in this picture book based on a Shona folktale. (Rev: HBG 4/04; SLJ 1/04)

5589 Roop, Peter, and Connie Roop. *Buttons for General Washington* (2–3). Illus. by Peter E. Hanson. 1986, Carolrhoda LB $23.93 (978-0-87614-294-3); paper $5.95 (978-0-87614-476-3). 48pp. Based on incidents from the life of John Darragh, this is the story of a 14-year-old boy who carries secret messages to George Washington hidden in his coat buttons during the Revolution. (Rev: BCCB 12/86; BL 12/1/86)

5590 Ruelle, Karen Gray. *The Tree* (K–3). Illus. by Deborah Durland DeSaix. 2008, Holiday $16.95

(978-0-8234-1904-3). 32pp. A New York City neighborhood's history comes to life through this story of a single elm tree. (Rev: BL 9/15/08; LMC 3/09)

5591 Rumford, James. *Silent Music* (1–3). Illus. by author. 2008, Roaring Brook $17.95 (978-1-59643-276-5). 32pp. A boy named Ali finds comfort in calligraphy during the bombing of Baghdad in 2003. (Rev: BCCB 4/08; BL 4/15/08; HB 3/08; LMC 5/08; SLJ 4/08)

5592 Russell, Margaret Timberlake. *Maggie's Amerikay* (K–3). Illus. by Jim Burke. 2006, Farrar $17.00 (978-0-374-34722-2). 40pp. An African American boy and an Irish American girl befriend each other while enduring hard times in a late-19th-century New Orleans rich in ragtime. (Rev: BL 5/1/06; SLJ 4/06)

5593 Ryan, Pam Muñoz. *Amelia and Eleanor Go for a Ride: Based on a True Story* (2–4). Illus. by Brian Selznick. 1999, Scholastic $17.99 (978-0-590-96075-5). 40pp. An interesting, if exaggerated, variation on the story of Amelia Earhart and Eleanor Roosevelt's shared plane ride. (Rev: BL 10/15/99; HBG 3/00; SLJ 9/99)

5594 Saint-Lot, Katia Novet. *Amadi's Snowman* (PS–1). Illus. by Dimitrea Tokunbo. 2008, Tilbury House $16.95 (978-0-88448-298-7). 32pp. A young Nigerian boy's first glimpse of a snowman prompts a new interest in reading and knowledge. (Rev: BL 7/08; LMC 1/09)

5595 Saltzman, David. *The Jester Has Lost His Jingle* (1–3). Illus. 1995, Jester $20.00 (978-0-9644563-0-3). 64pp. A jester who is out of work because he isn't funny sets out to discover laughter in the world. (Rev: BL 10/15/95; SLJ 10/95)

5596 Sandin, Joan. *The Long Way to a New Land* (1–3). Illus. by author. 1981, HarperCollins paper $3.99 (978-0-06-444100-1). 64pp. An easy-to-read account of a Swedish family's journey to New York in the late 1860s.

5597 Santore, Charles. *The Silk Princess* (1–3). Illus. by author. 2007, Random $17.99 (978-0-375-83664-0). 32pp. A Chinese princess fascinated by a cocoon sets off on a journey that leads her to a wise man who teaches her how to make silk from the thread. (Rev: BL 11/15/07; LMC 3/08; SLJ 2/08)

5598 Sasso, Sandy Eisenberg. *Butterflies Under Our Hats* (PS–2). Illus. by Joani Keller Rothenberg. 2006, Paraclete $16.95 (978-1-55725-474-0). 32pp. In the town of Chelm — a place famously without luck — a visitor who believes in hope arrives in a cloud of butterflies. (Rev: BL 6/1–15/06; SLJ 8/06)

5599 Say, Allen. *The Bicycle Man* (K–3). Illus. by author. 1982, Houghton $11.95 (978-0-685-05704-9); paper $6.95 (978-0-395-50652-3). 48pp. Two American soldiers in Japan put on a show for a school.

5600 Schick, Eleanor. *Navajo Wedding Day: A Dine Marriage Ceremony* (1–3). Illus. 1999, Marshall Cavendish $15.95 (978-0-7614-5031-3). 40pp. A realistic picture book that describes a marriage ceremony in Navajo country. (Rev: BL 4/15/99; HBG 10/99; SLJ 4/99)

5601 Scott, Ann H. *On Mother's Lap* (PS–K). Illus. by Glo Coalson. 1992, Houghton $16.00 (978-0-395-58920-5); paper $6.95 (978-0-395-62976-5). 32pp. A warm, tender story of an Eskimo family and of a young boy's realization that there is enough room on mother's lap for both him and his sister.

5602 Seabrooke, Brenda. *The Boy Who Saved the Town* (2–4). Illus. by Howard M. Burns. 1990, Tidewater $8.95 (978-0-87033-405-4). 28pp. This legend tells how the town of St. Michaels escaped bombardment by the British in the War of 1812. (Rev: BL 9/1/90; HBG 4/04; SLJ 2/04)

5603 Shank, Ned. *The Sanyasin's First Day* (K–3). Illus. by Catherine Stock. 1999, Marshall Cavendish $15.95 (978-0-7614-5055-9). 32pp. The lives of several people intersect in this story set in modern India about a holy man who begs on the streets and is given alms by a child. (Rev: BL 10/1/99; HBG 3/00; SLJ 11/99)

5604 Shulevitz, Uri. *How I Learned Geography* (K–3). Illus. by author. 2008, Farrar $16.95 (978-0-374-33499-4). 32pp. A small refugee boy discovers new horizons and forgets his hunger when his father brings home a map of the world; set in 1939, this is based on the author's experiences. Caldecott Honor Book, 2009. (Rev: BL 5/1/08; HB 3/08; SLJ 5/08)

5605 Siebert, Diane. *Rhyolite: The True Story of a Ghost Town* (2–4). Illus. by David Frampton. 2003, Clarion $16.00 (978-0-618-09673-2). 32pp. Woodcut illustrations and simple narrative verse chronicle the brief history of Rhyolite, Nevada, a gold-mining town that enjoyed a brief heyday in the early 1900s. (Rev: BL 4/15/03; HB 7/03; HBG 10/03; SLJ 5/03) [811]

5606 Siemiatycki, Jack, and Avi Slodovnick. *The Hockey Card* (1–3). Illus. by Doris Barrette. 2002, Lobster $16.95 (978-1-894222-65-5). 32pp. Uncle Jack tells his nephew about an exciting game during recess many years ago in which he bet everything on his treasured Maurice "The Rocket" Richard card. (Rev: BL 1/1–15/03)

5607 Simon, Norma. *All Kinds of Children* (PS–K). Illus. by Diane Paterson. 1999, Whitman $16.95 (978-0-8075-0281-5). 32pp. This book emphasizes how children around the world have different lifestyles and homes but similar needs. (Rev: BL 3/15/99; HBG 10/99; SLJ 6/99) [305.23]

5608 Slate, Joseph. *The Great Big Wagon That Rang: How the Liberty Bell Was Saved* (PS–2). Illus. by Craig Spearing. 2002, Marshall Cavendish $16.95 (978-0-7614-5108-2). 32pp. The story of a farmer's role in saving the Liberty Bell from the British. (Rev: BL 11/1/02; HBG 3/03; SLJ 11/02)

5609 Slate, Joseph. *I Want to Be Free* (2–4). Illus. by E. B. Lewis. 2009, Putnam $16.99 (978-0-399-24342-4). 32pp. A compelling story of a young escaped slave who saves a slave child who eventually frees him from his shackle; based on a tale retold by Rudyard Kipling in *Kim*. (Rev: BCCB 1/09; BL 12/1/08; LMC 5/09; SLJ 1/09)

5610 Smalls, Irene. *Don't Say Ain't* (1–3). Illus. by Colin Bootman. 2003, Charlesbridge $15.95 (978-1-57091-381-5). 32pp. A gifted African American student attending an integrated school in 1957 learns to "speak proper" when appropriate. (Rev: BL 2/15/03; HBG 10/03; SLJ 3/03)

5611 Smith, Lane. *John, Paul, George and Ben* (K–3). Illus. 2006, Hyperion $16.99 (978-0-7868-4893-5). 40pp. A humorous look at the contributions of five of America's founding fathers — John Hancock, Paul Revere, George Washington, Benjamin Franklin, and Thomas Jefferson — with facts appended; best suited to readers who already are familiar with the history. (Rev: BL 2/15/06; SLJ 3/06*) ⌒

5612 Sockabasin, Allen. *Thanks to the Animals* (PS–2). Illus. by Rebekah Raye. 2005, Tilbury House $16.95 (978-0-88448-270-3). When Joo Tum's infant son tumbles off the family's sled, the baby is lovingly tended by an assortment of animals until his father returns for him. (Rev: SLJ 10/05)

5613 Spinelli, Eileen. *Heat Wave* (PS–2). Illus. by Betsy Lewin. 2007, Harcourt $16.00 (978-0-15-216779-0). 32pp. The residents of Lumberville suffer through a hot spell in the days before air conditioning. (Rev: BL 5/1/07; HB 11/07; SLJ 6/07)

5614 Spiotta-Dimare, Loren. *Rockwell: A Boy and His Dog* (1–4). Illus. by Cliff Miller. 2005, Barron's $14.95 (978-0-7641-5790-5). 28pp. A fictional conversation between the painter and his model, Scotty, gives the reader a feel for the artist's inspirations and times. (Rev: SLJ 8/05)

5615 Steig, William. *When Everybody Wore a Hat* (K–3). Illus. 2003, HarperCollins LB $18.89 (978-0-06-009701-1). 40pp. Steig looks back at the Bronx of 1916 — the year he was 8 years old. (Rev: BL 5/1/03; HB 5/03; HBG 10/03; SLJ 5/03) [813.5]

5616 Stengel, Joyce A. *St. Patrick and the Three Brave Mice* (K–3). Illus. by Herb Leonhard. 2009, Pelican $15.95 (978-1-58980-663-4). 32pp. Ireland's last snake tries to steal St. Patrick's famous bell but is spotted by a little mouse named Tulla; a tense story with Celtic motifs and evocative illustrations. (Rev: BLO 2/9/09; LMC 10/09)

5617 Stevens, Jan R. *Carlos and the Cornfield / Carlos y la Milpa de Maiz* (K–3). Illus. by Jeanne Arnold. 1995, Northland LB $14.95 (978-0-87358-596-5). 32pp. Carlos learns some truths about gardening when he plants corn to earn enough money to buy a pocketknife. (Rev: BL 9/1/95; SLJ 9/95)

5618 Stewart, Sarah. *The Gardener* (K–3). Illus. by David Small. 1997, Farrar $16.00 (978-0-374-32517-6). 40pp. During the Depression, a little girl is sent off to live with a cold, somber uncle, but gradually she wins him over. (Rev: BL 6/1–15/97; HB 11/97; HBG 3/98; SLJ 8/97*)

5619 Stock, Catherine. *Gugu's House* (1–3). Illus. 2001, Clarion $16.00 (978-0-618-00389-1). 32pp. Set in Zimbabwe, this is the story of a loving grandmother whose talents include creating paintings and sculptures, as well as telling stories to granddaughter Kukamba. (Rev: BL 2/15/01*; HBG 10/01)

5620 Stroud, Bettye. *The Leaving* (K–3). Illus. by Cedric Lucas. 2001, Marshall Cavendish $15.95 (978-0-7614-5067-2). 32pp. Five years after emancipation, a young girl helps her parents escape from bondage. (Rev: BL 2/15/01; HBG 10/01)

5621 Stroud, Bettye. *The Patchwork Path: A Quilt Map to Freedom* (K–3). Illus. by Erin Susanne Bennett. 2005, Candlewick $15.99 (978-0-7636-2423-1). 32pp. On her way with her father to Canada and freedom, 10-year-old slave Hannah thinks of the quilt her mother used to teach her the necessary code. (Rev: BL 2/1/05; SLJ 1/05)

5622 Stryer, Andrea Stenn. *Kami and the Yaks* (K–3). Illus. by Bert Dodson. 2007, Bay Otter $15.95 (978-0-977896-10-3). When a deaf Sherpa boy finds one of his family's herd of yaks in distress in a storm, he must climb all the way down to his village to get help. (Rev: BL 2/1/07; SLJ 4/07)

5623 Stuve-Bodeen, Stephanie. *Babu's Song* (PS–2). Illus. by Aaron Boyd. 2003, Lee & Low $16.95 (978-1-58430-058-8). Set in Tanzania, this heartwarming story tells of the close relationship between Babu and his mute grandfather and the choices they must make about possessions and expenditures. (Rev: BL 6/1–15/03; HBG 10/03; SLJ 12/03)

5624 Stuve-Bodeen, Stephanie. *Elizabeti's Doll* (PS–1). Illus. by Christy Hale. 1998, Lee & Low $19.95 (978-1-880000-70-0). 32pp. In Tanzania, Elizabeti lacks a doll to copy her mother's activities with her new baby, so the little girl uses a rock instead. (Rev: BL 10/1/98; HB 11/98; HBG 3/99; SLJ 9/98)

5625 Stuve-Bodeen, Stephanie. *Mama Elizabeti* (1–3). Illus. by Christy Hale. 2000, Lee & Low $15.95 (978-1-58430-002-1). 32pp. Set in contemporary Tanzania, this story involves Elizabeti and her problems caring for her toddler brother. (Rev: BCCB 9/00; BL 8/00; HB 7/00; HBG 10/00; SLJ 7/00)

5626 Swain, Gwenyth. *Riding to Washington* (K–3). Illus. by David Geister. 2008, Sleeping Bear $17.95 (978-1-58536-324-7). 40pp. The story of a young girl's bus trip to hear Martin Luther King's historic I Have a Dream speech in August 1963. (Rev: BL 3/1/08; SLJ 6/08)

5627 Sweeney, Joan. *Suzette and the Puppy: A Story About Mary Cassatt* (PS–3). Illus. by Jennifer Heyd Wharton. 2000, Barron's $14.99 (978-0-7641-5294-8). A fictionalized story of a little French girl and how Mary Cassatt came to paint her as the "Little Girl in a Blue Armchair." (Rev: SLJ 1/01)

5628 Tafolla, Carmen. *What Can You Do with a Rebozo?* (K–1). Illus. by Amy Córdova. 2008, Tricycle $14.95 (978-1-58246-220-2). 32pp. A young girl explores the various uses of the traditional Mexican *rebozo* — wearing it as an accessory, making a tunnel with it, framing a cradle for her baby brother, and even seeing it as a superhero's cape. Belpré Honor Book. (Rev: SLJ 1/08)

5629 Tankard, Jeremy. *Me Hungry!* (PS–K). Illus. by author. 2008, Candlewick $15.99 (978-0-7636-3360-8). 40pp. A prehistoric boy is hungry and his parents are busy, so he heads off on a hunt and on the way makes a new friend — a mammoth. (Rev: BCCB 4/08; BL 5/15/08; HB 5/08; SLJ 9/08)

5630 Taulbert, Clifton L. *Little Cliff and the Cold Place* (K–2). Illus. by E. B. Lewis. 2002, Dial $16.99 (978-0-8037-2558-4). 32pp. Little Cliff lives in Mississippi in the 1950s and longs to go to the Arctic, so his great-grandfather comes up with a compromise — a fishing expedition at the icehouse. (Rev: BL 11/1/02; HBG 3/03; SLJ 9/02)

5631 Tavares, Matt. *Mudball* (K–3). Illus. 2005, Candlewick $15.99 (978-0-7636-2387-6). 32pp. The entertaining story of a baseball game long ago that, thanks to a mud puddle, gained renown for the game's shortest home run. (Rev: BL 3/1/05; SLJ 3/05)

5632 Taylor, Debbie. *Sweet Music in Harlem* (1–3). Illus. by Frank Morrison. 2004, Lee & Low $16.95 (978-1-58430-165-3). 32pp. A famous 1958 photograph inspired this story about young C.J. scrambling to find his jazz-playing uncle's hat for a photo shoot and in the process attracting some of Harlem's most notable jazzmen, who want to join in. (Rev: BL 5/1/04; SLJ 7/04)

5633 Taylor, Joanne. *Making Room* (1–3). Illus. by Peter Rankin. 2004, Tundra $15.95 (978-0-88776-651-0). In 1800s Nova Scotia, a man gradually adds to his one-room house as his family grows. (Rev: SLJ 11/04)

5634 Thaxter, Celia. *Celia's Island Journal* (PS–3). Illus. by Loretta Krupinski. 1992, Little, Brown $15.95 (978-0-316-83921-1). 32pp. The author's life on White Island off the New England coast. (Rev: BL 12/1/92; HB 11/92; SLJ 10/92) [974.1]

5635 Thermes, Jennifer. *Sam Bennett's New Shoes* (K–2). 2006, Carolrhoda $15.95 (978-1-57505-822-1). 32pp. In this story based on an 18th-century custom, Sam Bennett gets new shoes and his father takes the old shoes and hides them in the wall to bring good fortune. (Rev: BL 6/1–15/06; SLJ 3/06)

5636 Thong, Roseanne. *The Wishing Tree* (PS–2). Illus. by Connie McLennan. 2004, Shen's $16.95 (978-1-885008-26-8). 30pp. After years of visits to the Wishing Tree, Ming turns his back on the annual tradition when his grandmother dies. (Rev: BL 2/1/05)

5637 Tompert, Ann. *The Pied Piper of Peru* (K–2). Illus. by Kestutis Kasparavicius. 2002, Boyds Mills $15.95 (978-1-56397-949-1). 32pp. A 16th-century Peruvian saint tries to rid the priory of a colony of mice in this story about Saint Martin de Porres. (Rev: BCCB 4/02; BL 3/15/02; HBG 10/02) [270.6]

5638 Tran, Truong. *Going Home, Coming Home / Ve Nha Tham Que Hu'O'Ng* (1–3). Illus. by Ann Phong. 2003, Children's Book Pr. $16.95 (978-0-89239-179-0). 32pp. Eight-year-old Vietnamese American Ami Chi visits the homeland of her parents in this poignant bilingual tale. (Rev: BL 9/1/03; SLJ 9/03)

5639 Trottier, Maxine. *Flags* (1–4). Illus. by Paul Morin. 1999, Stoddart $16.95 (978-0-7737-3136-3). When their Japanese American neighbor, Mr. Hiroshi, is sent to an internment camp after Pearl Harbor, Mary saves some stones and some bulbs from his garden to start one of her own. (Rev: SLJ 3/00)

5640 Trottier, Maxine. *Little Dog Moon* (K–5). Illus. by Laura Fernandez and Rick Jacobson. 2000, Stoddart $14.95 (978-0-7737-3220-9). Moon, a young Tibetan terrier, helps guide two Tibetan children across the border to freedom in Nepal. (Rev: SLJ 3/01)

5641 Trottier, Maxine. *The Walking Stick* (K–3). Illus. by Annouchka Gravel Galouchko. 1999, Stoddart $15.95 (978-0-7737-3101-1). A story about a walking stick fashioned by a Buddhist monk in Vietnam for a young boy who carries it throughout his life, even when he must leave his native land and come to America. (Rev: SLJ 9/99)

5642 Uhlberg, Myron. *Dad, Jackie, and Me* (2–5). Illus. by Colin Bootman. 2005, Peachtree $16.95 (978-1-56145-329-0). In Brooklyn in 1947, a boy and his deaf father admire Jackie Robinson's baseball prowess. (Rev: BCCB 5/05; BL 8/05; SLJ 5/05)

5643 Ulmer, Mike. *The Gift of the Inuksuk* (PS–2). Illus. by Melanie Rose. 2004, Sleeping Bear $17.95 (978-1-58536-214-1). 32pp. This sparely worded, original pourquoi tale offers an explanation for the *Inuksuk*, sculptures of piled stones, that dot the Arctic landscape. (Rev: BL 1/1–15/05; SLJ 4/05)

5644 U'Ren, Andrea. *Mary Smith* (PS–2). Illus. by author. 2003, Farrar $16.00 (978-0-374-34842-7). The colorful story of a day in the life of pre-alarm-clock Mary Smith, who uses a peashooter to wake the people of her town; an afterword gives historical context. (Rev: HB 9/03; HBG 4/04; SLJ 9/03)

5645 Usher, M. D. *Diogenes* (1–3). Illus. by Michael Chesworth. 2009, Farrar $16.95 (978-0-374-31785-0). 32pp. In ancient Greece, a dog named Diogenes is determined to be his own master in this appealing story based on the views of the classical philosopher; with biographical information on Diogenes and his beliefs. (Rev: BLO 5/27/09; SLJ 6/09)

5646 Vander Zee, Ruth. *Always with You* (2–4). Illus. by Ronald Himler. 2008, Eerdmans $17.00 (978-0-8028-5295-3). 32pp. Based on a true story, this picture book follows the story of 4-year-old Kim, orphaned in the Vietnam War. (Rev: BL 2/15/08; SLJ 9/08)

5647 Van West, Patricia E. *The Crab Man* (1–3). Illus. by Cedric Lucas. 1998, Turtle $15.95 (978-1-890515-08-9). 40pp. A young Jamaican boy must decide whether or not he should continue to sell hermit crabs after he discovers that they are being cruelly treated. (Rev: BL 10/1/98; HBG 3/99; SLJ 11/98)

5648 Vaughan, Marcia. *The Secret to Freedom* (K–3). Illus. by Larry Johnson. 2001, Lee & Low $16.95 (978-1-58430-021-2). 32pp. Great Aunt Lucy talks about her days as a slave and the secret quilt code that directed her brother Albert and other slaves on the road to freedom. (Rev: BL 6/1–15/01; HBG 10/01; SLJ 6/01)

5649 Vaughan, Marcia. *Up the Learning Tree* (K–3). Illus. by Derek Blanks. 2003, Lee & Low $16.96 (978-1-58430-049-6). A schoolteacher risks everything to help a brave young slave gain an education. (Rev: BL 11/1/03; HBG 4/04; SLJ 11/03)

5650 Villaseñor, Victor. *The Frog and His Friends Save Humanity / La rana y sus amigos salvan a la humanidad* (PS–3). Trans. by Edna Ochoa. Illus. by José Ramírez. 2005, Arte Publico $15.95 (978-1-55885-429-1). 32pp. In this captivating bilingual children's tale, set at the dawn of creation, other animals puzzle over the role of a human child. (Rev: BL 8/05; SLJ 6/06)

5651 Von Ahnen, Katherine. *Charlie Young Bear* (2–3). Illus. by Paulette L. Lambert. Series: Council for Indian Education. 1994, Roberts Rinehart paper $4.95 (978-1-57098-001-5). 42pp. After the U.S. government agrees on a cash settlement with the Mesquakie Indians in 1955, Charlie Young Bear hopes his share will be a bike. (Rev: SLJ 4/95)

5652 Wallace, Ian. *Mavis and Merna* (K–3). Illus. 2005, Douglas & McIntyre $16.95 (978-0-88899-647-3). 40pp. Gully's, the general store in her 1960s Canadian town, has always been one of Mavis's favorite places, and when owner Joe Gully dies, Mavis becomes friends with his widow even though the store is closed. (Rev: BL 5/1/05; SLJ 6/05)

5653 Walton, Rick. *Dance, Pioneer, Dance!* (K–3). Illus. by Brad Teare. 1998, Deseret $14.95 (978-1-57345-243-4). 28pp. Brigham Young calls a square dance in which humans and animals take part. His whimsical verses recall the journey of the first Mormons to Utah in 1847. (Rev: BL 9/15/98; SLJ 8/98)

5654 Ward, Leila. *I Am Eyes Ni Macho* (PS–1). Illus. by Nonny Hogrogian. 1987, Scholastic paper $3.95 (978-0-590-40990-2). 32pp. A new day and all of nature's wonders are greeted by a Kenyan child. A reissue of the 1978 edition.

5655 Waterton, Betty. *Pettranella* (K–3). Illus. by Ann Blades. 1991, Firefly paper $4.95 (978-0-88899-108-9). 32pp. An immigrant girl grows flowers from seeds she brought from Europe.

5656 Watkins, Sherrin. *Green Snake Ceremony* (PS–2). Illus. by Kim Doner. Series: The Greyfeather. 1996, Council Oak $17.95 (978-0-933031-89-0). Neither a Shawnee girl nor the green snake that lives under the porch want to participate in the traditional snake ceremony that involves the young girl putting the snake in her mouth. (Rev: SLJ 12/96)

5657 Watson, Mary. *The Paper Dragonfly* (K–3). Illus. by author. 2007, Shenanigan $15.95 (978-0-9726614-3-0). 32pp. Instead of learning about growing rice, Kiyoshi makes paper lanterns; however, when the Emperor sees his dragonfly lantern, Kiyoshi's artistic skills are rewarded. (Rev: BL 12/15/07)

5658 Weinstein, Muriel Harris. *When Louis Armstrong Taught Me Scat* (PS–2). Illus. by R. Gregory Christie. 2009, Chronicle $16.99 (978-0-8118-5131-2). 32pp. A rhythmic story about a little girl who dreams about singing scat with Louis Armstrong. (Rev: BL 2/1/09; LMC 5/09)

5659 Wells, Rosemary. *The Miraculous Tale of the Two Maries* (K–2). Illus. by Petra Mathers. 2006, Viking $16.99 (978-0-670-05960-7). 32pp. Two teenage girls, both named Marie, drown in the ocean but persuade God to allow them to return to their town to do good deeds; inspired by a story of 19th-century France. (Rev: BL 3/1/06*; HB 3/06; HBG 10/06; SLJ 3/06)

5660 Wenberg, Michael. *Elizabeth's Song* (1–4). Illus. by Cornelius Van Wright. 2002, Beyond Words $15.95 (978-1-58270-069-4). 32pp. The fictionalized story of African American folk singer Elizabeth Cotton, 11-year-old author of "Freight Train Comin'." (Rev: BL 2/15/03; HBG 10/03)

5661 Weston, Anne. *My Brother Needs a Boa* (2–4). Illus. by Cheryl Nathan. 2005, Star Bright $15.95 (978-1-932065-96-1). To rid his shop of a pesky mouse, Benito heeds his sister's advice and goes in search of a rodent-catching snake. (Rev: SLJ 10/05)

5662 Whelan, Gloria. *Yuki and the One Thousand Carriers* (1–3). Illus. by Yan Nascimbene. Series: Tales of the World. 2008, Sleeping Bear $17.95 (978-1-58536-352-0). 32pp. In 17th-century Japan Yuki, young daughter of a governor, describes in haiku her family's long journey from Kyoto to Edo escorted by more than 1,000 helpers. (Rev: BL 4/15/08; LMC 1/09; SLJ 7/08)

5663 Whitaker, Zai. *Kali and the Rat Snake* (1–3). Illus. by Srividya Natarajan. 2006, Kane $15.95 (978-1-933605-10-4). Kali's classmates are unkind because his father is a snake catcher, but Kali wins their respect and gratitude when he captures a six-foot snake that invades their classroom; with handsome illustrations and endpapers. (Rev: SLJ 10/06)

5664 Wiebe, Rudy. *Hidden Buffalo* (1–3). Illus. by Michael Lonechild. 2004, Red Deer $17.95 (978-0-88995-285-0). 32pp. Based on a traditional tale, this book tells how a dream inspires the starving Cree people to brave dangers and journey to the Badlands in search of buffalo herds. (Rev: BL 3/1/04; SLJ 7/04)

5665 Williams, Karen L. *Painted Dreams* (PS–1). Illus. by Catherine Stock. 1998, Lothrop LB $15.89 (978-0-688-13902-5). 40pp. Set in the slums of Haiti, this picture book tells of little Ti Marie, who finds some discarded paints in an artist's trash and, with his help, cultivates her artistic talent. (Rev: BL 9/15/98; HBG 3/99; SLJ 10/98)

5666 Williams, Karen L. *When Africa Was Home* (PS–2). Illus. by Floyd Cooper. 1991, Orchard LB $16.99 (978-0-531-08525-7). 32pp. A white boy is so at home in Africa with his black friends that he feels lost when he has to go to America. (Rev: BCCB 2/92; BL 1/15/91*; SLJ 4/91)

5667 Williams, Laura E. *Torch Fishing with the Sun* (K–3). Illus. by Fabricio Vandenbroeck. 1999, Boyds Mills $15.95 (978-1-56397-685-8). 32pp. Young Makoa's grandfather tells him that he uses the sun as a torch while he fishes, but the boy has doubts when others claim that the old man actually buys his catch from another fisherman. (Rev: BL 3/15/99; HBG 10/99; SLJ 6/99)

5668 Willow, Diane. *At Home in the Rain Forest* (PS–3). Illus. by Laura Jacques. 1991, Charlesbridge $14.95 (978-0-88106-485-8). 32pp. The flora and fauna of the Amazon rain forest are explored in text and color paintings. (Rev: BL 6/1/91) [574]

5669 Winch, John. *Fly, Kite, Fly! A Story of Leonardo and a Bird Catcher* (PS–2). Illus. 2009, Trafalgar

$15.95 (978-1-921049-81-1). 40pp. On a mission to catch a red-tailed kite, 10-year-old Giacomo meets Leonardo da Vinci and learns why the elderly artist has been releasing his birds from traps. (Rev: BLO 10/7/08)

5670 Winnick, Karen B. *Mr. Lincoln's Whiskers* (1–3). Illus. 1996, Boyds Mills $16.95 (978-1-56397-485-4). 32pp. A young girl writes to Lincoln to suggest that he would gain votes if he grew whiskers. (Rev: BL 12/15/96; SLJ 1/97)

5671 Winnick, Karen B. *Sybil's Night Ride* (K–3). Illus. 2000, Boyds Mills $15.95 (978-1-56397-697-1). 32pp. This picture book re-creates the historic ride of 16-year-old Sybil Ludington who, during the American Revolution, raced on her horse to warn her father's troops that the British were burning Danbury, New York. (Rev: BL 3/1/00; HBG 10/00)

5672 Winter, Jeanette. *Elsina's Clouds* (PS–3). Illus. 2004, Farrar $16.00 (978-0-374-32118-5). 40pp. In Basotho tradition, Elsina paints the outside walls of her house, decorating them with bright colors and scenes of nature. (Rev: BL 3/1/04; HB 3/04; SLJ 4/04)

5673 Winter, Jeanette. *Follow the Drinking Gourd* (K–3). Illus. by author. 1988, Knopf paper $5.99 (978-0-679-81997-4). 48pp. The story of Peg Leg Pete who helps slaves escape to the North. (Rev: BCCB 1/89; BL 12/15/88; SLJ 5/89)

5674 Winter, Jonah. *The Fabulous Feud of Gilbert and Sullivan* (K–3). Illus. by Richard Egielski. 2009, Scholastic $16.99 (978-0-439-93050-5). 40pp. An entertaining story about the famous musical team and their sometimes troubled collaboration in the Victorian era. (Rev: BL 4/1/09; HB 5/09; SLJ 6/09)

5675 Winter, Jonah. *Steel Town* (1–3). Illus. by Terry Widener. 2008, Atheneum $16.99 (978-1-4169-4081-4). 40pp. A moving, oversized look at the lives of workers in a 1930s steel town, with rhythmic text, evocative illustrations, and lots of details on the production process. (Rev: BCCB 7–8/08; BL 4/1/08; HB 7/08; LMC 8/08; SLJ 5/08)

5676 Wisniewski, David. *Rain Player* (K–3). Illus. 1991, Houghton $17.00 (978-0-395-55112-7). 32pp. Young Pik challenges the rain god in this story based on Mayan folklore. (Rev: BCCB 11/91; BL 10/15/91*; HB 1/92; SLJ 10/91)

5677 Wittmann, Patricia. *Buffalo Thunder* (K–4). Illus. by Bert Dodson. 1997, Marshall Cavendish $15.95 (978-0-7614-5001-6). 32pp. A young boy and his family share many adventures when they travel west in their prairie schooner. (Rev: BL 9/15/97; HBG 3/98; SLJ 9/97)

5678 Wolff, Ferida, and Harriet May Savitz. *The Story Blanket* (PS–2). Illus. by Elena Odriozola. 2008, Peachtree $16.95 (978-1-56145-466-2). 32pp. Elderly storyteller Babba Zarrah sacrifices wool from her blanket to provide, secretly, needed socks, scarves, mittens, and so forth for the residents of her chilly mountain village; when the villagers work out who has left these gifts they respond in kind. (Rev: BCCB 10/08; BL 10/15/08; LMC 3/09; SLJ 11/08)

5679 Wong, Janet S. *The Trip Back Home* (PS–2). Illus. by Bo Jia. 2000, Harcourt $16.00 (978-0-15-200784-3). 32pp. The food and fun involved when the author visited her grandparents in rural Korea when she was a child are recalled in this tender story of family love. (Rev: BL 11/15/00; HBG 3/01; SLJ 12/00)

5680 Woodruff, Elvira. *The Memory Coat* (K–4). Illus. by Michael Dooling. 1999, Scholastic $16.95 (978-0-590-67717-2). 32pp. This story of a Jewish family's migration from Russia to America focuses on Rachel and her orphaned cousin, Grisha. (Rev: BL 1/1–15/99; HBG 10/99; SLJ 3/99)

5681 Woodruff, Elvira. *Small Beauties: The Journey of Darcy Heart O'Hara* (K–3). Illus. by Adam Rex. 2006, Knopf $15.95 (978-0-375-82686-3). 32pp. Darcy's precious mementoes of her home in Ireland — a pebble, a flower, a chip of stone — give her strength during the family's difficult journey to America. (Rev: BL 8/06)

5682 Woodson, Jacqueline. *Coming on Home Soon* (K–3). Illus. by E. B. Lewis. 2004, Putnam $16.99 (978-0-399-23748-5). Living with her grandmother, young African American Ada Ruth waits for her mother to return from her work in Chicago during World War II. Caldecott Honor Book. (Rev: BL 8/04*; HB 9/04; SLJ 10/04*)

5683 Wormell, Christopher. *The Wild Girl* (PS–1). Illus. by author. 2006, Eerdmans $17.00 (978-0-8028-5311-0). A young girl who survives a hard and lonely life in a cave with her dog — eating fruit, nuts, and fish — at first tries to chase a bear away, but realizing it has a cub she allows it to come into the cave and they all share what they have. (Rev: SLJ 11/06)

5684 Would, Nick. *The Scarab's Secret* (K–3). Illus. by Christina Balk. 2006, Walker $16.95 (978-0-8027-9561-8). 32pp. A scarab beetle tells how it saved the life of an Egyptian prince and thus secured for itself an important place in the mythology of ancient Egypt. (Rev: BL 3/15/06; SLJ 4/06)

5685 Wright, Courtni C. *Jumping the Broom* (K–3). Illus. by Gershom Griffith. 1994, Holiday House LB $15.95 (978-0-8234-1042-2). A picture book set in the days of slavery about the marriage celebration known as "jumping the broom." (Rev: BCCB 7–8/94; SLJ 4/94)

5686 Xiong, Kim. *Little Stone Lion* (PS–2). Illus. 2005, Heryin $13.99 (978-0-9762056-1-6). 32pp. A small stone lion reflects on the people and history of the small Chinese village over which he stands guard. (Rev: BL 11/1/05)

5687 Yacowitz, Caryn. *Pumpkin Fiesta* (PS–1). Illus. by Joe Cepeda. 1998, HarperCollins $16.99 (978-0-06-027658-4). 32pp. Foolish Fernando tries by fair and foul means to rob Old Juana of the glory of winning the fiesta's special prize for her extraordinary pumpkins, but justice triumphs. (Rev: BL 9/1/98; HB 11/98; HBG 3/99; SLJ 9/98)

5688 Yang, Belle. *Always Come Home to Me* (PS–2). Illus. by author. 2007, Candlewick $16.99 (978-0-7636-2899-4). 32pp. Vibrant illustrations add to this story of Chinese twins Mei-Mei and her brother

DiDi and their love for their white doves. (Rev: BL 9/1/07; SLJ 11/07)

5689 Yin. *Brothers* (2–4). Illus. by Chris Soentpiet. 2006, Philomel $17.99 (978-0-399-23406-4). 40pp. Newly arrived in 19th century San Francisco, Ming ignores his older brothers' warnings not to venture outside Chinatown and strikes up a friendship with Patrick, a young Irish immigrant; a sequel to *Coolies* (2000). (Rev: BL 8/06; SLJ 11/06)

5690 Yin. *Coolies* (K–4). Illus. by Chris K. Soentpiet. 2001, Penguin $16.99 (978-0-399-23227-5). 40pp. The experiences of two Chinese brothers who migrate to America to work on the Transcontinental Railroad reveal the courage and integrity of these Chinese Americans and the racism they endured. (Rev: BCCB 2/01; BL 2/1/01; HB 3/01; HBG 10/01; SLJ 3/01)

5691 Yolen, Jane. *My Uncle Emily* (K–3). Illus. by Nancy Carpenter. 2009, Philomel $17.99 (978-0-399-24005-8). 32pp. A free-verse, fictionalized story about Emily Dickinson's nephew Gib, who calls his aunt an "uncle" and appreciates their close relationship. (Rev: BL 5/1/09; HB 7/09; LMC 10/09; SLJ 6/09)

5692 Yolen, Jane. *Naming Liberty* (1–3). Illus. by Jim Burke. 2008, Philomel $16.99 (978-0-399-24250-2). 32pp. Yolen interweaves the story of the creation of the Statue of Liberty with a Russian Jewish family's journey to America. (Rev: BL 4/15/08; LMC 10/08)

5693 Yong Yi, Hu. *Good Morning China* (PS–2). Illus. by author. 2007, Roaring Brook $16.95 (978-1-59643-240-6). 32pp. In China, people enjoy the morning in the park with activities such as cycling, playing chess, and doing tai chi. (Rev: BL 12/15/07; LMC 3/08; SLJ 1/08)

PERSONAL PROBLEMS

5694 Adams, Eric J., and Kathleen Adams. *On the Day His Daddy Left* (1–3). Illus. by Layne Johnson. 2000, Whitman $16.99 (978-0-8075-6072-3). Danny worries that his parents' divorce is his fault. (Rev: BL 3/1/03; HBG 3/01; SLJ 12/00)

5695 Allen, Debbie. *Dancing in the Wings* (K–3). Illus. by Kadir Nelson. 2000, Dial $16.99 (978-0-8037-2501-0). 32pp. Sassy is afraid that she is too tall and lanky to become a ballerina, but a Russian ballet master chooses her to dance in a festival. (Rev: BCCB 11/00; BL 11/15/00; HBG 3/01; SLJ 9/00)

5696 Altman, Linda J. *Amelia's Road* (PS–3). Illus. by Enrique O. Sánchez. 1993, Lee & Low $15.95 (978-1-880000-04-5). 32pp. Amelia, the daughter of migrant workers, cries every time her father takes out a map because it means her family will move again. (Rev: BL 9/15/93; SLJ 12/93)

5697 Bahr, Mary. *If Nathan Were Here* (K–2). Illus. by Karen A. Jerome. 2000, Eerdmans $16.00 (978-0-8028-5187-1). 32pp. A boy imagines all the things he could do if Nathan were there but, as the reader learns, Nathan is dead and his friend misses him. (Rev: BL 4/15/00; HBG 10/00; SLJ 8/00)

5698 Bang, Molly. *When Sophie Gets Angry — Really, Really Angry* (PS–3). Illus. 1999, Scholastic $16.99 (978-0-590-18979-8). 40pp. This book describes in drawings and text what happens to Sophie when she is truly discontented. Caldecott Honor Book, 2000. (Rev: BCCB 4/99; BL 2/1/99; HBG 10/99; SLJ 1/99*)

5699 Barnholdt, Lauren. *The Secret Identity of Devon Delaney* (4–7). 2007, Aladdin Mix paper $5.99 (978-1-4169-3503-2). 264pp. The lies that Devon tells while spending the summer at her grandmother's house come back to bite her when her new friend Lexi moves to Devon's town and attends Devon's middle school. (Rev: BL 8/07; SLJ 8/07)

5700 Barron, T. A. *Where Is Grandpa?* (PS–3). Illus. by Chris K. Soentpiet. 2000, Penguin $16.99 (978-0-399-23037-0). 32pp. A young boy believes his dead grandfather is enjoying all the beauties of nature that he loved. (Rev: BL 5/1/00; HBG 10/00; SLJ 2/00)

5701 Bateman, Teresa. *Hamster Camp: How Hany Got Fit* (K–3). Illus. by Nancy Cote. 2005, Whitman $16.99 (978-0-8075-3139-6). 32pp. Harry, an indolent boy with a craving for unhealthy foods, accompanies his pet to Hamster Camp, where Harry is promptly transformed into a hamster and learns to eat properly. (Rev: BL 5/15/05)

5702 Battle-Lavert, Gwendolyn. *Off to School* (K–3). Illus. by Gershom Griffith. 1995, Holiday House LB $15.95 (978-0-8234-1185-6). 32pp. A migrant worker's child, Wezielee, longs to go to school but must stay at the camp and cook for the laborers. (Rev: BL 10/15/95; SLJ 1/96)

5703 Baumgart, Klaus. *Don't Be Afraid, Tommy* (PS–1). Illus. by author. 1998, Little Tiger $14.95 (978-1-888444-32-2). Tommy learns to conquer his own fears when he is given a toy dog and told to teach him not to be afraid. (Rev: HBG 10/98; SLJ 7/98)

5704 Bernstein, Sharon C. *A Family That Fights* (PS–3). Illus. by Karen Ritz. 1991, Whitman LB $15.99 (978-0-8075-2248-6). 32pp. A quiet story that deals with three children who live in a family where the father hits their mother and threatens them when he is angry. (Rev: BL 11/15/91; SLJ 2/92)

5705 Best, Cari. *Getting Used to Harry* (PS–3). Illus. by Diane Palmisciano. 1996, Orchard LB $16.99 (978-0-531-08794-7). 32pp. Cynthia gradually adjusts to her mother's new husband, Harry the shoe man. (Rev: BCCB 10/96; BL 11/1/96; SLJ 10/96)

5706 Bottner, Barbara. *Bootsie Barker Bites* (PS–3). Illus. by Peggy Rathmann. 1992, Penguin $17.99 (978-0-399-22125-5). 32pp. The young narrator stands just so much from bully Bootsie Barker and finally stands up for herself. (Rev: BCCB 9/92; BL 10/1/92*; HB 3/93; SLJ 2/93*)

5707 Browne, Anthony. *Silly Billy* (PS–2). Illus. 2006, Candlewick $15.99 (978-0-7636-3124-6). 32pp. Billy's Grandma gives him some Guatemalan worry dolls to help him reduce his burden of fears in this beautifully illustrated picture book. (Rev: BL 10/15/06; SLJ 11/06)

5708 Buckley, James. *The Very Ordered Existence of Merilee Marvelous* (5–8). 2007, Greenwillow $16.99 (978-0-06-123197-1). 384pp. Marilee, a bright young girl with Asperger's syndrome, enjoys order in her life until a new boy in town — Biswick, who has fetal alcohol syndrome — decides to attach himself to her. (Rev: BL 9/1/07; SLJ 10/07)

5709 Buehner, Caralyn. *Would I Ever Lie to You?* (K–4). Illus. by Jack E. Davis. 2007, Dial $16.99 (978-0-8037-2793-9). An older cousin is full of scary tales that the narrator must sort out (Which are true and which are lies?) in this reassuring story that will help readers deal with teasing. (Rev: SLJ 5/07)

5710 Bulla, Clyde Robert. *The Chalk Box Kid* (2–3). Illus. by Thomas B. Allen. 1987, Random LB $11.99 (978-0-394-99102-3); paper $3.99 (978-0-394-89102-6). 64pp. Miffed because Uncle Max is sharing his room, Gregory sets out to explore his new neighborhood. (Rev: BCCB 9/87; BL 12/1/87; SLJ 12/87)

5711 Bunnett, Rochelle. *Friends in the Park* (PS–K). Illus. by Carl Sahlhoff. 1993, Checkerboard $7.95 (978-1-56288-347-8). 32pp. In this book of photographs and text, disabled kids are shown enjoying all the activities that youngsters like. (Rev: BL 4/15/93) [305.9]

5712 Bunting, Eve. *The Days of Summer* (PS–3). Illus. by William Low. 2001, Harcourt $16.00 (978-0-15-201840-5). 32pp. In this moving picture book, a girl and her younger sister are bewildered when their grandparents divorce. (Rev: BL 4/1/01; HBG 10/01; SLJ 5/01)

5713 Bunting, Eve. *Fly Away Home* (K–3). Illus. by Ronald Himler. 1991, Houghton $16.00 (978-0-395-55962-8). 32pp. The airport serves as a home for two homeless people — a boy and his father. (Rev: BCCB 5/92; BL 4/1/91*; HB 7/91; SLJ 6/91*)

5714 Bunting, Eve. *On Call Back Mountain* (1–3). Illus. by Barry Moser. 1997, Scholastic $15.95 (978-0-590-25929-3). Two young brothers adjust to the death of an elderly man who has worked as a fire spotter in a tower close to their home. (Rev: SLJ 3/97)

5715 Burnett, Frances Hodgson. *A Little Princess* (K–2). Illus. by Barbara McClintock. 2000, HarperCollins LB $16.89 (978-0-06-029010-8). 32pp. A retelling in a shortened form of Burnett's beloved classic story of a privileged child who turned pauper and back again. (Rev: BL 1/1–15/01; HBG 3/01)

5716 Campbell, Bebe Moore. *I Get So Hungry* (PS–2). Illus. by Amy Bates. 2008, Putnam $16.99 (978-0-399-24311-0). 32pp. Nikki, a young African American girl, learns to control her eating with the help of her teacher, who has herself suffered health problems because of her weight. (Rev: BCCB 6/08; BL 5/1/08; LMC 10/08; SLJ 5/08)

5717 Canfield, Jack, and Mark V. Hansen. *Chicken Soup for Little Souls: The Best Night Out with Dad* (K–4). Illus. by Bert Dodson. Series: Chicken Soup for Little Souls. 1997, Health Communications $14.95 (978-1-55874-508-7). 32pp. This slight story

teaches the value of being unselfish and giving to others. Also use *Chicken Soup for Little Souls: The Goodness Gorilla* and *Chicken Soup for Little Souls: The Never-Forgotten Doll* (1997). (Rev: BL 11/15/97; HBG 3/98; SLJ 1/98)

5718 Carlson, Nancy. *Arnie and the New Kid* (PS–2). Illus. 1992, Puffin paper $5.99 (978-0-14-050945-8). 32pp. When Arnie has an accident, he realizes what life is like for newcomer Philip, who is confined to a wheelchair. (Rev: BCCB 5/90; BL 5/15/90)

5719 Carr, Jan. *Dark Day, Light Night* (PS–2). Illus. by James Ransome. 1996, Hyperion LB $15.49 (978-0-7868-2014-6). 32pp. When 'Manda claims there is nothing in the world she really likes, Aunt Ruby compiles a list of her own favorite things. (Rev: BL 2/15/96; HB 5/96; SLJ 6/96)

5720 Carrick, Carol. *Patrick's Dinosaurs* (PS–3). Illus. by Donald Carrick. 1983, Houghton $16.00 (978-0-89919-189-8); paper $5.95 (978-0-89919-402-8). 32pp. Patrick is frightened when his brother tells him about dinosaurs.

5721 Caseley, Judith. *Priscilla Twice* (K–2). Illus. 1995, Greenwillow LB $14.93 (978-0-688-13306-1). 32pp. After her parents divorce, Priscilla finds that she now has two of everything, including two sets of clothes. (Rev: BL 8/95; SLJ 9/95)

5722 Cave, Kathryn. *You've Got Dragons* (K–3). Illus. by Nick Maland. 2003, Peachtree $16.95 (978-1-56145-284-2). Young Ben explains about the dragons he gets when in stressful situations, and what he does to get rid of them. (Rev: BCCB 11/03; BL 10/15/03; HBG 4/04; SLJ 12/03)

5723 Chapra, Mimi. *Sparky's Bark / El ladrido de Sparky* (PS–2). Illus. by Vivi Escriva. 2006, HarperCollins $16.99 (978-0-06-053172-0). 32pp. A Hispanic girl visiting relatives in Ohio overcomes her culture shock and begins to learn English in this bilingual picture book. (Rev: BL 5/1/06; SLJ 6/06)

5724 Clark, Emma Chichester. *What Shall We Do, Blue Kangaroo?* (PS–1). Illus. by author. 2003, Doubleday LB $17.99 (978-0-385-90866-5). Lily is delighted to realize she doesn't have to depend on adults for things to do, but glad that stuffed toy Blue Kangaroo is still around to help. (Rev: BL 5/15/03; HB 9/03; HBG 4/04; SLJ 7/03)

5725 Cohn, Janice. *Molly's Rosebush* (PS–2). Illus. by Gail Owens. 1994, Whitman LB $14.95 (978-0-8075-5213-1). 32pp. Grandma helps Molly get over her grief at the loss of her mother's baby by miscarriage. (Rev: BL 1/15/95; SLJ 3/95)

5726 Cooper, Helen. *Tatty Ratty* (PS–K). Illus. 2002, Farrar $16.00 (978-0-374-37386-3). 32pp. When Molly accidentally leaves her favorite stuffed animal on the bus, she is comforted by thoughts of the grand adventures he is having. (Rev: BL 2/15/02; HBG 10/02; SLJ 4/02)

5727 Cooper, Ilene. *Jake's Best Thumb* (PS–1). Illus. by Claudio Munoz. 2008, Dutton $16.99 (978-0-525-47788-4). 32pp. Jake's kindergarten classmate Cliff denounces Jake as as thumb-sucker, but does Cliff have his own security need? (Rev: BCCB 9/08; BLO 8/1/08; SLJ 3/09)

5728 Cote, Nancy. *Jackson's Blanket* (PS). Illus. by author. 2008, Putnam $16.99 (978-0-399-24694-4). 32pp. Jackson won't be parted from his blanket until the day he finds a kitten in the snow and realizes it needs the blanket more than he does. (Rev: BLO 9/24/08)

5729 Cottin, Menena. *The Black Book of Colors* (K–3). Trans. by Elisa Amado. Illus. by Rosana Faria. 2008, Groundwood $17.95 (978-0-88899-873-6). 24pp. This unusual book challenges readers to imagine being blind and to experience colors through touch, as blind people do; with a guide to the Braille alphabet. (Rev: BL 10/1/08; LMC 11/08; SLJ 9/08)

5730 Cowley, Joy. *Big Moon Tortilla* (PS–3). Illus. by Dyanne Strongbow. 1998, Boyds Mills $14.95 (978-1-56397-601-8). When Marta Enos has a bad day at home on the Papago reservation in southern Arizona, her grandmother tells her a traditional tale to help her cope with problems. (Rev: BL 10/15/98; HBG 10/99; SLJ 11/98)

5731 Cox, Judy. *Puppy Power* (2–4). Illus. by Steve Björkman. 2008, Holiday $15.95 (978-0-8234-2073-5). 96pp. Fran, an overbearing 3rd-grader, learns a little about self-control while taking her rambunctious Newfoundland puppy to obedience class. (Rev: BCCB 6/08; BL 5/1/08; LMC 10/08; SLJ 6/08)

5732 Crary, Elizabeth. *I'm Frustrated* (PS–1). Illus. by Jean Whitney. 1992, Parenting LB $16.95 (978-0-943990-65-1). 30pp. In this slim book, a child is faced with a difficult situation and must work through his feelings. Others in this series are: *I'm Mad; I'm Proud* (both 1992). (Rev: SLJ 6/92)

5733 Cristaldi, Kathryn. *Samantha the Snob* (1–3). Illus. by Denise Brunkus. Series: Step into Reading. 1994, Random paper $3.99 (978-0-679-84640-6). 48pp. Everyone thinks that the new girl in their class is a snob and showoff, but her birthday party shows that they are wrong. (Rev: SLJ 11/94)

5734 Crocker, Nancy. *Betty Lou Blue* (PS–2). Illus. by Boris Kulikov. 2006, Dial $16.99 (978-0-8037-2937-7). 32pp. Poor Betty Lou Blue is taunted mercilessly by classmates because of her large feet, but those appendages come to the rescue when an avalanche traps her tormentors in snowdrifts. (Rev: BL 8/06; SLJ 12/06)

5735 Curtis, Jamie Lee. *Today I Feel Silly: And Other Moods That Make My Day* (PS–2). Illus. by Laura Cornell. 1998, HarperCollins $16.99 (978-0-06-024560-3). 32pp. In this lighthearted picture book, the young narrator describes how she feels on different days and the ways she copes with emotional ups and downs. (Rev: BL 10/15/98; HBG 3/99; SLJ 12/98)

5736 Czech, Jan M. *An American Face* (PS–2). Illus. by Frances Clancy. 2000, Child & Family paper $8.95 (978-0-87868-718-3). 32pp. Korean-born Jessie believes that when he becomes an American citizen he will get a new face like his adoptive American parents. (Rev: BL 5/15/00; SLJ 8/00)

5737 Davies, Sally J. K. *Why Did We Have to Move Here?* (K–3). Illus. 1997, Carolrhoda $15.95 (978-1-57505-046-1). 32pp. After William and his family move to a new home, he has difficulty making friends. (Rev: BL 12/15/97; HBG 3/98)

5738 dePaola, Tomie. *Oliver Button Is a Sissy* (K–3). Illus. by author. 1979, Harcourt $14.00 (978-0-15-257852-7); paper $6.00 (978-0-15-668140-7). 48pp. People think Oliver is a sissy until he shines in a talent show as a fine tap dancer.

5739 Dierssen, Andreas. *The Old Red Tractor* (PS–K). Trans. by Marianne Martens. Illus. by Daniel Sohr. 2006, North-South $16.95 (978-0-7358-2088-3). 32pp. Towhead Tony loves his old red tractor until a friend shows up with a brand-new tractor that has a horn. (Rev: BL 9/15/06; SLJ 10/06)

5740 Edwards, Becky. *My Brother Sammy* (PS–2). Illus. by David Armitage. 1999, Millbrook LB $23.90 (978-0-7613-1417-2). An older boy has troubles adjusting to the erratic behavior of his autistic younger brother, Sammy. (Rev: HBG 10/99; SLJ 7/99)

5741 Ehrlich, H. M. *Gotcha, Louie!* (PS–K). Illus. by Emily Bolam. 2002, Houghton $15.00 (978-0-618-19549-7). 32pp. Young Louie gets lost in the tall grass close to the beach, but his mother very cleverly finds him. (Rev: BL 4/15/02; HBG 10/02; SLJ 4/02)

5742 Ehrlich, H. M. *Louie's Goose* (PS–3). Illus. by Emily Bolam. 2000, Houghton $15.00 (978-0-618-03023-1). 32pp. Louie is so attached to his stuffed goose, Rosie, that, although it is falling apart and needs constant repair, he can't part with it. (Rev: BL 3/1/00; HBG 10/00; SLJ 3/00)

5743 Elliott, David. *Finn Throws a Fit!* (PS–1). Illus. by Timothy Basil Ering. 2009, Candlewick $16.99 (978-0-7636-2356-2). 32pp. The emotional rollercoaster of toddler life is depicted in this tale of Finn who definitely does not want his peaches, but after his "fit" subsides he changes his mind. (Rev: BL 7/09; SLJ 9/09)

5744 Ellis, Sarah. *Ben Over Night* (PS–2). Illus. by Kim LaFave. 2005, Fitzhenry & Whiteside $16.95 (978-1-55041-807-1). 32pp. Peter's house is only across the street, but even though Ben loves to play there, he's scared to stay there overnight. (Rev: BL 5/1/05; SLJ 6/05)

5745 Elya, Susan Middleton. *Home at Last* (K–3). Illus. by Felipe Davalos. 2002, Lee & Low $16.95 (978-1-58430-020-5). 32pp. Ana, who has recently arrived from Mexico with her family, helps persuade her mother to attend English-language classes. (Rev: BCCB 9/02; BL 5/1/02; HBG 10/02; SLJ 7/02)

5746 Fernandes, Eugenie. *A Difficult Day* (K–2). Illus. 1999, Kids Can $14.95 (978-0-921103-17-2). 32pp. Poor Melinda has a bad day and a temper tantrum, but it ends with cookies and hugs from an understanding mom. (Rev: BL 5/15/99; HBG 10/99)

5747 Figueredo, D. H. *When This World Was New* (PS–3). Illus. by Enrique O. Sánchez. 1999, Lee & Low $15.95 (978-1-880000-86-1). 32pp. Danilito leaves his warm Caribbean island to migrate with his parents to the U.S., and there he has many unsettling experiences but one outstanding joy — seeing the city transformed by snow. (Rev: BL 6/1–15/99; HBG 10/99; SLJ 7/99)

5748 Fine, Edith Hope. *Under the Lemon Moon* (K–3). Illus. by Rene King Moreno. 1999, Lee & Low $16.95 (978-1-880000-69-4). 32pp. Young Rosalinda learns to cope with loss when a thief steals all the lemons from her pet tree and damages it as well. (Rev: BL 5/15/99; HBG 10/99; SLJ 4/99)

5749 Fitzpatrick, Marie-Louise. *I Am I* (K–3). Illus. by author. 2006, Roaring Brook $16.95 (978-1-59643-054-9). Two children compete for dominance and their hateful words destroy the landscape around them; they eventually work out that peaceful coexistence is a much better strategy. (Rev: SLJ 6/06*)

5750 Fleming, Virginia. *Be Good to Eddie Lee* (K–3). Illus. by Floyd Cooper. 1993, Penguin $16.99 (978-0-399-21993-1). 30pp. Eddie Lee, a boy with Down's syndrome, teaches his neighbor, Christy, to look at the world differently. (Rev: BL 1/15/94; SLJ 2/94)

5751 Foreman, Michael. *A Child's Garden: A Story of Hope* (K–3). Illus. by author. 2009, Candlewick $17.99 (978-0-7636-4271-6). 32pp. In a time of conflict, children from opposing sides find hope and joy in a garden. (Rev: BL 5/1/09; SLJ 6/09)

5752 Fox, Mem. *Harriet, You'll Drive Me Wild!* (PS). Illus. by Marla Frazee. 2000, Harcourt $16.00 (978-0-15-201977-8). 32pp. Harriet is such a pest that her usually patient mother begins to shout at her but then they kiss and make up. (Rev: BCCB 6/00; BL 3/1/00; HB 3/00; HBG 10/00; SLJ 4/00)

5753 Frame, Jeron Ashford. *Yesterday I Had the Blues* (K–2). Illus. by R. Gregory Christie. 2003, Tricycle $14.95 (978-1-58246-084-0). A young African American boy, who's suffered a bout of the blues, ponders the varied moods of his family members and assigns each a color; vibrant illustrations add to the engaging text. (Rev: HBG 4/04; SLJ 10/03)

5754 Freymann, Saxton, and Joost Elffers. *How Are You Peeling? Foods with Moods* (PS–1). Illus. 1999, Scholastic $16.95 (978-0-439-10431-9). 48pp. Collages of fruits and vegetables are used to portray human emotions. (Rev: BL 2/1/00; HBG 3/00; SLJ 1/00) [152.4]

5755 Gehret, Jeanne. *The Don't-Give-Up-Kid and Learning Differences* (K–3). Illus. by Sandra A. DePauw. 1992, Verbal Images paper $9.95 (978-0-88428-110-8). 32pp. A 1st-grader receives special attention to help his dyslexia. (Rev: BL 6/1/90)

5756 Gifaldi, David. *Ben, King of the River* (K–3). Illus. by Layne Johnson. 2001, Whitman $16.99 (978-0-8075-0635-6). 32pp. An older boy is afraid his disabled brother will spoil the family's first camping trip. (Rev: BL 3/1/01; HBG 10/01)

5757 Giff, Patricia Reilly. *Ronald Morgan Goes to Bat* (PS–3). Illus. by Susanna Natti. 1988, Puffin paper $5.99 (978-0-14-050669-3). 32pp. Ronald is so bad a batter that he closes his eyes when the ball comes, but his spirit is unbeatable. Also use: *Watch Out, Ronald Morgan!* (1985). (Rev: BL 6/1/88; HB 9/88; SLJ 9/88)

5758 Gilmore, Rachna. *Grandpa's Clock* (2–4). Illus. by Amy Meissner. 2006, Orca $17.95 (978-1-55143-333-2). Cayley's grandfather promises to make her a special clock, but the project must be put on hold when he has a heart attack and goes to the hospital. (Rev: SLJ 6/06)

5759 Golding, Theresa Martin. *Abby's Asthma and the Big Race* (K–3). Illus. by Margeaux Lucas. 2009, Albert Whitman $16.99 (978-0-8075-0465-9). 32pp. Abby is a fast runner but she has asthma, and this book shows just what she goes through to succeed. (Rev: BL 3/15/09; SLJ 4/09)

5760 Grant, Karima. *Sofie and the City* (PS–2). Illus. by Janet Montecalvo. 2006, Boyds Mills $15.95 (978-1-59078-273-6). A little girl from Senegal yearns for home but learns to appreciate life in the United States when she makes a friend. (Rev: SLJ 5/06)

5761 Gravett, Emily. *Little Mouse's Big Book of Fears* (2–4). Illus. by author. 2008, Simon & Schuster $17.99 (978-1-4050-8948-7). 32pp. Little Mouse talks about his many fears — which include ablutophobia (fear of bathing) and sciaphobia (fear of shadows) — in this sensitive yet humorous book. (Rev: BL 12/1/08; HB 1/09; LMC 3/09; SLJ 10/08*)

5762 Gregory, Nan. *Pink* (K–2). Illus. by Luc Melanson. 2007, Groundwood $17.95 (978-0-88899-781-4). 32pp. Vivi works hard to earn enough to buy the pink doll she covets, and is distressed to find it's already been sold. (Rev: BCCB 10/07; BL 10/1/07; SLJ 11/07)

5763 Grifalconi, Ann. *Tiny's Hat* (K–3). Illus. by author. 1999, HarperCollins LB $14.89 (978-0-06-027655-3). When Tiny's father, a blues player, goes away, the little girl dons her daddy's big black hat and begins to sing the blues. (Rev: HBG 10/99; SLJ 1/99)

5764 Grimm, Edward. *The Doorman* (K–3). Illus. by Ted Lewin. 2000, Orchard LB $17.99 (978-0-531-33280-1). 32pp. Residents in a New York City apartment building mourn the death of the doorman who meant so much to them. (Rev: BCCB 7–8/00; BL 7/00; HBG 3/01; SLJ 10/00)

5765 Gunning, Monica. *A Shelter in Our Car* (K–3). Illus. by Elaine Pedlar. 2004, Children's Book Pr. $16.95 (978-0-89239-183-7). 32pp. Jamaican-born Zettie and her mother live in the backseat of their car while they try to make a real life for themselves. (Rev: BL 4/1/04)

5766 Harrison, Troon. *Aaron's Awful Allergies* (PS–1). Illus. by Eugenie Fernandes. 1998, Kids Can $14.95 (978-1-55074-299-2). Aaron is unhappy when he has to get rid of his pets because of his allergies. (Rev: HBG 10/98; SLJ 3/98)

5767 Headley, Justina Chen. *The Patch* (PS–2). Illus. by Mitch Vane. 2006, Charlesbridge $15.95 (978-1-58089-049-6). 32pp. Five-year-old Becca, an aspiring ballerina, at first balks at wearing an eye patch to correct her lazy eye but finds a way to turn the patch into a fashion asset. (Rev: BL 2/1/06; SLJ 2/06)

5768 Heide, Florence Parry, and Roxanne H. Pierce. *Oh, Grow Up!* (K–4). Illus. by Nadine Bernard Westcott. 1996, Orchard LB $16.99 (978-0-531-08771-8). 32pp. Humorous verses and imaginative drawings illustrate everyday problems in growing up, such as dealing with brothers and sisters. (Rev: BCCB 3/96; BL 3/1/96; SLJ 4/96)

5769 Heitler, Susan M. *David Decides About Thumb-sucking: A Motivating Story for Children and an Informative Guide for Parents* (PS–3). Illus. by Paula Singer. 1996, Reading Matters paper $13.95 (978-0-9614780-2-5). 52pp. This photo-essay con-centrates on David and his decision to give up his thumb sucking. (Rev: BL 11/1/85; SLJ 2/86)

5770 Henkes, Kevin. *Bird Lake Moon* (5–7). 2008, Greenwillow $15.99 (978-0-06-147076-9). 192pp. Unsettled because his parents are divorcing, Mitch hopes to move into the empty house next door and is annoyed when the family who owns it turns up; he decides to trick them into thinking their dead son is haunting them, a choice that has consequences when he becomes friends with the son. (Rev: BL 3/15/08; SLJ 3/08) ⌒

5771 Holcomb, Nan. *Andy Finds a Turtle* (K–3). Illus. by Dot Yoder. Series: Turtle Books. 1992, Jason LB $15.95 (978-0-944727-13-3); paper $9.95 (978-0-944727-02-7). 32pp. The story of Andy, a young boy with cerebral palsy. Two other books about children with physical problems are: *Danny and the Merry-Go-Round* and *How about a Hug* (both 1992). All three are reissues.

5772 Hopkins, Beverly H. *Changes: My Family and Me* (PS–2). Illus. by Sarah K. Hoctor. 1999, Child & Family $8.95 (978-0-87868-723-7). As seen through the eyes of the oldest child in a family, this account tells of the changes that a family experi-ences when parents divorce, remarry, and have both stepchildren and children of their own. (Rev: SLJ 6/99)

5773 Howard, Arthur. *The Hubbub Above* (K–2). Illus. by author. 2005, Harcourt $16.00 (978-0-15-204592-0). Sydney is very happy living on the 52nd floor of Ivory Towers until elephant neighbors called the Kabooms move in and destroy her peace. (Rev: SLJ 5/05)

5774 Howard, Elizabeth F. *Virgie Goes to School with Us Boys* (K–2). Illus. by E. B. Lewis. 2000, Simon & Schuster $16.00 (978-0-689-80076-4). 32pp. Virgie, youngest in a family of boys, vows that she will accompany her brothers when they walk the seven miles to school every Monday morn-ing. (Rev: BCCB 2/00; BL 11/1/99*; HBG 10/00; SLJ 3/00)

5775 Hughes, Shirley. *Alfie and the Birthday Sur-prise* (PS–K). Illus. 1998, Lothrop $16.00 (978-0-688-15187-4). 32pp. Alfie, an English toddler, helps his neighbors adjust to the death of their pet cat, Smoky. (Rev: BCCB 3/98; BL 3/1/98; HB 5/98; HBG 10/98; SLJ 3/98)

5776 Hutchins, Hazel. *Believing Sophie* (K–3). Illus. by Dorothy Donohue. 1995, Whitman LB $14.95 (978-0-8075-0625-7). 32pp. Sophie is falsely accused of stealing cough drops from her local store. (Rev: BL 9/1/95; SLJ 1/96)

5777 Isadora, Rachel. *Ben's Trumpet* (K–3). Illus. by author. 1979, Greenwillow $17.99 (978-0-688-80194-6); Morrow paper $6.99 (978-0-688-10988-2). 32pp. A young African American boy dreams of becoming a trumpet player and eventually is taken to a jazz club by a musician.

5778 Isherwood, Shirley. *Flora the Frog* (K–3). Illus. by Anna C. Leplar. 2000, Peachtree $16.95 (978-1-56145-223-1). 32pp. Flora is so upset at playing a frog in the class play, that she throws away the frog costume that her mother and aunt have made. (Rev: BCCB 11/00; BL 9/15/00; HBG 3/01; SLJ 10/00)

5779 Jenkins, Emily. *The Little Bit Scary People* (PS–2). Illus. by Alexandra Boiger. 2008, Hyperion $16.99 (978-1-4231-0075-1). 32pp. A little girl dis-covers that people are less scary if she imagines how they behave in other situations. (Rev: BCCB 11/08; BL 12/15/08; HB 11/08; LMC 1/09; SLJ 9/08)

5780 Jennings, Patrick. *The Lightning Bugs* (2–4). Illus. by Anna Alter. 2003, Holiday House $15.95 (978-0-8234-1673-8). 55pp. Ike and his sister Mem join their friends in catching lightning bugs, but Ike becomes distressed when there is cruelty involved. (Rev: HBG 4/04; SLJ 8/03)

5781 Jimenez, Francisco. *La Mariposa* (K–3). Illus. by Simon Silva. 1998, Houghton $16.00 (978-0-395-81663-9). 40pp. Francisco becomes adept at drawing butterflies and, as a gesture of reconcilia-tion, offers one of his drawings to the boy who beat him up on the playground. (Rev: BL 3/1/99; HBG 3/99; SLJ 11/98)

5782 Johnson, Vincent L. *Of Corn Silk and Black Braids* (K–3). Illus. by Linda Crockett. 2005, Marzetta $17.95 (978-0-9657033-2-1). Sarah, a young African American girl, envies Mary Beth who has lovely blond hair, but with a little help from her mother and aunt, the girl learns to like her-self just the way she is. (Rev: SLJ 12/05)

5783 Jordan, Deloris, and Roslyn M. Jordan. *Salt in His Shoes: Michael Jordan in Pursuit of a Dream* (K–4). Illus. by Kadir Nelson. 2000, Simon & Schuster $16.95 (978-0-689-83371-7). 32pp. A fic-tionalized tale about a youthful Michael Jordan whose mother (the author) encourages him to pur-sue his basketball dreams even though he's the shortest boy on the team. (Rev: BL 2/1/01; HBG 3/01)

5784 Joslin, Sesyle. *What Do You Say, Dear?* (1–3). Illus. by Maurice Sendak. 1958, HarperCollins LB $17.89 (978-0-06-023074-6); paper $6.95 (978-0-06-443112-5). 48pp. Humorous handbook on man-ners for young ladies and gentlemen of 6 to 8. Also use: *What Do You Do, Dear?* (1958).

5785 Karkowsku, Nancy. *Grandma's Soup* (PS–3). Illus. by Shelly O. Haas. 1989, Kar-Ben paper $5.95 (978-0-930494-99-5). Several grandchildren gradu-ally adjust to the fact that their grandmother has Alzheimer's disease. (Rev: SLJ 12/89)

5786 Keats, Ezra Jack. *Louie* (PS–K). Illus. by author. 1983, Greenwillow $15.89 (978-0-688-02383-6). 32pp. Louie, a silent child, makes his first friend, a puppet, and is allowed to keep it for his very own.

5787 Kelley, Marty. *Winter Woes* (PS–2). Illus. by author. 2005, Zino $12.95 (978-1-55933-306-1). A little boy imagines in humorous detail the myriad dangers that might befall him should he go out into the snow. (Rev: SLJ 4/05)

5788 Kibbey, Marsha. *My Grammy: A Book About Alzheimer's Disease* (1–3). Illus. by Karen Ritz. 1988, Carolrhoda paper $4.95 (978-0-87614-544-9). 32pp. Eight-year-old Amy and her family must cope with Grammy's worsening Alzheimer's disease. (Rev: BL 7/88; SLJ 10/88)

5789 Klassen, Heather. *I Don't Want to Go to Justin's House Anymore* (PS–2). Illus. by Beth Jepson. 1999, Child & Family paper $6.95 (978-0-87868-724-4). Collin witnesses child abuse at friend Justin's house, and gets his mother to promise to get help. (Rev: SLJ 3/00)

5790 Kolbisen, Irene M. *Wiggle-Butts and Up-Faces* (PS–K). Illus. by Sandy D. Zmolek. 1989, I Think I Can LB $14.95 (978-1-877863-00-4). 32pp. Ingrid's young brother is afraid of taking beginner swimming lessons. (Rev: BL 12/1/89)

5791 Kostecki-Shaw, Jenny Sue. *My Travelin' Eye* (K–2). Illus. by author. 2008, Holt $16.95 (978-0-8050-8169-5). 40pp. When Jenny Sue's eye problems mean she has to wear a patch, her mother helps her create bright, imaginative eyewear. (Rev: BL 4/1/08; SLJ 6/08)

5792 Kraus, Jeanne R. *Annie's Plan: Taking Charge of Schoolwork and Homework* (2–5). Illus. by Charles Beyl. 2007, Magination $14.95 (978-1-59147-481-4). 47pp. Annie is a smart girl but she has trouble staying focused, so her parents and teacher help her organize herself for more efficient homework; includes a note for adults. (Rev: SLJ 4/07)

5793 Krauss, Ruth. *A Very Special House* (PS–K). Illus. by Maurice Sendak. 1953, HarperCollins LB $17.89 (978-0-06-023456-0). 32pp. A little boy tells what it would be like in his very special house — no one would ever say "Stop, Stop."

5794 Krisher, Trudy. *Kathy's Hats: A Story of Hope* (PS–3). Illus. by Nadine Bernard Westcott. 1992, Whitman LB $16.99 (978-0-8075-4116-6). 32pp. When Kathy undergoes chemotherapy for cancer, she finds a new reason to wear her hats. (Rev: BCCB 10/92; BL 10/1/92; SLJ 6/91)

5795 Krishnaswami, Uma. *The Closet Ghosts* (PS–2). Illus. by Shiraaz Bhabha. 2006, Children's Book Pr. $16.95 (978-0-89239-208-7). 32pp. Anu has just moved and is distressed to find ghosts in her closet; with the help of a Hindu god and the friends she finds at her new school, all ends well. (Rev: SLJ 6/06)

5796 Kroll, Virginia. *Brianna Breathes Easy: A Story About Asthma* (1–3). Illus. by Jayoung Cho. 2005, Whitman $16.99 (978-0-8075-0880-0). 32pp. Brianna learns she has asthma and how to control it in this informative story that will ease the fears of children with this condition. (Rev: BL 3/1/05)

5797 Kroll, Virginia. *Ryan Respects* (K–2). Illus. by Paige Billin-Frye. Series: The Way I Act. 2006, Albert Whitman $15.99 (978-0-8075-6946-7). 24pp. After unkindly teasing his friend Doug, young Ryan gets his comeuppance and also learns some important lessons about the importance of respecting others' feelings. (Rev: BL 4/15/06; SLJ 3/06)

5798 Lagercrantz, Rose, and Samuel Lagercrantz. *Is It Magic?* (K–3). Trans. by Paul Norlen. Illus. by Eva Eriksson. 1991, R&S $13.95 (91-29-59182-1). Young Pete and Cilla are in love until the class bully steps in. (Rev: SLJ 3/91)

5799 Laguna, Sofie. *Bad Buster* (1–2). Illus. by Leigh Hobbs. Series: Nibbles. 2006, Running Pr. paper $3.95 (978-0-7624-2626-3). 60pp. Buster is very good at being bad but when he stops a burglary and is praised for his good deed, will he decide to change or go back to his bad ways? An easy chapter book that may appeal to reluctant readers. (Rev: SLJ 3/07)

5800 Lampert, Emily. *A Little Touch of Monster* (PS–1). Illus. by Melanie Kroupa. 1986, Little, Brown LB $12.95 (978-0-316-51287-9). 32pp. No one listens to Parker, so he turns into a bit of a monster; then they listen to him too much, granting almost his every wish. (Rev: BCCB 5/86; BL 3/15/86; HB 5/86)

5801 Lears, Laurie. *Ian's Walk: A Story About Autism* (2–3). Illus. by Karen Ritz. 1998, Whitman $16.99 (978-0-8075-3480-9). 32pp. Narrator Julie and her sister Tara take their autistic younger brother, Ian, for a walk. Although they are disturbed by his unusual reactions to events and have ambivalent feelings toward him, they show their love by rescuing him when he wanders away. (Rev: BL 4/1/98; HB 5/98; HBG 10/98; SLJ 9/98)

5802 Lears, Laurie. *Nathan's Wish: A Story About Cerebral Palsy* (1–3). Illus. by Stacey Schuett. 2005, Albert Whitman $16.99 (978-0-8075-7101-9). Nathan, who has cerebral palsy, is encouraged when his neighbor finds a way to help an injured owl. (Rev: SLJ 7/05)

5803 Leonetti, Mike. *The Goalie Mask* (2–4). Illus. by Shayne Letain. Series: Hockey Heroes. 2004, Raincoast $15.95 (978-1-55192-703-9). A young player learns from his grandfather about the invention of the mask that protects players' faces from hockey pucks. (Rev: SLJ 2/05)

5804 Leonetti, Mike. *Gretzky's Game* (1–3). Illus. by Greg Banning. 2006, Raincoast $15.95 (978-1-55192-851-7). 32pp. Ryan, a young hockey player who's small for his age, patterns his playing style after that of his idol, Wayne Gretzky. (Rev: BL 2/15/06)

5805 Levy, Janice. *Alley Oops* (1–4). Illus. by Cynthia B. Decker. 2005, Flashlight $15.95 (978-0-9729225-4-8). J.J. has been bullying an overweight boy called Patrick, so J.J.'s father sits down with him and tells him a story about his own behavior as a boy. (Rev: SLJ 8/05)

5806 Levy, Janice. *Totally Uncool* (K–3). Illus. by Chris Monroe. 1998, Carolrhoda $15.95 (978-1-57505-306-6). 32pp. Alex is not impressed with Elizabeth, Dad's new girlfriend, until Elizabeth helps cure her headaches and designs a prize-winning costume for her. (Rev: BCCB 2/99; BL 2/15/99; HBG 10/99; SLJ 3/99)

5807 Liao, Jimmy. *The Sound of Colors: A Journey of the Imagination* (1–5). Adapted by Sarah L. Thomson. Illus. by author. 2005, Little, Brown $16.99 (978-0-316-93992-8). A blind girl imagines a colorful journey over land and sea as she makes her way through the subway. (Rev: SLJ 9/05)

5808 Lichtenheld, Tom. *What Are You So Grumpy About?* (K–3). Illus. 2003, Little, Brown $15.95 (978-0-316-59236-9). 32pp. Humorous double-spread cartoons show situations that could provoke a bad temper. (Rev: BL 3/15/03; HBG 10/03; SLJ 4/03)

5809 Lindgren, Barbro. *Sam's Ball* (PS). Illus. by Eva Eriksson. 1983, Morrow paper $7.99 (978-0-688-02359-1). 32pp. A book in which a toddler shares his toy with a kitty. Four others in this series are: *Sam's Car; Sam's Cookie; Sam's Teddy Bear* (all 1982); *Sam's Bath* (1983).

5810 Lobby, Ted. *Jessica and the Wolf: A Story for Children Who Have Bad Dreams* (PS–1). Illus. by Tennessee Dixon. 1990, Brunner $11.95 (978-0-945354-22-2); paper $8.95 (978-0-945354-21-5). 32pp. Parents help their daughter when she has a recurring nightmare about a wolf. (Rev: BL 9/1/90)

5811 Lottridge, Celia B. *Something Might Be Hiding* (PS–K). Illus. by Paul Zwolak. 1996, Douglas & McIntyre $14.95 (978-0-88899-176-8). 24pp. A child feels the stress of moving to a new house. (Rev: BL 8/96; SLJ 6/96)

5812 Ludwig, Trudy. *Just Kidding* (K–3). Illus. by Adam Gustavson. 2006, Tricycle $15.95 (978-1-58246-163-2). 32pp. D.J. gets help from his father and a teacher when Vince's bullying becomes upsetting; front matter offers advice to adults and back matter provides tips for children. (Rev: BL 4/15/06; SLJ 6/06)

5813 McCourt, Lisa. *Chicken Soup for Little Souls: The New Kid and the Cookie Thief* (K–2). Illus. by Mary O. Young. Series: Chicken Soup for Little Souls. 1998, Health Communications $14.95 (978-1-55874-588-9). 32pp. Julie mistakenly thinks that the boy next to her on the school bus has eaten her cookies and forces herself to apologize. (Rev: BL 2/1/99; HBG 3/99; SLJ 12/98)

5814 McKissack, Patricia C. *The Honest-to-Goodness Truth* (PS–3). Illus. by Giselle Potter. 2000, Simon & Schuster $16.00 (978-0-689-82668-9). 32pp. When Libby tells the honest truth to her friends and classmates, she finds that she can hurt their feelings. (Rev: BCCB 2/00; BL 12/15/99; HBG 10/00; SLJ 1/00)

5815 McNamara, Margaret. *The Pumpkin Patch* (PS–1). Illus. by Mike Gordon. Series: Robin Hill School. 2003, Simon & Schuster paper $3.99 (978-0-689-85874-1). 32pp. Katie's classmates laugh at her pumpkin, saying it's too small, but it's just the right size for a pie. (Rev: HBG 4/04; SLJ 10/03)

5816 Magorian, Michelle. *Who's Going to Take Care of Me?* (PS–K). Illus. by James G. Hale. 1990, HarperCollins $13.95 (978-0-06-024105-6). 32pp. When Eric's older sister starts school, he wonders who will take care of him. (Rev: BL 11/15/90; HB 1/91; SLJ 12/90)

5817 Mauser, Pat Rhoads. *Patti's Pet Gorilla* (2–4). Illus. by Diane Palmisciano. 1991, Avon paper $2.95 (978-0-380-71039-3). 64pp. Patti wants to impress her classmates at show-and-tell, so she tells them she has a pet gorilla. (Rev: BCCB 9/87; BL 3/15/87; SLJ 8/87)

5818 Mayer, Mercer. *There Are Monsters Everywhere* (PS–2). Illus. by author. 2005, Dial $15.99 (978-0-8037-0621-7). Fearful of the monsters that follow him everywhere he goes, a young boy takes karate lessons. (Rev: SLJ 12/05)

5819 Mayer, Mercer. *You're the Scaredy-Cat* (K–2). Illus. by author. 1991, Rain Bird paper $5.95 (978-1-879920-01-9). 40pp. Two young boys decide to spend the night camping out in the backyard.

5820 Meddaugh, Susan. *Just Teenie* (PS–2). Illus. 2006, Houghton $16.00 (978-0-618-68565-3). 32pp. Justine is totally frustrated by her tininess until an out-of-control plant gives her a different perspective on life. (Rev: BL 4/15/06; SLJ 6/06)

5821 Medearis, Angela Shelf. *Annie's Gifts* (K–3). Illus. by Anna Rich. 1995, Just Us Bks. $14.95 (978-0-940975-30-9); paper $6.95 (978-0-940975-31-6). Annie is upset because everyone in her family except her is musically talented. (Rev: BCCB 4/95; SLJ 9/95)

5822 Miller, Elizabeth I. *Just Like Home: Como en Mi Tierra* (PS–3). Illus. by Mira Reisberg. 1999, Whitman $16.99 (978-0-8075-4068-8). 32pp. A Hispanic girl gradually fits into American life in this bilingual picture book. (Rev: BL 12/1/99; HBG 3/00; SLJ 12/99)

5823 Miller, Kathryn Ann. *Did My First Mother Love Me? A Story for an Adopted Child* (K–3). Illus. by Jami Moffett. 1994, Morning Glory $12.95 (978-0-930934-85-9). 47pp. A girl learns the reasons why her real mother put her up for adoption and is comforted by this knowledge. (Rev: SLJ 7/94)

5824 Miller, William. *Night Golf* (1–3). Illus. by Cedric Lucas. 1999, Lee & Low $15.95 (978-1-880000-79-3). This is the story of an African American boy in the late 1950s, the prejudice he encounters when he wants to play golf on an all-white course, and how he perseveres and overcomes this problem. (Rev: HBG 10/99; SLJ 6/99)

5825 Millman, Isaac. *Moses Goes to a Concert* (K–4). Illus. 1998, Farrar $16.00 (978-0-374-35067-3). 40pp. This picture book, written in both English and American Sign Language, portrays the everyday experiences of a deaf child, Moses, and of a special occasion when he and his classmates go to a concert. (Rev: BL 4/15/98*; HBG 10/98; SLJ 4/98)

5826 Millman, Isaac. *Moses Goes to School* (PS–3). Illus. 2000, Farrar $16.00 (978-0-374-35069-7).

32pp. This story, written in both English and sign language, tells how Moses and his friends learn at their special school for the deaf. (Rev: BL 8/00; HBG 3/01; SLJ 8/00)

5827 Millman, Isaac. *Moses Goes to the Circus* (PS–2). Illus. by author. 2003, Farrar $16.00 (978-0-374-35064-2). Moses, who is deaf, and his family go to a circus for vision- and hearing-impaired children. (Rev: BL 4/15/03; HBG 10/03; SLJ 3/03)

5828 Mochizuki, Ken. *Baseball Saved Us* (2–4). Illus. by Dom Lee. 1993, Lee & Low $15.95 (978-1-880000-01-4). 32pp. A Japanese American boy gains acceptance playing an excellent game of baseball learned while an internee during World War II. (Rev: BCCB 5/93; BL 4/15/93; HB 7/93; SLJ 6/93)

5829 Montserrat, Pep. *Ms. Rubinstein's Beauty* (K–3). Illus. 2006, Sterling $14.95 (978-1-4027-3063-4). 32pp. A bearded lady and a man with an elephantine nose — who appear as freaks in different circuses — discover the inner beauty in each other during an encounter in the park. (Rev: BL 9/15/06; SLJ 1/07)

5830 Moore, Julianne. *Freckleface Strawberry* (PS–2). Illus. by LeUyen Pham. 2007, Bloomsbury $16.95 (978-1-59990-107-7). 32pp. A 7-year-old girl is unhappy with her many freckles. (Rev: SLJ 10/07)

5831 Munsch, Robert, and Saoussan Askar. *From Far Away* (K–3). Illus. by Michael Martchenko. 1995, Firefly LB $16.95 (978-1-55037-397-4); paper $5.95 (978-1-55037-396-7). 24pp. Saoussan, a war refugee, has problems adjusting to her new home in Canada. (Rev: BL 1/1–15/96; SLJ 3/96)

5832 Napoli, Donna Jo. *Flamingo Dream* (K–3). Illus. by Cathie Felstead. 2002, HarperCollins LB $16.89 (978-0-688-17863-5). 32pp. A young narrator suffers the loss of her beloved father to cancer. (Rev: BL 4/15/02; HB 7/02; HBG 10/02; SLJ 5/02)

5833 Ness, Evaline. *Sam, Bangs and Moonshine* (K–2). Illus. by author. 1966, Holt $15.95 (978-0-8050-0314-7); paper $6.95 (978-0-8050-0315-4). 48pp. A little girl learns to distinguish truth from "moonshine" only after her cat and playmate nearly meet tragedy. Caldecott Medal winner, 1967.

5834 Newman, Leslea. *Saturday Is Pattyday* (PS–3). Illus. by Annette Hegel. 1993, New Victoria LB $14.95 (978-0-934678-52-0); paper $6.95 (978-0-934678-51-3). 24pp. Frankie is unhappy when his two moms break up and one moves to her own apartment. (Rev: BCCB 11/93; BL 11/1/93)

5835 Newsome, Jill. *Dream Dancer* (PS–2). Illus. by Claudio Munoz. 2002, HarperCollins LB $15.89 (978-0-06-001322-6). 48pp. A ballerina doll given to her by her grandmother helps Lily through her long recovery after an injury leaves her unable to dance. (Rev: BL 1/1–15/02; HBG 10/02; SLJ 3/02)

5836 Old, Wendie. *Stacy Had a Little Sister* (PS–2). Illus. by Judith Friedman. 1995, Whitman LB $16.99 (978-0-8075-7598-7). 32pp. When Stacy's baby sister dies of SIDS, she feels confused and guilty. (Rev: BCCB 5/95; BL 1/1/95; SLJ 2/95)

5837 Osilaja, Peter. *My Body Is Mine!* (K–2). Illus. by Gary Phillips. 2007, KidSafety of America LB

$14.95 (978-1-884413-83-4); paper $8.95 (978-1-884413-84-1). Michael's first sleepover is the setting for this story with lessons on good and bad touching and Internet safety. (Rev: SLJ 8/07)

5838 Paterson, Katherine. *The Smallest Cow in the World* (PS–2). Illus. by Jane Brown. 1991, HarperCollins paper $3.99 (978-0-06-444164-3). 64pp. When he and his family move to another farm, Marvin misses Rosie, the cow he left behind. (Rev: BCCB 1/92*; BL 9/15/91; HB 9/91; SLJ 1/92*)

5839 Peacock, Carol Antoinette. *Mommy Far, Mommy Near: An Adoption Story* (K–2). Illus. by Shawn Costello Brownell. 2000, Whitman $16.99 (978-0-8075-5234-6). 32pp. In spite of her loving Caucasian American family, Elizabeth, an adopted Chinese girl, sometimes wonders why her real mother gave her up and why there wasn't enough room for her in China. (Rev: BL 3/15/00; HBG 10/00; SLJ 5/00)

5840 Peterson, Jeanne Whitehouse. *I Have a Sister, My Sister Is Deaf* (1–3). Illus. by Deborah Kogan Ray. 1977, HarperCollins LB $15.89 (978-0-06-024702-7); paper $6.99 (978-0-06-443059-3). 32pp. About a young girl's adjustment to deafness.

5841 Polacco, Patricia. *Thank You, Mr. Falker* (K–4). Illus. 1998, Penguin $16.99 (978-0-399-23166-7). 40pp. Based on the author's personal experiences, this is the story of Trisha, who was able to draw beautifully but hid the fact that she couldn't read until she got special help in the 5th grade. (Rev: BCCB 6/98; BL 5/1/98; HBG 10/98; SLJ 6/98)

5842 Pollack, Eileen. *Whisper Whisper Jesse, Whisper Whisper Josh: A Story About AIDS* (K–4). Illus. by Bruce Gilfoy. 1992, Advantage LB $16.95 (978-0-9624828-4-7); paper $5.95 (978-0-9624828-3-0). 32pp. Jesse's uncle, Josh, who is dying of AIDS, comes to stay with Jesse's family. (Rev: BL 3/15/93)

5843 Prats, Joan de Déu. *Sebastian's Roller Skates* (PS–2). Illus. by Francesc Rovira. 2005, Kane $15.95 (978-1-929132-81-2). 40pp. Shy Sebastian finds his self-confidence and ability to express himself growing after he masters roller skating. (Rev: BL 11/1/05; SLJ 10/05)

5844 Ransom, Jeanie Franz. *I Don't Want to Talk About It* (K–3). Illus. by Kathryn Kunz Finney. 2000, Magination $14.95 (978-1-55798-664-1); paper $9.95 (978-1-55798-703-7). 28pp. A young girl whose parents are divorcing talks about her feelings and means of coping. (Rev: SLJ 2/01)

5845 Raschka, Chris. *The Purple Balloon* (1–3). Illus. 2007, Random $16.99 (978-0-375-84146-0). 32pp. Designed primarily for terminally ill children and their friends and family members, this book deals sensitively with the issues that face those who are dying and the people who love them, emphasizing how many people are there to help. (Rev: BL 4/1/07)

5846 Recorvits, Helen. *My Name Is Yoon* (K–2). Illus. by Gabi Swiatkowska. 2003, Farrar $16.00 (978-0-374-35114-4). 32pp. Yoon, a Korean immigrant child, is unhappy in America until she begins to feel at home in her new and different surroundings. (Rev: BL 3/15/03; HBG 10/03; SLJ 5/03)

5847 Reynolds, Marilynn. *Goodbye to Griffith Street* (K–2). Illus. by Renn Benoit. 2004, Orca $16.95 (978-1-55143-285-4). It snows on John's last day on Griffith Street (his parents are getting divorced and he and his mother must move), and John decides to leave his friends and neighbors with the gift of snow angels and stars. (Rev: SLJ 1/05)

5848 Riggs, Shannon. *Not in Room 204* (1–3). Illus. by Jaime Zollars. 2007, Albert Whitman $16.99 (978-0-8075-5764-8). 32pp. A class about "stranger danger" gives Regina the courage to tell her teacher about her father's inappropriate behavior; a sensitive story that provides no details. (Rev: BL 2/1/07)

5849 Robberecht, Thierry. *Angry Dragon* (PS–2). Illus. by Philippe Goossens. 2004, Clarion $15.00 (978-0-618-47430-1). 32pp. A little boy pictures himself transformed into a fire-breathing dragon every time his anger gets out of control. (Rev: BL 1/1–15/05)

5850 Robberecht, Thierry. *Sam Is Never Scared* (PS–2). Illus. by Philippe Goossens. 2006, Clarion $12.00 (978-0-618-73278-4). 29pp. Sam acts brave in public but hides his fears of monsters and ghosts until the day a huge spider lands on his hand; his father reassures him that everyone is afraid of something. (Rev: SLJ 10/06)

5851 Rodriguez, Luis J. *America Is Her Name* (2–4). Illus. by Carlos Vazquez. 1998, Curbstone $15.95 (978-1-880684-40-5). Lonely in her barrio home in Chicago, America Soliz learns to express herself in poetry. (Rev: HBG 10/98; SLJ 9/98)

5852 Rosenberry, Vera. *Vera Runs Away* (PS–3). Illus. 2000, Holt $16.00 (978-0-8050-6267-0). 32pp. Vera feels so underappreciated at home when she receives a straight-A report card that she decides to run away. (Rev: BL 10/15/00; HBG 3/01; SLJ 11/00)

5853 Rosenthal, Amy Krouse. *It's Not Fair!* (PS–3). Illus. by Tom Lichtenheld. 2008, HarperCollins $16.99 (978-0-06-115257-3). 40pp. "Why'd I get the smaller half?" "Why does my team always lose?" Children, but also animals and inanimate objects, air their complaints. (Rev: BCCB 6/08; BL 4/15/08; SLJ 4/08)

5854 Rotner, Shelley, and Sheila Kelly. *Something's Different* (K–3). Illus. 2002, Millbrook LB $22.90 (978-0-7613-1923-8). 32pp. A boy tries to understand his parents' marital problems. (Rev: BL 3/1/02; HBG 10/02; SLJ 8/02)

5855 Say, Allen. *Allison* (PS–3). Illus. 1997, Houghton $17.00 (978-0-395-85895-0). 32pp. Little Allison, an Asian girl, is upset when she learns that she has been adopted by her Caucasian parents. (Rev: BL 12/15/97*; HBG 3/98; SLJ 10/97)

5856 Say, Allen. *Emma's Rug* (PS–3). Illus. 1996, Houghton $16.95 (978-0-395-74294-5). 32pp. Emma is inconsolable when she loses the rug that has been the inspiration for her art. (Rev: BCCB 11/96; BL 10/1/96; HB 9/96; SLJ 9/96)

5857 Scacco, Linda. *Always My Grandpa: A Story for Children About Alzheimer's Disease* (1–3). Illus.

by Nicole Wong. 2006, Magination $14.95 (978-1-59147-311-4); paper $8.95 (978-1-59147-312-1). 48pp. Daniel is sad to see his grandfather changing during one summer at the beach house, and he is encouraged to discuss his feelings with his family. (Rev: SLJ 6/07)

5858 Schick, Eleanor. *Mama* (K–3). Illus. 2000, Marshall Cavendish $15.95 (978-0-7614-5060-3). 32pp. A mother's death and the ensuing sorrow, acceptance, and cherishing of memories are the subjects of this picture book, seen through a young daughter's eyes. (Rev: BL 2/15/00; HBG 10/00; SLJ 5/00)

5859 Schotter, Roni. *Room for Rabbit* (PS–2). Illus. by Cyd Moore. 2003, Clarion $15.00 (978-0-618-18183-4). 32pp. Kara finds that her father's new wife is taking up too much space and uses her rabbit as her spokesperson. (Rev: BL 3/1/03; HBG 10/03; SLJ 4/03)

5860 Seeger, Pete, and Paul Dubois Jacobs. *The Deaf Musicians* (K–3). Illus. by R. Gregory Christie. 2006, Putnam $16.99 (978-0-399-24316-5). When jazz pianist Lee loses his hearing, he has to leave the group he's been playing with, but while studying sign language at a school for the deaf he meets Max, a sax player, and together they start up a sign-language band. (Rev: SLJ 11/06*)

5861 Sendak, Maurice. *Pierre: A Cautionary Tale in Five Chapters and a Prologue* (K–3). Illus. by author. 1962, HarperCollins LB $16.89 (978-0-06-025965-5). 48pp. The story about a young boy whose motto is "I don't care."

5862 Senisi, Ellen B. *All Kinds of Friends, Even Green!* (K–4). Photos by author. 2002, Woodbine $15.95 (978-1-890627-35-5). Wheelchair-bound Zaki chooses a neighbor's iguana for his school assignment, because the plucky animal manages to cope despite missing toes. (Rev: HBG 10/03; SLJ 11/02)

5863 Shange, Ntozake. *White Wash* (PS–2). Illus. by Michael Sporn. 1997, Walker $15.95 (978-0-8027-8490-2). Helene-Angel and her brother are attacked by a group of white thugs who cover her face with white paint and traumatize her so much that she doesn't want to return to school. (Rev: HBG 3/98; SLJ 5/98)

5864 Shannon, David. *A Bad Case of Stripes* (1–3). Illus. 1998, Scholastic $16.99 (978-0-590-92997-4). 32pp. Camilla's desire to please and be popular causes her some problems. (Rev: BCCB 3/98; BL 1/1–15/98; HBG 10/98; SLJ 3/98)

5865 Shannon, David. *Too Many Toys* (PS–3). Illus. by author. 2008, Scholastic $16.99 (978-0-439-49029-0). 32pp. Spencer's room looks like a Toys R Us aisle and his mom rules that some of them have got to go, forcing Spencer to make some difficult decisions. (Rev: BL 10/1/08; LMC 1/09; SLJ 1/09)

5866 Shavick, Andrea. *You'll Grow Soon, Alex* (PS–1). Illus. by Russell Ayto. 2000, Walker $15.95 (978-0-8027-8736-1). 32pp. Alex tries everything including diet and exercise to hasten his growth but later decides that being tall has its disadvantages. (Rev: BL 10/15/00; HBG 10/01; SLJ 10/00)

5867 Shin, Sun Yung. *Cooper's Lesson* (PS–3). Trans. by Min Paek. Illus. by Kim Cogan. 2004, Children's Book Pr. $16.95 (978-0-89239-193-6). 32pp. Cooper's mother is Korean and his father is white, resulting in some confusion for the young boy; the story is told in English and Korean. (Rev: BL 3/15/04*; SLJ 5/04)

5868 Simon, Norma. *I Wish I Had My Father* (2–4). Illus. by Arieh Zeldich. 1983, Whitman LB $13.95 (978-0-8075-3522-6). 32pp. A young boy wishes his divorced father was back with him.

5869 Smothers, Ethel Footman. *The Hard-Times Jar* (1–3). Illus. by John Holyfield. 2003, Farrar $16.00 (978-0-374-32852-8). 32pp. Emma, the dark-skinned daughter of migrant workers, finds the strength to face her new 3rd-grade classroom in Pennsylvania, and learns to appreciate reading and books. (Rev: BL 8/03; HBG 4/04; SLJ 10/03)

5870 Soto, Gary. *My Little Car* (PS–2). Illus. by Pam Paparone. 2006, Putnam $15.99 (978-0-399-23220-6). 32pp. Teresa loves the low-rider pedal-car that her grandfather gives her, but over time its allure fades and she starts to neglect it. (Rev: BL 3/1/06; SLJ 6/06)

5871 Spalding, Andrea, and Janet Wilson. *Me and Mr. Mah* (PS–2). Illus. 2000, Orca $14.95 (978-1-55143-168-0). Ian misses his father after his parents divorce but finds a friend and kindred spirit in Mr. Mah, a neighbor who misses his family in China. (Rev: BL 3/1/03; HBG 9/00; SLJ 3/00)

5872 Spelman, Cornelia Maude. *After Charlotte's Mom Died* (K–2). Illus. by Judith Friedman. 1996, Whitman LB $15.99 (978-0-8075-0196-2). 32pp. Charlotte feels conflicting emotions, such as anger and fear, as she adjusts to her mother's death. (Rev: BL 4/15/96; SLJ 8/96)

5873 Spelman, Cornelia Maude. *Mama and Daddy Bear's Divorce* (PS–1). Illus. by Kathy Parkinson. 1998, Whitman $15.99 (978-0-8075-5221-6). 32pp. Though animals are used as characters, this is a realistic story about the effects of divorce. It offers the comforting message that love continues even through separation. (Rev: BL 12/1/98; HBG 3/99; SLJ 9/98)

5874 Spelman, Cornelia Maude. *When I Feel Jealous* (PS–1). Illus. by Kathy Parkinson. Series: The Way I Feel. 2003, Whitman LB $15.99 (978-0-8075-8886-4). A little bear talks about the sorts of things that make her jealous and what she does to cope with such feelings. (Rev: HBG 4/04; SLJ 10/03)

5875 Spinelli, Eileen. *Wanda's Monster* (K–2). Illus. by Nancy Hayashi. 2002, Whitman $15.95 (978-0-8075-8656-3). 32pp. Granny is the only one who believes there's a monster in Wanda's closet, but points out that it can't be much fun for the monster. (Rev: BL 12/1/02; HB 1/03; HBG 3/03; SLJ 10/02)

5876 Stauffacher, Sue. *Harry Sue* (5–8). 2005, Knopf LB $17.99 (978-0-375-93274-8). 272pp. Both her parents are in prison and 11-year-old Harry Sue Clotkin acts as tough as she can in the face of a difficult life with her grandmother. (Rev: BL 5/1/05; SLJ 8/05)

5877 Steig, William. *Spinky Sulks* (K–3). Illus. 1988, Farrar paper $4.95 (978-0-374-46990-0). 32pp. Spinky is a first-class sulker but is forced to reconsider his position. (Rev: BCCB 12/88; BL 1/15/89; HB 3/89)

5878 Stein, Sara Bonnett. *About Dying* (1–3). Illus. by author. 1974, Walker $10.95 (978-0-8027-6172-9); paper $8.95 (978-0-8027-7223-7). 48pp. Sensitive portrayal of the death of a bird and of a grandfather. Also use: *About Handicaps* (1974); *Making Babies* (1974); *About Phobias; The Adopted One; On Divorce* (all 1979).

5879 Stier, Catherine. *Bugs in My Hair?!* (K–3). Illus. by Tammie Lyon. 2008, Albert Whitman $16.99 (978-0-8075-0908-1). 32pp. Third-grader Ellie, who's a bit of a perfectionist, is devastated to find she has lice in her hair, but once she's accepted the fact decides to take steps to help others. (Rev: BL 7/08; SLJ 5/08)

5880 Stolz, Mary. *Storm in the Night* (K–3). Illus. by Pat Cummings. 1988, HarperCollins paper $6.99 (978-0-06-443256-6). 32pp. Grandfather tells Thomas, a young African American boy, of a time when he was afraid, in order to calm the child's fears about a dark, stormy night. (Rev: BL 2/1/88; HB 7/88; SLJ 3/88)

5881 Taback, Simms. *I Miss You Every Day* (PS–1). Illus. by author. 2007, Viking $16.99 (978-0-670-06192-1). 40pp. In this picture book with rhyming lines, a young girl wraps herself up and mails herself to a far-away loved one. (Rev: BL 9/1/07; SLJ 8/07)

5882 Tarpley, Natasha Anastasia. *Joe-Joe's First Flight* (PS–2). Illus. by E. B. Lewis. 2003, Knopf $15.95 (978-0-375-81053-4). 40pp. In the 1920s, young Joe-Joe dreams of flying a plane but fears that, as an African American, he won't be allowed to. (Rev: BL 2/15/04; HBG 10/03; SLJ 7/03)

5883 Thiel, Annie. *Danny Is Moving* (1–4). Illus. by William M. Edwards. 2006, Playdate Kids $14.95 (978-1-933721-02-6). Danny worries about leaving his old friends and moving to a new neighborhood, but he soon discovers how easy it is to make new friends. (Rev: SLJ 9/06)

5884 Thompson, Mary. *Andy and His Yellow Frisbee* (1–3). Illus. by author. 1996, Woodbine $14.95 (978-0-933149-83-0). The story of an autistic child as seen through the eyes of a young classmate. (Rev: SLJ 1/97)

5885 Thompson, Richard. *The Night Walker* (K–3). Illus. by Martin Springett. 2002, Fitzhenry & Whiteside $16.95 (978-1-55041-672-5). A tense tale about a young boy out walking near dark who suspects he's being followed by the Night Walker. (Rev: BL 9/1/03; SLJ 4/03)

5886 Tinkham, Kelly A. *Hair for Mama* (K–3). Illus. by Amy June Bates. 2007, Dial $16.99 (978-0-8037-2955-1). Marcus tries to help out when his mother is reluctant to have her picture taken after losing her hair to cancer treatment. (Rev: HB 7/07; SLJ 7/07)

5887 Vail, Rachel. *Sometimes I'm Bombaloo* (PS–2). Illus. by Yumi Heo. 2002, Scholastic $16.95 (978-

0-439-08755-1). 32pp. Katie is a mostly-good kid who sometimes turns into an angry "Bombaloo." (Rev: BCCB 4/02; BL 2/1/02; HBG 10/02; SLJ 3/02)

5888 Verniero, Joan C. *You Can Call Me Willy: A Story for Children About AIDS* (K–3). Illus. by Verdon Flory. Series: Books to Help Parents Help Their Children. 1995, Magination paper $9.95 (978-0-945354-60-4). A touching story of a 3rd-grader who has AIDS and the intolerance and misunderstandings she faces at school. (Rev: SLJ 9/95)

5889 Vettiger, Susanne. *Basghetti Spaghetti* (K–2). Illus. by Marie-Anne Räber. 2005, North-South LB $16.50 (978-0-7358-1992-4). Oscar, a crab, has some trouble pronouncing words correctly when he's nervous but improves after visiting Doctor Octopus. (Rev: SLJ 8/05)

5890 Vigna, Judith. *I Wish Daddy Didn't Drink So Much* (PS). Illus. by author. 1988, Whitman paper $6.95 (978-0-8075-3526-4). 32pp. A Christmas story told by a little girl whose father is an alcoholic. (Rev: BL 10/1/88; SLJ 1/89)

5891 Vigna, Judith. *Saying Goodbye to Daddy* (K–2). Illus. 1991, Whitman LB $16.99 (978-0-8075-7253-5). 32pp. When her father is killed in a car accident, Clare goes through the phases of grieving. (Rev: BL 2/1/91; SLJ 3/91)

5892 Viorst, Judith. *The Tenth Good Thing About Barney* (K–2). Illus. by Erik Blegvad. 1971, Macmillan $14.00 (978-0-689-20688-7); paper $4.99 (978-0-689-71203-6). 32pp. At a backyard funeral, a little boy tries to think of 10 good things to say about his cat, Barney — but can come up with only nine.

5893 Waber, Bernard. *Ira Sleeps Over* (PS–2). Illus. by author. 1973, Houghton $16.00 (978-0-395-13893-9); paper $6.95 (978-0-395-20503-7). 48pp. When Ira is invited to sleep overnight at Reggie's house, he wants to go, but should he or shouldn't he take along his teddy bear?

5894 Wahl, Jan. *Candy Shop* (K–3). Illus. by Nicole Wong. 2004, Charlesbridge $15.95 (978-1-57091-508-6). 32pp. Daniel, a young African American boy, not only dresses as a cowboy but also tries to act like one, and he takes action when hateful words are written in front of his favorite candy store. (Rev: BL 4/15/04; SLJ 3/04)

5895 Watts, Jeri Hanel. *Keepers* (K–3). Illus. by Felicia Marshall. 1997, Lee & Low $15.95 (978-1-880000-58-8). 32pp. Kenyon feels guilty because he has bought a baseball glove with the money intended for Grandmother's 90th birthday present. (Rev: BL 1/1–15/98; HBG 3/98; SLJ 1/98)

5896 Weigelt, Udo. *Becky the Borrower* (PS–2). Illus. by Astrid Henn. 2008, North-South $16.95 (978-0-7358-2205-4). 32pp. Becky borrows and borrows from her kindergarten classmates until she does not know what is whose any more. (Rev: BLO 12/30/08; LMC 5/09; SLJ 9/08)

5897 Weiss, Ellen. *The Nose Knows* (1–3). Illus. by Margeaux Lucas. Series: Science Solves It! 2002, Kane paper $4.99 (978-1-57565-120-0). 32pp. Peter's acute nose is useful when everyone has a cold in this story that interweaves scientific facts. (Rev: SLJ 1/03)

5898 Willis, Jeanne. *Susan Laughs* (PS–K). Illus. 2000, Holt $15.00 (978-0-8050-6501-5). 32pp. Susan is presented in a series of activities — laughing, singing, and swimming, for example — and on the last page is shown in her wheelchair. (Rev: BCCB 10/00; BL 8/00; HBG 3/01; SLJ 11/00)

5899 Winter, Jeanette. *Angelina's Island* (PS–2). 2007, Farrar $16.00 (978-0-374-30349-5). 320pp. Living in New York City with her parents, Angelina longs for the sun, food, and friends of her former home in Jamaica. (Rev: BL 2/1/07)

5900 Winton, Tim. *The Deep* (PS–2). Illus. by Karen Louise. 2000, Tricycle $14.95 (978-1-58246-024-6). 32pp. Alice is afraid to swim in the deep water near her home until some playful dolphins help her to overcome her fears. (Rev: BL 5/15/00; HBG 10/00; SLJ 7/00)

5901 Wishinsky, Frieda. *Each One Special* (PS–2). Illus. by H. Werner Zimmermann. 1999, Orca $14.95 (978-1-55143-122-2). 32pp. When a creative cake decorator is fired from his job, he takes up a related field — sculpting. (Rev: BL 1/1–15/99; HBG 10/99; SLJ 7/99)

5902 Zolotow, Charlotte. *The Three Funny Friends* (PS–2). Illus. by Linda Bronson. 2003, Running Pr. $15.95 (978-0-7624-1553-3). A lonely young girl, who has just moved to a new town, comforts herself with three imaginary friends — Guy-Guy, Bickerina, and Mr. Dobie — until a real-life friend comes along. (Rev: SLJ 12/03)

REAL AND ALMOST REAL ANIMALS

5903 Abley, Mark. *Ghost Cat* (PS–K). Illus. by Karen Reczuch. 2001, Groundwood $16.95 (978-0-88899-433-2). 32pp. Elderly Miss Wilkinson depends on her cat for companionship and is bereft when he becomes ill and dies, but comforted when the rose bush she plants on his grave blooms. (Rev: HBG 3/02; SLJ 9/01)

5904 Adlerman, Daniel. *Africa Calling: Nighttime Falling* (PS–1). Illus. by Kimberly Adlerman. 1996, Whispering Coyote $15.95 (978-1-879085-98-5). 32pp. A young girl tries to imagine her stuffed animals in their native African habitats. (Rev: BL 10/1/96; SLJ 9/96)

5905 Alsenas, Linas. *Peanut* (PS–1). Illus. by author. 2007, Scholastic $16.99 (978-0-439-77980-7). 32pp. A lonely old woman named Mildred adopts a stray "puppy" (actually an elephant) and names him Peanut; when a man from the circus finally comes to take him away, she is sad until she spots a stray "kitten" (actually a camel). (Rev: LMC 10/07*; SLJ 12/07)

5906 Anderson, Sara. *Octopus Oyster Hermit Crab Snail: A Poem of the Sea* (1–3). Illus. by author. 2005, Handprint $16.95 (978-1-59354-079-1). Eye-catching illustrations and rhyming text introduce a variety of marine creatures. (Rev: HBG 4/06; SLJ 12/05)

5907 Appelt, Kathi. *Where, Where Is Swamp Bear?* (PS–1). Illus. by Megan Halsey. 2002, Harper-

Collins LB $15.89 (978-0-688-17103-2). 32pp. A young Louisiana boy called Pierre goes fishing with his Granpere, but the boy's main preoccupation is looking for the elusive Swamp Bear and learning about the bear's life. (Rev: BL 2/15/02; HBG 10/02; SLJ 1/02*)

5908 Araki, Mie. *Kitten's Big Adventure* (PS). Illus. 2005, Harcourt $15.00 (978-0-15-216738-7). 40pp. A small kitten enjoys chasing a butterfly but is quick to hurry back to its mother's side. (Rev: BL 5/1/05; SLJ 6/05)

5909 Arnosky, Jim. *Babies in the Bayou* (PS–2). Illus. by author. 2007, Putnam $16.99 (978-0-399-22653-3). 32pp. A look at the young animals of the bayou and their mothers, with simple text and lush illustrations. (Rev: BL 12/1/06; SLJ 1/07)

5910 Arnosky, Jim. *Dolphins on the Sand* (PS–2). Illus. by author. 2008, Putnam $16.99 (978-0-399-24606-7). 32pp. A young boy is among the rescuers who work through a night to save dolphins stranded on a sandbar; this moving story also delivers a message about nature and the environment. (Rev: BL 7/08; SLJ 9/08)

5911 Arnosky, Jim. *Gobble It Up! A Fun Song About Eating!* (PS). Illus. by author. 2008, Scholastic $16.99 (978-0-439-90362-2). 32pp. This simple rhyming picture book introduces a variety of animals and their eating habits; an accompanying CD holds a catchy song sung by the author. (Rev: BL 9/1/08; SLJ 9/08)

5912 Arnosky, Jim. *Grandfather Buffalo* (PS–2). Illus. 2006, Putnam $16.99 (978-0-399-24169-7). 32pp. A heartwarming story about an aging buffalo, unable to keep up with the herd, that finds renewed interest in life when he saves a newborn calf in a dust storm. (Rev: BL 2/1/06; HBG 10/06; SLJ 2/06*)

5913 Arnosky, Jim. *Little Lions* (PS). Illus. 1998, Penguin $17.99 (978-0-399-22944-2). 32pp. A simple picture book that reports on the playful activities of two mountain lion cubs and their ever-watchful mother. (Rev: BL 3/1/98; HBG 10/98; SLJ 3/98)

5914 Arnosky, Jim. *Turtle in the Sea* (PS–2). Illus. 2002, Penguin $16.99 (978-0-399-22757-8). 32pp. A sea turtle survives the dangers surrounding her in the ocean. (Rev: BL 9/1/02; HBG 3/03; SLJ 8/02)

5915 Arrigoni, Patricia. *Harpo: The Baby Harp Seal* (2–3). Illus. 1995, Travel Publishers $16.95 (978-0-9625468-8-4). 32pp. Harpo, a baby harp seal, is rescued by a little girl when he is separated from his mother. (Rev: BL 2/1/96)

5916 Aruego, Jose, and Ariane Dewey. *The Last Laugh* (PS). Illus. 2006, Dial $12.99 (978-0-8037-3093-9). 24pp. A bullying snake gets his comeuppance from a clever duck in this nearly wordless humorous story. (Rev: BCCB 5/06; BL 2/1/06; HBG 10/06; SLJ 3/06)

5917 Asch, Frank. *The Last Puppy* (PS–2). Illus. by author. 1989, Simon & Schuster paper $4.95 (978-0-671-66687-3). 32pp. An enchanting story of the puppy born last in a large litter.

5918 Ashman, Linda. *Castles, Caves, and Honeycombs* (PS–K). Illus. by Lauren Stringer. 2001, Har-

court $16.00 (978-0-15-202211-2). 32pp. Animal homes — nests, shells, dens, or hollow logs — are pictured in drawings and rhyming verse. (Rev: BL 3/15/01*; HB 7/01; HBG 10/01)

5919 Ashman, Linda. *Stella, Unleashed: Notes from the Doghouse* (PS–K). Illus. by Paul Meisel. 2008, Sterling $14.95 (978-1-4027-3987-3). 40pp. In a series of poems a mongrel named Stella describes the joys (and puzzles) of life with the human family that has adopted her. (Rev: BL 5/1/08; SLJ 4/08)

5920 Austin, Patricia. *The Cat Who Loved Mozart* (1–3). Illus. by Henri Sorenson. 2001, Holiday House $16.95 (978-0-8234-1535-9). 32pp. Nine-year-old Jennifer adopts a stray cat that resists her affection until it hears her practicing for a piano recital. (Rev: BL 5/1/01; HBG 10/01; SLJ 6/01)

5921 Bailey, Linda. *Stanley at Sea* (PS–2). Illus. by Bill Slavin. 2008, Kids Can $16.95 (978-1-55453-193-6). 32pp. The appealing Stanley and his pack of hungry doggy friends return for another adventure as they set off to sea in a rowboat. (Rev: SLJ 4/08)

5922 Bailey, Linda. *Stanley's Party* (PS–3). Illus. by Bill Slavin. 2003, Kids Can $14.95 (978-1-55337-382-7). Stanley the dog samples forbidden pleasures while his owners are out. (Rev: HBG 10/03; SLJ 7/03)

5923 Bailey, Linda. *Stanley's Wild Ride* (PS–2). Illus. by Bill Slavin. 2006, Kids Can $14.95 (978-1-55337-960-7). 32pp. Stanley the dog escapes from his backyard and liberates his canine friends for a wild time on the town. (Rev: BL 3/1/06; SLJ 6/06)

5924 Banks, Kate. *The Cat Who Walked Across France* (PS–2). Illus. by Georg Hallensleben. 2004, Farrar $16.00 (978-0-374-39968-9). 40pp. A French cat who has been uprooted after the death of his owner decides to head back to the house he loves; beautiful paintings document his long and difficult journey. (Rev: BL 3/15/04; HB 3/04; SLJ 3/04)

5925 Barner, Bob. *Fish Wish* (PS–K). Illus. 2000, Holiday House $16.95 (978-0-8234-1482-6). 32pp. Collages are used to illustrate this fanciful picture book about a boy who dreams of being a fish and encountering all the creatures in a coral reef. (Rev: BL 2/1/00; HBG 10/00; SLJ 5/00)

5926 Barton, Byron. *Bones, Bones, Dinosaur Bones* (PS–K). Illus. 1990, HarperCollins LB $15.89 (978-0-690-04827-8). 32pp. Paleontologists collect a number of bones and reconstruct a dinosaur. (Rev: BL 10/15/90; HB 11/90*; SLJ 9/90)

5927 Base, Graeme. *The Water Hole* (PS–1). Illus. 2001, Abrams $18.95 (978-0-8109-4568-5). 30pp. Part counting book, part introduction to animal species, and part overview of the water cycle, this richly illustrated picture book shows various animals — from 1 rhino to 10 kangaroos — gathering at a water hole. (Rev: BL 10/1/01; HBG 3/02; SLJ 12/01)

5928 Beames, Margaret. *Night Cat* (K–4). Illus. by Sue Hitchcock. 2003, Scholastic $15.95 (978-0-439-38576-3). Menacing creatures and a shower of rain persuade Oliver the cat of the benefits of home. (Rev: HBG 4/04; SLJ 9/03)

5929 Bennett, Dean. *Finding a Friend in the Forest: A True Story* (PS–3). Illus. by author. 2005, Down East $15.95 (978-0-89272-662-2). A beagle and a doe become fast friends in this appealing picture book set in northern Maine. (Rev: SLJ 1/06)

5930 Bennett, Kelly. *Not Norman: A Goldfish Story* (K–3). Illus. by Noah Z. Jones. 2005, Candlewick $15.99 (978-0-7636-2384-5). 32pp. A goldfish isn't the kind of pet the narrator initially wants in this entertaining and eye-catching story. (Rev: BL 2/15/05; SLJ 3/05)

5931 Berenzy, Alix. *Sammy: The Classroom Guinea Pig* (PS–2). Illus. 2005, Holt $16.95 (978-0-8050-4024-1). 32pp. Lots of information about guinea pigs is conveyed as Ms. B.'s class investigates why Sammy is making so much noise. (Rev: BL 5/15/05)

5932 Bergman, Mara. *Yum, Yum! What Fun!* (PS–2). Illus. by Nick Maland. 2009, Greenwillow $17.99 (978-0-06-168860-7). 32pp. When young Katie and James bake bread, the smell attracts a menagerie of unexpected visitors from the zoo next door. (Rev: BL 2/1/09; SLJ 4/09)

5933 Berkes, Marianne. *Marsh Morning* (2–4). Illus. by Robert Noreika. 2003, Millbrook LB $22.90 (978-0-7613-2568-0). 32pp. Watercolor illustrations and short rhymes tell the stories of 15 species of birds and their morning songs. (Rev: BL 3/15/03; HBG 10/03; SLJ 4/03)

5934 Best, Cari. *Goose's Story* (PS–3). Illus. by Holly Meade. 2002, Farrar $16.00 (978-0-374-32750-7). 32pp. A young girl witnesses how an injured goose copes with his disability and tries to survive though left behind by the flock. (Rev: BCCB 9/02; BL 5/1/02*; HB 5/02; HBG 10/02; SLJ 7/02)

5935 Bevis, Mary. *Wolf Song* (K–3). Illus. by Consie Powell. 2007, Raven $18.95 (978-0-9794202-0-7); paper $12.95 (978-0-9794202-1-4). 32pp. Young Nell and her uncle go into the north woods and enjoy the song of the wolves; with facts about wolves and about howling expeditions. (Rev: SLJ 12/07)

5936 Blackford, Harriet. *Elephant's Story* (PS–2). Illus. by Manja Stojic. 2008, Sterling $14.95 (978-1-905417-75-9). 32pp. Large text, effective illustrations, and a factual note at the end introduce elephants through the fictional story of one baby elephant on the African savanna. (Rev: BCCB 5/08; BL 4/1/08; SLJ 10/08)

5937 Blackford, Harriet. *Tiger's Story* (1–3). Illus. by Manya Stojic. 2007, Boxer Bks. LB $12.95 (978-1-905417-39-1). A young tiger searches through the forest for a place to call home. Beautiful illustrations and tiger facts add interest. (Rev: SLJ 5/07)

5938 Blackstone, Stella. *I Dreamt I Was a Dinosaur* (PS–2). Illus. by Clare Beaton. 2005, Barefoot Books $15.99 (978-1-84148-238-5). A child dreams of being a dinosaur and cavorting with all sorts of prehistoric creatures; factual information is appended. (Rev: SLJ 1/06)

5939 Blackstone, Stella. *Secret Seahorse* (PS–2). Illus. by Clare Beaton. 2004, Barefoot Books $15.99 (978-1-84148-704-5). 32pp. A fast-moving seahorse weaves in and out of sight through the coral reefs and caves beneath the sea. (Rev: BL 4/15/04; SLJ 1/05)

5940 Blackstone, Stella. *Who Are You, Baby Kangaroo?* (PS–K). Illus. by Clare Beaton. 2004, Barefoot Books $14.99 (978-1-84148-217-0). A puppy determined to find out the word for a baby kangaroo travels far and wide asking other animals. (Rev: SLJ 11/04)

5941 Blades, Ann. *Mary of Mile 18* (K–3). Illus. 2001, Tundra $14.95 (978-0-88776-581-0). 48pp. This 30th anniversary reissue of the classic story of a Canadian girl who takes in a part-wolf pup has a larger format and slight redesign. (Rev: BL 10/15/01; HBG 10/02)

5942 Blake, Robert J. *Akiak: A Tale from the Iditarod* (PS–3). Illus. 1997, Penguin $16.99 (978-0-399-22798-1). 32pp. An aging sled dog named Akiak participates in the Iditarod sled race for the last time. (Rev: BL 9/1/97; HBG 3/98; SLJ 9/97*)

5943 Blake, Robert J. *Togo* (2–4). Illus. 2002, Penguin $16.99 (978-0-399-23381-4). 48pp. Blake's brilliantly illustrated story is a gripping tribute to Togo, the dog that should have got credit for the famous serum run during the diphtheria epidemic in Nome in 1925. (Rev: BL 9/15/02; HBG 3/03; SLJ 9/02*)

5944 Blanc, Esther S. *Berchick* (1–3). Illus. by Tennessee Dixon. 1989, Volcano $14.95 (978-0-912078-81-6). Mama takes care of a colt found beside its dead mother. (Rev: SLJ 11/89)

5945 Bloom, Suzanne. *No Place for a Pig* (K–3). Illus. by author. 2003, Boyds Mills $15.95 (978-1-59078-047-3). When her apartment becomes too small for her rapidly growing pig, Ms. Taffy's neighbors come to the rescue. (Rev: BL 1/1–15/04; HBG 4/04; SLJ 11/03)

5946 Bloxam, Frances. *Little Tom Turkey* (PS–2). Illus. by Jim Sollers. 2005, Down East $15.95 (978-0-89272-671-4). In rhyming verse with dollops of humor and fact, Bloxam tells the story of an appealing and ambitious young wild turkey. (Rev: SLJ 6/05)

5947 Blumenthal, Deborah. *Black Diamond and Blake* (1–3). Illus. by Miles Hyman. 2009, Knopf $16.99 (978-0-375-84003-6). 40pp. This picture-book story is told from the point of view of a racehorse who, after an injury, finds himself in a prison rehabilitation program, where he eventually finds happiness. (Rev: BL 12/15/08; LMC 5/09; SLJ 2/09)

5948 Boelts, Maribeth. *Before You Were Mine* (PS–2). Illus. by David Walker. 2007, Putnam $15.99 (978-0-399-24526-8). 32pp. A young boy wonders about the life his new dog may have led before the boy and his family chose the dog from an animal shelter. (Rev: BCCB 12/07; BL 12/1/07; SLJ 10/07)

5949 Bradford, Karleen. *You Can't Rush a Cat* (2–3). Illus. by Leslie Elizabeth Watts. 2003, Orca $16.95 (978-1-55143-247-2). 32pp. Jessica helps her grandfather coax a shy stray kitten out of the bushes in this charming story. (Rev: BL 2/1/04; HBG 4/04; SLJ 2/04)

5950 Bradley, Kimberly Brubaker. *The Perfect Pony* (K–2). Illus. by Shelagh McNicholas. 2007, Dial $16.99 (978-0-8037-2851-6). 32pp. A young girl talks about learning to ride and her search for just the right pony. (Rev: BL 4/1/07)

5951 Braeuner, Shellie. *The Great Dog Wash* (PS–K). Illus. by Robert Neubecker. 2009, Simon & Schuster $15.99 (978-1-4169-7116-0). 32pp. A dog wash bubbles out of control when a cat strolls by. (Rev: BL 5/15/09)

5952 Broach, Elise. *Wet Dog!* (PS–2). Illus. by David Catrow. 2005, Dial $16.99 (978-0-8037-2809-7). After he is turned away from nearly every source of water in town, a very hot dog interrupts a wedding party by a cool lake. (Rev: SLJ 7/05)

5953 Broome, Errol. *Drusilla the Lucky Duck* (3–4). Illus. by Sharon Thompson. 2003, Annick $16.95 (978-1-55037-799-6); paper $4.95 (978-1-55037-798-9). 72pp. The story of young Carrie and her pet duckling Drusilla, and how Carrie races to save Drusilla from becoming someone's dinner. (Rev: SLJ 3/04)

5954 Brown, Margaret Wise. *Big Red Barn* (PS–1). Illus. by Felicia Bond. 1989, HarperCollins LB $17.89 (978-0-06-020749-6). 32pp. The big red barn contains lots and lots of animals and their offspring. (Rev: BL 3/1/89; SLJ 6/89)

5955 Brown, Margaret Wise. *Wheel on the Chimney* (PS–3). Illus. by Tibor Gergely. 1954, Harper-Collins LB $13.89 (978-0-397-30296-3). 32pp. Hungarian storks return each spring from Africa to nest on farmers' chimneys. A 1955 Caldecott Honor Book.

5956 Brown, Ruth. *The Tale of Two Mice: A Cat-and-Mouse Tale* (PS–3). Illus. by author. 2008, Candlewick $16.99 (978-0-7636-4015-6). 32pp. Two very hungry little mice mount an assault on a human kitchen all the while on the lookout for the cat; lift-up flaps add to the fun. (Rev: BL 12/15/08; SLJ 1/09)

5957 Brown, Tricia. *Groucho's Eyebrows* (K–2). Illus. by Barbara Lavallee. 2003, Alaska Northwest $15.95 (978-0-88240-556-8). Enticing illustrations grace this story of an Alaskan girl named Kristie and her white cat with magnificent black eyebrows. (Rev: HBG 4/04; SLJ 6/04)

5958 Bruel, Nick. *Little Red Bird* (PS–2). Illus. by author. 2008, Roaring Brook $16.95 (978-1-59643-339-7). 32pp. After a day free from her cage, Little Red Bird must decide whether to continue exploring or return to the comforts of home. (Rev: BL 4/15/08; LMC 5/08; SLJ 6/08)

5959 Bruel, Robert O. *Bob and Otto* (PS–K). Illus. by Nick Bruel. 2007, Roaring Brook $15.95 (978-1-59643-203-1). 32pp. In their early years, worms Bob and Otto are inseparable, but the two must part ways when Bob's metamorphosis into a butterfly approaches. (Rev: BL 4/1/07)

5960 Buck, Nola. *Oh, Cats!* (PS–1). Illus. by Nadine Bernard Westcott. 1997, HarperCollins LB $16.89 (978-0-06-025374-5). 32pp. A little girl tries to

befriend three very independent cats. (Rev: BL 11/15/96; SLJ 2/97)

5961 Bunting, Eve. *Emma's Turtle* (PS–2). Illus. by Marsha Winborn. 2007, Boyds Mills $15.95 (978-1-59078-350-4). 32pp. Emma's turtle has a yen for foreign travel and imagines himself in Africa, Australia, and India when he escapes from his pen. (Rev: BL 10/1/07; SLJ 9/07)

5962 Bunting, Eve. *Whales Passing* (PS–2). Illus. by Lambert Davis. 2003, Scholastic $15.95 (978-0-590-60358-4). A gentle — and fact-filled — story of a boy being introduced by his father to the wonders of orcas and nature in general. (Rev: HBG 10/03; SLJ 6/03)

5963 Burke, Tina. *Fly, Little Bird* (PS–K). Illus. by author. 2006, Kane $14.95 (978-1-933605-02-9). 32pp. A nearly wordless book that depicts a little girl, accompanied by her puppy, capturing and then setting free a baby wild parrot. (Rev: BL 5/15/06)

5964 Burningham, John. *Hey! Get Off Our Train* (K–3). Illus. 1990, Crown paper $7.99 (978-0-517-88204-7). 48pp. A boy's dream takes him on a train trip around the world where he sees environmental dangers. (Rev: BCCB 4/90; BL 5/15/90; HB 5/90; SLJ 5/90)

5965 Bushey, Jeanne. *A Sled Dog for Moshi* (K–3). Illus. by Germaine Arnaktauyok. 1994, Hyperion LB $15.49 (978-1-56282-632-1). 40pp. A sled dog saves two Inuit children during a storm. (Rev: BL 1/15/95; SLJ 1/95)

5966 Bushnell, Jack. *Sky Dancer* (K–3). Illus. by Jan Ormerod. 1996, Lothrop LB $15.93 (978-0-688-05289-8). 32pp. Jenny tries to save a red-tailed hawk from being shot by local farmers. (Rev: BL 9/15/96; SLJ 9/96)

5967 Butler, John. *Pi-Shu, the Little Panda* (K–2). Illus. 2001, Peachtree $15.95 (978-1-56145-242-2). 32pp. The daily activities of a baby panda named Pi-shu are recounted in this picture book that also gives information on why this is an endangered species. (Rev: BL 3/15/01; HBG 10/01)

5968 Buxton, Jane. *The Littlest Llama* (PS–2). Illus. by Jenny Cooper. 2008, Sterling $9.95 (978-1-4027-5277-3). 32pp. Rhyming couplets tell the story of a little llama who has nobody to play with; the detailed illustrations show typical llama behaviors. (Rev: BL 4/15/08; SLJ 4/08)

5969 Buzzeo, Toni. *Little Loon and Papa* (PS–2). Illus. by Margaret Spengler. 2004, Dial $16.99 (978-0-8037-2958-2). Despite his father's patient advice, Little Loon is having trouble learning to dive until outside pressures force him to take the plunge. (Rev: SLJ 6/04)

5970 Byars, Betsy, and Betsy Duffey. *Dog Diaries: Secret Writings of the WOOF Society* (3–4). Illus. by Erik Brooks. 2007, Holt $15.95 (978-0-8050-7657-9). 72pp. Eleven stories by dogs are presented at a book club for dogs called the WOOF Society. Dog-lovers will enjoy reading these brief, varied tales by dogs in all sorts of situations. (Rev: SLJ 6/07)

5971 Campbell, Rod. *Dear Zoo* (PS). Illus. by author. 1983, Puffin paper $4.95 (978-0-317-62180-

8). 22pp. A youngster keeps sending back the pets requested from a zoo until a puppy arrives.

5972 Capucilli, Alyssa Satin. *Inside a Barn in the Country: A Rebus Read-Along Story* (PS–K). Illus. by Tedd Arnold. 1995, Scholastic $10.95 (978-0-590-46999-9). 32pp. Using simple verses, this game book also teaches the sounds that animals make. (Rev: BL 1/15/95; SLJ 4/95)

5973 Carle, Eric. *Does a Kangaroo Have a Mother, Too?* (PS–1). Illus. 2000, HarperCollins LB $17.89 (978-0-06-028767-2). 32pp. In this simple book about wildlife, 12 young animals are presented along with their mothers. (Rev: BCCB 4/00; BL 1/1–15/00; HBG 10/00; SLJ 4/00) [591.3]

5974 Carle, Eric. *Have You Seen My Cat?* (PS–2). Illus. by author. 1991, Picture Book $16.00 (978-0-88708-054-8). A small boy loses his cat, sees many other felines, and returns home to find that his cat has had kittens. A reissue of a 1973 title.

5975 Carle, Eric. *Mister Seahorse* (PS–3). Illus. 2004, Penguin $17.99 (978-0-399-24269-4). 40pp. Imaginative tissue-paper collages with occasional overlays show Mr. Seahorse as he keeps vigil over Mrs. Seahorse's eggs in his pouch and encounters other marine fathers who play a role in caring for their young. (Rev: BL 4/1/04*; SLJ 5/04)

5976 Carrick, Carol. *Mothers Are Like That* (PS–1). Illus. by Paul Carrick. 2000, Clarion $15.00 (978-0-395-88351-8). 32pp. This tender picture book shows how various animals keep their offspring clean including a human mother and child. (Rev: BL 3/15/00; HB 3/00; HBG 10/00; SLJ 5/00)

5977 Carrick, Carol. *The Polar Bears Are Hungry* (PS–2). Illus. by Paul Carrick. 2002, Clarion $14.00 (978-0-618-15962-8). 32pp. A polar bear mother finds it more and more difficult to feed her cubs as spring and summer arrive, in this fictional presentation that will prompt discussion of human impact on animals. (Rev: BL 10/15/02; HBG 3/03; SLJ 11/02)

5978 Cartwright, Reg. *What We Do* (PS–1). Illus. by author. 2005, Holt $7.95 (978-0-8050-7671-4). In rhyming text and bright illustrations, a variety of animals explain the way the move and behave. (Rev: SLJ 10/05)

5979 Casanova, Mary. *Utterly Otterly Day* (PS–1). Illus. by Ard Hoyt. 2008, Simon & Schuster $16.99 (978-1-4169-0868-5). 40pp. Brave Little Otter has some scary adventures when he spends a day by himself. (Rev: BL 5/15/08; SLJ 6/08)

5980 Cate, Annette LeBlanc. *The Magic Rabbit* (K–3). Illus. by author. 2007, Candlewick $15.99 (978-0-7636-2672-3). 32pp. Street magician Ray and his sidekick, a white rabbit called Bunny, become separated in an accident and spend the day searching for each other. (Rev: BL 9/15/07; SLJ 9/07)

5981 Cecka, Melanie. *Violet Goes to the Country* (K–2). Illus. by Emily Arnold McCully. 2007, Viking $15.99 (978-0-670-06181-5). 36pp. The adventures of Violet, a little white cat, on her first trip to a farm; a gentle story based on characters in Jan Karon's Milford Years series for adults. (Rev: BL 9/1/07; SLJ 10/07)

5982 Chamberlain, Margaret. *Please Don't Tease Tootsie* (PS–2). Illus. by author. 2008, Dutton $16.99 (978-0-525-47982-6). 32pp. This playful story told in verse focuses on the proper care of pets and is illustrated with bright artwork. (Rev: BLO 8/28/08; SLJ 8/08)

5983 Chess, Victoria. *The Costume Party* (K–2). Illus. 2005, Kane $15.95 (978-1-929132-87-4). 32pp. Trapped indoors by several days of bad weather, Madame Coco throws a costume party to entertain her five pet dogs. (Rev: BL 10/15/05; SLJ 9/05)

5984 Chitwood, Suzanne Tanner. *Wake Up, Big Barn!* (PS–1). Illus. 2002, Scholastic $15.95 (978-0-439-26627-7). 40pp. Farm animals are introduced in lively collage in this rhythmic book for preschoolers. (Rev: BL 2/1/02; HBG 10/02; SLJ 4/02)

5985 Christian, Peggy. *Chocolate, a Glacier Grizzly* (K–3). Illus. by Carol Cottone-Kolthoff. 1997, Benefactory $12.95 (978-1-882728-63-3). 32pp. The story of a female grizzly bear in Glacier National Park from her birth to the birth of her own cubs years later. (Rev: SLJ 11/97)

5986 Cimarusti, Marie Torres. *Peek-a-Moo!* (PS). Illus. by Stephanie Peterson. 1998, Dutton $10.99 (978-0-525-46083-1). A flap book that introduces seven familiar farm animals and the sounds they make. (Rev: SLJ 11/98)

5987 Clark, Emma Chichester. *Piper* (PS–2). Illus. 2007, Eerdmans $17.00 (978-0-8028-5314-1). 32pp. Piper, a good-natured black dog, angers his new owner by cavorting with rabbits instead of getting rid of them; running away after a beating, he helps an old woman who provides him with a happy new home. (Rev: BL 1/1–15/07)

5988 Clark, Emma Chichester. *Will and Squill* (PS–2). Illus. 2006, Carolrhoda $15.95 (978-1-57505-936-5). 32pp. A boy named Will and a squirrel called Squill are great friends despite their mothers' disapproval. (Rev: BL 3/1/06; SLJ 3/06)

5989 Clarke, Jane. *Only Tadpoles Have Tails* (PS–2). Illus. by Jane Gray. Series: Flying Foxes. 2004, Crabtree LB $22.60 (978-0-7787-1484-2); paper $4.95 (978-0-7787-1530-6). 46pp. Kicky the frog is embarrassed about his tadpole tail until it helps him swim fast enough to escape piranhas. (Rev: SLJ 8/04)

5990 Clarke, Jane. *Stuck in the Mud* (PS–1). Illus. by Garry Parsons. 2008, Walker $16.95 (978-0-8027-9758-2). 32pp. A cumulative tale in which Hen discovers that one of her chicks is stuck in the mud and is helped by a succession of animals that all become stuck too; a final gatefold brings a surprise. (Rev: BL 2/15/08; SLJ 2/08)

5991 Clayton, Elaine. *A Blue Ribbon for Sugar* (K–2). 2006, Roaring Brook $16.95 (978-1-59643-157-7). 32pp. When Bonnie's beloved rocking horse breaks, she's treated to riding lessons on a real pony and eventually wins a blue ribbon at a horse show. (Rev: BL 6/1–15/06; SLJ 5/06)

5992 Clements, Andrew. *Naptime for Slippers* (PS–1). Illus. by Janie Bynum. 2005, Dutton $12.99 (978-0-525-47287-2). 32pp. Slippers the puppy is active and interested in everything going on around him, so much so that he misses naptime and is exhausted when it's time for a walk. (Rev: BL 2/1/05; SLJ 2/05)

5993 Clements, Andrew. *Slippers at Home* (PS–2). Illus. by Janie Bynum. 2004, Dutton $14.99 (978-0-525-47138-7). 32pp. Slippers is a happy puppy who enjoys the differences among his human family members. (Rev: SLJ 1/05)

5994 Clements, Andrew. *Slippers at School* (PS–2). Illus. by Janie Bynum. 2005, Dutton $14.99 (978-0-525-47189-9). 32pp. Slippers, Laura's puppy, hides in the girl's backpack on her first day at school and manages to evade ejection through a series of funny misunderstandings. (Rev: BL 8/05; SLJ 9/05)

5995 Clements, Andrew. *Slippers Loves to Run* (PS–2). Illus. by Janie Bynum. Series: Slippers. 2006, Dutton $12.99 (978-0-525-47648-1). 32pp. Restless puppy Slippers runs from his back yard to explore the big world before running home for a hug from his owners. (Rev: SLJ 6/06)

5996 Cochran, Bill. *The Forever Dog* (PS–2). Illus. by Dan Andreasen. 2007, HarperCollins $16.99 (978-0-06-053939-9). 32pp. A young boy tries to forgive his dead dog for deserting him. (Rev: BL 4/1/07; SLJ 3/07)

5997 Coffelt, Nancy. *Good Night, Sigmund* (PS–1). Illus. 1992, Harcourt $13.95 (978-0-15-200464-4). 40pp. The artwork is a show stealer in this story of a young boy and his pet cat. (Rev: BL 2/15/92; SLJ 5/92)

5998 Coffey, Maria. *A Cat Adrift* (PS–1). Illus. by Eugenie Fernandes. 2002, Annick LB $18.95 (978-1-55037-727-9). 32pp. Teelo the cat makes friends with a little girl and her grandfather when they rescue him from the ocean. (Rev: BL 7/02; HBG 10/02; SLJ 8/02)

5999 Cohen, Barbara S. *Forever Friends* (PS–2). Illus. by Dorothy Louise Hall. 2002, Tallfellow/Smallfellow $16.95 (978-1-931290-12-8). 32pp. Petey the dog describes all he does for his owner, Skip, in this playful picture book. (Rev: BL 7/02)

6000 Cole, Henry. *Trudy* (PS–1). Illus. by author. 2009, Greenwillow $17.99 (978-0-06-154267-1). 32pp. Esme's goat Trudy seems to have an unusual talent — she can predict snow? (Rev: BL 12/1/08; SLJ 12/08)

6001 Collard, Sneed B., III. *Butterfly Count* (1–3). Illus. by Paul Kratter. 2002, Holiday House $16.95 (978-0-8234-1607-3). 32pp. Amy's great-great-grandmother gave her prairie land to help restore the regal fritillary butterfly to its rightful home, and now Amy awaits its return. (Rev: BL 4/1/02; HBG 10/02; SLJ 6/02)

6002 Cooper, Elisha. *Magic Thinks Big* (PS–1). Illus. 2004, Greenwillow LB $15.89 (978-0-06-058165-7). 32pp. Readers are invited into the musings of an imaginative but idle tabby cat named Magic. (Rev: BL 5/15/04; HB 5/04; SLJ 4/04)

6003 Cowcher, Helen. *Jaguar* (K–2). Illus. 1997, Scholastic $15.95 (978-0-590-29937-4). 32pp. When an armed hunter finally corners the jaguar

that has been killing his cattle, he is so enthralled by its beauty that he cannot shoot it. (Rev: BL 10/15/97; HBG 3/98; SLJ 8/97)

6004 Crum, Shutta. *Click!* (K–2). Illus. by John Beder. 2003, Fitzhenry & Whiteside $14.95 (978-1-55005-074-5). 24pp. A nicely illustrated story told in parallel about a boy and his mother (who are wildlife photographers) and a bear and her cub. (Rev: BL 2/15/04; SLJ 2/04)

6005 Crum, Shutta. *A Family for Old Mill Farm* (1–3). Illus. by Niki Daly. 2007, Clarion $16.00 (978-0-618-42846-5). 32pp. A house-hunting family rejects one house after another, finally selecting on an old farm that many animal families call home as well. (Rev: SLJ 6/07)

6006 Cutler, Jane. *Mr. Carey's Garden* (K–3). Illus. by G. Brian Karas. 1996, Houghton $16.00 (978-0-395-68191-6). 32pp. Eveyone offers free advice on how Mr. Carey can rid his garden of snails. (Rev: BL 3/15/96; HB 5/96; SLJ 5/96)

6007 Dalgliesh, Alice. *The Bears on Hemlock Mountain* (1–4). Illus. by Helen Sewell. 1990, Macmillan paper $4.99 (978-0-689-71604-1). 64pp. Jonathan ventured over the mountain by himself after dark and discovered the reality of bear existence!

6008 Davies, Nicola. *White Owl, Barn Owl* (K–3). Illus. by Michael Foreman. 2007, Candlewick $16.99 (978-0-7636-3364-6). 32pp. A story about a barn owl who nests in a child's homemade box includes basic facts about the bird and its characteristics. (Rev: BL 5/15/07; SLJ 7/07*)

6009 Davis, Katie. *Who Hoots?* (PS–K). Illus. 2000, Harcourt $14.00 (978-0-15-202312-6). 36pp. This fun book delightfully presents animals that hoot, buzz, squeak, roar, and quack, and those that don't. (Rev: BL 10/1/00; HBG 3/01; SLJ 12/00)

6010 Day, Alexandra. *Carl's Sleepy Afternoon* (K–2). Illus. 2005, Farrar $12.95 (978-0-374-31088-2). 40pp. Rottweiler Carl is left at home for a good nap but ends up having a very busy afternoon. (Rev: BL 9/1/05; SLJ 10/05)

6011 Day, Alexandra. *Carl's Summer Vacation* (PS–K). Illus. by author. 2008, Farrar $12.95 (978-0-374-31085-1). 32pp. Madeleine and Carl the rottweiler have an enjoyable afternoon exploring around the summer cottage while they are supposed to be napping. (Rev: BL 8/08; HB 7/08; SLJ 5/08)

6012 De Cock, Nicole. *The Girl and the Elephant* (K–2). Illus. by author. 2004, Tricycle $15.95 (978-1-58246-133-5). A girl misses the elephant when he leaves the zoo and decides to go to Africa in pursuit. (Rev: SLJ 11/04)

6013 Delaney, Michael. *Obi, Gerbil on the Loose!* (2–4). Illus. by author. 2008, Dutton $15.99 (978-0-525-47890-4). 160pp. Obi the gerbil has a scary time when her family goes away and the neighbor looking after the pets seems to be unaware of her existence. (Rev: BL 6/1–15/08; SLJ 11/08)

6014 Demas, Corinne. *Always in Trouble* (K–2). Illus. by Noah Z. Jones. 2009, Scholastic $16.99 (978-0-545-02453-2). 40pp. Toby, a bouncy unruly dog who belongs to an African American family, goes to obedience school not just once but twice. (Rev: BCCB 1/09; BL 1/1–15/09; SLJ 1/09)

6015 Dennard, Deborah. *Bullfrog at Magnolia Circle* (K–4). Illus. by Kristin Kest. Series: Smithsonian Backyard. 2002, Soundprints $15.95 (978-1-931465-04-5); paper $6.95 (978-1-931465-39-7). 32pp. A young bullfrog who has reached maturity looks for a stretch of bayou to call his own in this accurate portrayal of a bullfrog's life. (Rev: HBG 3/03; SLJ 12/02)

6016 Denslow, Sharon Phillips. *In the Snow* (PS–K). Illus. by Nancy Tafuri. 2005, Greenwillow $15.99 (978-0-06-059683-5). 40pp. A young child puts out seeds to feed hungry woodland animals in this gentle story that introduces animals and the idea of animal footprints. (Rev: BL 10/15/05; SLJ 3/06)

6017 Díaz, Katacha. *Badger at Sandy Ridge Road* (K–3). Illus. by Kristin Kest. Series: Smithsonian's Backyard. 2005, Soundprints $15.95 (978-1-59249-420-0). 31pp. The story of a desert badger looking for a place to give birth is followed by facts about the North American badger. (Rev: SLJ 7/05)

6018 Diehl, Jean Heilprin. *Loon Chase* (1–3). Illus. by Kathryn Freeman. 2006, Sylvan Dell $15.95 (978-0-9764943-8-6). When their bird dog's hunting instincts send it in pursuit of a mother loon and her babies, a boy and his mother worry that their pet will hurt the endangered birds. (Rev: SLJ 4/06)

6019 Disalvo-Ryan, DyAnne. *A Dog Like Jack* (PS–2). Illus. 1999, Holiday House $16.95 (978-0-8234-1369-0). 32pp. Mike and his dog Jack share many years together, and when the dog dies, Mike grieves but learns to celebrate his friend's life. (Rev: BL 3/1/99; HBG 10/99; SLJ 4/99)

6020 Dixon, Ann. *Blueberry Shoe* (PS–3). Illus. by Evon Zerbetz. 1999, Alaska Northwest $22.95 (978-0-88240-518-6); paper $8.95 (978-0-88240-519-3). 32pp. Several Alaskan animals are introduced in this story of a lost red sneaker and how each of the animals that finds it changes it. (Rev: BL 10/15/99; HBG 3/00; SLJ 12/99)

6021 Dodd, Emma. *I Don't Want a Posh Dog* (PS–1). Illus. by author. 2009, Little, Brown $15.99 (978-0-316-03390-9). 32pp. In simple verses accompanied by colorful art, a young girl surveys a number of dog options and finally identifies the kind of dog she wants. (Rev: BL 4/15/09; SLJ 6/09)

6022 Dodd, Emma. *What Pet to Get?* (PS–2). Illus. by author. 2008, Scholastic $16.99 (978-0-545-03570-5). 32pp. Jack needs a pet and after considering everything from an elephant (too big) to a Tyrannosaurus rex (too extinct), he finally decides a dog will do just fine. (Rev: BL 3/1/08; SLJ 3/08)

6023 Doherty, Berlie. *Paddiwak and Cozy* (PS–1). Illus. by Alison Bartlett. 1999, Orchard $14.95 (978-0-531-30180-7). 32pp. Instant dislike develops when new cat Cozy is introduced into Sally's house and meets Paddiwak, the cat-in-residence. (Rev: BL 8/99; HBG 3/00; SLJ 10/99)

6024 Doner, Kim. *Buffalo Dreams* (K–4). 1999, Graphic Arts $16.95 (978-1-55868-475-1); paper $9.95 (978-1-55868-476-8). 40pp. When her little brother angers the mother of a rare white buffalo, Sarah must summon up the courage to rescue him. (Rev: BL 1/1–15/00; HBG 3/00; SLJ 2/00)

6025 Dowson, Nick. *Tracks of a Panda* (PS–2). Illus. by Yu Rong. 2007, Candlewick $16.99 (978-0-7636-3146-8). 32pp. Facts about pandas are interwoven into a story about a mother panda rearing her cub in the face of humans taking over their habitat. (Rev: BL 10/15/07; HB 11/07; SLJ 2/08)

6026 Doyle, Malachy. *Horse* (K–2). Illus. by Angelo Rinaldi. 2008, Simon & Schuster $16.99 (978-1-4169-2467-8). 32pp. This companion to *Cow* (2002) follows a foal from birth through the first year of life, featuring realistic paintings and a simple text. (Rev: BCCB 7–8/08; BL 6/1–15/08; SLJ 7/08)

6027 Doyle, Malachy. *Well, a Crocodile Can! Flip-up Flaps and Pop-up Tricks* (PS–K). Illus. by Britta Teckentrup. 1999, Millbrook $12.95 (978-0-7613-1032-7). Pop-ups and flaps are used to show a variety of different animals performing amazing tricks that are true to their nature — like an elephant wiggling its ears. (Rev: SLJ 3/00)

6028 Drachman, Eric. *A Frog Thing* (PS–2). Illus. by James Muscarello. 2006, Kidwick $18.95 (978-0-9703809-3-7). A frog named Frank who longs to fly finally gets his chance but comes to recognize that flying really isn't a frog thing; with beautiful illustrations and CD. (Rev: SLJ 6/06)

6029 Dunbar, Joyce. *Four Fierce Kittens* (PS–K). Illus. by Jakki Wood. 1992, Scholastic $13.95 (978-0-590-45535-0). 32pp. Four kittens think they are fierce but cannot frighten the other farm animals. (Rev: BL 6/1/92; SLJ 4/92)

6030 Dunn, Judy. *The Little Puppy* (PS–K). Illus. by Phoebe Dunn. 1984, Random paper $3.25 (978-0-394-86595-9). 32pp. The story of a little boy who must care for his first puppy.

6031 Edwards, Becky. *My Cat Charlie* (K–3). Illus. by David Armitage. 2001, Bloomsbury $17.95 (978-0-7475-4465-4). A little girl and her beloved cat must separate when her family moves to an apartment. (Rev: SLJ 12/01)

6032 Edwards, Pamela Duncan. *Muldoon* (PS–K). Illus. by Henry Cole. 2002, Hyperion $14.99 (978-0-7868-0360-6). 32pp. Muldoon, a dog, is convinced that he "works" for the West family — but he's actually a much-loved pet. (Rev: BL 2/15/03; HBG 3/03; SLJ 12/02)

6033 Ehlert, Lois. *Oodles of Animals* (PS–1). Illus. by author. 2008, Harcourt $17.00 (978-0-15-206274-3). 56pp. Inventive illustrations of animals are paired with brief, humorous poems. (Rev: BCCB 5/08; BL 7/08; LMC 10/08; SLJ 5/08)

6034 Ehlert, Lois. *Wag a Tail* (PS–2). 2007, Harcourt $16.00 (978-0-15-205843-2). 40pp. Ehlert's colorful paper collages portray happy dogs as they first visit a farmer's market with their humans, then cavort leash-free at a dog park. (Rev: BL 1/1–15/07)

6035 Erlbruch, Wolf. *Mrs. Meyer the Bird* (PS–2). Illus. 1997, Orchard LB $15.99 (978-0-531-33017-3). 32pp. Mrs. Meyer is a born worrier until she finds an injured bird to take care of and take her mind off her problems. (Rev: BCCB 5/97; BL 4/1/97; SLJ 4/97)

6036 Ets, Marie Hall. *Play with Me* (PS–K). Illus. by author. 1955, Puffin paper $5.99 (978-0-14-050178-0). 32pp. A little girl finds a playmate among the meadow creatures when she finally learns to sit quietly and not frighten them.

6037 Falwell, Cathryn. *Scoot!* (PS). Illus. by author. 2008, Greenwillow $16.99 (978-0-06-128882-1). 32pp. As all manner of animals frolic around a pond, the six turtles on a log remain still and silent — until a strong wind comes up; end matter includes additional information and advice on making painted textures on paper. (Rev: BL 1/1–15/08; SLJ 1/08)

6038 Faulkner, Keith. *David Dreaming of Dinosaurs* (K–2). Illus. by Jonathan Lambert. 1992, Fantasy $13.00 (978-1-56021-182-2). 12pp. David dreams of dinosaurs and they appear in foldout illustrations. (Rev: BL 11/15/92)

6039 Feder, Jane. *A Little Puppy* (PS). Illus. by Amy Schwartz. 2009, Candlewick $4.99 (978-0-7636-2651-8). 14pp. A simple board-book story about a little puppy exploring its surroundings. (Rev: BL 5/1/09)

6040 Flack, Marjorie. *Angus and the Ducks* (K–2). Illus. by author. 1997, Farrar paper $5.95 (978-0-374-40385-0). 40pp. Angus, the Scottish terrier, and his amusing adventures. Other titles in this series are: *Angus and the Cat* and *Angus Lost* (both 1989).

6041 Fleming, Denise. *Barnyard Banter* (PS–1). Illus. 1994, Holt $16.95 (978-0-8050-1957-5). 32pp. All the farm animals greet Goose with their appropriate sounds as she tours the farmyard. (Rev: BCCB 5/94; BL 5/1/94; HB 5/94; SLJ 5/94*)

6042 Fleming, Denise. *Buster* (PS–1). Illus. by author. 2003, Holt $15.95 (978-0-8050-6279-3). The idyllic life of Buster the dog is threatened by the arrival of Betty the kitten, but when he runs away and gets lost, it's Betty who comes to the rescue. (Rev: HB 9/03; HBG 4/04; SLJ 9/03)

6043 Fleming, Denise. *Buster Goes to Cowboy Camp* (PS–3). Illus. by author. 2008, Holt $8.95 (978-0-8050-7892-3). 40pp. Buster the dog (last seen in *Buster*, 2003) has a great time at "camp" in this story with a Wild West flavor. (Rev: BCCB 7–8/08; BL 5/15/08; SLJ 7/08)

6044 Fleming, Denise. *In the Tall, Tall Grass* (PS–1). Illus. 1991, Holt $16.95 (978-0-8050-1635-2). 32pp. An excellent story-hour book in which a caterpillar munches through the tall, tall grass, watching nature along the way. (Rev: BL 10/1/91*; HB 1/92*; SLJ 9/91*)

6045 Ford, Christine, and Trish Holland. *Ocean's Child* (PS–2). Illus. by David Diaz. 2009, Golden $15.99 (978-0-375-84752-3). 40pp. A pregnant Inuit mother and her young child canoe along the seacoast enjoying the baby animals they see. (Rev: BL 4/1/09; LMC 8/09; SLJ 7/09)

6046 Fox, Mem. *Zoo-Looking* (PS–1). Illus. by Candace Whitman. 1996, Mondo $15.95 (978-1-57255-010-0). 28pp. Flora is happy when the animals at the zoo seem to look back at her. (Rev: BCCB 7–8/96; BL 6/1–15/96; SLJ 7/96)

6047 Frazier, Craig. *Hank Finds Inspiration* (K–3). Illus. by author. 2008, Roaring Brook $16.95 (978-1-59643-358-8). 32pp. Unhappy with their "flat and boring yard," Stanley the boy and Hank the snake seek inspiration in the big city. (Rev: BLO 9/24/08; SLJ 9/08)

6048 Freedman, Claire. *Gooseberry Goose* (PS–2). Illus. by Vanessa Cabban. 2003, Tiger Tales $15.95 (978-1-58925-030-7). Gooseberry the gosling practices his flying techniques in preparation for migration south, while animals are busy getting ready for the coming of winter. (Rev: SLJ 12/03)

6049 Freedman, Claire. *One Magical Morning* (PS). Illus. by Louise Ho. 2005, Good Bks. $16.00 (978-1-56148-472-0). A mother bear and her baby watch morning arrive and the animals waking up. (Rev: SLJ 5/05)

6050 French, Vivian. *Caribou Journey* (1–3). Illus. by Lisa Flather. Series: Fantastic Journeys. 2001, Zero to Ten $15.95 (978-1-84089-216-1). 32pp. Animal migration is explored in this story about a pregnant caribou, Ragged Ear, and the herd's annual march to the calving grounds. (Rev: BL 4/1/02; SLJ 12/01)

6051 French, Vivian. *Whale Journey* (K–3). Illus. by Lisa Flather. 1998, Zero to Ten $14.95 (978-1-84089-022-8). 32pp. Beginning with his birth, this book traces the journey north to Alaskan waters of gray whale Little Grey and his mother and a friend. (Rev: BL 1/1–15/99; HBG 3/99)

6052 Friedman, Mel, and Ellen Weiss. *Kitten Castle* (K–3). Illus. by Lynn Adams. 2001, Kane paper $4.95 (978-1-57565-103-3). 32pp. Anna and her friend Tom use everyday items to build a castle for four lively kittens in this book that introduces shapes. (Rev: SLJ 9/01)

6053 Galvin, Laura Gates. *Bumblebee at Apple Tree Lane* (1–3). Illus. by Kristin Kest. 2000, Soundprints $15.95 (978-1-56899-820-6). 31pp. This fictional account of the queen bumblebee follows her life from waking from hibernation in the spring to crawling underground when winter approaches. (Rev: HBG 3/01; SLJ 3/01)

6054 Galvin, Laura Gates. *River Otter at Autumn Lane* (PS–2). Illus. by Christopher Leeper. 2002, Soundprints $4.95 (978-1-931465-62-5); paper $6.95 (978-1-931465-70-0). 32pp. A fictional introduction to the behavior, diet, and habitat of a mother otter and her young, with appealing realistic paintings. (Rev: BL 2/1/03)

6055 Gannij, Joan. *Elusive Moose* (PS–2). Illus. by Clare Beaton. 2006, Barefoot Books $15.99 (978-1-905236-75-6). 32pp. An invisible narrator lists all the animals he has seen in the north woods, except for the moose that's hiding in each scene. (Rev: BL 11/15/06; SLJ 11/06)

6056 Gannij, Joan. *Hidden Hippo* (PS–2). Illus. by Clare Beaton. 2008, Barefoot Books $15.99 (978-1-84686-170-3). 32pp. A young, unseen narrator searches an African plain for a hippo but only finds other animals — elephants, lions, leopards; readers will spot the hippo hidden on each spread and will appreciate the information on endangered species at the end. (Rev: BLO 9/24/08; LMC 3/09) [590]

6057 George, Jean Craighead. *The Cats of Roxville Station* (4–6). Illus. by Tom Pohrt. 2009, Dutton $16.99 (978-0-525-42140-5). 192pp. A young cat named Ratchet, throw into a river by her owner, must learn to survive in the wild. (Rev: BL 3/15/09; HB 7/09; SLJ 6/09)

6058 George, Jean Craighead. *Frightful's Daughter* (1–3). Illus. by Daniel San Souci. 2002, Dutton $16.99 (978-0-525-46907-0). 32pp. Sam Gribley (of *My Side of the Mountain* and its sequels) must rescue a chick of the falcon he calls Frightful. (Rev: BL 9/1/02; HBG 3/03; SLJ 9/02)

6059 George, Jean Craighead. *Frightful's Daughter Meets the Baron Weasel* (2–4). Illus. by Daniel San Souci. 2007, Dutton $16.99 (978-0-525-47202-5). 48pp. A predatory weasel has its eye on the chicks of peregrine falcon Oksi in this sequel to *Frightful's Daughter* (2002). (Rev: BL 9/1/07)

6060 George, Jean Craighead. *Look to the North: A Wolf Pup Diary* (K–4). Illus. by Lucia Washburn. 1997, HarperCollins LB $15.89 (978-0-06-023640-3). 32pp. A description of a year in the lives of three wolf cubs and how they adjust to each of the seasons. (Rev: BL 4/15/97; SLJ 4/97)

6061 George, Lindsay Barrett. *In the Garden: Who's Been Here?* (PS–2). Illus. 2006, Greenwillow $16.99 (978-0-06-078762-2). 48pp. While picking vegetables in the garden, Christina and Jeremy wonder about the animals that got there first. (Rev: BL 4/15/06; SLJ 5/06)

6062 George, Twig C. *Seahorses* (K–3). 2003, Millbrook LB $24.90 (978-0-7613-2869-8). 32pp. Seahorses and their lives are presented in eye-catching illustrations and poetic but informative text. (Rev: HBG 4/04; SLJ 4/04) [597]

6063 Gill, Shelley. *Alaska's Three Bears* (PS–2). Illus. by Shannon Cartwright. 1990, Paws Four $15.95 (978-0-934007-10-8); paper $8.95 (978-0-934007-11-5). 32pp. In a folklike tale, three types of Alaskan bears — polar bears, black bears, and grizzlies — are introduced. (Rev: BL 3/1/91)

6064 Gill, Shelley. *Big Blue* (1–3). Illus. by Ann Barrow. 2003, Charlesbridge LB $15.95 (978-1-57091-352-5). In this delightful tale based on a real-life experience of the author, a young girl's dream of swimming with a blue whale is fulfilled when her mother takes her on a trip to Baja California in Mexico. (Rev: HBG 4/04; SLJ 8/03)

6065 Gliori, Debi. *The Snow Lambs* (PS–3). Illus. 1996, Scholastic $15.95 (978-0-590-20304-3). 40pp. Young Sam worries about the safety of the family's sheepdog during severe winter weather. (Rev: BCCB 2/97; BL 11/15/96*; SLJ 10/96)

6066 Goldfinger, Jennifer P. *My Dog Lyle* (K–2). Illus. by author. 2007, Clarion $16.00 (978-0-618-63983-0). 32pp. An amusing child's view of why her beloved pet dog is so special. (Rev: BCCB 9/07; BL 6/1–15/07; SLJ 6/07)

6067 Golembe, Carla. *Annabelle's Big Move* (PS–1). Illus. 1999, Houghton $16.00 (978-0-395-91543-1). 32pp. When the family she lives with moves, Annabelle the dog is confused and a little frightened by all the activity, including being put in a crate that goes on an airplane. (Rev: BL 4/15/99; HBG 10/99; SLJ 5/99)

6068 Golson, Terry. *Tillie Lays an Egg* (PS–2). Illus. by Ben Fink. 2009, Scholastic $14.99 (978-0-545-00537-1). 32pp. Tillie the hen likes to lay her eggs in inventive places in this I-spy story that also provides basic information about chickens plus opportunities for counting and reviewing days of the week. (Rev: BCCB 1/09; BL 1/1–15/09; SLJ 1/09)

6069 Gore, Leonid. *Danny's First Snow* (PS–K). Illus. by author. 2007, Atheneum $16.99 (978-1-4169-1330-6). 32pp. A little bunny wakes up to find his world transformed by a snowfall. (Rev: BL 10/1/07; SLJ 12/07)

6070 Graber, Janet. *Muktar and the Camels* (PS–3). Illus. by Scott Mack. 2009, Holt $16.99 (978-0-8050-7834-3). 32pp. Muktar, an 11-year-old orphan on Kenya's border with Somalia who remembers his librarian father delivering books by camel, tends an injured camel and wins himself a job. (Rev: BL 6/1–15/09; LMC 10/09; SLJ 8/09)

6071 Graham, Bob. *How to Heal a Broken Wing* (PS–1). Illus. by author. 2008, Candlewick $16.99 (978-0-7636-3903-7). 40pp. A kind boy rescues an injured bird on a busy city street and nurses it back to health; the illustrations extend and highlight the poignant moments. (Rev: BCCB 10/08; BL 9/15/08*; SLJ 10/08*)

6072 Graham, Bob. *"The Trouble with Dogs . . ." Said Dad* (PS–2). Illus. by author. 2007, Candlewick $12.99 (978-0-7636-3316-5). 32pp. Kate's family sends hyper dog Dave to a trainer, but has he learned obedience at the expense of his fun personality? A sequel to 2001's *"Let's Get a Pup!" Said Kate*. (Rev: BCCB 9/07; BL 7/07; HB 9/07; SLJ 10/07)

6073 Gray, Rita. *The Wild Little Horse* (PS–2). Illus. by Ashley Wolff. 2005, Dutton $15.99 (978-0-525-47455-5). A young colt takes pleasure in his surroundings — and in his independence — as his parents allow him the freedom to run and explore. (Rev: SLJ 9/05)

6074 Greco, Francesca. *Cyril the Mandrill* (PS–2). Illus. by author. 2005, Star Bright $16.95 (978-1-932065-92-3). Lonely Cyril, derided by other animals in the zoo who are jealous of his bright, distinctive markings, finally wins them over. (Rev: SLJ 7/05)

6075 Grimes, Nikki. *When Gorilla Goes Walking* (PS–2). Illus. by Shane Evans. 2007, Scholastic $16.99 (978-0-439-31770-2). 32pp. Cecelia, a young African American girl, describes in interconnected poems the exploits of her assertive cat called Gorilla. (Rev: BL 4/15/07; HBG 10/07)

6076 Grindley, Sally. *Little Elephant Thunderfoot* (K–2). Illus. by John Butler. 1999, Peachtree $15.95 (978-1-56145-180-7). After his grandmother is killed by poachers in an African savanna, Little Elephant must find a new home and adjust to a new herd. (Rev: HBG 3/00; SLJ 2/00)

6077 Grindley, Sally. *Little Sibu: An Orangutan Tale* (PS–2). Illus. by John Butler. 1999, Peachtree $15.95 (978-1-56145-196-8). Little Sibu is now 7 and his mother must force him to leave her and live on his own as other male orangutans do. (Rev: HBG 10/99; SLJ 5/99)

6078 Grindley, Sally. *Polar Star* (K–3). Illus. by John Butler. 1998, Peachtree $15.95 (978-1-56145-181-4). A beautifully illustrated story about Polar Star, her cubs, and their activities in the cold land they call home. (Rev: HBG 3/99; SLJ 12/98)

6079 Grogan, John. *Bad Dog, Marley!* (PS–2). Illus. by Richard Cowdrey. 2007, HarperCollins $16.99 (978-0-06-117114-7). A yellow lab gets into all kinds of trouble but proves himself an important member of the family in this adaptation of the author's adult novel *Marley & Me*. (Rev: SLJ 8/07)

6080 Grooms, Molly. *We Are Bears* (PS–1). Illus. by Lucia Guarnotta. 2000, NorthWord $12.95 (978-1-55971-747-2). 32pp. A mother bear takes her two cubs out on a nature walk. (Rev: BL 12/15/00)

6081 Guilloppe, Antoine. *One Scary Night* (2–4). Illus. 2005, Milk & Cookies $15.95 (978-0-689-04636-0). 32pp. In this scary, wordless picture book, a young boy wandering through the snowy woods alone at night is being followed by a creature that in the last spread turns out to be a friendly dog. (Rev: BL 11/1/05; SLJ 11/05)

6082 Guthrie, Arlo. *Mooses Come Walking* (PS–K). Illus. by Alice M. Brock. 1995, Chronicle $11.95 (978-0-8118-1051-7). 32pp. A picture book that gives advice to youngsters when moose come visiting at night. (Rev: BL 12/15/95)

6083 Haas, Jessie. *No Foal Yet* (1–3). Illus. by Joseph A. Smith. 1995, Greenwillow LB $15.93 (978-0-688-12956-9). 24pp. Nora becomes impatient waiting for her horse Bonnie to give birth; but when it finally happens, no one is around. (Rev: BL 5/15/95; HB 5/95; SLJ 6/95)

6084 Hale, Irina. *The Naughty Crow* (K–3). Illus. 1992, Macmillan LB $14.95 (978-0-689-50546-1). 32pp. In a story set in czarist Russia, a naughty crow is banished from the household that has adopted him. (Rev: BL 11/5/92; SLJ 10/92)

6085 Halfmann, Janet. *Little Skink's Tail* (2–4). Illus. by Laurie Allen Klein. 2007, Sylvan Dell $15.95 (978-0-9768823-8-1); paper $8.95 (978-1-934359-20-4). Little Skink quickly jettisons her tail when attacked by a crow and then tries on some other ones for size; this humorous story also offers information about animals and their appendages. (Rev: LMC 1/08; SLJ 1/08)

6086 Hammerle, Susa. *Let's Try Horseback Riding* (PS–2). Trans. by Marisa Miller. Illus. by Kyrima Trapp. 2006, North-South $12.95 (978-0-7358-2093-7). 24pp. Rebecca is thrilled to receive riding lessons for her birthday, and learns all about caring for horses, horseback riding, and equine behavior. (Rev: BL 9/15/06; SLJ 11/06)

6087 Harjo, Joy. *The Good Luck Cat* (PS–3). Illus. by Paul Lee. 2000, Harcourt $16.00 (978-0-15-232197-0). Having used up eight of her nine lives, Woogie, a cat, disappears and everyone fears the worse. (Rev: BCCB 4/00; BL 6/1–15/03; HBG 10/00; SLJ 4/00)

6088 Harper, Isabelle. *My Cats Nick and Nora* (PS–1). Illus. by Barry Moser. 1995, Scholastic $14.95 (978-0-590-47620-1). 32pp. Isabelle and cousin Emmie spend every Sunday taking care of the family pets, Nick and Nora. A sequel to *My Dog Rosie* (1994). (Rev: BL 10/1/95; SLJ 10/95)

6089 Harper, Isabelle. *Our New Puppy* (PS–1). Illus. by Barry Moser. 1996, Scholastic $14.95 (978-0-590-56926-2). 32pp. Rosie gradually grows to love the family's new puppy. (Rev: BL 9/1/96; SLJ 10/96)

6090 Harrison, David L. *Piggy Wiglet* (K–2). Illus. by Karen Stormer Brooks. 2007, Boyds Mills $16.95 (978-1-59078-386-3). A farm pig sees a little of the world on his way to catch the sun. He returns home at bedtime, tired from outrunning his pursuers on his adventure through town. (Rev: SLJ 5/07)

6091 Harshman, Terry Webb. *Bessie's Bed* (PS–2). Illus. by Sharon Hawkins Vargo. Series: Silly Millies. 2003, Millbrook LB $17.90 (978-0-7613-2742-4). 32pp. In this cumulative tale for beginning readers, a variety of creatures climb into Bessie's bed on a stormy night, but they all make too much noise for sleep. (Rev: HBG 4/04; SLJ 3/04)

6092 Hassett, John, and Ann Hassett. *The Nine Lives of Dudley Dog* (PS–2). Illus. by John Hassett. 2008, Houghton $16.00 (978-0-618-81153-3). 32pp. A little girl who wants a cat instead finds herself the owner of a dog that will chase cats over hill and dale, through thick and thin. (Rev: BL 6/1–15/08)

6093 Hazen, Barbara S. *Tight Times* (2–3). Illus. by Trina S. Hyman. 1979, Puffin paper $5.99 (978-0-14-050442-2). 32pp. A child is allowed to keep a stray kitten even though there are hard times in the household.

6094 Heiligman, Deborah. *Fun Dog, Sun Dog* (K–3). Illus. by Tim Bowers. 2005, Marshall Cavendish $14.95 (978-0-7614-5162-4). 32pp. Tinka, an energetic golden retriever, and her boy enjoy a day at the beach, described in catchy rhymes. (Rev: BL 5/1/05; SLJ 5/05)

6095 Helmer, Marilyn. *Fog Cat* (PS–2). Illus. by Paul Mombourquette. 1999, Kids Can $14.95 (978-1-55074-460-6). 32pp. Hannah manages, in foggy weather, to get a wild cat to come indoors — but only long enough to have her litter and leave again. (Rev: BL 3/15/99; HBG 10/99; SLJ 5/99)

6096 Helmer, Marilyn. *Mr. McGratt and the Ornery Cat* (PS–3). Illus. by Martine Gourbault. 1999, Kids Can $14.95 (978-1-55074-564-1). At first Mr. McGratt wants to get rid of the cat that has moved in but, in time, he realizes he has found the perfect pet. (Rev: HBG 3/00; SLJ 12/99)

6097 Henderson, Kathy. *Dog Story* (PS–K). Illus. 2005, Bloomsbury $16.99 (978-0-7475-5071-6). 32pp. Jo eventually gets the dog she wants, but only after she has been offered various substitutes — a mouse, a cat, a brother, and so forth. (Rev: BL 2/15/05; SLJ 4/05)

6098 Henkes, Kevin. *Birds* (PS–K). Illus. by Laura Dronzek. 2009, Greenwillow $17.99 (978-0-06-136304-7). 32pp. A little girl is fascinated by birds — their colors, shapes, sizes, movements, and so forth. (Rev: BL 1/1–15/09; SLJ 2/09)

6099 Henkes, Kevin. *A Good Day* (PS–K). Illus. by author. 2007, Greenwillow $16.99 (978-0-06-114018-1). 32pp. Four animals start off having a bad day, but luckily things turn around before the day is over. (Rev: BL 12/15/06; SLJ 3/07*)

6100 Henkes, Kevin. *Old Bear* (PS). Illus. by author. 2008, Greenwillow $17.99 (978-0-06-155205-2). 32pp. Throughout his long hibernation Old Bear dreams that he is a young cub enjoying the changing seasons. (Rev: BCCB 11/08; BL 6/1–15/08; HB 11/08; SLJ 9/08)

6101 Herriot, James. *Only One Woof* (2–4). Illus. by Peter Barrett. 1985, St. Martin's $13.00 (978-0-312-58583-9). 32pp. The sentimental story of two sheepdogs and the one and only time one of them barks. (Rev: BL 1/1/86; HB 3/86; SLJ 1/86)

6102 Hest, Amy. *The Dog Who Belonged to No One* (PS–1). Illus. by Amy Bates. 2008, Abrams $15.95 (978-0-8109-9483-6). 32pp. A lonely girl named Lia and a stray dog caught out in a storm find happiness and friendship. (Rev: BL 8/08; SLJ 8/08)

6103 Himler, Ronald. *Six Is So Much Less Than Seven* (K–2). Illus. by author. 2002, Star Bright $16.95 (978-1-887734-91-2). An old man mourns the death of his cat, which leaves him with only six. (Rev: HBG 10/02; SLJ 12/02)

6104 Himmelman, John. *Katie Loves the Kittens* (PS–2). Illus. by author. 2008, Holt $14.95 (978-0-8050-8682-9). 32pp. Katie the dog is much too rambunctious for the three new kittens until she learns that her joy is scaring them. (Rev: BLO 8/28/08; SLJ 9/08)

6105 Hirschi, Ron. *What Is a Cat?* (PS–K). Illus. by Linda Q. Younker. 1991, Walker LB $14.85 (978-0-8027-8123-9). 32pp. An attractive book for young browsers to enjoy. (Rev: BL 1/15/92; SLJ 11/91) [599.7]

6106 Hirschi, Ron. *What Is a Horse?* (PS–2). Illus. by Linda Q. Younker and Ron Hirschi. 1989, Walker LB $12.85 (978-0-8027-6877-3). 32pp. This introduction includes material on structure, habits, and uses of the horse. Also use: *Where Do Horses Live?* (1989). (Rev: BL 8/89; SLJ 1/90) [636.1]

6107 Hirschi, Ron. *Where Do Cats Live?* (PS–K). Illus. by Linda Q. Younker. 1991, Walker LB $14.85 (978-0-8027-8110-9). 32pp. A visually appealing book that shows cats living alone, together, indoors, outdoors, everywhere. (Rev: BL 1/15/92; SLJ 11/91) [636.8]

6108 Hiscock, Bruce. *Coyote and Badger: Desert Hunters of the Southwest* (2–4). Illus. 2001, Boyds Mills $15.95 (978-1-56397-848-7). 32pp. Coyote and Badger discover that each can use the other's talents to make hunting more efficient. (Rev: BL 4/15/01; HBG 10/01; SLJ 7/01)

6109 Hobbs, Leigh. *Old Tom, Man of Mystery* (K–2). Illus. by author. 2005, Peachtree $16.95 (978-1-56145-346-7). Angry when his mistress assigns him

a number of chores, Old Tom the cat decides to play a trick on her; a sequel to *Old Tom's Holiday* (2004). (Rev: SLJ 12/05)

6110 Hobbs, Leigh. *Old Tom's Holiday* (K–3). Illus. by author. 2004, Peachtree $16.95 (978-1-56145-316-0). Angela Throgmorton believes she left her cat at home but she is lonely on holiday and is thrilled to find out that he came along after all. (Rev: SLJ 11/04)

6111 Hodgkins, Fran. *The Cat of Strawberry Hill: A True Story* (PS–2). Illus. by Lesia Sochor. 2005, Down East $15.95 (978-0-89272-684-4). 32pp. A playful kitten that goes astray from its owners at a highway rest stop is adopted by innkeepers and has a satisfying life thereafter. (Rev: BL 12/15/05; SLJ 3/06)

6112 Hodgkins, Fran. *Who's Been Here? A Tale in Tracks* (PS–2). Illus. by Karel Hayes. 2008, Down East $15.95 (978-0-89272-714-8). Three siblings follow their dog on a winter's day and inspect the various tracks left in the snow. (Rev: SLJ 12/08)

6113 Hodgkinson, Leigh. *Boris and the Snoozebox* (PS–2). Illus. by author. 2008, Tiger Tales $15.95 (978-1-58925-071-0). 32pp. When Boris the cat is tired he climbs into a cardboard box for a nap, only to find himself being shipped overseas. (Rev: BL 4/1/08; SLJ 7/08)

6114 Hollenbeck, Kathleen M. *Islands of Ice: The Story of a Harp Seal* (PS–3). Illus. by John Paul Genzo. Series: Smithsonian Backyard. 2001, Smithsonian Institution $15.95 (978-1-56899-965-4). 32pp. This fictional story about a harp seal focuses on true facts about the animal's life and habitat. (Rev: BL 2/1/02)

6115 Holsonback, Anita. *Monkey See, Monkey Do: An Animal Exercise Book for You!* (PS–K). Illus. by Leo Timmers. 1997, Millbrook LB $20.90 (978-0-7613-0260-5). Each page features an animal in its natural habitat along with a drawing of a boy and girl who mimic the way the creature moves and a verse. (Rev: HBG 3/98; SLJ 1/98)

6116 Holtei, Christa. *Nanuk Flies Home* (K–2). Illus. by Astrid Vohwinkel. 2008, Eerdmans $16.00 (978-0-8028-5342-4). 26pp. A baby polar bear's dream of flying comes true in a most unusual way. (Rev: SLJ 9/08)

6117 Hornsey, Chris. *Why Do I Have to Eat off the Floor?* (PS–1). Illus. by Gwyn Perkins. 2007, Walker $15.95 (978-0-8027-9617-2). 24pp. Murphy, a fun-loving beagle, poses all sorts of questions about his life to his young owner. (Rev: BL 4/1/07; SLJ 3/07)

6118 Houk, Randy. *Chessie, the Travelin' Man* (K–3). Illus. by Paula Bartlett. 1997, Benefactory $12.95 (978-1-882728-56-5). 32pp. The story of a Florida manatee and his trips from the South to Port Judith, Rhode Island, in 1994 and 1995. (Rev: SLJ 11/97)

6119 Hubbell, Patricia. *Bouncing Time* (PS). Illus. by Melissa Sweet. 2000, HarperCollins LB $15.89 (978-0-688-17377-7). 32pp. A delightful rhyming poem about a mother with a child in a backpack who visit a zoo and watch the animals at play. (Rev: BCCB 5/00; BL 4/1/00; HBG 10/00; SLJ 7/00)

6120 Hucke, Johannes. *Pip in the Grand Hotel* (PS–2). Illus. by Daniel Muller. 2009, North-South $16.95 (978-0-7358-2225-2). 32pp. A pet mouse named Pip's escape prompts a boisterous chase through an exclusive hotel; detailed illustrations add to the fun. (Rev: BL 3/1/09; SLJ 5/09)

6121 Huggins-Cooper, Lynn. *Alien Invaders / Invasores extraterrestres* (1–3). Trans. by Eida de la Vega. Illus. by Bonnie Leick. 2005, Raven Tree $16.95 (978-0-9724973-9-8). 32pp. In this attractive bilingual picture book, a little boy becomes convinced that the insects he sees all around him are alien invaders from outer space. (Rev: SLJ 10/05)

6122 Huneck, Stephen. *Sally Gets a Job* (PS–2). Illus. by author. 2008, Abrams $16.95 (978-0-8109-9493-5). 32pp. Sally the black lab imagines herself in a variety of jobs — teacher, archaeologist, hip hop star, chef, and so forth. (Rev: BL 4/1/08; SLJ 4/08)

6123 Huneck, Stephen. *Sally Goes to the Beach* (K–3). Illus. 2000, Abrams $17.95 (978-0-8109-4186-1). 38pp. Simple color woodcuts are used to illustrate this dog's-eye view of a day at the beach. (Rev: BCCB 11/00; BL 5/15/00; HBG 10/00; SLJ 6/00)

6124 Huneck, Stephen. *Sally Goes to the Mountains* (PS–1). Illus. by author. 2001, Abrams $17.95 (978-0-8109-4485-5). Sally the black Lab has a wonderful dream in which she goes to the mountains and meets all kinds of animals. (Rev: HBG 10/01; SLJ 7/01)

6125 Huneck, Stephen. *Sally Goes to the Vet* (PS–2). Illus. 2004, Abrams $17.95 (978-0-8109-4813-6). 32pp. Sally, a good-natured black Labrador, finds that a visit to the vet's office can be fun. (Rev: BL 5/15/04; SLJ 11/04)

6126 Huneck, Stephen. *Sally's Snow Adventure* (PS–2). 2006, Abrams $15.95 (978-0-8109-7061-8). 32pp. While on a ski trip to a dog-friendly resort, Sally the black Labrador retriever gets lost but is finally saved by a pair of rescue dogs that she befriended earlier. (Rev: BL 9/1/06; SLJ 10/06)

6127 Hutchins, Hazel. *One Duck* (K–2). Illus. by Ruth Ohi. 1999, Annick LB $18.95 (978-1-55037-561-9); paper $6.95 (978-1-55037-560-2). A duck whose nest is in the way of an oncoming tractor is helped by a considerate farmer. (Rev: HBG 3/00; SLJ 10/99)

6128 Imai, Ayano. *Chester* (PS–1). Illus. by author. 2007, Penguin $16.99 (978-0-698-40062-7). 32pp. Chester the dog runs away because he feels neglected by his human family, and his fruitless quest for a new home makes him appreciate his owners, who had never stopped searching for him. (Rev: BL 6/1–15/07; SLJ 12/07)

6129 Isadora, Rachel. *A South African Night* (PS–K). Illus. 1998, Greenwillow $14.89 (978-0-688-11390-2). 24pp. As the people of Johannesburg go home after a day's work and prepare for bed, many of the animals in the Kruger National Park begin their noc-

turnal activities. (Rev: BCCB 4/98; BL 2/15/98; HBG 10/98; SLJ 8/98)

6130 Jagtenberg, Yvonne. *Jack's Rabbit* (PS–1). Illus. 2003, Millbrook $15.95 (978-0-7613-1544-5). 32pp. Jack's rabbit escapes while Jack is trying to draw him and Jack hunts for him all over the place. (Rev: BL 3/1/03)

6131 Janisch, Heinz. *Heave Ho!* (PS–K). Illus. by Carola Holland. 2006, North-South $16.95 (978-0-7358-2091-3). In only 12 sentences, this entertaining tale shows a dog, a cat, and a few mice banding together to raid the refrigerator. (Rev: SLJ 11/06)

6132 Jeffers, Susan. *My Chincoteague Pony* (PS–3). Illus. by author. 2008, Hyperion $16.99 (978-1-4231-0023-2). 40pp. Young Julie, a fan of *Misty of Chincoteague*, is desperate to get a pony and finally succeeds through the generosity of others. (Rev: BCCB 7–8/08; BL 4/15/08; HB 7/08; LMC 3/08; SLJ 6/08)

6133 Jenkins, Emily. *Skunkdog* (PS–2). Illus. by Pierre Pratt. 2008, Farrar $16.95 (978-0-374-37009-1). 32pp. Dumpling is a lonely dog because she's different — she has no sense of smell — and to her family's dismay she makes friends with a skunk. (Rev: BL 5/1/08; SLJ 4/08)

6134 Jenkins, Emily. *Sugar Would Not Eat It* (PS–2). Illus. by Giselle Potter. 2009, Random $16.99 (978-0-375-83603-9). 40pp. Leo has adopted a stray cat he calls Sugar and he cannot understand why it won't eat a piece of his birthday cake. (Rev: BCCB 7–8/09; BL 3/15/09; SLJ 5/09)

6135 Jennings, Linda. *Little Puppy Lost* (PS–K). Illus. by Alison Edgson. 2008, Good Bks. $16.95 (978-1-56148-635-9). 32pp. Ollie, a little golden puppy, finds himself lost and alone in a snowy field and must bravely try to find his way home. (Rev: BL 12/1/08; SLJ 12/08)

6136 Jennings, Sharon. *Bearcub and Mama* (PS). Illus. by Melanie Watt. 2005, Kids Can $15.95 (978-1-55337-556-2). 32pp. Bearcub has learned well from his mother, and when he is separated from her in a storm, he knows what to do. (Rev: BL 2/15/05)

6137 Johnson, Herschel. *A Visit to the Country* (1–3). Illus. by Romare Bearden. 1989, HarperCollins $13.95 (978-0-06-022849-1). 32pp. Mike nurses an injured cardinal back to health but knows he must return it to the wild. (Rev: BL 9/15/89; SLJ 12/89)

6138 Johnson, Paul B., and Celeste Lewis. *Lost* (PS–2). Illus. by Paul Johnson. 1996, Orchard LB $16.99 (978-0-531-08851-7). 32pp. While camping out in Arizona's Tonto National Forest, a young girl's dog wanders off and gets lost. (Rev: BCCB 3/96; BL 4/1/96; SLJ 4/96*)

6139 Johnson, Rebecca. *The Proud Pelican's Secret* (K–2). Photos by Steve Parish. Series: Animal Storybooks. 2005, Gareth Stevens LB $22.00 (978-0-8368-5974-4). 24pp. A pelican who seems more interested in his looks than in fishing nonetheless always seems well fed; facts and photographs round out this nice combination of fiction and nonfiction. (Rev: SLJ 2/06)

6140 Johnson, Rebecca. *Sea Turtle's Clever Plan* (K–2). Photos by Steve Parish. 2005, Gareth Stevens LB $22.00 (978-0-8368-5975-1). 24pp. A clever, newly hatched sea turtle finds a way to avoid danger on her trip to the sea; facts and photographs round out this nice combination of fiction and nonfiction. (Rev: SLJ 2/06)

6141 Johnson, Rebecca. *Tree Frog Hears a Sound* (K–2). Photos by Steve Parish. Series: Animal Storybooks. 2005, Gareth Stevens LB $22.00 (978-0-8368-5976-8). 24pp. A female tree frog hops through the forest in search of the male whose call she has heard; facts and photographs round out this nice combination of fiction and nonfiction. (Rev: SLJ 2/06)

6142 Johnston, Tony. *The Barn Owls* (PS–3). Illus. by Deborah Kogan Ray. 2000, Charlesbridge $15.95 (978-0-88106-981-5). 32pp. Eloquent pictures and text describe the activities of a family of barn owls. (Rev: BL 2/15/00; HBG 10/00; SLJ 3/00)

6143 Jonas, Ann. *Bird Talk* (K–2). Illus. 1999, Greenwillow LB $14.89 (978-0-688-14173-8). 32pp. About 65 different species of birds comment on a garden being seeded, with each bird identified by name at the back of this imaginative nature book. (Rev: BCCB 5/99; BL 6/1–15/99; HBG 10/99; SLJ 4/99)

6144 Jones, Jolie. *Little Kisses* (K–2). Illus. by Julie Downing. Series: The Julie Andrews Collection. 2005, HarperCollins LB $16.89 (978-0-06-058699-7). Bejinhos the dog and Jolie enjoy each other's company and know the rules, but Bejinhos gets into trouble while his mistress is spending at school; appealing illustrations enhance the meandering text. (Rev: SLJ 1/06)

6145 Joosse, Barbara M. *Bad Dog School* (K–3). Illus. by Jennifer Plecas. 2004, Clarion $15.00 (978-0-618-13331-4). 32pp. After going to obedience school, formerly over-zesty puppy Zippy becomes too restrained and his family decides to untrain him a bit. (Rev: SLJ 9/04)

6146 Joosse, Barbara M. *Wind-Wild Dog* (1–3). Illus. by Kate Kiesler. 2006, Holt $16.95 (978-0-8050-7053-8). 32pp. Sled-dog Ziva faces a difficult choice between remaining with the man who has shown his faith in her and running free with the wolves she hears at night. (Rev: BL 10/1/06; SLJ 11/06)

6147 Karon, Jan, and Melanie Cecka. *Violet Comes to Stay* (K–2). Illus. by Emily Arnold McCully. 2006, Viking $15.99 (978-0-670-06073-3). Violet the kitten fails to remember her mother's mousing advice and has problems finding a suitable home. (Rev: SLJ 11/06)

6148 Kasperson, James. *Little Brother Moose* (PS–3). Illus. by Karlyn Holman. 1995, Dawn paper $7.95 (978-1-883220-33-4). 32pp. A young moose who wanders into town finds his way home by following migrating geese. (Rev: BL 7/95; SLJ 10/95)

6149 Kasza, Keiko. *The Dog Who Cried Wolf* (PS–2). Illus. 2005, Putnam $15.99 (978-0-399-24247-2). 32pp. When his owner reads him a book about wolves, Moka the dog decides to run away to the wilds and live free, but eventually discovers a wolf's life is not quite what he expected. (Rev: BL 9/1/05; SLJ 12/05*)

6150 Katz, Susan. *Oh, Theodore!* (PS–2). Illus. by Stacey Schuett. 2007, Clarion $16.00 (978-0-618-70222-0). 32pp. Told in short poems and free verse, this is an appealing story about a Latino boy and his guinea pig. (Rev: BL 9/1/07; SLJ 10/07) [811.54]

6151 Keller, John G. *The Rubber-Legged Ducky* (K–2). Illus. by Henry Cole. 2008, Harcourt $16.00 (978-0-15-205289-8). 32pp. Five the duckling was born with a rubber leg (his mother accidentally swallowed a rubber band) and says "bing-boing" instead of quacking; but his strange physique proves useful when a fox comes prowling. (Rev: BL 5/15/08; SLJ 4/08)

6152 Kelly, Irene. *A Small Dog's Big Life: Around the World with Owney* (PS–2). Illus. 2005, Holiday $16.95 (978-0-8234-1863-3). 32pp. This engaging picture book chronicles in fictionalized letters and newspaper accounts the story of Owney, a stray dog that became a post office mascot in the late 19th century and traveled around the world. (Rev: BL 7/05; SLJ 8/05)

6153 Kerby, Mona. *Owney, the Mail-Pouch Pooch* (K–3). Illus. by Lynne Barasch. 2008, Farrar $16.95 (978-0-374-35685-9). 40pp. A stray dog called Owney finds a home at the post office, traveling all the way across the country and even further afield as he guards the mail; based on the true story of a late 19th-century dog whose body is preserved at the Smithsonian. (Rev: BCCB 6/08; BL 4/1/08; HB 7/08; SLJ 4/08)

6154 Kerr, Judith. *Goodbye Mog* (K–3). Illus. by author. 2003, HarperCollins $17.95 (978-0-00-714968-1). Mog the cat dies early in this book but lingers around in spirit to watch over her family's recovery and acceptance of a new kitten. (Rev: SLJ 4/03)

6155 Kerr, Judith. *Goose in a Hole* (PS–2). Illus. by author. 2006, Collins $15.99 (978-0-00-720793-0). In search of the water that has mysteriously gone missing from the village pond, Katerina the goose fearlessly sets off down a hole, family in tow. (Rev: SLJ 7/06)

6156 Kimmel, Haven. *Orville: A Dog Story* (K–3). Illus. by Robert Andrew Parker. 2003, Clarion $15.00 (978-0-618-15955-0). 32pp. A moving story about a stray dog trying to find a comfortable home. (Rev: BCCB 11/03; BL 9/15/03; HBG 4/04; LMC 1/04; SLJ 11/03)

6157 King, Deborah. *The Flight of the Snow Geese* (K–2). Illus. 1998, Orchard $15.95 (978-0-531-30088-6). 32pp. In verses accompanied by watercolor paintings, the author tells of the annual journey of snow geese from their tundra home to warmer climates. (Rev: BL 9/15/98; HBG 3/99; SLJ 11/98)

6158 King, Stephen Michael. *Mutt Dog!* (PS–2). Illus. 2005, Harcourt $16.00 (978-0-15-205561-5). 32pp. Mutt Dog struggles to survive on the city streets until he is adopted by a worker at the local homeless shelter. (Rev: BL 10/1/05; SLJ 11/05)

6159 Kirk, David. *Little Bunny, Biddle Bunny* (PS). Illus. by author. 2002, Scholastic $9.95 (978-0-439-33819-6). A gentle story of a little rabbit's adventures in sunny meadows. (Rev: HBG 10/02; SLJ 4/02)

6160 Koldofsky, Eleanor. *Clip-Clop* (K–3). Illus. by David Parkins. 2005, Tundra $15.95 (978-0-88776-681-7). In this nostalgia-filled picture book set in the early 20th century, young Consuela lives for her encounters with the workhorses that pass through her neighborhood each day; an Author's Note provides additional information. (Rev: SLJ 11/05)

6161 Koralek, Jenny. *Cat and Kit* (PS–2). Illus. by Patricia MacCarthy. 1995, Hyperion LB $14.49 (978-0-7868-2030-6). 32pp. Cat rescues Kit, but in time the young kitten returns to the wild where he belongs. (Rev: BL 7/95; SLJ 9/95)

6162 Kotzwinkle, William, and Glenn Murray. *Walter the Farting Dog* (K–3). Illus. by Audrey Colman. 2001, Frog $14.95 (978-1-58394-053-2). 32pp. Poor Walter's flatulence almost causes his new family to return him to the pound, until he uses his unique "gift" to save them from burglars. (Rev: BL 2/15/02)

6163 Kotzwinkle, William, and Glenn Murray. *Walter the Farting Dog: Trouble at the Yard Sale* (K–3). Illus. by Audrey Colman. 2004, Dutton $16.99 (978-0-525-47217-9). 32pp. Walter proves himself a hero in this grossly amusing second book about his flatulent tendencies. (Rev: BL 4/15/04; SLJ 4/04)

6164 Krebs, Laurie. *We're Sailing to Galapagos: A Week in the Pacific* (PS–3). Illus. by Grazia Restelli. 2005, Barefoot Books $16.99 (978-1-84148-902-5). During a visit to the Galapagos, readers are introduced to the various animals found there, with informative text following a rhyming story. (Rev: SLJ 5/05)

6165 Kroll, Steven. *Patches Lost and Found* (K–3). Illus. by Barry Gott. 2001, Winslow $15.95 (978-1-890817-53-4). 32pp. Jenny loves to draw pictures but can't write stories, so she draws pictures of her pet hamster and fills in the words of a story afterward. (Rev: BL 3/1/01*; HBG 10/01)

6166 Kroll, Steven. *A Tale of Two Dogs* (PS–1). Illus. by Mike Reed. 2004, Marshall Cavendish $16.95 (978-0-7614-5161-7). 32pp. When the Morrisons return puppy Morgan to the pound and come home with a less unruly dog, are they really further ahead? (Rev: BL 4/15/04; SLJ 7/04)

6167 Kroll, Virginia. *Motherlove* (PS–2). Illus. by Lucia Washburn. 1998, Dawn $16.95 (978-1-883220-81-5); paper $7.95 (978-1-883220-80-8). In rhyming text, the role of mothers in the animal kingdom is explored with paintings of various animal mothers and their offspring. (Rev: HBG 3/99; SLJ 3/99) [591.56]

6168 Kuskin, Karla. *So, What's It Like to Be a Cat?* (PS–2). Illus. by Betsy Lewin. 2005, Simon & Schuster $15.95 (978-0-689-84733-2). 32pp. A self-confident cat happily answers in graceful lyrics the questions posed by a young interviewer. (Rev: BL 5/1/05)

6169 Kutner, Merrily. *Down on the Farm* (PS). Illus. by Will Hillenbrand. 2004, Holiday House $16.95 (978-0-8234-1721-6). Barnyard animals are introduced in bouncy rhymes and lots of caws, honks, and oinks. (Rev: SLJ 3/04)

6170 Kwon, Yoon-duck. *My Cat Copies Me* (K–3). Illus. 2007, Kane $15.95 (978-1-933605-26-5). 32pp. A young girl and her cat have fun together, copying each other's movements at play. (Rev: BL 4/15/07)

6171 Labatt, Mary. *Sam Gets Lost* (PS). Trans. and illus. by Marisol Sarrazin. Series: Kids Can Read. 2004, Kids Can paper $3.95 (978-1-55337-563-0). 32pp. Puppy Sam gets lost — and then found — in this simple story. Also use *Sam Goes to School* (2004). (Rev: BL 7/04)

6172 Lacombe, Benjamin. *Cherry and Olive* (PS–2). Illus. by author. 2007, Walker $16.95 (978-0-8027-9707-0). 32pp. In desperate need of a friend, lonely Cherry falls in love with a wrinkly dog at the animal shelter where her father works. (Rev: BL 11/1/07; SLJ 12/07)

6173 Lang, Glenna. *Looking Out for Sarah* (PS–3). Illus. 2001, Charlesbridge $15.95 (978-0-88106-647-0). 32pp. Based on a true story, this book presents a typical day in the life of a blind woman through the eyes of her guide dog, Perry. (Rev: BL 11/1/01; HB 9/01; HBG 3/02; SLJ 9/01)

6174 Lange, Willem. *John and Tom* (K–3). Illus. by Burt Dodson. Series: Family Heritage. 2001, Vermont Folklife Center $14.95 (978-0-916718-17-6). 32pp. A young logger named John is pinned beneath a tree and is rescued by his horse in this based-in-truth tale set in 1950s Vermont. (Rev: BL 11/1/01; SLJ 12/01)

6175 Lareau, Kara. *Ugly Fish* (1–4). Illus. by Scott Magoon. 2006, Harcourt $16.00 (978-0-15-205082-5). Ugly Fish, who would rather eat other fish than make friends, gets his comeuppance when Shiny Fish is introduced into his tank. (Rev: SLJ 7/06) ⊙

6176 Lawson, Julie. *Bear on the Train* (PS–2). Illus. by Brian Deines. 1999, Kids Can $15.95 (978-1-55074-560-3). 32pp. Bear enters the hopper of a train to eat some grain and becomes so comfortable that he hibernates there all winter. (Rev: BL 10/15/99; HBG 3/00; SLJ 11/99)

6177 Lears, Laurie. *Stay Away from Rat Boy!* (PS–3). Illus. by Red Hansen. 2009, Albert Whitman $16.99 (978-0-8075-6789-0). 32pp. A bully reforms through his close connection to the class rat. (Rev: BL 4/1/09; SLJ 4/09)

6178 Lechner, John. *A Froggy Fable* (PS–2). Illus. 2005, Candlewick $14.99 (978-0-7636-2123-0). 32pp. Accepting change is the message of this fable about a frog who is dismayed when his cozy home under a rock is disturbed. (Rev: BL 6/1–15/05; SLJ 5/05)

6179 Lee, Spike, and Tonya Lewis Lee. *Please, Puppy, Please* (PS–1). Illus. by Kadir Nelson. 2005, Simon & Schuster $16.95 (978-0-689-86804-7). 32pp. Two African American children give their high-energy puppy lots of instructions he fails to heed. (Rev: BL 11/1/05; SLJ 11/05)

6180 Leedy, Loreen. *Mapping Penny's World* (PS–2). Illus. 2000, Holt $17.00 (978-0-8050-6178-9). 32pp. Using her newly learned map skills, Penny draws maps of the territory covered by her pet boxer, Lisa. (Rev: BCCB 9/00; BL 7/00; HBG 3/01; SLJ 9/00)

6181 Lerner, Sharon. *Black Beauty* (K–2). Illus. by Susan Jeffers. 2009, Random $16.99 (978-0-375-85892-5). 40pp. This adaptation of the classic story excludes many details yet still retains the plot to create a shorter yet gratifying read with fine illustrations. (Rev: BLO 6/17/09; LMC 11/09)

6182 Lewin, Ted. *Nilo and the Tortoise* (K–3). Illus. by author. 1999, Scholastic $16.95 (978-0-590-69004-1). Young Nilo is stranded overnight on one of the Galapagos Islands and shares sleeping quarters with a giant tortoise. (Rev: BL 8/99; SLJ 4/99)

6183 Lewis, Kim. *A Puppy for Annie* (PS–2). Illus. by author. 2006, Candlewick $15.99 (978-0-7636-3200-7). Annie loves her Border collie Bess and gradually learns to understand what Bess is trying to convey as the two roam together in the English countryside. (Rev: BL 11/15/06; SLJ 2/07)

6184 Lewis, Wendy A. *In Abby's Hands* (1–4). Illus. by Marilyn Mets and Peter Ledwon. 2004, Red Deer $17.95 (978-0-88995-282-9). Abby is home alone when her Labrador retriever goes into labor, and she gains confidence as she offers the dog comfort and aid. (Rev: SLJ 3/04)

6185 Lindgren, Barbro. *Julia Wants a Pet* (K–2). Trans. from Swedish by Elisabeth Kallick Dyssegaard. Illus. by Eva Eriksson. 2003, R&S $15.00 (91-29-65940-X). Seven-year-old Julia travels far and wide in her search for the perfect pet. (Rev: HB 9/03; HBG 4/04; SLJ 11/03)

6186 Lindgren, Barbro. *Rosa: Perpetual Motion Machine* (PS–2). Illus. by Eva Eriksson. 1996, Douglas & McIntyre $14.95 (978-1-55054-241-7). 32pp. A mischievous pup breaks her lease, runs away, and gets lost. (Rev: BL 6/1–15/96; SLJ 7/96)

6187 Liwska, Renata. *Little Panda* (PS–2). Illus. by author. 2008, Houghton $12.95 (978-0-618-96627-1). 32pp. Alone for a time — and despite warnings from his mother and grandfather — little panda Bao Bao finds himself facing a hungry tiger in this charming picture book. (Rev: BL 12/1/08; HB 1/09; SLJ 11/08)

6188 Lobel, Anita. *Hello, Day!* (PS). Illus. by author. 2008, Greenwillow $16.99 (978-0-06-078765-3). 32pp. The animals of the farmyard greet the sun with various noises but only the owl signals its departure with a "Whoo-ooo." (Rev: BCCB 7–8/08; BL 4/1/08; HB 3/08; SLJ 3/08)

6189 Lobel, Anita. *Nini Here and There* (PS–K). Illus. 2007, Greenwillow $16.99 (978-0-06-078767-7). 32pp. Watching her family pack, Nini the cat fears she will be left behind but instead finds herself in a new and wonderful place. (Rev: BCCB 9/07; BL 5/1/07; SLJ 6/07)

6190 Lobel, Arnold. *The Rose in My Garden* (PS–3). Illus. by Anita Lobel. 1984, Morrow paper $7.99 (978-0-688-12265-2). 40pp. A cumulative tale that starts with a bee sleeping on a rose.

6191 London, Jonathan. *Baby Whale's Journey* (1–3). Illus. by Jon Van Zyle. 1999, Chronicle $14.95 (978-0-8118-2496-5). 35pp. A poetic introduction to the life of a sperm whale from its birth through weaning to final acceptance by the pod as they feed on a giant squid. (Rev: BL 11/1/99; HBG 3/00; SLJ 1/00)

6192 London, Jonathan. *Little Swan* (PS–3). Illus. by Kristina Rodanas. 2009, Marshall Cavendish $17.99 (978-0-7614-5523-3). 32pp. London follows a trumpeter swan's development from breaking out of its shell to its first migration. (Rev: BL 5/1/09; SLJ 4/09)

6193 Love, Donna. *Henry the Impatient Heron* (PS–3). Illus. by Christina Wald. 2009, Sylvan Dell $16.95 (978-1-934359-90-7); paper $8.95 (978-1-607180-35-7). 32pp. A simple story with happy illustrations tell this heron's tale; fact boxes and lesson plans. (Rev: SLJ 6/09)

6194 Luthardt, Kevin. *Larabee* (PS–1). Illus. 2004, Peachtree $15.95 (978-1-56145-300-9). 32pp. Larabee, an amiable puppy who likes to help deliver the mail, longs to receive a letter of his own. (Rev: BL 3/15/04; SLJ 4/04)

6195 Luthardt, Kevin. *Peep!* (PS–2). Illus. by author. 2003, Peachtree $15.95 (978-1-56145-046-6). A young boy and a hatchling duck become fast friends; when the bird eventually flies away, the youngster is sad until one day, on a walk, he hears a "mew." (Rev: BL 5/03; HB 7/03; HBG 10/03; SLJ 5/03)

6196 Lyon, George E. *Ada's Pal* (PS–1). Illus. by Marguerite Casparian. 1996, Orchard LB $15.99 (978-0-531-08878-4). 32pp. Ada pines away when her companion, the other dog in the family, dies. (Rev: BL 9/15/96; SLJ 9/96)

6197 Lyon, George E. *A Traveling Cat* (PS–1). Illus. by Paul Johnson. 1998, Orchard $15.95 (978-0-531-30102-9). 32pp. A little girl cares for a stray cat and tends to her litter. When the cat later disappears, the girl realizes that she is a born traveler. (Rev: BL 11/15/98; HB 11/98; HBG 3/99; SLJ 9/98)

6198 Macaulay, David. *Angelo* (K–3). Illus. 2002, Houghton $16.00 (978-0-618-16826-2). 48pp. An Italian artist and a wounded pigeon share an unlikely friendship in this beautifully illustrated picture book that gives a bird's-eye view of Rome. (Rev: BCCB 6/02; BL 7/02; HB 5/02; HBG 10/02; SLJ 5/02)

6199 McBratney, Sam. *I Love It When You Smile* (PS–1). Illus. by Charles Fuge. 2006, HarperCollins $15.99 (978-0-06-084245-1). Lively illustrations incorporating an onlooking mouse and duck add to the simple text about a mother kangaroo trying to cheer up her grumpy child. (Rev: SLJ 5/06)

6200 McCarty, Peter. *Fabian Escapes* (PS–K). Illus. 2007, Holt $16.95 (978-0-8050-7713-1). 32pp. In this colorful sequel to *Hondo and Fabian* (2002), Fabian the cat leads a canine trio on a merry chase while Hondo the dog is stuck at home playing with the toddler. (Rev: BL 3/15/07)

6201 McCarty, Peter. *Hondo and Fabian* (PS–K). Illus. 2002, Holt $16.95 (978-0-8050-6352-3). 32pp.

Captivating illustrations and simple text portray a day in the life of two family pets, Hondo the dog and Fabian the cat. Caldecott Honor Book, 2003. (Rev: BL 2/15/02; HBG 10/02; SLJ 6/02)

6202 McDonald, Megan. *Insects Are My Life* (PS–2). Illus. by Paul Johnson. 1995, Orchard LB $16.99 (978-0-531-08724-4). 32pp. No one seems to understand Amanda's fascination with insects. (Rev: BCCB 4/95; BL 3/1/95; HB 3/95; SLJ 3/95*)

6203 McDonald, Megan. *Whoo-oo Is It?* (PS–1). Illus. by S. D. Schindler. 1992, Orchard LB $16.99 (978-0-531-08574-5). 32pp. A mother owl oversees the hatching of her egg in this book that explores the sounds of the night. (Rev: BL 2/1/92; HB 5/92; SLJ 4/92)

6204 McFarland, Lyn Rossiter. *Widget* (PS–1). Illus. by Jim McFarland. 2001, Farrar $16.00 (978-0-374-38428-9). 32pp. Preschoolers will love the charming illustrations and humorous story about a stray dog who pretends to be a cat in order to fit in at his new home. (Rev: BL 11/1/01; HBG 3/02; SLJ 8/01*)

6205 McFarland, Lyn Rossiter. *Widget and the Puppy* (PS–2). Illus. by Jim McFarland. 2004, Farrar $16.00 (978-0-374-38429-6). Widget the dog falls asleep while babysitting a puppy and it is the six cats of the household that save the day, although they get none of the praise. (Rev: SLJ 9/04)

6206 McFarlane, Sheryl. *This Is the Dog* (PS–2). Illus. by Chrissie Wysotski. 2003, Fitzhenry & Whiteside $15.95 (978-1-55041-551-3). Rhythmic text and striking illustrations highlight this story of a wayward golden retriever puppy. (Rev: SLJ 10/03)

6207 McGhee, Alison. *Always* (PS–1). Illus. by Pascal LeMaitre. 2009, Simon & Schuster $15.99 (978-1-4169-7481-9). 40pp. A lovable dog explains, through words and sweet illustrations, the many ways he will keep the "castle" safe because he loves his young owner so much. (Rev: LMC 10/09; SLJ 5/09)

6208 McGraw, Sheila. *Pussycats Everywhere!* (PS–2). Illus. by author. 2000, Firefly LB $19.95 (978-1-55209-346-7); paper $6.95 (978-1-55209-348-1). When Karen's cat wanders away and she places lost-cat posters everywhere, 37 cats are brought to her house. (Rev: HBG 3/01; SLJ 12/00)

6209 McGrory, Anik. *Kidogo* (PS–1). Illus. by author. 2005, Bloomsbury $15.95 (978-1-58234-974-9). Kidogo, a young elephant, is feeling very small until he encounters a colony of ants. (Rev: SLJ 9/05*)

6210 McHenry, E. B. *Has Anyone Seen Winnie and Jean?* (PS–1). Illus. by author. 2007, Bloomsbury $16.95 (978-1-58234-999-2). 32pp. Corgis Winnie and Jean escape from their yard and have a great deal of fun before being captured. (Rev: BL 6/1–15/07; SLJ 7/07)

6211 McHenry, E. B. *Poodlena* (PS–1). Illus. 2004, Bloomsbury $16.95 (978-1-58234-824-7). 32pp. Poodlena, a pampered pink poodle, takes pains to preserve her pristine appearance until an encounter with a playful canine persuades her that she's been missing out on a lot of fun. (Rev: BL 5/1/04; SLJ 11/04)

6212 McKenna, Virginia. *Back to the Blue* (K–3). Illus. by Ian Andrew. Series: Born Free Wildlife Book/Templar Book. 1998, Millbrook LB $21.40 (978-0-7613-0409-8). Based on fact, these are accounts of real animal rescue and relocation projects run by the conservation charity Born Free Foundation. (Rev: BL 8/98; HBG 10/98; SLJ 3/98)

6213 McKinlay, Penny. *Flabby Tabby* (PS–1). Illus. by Britta Teckentrup. 2006, Frances Lincoln $15.95 (978-1-84507-090-8). 32pp. Tabby, an overweight cat, embarks on a secret fitness program when a new kitten arrives in the house and keeps beating her to the food bowl. (Rev: BL 1/1–15/06; SLJ 2/06)

6214 McLellan, Stephanie Simpson. *Leon's Song* (PS–3). Illus. by Dianna Bonder. 2004, Fitzhenry & Whiteside $15.95 (978-1-55041-813-2). Leon, a 40-year-old frog who lacks a sense of fulfillment, comes into his own when he alerts the pond creatures to the presence of danger. (Rev: SLJ 1/05)

6215 MacLeod, Elizabeth. *I Heard a Little Baa* (PS). Illus. by Louise Phillips. 1998, Kids Can $10.95 (978-1-55074-496-5). 24pp. An animal guessing game in which different animal riddles-in-rhyme are solved by unfolding pages. (Rev: HBG 3/99; SLJ 12/98)

6216 McMillan, Bruce. *Gletta the Foal* (PS–2). Illus. 1998, Marshall Cavendish $14.95 (978-0-7614-5039-9). 32pp. An Icelandic foal tells her own story as she plays with other horses, adjusts to her family, and experiences new emotions. Captivating photos accompany the imaginative text. (Rev: BL 9/15/98; HBG 3/99; SLJ 12/98)

6217 McNulty, Faith. *The Lady and the Spider* (K–3). Illus. by Bob Marstall. 1986, HarperCollins $15.00 (978-0-06-024191-9). 48pp. The reader enters the small world of the spider, who lives on a head of lettuce in a garden and feels part of it. (Rev: BL 3/15/86; SLJ 9/86)

6218 McPhail, David. *The Searcher and Old Tree* (PS–K). Illus. by author. 2008, Charlesbridge $15.95 (978-1-58089-223-0). 32pp. After a night of searching for food, a raccoon climbs into his usual old tree and manages to sleep through a raging thunderstorm. (Rev: BL 2/15/08; LMC 10/08; SLJ 2/08)

6219 Madison, Alan. *Velma Gratch and the Way Cool Butterfly* (PS–2). Illus. by Kevin Hawkes. 2007, Schwartz & Wade $16.99 (978-0-375-83597-1). 40pp. A monarch butterfly rescues 1st-grader Velma from the long shadows cast by her talented older sisters in this story full of butterfly facts. (Rev: BL 10/15/07; SLJ 12/07)

6220 Madrigal, Antonio H. *Blanca's Feather* (1–4). Illus. by Gerardo Suzan. 2000, Rising Moon $15.95 (978-0-87358-743-3). 32pp. On Saint Francis of Assisi's Day, Rosalia can't find her hen to take to church to be blessed and brings one of her feathers instead. (Rev: BL 4/15/00; HBG 10/00; SLJ 7/00)

6221 Mahy, Margaret. *Dashing Dog!* (PS–2). Illus. by Sarah Garland. 2002, HarperCollins LB $15.89 (978-0-06-000457-6). 32pp. Rhyming verse and lively illustrations present a poodle's day at the beach, during which the rambunctious pup ruins his nice hairdo, chases birds and Frisbees . . . and rescues the baby. (Rev: BL 10/1/02; HBG 3/03; SLJ 9/02)

6222 Mallat, Kathy. *Trouble on the Tracks* (PS–K). Illus. 2001, Walker LB $16.85 (978-0-8027-8773-6). 24pp. A train is derailed by trouble — then it's revealed that Trouble is a cat, and the train is a toy. (Rev: BL 9/1/01; HBG 3/02; SLJ 9/01)

6223 Maltbie, P. I. *Picasso and Minou* (PS–2). Illus. by Pau Estrada. 2005, Charlesbridge $15.95 (978-1-57091-620-5). 32pp. Minou, a cat of strong artistic tastes who lives with Picasso, is pleased when the artist leaves his Blue Period in this beautifully illustrated picture book that blends fact and fiction. (Rev: BL 2/15/05; SLJ 4/05)

6224 Manning, Mick. *Cock-a-Doodle-Hooooooo!* (PS–2). Illus. by Brita Granström. 2007, Good Bks. $16.95 (978-1-56148-568-0). An owl makes himself at home on a farm that needs a rooster and finds that his talent for rodent-catching comes in handy. (Rev: SLJ 5/07)

6225 Mansfield, Howard. *Hogwood Steps Out: A Good, Good Pig Story* (K–2). Illus. by Barry Moser. 2008, Roaring Brook $16.95 (978-1-59643-269-7). 32pp. A huge pig named Christopher Hogwood narrates his adventures as he unlocks the gate and heads off into an exciting spring day. (Rev: BL 3/1/08; LMC 3/08; SLJ 6/08)

6226 Manuel, Lynn. *The Trouble with Tilly Trumble* (K–2). Illus. by Diane Greenseid. 2006, Abrams $16.95 (978-0-8109-5972-9). 32pp. Tilly Trumble is preoccupied by chairs and particularly by finding the right one for the comfortable spot by her fire, but the stray dog that appears on her doorstep seems to solve the problem. (Rev: BL 4/15/06; SLJ 12/06)

6227 Markle, Sandra. *Little Lost Bat* (2–4). Illus. by Allan Marks. 2006, Charlesbridge $15.95 (978-1-57091-656-4). 32pp. This picture-book tale about a newborn bat left to fend for itself after its mother is killed by a predator is full of bat facts and lore. (Rev: BL 6/1–15/06; HB 7/07; HBG 4/07; LMC 1/07; SLJ 8/06*)

6228 Marsh, T. J., and Jennifer Ward. *Way Out in the Desert* (PS–2). Illus. by Kenneth J. Spengler. 1998, Rising Moon $15.95 (978-0-87358-687-0). 32pp. Using double-page spreads, familiar animals of the desert are presented in a delightful takeoff on "Over in the Meadow." (Rev: BCCB 5/98; HBG 10/98; SLJ 6/98)

6229 Martin, Bill, Jr. *Baby Bear, Baby Bear, What Do You See?* (PS–K). Illus. by Eric Carle. 2007, Holt $16.95 (978-0-8050-8336-1). 32pp. Searching for his mother, a baby bear meets many native American animals. (Rev: BL 6/1–15/07; SLJ 8/07)

6230 Martin, Bill, Jr. *Panda Bear, Panda Bear, What Do You See?* (PS–2). Illus. by Eric Carle. 2003, Holt $15.95 (978-0-8050-1758-8). Ten endangered animals — including the bald eagle, red wolf, and black panther — are introduced in Martin and Carle's familiar format. (Rev: HBG 4/04; SLJ 8/03)

6231 Martin, Bill, Jr. *Polar Bear, Polar Bear, What Do You Hear?* (PS–K). Illus. by Eric Carle. 1991, Holt $15.95 (978-0-8050-1759-5). 32pp. Animal

sounds from 10 different animals are featured in this picture book. (Rev: BCCB 12/91; BL 11/15/91; HB 1/92; SLJ 11/91*)

6232 Martin, Jacqueline B. *Washing the Willow Tree Loon* (2–4). Illus. by Nancy Carpenter. 1995, Simon & Schuster $16.00 (978-0-689-80415-1). 40pp. A fictionalized account of how an oil-slicked loon is saved by a woman who, with others, tries to save animals after an oil barge hits a bridge. (Rev: BL 12/15/95; HB 9/95; SLJ 10/95)

6233 Marzollo, Jean. *Mama Mama* (PS). Illus. by Laura Regan. Series: Harper Growing Tree. 1999, HarperCollins $6.99 (978-0-694-01245-9). This board book celebrates the tender mother-child relations that exist with such animals as a lioness, leopard, chimpanzee, panda, elephant, and sea otter. (Rev: SLJ 11/99)

6234 Masurel, Claire. *¡No, Tito, no! / No, No, Titus!* (K–2). Trans. by Diego Lasconi. Illus. by Shari Halpern. 2006, North-South LB $16.50 (978-0-7358-2074-6); paper $6.95 (978-0-7358-2075-3). An endearing puppy, newly adopted by a farm family, tries to figure out where he fits in the overall scheme of things. (Rev: SLJ 10/06)

6235 Masurel, Eric. *Un gato y un perro / A Cat and a Dog* (PS–1). Trans. by Andres Antreasyan. Illus. by Bob Kolar. 2003, North-South paper $6.95 (978-0-7358-1784-5). A cat and dog, normally antagonistic toward each other, decide to band together to solve each other's problems in this bilingual tale. (Rev: BL 3/1/04)

6236 Meade, Holly. *A Place to Sleep* (PS–2). Illus. 2001, Marshall Cavendish $15.95 (978-0-7614-5096-2). 32pp. Facts about where and how different animals sleep, playfully conveyed through colorful illustrations and amusing text. (Rev: BCCB 12/01; BL 9/1/01; HBG 3/02; SLJ 9/01)

6237 Meister, Cari. *My Pony Jack at Riding Lessons* (PS–K). Illus. by Amy Young. Series: Viking Easy-to-Read. 2005, Viking $13.99 (978-0-670-05918-8). 32pp. In this sequel to *My Pony Jack* (2005) suitable for beginning readers, Lacy takes riding lessons. (Rev: BL 10/15/05; SLJ 10/05)

6238 Meister, Cari. *My Pony Jack at the Horse Show* (PS–2). Illus. by Amy Young. Series: Viking Easy-to-Read. 2006, Viking $13.99 (978-0-670-05919-5). 32pp. Lacy gets her pony Jack ready for a show, suffers some nerves when she arrives at the ring, and comes home with second prize; for beginning readers. (Rev: SLJ 8/06)

6239 Meister, Cari. *Tiny on the Farm* (K–1). Illus. by Rich Davis. 2008, Viking $16.99 (978-0-670-06246-1). 32pp. Tiny, the gigantic dog, helps to find kittens in this simple picture-book story that will have readers searching the images. (Rev: SLJ 5/08)

6240 Meyers, Susan. *Kittens! Kittens! Kittens!* (PS–K). Illus. by David Walker. 2007, Abrams $15.95 (978-0-8109-1218-2). 32pp. Rhyming text and cheerful pictures track kittens as they play, explore, and grow. (Rev: BL 1/1–15/07)

6241 Miles, Victoria. *Old Mother Bear* (PS–3). Illus. by Molly Bang. 2007, Chronicle $16.95 (978-0-8118-5033-9). 32pp. This strikingly illustrated picture book based on true events follows an aging female grizzly bear as she guides her final set of cubs along the path to adulthood. (Rev: BL 4/15/07)

6242 Miller, Edna. *Patches Finds a New Home* (K–2). Illus. by author. 1989, Simon & Schuster paper $12.95 (978-0-671-66266-0). 40pp. A mother cat searches for a new home for herself and her kittens. (Rev: BL 6/15/89; SLJ 6/89)

6243 Miller, Ruth. *I Went to the Bay* (PS–1). Illus. by Martine Gourbault. 1999, Kids Can $12.95 (978-1-55074-498-9). 24pp. A young boy searches above and below water for frogs but finds only a variety of other marine animals. (Rev: BL 3/15/99; HBG 10/99; SLJ 6/99) [629]

6244 Minor, Florence. *If You Were a Penguin* (PS). Illus. by Wendell Minor. 2009, HarperCollins $17.99 (978-0-06-113097-7). 32pp. Rhyming text presents all the things you could do if you were a penguin in this happy, fact-filled volume. (Rev: BL 1/1–15/09; SLJ 4/09)

6245 Minshull, Evelyn. *Eaglet's World* (PS–2). Illus. by Andrea Gabriel. 2002, Whitman $16.95 (978-0-8075-8929-8). 32pp. An eaglet ventures first from his egg and then from his nest in this story about growth and independence. (Rev: BL 3/1/02; HBG 10/02; SLJ 5/02)

6246 Mitchell, Adrian, and Daniel Pudles. *Twice My Size* (PS–1). Illus. 1999, Millbrook LB $22.90 (978-0-7613-1423-3). 32pp. A series of animals each introduces another animal friend that is bigger than it is. (Rev: BL 4/15/99; HBG 10/99; SLJ 6/99)

6247 Mitton, Tony. *All Afloat on Noah's Boat!* (PS–2). Illus. by Guy Parker-Rees. 2007, Scholastic $16.99 (978-0-439-87397-0). During the animal talent show on the ark, the two caterpillars on board are busy in their cocoons. They display their special "talent" at the end of this rhyming story, when they turn into butterflies. (Rev: SLJ 5/07)

6248 Mockford, Caroline. *Cleo the Cat* (PS). Illus. by author. 2000, Barefoot Books $14.99 (978-1-84148-259-0). A charming story about a cat named Cleo who finds a home and a friend. (Rev: HBG 3/01; SLJ 12/00)

6249 Mockford, Caroline. *Come Here, Cleo!* (PS–1). Illus. by author. 2001, Barefoot Books $14.99 (978-1-84148-329-0). A cat has simple adventures such as climbing a tree and chasing a butterfly. (Rev: HBG 10/01; SLJ 4/01)

6250 Molski, Carol. *Swimming Sal* (K–2). Illus. by Mary Newell Depalma. 2009, Eerdmans $17.00 (978-0-8028-5327-1). 32pp. A Portuguese water dog with ambition finally gets to display her swimming skills. (Rev: BL 4/15/09; SLJ 3/09)

6251 Montenegro, Laura Nyman. *A Poet's Bird Garden* (PS–3). Illus. by author. 2007, Farrar $16.00 (978-0-374-36038-2). 32pp. Natalie's pet bird has escaped, and even some local poets can't find the words to coax the bird out of a tree. (Rev: BL 7/07; SLJ 12/07)

6252 Murphy, Yannick. *Ahwooooooooo!* (PS–2). 2006, Clarion $16.00 (978-0-618-11762-8). 32pp. Little Wolf's parents are too busy to teach him how

to howl, so he turns to his grandfather for help. (Rev: BL 8/06; SLJ 6/06)

6253 Nethery, Mary. *Mary Veronica's Egg* (PS–2). Illus. by Paul Yalowitz. 1999, Orchard LB $16.99 (978-0-531-33134-7). 32pp. Mary Veronica finds a large egg that, to her delight, later hatches into a duckling. (Rev: BCCB 2/99; BL 7/99; HBG 10/99; SLJ 3/99)

6254 Newman, Leslea. *The Best Cat in the World* (PS–2). Illus. by Ronald Himler. 2004, Eerdmans $16.00 (978-0-8028-5252-6). 32pp. Mourning for his dead cat Charlie, Victor is reluctant to bring a new kitten into his life. (Rev: BL 1/1–15/04; SLJ 2/04)

6255 Niland, Deborah. *Annie's Chair* (PS–K). Illus. by author. 2006, Walker $16.95 (978-0-8027-8082-9). Annie initially has a very big problem when she finds the dog sitting in her special chair, but a kindly lick reminds her how to share. (Rev: SLJ 6/06)

6256 Nodset, Joan L. *Come Back, Cat* (PS–2). Illus. by Steven Kellogg. 2008, HarperCollins $16.99 (978-0-06-028081-9). 40pp. It takes some doing, but a little girl finally succeeds in making friends with a jumpy cat; originally published in 1973, this edition has new mixed-media illustrations. (Rev: BLO 8/28/08)

6257 Nolan, Lucy. *Bad to the Bone* (1–3). Illus. by Mike Reed. Series: Down Girl and Sit. 2008, Marshall Cavendish $14.99 (978-0-7614-5439-7). 64pp. A funny dog's-eye view of life, featuring Down Girl, her best friend Sit, and their efforts to train their humans. (Rev: BL 11/15/08; SLJ 1/09)

6258 Oates, Joyce Carol. *Naughty Chérie!* (PS–K). Illus. by Mark Graham. 2008, HarperCollins $16.99 (978-0-06-074358-1). 32pp. After a visit to an animal "kindercare," Little Chérie, a naughty kitten, learns to be better behaved and returns to her happy family. (Rev: BL 12/15/07; SLJ 1/08)

6259 Ochiltree, Dianne. *Pillow Pup* (PS–1). Illus. by Mireille D'Allance. 2002, Simon & Schuster $14.95 (978-0-689-83408-0). 32pp. Puppy Maggie and her owner enjoy a friendly pillow fight. (Rev: BL 5/15/02; HBG 10/02)

6260 O'Connor, Jane, and Jessie Hartland. *The Perfect Puppy for Me!* (1–3). Illus. by Jessie Hartland. 2003, Viking $15.99 (978-0-670-03614-1). A young boy who loves dogs researches the breeds that will be available on his birthday, conveying lots of information along with the endearing story. (Rev: BL 5/15/03; HBG 10/03; SLJ 7/03)

6261 O'Connor, Sandra Day. *Finding Susie* (PS–2). Illus. by Tom Pohrt. 2009, Knopf $16.99 (978-0-375-84103-3). 40pp. Longing for a pet, Sandra takes in a number of wild animals and then sets them free before deciding that what she needs is a dog; based on the childhood of the Supreme Court justice. (Rev: BLO 6/23/09; SLJ 5/09)

6262 O'Hair, Margaret. *My Pup* (PS). Illus. by Tammie Lyon. 2008, Marshall Cavendish $14.99 (978-0-7614-5389-5). 32pp. A little girl and her puppy pass a happy day together in this simple read-aloud with lots of repetition. (Rev: BL 4/1/08; SLJ 6/08)

6263 Okimoto, Jean D. *Blumpoe the Grumpoe Meets Arnold the Cat* (PS–3). Illus. by Howie Schneider. 1990, Little, Brown $13.95 (978-0-316-63811-1). 32pp. In an accommodating hotel, a grumpy old man is offered a cat to keep him company. (Rev: BL 5/15/90; HB 7/90; SLJ 7/90)

6264 Oliver, Narelle. *Twilight Hunt: A Seek-and-Find Book* (PS–K). Illus. by author. 2007, Star Bright $16.95 (978-1-59572-107-5). 33pp. As a mother screech owl sets out on her evening hunt to feed her babies, the illustrations clearly show the challenges she faces. (Rev: SLJ 12/07)

6265 Orr, Katherine. *Story of a Dolphin* (K–4). Illus. 1993, Carolrhoda LB $15.95 (978-0-87614-777-1). 32pp. Tourists on a Caribbean island mistreat the dolphin that Laura and her father have grown to love and understand. (Rev: BL 9/15/93; SLJ 10/93)

6266 Page, Gail. *How to Be a Good Dog* (PS–2). Illus. by author. 2006, Bloomsbury $15.95 (978-1-58234-683-0). Bobo wants to be a good dog, so the cat teaches him how to behave, with mixed results. (Rev: SLJ 6/06)

6267 Park, Linda Sue. *Mung-Mung: A Foldout Book of Animal Sounds* (PS). Illus. by Diane Bigda. 2004, Charlesbridge $9.95 (978-1-57091-486-7). This guessing game for preschoolers involves animal sounds in several languages — first the onomatopoeic sound in lettering, then, overleaf, a drawing of the animal who makes it. (Rev: SLJ 6/04) [418]

6268 Parker, Marjorie Blain. *Jasper's Day* (1–3). Illus. by Janet Wilson. 2002, Kids Can $15.95 (978-1-55074-957-1). 32pp. A touching but realistic story of a family's last day with their pet dog, before he is put to sleep. (Rev: BL 12/15/02; HBG 3/03; SLJ 1/03)

6269 Partridge, Elizabeth. *Big Cat Pepper* (K–3). Illus. by Lauren Castillo. 2009, Bloomsbury $16.99 (978-1-59990-024-7). 32pp. Pepper the cat becomes ill and dies in this story about loss. (Rev: BL 4/15/09; SLJ 6/09)

6270 Patent, Dorothy Hinshaw. *Baby Horses* (PS–1). Illus. by William Muñoz. 1991, Carolrhoda LB $22.60 (978-0-87614-690-3). 56pp. A new edition presenting the first months of a foal's life in simple text and color photos. (Rev: BL 1/1/92) [636.1]

6271 Pedersen, Janet. *Houdini the Amazing Caterpillar* (PS–2). Illus. by author. 2008, Clarion $16.00 (978-0-618-89332-4). 32pp. Houdini the caterpillar wows his classroom with his amazing transformations, especially the one to a butterfly; includes facts about the life cycle of a monarch butterfly. (Rev: BL 9/1/08)

6272 Penner, Lucille R. *Dinosaur Babies* (PS–1). Illus. by Peter Barrett. Series: Step into Reading. 1991, Random paper $3.99 (978-0-679-81207-4). 32pp. An easily read introduction to dinosaurs and their babies in large type with many illustrations. (Rev: BL 2/1/92; SLJ 1/92) [567.9]

6273 Perrow, Angeli. *Lighthouse Dog to the Rescue* (K–3). Illus. by Emily Harris. 2000, Down East $14.95 (978-0-89272-487-1). 32pp. Based on a real incident in Maine during the 1930s, a dog that lives in a lighthouse brings a mail boat's captain safely home during a terrible blizzard. (Rev: BL 3/1/01; HBG 10/01)

6274 Pfeffer, Wendy. *Mallard Duck at Meadow View Pond* (PS–3). Illus. by Taylor Oughton. Series: Smithsonian Backyard. 2001, Smithsonian Institution $15.95 (978-1-56899-956-2). 32pp. This fictional story about a duck focuses on true facts about the animal's life and habitat. (Rev: BL 2/1/02)

6275 Pichon, Liz. *Penguins* (PS–K). Illus. by author. 2008, Scholastic $12.99 (978-0-545-02215-6). 24pp. Penguins at the zoo find a camera and have a wonderful time mugging for it. (Rev: BL 9/1/08)

6276 Pierce, Terry. *Blackberry Banquet* (K–3). Illus. by Lisa Downey. 2008, Sylvan Dell $16.95 (978-1-934359-70-9); paper $8.95 (978-1-934359-28-0). 32pp. Forest animals feast on wild blackberries — until the bear comes; a "For Creative Minds" section features interesting facts. (Rev: LMC 11/08; SLJ 9/08)

6277 Pilkey, Dav. *Dogzilla* (K–3). Illus. 1993, Harcourt paper $7.00 (978-0-15-223945-9). 32pp. Using retouched photos of the author's pets as illustrations, this zany story tells of Dreadful Dogzilla, whose breath could send everyone running. Also use *Kat Kong* (1993). (Rev: BL 9/1/93; SLJ 12/93)

6278 Pinkney, Jerry. *The Lion and the Mouse* (PS–1). Illus. by author. 2009, Little, Brown $16.99 (978-0-316-01356-7). 40pp. Jerry Pinkney's lively, wordless retelling of Aesop's famous fable unfolds through beautiful watercolor illustrations. (Rev: BCCB 11/09; BL 7/09*; HB 11/09; SLJ 9/09)

6279 Pitzer, Susanna. *Not Afraid of Dogs* (PS–2). Illus. by Larry Day. 2006, Walker $16.95 (978-0-8027-8067-6). 32pp. Daniel is not scared of dogs although he does everything he can to avoid them, but when he finds his visiting aunt's dog cowering in the bathroom during a thunderstorm, he can't resist offering comfort. (Rev: BL 6/1–15/06; SLJ 7/06*)

6280 Plowden, Sally Hartmam. *Turtle Tracks* (PS–2). Illus. by Tee Plowden. 2002, PCF $14.95 (978-0-9679016-6-4). 32pp. At the beach one day, a girl learns all about sea turtles in this book that includes turtle facts and wildlife resources. (Rev: BL 7/02)

6281 Polacco, Patricia. *Mrs. Mack* (K–4). Illus. 1998, Penguin $16.99 (978-0-399-23167-4). 40pp. Drawing on incidents in the author's childhood, this is the story of Mrs. Mack, who allowed the author to work around horses and gain self-confidence. (Rev: BL 11/15/98; HBG 3/99; SLJ 12/98)

6282 Poppenhäger, Nicole. *Snow Leopards* (K–3). Trans. from German by J. Alison James. Illus. by Ivan Gantschev. 2006, North-South $15.95 (978-0-7358-2087-6). Two young snow leopards separated by an avalanche search for each other and are eventually reunited; a moving story with dramatic artwork. (Rev: SLJ 11/06)

6283 Porte, Barbara Ann. *Tale of a Tadpole* (PS–3). Illus. by Annie Cannon. 1997, Orchard LB $16.99 (978-0-531-33049-4). 32pp. Francine watches the changes that occur to a tadpole until it becomes a toad. (Rev: BL 8/97; HBG 3/98; SLJ 9/97)

6284 Posey, Lee. *Night Rabbits* (PS–3). Illus. by Michael G. Montgomery. 1999, Peachtree $15.95 (978-1-56145-164-7). 32pp. A little girl who can't get to sleep watches the rabbits on the lawn, but in the morning she's always ready for her father's arms. (Rev: BL 5/1/99; HBG 10/99; SLJ 5/99)

6285 Postgate, Daniel. *Smelly Bill* (PS–2). Illus. by author. 2007, North-South $16.95 (978-0-7358-2135-4). Great Aunt Bleach manages to catch and bathe a very dirty dog named Bill, but only after a messy battle described in humorous rhyme. (Rev: SLJ 8/07)

6286 Prince, Joshua. *I Saw an Ant on the Railroad Track* (PS–1). Illus. by Macky Pamintuan. 2006, Sterling $14.95 (978-1-4027-2183-0). 24pp. Jack, a brawny switchman, tries to avoid a collision between an oncoming train and an ant that's on the tracks. (Rev: BL 2/1/06; SLJ 7/06)

6287 Pringle, Laurence. *Naming the Cat* (K–3). Illus. by Katherine Potter. 1997, Walker LB $16.85 (978-0-8027-8622-7). 32pp. A family ponders what the best name would be for their new cat. After watching its escapades, they decide to call him Lucky. (Rev: BL 10/1/97; HBG 3/98; SLJ 11/97)

6288 Prosek, James. *Bird, Butterfly, Eel* (K–3). Illus. by author. 2009, Simon & Schuster $16.99 (978-0-689-86829-0). 40pp. This nicely illustrated volume follows the long migratory journeys of a monarch butterfly, a barn swallow, and an eel. (Rev: BL 1/1–15/09; SLJ 2/09)

6289 Provensen, Alice. *A Day in the Life of Murphy* (PS–2). Illus. by author. 2003, Simon & Schuster $16.95 (978-0-689-84884-1). Murphy, a fun-loving terrier who lives on a farm, describes a typical day in his life. (Rev: BL 5/15/03; HB 7/03; HBG 10/03; SLJ 7/03)

6290 Radunsky, Vladimir. *You?* (PS–2). Illus. by author. 2009, Harcourt $16.00 (978-0-15-205177-8). 40pp. A little girl who wants a dog meets a little dog who wants a girl. (Rev: BL 5/15/09; SLJ 6/09)

6291 Raff, Courtney Granet. *Giant of the Sea: A Story of a Sperm Whale* (PS–2). Illus. by Shawn Gould. 2002, Soundprints $4.95 (978-1-931465-72-4); paper $6.95 (978-1-931465-80-9). 32pp. A fictional look at the behavior, diet, and habitat of a mother sperm whale and her young, with attractive illustrations that often show the animal's perspective. (Rev: BL 2/1/03)

6292 Rammell, S. Kelly. *City Beats: A Hip-Hoppy Pigeon Poem* (PS–2). Illus. by Jeanette Canyon. 2006, Dawn $16.95 (978-1-58469-076-4); paper $8.95 (978-1-58469-077-1). A hip-hop-style poem describes a city pigeon's life from dawn to dusk. (Rev: SLJ 8/06)

6293 Rand, Gloria. *Little Flower* (PS–1). Illus. by R. W. Alley. 2002, Holt $16.95 (978-0-8050-6480-3). 32pp. Miss Pearl takes a fall and is saved in a unique way by her potbellied pig, Little Flower. (Rev: BL 3/15/02; HBG 10/02; SLJ 8/02)

6294 Rand, Gloria. *Mary Was a Little Lamb* (PS–1). Illus. by Ted Rand. 2004, Holt $16.95 (978-0-8050-

6816-0). 32pp. Based on truth, this is the story of a lovable lamb named Mary who becomes such a distraction that she is banished to a petting zoo. (Rev: BL 4/15/04; SLJ 6/04)

6295 Rankin, Laura. *Fluffy and Baron* (PS–1). Illus. by author. 2006, Dial $16.99 (978-0-8037-2953-7). The story of an unlikely friendship between a large dog and a wild duck, with beautiful illustrations. (Rev: SLJ 7/06)

6296 Rathmann, Peggy. *Officer Buckle and Gloria* (PS–2). Illus. 1995, Penguin $16.99 (978-0-399-22616-8). 32pp. A police dog named Gloria steals the show when Officer Buckle gives a presentation on safety to local school children. Caldecott Medal winner, 1996. (Rev: BCCB 10/95; BL 11/1/95*; HB 11/95; HBG 4/04; SLJ 9/95*)

6297 Ravishankar, Anushka. *Elephants Never Forget!* (PS–K). Illus. by Christiane Pieper. 2008, Houghton $16.00 (978-8-1862-1104-5). 32pp. A young elephant is separated from his family in a storm and finds a new home with a herd of water buffalo but later must make a difficult decision. (Rev: BL 6/1–15/08; HB 3/08)

6298 Raye, Rebekah. *The Very Best Bed* (PS–2). Illus. by author. 2006, Tilbury House $16.95 (978-0-88448-284-0). A squirrel searching for the perfect place to sleep tries out various other animals' solutions. (Rev: SLJ 1/07)

6299 Rayner, Catherine. *Harris Finds His Feet* (PS–2). Illus. by author. 2008, Good Bks. $16.95 (978-1-56148-616-8). 28pp. Worried about his large feet, young hare Harris consults his grandfather and learns all the advantages of these appendages. (Rev: BL 6/1–15/08; SLJ 8/08)

6300 Rice, Eve. *Sam Who Never Forgets* (PS–1). Illus. by author. 1977, Morrow paper $6.99 (978-0-688-07335-0). 32pp. Sam, the zookeeper, feeds all the animals each day, but one day there appears to be nothing for the elephant.

6301 Richardson, Justin, and Peter Parnell. *And Tango Makes Three* (PS–2). Illus. by Henry Cole. 2005, Simon & Schuster $14.95 (978-0-689-87845-9). 32pp. This warm story of two male penguins who prefer each other's company to that of females and who together raise a chick called Tango is based on a true story. (Rev: BL 5/15/05)

6302 Robertus, Polly M. *The Dog Who Had Kittens* (PS–2). Illus. by Janet Stevens. 1991, Holiday House LB $16.95 (978-0-8234-0860-3). 32pp. Baxter, a basset hound, decides that he can help raise the new family of Eloise the cat. (Rev: BL 3/15/91; SLJ 5/91)

6303 Rockwell, Anne. *Backyard Bear* (PS–2). Illus. by Megan Halsey. 2006, Walker $15.95 (978-0-8027-9573-1). 32pp. A young bear finds itself roaming through a human neighborhood in this realistic story about the effects of development on animal habitats. (Rev: BL 10/15/06; SLJ 10/06)

6304 Root, Phyllis. *Flip, Flap, Fly!* (PS). Illus. by David Walker. 2009, Candlewick $14.99 (978-0-7636-3109-3). 32pp. A procession of baby animals demonstrate how they move as they spot other baby animals all around. (Rev: BL 4/15/09; HB 5/09; SLJ 5/09)

6305 Root, Phyllis. *Looking for a Moose* (PS–K). Illus. by Randy Cecil. 2006, Candlewick $15.99 (978-0-7636-2005-9). 32pp. Bouncy text and appealing hide-and-seek illustrations follow a group of children on an adventurous search for an elusive moose. (Rev: BL 10/1/06; SLJ 10/06)

6306 Rostoker-Gruber, Karen. *Bandit* (PS–1). Illus. by Vincent Nguyen. 2008, Marshall Cavendish $15.99 (978-0-7614-5382-6). 40pp. Moved against his will to a new house, Bandit the cat returns immediately to the old one only to find that new people are living there; all turns out well in this humorous and well illustrated story. (Rev: BL 5/15/08; SLJ 5/08)

6307 Rostoker-Gruber, Karen. *Rooster Can't Cock-a-Doodle-Doo* (PS–2). Illus. by Paul Rátz de Tagyos. 2004, Dial $15.99 (978-0-8037-2877-6). All the animals band together to wake Farmer Ted when the rooster has a sore throat. (Rev: HB 7/04; SLJ 7/04)

6308 Rotner, Shelley, and Cheo Garcia. *Pick a Pet* (PS–1). Illus. 1999, Orchard LB $16.99 (978-0-531-33147-7). 32pp. Using alliteration, this story involves Patty's search for a pet, such as a freckled frog, or a plump pig, or even one of the fanciful creatures Patty imagines. (Rev: BL 7/99; HBG 10/99; SLJ 4/99)

6309 Rounds, Glen. *Once We Had a Horse* (K–2). Illus. 1996, Holiday House $16.95 (978-0-8234-1241-9). 32pp. One summer, a boy and his sister learn to ride a gentle farm horse. (Rev: BL 6/1–15/96; SLJ 7/96*)

6310 Rounds, Glen. *Wild Horses* (1–4). Illus. 1993, Holiday House LB $14.95 (978-0-8234-1019-4). 32pp. The lives of wild horses in the West are explored in text and beautiful drawings. (Rev: BL 4/1/93) [599.72]

6311 Roy, Ron. *Three Ducks Went Wandering* (PS–1). Illus. by Paul Galdone. 1987, Ticknor paper $5.95 (978-0-89919-494-3). Three ducks are oblivious to the dangers all around them when they take a walk.

6312 Ruelle, Karen Gray. *Bark Park* (PS–2). Illus. by author. 2008, Peachtree $15.95 (978-1-56145-434-1). 32pp. Dogs of all kinds congregate at the dog park, described in simple rhymes and bright collages. (Rev: BL 4/1/08; SLJ 5/08)

6313 Ruepp, Krista. *Anna's Prince* (K–3). Trans. from German by J. Alison James. Illus. by Ulrike Heyne. 2006, North-South $15.95 (978-0-7358-2081-4). Young Anna trains her beloved pony, Prince, to carry a rider in this sequel, set in Iceland, to *Winter Pony* (2002) and *Runaway Pony* (2005). (Rev: SLJ 11/06)

6314 Ruepp, Krista. *Runaway Pony* (PS–2). Illus. by Ulrike Heyne. 2005, North-South $15.95 (978-0-7358-1985-6). 32pp. Anna's pony, Prince, is back home from the herd, but Anna must work to regain his trust when he is spooked by a loud tractor in this sequel to *The Winter Pony* (2002). (Rev: BL 6/1–15/05)

6315 Rumford, James. *Chee-Lin: A Giraffe's Journey* (1–3). Illus. by author. 2008, Houghton $17.00 (978-0-618-71720-0). 40pp. This vividly imagined story follows an East African giraffe who survives a dangerous trip to China and finally lands in the emperor's palace; inspired by a 15th-century Chinese painting. (Rev: BL 9/15/08)

6316 Rush, Ken. *What About Emma?* (PS–3). Illus. 1996, Orchard LB $16.99 (978-0-531-08884-5). 32pp. Even though her farm family must sell their stock to survive, Sue is allowed to keep her favorite cow, Emma. (Rev: BL 9/1/96; SLJ 9/96)

6317 Rylant, Cynthia. *The Bookshop Dog* (PS–K). Illus. 1996, Scholastic $17.99 (978-0-590-54331-6). 40pp. A dog named Martha Jane becomes the mascot at her owner's bookshop. (Rev: BL 9/1/96; SLJ 9/96)

6318 Rylant, Cynthia. *Cat Heaven* (PS–3). Illus. 1997, Scholastic $16.95 (978-0-590-10054-0). 40pp. A picture book about activities in cat heaven. (Rev: BL 9/1/97; HBG 3/98; SLJ 10/97)

6319 Rylant, Cynthia. *The Old Woman Who Named Things* (PS–3). Illus. by Kathryn Brown. 1996, Harcourt $16.00 (978-0-15-257809-1). 32pp. An old lady who only names things that will outlive her doesn't name the pup she adopts. (Rev: BL 5/1/96*; HB 5/98; SLJ 10/96*)

6320 Rylant, Cynthia. *Puppies and Piggies* (PS). Illus. by Ivan Bates. 2008, Harcourt $16.00 (978-0-15-202321-8). 32pp. Puppy, Piggy, Chicky, and other farm animals describe the things they love. (Rev: BL 4/1/08; SLJ 4/08)

6321 Sabates, Berta Garcia, and Merce Segarra. *Let's Take Care of Our New Hamster* (PS–2). Trans. by Sally-Ann Hopwood. Illus. by Rosa M. Curto. Series: Let's Take Care of. 2008, Barron's paper $6.99 (978-0-7641-3872-0). 32pp. A family brings home a new hamster in this fictional story that provides plenty of useful information on the care of these pets. (Rev: BL 4/15/08; SLJ 7/08)

6322 Sackett, Hannah Kate. *Animal Faces in the Forest* (2–4). Illus. by Martin Camm. Series: Animal Faces. 2003, McGraw-Hill $16.95 (978-1-57768-428-2). 32pp. Thirteen forest animals, from beetles to beavers, are pictured and described, with explanations of how facial characteristics help the animal to survive. (Rev: HBG 4/04; SLJ 3/04) [591]

6323 Sáez Castán, Javier. *The Three Hedgehogs* (K–3). Illus. by Javier Saez Caston. 2004, Groundwood $15.95 (978-0-88899-595-7). 32pp. In this colorfully illustrated tale told in two acts, three hungry hedgehogs steal apples from an orchard and must undergo a trial. (Rev: SLJ 7/04)

6324 Salerno, Steven. *Little Tumbo* (PS–2). Illus. by author. 2003, Marshall Cavendish $14.95 (978-0-7614-5136-5). Little Tumbo is a very small elephant and his squeaks initially fail to raise an alarm, but when he is captured for a second time he manages a full-blown trumpet. (Rev: HBG 4/04; SLJ 12/03)

6325 Saltzberg, Barney. *I Love Cats* (PS). Illus. by author. 2005, Candlewick $8.99 (978-0-7636-2588-7). Good reasons to love cats, in rhyming text with sweet illustrations. (Rev: SLJ 8/05)

6326 Saltzberg, Barney. *I Love Dogs* (PS). Illus. by author. 2005, Candlewick $8.99 (978-0-7636-2587-0). Good reasons to love dogs, in rhyming text with sweet illustrations. (Rev: SLJ 8/05)

6327 Scamell, Ragnhild. *Wish Come True Cat* (K–2). Illus. by Gaby Hansen. 2001, Barron's $13.95 (978-0-7641-5392-1). A little girl comes to love a scruffy cat who turns up after she had wished for a cute kitten. (Rev: HBG 3/02; SLJ 1/02)

6328 Schachner, Judy. *Skippyjon Jones* (K–3). Illus. by author. 2003, Dutton $15.99 (978-0-525-47134-9). Young readers will fall in love with Skippyjon Jones, a rambunctious Siamese kitten who would rather play at being a bird or dog than accept his true identity as a cat. (Rev: HBG 4/04; SLJ 1/04)

6329 Schaefer, Lola M. *Arrowhawk* (2–3). Illus. by Gabi Swiatkowska. 2004, Holt $16.95 (978-0-8050-6371-4). 32pp. Based on real events, this is a beautifully illustrated story, told from the bird's point of view, of a young red-tailed hawk that was nursed back to health after being shot by an arrow. (Rev: BL 5/15/04; SLJ 5/04)

6330 Schertle, Alice. *Very Hairy Bear* (PS–K). Illus. by Matt Phelan. 2007, Harcourt $16.00 (978-0-15-216568-0). 32pp. A big, brown, hairy bear (apart from his nose) frolics through the seasons before settling down for the winter. (Rev: BCCB 12/07; BL 10/1/07; SLJ 12/07)

6331 Schindel, John. *Busy Penguins* (PS). Illus. by Jonathan Chester. 2000, Tricycle $6.95 (978-1-58246-016-1). 20pp. A board book that shows penguins in various activities — jumping, sliding, diving, bumping, and even pooping. (Rev: BL 3/15/00; SLJ 8/00)

6332 Schmidt, Karen Lee. *Carl's Nose* (PS–2). Illus. by author. 2006, Harcourt $16.00 (978-0-15-205049-8). Carl the dog has a nose for bad weather and provides reliable forecasts to the citizens of Grimsville until the climate suddenly turns sunny and he must seek a new occupation, now using his nose to search for lost souls. (Rev: SLJ 11/06)

6333 Schoenherr, Ian. *Cat and Mouse* (PS–2). Illus. by author. 2008, HarperCollins $16.99 (978-0-06-136313-9). 40pp. A friendship between Cat and Mouse explodes into animated cat and mouse play. (Rev: SLJ 9/08)

6334 Schulman, Janet. *A Bunny for All Seasons* (PS–K). Illus. by Meilo So. 2003, Knopf $9.95 (978-0-375-82256-8). 32pp. A gentle story of a bunny enjoying a wonderful garden full of food, meeting another rabbit, getting cozy for the winter, and the pair returning to the garden with their young in the spring. (Rev: BL 3/1/03; HBG 10/03; SLJ 2/03)

6335 Seeger, Laura Vaccaro. *Dog and Bear* (PS–K). Illus. 2007, Roaring Brook $12.95 (978-1-59643-053-2). 32pp. Three simple stories with minimal text depict the friendship between Dog, a fun-loving dachshund, and Bear, a stuffed animal. (Rev: BCCB 6/07; BL 3/15/07; HB 5/07; HBG 10/07; LMC 8/07)

6336 Segal, John. *The Lonely Moose* (PS–2). Illus. by author. 2007, Hyperion $15.99 (978-1-4231-0173-4). 40pp. Used to a life by himself, Moose helps Bird, who has fallen into the lake, and the two learn to enjoy each other's friendship. (Rev: BL 11/1/07; LMC 11/07; SLJ 10/07)

6337 Seymour, Tres. *Hunting the White Cow* (PS–3). Illus. by Wendy A. Halperin. 1993, Orchard LB $17.99 (978-0-531-08646-9). 32pp. After a white cow has escaped from the farm, several people try unsuccessfully to catch her. (Rev: BCCB 10/93; BL 9/1/93; HB 11/93; SLJ 12/93*)

6338 Shannon, David. *Good Boy, Fergus!* (K–2). Illus. 2006, Scholastic $15.99 (978-0-439-49027-6). 40pp. West Highland terrier Fergus has a great day, encouraged in his chasing and scratching and munching by his young master. (Rev: BL 1/1–15/06; SLJ 3/06)

6339 Shapiro, Arnold L. *Mice Squeak, We Speak* (PS–K). Illus. by Tomie dePaola. 1997, Penguin $14.99 (978-0-399-23202-2). 32pp. Three friends introduce the different sounds made by a variety of animals. (Rev: BL 9/15/97*; HBG 3/98; SLJ 10/97)

6340 Shaw, Nancy. *Raccoon Tune* (PS–2). Illus. by Howard Fine. 2003, Holt $15.95 (978-0-8050-6544-2). A family of raccoons have a splendid (and noisy) time raiding trash cans and feasting on a surprise haul of trout. (Rev: HBG 10/03; SLJ 7/03)

6341 Sheehan, Patty. *Shadow and the Ready Time* (K–3). Illus. by Itoko Maeno. 1994, Advocacy $14.95 (978-0-911655-13-1). 38pp. A wolf cub is raised by an older, lame wolf when he is separated from his pack. (Rev: SLJ 12/94)

6342 Shields, Gillian. *DogFish* (PS–2). Illus. by Dan Taylor. 2008, Atheneum $16.99 (978-1-4169-7127-6). 32pp. A little boy who really wants a dog learns to make the most out of his goldfish. (Rev: BL 11/15/08; SLJ 12/08)

6343 Sillifant, Alec. *Farmer Ham* (K–3). Illus. by Mike Spoor. 2007, North-South $15.95 (978-0-7358-2134-7). 24pp. This farmer is not as silly as the crows think he is. (Rev: SLJ 10/07)

6344 Simmons, Jane. *Ebb and Flo and the Baby Seal* (PS–2). Illus. 2002, Simon & Schuster $16.00 (978-0-689-84368-6). 32pp. A dog named Ebb helps reunite a baby seal with its mother. (Rev: BL 1/1–15/02; HBG 10/02; SLJ 3/02*)

6345 Simon, Norma. *Oh, That Cat!* (K–3). Illus. by Dora Leder. 1986, Whitman LB $15.99 (978-0-8075-5919-2). 32pp. Max may be obnoxious in some ways, but he's special too. (Rev: BL 4/15/86; SLJ 8/86)

6346 Simont, Marc. *The Stray Dog* (PS–3). Illus. 2001, HarperCollins LB $17.89 (978-0-06-028934-8). 32pp. A family goes back to a picnic ground to bring home the stray dog they saw the week before in this tender animal story. Caldecott Honor Book, 2002. (Rev: BCCB 3/01; BL 1/1–15/01; HBG 10/01; SLJ 2/01)

6347 Singer, Marilyn. *Good Day, Good Night* (PS–2). Illus. by Ponder Goembel. 1998, Marshall Cavendish $15.95 (978-0-7614-5018-4). An interesting book that describes, in rhyme, how various animals spend their days and nights. (Rev: BCCB 7–8/98; HBG 10/98; SLJ 6/98)

6348 Siomades, Lorianne. *Katy Did It!* (PS–2). Illus. by author. 2009, Boyds Mills $16.95 (978-1-59078-602-4). 32pp. An overly energetic katydid named Katy has an annoying little brother who blames everything on her, but his cry of "Katy did it!" is finally appropriately pleasing. (Rev: BLO 5/15/09; SLJ 3/09)

6349 Slier, Deborah. *Farm Animals* (PS). Illus. 1988, Checkerboard $2.95 (978-1-56288-084-2). 12pp. Farm creatures for the toddler to admire. (Rev: BCCB 7–8/88; BL 7/88)

6350 Sloat, Teri. *I'm a Duck!* (PS–2). Illus. 2006, Putnam $15.99 (978-0-399-24274-8). 32pp. A happy duck celebrates its duck-ness and in the process introduces readers to its life cycle. (Rev: BL 3/1/06; SLJ 2/06)

6351 Smath, Jerry. *Sammy Salami* (PS–2). Illus. by author. 2007, Abrams $18.95 (978-0-8109-9350-1). 40pp. A story about a salami-loving cat and his adventures in pursuit of his owner Pete, who has departed on vacation. (Rev: BL 1/1–15/08; SLJ 10/07)

6352 Smith, Linda. *Mrs. Crump's Cat* (2–4). Illus. by David Roberts. 2006, HarperCollins $16.99 (978-0-06-028302-5). When a stray cat shows up on her porch, the life of cranky Mrs. Crump takes a turn for the better. (Rev: SLJ 4/06)

6353 Smith, Maggie. *Desser the Best Ever Cat* (PS–1). Illus. 2001, Knopf $14.95 (978-0-375-81056-5). 32pp. An engaging picture book arranged like a scrapbook of memories that tells the life story of a family's beloved cat from the day he was adopted as a stray. (Rev: BL 2/15/01; HBG 10/01)

6354 Spinelli, Eileen. *Hero Cat* (PS–2). Illus. by Jo Ellen McAllister Stammen. 2006, Marshall Cavendish $16.95 (978-0-7614-5223-2). 32pp. A mother cat rescues her kittens from a fire in this story based on truth. (Rev: BL 3/1/06; SLJ 4/06)

6355 Spirin, Gennady. *Martha* (PS–K). Illus. by author. 2005, Philomel $15.99 (978-0-399-23980-9). Spirin's son brings to their home in Moscow a crow with a broken wing and insists that they keep it alive. (Rev: BCCB 4/05; BL 7/05; SLJ 4/05)

6356 Stainton, Sue. *I Love Cats* (PS–1). Illus. by Anne Mortimer. 2007, HarperCollins $15.99 (978-0-06-085154-5). 24pp. A colorful celebration of cats of all kinds. (Rev: BL 3/15/07; SLJ 3/07)

6357 Stanley, Mandy. *What Do You Do?* (PS). Illus. by author. 2005, Simon & Schuster $7.99 (978-1-4169-0499-1). A number of animals answer the title's question in this book, which is similar to the author's *What Do You Say?* (2003). (Rev: SLJ 7/05)

6358 Stein, David Ezra. *Leaves* (PS–1). Illus. by author. 2007, Putnam $15.99 (978-0-399-24636-4). 32pp. What's a young bear to think when the leaves start falling off the trees? Simple text and lovely illustrations follow him through the changes of season. (Rev: BL 9/1/07; SLJ 8/07)

6359 Stein, David Ezra. *Ned's New Friend* (PS–2). Illus. by author. 2007, Simon & Schuster $14.99 (978-1-4169-2490-6). 32pp. Jealous at first of Cowboy Ned's new lady friend, Andy the horse soon realizes that he and Ned will always be friends. (Rev: BL 6/1–15/07; SLJ 11/07)

6360 Stevens, Janet, and Susan Stevens Crummel. *The Great Fuzz Frenzy* (PS–2). Illus. 2005, Harcourt $17.00 (978-0-15-204626-2). 56pp. Chaos erupts when a green tennis ball drops into a prairie dog burrow; an exciting read with inventive illustrations enhanced by the oversize format. (Rev: BL 9/1/05; SLJ 9/05*)

6361 Stockdale, Susan. *Some Sleep Standing Up* (PS–K). Illus. 1996, Simon & Schuster paper $13.00 (978-0-689-80509-7). 32pp. Two-page spreads illustrate the ways in which various animals sleep. (Rev: BL 9/1/96; SLJ 4/96) [591.52]

6362 Stohner, Anu. *Brave Charlotte* (PS–2). Illus. by Henrike Wilson. 2005, Bloomsbury $16.95 (978-1-58234-690-8). 32pp. Charlotte, an adventurous sheep, comes to the rescue when the shepherd breaks his leg in this picture book featuring excellent illustrations. (Rev: BL 8/05; SLJ 1/06)

6363 Sutherland, T. T. *Runaway Retriever* (4–6). Series: Pet Trouble. 2009, Scholastic paper $5.99 (978-0-545-10241-4). 176pp. Merlin the golden retriever, a real escape artist, is devoted to Parker and breaks out to be with him wherever he goes. (Rev: BLO 5/15/09)

6364 Swaim, Jessica. *The Hound from the Pound* (K–2). Illus. by Jill McElmurry. 2007, Candlewick $15.99 (978-0-7636-2330-2). 32pp. Adopting a naughty basset hound changes life for lonely Miss Mary in this lively book full of humor and wordplay. (Rev: BL 10/1/07; HB 1/08; SLJ 10/07) [811]

6365 Swanson, Diane. *Animals Can Be So Sleepy* (PS–K). Illus. 2001, Sterling $10.95 (978-1-55054-837-2). 24pp. Each spread in this simple picture book features a sleeping animal on one page and a short poem about it on the other. (Rev: BL 1/1–15/02)

6366 Sweet, Melissa. *Tupelo Rides the Rails* (K–3). Illus. by author. 2008, Houghton $17.00 (978-0-618-71714-9). 40pp. After being dumped by the wayside, courageous dog Tupelo meets up with other strays and finds herself on a train to a new life in this story full of doggy lore. (Rev: BL 1/1–15/08; SLJ 3/08)

6367 Taback, Simms. *Simms Taback's City Animals* (PS). Illus. by author. 2009, Blue Apple $12.99 (978-1-934706-52-7). 20pp. This board book neatly unfolds to reveal six animals clue by clue. (Rev: BLO 5/15/09; SLJ 6/09)

6368 Tafuri, Nancy. *Five Little Chicks* (PS). Illus. 2006, Simon & Schuster $14.95 (978-0-689-87342-3). 32pp. A mother hen teaches her five newborn chicks where to find a good meal. (Rev: BL 12/15/05; SLJ 2/06)

6369 Tafuri, Nancy. *Whose Chick Are You?* (PS–K). Illus. by author. 2007, HarperCollins $16.99 (978-0-06-082514-0). When a baby swan hatches, nobody seems to know who it belongs to. (Rev: BL 12/15/06; SLJ 2/07)

6370 Taha, Karen T. *Hotdog on TV* (PS–2). Illus. by Hideko Takahashi. Series: Dial Easy-to-Read. 2005, Dial $14.99 (978-0-8037-2933-9). 40pp. Hotdog, a dachshund, is so appealing that a new variety of ice cream is invented for him to advertise on TV. (Rev: BL 6/1–15/05)

6371 Teckentrup, Britta. *Grumpy Cat* (PS–K). Illus. by author. 2008, Boxer $14.95 (978-1-905417-69-8). 32pp. A lovable kitten manages to break through Grumpy Cat's defenses and the two become fast friends. (Rev: BL 4/1/08; SLJ 5/08)

6372 Thompson, Colin. *Unknown* (2–3). Illus. by Anna Pignataro. 2000, Walker LB $16.85 (978-0-8027-8731-6). 32pp. A small stray dog labeled "Unknown" in the animal shelter is able to warn the keeper about a dangerous fire. (Rev: BCCB 5/00; BL 5/1/00; HBG 10/00; SLJ 7/00)

6373 Thompson, Lauren. *Little Quack* (PS–K). Illus. by Derek Anderson. 2003, Simon & Schuster $14.95 (978-0-689-84723-3). 32pp. Five little ducklings follow their mother — the last very reluctantly — into the pond in this charming picture book. (Rev: BL 2/1/03; HBG 10/03; SLJ 6/03)

6374 Tildes, Phyllis L. *Animals: Black and White* (PS–2). Illus. by author. 1996, Charlesbridge paper $6.95 (978-0-88106-959-4). This picture puzzle book consists of guessing games in which several black-and-white animals describe themselves and show parts of their bodies before their identities are revealed. (Rev: SLJ 1/97)

6375 Tildes, Phyllis L. *Calico's Curious Kittens* (PS). Illus. 2003, Charlesbridge $16.95 (978-1-57091-511-6); paper $6.95 (978-1-57091-512-3). 32pp. Calico's kittens are full of mischief, but as cute as can be. (Rev: BL 2/1/03; HBG 10/03; SLJ 2/03)

6376 Timmel, Carol Ann. *Tabitha: The Fabulous Flying Feline* (PS–1). Illus. by Laura Kelly. 1996, Walker paper $16.85 (978-0-8027-8449-0). 32pp. Tabitha the cat remains undiscovered for 13 days in the cargo hold of a large airplane. (Rev: BL 10/15/96; SLJ 11/96)

6377 Townsend, Una Belle. *Grady's in the Silo* (1–4). Illus. by Bob Artley. 2003, Pelican $15.95 (978-1-58980-098-4). Based on a real-life event, this is an entertaining story about Grady, a cow that gets stuck in a silo while trying to avoid an injection. (Rev: HBG 10/03; SLJ 5/03)

6378 Tsubakiyama, Margaret. *Mei-Mei Loves the Morning* (PS–3). Illus. by Cornelius Van Wright and Ying-Hwa Hu. 1999, Whitman $15.95 (978-0-8075-5039-7). In modern, urban China, Mei-Mei and her grandfather participate in the family's daily routines, such as feeding the bird, eating breakfast, going to the park, and shopping at the market. (Rev: BCCB 5/99; BL 3/15/99; HBG 10/99; SLJ 5/99)

6379 Turner, Sandy. *Cool Cat, Hot Dog* (PS–2). Illus. by author. 2005, Simon & Schuster $16.95 (978-0-689-84946-6). Imaginative torn-paper artwork is the highlight of this discussion — between a dog and cat — of their different characteristics. (Rev: SLJ 8/05)

6380 Umansky, Kaye. *I Don't Like Gloria!* (PS–1). Illus. by Margaret Chamberlain. 2007, Candlewick $15.99 (978-0-7636-3202-1). Calvin, a dog, is not at all fond of Gloria, the new cat in the house, and both of them are distraught when a third pet comes on the scene. (Rev: SLJ 5/07)

6381 Van Camp, Richard. *What's the Most Beautiful Thing You Know About Horses?* (K–3). Illus. by George Littlechild. 1998, Children's Book Pr. $15.95 (978-0-89239-154-7). A little child living in Canada's Northwest Territories asks about the beauty of horses. (Rev: HBG 3/99; SLJ 10/98)

6382 Van Laan, Nancy. *When Winter Comes* (PS–2). Illus. by Susan Gaber. 2000, Simon & Schuster $16.00 (978-0-689-81778-6). As a family walks through the woods during an early snowfall, they wonder about the animals cope during the winter; the illustrations reveal the answers. (Rev: HBG 3/01; SLJ 11/00)

6383 Vargo, Vanessa. *Zebra Talk* (PS–1). Illus. 1991, Child's Play paper $5.99 (978-0-85953-395-9). 20pp. A mother zebra explains how life was years ago when thousands of zebras roamed the plains of Africa. (Rev: BL 3/1/91)

6384 Vernick, Audrey Glassman, and Ellen Glassman Gidaro. *Bark and Tim: A True Story of Friendship Based on the Paintings of Tim Brown* (K–3). Illus. by Tim Brown. 2003, Overmountain $14.95 (978-1-57072-271-4). This charming story, based on the Mississippi childhood of African American folk artist Tim Brown, tells about a young boy's loving relationship with a dog named Bark. (Rev: HBG 4/04; SLJ 1/04)

6385 Von Buhler, Cynthia. *The Cat Who Wouldn't Come Inside: Based on a True Story* (PS–2). Photos by author. Illus. by author. 2006, Houghton $16.00 (978-0-618-56314-2). In an effort to convince a stray cat to stay, a woman adds more and more attractions to her front porch, until it's just as nice outside as inside. (Rev: SLJ 11/06)

6386 Votaw, Carol. *Good Morning, Little Polar Bear* (PS–2). Illus. by Susan Banta. 2005, NorthWord $15.95 (978-1-55971-932-2). In this appealing picture book, a young Inuit child celebrates the arrival of summer by making the rounds of the creatures that call the Arctic home. (Rev: SLJ 11/05)

6387 Waddell, Martin. *It's Quacking Time!* (PS–K). Illus. by Jill Barton. 2005, Candlewick $15.99 (978-0-7636-2738-6). 32pp. Young Duckling learns a lot about nature as his family waits for a new egg to hatch. (Rev: BL 2/1/05; SLJ 4/05)

6388 Waldron, Kathleen Cook. *Roundup at the Palace* (K–3). Illus. by Alan Daniel and Lea Daniel. 2006, Red Deer $17.95 (978-0-88995-319-2). A bull escapes from a truck on the way to a stock show in Denver, and Zack and Alice must coax him back to safety in this story based on an actual event. (Rev: SLJ 7/06)

6389 Walsh, Alice. *Heroes of the Isle aux Morts* (PS–3). Illus. by Geoff Butler. 2001, Tundra $14.95 (978-0-88776-501-8). 32pp. Based on truth, this is the story of a dramatic rescue at sea in 1832, in which a Newfoundland dog plays a major role. (Rev: BL 6/1–15/01; HBG 10/01; SLJ 10/01)

6390 Walsh, Melanie. *Do Lions Live on Lily Pads?* (PS). 2006, Houghton $15.00 (978 0 618-47300-7). 32pp. Using questions and answers, this simple picture book reveals the distinctive habitats of animals including lions, parakeets, giraffes, and crocodiles. (Rev: BL 6/1–15/06; SLJ 7/06)

6391 Ward, Helen. *Old Shell, New Shell: A Coral Reef Tale* (K–3). Illus. 2002, Millbrook LB $24.90 (978-0-7613-2708-0). 40pp. A hermit crab seeks a bigger home in this boldly illustrated tale, which also includes a detailed key identifying life on a coral reef. (Rev: BL 1/1–15/02; HBG 10/02; SLJ 2/02)

6392 Warhola, James. *Uncle Andy's Cats* (PS–1). Illus. by author. 2009, Putnam $16.99 (978-0-399-25180-1). 32pp. An amusingly illustrated story of Andy Warhol's 25 cats, written by his nephew, who visited the house and the cats frequently. (Rev: BL 7/09)

6393 Waring, Geoff. *Oscar and the Bat: A Book About Sound* (PS–2). Illus. by author. Series: Start with Science. 2008, Candlewick $14.99 (978-0-7636-4025-5). 32pp. In this fiction and science hybrid title, a cat named Oscar and his bat friend explore how animals make sounds and how we hear them. (Rev: BL 12/1/08; SLJ 12/08)

6394 Warnes, Tim. *Mommy Mine* (PS). Illus. by Jane Chapman. 2005, HarperCollins $16.99 (978-0-06-058947-9). 32pp. Contrasting mothers and their babies — mice and elephants, for example — are juxtaposed in bright pictures with a simple rhyme. (Rev: BL 5/15/05)

6395 Warrick, Karen Clemens. *If I Had a Tail* (PS–2). Illus. by Sherry Neidigh. 2001, Rising Moon LB $15.95 (978-0-87358-781-5). 32pp. An amusing picture book in which the tails of various animals and their uses are explored. (Rev: BL 4/1/01; HBG 10/01; SLJ 6/01)

6396 Weaver, Tess. *Cat Jumped In!* (PS–2). Illus. by Emily Arnold McCully. 2007, Clarion $16.00 (978-0-618-61488-2). 32pp. A lively and curious cat creates havoc as it moves through an artist's house. (Rev: BL 12/15/07; SLJ 12/07)

6397 Weller, Frances W. *The Day the Animals Came: A Story of Saint Francis Day* (PS–2). Illus. by Loren Long. 2003, Philomel $16.99 (978-0-399-23630-3). The blessing of the animals at the Cathedral of St. John the Divine in New York City makes a young Caribbean girl named Ria feel more at home. (Rev: BL 10/1/03; HBG 4/04; SLJ 11/03)

6398 Weller, Frances W. *Riptide* (PS–3). Illus. by Robert J. Blake. 1990, Penguin $17.99 (978-0-399-21675-6). 32pp. A dog named Riptide acts as a lifeguard on Cape Cod. (Rev: BL 3/15/90*; HB 7/90; HBG 4/04; SLJ 4/90*)

6399 Wells, Rosemary. *McDuff's Wild Romp* (PS). Illus. by Susan Jeffers. Series: McDuff Stories. 2005, Hyperion $9.99 (978-0-7868-1930-0). 32pp. The adorable West Highland terrier ends up in disgrace after a scrap with a cat over a piece of turkey. (Rev: BL 6/1–15/05; SLJ 4/05)

6400 West, Jim, and Marshall Izen. *The Dog Who Sang at the Opera* (1–3). Illus. by Erika Oller. 2004, Abrams $16.95 (978-0-8109-4928-7). 32pp. A Russian wolfhound's operatic debut ends ignomin-

iously in this story based on a real incident. (Rev: BL 1/1–15/05; SLJ 2/05)

6401 Wheeler, Lisa. *Sixteen Cows* (PS–2). Illus. by Kurt Cyrus. 2002, Harcourt $16.00 (978-0-15-202676-9). 32pp. After their herds of cows mingle when a dividing fence is blown down, Cowboy Gene and Cowgirl Sue decide they should also, and so they get married. (Rev: BL 6/1–15/02; HBG 10/02; SLJ 4/02)

6402 White, Amanda. *Rip and Rap* (PS). Illus. by Debbie Harter. 2002, Barefoot Books $14.99 (978-1-84148-944-5). Sheepdog puppies Rip and Rap become indistinguishable when Rap gets covered in mud. (Rev: HBG 3/03; SLJ 1/03)

6403 White, Kathryn. *The Nutty Nut Chase* (PS–3). Illus. by Vanessa Cabban. 2004, Good Bks. $16.00 (978-1-56148-446-1). Two quarrelsome squirrels are among the animals much surprised by a disappearing nut. (Rev: SLJ 1/05)

6404 Wieler, Diana. *To the Mountains by Morning* (K–3). Illus. by Ange Zhang. 1996, Douglas & McIntyre $14.95 (978-0-88899-227-7). 32pp. Knowing she is going to be disposed of because of her age, Old Bailey the mare runs away. (Rev: BL 7/96; SLJ 6/96)

6405 Wildsmith, Brian, and Rebecca Wildsmith. *Wake Up, Wake Up!* (PS–1). Illus. 1993, Harcourt $6.95 (978-0-15-200685-3). 16pp. One by one, the animals wake up until, finally, the farmer also wakes up to feed them. (Rev: BL 3/15/93)

6406 Willis, Nancy Carol. *Raccoon Moon* (PS–2). Illus. 2002, Birdsong $15.95 (978-0-9662761-2-1); paper $6.95 (978-0-9662761-3-8). 32pp. Three raccoon cubs are born and grow up in this wonderfully illustrated introduction to a raccoon's lifecycle. (Rev: BL 12/15/02; SLJ 1/03)

6407 Wilson, Sarah. *A Nap in a Lap* (PS). Illus. by Akemi Gutierrez. 2003, Holt $15.95 (978-0-8050-6973-0). A little girl and her dog observe the diverse places and ways in which various animals nap before heading home where, the child herself takes a nap on her mother's lap. (Rev: BL 1/1–15/04; SLJ 1/04)

6408 Winstead, Rosie. *Ruby and Bubbles* (K–2). Illus. by author. 2006, Dial $15.99 (978-0-8037-3024-3). Ruby's love for her pet bird Bubbles is shaken when bullies mock the bird and its inability to fly. (Rev: SLJ 2/06)

6409 Wittbold, Maureen. *Mending Peter's Heart* (K–6). Illus. by Larry Salk. 1995, Portunus paper $8.95 (978-0-9641330-2-0). 32pp. Peter needs consolation when his pet husky, Mishka, dies. (Rev: SLJ 11/95)

6410 Wood, Audrey. *A Dog Needs a Bone!* (PS–2). Illus. by author. 2007, Scholastic $16.99 (978-0-545-00005-5). 32pp. A dog who desperately wants a bone has a mistress who loves to tease. (Rev: BL 10/15/07; SLJ 9/07)

6411 Wood, Ellen. *Hundreds of Fish* (1–4). Illus. by Monique Felix. 2000, Creative $17.95 (978-1-56846-162-5). 40pp. The food chain is explored in this picture book set in Alaska about a young girl who, while ice fishing, catches a pike that she saw eating three ducklings months before. (Rev: HBG 10/00; SLJ 9/00)

6412 Wright, Cliff. *Bear and Ball* (PS). Illus. by author. 2005, Chronicle $5.95 (978-0-8118-4819-0). A simple board book rhyming story about two bear cubs playing with a ball. Also use *Bear and Kite* (2005). (Rev: SLJ 7/05)

6413 Yang, James. *Joey and Jet* (PS–2). Illus. 2004, Simon & Schuster $15.95 (978-0-689-86926-6). 32pp. A boy and a dog have fun with a ball in this attractive volume that highlights the use of prepositions. (Rev: BL 1/1–15/05)

6414 Yolen, Jane. *Hoptoad* (PS–K). Illus. by Karen Lee Schmidt. 2003, Harcourt $16.00 (978-0-15-216352-5). In this simple, appealing tale told in rhyming text, a man and his son stop their camper to rescue a toad from a dangerous trip across the road. (Rev: BL 5/15/03; HBG 10/03; SLJ 6/03)

6415 Yolen, Jane. *Owl Moon* (PS–2). Illus. by John Schoenherr. 1987, Penguin $16.99 (978-0-399-21457-8). 32pp. Winner of the 1988 Caldecott Medal, this is the poetic story of a little girl and her father on an owl adventure in winter. (Rev: BL 12/15/87; SLJ 12/87)

6416 Zagwyn, Deborah Turney. *Turtle Spring* (PS–1). Illus. 1998, Tricycle $15.95 (978-1-883672-53-9). 32pp. Clee is happy to have a pet turtle to play with instead of her baby brother. Over the winter, though, she thinks the turtle has died, and she comes to love her brother. In spring, Clee's turtle wakes from its hibernation and she has both brother and turtle to love. (Rev: BL 7/98*; HBG 10/98; SLJ 8/98)

6417 Ziefert, Harriet. *Beach Party!* (PS). Illus. by Simms Taback. 2005, Blue Apple $8.95 (978-1-59354-067-8). A board book featuring adorable sea animals on their way to the ocean for a swim. (Rev: SLJ 8/05)

6418 Ziefert, Harriet. *Birdhouse for Rent* (PS–K). Illus. by Donald Dreifuss. 2001, Houghton $16.00 (978-0-618-04881-6). A birdhouse is used by bees and chipmunks before Mrs. Chickadee moves in, lays her eggs, and sees her chicks hatch. (Rev: HBG 3/02; SLJ 9/01)

6419 Ziefert, Harriet. *Murphy Jumps a Hurdle* (K–3). Illus. by Emily Bolam. 2006, Blue Apple $15.95 (978-1-59354-174-3). 40pp. Murphy the yellow Lab and his owner Cheryl tackle agility training in this entertaining book with cartoonlike illustrations. (Rev: BL 11/1/06)

6420 Ziefert, Harriet. *One Smart Skunk* (PS–3). Illus. by Santiago Cohen. 2004, Blue Apple $15.95 (978-1-59354-064-7). Rebecca the skunk's life under the deck becomes unbearable as she suffers from a combination of moth balls and rap music. (Rev: SLJ 1/05)

SCHOOL STORIES

6421 Abercrombie, Barbara. *The Show-and-Tell Lion* (K–2). Illus. by Lynne Avril Cravath. 2006, Simon & Schuster $16.95 (978-0-689-86408-7). 32pp. Unprepared for show-and-tell, young Matthew makes up a story about having a lion but faces a real dilemma when his classmates want to see it. (Rev: BL 9/15/06; HBG 4/07; SLJ 7/06)

6422 Alexander, Martha, and James Rumford. *Max and the Dumb Flower Picture* (PS–K). Illus. by Martha Alexander. 2009, Charlesbridge $9.95 (978-1-58089-156-1). 32pp. Max refuses to cooperate with his teacher by coloring in the lines and instead creates an original work of art. (Rev: BL 7/09)

6423 Aliki. *A Play's the Thing* (2–4). Illus. 2005, HarperCollins $16.99 (978-0-06-074355-0). 32pp. José is less than thrilled when his teacher, Miss Brilliant, decides the class will put on a dramatization of "Mary Had a Little Lamb"; cartoon panels and a running narrative tell the story. (Rev: BL 10/15/05; HB 9–1/05; HBG 4/06; LMC 5/06; SLJ 8/05*)

6424 Allard, Harry. *Miss Nelson Has a Field Day* (1–3). Illus. by James Marshall. 1985, Houghton $16.00 (978-0-395-36690-5); paper $5.95 (978-0-395-48654-2). 32pp. The plucky Miss Nelson gets a losing football team into shape. (Rev: BCCB 7–8/85; BL 5/15/85; HB 5/85)

6425 Allard, Harry. *Miss Nelson Is Missing!* (K–2). Illus. by James Marshall. 1985, Houghton $16.00 (978-0-395-25296-3); paper $6.99 (978-0-395-40146-0). When Miss Nelson's students in Room 207 misbehave, she disappears and is replaced by a martinet. A sequel is: *Miss Nelson Is Back* (1985).

6426 Ashley, Bernard. *Cleversticks* (PS–1). Illus. by Derek Brazell. 1995, Crown paper $6.99 (978-0-517-88332-7). 32pp. Ling Sung is a nobody at school until he reveals he can use chopsticks. (Rev: BCCB 7–8/92; BL 11/15/92; SLJ 3/93)

6427 Aston, Dianna. *Not So Tall for Six* (1–2). Illus. by Frank W. Dormer. 2008, Charlesbridge $14.95 (978-1-57091-705-9). 32pp. Kylie Bell, in 1st grade, may not be tall in stature but she's big on courage when she's being bullied. (Rev: BCCB 4/08; SLJ 4/08)

6428 Barnes, Derrick. *Ruby and the Booker Boys: Brand New School, Brand New Ruby* (2–4). Illus. by Vanessa Brantley Newton. 2008, Scholastic paper $4.99 (978-0-545-01760-2). 144pp. About to start 3rd grade at her new school, which her three brothers already attend, African American Ruby Booker aims to make her own mark. (Rev: BLO 3/19/09)

6429 Bateman, Teresa. *The Bully Blockers Club* (PS–3). Illus. by Jackie Urbanovic. 2004, Whitman LB $16.99 (978-0-8075-0918-0). Lotty Raccoon is determined not to put up with being bullied by classmate Grant Grizzly, so she starts an anti-bully club. (Rev: SLJ 11/04)

6430 Beaty, Andrea. *Iggy Peck, Architect* (K–2). Illus. by David Roberts. 2007, Abrams $16.95 (978-0-8109-1106-2). 32pp. Iggy's teacher doesn't appreciate the 2nd-grader's precocious talent for building until the class needs an emergency suspension bridge. (Rev: LMC 1/08; SLJ 11/07)

6431 Best, Cari. *Shrinking Violet* (K–3). Illus. by Giselle Potter. 2001, Farrar $16.00 (978-0-374-36882-1). 40pp. Shy Violet has her moment in the limelight when she's cast in an offstage speaking role. (Rev: BCCB 10/01; BL 8/01; HB 9/01; HBG 3/02; SLJ 8/01*)

6432 Blake, Stephanie. *I Don't Want to Go to School!* (PS–1). Illus. by author. 2009, Random $12.99 (978-0-375-85688-4). 32pp. Simon is certain that he doesn't want to go to school, but after a day of learning and playing he changes his mind. (Rev: BL 7/09)

6433 Boelts, Maribeth. *Little Bunny's Preschool Countdown* (PS). Illus. by Kathy Parkinson. 1996, Whitman LB $16.99 (978-0-8075-4582-9). 32pp. LB, a rabbit, begins to dread his first day at preschool. (Rev: BL 9/15/96; SLJ 11/96)

6434 Boelts, Maribeth. *When It's the Last Day of School* (K–2). Illus. by Hanako Wakiyama. 2004, Penguin $15.99 (978-0-399-23498-9). 32pp. Full of anticipation about summer vacation, James vows to be on his best behavior on the very last day of school. (Rev: BL 4/15/04; SLJ 4/04)

6435 Borden, Louise. *The John Hancock Club* (2–4). Illus. by Adam Gustavson. 2007, Simon & Schuster $16.99 (978-1-4169-1813-4). 48pp. Sean is not looking forward to learning cursive writing but his 3rd-grade teacher provides motivation. (Rev: BL 5/1/07; LMC 10/07; SLJ 6/07)

6436 Borden, Louise. *The Last Day of School* (1–3). Illus. by Adam Gustavson. 2006, Simon & Schuster $15.95 (978-0-689-86869-6). 40pp. It's the last day of school, and one of Mrs. Mallory's 3rd-grade students has a special surprise for her. (Rev: BL 2/1/06; SLJ 3/06)

6437 Bowen, Anne. *The Great Math Tattle Battle* (1–3). Illus. by Jaime Zollars. 2006, Albert Whitman $15.99 (978-0-8075-3163-1). 32pp. Math whiz Harley Harrison is the scourge of his 2nd-grade class, constantly tattling on his classmates until a newcomer called Emma Jean turns the tables on him. (Rev: BL 4/15/06; SLJ 6/06)

6438 Brisson, Pat. *I Remember Miss Perry* (K–3). Illus. by Stephanie Jorisch. 2006, Dial $16.99 (978-0-8037-2981-0). 32pp. Stevie fondly remembers Miss Perry — his first teacher — when she is killed in a car accident. (Rev: BL 2/1/06; SLJ 3/06)

6439 Brown, Marc. *D.W.'s Guide to Preschool* (PS). Illus. by author. 2003, Little, Brown $15.95 (978-0-316-12069-2). D. W., Arthur's little sister, offers advice on virtually every aspect of preschool life, covering such important topics as bathroom breaks, circle time, and snack time. (Rev: HBG 4/04; SLJ 12/03)

6440 Bunting, Eve. *My Special Day at Third Street School* (K–3). Illus. by Suzanne Bloom. 2004, Boyds Mills $15.95 (978-1-59078-075-6). 32pp. A boy explains in engaging detail the class preparations for an author visit by Amanda Drake — and the successes of the day itself. (Rev: BL 3/15/04*; SLJ 3/04)

6441 Bunting, Eve. *One Green Apple* (1–3). Illus. by Ted Lewin. 2006, Clarion $16.00 (978-0-618-43477-0). 32pp. Farah, a young Muslim immigrant, feels uncomfortable in her new school until she joins classmates on a field trip to an apple orchard where she discovers that some things are the same no matter where you are. (Rev: BL 6/1–15/06; HBG 10/06; LMC 8/06; SLJ 6/06)

6442 Bunting, Eve. *Our Teacher's Having a Baby* (K–2). Illus. by Diane deGroat. 1992, Houghton $15.00 (978-0-395-60470-0). 32pp. Mrs. Neal explains to her class that she is going to have a baby, and together they prepare for the event. (Rev: BL 9/15/92; HB 5/04; SLJ 3/93)

6443 Bush, Laura, and Jenna Bush. *Read All About It!* (K–3). Illus. by Denise Brunkus. 2008, HarperCollins $17.99 (978-0-06-156075-0). 32pp. Tyrone is popular and enjoys school except for reading until he finally listens to a story and discovers a whole new world. (Rev: BL 5/1/08; SLJ 6/08)

6444 Buzzeo, Toni. *The Library Doors* (PS–1). Illus. by Nadine Bernard Westcott. 2008, Upstart $17.95 (978-1-60213-037-1). 32pp. Using the well-known children's song "The Wheels on the Bus" as a framework, this is a rhythmic introduction to various activities at the library. (Rev: BLO 1/7/09)

6445 Calmenson, Stephanie. *Late for School!* (K–2). Illus. by Sachiko Yoshikawa. 2008, Carolrhoda $16.95 (978-1-57505-935-8). 32pp. Mr. Bungles, the teacher, is late for school and tries many options in his zeal to get there; illustrations full of motion add to the fun. (Rev: BL 8/08; LMC 1/09; SLJ 9/08)

6446 Carlson, Nancy. *Hooray for Grandparents' Day!* (PS–2). Illus. 2000, Viking $15.99 (978-0-670-88876-4). 32pp. Arnie has no grandparents to bring to school on Grandparents' Day and he feels left out. (Rev: BL 6/1–15/00; HBG 3/01; SLJ 8/00)

6447 Carlson, Nancy. *Look Out Kindergarten, Here I Come!* (PS–K). Illus. 1999, Viking $15.99 (978-0-670-88378-3). 32pp. Henry is excited about his first day in kindergarten, particularly after he makes a new friend. (Rev: BL 6/1–15/99; HBG 10/99; SLJ 7/99)

6448 Carson, Jana. *Stop Teasing Taylor!* (K–2). Illus. by Meryl Treatner. Series: We Both Read. 2005, Treasure Bay $7.99 (978-1-891327-61-2); paper $3.99 (978-1-891327-62-9). Designed to be read in tandem by a beginning reader and one who's more advanced, this is a simple story about a young boy's first day at school. (Rev: SLJ 4/06)

6449 Carter, Alden R. *Dustin's Big School Day* (K–2). Illus. by Dan Young and Carol S. Carter. 1999, Whitman $14.95 (978-0-8075-1741-3). 32pp. Photographs are used to document Dustin's day in school, when a ventriloquist visits as a special treat. (Rev: BCCB 3/99; BL 4/15/99; HBG 10/99; SLJ 6/99)

6450 Caseley, Judith. *Field Day Friday* (PS–2). Illus. 2000, Greenwillow LB $16.89 (978-0-688-16762-2). 32pp. At his school's field day, Mickey's sneaker comes off during the 50-yard dash and the wretched youngster comes in last. (Rev: BL 5/1/00; HBG 10/00; SLJ 5/00)

6451 Chapra, Mimi. *Amelia's Show-and-Tell Fiesta / Amelia y la fiesta de "muestra y cuenta"* (K–2). 2004, HarperCollins LB $17.89 (978-0-06-050256-0). When she gets to school, Amelia worries that her Cuban fiesta dresses are not suitable for show-and-tell in this book with lively English text and a more pedestrian Spanish translation. (Rev: SLJ 9/04)

6452 Chardiet, Bernice, and Grace Maccarone. *The Best Teacher in the World* (PS–2). Illus. by G. Brian Karas. 1991, Scholastic paper $2.50 (978-0-590-43307-5). 32pp. Bunny is selected by her favorite teacher to run an errand. (Rev: BL 1/1/90; SLJ 10/90)

6453 Choldenko, Gennifer. *How to Make Friends with a Giant* (K–2). Illus. by Amy Walrod. 2006, Putnam $16.99 (978-0-399-23779-9). Tiny Jake and giant Jacomo become unlikely friends in this story about the advantages of being different. (Rev: SLJ 7/06)

6454 Cocca-Leffler, Maryann. *Jack's Talent* (PS–2). Illus. by author. 2007, Farrar $16.00 (978-0-374-33681-3). 32pp. In this reassuring book, Jack overcomes his insecurity on the first day of school as he discovers a talent for remembering names and facts. (Rev: BL 6/1–15/07; HB 9/07; SLJ 11/07)

6455 Cocca-Leffler, Maryann. *Mr. Tanen's Tie Trouble* (K–3). Illus. by author. 2003, Whitman LB $16.99 (978-0-8075-5305-3). Mr. Tanen the school principal puts his collection of wondrous ties up for auction when he discovers the playground has no funds. (Rev: BL 6/03; SLJ 5/03)

6456 Cocca-Leffler, Maryann. *Mr. Tanen's Ties* (PS–2). Illus. 1999, Whitman LB $16.99 (978-0-8075-5301-5). 32pp. Mr. Tanen wears different ties to school each day to mark various occasions, but Mr. Apple, the superintendent of schools, doesn't like it. (Rev: BL 5/15/99; HBG 10/99; SLJ 3/99)

6457 Cocca-Leffler, Maryann. *Princess K.I.M. and the Lie That Grew* (PS–2). Illus. by author. 2009, Albert Whitman $16.99 (978-0-8075-4178-4). 32pp. The rise and fall of a royal princess named Kim hinges on a small lie. (Rev: BCCB 6/09; SLJ 6/09)

6458 Cohen, Miriam. *First Grade Takes a Test* (K–1). Illus. by Ronald Himler. 2006, Star Bright $15.95 (978-1-59572-054-2); paper $5.95 (978-1-59572-055-9). 32pp. A newly illustrated version of Cohen's story about a 1st-grade class and what they learn about aptitude when they take an intelligence test. (Rev: BL 11/15/06)

6459 Cohen, Miriam. *Will I Have a Friend?* (PS–2). Illus. by Ronald Himler. 2009, Star Bright $15.95 (978-1-59572-069-6). 32pp. Jim worries about making friends on his first day of school in this updated version of a classic story with new illustrations. (Rev: BL 4/1/09)

6460 Conlin, Susan, and Susan L. Friedman. *All My Feelings at Preschool: Nathan's Day* (PS–K). Illus. by Kathryn M. Smith. 1991, Parenting LB $17.95 (978-0-943990-61-3); paper $7.95 (978-0-943990-60-6). 32pp. This picture book describes a day in the life of Nathan at his nursery school. (Rev: BL 6/1/91)

6461 Corey, Shana. *First Graders from Mars: Episode 1 — Horus's Horrible Day* (K–2). Illus. by Mark Teague. 2001, Scholastic $14.95 (978-0-439-26220-0). 32pp. Horus, a Martian lad, is having a horrible time getting used to 1st grade until he meets another scared student. (Rev: BL 8/01; HBG 3/02; SLJ 9/01)

6462 Couric, Katie. *The Blue Ribbon Day* (K–2). Illus. by Marjorie Priceman. 2004, Doubleday $15.95 (978-0-385-50142-2). Carrie O'Toole is disappointed when she fails to make the Brookhaven School soccer team. (Rev: SLJ 1/05)

6463 Couric, Katie. *The Brand New Kid* (K–2). Illus. by Marjorie Priceman. 2000, Doubleday $15.95 (978-0-385-50030-2). Lazlo S. Gasky is unhappy and friendless at his new school, until a classmate decides to help him. (Rev: SLJ 2/01)

6464 Cox, Judy. *Don't Be Silly, Mrs. Millie!* (PS–K). Illus. by Joe Mathieu. 2005, Marshall Cavendish $14.95 (978-0-7614-5166-2). 32pp. Kindergarten teacher Mrs. Millie is prone to confusing her words — "coats" become "goats" — and the illustrations add to the general zaniness. (Rev: BL 8/05; SLJ 10/05)

6465 Creech, Sharon. *A Fine, Fine School* (K–3). Illus. by Harry Bliss. 2001, HarperCollins LB $17.89 (978-0-06-027737-6). 32pp. A wonderfully illustrated, very funny story about a school principal who just doesn't know when to quit. (Rev: BL 8/01; HBG 3/02; SLJ 8/01)

6466 Cuyler, Margery. *Bullies Never Win* (PS–2). Illus. by Arthur Howard. 2009, Simon & Schuster $16.99 (978-0-689-86187-1). 32pp. In 1st grade, Jessica is bullied by classmate Brenda until Jessica finally tells her mother, who helps her deal with the problem. (Rev: BL 7/09; SLJ 6/09)

6467 Cuyler, Margery. *Hooray for Reading Day!* (PS–1). Illus. by Arthur Howard. Series: Jessica Worries. 2008, Simon & Schuster $15.99 (978-0-689-86188-8). 32pp. First-grader Jessica is terrified of reading aloud on Reading Theater Day and practices with her dog Wiggles. (Rev: BL 8/08; LMC 11/08; SLJ 8/08)

6468 Cuyler, Margery. *Stop, Drop, and Roll* (K–3). Illus. by Arthur Howard. 2001, Simon & Schuster $16.00 (978-0-689-84355-6). 32pp. Jessica agonizes over her role in a play for Fire Prevention Week. (Rev: BCCB 11/01; BL 9/15/01; HBG 3/02; SLJ 10/01)

6469 Cuyler, Margery. *We're Going on a Lion Hunt* (PS–2). Illus. by Joe Mathieu. 2008, Marshall Cavendish $14.99 (978-0-7614-5454-0). 32pp. An intrepid teacher and students set off on a make-believe safari and meet a variety of animals before they come across one with a cold nose and sharp teeth. (Rev: BL 9/1/08)

6470 Daniels, Teri. *The Feet in the Gym* (K–3). Illus. by Travis Foster. 1999, Winslow $15.95 (978-1-890817-12-1). 32pp. The humorous story of how a poor school custodian tries to keep the school clean, in spite of different groups of children, each producing its own terrible mess. (Rev: BL 7/99; SLJ 6/99)

6471 Danneberg, Julie. *First Year Letters* (K–3). Illus. by Judy Love. 2003, Charlesbridge $16.95 (978-1-58089-084-7); paper $6.95 (978-1-58089-085-4). 32pp. Letters exchanged by a fictional new teacher and her students reveal how they learn together during the course of a school year. (Rev: BL 2/1/03; HBG 10/03; SLJ 4/03)

6472 Danneberg, Julie. *Last Day Blues* (K–2). Illus. by Judy Love. 2006, Charlesbridge $16.95 (978-1-58089-046-5); paper $6.95 (978-1-58089-104-2). 32pp. Mrs. Hartwell's class worries that she will be lonely during the summer and tries to think of a suitable gift; meanwhile, Mrs. Hartwell can be seen celebrating the end of school with other teachers. (Rev: BL 1/1–15/06; SLJ 2/06)

6473 Davis, Gibbs. *The Other Emily* (K–2). Illus. by Linda Shute. 1990, Harcourt paper $4.95 (978-0-395-54947-6). 32pp. Emily loves her name until she encounters another Emily in her class.

6474 Davis, Katie. *Kindergarten Rocks!* (PS–K). Illus. by author. 2005, Harcourt $15.00 (978-0-15-204932-4). Dexter isn't nervous at all during his first day of kindergarten, but his stuffed dog Rufus is quite apprehensive. (Rev: SLJ 9/05)

6475 dePaola, Tomie. *The Art Lesson* (K–3). Illus. by author. 1989, Penguin $16.99 (978-0-399-21688-6). 32pp. Tommy just keeps on drawing and drawing and drawing. (Rev: BCCB 3/89; BL 3/1/89; SLJ 4/89)

6476 dePaola, Tomie. *Stagestruck* (PS–2). Illus. 2005, Penguin $16.99 (978-0-399-24338-7). 32pp. When Tommy fails to win the starring role in his kindergarten production of Peter Rabbit, he decides to steal the show anyway, and ends up apologizing. (Rev: BL 1/1–15/05; SLJ 1/05)

6477 Derby, Sally. *The Wacky Substitute* (K–3). Illus. by Jennifer Herbert. 2005, Marshall Cavendish $14.95 (978-0-7614-5219-5). When substitute teacher Mr. Wuerst loses his eyeglasses, it sets the stage for some entertaining mishaps in the classroom. (Rev: SLJ 10/05)

6478 DiPucchio, Kelly S. *Mrs. McBloom, Clean Up Your Room!* (K–2). Illus. by Guy Francis. 2005, Hyperion $15.99 (978-0-7868-0932-5). 32pp. Mrs. McBloom is retiring after a half century of teaching, and her students help to clean up the amazingly diverse clutter in her classroom. (Rev: BL 8/05; SLJ 9/05)

6479 Dodds, Dayle Ann. *Teacher's Pets* (PS–2). Illus. by Marylin Hafner. 2006, Candlewick $15.99 (978-0-7636-2252-7). 40pp. Miss Fry's classroom becomes home to her students' pets in this story of a happy menagerie. (Rev: BL 5/15/06; SLJ 5/06)

6480 Driscoll, Laura. *Lila the Fair* (1–3). Illus. by Blanche Sims. 2005, Kane paper $4.99 (978-1-57565-148-4). 32pp. Lila calls herself "fair" because of her abilities as a peacemaker, which she exercises often as a middle child. (Rev: BL 3/1/05)

6481 Dubosarsky, Ursula. *Rex* (K–2). Illus. by David Mackintosh. 2006, Roaring Brook $16.95 (978-1-59643-186-7). 32pp. In words and art, various students describe what happened when they took Rex the class chameleon home for the night. (Rev: BL 11/15/06; SLJ 9/06)

6482 Edwards, Becky. *My First Day at Nursery School* (PS–1). Illus. by Anthony Flintoft. 2002, Bloomsbury $15.95 (978-1-58234-761-5). 32pp. A reassuring tale of a child's first day at nursery school. (Rev: BL 8/02; SLJ 8/02)

6483 Elschner, Géraldine. *Max's Magic Seeds* (PS–1). Illus. by Jean Pierre Corderoch. 2007, Penguin $16.99 (978-0-698-40059-7). 32pp. Detailed drawings of European village life will attract readers to this story of a boy who plants flowers along his daily walk to school. (Rev: BL 5/15/07; SLJ 7/07)

6484 Ely, Lesley. *Looking After Louis* (1–3). Illus. by Polly Dunbar. 2004, Whitman $16.99 (978-0-8075-4746-5). 32pp. Through the eyes of a little girl, this story looks at the experiences of an autistic boy and his treatment by his classmates. (Rev: BL 4/15/04; SLJ 4/04)

6485 Esham, Barbara. *Last to Finish: A Story About the Smartest Boy in Math Class* (1–3). Illus. by Mike Gordon. Series: The Adventures of Everyday Geniuses. 2008, Mainstream $16.99 (978-1-60336-456-0). 32pp. Max's enjoyment of math is jeopardized when the teacher starts timing tests. (Rev: BL 7/08)

6486 Esham, Barbara. *Stacey Coolidge's Fancy-Smancy Cursive Handwriting* (1–3). Illus. by Mike Gordon. Series: Adventures of Everyday Geniuses. 2008, Mainstream $16.95 (978-1-60336-462-1). 32pp. Carolyn enjoys 2nd grade until they start cursive writing. (Rev: BL 6/1–15/08)

6487 Fain, Moira. *Snow Day* (K–3). Illus. 1996, Walker LB $16.85 (978-0-8027-8410-0). 32pp. Maggie Murphy escapes a school punishment when a snow day is declared the following day. (Rev: BCCB 10/96; BL 10/15/96; SLJ 10/96*)

6488 Falwell, Cathryn. *David's Drawings* (PS–2). Illus. 2001, Lee & Low $16.00 (978-1-58430-031-1). 32pp. Collages of cut-paper and fabric illustrate this story of how one boy's drawing of a bare tree becomes a classroom's cooperative masterpiece. (Rev: BL 11/15/01; HBG 10/02; SLJ 10/01)

6489 Finchler, Judy. *Testing Miss Malarkey* (1–4). Illus. by Kevin O'Malley. 2000, Walker LB $16.85 (978-0-8027-8737-8). 32pp. A humorous story in which kids are being prepared for standardized tests that they eventually pass with flying colors. (Rev: BL 10/1/00)

6490 Finchler, Judy, and Kevin O'Malley. *Miss Malarkey Leaves No Reader Behind* (1–3). Series: Miss Malarkey. 2006, Walker $16.95 (978-0-8027-8084-3). 32pp. Miss Malarkey finally finds a book that's just right for a guy who's not too fond of reading. (Rev: BL 7/06; SLJ 8/06)

6491 French, Simon. *Guess the Baby* (PS–1). Illus. by Donna Rawlins. 2002, Clarion $14.00 (978-0-618-25989-2). 32pp. Classmates bring in their baby pictures and try to guess who's who. (Rev: BL 12/15/02; HBG 3/03; SLJ 12/02)

6492 Giff, Patricia Reilly. *Today Was a Terrible Day* (2–3). Illus. by Susanna Natti. 1980, Puffin paper $5.99 (978-0-14-050453-8). 32pp. Ronald is having a terrible day until his teacher writes him an understanding note. (Rev: SLJ 3/04)

6493 Grindley, Sally. *It's My School* (PS–2). Illus. by Margaret Chamberlain. 2006, Walker $15.95 (978-0-8027-8086-7). 32pp. Tom is not pleased when his little sister starts school but he is quick to protect her when necessary. (Rev: BL 8/06; SLJ 7/06*)

6494 Gutman, Dan. *Mr. Klutz Is Nuts!* (2–3). Illus. by Jim Paillot. Series: My Weird School. 2004, HarperCollins LB $15.89 (978-0-06-050703-9); paper $3.99 (978-0-06-050702-2). 96pp. The school principal is an eccentric character who uses unusual incentives in this humorous easy chapter book that will appeal to reluctant readers. (Rev: SLJ 11/04)

6495 Harper, Jessica. *A Place Called Kindergarten* (PS–K). Illus. by G. Brian Karas. 2006, Putnam $15.99 (978-0-399-24226-7). 32pp. The barnyard animals worry when Tommy doesn't turn up as usual, but he has only gone to kindergarten and returns to tell them all about it. (Rev: BL 8/06; SLJ 8/06)

6496 Harris, Robie H. *I Am Not Going to School Today!* (PS–K). Illus. by Jan Ormerod. 2003, Simon & Schuster $16.95 (978-0-689-83913-9). All the worries of the first day of school are captured in this story that ends happily. (Rev: HBG 4/04; SLJ 7/03)

6497 Hathorn, Libby. *Freya's Fantastic Surprise* (1–3). Illus. by Sharon Thompson. 1989, Scholastic $12.95 (978-0-590-42442-4). 32pp. Freya makes up so many surprises at News Time in school that her classmates become hostile. (Rev: HB 3/89)

6498 Havill, Juanita. *Jamaica and the Substitute Teacher* (PS–3). Illus. by Anne S. O'Brien. 1999, Houghton $15.00 (978-0-395-90503-6). 32pp. Jamaica is so ashamed of cheating on a spelling test that she can't cope with the guilt and decides to confess. (Rev: BL 2/15/99; HB 5/99; HBG 10/99; SLJ 5/99)

6499 Hays, Anna Jane. *Ready, Set, Preschool!* (PS). Illus. by True Kelley. 2005, Knopf $16.95 (978-0-375-82519-4). 40pp. This collection of rhymes, stories, and interactive games offers lots of concepts and ideas for preschoolers and their parents. (Rev: BL 8/05; SLJ 9/05)

6500 Heck, Ed. *Monkey Lost* (PS–2). Illus. by author. 2005, Milk & Cookies $15.95 (978-0-689-04633-9). Eric's teacher and classmates pitch in to help find the monkey he brought to school for show-and-tell, unaware that it is only a stuffed animal. (Rev: SLJ 11/05)

6501 Henkes, Kevin. *Lilly's Purple Plastic Purse* (PS–K). Illus. 1996, Greenwillow $17.89 (978-0-688-12898-2). 32pp. Lilly runs afoul of her teacher, Mr. Slinger, whom she adores. A sequel to *Julius, the Baby of the World* (1990). (Rev: BCCB 10/96; BL 8/96*; HB 9/96; SLJ 8/96*)

6502 Hennessy, B. G. *Mr. Ouchy's First Day* (K–2). Illus. by Paul Meisel. 2006, Putnam $15.99 (978-0-399-24248-9). 32pp. Mr. Ouchy is nervous about his first day as a teacher until he actually interacts with the class. (Rev: BL 8/06; SLJ 7/06)

6503 Hobbie, Nathaniel. *Priscilla Superstar!* (1–3). Illus. by Jocelyn Hobbie. 2006, Little, Brown $16.99 (978-0-316-01386-4). 32pp. Even though Priscilla doesn't get the lead in her roller-skating school's play she still shows off her talent and learns what it means to be a real star. (Rev: BL 2/1/07; SLJ 10/06)

6504 Hoffman, Mary. *Princess Grace* (K–3). Illus. by Cornelius Van Wright. 2008, Dial $16.99 (978-0-8037-3260-5). 32pp. On parade day, Grace and her classmates portray royalty from different cultures, Grace in West African Kente robes. (Rev: BL 2/15/08; HB 3/08; SLJ 1/08)

6505 Hole, Stian. *Garmann's Summer* (1–3). Trans. by Don Bartlett. Illus. by author. 2008, Eerdmans $17.50 (978-0-8028-5339-4). 42pp. Fall is coming and with it the beginning of 1st grade, which Garmann, a thoughtful boy, views with some trepidation; but discussions with various adults make it clear that everyone has to deal with fears. (Rev: BL 5/1/08; SLJ 6/08)

6506 Howlett, Bud. *I'm New Here* (K–4). Illus. 1993, Houghton $17.00 (978-0-395-64049-4). 32pp. A photo-essay about a 5th-grader from El Salvador and her first experiences in an American school. (Rev: BL 10/1/93; SLJ 9/93)

6507 Hurwitz, Johanna. *Mostly Monty* (1–3). Illus. by Anik McGrory. 2007, Candlewick $15.99 (978-0-7636-2831-4). 96pp. Monty is a 1st-grader with asthma who learns to overcome his physical limits by discovering his many unique talents and sharing them with others. Also use *Mighty Monty* (2008). (Rev: BCCB 9/07; BL 6/1–15/07; LMC 11/07; SLJ 7/07)

6508 Jacobson, Jennifer. *Andy Shane and the Queen of Egypt* (K–2). Illus. by Abby Cater. Series: Andy Shane. 2008, Candlewick $13.99 (978-0-7636-3211-3). 64pp. Andy must make a choice when both he and the bossy Dolores want Egypt for their African country project; will he decide to work with her? (Rev: BL 4/1/08; SLJ 7/08)

6509 Johnson, Dolores. *My Mom Is My Show-and-Tell* (K–3). Illus. 1999, Marshall Cavendish $15.95 (978-0-7614-5041-2). 32pp. Brian, an African American boy who is the class clown, is anxious about his mother's visit on Parents' Day. (Rev: BL 4/15/99; HBG 10/99; SLJ 5/99)

6510 Johnson, Doug. *Substitute Teacher Plans* (1–3). Illus. by Tammy Smith. 2002, Holt $16.95 (978-0-8050-6520-6). 32pp. An exhausted teacher mixes up the instructions for her substitute with her list of things to do on her day off, sending her students on an adventure. (Rev: BL 9/15/02; HBG 3/03; SLJ 8/02)

6511 Jules, Jacqueline. *No English* (PS–2). Illus. by Amy Huntington. 2007, Mitten $17.95 (978-1-58726-474-0). 32pp. Second-grader Diane befriends a new student, Blanca, when she discovers that she cannot speak English, and they use drawings to get to know one another. (Rev: BL 11/1/07; LMC 1/08; SLJ 1/08)

6512 Karas, G. Brian. *The Class Artist* (K–3). Illus. 2001, Greenwillow LB $15.89 (978-0-688-17815-4). 32pp. A boy struggles with an art assignment until his teacher suggests that he draw a picture of how he feels. (Rev: BCCB 9/01; BL 11/15/01; HBG 3/02; SLJ 9/01)

6513 Kelley, True. *School Lunch* (K–2). Illus. 2005, Holiday $16.95 (978-0-8234-1894-7). 32pp. When Harriet, the school cook, takes a vacation, students and faculty are disappointed in her replacements and write letters begging her to return. (Rev: BL 9/15/05; SLJ 11/05)

6514 Kirk, Daniel. *Keisha Ann Can!* (PS–1). Illus. by author. 2008, Putnam $15.99 (978-0-399-24179-6). 32pp. African American Keisha Ann loves everything about school and is proud of her achievements in this brightly illustrated story with rhyming text. (Rev: BL 6/1–15/08; SLJ 7/08)

6515 Kline, Suzy. *Herbie Jones Sails into Second Grade* (1–3). Illus. by Sami Sweeten. 2006, Putnam $14.99 (978-0-399-22665-6). 64pp. On his first day of 2nd grade, Herbie Jones meets a new friend and learns that his teacher is a man who has a sense of humor. (Rev: BL 8/06)

6516 Kline, Suzy. *Horrible Harry and the Dragon War* (1–3). Illus. by Frank Remkiewicz. 2002, Viking $13.99 (978-0-670-03559-5). 64pp. Harry and classmate Song Lee quarrel over a school project on dragons but finally become friends again. (Rev: BL 6/1–15/02; HBG 3/03; SLJ 8/02)

6517 Kline, Suzy. *Horrible Harry Bugs the Three Bears* (2–4). Illus. by Frank Remkiewicz. 2008, Viking $13.99 (978-0-670-06293-5). 80pp. Horrible Harry gives Edward the earwig a proper burial and along with his classmates performs "Goldilocks and the Three Bugs." (Rev: BL 2/1/08)

6518 Kline, Suzy. *Horrible Harry Goes to the Moon* (2–3). Illus. by Frank Remkiewicz. 2000, Viking $13.99 (978-0-670-88764-4). 64pp. In this story about Horrible Harry, Miss Mackle's 3rd-grade class decides to hold a bake sale to buy a used telescope. (Rev: HBG 10/00; SLJ 2/00)

6519 Koster, Gloria. *The Peanut-Free Café* (K–2). Illus. by Maryann Cocca-Leffler. 2006, Albert Whitman $16.99 (978-0-8075-6386-1). 32pp. Food allergies take center stage in this story about the steps a classmate takes to make life more comfortable for a student with a peanut allergy. (Rev: BL 2/1/06; SLJ 9/06)

6520 Krishnaswami, Uma. *The Happiest Tree: A Yoga Story* (PS–2). Illus. by Ruth Jeyaveeran. 2005, Lee & Low $16.95 (978-1-58430-237-7). 32pp. Meena signs up for a children's yoga class that she hopes will help her to overcome her clumsiness. (Rev: BL 10/1/05; SLJ 11/05)

6521 Laminack, Lester L. *Jake's 100th Day of School* (1–3). Illus. by Judy Love. 2006, Peachtree $16.95 (978-1-56145-355-9). 32pp. Jake has prepared 100 family photographs for the 100th day of school but leaves them at home in his excitement; his principal and a 100-year-old woman rescue the day. (Rev: BL 2/1/06; SLJ 3/06)

6522 Laminack, Lester L. *Snow Day!* (K–2). Illus. by Adam Gustavson. 2007, Peachtree $16.95 (978-1-56145-418-1). 32pp. A narrator gleefully fantasizes about the various ways to spend a snow day — from snuggling on the sofa to building a snow fort — and the reader is surprised at the end to learn the narrator is in fact the father, a teacher. (Rev: BL 10/1/07; SLJ 10/07)

6523 Larsen, Andrew. *Bella and the Bunny* (PS–K). Illus. by Kate Endle. 2007, Kids Can $14.95 (978-1-55337-970-6). Bella loses her favorite grandma-made sweater at preschool, but is happy to find it again. (Rev: SLJ 5/07)

6524 Larsen, Kirsten. *The Ghost Town Mystery* (K–3). Illus. by Jerry Smath. 2008, Kane paper $5.95 (978-1-57565-257-3). 32pp. On a field trip to a ghost town, Max learns American history, solves a mystery and successfully faces down his fear. (Rev: BLO 2/8/08; SLJ 7/08)

6525 Lee, Hyun Young. *Something for School* (PS–1). Illus. by author. 2008, Kane $15.95 (978-1-933605-85-2). 40pp. It's the first day of kindergarten and everyone thinks Yoon is a boy. (Rev: SLJ 9/08)

6526 Lehn, Barbara. *What Is a Teacher?* (K–2). Photos by Carol Krauss. 2000, Millbrook LB $21.90 (978-0-7613-1713-5). The characteristics of a good teacher are acted out in a series of captioned photos showing children in the teacher's role. (Rev: HBG 3/01; SLJ 1/01)

6527 Levert, Mireille. *Eddie Longpants* (K–1). Illus. by author. 2005, Groundwood $16.95 (978-0-88899-671-8). Teased by his classmates about being so tall, Eddie Longpants must decide whether to retaliate in kind or show his tormentors that he knows a better way to behave. (Rev: SLJ 10/05)

6528 Lin, Grace. *Lissy's Friends* (PS–2). Illus. by author. 2007, Viking $15.99 (978-0-670-06072-6). 32pp. Lonely at her new school, Lissy makes origami friends that lead to a real-life friendship. (Rev: BL 5/15/07; SLJ 7/07)

6529 Lovell, Patty. *Stand Tall, Molly Lou Melon* (K–3). Illus. by David Catrow. 2001, Penguin $15.99 (978-0-399-23416-3). First-grader Molly Lou's grandmother has told her to believe in herself, and Molly Lou puts this successfully into action when she moves to a new school and must deal with the bully. (Rev: BCCB 10/01; HBG 3/02; SLJ 10/01)

6530 Lowry, Lois. *Gooney Bird Is So Absurd* (2–4). Illus. by Middy Thomas. 2009, Houghton $15.00 (978-0-547-11967-0). 112pp. Gooney Bird Greene and her 2nd-grade classmates try to comfort their poetry teacher when her mother dies in this story full of humor, poems, and poignancy. (Rev: BL 2/1/09; HB 5/09; SLJ 3/09) ☊

6531 McCain, Becky Ray. *Nobody Knew What to Do: A Story About Bullying* (K–3). Illus. by Todd Leonardo. 2001, Whitman $16.99 (978-0-8075-5711-2). 32pp. When a boy sees bullies bothering one of his classmates, he decides to ask the teacher for help. (Rev: BL 5/15/01; HBG 10/01; SLJ 5/01)

6532 McGhee, Alison. *Countdown to Kindergarten* (PS–K). Illus. by Harry Bliss. 2002, Harcourt $16.00 (978-0-15-202516-8). 32pp. A soon-to-be kindergartner fears starting school because she's heard that, among other things, you must be able to tie your shoes. (Rev: BCCB 10/02; BL 8/02; HBG 3/03; SLJ 9/02)

6533 McGhee, Alison. *Mrs. Watson Wants Your Teeth* (K–2). Illus. by Harry Bliss. 2004, Harcourt $16.00 (978-0-15-204931-7). A rumor that her teacher is a 300-year-old alien with a purple tongue and a liking for baby teeth scares a 1st-grader on her first day of school. (Rev: SLJ 9/04)

6534 MacKall, Dandi Daley. *First Day* (PS–K). Illus. by Tiphanie Beeke. 2003, Harcourt $16.00 (978-0-15-216577-2). Told in rhyming text, this story of a little girl's first day of school is a good choice for children facing the transition from family room to classroom. (Rev: HBG 4/04; SLJ 9/03)

6535 McNamara, Margaret. *How Many Seeds in a Pumpkin?* (K–3). Illus. by G. Brian Karas. 2007, Random $14.99 (978-0-375-84014-2). 40pp. The smallest boy in the class gains confidence by correctly guessing the number of seeds in three pumpkins, and everyone learns some basic math and science concepts in the process. (Rev: BL 6/1–15/07; SLJ 7/07)

6536 McNamara, Margaret. *Martin Luther King Jr. Day* (K–1). Illus. by Mike Gordon. Series: Robin Hill School. Ready-to-Read. 2007, Simon & Schuster LB $13.89 (978-1-4169-3495-0); paper $3.99 (978-1-4169-3494-3). 32pp. On a trip to a museum, 1st-graders learn about Dr. King and his importance. (Rev: SLJ 4/08)

6537 McNaughton, Colin. *When I Grow Up* (PS–1). Illus. by author. 2005, Candlewick $12.99 (978-0-7636-2675-4). Children putting on a school play tell what they want to be one day — except for one little boy, who is reassured when he says he doesn't want to grow up. (Rev: SLJ 7/05)

6538 Marsh, Carole. *The Case of the Crybaby Cowboy* (1–3). Illus. by Cecil Anderson. Series: Three Amigos. 2006, paper $3.99 (978-0-635-06166-9). 54pp. The Three Amigos, boy detectives, try to find out why one of their classmates — dressed like a cowboy — cries all the time. Also use *The Riddle of the Ooglie Booglie* (2006). (Rev: SLJ 11/06)

6539 Mills, Claudia. *Ziggy's Blue-Ribbon Day* (K–3). Illus. by R. W. Alley. 2005, Farrar $16.00 (978-0-374-32352-3). 32pp. Ziggy's artistic talent makes up for his lack of athletic ability at the track-and-field meet. (Rev: BL 9/1/05; SLJ 11/05)

6540 Milord, Susan. *Happy School Year!* (PS–1). Illus. by Mary Newell Depalma. 2008, Scholastic $15.99 (978-0-439-88280-4). 40pp. All over town a great variety of multicultural children prepare for their first day of school in a variety of different ways. (Rev: BL 8/08; LMC 10/08; SLJ 7/08)

6541 Moon, Nicola. *Something Special* (K–2). Illus. by Alex Ayliffe. 1997, Peachtree $14.95 (978-1-56145-137-1). 32pp. Charlie decides to bring his new baby sister to school for a special show-and-tell. (Rev: BL 6/1–15/97; SLJ 6/97)

6542 Moore-Mallinos, Jennifer. *My Brother Is Autistic* (1–3). Illus. by Marta Fàbrega. 2008, Barron's paper $6.99 (978-0-7641-4044-0). 32pp. A young boy is ashamed of his autistic brother's behavior at school until an observant teacher steps in. (Rev: SLJ 6/09)

6543 Moss, Miriam. *Wibble Wobble* (K–2). Illus. by Joanna Mockler. 2001, ME Media $14.95 (978-1-58925-013-0). 32pp. William is elated to lose his first tooth, and when it goes missing he enlists the

help of the class to find it. (Rev: BL 2/1/02; SLJ 11/01)

6544 Munsch, Robert. *We Share Everything!* (PS–1). Illus. by Michael Martchenko. 1999, Scholastic $11.95 (978-0-590-89600-9). 32pp. In kindergarten, the high jinks of Amanda and Jeremiah prove to be too much for their long-suffering teacher. (Rev: BCCB 11/99; BL 9/1/99; HBG 3/00; SLJ 9/99)

6545 Musgrave, Susan, and Marie-Louise Gay. *Dreams Are More Real than Bathtubs* (K–3). Illus. 1999, Orca $14.95 (978-1-55143-107-9). 32pp. A little girl shares her thoughts about her family, her pet stuffed lion, fears, and starting 1st grade. (Rev: BL 7/99; HBG 10/99; SLJ 8/99)

6546 Nagda, Ann Whitehead. *The Valentine Cat* (2–4). Illus. by Stephanie Roth. 2008, Holiday $16.95 (978-0-8234-2123-7). 128pp. Jenny's brother develops asthma and she must find a new home for her cat Munchkin; keeping at school seems to be a good option. (Rev: BLO 12/18/08; SLJ 2/09)

6547 Nobisso, Josephine. *In English of Course* (2–4). Illus. by Dasha Ziborova. 2002, Gingerbread House $16.95 (978-0-940112-07-0); paper $8.95 (978-0-940112-08-7). 32pp. Young Josephine, a new immigrant from Italy, manages to communicate with her New York City classmates despite her limited knowledge of English. (Rev: BL 2/15/03; HBG 3/03; SLJ 2/03)

6548 Northway, Jennifer. *See You Later, Mom!* (PS). Illus. by author. 2006, Frances Lincoln $15.95 (978-1-84507-537-8). William takes his time separating from Mom and making friends at preschool. (Rev: SLJ 6/06)

6549 O'Neill, Alexis. *The Recess Queen* (PS–1). Illus. by Laura Huliska-Beith. 2002, Scholastic $16.99 (978-0-439-20637-2). 32pp. Mean Jean, the recess queen, has a change in attitude when the new girl at school asks her to play in this brightly illustrated, energetic tale. (Rev: BCCB 3/02; BL 3/1/02; HBG 10/02; SLJ 3/02)

6550 O'Neill, Alexis. *The Worst Best Friend* (PS–K). Illus. by Laura Huliska-Beith. 2008, Scholastic $16.99 (978-0-545-01023-8). 32pp. A tale of preschool friendship, betrayal, and making up that children will recognize. (Rev: BL 9/1/08)

6551 Pak, Soyung. *Sumi's First Day of School Ever* (PS–1). Illus. by Joung Un Kim. 2003, Viking $15.99 (978-0-670-03522-9). Sumi, a little Korean girl, is afraid on her first day of school, but the kindness of a teacher and friendliness of a classmate make her feel more comfortable. (Rev: HB 7/03; HBG 4/04; SLJ 8/03)

6552 Park, Barbara. *Junie B., First Grader: One Man Band* (1–3). Illus. by Denise Brunkus. Series: Junie B. Jones. 2003, Random LB $13.99 (978-0-375-92522-1). 87pp. Junie B. debuts as a cheerleader in this entry in the popular series. Also use *Shipwrecked* (2004). (Rev: HBG 4/04; SLJ 3/04)

6553 Pattison, Darcy. *19 Girls and Me* (PS–2). Illus. by Steven Salerno. 2006, Philomel $16.99 (978-0-399-24336-3). John Hercules is dismayed to learn he is the only boy in his kindergarten class, but soon sets aside his assumptions about girls and thinks of his 19 classmates as friends. (Rev: SLJ 7/06)

6554 Pennypacker, Sara. *Clementine's Letter* (2–4). Illus. by Marla Frazee. 2008, Hyperion $14.99 (978-0-7868-3884-4). 160pp. Third-grader Clementine is not happy that she may lose her beloved teacher and is not inclined to write a letter supporting his nomination for the program that will take him away. (Rev: BL 4/1/08; HB 7/08; SLJ 7/08) ∩

6555 Pérez, L. King. *First Day in Grapes* (1–3). Illus. by Robert Casilla. 2002, Lee & Low $16.95 (978-1-58430-045-8). 32pp. Chico, the son of migrant workers, starts 3rd grade in yet another school with trepidation, but his first day goes well despite bullies and a surly bus driver. (Rev: BL 11/15/02; HBG 3/03; SLJ 10/02)

6556 Plourde, Lynn. *Book Fair Day* (1–3). Illus. by Thor Wickstrom. 2006, Dutton $16.99 (978-0-525-47696-2). 40pp. It's Book Fair Day in the school library, and Dewey Booker is worried that all the good books will be gone by the time his class gets its turn. (Rev: BL 8/06; SLJ 7/06)

6557 Plourde, Lynn. *Pajama Day* (PS–2). Illus. by Thor Wickstrom. 2005, Dutton $16.99 (978-0-525-47355-8). 40pp. When Drew A. Blank shows his inventiveness when he arrives at school unprepared for Pajama Day. (Rev: BL 1/1–15/05; SLJ 2/05)

6558 Plourde, Lynn. *School Picture Day* (K–2). Illus. by Thor Wickstrom. 2002, Dutton $16.99 (978-0-525-46886-8). 40pp. Josephina Caroleena Wattasheena's curious nature causes calamity at her school on picture day. (Rev: BL 8/02; HBG 3/03; SLJ 7/02)

6559 Plourde, Lynn. *Science Fair Day* (PS–3). Illus. by Thor Wickstrom. 2008, Dutton $16.99 (978-0-525-47878-2). 40pp. On the final day of science fair preparations Ima Kindanozee creates havoc as she investigates her fellow students' projects. (Rev: BL 11/15/07; SLJ 3/08)

6560 Polacco, Patricia. *Mr. Lincoln's Way* (K–3). Illus. 2001, Penguin $16.99 (978-0-399-23754-6). 40pp. A school principal uses a bully's interest in birds to teach him about tolerance and kindness. (Rev: BL 9/1/01; HBG 3/02; SLJ 8/01)

6561 Poydar, Nancy. *The Bad-News Report Card* (K–3). Illus. 2006, Holiday $16.95 (978-0-8234-1992-0). 32pp. Stricken by an attack of report card anxiety, Isabel hides the card away and tries to forget about it; when she finally checks it out, she discovers that all her worries were unwarranted. (Rev: BL 9/1/06)

6562 Poydar, Nancy. *The Biggest Test in the Universe* (1–3). Illus. by author. 2005, Holiday House $16.95 (978-0-8234-1944-9). Sam is apprehensive about taking the "big test" after hearing horror stories about it from the older kids, but he discovers these stories are exaggerated. (Rev: SLJ 9/05)

6563 Poydar, Nancy. *Bunny Business* (PS–3). Illus. by author. 2003, Holiday House $16.95 (978-0-8234-1771-1). Harry turns out to be a good listener despite his fellow students' low opinion. (Rev: HBG 10/03; SLJ 4/03)

6564 Poydar, Nancy. *First Day, Hooray!* (PS–1). Illus. 1999, Holiday House $16.95 (978-0-8234-1437-6). 32pp. Young Ivy Green is worried about her first day at school, but so are others involved in the school's opening, including the bus driver and the principal. (Rev: BL 10/15/99; HBG 3/00; SLJ 8/99)

6565 Poydar, Nancy. *Fish School* (1–3). Illus. by author. 2009, Holiday $16.95 (978-0-8234-2140-4). 32pp. Charlie hopes to educate his treasured pet goldfish on a class trip to the aquarium; however, when Charlie's backpack and the bag containing his goldfish goes missing, it is Charlie who learns a lesson; includes information on caring for goldfish. (Rev: BL 7/09; SLJ 8/09)

6566 Poydar, Nancy. *Last Day, Hooray!* (K–2). Illus. 2004, Holiday House $16.95 (978-0-8234-1807-7). 32pp. With visions of summer dancing in their heads, students and staff celebrate the final day of the school year. (Rev: BL 4/15/04; SLJ 4/04)

6567 Poydar, Nancy. *Snip, Snip . . . Snow!* (PS–1). Illus. 1997, Holiday House LB $16.95 (978-0-8234-1328-7). 32pp. Sophie is so disappointed at the lack of snow that she persuades her teacher to let the class make paper snowflakes. (Rev: BL 11/1/97; HBG 3/98; SLJ 10/97)

6568 Poydar, Nancy. *Zip, Zip . . . Homework* (PS–2). Illus. by author. 2008, Holiday $16.95 (978-0-8234-2090-2). 32pp. Violet is so absorbed in the organization of her efficient new backpack that she leaves her assignment at school and finds herself weaving a tangled web. (Rev: BL 9/1/08; SLJ 9/08)

6569 Pulver, Robin. *Author Day for Room 3T* (K–3). Illus. by Chuck Richards. 2005, Clarion $16.00 (978-0-618-35406-1). 32pp. It's Author Day and the class has been eagerly anticipating someone "new and different," so when a chimp turns up (the librarian is very near-sighted), they are not taken aback. (Rev: BL 5/1/05; SLJ 4/05)

6570 Radabaugh, Melinda. *Going to School* (PS–1). Series: First Time. 2003, Heinemann LB $18.50 (978-1-4034-0227-1). 24pp. A reassuring, simple introduction to what happens during a typical day at school. (Rev: HBG 10/03; SLJ 6/03) [372.12]

6571 Reiser, Lynn. *Earthdance* (PS–3). Illus. 1999, Greenwillow LB $15.89 (978-0-688-16327-3). 32pp. While Terra is at school preparing for a show, her astronaut mother is traveling to the end of the universe. (Rev: BL 12/1/99; HBG 3/00; SLJ 10/99)

6572 Reynolds, Peter H. *The Dot* (K–2). Illus. by author. 2003, Candlewick $14.00 (978-0-7636-1961-9). A young girl who is sure she can't draw finds success when she heeds her teacher's advice to "make a mark and see where it takes you." (Rev: HBG 4/04; SLJ 11/03)

6573 Rockwell, Anne. *Career Day* (PS–K). Illus. by Lizzy Rockwell. 2000, HarperCollins $16.99 (978-0-06-027565-5). 32pp. During Mrs. Madoff's classroom Career Day presentations, 10 children introduce a parent or grandparent who talks about his or her occupation. (Rev: BL 5/1/00; HBG 10/00; SLJ 7/00)

6574 Rockwell, Anne. *My Preschool* (PS). Illus. by author. 2008, Holt $16.95 (978-0-8050-7955-5).

32pp. This picture book follows little Fred's day at preschool, looking at both the fun and the difficult parts. (Rev: BL 8/08; SLJ 4/08)

6575 Rodman, Mary Ann. *First Grade Stinks!* (PS–1). Illus. by Beth Spiegel. 2006, Peachtree $15.95 (978-1-56145-377-1). 32pp. Haley pretty quickly decides that 1st grade is no fun in comparison with kindergarten. (Rev: BL 8/06; SLJ 8/06)

6576 Rogers, Jacqueline. *Tiptoe into Kindergarten* (PS–1). Illus. 1999, Scholastic $10.95 (978-0-590-46653-0). 32pp. A preschooler steals into her brother's kindergarten class and soon becomes part of the activities. (Rev: BL 8/99; HBG 3/00; SLJ 9/99)

6577 Rosen, Michael. *Totally Wonderful Miss Plumberry* (PS–K). Illus. by Chinlun Lee. 2006, Candlewick $15.99 (978-0-7636-2744-7). 40pp. Molly's teacher recognizes Molly's huge disappointment when Russell's stegosaurus seems to be stealing the show and she refocuses the class on Molly's crystal. (Rev: BL 8/06)

6578 Rousaki, Maria. *Unique Monique* (PS–2). Illus. by Polina Papanikolaou. 2003, Kane $15.95 (978-1-929132-51-5). Monique experiments with various ways to enhance her drab school uniform, but they all meet with the principal's disapproval until she thinks of her teeth. (Rev: HBG 4/04; SLJ 11/03)

6579 Russo, Marisabina. *I Don't Want to Go Back to School* (PS–2). Illus. 1994, Greenwillow $15.89 (978-0-688-04602-6). 32pp. A little boy worries about his reception when he returns to school after summer vacation. (Rev: BL 9/1/94; SLJ 7/94*)

6580 Rylant, Cynthia. *The Ticky-Tacky Doll* (PS–1). Illus. by Harvey Stevenson. 2002, Harcourt $16.00 (978-0-15-201078-2). 32pp. A little girl, sad to leave her doll behind when she goes to school, is cheered when her grandmother makes her a smaller doll to take with her. (Rev: BL 9/1/02; HBG 3/03; SLJ 11/02)

6581 Saltzberg, Barney. *Show-and-Tell* (K–3). Illus. 1994, Hyperion LB $15.49 (978-0-7868-2016-0). 32pp. Young Phoebe's parents always interfere with her school plans and create something grand out of a simple assignment. (Rev: BL 10/15/94; SLJ 10/94)

6582 Schaefer, Carole Lexa. *Kids Like Us* (PS). Illus. by Pierr Morgan. 2008, Viking $15.99 (978-0-670-06290-4). 32pp. On a gray and rainy day, children in a classroom use their imaginations to fuel their play. (Rev: BL 5/1/08; SLJ 5/08)

6583 Schwartz, Amy. *Annabelle Swift, Kindergartner* (PS–K). Illus. by author. 1988, Orchard paper $6.99 (978-0-531-07027-7). 32pp. A good match of art and text tells the story of Annabelle, who finds that school isn't as much fun as she had thought — until it's time to count the milk money. (Rev: BCCB 5/88; BL 2/1/88; HB 3/88)

6584 Schwartz, Amy. *Begin at the Beginning: A Little Artist Learns About Life* (PS–2). Illus. 2005, HarperCollins LB $16.89 (978-0-06-000112-4). 40pp. Sara struggles to pick a subject and get started on her art fair project. (Rev: BL 5/15/05)

6585 Scieszka, Jon. *Math Curse* (1–4). Illus. by Lane Smith. 1995, Viking $17.99 (978-0-670-86194-1).

32pp. All sorts of math problems and riddles, from the practical to the absurd are presented in this school story. (Rev: BCCB 10/95; BL 11/1/95*; HB 11/95; SLJ 9/95*)

6586 Senisi, Ellen B. *Kindergarten Kids* (PS–K). Illus. 1994, Scholastic paper $3.25 (978-0-590-47614-0). 32pp. A photo-essay that describes a typical day in a kindergarten class in Schenectady, New York. (Rev: BL 11/1/94) [372.21]

6587 Shannon, David. *David Goes to School* (PS–K). Illus. 1999, Scholastic $16.99 (978-0-590-48087-1). 32pp. David, an imaginative nonconformist, has difficulty doing the right thing when he begins school. (Rev: BCCB 1/00; BL 8/99*; HBG 3/00; SLJ 9/99)

6588 Shaw, Mary. *Brady Brady and the Big Mistake* (K–3). Illus. by Chuck Temple. 2003, Stoddart paper $4.95 (978-0-7737-6304-3). The entertaining, sports-based adventures of Brady Brady and the Ice Hogs continue. Also use *Brady Brady and the Singing Tree* and *Brady Brady and the Twirlin' Torpedo* (both 2003). (Rev: SLJ 8/03)

6589 Shaw, Mary. *Brady Brady and the Great Rink* (1–3). Illus. by Chuck Temple. Series: Brady Brady. 2002, Stoddart paper $4.95 (978-0-7737-6224-4). Brady Brady builds a skating rink in his backyard that comes in handy when the school's power fails. Also use *Brady Brady and the Runaway Goalie* (2002). (Rev: SLJ 10/02)

6590 Slate, Joseph. *Miss Bindergarten Celebrates the Last Day of Kindergarten* (PS–K). Illus. by Ashley Wolff. 2006, Button $16.99 (978-0-525-47744-0). 48pp. The school year comes to an end for Miss Bindergarten and her 26 alphabetical kindergarten students. (Rev: BL 2/15/06; SLJ 3/06)

6591 Slate, Joseph. *Miss Bindergarten Has a Wild Day in Kindergarten* (PS–2). Illus. by Ashley Wolff. 2005, Button $16.99 (978-0-525-47084-7). Miss Bindergarten and her students are having a wild day as water spills, hats fly, and butterflies are set free — a fine finale. (Rev: SLJ 2/05)

6592 Slate, Joseph. *Miss Bindergarten Stays Home from Kindergarten* (PS–2). Illus. by Ashley Wolff. 2000, Dutton $16.99 (978-0-525-46396-2). Miss Bindergarten catches the flu and has to stay home; progressively the students and even the substitute, Mr. Tusky, are also infected. (Rev: HBG 3/01; SLJ 11/00)

6593 Slate, Joseph. *Miss Bindergarten Takes a Field Trip* (PS–K). Illus. by Ashley Wolff. 2001, Dutton $16.99 (978-0-525-46710-6). 32pp. Miss Bindergarten takes her kindergartners on an interesting field trip that subtly introduces all sorts of shapes. (Rev: BL 10/1/01; HBG 3/02; SLJ 9/01)

6594 Stampler, Ann R. *Go Home, Mrs. Beekman!* (PS). Illus. by Marsha Carrington. 2008, Dutton $16.99 (978-0-525-46933-9). 32pp. Emily asks her mother to stay with her when she gets to preschool but then finds that her mother won't leave. (Rev: BL 8/08; LMC 11/08)

6595 Stoeke, Janet Morgan. *The Bus Stop* (PS–1). Illus. by author. 2007, Dutton $12.99 (978-0-525-47805-8). 24pp. This charming, reassuring picture book focuses on three young children as they prepare to ride the school bus for the very first time. (Rev: BL 5/15/07; SLJ 7/07)

6596 Stoeke, Janet Morgan. *It's Library Day* (K–2). Illus. by author. 2008, Dutton $12.99 (978-0-525-47944-4). 24pp. A multicultural group of children enjoy visiting the school library and finding just the right books to read. (Rev: BL 7/08; SLJ 7/08)

6597 Stuve-Bodeen, Stephanie. *Elizabeti's School* (PS–1). Illus. by Christy Hale. 2002, Lee & Low $16.95 (978-1-58430-043-4). 32pp. Elizabeti tackles her first day at school and comes home to tell her loving family all about it in this story set in Tanzania. (Rev: BCCB 12/02; BL 9/15/02; HB 11/02; HBG 3/03; SLJ 9/02)

6598 Tester, Sylvia Root. *We Laughed a Lot, My First Day of School* (PS–1). Illus. by Frances Hook. 1979, Child's World LB $14.95 (978-0-685-55556-9). A Mexican American boy has an unexpectedly pleasant first day at school.

6599 Thomson, Melissa. *Keena Ford and the Second-Grade Mix-Up* (2–4). Illus. by Frank Morrison. 2008, Dial $14.99 (978-0-8037-3263-6). 112pp. In Washington, D.C., a 2nd-grade African American girl records in her diary her problems at school, where she seems to invite problems. (Rev: BCCB 7–8/08; BLO 12/30/08; LMC 1/09; SLJ 10/08)

6600 Trice, Linda. *Kenya's Word* (1–3). Illus. by Pamela Johnson. 2006, Charlesbridge $16.95 (978-1-57091-887-2); paper $6.95 (978-1-57091-888-9). 32pp. After a series of homework assignments that went awry, Kenya is determined to impress her teacher and classmates with her "favorite describing word." (Rev: BL 2/1/06; SLJ 3/06)

6601 Uegaki, Chieri. *Suki's Kimono* (K–3). Illus. by Stephane Jorisch. 2003, Kids Can $15.95 (978-1-55337-084-0). Undeterred by her older sisters' opposition, young Suki proudly wears her favorite garment — a kimono — on the first day of school. (Rev: HBG 4/04; SLJ 12/03)

6602 Veldkamp, Tjibbe. *The School Trip* (PS–3). Illus. by Philip Hopman. 2001, Front St. $15.95 (978-1-886910-70-6). 32pp. Afraid of attending school, Davy opts to build his own, and when he adds wheels the fun really starts. (Rev: BL 8/01; HBG 10/01; SLJ 7/01)

6603 Warner, Sally. *Excellent Emma* (2–4). Illus. by Jamie Harper. 2009, Viking $14.99 (978-0-670-06310-9). 144pp. Third-grader Emma tries to get her father's attention by entering a school sports competition in this lively story about divorce and school life. (Rev: BLO 2/9/09; SLJ 3/09)

6604 Wells, Rosemary. *Yoko's World of Kindness: Golden Rules for a Happy Classroom* (PS–2). Illus. by John Nez and Jody Wheeler. 2005, Hyperion $19.99 (978-0-7868-5109-6). 154pp. An anthology of previously published stories about Yoko, Noisy Nora, and other children in Mrs. Jenkins's class. (Rev: SLJ 10/05)

6605 Wheatley, Nadia. *Luke's Way of Looking* (K–4). Illus. by Matt Ottley. 2001, Kane $15.95 (978-1-929132-18-8). Appealing illustrations extend this story of a young boy who doesn't match his art teacher's expectations. (Rev: HBG 3/02; SLJ 6/02)

6606 Winkler, Henry, and Lin Oliver. *I Got a "D" in Salami* (3–5). Illus. 2003, Grosset $13.99 (978-0-448-43233-5); paper $4.99 (978-0-448-43163-5). 167pp. When Hank Zipzer gets three Ds on his report card, he goes to great lengths to keep this bad news from his parents. (Rev: HBG 4/04; SLJ 10/03)

6607 Yashima, Taro. *Crow Boy* (K–3). Illus. by author. 1955, Puffin paper $6.99 (978-0-14-050172-8). 40pp. Distinguished picture book about a shy little Japanese boy who feels like an outsider at school.

6608 Zemach, Kaethe. *Ms. McCaw Learns to Draw* (K–3). Illus. by author. 2008, Scholastic $16.99 (978-0-439-82914-4). 32pp. Dudley's teacher, Ms. McCaw, is patient with his learning disabilities and Dudley happily comes to her rescue with his artistic talent. (Rev: BL 2/1/08; LMC 1/08; SLJ 1/08)

6609 Ziefert, Harriet. *Schools Have Learn* (PS–2). Illus. by Amanda Haley. 2004, Blue Apple $15.95 (978-1-59354-056-2). Inventive wordplay — "good-byes have hugs, backpacks have lugs" — accompanies children through a typical day. (Rev: BCCB 12/04; SLJ 2/05)

TRANSPORTATION AND MACHINES

6610 Baer, Edith. *This Is the Way We Go to School* (PS–2). Illus. by Steve Björkman. 1994, Scholastic paper $5.99 (978-0-590-49443-4). 40pp. How children around the world go to school is told in rhyming couplets. (Rev: BCCB 10/90; BL 10/1/90; SLJ 7/90*) [629]

6611 Barton, Byron. *Airport* (PS–1). Illus. by author. 1982, HarperCollins LB $17.89 (978-0-690-04169-9); paper $6.99 (978-0-06-443145-3). 32pp. Common sights at an airport, reproduced in drawings and text.

6612 Bee, William. *And the Train Goes . . . .* (PS–K). Illus. by author. 2007, Candlewick $15.99 (978-0-7636-3248-9). There's a lot going on in this train. People off to various destinations are portrayed in lovely illustrations and described in entertaining text. (Rev: SLJ 6/07)

6613 Bell, Babs. *The Bridge Is Up!* (PS). Illus. by Rob Hefferan. 2004, HarperCollins LB $13.89 (978-0-06-053794-4). A colorfully illustrated cumulative tale about a long line of vehicles (driven by various animals) all waiting to cross a drawbridge. (Rev: SLJ 3/04)

6614 Borden, Louise. *The Neighborhood Trucker* (PS–2). Illus. by Sandra Speidel. 1997, Scholastic paper $3.95 (978-0-590-46037-8). 32pp. A boy is entranced with trucks, particularly a cement truck driven by Slim. (Rev: BCCB 12/90; BL 9/1/90; SLJ 10/90)

6615 Brown, Margaret Wise. *Two Little Trains* (PS–K). Illus. by Diane Dillon. 2001, HarperCollins $16.99 (978-0-06-028376-6). 40pp. Using double-page spreads, this book shows two parallel journeys, one by a streamlined diesel train as it travels across the country and the other by a toy train as it moves around a house. (Rev: BL 4/15/01*; HB 5/01*; HBG 10/01; SLJ 5/01)

6616 Burton, Virginia Lee. *Mike Mulligan and His Steam Shovel* (1–3). Illus. by author. 1939, Houghton LB $11.95 (978-0-395-06681-2); paper $7.99 (978-0-395-25939-9). Thrilling race against time as Mike Mulligan and his steam shovel dig a cellar in one day. Also use: *Katy and the Big Snow* (1973).

6617 Cohen, Deborah Bodin. *Engineer Ari and the Rosh Hashanah Ride* (K–3). Illus. by Shahar Kober. 2008, Lerner $17.95 (978-0-8225-8648-7); paper $7.95 (978-0-8225-8650-0). 32pp. In 1892 Israel's first train makes its way — on Rosh Hashanah, the Jewish New Year — from Jaffa to Jerusalem with Engineer Ari at the wheel, a boastful man who takes time on this holy day to reconsider his treatment of his friends. (Rev: BL 9/1/08; SLJ 9/08)

6618 Cowley, Joy. *The Rusty, Trusty Tractor* (K–2). Illus. by Olivier Dunrea. 1999, Boyds Mills $15.95 (978-1-56397-565-3). 40pp. In spite of a tractor salesman's dire predictions, Micah's grandfather's 50-year-old tractor takes the old man through another season on the farm. (Rev: BCCB 3/99; BL 3/15/99; HBG 10/99; SLJ 5/99)

6619 Crews, Donald. *Bicycle Race* (PS–K). Illus. by author. 1985, Greenwillow $17.89 (978-0-688-05172-3). 24pp. A counting book that features 12 bicyclists in yellow numbered helmets, with a flat tire added for drama. (Rev: BL 9/15/85; SLJ 11/85)

6620 Crews, Donald. *Flying* (PS). Illus. by author. 1986, Greenwillow $17.89 (978-0-688-04319-3); Morrow paper $6.99 (978-0-688-09235-1). 32pp. Brief text and full-color art highlight this study in movement as a plane takes off, flies over different landscapes, and lands. (Rev: BL 9/1/86; SLJ 10/86)

6621 Crews, Donald. *Freight Train / Tren de carga* (PS–2). Trans. by M. J. Infante. Illus. by author. 2003, Greenwillow $16.99 (978-0-06-056202-1). A lively bilingual book version of the 1979 Caldecott Honor Book showing a multicolored freight train as it makes its journey through tunnels, over bridges, and around big cities. (Rev: HBG 4/04; SLJ 12/03)

6622 Crews, Donald. *Inside Freight Train* (PS). Illus. 2001, HarperCollins $9.99 (978-0-688-17087-5). 12pp. A well-designed board book that makes Crews's famous 1978 book interactive by using split pages that slip sideways to reveal smaller pages. (Rev: BL 12/15/00*; HBG 10/01)

6623 Crews, Donald. *School Bus* (PS–1). Illus. by author. 1984, Greenwillow $17.89 (978-0-688-02808-4); Morrow paper $6.99 (978-0-688-12267-6). 32pp. Many kinds of school buses pick up children for school.

6624 Delafosse, Claude. *Tools* (PS–1). Trans. from French by Wendy Barish. Illus. by Daniel Moignot. Series: First Discovery. 1999, Scholastic $12.95 (978-0-439-04404-2). This book covers such common tools as pliers, wall anchors, saws, and hammers. (Rev: HBG 3/00; SLJ 1/00)

6625 Frazee, Marla. *Roller Coaster* (PS–1). Illus. by author. 2003, Harcourt $16.00 (978-0-15-204554-8). A young boy who is just tall enough to ride the giant coaster for the first time has a breath-taking experience. (Rev: HB 5/03; HBG 10/03; SLJ 7/03)

6626 Freymann, Saxton, and Joost Elffers. *Fast Food* (PS–2). Illus. by Saxton Freymann. 2006, Scholastic $12.99 (978-0-439-11019-8). 32pp. In this volume, Freymann and Effers turn their ordinary fruits and vegetables into a variety of modes of transportation. (Rev: BL 2/1/06*; LMC 5/06; SLJ 4/06) [641.8]

6627 Gall, Chris. *Dinotrux* (PS–1). Illus. by author. 2009, Little, Brown $16.99 (978-0-316-02777-9). 32pp. A funny tale of ferocious prehistoric trucks — Craneosaurus, Dumploducus — that roamed with the dinosaurs. (Rev: BL 7/09; SLJ 6/09)

6628 Garcia, Emma. *Tip Tip Dig Dig* (PS–K). Illus. by author. 2007, Sterling $14.95 (978-1-905417-58-2). 32pp. From hole in the ground to finished playground, a variety of construction vehicles are called into action. (Rev: SLJ 11/07)

6629 Gibbons, Faye. *Full Steam Ahead* (K–3). Illus. by Sherry Meidell. 2002, Boyds Mills $15.95 (978-1-56397-858-6). 32pp. Sammy and his family experience the excitement of seeing the first train to roll through their home town in Georgia. (Rev: BL 4/1/02; HBG 10/02; SLJ 7/02)

6630 Gibbons, Gail. *Boat Book* (PS–1). Illus. by author. 1983, Holiday House LB $16.95 (978-0-8234-0478-0); paper $5.95 (978-0-8234-0709-5). 32pp. An illustration of all sorts of boats in simple drawings.

6631 Gibbons, Gail. *Emergency!* (PS–1). Illus. 1994, Holiday House LB $16.95 (978-0-8234-1128-3). 32pp. This picture book shows how a number of people are saved through the use of such vehicles as fire engines, Coast Guard boats, and police cars. (Rev: BCCB 11/94; BL 10/15/94; SLJ 11/94) [363.3]

6632 Gramatky, Hardie. *Little Toot* (K–3). Illus. by author. 1939, Penguin paper $7.99 (978-0-698-11576-7). 96pp. Little Toot, son of the mightiest tug in the harbor, had no ambition until he became a hero during a raging storm.

6633 Hamilton, Kersten. *Red Truck* (PS–K). Illus. by Valeria Petrone. 2008, Viking $15.99 (978-0-670-06275-1). 32pp. Can the little red tow truck make it through the mud to rescue the children on the school bus? We think he can. (Rev: BL 1/1–15/08; SLJ 4/08)

6634 Hennessy, B. G. *Road Builders* (PS–1). Illus. by Simms Taback. 1994, Viking $16.99 (978-0-670-83390-0). 32pp. A picture book that shows how different kinds of machines and vehicles are used in building a road. (Rev: BL 5/1/94; SLJ 9/94) [625.7]

6635 Hill, Lee S. *Earthmovers* (2–3). Illus. Series: Pull Ahead Books. 2002, Lerner LB $22.60 (978-0-8225-0689-8); paper $5.95 (978-0-8225-0603-4). 32pp. A small-format book for younger readers about how earthmovers and their drivers accomplish their tasks. Also use *Trains* (2002). (Rev: BL 8/02; HBG 3/03; SLJ 10/02)

6636 Hill, Lee S. *Get Around in the City* (1–3). Series: Get Around Book. 1999, Carolrhoda LB $14.60 (978-1-57505-307-3). 32pp. An attractive, practical book that depicts in photos and text different kinds of urban transportation including cars, buses, gondolas, and elephants. A companion volume is *Get Around in the Country* (1999). (Rev: HBG 10/99; SLJ 7/99) [629.04]

6637 Hoban, Tana. *Construction Zone* (PS–1). Illus. 1997, Greenwillow $15.89 (978-0-688-12285-0). 32pp. Thirteen construction machines like the bulldozer, backhoe, and forklift are introduced in pictures and a simple text. (Rev: BCCB 4/97; BL 4/1/97; SLJ 3/97) [624]

6638 Horacek, Petr. *Choo Choo* (PS). Illus. by author. 2008, Candlewick $5.99 (978-0-7636-3477-3). 16pp. A trainful of children head for the beach in this bright and rhythmic board book. (Rev: BL 7/08)

6639 Hubbell, Patricia. *Airplanes: Soaring! Diving! Turning!* (PS–2). Illus. by Megan Halsey. Series: Things That Go! 2008, Marshall Cavendish $16.99 (978-0-7614-5388-8). 32pp. Paired with simple rhyming text, planes of all kinds — cargo, military, modern, vintage — fly across the pages of this attractive book. (Rev: BL 4/1/08; SLJ 7/08)

6640 Hubbell, Patricia. *My First Airplane Ride* (PS–1). Illus. by Nancy Speir. 2008, Marshall Cavendish $16.99 (978-0-7614-5436-6). 40pp. A boy's first trip by plane is chronicled in rhyming text and detailed illustrations of pre-departure procedures such as getting boarding passes and clearing security. (Rev: BL 9/1/08)

6641 Hubbell, Patricia. *Trains: Huffing! Puffing! Pulling!* (1–3). 2005, Marshall Cavendish $14.95 (978-0-7614-5194-5). 32pp. With an appealing blend of rhyming text and intricate collage illustrations, this picture book introduces young readers to different types of trains. (Rev: BL 10/1/05; SLJ 9/05)

6642 Hundal, Nancy. *Number 21* (PS–3). Illus. by Brian Denes. 2001, Fitzhenry & Whiteside $16.95 (978-1-55041-543-8). 32pp. Three children are excited to see Dad's new dump truck, especially when he fills the dump box with water to make an instant swimming pool. (Rev: BL 8/01; SLJ 4/01)

6643 Johnson, Angela. *Those Building Men* (1–4). Illus. by Barry Moser. 2001, Scholastic $16.95 (978-0-590-66521-6). 32pp. This poem pays tribute to builders and construction workers who move earth for canals, lay steel for railroads, and cut down trees for building. (Rev: BCCB 2/01; BL 2/1/01; HBG 10/01; SLJ 3/01)

6644 Jorgensen, Norman. *The Call of the Osprey* (K–3). Illus. by Brian Harrison-Lever. 2004, Fremantle Arts Centre $22.50 (978-1-920731-85-4). A young boy named Tom and a retired sea captain lovingly restore a steamboat, which Tom then inherits, in a simple story full of sea lore. (Rev: SLJ 2/05)

6645 Katz, Bobbi. *Truck Talk: Rhymes on Wheels* (PS–1). Illus. 1997, Scholastic $10.95 (978-0-590-69328-8). 32pp. Each of the trucks pictured — e.g., tow trucks, ambulances, and garbage trucks — describes its function in its own words. (Rev: BL 4/1/97; SLJ 3/97) [811]

6646 Kuklin, Susan. *All Aboard! A True Train Story* (PS–1). Illus. 2003, Scholastic $16.99 (978-0-439-45583-1). 32pp. An eye-catching visit to the Durango & Silverton narrow-gauge steam railway in

Colorado, with minimal text. (Rev: BL 2/1/04; HBG 4/04; SLJ 12/03)

6647 Liebman, Dan. *I Want to Be a Mechanic* (K–2). Series: I Want to Be. 2003, Firefly LB $14.95 (978-1-55297-695-1); paper $3.99 (978-1-55297-693-7). A photo-filled inside look at a day in the life of an auto mechanic. (Rev: SLJ 8/03) [629.28]

6648 London, Jonathan. *My Big Rig* (PS–K). Illus. by Viviana Garofoli. 2007, Marshall Cavendish $14.99 (978-0-7614-5346-8). 32pp. Inspired by his toy truck, a young boy imagines a cross-country trip at the wheel of a tractor-trailer. (Rev: BL 4/15/07)

6649 London, Jonathan. *A Train Goes Clickety-Clack* (PS–K). Illus. by Denis Roche. 2007, Holt $15.95 (978-0-8050-7972-2). 32pp. This choo-choo title is right on track with its rhythmic and colorful look at trains old and new. (Rev: SLJ 10/07)

6650 London, Jonathan. *A Truck Goes Rattley-Bumpa* (PS). Illus. by Denis Roche. 2005, Holt $14.95 (978-0-8050-7233-4). 32pp. Trucks of all shapes and sizes performing different tasks are shown in simple illustrations with short rhyming couplets. (Rev: BL 10/1/05; SLJ 9/05)

6651 Lyon, George E. *Trucks Roll!* (PS). Illus. by Craig Frazier. 2007, Atheneum $14.99 (978-1-4169-2435-7). 40pp. Rhyming verses and eye-catching illustrations show how trucks carry many different cargos. (Rev: BL 5/1/07; HB 7/07; SLJ 9/07)

6652 McCarty, Peter. *Moon Plane* (PS–K). 2006, Holt $16.95 (978-0-8050-7943-2). 32pp. Gazing up at a plane in the sky, a young boy imagines what it would be like to board such an aircraft and fly all the way to the moon; the simple, effective text and illustrations encourage imagination. (Rev: BL 9/1/06; HBG 4/07)

6653 McGough, Roger. *Until I Met Dudley: How Everyday Things Really Work* (K–4). Illus. by Chris Riddell. 1997, Walker $15.95 (978-0-8027-8623-4). An amusing story that explains how five common appliances, like a toaster, work. (Rev: HBG 3/98; SLJ 11/97)

6654 McMullen, Kate. *I'm Dirty!* (PS–2). Illus. by Jim McMullen. 2006, HarperCollins $16.99 (978-0-06-009293-1). 40pp. A spirited backhoe loader groans aloud as it works, counting the items it is moving and generally enjoying getting good and dirty. (Rev: BCCB 10/06; BL 9/15/06; HB 11/06; HBG 4/07)

6655 Maestro, Betsy, and Ellen DelVecchio. *Big City Port* (PS–2). Illus. by Giulio Maestro. 1984, Macmillan LB $14.95 (978-0-02-762110-5); Scholastic paper $4.95 (978-0-590-41577-4). 32pp. A picture book that shows activities in a big-city port.

6656 Mayo, Margaret. *Emergency!* (PS–1). Illus. by Alex Ayliffe. 2002, Carolrhoda $14.95 (978-0-87614-922-5). 32pp. Arresting artwork details emergency vehicles and their uses in this exciting, large-format picture book. (Rev: BL 8/02; HBG 3/03; SLJ 10/02)

6657 Milusich, Janice. *Off Go Their Engines, Off Go Their Lights* (K–1). Illus. by David Gordon. 2008, Dutton $15.99 (978-0-525-47940-6). 32pp. On their way home in a yellow taxi, a mother and son watch vehicles of all kinds parking at the end of their working day. (Rev: BL 6/1–15/08; SLJ 8/08)

6658 Miranda, Anne. *Beep! Beep!* (PS). Illus. by David Murphy. 1999, Turtle $15.95 (978-1-890515-14-0). All kinds of vehicles are shown in this picture book about a boy who imagines that he is riding in each of them. (Rev: HBG 3/00; SLJ 6/99)

6659 Moignot, Daniel. *Fire Fighting* (PS–1). Trans. from French by Wendy Barish. Illus. by author. Series: First Discovery. 1999, Scholastic $12.95 (978-0-439-04403-5). Using one sentence per page, this simple account introduces fire fighting equipment such as trucks, ladders, and protective clothing. (Rev: HBG 3/00; SLJ 1/00)

6660 Moore, Patrick. *The Mighty Street Sweeper* (PS). Illus. 2006, Holt $15.95 (978-0-8050-7789-6). 32pp. A colorful celebration of the street sweeper, a little truck with a very big responsibility. (Rev: BL 10/15/06; SLJ 10/06)

6661 Mortensen, Denise Dowling. *Wake Up Engines* (PS–K). Illus. by Melissa Iwai. 2007, Clarion $16.00 (978-0-618-51736-7). 32pp. Morning traffic outside parallels the activities of a little boy playing with his toys inside. (Rev: BL 7/07; SLJ 7/07)

6662 Mott, Evelyn Clarke. *Steam Train Ride* (PS–K). Illus. 1991, Walker LB $14.85 (978-0-8027-6996-1). A delightful ride for train lovers on Engine 89. (Rev: BL 5/15/91; SLJ 8/91) [625.2]

6663 Munro, Roxie. *Go! Go! Go!* (PS–2). Illus. by author. 2009, Sterling LB $15.95 (978-1-4027-3773-2). 24pp. With folds, flaps, and lots of energy, Munro presents many people on the go — firemen heading to an emergency, riders on horseback, race car pit crews, and so forth. (Rev: HB 7/09; SLJ 6/09)

6664 Neitzel, Shirley. *I'm Taking a Trip on My Train* (PS–1). Illus. by Nancy W. Parker. 1999, Greenwillow LB $14.89 (978-0-688-15834-7). 32pp. A boy pretends he is an engineer on his toy train in this picture book, which uses rebus drawings to introduce parts of a train and a freight yard. (Rev: BL 4/15/99; HBG 10/99; SLJ 3/99)

6665 Parker, Neal Evan. *Captain Annabel* (PS–4). Illus. by Emily Harris. 2005, Down East $15.95 (978-0-89272-653-0). Encouraged by her father, Annabel has always loved sailing, and she grows up to be a tugboat captain. (Rev: SLJ 5/05)

6666 Piper, Watty. *The Little Engine That Could* (PS–1). Illus. by Loren Long. 2005, Philomel $17.99 (978-0-399-24467-4). 48pp. This new edition of the beloved children's classic, originally published in 1930, about a diminutive but determined train engine is beautifully illustrated in rich, warm colors. (Rev: BL 9/1/05; SLJ 9/05)

6667 Pulver, Robin. *Axle Annie and the Speed Grump* (K–3). Illus. 2005, Dial $16.99 (978-0-8037-2787-8). 32pp. Axle Annie, Burskyville's beloved and very skilled school bus driver, saves the life of dangerous driver Rush Hotfoot with the help of her passengers. (Rev: BL 11/1/05; SLJ 12/05)

6668 Ransom, Candice F. *The Old Blue Pickup Truck* (PS–1). Illus. by Jenny Mattheson. 2009, Walker $16.99 (978-0-8027-9591-5). 32pp. A

daughter notices how many different uses the pickup has as she and her father run several errands together. (Rev: BL 7/09; SLJ 5/09)

6669 Ransom, Candice F. *Tractor Day* (PS). Illus. by Laura J. Bryant. 2007, Walker $16.95 (978-0-8027-8090-4). 32pp. This cozy, rhyming tribute to farming depicts a cheerful family hard at work, with dad and daughter riding the big red tractor all day. (Rev: BL 1/1–15/07; SLJ 3/07)

6670 Rex, Michael. *My Race Car* (PS–2). Illus. 2000, Holt $15.95 (978-0-8050-6101-7). 32pp. In this fantasy, a young boy imagines being on a racetrack in his car and, after checking the car, participating in an exciting race at top speed. (Rev: BCCB 9/00; BL 5/1/00; HBG 10/00; SLJ 7/00) [629.228]

6671 Richards, Laura E. *Jiggle Joggle Jee!* (PS). Illus. by Sam Williams. 2001, HarperCollins LB $15.89 (978-0-688-17833-8). 32pp. A newly illustrated version of an early-20th-century fantasy poem about a train. (Rev: BL 7/01; HBG 10/01; SLJ 5/01)

6672 Scieszka, Jon. *Melvin Might?* (PS–K). Illus. by Juan Pablo Navas. Series: Trucktown. 2008, Simon & Schuster $16.99 (978-1-4169-4134-7). 44pp. Melvin the cement mixer is not at all brave, even in front of Payloader Pete and Jack Truck, but finds unexpected courage when Rescue Rita is in trouble. (Rev: BL 8/08)

6673 Siebert, Diane. *Train Song* (PS–2). Illus. by Mike Wimmer. 1990, HarperCollins LB $16.89 (978-0-690-04728-8). 32pp. This poem portrays trains as they travel across America. (Rev: BCCB 12/90; BL 10/1/90; SLJ 9/90*)

6674 Singer, Marilyn. *I'm Your Bus* (PS–K). Illus. by Evan Polenghi. 2009, Scholastic $16.99 (978-0-545-08918-0). 32pp. A rhythmic romp with a friendly school bus explains the ins and outs of a bus's day. (Rev: BL 7/09)

6675 Sís, Peter. *Trucks Trucks Trucks* (PS). Illus. 1999, Greenwillow $16.99 (978-0-688-16276-4). 24pp. Matt enters an imaginary world where he operates a number of massive trucks and oversees their many operations. (Rev: BCCB 5/99; BL 6/1–15/99; HB 5/99; HBG 10/99; SLJ 5/99)

6676 Suen, Anastasia. *Red Light, Green Light* (PS). Illus. by Ken Wilson-Max. 2005, Harcourt $16.00 (978-0-15-202582-3). 40pp. Minimal text and bold illustrations blend to depict a toddler deploying his toy vehicles on a busy traffic grid. (Rev: BL 11/15/05; SLJ 10/05)

6677 Sutton, Sally. *Roadwork* (PS–1). Illus. by Brian Lovelock. 2008, Candlewick $15.99 (978-0-7636-3912-9). 32pp. A boisterous, rhyming look at all the machines and people involved in building a new road. (Rev: BL 6/1–15/08; SLJ 8/08)

6678 Vetter, Jennifer Riggs. *Down by the Station* (PS–K). Illus. by Frank Remkiewicz. 2009, Ten Speed $15.99 (978-1-58246-243-1). 32pp. All sorts of modes of transportation are included in this expanded version of the traditional children's song with energetic illustrations. (Rev: BL 4/1/09; SLJ 4/09)

6679 Weatherby, Brenda. *The Trucker* (PS–2). Illus. by Mark Alan Weatherby. 2004, Scholastic $15.95

(978-0-439-39877-0). 32pp. A little boy dreams he's driving a tractor-trailer in this well-illustrated book, and wakes to find that he's been riding along in his father's big rig. (Rev: BL 2/15/04; SLJ 4/04)

6680 *Wheels on the Go!* (PS). Illus. by La Coccinella. Series: Look and See. 2008, Sterling $6.95 (978-1-4027-5826-3). 26pp. A rhyming riddle introduces the vehicles featured in this rugged board book with die-cut holes. (Rev: BL 9/1/08)

6681 Wickberg, Susan. *Hey Mr. Choo-Choo, Where Are You Going?* (PS–K). Illus. by Yumi Heo. 2008, Putnam $16.99 (978-0-399-23993-9). 32pp. Mister Choo-choo travels far and wide to reach the bright blue sea; children will want to chant along to the rhythmic narrative. (Rev: SLJ 4/08)

6682 Willems, Mo. *The Pigeon Loves Things That Go!* (PS). Illus. by author. 2005, Hyperion $6.99 (978-0-7868-3651-2). A board book featuring the beloved pigeon from *Don't Let the Pigeon Drive the Bus* (2003) and another children's favorite: things that move. (Rev: SLJ 8/05)

6683 Wilson-Max, Ken. *Little Green Tow Truck* (PS–2). Illus. 1997, Scholastic paper $14.95 (978-0-590-89802-7). 14pp. Tabs and flaps are featured in this book about the parts and uses of tow trucks. Also use *Big Red Fire Truck* (1997). (Rev: BL 12/15/97) [629]

6684 Wolf, Sallie. *Truck Stuck* (PS). Illus. by Andy Robert Davies. 2008, Charlesbridge $14.95 (978-1-58089-119-6). 32pp. An 18-wheeler gets stuck under a viaduct, and the ensuing traffic jam boosts sales at lemonade stand. (Rev: BL 3/1/08; SLJ 2/08)

6685 Ziefert, Harriet. *Train Song* (PS). Illus. by Donald Saaf. 2000, Orchard $14.95 (978-0-531-30204-0). 32pp. A little boy watches a freight train go by and sees the contents of all the cars: logs, pigs, ducks, cows, and so on. (Rev: BL 4/1/00; HBG 10/00; SLJ 4/00)

6686 Zimmerman, Andrea, and David Clemesha. *Dig!* (PS–K). Illus. by Marc Rosenthal. 2004, Harcourt $16.00 (978-0-15-216785-1). Mr. Rally and his dog, Lightning, really enjoy digging — with a backhoe or without. (Rev: BL 5/15/04; SLJ 7/04)

Graphic Novels

6687 Barba, Corey. *Yam: Bite-Size Chunks* (K–3). Illus. by author. 2008, Top Shelf paper $10.00 (978-1-60309-014-8). 88pp. This wordless graphic novel follows a young boy who lives on a remote island through a series of magical adventures. (Rev: BLO 9/17/08)

6688 Bliss, Harry. *Luke on the Loose* (PS–2). Illus. by author. 2009, Raw Junior/TOON $12.95 (978-1-935179-00-9). 32pp. An African American boy called Luke chases a pigeon all around New York City; the simple text makes this graphic novel suitable for beginning readers. (Rev: BCCB 6/09; BL 3/1/09; LMC 5/09)

6689 Davis, Eleanor. *Stinky* (K–2). Illus. by author. 2008, Raw Junior/TOON $12.95 (978-0-9799238-4-5). 40pp. Stinky the swamp monster becomes friends with a much-too-clean little boy in this

graphic novel full of repetition. (Rev: BL 9/1/08; SLJ 9/08)

6690 Faller, Regis. *Polo and the Magic Flute* (PS–2). Illus. by author. 2009, Roaring Brook $9.95 (978-1-59643-495-0). 32pp. Polo the dog's fishing trip turns into a magical adventure in this wordless book. (Rev: BL 3/1/09; SLJ 7/09)

6691 Hayes, Geoffrey. *Benny and Penny in the Big No-No!* (K–1). Illus. by author. 2009, Raw Junior/TOON $12.95 (978-0-9799238-9-0). 32pp. Is their new neighbor a thief? Mice Benny and Penny bravely investigate and discover they totally misjudged her. (Rev: BL 3/1/09)

6692 Hoena, Blake A. *Eek and Ack vs. the Wolfman* (1–3). Illus. by Steve Harpster. Series: Graphic Sparks. 2009, Stone Arch LB $16.99 (978-1-4342-1189-7). 40pp. Aliens Eek and Ack arrive on Earth on Halloween and find themselves facing a werewolf. (Rev: BL 3/1/09)

6693 Hoena, Blake A. *Jack and the Beanstalk* (K–2). Illus. by Ricardo Tercio. 2008, Stone Arch $15.95 (978-1-4342-0766-1). 40pp. A snappy new graphic novel version of the suspenseful classic. (Rev: BLO 9/17/08; LMC 5/09)

6694 Kochalka, James. *Johnny Boo: Twinkle Power* (K–3). Illus. by author. 2008, Top Shelf paper $9.95 (978-1-60309-015-5). 40pp. A silly adventure in which ghost Johnny Boo and his sidekick Squiggle consider the potential of stars' Twinkle Power, then wonder about wiggle power, and find some fun in Johnny Boo's hair. (Rev: BL 3/1/09)

6695 Kovac, Tommy. *Wonderland* (4–8). Illus. by Sonny Liew. 2009, Disney $19.99 (978-1-4231-0451-3). 160pp. A chaotic graphic Alice in Wonderland novel from the point of view of the terribly tidy maid, Mary Ann. (Rev: BCCB 6/09; BL 5/15/09; SLJ 5/09)

6696 Labatt, Mary. *Dracula Madness* (2–4). Illus. by Jo Rioux. Series: Sam and Friends Mystery. 2009, Kids Can $16.95 (978-1-55453-418-0); paper $7.95 (978-1-55337-303-2). 96pp. Based on *Spying on Dracula* (1999), this graphic novel features Sam the independent-minded sheepdog detective and 10-year-old Jennie, who can hear Sam's thoughts, as they investigate a neighbor's suspicious behavior. (Rev: BL 3/1/09)

6697 Lynch, Jay. *Mo and Jo: Fighting Together Forever* (K–2). Illus. by Dean Haspiel. 2008, Raw Junior/TOON LB $12.95 (978-0-9799238-5-2). 40pp. Twins Mona and Joey, usually at odds with one another, learn to cooperate when they acquire superhero powers. (Rev: BL 9/15/08; LMC 1/09; SLJ 9/08)

6698 Spiegelman, Art. *Jack and the Box* (K–1). Illus. by author. 2008, Raw Junior/TOON $12.95 (978-0-9799238-3-8). 32pp. A young bunny wrestles with a jack-in-the-box that seems to have a mind of its own in this bouncy graphic novel. (Rev: BL 9/1/08; HB 11/08)

6699 Sturm, James, and Andrew Arnold. *Adventures in Cartooning: How to Turn Your Doodles into Comics* (PS–5). Illus. by James Sturm. 2009, Roaring Brook paper $12.95 (978-1-59643-369-4).

112pp. An adventure featuring a princess, a knight, an elf, and a dragon serves as the backdrop for instruction in the art of cartooning. (Rev: BL 3/1/09; SLJ 4/09)

6700 Townsend, Michael. *Billy Tartle in Say Cheese!* (1–3). Illus. by author. 2007, Knopf $15.99 (978-0-375-83932-0). Billy adds some color to class picture day in this comic-book style story with zany-looking characters. (Rev: BCCB 9/07; LMC 11/07; SLJ 7/07)

Stories About Holidays and Holy Days

GENERAL AND MISCELLANEOUS

6701 Bertrand, Diane Gonzales. *Uncle Chente's Picnic / El Picnic de Tio Chente* (K–2). Trans. by Julia Mercedes Castilla. Illus. by Pauline Rodriguez Howard. 2001, Piñata $15.95 (978-1-55885-337-9). Uncle Chente arrives for a Fourth of July picnic, but plans must be changed when there is a huge storm. (Rev: SLJ 1/02)

6702 Bouchard, David. *The Dragon New Year: A Chinese Legend* (PS–3). Illus. by Zhong-Yang Huang. 1999, Peachtree $16.95 (978-1-56145-210-1). 32pp. A Chinese grandmother explains to her frightened grandchild the origin of the noisy Dragon Dance at New Year's and how it was intended to frighten a real dragon who lived at the bottom of the sea. (Rev: BL 9/1/99; HBG 3/00; SLJ 11/99)

6703 Bourgeois, Paulette. *Franklin's Holiday Treasury* (PS–1). Illus. by Brenda Clark. 2002, Kids Can $15.95 (978-1-55337-045-1). 128pp. Four holiday adventures of Franklin the turtle are gathered here: Halloween, Thanksgiving, Christmas, and Valentine's Day. (Rev: BL 1/1–15/03; HBG 3/03)

6704 Brown, Marc. *Arthur's April Fool* (PS–2). Illus. by author. 1985, Little, Brown paper $5.95 (978-0-316-11234-5). 32pp. Arthur is afraid he will forget his magic tricks prepared for the April Fools' Day show.

6705 Bunting, Eve. *The Mother's Day Mice* (PS–1). Illus. by Jan Brett. 1986, Houghton $15.00 (978-0-89919-387-8); paper $5.95 (978-0-89919-702-9). Three little mice go out to seek presents for Mother's Day; the smallest one brings home a song he heard a human sing. (Rev: BCCB 4/86; BL 4/1/86; SLJ 3/86)

6706 Bunting, Eve. *A Perfect Father's Day* (PS–1). Illus. by Susan Meddaugh. 1993, Houghton paper $5.95 (978-0-395-66416-2). 32pp. Susie plans a perfect time for her father on Father's Day. (Rev: BL 4/15/91; SLJ 5/91)

6707 Bunting, Eve. *St. Patrick's Day in the Morning* (PS–2). Illus. by Jan Brett. 1983, Houghton $16.00 (978-0-395-29098-9); paper $5.95 (978-0-89919-162-1). 32pp. Jamie is too small to parade to the top of the hill with the rest of his family, so he rises early and has a St. Patrick's Day adventure of his own.

6708 Carrier, Roch. *A Happy New Year's Day* (2–4). Illus. by Gilles Pelletier. 1991, Tundra $14.95 (978-0-88776-267-3). This is a happy recollection of a New Year's Day spent in a French Canadian town during World War II. (Rev: SLJ 2/92)

6709 Chin, Steven A. *Dragon Parade: A Chinese New Year Story* (PS–3). Illus. by Mou-Sien Tseng. 1993, Raintree LB $22.83 (978-0-8114-7215-9). 32pp. This is a fictionalized account of the Chinese immigrant Noram Ah Sing, who started the first big New Year's Parade in San Francisco. (Rev: BL 5/1/93; SLJ 7/93)

6710 Compestine, Ying Chang. *The Runaway Rice Cake* (PS–3). Illus. by Tungwai Chau. 2001, Simon & Schuster $16.95 (978-0-689-82972-7). 40pp. As part of the Chinese New Year's Eve celebration, Mooma Chang cooks a rice cake that comes to life and runs away. (Rev: BL 2/1/01; HBG 3/02; SLJ 2/01)

6711 deGroat, Diane. *April Fool! Watch Out at School!* (PS–2). Illus. by author. Series: Gilbert and Friends. 2009, HarperCollins $17.99 (978-0-06-143042-8). 32pp. Gilbert the possum is annoyed to be fooled so many times and plots revenge on the much-disliked Lewis. (Rev: BL 12/1/08; SLJ 5/09)

6712 deGroat, Diane. *Mother, You're the Best (But Sister, You're a Pest!)* (PS–2). Illus. by author. 2008, HarperCollins $16.99 (978-0-06-123899-4). 32pp. On Mother's Day, Gilbert the possum entertains his little sister, thereby giving mom some much-appreciated time to herself. (Rev: BL 2/15/08; SLJ 3/08)

6713 dePaola, Tomie. *The Lady of Guadalupe* (K–3). Illus. by author. 1980, Holiday House LB $18.95 (978-0-8234-0373-8); paper $8.95 (978-0-8234-0403-2). 48pp. The legend of the patron saint of Mexico is retold in this excellent picture book.

6714 Dillon, Jana. *Lucky O'Leprechaun* (K–2). Illus. by author. 1998, Pelican $15.95 (978-1-56554-333-1). On St. Patrick's Day weekend, Meg and Sean are determined to catch the leprechaun that lives under a thorn bush in the garden. (Rev: HBG 3/99; SLJ 1/99)

6715 *The 11th Commandment: Wisdom from Our Children* (PS–3). Illus. 1996, Jewish Lights $16.95 (978-1-879045-46-0). 48pp. The results of a survey of a group of children from different faiths who were asked to suggest an 11th commandment. (Rev: BL 10/1/96) [170]

6716 English, Karen. *Nadia's Hands* (K–4). Illus. by Jonathan Weiner. 1999, Boyds Mills $16.95 (978-1-56397-667-4). 32pp. A Pakistani American girl learns to appreciate the rich traditions of marriage in her faith when she is asked to be a flower girl at her aunt's wedding. (Rev: BCCB 4/99; BL 3/1/99; HBG 10/99; SLJ 4/99)

6717 Ford, Juwanda G. *K Is for Kwanzaa: A Kwanzaa Alphabet Book* (K–3). Illus. by Ken Wilson-Max. 1997, Scholastic $10.95 (978-0-590-92200-5). 32pp. Arranged alphabetically various objects, customs, and rituals connected with Kwanzaa are introduced. (Rev: BL 9/1/97; HBG 3/98; SLJ 10/97) [394.261]

6718 Garcia, Aurora Colon. *Cinco de Mayo* (1–3). Series: Holiday Histories. 2003, Heinemann LB $22.79 (978-1-4034-3501-9). 32pp. The annual celebration marking Mexico's battlefield victory over French forces on May 5, 1862, is explained for younger readers in this well-illustrated book. (Rev: SLJ 5/04) [394.262]

6719 Ghazi, Suhaib Hamid. *Ramadan* (K–4). Illus. by Omar Rayyan. 1996, Holiday House $17.95 (978-0-8234-1254-9). 32pp. The Islamic month of Ramadan, with its fasting and prayers, as seen through the eyes of a young boy. (Rev: BCCB 12/96; BL 10/1/96; SLJ 10/96) [297]

6720 Gower, Catherine. *Long-Long's New Year* (K–3). Illus. by He Zhihong. 2005, Tuttle $16.95 (978-0-8048-3666-1). 32pp. Long-Long and his grandfather sell cabbages at the market to raise money for the upcoming Spring Festival, also known as Chinese New Year. (Rev: BL 2/15/05; SLJ 6/05)

6721 Katz, Karen. *My First Kwanzaa* (PS). Illus. by author. 2003, Holt $14.95 (978-0-8050-7077-4). Double-page spreads with colorful illustrations introduce the seven days of Kwanzaa and the associated traditions. (Rev: HBG 4/04; SLJ 10/03) [394.2]

6722 Keep, Richard. *Clatter Bash! A Day of the Dead Celebration* (K–3). Illus. by author. 2004, Peachtree $15.95 (978-1-56145-322-1). After the people leave the graveyards, the skeletons emerge and have a party, enjoying the food left behind for them. (Rev: SLJ 2/05)

6723 Khan, Hena. *Night of the Moon: A Muslim Holiday Story* (K–2). Illus. by Julie Paschkis. 2008, Chronicle $16.99 (978-0-8118-6062-8). 32pp. Seven-year-old Pakistani American Yasmeen and her family celebrate the month of Ramadan, ending with the "night of the moon." (Rev: BL 10/1/08; LMC 5/09; SLJ 9/08)

6724 Kimmelman, Leslie. *Happy 4th of July, Jenny Sweeney!* (PS–1). Illus. by Nancy Cote. 2003, Whitman LB $16.99 (978-0-8075-3152-5). Young Jenny observes the Fourth of July celebrations of her ethnically diverse community. (Rev: BL 5/15/03; HBG 10/03; SLJ 7/03)

6725 Klein, Adria F. *Max Celebrates Chinese New Year* (K–2). Illus. by Mernie Gallagher-Cole. Series: Max. 2007, Picture Window LB $19.93 (978-1-4048-3147-6). 24pp. Max celebrates Chinese New Year with his friend Lily in this easy reader. (Rev: SLJ 7/07)

6726 Levy, Janice. *The Spirit of Tio Fernando: A Day of the Dead Story/El Espiritu de Tio Fernando: Una Historia del Dia de los Muertos* (1–3). Trans. by Teresa Mlawer. Illus. by Morella Fuenmayor. 1995, Whitman $14.95 (978-0-8075-7585-7); paper $6.95 (978-0-8075-7586-4). 32pp. On the Day of the Dead, Nando remembers his Uncle Fernando, who died six months before. (Rev: BL 11/15/95; SLJ 11/95)

6727 Lin, Grace. *Bringing in the New Year* (PS–1). Illus. by author. 2008, Knopf $15.99 (978-0-375-83745-6). 32pp. A Chinese family prepares to celebrate the Chinese New Year in this colorful and informative picture book. (Rev: BL 12/15/07; SLJ 3/08)

6728 Low, William. *Chinatown* (K–1). Illus. 1997, Holt paper $15.95 (978-0-8050-4214-6). 32pp. At Chinese New Year's, a boy and his grandmother take a tour through their Chinatown. (Rev: BL 9/15/97; HBG 3/98; SLJ 9/97)

6729 Luenn, Nancy. *A Gift for Abuelita: Celebrating the Day of the Dead / Un regalo para Abuelita: En celebración del Día de los Muertos* (K–3). Illus. by Robert Chapman. 1998, Rising Moon $15.95 (978-0-87358-688-7). 32pp. Told in English and Spanish, this picture book relates Rosita's tribute to her grandmother on the Day of the Dead. (Rev: BCCB 1/99; BL 3/15/99; HBG 3/99; SLJ 3/99)

6730 Medearis, Angela Shelf. *Seven Spools of Thread: A Kwanzaa Story* (K–3). Illus. by Daniel Minter. 2000, Whitman $15.95 (978-0-8075-7315-0). 40pp. An original folktale that takes place in a Ghanaian village and effectively introduces the seven principles of Kwanzaa. (Rev: BL 9/15/00; HBG 3/01)

6731 Mobin-Uddin, Asma. *A Party in Ramadan* (1–3). Illus. by Laura Jacobsen. 2009, Boyds Mills $16.95 (978-1-59078-604-8). 32pp. It's Ramadan, and Leena is invited to a party on the day she plans to fast. Will she be able to resist the chocolate cake? (Rev: BCCB 5/09; BL 3/15/09; SLJ 4/09)

6732 Moore, Elizabeth, and Alice Couvillon. *Mimi and Jean-Paul's Cajun Mardi Gras* (1–3). Illus. by Marilyn C. Rougelot. 1996, Pelican $15.95 (978-1-56554-069-9). The unique Courir (Run) de Mardi Gras celebrated in Cajun country is experienced by a young girl. (Rev: SLJ 3/96)

6733 Moorman, Margaret. *Light the Lights! A Story About Celebrating Hanukkah and Christmas* (K–3). Illus. 1994, Scholastic $12.95 (978-0-590-47003-2). 32pp. This book celebrates the spirit of both Christmas and Hanukkah and shows similarities in these holidays and their traditions. (Rev: BL 8/94) [394.26]

6734 Mora, Pat. *Book Fiesta! Celebrate Children's Book Day/Book Day / Celebremos El día de los niños/El día de los libros* (PS–2). Illus. by Rafael Lopez. 2009, HarperCollins $17.99 (978-0-06-128877-7). 40pp. Written in Spanish and English, this brightly illustrated book about Children's Day/Book Day features multicultural children playing, reading, and listening to stories; written by the founder of this holiday. (Rev: BL 1/1–15/09; SLJ 2/09)

6735 Nielsen, Laura. *Mrs. Muddle's Holidays* (PS–2). Illus. by Thomas Yezerski. 2008, Farrar $16.95 (978-0-374-35094-9). 32pp. Maple Street's diverse residents already celebrate a bunch of holidays, but when Mrs. Muddle moves in they discover more — First Robin Day, Earthworm Appreciation Day, and so forth. (Rev: BL 5/1/08; SLJ 4/08)

6736 Nolan, Janet. *The St. Patrick's Day Shillelagh* (2–4). Illus. by Ben F. Stahl. 2002, Whitman $16.95 (978-0-8075-7344-0). 32pp. On his trip from Ireland to America during the potato famine, Fergus carved a beautiful shillelagh that is passed from generation to generation. (Rev: BL 1/1–15/03; HBG 3/03; SLJ 12/02)

6737 Patrick, Diane. *Family Celebrations* (2–5). Illus. by Michael Bryant. 1993, Silver Moon LB $14.95 (978-1-881889-04-5). 62pp. Portrays a variety of family gatherings that are associated with such occasions as birth, marriage, and death as they are observed in many cultures. (Rev: BL 6/1–15/93) [392]

6738 Piernas-Davenport, Gail. *Shante Keys and the New Year's Peas* (K–2). Illus. by Marion Eldridge. 2007, Albert Whitman $16.95 (978-0-8075-7330-3). 32pp. When Grandma discovers there are no black-eyed peas, Shanté is sent in search of the ingredient that will bring her African American family luck and in her diverse neighborhood encounters a Chinese lady, a Scottish grocer, a Mexican restaurant keeper, and a Hindu family. (Rev: BL 11/15/07; SLJ 1/08)

6739 Rahaman, Vashanti. *Divali Rose* (K–3). Illus. by Jamel Akib. 2008, Boyds Mills $16.95 (978-1-59078-524-9). 32pp. In Trinidad Ricki's family is preparing for the Hindu festival of lights when Ricki accidentally snaps a rosebud off a bush; his grandfather blames their new neighbors from India and Ricki must decide whether to confess. (Rev: BL 10/1/08; LMC 11/09; SLJ 9/08)

6740 Roberts, Bethany. *Fourth of July Mice!* (PS–1). Illus. by Doug Cushman. Series: Holiday Mice. 2004, Clarion $13.00 (978-0-618-31367-9). 32pp. The family of mice featured in other holiday titles celebrate Independence Day in fine style. (Rev: BL 5/15/04)

6741 Rockwell, Anne. *Mother's Day* (PS–1). Illus. by Lizzy Rockwell. 2004, HarperCollins $16.99 (978-0-06-051374-0). 40pp. Looking forward to Mother's Day, the children in Mrs. Madoff's classroom explain how they will celebrate the occasion. (Rev: BL 2/15/04; SLJ 3/04)

6742 Rockwell, Anne. *President's Day* (K–2). Illus. by Lizzy Rockwell. 2008, HarperCollins $16.99 (978-0-06-050194-5). 40pp. It's Presidents' Day, and Mrs. Madoff's class learns about Washington and Lincoln plus Jefferson and Teddy Roosevelt for good measure. (Rev: BL 2/15/08; SLJ 1/08)

6743 Sasso, Sandy Eisenberg. *A Prayer for the Earth: The Story of Naamah, Noah's Wife* (PS–2). Illus. by Bethanne Andersen. 1997, Jewish Lights $16.95 (978-1-879045-60-6). 32pp. Noah's wife, Naamah, is given the job of bringing samples of each of the earth's plants into Noah's Ark. (Rev: BCCB 7–8/97; BL 2/15/97; SLJ 6/97)

6744 Schnetzler, Pattie. *Earth Day Birthday* (PS–4). Illus. by Chad Wallace. Series: Sharing Nature with Children. 2004, Dawn $16.95 (978-1-58469-053-5); paper $8.95 (978-1-58469-054-2). Set to the melody of "The Twelve Days of Christmas," the lyrics in this attractively illustrated song showcase 12 animal species from different parts of the world; information on Earth Day follows the text. (Rev: SLJ 7/04) [782.42]

6745 Shragg, Karen I. *A Solstice Tree for Jenny* (K–3). Illus. by Heidi Schwabacher. 2001, Prometheus paper $13.98 (978-1-57392-930-1). 50pp. Jenny wants to know why her family doesn't celebrate any religious holidays. (Rev: BL 12/15/01)

6746 Swartz, Nancy Sohn. *In Our Image: God's First Creatures* (PS–2). Illus. by Melanie Hall. 1998, Jewish Lights $16.95 (978-1-879045-99-6). 32pp. Several animals reveal characteristics that God would want humans to possess, such as the bravery of the tiger and the gentleness of the lamb. (Rev: BL 10/1/98; HBG 3/99; SLJ 3/99) [296.3]

6747 Tucker, Kathy. *The Leprechaun in the Basement* (PS–2). Illus. by John Sandford. 1999, Whitman $15.95 (978-0-8075-4450-1). 32pp. On St. Patrick's Day, Michael meets a leprechaun and the two learn a lesson from each other about relationships. (Rev: BL 1/1–15/99; HBG 10/99; SLJ 12/98)

6748 Vaughan, Marcia. *The Dancing Dragon* (K–2). Illus. by Stanley Wong Hoo Foon. 1996, Mondo paper $5.95 (978-1-57255-134-3). In rhyming couplets, a Chinese American child describes preparations for Chinese New Year celebrations, including the dragon parade. (Rev: SLJ 12/96)

6749 Whitehead, Kathy. *Looking for Uncle Louie on the 4th of July* (K–3). Illus. by Pablo Torrecilla. 2005, Boyds Mills $15.95 (978-1-59078-061-9). 32pp. On the 4th of July in Texas, young Joe watches the parade, waiting with bated breath for the arrival of his Uncle Louie's spectacular car. (Rev: BL 5/15/05; SLJ 5/05)

6750 Wong, Janet S. *Apple Pie Fourth of July* (PS–2). Illus. by Margaret Chodos-Irvine. 2002, Harcourt $16.00 (978-0-15-202543-4). 40pp. A young Chinese American girl working in her parents' grocery is convinced no one will want to eat their Chinese food on the Fourth of July. (Rev: BL 8/02; HBG 10/02; SLJ 5/02)

6751 Wong, Janet S. *This Next New Year* (PS–3). Illus. by Yangsook Choi. 2000, Farrar $16.00 (978-0-374-35503-6). 32pp. A little boy who is half Korean prepares to celebrate Chinese New Year and describes the traditional and modern customs involved. (Rev: BCCB 9/00; BL 9/15/00; HB 11/00; HBG 3/01; SLJ 10/00)

BIRTHDAYS

6752 Bailey, Debbie. *Happy Birthday* (PS). Photos by Susan Huszar. Series: Talk-About-Books. 1999, Annick $5.95 (978-1-55037-559-6). In this board book, full-color illustrations are used to show different ways of celebrating children's birthdays. (Rev: SLJ 9/99)

6753 Barker, Marjorie. *Magical Hands* (2–4). Illus. by Yoshi. 1989, Picture Book $16.00 (978-0-88708-103-3). 28pp. William does his friends' work, hoping they will think it is magic, and then finds that his work is done too! (Rev: BL 2/1/90)

6754 Beck, Andrea. *Elliot Bakes a Cake* (PS–1). Illus. 1999, Kids Can $12.95 (978-1-55074-443-9). 32pp. Elliot Moose and his stuffed toy friends converge on the kitchen to bake a birthday cake for their pal Lionel Lion. (Rev: BL 10/1/99; HBG 3/00; SLJ 12/99)

6755 Bertrand, Diane Gonzales. *The Last Doll / La Ultima Muneca* (PS–3). Illus. by Anthony Accardo.

2001, Arte Publico $14.95 (978-1-55885-290-7). 32pp. A special doll dressed in white lace is chosen to be a gift for Teresa at her *quinceanera* coming-of-age party. (Rev: BL 10/1/01; SLJ 4/01)

6756 Brown, Marc. *Arthur's Birthday* (K–2). Illus. 1989, Little, Brown $15.95 (978-0-316-11073-0); paper $5.95 (978-0-316-11074-7). Muffy is upset to learn that Arthur's birthday is the same day as hers. (Rev: BL 4/15/89; HB 5/89)

6757 Cameron, Ann. *Julian, Dream Doctor* (2–4). Illus. by Ann Strugnell. Series: Stepping Stone. 1990, Random LB $11.99 (978-0-679-90524-0); paper $3.99 (978-0-679-80524-3). 40pp. In this warm story of an African American family, Julian wants to discover Dad's idea of a dream birthday present. (Rev: BCCB 3/90; BL 5/15/90; HB 9/90; SLJ 7/90)

6758 Capucilli, Alyssa Satin. *Happy Birthday, Biscuit!* (PS). Illus. by Pat Schories. Series: I Can Read. 1999, HarperCollins LB $16.89 (978-0-06-028361-2). 24pp. A frisky puppy named Biscuit enjoys a birthday romp with his friends in this book for beginning readers. (Rev: BL 6/1–15/99; HBG 10/99; SLJ 6/99)

6759 Carle, Eric. *The Secret Birthday Message* (PS–1). Illus. by author. 1972, HarperCollins LB $17.89 (978-0-690-72348-9); paper $6.99 (978-0-06-443099-9). 26pp. In a brightly illustrated picture book with intriguing cutouts, a little boy has to decipher the coded message to find his birthday present.

6760 Chavarria-Chairez, Becky. *Magda's Pinata Magic / Magda y el Piñata Magica* (K–3). Trans. by Gabriela Baeza Ventura. Illus. by Anne Vega. 2001, Arte Publico $14.95 (978-1-55885-320-1). 32pp. Gabriel is upset by the idea of destroying his birthday pinata, so his sister Magda comes up with a solution in this bilingual picture book. (Rev: BL 10/15/01; SLJ 1/02)

6761 Chavarria-Chairez, Becky. *Magda's Tortillas / Las tortillas de Magda* (K–2). Trans. by Julia Mercedes Castilla. Illus. by Anne Vega. 2000, Piñata $14.95 (978-1-55885-286-0). On her birthday, Magda produces tortillas in different shapes in this bilingual book. (Rev: SLJ 10/00)

6762 Day, Alexandra. *Carl's Birthday* (PS–2). Illus. 1995, Farrar $12.95 (978-0-374-31144-5). 32pp. In this almost wordless picture book, Madeline and her beloved Rottweiler, Carl, secretly help prepare a surprise birthday party for the dog. (Rev: BL 1/1–15/96; SLJ 12/95)

6763 Dokas, Dara Sanders. *Muriel's Red Sweater* (PS–K). Illus. by Bernadette Pons. 2009, Dutton $16.99 (978-0-525-47962-8). 32pp. Unbeknownst to Muriel, her red sweater slowly comes apart as she visits her friends' houses with birthday party invitations, but her resourceful friends use the red yarn in many ways including a bow for her gift — a new sweater! (Rev: SLJ 2/09)

6764 Dominguez, Kelli Kyle. *The Perfect Pinata / La Piñata Perfecta* (PS–2). Trans. by Teresa Mlawer. Illus. by Diane Patterson. 2002, Whitman $16.99 (978-0-8075-6495-0). 32pp. This bilingual text describes Marisa's reluctance to break her beautiful

sixth-birthday pinata and her parents' happy solution. (Rev: BL 4/15/02; HBG 10/02)

6765 Dorflinger, Carolyn. *Tomorrow Is Mom's Birthday* (PS–1). Illus. by Iza Trapani. 1994, Whispering Coyote $14.95 (978-1-879085-84-8). 32pp. Tyler thinks of all sorts of things to give to his mother on her birthday, but he decides to paint a family portrait. (Rev: BCCB 4/94; BL 5/1/94)

6766 Edmiston, Jim. *The Emperor Who Forgot His Birthday* (PS–1). Illus. by author. Series: A Barefoot Beginner Book. 1999, Barefoot Books $14.95 (978-1-84148-015-2). An emperor wakes up and finds that his cat, family, and servants are all missing, little knowing that they are preparing a surprise birthday party for him. (Rev: SLJ 12/99)

6767 Falwell, Cathryn. *Butterflies for Kiri* (K–3). Illus. by author. 2003, Lee & Low $16.95 (978-1-58430-100-4). Kiri, a young Japanese-American girl, overcomes her initial frustrations as she struggles to make sense of the origami kit she's received as a birthday gift. (Rev: BL 5/15/03; HBG 10/03; SLJ 5/03)

6768 Fox, Mem. *Night Noises* (PS–2). Illus. by Terry Denton. 1989, Harcourt $16.00 (978-0-15-200543-6); paper $4.95 (978-0-15-257421-5). 32pp. An old lady's dog becomes agitated at the commotion he hears outside while the woman sleeps, which turns out to be relatives arriving for a surprise ninetieth birthday party. (Rev: BL 11/15/89; HB 11/89*; SLJ 9/89*)

6769 Geras, Adele. *Little Ballet Star* (PS–2). Illus. by Shelagh McNicholas. 2008, Dial $16.99 (978-0-8037-3237-7). 32pp. Aunt Gina, a ballerina, takes Tilly backstage to see the dancers warming up for their roles and then — as a birthday surprise — invites her onstage to dance. (Rev: BL 3/1/08; SLJ 3/08)

6770 Graham, Bob. *Oscar's Half Birthday* (PS–K). Illus. 2005, Candlewick $16.99 (978-0-7636-2699-0). 32pp. A happy interracial family goes to the park to celebrate little Oscar's birthday. (Rev: BL 5/1/05)

6771 Griffith, Helen V. *How Many Candles?* (K–3). Illus. by Sonja Lamut. 1999, Greenwillow $16.00 (978-0-688-16258-0). 24pp. Different animals help celebrate Robbie's tenth birthday, although each realizes that its life cycle span differs from that of humans. (Rev: BL 10/15/99; HBG 3/00; SLJ 9/99)

6772 Hershenhorn, Esther. *There Goes Lowell's Party!* (K–3). Illus. by Jacqueline Rogers. 1998, Holiday House LB $15.95 (978-0-8234-1313-3). In this tale set in the Ozarks, Lowell is afraid that rain will spoil his birthday party. (Rev: BCCB 4/98; HBG 10/98; SLJ 3/98)

6773 Hobbie, Holly. *Toot and Puddle: A Present for Toot* (PS–1). Illus. 1998, Little, Brown $12.95 (978-0-316-36556-7). 32pp. Puddle, a pig, is in a quandary about buying a birthday present for friend Toot, another pig. (Rev: BL 11/1/98; HBG 3/99; SLJ 10/98)

6774 Hutchins, Pat. *Happy Birthday, Sam* (1–3). Illus. by author. 1978, Morrow paper $6.99 (978-0-688-10482-5). 32pp. Sam is disappointed on his birthday morning to discover that he hasn't grown at all.

6775 Hutchins, Pat. *It's My Birthday* (PS–2). 1999, Greenwillow LB $14.89 (978-0-688-09664-9). 32pp. Monster Billy acts so selfishly about his birthday presents that he finds it difficult to get anyone to play with him. (Rev: BL 6/1–15/99; HBG 10/99; SLJ 3/99)

6776 Javernick, Ellen. *The Birthday Pet* (PS–2). Illus. by Kevin O'Malley. 2009, Marshall Cavendish $16.99 (978-0-7614-5522-6). 32pp. Danny's birthday wish is to have a pet turtle and he persists despite suggestions that he consider a dog, a cat, a rat, a bird. (Rev: BL 4/1/09; SLJ 3/09)

6777 Kromhout, Rindert. *Little Donkey and the Birthday Present* (K–2). Trans. from Dutch by Marianne Martens. Illus. by Annemarie van Haeringen. 2007, North-South $15.95 (978-0-7358-2132-3). Little Donkey chooses a beautiful kite as a present for his friend Jackie the yak, but then decides he wants to keep it himself. (Rev: SLJ 4/07)

6778 Kulling, Monica. *Edgar Badger's Balloon Day* (K–3). Illus. by Carol O'Malia. 1997, Mondo paper $4.50 (978-1-57255-220-3). 46pp. Edgar Badger is afraid that his friends have forgotten that his birthday is approaching. (Rev: SLJ 1/98)

6779 Lewis, Rose. *Every Year on Your Birthday* (PS–K). Illus. by Jane Dyer. 2007, Little, Brown $16.99 (978-0-316-52552-7). 32pp. A single mother shares with her adopted Asian daughter why her birthday is so special, and recounts the many fun experiences they share together each year on that day. (Rev: BL 6/1–15/07; SLJ 6/07)

6780 Look, Lenore. *Henry's First-Moon Birthday* (PS–3). Illus. by Yumi Heo. 2001, Simon & Schuster $16.00 (978-0-689-82294-0). 40pp. Young Jen, a Chinese American girl, helps her grandmother in the preparation of her young brother's first-moon birthday party. (Rev: BCCB 3/01; BL 4/1/01*; HBG 10/01; SLJ 6/01*)

6781 Lopez, Loretta. *The Birthday Swap* (PS–3). Illus. 1997, Lee & Low $15.95 (978-1-880000-47-2). 32pp. A young Mexican American girl enjoys the annual reunion of family from both sides of the border, when everyone comes to celebrate her older sister's birthday. (Rev: BCCB 6/97; BL 5/1/97; SLJ 6/97)

6782 McCourt, Lisa, adapt. *Della Splatnuk, Birthday Girl* (K–3). Illus. by Pat G. Porter. Series: Chicken Soup for Little Souls. 1999, Health Communications $14.95 (978-1-55874-600-8). Carrie realizes how cruel her classmates are when she is the only one to attend Della's birthday party because the others think she is weird. (Rev: BL 5/1/99; HBG 10/99; SLJ 9/99)

6783 McLarey, Kristina Thermaenius, and Myra McLarey. *When You Take a Pig to a Party* (PS–3). Illus. by Marjory Wunsch. 2000, Orchard LB $16.99 (978-0-531-33257-3). 32pp. When Adelaide is invited to Ethan's birthday party she makes the mistake of bringing her pet pig, Sherman, along. (Rev: BL 4/15/00; HBG 10/00; SLJ 4/00)

6784 McPhail, David. *Big Brown Bear's Birthday Surprise* (K–2). Illus. 2007, Harcourt $16.00 (978-0-15-206098-5). 32pp. Although he's forgotten this, it's Bear's birthday — and more surprises are to come during this day he shares with Rat. (Rev: BL 5/1/07; SLJ 6/07)

6785 Moon, Nicola. *Happy Birthday, Amelia* (K–2). Illus. by Jenny Jones. 2000, Pavilion $17.95 (978-1-86205-208-6). 32pp. On her birthday, Amelia follows clues that take her around her farmyard home and eventually to the orchard where everyone is waiting for her party to begin. (Rev: BL 7/00)

6786 Mueller, Virginia. *Monster's Birthday Hiccups* (PS–K). Illus. by Lynn Munsinger. 1992, Whitman LB $13.95 (978-0-8075-5267-4). 24pp. Monster cures his hiccups at his birthday party by blowing out the candles on his cake and granting his own wish. (Rev: BL 1/15/92)

6787 Nakagawa, Chihiro. *Who Made This Cake?* (PS–1). Trans. by Chihiro Nakagawa. Illus. by Junji Koyose. 2008, Front St. $16.95 (978-1-59078-595-9). 32pp. A birthday cake is made by a crew of tiny yet happy people who must use dump trucks, cranes, and other equipment. (Rev: BL 9/1/08; HB 1/09)

6788 Oram, Hiawyn. *Badger's Bring Something Party* (PS–2). Illus. by Susan Varley. 1995, Lothrop $15.00 (978-0-688-14082-3). 32pp. Mole feels out of place at Badger's birthday party because he didn't have a gift to bring. A prequel to *Badger's Parting Gifts* (1984). (Rev: BL 4/15/95; HB 5/95; SLJ 7/95)

6789 Patricelli, Leslie. *The Birthday Box* (PS). Illus. by author. 2007, Candlewick $15.99 (978-0-7636-2825-3). A young child is just as thrilled with the box that holds a birthday present as he is with what's inside in this picture book that encourages imaginative play. (Rev: SLJ 5/07)

6790 Rempt, Fiona. *Snail's Birthday Wish* (PS–1). Illus. by Noëlle Smit. 2007, Sterling LB $14.95 (978-1-905417-52-0). 32pp. Snail's friends, sensitive to his dream of moving faster, bring him puzzling presents that fit together for a surprise ending — a car. (Rev: SLJ 11/07)

6791 Rose, Deborah L. *Birthday Zoo* (PS–2). Illus. by Lynn Munsinger. 2002, Whitman $15.95 (978-0-8075-0776-6). 32pp. A little boy is treated to a rollicking birthday party hosted by the animals at the zoo in this rhyming picture book. (Rev: BL 9/15/02; HB 11/02; HBG 3/03; SLJ 10/02)

6792 Roth, Susan L. *Happy Birthday Mr. Kang* (2–4). Illus. 2001, National Geographic $16.95 (978-0-7922-7723-1). 32pp. When Mr. Kang's grandson Sam asks if the old man's hua mei bird wants its freedom, Mr. Kang releases it with surprising results in this birthday story. (Rev: BL 1/1–15/01; HBG 10/01; SLJ 2/01)

6793 Scamell, Ragnhild. *Toby's Doll's House* (PS–3). Illus. by Adrian Reynolds. 1999, Levinson $14.95 (978-1-86233-026-9). Toby takes all the boxes in which his birthday gifts were packed and turns them into the doll's house that he really wanted. (Rev: SLJ 9/99)

6794 Schaefer, Carole Lexa. *Dragon Dancing* (PS–1). Illus. by Pierr Morgan. 2007, Viking $16.99 (978-0-670-06084-9). For Mei Lin's birthday, the class decorates dragons and enjoys a boisterous and colorful dragon dance. (Rev: BL 1/1–15/07; SLJ 3/07*)

6795 Segal, Lore. *Morris the Artist* (PS–2). Illus. by Boris Kulikov. 2003, Farrar $16.00 (978-0-374-35063-5). Morris, an aspiring artist, takes a gift of a paint set to Benjamin's birthday party but finds he cannot part with it and eventually opens it up himself. (Rev: HBG 4/04; SLJ 6/03)

6796 Shaw, Nancy. *Sheep in a Shop* (PS–1). Illus. by Margot Apple. 1991, Houghton $15.00 (978-0-395-53681-0). 32pp. Five sheep are a little short of cash when they shop for a present for a friend. (Rev: HB 5/91*; SLJ 2/91)

6797 Soto, Gary. *Chato and the Party Animals* (PS–3). Illus. by Susan Guevara. 2000, Penguin $16.99 (978-0-399-23159-9). 32pp. Because he is from a pound, Novio Boy doesn't know his birthday, so Chato the Cat organizes a special surprise birthday party for him. (Rev: BL 8/00; HBG 3/01; SLJ 7/00)

6798 Sperring, Mark. *The Fairytale Cake* (PS–K). Illus. by Jonathan Langley. 2005, Scholastic $15.95 (978-0-439-68329-6). 32pp. Detailed drawings add to the fun in this story of a parade of nursery rhyme and fairy tale characters delivering a little boy's birthday cake. (Rev: BL 7/05; SLJ 9/05)

6799 Spinelli, Eileen. *In My New Yellow Shirt* (PS). Illus. by Hideko Takahashi. 2001, Holt $15.95 (978-0-8050-6242-7). 32pp. A birthday boy sees lots of potential in his new yellow shirt, despite his friend's dismissal of the gift. (Rev: BCCB 9/01; BL 6/1–15/01; HBG 3/02; SLJ 8/01)

6800 Starr, Meg. *Alicia's Happy Day* (PS–1). Illus. by Ying-Hwa Hu. 2003, Star Bright $15.95 (978-1-887724-85-2). 32pp. Alicia's birthday is a happy, special day thanks to her friends, neighbors, and family. (Rev: BL 2/1/03)

6801 Stein, David Ezra. *Cowboy Ned and Andy* (PS–2). Illus. by author. 2006, Simon & Schuster $14.95 (978-1-4169-0041-2). Andy, a horse, wants to get Cowboy Ned a cake for his birthday, but when he can't find one in the desert, he gives Ned a hug instead. (Rev: SLJ 7/06)

6802 Stevens, Jan R. *Carlos and the Carnival: Carlos y la Feria* (K–3). Illus. by Jeanne Arnold. 1999, Northland $15.95 (978-0-87358-733-4). 32pp. In this bilingual book, Carlos receives some money for his birthday but does not need his father's advice about spending it wisely. (Rev: BL 8/99; HBG 3/00; SLJ 7/99)

6803 Uff, Caroline. *Happy Birthday, Lulu!* (PS). Illus. 2000, Walker $14.95 (978-0-8027-8751-4). 24pp. Lulu celebrates her birthday in many ways, receiving cards, opening presents, getting a special phone call from Grandpa, and having a big party. (Rev: BL 12/1/00)

6804 Wallace, John. *Tiny Rabbit Goes to a Birthday Party* (PS–K). Illus. 2000, Holiday House $16.95 (978-0-8234-1489-5). 32pp. Tiny Rabbit is worried about going to his first birthday party but, when he has a good time, he starts to make plans for his own party. (Rev: BL 2/1/00; HBG 10/00; SLJ 4/00)

6805 Wallace, Nancy E. *Tell-A-Bunny* (PS–1). Illus. 2000, Winslow $15.95 (978-1-890817-29-9). 32pp. When bunnies phone each other about a surprise birthday party, the message gets garbled as it is passed from one bunny to another. (Rev: BL 5/15/00; HBG 10/00; SLJ 5/00)

6806 Wardlaw, Lee. *Bow-Wow Birthday* (PS–3). Illus. by Arden Johnson-Petrov. 1998, Boyds Mills $14.95 (978-1-56397-489-2). A humorous story about a group of children who hold a birthday party for an ancient dog who only wants to sleep in his favorite closet. (Rev: BCCB 4/98; BL 3/1/98; HBG 10/98; SLJ 5/98)

6807 Whittington, Mary K. *The Patchwork Lady* (K–2). Illus. by Jane Dyer. 1991, Harcourt $13.95 (978-0-15-259580-7). A woman whose house and dress look like a patchwork quilt decides to hold a birthday party for herself. (Rev: SLJ 6/91)

6808 Wilson, Karma. *Whopper Cake* (PS–2). Illus. by Will Hillenbrand. 2007, Simon & Schuster $16.99 (978-0-689-83844-6). 40pp. Exaggerated illustrations complement this funny, larger-than-life story about Grandpa, who decides to make a birthday cake as big as a house for his wife, Grandma. (Rev: BL 6/1–15/07; SLJ 7/07)

6809 Wright, Betty R. *The Blizzard* (PS–2). Illus. by Ronald Himler. 2003, Holiday House $16.95 (978-0-8234-1656-1). It's Billy's birthday and a snowstorm means his cousins can't come to celebrate, but his disappointment disappears when a full-blown blizzard means his whole class must spend the night at his house. (Rev: BL 7/03*; HBG 4/04; SLJ 10/03)

CHRISTMAS

6810 Aliki. *Christmas Tree Memories* (PS–2). Illus. 1991, HarperCollins LB $14.89 (978-0-06-020008-4). 32pp. This is a remembrance of Christmases past and the activities associated with celebrations years ago. (Rev: BL 7/91; HB 11/91)

6811 Alsenas, Linas. *Mrs. Claus Takes a Vacation* (K–3). Illus. by author. 2006, Scholastic $16.99 (978-0-439-77978-4). Feeling restricted, Mrs. Claus decides to take a world tour of her own, leaving Mr. Claus at home to worry about her. (Rev: HB 11/06; HBG 4/07; SLJ 10/06)

6812 Appelt, Kathi. *Merry Christmas, Merry Crow* (PS–2). Illus. by Jon Goodell. 2005, Harcourt $16.00 (978-0-15-202651-6). 32pp. In this charming rhyming Christmas tale, a clever crow flies around town collecting odds and ends with which to decorate a Christmas tree. (Rev: BL 10/15/05; HBG 4/06; SLJ 10/05)

6813 Arnold, Katya. *The Adventures of Snowwoman* (PS–3). Illus. 1998, Holiday House $15.95 (978-0-8234-1390-4). 32pp. Children build Snowwoman to take a message to Santa to bring them a tree. (Rev: BL 12/1/98; HBG 3/99; SLJ 3/99)

6814 Auch, Mary Jane. *The Nutquacker* (K–3). Illus. 1999, Holiday House $17.95 (978-0-8234-1524-3).

32pp. Clara the duck wanders off to find something called "Christmas," which she hears is on its way, only to find that Christmas is a time for being with people who love you. (Rev: BL 11/1/99; HBG 3/00; SLJ 10/99)

6815 Autry, Gene, and Oakley Haldeman. *Here Comes Santa Claus* (PS–1). Illus. by Bruce Whatley. 2002, HarperCollins LB $18.89 (978-0-06-028269-1). 32pp. The 1947 song coauthored by Gene Autry forms the basis of this picture book that follows parallel stories of Santa's preparations and a family readying for his arrival. (Rev: BL 10/1/02; HBG 3/03; SLJ 10/02)

6816 Barry, Robert. *Mr. Willowby's Christmas Tree* (PS–2). Illus. 2000, Doubleday $15.95 (978-0-385-32721-3). 32pp. A Christmas tree makes the rounds of seven different homes. In each case it is chopped down a little to fit the house, until the last part is so small that three little mice find it just right. (Rev: BL 9/1/00; HBG 10/01)

6817 Bauer, Marion Dane. *Christmas in the Forest* (2–3). Illus. 1998, Holiday House $15.95 (978-0-8234-1371-3). 48pp. The spirit of Christmas pervades the animal kingdom and makes friends out of traditional enemies in this beginning reader. (Rev: BL 12/1/98; HBG 3/99; SLJ 10/98)

6818 Bauer, Marion Dane. *Christmas Lights* (PS–1). Illus. by Susan Mitchell. 2006, Simon & Schuster $14.95 (978-0-689-86942-6). This colorful light-up book celebrates the joys of Christmas. (Rev: SLJ 10/06)

6819 Bauer, Sepp. *The Christmas Rose* (1–4). Illus. by Else Wenz-Vietor. 2008, Charlesbridge $12.95 (978-1-58089-232-2). 48pp. Arranged in parts like an Advent calendar, this story about children Fritz and Gretel, who ask Saint Nikolaus for help in healing their sick father, can be read a day at a time. (Rev: BLO 8/28/08)

6820 Baumgart, Klaus. *Laura's Christmas Star* (1–3). Trans. from German by Judy Waite. Illus. by author. 1999, Little Tiger $16.95 (978-1-888444-59-9). Facing a treeless Christmas, young Laura finds a small, raggedy tree in the street and brings it home. (Rev: HBG 3/00; SLJ 10/99)

6821 Beck, Andrea. *Elliot's Christmas Surprise* (PS–1). Illus. by author. Series: An Elliot Moose Story. 2003, Kids Can $12.95 (978-1-55337-474-9); paper $5.95 (978-1-55337-661-3). Elliot, the stuffed moose, scrambles to get Christmas gifts for all his friends after he receives a big red box. (Rev: HBG 4/04; SLJ 10/03)

6822 Bedford, David. *I've Seen Santa!* (PS–1). Illus. by Tim Warnes. 2006, Tiger Tales $15.95 (978-1-58925-058-1). Little Bear, Big Bear, and Mommy Bear try to stay awake for Santa. (Rev: SLJ 10/06)

6823 Berger, Barbara Helen. *The Donkey's Dream* (K–3). Illus. by author. 1985, Penguin $17.99 (978-0-399-21233-8). 32pp. The story of a donkey who at Christmas time carried "a lady full of heaven" to a stable. (Rev: HB 11/85; SLJ 10/85)

6824 Bond, Michael. *Paddington Bear and the Christmas Surprise* (K–2). Illus. by R. W. Alley. 1997, HarperCollins $11.95 (978-0-694-00897-1).

Paddington's visit with his family to a department store at Christmas is not the joyful occasion he had hoped for. (Rev: BL 9/15/97; SLJ 10/97)

6825 Bowen, Anne. *Christmas Is Coming* (PS–2). Illus. by Tomek Bogacki. 2007, Carolrhoda $16.95 (978-1-57505-934-1). 32pp. A little girl tells her baby brother that Christmas is coming and describes the family traditions. (Rev: BL 9/15/07)

6826 Boynton, Sandra. *Bob: And 6 More Christmas Stories* (PS–K). Illus. by author. 1999, Simon & Schuster $7.99 (978-0-689-82568-2). A humorous book that consists of seven double-page stories about animals celebrating Christmas. (Rev: SLJ 10/99)

6827 Brett, Jan. *Christmas Trolls* (K–3). Illus. 1993, Penguin LB $16.99 (978-0-399-22507-9). 32pp. Treva discovers that the mysterious disappearance of objects from her house is the work of trolls. (Rev: BL 7/93)

6828 Brett, Jan. *The Wild Christmas Reindeer* (K–2). Illus. 1990, Penguin $17.99 (978-0-399-22192-7). 32pp. Santa has a whole new crew of wild reindeer that might not want to work on Christmas Eve. (Rev: BL 9/15/90*)

6829 Brown, Elizabeth Ferguson. *Coal Country Christmas* (PS–2). Illus. by Harvey Stevenson. 2003, Boyds Mills $15.95 (978-1-59078-020-6). A bittersweet Christmas story about a young girl visiting her grandmother's home in Pennsylvania's depressed coal country. (Rev: HBG 4/04; SLJ 10/03)

6830 Brown, Marc. *Arthur's Christmas* (K–2). Illus. by author. 1984, Little, Brown $15.95 (978-0-316-11180-5). Arthur, an anteater, has a series of Christmas adventures.

6831 Brown, Margaret Wise. *The Little Fir Tree* (K–2). Illus. by Jim LaMarche. 2005, HarperCollins $15.99 (978-0-06-028189-2). 32pp. LaMarche's art breathes new life into the classic tale, first published in 1954, of a little fir tree and how it helped to brighten Christmas for a lame boy. (Rev: BL 9/15/05; SLJ 10/05)

6832 Brown, Rachel W.N. *Small Camel Follows the Star* (PS–2). Illus. by Giuliano Ferri. 2007, Albert Whitman $16.95 (978-0-8075-7453-9). 32pp. Small Camel tells the Nativity story from his perspective as the animal who carries precious gifts for the baby Jesus. (Rev: BL 9/15/07)

6833 Buehner, Caralyn. *Snowmen at Christmas* (PS–K). Illus. by Mark Buehner. 2005, Dial $16.99 (978-0-8037-2995-7). 32pp. First seen in *Snowmen at Night* (2002), these jolly characters return to show how snow families celebrate Christmas. (Rev: BL 9/1/05; SLJ 10/05)

6834 Bunting, Eve. *Christmas Cricket* (PS–2). Illus. by Timothy Bush. 2002, Clarion $15.00 (978-0-618-06554-7). 32pp. A cricket perched among the branches of a Christmas tree is heartened to hear his chirping described as an angel's song. (Rev: BL 9/15/02; HBG 3/03; SLJ 10/02)

6835 Bunting, Eve. *December* (K–3). Illus. by David Diaz. 1997, Harcourt $16.00 (978-0-15-201434-6). 40pp. A miracle occurs when a homeless mother and her son allow an old lady to sleep in their cardboard home at Christmas time. (Rev: BL 9/1/97*; HBG 3/98; SLJ 10/97*)

6836 Bunting, Eve. *Night Tree* (PS–3). Illus. by Ted Rand. 1991, Harcourt $13.95 (978-0-15-257425-3). 32pp. On the night before Christmas, a family drives into the woods and decorates a tree. (Rev: BCCB 10/91; BL 9/15/91; HB 11/91)

6837 Bunting, Eve. *We Were There: A Nativity Story* (PS–3). Illus. by Wendell Minor. 2001, Clarion $16.00 (978-0-395-82265-4). 32pp. A variety of creatures including the rat, spider, toad, and snake claim they too were present at Jesus' birth. (Rev: BL 9/1/01; HBG 3/02; SLJ 10/01)

6838 Carle, Eric. *Dream Snow* (PS–1). Illus. 2000, Philomel $21.99 (978-0-399-23579-5). 32pp. In this counting book set at Christmastime, a farmer dreams that a gentle snow covers all his animals. (Rev: BCCB 10/00; BL 9/1/00; HBG 3/01)

6839 Carlson, Lori M. *Hurray for Three Kings' Day!* (PS–3). Illus. by Ed Martinez. 1999, Morrow LB $15.89 (978-0-688-16240-5). 32pp. The traditional Latin American holiday is the setting for this story about Anita and her older brothers, who dress as the Christmas kings and carry make-believe gifts around the town. (Rev: BL 9/1/99; HBG 3/00; SLJ 10/99)

6840 Carlson, Nancy. *Harriet and George's Christmas Treat* (PS–2). Illus. 2001, Carolrhoda $15.95 (978-1-57505-506-0). 32pp. Harriet and George try unsuccessfully to avoid eating Mrs. Hoozit's Christmas fruitcake. (Rev: BL 10/1/01; HBG 3/02; SLJ 10/01)

6841 Catalano, Dominic. *Santa and the Three Bears* (PS–K). Illus. 2000, Boyds Mills $15.95 (978-1-56397-864-7). 32pp. Mama, Papa, and Baby Bear seek shelter in Santa's house while he is out delivering gifts and the three intruders wreak mayhem before falling asleep. (Rev: BL 9/1/00; HBG 3/01)

6842 Chaconas, Dori. *Christmas Mouseling* (PS–2). Illus. by Susan Kathleen Hartung. 2005, Viking $15.99 (978-0-670-05984-3). 32pp. When a wintry wind destroys their nest, a mother mouse finds shelter for her newborn in the manger in which Jesus Christ was just born. (Rev: BL 10/15/05; SLJ 10/05)

6843 Chaconas, Dori. *When Cows Come Home for Christmas* (PS–2). Illus. by Lynne Chapman. 2005, Albert Whitman $15.95 (978-0-8075-8877-2). 32pp. In this romp of a Christmas tale, members of an extended bovine family try to squeeze together in a small house to celebrate the holiday. (Rev: BL 10/15/05; SLJ 10/05)

6844 Chen, Chih-Yuan. *The Best Christmas Ever* (PS–2). Illus. 2005, Heryin $13.99 (978-0-9762056-2-3). In this gentle Christmas tale, Little Bear works behind the scenes to ensure that the holiday is a happy one for everyone in his family despite the lack of money. (Rev: BL 12/1/05)

6845 Chen, Pauline. *Peiling and the Chicken-Fried Christmas* (4–6). 2007, Bloomsbury $15.95 (978-1-59990-122-0). 142pp. Eleven-year-old Peiling and her family, immigrants from Taiwan, experiment

with celebrating Christmas. (Rev: BL 10/15/07; HB 11/07; LMC 11/07)

6846 Chorao, Kay. *The Christmas Story* (PS–3). Illus. 1996, Holiday House LB $16.95 (978-0-8234-1251-8). 28pp. The biblical account of Christmas from the King James version is illustrated in Renaissance-like paintings. (Rev: BL 9/1/96)

6847 Clark, Emma Chichester. *Melrose and Croc: A Christmas Story to Remember* (PS–2). Illus. 2006, Walker $16.95 (978-0-8027-9597-7). 32pp. A simple, beautifully illustrated story about Melrose the dog and Croc the crocodile, lonely souls who meet in the big city on Christmas Eve. (Rev: BL 11/1/06; SLJ 10/06)

6848 Climo, Shirley. *The Cobweb Christmas* (K–3). Illus. by Joe Lasker. 1982, HarperCollins LB $15.89 (978-0-690-04216-0); paper $5.95 (978-0-06-443110-1). 32pp. Spiders turn Tante's Christmas tree into a glistening thing of beauty.

6849 Coffey, Tim. *Christmas at the Top of the World* (PS). Illus. by author. 2003, Whitman LB $16.95 (978-0-8075-5762-4). Little Reindeer, joined by his mother and other animals, travels to the North Pole to find his father and see the wonders "at the top of the world." (Rev: HBG 4/04; SLJ 10/03)

6850 Conover, Chris. *The Christmas Bears* (PS–2). Illus. by author. 2008, Farrar $16.95 (978-0-374-33275-4). 32pp. A happy and beautifully illustrated Christmas story featuring a father (Santa Bear) and seven little cubs who make cookies, decorate a tree, and anticipate. (Rev: BL 10/1/08; HB 11/08; SLJ 10/08)

6851 Conrad, Pam. *The Tub People's Christmas* (PS–K). Illus. by Richard Egielski. 1999, HarperCollins LB $15.89 (978-0-06-026029-3). 32pp. Small wooden toys named the Tub People are confused when they become ornaments on a Christmas tree. (Rev: BL 9/1/99; HBG 3/00; SLJ 10/99)

6852 Corrin, Sara, and Stephen Corrin, eds. *Round the Christmas Tree* (K–4). Illus. by Jill Bennett. 1983, Puffin paper $3.95 (978-0-317-62263-8). Sixteen stories, many of them fairy tales, about Christmas.

6853 Cotten, Cynthia. *This Is the Stable* (PS–2). Illus. by Delana Bettoli. 2006, Holt $16.95 (978-0-8050-7556-4). 32pp. Using a "This Is the House that Jack Built" style, this rhyming retelling of the Nativity story is a good choice for read-alouds. (Rev: BL 11/1/06; SLJ 10/06)

6854 Cowley, Joy. *Mrs. Wishy-Washy's Christmas* (PS–1). Illus. by Elizabeth Fuller. 2005, Philomel $15.99 (978-0-399-24344-8). 32pp. When Mrs. Wishy-Washy orders the farm animals to get cleaned up for Christmas, the creatures balk at using the icy tub in the barnyard and instead go inside to use her tub. (Rev: BL 9/15/05; SLJ 10/05)

6855 Crisp, Marty. *The Most Precious Gift: A Story of the Nativity* (PS–2). 2006, Philomel $16.99 (978-0-399-24296-0). 32pp. A poor boy named Ameer joins a caravan to go see the baby Jesus and must decide what gift he can offer the newborn king. (Rev: BL 11/15/06; SLJ 10/06)

6856 Czernecki, Stefan, and Timothy Rhodes. *Pancho's Pinata* (PS–2). Illus. by Stefan Czernecki. 1992, Hyperion $14.95 (978-1-56282-277-4); paper $4.95 (978-0-7868-1007-9). 40pp. The fanciful story of how the first pinata was invented, in the village of San Miguel. (Rev: BL 11/1/92) [398.2]

6857 D'Allance, Mireille. *Bear's Christmas Star* (PS–1). Illus. 2000, Simon & Schuster $12.95 (978-0-684-83826-7). 28pp. Bear wants to help trim the Christmas tree but Papa says he is just too small; however, at the end, it takes both of them to put the star on the top of the tree. (Rev: BL 11/1/00)

6858 Demas, Corinne. *Two Christmas Mice* (PS–2). Illus. by Stephanie Roth. 2005, Holiday $16.95 (978-0-8234-1785-8). 32pp. Neighbors Annamouse and Willamouse join forces to celebrate Christmas. (Rev: BL 10/15/05; SLJ 10/05)

6859 dePaola, Tomie, ed. *The Clown of God* (K–3). Illus. by Tomie dePaola. 1978, Harcourt $16.00 (978-0-15-219175-7); paper $7.00 (978-0-15-618192-1). 45pp. On Christmas Eve, a juggler gives to a statue of Christ his only possession, the gift of his art.

6860 dePaola, Tomie. *An Early American Christmas* (K–2). Illus. by author. 1987, Holiday House $17.95 (978-0-8234-0617-3); paper $6.95 (978-0-8234-0979-2). 32pp. What it might have been like for a German family of long ago to move to a New England village where most of the people did not celebrate Christmas. (Rev: BCCB 11/87; BL 9/1/87)

6861 dePaola, Tomie, retel. *The Legend of Old Befana* (PS–3). Illus. by Tomie dePaola. 1980, Harcourt $16.00 (978-0-15-243816-6); paper $6.00 (978-0-15-243817-3). 32pp. The legend of the old lady who is still searching for the Christ child.

6862 dePaola, Tomie. *Merry Christmas, Strega Nona* (PS–3). Illus. by author. 1986, Harcourt paper $7.00 (978-0-15-253184-3). 32pp. Strega Nona is worried because her helper Big Anthony doesn't seem to be helping her to prepare for Christmas at all. (Rev: BL 11/1/86; HB 11/86)

6863 dePaola, Tomie. *The Night of Las Posadas* (K–4). Illus. 1999, Penguin $16.99 (978-0-399-23400-2). 32pp. During the festival of Las Posadas, a Spanish custom that celebrates the search for shelter by Joseph and Mary, a miracle occurs in this fantasy set in Santa Fe, New Mexico. (Rev: BL 9/1/99; HBG 3/00; SLJ 10/99)

6864 DiCamillo, Kate. *Great Joy* (PS–2). Illus. by Bagram Ibatoulline. 2007, Candlewick $16.99 (978-0-7636-2920-5). 32pp. With illustrations that evoke the 1940s, this is a gentle Christmas story about a young girl, Frances, who is distressed by the thought that an organ grinder and his monkey have no home to go to. (Rev: BCCB 12/07; BL 10/15/07; LMC 3/08)

6865 Dooley, Norah. *Everybody Serves Soup* (2–4). Illus. by Peter J. Thornton. 2000, Carolrhoda $15.95 (978-1-57505-422-3). 40pp. When Carrie tastes her neighbors' soups, she gets an idea for a unique Christmas present for her mother. (Rev: BL 1/1–15/01; HBG 3/01)

6866 Dunbar, Joyce. *This Is the Star* (K–3). Illus. by Gary Blythe. 1996, Harcourt $16.00 (978-0-15-200851-2). 36pp. A cumulative talc using the story of the Nativity as a framework. (Rev: BL 9/1/96; HBG 4/04; SLJ 4/04)

6867 Duval, Kathy. *The Three Bears' Christmas* (PS–K). Illus. by Paul Meisel. 2005, Holiday $16.95 (978-0-8234-1871-8). 32pp. The three bears return from a Christmas Eve walk to find that someone has been in their house — even tried out the beds — and left a red coat and presents under the tree. (Rev: BL 9/1/05*; HB 11/05; HBG 4/06; SLJ 10/05)

6868 Elschner, Géraldine. *Pashmina the Little Christmas Goat* (PS–2). Illus. by Angela Kehlenbeck. 2006, Penguin $16.99 (978-0-698-40046-7). 32pp. When father brings home a small white goat to eat for Christmas dinner the family decides instead to keep it and raise it, and the rewards continue year after year; rich illustrations add to the warmth of the story. (Rev: BL 12/1/06; SLJ 10/06)

6869 Engelbreit, Mary. *Mary Engelbreit's A Merry Little Christmas: Celebrate from A to Z* (PS–3). Illus. by author. 2006, HarperCollins LB $17.89 (978-0-06-074159-4). Celebrates a mouse family's Christmas, and all the delights from A to Z. (Rev: SLJ 10/06)

6870 Evans, Richard Paul. *The Light of Christmas* (K–2). Illus. by Daniel Craig. 2002, Simon & Schuster $16.95 (978-0-689-83468-4). 32pp. A boy called Alexander does a good deed and is rewarded with the special right to light the flame on Christmas Eve. (Rev: BL 10/1/02; HBG 3/03; SLJ 10/02)

6871 Falconer, Ian. *Olivia Helps with Christmas* (PS–1). Illus. by author. 2007, Atheneum $18.99 (978-1-4169-0786-2). 58pp. Little pig Olivia tries — really! — to help with Christmas preparations. (Rev: BL 9/15/07; HB 11/07) ∩

6872 Fine, Edith Hope. *Cricket at the Manger* (PS–2). Illus. by Winslow Pels. 2005, Boyds Mills $15.95 (978-1-56397-993-4). 32pp. Awakened by strange noises, an initially grouchy cricket witnesses the birth of Jesus in a manger. (Rev: BL 9/1/05; SLJ 10/05)

6873 Foreman, Michael. *Cat in the Manger* (PS–3). Illus. 2001, Holt $16.95 (978-0-8050-6677-7). 24pp. A cat is displaced from his bed to make room for a baby in the manger. (Rev: BCCB 11/01; BL 9/15/01; HBG 3/02; SLJ 10/01)

6874 Fox, Mem. *Wombat Divine* (PS–3). Illus. by Kerry Argent. 1996, Harcourt $15.00 (978-0-15-201416-2). 32pp. A sleepy wombat gets to play baby Jesus in the Christmas Nativity play. (Rev: BL 10/15/96; SLJ 10/96*)

6875 Frazee, Marla. *Santa Claus: The World's Number One Toy Expert* (PS–K). Illus. 2005, Harcourt $16.00 (978-0-15-204970-6). 40pp. A portrait of Santa hard at work, taking requests and testing toys. (Rev: BCCB 12/05; BL 11/1/05*; HB 11/05; HBG 4/06; SLJ 10/05*)

6876 Gackenbach, Dick. *Claude the Dog: A Christmas Story* (K–3). Illus. by author. 1984, Houghton paper $5.95 (978-0-89919-124-9). 32pp. Claude gives away all his presents but gets an even better one from his master. A related title is: *What's Claude Doing?* (1984).

6877 Gammell, Stephen. *Wake Up, Bear . . . It's Christmas!* (PS–1). Illus. by author. 1981, Morrow paper $4.95 (978-0-688-09934-3). 32pp. A bear is afraid he will sleep through Christmas.

6878 Gantos, Jack. *Rotten Ralph's Rotten Christmas* (K–2). Illus. by Nicole Rubel. 1984, Houghton $16.00 (978-0-395-35380-6); paper $7.95 (978-0-395-45685-9). 32pp. This miserable cat is determined that Sarah's Christmas will also be miserable.

6879 Garland, Michael. *Christmas Magic* (PS–3). Illus. 2001, Dutton $16.99 (978-0-525-46797-7). 32pp. Arresting artwork shows how Emily's Christmas Eve was a night of real enchantment. (Rev: BCCB 11/01; BL 9/1/01; HBG 3/02; SLJ 10/01)

6880 Gillmor, Don. *The Christmas Orange* (K–2). Illus. by Marie-Louise Gay. 1999, Stoddart $15.95 (978-0-7737-3100-4). 32pp. When Anton receives only an orange for Christmas, he sues Santa for breach of promise. (Rev: BL 1/1–15/00)

6881 Gliori, Debi. *What Can I Give Him?* (PS–3). Illus. 1998, Holiday House $15.95 (978-0-8234-1392-8). 32pp. Using double-page spreads — one depicting a contemporary girl with her loving family at Christmastime and the other a poor servant girl in the stable where Jesus was born -- this book explores the question of what one should give as a loving present. (Rev: BL 9/1/98; HBG 3/99; SLJ 10/98)

6882 Gutman, Anne. *Gaspard and Lisa's Christmas Surprise* (PS–K). Illus. by Georg Hallensleben. Series: The Misadventures of Gaspard and Lisa. 2002, Knopf $9.95 (978-0-375-82229-2). Gaspard and Lisa, young animals, set out to make a raincoat for their teacher. (Rev: HBG 3/03; SLJ 10/02)

6883 Hague, Michael. *The Perfect Present* (PS–1). Illus. 1996, Morrow $16.00 (978-0-688-10880-9). 48pp. Jack, a rabbit, goes to Big Bear's Toy Shoppe to find a Christmas present for his girlfriend. (Rev: BL 9/1/96; SLJ 4/04)

6884 Harley, Bill. *Dear Santa: The Letters of James B. Dobbins* (PS–2). Illus. by R. W. Alley. 2005, HarperCollins $15.99 (978-0-06-623778-7). 32pp. In a series of letters to Santa Claus, Jimmy Dobbins places orders for some pretty outrageous Christmas gifts and also offers explanations for some of his lapses in behavior over the past year. (Rev: BL 10/1/05; SLJ 10/05)

6885 Harvey, Brett. *My Prairie Christmas* (1–3). Illus. by Deborah Kogan Ray. 1990, Holiday House LB $16.95 (978-0-8234-0827-6). 32pp. Young Eleanor wonders what sort of Christmas her pioneering family can have in their new Dakota home. (Rev: BCCB 11/90; BL 10/1/90)

6886 Hassett, Ann, and John Hassett. *The Finest Christmas Tree* (K–2). Illus. 2005, Houghton $16.00 (978-0-618-50901-0). 32pp. Things look bleak for Farmer Tuttle when the demand for his Christmas trees drops as more and more of his customers opt for the artificial variety. (Rev: BL 11/1/05; SLJ 10/05)

6887 Heath, Amy. *Sofie's Role* (PS–2). Illus. 1992, Macmillan LB $14.95 (978-0-02-743505-4). 36pp. On the day before Christmas, a young girl helps her parents in their bakery. (Rev: BCCB 12/92; BL 7/92)

6888 Helmer, Marilyn. *One Splendid Tree* (K–2). Illus. by Dianne Eastman. 2005, Kids Can $15.95 (978-1-55337-683-5). With their father off fighting in World War II, siblings Junior and Hattie try to give their tiny apartment a bit of Christmas spirit by decorating a discarded plant; the illustrations offer lots of period details. (Rev: SLJ 10/05)

6889 High, Linda O. *A Christmas Star* (K–3). Illus. by Ronald Himler. 1997, Holiday House LB $15.95 (978-0-8234-1301-0). 32pp. Stolen gifts are miraculously returned to a church in this Christmas tale set during the Depression. (Rev: BL 9/1/97; HBG 3/98; SLJ 10/97)

6890 High, Linda Oatman. *The Last Chimney of Christmas Eve* (PS–2). Illus. by Kestutis Kasparavicius. 2001, Boyds Mills $15.95 (978-1-56397-804-3). 32pp. Nicholas, a chimney sweep, repays a kind stranger by growing up to be Santa Claus. (Rev: BL 9/15/01; HBG 3/02; SLJ 10/01)

6891 Hoban, Lillian. *Arthur's Christmas Cookies* (1–2). Illus. by author. 1972, HarperCollins paper $3.99 (978-0-06-444055-4). 64pp. What can Arthur give his parents for Christmas? Christmas cookies such as he learned to bake in Cub Scouts are the answer, but a hilarious mix-up occurs when salt is used instead of sugar.

6892 Holland, Trish, and Christine Ford. *The Soldiers' Night Before Christmas* (K–3). Illus. by John Manders. 2006, Random $8.99 (978-0-375-83795-1). Using the structure of Clement Moore's classic Christmas poem, this story in rhyme is set on a U.S. Army base in the desert, and the gifts arrive not in a sleigh but by Humvee. (Rev: SLJ 10/06)

6893 Hooks, William H. *The Legend of the Christmas Rose* (K–4). Illus. by Richard A. Williams. 1999, HarperCollins LB $14.89 (978-0-06-027103-9). 32pp. Dorothy has no presents to offer the infant Jesus, but an angel provides her with the flower now known as the Christmas Rose. (Rev: BL 9/1/99; HBG 3/00)

6894 Hooper, Maureen Brett. *Silent Night: A Christmas Carol Is Born* (1–3). Illus. by Kasi Kubiak. 2001, Boyds Mills $15.95 (978-1-56397-782-4). 32pp. The fictionalized story behind the carol "Silent Night." (Rev: BL 9/15/01; HBG 3/02; SLJ 10/01)

6895 Horn, Sandra Ann. *Babushka* (K–3). Illus. by Sophie Fatus. 2002, Barefoot Books $16.99 (978-1-84148-353-5). 32pp. In this version of a Russian tale, Babushka travels to visit the newly born Christ child, but gives away the gifts she brought to needy people along the way. (Rev: BL 12/15/02; HBG 3/03; SLJ 10/02)

6896 Horse, Harry. *Little Rabbit's Christmas* (PS–1). Illus. by author. 2007, Peachtree $15.95 (978-1-56145-419-8). 32pp. Little Rabbit learns a lesson on Christmas morning when his friends help him fix the little red sled he refused to share. (Rev: BL 9/15/07; HB 11/07)

6897 Howard, Ellen. *The Log Cabin Christmas* (K–3). Illus. by Ronald Himler. 2000, Holiday House $16.95 (978-0-8234-1381-2). 32pp. Set in Michigan during pioneer times, Elvirey and her family are afraid there will be no Christmas now that Mam's dead, but the young girl decides she can save the day. (Rev: BCCB 11/00; BL 11/15/00; HBG 3/01)

6898 Hudson, Cheryl W. *Hold Christmas in Your Heart: African-American Songs, Poems, and Stories for the Holidays* (K–2). Illus. 1995, Scholastic $10.95 (978-0-590-48024-6). 32pp. Poems, stories, and songs from African American authors are found in this fine anthology. (Rev: BL 9/15/95)

6899 Hughes, Langston. *Carol of the Brown King* (PS–3). Illus. by Ashley Bryan. 1998, Simon & Schuster $16.00 (978-0-689-81877-6). 32pp. A colorful picture book that presents six short poems about Christmas — five by Langston Hughes plus one poem he translated from a Puerto Rican Christmas card. (Rev: BL 9/1/98; HB 9/98; HBG 3/99; SLJ 10/98) [811]

6900 Jeffs, Stephanie. *Christopher Bear's First Christmas* (PS–K). Illus. by Jacqui Thomas. Series: Christopher Bear. 2002, Augsburg $5.99 (978-0-8066-4349-6). 29pp. Joe and his bear participate in the preschool's presentation of the first Christmas. (Rev: SLJ 10/02)

6901 Jimenez, Francisco. *The Christmas Gift: El regalo de Navidad* (K–4). Illus. by Claire B. Cotts. 2000, Houghton $16.00 (978-0-395-92869-1). 32pp. In this bilingual book, Panchito is disappointed because there is no money to buy him the red ball he wants for Christmas. (Rev: BCCB 12/00; BL 9/1/00; HBG 3/01)

6902 Johnston, Tony. *A Kenya Christmas* (K–2). Illus. by Leonard Jenkins. 2003, Holiday House $16.95 (978-0-8234-1623-3). A Kenya man tells his grandchildren about a wondrous Christmas from his past, involving snow made from chicken feathers and a Santa carried on an elephant. (Rev: HBG 4/04; SLJ 10/03)

6903 Kastner, Jill. *Merry Christmas, Princess Dinosaur!* (PS). Illus. 2002, HarperCollins LB $17.89 (978-0-06-000472-9). 32pp. Princess Dinosaur is so excited by the prospect of Santa's visit that she falls asleep in the Christmas tree. (Rev: BL 9/1/02; HBG 3/03; SLJ 10/02)

6904 Katz, Karen. *Counting Christmas* (PS). Illus. by author. 2003, Simon & Schuster $14.95 (978-0-689-84925-1). Counting from 10 down to one, this holiday book features double-page spreads full of Christmas details. (Rev: HBG 4/04; SLJ 10/03)

6905 Kennedy, Pamela. *A Christmas Carol* (K–3). Illus. by Carol Heyer. 1995, Ideals $14.95 (978-1-57102-047-5). 32pp. With vibrant paintings and a simple text, the classic story is retold for a young audience. (Rev: BL 11/15/95)

6906 Kidslabel. *Spot 7 Christmas* (1–4). 2006, Chronicle $12.95 (978-0-8118-5323-1). Readers are challenged to identify what's out of place in each of these 13 Christmas-themed photo spreads. (Rev: SLJ 10/06)

6907 Knott, Anthony. *An Angel Came to Nazareth: A Story of the First Christmas* (K–5). Illus. by Maggie Kneen. 2005, Chronicle $15.95 (978-0-8118-4798-8). An angel offers four beasts of burden — horse, donkey, camel, and ox — the option of choosing their riders for a trip from Nazareth to Bethlehem; a simple story with lush illustrations. (Rev: SLJ 10/05)

6908 Knowlton, Laurie L. *The Nativity: Mary Remembers* (K–3). Illus. by Kasi Kubiak. 1998, Boyds Mills $14.95 (978-1-56397-714-5). 32pp. The story of the Nativity is retold through the eyes of Mary, who wonders how she could have been chosen to bear the child who will be the Messiah. (Rev: BCCB 11/98; BL 9/15/98; HBG 10/99; SLJ 10/98)

6909 Kroeber, Theodora. *A Green Christmas* (K–3). Illus. by John Larrecq. 1967, Houghton $6.95 (978-0-87466-047-0). Children new to California discover that Santa Claus will visit places without snow.

6910 Kroll, Steven. *Pooch on the Loose: A Christmas Adventure* (PS–1). Illus. by Michael Garland. 2005, Marshall Cavendish $14.95 (978-0-7614-5239-3). 32pp. Bart the dog escapes from his master and visits the sights of New York City; Photoshop art gives a realistic view of the city and Christmas. (Rev: BL 9/1/05; SLJ 10/05)

6911 Kroll, Virginia. *Uno, Dos, Tres, Posada! Let's Celebrate Christmas* (PS–2). Illus. by Loretta Lopez. 2006, Viking $17.99 (978-0-670-05923-2). Readers learn vocabulary and numbers in Spanish as a little girl introduces each step of a posada, a Hispanic holiday tradition celebrated on the nine nights before Christmas. (Rev: SLJ 10/06)

6912 Krupinski, Loretta. *Christmas in the City* (PS–2). Illus. 2002, Hyperion $15.99 (978-0-7868-0834-2). 40pp. This beautifully illustrated book tells the tale of Mr. and Mrs. Mouse and their Christmas trip to New York during which they explore the city and Mrs. Mouse gives birth in a manger. (Rev: BL 9/15/02; HBG 3/03; SLJ 10/02)

6913 Krykorka, Ian. *Carl, the Christmas Carp* (K–3). Illus. by Vladyana Krykorka. 2006, Orca $17.95 (978-1-55143-329-5). 32pp. Radim's Czech family usually eats carp for Christmas but when he feels sorry for the fish and releases it into the river, his family learns a new tradition for the holiday. (Rev: BL 11/15/06)

6914 Landa, Norbert. *Little Bear's Christmas* (PS–K). Illus. by Marlis Scharff-Kniemeyer. 1999, Little Tiger $14.95 (978-1-888444-60-5). 32pp. Little Bear sets the alarm clock so he will not hibernate through Christmas and miss seeing Santa Claus. (Rev: BL 10/1/99; HBG 3/00; SLJ 10/99)

6915 Leeson, Christine. *The Magic of Christmas* (PS–3). Illus. by Gaby Hansen. 2001, ME Media $14.95 (978-1-58925-011-6). 30pp. In this charming picture book, Molly Mouse and her brothers and sisters decorate a Christmas tree with help from forest friends usually considered enemies. (Rev: BL 9/15/01; SLJ 10/01)

6916 Leuck, Laura. *Santa Claws* (1–4). Illus. by Gris Grimly. 2006, Chronicle $16.95 (978-0-8118-4992-0). In this offbeat Christmas tale, Mack and Zack, two young monsters, prepare for the arrival of Santa Claws. (Rev: SLJ 10/06)

6917 Lewis, J. Patrick. *The Snowflake Sisters* (PS–2). Illus. by Lisa Desimini. 2003, Simon & Schuster $16.95 (978-0-689-85029-5). Crystal and Ivory, two snowflake siblings, find themselves in New York and settle on a snowman in Central Park in this Christmas-related story with wonderful collage illustrations. (Rev: HBG 4/04; SLJ 10/03)

6918 Love, Maryann Cusimano. *You Are My Miracle* (PS–K). Illus. by Satomi Ichikawa. 2005, Philomel $15.99 (978-0-399-24037-9). A mother bear and her child celebrate Christmas in rhyming text that emphasizes togetherness. (Rev: SLJ 10/05)

6919 McCaughrean, Geraldine. *How the Reindeer Got Their Antlers* (1–3). Illus. by Heather Holland. 2000, Holiday House $16.95 (978-0-8234-1562-5). 32pp. The reindeer is ashamed of its twisted antlers, until Santa uses them to save the day when his sleigh slips on ice. (Rev: BL 9/1/00; HBG 3/01)

6920 McCourt, Frank. *Angela and the Baby Jesus* (K–3). Illus. by Raúl Colón. 2007, Simon & Schuster $17.99 (978-1-4169-3789-0). 32pp. Warm illustrations enhance this story about 6-year-old Angela's misguided effort to keep the baby Jesus in the church creche warm. (Rev: BCCB 12/07; BL 9/15/07)

6921 McCutcheon, John. *Christmas in the Trenches* (2–4). Illus. by Henri Sorenson. 2006, Peachtree $18.95 (978-1-56145-374-0). 32pp. On Christmas Day, a World War I veteran tells his grandchildren about the incredible Christmas truce of 1914; McCutcheon's song by the same name is printed at the end. (Rev: BL 8/06; SLJ 10/06)

6922 McDonald, Megan. *Tundra Mouse: A Storyknife Tale* (PS–2). Illus. by S. D. Schindler. 1997, Orchard LB $16.99 (978-0-531-33047-0). 32pp. Tundra Mouse and House Mouse think they are doing people a favor when they tidy up by stripping a Christmas tree of its ornaments, little knowing it's the night before Christmas. (Rev: BL 1/1–15/98; HBG 3/98; SLJ 10/97)

6923 McGovern, Ann. *The Lady in the Box* (K–3). Illus. by Marni Backer. 1997, Turtle $14.95 (978-1-890515-01-0). 32pp. At Christmas time, two youngsters help a homeless woman who is living over a hot-air vent. (Rev: BL 9/1/97; SLJ 10/97)

6924 McKissack, Patricia C. *The All-I'll-Ever-Want Christmas Doll* (K–3). Illus. by Jerry Pinkney. 2007, Random $16.99 (978-0-375-83759-3). 40pp. During the depression, Nella and her African American sisters must share a single Christmas doll. (Rev: BCCB 12/07; BL 9/15/07; HB 11/07; LMC 11/07)

6925 Major, Kevin. *Aunt Olga's Christmas Postcards* (K–3). Illus. by Bruce Roberts. 2005, Groundwood $18.95 (978-0-88899-593-3). 40pp. Anna and her 95-year-old great-great-Aunt Olga write Christmas verses together and share historic postcards and memories. (Rev: BL 11/1/05; SLJ 10/05)

6926 Manushkin, Fran. *The Perfect Christmas Picture* (PS–3). Illus. by Karen Ann Weinhaus. 1980, HarperCollins $11.95 (978-0-06-024068-4). 64pp. An easily read story of Mr. Green, who wants to photograph his family for a Christmas picture.

6927 Martín, Hugo C. *Pablo's Christmas* (K–4). Illus. by Lee Chapman. 2006, Sterling LB $14.95 (978-1-4027-2560-9). Left behind to watch over his expectant mother when his father leaves Mexico to find work in the United States, Pablo does his best to prepare for Christmas. (Rev: SLJ 10/06)

6928 Marzollo, Jean. *I Spy Christmas: A Book of Picture Riddles* (PS–3). Illus. by Walter Wick. 1992, Scholastic $13.99 (978-0-590-45846-7). 40pp. Full-color photos illustrate 13 scenes of Christmas. (Rev: BCCB 11/92; BL 11/1/92) [793.73]

6929 May, Robert L. *Rudolph the Red-Nosed Reindeer: The Original Story of Rudolph* (K–3). Illus. by David Wenzel. 2001, Grosset $9.99 (978-0-448-42534-4). The original text of Rudolph is presented with new illustrations that convey a warm, nostalgic feeling. (Rev: HBG 3/02; SLJ 10/01)

6930 Mayer, Mercer. *The Little Drummer Mouse* (K–3). Illus. by author. 2006, Dial $16.99 (978-0-8037-3147-9). A little mouse, playing on his acorn drum, helps to celebrate the birth of Jesus Christ. (Rev: SLJ 10/06)

6931 Medearis, Angela Shelf. *Poppa's Itchy Christmas* (PS–1). Illus. by John Ward. 1998, Holiday House $15.95 (978-0-8234-1298-3). 32pp. George, an African American youngster, is not happy with the scarf and red long underwear he receives for Christmas, but when he falls through the ice while trying out his new skates, they are the two items that help save his life. (Rev: BL 9/1/98; HBG 10/99; SLJ 10/98)

6932 Menotti, Gian Carlo. *Amahl and the Night Visitors* (K–3). Illus. by Michele Lemieux. 1986, Morrow LB $19.88 (978-0-688-05427-4). 64pp. A lavish edition of the story of this touching opera. (Rev: BCCB 10/86; HB 11/86)

6933 Milgrim, David. *Santa Duck* (K–2). Illus. by author. 2008, Putnam $16.99 (978-0-399-25018-7). 32pp. When Nicholas the duck puts on a Santa suit, he is deluged with gift lists and becomes a Santa's helper who forgets to ask for a gift for himself. (Rev: BCCB 10/08; BLO 10/7/08; HB 11/08)

6934 Minor, Wendell, and Florence Minor. *Christmas Tree!* (PS–2). Illus. by authors. 2005, HarperCollins $16.99 (978-0-06-056034-8). Christmas trees of all kinds and sizes are celebrated in rhyming text and colorful illustrations. (Rev: SLJ 10/05)

6935 Moore, Clement C., and Carter Goodrich. *A Creature Was Stirring: One Boy's Night Before Christmas* (PS–2). Illus. by Carter Goodrich. 2006, Simon & Schuster $16.95 (978-0-689-86399-8). 40pp. Moore's classic Christmas poem is presented here along with a young boy's account of what he did that night when he could not sleep. (Rev: BL 11/15/06; SLJ 10/06)

6936 Morpurgo, Michael. *On Angel Wings* (K–2). Illus. by Quentin Blake. 2007, Candlewick paper $8.99 (978-0-7636-3466-7). 48pp. The Angel

Gabriel makes it possible for a young shepherd to see the newborn Christ in this small-format Nativity story. (Rev: BL 10/15/07; HB 11/07)

6937 Morrissey, Dean. *The Christmas Ship* (K–4). Illus. 2000, HarperCollins LB $16.89 (978-0-06-028576-0). 40pp. On Christmas Eve, toy maker Sam Thatcher helps Santa by delivering toys from his boat, which soars through the night sky. (Rev: BL 10/1/00; HBG 3/01)

6938 Moses, Will. *Silent Night* (1–4). Illus. 1997, Penguin $16.99 (978-0-399-23100-1). 40pp. Using the words of the carol as chapter headings, this is the story of a family's exciting Christmas in rural Vermont. (Rev: BL 9/1/97; HBG 3/98; SLJ 10/97)

6939 Moulton, Mark Kimball. *Reindeer Christmas* (PS–2). Illus. by Karen Hillard Good. 2008, Simon & Schuster $15.99 (978-1-4169-6108-6). 40pp. A warm, rhyming tale about a family that cares for an injured reindeer and later discovers that it was Donner; Santa is grateful. (Rev: BL 9/1/08)

6940 O'Brien, John. *Mother Hubbard's Christmas* (K–2). Illus. 1996, Boyds Mills $14.95 (978-1-56397-139-6). 28pp. This hilarious variation on the standard nursery rhyme tells how Mother Hubbard prepares for Christmas. (Rev: BL 10/15/96)

6941 Oppenheim, Joanne. *The Miracle of the First Poinsettia: A Mexican Christmas Story* (K–2). Illus. by Fabian Negrin. 2003, Barefoot Books $16.99 (978-1-84148-245-3). Young Juanita has no money to give to the church so she follows the advice of a stone angel and gathers weeds, which are miraculously transformed into the beautiful scarlet blossoms of a poinsettia. (Rev: HBG 4/04; SLJ 10/03)

6942 Palatini, Margie. *Moosletoe* (PS–1). Illus. by Henry Cole. 2000, Hyperion $15.99 (978-0-7868-0567-9). 32pp. The moose with the remarkable mustache allows it to be decked with ornaments to preserve the spirit of the Christmas season. (Rev: BL 9/1/00; HBG 3/01)

6943 Pallotta, Jerry. *Who Will Guide My Sleigh Tonight?* (PS–2). Illus. by David Biedrzycki. 2006, Scholastic paper $5.99 (978-0-439-85369-9). Santa Claus, searching for animals to pull his gift-laden sleigh, considers a wide array of possibilities — from skunks and giraffes to kangaroos and snakes — before finally settling on reindeer. (Rev: SLJ 10/06)

6944 Parish, Peggy. *Merry Christmas, Amelia Bedelia* (1–2). Illus. by Lynn Sweat. Series: Amelia Bedelia. 1986, Greenwillow $17.89 (978-0-688-06102-9); Avon paper $3.99 (978-0-380-70325-8). 64pp. Christmas fun with silly Amelia Bedelia, the maid with nonsensical assumptions. (Rev: BCCB 10/86; BL 10/1/86)

6945 Parker, Toni Trent. *Snowflake Kisses and Gingerbread Smiles* (PS–2). Photos by Earl Anderson. 2002, Scholastic $6.95 (978-0-439-33872-1). Photographs of seasonal items and African American children emphasize the delights of Christmas. (Rev: HBG 3/03; SLJ 10/02)

6946 Paterson, Katherine. *Marvin's Best Christmas Present Ever* (1–2). Illus. by Jane Brown. 1997, HarperCollins LB $15.89 (978-0-06-027160-2).

48pp. Marvin is so happy with the Christmas wreath he has made for the family's trailer door that he doesn't want to take it down. (Rev: BL 9/1/97; HB 11/97; HBG 3/98; SLJ 10/97*)

6947 Pilkey, Dav. *Dragon's Merry Christmas* (1–2). Illus. 1991, Orchard LB $16.99 (978-0-531-08557-8). 48pp. The Christmas tree that Dragon finds in the forest is too perfect to cut down. (Rev: BL 7/91)

6948 Pinkwater, Daniel. *Wolf Christmas* (PS–3). Illus. by Jill Pinkwater. 1998, Marshall Cavendish $15.95 (978-0-7614-5030-6). 32pp. On the longest night of the year, three wolf pups are taken by their Uncle Louis to see a human village and witness how this other animal species acts during their winter holidays. (Rev: BL 9/1/98; HBG 3/99; SLJ 10/98)

6949 Polacco, Patricia. *Welcome Comfort* (K–3). Illus. by author. 1999, Philomel LB $16.99 (978-0-399-23169-8). Welcome Comfort, an overweight foster child, gets a special surprise at Christmas. (Rev: BCCB 11/99; HBG 3/00; SLJ 10/99)

6950 Price, Moe. *The Reindeer Christmas* (K–3). Illus. by Atsuko Morozumi. 1993, Harcourt $15.95 (978-0-15-266199-1). 32pp. A delightful Christmas story that tells why Santa decided that reindeer should be the animals to pull his sleigh. (Rev: BL 9/15/93)

6951 Primavera, Elise. *Auntie Claus* (PS–2). Illus. 1999, Harcourt $16.00 (978-0-15-201909-9). 40pp. Sophie Crinkle follows her Aunt Claus to a snowy land and there discovers that her relative is the real force behind Christmas. (Rev: BCCB 12/99; BL 9/1/99; HBG 3/00; SLJ 10/99)

6952 Primavera, Elise. *Auntie Claus and the Key to Christmas* (K–2). 2002, Harcourt $16.00 (978-0-15-202441-3). 40pp. Christopher, trying to get on Santa's "bad" list, journeys to the North Pole and becomes a believer after meeting the bad boys and girls on the list. (Rev: BCCB 11/02; BL 9/15/02; HBG 3/03; SLJ 10/02)

6953 Pulver, Robin. *Christmas for a Kitten* (PS–2). Illus. by Layne Johnson. 2003, Whitman LB $16.95 (978-0-8075-1151-0). Santa adopts a tiny abandoned kitten that has been having a tough time. (Rev: HBG 4/04; SLJ 10/03)

6954 Rahaman, Vashanti. *O Christmas Tree* (K–3). Illus. by Frane Lessac. 1996, Boyds Mills $14.95 (978-1-56397-237-9). 26pp. Anslem has problems believing in a traditional Christmas with snow and Christmas trees in his Caribbean home. (Rev: BCCB 11/96; BL 9/1/96*)

6955 Ransom, Candice F. *The Christmas Dolls* (K–3). Illus. by Moira Fain. 1998, Walker LB $16.85 (978-0-8027-8661-6). 32pp. Claire is sad because her father will be absent for Christmas. She is comforted by helping her mother repair dolls to give to poor children and by making a rag doll that she will give her mother on Christmas morning. (Rev: BL 9/1/98; HBG 3/99; SLJ 10/98)

6956 Recorvits, Helen. *Yoon and the Christmas Mitten* (PS–2). Illus. by Gabi Swiatkowska. 2006, Farrar $16.00 (978-0-374-38688-7). 32pp. Yoon, a young Korean American girl, learns about the Christmas holiday in her American school and tries to persuade her family that they can celebrate the holiday and still be true to their Korean customs; a sequel to *My Name Is Yoon* (2003). (Rev: BL 12/1/06; SLJ 10/06)

6957 Reiss, Mike. *Merry Un-Christmas* (1–3). Illus. by David Catrow. 2006, HarperCollins $15.99 (978-0-06-059126-7). Noelle and her family live in Texmas, where it's Christmas 364 days of the year and the one day they look forward to eagerly is Un-Christmas, when there are no gifts and the kids can go to school. (Rev: SLJ 10/06)

6958 Reiss, Mike. *Santa Claustrophobia* (2–5). Illus. by David Catrow. 2002, Price Stern Sloan $10.99 (978-0-8431-7756-5). Santa is suffering from claustrophobia and Doc Holiday recommends some time off. (Rev: BCCB 12/02; HBG 3/03; SLJ 10/02)

6959 Repchuk, Caroline. *The Snow Tree* (PS–1). Illus. by Josephine Martin. 1997, Dutton $15.99 (978-0-525-45903-3). 32pp. Animals offer to a little bear many colorful objects to decorate his Christmas tree. (Rev: BL 9/1/97; HBG 3/98)

6960 Roberts, Bethany. *Cookie Angel* (PS–2). Illus. by Vladimir Vagin. 2007, Holt $16.95 (978-0-8050-6974-7). 32pp. When the clock strikes midnight on Christmas Eve, a cookie angel atop the tree and toys arrayed around the bottom come alive and have a wild time. (Rev: BL 9/15/07)

6961 Rowlands, Avril. *The Christmas Sheep and Other Stories* (2–4). Illus. by Rosslyn Moran. 2001, Good Bks. $16.00 (978-1-56148-336-5). 48pp. Four stories about the animals that were part of the first Christmas. (Rev: BL 9/15/01; SLJ 10/01)

6962 Rox, John. *I Want a Hippopotamus for Christmas* (K–3). Illus. by Bruce Whatley. 2005, HarperCollins $17.99 (978-0-06-052942-0). A girl's Christmas wish is granted when a hippo arrives at her house in this funny version of a 1953 song. (Rev: SLJ 10/05)

6963 Rylant, Cynthia. *Christmas in the Country* (K–2). Illus. by Diane Goode. 2002, Scholastic $15.95 (978-0-439-07334-9). 32pp. A story of a loving family's beautiful white Christmas, full of tradition and celebration. (Rev: BL 9/15/02; HB 11/02; HBG 3/03; SLJ 10/02)

6964 Rylant, Cynthia. *Mr. Putter and Tabby Bake the Cake* (1–3). Illus. by Arthur Howard. 1994, Harcourt $13.00 (978-0-15-200205-3); paper $6.00 (978-0-15-200214-5). 44pp. Mr. Putter bakes a Christmas cake for his neighbor, Mrs. Teaberry, in this easily read book. (Rev: BL 10/15/94; HB 9/94; SLJ 12/94)

6965 Rylant, Cynthia. *Silver Packages: An Appalachian Christmas Story* (K–3). Illus. by Chris K. Soentpiet. 1997, Orchard LB $17.99 (978-0-531-33051-7). 32pp. At Christmas time, a young doctor tries to repay an Appalachian community for the gifts that were given to him in the past. (Rev: BL 9/1/97; HBG 3/98; SLJ 10/97)

6966 Santiago, Esmeralda. *A Doll for Navidades* (K–2). Illus. by Enrique O. Sánchez. 2005, Scholastic $16.99 (978-0-439-55398-8). 32pp. Seven-year-old Esmeralda desperately wants a doll for Three Kings' Day and she is deeply disappointed when her younger sister receives one instead in this picture book set in Puerto Rico. (Rev: BL 11/1/05; SLJ 10/05)

6967 Say, Allen. *Tree of Cranes* (PS–3). Illus. 1991, Houghton $17.95 (978-0-395-52024-6). 32pp. A Japanese woman brings a tree indoors because it reminds her of the Christmas she spent years ago in California. (Rev: BCCB 9/91*; BL 9/15/91; HB 11/91*)

6968 Schneider, Antonie. *Advent Storybook: 24 Stories to Share Before Christmas* (K–3). Trans. by Marisa Miller. Illus. by Maja Dusikova. 2005, North-South $17.95 (978-0-7358-1963-4). Benjamin Bear's mother tells him a Christmas-related story for each of the 24 days in the little bear's Advent calendar; each parable features Little Bear and ends with a moral. (Rev: SLJ 10/05)

6969 Sharkey, Niamh. *Santasaurus* (PS–2). Illus. by author. 2005, Candlewick $15.99 (978-0-7636-2671-6). Full of Christmas spirit, dinosaur siblings Milo, Mollie, and Ollie eagerly await the arrival of Santasaurus. (Rev: SLJ 10/05)

6970 Slate, Joseph. *The Secret Stars* (PS–2). Illus. by Felipe Davalos. 1998, Marshall Cavendish $15.95 (978-0-7614-5027-6). 32pp. On the Night of the Three Kings holiday, the weather in New Mexico is so bad that Pepe and Sila worry that the kings will not be able to deliver their presents. (Rev: BL 9/15/98; HBG 3/99; SLJ 10/98)

6971 Smith, Cynthia Leitich, and Greg Leitich Smith. *Santa Knows* (K–3). Illus. by Steve Björkman. 2006, Dutton $16.99 (978-0-525-47757-0). Alfie F. Snorklepuss is convinced there's no Santa, so it's an eye-opening experience for this Santa-doubter when the man himself shows up to take Alfie on a trip to the North Pole. (Rev: SLJ 10/06)

6972 Soto, Gary. *Too Many Tamales* (PS–1). Illus. by Ed Martinez. 1993, Penguin $16.99 (978-0-399-22146-0). 32pp. A Hispanic child enthusiastically enters into the cooking and other rituals that surround her family's celebration of Christmas. (Rev: BCCB 10/93; BL 9/15/93; HB 11/93)

6973 Speirs, John. *The Little Boy's Christmas Gift* (PS–3). Illus. 2001, Abrams $16.95 (978-0-8109-4399-5). 32pp. A boy's gift to the Holy Family is a decorated tree in this lavishly illustrated picture book. (Rev: BL 10/15/01; HBG 3/02)

6974 Spirin, Gennady. *The Christmas Story: According to the Gospels of Matthew and Luke from the King James Bible* (1–6). Illus. 1998, Holt $19.95 (978-0-8050-5292-3). 32pp. A beautifully illustrated version of the Nativity that incorporates verses from the Gospels of Matthew and Luke from the King James version of the Bible. (Rev: BL 11/15/98; HBG 3/99; SLJ 10/98) [232.9]

6975 Spowart, Robin. *Inside, Outside Christmas* (PS). Illus. 1998, Holiday House $15.95 (978-0-8234-1370-6). 32pp. Using double-page spreads and short rhyming phrases, this picture book depicts inside and outside activities of a loving mouse family at Christmas. (Rev: BL 9/1/98; HBG 3/99; SLJ 10/98)

6976 Stevenson, James. *Christmas at Mud Flat* (1–3). Illus. 2000, HarperCollins LB $15.89 (978-0-688-17302-9). 48pp. It's a week before Christmas and everyone in Mud Flat is making hasty preparations for the big event. (Rev: BCCB 11/00; BL 9/1/00; HBG 3/01)

6977 Stoeke, Janet Morgan. *Minerva Louise on Christmas Eve* (PS–2). Illus. by author. 2007, Dutton $15.99 (978-0-525-47857-7). 32pp. Chicken Minerva Louise comes to her usual strange conclusions while following Santa down a chimney on Christmas Eve. (Rev: BL 9/15/07; HB 11/07)

6978 Sykes, Julie. *Hurry, Santa!* (PS–K). Illus. by Tim Warnes. 1998, Little Tiger $14.95 (978-1-888444-37-7). 32pp. Santa oversleeps and Christmas Eve becomes a big rush, rush, rush to get everything done in time. (Rev: BL 9/1/98; HBG 3/99; SLJ 10/98)

6979 Tafuri, Nancy. *The Donkey's Christmas Song* (PS). Illus. 2002, Scholastic $16.95 (978-0-439-27313-8). 32pp. A donkey is reluctant to add his braying to the manger lullaby. (Rev: BL 9/15/02; HBG 3/03; SLJ 10/02)

6980 Tews, Susan. *The Gingerbread Doll* (K–3). Illus. by Megan Lloyd. 1993, Clarion $16.00 (978-0-395-56438-7). 32pp. Starting as a poor youngster during the Great Depression when she gets a gingerbread doll, Rebecca finds that her Christmas presents change as her family gets more prosperous. (Rev: BL 9/1/93)

6981 Thayer, Jane. *The Puppy Who Wanted a Boy* (1–3). Illus. by Lisa McCue. 1986, Morrow paper $5.95 (978-0-688-08293-2). 48pp. Petey the puppy doesn't get a boy for Christmas as he wished, but he does find 50 boys in a Home for Boys to whom he can give his love. (Rev: BL 4/1/86; SLJ 5/86)

6982 Thompson, Kay. *Eloise at Christmastime* (PS–3). Illus. by Hilary Knight. 199, Simon & Schuster $17.50 (978-0-689-83039-6). A reissue of the book about the little girl who lives in the Plaza Hotel in New York City and her adventures at Christmas. (Rev: BL 11/15/99; HBG 3/00)

6983 Thomson, Pat. *Beware of the Aunts!* (PS–2). Illus. by Emma Chichester Clark. 1992, Macmillan $14.95 (978-0-689-50538-6). Nine unusual aunts and Christmas gift giving are the subjects of this humorous book. (Rev: SLJ 7/92)

6984 Trivas, Irene. *Emma's Christmas* (PS–4). Illus. 1988, Orchard paper $6.95 (978-0-531-07022-2). 32pp. When Emma, the farmer's daughter, declines the prince's offer of marriage, he begins to send her gifts. (Rev: BCCB 10/88; BL 9/15/88; HB 11/88)

6985 Tudor, Tasha. *Corgiville Christmas* (K–2). Illus. by author. 2003, Front St. $15.95 (978-1-932425-00-0). Corgiville, a 1920s New England village populated by corgis, cats, rabbits, and other animals, is buzzing with activity as its residents prepare for the Christmas holiday. (Rev: HBG 4/04; SLJ 10/03)

6986 Van Allsburg, Chris. *The Polar Express* (K–2). Illus. by author. 1985, Houghton $18.95 (978-0-395-38949-2). 32pp. Whisked aboard the Polar Express to the North Pole on Christmas Eve, a young boy gets to receive the first gift of Christmas. Caldecott Medal winner, 1986. (Rev: BCCB 10/85; BL 10/1/85; SLJ 10/85)

6987 Van Steenwyk, Elizabeth. *Prairie Christmas* (K–3). Illus. by Ronald Himler. 2006, Eerdmans $17.00 (978-0-8028-5280-9). 32pp. In 1880s Nebraska, 11-year-old Emma experiences a very special Christmas on a trip with her mother to deliver a new baby. (Rev: BL 9/15/06; SLJ 10/06)

6988 Wallner, Alexandra. *An Alcott Family Christmas* (K–2). Illus. 1996, Holiday House LB $15.95 (978-0-8234-1265-5). 30pp. A fictionalized account of how Louisa May Alcott's family might have observed Christmas as the March family did in *Little Women.* (Rev: BL 9/1/96)

6989 Walsh, Vivian, and J. Otto Seibold. *Olive, the Other Reindeer* (1–3). Illus. 1997, Chronicle $13.95 (978-0-8118-1807-0). 32pp. A little dog believes that she is really a reindeer and heads to the North Pole to give Santa a hand. (Rev: BL 10/15/97; HBG 3/98)

6990 Ward, Helen. *The Animals' Christmas Carol* (PS–3). Illus. 2001, Millbrook LB $24.90 (978-0-7613-2408-9). 40pp. A beautifully illustrated book based on the Christmas carol "The Friendly Beasts," in which animals bring gifts to baby Jesus in the manger. (Rev: BCCB 11/01; BL 9/15/01; HBG 3/02)

6991 Weigelt, Udo. *Little Donkey's Wish* (K–2). Trans. by Marianne Martens. Illus. by Pirkko Vainio. 2005, North-South $15.95 (978-0-7358-2031-9). A shy donkey gets her Christmas wish when Santa chooses her to fill in for one of his reindeer. (Rev: SLJ 10/05)

6992 Westerlund, Kate. *Sharing Christmas* (PS–2). Illus. by Eve Tharlet. 2007, Penguin $16.99 (978-0-698-40074-0). 32pp. A wish upon a star and the sound of bells lead the young deer Clara, her mother, and a variety of forest creatures to the farm for a joyous Christmas. (Rev: BL 9/15/07)

6993 Wild, Margaret. *Thank You, Santa* (PS–3). Illus. by Kerry Argent. 1992, Scholastic $12.95 (978-0-590-45805-4). 32pp. After Christmas, a young girl in Australia begins a correspondence with Santa Claus. (Rev: BCCB 11/92; BL 11/1/92)

6994 Willey, Margaret. *A Clever Beatrice Christmas* (PS–2). Illus. by Heather Solomon. 2006, Simon & Schuster $16.95 (978-0-689-87017-0). 40pp. To prove the existence of Père Noël to some skeptical friends, clever Beatrice promises to bring some irrefutable evidence, such as a clipping from his beard or a bell from his sleigh. (Rev: BL 10/15/06; SLJ 10/06)

6995 Wilson, Karma. *Mortimer's Christmas Manger* (PS–2). Illus. by Jane Chapman. 2005, Simon & Schuster $15.95 (978-0-689-85511-5). Tired of his home in a dark hole under the stairs, Mortimer the mouse takes up residence in a Nativity scene. (Rev: SLJ 10/05)

6996 Winthrop, Elizabeth. *Bear's Christmas Surprise* (PS–2). Illus. by Patience Brewster. 1991, Holiday House LB $14.95 (978-0-8234-0888-7). 32pp. While playing hide-and-seek, Bear accidentally discovers some Christmas presents hidden in a closet and opens them. (Rev: BL 9/15/91)

6997 Winthrop, Elizabeth. *The First Christmas Stocking* (2–4). Illus. by Bagram Ibatoulline. 2006, Random $15.95 (978-0-385-32804-3). 40pp. On Christmas Eve, Claire gives the stockings she's knitted to a poor boy on the street instead of to the rich customer who ordered them, and wakes up on Christmas morning to find a miracle of her own. (Rev: BL 11/15/06)

6998 Wolfe, Frances. *The Little Toy Shop* (PS–2). Illus. by author. 2008, Tundra $19.95 (978-0-88776-865-1). 32pp. When a little stuffed bunny is accidentally sold from the toy shop, it takes a Christmas miracle to restore him to good health and get him to his intended child. (Rev: BLO 10/7/08; SLJ 10/08)

6999 Wolff, Patricia Rae. *A New Improved Santa* (K–3). Illus. by Lynne W. Cravath. 2002, Scholastic $15.95 (978-0-439-35249-9). Santa spends the year on self-improvement — diet, exercise, new hairstyle — only to find the children prefer him the old way. (Rev: BCCB 11/02; HBG 3/03; SLJ 10/02)

7000 Wood, Audrey. *The Christmas Adventure of Space Elf Sam* (PS–3). Illus. by Bruce Robert Wood. 1998, Scholastic $15.95 (978-0-590-03143-1). 40pp. When families from Earth colonize outer space, Santa Claus needs help to perform his Christmas Eve duties. (Rev: BL 9/1/98; HBG 3/99; SLJ 10/98)

7001 Wood, Don, and Audrey Wood. *Merry Christmas, Big Hungry Bear!* (PS–2). Illus. 2002, Scholastic $16.99 (978-0-439-32092-4). 48pp. Little Mouse decides to share his Christmas with Big Hungry Bear, who never gets any presents. (Rev: BCCB 11/02; BL 9/15/02; HBG 3/03; SLJ 10/02)

7002 Wright, Cliff. *Santa's Ark* (K–3). Illus. 1997, Millbrook LB $23.90 (978-0-7613-0314-5). 36pp. Different animals from around the world stow away in Santa's sleigh when he makes his stops. (Rev: BL 12/15/97; HBG 3/98; SLJ 10/97)

7003 Yin. *Dear Santa, Please Come to the 19th Floor* (1–3). Illus. by Chris Soentpiet. 2002, Philomel $17.99 (978-0-399-23636-5). Willy asks Santa for a special present for his friend Carlos, who is in a wheelchair and living in poverty. (Rev: HBG 3/03; SLJ 10/02)

7004 Zagwyn, Deborah Turney. *The Winter Gift* (K–3). Illus. 2000, Tricycle $15.95 (978-1-883672-93-5). 32pp. Grandma is selling all her furniture before moving into an apartment, but she gives her piano to her grandchildren to continue the tradition of playing it at Christmas. (Rev: BL 9/1/00*; HBG 3/01)

7005 Ziefert, Harriet. *Home for Navidad* (PS–3). Illus. by Santiago Cohen. 2003, Houghton $15.00 (978-0-618-34976-0). Ten-year-old Rosa, who lives with her grandmother and uncle in Mexico, hopes her mother will finally make it back from New York to spend Christmas with them. (Rev: HB 9/03; HBG 4/04; SLJ 10/03)

EASTER

7006 Berlin, Irving. *Easter Parade* (PS–1). Illus. by Lisa McCue. 2003, HarperCollins LB $16.89 (978-0-06-029126-6). 32pp. Father Rabbit and his behatted young daughter parade down the street with all the other finely dressed animals in this cheerful rendition of the famous Irving Berlin song. (Rev: BL 3/15/03; HBG 4/04; SLJ 2/03) [782.42164]

7007 Bishop, Adela. *The Easter Wolf* (PS–2). Illus. by Carole Dzapla. 1991, Dot $12.95 (978-0-9625620-1-3). 28pp. When he is saved from drowning by the Easter Rabbit, a hungry wolf reforms. (Rev: BL 3/15/91)

7008 Bostrom, Kathleen Long. *Sunrise Hill: An Easter Story of Faith, Inspiration, and Courage* (K–3). Illus. by Rick Johnson. 2004, Zondervan $14.99 (978-0-310-70508-6). 32pp. Despite the loss of their church, the people of a 19th-century farming community celebrate a special Easter service on Sunrise Hill, affirming their faith in rebirth. (Rev: BL 3/1/04)

7009 deGroat, Diane. *Last One in Is a Rotten Egg!* (PS–2). Illus. by author. Series: Gilbert. 2007, HarperCollins $15.99 (978-0-06-089294-4). A much-anticipated visit from their cousin turns out to be far less fun than expected for Gilbert the opossum and his sister. (Rev: BL 1/1–15/07; SLJ 2/07)

7010 Elschner, Géraldine. *The Easter Chick* (PS–2). Trans. by Marianne Martens. Illus. by Alexandra Junge. 2004, North-South $15.95 (978-0-7358-1855-2). 32pp. The fact that Easter is a movable feast is underlined in this story in which an owl helps a mother hen to schedule the hatching of her chick. (Rev: BL 3/1/04; SLJ 5/04)

7011 Engelbreit, Mary. *Queen of Easter* (PS–K). Illus. by author. Series: Ann Estelle Stories. 2006, HarperCollins $15.99 (978-0-06-008184-3). Disappointed with the plain straw hat she is given for the Easter parade, Ann Estelle leaves it outside, where robins adopt it as a nest; Ann Estelle enjoys redecorating last year's hat and the new family in this year's. (Rev: SLJ 2/06)

7012 Friedrich, Priscilla, and Otto Friedrich. *The Easter Bunny That Overslept* (PS–2). Illus. by Donald Saaf. 2002, HarperCollins LB $17.89 (978-0-06-029646-9). 32pp. In this bright new version of a 1950s classic, the Easter Bunny oversleeps and discovers that no one wants Easter eggs on the Fourth of July or Halloween. (Rev: BL 2/15/02; HBG 10/02; SLJ 1/02)

7013 Gibbons, Gail. *Easter* (PS–2). Illus. by author. 1989, Holiday House LB $17.95 (978-0-8234-0737-8); paper $6.95 (978-0-8234-0866-5). 32pp. Biblical, pagan, and modern aspects of the holiday are described. (Rev: BL 4/1/89; SLJ 3/89)

7014 Heyward, DuBose. *The Country Bunny and the Little Gold Shoes* (K–3). Illus. by Marjorie Flack. 1939, Houghton $15.00 (978-0-395-15990-3); paper $6.95 (978-0-395-18557-5). 48pp. Cottontail, the mother of 21 bunnies, finally realizes her great ambition to be an Easter Bunny.

7015 Houselander, Caryll. *Petook: An Easter Story* (K–3). Illus. by Tomie dePaola. 1988, Holiday

House LB $16.95 (978-0-8234-0681-4). 32pp. The rooster, Petook, and a simple story of Easter. (Rev: BL 4/15/88; SLJ 5/88)

7016 Nerlove, Miriam. *Easter* (PS–1). Illus. 1989, Whitman paper $4.95 (978-0-8075-1872-4). 24pp. This major religious holiday is described in rhyming text. (Rev: BL 1/15/90; SLJ 4/90)

7017 Polacco, Patricia. *Chicken Sunday* (PS–3). Illus. 1992, Penguin $16.99 (978-0-399-22133-0). 32pp. Three youngsters of different races and religions unite to help Miss Eula have a good Easter. (Rev: BCCB 7–8/92; BL 3/15/92*; SLJ 5/92*)

7018 Stoeke, Janet Morgan. *Minerva Louise and the Colorful Eggs* (PS–2). 2006, Dutton $15.99 (978-0-525-47633-7). It's spring, but Minerva Louise the chicken doesn't know what to make of the brightly colored eggs she discovers hidden in odd places around the farmyard. (Rev: BL 2/1/06; SLJ 2/06)

7019 Tegen, Katherine. *The Story of the Easter Bunny* (PS–1). Illus. by Sally Anne Lambert. 2005, HarperCollins LB $14.89 (978-0-06-050712-1). 40pp. A pet white rabbit takes over the Easter preparations — basket weaving, candy making, and egg coloring — when the elderly couple who own him become too old to continue. (Rev: BL 2/1/05; SLJ 2/05)

7020 Wells, Rosemary. *Max Counts His Chickens* (PS–K). Illus. 2007, Viking $15.99 (978-0-670-06222-5). 32pp. Combining a counting lesson with Max and Ruby's familiar sibling tussles, this charming tale features a marshmallow chick hunt and a special delivery from the Easter bunny. (Rev: BL 1/1–15/07)

7021 Zolotow, Charlotte. *The Bunny Who Found Easter* (PS–2). Illus. by Helen Craig. 1998, Houghton $16.00 (978-0-395-86265-0). 32pp. A new edition of the story about a bunny who wanders through a year searching for Easter so he can enjoy the company of other bunnies. The 1959 edition is illustrated by Betty Peterson. (Rev: BL 3/1/98; HBG 3/99; SLJ 9/98)

HALLOWEEN

7022 Atwell, Debby. *The Warthog's Tail* (K–3). 2005, Houghton $16.00 (978-0-618-50781-8). 32pp. When a young witch is unable to conjure up a spell powerful enough to remove a sleeping warthog from her path, she decides instead to try her powers of persuasion. (Rev: BL 10/1/05; SLJ 11/05)

7023 Bauer, Marion Dane. *I'm Not Afraid of Halloween! A Pop-up and Flap Book* (PS–K). Illus. by Rusty Fletcher. 2006, Simon & Schuster $7.99 (978-0-689-85050-9). This colorful pop-up book, which includes lift-the-flap features, showcases a host of costumed trick-or-treaters who come calling at a young vampire's door on Halloween night. (Rev: SLJ 9/06)

7024 Behn, Harry. *Halloween* (2–3). 2003, Cheshire Studio Bks. $15.95 (978-0-7358-1609-1). 32pp. Three children costumed as a devil, skeleton, and witch find trick-or-treating can become very spooky as the evening progresses. (Rev: BL 9/1/03; HBG 4/04; SLJ 8/03)

7025 Bollinger, Peter. *Algernon Graeves Is Scary Enough* (K–2). Illus. by author. 2005, HarperCollins LB $15.89 (978-0-06-052269-8). Algernon can't decide between spooky costumes for Halloween and decides to combine them all. (Rev: SLJ 8/05)

7026 Bridwell, Norman. *Clifford's Halloween* (PS–1). Illus. by author. 1970, Scholastic paper $3.99 (978-0-590-44287-9). 32pp. Halloween adventures of a big red dog.

7027 Broyles, Anne. *Shy Mama's Halloween* (2–4). Illus. by Leane Morin. 2000, Tilbury House $16.95 (978-0-88448-218-5). 40pp. Recently arrived from Russia, Anya and her siblings are taken out on Halloween by their mother and suddenly feel more at home in their new country. (Rev: BL 11/15/00; HBG 3/01; SLJ 1/01)

7028 Bullard, Lisa. *Trick-or-Treat on Milton Street* (K–2). Illus. by Joni Oeltjenbruns. 2001, Carolrhoda LB $15.95 (978-1-57505-158-1). Charley gets a big surprise on Halloween that makes him look at his new neighborhood in quite a different way. (Rev: HBG 3/02; SLJ 9/01)

7029 Bunting, Eve. *Scary, Scary Halloween* (PS–1). Illus. by Jan Brett. 1986, Houghton $16.00 (978-0-89919-414-1); paper $6.95 (978-0-89919-799-9). 32pp. A scary poem tells of a parade of creatures on Halloween night. (Rev: BCCB 9/86; BL 9/1/86; HB 11/86)

7030 Carlson, Nancy. *Harriet's Halloween Candy* (PS–K). Illus. by author. 1982, Carolrhoda LB $15.95 (978-0-87614-182-3); Lerner paper $4.95 (978-0-87614-850-1). 32pp. A childlike dog overeats on Halloween candy.

7031 Caseley, Judith. *Witch Mama* (PS–2). Illus. 1996, Greenwillow LB $14.93 (978-0-688-14458-6). 32pp. On Halloween, Mama becomes Witch Mama, but she still cares for her two children. (Rev: BL 9/1/96; SLJ 8/96)

7032 Cazet, Denys. *Minnie and Moo: The Night of the Living Bed* (1–2). Illus. by author. Series: I Can Read Book. 2003, HarperCollins LB $16.99 (978-0-06-000503-0). 48pp. It's Halloween, and cows Minnie and Moo team up to collect as much chocolate as possible in this book for beginning readers. (Rev: BL 9/1/03; HBG 4/04; SLJ 9/03)

7033 Cazet, Denys. *The Perfect Pumpkin Pie* (PS–2). Illus. 2005, Simon & Schuster $15.95 (978-0-689-86467-4). 32pp. In this lively Halloween tale, a boy and his grandmother are visited by a ghost who's searching for some pumpkin pie. (Rev: BL 10/15/05; SLJ 10/05)

7034 Choi, Yangsook. *Behind the Mask* (K–3). Illus. 2006, Farrar $16.00 (978-0-374-30522-2). 40pp. A young Korean American boy, still grieving over his grandfather's death, gains cachet among his classmates when he wears his grandfather's scary mask dance costume for Halloween. (Rev: BL 10/15/06; SLJ 12/06)

7035 Crimi, Carolyn. *Boris and Bella* (K–2). Illus. by Gris Grimly. 2004, Harcourt $15.00 (978-0-15-202528-1). 32pp. Messy monster Bella Lagrossi and her fastidious neighbor Boris Kleanitoff find they have something in common in this entertaining Halloween tale full of wordplay. (Rev: BL 1/1–15/05; SLJ 9/04)

7036 Cushman, Doug. *Aunt Eater's Mystery Halloween* (1–2). Illus. Series: I Can Read. 1998, HarperCollins LB $14.89 (978-0-06-027804-5). 64pp. Four short mysteries about Halloween are solved by Aunt Eater, the anteater who dresses like Sherlock Holmes. (Rev: BL 9/1/98; HBG 3/99; SLJ 10/98)

7037 Cuyler, Margery. *The Bumpy Little Pumpkin* (PS–2). Illus. by Will Hillenbrand. 2005, Scholastic $15.95 (978-0-439-52835-1). 32pp. Her older siblings scoff when Little Nell (first seen in *The Biggest, Best Snowman*, published in 1998) selects an ugly little pumpkin at harvest time, but the girl manages to transform the gourd into a nice-looking jack-o'-lantern with the help of a few animal friends. (Rev: BL 9/1/05; SLJ 8/05)

7038 deGroat, Diane. *Trick or Treat, Smell My Feet* (PS–3). Illus. Series: Gilbert. 1998, Morrow LB $14.89 (978-0-688-15767-8). 32pp. Gilbert takes his sister's Halloween costume to the school parade instead of his own by mistake and finds that he has to dress as a ballerina instead of a Martian space pilot. (Rev: BL 9/1/98; HBG 3/99; SLJ 10/98)

7039 Desimini, Lisa. *Trick-or-Treat, Smell My Feet!* (PS–2). Illus. 2005, Scholastic $16.95 (978-0-439-23323-1). 40pp. Delia and Ophelia, twin witches, cast a spell over the neighborhood trick-or-treaters. (Rev: BL 9/15/05; SLJ 8/05)

7040 Druce, Arden. *Halloween Night* (PS–K). Illus. by David Wenzel. 2001, Rising Moon $14.95 (978-0-87358-797-6); paper $6.95 (978-0-87358-762-4). 32pp. Rhyming riddles about a spooky Halloween night are accompanied by illustrations that suit the mood and contain clues. (Rev: BCCB 9/01; BL 9/1/01; HBG 3/02; SLJ 9/01)

7041 Egan, Tim. *The Experiments of Doctor Vermin* (K–3). Illus. 2002, Houghton $15.00 (978-0-618-13224-9). 32pp. Sheldon the pig stumbles into Dr. Vermin's spooky mansion on Halloween night, but finds refuge with the wolves next door in this amusing story. (Rev: BL 9/1/02; HBG 3/03; SLJ 10/02)

7042 *Five Little Pumpkins* (PS). Illus. by Dan Yaccarino. 1998, HarperCollins $5.99 (978-0-694-01177-3). 16pp. A board book that illustrates the old rhyme about five little pumpkins sitting on a gate. (Rev: BL 12/15/98; HBG 3/99; SLJ 2/99)

7043 Fleming, Denise. *Pumpkin Eye* (1–3). Illus. 2001, Holt $15.95 (978-0-8050-6681-4). 32pp. Lightly scary Halloween excitement is captured in rhyming text and inventive artwork. (Rev: BCCB 10/01; BL 9/15/01; HBG 3/02; SLJ 9/01)

7044 Friedman, Laurie. *I'm Not Afraid of This Haunted House* (K–2). Illus. by Teresa Murfin. 2005, Carolrhoda $15.95 (978-1-57505-751-4). 32pp. In this spine-tingling Halloween tale, told in rhyming couplets, young Simon Lester Henry Strauss takes friends on a tour of a haunted house. (Rev: BL 9/1/05; SLJ 9/05)

7045 Grambling, Lois G. *T. Rex Trick-or-Treats* (K–2). Illus. by Jack E. Davis. 2005, HarperCollins $12.99 (978-0-06-050252-2). 32pp. T. Rex can't

decide what he wants to wear when he goes trick-or-treating. (Rev: BL 9/1/05; SLJ 8/05)

7046 Hall, Zoe. *It's Pumpkin Time!* (K–3). Illus. by Shari Halpern. 1994, Scholastic $13.95 (978-0-590-47833-5). This picture book describes how two children plant a pumpkin seed and care for it so that it will be useful at Halloween. (Rev: SLJ 11/94)

7047 Hatch, Elizabeth. *Halloween Night* (PS–1). Illus. by Jimmy Pickering. 2005, Doubleday $15.95 (978-0-385-74622-9). A cumulative, mildly scary story in which a timid little mouse winds up with the treats. (Rev: SLJ 8/05)

7048 Hautzig, Deborah. *Little Witch's Big Night* (1–2). Illus. by Marc Brown. 1984, Random paper $3.99 (978-0-394-86587-4). 48pp. Little Witch has a better Halloween than she expected.

7049 Hennessy, B. G. *Corduroy's Halloween: A Lift-the-Flap Book* (PS–K). Illus. by Lisa McCue. 1995, Viking $11.99 (978-0-670-86193-4). Flaps that lift add surprise to this story of how a little bear spends his Halloween. (Rev: SLJ 10/95)

7050 Holub, Joan. *Boo Who? A Spooky Lift-the-Flap Book* (PS–1). Illus. by author. Series: Spooky Lift-the-Flap Book. 1997, Scholastic $6.95 (978-0-590-05905-3). Rhymes and flaps are used to introduce the objects and creatures associated with Halloween. (Rev: SLJ 10/97)

7051 Horowitz, Dave. *The Ugly Pumpkin* (K–2). Illus. by author. 2005, Putnam $16.99 (978-0-399-24267-0). A misshapen pumpkin feels out of place as Halloween nears. (Rev: SLJ 8/05)

7052 Hubbard, Patricia. *Trick or Treat Countdown* (PS). Illus. by Michael Letzig. 1999, Holiday House $16.95 (978-0-8234-1367-6). A simple counting rhyme goes from one to 12 and back again, using Halloween symbols and general spookiness. (Rev: BCCB 10/99; BL 9/1/99; HBG 3/00; SLJ 9/99)

7053 Hubbell, Patricia. *Boo! Halloween Poems and Limericks* (K–4). Illus. by Jeff Spackman. 1998, Marshall Cavendish $15.95 (978-0-7614-5023-8). 32pp. Witty original poems and limericks about Halloween are presented with suitably lurid illustrations. (Rev: BL 9/1/98; HBG 3/99; SLJ 9/98) [811]

7054 Hulme, Joy N. *Eerie Feary Feeling: A Hairy Scary Pop-Up Book* (K–2). Illus. by Paul Ely. 1998, Orchard $13.95 (978-0-531-30086-2). Cats, bats, witches, ghosts, and ghouls are all featured in this interactive pop-up book. (Rev: SLJ 12/98)

7055 Hutchins, Pat. *Which Witch Is Which?* (PS–K). Illus. 1989, Greenwillow $17.89 (978-0-688-06358-0). 24pp. Identical twins dress as witches on Halloween. (Rev: BL 9/1/89; SLJ 8/89*)

7056 Johnston, Tony. *The Vanishing Pumpkin* (PS–2). Illus. by Tomie dePaola. 1996, Penguin paper $6.99 (978-0-698-11414-2). 32pp. An old man and an old woman set out on Halloween to find their pumpkin.

7057 Johnston, Tony. *Very Scary* (PS–K). Illus. by Douglas Florian. 1995, Harcourt $13.00 (978-0-15-293625-9). 32pp. When a girl carves a pumpkin into a jack-o'-lantern, it shouts "Boo" and frightens everyone. (Rev: BL 9/15/95; SLJ 11/95)

7058 Keats, Ezra Jack. *The Trip* (1–3). Illus. by author. 1978, Greenwillow $16.89 (978-0-688-84123-2); Morrow paper $5.99 (978-0-688-07328-2). 32pp. Halloween proves to be a time when Louis isn't lonely anymore.

7059 Kimball, Linda Hoffman. *Come with Me on Halloween* (PS–1). Illus. by Mike Reed. 2005, Albert Whitman $16.95 (978-0-8075-3132-7). The father-son relationship is reversed as the two meet fearsome characters while trick-or-treating. (Rev: SLJ 10/05)

7060 Kovalski, Maryann. *Omar's Halloween* (PS–K). 2006, Fitzhenry & Whiteside $16.95 (978-1-55041-559-9). 32pp. As Halloween nears, Omar the bear has terrible trouble with costume selection, but on the day his ghost outfit finally comes into its own. (Rev: BL 9/1/06; SLJ 9/06)

7061 Kraus, Robert. *How Spider Saved Halloween* (K–3). Illus. by author. 1988, Scholastic paper $2.99 (978-0-590-42117-1). 32pp. Spider saves the fun of Halloween by creating an ingenious disguise.

7062 Krieb, Mr. *We're Off to Find the Witch's House* (PS–2). Illus. by R. W. Alley. 2005, Dutton $14.99 (978-0-525-47003-8). 32pp. In this fun-filled Halloween tale told in rhyming text, four trick-or-treaters encounter all sorts of frightening ghosts and ghouls when they set off in search of a witch's house. (Rev: BL 9/15/05; SLJ 8/05)

7063 Kroll, Steven. *The Biggest Pumpkin Ever* (PS–2). Illus. by Jeni Bassett. 1984, Holiday House LB $17.95 (978-0-8234-0505-3); Scholastic paper $2.50 (978-0-590-41113-4). 32pp. Two mice hope to grow the largest pumpkin ever for Halloween.

7064 Lattimore, Deborah N. *Cinderhazel: The Cinderella of Halloween* (PS–2). Illus. 1997, Scholastic $15.95 (978-0-590-20232-9). 32pp. A parody on the famous fairy tale, with a feminist twist and a Halloween setting. (Rev: BL 9/1/97; HBG 3/98; SLJ 10/97)

7065 Leedy, Loreen. *The Dragon Halloween Party* (PS–2). Illus. by author. 1986, Holiday House paper $5.95 (978-0-8234-0765-1). 32pp. Ten children and their mother Ma Dragon get ready for their Halloween party, in short rhyming verse. (Rev: BL 9/15/86; SLJ 12/86)

7066 Leedy, Loreen. *2 x 2=Boo! A Set of Spooky Multiplication Stories* (1–4). Illus. 1995, Holiday House LB $17.95 (978-0-8234-1190-0). 32pp. Halloween creatures and objects are used in a series of scary stories to demonstrate the principles of multiplication. (Rev: BL 9/15/95; SLJ 11/95)

7067 Lewis, Kevin. *The Runaway Pumpkin* (PS–2). Illus. by S. D. Schindler. 2003, Scholastic $15.95 (978-0-439-43974-9). A giant pumpkin on the rampage is finally brought under control in this Halloween story with a repetitive chorus. (Rev: HBG 4/04; SLJ 10/03)

7068 McGhee, Alison. *Only a Witch Can Fly* (K–2). Illus. by Taeeun Yoo. 2009, Feiwel & Friends $16.99 (978-0-312-37503-4). 32pp. On Halloween, a young witch finally masters her broom. (Rev: BL 5/1/09; HB 9/09)

7069 McGhee, Alison. *A Very Brave Witch* (K–2). Illus. by Harry Bliss. 2006, Simon & Schuster $12.95 (978-0-689-86730-9). On Halloween night, a young witch has an eye-opening encounter with some colorfully costumed trick-or-treaters. (Rev: SLJ 8/06)

7070 McGrath, Barbara Barbieri. *The Little Green Witch* (K–2). Illus. by Martha Alexander. 2005, Charlesbridge $14.95 (978-1-58089-042-7). In a Halloween twist on "The Little Red Hen," a little witch grows a pumpkin and no one wants to help her until it's time to eat pumpkin pie. (Rev: SLJ 8/05)

7071 Mayr, Diane. *Littlebat's Halloween Story* (PS–1). Illus. by Gideon Kendall. 2001, Whitman $16.99 (978-0-8075-7629-8). 32pp. Littlebat loves story time but his mother tells him he must remain hidden until he can make an appearance without scaring the children. (Rev: BL 9/1/01; HBG 3/02; SLJ 9/01)

7072 Meddaugh, Susan. *The Witches' Supermarket* (PS–3). Illus. 1991, Houghton $16.00 (978-0-395-57034-0). 32pp. On Halloween, Helen finds herself in a strange supermarket offering such goodies as scum milk and bug bars. (Rev: BCCB 9/91; BL 8/91; SLJ 11/91)

7073 Mills, Claudia. *Gus and Grandpa and the Halloween Costume* (2–3). Illus. by Catherine Stock. Series: Gus and Grandpa. 2002, Farrar $15.00 (978-0-374-32816-0). 48pp. It's Grandpa who solves Gus's Halloween costume crisis, producing a Mounties uniform that Gus's father wore when he was a boy. (Rev: BL 9/1/02; HBG 3/03)

7074 Mitton, Tony. *Spooky Hour* (PS–2). Illus. by Guy Parker-Rees. 2004, Scholastic $16.95 (978-0-439-60373-7). A bouncy Halloween book featuring witches, ghosts, skeletons, and other characters on their way to a great feast. (Rev: SLJ 8/04)

7075 Montes, Marisa. *Los Gatos Black on Halloween* (K–2). Illus. by Yuri Morales. 2006, Holt $16.95 (978-0-8050-7429-1). 32pp. There's a Monster's Ball at Haunted Hall and a rhythmic English/Spanish text describes the antics of los gatos, los muertos, las brujas, and their friends, all enjoying themselves until the arrival of the scary trick-or-treaters. (Rev: BL 8/06)

7076 Neitzel, Shirley. *Who Will I Be? A Halloween Rebus Story* (PS–2). Illus. by Nancy W. Parker. 2005, Greenwillow LB $13.89 (978-0-06-056068-3). 32pp. In this engaging rebus tale, a young girl tries to decide what sort of costume to wear for Halloween. (Rev: BL 8/05; SLJ 9/05)

7077 Nikola-Lisa, W. *Shake Dem Halloween Bones* (PS–2). Illus. by Mike Reed. 1997, Houghton $16.00 (978-0-395-73095-9). 32pp. Fairy tale characters shake, rattle, and roll at a super Halloween party. (Rev: BL 10/1/97; HBG 3/98)

7078 Parish, Herman. *Happy Haunting, Amelia Bedelia* (K–2). Illus. by Lynn Sweat. Series: Amelia Bedelia. 2004, Greenwillow LB $16.89 (978-0-06-051894-3). 64pp. Amelia Bedelia is supposed to be helping Mr. and Mrs. Rogers with their Halloween party. (Rev: SLJ 8/04)

7079 Passen, Lisa. *Attack of the 50-Foot Teacher* (K–3). Illus. 2000, Holt $16.00 (978-0-8050-6100-0). 32pp. Miss Birmbaum assigns homework on Halloween but, after an encounter with space aliens and a visit with her principal, she realizes that nobody gives homework on a holiday like this. (Rev: BL 11/15/00; HBG 3/01; SLJ 12/00)

7080 Pilkey, Dav. *The Hallo-Wiener* (PS–2). Illus. 1995, Scholastic $16.95 (978-0-590-41703-7). 32pp. At Halloween, Oscar the dachshund earns a change in his nickname from Wiener Dog to Hero Sandwich. (Rev: BCCB 10/95; BL 9/15/95; SLJ 10/95*)

7081 Polacco, Patricia. *Picnic at Mudsock Meadow* (K–3). Illus. 1992, Penguin $16.99 (978-0-399-21811-8). 32pp. During the Halloween festivities, William is a failure until he has courage enough to investigate a scary swamp. (Rev: BL 11/15/92; HB 11/92; SLJ 10/92)

7082 Poydar, Nancy. *The Perfectly Horrible Halloween* (PS–3). Illus. 2001, Holiday House $16.95 (978-0-8234-1592-2). 32pp. Arnold successfully improvises for the Halloween contest after forgetting his costume. (Rev: BL 9/1/01; HBG 3/02; SLJ 9/01)

7083 Reiner, Carl. *Tell Me a Scary Story . . . But Not Too Scary!* (PS–2). Illus. by James Bennett. 2003, Little, Brown $18.95 (978-0-316-83329-5). In this suspenseful Halloween tale, a curious boy finds more than he bargained for when he goes exploring in the basement of a mysterious neighbor. (Rev: HBG 4/04; SLJ 10/03)

7084 Roberts, Bethany. *Halloween Mice!* (PS–1). Illus. by Doug Cushman. 1995, Clarion $13.00 (978-0-395-67064-4). 32pp. At Halloween, a group of mice turn the tables and frighten a cat. (Rev: BL 9/15/95; SLJ 9/95)

7085 Rosenberry, Vera. *Vera's Halloween* (K–2). Illus. by author. 2008, Holt $16.95 (978-0-8050-8144-2). 32pp. Vera's Halloween starts out well with her toilet-paper mummy costume, but when she stops to adjust a bandage she finds herself alone. (Rev: BL 9/1/08)

7086 Ross, Eileen. *The Halloween Showdown* (K–2). Illus. by Lynn Rowe Reed. 1999, Holiday House $15.95 (978-0-8234-1395-9). At Halloween, Grandmother Katt enlists the help of her animal friends to save a kitty that has been stolen by a witch named Grizzorka. (Rev: BCCB 10/99; HBG 3/00; SLJ 9/99)

7087 Roy, Ron. *The Bald Bandit* (2–4). Illus. by John S. Gurney. Series: A to Z Mysteries. 1997, Random LB $11.99 (978-0-679-98449-8); paper $3.99 (978-0-679-88449-1). 70pp. A short Halloween story about three youngsters who are trying to find a videotape of a bank robbery. (Rev: HBG 3/98; SLJ 1/98)

7088 Ruelle, Karen Gray. *Spookier Than a Ghost* (1–2). Illus. 2001, Holiday House $14.95 (978-0-8234-1667-7). 32pp. Kitten Emily's Halloween costume doesn't turn out quite as she had hoped, but she and brother Harry still have fun trick-or-treating

in this easy reader. (Rev: BL 9/15/01; HBG 3/02; SLJ 9/01)

7089 Rylant, Cynthia. *Moonlight: The Halloween Cat* (PS–K). Illus. by Melissa Sweet. 2003, HarperCollins LB $17.89 (978-0-06-029712-1). Moonlight the black cat serves as tour guide for this nonspooky celebration of Halloween. (Rev: HBG 4/04; SLJ 9/03)

7090 Shaw, Nancy. *Sheep Trick or Treat* (PS–1). Illus. by Margot Apple. 1997, Houghton $14.00 (978-0-395-84168-6). 32pp. Sheep in costumes go trick-or-treating at Halloween and have unexpected adventures. (Rev: BL 9/1/97; HB 9/97; HBG 3/98; SLJ 9/97)

7091 Smalls, Irene. *Jenny Reen and the Jack Muh Lantern* (PS–3). Illus. by Keinyo White. 1996, Simon & Schuster $16.00 (978-0-689-31875-7). 32pp. Jenny Reen, a slave child, is frightened by a wild creature she sees in the woods in this Halloween tale. (Rev: BCCB 12/96; BL 9/1/96; SLJ 12/96)

7092 Spirn, Michele. *A Know-Nothing Halloween* (1–2). Illus. Series: I Can Read. 2000, HarperCollins LB $15.99 (978-0-06-028186-1). 48pp. Four friends and a dog named Floris learn some Halloween tricks and scare themselves in this book for beginning readers. (Rev: BL 9/1/00)

7093 Spurr, Elizabeth. *Halloween Sky Ride* (PS–3). Illus. by Ethan Long. 2005, Holiday House $16.95 (978-0-8234-1870-1). A not-too-scary witch takes too many friends on a broom ride to a Halloween party. (Rev: SLJ 8/05)

7094 Spurr, Elizabeth. *Pumpkin Hill* (PS–2). Illus. by Whitney Martin. 2006, Holiday House $16.95 (978-0-8234-1869-5). There's an orange avalanche in this rollicking Halloween tale as hundreds of plump pumpkins roll down a hill into town, causing confusion at first but paving the way for festive holiday decorations. (Rev: SLJ 10/06)

7095 Thompson, Lauren. *Mouse's First Halloween* (PS–K). Illus. by Buket Erdogan. 2000, Simon & Schuster $12.95 (978-0-689-83176-8). 32pp. On his first Halloween, Mouse has a few scary adventures. (Rev: BL 9/1/00; HBG 3/01; SLJ 8/00)

7096 Updike, David. *An Autumn Tale* (2–4). Illus. by Robert Andrew Parker. 1988, Pippin $15.95 (978-0-945912-02-6). 40pp. A magical Halloween tale of young Homer and his dog Sophocles. (Rev: BCCB 5/89; BL 10/15/88; SLJ 11/88)

7097 Vaughan, Marcia. *We're Going on a Ghost Hunt* (PS–3). Illus. by Ann Schweninger. 2001, Harcourt $15.00 (978-0-15-202353-9). 32pp. A lighthearted rhyming Halloween story of two children who go out hunting for a ghost, only to become frightened and run home. (Rev: BL 9/15/01; HBG 3/02; SLJ 9/01)

7098 Walton, Rick. *Mrs. McMurphy's Pumpkin* (PS–3). Illus. by Delana Bettoli. 2004, HarperCollins $8.99 (978-0-06-053409-7). An uppity pumpkin challenges an unafraid Mrs. Murphy. (Rev: SLJ 8/04)

7099 West, Kipling. *A Rattle of Bones: A Halloween Book of Collective Nouns* (K–2). Illus. 1999,

Orchard $15.95 (978-0-531-30196-8). 32pp. In a series of rhyming couplets, collective nouns are effectively introduced to describe groups of creatures associated with Halloween, such as a cloud of bats, a venom of spiders, and a wake of vultures. (Rev: BL 9/1/99; HBG 3/00; SLJ 9/99)

7100 Weston, Martha. *Tuck's Haunted House* (PS–2). Illus. 2002, Clarion $14.00 (978-0-618-15966-6). 32pp. Tuck the pig stages a haunted house for his friends, and his little sister Bunny adds to the scariness of Halloween. (Rev: BL 9/1/02; HBG 3/03; SLJ 10/02)

7101 Winters, Kay. *The Teeny Tiny Ghost* (PS–1). Illus. by Lynn Munsinger. 1997, HarperCollins LB $14.89 (978-0-06-025684-5). 32pp. A tiny ghost passes the test of not being frightened on Halloween. (Rev: BL 9/1/97; HBG 3/98; SLJ 11/97)

7102 Winters, Kay. *Whooo's Haunting the Teeny Tiny Ghost?* (PS–1). Illus. by Lynn Munsinger. 1999, HarperCollins $14.95 (978-0-06-027358-3). 32pp. The teeny tiny ghost finds that someone is haunting his house and later discovers that it is his cousin practicing his haunting techniques. (Rev: BL 9/1/99; HBG 3/00; SLJ 9/99)

7103 Ziefert, Harriet. *On Halloween Night* (PS–2). Illus. by Renée Andriani. 2001, Puffin paper $5.99 (978-0-14-056820-2). Emily's costume grows in "The House That Jack Built" fashion as her whole family pitches in to help. (Rev: SLJ 9/01)

JEWISH HOLY DAYS

7104 Adler, Tzivia. *The Sefer Torah Parade* (PS). Illus. by Ito Esther Perez. 2005, Hachai $11.95 (978-1-929628-26-1). A Jewish girl describes the festivities as a new Torah is brought into her family's temple. (Rev: HBG 4/06; SLJ 9/05)

7105 Biers-Ariel, Matt. *Solomon and the Trees* (K–3). Illus. by Esti Silverberg-Kiss. 2001, UAHC $13.95 (978-0-8074-0749-3). 32pp. King Solomon rues the day that he inadvertently allowed his forest to be cut down to build the Temple, in the legend said to have inspired the Jewish holiday of Tu Bish'vat. (Rev: BL 8/01)

7106 Carter, David A. *Chanukah Bugs: A Pop-Up Celebration* (PS–K). Illus. by author. 2002, Simon & Schuster $10.95 (978-0-689-81860-8). Flaps that resemble gift boxes open to reveal the "Shammash Bug," the "Dizzy Dreidel Bug," and so forth, one for each of the eight nights. (Rev: SLJ 10/02)

7107 Cleary, Brian P. *Eight Wild Nights: A Family Hanukkah Tale* (K–3). Illus. by David Udovic. 2006, Lerner LB $16.95 (978-1-58013-152-0). The members of an extended and rambunctious family gather for Festival of Lights. (Rev: SLJ 10/06)

7108 Cohen, Barbara. *Here Come the Purim Players!* (K–3). Illus. by Shoshana Mekibel. 1998, UAHC $13.95 (978-0-8074-0645-8). In medieval Prague, the Jews in the ghetto celebrate Purim at the rabbi's house with a performance of the story of Esther. (Rev: SLJ 6/98)

7109 Da Costa, Deborah. *Hanukkah Moon* (K–3). Illus. by Gosia Mosz. 2007, Kar-Ben $17.95 (978-1-58013-244-2); paper $7.95 (978-1-58013-245-9).

32pp. Isobel spends Hanukkah with her Aunt Luisa and learns that the holiday can be celebrated in various different ways. (Rev: BCCB 10/07; BL 9/15/07)

7110 Gelman, Rita G. *Queen Esther Saves Her People* (K–3). Illus. by Frane Lessac. 1998, Scholastic $15.95 (978-0-590-47025-4). 40pp. A personalized account of the Jewish girl Esther and how she saved her people at the court of the Persian king. (Rev: BCCB 3/98; BL 3/1/98; HBG 10/98; SLJ 2/98) [222]

7111 Gold-Vukson, Marji. *The Colors of My Jewish Year* (PS). Illus. by Madeline Wikler. 1998, Kar-Ben $4.95 (978-1-58013-011-0). This concept book introduces the colors of the rainbow (plus a few others) while describing the Jewish holidays associated with each. (Rev: SLJ 11/98)

7112 Goldin, Barbara D. *The World's Birthday: A Rosh Hashanah Story* (PS–3). Illus. by Jeanette Winter. 1990, Harcourt $13.95 (978-0-15-299648-2). 32pp. On Rosh Hashanah, the celebration of the birth of the world, Daniel wants to invite the world over to its birthday party. (Rev: BL 9/1/90; HB 11/90; SLJ 2/91)

7113 Groner, Judye, and Madeline Wikler. *All About Hanukkah: In Story and Song*. Rev. ed. (K–3). Illus. by Kinny Kreiswirth. 1999, Kar-Ben paper $12.95 (978-1-58013-057-8). 32pp. This story on the origins of Hanukkah tells of struggles of the Jewish people of 2000 years ago to regain their religious freedom by opposing the power of a Syrian king. (Rev: SLJ 10/99) [286]

7114 Hanft, Josh. *The Miracles of Passover* (K–3). Illus. by Seymour Chwast. 2007, Blue Apple $15.95 (978-1-59354-600-7). This is an attractive book that explains Passover traditions in engaging text and imaginative lift-the-flaps. (Rev: SLJ 4/07) [296.4]

7115 Howland, Naomi. *Latkes, Latkes, Good to Eat: A Chanukah Story* (PS–1). Illus. 1999, Clarion $16.00 (978-0-395-89903-8). 32pp. As a reward for helping an old lady, Sadie is given a magic frying pan, which will produce as many latkes at Hanukkah as she wants. (Rev: BL 9/1/99; HBG 3/00; SLJ 10/99)

7116 Howland, Naomi. *The Matzah Man: A Passover Story* (PS–1). Illus. 2002, Clarion $16.00 (978-0-618-11750-5). 32pp. Matzah Man attempts to escape the Passover seder in this version of the story of the gingerbread boy filled with familiar Jewish references. (Rev: BL 2/15/02; HBG 10/02; SLJ 3/02)

7117 Jules, Jacqueline. *Clap and Count! Action Rhymes for the Jewish New Year* (PS). Illus. by Sally Springer. 2001, Kar-Ben $17.95 (978-1-58013-067-7). 56pp. Nursery rhymes and finger plays with a Jewish twist take children through the holidays and holy days of the Jewish year. (Rev: BL 11/1/01)

7118 Kimmel, Eric A. *Asher and the Capmakers: A Hanukkah Story* (K–3). Illus. by Will Hillenbrand. 1993, Holiday House LB $16.95 (978-0-8234-1031-6). 32pp. Asher has many adventures when he sets out to borrow an egg for the family's latkes. (Rev: BL 7/93)

7119 Kimmel, Eric A. *The Chanukkah Guest* (PS–2). Illus. by Giora Carmi. 1990, Holiday House LB $17.95 (978-0-8234-0788-0); paper $6.95 (978-0-8234-0978-5). 32pp. Bubba Brayna is making potato latkes for the rabbi. (Rev: BCCB 12/90; BL 9/15/90*)

7120 Kimmel, Eric A. *Hershel and the Hanukkah Goblins* (K–3). Illus. by Trina S. Hyman. 1989, Holiday House LB $17.95 (978-0-8234-0769-9). 32pp. In this tale set in Eastern Europe, Hershel is looking forward to Hanukkah until he finds that the synagogue is haunted by goblins. (Rev: BCCB 10/89; BL 9/1/89; HB 1/90)

7121 Kimmel, Eric A. *The Magic Dreidels: A Hanukkah Story* (PS–3). Illus. by Katya Krenina. 1996, Holiday House LB $16.95 (978-0-8234-1256-3). 28pp. In this Hanukkah story, Jacob receives a magic dreidel from a goblin. (Rev: BCCB 11/96; BL 9/1/96)

7122 Kimmel, Eric A. *Zigazak! A Magical Hanukkah Night* (PS–4). Illus. by Jon Goodell. 2001, Doubleday $15.95 (978-0-385-32652-0). 32pp. A rabbi outwits two playful devils who are disrupting a small town's Hanukkah celebration. (Rev: BCCB 10/01; BL 10/1/01; HBG 3/02; SLJ 10/01)

7123 Kimmelman, Leslie. *The Runaway Latkes* (PS). Illus. by Paul Yalowitz. 2000, Whitman $15.95 (978-0-8075-7176-7). 32pp. In this humorous Hanukkah version of "The Gingerbread Man," three latkes jump out of the pan and roll off to see the town. (Rev: BL 9/1/00; HBG 3/01)

7124 Kimmelman, Leslie. *Sound the Shofar! A Story for Rosh Hashanah and Yom Kippur* (PS–1). Illus. by John Himmelman. 1998, HarperCollins $15.99 (978-0-06-027501-3). 32pp. A young girl describes the family's activities during Rosh Hashanah and Yom Kippur while her uncle blows the ram's horn, known as the shofar. (Rev: BL 10/1/98; HBG 3/99; SLJ 1/99)

7125 Kobre, Faige. *A Sense of Shabbat* (PS–K). Illus. 1990, Torah $11.95 (978-0-933873-44-5). 32pp. This Jewish holiday is shown from a preschooler's sensory perspective. (Rev: BCCB 3/91; BL 1/1/91) [296.4]

7126 Krensky, Stephen. *Hanukkah at Valley Forge* (2–4). Illus. by Greg Harlin. 2006, Dutton $17.99 (978-0-525-47738-9). 32pp. In this fact-based historical tale, a young Jewish soldier explains to General George Washington the meaning of the Hanukkah celebration. (Rev: BL 9/1/06; SLJ 10/06)

7127 Kress, Camille. *Purim!* (PS). Illus. by author. 1999, UAHC $5.95 (978-0-8074-0654-0). A brief text and quiet illustrations depict a group of children acting out the story of Purim. (Rev: SLJ 8/99)

7128 Kress, Camille. *Tot Shabbat* (PS). Illus. 1996, UAHC $5.95 (978-0-8074-0607-6). 7pp. In this simple board book, the Jewish Sabbath is introduced. (Rev: BL 2/1/97; SLJ 9/97)

7129 Kroll, Steven. *The Hanukkah Mice* (PS–2). Illus. by Michelle Shapiro. 2008, Marshall Cavendish $14.99 (978-0-7614-5428-1). 40pp. A family of mice enjoys Rachel's Hanukkah dollhouse and celebrates the holiday along with her. (Rev: BL 9/1/08)

7130 Kropf, Latifa Berry. *Happy Birthday, World: A Rosh Hashanah Celebration* (PS). Illus. by Lisa Carlson. 2005, Lerner $5.95 (978-0-929371-32-0). This attractive board book introduces young readers to Rosh Hashanah by comparing the rituals of the Jewish holiday to those of a child's birthday. (Rev: SLJ 11/05)

7131 Lamstein, Sarah Marwil. *Letter on the Wind* (K–3). Illus. by Neil Waldman. 2007, Boyds Mills $16.95 (978-1-932425-74-1). 32pp. Hayim asks the Almighty for help when his village has no oil for the Hanukkah lights; based on a folktale. (Rev: BL 9/15/07; LMC 11/07)

7132 Lanton, Sandy. *Lots of Latkes: A Hanukkah Story* (K–3). Illus. by Vicki Jo Redenbaugh. 2003, Lerner $14.95 (978-1-58013-091-2); paper $6.95 (978-1-58013-061-5). Despite the fact that everyone brought latkes instead of the varied spread that had been planned, the guests at Rivka Leah's Hanukkah party have a wonderful time. (Rev: HBG 4/04; SLJ 10/03)

7133 Levine, Abby. *This Is the Dreidel* (PS–2). Illus. by Paige Billin-Frye. 2003, Whitman LB $16.99 (978-0-8075-7884-1). Simple rhyming couplets and bright illustrations show Max and his younger sister Ruth preparing for and participating in the fun of Hanukkah. (Rev: HBG 4/04; SLJ 10/03)

7134 Levine, Abby. *This Is the Matzah* (PS–2). Illus. by Paige Billin-Frye. 2005, Whitman $16.99 (978-0-8075-7885-8). 32pp. Max and his sister Ruth help their parents prepare for the Seder celebration in this introduction to the traditions of Passover told in rhyming couplets. (Rev: BL 2/15/05; SLJ 5/05)

7135 Manushkin, Fran. *The Matzah That Papa Brought Home* (PS–1). Illus. by Ned Bittinger. 1995, Scholastic $14.95 (978-0-590-47146-6). 32pp. A cumulative tale that introduces symbols associated with Passover. (Rev: BL 1/15/95; SLJ 2/95)

7136 Medoff, Francine. *The Mouse in the Matzah Factory* (K–3). Illus. by Nicole In den Bosch. 2003, Kar-Ben paper $6.95 (978-1-58013-048-6). 32pp. A curious mouse follows a harvest of wheat from field to mill to bakery, where it is made into matzohs for Passover. (Rev: BL 3/15/03; SLJ 10/03)

7137 Melmed, Laura K. *Moishe's Miracle: A Hanukkah Story* (K–3). Illus. by David Slonim. 2000, HarperCollins LB $15.89 (978-0-688-14683-2). 32pp. Moishe's generosity at Hanukkah results in a gift of a magical pan that makes pancakes for all. (Rev: BL 9/1/00; HB 9/00; HBG 3/01)

7138 Michelson, Richard. *Grandpa's Gamble* (PS–4). Illus. by Barry Moser. 1999, Marshall Cavendish $15.95 (978-0-7614-5034-4). 32pp. At Passover, Grandpa, a Jewish immigrant of many years ago, regrets that he lied and cheated to get ahead and tells how he changed his wicked ways. (Rev: BCCB 4/99; BL 3/15/99; HBG 10/99; SLJ 6/99)

7139 Modesitt, Jeanne. *It's Hanukkah!* (PS–1). Illus. by Robin Spowart. 1999, Holiday House $15.95

(978-0-8234-1451-2). A family of mice enjoy all the activities associated with Hanukkah, including lighting the Menorah and eating latkes. (Rev: HBG 3/00; SLJ 10/99)

7140 Nerlove, Miriam. *Hanukkah* (PS–1). Illus. 1989, Whitman paper $5.95 (978-0-8075-3142-6). 24pp. A brief history and explanation of the customs and activities of Hanukkah in verse. (Rev: BL 7/89; SLJ 9/89)

7141 Nerlove, Miriam. *Passover* (PS–1). Illus. 1989, Whitman LB $15.99 (978-0-8075-6360-1). 24pp. A description of this Jewish holy day in rhyming text. (Rev: BL 1/15/90; SLJ 4/90)

7142 Nerlove, Miriam. *Shabbat* (PS–1). Illus. 1998, Whitman $15.99 (978-0-8075-7324-2). 24pp. Using a simple rhyming text and gentle watercolors, this book shows how a happy, traditional family observes Shabbat, the Jewish Sabbath, both at home and at the synagogue. (Rev: BL 10/1/98; HBG 3/99; SLJ 10/98) [296.4]

7143 Newman, Leslea. *The Eight Nights of Chanukah* (K–2). Illus. by Elivia Savadier. 2005, Abrams $12.95 (978-0-8109-5785-5). 24pp. Newman gives "The Twelve Days of Christmas" a new twist with a version that celebrates Hanukkah; a note and a glossary follow the text. (Rev: BL 10/15/05; SLJ 10/05)

7144 Newman, Leslea. *Matzo Ball Moon* (PS–3). Illus. by Elaine Greenstein. 1998, Clarion $15.00 (978-0-395-71530-7). 32pp. At Passover, all of Eleanor's family enjoy the matzo balls of her grandmother, Bubbe, and when Eleanor opens the door to welcome the prophet Elijah, she sees a full moon and imagines it to be another of Bubbe's yummy creations. (Rev: BL 4/1/98; HBG 10/98; SLJ 6/98)

7145 Newman, Leslea. *Runaway Dreidel!* (PS–2). Illus. by Krysten Brooker. 2002, Holt $17.95 (978-0-8050-6237-3). 32pp. A rhyming fantasy about a dreidel that takes off, zooming into space to become a star. (Rev: BCCB 11/02; BL 9/1/02; HBG 3/03; SLJ 10/02)

7146 Oberman, Sheldon. *By the Hanukkah Light* (1–4). Illus. by Neil Waldman. 1997, Boyds Mills $15.95 (978-1-56397-658-2). 32pp. As Rachel and her grandfather polish the menorah at Hanukkah, he tells her about the Holocaust and its meaning for the Jewish people. (Rev: BL 9/1/97*; HBG 3/98; SLJ 10/97)

7147 Olswanger, Anna. *Shlemiel Crooks* (2–4). Illus. by Paula Goodman Koz. 2005, NewSouth paper $14.95 (978-1-58838-165-1). 36pp. Based on a true incident, this humorous story tells of the hapless thieves who plan to steal Reb Elias's special Passover wine. (Rev: BL 5/15/05; SLJ 6/05)

7148 Portnoy, Mindy A. *Matzah Ball: A Passover Story* (PS–3). Illus. by Katherine J. Kahn. 1994, Kar-Ben paper $6.95 (978-0-929371-69-6). While attending a baseball game during Passover, Aaron meets an elderly man (Elijah perhaps?) who tells him about Jewish fans going to games at Ebbets Field. (Rev: SLJ 8/94)

7149 Pushker, Gloria Teles. *Toby Belfer and the High Holy Days* (K–3). Illus. by Judith Hierstein. Series: Toby Belfer. 2001, Pelican $15.95 (978-1-

56554-765-0). 32pp. Toby explains the meaning of the Jewish holidays of Rosh Hashanah and Yom Kippur to her friend Donna. (Rev: BL 10/1/01; HBG 3/02; SLJ 1/02)

7150 Rauchwerger, Diane Levin. *Dinosaur on Passover* (PS–K). Illus. by Jason Wolff. 2006, Lerner LB $15.95 (978-1-58013-156-8); paper $6.95 (978-1-58013-161-2). A dinosaur joins in the Passover seder in this story with rhyming text that covers all the usual rituals. (Rev: SLJ 4/06)

7151 Rosen, Michael J. *Our Eight Nights of Hanukkah* (K–3). Illus. by DyAnne Disalvo-Ryan. 2000, Holiday House $16.95 (978-0-8234-1476-5). 32pp. The activities of a Jewish family are chronicled as they celebrate the eight nights of Hanukkah. (Rev: BL 9/1/00; HBG 3/01)

7152 Rothenberg, Joan. *Inside-Out Grandma* (K–3). Illus. 1995, Hyperion LB $15.49 (978-0-7868-2092-4). 32pp. A circuitous story about the relationship between a grandmother wearing her clothes inside out and making potato pancakes at Hanukkah. (Rev: BCCB 11/95; BL 9/15/95)

7153 Rouss, Sylvia. *Sammy Spider's First Passover* (PS–K). Illus. by Katherine J. Kahn. 1995, Kar-Ben paper $7.95 (978-0-929371-82-5). A pleasant story about a little spider that watches the Shapiro family make preparations for Passover. (Rev: SLJ 7/95)

7154 Rouss, Sylvia. *Sammy Spider's First Rosh Hashanah* (PS–1). Illus. by Katherine J. Kahn. 1996, Kar-Ben paper $7.95 (978-0-929371-99-3). Mother Spider explains to her son Sammy the holiday customs and symbols associated with the Jewish New Year. (Rev: SLJ 5/97)

7155 Rouss, Sylvia. *Sammy Spider's First Shabbat* (K–2). Illus. by Katherine J. Kahn. 1998, Kar-Ben $14.95 (978-1-58013-007-3); paper $7.95 (978-1-58013-006-6). Sammy Spider observes the Shapiro family's preparations for the Shabbat, including braiding the challah. (Rev: SLJ 6/98)

7156 Schotter, Roni. *Passover!* (PS–1). Illus. by Erin Eitter Kono. 2006, Little, Brown $12.99 (978-0-316-93991-1). 32pp. A Jewish family's preparations for Passover are described in rhyming text with cartoon illustrations. (Rev: BL 2/15/06; SLJ 4/06)

7157 Shulman, Goldie. *Way Too Much Challah Dough* (PS–2). Illus. by Vitaliy Romanenko. 2006, Hachai $12.95 (978-1-929628-23-0). 32pp. When Mindy uses too much yeast, her challah dough grows out of control and her grandmother must come to the rescue. (Rev: BL 10/1/06)

7158 Simpson, Lesley. *The Shabbat Box* (PS–1). Illus. by Nicole In den Bosch. 2001, Kar-Ben paper $6.95 (978-1-58013-027-1). 32pp. Ira must come up with a solution when he loses the treasured class Shabbat box on his way home from school. (Rev: BL 10/1/01; SLJ 12/01)

7159 Spinner, Stephanie. *It's a Miracle: A Hanukkah Storybook* (K–2). Illus. by Jill McElmurry. 2003, Simon & Schuster $16.95 (978-0-689-84493-5). Owen lights the candles each night of the holiday and his Grandma Karen tells a story of Jewish family life. (Rev: HBG 4/04; SLJ 10/03)

7160 Stillerman, Marci. *Nine Spoons: A Chanukah Story* (K–2). Illus. by Pesach Gerber. 1998, Hachai $12.95 (978-0-922613-84-7). In a Nazi concentration camp, Raizel shows her ingenuity by fashioning a menorah out of nine spoons so that Hanukkah can be celebrated. (Rev: HB 1/99; HBG 3/99; SLJ 10/98)

7161 Terwilliger, Kelly. *Bubbe Isabella and the Sukkot Cake* (PS–K). Illus. by Phyllis Hornung. 2005, Kar-Ben $15.95 (978-1-58013-187-2); paper $6.95 (978-1-58013-128-5). 24pp. A Jewish grandmother makes a lemon cake and a beautiful sukkah for the Sukkot holiday, but at first the only guests are animals that prefer the decoration to the cake. (Rev: BL 9/1/05; SLJ 10/05)

7162 Topek, Susan Remick. *A Costume for Noah: A Purim Story* (PS–K). Illus. by Sally Springer. 1996, Kar-Ben $13.95 (978-0-929371-91-7); paper $5.95 (978-0-929371-90-0). Traditional terms and customs are introduced in this simple story of a boy preparing with his friends to celebrate Purim. (Rev: SLJ 5/96)

7163 Topek, Susan Remick. *Shalom Shabbat: A Book for Havdalah* (PS). Illus. by Shelly Schonebaum Ephraim. 1998, Kar-Ben $5.95 (978-1-58013-010-3). This simple board book celebrates the ceremony of Havdalah that takes place at the end of the Jewish Sabbath. (Rev: SLJ 2/99)

7164 Ungar, Richard. *Rachel's Gift* (K–3). Illus. 2003, Tundra $16.95 (978-0-88776-616-9). 32pp. With humor and style, Ungar describes a Chelm family's preparations for its Passover seder. (Rev: BL 5/1/03; HBG 10/03; SLJ 5/03)

7165 Vorst, Rochel Groner. *The Sukkah That I Built* (PS–2). Illus. by Elizabeth Victor-Elsby. 2002, Hachai $10.95 (978-1-929628-07-0). 26pp. A young boy (with help from his family) builds a sukkah — a temporary structure used in the celebration of Sukkot — to the refrain of "The House that Jack Built." (Rev: BL 10/1/02; HBG 3/03)

7166 Wayland, April Halprin. *New Year at the Pier: A Rosh Hashanah Story* (PS–3). Illus. by Stephane Jorisch. 2009, Dial $16.99 (978-0-8037-3279-7). 32pp. Izzy and his parents prepare to make amends for mistakes during the Jewish New Year tradition of Tashlich. (Rev: BL 6/1–15/09; SLJ 7/09)

7167 Weber, Elka. *The Yankee at the Seder* (1–3). Illus. by Adam Gustavson. 2009, Tricycle $16.99 (978-1-58246-256-1). 32pp. Loosely based on a true event detailed in the endnote, this unusual story tells how a Confederate family shares a Seder dinner with a Jewish Yankee soldier. (Rev: BCCB 5/09; BLO 1/7/09; SLJ 1/09)

7168 Wilkowski, Susan. *Baby's Bris* (PS–1). Illus. by Judith Friedman. 1999, Karben $16.95 (978-1-58013-052-3); paper $6.95 (978-1-58013-053-0). 32pp. A young girl grows to love her baby brother particularly through an understanding of the bris ceremony when the boy is circumcised. (Rev: BL 1/1–15/00; HBG 3/00; SLJ 1/00)

7169 Zalben, Jane Breskin. *Pearl's Passover: A Family Celebration Through Stories, Recipes, Crafts, and Songs* (K–3). Illus. 2002, Simon &

Schuster $16.00 (978-0-689-81487-7). 48pp. A lamb named Pearl and her family prepare for Passover in this volume that interweaves fictional characters with recipes, crafts, and basic information about the holiday. (Rev: BL 2/15/02; HB 3/02; HBG 10/02; SLJ 2/02)

7170 Zolkower, Edie Stoltz. *Too Many Cooks: A Passover Parable* (PS–2). Illus. by Shauna Mooney Kawasaki. 2000, Kar-Ben paper $5.95 (978-1-58013-063-9). At Passover, everyone in the family decides to add a special ingredient to Bubbie's charoses for the seder. (Rev: SLJ 12/00)

THANKSGIVING

7171 Anderson, Derek. *Over the River: A Turkey's Tale* (PS–K). Illus. 2005, Simon & Schuster $14.95 (978-0-689-87635-6). 40pp. The popular Thanksgiving song is given a new twist in this tale of a turkey family on its way to celebrate the holiday with Grandma. (Rev: BL 9/15/05; HBG 4/06; SLJ 10/05)

7172 Archer, Peggy. *Turkey Surprise* (PS–K). Illus. by Thor Wickstrom. 2005, Dial $10.99 (978-0-8037-2969-8). 32pp. A turkey succeeds in eluding two Pilgrim brothers, who settle for a vegetarian Thanksgiving feast. (Rev: BL 9/1/05; HBG 4/06)

7173 Auch, Mary Jane, and Herm Auch. *Beauty and the Beaks: A Turkey's Cautionary Tale* (K–3). Illus. by Mary Jane Auch. 2007, Holiday $16.95 (978-0-8234-1990-6). 32pp. "Wattle I do?" asks pretentious turkey Lance when he discovers he's been invited to be the main dish in this funny story full of wordplay. (Rev: BL 9/15/07; SLJ 9/07)

7174 Bateman, Teresa. *Gus, the Pilgrim Turkey* (PS–2). Illus. by Ellen Sasaki. 2008, Albert Whitman $16.99 (978-0-8075-1266-1). 32pp. Gus is a happy young turkey until he learns that his life might be in danger toward Thanksgiving, and he sets off for points south. (Rev: BL 9/15/08; SLJ 9/08)

7175 Bateman, Teresa. *A Plump and Perky Turkey* (PS–2). Illus. by Jeff Shelly. 2001, Winslow $15.95 (978-1-890817-91-6). 40pp. Pete the turkey cleverly escapes hungry townspeople on Thanksgiving. (Rev: BCCB 11/01; BL 9/1/01; HBG 3/02; SLJ 9/01)

7176 Bildner, Phil. *Turkey Bowl* (1–3). Illus. by C. F. Payne. 2008, Simon & Schuster $15.99 (978-0-689-87896-1). 32pp. Ethan's dream of playing in his family's annual Thanksgiving football game melts away when a big snowstorm comes. (Rev: BL 9/15/08)

7177 Brown, Marc. *Arthur's Thanksgiving* (K–3). Illus. by author. 1983, Little, Brown paper $5.95 (978-0-316-11232-1). 32pp. Arthur is made director of his class Thanksgiving play.

7178 Bunting, Eve. *How Many Days to America? A Thanksgiving Story* (2–4). Illus. by Beth Peck. 1988, Houghton $16.00 (978-0-89919-521-6); paper $6.95 (978-0-395-54777-9). 32pp. A family flees oppression on a Caribbean island and heads for the United States. (Rev: BL 11/1/88; SLJ 10/88)

7179 Bunting, Eve. *A Turkey for Thanksgiving* (PS–1). Illus. by Diane deGroat. 1991, Houghton $16.00 (978-0-89919-793-7). 32pp. After bringing a live turkey home at Thanksgiving, Mr. and Mrs. Moose decide to have a vegetarian meal. (Rev: BCCB 9/91; BL 10/1/91; SLJ 9/91)

7180 Capucilli, Alyssa Satin. *Happy Thanksgiving, Biscuit!* (PS). Illus. by Pat Schories. 1999, Harper-Collins paper $6.99 (978-0-694-01221-3). In this flap book, Biscuit, an endearing puppy, enjoys the fuss surrounding Thanksgiving. (Rev: SLJ 12/99)

7181 Cazet, Denys. *Minnie and Moo and the Thanksgiving Tree* (1–2). Illus. 2000, DK $12.99 (978-0-7894-2654-3); paper $3.99 (978-0-7894-2655-0). 418pp. At Thanksgiving, Minnie and Moo help the animals (starting with the turkeys) escape by hiding them in a tree only to discover that the farmer and his family are vegetarians. (Rev: BL 9/1/00; HB 9/00; HBG 3/01; SLJ 9/00)

7182 Cowley, Joy. *Gracias, the Thanksgiving Turkey* (PS–2). Illus. by Joe Cepeda. 1996, Scholastic $15.95 (978-0-590-46976-0). 32pp. A New York City boy dreads Thanksgiving, when his pet turkey, Gracias, will be killed. (Rev: BCCB 11/96; BL 9/1/96; SLJ 12/96)

7183 Cox, Judy. *One Is a Feast for Mouse: A Thanksgiving Tale* (PS–2). Illus. by Jeffrey Ebbeler. 2008, Holiday $16.95 (978-0-8234-1977-7). 32pp. A little mouse who has amassed a feast from the Thanksgiving leftovers loses almost all of it when the cat pounces — but one luscious pea remains. (Rev: BL 10/1/08; HB 11/08; SLJ 9/08)

7184 Dalgliesh, Alice. *The Thanksgiving Story* (K–3). Illus. by Helen Sewell. 1988, Macmillan paper $5.99 (978-0-689-71053-7). 32pp. This reissued 1954 Caldecott Honor Book tells of the Hopkins family's experiences from the Mayflower voyage to the first Thanksgiving.

7185 deGroat, Diane. *We Gather Together . . . Now Please Get Lost!* (PS–2). Illus. Series: Gilbert. 2001, North-South LB $15.88 (978-1-58717-096-6). 32pp. Gilbert and his animal classmates take an entertaining, mishap-filled field trip to Pilgrim Town. (Rev: BL 9/1/01; HBG 3/02; SLJ 8/01)

7186 Gibbons, Gail. *Thanksgiving Is . . .* (PS–2). Illus. by author. 2004, Holiday House $17.95 (978-0-8234-1849-7). Brief text introduces the holiday and its relation to harvest time, Pilgrims, and Native Americans. (Rev: SLJ 9/04) [394.2]

7187 Goode, Diane. *Thanksgiving Is Here!* (PS–2). Illus. by author. 2003, HarperCollins LB $16.89 (978-0-06-051589-8). An appealing portrait of an extended family gathering for its annual Thanksgiving feast. (Rev: HBG 4/04; SLJ 9/03)

7188 Jackson, Alison. *I Know an Old Lady Who Swallowed a Pie* (PS–2). Illus. by Judith Byron Schachner. 1997, Dutton $15.99 (978-0-525-45645-2). 32pp. This favorite folk song is given a new twist by using foods associated with Thanksgiving. (Rev: BL 9/1/97; HBG 3/98; SLJ 11/97)

7189 Jennings, Sharon. *Franklin's Thanksgiving* (PS–1). Illus. by Brenda Clark. Series: Franklin. 2001, Kids Can $10.95 (978-1-55074-798-0). 32pp. Franklin the turtle's family Thanksgiving dinner becomes so overcrowded that the feast is moved outdoors. (Rev: BL 9/15/01; HBG 3/02; SLJ 9/01)

7190 Kroll, Steven. *Oh, What a Thanksgiving!* (K–2). Illus. by S. D. Schindler. 1988, Scholastic paper $3.95 (978-0-590-40616-1). 32pp. David imagines himself at Plymouth in 1620. (Rev: BL 9/15/88; SLJ 9/88)

7191 Kroll, Virginia. *The Thanksgiving Bowl* (PS–2). Illus. by Philomena O'Neill. 2007, Pelican $15.95 (978-1-58980-365-7). 32pp. Grandma Grace's yellow plastic gratitude bowl is the central image in this Thanksgiving story. (Rev: BL 10/1/07)

7192 Mayr, Diane. *Run, Turkey, Run!* (PS–2). Illus. by Laura Rader. 2007, Walker $15.95 (978-0-8027-9630-1). 32pp. Turkey's frantic attempts to avoid becoming Thanksgiving dinner end in success when the family eats grilled cheese sandwiches. (Rev: BL 9/15/07; LMC 11/07; SLJ 10/07)

7193 Milgrim, David. *Thank You, Thanksgiving* (PS–K). Illus. by author. 2003, Clarion $9.95 (978-0-618-27466-6). 32pp. A little girl walks through town expressing in simple words her thanks to all the animals and objects that enrich her life. (Rev: HBG 4/04; SLJ 9/03)

7194 Parish, Herman. *Amelia Bedelia Talks Turkey* (1–3). Illus. by Lynn Sweat. 2008, HarperCollins $16.99 (978-0-06-084352-6). 64pp. Wordplay and hilarity abound when Amelia Bedelia is put in charge of the 3rd-grade Thanksgiving play. (Rev: SLJ 3/09)

7195 Pomeranc, Marion Hess. *The Can-Do Thanksgiving* (K–2). Illus. by Nancy Cote. 1998, Whitman $16.99 (978-0-8075-1054-4). 32pp. Through a school food drive and a contribution of a can of peas, Dee is chosen to help serve a Thanksgiving meal and, there, meets a new friend. (Rev: BL 11/1/98; HBG 3/99; SLJ 9/98)

7196 Reed, Lynn Rowe. *Thelonius Turkey Lives!* (PS–2). Illus. by author. 2005, Knopf $15.95 (978-0-375-83126-3). The other farm animals gang up on their keeper when Thelonious becomes convinced she wants to eat him for Thanksgiving. (Rev: SLJ 8/05)

7197 Roberts, Bethany. *Thanksgiving Mice!* (PS–1). Illus. by Doug Cushman. 2001, Clarion $13.00 (978-0-618-12040-6). 32pp. Mice put on a play about the trials of the Pilgrims and the first Thanksgiving. (Rev: BL 9/1/01; HBG 3/02; SLJ 9/01)

7198 Roop, Peter, and Connie Roop. *Let's Celebrate Thanksgiving* (1–4). Illus. by Gwen Connelly. 1999, Millbrook LB $22.90 (978-0-7613-0973-4); paper $7.95 (978-0-7613-0429-6). 32pp. An easy-to-read explanation of Thanksgiving's origination and how it is celebrated, along with some related jokes and projects. (Rev: BL 9/15/99; HBG 3/00; SLJ 11/99) [394.2649]

7199 Ruelle, Karen G. *The Thanksgiving Beast Feast* (1–2). Illus. 1999, Holiday House $15.95 (978-0-8234-1511-3). 32pp. At Thanksgiving, Harry Cat and his sister, Emily, decide to show their thanks by preparing food for the birds, squirrels, and chipmunks in their neighborhood. (Rev: BL 9/1/99; HB 9/99; HBG 3/00; SLJ 9/99)

7200 Scheer, Julian. *A Thanksgiving Turkey* (PS–3). Illus. by Ronald Himler. 2001, Holiday House $16.95 (978-0-8234-1674-5). 32pp. A boy learns to know his grandfather and Virginia farm life in a beautifully illustrated and sensitive story that culminates with the capture and release of a wild turkey. (Rev: BCCB 10/01; BL 9/1/01; HBG 3/02; SLJ 9/01)

7201 Shore, Diane Z. *This Is the Feast* (PS–2). Illus. by Megan Lloyd. 2008, HarperCollins $16.99 (978-0-06-623794-7). 32pp. The story of the Pilgrims' voyage, arrival in America, and the first celebratory Thanksgiving feast is told in poetic text and bright illustrations. (Rev: BL 9/15/08)

7202 Spirn, Michele. *The Know-Nothings Talk Turkey* (1–2). Illus. Series: I Can Read. 2000, HarperCollins $14.95 (978-0-06-028183-0). 48pp. In his easy-to-read book, four friends and their dog Floris decide to serve a turkey at Thanksgiving so they invite one to their dinner. (Rev: BL 9/1/00; HBG 3/01; SLJ 10/00)

7203 Willey, Margaret. *Thanksgiving with Me* (PS–2). Illus. by Lloyd Bloom. 1998, HarperCollins $15.95 (978-0-06-027113-8). 32pp. While her mother describes each of her six brothers, a little girl waits with great anticipation for the arrival of her uncles at Thanksgiving time. (Rev: BCCB 11/98; BL 9/1/98; HBG 3/99; SLJ 9/98)

7204 Wilson, Karma. *Give Thanks to the Lord: Celebrating Psalm 92* (PS–2). Illus. by Amy June Bates. 2007, Zondervan $14.99 (978-0-310-71118-6). 32pp. A young boy gives thanks for the wonders of Thanksgiving Day. (Rev: BL 10/1/07) [242]

VALENTINE'S DAY

7205 Bond, Felicia. *The Day It Rained Hearts* (PS–K). 2001, HarperCollins LB $17.89 (978-0-06-001078-2). 63pp. When it rains hearts, Cornelia catches them and makes unique, individualized valentines for her friends. (Rev: BL 12/1/01; HBG 3/02)

7206 Bunting, Eve. *The Valentine Bears* (K–3). Illus. by Jan Brett. 1983, Houghton $16.00 (978-0-89919-138-6); paper $5.95 (978-0-89919-313-7). 32pp. Mr. and Mrs. Bear decide not to sleep through Valentine's Day this year.

7207 Capucilli, Alyssa Satin. *Biscuit's Valentine's Day* (PS). Illus. by Pat Schories. 2000, HarperCollins $6.99 (978-0-694-01222-0). 20pp. While his young owner is preparing for Valentine's Day, Biscuit the dog is engaged in all sorts of activities that are revealed when the reader lifts the flaps in this interactive book. (Rev: BL 2/15/01)

7208 Carlson, Nancy. *Henry and the Valentine Surprise* (PS–1). Illus. by author. 2008, Viking $15.99 (978-0-670-06267-6). 32pp. Does Henry the mouse's teacher have a girlfriend? Henry and his classmates investigate. (Rev: BL 2/1/09; SLJ 12/08)

7209 Carr, Jan. *Sweet Hearts* (PS–2). Illus. by Dorothy Donohue. 2002, Holiday House $16.95 (978-0-8234-1732-2). 32pp. Elaborately constructed collage valentines star in this story in which a little panda creates and decorates paper hearts for his parents. (Rev: BL 12/1/02; HBG 3/03; SLJ 11/02)

7210 Demas, Corinne. *Valentine Surprise* (PS–1). Illus. by R. W. Alley. 2008, Walker $12.95 (978-0-8027-9664-6). 32pp. Lily's disappointment with her efforts to make a perfect heart-shaped Valentine for her mother leads her to a lovely solution. (Rev: BL 1/1–15/08; SLJ 3/08)

7211 Friedman, Laurie. *Love, Ruby Valentine* (K–4). Illus. by Lynne Avril Cravath. 2006, Carolrhoda $15.95 (978-1-57505-899-3). Ruby Valentine works so hard to prepare for Valentine's Day that when the big day comes, she sleeps through it and must deliver her gifts a day late. (Rev: SLJ 11/06)

7212 Gregory, Valiska. *A Valentine for Norman Noggs* (PS–2). Illus. by Marsha Winborn. 1999, HarperCollins LB $15.89 (978-0-06-027657-7). 32pp. Hamster Norman faces possible trouble when he ignores the threats of bullies Richard and Arthur and delivers a valentine to Wilhemina. (Rev: BCCB 2/99; BL 4/1/99; HBG 10/99; SLJ 1/99)

7213 Hoban, Lillian. *Silly Tilly's Valentine* (K–2). Illus. by author. Series: I Can Read. 1998, HarperCollins LB $16.89 (978-0-06-027401-6). 47pp. Tilly the mole is so excited about a snowfall that she forgets it is Valentine's Day. (Rev: HBG 10/98; SLJ 2/98)

7214 Poydar, Nancy. *Rhyme Time Valentine* (PS–3). Illus. 2002, Holiday House $16.95 (978-0-8234-1684-4). 32pp. Poor little Ruby is dismayed when the valentines she made are blown away by a strong wind. (Rev: BL 1/1–15/03; HBG 3/03; SLJ 11/02)

7215 Roberts, Bethany. *Valentine Mice!* (PS–K). Illus. by Doug Cushman. 1998, Clarion $13.00 (978-0-395-77518-9). 32pp. A group of mice are so busy delivering valentines in a snowy forest that they don't realize the smallest one of them is missing. (Rev: BL 12/15/97; HBG 10/98; SLJ 1/98)

7216 Roop, Peter, and Connie Roop. *Let's Celebrate Valentine's Day* (2–4). Illus. by Katy K. Arnsteen. Series: Let's Celebrate. 1999, Millbrook LB $22.90 (978-0-7613-0972-7); paper $5.95 (978-0-7913-0428-0). 32pp. Discusses the origins of Valentine's Day, describes how it is celebrated, and includes many related jokes and riddles. (Rev: BL 2/15/99; HBG 10/99; SLJ 4/99) [394.2618]

7217 Ruelle, Karen G. *Snow Valentines* (1–2). Illus. Series: Holiday House Reader. 2000, Holiday House $15.95 (978-0-8234-1533-5). 32pp. A book for beginning readers that describes how two little cats solve the problem of what to get their parents for Valentine's Day. (Rev: BL 7/00; HBG 10/01; SLJ 9/00)

7218 Weeks, Sarah. *Be Mine, Be Mine, Sweet Valentine* (PS–K). Illus. by Fumi Kosaka. 2005, HarperCollins $9.99 (978-0-694-01514-6). A rhyming guessing game in which the reader must supply the name of the Valentine's Day gift. (Rev: SLJ 1/06)

Books for Beginning Readers

7219 Adler, David A. *Bones and the Birthday Mystery* (K–2). Illus. by Barbara Johansen Newman. Series: Jeffrey Bones. 2007, Viking $13.99 (978-0-670-06164-8). 32pp. Bones solves the mystery of a missing birthday card in this funny, accessible fifth volume in the series. Other installments include *Bones and the Cupcake Mystery, Bones and the Dinosaur Mystery* (2005), and *Bones and the Math Test Mystery* (2008). (Rev: BL 5/1/07; SLJ 5/07)

7220 Adler, David A. *Young Cam Jansen and the 100th Day of School Mystery* (1–2). Illus. by Susanna Natti. Series: Viking Easy-to-Read. 2009, Viking $13.99 (978-0-670-06172-3). 32pp. Cam Jansen is back, working on a case involving pizzas missing from the class's "Letter P" party. Earlier volumes in the series include *Young Cam Jansen and the Dinosaur Game* (1996), *Young Cam Jansen and the Baseball Mystery* (1999), *Young Cam Jansen and the Library Mystery* (2001), *Young Cam Jansen and the Double Beach Mystery* (2002), *Young Cam Jansen and the New Girl Mystery* (2004), *Young Cam Jansen and the Substitute Mystery* (2005), *Young Cam Jansen and the Lions' Lunch Mystery* (2007), and *Young Cam Jansen and the Molly Shoe Mystery* (2008). (Rev: BL 7/09)

7221 Albee, Sarah. *The Dragon's Scales* (1–2). Illus. by John Manders. Series: Step into Reading + Math. 1998, Random LB $11.99 (978-0-679-98381-1); paper $3.99 (978-0-679-88381-4). 48pp. While telling an exciting story about a clever girl who outwits a dragon, this book also explains the concept of weights and measures. (Rev: BL 7/98)

7222 Albert, Shirley. *Doll Party* (1–2). Illus. by Amy Flynn. 1994, Penguin paper $3.99 (978-0-448-40182-9). 32pp. An easy-to-read book about Becky and her new doll. (Rev: BL 1/1/95)

7223 Alexander, Sue. *World Famous Muriel and the Magic Mystery* (2–3). Illus. by Marla Frazee. 1990, HarperCollins LB $12.89 (978-0-690-04789-9). 32pp. Muriel, known for her tightrope walking and incredible smarts, is after a missing magician. (Rev: BL 3/15/90; SLJ 7/90)

7224 Allen, Laura J. *Rollo and Tweedy and the Ghost at Dougal Castle* (1–2). Illus. Series: I Can Read. 1992, HarperCollins LB $15.89 (978-0-06-020107-4). 64pp. A mouse detective and his assistant catch the ghost that is haunting a Scottish castle. (Rev: BCCB 9/92*; BL 6/15/92; HB 9/92; SLJ 10/92)

7225 Alphin, Elaine M. *Dinosaur Hunter* (1–2). Illus. by Don Bolognese. Series: I Can Read Book. 2003, HarperCollins LB $16.89 (978-0-06-028304-9). 48pp. After discovering dinosaur bones on his family's Wyoming ranch in the late 19th century, Ned foils the attempts of a fossil hunter to swindle him out of them. (Rev: BL 9/1/03; HBG 4/04; SLJ 12/03)

7226 Armstrong, Jennifer. *Sunshine, Moonshine* (1–2). Illus. by Lucia Washburn. 1997, Random paper $3.99 (978-0-679-86442-4). 32pp. A busy day in the life of a young boy is chronicled in this easy-to-read book. (Rev: BL 5/1/97; SLJ 8/97)

7227 Arnold, Caroline. *Wiggle and Waggle* (K–2). Illus. by Mary Peterson. 2007, Charlesbridge $12.95 (978-1-58089-306-0). 48pp. Two worm friends have amusing adventures in this well-designed easy-reader that conveys some information about worms. (Rev: BL 7/07; LMC 1/08; SLJ 11/07)

7228 Arnold, Tedd. *Hi! Fly Guy!* (K–2). Illus. by author. 2005, Scholastic $5.99 (978-0-439-63903-3). 30pp. Buzz enters a fly in a pet competition, and the gifted insect impresses everyone with its multiple talents. Theodor Seuss Geisel Honor Book. The insect's subsequent feats are recorded in *Shoo, Fly Guy!* and *Super Fly Guy* (2006), *There Was an Old Lady Who Swallowed Fly Guy* (2007), and *Hooray for Fly Guy!* and *Fly High, Fly Guy!* (2008). (Rev: BCCB 10/05; HBG 4/06; LMC 1/06; SLJ 2/06) ∩

7229 Backstein, Karen. *The Blind Men and the Elephant* (1–2). Illus. by Annie Mitra. 1992, Scholastic paper $3.99 (978-0-590-45813-9). 48pp. The Indian folktale about the blind men who each see the nature of the elephant in a different way. (Rev: BL 3/1/93) [398.2]

7230 Bader, Bonnie. *Benny the Big Shot Goes to Camp* (1–2). Illus. by Shari Warren. Series: All Aboard Reading. 2003, Grosset paper $3.99 (978-0-448-42894-9). 48pp. Benny's bragging fails to impress his campmates and they steal his "blankie." (Rev: BL 5/15/03; HBG 10/03)

7231 Baker, Barbara. *N-O Spells No!* (1–3). Illus. by Nola L. Malone. 1993, Scholastic paper $3.99 (978-0-590-44186-5). 64pp. In this book illustrated with cartoons, there are five short stories about Annie and her big brother. (Rev: BL 6/1/91; SLJ 8/91) ∩

7232 Baker, Keith. *Little Green* (PS–1). Illus. 2001, Harcourt $16.00 (978-0-15-292859-9). 32pp. In this easy reader, a boy is fascinated by the behavior of a hummingbird. (Rev: BCCB 4/01; BL 4/15/01; HBG 10/01; SLJ 4/01)

7233 Baker, Keith. *Lucky Days with Mr. and Mrs. Green* (K–2). Illus. by author. 2005, Harcourt $16.00 (978-0-15-216500-0). 72pp. Mr. Green looks for his wife's lost pearls, guesses the number of gumballs in a jar, and enters a singing contest in the three stories in this chapter book. (Rev: BCCB 4/05; HB 5/05; SLJ 3/05)

7234 Baker, Keith. *On the Go with Mr. and Mrs. Green* (PS–2). Series: Mr. and Mrs. Green. 2006, Harcourt $16.00 (978-0-15-205762-6). 72pp. The further adventures of the affectionate alligators include magic tricks and high technology. (Rev: BL 5/1/06; SLJ 6/06)

7235 Bang-Campbell, Monika. *Little Rat Rides* (2–4). Illus. by Molly Bang. 2004, Harcourt $15.00 (978-0-15-204667-5). 48pp. Although she has long dreamed of riding a horse, just as her father once did, Little Rat is consumed by misgivings when the opportunity to ride finally arrives. Little Rat struggles with learning the violin in a sequel, *Little Rat Makes Music* (2007). (Rev: BL 5/1/04; HB 5/04; SLJ 5/04)

7236 Banks, Kate. *Monkeys and the Universe* (PS–2). Illus. by Tomek Bogacki. 2009, Farrar $14.95 (978-0-374-35028-4). 48pp. With some mutual disagreement, Max the monkey and his big brother Pete learn about the solar system and the stars; for beginning readers. (Rev: BL 4/1/09; HB 7/09; SLJ 3/09)

7237 Bauer, Marion Dane. *Bear's Hiccups* (1–2). Illus. by Diane D. Hearn. Series: Holiday House Reader. 1998, Holiday House $15.95 (978-0-8234-1339-3). 48pp. A group of animals demands to know if Bear, a grouch who wants to dominate the forest pond, is responsible for the disappearance of Frog. (Rev: BCCB 6/98; BL 5/1/98; HBG 10/98; SLJ 6/98)

7238 Bauer, Marion Dane. *Turtle Dreams* (1–2). Illus. by Diane D. Hearn. Series: Holiday House Reader. 1997, Holiday House LB $14.95 (978-0-8234-1322-5). 48pp. In this easy reader, Turtle goes to sleep for the winter and finds that he has wonderful dreams. (Rev: BL 2/1/98; HBG 3/98; SLJ 1/98)

7239 Benchley, Nathaniel. *A Ghost Named Fred* (1–3). Illus. by Ben Shecter. 1968, HarperCollins LB $17.89 (978-0-06-020474-7). 64pp. To get out of the rain, George enters an empty house and meets Fred, an absentminded ghost.

7240 Benchley, Nathaniel. *Oscar Otter* (K–2). Illus. by Arnold Lobel. 1966, HarperCollins paper $3.99 (978-0-06-444025-7). 64pp. Hilarious words and pictures describe Oscar's fun on the long and perilous slide he builds to get to his pool.

7241 Berenstain, Stan, and Jan Berenstain. *The Berenstain Bears' New Pup* (K–2). Illus. by authors. Series: Berenstain Bears. 2005, HarperCollins paper $3.99 (978-0-06-058344-6). 32pp. A rhyming easy-reader about a new pet, in the Berenstain tradition. (Rev: SLJ 7/05)

7242 Bernstein, Margery. *My Brother, the Pest* (1–2). Illus. by Dorothy Handelman. Series: Real Kids Readers. 1999, Millbrook LB $18.90 (978-0-7613-2055-5); paper $4.99 (978-0-7613-2080-7). 32pp. A rhyming story of sibling rivalry involving two sisters who quarrel and make up. (Rev: BL 5/15/99; SLJ 8/99)

7243 Black, Sonia. *Hanging Out with Mom* (1–2). Illus. by George Ford. 2000, Scholastic paper $3.99 (978-0-590-86636-1). 32pp. A beginning reader about a day that an African American boy and his mother spend in the park. (Rev: BL 10/1/00)

7244 Blackwood, Gary L. *The Just-So-Woman* (1–3). Illus. by Jane Manning. 2006, HarperCollins $15.99 (978-0-06-057727-8). 48pp. Once upon a time in the days before electricity, the Just-So Woman ran out of soap, butter, and other farm essentials and asked her neighbor, the Any-Way Man, for help, learning an important lesson in the process; a funny book for beginning readers. (Rev: BL 12/1/06; SLJ 11/06)

7245 Blair, Eric, retel. *Belling the Cat: A Retelling of Aesop's Fable* (K–3). Illus. by Dianne Silverman. Series: Read-It! Readers Fairy Tales. 2004, Picture Window LB $19.93 (978-1-4048-0321-3). 24pp. A simple retelling for beginning readers, with brief material on Aesop and on the nature of a fable. Also use *The Shoemaker and His Elves: A Retelling of the Grimms' Fairy Tale*. (Rev: SLJ 8/04)

7246 Bonsall, Crosby. *Mine's the Best* (1–2). Illus. by author. 1997, HarperCollins paper $3.99 (978-0-06-444213-8). 32pp. Two small boys discover they have identical balloons, and then begins the argument — whose is the best?

7247 Bonsall, Crosby. *Piggle* (1–2). Illus. by author. 1973, HarperCollins LB $15.89 (978-0-06-020580-5). 64pp. Homer goes in search of someone to play games with and finds Bear, who enjoys "Piggle" with him. This rhyming spree of nonsense words will please beginning readers. (Rev: HBG 10/02)

7248 Bonsall, Crosby. *Who's a Pest?* (1–3). Illus. by author. 1962, HarperCollins paper $3.99 (978-0-06-444099-8). 64pp. Even though his four sisters, a lizard, a rabbit, and a chipmunk insist that he's a pest, Homer refuses to believe it. (Rev: HBG 10/02)

7249 Bonsall, Crosby. *Who's Afraid of the Dark?* (1–3). Illus. by author. 1980, HarperCollins paper $3.99 (978-0-06-444071-4). 32pp. A little boy talks about how Stella, his dog, is afraid of the dark. (Rev: HBG 10/02)

7250 Bottner, Barbara. *Bootsie Barker Ballerina* (1–2). Illus. by G. Brian Karas. 1997, HarperCollins LB $15.89 (978-0-06-027101-5). 40pp. Bootsie Barker gets her comeuppance when she tries to bully everyone in her ballet class, including the teacher. (Rev: BL 5/1/97; SLJ 6/97)

7251 Bottner, Barbara. *Two Messy Friends* (K–2). Illus. by author. Series: Hello Reader! 1999, Scholastic paper $3.50 (978-0-590-63285-0). In this beginning reader, two very different friends accommodate their differences because they value their friendship. (Rev: SLJ 8/99)

7252 Bottner, Barbara, and Gerald Kruglik. *Pish and Posh Wish for Fairy Wings* (K–2). Illus. by Barbara Bottner. 2006, HarperCollins $15.99 (978-0-06-051419-8). 48pp. Trainee fairies Pish and Posh learn to cooperate (with a little help from the Monster Under the Bed) in order to make a wise wish and earn their fairy wings. (Rev: BL 12/1/06)

7253 Brenner, Barbara. *Wagon Wheels* (1–3). Illus. by Don Bolognese. 1993, HarperCollins paper $3.99 (978-0-06-444052-3). 64pp. The adventures of an African American family in Kansas in the 1870s.

7254 Bridwell, Norman. *Clifford Makes a Friend* (1). Illus. Series: Hello Reader! 1998, Scholastic paper $3.99 (978-0-590-37930-4). 32pp. Clifford, the beloved shaggy dog, meets a boy and, after copying his actions, becomes his friend. (Rev: BL 3/15/99)

7255 Brill, Marlene T. *Allen Jay and the Underground Railroad* (1–2). Illus. by Janice L. Porter. Series: On My Own. 1993, Carolrhoda LB $23.93 (978-0-87614-776-4); paper $5.95 (978-0-87614-605-7). 48pp. This story, which is based on fact, tells how a young Quaker child helped a slave to freedom. (Rev: BL 7/93; SLJ 8/93)

7256 Brimner, Larry Dane. *Cats!* (1). Illus. by Tom Payne. Series: Rookie Readers. 2000, Children's Book Pr. paper $4.95 (978-0-516-27075-3). 24pp.

After a little girl lets nine cats into her room, they oblige by playing with her in this book for beginning readers. (Rev: BL 2/15/01)

7257 Brimner, Larry Dane. *Twelve Plump Cookies* (1–2). Illus. by Sharon L. Holm. Series: Magic Door to Learning. 2005, The Child's World LB $21.36 (978-1-59296-523-6). 24pp. A young boy bakes a dozen cookies for guests, but when more people than expected show up, he must use his ingenuity to see that everyone gets at least part of a cookie. (Rev: SLJ 12/05)

7258 Brisson, Pat. *Little Sister, Big Sister* (2–3). Illus. 1999, Holt $15.95 (978-0-8050-5887-1). 56pp. Two sisters, Zelda and Ivy, are sometimes friends and sometimes enemies in these four stories for beginning readers. (Rev: BCCB 3/99; BL 4/15/99; HBG 10/99; SLJ 7/99)

7259 Brown, Charlotte Lewis. *Beyond the Dinosaurs: Monsters of the Air and Sea* (K–3). Illus. by Phil Wilson. 2007, HarperCollins $15.99 (978-0-06-053056-3). 32pp. Prehistoric creatures are featured in this simple illustrated book for beginning readers. (Rev: SLJ 6/07)

7260 Brown, Marc. *There's No Place Like Home* (1–3). Illus. Series: Step into Reading. 1991, Parents $5.95 (978-0-8193-1125-2). 40pp. In this easy reader, various kinds of homes are introduced in verse. (Rev: BL 12/1/91)

7261 Brown, Margaret Wise. *I Like Stars* (1). Illus. by Joan Paley. Series: Road to Reading. 1998, Golden paper $3.99 (978-0-307-26105-2). 32pp. A little rabbit leaves his bed and joins in play with a frog, a bird, and a mouse in this easy-to-read book. (Rev: BL 3/15/99)

7262 Brust, Beth Wagener. *The Great Tulip Trade* (K–2). Illus. by Jenny Mattheson. Series: Step into Reading. 2005, Random LB $11.99 (978-0-375-92573-3); paper $3.99 (978-0-375-82573-6). 48pp. In tulip-crazy 1636 Holland, Anna refuses to trade her most cherished bloom even in exchange for gold and diamonds. (Rev: BL 6/1–15/05)

7263 Buck, Nola. *Sid and Sam* (PS–K). Illus. Series: My First I Can Read Book. 1996, HarperCollins LB $14.89 (978-0-06-025372-1). 32pp. Sid's song is so long that his friend Sam says, "So long." (Rev: BCCB 7–8/96; BL 8/96; SLJ 6/96)

7264 Bulla, Clyde Robert. *Daniel's Duck* (1–3). Illus. by Joan Sandin. 1979, HarperCollins paper $3.99 (978-0-06-444031-8). 64pp. In this story for beginning readers, a young boy is hurt when people make fun of his wood carving of a duck.

7265 Byars, Betsy. *Boo's Dinosaur* (1–3). Illus. by Erik Brooks. 2006, Holt $15.95 (978-0-8050-7958-6). 41pp. Boo convinces her older brother to join in the fun as she entertains a dinosaur that only she can see in this appealing early chapter book. (Rev: SLJ 9/06)

7266 Calmenson, Stephanie. *My Dog's the Best!* (1–2). Illus. by Marcy Ramsey. 1997, Scholastic $3.99 (978-0-590-33072-5). 32pp. An easy-to-read book in which a number of children tell why they think their dog is best. (Rev: BL 2/1/98)

7267 Cameron, Ann. *Julian's Glorious Summer* (2–3). Illus. by Dora Leder. 1987, Random paper $3.99 (978-0-394-89117-0). 64pp. Troubles begin for Julian when he lies because he is afraid to ride a bike. Also use two other stories about the ups and downs of this warm African American family: *More Stories Julian Tells* (Knopf 1986); *Julian, Secret Agent* (Random 1988). (Rev: BCCB 12/87; BL 12/15/87; SLJ 12/87)

7268 *Can You Play?* (PS–1). Illus. by Emily Bolam. Series: I'm Going to Read! 2005, Sterling paper $3.95 (978-1-4027-2094-9). Stella and her dog romp through the pages of this curriculum-oriented beginning reader. (Rev: SLJ 9/05)

7269 Caple, Kathy. *The Friendship Tree* (1–2). Illus. Series: Holiday House Reader. 2000, Holiday House $15.95 (978-0-8234-1376-8). 32pp. Blanche and Otis are sheep in this easy reader that consists of four stories about trees and forests. (Rev: BL 2/15/00; HB 7/00; HBG 10/00; SLJ 4/00)

7270 Caple, Kathy. *Worm Gets a Job* (PS–2). Illus. by author. 2004, Candlewick $15.99 (978-0-7636-1694-6). Worm's efforts to earn money for painting supplies have unexpected consequences. (Rev: SLJ 7/04)

7271 Capucilli, Alyssa Satin. *Bathtime for Biscuit* (1). Illus. by Pat Schories. 1998, HarperCollins LB $17.89 (978-0-06-027938-7). 32pp. A simple story about the problems a little boy has getting his little dog, Biscuit, into the bath. (Rev: BL 11/1/98; HBG 3/99; SLJ 10/98)

7272 Capucilli, Alyssa Satin. *Biscuit* (K–1). Illus. 1996, HarperCollins LB $17.89 (978-0-06-026198-6). 32pp. A dog named Biscuit tries to make his wants known. Also use *Biscuit Finds a Friend* (1997), *Biscuit's New Trick* (2000), *Biscuit Wants to Play* (2001), *Biscuit Goes to School* (2002), and *Biscuit Takes a Walk* (2009). (Rev: BL 8/96; SLJ 7/96)

7273 Capucilli, Alyssa Satin. *Inside a Zoo in the City: A Rebus Read-Along Story* (PS–K). Illus. by Tedd Arnold. 2000, Scholastic $11.95 (978-0-590-99715-7). 32pp. Told with pictures that substitute for the names of various animals, this simple rebus book tells how the animals in a zoo actually live in apartments and have to get up in the morning and go to work like other people. (Rev: BL 12/15/00; HBG 10/01; SLJ 3/01)

7274 Capucilli, Alyssa Satin. *Pedro's Burro* (PS–1). Illus. by Pau Estrada. Series: My First I Can Read. 2007, HarperCollins $15.99 (978-0-06-056031-7). 32pp. Pedro and Papa set off to buy a burro, but none of them are quite right until they meet the one wearing a hat. (Rev: SLJ 11/07)

7275 Carris, Joan. *Welcome to the Bed and Biscuit* (1–3). Illus. by Noah Z. Jones. 2006, Candlewick $15.99 (978-0-7636-2151-3). 128pp. Grandpa Bender runs an animal boardinghouse but his personal pets — a mynah, a cat, and a small pig — have extra privileges and are miffed when Grandpa brings home a tiny puppy. (Rev: BL 10/1/06; SLJ 10/06)

7276 Carter, Candace. *Sid's Surprise* (PS–K). Illus. by Joung Un Kim. Series: Green Light Reader.

2005, Harcourt $12.95 (978-0-15-205183-9); paper $3.95 (978-0-15-205182-2). 32pp. This easy chapter book features a little snake who is thrilled to finally have a rattle — just like the big snakes. (Rev: BL 3/1/05)

7277 Catalanotto, Peter, and Pamela Schembri. *The Veterans Day Visitor* (1–2). Illus. by Peter Catalanotto. Series: 2nd-Grade Friends. 2008, Holt $15.95 (978-0-8050-7840-4). 64pp. This beginning chapter book touches on both Veterans Day and narcolepsy as Emily worries that her grandfather will fall asleep in front of her class. (Rev: BLO 7/31/08; HB 9/08)

7278 Cazet, Denys. *The Case of the Missing Jelly Donut* (1–3). Illus. Series: An I Can Read Book. 2005, HarperCollins $15.99 (978-0-06-073007-9). 48pp. Minnie and Moo, bovine detectives, go undercover to track down a suspected donut thief in this entertaining easy chapter book. (Rev: BL 9/1/05; SLJ 10/05)

7279 Cazet, Denys. *Minnie and Moo: Wanted Dead or Alive* (K–2). Series: I Can Read. 2006, HarperCollins $15.99 (978-0-06-073010-9). 48pp. Cows Minnie and Moo go to the bank to try to arrange a loan for Mr. Farmer but are mistaken for notorious bank robbers. Also recommended are *Minnie and Moo Go Dancing* and *Minnie and Moo Go to the Moon* (both 1998), *Minnie and Moo Go to Paris* and *Minnie and Moo Save the Earth* (both 1999), *Minnie and Moo and the Musk of Zorro* (2000), and *Minnie and Moo Meet Frankenswine* (2001). (Rev: BL 8/06; SLJ 8/06)

7280 Cazet, Denys. *The Octopus* (1–3). Illus. Series: I Can Read. 2005, HarperCollins LB $16.89 (978-0-06-051089-3). 48pp. Barney the puppy is miserable with chicken pox, so Grandpa tells him an elaborate tall tale about his triumph over an octopus. (Rev: BL 1/1–15/05; SLJ 1/05)

7281 Cazet, Denys. *A Snout for Chocolate* (K–2). Illus. by author. Series: Grandpa Spanielson's Chicken Pox Stories. 2006, HarperCollins $15.99 (978-0-06-051093-0). 48pp. To distract his grandson from a continuing itchy case of chicken pox, Grandpa Spanielson tells the boy how he saved Mrs. Piggerman's life when he was fire chief. Also use *The Shrunken Head* (2007). (Rev: SLJ 1/06)

7282 Chaconas, Dori. *The Collectors* (K–2). Illus. by Lisa McCue. 2008, Viking $13.99 (978-0-670-06286-7). 32pp. When possum Fuzz's "stones" hatch into ducklings, mother duck pushes him into her nest and sits on him and Cork, the muskrat, must come to the rescue. (Rev: BL 3/1/08; SLJ 3/08)

7283 Chaconas, Dori. *Cork and Fuzz* (K–2). Illus. by Lisa McCue. 2005, Viking $13.99 (978-0-670-03602-8). 32pp. Cork and Fuzz, a muskrat and a possum, both bored and lonely, try to overlook their differences and find a common interest. (Rev: SLJ 5/05)

7284 Chaconas, Dori. *Cork and Fuzz: Finders Keepers* (PS–2). Illus. by Lisa McCue. Series: Viking Easy-to-Read. 2009, Viking $13.99 (978-0-670-01113-1). 32pp. This friendship story has the short muskrat and the tall possum arguing over a green stone, but harmony is soon restored. (Rev: BL 2/1/09; SLJ 1/09)

7285 Chaconas, Dori. *Cork and Fuzz: Short and Tall* (PS–2). Illus. by Lisa McCue. Series: Viking Easy-to-Read. 2006, Viking $13.99 (978-0-670-05985-0). 32pp. The friendship between Cork the muskrat and Fuzz the possum is tested over their differences in size. Also use *Cork and Fuzz: Good Sports* (2007). (Rev: BL 1/1–15/06; SLJ 4/06)

7286 Charles, Veronika M. *Don't Go into the Forest!* (2–3). Illus. by Leanne Franson. Series: Easy-to-Read Spooky Tales. 2001, Stoddart paper $5.95 (978-0-7737-6190-2). 56pp. Young boys tell each other scary stories while they contemplate entering a forest at night. (Rev: SLJ 1/02)

7287 Charles, Veronika M. *Don't Open the Door!* (2–3). Illus. by Leanne Franson. 2001, Stoddart paper $5.95 (978-0-7737-6137-7). 56pp. During a sleepover at the narrator's house, the guests enjoy telling each other scary stories. (Rev: BL 4/15/01; SLJ 9/01)

7288 *A Class Play with Ms. Vanilla* (PS–2). Illus. by Martha Gradisher. Series: I'm Going to Read! 2005, Sterling LB $11.95 (978-1-4027-2087-1); paper $3.95 (978-1-4027-2108-3). A class production of Little Red Riding Hood doesn't turn out quite as the students expected in this easy reader. (Rev: SLJ 9/05)

7289 Cleary, Beverly. *Muggie Maggie* (2–3). Illus. by Kay Life. 1990, Avon paper $5.99 (978-0-380-71087-4). 80pp. Third-grader Maggie decides that learning to write is not necessary for a girl who can use a computer. (Rev: BCCB 6/90; BL 3/15/90; HB 11/90; SLJ 6/90)

7290 Clements, Andrew. *Dolores and the Big Fire: A True Story* (1–2). Illus. by Ellen Beier. Series: Pets to the Rescue. 2002, Simon & Schuster $15.00 (978-0-689-82916-1). 32pp. Dolores, a cat who is afraid of the dark, manages to save her master when their house catches fire. (Rev: BL 6/1–15/02; HBG 10/02; SLJ 5/02)

7291 Clifford, Eth. *Flatfoot Fox and the Case of the Missing Schoolhouse* (2–3). Illus. by Brian Lies. 1997, Houghton $15.00 (978-0-395-81446-8). 48pp. An easy read in which Flatfoot Fox and sidekick Secretary Bird foil the schemes of Wacky Weasel. (Rev: BL 3/15/97; SLJ 4/97)

7292 Cocca-Leffler, Maryann. *Ice-Cold Birthday* (K–1). Illus. Series: All Aboard Reading. 1992, Penguin paper $3.99 (978-0-448-40380-9). 32pp. A young girl has a delightful birthday in spite of a power blackout. (Rev: BL 10/1/92; SLJ 9/92)

7293 Coerr, Eleanor. *The Big Balloon Race* (1–3). Illus. by Carolyn Croll. 1992, HarperCollins paper $3.99 (978-0-06-444053-0). 64pp. Arill and her mother fly their balloon in a suspenseful race.

7294 Coerr, Eleanor. *Buffalo Bill and the Pony Express* (2–4). Illus. by Don Bolognese. 1995, HarperCollins LB $15.89 (978-0-06-023373-0). 64pp. Billy outsmarts some Indians and scares off a pack of wolves in this easily read adventure. (Rev: BCCB 4/95; BL 4/15/95; HB 7/95; SLJ 5/95)

7295 Coerr, Eleanor. *Chang's Paper Pony* (1–3). Illus. by author. 1988, HarperCollins paper $3.99 (978-0-06-444163-6). 64pp. A young Chinese boy longs for a pony in the California Gold Rush days. (Rev: BL 7/88; SLJ 12/88)

7296 Coerr, Eleanor. *The Josefina Story Quilt* (1–3). Illus. by Bruce Degen. 1986, HarperCollins LB $16.89 (978-0-06-021349-7); paper $3.99 (978-0-06-444129-2). 64pp. Faith's sorrow at the death of her pet hen during their trip west to California is softened by the quilt she sews in remembrance. (Rev: BCCB 5/86; BL 3/15/86; SLJ 5/86)

7297 Cohen, Caron L. *How Many Fish?* (1–2). Illus. by S. D. Schindler. Series: My First I Can Read Book. 1998, HarperCollins paper $12.95 (978-0-06-027713-0). 32pp. A fish is trapped under a child's upside-down pail, but later it is freed in this easy-to-read adventure. (Rev: BL 2/1/98; HBG 10/98; SLJ 2/98)

7298 Cole, Joanna. *The Missing Tooth* (1–3). Illus. by Marylin Hafner. 1989, Random paper $3.99 (978-0-394-89279-5). 48pp. Arlo is upset when best friend Robby loses a second tooth and he doesn't. (Rev: BL 3/1/89; SLJ 5/89)

7299 Cole, Joanna. *Norma Jean, Jumping Bean* (1–3). Illus. 1987, Random paper $3.99 (978-0-394-88668-8). 48pp. Norma Jean, a kangaroo child, stops jumping when her feelings are ruffled, until field day at school. (Rev: BCCB 6/87; BL 6/1/87; SLJ 6–7/87)

7300 Cole, Joanna, and Stephanie Calmenson, eds. *Ready . . . Set . . . Read! The Beginning Reader's Treasury* (K–2). Illus. 1990, Doubleday $17.95 (978-0-385-41416-6). 144pp. This is an easily read collection of stories by such writers as Dr. Seuss and Maurice Sendak. (Rev: BL 12/1/90; SLJ 9/90*)

7301 Collicott, Sharleen. *Mildred and Sam and Their Babies* (PS–2). Illus. Series: I Can Read! 2005, HarperCollins LB $16.89 (978-0-06-058112-1). 48pp. For beginning readers, this is a simple story about eight baby mice growing up in a safe and loving home. (Rev: BL 5/15/05)

7302 Cooper, Susan. *The Magician's Boy* (2–4). Illus. by Serena Riglietti. 2005, Simon & Schuster $15.95 (978-0-689-87622-6). 112pp. The Boy, apprenticed to a master magician, is dispatched to find a missing puppet and in the course of his search ends up in a land filled with characters from familiar fairy tales and nursery rhymes. (Rev: BL 1/1–15/05; SLJ 3/05)

7303 Cosby, Bill. *One Dark and Scary Night* (K–2). Illus. by Varnette P. Honeywood. Series: Little Bill. 1999, Scholastic $13.95 (978-0-590-51475-0); paper $3.99 (978-0-590-51476-7). In this beginning reader, Little Bill learns to conquer his fears concerning noises he hears in the night. (Rev: HBG 10/99; SLJ 7/99)

7304 Cosby, Bill. *Shipwreck Saturday* (2–4). Illus. Series: Little Bill. 1998, Scholastic $13.95 (978-0-590-16400-9); paper $3.99 (978-0-590-95620-8). 40pp. Although Little Bill's boat is destroyed on its first voyage, a friend uses its parts for a kite. (Rev: BL 5/15/98; SLJ 6/98)

7305 Cosby, Bill. *Super-Fine Valentine* (2–4). Illus. Series: Little Bill. 1998, Scholastic $13.95 (978-0-590-16401-6). 40pp. Using eye-catching artwork, this is the simple story of Little Bill who is reluctant to give his friend Mia a Valentine until some of his other friends give her one first. (Rev: BL 5/15/98; SLJ 6/98)

7306 Cottringer, Anne. *Movie Magic: A Star Is Born* (2–4). Illus. by Roger Stewart. Series: Eyewitness Reader. 1999, DK $12.99 (978-0-7894-4009-9); paper $3.99 (978-0-7894-4008-2). 48pp. In this easy reader, which uses color photos to show the movie-making process, a young African American girl gets a part in a science fiction movie. (Rev: SLJ 8/99)

7307 Coxe, Molly. *Big Egg* (1–2). Illus. 1997, Random LB $11.99 (978-0-679-98126-8); paper $3.99 (978-0-679-88126-1). 32pp. For the beginning reader, this story tells what happens after Hen finds a huge egg among her little ones. (Rev: BL 5/1/97)

7308 Coxe, Molly. *Hot Dog* (1). Illus. Series: Road to Reading. 1998, Golden paper $3.99 (978-0-307-26101-4). 32pp. A dog who is trying to fight the heat, irritates a cat, skunk, pig, and others in this beginning reader. (Rev: BCCB 2/99; BL 3/15/99)

7309 Cristaldi, Kathryn. *Baseball Ballerina* (1–3). Illus. by Abby Carter. Series: Step into Reading. 1992, Random paper $3.99 (978-0-679-81734-5). 48pp. A young girl who loves baseball is afraid that her friends will find out she is taking ballet lessons. (Rev: BCCB 6/92; BL 6/1/92; SLJ 9/92)

7310 Cristaldi, Kathryn. *Princess Lulu Goes to Camp* (1–2). Illus. by Heather H. Maione. 1997, Penguin paper $3.99 (978-0-448-41125-5). 48pp. An easy reader about the obnoxious Princess Lulu at a summer camp. (Rev: BL 8/97; SLJ 12/97)

7311 Cushman, Doug. *Aunt Eater Loves a Mystery* (1–2). Illus. by author. 1987, HarperCollins paper $3.99 (978-0-06-444216-1). 64pp. Grandmotherly Aunt Eater, an anteater, loves to solve mysteries. (Rev: BL 10/1/87; SLJ 12/87)

7312 Cushman, Doug. *Aunt Eater's Mystery Vacation* (1–2). Illus. 1992, HarperCollins LB $15.89 (978-0-06-020514-0). 64pp. Amateur detective Aunt Eater finds mystery and adventure on what was promised to be a relaxing cruise. (Rev: BL 4/1/92; SLJ 6/92)

7313 Cushman, Doug. *Dirk Bones and the Mystery of the Haunted House* (K–2). Series: I Can Read! 2006, HarperCollins $16.99 (978-0-06-073764-1). 32pp. Dirk Bones, a skeleton reporter for the "Ghostly Tombs," investigates a haunted house whose ghostly residents are spooked by unexplained noises. (Rev: BL 8/06; SLJ 7/06)

7314 Cushman, Doug. *Dirk Bones and the Mystery of the Missing Books* (K–2). Illus. by author. Series: I Can Read. 2009, HarperCollins $16.99 (978-0-06-073768-9). 32pp. Dirk, the skeleton detective, is looking into the case of a missing manuscript when he discovers that even more books have disappeared and there is a suspicious plant in the area. (Rev: BL 5/1/09; SLJ 5/09)

7315 Cushman, Doug. *Inspector Hopper's Mystery Year* (1–3). Illus. by author. Series: I Can Read.

2003, HarperCollins LB $16.89 (978-0-06-008963-4). 64pp. Grasshopper Inspector Hopper and his assistant, McBugg, are kept busy throughout the year with seasonal mysteries to solve. (Rev: HBG 10/03; SLJ 5/03)

7316 Cutler, Jane. *Rose and Riley Come and Go* (K–2). Illus. by Thomas F. Yezerski. 2005, Farrar $15.00 (978-0-374-36341-3). 48pp. Friends Rose, a tiny vole, and Riley, a lively groundhog, make discoveries about nature in three episodic stories for beginning readers that feature silly wordplay and detailed illustrations. (Rev: BL 6/1–15/05)

7317 Dahl, Michael. *The Tall, Tall Slide* (K–2). Illus. by Sara Gray. Series: Read It! Readers. 2006, Picture Window LB $19.93 (978-1-4048-1186-7). 32pp. On a hot summer day, new friends help Tina to overcome her fears of the tall slide at the local swimming pool. (Rev: BL 3/1/06)

7318 Danziger, Paula. *Get Ready for Second Grade, Amber Brown* (1–3). Illus. by Tony Ross. 2002, Penguin $13.99 (978-0-399-23607-5). 48pp. Amber's concerns about the new 2nd-grade teacher turn out to be unfounded in this prequel for beginning readers. (Rev: BL 11/1/02; HBG 10/02; SLJ 7/02)

7319 Danziger, Paula. *It's a Fair Day, Amber Brown* (1–3). Illus. by Tony Ross. 2002, Penguin $14.99 (978-0-399-23606-8). 48pp. Amber and her family spend an enjoyable day at the fair despite some arguments and Amber getting lost. (Rev: BL 11/1/02; HBG 10/02; SLJ 7/02)

7320 Danziger, Paula. *It's Justin Time, Amber Brown* (1–3). Illus. by Tony Ross. 2001, Penguin $13.99 (978-0-399-23470-5). 48pp. In this beginning reader, Amber Brown, age 7, gets her wish of a watch for her birthday now that she has learned to tell the time. (Rev: HBG 10/01; SLJ 3/01)

7321 Danziger, Paula. *Orange You Glad It's Halloween, Amber Brown?* (1–3). Illus. by Tony Ross. 2005, Penguin $13.99 (978-0-399-23471-2). 48pp. In addition to planning for Halloween, Amber has concerns about school and family life in this easy-reader that also features her best friend Justin. (Rev: BL 5/15/05)

7322 Danziger, Paula. *What a Trip, Amber Brown* (K–3). Illus. by Tony Ross. Series: A Is for Amber. 2001, Penguin $13.99 (978-0-399-23469-9). 48pp. Amber and Justin enjoy an on-again off-again friendship on a vacation in the "Poke a nose." (Rev: HBG 10/01; SLJ 4/01)

7323 Davis, Tim. *Mice of the Westing Wind: Book One* (2–3). Illus. by author. 1998, Journey Bks. paper $7.49 (978-1-57924-065-3). 114pp. Two mouse spies, Charles and Oliver, join a group out to capture a crew of pirate sea dogs who have escaped from prison. Also use *The Mouse of the Westing Wind: Book Two* (1998). (Rev: SLJ 5/99)

7324 deGroat, Diane. *Gilbert, the Surfer Dude* (K–2). Illus. by author. Series: I Can Read Book: Gilbert and Friends. 2009, HarperCollins $16.99 (978-0-06-125211-2). 32pp. Gilbert the possum has forgotten his bathing suit and buys some too-large "Surfer Dude" trunks only to discover that oversize

trunks and surfing don't mix well. (Rev: BL 3/15/09; SLJ 6/09)

7325 Delton, Judy. *Cookies and Crutches* (1–2). Illus. by Alan Tiegreen. 1988, Dell paper $3.99 (978-0-440-40010-3). 80pp. Molly and her friends find out that baking at home isn't quite as easy as it looks. (Rev: BL 6/1/88)

7326 Denton, Kady M. *Watch Out, William!* (K–2). Series: I Am Reading. 2006, Kingfisher paper $3.95 (978-0-7534-5960-7). 48pp. Three short chapters recount everyday adventures of William and his little sister Jane. (Rev: BL 5/1/06; SLJ 8/06)

7327 dePaola, Tomie. *Hide-and-Seek All Week* (1–2). Illus. Series: The Barkers. 2001, Penguin paper $3.99 (978-0-448-42545-0). 32pp. Moffie and Morgie and friends decide they want to play hide-and-seek during recess, but can't decide on the rules. (Rev: BL 2/1/02; HBG 3/02; SLJ 2/02)

7328 dePaola, Tomie. *Kit and Kat* (1–2). Illus. 1994, Penguin paper $3.99 (978-0-448-40748-7). 32pp. Three easily read stories about the everyday adventures of Kit and Kat, the Kitten Kids. (Rev: BL 1/1/95)

7329 deRubertis, Barbara. *Deena's Lucky Penny* (1–2). Illus. by Joan Holub and Cynthia Fisher. Series: Math Matters. 1999, Kane paper $4.95 (978-1-57565-091-3). 32pp. This easy reader introduces the simple arithmetic of counting money, through the story of a young girl who saves to buy her mother a birthday present. (Rev: BL 12/1/99)

7330 DiCamillo, Kate. *Mercy Watson Fights Crime* (PS–2). Illus. by Chris Van Dusen. 2006, Candlewick $12.99 (978-0-7636-2590-0). 70pp. Mercy Watson, the crime-fighting pig, nabs a toaster thief red-handed. (Rev: SLJ 11/06*)

7331 DiCamillo, Kate. *Mercy Watson Princess in Disguise* (PS–2). Illus. by Chris Van Dusen. 2007, Candlewick $12.99 (978-0-7636-3014-0). 80pp. Mercy the pig is up to her old shenanigans as she pursues the promise of goodies while trick-or-treating in her Halloween princess costume. (Rev: BL 7/07; SLJ 8/07)

7332 DiCamillo, Kate. *Mercy Watson to the Rescue* (PS–2). Illus. by Chris Van Dusen. 2005, Candlewick $12.99 (978-0-7636-2270-1). 80pp. The Watsons love Mercy, their pig, so much that they invite her to share their bed, a decision with disastrous consequences; the first in a new series of chapter books for beginning readers. (Rev: BCCB 12/05; BL 8/05*; HBG 4/06; LMC 1/06; SLJ 10/05)

7333 Donahue, Jill L. *Benny and the Birthday Gift* (1–2). Illus. by Burak Senturk. 2007, Picture Window LB $19.93 (978-1-4048-3164-3). 24pp. Beginning readers will build their confidence with this simple story about Benny's search for a friend's birthday gift. (Rev: SLJ 7/07)

7334 Donnelly, Judy. *The Titanic: Lost . . . and Found* (2–4). Illus. by Keith Kohler. 1987, Random paper $3.99 (978-0-394-88669-5). 48pp. In a simple account the author describes the sinking of the *Titanic* and its rediscovery. (Rev: BCCB 6/87; BL 6/1/87; SLJ 6–7/87)

7335 Donnelly, Judy. *Tut's Mummy: Lost . . . and Found* (2–3). Illus. by James Watling. 1988, Random paper $3.99 (978-0-394-89189-7). 48pp. The story of the 20th-century discovery of King Tut's tomb. (Rev: BL 10/1/88; SLJ 10/88)

7336 Dotlich, Rebecca. *Away We Go!* (PS). Illus. by Dan Yaccarino. Series: Growing Tree. 2000, HarperCollins $9.95 (978-0-694-01393-7). 24pp. All kinds of vehicles — from a school bus and jumbo jet to a wheelchair and sled — are pictured along with people in motion in this easy-to-read book. (Rev: BL 9/1/00; HBG 3/01; SLJ 11/00)

7337 Dotlich, Rebecca Kai. *Peanut and Pearl's Picnic Adventure* (PS–1). Illus. by R. W. Alley. Series: I Can Read. 2007, HarperCollins $15.99 (978-0-06-054920-6). 32pp. Peanut and Pearl set off on a picnic but then become separated and cannot find each other. (Rev: BL 5/1/07; SLJ 10/07)

7338 Dubowski, Cathy E. *Pirate School* (1–3). Illus. by Mark Dubowski. Series: All Aboard Reading. 1996, Grosset paper $3.99 (978-0-448-41132-3). 48pp. An easy-to-read adventure about a boy who attends pirate school. (Rev: SLJ 4/97)

7339 Dubowski, Cathy E., and Mark Dubowski. *Snug Bug* (PS–1). Illus. 1995, Penguin paper $3.99 (978-0-448-40849-1). 32pp. An easily read book about a little bug that prepares for bed. (Rev: BL 7/95)

7340 Duey, Kathleen. *Moonsilver: The Unicorn's Secret #1* (2–4). Illus. by Omar Rayyan. 2001, Simon & Schuster paper $3.99 (978-0-689-84269-6). 80pp. This alluring fantasy tale for younger readers introduces a young girl who finds a mysterious white mare with a scar on its forehead. (Rev: BL 1/1–15/02; SLJ 12/01)

7341 Duey, Kathleen. *The Mountains of the Moon* (2–4). Illus. by Omar Rayyan. Series: Ready-for-Chapters Unicorn's Secret. 2002, Simon & Schuster paper $3.99 (978-0-689-84272-6). 80pp. The fourth episode in the continuing magical story of Heart and her unicorns, for beginning readers. Also use the third book in the series, *The Silver Bracelet* (2002). (Rev: BL 9/1/02; HBG 3/03)

7342 Duey, Kathleen. *The Sunset Gates* (2–4). Illus. by Omar Rayyan. Series: Unicorn's Secret. 2002, Simon & Schuster paper $3.99 (978-0-689-85346-3). 80pp. The adventures of Heart Avamir, who is on the run in an effort to save two unicorns, continue in this easy-reader as she travels with gypsies and learns to read. Also use *True Heart* (2003). (Rev: BL 3/1/03; HBG 10/03)

7343 Durant, Alan. *Brown Bear Gets in Shape* (K–2). Illus. by Annabel Hudson. Series: I Am Reading. 2004, Kingfisher paper $3.95 (978-0-7534-5797-9). 45pp. Brown Bear is determined to get in shape, and tries copying Bunny and Chimp's diet and exercise regimens. (Rev: SLJ 8/04)

7344 Dussling, Jennifer. *Fair Is Fair!* (1–2). Illus. by Diane Palmisciano. Series: Math Matters. 2003, Kane paper $4.99 (978-1-57565-131-6). 32pp. Marco's skill with bar graphs helps him persuade his father to raise his allowance. (Rev: SLJ 2/04)

7345 Eastman, P. D. *Are You My Mother?* (1–3). Illus. by author. 1960, Random LB $13.99 (978-0-394-90018-6). 64pp. A bird falls from the nest and looks for its mother.

7346 Eastman, Peter. *Fred and Ted Go Camping* (PS–2). Illus. by author. Series: Beginner Books. 2005, Random $8.99 (978-0-375-82965-9). Two dog friends enjoy each other's company on a camping trip in this book for beginning readers. (Rev: SLJ 7/05)

7347 Eaton, Deborah. *My Wild Woolly* (K–2). Illus. by G. Brian Karas. Series: Green Light Readers. 2005, Harcourt $12.95 (978-0-15-205148-8). 24pp. A young boy spends an entertaining afternoon playing in his backyard with a "wild woolly," a creature the boy's mother claims does not exist. (Rev: BL 11/1/05)

7348 Eaton, Deborah. *The Rainy Day Grump* (K–2). Illus. by Dorothy Handelman. Series: Real Kids Readers. 1998, Millbrook LB $18.90 (978-0-7613-2018-0); paper $4.99 (978-0-7613-2043-2). 32pp. In this easy reader illustrated by color photographs, Rosie tries to amuse her brother Clay who is grumpy because it's raining and he can't go out to play. (Rev: BL 11/1/98)

7349 Egan, Tim. *Dodsworth in New York* (1–2). Illus. by author. 2007, Houghton $15.00 (978-0-618-77708-2). 48pp. Dodsworth the mouse sets off for New York only to find that his friend Hodges's duck has come along for the ride. (Rev: BCCB 10/07; BL 10/15/07; HB 9/07; SLJ 11/07)

7350 Ehrlich, Amy. *Bravo, Kazam!* (PS–K). Illus. by Barney Saltzberg. Series: Brand New Readers. 2002, Candlewick paper $4.99 (978-0-7636-1316-7). 40pp. In this beginning reader illustrated with cartoons, a rabbit is chased by a pack of magical cards. (Rev: BL 4/15/02)

7351 Elste, Joan. *True Blue* (2–3). Illus. by DyAnne Disalvo-Ryan. 1996, Penguin paper $3.99 (978-0-448-41264-1). 48pp. J.D. worries when his faithful dog Blue disappears. (Rev: BL 11/15/96)

7352 Emerson, Carl. *The Autumn Leaf* (K–2). Illus. by Cori Doerrfeld. Series: Read-It! Readers: Science. 2008, Picture Window LB $19.93 (978-1-4048-2624-3); paper $3.95 (978-1-4048-4755-2). 32pp. Owen and Emma explore how a change of weather changes a tree in this book for beginning readers. Also use *The Busy Spring, The Cold Winter Day,* and *The Summer Playground* (all 2008). (Rev: SLJ 12/08)

7353 Erickson, John R. *Hank the Cowdog: The Case of the Haystack Kitties* (2–3). Illus. by Gerald L. Holmes. Series: Hank the Cowdog. 1998, Gulf $14.95 (978-0-87719-338-8). 113pp. Hank's many adventures on the ranch include being threatened by a bull and saving a family of kittens. (Rev: SLJ 11/98)

7354 Finch, Margo. *The Lunch Bunch* (K–2). Photos by Dorothy Handelman. Series: Real Kids Readers. 1998, Millbrook LB $16.90 (978-0-7613-2005-0); paper $4.99 (978-0-7613-2030-2). 32pp. A new girl at school searches for friends in this enjoyable beginning reader. (Rev: SLJ 7/98)

7355 Fine, Anne. *The Jamie and Angus Stories* (2–4). Illus. by Penny Dale. 2002, Candlewick $15.99 (978-0-7636-1862-9). 112pp. Jamie and toy bull Angus have a variety of gentle adventures in these six stories for beginning chapter-book readers. (Rev: BCCB 10/02; BL 11/15/02; HB 1/03*; HBG 3/03; SLJ 9/02)

7356 Fine, Annie. *Jamie and Angus Together* (PS–2). Illus. by Penny Dale. 2007, Candlewick $15.99 (978-0-7636-3374-5). 112pp. The six short stories in this engaging chapter book follow Jamie as he plays with his beloved stuffed animal Angus; a sequel to *The Jamie and Angus Stories* (2002). (Rev: BL 6/1–15/07; SLJ 8/07)

7357 Florie, Christine. *Lara Ladybug* (PS–1). Illus. by Danny Brooks Dalby. Series: Rookie Reader. 2005, Children's Pr. LB $19.50 (978-0-516-25137-0); paper $4.95 (978-0-516-25281-0). 23pp. Lara has lost her spots in this book for beginning readers illustrated with collages. (Rev: SLJ 7/05)

7358 Floyd, Lucy. *A Place for Nicholas* (PS–2). Illus. by David McPhail. Series: Green Light Reader. 2005, Harcourt paper $3.95 (978-0-15-205149-5). 24pp. Nicholas longs for a space of his own in this reprint of a 1997 title. (Rev: BL 2/15/05)

7359 Ford, Bernette. *Don't Hit Me!* (K–1). Illus. by Gary Grier. Series: Just for You! 2004, Scholastic paper $3.99 (978-0-439-56860-9). 32pp. A simple easy-reader story about friends agreeing to disagree, featuring African Americans. Also use *Hurry Up!!* (2004). (Rev: SLJ 1/05)

7360 Ford, Juwanda G. *Shop Talk* (K–3). Illus. by Jim Hoston. Series: Just for You! 2004, Scholastic paper $3.99 (978-0-439-56873-9). 32pp. A simple easy-reader story about a visit to the barbershop, featuring African Americans. (Rev: SLJ 1/05)

7361 Ford, Juwanda G. *Sunday Best* (K–3). Illus. by Colin Bootman. Series: Just for You! 2004, Scholastic paper $3.99 (978-0-439-56854-8). 32pp. An African American family enjoys a weekend together. (Rev: SLJ 1/05)

7362 Freeman, Martha. *Mrs. Wow Never Wanted a Cow* (K–2). Illus. by Steven Salerno. 2006, Random $8.99 (978-0-375-83418-9). Mrs. Wow's pets change their ways when a cow becomes a member of the family in this humorous brightly illustrated book for beginning readers. (Rev: SLJ 6/06)

7363 Gantos, Jack. *Rotten Ralph Helps Out* (1–2). Illus. by Nicole Rubel. Series: Rotten Ralph Rotten Reader. 2001, Farrar $14.00 (978-0-374-36355-0). 48pp. Ralph the rotten cat helps — or rather hinders — Sarah with her project on ancient Egypt. Also use *Practice Makes Perfect for Rotten Ralph* (2002) and *Best in Show for Rotten Ralph* (2005). (Rev: BL 7/01; HB 9/01; HBG 3/02; SLJ 8/01)

7364 Gauthier, Gail. *A Girl, a Boy, and Three Robbers* (2–4). Illus. by Joe Cepeda. 2008, Putnam $14.99 (978-0-399-24690-6). 87pp. Imaginative Hannah forces Brandon, who would prefer to watch television, to go along with her ideas; but then her wild stories about the children next door seem to come true and Hannah's cat must be rescued. (Rev: HB 9/08; LMC 11/08; SLJ 11/08)

7365 George, Jean Craighead. *Goose and Duck* (PS–2). Illus. by Priscilla Lamont. 2008, HarperCollins $16.99 (978-0-06-117076-8). 48pp. In this humorous book for beginning readers, a goose imitates the actions of a boy while a duck follows the behavior of the goose. (Rev: BCCB 2/08; BL 12/1/07; SLJ 2/08)

7366 George, Olivia. *My Birthday Cake* (K–2). Illus. by Martha Aviles. Series: My First Reader. 2005, Children's Pr. LB $18.50 (978-0-516-25178-3). 31pp. A birthday girl tries to make her own cake, covering it with blue icing, in this book for beginning readers with a list of words. (Rev: SLJ 5/05)

7367 Ghigna, Charles. *Mice Are Nice* (1). Illus. by Jon Goodell. Series: Step into Reading. 1999, Random paper $3.99 (978-0-679-88929-8). 32pp. In a pet store, a small mouse tells a little girl why mice make the best pets compared with other animals. (Rev: BL 10/1/99; HBG 3/00)

7368 Gibala-Broxholm, Scott. *Scary Fright, Are You All Right?* (K–3). Illus. 2002, Dial $14.99 (978-0-8037-2588-1). 48pp. Scary Fright, a little monster, alarms her parents by acting too much like a human girl. (Rev: BL 9/15/02; HBG 3/03; SLJ 8/02)

7369 Giff, Patricia Reilly. *The Beast in Ms. Rooney's Room* (2–4). Illus. by Blanche Sims. 1984, Dell paper $4.50 (978-0-440-40485-9). 80pp. A volume in the Kids of the Polk Street School series. Another title is: *Fish Face* (1984).

7370 Giff, Patricia Reilly. *In the Dinosaur's Paw* (2–4). Illus. by Blanche Sims. 1985, Dell paper $3.99 (978-0-440-44150-2). 80pp. The Polk Street School kids in the month of February. Also use: *The Candy Corn Contest* (1984); *December Secrets* (1984); *The Valentine Star* (1985); *All about Stacy* (1988). (Rev: BL 4/15/85)

7371 Giff, Patricia Reilly. *Next Stop, New York City! The Polk Street Kids on Tour* (2–4). Illus. by Blanche Sims. Series: Polk Street Special. 1997, Dell paper $3.99 (978-0-440-41362-2). 119pp. When Ms. Rooney and the Polk Street crowd visit New York City, Emily Arrow is upset because she has been dubbed an expert on the Big Apple, but she really knows nothing about it. (Rev: SLJ 10/97)

7372 Giff, Patricia Reilly. *Purple Climbing Days* (1–3). Illus. by Blanche Sims. 1985, Bantam paper $3.99 (978-0-440-47309-1). 80pp. Richard "Beast" Best of the Polk Street School is afraid to climb the floor-to-ceiling rope in gym. Two others in this series are: *Lazy Lions, Lucky Lambs; Snaggle Doodles* (both 1985). (Rev: BL 8/85; SLJ 11/85)

7373 Giff, Patricia Reilly. *Sunny-Side Up* (1–3). Illus. by Blanche Sims. 1986, Dell paper $3.99 (978-0-440-48406-6). 74pp. The Polk Street School kids are in summer school and have to deal with Matthew's announcement that he is moving away. Another in this series is: *Spectacular Stone Soup* (1989). (Rev: BL 10/1/86; SLJ 3/87)

7374 Gikow, Louise A. *A Day with Daddy* (PS–2). Illus. by Gustavo Mazali. Series: My First Reader. 2004, Children's Pr. LB $18.50 (978-0-516-24410-5). 31pp. Daddy is the one exhausted by a day out in this rhyming book for beginning readers with cartoon illustrations and a word list. (Rev: SLJ 7/04)

7375 *Go Away, Crows!* (PS–2). Illus. by Santiago Cohen. Series: I'm Going to Read! 2005, Sterling LB $11.95 (978-1-4027-2080-2); paper $3.95 (978-1-4027-2103-8). A brother and sister find a way to scare the crows away from their garden in this easy reader. (Rev: SLJ 9/05)

7376 Gorbachev, Valeri. *Ms. Turtle the Babysitter* (K–1). Illus. by author. 2005, HarperCollins $15.99 (978-0-06-058073-5). 64pp. Simple chapters describe the ways three little frogs try their turtle babysitter's patience. (Rev: SLJ 8/05)

7377 Graham, Bob. *Tales from the Waterhole* (K–3). Illus. by author. 2004, Candlewick $16.99 (978-0-7636-2324-1). 62pp. The animals of the savannah enjoy playing around the waterhole — soccer, skateboarding, and so forth — in this series of five short stories for beginning readers. (Rev: SLJ 7/04)

7378 Grant, Judyann Ackerman. *Chicken Said, "Cluck!"* (K–2). Illus. by Sue Truesdell. Series: I Can Read! 2008, HarperCollins $16.99 (978-0-06-028723-8). 32pp. Earl and Pearl banish the pesky Chicken when they plant a pumpkin patch, but Chicken proves very useful when the grasshoppers turn up. (Rev: HB 1/09; SLJ 11/08)

7379 Greco, Francesca. *Gideon* (2–4). Illus. by author. 2003, Star Bright $16.95 (978-1-932065-02-2). Poor Gideon the chameleon — always invisible to his jungle neighbors — comes into his own when he warns them of an approaching tiger. (Rev: HBG 10/03; SLJ 5/03)

7380 Greenburg, Dan. *Dude, Where's My Spaceship?* (2–3). Illus. by Dave Calver. Series: Weird Planet. 2006, Random LB $11.99 (978-0-375-93344-8); paper $3.99 (978-0-375-83344-1). 81pp. After crashing their spaceship on Earth, alien Klatu and his brother Lek try to rescue their sister Ploo, who's been taken captive by a band of earthlings; humor and large print make this suitable for emerging readers. (Rev: SLJ 3/06)

7381 Greene, Carol. *Hi, Clouds* (K–2). Illus. by Gene Sharp. 1983, Children's Book Pr. LB $19.50 (978-0-516-02036-5); paper $4.95 (978-0-516-42036-3). 32pp. Two children see many objects in clouds in this easy-to-read book. Two others in this series are: *Ice Is . . . Whee!; Shine, Sun!* (both 1983).

7382 Greene, Stephanie. *Moose Crossing* (1–3). Illus. by Joe Mathieu. Series: Moose and Hildy. 2005, Marshall Cavendish $14.95 (978-0-7614-5233-1). 56pp. In this easy-reader chapter book, Moose finds that celebrity is not as much fun as he expected. (Rev: SLJ 3/06)

7383 Greene, Stephanie. *Moose's Big Idea* (1–3). Illus. by Joe Mathieu. Series: Moose and Hildy. 2005, Marshall Cavendish $14.95 (978-0-7614-5212-6). 51pp. In this easy-reader chapter book, Moose bemoans his lost antlers, draws pictures at home during hunting season, and later sells puts on a disguise and sells doughnuts, coffee, and original artwork to unsuspecting hunters; all this in the company of his pig friend Hildy. (Rev: SLJ 10/05)

7384 Greene, Stephanie. *Owen Foote, Super Spy* (2–4). Illus. by Martha Weston. 2001, Clarion $15.00 (978-0-618-11752-9). 90pp. Owen and his friends spy on their elementary-school principal in this funny adventure. (Rev: BL 1/1–15/02; HB 11/01; HBG 3/02; SLJ 10/01)

7385 Greene, Stephanie. *The Show-Off* (1–3). Illus. by Joe Mathieu. Series: Moose and Hildy. 2007, Marshall Cavendish $14.99 (978-0-7614-5374-1). 53pp. Hildy the pig and her friend Moose help boring cousin Vincent learn how to behave; a short chapter book for transitional readers. (Rev: SLJ 10/07)

7386 Gregorich, Barbara. *Waltur Buys a Pig in a Poke and Other Stories* (2–4). Illus. by Kristin Sorra. 2006, Houghton $15.00 (978-0-618-47306-9). 64pp. In this easy-reader chapter book full of wordplay, Waltur the bear learns the truth behind three widely held maxims. (Rev: BL 6/1–15/06; SLJ 7/06)

7387 Gregorich, Barbara. *Waltur Paints Himself into a Corner and Other Stories* (K–3). Illus. by Kristin Sorra. 2007, Houghton $15.00 (978-0-618-74796-2). 48pp. Each story in this humorous easy-reader features Waltur the bear learning the meaning of a different idiom, such as "putting the cart before the horse." (Rev: BL 12/1/07; SLJ 10/07)

7388 Griffiths, Andy. *The Cat on the Mat Is Flat* (2–4). Illus. by Terry Denton. 2007, Feiwel & Friends paper $9.95 (978-0-312-36787-9). 176pp. Nine action-packed rhyming stories are full of fun and wordplay. (Rev: SLJ 1/08)

7389 Grimes, Nikki. *A Day With Daddy* (K–2). Illus. by Nicole Tadgell. Series: Just for You! 2004, Scholastic paper $3.99 (978-0-439-56850-0). 32pp. An African American who lives with his mother looks forward to an outing with his father in this easy-reader. (Rev: BL 10/15/04; SLJ 2/05)

7390 Grimes, Nikki. *Wild, Wild Hair* (1–2). Illus. by George Ford. Series: Hello Reader! 1997, Scholastic $3.99 (978-0-590-26590-4). A young African American girl dreads Monday, when her hair is braided, in this easy-to-read book. (Rev: BL 5/1/97; SLJ 4/97)

7391 Grindley, Sally. *Poppy and Max and the Fashion Show* (K–2). Illus. by Lindsey Gardiner. Series: Poppy and Max. 2009, Orchard paper $6.95 (978-1-84362-393-9). 32pp. Amiable Poppy and her talking dog Max have a chance to be in a fashion show and while Poppy is excited to volunteer, Max is hesitant at first. (Rev: SLJ 5/09)

7392 Grindley, Sally. *Poppy and Max and the Lost Puppy* (K–2). Illus. by Lindsey Gardiner. Series: Poppy and Max. 2009, Orchard paper $6.95 (978-1-84362-394-6). 32pp. Poppy's talking dog Max must deal with some jealousy when Poppy finds a lost puppy. Also use *Poppy and Max and the River Picnic, Poppy and Max and the Noisy Night,* and *Poppy and Max and the Snow Dog* (all 2009). (Rev: SLJ 5/09)

7393 Guest, Elissa Haden. *Iris and Walter: The School Play* (K–2). Illus. by Christine Davenier. Series: Iris and Walter. 2003, Harcourt $15.00 (978-

0-15-216481-2). 44pp. Iris and Walter are excited to have roles in the school play, but when the big day finally arrives, Iris is sick. Also use *Iris and Walter: Lost and Found* (2004). (Rev: HB 5/03; HBG 10/03; SLJ 4/03)

7394 Guest, Elissa Haden. *Iris and Walter: The Sleepover* (K–1). Illus. by Christine Davenier. 2002, Harcourt $14.00 (978-0-15-216487-4). 44pp. Iris can't wait for the sleepover at Walter's house, but when it arrives she can't sleep and has to be taken home to bed. (Rev: BL 11/1/02; HBG 3/03; SLJ 10/02)

7395 Guest, Elissa Haden. *Iris and Walter and the Birthday Party* (1–3). Illus. by Christine Davenier. Series: Iris and Walter. 2006, Harcourt $15.00 (978-0-15-205015-3). 44pp. Walter and Iris's friends will get to ride Walter's horse on his birthday, but there is a surprise — a foal — awaiting them. (Rev: BL 2/1/06; SLJ 3/06)

7396 Guest, Elissa Haden. *Iris and Walter and the Field Trip* (1–3). Illus. by Christine Davenier. 2005, Harcourt $15.00 (978-0-15-205014-6). 44pp. Despite his teacher's warnings to stay together, Walter is so entranced by the coral reef exhibit at the aquarium that the class has to go back to get him. (Rev: BL 5/15/05; SLJ 6/05)

7397 Guilfoile, Elizabeth. *Nobody Listens to Andrew* (1–3). Illus. by Mary Stevens. 1957, Modern Curriculum paper $7.50 (978-0-8136-5959-6). The reaction of Andrew's elders when he tells them there is a bear in his bed.

7398 Gunderson, Jessica. *The Emperor's Painting: A Story of Ancient China* (2–5). Illus. by Caroline Hu. Series: Read-it! Chapter Books: Historical Tales. 2008, Picture Window LB $21.26 (978-1-4048-4734-7). 64pp. Eye-catching illustrations add appeal to this historical fiction chapter book for newly independent readers about an artist's apprentice who learns a valuable lesson along with the art of scroll painting. (Rev: SLJ 2/09)

7399 Gunderson, Jessica. *The Jade Dragon: A Story of Ancient China* (2–5). Illus. by Caroline Hu. Series: Read-it! Chapter Books: Historical Tales. 2008, Picture Window LB $21.26 (978-1-4048-4735-4). 64pp. A young boy's fortune changes when he finds a jade dragon and learns an important lesson about luck. Also use *Stranger on the Silk Road* and *The Terracotta Girl* (both 2008). (Rev: SLJ 2/09)

7400 Gutierrez, Akemi. *The Mummy and Other Adventures of Sam and Alice* (K–2). Illus. by author. 2005, Houghton $16.00 (978-0-618-50761-0). Siblings Sam and Alice show — in three short stories — how the power of imagination can turn a humdrum day into a fascinating adventure. (Rev: SLJ 11/05)

7401 Haddix, Margaret P. *Say What?* (2–4). Illus. by James Bernardin. 2004, Simon & Schuster $12.95 (978-0-689-86255-7). 96pp. Sukie is much confused when her parents start talking nonsense, and she and her siblings retaliate in kind when they discover their parents' real motive. (Rev: BL 2/15/04; SLJ 2/04)

7402 Hall, Kirsten. *At the Carnival* (K–1). Illus. by Laura Rader. 1996, Scholastic $3.99 (978-0-590-68994-6). 32pp. An easy reader that uses detachable pages and a trip to the carnival to introduce language. (Rev: BL 2/1/97)

7403 Hapka, Cathy, and Ellen Titlebaum. *How Not to Babysit Your Brother* (K–3). Illus. by Debbie Palen. Series: Step into Reading. 2005, Random LB $11.99 (978-0-375-92856-7); paper $3.99 (978-0-375-82856-0). 48pp. A humorous early chapter book about two brothers who create quite a stir while their grandmother is sleeping. (Rev: SLJ 8/05)

7404 Hapka, Cathy, and Ellen Titlebaum. *How Not to Start Third Grade* (1–3). Illus. by Debbie Palen. 2007, Random LB $11.99 (978-0-375-93904-4); paper $3.99 (978-0-375-83904-7). 48pp. Will's first day of 3rd grade is seriously disrupted by the antics of his little brother Steve, who is starting kindergarten. (Rev: BL 9/1/07; SLJ 7/07)

7405 Harrison, David L. *Johnny Appleseed: My Story* (1–2). Illus. by Mike Wohnoutka. Series: Step into Reading. 2001, Random paper $3.99 (978-0-375-81247-7). 48pp. Johnny Appleseed tells the story of his life to a pioneer family. (Rev: BL 2/1/02; HBG 3/02) [634]

7406 *Harry's Bath* (K–1). Illus. by Seymour Chwast. Series: I'm Going to Read! 2005, Sterling paper $3.95 (978-1-4027-2100-7). Harry claims he can't get in the tub because it's already full of animals in this beginning reader. (Rev: SLJ 9/05)

7407 Hautzig, Deborah. *Little Witch Goes to School* (K–3). Illus. by Sylvie Wickstrom. Series: Step into Reading. 1998, Random paper $3.99 (978-0-679-88738-6). 47pp. When she promises to be bad, Little Witch is allowed to go to school, where she breaks her promise by being a good and cooperative student. (Rev: SLJ 1/99)

7408 Hautzig, Deborah. *The Nutcracker Ballet* (1–3). Illus. by Carolyn Ewing. 1992, Random paper $3.99 (978-0-679-82385-8). 48pp. In a simple narrative, this is the story of the Nutcracker. (Rev: BL 12/1/92)

7409 Hay, Samantha. *Hocus-Pocus Hound* (1–3). Illus. by Nathan Reed. Series: I Am Reading. 2006, Kingfisher paper $3.95 (978-0-7534-5957-7). 48pp. A scruffy-looking hound becomes an unexpectedly helpful assistant to Marvo the Magician. (Rev: SLJ 1/07)

7410 Hayes, Geoffrey. *Benny and Penny: In Just Pretend* (PS–1). Illus. by author. 2008, Raw Junior/TOON $12.95 (978-0-9799238-0-7). 32pp. An easy-reader graphic novel in which Benny the pirate mouse has a falling-out with his sister followed by a change of heart at the end. (Rev: BL 3/15/08; SLJ 5/08)

7411 Hays, Anna Jane. *The Secret of the Circle-K Cave* (2–4). Illus. by Jerry Smath. Series: Science Solves It. 2006, Kane paper $4.99 (978-1-57565-189-7). 32pp. While visiting his aunt and uncle in New Mexico, Rick and his cousins explore a cave where they discover clues to an unsolved 19th-century robbery; scientific aspects are covered in sidebars. (Rev: BL 8/06)

7412 Hays, Anna Jane. *Smarty Sara* (1–2). Illus. by Sylvie Wickstrom. Series: Step into Reading. 2008, Random LB $11.99 (978-0-375-95054-4); paper $3.99 (978-0-375-83512-4). 32pp. Sara enjoys reading and writing as well as planning entertainment for her friends. (Rev: BL 7/08)

7413 Hayward, Linda. *What Homework?* (1–3). Illus. by Page Eastburn O'Rourke. 2002, Kane paper $4.99 (978-1-57565-116-3). 32pp. Andy succeeds in completing his assignment in the nick of time. (Rev: SLJ 11/02)

7414 Hazen, Lynn E. *Cinder Rabbit* (K–2). Illus. by Elyse Pastel. 2008, Holt $15.95 (978-0-8050-8194-7). 64pp. A little bunny who's lost her hop must face her fears when she is chosen for the role of Cinder Rabbit in the class play. (Rev: BL 6/1/08; SLJ 3/08)

7415 Head, Judith. *Mud Soup* (1–2). Series: Step into Reading. 2003, Random LB $11.99 (978-0-375-81087-9). 48pp. In this charming cross-cultural tale for beginning readers, Josh learns from a Latina friend that different doesn't mean bad. (Rev: BL 8/03; HBG 4/04)

7416 Heling, Kathryn, and Deborah Hembrook. *Mouse Makes Words: A Phonics Reader* (1–2). Illus. by Patrick Joseph. Series: Step into Reading. 2002, Random paper $3.99 (978-0-375-81399-3). 32pp. By changing the first letter in a series of words, new words are formed in this beginning reader. (Rev: BL 4/1/02; HBG 10/02; SLJ 7/02)

7417 Herman, Gail. *Double-Header* (1–2). Illus. by Jerry Smath. 1993, Penguin paper $3.99 (978-0-448-40157-7). 32pp. Monsters Bob and Rob, who share the same body, but with two heads, discuss their dilemma. (Rev: BL 12/1/93; SLJ 2/94)

7418 Herman, R. A. *Pal the Pony* (1–2). Illus. 1996, Penguin paper $3.99 (978-0-448-41257-3). 32pp. A pony named Pal shows his true talents at a rodeo. (Rev: BL 8/96; SLJ 7/96)

7419 Hicks, Betty. *Basketball Bats* (2–4). Illus. by Adam McCauley. Series: Gym Shorts. 2008, Roaring Brook $14.95 (978-1-59643-243-7). 64pp. Henry has trouble sharing the ball when his team is challenged by the rival Tigers. (Rev: BL 6/1–15/08; HB 7/08; LMC 5/08; SLJ 7/08)

7420 Hicks, Betty. *Goof-off Goalie* (2–4). Illus. by Adam McCauley. Series: Gym Shorts. 2008, Roaring Brook $14.95 (978-1-59643-244-4). 64pp. Goose must overcome his reputation as a dreamer and convince the soccer coach that he's a good candidate for goalie. (Rev: BLO 7/31/08; HB 7/08; LMC 5/08; SLJ 7/08)

7421 Hicks, Betty. *Swimming with Sharks* (1–3). Illus. by Adam McCauley. Series: Gym Shorts. 2008, Roaring Brook $15.95 (978-1-59643-245-1). 64pp. Rita is disappointed when she can't join her friends on the Sharks swimming team. (Rev: BL 9/15/08; HB 9/08)

7422 Hill, Susan. *Ruby Bakes a Cake* (K–3). Illus. by Margie Moore. Series: An I Can Read Book. 2004, HarperCollins LB $16.89 (978-0-06-008976-4). 28pp. Ruby, a raccoon, consults her friends before making a cake and includes all the ingredients they suggest. (Rev: SLJ 6/04)

7423 Hill, Susan. *Ruby's Perfect Day* (PS–K). Illus. by Margie Moore. 2006, HarperCollins $15.99 (978-0-06-008982-5). 32pp. Ruby Raccoon learns that playing by herself can be just as much fun as playing with all her woodland friends. (Rev: BL 12/1/06; SLJ 10/06)

7424 Himmelman, John. *The Animal Rescue Club* (1–3). Illus. by author. Series: An I Can Read Book. 1998, HarperCollins LB $15.89 (978-0-06-027409-2). 46pp. In this easy reader, members of the Animal Rescue Club take a number of creatures in distress to a hospital and later return them to their natural habitats. (Rev: HBG 10/98; SLJ 6/98)

7425 Hindley, Judy. *Princess Rosa's Winter* (1–2). Illus. by Margaret Chamberlain. Series: I Am Reading. 2005, Kingfisher paper $3.95 (978-0-7534-5859-4). 48pp. Princess Rosa and her family remember what they enjoy about winter when Hoda the jester entertains them in their castle. (Rev: BL 3/15/05)

7426 Hoban, Lillian. *Arthur's Birthday Party* (1–2). Illus. 1999, HarperCollins $14.95 (978-0-06-027798-7). 64pp. As expected at Arthur's birthday party, all his friends perform amazing gymnastic tricks, but Arthur wins the best all-round gymnast award. (Rev: BL 3/15/99; HB 1/99; HBG 10/99; SLJ 2/99)

7427 Hoban, Lillian. *Arthur's Loose Tooth* (1–3). Illus. by author. 1985, HarperCollins LB $17.89 (978-0-06-022354-0); paper $3.99 (978-0-06-444093-6). 64pp. Brave Arthur the chimp is afraid of blood, so how does he get rid of his loose tooth in order to eat taffy apples? (Rev: BL 10/15/85; HB 11/85; SLJ 12/85)

7428 Hoban, Lillian, and Phoebe Hoban. *Ready . . . Set . . . Robot!* (2–3). Illus. by Lillian Hoban. 1982, HarperCollins $11.95 (978-0-06-022345-8). 64pp. A robot, Sol-1, competes in a space race.

7429 Hoban, Russell. *Bedtime for Frances* (1–2). Illus. by Garth Williams. 1960, HarperCollins LB $13.89 (978-0-06-022351-9); paper $6.99 (978-0-06-443451-5). 32pp. Frances, a badger, tries every familiar trick to tease her way past bedtime. Others in the series: *Bread and Jam for Frances* (1965); *A Bargain for Frances* (1970).

7430 Hoban, Russell. *Best Friends for Frances* (1–2). Illus. by Lillian Hoban. 1969, HarperCollins LB $17.89 (978-0-06-022328-1); paper $6.99 (978-0-06-443008-1). 32pp. When friend Albert decides that he must exclude girls from his "wondering day" and baseball game, Frances chooses younger sister Gloria as a companion. Also use: *A Baby Sister for Frances* (1964).

7431 Hoff, Syd. *Barkley* (1–3). Illus. by author. 1975, HarperCollins LB $15.89 (978-0-06-022448-6). 32pp. An easily read story about a forcibly retired, aging circus dog.

7432 Hoff, Syd. *Barney's Horse* (1–3). Illus. by author. 1987, HarperCollins LB $16.89 (978-0-06-022450-9); paper $3.99 (978-0-06-444142-1). 32pp. Barney the peddler and his horse delight children, but elevated trains soon begin to rumble overhead. (Rev: BCCB 11/87; BL 10/1/87)

7433 Hoff, Syd. *Danny and the Dinosaur* (K–2). Illus. by author. 1958, HarperCollins LB $17.89 (978-0-06-022466-0); paper $3.99 (978-0-06-444002-8). 64pp. Danny wanted to play and so did the dinosaur. What could have been more natural than for them to leave the museum together? Also from the same author and publisher: *Sammy the Seal* (1959).

7434 Hoff, Syd. *Danny and the Dinosaur Go to Camp* (1–3). Illus. 1996, HarperCollins LB $17.89 (978-0-06-026440-6). 32pp. At summer camp, a dinosaur provides transportation for tired boys and girls. (Rev: BL 8/96; SLJ 6/96)

7435 Hoff, Syd. *Grizzwold* (1–2). Illus. by author. 1963, HarperCollins LB $17.89 (978-0-06-022481-3); paper $3.99 (978-0-06-444057-8). 64pp. After foresters have destroyed his home, a bear sets out to find a new one.

7436 Hoff, Syd. *The Lighthouse Children* (1–2). Illus. Series: I Can Read. 1994, HarperCollins LB $15.89 (978-0-06-022959-7). 32pp. After a storm destroys their lighthouse, two children must leave the seagulls they feed in this easy-to-read book. (Rev: BL 2/1/94; SLJ 4/94)

7437 Hoff, Syd. *Mrs. Brice's Mice* (PS–2). Illus. by author. 1988, HarperCollins paper $3.99 (978-0-06-444145-2). 32pp. Mrs. Brice has 25 mice — one is an individualist. (Rev: BCCB 12/88; BL 12/1/88; SLJ 4/89)

7438 Hoff, Syd. *Stanley* (1–3). Illus. by author. 1992, HarperCollins paper $3.99 (978-0-06-444010-3). 64pp. A caveman finds a new home in this inventive tale.

7439 Hood, Susan. *I Am Mad!* (PS–1). Photos by Dorothy Handelman. Series: Real Kids Readers. 1999, Millbrook LB $18.90 (978-0-7613-2061-6); paper $4.99 (978-0-7613-2086-9). 28pp. For very beginning readers, this is a simple story of a bullying older sister. (Rev: SLJ 1/00)

7440 Hood, Susan. *Meet Trouble* (PS–1). Illus. by Kristina Stephenson. Series: First Friends First Readers. 2001, Grosset paper $3.99 (978-0-448-42455-2). Trouble the cat didn't come by his name by accident, and lives up to it in the first of the two stories in this humorous book. (Rev: SLJ 12/01)

7441 Hood, Susan. *The New Kid* (K–1). Illus. by Dorothy Handelman. Series: Real Kids Readers. 1998, Millbrook LB $18.90 (978-0-7613-2014-2); paper $4.99 (978-0-7613-2039-5). 32pp. Sid, a newcomer at school, acts strangely because he is uncomfortable, but one boy, who understands the situation, makes the effort to become his friend. (Rev: BL 11/1/98; SLJ 1/99)

7442 Hood, Susan. *Pup and Hound Hatch an Egg* (PS–1). Illus. by Linda Hendry. Series: Pup and Hound. 2007, Kids Can $14.95 (978-1-55337-974-4); paper $3.95 (978-1-55337-975-1). 32pp. Whose egg have Pup and Hound found? Readers will be surprised when a baby turtle emerges, ready for fun with the two friends. Also use *Pup and Hound Stay Up Late* and *Pup and Hound in Trouble* (both 2005)

and *Pup and Hound Catch a Thief* (2007). (Rev: SLJ 6/07)

7443 Hooks, Gwendolyn. *The Mystery of the Missing Dog* (K–3). Illus. by Nancy Devard. Series: Just for You! 2004, Scholastic paper $3.99 (978-0-439-56864-7). 32pp. Alex, an African American boy, searches his apartment looking for his dog in this easy-reader. Also use *Three's a Crowd* (2004), about jealousy. (Rev: SLJ 1/05)

7444 Hooks, Gwendolyn. *Nice Wheels* (K–2). Illus. by Renée Andriani. Series: My First Reader. 2005, Children's Pr. LB $18.50 (978-0-516-25179-0). 31pp. The new boy in class has a wheelchair in this book for beginning readers with a list of words. (Rev: SLJ 5/05)

7445 Horowitz, Ruth. *Big Surprise in the Bug Tank* (1–3). Illus. by Joan Holub. Series: Dial Easy-to-Read. 2005, Dial $14.99 (978-0-8037-2874-5). 46pp. The two boys first seen in *Breakout at the Bug Lab* (2001) adopt two giant cockroaches from the mother's lab and, of course, the population soon expands from two. (Rev: BCCB 1/05; HB 5/05; SLJ 2/05)

7446 Howe, James. *Houndsley and Catina* (2–4). Illus. by Marie-Louise Gay. 2006, Candlewick $14.99 (978-0-7636-2404-0). 40pp. Best friends Houndsley the dog and Catina the cat try to find goals that fit their talents; an early chapter book with watercolor-and-pencil illustrations. (Rev: BL 2/15/06; SLJ 5/06)

7447 Howe, James. *Houndsley and Catina: Plink and Plunk* (PS–2). Illus. by Marie-Louise Gay. 2009, Candlewick $15.99 (978-0-7636-3385-1). 48pp. Catina the cat teaches Houndsley the dog to ride a bike and he teaches her to swim in this easy reader about conquering fears. (Rev: BL 5/1/09)

7448 Howe, James. *Houndsley and Catina and the Birthday Surprise* (PS–2). Illus. by Marie-Louise Gay. 2006, Candlewick $14.99 (978-0-7636-2405-7). 48pp. Houndsley the dog and Catina the cat are sad that they do not know their birthdays but they find a creative way to get around this; an easy-reader sequel to *Houndsley and Catina* (2006). (Rev: BL 10/1/06; SLJ 11/06)

7449 Howe, James. *Pinky and Rex and the New Baby* (K–3). Illus. by Melissa Sweet. 1994, Avon paper $3.99 (978-0-380-12083-3). 48pp. Rex and her best friend are nervous about the new baby Rex's parents are planning to adopt. (Rev: BL 3/1/93; SLJ 6/93)

7450 Howe, James. *Pinky and Rex Get Married* (K–3). Illus. by Melissa Sweet. 1990, Simon & Schuster LB $11.95 (978-0-685-58512-2). 48pp. Two young friends, a 7-year-old girl and a boy named Pinky, are so close that they decide to get married. Also use: *Pinky and Rex* (1990). (Rev: BCCB 4/90; BL 4/15/90*; HB 3/90; SLJ 5/90)

7451 Howe, James. *The Vampire Bunny* (1–3). Illus. by Jeff Mack. 2004, Simon & Schuster $14.95 (978-0-689-85724-9). 41pp. Chester the cat and Harold the dog disagree over whether the baby bunny they have found is a vampire in this adaptation for beginning readers. (Rev: SLJ 6/04)

7452 Hsu, Stacey W. *Old Mo* (PS–1). Illus. by Adam Ritter. Series: Rookie Reader. 2006, Children's Pr. LB $19.50 (978-0-516-24981-0). 32pp. A boy and his beloved pet cat enjoy each other's company throughout the day in this easy reader. (Rev: SLJ 6/06)

7453 Hudson, Wade. *Jamal's Busy Day* (PS–1). Illus. by George Ford. 1991, Just Us Bks. LB $12.95 (978-0-940975-21-7); paper $6.95 (978-0-940975-24-8). Jamal, an African American boy, prepares with his parents for a busy day — he will spend his at school and they at work. (Rev: SLJ 2/92)

7454 Hudson, Wade. *The Two Tyrones* (K–3). Illus. by Mark Page. 2004, Scholastic paper $3.99 (978-0-439-56866-1). 32pp. School is starting and it turns out there will be two Tyrones this year. (Rev: SLJ 1/05)

7455 Hulme, Joy N. *Mary Clare Likes to Share: A Math Reader* (K–1). Illus. by Lizzy Rockwell. Series: Step into Reading. 2006, Random LB $11.99 (978-0-375-93421-6); paper $3.99 (978-0-375-83421-9). 32pp. A humorous, rhyming easy-reader that uses Mary Clare's sharing of food to introduce fractions. (Rev: SLJ 2/07)

7456 Hurwitz, Johanna. *The Adventures of Ali Baba Bernstein* (2–4). Illus. 1985, Morrow $16.95 (978-0-688-04161-8); Avon paper $4.99 (978-0-380-72349-2). 96pp. Episodes in the life of David Bernstein, an 8-year-old who changes what he thinks is his boring name. Also use: *Hurray for Ali Baba Bernstein* (1989). (Rev: BCCB 6/85; BL 5/15/85; HB 5/85)

7457 Hutchins, Hazel. *Robyn's Art Attack* (K–3). Illus. by Yvonne Cathcart. Series: First Novels. 2002, Formac paper $3.99 (978-0-88780-564-6). 59pp. Robyn's classmates expect a boring day when she chooses an art gallery for their field trip. (Rev: SLJ 1/03)

7458 *I Am Sick* (K–2). Illus. by Johanna Hantel. Series: My First Reader. 2005, Children's Pr. LB $18.50 (978-0-516-24878-3); paper $3.95 (978-0-516-24970-4). 32pp. A young girl is nervous about going to the doctor, but her father goes with her and the doctor is kind, giving her medicine that makes her headache and sore throat better; for beginning readers. (Rev: SLJ 1/06)

7459 Inches, Alison. *Corduroy Writes a Letter* (K–2). Illus. by Allan Eitzen. Series: Viking Easy-to-Read. 2002, Viking $13.99 (978-0-670-03548-9). 32pp. Corduroy the teddy bear and Lisa, an African American girl, find out how much they can accomplish by writing letters. Also use *Corduroy's Garden* (2002). (Rev: BL 1/1–15/03; HBG 3/03)

7460 Jacobson, Jennifer. *Andy Shane and the Pumpkin Trick* (1–3). Illus. by Abby Carter. 2006, Candlewick $13.99 (978-0-7636-2605-1). 64pp. Andy is reluctant to spend so much time on bossy Dolores's birthday party, especially as it's on Halloween, but in the end he saves the day, confounding pranksters. (Rev: BL 9/1/06; SLJ 10/06)

7461 Jane, Pamela. *Milo and the Flapjack Fiasco* (K–3). Illus. by Meredith Johnson. 2004, Mondo $13.95 (978-1-59336-113-6). 32pp. Milo and his sister Sam try to make flapjacks for the visiting teacher in this easy-reader. (Rev: SLJ 6/04)

7462 Jarman, Julia. *The Magic Backpack* (PS–2). Illus. by Adriano Gon. Series: Flying Foxes. 2004, Crabtree LB $22.60 (978-0-7787-1487-3); paper $4.95 (978-0-7787-1533-7). 48pp. Josh forgets to bring a key ingredient for the class cake, but fortunately his magic backpack flies him to a cocoa plantation in Ghana. (Rev: SLJ 8/04)

7463 Jennings, Patrick. *The Tornado Watches: An Ike and Mem Story* (2–5). Illus. by Anna Alter. 2002, Holiday House $15.95 (978-0-8234-1672-1). 64pp. A young boy named Ike fears his family is in danger after a tornado warning causes them to spend the night in their basement. (Rev: BL 8/02; HB 1/03; HBG 3/03; SLJ 12/02)

7464 Jennings, Patrick. *The Weeping Willow* (2–4). Illus. by Anna Alter. 2002, Holiday House $15.95 (978-0-8234-1671-4). 56pp. Friends Ike and Buzzy decide to build a tree house, only to find themselves embroiled in arguments. (Rev: BL 12/15/02; HB 1/03*; HBG 3/03; SLJ 2/03)

7465 Jinkins, Jim. *Pinky Dinky Doo: Back to School Is Cool* (K–3). Illus. by author. Series: Step into Reading. 2005, Random $12.95 (978-0-375-83236-9); paper $3.99 (978-0-375-83237-6). 48pp. Pinky makes up a funny story about picture day at school to tell to her little brother. (Rev: SLJ 9/05)

7466 Johansen, K. V. *Pippin and the Bones* (PS–2). Illus. by Bernice Lum. 2000, Kids Can $12.95 (978-1-55074-629-7). 32pp. For beginning readers, this is the story of a dog named Pippin who digs up some huge bones that his master gives to the museum. (Rev: BL 8/00; HBG 10/00; SLJ 8/00)

7467 Johnson, Crockett. *Harold and the Purple Crayon* (K–2). Illus. by author. 1958, HarperCollins paper $6.99 (978-0-06-443022-7). 64pp. A little boy draws all of the things necessary for him to go for a walk. Three sequels are: *Harold's Trip to the Sky* (1957); *Harold's Circus* (1959); *A Picture for Harold's Room* (1960).

7468 Johnston, Tony. *The Bull and the Fire Truck* (1–2). Illus. by R. W. Alley. 1996, Scholastic $3.99 (978-0-590-47597-6). 32pp. An easily read book about how a community accommodates a bull that hates the color red. (Rev: BL 2/1/97)

7469 Johnston, Tony. *Sparky and Eddie: The First Day of School* (1–2). Illus. by Susannah Ryan. Series: Hello Reader! 1997, Scholastic paper $3.99 (978-0-590-47979-0). 32pp. In this easy reader, friends Sparky and Eddie decide that they won't start school if they can't be in the same rooms. (Rev: BL 8/97; HBG 3/98; SLJ 9/97)

7470 Jones, Christianne C. *Emma's New Look* (1–2). Illus. by Necdet Yilmaz. 2007, Picture Window LB $19.93 (978-1-4048-3138-4). 24pp. This easy reader with a simple story and fun illustrations will help build skills. (Rev: SLJ 7/07)

7471 Karlin, Nurit. *The Fat Cat Sat on the Mat* (1–2). Illus. 1996, HarperCollins LB $14.89 (978-0-06-026674-5). 32pp. A witch's rat can't budge a cat from a favorite resting place, the mat. (Rev: BCCB 10/96; BL 9/15/96; SLJ 12/96)

7472 Keenan, Sheila. *More or Less a Mess* (1–2). Illus. by Patrick Girouard. Series: Hello Math Reader. 1997, Scholastic $3.99 (978-0-590-60248-8). When a girl is told by her mother to tidy up her room, she doesn't know where to begin, so she puts everything under the covers of her bed. (Rev: BL 5/1/97)

7473 Kenah, Katharine. *The Best Chef in Second Grade* (K–2). Illus. by Abby Carter. 2007, HarperCollins $15.99 (978-0-06-053561-2). 48pp. Ollie jumps at the opportunity to showcase his hidden cooking talents when a TV chef visits Mr. Hopper's class; for beginning readers. (Rev: BCCB 1/08; BL 11/1/07; SLJ 12/07)

7474 Kenah, Katharine. *The Best Seat in Second Grade* (K–2). Illus. by Abby Carter. Series: I Can Read! 2005, HarperCollins $16.99 (978-0-06-000734-8). 64pp. Sam, a 2nd-grader, gets more than he bargained for when he takes the class hamster along on a school field trip. (Rev: BL 8/05; SLJ 7/05)

7475 Kenah, Katharine. *The Best Teacher in Second Grade* (K–2). Illus. by Abby Carter. Series: I Can Read! 2006, HarperCollins $16.99 (978-0-06-053564-3). 48pp. Luna's teacher supports the new girl's idea for a special night sky program even though her classmates are cool to the suggestion. (Rev: BL 6/1–15/06; SLJ 7/06)

7476 Kerrin, Jessica Scott. *Martin Bridge on the Lookout!* (2–4). Illus. by Joseph Kelly. 2005, Kids Can $14.95 (978-1-55337-689-7); paper $4.95 (978-1-55337-773-3). 142pp. In this beginning chapter book, Martin Bridge returns in a trio of short stories about minor misadventures that turn out well. (Rev: SLJ 11/05)

7477 Kerrin, Jessica Scott. *Martin Bridge, Ready for Takeoff!* (2–4). Illus. by Joseph Kelly. 2005, Kids Can $14.95 (978-1-55337-688-0). 120pp. Martin must deal with typical 3rd-grade dilemmas in this three-chapter book with pencil illustrations. (Rev: BL 3/15/05; SLJ 5/05)

7478 Kessler, Leonard. *Here Comes the Strikeout* (1–2). Illus. by author. 1992, HarperCollins paper $3.99 (978-0-06-444011-0). 64pp. Bobby always strikes out at bat until his friend Willie helps him to improve his game. Two other sports stories by the same author and publisher are: *Kick, Pass and Run* (1966); *Last One in Is a Rotten Egg* (1969). (Rev: BL 12/1/92)

7479 Kimmelman, Leslie. *In the Doghouse* (K–2). Illus. by True Kelley. Series: Holiday House Reader. 2006, Holiday $14.95 (978-0-8234-1882-4). 32pp. Emma's dog Bo disappears after she is angry with him, causing much anguish but ending in a joyous reunion in this well-rounded book for beginning readers. (Rev: BL 4/15/06; SLJ 5/06)

7480 King-Smith, Dick. *The Twin Giants* (1–3). Illus. by Mini Grey. 2008, Candlewick $16.99 (978-0-7636-3529-9). 80pp. Identical twin giants Normous and Lottavim have an enjoyable childhood and adolescence and decide at the age of 20 that they each need a wife, a task that poses challenges; attractive illustrations add to the humor. (Rev: BL 7/08; SLJ 7/08)

7481 Klein, Adria F. *Max Goes to School* (PS–1). Illus. by Mernie Gallagher-Cole. Series: Read-it! Readers. 2005, Picture Window LB $19.93 (978-1-4048-1179-9). 24pp. Max, a young African American boy, spends an enjoyable first day at school in this simple easy reader. Also use *Max Goes to the Barber* and *Max Goes to the Dentist* (both 2005), *Max and the Adoption Day Party* and *Max Learns Sign Language* (both 2007), and *Max Goes to the Farmers' Market* (2009). (Rev: SLJ 1/06)

7482 Kline, Suzy. *Horrible Harry and the Locked Closet* (2–4). Illus. by Frank Remkiewicz. 2004, Viking $13.99 (978-0-670-05944-7). 80pp. Bored after four days of indoor recess and not completely diverted by their study of volcanoes, Horrible Harry and other students in Miss Mackle's class investigate what's behind a locked closet door. (Rev: BL 5/1/04; SLJ 11/04)

7483 Kline, Suzy. *Horrible Harry and the Mud Gremlins* (2–4). Illus. by Frank Remkiewicz. Series: Horrible Harry. 2003, Viking $13.99 (978-0-670-03617-2). 64pp. Horrible Harry encourages his classmates to break a school rule and go under the playground fence to see fungi with his mini-microscope. (Rev: BL 3/15/03; HBG 10/03)

7484 Kline, Suzy. *Horrible Harry Goes to Sea* (2–4). Illus. by Frank Remkiewicz. 2001, Viking $13.99 (978-0-670-03516-8). 64pp. After hearing a student's story of an ancestor who sailed on the *Titanic*, the teacher arranges a class riverboat trip and many humorous adventures ensue. (Rev: BL 12/1/01; HBG 3/02; SLJ 11/01)

7485 Kline, Suzy. *Horrible Harry Takes the Cake* (1–3). Illus. by Frank Remkiewicz. Series: Horrible Harry. 2006, Viking $13.99 (978-0-670-06075-7). 64pp. Harry tries to find out who their teacher is marrying; the nineteenth book in this humorous series. (Rev: BL 2/1/06; SLJ 5/06)

7486 Knudsen, Michelle. *Fish and Frog* (PS). Illus. by Valeria Petrone. Series: Brand New Readers. 2005, Candlewick paper $5.99 (978-0-7636-2457-6). 40pp. An enjoyable beginning reader with a simple story line and bright illustrations portraying a fish and frog that live in the same pond. (Rev: SLJ 8/05)

7487 Konrad, Marla Stewart. *Mom and Me* (PS–K). Illus. Series: World Vision Early Reader. 2009, Tundra $12.95 (978-0-88776-866-8). 24pp. Accompanied by minimal text, color photographs show mothers and children around the world in everyday activities. (Rev: BL 5/1/09; SLJ 5/09)

7488 Krensky, Stephen. *Buster's Dino Dilemma* (1–3). Illus. by Marc Brown. Series: A Marc Brown Arthur Chapter Book. 1998, Little, Brown paper $3.95 (978-0-316-11560-5). 58pp. Based on scripts used in the PBS series, this easy chapter book involves Arthur and a fossil he has found during a school field trip. Also use *Locked in the Library!* (1998). (Rev: HBG 10/98; SLJ 11/98)

7489 Krensky, Stephen. *Lionel's Birthday* (1–3). Illus. by Susanna Natti. Series: Dial Easy-to-Read. 2003, Penguin $13.99 (978-0-8037-2752-6). 48pp. In this ninth easy-reader about Lionel, he prepares for an upcoming birthday and buries a time capsule. (Rev: BL 7/03; HBG 4/04; SLJ 10/03)

7490 Krensky, Stephen. *We Just Moved!* (1–2). Illus. by Larry DiFiori. Series: Hello Reader! 1998, Scholastic paper $3.99 (978-0-590-33127-2). 32pp. Set during the Middle Ages, this humorous story tells of a young boy's move to a new castle and how this compares with a change of homes in modern times. (Rev: BL 7/98)

7491 Kroll, Virginia. *Honest Ashley* (K–3). Illus. by Nancy Cote. Series: The Way I Act. 2005, Albert Whitman $15.99 (978-0-8075-3371-0). 32pp. The virtues of honesty are explored in this tale of a girl trying to decide whether to copy an old essay of her brother's or to do the school assignment on her own. (Rev: BL 6/1–15/06; SLJ 3/06)

7492 Kvasnosky, Laura McGee. *Zelda and Ivy: The Runaways* (K–3). 2006, Candlewick $14.99 (978-0-7636-2689-1). 48pp. Fox sisters Zelda and Ivy decide to run away from home, bury a time capsule, and experiment with a creative juice. (Rev: BL 6/1–15/06; SLJ 7/06*)

7493 Labatt, Mary. *A Parade for Sam* (PS–2). Illus. by Marisol Sarrazin. Series: Kids Can Read. 2005, Kids Can $14.95 (978-1-55337-787-0); paper $3.95 (978-1-55337-788-7). 32pp. Not content to watch the carnival parade from the sidelines, Sam, a fluffy puppy, wants to be a part of it; suitable for beginning readers. (Rev: BL 10/15/05)

7494 Labatt, Mary. *Pizza for Sam* (PS–1). Illus. by Marisol Sarrazin. Series: Kids Can Read. 2003, Kids Can $14.95 (978-1-55337-329-2); paper $3.95 (978-1-55337-331-5). 32pp. Sam does not want to eat dog food and greets a pizza with joy. (Rev: BL 3/1/03; HBG 10/03; SLJ 5/03)

7495 Labatt, Mary. *Sam at the Seaside* (PS–2). Illus. by Marisol Sarrazin. Series: Kids Can Read. 2006, Kids Can $14.95 (978-1-55337-876-1). 32pp. On a visit to the seashore with her owners, Sam the puppy's exuberance gets her into all sorts of problems. Also use *Sam Goes Next Door* (2006). (Rev: SLJ 11/06)

7496 Labatt, Mary. *Sam Finds a Monster* (PS–2). Illus. by Marisol Sarrazin. Series: Kids Can Read. 2003, Kids Can $14.95 (978-1-55337-351-3); paper $3.95 (978-1-55337-352-0). 32pp. A lovable puppy named Sam tries to track down a monster she believes has escaped from the television into her owners' house. (Rev: HBG 10/03; SLJ 5/03)

7497 Lachtman, Ofelia Dumas. *Pepita Finds Out / Lo Que Pepita Descubre* (1–3). Trans. by Carolina Villarroel. Illus. by Alex P. DeLange. 2002, Piñata $15.95 (978-1-55885-375-1). Pepita frets because she can't find a suitable subject for her school report in this novel with the English text above the Spanish. (Rev: HBG 10/03; SLJ 3/03)

7498 Landry, Leo. *Sea Surprise* (2–4). Illus. 2005, Holt $15.95 (978-0-8050-6645-6). 64pp. The plan-

ning for Eel's surprise party involves lots of underwater suspense. (Rev: BL 5/15/05)

7499 Larson, Kirby. *Cody and Quinn, Sitting in a Tree* (2–3). Illus. 1996, Holiday House $14.95 (978-0-8234-1227-3). 64pp. Cody is teased by a bully because of his friendship with a girl, Quinn. (Rev: BCCB 9/96; BL 4/1/96; SLJ 4/96)

7500 Laurence, Daniel. *Captain and Matey Set Sail* (K–2). Illus. by Claudio Munoz. Series: An I Can Read Book. 2001, HarperCollins LB $15.89 (978-0-06-028957-7). 64pp. Two pirates bicker constantly about everything — what to call their parrot, what to do with the treasure if they ever find it, which song to sing while scrubbing the deck, and so forth. (Rev: BCCB 9/01; BL 7/01; HB 1/02; HBG 3/02; SLJ 11/01)

7501 Lavis, Steve. *Little Mouse Has a Busy Day* (PS–K). Illus. by author. 2000, Ragged Bear $6.95 (978-1-929766-10-9). This book for beginning readers traces the hour-by-hour activities of Little Mouse from getting up at 8 A.M. to bedtime at 6. Also use *Little Mouse Has an Adventure*. (Rev: SLJ 1/01)

7502 Lawlor, Laurie. *The Worst Kid Who Ever Lived on Eighth Avenue* (1–2). Illus. by Cynthia Fisher. 1998, Holiday House $14.95 (978-0-8234-1350-8). 48pp. Mary Lou and her friends are convinced that big bad Leroy is up to no good when he buries a large bag in his backyard. (Rev: BL 5/1/98; HBG 10/98; SLJ 4/98)

7503 Leonard, Marcia. *Best Friends* (PS–1). Photos by Dorothy Handelman. Series: Real Kids Readers. 1999, Millbrook LB $18.90 (978-0-7613-2064-7); paper $4.99 (978-0-7613-2089-0). 30pp. In this simple story for very beginning readers that is illustrated with photographs, two girls describe their similarities and differences. (Rev: SLJ 1/00)

7504 Leonard, Marcia. *Dan and Dan* (PS–1). Photos by Dorothy Handelman. Series: Real Kids Readers. 1998, Millbrook LB $18.90 (978-0-7613-2003-6); paper $4.99 (978-0-7613-2028-9). 31pp. A beginning reader that tells of the loving relationship between a young boy and his namesake and grandfather. (Rev: SLJ 6/98)

7505 Leonard, Marcia. *Get the Ball, Slim* (1). Illus. by Dorothy Handelman. Series: Real Kids Readers. 1998, Millbrook LB $18.90 (978-0-7613-2000-5); paper $4.99 (978-0-7613-2025-8). 32pp. Using photographs for illustrations, this simple reader tells about African American twins Tim and Jim and their dog Slim. (Rev: BL 5/1/98; HBG 10/98; SLJ 6/98)

7506 Leonard, Marcia. *I Like Mess* (1). Illus. by Dorothy Handelman. Series: Real Kids Readers. 1998, Millbrook LB $18.90 (978-0-7613-2002-9); paper $4.99 (978-0-7613-2027-2). 32pp. In this simple reader illustrated with photographs, a young girl tries to please her mother by cleaning up the mess she has created. (Rev: BL 5/1/98; SLJ 6/98)

7507 Leonard, Marcia. *My Pal Al* (PS–1). Photos by Dorothy Handelman. Series: Real Kids Readers. 1998, Millbrook LB $18.90 (978-0-7613-2001-2); paper $4.99 (978-0-7613-2026-5). 31pp. A beginning reader that describes how a little African American girl loves her favorite toy. (Rev: SLJ 6/98)

7508 Leonard, Marcia. *No New Pants!* (1). Illus. by Dorothy Handelman. Series: Real Kids Readers. 1999, Millbrook LB $18.90 (978-0-7613-2063-0); paper $4.99 (978-0-7613-2088-3). 32pp. A young African American child doesn't want to go shopping for pants with his mother, but he enjoys getting a pair of hand-me-downs from his brother. (Rev: BL 12/1/99; HBG 3/00)

7509 Le Sieg, Theo. *Ten Apples Up on Top* (K–2). Illus. 1961, Random LB $11.99 (978-0-394-90019-3). 72pp. Three bears try to pile apples on their heads in this nonsense story. Also from the same author and publisher: *I Wish That I Had Duck Feet* (1965); *Eye Book* (1968).

7510 Levinson, Nancy S. *Clara and the Bookwagon* (1–2). Illus. by Carolyn Croll. 1988, HarperCollins LB $15.89 (978-0-06-023838-4); paper $3.99 (978-0-06-444134-6). 64pp. A real-life story about a young girl who wants to read despite her father's objections. (Rev: BL 4/1/88; SLJ 7/88)

7511 Levinson, Nancy S. *Prairie Friends* (2–4). Illus. by Stacey Schuett. Series: An I Can Read Book. 2003, HarperCollins LB $16.89 (978-0-06-028002-4). 64pp. Betsy is thrilled when a girl her age moves into the neighborhood, but the city girl takes time to adapt to her new surroundings in this story that includes lots of interesting facts about prairie life in the middle 1800s. (Rev: BL 1/1–15/03; HBG 10/03; SLJ 3/03)

7512 Levy, Elizabeth. *A Hare-Raising Tail* (2–5). Illus. by Mordicai Gerstein. Series: Ready-for-Chapters. 2002, Simon & Schuster paper $3.99 (978-0-689-84626-7). 64pp. Fletcher the basset hound finds a new home with Jill, and all goes well until Jill takes him to school for show-and-tell. (Rev: BL 9/1/02; HBG 10/02; SLJ 1/03)

7513 Levy, Elizabeth. *The Karate Class Mystery* (2–4). Illus. by Denise Brunkus. 1996, Scholastic $3.99 (978-0-590-60323-2). 48pp. A mystery in which Justin's karate belt disappears and the culprit must be caught. (Rev: BL 2/1/97)

7514 Levy, Elizabeth. *Parents' Night Fright* (2–4). Illus. by Denise Brunkus. 1998, Scholastic paper $3.99 (978-0-590-60324-9). 48pp. When Charlene's prize-winning story disappears, she and buddies Justin, who is deaf, and the invisible Chip set out to solve the mystery. (Rev: BL 7/98; SLJ 9/98)

7515 Lewin, Betsy. *Wiley Learns to Spell* (PS–1). Illus. by author. Series: Hello Reader! 1998, Scholastic paper $3.99 (978-0-590-10835-5). In this easy reader, Wiley, a mischievous monster, makes words out of an armload of colorful block letters. (Rev: SLJ 2/99)

7516 Lewis, Rob. *Grandpa at the Beach* (2–3). Illus. 1998, Mondo paper $4.50 (978-1-57255-552-5). 47pp. A grandfather bear and his grandson, Finley, investigate the reports that a beach house contains a monster and discover it is only Dad. (Rev: BL 7/98)

7517 Lewis, Rob. *Too Much Trouble for Grandpa* (2–3). Illus. 1998, Mondo paper $4.50 (978-1-

57255-551-8). 47pp. Grandpa Bear brings home things he believes will not cause problems, such as a cat and a girlfriend, but in each case he is wrong. (Rev: BL 7/98)

7518 Lindeen, Mary. *Ships* (PS–3). Series: Mighty Machines. 2007, Children's Pr. LB $18.50 (978-1-60014-060-0). 24pp. The basics about ships for young readers, clearly presented and accompanied by engaging photographs. (Rev: SLJ 7/07)

7519 Little, Jean. *Emma's Magic Winter* (1–2). Illus. by Jennifer Plecas. 1998, HarperCollins $15.95 (978-0-06-025389-9). 64pp. Though Emma is basically very shy, she is brave enough to make a good friend of Sally, the new girl next door. (Rev: BCCB 10/98; BL 11/1/98; HB 9/98*; HBG 3/99; SLJ 10/98)

7520 Lobel, Arnold. *Frog and Toad Are Friends* (K–2). Illus. by author. 1970, HarperCollins LB $17.89 (978-0-06-023958-9); paper $3.99 (978-0-06-444020-2). 64pp. Two new friends for the independent reader. Three sequels are: *Frog and Toad Together* (1972); *Frog and Toad All Year* (1976); *Days with Frog and Toad* (1979).

7521 Lobel, Arnold. *Grasshopper on the Road* (1–2). Illus. by author. 1978, HarperCollins LB $17.89 (978-0-06-023962-6); paper $3.99 (978-0-06-444094-3). 64pp. A series of short stories, each with a vital message.

7522 Lobel, Arnold. *Mouse Soup* (1–2). Illus. by author. 1977, HarperCollins LB $17.89 (978-0-06-023968-8); paper $3.99 (978-0-06-444041-7). 64pp. When Mouse is caught by Weasel, who plans to use him for soup, he convinces his captor that "mouse soup must be mixed with stones to make it taste really good."

7523 Lobel, Arnold. *Mouse Tales* (1–2). Illus. by author. 1972, HarperCollins LB $17.89 (978-0-06-023942-8); paper $3.99 (978-0-06-444013-4). 64pp. Seven bedtime stories told by Papa Mouse to his seven sons. Lively little drawings add to the humor.

7524 Lobel, Arnold. *Owl at Home* (1–2). Illus. by author. 1975, HarperCollins LB $17.89 (978-0-06-023949-7); paper $3.99 (978-0-06-444034-9). 64pp. Five stories dealing with the humorous and bungling attempts of Owl to be helpful.

7525 Lobel, Arnold. *Small Pig* (K–2). Illus. by author. 1969, HarperCollins LB $17.89 (978-0-06-023932-9); paper $3.99 (978-0-06-444120-9). 64pp. A dirty little pig in a search for mud ends up in cement.

7526 Lobel, Arnold. *Uncle Elephant* (K–3). Illus. by author. 1981, HarperCollins LB $17.89 (978-0-06-023980-0); paper $3.99 (978-0-06-444104-9). 64pp. A nephew and uncle elephant form a friendship.

7527 Lodge, Bernard. *Custard Surprise* (K–2). Illus. by Tim Bowers. 2007, HarperCollins $15.99 (978-0-06-073687-3). 48pp. Dinah and Rufus, two chickens, serve up tasty meals for animal customers in their diner but refuse to give a fox what he wants — a chicken dinner. (Rev: SLJ 8/07)

7528 Loehr, Mallory. *Dragon Egg* (PS–K). Illus. by Hala Wittwer. 2007, Random LB $11.99 (978-0-375-94350-8); paper $3.99 (978-0-375-84350-1).

32pp. A cumulative story about a dragon egg that is chased by a trail of characters as it rolls down a hill, only to have the procession reversed when the newborn heads back home. (Rev: BL 9/1/07)

7529 Lofting, Hugh. *Doctor Dolittle's Great Adventure* (1–2). Adapted by Diane Namm. Illus. by John Kanzler. Series: The Story of Doctor Dolittle. 2007, Sterling paper $3.95 (978-1-4027-4122-7). 32pp. In this third installment, the doctor and his friends are trying to take Circus Crocodile home when they are shipwrecked and then imprisoned, but in the end, of course, they do succeed. Also use *Doctor Dolittle's Magical Cure* (2007), the fourth book in the series. (Rev: SLJ 1/08)

7530 Lopshire, Robert. *Put Me in the Zoo* (1–3). Illus. by author. 1960, Beginner Books $7.99 (978-0-394-80017-2). 72pp. An unusual dog thinks he should be in the zoo, but his talents really mean he should be in a circus.

7531 Lucas, Sally. *Dancing Dinos Go to School* (PS–K). Illus. by Margeaux Lucas. Series: Step into Reading. 2006, Random LB $11.99 (978-0-375-93241-0); paper $Random,.00 (978-0-375-83241-3). 32pp. A group of dinosaurs leap from the pages of a book and spend a wild day disrupting the school. (Rev: BL 8/06; SLJ 10/06)

7532 Maccarone, Grace. *The Gym Day Winner* (PS–1). Illus. 1996, Scholastic paper $3.99 (978-0-590-26263-7). 32pp. A youngster finds a sport at which he excels. (Rev: BL 8/96; SLJ 1/97)

7533 Maccarone, Grace. *I Shop with My Daddy* (1). Illus. by Denise Brunkus. Series: Hello Reader! 1998, Scholastic paper $3.99 (978-0-590-50196-5). 32pp. A little girl and her father go shopping, and as a last item, he allows her something sweet — a frozen yogurt. (Rev: BL 7/98)

7534 Maccarone, Grace. *My Tooth Is About to Fall Out* (1–2). Illus. by Betsy Lewin. 1995, Scholastic $3.99 (978-0-590-48376-6). 32pp. An easy-to-read book about the problems of having a loose tooth. (Rev: BL 7/95)

7535 McCully, Emily Arnold. *The Grandma Mix-Up* (1–3). Illus. by author. 1988, HarperCollins LB $15.89 (978-0-06-024202-2); paper $3.99 (978-0-06-444150-6). 64pp. Two grandmothers with very different ways arrive to baby-sit. (Rev: BL 12/1/89; SLJ 3/89)

7536 McCully, Emily Arnold. *Grandmas at Bat* (1–2). Illus. 1993, HarperCollins paper $3.99 (978-0-06-444193-3). 64pp. Pip's two grandmothers, last-minute replacements, coach his baseball team. (Rev: BL 3/1/93; HB 7/93; SLJ 6/93)

7537 McDonald, Megan. *Beezy and Funnybone* (1–2). Illus. by Nancy Poydar. Series: Beezy. 2000, Orchard LB $15.99 (978-0-531-33211-5); paper $4.95 (978-0-531-07161-8). 48pp. A book for beginning readers that contains three simple stories about a little girl and her dog Funnybone. (Rev: BL 7/00; HBG 10/00; SLJ 9/00)

7538 McDonald, Megan. *Beezy at Bat* (1–2). Illus. by Nancy Poydar. 1998, Orchard LB $14.99 (978-0-531-33085-2). 48pp. In this, the third book about Beezy, she plays baseball, exchanges riddles with

Gran, and scares a friend with a snake. (Rev: BL 11/1/98; HBG 3/99; SLJ 9/98)

7539 McDonald, Megan. *Beezy Magic* (2–4). Illus. by Nancy Poydar. 1997, Orchard LB $14.99 (978-0-531-33064-7). 48pp. Three easily read short stories involving carrot-haired Beezy, her family, and her dog. (Rev: BL 7/98; HBG 10/98; SLJ 4/98)

7540 McDonald, Megan. *Stink: The Incredible Shrinking Kid* (2–4). Illus. by Peter H. Reynolds. Series: Judy Moody. 2005, Candlewick $12.99 (978-0-7636-2025-7). 112pp. Stink, Judy Moody's younger brother, is convinced he's shrinking and decides to make the best of it in this beginning chapter book. (Rev: BL 3/1/05; SLJ 4/05)

7541 McDonald, Megan. *Stink and the Great Guinea Pig Express* (2–4). Illus. by Peter H. Reynolds. 2008, Candlewick $12.99 (978-0-7636-2835-2). 128pp. Stink, Sophie, and Webster are on a mission to find homes for 101 rescued guinea pigs in this easy-to-read chapter book. (Rev: BL 3/1/08; SLJ 3/08)

7542 McEwan, Jamie. *Whitewater Scrubs* (K–2). Illus. by John Margeson. 2005, Darby Creek $14.99 (978-1-58196-038-9). 64pp. Accustomed to athletic success, Clara must conquer her fears when she joins Willie and the football scrubs for a kayaking class; suitable for beginning chapter-book readers. (Rev: BL 9/1/05; SLJ 11/05)

7543 McKay, Sindy. *Ben and Becky in the Haunted House* (1–3). Illus. by Meredith Johnson. Series: We Both Read. 1999, Treasure Bay $7.99 (978-1-891327-14-8); paper $3.99 (978-1-891327-18-6). The story of two children who are forced to spend a night in a haunted house is told with two texts, one for adults and the other for beginning readers. (Rev: SLJ 11/99)

7544 McKenna, Colleen O'Shaughnessy. *Doggone . . . Third Grade!* (2–3). Illus. by Stephanie Roth. 2002, Holiday House $15.95 (978-0-8234-1696-7). 80pp. Third-grader Gordie comes up with a trick for his dog to perform in the class talent show. (Rev: BL 7/02; HBG 10/02; SLJ 7/02)

7545 McKenna, Colleen O'Shaughnessy. *Third Grade Ghouls* (2–4). Illus. by Stephanie Roth. 2001, Holiday House $15.95 (978-0-8234-1652-3). 80pp. This simple beginning chapter book finds 3rd-grader Gordie searching for the perfect costume to wear for the Halloween parade. (Rev: BL 1/1–15/02; HBG 10/02; SLJ 2/02)

7546 McKenna, Colleen O'Shaughnessy. *Third Grade Wedding Bells* (2–4). Illus. by Stephanie Roth. Series: Third Grade. 2006, Holiday $15.95 (978-0-8234-1943-2). 160pp. Gordie, Lucy, and Lamont are distressed to hear their teacher is getting married — will they lose her? (Rev: BL 5/1/06; SLJ 4/06)

7547 McKissack, Patricia C. *Tippy Lemmey* (2–4). Illus. by Susan Keeter. Series: Ready-for-Chapters. 2003, Simon & Schuster paper $3.99 (978-0-689-85019-6). 64pp. Mischievous Tippy the dog is a source of annoyance to Leandra and her friends, but when the pup is kidnapped, they come to his rescue in this story set in Tennessee in 1951. (Rev: BCCB

3/03; BL 1/1–15/03; HB 3/03; HBG 10/03; SLJ 1/03)

7548 McKissack, Patricia C., and Fredrick McKissack. *Messy Bessey's Family Reunion* (K–1). Illus. by Dana Regan. Series: Rookie Readers. 2000, Children's Book Pr. LB $19.50 (978-0-516-20830-5); paper $4.95 (978-0-516-26552-0). 32pp. In this easy reader, Messy Bessey is so upset at the mess she and her relatives have made at an outdoor picnic that she organizes them into a clean-up squad. (Rev: BL 12/1/00)

7549 McKissack, Patricia C., and Fredrick McKissack. *Messy Bessey's Holidays* (PS–2). Illus. by Dana Regan. Series: Rookie Readers. 1999, Children's Book Pr. LB $19.50 (978-0-516-20829-9). 30pp. In this beginning reader, a child bakes cookies for her friends for Hanukkah, Christmas, and Kwanzaa. (Rev: HBG 10/99; SLJ 8/99)

7550 McKissack, Patricia C., and Fredrick McKissack. *Miami Makes the Play* (2–4). Illus. Series: Road to Reading. 2001, Golden paper $3.99 (978-0-307-26505-0). 92pp. Miami and friends head for baseball camp for a summer of fun and play but must make some decisions, such as whether to support a coed team. (Rev: BL 5/1/01; HBG 10/01)

7551 McMullan, Kate. *Pearl and Wagner: One Funny Day* (K–2). Illus. by R. W. Alley. 2009, Dial $14.99 (978-0-8037-3085-4). 40pp. An easy-reader featuring Wagner and Pearl on April Fools' day. (Rev: BCCB 6/09; BL 11/15/08; HB 3/09; SLJ 3/09)

7552 McNamara, Margaret. *The Counting Race* (PS–1). Illus. by Mike Gordon. Series: Ready-to-Read. 2003, Simon & Schuster paper $3.99 (978-0-689-85539-9). 31pp. The concept of counting by twos is introduced in this easy-reader story about 1st-graders at Robin Hill School. (Rev: HBG 4/04; SLJ 7/03)

7553 McNamara, Margaret. *Fall Leaf Project* (PS–K). Illus. by Mike Gordon. Series: Ready-to-Read. 2006, Simon & Schuster paper $3.99 (978-1-4169-1537-9). 32pp. Mrs. Connor's class collects leaves in a variety of fall colors and sends them to a 1st-grade class in the Southwest. (Rev: BL 1/1–15/07)

7554 McNamara, Margaret. *The First Day of School* (K–2). Illus. by Mike Gordon. Series: Ready-to-Read. 2005, Aladdin LB $11.89 (978-0-689-86915-0); paper $3.99 (978-0-689-86914-3). 32pp. Michael can't wait to start 1st grade until he learns that he won't be able to take his dog to class; suitable for beginning readers. (Rev: BL 8/05; SLJ 8/05)

7555 McNamara, Margaret. *One Hundred Days (Plus One)* (K–3). Illus. by Mike Gordon. Series: Robin Hill School. 2003, Simon & Schuster paper $3.99 (978-0-689-85535-1). 32pp. Hannah is miserable when she misses the 100th day of school, for which she has been collecting buttons, but gets a happy surprise when she returns to class. (Rev: HBG 10/03; SLJ 4/03)

7556 McPhail, David. *A Bug, a Bear, and a Boy* (1–2). Illus. 1998, Scholastic paper $3.99 (978-0-590-14904-4). 32pp. A young boy spends an enjoy-able day with his two companions, a bear and a bug. (Rev: BL 11/1/98)

7557 McPhail, David. *The Day the Sheep Showed Up* (1–2). Illus. Series: Hello Reader! 1998, Scholastic paper $3.99 (978-0-590-84910-4). 32pp. An uproarious farce in which the other animals try to find out what sort of being is a sheep after it unexpectedly joins the farm community. (Rev: BL 5/1/98)

7558 McPhail, David. *The Great Race* (1–2). Illus. Series: Hello Reader! 1998, Scholastic paper $3.99 (978-0-590-84909-8). 32pp. In this humorous easy reader, the animals have a race and, in spite of many mistakes, end together — each one a winner! (Rev: BL 5/1/98)

7559 McPhail, David. *Rick Is Sick* (PS–1). Illus. Series: Green Light Reader. 2004, Harcourt $11.95 (978-0-15-205091-7). 24pp. Bunny Jack finds Rick the bear sick in bed and does what he can to help in this simple story for very early readers. (Rev: BL 3/15/04; SLJ 5/04)

7560 McPhail, David. *Snow Lion* (PS–2). Illus. by author. 1983, Parents LB $5.95 (978-0-8193-1098-9). 48pp. A lion finds it's too hot for him to stay in the jungle.

7561 Marshall, Edward. *Three by the Sea* (1–3). Illus. by James Marshall. 1981, Puffin paper $3.99 (978-0-14-037004-1). 48pp. Three friends, Lolly, Spider, and Sam, tell stories by the seashore.

7562 Marshall, James. *Fox Outfoxed* (2–3). Illus. 1992, Viking paper $3.99 (978-0-14-038113-9). 48pp. Three easily read stories about Fox and how his careful plans misfire. (Rev: BCCB 4/92; BL 4/1/92; HB 7/92; SLJ 5/92*)

7563 Marzollo, Jean. *I Am an Apple* (PS–1). Illus. by Judith Moffatt. Series: Hello Reader! 1997, Scholastic $3.99 (978-0-590-37223-7). A beginning reader that details the life of an apple from flower to fruit to market to table. (Rev: SLJ 1/98)

7564 Marzollo, Jean. *I'm a Caterpillar* (K–2). Illus. by Judith Moffatt. Series: Hello Reader! 1997, Scholastic $3.99 (978-0-590-84779-7). A beginning reader that presents, in story form, the life cycle of a caterpillar. (Rev: SLJ 11/97)

7565 Marzollo, Jean. *Once upon a Springtime* (1–2). Illus. by Jacqueline Rogers. Series: Hello Reader! 1998, Scholastic paper $3.99 (978-0-590-46017-0). 30pp. A fawn and its mother stay together during the first year of its life and observe humans and their comparable annual activities. (Rev: BL 5/1/98)

7566 Marzollo, Jean. *Soccer Sam* (1–2). Illus. by Blanche Sims. 1987, Random paper $3.99 (978-0-394-88406-6). 48pp. Marco from Mexico spends a year with his friend Sam in the United States, and the boys organize a soccer team. (Rev: BL 8/87; SLJ 9/87)

7567 Marzollo, Jean, et al. *Football Friends* (1–2). Illus. by True Kelley. Series: Hello Reader! 1997, Scholastic $3.99 (978-0-590-38395-0). 32pp. Freddy becomes so angry with his friend Mark when they choose teams for playing football that he begins using his fists and feet in this easy-to-read sports book. (Rev: BL 2/1/98; SLJ 3/98)

7568 Mason, Jane B. *Hello, Two-Wheeler!* (1–2). Illus. by David Monteith. 1995, Penguin paper $3.99 (978-0-448-40853-8). 48pp. A boy accidentally learns to ride his bike without its training wheels. (Rev: BL 7/95)

7569 Masters, Anthony. *Ricky's Rat Gang* (1–3). Illus. by Chris Fisher. Series: I Am Reading. 2004, Kingfisher paper $3.95 (978-0-7534-5800-6). 41pp. Three mice plot to drive bullying rats from the supermarket storeroom in this book for beginning readers. (Rev: SLJ 9/04)

7570 Masurel, Claire. *That Bad, Bad Cat* (1). Illus. by True Kelley. Series: All Aboard Reading. 2002, Penguin paper $3.99 (978-0-448-42622-8). 32pp. The family cat is always misbehaving, but when he fails to show up for dinner everyone misses him. (Rev: BL 6/1–15/02; HBG 10/02)

7571 Matthias, Catherine. *I Love Cats* (K–1). Illus. by Tom Dunnington. 1983, Children's Book Pr. LB $19.50 (978-0-516-02041-9); paper $4.95 (978-0-516-42041-7). 32pp. The narrator likes many things, but cats are best.

7572 Mayfield, Sue. *Shoot!* (1–2). Illus. by Ken Cox. Series: Blue Bananas. 2001, Crabtree LB $22.60 (978-0-7787-0847-6). 48pp. Shoot the dog, the team mascot, helps Jamie and his friends win the soccer game. (Rev: SLJ 7/02)

7573 Medearis, Angela Shelf. *Here Comes the Snow* (1). Illus. 1996, Scholastic paper $3.99 (978-0-590-26266-8). 32pp. Kids enjoy all of the fun of a first snowfall. (Rev: BL 8/96; SLJ 9/96)

7574 Medearis, Angela Shelf. *On the Way to the Pond* (K–2). Illus. by Lorinda Bryan Cauley. 2006, Harcourt $12.95 (978-0-15-205599-8); paper $3.95 (978-0-15-205623-0). Tess Tiger and Herbert Hippo have a picnic by a cool pond in this easy reader. (Rev: SLJ 6/06)

7575 Medearis, Angela Shelf. *Singing for Dr. King* (K–3). Illus. by Cornelius Van Wright and Ying-Hwa Hu. Series: Just for You! 2004, Scholastic paper $3.99 (978-0-439-56855-5). 32pp. An African American 3rd-grader becomes involved in civil rights in this easy-reader. (Rev: SLJ 1/05)

7576 Meister, Cari. *My Pony Jack* (PS–K). Illus. by Amy Young. Series: Viking Easy-to-Read. 2005, Viking $13.99 (978-0-670-05917-1). 32pp. In simple rhyming couplets suitable for beginning readers, Lacy talks about her pony and how she grooms him. (Rev: BL 5/1/05)

7577 Meister, Cari. *Skinny and Fats, Best Friends* (K–2). Illus. by Steve Björkman. Series: Holiday House Reader. 2002, Holiday House $14.95 (978-0-8234-1692-9). 32pp. Skinny, a rabbit, and Fats, a pig, enjoy spending time fishing, making marshmallows, and building rockets. (Rev: HBG 3/03; SLJ 10/02)

7578 Meister, Cari. *Tiny Goes Camping* (PS). Illus. by Rich Davis. Series: Viking Easy-to-Read. 2006, Viking $13.99 (978-0-670-89250-1). 32pp. A boy and his huge dog ("Tiny" of the title) plan to camp out in their back yard in this easy reader. (Rev: BL 5/1/06; SLJ 6/06)

7579 Michalak, Jamie. *Joe and Sparky Get New Wheels* (1–3). Illus. by Frank Remkiewicz. 2009, Candlewick $15.99 (978-0-7636-3387-5). 48pp. Unlikely friends Joe the giraffe and Sparky the turtle enjoy a day out of the zoo. (Rev: BCCB 4/09; SLJ 4/09)

7580 Miller, Sara S. *Cat in the Bag* (1). Illus. by Benton Mahan. Series: Rookie Readers. 2001, Children's Book Pr. $19.50 (978-0-516-22014-7). 32pp. While trying to pack, a little girl must keep chasing her cat out of her suitcase in this easy reader. (Rev: BL 11/1/01)

7581 Miller, Sara S. *Three More Stories You Can Read to Your Cat* (1–3). Illus. by True Kelley. 2002, Houghton $15.00 (978-0-618-11035-3). 48pp. These simple, playful stories are about cats who face such problems as wanting to come inside during a snow storm and finding entertainment on a particularly boring birthday. (Rev: BL 4/15/02; HBG 10/02; SLJ 5/02)

7582 Miller, Sara S. *Three More Stories You Can Read to Your Dog* (2–3). Illus. 2000, Houghton $15.00 (978-0-395-92293-4). 48pp. Three amusing easy-to-read stories that will amuse children, even if they don't have a dog. (Rev: BL 3/15/00; HBG 10/00; SLJ 4/00)

7583 Miller, Sara S. *Three Stories You Can Read to Your Cat* (1–3). Illus. by True Kelley. 1997, Houghton $15.00 (978-0-395-78831-8). 48pp. An easy-to-read book about Kelley's playful, adventurous cat. (Rev: BL 3/1/97; SLJ 5/97)

7584 Miller, Sara S. *Three Stories You Can Read to Your Dog* (2–4). Illus. by True Kelley. 1995, Houghton $15.00 (978-0-395-69938-6). 42pp. Three easy-to-read stories that feature a muddle-headed dog that doesn't know how to behave. (Rev: BCCB 3/95; BL 4/15/95; SLJ 4/95)

7585 Miller, Sara S. *Three Stories You Can Read to Your Teddy Bear* (1–3). Illus. by True Kelley. 2004, Houghton $15.00 (978-0-618-30397-7). 48pp. In this companion to *Three Stories You Can Read to Your Cat* (1993) and *Three Stories You Can Read to Your Dog* (1995), three entertaining stories are designed to be read to a teddy bear. (Rev: BL 3/1/04; SLJ 6/04)

7586 Mills, Claudia. *Gus and Grandpa Go Fishing* (1–3). Illus. by Catherine Stock. Series: Gus and Grandpa. 2003, Farrar $15.00 (978-0-374-32815-3). 48pp. Grandpa shows Gus how to fish in this installment in the long-running series. (Rev: BL 9/1/03; HBG 4/04; SLJ 10/03)

7587 Milton, Joyce. *Whales: The Gentle Giants* (2–3). Illus. by Alton Langford. 1989, Random paper $3.99 (978-0-394-89809-4). 48pp. A sailor named Brendan steps on the back of a whale. (Rev: BL 6/1/89)

7588 Minarik, Else Holmelund. *Little Bear* (K–2). Illus. by Maurice Sendak. 1957, HarperCollins LB $16.89 (978-0-06-024241-1); paper $3.95 (978-0-06-444004-2). 64pp. Humorous adventure stories of Mother Bear and Little Bear. Others in the series: *Little Bear's Friend* (1960); *Little Bear's Visit* (1961); *A Kiss for Little Bear* (1968).

7589 Minarik, Else Holmelund. *No Fighting, No Biting!* (PS–3). Illus. by Maurice Sendak. 1958, HarperCollins LB $17.89 (978-0-06-024291-6); paper $3.95 (978-0-06-444015-8). 64pp. Light-foot and Quick-foot, two little alligators, teach Rosa and Willy a lesson.

7590 Moffatt, Judith. *Who Stole the Cookies?* (1–2). Illus. 1996, Penguin paper $3.99 (978-0-448-41127-9). 32pp. A cast of animal characters ask who stole the cookies in this rhyming first reader. (Rev: BL 8/96; SLJ 9/96)

7591 Morris, Jennifer E. *May I Please Have a Cookie?* (K–1). Illus. Series: Scholastic Reader. 2005, Scholastic paper $3.99 (978-0-439-73819-4). 32pp. A young alligator learns the right way to get a cookie from his mother in this beginning reader. (Rev: BL 1/1–15/06)

7592 Morris, Kim. *Mølly in the Middle* (2–3). Illus. by Dorothy Handelman. Series: Real Kids Readers. 1999, Millbrook LB $18.90 (978-0-7613-2059-3); paper $4.99 (978-0-7613-2084-5). 48pp. Molly, a middle child, decides that if she can't be the youngest or oldest, she will be the "est" in some other way, such as being the loudest or funniest. (Rev: BL 5/15/99; SLJ 8/99)

7593 Namm, Diane. *Guess Who?* (PS–2). Illus. by David Sheldon. Series: My First Reader. 2004, Children's Pr. LB $18.50 (978-0-516-24412-9). 31pp. Potential visitors are the subject of this rhyming book for beginning readers with cartoon illustrations and a word list. (Rev: SLJ 7/04)

7594 Napoli, Donna Jo, and Robert Furrow. *Sly the Sleuth and the Food Mysteries* (2–4). Illus. by Heather Maione. 2007, Dial $16.99 (978-0-8037-3119-6). 144pp. Sly and her friends explore three food-related mysteries presented in short sentences and basic vocabulary. (Rev: BL 5/1/07; SLJ 6/07)

7595 Napoli, Donna Jo, and Robert Furrow. *Sly the Sleuth and the Pet Mysteries* (2–4). Illus. by Heather Maione. Series: Sly the Sleuth. 2005, Dial $15.99 (978-0-8037-2993-3). 96pp. Sylvia (a.k.a. "Sly the Sleuth") solves her friends' pet mysteries in this illustrated easy reader, the first in a series. (Rev: BL 3/1/05)

7596 Nelson, Vaunda Micheaux. *Ready? Set. Raymond!* (K–1). Illus. by Derek Anderson. Series: Step into Reading. 2002, Random LB $11.99 (978-0-375-91363-1); paper $3.99 (978-0-375-81363-4). 32pp. Raymond, an appealing African American boy, "does things fast," including making a friend and running a race, in this collection of three short, nicely illustrated stories. (Rev: BL 9/15/02; HBG 3/03; SLJ 12/02)

7597 Nodset, Joan L. *Come Here, Cat* (K–3). Illus. by Steven Kellogg. 1973, HarperCollins $10.00 (978-0-06-024557-3). 32pp. A young girl chases a cat around her house and onto the roof in this simple but enjoyable story.

7598 Nodset, Joan L. *Go Away, Dog* (1–2). Illus. by Paul Meisel. 1997, HarperCollins LB $14.89 (978-0-06-027503-7). 32pp. A boy finds that he can't get rid of the dog that is following him in this easy-to-read book. (Rev: BL 8/97; HBG 3/98; SLJ 10/97)

7599 Nodset, Joan L. *Who Took the Farmer's Hat?* (1–2). Illus. by Fritz Siebel. 1963, HarperCollins LB $17.89 (978-0-06-024566-5); paper $6.99 (978-0-06-443174-3). 32pp. When the wind blows away the farmer's hat, all of the animals think they saw it.

7600 O'Connor, Jane. *Fancy Nancy Sees Stars* (K–2). Illus. by Robin P. Glasser. Series: I Can Read. 2008, HarperCollins $16.99 (978-0-06-123612-9); paper $3.99 (978-0-06-123611-2). 32pp. The drama of the frilly child continues as Nancy looks forward excitedly to a trip to the planetarium. (Rev: BL 2/1/09)

7601 O'Connor, Jane. *Kate Skates* (PS–1). Illus. by DyAnne Disalvo-Ryan. 1995, Penguin paper $3.99 (978-0-448-40935-1). 48pp. Tiny Jen easily learns to skate on her double blades, but older sister Kate has problems with her grownup single blades. (Rev: BL 1/1–15/96; SLJ 5/96)

7602 O'Connor, Jane. *Molly the Brave and Me* (1–3). Illus. by Sheila Hamanaka. 1990, Random paper $3.99 (978-0-394-84175-5). 48pp. Molly seems fearless, but in time of trouble Beth leads the way. (Rev: BCCB 6/90; BL 6/1/90; SLJ 8/90)

7603 O'Connor, Jane. *Nina, Nina Ballerina* (PS–1). Illus. by DyAnne Disalvo-Ryan. 1993, Penguin paper $3.99 (978-0-448-40511-7). 32pp. When Nina breaks her arm, she worries that she will not be able to perform in her ballet class show. (Rev: BL 7/93; SLJ 8/93)

7604 O'Connor, Jane. *Poison Ivy Expert* (K–2). Illus. by Ted Enik. Series: Fancy Nancy. I Can Read! 2009, HarperCollins $16.99 (978-0-06-123614-3); paper $3.99 (978-0-06-123613-6). 32pp. Nancy thinks she can recognize poison ivy, but gathering wildflowers for her teacher proves otherwise; for beginning readers. (Rev: SLJ 3/09)

7605 O'Connor, Jane. *The Teeny Tiny Woman* (K–2). Illus. by R. W. Alley. 1986, Random paper $3.99 (978-0-394-88320-5). 32pp. The familiar folktale retold. By the same author, another easy reader, *Sir Small and the Dragonfly* (1988). (Rev: BL 12/1/86)

7606 Ormerod, Jan. *The Newest Dancer* (PS–1). Illus. by author. Series: Ballet Sisters. 2008, Scholastic paper $5.99 (978-0-439-82282-4). 32pp. Bonnie's little sister Sylvie has her first ballet class. (Rev: BL 2/15/08; SLJ 5/08)

7607 Osborne, Mary Pope. *Dinosaurs Before Dark* (1–2). Illus. by Sal Murdocca. 1992, Random LB $11.99 (978-0-679-92411-1). 68pp. Jack and his sister time-travel to the days of the dinosaurs. (Rev: BL 10/1/92; SLJ 9/92)

7608 Osborne, Mary Pope. *Mummies in the Morning* (1–4). Illus. Series: Magic Tree House. 1993, Random LB $11.99 (978-0-679-92424-1); paper $3.99 (978-0-679-82424-4). 72pp. Jack and Annie time-travel to ancient Egypt to help a queen find a copy of the Book of the Dead. (Rev: BL 4/1/94)

7609 Packard, Mary. *The Very Bad Day* (PS–2). Illus. by Joy Allen. 2004, Children's Pr. LB $18.50 (978-0-516-24415-0). 31pp. Things do not start off well for the young heroine of this rhyming book for beginning readers, with cartoon illustrations and a word list. (Rev: SLJ 7/04)

7610 Papademetriou, Lisa. *My Pen Pal, Pat* (1–3). Photos by Dorothy Handelman. Series: Real Kids Readers. 1998, Millbrook LB $18.90 (978-0-7613-2023-4); paper $4.99 (978-0-7613-2048-7). 45pp. Two pen pals named Pat finally meet and discover that one is a boy and the other a girl. (Rev: HBG 3/99; SLJ 12/98)

7611 Papademetriou, Lisa. *You're in Big Trouble, Brad!* (1–3). Photos by Dorothy Handelman. Series: Real Kids Readers. 1998, Millbrook LB $18.90 (978-0-7613-2022-7); paper $4.99 (978-0-7613-2047-0). 44pp. When Brad is called to the principal's office, he thinks that he is facing big trouble, but actually he just forgot his lunch. (Rev: SLJ 12/98)

7612 Parish, Herman. *Amelia Bedelia's Masterpiece* (1–3). Illus. by Lynn Sweat. Series: Amelia Bedelia. 2007, Greenwillow $15.99 (978-0-06-084355-7). 64pp. The literal-minded housekeeper visits an art museum and suffers many misinterpretations. Other recent titles in this funny, long-running series include *Calling Doctor Amelia Bedelia* (2002), *Amelia Bedelia, Rocket Scientist?* (2005), *Amelia Bedelia Under Construction* (2006), and *Amelia Bedelia's Masterpiece* (2007). (Rev: BL 6/1–15/07)

7613 Parish, Peggy. *No More Monsters for Me!* (K–3). Illus. by Marc Simont. 1981, HarperCollins LB $17.89 (978-0-06-024658-7); paper $3.99 (978-0-06-444109-4). 64pp. A young girl wants to keep a monster for a pet.

7614 Parish, Peggy. *Scruffy* (1–2). Illus. by Kelly Oechsli. 1988, HarperCollins paper $3.99 (978-0-06-444137-7). 64pp. A small boy learns how to choose and care for his first pet — a kitten. (Rev: BL 2/1/88; SLJ 7/88)

7615 Park, Barbara. *Junie B., First Grader (at Last!)* (2–3). Illus. by Denise Brunkus. 2001, Random LB $13.99 (978-0-375-81516-4). 96pp. When her best friend deserts her and she finds out she needs glasses, Junie B. Jones discovers that 1st grade is not what she expected. (Rev: BL 11/15/01; HBG 3/02; SLJ 1/02)

7616 Park, Barbara. *Junie B. Jones Has a Monster Under Her Bed* (2–3). Illus. by Denise Brunkus. Series: Stepping Stone. 1997, Random $11.99 (978-0-679-96697-5). 80pp. An easy reader in which little Junie is convinced that an invisible monster lives under her bed. Also use *Junie B. Jones Is Not a Crook* (1997). (Rev: HB 7/97; SLJ 11/97)

7617 Park, Barbara. *Junie B. Jones Loves Handsome Warren* (1–2). Illus. by Denise Brunkus. 1996, Random LB $11.99 (978-0-679-96696-8); paper $3.99 (978-0-679-86696-1). 71pp. Junie falls in love with a new boy in her kindergarten class in this easy-to-read book. (Rev: BL 2/1/97)

7618 Parker, Marjorie Blain. *Hello, Freight Train!* (PS–K). Illus. by Bob Kolar. Series: Scholastic Reader. 2005, Scholastic paper $3.99 (978-0-439-59891-0). 32pp. A dog tells his puppy about the different types of wagons on the passing freight train. (Rev: BL 5/15/05)

7619 Paul, Ann Whitford. *Hop! Hop! Hop!* (PS–K). Illus. by Jan Gerardi. Series: Step into Reading. 2005, Random LB $11.99 (978-0-375-92857-4); paper $3.99 (978-0-375-82857-7). 32pp. An early reader featuring Little Rabbit, who tries to do what Big Rabbit does but can't always keep up. (Rev: SLJ 8/05)

7620 Paul, Ann Whitford. *Snail's Good Night* (PS–1). Illus. by Rosanne Litzinger. 2008, Holiday $14.95 (978-0-8234-1912-8). 32pp. Snail slides — very slowly — from friend to friend to bid them each good night, usually arriving far too late. (Rev: BL 3/1/08; SLJ 2/08)

7621 Pearson, Susan. *Eagle-Eye Ernie Comes to Town* (2–3). Illus. by Gioia Fiammenghi. 1990, Simon & Schuster paper $11.95 (978-0-671-70564-0). 70pp. Ernestine earns the admiration of her classmates when she solves the mystery of items missing from lunch bags. (Rev: BCCB 12/92; BL 10/1/90; SLJ 4/91)

7622 Pearson, Susan. *The Green Magician Puzzle* (1–3). Illus. by Gioia Fiammenghi. 1991, Simon & Schuster paper $11.95 (978-0-671-74054-2). 88pp. Ernie and her classmates must solve a series of riddles to become the Green Magicians of the Earth Day parade. (Rev: SLJ 12/91)

7623 *Pet Stories: You Don't Have to Walk* (1–2). Illus. 2000, North-South LB $14.88 (978-1-58717-032-4). 64pp. A book for beginning readers that features stories and excerpts from well-known easy-to-read books like Cynthia Rylant's Henry and Mudge stories. A companion book is *School Stories: Your Dog Didn't Eat* (2000). (Rev: BL 7/00; HBG 3/01)

7624 Phillips, Joan. *My New Boy* (K–2). Illus. by Lynn Munsinger. 1986, Random paper $3.99 (978-0-394-88277-2). 32pp. A pet store puppy searches for just the right owner. Also use: *Lucky Bear* (1986). (Rev: BCCB 1/87; BL 12/1/86)

7625 Pierce, Terry. *Tae Kwon Do!* (PS–K). Illus. by Todd Bonita. Series: Step into Reading. 2006, Random $3.99 (978-0-375-83448-6). 32pp. For beginning readers, this is a simple rhyming account of a brother and sister's tae kwon do class. (Rev: SLJ 5/06)

7626 Pilkey, Dav. *Big Dog and Little Dog Making a Mistake* (PS–K). Illus. by author. Series: A Big Dog and Little Dog Book. 1999, Harcourt $5.95 (978-0-15-200354-8). This board book for beginning readers tells what happens when two doggy friends mistake a skunk for a kitten. (Rev: SLJ 6/99)

7627 Pinkwater, Daniel. *Mush's Jazz Adventure* (2–4). Illus. by Jill Pinkwater. Series: Ready-for-Chapters. 2002, Simon & Schuster paper $3.99 (978-0-689-84572-7). 37pp. Mush, an alien dog, tells the story of her arrival on Earth and how she and three other animals saved a dance hall owner from robbers in this entertaining and improbable beginning chapter book. (Rev: HBG 3/03; SLJ 2/03)

7628 Platt, Kin. *Big Max* (1–2). Illus. by Robert Lopshire. Series: I Can Read. 1992, HarperCollins paper $3.99 (978-0-06-444006-6). 64pp. A modest detective unravels the case of the king's missing elephant in this newly illustrated I Can Read Book.

7629 Platt, Kin. *Big Max and the Mystery of the Missing Giraffe* (K–2). Illus. by Lynne Cravath.

Series: I Can Read. 2005, HarperCollins $15.99 (978-0-06-009918-3). 64pp. Big Max continues his detective work in this entertaining mystery for beginning readers. (Rev: SLJ 7/05)

7630 Pomerantz, Charlotte. *The Outside Dog* (1–3). Illus. by Jennifer Plecas. 1993, HarperCollins LB $15.89 (978-0-06-024783-6). 64pp. An easy-reader that tells how Marisol gradually breaks down her grandfather's opposition to having a dog as a pet. (Rev: BCCB 10/93; BL 9/15/93*; SLJ 11/93*)

7631 Porte, Barbara Ann. *Harry in Trouble* (1–3). Illus. by Yossi Abolafia. 1989, Dell paper $4.99 (978-0-440-80210-5). 48pp. Harry's third library card has disappeared! (Rev: BCCB 2/89; BL 3/1/89; SLJ 3/89)

7632 *The Prince Has a Boo-Boo!* (K–1). Illus. by R. W. Alley. Series: I'm Going to Read. 2005, Sterling paper $3.95 (978-1-4027-2089-5). 28pp. This beginning reader featuring a cumulative story about a prince in need of a bandage introduces 50 basic vocabulary words. (Rev: BL 9/1/05; SLJ 9/05)

7633 Proimos, James. *Mutton Soup: More Adventures of Johnny Mutton* (2–4). Illus. 2004, Harcourt $16.00 (978-0-15-216772-1). 48pp. In these five graphic-novel-style stories, Johnny Mutton — the lamb adopted by humans — gets etiquette lessons, goes on the rollercoast, and has other adventures. (Rev: BL 3/1/04; HB 3/04; SLJ 4/04)

7634 Proimos, James, and Andy Rheingold. *When Guinea Pigs Fly!* (2–5). Illus. by James Proimos. 2005, Scholastic paper $3.99 (978-0-439-51902-1). 105pp. Brooks the guinea pig dreams of freedom from his pet shop, so he is initially ecstatic when he and friends Leone and Allen are accidentally set free in a park; a beginning chapter book with black-and-white cartoon drawings. (Rev: SLJ 11/05)

7635 Ransom, Candice F. *Danger at Sand Cave* (1–3). Illus. by Den Schofield. Series: On My Own History. 2000, Carolrhoda LB $21.27 (978-1-57505-379-0); paper $23.93 (978-1-57505-454-4). 46pp. A fictitious 10-year-old boy helps in the unsuccessful efforts to rescue Floyd Collins from a cave in 1925. (Rev: HB 7/00; HBG 10/00; SLJ 8/00)

7636 Rau, Dana Meachen. *Chilly Charlie* (K–1). Illus. by Martin Lemelman. Series: Rookie Readers. 2001, Children's Book Pr. paper $4.95 (978-0-516-27288-7). 24pp. Charlie feels that he is getting cold and needs a hug to keep him warm. (Rev: BL 4/15/01)

7637 Rau, Dana Meachen. *In the Yard* (K–1). Illus. by Elizabeth Wolf. Series: Compass Point Early Reader. 2001, Compass Point LB $14.95 (978-0-7565-0116-7). 24pp. A brief, simple text and bold illustrations depict an African American family enjoying their backyard. (Rev: SLJ 2/02)

7638 Rau, Dana Meachen. *Shoo, Crow! Shoo!* (1). Illus. by Mary Galan Rojas. 2001, Compass Point Early Reader. 2001, Compass Point LB $14.95 (978-0-7565-0072-6). 24pp. Two children make a scarecrow from old clothes, hay, and a pumpkin. (Rev: BL 7/01; SLJ 8/01)

7639 Reggier, DeMar. *Gooci Food* (K–2). Illus. by David Austin Clar. Series: My First Reader. 2005, Children's Pr. LB $18.50 (978-0-516-24879-0); paper $3.95 (978-0-516-24969-8). 32pp. In this easy-reader, a young boy accompanies his father to the grocery store where they buy ingredients for a special meal for Mom. (Rev: SLJ 1/06)

7640 Ries, Lori. *Aggie and Ben: Three Stories* (K–2). Illus. by Frank W. Dormer. 2006, Charlesbridge $12.95 (978-1-57091-594-9). 48pp. A beginning chapter book in which Ben takes home a new pet dog, Aggie, and the two get to know each other. (Rev: SLJ 7/06)

7641 Ries, Lori. *Good Dog, Aggie* (1–3). Illus. by Frank W. Dormer. 2009, Charlesbridge $12.95 (978-1-57091-645-8). 48pp. When Ben's dog Aggie gets kicked out of obedience school, Ben teaches her with help from a friendly neighbor. (Rev: BCCB 3/09; BLO 5/27/09; SLJ 5/09)

7642 Ritchie, Alison. *Horrible Haircut* (1–2). Illus. by Ian Newsham. Series: Blue Bananas. 2001, Crabtree LB $22.60 (978-0-7787-0844-5); paper $4.95 (978-0-7787-0890-2). 45pp. Lucy and her mother make a deal — if Lucy doesn't like the cut her mother gives her, she gets to cut her mother's hair — in this book for fluent beginning readers. (Rev: SLJ 7/02)

7643 Robins, Joan. *Addie Meets Max* (1–3). Illus. by Sue Truesdell. 1985, HarperCollins $9.95 (978-0-06-025063-8). 32pp. Addie is sure she won't like her new neighbor until mother invites him in for pizza. Also use: *Addie Runs Away* (1989). (Rev: BCCB 5/85; BL 4/15/85; SLJ 5/85)

7644 Rocklin, Joanne. *This Book Is Haunted* (K–2). Illus. by JoAnn Adinolfi. 2002, HarperCollins LB $17.89 (978-0-06-028457-2). 46pp. A selection of not-very-frightening Halloween stories for beginning readers. (Rev: BCCB 10/02; HBG 3/03; SLJ 9/02)

7645 Roop, Peter, and Connie Roop. *Keep the Lights Burning, Abbie* (1–3). Illus. by Peter E. Hanson. 1985, Carolrhoda LB $23.93 (978-0-87614-275-2); paper $5.95 (978-0-87614-454-1). 40pp. The true story of Abbie Burgess, who keeps the lighthouse lights ablaze for four storm-filled weeks while her father is on the mainland. (Rev: BCCB 1/86; BL 1/15/86) [387.1]

7646 Ross, Alice, and Kent Ross. *The Copper Lady* (1–3). Illus. by Leslie Bowman. 1997, Carolrhoda LB $23.93 (978-0-87614-934-8). 48pp. An easy-to-read book about a young Parisian who watches the construction of the Statue of Liberty and stows away on the ship that is taking it to the United States. (Rev: BCCB 7–8/97; BL 8/97; HB 5/04; SLJ 9/97)

7647 Roy, Ron. *Kidnapped at the Capital* (2–4). Illus. by Liza Woodruff. Series: Capital Mysteries. 2002, Golden paper $3.99 (978-0-307-26514-2). 80pp. A mystery takes K.C. Corcoran and Marshall Li on a lively hunt through Washington, D.C. (Rev: BL 9/1/02)

7648 Ruelle, Karen Gray. *April Fool!* (1–2). Series: Holiday House Reader. 2002, Holiday House

$14.95 (978-0-8234-1686-8). 32pp. Two little kittens try to come up with April Fool's jokes to play on their parents and each other. (Rev: BL 2/1/02; HBG 10/02; SLJ 6/02)

7649 Ruelle, Karen Gray. *The Crunchy, Munchy Christmas Tree* (1–2). Illus. by author. Series: Holiday House Reader. 2004, Holiday House $14.95 (978-0-8234-1787-2). 32pp. Kitten siblings Harry and Emily's find a way to entertain themselves when their Christmas plans are disrupted by a snowstorm. (Rev: BL 9/1/03; HBG 4/04; SLJ 10/03)

7650 Ruelle, Karen Gray. *Easter Egg Disaster* (1–2). Illus. Series: Holiday House Reader. 2004, Holiday House $14.95 (978-0-8234-1806-0). 32pp. In four short chapters suitable for beginning readers, kittens Harry and Emily have various misadventures with eggs. (Rev: BL 3/15/04; SLJ 4/04)

7651 Ruelle, Karen Gray. *Easy as Apple Pie: A Harry and Emily Adventure* (K–2). Illus. by author. Series: Holiday House Reader. 2002, Holiday House $14.95 (978-0-8234-1759-9). 32pp. Kittens Harry and Emily have different reactions when invited to pick apples with their grandparents. (Rev: BL 8/02; HBG 3/03; SLJ 10/02)

7652 Rylant, Cynthia. *Annie and Snowball and the Cozy Nest* (PS–2). Illus. by Sucie Stevenson. Series: Annie and Snowball Ready-to-Read. 2009, Simon & Schuster $15.99 (978-1-4169-3943-6). 40pp. Annie and her bunny and other friends watch a mother robin sitting on her eggs and eventually hear the sound of baby birds. (Rev: BL 4/1/09)

7653 Rylant, Cynthia. *Annie and Snowball and the Dress-up Birthday* (K–2). Illus. by Sucie Stevenson. Series: Ready-to-Read. 2007, Simon & Schuster $14.99 (978-1-4169-0938-5). 40pp. Annie (cousin of Henry of Henry and Mudge) likes wearing nice ribbons and bows, so she and her pet rabbit Snowball invite Henry and Mudge to a "Dress-up Birthday," but that term can be misinterpreted . . . . (Rev: SLJ 4/07)

7654 Rylant, Cynthia. *The Case of the Climbing Cat* (1–2). Illus. by G. Brian Karas. Series: High Rise Private Eyes. 2000, Greenwillow LB $14.89 (978-0-688-16309-9). 48pp. An easy-to-read mystery in which Bunny, a rabbit, and Jack, a raccoon, help a neighbor find her stolen binoculars. Also use *The Case of the Missing Monkey* (2000). (Rev: BCCB 11/00; BL 10/1/00; HBG 3/01; SLJ 8/00)

7655 Rylant, Cynthia. *The Case of the Desperate Duck* (1–3). Illus. by G. Brian Karas. Series: The High-Rise Private Eyes. 2005, HarperCollins $14.99 (978-0-06-053451-6). 48pp. A rabbit and a raccoon solve the mystery of the missing sugar cubes in this easy-reader. (Rev: SLJ 8/05)

7656 Rylant, Cynthia. *Henry and Mudge and Annie's Good Move* (2–3). Illus. by Sucie Stevenson. 1998, Simon & Schuster $14.00 (978-0-689-81174-6). 40pp. Henry and his dog Mudge are both excited to hear that Henry's cousin, Annie, is going to move next door. (Rev: BL 7/98; HBG 3/99; SLJ 10/98)

7657 Rylant, Cynthia. *Henry and Mudge and the Big Sleepover* (K–2). Illus. by Sucie Stevenson. 2006, Simon & Schuster $14.95 (978-0-689-81171-5).

40pp. Henry and his dog Mudge enjoy a variety of typical sleepover activities at Patrick's house. (Rev: BL 8/06; SLJ 7/06)

7658 Rylant, Cynthia. *Henry and Mudge and the Great Grandpas* (K–2). Illus. by Sucie Stevenson. Series: Ready-to-Read. 2005, Simon & Schuster $14.95 (978-0-689-81170-8). 40pp. Henry and Mudge the dog visit Great Grandpa Bill, and all the other grandpas who live there too. (Rev: BL 5/1/05) ∩

7659 Rylant, Cynthia. *Henry and Mudge and the Tumbling Trip* (1–3). Illus. by Carolyn Bracken. Series: Ready-to-Read. 2005, Simon & Schuster $14.95 (978-0-689-81180-7). 40pp. Henry and his dog Mudge take a trip out west. (Rev: BL 2/1/06)

7660 Rylant, Cynthia. *The High-Rise Private Eyes: The Case of the Troublesome Turtle* (2–4). Illus. 2001, Greenwillow LB $14.89 (978-0-688-16311-2). 48pp. Bunny Brown and her partner Jack Jones, a raccoon, investigate the disappearance of some balloons. (Rev: BL 5/15/01; HB 5/01; HBG 10/01; SLJ 7/01)

7661 Rylant, Cynthia. *Mr. Putter and Tabby Run the Race* (K–2). Illus. by Arthur Howard. 2008, Harcourt $15.00 (978-0-15-206069-5). 44pp. Mr. Putter agrees to run in a senior marathon when he learns that one of the prizes is a train set. Earlier installments in this long-running series featuring Tabby the cat and neighbor Mrs. Teaberry and her dog Zeke include *Mr. Putter and Tabby Paint the Porch* (2000), *Mr. Putter and Tabby Stir the Soup* (2003), *Mr. Putter and Tabby Make a Wish* (2005), and *Mr. Putter and Tabby Spin the Yarn* (2006). (Rev: BL 4/1/08; SLJ 2/08) ∩

7662 Rylant, Cynthia. *Poppleton and Friends* (1–3). Illus. by Mark Teague. 1997, Scholastic $15.95 (978-0-590-84786-5). 48pp. Three stories about the friendship of Poppleton pig with his buddies Hudson and Cherry Sue. (Rev: BL 8/97; HBG 3/98; SLJ 9/97)

7663 Rylant, Cynthia. *Poppleton Everyday* (PS–2). Illus. by Mark Teague. 1998, Scholastic $15.95 (978-0-590-84845-9). 48pp. A beginning reader that presents Poppleton the pig in three humorous stories about his misadventures. (Rev: BCCB 4/98; HBG 10/98; SLJ 5/98)

7664 Rylant, Cynthia. *Poppleton Forever* (1–2). Illus. by Mark Teague. 1998, Scholastic $14.95 (978-0-590-84843-5). 56pp. In this easy reader, Poppleton the pig and friend Cherry Pie, a llama, share three adventures — one involving getting Poppleton's newly planted tree to grow. (Rev: BL 7/98; HBG 3/99; SLJ 9/98)

7665 Rylant, Cynthia. *Poppleton in Fall* (1–2). Illus. by Mark Teague. 1999, Scholastic $14.95 (978-0-590-84789-6). 56pp. In these three episodes, Poppleton Pig is always helped out of troubling situations by his dear friend Cherry Sue, the llama. (Rev: BL 10/15/99; HBG 3/00; SLJ 9/99)

7666 Rylant, Cynthia. *Puppy Mudge Wants to Play* (PS–K). Illus. by Sucie Stevenston. Series: Ready-to-Read Puppy Mudge. 2005, Simon & Schuster $14.95 (978-0-689-83984-9). 32pp. Puppy Mudge finally succeeds in distracting Henry from his book and getting him to play. (Rev: BL 5/15/05)

7667 Sachar, Louis. *Marvin Redpost: Kidnapped at Birth?* (1–3). Illus. by Neal Hughes. Series: Stepping Stone. 1992, Random LB $11.99 (978-0-679-91946-9); paper $3.99 (978-0-679-81946-2). 68pp. Marvin Redpost secretly believes that he is the kidnapped son of the king. (Rev: BCCB 10/92; BL 12/1/92; SLJ 3/93)

7668 Scarry, Richard. *Mr. Fixit's Magnet Machine* (1–2). Illus. Series: Ready-to-Read. 1998, Simon & Schuster paper $3.99 (978-0-671-81624-7). 32pp. When Huckle, Lowly, and Mr. Frumble notice metal objects flying into the air, they trace this phenomenon to Mr. Fixit's new magnet machine. (Rev: BL 7/98)

7669 Schaefer, Lola M. *Follow Me, Mittens* (PS–2). Illus. by Susan Kathleen Hartung. Series: My First I Can Read. 2007, HarperCollins $15.99 (978-0-06-054665-6). 25pp. A companion to *What's That, Mittens?*, this simple story of Nick and Mittens on a walk will build the confidence of young readers. (Rev: SLJ 7/07)

7670 Schaefer, Lola M. *Mittens* (PS–K). Illus. by Susan Kathleen Hartung. Series: My First I Can Read. 2006, HarperCollins $14.99 (978-0-06-054659-5). 32pp. A simple book for beginning readers about Mittens the kitten's fears about his new home. (Rev: BL 4/15/06; SLJ 6/06)

7671 Schmauss, Judy Kentor. *Parade Day* (K–1). Illus. by Randy Chewning. Series: Reader's Clubhouse. 2006, Barron's paper $3.99 (978-0-7641-3293-3). 24pp. This simple tale of friends gathering for a parade is designed to help children practice their phonics skills, focusing in this title on the long "a" sound. Part of a series that includes *Too, Too Hot!* and *Luke's Mule* (both 2006). (Rev: SLJ 11/06)

7672 Schulte, Mary. *Who Do I Look Like?* (PS–1). Illus. by Maryn Roos. Series: A Rookie Reader. 2006, Children's Pr. LB $19.50 (978-0-516-24978-0). 32pp. An easy reader that features a child in a racially mixed family wondering whom he most resembles. (Rev: SLJ 6/06)

7673 Schwartz, Alvin. *Ghosts! Ghostly Tales from Folklore* (K–2). Illus. by Victoria Chess. 1991, HarperCollins LB $17.89 (978-0-06-021797-6); paper $3.99 (978-0-06-444170-4). 64pp. Contains a number of suspenseful ghost stories written for the beginning reader. (Rev: BCCB 9/91; BL 9/15/91; HB 9/91; SLJ 9/91)

7674 Schwartz, Alvin. *I Saw You in the Bathtub and Other Folk Rhymes* (1–3). Illus. by Syd Hoff. 1989, HarperCollins paper $3.99 (978-0-06-444151-3). 64pp. An amusing assortment of folk rhymes. Also use: *All of Our Noses Are Here and Other Noodle Tales* (1985). (Rev: BCCB 4/89; BL 3/1/89; SLJ 5/89)

7675 Seeger, Laura Vaccaro. *Two's Company* (PS–1). Illus. by author. 2008, Roaring Brook $12.95 (978-1-59643-273-4). 32pp. The teddy bear and dachshund friends first seen in *Dog and Bear* (2007) return in three brief stories paired with sim-

ple paintings. (Rev: BCCB 4/08; BL 4/1/08; HB 3/08; LMC 8/08; SLJ 4/08)

7676 Seuss, Dr. *The Cat in the Hat* (1–3). Illus. by author. 1957, Random LB $11.99 (978-0-394-90001-8). 72pp. The story of the fabulous cat that came to visit one rainy day when Mother was away. Also from the same author and publisher: *The Cat in the Hat Comes Back!* (1958); *Foot Book* (1968).

7677 Seuss, Dr. *Green Eggs and Ham* (K–3). Illus. by author. 1960, Random $11.99 (978-0-394-90016-2). 72pp. A charming nonsense book.

7678 Seuss, Dr. *Hop on Pop* (1–2). Illus. by author. 1963, Random LB $11.99 (978-0-394-90029-2). 72pp. One of the many entertaining, controlled vocabulary stories of Dr. Seuss. Also use: *One Fish, Two Fish, Red Fish, Blue Fish* (1960); *Fox in Socks* (1965).

7679 Seuss, Dr. *I Am Not Going to Get Up Today!* (1–2). Illus. by James Stevenson. 1987, Random LB $11.99 (978-0-394-99217-4). 48pp. A rhyming story about a little boy who refuses to get up in the morning. (Rev: BL 12/1/87)

7680 Seuss, Dr. *I Can Lick Thirty Tigers Today and Other Stories* (K–3). Illus. by author. 1969, Random $14.95 (978-0-394-80094-3). The Cat in the Hat tells three zany stories.

7681 Seuss, Dr. *I Can Read with My Eyes Shut!* (1–2). Illus. by author. 1978, Random LB $11.99 (978-0-394-93912-4). The Cat in the Hat tells us of all the joys of reading.

7682 Seuss, Dr. *Oh Say Can You Say?* (1–3). Illus. by author. 1979, Random LB $11.99 (978-0-394-94255-1). Tongue-twisting verses presented by a variety of imaginative creatures.

7683 Sharmat, Marjorie W. *Nate the Great* (1–3). Illus. by Marc Simont. 1986, Dell paper $4.50 (978-0-440-46126-5). 48pp. Nate, a boy detective, puts on his Sherlock Holmes outfit and sets out confidently to solve the mystery of the missing painting. Other titles in the series: *Nate the Great Goes Undercover* (1977); *Nate the Great and the Lost List* (1976); *Nate the Great and the Phony Clue* (1981); *Nate the Great and the Sticky Case* (1981); *Nate the Great and the Missing Key* (1981); *Nate the Great and the Snowy Trail* (1982).

7684 Sharmat, Marjorie W. *Nate the Great and the Fishy Prize* (1–3). Illus. by Marc Simont. 1988, Dell paper $4.50 (978-0-440-40039-4). Nate the Great and his dog Sludge solve the mystery of the stolen prize. Also use: *Nate the Great Stalks Stupidweed* (1986); *Nate the Great Goes Down in the Dumps* (1989). (Rev: BL 8/85; SLJ 9/85)

7685 Sharmat, Marjorie W., and Craig Sharmat. *Nate the Great and the Tardy Tortoise* (1–3). Illus. by Marc Simont. 1995, Delacorte $13.95 (978-0-385-32111-2). 48pp. Using a trail of half-eaten plants as a guide, Nate the Great is able to return a lost turtle to its owner. (Rev: BL 10/1/95; SLJ 10/95)

7686 Sharmat, Marjorie W., and Mitchell Sharmat. *Nate the Great Talks Turkey* (K–2). Illus. by Jody Wheeler. 2006, Delacorte $11.95 (978-0-385-73336-6). 80pp. Boy detective Nate the Great decides to pass on the case of the missing turkey until he uncovers a clue that just cannot be ignored; his cousin Olivia meanwhile is doing her own sleuthing. (Rev: BL 10/15/06; SLJ 10/06)

7687 Shaw, Nancy. *Sheep in a Jeep* (K–2). Illus. by Margot Apple. 1986, Houghton $15.00 (978-0-395-41105-6); paper $5.95 (978-0-395-47030-5). 32pp. Silly sheep in a silly tale; they fall down, Jeep and all, and land in a muddy pool. Also use: *Sheep on a Ship* (1989). (Rev: BL 9/15/86; HB 11/86)

7688 Shaw, Nancy. *Sheep Out to Eat* (PS–1). Illus. by Margot Apple. 1992, Houghton $15.00 (978-0-395-61128-9). 32pp. Several sheep are asked to leave a tea shop after they misbehave in this amusing story in rhyme. (Rev: BL 9/15/92; SLJ 9/92)

7689 Shea, George. *First Flight: The Story of Tom Tate and the Wright Brothers* (2–3). Illus. by Don Bolognese. Series: I Can Read. 1997, HarperCollins LB $15.89 (978-0-06-024504-7). 48pp. A fictional account of a boy who is a friend of Orville and Wilbur Wright and participates in their flights. (Rev: BL 11/15/96; HB 3/97; SLJ 1/97)

7690 Shreeve, Elizabeth. *Hector Springs Loose* (2–4). Illus. by Pamela Levy. Series: The Adventures of Hector Fuller. 2004, Simon & Schuster paper $3.99 (978-0-689-86414-8). 67pp. Hector the wumblebug loses his home to a flea circus and goes off in search of a new one in this work for new chapter-book readers. (Rev: SLJ 3/04)

7691 Silverman, Erica. *Cowgirl Kate and Cocoa* (PS–2). Illus. by Betsy Lewin. 2005, Harcourt $15.00 (978-0-15-202124-5). 48pp. Four easy-to-read chapters about the fun-filled friendship between a cowgirl and her talking horse. (Rev: BL 3/1/05; SLJ 3/05)

7692 Silverman, Erica. *Partners* (1–3). Illus. by Betsy Lewin. 2006, Harcourt $15.00 (978-0-15-202125-2). 44pp. Kate and her faithful horse Cocoa continue their happy friendship in four new episodes; a sequel to *Cowboy Kate and Cocoa* (2005). (Rev: BL 2/15/06; SLJ 8/06)

7693 Silverman, Erica. *Rain or Shine* (PS–2). Illus. by Betsy Lewin. Series: Cowgirl Kate and Cocoa. 2008, Harcourt $15.00 (978-0-15-205384-0). 44pp. The affectionate relationship between Cowgirl Kate and her horse Cocoa continues through four more adventures — mainly in the rain. (Rev: BL 4/15/08; SLJ 4/08)

7694 Silverman, Erica. *School Days* (PS–2). Illus. by Betsy Lewin. Series: Cowgirl Kate and Cocoa. 2007, Harcourt $15.00 (978-0-15-205378-9). 48pp. Cocoa the horse suffers separation anxiety when Kate starts school and seems to be preoccupied with homework and her new friend. (Rev: BL 3/15/07)

7695 Simon, Charnan. *I Like to Win!* (PS–1). Photos by Dorothy Handelman. Series: Real Kids Readers. 1999, Millbrook LB $16.90 (978-0-7613-2062-3); paper $4.99 (978-0-7613-2087-6). 31pp. An African American girl and boy resolve their differences about winning at board games in this book for the very beginning reader. (Rev: SLJ 1/00)

7696 Simon, Charnan. *Mud!* (1). Illus. by Dorothy Handelman. Series: Real Kids Readers. 1999, Millbrook LB $18.90 (978-0-7613-2051-7); paper $4.99

(978-0-7613-2076-0). 32pp. Color photographs are used to illustrate this easy-to-read story about three boys playing in the mud. (Rev: BL 5/15/99)

7697 Simon, Francesca. *Horrid Henry* (1–3). Illus. by Tony Ross. 2009, Sourcebooks paper $4.99 (978-1-4022-1775-3). 112pp. In four short and funny chapters, Horrid Henry unsettles his brother Perfect Peter, disrupts a dance recital, spars with his neighbor Moody Margaret, and ruins a camping trip. (Rev: BCCB 6/09; BL 5/15/09; SLJ 4/09)

7698 Singer, Bill. *The Fox with Cold Feet* (K–2). Illus. by Dennis Kendrick. 1980, Parents LB $5.95 (978-0-8193-1022-4). 48pp. A fox sets out to get a pair of boots to help cure his cold feet.

7699 Singer, Marilyn. *Solomon Sneezes* (PS–1). Illus. by Brian Floca. Series: Harper Growing Tree. 1999, HarperCollins $9.95 (978-0-694-01748-5). In this beginning reader, Solomon Snorkel's sneezes are so powerful they can knock down skiers and topple a giant. (Rev: HBG 3/00; SLJ 9/99)

7700 Skofield, James. *Detective Dinosaur* (1–3). Illus. 1996, HarperCollins LB $15.89 (978-0-06-024908-3). 48pp. Three uncomplicated mysteries are included in this easily read book. (Rev: BL 8/96; SLJ 8/96)

7701 Slaughter, Hope. *Buckley and Wilberta* (2–3). Illus. Series: I'm Reading Now. 1996, Red Hen LB $14.95 (978-0-931093-15-9). 64pp. Two friends, Buckley the Hedgehog and Wilberta Rabbit, are featured in four stories. (Rev: BL 4/1/96)

7702 Smith, Charles R., Jr. *Let's Play Baseball!* (PS–1). Illus. by Terry Widener. 2006, Candlewick $8.99 (978-0-7636-1646-5). A little boy can't resist the call of a baseball wanting to play. (Rev: SLJ 7/06)

7703 Smith, Janice Lee. *Wizard and Wart in Trouble* (1–2). Illus. by Paul Meisel. Series: I Can Read. 1998, HarperCollins LB $15.89 (978-0-06-027762-8). 48pp. Wizard and his dog Wart straighten out problems with the use of magic spells. (Rev: BL 5/1/98; HBG 10/98; SLJ 6/98)

7704 Spohn, Kate. *Turtle and Snake's Spooky Halloween* (PS–1). Illus. by author. 2002, Viking $13.99 (978-0-670-03560-1). 32pp. Turtle and Snake plan a really good Halloween party and follow their checklist. (Rev: HBG 3/03; SLJ 9/02)

7705 Stamper, Judith B. *Breakfast at Danny's Diner: A Book About Multiplication* (K–2). Illus. by Chris Demarest. Series: All Aboard Math. 2003, Grosset paper $3.99 (978-0-448-43210-6). 45pp. Basic multiplication skills are conveyed in this entertaining book about two youngsters helping out at their uncle's diner. (Rev: BL 1/1–15/04; HBG 4/04; SLJ 3/04)

7706 Stamper, Judith B. *Five Goofy Ghosts* (2–3). Illus. by Tim Raglin. Series: Hello Reader! 1997, Scholastic $3.99 (978-0-590-92152-7). 32pp. Five horror stories that are also humorous are contained in this simple beginning reader. (Rev: BL 2/1/98)

7707 Stamper, Judith B. *The Wild Leaf Ride* (PS–2). Illus. by Carolyn Bracken. Series: Scholastic Reader. 2004, Scholastic paper $3.99 (978-0-439-56998-9). Ms. Frizzle's students have an exciting time on the Magic School Bus as they set off in search of a leaf in this book for beginning readers. (Rev: SLJ 3/05)

7708 Standford, Natalie. *The Bravest Dog Ever: The True Story of Balto* (1–3). Illus. by Donald Cook. 1989, Random paper $3.99 (978-0-394-89695-3). 48pp. In easy-to-read format, this is the true story of an amazing dog who guided a sled team carrying medicine to Nome, Alaska. (Rev: BCCB 1/90; BL 2/1/90; SLJ 2/90) [636.7]

7709 Stanley, George E. *Ghost Horse* (1–3). Illus. by Ann Barrow. Series: Road to Reading. 2000, Golden paper $3.99 (978-0-307-26500-5). 69pp. With the help of a new friend, Emily solves the mystery of a ghost horse she spies from her bedroom window. (Rev: SLJ 3/01)

7710 Stanley, George E. *Snake Camp* (1–2). Illus. by Jared Lee. Series: Road to Reading. 2000, Golden $10.99 (978-0-307-46406-4); paper $3.99 (978-0-307-26406-0). 32pp. In this easy-reader, Stevie mistakenly is sent to a snake camp instead of a computer camp and, unfortunately, Stevie is terrified of snakes. (Rev: BL 12/1/00; HBG 3/01)

7711 Stauffacher, Sue. *Bessie Smith and the Night Riders* (2–4). Illus. by John Holyfield. 2006, Putnam $16.99 (978-0-399-24237-3). 32pp. A fictionalized, dramatically illustrated account of a real-life confrontation between singer Bessie Smith and Ku Klux Klan members in 1927. (Rev: BL 2/1/06; SLJ 1/06)

7712 Stevenson, James. *Mud Flat April Fool* (1–3). Illus. 1998, Greenwillow $15.89 (978-0-688-15164-5). 48pp. A humorous book for beginning readers in which the animal residents of Mud Flat have fun playing jokes on April Fools' Day. (Rev: BL 2/15/98; HB 5/98; HBG 10/98; SLJ 3/98)

7713 Suen, Anastasia. *Willie's Birthday* (K–2). Illus. by Allan Eitzen. 2001, Viking $13.99 (978-0-670-88943-3). 32pp. A beginning reader in which mayhem results when Peter invites his friends and their pets to help celebrate the birthday of his dachshund, Willie. (Rev: HBG 10/01; SLJ 3/01)

7714 Suen, Anastasia, and Ezra Jack Keats. *The Clubhouse* (K–2). Illus. by Allan Eitzen. Series: Viking Easy-to-Read. 2002, Viking $13.99 (978-0-670-03537-3). 32pp. Peter, an African American boy, and his friends find a pile of wood and build a place to play. (Rev: BL 4/15/02; HBG 10/02; SLJ 8/02)

7715 Sullivan, Paula. *Todd's Box* (PS–1). Illus. by Nadine Bernard Westcott. Series: Green Light Reader. 2004, Harcourt $11.95 (978-0-15-205093-1). 24pp. Todd ignores his mother's scolding and continues to pick up items of interest, presenting them all to her once they are on the bus. (Rev: BL 3/15/04; SLJ 5/04)

7716 Swanson, June. *I Pledge Allegiance* (1–3). Illus. by Rick Hanson. 1990, Carolrhoda LB $21.27 (978-0-87614-393-3). 40pp. The difficult words in the Pledge of Allegiance are explained and its history is traced. (Rev: BCCB 6/90; BL 6/1/90; SLJ 7/90) [323.6]

7717 Sweeney, Jacqueline. *Critter Day* (K–2). Series: We Can Read! 2000, Marshall Cavendish $21.36 (978-0-7614-1119-2). After a day of games, each animal has won one of the events. Also use *Molly's Store*, *Homesick*, and *What About Bettie*, all in the same series for beginning readers (all 2000). (Rev: HBG 3/01; SLJ 11/00)

7718 Tafuri, Nancy. *Spots, Feathers, and Curly Tails* (PS). Illus. by author. 1988, Greenwillow $17.89 (978-0-688-07537-8). 32pp. A concept book that makes a mystery of identifying familiar animals from the barnyard. (Rev: BL 8/88; HB 11/88; SLJ 12/88)

7719 Tafuri, Nancy. *Will You Be My Friend?* (PS–K). Illus. 2000, Scholastic $16.95 (978-0-590-63782-4). 32pp. In this easy reader, a young bunny and his friends help Bird rebuild his home when his nest is ruined in a rainstorm. (Rev: BL 1/1–15/00; HBG 10/00; SLJ 3/00)

7720 Tate, Lindsey. *Kate Larkin, the Bone Expert* (1–4). Illus. by Diane Palmisciano. 2008, Holt $16.95 (978-0-8050-7901-2). 80pp. Eight-year-old Kate tells the story of her broken arm and how it healed in this book for beginning readers with large type, many illustrations, and two activities. (Rev: LMC 3/09; SLJ 4/08)

7721 Taylor, Sean. *Small Bad Wolf* (K–2). Illus. by Jan Lewis. Series: I Am Reading. 2004, Kingfisher paper $3.95 (978-0-7534-5801-3). 45pp. Small Bad Wolf wants to emulate his father, but his father's lessons leave something to be desired. (Rev: SLJ 8/04)

7722 Taylor-Butler, Christine. *Ah-Choo* (K–2). Illus. by Carol Koeller. Series: My First Reader. 2005, Children's Pr. LB $18.50 (978-0-516-25175-2). 31pp. A girl at home with a cold finds ways to amuse herself in this book for beginning readers with a list of words. (Rev: SLJ 5/05)

7723 Taylor-Butler, Christine. *Step-by-Step* (K–2). Illus. by Susan Miller. Series: My First Reader. 2005, Children's Pr. LB $18.50 (978-0-516-24875-2); paper $3.95 (978-0-516-24974-2). 32pp. A young boy makes a beautiful bouquet for his grandmother by dyeing white flowers using bright colors. (Rev: SLJ 1/06)

7724 Taylor-Butler, Christine. *Who Needs Friends?* (PS–1). Illus. by Susan Havice. Series: A Rookie Reader. 2006, Children's Pr. LB $19.50 (978-0-516-24979-7). 32pp. A young boy decides to throw himself a birthday party when it seems no one has remembered the special day. (Rev: SLJ 6/06)

7725 Thiesing, Lisa. *A Dark and Noisy Night* (PS–1). Illus. Series: Dutton Easy Reader. 2005, Dutton $13.99 (978-0-525-47388-6). 32pp. Peggy the Pig cannot fall asleep because of the scary noises that seem to be everywhere. (Rev: BL 9/15/05; SLJ 1/06)

7726 Thomas, Shelley Moore. *Get Well, Good Knight* (K–2). Illus. by Jennifer Plecas. Series: Dutton Easy Reader. 2002, Dutton $13.99 (978-0-525-46914-8). 48pp. The Good Knight rides off on a quest to cure three little dragons with horrible colds, in this appealing easy reader. (Rev: BCCB 12/02; BL 1/1–15/03; HB 9/02; HBG 3/03; SLJ 11/02)

7727 Thomas, Shelley Moore. *Good Night, Good Knight* (1–3). Illus. by Jennifer Plecas. Series: Dutton Easy Reader. 2000, Dutton $13.99 (978-0-525-46326-9). 48pp. A gentle knight discovers three young dragons who want to be tucked in for the night in this charming bedtime book for beginning readers. (Rev: BCCB 2/00; BL 2/15/00; HBG 10/00; SLJ 3/00)

7728 Thomas, Shelley Moore. *Happy Birthday, Good Knight* (K–2). Illus. by Jennifer Plecas. Series: Dutton Easy Reader. 2006, Dutton $13.99 (978-0-525-47184-4). 48pp. Things go badly when the Good Knight's three little dragon friends try to create a birthday gift. (Rev: BL 1/1–15/06; SLJ 3/06)

7729 Tidd, Louise Vitellaro. *The Best Pet Yet* (K–2). Photos by Dorothy Handelman. Series: Real Kids Readers. 1998, Millbrook LB $18.90 (978-0-7613-2006-7); paper $4.99 (978-0-7613-2031-9). 32pp. A boy selects his first pet in this beginning reader with photographs. (Rev: HBG 10/98; SLJ 7/98)

7730 Tidd, Louise Vitellaro. *I'll Do It Later* (1–2). Illus. by Dorothy Handelman. Series: Real Kids Readers. 1999, Millbrook LB $18.90 (978-0-7613-2066-1); paper $4.99 (978-0-7613-2091-3). 32pp. In this easy reader, a snow day provides a lazy boy with a reprieve from submitting a school assignment. (Rev: BL 12/1/99; SLJ 11/99)

7731 Tidd, Louise Vitellaro. *Let Me Help!* (1–2). Illus. by Dorothy Handelman. Series: Real Kids Readers. 1999, Millbrook LB $18.90 (978-0-7613-2067-8); paper $4.99 (978-0-7613-2092-0). 32pp. In spite of Tara's good intentions, her efforts to help her father always end disastrously. (Rev: BL 10/1/99; HBG 3/00)

7732 Tidd, Louise Vitellaro. *Lost and Found* (PS–2). Photos by Dorothy Handelman. Series: Real Kids Readers. 1998, Millbrook LB $18.90 (978-0-7613-2020-3); paper $4.99 (978-0-7613-2045-6). 31pp. Using engaging photos and double-page spreads, this easy-reader tells about the search for a lost sneaker. (Rev: SLJ 1/99)

7733 Torrey, Richard. *Beans Baker's Best Shot* (1–3). Series: Step into Reading. 2006, Random LB $11.99 (978-0-375-92839-0); paper $3.99 (978-0-375-82839-3). 48pp. An injury sidelines Beans Baker from his soccer team's championship game, but he tries to do his part by cheering on his teammates. (Rev: BL 8/06; SLJ 10/06)

7734 Twain, Mark. *The Best Fence Painter*. Bk. 2 (K–2). Adapted by Catherine Nichols. Illus. by Amy Bates. Series: The Adventures of Tom Sawyer. 2006, Sterling paper $3.95 (978-1-4027-3288-1). 32pp. For beginning readers, this chapter book with simple vocabulary and short sentences retells the fence-painting episode. Also use *A Song for Aunt Polly* (2006). (Rev: SLJ 8/06)

7735 Underwood, Deborah. *Pirate Mom* (PS–2). Illus. by Stephen Gilpin. Series: Step into Reading. 2006, Random LB $11.99 (978-0-375-93323-3); paper $3.99 (978-0-375-83323-6). 48pp. When

Pete's mother is hypnotized into thinking she is a pirate, it's up to Pete to try to stop her zany behavior. (Rev: BL 5/1/06)

7736 Vail, Rachel. *Mama Rex and T: Homework Trouble* (2–4). Illus. by Steve Björkman. 2002, Scholastic $14.95 (978-0-439-40628-4). 32pp. Mama Rex and T, a young dinosaur, finish the project he's neglected in this challenging beginning chapter book. Also use *Mama Rex and T: The Horrible Play Date* (2002), about friendship. (Rev: HBG 3/03; SLJ 10/02)

7737 Vail, Rachel. *Mama Rex and T: The Reading Champion* (1–3). Illus. by Steve Bjarkman. 2004, Scholastic paper $3.99 (978-0-439-57822-6). A young dinosaur initially has trouble reading in this appealing easy-reader. (Rev: SLJ 8/04)

7738 Van Leeuwen, Jean. *Amanda Pig and the Really Hot Day* (K–2). Illus. by Ann Schweninger. Series: Dial Easy-to-Read. 2005, Dial $14.99 (978-0-8037-2887-5). 48pp. Four episodic easy-reader stories show Amanda Pig and her family coping with hot weather. (Rev: BL 6/1–15/05)

7739 Van Leeuwen, Jean. *Amanda Pig and the Wiggly Tooth* (K–2). Illus. by Ann Schweninger. Series: Oliver and Amanda. 2008, Dial $14.99 (978-0-8037-3104-2). 40pp. Amanda Pig won't let her father pull out her wiggly tooth, but then it falls out by itself and she loses it! (Rev: BL 5/15/08; SLJ 4/08)

7740 Van Leeuwen, Jean. *Oliver Pig and the Best Fort Ever* (K–2). Illus. by Ann Schweninger. Series: Dial Easy-to-Read. 2006, Dial $15.99 (978-0-8037-2888-2). 40pp. Oliver Pig calls on his friends to help him build "the best fort ever" in four chapters suited to beginning readers. (Rev: BL 4/15/06; SLJ 7/06)

7741 Van Leeuwen, Jean. *Oliver the Mighty Pig* (PS–2). Illus. by Ann Schweninger. Series: Dial Easy-to-Read. 2004, Dial $14.99 (978-0-8037-2886-8). 48pp. Oliver really enjoys the superhero powers imparted by his Mighty Pig cape, and feels very weak while it's in the wash in this easy-reader. (Rev: BL 3/1/04; SLJ 3/04)

7742 Viorst, Judith. *Alexander, Who Used to Be Rich Last Sunday* (K–2). Illus. by Ray Cruz. 1978, Macmillan LB $16.00 (978-0-689-30602-0); paper $4.99 (978-0-689-71199-2). 32pp. Alexander spends his dollar gift foolishly penny by penny. (Rev: SLJ 6/04)

7743 Wallace, Carol. *Easter Bunny Blues* (1–2). Illus. by Steve Björkman. 2009, Holiday $15.95 (978-0-8234-2162-6). 32pp. The Easter Bunny is sick and two dogs enlist an engaging assemblage of kindly animals to collect eggs, paint them, and distribute Easter baskets. (Rev: BLO 2/9/09; SLJ 2/09)

7744 Wallace, Carol. *One Nosy Pup* (PS–2). Illus. by Steve Björkman. Series: Holiday House Reader. 2005, Holiday House $15.95 (978-0-8234-1917-3). 40pp. A beagle puppy discovers a new friend, Charlie the hamster, in the kitchen of his owners' new house. (Rev: BL 3/1/05; SLJ 4/05)

7745 Wallace, Carol. *Turkeys Together* (K–2). Illus. by Jacqueline Rogers. Series: Holiday House Reader. 2005, Holiday House $15.95 (978-0-8234-1895-4). 40pp. A hunting dog befriends two mother turkeys in this easy-reader. (Rev: SLJ 8/05)

7746 Wallace, Karen. *A Bed for the Winter* (PS–3). Series: DK Readers. 2000, DK $12.99 (978-0-7894-5706-6); paper $3.99 (978-0-7894-5707-3). 32pp. In this beginning reader, a dormouse searches for a winter home and sees other animals doing the same thing. (Rev: HBG 3/01; SLJ 1/01)

7747 Walsh, Vivian. *Gluey: A Snail Tale* (K–3). Illus. by J. Otto Seibold. 2002, Harcourt $15.00 (978-0-15-216620-5). 48pp. Celerina the rabbit moves into Gluey the snail's home, believing it to be abandoned, and hosts a disastrous party in this complex tale for beginning readers. (Rev: BL 10/15/02; HBG 3/03; SLJ 12/02)

7748 Weeks, Sarah. *Pip Squeak* (PS–2). Illus. by Jane Manning. 2007, HarperCollins $15.99 (978-0-06-075635-2). 32pp. Pip Squeak the mouse (first seen in the 2000 publication *Drip, Drop*) busies himself cleaning for his friend Max only to find that Max is one of the messiest people ever. (Rev: HB 7/07; SLJ 2/08)

7749 Weeks, Sarah. *Splish, Splash!* (1). Illus. by Ashley Wolff. 1999, HarperCollins $12.95 (978-0-06-027892-2). 32pp. In his bathtub, Chub the fish is joined by many friends who want to frolic with him. (Rev: BL 3/15/99; HBG 10/99; SLJ 2/99)

7750 West, Colin. *Moose and Mouse* (K–2). Illus. by author. Series: I Am Reading. 2004, Kingfisher paper $3.95 (978-0-7534-5715-3). 45pp. Moose and mouse are friends despite their differences. (Rev: SLJ 8/04)

7751 Weston, Martha. *Cats Are Like That* (1–2). Illus. 1999, Holiday House LB $15.95 (978-0-8234-1419-2). 32pp. Fuzzy the cat is jealous when Dot begins showering her attentions on her new pet fish. (Rev: BL 3/15/99; HBG 10/99; SLJ 6/99)

7752 Weston, Martha. *Jack and Jill and Big Dog Bill: A Phonics Reader* (1). Illus. Series: Early Step into Reading. 2002, Random paper $3.99 (978-0-375-81248-4). 32pp. Two small children, Jack and Jill, along with their dog, try to slide down a snow-covered hillside on their sled with amusing results in this easy reader. (Rev: BL 4/15/02; HBG 10/02; SLJ 7/02)

7753 Weston, Martha. *Space Guys* (K–1). Illus. Series: Holiday House Reader. 2000, Holiday House $14.95 (978-0-8234-1487-1). 32pp. A group of space travelers spend a riotous night in an average American home in this science fiction easy-reader. (Rev: BL 4/15/00; HBG 10/00; SLJ 5/00)

7754 Wetterer, Margaret K. *Kate Shelley and the Midnight Express* (2–3). Illus. by Karen Ritz. 1990, Carolrhoda LB $23.93 (978-0-87614-425-1). 48pp. Based on a true story, the tale of a young girl who saved a train from disaster. (Rev: BCCB 11/90; BL 9/15/90; SLJ 1/91)

7755 Wheeler, Lisa. *Who's Afraid of Granny Wolf?* (1–2). Illus. by Frank Ansley. 2004, Simon & Schuster $14.95 (978-0-689-84952-7). 47pp. Tradi-

tional enemies — the wolf and the pig — are best of friends in this humorous original story. (Rev: SLJ 8/04)

7756 Wilhelm, Hans. *I Lost My Tooth!* (PS–1). Illus. by author. Series: Hello Reader! 1999, Scholastic paper $3.99 (978-0-590-64230-9). A little puppy plans to leave his loose tooth for the Tooth Fairy when it falls out, but he accidentally swallows it. (Rev: SLJ 9/99)

7757 Wilhelm, Hans. *It's Too Windy!* (1). 2000, Scholastic paper $3.99 (978-0-439-10849-2). 32pp. An easy-to-read book about a shaggy white dog who saves a baby when its stroller rolls away. (Rev: BL 7/00)

7758 Willems, Mo. *Are You Ready to Play Outside?* (PS–2). Illus. by author. 2008, Hyperion $8.99 (978-1-4231-1347-8). 64pp. Rain dampens Piggie's happy disposition until Gerald the elephant lends her an ear. (Rev: BL 11/15/08; SLJ 12/08)

7759 Willis, Jeanne. *Be Quiet, Parrot!* (1–2). Illus. by Mark Birchall. 2000, Carolrhoda $7.25 (978-1-57505-492-6). 32pp. In this beginning reader, a noisy parrot interrupts everyone and everything with his constant talking. Also use *Take Turns, Penguin!* (2000), an additional story about sharing and self-ishness. (Rev: BL 12/1/00; HBG 3/01; SLJ 1/01)

7760 Wiseman, Bernard. *Barber Bear* (2–3). Illus. by author. 1987, Little, Brown paper $11.95 (978-0-316-94859-3). 48pp. Puns aplenty in this story of Barber Bear. (Rev: BL 8/87; SLJ 8/87)

7761 Wiseman, Bernard. *Morris and Boris at the Circus* (1–2). Illus. by author. 1988, HarperCollins paper $3.99 (978-0-06-444143-8). 64pp. Two friends, a moose and a bear, attend the circus. Also use: *Morris Goes to School* (1983). (Rev: BL 12/1/88; SLJ 2/89)

7762 Wishinsky, Frieda. *A Bee in Your Ear* (2–4). Illus. by Louise-Andree Laliberte. 2005, Orca paper $4.99 (978-1-55143-324-0). 64pp. Kate must contend with spelling-bee pressure, a bully named Violet, and problems with her friend Jake in this beginning chapter book. (Rev: BL 3/15/05)

7763 Wishinsky, Frieda. *Just Mabel* (1–3). Illus. by Sue Heap. Series: I Am Reading. 2004, Kingfisher paper $3.95 (978-0-7534-5742-9). 45pp. Mabel finds a way to stop the teasing about her name and her clothes in this book for beginning readers. (Rev: SLJ 9/04)

7764 Ziefert, Harriet. *Sometimes I Share* (PS–1). Illus. by Carol Nicklaus. Series: I'm Going to Read! 2005, Sterling $11.95 (978-1-4027-2068-0); paper $3.95 (978-1-4027-2090-1). 28pp. Simple first-person text chronicles the ups and downs of a girl's relationship with her little brother; suitable for early beginning readers. (Rev: BL 8/05)

7765 Ziefert, Harriet. *Toes Have Wiggles Kids Have Giggles* (K–3). Illus. by Rebecca Doughty. 2002, Penguin $13.99 (978-0-399-23617-4). 32pp. Clever wordplays and amusing rhymes introduce readers to what words can do. (Rev: BL 6/1–15/02)

Fiction for Older Readers

General

7766 Adler, C. S. *Always and Forever Friends* (5–7). 1990, Avon paper $3.99 (978-0-380-70687-7). 176pp. Wendy, at 11, is having a painful struggle making new friends after Meg moves away until she meets Honor, who is African American and very hesitant about accepting Wendy. (Rev: BCCB 4/88; BL 4/1/88; SLJ 4/88)

7767 Adler, C. S. *The Magic of the Glits* (5–7). Illus. by Ati Forberg. 1987, Avon paper $2.50 (978-0-380-70403-3). 96pp. Jeremy, age 12, takes care of 7-year-old Lynette for the summer. A reissue of the 1979 edition. Also use *Some Other Summer* (1988).

7768 Amesse, Susan. *Kissing Brendan Callahan* (4–6). 2005, Roaring Brook $15.95 (978-1-59643-015-0). 160pp. Twelve-year-old Sarah, an aspiring romance writer, is devastated when her mother won't let her enter a writing contest to be judged by the girl's favorite author; meanwhile kissable Brendan offers a questionable alternative. (Rev: BL 11/15/05; HBG 4/06; SLJ 12/05; VOYA 12/05)

7769 Anderson, M. T. *Me, All Alone, at the End of the World* (4–6). Illus. by Kevin Hawkes. 2005, Candlewick $16.99 (978-0-7636-1586-4). 40pp. A boy's solitary but idyllic life at the End of the World is threatened by the arrival of an elderly entrepreneur who proposes to turn the area into a massive theme park. (Rev: BL 11/15/05; HBG 4/06; LMC 1/06; SLJ 12/05)

7770 Anderson, M. T. *The Serpent Came to Gloucester* (2–4). Illus. by Bagram Ibatoulline. 2005, Candlewick $16.99 (978-0-7636-2038-7). 40pp. In poetic narrative, Anderson tells, from the point of view of a young boy, the story of continued sightings of a supposed sea serpent on the coast of Massachusetts in 1817. (Rev: BL 6/1–15/05; SLJ 6/05)

7771 Bair, Sheila. *Rock, Brock, and the Savings Shock* (3–5). Illus. by Barry Gott. 2006, Albert Whitman $16.99 (978-0-8075-7094-4). While Brock saves his money, his twin brother Rock squanders it, and learns a lesson about the value of a dollar; saving tips and a brief math lesson at the end explain the underlying concepts. (Rev: SLJ 7/06)

7772 Bateson, Catherine. *Stranded in Boringsville* (5–8). 2005, Holiday House $16.95 (978-0-8234-1969-2). 138pp. Twelve-year-old Rain's life is turned upside down when she and her mother move from cosmopolitan Melbourne to a small Australian town in the middle of nowhere; but she finds a good friend in her neighbor Daniel. (Rev: BL 12/1/05; SLJ 2/06; VOYA 2/06)

7773 Bauer, A. C. E. *No Castles Here* (4–7). 2007, Random $15.99 (978-0-375-83921-4). 288pp. A magical book, a Big Brother, and a school chorus rescue 11-year-old Augie Boretski from feeling completely lost in his life of poverty and loneliness in Camden, New Jersey. (Rev: BL 12/1/07; SLJ 10/07)

7774 Bauer, Marion Dane. *On My Honor* (5–7). 1986, Houghton $15.00 (978-0-89919-439-4); Dell paper $4.99 (978-0-440-46633-8). 96pp. A powerful story in which 12-year-old Joel faces telling his parents that his friend Tony has drowned in the river they promised never to swim. (Rev: BCCB 10/86; BL 9/1/86; SLJ 11/86)

7775 Bell, Alison. *Zibby Payne and the Party Problem* (3–6). 2008, Lobster paper $6.95 (978-1-897073-69-8). 95pp. Sixth-grader Zibby wants to have an inclusive party — unlike the exclusive party her friend Amber is having — but realizes she'll have to invite the losers too. (Rev: BL 4/15/08)

7776 Bell, Alison. *Zibby Payne and the Wonderful, Terrible Tomboy Experiment* (3–5). Series: Zibby Payne. 2006, Lobster paper $6.95 (978-1-897073-39-1). 96pp. When her longtime friend Sarah shows more interest in fashion and boy-watching than sports, 6th-grader Zibby reacts by becoming a total tomboy. (Rev: SLJ 12/06)

7777 Bell, Joanne. *Breaking Trail* (5–7). 2005, Groundwood $15.95 (978-0-88899-630-5); paper $6.95 (978-0-88899-662-6). 135pp. Becky's dreams of training a dog team to participate in the Junior

Quest fade when her father grows increasingly depressed, but a sled trip back to the family's cabin offers a chance to make those dreams come true. (Rev: SLJ 10/05)

7778 Belton, Sandra. *The Tallest Tree* (3–5). 2008, Greenwillow $16.99 (978-0-06-052749-5). 160pp. Paul Robeson serves as a source of inspiration for African Americans young and old in a depressed neighborhood. (Rev: BL 2/1/08; SLJ 3/08)

7779 Bernard, Virginia. *Eliza Down Under: Going to Sydney* (5–8). Series: Going To. 2000, Four Corners paper $7.95 (978-1-893577-02-2). 96pp. This novel deals with Eliza's adventures in Australia when she accompanies her mother to the 2000 Olympic Games in Sydney. (Rev: SLJ 3/00)

7780 Blatchford, Claire H. *Nick's Secret* (5–7). 2000, Lerner LB $14.95 (978-0-8225-0743-7). 168pp. When 13-year-old Nick, who is deaf, is summoned to a motel by Darryl Smythe and his gang of vandals, the boy knows he is in for trouble. (Rev: BL 9/15/00; HBG 3/01; SLJ 12/00; VOYA 2/01)

7781 Boles, Philana Marie. *Little Divas* (5–8). 2006, HarperCollins LB $16.89 (978-0-06-073300-1). 176pp. Twelve-year-old Cass is facing a lot of change in her life: her parents' divorce, living with her father, a new friend, a first kiss, and perhaps a new school. (Rev: BL 4/1/06; SLJ 1/06)

7782 Brooks, Bruce. *Everywhere* (5–8). 1990, HarperCollins LB $16.89 (978-0-06-020729-8). 80pp. Eleven-year-old Dooley, who is African American, helps a 10-year-old white boy live through the emotional trauma of waiting to see if his beloved grandfather will recover from a heart attack. (Rev: BCCB 10/90; BL 10/15/90*; SLJ 9/90*)

7783 Butcher, Kristin. *The Runaways* (5–8). 1998, Kids Can $16.95 (978-1-55074-413-2). During an unsuccessful attempt to run away from home, young Nick Battle meets Luther, a homeless man, and through this friendship gains insights into poverty in America. (Rev: BL 4/15/98; HBG 10/98; SLJ 4/98)

7784 Butler, Don Hillestad. *Tank Talbott's Guide to Girls* (4–6). 2006, Albert Whitman $15.99 (978-0-8075-7761-5). 178pp. As part of his effort to move on to 6th grade, Tank Talbott writes a guide to girls, filled with advice he'll need himself if he's to survive a summer-long visit from his stepsisters; a sequel to *Trading Places with Tank Talbott* (2003). (Rev: BL 4/15/06; SLJ 5/06)

7785 Byars, Betsy. *The Pinballs* (5–7). 1977, Harper-Collins LB $16.89 (978-0-06-020918-6). 144pp. Three misfits in a foster home band together to help lessen their problems.

7786 Byrd, Sandra. *Island Girl* (5–8). Series: Friends for a Season. 2005, Bethany House paper $9.99 (978-0-7642-0020-5). 125pp. Confused by changes in her family situation, 13-year-old Meg spends a summer with her grandparents on an Oregon island where she meets and befriends Tia. (Rev: BL 10/1/05)

7787 Cabot, Meg. *Allie Finkle's Rules for Girls: Moving Day* (3–5). 2008, Scholastic $15.99 (978-0-545-03947-5). 240pp. Nine-year-old Allie, whose

rules usually result from her somewhat reckless behavior ("Don't Stick a Spatula Down Your Best Friend's Throat"), now faces moving to a new neighborhood and school. (Rev: BL 6/1–15/08; SLJ 6/08) ∩

7788 Carlson, Ron. *The Speed of Light* (4–7). 2003, HarperTempest LB $16.89 (978-0-06-029825-8). 288pp. Baseball, science experiments, and the mysteries of the universe occupy Larry and his two best friends during the summer before junior high. (Rev: BL 8/03; HBG 4/04; SLJ 7/03; VOYA 10/03)

7789 Carlyle, Carolyn. *Mercy Hospital: Crisis!* (5–8). 1993, Avon paper $3.50 (978-0-380-76846-2). 128pp. Three friends volunteer at a local hospital. (Rev: SLJ 7/93)

7790 Caseley, Judith. *The Kissing Diary* (5–8). 2007, Farrar $16.00 (978-0-374-36346-8). 208pp. After her parents' divorce, 12-year-old Rosie keeps a diary in which she describes problems at home and at school and her crush on Robbie Romano. (Rev: BL 8/07; SLJ 11/07)

7791 Cassidy, Cathy. *Scarlett* (5–8). 2006, Viking $16.99 (978-0-670-06068-9). 272pp. Much to her surprise (and with some help from a mysterious boy), 12-year-old Scarlett actually enjoys living in Ireland with her father and his new family. (Rev: BL 12/1/06)

7792 Chocolate, Deborah N. *NEATE to the Rescue!* (4–7). 1992, Just Us Bks. paper $3.95 (978-0-940975-42-2). 98pp. A 13-year-old African American girl and her friends help out when her mother's seat on the local council is put in doubt by a racist. (Rev: BCCB 3/93; BL 3/15/93)

7793 Clements, Andrew. *The School Story* (4–7). Illus. 2001, Simon & Schuster $16.00 (978-0-689-82594-1). 160pp. Two 12-year-old girls tackle the task of getting a book by a new author published. (Rev: BCCB 7–8/01; BL 6/1–15/01; HB 7/01; HBG 10/01; SLJ 6/01)

7794 Clements, Andrew. *A Week in the Woods* (4–8). 2002, Simon & Schuster $16.95 (978-0-689-82596-5). 208pp. Mark, a lonely 5th-grader, and a forceful teacher test each other — and Mark's survival skills — on a weeklong camping trip. (Rev: BCCB 1/03; BL 10/1/02; HBG 3/03; SLJ 11/02)

7795 Codell, Esmé Raji. *Vive la Paris* (4–6). 2006, Hyperion $15.99 (978-0-7868-5124-9). 192pp. Paris McCray, an African American fifth grader, develops a very special relationship with her piano teacher, a Holocaust survivor; a companion to *Sahara Special* (2003). (Rev: BL 9/15/06; SLJ 10/06)

7796 Cohen, Tish. *The Invisible Rules of the Zoe Lama* (4–7). 2007, Dutton $15.99 (978-0-525-47810-2). 208pp. This playfully illustrated story about 7th-grader Zoë describes her busy life at home and at school, offering advice and organizing projects and lives. (Rev: BL 10/1/07; SLJ 8/07)

7797 Cole, Sheila. *The Canyon* (4–6). 2002, Harper-Collins LB $15.89 (978-0-06-029496-0). 144pp. A California sixth-grader named Zach fights to preserve the canyon near his home when he discovers it is targeted for development. (Rev: BL 8/02; HBG 10/02; SLJ 6/02)

7798 Colfer, Eoin. *Benny and Omar* (5–8). 2001, O'Brien paper $7.95 (978-0-86278-567-3). 240pp. Benny, a young Irish lad, has trouble adjusting to his new life in Tunisia until he befriends Omar, a local orphan without a home, and the two have some exciting and amusing adventures. (Rev: BL 8/01; SLJ 12/01)

7799 Conrad, Pam. *Our House: The Stories of Levittown* (4–7). Illus. by Brian Selznick. 1995, Scholastic paper $14.95 (978-0-590-46523-6). 96pp. A series of fictional vignettes trace the history of the middle-class community of Levittown, New York. (Rev: BCCB 12/95; BL 1/1–15/96; HB 11/95; SLJ 11/95)

7800 Creech, Sharon. *Granny Torrelli Makes Soup* (4–6). Illus. by Chris Raschka. 2003, HarperCollins LB $16.89 (978-0-06-029291-1). 160pp. Food, warmth, and wisdom blend as 12-year-old Rosie spends time with her grandmother and talks about her blind friend Bailey and other life experiences. (Rev: BL 9/1/03*; HB 11/03; HBG 4/04; SLJ 8/03*)

7801 Danziger, Paula, and Ann M. Martin. *P. S. Longer Letter Later* (5–8). 1998, Scholastic paper $16.95 (978-0-590-21310-3). This novel consists of letters between two recently separated girlfriends — one who is adjusting well and the other who is facing family problems after her father loses his job and the family must change its lifestyle. (Rev: BL 6/1–15/98; HBG 10/98; SLJ 5/98; VOYA 8/98)

7802 DeFelice, Cynthia. *The Light on Hogback Hill* (4–8). 1993, Macmillan paper $15.00 (978-0-02-726453-1). 144pp. When 11-year-olds Hadley and Josh discover that the Witch Woman of Hogback Hill is really a shy, deformed woman, they help her find the courage to return to town. (Rev: BCCB 12/93; BL 11/1/93; SLJ 11/93)

7803 Draper, Sharon M. *The Space Mission Adventure* (3–6). Illus. by Jesse Joshua Watson. Series: Ziggy and the Black Dinosaurs. 2006, Simon & Schuster paper $4.99 (978-0-689-87914-2). 121pp. While attending Space Camp in Huntsville, Alabama, Ziggy and his friends (African American boys from Ohio) cooperate with other campers and experience the weightlessness of space travel during a simulated shuttle mission; lots of scientific information is interwoven. (Rev: SLJ 1/07)

7804 Dunlop, Eileen. *Finn's Search* (4–7). 1994, Holiday $14.95 (978-0-8234-1099-6). 128pp. Two Scottish boys try to save a gravel pit from local developers. (Rev: BCCB 12/94; BL 10/1/94; SLJ 10/94)

7805 Eduar, Gilles. *Gigi and Zachary's Around-the-World Adventure: A Seek-and-Find Game* (2–4). Illus. by author. 2003, Chronicle $16.95 (978-0-8118-3909-9). Young readers follow Gigi the giraffe and Zachary the zebra on a trip to far-flung countries, learning about exotic destinations and searching for specific items in the accompanying illustrations. (Rev: HBG 10/03; SLJ 6/03)

7806 Ekeland, Ivar. *The Cat in Numberland* (3–5). Illus. by John O'Brien. 2006, Cricket $19.95 (978-0-8126-2744-2). 59pp. Is zero a number? What is infinity? The answers are found at Hotel Infinity, where there is always room . . . even though all the rooms are full; a clever book introducing complex ideas. (Rev: SLJ 7/06)

7807 Ellerbee, Linda. *Girl Reporter Blows Lid Off Town!* (4–7). Series: Get Real. 2000, HarperCollins LB $14.89 (978-0-06-028245-5). 224pp. Casey Smith, a 6th-grade reporter, discovers the thrill of tracking down stories and getting at the truth in this lighthearted story set in a small town in the Berkshires. Also use *Girl Reporter Sinks School!* (Rev: BL 3/1/00; HBG 10/00; SLJ 6/00)

7808 Ellison, James Whitfield. *Akeelah and the Bee* (4–6). 2006, Newmarket paper $6.95 (978-1-55704-729-8). 186pp. A novelization of the movie about Akeelah, an 11-year-old student at a middle school in South Central Los Angeles, who is pushed into participating in her school's spelling bee and wins, qualifying her for the district competition. (Rev: SLJ 11/06)

7809 Emerson, Kevin. *Carlos Is Gonna Get It* (4–7). 2008, Scholastic $16.99 (978-0-439-93525-8). 291pp. A group of 7th-graders plan a prank on their special-needs classmate during a wilderness trip, but their plan backfires when they become lost in the forest during a lightning storm. (Rev: BCCB 11/08; BL 10/1/08; SLJ 12/08)

7810 Feldman, Jody. *The Gollywhopper Games* (4–7). Illus. by Victoria Jamieson. 2008, Greenwillow $16.99 (978-0-06-121450-9). 320pp. Gil Goodson is determined to win the Gollywhopper Games, sponsored by the Golly Toy and Game Company, in this engaging novel that includes the puzzles that Gil must solve to be victorious. (Rev: BL 12/1/07; SLJ 3/08)

7811 Fellowes, Julian. *The Curious Adventures of the Abandoned Toys* (3–5). Illus. by S. D. Schindler. 2007, Holt $17.95 (978-0-8050-7526-7). 64pp. Replaced by newer toys at the children's hospital, a teddy bear named Doc finds himself in the junkyard but soon makes a new life with new rewards. (Rev: BL 10/1/07; SLJ 1/08)

7812 Fletcher, Ralph. *Flying Solo* (5–8). 1998, Clarion $16.00 (978-0-395-87323-6). This novel answers the question, "What would a 6th-grade class do if their substitute teacher fails to appear and they are left alone for a whole day?" (Rev: BCCB 9/98; BL 8/98*; HB 11/98; HBG 3/99; SLJ 10/98)

7813 Frank, Lucy. *Lucky Stars* (4–7). 2005, Simon & Schuster $16.95 (978-0-689-85933-5). 304pp. Kira, a talented singer with a feisty character, arrives in New York City to find that her father has plans that don't fit in with her own. (Rev: BL 5/15/05; SLJ 7/05)

7814 Frederick, Heather Vogel. *The Mother-Daughter Book Club* (4–7). 2007, Simon & Schuster $15.99 (978-0-689-86412-4). 256pp. Four very different 6th-grade girls join a book club where they will read *Little Women* with their mothers. (Rev: BL 6/1–15/07; SLJ 8/07)

7815 Frederick, Heather Vogel. *Much Ado About Anne* (5–8). 2008, Simon & Schuster $15.99 (978-0-689-85566-5). 324pp. Seventh-graders Cassidy,

Megan, Jess, and Emma are reading books by Lucy Maud Montgomery with their mothers and using insights gained there in dealing with various problems; a sequel to *The Mother-Daughter Book Club* (2007). (Rev: SLJ 11/08)

7816 Fredericks, Mariah. *Fame* (5–8). Illus. by Liselotte Watkins. Series: In the Cards. 2008, Atheneum $15.99 (978-0-689-87656-1). 288pp. Eve tries out for the 8th-grade play only after the tarot cards tell her it could lead to fame in this sequel to *In the Cards: Love* (2007). (Rev: BL 1/1–15/08; SLJ 8/08)

7817 French, S. Terrell. *Operation Redwood* (5–7). 2009, Abrams $16.95 (978-0-8109-8354-0). 368pp. Twelve-year-old Julian tries to save historic redwoods with a little help from his friends. (Rev: BLO 5/28/09; HB 7/09; SLJ 7/09)

7818 Friedman, Laurie. *Heart to Heart with Mallory* (2–4). Illus. by Barbara Pollak. 2006, Carolrhoda LB $15.95 (978-1-57505-932-7). 159pp. In diary format, Mallory worries that Joey's father and Mary Ann's mother will get married, and that Joey and Mary Ann will forget about Mallory. (Rev: SLJ 1/07)

7819 Friedman, Laurie. *Red, White and True Blue Mallory* (2–4). Illus. by Jennifer Kalis. 2009, Carolrhoda $15.95 (978-0-8225-8882-5). 184pp. Fourthgrader Mallory journals her way through a class trip to Washington, D.C., describing the things she sees and her relationships with her classmates. (Rev: BL 4/1/09; SLJ 9/09)

7820 Gantos, Jack. *Heads or Tails: Stories from the Sixth Grade* (5–8). 1994, Farrar $16.00 (978-0-374-32909-9). 176pp. A collection of eight unusual short stories about 6th-grader Jack, a born survivor who overcomes amazing obstacles in this book set in Fort Lauderdale. (Rev: BCCB 7–8/94; HB 7/94; SLJ 6/94*)

7821 Gantos, Jack. *Jack on the Tracks: Four Seasons of Fifth Grade* (5–7). 1999, Farrar $16.00 (978-0-374-33665-3). 192pp. An episodic novel (the fourth about Jack Henry) in which Jack, a preadolescent, has several innocent adventures while growing up. (Rev: BCCB 9/99; BL 9/1/99; HB 11/99; HBG 3/00; SLJ 10/99; VOYA 2/00)

7822 Gibson, Sarah. *The Truth About Horses, Friends, and My Life as a Coward* (2–5). Illus. by Glin Dibley. 2008, Marshall Cavendish $15.99 (978-0-7614-5459-5). 160pp. Living on an island in Maine, Sophie acquires some true friends as she struggles to overcome her fear of the horses her family owns. (Rev: BLO 8/28/08; LMC 3/09)

7823 Gilson, Jamie. *Thirteen Ways to Sink a Sub* (4–7). Illus. by Linda Strauss Edwards. 1982, Lothrop $15.95 (978-0-688-01304-2). 144pp. The girls in Room 4A challenge the boys to see who can first make their substitute teacher cry. A sequel is *4B Goes Wild* (1983).

7824 Givner, Joan. *Ellen Fremedon, Journalist* (5–7). 2005, Groundwood $15.95 (978-0-88899-668-8). 192pp. In this appealing sequel to *Ellen Fremedon* (2004), young Ellen uncovers some

shocking stories when she starts a newspaper in quiet Partridge Cove. (Rev: BL 11/1/05; SLJ 2/06)

7825 Goldberg, Whoopi, and Deborah Underwood. *Plum Fantastic: Sugar Plum Ballerinas* (3–5). Illus. by Maryn Roos. 2008, Hyperion paper $4.99 (978-0-7868-5260-4). 160pp. Alexandrea's recent move to Harlem is stressing her enough without her mother's dream that she become a ballet dancer (instead of the speed skater Alex would like to be). (Rev: BL 1/1–15/09; SLJ 12/08)

7826 Greene, Constance C. *A Girl Called Al* (5–7). Illus. by Byron Barton. 1991, Puffin paper $5.99 (978-0-14-034786-9). 128pp. The friendship between two 7th-graders and their apartment building superintendent is humorously and deftly recounted.

7827 Greenwald, Sheila. *Rosy Cole's Worst Ever, Best Yet Tour of New York City* (3–5). 2003, Farrar $16.00 (978-0-374-36349-9). 128pp. Rosy takes her cousin on a tour of New York City and, despite her plans constantly going awry, the two have wonderful adventures. (Rev: BL 7/03; HB 7/03; HBG 4/04; SLJ 11/03)

7828 Gregory, Deborah. *Wishing on a Star* (5–8). Series: The Cheetah Girls. 1999, Hyperion paper $3.99 (978-0-7868-1384-1). 120pp. A light novel about five girls in New York City who form a singing group, the Cheetah Girls, and are soon signed up for an important gig. (Rev: SLJ 1/00)

7829 Grunwell, Jeanne Marie. *Mind Games* (5–8). 2003, Houghton $15.00 (978-0-618-17672-4). 144pp. Six very different 7th-graders get to know each other as they collaborate on a science fair project in this inventive novel sprinkled with press clippings and project notes. (Rev: BL 5/15/03; HB 5/03; HBG 10/03; LMC 10/03; SLJ 5/03)

7830 Gutman, Dan. *Nightmare at the Book Fair* (4–6). 2008, Simon & Schuster $15.99 (978-1-4169-2438-8). 230pp. A bang on the head sends 5th-grader Trip Dinkleman into a totally unexpected world of literary adventures, and he discovers that reading might not be so bad after all. (Rev: LMC 11/08; SLJ 9/08)

7831 Hächler, Bruno. *Hubert and the Apple Tree* (2–4). Trans. by Rosemary Lanning. Illus. by Albrecht Rissler. 2006, North-South $15.95 (978-0-7358-2044-9). 32pp. Hubert loves the apple tree he has grown up with, and is distressed when it is hit by lightning; a challenging, beautifully illustrated, picture book for older children. (Rev: BL 4/15/06)

7832 Haddix, Margaret P. *Dexter the Tough* (2–5). Illus. by Mark Elliott. 2007, Simon & Schuster $15.99 (978-1-4169-1159-3). 139pp. After getting off on the wrong foot at his new school, Dexter puts on a tough exterior to hide his anxieties, but a persistent teacher and a would-be friend manage to break through to the uncertain young boy inside. (Rev: SLJ 1/07)

7833 Hahn, Mary Downing. *Janey and the Famous Author* (2–4). Illus. by Timothy Bush. 2005, Clarion $15.00 (978-0-618-35408-5). 48pp. Devastated when she gets separated from her class and misses an opportunity to meet her favorite author at a literary festival, Janey is comforted by a kindly older woman. (Rev: BL 12/1/05)

7834 Hall, Katy, and Lisa Eisenberg. *The Paxton Cheerleaders: Go for It, Patti!* (4–7). 1994, Simon & Schuster paper $3.50 (978-0-671-89490-0). 137pp. Four 7th-grade girls from different backgrounds make the cheerleading team in their junior high school. (Rev: BL 2/1/95)

7835 Han, Jenny. *Shug* (5–8). 2006, Simon & Schuster $14.95 (978-1-4169-0942-2). 256pp. Annemarie Wilcox, a 7th-grader better known as Shug, faces numerous challenges in addition to the usual middle-school problems: a gorgeous older sister, squabbling parents, a fight with her best friend, and a crush on Mark that doesn't seem to be reciprocated. (Rev: BL 2/15/06; SLJ 5/06)

7836 Harley, Bill. *The Amazing Flight of Darius Frobisher* (4–6). 2006, Peachtree $14.95 (978-1-56145-381-8). 160pp. When his father disappears on a hot-air balloon trip and is presumed dead, 11-year-old Darius Frobisher is sent to live with his cranky Aunt Inga, a situation lightened when he meets a man who may have built a bicycle that will fly. (Rev: SLJ 12/06)

7837 Harrington, Jane. *Four Things My Geeky-Jock-of-a-Best-Friend Must Do in Europe* (5–8). 2006, Darby Creek LB $15.95 (978-1-58196-041-9). 160pp. From the European cruise she is taking with her mother, 13-year-old Brady reports via letter on her progress in meeting her must-dos — which include wearing a revealing bikini and meeting a "code-red Euro-hottie." (Rev: SLJ 6/06)

7838 Hathaway, Barbara. *Missy Violet and Me* (3–5). 2004, Houghton $15.00 (978-0-618-37163-1). 112pp. Stories of growing up in a southern town in the 1930s are told from the viewpoint of an 11-year-old girl. (Rev: BL 2/15/04; SLJ 5/04)

7839 Havill, Juanita. *Grow: A Novel in Verse* (2–5). Illus. by Stanislawa Kodman. 2008, Peachtree $14.95 (978-1-56145-441-9). 160pp. A community garden in Minneapolis brings together a diverse group, including unhappy 12-year-old Kate. (Rev: BL 6/1–15/08; SLJ 5/08)

7840 Hawking, Lucy, and Stephen Hawking. *George's Secret Key to the Universe* (3–6). Illus. by Garry Parsons. 2007, Simon & Schuster $17.99 (978-1-4169-5220-6). 304pp. Stephen Hawking and his daughter weave scientific information into this fictional story of George's adventures traveling through a computer portal and learning about the universe. (Rev: BL 12/1/07; LMC 5/08)

7841 Hemingway, Edith M. *Road to Tater Hill* (5–8). 2009, Delacorte $16.99 (978-0-385-73677-0). 224pp. In the mountains of North Carolina in 1963, 10-year-old Annie must deal with her baby sister's death, her mother who is silent and absent with grief, and her father who is overseas. (Rev: BCCB 10/09; BL 7/09)

7842 Hemphill, Helen. *Runaround* (5–8). 2007, Front St. $16.95 (978-1-932425-83-3). 117pp. In 1960s Kentucky, motherless 11-year-old Sassy needs more information about love but has trouble finding a source as her Dad is busy with other things, her

housekeeper wants her just to act like a young lady, and her sister may be involved with the same handsome neighbor. (Rev: BL 3/1/07*; SLJ 4/07)

7843 Henkes, Kevin. *Olive's Ocean* (5–8). 2003, Greenwillow LB $16.89 (978-0-06-053544-5). 224pp. During a summer at the beach, Martha, an aspiring writer, wrestles with a classmate's sudden death, has her first whiff of romance, and gets to know her family and herself better. Newbery Honor Book, 2004. (Rev: BL 9/1/03*; HB 11/03*; HBG 4/04; SLJ 8/03*)

7844 Hiaasen, Carl. *Flush* (5–8). 2005, Knopf LB $18.99 (978-0-375-92182-7). 272pp. Noah Underwood and his younger sister Abbey set out to prove their father was justified in sinking a floating casino because it was polluting. (Rev: BL 8/05; SLJ 9/05)

7845 Hiaasen, Carl. *Hoot* (5–8). 2002, Knopf $15.95 (978-0-375-82181-3). 272pp. Roy Eberhart, the new kid in Coconut Cove, finds himself embroiled in a battle to save some owls. Newbery Honor Book, 2003. (Rev: BCCB 11/02; BL 10/15/02; HB 11/02; HBG 3/03; SLJ 8/02)

7846 Hill, David. *Running Hot* (5–8). 2007, Simply Read paper $9.95 (978-1-894965-52-1). 116pp. A group of students clearing forest trees in rural New Zealand suddenly find themselves threatened by a raging fire. (Rev: SLJ 4/07)

7847 Hirsch, Odo. *Have Courage, Hazel Green!* (4–7). 2006, Bloomsbury $15.95 (978-1-58234-659-5). 256pp. Independent-minded Hazel Green and her friends must mend some fences when her plan to shame a neighbor into apologizing for a blatant act of ethnic prejudice backfires. (Rev: BL 6/1–15/06; SLJ 8/06)

7848 Hirsch, Odo. *Hazel Green* (3–6). 2003, Bloomsbury $15.95 (978-1-58234-820-9). 188pp. The title character in this appealing tale takes on the adult establishment in her community as she fights for the right of children to march in the annual Frogg Day parade. (Rev: BL 6/1–15/03; HBG 10/03; SLJ 6/03)

7849 Hobbs, Valerie. *Defiance* (4–7). 2005, Farrar $16.00 (978-0-374-30847-6). 128pp. An elderly neighbor named Pearl — and her cow — become valuable friends to 11-year-old Toby, who does not want to tell his parents that his cancer is back. (Rev: BL 8/05; SLJ 9/05)

7850 Holm, Jennifer. *Middle School Is Worse Than Meatloaf: A Year Told Through Stuff* (5–8). Illus. by Elicia Castaldi. 2007, Atheneum $12.99 (978-0-689-85281-7). 128pp. Receipts, notes, cards, magazine clippings, and other "stuff" tell of an eventful year in Ginny's life that includes bad hair days, iffy report cards, her mother's remarriage, and other tragedies. (Rev: BL 10/15/07; SLJ 9/07)

7851 Holt, Kimberly Willis. *When Zachary Beaver Came to Town* (5–9). 1999, Holt $16.95 (978-0-8050-6116-1). 227pp. Thirteen-year-old Toby Wilson learns the value of love and friendship when he gets to know Zachary Beaver, a 643-pound teen who has been abandoned by his guardian. (Rev: BCCB 12/99; BL 9/15/99; HB 11/99; HBG 3/00; SLJ 11/99*; VOYA 12/99)

7852 Honeycutt, Natalie. *Josie's Beau* (5–7). 1988, Avon paper $2.95 (978-0-380-70524-5). 128pp. Beau's mother doesn't want him fighting, so Josie offers to say she's the one who fights — but the lie backfires. (Rev: BCCB 12/87; BL 12/1/87; SLJ 12/87)

7853 Horvath, Polly. *My One Hundred Adventures* (4–6). 2008, Random $16.99 (978-0-375-84582-6). 272pp. Twelve-year-old Jane lives at the beach with her mother and younger siblings, and longs for adventures; although she does not reach the desired 100, she does indeed have a busy summer with many new experiences. (Rev: BCCB 10/08; BL 6/1–15/08; HB 9/08; LMC 11/08; SLJ 9/08) ⌒

7854 Hossack, Sylvie. *Green Mango Magic* (4–7). 1999, Avon $14.00 (978-0-380-97613-3). 128pp. Maile, who lives alone with her grandmother in Hawaii since her father abandoned her, finds a friend in Brooke, from Seattle, who is a recovering cancer patient. (Rev: BCCB 12/98; BL 5/1/99; HBG 10/99; SLJ 2/99; VOYA 8/99)

7855 Howe, James. *The Misfits* (5–8). 2001, Simon & Schuster $16.00 (978-0-689-83955-9). 288pp. A group of 7th-grade social misfits challenge the so-called norms at their school by running for student council and instituting a no-names-calling day. (Rev: BCCB 1/02; BL 11/15/01; HB 11/01; HBG 3/02; SLJ 11/01; VOYA 12/01)

7856 Hudson, Wade. *Anthony's Big Surprise* (5–7). Series: NEATE. 1998, Just Us Bks. paper $3.95 (978-0-940975-42-2). 89pp. Interracial tensions erupt in junior high school when some African American students are suspended and Anthony, who is also trying to cope with a family crisis, must deal with both problems. (Rev: SLJ 6/99)

7857 Jaramillo, Ann. *La Línea* (5–8). 2006, Roaring Brook $16.95 (978-1-59643-154-6). 144pp. Miguel, 15, and his sister Elena, 13, survive a terrifying journey across the border (la linea) from Mexico to California to join their parents. (Rev: BCCB 5/06; BL 3/15/06*; HBG 10/06; LMC 10/06; SLJ 4/06; VOYA 4/06)

7858 Jennings, Patrick. *The Beastly Arms* (5–7). 2001, Scholastic paper $16.95 (978-0-439-16589-1). 288pp. A dreamy 6th-grader who pictures animals in everything he sees, discovers a world of real beasts when he and his mother move to the Beastly Arms. (Rev: BCCB 10/01; BL 5/1/01; HB 7/01; HBG 10/01; SLJ 4/01)

7859 Jennings, Richard W. *The Great Whale of Kansas* (5–9). 2001, Houghton $15.00 (978-0-618-10228-0). 160pp. When a boy finds a prehistoric whale fossil in his backyard, the discovery brings unexpected consequences. (Rev: HB 9/01; HBG 3/02; SLJ 8/01; VOYA 2/02)

7860 Jennings, Richard W. *Stink City* (5–8). 2006, Houghton $16.00 (978-0-618-55248-1). 192pp. Cade Carlsen, heir to his family's successful — but smelly — catfish bait business, becomes an anti-fishing activist. (Rev: BL 10/15/06)

7861 Jones, Diana Wynne. *Unexpected Magic: Collected Stories* (5–10). 2004, Greenwillow $16.99 (978-0-06-055533-7). An exciting anthology of 16 tales of mystery and magic by a master of fantasy. (Rev: BL 4/15/04; SLJ 9/04)

7862 Jukes, Mavis. *Getting Even* (5–7). 1988, Knopf paper $4.50 (978-0-679-86570-4). 160pp. Maggie seems unable to stop the nasty pranks of classmate Corky, and receives differing advice from her divorced parents. (Rev: BCCB 5/88; BL 4/1/88; SLJ 5/88)

7863 Kehret, Peg. *Trapped* (4–6). 2006, Dutton $17.99 (978-0-525-47728-0). 192pp. A cat called Pete participates in this exciting story about efforts to track down the man who's setting illegal traps. (Rev: BL 12/1/06; SLJ 11/06)

7864 Kelsey, Marybeth. *Tracking Daddy Down* (4–7). 2008, HarperCollins $16.99 (978-0-06-128842-5). 292pp. Eleven-year-old Billie knows her father and uncle have robbed a bank and she hopes to persuade them to surrender. (Rev: LMC 3/09; SLJ 12/08)

7865 Kerrin, Jessica Scott. *Martin Bridge: Onwards and Upwards!* (2–4). Illus. by Joseph Kelly. 2009, Kids Can $16.95 (978-1-55453-160-8). 112pp. Martin's mother takes up the electronic keyboard in the first of these two stories; in the second, Laila wants to join the boys' Junior Badgers club but meets resistance. (Rev: BL 5/1/09)

7866 Kerrin, Jessica Scott. *Martin Bridge Blazing Ahead!* (2–4). Illus. by Joseph Kelly. 2006, Kids Can $14.95 (978-1-55337-961-4); paper $4.95 (978-1-55337-962-1). 109pp. Martin Bridge is back in a funny early chapter book with two new slice-of-life tales: an overnight camping trip with the Junior Badgers and a lawnmower repair session with his dad. (Rev: SLJ 11/06)

7867 Kherdian, David. *The Revelations of Alvin Tolliver* (5–7). 2001, Hampton Roads paper $7.95 (978-1-57174-255-1). 48pp. Twelve-year-old Alvin is fascinated with nature and the great outdoors, and finds some unusual adult friends who introduce him to nature's charms. (Rev: BL 12/1/01; SLJ 3/02)

7868 Kimmel, Elizabeth C. *Lily B. on the Brink of Paris* (5–8). 2006, HarperCollins $16.99 (978-0-06-083948-2). 192pp. Lily B.'s latest diary entries record the cultural sights of Paris, where the 13-year-old travels with her French class. (Rev: BL 1/1–15/07; SLJ 1/07)

7869 King, Daren. *Mouse Noses on Toast* (2–4). Illus. by David Roberts. 2008, Putnam $15.99 (978-0-399-25037-8). 128pp. When Paul Mouse discovers that a restaurant is serving mouse noses on toast, he and his friends campaign to change the menu. (Rev: BL 12/1/07)

7870 King-Smith, Dick. *The Catlady* (3–5). Illus. by John Eastwood. 2006, Knopf LB $17.99 (978-0-375-92985-4). 80pp. In 1901 England, Muriel Ponsonby has a house full of cats, many of whom she believes are reincarnated — including Queen Victoria. (Rev: BL 1/1–15/06; SLJ 1/06)

7871 Kline, Lisa Williams. *The Princesses of Atlantis* (5–7). 2002, Cricket $16.95 (978-0-8126-2855-5). 184pp. Twelve-year-old Arlene experiences ups and downs in her friendship with Carly, with whom she is writing a novel about two princesses. (Rev: BL 4/15/02; HBG 10/02; SLJ 7/02)

7872 Koertge, Ron. *The Heart of the City* (5–7). 1998, Orchard LB $16.99 (978-0-531-33078-4). 144pp. Apprehensive about moving to the big city of Los Angeles, 10-year-old Joy soon finds a friend in a young African American girl and together they fight the takeover of an abandoned house by hoods. (Rev: BCCB 4/98; BL 4/1/98; HBG 10/98)

7873 Kompaneyets, Marc. *The Squishiness of Things* (2–5). Illus. 2005, Knopf $15.95 (978-0-375-82750-1). 40pp. Hieronymus, an eccentric scholar, embarks on an epic journey to discover the origin of a single strand of hair that appears one morning on his desktop. (Rev: BL 7/05; SLJ 8/05)

7874 Konigsburg, E. L. *The Mysterious Edge of the Heroic World* (5–7). 2007, Simon & Schuster $16.99 (978-1-4169-4972-5). 240pp. Amedeo Kaplan hopes to make a name for himself by discovering something important; could he have the opportunity as he and his new friend William help to clean out the home of Mrs. Aida Zender, a former opera singer? Blending humor and mystery, this story has an added layer of Holocaust history. (Rev: BL 9/15/07; SLJ 9/07) ∩

7875 Konigsburg, E. L. *The Outcasts of 19 Schuyler Place* (4–8). 2004, Simon & Schuster $16.95 (978-0-689-86636-4). 304pp. Rescued from summer camp by aging uncles, Margaret is dismayed to find that their prized garden sculptures are endangered in this absorbing, amusing, and thought-provoking novel. (Rev: BL 12/15/03*; HB 3/04; SLJ 1/04*)

7876 Konigsburg, E. L. *The View from Saturday* (5–7). 1996, Simon & Schuster $16.00 (978-0-689-80993-4). 163pp. A complicated tale about four 6th-graders who are contestants in an Academic Bowl competition. Newbery Medal winner, 1997. (Rev: BCCB 11/96; BL 10/15/96; SLJ 9/96*)

7877 Korman, Gordon. *The Twinkie Squad* (5–7). 1992, Scholastic paper $13.95 (978-0-590-45249-6). 160pp. A bossy, insecure 6th-grader and a defender of weaker kids are sentenced to the school's Special Discussion Group. (Rev: BCCB 11/92; BL 9/15/92; SLJ 9/92)

7878 Lantz, Francess. *The Day Joanie Frankenhauser Became a Boy* (4–6). 2005, Dutton $16.99 (978-0-525-47437-1). 208pp. When she moves to a new school and finds her name has been listed as John, Joanie decides to try life as a boy. (Rev: BL 6/1–15/05)

7879 Lasky, Kathryn. *Georgia Rises* (2–4). Illus. by Ora Eitan. 2009, Farrar $16.95 (978-0-374-32529-9). 40pp. This narrative follows artist Georgia O'Keeffe through a day of painting in her later life on a ranch in New Mexico. (Rev: BCCB 9/09; BL 5/15/09; SLJ 6/09)

7880 Lee, Milly. *Landed* (3–5). Illus. by Yangsook Choi. 2006, Farrar $16.00 (978-0-374-34314-9). 40pp. Twelve-year-old Sun must study hard to prepare for the tests he will face from American immigration officials. (Rev: BCCB 5/06; BL 1/1–15/06*; HBG 10/06; LMC 11/06; SLJ 2/06)

7881 Lewis, Maggie. *Morgy Coast to Coast* (3–5). Illus. by Michael Chesworth. 2005, Houghton $15.00 (978-0-618-44896-8). 80pp. Morgy describes life at school and at home — hockey, the trumpet, and a retired greyhound figure large — through narrative and emails to his friend in California in this sequel to *Morgy Makes His Move* (2002). (Rev: BL 6/1–15/05; SLJ 5/05)

7882 Lewis, Maggie. *Morgy's Musical Summer* (3–5). Illus. by Michael Chesworth. 2008, Houghton $15.00 (978-0-618-77707-5). 112pp. Morgy goes to summer music camp in this third installment in the chapter book series. (Rev: BL 4/1/08; SLJ 5/08)

7883 Lichtman, Wendy. *Do the Math: Secrets, Lies, and Algebra* (5–9). 2007, HarperCollins $16.99 (978-0-06-122955-8). 183pp. Tess, 13, applies mathematical principles to all situations in her life including a cheating classmate, untrustworthy friends, and a potential murder. (Rev: BCCB 9/07; SLJ 12/07)

7884 Lindo, Elvira. *Manolito Four-Eyes* (4–6). Trans. by Joanne Moriarity. Illus. by Emilio Urberuaga. 2008, Marshall Cavendish $15.99 (978-0-7614-5303-1). 160pp. Ten-year-old Manolito, who is unfazed by his thick glasses and happy with the nickname "Four Eyes," shares with humor the activities of his life in a Madrid suburb. (Rev: BL 5/1/08; LMC 10/08; SLJ 7/08)

7885 Littman, Sarah Darer. *Confessions of a Closet Catholic* (4–7). 2005, Dutton $15.99 (978-0-525-47365-7). 193pp. Since she made friends with Mac, a Catholic girl, 11-year-old Justine has been questioning her Jewish faith. (Rev: SLJ 1/05)

7886 Lord, Cynthia. *Rules* (4–7). 2006, Scholastic $15.99 (978-0-439-44382-1). 208pp. Catherine is a likable 12-year-old struggling to cope with the family challenges posed by her younger autistic brother. Newbery Honor Book, 2007. (Rev: BL 2/15/06; SLJ 4/06)

7887 Lowery, Linda. *Truth and Salsa* (4–7). 2006, Peachtree $14.95 (978-1-59145-366-6). 176pp. Staying with her grandmother in Mexico after her parents separate, Haley makes a new friend and learns about people living on the edge of poverty. (Rev: SLJ 7/06)

7888 Lubar, David. *Hidden Talents* (5–9). 1999, Tor $16.95 (978-0-312-86646-4). 224pp. Five misfits, who are attending the last-resort Edgeview Alternative School, become friends and discover extrasensory talents they can use against the school bully. (Rev: BL 9/15/99; HBG 10/99; SLJ 11/99; VOYA 10/99)

7889 MacDonald, Amy. *Too Much Flapdoodle!* (5–8). Illus. by Cat B. Smith. 2008, Farrar $16.95 (978-0-374-37671-0). 192pp. Parker, 12, suffers a severe shock to his urban self when he goes to spend the summer on a ramshackle farm without Internet and cell service and nothing to do but chores. (Rev: BL 12/15/08; SLJ 11/08)

7890 McDonald, Megan. *Judy Moody Declares Independence* (2–4). Illus. by Peter Reynolds. 2005, Candlewick $15.99 (978-0-7636-2361-6). 150pp. A visit to historic sites in Boston provokes a spirited uprising against various parental rules and requirements. (Rev: BL 6/1–15/05)

7891 McGhee, Alison. *Julia Gillian (and the Art of Knowing)* (3–5). Illus. by Drazen Kozjan. 2008, Scholastic $15.99 (978-0-545-03348-0). 281pp. Over the summer, 9-year-old Julia explores her Minneapolis neighborhood with her dog, reflects on changes in her life, and resists finishing a book that may have an unhappy ending. (Rev: BL 8/08; HB 7/08; LMC 11/08; SLJ 7/08)

7892 MacLean, Jill. *The Nine Lives of Travis Keating* (5–8). 2008, Fitzhenry & Whiteside paper $11.95 (978-1-55455-104-0). 215pp. Eleven-year-old Travis misses his mother and his old life but soon finds new purpose when he finds a tribe of feral cats who need care and protection. (Rev: BLO 11/19/08; SLJ 3/09)

7893 Margolis, Leslie. *Boys Are Dogs* (4–7). 2008, Bloomsbury $15.99 (978-1-59990-221-0). 208pp. Sixth-grader Annabelle is struggling to cope at her new school and discovers that the training manual that came with her new, rambunctious puppy offers useful advice. (Rev: BCCB 11/08; SLJ 11/08) ∩

7894 Martinez, Arturo O. *Pedrito's World* (5–7). 2007, Texas Tech Univ. $16.95 (978-0-89672-600-0). 130pp. In rural south Texas in 1941, 6-year-old Pedrito describes the important things in his life — his first day of school, the death of a friend, a Christmas celebration, his first words of English. (Rev: BL 5/1/07)

7895 Mason, Jane. *Bella Baxter Inn Trouble* (2–4). Illus. by John Shelley. 2005, Simon & Schuster paper $3.99 (978-0-689-86280-9). 80pp. Seven-year-old Bella is proud to be able to contribute when her family buys an old house, planning to turn it into an inn. (Rev: BL 5/15/05)

7896 Mason, Jane B., and Sarah Hines Stephens. *Bella Baxter and the Itchy Disaster* (2–4). Illus. by John Shelley. 2005, Simon & Schuster paper $3.95 (978-0-689-86281-6). 80pp. Bella Baxter's special preparations for the arrival of a visiting botanist at the Sea Inn take a dangerous turn. (Rev: BL 12/15/05)

7897 Mass, Wendy. *Every Soul a Star* (5–8). 2008, Little, Brown $16.99 (978-0-316-00256-1). 322pp. Three quite different young teens meet at a wilderness camp to view a spectacular solar eclipse and find themselves much changed by the experience. (Rev: BL 12/1/08; HB 11/08; LMC 5/09; SLJ 11/08) ∩

7898 Matthews, L. S. *A Dog for Life* (5–7). 2006, Delacorte $14.95 (978-0-385-73366-3). 144pp. Tom is sick and Mouse the dog is banished on grounds of possible infection, so John and Mouse, who can communicate psychically, set out to find Mouse a new home. (Rev: BL 12/1/06*; SLJ 10/06) ∩

7899 Mazer, Norma Fox. *10 Ways to Make My Sister Disappear* (3–5). 2007, Scholastic $16.99 (978-0-439-83983-9). 143pp. Ten-year-old Sprig must cope with her 12-year-old sister Dakota, unsettled friendships, boys, and a father who is away in Afghanistan. (Rev: BCCB 10/07; BL 9/1/07; HB 11/07; SLJ 11/07)

7900 Milky, D. J., and Mark Seidenberg. *Kung Fu Klutz and Karate Cool* (2–4). Illus. by Erich Owen. 2007, TokyoPop paper $4.99 (978-1-59816-052-9). 85pp. The well-named Marvin Klutzer, a 3rd-grader, takes up karate in hopes of defending himself against the class bully; a chapter book with manga-style illustrations. (Rev: SLJ 11/07)

7901 Mills, Claudia. *How Oliver Olson Changed the World* (2–4). Illus. by Heather Maione. 2009, Farrar $15.95 (978-0-374-32487-1). 112pp. Oliver is worried that his hovering parents will nix the 3rd-grade space sleepover, but his diorama partner Crystal helps him find a way to display some independence. (Rev: BL 2/15/09; HB 3/09; SLJ 3/09)

7902 Moloney, James. *Trapped* (4–8). Illus. by Shaun Tan. 2008, Stone Arch LB $16.95 (978-1-59889-863-7). 73pp. David, a skateboarder, can't resist exploring a huge drainpipe even though he knows that two boys once died there in this illustrated book that will appeal to reluctant readers. (Rev: BL 12/15/07; SLJ 2/08)

7903 Morgan, Melissa J. *Natalie's Secret* (4–6). Series: Camp Confidential. 2005, Grosset paper $4.99 (978-0-448-43737-8). 160pp. Eleven-year-old Natalie is a city girl and finds adjusting to camp challenging, especially when her famous father is arriving and she will have to tell her new friends the truth. (Rev: SLJ 4/05)

7904 Morpurgo, Michael. *I Believe in Unicorns* (3–5). Illus. by Gary Blythe. 2006, Candlewick $12.99 (978-0-7636-3050-8). 80pp. A moving story about a boy's love of books and storytelling and his and others' efforts to save the contents of the library when war arrives. (Rev: BL 12/1/06; SLJ 12/06)

7905 Morris, Taylor. *Class Favorite* (5–8). 2007, Simon & Schuster paper $5.99 (978-1-4169-3598-8). 295pp. It's hard enough being an 8th-grader, but Sara has to endure countless public embarrassments at her school — still, this hilarious book shows how this unflappable girl keeps trying to climb the social ladder in spite of it all. (Rev: SLJ 3/08)

7906 Murphy, Pat. *The Wild Girls* (5–8). 2007, Viking $16.99 (978-0-670-06226-3). 272pp. Joan and best friend Sarah (who calls herself Fox) love to explore in the woods and to write — a pastime that wins them spots at a writing camp and an outlet for their frustrations with their family lives. (Rev: BL 10/1/07; SLJ 11/07) ∩

7907 Naylor, Phyllis Reynolds. *Anyone Can Eat Squid!* (2–4). Illus. by Marcy Ramsey. Series: Simply Sarah. 2005, Marshall Cavendish $14.95 (978-0-7614-5182-2). 76pp. Sarah, hoping to be recognized as "special," tries to help a classmate whose parents own a Chinese restaurant. (Rev: SLJ 7/05)

7908 Naylor, Phyllis Reynolds. *Faith, Hope, and Ivy June* (5–8). 2009, Delacorte $16.99 (978-0-385-73615-2). 288pp. Seventh-graders Ivy June and Catherine trade lives for two weeks — Kentucky mountain vs. modern suburb — and track their experiences in journals. (Rev: BCCB 9/09; BL 5/15/09; HB 9/09; LMC 10/09; SLJ 10/09; VOYA 8/09) ∩

7909 Naylor, Phyllis Reynolds. *Patches and Scratches* (2–4). Illus. by Marcy Ramsey. Series: Simply Sarah. 2007, Marshall Cavendish $14.99 (978-0-7614-5347-5). 77pp. Sarah helps out her friend Peter when his grandmother says Peter can't keep a pet in their apartment. (Rev: SLJ 6/07)

7910 Naylor, Phyllis Reynolds. *Roxie and the Hooligans* (3–5). Illus. by Alexandra Boiger. 2006, Simon & Schuster $15.95 (978-1-4169-0243-0). 128pp. Fantasy and reality become blurred in this multilayered story about 9-year-old Roxie Warbler, who applies her book-learned knowledge to survive and conquer when stranded on a desert island with bullies and robbers. (Rev: BL 2/15/06; SLJ 4/06)

7911 Nuzum, K. A. *The Leanin' Dog* (4–7). 2008, HarperCollins $15.99 (978-0-06-113934-5). 176pp. A starving dog appears at the door of an unhappy 11-year-old girl's wilderness home. (Rev: BCCB 11/08; BL 11/15/08; SLJ 10/08) ∩

7912 O'Connor, Barbara. *Greetings from Nowhere* (4–6). 2008, Farrar $16.00 (978-0-374-39937-5). 208pp. Set in a motel in the Smoky Mountains, this appealing novel interweaves the stories of four groups of individuals looking for change in their lives. (Rev: BL 1/1–15/08; SLJ 3/08)

7913 Paratore, Coleen Murtagh. *The Cupid Chronicles* (5–9). 2006, Simon & Schuster $15.95 (978-1-4169-0867-8). 207pp. Now that her mother is married, Willa puts her considerable energies into the campaign to save the town library, and somehow romance keeps intruding; a sequel to *The Wedding Planner's Daughter* (2005). (Rev: SLJ 4/07) ∩

7914 Park, Linda Sue. *Project Mulberry* (5–8). 2005, Clarion $16.00 (978-0-618-47786-9). Working on a silkworm project with her friend Patrick, Korean American Julia also learns about prejudices and friendship. (Rev: BL 8/05; SLJ 5/05)

7915 Parkinson, Siobhan. *Blue like Friday* (4–7). 2008, Roaring Brook $16.95 (978-1-59643-340-3). 160pp. In Ireland, tweens Olivia and Hal are unlikely friends but Olivia helps Hal to accept his mother's fiancé. (Rev: BL 3/1/08; SLJ 6/08)

7916 Parkinson, Siobhan. *Something Invisible* (4–7). 2006, Roaring Brook $16.95 (978-1-59643-123-2). 160pp. Jake, a self-absorbed 11-year-old, learns a lot about family and friendship over a summer that involves tragedy. (Rev: BL 3/1/06; SLJ 4/06; VOYA 6/06)

7917 Patron, Susan. *Lucky Breaks* (3–6). Illus. by Matt Phelan. 2009, Atheneum $16.99 (978-1-4169-3998-6). 192pp. In this sequel to *The Higher Power of Lucky* (2006), Lucky and her mother have found a home in the desert community of Hard Pan (population 43) and Lucky is busy learning how to make a best friend, figuring out if she might almost be in love, and getting herself into a very deep hole. (Rev: BCCB 5/09; BL 1/1–15/09; HB 9/09; SLJ 3/09) ∩

7918 Patterson, Nancy Ruth. *The Winner's Walk* (3–5). Illus. by Thomas F. Yezerski. 2006, Farrar $16.00 (978-0-374-38445-6). 128pp. Nine-year-old Case Callahan, fearful he'll be a loser all his life, takes in a stray dog so talented that it makes the boy

look good, but Case soon discovers that the dog's rightful owner is a disabled girl. (Rev: BL 8/06; SLJ 10/06)

7919 Pavlcin, Karen. *Perch, Mrs. Sackets, and Crow's Nest* (4–7). 2007, Alma Little $16.95 (978-1-934617-00-7). 133pp. Ten-year-old Andy Parker dreads the idea of a summer in the country but in the end finds he really enjoys it. (Rev: SLJ 12/07)

7920 Payne, C. C. *Something to Sing About* (4–6). 2008, Eerdmans paper $8.50 (978-0-8028-5344-8). 176pp. Ten-year-old Jamie Jo, who lives in Kentucky, is capital-T-terrified of bees but must confront her fear when the possibility of a puppy arises, in this novel that includes Christian themes. (Rev: BL 10/1/08; SLJ 3/09)

7921 Perkins, Lynne Rae. *All Alone in the Universe* (5–8). 1999, Greenwillow $16.99 (978-0-688-16881-0). 160pp. Debbie is crushed when her friend of many years drops her for another, but she has the courage to adjust and reach out to others. (Rev: BCCB 10/99; BL 9/1/99*; HB 9/99; HBG 3/00; SLJ 10/99)

7922 Potter, Ellen. *Slob* (4–7). 2009, Philomel $16.99 (978-0-399-24705-7). 208pp. Twelve-year-old Owen is smart and fat and carries around a tragic memory. (Rev: BCCB 9/09; BL 6/1–15/09; SLJ 7/09)

7923 Rayban, Chloe. *Hollywood Bliss: My Life So Far* (5–8). Series: Hollywood Bliss. 2007, Bloomsbury $16.95 (978-1-59990-093-3). 288pp. Hollywood's famous and super-rich mom is getting married in an over-the-top ceremony — and Hollywood is gaining a new stepbrother in this glamorous and funny sequel to *Hollywood Bliss: My Life Starring Mum* (2006). (Rev: BL 7/07; SLJ 2/08)

7924 Regan, Dian C. *The World According to Kaley* (3–5). 2005, Darby Creek $14.99 (978-1-58196-039-6). 112pp. Kaley's fourth-grade World History assignments include a lot of commentary about her personal life, plus some rather hazy understanding of world history with an emphasis on interpretation. (Rev: BL 11/1/05)

7925 Richter, Jutta. *The Summer of the Pike* (4–7). Trans. by Anna Brailovsky. Illus. by Quint Buchholz. 2006, Milkweed $16.95 (978-1-57131-671-4); paper $6.95 (978-1-57131-672-1). 91pp. Anna, Daniel, and Lucas, who live on the grounds of a German manor, spend a difficult summer as Anna wishes for a closer relationship with her mother and the boys' mother is slowly dying of cancer; translated from German. (Rev: BL 1/1–15/07; SLJ 12/06)

7926 Roberts, Diane. *Puppet Pandemonium* (3–5). 2006, Delacorte $15.95 (978-0-385-73309-0). 115pp. Still recovering from the trauma of moving from Seattle to small-town Texas, fifth-grader Baker gains recognition with his ventriloquist skills. (Rev: SLJ 12/06)

7927 Robinson, Sharon. *Safe at Home* (4–7). 2006, Scholastic $16.99 (978-0-439-67197-2). 151pp. Still shaken by the sudden death of his father, 10-year-old Elijah Breeze must cope with culture shock when his mother moves him from suburban Connecticut to New York City's Harlem and he attends a coed summer baseball camp. (Rev: SLJ 10/06)

7928 Romain, Trevor. *Under the Big Sky* (4–7). Illus. 2001, HarperCollins LB $14.89 (978-0-06-029495-3). 48pp. Encouraged by his grandfather, a young boy searches far and wide for the secret of life. (Rev: BL 8/01; HBG 10/01; SLJ 8/01)

7929 Rylant, Cynthia. *God Went to Beauty School* (4–8). 2003, HarperCollins LB $15.89 (978-0-06-009434-8). 64pp. God indulges in a lot of mortal activities, some fairly wacky, in this collection of thought-provoking poems. (Rev: BL 8/03; HB 7/03*; HBG 10/03; SLJ 6/03; VOYA 8/03)

7930 Sachar, Louis. *Small Steps* (5–8). 2006, Delacorte LB $18.99 (978-0-385-90333-2). 272pp. Two years after being released from Camp Green Lake, African American 17-year-old Armpit is home in Texas and trying to find good work, which is hard when you have a record, when X-Ray turns up with an interesting proposal; a sequel to *Holes* (1998). (Rev: BL 1/1–15/06*; SLJ 1/06; VOYA 2/06)

7931 Sachs, Marilyn. *The Bears' House* (4–7). Illus. by Louis Glanzman. 1987, Avon paper $2.99 (978-0-380-70582-5). 80pp. A poor girl escapes from reality by living in a fantasy in her classroom. A reissue of the 1971 edition.

7932 Salisbury, Graham. *Calvin Coconut: Trouble Magnet* (3–5). Illus. by Jacqueline Rogers. 2009, Random $12.99 (978-0-385-73701-2). 160pp. Calvin leaves the Hawaiian beach behind and starts 4th grade — walking right into the arms of bullies, tough teachers, new girls, and family troubles. (Rev: BCCB 4/09; BL 1/1–15/09; SLJ 5/09)

7933 San Souci, Daniel. *Space Station Mars* (1–4). Illus. by author. Series: A Clubhouse Book. 2005, Tricycle $15.95 (978-1-58246-142-7). When they find a strange-looking rock in their neighbor's yard, the San Souci brothers and their friends become convinced that it's a meteor from Mars; a sequel to *The Dangerous Snake and Reptile Club* (2004). (Rev: SLJ 10/05)

7934 Schaefer, Laura. *The Teashop Girls* (5–8). Illus. by Sujean Rim. 2008, Simon & Schuster $15.99 (978-1-4169-6793-4). 256pp. Annie and her friends try a variety of business strategies to help save Annie's grandmother's teashop in this book full of tea trivia. (Rev: BL 12/1/08)

7935 Schwartz, Ellen. *Stealing Home* (4–7). 2006, Tundra $8.95 (978-0-88776-765-4). 217pp. Joey, a biracial 9-year-old baseball fan living in the Bronx, is orphaned with his mother's death and moved to live with his Jewish maternal grandparents in Brooklyn, where he must cope with a startlingly different world. (Rev: BL 9/1/06; SLJ 10/06)

7936 Shafer, Audrey. *The Mailbox* (5–7). 2006, Delacorte $15.95 (978-0-385-73344-1). 178pp. Twelve-year-old Gabe, who has been happy with Uncle Vernon after years in foster care, is shocked when he comes home to find Uncle Vernon dead. (Rev: SLJ 11/06) ∩

7937 Shura, Mary Francis. *The Josie Gambit* (5–7). 1986, Avon paper $2.50 (978-0-380-70497-2). 160pp. Josie's friend Tory behaves in an inexplica-

ble way to his new friend Greg. (Rev: BCCB 5/86; SLJ 9/86)

7938 Smith, Anne Warren. *Tails of Spring Break* (4–6). 2005, Whitman $15.99 (978-0-8075-6358-8). 128pp. Things don't go well for Katie and her little brother when they decide to start a pet-sitting business. (Rev: BL 5/15/05; SLJ 5/05)

7939 Snyder, Zilpha Keatley. *The Egypt Game* (5–7). Illus. by Alton Raible. 1967, Dell paper $5.99 (978-0-440-42225-9). 224pp. Humor and suspense mark an outstanding story of city children whose safety, while playing at an unsupervised re-creation of an Egyptian ritual, is threatened by a violent lunatic.

7940 Stolz, Mary. *The Bully of Barkham Street* (4–8). Illus. by Leonard Shortall. 1963, Harper-Collins paper $6.99 (978-0-06-440159-3). 224pp. Eleven-year-old Martin goes through a typical phase of growing up — feeling misunderstood. Also use *A Dog on Barkham Street* (1960).

7941 Talbott, Hudson. *Safari Journal* (3–6). Illus. by author. 2003, Harcourt $18.00 (978-0-15-216393-8). 64pp. Twelve-year-old Carey is not happy when his aunt drags him off for a two-week safari in East Africa, but once he arrives he is enchanted by the new people, customs, and sights and records them all in his diary. (Rev: HBG 10/03; SLJ 4/03)

7942 Tarshis, Lauren. *Emma-Jean Lazarus Fell in Love* (5–7). 2009, Dial $16.99 (978-0-8037-3321-3). 176pp. Emma-Jean is a bright 7th-grader who applies logic even to matters of the heart. (Rev: BL 5/15/09; SLJ 7/09)

7943 Thomas, Frances. *Polly's Absolutely Worst Birthday Ever* (2–4). 2003, Delacorte $14.95 (978-0-385-73025-9). 96pp. In her diary, 9-year-old Polly confides in detail the disappointments and triumphs of her life. (Rev: BL 7/03; HBG 10/03; SLJ 11/03)

7944 Trueit, Trudi. *Julep O'Toole: What I Really Want to Do Is Direct* (5–7). 2007, Dutton $16.99 (978-0-525-47781-5). 166pp. Julep auditions for the school play to earn extra English credit but ends up as assistant director in this enjoyable third installment in the series. (Rev: SLJ 6/07)

7945 Tulloch, Richard. *Freaky Stuff* (5–8). Illus. by Shane Nagle. 2007, Walker $16.95 (978-0-8027-9623-3). 193pp. Funny illustrations are included in this sequel to *Weird Stuff* (2006), in which Brian is unhappy with a TV series based on his favorite books and the effect the show has on his little brother. (Rev: SLJ 6/07)

7946 Urban, Linda. *A Crooked Kind of Perfect* (3–5). 2007, Harcourt $16.00 (978-0-15-206007-7). 224pp. Zoe, 10, dreams of becoming a classical pianist and performing at Carnegie Hall, but she settles for the Perfectone D-60 electric organ her father gives her and sets out to succeed on this instrument. (Rev: BCCB 2/08; BL 11/15/07; HB 1/08; SLJ 9/07)

7947 Vail, Rachel. *If You Only Knew* (4–7). Series: Friendship Ring. 1998, Scholastic paper $14.95 (978-0-590-03370-1). 240pp. In this book shaped like a CD, Zoe Grandon, a 7th grader, gives up a boy she likes to pursue a friendship. (Rev: BCCB 10/98; BL 10/15/98; HBG 3/99; SLJ 10/98; VOYA 6/99)

7948 Vail, Rachel. *Not That I Care* (4–7). Series: Friendship Ring. 1998, Scholastic paper $14.95 (978-0-590-03476-0). 240pp. For a classroom presentation on 10 items that reveal who you are, Morgan Miller remembers crucial incidents in her life but, in her final report, glosses over the truth. (Rev: BCCB 12/98; BL 11/15/98; HBG 3/99; SLJ 12/98; VOYA 6/99)

7949 Vail, Rachel. *Please, Please, Please* (4–7). Series: Friendship Ring. 1998, Scholastic paper $14.95 (978-0-590-00327-8). 288pp. CJ Hurley has to overcome a controlling mother in order to hang out with her friends in this book shaped like a CD. (Rev: BCCB 10/98; BL 10/15/98; HBG 3/99; SLJ 12/98; VOYA 6/99)

7950 Van Draanen, Wendelin. *Flipped* (5–8). 2001, Knopf $14.95 (978-0-375-81174-6). 212pp. In 2nd grade Julianna was infatuated with Bryce, but now, six years later, the situation is reversed in this story told from each viewpoint in alternating chapters. (Rev: BCCB 1/02; BL 12/15/01; HBG 3/02; SLJ 11/01*; VOYA 12/01)

7951 Vaupel, Robin. *My Contract with Henry* (5–8). 2003, Holiday $16.95 (978-0-8234-1701-8). 192pp. An 8th-grade Thoreau project brings a group of outsider students together as they learn about the environment, the simple life, and each other. (Rev: BL 7/03; HBG 10/03; SLJ 7/03; VOYA 10/03)

7952 Viau, Nancy. *Samantha Hansen Has Rocks in Her Head* (3–6). Illus. by LeUyen Pham. 2008, Abrams $15.95 (978-0-8109-7299-5). 178pp. Samantha, a 10-year-old with a passion for science and rocks in particular, struggles to master her temper so that her mother will take her on a trip to the Grand Canyon. (Rev: LMC 3/09; SLJ 3/09)

7953 Wallace, Karen. *Something Slimy on Primrose Drive* (2–4). Illus. by Helen Flook. 2006, Stone Arch LB $22.60 (978-1-59889-113-3). 65pp. Pearl Wolfbane hopes life will become more normal when her Munsters-like family moves to Primrose Drive, but her new, conservative neighbors surprise her when they all join forces to track down a thief. (Rev: BL 11/15/06)

7954 Warner, Sally. *It's Only Temporary* (5–7). Illus. by author. 2008, Viking $15.99 (978-0-670-06111-2). 160pp. With sketches and lists, 12-year-old Skye reviews her problems in her journal when she is sent to live with her grandmother after her brother has a bad accident. (Rev: BL 6/1–15/08; SLJ 8/08)

7955 Watson, Stephanie. *Elvis and Olive* (3–5). 2008, Scholastic $15.99 (978-0-545-03183-7). 205pp. Dependable Natalie, 10, and an unruly new girl called Annie become friends despite their differences, rename themselves Olive and Elvis, and spend the summer spying on their neighbors with predictably unhappy results. (Rev: BL 4/1/08; SLJ 4/08)

7956 Waysman, Dvora. *Back of Beyond: A Bar Mitzvah Journey* (5–7). Illus. 1996, Pitspopany paper $4.95 (978-0-943706-54-2). 140pp. On a trip to Australia, a 12-year-old Jewish boy becomes involved in the Aborigine culture and witnesses a ritual of manhood similar to a bar mitzvah. (Rev: SLJ 5/96)

7957 Weatherford, Carole Boston. *Princeville: The 500-Year Flood* (3–5). Illus. by Douglas Alvord. 2001, Coastal Carolina LB $14.95 (978-1-928556-32-9). 32pp. An African American family in North Carolina is forced to leave home as the waters caused by Hurricane Floyd rise. (Rev: BL 2/15/02)

7958 Wedekind, Annie. *A Horse of Her Own* (5–7). 2008, Feiwel & Friends $16.95 (978-0-312-36927-9). 288pp. At horse camp, Jane is surrounded by girls who come from wealthy families and who have horses of their own, a fact that bothers her until she wins an important competition. (Rev: BL 5/15/08; SLJ 8/08)

7959 Weston, Carol. *Melanie in Manhattan* (3–6). 2005, Knopf LB $17.99 (978-0-375-93028-7). 266pp. Romance — with Miguel, who is coming from Spain to visit — and friendship with Cecily preoccupy the thoughts of fifth grader Melanie. (Rev: SLJ 1/05)

7960 Whitehouse, Howard. *The Faceless Fiend: Being the Tale of a Criminal Mastermind, His Masked Minions and a Princess with a Butter Knife, Involving Explosives and a Certain Amount of Pushing and Shoving* (4–7). Illus. by Bill Slavin. 2007, Kids Can $16.95 (978-1-55453-130-1); paper $7.95 (978-1-55453-180-6). 272pp. In this sequel to *The Strictest School in the World* (2006), Emmaline and her friend Princess Purnah escape from St. Grimelda's School for Young Ladies and — with a motley crew of supporters and many comical mishaps along the way — manage to foil a kidnapping. (Rev: LMC 1/08; SLJ 11/07)

7961 Whitehouse, Howard. *The Strictest School in the World: Being the Tale of a Clever Girl, a Rubber Boy and a Collection of Flying Machines, Mostly Broken* (5–8). Illus. by Bill Slavin. 2006, Kids Can $16.95 (978-1-55337-882-2); paper $6.95 (978-1-55337-883-9). 252pp. Raised in India where her father is a British colonial official, Emmaline Cayley is upset when her parents send her to a strict school in England, so she hatches a plan to escape; an appealing blend of humor, fantasy, and Gothic atmosphere. (Rev: SLJ 11/06)

7962 Wiles, Deborah. *The Aurora County All-Stars* (4–6). 2007, Harcourt $16.00 (978-0-15-206068-8). 272pp. Among other worries, 12-year-old House Jackson, captain of the Aurora County All-Stars, faces a conflict between his big game and a July 4th pageant in this humorous novel set in the same small Mississippi town as *Love, Ruby Lavender* (2001) and *Each Little Bird That Sings* (2005). (Rev: BCCB 12/07; BL 9/1/07; HB 9/07; SLJ 10/07) ∩

7963 Wilson, Jacqueline. *Candyfloss* (4–7). Illus. by Nick Sharratt. 2007, Roaring Brook $14.95 (978-1-59643-241-3). 352pp. Flossie, busy helping her divorced dad at his restaurant while her mother and stepfather are in Australia, must also deal with old and new friends at school in this story set in England. (Rev: BL 10/1/07; HB 9/07; LMC 11/07; SLJ 9/07)

7964 Winerip, Michael. *Adam Canfield, Watch Your Back!* (5–8). Series: Adam Canfield. 2007, Candlewick $15.99 (978-0-7636-2341-8). 256pp. Adam of *Adam Canfield of the Slash* has even more on his plate in this sequel: writing for the school newspaper, exposing an unfair science fair, and even facing down high school muggers. (Rev: BL 4/1/08; SLJ 12/07)

7965 Wittlinger, Ellen. *Gracie's Girl* (4–7). 2000, Simon & Schuster $16.95 (978-0-689-82249-0). 192pp. Bess and her best friend Ethan, both middle schoolers, get involved with a homeless old lady. (Rev: BCCB 2/01; BL 9/15/00; HBG 3/01; SLJ 11/00; VOYA 10/01)

7966 Woodson, Jacqueline. *Feathers* (4–6). 2007, Putnam $15.99 (978-0-399-23989-2). 118pp. When a white boy joins Frannie's 1971 sixth-grade class, and is sometimes called the "Jesus Boy," Frannie examines her own faith and the problems in her home. Newbery Medal, 2008. (Rev: BL 11/15/06; SLJ 4/07*)

7967 Wynne-Jones, Tim. *Rex Zero, King of Nothing* (4–6). 2008, Farrar $16.95 (978-0-374-36259-1). 224pp. In early 1960s Ottawa, 6th-grader Rex struggles with a mean teacher, a father with postwar terrors, and several puzzling mysteries. (Rev: BL 3/15/08; HB 3/08; SLJ 5/08)

Adventure and Mystery

7968 Abbott, Kate. *Mystery at Echo Cliffs* (4–6). Illus. by Faith DeLong. 1994, Red Crane paper $11.95 (978-1-878610-37-9). 183pp. After the death of their parents, two Navajo youngsters move back to the reservation, where they help track down a gang of pottery thieves. (Rev: SLJ 12/94)

7969 Abela, Deborah. *Mission: The Nightmare Vortex* (4–6). Illus. by George O'Connor. Series: Spy Force. 2005, Simon & Schuster $9.95 (978-0-689-87359-1). 246pp. Eleven-year-old Max Remy and her best friend Linden, Spy Force agents, spring into action to foil the evil plans of Mr. Blue to activate a dormant volcano and destroy all the spies at a secret awards ceremony. (Rev: HBG 4/06; SLJ 4/06)

7970 Abrahams, Peter. *Into the Dark* (5–12). Series: Echo Falls. 2008, HarperCollins $15.99 (978-0-06-073708-5). 304pp. Ingrid's grandfather, a World War II veteran, is a suspect in a murder committed using a World War II-era rifle. Can Ingrid solve the mystery and clear her grandfather's name? (Rev: BL 5/1/08; SLJ 3/08)

7971 Adams, W. Royce. *Me and Jay* (5–8). 2001, Rairarubia paper $10.99 (978-1-58832-021-6). 125pp. Two 13-year-olds meet with trouble at every turn when they venture into forbidden territory in search of a hidden pond. (Rev: BL 1/1–15/02)

7972 Adler, David A. *Andy Russell, NOT Wanted by the Police* (3–5). Illus. by Leanne Franson. 2001, Harcourt $14.00 (978-0-15-216474-4). 128pp. Andy and Tamika solve the mystery of an intruder at a neighbor's house in this beginning chapter book. (Rev: BL 1/1–15/02; HBG 3/02; SLJ 1/02)

7973 Adler, David A. *Cam Jansen: The Summer Camp Mysteries* (3–5). Illus. by Joy Allen. 2007, Viking $13.99 (978-0-670-06218-8); Penguin paper $4.99 (978-0-14-240742-4). 128pp. Cam sleuthes her way through three separate summer camp cases, including the mystery of the missing snack money. (Rev: BL 5/15/07)

7974 Adler, David A. *Cam Jansen and the Barking Treasure Mystery* (2–4). Illus. 1999, Viking $13.99 (978-0-670-88516-9). 64pp. Cam and her best friend solve the mystery of a missing dog. (Rev: BL 10/15/99; HBG 3/00; SLJ 12/99)

7975 Adler, David A. *Cam Jansen and the Birthday Mystery* (2–4). Illus. 2000, Viking $13.99 (978-0-670-88877-1). 64pp. In this beginning chapter book, Cam, with her photographic memory, solves the mystery of who stole her grandparents' luggage at the airport. (Rev: BL 11/1/00; HBG 3/01; SLJ 1/01)

7976 Adler, David A. *Cam Jansen and the Catnapping Mystery* (2–3). Illus. 1998, Viking $13.99 (978-0-670-88044-7). 47pp. Cam Jansen, super girl detective, helps police track down the thief who posed as a bellhop and stole an elderly woman's luggage and pet cat from the Royal Hotel. (Rev: BL 11/15/98; HBG 3/99; SLJ 1/99)

7977 Adler, David A. *Cam Jansen and the First Day of School Mystery* (2–4). Illus. by Susanna Natti. 2002, Viking $13.99 (978-0-670-03575-5). 64pp. Cam's great memory comes into play when her teacher is arrested and taken away on the first day of school. (Rev: BL 12/1/02; HBG 3/03; SLJ 1/03)

7978 Adler, David A. *Cam Jansen and the Ghostly Mystery* (2–4). Illus. 1996, Viking $13.99 (978-0-670-86872-8). 64pp. Cam Jansen and her friend Eric are involved in the robbery of a ticket booth at a rock concert. (Rev: BL 1/1–15/97; HBG 3/98; SLJ 12/96)

7979 Adler, David A. *Cam Jansen and the Mystery of the Chocolate Fudge Sale* (2–4). Illus. by Susanna Natti. 1993, Viking $13.99 (978-0-670-84968-0). 64pp. Cam springs into action when she spots a suspicious woman around a vacant house. (Rev: BL 10/15/93; SLJ 9/93)

7980 Adler, David A. *Cam Jansen and the Scary Snake Mystery* (2–4). Illus. 1997, Viking $13.99 (978-0-670-87517-7). 64pp. Cam solves a mystery in which her mother's video camera is stolen after it had been used to photograph someone's pet snake. (Rev: BL 11/15/97; SLJ 12/97)

7981 Adler, David A. *Cam Jansen and the School Play Mystery* (2–4). Illus. 2001, Viking $14.99 (978-0-670-89280-8). 64pp. Readers already familiar with Cam's exploits will enjoy this story in which Cam uses her photographic memory to solve the mystery of the missing admission money while her friends act onstage in a play about Honest Abe. (Rev: BL 8/01; HBG 3/02; SLJ 1/02)

7982 Adler, David A. *Cam Jansen and the Secret Service Mystery* (2–4). Illus. by Susanna Natti. 2006, Viking $13.99 (978-0-670-06092-4). 64pp. When the pearls belonging to a school donor are stolen, Cam Jansen, girl detective, teams up with the Secret Service to try to track them down. (Rev: BL 10/15/06; HBG 4/07)

7983 Adler, David A. *Cam Jansen and the Tennis Trophy Mystery* (2–4). Illus. by Susanna Natti. Series: Cam Jansen. 2003, Viking $13.99 (978-0-670-03643-1). 56pp. In this 23rd adventure for young detective Cam Jansen, a teacher falls under suspicion in the theft of a tennis trophy. (Rev: HBG 4/04; SLJ 3/04)

7984 Adler, David A. *Cam Jansen and the Triceratops Pops Mystery* (2–4). Illus. 1995, Viking $13.99 (978-0-670-86027-2). 64pp. Cam and her friend Eric solve the mystery of the missing CDs. (Rev: BL 11/1/95; SLJ 12/95)

7985 Adler, David A. *Cam Jansen and the Valentine Baby Mystery* (2–4). Illus. by Susanna Natti. Series: Cam Jansen. 2005, Viking $13.99 (978-0-670-06009-2). 80pp. Girl detective Cam Jansen and her friend Eric investigate the disappearance of Eric's mother's purse from a hospital waiting room; the 25th installment in this popular series. (Rev: BL 1/1–15/06; HBG 4/06)

7986 Aiken, Joan. *Midwinter Nightingale* (5–8). Series: Wolves Chronicles. 2003, Delacorte $15.95 (978-0-385-73081-5). 224pp. Dido Twite and Simon, Duke of Battersea, continue their adventures in this eighth installment in the series, protecting a dying king, searching for a missing coronet, and defeating an evil baron. (Rev: BL 6/1–15/03; HBG 10/03; SLJ 6/03)

7987 Aiken, Joan. *The Wolves of Willoughby Chase* (4–6). Illus. by Pat Marriott. 1987, Dell paper $4.99 (978-0-440-49603-8). 168pp. A Victorian melodrama about two little girls who outwit their wicked governess-guardian. A reissue of the 1963 edition. Two sequels are: *Black Hearts in Battersea* (1981) and *Nightbirds on Nantucket* (1969).

7988 Alexander, Lloyd. *The Golden Dreams of Carlo Chuchio* (5–8). 2007, Holt $17.95 (978-0-8050-8333-0). 306pp. The final book by the late Alexander takes Carlo along the Road of Golden Dreams in search of treasure. (Rev: BCCB 10/07; BL 7/07; HB 9/07; LMC 1/08; SLJ 8/07)

7989 Alexander, Lloyd. *The Xanadu Adventure* (5–8). 2005, Button $16.99 (978-0-525-47371-8). 160pp. Vesper Holly, accompanied by friends and guardians, sets off for Asia Minor to search for an artifact in the ancient city of Troy but soon finds herself in the clutches of her nemesis, Dr. Desmond Helvitius. (Rev: BL 2/1/05*; SLJ 2/05)

7990 Allison, Jennifer. *Gilda Joyce: Psychic Investigator* (5–7). 2005, Dutton $13.99 (978-0-525-47375-6). 336pp. Thirteen-year-old Gilda Joyce and a new friend, Juliet, look into the suicide of Juliet's aunt in this richly layered mystery. (Rev: BL 5/1/05*; SLJ 7/05*)

7991 Allison, Jennifer. *Gilda Joyce: The Ghost Sonata* (5–8). 2007, Dutton $15.99 (978-0-525-47808-9). 344pp. Gilda's psychic abilities come in handy as she accompanies her friend Wendy to a piano competition in England and discovers that Wendy is being haunted. (Rev: SLJ 8/07) ∩

7992 Allison, Jennifer. *Gilda Joyce: The Ladies of the Lake* (5–8). 2006, Dutton $16.99 (978-0-525-47693-1). 256pp. Thirteen-year-old Gilda Joyce — introduced in *Gilda Joyce: Psychic Investigator* (2005) — uses all her psychic abilities to unravel the mystery surrounding a drowning death at her school. (Rev: BL 10/15/06; HBG 4/07; SLJ 9/06)

7993 Anastasio, Dina. *The Case of the Glacier Park Swallow* (4–7). Illus. 1994, Roberts Rinehart paper $6.95 (978-1-879373-85-3). 80pp. Juliet, who wants to be a veterinarian, stumbles upon a drug-smuggling ring in this tightly knit mystery. (Rev: BL 12/1/94; SLJ 10/94)

7994 Anastasio, Dina. *The Case of the Grand Canyon Eagle* (5–8). Series: Juliet Stone Environmental Mystery. 1994, Roberts Rinehart paper $6.95 (978-1-879373-84-6). 73pp. In this ecological mystery, 17-year-old Juliet Stone investigates the disappearance of eagle eggs. (Rev: SLJ 10/94)

7995 Anderson, Mary. *Suzy's Secret Snoop Society* (4–6). 1990, Avon paper $2.95 (978-0-380-75917-0). 112pp. Two new friends accidentally uncover a criminal plot. (Rev: BL 12/15/90)

7996 Andrews, Jean F. *The Secret in the Dorm Attic* (3–5). 1990, Gallaudet Univ. paper $4.95 (978-0-930323-66-0). 100pp. At a school for the deaf, some boys uncover stolen jewels and become the victims of a kidnapping. (Rev: BL 10/1/90)

7997 Avi. *Captain Grey* (5–8). 1993, Morrow paper $4.95 (978-0-688-12234-8). 160pp. In 1783, young Kevin is captured by pirates. A reissue.

7998 Avi. *Who Stole the Wizard of Oz?* (4–6). Illus. by Derek James. 1990, McKay paper $4.99 (978-0-394-84992-8). 128pp. Several books disappear from the Chickertown Library book sale.

7999 Avi. *Windcatcher* (4–7). 1991, Avon paper $4.99 (978-0-380-71805-4). 128pp. Eleven-year-old Tony dreads a summer by the sea, but ends up finding a sailing adventure. (Rev: BCCB 5/91; BL 3/1/91; HB 5/91; SLJ 4/91)

8000 Baccalario, Pierdomenico. *The Door to Time* (4–6). Illus. by Iacopo Bruno. Series: Ulysses Moore. 2006, Scholastic $12.99 (978-0-439-77438-3). 240pp. After moving to a home on the English coast, Jason and Julia, 11-year-old twins, along with a new friend, try to unravel the mysteries surrounding their new house. (Rev: BL 12/15/05; SLJ 1/06)

8001 Balliett, Blue. *Chasing Vermeer* (5–8). Illus. by Brett Helquist. 2004, Scholastic $16.95 (978-0-439-37294-7). 272pp. Petra and Calder, brainy 12-year-old classmates at the University of Chicago Lab School, join forces to find out what happened to a missing Vermeer painting. (Rev: BL 4/1/04*; HB 7/04; SLJ 7/04)

8002 Barrett, Tracy. *The Beast of Blackslope* (4–6). Series: Sherlock Files. 2009, Holt $15.95 (978-0-8050-8341-5). 160pp. Xander and Xena Holmes are in England and investigate a mysterious beast in the woods, with some help from their ancestor Sherlock's files. (Rev: BLO 4/23/09; SLJ 6/09)

8003 Barrett, Tracy. *The 100-Year-Old Secret* (4–6). Series: Sherlock Files. 2008, Holt $15.95 (978-0-8050-8340-8). 160pp. Arriving in London from

Florida, 12-year-old Xena Holmes and her younger brother Xander discover they are descendants of Sherlock Holmes and receive his notebook of unsolved cases. (Rev: BL 5/1/08; LMC 3/09; SLJ 6/08)

8004 Base, Graeme. *The Eleventh Hour: A Curious Mystery* (4–6). Illus. 1989, Abrams $18.95 (978-0-8109-0851-2). 32pp. An elaborate picture-book mystery written in verse. (Rev: BL 11/1/89; SLJ 2/90)

8005 Base, Graeme. *Enigma: A Magical Mystery* (2–4). Illus. by author. 2008, Abrams $19.95 (978-0-8109-7245-2). 48pp. A retirement home for magicians is the setting for this mystery story that asks readers to participate as Bertie Badger sets off to find stolen magic props; a fold-out decoder appears in the back of the book. (Rev: BL 10/1/08; SLJ 11/08)

8006 Beil, Michael D. *The Red Blazer Girls: The Ring of Rocamadour* (5–8). 2009, Knopf $15.99 (978-0-375-84814-8). 304pp. In this snappy title, a quirky bunch of schoolgirls from St. Veronica's in Manhattan attempt to solve a mystery while also dealing with almost-boyfriends and other daily challenges. (Rev: BL 1/1–15/09; SLJ 6/09)

8007 Berlin, Eric. *The Potato Chip Puzzles* (4–6). 2009, Putnam $16.99 (978-0-399-25198-6). 256pp. Winston and his friends enter a puzzle contest that is enlivened by a mysterious cheater in this readable book full of puzzles. (Rev: BL 5/1/09; SLJ 8/09)

8008 Berlin, Eric. *The Puzzling World of Winston Breen* (4–6). 2007, Putnam $16.99 (978-0-399-24693-7). 224pp. Puzzle fan Winston Breen, 12, and his younger sister Kate find themselves embroiled in a group treasure hunt in this mystery story full of brainteasers to solve along the way. (Rev: BCCB 11/07; BL 11/15/07; LMC 11/07; SLJ 11/07)

8009 Biedrzycki, David. *Ace Lacewing: Bug Detective* (2–4). Illus. 2005, Charlesbridge $15.95 (978-1-57091-569-7). 40pp. Full of funny wordplay and cartoon-style art, this is the story of bug detective Ace Lacewing's efforts to find the missing Queenie Bee. Also use *Bad Bugs Are My Business* (2009). (Rev: BL 9/1/05; SLJ 8/05)

8010 Blades, Ann. *A Boy of Tache* (3–5). Illus. 1995, Tundra paper $5.95 (978-0-88776-350-2). A novel of life in Tache, an Indian reservation in northwest Canada, which focuses on a young boy and a trapping expedition.

8011 Blatchford, Claire H. *Nick's Mission* (4–6). 1995, Lerner LB $14.95 (978-0-8225-0740-6). 144pp. A hearing-impaired boy happens on a gang of smugglers who are illegally bringing macaws into the United States from Mexico. (Rev: BL 11/15/95; SLJ 10/96)

8012 Bledsoe, Lucy Jane. *The Antarctic Scoop* (4–7). 2003, Holiday House $16.95 (978-0-8234-1792-6). 168pp. In this fast-paced adventure story, 12-year-old Victoria, a shy girl with ambitious dreams, wins a trip to Antarctica but discovers during her travels that the real goal of the contest sponsor is to develop and exploit the icy continent. (Rev: BL 1/1–15/04; SLJ 1/04)

8013 Bledsoe, Lucy Jane. *Tracks in the Snow* (3–6). 1997, Holiday House paper $16.95 (978-0-8234-1309-6). 96pp. A survival story about two girls caught in the woods during a violent snowstorm. (Rev: BL 8/97; HBG 3/98; SLJ 7/97)

8014 Bloor, Edward. *Taken* (5–8). 2007, Knopf $16.99 (978-0-375-83636-7). 256pp. In Florida in the year 2035, where kidnapping has become a common crime with recognized procedures, 13-year-old Charity must find a way to escape and survive when her wealthy family's payoff to the kidnappers goes wrong. (Rev: BL 9/1/07; SLJ 12/07)

8015 Bodett, Tom. *Williwaw* (5–8). 1999, Random paper $5.50 (978-0-375-80687-2). The story of two youngsters — 13-year-old September Crane and her 12-year-old brother Ivan — and their life in the wilds of Alaska, where they are often left alone by their fisherman father. (Rev: BCCB 6/99; BL 4/1/99; HBG 10/99; SLJ 5/99)

8016 Boie, Kirsten. *The Princess Plot* (4–8). 2009, Scholastic $17.99 (978-0-545-03220-9). 384pp. Fourteen-year-old Jenna soon realizes her "acting test" assignment — impersonating the princess of a government in dangerous turmoil — involves more than she was told. (Rev: BCCB 9/09; BLO 5/28/09; SLJ 10/09; VOYA 10/09) ∩

8017 Bosch, Pseudonymous. *The Name of This Book Is Secret* (4–7). Illus. 2007, Little, Brown $16.99 (978-0-316-11366-3). 247pp. What's inside this book is secret, too, and only after much cautioning does the narrator begin to tell the story of a group trying to discover the key to immortality. (Rev: BL 7/07; SLJ 1/08) ∩

8018 Bracegirdle, P. J. *Fiendish Deeds* (5–7). Series: The Joy of Spooking. 2008, Simon & Schuster $15.99 (978-1-4169-3416-5). 215pp. When 11-year-old Joy learns that there are plans to build a water park on Spooking's bog — where she believes a monster resides — the young fan of horror stories sets out to stop this; the spooky setting and dark humor add to the appeal. (Rev: LMC 3/09; SLJ 3/09)

8019 Brittain, Bill. *Dr. Dredd's Wagon of Wonders* (4–6). Illus. by Andrew Glass. 1987, HarperCollins LB $15.89 (978-0-06-020714-4). 160pp. Set in a remote New England town. Dr. Dredd comes to Coven Tree to cure the drought and causes havoc in this spooky tale. (Rev: SLJ 8/87)

8020 Brittain, Bill. *Who Knew There'd Be Ghosts?* (4–6). Illus. by Michele Chessare. 1985, HarperCollins paper $5.99 (978-0-06-440224-8). 128pp. Tommy, the narrator, relates how he discovers ghosts Essie and Horace and how they help him solve a mystery. (Rev: BL 6/1/85; HB 7/85; SLJ 5/85)

8021 Broach, Elise. *Masterpiece* (3–6). Illus. by Kelly Murphy. 2008, Holt $16.95 (978-0-8050-8270-8). 304pp. A lonely artistic boy and an overprotected artistic beetle become unlikely friends and solve a mystery. (Rev: BL 9/15/08; HB 11/08; LMC 5/09)

8022 Bruchac, Joseph. *Bearwalker* (5–8). Illus. by Sally Wern Comport. 2007, HarperCollins $15.99 (978-0-06-112309-2). 224pp. Thirteen-year-old Baron, Native American and not as tall as he would like, comes into his own on a class trip to the Adirondacks as he draws on strengths that were not apparent to his classmates. (Rev: BL 9/15/07; SLJ 8/07)

8023 Bruchac, Joseph. *Night Wings* (5–8). Illus. by Sally Wern Comport. 2009, HarperCollins $15.99 (978-0-06-112318-4). 208pp. Indian lore gives this thriller an additional layer of meaning. (Rev: BL 6/1–15/09; SLJ 7/09)

8024 Bruchac, Joseph. *The Return of Skeleton Man* (5–8). Illus. by Sally Wern Comport. 2006, Harper-Collins $15.99 (978-0-06-058090-2). 144pp. Molly, the Mohawk teen who survived a terrifying kidnapping in *Skeleton Man* (2001), discovers her nemesis is back. (Rev: BL 9/15/06; SLJ 8/06)

8025 Buckey, Sarah Masters. *The Stolen Sapphire: A Samantha Mystery* (2–4). Series: American Girl Mysteries. 2006, American Girl paper $6.95 (978-1-59369-099-1). 181pp. Traveling to Europe on an ocean liner in the early 1900s, Samantha and her adopted sister Nellie try to prove the innocence of their French tutor, who's been accused of stealing a valuable gem. (Rev: SLJ 4/06)

8026 Buckley, Michael. *The Unusual Suspects* (4–6). Illus. by Peter Ferguson. Series: Sisters Grimm. 2005, Abrams $14.95 (978-0-8109-5926-2). 290pp. Sabrina and Daphne Grimm, descendants of Wilhelm and living in a community full of fairy-tale figures, investigate the mysterious death of Sabrina's teacher; a multilayered, fast-paced second installment in the series. Also use *Magic and Other Misdemeanors* (2007). (Rev: SLJ 1/06; VOYA 8/06)

8027 Bunting, Eve. *Coffin on a Case* (4–6). 1992, HarperCollins $15.95 (978-0-06-020273-6). 108pp. The daughter of a woman who has disappeared enlists the aid of a private detective's son to find her. (Rev: BCCB 11/92; BL 10/1/92; SLJ 10/92)

8028 Bunting, Eve. *Someone Is Hiding on Alcatraz Island* (5–8). 1986, Berkley paper $5.99 (978-0-425-10294-7). 144pp. A boy and a young woman ranger are trapped by a gang of thugs on Alcatraz. (Rev: BL 7/88)

8029 Butler, Dori. *Do You Know the Monkey Man?* (5–7). 2005, Peachtree $14.95 (978-1-56145-340-5). 224pp. After a psychic says that her twin sister — believed drowned 10 years before — is not dead at all, 13-year-old Samantha sets off with a friend to investigate. (Rev: BL 5/1/05; SLJ 6/05)

8030 Byars, Betsy. *The Black Tower* (4–6). 2006, Viking $12.99 (978-0-670-06174-7). 144pp. Herculeah Jones tries to unravel the suspenseful mystery surrounding the dark past of a neighborhood mansion. (Rev: BL 10/15/06; SLJ 12/06)

8031 Byars, Betsy. *King of Murder* (4–6). Series: A Herculeah Jones Mystery. 2006, Sleuth $10.99 (978-0-670-06065-8). 115pp. Herculeah finds herself in grave danger as she tries to unmask suspected murderer Mathias King. (Rev: SLJ 6/06)

8032 Cadwallader, Sharon. *Cookie McCorkle and the Case of the Emerald Earrings* (3–5). Illus. by Patrick Chapin. 1991, Avon paper $2.95 (978-0-380-76098-5). 128pp. Ten-year-old Cookie and her dog Moriarity solve a mystery in the Holmesian manner. Followed by: *Cookie McCorkle and the Case of the Polka-Dot Safecracker* (1991). (Rev: BL 9/15/91)

8033 Capeci, Anne. *Danger: Dynamite!* (3–6). Illus. by Paul Casale. Series: Cascade Mountain Railroad Mysteries. 2003, Peachtree $12.95 (978-1-56145-288-0). 127pp. In this engaging mystery tale set in the 1920s, 10-year-old Billy and his best friend Finn investigate the mysterious disappearance of a crate of dynamite. (Rev: HBG 4/04; SLJ 1/04)

8034 Capeci, Anne. *Ghost Train* (3–5). Illus. by author. Series: Cascade Mountain Railroad Mysteries. 2004, Peachtree $12.95 (978-1-56145-324-5). 144pp. Billy, Finn, and Dannie are instrumental in preventing a train robbery in this fast-paced mystery full of historical detail. (Rev: SLJ 1/05)

8035 Carman, Patrick. *Skeleton Creek* (5–8). 2009, Scholastic $14.99 (978-0-545-07566-4). 192pp. Sidelined by a broken leg, teenage Ryan nevertheless keeps in touch with his friend Sarah as she continues to investigate a mystery and documents her adventures on film; readers can view the videos on an accompanying Web site. (Rev: BL 12/1/08; LMC 5/09; SLJ 3/09)

8036 Casanova, Mary. *Jess* (3–5). Series: American Girl Today. 2005, Pleasant paper $6.95 (978-1-59369-016-8). 126pp. While accompanying her parents on an archaeological expedition to Belize, 10-year-old Jess meets a new friend who invites her on an eco-adventure in the nearby rain forest; factual information is interwoven and an afterword adds relevance. (Rev: SLJ 9/06)

8037 Casanova, Mary. *Moose Tracks* (4–6). 1995, Hyperion LB $15.49 (978-0-7868-2035-1). 128pp. During a moose hunt, Seth and friend Matt stumble onto a pair of dangerous poachers. (Rev: BCCB 7–8/95; BL 7/95; SLJ 6/95)

8038 Catanese, P. W. *The Thief and the Beanstalk* (4–6). 2005, Simon & Schuster paper $4.99 (978-0-689-87173-3). 272pp. An exciting adventure in which Nick, with greed in his heart, climbs a giant beanstalk and finds at the top the giant's wife and her evil sons — and a moral dilemma. (Rev: SLJ 7/05)

8039 Cavanagh, Helen. *Panther Glade* (5–8). 1993, Simon & Schuster paper $16.00 (978-0-671-75617-8). Bill spends a summer in Florida with his great-aunt Cait. He's afraid of the Everglades and alligators, but he comes to appreciate Indian history and crafts. (Rev: BL 6/1–15/93; SLJ 6/93; VOYA 10/93)

8040 Cheshire, Simon. *The Curse of the Ancient Mask and Other Case Files* (3–5). Illus. by R. W. Alley. 2009, Roaring Brook $13.95 (978-1-59643-474-5). 176pp. Saxby Smart, 10, has his Crime Headquarters in a shed in his backyard and from there conducts three investigations. (Rev: BL 5/1/09; LMC 10/09; SLJ 6/09)

8041 Christian, Mary Blount. *Sebastian (Super Sleuth) and the Copycat Crime* (3–5). 1993, Macmillan LB $13.00 (978-0-02-718211-8). 64pp. Sebastian the dog detective once again comes to the rescue and this time solves the mystery of the stolen manuscript. (Rev: BL 1/1/94; SLJ 3/94)

8042 Cirrone, Dorian. *The Missing Silver Dollar* (2–4). Illus. by Liza Woodruff. Series: Lindy Blues. 2006, Marshall Cavendish $14.95 (978-0-7614-5284-3). 74pp. Lindy Blues, a fourth grader and self-appointed investigative reporter for her neighborhood, tracks down a neighbor's missing silver dollar. (Rev: SLJ 9/06)

8043 Clements, Andrew. *Room One* (3–5). Illus. by Chris Blair. 2006, Simon & Schuster $15.95 (978-0-689-86686-9). 176pp. Ted, the only 6th grader in his one-room school, discovers a mystery while delivering papers one morning in this story set in rural Nebraska. (Rev: BL 5/1/06; SLJ 7/06) ⌒

8044 Clifford, Eth. *Help! I'm a Prisoner in the Library* (3–5). Illus. by George Hughes. 1979, Houghton $16.00 (978-0-395-28478-0); Scholastic paper $5.99 (978-0-590-44351-7). 112pp. Two youngsters are locked in a library after it closes. Two sequels are: *The Dastardly Murder of Dirty Pete* (1981); *Just Tell Me When We're Dead!* (1983).

8045 Clifford, Eth. *Scared Silly* (3–5). Illus. by George Hughes. 1989, Scholastic paper $2.75 (978-0-590-42382-3). 128pp. Mary Rose and Jo-Beth encounter a mysterious Walk-Your-Way-Around-the-World Museum. (Rev: BCCB 4/88; BL 4/1/88; SLJ 6–7/88)

8046 Colfer, Eoin. *Half Moon Investigations* (4–6). 2006, Hyperion $16.95 (978-0-7868-4957-4). 304pp. Fletcher ("Half") Moon, an aspiring private investigator, finds himself in all sorts of trouble when pretty April Devereux asks him to nab a thief in their Irish town; this story is full of jargon and humor. (Rev: BL 5/1/06; SLJ 4/06) ⌒

8047 Collard, Sneed B. *Double Eagle* (5–8). 2009, Peachtree $15.95 (978-1-56145-480-8). 245pp. In 1973 13-year-old Mike and a friend find a rare coin and rush to see if there are more before an approaching hurricane arrives. (Rev: BL 5/1/09)

8048 Collier, James Lincoln. *The Dreadful Revenge of Ernest Gallen* (5–8). 2008, Bloomsbury $16.95 (978-1-59990-220-3). 192pp. Gene, the main character in this Depression-era mystery, is haunted by a ghost looking for revenge and searches for the role his family and neighbors played in a horrible crime. (Rev: BL 8/08; SLJ 9/08)

8049 Comino, Sandra. *The Little Blue House* (4–7). 2003, Douglas & McIntyre $15.95 (978-0-88899-504-9). 155pp. Young Cintia and her friend Bruno investigate why an abandoned house in their small town in Argentina turns blue for one day each year in this suspenseful novel that contains some violence. (Rev: BL 2/15/04)

8050 Conrad, Hy. *Kids' Whodunits 2: Crack the Cases!* (4–7). Illus. by Sue Blanchard. 2009, Sterling paper $6.95 (978-1-4027-5398-5). 96pp. Twelve-year-old Jonah Bixby, who has learned

much at the Fifth Precinct, solves 20 varied cases while giving readers plenty of clues. (Rev: BL 5/1/09)

8051 Copeland, Mark. *The Bundle at Blackthorpe Heath* (4–7). 2006, Houghton $15.00 (978-0-618-56302-9). 224pp. With the help of a spyglass he receives as a birthday present, 12-year-old Arthur Piper uncovers a conspiracy to undermine his grandfather's traveling insect circus. (Rev: BL 6/1–15/06; SLJ 7/06)

8052 Couloumbis, Audrey. *Maude March on the Run! or, Trouble Is Her Middle Name* (5–7). 2007, Random $15.99 (978-0-375-83246-8). 308pp. In this action-packed sequel to *The Misadventures of Maude March*, 16-year-old Maude and her 12-year-old sister, both orphans, are pursued by the law after Maude is unjustly accused of multiple crimes. (Rev: SLJ 1/07)

8053 Cray, Jordan. *Dead Man's Hand* (5–9). Series: danger.com. 1998, Simon & Schuster paper $3.99 (978-0-689-82383-1). In this light read, Nick Annunciato and his stepsister, Annie Hanley, use their brains and a computer to solve a murder and escape a biological-weapons smuggling ring. (Rev: SLJ 2/99)

8054 Cray, Jordan. *Shiver* (5–8). Series: danger.com. 1998, Simon & Schuster paper $3.99 (978-0-689-82384-8). 203pp. Six drama students are spending a weekend in the Green Mountains of Vermont, when one of the group is murdered. (Rev: SLJ 2/99)

8055 Creech, Sharon. *The Wanderer* (5–9). Illus. by David Diaz. 2000, HarperCollins LB $17.89 (978-0-06-027731-4). 288pp. In this Newbery Honor Book, 13-year-old Sophie, her two cousins, and three uncles sail across the Atlantic to England in a 45-foot yacht. (Rev: BCCB 4/00*; BL 4/1/00; HB 5/00; HBG 10/00; SLJ 4/00*)

8056 Crossman, David A. *The Mystery of the Black Moriah* (5–8). Series: A Bean and Ab Mystery. 2002, Down East $16.95 (978-0-89272-536-6). 234pp. The ever-curious Bean and Ab become caught up in a mystery adventure involving pirates, kidnappers, and a legendary ghost. (Rev: HBG 3/03; SLJ 12/02)

8057 Crossman, David A. *The Secret of the Missing Grave* (5–8). Series: A Bean and Ab Mystery. 1999, Down East $16.95 (978-0-89272-456-7). 184pp. Two girls investigate a haunted house and become involved in a mystery concerning a missing treasure and stolen paintings in this fast-paced novel set in Maine. (Rev: HBG 3/00; SLJ 1/00)

8058 Curtis, Christopher Paul. *Mr. Chickee's Funny Money* (4–6). Series: Flint Future Detectives. 2005, Random $15.95 (978-0-385-32772-5). 160pp. Nine-year-old Steven and his friends try to find out if the quadrillion dollar bill he was given by his blind neighbor is the real thing in this fast-paced and humorous mystery. A sequel is *Mr. Chickee's Messy Mission* (2007). (Rev: BL 8/05; SLJ 10/05*)

8059 Cushman, Doug. *The Mystery of the Monkey's Maze* (1–4). Illus. 1999, HarperCollins LB $15.89 (978-0-06-027720-8). 32pp. After receiving threatening notes, Dr. Irene A. Tann, who is in Borneo on the trail of a flower that will cure hiccups, asks Seymour Sleuth and his sidekick Abbott Moggs to crack the case. (Rev: BL 6/1–15/99; HBG 10/99; SLJ 5/99)

8060 Deedy, Carmen A. *The Secret of Old Zeb* (2–3). Illus. by Michael P. White. 1997, Peachtree $16.95 (978-1-56145-115-9). An adventure novel in which Uncle Walter tells his niece about a summer when he found that his next-door neighbor was building a ship in his basement. (Rev: HBG 3/98; SLJ 3/98)

8061 DeFelice, Cynthia. *Lostman's River* (5–7). 1994, Macmillan LB $15.00 (978-0-02-726466-1). 160pp. Tyler's trust is betrayed when he takes an eccentric scientist to a secret rookery in the Everglades and the man reveals himself to be an unscrupulous plume hunter. (Rev: BCCB 6/94; BL 5/15/94; HB 9/94; SLJ 7/94)

8062 DeFelice, Cynthia. *The Missing Manatee* (5–8). 2005, Farrar $16.00 (978-0-374-31257-2). 192pp. Skeet Waters sets out to solve the mystery of a murdered manatee he finds near his Florida home. (Rev: BL 3/1/05; SLJ 6/05)

8063 Delaney, Mark. *The Protester's Song* (5–9). Series: Misfits, Inc. 2001, Peachtree paper $5.95 (978-1-56145-244-6). 214pp. Four teens keep themselves busy investigating an incident that occurred during riots in Ohio in 1970 and, in a subplot, try to stop the new principal from removing books from the library. (Rev: SLJ 8/01)

8064 Delaney, Mark. *The Vanishing Chip* (5–8). Series: Misfits, Inc. 1998, Peachtree paper $5.95 (978-1-56145-176-0). 188pp. Four teens who don't fit in at school investigate the disappearance of the world's most powerful computer chip. (Rev: BL 12/15/98; SLJ 2/99)

8065 Demers, Barbara. *Willa's New World* (5–8). 2000, Coteau paper $6.95 (978-1-55050-150-6). 192pp. An adventure story set in Canada around 1800 in which 15-year-old Willa is sent to a trading post on Hudson's Bay. (Rev: BL 9/15/00; SLJ 9/00)

8066 Doder, Joshua. *A Dog Called Grk* (5–8). 2007, Delacorte $14.99 (978-0-385-73359-5). 272pp. In this fast-paced adventure, 12-year-old Londoner Tim, trying to help the Stanislavian ambassador's family — and dog — becomes enmeshed in international political intrigue. A sequel is *Grk and the Pelotti Gang* (2007). (Rev: BL 1/1–15/07; SLJ 3/07)

8067 Doder, Joshua. *Operation Tortoise* (5–8). Series: The Grk Books. 2009, Random $15.99 (978-0-385-73362-5). 240pp. Tim, 12, and his dog Grk are in the Seychelles and find themselves investigating a sinister laboratory in this fast-paced suspense story. (Rev: BL 3/1/09)

8068 Dowd, Siobhan. *The London Eye Mystery* (5–8). 2008, Random $15.99 (978-0-375-84976-3). 336pp. Ted and Kat's cousin Salim disappears after entering a ride called the London Eye, and Ted relies on his unusual intellectual abilities to try to find him. (Rev: BL 1/1–15/08; HB 5/08; LMC 3/08; SLJ 2/08)

8069 Dowswell, Paul. *Battle Fleet* (5–8). 2008, Bloomsbury $16.95 (978-1-59990-080-3). 300pp. Young Sam is again on the high seas, this time on

Lord Nelson's ship for the battle of Trafalgar. A follow-up to *Powder Monkey* and *Prison Ship*. (Rev: BL 4/15/08; SLJ 9/08)

8070 Doyle, Roddy. *Wilderness* (5–7). 2007, Scholastic $16.99 (978-0-439-02356-6). 224pp. Johnny and Tom must find their mother in frozen Lapland when her dogsled team is lost; meanwhile the boys' half sister is reunited with her own mother, who left her family long ago. (Rev: BL 11/15/07; HB 1/08; SLJ 11/07)

8071 Draanen, Wendelin Van. *Sammy Keyes and the Skeleton Man* (5–8). 1998, Knopf paper $4.99 (978-0-375-80054-2). Sammy, the youthful sleuth, is challenged when she tries to solve the mystery of a man dressed in a skeleton costume. (Rev: BL 9/1/98; HBG 3/99; SLJ 9/98)

8072 Draper, Penny. *Terror at Turtle Mountain* (4–7). 2006, Coteau paper $7.95 (978-1-55050-343-2). 160pp. In Canada's Northwest Territory in 1903, a 13-year-old girl participates in frantic efforts to rescue victims of a rock slide; an action-packed novel based on a real-life incident. (Rev: SLJ 10/06)

8073 Draper, Sharon M. *Lost in the Tunnel of Time* (3–6). Illus. by Michael Bryant. Series: Ziggy and the Black Dinosaurs. 1996, Just Us Bks. paper $6.00 (978-0-940975-63-7). 96pp. While exploring tunnels used by the Underground Railroad, boys are trapped underground when one of the tunnels collapses. (Rev: SLJ 8/96)

8074 Draper, Sharon M. *Shadows of Caesar's Creek* (3–5). Series: Ziggy and the Black Dinosaurs. 1997, Just Us Bks. paper $6.00 (978-0-940975-76-7). 91pp. A group of African American kids get lost in a state park and are rescued by a Shawnee chief. (Rev: SLJ 6/98)

8075 Duey, Kathleen, and Karen A. Bale. *Flood: Mississippi, 1927* (4–6). Series: Survival! 1998, Simon & Schuster paper $3.99 (978-0-689-82116-5). 169pp. Two children living on the banks of the Mississippi set out to rescue their hard-earned, hidden money before it is swept away in a flood. (Rev: SLJ 12/98)

8076 Duncan, Lois. *News for Dogs* (3–5). 2009, Scholastic $16.99 (978-0-545-10853-9). 224pp. Andi and her older, middle-school brother Bruce start a newspaper for dogs and take on a dog-napping case. (Rev: BL 4/1/09) ◐

8077 Easley, Maryann. *I Am the Ice Worm* (4–6). 1996, Boyds Mills $16.95 (978-1-56397-412-0). 127pp. A California girl is rescued by Inupiats when she is stranded in Alaska after a plane crash. (Rev: BL 10/15/96; SLJ 11/96)

8078 Easton, Patricia H. *A Week at the Fair: A Country Celebration* (2–5). Photos by Herb Ferguso. 1995, Millbrook LB $22.90 (978-1-56294-527-5). A week's activities at a county fair in western Pennsylvania are seen through the eyes of a 12-year-old girl. (Rev: SLJ 2/96)

8079 Eden, Alexandra. *Holy Smoke: A Bones and Duchess Mystery* (5–7). 2004, Alien A. Knoll $16.00 (978-1-888310-46-7). 112pp. Ex-cop Bones Fatzinger and Verity Buscador, a 12-year-old girl with Asperger's syndrome, work together to track down the person responsible for setting fire to a local church. (Rev: BL 5/1/04)

8080 Ellis, Mary. *Lily Dragon* (3–5). Illus. by Rachael Phillips. 2001, HarperCollins paper $7.50 (978-0-00-675458-9). 139pp. Lily sets off on a trip to visit her mother's family in China, determined to hunt for the hidden treasure she's heard about so often. (Rev: SLJ 8/01)

8081 Elmer, Robert. *Far from the Storm* (4–7). Series: Young Underground. 1995, Bethany paper $5.99 (978-0-556-61377-0). 174pp. At the end of World War II, Danish twins Peter and Elise set out to find the culprit who set their uncle's boat on fire. (Rev: BL 2/15/96)

8082 Emerson, Kathy L. *The Mystery of the Missing Bagpipes* (5–7). 1991, Avon paper $2.95 (978-0-380-76138-8). 128pp. Kim tries to find the real culprit when a young boy is wrongfully accused of stealing a set of ancient bagpipes and some precious daggers. (Rev: BL 9/15/91)

8083 Emerson, Scott. *The Case of the Cat with the Missing Ear: From the Notebooks of Edward R. Smithfield, D.V.M.* (5–7). 2003, Simon & Schuster LB $15.95 (978-0-689-85861-1). This canine take-off of the Sherlock Holmes format features Yorkshire terrier Samuel Blackthorne and his sidekick and chronicler Dr. Edward Smithfield, who investigate mysteries with humor and deductive prowess. (Rev: BCCB 10/02; BL 12/1/03; HBG 4/04; SLJ 3/04)

8084 Engh, M. J. *The House in the Snow* (4–6). Illus. 1990, Scholastic paper $2.75 (978-0-590-42658-9). 144pp. Orphan Benjamin lands in a house of robbers who have cloaks that make them invisible. With the help of the other boys, he plans to take over the house. (Rev: BL 11/1/87; SLJ 9/87)

8085 Erickson, John R. *Discovery at Flint Springs* (5–8). 2004, Viking $16.99 (978-0-670-05946-1). 192pp. In 1927, 14-year-old Riley and his younger brother Coy join in an exciting search for archaeological sites on their Texas ranch. (Rev: BL 2/1/05; SLJ 12/04)

8086 Ernst, Kathleen. *Midnight in Lonesome Hollow* (4–6). 2007, Pleasant $10.95 (978-1-59369-161-5); paper $6.95 (978-1-59369-160-8). 180pp. In rural Kentucky during the Depression, Kit investigates threats to a professor researching local traditions and worried about her friend Fern, who may end up in an orphanage. (Rev: BL 5/15/07; SLJ 5/07)

8087 Ernst, Kathleen. *Secrets in the Hills: A Josefina Mystery* (4–7). Series: American Girl Mystery. 2006, Pleasant paper $6.95 (978-1-59369-097-7). 184pp. In 1820s New Mexico, Josefina decides to investigate the possibility that there is treasure buried near her home. (Rev: BL 5/15/06; SLJ 4/06)

8088 Ewing, Lynne. *Drive-By* (5–8). 1996, HarperCollins paper $4.99 (978-0-06-440649-9). When Tito's brother is killed in a gang-related shooting, he is bullied and threatened by the gang to reveal where his brother hid a cache of stolen money. (Rev: SLJ 8/96)

8089 Fagan, Deva. *Fortune's Folly* (5–7). 2009, Holt $17.95 (978-0-8050-8742-0). 272pp. Seventeen-

year-old Fortunata becomes a fortune teller to support herself and her father and finds herself in a pickle when her predictions threaten her father's life. (Rev: BCCB 9/09; BL 4/1/09; SLJ 7/09)

8090 Falcone, L. M. *The Mysterious Mummer* (5–7). 2003, Kids Can $16.95 (978-1-55337-376-6). 192pp. When Joey, 13, arrives in Newfoundland to spend Christmas with his aunt, he finds some very mysterious goings-on. (Rev: HBG 4/04; SLJ 10/03)

8091 Fama, Elizabeth. *Overboard* (4–8). 2002, Cricket $15.95 (978-0-8126-2652-0). 176pp. Fourteen-year-old Emily struggles to save her own life and that of a boy named Isman when a ferry sinks off the coast of Sumatra. (Rev: BCCB 6/02; BL 7/02; HBG 10/02; SLJ 7/02)

8092 Fardell, John. *The Flight of the Silver Turtle* (5–8). 2006, Putnam $15.99 (978-0-399-24382-0). 256pp. The same crew from *The 7 Professors of the Far North* (2005) must find an antigravity machine before the villains discover it, in an exciting chase around Europe. (Rev: BL 12/15/06; SLJ 10/06)

8093 Farley, Carol. *The Case of the Haunted Health Club* (4–6). 1991, Avon paper $2.95 (978-0-380-75918-7). 112pp. Two sisters solve a mystery involving a health club. (Rev: BL 3/15/91)

8094 Farley, Carol. *The Case of the Vanishing Villain* (5–6). Illus. 1986, Avon paper $2.95 (978-0-380-89959-3). 80pp. A 10-year-old solves the mystery of an escaped convict's disappearance. Also use *Mystery of the Melted Diamonds* (1986) and *The Case of the Lost Lookalike* (1988). (Rev: BL 9/15/86; SLJ 11/86)

8095 Ferguson, Dwayne J. *Case of the Missing Ankh* (2–4). Series: Kid Caramel. 1997, Just Us Bks. paper $4.50 (978-0-940975-71-2). 59pp. Two junior detectives solve the mystery of the stolen museum treasure. (Rev: SLJ 9/97)

8096 Ferguson, Dwayne J. *Kid Caramel, Private Investigator: The Werewolf of PS 40* (3–5). Series: Kid Caramel. 1998, Just Us Bks. paper $4.50 (978-0-940975-82-8). 68pp. When animals begin to disappear from his town, Kid Caramel and his sidekick, Earnie, set out to find the culprit. (Rev: SLJ 3/99)

8097 Ferraiolo, Jack D. *The Big Splash* (5–7). 2008, Abrams $15.95 (978-0-8109-7067-0). 288pp. Matt Stevens, an average middle-schooler with a glib tongue and a knack for solving crimes, uncovers a mystery while working with "the organization," a mafia-like syndicate run by 7th-grader Vincent "Mr. Biggs" Biggio, and specializing in forged hall passes, test-copying rings, black market candy selling, and so forth. (Rev: BCCB 11/08; BLO 10/7/08; LMC 3/09; SLJ 11/08; VOYA 10/08) ∩

8098 Fields, T. S. *Danger in the Desert* (5–7). 1997, Rising Moon $12.95 (978-0-87358-666-5); paper $6.95 (978-0-87358-664-1). 126pp. A survival story about two boys who endure great hardships when they are left without food or supplies in the desert. (Rev: HBG 3/98; SLJ 11/97)

8099 Fienberg, Anna. *Horrendo's Curse* (3–6). Illus. by Kim Gamble. 2002, Annick $18.95 (978-1-55037-773-6); paper $6.95 (978-1-55037-772-9). 160pp. Twelve-year-old Horrendo, whose curse is an inability to say anything cruel although surrounded by rude foul-mouths, manages to persuade his pirate kidnappers that politeness is the best policy. (Rev: BL 12/1/02; HBG 10/03; SLJ 2/03)

8100 Figley, Marty Rhodes. *The Schoolchildren's Blizzard* (1–3). Illus. by Shelly O. Haas. Series: On My Own History. 2004, Carolrhoda LB $27.93 (978-1-57505-586-2). 48pp. A teacher rescues 16 students after the roof of the school is blown off during a severe blizzard in 1888 in this story based on a Nebraska storm. (Rev: BL 3/1/04)

8101 Fleck, Earl. *Chasing Bears: A Canoe-Country Adventure* (5–8). Illus. by author. 1999, Holy Cow paper $12.95 (978-0-930100-90-2). 135pp. An adventure story set near the Minnesota-Canada border that involves Danny, a 12-year-old who is on a canoe trip with his father and older brother. (Rev: SLJ 12/99)

8102 Fleischman, Paul. *The Half-a-Moon Inn* (5–7). Illus. by Kathryn Jacobi. 1991, HarperCollins paper $5.99 (978-0-06-440364-1). 96pp. A young mute boy sets out to find his mother in a violent snowstorm.

8103 Fleischman, Sid. *The Ghost in the Noonday Sun* (5–7). Illus. by Warren Chappell. 1989, Scholastic paper $3.50 (978-0-590-43662-5). 144pp. This pirate story features all the standard ingredients — a shanghaied boy, a villainous captain, and buried treasure. (Rev: VOYA 8/89)

8104 Fleischman, Sid. *The Giant Rat of Sumatra or Pirates Galore* (4–6). Illus. by John Hendrix. 2005, Greenwillow LB $16.89 (978-0-06-074239-3). 208pp. In a fast-paced adventure, 12-year-old cabin boy Edmund Amos Peters, who's been shipwrecked and captured by pirates, arrives in mid-19th-century San Diego to find his adventures are not over. (Rev: BL 2/1/05; SLJ 1/05)

8105 Fleischman, Sid. *The Whipping Boy* (5–7). Illus. 1986, Greenwillow $16.99 (978-0-688-06216-3). 96pp. Prince Brat and his whipping boy, Jemmy, who takes the blame for all the bad things the prince does, find their roles reversed when they meet up with CutWater and Hold-Your-Nose Billy. Newbery Medal winner, 1987. (Rev: BCCB 3/86; BL 3/1/86; SLJ 5/86)

8106 Fontes, Justine, and Ron Fontes. *Captured by Pirates* (4–6). Illus. by David Witt. Series: Twisted Journey. 2007, Lerner $27.93 (978-0-8225-6201-6); paper $7.95 (978-0-8225-6202-3). 112pp. Will you be captured by pirates? Set sail from England as a boy in 1635 and make your own choices in this part-text part-graphic novel book. (Rev: BL 10/1/07; SLJ 9/07)

8107 Freeman, Martha. *Who Stole Halloween?* (4–6). 2005, Holiday $16.95 (978-0-8234-1962-3). 232pp. Alex, boy detective, asks his friend Yasmeen to help him track down a missing cat named Halloween. (Rev: BL 8/05; SLJ 10/05)

8108 Freeman, Martha. *Who Stole Uncle Sam?* (4–6). 2008, Holiday $16.95 (978-0-8234-2091-9). 256pp. Alex and his friend Yasmeen investigate the disappearance of a baseball coach/Uncle Sam imperson-

ator; a humorous read with lots of background information. (Rev: BLO 8/28/08)

8109 Fusilli, Jim. *Marley Z. and the Bloodstained Violin* (5–8). 2008, Dutton $16.99 (978-0-525-47907-9). 208pp. Marley's musician friend Marisol is accused of stealing a valuable violin, and Marley is determined to prove her innocence in this mystery set in New York City. (Rev: BL 5/1/08; SLJ 9/08)

8110 Gaetz, Dayle Campbell. *Alberta Alibi* (4–6). 2005, Orca paper $6.95 (978-1-55143-404-9). When Sheila's divorced father is accused of sabotaging a housing development near his Canadian ranch, the 12-year-old and her friends Katie and Rusty try to prove him innocent and identify the real culprits; the third installment in a series. (Rev: SLJ 4/06; VOYA 4/06)

8111 Galbraith, Kathryn O. *Something Suspicious* (4–6). 1987, Avon paper $2.50 (978-0-380-70253-4). 128pp. Lizzie and her friend Ivy are on the trail of the bank robber known as the Green Pillowcase Bandit. (Rev: BCCB 1/86; BL 10/1/85)

8112 Garden, Nancy. *The Case of the Stolen Scarab* (4–6). Illus. by Danamarie Hosler. Series: Candlestone Inn Mystery. 2004, Two Lives paper $8.95 (978-0-9674468-7-5). 205pp. Nikki and Travis, with their mothers, have only just arrived at their new inn when a mystery presents itself — a scarab has been stolen and the thief may be in the area. (Rev: SLJ 3/05)

8113 Garland, Sherry. *The Silent Storm* (4–7). 1993, Harcourt $14.95 (978-0-15-274170-9). 240pp. Alyssa, who has lost both of her parents in a violent storm and has become mute because of the trauma, hears that another hurricane is approaching. (Rev: BCCB 4/93; BL 6/1–15/93; SLJ 7/04)

8114 George, Jean Craighead. *Julie of the Wolves* (5–8). Illus. by John Schoenherr. 1974, HarperCollins LB $16.89 (978-0-06-021944-4); paper $5.99 (978-0-06-440058-9). 180pp. Julie (Inuit name, Miyax) begins a trek across frozen Alaska and is saved only by the friendship of a pack of wolves. Newbery Medal winner, 1973.

8115 George, Jean Craighead. *Julie's Wolf Pack* (5–7). Illus. Series: Julie of the Wolves. 1997, HarperCollins LB $18.89 (978-0-06-027407-8). 208pp. Kapu, leader of the pack, is captured by researchers in this continuing story of Julie and her wolf friends. (Rev: BL 9/1/97; HBG 3/98; SLJ 9/97; VOYA 6/98)

8116 George, Twig C. *Swimming with Sharks* (4–6). Illus. 1999, HarperCollins LB $14.89 (978-0-06-027758-1). 96pp. Sarah and her grandfather, a shark expert, are on the trail of a "finner" — someone who cuts off sharks' fins and leaves them to die. (Rev: BL 7/99; HBG 10/99; SLJ 7/99)

8117 Gerson, Corrine. *My Grandfather the Spy* (5–7). 1990, Walker $14.95 (978-0-8027-6955-8). 120pp. When a man arrives on the family farm in Vermont with a briefcase full of money, Danny suspects his grandfather is a spy. (Rev: BL 6/15/90; SLJ 8/90)

8118 Giff, Patricia Reilly. *Eleven* (3–6). 2008, Random $15.99 (978-0-385-73069-3). 144pp. Sam, 10, finds a newspaper article with his picture and the word "missing" and, with the help of a new classmate, Caroline, he begins to uncover the complex mystery of his past. (Rev: BL 12/1/07; HB 9/08; LMC 1/08; SLJ 1/08) ☊

8119 Givner, Joan. *Ellen Fremedon* (5–7). 2004, Groundwood $15.95 (978-0-88899-557-5). 176pp. When her family seeks to block a proposed housing development, 12-year-old Ellen Fremedon, an aspiring novelist, must set aside her summer project to cope with the repercussions. (Rev: BL 11/15/04)

8120 Givner, Joan. *Ellen Fremedon, Volunteer* (4–6). 2007, Groundwood $16.95 (978-0-88899-743-2). 184pp. Thirteen-year-old Ellen, at loose ends with her best friend away at summer camp, volunteers to help out a local retirement center and gets drawn into the mystery surrounding the disappearance of a new friend's mother. (Rev: BL 4/1/07)

8121 Godden, Rumer. *The Rocking Horse Secret* (4–6). Illus. by Juliet Stanwell Smith. 1988, Puffin paper $3.95 (978-0-317-69650-9). 64pp. Tibby solves many problems when she finds a will hidden in a rocking horse.

8122 Gordon, Amy. *Return to Gill Park* (5–8). Series: Gill Park. 2006, Holiday $16.95 (978-0-8234-1998-2). 234pp. This oddball sequel to *The Gorillas of Gill Park* (2006) finds Willy Wilson on the trail of vandals determined to destroy the beauty of the park he now owns. (Rev: BL 5/15/06; SLJ 4/06)

8123 Gourley, Catherine, ed. *Read for Your Life: Tales of Survival from the Editors of Read Magazine* (5–8). Series: Best of Read. 1998, Millbrook paper $5.95 (978-0-7613-0344-2). This is a collection of excellent survival stories from 50 years of *Read,* a literary magazine for middle and high school students. (Rev: BL 8/98)

8124 Graf, Mike. *Bryce and Zion: Danger in the Narrows* (5–8). Illus. by Marjorie Leggitt. Series: Adventures with the Parkers. 2006, Fulcrum paper $9.95 (978-1-55591-532-2). 94pp. On a vacation in the national parks of southern Utah, 10-year-old twins James and Morgan Parker learn about the delicate ecology of the area, rescue an injured hiker, and come to the aid of their father when he slips and falls in the Narrows; a fact-filled adventure story with full-color photographs and nature sketches. (Rev: SLJ 12/06)

8125 Greenburg, Dan. *Treachery and Betrayal at Jolly Days* (4–6). Illus. by Scott M. Fischer. Series: Secrets of the Dripping Fang. 2006, Harcourt $11.95 (978-0-15-205463-2). 144pp. Once again fleeing the evil Mandible sisters, the Schluffmuffin twins find themselves in a swamp and encounter a zombie who just might be their long-lost father. (Rev: BL 2/15/06; SLJ 6/06)

8126 Greene, Stephanie. *Owen Foote, Frontiersman* (2–4). Illus. 1999, Clarion $14.00 (978-0-395-61578-2). 96pp. In this beginning chapter book, Owen and his pal Joseph must rescue their tree fort from two older boys who threaten to destroy it. (Rev: BL 10/15/99; HB 9/99; HBG 3/00; SLJ 10/99)

8127 Gregory, Kristiana. *The Secret of Robber's Cave* (3–5). Illus. by Patrick Faricy. Series: Cabin Creek Mysteries. 2008, Scholastic paper $4.99 (978-0-439-92950-9). 176pp. A fast-moving mystery adventure about two brothers who set off for Lost Island to solve a mystery from the 1880s. (Rev: BLO 3/3/08; SLJ 3/08)

8128 Grover, Wayne. *Dolphin Freedom* (3–5). Illus. 1999, Greenwillow $15.00 (978-0-688-16010-4). 112pp. Diver Wayne Grover tries to save dolphins that are the target of a poaching ring working off the coast of Florida. (Rev: BL 5/15/99; HBG 10/99; SLJ 6/99)

8129 Gutman, Dan. *Getting Air* (5–8). 2007, Simon & Schuster $15.99 (978-0-689-87680-6). 224pp. Thirteen-year-old Jimmy and five others prevent a hijacking, survive a plane crash, and find themselves faced with surviving in a Canadian forest; girl scout lore comes to their aid and they even find time to build a half-pipe for skateboarding. (Rev: BL 7/07; SLJ 6/07)

8130 Gutman, Dan. *Shoeless Joe and Me* (4–7). Series: Baseball Card Adventure. 2002, HarperCollins LB $17.89 (978-0-06-029254-6). 144pp. Thirteen-year-old Joe travels back in time to remedy the 1919 Black Sox scandal and save Shoeless Joe's reputation. (Rev: BL 1/1–15/02; HBG 10/02; SLJ 3/02)

8131 Hale, Bruce. *From Russia with Lunch* (3–5). Illus. by author. Series: Chet Gecko Mystery. 2009, Houghton $15.00 (978-0-15-205488-5). 144pp. The wisecracking and very punny Chet Gecko leaps to solve a new mystery at school in this 14th volume in the series. (Rev: BL 2/1/09)

8132 Harlow, Joan Hiatt. *Star in the Storm* (4–7). Illus. 2000, Simon & Schuster $16.00 (978-0-689-82905-5). 160pp. This novel, set in Newfoundland in 1912, tells how a girl and her dog save a ship full of stranded passengers. (Rev: BCCB 3/00; BL 1/1–15/00; HB 3/00; HBG 10/00; SLJ 4/00)

8133 Harrison, Ted. *Children of the Yukon* (2–4). Illus. by author. 1977, Tundra paper $6.95 (978-0-88776-163-8). Life in present-day Yukon with a little historical material.

8134 Haugaard, Erik C. *Under the Black Flag* (5–7). 1994, Roberts Rinehart paper $8.95 (978-1-879373-63-1). 170pp. Fourteen-year-old William is captured by the pirate Blackbeard and held for ransom in this 18th-century yarn. (Rev: BL 4/1/94; HB 9/94; SLJ 5/94)

8135 Haven, Paul. *The Seven Keys of Balabad* (5–8). Illus. by Mark Zug. 2009, Random $16.99 (978-0-375-83350-2). 288pp. Twelve-year-old Oliver, whose father is a foreign correspondent assigned to Balabad, finds himself pulled out of Manhattan and into the middle of an exotic and dangerous mystery surrounding a 500-year-old sacred carpet. (Rev: BCCB 2/09; BL 1/1–15/09; SLJ 4/09)

8136 Hawks, Robert. *The Richest Kid in the World* (4–8). 1992, Avon paper $2.99 (978-0-380-76241-5). 136pp. Josh is kidnapped and taken to the estate of billionaire Grizzle Welch. (Rev: SLJ 5/92)

8137 Hayes, Daniel. *The Trouble with Lemons* (5–8). 1991, Random paper $5.99 (978-0-449-70416-5). Tyler, 14, has all kinds of problems — allergies, asthma, and nightmares — and then he finds a dead body. (Rev: BL 5/1/91; SLJ 6/91)

8138 Hearne, Betsy. *Who's in the Hall? A Mystery in Four Chapters* (2–4). Illus. 2000, Greenwillow LB $16.89 (978-0-688-16262-7). 32pp. Three different sets of kids in the same apartment building are troubled by a stranger who knocks at their doors asking to be let in. (Rev: BCCB 1/01; BL 9/15/00; HBG 3/01; SLJ 8/00)

8139 Henderson, Aileen K. *The Summer of the Bonepile Monster* (3–5). Illus. 1995, Milkweed paper $6.95 (978-1-57131-602-8). 140pp. Hollis changes into a self-reliant young man during a summer spent in the country during which he solves a community mystery. (Rev: BCCB 7–8/95; BL 5/1/95; SLJ 7/95)

8140 Herndon, Ernest. *The Secret of Lizard Island* (3–5). 1994, HarperCollins paper $5.99 (978-0-310-38251-5). 128pp. Through a misunderstanding, Eric, a typical 12-year-old, is sent to a South Pacific island where scientists are growing huge lizards. (Rev: BL 9/1/94)

8141 Hesse, Karen. *Stowaway* (5–8). Illus. 2000, Simon & Schuster $17.95 (978-0-689-83987-0). 319pp. Told by an 11-year-old stowaway, this adventurous sea story tells of Captain Cook's two-and-a-half-year voyage around the world beginning in 1768. (Rev: BL 12/15/00; HB 1/01; HBG 3/01; SLJ 11/00; VOYA 4/01)

8142 Heyes, Eileen. *O'Dwyer and Grady Starring in Tough Act to Follow* (4–7). Illus. by Eric Bowman. Series: O'Dwyer and Grady. 2003, Simon & Schuster paper $4.99 (978-0-689-84920-6). 176pp. Young actors Billy and Virginia stumble into a mystery while searching for props for a show in this action-packed story set in the 1930s. (Rev: BL 5/15/03; SLJ 7/03)

8143 Heyman, Alissa, adapt. *The Big Book of Adventure* (3–6). Illus. by Pedro Rodriguez. 2008, Sterling LB $12.95 (978-1-4027-5156-1). 109pp. A collection of classic adventure stories — some well-known, others less familiar — prefaced with author biographies and integrated with cartoon graphics. (Rev: SLJ 9/08)

8144 Higgins, F. E. *The Black Book of Secrets* (5–7). 2007, Feiwel & Friends $14.95 (978-0-312-36844-9). 288pp. Joe Zabbidou takes the confessions of everyone in the remote village of Pagus Parvus, collecting them in a black book. Ludlow Fitch, a desperate boy on the run from cruel parents, acts as Joe's scribe, a dangerous position in a dangerous world. (Rev: BL 10/15/07; HB 1/08; LMC 5/08; SLJ 4/08)

8145 Higson, Charlie. *Blood Fever: A James Bond Adventure* (5–8). Series: Young Bond. 2006, Hyperion $16.95 (978-0-7868-3662-8). 347pp. Even at 13, Bond is having adventures: this one finds him on the island of Sardinia, caught up in an art-theft mystery and rescuing a girl in peril. (Rev: SLJ 6/06)

8146 Hildick, E. W. *The Purloined Corn Popper* (4–6). 1997, Marshall Cavendish $14.95 (978-0-7614-5010-8). 160pp. In this new mystery series, Tim Kowalski and his friend investigate the disappearance of a corn popper that contained Mrs. Kowalski's money. Also use *Sneak Thief* (1997). (Rev: BL 1/1–15/98; HBG 10/98; SLJ 2/98)

8147 Hilgartner, Beth. *A Murder for Her Majesty* (5–8). 1986, Houghton paper $6.95 (978-0-395-61619-2). 256pp. Alice disguises herself as a boy to escape her father's murderers. (Rev: BCCB 9/86; SLJ 10/86)

8148 Hobbs, Will. *Jackie's Wild Seattle* (5–8). 2003, HarperCollins LB $16.89 (978-0-06-051631-4). 192pp. In the aftermath of September 11, 2001, Shannon, 14, and her younger brother spend an exciting and healing summer in Seattle with their animal rescuer uncle. (Rev: BL 6/1–15/03; HBG 4/04; SLJ 5/03; VOYA 8/03)

8149 Hobbs, Will. *Jason's Gold* (5–9). 1999, Morrow $17.99 (978-0-688-15093-8). 192pp. In this sharply realistic novel, 15-year-old Jason leaves Seattle in 1897 and, with a dog he has saved, heads for the Klondike and gold. (Rev: BL 8/99; HB 9/99; HBG 3/00; SLJ 11/99)

8150 Holm, Jennifer, and Jonathan Hamel. *You Only Have Nine Lives* (3–5). Illus. by Brad Weinman. Series: The Stink Files. 2005, HarperCollins $14.99 (978-0-06-052985-7). 128pp. Traveling to France as the winner of a cat food competition, cat sleuth Mr. Stink is mistaken as a prince and uncovers secrets about his own origins. (Rev: SLJ 12/05)

8151 Holman, Felice. *Slake's Limbo* (5–9). 1974, Macmillan paper $4.99 (978-0-689-71066-7). 126pp. Thirteen-year-old Artemis Slake finds an ideal hideaway for four months in the labyrinth of the New York City subway. (Rev: BL 6/1/88)

8152 Hopper, Nancy J. *Ape Ears and Beaky* (4–7). 1987, Avon paper $2.50 (978-0-380-70270-1). 112pp. Scott and Beaky solve the mystery of the robberies in a condominium.

8153 Horowitz, Anthony. *Alex Rider: The Gadgets* (5–8). Illus. by John Lawson. 2006, Philomel $15.99 (978-0-399-24486-5). 44pp. A look at all the gadgets used in the first five Alex Rider mysteries — including such wonders as a radio mouth brace, exploding ear stud, and pizza delivery assassin kit — with diagrams and details of how they were used. (Rev: BL 4/1/06; SLJ 4/06)

8154 Horowitz, Anthony. *South by Southeast* (4–7). Series: Diamond Brothers. 2005, Philomel $16.99 (978-0-399-24155-0); paper $5.99 (978-0-14-240374-7). 148pp. Hapless private eye Tim Diamond and his brother Nick find themselves drawn into a labyrinthine mystery after a visit from a stranger. (Rev: BL 12/1/05; SLJ 12/05)

8155 Horowitz, Anthony. *Stormbreaker* (5–9). Series: Alex Rider. 2001, Philomel $17.99 (978-0-399-23620-4). 208pp. Fourteen-year-old Alex becomes embroiled in dangerous undercover exploits when his MI6 uncle is murdered. (Rev: BCCB 9/01; BL 9/1/01; HBG 10/01; SLJ 6/01; VOYA 8/01)

8156 Horowitz, Anthony. *Three of Diamonds* (5–8). Series: Diamond Brothers. 2005, Philomel $16.99 (978-0-399-24157-4). 240pp. Tim and Nick succeed in solving crimes despite Tim's blunderings in these three fast-paced and entertaining mystery stories full of wordplay. (Rev: BL 5/15/05; SLJ 5/05)

8157 Horse, Harry. *The Last Castaways* (2–5). Illus. by author. 2009, Peachtree $12.95 (978-1-56145-439-6). 128pp. Letters, logs, and diaries tell the story of Grandfather's adventures at sea — and marooned on land — with his dog Roo. (Rev: BL 4/1/09)

8158 Horse, Harry. *The Last Gold Diggers* (2–4). Illus. by author. 2008, Peachtree $12.95 (978-1-56145-435-8). 136pp. In letters and journal entries Grandfather describes a series of zany adventures in Australia with his talented dog Roo as they search for Grandfather's missing brother. (Rev: BL 4/15/08)

8159 Howard, Milly. *The Case of the Dognapped Cat* (2–4). Illus. 1997, Bob Jones Univ. paper $6.49 (978-0-89084-936-1). 144pp. Three Florida youngsters call themselves Crimebusters and, in this adventure, solve the mystery of a cat that has been kidnapped. (Rev: BL 1/1–15/98)

8160 Hunt, L. J. *The Abernathy Boys* (5–7). 2004, HarperCollins LB $16.89 (978-0-06-029259-1). 208pp. Young Bud and Temple Abernathy survive an eventful journey through the desert in this fictionalized version of a real expedition in the early 20th century. (Rev: BL 1/1–15/04; SLJ 3/04)

8161 Hyde, Dayton O. *Mr. Beans* (5–7). 2000, Boyds Mills $14.95 (978-1-56397-866-1). 160pp. In a small town in Oregon in the early 1940s, bully Mugsy wrongfully accuses a tame bear of attacking him, and timid Chirp frees the bear and takes off with him on a wilderness journey. (Rev: BL 11/15/00; HBG 10/01; SLJ 1/01; VOYA 4/01)

8162 Hyland, Hilary. *The Wreck of the Ethie* (4–7). Illus. by Paul Bachem. 1999, Peachtree paper $7.95 (978-1-56145-198-2). 115pp. Told through the eyes of two youngsters, this is a novelization of a true incident in which a dog saved passengers after their ship sank off the coast of Newfoundland. (Rev: SLJ 4/00)

8163 Jackson, Melanie. *Queen of Disguises* (4–6). 2009, Orca paper $9.95 (978-1-55469-037-4). 160pp. A funny mystery in which young sleuth and singer Dinah Galloway is threatened by a vengeful actress. (Rev: BL 5/1/09)

8164 Jam, Teddy. *ttuM* (2–4). Illus. by Harvey Chan. Series: A Charlotte Novel. 1999, Groundwood $14.95 (978-0-88899-373-1); paper $5.95 (978-0-88899-374-8). 109pp. In this beginning chapter book, a little girl who speaks to her dog, ttuM, in reverse, solves a mystery about a strange person in black seen canoeing on the village lake. (Rev: SLJ 3/00)

8165 Jennings, Patrick. *The Bird Shadow: An Ike and Mem Story* (2–4). Illus. by Anna Alter. 2001, Holiday House $15.95 (978-0-8234-1670-7). 55pp. Ike and little sister Mem end up making a new friend when they dare to investigate a spooky old house. (Rev: HBG 10/02; SLJ 3/02)

8166 Jennings, Richard W. *The Pirates of Turtle Rock* (5–8). 2008, Houghton $16.00 (978-0-618-98793-1). 160pp. A modern-day Florida girl falls for a young pirate and the two embark on a treasure hunt for an ancient Caribbean artifact; a novel full of humor and adventure. (Rev: BL 4/15/08; SLJ 8/08)

8167 Johns, Linda. *Hannah West in Deep Water* (5–8). 2006, Puffin paper $5.99 (978-0-14-240700-4). 160pp. Hannah investigates environmental shenanigans while she and her mother are house-sitting a houseboat and a dog. (Rev: BL 12/15/06)

8168 Johns, Linda. *Hannah West in the Belltown Towers: A Mystery* (5–8). 2006, Sleuth paper $5.99 (978-0-14-240637-3). 160pp. Hannah, an adopted Chinese girl with lots of nerve and curiosity, moves with her mother to Seattle and soon finds herself embroiled in an art theft. (Rev: BL 5/1/06)

8169 Johns, Linda. *Hannah West on Millionaire's Row* (5–8). Series: Hannah West. 2007, Puffin paper $5.99 (978-0-14-240824-7). 160pp. Girl sleuth Hannah West, who was adopted from China, solves a mystery involving feng shui, antiques, and old mansions in this fourth installment in the series. (Rev: BL 10/1/07)

8170 Johnson, Annabel, and Edgar Johnson. *The Grizzly* (5–7). Illus. by Gilbert Riswold. 1964, HarperCollins paper $4.95 (978-0-06-440036-7). 194pp. A perceptive story of a father-son relationship in which David, on a camping trip, saves his father's life when a grizzly bear attacks.

8171 Johnson, Henry, and Paul Hoppe. *Travis and Freddy's Adventures in Vegas* (5–8). 2006, Dutton $15.99 (978-0-525-47646-7). 176pp. A lighthearted, fast-paced adventure in which preteens Travis and Freddy head to Las Vegas to win enough money to save Travis's home; there they win big but soon find they have the mob at their heels. (Rev: BL 2/15/06; SLJ 4/06; VOYA 4/06)

8172 Johnson, Rodney. *The Secret of Dead Man's Mine* (5–7). Illus. by Jill Thompson. Series: Rinnah Two Feathers Mystery. 2001, Uglytown paper $12.00 (978-0-9663473-3-3). 241pp. Rinnah Two Feathers and two friends set out to solve the mystery of a suspicious stranger and find themselves in danger. (Rev: SLJ 9/01)

8173 Jones, Elizabeth McDavid. *Traitor in Williamsburg* (3–5). Series: Felicity Mystery. 2008, American Girl paper $6.95 (978-1-59369-296-4). 180pp. In 1776 Williamsburg, Felicity and Elizabeth investigate mysterious anonymous notices accusing Felicity's father, among others, of helping the British. (Rev: BL 4/15/08)

8174 Joosse, Barbara M. *Dead Guys Talk: A Wild Willie Mystery* (3–5). Illus. by Abby Carter. 2006, Clarion $15.00 (978-0-618-30666-4). 112pp. A puzzle at the cemetery tasks the nerve and sleuthing skills of Scarface Detectives Willie, Lucy, and Kyle. (Rev: BL 5/1/06; SLJ 9/06)

8175 Joosse, Barbara M. *Ghost Trap: A Wild Willie Mystery* (3–5). Illus. 1998, Clarion $15.00 (978-0-

395-66587-9). 69pp. An easily read mystery about three friends, Willie, Kyle, and Lucy, and mysterious happenings that occur in a house formerly owned by an amateur detective and now the home of Kyle and his family. (Rev: BCCB 7–8/98; BL 6/1–15/98; HB 7/98; HBG 10/98; SLJ 6/98)

8176 Keane, Dave. *The Haunted Toolshed* (2–5). Illus. by author. Series: Joe Sherlock, Kid Detective. 2006, HarperCollins paper $3.99 (978-0-06-076188-2). 120pp. Goofy boy detective Joe Sherlock gets to the bottom of a tricky mystery in this first installment in a series that will entertain the flatulence gang. (Rev: SLJ 7/06)

8177 Keene, Carolyn. *Where's Nancy?* (4–7). Series: Nancy Drew Super Mystery. 2005, Simon & Schuster paper $4.99 (978-0-416-90034-7). 176pp. Nancy herself is missing in this first installment of a new series. (Rev: BL 5/1/05)

8178 Kehret, Peg. *Earthquake Terror* (4–7). 1998, Puffin paper $5.99 (978-0-14-038343-0). 144pp. A violent earthquake strikes the small island on which 12-year-old Jonathan is alone with his younger sister, Abby. (Rev: BCCB 3/96; BL 1/1–15/96; SLJ 2/96)

8179 Kehret, Peg. *Stolen Children* (4–7). 2008, Dutton $16.99 (978-0-525-47835-5). 208pp. Fourteen-year-old Amy is babysitting for a wealthy family when she and 3-year-old Kendra are kidnapped in this fast-paced, dramatic story. (Rev: BL 12/15/08; SLJ 12/08)

8180 Kehret, Peg. *The Stranger Next Door* (4–6). 2002, Dutton $15.99 (978-0-525-46829-5). 160pp. Twelve-year-old Alex discovers who's behind a spate of vandalism and arson in his new neighborhood, with the help of his feline friend Pete. (Rev: BL 2/1/02; HBG 10/02; SLJ 3/02)

8181 Kelsey, Marybeth. *A Recipe 4 Robbery* (4–6). 2009, HarperCollins $16.99 (978-0-06-128843-2). 288pp. Sixth-grader Lindy finds a stolen locket and, with her friends Margaret and Gus, sets out to find the robber and clear all suspicion from Granny Goose. (Rev: BL 5/1/09; SLJ 7/09)

8182 Kidd, Ronald. *The Year of the Bomb* (4–7). 2009, Simon & Schuster $15.99 (978-1-4169-5892-5). 208pp. In 1955 California as *Invasion of the Body Snatchers* is being filmed, four 7th-grade boys face danger as they learn about Cold War tensions and spies. (Rev: BL 5/1/09; LMC 10/09; SLJ 7/09; VOYA 10/09)

8183 King-Smith, Dick. *Harry's Mad* (4–6). Illus. 1990, Macmillan $15.95 (978-0-7451-1101-8); Knopf paper $4.99 (978-0-679-88688-4). Mad the talking parrot is stolen, but the sharp-witted bird finally makes it back home. (Rev: BCCB 5/87; BL 7/87; SLJ 5/87)

8184 Klise, Kate. *Trial by Jury Journal* (5–8). Illus. by M. Sarah Klise. 2001, HarperCollins LB $16.89 (978-0-06-029541-7). 256pp. When she is given the opportunity to serve as her state's first juvenile juror, 12-year-old Lily's sleuthing skills solve a murder mystery and save the day. (Rev: BCCB 4/01; BL 9/1/01; HB 5/01; HBG 10/01; SLJ 6/01)

8185 Konigsburg, E. L. *From the Mixed-Up Files of Mrs. Basil E. Frankweiler* (5–7). Illus. by author. 1967, Macmillan $17.00 (978-0-689-20586-6). 168pp. Adventure, suspense, detection, and humor are involved when 12-year-old Claudia and her younger brother elude the security guards and live for a week in New York's Metropolitan Museum of Art. Newbery Medal winner, 1968.

8186 Konigsburg, E. L. *Silent to the Bone* (5–9). 2000, Simon & Schuster $16.00 (978-0-689-83601-5). 272pp. A mystery story filled with suspense about a baby who's been dropped and a 13-year-old suspect who has lost his ability to speak. (Rev: BL 8/00*; HB 11/00; HBG 3/01; SLJ 9/00; VOYA 12/00)

8187 Korman, Gordon. *The Abduction* (4–7). Series: Kidnapped. 2006, Scholastic paper $4.99 (978-0-439-84777-3). 138pp. A fast-paced thriller, the opening volume of a new series, in which 15-year-old Aiden works with the FBI to rescue his 11-year-old sister Meg, who was abducted while on her way home from school and is meanwhile resisting her captors. The second volume is *The Search* (2006). (Rev: BL 8/06; SLJ 9/06)

8188 Korman, Gordon. *Chasing the Falconers* (4–7). 2005, Scholastic paper $4.99 (978-0-439-65136-3). 144pp. In this fast-paced adventure, Aiden and Meg Falconer must evade pursuers as they work to gather evidence that will prove their parents' innocence of treason. (Rev: BL 5/15/05; SLJ 8/05)

8189 Korman, Gordon. *One False Note* (4–8). Series: The 39 Clues. 2008, Scholastic $12.99 (978-0-545-06042-4). 176pp. Amy and Dan Cahill's arguments continue as they race to stay ahead of their cousins in hunting down the next clue that will solve their family mystery; a sequel to Rick Riordan's *The Maze of Bones* (2008). (Rev: BL 2/1/09; SLJ 7/09; VOYA 4/09) ∩

8190 Korman, Gordon. *Swindle* (3–6). 2008, Scholastic $16.99 (978-0-439-90344-8). 252pp. Griffin Bings organizes a 6th-grade effort to rescue a rare baseball card and save the family business. (Rev: BL 1/1–15/08; SLJ 2/08)

8191 Krupinski, Loretta. *Lost in the Fog* (3–4). Illus. 1990, Little, Brown $14.95 (978-0-316-07462-9). 32pp. When their boat loaded with geese overturns, Mother Tipton thinks of a novel plan to save herself and Willie. (Rev: BL 5/1/90)

8192 Labatt, Mary. *The Ghost of Captain Briggs* (3–5). Illus. by Troy Hill-Jackson. Series: Sam, Dog Detective. 1999, Kids Can $12.95 (978-1-55074-638-9); paper $4.95 (978-1-55074-636-5). 116pp. Jenny learns to read the thoughts of sheepdog Samantha, and together they investigate a haunted house. Also use *Spying on Dracula* (1999). (Rev: HBG 3/00; SLJ 2/00)

8193 Lachtman, Ofelia Dumas. *Call Me Consuelo* (4–6). 1997, Arte Publico paper $9.95 (978-1-55885-187-0). 147pp. Consuelo, a recent arrival in Los Angeles, becomes involved in finding the criminals who are committing mysterious local robberies. (Rev: SLJ 7/97)

8194 Lafevers, R. L. *Theodosia and the Serpents of Chaos* (5–8). Illus. by Yoko Tanaka. 2007, Houghton $16.00 (978-0-618-75638-4). 344pp. In the early 20th century, precocious 11-year-old Theodosia finds herself embroiled in a supernatural mystery involving Egyptian artifacts. (Rev: BL 5/1/07*; SLJ 4/07)

8195 Lalicki, Tom. *Danger in the Dark: A Houdini and Nate Mystery* (3–6). 2006, Farrar $14.95 (978-0-374-31680-8). 192pp. With the help of Harry Houdini, 12-year-old Nate plans to uncover suspected swindling by the strange man who's been holding séances with Nate's rich great-aunt in this historical mystery set in 1911 Manhattan. (Rev: BL 11/15/06; SLJ 10/06)

8196 Lalicki, Tom. *Shots at Sea: A Houdini and Nate Mystery* (4–7). Series: Houdini and Nate. 2007, Farrar $15.95 (978-0-374-31679-2). 208pp. In the second book in the series, Nate, 13, is aboard the *Lusitania* and finds among his fellow-passengers both Harry Houdini and Teddy Roosevelt; Nate and the former rescue the latter from an assassination attempt. (Rev: BL 1/1–15/08; SLJ 11/07)

8197 Landon, Lucinda. *Meg Mackintosh and the Mystery at the Medieval Castle: A Solve-It-Yourself Mystery* (3–6). Illus. by author. 1989, Little, Brown paper $4.95 (978-0-316-51376-0). 64pp. While Meg and her class visit a castle, a jewel-encrusted chalice is stolen. Also use: *Meg Mackintosh and the Case of the Curious Whale Watch* (1987). (Rev: BL 6/15/89)

8198 Landon, Lucinda. *Meg Mackintosh and the Mystery at the Soccer Match* (3–6). Illus. by author. Series: Solve-It-Yourself Mystery. 1997, Secret Passage paper $4.95 (978-1-888695-05-2). 48pp. Detective Meg and her soccer team are competing for a gold medal that suddenly disappears from the awards table. (Rev: SLJ 3/98)

8199 Landon, Lucinda. *Meg Mackintosh and the Mystery in the Locked Library: A Solve-It-Yourself Mystery* (3–6). Illus. 1996, Secret Passage paper $4.95 (978-1-888695-04-5). 48pp. Along with Meg Mackintosh, readers are asked to solve the mystery of the stolen rare book. (Rev: BL 2/1/93; SLJ 3/93)

8200 Lane, Kathleen. *Nana Cracks the Case!* (2–4). Illus. by Sarah Horne. 2009, Chronicle $14.99 (978-0-8118-6258-5). 120pp. Feisty Nana and her lively grandchildren Eufala and Bog investigate missing candy in this funny mystery loaded with visual jokes. (Rev: LMC 8/09; SLJ 6/09)

8201 Lasky, Kathryn. *Born to Rule* (3–6). Series: Camp Princess. 2006, HarperCollins $15.99 (978-0-06-058761-1). 143pp. This first book in the Camp Princess series has Princess Alicia of All the Belgravias reluctantly attending princess training camp and stumbling upon a ghost story. (Rev: SLJ 5/06)

8202 Latta, Sara. *Stella Brite and the Dark Matter Mystery* (2–4). Illus. by Meredith Johnson. 2006, Charlesbridge paper $6.95 (978-1-57091-884-1). 32pp. To give their fledgling detective agency a higher profile, Stella Brite and her brother Max try to unravel the mystery of invisible dark matter in the universe. (Rev: SLJ 4/06)

8203 Lawrence, Iain. *The Séance* (5–7). 2008, Delacorte $15.99 (978-0-385-73375-5). 272pp. Scooter, whose spiritualist mother performs fake séances, is caught up in a murder mystery involving his idol, Houdini, in this novel that captures the tone of 1920s New York City. (Rev: BL 5/1/08; SLJ 8/08)

8204 Leavey, Peggy Dymond. *The Deep End Gang* (3–7). 2003, Napoleon paper $7.95 (978-0-929141-89-3). 125pp. Twelve-year-old Martin joins forces with two friends to investigate suspicious events at a deserted house in his neighborhood. (Rev: SLJ 9/03)

8205 Lee, Norman. *Camel Rider* (5–7). 2007, Charlesbridge $15.95 (978-1-58089-314-5). 204pp. Two boys — a 12-year-old Australian named Adam and Walid, a camel driver from Bangladesh — find themselves alone in the desert during a Middle Eastern war and must struggle to survive; told in alternating first-person narratives, this is an exciting story that also shows how people with no common language can learn to communicate. (Rev: BL 9/1/07; SLJ 7/07)

8206 Leroux, Gaston. *The Phantom of the Opera* (3–6). Illus. by Paul Jennis. 1989, Random paper $3.99 (978-0-394-83847-2). 48pp. An abridgment of this horror story about a defaced man who lives in the depths of an opera house. (Rev: SLJ 1/90)

8207 Lisle, Janet T. *A Message from the Match Girl* (4–6). Series: Investigators of the Unknown. 1995, Orchard LB $16.99 (978-0-531-08787-9). 128pp. Georgina and Poco wonder if the messages and mementos that Walter is receiving from the past are genuine. (Rev: BCCB 11/95; BL 10/1/95; SLJ 10/95*)

8208 Little, Kimberly Griffiths. *Enchanted Runner* (5–7). 1999, Avon $15.00 (978-0-380-97623-2). 160pp. Twelve-year-old Kendall, who is half Native American, hopes to excel in running as his ancestors did, and is given an unusual opportunity to test himself. (Rev: BCCB 9/99; BL 9/1/99; HBG 3/00; SLJ 12/99)

8209 Lloyd, Emily. *Catch of the Day: The Case of the Helpless Humpbacks* (4–6). Series: Kinetic City Super Crew. 1997, McGraw-Hill paper $4.25 (978-0-07-006390-7). 166pp. The Kinetic City Super Crew faces opposition from some fishermen when its members try various methods to discourage whales from swimming into fishing nets off the coast of Nova Scotia. (Rev: SLJ 7/98)

8210 Lloyd, Emily. *Forest Slump: The Case of the Pilfered Pine Needles* (3–5). 1997, McGraw-Hill paper $4.25 (978-0-07-006388-4). 150pp. Using a message from science as a basis, this novel tells how four youngsters solve the mystery of who has stolen the pine needles from the forest floor. (Rev: BL 2/15/98; SLJ 4/98)

8211 Lourie, Peter. *The Lost Treasure of Captain Kidd* (5–8). Illus. 1996, Shawangunk Pr. paper $10.95 (978-1-885482-03-7). 136pp. Friends Killian and Alex set out to discover Captain Kidd's treasure buried on the banks of the Hudson River centuries ago. (Rev: BL 2/15/96; SLJ 6/96)

8212 Low, Dene. *The Entomological Tales of Augustus T. Percival: Petronella Saves Nearly Everyone*

(5–8). Illus. by Jen Corace. 2009, Houghton $16.00 (978-0-547-15250-9). 196pp. In Victorian London, 16-year-old Petronella must deal with her embarrassing, bug-eating uncle and save an international dignitary who has been kidnapped. (Rev: BL 7/09)

8213 Mac. *Anna Smudge: Professional Shrink* (4–6). Illus. by Glenn Fabry. 2008, Toasted Coconut paper $9.99 (978-1-934906-00-2). 256pp. While dealing with the usual problems of her age, Anna, an 11-year-old who is good at listening, sets herself up as a psychologist and soon finds herself drawn into a complex mystery. (Rev: BL 6/1–15/08; SLJ 6/08)

8214 McCall Smith, Alexander. *The Cowgirl Aunt of Harriet Bean* (2–4). Illus. by Laura Rankin. 2006, Bloomsbury $9.95 (978-1-58234-977-0). 67pp. Out West to meet her Aunt Formica for the first time, girl detective Harriet Bean, accompanied by Aunts Thessalonika and Japonica, uses her sleuthing skills to help track down some cattle rustlers. (Rev: SLJ 1/07)

8215 McCall Smith, Alexander. *Max and Maddy and the Chocolate Money Mystery* (2–4). Illus. by Macky Pamintuan. 2007, Bloomsbury $9.95 (978-1-59990-036-0). 80pp. Child detectives Max and Maddy solve the mystery of why dogs are robbing Swiss banks. (Rev: BL 7/07; LMC 5/07)

8216 McClain, Margaret S. *Bellboy: A Mule Train Journey* (4–6). Illus. by Sara Brown Stuart. 1989, New Mexico Publg. $17.95 (978-0-9622468-1-4). 192pp. A young boy takes a job leading a mule train into isolated towns in northern California in the 1870s. (Rev: BL 3/1/90)

8217 MacDonald, Bailey. *Wicked Will* (4–7). 2009, Aladdin $16.99 (978-1-4169-8660-7). 208pp. In Stratford in the 16th century, Viola, an actress disguised as a boy, meets 12-year-old Will Shakespeare and together they try to trap a murderer. (Rev: BL 5/1/09; LMC 10/09)

8218 McFadden, Deanna. *Robinson Crusoe: Retold from the Daniel Defoe Original* (4–7). Illus. by Jamel Akib. Series: Classic Starts. 2006, Sterling $4.95 (978-1-4027-2664-4). 160pp. The 1719 original text is retold in brief, accessible sentences that portray Crusoe and Friday as equals. (Rev: BL 2/15/06)

8219 Machado, Ana Maria. *From Another World* (4–7). Illus. by Lucia Brandao. 2005, Douglas & McIntyre $15.95 (978-0-88899-597-1). 128pp. Spending a night in an outbuilding of an old farmhouse, Mariano and his three friends meet the ghost of a 19th-century slave girl and promise to help in this story set in Brazil. (Rev: BL 5/1/05; SLJ 6/05)

8220 Mack, Tracy, and Michael Citrin. *The Fall of the Amazing Zalindas* (4–7). Illus. by Greg Ruth. Series: Sherlock Holmes and the Baker Street Irregulars. 2006, Scholastic $16.99 (978-0-439-82836-9). 256pp. Sherlock Holmes calls on a gang of street children to help him investigate the mysterious deaths of a family of trapeze artists. (Rev: BL 11/1/06; SLJ 1/07)

8221 Mack, Tracy, and Michael Citrin. *The Mystery of the Conjured Man* (5–7). Series: Sherlock Holmes and the Baker Street Irregulars. 2009,

Scholastic paper $6.99 (978-0-439-83667-8). 208pp. This second fast-paced installment in the series contains séances, death, hidden passages, fraud, and a twist at the end. (Rev: BLO 6/16/09; SLJ 6/09)

8222 Mahy, Margaret. *Tangled Fortunes* (4–6). Illus. 1994, Delacorte $14.95 (978-0-385-32066-5). 105pp. The friendship between a brother and sister is explored in this mystery set in New Zealand. (Rev: BL 10/1/94; SLJ 11/94*)

8223 Maifair, Linda Lee. *The Case of the Bashed-Up Bicycle* (2–4). 1996, Zondervan paper $3.99 (978-0-310-20736-8). 64pp. Tomboy Darcy solves the mystery of who stripped down her brother's new bicycle. Also use *The Case of the Nearsighted Neighbor* (1996). (Rev: BL 11/15/96)

8224 Markham, Marion M. *The April Fool's Day Mystery* (2–4). Illus. by Pau Estrada. 1991, Avon paper $3.50 (978-0-380-71716-3). 42pp. The detective twins Kate and Micky Dixon try to clear the name of Billy Wade, wrongfully accused of putting a snake in the school cafeteria's flour bin. (Rev: BL 7/91; SLJ 9/91)

8225 Markham, Marion M. *The Halloween Candy Mystery* (2–4). Illus. by Emily Arnold McCully. 1982, Avon paper $2.95 (978-0-380-70965-6). 48pp. The Dixon twins and their brother solve the mystery of a Halloween thief. Another mystery is: *The Christmas Present Mystery* (1984).

8226 Markham, Marion M. *The Thanksgiving Day Parade Mystery* (3–4). Illus. 1986, Avon paper $2.95 (978-0-380-70967-0). 48pp. Twins Kate and Mickey track down the disappearance of the school band on the way to the Macy's Thanksgiving Day Parade. Also use: *The Birthday Party Mystery* (1989). (Rev: BCCB 11/86; BL 9/15/86; SLJ 11/86)

8227 Martin, Terri. *A Family Trait* (5–7). 1999, Holiday $15.95 (978-0-8234-1467-3). 156pp. In this fast-paced story, Iris, 11 years old and incurably curious, has a number of mysteries to solve while trying to finish a book report. (Rev: BL 10/1/99; HBG 3/00; SLJ 10/99)

8228 Mason, Jane B., and Sarah Hines Stephens. *Bella Baxter and the Lighthouse Mystery* (2–4). Illus. by John Shelley. Series: Bella Baxter. 2006, Simon & Schuster paper $3.99 (978-0-689-86282-3). 80pp. Bella Baxter, excited when a popular filmmaker pays a visit to her family's inn, volunteers to guide him to a local lighthouse that may be haunted. (Rev: BL 2/15/06)

8229 Mass, Wendy. *Jeremy Fink and the Meaning of Life* (5–8). 2006, Little, Brown $15.99 (978-0-316-05829-2). 290pp. Just before his 13th birthday, Jeremy Fink receives a package from his dead father containing a locked box but no keys; Jeremy and Liz set off on a tour of New York City in search of the keys and meet a number of characters with different views on the meaning of life. (Rev: BL 12/15/06; SLJ 12/06)

8230 Matas, Carol. *Rosie in Los Angeles: Action!* (3–6). 2004, Simon & Schuster paper $4.99 (978-0-689-85716-4). 128pp. An action story set in California in the early 20th century and starring the same lively young Rosie as two earlier books. (Rev: SLJ 3/04)

8231 Mazer, Harry. *Snow Bound* (5–7). 1987, Dell $21.50 (978-0-8446-6240-4); paper $5.50 (978-0-440-96134-5). Tony and Cindy survive for several days after being trapped in a snow storm. (Rev: BL 9/1/89)

8232 Meacham, Margaret. *Oyster Moon* (3–6). Illus. by Marcy Ramsey. 1996, Cornell Maritime paper $9.95 (978-0-87033-459-7). 112pp. Anna, who is able to communicate through telepathy with her twin brother, Toby, receives messages indicating that he is in danger. (Rev: SLJ 11/96)

8233 Medearis, Angela Shelf. *The Spray-Paint Mystery* (3–5). 1996, Scholastic paper $2.99 (978-0-590-48474-9). 102pp. A young African American third-grader sets out to find the culprit who is spray-painting a wall in his school. (Rev: BL 2/15/97; SLJ 4/97)

8234 Miller, Kirsten. *Kiki Strike: Inside the Shadow City* (5–8). 2006, Bloomsbury $16.95 (978-1-58234-960-2). 250pp. A complex story featuring adventurous and multitalented 12-year-old girls exploring the subterranean levels of New York City. (Rev: BL 7/06; HBG 10/06; LMC 10/06; SLJ 6/06; VOYA 8/06)

8235 Miller, Kirsten. *Kiki Strike: The Empress's Tomb* (5–8). 2007, Bloomsbury $16.95 (978-1-59990-047-6). 369pp. Kiki and the Irregulars tackle assorted bad guys in this sequel to *Kiki Strike: Inside the Shadow City,* again set in the world under New York City. (Rev: SLJ 12/07)

8236 Milway, Alex. *The Mousehunter* (4–7). Illus. by author. 2009, Little, Brown $15.99 (978-0-316-02454-9). 422pp. Twelve-year-old Emiline is a mousekeeper in a world where many breeds of mice are prized, and she bravely sets out to defeat a pirate named Mousebeard. (Rev: BL 12/15/08; SLJ 3/09)

8237 Mitchelhill, Barbara. *The Graffiti Mystery* (2–4). Illus. by Tony Ross. Series: Damian Drooth Supersleuth. 2009, Stone Arch $17.99 (978-1-4342-1215-3). 72pp. A misspelling in the graffiti in the boys' bathroom leads Damian to hold a contest that will reveal the culprit; a funny, light story. (Rev: BL 5/1/09; LMC 10/09; SLJ 6/09)

8238 Mitchell, Marianne. *Finding Zola* (5–8). 2003, Boyds Mills $16.95 (978-1-59078-070-1). 144pp. A 13-year-old girl in a wheelchair investigates the disappearance of an elderly woman who has been staying with her. (Rev: BL 5/15/03; HBG 10/03; SLJ 2/03; VOYA 10/03)

8239 Mitchell, Marianne. *Firebug* (5–8). 2004, Boyds Mills $16.95 (978-1-59078-170-8). 164pp. Twelve-year-old Haley investigates a suspicious fire at her Uncle Jake's Arizona ranch. (Rev: BL 3/15/04; SLJ 2/04)

8240 Mitchell, Nancy. *Global Warning: Attack on the Pacific Rim!* (5–8). Illus. by Darren Wiebe and Ryan T. Fong. Series: The Changing Earth Trilogy. 1999, Lightstream paper $5.95 (978-1-892713-02-5). 191pp. A thrilling adventure story about Jenny Powers, a wheelchair-bound youngster, who must warn the authorities of an impending biological disaster at her school. (Rev: SLJ 10/99)

8241 Montgomery, Lewis B. *The Case of the Poisoned Pig.* Bk. 2 (1–4). Illus. by Amy Wummer. Series: Milo and Jazz Mysteries. 2009, Kane LB $22.60 (978-1-57565-289-4); paper $6.95 (978-1-57565-286-3). 96pp. Jazz's pig is sick and the veterinarian suspects poisoning; Milo and Jazz investigate. (Rev: SLJ 7/09)

8242 Montgomery, Lewis B. *The Case of the Stinky Socks* (2–4). Illus. by Amy Wummer. Series: Milo and Jazz Mysteries. 2009, Kane $22.60 (978-1-57565-288-7); paper $6.95 (978-1-57565-285-6). 96pp. Where are Jazz's brother's lucky socks? Milo and Jazz investigate in this first volume in a new early chapter-book series. (Rev: BL 5/1/09; SLJ 7/09)

8243 Morpurgo, Michael. *Kensuke's Kingdom* (4–7). 2003, Scholastic paper $16.95 (978-0-439-38202-1). 176pp. A boy washed onto a seemingly deserted island finds a friend in a Japanese soldier who has lived there since World War II. (Rev: BL 2/15/03; HB 5/03; HBG 10/03; SLJ 3/03; VOYA 6/03)

8244 Mundis, Hester. *My Chimp Friday* (4–7). 2002, Simon & Schuster $16.00 (978-0-689-83837-8). 176pp. Rachel and her family grow to love their new pet, a chimp named Friday, but when kidnappers try to steal Friday, Rachel realizes he is not an ordinary chimp. (Rev: BL 6/1–15/02; HBG 10/02; SLJ 6/02)

8245 Murphy, T. M. *The Secrets of Code Z* (4–8). Series: A Belltown Mystery. 2001, J. N. Townsend paper $9.95 (978-1-880158-33-3). 144pp. Orville Jacques becomes embroiled in a fast-paced mystery involving CIA cover-ups, a death powder, and an evil Russian. (Rev: BL 5/15/01; SLJ 7/01)

8246 Murrow, Liza Ketchum. *The Ghost of Lost Island* (4–6). 1991, Holiday House $16.95 (978-0-8234-0874-0). 176pp. Gabe and his sister try to solve the mystery of a drowned dairymaid on Lost Island. (Rev: BCCB 5/91; BL 4/15/91; SLJ 5/91)

8247 Napoli, Donna Jo. *North* (4–7). 2004, Greenwillow $16.99 (978-0-06-057987-6). 352pp. Twelve-year-old Alvin, an African American boy fascinated by explorer Matthew Henson, sets off for the Arctic and, with the help of several adults along the way, makes the long and complex journey safely. (Rev: BL 3/1/04; SLJ 5/04)

8248 Naylor, Phyllis Reynolds. *Bernie Magruder and the Bats in the Belfry* (4–7). 2003, Simon & Schuster $16.95 (978-0-689-85066-0). 144pp. Bernie is investigating a bat with a fatal bite; could it be connected to the fact that the bells in the belfry are annoyingly stuck on the same tune? (Rev: BL 1/1–15/03; HBG 10/03; SLJ 4/03)

8249 Nickerson, Sara. *How to Disappear Completely and Never Be Found* (4–8). Illus. by Sally Wern Comport. 2002, HarperCollins LB $17.89 (978-0-06-029772-5). 288pp. Two youngsters with problems, 12-year-old Margaret and her friend Boyd, explore a deserted mansion and solve the mystery of the supernatural terrors it supposedly contains.

(Rev: BCCB 5/02; BL 4/1/02; HB 7/02; HBG 10/02; SLJ 4/02)

8250 Nolan, Peggy. *The Spy Who Came in from the Sea* (4–8). 1999, Pineapple $14.95 (978-1-56164-186-4). 129pp. In this adventure story set in World War II Florida, 14-year-old Frank, who has a reputation for lying, is not believed when he claims to have seen a German sub off the coast. (Rev: HBG 3/00; SLJ 1/00)

8251 Nordin, Sofia. *In the Wild* (4–7). Trans. from Swedish by Maria Lundin. 2005, Groundwood $15.95 (978-0-88899-648-0). 119pp. Set in Sweden, this is an adventure story featuring 6th-grade outcast Amanda and bully Philip, who become lost and must rely on their own resources to survive. (Rev: SLJ 10/05)

8252 Obrist, Jürg. *Case Closed?! 40 Mini-Mysteries for You to Solve* (2–5). Illus. 2003, Millbrook LB $22.90 (978-0-7613-2739-4). 80pp. Readers help young detectives Daisy and Ridley solve mysteries involving puzzles, codes, and other challenges. (Rev: BL 2/15/04; HBG 4/04; SLJ 2/04)

8253 Obrist, Jürg. *Complex Cases: Three Major Mysteries for You to Solve* (3–6). Illus. by author. Series: Mini-Mysteries. 2006, Millbrook LB $23.93 (978-0-7613-3419-4); paper $6.95 (978-0-8225-5975-7). 93pp. This new volume in the series presents three longer mysteries, challenging readers to solve them using deduction and the clues in the many illustrations. (Rev: SLJ 6/06)

8254 O'Dell, Scott. *Black Star, Bright Dawn* (5–8). 1988, Houghton $18.00 (978-0-395-47778-6). 144pp. An Inuit girl decides to run the 1,197-mile sled dog race called the Iditarod. (Rev: BCCB 6/88; BL 4/1/88; SLJ 5/88; VOYA 6/88)

8255 O'Dell, Scott. *Island of the Blue Dolphins* (5–8). 1960, Houghton $16.00 (978-0-395-06962-2); Dell paper $6.50 (978-0-440-43988-2). 192pp. An Indian girl spends 18 years alone on an island off the coast of California in the 1800s. Newbery Medal winner, 1961. A sequel is *Zia* (1976). (Rev: BL 3/1/88)

8256 Oliver, Andrew. *If Photos Could Talk* (4–7). Series: A Sam and Stephanie Mystery. 2005, Adams-Pomeroy paper $12.95 (978-0-9661009-6-9). 259pp. Twelve-year-olds Sam and Stephanie investigate the disappearance of an elderly man in their small Wisconsin town in this well-plotted novel. (Rev: SLJ 1/06)

8257 Orr, Wendy. *Nim at Sea* (3–6). Illus. by Kerry Millard. 2008, Knopf LB $15.99 (978-0-385-90535-0). 128pp. When a dastardly poacher kidnaps her sea lion friend, Selkie, Nim and her family members each set out on individual rescue adventures. (Rev: BL 3/1/08; SLJ 5/08)

8258 Otis, James. *Toby Tyler: Or Ten Weeks with a Circus* (4–6). 1981, Buccaneer LB $25.95 (978-0-89966-363-0). 152pp. A perennial favorite about a subject popular with most children.

8259 Parkinson, Curtis. *Storm-Blast* (4–8). 2003, Tundra paper $7.95 (978-0-88776-630-5). 156pp. On a sailing trip in the Caribbean, three teens become stranded in a small dinghy and must use their resources to survive. (Rev: SLJ 10/03; VOYA 8/03)

8260 Patneaude, David. *The Last Man's Reward* (5–8). 1996, Albert Whitman LB $15.99 (978-0-8075-4370-2). 185pp. In this adventure, a group of boys agree to a pact rewarding the last to leave the neighborhood. (Rev: BL 6/1–15/96; SLJ 7/96)

8261 Paulsen, Gary. *Brian's Winter* (5–9). 1996, Delacorte $15.95 (978-0-385-32198-3). In a reworking of the ending of *Hatchet,* in which Brian Robeson is rescued after surviving a plane crash, this novel tells what would have happened had Brian had to survive a harsh winter in the wilderness. (Rev: BL 12/15/95; SLJ 2/96; VOYA 2/97)

8262 Paulsen, Gary. *Escape from Fire Mountain* (4–6). Series: Culpepper Adventure. 1995, Dell paper $3.99 (978-0-440-41025-6). 67pp. An adventure story in which a young girl faces incredible challenges to rescue two lost children. (Rev: SLJ 7/95)

8263 Paulsen, Gary. *The River* (5–10). 1991, Delacorte $15.95 (978-0-385-30388-0). In this sequel to *Hatchet,* Paulsen takes the wilderness adventure beyond self-preservation and makes teen Brian responsible for saving someone else. (Rev: BL 5/15/91)

8264 Pearson, Ridley. *The Challenge* (5–8). 2008, Disney $16.99 (978-1-4231-0640-1). 336pp. Steve is caught up in a terrorist kidnapping plot when he looks inside an abandoned briefcase in this fast-paced adventure. (Rev: BL 1/1–15/08; LMC 5/08)

8265 Philbrick, Rodman. *The Young Man and the Sea* (5–6). 2004, Scholastic $16.95 (978-0-439-36829-2). 192pp. With a nod to Hemingway, this is the story of Skiff, a 12-year-old boy living in Maine, who seeks to solve his problems by catching a giant bluefin tuna. (Rev: BL 1/1–15/04; HB 3/04; SLJ 2/04)

8266 Pilling, Ann. *The Year of the Worm* (5–7). 2000, Lion paper $7.50 (978-0-7459-4294-0). 172pp. Lonely Peter Wrigley, who is mourning his father's death, gets his chance to become a hero when he uncovers a group of birds'-nest poachers in this English novel set in the Lake District. (Rev: SLJ 3/01)

8267 Potter, Ellen. *Pish Posh* (4–6). 2006, Philomel $15.99 (978-0-399-23995-3). 240pp. Eleven-year-old Clara Frankofile is a horrible snob who rules the roost at her parents' posh New York City restaurant, but she finds herself in new territory when she investigates a mystery about the soup chef. (Rev: BL 2/1/06; SLJ 4/06)

8268 Pullman, Philip. *The Scarecrow and His Servant* (4–6). Illus. by Peter Bailey. 2005, Knopf $15.95 (978-0-375-81531-7). 240pp. A multilayered tale in which a scarecrow and his orphan-boy servant embark on a series of adventures. (Rev: BCCB 9/05; BL 9/1/05*; HB 9/05; LMC 1/06; SLJ 9/05)

8269 Quattlebaum, Mary. *Jackson Jones and the Curse of the Outlaw Rose* (3–5). 2006, Delacorte $14.95 (978-0-385-73349-6). 112pp. Jackson and friends, who garden in an inner-city community patch, tussle with mystery when a rose twig, removed from an old cemetery, seems to bring bad luck; the third installment in the series. (Rev: BL 1/1–15/07; SLJ 11/06)

8270 Ransome, Arthur. *Swallows and Amazons* (4–7). Illus. by author. 1985, Godine paper $14.95 (978-0-87923-573-4). 352pp. These adventures of the four Walker children have been read for many years. A reissue. Others in the series *Swallowdale* (1985); *Peter Duck* (1987).

8271 Ransome, Arthur. *Winter Holiday* (4–7). Illus. by author. 1989, Godine paper $14.95 (978-0-87923-661-8). Further adventures of the Swallows and Amazons. A reissue. A sequel is *Coot Club*.

8272 Rau, Dana Meachen. *One Giant Leap* (3–5). Illus. by Thomas Buchs. Series: Odyssey. 1996, Smithsonian Institution $14.95 (978-1-56899-343-0); paper $5.95 (978-1-58899-344-1). 32pp. The first moon landing is described in a fictional account in which a young boy believes he is Neil Armstrong. (Rev: BL 10/15/96)

8273 Repp, Gloria. *Mik-Shrok* (4–8). Illus. by Jim Brooks. 1998, Bob Jones Univ. paper $7.49 (978-1-57924-069-1). 133pp. A married missionary couple journey to a remote Alaska village in 1950, where they begin their work and, in time, acquire a dog team led by Mik-Shrok. (Rev: BL 3/1/99)

8274 Richardson, V. A. *The Moneylender's Daughter* (5–8). 2006, Bloomsbury $17.95 (978-1-58234-885-8). 300pp. In this exciting sequel to *The House of Windjammer* (2003), Adam Windjammer sets sail for America, finds himself burdened with more responsibility on the death of his uncle, and is pre-occupied with thoughts of Jade van Helsen, daughter of the man who brought his family to the brink of ruin. (Rev: BL 6/1–15/06; SLJ 9/06)

8275 Riehecky, Janet. *The Mystery of the Missing Money* (4–6). Illus. 1996, Forest House LB $12.95 (978-1-56674-087-6); paper $5.95 (978-1-56674-701-1). 120pp. Twins Karen and Kyle investigate strange lights and noises in an empty old house. (Rev: BL 7/96; SLJ 7/96)

8276 Riehecky, Janet. *The Mystery of the UFO* (4–6). Illus. 1996, Forest House LB $12.95 (978-1-56674-088-3); paper $6.95 (978-1-56674-702-8). 128pp. Rumors of UFO sightings bring twins Karen and Kyle to a campground to investigate. (Rev: BL 7/96; SLJ 7/96)

8277 Roberts, Willo Davis. *Baby-Sitting Is a Dangerous Job* (5–7). 1987, Fawcett paper $6.50 (978-0-449-70177-5). 192pp. Darcy tries to cope with three bratty children, but a kidnapping puts her and her charges in the hands of three dangerous men. (Rev: BCCB 3/85; BL 5/1/85; SLJ 5/85)

8278 Roberts, Willo Davis. *The One Left Behind* (4–7). 2006, Simon & Schuster $16.95 (978-0-689-85075-2). 144pp. Mandy, an 11-year-old mourning her dead twin sister, is accidentally left home alone for the weekend and pluckily investigates when there's a break-in downstairs. (Rev: BL 4/1/06; SLJ 5/06)

8279 Robinson, Mary. *The Amazing Valvano and the Mystery of the Hooded Rat* (4–6). 1990, Avon paper $2.75 (978-0-380-70713-3). 168pp. Maria's plans

for her great magic act go astray when Lester the rat is stolen. (Rev: BL 6/15/88; SLJ 4/88)

8280 Rocklin, Joanne. *Sonia Begonia* (4–6). Illus. by Julie Downing. 1986, Avon paper $2.50 (978-0-380-70307-4). 96pp. Sonia Begley wants to follow in her family's footsteps and open her own business, which she does with some amusing results. (Rev: BCCB 3/86; BL 3/15/86; SLJ 5/86)

8281 Rogan, S. Jones. *The Daring Adventures of Penhaligon Brush* (3–5). Illus. by Christian Slade. 2007, Knopf $15.99 (978-0-375-84344-0). 224pp. Heroic fox Penhaligon Brush finds himself on a mission to rescue his brother and an entire village from the evil paws of the feline Sir Derek in this humorous adventure with elements of mystery and romance. (Rev: BCCB 12/07; BL 11/15/07; LMC 11/07; SLJ 11/07)

8282 Rose, Malcolm. *Blood Brother* (4–7). Series: Traces. 2008, Kingfisher paper $5.95 (978-0-7534-6170-9). 219pp. Luke and his robot sidekick are investigating 26 mysterious deaths at York Hospital; could Luke's doctor father, the principal investigator on a clinical trial at the hospital, somehow be responsible? (Rev: BL 11/15/07)

8283 Rossell, Judith. *Jack Jones and the Pirate Curse* (4–7). 2007, Walker $15.95 (978-0-8027-9661-5). 176pp. Jack inherits the family curse and finds himself suddenly facing a band of vengeful pirates he knows he must fight with brain rather than brawn. (Rev: BL 4/1/07; SLJ 6/07)

8284 Roy, Ron. *The Deadly Dungeon* (2–4). Illus. by John S. Gurney. Series: A to Z Mysteries. 1998, Random LB $11.99 (978-0-679-98755-0); paper $3.99 (978-0-679-88755-3). 86pp. Dink, Josh, and Ruth Rose uncover a mystery when they travel to Maine to visit a castle. (Rev: SLJ 10/98)

8285 Roy, Ron. *The Goose's Gold* (2–4). Illus. by John S. Gurney. Series: Stepping Stone. 1999, Random paper $3.99 (978-0-679-89078-2). 86pp. An easy chapter book mystery in which three young sleuths overhear a man planning a robbery and set out to foil his plot. (Rev: BL 10/15/99; HBG 10/99; SLJ 7/99)

8286 Ruckman, Ivy. *Night of the Twisters* (4–6). 1984, HarperCollins LB $16.89 (978-0-690-04409-6); paper $5.99 (978-0-06-440176-0). 160pp. An 11-year-old boy witnesses a series of tornadoes that destroy his Nebraska town.

8287 Ruckman, Ivy. *Spell It M-U-R-D-E-R* (4–6). 1994, Bantam paper $3.50 (978-0-553-48175-4). 160pp. Two girls stumble upon a murderer when they try to escape from a summer camp they detest. (Rev: BL 7/94; SLJ 8/94)

8288 Runholt, Susan. *Rescuing Seneca Crane* (5–8). 2009, Viking $16.99 (978-0-670-06291-1). 288pp. Fourteen-year-old friends Kari and Lucas, first seen in *The Mystery of the Third Lucretia* (2008), are on a trip to Scotland and investigate the disappearance of a young piano player. (Rev: BLO 4/23/09)

8289 St. George, Judith. *The Ghost, The White House, and Me* (3–6). 2007, Holiday House $16.95 (978-0-8234-2045-2). 160pp. First daughters KayKay and Annie do their best to adapt to life in the less-than-homey White House and investigate some ghostly suspicions in the Lincoln bedroom while their mother is occupied with her presidential duties. (Rev: BCCB 2/08; BL 11/1/07; LMC 1/08; SLJ 11/07)

8290 Salisbury, Graham. *Night of the Howling Dogs* (5–8). 2007, Random $16.99 (978-0-385-73122-5). 208pp. Dylan, an 8th-grader from Hilo, Hawaii, goes on a trip to the coast with his scout troop to camp in the shadow of a volcano and faces a bully and natural disasters. (Rev: BL 8/07; HB 9/07; SLJ 8/07) ∩

8291 Santopolo, Jill. *The Nina, the Pinta, and the Vanishing Treasure* (3–5). Illus. by C. B. Canga. Series: Alec Flint. 2008, Scholastic $15.99 (978-0-439-90352-3). 208pp. With classmate Gina Rossi, 4th-grader Alec Flint investigates the disappearances of a Christopher Columbus exhibit and of the art teacher. (Rev: BL 5/1/08; LMC 10/08)

8292 Schade, Susan. *Faradawn* (3–5). Illus. by Jon Buller. Series: Fog Mound. 2007, Simon & Schuster $15.99 (978-0-689-87686-8). 208pp. Thelonious Chipmunk and his animal friends leave Fog Mound to explore further afield and perhaps find out what happened to the humans. (Rev: BL 9/15/07)

8293 Scieszka, Jon. *Knights of the Kitchen Table* (3–5). Illus. by Lane Smith. 1991, Viking $15.99 (978-0-670-83622-2). 64pp. The Time Warp Trio hangs out with Lancelot and his pals. Also use: *The Not-So-Jolly Roger* (1991). (Rev: BCCB 7–8/91; BL 5/1/91; SLJ 8/91*)

8294 Selznick, Brian. *The Invention of Hugo Cabret* (4–9). Illus. by author. 2007, Scholastic $22.99 (978-0-439-81378-5). 531pp. In 1930s Paris a young apprentice clock keeper, an orphan who struggles to make his way in life, finds himself drawn into a complex mystery that threatens the anonymity he treasures; part graphic novel, part flip book, the design is as compelling as the story. Caldecott Medal, 2008. (Rev: BL 1/1–15/07; SLJ 3/07*)

8295 Shahan, Sherry. *Death Mountain* (5–8). 2005, Peachtree $15.95 (978-1-56145-353-5). 178pp. In this gripping thriller, 14-year-old Erin uses her survival skills to rescue her new friend Mae and navigate their way through a mountain wilderness to safety. (Rev: SLJ 11/05; VOYA 2/06)

8296 Shands, Linda. *Wild Fire* (4–6). 2001, Revell paper $5.99 (978-0-8007-5746-5). 176pp. Wakara, a 15-year-old of American Indian and Irish parentage, is still mourning her mother's death when she and her brother become trapped by a forest fire. (Rev: BL 5/1/01)

8297 Shearer, Alex. *Sea Legs* (4–6). 2005, Simon & Schuster $15.95 (978-0-689-87143-6). 320pp. Twins Clive and Eric stow away on the cruise sip where their father works and end up fighting pirates in this entertaining story. (Rev: BL 3/15/05; SLJ 3/05)

8298 Shura, Mary Francis. *Don't Call Me Toad!* (4–6). Illus. by Jacqueline Rogers. 1987, Avon paper $2.95 (978-0-380-70496-5). Jane and Dinah have a rocky relationship at first and become

involved in a mystery about robberies that sweep a town. (Rev: BCCB 7–8/87; BL 5/15/87; SLJ 4/87)

8299 Simner, Janni Lee. *Secret of the Three Treasures* (3–5). 2006, Holiday $16.95 (978-0-8234-1914-2). 134pp. The irrepressible Tiernay, emulating her novelist father's heroes, sets out with her mother's boyfriend's son in search of buried treasure and finds herself in real danger; a humorous multilayered story that also tackles bullying and genealogy. (Rev: BL 5/1/06; SLJ 8/06)

8300 Simon, Seymour. *The On-Line Spaceman and Other Cases* (3–6). Illus. 1997, Morrow $14.95 (978-0-688-14433-3). 96pp. Using deduction and an advanced knowledge of science, 12-year-old Einstein Anderson solves ten short mysteries. (Rev: BL 5/1/97; SLJ 4/97)

8301 Singh, Vandana. *Younguncle Comes to Town* (3–5). Illus. by B. M. Kamath. 2006, Viking $14.99 (978-0-670-06051-1). 112pp. Three siblings in northern India are captivated by the real-life adventures of Younguncle, their father's youngest brother. (Rev: BL 4/1/06; SLJ 5/06)

8302 Skurzynski, Gloria, and Alane Ferguson. *Buried Alive* (4–7). Series: Mysteries in Our National Parks. 2003, National Geographic $15.95 (978-0-7922-6966-3). 146pp. A hit man and an avalanche are only two of the challenges Jack and Ashley face while on vacation with their parents in Denali National Park. (Rev: HBG 10/03; SLJ 12/03)

8303 Skurzynski, Gloria, and Alane Ferguson. *Cliff-Hanger* (4–7). Series: Mysteries in Our National Parks. 1999, National Geographic $15.95 (978-0-7922-7036-2). 152pp. In Mesa Verde National Park, the Landon family encounters two problems — a foster care girl named Lucky, who is deceitful, and a rampaging cougar. (Rev: BL 4/15/99; HBG 10/99; SLJ 5/99)

8304 Skurzynski, Gloria, and Alane Ferguson. *Deadly Waters* (4–7). Illus. Series: Mysteries in Our National Parks. 1999, National Geographic $15.95 (978-0-7922-7037-9). 160pp. The Landon kids — Jack, Ashley, and foster brother, Bridger — travel to the Florida Everglades where their parents are investigating the mysterious deaths of some manatees. (Rev: BL 10/15/99; HBG 3/00; SLJ 10/99)

8305 Skurzynski, Gloria, and Alane Ferguson. *Ghost Horses* (4–6). Illus. Series: National Parks Mystery. 2000, National Geographic $15.95 (978-0-7922-7055-3). 152pp. Horses that are behaving strangely, a flash flood, and interpersonal conflicts are three of the elements in this mystery story set in Utah's Zion National Park. (Rev: BL 12/15/00; HBG 3/01; SLJ 11/00)

8306 Skurzynski, Gloria, and Alane Ferguson. *The Hunted* (5–8). Illus. Series: Mysteries in Our National Parks. 2000, National Geographic $15.95 (978-0-7922-7053-9). 160pp. The Landon family sets out to discover why young grizzly bears are disappearing from Glacier National Park. (Rev: BL 6/1–15/00; HBG 10/00; SLJ 8/00)

8307 Skurzynski, Gloria, and Alane Ferguson. *Rage of Fire* (4–6). Illus. Series: National Parks Mystery. 1998, National Geographic $15.95 (978-0-7922-

7035-5). 160pp. While visiting Devastation Trail in Hawaii Volcanoes National Park, Jack Landon, his sister, and their friend, a Vietnamese youngster, realize they are being stalked by a mysterious woman in red. (Rev: BL 6/1–15/98; HBG 10/98; SLJ 7/98)

8308 Skurzynski, Gloria, and Alane Ferguson. *Wolf Stalker* (5–8). Series: Mysteries in Our National Parks. 1997, National Geographic $15.00 (978-0-7922-7034-8). Three youngsters solve the mystery of who is killing the wolves of Yellowstone Park. (Rev: HBG 3/98; SLJ 1/98)

8309 Smith, Roland. *Cryptid Hunters* (5–8). 2005, Hyperion $15.99 (978-0-7868-5161-4). 352pp. Thirteen-year-old twins Marty and Grace find themselves in an action-packed adventure in the Congo. (Rev: BL 2/1/05; SLJ 5/05)

8310 Smith, Roland. *Jack's Run* (5–8). 2005, Hyperion $15.99 (978-0-7868-5592-6). 288pp. Last seen adapting to being in the witness protection program in *Zach's Lie* (2001), Jack and Joanne are now in danger after Joanne has blown their cover in this fast-paced, suspenseful story. (Rev: BL 8/05; SLJ 12/05; VOYA 10/05)

8311 Snicket, Lemony. *The Ersatz Elevator* (3–6). Illus. Series: A Series of Unfortunate Events. 2001, HarperCollins LB $15.89 (978-0-06-028889-1). 266pp. Count Olaf soon finds the Baudelaire orphans at their new home, chez Mr. and Mrs. Squalor. (Rev: BL 8/01; HBG 10/01; SLJ 8/01)

8312 Snicket, Lemony. *The Hostile Hospital* (4–6). Illus. by Brett Helquist. Series: A Series of Unfortunate Events. 2001, HarperCollins LB $15.89 (978-0-06-028891-4). 272pp. The Baudelaire children face danger and intrigue in their quest to find out more about their dead parents. (Rev: BL 10/15/01; HBG 3/02; SLJ 11/01)

8313 Snicket, Lemony. *The Miserable Mill* (4–6). Series: A Series of Unfortunate Events. 2000, HarperCollins LB $15.89 (978-0-06-028315-5). 128pp. The unfortunate Baudelaire orphans are forced to work in a lumber mill in this entertaining segment of the ongoing melodrama set in mock-Victorian times. (Rev: BL 5/1/00; HBG 10/00; SLJ 7/00)

8314 Snicket, Lemony. *The Slippery Slope* (3–5). Illus. by Brett Helquist. 2003, HarperCollins LB $15.89 (978-0-06-029641-4). 337pp. In this episode in the continuing saga, Violet and Klaus get help from a stranger as they seek to free Sunny from the clutches of Count Olaf and find the "last safe place." (Rev: BL 1/1–15/04; HBG 4/04; SLJ 1/04)

8315 Snicket, Lemony. *The Vile Village* (3–6). Illus. Series: A Series of Unfortunate Events. 2001, HarperCollins LB $15.89 (978-0-06-028890-7). 272pp. Aphorisms abound as a village decides to raise three children and takes on the Baudelaire orphans. (Rev: BL 8/01; HBG 3/02; SLJ 8/01)

8316 Snyder, Zilpha Keatley. *The Treasures of Weatherby* (4–6). 2007, Simon & Schuster $15.95 (978-1-4169-1398-6). 213pp. Harleigh J. Weatherby, IV, an undersized 12-year-old, makes friends with Allegra, a mysterious stranger, and together

they set out to foil a plot to steal the long-lost Weatherby treasure. (Rev: SLJ 2/07)

8317 Sobol, Donald J. *Encyclopedia Brown and the Case of the Jumping Frogs* (4–6). Illus. 2003, Delacorte $14.95 (978-0-385-72931-4). 96pp. The 10-year-old sleuth cracks another bunch of not-so-easy cases in this new entry in a long series. (Rev: BL 2/1/04; HBG 4/04)

8318 Sobol, Donald J. *Encyclopedia Brown and the Case of the Mysterious Handprints* (3–5). Illus. 1985, Morrow $15.99 (978-0-688-04626-2). 96pp. Matching wits with the 10-year-old sleuth in ten more crime cases. Also use: *Encyclopedia Brown and the Case of the Secret Pitch* (1978, Bantam); *Encyclopedia Brown Lends a Hand* (1979, Dutton); *Encyclopedia Brown and the Case of the Treasure Hunt* (1988). (Rev: BL 11/15/85; SLJ 2/86)

8319 Soto, Gary. *Crazy Weekend* (4–7). 1994, Scholastic paper $13.95 (978-0-590-47814-4). 143pp. Two boys are being pursued by some crooks in this fast-moving adventure story. (Rev: BCCB 7–8/94; SLJ 3/94)

8320 Sperry, Armstrong. *Call It Courage* (5–8). Illus. by author. 1968, Macmillan $16.95 (978-0-02-786030-6); paper $4.99 (978-0-689-71391-0). 96pp. The "Crusoe" theme is interwoven with this story of a Polynesian boy's courage in facing the sea he feared. Newbery Medal winner, 1941.

8321 Spirn, Michele. *The Bridges in London: Going to London* (5–7). Series: Going To. 2000, Four Corners paper $7.95 (978-1-893577-00-8). 96pp. When two sisters fly to London with their parents, they become involved in a mystery when they find a suitcase full of knives. (Rev: SLJ 3/00)

8322 Spizman, Robyn Freedman, and Mark Johnston. *The Secret Agents Strike Back* (5–8). 2007, Simon & Schuster $16.99 (978-1-4169-0086-3). 152pp. Information about a possible cure for cancer is stolen and Kyle and his friends chase clues all over New York City in this entertaining mystery. (Rev: SLJ 6/07)

8323 Springer, Nancy. *The Case of the Cryptic Crinoline* (5–8). Series: Enola Holmes Mystery. 2009, Philomel $14.99 (978-0-399-24781-1). 176pp. Florence Nightingale may be able to help Sherlock's younger sister Enola Holmes as she investigates the disappearance of her landlady. (Rev: BLO 4/23/09; SLJ 7/09)

8324 Springer, Nancy. *The Case of the Missing Marquess: An Enola Holmes Mystery* (5–8). Series: Enola Holmes. 2006, Philomel paper $10.99 (978-0-399-24304-2). 224pp. Enola Holmes, the much younger sister of Sherlock and Mycroft, embarks on a search for her mother, who disappears on Enola's 14th birthday. (Rev: BCCB 2/06; BL 12/1/05*; HBG 10/06; SLJ 2/06*)

8325 Springer, Nancy. *Lionclaw* (5–8). Series: Tales of Rowan Hood. 2002, Putnam $16.99 (978-0-399-23716-4). 128pp. Gentle, music-loving Lionel abandons his timidity when Rowan Hood is captured, but, despite his newfound courage, his father still refuses to accept him in this sequel to *Rowan Hood:*

Outlaw Girl of Sherwood Forest (2001). (Rev: BL 10/1/02; HBG 10/03; SLJ 10/02; VOYA 12/02)

8326 Springer, Nancy. *Outlaw Princess of Sherwood* (4–7). Series: Tales of Rowan Hood. 2003, Putnam $16.99 (978-0-399-23721-8). 160pp. The third installment of this series features Princess Ettarde, whose father has hatched a dastardly plot to lure Etty away from Sherwood Forest. (Rev: BL 12/1/03; HBG 4/04; SLJ 9/03)

8327 Stanley, Diane. *The Mysterious Case of the Allbright Academy* (4–7). 2008, HarperCollins $15.99 (978-0-06-085817-9). 272pp. What's going on at Allbright Academy? Frannie suspects that her "perfect" classmates are being brainwashed and placed into positions of authority in the U.S. government, and she sets out to foil the plot. (Rev: BL 11/15/07; SLJ 3/08)

8328 Stanley, George E. *The Clue of the Left-Handed Envelope* (2–3). Illus. by Sal Murdocca. Series: Third-Grade Detectives. 2000, Simon & Schuster paper $3.99 (978-0-689-82194-3). 80pp. Noelle and Todd together with the other third graders and their teacher, Mr. Merlin, unmask the identity of the person who has sent Amber Lee a secret-admirer letter. (Rev: BCCB 12/00; SLJ 2/01)

8329 Stead, Rebecca. *When You Reach Me* (4–7). 2009, Random $15.99 (978-0-385-73742-5). 208pp. New York City — 1978. Sixth-grader Miranda receives notes from someone she believes knows the future. (Rev: BCCB 9/09; BL 6/1–15/09; HB 7/09; SLJ 7/09)

8330 Steiner, Barbara. *Foghorn Flattery and the Dancing Horses* (4–6). 1991, Avon paper $2.95 (978-0-380-76147-0). 108pp. Carly and brother Foghorn travel to Vienna and encounter a mystery. (Rev: BL 6/15/91)

8331 Stem, Jacqueline. *The Cellar in the Woods* (4–6). 1997, Eakin $14.95 (978-1-57168-115-7). 145pp. In East Texas, three cousins explore a deserted house and encounter danger. (Rev: SLJ 1/98)

8332 Stengel, Joyce A. *Mystery of the Island Jewels* (5–8). 2002, Simon & Schuster paper $4.99 (978-0-689-85049-3). 199pp. On a cruise to Martinique with her father and new stepfamily, 14-year-old Cassie and new friend Charles uncover a mystery. (Rev: SLJ 6/02)

8333 Stenhouse, Ted. *Murder on the Ridge* (5–8). 2006, Kids Can $16.95 (978-1-55337-892-1); paper $6.95 (978-1-55337-893-8). 240pp. Will and Arthur, a white boy and an Indian boy who are friends despite the prejudices of 1950s Canada, investigate a World War I mystery in the latest installment in the series that started with *Across the Steel River* (2001) and *A Dirty Deed* (2003). (Rev: BL 5/15/06)

8334 Stevenson, Robert Louis. *Treasure Island* (5–9). Adapted and illus. by Tim Hamilton. Series: Puffin Graphics. 2005, Puffin paper $10.99 (978-0-14-240470-6). 176pp. Robert Louis Stevenson's adventure classic springs to life in this striking graphic novel adaptation that remains faithful to the original text. (Rev: SLJ 11/05)

8335 Stevenson, Robert Louis. *Treasure Island* (5–9). Illus. by N. C. Wyeth. Series: Scribner Storybook Classic. 2003, Simon & Schuster $18.95 (978-0-689-85468-2). 64pp. This picture-book adaptation of the classic story features beautiful paintings by N. C. Wyeth. (Rev: BL 8/03; HBG 4/04)

8336 Stevenson, Robin. *Dead in the Water* (5–8). Series: Orca Sports. 2008, Orca paper $9.95 (978-1-55143-962-4). 176pp. While at sea as part of a sailing camp, Simon ends up a captive on a boat full of poachers in this thriller for reluctant readers. (Rev: BL 3/15/08)

8337 Stewart, Trenton Lee. *The Mysterious Benedict Society and the Perilous Journey* (4–7). Illus. by Diana Sudyka. Series: The Mysterious Benedict Society. 2008, Little, Brown $16.99 (978-0-316-05780-6). 440pp. Reynie, Kate, Sticky, and Constance have many adventures as they travel to rescue Mr. Benedict from the evil Mr. Curtain in this action-packed sequel to *The Mysterious Benedict Society* (2007). (Rev: BL 3/15/08; SLJ 5/08)

8338 Stine, R. L. *The Wrong Number* (5–9). 1990, Pocket paper $4.99 (978-0-671-69411-1). While making a crank telephone call, a teenager hears a murder being committed. (Rev: SLJ 6/90)

8339 Stolz, Mary. *Casebook of a Private (Cat's) Eye* (3–5). Illus. 1999, Front St. $14.95 (978-0-8126-2650-6). 128pp. Eileen O'Kelly, a cat detective from Boston, solves a number of short mysteries in this novel set in 1912. (Rev: BCCB 6/99; BL 4/15/99; HBG 10/99; SLJ 6/99)

8340 Strickland, Brad. *The House Where Nobody Lived* (5–8). Series: Lewis Barnavelt. 2006, Dial $16.99 (978-0-8037-3148-6). 176pp. Lewis befriends David, whose family has moved into a creepy, long-abandoned house, which may be haunted; with help from Uncle Jonathan and a neighborhood witch, Lewis confronts magic and danger. (Rev: BL 1/1–15/07; SLJ 1/07)

8341 Sukach, Jim. *Clever Quicksolve Whodunit Puzzles* (4–7). Illus. by Lucy Corvino. Series: Mini-Mysteries for You to Solve. 1999, Sterling $14.95 (978-0-8069-6569-7). 96pp. Thirty-five mini-mysteries are presented with answers appended. (Rev: SLJ 1/00)

8342 Tate, Nikki. *Venom* (5–8). 2009, Orca paper $9.95 (978-1-55469-071-8). 176pp. For reluctant readers, this suspenseful story set in the world of horse racing features 16-year-old Spencer, who challenges dangerous forces when he suspects the use of illegal drugs. (Rev: BL 5/1/09)

8343 Taylor, Cora. *Murder in Mexico* (4–7). Series: The Spy Who Wasn't There. 2007, Coteau paper $7.95 (978-1-55050-353-1). 162pp. In this second, fast-paced installment in the mystery series, twins Jennifer and Maggie are visiting ruins in the Yucatan when Jennifer must use her ability to become invisible to solve a crime. (Rev: SLJ 4/07)

8344 Taylor, Theodore. *The Cay* (5–8). 1987, Doubleday $16.95 (978-0-385-07906-8); Avon paper $4.95 (978-0-380-00142-2). 160pp. A blind boy and an old black sailor are shipwrecked on a coral island. (Rev: BL 9/1/89)

8345 Taylor, Theodore. *Ice Drift* (4–7). 2005, Harcourt $16.00 (978-0-15-205081-8). 240pp. Inuit brothers Alika, 14, and Sulu, 10, struggle to survive over the months that they are trapped on an ice floe that is slowly floating south in the Greenland Strait. (Rev: BL 2/1/05; SLJ 1/05)

8346 Taylor, William. *Numbskulls* (4–6). 1995, Scholastic $14.95 (978-0-590-22629-5). 144pp. To help his younger sister, Chas submits to the ordeal of being placed in evil Alice's learning machine. A sequel to *Knitwits* (1992). (Rev: BL 10/15/95; SLJ 10/95)

8347 Thomas, Jane Resh. *Courage at Indian Deep* (5–7). 1984, Houghton paper $6.95 (978-0-395-55699-3). 128pp. A young boy must help save a ship caught in a sudden storm.

8348 Thomas, Jane Resh. *Fox in a Trap* (3–5). Illus. by Troy Howell. 1987, Houghton paper $5.95 (978-0-395-54426-6). 96pp. Daniel changes his mind about trapping once he accompanies his Uncle Pete. (Rev: BCCB 4/87; BL 4/1/87; SLJ 6–7/87)

8349 Thompson, Kate. *Highway Robbery* (4–7). Illus. by Robert Dress. 2009, HarperCollins $15.99 (978-0-06-173034-4). 128pp. This story with a folktale feel features a boy who waits all the long night for the return of a horse's owner. (Rev: BCCB 7–8/09; BL 6/1–15/09; HB 7/09; SLJ 6/09)

8350 Torrey, Michele. *The Case of the Mossy Lake Monster and Other Super-Scientific Cases* (3–5). Illus. by Barbara Johansen Newman. Series: Doyle and Fossey, Science Detectives. 2002, Dutton $14.99 (978-0-525-46815-8). 112pp. Fifth-graders Drake Doyle and Nell Fossey solve a string of mysteries using scientific reasoning in this easy-to-read second book in the series. (Rev: BL 1/1–15/02; HBG 10/02; SLJ 2/02)

8351 Torrey, Michele. *Voyage of Ice* (4–7). Series: Chronicle of Courage. 2004, Knopf LB $17.99 (978-0-375-92381-4). 192pp. In 1851, 15-year-old Nick signs on as a hand aboard the whaler *Sea Hawk* and soon discovers unexpected hardships, including struggling to survive in the Arctic. (Rev: BL 5/15/04; SLJ 7/04)

8352 Trembath, Don. *Emville Confidential* (5–8). 2007, Orca paper $8.95 (978-1-55143-671-5). 192pp. A tongue-in-cheek hard-boiled detective novel featuring 7th-graders Baron, Myles, and Rebecca. (Rev: BL 11/1/07; SLJ 2/08)

8353 Trout, Richard E. *Czar of Alaska: The Cross of Charlemagne* (5–8). Series: MacGregor Family Adventure. 2005, Pelican $15.95 (978-1-58980-328-2). 248pp. In volume four of the series, the five MacGregors travel to Alaska to assess the environmental impact of drilling for oil and become entangled with ecoterrorists and priests seeking an ancient cross. (Rev: SLJ 12/05)

8354 Tuitel, Johnnie, and Sharon Lamson. *The Barn at Gun Lake* (4–6). Series: The Gun Lake Adventure. 1999, Cedar Tree paper $5.99 (978-0-9658075-0-0). 103pp. Wheelchair-bound Johnnie, who has cerebral palsy, stumbles onto a CD-pirating ring and tries to find its leader. Also use *Mystery Explosion!* (1999). (Rev: SLJ 8/99)

8355 Twain, Mark. *The Stolen White Elephant* (4–8). Illus. 1882, Ayer $19.95 (978-0-8369-3486-1). The tale of the elephant's guardian who naively is impressed by a corrupt police detective. (Rev: BL 5/1/88; SLJ 2/88)

8356 Umansky, Kaye. *Solomon Snow and the Stolen Jewel* (4–7). 2007, Candlewick $12.99 (978-0-7636-2793-5). 256pp. In this sequel to *Solomon Snow and the Silver Spoon* (2005), Solomon and Prudence set out to help Prudence's father escape from a prison ship and become caught up in a plot to steal a cursed ruby. (Rev: BL 4/15/07; SLJ 7/07)

8357 Updike, David. *A Spring Story* (3–5). Illus. by Robert Andrew Parker. 1989, Pippin LB $15.95 (978-0-945912-06-4). 40pp. When spring comes, the ice breaks up and two adventurous boys are stranded on an ice floe. (Rev: BCCB 3/90; BL 1/15/90; SLJ 1/90)

8358 Valgardson, W. D. *Winter Rescue* (4–6). Illus. by Ange Zhang. 1995, Simon & Schuster paper $15.00 (978-0-689-80094-8). An adventure story that involves a young boy and the Icelandic-Canadian fishermen around Lake Winnipeg. (Rev: BCCB 12/95; SLJ 11/95)

8359 Van Draanen, Wendelin. *The Greatest Power* (3–5). Illus. by Stephen Gilpin. 2009, Knopf $12.99 (978-0-375-84377-8). 208pp. Dave, 13, and his sidekick gecko Sticky investigate a bank robbery by the evil Damien Black. (Rev: BL 5/1/09; LMC 10/09; SLJ 4/09)

8360 Van Draanen, Wendelin. *Sammy Keyes and the Art of Deception* (5–8). Series: Sammy Keyes. 2003, Knopf $15.95 (978-0-375-81176-0). 272pp. Sammy (with some help from Grams) solves a mystery involving an art thief. (Rev: BL 2/1/03; HBG 10/03; SLJ 3/03; VOYA 8/03)

8361 Van Draanen, Wendelin. *Sammy Keyes and the Dead Giveaway* (5–8). 2005, Knopf LB $17.99 (978-0-375-92350-0). 304pp. Seventh-grade sleuth Sammy tackles personal problems — should she make a confession that would exonerate her archenemy? — and community ones as she investigates abuse of eminent domain. (Rev: BL 9/1/05; SLJ 11/05)

8362 Van Draanen, Wendelin. *Shredderman: Meet the Gecko* (3–5). 2005, Knopf LB $14.99 (978-0-375-92353-1). 176pp. Nerdy Nolan Byrd assumes his Shredderman superhero persona to help a young TV star chase off a pesky reporter. (Rev: BL 2/1/05; SLJ 1/05)

8363 Vazquez, Diana. *Lost in Sierra* (4–6). Illus. by German Jaramillo. 2002, Coteau paper $7.95 (978-1-55050-184-1). 173pp. On a visit to Spain, 13-year-old Ana discovers why her grandmother's brother never came back from Spain's civil war. (Rev: SLJ 8/02)

8364 Walden, Mark. *H.I.V.E: The Higher Institute of Villainous Education* (5–8). Series: H.I.V.E. 2007, Simon & Schuster $15.99 (978-1-4169-3571-1). 320pp. Kidnapped along with three of his friends and enrolled in an academy that grooms students in the villainous arts, 13-year-old brilliant orphan Otto maps a plan to escape, a feat never before accomplished. (Rev: BL 4/1/07; SLJ 6/07)

8365 Walden, Mark. *H.I.V.E: The Overlord Protocol* (5–8). Series: H.I.V.E. 2008, Simon & Schuster $15.99 (978-1-4169-6016-4). 384pp. Wing and Otto, students at the Higher Institute of Villainous Education (H.I.V.E.), travel to Japan for Wing's father's funeral and realize they have fallen into an evil trap. (Rev: BL 3/1/08)

8366 Wallace, Bill. *Blackwater Swamp* (4–6). Illus. 1994, Holiday House $16.95 (978-0-8234-1120-7). 185pp. A woman, known by all to be a witch, helps Ted catch a group of crooks responsible for some local robberies. (Rev: BCCB 5/94; BL 6/1–15/94; SLJ 4/94)

8367 Wallace, Bill. *Danger in Quicksand Swamp* (4–7). 1989, Holiday $16.95 (978-0-8234-0786-6). 181pp. While searching for buried treasure, Ben and Jake become stranded on an island near Quicksand Swamp. (Rev: BL 1/1/90; SLJ 10/89)

8368 Wallace, Bill. *Trapped in Death Cave* (5–8). 1984, Holiday $16.95 (978-0-8234-0516-9). 176pp. Gary is convinced his grandpa was murdered to secure a map indicating where gold is buried.

8369 Wallace, Karen. *The Secret of the Crocodiles* (4–6). Series: Lady Violet's Casebook. 2008, Simon & Schuster paper $9.95 (978-0-689-87483-3). 236pp. Lady Violet is a teen at the turn of the 20th century and in this volume travels with her family, governess, and pet monkey to Egypt, where they become entangled in intrigues and Violet longs for more freedom. (Rev: BL 7/08)

8370 Walters, Eric. *Northern Exposures* (5–8). 2008, Fitzhenry & Whiteside paper $11.95 (978-1-55455-107-1). 298pp. In this fast-paced novel, a 13-year-old boy finds himself on an adventure when he wins a trip to photograph polar bears and gets involved with poachers; this will appeal to reluctant readers. (Rev: SLJ 2/09)

8371 Weir, Joan. *The Mysterious Visitor* (5–7). Series: Lion and Bobbi. 2002, Raincoast paper $6.99 (978-1-55192-404-5). 176pp. Two Canadian youngsters, Lion and sister Bobbi, try to solve the mystery of strange events occurring on a friend's land. (Rev: BL 5/1/02)

8372 Weltman, June. *Mystery of the Missing Candlestick* (5–8). 2004, Mayhaven $23.95 (978-1-878044-98-3). 216pp. Miranda, 17, and her friends Leila and Rebecca join forces to solve the mystery of a valuable antique candlestick that has been stolen from Rebecca's grandfather. (Rev: BL 5/1/04)

8373 White, Ruth. *The Search for Belle Prater* (4–7). 2005, Farrar $16.00 (978-0-374-30853-7). 176pp. In this sequel to *Belle Prater's Boy,* 13-year-old Woodrow and his cousin Gypsy continue to search for Woodrow's missing mother against the backdrop of mid-1950s segregation. (Rev: BL 2/15/05*; SLJ 4/05)

8374 Wilson, Barbara. *A Clear Spring* (4–6). 2002, Feminist paper $12.50 (978-1-55861-277-8). 176pp. While working at a nature center with her aunt's lesbian partner, Willa teams up with her cousins to track down polluters. (Rev: BL 7/02; HBG 10/02)

8375 Wilson, Eric. *Murder on the Canadian: A Tom Austen Mystery* (4–8). Illus. by Richard Row. 2000, Orca paper $4.99 (978-1-55143-151-2). 95pp. A fast-moving mystery starring an intrepid hero who is also featured in *Vancouver Nightmare: A Tom Austen Mystery* (2000). (Rev: SLJ 1/01)

8376 Wilson, N. D. *Leepike Ridge* (4–7). 2007, Random $15.99 (978-0-375-83873-6). 240pp. Eleven-year-old Tom must use his survival skills when he finds himself trapped in a series of caves where he meets Reg, who's been trapped for three years, and discovers mysterious carvings on the wall. (Rev: BL 5/15/07; HB 5/07; LMC 10/07; SLJ 5/07)

8377 Woodruff, Elvira. *Ghosts Don't Get Goose Bumps* (4–6). Illus. by Joel Iskowitz. 1993, Holiday House $16.95 (978-0-8234-1035-4). 96pp. On her visit to West Virginia, Jenna befriends an impish girl and is soon involved in a haunted marble factory and a mysterious disappearance. (Rev: BL 11/15/93; SLJ 10/93)

8378 Wright, Betty R. *The Dollhouse Murders* (4–7). 1983, Holiday $16.95 (978-0-8234-0497-1). 160pp. Dolls in a dollhouse come to life in this mystery about long-ago murders.

8379 Wright, Betty R. *Princess for a Week* (3–5). Illus. by Jacqueline Rogers. 2006, Holiday $16.95 (978-0-8234-1945-6). 105pp. Roddy is already stressed when an overbearing girl called Princess comes to stay; she persuades him to investigate the goings-on at an abandoned house nearby. (Rev: BL 5/1/06; SLJ 5/06)

8380 Wright, Susan K. *Dead Letters* (4–6). Series: Dead-End Road Mysteries. 1996, Herald paper $6.99 (978-0-8361-9036-6). 176pp. Nellie and her friends set out to catch the culprit who is stealing mail from the boxes outside the Lucky Clover trailer park. (Rev: SLJ 9/96)

8381 Wyss, Johann D. *Swiss Family Robinson* (4–6). Illus. by Lynd Ward. 1949, Putnam $19.99 (978-0-448-06022-4). 400pp. The classic story of a shipwrecked family is presented for a younger audience.

8382 Yep, Laurence. *The Case of the Firecrackers* (4–7). 1999, HarperCollins LB $15.89 (978-0-06-024452-1). 144pp. In this Chinatown mystery, Tiger Lil and her great-niece Lily are on the trail of the murderer who killed the star of the television show in which they were extras. (Rev: BL 9/15/99; HBG 3/00; SLJ 9/99)

8383 Yep, Laurence. *The Case of the Lion Dance* (4–6). Series: Chinatown Mystery. 1998, HarperCollins LB $15.89 (978-0-06-024448-4). 224pp. Lily and her great aunt Tiger Lil, a public relations expert, try to find out who is responsible for ruining the opening of a new restaurant and stealing money meant for a charity. (Rev: BL 10/15/98; HBG 3/99; SLJ 11/98)

8384 Young, E. L. *The Black Sphere* (5–8). Illus. Series: STORM. 2009, Dial $16.99 (978-0-8037-3268-1). 320pp. Three 14-year-olds — Andrew, Will, and Gaia — save the day in this thriller featuring high-tech intrigue and budding romance. (Rev: BL 2/1/09; SLJ 9/09; VOYA 3/09)

8385 Young, E. L. *The Infinity Code* (5–8). 2008, Dial $16.99 (978-0-8037-3265-0). 336pp. Young computer whizzes Andrew, Will, Gaia, and Caspian make up the group STORM ("Science and Technology to Over-Rule Misery") and find themselves in a tech-driven battle against a group that has kidnapped Caspian's father. (Rev: BL 3/1/08; SLJ 5/08)

8386 Zambreno, Mary F. *Journeyman Wizard* (4–7). 1994, Harcourt $16.95 (978-0-15-200022-6). 240pp. Student wizard Jeremy is studying the casting of spells with Lady Allons when an unfortunate death occurs and he is accused of murder. (Rev: BL 5/1/94; SLJ 6/94)

Animal Stories

8387 Adler, C. S. *More Than a Horse* (5–7). 1997, Clarion $15.00 (978-0-395-79769-3). 192pp. Leeann and her mother move to a dude ranch in Arizona, where the young girl develops a love of horses. (Rev: BCCB 3/97; BL 3/15/97; SLJ 4/97)

8388 Adler, C. S. *One Unhappy Horse* (5–7). 2001, Clarion $16.00 (978-0-618-04912-7). 155pp. Set on a small ranch near Tucson, this novel features 12-year-old Jan, her horse, Dove, an old lady in a retirement home, and Jan's new friend, Lisa. (Rev: BL 3/1/01; HBG 10/01; SLJ 4/01)

8389 Ahlberg, Allan. *Half a Pig* (3–5). Trans. by Allan Ahlberg and Jessica Ahlberg. Illus. by Jessica Ahlberg. 2004, Candlewick $16.99 (978-0-7636-2373-9). 40pp. An amusing story of a married couple's conflict over the fate of their jointly owned pig, Esmeralda, also serves as the basis for tips on language and use of words. (Rev: BL 8/04; HB 7/04; SLJ 8/04)

8390 Alter, Judith. *Callie Shaw, Stable Boy* (5–8). 1996, Eakin $16.95 (978-1-57168-092-1). During the Great Depression, Callie, disguised as a boy, works in a stable and uncovers a race-fixing racket. (Rev: BL 2/1/97; SLJ 8/97)

8391 Alter, Judith. *Maggie and a Horse Named Devildust* (5–7). 1989, Ellen C. Temple paper $5.95 (978-0-936650-08-1). 160pp. Maggie is determined to ride her spirited horse in the Wild West show in this historical horse story. (Rev: BL 4/15/89)

8392 Alter, Judith. *Maggie and the Search for Devildust* (5–7). 1989, Ellen C. Temple paper $5.95 (978-0-936650-09-8). 159pp. Maggie, a gorgeous girl of the Old West, sets out to find her horse, which has been stolen. (Rev: BL 10/1/89)

8393 Appelt, Kathi. *The Underneath* (4–8). Illus. by David Small. 2008, Atheneum $16.99 (978-1-4169-5058-5). 314pp. Newborn kittens, a bloodhound named Ranger, and a water snake find safety together in this story set in the mysterious bayous of East Texas. Newbery Honor Book, 2009. (Rev: BL 5/15/08; SLJ 6/08)

8394 Avi. *The Good Dog* (3–6). 2001, Simon & Schuster $16.00 (978-0-689-83824-8). 256pp. A malamute dog reconsiders his position as a pet when a wolf comes to town. (Rev: BL 9/1/01; HB 1/02; HBG 3/02; SLJ 12/01)

8395 Bagnold, Enid. *National Velvet* (5–8). Illus. by Ted Lewin. 1985, Avon paper $4.99 (978-0-380-71235-9). 272pp. The now-classic story of Heather Brown and her struggle to ride in the Grand National. A reissue. (Rev: BL 12/15/85)

8396 Bastedo, Jamie. *Tracking Triple Seven* (5–7). 2001, Red Deer paper $9.95 (978-0-88995-238-6). 224pp. Benji, a teenage boy grieving his mother's death, becomes involved with biologists tracking grizzly bears near his father's mine in Canada. (Rev: BL 2/1/02)

8397 Bauer, Marion Dane. *Runt* (3–6). 2002, Clarion $14.00 (978-0-618-21261-3). 144pp. A tale of a wolf born the runt of the litter and his struggle to improve his position in the pack and earn his father's approval. (Rev: BL 10/15/02; SLJ 9/02)

8398 Baylor, Byrd. *Hawk, I'm Your Brother* (3–5). Illus. by Peter Parnall. 1976, Macmillan paper $5.99 (978-0-689-71102-2). 48pp. A desert boy captures a young hawk, hoping it will teach him how to fly.

8399 Bechtold, Lisze. *Buster and Phoebe: The Great Bone Game* (1–4). Illus. by author. 2003, Houghton $15.00 (978-0-618-20862-3). Phoebe, the resident dog, greets newcomer Buster with skepticism, but the two soon come to terms in this beginning chapter book. (Rev: HB 9/03; HBG 4/04; SLJ 7/03)

8400 Beha, Eileen. *Tango: The Tale of an Island Dog* (4–6). 2009, Bloomsbury $15.99 (978-1-59990-262-1). 272pp. A little Yorkie used to living in the lap of luxury suddenly finds himself washed up on Prince Edward Island where he must adapt to a new lifestyle. (Rev: SLJ 7/09) ∩

8401 Berends, Polly. *The Case of the Elevator Duck* (3–5). Illus. by Diane Allison. 1989, Random paper $3.99 (978-0-394-82646-2). 64pp. In spite of the rule that no pets are allowed in his housing development, little Gilbert decides to keep a duck in an elevator.

8402 Brandenburg, Jim. *Scruffy: A Wolf Finds His Place in the Pack* (2–4). Illus. 1996, Walker LB $16.85 (978-0-8027-8446-9). 32pp. A photo-essay about an outcast wolf that gradually finds status in the pack. (Rev: BCCB 10/96; BL 9/1/96; SLJ 12/96)

8403 Briggs-Bunting, Jane. *Laddie of the Light* (4–6). Illus. 1997, Black River Trading $17.00 (978-0-9649083-1-4). 43pp. Jessie adjusts to her parents' approaching divorce with the help of two dogs, one real and the other a fictitious one that her grandfather tells her about. (Rev: BL 7/97)

8404 Brooke, Lauren. *Heartland: Coming Home* (4–7). 2000, Scholastic paper $4.99 (978-0-439-13020-2). 144pp. When her mother dies, Amy works through her grief by helping horses with behavioral problems in this novel set on a Virginia horse farm. (Rev: BL 9/15/00)

8405 Brown, F. K. *Last Hurdle* (4–6). Illus. by Peter Spier. 1988, Shoe String LB $18.50 (978-0-208-02212-7). 202pp. Kathy spends her savings on a broken-down horse, but manages to restore him in this book originally published in 1953.

8406 Bryant, Bonnie. *Horse Crazy* (4–6). 1996, Bantam paper $4.50 (978-0-553-48402-1). 144pp. Three girls become friends at a riding stable. Also usc: *Horse Shy* (1996). (Rev: BL 2/15/89)

8407 Bunting, Eve. *Reggie* (1–3). Illus. by D. Brent Burkett. 2006, Cricket $16.95 (978-0-8126-2746-6). 112pp. Alex keeps a toy mouse he finds even though he knows another child is looking for it, but when his own dog Patch disappears, he questions his decision. (Rev: BL 10/1/06; SLJ 11/06)

8408 Burgess, Melvin. *The Cry of the Wolf* (5–8). 1994, Morrow $17.99 (978-0-397-30693-0). 128pp. Young Ben Tilley insists that wolves run past his farm in rural Surrey, even though they have supposedly been gone from England for 500 years. (Rev: BL 10/15/92; SLJ 9/92)

8409 Byars, Betsy. *The Midnight Fox* (4–6). Illus. by Ann Grifalconi. 1968, Puffin paper $5.99 (978-0-14-031450-2). 160pp. When Tom spends two months on a farm with his aunt and uncle, he never expects that a black fox will become the focus of his life.

8410 Byars, Betsy. *Tornado* (3–5). Illus. 1996, HarperCollins LB $15.89 (978-0-06-026452-9). 64pp. To pass the time during a tornado watch, Pete, a farmhand, tells about another Tornado, an unusual dog. (Rev: BCCB 11/96; BL 9/15/96; HB 11/96; SLJ 11/96)

8411 Byars, Betsy, et al. *My Dog, My Hero* (3–6). Illus. 2000, Holt $16.00 (978-0-8050-6327-1). 48pp. Author Byars and her two daughters collaborated on this collection of eight stories about heroic dogs. (Rev: BL 1/1–15/01; HBG 3/01; SLJ 1/01)

8412 Carlson, Nolan. *Summer and Shiner* (5–8). 1992, Hearth paper $6.95 (978-0-9627947-4-2). 160pp. In a small Kansas town in the 1940s, 12-year-old Carley adopts a raccoon called Shiner. (Rev: BL 9/15/92)

8413 Cleary, Beverly. *Strider* (5–9). Illus. 1991, Morrow LB $17.89 (978-0-688-09901-5). In this sequel to the 1984 Newbery winner *Dear Mr. Henshaw*, Leigh Botts is beginning high school and still writing in his diary, with his beloved dog, Strider, by his side. (Rev: BCCB 10/91; BL 7/91*; HB 9/91; SLJ 9/91)

8414 Cole, Joanna, and Stephanie Calmenson, eds. *Give a Dog a Bone: Stories, Poems, Jokes, and Riddles About Dogs* (2–3). Illus. 1996, Scholastic $16.95 (978-0-590-46374-4). 96pp. An anthology of writings, anecdotes, and jokes about dogs. (Rev: BL 2/1/96; SLJ 3/96)

8415 Crisp, Marty. *My Dog, Cat* (3–6). Illus. 2000, Holiday House $15.95 (978-0-8234-1537-3). 64pp. Even though he always wanted a big dog, Abbie finds that size doesn't matter when he takes care of a little Yorkie while its owner is away. (Rev: BCCB 12/00; BL 1/1–15/01; HBG 10/01; SLJ 1/01)

8416 Cuffe-Perez, Mary. *Skylar* (3–5). Illus. by Renata Liwska. 2008, Philomel $14.99 (978-0-399-24543-5). 144pp. Answering a plea for help from an injured heron, five out-of-shape pond geese set off on their first migration and meet many challenges, learning to work together and fly above their fears. (Rev: BL 1/1–15/08; SLJ 7/08)

8417 DeJong, Meindert. *Along Came a Dog* (4–7). Illus. by Maurice Sendak. 1958, HarperCollins paper $5.95 (978-0-06-440114-2). 192pp. The friendship of a timid, lonely dog and a toeless little red hen is the basis for a very moving story, full of suspense.

8418 DeJong, Meindert. *Hurry Home, Candy* (4–6). Illus. by Maurice Sendak. 1953, HarperCollins LB $17.89 (978-0-06-021486-9); paper $7.95 (978-0-06-440025-1). 244pp. Candy is a little dog who, after many adventures, finds a home.

8419 Erickson, John R. *The Case of the Vanishing Fishhook* (3–6). Illus. by Gerald L. Holmes. Series: Hank the Cowdog. 1999, Viking $14.99 (978-0-670-88438-4); paper $4.99 (978-0-14-130356-7). 144pp. When Hank, a lovable dog, eats the liver that his young owner is using for fish bait, he realizes that he has also eaten a fish hook. (Rev: HBG 10/99; SLJ 4/99)

8420 Farley, Terri. *The Wild One* (4–6). 2002, Avon paper $4.99 (978-0-06-441085-4). 224pp. Sam is determined to find her stallion, Blackie, who ran away after she fell off and hit her head. (Rev: BL 9/1/02; SLJ 12/02)

8421 Feiffer, Jules. *A Room with a Zoo* (3–5). Illus. 2005, Hyperion $16.95 (978-0-7868-3702-1). 192pp. Julie (daughter of author and cartoonist Feiffer) wants a dog, and the procession of intervening pets do not assuage this need. (Rev: BL 9/15/05; SLJ 11/05)

8422 Feldman, Eve B. *That Cat!* (2–4). Illus. 1994, Morrow $14.00 (978-0-688-13310-8). 112pp. Molly is devastated when her cat disappears, and she tries many tactics to get him home. (Rev: BL 10/1/94; SLJ 9/94)

8423 Fine, Anne. *The Diary of a Killer Cat* (2–4). Illus. by Steve Cox. 2006, Farrar $15.00 (978-0-374-31779-9). 64pp. Tuffy the cat cannot understand the reactions of his humans to what he views as totally normal feline behavior. (Rev: BL 1/1–15/06; SLJ 2/06)

8424 Fine, Anne. *Notso Hotso* (2–4). Illus. by Tony Ross. 2006, Farrar $15.00 (978-0-374-35550-0). 96pp. Anthony, a British dog with a sense of dignity but a bad skin condition, is initially mortified when his fur is shaved off, but then decides he looks like a lion; an easy chapter book that will appeal to reluctant readers. (Rev: BL 1/1–15/06; SLJ 3/06)

8425 Gallaz, Christophe. *The Wolf Who Loved Music* (3–6). Illus. by Marshall Arisman. 2003, Creative Editions $17.95 (978-1-56846-178-6). 32pp. In this bittersweet tale set in Switzerland, Anne is devastated when townspeople hunt down and kill a wolf that may have been attracted by the young's girl violin playing. (Rev: HBG 4/04; SLJ 12/03)

8426 George, Jean Craighead. *The Cry of the Crow* (5–7). 1980, HarperCollins paper $5.99 (978-0-06-440131-9). 160pp. Mandy finds a helpless baby crow in the woods and tames it.

8427 George, Jean Craighead. *Frightful's Mountain* (5–8). 1999, Dutton $18.99 (978-0-525-46166-1).

176pp. Frightful, the falcon in *My Side of the Mountain,* is the central character in this novel in which she has difficult and enjoyable adventures in the wild. (Rev: BL 9/1/99; HBG 3/00; SLJ 9/99; VOYA 6/00)

8428 George, Twig C. *A Dolphin Named Bob* (2–5). Illus. 1996, HarperCollins LB $13.89 (978-0-06-025363-9). 64pp. Presents, in a fictional format, the life cycle of a dolphin at the Maryland State Aquarium. (Rev: BL 2/1/96; SLJ 5/96)

8429 Ghent, Natale. *No Small Thing* (5–8). 2005, Candlewick $15.00 (978-0-7636-2422-4). 256pp. Nathaniel and his siblings struggle to keep their horse while their single mother struggles to keep her family afloat. (Rev: BL 3/1/05; SLJ 4/05)

8430 Ghent, Natale. *Piper* (5–7). 2001, Orca paper $6.95 (978-1-55143-167-3). 176pp. The love and attention young Wesley showers on a tiny Australian shepherd puppy helps her recover from the death of her father. (Rev: BL 3/1/01)

8431 Giff, Patricia Reilly. *Wild Girl* (3–6). 2009, Random $15.99 (978-0-375-83890-3). 160pp. After a long separation, 12-year-old Lydie is reunited with her father and brother only to find it hard going until she comes upon a horse who helps her through. (Rev: BL 6/1–15/09; HB 9/09)

8432 Haas, Jessie. *A Blue for Beware* (2–4). Illus. 1995, Greenwillow $14.00 (978-0-688-13678-9). 64pp. Lily and her horse Beware compete in their first horse show. A sequel to *Beware the Mare* (1993). (Rev: BCCB 3/95; BL 5/15/95; HB 5/95; SLJ 5/95)

8433 Haas, Jessie. *Jigsaw Pony* (2–4). Illus. by Ying-Hwa Hu. 2005, Greenwillow $15.99 (978-0-06-078245-0). 112pp. Sharing isn't easy for twins Fran and Kiera, but they eventually come together over their adopted pony Jigsaw. (Rev: BL 9/1/05; SLJ 12/05)

8434 Hall, Elizabeth. *Child of the Wolves* (4–7). 1996, Houghton $16.00 (978-0-395-76502-9). 176pp. Granite, a Siberian husky pup, must survive in the wilderness when he is separated from his family. (Rev: BCCB 3/96; BL 4/1/96; VOYA 6/96)

8435 Hall, Lynn. *The Soul of the Silver Dog* (5–8). 1992, Harcourt $16.95 (978-0-15-277196-6). A handicapped dog bonds with his new teenage owner living in a troubled family. (Rev: BL 4/15/92; SLJ 6/92)

8436 Heinz, Brian. *Cheyenne Medicine Hat* (4–8). Illus. by Gregory Manchess. 2006, Creative Editions $18.95 (978-1-56846-181-6). 32pp. The story of a summer in the life of a wild mustang mare as she tries to keep her band safe from predators — both animal and human. (Rev: SLJ 11/06)

8437 Henkes, Kevin. *Protecting Marie* (5–7). 1995, Greenwillow $19.99 (978-0-688-13958-2). 208pp. Fanny is afraid that she will lose her pet dog if her temperamental father decides the dog must go. (Rev: BCCB 3/95; BL 3/15/95; HB 7/95; SLJ 5/95*)

8438 Henry, Marguerite. *King of the Wind* (5–8). Illus. by Wesley Dennis. 1990, Macmillan $17.95 (978-0-02-743629-7). 176pp. The story of the famous stallion Godolphin Arabian, ancestor of Man O'War and founder of the Thoroughbred breed. Newbery Medal winner, 1949. Also use *Black Gold* and *Born to Trot* (both 1987).

8439 Henry, Marguerite. *San Domingo: The Medicine Hat Stallion* (4–6). Illus. by Robert Lougheed. 1992, Macmillan paper $4.99 (978-0-689-71631-7). 240pp. Set in the West during the mid-19th century, this is the story of a young man who rights a wrong inflicted on his father. Also from the same author and publisher: *Brighty of the Grand Canyon; Justin Morgan Had a Horse* (both 1991).

8440 Hesse, Karen. *Sable* (2–4). Illus. by Marcia Sewall. 1994, Holt $15.95 (978-0-8050-2416-6). 60pp. Tate is sure that her dog, Sable, who has been given away for misbehaving, will return. (Rev: BCCB 5/94; BL 6/1–15/94; HB 7/94; SLJ 5/94*)

8441 High, Linda O. *Hound Heaven* (5–8). 1995, Holiday $15.95 (978-0-8234-1195-5). More than anything in the world, Silver Iris wants a dog, but her grandfather won't allow it. (Rev: BCCB 12/95; SLJ 11/95; VOYA 2/96)

8442 Hobbs, Valerie. *Sheep* (4–6). 2006, Farrar $16.00 (978-0-374-36777-0). 128pp. A poignant tale of a smart and sensitive border collie desperately searching for a home and the chance to herd sheep. (Rev: BL 2/1/06; SLJ 3/06)

8443 Hosler, Jay. *Clan Apis* (5–7). Illus. 2001, Active Synapse paper $15.00 (978-0-9677255-0-5). 158pp. Nyuki, a honeybee, describes his hive's history and migration to a new location in a text presented in graphic novel style that includes information about bees and their environment. (Rev: BL 7/01)

8444 Hunter, Erin. *Seekers: The Quest Begins* (5–8). Series: Seekers. 2008, HarperCollins $16.99 (978-0-06-087122-2). 304pp. Readers are introduced to three bear cubs — a polar bear, a black bear, and a grizzly — in this first installment in a series about survival and the realities of bear life in the wild and in captivity. (Rev: BL 5/15/08)

8445 Hurwitz, Johanna. *One Small Dog* (3–5). 2000, HarperCollins LB $15.89 (978-0-06-029220-1). 128pp. Curtis has always wanted a dog and finally gets one, but the small cocker spaniel causes enormous problems. (Rev: BCCB 9/00; BL 10/15/00; HB 9/00; HBG 3/01; SLJ 11/00)

8446 Hutchins, Hazel. *T J and the Cats* (2–4). 2002, Orca paper $5.95 (978-1-55143-205-2). 112pp. A beginning chapter book about a boy who doesn't like cats, but agrees to care for his grandmother's four while she's on vacation and slowly changes his mind. (Rev: BL 12/15/02; SLJ 2/03)

8447 Jimenez, Juan Ramon. *Platero y Yo / Platero and I* (5–7). Trans. by Myra Cohn Livingston and Joseph F. Dominguez. Illus. by Antonio Frasconi. 1994, Clarion $16.00 (978-0-395-62365-7). 47pp. Using both Spanish and English texts, this book contains excerpts from the prose poem about a writer and his donkey. (Rev: BL 6/1–15/94) [863]

8448 Joyce, William. *Buddy* (4–6). Illus. 1997, HarperCollins LB $15.89 (978-0-06-027661-4).

96pp. Gertrude Lintz buys a gorilla and treats it like a human. (Rev: BL 8/97; SLJ 8/97)

8449 Kehret, Peg. *Saving Lilly* (3–6). 2001, Pocket $16.00 (978-0-671-03422-1). 160pp. Two sixth-graders boycott a class trip to the circus because of animal cruelty and persuade the class to raise funds to send performer Lilly to an elephant sanctuary. (Rev: BL 12/1/01; HBG 10/02; SLJ 11/01)

8450 Keith, Harold. *Chico and Dan* (4–6). Illus. by Scott Arbuckle. 1998, Eakin $16.95 (978-1-57168-216-1). In 1915, eleven-year-old Dan gets a job working on his great-uncle's cattle ranch in Nevada, where he tames a wild colt and teaches him to be a cow horse. (Rev: HBG 3/99; SLJ 10/98)

8451 King-Smith, Dick. *The Cuckoo Child* (3–6). Illus. by Leslie Bowman. 1995, Hyperion paper $3.95 (978-0-7868-1001-7). 128pp. Jack oversees the hatching of an ostrich egg and tends the offspring, Oliver, for two years in this humorous story. (Rev: BL 4/15/93; SLJ 4/93*)

8452 King-Smith, Dick. *Dinosaur Trouble* (2–4). Illus. by Nick Bruel. 2008, Roaring Brook $14.95 (978-1-59643-324-3). 128pp. Two young dinosaurs from opposing families join forces to end the Tyrannosaurus rex's reign of terror. (Rev: BL 3/1/08; LMC 3/08; SLJ 3/08)

8453 King-Smith, Dick. *Hairy Hezekiah* (2–4). Illus. by Nick Bruel. 2007, Roaring Brook $12.95 (978-1-59643-318-2). 89pp. A lonely zoo camel figures out how to unlock his gate and ambles off on an adventure. (Rev: BCCB 10/07; SLJ 10/07)

8454 King-Smith, Dick. *The Invisible Dog* (2–4). Illus. by Roger Roth. 1995, Random paper $4.99 (978-0-679-87041-8). Janie can't have a pet dog so she invents one. (Rev: BCCB 4/93; BL 3/1/93; HB 5/93; SLJ 5/93)

8455 Kipling, Rudyard. *The Jungle Book: Mowgli's Story* (2–4). Illus. by Nicola Bayley. 2005, Candlewick $19.99 (978-0-7636-2317-3). 160pp. An appealing presentation of unabridged Mowgli adventures. (Rev: BL 5/1/05; SLJ 6/05)

8456 Kipling, Rudyard. *The Jungle Book: The Mowgli Stories* (4–7). Illus. by Jerry Pinkney. 1995, Morrow $25.99 (978-0-688-09979-4). 272pp. Eight stories about Mowgli are reprinted with 18 handsome watercolors. (Rev: BCCB 6/96; BL 10/15/95; SLJ 11/95)

8457 Kipling, Rudyard. *Just So Stories* (3–5). Illus. by David Frampton. 1991, HarperCollins $19.95 (978-0-06-023294-8). 128pp. Woodcuts enhance the retelling of these old favorites. (Rev: BL 11/15/91; HB 1/92; SLJ 11/91)

8458 Kipling, Rudyard. *Just So Stories* (4–6). Illus. by Barry Moser. 1996, Morrow $24.99 (978-0-688-13957-5). 160pp. Twelve classic stories are featured in this well-illustrated edition of Kipling favorites. (Rev: BL 11/1/96)

8459 Lantz, Francess. *Mom, There's a Pig in My Bed!* (4–6). 1992, Avon paper $3.50 (978-0-380-76112-8). 144pp. Mr. Ewing, fired from his job, moves to rural Kansas to raise seeing-eye pigs for blind people who are allergic to dogs, not realizing that pigs have poor eyesight too. (Rev: BL 4/15/92; SLJ 1/93)

8460 Lattimore, Deborah N. *Frida María: A Story of the Old Southwest* (2–4). Illus. by author. 1994, Harcourt $14.95 (978-0-15-276636-8). In this horse story set in Old California, Frida tries to be a conventional girl to please her mother, but her adventurous spirit prevails. (Rev: SLJ 5/94)

8461 Lawson, Julie. *Cougar Cove* (4–6). Illus. by David Powell. 1996, Orca paper $6.95 (978-1-55143-072-0). 138pp. An animal adventure involving a girl who is visiting relatives on Vancouver Island, Canada. (Rev: SLJ 9/96)

8462 Lester, Alison. *The Circus Horse* (1–3). Illus. by Roland Harvey. Series: Horse Crazy. 2009, Chronicle paper $4.99 (978-0-8118-6656-9). 64pp. For horse lovers who are graduating from easy readers, this tale set in Australia is a satisfying story about trick riding. (Rev: BL 3/15/09; LMC 8/09; SLJ 7/09)

8463 Levin, Betty. *Look Back, Moss* (5–8). 1998, Greenwillow $15.00 (978-0-688-15696-1). Young Moss, disturbed by his mother's lack of attention and his own weight problems, welcomes an injured sheepdog into the family. (Rev: BCCB 10/98; BL 8/98; HB 1/99; HBG 3/99; SLJ 11/98)

8464 Levin, Betty. *That'll Do, Moss* (4–6). 2002, HarperCollins LB $15.89 (978-0-06-000532-0). 128pp. Moss the Border collie and a girl named Diane, who works at the farm where Moss lives, rescue one of the farmer's sons who has run away. (Rev: BL 8/02; HBG 10/02; SLJ 10/02)

8465 Loizeaux, William. *Wings* (4–6). Illus. by Leslie Bowman. 2006, Farrar $16.00 (978-0-374-34802-1). 160pp. In 1960, 10-year-old Nick finds a baby mockingbird that's been abandoned by its mother and nurses it back to health. (Rev: BL 9/1/06; SLJ 9/06)

8466 Lowry, Lois. *Stay! Keeper's Story* (5–8). Illus. 1997, Houghton $16.00 (978-0-395-87048-8). 128pp. A dog named Keeper narrates this story about his puppyhood and the three different masters he has had. (Rev: BL 11/1/97; HBG 3/98; SLJ 10/97)

8467 Lubar, David. *Dog Days* (3–6). 2004, Darby Creek $15.95 (978-1-58196-013-6). 112pp. Larry Haskins passes his summer playing baseball and taking care of three stray dogs; his worries about the rising price of dog food are resolved when he finds the solution to a mysterious stain. (Rev: BL 4/1/04; SLJ 5/04)

8468 Malone, Geoffrey. *Torn Ear* (4–6). 2003, Hodder paper $8.95 (978-0-340-86057-1). 144pp. Readers follow Torn Ear, a fox, as he grows to adulthood, survives dangers, mates, and has his own cubs. (Rev: BL 3/1/03)

8469 Malterre, Elona. *The Last Wolf of Ireland* (5–7). 1990, Houghton $15.00 (978-0-395-54381-8). 124pp. Devin and his friend Katey hide wolf pups when the pups are threatened. (Rev: BCCB 10/90; BL 9/15/90*; SLJ 10/90)

8470 Martin, Ann M. *A Dog's Life: The Autobiography of a Stray* (4–6). 2005, Scholastic $16.99 (978-

0-439-71559-1). 192pp. Squirrel the dog looks back on the difficult years she spent as a stray before she was finally adopted by a loving human family. (Rev: BL 12/1/05; SLJ 11/05; VOYA 12/05)

8471 Martin, Ann M. *Everything for a Dog* (5–8). 2009, Feiwel & Friends $16.99 (978-0-312-38651-1). 224pp. Three separate story lines introduce Bone, a dog who has suffered through losing more than one home; Sunny, a dog who comforts her young master after his brother's death; and a boy named Henry who longs to have a dog. (Rev: BL 6/1–15/09)

8472 Michaels, Vaughn. *Dodi's Prince* (3–5). Illus. by Jacqueline Rogers. 2003, Dutton $15.99 (978-0-525-47034-2). 96pp. Life in a trailer park in a remote Texas town is lonely for 8-year-old Dodi until a stray dog appears. (Rev: BL 3/15/03; HBG 10/03; SLJ 3/03)

8473 Moeyaert, Bart. *Bare Hands* (3–7). Trans. by David Colmer. 1999, Front St. $14.95 (978-1-886910-32-4). 112pp. In this translation of a powerful novel from the Netherlands, Young Ward seeks revenge when the village loner, who is also his mother's suitor, kills his dog. (Rev: BL 12/15/98*; HBG 10/99; SLJ 2/99)

8474 Morehead, Debby. *A Special Place for Charlee: A Child's Companion Through Pet Loss* (3–6). Illus. by Karen Cannon. 1996, Partners in Publishing paper $6.95 (978-0-9654049-0-7). 36pp. Mark gets help and counseling when the dog he has grown up with dies. (Rev: BL 11/15/96)

8475 Morey, Walt. *Gentle Ben* (5–8). Illus. 1991, Puffin paper $6.99 (978-0-14-036035-6). A warm story of deep trust and friendship between a boy and an Alaskan bear.

8476 Morey, Walt. *Scrub Dog of Alaska* (4–8). 1989, Blue Heron paper $7.95 (978-0-936085-13-5). 160pp. A pup, abandoned because of his small size, turns out to be a winner. Also use *Kavik the Wolf Dog* (1977, Dutton).

8477 Morey, Walt. *Year of the Black Pony* (5–8). Illus. by Fredrika Spillman. 1989, Blue Heron paper $6.95 (978-0-936085-14-2). 160pp. A family story about a boy's love for his pony in rural Oregon at the turn of the 20th century.

8478 Morgan, Clay. *The Boy Who Spoke Dog* (5–8). 2003, Dutton $15.99 (978-0-525-47159-2). 166pp. Marooned on an island dominated by two warring dog packs, Jack, a young cabin boy, feels very much alone until he develops a friendship with a border collie named Moxie. (Rev: BL 1/1–15/04; SLJ 1/04; VOYA 6/04)

8479 Mowat, Farley. *The Dog Who Wouldn't Be* (4–7). Illus. by Paul Galdone. 1957, Bantam paper $4.99 (978-0-553-27928-3). 208pp. The humorous story of Mutt, a dog of character and personality, and his boy.

8480 Mukerji, Dhan Gopal. *Gay-Neck: The Story of a Pigeon* (4–8). Illus. by Boris Artzybasheff. 1968, Dutton $16.99 (978-0-525-30400-5). 192pp. A boy from India's brave carrier pigeon is selected to perform dangerous missions during World War I. Newbery Medal winner, 1928.

8481 Myers, Anna. *Red-Dirt Jessie* (4–7). 1992, Walker $13.95 (978-0-8027-8172-7). 120pp. In this tale of the Depression era in Oklahoma, 12-year-old Jessie helps keep her family together. (Rev: BCCB 10/92; BL 1/15/93; HB 1/93; SLJ 11/92*)

8482 Myers, Christopher. *Black Cat* (3–8). Illus. 1999, Scholastic $16.95 (978-0-590-03375-6). 40pp. An intriguing picture book with rap rhythm that tells of a black cat's progress walking through a city's streets. (Rev: BCCB 2/99; BL 4/15/99; HB 3/99; HBG 10/99; SLJ 3/99)

8483 Napoli, Donna Jo. *Mogo, The Third Warthog* (3–5). Illus. by Lita Judge. 2008, Hyperion $15.99 (978-1-4231-0816-0). 208pp. Mogo the warthog is the runt of his litter but is determined to survive on the scary and dangerous savanna, and with the help of a young baboon he manages to do just that. (Rev: BL 6/1–15/08; LMC 3/08; SLJ 8/08)

8484 Naylor, Phyllis Reynolds. *Cuckoo Feathers* (3–5). Illus. by Marcy Ramsey. 2006, Marshall Cavendish $14.95 (978-0-7614-5285-0). 96pp. When the two pigeons Sarah has regarded as her own decamp for a neighboring Chicago apartment, she is reluctant to give them up. (Rev: BL 5/1/06; SLJ 6/06)

8485 Naylor, Phyllis Reynolds. *Saving Shiloh* (4–7). 1997, Simon & Schuster $15.00 (978-0-689-81460-0). 144pp. In this sequel to the Newbery Medal-winning *Shiloh* and *Shiloh Season*, Marty again encounters the evil Judd Travers, who has been accused of murder. (Rev: BL 9/1/97*; HB 9/97; HBG 3/98; SLJ 9/97)

8486 Naylor, Phyllis Reynolds. *Shiloh* (4–8). 1991, Macmillan $16.00 (978-0-689-31614-2). 144pp. When a beagle follows him home, Marty, from a West Virginia family with a strict code of honor, learns a painful lesson about right and wrong. Newbery Medal winner, 1992. (Rev: BCCB 10/91; BL 12/1/91*; HB 1/92; SLJ 9/91)

8487 Naylor, Phyllis Reynolds. *Shiloh Season* (4–8). 1996, Simon & Schuster $15.00 (978-0-689-80647-6). 120pp. The evil Judd Travers wants his dog back from the Prestons in this sequel to *Shiloh* (1991). (Rev: BCCB 12/96; BL 11/15/96*; HB 11/96; SLJ 11/96)

8488 Newman, Leslea. *Hachiko Waits* (3–5). Illus. by Machiyo Kodaira. 2004, Holt $15.95 (978-0-8050-7336-2). 112pp. This is the fictionalized story of a Japanese Akita who continued — for ten years — to wait at the station for his master's return. (Rev: BL 1/1–15/05; SLJ 11/04)

8489 Nielsen, Virginia. *Batty Hattie* (4–6). 1999, Marshall Cavendish $14.95 (978-0-7614-5047-4). 142pp. When her mother goes on tour with a jazz band, Harriet is left alone with her uncle and feels extreme loneliness until she rescues a helpless baby bat she finds on the ground. (Rev: BCCB 4/99; BL 3/1/99; HBG 10/99; SLJ 4/99)

8490 Nolan, Lucy. *On the Road* (1–3). Illus. by Mike Reed. 2005, Marshall Cavendish $14.95 (978-0-7614-5234-8). 64pp. The dog who thinks her name is Down Girl relates an exciting car ride to the beach with her friend Sit, fun camping in the woods, and a trip to the vet, all the while commenting on life and owners. (Rev: BL 11/15/05; SLJ 3/06)

8491 Parker, Cam. *A Horse in New York* (4–8). 1989, Avon paper $2.75 (978-0-380-75704-6). 135pp. To save Blue, the horse she rode at summer camp, from destruction, Tiffin has to convince her parents to board him for the winter. (Rev: BL 12/15/89)

8492 Parker, Marjorie Hodgson. *Assault: The Crippled Champion: The King Ranch Racehorse* (2–4). Illus. by Charles Shaw. 2004, Bright Sky $14.95 (978-1-931721-34-9). 80pp. A colt called Assault describes his triumphant winning of the Triple Crown in 1946 despite the lameness he suffers. (Rev: SLJ 11/04)

8493 Patent, Dorothy Hinshaw. *Return of the Wolf* (4–6). Illus. by Jared T. Williams. 1995, Clarion $15.95 (978-0-395-72100-1). 67pp. A female wolf banished from her pack finds a new mate and a territory where she can begin a new pack. (Rev: BCCB 7–8/95; SLJ 7/95)

8494 Platt, Chris. *Moon Shadow* (4–7). 2006, Peachtree $14.95 (978-1-56145-382-5). 176pp. When a wild mustang mare dies giving birth near her Nevada home, 13-year-old Callie vows to raise and train the foal. (Rev: BL 11/1/06; SLJ 1/07)

8495 Popp, Monika. *Farm Year* (2–4). Illus. by Monika Popp and Regine Frick von Schmuck. 2002, Groundwood $18.95 (978-0-88899-452-3). A young farm boy takes special interest in a Holstein heifer and shepherds her tenderly through her first year of life. (Rev: HBG 10/02; SLJ 6/02)

8496 Reinhart, Matthew. *The Jungle Book: A Pop-up Adventure* (2–4). Illus. by author. 2006, Simon & Schuster $26.95 (978-1-4169-1824-0). The stories of Mowgli, Shere Khan, and other jungle inhabitants unfold in dramatic fold-outs and pop-ups. (Rev: SLJ 11/06)

8497 Rounds, Glen. *The Blind Colt* (3–6). Illus. by author. 1989, Holiday House $16.95 (978-0-8234-0010-2); paper $5.95 (978-0-8234-0758-3). 84pp. The story of the colt that overcame his blindness and the boy who saved him. A reissue.

8498 Sachar, Louis. *Marvin Redpost: Alone in His Teacher's House* (2–4). 1994, Random LB $11.99 (978-0-679-91949-0); paper $3.99 (978-0-679-81949-3). 83pp. Marvin is upset and confused when the dog he is taking care of dies. (Rev: BL 6/1–15/94)

8499 Sachs, Betsy. *The Boy Who Ate Dog Biscuits* (2–4). Illus. by Margot Apple. 1989, Random paper $3.99 (978-0-394-84778-8). 64pp. Billy, who helps out at the vet's office and likes dog biscuits, prefers dogs to his baby sister. (Rev: BL 1/15/90)

8500 Salten, Felix. *Bambi: A Life in the Woods* (5–8). 1926, Pocket paper $4.99 (978-0-671-66607-1). The growing to maturity of an Austrian deer.

8501 Saunders, Susan. *Lucky Lady* (3–7). 2000, HarperCollins $14.95 (978-0-380-97784-0). 144pp. The lives of 12-year-old Jennie and her dispirited grandfather change for the better when the girl buys a wild buckskin filly named Lucky Lady. (Rev: BCCB 5/00; BL 8/00; HBG 10/00; SLJ 7/00)

8502 Schlein, Miriam. *The Year of the Panda* (3–5). Illus. by Kam Mak. 1990, HarperCollins LB $15.89

(978-0-690-04866-7). 96pp. A Chinese farm boy cares for an orphaned baby panda. (Rev: BCCB 11/90; BL 9/15/90; HB 11/90; SLJ 10/90)

8503 Seuling, Barbara. *Robert and the Great Pepperoni* (2–3). Illus. by Paul Brewer. 2001, Cricket $14.95 (978-0-8126-2825-8). 118pp. Second-grader Robert really wants a dog and he starts a pet-sitting service that eventually but temporarily gives him a chance to look after one. (Rev: HB 1/02; HBG 3/02; SLJ 10/01)

8504 Sherlock, Patti. *Four of a Kind* (5–9). 1991, Holiday $13.95 (978-0-8234-0913-6). Andy's grandfather agrees to lend him money to buy a pair of horses, and he sets his sights on winning the horse-pulling contest at a state fair. (Rev: BL 12/1/91; SLJ 10/91)

8505 Silverstein, Shel. *Lafcadio, the Lion Who Shot Back* (3–6). Illus. by author. 1963, HarperCollins LB $16.89 (978-0-06-025676-0). 112pp. His marksmanship makes him a success, but Lafcadio discovers it's not to his liking.

8506 Smith, Susan M. *The Booford Summer* (3–6). Illus. 1994, Clarion $15.00 (978-0-395-66590-9). 144pp. A girl takes pity on Booford, a neighbor's dog, and begins taking him for walks. (Rev: BL 9/15/94; SLJ 11/94)

8507 Snelling, Lauraine. *The Winner's Circle* (5–8). Series: Golden Filly. 1995, Bethany House paper $5.99 (978-1-55661-533-7). In this horse story, Trish Evanston, a high school senior who is also a jockey and Triple Crown winner, is being stalked by a mystery man who sends her threatening notes. (Rev: SLJ 10/95; VOYA 4/96)

8508 Springer, Nancy. *A Horse to Love* (4–8). 1987, HarperCollins $11.95 (978-0-06-025824-5). Erin's parents buy her a horse hoping that this will help cure her shyness. (Rev: BL 3/87; SLJ 3/87)

8509 Taylor, Theodore. *Tuck Triumphant* (4–7). 1991, Avon paper $5.99 (978-0-380-71323-3). 150pp. A 1950s novel about a blind dog in a loving family and the deaf Korean boy they adopt. (Rev: BL 2/1/91)

8510 Tolan, Stephanie S. *Listen!* (4–7). 2006, HarperCollins $15.99 (978-0-06-057925-8). 208pp. Lonely after the death of her mother and the departure of her best friend for the summer, 12-year-old Charley finds solace in a stray dog. (Rev: BL 4/1/06)

8511 Updike, David. *The Sounds of Summer* (3–5). Illus. by Robert Andrew Parker. 1993, Pippin $15.95 (978-0-945912-20-0). 40pp. After Homer's dog, Sophocles, dies, the boy remembers the good times they had together. (Rev: BCCB 10/93; BL 9/1/93; SLJ 10/93)

8512 Ure, Jean. *Muddy Four Paws* (4–6). Series: We Love Animals. 1999, Barron's paper $3.95 (978-0-7641-0968-3). 128pp. In this English story, 11-year-old Clara is upset when her mother will not let her adopt a puppy she has found in a ditch. (Rev: SLJ 6/99)

8513 Van Laan, Nancy. *Busy, Busy Moose* (1–2). Illus. by Amy Rusch. 2003, Houghton $15.00 (978-0-395-96091-2). 48pp. In this sequel to *Moose Tales*

(2001), the title character and his friends experience the changing seasons. (Rev: BL 7/03; HB 9/03; HBG 4/04; SLJ 9/03)

8514 Wallace, Bill. *Coyote Autumn* (4–6). 2000, Holiday House $16.95 (978-0-8234-1628-8). 201pp. During his first autumn in rural Oklahoma, Brad finds an orphan coyote pup that he raises. (Rev: BCCB 11/00; BL 12/15/00; HBG 10/01; SLJ 10/00)

8515 Wallace, Bill. *Goosed!* (2–4). Illus. by Jacqueline Rogers. 2002, Holiday House $16.95 (978-0-8234-1757-5). 128pp. T.P. the dog does not welcome the arrival of a Labrador puppy in his life in this beginning chapter book. (Rev: HBG 3/03; SLJ 12/02)

8516 Wallace, Carol, and Bill Wallace. *The Meanest Hound Around* (2–4). Illus. by John Steven Gurney. 2003, Simon & Schuster $15.95 (978-0-7434-3785-1). 160pp. In this heartwarming story of canine friendship, Freddie, an abandoned dog, befriends a watchdog named Spike and helps him to escape from his abusive owner. (Rev: HBG 10/03; SLJ 4/03)

8517 Wedekind, Annie. *Wild Blue: The Story of a Mustang Appaloosa* (4–7). 2009, Feiwel & Friends $12.99 (978-0-312-38424-1). 128pp. Josiah helps a mustang return to her Idaho home. (Rev: BL 6/1–15/09; SLJ 5/09)

8518 Whelan, Gloria. *Silver* (2–4). Illus. by Stephen Marchesi. 1988, Random paper $3.99 (978-0-394-89611-3). 64pp. Rachel wants to compete in the Alaska Iditarod sled race, and she thinks she can win with her lead dog, Silver. (Rev: BCCB 7–8/88; BL 7/88; SLJ 10/88)

8519 Wiebe, Trina. *Hamsters Don't Glow in the Dark* (2–4). Illus. by Marisol Sarrazin. 2000, Lobster paper $5.95 (978-1-894222-15-0). 32pp. Abby brings the class hamster home for spring break and discovers that Mr. Nibbles was misnamed because she has given birth to eight babies. (Rev: SLJ 2/01)

8520 Wilbur, Frances. *The Dog with Golden Eyes* (4–7). Illus. 1998, Milkweed paper $6.95 (978-1-57131-615-8). 160pp. Cassie befriends a white dog that turns out to be an arctic wolf, and she must find his owners before he becomes a target for the police or hunters. (Rev: BCCB 9/98; BL 9/1/98; HBG 3/99; SLJ 7/98; VOYA 8/98)

8521 Woods, Shirley. *Jack: The Story of a Beaver* (3–5). Illus. by Celia Godkin. 2002, Fitzhenry & Whiteside $14.95 (978-1-55041-733-3). 96pp. Nature lovers will enjoy the story of the first two years of life for Jack the Beaver, who evades predators, learns to avoid traps, and finally finds a mate. (Rev: BL 1/1–15/03; SLJ 3/03)

8522 Woods, Shirley. *Tooga: The Story of a Polar Bear* (4–6). Illus. by Muriel Wood. 2004, Fitzhenry & Whiteside $14.95 (978-1-55041-898-9). 96pp. Facts are interwoven into this story of a polar bear cub who makes his long and dangerous way home after floating hundreds of miles on an ice flow. (Rev: SLJ 4/05)

8523 Wright, Lynn F. *Flick* (3–5). Illus. by Tony Waters. 1995, Worry Wart $13.95 (978-1-881519-02-7); paper $7.95 (978-1-881519-03-4). 68pp. Jack

nurses back to health a badly injured puppy he has found on the railroad tracks. (Rev: SLJ 2/96)

Ethnic Groups

8524 Abraham, Susan Gonzales, and Denise Gonzales Abraham. *Cecilia's Year* (4–7). 2004, Cinco Puntos $16.95 (978-0-938317-87-6). 216pp. Inspired by the real-life story of the authors' mother, this is the story of a 14-year-old Hispanic American girl's determination to defy cultural tradition and continue her schooling in Depression-era New Mexico. (Rev: BL 1/1–15/05; SLJ 4/05)

8525 Baskin, Nora Raleigh. *The Truth About My Bat Mitzvah* (5–8). 2008, Simon & Schuster $15.99 (978-1-4169-3558-2). 144pp. Caroline, daughter of a Jewish mother and Christian father, has never been a practicing Jew but when her grandmother dies and leaves her a Star of David necklace — and her best friend Rachel is preparing for her bat mitzvah at the same time — she begins to acknowledge this part of her identity. (Rev: BL 3/15/08; SLJ 4/08)

8526 Bernardo, Anilú. *Un día con mis tías / A Day with My Aunts* (2–4). Illus. by Christina Rodriguez. 2006, Piñata $15.95 (978-1-55885-374-4). A young Latina girl spends a fun-filled day with her aunts in this appealing bilingual book that includes empanada recipes. (Rev: SLJ 10/06)

8527 Bernier-Grand, Carmen. *In the Shade of the Nispero Tree* (4–7). 1999, Orchard LB $16.99 (978-0-531-33154-5). 192pp. Prejudice and racism separate two friends in this story set in Ponce, Puerto Rico, during 1961. (Rev: BCCB 3/99; BL 4/1/99; HBG 10/99; SLJ 3/99)

8528 Bertrand, Diane Gonzales. *The Ruiz Street Kids / Los muchachos de la calle Ruiz* (3–6). 2006, Piñata paper $9.95 (978-1-55885-321-8). 240pp. Joe Silva and his friends shun David until they realize he's just insecure; Spanish text follows the English. (Rev: SLJ 10/06)

8529 Blume, Judy. *Iggie's House* (4–7). 1970, Dell paper $4.99 (978-0-440-44062-8). 128pp. An African American family moves into Iggie's old house.

8530 Caraballo, Samuel. *Estrellita Says Good-bye to Her Island / Estrellita se despide de su isla* (3–5). Illus. by Pablo Torrecilla. 2002, Arte Publico $15.95 (978-1-55885-338-6). 32pp. In this bilingual book, a young girl bids good-bye to her island home and all the sights and sounds that are important to her. (Rev: BL 5/1/02)

8531 Cheng, Andrea. *Eclipse* (5–8). 2006, Front St. $16.95 (978-1-932425-21-5). 136pp. In 1952 Cincinnati, 8-year-old immigrant Peti is disappointed when his relatives arrive to live with them; his cousin is a bully and his mother still worries about her father, who cannot get out of Hungary. (Rev: BL 11/1/06)

8532 Cheng, Andrea. *Honeysuckle House* (4–7). 2004, Front St. $16.95 (978-1-886910-99-7). 136pp.

The problems of immigration and adjustment to new cultures are shown in this story of two girls of Chinese heritage, told in the girls' alternating voices. (Rev: BL 4/1/04; HB 7/04; SLJ 6/04)

8533 Cheng, Andrea. *Shanghai Messenger* (4–6). Illus. by Ed Young. 2005, Lee & Low $17.95 (978-1-58430-238-4). 40pp. Xiao Mei, an 11-year-old Chinese American girl, learns about the Chinese half of her heritage on a summer trip to Shanghai. (Rev: BL 8/05; SLJ 9/05)

8534 Cruz, Maria Colleen. *Border Crossing* (4–8). 2003, Arte Publico paper $9.95 (978-1-55885-405-5). 128pp. Ceci, 12, can't understand why her Mexican father won't speak Spanish or talk about his home, so she decides to go and investigate. (Rev: BL 11/15/03; SLJ 2/04)

8535 Cummings, Mary. *Three Names of Me* (2–5). Illus. by Lin Wang. 2006, Albert Whitman $15.95 (978-0-8075-7903-9). A young Chinese American girl tells the story behind her three names — one from her birth mother, another she received at the orphanage, and a third given by her adoptive parents. (Rev: SLJ 10/06)

8536 Curtis, Christopher Paul. *The Watsons Go to Birmingham — 1963* (4–8). 1995, Delacorte $16.95 (978-0-385-32175-4); Dell paper $6.50 (978-0-440-41412-4). 210pp. An African American family returns to Alabama from Michigan to place their troubled son with his grandmother in this novel set in the 1960s. (Rev: BL 8/95; SLJ 10/95*; VOYA 12/95)

8537 Dole, Mayra L. *Drum, Chavi, Drum ! / Toca, Chavi, Toca!* (2–3). Illus. by Tonel. 2003, Children's Book Pr. $16.95 (978-0-89239-186-8). 32pp. In this charming and rhythmic bilingual book, Chavi sets out to prove that being a girl doesn't mean she can't be a great drummer. (Rev: BL 8/03; HBG 4/04; SLJ 12/03)

8538 English, Karen. *Francie* (5–8). 1999, Farrar $17.00 (978-0-374-32456-8). Francie, a black girl growing up in segregated Alabama, places her family in danger when she helps a friend who is escaping a racist employer. (Rev: BCCB 10/99; BL 10/15/99; HB 9/99; HBG 3/00; SLJ 9/99; VOYA 2/00)

8539 Fleischman, Paul. *Seedfolks* (4–8). Illus. 1997, HarperCollins LB $15.89 (978-0-06-027472-6). Thirteen people from many cultures explain why they have planted gardens in a vacant lot in Cleveland, Ohio. (Rev: BCCB 7–8/97; BL 5/15/97; HB 5/97; SLJ 5/97*; VOYA 6/97)

8540 Fleming, Candace. *Lowji Discovers America* (3–5). 2005, Simon & Schuster $15.95 (978-0-689-86299-1). 160pp. Lowji, newly arrived in Illinois from his native India, convinces the landlady to keep animals at his apartment building and gets to know his new neighbors. (Rev: BL 3/15/05; SLJ 4/05)

8541 Flood, Pansie Hart. *It's Test Day, Tiger Turcotte* (2–3). Illus. by Amy Wummer. 2004, Carolrhoda LB $19.93 (978-1-57505-056-0); paper $6.95 (978-1-57505-670-8). 72pp. Tiger—a boy of multiracial heritage—is already nervous about taking a test, but when it comes to filling in his race, he's genuinely puzzled. (Rev: BCCB 4/04; SLJ 7/04)

8542 Fogelin, Adrian. *Crossing Jordan* (5–8). Illus. by Suzy Schultz. 2000, Peachtree $14.95 (978-1-56145-215-6). 140pp. Set in contemporary Florida, this novel tells how 12-year-old Cass must keep her friendship with African American Jemmie a secret from her racist father. (Rev: BCCB 4/00; HBG 10/00; SLJ 6/00)

8543 Gardiner, John Reynolds. *Stone Fox* (3–6). Illus. by Marcia Sewall. 1980, HarperCollins LB $16.89 (978-0-690-03984-9); paper $5.50 (978-0-06-440132-6). 96pp. Ten-year-old Willy competes against the Indian mountain man, Stone Fox, in the national dogsled races.

8544 Garland, Sherry. *The Lotus Seed* (K–5). Illus. by Tatsuro Kluchi. 1993, Harcourt $16.00 (978-0-15-249465-0). 32pp. A young narrator tells of fleeing her Vietnamese homeland to settle with her family in America. (Rev: BL 3/15/93*; HB 5/93; SLJ 7/93)

8545 Giff, Patricia Reilly. *Maggie's Door* (3–6). 2003, Random LB $17.99 (978-0-385-90095-9). 160pp. In this poignant sequel to *Nory Ryan's Song*, Nory and her friend Sean describe in alternating chapters the horrors of their voyages — and their enduring spirit and optimism — from their native Ireland to join relatives in America. (Rev: BL 9/15/03; HB 9/03; HBG 4/04; SLJ 9/03)

8546 Greenfield, Eloise. *Koya DeLaney and the Good Girl Blues* (4–6). 1995, Scholastic paper $2.95 (978-0-590-43299-3). 176pp. Sixth-grader Koya DeLaney, whose talent is a gift of laughter, has some growing up to do when family conflicts arise. (Rev: BCCB 3/92; BL 2/15/92; SLJ 3/92)

8547 Haugaard, Kay. *No Place* (4–6). 1998, Milkweed $15.95 (978-1-57131-616-5). 175pp. Based on fact, this is the story of a yearlong project in which Arturo and his friends turn a junk-filled barrio lot in Los Angeles into a park. (Rev: BL 11/15/98; HBG 3/99)

8548 Herrera, Juan Felipe. *Downtown Boy* (5–8). 2005, Scholastic $16.99 (978-0-439-64489-1). 304pp. This poignant free-verse novel, narrated by 10-year-old Juanito, offers an unflinching look at what life was like for Chicano migrant workers and their families in 1950s California. (Rev: BL 12/15/05; SLJ 1/06; VOYA 4/06)

8549 Hobbs, Will. *Crossing the Wire* (5–8). 2006, HarperCollins $15.99 (978-0-06-074138-9). 224pp. Victor, a teenage Mexican boy who is the sole support for his family, decides to risk the dangerous crossing into the United States in search of work. (Rev: BL 5/1/06; SLJ 5/06; VOYA 4/06) ∩

8550 Hoyt-Goldsmith, Diane. *Day of the Dead: A Mexican-American Celebration* (4–6). Illus. 1994, Holiday House LB $17.95 (978-0-8234-1094-1). 32pp. The Hispanic Day of the Dead celebration as seen through the experiences of an American family living in a Mexican American community. (Rev: BL 7/94; SLJ 9/94)

8551 Jimenez, Francisco. *The Circuit: Stories from the Life of a Migrant Child* (5–10). 1997, Univ. of

New Mexico paper $11.95 (978-0-8263-1797-1). Eleven moving stories about the lives, fears, hopes, and problems of children in Mexican migrant worker families. (Rev: BL 12/1/97)

8552 Johnston, Tony. *Any Small Goodness: A Novel of the Barrio* (4–7). Illus. by Raúl Colón. 2001, Scholastic paper $16.95 (978-0-439-18936-1). 128pp. Eleven-year-old Arturo Rodriguez, whose Mexican family is new to Los Angeles, describes family life, school, celebrations, and dangers. (Rev: BL 9/15/01; HBG 3/02; SLJ 9/01; VOYA 10/01)

8553 Lee, Lauren. *Stella: On the Edge of Popularity* (5–7). 1994, Polychrome $10.95 (978-1-879965-08-9). 178pp. A Korean American girl has to choose between being popular and being loyal to her Korean culture. (Rev: BCCB 7–8/94; SLJ 9/94)

8554 Lester, Julius. *The Old African* (4–7). Illus. by Jerry Pinkney. 2005, Dial $19.99 (978-0-8037-2564-5). 80pp. An elderly slave who never speaks uses his acute mental powers to relieve the pain of his people on a Georgia plantation. (Rev: BL 7/05*; SLJ 9/05; VOYA 12/05)

8555 Lin, Grace. *The Year of the Dog* (3–5). Illus. 2006, Little, Brown $14.99 (978-0-316-06000-4). 136pp. A 12-year-old Taiwanese American girl chronicles the events of a year that includes a new friend, academic achievements, growing awareness of cultural differences, and a touch of romance. (Rev: BCCB 2/06; BL 1/1–15/06*; HB 3/06; HBG 10/06; SLJ 3/06)

8556 Lin, Grace. *The Year of the Rat* (3–5). Illus. by author. 2008, Little, Brown $14.99 (978-0-316-11426-4). 176pp. Grace's Taiwanese American family celebrates Chinese New Year as Grace tackles such changes as her best friend moving away and a Chinese boy arriving at her school in this sequel to *The Year of the Dog* (2006). (Rev: BL 11/15/07; HB 5/08; SLJ 3/08)

8557 Littlesugar, Amy. *A Portrait of Spotted Deer's Grandfather* (2–4). Illus. 1997, Whitman LB $15.95 (978-0-8075-6622-0). 32pp. Spotted Deer's grandfather, Moose Horn, is afraid that if he has his portrait painted he will lose his spirit. (Rev: BL 1/1–15/98; HBG 3/98; SLJ 9/97)

8558 Look, Lenore. *Ruby Lu, Empress of Everything* (2–4). Illus. by Anne Wilsdorf. 2006, Simon & Schuster $15.95 (978-0-689-86460-5). 176pp. Ruby Lu faces new challenges as she helps her deaf cousin Flying Duck, newly arrived from China, to adjust to school and life in America; a sequel to *Ruby Lu, Brave and True* (2004). (Rev: BL 2/15/06; SLJ 7/06*)

8559 Lord, Bette Bao. *In the Year of the Boar and Jackie Robinson* (4–6). Illus. by Marc Simont. 1984, HarperCollins paper $5.99 (978-0-06-440175-3). 176pp. The story of a Chinese girl who leaves China to join her father in New York in 1947.

8560 Marsden, Carolyn. *Bird Springs* (3–5). 2007, Viking $14.99 (978-0-670-06193-8). 128pp. Gregory, a 10-year-old Navajo boy, must cope with moving to a new place and missing his estranged father. (Rev: BCCB 9/07; BL 5/15/07; HB 7/07; LMC 11/07; SLJ 5/07)

8561 Marsden, Carolyn, and Virginia Shin-Mui Loh. *The Jade Dragon* (2–4). 2006, Candlewick $15.99 (978-0-7636-3012-6). 176pp. Ginny, a young Chinese American girl, and Stephanie, adopted by a Caucasian American couple, become friends after a few false starts. (Rev: BL 11/1/06; SLJ 11/06)

8562 Martin, Bill, Jr., and John Archambault. *Knots on a Counting Rope* (PS–5). Illus. by Ted Rand. 1987, Holt $16.95 (978-0-8050-0571-4). 32pp. Each time his grandson asks him to repeat the story of Boy-Strength of Blue-Horses, Grandfather adds another knot in the counting rope, a metaphor for the passage of time. (Rev: BCCB 11/87; BL 11/15/87; SLJ 12/87)

8563 Medearis, Michael, and Angela Shelf Medearis. *Daisy and the Doll* (2–4). Illus. 2000, Vermont Folklife Center $14.95 (978-0-916718-15-2). 32pp. Daisy, an African American girl, is embarrassed when her classroom teacher gives her a black doll to hold during a program on different countries and nationalities. (Rev: BL 9/15/00; SLJ 9/00)

8564 Mobin-Uddi, Asma. *My Name Is Bilal* (4–7). Illus. by Barbara Kiawk. 2005, Boyds Mills $15.95 (978-1-59078-175-3). 32pp. When they start at a new school, Muslim Bilal and his sister Ayesha balance pride in their own heritage and their desire to blend in. (Rev: BL 8/05; SLJ 8/05)

8565 Mochizuki, Ken. *Heroes* (2–4). Illus. by Dom Lee. 1995, Lee & Low $15.95 (978-1-880000-16-8). 32pp. During the Vietnam War, a Japanese American child becomes the butt of other children's bullying. (Rev: BL 3/15/95; HB 5/95; SLJ 7/95)

8566 Montes, Marisa. *Get Ready for Gabi! A Crazy Mixed-Up Spanglish Day* (3–6). Illus. by Joe Cepeda. 2003, Scholastic $12.95 (978-0-439-51710-2); paper $3.99 (978-0-439-47519-8). 124pp. Third-grader Gabi speaks Spanish at home and English at school, but when a classmate starts causing problems, what comes out of her mouth is a mixture of the two. (Rev: BL 9/1/03; HBG 10/03; SLJ 11/03)

8567 Myers, Walter Dean. *The Dream Bearer* (5–8). 2003, HarperCollins LB $24.00 (978-0-06-054277-1). 240pp. David, 12 and living in Harlem, gains valuable insights about his heritage and his ambitions when he gets to know an old man who calls himself a "dream bearer." (Rev: BL 7/03; HBG 4/04; SLJ 6/03; VOYA 6/03)

8568 Myers, Walter Dean. *145th Street: Stories* (5–9). 2000, Delacorte $15.95 (978-0-385-32137-2). 150pp. A Harlem neighborhood is the setting for this collection of short stories dealing with a wide range of human emotions. (Rev: BL 12/15/99; HB 3/00; HBG 10/00; SLJ 4/00)

8569 Naidoo, Beverley. *Journey to Jo'burg: A South African Story* (4–6). Illus. by Eric Velasquez. 1986, HarperCollins paper $4.99 (978-0-06-440237-8). 96pp. The story of Naledi, from a South African village, who travels to the city with her brother to seek their mother, who works in the home of whites, because their baby sister is dying. (Rev: BCCB 5/86; BL 3/25/86; SLJ 8/86)

8570 Namioka, Lensey. *Yang the Third and Her Impossible Family* (4–7). Illus. by Kees de Kiefte.

1996, Bantam paper $4.50 (978-0-440-41231-1). 144pp. Mary, part of a Chinese family newly arrived in Seattle, is embarrassed by her parents' old-country ways in this humorous story. (Rev: BCCB 5/95; BL 4/15/95; SLJ 8/95)

8571 Nislick, June Levitt. *Zayda Was a Cowboy* (4–7). 2005, Jewish Publication Soc. paper $9.95 (978-0-8276-0817-7). 128pp. A Jewish grandfather tells his grandchildren about his exploits as a cowboy when he first arrived in America from Eastern Europe; an epilogue gives background and there is a glossary and a bibliography. (Rev: BL 8/05*)

8572 O'Connell, Rebecca. *Penina Levine Is a Hard-Boiled Egg* (4–6). Illus. by Majella Lue Sue. 2007, Roaring Brook $16.95 (978-1-59643-140-9). 176pp. Penina, a feisty Jewish sixth grader troubled by a school assignment involving the Easter bunny, worries that confiding in her parents will only cause more trouble. (Rev: BL 3/15/07)

8573 Parker, Toni Trent. *Sienna's Scrapbook: Our African American Heritage Trip* (3–6). Illus. by Janell Genovese. 2005, Chronicle $15.95 (978-0-8118-4300-3). 61pp. Sienna, a young African American girl, keeps a scrapbook of her family's summer trip to important sites in the history of black Americans; Sienna's humorous comments, varied ephemera, and appealing illustrations add to the appeal. (Rev: SLJ 1/06)

8574 Perry, Michael. *Daniel's Ride* (2–4). Illus. by Lee Ballard. 2001, Free Will $16.00 (978-0-9701771-9-3). 32pp. In this colorful glimpse of Latino culture, Daniel enjoys a ride in his big brother Hector's convertible and makes an important promise. (Rev: BL 9/1/01; SLJ 1/02)

8575 Pinkney, Andrea D. *Hold Fast to Dreams* (5–8). 1995, Morrow $16.00 (978-0-688-12832-6). 112pp. A bright, resourceful African American girl faces problems when she finds she is the only black student in her new middle school. (Rev: BCCB 5/95; BL 2/15/95; HB 9/95; SLJ 4/95)

8576 Pitts, Paul. *Racing the Sun* (5–7). 1988, Avon paper $6.99 (978-0-380-75496-0). 160pp. Brandon begins to understand his Navajo heritage after his grandfather comes to live with him. (Rev: BL 9/15/88; SLJ 2/89)

8577 Robles, Anthony D. *Lakas and the Makibaka Hotel* (2–4). Trans. by Eloisa D. de Jesus. Illus. by Carl Angel. 2006, Children's Book Pr. $16.95 (978-0-89239-213-1). 32pp. Based on a real-life incident, this lively bilingual (English and Tagalog) picture book tells the story of a group of Filipino Americans fighting to prevent the sale of the hotel in which they live. (Rev: BL 2/15/06; SLJ 4/06)

8578 Roseman, Kenneth. *The Other Side of the Hudson: A Jewish Immigrant Adventure* (5–8). Illus. Series: Do-It-Yourself Adventure. 1993, UAHC paper $11.95 (978-0-8074-0506-2). 140pp. Using an interactive format, readers can choose various destinations for a young male Jewish immigrant after he arrives in New York City from Germany in 1851. (Rev: SLJ 6/94)

8579 Sebestyen, Ouida. *Words by Heart* (5–7). 1979, Little, Brown $15.95 (978-0-316-77931-9). 144pp. Race relations are explored when an African American family moves to an all-white community during the Reconstruction era. (Rev: BL 6/1/88)

8580 Sing, Rachel. *Chinese New Year's Dragon* (3–5). Illus. by Shao Wei Liu. 1994, Simon & Schuster paper $5.99 (978-0-671-88602-8). 23pp. A young girl works with her family to prepare for the Chinese New Year and then enjoys participating in the joyous festival. (Rev: BL 4/15/94)

8581 Skrypuch, Marsha Forchuk. *Silver Threads* (2–4). Illus. by Michael Martchenko. 2004, Fitzhenry & Whiteside $16.95 (978-1-55041-901-6). 32pp. This picture-book story of Ukrainian immigrants' bittersweet experiences in early-20th-century Canada is based on the lives of the author's grandparents. (Rev: BL 12/1/04; SLJ 1/05)

8582 Son, John. *Finding My Hat* (4–8). Series: First Person Fiction. 2003, Scholastic $16.95 (978-0-439-43538-3). 192pp. Autobiography plays a large part in this frank, often funny novel about the son of Korean immigrants growing up in America in the 1970s and 1980s. (Rev: BL 11/15/03; HBG 4/04; LMC 11/03; SLJ 10/03)

8583 Soto, Gary. *Local News* (4–7). 1993, Harcourt $14.00 (978-0-15-248117-9). 144pp. This collection of 13 short stories deals with a number of Mexican American youngsters at home, school, and play. (Rev: BL 4/15/93; HB 7/93*)

8584 Soto, Gary. *Petty Crimes* (5–8). 1998, Harcourt $17.00 (978-0-15-201658-6). Ten short stories about Mexican American teenagers in California's Central Valley deal with some humorous situations but more often with gangs, violence, and poverty. (Rev: BL 3/15/98; HBG 10/98; SLJ 5/98)

8585 Spinelli, Jerry. *Maniac Magee* (5–7). 1990, Little, Brown $15.95 (978-0-316-80722-7). 192pp. This thought-provoking Newbery Medal winner (1991) tells the story of an amazing white boy who runs away from home and suddenly becomes aware of the racism in his town. (Rev: BL 6/1/90*; SLJ 6/90)

8586 Stering, Shirley. *My Name Is Seepeetza* (5–10). 1997, Douglas & McIntyre paper $5.95 (978-0-88899-165-2). Told in diary form, this autobiographical novel about a 6th-grade Native American girl tells of her heartbreak at the terrible conditions at her school, where she is persecuted because of her race. (Rev: BL 3/1/97)

8587 Tolliver, Ruby C. *Sarita, Be Brave* (3–6). 1999, Eakin $14.95 (978-1-57168-184-3). 144pp. After the deaths of her grandmother and mother, 12-year-old Sara leaves Honduras for an eventful truck trip to Texas where she encounters problems and hardships before making a good adjustment. (Rev: HBG 3/00; SLJ 8/99)

8588 Vogiel, Eva. *Invisible Chains* (5–8). 2000, Judaica $19.95 (978-1-880582-57-2). 280pp. In 1948, 14-year-old Frumie is sent with her crippled younger sister, Judy, to a boarding school for religiously observant Jewish girls. (Rev: BL 7/00; HBG 10/00)

8589 Walters, Eric. *War of the Eagles* (5–7). 1998, Orca $14.00 (978-1-55143-118-5); paper $7.95

(978-1-55143-099-7). 224pp. During the opening months of the war against Japan, a West Coast Canadian boy witnesses the growing prejudice against Japanese Canadians and also becomes aware of his own Indian heritage. (Rev: BL 12/15/98; HBG 3/99; SLJ 12/98)

8590 Weatherford, Carole Boston. *Dear Mr. Rosenwald* (2–4). Illus. by R. Gregory Christie. 2006, Scholastic $16.99 (978-0-439-49522-6). 32pp. In this fact-based tale from the rural South of the 1920s, 10-year-old Ovella describes her community's efforts to build a new school with seed money from Julius Rosenwald, president of Sears, Roebuck. (Rev: BL 10/1/06; SLJ 10/06*)

8591 Winston, Sherri. *The Kayla Chronicles* (5–9). 2008, Little, Brown $16.99 (978-0-316-11430-1). 188pp. African American Kayla alienates her friend Rosalie when she joins her Florida high school's hip-hop dance team. (Rev: BL 2/1/08; SLJ 4/08)

8592 Wiseman, Eva. *No One Must Know* (4–7). 2004, Tundra paper $8.95 (978-0-88776-680-0). 208pp. Thirteen-year-old Alexandra, who's been raised as a Catholic in Canada, learns that her parents are really Jewish Holocaust survivors. (Rev: BL 1/1–15/05; SLJ 6/05)

8593 Yee, Paul. *A Song for Ba* (2–5). Illus. by Jan Peng Wang. 2004, Douglas & McIntyre $16.95 (978-0-88899-492-9). 32pp. Singing Chinese opera is the forte of three generations of an immigrant family, and even though his father doesn't want him to follow in these footsteps, young Wei Lim is secretly tutored by his grandfather. (Rev: BL 4/1/04; SLJ 6/04)

8594 Yep, Laurence. *Dream Soul* (5–8). 2000, HarperCollins LB $14.89 (978-0-06-028309-4). 256pp. In this sequel to *Star Fisher* (1991), the Lees, a family of Chinese immigrants who live in Clarksburg, West Virginia, in 1927, face conflicts when the children want to celebrate Christmas. (Rev: BCCB 12/00; BL 12/1/00)

Family Stories

8595 Adler, C. S. *Ghost Brother* (5–8). 1990, Houghton $15.00 (978-0-395-52592-0). 150pp. After his older brother dies in an accident, 11-year-old Wally finds comfort in his ghost. (Rev: BCCB 5/90; BL 5/15/90; SLJ 5/90; VOYA 8/90)

8596 Adler, C. S. *The No Place Cat* (5–8). 2002, Clarion $15.00 (978-0-618-09644-2). 153pp. Twelve-year-old Tess runs away from home only to find that life with her father and new stepfamily had its good side after all. (Rev: BCCB 4/02; HBG 10/02; SLJ 3/02)

8597 Adler, C. S. *One Sister Too Many* (5–7). 1989, Macmillan paper $3.95 (978-0-689-71521-1). 176pp. Casey and her reunited family are being driven crazy by the newest addition — a colicky baby. (Rev: BCCB 3/89; BL 3/15/89; SLJ 4/89)

8598 Alcott, Louisa May. *Little Women* (5–9). 1947, Putnam $21.99 (978-0-448-06019-4). One of the many fine editions of this enduring story. Two sequels are *Little Men* and *Jo's Boys*.

8599 Almond, David. *My Dad's a Birdman* (4–6). Illus. by Polly Dunbar. 2008, Candlewick $15.99 (978-0-7636-3667-8). 128pp. Lizzie's father might be crazy but nonetheless she will help him make wings to fly across the River Tyne and win the Great Human Bird Competition. (Rev: BL 3/15/08; HB 5/08; LMC 10/08; SLJ 5/08)

8600 Alvarez, Julia. *How Tia Lola Came to Visit Stay* (4–7). 2001, Knopf $15.95 (978-0-375-80215-7). 160pp. Aunt Lola from the Dominican Republic comes to visit 10-year-old Miguel and his family in Vermont and everywhere she goes she spreads friendliness, enthusiasm, stories, and surprise parties. (Rev: BCCB 4/01; BL 2/15/01; HBG 10/01; SLJ 3/01)

8601 Baker, Deirdre. *Becca at Sea* (4–6). 2007, Groundwood $16.95 (978-0-88899-737-1). 165pp. Ten-year-old Becca learns to love her grandmother's rough character as well as the choppy waters that surround her British Columbia island home in this episodic novel. (Rev: HB 1/08; LMC 1/08; SLJ 10/07)

8602 Barshaw, Ruth McNally. *Ellie McDoodle: Have Pen, Will Travel* (3–6). Illus. by author. 2007, Bloomsbury $11.95 (978-1-58234-745-5). 170pp. Ellie survives a summer camping trip with her annoying cousins by playing games and pranks and recording it all in her diary/sketchbook. (Rev: SLJ 6/07)

8603 Bateson, Catherine. *Being Bee* (3–6). 2007, Holiday $16.95 (978-0-8234-2104-6). 144pp. Making a new family is hard for Bee when her father's girlfriend, Jazzi, moves in and begins redecorating; set in Australia. (Rev: BL 10/1/07; HB 11/07; SLJ 10/07)

8604 Bauer, Joan. *Stand Tall* (5–7). 2002, Putnam $16.99 (978-0-399-23473-6). 192pp. Tree, a tall 7th grader, has a lot of challenges in this nonetheless humorous novel: his height, his lack of athletic ability, shuffling between his divorced parents' homes, and his veteran grandfather's ailments, to name just a few. (Rev: BCCB 10/02; BL 9/15/02; HB 11/02; HBG 3/03; SLJ 8/02)

8605 Bauer, Jutta. *Grandpa's Angel* (1–3). Illus. 2005, Candlewick $12.99 (978-0-7636-2743-0). 48pp. The illustrations — most notably the images of a guardian angel — add another dimension to this captivating tale about an elderly man telling his grandson about the ups and downs of his life; a German import, this includes stories of World War II. (Rev: BL 10/15/05; SLJ 10/05)

8606 Bawden, Nina. *Granny the Pag* (5–8). 1996, Clarion $16.00 (978-0-395-77604-9). Catriona is embarrassed by her grandmother's eccentric ways, such as riding motorbikes and wearing leather jackets, but that doesn't mean she wants to live with her parents instead. (Rev: BCCB 3/96; BL 4/1/96; HB 9/96; SLJ 4/96*; VOYA 6/96)

8607 Beaty, Andrea. *Cicada Summer* (4–6). 2008, Abrams $15.95 (978-0-8109-9472-0). 176pp. In small-town Illinois, 12-year-old Lilly, who has not spoken since her brother died two years ago, tries to retain her protective silence. (Rev: BL 6/1–15/08; HB 5/08; LMC 10/08; SLJ 6/08)

8608 Beiton, Sandra. *Beauty, Her Basket* (1–4). Illus. by Cozbi A. Cabrera. 2004, Greenwillow $16.99 (978-0-688-17821-5). 32pp. As she learns from her grandmother how to weave baskets from the grasses of the Sea Islands off the coast of Georgia, a young girl also becomes more familiar with her African ancestry. (Rev: BL 3/1/04; SLJ 6/04)

8609 Bertrand, Diane Gonzales. *Alicia's Treasure* (4–6). 1996, Arte Publico paper $7.95 (978-1-55885-086-6). 125pp. Ten-year-old Alicia spends her first weekend at the beach, thanks to her brother's girlfriend. (Rev: BL 5/1/96; SLJ 7/96)

8610 Betancourt, Jeanne. *Puppy Love* (5–6). Illus. 1986, Avon paper $2.50 (978-0-380-89958-6). Aviva is having trouble dealing with her divorced parents' new lives and her own crush on Bob Hanley. (Rev: BL 8/86; SLJ 12/86)

8611 Birdsall, Jeanne. *The Penderwicks: A Summer Tale of Four Sisters, Two Rabbits, and a Very Interesting Boy* (3–6). 2005, Knopf LB $17.99 (978-0-375-93143-7). 192pp. Four sisters, ages 4 to 12, spend a wonderful summer in the Berkshires with their father. (Rev: BL 4/1/05)

8612 Birdsall, Jeanne. *The Penderwicks on Gardam Street* (4–7). Series: The Penderwicks. 2008, Knopf $15.99 (978-0-375-84090-6). 00pp. The loving, close Penderwick sisters, who were introduced in *The Penderwicks*, are loath to see their widower father start dating again and come up with a plan to discourage him. (Rev: BL 5/1/08; SLJ 3/08)

8613 Birdseye, Tom. *A Tough Nut to Crack* (3–5). 2006, Holiday $16.95 (978-0-8234-1967-8). 124pp. Cassie, sent from the city to help out at her grandfather's farm after he's injured, is determined to mend a long-standing feud between her father and grandfather. (Rev: BL 1/1–15/07; SLJ 1/07)

8614 Birdseye, Tom. *Tucker* (5–8). 1990, Holiday $16.95 (978-0-8234-0813-9). A story set in rural Kentucky of a young boy reunited with his younger sister after seven years of separation caused by divorce. (Rev: BL 7/90; SLJ 6/90)

8615 Bledsoe, Lucy Jane. *Cougar Canyon* (5–8). 2001, Holiday $16.95 (978-0-8234-1599-1). 130pp. A family story and environmental tale about a 13-year-old girl named Izzy who fights to save a cougar in the local park. (Rev: BCCB 2/02; BL 2/1/02; HBG 3/02; SLJ 2/02; VOYA 4/02)

8616 Blume, Judy. *Cool Zone with the Pain and the Great One* (3–5). Illus. by James Stevenson. 2008, Delacorte LB $19.99 (978-0-385-90325-7); paper $12.95 (978-0-385-73306-9). 128pp. In alternating chapters, 1st-grader Jake (the Pain) and his 3rd-grader sister Abigail (the Great One) tell stories of sibling rivalry, bullies, stuffed animals, and loose teeth. (Rev: BL 3/1/08; SLJ 6/08) ⌒

8617 Blume, Judy. *Double Fudge* (4–6). Series: Fudge. 2002, Dutton $15.99 (978-0-525-46926-1). 160pp. Twelve-year-old Peter Hatcher suffers many trials in this novel, as his younger brother Fudge (Farley) becomes obsessed with money, and a fami-

ly of long-lost relatives arrives for an extended stay in New York. (Rev: BCCB 11/02; BL 9/15/02; HB 11/02; HBG 3/03; SLJ 9/02)

8618 Blume, Judy. *It's Not the End of the World* (5–8). 1972, Dell paper $5.50 (978-0-440-44158-8). Twelve-year-old Karen's world seems to end when her parents are divorced and her older brother runs away.

8619 Borders, Christine. *Gram Makes a House Call* (2–4). Illus. by author. 1999, Greenhills paper $5.95 (978-0-9671160-0-6). 77pp. A simple chapter book about the good times a boy has with his unconventional grandmother. (Rev: SLJ 1/00)

8620 Brand, Christianna. *Nurse Matilda* (3–5). Illus. by Edward Ardizzone. 2005, Bloomsbury $16.95 (978-1-58234-670-0). 384pp. Nurse Matilda tries to bring order to a family with innumerable children in this inspiration for the movie "Nanny McPhee." (Rev: BL 3/1/05)

8621 Brokaw, Nancy Steele. *Leaving Emma* (4–7). 1999, Clarion $15.00 (978-0-395-90699-6). 144pp. When Emma's best friend moves away and her father is sent to work overseas, the young girl is left with a mother who suffers from bouts of depression. (Rev: BCCB 3/99; BL 3/1/99; HBG 10/99; SLJ 5/99)

8622 Bryant, Ann. *One Mom Too Many!* Bk. 1 (4–7). Series: Step-Chain. 2003, Lobster paper $3.95 (978-1-894222-78-5). 190pp. Sarah, 12, is not pleased to discover that both her divorced parents have found new romantic interests. (Rev: SLJ 5/04)

8623 Bunting, Eve. *Is Anybody There?* (4–7). 1990, HarperCollins paper $6.99 (978-0-06-440347-4). 176pp. Marcus is both scared and angry after his latchkey disappears and things are stolen. (Rev: BCCB 10/88; BL 12/15/88; SLJ 12/88)

8624 Burch, Robert. *Ida Early Comes over the Mountain* (4–8). 1990, Puffin paper $5.99 (978-0-14-034534-6). 140pp. The four motherless Sutton children find a new and most unusual housekeeper in Ida.

8625 Burnett, Frances Hodgson. *A Little Princess* (4–6). Illus. by Tasha Tudor. 1987, HarperCollins paper $6.99 (978-0-06-440187-6). 240pp. Sad story of a penniless orphan whose fortune is finally restored.

8626 Butcher, Kristin. *The Gramma War* (4–6). 2001, Orca paper $6.95 (978-1-55143-183-3). 170pp. Annie's life isn't enhanced when her difficult grandmother moves in and takes Annie's room, but an interest in genealogy brings them closer. (Rev: BCCB 1/02; BL 10/1/01; SLJ 9/01)

8627 Byars, Betsy. *Beans on the Roof* (3–5). Illus. 1990, Dell paper $3.99 (978-0-440-40314-2). 80pp. George's sister and the whole family are writing roof poems and George feels awful until he can write one too. (Rev: BCCB 11/88; BL 11/1/88; SLJ 11/88)

8628 Byars, Betsy. *Cracker Jackson* (5–6). 1986, Puffin paper $5.99 (978-0-14-031881-4). 168pp. Eleven-year-old Cracker proves a caring friend to his ex-baby-sitter when he suspects she is a victim of wife beating. (Rev: BL 4/1/85; HB 5/85; SLJ 5/85)

8629 Canfield, Dorothy. *Understood Betsy* (4–6). Illus. by Martha Alexander. 1981, Buccaneer LB $12.95 (978-0-89966-342-5). 219pp. A new edition of the old favorite about Elizabeth Ann and the fearful new way of life that awaits her when she goes to live in the wilds of Vermont.

8630 Carlson, Margaret. *The Canning Season* (4–6). Illus. 1999, Carolrhoda paper $7.95 (978-1-57505-283-0). Peggie's family's prejudice threatens her friendship with an African American girl in 1950s Minnesota. (Rev: BL 2/15; HBG 3/00; SLJ 3/99)

8631 Carmichael, Clay. *Wild Things* (5–8). 2009, Front St. $18.95 (978-1-59078-627-7). 248pp. After her mother dies, 11-year-old Zoe goes to live with her sculptor uncle Henry and gradually learns to trust people with the help of a feral cat who alternates narrating with Zoe. (Rev: BL 4/15/09; VOYA 8/09)

8632 Cassidy, Cathy. *Indigo Blue* (5–8). 2005, Viking $15.99 (978-0-670-05927-0). 256pp. As her family life slowly disintegrates, 11-year-old Indigo tries her best to conceal the truth from her friends at school in this realistic story set in Britain. (Rev: BL 10/1/05; SLJ 11/05)

8633 Chambers, Veronica. *Marisol and Magdalena: The Sound of Our Sisterhood* (5–9). 1998, Hyperion LB $15.49 (978-0-7868-2385-7). 141pp. Hispanic American Marisol is sent to live with her grandmother in Panama for a year, and hopes to track down her absent father. (Rev: BL 10/1/98; SLJ 12/98)

8634 Chase, Diana. *The Lighthouse Kids* (4–6). 2004, Fremantle Arts Centre paper $13.50 (978-1-86368-346-3). 271pp. When their mother dies, Ellen and Davey are sent to live with the lighthouse keeper grandfather they have never met. (Rev: SLJ 11/04)

8635 Cleary, Beverly. *Socks* (4–6). Illus. by Beatrice Darwin. 1973, Avon paper $5.99 (978-0-380-70926-7). 160pp. What happens when the family cat Socks realizes that his position of importance is threatened by the arrival of a baby.

8636 Clifton, Lucille. *The Lucky Stone* (3–5). Illus. by Dale Payson. 1986, Dell paper $3.99 (978-0-440-45110-5). 64pp. Several stories in the life of a girl's great-grandmother linked by the power of a stone.

8637 Clough, B. W. *An Impossumble Summer* (4–6). 1992, Walker $14.95 (978-0-8027-8150-5). 146pp. Rianne and her siblings discover their grumpy opossum can speak and grant wishes. (Rev: BL 3/1/92; SLJ 4/92)

8638 Cohen, Barbara. *The Carp in the Bathtub* (3–4). Illus. by Joan Halpern. 1972, Kar-Ben paper $5.95 (978-0-930494-67-4). 48pp. Two Jewish children decide that the carp in the bathtub should be rescued before it becomes Passover gefilte fish.

8639 Cohen, Miriam. *Mimmy and Sophie All Around the Town* (2–3). Illus. by Thomas F. Yezerski. 2004, Farrar $16.00 (978-0-374-34989-9). 80pp. Two girls living in Brooklyn during the Depression experience

all the joys and irritations of sisterhood. (Rev: BL 1/1–15/04; SLJ 5/04)

8640 Cohn, Rachel. *The Steps* (4–7). 2003, Simon & Schuster $16.95 (978-0-689-84549-9). 144pp. Annabel resents the complexity of her family life as she reluctantly sets out to visit her father and his new wife, baby, and stepchildren in Australia, but she gradually learns to accept the situation in this humorous portrayal. (Rev: BCCB 2/03; BL 1/1–15/03; HB 5/03; HBG 10/03; SLJ 2/03*)

8641 Coman, Carolyn. *Sneaking Suspicions* (4–6). Illus. by Rob Shepperson. 2007, Front St. $16.95 (978-1-59078-491-4). 248pp. After Ivy's parents are released from prison, she attempts to keep everyone honest as the family sets off to the Florida Everglades to find a long-lost cousin; a sequel to *The Big House* (2004). (Rev: BL 9/15/07; LMC 1/08; SLJ 10/07)

8642 Coman, Carolyn. *What Jamie Saw* (5–8). 1995, Front St. $15.95 (978-1-886910-02-7). 128pp. In this novel seen through the eyes of a young boy, a mother and her family flee her physically abusive husband. (Rev: BCCB 12/95; BL 12/15/95*; SLJ 12/95*)

8643 Conford, Ellen. *And This Is Laura* (4–6). 1992, Little, Brown paper $4.95 (978-0-316-15354-6). 192pp. A very ordinary girl discovers that she possesses psychic powers.

8644 Connor, Leslie. *Waiting for Normal* (5–7). 2008, HarperCollins $15.99 (978-0-06-089088-9). 304pp. Addie lives in a trailer with her mother and looks forward to visits with her stepfather and half sisters, whose life is far more "normal." (Rev: BL 4/1/08; SLJ 2/08)

8645 Corcoran, Barbara. *The Potato Kid* (5–8). 1993, Avon paper $3.50 (978-0-380-71213-7). 192pp. In spite of her protests, Ellis must look after an underprivileged girl her mother takes in for the summer. (Rev: BCCB 11/89; BL 11/15/89; HB 1/90; SLJ 10/89; VOYA 2/90)

8646 Cotten, Cynthia. *Fair Has Nothing to Do with It* (4–7). 2007, Farrar $16.00 (978-0-374-39935-1). 160pp. Upset by the death of his grandfather, 12-year-old Michael focuses his energies on an art project to honor his memory. (Rev: BL 4/1/07; SLJ 6/07)

8647 Couloumbis, Audrey. *Getting Near to Baby* (5–9). 1999, Putnam $17.99 (978-0-399-23389-0). 224pp. When their baby sister dies and their mother sinks into a depression, 12-year-old Willa Jo and Little Sister go to live with a bossy aunt in this story set in North Carolina. Newbery Honor Book, 2000. (Rev: BCCB 11/99; BL 11/1/99; HB 11/99; HBG 3/00; SLJ 10/99; VOYA 2/00)

8648 Couloumbis, Audrey. *Love Me Tender* (5–8). 2008, Random $16.99 (978-0-375-83839-2). 224pp. Thirteen-year-old Elvira initially questions her future when after a fight, her father leaves for Vegas to compete in an Elvis-impersonation contest and her pregnant mother takes Elvira and her younger sister to Memphis to reunite with her family. (Rev: BL 2/15/08; SLJ 4/08)

8649 Creech, Sharon. *Heartbeat* (3–6). 2004, Harper-Collins $15.99 (978-0-06-054022-7). 192pp. Thoughtful 12-year-old Annie, who enjoys running but not competing, faces numerous personal challenges in this story told in free verse. (Rev: BL 2/1/04; HB 5/04; SLJ 2/04)

8650 Creech, Sharon. *Replay* (4–7). 2005, Harper-Collins LB $16.89 (978-0-06-054020-3). 240pp. Twelve-year-old Leo untangles some of the secrets of his boisterous Italian American family when he finds his father's boyhood journal. (Rev: BCCB 11/05; BL 9/1/05*; HBG 4/06; LMC 3/06; SLJ 9/05; VOYA 12/05)

8651 Cutler, Jane. *Leap, Frog* (3–5). Illus. by Tracey Campbell Pearson. 2002, Farrar $16.00 (978-0-374-34362-0). 208pp. Third-grader Edward has a busy time participating in a variety of projects, particularly the frog-jumping contest that honors Mark Twain, and dealing with newcomer Charlie, a first-grader who regards Edward with awe. (Rev: BCCB 12/02; BL 11/1/02; HB 9/02; HBG 3/03; SLJ 10/02)

8652 Danziger, Paula. *Amber Brown Is Green with Envy* (2–4). Illus. by Tony Ross. 2003, Penguin $15.99 (978-0-399-23181-0). 160pp. Amber's divorced parents are moving in new directions and the fourth grader finds the tensions difficult to cope with. (Rev: BL 9/1/03; HBG 4/04; SLJ 9/03)

8653 Davies, Jacqueline. *The Lemonade War* (3–5). 2007, Houghton $16.00 (978-0-618-75043-6). 192pp. Evan and his younger sister Jessie — who has just skipped third grade and will be in Evan's class next year — now find themselves in constant conflict, even over their money-raising activities; includes tips for running a lemonade stand. (Rev: BL 3/15/07)

8654 de Anda, Diane. *The Ice Dove and Other Stories* (3–5). 1997, Arte Publico paper $7.95 (978-1-55885-189-4). 72pp. In these four stories, two involving Christmas and two the classroom, Hispanic American youngsters gain the strength to face problems through help from their loving extended families. (Rev: BL 10/1/97)

8655 Delacre, Lulu. *Salsa Stories* (4–7). Illus. 2000, Scholastic paper $16.99 (978-0-590-63118-1). 112pp. After each of her relatives tells a childhood story about a favorite food, Carmen Teresa records them and supplies appropriate recipes. (Rev: BCCB 5/00; BL 5/1/00; HBG 10/00; SLJ 3/00; VOYA 6/00)

8656 Delton, Judy. *Angel Bites the Bullet* (3–5). Illus. 2000, Houghton $15.00 (978-0-618-04085-8). 144pp. Angel and her best friend try everything to get rid of the unwanted guest who's sharing Angel's room. (Rev: BL 11/1/00; HBG 3/01; SLJ 10/00)

8657 Delton, Judy. *Angel's Mother's Boyfriend* (3–5). Illus. by Margot Apple. 1986, Houghton $16.00 (978-0-395-39968-2). 176pp. Angel and brother Rags are dismayed to discover that their mother has a boyfriend, and doubly dismayed to discover that he is a clown — a real one! Also use: *Angel in Charge* (1985); *Angel's Mother's Wedding* (1987). (Rev: BL 4/1/86; HB 7/86; SLJ 8/86)

8658 Deuker, Carl. *High Heat* (5–8). 2003, Houghton $16.00 (978-0-618-31117-0). 288pp. Even his baseball prowess seems to desert Shane when his father commits suicide and he must move to a tough new neighborhood and school. (Rev: BL 8/03; HBG 10/03; SLJ 7/03; VOYA 8/03)

8659 Doucet, Sharon Arms. *Fiddle Fever* (4–7). 2000, Clarion $15.00 (978-0-618-04324-8). 176pp. Felix disobeys his mother, who hates fiddle playing, and builds one out of a cigar box and practices in secret. (Rev: BL 9/1/00; HB 9/00; HBG 3/01; SLJ 10/00)

8660 Dowell, Frances O'Roark. *Dovey Coe* (4–7). 2000, Simon & Schuster $16.00 (978-0-689-83174-4). 192pp. The mountain country of North Carolina in 1928 is the setting of this story of a plucky girl who cares for her siblings and who gets involved in a murder trial. (Rev: BL 4/15/00; HBG 10/00; SLJ 5/00; VOYA 6/00)

8661 Doyle, Eugenie. *Stray Voltage* (5–7). 2002, Front St. $16.95 (978-1-886910-86-7). 136pp. The electrical problems in Ian's family barn reflect the flickering, unpredictable relationships at home, but a wise teacher helps Ian to cope with his circumstances. (Rev: BCCB 1/03; BL 1/1–15/03*; HBG 3/03; SLJ 10/02*; VOYA 2/03)

8662 Draper, Sharon M. *Little Sister Is Not My Name* (2–4). 2009, Scholastic $16.99 (978-0-545-07151-2). 112pp. Sassy is the youngest and smallest in her African American family and often feels left out until the day when her size proves useful. (Rev: BL 4/15/09; SLJ 3/09)

8663 Duble, Kathleen Benner. *Bravo Zulu, Samantha!* (5–8). 2007, Peachtree $14.95 (978-1-56145-401-3). 144pp. Twelve-year-old Samantha unwillingly spends the summer with her grandparents but her retired Air Force grandfather turns out to have an exciting secret. (Rev: BL 6/1–15/07; SLJ 6/07)

8664 Duncan, Jane. *Brave Janet Reachfar* (4–6). Illus. by Mairi Hedderwick. 1975, Houghton $7.95 (978-0-8164-3130-4). 32pp. Scottish farm life is depicted through the adventures of young Janet and her relationship with her tyrannical grandmother.

8665 Dunlop, Eileen. *Finn's Island* (4–6). 1992, Holiday House $13.95 (978-0-8234-0910-5). 128pp. Bored and grieving, Finn takes a trip from Scotland to the Hebrides island of his grandfather's birth, where he learns to see the man more realistically. (Rev: BL 2/1/92; SLJ 6/92)

8666 Dunmore, Helen. *Brother Brother, Sister Sister* (5–8). 2000, Scholastic paper $4.50 (978-0-439-11322-9). 116pp. Written in diary format, this is the story of Tanya, once an only child and now surrounded by babies after her mother has quadruplets. (Rev: SLJ 8/00)

8667 Edwards, Nancy. *Mom for Mayor* (3–5). Illus. by Michael Chesworth. 2006, Cricket $15.95 (978-0-8126-2743-5). 144pp. In a last-ditch effort to prevent the sale of a local playground to developers, fifth-grader Eric convinces his mother to run for mayor against the man who engineered the sale plan; an entertaining chapter book with humorous illustrations. (Rev: BL 3/15/06; SLJ 3/06)

8668 Ellis, Sarah. *Odd Man Out* (4–6). 2006, Groundwood $16.95 (978-0-88899-702-9). 160pp. Twelve-year-old Kip spends a summer with his grandmother and five female cousins and learns — from a binder he finds in the attic — about the father he never knew. (Rev: BL 12/1/06; SLJ 12/06)

8669 Ellis, Sarah. *Out of the Blue* (5–7). Illus. 1995, Simon & Schuster paper $15.00 (978-0-689-80025-2). 120pp. Twelve-year-old Megan discovers that she has a 24-year-old half-sister whom her mother gave up for adoption years ago. (Rev: BCCB 4/95; BL 5/1/95; HB 7/95; SLJ 5/95)

8670 Encinas, Carlos. *The New Engine / La Maquina Nueva* (1–5). Illus. by author. 2001, Kiva $15.95 (978-1-885772-24-4). A man worried that a computer may replace him remembers his family's fear that the arrival of a diesel locomotive would put his own father out of work. (Rev: SLJ 1/02)

8671 Engel, Diana. *Holding On* (4–6). 1997, Marshall Cavendish $14.95 (978-0-7614-5016-0). 96pp. Tommy is fearful about spending two weeks with his erratic great-uncle, but slowly they become friends. (Rev: BL 9/15/97; HBG 3/98; SLJ 11/97)

8672 Enright, Elizabeth. *Thimble Summer* (4–6). Illus. by author. 1938, Holt $17.95 (978-0-8050-0306-2). 124pp. A small girl on a Wisconsin farm finds a magic thimble. Newbery Award winner, 1939.

8673 Fenner, Carol. *Yolonda's Genius* (4–6). 1995, Simon & Schuster paper $17.00 (978-0-689-80001-6). 153pp. African American Yolanda tries to prove that her young brother, who does poorly at school, is really a musical genius. (Rev: BL 6/1–15/95; SLJ 7/95)

8674 Fleischman, Sid. *Bo and Mzzz Mad* (5–7). 2001, Greenwillow LB $15.89 (978-0-06-029398-7). 112pp. When his father dies, 12-year-old Bo accepts an invitation from relatives despite a long-standing family feud. (Rev: BL 5/15/01*; HB 5/01; HBG 10/01; SLJ 5/01)

8675 Fletcher, Brian. *Uncle Daddy* (4–6). 2001, Holt $15.95 (978-0-8050-6663-0). 133pp. Nine-year-old Rivers's peaceful life is upset when his long-absent father turns up without warning. (Rev: BCCB 5/01; BL 8/01; HB 7/01; HBG 10/01; SLJ 5/01)

8676 Fletcher, Ralph. *Fig Pudding* (5–7). 1995, Clarion $15.00 (978-0-395-71125-5). 160pp. A year that brings both tragedy and hilarity in the life of a family of six children. (Rev: BCCB 5/95; BL 5/15/95; SLJ 7/95)

8677 Flood, Pansie Hart. *Secret Holes* (4–6). Illus. by Felicia Marshall. 2003, Carolrhoda LB $15.95 (978-0-87614-923-2). 122pp. After moving with her mother from Florida to a farm in rural South Carolina, 10-year-old Sylvia discovers that her new best friend — 100-year-old Lula Maye — is also her great-grandmother and that the father she'd long believed was dead is very much alive. (Rev: HBG 4/04; SLJ 1/04)

8678 Flood, Pansie Hart. *Sometimey Friend* (3–5). Illus. by Felicia Marshall. 2005, Carolrhoda $15.95 (978-1-57505-866-5). 128pp. While the aunt who raised her travels to Florida, 10-year-old Sylvia

Freeman stays in South Carolina with her elderly great-grandmother, an arrangement that suits her fine until her classmates begin poking fun at the old woman. (Rev: BL 11/15/05; SLJ 12/05)

8679 Fogelin, Adrian. *My Brother's Hero* (5–8). 2002, Peachtree $14.95 (978-1-56145-274-3). 224pp. When Ben and his family travel to Florida for a vacation, Ben meets a girl named Mica, whose life he finds exciting and mysterious. (Rev: BL 2/1/03; HBG 10/03; SLJ 2/03)

8680 Foggo, Cheryl. *One Thing That's True* (5–8). 1998, Kids Can $16.95 (978-1-55074-411-8). 128pp. Roxanne is heartbroken when her older brother runs away after learning that he is adopted. (Rev: BCCB 5/98; BL 2/15/98; HBG 10/98; SLJ 4/98)

8681 Fox, Paula. *The Village by the Sea* (5–8). 1988, Orchard $15.95 (978-0-531-05788-9). Emma is staying with an aunt and uncle while her father has heart surgery, and the three interact in complex ways. Also use the reissued *A Likely Place* (1997). (Rev: BCCB 7–8/88; BL 9/1/88; HB 9/88; SLJ 8/88; VOYA 10/88)

8682 Frazier, Sundee T. *Brendan Buckley's Universe and Everything in It* (4–6). 2007, Delacorte $14.99 (978-0-385-73439-4). 199pp. Brendan's love of rocks leads the mixed-race boy to a relationship with his estranged white grandfather. (Rev: BL 1/1–15/08; LMC 1/08; SLJ 10/07) ⌒

8683 Freeman, Martha. *The Trouble with Twins* (3–5). Illus. by Cat B. Smith. 2007, Holiday $16.95 (978-0-8234-2025-4). 85pp. Two previous books featuring Holly introduced this lively, caring girl who is now coping with her energetic 2-year-old twin brothers. (Rev: BCCB 1/08; BL 12/1/07; SLJ 3/08)

8684 French, Simon. *Where in the World* (5–8). 2003, Peachtree $14.95 (978-1-56145-292-7). 208pp. A move from Germany to Australia is difficult for Ari, a talented young violinist who spends time living in the past while trying to find ways to cope with the present. (Rev: BL 12/1/03; HBG 4/04; SLJ 12/03*)

8685 Friedman, Laurie. *Mallory vs. Max* (2–4). Illus. by Tamara Schmitz. 2005, Carolrhoda LB $15.95 (978-1-57505-795-8). 159pp. Eight-year-old Mallory is not pleased when her brother Max's new puppy gets all the attention. (Rev: SLJ 4/05)

8686 Gantos, Jack. *Jack Adrift: Fourth Grade Without a Clue* (4–7). 2003, Farrar $16.00 (978-0-374-39987-0). 208pp. In this prequel to the four previous books, Jack Henry is 9 and has just moved to Cape Hatteras where he has comic experiences and more serious conversations with his dad. (Rev: BL 8/03; HB 11/03; HBG 4/04; SLJ 9/03)

8687 Garcia, Cristina. *I Wanna Be Your Shoebox* (5–8). 2008, Simon & Schuster $16.99 (978-1-4169-6229-8). 208pp. Thirteen-year-old Yumi is part Cuban, part Japanese, and part Jewish, and it is only when her terminally ill grandfather, a Russian Jew, tells her his life story that she begins to understand her own identity. (Rev: BL 8/08)

8688 Gates, Doris. *Blue Willow* (5–8). 1940, Penguin paper $6.99 (978-0-14-030924-9). An easily read novel about a poor girl and the china plate that belonged to her mother. (Rev: BCCB 12/99)

8689 Gates, Susan. *Beyond the Billboard* (5–8). 2007, Harcourt $16.00 (978-0-15-205983-5). 224pp. Ford and Firebird, 13-year-old twins, have grown up secluded from the modern world but their lives are about to change as secrets are revealed. (Rev: BL 6/1–15/07; SLJ 8/07)

8690 Gay, Marie-Louise, and David Homel. *Travels with My Family* (3–5). 2006, Groundwood $15.95 (978-0-88899-688-6). 80pp. Adventures are guaranteed in this family, which takes unusual (and sometimes dangerous) vacations — observed by an older brother with a dry sense of humor. (Rev: BL 5/15/06; SLJ 8/06)

8691 Gifaldi, David. *Listening for Crickets* (3–5). 2008, Holt $16.95 (978-0-8050-7385-0). 192pp. Jake, about to start 5th grade, describes his difficulties at home (feuding parents and a Dad out of work and drinking) and at school and the comfort he gets from telling stories to his younger sister. (Rev: BL 5/15/08; HB 9/08; LMC 3/09)

8692 Giff, Patricia Reilly. *Pictures of Hollis Woods* (5–7). 2002, Random $15.95 (978-0-385-32655-1). 160pp. Twelve-year-old Hollis Woods has finally found a foster home where she feels safe, but when the artist who takes her in begins to suffer from dementia, Hollis finds herself in the position of caregiver. Newbery Honor Book, 2003. (Rev: BCCB 12/02; BL 10/15/02; HB 1/03; HBG 3/03; SLJ 9/02)

8693 Gilliland, Hap, and William Walters. *Flint's Rock* (5–7). 1996, Roberts Rinehart paper $8.95 (978-1-879373-82-2). 144pp. Flint, a young Cheyenne, faces problems when he moves with his parents from the reservation to Butte, Montana. (Rev: BCCB 5/96; BL 5/1/96)

8694 Gilmore, Rachna. *Mina's Spring of Colors* (4–7). 2000, Fitzhenry & Whiteside $14.95 (978-1-55041-549-0); paper $8.95 (978-1-55041-534-6). 150pp. Mina is happy when her grandfather comes from India, but with his arrival comes a culture clash that troubles the girl. (Rev: BL 6/1–15/00; SLJ 9/00; VOYA 12/00)

8695 Glatt, Lisa, and Suzanne Greenberg. *Abigail Iris: The One and Only* (2–4). Illus. by Joy Allen. 2009, Walker $14.99 (978-0-8027-9782-7). 160pp. After spending a vacation with her friend Genevieve, who is an "only," Abigail Iris appreciates her own siblings more. (Rev: BCCB 4/09; BL 3/1/09; SLJ 3/09)

8696 Golding, Theresa Martin. *The Secret Within* (5–8). 2002, Boyds Mills $16.95 (978-1-56397-995-8). 240pp. Eighth-grader Carly's secret is that her father is abusive and a criminal; the neighbors in the family's new town help her and her mother to finally escape his grip. (Rev: BL 9/15/02; HBG 3/03; SLJ 8/02; VOYA 2/03)

8697 Goobie, Beth. *Something Girl* (5–8). 2005, Orca paper $7.95 (978-1-55143-347-9). 112pp. Fifteen-year-old Sophie tries to hide the fact that her mother is an alcoholic and her father abusive in this book for reluctant readers. (Rev: BL 7/05; SLJ 12/05)

8698 Goodman, Joan E. *Songs from Home* (5–7). Illus. 1994, Harcourt paper $4.95 (978-0-15-203591-4). 224pp. Anna discovers the truth about her father, who has become a drifter in Italy singing for tips in restaurants. (Rev: BCCB 12/94; BL 9/1/94; SLJ 10/94)

8699 Greene, Stephanie. *Sophie Hartley, on Strike* (3–5). 2006, Clarion $15.00 (978-0-618-71960-0). 152pp. Ten-year-old Sophie and her older sister Nora feel their share of the household chores is too heavy and decide to go on strike. (Rev: BL 1/1–15/07; SLJ 1/07)

8700 Greenfield, Eloise. *Sister* (5–7). Illus. by Moneta Barnett. 1974, HarperCollins $15.99 (978-0-690-00497-7); paper $5.99 (978-0-06-440199-9). 96pp. Four years in an African American girl's life, as revealed through scattered diary entries, during which she shows maturation, particularly in her attitude toward her sister.

8701 Griffith, Helen V. *Grandaddy and Janetta Together: The Three Stories in One Book* (2–5). Illus. 2001, Greenwillow LB $15.89 (978-0-06-029238-6). 80pp. Three great picture books — *Grandaddy's Place* (1987), *Grandaddy and Janetta* (1993), and *Grandaddy's Stars* (1995) — are reprinted in one volume that tells the continuing story of the bond between a city girl and her country grandfather. (Rev: BL 12/15/00; HBG 10/01)

8702 Grimes, Nikki. *Dark Sons* (5–8). 2005, Hyperion $15.99 (978-0-7868-1888-4). 218pp. Alternating between biblical times and contemporary New York, free-verse narratives express the frustrations of Ishmael — son of Abraham, who must wander the desert with his rejected mother — and of Sam, whose father has left his mother for a young white woman. (Rev: BL 8/05*; SLJ 11/05; VOYA 10/05)

8703 Hahn, Mary D. *As Ever, Gordy* (5–8). 1998, Houghton $15.00 (978-0-395-83627-9). After his grandmother's death, 13-year-old Gordy must move back to his hometown to live with his older brother, and there he finds himself in a downward spiral. A sequel to *Stepping on Cracks* and *Following My Own Footsteps*. (Rev: BCCB 6/98; BL 5/1/98; HBG 10/98; SLJ 7/98; VOYA 4/99)

8704 Hall, Donald. *Old Home Day* (3–6). Illus. by Emily Arnold McCully. 1996, Harcourt $16.00 (978-0-15-276896-6). 48pp. The changes in Blackwater Pond in New Hampshire from the Ice Age to the present, with emphasis on the time after the first settlers arrived in 1799. (Rev: BCCB 10/96; BL 9/1/96*; HB 11/96; SLJ 10/96)

8705 Hamilton, Virginia. *Bluish* (4–6). 1999, Scholastic $16.95 (978-0-590-28879-8). 128pp. Dreenie tries to become friends with a girl nicknamed Bluish, wheelchair-ridden and suffering from cancer, who is in Dreenie's fifth-grade class. (Rev: BCCB 10/99; BL 9/15/99; HBG 3/00; SLJ 11/99)

8706 Hamilton, Virginia. *Plain City* (5–7). 1993, Scholastic paper $13.95 (978-0-590-47364-4). 194pp. Buhlaire's life changes dramatically when the father she believed to be dead unexpectedly arrives in town. (Rev: BCCB 11/93; BL 9/15/93*; SLJ 11/93*)

8707 Hamilton, Virginia. *Second Cousins* (5–8). 1998, Scholastic paper $14.95 (978-0-590-47368-2). In this sequel to *Cousins,* 12-year-old Cammy learns a secret during a family reunion in her small Ohio town. (Rev: BCCB 11/98; BL 8/98; HB 1/99; HBG 3/99; SLJ 11/98; VOYA 2/99)

8708 Hansen, Joyce. *One True Friend* (4–7). 2001, Clarion $14.00 (978-0-395-84983-5). 151pp. Amir's correspondence with his friend Doris comforts him as he tries to fulfill a deathbed promise to his mother to keep his family together. (Rev: BCCB 12/01; BL 12/15/01; HBG 3/02; SLJ 12/01; VOYA 10/01)

8709 Harrison, Mette Ivie. *The Monster in Me* (5–8). 2003, Holiday $16.95 (978-0-8234-1713-1). 176pp. A caring foster family and her growing enjoyment in running make Natalie, 13, more optimistic about life. (Rev: BL 4/1/03; HBG 10/03; SLJ 6/03; VOYA 10/03)

8710 Hausman, Gerald, and Uton Hinds. *The Jacob Ladder* (5–8). 2001, Orchard paper $15.95 (978-0-531-30331-3). 119pp. This story of a young Jamaican who struggles valiantly to cope with poverty, a charismatic but neglectful father, and the problems of growing up is based on the youth of coauthor Uton Hinds. (Rev: BL 5/1/01; HBG 3/02; SLJ 4/01; VOYA 6/01)

8711 Henkes, Kevin. *The Birthday Room* (5–7). 1999, Greenwillow $19.99 (978-0-688-16733-2). 176pp. Ben travels to Oregon with his mother to visit Uncle Ian who was responsible for Ben's losing his little finger in an accident. (Rev: BCCB 9/99; BL 7/99; HB 9/99; HBG 3/00; SLJ 10/99)

8712 Hermes, Patricia. *Emma Dilemma and the Camping Nanny* (3–6). 2009, Marshall Cavendish $15.99 (978-0-7614-5534-9). 144pp. Nine-year-old Emma is frustrated by her nanny's affection for her boyfriend and by her friend Luisa's defection. What can she do, and will it work? (Rev: BL 3/15/09; SLJ 5/09)

8713 Hermes, Patricia. *Emma Dilemma and the New Nanny* (3–5). 2006, Marshall Cavendish $15.95 (978-0-7614-5286-7). 112pp. Accident-prone Emma, 8, is trying to keep her ferret under control and the new nanny from being fired, but somehow things keep going wrong. (Rev: BL 4/15/06; SLJ 5/06)

8714 Hermes, Patricia. *Emma Dilemma and the Soccer Nanny* (3–5). 2008, Marshall Cavendish $15.99 (978-0-7614-5301-7). 112pp. Emma, now 9, would like her nanny to chaperone the soccer trip to Washington, not her mother. (Rev: BL 7/08; SLJ 6/08)

8715 Hermes, Patricia. *Emma Dilemma and the Two Nannies* (2–4). 2007, Marshall Cavendish $15.99 (978-0-7614-5353-6). 116pp. Emma's nanny is taking a three-week vacation and, worried that her parents may prefer the substitute nanny, Emma plots against this eventuality while also coping with crises such as her ferret eating a classmate's book. (Rev: SLJ 4/07)

8716 Hermes, Patricia. *You Shouldn't Have to Say Good-bye* (5–8). 1982, Scholastic paper $3.25 (978-0-590-43174-3). 117pp. A moving novel about a girl whose mother is dying of cancer.

8717 Herschler, Mildred Barger. *The Darkest Corner* (5–9). 2000, Front St. $17.95 (978-1-886910-54-6). 240pp. In this novel set in the Deep South of the 1960s, 10-year-old Teddy is shocked to discover that her beloved dad participated in the lynching of her best friend's father. (Rev: BL 1/1–15/01; HBG 3/01; SLJ 2/01; VOYA 2/01)

8718 Hicks, Betty. *Out of Order* (4–7). 2005, Roaring Brook $15.95 (978-1-59643-061-7). 176pp. In alternating chapters, four new stepsiblings relate the problems — and the fun — they have had adjusting to life together. (Rev: BL 9/15/05; SLJ 10/05; VOYA 12/05)

8719 High, Linda O. *Maizie* (4–8). 1995, Holiday $14.95 (978-0-8234-1161-0). 177pp. Maizie, a survivor, succeeds in spite of being abandoned by her mother and left with an alcoholic father. (Rev: BCCB 4/95; BL 4/15/95; HB 5/95; SLJ 4/95)

8720 Hirahara, Naomi. *1001 Cranes* (4–7). 2008, Delacorte $15.99 (978-0-385-73556-8). 240pp. Twelve-year-old Angela reluctantly spends the summer with her Japanese American grandparents, where she learns to cope with her parents' separation while creating origami for the family business. (Rev: BL 8/08; SLJ 8/08)

8721 Hogeweg, Margriet. *The God of Grandma Forever* (4–6). 2001, Front St. $14.95 (978-1-886910-69-0). 112pp. Maria has a difficult relationship with her religious grandmother in this story translated from Dutch. (Rev: BCCB 6/01; BL 9/15/01; HBG 10/01; SLJ 7/01)

8722 Holcomb, Jerry Kimble. *The Chinquapin Tree* (5–9). 1998, Marshall Cavendish $14.95 (978-0-7614-5028-3). 189pp. Faced with being sent back to their abusive mother, three youngsters head for the wilderness in this survival story set in Oregon. (Rev: BL 5/1/98; HBG 10/98; SLJ 5/98)

8723 Holm, Jenni. *Our Only May Amelia* (4–6). 1999, HarperCollins LB $15.89 (978-0-06-028354-4). 160pp. Told in diary form, this is the story of 12-year-old May Amelia, who lives with her large family in Washington State in the late 1800s, and of her troubles when her grandmother comes to stay. Newbery Honor Book, 2000. (Rev: BCCB 9/99; BL 9/1/99; HBG 10/99; SLJ 6/99)

8724 Holt, Kimberly Willis. *Piper Reed, the Great Gypsy* (3–5). Illus. by Christine Davenier. 2008, Holt $14.95 (978-0-8050-8198-5). 160pp. In this sequel to *Piper Reed, Navy Brat* (2007), 9-year-old Piper, a dyslexic, continues her entertaining descriptions of her family life. Her father is away at sea but Piper enjoys various events including a Gypsy Club pet show. (Rev: BL 7/08; HB 9/08) ⌒

8725 Honeycutt, Natalie. *Twilight in Grace Falls* (5–9). 1997, Orchard LB $17.99 (978-0-531-33007-4). A moving novel about the closing of a lumber mill that brings unemployment to 11-year-old Dasie Jenson's father. (Rev: BCCB 6/97; BL 3/15/97*; HB 7/97; SLJ 5/97; VOYA 8/97)

8726 Hunter, Evan. *Me and Mr. Stenner* (5–8). 1976, HarperCollins $11.95 (978-0-397-31689-2). 128pp. Abby's attitudes toward her new stepfather gradually change from resentment to love.

8727 Jarrow, Gail. *If Phyllis Were Here* (5–7). 1989, Avon paper $2.75 (978-0-380-70634-1). 144pp. Libby, age 11, has to learn to adjust to living without her best friend — her grandmother who moves to Florida. (Rev: BL 10/15/87; SLJ 9/87)

8728 Johnson, Angela. *Songs of Faith* (5–8). 1998, Orchard LB $16.99 (978-0-531-33023-4). Doreen is a child of divorce who is particularly upset by her younger brother's problems adjusting after their father moves away. (Rev: BCCB 6/98; BL 2/15/98; HBG 10/98; SLJ 3/98; VOYA 6/98)

8729 Johnston, Lindsay Lee. *Soul Moon Soup* (5–7). 2002, Front St. $15.95 (978-1-886910-87-4). 134pp. When homeless Phoebe and her mother hit bottom, Phoebe goes to live with her grandmother and slowly learns to value her own resources in this story told in verse. (Rev: BCCB 2/03; BL 11/15/02; HB 1/03; HBG 3/03; SLJ 11/02)

8730 Johnston, Tony. *Angel City* (2–4). Illus. by Carole Byard. 2006, Philomel $15.99 (978-0-399-23405-7). 40pp. An elderly African American man discovers a Latino baby abandoned in a dumpster and takes the child home to raise as his own. (Rev: BL 6/1–15/06; SLJ 6/06)

8731 Jones, Kimberly K. *Sand Dollar Summer* (5–8). 2006, Simon & Schuster $15.95 (978-1-4169-0362-8). 224pp. Annalise's summer in Maine with her mother and younger, often-mute brother Free takes a dramatic turn when a hurricane hits their island. (Rev: BL 5/15/06; HBG 10/06; LMC 1/07; SLJ 6/06*)

8732 Joosse, Barbara M. *Pieces of the Picture* (5–8). 1989, HarperCollins LB $12.89 (978-0-397-32343-2); paper $3.50 (978-0-06-440310-8). 144pp. Emily is not happy when she and her mother move to Wisconsin after her father's death to earn a livelihood running an inn. (Rev: BL 6/1/89; SLJ 4/89)

8733 Kehret, Peg. *Sisters Long Ago* (5–8). 1992, Pocket paper $3.99 (978-0-671-78433-1). 149pp. While surviving a near drowning, Willow has a glimpse of herself living another life in ancient Egypt. (Rev: SLJ 3/90)

8734 Kelly, Katy. *Lucy Rose: Big on Plans* (2–4). Illus. by Adam Rex. 2005, Delacorte $12.95 (978-0-385-73204-8). 128pp. Lucy Rose, a precocious 8-year-old, chronicles her busy plans for the summer in her journal. (Rev: BL 8/05; SLJ 6/05)

8735 Kelly, Katy. *Lucy Rose: Busy Like You Can't Believe* (2–4). Illus. by Adam Rex. Series: Lucy Rose. 2006, Delacorte $12.95 (978-0-385-73319-9). 176pp. Now in fourth grade, Lucy Rose reveals in her diary her struggles with her mother's romantic life and learns some important lessons about the perils of eavesdropping. (Rev: BL 10/15/06; SLJ 10/06)

8736 Kennedy, Marlane. *Me and the Pumpkin Queen* (4–6). 2007, Greenwillow $15.99 (978-0-06-114022-8). 192pp. In homage to her late mother, 11-year-old Mildred tries for years to grow giant pumpkins to win a contest, and her family and friends provide support along the way. (Rev: BCCB 9/07; BL 7/07; SLJ 8/07)

8737 Kirby, Susan E. *Ida Lou's Story* (4–6). Series: American Quilts. 2001, Simon & Schuster paper $4.99 (978-0-689-80972-9). 170pp. Lacey likes to hear stories of times past and her great-great-aunt Ida Lou who dreamed of becoming a trapeze artist. (Rev: SLJ 12/01)

8738 Klein, Norma. *Mom, the Wolfman and Me* (5–8). 1972, Avon paper $3.50 (978-0-380-00791-2). 160pp. Brett's mother is single but the Wolfman is becoming more than a steady boyfriend.

8739 Klise, Kate. *Far from Normal* (5–8). 2006, Scholastic $16.99 (978-0-439-79447-3). 256pp. In this sequel to *Deliver Us from Normal* (2005), the Harrisong family makes a deal with the devil when a retailing giant threatens to sue over disparaging remarks made about the chain in a book written by Charles. (Rev: BL 10/15/06; VOYA 4/07)

8740 Levoy, Myron. *The Witch of Fourth Street and Other Stories* (4–7). Illus. 1991, Peter Smith $19.75 (978-0-8446-6450-7); HarperCollins paper $5.99 (978-0-06-440059-6). 128pp. Eight stories about growing up poor on the Lower East Side of New York City.

8741 Levy, Elizabeth. *Big Trouble in Little Twinsville* (3–6). 2001, HarperCollins LB $15.89 (978-0-06-028591-3). 96pp. Ten-year-old Eve finds her twin younger sisters a source of great annoyance, but her attitude changes when the two do badly in a talent contest. (Rev: BCCB 7–8/01; BL 7/01; HBG 10/01; SLJ 5/01)

8742 Levy, Elizabeth. *Night of the Living Gerbil* (3–5). Illus. by Bill Basso. 2001, HarperCollins LB $15.89 (978-0-06-028589-0). 96pp. When Robert's hamster dies, he has it stuffed by a taxidermist who puts the hamster in such a frightful pose that Robert and his brother fear he has been turned into a Zombie. (Rev: BL 11/1/01; HBG 3/02; SLJ 11/01)

8743 Lewis, Beverly. *The Chicken Pox Panic* (2–4). Illus. Series: Cul-de-Sac Kids. 1995, Bethany House paper $3.99 (978-1-55661-626-6). 80pp. While recovering from chicken pox, Abby plans a birthday party for her Korean brother; but when he arrives, everyone has chicken pox. Also in the series: *The Double Dabble Surprise* (1995). (Rev: BL 9/1/95)

8744 Lewis, Beverly. *Whispers down the Lane* (5–8). Series: Summerhill Secrets. 1995, Bethany paper $5.99 (978-1-55661-476-7). 144pp. An Amish girl agrees to hide Lissa, who has run away from her father's abusive treatment. (Rev: BL 9/1/95; SLJ 2/96)

8745 Lindbergh, Anne. *The Worry Week* (5–7). Illus. by Kathryn Hewitt. 1985, Harcourt $12.95 (978-0-15-299675-8); Avon paper $2.95 (978-0-380-70394-4). 144pp. Left alone with her sisters for a week in Maine, 11-year-old "Legs" spends most of her time tending to and worrying about her siblings. (Rev: BL 6/1/85; HB 9/85; SLJ 8/85)

8746 Lindquist, Jennie D. *The Little Silver House* (3–5). Illus. by Garth Williams. 1986, Peter Smith $16.00 (978-0-8446-6190-2). A 9-year-old girl is intrigued by a mysterious boarded-up house. A reissue of a 1959 title.

8747 Little, Jean. *Emma's Strange Pet* (1–2). Illus. by Jennifer Plecas. Series: I Can Read. 2003, HarperCollins $15.99 (978-0-06-028350-6). 64pp. In a concession to his sister Emma's allergies, Max gives up his quest for a dog and accepts a lizard in this sweet but challenging book for beginning readers. (Rev: BL 7/03; HBG 4/04; SLJ 10/03)

8748 Loredo, Betsy. *Faraway Families* (2–4). Illus. by Monisha Raja. Series: Family Ties. 1995, Silver Moon LB $14.95 (978-1-881889-61-8). 56pp. Five short stories, each dealing with a different racial minority, explore the emotional problems that result after families are separated. (Rev: SLJ 8/95)

8749 Lowry, Lois. *Us and Uncle Fraud* (4–6). 1984, Houghton $16.00 (978-0-395-36633-2). 192pp. Two children become disillusioned with their Uncle Claude.

8750 Luger, Harriett M. *Bye, Bye, Bali Kai* (5–7). 1996, Harcourt paper $5.00 (978-0-15-200863-5). 192pp. Suzie's family hits rock bottom when they are evicted and forced to live in an abandoned building. (Rev: BCCB 3/96; BL 6/1–15/96; SLJ 6/96; VOYA 6/96)

8751 Lupica, Mike. *Miracle on 49th Street* (5–8). 2006, Philomel $17.99 (978-0-399-24488-9). 288pp. The life of pro basketball star Josh Cameron is turned upside down when 12-year-old Molly Parker turns up claiming to be his daughter. (Rev: BL 9/1/06; SLJ 11/06) 🎧

8752 Lurie, April. *Dancing in the Streets of Brooklyn* (5–9). 2002, Delacorte LB $17.99 (978-0-385-90066-9). 192pp. Judy, from a Norwegian immigrant family, is devastated to learn that the man she knows as "Pa" is not her birth father in this novel set in 1944. (Rev: BCCB 12/02; BL 11/15/02; HBG 3/03; SLJ 9/02)

8753 Lyon, Annabel. *All-Season Edie* (5–7). 2008, Orca paper $8.95 (978-1-55143-713-2). 179pp. Edie, 11, flirts with witchcraft as a solution to her family's problems and to aid her in her quest for coolness; this is a fast-paced first-person narrative full of humor. (Rev: BL 3/1/08)

8754 Lyons, Kelly Starling. *Eddie's Ordeal* (5–8). Illus. 2004, Just Us Bks. paper $3.95 (978-0-940975-16-3). 85pp. When Eddie's grades slip, his father makes him quit baseball. (Rev: BL 2/1/05)

8755 McDonough, Alison. *Do the Hokey Pokey* (3–5). Illus. 2001, Front St. $14.95 (978-0-8126-2699-5). 120pp. Shy, friendless Brendan is afraid he will be embarrassed by his boisterous mother when she is chosen to be DJ for the all-school party. (Rev: BCCB 9/01; BL 4/1/01; HBG 10/01; SLJ 5/01)

8756 Machado, Ana Maria. *Me in the Middle* (4–6). Trans. from Portuguese by David Unger. Illus. by Caroline Merola. 2002, Groundwood $14.95 (978-0-88899-463-9); paper $5.95 (978-0-88899-467-7). 110pp. Young Bel feels close to her late great-grandmother and hears in her mind her accounts of life in Brazil at the turn of the 20th century, but finds her admonitions on behavior difficult to accept. (Rev: BCCB 7–8/02; HBG 10/02; SLJ 8/02)

8757 McKay, Hilary. *Forever Rose* (4–7). 2008, Simon & Schuster $16.99 (978-1-4169-5486-6). 304pp. Rose, part of the flighty and dramatic Casson family, gets her own book in the series, in which she and her friends cook up a dangerous adventure and her family unveils a series of surprises. (Rev: BL 4/1/08; SLJ 5/08)

8758 McKay, Hilary. *Saffy's Angel* (4–7). 2002, Simon & Schuster $16.00 (978-0-689-84933-6). 160pp. Saffron learns she was adopted into her artistic family and travels to Italy in search of her roots. (Rev: BCCB 5/02; BL 5/15/02; HB 7/02*; HBG 10/02; SLJ 5/02)

8759 McKissack, Patricia C. *Stitchin' and Pullin': A Gee's Bend Quilt* (3–5). Illus. by Cozbi A. Cabrera. 2008, Random $17.99 (978-0-375-83163-8). 48pp. The free-verse story of a young African American girl choosing fabrics for her quilt draws in details of her personal history and heritage. (Rev: BL 12/15/08; HB 11/08; LMC 11/08; SLJ 11/08)

8760 MacLachlan, Patricia. *All the Places to Love* (5–8). Illus. 1994, HarperCollins LB $18.89 (978-0-06-021099-1). This picture book celebrates the love found in an extended rural family and the joy that a new arrival brings. (Rev: BCCB 7–8/94; BL 6/1–15/94*; SLJ 6/94)

8761 MacLachlan, Patricia. *Cassie Binegar* (4–7). 1982, HarperCollins paper $5.99 (978-0-06-440195-1). 128pp. Cassie is not happy with the disorder in her family situation.

8762 MacLachlan, Patricia. *Seven Kisses in a Row* (2–4). Illus. by Maria Pia Marrella. 1983, Harper-Collins paper $4.99 (978-0-06-440231-6). 64pp. Seven stories about two youngsters who are cared for by an aunt and uncle.

8763 MacLean, Christine Cole. *Mary Margaret and the Perfect Pet Plan* (3–5). 2004, Dutton $15.99 (978-0-525-47183-7). 168pp. Nearly 9 years old, Mary Margaret wants a pet and makes many efforts to get one, but it's a long time before her allergic father and pregnant mother can see reason. (Rev: BCCB 6/04; SLJ 7/04)

8764 Madison, Alan. *100 Days and 99 Nights* (3–5). Illus. by Julia Denos. 2008, Little, Brown $14.99 (978-0-316-11354-0). 144pp. In this book that combines humor with a stressful situation, 7-year-old Esme tries to remain brave while her military father is away on a tour of duty; she communes with her "bedzoo" of stuffed animals and takes part in a scrap metal drive. (Rev: BL 5/1/08; LMC 1/09; SLJ 6/08)

8765 Mansfield, Creina. *Cherokee* (5–8). 2001, O'Brien paper $7.95 (978-0-86278-368-6). 127pp. Gene's wonderful life with his jazz musician grandfather, Cherokee, comes to an end when his aunt decides he needs a home and an education. (Rev: SLJ 11/01)

8766 Marino, Jan. *For the Love of Pete* (5–8). 1994, Avon paper $3.50 (978-0-380-72281-5). 197pp. Three devoted servants take Phoebe on a journey to find the father she has never met. (Rev: BCCB 7–8/93; BL 6/1–15/93; SLJ 5/93*)

8767 Marsden, Carolyn. *Silk Umbrellas* (3–6). 2004, Candlewick $14.99 (978-0-7636-2257-2). 144pp. Eleven-year-old Noi hopes to be able to support her family by creating and selling painted silk umbrellas in this story set in a small Thai village. (Rev: BL 2/1/04*; SLJ 3/04)

8768 Martin, Patricia. *Lulu Atlantis and the Quest for True Blue Love* (2–4). Illus. by Marc Boutavant. 2008, Random $15.99 (978-0-375-84016-6). 228pp. With the arrival of a new baby in the house, Lulu — who is seeking True Blue Love — turns more and more to her daddy longlegs friend Harry. (Rev: LMC 3/08; SLJ 3/08)

8769 Martin, Patricia A. *Travels with Rainie Marie* (5–7). 1997, Hyperion LB $16.49 (978-0-7868-2212-6). 192pp. When there is no one to care for her and her five brothers and sisters, Rainie Marie is afraid that her bossy aunt will try to split up the family among various relatives. (Rev: BL 5/15/97; SLJ 7/97)

8770 Matas, Carol. *Sparks Fly Upward* (4–8). 2002, Clarion $15.00 (978-0-618-15964-2). 192pp. Set in Manitoba in the early 20th century, this is the story of 12-year-old Rebecca, a Jewish girl, and her life with a Ukrainian foster family. (Rev: BCCB 7–8/02; BL 4/1/02; HBG 10/02; SLJ 3/02)

8771 Matthews, Kezi. *Flying Lessons* (5–7). 2002, Cricket $16.95 (978-0-8126-2671-1). 168pp. A girl in a small southern town bonds with an eclectic bunch of adults after the airplane in which her mother was traveling disappears. (Rev: BL 12/15/02; HB 1/03; HBG 3/03; SLJ 12/02; VOYA 6/03)

8772 Mazer, Norma Fox. *What I Believe* (5–8). 2005, Harcourt $16.00 (978-0-15-201462-9). 176pp. When Vicki's father loses his job and the family's fortunes go into free fall, Vicki finds the resulting changes hard to accept and reveals in her poems and journal her coping strategies. (Rev: BL 9/15/05; SLJ 10/05)

8773 Mead, Alice. *Isabella's Above-Ground Pool* (2–4). Illus. by Maryann Cocca-Leffler. 2006, Farrar $16.00 (978-0-374-33617-2). 112pp. Nine-year-old Isabella learns some important lessons about sharing after a tornado sweeps through her small Texas town. (Rev: BL 4/1/06; SLJ 5/06)

8774 Mead, Alice. *Junebug in Trouble* (5–8). 2002, Farrar $16.00 (978-0-374-33969-2). 144pp. Young Junebug and his mother move out of the housing projects, but Junebug continues to get into the trouble his mother was hoping to avoid. (Rev: BCCB 6/02; BL 4/15/02; HB 5/02; HBG 10/02; SLJ 3/02)

8775 Medearis, Angela Shelf. *What Did I Do to Deserve a Sister Like You?* (3–5). Illus. by Don Tate and Mark Galbreath. 2002, Eakin $13.95 (978-1-57168-471-4); paper $7.95 (978-1-57168-642-8). 123pp. Sharie, 10, juggles her dislike of her older sister, her problems with her piano teacher, and a longing to ride on a roller-coaster. (Rev: HBG 10/02; SLJ 5/02)

8776 Meehl, Brian. *Out of Patience* (4–6). 2006, Delacorte LB $17.95 (978-0-385-90320-2). 304pp. Twelve-year-old Jake's dream of escaping his boring Kansas hometown, where his plumber father hopes to open a toilet museum, is put on the back burner when his dad brings home a cursed toilet plunger. (Rev: BL 4/1/06; SLJ 11/06; VOYA 6/06)

8777 Mills, Claudia. *Trading Places* (4–6). 2006, Farrar $16.00 (978-0-374-31798-0). 138pp. Twins Todd and Amy must relinquish their familiar roles when things get tough at home and at school. (Rev: BL 2/1/06; SLJ 5/06)

8778 Modiano, Patrick. *Catherine Certitude* (4–7). Trans. by William Rodarmor. Illus. by Jean-Jacques Sempé. 2001, Godine $17.95 (978-0-87923-959-6). 64pp. An adult Catherine reminisces about her life as a youngster in Paris — living with her father, puzzling over his job, going to ballet classes, eating in restaurants — in this stylishly illustrated chapter book delivered in picture-book format. (Rev: BL 12/15/01; HBG 3/02; SLJ 2/02)

8779 Montgomery, L. M. *Christmas with Anne and Other Holiday Stories* (4–7). 1996, McClelland & Stewart $12.95 (978-0-7710-6204-9). 214pp. A collection of 16 short pieces and stories (two from the Anne of Green Gables books) that deal with Christmas. (Rev: BL 9/1/96)

8780 Morris, Jennifer. *Come, Llamas* (4–6). 2005, Delacorte LB $17.99 (978-0-385-90229-8). 208pp. Nine-year-old JT describes the summer he plays a growing role in his family's Alaska llama ranch and must deal with his grandfather's illness. (Rev: BL 2/1/05; SLJ 1/05)

8781 Moss, Marissa. *Amelia's Longest, Biggest, Most-Fights-Ever Family Reunion* (3–5). Illus. Series: Amelia. 2006, Simon & Schuster $9.95 (978-0-689-87447-5). 80pp. Amelia first steels herself for a reunion with her father's extended family and then records her experiences. (Rev: BL 8/06; SLJ 9/06)

8782 Mourlevat, Jean-Claude. *The Pull of the Ocean* (5–8). Trans. by Y. Mauder. 2006, Delacorte $15.95 (978-0-385-73348-9). 208pp. In this modern version of "Tom Thumb," Yann — the smallest and youngest of seven — leads his six older brothers (three sets of twins) away from their dismal home to the ocean that's far to the west, meeting many characters along the way. (Rev: BL 12/1/06; SLJ 1/07*)

8783 Mulford, Philippa Greene. *The Holly Sisters on Their Own* (4–6). 1998, Marshall Cavendish $14.95 (978-0-7614-5022-1). 158pp. Charmaine, age 11, is not happy at the prospect of her older half sister's arrival to spend the summer in New York City, but time produces a friendship. (Rev: BCCB 7–8/98; BL 5/1/98; HBG 10/98; SLJ 4/98)

8784 Nelson, Rosemary. *Hubcaps and Puppies* (3–6). 2002, Napoleon paper $8.95 (978-0-929141-98-5). 184pp. Thirteen-year-old Nikki faces difficult choices, such as whether to allow herself to love a stray puppy so soon after the death of her dog. (Rev: BL 3/1/03)

8785 Nelson, Theresa. *Earthshine* (5–9). 1994, Orchard LB $17.99 (978-0-531-08717-6). "Slim" decides to live with her father and his lover, who is dying of AIDS. At a support group, she meets Isaiah, whose pregnant mother also has AIDS. (Rev: BL 9/1/94; SLJ 9/94*; VOYA 10/94)

8786 Nelson, Theresa. *Ruby Electric* (5–8). 2003, Simon & Schuster $16.95 (978-0-689-83852-1). 272pp. The movie script she is writing brings 12-year-old Ruby needed relief from the realities of her life. (Rev: BL 7/03; HB 7/03; HBG 10/03; SLJ 6/03*; VOYA 10/03)

8787 Nixon, Joan Lowery. *Maggie Forevermore* (5–8). 1987, Harcourt $13.95 (978-0-15-250345-1). In this sequel to *Maggie, Too* and *And Maggie Makes Three* (both o.p.), 13-year-old Maggie resents spending Christmas with her father and his new wife in California. (Rev: BCCB 4/87; BL 3/1/87; SLJ 3/87)

8788 Orr, Wendy. *Mokie and Bik* (2–4). Illus. by Jonathan Bean. 2007, Holt $15.95 (978-0-8050-7979-1). 74pp. Fraternal twins Mokie and Bik live with their mother on a houseboat, enjoy their own private language, and have many adventures. (Rev: BL 6/1–15/07; SLJ 7/07)

8789 Paratore, Coleen Murtagh. *Mack McGinn's Big Win* (4–7). 2007, Simon & Schuster $15.99 (978-1-4169-1613-0). 192pp. Mack is unhappy about his family's move to a new neighborhood and jealous of the attention his older brother gets for his athletic abilities, until a heroic act on Mack's part changes perceptions. (Rev: BL 7/07; SLJ 8/07)

8790 Park, Barbara. *The Graduation of Jake Moon* (5–8). 2000, Simon & Schuster $15.00 (978-0-689-83912-2). 115pp. Jake Moon finds it impossible to cope with his grandfather's gradual disintegration from Alzheimer's disease. (Rev: BCCB 12/00; BL 6/1–15/00; HB 9/00; HBG 3/01; SLJ 9/00)

8791 Paros, Jennifer. *Violet Bing and the Grand House* (2–4). Illus. 2007, Viking $14.99 (978-0-670-06151-8). 112pp. Despite her determination not to, Violet Bing finds some things that pique her interest during a summer stay with her Great-Aunt Astrid. (Rev: BL 3/15/07)

8792 Paterson, Katherine. *Park's Quest* (4–7). 1989, Puffin paper $5.99 (978-0-14-034262-8). 160pp. A boy searches for the cause of his father's death in Vietnam. (Rev: BCCB 4/88; HB 7/88; SLJ 5/88)

8793 Paterson, Katherine. *The Same Stuff as Stars* (5–7). 2002, Clarion $15.00 (978-0-618-24744-8). 256pp. An unhappy 11-year-old Angel and her younger brother Bernie are sent to live with their father's grandmother, where Angel finds comfort in a mysterious man who introduces her to astronomy. (Rev: BCCB 10/02; BL 9/15/02; HB 9/02; HBG 3/03; SLJ 8/02*)

8794 Pearce, Emily Smith. *Isabel and the Miracle Baby* (2–4). 2007, Front St. $15.95 (978-1-932425-44-4). 125pp. Eight-year-old Isabel has her hands full with a new baby in the house, her mother recovering from cancer and her father gone much of the time. (Rev: BL 10/1/07; SLJ 10/07)

8795 Pearsall, Shelley. *All Shook Up* (5–8). 2008, Knopf $15.99 (978-0-375-83698-5). 272pp. Josh's divorced dad has a new girlfriend and a new job as an Elvis impersonator, much to Josh's horror. (Rev: BL 5/1/08; SLJ 7/08)

8796 Perez, Amada Irma. *My Diary from Here to There / Mi Diario de Aqui Hasta Alla* (2–4). Trans. by Consuelo Hernandez. Illus. by Maya Christina Gonzalez. 2002, Children's Book Pr. $16.95 (978-0-89239-175-2). 32pp. Amada tells her diary her worries about moving from Mexico to California in this bilingual book with appealing illustrations. (Rev: BL 11/1/02; HB 9/02; HBG 3/03)

8797 Pfeffer, Susan Beth. *Devil's Den* (4–7). 1998, Walker $15.95 (978-0-8027-8650-0). 128pp. Joey faces the pain of rejection when he seeks out his real father, discovers he is not wanted by him, and must accept living permanently with his mom and loving stepfather. (Rev: BCCB 5/98; BL 5/15/98; HBG 10/98; SLJ 6/98)

8798 Pfeffer, Susan Beth. *Kid Power* (4–6). Illus. by Leigh Grant. 1991, Scholastic paper $2.99 (978-0-590-42607-7). 121pp. A spunky young girl organizes an employment agency for herself and friends when her mother loses her job.

8799 Porte, Barbara Ann. *Fat Fanny, Beanpole Bertha and the Boys* (4–6). Illus. by Maxie Chambliss. 1991, Orchard LB $16.99 (978-0-531-08528-8). 112pp. Fanny and Bertha are best friends despite their differences. (Rev: BCCB 4/91*; BL 3/1/91; HB 7/91; SLJ 2/91*)

8800 Pryor, Bonnie. *Toenails, Tonsils, and Tornadoes* (3–5). Illus. 1997, Morrow $15.00 (978-0-688-14885-0). 160pp. Fourth-grader Martin is not too happy when his Aunt Henrietta visits, principally because he has to give up his room. (Rev: BCCB 6/97; BL 5/15/97; SLJ 5/97)

8801 Ransom, Candice F. *Finding Day's Bottom* (4–6). 2006, Carolrhoda $15.95 (978-1-57505-933-4). 168pp. In this poignant tale set in the Blue Ridge Mountains of Virginia, 11-year-old Jane-Ery slowly comes to appreciate her Grandpap's love after her father's death in an accident. (Rev: BL 10/15/06; SLJ 9/06)

8802 Ransom, Candice F. *Seeing Sky-Blue Pink* (3–5). 2007, Carolrhoda $16.95 (978-0-8225-7142-1). 128pp. Eight-year-old Maddie adjusts to her new home on a farm after her mother marries a nice man named Sam. (Rev: BCCB 11/07; BL 10/15/07; LMC 1/08; SLJ 10/07)

8803 Rinn, Miriam. *The Saturday Secret* (4–7). Illus. 1998, Alef Design Group paper $7.95 (978-1-881283-26-3). 144pp. Jason's resentment and anger at having to obey the strict rules imposed by his devout Orthodox Jewish stepfather are made more intense because of his grief at the death of his beloved father. (Rev: BL 10/1/98; SLJ 2/99)

8804 Rodowsky, Colby. *Ben and the Sudden Too-Big Family* (3–5). 2007, Farrar $16.00 (978-0-374-30658-8). 120pp. Ben, 10, likes to divide events in his life into "all right" and "not all right," and although his new stepmother and even the arrival of his new adopted sister from China fell into the former category, he's not at all sure about the prospect of a houseful of his stepmother's relatives. (Rev: SLJ 4/07)

8805 Rodowsky, Colby. *That Fernhill Summer* (5–8). 2006, Farrar $16.00 (978-0-374-37442-6). 176pp. When her grandmother becomes ill, biracial teen Kiara confronts family problems and develops relationships with two white cousins she didn't know existed. (Rev: BL 4/15/06; SLJ 6/06)

8806 Ryan, Pam Muñoz. *Paint the Wind* (4–7). 2007, Scholastic $16.99 (978-0-439-87362-8). 326pp. On the death of her grandmother — who has been a distant and strict guardian — orphaned 11-year-old Maya is sent to relatives in Wyoming, where she learns about the love of horses and family. (Rev: BL 11/15/07; LMC 1/08; SLJ 11/07)

8807 Salmansohn, Karen. *One Puppy, Three Tales* (4–6). Illus. by author. Series: Alexandra Rambles On! 2001, Tricycle $12.95 (978-1-58246-044-4). Twelve-year-old Alexandra shares vivid details of her life and her relationships with her mother, father, and friends. (Rev: HBG 10/01; SLJ 6/01)

8808 Salmansohn, Karen. *Wherever I Go, There I Am* (4–7). Illus. by author. Series: Alexandra Rambles On! 2002, Tricycle $12.95 (978-1-58246-079-6). Alexandra's journal reveals her angst about issues such as scary movies and becoming a teenager. (Rev: HBG 3/03; SLJ 2/03)

8809 Schirripa, Steven R., and Charles Fleming. *Nicky Deuce: Welcome to the Family* (4–6). 2005, Delacorte $15.95 (978-0-385-73257-4). 176pp. When his summer camp is abruptly closed, Nicholas Borelli II is sent to Brooklyn for a two-week stay with his Grandma Tutti and learns about his Italian American roots. (Rev: BL 10/1/05; SLJ 8/05)

8810 Seidler, Tor. *Brothers Below Zero* (5–8). 2002, HarperCollins LB $15.89 (978-0-06-029180-8). 137pp. Artistic Tim, overwhelmed by his athletic younger brother, eventually runs away to the place he has felt most valued. (Rev: BCCB 3/02; BL 1/1–15/02; HBG 10/02; SLJ 4/02)

8811 Shearer, Alex. *The Great Blue Yonder* (5–8). 2002, Clarion $15.00 (978-0-618-21257-6). 192pp. Twelve-year-old Harry, who has died in an accident, experiences afterlife on the Other Side and has the opportunity to review his relations with other family members. (Rev: BCCB 6/02; HBG 10/02; SLJ 4/02; VOYA 6/02)

8812 Sidney, Margaret. *The Five Little Peppers and How They Grew* (4–6). 1981, Buccaneer LB $27.95 (978-0-89966-340-1). 302pp. The classic of five children growing up many decades ago.

8813 Slate, Joseph. *Crossing the Trestle* (5–8). 1999, Marshall Cavendish $14.95 (978-0-7614-5053-5). 144pp. Set in West Virginia in 1944, this novel centers on 11-year-old Petey and the problems he and his family face after their father is killed in an accident. (Rev: BCCB 12/99; BL 1/1–15/00; HBG 3/00; SLJ 10/99)

8814 Smith, Emily. *Joe vs. the Fairies* (2–4). Illus. by Georgie Birkett. 2006, Trafalgar paper $7.50 (978-0-552-55174-8). 92pp. Joe isn't pleased when his cousins arrive and monopolize his sisters with girlish games, but then he meets a girl who enjoys climbing trees. (Rev: BL 1/1–15/06)

8815 Smith, Janice Lee. *The Monster in the Third Dresser Drawer and Other Stories About Adam Joshua* (3–5). Illus. by Dick Gackenbach. 1981, HarperCollins LB $15.89 (978-0-06-025739-2). 96pp. Adam Joshua faces many everyday problems,

including a new baby sister, in these six stories. A sequel is: *The Kid Next Door and Other Headaches: Stories about Adam Joshua* (1984).

8816 Smith, Robert K. *The War with Grandpa* (4–6). Illus. by Richard Lauter. 1984, Dell paper $4.99 (978-0-440-49276-4). 128pp. Peter resents giving up his bedroom to his grandfather.

8817 Smith, Sherri L. *Hot, Sour, Salty, Sweet* (5–7). 2008, Delacorte $15.99 (978-0-385-73417-2). 176pp. As her grandmothers, one Chinese American and one African American, argue over food and family, Ana's junior high graduation party gets more and more complicated. (Rev: BL 2/1/08; SLJ 4/08)

8818 Springer, Nancy. *Separate Sisters* (5–7). 2001, Holiday $16.95 (978-0-8234-1544-1). 84pp. Two teenage girls deal with the divorce of their parents in different ways. (Rev: BCCB 2/02; BL 2/1/02; HB 3/02; HBG 10/02; SLJ 2/02; VOYA 4/02)

8819 Stacey, Cherylyn. *How Do You Spell Abducted?* (4–8). 1996, Red Deer paper $7.95 (978-0-88995-148-8). When their divorced father abducts Deb, Paige, and Cory, the three youngsters must escape from his home in the U.S. and make their way back to their mother in Canada. (Rev: SLJ 12/96)

8820 Stewart, Sarah. *The Journey* (2–4). Illus. by David Small. 2001, Farrar $16.00 (978-0-374-33905-0). 40pp. A young Amish girl from the country keeps a diary about her exciting visit to Chicago with her mother. (Rev: BL 3/15/01; HB 3/01; HBG 10/01; SLJ 3/01)

8821 Stolz, Mary. *Go Fish* (3–5). Illus. by Pat Cummings. 1991, HarperCollins LB $14.89 (978-0-06-025822-1). 80pp. Thomas and his grandfather spend warm times together. (Rev: BCCB 5/91; BL 5/15/91; HB 7/91; SLJ 5/91*)

8822 Talbert, Marc. *The Purple Heart* (5–8). 1992, HarperCollins $14.95 (978-0-06-020428-0); Avon paper $3.50 (978-0-380-71985-3). Luke's father has returned from Vietnam an anguished, brooding war hero, and Luke loses his father's Purple Heart, leading to confrontation and reconciliation. (Rev: BL 12/15/91*; SLJ 2/92)

8823 Taylor, Sydney. *All-of-a-Kind Family* (3–6). Illus. by Helen John. 1980, Peter Smith $21.25 (978-0-8446-6253-4); Dell paper $4.99 (978-0-440-40059-2). 192pp. Warm and moving stories of Jewish family life in New York City. Also use: *Ella of All-of-a-Kind Family* (1980, Dell paper).

8824 Thomas, Jane Resh. *Blind Mountain* (4–7). 2006, Clarion $15.00 (978-0-618-64872-6). 128pp. Forced to go on a hiking trip with his bossy father in the mountainous Montana wilderness, 12-year-old Sam finds himself in charge of their survival when his father is temporarily blinded by a branch. (Rev: BL 12/1/06; SLJ 12/06)

8825 Thomson, John. *A Small Boat at the Bottom of the Sea* (5–7). 2005, Milkweed $16.95 (978-1-57131-657-8); paper $6.95 (978-1-57131-656-1). 148pp. Upset and angry when he's sent to spend the summer with his ex-con uncle and dying aunt on Puget Sound, 12-year-old Donovan begins to develop a closer relationship with his uncle as his vacation progresses. (Rev: SLJ 10/05; VOYA 4/06)

8826 Tilly, Meg. *Porcupine* (5–8). 2007, Tundra $15.95 (978-0-88776-810-1). 192pp. Jacqueline and her younger brother and sister go to Canada to live with a great-grandmother after their father dies in Afghanistan. (Rev: BL 11/15/07; SLJ 12/07)

8827 Uhlberg, Myron. *The Printer* (2–4). Trans. and illus. by Henri Sorensen. 2003, Peachtree $16.95 (978-1-56145-221-7). 32pp. In 1940 New York City, a young boy describes how his deaf father, a printer, alerted his hearing co-workers to a deadly fire in the pressroom; an endnote supplies historical details. (Rev: BL 9/1/03; HBG 4/04; SLJ 12/03)

8828 Van Steenwyk, Elizabeth. *Three Dog Winter* (5–8). 1987, Walker $13.95 (978-0-8027-6718-9). A story of dog racing, this family tale tells of 12-year-old Scott and his Malamute, Kaylah. (Rev: BL 2/1/88; SLJ 12/87)

8829 Viglucci, Patricia C. *Sun Dance at Turtle Rock* (5–7). 1996, Patri paper $4.95 (978-0-9645914-9-3). 128pp. The child of a racially mixed marriage feels uncomfortable when he visits his white grandfather. (Rev: BL 4/15/96)

8830 Voigt, Cynthia. *Dicey's Song* (5–9). 1982, Macmillan $17.95 (978-0-689-30944-1). 204pp. This story of Dicey's life with her "Gram" in Maryland won a Newbery Medal (1983). Preceding it was *Homecoming* (1981) and a sequel is *A Solitary Blue* (1983). (Rev: BL 12/15/89)

8831 Walker, Pamela. *Pray Hard* (5–8). 2001, Scholastic paper $15.95 (978-0-439-21586-2). 177pp. After Amelia Forest's father dies in an airplane accident for which she feels responsible, her life and that of her family fall apart. (Rev: BL 3/1/01; HBG 10/01; SLJ 7/01; VOYA 8/01)

8832 Wallace, Bill. *Beauty* (5–7). 1988, Holiday $16.95 (978-0-8234-0715-6). 192pp. Luke finds the adjustment difficult when he and his mother go to live on his grandfather's Oklahoma farm. (Rev: BCCB 11/88; BL 2/1/89; SLJ 10/88)

8833 Wallace, Bill. *True Friends* (4–7). 1994, Holiday $15.95 (978-0-8234-1141-2). 160pp. Everything in Courtney's life becomes a shambles and she must rely on her new friend Judy to help her. (Rev: BCCB 11/94; BL 10/15/94; SLJ 10/94)

8834 Weeks, Sarah. *My Guy* (4–7). 2001, HarperCollins LB $14.89 (978-0-06-028370-4). 192pp. Guy and Lana agree on only one thing — they don't want to become part of a blended family — and they set out to make sure it won't happen. (Rev: BCCB 6/01; BL 8/01; HB 7/01; HBG 10/01; SLJ 5/01)

8835 Welch, Sheila K. *The Shadowed Unicorn* (4–6). 2000, Front St. $15.95 (978-0-8126-2895-1). 192pp. Identical twins Brendan and Nick join their older, bossy sister Arni on a hunt for a black unicorn in this family story that borders on fantasy. (Rev: BCCB 10/00; BL 4/15/00; HBG 10/00; SLJ 7/00)

8836 White, Ruth. *Belle Prater's Boy* (5–9). 1996, Farrar $17.00 (978-0-374-30668-7). Set in Appalachia in the 1950s, this moving, often humorous story tells about Gypsy and her unusual cousin Woodrow, who hides a secret involving his mother's disappearance. (Rev: BL 4/15/96; SLJ 4/96*)

8837 White, Ruth. *Tadpole* (5–8). 2003, Farrar $16.00 (978-0-374-31002-8). 208pp. In this novel set in 1950s Appalachia, uncertain 10-year-old Carolina finds her own strengths when her 13-year-old cousin Tadpole arrives, running away from an abusive uncle. (Rev: BL 5/1/03; HB 5/03; HBG 10/03; SLJ 3/03*)

8838 Wilder, Laura Ingalls. *Little House in the Big Woods* (4–7). Illus. by Garth Williams. 1953, HarperCollins LB $17.89 (978-0-06-026431-4); paper $6.99 (978-0-06-440001-5). 238pp. Outstanding story of a log-cabin family in Wisconsin in the late 1800s. Also use *By the Shores of Silver Lake; Farmer Boy; Little House on the Prairie; Long Winter; On the Banks of Plum Creek; These Happy Golden Years* (all 1953); *Little Town on the Prairie* (1961); *The First Four Years* (1971).

8839 Wiles, Deborah. *Each Little Bird That Sings* (4–6). 2005, Harcourt $16.00 (978-0-15-205113-6). 264pp. Comfort Snowberger, the daughter of undertakers, faces death in her own family for the first time in this engaging and sometimes funny novel set in rural Mississippi. (Rev: BL 3/1/05; SLJ 3/05)

8840 Wiles, Deborah. *Love, Ruby Lavender* (4–6). 2001, Harcourt $16.00 (978-0-15-202314-0). 128pp. Ruby misses her grandmother terribly when she goes to Hawaii on vacation, but over the course of the summer she finds that life goes on and that diversions arise. (Rev: BCCB 9/01; BL 5/1/01; HBG 10/01; SLJ 4/01*)

8841 Williams, Dar. *Lights, Camera, Amalee* (5–7). 2006, Scholastic $16.99 (978-0-439-80352-6). 311pp. A modest inheritance from a grandmother she barely knew gives 12-year-old Amalee the funds she needs to make a documentary about endangered species. (Rev: SLJ 9/06)

8842 Willis, Patricia. *The Barn Burner* (5–8). 2000, Clarion $15.00 (978-0-395-98409-3). 208pp. In 1933, 14-year-old Ross, a runaway, becomes involved with the Warfield family whose father is away looking for work. (Rev: BCCB 5/00; BL 4/15/00; HBG 10/00; SLJ 7/00)

8843 Wilson, Nancy Hope. *Mountain Pose* (5–7). 2001, Farrar $17.00 (978-0-374-35078-9). 240pp. Ellie is surprised to inherit her grandmother's farm, but when she reads the diaries left for her she begins to understand more about her family. (Rev: BCCB 6/01; BL 8/01; HB 7/01; HBG 10/01; SLJ 4/01*; VOYA 6/01)

8844 Wishinsky, Frieda. *Just Call Me Joe* (2–4). 2004, Orca paper $4.99 (978-1-55143-249-6). 101pp. Ten-year-old Joseph and his teenage sister have migrated to New York from Russia in 1910 and face many difficulties as they wait for their parents to join them. (Rev: SLJ 5/04)

8845 Woodruff, Elvira. *"Dear Napoleon, I Know You're Dead, But . . ."* (3–5). Illus. 1992, Holiday House $16.95 (978-0-8234-0962-4). 220pp. Marty is astounded when he receives a reply to his letter to Napoleon, after Gramps tells him about a courier at his nursing home who can deliver messages to the dead. (Rev: BCCB 12/92; BL 12/15/92; SLJ 10/92)

8846 Woodson, Jacqueline. *Hush* (5–9). 2002, Putnam $15.99 (978-0-399-23114-8). 192pp. A girl and her family are relocated in the witness protection program after her father, a police officer, testifies against fellow cops in a case that involves racial prejudice. (Rev: BCCB 3/02; BL 1/1–15/02; HB 1/02; HBG 10/02; SLJ 2/02*; VOYA 2/02)

8847 Woodson, Jacqueline. *Peace, Locomotion* (4–7). 2009, Putnam $15.99 (978-0-399-24655-5). 144pp. In letters to his little sister Lili, who is living in a separate foster home, 12-year-old Lonnie describes his life and his fears for his foster brother who is away at war. (Rev: BCCB 1/09; BL 12/15/08; HB 1/09; LMC 5/09; SLJ 1/09) ⌒

8848 Woodworth, Chris. *When Ratboy Lived Next Door* (4–8). 2005, Farrar $16.00 (978-0-374-34677-5). 192pp. Twelve-year-old Lydia takes an instant dislike to her new neighbor Willis and his pet raccoon, but as she gains a better understanding of the family dynamics that make the boy who he is, she also gains valuable insights into her strained relationship with her mother. (Rev: BCCB 2/05; BL 1/1–15/05; SLJ 3/05)

8849 Yep, Laurence, and Katherine S. Yep. *The Dragon's Child: A Story of Angel Island* (3–6). Illus. 2008, HarperCollins $15.99 (978-0-06-027692-8). 144pp. Yep and his niece blend fact and fiction in this account of Yep's father's journey to America in 1922. (Rev: BCCB 6/08; BL 4/1/08; SLJ 6/08)

8850 Zalben, Jane Breskin. *Brenda Berman, Wedding Expert* (2–4). Illus. by Victoria Chess. 2009, Clarion $16.00 (978-0-618-31321-1). 48pp. Brenda is not at all sure about the woman named Florrie, who will marry Brenda's favorite uncle, and as for Florrie's niece Lucy . . . (Rev: BCCB 9/09; SLJ 6/09)

Fantasy and the Supernatural

8851 Abbott, Tony. *City of the Dead* (5–8). Series: The Haunting of Derek Stone. 2009, Scholastic paper $4.99 (978-0-545-03429-6). 160pp. Derek Stone's normal life ends when his father and brother Ronny are supposedly killed in a train accident; but Ronny then turns up — a changed person — and Derek learns about a similar accident many years before that has sinister overtones. (Rev: BCCB 1/09; BL 1/1–15/09; LMC 5/09)

8852 Abbott, Tony. *Kringle* (5–8). 2005, Scholastic $14.99 (978-0-439-74942-8). 352pp. In early Britain a 12-year-old orphan named Kringle battles dark forces and discovers his true destiny. (Rev: BCCB 12/05; BL 10/15/05; HBG 4/06; SLJ 10/05; VOYA 2/06)

8853 Adler, C. S. *Good-bye Pink Pig* (5–7). 1986, Avon paper $2.75 (978-0-380-70175-9). 176pp. Shy Amanda takes comfort in the make-believe world of her miniature pink pig — away from the elegant

world of her mother and easygoing life of her brother — until trouble enters her real and imaginary worlds and she learns to assert herself. (Rev: BCCB 2/86; BL 12/15/85)

8854 Adler, C. S. *Help, Pink Pig!* (5–7). 1991, Avon paper $2.95 (978-0-380-71156-7). 176pp. Unsure of herself with her mother, Amanda retreats into the world of her miniature pink pig. (Rev: BL 5/1/90; SLJ 5/90)

8855 Ahlberg, Allan. *The Improbable Cat* (4–6). Illus. by Peter Bailey. 2004, Delacorte $9.95 (978-0-385-73186-7). 128pp. The kitten that they adopt grows ever bigger and more powerful, taking over the household, and David and his dog, Billy, are the only ones that can stop it. (Rev: SLJ 8/04)

8856 Alcock, Vivien. *The Haunting of Cassie Palmer* (5–8). 1997, Houghton paper $6.95 (978-0-395-81653-0). 160pp. Cassie finds she is blessed with second sight.

8857 Alexander, Lloyd. *The Rope Trick* (4–7). 2002, Dutton $16.99 (978-0-525-47020-5). 256pp. A young magician sets out on a challenging journey to master the difficult rope trick. (Rev: BCCB 1/03; BL 10/15/02; HB 11/02; HBG 3/03; SLJ 9/02; VOYA 12/02)

8858 Alexander, Lloyd. *Time Cat: The Remarkable Journeys of Jason and Gareth* (4–6). Illus. by Bill Sokol. 1996, Puffin paper $6.99 (978-0-14-037827-6). Jason's cat takes him to various times and places.

8859 Allen, Will. *Swords for Hire: Two of the Most Unlikely Heroes You'll Ever Meet* (5–8). Illus. by David Michael Beck. 2003, CenterPunch paper $6.95 (978-0-9724882-0-4). 168pp. A spoof of a fantasy in which inexperienced warrior 16-year-old Sam Hatcher and his eccentric mentor Rigby Skeet set off to rescue King Olive, who has been unseated by his evil brother. (Rev: BCCB 6/03; SLJ 8/03)

8860 Almond, David. *Skellig* (5–8). 1999, Delacorte $16.95 (978-0-385-32653-7). Michael discovers a ragged man in his garage existing on dead flies in this novel that is part fantasy, part mystery, and part family story. (Rev: BL 2/1/99*; HB 5/99; HBG 10/99; SLJ 2/99)

8861 Alphin, Elaine M. *Ghost Soldier* (5–7). 2001, Holt $16.95 (978-0-8050-6158-1). 216pp. Alex, who has special powers, meets a Civil War ghost and helps him discover what happened to his family. (Rev: BCCB 7–8/01; BL 8/01; HBG 10/02; SLJ 8/01; VOYA 8/01)

8862 Alphin, Elaine M. *Tournament of Time* (4–6). 1994, Bluegrass paper $3.95 (978-0-9643683-0-9). 125pp. A young American girl in York, England, solves a historic murder mystery with the help of ghosts. (Rev: BL 3/15/95)

8863 Alter, Stephen. *Ghost Letters* (5–8). 2008, Bloomsbury $16.95 (978-1-58234-739-4). 250pp. Gil tosses a message in a bottle into the sea off the Massachusetts coast and receives a reply from a boy living 100 years in the past; fantasy and the supernatural combine for a chilling and thrilling story. (Rev: BL 1/1–15/08; SLJ 5/08)

8864 Alter, Stephen. *The Phantom Isles* (4–7). Illus. 2007, Bloomsbury $16.95 (978-1-58234-738-7). 224pp. Sixth-graders Courtney, Orion, and Ming join with the librarian of their Massachusetts town in an effort to free ghosts that have become trapped in books. (Rev: BL 2/1/07; SLJ 3/07)

8865 Alton, Steve. *The Malifex* (5–8). 2002, Carolrhoda LB $14.95 (978-0-8225-0959-2). 182pp. Sam's vacation in contemporary England is complicated by a Wiccan's daughter, the release of the ghost of Merlin's apprentice, and a battle between good and evil. (Rev: BL 9/1/02; HBG 10/03; SLJ 11/02)

8866 Amato, Mary. *The Word Eater* (4–6). Illus. 2000, Holiday House $15.95 (978-0-8234-1468-0). 146pp. Lerner's pet worm Fip likes eating paper, but when he eats paper with an object's name on it, the object itself disappears in this comic fantasy. (Rev: BCCB 9/00; BL 10/15/00; HBG 3/01; SLJ 10/00)

8867 Amoss, Berthe. *Lost Magic* (5–7). 1993, Hyperion $14.95 (978-1-56282-573-7). 192pp. Fantasy and history mingle in this story set in the Middle Ages about a young girl who knows how to use both healing herbs and magic. (Rev: BL 11/1/93)

8868 Andersen, Jodi. *May Bird and the Ever After* (4–7). Illus. by Leonid Gore. 2005, Simon & Schuster $15.95 (978-0-689-86923-5). 336pp. After falling into a lake near her home, 10-year-old May Bird finds herself in Ever After, a fantasy underworld inhabited by the souls of the dead. (Rev: BCCB 12/05; BL 10/15/05; HBG 4/06; SLJ 12/05; VOYA 12/05) 🎧

8869 Anderson, Jodi Lynn. *May Bird Among the Stars* (4–7). 2006, Simon & Schuster $16.95 (978-0-689-86924-2). 272pp. In this sequel to *May Bird and the Ever After*, 10-year-old May Bird and her cat Somber Kitty remain trapped in the Afterlife torn between finding a way home and helping to save Ever After from the villainous Bo Cleevil. (Rev: BL 12/1/06; SLJ 11/06)

8870 Anderson, Jodi Lynn. *May Bird, Warrior Princess* (4–7). Series: May Bird. 2007, Atheneum $16.99 (978-0-689-86925-9). 256pp. Three years after returning from the land of the dead, May Bird and Somber Kitty return to Ever After after falling from a rooftop in the final installment in this inventive fantasy series. (Rev: BL 11/1/07; SLJ 10/07)

8871 Anderson, M. T. *The Game of Sunken Places* (5–8). 2004, Scholastic $16.95 (978-0-439-41660-3). 272pp. Brian and Gregory, both 13, find themselves embroiled in a dangerous and suspenseful game during a stay at the spooky mansion of Gregory's eccentric Uncle Max. (Rev: BL 4/15/04*; SLJ 9/04; VOYA 6/04)

8872 Anderson, M. T. *Jasper Dash and the Flame-Pits of Delaware* (4–7). 2009, Simon & Schuster $16.99 (978-1-4169-8639-3). 432pp. Jasper Dash, Boy Technonaut, and his sidekicks Lily and Katie delve into an alternate Delaware, find art thieves, and battle strange enemies; a funny parody. (Rev: BL 7/09; HB 9/09; SLJ 9/09) 🎧

8873 Anderson, M. T. *Whales on Stilts!* (5–7). 2005, Harcourt $15.00 (978-0-15-205340-6). 192pp. Twelve-year-old Lily Gefelty enlists the help of two friends to foil a plan to take over the world using an army of mind-controlled whales on stilts; a fast-paced adventure full of tongue-in-cheek fun. (Rev: BL 2/15/05*; SLJ 5/05)

8874 Appelbaum, Susannah. *The Hollow Bettle* (4–7). 2009, Knopf $16.99 (978-0-375-85173-5). 416pp. Eleven-year-old Ivy sets out to find her missing uncle, a healer, in this first installment in a fantasy involving magic, herbs, and poisons. (Rev: BL 6/1–15/09; LMC 10/09)

8875 Arkin, Alan. *The Lemming Condition* (4–7). Illus. by Joan Sandin. 1989, HarperCollins paper $9.95 (978-0-06-250048-9). 64pp. Bubber opposes the mass suicide of his companions in this interesting fable.

8876 Arnold, Louise. *Golden and Grey: The Nightmares That Ghosts Have* (4–6). 2006, Simon & Schuster $15.95 (978-0-689-87586-1). 304pp. In this sequel to *Golden and Grey: An Unremarkable Boy and a Rather Remarkable Ghost*, 11-year-old Tom Golden and his ghostly friend Grey Arthur try to figure out what's causing ghosts to disappear. (Rev: BL 10/15/06; HBG 4/07; LMC 1/07; SLJ 9/06)

8877 Arnold, Louise. *Golden and Grey (An Unremarkable Boy and a Rather Remarkable Ghost)* (4–6). 2005, Simon & Schuster $15.95 (978-0-689-87473-4). 272pp. Two misfits — a ghost and an 11-year-old boy — become friends and help each other in their respective communities. (Rev: BL 6/1–15/05)

8878 Arold, Marliese. *Ghost Park: The Vanishing Gate/The Imposter*. Bks. 1 and 2 (4–6). Trans. from German by Alexis L. Spry. Illus. by Barbara Scholz. 2007, North-South $12.95 (978-0-7358-2099-9). 216pp. Max and Sophie encounter magic and spirits as caretakers of an odd estate in these stories originally published in German. (Rev: SLJ 8/07)

8879 Asch, Frank. *Mrs. Marlowe's Mice* (2–4). Illus. by David Asch. 2007, Kids Can $17.95 (978-1-55453-022-9). 32pp. Mrs. Marlowe, a cat who works as a librarian, hides a large and happy family of mice in her apartment in this beautifully illustrated book. (Rev: BL 10/1/07; SLJ 10/07)

8880 Auch, Mary Jane. *I Was a Third Grade Spy* (2–4). Illus. 2001, Holiday House $15.95 (978-0-8234-1576-2). 96pp. Young Josh and Artful the dog who can now speak take turns narrating their entertaining efforts to win the talent show. (Rev: BCCB 7–8/01; BL 5/1/01; HBG 10/01; SLJ 7/01)

8881 Augarde, Steve. *The Various* (4–8). 2004, Random LB $17.99 (978-0-385-75037-0). 448pp. Midge, a 12-year-old girl on vacation in the countryside, discovers a tribe of little people known as the Various, who are not as helpless as they seem. (Rev: BL 12/15/03; SLJ 3/04)

8882 Avi. *Bright Shadow* (5–8). 1994, Simon & Schuster paper $4.99 (978-0-689-71783-3). At the death of the great wizard, Morenna finds she possesses the last five wishes in the world. (Rev: SLJ 12/85)

8883 Avi. *Ereth's Birthday: A Tale from Dimwood Forest* (3–5). 2000, HarperCollins $17.99 (978-0-380-97734-5). 192pp. Ereth, a cranky porcupine, gets more than he bargained for when he looks after three little foxes after their mother dies. (Rev: BCCB 7–8/00; BL 4/1/00; HB 5/00; HBG 10/00; SLJ 5/00)

8884 Avi. *The Mayor of Central Park* (3–6). Illus. by Brian Floca. 2003, HarperCollins LB $16.89 (978-0-06-051556-0). 208pp. In New York City's Central Park in 1900, Oscar the squirrel leads the fight against an invading rat pack led by Big Daddy Duds. (Rev: BL 8/03; HBG 4/04; SLJ 12/03)

8885 Avi. *Poppy* (4–6). Illus. 1995, Orchard LB $16.99 (978-0-531-08783-1). 160pp. Tragedy occurs when a young deer mouse named Poppy disobeys her father and ventures out into the night with her boyfriend. (Rev: BCCB 1/96; BL 10/15/95*; SLJ 12/95*)

8886 Avi. *Poppy and Rye* (4–6). Illus. 1998, Avon $16.99 (978-0-380-97638-6). 160pp. Fearless deer mouse Poppy travels to visit another mouse family, where she foils the plans of some beavers to build a dam and also falls in love with another mouse named Rye. (Rev: BL 5/15/98; HB 7/98; HBG 10/98; SLJ 6/98)

8887 Avi. *Ragweed* (4–6). Illus. 1999, Avon $17.99 (978-0-380-97690-4). 192pp. Ragweed, a brave young mouse, becomes friends with members of a hip band and leads the opposition against Silversides, an angry white cat. (Rev: BCCB 10/99; BL 5/15/99; HBG 10/99; SLJ 7/99)

8888 Avi. *The Seer of Shadows* (4–7). 2008, HarperCollins $16.99 (978-0-06-000015-8). 208pp. Horace, a photographer's apprentice in 1872, is told by his boss to fake photographs of ghosts, but discovers that he has the ability to conjure actual ghosts with his camera. (Rev: BL 2/15/08; SLJ 2/08) 🎧

8889 Avi. *Something Upstairs: A Tale of Ghosts* (5–7). 1988, Orchard LB $16.99 (978-0-531-08382-6); Avon paper $5.99 (978-0-380-70853-6). 128pp. Kenny moves into a house in Rhode Island that is haunted by the ghost of a slave who was murdered in 1800. (Rev: BCCB 9/88; BL 11/1/88; SLJ 10/88)

8890 Avi. *Strange Happenings: Five Tales of Transformation* (4–7). 2006, Harcourt $15.00 (978-0-15-205790-9). 160pp. Shape-shifting and invisibility are among the transformations in this collection of five fantasy tales. (Rev: BL 3/15/06; SLJ 5/06)

8891 Babbitt, Natalie. *The Devil's Other Storybook* (4–6). Illus. by author. 1987, Farrar paper $4.95 (978-0-374-41704-8). 112pp. The devil generally fouls up things in these humorous tales, but sometimes does an unintentional good deed. (Rev: BCCB 7–8/87; BL 8/87; SLJ 8/87)

8892 Babbitt, Natalie. *The Search for Delicious* (4–7). Illus. by author. 1969, Farrar $17.00 (978-0-374-36534-9). 176pp. The innocent task of polling the kingdom's subjects for personal food preferences provokes civil war in a zestful spoof of taste and society.

8893 Babbitt, Natalie. *Tuck Everlasting* (4–6). 1975, Farrar $16.00 (978-0-374-37848-6). 160pp. Violence erupts when the Tuck family members discover that their secret about a spring that brings immortality has been discovered.

8894 Baccalario, Pierdomenico. *The Long-Lost Map* (4–6). Trans. by Leah Janeczko. Series: Ulysses Moore. 2006, Scholastic $12.99 (978-0-439-77439-0). 272pp. Jason and Rick are investigating in ancient Egypt while Jason's twin Julia, back in Cornwall, deals with Oblivia Newton in this exciting, fast-paced sequel to *Door to Time* (2005). (Rev: BL 7/06; SLJ 8/06)

8895 Baggott, Julianna. *The Prince of Fenway Park* (5–8). 2009, HarperCollins $16.99 (978-0-06-087242-7). 336pp. Twelve-year-old Oscar Egg holds the power to lift the curse affecting the Boston Red Sox. (Rev: BL 5/15/09; SLJ 5/09)

8896 Bailey, Carolyn Sherwin. *Miss Hickory* (4–6). Illus. by Ruth Gannett. 1946, Puffin paper $5.99 (978-0-14-030956-0). 128pp. The adventures of a doll made from an apple branch with a hickory nut head. Newbery Award winner, 1947.

8897 Bailey, Len. *Clabbernappers* (4–6). 2005, Tor $17.95 (978-0-7653-0981-5). 240pp. An exciting land of pirates and chess characters awaits junior rodeo champ Danny Ray when he ventures through a mysterious door at an amusement park. (Rev: BL 1/1–15/05; SLJ 6/05)

8898 Bailey, Linda. *Adventures in the Middle Ages* (3–6). Illus. by Bill Slavin. 2000, Kids Can $14.95 (978-1-55074-538-2); paper $8.95 (978-1-55074-540-5). 48pp. A slapstick story about twins Josh and Emma and their trip to the Middle Ages via a yellowing guidebook that gives basic information about the period. (Rev: BL 9/15/03; HBG 3/01; SLJ 12/00)

8899 Baker, E. D. *Dragon's Breath* (5–7). 2003, Bloomsbury $15.95 (978-1-58234-858-2). 292pp. Esmeralda and Eadric help Aunt Grassina find ingredients needed to break the spell that turned Grassina's true love, Haywood, into an otter in this humorous sequel to *The Frog Princess* (2002). (Rev: BL 4/15/04; SLJ 12/03; VOYA 4/04)

8900 Baker, E. D. *The Frog Princess* (5–8). 2002, Bloomsbury $15.95 (978-1-58234-799-8). 220pp. When Princess Esmeralda kisses the frog, she turns into one herself in this humorous twist on the traditional saga. (Rev: BCCB 2/03; BL 11/15/02; SLJ 1/03; VOYA 12/02)

8901 Baker, E. D. *The Salamander Spell* (4–7). 2007, Bloomsbury $16.95 (978-1-59990-018-6). 250pp. In this prequel to *The Frog Princess* (2002), 13-year-old Grassina is tired of being overshadowed by her older sister Chartreuse and, accompanied by her snake friend Pippa, runs away to the swamp where she discovers her powers, meets a young magician, and saves the kingdom from werewolves. (Rev: BL 9/15/07; SLJ 12/07)

8902 Baker, E. D. *Wings: A Fairy Tale* (5–8). 2008, Bloomsbury $16.95 (978-1-59990-193-0). 250pp. Could Tamisin really be a goblin? When she grows wings, she realizes she must be from another world. (Rev: BL 5/15/08)

8903 Baker, Jeannie. *The Hidden Forest* (2–4). Illus. 2000, Greenwillow LB $16.89 (978-0-688-15761-6). 32pp. In this fantasy, Ben is led by his friend Sophie into the underwater world of a kelp forest where they encounter a whale. (Rev: BL 9/1/00; HB 7/00; HBG 10/00; SLJ 5/00)

8904 Ball, Justin, and Evan Croker. *Space Dogs* (4–7). 2006, Knopf $15.95 (978-0-375-83256-7). 250pp. When a powerful force threatens to destroy Gersbach, the planet's inhabitants dispatch dog-shaped vehicles to Earth in a desperate attempt to head off disaster; they end up battling in the front yard of Amy and Lucy Buckley in this humorous, action-packed story. (Rev: BL 6/1–15/06; SLJ 8/06)

8905 Banks, Lynne Reid. *Angela and Diabola* (5–8). 1997, Avon $15.95 (978-0-380-97562-4). A wicked romp that chronicles the lives of twins, the angelic Angela and the truly horrible and destructive Diabola. (Rev: SLJ 7/97)

8906 Banks, Lynne Reid. *Harry the Poisonous Centipede's Big Adventure* (3–5). Illus. 2001, HarperCollins LB $14.89 (978-0-06-029394-9). 192pp. Young centipede Harry finds himself trapped with many of his friends, and they have great adventures finding their way home after escaping. (Rev: BL 6/1–15/01; HBG 10/01; SLJ 5/01)

8907 Banks, Lynne Reid. *The Indian in the Cupboard* (3–5). Illus. by Brock Cole. 1985, Doubleday $16.95 (978-0-385-17051-2); Avon paper $5.99 (978-0-380-60012-0). 192pp. A magical cupboard turns toys into living things.

8908 Banks, Lynne Reid. *The Key to the Indian* (4–8). Illus. Series: Indian in the Cupboard. 1998, Avon $16.00 (978-0-380-97717-8). 240pp. In the fifth book of the Indian in the Cupboard series, Omri and Dad return to the time of Little Bear to help the Iroquois deal with European meddlers. (Rev: BL 11/15/98; HBG 3/99; SLJ 12/98)

8909 Banks, Lynne Reid. *The Mystery of the Cupboard* (4–8). Illus. Series: Indian in the Cupboard. 1993, HarperCollins paper $5.99 (978-0-380-72013-2). In this, the fourth book in the series, the young hero Omri uncovers a diary that reveals secrets about his magical cupboard. (Rev: BCCB 6/93; BL 4/1/93; HB 7/93; SLJ 6/93; VOYA 10/93)

8910 Banks, Lynne Reid. *The Return of the Indian* (5–7). Illus. by William Celdart. Series: Indian in the Cupboard. 1986, Doubleday $16.95 (978-0-385-23497-9); Avon paper $5.99 (978-0-380-70284-8). 192pp. Omri brings his plastic Indian figures to life and discovers that his friend Little Bear has been wounded and needs his help. (Rev: BL 9/15/86; HB 11/86; SLJ 11/86)

8911 Barlow, Steve, and Steve Skidmore. *Whizzard!* (4–6). Illus. by Fiona Land. Series: Tales of the Dark Forest. 2003, Collins paper $8.95 (978-0-00-710864-0). 252pp. In this fast-paced comic fantasy, Tym, the bumbling apprentice to the local wizard, cooks up a magical potion that endows him with the power to travel at super-fast speed. (Rev: SLJ 2/04)

8912 Barrett, Tracy. *Cold in Summer* (4–7). 2003, Holt $16.95 (978-0-8050-7052-1). 208pp. An enjoyable story about a lonely girl who slowly comes to realize that her new friend is a ghost. (Rev: BL 4/1/03; HB 5/03; HBG 10/03; SLJ 7/03; VOYA 6/03)

8913 Barrett, Tracy. *On Etruscan Time* (5–8). 2005, Holt $16.95 (978-0-8050-7569-4). 176pp. Hector, 11, finds himself struggling to rescue an Etruscan boy from execution, in this time-travel fantasy set on an archaeological dig in Italy. (Rev: BL 6/1–15/05; SLJ 7/05)

8914 Barrie, J. M. *Peter Pan* (5–7). Illus. 2000, Chronicle $19.95 (978-0-8118-2297-8). 173pp. Using illustrations from 15 different artists, this is an unusual, unabridged edition of Barrie's classic fantasy. (Rev: BL 11/1/00; HBG 3/01; SLJ 12/00)

8915 Barron, T. A. *Tree Girl* (4–8). 2001, Putnam $14.99 (978-0-399-23457-6). 128pp. Rowanna, 9, discovers she is descended from tree spirits after she is lured into the woods by a shape-shifting bear cub in this book for middle-graders. (Rev: BCCB 10/01; BL 11/1/01; HBG 3/02; SLJ 10/01; VOYA 10/01)

8916 Barrows, Annie. *Ivy and Bean* (1–3). Illus. by Sophie Blackall. 2006, Chronicle $14.95 (978-0-8118-4903-6). 116pp. Seven-year-old Bean takes an instant dislike to Ivy when she moves in across the street, but when Ivy comes to Bean's rescue the two begin to develop a friendship; excellent artwork adds to the story. (Rev: BCCB 6/06; BL 4/1/06*; HBG 10/06; LMC 1/07; SLJ 7/06)

8917 Barrows, Annie. *Ivy and Bean and the Ghost That Had to Go* (1–3). Illus. by Sophie Blackall. 2006, Chronicle $14.95 (978-0-8118-4910-4). 102pp. Best friends Ivy and Bean try to run off the ghost that's haunting the girls' bathroom at school. (Rev: BL 10/15/06; SLJ 2/07)

8918 Barry, Dave, and Ridley Pearson. *Peter and the Secret of Rundoon* (4–7). Illus. by Greg Call. Series: Starcatchers. 2007, Hyperion $18.99 (978-0-7868-3788-5). 496pp. In this action-packed conclusion to the Starcatchers trilogy, Peter (Pan, that is) saves the world long before ever meeting Wendy and her siblings. (Rev: BL 11/15/07; SLJ 10/07)

8919 Barry, Dave, and Ridley Pearson. *Peter and the Shadow Thieves* (5–8). Illus. by Greg Call. 2006, Hyperion $18.99 (978-0-7868-3787-8). 464pp. In this sequel to *Peter and the Starcatchers* (2005), the forever-young Peter and Tinker Bell race to foil the evil plans of Lord Ombra. (Rev: BL 6/1–15/06; SLJ 8/06; VOYA 8/06)

8920 Base, Graeme. *TruckDogs* (4–6). Illus. 2004, Abrams $16.95 (978-0-8109-5031-3). 192pp. Creatures that are part animal, part vehicle — such as TruckSheep and TruckDogs — star in this story about an assault on their town by the RottWheeler gang. (Rev: BL 2/15/04; SLJ 3/04)

8921 Bateman, Colin. *Running with the Reservoir Pups* (4–7). 2005, Delacorte LB $17.99 (978-0-440-42048-4). 272pp. Eddie becomes involved with a gang of tough Belfast kids and ends up rescuing kidnapped babies from a horrible fate in this action-packed fantasy, the first installment in a trilogy. (Rev: BL 3/1/05; SLJ 1/05)

8922 Bauer, Marion Dane. *The Blue Ghost* (2–4). Illus. by Suling Wang. 2005, Random $11.95 (978-0-375-83179-9). 96pp. Nine-year-old Liz is summoned into the past to help a family of children and a blue ghost. (Rev: BL 9/1/05; SLJ 8/05)

8923 Bauer, Marion Dane. *The Red Ghost* (2–4). Illus. by Peter Ferguson. 2008, Random $11.99 (978-0-375-84081-4). 96pp. A doll that seemed perfect for Jenna's little sister turns out to have sad associations in this companion to *The Blue Ghost* (2005). (Rev: BL 4/15/08; SLJ 4/08)

8924 Bauer, Marion Dane. *The Secret of the Painted House* (3–5). Illus. by Leonid Gore. 2007, Random $11.99 (978-0-375-84079-1). 112pp. Nine-year-old Emily discovers an old playhouse in the woods inhabited by a little girl ghost who tries to hold Emily and her brother captive. (Rev: BCCB 10/07; BL 5/1/07; SLJ 8/07)

8925 Bauer, Marion Dane. *Touch the Moon* (5–7). Illus. by Alix Berenzy. 1987, Houghton $15.00 (978-0-89919-526-1). 96pp. Angry when she doesn't get a real horse, Jennifer throws away her toy horse gift and learns a lesson in responsibility. (Rev: BCCB 9/87; BL 9/15/87; HB 9/87)

8926 Baum, L. Frank. *The Marvelous Land of Oz* (4–6). Illus. by John R. Neill. 1985, Morrow $25.99 (978-0-688-05439-7). 288pp. This is a facsimile of the original 1904 edition with the illustrations in both color and black and white. Other titles in this series are published by Peter Smith and Amereon in hard cover and Dover and Puffin in paperback.

8927 Baum, L. Frank. *The Wizard of Oz* (PS–4). Illus. by Charles Santore. 1986, Ballantine paper $5.99 (978-0-345-33590-6). 96pp. For a younger audience than the original, this is an abridged, heavily illustrated version of the Baum classic. (Rev: SLJ 12/91)

8928 Baum, L. Frank. *The Wonderful Wizard of Oz* (2–7). Illus. by Michael Foreman. 2005, Sterling LB $12.95 (978-1-4027-2535-7). 160pp. The lustrous watercolor artwork of Michael Foreman brings new life and humorous details to this classic fantasy. (Rev: SLJ 12/05)

8929 Baum, L. Frank. *The Wonderful Wizard of Oz* (4–8). Illus. by W. W. Denslow. 2000, HarperCollins $24.99 (978-0-06-029323-9). 267pp. A handsome facsimile of the 1900 publication on high-quality paper and featuring 24 original color plates and 130 two-color drawings. (Rev: BL 12/1/00)

8930 Baum, L. Frank. *The Wonderful Wizard of Oz: A Commemorative Pop-Up* (4–8). Illus. by Robert Sabuda. 2001, Simon & Schuster $24.95 (978-0-689-81751-9). An extraordinary pop-up version of the classic fantasy told in a condensed text. (Rev: BL 12/1/00; HB 9/00; HBG 3/01; SLJ 11/00)

8931 Baum, Roger S. *Dorothy of Oz* (4–6). Illus. by Elizabeth Miles. 1989, Morrow $26.99 (978-0-688-07848-5). 176pp. A story true to the original in which Dorothy is called back to Oz because the Tin Woodman, the Scarecrow, and the Cowardly Lion need help. (Rev: BL 1/1/90; SLJ 10/89)

8932 Beck, Ian. *The Secret History of Tom Trueheart* (4–7). Illus. 2007, HarperCollins $16.99 (978-0-06-115210-8). 341pp. Twelve-year-old Tom Trueheart must try to track down his six older brothers when they mysteriously disappear, suspected victims of the enemy of storytelling. (Rev: SLJ 2/07) ∩

8933 Becker, Bonny. *Holbrook: A Lizard's Tale* (4–6). Illus. by Abby Carter. 2006, Clarion $15.00 (978-0-618-71458-2). 148pp. Holbrook the lizard takes his best painting to the city in hopes of artistic recognition; this complex animal adventure features take-offs on art world luminaries, the outwitting of the carnivorous Count Rumolde, and revelations about city life. (Rev: BL 1/1–15/07; SLJ 12/06)

8934 Becker, Tom. *Lifeblood* (5–8). Series: Darkside. 2008, Scholastic $16.99 (978-0-545-03742-6). 279pp. In this second action-packed installment in the series, Jonathan, born of a Darkside mother and Lightside father, travels between these contemporary and fantasy worlds as he tries to solve a series of murders. (Rev: LMC 3/08; SLJ 3/09)

8935 Bell, Hilari. *Shield of Stars* (5–8). Series: The Shield, the Sword and the Crown. 2007, Simon & Schuster $16.99 (978-1-4169-0594-3). 272pp. Weasel, 14 and a reformed pickpocket, sets out to rescue Justice Holis, who has given him a home and a job, from the wicked ruler of Deorthas. The second book is *Sword of Waters* (2008). (Rev: BL 5/15/07; SLJ 5/07)

8936 Bell, Hilari. *The Wizard Test* (5–8). 2005, HarperCollins LB $16.89 (978-0-06-059941-6). 176pp. Fourteen-year-old Dayven is not thrilled when he learns he has magical abilities until he undergoes wizard training. (Rev: BL 2/1/05; SLJ 3/05)

8937 Bell, Ted. *Nick of Time* (5–8). 2008, St. Martin's $17.95 (978-0-312-38068-7). 432pp. Villains from the past and present (that is, 1939) show up when plucky young Nick opens a sea chest washed up near his family's lighthouse. (Rev: BL 4/1/08; SLJ 5/08)

8938 Bellairs, John. *The Ghost in the Mirror* (5–8). 1994, Puffin paper $5.99 (978-0-14-034934-4). 176pp. Fourteen-year-old Rose and white witch Mrs. Zimmerman are transported in time to 1828 on a secret mission. (Rev: SLJ 3/93)

8939 Bender, Robert, comp. *Lima Beans Would Be Illegal: Children's Ideas of a Perfect World* (2–5). Illus. by Robert Bender. 2000, Dial $12.00 (978-0-8037-2532-4). An appealing fantasy in which children describe what a perfect world would be like. (Rev: HBG 10/00; SLJ 7/00)

8940 Berkeley, Jon. *The Lightning Key* (4–7). Illus. by Brandon Dorman. Series: The Wednesday Tales. 2009, HarperCollins $16.99 (978-0-06-075513-3). 399pp. In this fast-moving conclusion to the trilogy Miles sets off in hot pursuit of the thieves who stole the powerful Tiger's Egg, having many adventures on the way. (Rev: SLJ 7/09; VOYA 2/09)

8941 Berkeley, Jon. *The Palace of Laughter: The Wednesday Tales No. 1* (4–7). Illus. by Brandon

Dorman. Series: Julie Andrews Collection. 2006, HarperCollins $16.99 (978-0-06-075507-2). 418pp. Miles Wednesday, an 11-year-old orphan, joins forces with a talking tiger and a diminutive angel named Little to rescue Little's mentor from the Palace of Laughter. (Rev: SLJ 8/06)

8942 Berryhill, Shane. *Chance Fortune and the Outlaws* (5–8). Series: Adventures of Chance Fortune. 2006, Tom Doherty Assoc. $17.95 (978-0-7653-1468-0). 269pp. Despite his lack of superpowers, 14-year-old Josh Blevins manages to bluff his way into Burlington Academy for the Superhuman, and there discovers that evil is afoot. (Rev: SLJ 1/07)

8943 Betancourt, Jeanne. *Ava Tree and the Wishes Three* (2–4). Illus. by Angela Dominguez. 2009, Feiwel & Friends $14.99 (978-0-312-37760-1). 144pp. It's 8-year-old Ava's birthday and she suddenly realizes that she has a wishing power, but it only allows three wishes a day. (Rev: BL 3/15/09; HB 5/09; LMC 8/09; SLJ 5/09)

8944 Bial, Raymond. *The Fresh Grave: And Other Ghostly Stories* (5–7). 1997, Midwest Traditions paper $13.95 (978-1-883953-22-5). 162pp. A series of ten short, humorous ghost stories featuring two teenage heroes and their escapades in a small midwestern town. (Rev: SLJ 12/97)

8945 Bial, Raymond. *The Ghost of Honeymoon Creek* (5–8). Illus. 1999, Midwest Traditions paper $13.95 (978-1-883953-27-0). 176pp. While investigating a strange light in a neighboring farm, 15-year-old Hank encounters a ghost. (Rev: BL 9/1/00; HBG 3/01; SLJ 1/01)

8946 Bildner, Phil, and Loren Long. *The Barnstormers: Tales of Travelin' Nine Game 1* (4–7). Illus. by Loren Long. 2007, Simon & Schuster $9.99 (978-1-4169-1863-9). 144pp. On the road with their late father's traveling baseball team, siblings Griffith, Ruby, and Graham discover a ragged baseball with magical powers. (Rev: BL 4/1/07; SLJ 4/07)

8947 Billingsley, Franny. *The Folk Keeper* (5–8). 1999, Simon & Schuster $16.00 (978-0-689-82876-8); Aladdin paper $4.99 (978-0-689-84461-4). 162pp. Orphaned Corinna disguises herself as a boy to become a Folk Keeper, one who guards the fierce Folk who live underground. (Rev: BCCB 10/99; BL 9/1/99; HB 11/99; HBG 3/00; SLJ 10/99; VOYA 12/99)

8948 Binding, Tim. *Sylvie and the Songman* (5–8). Illus. by Angela Barrett. 2009, Random $15.99 (978-0-385-75157-5). 224pp. Sylvie's composer father disappears, the animals lose their voices, and a villain arrives. (Rev: BL 6/1–15/09)

8949 Birdseye, Tom. *The Eye of the Stone* (4–6). 2000, Holiday House $15.95 (978-0-8234-1564-9). 165pp. Jackson, a fearful 13-year-old boy, is transported to a primitive society where he must find the courage to fight a monster and bring peace to his people. (Rev: BL 2/15/01; HBG 10/01; SLJ 12/00)

8950 Birney, Betty. *The Princess and the Peabodys* (5–8). 2007, HarperCollins $15.99 (978-0-06-084720-3). 249pp. Casey Peabody, a no-nonsense sports-loving 8th grader, is an unlikely constant companion for Princess Eglantine, who is acciden-

tally released from 700 years of imprisonment, but the two do become good friends while efforts are made to return Egg to her medieval home. (Rev: BCCB 11/07; SLJ 1/08)

8951 Black, Holly. *The Ironwood Tree* (3–6). Illus. by Tony DiTerlizzi. Series: The Spiderwick Chronicles. 2004, Simon & Schuster $9.95 (978-0-689-85939-7). 128pp. In the fourth installment in the series, Jared and Simon must rescue Mallory from evil dwarves. (Rev: SLJ 6/04)

8952 Black, Holly. *Lucinda's Secret* (3–6). Illus. by Tony DiTerlizzi. Series: Spiderwick Chronicles. 2003, Simon & Schuster $9.95 (978-0-689-85938-0). 128pp. The Grace siblings visit their Aunt Lucinda to learn more about Arthur Spiderwick's *Field Guide to the Fantastical World Around You*. (Rev: HBG 4/04; SLJ 11/03)

8953 Blair, Margaret Whitman. *Brothers at War* (4–7). 1997, White Mane paper $7.95 (978-1-57249-049-9). 145pp. Two brothers and their friend Sarah find themselves transported back in time to the Battle of Antietam in 1862. (Rev: BL 8/97)

8954 Block, Francesca Lia. *The Waters and the Wild* (5–8). 2009, HarperTeen $16.99 (978-0-06-145244-4). 128pp. Bee, 13 and a lonely misfit, believes she was switched at birth with the real Bee. (Rev: BL 3/15/09; SLJ 7/09)

8955 Bode, N. E. *The Slippery Map* (5–8). 2007, HarperCollins $16.99 (978-0-06-079108-7). 288pp. Orphan Oyster R. Motel, 10, enters the imaginary world of Boneland and discovers that his parents are in danger and that the slippery map has fallen into the hands of evil Dark Mouth. (Rev: BL 11/1/07; SLJ 12/07)

8956 Bode, N. E. *The Somebodies* (5–8). Illus. by Peter Ferguson. 2006, HarperCollins $16.99 (978-0-06-079111-7). 284pp. Fern and her best friend Howard are determined to foil the Blue Queen's plan to destroy the home of the Anybodies who live in a city beneath Manhattan; the final book in a fast-paced trilogy. (Rev: SLJ 9/06)

8957 Bondoux, Anne-Laure. *Vasco: Leader of the Tribe* (4–7). 2007, Delacorte $15.99 (978-0-385-73363-2). 256pp. Vasco, a rat with hopes for the future, escapes extermination by humans and boards an ocean liner, where he encounters more obstacles before tackling a dangerous rainforest. (Rev: BL 12/1/07; LMC 1/08; SLJ 3/08)

8958 Boniface, William. *The Hero Revealed* (3–5). Illus. by Stephen Gilpin. Series: Extraordinary Adventures of Ordinary Boy. 2006, HarperCollins $15.99 (978-0-06-077464-6). 320pp. Ordinary Boy is the only resident with no superpowers, but when Superopolis is threatened by the evil Professor Brain-Drain it looks as if Ordinary Boy may be the only one who can save the day. (Rev: BL 6/1–15/06; SLJ 6/06)

8959 Borsky, Mary. *Benny Bensky and the Perogy Palace* (2–4). Illus. by Linda Hendry. 2001, Tundra paper $7.95 (978-0-88776-523-0). 120pp. Benny the dog plays an important role in solving the mystery of the downturn in the perogy business. (Rev: SLJ 8/01)

8960 Bouwman, H. M. *The Remarkable and Very True Story of Lucy and Snowcap* (5–7). 2008, Marshall Cavendish $16.99 (978-0-7614-5441-0). 288pp. In 1787 on the fictional island of Tatenland, two 12-year-old girls — Lucy, a native Colay, and Snowcap, daughter of a British governor — investigate why the men have all been turned to stone. (Rev: BLO 10/7/08; LMC 3/09; SLJ 11/08)

8961 Bradman, Tony. *Voodoo Child* (4–7). Illus. by Martin Chatterton. Series: Tales of Terror. 2005, Egmont paper $7.50 (978-1-4052-1126-0). 88pp. Megan hopes a voodoo doll will get rid of her father's girlfriend. Other scary titles in this series are *Deadly Game* and *Final Cut* (both 2005). (Rev: SLJ 6/05)

8962 Breathed, Berkeley. *The Last Basselope: One Ferocious Story* (4–7). Illus. 2001, Little, Brown paper $5.95 (978-0-316-12664-9). 32pp. In this imaginative picture book for older readers, Opus and his reluctant adventurers are after the nearly extinct basselope. (Rev: BCCB 1/93; BL 12/15/92; SLJ 1/93)

8963 Breen, M. E. *Darkwood* (5–8). 2009, Bloomsbury $16.99 (978-1-59990-259-3). 288pp. Twelve-year-old Annie flees the home she has shared with her aunt and uncle and finds herself in an even less inviting world that is full of danger but may offer clues to her heritage. (Rev: BCCB 9/09; BL 5/15/09; SLJ 6/09; VOYA 10/09)

8964 Brittain, Bill. *All the Money in the World* (4–6). Illus. by Charles Robinson. 1992, HarperCollins paper $4.95 (978-0-06-440128-9). 160pp. A leprechaun grants Quentin Stowe his wish for all the money in the world.

8965 Brown, Calef. *Polkabats and Octopus Slacks: 14 Stories* (3–5). Illus. 1998, Houghton $16.00 (978-0-395-85403-7). 32pp. Nonsense verses introduce some wacky characters, including Kansas City Octopus, who goes out on the town in four-legged bell bottoms. (Rev: BL 3/15/98; HBG 10/98; SLJ 5/98)

8966 Brown, Jeff. *Stanley, Flat Again!* (2–4). Illus. by Scott Nash. Series: Flat Stanley. 2003, HarperCollins LB $16.89 (978-0-06-029826-5). 87pp. Stanley, first seen in *Flat Stanley* (1964), is flat once more and has a series of adventures in this entertaining early chapter book. (Rev: HBG 10/03; SLJ 3/03)

8967 Brown, Jeff, and Sara Pennypacker. *The Mount Rushmore Calamity* (2–4). Illus. by Macky Pamintuan. Series: Flat Stanley's Worldwide Adventures. 2009, HarperTrophy $15.99 (978-0-06-142991-0); paper $4.99 (978-0-06-142990-3). 96pp. In this first installment in a new series, Flat Stanley goes to Mount Rushmore, saves Lincoln, then goes hunting for gold; historical and geographical information are woven into the entertaining story. (Rev: BL 5/15/09; SLJ 8/09)

8968 Bruchac, Joseph. *Whisper in the Dark* (5–8). 2005, HarperCollins $16.99 (978-0-06-058087-2). 192pp. A frightening Native American legend seems to be coming true for 13-year-old Maddie, descended from a Narragansett chief. (Rev: BL 9/1/05; SLJ 8/05)

8969 Buckingham, Royce. *Demonkeeper* (4–7). 2007, Putnam $15.99 (978-0-399-24649-4). 214pp. Nat lives in Seattle and looks after mostly harmless demons in his creaky old house — until the day when the scary Beast gets loose and Nat must try to retrieve this orphan-eating demon; this fast-paced romp will please reluctant readers. (Rev: SLJ 9/07)

8970 Buckingham, Royce. *Goblins! An UnderEarth Adventure* (5–8). 2008, Putnam $16.99 (978-0-399-25002-6). 232pp. Twelve-year-old Sam and his 17-year-old friend PJ, son of the only police officer in their small town, discover a scary underworld where goblins live. (Rev: SLJ 11/08)

8971 Buckley, Michael. *The Fairy-Tale Detectives* (4–6). Illus. by Peter Ferguson. Series: Sisters Grimm. 2005, Abrams $14.95 (978-0-8109-5925-5). 304pp. Sent to live with their grandmother after their parents disappear, sisters Daphne and Sabrina Grimm find themselves in a magical town full of fairy tale characters known as Everafters. (Rev: BL 11/15/05; SLJ 1/06; VOYA 8/06) ∩

8972 Buffie, Margaret. *The Seeker* (5–8). 2002, Kids Can $16.95 (978-1-55337-358-2). 384pp. Emma is involved in a quest to reunite her family and becomes embroiled in interplanetary intrigue and gaming in this sequel to *The Watcher* (2000). (Rev: BL 10/1/02; HBG 10/03; SLJ 11/02; VOYA 4/03)

8973 Buffie, Margaret. *The Watcher* (5–8). 2000, Kids Can $16.95 (978-1-55074-829-1). 264pp. Sixteen-year-old Emma discovers that she is really a changeling, a Watcher, whose mission is to protect her younger sister from warring factions. (Rev: BL 11/1/00; HBG 3/01; SLJ 10/00; VOYA 2/01)

8974 Burden, Meg. *Northlander: Tales of the Borderlands* (5–8). Series: Tales of the Borderlands. 2007, Brown Barn paper $8.95 (978-0-9768126-8-5). 280pp. Ellin, a Southling with healing powers and other mystical abilities, is torn between her homeland and her friends in the Northlands. (Rev: BL 1/1–15/08; SLJ 2/08)

8975 Bush, Lawrence. *Emma Ansky-Levine and Her Mitzvah Machine* (4–6). Illus. by Joel Iskowitz. 1991, UAHC paper $7.95 (978-0-8074-0458-4). 115pp. Emma receives a machine from her uncle in Jerusalem that gives her personal guidance. (Rev: SLJ 7/91)

8976 Buzbee, Lewis. *Steinbeck's Ghost* (5–8). 2008, Feiwel & Friends $17.95 (978-0-312-37328-3). 352pp. Thirteen-year-old Travis is unhappy when his family moves to a new subdivision and he drifts back to his old neighborhood in Salinas, California, John Steinbeck's hometown; there he works to save the Steinbeck Library from closure and finds that characters from Steinbeck novels are coming to life. (Rev: BL 8/08; SLJ 9/08) ∩

8977 Byars, Betsy. *Little Horse* (2–4). Illus. by David McPhail. 2002, Holt $15.95 (978-0-8050-6413-1). 64pp. A tiny horse gets lost in a land where the flowers are as big as trees in this beginning chapter book. (Rev: BCCB 6/02; BL 3/15/02; HB 5/02; HBG 10/02; SLJ 4/02)

8978 Byars, Betsy. *The Winged Colt of Casa Mia* (4–6). Illus. by Richard Cuffari. 1981, Avon paper $2.95 (978-0-380-00201-6). 132pp. In this fantasy, a young boy visits the Texas ranch of his uncle, an ex-stuntman, and encounters a colt with supernatural powers.

8979 Byng, Georgia. *Molly Moon Stops the World* (5–8). 2004, HarperCollins LB $18.89 (978-0-06-051413-6). 384pp. Molly Moon, a girl of unusual hypnotic powers, is dispatched to California to foil a power-mad hypnotist called Primo Cell. (Rev: BL 5/1/04; SLJ 5/04)

8980 Byng, Georgia. *Molly Moon's Hypnotic Time Travel Adventure* (4–6). 2005, HarperCollins $16.99 (978-0-06-075032-9). 392pp. When her beloved dog is kidnapped, Molly Moon travels back in time to late 19th-century India where she matches wits the villainous Maharaja of Waqt and meets former versions of herself. (Rev: SLJ 1/06)

8981 Cameron, Eleanor. *The Court of the Stone Children* (5–7). 1990, Puffin paper $6.99 (978-0-14-034289-5). 192pp. Nina's move with her family to San Francisco is a disaster until she encounters a young ghost in a small museum.

8982 Cardo, Horacio. *The Story of Chess* (3–5). Illus. 1998, Abbeville $16.95 (978-0-7892-0250-5). 45pp. After their countries destroyed each other in a war, two kings listen to a war historian who uses the first chess set to explain every participant and every move. (Rev: BL 11/15/98; HBG 3/99; SLJ 4/99)

8983 Carman, Patrick. *Beyond the Valley of Thorns* (4–6). Series: The Land of Elyon. 2005, Scholastic $11.99 (978-0-439-70094-8). 221pp. In the second installment of this fantasy series, Alexa and her companions confront a host of new dangers as they battle the ogre Abaddon. (Rev: SLJ 10/05; VOYA 12/05)

8984 Carman, Patrick. *The Dark Hills Divide* (4–6). Series: Land of Elyon. 2005, Scholastic $11.95 (978-0-439-70093-1). 272pp. Alexa, 12, discovers the secrets of her walled city and a plan to destroy it in this fantasy, the first volume in a trilogy. (Rev: BL 3/1/05; SLJ 4/05)

8985 Carman, Patrick. *Rivers of Fire* (5–8). Series: Atherton. 2008, Little, Brown $16.99 (978-0-316-16672-0). 352pp. The planet of Atherton is still in trouble, and Edgar, Samuel, and Isabel fight to save it in this continuation of the story that began in *The House of Power*. (Rev: BL 5/15/08; SLJ 8/08)

8986 Carman, Patrick. *The Tenth City* (4–6). Series: The Land of Elyon. 2006, Scholastic $11.99 (978-0-439-70095-5). 186pp. In the conclusion of this fantasy series, Alexa and her band of supporters face off against Grindall who has kidnapped Yipes, Alexa's diminutive friend. (Rev: SLJ 8/06)

8987 Carmody, Isobelle. *Little Fur: The Legend Begins* (3–5). 2006, Random $12.95 (978-0-375-83854-5). 208pp. Little Fur (who is half elf, half troll) sets out on a journey through the human world to save the trees that she calls home as well as the earth spirit. (Rev: BL 11/15/06; SLJ 11/06)

8988 Carmody, Isobelle. *A Mystery of Wolves* (3–5). Illus. by author. 2008, Random $12.99 (978-0-375-83858-3). 240pp. Little Fur, a half-elf and half-troll girl, sets out on a classic discovery search during which she must uncover the Mystery of Wolves. (Rev: BL 2/1/08)

8989 Carroll, Lewis. *Alice in Wonderland and Through the Looking Glass* (4–7). Illus. by John Tenniel. 1963, Putnam $18.99 (978-0-448-06004-0). One of many recommended editions of these enduring fantasies.

8990 Carroll, Lewis. *Alice Through the Looking-Glass* (4–7). Illus. by Helen Oxenbury. 2005, Candlewick $24.99 (978-0-7636-2892-5). 226pp. Faithful to the original text, Oxenbury's inviting artwork will draw young readers; a companion to her award-winning *Alice's Adventures in Wonderland* (1999). (Rev: BL 12/15/05*; HBG 4/06; SLJ 12/05)

8991 Carroll, Lewis. *Alice's Adventures in Wonderland* (3–5). Illus. by Alison Jay. 2006, Dial $25.99 (978-0-8037-2940-7). 224pp. A handsomely illustrated, faithful retelling of the classic story, with glowing paintings of diverse sizes. (Rev: BL 11/1/06)

8992 Carroll, Lewis. *Alice's Adventures in Wonderland* (5–7). Illus. 2000, Chronicle $19.95 (978-0-8118-2274-9). 140pp. This oversize edition of the complete text of Carroll's classic features illustrations from 29 artists. (Rev: BL 11/1/00; HBG 3/01; SLJ 11/00)

8993 Carroll, Lewis. *Through the Looking Glass, and What Alice Found There* (4–7). Illus. by John Tenniel. 1977, St. Martin's $14.95 (978-0-312-80374-2). 224pp. The sequel to *Alice's Adventures in Wonderland*. One of many editions.

8994 Carroll, Thomas. *The Colony* (4–7). 2000, Sunstone $18.95 (978-0-86534-295-8). 152pp. Fifth-grader Tony and his bullying arch-enemy Lawrence are shrunk to the size of ants by a Navajo charm and in their new environment join opposing forces. (Rev: HBG 3/01; SLJ 7/00)

8995 Carus, Marianne, ed. *That's Ghosts for You: 13 Scary Stories* (4–7). Illus. by YongSheng Xuan. 2000, Front St. $15.95 (978-0-8126-2675-9). 131pp. A fine collection of 13 chilling stories set in locations around the world, each with a supernatural twist. (Rev: BL 12/1/00; HBG 3/01; SLJ 12/00)

8996 Catanese, P. W. *The Mirror's Tale: A Further Tales Adventure* (4–7). 2006, Simon & Schuster paper $4.99 (978-1-4169-1251-4). 274pp. When their father decides to separate his mischievous 13-year-old twin sons for the summer, they switch places and one is sent to the castle of his aunt and uncle where he discovers and falls under the spell of a bewitching mirror. (Rev: SLJ 8/06)

8997 Cazet, Denys. *Minnie and Moo and the Seven Wonders of the World* (2–4). Illus. by author. 2003, Simon & Schuster $16.95 (978-0-689-85330-2). 134pp. A chapter book in which bovine friends Minnie and Moo seek to save the farm by conducting tours of the "Seven Wonders of the World." (Rev: HBG 4/04; SLJ 11/03)

8998 Chan, Gillian. *The Carved Box* (5–8). 2001, Kids Can $16.95 (978-1-55074-895-6). 232pp. The acquisition of a dog and a carved box ease the transition for orphaned Callum, 15, who has moved from Scotland to Canada to live with his uncle, in this novel which has an element of fantasy that comes to the fore in the dramatic ending. (Rev: BL 10/01; HBG 3/02; SLJ 10/01; VOYA 4/02)

8999 Chocolate, Deborah N. *Pigs Can Fly* (2–4). Illus. by Leslie Tryon. 2004, Cricket $15.95 (978-0-8126-2706-0). 64pp. In this engaging collection of four stories, Harriet the potbellied pig realizes her dream of flying, helps a friend overcome her fear of heights, competes in a swimming contest, and nearly kills Homer Mouse with kindness. (Rev: BL 5/1/04; SLJ 5/04)

9000 Clark, Margaret, comp. *A Treasury of Dragon Stories* (2–5). Illus. by Mark Robertson. Series: Treasury. 1997, Kingfisher paper $6.95 (978-0-7534-5114-4). 156pp. A collection of 15 previously published stories or excerpts from books that deal with dragons. (Rev: SLJ 1/98)

9001 Clarke, Judith. *Starry Nights* (5–9). 2003, Front St. $15.95 (978-1-886910-82-9). 152pp. When Jess's family moves to a new house, a ghost seems to be involved in the family's emotional upheavals. (Rev: BL 6/1–15/03; HB 9/03; HBG 4/04)

9002 Coleman, Alice Scovell. *Engraved in Stone* (4–7). Illus. by Anjal R. Armand. 2003, Tiara Bks. $14.95 (978-0-9729846-0-7). 147pp. A prince and princess who will do anything to avoid their planned marriage set off on a quest to get their fate changed in this humorous fantasy. (Rev: SLJ 12/03)

9003 Coleman, Janet W. *Fast Eddie* (3–4). Illus. by Alec Gillman. 1993, Macmillan LB $13.95 (978-0-02-722815-1). 144pp. Eddie the raccoon faces danger when he plays tricks on humans. (Rev: SLJ 6/93)

9004 Colfer, Eoin, and Andrew Donkin. *Artemis Fowl: The Graphic Novel* (5–7). Illus. by Giovanni Rigano. 2007, Hyperion $18.99 (978-0-7868-4881-2); paper $9.99 (978-0-7868-4882-9). 112pp. A well-illustrated graphic novel rendering of the 2001 novel about the 12-year-old genius and adventurous criminal entrepreneur Artemis Fowl. (Rev: BL 11/15/07; LMC 1/08; SLJ 1/08)

9005 Collins, Suzanne. *Gregor and the Code of Claw* (5–9). Series: The Underland Chronicles. 2007, Scholastic $17.99 (978-0-439-79143-4). 412pp. A mysterious prophecy makes Gregor question himself in this adventure-filled fifth title in the series. (Rev: SLJ 7/07)

9006 Collins, Suzanne. *Gregor and the Curse of the Warmbloods* (4–6). Series: Underland Chronicles. 2005, Scholastic $16.95 (978-0-439-65623-8). 368pp. In this third volume in the series, Gregor, his sister Boots, and his mother travel to the Underland to deal with the terrible plague spreading there. (Rev: BL 7/05; SLJ 7/05; VOYA 10/05)

9007 Collins, Suzanne. *Gregor and the Marks of Secret* (5–8). Series: The Underland Chronicles. 2006, Scholastic $16.99 (978-0-439-79145-8). 341pp. Gregor, accompanied by his little sister Boots, joins forces with Queen Luxa to defend Underland from attacks by the rat army. (Rev: SLJ 9/06; VOYA 8/06)

9008 Collins, Suzanne. *Gregor the Overlander* (4–7). 2003, Scholastic $17.99 (978-0-439-43536-9). 320pp. When his baby sister disappears into an air vent, 11-year-old Gregor doesn't hesitate to follow and finds himself in a whole new world, an Underland where an unexpected role awaits him. (Rev: BCCB 1/04; BL 11/15/03*; HB 9/03; HBG 9–10/03; LMC 11/03; SLJ 11/03; VOYA 10/03)

9009 Collodi, Carlo. *The Adventures of Pinocchio*. Rev. ed. (4–10). Trans. from Italian by M. A. Murray. Illus. by Roberto Innocenti. 2005, Creative Editions $19.95 (978-1-56846-190-8). 191pp. Nineteenth-century European landscapes provide the backdrop for this appealing retelling of the classic story about the puppet that longed to become a little boy; a revision of the 1988 edition. (Rev: SLJ 12/05)

9010 Conly, Jane L. *R-T, Margaret, and the Rats of NIMH* (4–6). Illus. by Leonard Lubin. 1990, HarperCollins LB $14.89 (978-0-06-021364-0); paper $6.99 (978-0-06-440387-0). 288pp. The third installment of the brilliant rodents, in which two human children star. (Rev: BCCB 6/90; BL 5/15/90; SLJ 6/90)

9011 Conly, Jane L. *Racso and the Rats of NIMH* (5–7). Illus. by Leonard Lubin. 1986, HarperCollins LB $17.89 (978-0-06-021362-6). 288pp. This sequel to the Newbery Medal winner involves once again the smart rodents who wish to live in peace in Thorn Valley. (Rev: BCCB 6/86; BL 6/1/86; SLJ 4/86)

9012 Conly, Jane Leslie. *Impetuous R., Secret Agent* (4–6). Illus. by Bonnie Leick. 2008, Hyperion $17.99 (978-1-4231-0418-6). 288pp. This deft tale follows three cockroach kids and their friendly people as they work to raise enough cash to keep their jazz club home intact. (Rev: BL 9/1/08)

9013 Cooper, Susan. *The Boggart* (4–6). 1993, Macmillan $15.00 (978-0-689-50576-8). 200pp. An old desk unleashes the Boggart, a mischievous spirit who has lived in a Scottish castle for centuries. (Rev: BCCB 3/93; BL 1/15/93; HB 5/93*; SLJ 1/93)

9014 Cooper, Susan. *The Boggart and the Monster* (4–6). 1997, Simon & Schuster paper $16.00 (978-0-689-81330-6). 192pp. The Boggart, a Scottish spirit-creature, wants to accompany young Jessup and Emily when they go to Loch Ness to find the monster. (Rev: BCCB 5/97; BL 3/1/97; HB 5/97; SLJ 5/97)

9015 Cooper, Susan. *Green Boy* (4–8). 2002, Simon & Schuster $16.00 (978-0-689-84751-6). 208pp. Two young boys discover a futuristic world in which natural resources are depleted and a war to save the environment is being waged. (Rev: BCCB 5/02; BL 3/1/02; HB 5/02; HBG 10/02; SLJ 2/02)

9016 Cooper, Susan. *King of Shadows* (5–8). Illus. by John Clapp. 1999, Simon & Schuster $16.00 (978-0-689-82817-1). 192pp. Nat Field time-travels to 1599 London and assumes the child-actor role of Puck in *A Midsummer Night's Dream*. (Rev: BL 10/15/99*; HB 11/99; HBG 3/00; SLJ 11/99)

9017 Cooper, Susan. *Silver on the Tree* (5–7). 1980, Macmillan $18.00 (978-0-689-50088-6). 256pp. In this fifth and last volume of a series, Will Stanton and his friends wage a final battle against the Dark, the powers of evil. The first four volumes are *Over Sea, Under Stone* (1966), *The Dark Is Rising* (1973), *The Grey King* (1975), and *Greenwitch* (1985). *The Grey King* won the 1976 Newbery Medal.

9018 Corder, Zizou. *Lionboy: The Truth* (5–8). 2005, Dial $16.99 (978-0-8037-2985-8). 240pp. In the final installment in the trilogy, Charlie Ashanti, reunited with his parents in Morocco, is kidnapped by the Corporacy and put on a boat bound for the Caribbean, but the boy wonder calls on his animal friends for help. (Rev: BL 10/1/05; SLJ 9/05; VOYA 12/05)

9019 Coville, Bruce. *The Dragon of Doom* (2–4). Illus. by Katherine Coville. Series: Moongobble and Me. 2003, Simon & Schuster $14.95 (978-0-689-85754-6). 69pp. Young Edward finds life in his hometown of Pigbone terribly boring until a magician named Moongobble arrives and asks the boy to be his assistant. (Rev: HBG 4/04; SLJ 1/04)

9020 Coville, Bruce. *The Ghost in the Big Brass Bed* (4–6). 1991, Bantam paper $4.50 (978-0-553-15827-4). 184pp. Two ghosts appeal for help to Chris and Nina, who try to solve the mystery surrounding them. (Rev: SLJ 1/92)

9021 Coville, Bruce, ed. *A Glory of Unicorns* (5–8). Illus. 1998, Scholastic paper $16.95 (978-0-590-95943-8). A collection of stories by fantasy authors, including the editor and his wife, that deal with unicorns. (Rev: BL 6/1–15/98; HBG 10/98; SLJ 5/98; VOYA 8/98)

9022 Coville, Bruce. *Goblins in the Castle* (5–7). Illus. 1992, Pocket paper $4.99 (978-0-671-72711-6). 166pp. William, now 11, has grown up in Toad-in-a-Cage Castle and knows many of its secret passages. (Rev: BL 2/1/93)

9023 Coville, Bruce. *Juliet Dove, Queen of Love: A Magic Shop Book* (4–8). 2003, Harcourt $17.00 (978-0-15-204561-6). 190pp. Life changes for shy Juliet, 12, when she is given an amulet and the boys suddenly come flocking to her side. (Rev: BL 1/1–15/04; HBG 4/04; SLJ 12/03)

9024 Coville, Bruce. *The Prince of Butterflies* (3–5). Illus. by John Clapp. 2002, Harcourt $16.00 (978-0-15-201454-4). 40pp. Migrating monarchs turn a boy into a butterfly so he can help them on their journey in this socially conscious story. (Rev: BL 3/15/02; HBG 10/02; SLJ 5/02)

9025 Cowell, Cressida. *How to Speak Dragonese: By Hiccup Horrendous Haddock III* (3–5). Illus. by author. 2006, Little, Brown $10.99 (978-0-316-15600-4). 221pp. Young Viking Hiccup is joined by a friend and his dragon as they fight Roman invaders in this entertaining sequel to *How to Train Your Dragon* (2004) and *How to Be a Pirate* (2005). (Rev: SLJ 6/06)

9026 Cowell, Cressida. *How to Train Your Dragon: By Hiccup Horrendous Haddock III: Translated from an Old Norse Legend by Cressida Cowell* (4–8). Illus. 2004, Little, Brown paper $10.95 (978-0-316-73737-1). 224pp. The hilarious account of the fumbling efforts of nerdy Hiccup to capture and train a dragon and to take his rightful place as the next Warrior Chief. Also use *How to Be a Pirate: By Hiccup Horrendous Haddock III* (2005). (Rev: BL 4/15/04; SLJ 7/04)

9027 Cox, Judy. *The Mystery of the Burmese Bandicoot: The Tails of Frederick and Ishbu* (4–7). Illus. by Omar Rayyan. Series: The Tails of Frederick and Ishbu. 2007, Marshall Cavendish $16.99 (978-0-7614-5376-5). 256pp. Rats Frederick and Ishbu escape their schoolroom cage and embark on an adventure that involves a shipwreck and a statue with the power to end the world. (Rev: BL 10/1/07; SLJ 12/07)

9028 Crane, Jordan. *The Clouds Above* (2–4). Illus. 2005, Fantagraphics $18.95 (978-1-56097-627-1). 216pp. Simon skips school and with his cat, Jack, climbs a magic staircase into a world of adventure. (Rev: BL 10/1/05) [741.5]

9029 Creech, Sharon. *The Unfinished Angel* (4–6). 2009, HarperCollins $15.99 (978-0-06-143095-4). 176pp. Zola, a young American girl, moves to a small Swiss village with her father, meets an angel, aids a group of orphans, and helps to restore life to the aging community. (Rev: BL 7/09; SLJ 9/09) ∩

9030 Creedon, Catherine. *Blue Wolf* (4–8). 2003, HarperCollins LB $16.89 (978-0-06-050869-2). 192pp. Fantasy lurks around each corner of this story of Jamie, a 14-year-old for whom running is a retreat from life and who sometimes feels that wolves are right at his heels. (Rev: BCCB 1/04; BL 11/15/03; SLJ 10/03)

9031 Crew, Gary. *The Viewer* (5–9). Illus. by Shaun Tan. 2003, Lothian $16.95 (978-0-85091-828-1). A well-illustrated dark fantasy linked to world catastrophes caused by mankind, from religious persecution to atomic war. (Rev: SLJ 3/04)

9032 Crilley, Mark. *Akiko and the Journey to Toog* (3–5). Illus. by author. 2003, Delacorte $9.95 (978-0-385-73042-6). 164pp. In this comic-style intergalactic fantasy, fifth grader Akiko and a number of her friends journey to the planet Toog on a rescue mission. (Rev: HBG 4/04; SLJ 12/03)

9033 Cross, Gillian. *Pictures in the Dark* (5–8). 1996, Holiday $16.95 (978-0-8234-1267-9). A boy whose life is miserable uses supernatural means to escape the pressures. (Rev: BCCB 1/97; BL 1/1–15/97)

9034 Crosse, Joanna. *A Child's Book of Angels* (3–5). Illus. by Olwyn Whelan. 2000, Barefoot Books LB $19.99 (978-1-84148-082-4). 64pp. A young boy's guardian angel takes him on a tour of heaven where he meets different kinds of angels and learns about their responsibilities — looking after the seasons, for example, or healing. (Rev: HBG 10/01; SLJ 2/01)

9035 Crowley, Bridget. *Step into the Dark* (5–7). 2003, Hodder & Stoughton paper $8.95 (978-0-340-84416-8). 172pp. This ghost story is set in a theater and conveys the attraction of the stage. (Rev: BL 12/1/03)

9036 Curry, Jane Louise. *The Black Canary* (5–8). 2005, Simon & Schuster $16.95 (978-0-689-86478-0). 288pp. Twelve-year-old James, from a biracial family of musicians, resists pressure to develop his own musical abilities until he travels back in time to Elizabethan London and discovers he is also talented. (Rev: BL 2/15/05*; SLJ 3/05)

9037 Cuyler, Margery. *Weird Wolf* (3–6). Illus. by Dirk Zimmer. 1991, Holt paper $6.95 (978-0-8050-1643-7). 72pp. Nine-year-old Harry Walpole has to find out how to rid himself of being a werewolf, just like his grandfather. (Rev: BCCB 1/90; BL 12/1/89; SLJ 4/90)

9038 Dadey, Debbie, and Marcia T. Jones. *Leprechauns Don't Play Basketball* (5–8). Illus. by John S. Gurney. 1992, Scholastic paper $3.99 (978-0-590-44822-2). 70pp. The Bailey Elementary 3rd grade thinks the gym teacher is a leprechaun. (Rev: BL 9/15/92)

9039 Dadey, Debbie, and Marcia T. Jones. *This Side of Magic* (2–5). Illus. by Adam Stower. 2009, Starscape paper $3.99 (978-0-7653-5982-7). 136pp. Two children discover a magical land hidden right next door. (Rev: BL 6/1–15/09)

9040 Dahl, Michael. *Last Son of Krypton* (2–4). Illus. by John Delaney. Series: DC Super Heroes. 2009, Stone Arch $18.99 (978-1-4342-1155-2). 56pp. This action-packed, illustrated chapter book gives the story of Superman's arrival on Earth. (Rev: BLO 4/9/09; SLJ 6/09)

9041 Dahl, Michael. *The Museum Monsters* (2–5). Illus. by Dan Schoening. Series: DC Super Heroes: Superman. 2009, Stone Arch LB $25.32 (978-1-4342-1157-6); paper $5.95 (978-1-4342-1372-3). 56pp. A highly illustrated chapter book introduction to Clark Kent, Lois Lane, and Jimmy Olsen. (Rev: LMC 10/09*; SLJ 6/09)

9042 Dahl, Roald. *The Witches* (3–6). Illus. by Quentin Blake. 1983, Farrar $16.00 (978-0-374-38457-9). 208pp. A boy and his grandmamma save English children from being turned into mice by witches.

9043 Dale, Anna. *Whispering to Witches* (4–6). 2004, Bloomsbury $16.95 (978-1-58234-890-2). 304pp. Twelve-year-old Joe Binks's Christmas-time encounter with a novice witch named Twiggy sweeps him into a mission to retrieve a book of potions and spells before it can be put to evil use. (Rev: BL 11/15/04; SLJ 11/04)

9044 Daley, Michael J. *Space Station Rat* (4–6). 2005, Holiday $15.95 (978-0-8234-1866-4). 182pp. An escaped lab rat and a lonely boy, both residents of an orbiting space station, become friends and together face many challenges; the fast-paced texts switches from one character to the other. (Rev: BL 8/05; SLJ 8/05)

9045 Datlow, Ellen, and Terri Windling, eds. *Swan Sister: Fairy Tales Retold* (5–10). 2003, Simon & Schuster $16.95 (978-0-689-84613-7). 176pp. Retellings by well-known authors of traditional stories are inventive and entertaining. (Rev: BCCB 11/03; BL 9/15/03; HBG 4/04; SLJ 12/03)

9046 DeFelice, Cynthia. *The Ghost and Mrs. Hobbs* (4–6). 2001, Farrar $16.00 (978-0-374-38046-5). 192pp. A ghost asks 11-year-old Allie for help, but scary and mysterious happenings hamper her efforts. (Rev: BL 9/1/01; HB 11/01; HBG 3/02; SLJ 8/01)

9047 DeFelice, Cynthia. *The Ghost of Fossil Glen* (4–6). 1998, Farrar $16.00 (978-0-374-31787-4). 176pp. Allie has been chosen by the ghost of a young girl to avenge her death in this tense thriller. (Rev: BCCB 3/98; BL 3/15/98; HB 9/98; HBG 10/98; SLJ 7/98)

9048 De Fombelle, Timothée. *Toby Alone* (4–8). Trans. by Sarah Ardizzone. Illus. by François Place. 2009, Candlewick $16.99 (978-0-7636-4181-8). 384pp. In this gripping eco-fantasy, tiny Toby Lolness, 13, must struggle alone to beat the big corporation that threatens the survival of his tree world. (Rev: BCCB 5/09; HB 5/09; LMC 8/09; SLJ 5/09)

9049 Del Negro, Janice M. *Passion and Poison: Tales of Shape-Shifters, Ghosts, and Spirited Women* (5–8). Illus. by Vince Natale. 2007, Marshall Cavendish $16.99 (978-0-7614-5361-1). 64pp. A collection of seven creepy supernatural tales, each featuring females who face peril and challenges. (Rev: BL 9/1/07; SLJ 12/07)

9050 Delaney, Joseph. *Revenge of the Witch* (5–8). Illus. by Patrick Arrasmith. Series: The Last Apprentice. 2005, Greenwillow LB $17.89 (978-0-06-076619-1). 336pp. A scary story in which young Tom, seventh son of a seventh son, becomes an apprentice spook and must protect the people from ghouls, boggarts, and beasties. (Rev: BCCB 10/05; BL 8/05*; HB 11/05; HBG 4/06; LMC 3/06; SLJ 11/05; VOYA 8/06)

9051 De Mari, Silvana. *The Last Dragon* (5–8). Trans. by Shaun Whiteside. 2006, Hyperion $16.95 (978-0-7868-3636-9). 320pp. To fulfill a prophecy in which he will play a key role, a young elf named Yorsh, the last of his kind in a world hostile to elves, sets off in search of the last dragon. (Rev: BL 11/1/06; SLJ 1/07)

9052 Deming, Sarah. *Iris, Messenger* (5–8). 2007, Harcourt $16.00 (978-0-15-205823-4). 209pp. Iris is a miserable outcast whose life takes a turn for the better when the mythology book she gets for her birthday leads her to an amazing discovery. (Rev: SLJ 7/07)

9053 Derby, Sally. *Two Fools and a Horse: An Original Tale* (1–4). Illus. by Robert Rayevsky. 2003, Marshall Cavendish $16.95 (978-0-7614-5119-8). Janski and Wilhelm, two simple-minded peasants, track a suspicious-looking peddler, convinced that he has concealed a stolen horse in a sack on his back. (Rev: HBG 10/03; SLJ 5/03)

9054 Desplechin, Marie. *Poor Little Witch Girl* (4–6). 2006, Bloomsbury $15.95 (978-1-58234-898-8). 128pp. Eleven-year-old Verbena is learning to deal with the fact that she's a witch even though she longs for a normal life, but when one of her Grandma's spell lessons involves the cutest boy at school she feels her social life is doomed. (Rev: BL 12/1/06; SLJ 12/06)

9055 Deutsch, Stacia, and Rhody Cohon. *King's Courage* (2–4). Illus. by David Wenzel. Series: Blast to the Past. 2006, Simon & Schuster paper $3.99 (978-1-4169-1269-9). 112pp. Abigail and her friends travel back in time on a mission to convince Dr. Martin Luther King, Jr. to continue his civil rights campaign. (Rev: BL 2/1/06)

9056 DiCamillo, Kate. *The Magician's Elephant* (4–7). Illus. by Yoko Tanaka. 2009, Candlewick $16.99 (978-0-7636-4410-9). 208pp. Young orphan Peter Augustus Duchene learns from a fortune-teller that his younger sister Adele is still alive and sets off, with an elephant, to find her, facing many challenges along the way. (Rev: BCCB 11/09; BL 7/09; HB 9/09; SLJ 8/09*; VOYA 8/09)

9057 DiCamillo, Kate. *The Miraculous Journey of Edward Tulane* (2–4). Illus. by Bagram Ibatoulline. 2006, Candlewick $18.99 (978-0-7636-2589-4). 200pp. Edward Tulane, a china rabbit, learns the meaning of love on an odyssey that begins when he falls into the sea during an ocean voyage. (Rev: BCCB 4/06; BL 1/1–15/06*; HB 3/06; LMC 5/06; SLJ 2/06*) ∩

9058 DiCamillo, Kate. *The Tale of Despereaux: Being the Story of a Mouse, a Princess, Some Soup, and a Spool of Thread* (3–7). Illus. 2003, Candlewick $17.99 (978-0-7636-1722-6). 272pp. The diminutive mouse named Despereaux inspires confidence despite his odd appearance in this multilayered story involving Princess Pea, peasant girl Miggery Sow, and a rat named Roscuro. Newbery Medal winner, 2004. (Rev: BL 7/03; HB 5/04; SLJ 8/03)

9059 DiTerlizzi, Tony, and Holly Black. *Arthur Spiderwick's Field Guide to the Fantastical World Around You* (4–6). Illus. 2005, Simon & Schuster $24.95 (978-0-689-85941-0). 122pp. This large-format, beautifully illustrated volume is the guide to the inhabitants of the "Invisible World" that is featured in the Spiderwick series. (Rev: BL 2/1/06; SLJ 3/06)

9060 DiTerlizzi, Tony, and Holly Black. *The Nixie's Song* (3–6). Illus. by Tony DiTerlizzi. Series: Beyond the Spiderwick Chronicles. 2007, Simon & Schuster $10.99 (978-0-689-87131-3). XXpp. Nick think his life has changed dramatically when he gains a new stepsister, Laurie, but there's much more to come in this first installment in a new fantasy series by the creators of The Spiderwick Chronicles. (Rev: BL 10/15/07) ∩

9061 Divakaruni, Chitra Banerjee. *The Mirror of Fire and Dreaming* (5–8). 2005, Roaring Brook $16.95 (978-1-59643-067-9). 336pp. In this sequel to *The Conch Bearer* (2003), 12-year-old Anand continues his magic studies and travels back to Moghul times, where he encounters powerful sorcerers and evil jinns. (Rev: BL 9/1/05; SLJ 12/05)

9062 D'Lacey, Chris. *The Fire Within* (5–8). 2005, Scholastic $12.95 (978-0-439-67343-3). 340pp. A multilayered fantasy in which British college student David Rain comes to board at the home of Liz Pennykettle and her daughter, Lucy, and discovers that the clay dragons crafted by Liz have magical properties. (Rev: SLJ 10/05)

9063 Doherty, Berlie. *The Goblin Baby* (1–4). Illus. by Lesley Harker. Series: Stepping Stones Fantasy. 2009, Random LB $11.99 (978-0-375-95841-0); paper $4.99 (978-0-375-85841-3). 128pp. When Tam's baby sister is replaced with a changeling, he must go to the land of faeries to set things straight. (Rev: BCCB 6/09; BL 5/15/09; LMC 8/09; SLJ 5/09)

9064 Donaldson, Julia. *The Giants and the Joneses* (3–5). Illus. by Greg Swearingen. 2005, Holt $14.95 (978-0-8050-7805-3). 215pp. In this twist on the tale of Jack and the Beanstalk, filled with invented words, Jumbeelia, a young giantess who lives in Groil, climbs down a "bimplestonk" to a miniature world below where she kidnaps three "iggly plops." (Rev: SLJ 10/05) ∩

9065 Downer, Ann. *The Dragon of Never-Was* (4–7). Illus. by Omar Ryyan. 2006, Simon & Schuster $16.95 (978-0-689-85571-9). 305pp. In this lively sequel to *Hatching Magic* (2003), 12-year-old Theodora Oglethorpe accompanies her father to Scotland to investigate the origin of a mysterious scale and there learns more about her own magical powers. (Rev: BL 6/1–15/06; SLJ 12/06)

9066 Downer, Ann. *Hatching Magic* (4–7). Illus. by Omar Rayyan. 2003, Simon & Schuster $16.95 (978-0-689-83400-4). 242pp. A procession of a pet dragon, a wizard, and his archenemy travel through time from the 13th century to the 21st century, where an 11-year-old Bostonian becomes involved in their disputes. (Rev: BL 4/15/03; HB 7/03; HBG 10/03; SLJ 8/03)

9067 Doyle, Roddy. *Rover Saves Christmas* (2–5). Illus. by Brian Ajhar. 2001, Scholastic $14.95 (978-0-439-30530-3). 160pp. The lively crew from *The Giggler Treatment* (2000) return in an irreverent romp that takes Rover to the North Pole to sub for Rudolph. (Rev: HBG 3/02; SLJ 10/01)

9068 *Dr. Ernest Drake's Dragonology: The Complete Book of Dragons* (5–12). Illus. 2003, Candlewick $18.99 (978-0-7636-2329-6). Presented as the recently discovered research of a 19th-century scientist, this richly illustrated volume presents a very realistic encyclopedia of dragon facts and figures. (Rev: BL 4/15/04; SLJ 4/04)

9069 Drake, Salamanda. *Dragonsdale* (3–6). Illus. by Gilly Marklew. 2007, Scholastic $16.99 (978-0-439-87173-0). 288pp. A teen girl yearns to ride the dragons she cares for. (Rev: BCCB 9/07; BL 6/1–15/07; LMC 11/07; SLJ 6/07)

9070 Drexler, Sam, and Fay Shelby. *Lost in Spillville* (5–9). Series: Erika and Oz Adventures in American History. 2000, Aunt Strawberry paper $6.99 (978-0-9669988-1-8). 150pp. Two teenagers accidentally are transported to the 1930s and must locate an important clock maker to be returned to the 1990s. (Rev: SLJ 11/00; VOYA 12/00)

9071 Driscoll, Laura. *Beck and the Great Berry Battle* (1–3). Illus. by Judith Clarke. Series: Disney Fairies. 2006, Random paper $5.99 (978-0-7364-2373-1). 128pp. When conflict breaks out between the hummingbirds and the chipmunks in Never Land's Pixie Hollow, Beck the fairy steps in to mediate the dispute. (Rev: BL 2/1/06; SLJ 3/06)

9072 Driscoll, Laura. *Vidia and the Fairy Crown* (2–3). Illus. by Judith Clarke, et al. Series: Disney Fairies. 2006, Random paper $5.99 (978-0-7364-2372-4). 128pp. Vidia, a temperamental fairy who lives in Never Land's Pixie Hollow, struggles to clear her name after she's falsely accused of stealing Queen Clarion's crown. (Rev: SLJ 3/06)

9073 Duane, Diane. *Deep Wizardry* (5–8). Series: Young Wizards. 2001, Magic Carpet Bks. LB $15.25 (978-0-613-36059-3); Harcourt paper $6.95 (978-0-15-216257-3). 288pp. Nita and Kit, the two young wizards of *So You Want to Be a Wizard,* again use their powers to prevent a great catastrophe. (Rev: HB 5/85)

9074 Duane, Diane. *So You Want to Be a Wizard* (5–8). Series: Young Wizards. 2003, Harcourt $16.95 (978-0-15-204738-2); paper $6.95 (978-0-15-216250-4). 288pp. Nita and friends embark on a journey to retrieve the Book of Night with Moon.

9075 Duel, John. *Wide Awake in Dreamland* (5–8). Illus. 1992, Stargaze $15.95 (978-0-9630923-0-4). An evil warlock threatens to steal a 9-year-old's imagination unless the young boy can find a friendly wizard first. (Rev: BL 3/1/92; SLJ 5/92)

9076 Duey, Kathleen. *The Silver Thread: The Unicorn's Secret #2* (2–4). 2001, Simon & Schuster paper $3.99 (978-0-689-84270-2). 80pp. A young girl must rescue a unicorn child who has been shot by a hunter's arrow in this second volume of a four-part fantasy. (Rev: BL 3/1/02)

9077 Dunkle, Clare B. *The Hollow Kingdom* (5–8). 2003, Holt $16.95 (978-0-8050-7390-4). 230pp. A beauty-and-the-beast story with a twist, in which Kate is persuaded to marry a goblin king and move to his underground world. (Rev: BL 11/15/03; HBG 4/04; SLJ 12/03)

9078 Dunlop, Eileen. *The Ghost by the Sea* (4–6). 1996, Holiday House $15.95 (978-0-8234-1264-8). 192pp. Robin uncovers details of a death that occurred 80 years ago and is haunted by a restless ghost. (Rev: BCCB 3/97; BL 1/1–15/97; SLJ 3/97)

9079 Dunlop, Eileen. *Websters' Leap* (4–7). 1995, Holiday $15.95 (978-0-8234-1193-1). 160pp. In this time-slip fantasy, Jill gets involved with people who owned a Scottish castle 400 years before. (Rev: BL 10/1/95; SLJ 10/95)

9080 Dunmore, Helen. *Ingo* (5–8). 2006, HarperCollins $16.99 (978-0-06-081852-4). 336pp. As they search for their missing father, 11-year-old Sapphire and her brother Conor find themselves torn between their home on England's Cornish coast and the Mer people and magical sea world of Ingo. (Rev: BCCB 10/06; BL 9/1/06; HBG 4/07; SLJ 8/06; VOYA 4/06)

9081 Dunmore, Helen. *The Tide Knot* (5–8). 2008, HarperCollins $16.99 (978-0-06-081855-5). 336pp. Part-mermaid siblings Sapphire and Conor, introduced in *Ingo* (2006), must save humans from a huge tidal wave. (Rev: BL 1/1–15/08; HB 1/08; SLJ 2/08)

9082 Dunrea, Olivier. *Hanne's Quest* (2–4). Illus. 2006, Philomel $16.99 (978-0-399-24216-8). 112pp. Hanne, a young hen in Mem Pockets's henhouse, sets off on a heroic quest to save her owners' farm; excellent illustrations enhance this chapter book. (Rev: BCCB 4/06; BL 2/1/06*; HB 3/06; HBG 10/06; SLJ 2/06)

9083 DuPrau, Jeanne. *The Diamond of Darkhold* (4–9). Series: Ember. 2008, Random $16.99 (978-0-375-85571-9). 285pp. Lima and Doon return to Ember to search for a device that may offer hope, and to find food to support the residents of Sparks through the hard winter; the final installment in the series. (Rev: HB 9/08; SLJ 11/08) ⌒

9084 DuPrau, Jeanne. *The People of Sparks* (5–7). Series: Books of Ember. 2004, Random $15.95 (978-0-375-82824-9). 352pp. In this sequel to *The City of Ember,* Doon and Lina, plus the 400 people they have led from Ember to the surface of the Earth, seek aid from the people of Sparks. (Rev: BL 4/15/04; HB 7/04; SLJ 5/04)

9085 DuPrau, Jeanne. *The Prophet of Yonwood* (4–7). Series: Books of Ember. 2006, Random $15.95 (978-0-375-87526-7). 304pp. About 50 years before the time of the Embers series, 11-year-old Nickie hides out at her great-grandfather's estate in Yonwood, North Carolina, and thinks about good and evil as she watches her neighbors react to predictions of doom. (Rev: BL 5/15/06; SLJ 6/06; VOYA 4/06) ⌒

9086 Dyer, Heather. *The Girl with the Broken Wing* (2–4). Illus. by Peter Bailey. 2005, Scholastic $15.99 (978-0-439-74827-8). 160pp. An angel with a broken wing leads twins James and Amanda on some merry adventures. (Rev: BL 11/1/05; SLJ 1/06)

9087 Easton, Patricia Harrison. *Davey's Blue-Eyed Frog* (2–4). Illus. by Mike Wohnoutka. 2003, Clarion $14.00 (978-0-618-18185-8). 104pp. Davey catches a blue-eyed frog that turns out to be a princess in this illustrated chapter book. (Rev: BL 3/1/03; HBG 10/03; SLJ 7/03)

9088 Eaton, Jason Carter. *The Facttracker* (4–7). Illus. by Pascale Constantin. 2008, HarperCollins $15.99 (978-0-06-056434-6). 272pp. The library turns into the "liebrary" when the town of Traäkerfaxx decides to deal in lies rather than facts in this imaginative and clever story. (Rev: BL 1/1–15/08; SLJ 3/08)

9089 Edwards, Julie Andrews, and Emma Walton Hamilton. *The Great American Mousical* (4–6). Illus. by Tony Walton. 2006, HarperCollins $15.99 (978-0-06-057918-0). 160pp. In this spoof by actress Julie Andrews and her daughter, a troupe of mice in a condemned Broadway theater are feverishly rehearsing a musical revue when their star goes missing. (Rev: BL 1/1–15/06; SLJ 2/06)

9090 Einhorn, Edward. *Paradox in Oz* (4–6). Illus. 2000, Hungry Tiger $24.95 (978-1-929527-01-4). 240pp. This new Oz adventure is true to the famous series and contains familiar characters including Ozma and Glinda, the Good Witch of the South. (Rev: BL 4/15/00; SLJ 8/00)

9091 Elliott, David. *Jeremy Cabbage and the Living Museum of Human Oddballs and Quadruped Delights* (4–6). 2008, Knopf $15.99 (978-0-375-84333-4). 336pp. A humorous fast-paced fantasy about 11-year-old orphan Jeremy, who becomes embroiled in a dispute between the autocratic Baron von Strompie and the outcast cloons of the Living Museum of Human Oddballs and Quadruped Delights. (Rev: BL 3/15/08; SLJ 6/08)

9092 Enthoven, Sam. *The Black Tattoo* (5–8). 2006, Penguin $19.99 (978-1-59514-114-9). 512pp. In this action-packed fantasy epic set in London and Hell, three teenage friends — Esme, Charlie, and Jack — work together to defeat a demonic entity that has taken possession of Charlie. (Rev: BL 9/1/06; SLJ 1/07) ∩

9093 Etchemendy, Nancy. *The Power of Un* (4–7). 2000, Front St. $14.95 (978-0-8126-2850-0). 160pp. Gib, a young boy, meets a strange old man who gives him an "unner," which can send him back in time in this thought-provoking fantasy. (Rev: BCCB 7–8/00; BL 5/1/00; HBG 10/00; SLJ 6/00; VOYA 6/00)

9094 Falcone, L. M. *Walking with the Dead* (5–8). 2005, Kids Can $16.95 (978-1-55337-708-5). 196pp. Alex finds himself entangled in the world of Greek mythology when a mummy in his father's museum awakens to take care of some unfinished business in the underworld. (Rev: BL 3/15/05; SLJ 6/05)

9095 Farland, David. *Of Mice and Magic* (5–8). Illus. by Howard Lyon. Series: Ravenspell. 2005, Covenant Communications $16.95 (978-1-57734-918-1). 276pp. Ben's magical mouse Amber turns Ben into a mouse and together the two set out to rescue the animals from the pet store. (Rev: SLJ 1/06)

9096 Favole, Robert J. *Through the Wormhole* (5–8). 2001, Flywheel $17.95 (978-1-930826-00-7). 192pp. Detailed endnotes add historical weight to this story of Michael and Kate, who travel through time to 1778 to aid the Marquis de Lafayette and rescue one of Michael's ancestors. (Rev: BL 3/1/01; SLJ 4/01; VOYA 4/01)

9097 Fawcett, Melissa Jayne, and Joseph Bruchac. *Makiawisug: The Gift of the Little People* (3–5). Illus. by David Wagner. 1997, Little People $19.95 (978-0-9656933-2-5). 28pp. The story of the antics of the American Indian "little people," the Makiawisug. (Rev: BL 9/15/97)

9098 Fienberg, Anna. *The Witch in the Lake* (5–8). 2002, Annick LB $18.95 (978-1-55037-723-1); paper $7.95 (978-1-55037-722-4). 216pp. This story of magic and suspense in 16th-century Italy interweaves fantasy with facts about the time. (Rev: HBG 3/03; SLJ 8/02; VOYA 8/02)

9099 Findon, Joanne. *When Night Eats the Moon* (4–7). 2000, Red Deer paper $7.95 (978-0-88995-212-6). 176pp. Her flute music and some magic take Holly, a Canadian girl visiting England, back to prehistoric times at Stonehenge when the locals are being threatened with a Celtic invasion. (Rev: BL 8/00; VOYA 6/00)

9100 Fischbein, Dina. *Really Raoulino* (4–6). Illus. by Bill Crews. 2006, Handprint $15.95 (978-1-59354-151-4). 150pp. Neither Raoulino, a newcomer at the Metropolitan Zoo, nor his keepers know what kind of animal he is, but he knows that what really matters is getting out of the zoo and back to his island home. (Rev: BL 4/15/06; SLJ 6/06)

9101 Fisher, Catherine. *The Oracle Betrayed* (5–8). 2004, Greenwillow $16.99 (978-0-06-057157-3). 352pp. This suspenseful story set in an imaginary country that combines aspects of ancient Greece and ancient Egypt involves a young heroine, Mirany, on a dangerous quest. (Rev: BL 2/15/04; HB 3/04; SLJ 3/04; VOYA 4/04)

9102 Fisher, Catherine. *The Sphere of Secrets* (5–8). Series: Oracle Prophecies Trilogy. 2005, Greenwillow LB $18.89 (978-0-06-057162-7). 384pp. Alexos, introduced in *The Oracle Betrayed* (2004), embarks on a journey to the Well of Songs while his friend Mirany serves the Oracle. (Rev: BL 3/15/05; SLJ 3/05)

9103 Flanagan, John. *The Battle for Skandia* (4–7). Series: Ranger's Apprentice. 2008, Philomel $16.99 (978-0-399-24457-5). 292pp. In book four of the series, Will is saved from death by Halt and Horace, Evanlyn is captured, and the Temujai army closes in. (Rev: BL 4/1/08)

9104 Flanagan, John. *The Burning Bridge* (5–8). Series: Ranger's Apprentice. 2006, Philomel $16.99 (978-0-399-24455-1). 256pp. Will and his friend Horace again face war and find the safety of the kingdom depends on them. (Rev: BL 5/15/06; SLJ 8/06)

9105 Flanagan, John. *The Icebound Land* (4–7). Series: Ranger's Apprentice. 2007, Philomel $16.99 (978-0-399-24456-8). 256pp. Will, the ranger's apprentice, and Princess Evanlyn are captives on a ship that takes them to Skandia to work as slaves; while the ranger Halt and knight-in-training Horace journey to rescue them but face many obstacles. (Rev: BL 6/1–15/07; SLJ 8/07)

9106 Flanagan, John. *The Ruins of Gorlan* (5–8). 2005, Philomel $15.99 (978-0-399-24454-4). 256pp. Will becomes an apprentice ranger and plays a key role in protecting his kingdom in this memorable first installment in a new fantasy series. (Rev: BL 6/1–15/05*; SLJ 6/05)

9107 Fleischman, Sid. *The 13th Floor: A Ghost Story* (4–6). Illus. 1995, Greenwillow $16.99 (978-0-688-14216-2). 144pp. When a ghost who lived in the 17th century asks for his help, Bud obligingly travels back in time. (Rev: BL 10/1/95; HB 11/95; SLJ 10/95)

9108 Fleming, Ian. *Chitty Chitty Bang Bang* (4–6). Illus. by John Burningham. 1964, Amereon LB $19.95 (978-0-88411-983-8). 159pp. Chitty Chitty Bang Bang, a magical racing car, flies, floats, and has a real talent for getting the Pott family in and out of trouble.

9109 Fletcher, Charlie. *Ironhand* (5–8). Series: The Stoneheart Trilogy. 2008, Hyperion $16.99 (978-1-4231-0177-2). 400pp. In this sequel to *Stoneheart*, George races against three gruesome veins that have appeared on his body as he takes the Hard Way and searches for the Stoneheart. (Rev: BL 4/15/08; SLJ 6/08)

9110 Fletcher, Charlie. *Stoneheart* (5–8). 2007, Hyperion $16.99 (978-1-4231-0175-8). 464pp. At the Natural History Museum in London 12-year-old George stumbles upon a parallel world where good statues (or spits) and evil taints are at war. (Rev: BL 5/15/07; SLJ 8/07)

9111 Foon, Dennis. *The Dirt Eaters* (5–10). Series: Longlight Legacy Trilogy. 2003, Annick $19.95 (978-1-55037-807-8); paper $9.95 (978-1-55037-806-1). 320pp. In this well-written first installment of a trilogy, 15-year-old Roan finds himself torn between the peaceful ways of his upbringing and a desire to avenge a murderous attack on his village. (Rev: SLJ 1/04; VOYA 2/04)

9112 Forester, Victoria. *The Girl Who Could Fly* (4–7). 2008, Feiwel & Friends $16.95 (978-0-312-37462-4). 208pp. Piper McCloud can fly — an ability that unsettles her community — and she is taken to a school for children with unusual abilities, which she soon senses is not quite what it seems. (Rev: BL 6/1–15/08; SLJ 9/08)

9113 Foster, Evelyn, and Olwyn Whelan. *The Mermaid of Cafur* (1–5). 1999, Barefoot Books LB $15.95 (978-1-902283-40-1). Through the courage of Meaghan, the evil power of the mermaid queen of Cafur is broken and her captive children are set free. (Rev: SLJ 3/99)

9114 Fox, Helen. *Eager's Nephew* (5–8). 2006, Random LB $17.99 (978-0-385-90904-4). 208pp. In this sequel to *Eager* (2004), Eager the robot and his nephew Jonquil pay a forbidden visit to Eager's human friends, the Bells; mystery and adventure ensue. (Rev: BL 10/15/06; SLJ 1/07)

9115 Frederick, Heather. *For Your Paws Only* (4–6). Illus. by Sally Wern Comport. Series: Spy Mice. 2005, Simon & Schuster $9.95 (978-1-4169-0573-8). 258pp. Morning Glory Goldenleaf, lead operative of the Spy Mice Agency, uncovers a plot by evil rat leader Roquefort Dupont to rid the world of mice. (Rev: SLJ 12/05)

9116 Freeman, Martha. *The Spy Wore Shades* (4–6). 2001, HarperCollins LB $15.89 (978-0-06-029270-6). 235pp. Eleven-year-old Dougie helps a girl from an underground civilization to save her family's home from land developers. (Rev: BL 10/1/01; HBG 3/02; SLJ 8/01)

9117 French, Jackie. *My Dad the Dragon* (2–4). Illus. by Stephen Michael King. Series: Funny Families. 2007, Stone Arch LB $22.60 (978-1-59889-343-4); paper $7.95 (978-1-59889-436-3). 107pp. Horace receives an assignment from his teacher at knight school to slay a dragon in this chapter book packed with fantasy elements. (Rev: SLJ 7/07)

9118 French, Jackie. *My Mom the Pirate* (2–4). Illus. by Stephen Michael King. Series: Funny Families. 2007, Stone Arch LB $22.60 (978-1-59889-345-8); paper $7.95 (978-1-59889-438-7). 107pp. Cecil time-warps to school every day from a pirate ship roaming the seas 200 years in the past. (Rev: SLJ 7/07)

9119 French, Vivian. *The Bag of Bones* (3–5). Illus. by Ross Collins. Series: Tales from the Five Kingdoms. 2009, Candlewick $14.99 (978-0-7636-4255-6). 256pp. Will Trueheart Gracie Gillypot be able to stop the witch Truda Hangnail's evil plans? (Rev: BL 5/1/09)

9120 French, Vivian. *Princess Daisy and the Dazzling Dragon* (2–4). Illus. by Sarah Gibb. Series: Tiara Club. 2007, HarperCollins $15.99 (978-0-06-112434-1); paper $3.99 (978-0-06-112433-4). 70pp. Princess Daisy, who attends a special school to perfect her princess skills, has a stressful day in which she must deal with mean Princess Floreen and a baby dragon on the roof. (Rev: SLJ 7/07)

9121 French, Vivian. *The Robe of Skulls* (3–5). Series: Tales from the Five Kingdoms. 2008, Candlewick $14.99 (978-0-7636-3531-2). 208pp. This funny, multilayered story, the first in a series, features — among others — a sorceress who absolutely must have a new gown, a talking bat, and a girl called Gracie who has been locked in the cellar for being too cheerful. (Rev: BCCB 7–8/08; BL 9/1/08; HB 7/08)

9122 Fromental, Jean-Luc. *Broadway Chicken* (5–8). Trans. by Suzi Baker. Illus. 1995, Hyperion LB $15.49 (978-0-7868-2048-1). A tale of success and failure with, yes, a dancing chicken as the protagonist. (Rev: BL 12/15/95; SLJ 2/96)

9123 Froud, Wendy, and Terri Windling. *A Midsummer Night's Faery Tale* (4–6). Illus. 1999, Simon & Schuster $18.00 (978-0-684-85559-2). 52pp. A young fairy named Sneezle sets out on a dangerous quest to save the life of his queen, Titania. (Rev: BL 2/1/00)

9124 Funke, Cornelia. *Igraine the Brave* (3–5). Trans. by Anthea Bell. Illus. by author. 2007, Scholastic $16.99 (978-0-439-90379-0). 224pp. A medieval fantasy featuring lots of magic and a brave 12-year-old girl named Igraine who longs to be a knight. (Rev: BCCB 2/08; BL 10/1/07; LMC 1/08; SLJ 11/07)

9125 Gaiman, Neil. *Coraline* (5–8). Illus. by Dave McKean. 2002, HarperCollins LB $17.89 (978-0-06-623744-2). 176pp. An Alice-in-Wonderland type of tale for older readers in which a girl finds an alternate world in the empty apartment next door. (Rev: BCCB 11/02; BL 8/02; HB 11/02; HBG 3/03; SLJ 8/02*)

9126 Gaiman, Neil. *The Dangerous Alphabet* (1–4). Illus. by Gris Grimly. 2008, HarperCollins $17.99 (978-0-06-078333-4). 32pp. This unusual alphabet story follows two Victorian children and their gazelle on a treasure hunt through darkly funny sewers. (Rev: BL 3/1/08; HB 7/08; SLJ 5/08)

9127 Gaiman, Neil. *Odd and the Frost Giants* (3–6). Illus. by Brett Helquist. 2009, Harper $14.99 (978-0-06-167173-9). 128pp. Odd, a young Viking, takes off alone to seek adventure and meets three mythological Norse characters who need help defeating a giant in order to return home. (Rev: BL 7/09; HB 11/09) ⌒

9128 Gaiman, Neil. *The Wolves in the Walls* (3–6). Illus. by Dave McKean. 2003, HarperCollins $16.99

(978-0-380-97827-4). Lucy says there are wolves in the walls of her house, but her family doesn't believe her — until the wolves come out — in this imaginatively illustrated story. (Rev: BL 2/1/04; HBG 4/04; SLJ 9/03)

9129 García, Laura Gallego. *The Valley of the Wolves* (5–8). Trans. by Margaret Sayers Peden. 2006, Scholastic $16.99 (978-0-439-58553-8). 248pp. Dana, 10, learns to use her magical powers at an academy of sorcery and wonders about the origins of her best friend and constant companion Kai, visible only to Dana. (Rev: BL 5/15/06; SLJ 6/06; VOYA 6/06)

9130 Gardner, Lyn. *Into the Woods* (4–7). Illus. by Mini Grey. 2007, Random $16.99 (978-0-385-75115-5). 448pp. After their mother's death, Storm and her sisters flee the evil Dr. DeWilde and his pack of wolves and find themselves facing many dangers that will be familiar to readers of fairy tales. (Rev: BL 5/1/07; HB 7/07; LMC 10/07; SLJ 6/07)

9131 Gardner, Sally. *Magical Kids: The Smallest Girl Ever / The Boy Who Could Fly* (3–6). Illus. by author. 2008, Dial $16.99 (978-0-8037-3159-2). 224pp. This "flip-over" volume holds two short back-to-back novels about children whose lives are changed for the better by magic. (Rev: BL 12/15/08; SLJ 2/09)

9132 Gardner, Sally. *Magical Kids: The Strongest Girl in the World and The Invisible Boy* (2–5). Illus. by author. 2007, Dial $15.99 (978-0-8037-3158-5). 196pp. After reading about Josie Jenkins and her amazing feats of strength, readers can flip this book over to read about Sam, who can become invisible using a patch he received from an alien. (Rev: SLJ 7/07)

9133 Garland, Michael. *Miss Smith and the Haunted Library* (1–3). Illus. by author. 2009, Dutton $16.99 (978-0-525-42139-9). 32pp. The magical storybook first seen in *Miss. Smith's Incredible Storybook* (2003) comes to life again in a spooky library generating characters such as Count Dracula and Captain Hook causing chaos, delight, and suspense. (Rev: BLO 6/16/09; SLJ 7/09)

9134 Garland, Michael. *Miss Smith's Incredible Storybook* (1–4). Illus. by author. 2003, Dutton $16.99 (978-0-525-47133-2). A magic story book that brings the characters to life proves too much for the substitute teacher. (Rev: HBG 4/04; SLJ 10/03)

9135 Garza, Xavier. *Juan and the Chupacabras / Juan y el Chupacabras* (2–4). Trans. by Carolina Villarroel. Illus. by April Ward. 2006, Piñata $15.95 (978-1-55885-454-3). Cousins Luz and Juan don't know whether to believe their grandfather's tales of confrontations with the dreaded Chupacabras, so they decide to search out one of the bloodsucking demons themselves. (Rev: SLJ 10/06)

9136 Gear, W. Michael, and Kathleen O'Neal Gear. *Children of the Dawnland* (5–8). 2009, Starscape $17.95 (978-0-7653-2019-3). 304pp. Twig dreams the future and sees danger for her world so she takes off on a daring journey to save her people. (Rev: BL 7/09)

9137 Gerstein, Mordicai. *The Giant* (3–5). Illus. 1995, Hyperion LB $14.49 (978-0-7868-2104-4). 40pp. When three children rebuff a giant's attempts to become friends with them, later that night they hear him sobbing. (Rev: BL 10/15/95; SLJ 11/95)

9138 Gibbons, Faye. *Hook Moon Night: Spooky Stories from the Georgia Mountains* (3–6). Illus. 1997, Morrow $14.95 (978-0-688-14504-0). 128pp. In his Georgia home, Grandpa tells ghost stories, including one in which a sick woman is buried alive by her son-in-law. (Rev: BL 11/1/97; HBG 3/98; SLJ 10/97)

9139 Going, K. L. *The Garden of Eve* (5–8). 2007, Harcourt $17.00 (978-0-15-205986-6). 240pp. When Evie and her father move to a house with an enchanted apple orchard after Evie's mother dies, a ghost and a magical seed help to ease Evie's grief. (Rev: BL 10/1/07; HB 11/07; LMC 1/08; SLJ 12/07) ∩

9140 Golding, Julia. *The Gorgon's Gaze* (4–7). Series: Companions Quartet. 2007, Marshall Cavendish $16.99 (978-0-7614-5377-2). 320pp. This sequel to *Secret of the Sirens* finds both Connie and the Society for the Protection of Mythical Creatures in danger. (Rev: BL 1/1–15/08)

9141 Goldsmith, Howard. *The Twiddle Twins' Haunted House* (2–3). Illus. 1997, Mondo paper $4.50 (978-1-57255-222-7). 40pp. Hippo twins suspect a ghost when they are awakened one night by a tapping sound. Also use *Twiddle Twins' Music Box Mystery* (1997). (Rev: BL 2/1/98)

9142 Gonick, Larry. *Attack of the Smart Pies* (4–7). Illus. by author. 2005, Cricket $15.95 (978-0-8126-2740-4). 185pp. This complex novel with graphic elements blends fantasy, horror, mystery, and humor in the story of Emma, a 12-year-old orphan who flees from her threatening foster father and finds herself in Kokonino County, land of the New Muses. (Rev: SLJ 6/05)

9143 Gopnik, Adam. *The King in the Window* (5–8). 2005, Hyperion $19.95 (978-0-7868-1862-4). 416pp. Mistaken by window wraiths as their king, 11-year-old Oliver Parker struggles to resist their efforts to pull him into their world. (Rev: BL 10/1/05; SLJ 11/05; VOYA 2/06)

9144 Gormley, Beatrice. *Best Friend Insurance* (5–7). Illus. by Emily Arnold McCully. 1988, Avon paper $2.50 (978-0-380-69854-7). 160pp. Maureen finds that her mother has been transformed into a new friend named Kitty. (Rev: SLJ 8/04)

9145 Gormley, Beatrice. *Fifth Grade Magic* (4–6). Illus. by Emily Arnold McCully. 1982, Avon paper $3.50 (978-0-380-67439-8). 128pp. Gretchen uses the help of an inept fairy godmother to get the lead in the school play.

9146 Gormley, Beatrice. *Mail-Order Wings* (3–5). Illus. by Emily Arnold McCully. 1984, Avon paper $2.95 (978-0-380-67421-3). 164pp. Andrea finds her Wonda-Wings are gradually transforming her into a bird.

9147 Gormley, Beatrice. *More Fifth Grade Magic* (3–5). Illus. by Emily Arnold McCully. 1990, Avon paper $3.50 (978-0-380-70883-3). 128pp. Amy uses the magical powers she finds in a calendar to grant her wishes. (Rev: BL 8/89)

9148 Goto, Hiromi. *The Water of Possibility* (5–7). Illus. by Aries Cheung. Series: In the Same Boat. 2002, Coteau paper $8.95 (978-1-55050-183-4). 319pp. Sayuri, 12, and her younger brother discover a magical world full of danger in this fantasy that includes many elements of Japanese folklore. (Rev: SLJ 8/02)

9149 Grabenstein, Chris. *The Crossroads* (5–8). Illus. 2008, Random $16.99 (978-0-375-84697-7). 336pp. Zack sees creepy faces in trees in this ghost story full of action, suspense, and likable characters. (Rev: BL 5/1/08)

9150 Grahame, Kenneth. *The Reluctant Dragon* (2–4). Illus. by E. H. Shepard. 1938, Holiday House $15.95 (978-0-8234-0093-5); paper $6.95 (978-0-8234-0755-2). 58pp. Tongue-in-cheek story of a boy who makes friends with a peace-loving dragon. Another fine edition is illustrated by Michael Hague (1983, Holt), and a well-received picture-book version abridged and illustrated by Inga Moore was published in 2004 (Candlewick).

9151 Grahame, Kenneth. *The Wind in the Willows* (4–7). Illus. by E. H. Shepard. 1983, Macmillan $19.95 (978-0-684-17957-5). 256pp. The classic that introduced Mole, Ratty, and Mr. Toad. Two of many other editions arc: illus. by Michael Hague (1980, Henry Holt); illus. by John Burningham (1983, Viking).

9152 Grahame, Kenneth. *The Wind in the Willows: The Gates of Dawn, Vol. 3* (2–5). Trans. from French by Joe Johnson. Adapted by Michel Plessix. Illus. by author. 2000, NBM $15.95 (978-1-56163-245-9). 31pp. A graphic novel that retells key episodes from Chapters 7, 8, and 9 of *The Wind in the Willows*. (Rev: HBG 3/01; SLJ 7/00)

9153 Gray, Kes. *Nelly the Monster Sitter: Grerks, Squurms, and Water Greeps* (3–6). Illus. by Stephen Hanson. 2009, Penguin paper $7.99 (978-1-59514-259-7). 272pp. Nelly Morton likes the thrill and variety of monster sitting. (Rev: BLO 5/27/09)

9154 Gray, Luli. *Falcon and the Carousel of Time* (4–7). 2005, Houghton $15.00 (978-0-618-44895-1). 128pp. Falcon, 13, and her Aunt Emily travel back to 1903 New York City in this novel that blends elements of *Timespinners* (2003) and the two previous Falcon novels. (Rev: BL 6/1–15/05; SLJ 7/05)

9155 Gray, Luli. *Falcon and the Charles Street Witch* (4–7). 2002, Houghton $16.00 (978-0-618-16410-3). 144pp. In this fantasy follow-up to 1995's *Falcon's Egg*, a 12-year-old girl becomes reacquainted with a dragon she released over New York City and befriends a witch who lives in Greenwich Village. (Rev: BL 3/15/02*; HBG 10/02; SLJ 4/02; VOYA 4/02)

9156 Gray, Luli. *Timespinners* (4–6). 2003, Houghton $15.00 (978-0-618-16412-7). 160pp. While visiting the dioramas in the American Museum of Natural History, twins Allie and Fig Newton are transported backward in time to 1913 France and then to 35,000 B.C. (Rev: BL 3/1/03; HBG 10/03; SLJ 4/03)

9157 Greenburg, Dan. *A Ghost Named Wanda* (3–5). Illus. by Jack E. Davis. Series: Zack Files. 1996, Grosset paper $4.99 (978-0-448-41261-0). 59pp. The story of Zack, a 10-year-old with the knack of getting into unusual situations. Also use *Zap! I'm a Mind Reader* (1996). (Rev: SLJ 2/97)

9158 Greenburg, Dan. *Great-Grandpa's in the Litter Box* (3–5). Illus. 1996, Penguin paper $4.99 (978-0-448-41260-3). 61pp. Zack adopts a cat that not only talks but also claims to be a relative. Zack has further adventures in *Through the Medicine Cabinet* (1996). (Rev: BL 1/1–15/97; SLJ 2/97)

9159 Greenburg, Dan. *Secrets of Dripping Fang: The Onts* (3–5). Illus. by Scott M. Fischer. Series: The Onts. 2005, Harcourt $11.95 (978-0-15-205457-1). 131pp. Despite significant hygiene issues, the orphaned Shluffmuffin twins are adopted by the elderly Mandible sisters and welcomed to the old ladies' mansion in Dripping Fang Forest, where they discover that all is not as it seems. (Rev: SLJ 12/05)

9160 Greer, Gery, and Bob Ruddick. *Max and Me and the Time Machine* (5–8). 1983, HarperCollins paper $4.99 (978-0-06-440222-4). 140pp. Steve and Max travel back in time to England during the Middle Ages.

9161 Griffin, Adele. *Vampire Island* (4–7). 2007, Putnam $14.99 (978-0-399-23785-0). 144pp. Three Manhattan youngsters — vegetarian vampire siblings Lexington, Madison, and Hudson — try to behave like normal people but their respective vampire traits keep getting in the way in this lighthearted, action-packed story. (Rev: BL 8/07; LMC 11/08; SLJ 8/07)

9162 Griffin, Adele. *Witch Twins* (3–5). 2001, Hyperion $14.99 (978-0-7868-0739-0). 144pp. Fifth-grade twins Claire and Luna are given many opportunities both at home and at school to use their hidden powers as witches. (Rev: BL 4/15/01; HB 9/01; HBG 3/02; SLJ 7/01)

9163 Griffin, Peni R. *The Ghost Sitter* (4–6). 2001, Dutton $14.99 (978-0-525-46676-5). 128pp. A gentle ghost story in which Charlotte tries to help a girl who died 50 years ago to find peace. (Rev: BL 8/01; HB 5/01; HBG 10/01; SLJ 6/01)

9164 Griffin, Peni R. *Margo's House* (3–6). 1996, Simon & Schuster $16.00 (978-0-689-80944-6). 122pp. A girl and her father project themselves into the bodies of two dolls. (Rev: BCCB 11/96; BL 9/1/96; SLJ 10/96)

9165 Griffin, Peni R. *Switching Well* (5–9). 1993, Penguin paper $5.99 (978-0-14-036910-6). Two girls from different centuries trade places but soon regret their decisions. (Rev: BCCB 7–8/93; BL 6/1–15/93*; SLJ 6/93*; VOYA 8/93)

9166 Griffith, Helen V. *Cougar* (4–6). 1999, Greenwillow $15.00 (978-0-688-16337-2). 112pp. In this engaging fantasy, Nickel, a neglected youngster, gets help from a ghost horse to cope with bully Robbo. (Rev: BCCB 3/99; BL 4/1/99; HB 5/99; HBG 10/99; SLJ 5/99)

9167 Grindley, Sally. *Breaking the Spell: Tales of Enchantment* (3–5). Illus. 1997, Kingfisher $17.95 (978-0-7534-5002-4). 80pp. Seven original folk and fairy tales set in exotic locales and written by both established and new writers. (Rev: BL 1/1–15/98; HBG 3/98; SLJ 12/97)

9168 Guiberson, Brenda Z. *Tales of the Haunted Deep* (3–6). Illus. 2000, Holt $15.95 (978-0-8050-6057-7). 70pp. This collection of ghost stories of the sea contains tales of monsters, pirates, lighthouses, and ships, many of them from folklore. (Rev: BCCB 9/00; BL 6/1–15/00; HBG 10/00; SLJ 11/00)

9169 Gutman, Dan. *Abner and Me* (5–8). Series: Baseball Card Adventure. 2005, HarperCollins LB $17.89 (978-0-06-053444-8). 176pp. Stosh and his mother travel back to visit the Battle of Gettysburg in an effort to learn more about baseball's origins. (Rev: BL 1/1–15/05)

9170 Gutman, Dan. *Babe and Me* (4–7). Illus. 2000, Avon $16.99 (978-0-380-97739-0). 160pp. Joe and his dad time-travel to the 1932 World Series to witness a historic moment with hitter Babe Ruth. (Rev: BL 2/1/00; HBG 10/00; SLJ 2/00; VOYA 4/00)

9171 Gutman, Dan. *Honus and Me: A Baseball Card Adventure* (4–7). 1997, Avon paper $5.99 (978-0-380-78878-1). 160pp. Young Joe Stoshack finds a magical baseball card that allows him to travel through time and participate in the 1909 World Series. (Rev: BL 4/15/97; SLJ 6/97)

9172 Gutman, Dan. *Jackie and Me: A Baseball Card Adventure* (4–7). Illus. 1999, Avon $16.99 (978-0-380-97685-0). 144pp. While time-traveling to research a paper on Jackie Robinson, Joe Stoshack becomes an African American and experiences prejudice first hand. (Rev: BL 2/1/99; HBG 10/99; SLJ 3/99)

9173 Gutman, Dan. *Satch and Me* (4–7). Series: Baseball Card Adventure. 2005, HarperCollins LB $16.89 (978-0-06-059492-3). 173pp. Stosh travels back to 1942 to establish whether Satchel Paige was the fastest pitcher in history and learns about racial discrimination in the process. (Rev: SLJ 2/06; VOYA 4/06)

9174 Haddix, Margaret P. *Among the Brave* (4–7). Series: Shadow Children. 2004, Simon & Schuster $15.95 (978-0-689-85794-2). 240pp. This sequel to *Among the Barons* (2003) features Trey's efforts to rescue Luke and other third-born children. (Rev: BL 5/15/04; SLJ 6/04)

9175 Haddix, Margaret P. *Running Out of Time* (4–7). 1995, Simon & Schuster $16.95 (978-0-689-80084-9). 185pp. Living in a historical site where the time is the 1840s, Jessie escapes into the present in this fantasy. (Rev: BCCB 11/95; BL 10/1/95; SLJ 10/95*)

9176 Hague, Michael, ed. *The Book of Dragons* (4–7). Illus. by Michael Hague. 1995, Morrow $21.99 (978-0-688-10879-3). 160pp. Seventeen classic tales about dragons by such authors as Tolkien and Kenneth Grahame are included in this interesting anthology. (Rev: BL 10/1/95; SLJ 10/95)

9177 Hague, Michael, ed. *The Book of Fairies* (3–6). Illus. 2000, HarperCollins $21.99 (978-0-688-

10881-6). 128pp. Eight stories, songs, and poems celebrate this unworldly creature in a beautiful book illustrated by Michael Hague. (Rev: BL 12/15/00; HBG 3/01) [808.8]

9178 Hahn, Mary D. *The Doll in the Garden: A Ghost Story* (4–6). Illus. 1989, Houghton $16.00 (978-0-89919-848-4). 160pp. Ten-year-old Ashley and her mother try to start a new life in a house owned by a grouchy octogenarian. (Rev: BCCB 3/89; BL 3/15/89; SLJ 5/89)

9179 Hahn, Mary D. *Time for Andrew: A Ghost Story* (4–6). 1994, Clarion $15.00 (978-0-395-66556-5). 167pp. Drew changes places with his look-alike distant relative and travels back to 1910. (Rev: BCCB 4/94; BL 4/1/94; SLJ 5/94)

9180 Hahn, Mary D. *Wait Till Helen Comes: A Ghost Story* (5–7). 1986, Houghton $15.00 (978-0-89919-453-0); Avon paper $5.99 (978-0-380-70442-2). 192pp. Things go from bad to worse for Molly and Michael and their stepsister Heather when Heather becomes involved in a frightening relationship with the ghost of a dead child. (Rev: BCCB 10/86; BL 9/1/86; SLJ 10/86)

9181 Hahn, Mary Downing. *All the Lovely Bad Ones* (4–7). 2008, Clarion $16.00 (978-0-618-85467-7). 192pp. Travis and Corey encounter ghosts at their grandmother's bed-and-breakfast, which was a poor house long ago. (Rev: BL 5/1/08; SLJ 5/08)

9182 Hahn, Mary Downing. *Deep and Dark and Dangerous* (5–8). 2007, Clarion $16.00 (978-0-618-66545-7). 192pp. While spending the summer at her aunt's cottage in Maine, 13-year-old Ali meets a mysterious girl named Sissie who seems to know a great deal about a tragic accident that occurred three decades earlier. (Rev: BL 3/15/07; SLJ 5/07)

9183 Hahn, Mary Downing. *Witch Catcher* (4–7). 2006, Clarion $16.00 (978-0-618-50457-2). 240pp. When Jen and her widowed father move into a rambling old mansion, the 12-year-old girl disregards warnings and investigates an old stone tower behind the house. (Rev: BL 6/1–15/06; SLJ 8/06)

9184 Hale, Bruce. *The Big Nap* (2–6). Illus. Series: Chet Gecko Mystery. 2001, Harcourt $14.00 (978-0-15-202521-2). 112pp. Lizard detective Chet Gecko investigates why his classmates are turning into mindless model fourth-graders. (Rev: BL 12/1/01; HBG 3/02; SLJ 10/01)

9185 Hale, Bruce. *The Chameleon Wore Chartreuse* (3–6). Illus. Series: Chet Gecko Mystery. 2000, Harcourt $14.00 (978-0-15-202281-5). 112pp. Using a private-eye style of writing, this humorous mystery involves Chet Gecko, a fourth-grade lizard/investigator, who uncovers a plot to steal the team mascot. (Rev: BCCB 6/00; BL 5/15/00; HBG 3/01; SLJ 8/00)

9186 Hale, Bruce. *Farewell, My Lunchbag* (2–5). Illus. Series: Chet Gecko Mystery. 2001, Harcourt $14.00 (978-0-15-202275-4). 128pp. Detective Chet Gecko investigates the problem of the mystery food snatcher who is operating in his elementary school. (Rev: BL 3/15/01; HBG 10/01)

9187 Hale, Bruce. *Give My Regrets to Broadway* (3–5). Illus. Series: Chet Gecko Mystery. 2004,

Harcourt $14.00 (978-0-15-216700-4). 112pp. Chet Gecko and sidekick Natalie look for Scott Freeh, who was supposed to play the lead in the school play, *Omlet: The Prince of Denver*. (Rev: BL 5/1/04)

9188 Hale, Bruce. *The Mystery of Mr. Nice* (4–6). Series: Chet Gecko Mystery. 2000, Harcourt $14.00 (978-0-15-202271-6). 112pp. Chet Gecko, the lizard detective, sets out to discover why his school principal is suddenly acting very nicely toward everyone. (Rev: BL 11/1/00; HBG 3/01; SLJ 12/00)

9189 Hale, Bruce. *This Gum for Hire* (3–5). Illus. Series: Chet Gecko Mystery. 2002, Harcourt $14.00 (978-0-15-202491-8). 132pp. Lizard detective Chet Gecko investigates mysterious goings-on on the school football team. (Rev: BL 10/1/02; HBG 3/03; SLJ 9/02)

9190 Hale, Bruce. *Trouble Is My Beeswax: From the Tattered Casebook of Chet Gecko, Private Eye* (3–6). Illus. by author. Series: Chet Gecko Mystery. 2003, Harcourt $14.00 (978-0-15-216718-9). 111pp. Chet Gecko, junior detective, enlists the help of mockingbird sidekick Natalie Attired to investigate cheating at Emerson Hicky Elementary. (Rev: HBG 4/04; SLJ 11/03)

9191 Halpern, Jake, and Peter Kujawinski. *Dormia* (5–8). Illus. 2009, Houghton $17.00 (978-0-547-07665-2). 512pp. All the action takes place when 12-year-old Alphonso falls asleep and enters a world called Dormia where he must use his special powers and face dangers or Dormia will die. (Rev: BL 7/09)

9192 Hamilton, Richard. *Jack Bolt and the Highwaymen's Hideout* (2–4). Illus. by Sam Hearn. 2007, Bloomsbury Children's paper $5.95 (978-1-59990-091-9). 192pp. Jack, 10, connects with highwaymen from the 18th century when he discovers that his attic bedroom is a link to other eras. (Rev: BL 12/1/07)

9193 Hamilton, Virginia. *Jaguarundi* (2–5). Illus. by Floyd Cooper. 1994, Scholastic $14.95 (978-0-590-47366-8). 40pp. A wildcat (jaguarundi) persuades a coati to flee across the river to find a new home. (Rev: BCCB 2/95; BL 12/15/94; SLJ 12/94)

9194 Hanson, Mary. *How to Save Your Tail* (2–4). Illus. by John Hendrix. 2007, Random $15.99 (978-0-375-83755-5). 112pp. Captured by palace cats Brutus and Muffin, Bob the rat uses his baking and storytelling skills to keep himself off the dinner menu. (Rev: BL 4/1/07)

9195 Haptie, Charlotte. *Otto and the Flying Twins* (4–7). 2004, Holiday $17.95 (978-0-8234-1826-8). 304pp. In the City of Trees, Otto is shocked to discover his father is king of the magical Karmidee. The sequel is *Otto and the Bird Charmers* (2005). (Rev: BL 4/15/04; SLJ 6/04)

9196 Hardinge, Frances. *Well Witched* (5–8). 2008, HarperCollins LB $17.89 (978-0-06-088039-2); paper $16.99 (978-0-06-088038-5). 400pp. Ryan, Josh, and Chelle steal from a wishing well and discover that the act has given them undesirable wish-granting powers in this intriguing story. (Rev: BL 5/15/08; SLJ 8/08)

9197 Hartinger, Brent. *Dreamquest: Tales of Slumberia* (4–8). 2007, Tom Doherty Assoc. $16.95 (978-0-7653-1397-3). 168pp. Julie, 11, is suffering — her parents fight all day and she has nightmares every night — until she wakes up in Slumberia, where her dreams are created, and must escape while there's still a chance. (Rev: LMC 1/08*; SLJ 2/08)

9198 Haseley, Dennis. *Ghost Catcher* (3–5). Illus. by Lloyd Bloom. 1991, HarperCollins $15.95 (978-0-06-022244-4). 40pp. A man who can get close to ghosts without turning into one needs the help of his friends when he visits the shadow village. (Rev: BL 10/1/91; SLJ 11/91)

9199 Hatrick, Gloria. *Masks* (4–6). 1996, Orchard LB $16.99 (978-0-531-08864-7). 128pp. In this fantasy, Pete uses animal masks to communicate with his paralyzed older brother. (Rev: BCCB 3/96; BL 4/15/96; SLJ 5/96)

9200 Helgerson, Joseph. *Horns and Wrinkles* (4–7). 2006, Houghton $16.00 (978-0-618-61679-4). 368pp. Mysterious events are taking place in Blue Wing, Minnesota — the nose of a bully named Duke turns into a rhino horn, and his parents turn to stone — and 12-year-old Claire is drawn into an adventure involving fairies and trolls. (Rev: BL 9/1/06; SLJ 9/06) ∩

9201 Hemphill, Michael, and Sam Riddleburger. *Stonewall Hinkleman and the Battle of Bull Run* (5–7). 2009, Dial $16.99 (978-0-8037-3179-0). 192pp. At yet another boring Civil War reenactment, 12-year-old Stonewall Hinkleman finds himself whisked back to the First Battle of Bull Run, where he must stop a companion time traveler from reversing the outcome of the war. (Rev: BL 4/15/09; SLJ 5/09)

9202 Hennesy, Carolyn. *Pandora Gets Jealous* (4–7). Series: Mythic Misadventures. 2008, Bloomsbury $12.95 (978-1-59990-196-1). 256pp. A lighthearted take on the myth of Pandora in which Pandy takes a special box to school for show-and-tell. (Rev: BL 11/15/07; LMC 5/08; SLJ 3/08)

9203 Herbauts, Anne. *Monday* (3–5). Illus. by author. 2006, Enchanted Lion $16.95 (978-1-59270-057-8). 36pp. This unusual, almost-wordless book will appeal to thoughtful readers who follow a creature called Monday through a cycle of seasons, some shared with his friends Lester Day and Tom Morrow. (Rev: SLJ 4/07)

9204 Hess, Nina. *A Practical Guide to Monsters* (4–7). Illus. 2007, Mirrorstone $12.95 (978-0-7869-4809-3). 80pp. A tongue-in-cheek field guide to common monsters, this companion to the series Knights of the Silver Dragon is geared toward young wizards and features detailed illustrations. (Rev: BL 1/1–15/08)

9205 Hickman, Janet. *Ravine* (4–6). 2002, HarperCollins LB $15.89 (978-0-06-029367-3). 192pp. Jeremy enters a dangerous world of fantasy and adventure through a "time slip" in a ravine. (Rev: BCCB 9/02; BL 7/02; HB 5/02; HBG 10/02; SLJ 10/02)

9206 Highwater, Jamake. *Rama: A Legend* (5–9). 1997, Replica LB $24.95 (978-0-7351-0001-5).

When he's wrongfully banished from his father's kingdom and his wife, Sita, is kidnapped, valiant Prince Rama charges back to avenge the evil that's befallen his world. (Rev: BL 11/15/94; SLJ 12/94; VOYA 2/95)

9207 Hirsch, Odo. *Bartlett and the City of Flames* (3–6). Illus. by Andrew McLean. 2003, Bloomsbury $15.95 (978-1-58234-831-5). 201pp. In this gripping sequel to *Bartlett and the Ice Voyage,* the title character and Jacques le Grand try to free Darian, the son of the Pasha of the City of the Sun, from his captors in the underground City of Flames. (Rev: HBG 4/04; SLJ 12/03)

9208 Hiser, Constance. *Night of the Werepoodle* (2–4). Illus. 1994, Holiday House $14.95 (978-0-8234-1116-0). 122pp. After being bitten by a poodle, Jonathan turns into a "werepoodle" and must find some wolfbane to become a boy again. (Rev: BL 6/1–15/94; SLJ 6/94)

9209 Hoban, Russell. *The Mouse and His Child* (4–8). Illus. by David Small. 2001, Scholastic paper $16.99 (978-0-439-09826-7). 246pp. A toy mouse and his child embark on a quest to become "self-winding" and have sometimes scary, sometimes humorous adventures in this enchanting fantasy first published in 1967 and now updated with new illustrations. (Rev: BL 12/1/01; HBG 3/02)

9210 Hodges, Margaret, ed. *Comus* (4–6). Illus. by Trina S. Hyman. 1996, Holiday House $16.95 (978-0-8234-1146-7). 32pp. In this retelling of a work by John Milton, Alice resists the enchantment of the evil magician Comus. (Rev: BCCB 10/94; BL 3/1/96; SLJ 3/96)

9211 Hodges, Margaret. *Gulliver in Lilliput: From Gulliver's Travels by Jonathan Swift* (4–7). Illus. by Kimberly B. Root. 1995, Holiday $17.95 (978-0-8234-1147-4). 32pp. The story of Gulliver in the land of the little people is retold with bright, detailed illustrations. (Rev: BCCB 6/95; BL 4/15/95; HB 7/95; SLJ 6/95*)

9212 Hodges, Margaret, ed. *Hauntings: Ghosts and Ghouls from Around the World* (5–8). Illus. by David Wenzel. 1991, Little, Brown $16.95 (978-0-316-36796-7). 144pp. A diverse collection of 16 familiar and lesser-known tales about the supernatural. (Rev: BL 11/15/91; HB 11/91; SLJ 11/91) [398.2]

9213 Hoeye, Michael. *No Time Like Show Time* (5–8). Series: A Hermux Tantamoq Adventure. 2004, Putnam $14.99 (978-0-399-23880-2). 277pp. Hermux the mouse investigates who is responsible for sending threatening letters to famous director Fluster Varmint. (Rev: SLJ 11/04)

9214 Hoeye, Michael. *The Sands of Time* (5–8). Series: A Hermux Tantamoq Adventure. 2002, Putnam $14.99 (978-0-399-23879-6). 277pp. In this sequel to *Time Stops for No Mouse* (2002), the mouse watchmaker and a chipmunk friend believe that mice were once the slaves of cats. (Rev: HBG 3/03; SLJ 10/02; VOYA 12/02)

9215 Hoeye, Michael. *Time Stops for No Mouse* (5–9). Series: A Hermux Tantamoq Adventure. 2002, Putnam $14.99 (978-0-399-23878-9). 279pp.

Hermux Tantamoq, a mouse, leads a quiet life as a watchmaker until Linka Perflinger turns up and Hermux becomes entangled in mystery and suspense. (Rev: BL 3/15/02*; HB 7/02; HBG 10/02; SLJ 5/02; VOYA 6/02)

9216 Hoffman, Alice. *Aquamarine* (4–7). 2001, Scholastic paper $16.95 (978-0-439-09863-2). 112pp. Twelve-year-old friends Hailey and Claire find a lonely mermaid named Aquamarine, and they try to give her love and adventure. (Rev: BCCB 2/01; BL 3/1/01; HBG 10/01; SLJ 3/01; VOYA 4/01)

9217 Holm, Jennifer, and Jonathan Hamel. *The Stink Files, Dossier 001: The Postman Always Brings Mice* (3–5). Illus. by Brad Weinman. 2004, HarperCollins LB $15.89 (978-0-06-052980-2). 144pp. While trying to find out who murdered his owner, Sir Archibald, feline London-based sleuth James Edward Bristlefur is whisked away to New Jersey and a confusing new life amid middle-class children. (Rev: BL 5/1/04; SLJ 6/04)

9218 Holm, Jennifer, and Matthew Holm. *Babymouse: Beach Babe* (4–6). Illus. Series: Babymouse. 2006, Random LB $12.99 (978-0-375-93231-1); paper $5.95 (978-0-375-83231-4). 96pp. School is over for the year, and the lively Babymouse is headed to the beach for a summer of fun and adventure. (Rev: BL 3/15/06; SLJ 7/06)

9219 Holm, Jennifer, and Matthew Holm. *Babymouse: Rock Star* (2–4). 2006, Random LB $12.99 (978-0-375-93232-8); paper $5.95 (978-0-375-83232-1). 91pp. Babymouse may play the flute at school but in her dreams she's a wildly popular rock star. (Rev: SLJ 9/06)

9220 Horowitz, Anthony. *Evil Star* (5–8). Series: The Gatekeepers. 2006, Scholastic $17.99 (978-0-439-67996-1). 320pp. In the second installment of this action-packed fantasy series, 14-year-old Matt Freeman travels to Peru to learn more about the possible opening of another gate to the underworld. (Rev: BL 6/1–15/06; SLJ 7/06)

9221 Horowitz, Anthony. *Raven's Gate* (5–8). Series: The Gatekeepers. 2005, Scholastic $17.95 (978-0-439-67995-4). 256pp. Faced with a choice between jail and life in a remote Yorkshire village, 14-year-old Matt chooses the latter, unaware that he's about to enter a world of frightening evil. (Rev: BL 7/05*; SLJ 7/05; VOYA 10/05)

9222 Horowitz, Anthony. *The Switch* (5–8). 2009, Philomel $16.99 (978-0-399-25062-0). 192pp. Rich kid Tad Spencer, 13, is not pleased when he finds himself in the body of Bob Snarby, son of carnival workers, but then he starts to learn more about his old life. (Rev: BL 12/15/08; LMC 5/09; SLJ 3/09)

9223 Howe, James. *Invasion of the Mind Swappers from Asteroid 6!* (3–6). Illus. by Brett Helquist. 2002, Simon & Schuster $9.95 (978-0-689-83949-8). 96pp. Lessons about writing are hidden in the tale of a delightful dachshund named Howie, who keeps a journal detailing his writing experiences as he pens a story about an alien invasion. Also use *It Came from Beneath the Bed!* (2002). (Rev: BL 8/02; HBG 3/03; SLJ 11/02)

9224 Hughes, Carol. *Dirty Magic* (5–8). 2006, Random $17.95 (978-0-375-83187-4). 432pp. In a desperate attempt to save his little sister's life, 10-year-old Joe Brooks enters a shadowy world where ill children are held captive. (Rev: BL 10/1/06; SLJ 2/07)

9225 Hughes, Carol. *The Princess and the Unicorn* (3–6). 2009, Random $15.99 (978-0-375-85562-7). 288pp. This fantasy story follows Eleanor, an English princess who lays claim to a unicorn she discovers on a hunt, and Joyce, a courageous little forest fairy who sets out to rescue the unicorn and her forest village. (Rev: BL 1/1–15/09; SLJ 5/09)

9226 Hughes, Monica, sel. *What If? Amazing Stories* (5–10). 1998, Tundra paper $6.95 (978-0-88776-458-5). 199pp. Fourteen fantasy and science fiction short stories by noted Canadian writers are included in this anthology, plus a few related poems. (Rev: BL 2/15/99; SLJ 6/99; VOYA 6/99)

9227 Hughes, Shirley. *Enchantment in the Garden* (3–5). Illus. 1997, Lothrop $18.00 (978-0-688-14597-2). 64pp. In this fantasy, a rich little girl in Italy during the 1920s brings to life the statue of a sea god's son. (Rev: BCCB 7–8/97; BL 5/15/97; HB 3/97; SLJ 5/97)

9228 Hulme, John, and Michael Wexler. *The Glitch in Sleep* (5–8). Series: Seems. 2007, Bloomsbury $16.95 (978-1-59990-129-9). 288pp. When 12-year-old Becker gets a job at the Institute for Fixing and Repair, he discovers that the world as we know it is under the control of the Seems; a humorous and thought-provoking story with plenty of illustrations and lots of entertaining gadgets. (Rev: BL 11/15/07; LMC 1/08; SLJ 11/07)

9229 Hunter, Erin. *The Sight* (5–7). Series: Warriors: The Power of Three. 2007, HarperCollins $16.99 (978-0-06-089201-2). 384pp. Three kits — Hollypaw, Jaypaw, and Lionpaw — whose parents were members of the Thunderclan are endowed with special abilities in this series opener that follows the New Prophecy cycle. (Rev: BL 8/07; LMC 11/08)

9230 Hunter, Mollie. *The Mermaid Summer* (5–8). 1988, HarperCollins $15.89 (978-0-06-022628-2). 160pp. Eric Anderson refuses to recognize the power of the mermaid and leaves his Scottish fishing village after his boat is dashed to pieces on the rocks. (Rev: BCCB 5/88; BL 6/1/88; SLJ 6–7/88)

9231 Hurst, Carol Otis. *The Wrong One* (3–6). 2003, Houghton $15.00 (978-0-618-27599-1). 160pp. The Spencer children and their recently widowed mother move to a run-down farmhouse where strange things are happening. (Rev: BL 3/1/03; HBG 10/03; SLJ 5/03)

9232 Hurwitz, Johanna. *PeeWee's Tale* (2–5). Illus. 2000, North-South $13.95 (978-1-58717-027-0). 96pp. PeeWee is a little guinea pig whose intelligence and ability to read help him escape danger when he is left in a park. (Rev: BL 10/1/00; HBG 3/01; SLJ 10/00)

9233 Hussey, Charmain. *The Valley of Secrets* (4–7). Illus. by Christopher Crump. 2005, Simon & Schuster $16.95 (978-0-689-87862-6). 400pp. A detailed, multifaceted novel about an orphan who inherits his great-uncle's estate and, through his uncle's journal, learns about the plight of the Amazon Indians. (Rev: BL 3/1/05; SLJ 2/05)

9234 Hutchins, Hazel. *The Prince of Tarn* (3–5). Illus. 1997, Annick $14.95 (978-1-55037-439-1). 143pp. The spoiled prince created by his author mother in one of her fantasies comes to life and takes Fred to his kingdom. (Rev: BL 2/15/98; SLJ 2/98)

9235 Ibbotson, Eva. *The Great Ghost Rescue* (3–6). Illus. by Kevin Hawkes. 2002, Dutton $15.99 (978-0-525-46769-4). 144pp. A homeless ghost family moves into a boys' school and meets young Rick, who tries to establish a "sanctuary" for displaced ghosts in this humorous, scary, and sometimes gruesome book. (Rev: BCCB 11/02; BL 7/02; HB 9/02; HBG 3/03; SLJ 8/02)

9236 Icanberry, Mark. *Picnic on a Cloud* (3–5). Illus. by Mark Icanberry and Arthur Mount. Series: Look, Learn and Do. 2000, Tricycle $14.95 (978-1-893327-00-9); paper $7.95 (978-1-893327-02-3). 47pp. David, his dog Newton, and friend Jessica construct a blimp using 289 balloons and take a ride during which they picnic on a cloud. The trio build a greenhouse in *Super Salads* (2000). (Rev: SLJ 1/01)

9237 Irving, Washington. *The Legend of Sleepy Hollow* (4–6). Illus. by Gris Grimly. 2007, Atheneum $16.99 (978-1-4169-0625-4). 40pp. A faithful adaptation of Irving's classic story, with atmospheric illustrations. (Rev: BL 9/15/07; HB 11/07; LMC 11/07; SLJ 2/08)

9238 Irving, Washington. *The Legend of Sleepy Hollow: Found Among the Papers of the Late Diedrich Knickerbocker* (4–6). Illus. 1999, Ideals $16.95 (978-0-8249-4160-4). 64pp. A well-illustrated edition of this perennial favorite about Ichabod Crane, the Headless Horseman, and the heiress Katrina Van Tassel. (Rev: BL 10/1/99)

9239 Irving, Washington. *Rip Van Winkle and the Legend of Sleepy Hollow* (5–7). Illus. by Felix O. Darley. 1980, Sleepy Hollow $19.95 (978-0-912882-42-0). 152pp. A handsome edition of these two classics.

9240 Iserles, Inbali. *The Tygrine Cat* (5–8). 2008, Candlewick $15.99 (978-0-7636-3798-9). 256pp. Mati, the son of the slain queen of the Tygrine Cats, is being pursued by a killer sent by Suzerain in this feline fantasy. (Rev: BL 5/15/08)

9241 Jacques, Brian. *The Angel's Command: A Tale from the Castaways of the Flying Dutchman* (5–9). 2003, Putnam $23.99 (978-0-399-23999-1). 448pp. This action-packed fantasy, set in the 17th century, is the sequel to *Castaways of the Flying Dutchman*. (Rev: BL 2/1/03; HB 3/03; HBG 10/03; SLJ 3/03; VOYA 4/03)

9242 Jacques, Brian. *The Bellmaker* (5–7). Illus. Series: Redwall. 1995, Putnam $24.99 (978-0-399-22805-6). 352pp. This seventh tale in the series of animal fantasies features Mariel, a courageous, outspoken mouse. (Rev: BCCB 4/95; BL 4/1/95; HB 5/95; SLJ 8/95)

9243 Jacques, Brian. *Castaways of the Flying Dutchman* (5–9). 2001, Putnam $23.99 (978-0-399-23601-3). 318pp. A mute boy stows away on the *Flying Dutchman*, a ship that is condemned to sail the seas forever, and there he meets the ghostly crew and the crazed captain in this story in which the boy has many adventures and eventually gains the power of speech and the gift of staying young forever. (Rev: BCCB 3/01; BL 3/1/01; HB 3/01; HBG 10/01; SLJ 3/01; VOYA 4/01)

9244 Jacques, Brian. *Eulalia!* (5–8). Series: Redwall. 2007, Philomel $23.99 (978-0-399-24209-0). 400pp. Lord Asheye, Badger Lord of Salamandastron, wishes to find his successor in this satisfying installment in the long-running series. (Rev: BL 8/07; SLJ 5/08) ⌒

9245 Jacques, Brian. *The Great Redwall Feast* (4–6). Illus. by Christopher Denise. 1996, Penguin $21.99 (978-0-399-22707-3). 64pp. In this illustrated storybook, the creatures of Redwall prepare a magnificent feast. (Rev: BL 10/15/96; SLJ 12/96)

9246 Jacques, Brian. *High Rhulain* (5–8). Illus. by David Elliot. Series: Redwall. 2005, Philomel $23.99 (978-0-399-24208-3). 384pp. In this eighteenth installment, ottermaid Tiria bravely journeys to the Green Isle to rescue otter kinsmen from evil wildcats. (Rev: BL 9/1/05; SLJ 9/05)

9247 Jacques, Brian. *The Legend of Luke: A Tale from Redwall* (5–8). Illus. Series: Redwall. 2000, Putnam $23.99 (978-0-399-23490-3). 384pp. This book focuses on the building of the abbey, Martin's search for his father Luke, and Luke's heroic career. (Rev: BL 12/15/99; HBG 10/00; SLJ 2/00; VOYA 4/00)

9248 Jacques, Brian. *Loamhedge* (5–8). Series: Redwall. 2003, Putnam $23.99 (978-0-399-23724-9). 432pp. As Redwall stalwarts including Bragoon and Sarobando seek a cure for a haremaid's ills at Loamhedge Abbey, Redwall itself comes under attack. (Rev: BL 9/15/03; HB 11/03; HBG 4/04; SLJ 10/03)

9249 Jacques, Brian. *The Long Patrol* (5–8). Illus. Series: Redwall. 1998, Putnam $23.99 (978-0-399-23165-0). In this tenth adventure, the villainous Rapscallions decide to attack the peaceful Abbey of Redwall. (Rev: BCCB 4/98; BL 12/15/97; HB 3/98; HBG 10/98; SLJ 1/98)

9250 Jacques, Brian. *Lord Brocktree* (5–8). Series: Redwall. 2000, Putnam $23.99 (978-0-399-23590-0). 320pp. The villainous Ungatt Trunn and his Blue Hordes invade and capture the mountain fortress Salamandastron. (Rev: BCCB 9/00; BL 9/1/00; HB 9/00; HBG 3/01; SLJ 9/00)

9251 Jacques, Brian. *Mariel of Redwall* (5–7). Illus. by Gary Chalk. Series: Redwall. 1992, Putnam $24.99 (978-0-399-22144-6). 400pp. Fourth in the saga of the animals of Redwall Abbey, this story tells how the great Joseph Bell is brought to the abbey. (Rev: BCCB 3/92; BL 1/15/92*; HB 9/92; SLJ 3/92)

9252 Jacques, Brian. *Marlfox* (5–8). Illus. Series: Redwall. 1999, Putnam $22.99 (978-0-399-23307-4). 400pp. The famous tapestry depicting Martin

and Warrior has been stolen from Redwall Abbey, and four young would-be heroes set out to recover it. (Rev: BL 12/15/98; HB 1/99; HBG 10/99; SLJ 4/99; VOYA 2/99)

9253 Jacques, Brian. *Martin the Warrior* (5–7). Illus. by Gary Chalk. Series: Redwall. 1994, Putnam $23.99 (978-0-399-22670-0). 375pp. This volume tells how the mouse Martin the Warrior became the bold, courageous fighter that he is. (Rev: BCCB 1/94; BL 3/1/94; HB 9/94; SLJ 1/94)

9254 Jacques, Brian. *Mattimeo* (5–8). Series: Redwall. 1990, Putnam $23.99 (978-0-399-21741-8). The evil fox kidnaps the animal children of Redwall Abbey in this continuation of *Mossflower* (1988) and *Redwall* (1987). (Rev: BL 4/15/90; SLJ 9/90; VOYA 8/90)

9255 Jacques, Brian. *Mossflower* (5–7). Illus. by Gary Chalk. Series: Redwall. 1988, Putnam $24.99 (978-0-399-21549-0); Avon paper $5.99 (978-0-380-70828-4). 432pp. How a brave and resourceful mouse took power from the evil wildcat. (Rev: BCCB 12/88; BL 11/1/88; SLJ 11/88)

9256 Jacques, Brian. *Outcast of Redwall* (5–8). Illus. Series: Redwall. 1996, Philomel $24.99 (978-0-399-22914-5). This episode in the Redwall saga involves the badger Sunflash, his buddy Skarlath the kestrel, and their enemy the ferret Swartt Sixclaw. (Rev: BCCB 3/96; BL 3/1/96; SLJ 5/96; VOYA 10/96)

9257 Jacques, Brian. *The Pearls of Lutra* (5–8). Series: Redwall. 1997, Putnam $23.99 (978-0-399-22946-6). 408pp. The evil marten Mad Eyes threatens the peaceful Redwall Abbey in this ninth book in the series. (Rev: BCCB 4/97; BL 2/15/97; SLJ 3/97*; VOYA 6/97)

9258 Jacques, Brian. *Rakkety Tam* (5–8). Illus. by David Elliot. Series: Redwall. 2004, Putnam $23.99 (978-0-399-23725-6). 384pp. When Redwall is threatened by a murderous wolverine called Gulo the Savage, two warrior squirrels — Rakkety Tam McBurl and Wild Doogy Plumm — take action. (Rev: BL 9/15/04; SLJ 9/04)

9259 Jacques, Brian. *Redwall: The Graphic Novel* (4–7). Illus. by Bret Blevins. Series: Redwall. 2007, Philomel paper $12.99 (978-0-399-24481-0). 144pp. Redwall makes an effective transition to the graphic novel format with this spirited adaptation. (Rev: BL 9/1/07; SLJ 9/07)

9260 Jacques, Brian. *A Redwall Winter's Tale* (2–5). Illus. by Christopher Denise. 2001, Penguin $18.99 (978-0-399-23346-3). 80pp. The animals of Redwall Abbey gather once again to enjoy an end-of-autumn festival in this colorful picture book. (Rev: BL 9/1/01; HBG 3/02; SLJ 9/01)

9261 Jacques, Brian. *Salamandastron* (5–7). Illus. by Gary Chalk. Series: Redwall. 1993, Putnam $23.99 (978-0-399-21992-4). 400pp. These tales are centered on the badgers and hares of the castle of Salamandastron near the sea. (Rev: BCCB 7–8/93; BL 3/15/93; HB 5/93; SLJ 3/93)

9262 Jacques, Brian. *Seven Strange and Ghostly Tales* (4–7). 1991, Avon paper $3.99 (978-0-380-71906-8). 137pp. Seven genuinely scary stories with touches of humor. (Rev: BCCB 12/91; BL 1/1/91*; HB 5/92; SLJ 12/91)

9263 Jacques, Brian. *Taggerung* (5–8). Illus. Series: Redwall. 2001, Putnam $23.99 (978-0-399-23720-1). 448pp. The 14th book in the series features an otter named Taggerung who was kidnapped from the abbey as a baby and raised by an outlaw ferret. (Rev: BL 8/01; HB 11/01; HBG 3/02; SLJ 10/01; VOYA 10/01)

9264 Jacques, Brian. *The Tale of Urso Brunov* (2–4). Illus. by Alexi Natchev. 2003, Penguin $16.99 (978-0-399-23762-1). 48pp. When four little bears go astray, Urso Brunov embarks on an adventure-filled rescue journey. (Rev: BL 9/1/03; HBG 4/04; SLJ 9/03)

9265 Jacques, Brian. *Triss* (5–8). 2002, Putnam $23.99 (978-0-399-23723-2). 432pp. An action-packed installment in the Redwall series in which squirrel Triss, an escaped slave, meets up with the badger Sagax and his friend Scarum. (Rev: BL 9/1/02; HB 1/03; HBG 3/03; SLJ 10/02; VOYA 12/02)

9266 James, Mary. *Frankenlouse* (5–8). 1994, Scholastic paper $13.95 (978-0-590-46528-1). Nick, 14, is enrolled at Blister Military Academy, which is run by his father. He escapes into his own comic book creations featuring an insect named Frankenlouse. (Rev: BCCB 11/94; BL 10/15/94; SLJ 11/94; VOYA 12/94)

9267 James, Mary. *Shoebag* (3–7). 1990, Scholastic $13.95 (978-0-590-43029-6). 144pp. Shoebag, a cockroach named after his place of birth, turns into a boy. (Rev: BCCB 3/90; BL 4/15/90; SLJ 6/90*)

9268 James, Mary. *The Shuteyes* (4–7). 1994, Scholastic paper $3.25 (978-0-590-45070-6). 176pp. Chester has some unusual experiences when he journeys to Alert, a land where no one sleeps. (Rev: SLJ 4/93)

9269 Jarrell, Randall. *The Bat-Poet* (3–6). Illus. by Maurice Sendak. 1997, HarperCollins $17.95 (978-0-06-205084-7); paper $7.95 (978-0-06-205905-5). 44pp. A little-known bat makes up poems during the day to recite to his fellows.

9270 Jarvis, Robin. *Thomas: Book Three of the Deptford Histories* (5–8). 2006, Chronicle $17.95 (978-0-8118-5412-2). 400pp. This prequel to the Deptford Mice trilogy, written as the memoirs of an old sea mouse, contains plenty of battles, storms and heroic deeds and can be read as a stand-alone novel. (Rev: BL 1/1–15/07)

9271 Jarvis, Robin. *The Whitby Witches* (4–7). Illus. by Jess Petersen. 2006, Chronicle $17.95 (978-0-8118-5413-9). 296pp. Sent to live with their elderly Aunt Alice in the English seaside village of Whitby, 8-year-old Ben — who can see the invisible — and 12-year-old Jennet find themselves swept up in a struggle between good and evil. (Rev: BL 10/1/06; SLJ 10/06)

9272 Jenkins, Emily. *Toy Dance Party: Being the Further Adventures of a Bossyboots Stingray, a Courageous Buffalo, and a Hopeful Round Someone Called Plastic* (1–3). Illus. by Paul Zelinsky. 2008, Random $16.99 (978-0-375-83935-1). 176pp. When

their little girl, Honey, develops an interest in Barbie dolls, three old toys misbehave in six interconnected adventures in an attempt to get her to remember them. (Rev: BL 9/1/08)

9273 Jenkins, Emily. *Toys Go Out: Being the Adventures of a Knowledgeable Stingray, a Toughy Little Buffalo, and Someone Called Plastic* (1–3). Illus. by Paul Zelinsky. 2006, Random $16.95 (978-0-375-83604-6). 128pp. Three toys that belong to Little Girl have adventures, embarrassing situations, and scary moments that will be very familiar to young readers; a beginning chapter book. (Rev: BCCB 11/06; BL 10/1/06; HBG 10/07; SLJ 9/06*) ∩

9274 Jenkins, Jerry B., and Chris Fabry. *The Book of the King* (5–8). Series: The Wormling. 2007, Tyndale paper $5.99 (978-1-4143-0155-6). 228pp. Owen discovers that there is another world beneath his family's bookstore and that he must battle with dragons to overcome evil forces. (Rev: BL 10/15/07)

9275 Jenkins, Martin. *Jonathan Swift's Gulliver* (5–8). Illus. by Chris Riddell. 2005, Candlewick $19.99 (978-0-7636-2409-5). 144pp. A retelling of the classic tale using contemporary language and striking artwork. (Rev: BL 3/15/05; SLJ 3/05)

9276 Jennings, Patrick. *Wish Riders* (5–8). 2006, Hyperion $15.99 (978-1-4231-0010-2). 288pp. Combining historical fiction and fantasy, this tale of transformation focuses on Edith, 15, who slaves with four other foster children, cooking and cleaning in a Depression-era logging camp until a mysterious seed pod grows into five horses that spirit the children away to forest adventures. (Rev: BL 1/1–15/07)

9277 Jennings, Richard W. *Ghost Town* (5–8). 2009, Houghton $16.00 (978-0-547-19471-4). 176pp. A teenager discovers a camera with the ability to photograph the dearly departed. (Rev: BL 6/1–15/09; HB 7/09)

9278 Johansen, Hanna. *Dinosaur with an Attitude* (4–6). Trans. by Elisabetta Maccari. Illus. 1994, RDR $12.95 (978-1-57143-018-2). 144pp. In this fantasy, a boy faces problems caused by a dinosaur that hatched from one of his Easter eggs. (Rev: BL 8/94; SLJ 8/94)

9279 Johansen, K. V. *Nightwalker* (5–8). 2007, Orca paper $8.95 (978-1-55143-481-0). 144pp. Thrown into the dungeon when it's discovered that he possesses a powerful magical ring, young Maurey escapes with the help of a baroness and travels to Talverdin in an effort to find out if he is a nightwalker. (Rev: BL 4/1/07; SLJ 9/07)

9280 Johnson, Annabel. *I Am Leaper* (3–5). Illus. by Stella Ormai. 1992, Scholastic paper $2.99 (978-0-590-43399-0). 128pp. A talking kangaroo mouse leaves her burrow to warn humans that a monster is destroying the desert. (Rev: BL 11/15/90; SLJ 1/91)

9281 Johnson, Charles. *Pieces of Eight* (5–7). Illus. by Jennie Anne Nelson. 1989, Discovery $9.95 (978-0-944770-00-9). 110pp. David and Mitchell rouse a sea captain's ghost and get to meet Blackbeard the pirate. (Rev: BL 3/15/89)

9282 Johnson, Crockett. *Magic Beach* (1–3). Illus. 2005, Front St. $18.95 (978-1-932425-27-7). 64pp.

A boy and his sister conjure up a magical kingdom by writing words in the sand of a very special beach; originally published as *Castles in the Sand* in 1965. (Rev: BL 11/1/05; SLJ 6/06)

9283 Johnson, Gillian. *Thora: A Half-Mermaid Tale* (4–6). Illus. 2005, HarperCollins $15.99 (978-0-06-074378-9). 256pp. Ten-year-old Thora, half girl and half mermaid, on dry land after spending the first ten years of her life at sea, tries to foil the villainous plans of a fat-cat tycoon named Frooty de Mare. (Rev: BL 8/05)

9284 Johnson, Gillian. *Thora and the Green Sea-Unicorn* (3–5). Illus. by author. 2007, HarperCollins $15.99 (978-0-06-074381-9). 288pp. After her family's houseboat is destroyed, half-mermaid Thora and her fully human friend Louella try to track down Thora's missing sea-unicorn in this sequel to *Thora: A Half-Mermaid Tale* (2007). (Rev: BL 6/1–15/07; SLJ 6/07)

9285 Johnson, Jane. *The Shadow World: The Eidolon Chronicles* (4–7). Illus. by Adam Stower. Series: Eidolon Chronicles. 2007, Simon & Schuster $15.99 (978-1-4169-1783-0). 288pp. The second book in the series finds Ben entering Eidolon to bring back his sister Ellie, who is being held by the evil Dodman. (Rev: BL 12/1/07; SLJ 11/07)

9286 Johnston, Tony. *The Spoon in the Bathroom Wall* (3–4). 2005, Harcourt $16.00 (978-0-15-205292-8). 134pp. An Arthurian spoof in which fourth grader Martha Snapdragon discovers a jeweled spoon in the wall of the boys' bathroom. (Rev: SLJ 6/05)

9287 Jonell, Lynne. *The Secret of Zoom* (4–6). 2009, Holt $16.99 (978-0-8050-8856-4). 304pp. Christina, 10 years old and herself pitch-perfect, discovers that orphans with singing talent are being exploited to generate a fuel known as zoom. (Rev: BL 6/1–15/09; SLJ 11/09*)

9288 Jones, Diana Wynne. *The Game* (5–8). 2007, Penguin $11.99 (978-0-14-240718-9). 192pp. Hayley, an orphan who has been raised by her difficult grandparents, now finds herself amid a large, happy family in Ireland with cousins who love to play in the mythosphere, a land of stories where secrets about her past reside. (Rev: BL 12/1/06; SLJ 3/07)

9289 Jones, Diana Wynne. *The Pinhoe Egg* (5–8). Series: Chrestomanci. 2006, Greenwillow $18.89 (978-0-06-113125-7). 528pp. In this compelling addition to the Chrestomanci series, Marianne Pinhoe and Cat Chant find a strange egg with magical properties. (Rev: BL 9/15/06; SLJ 10/06) 🎧

9290 Jones, Kimberly K. *The Genie Scheme* (4–7). 2009, Simon & Schuster $15.99 (978-1-4169-5554-2). 192pp. When she acquires her personal genie, Janna, 12, learns that material possessions are not the best things to wish for. (Rev: BCCB 6/09; BL 3/15/09; SLJ 3/09)

9291 Juster, Norton. *The Phantom Tollbooth* (4–6). Illus. by Jules Feiffer. 1972, Knopf $19.95 (978-0-394-81500-8); paper $5.50 (978-0-394-82037-8). 256pp. When Milo receives a tollbooth as a gift, he finds that it admits him to a land where many adventures take place. A favorite fantasy.

9292 Kalman, Maira. *Smartypants (Pete in School)* (2–4). 2003, Penguin $15.99 (978-0-399-23478-1). 32pp. Pete the dog eats an encyclopedia and acquires superintelligence in this entertaining story. (Rev: BL 8/03*; HBG 4/04; SLJ 8/03)

9293 Kalman, Maira. *Swami on Rye: Max in India* (4–8). Illus. 1995, Viking $14.99 (978-0-670-84646-7). 40pp. A sophisticated comic novel about a dog who goes to India to find the meaning of life. (Rev: BL 10/15/95; SLJ 11/95)

9294 Karon, Jan. *Jeremy: The Tale of an Honest Bunny* (3–5). Illus. 2000, Viking $15.99 (978-0-670-88104-8). 82pp. A sweet tale about a toy bunny and his adventures traveling from a small English cottage to his new home in North Carolina. (Rev: BL 4/15/00; HBG 10/00; SLJ 9/00)

9295 Kassem, Lou. *A Summer for Secrets* (5–7). 1989, Avon paper $2.95 (978-0-380-75759-6). 105pp. Laura's ability to communicate with animals causes complications. (Rev: BL 10/1/89)

9296 Kay, Elizabeth. *The Divide* (5–9). 2003, Scholastic $15.95 (978-0-439-45696-8). 320pp. Felix, a 13-year-old with a heart problem, passes out while on a trip to Costa Rica and wakes up in a world full of mythical creatures. The sequel is *Back to the Divide* (2004). (Rev: BL 6/1–15/03; HBG 4/04; SLJ 9/03; VOYA 8/03)

9297 Kaye, Marilyn. *Out of Sight, Out of Mind* (5–8). Series: Gifted. 2009, Kingfisher paper $7.99 (978-0-7534-6283-6). 240pp. Eighth-grader Amanda, known for her critical aloofness, has a secret — any spark of sympathy causes her to "body snatch" against her will. Then one day she ends up in the body of nerdy Tracey and learns that the "gifted" class is not what it seems. (Rev: BL 5/15/09; LMC 10/09; SLJ 6/09; VOYA 10/09)

9298 Keehn, Sally M. *Gnat Stokes and the Foggy Bottom Swamp Queen* (5–8). 2005, Putnam $16.99 (978-0-399-24287-8). 160pp. This fantasy, set in the Appalachian mountains, features a 12-year-old girl named Gnat who faces swamp creatures and spells in her quest to rescue Goodlow Pryce. (Rev: BL 3/1/05; SLJ 4/05)

9299 Kehret, Peg. *Ghost's Grave* (5–8). 2005, Dutton $16.99 (978-0-525-46162-3). 192pp. Josh expects to be bored when he stays in his aunt's old house, but the ghost of a coal miner who died in 1903 livens things up. (Rev: BL 5/15/05; SLJ 10/05)

9300 Kehret, Peg. *Spy Cat* (4–6). 2003, Dutton $15.99 (978-0-525-47046-5). 192pp. Clever cat Pete, who understands everything but is frustrated by his inability to speak, plays a lead role in tracking down the neighborhood burglars. (Rev: BL 1/1–15/03; HBG 10/03; SLJ 1/03)

9301 Kempton, Kate. *The World Beyond the Waves: An Environmental Adventure* (5–7). Illus. 1995, Portunus $14.95 (978-0-9641330-6-8); paper $8.95 (978-0-9641330-1-3). 88pp. After being washed overboard during a violent storm, Sam visits a land where she meets ocean animals that have been misused by humans. (Rev: BL 4/15/95; SLJ 3/95)

9302 Kendall, Carol. *The Gammage Cup* (4–7). Illus. by Erik Blegvad. 1990, Harcourt paper $6.00 (978-0-15-230575-8). 283pp. A fantasy of the Minnipins, a small people of the "land between the mountains."

9303 Kerr, P. B. *The Blue Djinn of Babylon* (5–8). Series: Children of the Lamp. 2006, Scholastic $16.99 (978-0-439-67021-0). 384pp. Philippa Gaunt, 12, is wrongly convicted of cheating and her twin John must rescue her in this action-packed sequel to *The Akhenatan Adventure* (2005). (Rev: BL 3/15/06; SLJ 3/06; VOYA 2/06)

9304 Kessler, Liz. *Emily Windsnap and the Castle in the Mist* (3–6). Illus. by Ledwidge Natacha. 2007, Candlewick $15.99 (978-0-7636-3330-1). XXpp. Emily's problems as a typical elementary school mermaid take a turn for the worse when King Neptune puts a curse on her. (Rev: BL 9/15/07; SLJ 6/07)

9305 Kessler, Liz. *Emily Windsnap and the Monster from the Deep* (4–7). Series: Emily Windsnap. 2006, Candlewick $15.99 (978-0-7636-2504-7). 224pp. Half-human and half-mermaid, Emily Windsnap enjoys an idyllic life on Allpoints Island until she inadvertently awakens an evil monster named Kraken; a sequel to *The Tail of Emily Windsnap* (2004). (Rev: BL 6/1–15/06; SLJ 7/06)

9306 Kessler, Liz. *The Tail of Emily Windsnap* (4–7). Illus. by Sarah Gibb. Series: Emily Windsnap. 2004, Candlewick $15.99 (978-0-7636-2483-5). 224pp. Twelve-year-old Emily Windsnap, who turns into a mermaid when she gets into the water, learns the truth about her parents. (Rev: BL 5/1/04; SLJ 6/04; VOYA 6/04)

9307 Kilworth, Garry. *Attica* (4–8). 2009, IPG/Atom paper $11.95 (978-1-904233-56-5). 352pp. At the top of a house, step-siblings Jordy, Chloe, and Alex find themselves in a strange yet familiar — and threatening — new world. (Rev: BL 4/15/09; VOYA 10/09)

9308 Kimmel, Elizabeth C. *The Ghost of the Stone Circle* (5–8). 1998, Scholastic paper $15.95 (978-0-590-21308-0). Fourteen-year-old Cristyn, who is spending the summer in Wales with her historian father, discovers a ghost in the house her father has rented. (Rev: BCCB 3/98; BL 4/15/98; HBG 10/98; SLJ 4/98; VOYA 8/98)

9309 Kimmel, Elizabeth C. *Suddenly Supernatural: Scaredy Kat* (5–7). 2009, Little, Brown $10.99 (978-0-316-06685-3). 250pp. Can 13-year-old Kat, who can speak to the dead, and her friend Jac help the spirit of a young boy they find in an abandoned house? (Rev: HB 3/09; SLJ 3/09) ☊

9310 Kimmel, Eric A. *Don Quixote and the Windmills* (2–4). Illus. by Leonard Everett Fisher. 2004, Farrar $16.00 (978-0-374-31825-3). 32pp. Don Quixote is an appealing hero in this boldly illustrated adaptation in which he mistakes the windmills for giants. (Rev: BL 4/15/04; SLJ 4/04)

9311 King-Smith, Dick. *Animal Stories* (3–5). Illus. 1998, Orchard $18.95 (978-0-531-30099-2). 128pp. A collection of animal stories, including an excerpt from *Babe: the Gallant Pig* and a story involving Max, the heroic hedgehog. (Rev: BL 9/1/98; HBG 3/99; SLJ 11/98)

9312 King-Smith, Dick. *Lady Lollipop* (2–4). 2001, Candlewick $14.99 (978-0-7636-1269-6). 124pp. Spoiled Princess Penelope chooses a pig named Lollipop as her pet, and Lollipop's poor owner moves to the palace as the pig's keeper. (Rev: BCCB 9/01; BL 4/15/01; HB 5/01; HBG 10/01; SLJ 6/01*)

9313 King-Smith, Dick. *The Mouse Family Robinson* (3–5). Illus. by Nick Bruel. 2008, Roaring Brook $15.95 (978-1-59643-326-7). 80pp. After moving to the perfect catless home, house mouse John Robinson encounters class rivalry between the house mice and the fancy pet mice and suffers the loss of his old mouse friend. (Rev: BL 8/08; LMC 1/09)

9314 King-Smith, Dick. *Pigs Might Fly* (3–5). Illus. by Mary Rayner. 1990, Puffin paper $6.99 (978-0-14-034537-7). 168pp. A pig named Daggie Dogfoot saves the day because he can swim.

9315 King-Smith, Dick. *The Roundhill* (5–7). Illus. 2000, Random paper $4.99 (978-0-440-41844-3). 96pp. In the English countryside in 1936, 14-year-old Evan meets a mysterious girl who seems to be the Alice of *Alice in Wonderland*. (Rev: BL 1/1–15/01; HBG 3/01; SLJ 12/00)

9316 King-Smith, Dick. *The School Mouse* (3–5). Illus. 1995, Hyperion LB $14.49 (978-0-7868-2029-0). 124pp. Flora's ability to read saves her illiterate mouse parents from eating poison that has been placed around the school where they live. (Rev: BCCB 1/96; BL 10/15/95; SLJ 12/95*)

9317 Kipling, Rudyard. *Rikki-Tikki-Tavi* (3–5). Illus. by Jerry Pinkney. 1997, Morrow $15.89 (978-0-688-14321-3). 40pp. In this classic tale, a mongoose repays a debt of kindness after he has been saved from drowning. (Rev: BL 9/1/97*; HBG 3/98; SLJ 8/97*)

9318 Kirov, Erica. *Magickeepers: The Eternal Hourglass* (5–8). 2009, Sourcebooks $16.99 (978-1-4022-1501-8). 256pp. The son of a magician discovers magic is real in this melange of ancient underworld shadows and Las Vegas glitter. (Rev: LMC 10/09; SLJ 7/09)

9319 Kladstrup, Kristin. *The Book of Story Beginnings* (4–6). 2006, Candlewick $15.99 (978-0-7636-2609-9). 362pp. In this multilayered fantasy, 12-year-old Lucy tries with the help of a mysterious notebook to unravel the mystery surrounding the disappearance of her great-uncle Oscar in 1914. (Rev: BL 3/1/06; SLJ 4/06)

9320 Klimo, Kate. *The Dragon in the Sock Drawer* (4–6). Series: Dragon Keepers. 2008, Random $14.99 (978-0-375-85587-0). 176pp. Ten-year-old cousins Jesse and Daisy become the stand-in parents for a baby dragon and must figure out how to feed and take care of. (Rev: BLO 8/28/08; SLJ 7/08)

9321 Klise, Kate. *Dying to Meet You* (3–6). Illus. by M. Sarah Klise. Series: 43 Old Cemetery Road. 2009, Houghton $15.00 (978-0-15-205727-5). 160pp. An author named Ignatius B. Grumply moves into a Victorian mansion in a town called ghastly and finds he must share with a ghost named

Olive and an 11-year-old boy named Seymour; the action takes place in the form of letters between these three and there are many graphic elements. (Rev: BCCB 7–8/09; BL 4/1/09; HB 5/09; SLJ 5/09)

9322 Kluger, Jeffrey. *Nacky Patcher and the Curse of the Dry-Land Boats* (4–7). 2007, Philomel $18.99 (978-0-399-24604-3). 384pp. When thief Nacky Patcher and orphan Teedie find a sailing ship floating in the lake, they try to persuade the hapless inhabitants of Yole to rally together to rebuild the vessel and escape their oppression by the cruel Baloo family. (Rev: BL 6/1–15/07; SLJ 7/07)

9323 Knudsen, Michelle. *The Dragon of Trelian* (4–7). 2009, Candlewick $16.99 (978-0-7636-3455-1). 416pp. Calen, a lonely magician's apprentice, and Meg, who is secretly caring for a baby dragon, join forces when they find their kingdom is in danger. (Rev: BCCB 9/09; BL 4/1/09; HB 5/09; LMC 8/09; SLJ 6/09)

9324 Koller, Jackie F. *The Dragonling* (2–4). Illus. by Judith Mitchell. 1995, Pocket paper $3.99 (978-0-671-86790-4). 64pp. Darek befriends a young dragon that has been orphaned. (Rev: BL 1/1/91; SLJ 2/91)

9325 Koller, Jackie F. *If I Had One Wish . . .* (5–8). 1991, Little, Brown $14.95 (978-0-316-50150-7). 161pp. When 8th-grader Alec is granted his wish that his little brother had never been born, he learns a lesson about charity, kindness, and old-fashioned family values. (Rev: BCCB 12/91; BL 11/1/91; SLJ 11/91)

9326 Kortum, Jeanie. *Ghost Vision* (5–8). Illus. by Dugald Stermer. 1983, Scholastic paper $3.50 (978-0-614-19197-4). 160pp. A Greenland Inuit realizes that his son has special mystical powers.

9327 Kraan, Hanna. *Flowers for the Wicked Witch* (3–5). Trans. by Wanda Boeke. Illus. Series: Wicked Witch. 1998, Front St. $14.95 (978-1-886910-35-5). 128pp. A collection of charming stories about the relationship between a wicked witch and different forest animals, including a hare, a hedgehog, and an owl. (Rev: BL 11/15/98; HBG 10/99; SLJ 2/99)

9328 Kraan, Hanna. *Tales of the Wicked Witch* (3–5). Illus. by Annemarie van Haeringen. 1995, Front St. $13.95 (978-1-886910-04-1). 128pp. Fourteen short stories about several forest creatures who have problems with the resident witch. (Rev: BL 1/1–15/96; SLJ 1/96)

9329 Kraan, Hanna. *The Wicked Witch Is at It Again* (3–5). Trans. by Wanda Boeke. Illus. 1997, Front St. $14.95 (978-1-886910-18-8). 128pp. Fourteen brief stories about the relationship between a wicked witch and the forest animals that live nearby. (Rev: BL 9/15/97; SLJ 7/97*)

9330 Krensky, Stephen. *Arthur and the Big Blow-Up* (2–4). Illus. 2000, Little, Brown paper $3.95 (978-0-316-12203-0). 64pp. A quarrel between Francine and the Brain threatens the future of their soccer team, so Arthur intervenes to reconcile the two. (Rev: BL 6/1–15/00; HBG 10/00)

9331 Krulik, Nancy. *Girls Don't Have Cooties* (2–4). Illus. by John Wendy and Wendy. Series: Katie Kazoo, Switcheroo. 2002, Grosset paper $3.99 (978-0-448-42705-8). 76pp. Shape-changing Katie finds herself on both sides of the gender gap when the boys and girls at her school decide to hold competing sleep-over parties. (Rev: SLJ 4/03)

9332 Labatt, Mary. *Aliens in Woodford* (2–4). Illus. by Troy Hill-Jackson. 2000, Kids Can $12.95 (978-1-55074-611-2); paper $4.95 (978-1-55074-607-5). 110pp. Sam, a sheepdog, and her master, Jennie, who can understand the dog's thoughts, solve the mystery of strange nighttime activities at an abandoned airfield. (Rev: BL 9/15/03; HBG 3/01; SLJ 12/00)

9333 Labatt, Mary. *The Mummy Lives!* (3–5). Illus. by Troy Hill-Jackson. Series: Sam, Dog Detective. 2002, Kids Can $12.95 (978-1-55337-023-9); paper $4.95 (978-1-55337-042-0). 116pp. Telepathic Sam becomes convinced that she is the dog that an Egyptian mummy is seeking, in this novel suitable for reluctant readers. (Rev: HBG 10/02; SLJ 5/02)

9334 Labatt, Mary. *One Terrible Halloween* (2–5). Illus. by Troy Hill-Jackson. Series: Sam, Dog Detective. 2002, Kids Can $12.95 (978-1-55337-138-0); paper $4.95 (978-1-55337-139-7). 107pp. Sam the telepathic dog, with the help of owner Jennie and her friend Beth, investigates the mystery of the missing neighbors. (Rev: HBG 3/03; SLJ 10/02)

9335 Labatt, Mary. *The Secret of Sagawa Lake* (2–5). Series: Sam, Dog Detective. 2001, Kids Can $12.95 (978-1-55074-887-1); paper $4.95 (978-1-55074-889-5). 118pp. Ten-year-old Jennie, her telepathic dog Sam, and friend Beth investigate a mystery and become convinced there is a monster in the lake. (Rev: HBG 3/02; SLJ 11/01)

9336 Labatt, Mary. *Strange Neighbors* (2–4). 2000, Kids Can $12.95 (978-1-55074-605-1); paper $4.95 (978-1-55074-603-7). 116pp. Sam, the talking sheepdog who can only be understood by Jennie, is convinced that the three old ladies who have moved to their neighborhood are witches. (Rev: BL 5/1/00; HBG 10/00; SLJ 9/00)

9337 Labatt, Mary. *A Weekend at the Grand Hotel* (3–5). Illus. by Troy Hill-Jackson. Series: Sam, Dog Detective. 2001, Kids Can $12.95 (978-1-55074-883-3); paper $4.95 (978-1-55074-885-7). 104pp. Sam, the sheepdog detective, who can put thoughts in young Jennie's head, discovers a mystery on a weekend trip to the Grand Hotel. (Rev: HBG 10/01; SLJ 4/01)

9338 Landy, Derek. *Playing with Fire* (5–8). Series: Skulduggery Pleasant. 2008, HarperCollins $16.99 (978-0-06-124088-1). 400pp. Skulduggery and 13-year-old Valkyrie (formerly known as Stephanie) must curb the evil Baron Vengeous, who plans to bring back to life a terrifying monster called the Grotesquery. (Rev: BL 6/1–15/08; SLJ 7/08)

9339 Landy, Derek. *Skulduggery Pleasant* (5–8). Illus. Series: Skulduggery Pleasant. 2007, HarperCollins $17.99 (978-0-06-123115-5). 400pp. When she inherits her Uncle Gordon's property, plucky 12-year-old Stephanie finds herself swept into an adventure combining magic, mystery, and violence in which her companion is a skeleton named Skulduggery Pleasant. (Rev: BL 5/1/07; HB 7/07; SLJ 6/07)

9340 Langrish, Katherine. *Troll Fell* (5–7). 2004, HarperCollins $16.99 (978-0-06-058304-0). 272pp. Sent to live with his evil twin uncles after his father's death, 12-year-old Peer Ulfsson seeks a way to foil their plan to sell children to the trolls. (Rev: BL 4/15/04*; SLJ 7/04; VOYA 6/04)

9341 Langrish, Katherine. *Troll Mill* (5–8). 2006, HarperCollins LB $17.89 (978-0-06-058308-8). 288pp. In this sequel to *Troll Fell* (2004), 15-year-old Peer Ulfsson, who still worries about his cruel uncles and is increasingly involved with Hilde, must help protect a half-selkie baby from trolls and other threats. (Rev: BCCB 3/06; BL 2/1/06*; HBG 10/06; LMC 1/07; SLJ 3/06; VOYA 2/06)

9342 Langton, Jane. *The Dragon Tree* (3–5). Series: Hall Family Chronicles. 2008, HarperCollins $15.99 (978-0-06-082341-2). 176pp. Mortimer Moon, the new tree warden in Walden Pond, is fonder of cutting trees down than conserving them, and when he gets ready to fell a fast-growing new sapling the Hall children rally support to save it, little suspecting that it is in fact a magical Dragon Tree. (Rev: BL 4/1/08; SLJ 8/08)

9343 Langton, Jane. *The Fledgling* (5–7). 1980, HarperCollins LB $17.89 (978-0-06-023679-3); paper $6.99 (978-0-06-440121-0). 192pp. A young girl learns to fly with her Goose Prince. A sequel is *The Fragile Flag* (1984). Also use *The Diamond in the Window* (1962).

9344 Langton, Jane. *The Mysterious Circus* (3–5). 2005, HarperCollins LB $16.89 (978-0-06-009487-4). 224pp. Near Walden Pond, the Hall children are visited by an Indian relative bringing a seed that produces elephants. (Rev: BL 5/1/05; SLJ 5/05)

9345 Lansky, Bruce, ed. *Newfangled Fairy Tales, Book 1* (3–5). 1998, Meadowbrook LB $3.95 (978-0-671-57704-9). 110pp. These fractured fairy tales involve such characters as a backpacking Sleeping Beauty and King Midas as a workaholic banker. (Rev: BL 3/1/98)

9346 Larson, Kirsten. *Lily's Pesky Plant* (2–3). Illus. by Judith Clarke and the Disney Storybook Artists. Series: Disney Fairies. 2006, Random paper $5.99 (978-0-7364-2374-8). 128pp. Lily, a fairy who lives in Never Land's Pixie Hollow, has a green thumb, but the new plant in her garden has her neighbors very worried. (Rev: SLJ 3/06)

9347 Lasky, Kathryn. *The Capture* (5–8). 2003, Scholastic paper $5.99 (978-0-439-40557-7). 240pp. Soren, a happy, well-adjusted young barn owl, falls from his nest and is stolen away by a group of owlet thieves bent on reeducation. (Rev: BL 9/15/03; SLJ 10/03)

9348 Lauber, Patricia. *Purrfectly Purrfect: Life at the Acatemy* (3–6). Illus. by Betsy Lewin. 2000, HarperCollins LB $15.89 (978-0-06-029209-6). 78pp. A witty, well-illustrated story about cats who attend a school, the Acatemy, where they learn to be

"purrfect" by studying the "purriculum." (Rev: BCCB 12/00; HBG 3/01; SLJ 12/00)

9349 Law, Ingrid. *Savvy* (5–7). 2008, Dial $16.99 (978-0-8037-3306-0). 352pp. On her 13th birthday, Mississippi ("Mibs" for short) is to find out what her "savvy," or ability, will be, and she ends up in a series of adventures on the road to this discovery. Newbery Honor Book, 2009. (Rev: BL 5/15/08; HB 1/08; LMC 8/08; SLJ 5/08)

9350 Lawson, Robert. *The Fabulous Flight* (4–6). Illus. by author. 1984, Little, Brown paper $5.95 (978-0-316-51731-7). 152pp. Peter becomes so small he can take a trip via a pet seagull.

9351 Lawson, Robert. *Rabbit Hill* (4–7). Illus. by author. 1944, Puffin paper $5.99 (978-0-14-031010-8). 128pp. A warm and humorous story about the small creatures of a Connecticut countryside — each with a distinct personality. Newbery Medal winner, 1945.

9352 Laybourne, Emma. *Missing Magic* (4–7). 2007, Dial $16.99 (978-0-8037-3219-3). 193pp. Ned, 11, is one of the few students at Leodwych who has no magic, but his practical abilities prove useful when he and two of his classmates are kidnapped. (Rev: BL 7/07; SLJ 9/07)

9353 Layefsky, Virginia. *Impossible Things* (5–8). 1998, Marshall Cavendish $14.95 (978-0-7614-5038-2). 207pp. Twelve-year-old Brady has several personal and family problems to solve along with taking care of the dragonlike creature that he is hiding. (Rev: HBG 3/99; SLJ 11/98)

9354 Le Guin, Ursula K. *Jane on Her Own* (2–4). Illus. Series: Catwings. 1999, Orchard LB $15.99 (978-0-531-33133-0). 48pp. This fourth installment of the Catwings series features Jane, one of the winged cats, and her experiences when she leaves home to find adventure and friends. (Rev: BCCB 7–8/99; BL 2/1/99; HBG 10/99; SLJ 4/99)

9355 Le Guin, Ursula K. *Wonderful Alexander and the Catwings* (2–4). Illus. Series: Catwings. 1994, Orchard LB $15.99 (978-0-531-08701-5). 48pp. Alexander the kitten helps Jane — one of the flying cats called Catwings — regain her power of speech. (Rev: BL 9/15/94; SLJ 9/94)

9356 Lemke, Donald. *Emperor of the Airwaves* (2–5). Illus. by Erik Doescher and Mike DeCarlo. Series: DC Super Heroes: Batman. 2009, Stone Arch LB $25.32 (978-1-4342-1153-8); paper $5.95 (978-1-4342-1364-8). 56pp. A highly illustrated chapter book pitting Batman against the Penguin. (Rev: LMC 10/09*; SLJ 6/09)

9357 Lennon, Joan. *There's a Kangaroo in My Soup!* (2–3). Illus. by Wendy Rasmussen. 2000, Front St. $15.95 (978-0-8126-2898-2). 128pp. Gloria, a runaway circus kangaroo, brings young Kevin out of his shell in this beginning chapter book fantasy. (Rev: SLJ 12/00)

9358 Leonard, Elmore. *A Coyote's in the House* (5–8). 2004, HarperEntertainment $22.00 (978-0-06-072882-3). 149pp. A coyote named Antwan strikes up a friendship with a couple of pampered dogs from Hollywood. (Rev: BL 5/15/04*)

9359 Leszczynski, Diana. *Fern Verdant and the Silver Rose* (4–8). 2008, Knopf $15.99 (978-0-375-85213-8). 263pp. When her botanist mother Lily is kidnapped, Fern uses her newly discovered talent for communicating with plants to search for her. (Rev: LMC 3/09; SLJ 2/09)

9360 Lethcoe, Jason. *Amazing Adventures from Zoom's Academy* (3–6). Illus. by author. 2005, Ballantine paper $12.95 (978-0-345-48355-3). 151pp. Thirteen-year-old Summer Jones is amazed to find out that her father is a professor at Zoom's Academy for the Super-Gifted; while Summer's powers are being assessed, a move is afoot to attack the academy. (Rev: SLJ 1/06)

9361 Lethcoe, Jason. *Wings* (3–5). 2009, Grosset paper $6.99 (978-0-448-44653-0). 224pp. Fourteen-year-old Edward is sent to boarding school after his mother dies, and there finds that he has wings and is a Guardian with a mission to fulfill. (Rev: BLO 2/9/09; SLJ 8/09)

9362 Levine, Gail C. *Fairy Dust and the Quest for the Egg* (3–5). Illus. by David Christiana. Series: Disney Fairies. 2005, Disney $18.99 (978-0-7868-3491-4). 208pp. Prilla, a new arrival in the fairy community of Never Land, has trouble fitting in until she's assigned to help repair the magic egg that keeps the inhabitants of Never Land forever young. (Rev: BL 8/05*; HBG 10/06; SLJ 10/05)

9363 Levine, Gail C. *The Two Princesses of Bamarre* (4–7). 2001, HarperCollins LB $17.89 (978-0-06-029316-1). 256pp. Princess Addie sets out on a quest to find a cure for the Grey Death, a sickness that is destroying her older sister. (Rev: BCCB 10/01; BL 4/15/01; HB 5/01; HBG 10/01; SLJ 5/01)

9364 Levinson, Marilyn. *Rufus and Magic Run Amok* (3–5). 2001, Marshall Cavendish $14.25 (978-0-7614-5102-0). 96pp. Rufus Breckenridge, 10, just wants to be normal but instead inherits magical powers from his parents and grandparents and has to cope with a heap of new problems. (Rev: BCCB 1/02; HBG 3/02; SLJ 10/01)

9365 Levy, Elizabeth. *The Principal's on the Roof* (2–4). Illus. by Mordicai Gerstein. Series: Fletcher Mysteries. 2002, Simon & Schuster paper $3.99 (978-0-689-84627-4). 73pp. Fletcher the dog and Jasper the flea tackle the mystery of the sneezing principal. (Rev: HBG 3/03; SLJ 1/03)

9366 Lewis, C. S. *The Lion, the Witch and the Wardrobe* (5–8). Illus. Series: Narnia. 1988, Macmillan LB $22.95 (978-0-02-758200-0). Four children enter the kingdom of Narnia through the back of an old wardrobe. A special edition illustrated by Michael Hague. The other six volumes in this series are *Prince Caspian*, *The Voyage of the Dawn Treader*, *The Silver Chair*, *The Horse and His Boy*, *The Magician's Nephew*, and *The Last Battle*.

9367 Lewis, C. S. *The Lion, the Witch and the Wardrobe: A Story for Children* (4–7). Illus. by Pauline Baynes. 1988, Macmillan paper $7.95 (978-0-02-044490-9). 160pp. A beautifully written adventure featuring four children who go into the magical land of Narnia.

9368 Lichtenheld, Tom. *Everything I Know About Monsters: A Collection of Made-up Facts, Educated Guesses, and Silly Pictures About Creatures of Creepiness* (1–4). Illus. by author. 2002, Simon & Schuster $16.95 (978-0-689-84381-5). An appealingly silly guide to the kinds of monsters you find in various places (under the bed, in the closet), with practical tips on monster avoidance. (Rev: HBG 3/03; SLJ 9/02)

9369 Lin, Grace. *Where the Mountain Meets the Moon* (3–6). Illus. by author. 2009, Little, Brown $16.99 (978-0-316-11427-1). 288pp. On a quest to help her family, Minli encounters danger and magic in this story that draws on Chinese legend. (Rev: BL 5/1/09; HB 9/09; SLJ 7/09)

9370 Lindbergh, Anne. *The Hunky-Dory Dairy* (5–7). Illus. by Julie Brinckloe. 1986, Harcourt $14.95 (978-0-15-237449-5); Dell paper $2.75 (978-0-380-70320-3). 147pp. Zannah visits a community magically removed from the 20th century and enjoys introducing the people to bubble gum, tacos, and other "modern" things. (Rev: BCCB 9/86; BL 4/1/86; SLJ 8/86)

9371 Lindbergh, Anne. *The Prisoner of Pineapple Place* (5–7). 1988, Harcourt $13.95 (978-0-15-263559-6); Avon paper $2.95 (978-0-380-70765-2). 173pp. Pineapple Place is invisible to everyone except the inhabitants, and somehow finds itself landing in Connecticut. (Rev: BL 7/88; SLJ 8/88)

9372 Lindgren, Astrid. *Ronia, the Robber's Daughter* (4–7). 1985, Puffin paper $5.99 (978-0-14-031720-6). 176pp. Ronia becomes friendly with the son of her father's rival in this fantasy.

9373 Lisle, Holly. *The Silver Door* (5–8). Series: Moon and Sun. 2009, Scholastic $17.99 (978-0-545-00014-7). 386pp. In search of her birthright, Genna is thwarted by crazed dragons and other dangerous ephemera. (Rev: BLO 5/27/09; HB 7/09)

9374 Lisle, Janet T. *Afternoon of the Elves* (4–6). 1989, Orchard LB $16.99 (978-0-531-08437-3). 128pp. Hilary discovers that the strange girl named Sara-Kate has a garden inhabited by elves. (Rev: BCCB 10/89; BL 8/89*; HB 9/89; SLJ 9/89*)

9375 Lisle, Janet T. *The Gold Dust Letters* (4–6). 1994, Orchard LB $16.99 (978-0-531-08680-3). 128pp. Angela's father fools her into believing that she is receiving messages from a fairy in an effort to effect a reconciliation. (Rev: BCCB 7–8/94; BL 2/1/94; SLJ 4/94)

9376 Lisle, Janet T. *Looking for Juliette* (4–6). 1994, Orchard LB $16.99 (978-0-531-08720-6). 128pp. Georgina and her friend Poco believe that the strange Miss Bone is responsible for running down their cat Juliette. (Rev: BCCB 12/94; BL 9/15/94; SLJ 8/94*)

9377 Lisle, Janet Taylor. *Highway Cats* (4–7). Illus. by David Frankland. 2008, Philomel $14.99 (978-0-399-25070-5). 128pp. Against all odds, three kittens survive abandonment on the edge of a busy highway and meet up with a group of feral cats; the kittens' unusual abilities become apparent when the cats' scruffy piece of land comes under threat of development. (Rev: BL 7/08*; HB 9/08; LMC 1/09; SLJ 11/08) 🎧

9378 Llewellyn, Sam. *The Well Between the Worlds* (5–8). Series: Lyonesse. 2009, Scholastic $17.99 (978-0-439-93469-5). 352pp. Its policy of fishing for monsters in the Belowground has threatened the survival of the kingdom of Lyonesse, and 11-year-old Idris — a monstergroom — may be the only hope; the first installment in a series. (Rev: BCCB 2/09; BL 12/15/08; HB 3/09; LMC 5/09; SLJ 5/09; VOYA 2/09)

9379 Loizeaux, William. *Clarence Cochran, a Human Boy* (4–6). Illus. by Anne Wilsdorf. 2009, Farrar $16.00 (978-0-374-31323-4). 160pp. Inverting Kafka's *The Metamorphosis*, Loizeaux brings us the story of a young cockroach who wakes up to find himself a tiny boy and must struggle against extermination. (Rev: BCCB 6/09; SLJ 4/09)

9380 Loux, Lynn Crosbie. *The Day I Could Fly* (2–4). Illus. by Guy Porfirio. 2003, NorthWord $15.95 (978-1-55971-866-0). A young girl is transformed into a crow for a day. (Rev: SLJ 10/03)

9381 Lowry, Lois. *Gathering Blue* (5–9). 2000, Houghton $16.00 (978-0-618-05581-4). 224pp. In an inhospitable future world, young Kira must use her courage and her artistic talents. (Rev: BL 6/1–15/00*; HB 9/00; HBG 3/01; SLJ 8/00*)

9382 Lowry, Lois. *Gossamer* (5–8). 2006, Houghton $16.00 (978-0-618-68550-9). 144pp. A spirit called Littlest One learns to mix memories that will heal people while they sleep. (Rev: BL 2/15/06; SLJ 5/06*; VOYA 8/06)

9383 Lubar, David. *The Curse of the Campfire Weenies: And Other Warped and Creepy Tales* (5–7). 2007, Tor $15.95 (978-0-7653-1807-7). 208pp. Thirty-five creepy stories combine scariness and dark humor in a way that will attract reluctant readers. (Rev: SLJ 12/07)

9384 Lubar, David. *True Talents* (5–8). 2007, Tor $17.95 (978-0-7653-0977-8). 320pp. In this sequel to *Hidden Talents* (1999), the paranormally gifted student friends from Edgeview Alternative School flex their extraordinary powers in a series of interconnected adventures; memos, e-mails, and illustrations add to the action-packed narrative. (Rev: BL 3/15/07; SLJ 4/07)

9385 Lyons, Mary. *Knockabeg: A Famine Tale* (4–7). 2001, Houghton $15.00 (978-0-618-09283-3). 128pp. In order to protect the people of Knockabeg, faeries battle with the creatures who are causing the blight during the great Irish potato famine. (Rev: BL 11/15/01; HBG 3/02; SLJ 9/01; VOYA 10/01)

9386 Lytle, Robert A. *Three Rivers Crossing* (5–8). 2000, River Road $15.95 (978-0-938682-55-4). 208pp. After he suffers an accident while fishing, 7th-grader Walker wakes to find he is in the 1820s village of his ancestors. (Rev: BL 5/15/00; SLJ 6/00)

9387 McAllister, Angela. *Digory and The Lost King* (3–5). Illus. by Ian Beck. 2007, Bloomsbury $14.95 (978-1-59990-088-9); paper $5.95 (978-1-59990-089-6). 123pp. Digory sets off in search of his

father's missing twin and acquires a baby dragon in this sequel to *Digory the Dragon Slayer*. (Rev: SLJ 7/07)

9388 McAllister, Angela. *Digory the Dragon Slayer* (3–5). Illus. by Ian Beck. 2006, Bloomsbury $14.95 (978-1-58234-722-6); paper $5.95 (978-1-58234-912-1). 124pp. Digory is a gentle poetry-loving lad who is mistakenly considered knight material and sent off to slay dragons and marry princesses. (Rev: SLJ 8/06)

9389 McAllister, M. I. *Urchin of the Riding Stars* (5–8). Series: Mismantle Chronicles. 2005, Hyperion $17.95 (978-0-7868-5486-8). 288pp. When his mentor, Captain Crispin, is unjustly accused of slaying the infant prince of Mismantle, Urchin the squirrel is determined to find out who is responsible for the crime. (Rev: BL 10/1/05; SLJ 11/05; VOYA 2/06)

9390 McCaffrey, Laura Williams. *Alia Waking* (5–7). 2003, Clarion $16.00 (978-0-618-19461-2). 224pp. Alia, 12, and her best friend Kay long to become "keenten," or warrior women. (Rev: BL 3/1/03; HBG 10/03; SLJ 6/03; VOYA 10/03)

9391 McCaughrean, Geraldine. *A Pack of Lies* (5–7). 1990, Macmillan $16.95 (978-0-7451-1154-4). 168pp. Stories told by mysterious M.C.C. Berkshire, who wanders into an antique store run by adolescent Ailsa and her mother. (Rev: BCCB 5/89)

9392 MacDonald, Betty. *Hello, Mrs. Piggle-Wiggle* (3–5). Illus. by Hilary Knight. 1957, HarperCollins $16.99 (978-0-397-31715-8); paper $5.99 (978-0-06-440149-4). 132pp. Introducing the lady who loves all children, good or bad. Further adventures are: *Mrs. Piggle-Wiggle's Farm* (1954); *Mrs. Piggle-Wiggle* (1957); *Mrs. Piggle-Wiggle's Magic* (1957).

9393 McFarland, Lyn Rossiter. *The Pirate's Parrot* (2–4). Illus. 2000, Tricycle $14.95 (978-1-58246-014-7). 40pp. Near-blind pirate Captain Cur mistakes a bear for his new parrot in this farcical sea story. (Rev: BL 5/15/00; HBG 10/00; SLJ 5/00)

9394 McGraw, Eloise. *The Moorchild* (4–6). 1996, Simon & Schuster LB $17.00 (978-0-689-80654-4). 242pp. Set in the Middle Ages, this fantasy tells of Moql, who is born half human and half fairy, and her difficulties fitting into either world. (Rev: BCCB 6/96; BL 3/1/96*; HB 9/96; SLJ 4/96*)

9395 MacHale, D. J. *The Lost City of Faar* (5–8). Series: Pendragon. 2003, Simon & Schuster paper $5.99 (978-0-7434-3732-5). 385pp. After saving Denduron from Saint Dane in *The Merchant of Death* (2002), 14-year-old Bobby must confront the shape-changer again in Cloral, a world covered by water. (Rev: SLJ 5/03)

9396 MacHale, D. J. *The Rivers of Zadaa* (5–8). Series: Pendragon. 2005, Simon & Schuster $14.95 (978-1-4169-0710-7). 405pp. Bobby Pendragon teams up with Loor to foil the villainous Saint Dane's plan to cut off the water supply to Loor's people in Zadaa. (Rev: SLJ 7/05)

9397 McKissack, Patricia C. *The Dark-Thirty: Southern Tales of the Supernatural* (5–8). Illus. 1992, Knopf $17.99 (978-0-679-91863-9). Ten original stories, rooted in African American history and the oral-storytelling tradition, deal with such subjects as slavery, belief in "the sight," and the Montgomery bus boycott. (Rev: BCCB 12/92; BL 12/15/92; HB 3/93; SLJ 12/92*)

9398 McNamee, Eoin. *City of Time* (5–8). Series: The Navigator Trilogy. 2008, Random $16.99 (978-0-375-83912-2). 336pp. The moon is inching toward Owen's home planet, causing panic and environmental changes, and Owen travels to the City of Time to try to set things right. (Rev: BL 5/15/08; SLJ 8/08)

9399 McNish, Cliff. *Breathe: A Ghost Story* (4–8). 2006, Carolrhoda LB $15.95 (978-0-8225-6443-0). 261pp. After the death of his father, young Jack moves with his mother to an old farmhouse in the English countryside, a home that they share with the spirits of four children and the Ghost Mother who enslaved them. (Rev: SLJ 11/06)

9400 McNish, Cliff. *Silver City* (5–8). Series: Silver Sequence. 2006, Carolrhoda $15.95 (978-1-57505-926-6). 256pp. As the fearsome Roar draws closer to the Earth, Milo, Thomas, Helen, and their friends use their magical powers to keep the threat at bay; a sequel to *The Silver Child* (2005). (Rev: BL 6/1–15/06; SLJ 9/06)

9401 McNish, Cliff. *Silver World* (5–8). Series: The Silver Sequence. 2007, Carolrhoda LB $15.95 (978-1-57505-897-9). 247pp. In this third volume in the series, Milo and the other children of Coldharbour use their extraordinary powers to protect the Earth from being destroyed by the terrifying monster called "The Roar." (Rev: SLJ 6/07)

9402 Maguire, Gregory. *Four Stupid Cupids* (4–6). Series: Hamlet Chronicles. 2000, Clarion $16.00 (978-0-395-83895-2). 184pp. A far-fetched comedy about four cupids who are freed when the magical vase that Fawn Petros brings to her Vermont school breaks. (Rev: BL 12/1/00; HBG 3/01; SLJ 10/00)

9403 Maguire, Gregory. *Seven Spiders Spinning* (4–6). Illus. by Dirk Zimmer. 1994, Clarion $16.00 (978-0-395-68965-3). 144pp. In this farce, seven tarantulas invade a classroom and go on their separate quests. (Rev: BCCB 10/94; BL 9/15/94; SLJ 10/94)

9404 Mahy, Margaret. *The Blood-and-Thunder Adventure on Hurricane Peak* (4–6). Illus. by Wendy Smith. 1989, Macmillan $13.95 (978-0-689-50488-4). 132pp. Huxley and Zaza find fantastic adventures at Unexpected School on Hurricane Peak. (Rev: BCCB 10/89; BL 10/15/89; HB 11/89*; SLJ 10/89)

9405 Mahy, Margaret. *Maddigan's Fantasia* (5–8). 2007, Simon & Schuster $17.99 (978-1-4169-1812-7). 512pp. When 12-year-old Garland's father is killed, messengers from the future arrive to urge her to travel to a far-off town in search of a solar converter that will prevent future catastrophe. (Rev: BL 12/15/07; HB 11/07; LMC 1/08; SLJ 11/07)

9406 Mahy, Margaret. *A Tall Story and Other Tales* (3–5). Illus. by Jan Nesbitt. 1992, Macmillan $15.95 (978-0-689-50547-8). 96pp. Eleven stories combine

witches and monsters and such with everyday life. (Rev: BL 2/1/92; SLJ 3/92)

9407 Marsden, John. *The Rabbits* (2–8). Illus. by Shaun Tan. 2003, Simply Read $16.95 (978-0-9688768-8-6). In this allegory, native creatures welcome the newcomer rabbits, but the rabbits take over, devastate the landscape, and there is no happy ending. (Rev: SLJ 4/04)

9408 Martin, Ann M., and Laura Godwin. *The Doll People* (3–6). Illus. 2000, Hyperion $15.99 (978-0-7868-0361-3). 272pp. In this fantasy about dolls that are alive, Annabelle Doll tries to solve the mystery of the disappearance of Aunt Sarah Doll in 1955. (Rev: BCCB 1/01; BL 8/00; HBG 3/01; SLJ 11/00)

9409 Martin, Ann M., and Laura Godwin. *The Runaway Dolls* (3–6). Illus. by Brian Selznick. Series: Doll People. 2008, Disney $16.99 (978-0-7868-5584-1). 288pp. Annabelle Doll runs away with her long-lost sister and into a series of increasingly perilous situations. (Rev: BL 10/1/08; SLJ 10/08) ⌒

9410 Martin, George R. R. *The Ice Dragon* (3–5). Illus. by Yvonne Gilbert. 2006, Tom Doherty Assoc. $12.95 (978-0-7653-1631-8). 106pp. Seven-year-old Adara is a child who loves the cold, and her bond with the ice dragon allows her to rescue her home and family from marauding invaders. (Rev: SLJ 2/07)

9411 Martin, Rafe. *Birdwing* (5–8). 2005, Scholastic $16.99 (978-0-459-21167-7). 359pp. This appealing fantasy picks up where "The Six Swans" by the Brothers Grimm ends, chronicling the story of Ardwin, the prince who was turned into a swan and then restored to human form apart from his left arm, which remains a swan's wing. (Rev: BCCB 12/05 ; BL 11/15/05; HB 1/06; SLJ 12/05; VOYA 12/05)

9412 Martini, Clem. *The Mob* (5–8). Series: Feather and Bone: The Crow Chronicles. 2004, Kids Can $16.95 (978-1-55337-574-6). 240pp. As hundreds of crows of the Kinaar clan come together for their annual socialization at the Gathering Tree, internal conflicts threaten to tear the avian family apart in this first volume in a trilogy. (Rev: BL 10/1/04; SLJ 12/04)

9413 Mason, Timothy. *The Last Synapsid* (4–7). 2009, Delacorte $16.99 (978-0-385-73581-0). 288pp. Before there were dinosaurs, there were reptiles called synapsids and two of them — plus a villain named Jenkins — travel through time to a tiny town in Colorado where Rob and Phoebe try to figure out how to get them back where they came from before something terrible happens. (Rev: BCCB 1/09; BLO 2/9/09; LMC 5/09; SLJ 6/09)

9414 Masson, Sophie. *Serafin* (5–8). 2000, Saint Mary's paper $5.50 (978-0-88489-567-1). 140pp. After he saves Calou from being lynched as a witch, Frederick is forced to flee his 17th-century French village with Calou and soon afterward realizes that the girl is a matagot, a half-angel half-human creature. (Rev: SLJ 8/00)

9415 Matas, Carol, and Perry Nodelman. *Out of Their Minds* (5–8). Illus. Series: Minds. 1998, Simon & Schuster $16.00 (978-0-689-81946-9). In this fantasy (the third in the series), Princess Lenora and Prince Coren journey to Andilla to marry but find that some force is upsetting The Balance. (Rev: HBG 3/99; SLJ 9/98; VOYA 2/99)

9416 Mather, Karen Trella. *Silas: The Bookstore Cat* (2–4). Illus. by Chris Van Dusen. 1994, Down East $14.95 (978-0-89272-352-2). 32pp. Silas, the bookstore cat, helps his master find books about his favorite subject, soccer. (Rev: BL 2/1/95; SLJ 3/95)

9417 Mayes, Walter M. *Walter the Giant Storyteller's Giant Book of Giant Stories* (3–5). Illus. by Kevin O'Malley. 2005, Walker $18.95 (978-0-8027-8974-7). Captured by the tiny inhabitants of a Lilliputian-like island, Walter the Giant Storyteller tells a series of stories to convince his captors that giants are not bloodthirsty and mean but rather the victims of character assassination; an oversize volume with dramatic illustrations. (Rev: SLJ 11/05)

9418 Mazer, Anne. *Sister Magic: The Trouble with Violet* (2–4). Illus. by Bill Brown. 2007, Scholastic paper $3.99 (978-0-439-87246-1). 86pp. The magical aura surrounding her younger sister Violet makes the carefully organized Mabel quite uncomfortable. (Rev: BCCB 10/07; BL 9/1/07; SLJ 9/07)

9419 Mebus, Scott. *Gods of Manhattan* (5–8). Series: Gods of Manhattan. 2008, Dutton $17.99 (978-0-525-47955-0). 256pp. Rory discovers that he has the ability to see figures from New York history (such as Peter Stuyvesant and Babe Ruth) and that he must use this power to save Manhattan. (Rev: BL 5/15/08; SLJ 4/08)

9420 Mebus, Scott. *Spirits in the Park* (5–8). Series: Gods of Manhattan. 2009, Dutton $17.99 (978-0-525-42148-1). 384pp. In Mannahatta, the spirit city that exists parallel to the real city, Rory — reluctantly — must find his missing father. (Rev: BLO 4/24/09; SLJ 9/09; VOYA 8/09)

9421 Meddaugh, Susan. *Lulu's Hat* (3–5). Illus. 2002, Houghton $15.00 (978-0-618-15277-3). 64pp. Lulu's deep interest in magic leads her to follow a dog that has jumped into a top hat that has unusual powers. (Rev: BCCB 5/02; BL 5/1/02; HBG 10/02; SLJ 5/02)

9422 Medearis, Angela Shelf. *Haunts: Five Hair-Raising Tales* (4–7). Illus. by Trina S. Hyman. 1996, Holiday $15.95 (978-0-8234-1280-8). 37pp. Five stories that contain elements of horror and the supernatural. (Rev: BL 2/1/97; SLJ 4/97)

9423 Meehan, Kierin. *Hannah's Winter* (5–8). 2009, Kane $15.95 (978-1-933605-98-2). 212pp. Hannah, an Australian 12-year-old, finds herself enjoying her stay in Japan and, with her new friends Miki and Hiro, she investigates a mysterious riddle. (Rev: HB 5/09*; SLJ 3/09)

9424 Meyer, Kai. *The Stone Light* (5–7). Trans. from German by Elizabeth D. Crawford. Series: The Dark Reflections Trilogy. 2006, Simon & Schuster $16.95 (978-0-689-87789-6). 350pp. Desperately searching for help in their fight to free Venice from the evil Egyptian pharaoh, Merle travels on Vermithrax, the flying lion, to Hell in hopes of convincing Lucifer to ally himself with their cause; the sequel

to *The Water Mirror* (2005). (Rev: BL 3/15/07; SLJ 1/07)

9425 Meyer, Kai. *The Water Mirror* (4–7). Trans. by Elizabeth D. Crawford. Series: Dark Reflections. 2005, Simon & Schuster $15.95 (978-0-689-87787-2). 256pp. In an alternate Venice in danger of destruction, 14-year-old Merle, a plucky orphan, finds herself playing a central role; the first volume in a series noted for its setting; sequels are *The Stone Light* (2007) and *The Glass Word* (2008). (Rev: BL 1/1–15/06; SLJ 11/05*; VOYA 12/05) ∩

9426 Michael, Livi. *City of Dogs* (5–8). 2007, Putnam $16.99 (978-0-399-24356-1). 250pp. Sam has always wanted a dog and is happy when Jenny comes to live with him, but Jenny's mission becomes overarching and she must take on friends and foes in this fantasy full of mythological references. (Rev: BCCB 11/07; LMC 11/07; SLJ 11/07)

9427 Milne, A. A. *The World of Pooh: The Complete Winnie-the-Pooh; and the House at Pooh Corner* (1–4). Illus. by E. H. Shepard. 1988, Dutton $24.99 (978-0-525-44447-3). 320pp. A pleasing combination volume.

9428 Molloy, Michael. *The House on Falling Star Hill* (4–8). 2004, Scholastic $16.95 (978-0-439-57740-3). 384pp. While spending a vacation with his grandparents in a peaceful English village, Tim discovers an alternate world called Tallis and becomes involved in the turmoil taking place there. (Rev: BL 4/15/04; SLJ 4/04)

9429 Molloy, Michael. *The Time Witches* (5–8). 2002, Scholastic paper $4.99 (978-0-439-42090-7). 272pp. The characters from *The Witch Trade* (2002) return in this sequel in which Abby, a Light Witch, and her friends must travel into the past to foil a plot hatched by the nefarious Wolfbane. (Rev: BL 1/1–15/03; SLJ 8/03)

9430 Moloney, James. *The Book of Lies* (4–6). 2007, HarperCollins $16.99 (978-0-06-057842-8). 368pp. Kidnapped and brought to Mrs. Timmons's Home for Orphans and Foundlings, a young boy awakens with no memory of his former life, but a young girl offers him a single clue that sets him on the trail to his past. (Rev: BL 4/15/07)

9431 Monsell, Mary Elise. *Toohy and Wood* (3–5). Illus. 1992, Macmillan $12.95 (978-0-689-31721-7). 80pp. Toohy the lizard is devastated by the death of Pearl, a musical dove, in this story of a world inhabited by affectionate animals. (Rev: BCCB 12/92; BL 10/1/92; SLJ 10/92)

9432 Moonshower, Candie. *The Legend of Zoey* (4–6). 2006, Delacorte $15.95 (978-0-385-73280-2). 224pp. A multilayered story told in part through the diary entries of Zoey, a modern girl of Native American heritage, who travels back in time to 1811 and meets Prudence, the daughter of white settlers; the two endure the New Madrid earthquakes together. (Rev: BL 7/06; SLJ 12/06)

9433 Moredun, P. R. *The Dragon Conspiracy* (5–8). Series: World of Eldaterra. 2005, HarperCollins LB $17.89 (978-0-06-076664-1). 304pp. A complex first installment in which a British schoolboy in 1910 must battle female dragons to save both our world and the magical parallel world of Eldaterra. (Rev: BL 6/1–15/05; SLJ 10/05)

9434 Moroney, Lynn. *Moontellers: Myths of the Moon from Around the World* (3–5). Illus. by Greg Shed. 1995, Northland LB $14.95 (978-0-87358-601-6). A collection of stories that reflect the attitudes of various cultures — such as the Aztecs and the Chinese — toward the moon, with a final section on modern astronomers. (Rev: SLJ 9/95)

9435 Morris, Gerald. *Parsifal's Page* (5–8). 2001, Houghton $16.00 (978-0-618-05509-8). 240pp. Piers becomes a page to Parsifal and accompanies the innocent young man on his quest to become a knight. (Rev: BCCB 4/01; BL 4/15/01; HB 5/01; HBG 10/01; SLJ 4/01; VOYA 6/01)

9436 Morris, Gerald. *The Savage Damsel and the Dwarf* (5–8). 2000, Houghton $16.00 (978-0-395-97126-0). 224pp. Sixteen-year-old Lady Lynet travels to Camelot, in the company of a dwarf, to ask King Arthur's aid in defeating her sister's suitor. (Rev: BL 3/1/00; HB 5/00; HBG 10/00; SLJ 5/00; VOYA 6/00)

9437 Morris, Jackie. *The Seal Children* (2–5). Illus. by author. 2004, Frances Lincoln $16.95 (978-1-84507-040-3). The son of a Welsh fisherman and a selkie woman travels to his mother's world beneath the sea and returns with a box of pearls that the people in his village can use to finance a trip to the New World. (Rev: SLJ 7/04)

9438 Morrison, P. R. *Wind Tamer* (4–6). 2006, Bloomsbury $16.95 (978-1-58234-781-3). 336pp. A visit from his uncle convinces 10-year-old Archie Stringweed, who lives in a remote Scottish village, to confront the curse that has hung over his family for generations. (Rev: BL 10/15/06; SLJ 11/06)

9439 Morton-Shaw, Christine. *The Hunt for the Seventh* (5–8). 2008, HarperCollins $16.99 (978-0-06-072822-9). 288pp. Recently moved with his family to the stately Minerva Hall, young Jim finds himself haunted by the ghosts of children who have died in strange accidents. (Rev: BL 1/1–15/09; LMC 3/09; SLJ 5/09)

9440 Moses, Will. *The Legend of Sleepy Hollow* (3–5). Illus. 1995, Penguin $18.99 (978-0-399-22687-8). 48pp. A simple retelling of this classic tale, with paintings of various sizes and shapes. (Rev: BL 10/1/95; SLJ 10/95)

9441 Moses, Will. *Rip Van Winkle* (3–5). Illus. 1999, Penguin $17.99 (978-0-399-23152-0). 48pp. This large-format book is a handsome, somewhat simplified version of the classic fantasy by Washington Irving. (Rev: BCCB 12/99; BL 11/1/99; HBG 3/00; SLJ 10/99)

9442 Mould, Chris. *The Icy Hand* (4–6). Illus. by author. Series: Something Wickedly Weird. 2008, Roaring Brook $9.95 (978-1-59643-385-4). 174pp. With help from a talking fish and the ghost of his great-uncle Bartholomew, Stanley battles pirates searching to steal a family heirloom; the second installment in the series. (Rev: HB 11/08; LMC 3/09; SLJ 11/08)

9443 Muller, Rachel Dunstan. *The Solstice Cup* (5–8). 2009, Orca paper $9.95 (978-1-55469-017-

6). 144pp. On a visit in Northern Ireland, tween twins Breanne and Mackenzie ignore warnings about the fairies and find themselves transported into a scary Otherworld. (Rev: BL 5/15/09)

9444 Mullin, Caryl Cude. *A Riddle of Roses* (4–7). 2000, Second Story paper $6.95 (978-1-896764-28-3). 180pp. Meryl, who has been expelled from school for a year, goes on a quest to Avalon to find her own wisdom. (Rev: BL 2/15/01; VOYA 4/01)

9445 Murphy, Jill. *The Worst Witch* (4–6). 1982, Avon paper $2.50 (978-0-380-60665-8). 72pp. Mildred's first year at Miss Cackle's Academy for Witches is a disaster. A sequel is: *The Worst Witch Strikes Again* (1987).

9446 Murphy, Jill. *The Worst Witch Saves the Day* (3–5). Illus. by author. 2007, Candlewick $13.99 (978-0-7636-3319-4). 150pp. The famously disaster-prone, witch-in-training Mildred flies in for a brand-new adventure, in which a curling-iron catastrophe leads her to experiment with a hair-growing potion—with hair-raising results. Illustrations. (Rev: SLJ 11/07)

9447 Myers, Walter Dean. *Three Swords for Granada* (3–6). Illus. by John Spiers. 2002, Holiday House $15.95 (978-0-8234-1676-9). 80pp. Sword-wielding Spanish cats stand up to the dogs of the Fidorean Guard in this exciting fantasy set in 1420. (Rev: BL 7/02; HBG 10/03; SLJ 9/02)

9448 Naylor, Phyllis Reynolds. *The Healing of Texas Jake* (3–6). Illus. 1997, Simon & Schuster $15.00 (978-0-689-81124-1). 128pp. Each of the cats who are members of the Club of Mystery rally around their leader, Texas Jake, when he is injured in a brawl. (Rev: BL 5/1/97; SLJ 4/97)

9449 Naylor, Phyllis Reynolds. *Jade Green: A Ghost Story* (5–8). 2000, Simon & Schuster $16.00 (978-0-689-82005-2). 176pp. Set in South Carolina about 100 years ago, this ghost story involves Judith Sparrow, age 15, and the mystery surrounding the gruesome death of a girl named Jade Green. (Rev: BL 12/15/99; HBG 10/00; SLJ 2/00; VOYA 6/00)

9450 Naylor, Phyllis Reynolds. *Polo's Mother* (4–6). Illus. by Alan Daniel. Series: Cat Pack. 2005, Simon & Schuster $15.95 (978-0-689-86555-8). 176pp. Polo's mother finally turns up at the Club of Mysteries, but she is not what Polo expected. (Rev: BL 6/1–15/05; SLJ 5/05)

9451 Nelson, D. A. *Dark Isle* (4–6). 2008, Delacorte $15.99 (978-0-385-73630-5). 272pp. After being locked in the cellar by her foster parents, Morag, 10, goes off with a talking rat and a dodo bird to save the world. (Rev: BL 11/15/08; SLJ 1/09)

9452 Nesbit, E. *Lionel and the Book of Beasts* (2–4). Illus. by Michael Hague. 2006, HarperCollins $16.99 (978-0-688-14006-9). 48pp. This abridged retelling of Nesbit's classic book tells the story of new young king Lionel, who accidentally unleashes a dragon upon the land. (Rev: BL 12/1/06; SLJ 1/07)

9453 Nesbit, Edith. *The Enchanted Castle* (4–6). Illus. by Paul Zelinsky. 1992, Morrow $25.99 (978-0-688-05435-9). 304pp. A handsome volume that showcases Nesbit's fantasy about four English children and their adventures with a magic ring, first published in 1907. (Rev: BL 12/15/92)

9454 Nesbit, Edith. *Five Children and It* (4–6). Illus. by H. R. Miller. 1981, Buccaneer LB $21.95 (978-0-89966-362-3). 188pp. An enchanting story about a group of children who discover a Psammead, a sand fairy, who both enlivens and confuses their lives. Two more stories about the children: *The Phoenix and the Carpet* (1985); *The Story of the Amulet* (1986).

9455 Newbery, Linda. *Lost Boy* (5–8). 2008, Random $15.99 (978-0-375-84574-1). 208pp. New to the town of Hay-on-Wye in Wales, Matt feels the presence of a boy who died there several years before. (Rev: BCCB 3/08; BL 4/1/08; LMC 5/08; SLJ 3/08)

9456 Newman, Robert. *Merlin's Mistake* (4–6). Illus. by Richard Lebenson. 1986, Peter Smith $18.75 (978-0-8446-6187-2). Sixteen-year-old Brian and his friend Tertius set out to find Merlin in this fantasy originally published in 1970. Followed by: *The Testing of Tertius* (1986).

9457 Nigg, Joseph. *How to Raise and Keep a Dragon* (5–10). Illus. by Dan Malone. 2006, Barron's $18.99 (978-0-7641-5920-6). 128pp. This whimsical guide to the care and feeding of dragons offers tips for selecting just the right type of dragon, finding the correct equipment and supplies, establishing good modes of communication, and training for competitions. (Rev: SLJ 11/06)

9458 Nimmo, Jenny. *Charlie Bone and the Castle of Mirrors* (4–6). Series: Children of the Red King. 2005, Scholastic $9.95 (978-0-439-54528-0). 432pp. Back for another year at Bloor's Academy, Charlie Bone enlists the help of friends to save Billy Raven from his new adoptive parents. (Rev: BL 9/1/05; SLJ 10/05; VOYA 10/05)

9459 Nimmo, Jenny. *Charlie Bone and the Time Twister* (5–7). 2003, Scholastic $10.99 (978-0-439-49687-2). 416pp. In 1916 Henry Yewbeam finds a strange marble and is transported to the present-day Bloor's Academy, where Charlie Bone tests his magical abilities in an effort to send him home. A sequel to *Midnight for Charlie Bone* (2003). (Rev: BL 9/15/03; HBG 4/04; SLJ 10/03)

9460 Nimmo, Jenny. *The Chestnut Soldier* (4–6). Series: The Magician Trilogy. 2007, Scholastic $9.99 (978-0-439-84677-6). 203pp. Is a soldier visiting Gywn's Welsh town inhabited by the spirit of Efnisien, an evil prince of lore? The last volume in a trilogy that started with *The Snow Spider* (2006). (Rev: BCCB 5/07; BL 2/15/07) ∩

9461 Nimmo, Jenny. *The Dragon's Child* (2–4). Illus. by Alan Marks. 2008, Scholastic paper $6.99 (978-0-545-06468-2). 107pp. With the help of a slave-girl and a bird, a young dragon named Dando is able to fly. (Rev: BL 8/08; LMC 1/09)

9462 Nimmo, Jenny. *Emlyn's Moon* (3–5). Series: Magician Trilogy. 2007, Scholastic $9.99 (978-0-439-84676-9). 152pp. In this second installment in the trilogy, young magician Gwyn and his friend Nia find they hold the fate of Emlyn Llewelyn in their hands. (Rev: BL 12/15/06) ∩

9463 Nimmo, Jenny. *Griffin's Castle* (5–8). 1997, Orchard LB $17.99 (978-0-531-33006-7). When Dinah and her young mother, Rosalie, move into the rundown mansion owned by Rosalie's boyfriend, Dinah brings to life several carved animals for protection. (Rev: SLJ 6/97; VOYA 8/97)

9464 Nimmo, Jenny. *Midnight for Charlie Bone* (4–6). 2003, Scholastic paper $10.99 (978-0-439-47429-0). 416pp. Charlie Bone, who can look at photographs and hear the conversations and thoughts of the subjects, is sent to Bloor's Academy to enhance his skills and is drawn into a magical battle, makes friends, and becomes immersed in a mystery. (Rev: BL 1/1–15/03; HBG 10/03; SLJ 2/03)

9465 Nimmo, Jenny. *The Snow Spider* (3–5). Series: Magician Trilogy. 2006, Scholastic $9.99 (978-0-439-84675-2). 128pp. On Gwyn's 9th birthday his grandmother reveals to him that he's a magician, giving him five gifts to help him with his powers; set in Wales, this story incorporates elements of local folklore. (Rev: BL 11/15/06)

9466 Nitz, Kristin Wolden. *Saving the Griffin* (3–5). Illus. by Yoshiko Jaeggi. 2007, Peachtree $14.95 (978-1-56145-380-1). 192pp. During a trip to Italy, two American siblings try to keep their discovery of a baby griffin a secret from family members and others. (Rev: BL 5/15/07; LMC 10/07; SLJ 6/07)

9467 Nix, Garth. *Above the Veil* (5–7). Series: The Seventh Tower. 2001, Scholastic paper $5.99 (978-0-439-17685-9). 248pp. In episode four in this series, Tal and Milla continue their otherworldly adventures full of action, secrets, and surprising twists and turns. (Rev: SLJ 9/01)

9468 Nix, Garth. *Grim Tuesday* (5–8). Series: Keys to the Kingdom. 2004, Scholastic paper $7.99 (978-0-439-43655-7). 321pp. Arthur Penhaligon returns in this second installment in the series to the house that holds an alternate universe and there must challenge the evil Grim Tuesday, who threatens to destroy everything; later volumes include *Drowned Wednesday* (2005) and *Superior Saturday* (2008). (Rev: SLJ 8/04)

9469 Nix, Garth. *Mister Monday* (5–8). Series: The Keys to the Kingdom. 2003, Scholastic paper $6.99 (978-0-439-55123-6). 361pp. When 7th-grader Arthur Penhaligon receives a healing key from a mysterious stranger, the gift turns out to be a mixed blessing that brings illness and strange creatures seeking to reclaim the key. (Rev: BCCB 1/04; SLJ 12/03)

9470 Nix, Garth. *One Beastly Beast: Two Aliens, Three Inventors, Four Fantastic Tales* (5–7). Illus. by Brian Biggs. 2007, Eos $15.99 (978-0-06-084319-9). 176pp. Four short stories accompanied by cartoonish illustrations for readers who enjoy fantasy that's not too far out or too scary. (Rev: BCCB 10/07; BL 7/07; SLJ 9/07)

9471 Nixon, Joan Lowery. *Gus and Gertie and the Missing Pearl* (2–4). Illus. 2000, North-South LB $15.88 (978-1-58717-023-2). 48pp. When penguins Gertie and Gus enter a seedy hotel on a tropical island, Gertie's necklace is stolen and they must solve the mystery and catch the thief. (Rev: BL 11/1/00; HBG 3/01; SLJ 10/00)

9472 Nykko. *The Shadow Door* (4–7). Trans. by Carol Klio Burrell. Illus. by Bannister. Series: Elsewhere Chronicles. 2009, Lerner LB $27.93 (978-0-7613-4459-9); paper $6.95 (978-0-7613-3963-2). 48pp. Four friends find a door to a dangerous world peopled with shadowy creatures. (Rev: BL 3/1/09)

9473 Nyoka, Gail. *Mella and the N'anga: An African Tale* (5–8). 2006, Sumach paper $9.95 (978-1-894549-49-3). 160pp. Mella, the daughter of a king in ancient Zimbabwe, with the help of the magical powers she learns from the spiritual adviser called N'anga, strives to save her father's life and realm. (Rev: BL 3/1/06; SLJ 7/06)

9474 O'Brien, Robert C. *Mrs. Frisby and the Rats of NIMH* (5–7). Illus. by Zena Bernstein. 1971, Macmillan $18.00 (978-0-689-20651-1); paper $5.50 (978-0-689-71068-1). 240pp. Saga of a group of rats made literate and given human intelligence by a series of experiments, who escape from their laboratory to found their own community. Newbery Medal winner, 1972.

9475 Ogburn, Jacqueline. *The Bake Shop Ghost* (1–3). Illus. by Marjorie Priceman. 2005, Houghton $16.00 (978-0-618-44557-8). 32pp. The ghost of Cora Lee Merriweather, the bad-tempered owner of a bake shop, scares away all of the bakery's new owners until Annie Washington arrives, determined to stand her ground. (Rev: BCCB 9/05; BL 9/1/05*; HBG 4/06; LMC 5/06; SLJ 10/05)

9476 Okorafor-Mbachu, Nnedi. *The Shadow Speaker* (5–8). 2007, Hyperion $16.99 (978-1-4231-0033-1). 352pp. West Africa is a very different place in 2070 in this futuristic tale in which Muslim Ejii, 15, shadow-speaks with the queen who had her father killed years earlier. (Rev: BL 3/1/08; SLJ 2/08)

9477 Okorafor-Mbachu, Nnedi. *Zahrah the Windseeker* (5–8). 2005, Houghton $16.00 (978-0-618-34090-3). 320pp. In this appealing debut novel, 13-year-old Zahrah, a "dada girl" readily identifiable by her telltale vine-entwined dreadlocks, struggles to come to terms with her magical powers. (Rev: BL 11/15/05; SLJ 12/05)

9478 Oliver, Lin. *Attack of the Growling Eyeballs* (4–6). Illus. by Stephen Gilpin. Series: Who Shrunk Daniel Funk? 2008, Simon & Schuster $14.99 (978-1-4169-6225-0). 112pp. A sneeze causes Daniel Funk to shrink to toe-size and he then learns two things: that this is a family trait and that he has a twin brother Pablo, who is only an inch high but has a character at least twice his size; a funny action-packed novel. (Rev: BL 4/1/08; LMC 8/08)

9479 Olson, Arielle North, and Howard Schwartz, eds. *Ask the Bones: Scary Stories from Around the World* (5–9). 1999, Viking $16.99 (978-0-670-87581-8). A collection of 22 scary stories about subjects ranging from ghosts to witches and voodoo spells, accompanied by spooky illustrations. (Rev: BCCB 4/99; BL 5/1/99; HB 5/99; HBG 10/99; SLJ 4/99)

9480 Oram, Hiawyn. *My Unwilling Witch Goes to Ballet School* (2–4). Illus. by Sarah Warburton.

2009, Little, Brown paper $9.99 (978-0-316-03472-2). 112pp. Poor Rumblewick, a witch's familiar, describes in his diary how he must work overtime trying to get Haggy to behave like a witch when all Haggy wants to do is become a ballerina. (Rev: BL 7/09)

9481 Osborne, Mary Pope. *Moonlight on the Magic Flute* (2–4). Illus. by Sal Murdocca. Series: Magic Tree House. 2009, Random $11.99 (978-0-375-85646-4). 128pp. Transported back to 18th-century Vienna, Jack and Annie meet a young Mozart and help to save his life. (Rev: BLO 4/23/09) ∩

9482 Osborne, Mary Pope. *Night of the New Magicians* (2–4). Illus. by Sal Murdocca. Series: Magic Tree House. 2006, Random $11.95 (978-0-375-83035-8). 116pp. Jack and Annie are sent on a magician-searching mission at the 1889 World's Fair. (Rev: BL 5/1/06)

9483 Osterweil, Adam. *The Amulet of Komondor* (5–7). 2003, Front St. $15.95 (978-1-886910-81-2). 184pp. Finding themselves in a parallel world of "Japanimations," Joe and Katie face a mighty challenge, worry about how to get home, and continue their real-world romance in this lighthearted fantasy with *anime*-style illustrations. (Rev: BL 11/15/03; HBG 4/04; SLJ 12/03)

9484 Osterweil, Adam. *The Comic Book Kid* (4–6). Illus. 2001, Front St. $15.95 (978-1-886910-62-1). 152pp. Brian tries to travel back to 1939 and replace his father's prized Superman #1 comic book. (Rev: BL 5/15/01; HBG 10/01; SLJ 8/01)

9485 Park, Linda Sue. *Archer's Quest* (4–7). 2006, Clarion $16.00 (978-0-618-59631-7). 176pp. An ancient Korean ruler suddenly appears in the New York State bedroom of 12-year-old Kevin and the two must work out how to get him back home before the Year of the Tiger ends. (Rev: BL 3/15/06; SLJ 5/06)

9486 Paterson, Katherine. *The Field of the Dogs* (3–5). Illus. by Emily Arnold McCully. 2001, HarperCollins LB $14.89 (978-0-06-029475-5). 96pp. Josh, beset by bullies in the Vermont town where he has moved with his mother, discovers that he can understand the language of dogs. (Rev: BCCB 2/01; BL 10/15/01; HBG 10/01; SLJ 2/01)

9487 Paterson, Katherine. *The Wide-Awake Princess* (2–5). Illus. 2000, Clarion $15.00 (978-0-395-53777-0). 48pp. The story of a princess who leaves her castle to find out about the common people in her kingdom and how they live. (Rev: BL 3/15/00; HBG 10/00; SLJ 7/00)

9488 Paul, Donita K. *Dragonspell* (4–8). 2004, WaterBrook paper $12.99 (978-1-57856-823-9). 339pp. Fourteen-year-old Kale is the protagonist of this classic quest tale, set in the world of Amara, with Christian overtones reminiscent of C. S. Lewis. (Rev: SLJ 11/04)

9489 Pearce, Philippa. *A Finder's Magic* (3–5). Illus. by Helen Craig. 2009, Candlewick $15.99 (978-0-7636-4072-9). 128pp. When Till loses his dog Bess, he is happy to accept the help of a stranger who asks a variety of animals for pertinent information. (Rev: BCCB 5/09; BLO 5/27/09; SLJ 6/09)

9490 Pearce, Philippa. *Tom's Midnight Garden* (4–7). Illus. by Susan Einzig. 1959, Dell paper $6.99 (978-0-06-440445-7). 240pp. When the clock strikes 13, Tom visits his garden and meets Hatty, a strange mid-Victorian girl.

9491 Peck, Richard. *The Ghost Belonged to Me* (5–8). 1997, Viking paper $5.99 (978-0-14-038671-4). 184pp. Richard unwillingly receives the aid of his nemesis, Blossom Culp, in trying to solve the mystery behind the ghost of a young girl. Two sequels are *Ghosts I Have Been* (1977); *The Dreadful Future of Blossom Culp* (1983).

9492 Pemberton, Bonnie. *The Cat Master* (5–8). 2007, Marshall Cavendish $16.99 (978-0-7614-5340-6). 272pp. A dying Cat Master's telepathic message to his successor — indoor cat but formerly feral Buddy — is intercepted by the evil cat Jett, and Buddy and his friends must fight for justice to be fulfilled. (Rev: BL 6/1–15/07; SLJ 6/07)

9493 Pennypacker, Sara. *Stuart Goes to School* (2–4). Illus. by Martin Matje. 2003, Scholastic $15.95 (978-0-439-30182-4). 64pp. In this humorous sequel to *Stuart's Cape,* the title character enters the third grade at a new school and finds that having a magical cape can sometimes cause embarrassing problems. (Rev: BL 7/03; SLJ 9/03)

9494 Pérez, L. King. *Ghoststalking* (3–6). Illus. 1995, Carolrhoda LB $19.93 (978-0-87614-821-1). 56pp. Chuy and Emilio camp outdoors to find the ghost of La Llorona, a woman who has drowned her children in this Latino tale of the supernatural. (Rev: BL 9/15/95; SLJ 12/95)

9495 Perrin, Randy, et al. *Time Like a River* (5–7). 1997, RDR $14.95 (978-1-57143-061-8). 139pp. Margie travels back in time to find a cure for her mother's mysterious illness. (Rev: HBG 3/98; SLJ 3/98)

9496 Peterson, Will. *Triskellion* (5–9). Series: Triskellion. 2008, Candlewick $16.99 (978-0-7636-3971-6). 368pp. Telepathic twins Adam and Rachel, 14, are spending the summer in an ancient English village and find themselves swept into an adventure involving archaeology, folklore, and an ancient artifact; the first volume in a series. (Rev: BCCB 9/08; LMC 10/08; SLJ 11/08; VOYA 8-08)

9497 Pierce, Tamora. *Briar's Book* (5–9). Series: Circle of Magic. 1999, Scholastic paper $15.95 (978-0-590-55359-9). In this fantasy, Briar, a former street urchin and petty thief, and his teacher, Rosethorn, search for the cause of a deadly plague that is sweeping through their land. (Rev: BL 2/15/99; HBG 10/99; SLJ 3/99; VOYA 6/99)

9498 Pierce, Tamora. *Daja's Book* (5–9). Series: Circle of Magic. 1998, Scholastic paper $15.95 (978-0-590-55358-2). 234pp. Daja, a mage-in-training, uses her magical powers to create a living vine out of metal, and soon members of the nomadic Traders want to possess it. (Rev: BCCB 12/98; BL 12/1/98; HBG 3/99; SLJ 12/98; VOYA 2/99)

9499 Pierce, Tamora. *Magic Steps* (5–9). Series: The Circle Opens. 2000, Scholastic paper $16.95 (978-0-590-39588-5). 272pp. Fourteen-year-old Sandry and her friend Pasco use their magic to stop the murders of local merchants. (Rev: BCCB 3/00; BL 3/1/00; HB 5/00; HBG 10/00; SLJ 4/00)

9500 Pierce, Tamora. *Tris's Book* (5–9). Series: Circle of Magic. 1998, Scholastic paper $15.95 (978-0-590-55357-5). 251pp. Tris and her three fellow mages combine forces to fight the pirates who are threatening to destroy their home in this sequel to *Sandry's Book.* (Rev: BCCB 4/98; BL 8/98; HBG 10/98; SLJ 4/98; VOYA 8/98)

9501 Pilkey, Dav. *Captain Underpants and the Big, Bad Battle of the Bionic Booger Boy: Part 1: The Night of the Nasty Nostril Nuggets* (2–4). Illus. by author. 2003, Scholastic $16.95 (978-0-439-37609-9); paper $5.99 (978-0-439-37610-5). 173pp. The superhero and sidekicks George and Harold face off against Melvin Sneedley, who's transformed himself into the Bionic Booger Boy. A sequel is *Captain Underpants and the Big, Bad Battle of the Bionic Booger Boy, Part 2: The Revenge of the Ridiculous Robo-Boogers* (2003). (Rev: HBG 4/04; SLJ 1/04)

9502 Pilkey, Dav. *Ricky Ricotta's Giant Robot vs. the Voodoo Vultures from Venus* (2–4). Illus. by Martin Ontiveros. 2001, Scholastic $16.95 (978-0-439-23624-9). 125pp. Ricky the mouse and his giant robot friend tackle villains from Venus with dastardly plans. (Rev: HBG 10/01; SLJ 5/01)

9503 Pilkey, Dav. *Ricky Ricotta's Mighty Robot vs. the Jurassic Jackrabbits from Jupiter* (2–4). Illus. by Martin Ontiveros. 2002, Scholastic paper $3.99 (978-0-439-37643-3). 127pp. Ricky, his Mighty Robot, and cousin Lucy defeat General Jackrabbit, an invader from Jupiter with nefarious intent. (Rev: SLJ 12/02)

9504 Pilkey, Dav. *Ricky Ricotta's Mighty Robot vs. the Mecha-Monkeys from Mars* (2–4). Illus. by Martin Ontiveros. 2002, Scholastic paper $3.99 (978-0-439-25296-6). 143pp. Ricky and his robot friend battle the fiendish forces of an evil Martian monkey. (Rev: HBG 10/02; SLJ 4/02)

9505 Pilkey, Dav. *Ricky Ricotta's Mighty Robot vs. the Uranium Unicorns from Uranus* (1–3). Illus. by Martin Ricotta. Series: Ricky Ricotta. 2005, Scholastic $16.99 (978-0-439-37646-4); paper $4.99 (978-0-439-37647-1). 125pp. Ricky the mouse and his Mighty Robot must foil Uncle Unicorn's evil plot to take over the world. (Rev: SLJ 1/06)

9506 Pipe, Jim. *The Werewolf* (4–7). Illus. Series: In the Footsteps Of. 1996, Millbrook LB $24.90 (978-0-7613-0450-0). 40pp. A horror story in which Bernard, a werewolf, commits terrible acts under the influence of a full moon. (Rev: SLJ 7/96)

9507 Poblocki, Dan. *The Stone Child* (4–6). 2009, Random $15.99 (978-0-375-84254-2). 288pp. Strange things happen when 12-year-old Eddie and his family move to Gatesweed, where horror writer Nathaniel Olmstead lived before he went missing 13 years before. (Rev: BLO 5/27/09; SLJ 11/09)

9508 Porte, Barbara Ann. *Hearsay: Tales from the Middle Kingdom* (5–8). Illus. 1998, Greenwillow $15.00 (978-0-688-15381-6). Each of these 15 entertaining fantasies contains elements of Chinese folklore and culture. (Rev: BCCB 5/98; HBG 10/98; SLJ 6/98)

9509 Potter, Ellen. *Olivia Kidney* (4–6). Illus. by Peter Reynolds. 2003, Penguin $15.99 (978-0-399-23850-5). 160pp. When Olivia's father lands a job as superintendent of a New York City apartment block, the 12-year-old finds the building is full of strange and wonderful characters. (Rev: BL 6/1–15/03; HB 9/03; HBG 4/04; SLJ 6/03)

9510 Potter, Ellen. *Olivia Kidney and the Exit Academy* (4–7). Illus. by Peter H. Reynolds. Series: Olivia Kidney. 2005, Putnam $15.99 (978-0-399-24162-8). 256pp. After her brother's death, Olivia and her father move into a creepy apartment building where, she discovers, people go to rehearse their deaths. (Rev: BL 3/15/05; SLJ 5/05)

9511 Potter, Ellen. *Olivia Kidney and the Secret Beneath the City* (5–7). Series: Olivia Kidney. 2007, Philomel $16.99 (978-0-399-24701-9). 336pp. Twelve-year-old Olivia is starting 7th grade at a new arts school and also dealing with other problems real and surreal in this third book in the series. (Rev: BL 5/1/07; SLJ 6/07)

9512 Pratchett, Terry. *Johnny and the Dead* (5–8). Series: Johnny Maxwell. 2006, HarperCollins LB $16.89 (978-0-06-054189-7). 224pp. In the funny second volume of this trilogy, ghosts of the "post-senior citizens" buried in a local cemetery ask the title character to help block plans to bulldoze their final resting place. (Rev: BL 12/15/05; HB 1/06; SLJ 12/05; VOYA 2/06)

9513 Pratchett, Terry. *Only You Can Save Mankind* (5–8). 2005, HarperCollins LB $17.89 (978-0-06-054186-6). 224pp. It's up to Johnny to save the aliens in a new computer game, and the situation forces him to do some thinking about the very nature of war. (Rev: BL 4/15/05*; SLJ 10/05)

9514 Prevost, Guillaume. *The Book of Time* (5–8). Trans. by William Rodarmor. Series: The Book of Time. 2007, Scholastic $16.99 (978-0-439-88375-7). 215pp. Sam travels through time — to medieval Scotland, World War I France, and ancient Egypt — to find his missing father and finally discovers he's being held captive in Dracula's castle in this first installment in the series. The second installment is *The Gate of Days* (2008). (Rev: BCCB 9/07; BL 7/07; HB 9/07; SLJ 11/07) ⌒

9515 Primavera, Elise. *The Secret Order of the Gumm Street Girls* (4–7). Illus. 2006, HarperCollins $16.99 (978-0-06-056946-4). 464pp. Four girls who live on Gumm Street have little in common until a series of incidents appear to threaten their picturesque town of Sherbet and Franny, Pru, Cat, and Ivy find themselves on a very Oz-like adventure. (Rev: BL 12/15/06; SLJ 12/06)

9516 Prineas, Sarah. *The Magic Thief* (4–6). 2008, HarperCollins $16.99 (978-0-06-137587-3). 426pp. A young thief named Conn picks the pocket of the wizard Nevery and becomes the magician's apprentice; the first volume in a trilogy. (Rev: BCCB 7–8/08; BL 5/15/08; HB 9/08; SLJ 6/08)

9517 Prior, Natalie Jane. *Lily Quench and the Lighthouse of Skellig Mor* (3–5). Illus. by Janine Daw-son. 2004, Puffin paper $4.99 (978-0-14-240059-3). 160pp. Lily Quench and Dragon Queen continue to face danger and challenges in their efforts to save the land of Ashby in this fourth volume in the series. (Rev: SLJ 11/04)

9518 Proysen, Alf. *Little Old Mrs. Pepperpot and Other Stories* (3–5). 1960, Astor-Honor $14.95 (978-0-8392-3021-2). The story of a woman who can shrink to the size of a pepper pot.

9519 Prue, Sally. *Cold Tom* (4–8). 2003, Scholastic $15.95 (978-0-439-48268-4). 192pp. Tom has disabilities that make him an outcast, and he flees from his elfin tribe to the city inhabited by demons (humans), where he is confronted with his human side. (Rev: BL 9/15/03; HB 7/03*; HBG 10/03; SLJ 9/03*; VOYA 10/03)

9520 Pullman, Philip. *Lyra's Oxford* (5–8). Illus. by John Lawrence. 2003, Knopf $10.95 (978-0-375-82819-5). 64pp. This slim volume takes readers back to the world of Pullman's His Dark Materials trilogy, with maps, postcards, and other ephemera. (Rev: BL 2/1/04; SLJ 1/04; VOYA 6/04)

9521 Pyle, Howard. *The Garden Behind the Moon: A Real Story of the Moon Angel* (4–6). Illus. by author. 1988, Parabola paper $10.95 (978-0-930407-22-3). 180pp. A boy follows the path of the moonlight and visits the Moon-Angel and the Man-in-the-Moon in this fantasy. A reissue of the 1895 edition.

9522 Quinn, Zoe. *The Caped 6th Grader: Happy Birthday, Hero!* (4–6). Illus. by Brie Spangler. 2006, Random LB $11.99 (978-0-385-90304-2); paper $4.99 (978-0-440-42079-8). 135pp. Zoe Richards has just turned 12 when she finds out she has inherited a gene that gives her super powers; she now must work out how to keep this secret and live her normal life. (Rev: SLJ 9/06)

9523 Radunsky, Vladimir. *I Love You Dude* (2–4). Illus. 2005, Harcourt $16.00 (978-0-15-205176-1). 48pp. Dude, a young girl's doodle of a blue elephant on the wall of a New York City building, escapes cleanup by the anti-graffiti squad and sets off to find acceptance and a home. (Rev: BL 12/1/05; SLJ 10/05)

9524 Raham, Gary. *The Deep Time Diaries: As Recorded by Neesha and Jon Olifee* (4–6). Illus. by author. 2000, Fulcrum paper $17.95 (978-1-55591-415-8). 82pp. The author supplements the fictional diaries of a 22nd-century family of time travelers with notes, maps, interesting sites, and related activities. (Rev: SLJ 4/01)

9525 Ransom, Candice F. *Bones in the Badlands* (2–4). Illus. by Greg Call. Series: Time Spies. 2006, Wizards of the Coast paper $4.99 (978-0-7869-4028-8). (111pp. In the second volume of this time-travel series, Alex, Mattie, and Sophie find themselves in the Badlands at the close of the 19th century and help a paleontologist protect a cache of dinosaur bones from thieves. (Rev: SLJ 2/07)

9526 Ransom, Candice F. *Secret in the Tower* (2–4). Illus. by Greg Call. Series: Time Spies. 2006, Wizards of the Coast paper $4.99 (978-0-7869-4027-1). 112pp. In the opening book of this time-travel fantasy series, siblings Alex, Mattie, and Sophie find an antique spyglass that transports them back in time to the Revolutionary Battle of Yorktown in 1781. (Rev: SLJ 2/07)

9527 Ratnett, Michael. *Dracula Steps Out* (3–5). Illus. by June Goulding. 1998, Orchard $15.95 (978-0-531-30100-5). Dracula riddles and jokes are included in this interactive book where Dracula pops up in different places. (Rev: BL 1/1–15/99)

9528 Redmond, Shirley Raye. *Grampa and the Ghost* (3–5). 1994, Avon paper $3.50 (978-0-380-77382-4). 82pp. When Mark and Sibyl advertise for a ghost writer, they get an assistant from beyond the grave named Tallulah. (Rev: SLJ 7/94)

9529 Rees, Celia. *The Soul Taker* (5–8). 2004, Hodder paper $7.95 (978-0-340-87817-0). 152pp. Lewis, overweight and lacking confidence, finds himself in thrall to a sinister toy maker. (Rev: BL 1/1–15/04)

9530 Reiche, Dietlof. *Freddy in Peril* (2–5). Trans. by John Brownjohn. Illus. by Joe Cepeda. 2004, Scholastic $16.95 (978-0-439-53155-9). 208pp. When an evil professor threatens to kidnap Freddy, the golden hamster prodigy, an odd assortment of friends and strangers comes to the hamster's aid. (Rev: BL 4/1/04; SLJ 5/04)

9531 Reiche, Dietlof. *Freddy to the Rescue: Book Three in the Golden Hamster Saga* (3–5). Trans. from German by John Brownjohn. Illus. by Joe Cepeda. Series: Golden Hamster Saga. 2005, Scholastic $16.95 (978-0-439-53157-3). 235pp. It's up to talented golden hamster Freddy (and his cat and a few guinea pigs) to save a tribe of field hamsters in the third book in this funny series. (Rev: SLJ 9/05)

9532 Reiss, Kathryn. *Sweet Miss Honeywell's Revenge* (4–7). 2004, Harcourt $17.00 (978-0-15-216574-1). 288pp. A haunted dollhouse, a parallel story about the original owner of the antique, and the problems of blended family life are intertwined in this story about 12-year-old Zibby Thorne. (Rev: BL 5/1/04; SLJ 8/04)

9533 Richardson, Bill. *After Hamelin* (4–8). 2000, Annick $19.95 (978-1-55037-629-6). 144pp. In this entertaining fantasy that is a follow-up to the Pied Piper of Hamelin story, Penelope gets the gift of Deep Dreaming and is able to enter the Piper's secret world in the hope of rescuing the children. (Rev: BL 2/15/01; SLJ 4/01; VOYA 4/01)

9534 Richemont, Enid. *The Time Tree* (4–6). 1990, Little, Brown $12.95 (978-0-316-74452-2). 96pp. A girl from the 16th century visits the 20th and takes back the skills she has learned. (Rev: BCCB 5/90; BL 8/90; SLJ 6/90)

9535 Riddell, Chris. *Ottoline and the Yellow Cat* (2–4). Illus. by author. 2008, HarperCollins $10.99 (978-0-06-144879-9). 176pp. With extensive, engaging illustrations, this is the story of Ottoline Brown's investigation — with the help of her hairy sidekick Mr. Monroe — into the mystery of missing dogs. (Rev: BL 5/15/08; SLJ 7/08)

9536 Riordan, Rick. *The Last Olympian* (4–8). Series: Percy Jackson and the Olympians. 2009,

Hyperion $17.99 (978-1-4231-0147-5). 314pp. In this final installment in the series, demigod Percy is approaching his important 16th birthday as he moves to protect New York City. (Rev: BL 5/15/09; HB 7/09; SLJ 6/09; VOYA 6/09) ∩

9537 Roach, Marilynne K. *Encounters with the Invisible World* (5–9). Illus. by author. 1977, Amereon $18.95 (978-0-89190-874-6). Spooky stories about witches, demons, spells, and ghosts in New England.

9538 Roberts, Katherine. *Crystal Mask* (5–8). Series: The Echorium Sequence. 2002, Scholastic paper $15.95 (978-0-439-33864-6). 256pp. The Singers, a group of people who maintain peace in the world through their unusual powers, are confronted by evildoers known as the Frazhin. Also use *Dark Quetzal* (2003). (Rev: BL 4/15/02; HBG 10/02; SLJ 3/02)

9539 Robertson, Barbara. *Rosemary and the Island Treasure: Back to 1947* (3–6). Illus. Series: The Hourglass Adventures. 2001, Winslow paper $4.95 (978-1-890817-58-9). 113pp. Rosemary travels back in time to meet her grandmother — another Rosemary — on an island in the Bahamas, where together they search for treasure. Also use *Rosemary at Sea: Back to 1919*, which takes place on the *Mauretania*. (Rev: SLJ 2/02)

9540 Robertson, Barbara. *Rosemary Meets Rosemarie: Berlin in 1870* (4–6). Illus. 2001, Winslow paper $5.95 (978-1-890817-55-8). 125pp. For her tenth birthday, Rosemary Rita receives a magical hourglass that whisks her back in time to 1870 Berlin where she meets her 10-year-old great-great-great-grandmother and the two solve a mystery. Also use *Rosemary in Paris: Back to 1889* (2001). (Rev: SLJ 10/01)

9541 Rodda, Emily. *The Charm Bracelet* (2–5). Illus. by Raoul Vitale. Series: Fairy Realm. 2003, HarperCollins LB $15.89 (978-0-06-009584-0). 128pp. Queen Jessica must return from the mortal world to renew the magical powers of the realm; when the wicked Valda tries to stop her, Jessica's granddaughter Jessie uses her cleverness, a few helping hands, and some magic to save the day. (Rev: BL 1/1–15/03; HBG 10/03; SLJ 8/03)

9542 Rodda, Emily. *The Key to Rondo* (4–7). 2008, Scholastic $16.99 (978-0-545-03535-4). 333pp. A magic music box takes Leo and his cousin Mimi to the land of Rondo, home to fairy-tale characters and an evil queen. (Rev: BL 12/15/07; SLJ 4/08)

9543 Rodda, Emily. *The Pigs Are Flying* (4–6). Illus. by Noela Young. 1988, Greenwillow paper $2.95 (978-0-380-70555-9). 160pp. Rachel's friend Burt, who has come to cheer her when she has a cold, makes her believe in the impossible. (Rev: BL 10/1/88; HB 11/88)

9544 Rodda, Emily. *Rowan and the Keeper of the Crystal* (3–6). Series: Rowan of Rin. 2002, HarperCollins LB $16.89 (978-0-06-029777-0). 208pp. Rowan must take on his mother's duties to choose the next Keeper of the Crystal after she is poisoned in this third book in the series. (Rev: BCCB 4/02; BL 1/1–15/02; HB 3/02; HBG 10/02; SLJ 5/02)

9545 Roden, Katie. *The Mummy* (3–6). Illus. Series: In the Footsteps Of. 1996, Millbrook LB $21.90 (978-0-7613-0451-7). 40pp. Fiction and fact mix in this account of mummification and a horror story about King Tut's tomb. (Rev: SLJ 5/96)

9546 Rodgers, Mary, and Heather Hach. *Freaky Monday* (4–7). 2009, HarperCollins $15.99 (978-0-06-166478-6). 192pp. Switching bodies presents some challenges and some welcome changes for a 13-year-old-girl and her teacher; a successor to 1972's *Freaky Friday*. (Rev: BLO 4/14/09; SLJ 6/09)

9547 Rogers, Jonathan. *The Secret of the Swamp King* (4–6). 2005, Broadman & Holman $9.97 (978-0-8054-3132-2). 229pp. Worried that the giant-slaying hero Aidan may be growing too popular, King Darrow dispatches the teenager on an impossible mission. (Rev: SLJ 11/05)

9548 Rollins, James. *Jake Ransom and the Skull King's Shadow* (5–8). 2009, HarperCollins $16.99 (978-0-06-147379-1). 416pp. Jake Ransom and his older sister receive a package that may be linked to the disappearance of their archaeologist parents and find themselves transported into a strange and dangerous world. (Rev: BL 3/15/09) ∩

9549 Rowling, J. K. *Harry Potter and the Chamber of Secrets* (4–8). 1999, Scholastic $22.99 (978-0-439-06486-6). 352pp. During his second year at Hogwarts School of Witchcraft and Wizardry, Harry is baffled when he hears noises no one else can. (Rev: BCCB 9/99; BL 5/15/99*; HB 7/99; HBG 10/99; SLJ 7/99; VOYA 10/99)

9550 Rowling, J. K. *Harry Potter and the Goblet of Fire* (4–9). 2000, Scholastic $29.99 (978-0-439-13959-5). 734pp. This, the fourth installment of Harry Potter's adventures, begins when Voldemort tries to regain the power he lost in his failed attempt to kill Harry. (Rev: BL 8/00*; HB 11/00; HBG 3/01; SLJ 8/00)

9551 Rowling, J. K. *Harry Potter and the Half-Blood Prince* (5–12). Illus. by Mary GrandPré. 2005, Scholastic LB $34.99 (978-0-439-78677-5). 672pp. In this sixth and penultimate volume, Harry, now 16, begins mapping a strategy to defeat the evil Lord Voldemort. (Rev: BL 8/05*; SLJ 9/05; VOYA 10/05)

9552 Rowling, J. K. *Harry Potter and the Order of the Phoenix* (4–12). 2003, Scholastic LB $34.99 (978-0-439-56761-9). 870pp. Adolescence, adult hypocrisy, and the deadly threat of Voldemort and his evil supporters combine to make Harry's fifth year at Hogwarts as eventful as ever. (Rev: BL 7/03; HB 9/03; HBG 10/03; SLJ 8/03; VOYA 8/03)

9553 Rowling, J. K. *Harry Potter and the Prisoner of Azkaban* (4–8). Illus. by Mary GrandPré. 1999, Scholastic $22.99 (978-0-439-13635-8). 448pp. In this third thrilling adventure, a murderer has escaped from prison and is after our young hero. (Rev: BCCB 10/99; BL 9/1/99*; HB 11/99; HBG 3/00; SLJ 10/99)

9554 Rowling, J. K. *Harry Potter and the Sorcerer's Stone* (4–8). Illus. 1998, Scholastic $22.99 (978-0-590-35340-3). In this humorous and suspenseful story, 11-year-old Harry Potter attends the Hogwarts School for Witchcraft and Wizardry, where he discovers that he is a wizard just as his parents had been and that someone at the school is trying to steal a valuable stone with the power to make people immortal. (Rev: BCCB 11/98; BL 9/15/98; HB 1/99; HBG 3/99; SLJ 10/98; VOYA 12/98)

9555 Rowling, J. K. *The Tales of Beedle the Bard* (5–8). Illus. by author. 2008, Scholastic $12.99 (978-0-545-12828-5). 128pp. Professor Dumbledore's collection of five fairy tales, which he bequeathed to Hermione, will be enjoyed and then reevaluated as readers get to Dumbledore's accompanying commentary. (Rev: BCCB 3/09; BL 1/1–15/09; HB 3/09; SLJ 3/09)

9556 Ruby, Laura. *The Chaos King* (5–8). 2007, HarperCollins $16.99 (978-0-06-075258-3). 325pp. In this sequel to *The Wall and the Wing* (2006), Gurl — called Georgie now that she has been reunited with her parents — and her friend Bug must put aside their temporary differences and cope with myriad challenges. (Rev: BCCB 9/07; SLJ 11/07) ∩

9557 Ruiz, Joseph J. *The Little Ghost Who Wouldn't Go Away / El pequeño fantasma que no queria irse* (2–4). Trans. by Juan S. Lucero. Illus. by Kris Hotvedt. 2000, Sunstone paper $10.95 (978-0-86534-303-0). 95pp. The ghost of a young boy gets the help of Rebecca Garcia to locate his missing tombstone so he can rest in peace in this story in both Spanish and English. (Rev: SLJ 1/01)

9558 Runton, Andy. *Owly: Just a Little Blue* (3–5). Illus. Series: Owly. 2005, Top Shelf paper $10.00 (978-1-891830-64-8). 128pp. Owly and his friend Wormy try to help a bluebird whose habitat is endangered, but their overtures of friendship are at first rebuffed. (Rev: BL 7/05; SLJ 3/06)

9559 Runton, Andy. *Owly: The Way Home and the Bittersweet Summer* (3–5). Illus. 2004, Top Shelf paper $10.00 (978-1-891830-62-4). 160pp. Two sweet and simple graphic novellas feature lonely Owly the Owl and her new friend Wormy. (Rev: BL 2/1/05)

9560 Rupp, Rebecca. *Journey to the Blue Moon: In Which Time Is Lost and Then Found Again* (5–8). 2006, Candlewick $15.99 (978-0-7636-2544-3). 264pp. A multilayered story in which Alex loses his grandfather's pocket watch and takes a trip to the blue moon, where all things lost go; there he finds other searchers and a group that threatens his chances of returning home. (Rev: BL 12/1/06; SLJ 10/06)

9561 Rupp, Rebecca. *The Return of the Dragon* (3–6). 2005, Candlewick $15.99 (978-0-7636-2377-7). 160pp. In this engaging sequel to *The Dragon of Lonely Island* (1998), the Davis siblings return to the island and discover that their friend Fafnyr, a three-headed dragon, is being pursued by an unscrupulous billionaire named J. P. King. (Rev: BL 9/1/05; SLJ 12/05)

9562 Rylant, Cynthia. *The Bird House* (2–4). Illus. by Barry Moser. 1998, Scholastic $16.95 (978-0-590-47345-3). 32pp. In this charming fantasy, a young girl gradually forms a friendship with an old lady because of birds' intervention. (Rev: BL 10/15/98; HBG 3/99; SLJ 9/98)

9563 Rylant, Cynthia. *The Heavenly Village* (4–7). 1999, Scholastic paper $15.95 (978-0-439-04096-9). 96pp. A special book about the Heavenly Village — a place where some people stay who are not sure about going to heaven — and about some of the people who live in this in-between world. (Rev: BL 12/1/99*; HBG 3/00; SLJ 3/00; VOYA 2/00)

9564 Rylant, Cynthia. *The High-Rise Private Eyes: The Case of the Puzzling Possum* (2–4). Illus. by G. Brian Karas. 2001, Greenwillow $16.99 (978-0-688-16308-2). 48pp. In this beginning chapter book, the mystery of why a trombone is continually stolen and returned is solved by detective Bunny Brown and her bumbling sidekick, the raccoon named Jack. (Rev: BL 12/1/00; HB 3/01; HBG 10/01)

9565 Rylant, Cynthia. *The Whale* (2–4). Illus. by Preston McDaniels. Series: The Lighthouse Family. 2003, Simon & Schuster $14.95 (978-0-689-84881-0). 64pp. In this sequel to *The Lighthouse Family: The Storm*, mouse children Lila and Whistler, with the help of a grumpy cormorant, seek to reunite a lost baby whale with his mother. (Rev: BL 9/1/03; HBG 4/04; SLJ 11/03)

9566 Sage, Angie. *Book One: Magyk* (5–8). Illus. by Mark Zug. 2005, HarperCollins LB $18.89 (978-0-06-057732-2). 576pp. A fantasy of magic, spells, and evil forces, focusing on young Jenna, who was raised by Septimus Heap's family and who now must flee the evil Supreme Custodian. (Rev: BL 3/15/05; SLJ 4/05)

9567 Sage, Angie. *Flyte* (5–8). Illus. by Mark Zug. Series: Septimus Heap. 2006, HarperCollins $17.99 (978-0-06-057734-6). 544pp. In this fast-paced sequel to *Magyk* (2005), wizard Septimus must protect Princess Jenna from numerous dangers; a CD includes games. (Rev: BL 5/15/06; SLJ 6/06; VOYA 2/06)

9568 Sage, Angie. *My Haunted House* (2–4). Illus. by Jimmy Pickering. Series: Araminta Spookie. 2006, HarperCollins $8.99 (978-0-06-077481-3). 132pp. Living in a haunted house suits Araminta Spookie just fine, so she's understandably upset when her Aunt Tabby announces she plans to sell the house. (Rev: SLJ 2/07) ∩

9569 Sage, Angie. *Physik* (5–8). Series: Septimus Heap. 2007, HarperCollins $17.99 (978-0-06-057737-7). 560pp. When Septimus Heap, apprenticed to a wizard, inadvertently releases the spirit of an evil queen who lived centuries earlier, the ill-tempered monarch unleashes chaos in the kingdom; the third book in the series. (Rev: BL 4/1/07; SLJ 6/07) ∩

9570 Sage, Angie. *Queste* (5–8). Series: Septimus Heap. 2008, HarperCollins $17.99 (978-0-06-088207-5). 608pp. In the fourth book of the series, Septimus is sent on a dangerous Queste and tries to rescue his brother Nicko. (Rev: BL 5/15/08; SLJ 6/08)

9571 Sage, Angie. *The Sword in the Grotto* (2–4). Illus. by Jimmy Pickering. Series: Araminta Spook-ie. 2006, HarperCollins $8.99 (978-0-06-077484-4). 146pp. In the second book in the series, Araminta and her friend Wanda Wizzard run into trouble when they try to retrieve a sword from a grotto to present to the ghostly Sir Horace for his 500th birthday. (Rev: SLJ 2/07)

9572 St. John, Lauren. *The White Giraffe* (5–8). Illus. by David Dean. 2007, Dial $16.99 (978-0-8037-3211-7). 192pp. After the tragic death of her parents, 11-year-old Martine is sent to live with her grandmother on a large game preserve in South Africa, where she discovers her mystical gifts and exposes poachers who are hunting a rare white giraffe. (Rev: BL 6/1–15/07; LMC 11/07; SLJ 6/07)

9573 Sampson, Fay. *Pangur Ban: The White Cat* (5–8). Series: Pangur Ban. 2003, Lion paper $7.95 (978-0-7459-4763-1). 160pp. A Welsh cat and an Irish monk encounter princesses and mermaids in this fantasy set in the Middle Ages. (Rev: BL 5/15/03; SLJ 11/03)

9574 Sampson, Fay. *Shape-Shifter: The Naming of Pangur Ban* (5–8). Series: Pangur Ban. 2003, Lion paper $7.95 (978-0-7459-4762-4). 160pp. A Welsh cat pursued by witches befriends an Irish monk in this first book in the series. (Rev: BL 5/15/03)

9575 Sanderson, Brandon. *Alcatraz Versus the Evil Librarians* (5–8). 2007, Scholastic $16.99 (978-0-439-92550-1). 308pp. Alcatraz is a 13-year-old boy with unusual powers and a tendency to insert his own thoughts into the narrative, and the librarians are insidious censors of information; fast-paced antics ensure. (Rev: BCCB 2/08; HB 1/08; SLJ 11/07)

9576 Sanderson, Brandon. *Alcatraz Versus the Scrivener's Bones* (5–9). 2008, Scholastic $16.99 (978-0-439-92553-2). 320pp. Alcatraz Smedry and his companions face many obstacles as they try to rescue his father from the Library of Alexandria; a pun-filled, humorous fantasy. (Rev: HB 11/08; SLJ 12/08; VOYA 10/08)

9577 San Souci, Robert D. *Dare to Be Scared: Thirteen Stories to Chill and Thrill* (4–8). Illus. by David Ouimet. 2003, Cricket $15.95 (978-0-8126-2688-9). 168pp. A baker's dozen of spooky stories suitable for this age group that feature diverse characters. (Rev: BL 10/1/03; HBG 10/03; SLJ 9/03)

9578 Saunders, Kate. *The Little Secret* (3–6). Illus. by William Carman. 2009, Feiwel & Friends $16.99 (978-0-312-36961-3). 240pp. Eleven-year-old Jane's visit to her new friend's home on a Scottish island turns into adventure when she enters another dimension. (Rev: BL 5/15/09; LMC 10/09; SLJ 8/09)

9579 Say, Allen. *Stranger in the Mirror* (3–6). Illus. 1995, Houghton $16.95 (978-0-395-61590-4). 32pp. In this fantasy, Sam one morning discovers that he has the face of an old, wrinkled man. (Rev: BCCB 11/95; BL 10/1/95; SLJ 10/95*)

9580 Schade, Susan. *Travels of Thelonious* (4–7). Illus. by Jon Buller. 2006, Simon & Schuster $14.95 (978-0-689-87684-4). 208pp. This is the engaging, imaginative story of Thelonious, a squirrel who discovers the ruins of a city and searches for clues to the mystery of why humans disappeared. (Rev: BL 4/15/06; SLJ 7/06)

9581 Schaeffer, Susan F. *The Dragons of North Chittendon* (5–7). Illus. by Darcy May. 1986, Simon & Schuster paper $2.95 (978-0-685-14462-6). The story of Arthur, an unruly dragon, and his ESP relationship with the boy Patrick in a story of humans and dragons in and above North Chittendon, Vermont. (Rev: BL 8/86; SLJ 9/86)

9582 Schmidt, Gary D. *Pilgrim's Progress* (4–7). Illus. by Barry Moser. 1994, Eerdmans $22.00 (978-0-8028-5080-5). 88pp. A simple retelling of the classic in which Christian leaves his home to find the Celestial City. (Rev: BL 11/1/94; SLJ 12/94)

9583 Schmidt, Gary D. *Straw into Gold* (5–8). 2001, Clarion $15.00 (978-0-618-05601-9). 172pp. Two boys set off to find the answer to the king's riddle and thereby save the lives of rebels, only to discover much more than they had expected. (Rev: BCCB 9/01; HBG 10/01; SLJ 8/01; VOYA 2/02)

9584 Schwartz, Alvin. *Scary Stories 3: More Tales to Chill Your Bones* (4–7). Illus. by Stephen Gammell. 1991, HarperCollins LB $17.89 (978-0-06-021795-2); paper $5.99 (978-0-06-440418-1). 128pp. A modernized version of spooky tales handed down through the years. (Rev: BL 8/91; HB 11/91; SLJ 11/91)

9585 Scieszka, Jon. *Hey Kid, Want to Buy a Bridge?* (3–6). Illus. by Adam McCauley. 2002, Viking $15.99 (978-0-670-89916-6). 80pp. The Time Warp Trio is transported back to 1877 in their hometown of Brooklyn and gets to meet Thomas Edison and watch the building of the Brooklyn Bridge. (Rev: BL 2/1/02; HBG 10/02; SLJ 3/02)

9586 Scieszka, Jon. *Me Oh Maya* (2–6). Illus. by Adam McCauley. Series: Time Warp Trio. 2003, Penguin $14.99 (978-0-670-03629-5). 80pp. The Time Warp Trio turn up in Chichen Itza and must derail an evil high priest's plans to sacrifice them to please the harvest gods. (Rev: BL 9/15/03; HBG 4/04; SLJ 12/03)

9587 Scieszka, Jon. *Oh Say, I Can't See* (3–5). Illus. by Adam McCauley. Series: Time Warp Trio. 2005, Viking $14.99 (978-0-670-06025-2). 80pp. The three young time travelers play a key role in George Washington's decision to cross the Delaware River on Christmas Day in 1776. (Rev: BL 11/15/05; SLJ 11/05)

9588 Scieszka, Jon. *Sam Samurai* (4–6). Illus. by Adam McCauley. Series: Time Warp Trio. 2001, Viking $14.99 (978-0-670-89915-9). 80pp. While working on an assignment to write a haiku, the Time Warp Trio is accidentally transported back to 17th-century Japan in this wacky time-travel adventure. (Rev: BL 11/1/01; HBG 3/02; SLJ 11/01)

9589 Scieszka, Jon. *Summer Reading Is Killing Me* (3–6). Illus. by Lane Smith. 1998, Viking $15.99 (978-0-670-88041-6). 80pp. In this hilarious adventure, the Time Warp Trio get mixed up with characters from books on a summer reading list, such as Dracula, Winnie the Pooh, Long John Silver, and Frankenstein. (Rev: BL 6/1–15/98; HBG 3/99; SLJ 8/98)

9590 Scieszka, Jon. *Time Warp Trio: The High and the Flighty* (3–5). Adapted by Catherine Hapka & Lisa Rao. Illus. by author. Series: Time Warp Trio. 2007, HarperCollins $15.99 (978-0-06-111644-5); paper $3.99 (978-0-06-111643-8). 48pp. Based on a TV show made of the original series, this installment takes the time travelers back to Amelia Earhart's day. (Rev: SLJ 7/07)

9591 Scieszka, Jon. *Tut, Tut* (4–6). Illus. by Lane Smith. 1996, Viking $14.99 (978-0-670-84832-4). 80pp. The Time Warp Trio find themselves in ancient Egypt in the clutches of the pharaoh's evil priest. (Rev: BL 10/1/96; SLJ 9/04)

9592 Scieszka, Jon. *Viking It and Liking It* (2–4). Illus. by Adam McCauley. 2002, Viking $14.99 (978-0-670-89918-0). 80pp. The Time Warp Trio is thrown into the world of the Vikings and meets challenges including a feisty Leif Ericksson and meals of whale blubber. (Rev: BL 12/1/02; HBG 3/03; SLJ 1/03)

9593 Scieszka, Jon. *You Can't, but Genghis Khan* (2–5). Adapted by Jennifer Frantz. Illus. Series: Time Warp Trio. 2006, HarperTrophy paper $4.99 (978-0-06-111636-0). 74pp. The Time Warp Trio — Fred, Joe, and Sam — return in an adaptation from the TV series, in which they travel back to 13th-century Mongolia and are rescued from a battle by a young Genghis Khan. (Rev: SLJ 1/07)

9594 Scott, Deborah. *The Kid Who Got Zapped Through Time* (4–7). 1997, Avon $14.00 (978-0-380-97356-9). 160pp. In this humorous time-travel fantasy, Flattop Kincaid is transported to England during the Middle Ages, where he becomes a serf. (Rev: BL 11/1/97; SLJ 9/97)

9595 Seabrooke, Brenda. *Stonewolf* (5–8). 2005, Holiday $16.95 (978-0-8234-1848-0). 231pp. Young orphan Nicholas is taken captive by a group called the Synod but manages to escape, taking with him a sought-after secret formula. (Rev: BL 3/15/05; SLJ 3/05)

9596 Seabrooke, Brenda. *The Vampire in My Bathtub* (4–7). 1999, Holiday $16.95 (978-0-8234-1505-2). 150pp. After 13-year-old Jeff moves to a new home with his mother, he finds a friendly vampire hidden inside an old trunk. (Rev: BL 1/1–15/00; HBG 3/00; SLJ 12/99)

9597 Seidler, Tor. *Gully's Travels* (4–7). Illus. by Brock Cole. 2008, Scholastic $16.95 (978-0-5450-2506-5). 192pp. Spoiled dog Gulliver's life of luxury is turned upside-down when his master falls for an allergic Frenchwoman and hands the dog over to the doorman. (Rev: BL 9/1/08*; HB 9/08; LMC 1/09; SLJ 8/08)

9598 Seidler, Tor. *Mean Margaret* (4–6). Illus. by Jon Agee. 1997, HarperCollins LB $14.89 (978-0-06-205091-5). 176pp. Two newly married woodchucks decide to adopt a human child who has made her parents' life miserable. (Rev: BL 12/1/97; SLJ 11/97*)

9599 Selden, George. *The Cricket in Times Square* (3–6). Illus. by Garth Williams. 1960, Farrar $16.00 (978-0-374-31650-1). 160pp. A Connecticut cricket is transported in a picnic basket to New York's

Times Square. Two sequels are: *Tucker's Country-side* (1969); *Harry Cat's Pet Puppy* (1974).

9600 Selden, George. *The Genie of Sutton Place* (5–6). 1985, Farrar paper $7.95 (978-0-374-42530-2). The summer Tim lives with his Aunt Lucy on Sutton Place in New York City, he evokes his own magical genie who works not only miracles but mishaps.

9601 Selfors, Suzanne. *Fortune's Magic Farm* (4–7). Illus. by Catia Chien. 2009, Little, Brown $14.99 (978-0-316-01818-0). 264pp. Ten-year-old Isabelle lives in a soggy place called Runny Cove but knows she came from a place called Nowhere; she leaves her home and finds herself on a journey to a magical place called Fortune's Farm. (Rev: BCCB 5/09; BL 3/15/09; SLJ 3/09)

9602 Sellier, Marie. *Legend of the Chinese Dragon* (2–5). Illus. by Catherine Louis. 2008, North-South $15.95 (978-0-7358-2152-1). 40pp. In this legend, hostile Chinese tribes overcome their differences and create a creature to protect them — the dragon. (Rev: BL 12/15/07; SLJ 12/07)

9603 Sensel, Joni, and Christian Slade. *Reality Leak* (4–6). 2007, Holt $16.95 (978-0-8050-8125-1). 217pp. Very strange things start happening when Archibald Keen arrives in Bryan's town to repair a "reality leak." (Rev: SLJ 5/07)

9604 Sepulveda, Luis. *The Story of a Seagull and the Cat Who Taught Her to Fly* (3–6). Trans. by Margaret Sayers Peden. Illus. by Chris Sheban. 2003, Scholastic $15.95 (978-0-439-40186-9). 128pp. Zorba the cat finds himself charged with the responsibilities of raising a seagull chick and teaching it to fly. (Rev: BL 9/1/03; HBG 4/04; SLJ 12/03)

9605 Service, Pamela F. *Storm at the Edge of Time* (4–6). 1994, Walker $16.95 (978-0-8027-8306-6). 192pp. Three children from different time periods are summoned to help Urkar, a Neolithic wise man. (Rev: BL 10/15/94; SLJ 12/94)

9606 Shalant, Phyllis. *Bartleby of the Big Bad Bayou* (4–6). 2005, Dutton $17.99 (978-0-525-47366-4). 160pp. Bartleby the turtle and his alligator friend Seezer, both former pets, return to bayou country but find there have been some unwelcome changes while they were away; a sequel to *Bartleby of the Mighty Mississippi* (2000). (Rev: BL 7/05; SLJ 8/05)

9607 Shalant, Phyllis. *The Great Cape Rescue* (3–5). Series: The Society of Super Secret Heroes. 2007, Dutton $15.99 (978-0-525-47404-3). 128pp. A scruffy-looking cape gives Finch and his three best friends the power to deal with school bullies and family problems, so when the cape begins talking and suggests they use its powers to help others, the boys heed its message. (Rev: BL 4/1/07)

9608 Shan, Darren. *A Living Nightmare* (5–8). Series: Cirque du Freak. 2001, Little, Brown $15.95 (978-0-316-60340-9). 272pp. A supernatural story about a young boy who visits the Cirque Du Freak and is turned into a vampire. (Rev: BL 4/15/01; HBG 10/01; SLJ 5/01; VOYA 4/01)

9609 Shan, Darren. *Lord of the Shadows* (5–10). Series: Cirque du Freak. 2006, Little, Brown $15.99 (978-0-316-15628-8). 220pp. In the 11th book in the series, part-vampire Darren faces off against Steve Leopard, leader of the Vampaneze, in a battle to determine who will be the next Lord of the Shadows. (Rev: SLJ 9/06)

9610 Shan, Darren. *Tunnels of Blood* (5–8). Series: Cirque du Freak. 2002, Little, Brown $15.95 (978-0-316-60763-6). 240pp. Darren Shan, teenage half-vampire, sets out to investigate a spate of recent killings for which he believes his vampire master might be responsible. (Rev: BL 8/02; HBG 10/02; SLJ 5/02; VOYA 6/02)

9611 Shan, Darren. *Vampire Mountain* (5–8). Series: Cirque du Freak. 2002, Little, Brown $15.95 (978-0-316-60806-0). 208pp. Darren Shan, teenage half-vampire, and his mentor travel to Vampire Mountain. The fifth, sixth, and seventh installments in the series are *Trials of Death*, *The Vampire Prince* (both 2003), and *Hunters of the Dusk* (2004). (Rev: BL 8/02; HBG 3/03; SLJ 9/02; VOYA 12/02)

9612 Shan, Darren. *The Vampire's Assistant* (5–8). Series: Cirque du Freak. 2001, Little, Brown $15.95 (978-0-316-60610-3). 256pp. The creepy, suspenseful second installment about a boy who is "half vampire" and his efforts to adjust to the world of a traveling freak show. (Rev: BL 10/15/01; HBG 3/02; SLJ 8/01; VOYA 10/01)

9613 Shearer, Alex. *Professor Sniff and the Lost Spring Breezes* (4–6). Illus. 1998, Orchard $14.95 (978-0-531-30079-4). 112pp. Sam and Lorna discover that the wind cannot blow and seek the help of Professor Sniff who owns a hurricane he brought back from Florida. (Rev: BL 4/1/98; HBG 10/98; SLJ 4/98)

9614 Shearer, Alex. *The Summer Sisters and the Dance Disaster* (3–5). Illus. 1998, Orchard LB $15.99 (978-0-531-33080-7). 112pp. The three summer sisters decide to use magic to create different kinds of weather but unfortunately get their spells mixed up. (Rev: BL 4/15/98; HBG 10/98; SLJ 5/98)

9615 Sherman, Delia. *Changeling* (5–8). 2006, Viking $16.99 (978-0-670-05967-6). 292pp. Neef, kidnapped as a baby by fairies, faces exile from her home in New York Between — an alternate Manhattan inhabited by elves, pixies, fairies, and other spirits — when she breaks the rules. (Rev: SLJ 10/06)

9616 *Showcase Presents Superman, Vol. 1* (3–8). 2005, DC Comics paper $9.99 (978-1-4012-0758-8). 560pp. This impressive volume collects 29 Superman comics published between 1959 and 1963. (Rev: SLJ 1/06)

9617 Shreve, Susan. *Ghost Cats* (4–7). 1999, Scholastic paper $14.95 (978-0-590-37131-5). 128pp. A boy, who is trying to adjust to a new family home and the loss of his five cats, is helped when the cats return as ghosts. (Rev: BCCB 12/99; BL 9/1/99; HBG 3/00; SLJ 11/99; VOYA 6/00)

9618 Shusterman, Neal. *Darkness Creeping: Twenty Twisted Tales* (5–8). 2007, Penguin paper $6.99 (978-0-14 240721-9). 304pp. Four of these creepy stories were written for this collection; others have been published before but are not easily found. (Rev: BL 5/15/07; SLJ 7/07)

9619 Sierra, Judy. *The Gruesome Guide to World Monsters* (5–8). Illus. by Henrik Drescher. 2005, Candlewick $17.99 (978-0-7636-1727-1). 64pp. A wonderfully ghoulish field guide to more than 60 monsters from world folklore, complete with Gruesomeness Ratings and Survival Tips if appropriate. (Rev: BCCB 9/05; BL 9/15/05*; HBG 4/06; LMC 1/06; SLJ 9/05)

9620 Silberberg, Alan. *Pond Scum* (4–7). 2005, Hyperion $15.99 (978-0-7868-5634-3). 304pp. Ten-year-old Oliver gains a whole new appreciation for his animal neighbors after he finds a magical gem that allows him to assume the shape of various creatures. (Rev: BL 12/1/05; SLJ 11/05)

9621 Sims, J. Michael. *Young Claus: Legend of the Boy Who Became Santa* (2–4). 1995, Cygnet Trumpeter $12.95 (978-0-9645976-6-2). 112pp. A fantasy about a young orphan who encounters many adventures in his mission to be Santa. (Rev: BL 11/15/95)

9622 Sincic, Alan. *Edward Is Only a Fish* (3–5). Illus. 1996, Holt paper $4.95 (978-0-8050-4906-0). 56pp. When the Billingsly home is flooded because of running bathwater, Edward the goldfish has a field day and a free tour of the house. (Rev: BL 1/15/95; SLJ 2/95)

9623 Sinykin, Sheri. *Giving Up the Ghost* (5–8). 2007, Peachtree $15.95 (978-1-56145-423-5). 227pp. Davia is only 13, has asthma, is worried about her mother's cancer, and afraid of various things; now her dying Aunt Mari wants Davi to help Emilie, a young Creole ghost, to find peace. (Rev: LMC 1/08; SLJ 2/08)

9624 Sinykin, Sheri C. *A Matter of Time* (4–6). 1998, Marshall Cavendish $14.95 (978-0-7614-5019-1). 207pp. Jody, wanting to spend more time with his dad to understand him better, gets his wish when he time-travels back to 1958 and meets his father as a youngster. (Rev: BL 5/15/98; HBG 10/98; SLJ 5/98)

9625 Sleator, William. *Hell Phone* (5–8). 2006, Abrams $16.95 (978-0-8109-5479-3). 238pp. In this dark, suspenseful novel, 17-year-old Nick discovers that the cell phone he bought at a bargain price constantly rings with frightening requests. (Rev: BL 10/1/06; SLJ 11/06)

9626 Slepian, Jan. *Back to Before* (5–7). 1994, Scholastic paper $3.25 (978-0-590-48459-6). 144pp. Cousins Linny and Hilary travel back to a time before Linny's mother's death and Hilary's parents' separation. (Rev: BCCB 9/93; BL 9/1/93*; SLJ 10/93)

9627 Smith, Dodie. *The Hundred and One Dalmatians* (3–5). 1981, Avon paper $2.95 (978-0-380-00895-7). 208pp. Pongo and Missis must save the Dalmatian puppies captured by Cruella de Vil.

9628 Smith, Sherwood. *Wren's Quest* (5–8). 1993, Harcourt $16.95 (978-0-15-200976-2). Wren takes time out from magician school to search for clues to her parentage. Sequel to *Wren to the Rescue* (1990). (Rev: BL 4/1/93*; SLJ 6/93)

9629 Smith, Sherwood. *Wren's War* (5–8). 1995, Harcourt $17.00 (978-0-15-200977-9). In this sequel to *Wren to the Rescue* and *Wren's Quest*, Princess Teressa struggles to control herself and her destiny when she finds her parents murdered. (Rev: BL 3/1/95*; SLJ 5/95)

9630 Snow, Alan. *Here Be Monsters!* (4–6). Illus. by author. 2006, Simon & Schuster $17.95 (978-0-689-87047-7). 512pp. A complex, inventive, and humor-filled fantasy involving an amazing cast of eccentric characters and a resourceful hero called Arthur. (Rev: BL 5/15/06; SLJ 8/06)

9631 Snyder, Laurel. *Any Which Wall* (4–7). Illus. by LeUyen Pham. 2009, Random $16.99 (978-0-375-85560-3). 256pp. Four children discover a magic wall in a cornfield and have many adventures traveling through time. (Rev: BCCB 7–8/09; BL 5/15/09; HB 5/09; LMC 8/09; SLJ 6/09; VOYA 4/09)

9632 Snyder, Zilpha Keatley. *The Bronze Pen* (4–6). 2008, Atheneum $16.99 (978-1-4169-4201-6). 208pp. Twelve-year-old Audrey comes into the possession of a magic pen that helps her deal with her father's illness and her quirky new friend; set in the 1970s. (Rev: BL 2/15/08; LMC 10/08; SLJ 3/08)

9633 Snyder, Zilpha Keatley. *The Headless Cupid* (4–7). 1971, Dell paper $4.99 (978-0-440-43507-5). 208pp. Amanda, a student of the occult, upsets her new family. A sequel is *The Famous Stanley Kidnapping Case* (1985).

9634 Somary, Wolfgang. *Night and the Candlemaker* (4–8). Illus. 2000, Barefoot Books $16.99 (978-1-84148-137-1). 32pp. In this allegory, a candle maker continues with his trade in spite of threats he receives from Night. (Rev: BL 9/15/00; HBG 10/01; SLJ 1/01)

9635 Sonnenblick, Jordan. *Dodger and Me* (4–6). 2008, Feiwel & Friends $16.95 (978-0-312-37793-9). 176pp. Willie starts to understand what he really wants after he is granted three wishes by a large and magical blue chimpanzee. (Rev: BL 3/15/08; SLJ 6/08)

9636 Spalding, Andrea. *The Keeper and the Crows* (3–6). Illus. 2000, Orca paper $5.95 (978-1-55143-141-3). 119pp. Misha sets out to retrieve a key to a magic box that contains Hope, in this fantasy that is a spinoff on the Greek myth about Pandora's Box. (Rev: BL 11/15/00)

9637 Springer, Nancy. *Dussie* (5–8). 2007, Walker $16.95 (978-0-8027-9649-3). 176pp. When she hits puberty, Dussie, a New York City 13-year-old named for her aunt Medusa, discovers she is a gorgon — and that the talkative snakes that have sprouted from her head may be an inconvenience, as is her ability to turn people to stone. (Rev: BL 11/15/07; SLJ 12/07)

9638 Springer, Nancy. *Sky Rider* (5–8). 2000, HarperCollins paper $4.95 (978-0-380-79565-9). In this contemporary supernatural mystery, Dusty's beloved horse Tazz is cured by a visitor who turns out to be the angry ghost of a teenage boy recently killed on her father's property. (Rev: BCCB 10/99; HBG 3/00; SLJ 8/99)

9639 Stahler, David. *Truesight* (5–7). Series: The Truesight Trilogy. 2004, HarperCollins LB $16.89 (978-0-06-052286-5). 168pp. A race of blind people living in a colony on a distant planet includes one teenager who discovers he can see, and he sees all sorts of flaws in the people of his community. (Rev: SLJ 3/04; VOYA 4/04)

9640 Stahler, David, Jr. *The Seer* (5–7). Series: The Truesight Trilogy. 2007, HarperCollins $16.99 (978-0-06-052288-9). 248pp. Jacob, 13, leaves the colony of Harmony, where he is the only person who can see, and seeks both a new life and his childhood friend Delaney, who is a talented musician. (Rev: BCCB 5/07; SLJ 8/07)

9641 Stanley, Diane. *Bella at Midnight* (5–8). Illus. by Bagram Ibatoulline. 2006, HarperCollins LB $17.89 (978-0-06-077574-2). 288pp. A fine retelling of the Cinderella story featuring a plucky Bella and a storytelling format. (Rev: BCCB 4/06; BL 2/1/06*; HB 3/06; HBG 10/06; LMC 1/07; SLJ 3/06*; VOYA 2/06)

9642 Stanley, Diane. *The Trouble with Wishes* (2–4). Illus. by author. 2007, HarperCollins $16.99 (978-0-06-055451-4). In this humorous variation on the legend of Pygmalion, a sculptor named Pyg falls in love with a statue of a goddess and wishes she were real; his wish is granted and he soon comes to regret this. (Rev: BL 11/1/06; SLJ 2/07)

9643 Starkey, Dinah, ed. *Ghosts and Bogles* (5–10). Illus. 1987, David & Charles $17.95 (978-0-434-96440-6). A collection of 16 British ghost stories, each nicely presented with illustrations. (Rev: SLJ 9/87)

9644 Stead, Rebecca. *First Light* (5–8). 2007, Random $15.99 (978-0-375-84017-3). 336pp. On a scientific expedition to Greenland with his parents, 12-year-old Peter meets 14-year-old Thea, a member of a secret society that lives beneath the ice. (Rev: BL 4/15/07; SLJ 8/07)

9645 Steele, Mary. *Journey Outside* (5–8). Illus. by Rocco Negri. 1984, Peter Smith $21.75 (978-0-8446-6169-8); Puffin paper $5.99 (978-0-14-030588-3). 144pp. Young Dilar, believing that his Raft People have been circling endlessly in their quest for a "Better Place," sets out to discover the origin and fate of his kind.

9646 Steer, Dugald. *The Dragon's Eye* (5–8). Series: Dragonology Chronicles. 2006, Candlewick $15.99 (978-0-7636-2810-9). 256pp. In the late 19th century, Daniel Cook, 12, and his sister Beatrice attend a dragon school run by Dr. Ernest Drake and accompany him on search for the important Dragon's Eye. (Rev: BL 1/1–15/07; SLJ 1/07)

9647 Steig, William. *Abel's Island* (4–6). Illus. by author. 1976, Farrar $15.00 (978-0-374-30010-4). 128pp. A tale of a pampered mouse who must fend for himself after being marooned on an isolated island.

9648 Stevens, Eric. *The Revenge of Clayface* (2–5). Illus. by Gregg Schigiel and Lee Loughridge. Series: DC Super Heroes: Batman. 2009, Stone Arch LB $25.32 (978-1-4342-1149-1); paper $5.95 (978-1-4342-1369-3). 56pp. A highly illustrated

chapter book in which Batman faces Clayface and the Joker. (Rev: SLJ 6/09)

9649 Stewart, Jennifer J. *If That Breathes Fire, We're Toast!* (4–6). 1999, Holiday House $15.95 (978-0-8234-1430-7). 117pp. Mrs. Yang, a dragon, takes Rick and friend Natalie on several trips through time and imagination. (Rev: BCCB 9/99; BL 8/99; HBG 10/99; SLJ 12/99)

9650 Stewart, Paul. *Freeglader* (4–6). Illus. by Chris Riddell. Series: Edge Chronicles. 2006, Random LB $14.99 (978-0-385-75083-7). 416pp. Librarian knight Rook Barkwater and his friends face daunting challenges on their journey to reach a new home in the Free Glades; the final volume in this fast-paced and complex fantasy. (Rev: BL 12/1/05; SLJ 2/06; VOYA 12/05)

9651 Stewart, Paul. *Muddle Earth* (4–6). Illus. by Chris Riddell. 2007, Delacorte $16.99 (978-0-385-73316-8). 432pp. A funny fantasy in which young Joe Jefferson finds himself transported from his homework to become a saving hero in Muddle Earth. (Rev: BCCB 10/07; BL 6/1–15/07; LMC 10/07; SLJ 9/07)

9652 Stewart, Paul. *Return of the Emerald Skull* (4–6). Illus. by Chris Riddell. 2009, Random $15.99 (978-0-385-75128-5). 224pp. Barnaby Grimes, the messenger boy who travels by rooftop in 19th-century England, learns an ancient Chinese art and uses it when he investigates strange goings-on at Grassington Hall School. (Rev: BL 3/1/09; SLJ 4/09)

9653 Stewart, Paul. *Winter Knights* (4–6). Illus. by Chris Riddell. Series: Edge Chronicles. 2007, Random $12.99 (978-0-375-83741-8). 400pp. Quint and the other Knights Academy students encounter violent winter storms during training in this eighth volume in the series. (Rev: BL 7/07)

9654 Stewart, Paul, and Riddell Chris. *Hugo Pepper* (3–5). Illus. Series: Far-Flung Adventures. 2007, Random $14.99 (978-0-385-75092-9). 272pp. Ten-year-old Hugo Pepper, son of explorers who were eaten by polar bears, sets off on his parents' sled to learn more about his roots and finds himself in Firefly Square, where he finds adventure, intrigue, and eccentricity. (Rev: BL 4/1/07; SLJ 2/07)

9655 Stewart, Paul, and Chris Riddell. *Fergus Crane* (3–5). 2006, Random $14.95 (978-0-385-75088-2). 240pp. Nine-year-old Fergus Crane embarks on a series of magical adventures after a flying box and a winged horse enter his life. (Rev: BL 2/15/06; SLJ 6/06)

9656 Stewart, Sharon. *Raven Quest* (5–8). 2005, Carolrhoda LB $15.95 (978-1-57505-894-8). 320pp. Tok the raven seeks to restore his good name after being falsely accused of murder and sets off to find the legendary Grey Lords. (Rev: SLJ 1/06; VOYA 12/05)

9657 Stewart, Trenton Lee. *The Mysterious Benedict Society* (4–7). Illus. by Carson Ellis. 2007, Little, Brown $16.99 (978-0-316-05777-6). 485pp. Orphan Reynie Muldoon is one of a number of gifted children selected to take part in an effort to infiltrate the Learning Institute for the Very Enlightened; a complex story of mystery and adventure. (Rev: BL 1/1–15/07; SLJ 3/07*)

9658 Stine, R. L. *The Haunting Hour: Chill in the Dead of Night* (5–8). Illus. 2001, HarperCollins $14.89 (978-0-06-623605-6). 160pp. Ten chilling short stories, each with an introduction by the author. (Rev: BCCB 11/01; BL 1/1–15/02; HBG 3/02)

9659 Stine, R. L. *Nightmare Hour* (4–7). Illus. 1999, HarperCollins $16.99 (978-0-06-028688-0). 148pp. Ten scary stories by a master of mystery, with characters that include aliens, sorcerers, werewolves, witches, and ghosts. (Rev: BL 10/15/99; HBG 3/00; SLJ 12/99)

9660 Stone, David Lee. *The Yowler Foul-up* (5–8). 2006, Hyperion $16.99 (978-0-7868-5597-1). 304pp. A motley group of would-be heroes tries to stop a plot to turn the people of Dullitch into rocks in this sequel to *The Ratastrophe Catastrophe* (2004). (Rev: BL 4/15/06)

9661 Strasser, Todd. *Hey Dad, Get a Life!* (5–8). 1996, Holiday $15.95 (978-0-8234-1278-5). Twelve-year-old Kelly and her younger sister use the ghost of their dead father to accomplish their everyday chores and finally let their mother know about their secret helper. (Rev: BCCB 3/97; BL 2/15/97; SLJ 3/97)

9662 Strauss, Linda Leopold. *A Fairy Called Hilary* (2–4). Illus. 1999, Holiday House $15.95 (978-0-8234-1418-5). 113pp. Nine related stories about Caroline, her family, and their adopted fairy, Hilary. (Rev: BL 3/1/99; HBG 10/99; SLJ 3/99)

9663 Strickland, Brad. *The Curse of the Midions* (5–8). Series: Grimoire. 2006, Dial $12.99 (978-0-8037-3060-1). 160pp. A trip to London with his parents goes terribly awry when Jarvey Midion finds himself transported to an alternate universe where he must confront the villainous wizard Tantalus Mideon. (Rev: BL 6/1–15/06; SLJ 11/06)

9664 Strickland, Brad. *Tracked by Terror* (5–8). Series: Grimoire. 2007, Dial $15.99 (978-0-8037-3061-8). 192pp. This sequel to *Curse of the Midions* (2006) finds 12-year-old Jarvey and his friend Betsy navigating a haunted theater and being hunted by animals. (Rev: BL 11/15/07; LMC 11/07; SLJ 2/08)

9665 Strickland, Brad. *The Whistle, the Grave, and the Ghost* (5–8). Series: Lewis Barnevalt. 2003, Dial $16.99 (978-0-8037-2622-2). 160pp. A silver whistle frees a woman vampire, drawing Lewis Barnevalt and his friends into suspenseful adventures battling an ancient threat. (Rev: BL 8/03; HBG 4/04; SLJ 8/03)

9666 Sweet, J. H. *Dragonfly and the Web of Dreams* (2–4). Illus. by Tara Larsen Chang. Series: The Fairy Chronicles. 2007, Sourcebooks paper $6.99 (978-1-4022-0873-7). 119pp. Jennifer travels with her fairy friends to the home of the Dream Spider to rebuild the Web of Dreams and help everyone get a good night's sleep in the second book in the series. (Rev: SLJ 8/07)

9667 Tan, Shaun. *The Haunted Playground* (4–6). Illus. by author. 2008, Stone Arch LB $16.95 (978-1-59889-860-6). 64pp. For reluctant readers, this is a suspenseful tale in which Gavin, searching for

treasure in a playground one night with his metal detector, encounters sylphlike children. (Rev: BCCB 12/07; BL 11/1/07; SLJ 2/08)

9668 Taylor, Greg. *Killer Pizza* (5–8). 2009, Feiwel & Friends $14.99 (978-0-312-37379-5). 256pp. Fourteen-year-old Toby's first summer job involves making pizza and hunting monsters. (Rev: BL 5/15/09; SLJ 9/09; VOYA 8/09)

9669 Taylor, Laini. *Faeries of Dreamdark: Blackbringer* (5–8). 2007, Putnam $17.99 (978-0-399-24630-2). 368pp. With the help of her band of crows, a faerie named Magpie must hunt down devils that the humans have released and keep the dark from consuming the world. (Rev: BL 5/15/07; SLJ 8/07)

9670 Taylor, Theodore. *The Boy Who Could Fly Without a Motor* (3–6). 2002, Harcourt $15.00 (978-0-15-216529-1). 144pp. After Jon learns how to fly from a green-eyed magician, he becomes the center of attraction and even meets the President. (Rev: BL 6/1–15/02; HBG 10/02; SLJ 5/02)

9671 Teitelbaum, Michael. *The Scary States of America* (5–8). 2007, Delacorte LB $12.99 (978-0-385-90348-6); paper $7.99 (978-0-385-73331-1). 416pp. A collection of short stories about paranormal events that take place in each of the 50 states. (Rev: BL 6/1–15/07; SLJ 8/07)

9672 Thomas, Jane Resh. *The Princess in the Pigpen* (4–6). 1989, Houghton $16.00 (978-0-395-51587-7). 124pp. In a reverse time travel story, a girl is transported from 17th-century England to present-day America. (Rev: BL 9/15/89; SLJ 11/89)

9673 Thomas, Joyce C. *The Bowlegged Rooster and Other Tales That Signify* (2–5). Illus. 2000, HarperCollins LB $15.89 (978-0-06-025378-3). 112pp. Five original folktales in which animals mirror the human condition but solve their problems in a whimsical fashion. (Rev: BCCB 12/00; BL 10/1/00; HBG 3/01; SLJ 11/00)

9674 Thompson, Jill. *Magic Trixie* (3–5). Illus. by author. 2008, HarperCollins paper $7.99 (978-0-06-117045-4). 96pp. This graphic novel tells the story of Magic Trixie, a little witch who has used everything in her bag of tricks for show-and-tell and has just one more spell left: making something disappear, which might just be the new baby. (Rev: BL 9/1/08)

9675 Thomson, Sarah L. *Dragon's Egg* (3–6). 2007, Greenwillow $15.99 (978-0-06-128848-7). 272pp. Mella, a 12-year-old with a talent for looking after domestic dragons, and her friend Roger must deliver a "true dragon" egg to the Dragontooth Mountains. (Rev: BL 10/1/07; SLJ 1/08)

9676 Thomson, Sarah L. *Imagine a Day* (3–6). Illus. by Rob Gonsalves. 2005, Simon & Schuster $16.95 (978-0-689-85219-0). 40pp. Surrealist images are accompanied by brief text in this large-format volume that is a companion to *Imagine a Night* (2003). (Rev: BL 1/1–15/05; SLJ 4/05)

9677 Thornton, Duncan. *Kalifax* (5–9). Illus. by Yves Noblet. 2000, Coteau paper $8.95 (978-1-55050-152-0). 168pp. In this fantasy novel, young Tom, with the help of Grandfather Frost, saves the crew of his ship after it becomes trapped in ice. (Rev: SLJ 1/01)

9678 Thornton, Duncan. *The Star-Glass* (5–8). Illus. by Yves Noblet. 2004, Coteau paper $10.95 (978-1-55050-269-5). 402pp. Tom and Jenny face new challenges in this sequel to the fantasies *Kalifax* and *Captain Jenny and the Sea of Wonders.* (Rev: SLJ 4/04; VOYA 6/04)

9679 Thorpe, Kiki. *The Trouble with Tink* (2–3). Illus. by Judith Clarke and the Disney Storybook Artists. Series: Disney Fairies. 2006, Random paper $5.99 (978-0-7364-2371-7). 128pp. When Tinker Bell loses her hammer, she also loses her ability to mend the battered pots and pans of Never Land's Pixie Hollow. (Rev: SLJ 3/06)

9680 Tibo, Gilles. *The Cowboy Kid* (2–5). Illus. 2000, Tundra $16.95 (978-0-88776-511-7). 24pp. In this fantasy, a youngster named the Cowboy Kid finds a horse and together they ride through the sky rescuing other horses from statues and paintings. (Rev: BL 6/1–15/00)

9681 Titus, Eve. *Basil of Baker Street* (4–6). Illus. by Paul Galdone. 1958, Pocket paper $2.50 (978-0-318-37408-6). A clever mystery about a mouse who moves to 221 Baker Street out of admiration for Mr. Holmes. Another in the series: *Basil in the Wild West* (1990).

9682 Tolan, Stephanie S. *Who's There?* (5–8). 1994, Morrow $15.00 (978-0-688-04611-8); paper $4.95 (978-0-688-15289-5). 240pp. Fourteen-year-old Drew is convinced that there is a ghost in her crusty grandfather's house, where she and her brother Evan, who has been mute since their parents' deaths, are currently living. (Rev: BCCB 12/94; BL 9/1/94; SLJ 10/94)

9683 Tolkien, J. R. R. *Roverandom* (4–9). 1998, Houghton $17.00 (978-0-395-89871-0); paper $12.95 (978-0-395-95799-8). This fantasy deals with a dog named Roverandom who has the misfortune of insulting a wizard and having to pay the consequences. (Rev: BL 7/98; SLJ 6/98; VOYA 10/98)

9684 Townley, Roderick. *Into the Labyrinth* (5–7). 2002, Simon & Schuster $16.95 (978-0-689-84615-1). 272pp. In this sequel to *The Great Good Thing* (2001), Princess Sylvie and the other characters in their novel become exhausted as their popularity grows and they must rush from chapter to chapter; when the book goes digital, things spiral out of control and Sylvie must defeat an evil "bot" that threatens to destroy them. (Rev: BL 11/1/02; HBG 10/03; SLJ 10/02)

9685 Townsend, Tom. *The Trouble with an Elf* (5–8). Series: Fairie Ring. 1999, Royal Fireworks paper $9.99 (978-0-88092-525-9). 158pp. The adopted daughter of the king of the elves, Elazandra, journeys through a ring of mushrooms to the world of humans to stop the evil that will destroy both worlds. (Rev: SLJ 4/00)

9686 Trewellard, J. M. *Butterfingers* (4–6). Illus. by Ian Beck. 2007, Random $15.99 (978-0-385-75123-0). 224pp. Ned, a stable boy, is accompanied by many animals — including a dog, a pig, a pony and a mouse — as he endeavors to rescue Princess Bella. (Rev: BL 12/1/07; LMC 11/07; SLJ 9/07)

9687 Tripp, Jenny. *Pete and Fremont* (4–6). Illus. by John Manders. 2007, Harcourt $16.00 (978-0-15-205629-2). 192pp. Circus performers Pete the poodle and Fremont the grizzly bear form a mutually beneficial friendship in this story full of circus lore. (Rev: BL 3/15/07)

9688 Tunnell, Michael O. *School Spirits* (5–8). 1997, Holiday $15.95 (978-0-8234-1310-2). Three students at creepy Craven Hill School, including the son of the new principal, discover a ghost and solve a decades-old murder mystery involving an 8-year-old boy. (Rev: BCCB 3/98; BL 2/15/98; HBG 3/98; SLJ 3/98; VOYA 8/98)

9689 Turner, Ann. *Elfsong* (3–7). 1995, Harcourt $16.00 (978-0-15-200826-0). 208pp. Maddy and Grandpa discover a forest where elves live and they can hear birds and other animals speak. (Rev: BCCB 12/95; BL 10/1/95; SLJ 10/95)

9690 Turner, Ann. *Rosemary's Witch* (5–8). 1991, HarperCollins paper $3.95 (978-0-06-440494-5). Rosemary discovers that her new home is haunted by the spirit of a girl named Mathilda, who's become a witch because of her pain and anger. (Rev: BL 4/1/91; SLJ 5/91*)

9691 Turner, Megan W. *The Queen of Attolia* (5–8). 2000, Greenwillow $15.95 (978-0-688-17423-1). 288pp. In this sequel to *The Thief*, Gen, a slippery rogue, once more gets involved in the rivalry between two city states. (Rev: BL 4/15/00; HB 7/00; HBG 10/00; SLJ 5/00)

9692 Turner, Megan W. *The Thief* (5–8). 1996, Greenwillow $17.99 (978-0-688-14627-6). To escape life imprisonment, Gen must steal a legendary stone in this first-person fantasy set in olden days. (Rev: BCCB 11/96; BL 1/1–15/97; HB 11/96; SLJ 10/96; VOYA 6/97)

9693 Uhlberg, Myron. *Flying over Brooklyn* (3–6). Illus. 1999, Peachtree $15.95 (978-1-56145-194-4). 32pp. Set in Brooklyn in 1947, this dreamlike fantasy tells of a boy who dons a new coat that gives him the power to fly over the city's buildings. (Rev: BL 12/1/99; HBG 3/00; SLJ 12/99)

9694 Ullman, Barb Bentler. *The Fairies of Nutfolk Wood* (3–5). 2006, HarperCollins $16.99 (978-0-06-073614-9). 256pp. After her parents divorce, 10-year-old Willa and her mother move into a trailer in the woods; here Willa recovers from her stress and, with her elderly neighbor Hazel, befriends the local fairies. (Rev: BL 5/15/06; HBG 10/06; SLJ 7/06)

9695 Ure, Jean. *The Children Next Door* (4–6). 1996, Scholastic $14.95 (978-0-590-22293-8). 144pp. In this time-travel fantasy, Laura discovers the truth about two mysterious children who play in the garden next door. (Rev: BCCB 5/96; BL 1/1–15/96; SLJ 3/96)

9696 Ursu, Anne. *The Immortal Fire* (5–8). Series: Cronus Chronicles. 2009, Atheneum $16.99 (978-1-4169-0591-2). 528pp. Thirteen-year-olds Charlotte and Zee take on the task of saving mankind in this action-packed final installment in the series that features many classical references. (Rev: BLO 4/24/09; SLJ 9/09)

9697 Ursu, Anne. *The Shadow Thieves* (5–8). 2006, Simon & Schuster $16.95 (978-1-4169-0587-5). 416pp. A plot to reanimate the dead using the essence of living children is foiled by cousins Charlotte and Zee in this story of heroism and mythology that ranges from the Midwest to England to Hades. (Rev: BL 3/1/06; SLJ 4/06)

9698 Ursu, Anne. *The Siren Song* (5–8). Series: Cronus Chronicles. 2007, Atheneum $16.99 (978-1-4169-0589-9). 448pp. Charlotte, just back from the Underworld (in 2007's *The Shadow Thieves*), goes on a cruise with her cousin Zee and finds herself battling Poseidon and the sea monster Ketos; the second installment in the series that uses elements of Greek mythology. (Rev: BL 11/1/07; HB 7/07; SLJ 8/07)

9699 Van Allsburg, Chris. *The Sweetest Fig* (3–6). Illus. 1993, Houghton $18.95 (978-0-395-67346-1). 32pp. All of his wildest dreams come true when a cruel dentist eats the figs given him in payment by a poor woman. (Rev: BCCB 11/93; BL 10/1/93*; SLJ 11/93*)

9700 Van Allsburg, Chris. *The Wreck of the Zephyr* (2–5). Illus. by author. 1983, Houghton $18.95 (978-0-395-33075-3). 32pp. The story behind the wreck of a sailboat.

9701 Van Belkom, Edo. *Lone Wolf* (5–8). 2005, Tundra paper $8.95 (978-0-88776-741-8). 177pp. The four teen werewolves adopted by Ranger Brock in *Wolf Pack* (2004) defend their beloved woods against a corrupt developer. (Rev: SLJ 1/06; VOYA 4/06)

9702 Vande Velde, Vivian. *Ghost of a Hanged Man* (3–6). 1998, Marshall Cavendish $14.95 (978-0-7614-5015-3). 96pp. A town falls under the deathly curse placed on it by murderous Jake Barnett before he was hanged, and now 11-year-old Ben and his sister Annabelle believe they are next to be murdered by Jake's ghost. (Rev: BCCB 10/98; BL 11/15/98; HB 11/98; HBG 3/99; SLJ 10/98)

9703 Vande Velde, Vivian. *Now You See It . . .* (5–8). 2005, Harcourt $17.00 (978-0-15-205311-6). 288pp. Wendy, 15, puts on a pair of sunglasses and a whole new fantasy world is revealed. (Rev: BL 1/1–15/05; SLJ 1/05)

9704 Vande Velde, Vivian. *Witch Dreams* (5–8). 2005, Marshall Cavendish $15.95 (978-0-7614-5235-5). 128pp. Nyssa, a 16-year-old witch, seeks justice for her parents, who were murdered six years earlier. (Rev: BL 12/15/05; SLJ 11/05; VOYA 12/05)

9705 Vanderwal, Andrew H. *The Battle for Duncragglin* (5–7). 2009, Tundra $17.95 (978-0-88776-886-6). 336pp. On a visit to Scotland, 12-year-old Alex and three Scottish children are transported back to a chaotic and dangerous time. (Rev: BL 4/15/09; SLJ 7/09; VOYA 8/09)

9706 Van Leeuwen, Jean. *The Great Rescue Operation* (3–5). Illus. by Margot Apple. 1982, Dial LB $10.89 (978-0-685-01456-1). 144pp. Two mice try

to locate their friend who has disappeared in Macy's department store.

9707 Vansickle, Lisa. *The Secret Little City* (5–8). 2000, Palmae $15.95 (978-1-930167-11-7). 230pp. When 11-year-old Mackenzie moves with her family to a small town in Oregon, she discovers a whole civilization of inch-high people living beneath the floorboards of her new room. (Rev: SLJ 8/00)

9708 Vaugelade, Anais. *The War* (3–5). Trans. by Marie-Christine Rouffiac and Tom Streissguth. Illus. 2001, Carolrhoda $15.25 (978-1-57505-562-6). 32pp. In this picture-book allegory about the futility of war, a young idealist tricks the kings of the two warring sides into believing they have a common enemy and, therefore, must declare peace. (Rev: BL 3/15/01; HB 3/01; HBG 10/01)

9709 Vaupel, Robin. *The Rules of the Universe by Austin W. Hale* (5–8). 2007, Holiday $16.95 (978-0-8234-1811-4). 288pp. When Austin, 13, discovers that he can alter the molecular structures of people and animals, he conducts careful experiments to determine the limits of this power — and to see if he can save his dying grandfather. (Rev: BL 11/1/07)

9710 Velde, Vivian Vande. *Three Good Deeds* (3–5). 2005, Harcourt $16.00 (978-0-15-205382-6). 160pp. Transformed into a goose by a witch's curse, Howard must perform three good deeds to return to human form. (Rev: BL 10/15/05; SLJ 10/05)

9711 Velmans, Hester. *Isabel of the Whales* (4–6). 2005, Delacorte $15.95 (978-0-385-73202-4). 181pp. An informative fantasy in which a girl becomes a whale and learns about diving, feeding, and communication while she teaches the whales about such dangers as nets and ships. (Rev: SLJ 8/05)

9712 Vernon, Ursula. *Dragonbreath* (3–5). Illus. by author. 2009, Dial $12.99 (978-0-8037-3363-3). 144pp. After he gets a failing grade on his ocean report, Danny the dragon goes on an undersea adventure. (Rev: BCCB 9/09; BL 5/15/09)

9713 Vernon, Ursula. *Nurk: The Strange, Surprising Adventures of a (Somewhat) Brave Shrew* (3–5). Illus. by author. 2008, Harcourt $15.00 (978-0-15-206375-7). 144pp. Nurk the shrew finds unsuspected reserves of courage when he receives a cry for help. (Rev: BLO 7/30/08; SLJ 8/08) ∩

9714 Verrillo, Erica. *Elissa's Odyssey* (5–8). Series: Phoenix Rising. 2008, Random $16.99 (978-0-375-83948-1). 352pp. The second book in the trilogy, following *Elissa's Quest*, finds Elissa in Alhamazar, her mysterious power to speak to animals expanding. (Rev: BL 5/15/08)

9715 Verrillo, Erica. *Elissa's Quest* (5–8). Series: Phoenix Rising. 2007, Random $16.99 (978-0-375-83946-7). 352pp. Thirteen-year-old Elissa struggles to control her destiny when she finds out that she is the princess of Castlemar and that her father the king plans to trade her to a desert warlord. (Rev: BL 6/1–15/07; LMC 10/07; SLJ 8/07)

9716 Verrillo, Erica. *World's End* (5–8). Series: Phoenix Rising. 2009, Random $16.99 (978-0-375-83950-4). 336pp. Elissa must escape her father's plans for her in this satisfying final installment in the trilogy. (Rev: BLO 4/24/09; SLJ 9/09)

9717 Voake, Steve. *The Dreamwalker's Child* (5–8). 2006, Bloomsbury $16.95 (978-1-58234-661-8). 300pp. After being hit by a car, Sam Palmer finds himself in the alternate world of Aurobon, where he learns of a deadly plot to wipe out human life on Earth using a virus transmitted by mosquitoes. (Rev: SLJ 8/06; VOYA 6/06)

9718 Voelkel, Jon, and Pamela Voelkel. *Middleworld* (5–8). Illus. Series: Jaguar Stones Trilogy. 2007, Smith & Kraus $17.95 (978-1-57525-561-3). 390pp. Fourteen-year-old Max's parents disappear while working in Central America, and he searches for them with the help of local girl Lola and her knowledge of the mystical elements of Mayan culture. (Rev: BL 11/15/07; SLJ 10/07)

9719 Wade, Rebecca. *The Theft and the Miracle* (5–8). 2007, HarperCollins $16.99 (978-0-06-077493-6). 368pp. Mystery and supernatural are combined in this story of Hannah, a plain, overweight 12-year-old with artistic abilities, who — with her friend Sam — finds herself on a hunt for a missing religious statue. (Rev: BL 11/15/06; SLJ 1/07)

9720 Wallace, Bill. *The Legend of Thunderfoot* (3–5). 2006, Simon & Schuster $15.95 (978-1-4169-0691-9). 160pp. In this appealing animal fantasy, a young roadrunner finds ways to make the most of his oversized feet, swollen out of proportion by a snakebite. (Rev: BL 11/1/06; SLJ 10/06)

9721 Wallace, Bill. *Snot Stew* (4–6). Illus. by Lisa McCue. 1989, Holiday House $15.95 (978-0-8234-0745-3). 96pp. The amusing tale of how Mama Cat moves her kittens out into the world. (Rev: BL 5/15/89; SLJ 4/89)

9722 Wallace, Bill. *Totally Disgusting* (4–6). Illus. by Leslie Morrill. 1991, Holiday House $15.95 (978-0-8234-0873-3). 120pp. Feline Mewkiss wants to be brave and strong but isn't at all sure that he'll make it. (Rev: BCCB 6/91; BL 4/1/91; SLJ 6/91)

9723 Walsh, Jill Paton. *Pepi and the Secret Names* (3–5). Illus. by Fiona French. 1995, Lothrop $15.00 (978-0-688-13428-0). 32pp. In this fantasy set in ancient Egypt, Pepi gets animals to pose for her artist father by guessing their secret names. (Rev: BL 4/15/95; SLJ 4/95)

9724 Ward, David. *Escape the Mask* (5–8). Series: The Grassland Trilogy. 2008, Abrams $15.95 (978-0-8109-9477-5). 224pp. Coriko and Pippa escape the Spears, who have been keeping them as slaves, when the Spears are attacked by a mysterious group of warriors; but their adventures do not end there. (Rev: BL 4/15/08)

9725 Warfel, Elizabeth Stuart. *The Blue Pearls* (2–4). Illus. by Veronique Giarrusso. 2001, Barefoot Books $16.99 (978-1-902283-78-4). 32pp. In this fantasy, a group of angels are preparing a beautiful blue gown for a young mother who is about to die and be welcomed in heaven. (Rev: BL 4/15/01; HBG 10/01; SLJ 7/01)

9726 Watson, Patrick. *Ahmek* (5–6). Illus. by Tracy Thomson. 1999, Stoddart $14.95 (978-0-7737-3145-5). 167pp. Ahmek, a beaver, is forced to leave his beloved pond and travel north to find a new home and a mate for life. (Rev: SLJ 4/00)

9727 Waugh, Sylvia. *The Mennyms* (4–8). 1994, Greenwillow $16.00 (978-0-688-13070-1). 212pp. When their owner dies, a family of rag dolls comes to life and takes over her house in this beginning volume of an extensive series. (Rev: BCCB 5/94; HB 7/94; SLJ 4/94)

9728 Waugh, Sylvia. *Mennyms Alive* (4–6). 1997, Greenwillow $16.00 (978-0-688-15201-7). 224pp. The last book about the Mennyms, rag dolls who have problems finding a permanent home. (Rev: BL 9/15/97; HB 11/97; HBG 3/98; SLJ 9/97)

9729 Waxman, Sydell, retel. *The Rooster Prince* (2–5). Illus. by Giora Carmi. 2000, Pitspopany $16.95 (978-0-943706-45-0); paper $9.95 (978-0-943706-49-8). 40pp. In 18th-century Russia, a village boy is given the task of curing a prince who is behaving like rooster. (Rev: SLJ 1/01)

9730 Weatherill, Cat. *Barkbelly* (4–7). Illus. by Peter Brown. 2006, Knopf $15.95 (978-0-375-83327-4). 320pp. A wooden boy being raised by normal parents flees after he accidentally causes a tragedy and searches for his own family. (Rev: BL 5/15/06; SLJ 7/06)

9731 Weatherill, Cat. *Snowbone* (4–7). Illus. by Peter Brown. 2007, Knopf $15.99 (978-0-375-83328-1). 256pp. Snowbone rallies her fellow Ashenpeakers (a race of wooden beings that are used as slaves) to escape their bondage and end slavery; a companion to *Barkbelly* (2006). (Rev: BL 6/1–15/07; SLJ 12/07)

9732 Weatherill, Cat. *Wild Magic* (4–7). 2008, Walker $16.99 (978-0-8027-9799-5). 288pp. It seems that the Pied Piper (whose real name was Finn) was actually an elf and took the children from Hamelin in hopes of ridding himself of a curse. (Rev: BCCB 1/09; BL 12/1/08; LMC 1/09; SLJ 11/08)

9733 Weinberg, Karen. *Window of Time* (5–7). Illus. by Annelle W. Ratcliffe. 1991, White Mane paper $9.95 (978-0-942597-18-9). 166pp. Ben climbs through a window and finds himself 125 years back in time. (Rev: SLJ 7/91)

9734 Welch, R. C. *Scary Stories for Stormy Nights* (5–7). Illus. 1995, Lowell House paper $5.95 (978-1-56565-262-0). 128pp. Ten contemporary horror stories that involve such characters as a werewolf and some pirates. (Rev: BL 5/1/95)

9735 Welvaert, Scott R. *The Curse of the Wendigo: An Agate and Buck Adventure* (5–9). Illus. by Brann Garvey. 2006, Stone Arch LB $23.93 (978-1-59889-066-2). 105pp. Searching for their parents in the vast Canadian wilderness in the late 19th century, 16-year-old Buck and his younger sister Agate find themselves being pursued by the mythical Wendigo; suitable for reluctant readers. (Rev: SLJ 1/07)

9736 Wersba, Barbara. *Walter: The Story of a Rat* (4–7). Illus. by Donna Diamond. 2005, Front St. $16.95 (978-1-932425-41-3). 64pp. Miss Pomeroy, a children's author, develops a friendship with a literary rat named Walter who shares her house in this thoughtful and sophisticated book. (Rev: BCCB 2/06; BL 11/15/05; SLJ 12/05)

9737 West, Tracey. *Voyage of the Half Moon* (3–5). Illus. Series: Stories of the States. 1993, Silver Moon LB $14.95 (978-1-881889-18-2). 55pp. When Gwen is sent to live with a new foster family, she is haunted by a ghost that no one else can see. (Rev: SLJ 9/93)

9738 Westall, Robert. *Ghost Abbey* (5–9). 1990, Scholastic paper $3.25 (978-0-590-41693-1). Maggi realizes that the abbey her father is restoring seems to have a life of its own. (Rev: BCCB 2/89; BL 2/1/89; SLJ 3/89; VOYA 6/89)

9739 Westera, Marleen. *Sheep and Goat* (1–3). Illus. by Sylvia van Ommen. 2006, Front St. $16.95 (978-1-932425-81-9). 99pp. Sheep and Goat are very fond of each other despite their differences in these 18 short stories in an early-chapter-book format. (Rev: BL 2/1/07; SLJ 11/06)

9740 Westwood, Chris. *He Came from the Shadows* (5–8). 1991, HarperCollins LB $14.89 (978-0-06-021659-7). In a cautionary tale about the dangers of wishing for too much, odd things start to happen after a stranger comes to town. (Rev: BL 4/1/91; SLJ 6/91)

9741 Whelan, Gerard. *Dream Invader* (5–7). 2002, O'Brien paper $7.95 (978-0-86278-516-1). 176pp. Only Simon's grandmother can break the spell behind the bad dreams he's been having in this supernatural tale set in Ireland. (Rev: BL 9/1/02)

9742 White, E. B. *Charlotte's Web* (3–5). Illus. by Garth Williams. 1952, HarperCollins LB $17.89 (978-0-06-026386-7); paper $7.99 (978-0-06-440055-8). 184pp. Classic, whimsical barnyard fable about a spider who saves the life of Wilbur the pig. Read about the ever-engaging mouse in: *Stuart Little* (1945).

9743 White, E. B. *The Trumpet of the Swan* (3–6). Illus. by Edward Frascino. 1970, HarperCollins LB $14.89 (978-0-06-026398-0); paper $4.95 (978-0-06-440048-0). 222pp. Louis, a voiceless trumpeter swan, is befriended by Sam, learns to play a trumpet, and finds fame, fortune, and fatherhood.

9744 Whittemore, JoAnne. *Escape from Arylon* (5–8). Series: The Silverskin Legacy. 2006, Llewellyn paper $8.95 (978-0-7387-0869-0). 360pp. Ainsley and Megan, neighbors with an uneasy friendship, find themselves transported through a portal to Arylon, where they meet many magical characters and must save the Staff of Lexiam from thieves. (Rev: SLJ 6/06; VOYA 6/06)

9745 Whybrow, Ian. *Little Wolf's Diary of Daring Deeds* (2–4). Illus. by Tony Ross. 2000, Carolrhoda LB $14.95 (978-1-57505-411-7). 127pp. A beginning chapter book told in hilarious letters by Little Wolf, who is trying to found a school called Adventure Academy with his cousin Yeller. (Rev: HBG 10/00; SLJ 6/00)

9746 Whybrow, Ian. *Little Wolf's Haunted Hall for Small Horrors* (2–4). Illus. by Tony Ross. 2000, Carolrhoda $14.95 (978-1-57505-412-4). 128pp. Little Wolf, his friend Yeller, and younger brother Smellybreff encounter the ghost of Little Wolf's

uncle Bigbad Wolf in this amusing animal fantasy told through letters. (Rev: HBG 3/01; SLJ 9/00)

9747 Whybrow, Ian. *The Unvisibles* (4–6). 2006, Holiday $16.95 (978-0-8234-1972-2). 184pp. Oliver Gasper and Nicky Chew are 12-year-old boys with almost nothing in common, but their lives intersect when Oliver desperately needs a friend to help him reverse the magical chant that rendered him invisible. (Rev: BL 4/15/06; SLJ 5/06)

9748 Wilkinson, Carole. *Dragon Moon* (4–6). Series: Dragon Keeper. 2008, Hyperion $16.99 (978-1-4231-1143-6). 368pp. In this final volume in the trilogy set in ancient China, Ping must find a way to take her dragon Kai to the Dragon Haven. (Rev: BL 5/15/08; SLJ 6/08)

9749 Wilkinson, Carole. *Garden of the Purple Dragon* (4–6). 2007, Hyperion $16.99 (978-1-4231-0338-7). 354pp. Twelve-year-old Ping and her charge, baby dragon Kai, face trials and betrayals as Ping strives to protect the line of imperial dragons from dying out in this sequel to *Dragon Keeper* (2005). (Rev: BL 11/1/07; SLJ 9/07)

9750 Willard, Nancy. *The High Rise Glorious Skittle Skat Roarious Sky Pie Angel Food Cake* (3–5). Illus. by Richard J. Watson. 1990, Harcourt $15.95 (978-0-15-234332-3). 64pp. Grandma's cake has mysterious ingredients — an odd spell and the special help of angels. (Rev: BCCB 12/90; BL 9/1/90; SLJ 11/90*)

9751 Williams, Alex. *The Deep Freeze of Bartholomew Tullock* (5–8). 2008, Philomel $16.99 (978-0-399-25185-6). 304pp. Never-ending snow has ruined the Breeze family's fan business and they find themselves in debt to the tyrannical Bartholomew Tullock; with their parents young Madeline and Rufus succeed in finding the machine that has been causing the constant winter. (Rev: BCCB 11/08; BL 10/1/08; LMC 1/09; SLJ 1/09)

9752 Williams, Maiya. *The Golden Hour* (4–8). 2004, Abrams $16.95 (978-0-8109-4823-5). 272pp. Thirteen-year-old Rowan and his 11-year-old sister Nina are sent to live with two great-aunts after the death of their mother and find themselves — with their new friends Xanthe and Xavier — transported through a time portal to 1789 Paris. (Rev: BL 3/15/04; SLJ 4/04; VOYA 6/04)

9753 Williams, Maiya. *The Hour of the Cobra* (4–7). 2006, Abrams $16.95 (978-0-8109-5970-5). 300pp. Xanthe, Xavier, Rowan, and Nina time-travel to ancient Egypt and narrowly avoid altering history in this sequel to *The Golden Hour* (2004). (Rev: BL 5/15/06; SLJ 7/06; VOYA 6/06)

9754 Williams, Maiya. *The Hour of the Outlaw* (4–7). 2007, Abrams $16.95 (978-0-8109-9355-6). 352pp. Xavier and Xanthe, Rowan and Nina travel back in time again — this time to the Old West during the California Gold Rush. (Rev: BL 1/1–15/08; SLJ 1/08)

9755 Williams, Margery. *The Velveteen Rabbit: Or, How Toys Become Real* (2–4). Illus. by Michael Hague. 1983, Holt $16.95 (978-0-8050-0209-6). 48pp. Love brings a toy rabbit to life. One of many fine editions.

9756 Williams, Mark London. *Trail of Bones* (5–8). Series: Danger Boy. 2005, Candlewick $9.99 (978-0-7636-2154-4). 300pp. Eli, Thea, and Clyne — three characters of very different backgrounds — travel back in time from 2019 to early 19th-century America and become involved with Lewis and Clark and the plight of escaping slaves. (Rev: SLJ 7/05)

9757 Williams, Tad, and Deborah Beale. *The Dragons of Ordinary Farm* (4–7). Illus. by Greg Swearingen. 2009, HarperCollins $16.99 (978-0-06-154345-6). 416pp. Tyler and Lucinda are staying with their great-uncle for the summer and discover the farm is full of mythical animals — dragons, unicorns, and more. (Rev: BLO 4/24/09; LMC 10/09)

9758 Wilson, N. D. *Dandelion Fire* (4–7). 2008, Random $16.99 (978-0-375-83883-5). 480pp. In an attempt to learn more about his birth parents, Henry and his cousin Henrietta again explore in the magical cupboards that lead to other worlds and runs him right up against an evil witch and her powerful minion; a multilayered sequel to *100 Cupboards* (2007). (Rev: BLO 1/13/09; SLJ 1/09) ☊

9759 Wilson, N. D. *100 Cupboards* (4–7). Series: 100 Cupboards. 2007, Random $16.99 (978-0-375-83881-1). 304pp. Henry, a timid 12-year-old, and his braver cousin Henrietta discover a wall of cupboards that lead to alternate worlds. (Rev: BL 12/1/07; HB 1/08; LMC 5/08; SLJ 4/08)

9760 Winterson, Jeanette. *Tanglewreck* (4–7). 2006, Bloomsbury $16.95 (978-1-58234-919-0). 415pp. After "time tornadoes" upset the delicate balance of time and space in and around London, 11-year-old Silver embarks on a fantastic odyssey in search of the Timekeeper that, hopefully, can set things right again. (Rev: BL 10/1/06; SLJ 10/06; VOYA 8/06)

9761 Winthrop, Elizabeth. *The Battle for the Castle* (4–7). 1993, Holiday $16.95 (978-0-8234-1010-1). 216pp. William and friend Jason time-travel to the Middle Ages, where they become involved in a struggle to prevent the return of evil as a ruling power. A sequel to *The Castle in the Attic* (1985). (Rev: BL 9/1/93; HB 7/93; SLJ 5/93)

9762 Winthrop, Elizabeth. *The Castle in the Attic* (5–7). 1985, Holiday $16.95 (978-0-8234-0579-4). 192pp. In an effort to keep his sitter from returning to England, William miniaturizes her and then must find a way to undo the deed. (Rev: BCCB 10/85; BL 1/15/86; SLJ 2/86)

9763 Wojtowicz, Jen. *The Boy Who Grew Flowers* (1–3). Illus. by Steve Adams. 2005, Barefoot Books $16.99 (978-1-84148-686-4). 32pp. In this story of differences and self-acceptance, Rink Bowagon, a boy who sprouts flowers from his body during the full moon, courts Angelina Quiz, a new girl at school who has a short right leg. (Rev: BL 10/15/05; SLJ 2/06)

9764 Wollman, Jessica. *Tell Me Who* (4–6). 2009, Dutton $15.99 (978-0-525-42087-3). 224pp. Twelve-year-old Molly becomes extremely popular when she finds a magic machine that predicts who people will marry, but that doesn't ease her worries about her father's upcoming marriage to "the Claw." (Rev: BCCB 2/09; BL 1/1–15/09; SLJ 8/09)

9765 Wood, Beverley, and Chris Wood. *Dog Star* (5–8). 1998, Orca paper $6.95 (978-0-89609-537-3). On a cruise to Alaska with his family, 13-year-old Jeff Beacon encounters a magical pet bull terrier who transports him back in time to the Juneau of 1932. (Rev: VOYA 8/98)

9766 Wood, Beverley, and Chris Wood. *Jack's Knife* (5–9). Series: A Sirius Mystery. 2006, Raincoast paper $7.95 (978-1-55192-709-1). 293pp. This sequel to *Dog Star* (1998) finds Jack time-traveling with bull terrier Patsy Ann to 1930s Alaska to help solve a mystery at sea. (Rev: SLJ 5/06)

9767 Wood, David. *The Phantom Cat of the Opera* (2–5). Illus. by Peters Day. 2001, Watson-Guptill $16.95 (978-0-8230-4018-6). The classic story is retold with cats as characters, with sumptuous illustrations. (Rev: HBG 10/01; SLJ 11/01)

9768 Woodruff, Elvira. *Awfully Short for the Fourth Grade* (3–6). Illus. by Will Hillenbrand. 1989, Holiday House $15.95 (978-0-8234-0785-9). 112pp. Noah's toy soldiers and superheroes come to life and he becomes their size when he uses a special dust from his magic kit. (Rev: BL 1/1/90; SLJ 11/89)

9769 Woodruff, Elvira. *Orphan of Ellis Island* (4–7). 1997, Scholastic paper $15.95 (978-0-590-48245-5). 192pp. Left alone on Ellis Island, Dominic finds himself transported in time to the village in Italy his family came from. (Rev: BCCB 3/97; BL 6/1–15/97; SLJ 5/97)

9770 Wrede, Patricia C. *Thirteenth Child* (5–8). 2009, Scholastic $16.99 (978-0-545-03342-8). 352pp. Magical beasts appear on the western frontier in this American history fantasy with a global awareness vibe. (Rev: BCCB 9/09; BL 6/1–15/09; HB 7/09)

9771 Wright, Betty R. *Christina's Ghost* (4–6). 1985, Holiday House $16.95 (978-0-8234-0581-7). 128pp. Dismayed at having to spend the summer with grumpy Uncle Ralph in his Victorian mansion, Christina is even more dismayed to discover a ghost in the house. (Rev: BCCB 2/86; BL 2/1/86)

9772 Wright, Betty R. *Crandalls' Castle* (4–7). 2003, Holiday $16.95 (978-0-8234-1726-1). 192pp. This gripping suspense story combines supernatural elements with a look at teen girls' yearning to belong. (Rev: BL 4/1/03; HBG 10/03; SLJ 5/03)

9773 Wright, Betty R. *The Ghost in Room 11* (2–4). 1997, Holiday House $16.95 (978-0-8234-1318-8). 112pp. Matt can't convince his classmates that he is being visited by the ghost of an old school teacher. (Rev: BCCB 4/98; BL 3/1/98; HBG 10/98; SLJ 3/98)

9774 Wright, Betty R. *A Ghost in the House* (5–7). 1991, Scholastic paper $13.95 (978-0-590-43606-9). 160pp. Bizarre happenings take place when Sarah's elderly aunt moves in. (Rev: BCCB 11/91; BL 1/1/91; SLJ 11/91)

9775 Wright, Betty R. *The Ghost of Popcorn Hill* (2–4). Illus. by Karen Ritz. 1993, Holiday House $16.95 (978-0-8234-1009-5). 96pp. Martin and

Peter are frightened by the ghost who visits their bedroom each night in their rustic home on Popcorn Hill. (Rev: BCCB 6/93; BL 2/15/93; HB 7/93; SLJ 5/93)

9776 Wright, Randall. *The Silver Penny* (4–7). 2005, Holt $16.95 (978-0-8050-7391-1). 197pp. In this compelling fantasy set in the 19th century, Jacob — after breaking his leg and facing disability — receives from his great-grandfather a lucky silver penny that gives him access to a supernatural world. (Rev: BCCB 7–8/05; SLJ 8/05; VOYA 10/05)

9777 Wynne-Jones, Tim. *Some of the Kinder Planets* (5–8). 1995, Orchard LB $16.99 (978-0-531-08751-0). Nine imaginative stories about ordinary boys and girls in offbeat situations. (Rev: BCCB 5/95; BL 3/1/95*; HB 1/95, 5/95, 9/95; SLJ 4/95*)

9778 Yee, Paul. *Ghost Train* (3–5). Illus. by Harvey Chan. 1996, Douglas & McIntyre $15.95 (978-0-88899-257-4). 32pp. In this historical fantasy, a Chinese girl comes to the United States and discovers that her father has been killed while working as a railroad construction laborer. (Rev: BCCB 2/97; BL 11/1/96)

9779 Yep, Laurence. *Dragon of the Lost Sea* (5–8). 1982, HarperCollins paper $6.99 (978-0-06-440227-9). 224pp. Shimmer, a dragon, in the company of a boy, Thorn, sets out to destroy the villain Civet. (Rev: BL 4/15/04)

9780 Yolen, Jane. *Here There Be Dragons* (3–8). Illus. by David Wilgus. Series: Jane Yolen Books. 1993, Harcourt $16.95 (978-0-15-209888-9); paper $10.00 (978-0-15-201705-7). 160pp. This original collection of pieces about dragons contains eight stories and five poems. (Rev: SLJ 12/93)

9781 Yolen, Jane. *Merlin* (5–8). Series: Young Merlin Trilogy. 1997, Harcourt $16.00 (978-0-15-200814-7). In this concluding volume of a trilogy, Hawk-Hobby (Merlin) escapes from his enemies with a young friend who will later become King Arthur. (Rev: BL 4/15/97; SLJ 5/97)

9782 Yolen, Jane. *Passager* (4–7). Series: Young Merlin Trilogy. 1996, Harcourt $16.00 (978-0-15-200391-3). 96pp. In medieval England, an abandoned 8-year-old boy named Merlin is taken in by a friendly man who becomes his master. Book two of the trilogy is *Hobby* (1996). (Rev: BL 5/1/96; HB 7/96; SLJ 5/96*)

9783 Yolen, Jane. *The Pictish Child* (3–6). Series: Tartan Magic. 1999, Harcourt $15.00 (978-0-15-202261-7). 144pp. Molly receives a talisman that begins a series of events involving Jennifer, a young Pict girl, who has time-traveled to modern times from ninth-century Britain. (Rev: BL 11/15/99; HBG 3/00; SLJ 12/99)

9784 Yolen, Jane. *Wizard's Hall* (4–6). 1991, Harcourt $13.95 (978-0-15-298132-7). 144pp. Henry, an 11-year-old novice wizard, can't seem to get anything right. (Rev: BCCB 7–8/91; BL 3/15/91; SLJ 7/91)

9785 Yoshi. *The Butterfly Hunt* (5–8). Illus. 1991, Picture Book paper $14.95 (978-0-88708-137-8). In this fantasy, a young boy releases a butterfly and forevermore it becomes his own. (Rev: SLJ 6/91)

9786 Young, Steve. *15 Minutes* (5–8). 2006, HarperCollins $15.99 (978-0-06-072508-2). 172pp. Casey, a 7th-grader who's always late for almost everything, discovers that his grandfather's watch gives him the power to go back 15 minutes. (Rev: SLJ 9/06)

9787 Zadrzynska, Ewa. *The Peaceable Kingdom* (4–6). Illus. by Tomek Olbinski. 1994, M.M. Art Bks. $14.95 (978-0-9638904-0-5). 32pp. In this fantasy, visitors to Brooklyn find that the three animals pictured in Hicks's painting "The Peaceable Kingdom," hanging in the Brooklyn Museum, are sitting in the park. (Rev: BL 7/94; SLJ 9/94)

9788 Zahn, Timothy. *Dragon and Herdsman: The Fourth Dragonback Adventure* (5–8). 2006, Tom Doherty Assoc. $17.95 (978-0-7653-1417-8). 299pp. With the help of a shape-changing dragon and his friend Alison, 14-year-old Jack Morgan escapes from the Malison Ring. (Rev: SLJ 9/06; VOYA 6/06)

9789 Zappa, Ahmet. *The Monstrous Memoirs of a Mighty McFearless* (4–7). Illus. by author. 2006, Random $12.95 (978-0-375-83287-1). 224pp. Written and illustrated by the son of Frank Zappa, this rollicking fantasy follows Mini and Max McFearless, monsterminators who must rescue their father from kidnappers. (Rev: BL 5/15/06; SLJ 7/06) 🎧

Friendship Stories

9790 Abbott, Tony. *Firegirl* (5–8). 2006, Little, Brown $15.99 (978-0-316-01171-6). 145pp. Tom, already an outsider at his Catholic school, bravely befriends a girl scarred by burns even when his classmates ostracize and ridicule her. (Rev: BL 7/06; SLJ 7/06)

9791 Applebaum, Diana. *Cocoa Ice* (2–5). Illus. by Holly Meade. 1997, Orchard LB $17.99 (978-0-531-33040-1). 56pp. Two girls, one in Santo Domingo and the other in Maine, are linked by world trade, which brings chocolate to one and ice to the other. (Rev: BCCB 3/98; BL 11/1/97*; HBG 3/98; SLJ 1/98*)

9792 Bedard, Michael. *Emily* (3–5). Illus. by Barbara Cooney. 1992, Doubleday $16.95 (978-0-385-30697-3). A young girl visits her neighbor, the reclusive Emily Dickinson. (Rev: BCCB 1/93; BL 2/1/93; HB 1/93; SLJ 11/92)

9793 Bellingham, Brenda. *Lilly's Good Deed* (3–4). Illus. by Kathy Kaulbach. Series: First Novels. 1999, Formac paper $3.99 (978-0-88780-460-1). 64pp. A beginning chapter book from Canada in which Lilly discovers that first impressions can be wrong when she realizes the value of the friendship of a clumsy classmate. (Rev: SLJ 8/99)

9794 Blume, Lesley M. M. *Cornelia and the Audacious Escapades of the Somerset Sisters* (4–6). 2006, Knopf $15.95 (978-0-375-83523-0). 272pp. Cornelia befriends the elderly woman who moves in next door and finds her loneliness abated by the woman's fascinating stories of her life. (Rev: BL 7/06; SLJ 9/06)

9795 Bowe, Julie. *My New Best Friend* (2–4). 2008, Harcourt $16.00 (978-0-15-206498-3). 192pp. Fourth-grader Ida May has a new best friend, and together they try to exploit the potential of a mermaid nightlight to make wishes come true; Ida comes to recognize, however, that Stacey may not always be telling the truth. A sequel to *My Last Best Friend* (2007). (Rev: BLO 7/29/08)

9796 Bunting, Eve. *Summer Wheels* (3–5). Illus. by Thomas B. Allen. 1992, Harcourt $14.95 (978-0-15-207000-7). 48pp. Lawrence and Brady are annoyed by the new kid, who signs out a bike from the Bicycle Man with the clear intention of not returning it. (Rev: BCCB 3/92; BL 4/15/92; HB 7/92; SLJ 8/92)

9797 Burnett, Frances Hodgson. *The Secret Garden* (4–6). Illus. by Tasha Tudor. 1987, HarperCollins paper $6.99 (978-0-06-440188-3). 256pp. Three children find a secret garden and make it bloom again; the garden, in turn, changes the children. One of many fine editions.

9798 Burnett, Frances Hodgson. *The Secret Garden* (5–8). 1999, Scholastic paper $4.99 (978-0-439-09939-4). An easily read classic about a spoiled girl relocated to England and the unusual friendship she finds there.

9799 Buscaglia, Leo. *A Memory for Tino* (4–6). Illus. by Carol Newsom. 1988, Slack $12.95 (978-1-55642-020-7). 50pp. Tino becomes friends with elderly Mrs. Sunday, and gives her his family's TV set. (Rev: BL 4/1/88; SLJ 5/88)

9800 Butler, Dori. *Trading Places with Tank Talbott* (4–6). 2003, Whitman LB $15.99 (978-0-8075-1708-6). 139pp. Tank and Jason — who have similar looks but dissimilar interests — become unlikely friends when they decide to switch unwanted assignments; Jason takes Tank's dancing lessons and Tank takes Jason's swimming lessons. (Rev: HBG 4/04; SLJ 6/03)

9801 Campbell, Ellen Langas. *Raising the Roof* (3–6). Illus. by April D'Angelo. Series: Girls Know How. 2005, NouSoma paper $4.95 (978-0-9743604-1-6). 121pp. A group of fifth-grade girls decide to build a clubhouse with the help of a local construction firm's female CEO. (Rev: SLJ 1/06)

9802 Carlson, Natalie Savage. *The Family Under the Bridge* (3–5). Illus. by Garth Williams. 1958, HarperCollins LB $17.89 (978-0-06-020991-9); paper $5.99 (978-0-06-440250-7). 112pp. Old Armand, a Paris hobo, finds three children huddled in his hideaway under the bridge and befriends them.

9803 Choyce, Lesley. *Carrie's Crowd* (3–4). Illus. by Mark Thurman. Series: First Novels. 1999, Formac paper $3.99 (978-0-88780-464-9). 64pp. A beginning chapter book in which Carrie realizes that making a friend of Giselle, a member of the "in" crowd, was a mistake because Giselle is rude and lacks respect for others. (Rev: SLJ 8/99)

9804 Cosby, Bill. *The Best Way to Play* (2–4). Illus. 1997, Scholastic $13.95 (978-0-590-13756-0); paper $3.99 (978-0-590-95617-8). 40pp. Little Bill wants a $50 video game but finds that he can have more fun making up a game with his friends. Also use *The Meanest Thing To Say* and *The Treasure Hunt* (both 1997). (Rev: BL 2/15/98; HBG 3/98; SLJ 12/97)

9805 Cox, Judy. *Butterfly Buddies* (2–4). Illus. by Blanche Sims. 2001, Holiday House $15.95 (978-0-8234-1654-7). 80pp. Third-grader Robin learns about being herself — and about butterflies — from a new friend and a new teacher. (Rev: BCCB 1/02; BL 9/1/01; HBG 3/02; SLJ 10/01)

9806 Cox, Judy. *That Crazy Eddie and the Science Project of Doom* (2–4). Illus. by Blanche Sims. 2005, Holiday House $15.95 (978-0-8234-1931-9). 88pp. Matt and Eddie's friendship is severely strained, threatening the success of their volcano science fair project. (Rev: BL 6/1–15/05)

9807 Crabtree, Julie. *Discovering Pig Magic* (5–8). 2008, Milkweed $16.95 (978-1-57131-683-7); paper $6.95 (978-1-57131-684-4). 184pp. Thirteen-year-old Matilda and her friends Ariel and Nicki try using magic to resolve the problems they face. (Rev: BCCB 1/09; SLJ 6/09)

9808 Denman, K. L. *Mirror Image* (5–8). Series: Currents. 2007, Orca $14.95 (978-1-55143-667-8); paper $8.95 (978-1-55143-667-4). 112pp. Popular Lacey and Sable, an immigrant to Canada from Bosnia who is a loner, could not be more different, and the girls are initially disappointed to be paired for an art project. (Rev: BL 3/15/07)

9809 Dowell, Frances O'Roark. *The Kind of Friends We Used to Be* (4–7). 2009, Atheneum $16.99 (978-1-4169-5031-8). 240pp. Kate and Marylin, whose friendship fell apart in *The Secret Language of Girls* (2005), are now in 7th grade and still heading in separate directions. (Rev: BCCB 5/09; BL 3/1/09; SLJ 3/09) ∩

9810 Dower, Laura. *Only the Lonely: From the Files of Madison Finn* (4–6). Illus. 2001, Hyperion paper $4.99 (978-0-7868-1553-1). 144pp. Madison Finn spends an unexpectedly lonely summer before entering seventh grade and confides her concerns to her laptop computer. (Rev: BL 6/1–15/01; SLJ 8/01)

9811 Erlings, Fridrik. *Benjamin Dove* (5–8). 2007, North-South $15.95 (978-0-7358-2150-7); paper $7.95 (978-0-7358-2149-1). 206pp. Set in Iceland, this story of four boys' friendship ends in violence when some of the friends take tragically wrong turns in their lives. (Rev: BL 2/1/08; SLJ 12/07)

9812 Ferber, Brenda A. *Jemma Hartman, Camper Extraordinaire* (3–6). 2009, Farrar $16.95 (978-0-374-33672-1). 224pp. Jemma's hopes of a great summer sailing with her best friend Tammy are dashed when Tammy turns up with her irritating cousin Brooke. (Rev: BL 5/1/09; SLJ 5/09)

9813 Flake, Sharon G. *The Broken Bike Boy and the Queen of 33rd Street* (3–5). Illus. by Colin Bootman. 2007, Hyperion $15.99 (978-1-4231-0032-4). 144pp. Queen is a spoiled 5th-grader who thinks she is better than all her classmates until she develops a friendship with the new boy, Leroy. (Rev: BCCB 9/07; BL 6/1–15/07; HB 7/07; LMC 11/07; SLJ 6/07)

9814 Freeman, Martha. *The Trouble with Babies* (2–4). Illus. by Cat B. Smith. 2002, Holiday House $15.95 (978-0-8234-1698-1). 80pp. Holly must learn to adapt — to her new life in San Francisco with her mother and stepfather, to her new friends, and to the fact that she is going to have a new sibling. (Rev: BCCB 11/02; BL 7/02; HBG 3/03; SLJ 8/02)

9815 Friedman, Laurie. *Happy Birthday, Mallory!* (2–4). Illus. by Tamara Schmitz. Series: Mallory. 2005, Carolrhoda LB $15.95 (978-1-57505-823-8). 159pp. As a special treat, Mallory is allowed to have an old friend come to visit for her ninth birthday in this beginning chapter book. (Rev: SLJ 9/05)

9816 Friedman, Laurie. *Mallory on Board* (2–4). Illus. by Barbara Pollak. Series: Mallory. 2007, Carolrhoda LB $15.95 (978-0-8225-6194-1). 175pp. Mallory isn't sure that she likes the idea of her two best friends, Joey and Mary Ann, becoming step siblings in this story set on a cruise ship. (Rev: SLJ 6/07)

9817 Friedman, Laurie. *Mallory on the Move* (2–4). Illus. by Tamara Schmitz. 2004, Carolrhoda $15.95 (978-1-57505-538-1). 160pp. Mallory, 8, is nervous when her best friend Mary Ann comes to visit her new home and will no doubt meet Mallory's new friend Joey; told in the first person, this book will appeal to new chapter-book readers. (Rev: BL 4/15/04; SLJ 4/04)

9818 Gabhart, Ann. *Two of a Kind* (3–6). 1992, Avon paper $3.50 (978-0-380-76153-1). 170pp. Birdie decides it's better to be aloof, even with her likable aunt and uncle, so she won't feel so bad when she's sent to another foster home. (Rev: BL 8/92)

9819 Gonzalez, Rigoberto. *Soledad Sigh-Sighs / Soledad Suspiros* (1–3). Trans. by Jorge Argueta. Illus. by Rosa Ibarra. 2003, Children's Book Pr. $16.95 (978-0-89239-180-6). 32pp. Latchkey child Soledad lives a lonely life with an imaginary companion until two neighboring sisters befriend her and even envy her solitude, in this bilingual novel set in Brooklyn. (Rev: BL 5/15/03; HBG 10/03; SLJ 3/03)

9820 Greene, Bette. *I've Already Forgotten Your Name, Philip Hall!* (4–7). Illus. by Leonard Jenkins. 2004, HarperCollins $15.99 (978-0-06-051835-6). 176pp. A little white lie that strains her relationship with her best friend, Philip Hall, is only one of the dramas Beth Lambert must deal with in this story set in small-town Arkansas. (Rev: BL 5/1/04; HB 3/04; SLJ 3/04; VOYA 6/04)

9821 Greene, Carol. *The Jenny Summer* (2–4). Illus. by Ellen Eagle. 1988, HarperCollins $11.95 (978-0-06-022208-6). 80pp. Robin learns a lot about friendship during one summer. (Rev: BL 6/15/88; SLJ 8/88)

9822 Greenwald, Sheila. *Rosy Cole's Memoir Explosion: A Heartbreaking Story About Losing Friends, Annoying Family, and Ruining Romance* (3–5). Series: Rosy Cole. 2006, Farrar $16.00 (978-0-374-36347-5). 112pp. Rosy sets out to write a memoir and, in an effort to be entertaining, portrays her friends in a less-than-flattering light. (Rev: BL 5/1/06; SLJ 4/06)

9823 Gregory, Kristiana. *Bronte's Book Club* (3–6). 2008, Holiday $16.95 (978-0-8234-2136-7). 160pp. Lonely in a new town on the California coast, 12-year-old Bronte starts a book club and finds new friends. (Rev: BL 4/1/08)

9824 Grimes, Nikki. *Make Way for Dyamonde Daniel* (2–4). Illus. by R. Gregory Christie. 2009, Putnam $10.99 (978-0-399-25175-7). 96pp. African American 3rd-grader Dyamonde manages to befriend a new student despite his prickly character. (Rev: BL 5/1/09; LMC 10/09; SLJ 7/09)

9825 Grindley, Sally. *Dear Max* (2–4). Illus. by Tony Ross. 2006, Simon & Schuster $14.95 (978-1-4169-0392-5). 144pp. Max, a 9-year-old aspiring writer, sends a letter to his favorite author, D. J. Lucas, and the two develop an unusual friendship, sharing their problems with writing and life in often-humorous exchanges. Also use *Bravo, Max!* (2007). (Rev: BL 8/06; SLJ 8/06*)

9826 Herman, Charlotte. *Max Malone Makes a Million* (3–5). Illus. 1991, Holt paper $6.95 (978-0-8050-2328-2). 77pp. Max wants to make a fortune, but learns a lesson in generosity instead. Also use: *Max Malone and the Great Cereal Rip-Off* (1990). (Rev: BCCB 6/91; BL 3/1/91; SLJ 6/91)

9827 Hoffman, Mary. *Starring Grace* (2–4). Illus. by Caroline Binch. 2000, Penguin $14.99 (978-0-8037-2559-1). 96pp. A lively chapter book about young Grace and her many summer adventures with friends, culminating in walk-on roles in a theatrical production. (Rev: BCCB 9/00; BL 2/15/00; HB 3/00; HBG 10/00; SLJ 7/00)

9828 Hossack, Sylvie. *The Flying Chickens of Paradise Lane* (3–6). 1994, Avon paper $3.50 (978-0-380-72201-3). 144pp. Ten-year-old Brenda, who desperately wants to learn to fly, forms a secret club with friends and practices jumping from ever-increasing heights. (Rev: BL 3/1/93; SLJ 3/93)

9829 Hurwitz, Johanna. *Spring Break* (3–5). Illus. 1997, Morrow $15.95 (978-0-688-14937-6). 144pp. An appealing novel about Cricket and her adventures when she is unable to go with her class to Washington, D.C., during spring break because of a broken ankle. (Rev: BCCB 4/97; BL 4/15/97; SLJ 5/97)

9830 Jacobson, Jennifer. *Truly Winnie* (2–4). Illus. by Alissa Imre Geis. 2003, Houghton $15.00 (978-0-618-28008-7). 112pp. One lie leads to another as Winnie tries to hide the truth about her mother from her friends at camp in this sequel to *Winnie Dancing on Her Own* (2001). (Rev: BL 9/1/03; HBG 4/04; SLJ 11/03)

9831 Kaye, Marilyn. *Cabin Six Plays Cupid* (4–6). 1989, Avon paper $2.95 (978-0-380-75701-5). 116pp. Five friends in Cabin 6 at Camp Sunnyside try to help their counselor's love life. Also use: *No Boys Allowed* (1989). (Rev: BL 7/89; SLJ 9/89)

9832 Kaye, Marilyn. *A Friend Like Phoebe* (4–6). 1989, Harcourt $13.95 (978-0-15-200450-7). 144pp. Phoebe's best friend is chosen for an honor that Phoebe wanted, which causes a crisis in their friendship. A sequel to *Phoebe* (1987). (Rev: BL 8/89; SLJ 11/89)

9833 Kline, Suzy. *Herbie Jones Moves On* (3–5). 2003, Penguin $14.99 (978-0-399-23635-8). 78pp. Herbie Jones, the title character from eight previous children's books, is back, and this time he's lamenting the imminent departure of his best friend, Raymond. (Rev: HBG 10/03; SLJ 6/03)

9834 Koller, Jackie F. *Impy for Always* (2–4). Illus. by Carol Newsom. 1989, Little, Brown $9.95 (978-0-316-50147-7); paper $3.95 (978-0-316-50149-1). 64pp. Eight-year-old Imogene's thoughts of another fun summer are dashed when 12-year-old cousin Christina arrives all grown up. (Rev: BL 6/15/59)

9835 Lamb, Nancy. *The Great Mosquito, Bull, and Coffin Caper* (3–5). Illus. by Frank Remkiewicz. 1994, Morrow paper $4.95 (978-0-688-12944-6). 120pp. To make sure they will not forget each other when one moves away, two friends face three dares, each tougher than the last. (Rev: BL 10/15/92; SLJ 11/92)

9836 Lewis, Beverly. *Holly's First Love* (4–6). Series: Holly's Heart. 1993, Zondervan paper $6.99 (978-0-310-38051-1). 160pp. Holly and Andie's friendship is strained when they both find they are attracted to the new boy in town. Also use *Secret Summer Dreams* (1993). (Rev: SLJ 12/93)

9837 Lombard, Jenny. *Drita, My Homegirl* (3–5). 2006, Putnam $15.99 (978-0-399-24380-6). 112pp. Drita, a refugee from Kosovo, and Maxie, a motherless African American girl, connect despite their differences in this story set in a Brooklyn neighborhood. (Rev: BL 5/1/06; SLJ 3/06*)

9838 McDonald, Megan. *Judy Moody: Around the World in 8 1/2 Days* (3–4). Illus. by Peter H. Reynolds. 2006, Candlewick $15.99 (978-0-7636-2832-1). 157pp. In this new easy-chapter-book adventure, third-grader Judy Moody becomes so obsessed with new friend Amy Namey that she neglects some of her longtime pals. (Rev: SLJ 11/06)

9839 McGhee, Alison. *Snap* (4–6). 2004, Candlewick $15.99 (978-0-7636-2002-8). 132pp. Edwina Beckey, 11, who uses rubber bands to remember things, worries about her friend Sally, whose grandmother is dying. (Rev: BL 5/15/04; SLJ 4/04)

9840 Maguire, Gregory. *Six Haunted Hairdos* (4–6). Illus. 1997, Clarion $16.00 (978-0-395-78626-0). 148pp. A funny story about two rival school groups, the boys' Copycats and the girls' Tattletales, and how they amuse themselves by telling ghost stories. The sequel to *Seven Spiders Spinning* (1994). (Rev: BL 11/1/97; HBG 3/98; SLJ 9/97)

9841 Makris, Kathryn. *The Five Cat Club* (4–6). Series: Eco-Kids. 1994, Avon paper $3.50 (978-0-380-77049-6). 156pp. Three junior high girls find homes for five abandoned kittens and become interested in animal rights and environmental issues. Also use *The Green Team* and *The Clean-up Crew* (both 1994). (Rev: SLJ 9/94)

9842 Medearis, Angela Shelf. *The Adventures of Sugar and Junior* (2–3). Illus. by Nancy Poydar. 1995, Holiday House LB $15.95 (978-0-8234-1182-

5). 32pp. A simple story of a friendship between a Hispanic American and an African American youngster and their happy times together. (Rev: BL 10/15/95; SLJ 12/95)

9843 Myers, Laurie. *Surviving Brick Johnson* (3–5). Illus. 2000, Clarion $15.00 (978-0-395-98031-6). 80pp. Fifth-grader Alex believes that newcomer Brick is a big bully, but when they both sign up for karate classes, he finds that he is wrong. (Rev: BCCB 11/00; BL 9/15/00; HBG 3/01; SLJ 10/00)

9844 Myracle, Lauren. *The Fashion Disaster That Changed My Life* (5–8). 2005, Dutton $15.99 (978-0-525-47222-3). 160pp. Through her diary and instant messages, Allison relates the turmoil of 7th grade, from her humiliating first-day arrival with her mother's underwear clinging to her pants to her problems making and keeping friends. (Rev: BL 9/15/05; SLJ 7/05)

9845 Nagda, Ann Whitehead. *Dear Whiskers* (2–4). Illus. 2000, Holiday House $15.95 (978-0-8234-1495-6). 64pp. For a school assignment, Jenny writes to a younger Saudi Arabian girl in her school and gradually forms a friendship with this reclusive girl who knows little English. (Rev: BCCB 2/01; BL 11/15/00; HB 3/01; HBG 10/01; SLJ 1/01)

9846 Nemeth, Sally. *The Heights, the Depths, and Everything in Between* (5–8). 2006, Knopf LB $17.99 (978-0-375-93458-2). 272pp. Jake Little, a dwarf, and Lucy Small, who despite her name is unusually tall, become friends and navigate the rough waters of middle school and dealing with parents in this story set in the 1970s. (Rev: BL 7/06)

9847 Nicholson, Peggy, and John F. Warner. *The Case of the Furtive Firebug* (3–5). 1994, Lerner LB $13.27 (978-0-8225-0709-3). 120pp. Halley and her little brother Jason try to help a Vietnamese American girl who is falsely accused of arson. (Rev: BL 3/1/95)

9848 O'Connor, Barbara. *Fame and Glory in Freedom, Georgia* (4–6). 2003, Farrar $16.00 (978-0-374-32258-8). 112pp. Sixth-grader Bird finds difficulties and rewards in her campaign to befriend new-boy-at-school Harlem. (Rev: BL 7/03*; HB 7/03; HBG 10/03; SLJ 6/03)

9849 O'Dell, Kathleen. *Agnes Parker . . . Happy Camper?* (4–6). 2005, Dial $16.99 (978-0-8037-2962-9). 160pp. When Agnes and her best friend, Prejean, are assigned to different cabins at science camp, Agnes rightly worries that the two will grow apart. (Rev: BL 1/1–15/05; SLJ 3/05)

9850 O'Dell, Kathleen. *Agnes Parker. . . Keeping Cool in Middle School* (3–6). 2007, Dial $16.99 (978-0-8037-3078-6). 160pp. Now in 7th grade friends Agnes and Prejean take different approaches to the social life and try to cope with bullying and other challenges. (Rev: BL 7/07; SLJ 9/07)

9851 Pennypacker, Sara. *Clementine* (2–4). Illus. by Marla Frazee. 2006, Hyperion $14.99 (978-0-7868-3882-0). 144pp. Eight-year-old Clementine means well but seems to find herself spending a lot of time in the school principal's office. (Rev: BL 10/15/06; SLJ 10/06*)

9852 Preller, James. *Along Came Spider* (4–6). 2008, Scholastic $15.99 (978-0-545-03299-5). 144pp. Popular 5th-grader Spider finds it difficult to maintain his friendship with Trey, who displays some antisocial behaviors. (Rev: BL 12/1/08; SLJ 12/08)

9853 Robinson, Sharon. *Slam Dunk!* (4–6). 2007, Scholastic $16.99 (978-0-439-67199-6). 151pp. New to his Harlem school, 6th-grade Jumper struggles to discover if he can be a friend and competitor with a girl. (Rev: BL 9/1/07; SLJ 11/07)

9854 Sachar, Louis. *Sixth Grade Secrets* (4–6). 1987, Scholastic paper $4.99 (978-0-590-46075-0). 208pp. Laura starts a club called Pig City, which eventually ends up by telling everyone's secrets. (Rev: BL 11/1/87; SLJ 9/87)

9855 Salmansohn, Karen. *Oh, and Another Thing* (4–6). Illus. by author. Series: Alexandra Rambles On! 2001, Tricycle $12.95 (978-1-58246-045-1). Twelve-year-old Alexandra gets advice on how to handle boys. (Rev: SLJ 2/02)

9856 Spinelli, Jerry. *Eggs* (4–7). 2007, Little, Brown $15.99 (978-0-316-16646-1). 240pp. Two troubled children — 9-year-old David and 13-year-old Primrose — forge an unlikely friendship. (Rev: BL 4/1/07; SLJ 7/07)

9857 Stauffacher, Sue. *Donutheart* (4–6). 2006, Knopf $15.95 (978-0-375-83275-8). 208pp. In this sequel to *Donuthead* (2003), Franklin is having trouble making the adjustment to middle school but he sets aside his own preoccupations (hygiene and safety, among them) to come to the aid of Sarah, his best friend. (Rev: BL 11/1/06; SLJ 1/07)

9858 Staunton, Ted. *Two False Moves* (3–5). 2000, Red Deer paper $4.95 (978-0-88995-205-8). 64pp. Relations between classmates Nick and Lindsey deteriorate when Lindsey's parents become prospective buyers of the rented home where Nick and his family live. (Rev: BL 2/15/01)

9859 Steele, Mary. *Featherbys* (4–6). 1996, Peachtree paper $6.95 (978-1-56145-135-7). 180pp. Sixth-graders Jess and Vicky befriend two elderly sisters and help them fight a menacing relative. (Rev: BL 12/15/96)

9860 Stolz, Mary. *The Noonday Friends* (4–6). Illus. by Louis Glanzman. 1965, HarperCollins LB $16.89 (978-0-06-025946-4); paper $5.99 (978-0-06-440009-1). 192pp. Eleven-year-old Franny's unskilled father is out of work, and the demanded family teamwork leaves her free from chores only during lunch periods.

9861 Tarshis, Lauren. *Emma-Jean Lazarus Fell Out of a Tree* (4–6). 2007, Dial $16.99 (978-0-8037-3164-6). 208pp. Emma-Jean Lazarus is persuaded to use her analytical mind to help a classmate cope with a bully and discovers that social relationships are not always logical. (Rev: BL 3/15/07)

9862 Walsh, Jill Paton. *Gaffer Samson's Luck* (4–6). Illus. by Brock Cole. 1984, Farrar paper $4.95 (978-0-374-42513-5). 112pp. Out to retrieve a good luck stone for his elderly friend Gaffer, James runs into the school bully and learns about different kinds of friendship.

9863 Warner, Sally. *Not So Weird Emma* (2–4). Illus. by Jamie Harper. 2005, Viking $14.99 (978-0-670-06005-4). 128pp. The friendship of third graders Emma McGraw and Cynthia Harbison is fractured when the two start calling each other unflattering names; a sequel to *Only Emma* (2005). (Rev: BL 9/1/05; SLJ 11/05)

9864 Warner, Sally. *Only Emma* (2–4). Illus. by Jamie Harper. Series: Emma. 2005, Viking $14.99 (978-0-670-05979-9). 128pp. In this first book of a series, Emma must deal with a new school, a new apartment, and a week-long visit from 4-year-old Anthony Scarpetto. (Rev: BL 3/1/05; SLJ 4/05)

9865 Willner-Pardo, Gina. *Figuring Out Frances* (4–6). 1999, Clarion $14.00 (978-0-395-91510-3). 144pp. In middle school, Abigail, who is coping with personal problems such as her grandmother's Alzheimer's disease, is dismayed when her long-time friend Travis drifts away and prefers the company of boys. (Rev: BCCB 10/99; BL 9/15/99; HBG 3/00; SLJ 9/99)

9866 Willner-Pardo, Gina. *When Jane-Marie Told My Secret* (3–4). Illus. 1995, Clarion $14.95 (978-0-395-66382-0). 40pp. Carolyn can't forgive her dear friend Jane-Marie after she has given away one of their secrets. (Rev: BL 8/95; SLJ 9/95)

9867 Wong, Janet S. *Minn and Jake's Almost Terrible Summer* (3–6). Illus. by Genevieve Cote. 2008, Farrar $15.00 (978-0-374-34977-6). 112pp. Two friends, Minn and Jake, finally figure out how to get it better if not exactly right after a move separated them. (Rev: BCCB 9/08; BL 11/15/08; SLJ 8/08)

9868 Yee, Lisa. *Millicent Min, Girl Genius* (4–6). 2003, Scholastic $16.95 (978-0-439-42519-3). 256pp. Eleven-year-old Millicent Min, a child prodigy frustrated by her inability to find friends who are her intellectual equal, decides to hide her genius in order to win Emily as a friend. (Rev: BL 9/1/03; HB 9/03; HBG 4/04; SLJ 3/04)

9869 Yee, Lisa. *So Totally Emily Ebers* (5–8). 2007, Scholastic $16.99 (978-0-439-83847-4). 281pp. In this companion to *Millicent Min, Girl Genius* (2003) and *Stanford Wong Flunks Big-Time* (2005), Emily writes a series of letters to her absent father, telling him about her friends Millicent and Stanford and their tutoring arrangement. (Rev: BL 3/15/07; SLJ 4/07)

9870 Yee, Paul. *Shu-Li and Tamara* (2–4). Illus. by Shaoli Wang. 2008, Tradewind paper $7.95 (978-1-896580-93-7). 72pp. Fourth-grader Shu-li is happy to find a friend in her new school in Vancouver, but is it possible that Tamara has been stealing? (Rev: BL 4/1/08; SLJ 9/08)

Graphic Novels

9871 Akimoto, Nami. *Ultra Cute, Vol. 1* (5–8). Trans. from Japanese by Emi Onishi. Illus. by author. 2006, TokyoPop paper $9.99 (978-1-59532-956-1). 179pp. Ami and Noa, more rivals than friends, compete with each other over two guys who are not as nice as they seem. (Rev: SLJ 7/06)

9872 *The Amazing Spider-Man* (3–6). Illus. by Andy Mansfield. Series: Marvel Comics True Believers Retro Character Collection. 2007, Candlewick $24.99 (978-0-7636-3263-2). Pop-ups and pull tabs introduce young readers to the world of the classic superhero and his enemies. (Rev: SLJ 5/07)

9873 Baltazar, Art, and Franco Aureliani. *Patrick the Wolf Boy, Vol. 1* (2–8). Illus. by Art Baltazar. 2005, DDP paper $10.95 (978-1-932796-27-8). A graphic novel about the hilarious adventures of a young werewolf. (Rev: SLJ 7/05)

9874 Barker, Henry, and Shannon Lowry, adapts. *Historical Adventure* (4–8). Illus. by Dan Spiegle. Series: Bank Street Graphic Novels. 2007, World Almanac LB $29.27 (978-0-8368-7927-8). 56pp. Versions of *A Connecticut Yankee in King Arthur's Court*, *Around the World in Eighty Days*, and *The Prisoner of Zenda* are included here and act as good introductions to the classic stories. (Rev: SLJ 7/07)

9875 Baum, L. Frank. *The Wizard of Oz* (3–5). Adapted by Michael Cavallero. 2005, Puffin paper $10.99 (978-0-14-240471-3). 152pp. In this graphic adaptation that retains original dialogue, Dorothy wears jeans, the Good Witch of the North sports sunglasses, and the Tin Woodman has traded his ax for a buzz saw. (Rev: SLJ 11/05)

9876 Blackman, Haden, et al. *Clone Wars Adventures* (4–7). Series: Star Wars Clone Wars Adventures. 2006, Dark Horse paper $6.95 (978-1-59307-483-8). 96pp. This fifth volume of the fantasy series, based on the TV cartoon show, includes four fast-paced stories of graphic novel action and adventure. (Rev: BL 6/1–15/06)

9877 Brennan, Michael. *Electric Girl, Vol. 2* (5–8). Illus. 2002, Mighty Gremlin paper $13.95 (978-0-9703555-1-5). 160pp. In this graphic novel, Virginia, who can release bursts of electricity at will, locks horns with evil gremlin Oogleeoog. (Rev: BL 5/1/02; SLJ 5/02)

9878 Cammuso, Frank. *The Dodgeball Chronicles* (2–4). Illus. by author. 2008, Scholastic paper $9.99 (978-0-439-90322-6). 142pp. In this humorous graphic novel with an Arthurian flavor, our middle-school hero Artie King fights bullies and bad lunches. (Rev: BL 3/15/08; LMC 11/08; SLJ 7/08)

9879 Cammuso, Frank, and Jay Lynch. *Otto's Orange Day* (K–2). Illus. by Frank Cammuso. 2008, Raw Junior/TOON $12.95 (978-0-9799238-2-1). 40pp. Granting Otto's wish, a genie turns the world orange, which turns out not to have been the best choice of colors. (Rev: BL 3/15/08; HB 7/08; LMC 3/08; SLJ 5/08)

9880 Clugston, Chynna. *Queen Bee* (5–8). Illus. 2005, Scholastic paper $8.99 (978-0-439-70987-3). 112pp. In this humorous graphic novel about school cliques, Haley and Alexa, two middle school students with psychokinetic powers, battle each other to become the school's most popular girl. (Rev: BL 9/15/05; SLJ 1/06; VOYA 12/05)

9881 Craddock, Erik. *Stone Rabbit: BC Mambo* (3–5). Illus. by author. 2009, Random LB $11.99 (978-0-375-93922-8); paper $5.99 (978-0-375-84360-0). 96pp. A young rabbit finds himself transported first into a prehistoric world where he is seen as a god and then pursued for his barbecue sauce. (Rev: BL 11/15/08; LMC 5/09)

9882 *Creepy Creatures* (3–5). Illus. by Gabriel Hernandez, et al. Series: Goosebumps Graphix. 2006, Scholastic $16.99 (978-0-439-84124-5); paper $8.99 (978-0-439-84125-2). 144pp. Three Goosebumps stories — "The Werewolf of Fever Swamp," "The Scarecrow Walks at Midnight," and "The Abominable Snowman of Pasadena" — are presented in black-and-white graphic-novel format. (Rev: BL 10/1/06; SLJ 11/06)

9883 Davis, Eleanor. *The Secret Science Alliance and the Copycat Crook* (4–6). Illus. by author. 2009, Bloomsbury $18.99 (978-1-59990-142-8); paper $10.99 (978-1-59990-396-5). 160pp. The technology — some gadget instructions are included — will fascinate readers of this story about 10-year-old Julian Calendar who enters a new school hoping to create a new, popular personality for himself but finds that his scientific skills are actually appreciated. (Rev: BCCB 11/09; BL 7/09; LMC 11/09; SLJ 9/09)

9884 Davis, Jim. *Garfield: 30 Years of Laughs and Lasagna* (5–10). Illus. by author. 2008, Ballantine $35.00 (978-0-345-50379-4). 288pp. A collection of the popular comic strip that centers on a grumpy, overweight cat. (Rev: BL 10/15/08; SLJ 1/09)

9885 de Campi, Alex. *Kat and Mouse: Tripped* (3–5). Illus. by Federica Manfredi. 2007, TokyoPop paper $5.99 (978-1-59816-549-4). 96pp. In this second installment in the manga mystery series, Kat and Mouse are on a field trip to the art museum when a famous painting is stolen. (Rev: BL 3/15/07)

9886 Denton, Terry. *Storymaze 1: The Ultimate Wave* (3–6). Illus. 2003, Allen & Unwin paper $5.95 (978-1-86508-378-0). 144pp. An imaginative visit to a parallel universe, very similar to ours, where there is an ongoing battle between good and evil; a decoder glossary allows translation of digital speech. A recommended sequel is *Storymaze 2: The Eye of Ulam* (2003). (Rev: BL 5/15/03)

9887 Dezago, Todd. *Spider-Man: The Terrible Threat of the Living Brain!* (5–8). Illus. by Jonboy Meyers, et al. Series: Spider-Man. 2006, ABDO LB $21.35 (978-1-59961-008-5). Spider-Man, with a little help from Flash, foils the theft of the Living Brain, a powerful robot-like computer. (Rev: SLJ 11/06)

9888 Dezago, Todd. *Spider-Man and Captain America: Stars, Stripes, and Spiders!* (5–8). Series: Spider-Man Team Up. 2006, ABDO LB $21.35 (978-1-59961-001-6). In this action-packed comic-book fantasy, superheroes Spider-Man and Captain America team up to battle the Grey Gargoyle. (Rev: SLJ 11/06)

9889 *Fairy Tales of Oscar Wilde* (5–8). Illus. by P. Craig Russell. 1992, Nantier $15.95 (978-1-56163-056-1). 46pp. Graphic novel treatment enlivens this retelling of two of Wilde's short stories. (Rev: BL 1/15/93)

9890 Farshtey, Greg. *The Rise of the Toa Nuva* (3–6). Illus. by Carlos D'Anda. 2008, Papercutz $12.95 (978-1-59707-110-9). 112pp. Cyborgs defend a tropical island in this complex graphic novel based on a Lego game. (Rev: BL 8/08)

9891 Fisher, Jane Smith. *WJHC: Hold Tight* (4–7). Illus. 2005, Wilson Place paper $11.95 (978-0-9744235-1-7). 96pp. This graphic-novel sequel to *WJHC: On the Air* (2003) continues the adventures of six diverse teenage friends who launched a high school radio station, following them through a reality TV show, a celebrity fashion show, and a trip to a rock concert. (Rev: BL 11/1/05; SLJ 1/06)

9892 Fisher, Jane Smith. *WJHC: On the Air!* (4–8). Illus. 2003, Wilson Place paper $11.95 (978-0-9744235-0-0). 96pp. Six episodes catalog the entertaining misadventures of a diverse band of teens who launch a high school radio station. (Rev: BL 2/1/04; VOYA 12/03)

9893 Frampton, Otis. *Oddly Normal, Vol. 1* (4–7). Illus. 2006, Viper paper $11.95 (978-0-9777883-0-9). 128pp. Half-human and half-witch, unhappy 10-year-old Oddly Normal struggles to find a place where she fits in; a collection of four issues of a mini-series published by Viper Comics. Also use *Family Reunion* (2007). (Rev: BL 11/1/06)

9894 Friesen, Ray. *A Cheese Related Mishap and Other Stories* (5–8). Illus. 2005, Don't Eat Any Bugs paper $8.95 (978-0-9728177-6-9). 96pp. This collection of zany tales full of entertaining characters and situations was created by a teenage author/illustrator. (Rev: BL 11/15/05; SLJ 3/06)

9895 Friesen, Ray. *Cupcakes of Doom: A Collection of YARG! Piratey Comics* (4–6). Illus. by author. 2009, Don't Eat Any Bugs paper $12.95 (978-0-9802314-1-0). 100pp. Swashbuckling pirates are marooned on an island with a single Pirate Cookie at the beginning of this boisterous adventure full of wordplay. (Rev: BL 3/1/09)

9896 Friesen, Ray. *Yarg!* (3–5). Illus. Series: Lookit! 2007, Don't Eat Any Bugs paper $11.95 (978-0-972817-79-0). 102pp. Back for a new round of adventures in this madcap sequel to *A Cheese Related Mishap* (2005), Melville the penguin and his friends scramble for gold in an effort to pay the back rent on the castle of Pellmellia. (Rev: BL 3/15/07)

9897 Fuji, Machiko. *The Big Adventures of Majoko* (3–6). Illus. by Tomomi Mizuna. Series: Manga for Kids. 2009, Udon paper $7.99 (978-1-897376-81-2). 200pp. A young witch named Majoko and a shy girl named Nana team up in this magical adventure manga. (Rev: BL 4/1/09)

9898 Fujino, Moyamu. *The First King Adventure, Vol. 1* (4–8). Trans. from Japanese by Kay Bertrand. Illus. by author. 2004, ADV paper $9.99 (978-1-4139-0194-8). Prince Tiltu cannot succeed his father as king until he's made contracts with all of the spirit masters that inhabit the kingdom. (Rev: SLJ 7/05)

9899 Gaiman, Neil. *Coraline* (4–7). Illus. by P. Craig Russell. 2008, HarperCollins LB $19.89 (978-0-06-082544-7); paper $18.99 (978-0-06-082543-0). 192pp. This adaptation of the 2002 novel by the same name graphically captures Coraline's horror as her nightmares become real behind a strange door. (Rev: BL 3/15/08; SLJ 7/08)

9900 Gallardo, Adam. *Gear School* (4–7). Illus. by Nuria Peris. 2007, Dark Horse paper $7.95 (978-1-59307-854-6). 96pp. Teresa, 13, is being trained to operate huge robotic attack machines called Gear when aliens attack and she and her classmates must defend themselves. (Rev: BL 11/15/07)

9901 Gownley, Jimmy. *Amelia Rules! The Whole World's Crazy* (3–5). Illus. 2003, iBooks paper $14.95 (978-0-7434-7503-7). 160pp. This is a compilation of previously self-published comic-book episodes about the entertaining exploits, triumphs, and disappointments of fourth-grade Amelia. (Rev: BL 2/1/04)

9902 Gownley, Jimmy. *Superheroes* (4–7). Illus. by author. Series: Amelia Rules! 2007, Renaissance paper $14.95 (978-0-9712169-6-9). 176pp. Amelia's life is a blend of comedy and angst as she faces life after her parents' divorce, a new neighborhood, and new friends. (Rev: BL 9/1/07)

9903 Grant, Alan. *Kidnapped: The Graphic Novel* (5–8). Illus. by Cam Kennedy. 2007, Tundra paper $11.95 (978-0-88776-843-9). 64pp. A graphic novel adaptation of the story by Robert Louis Stevenson that captures the spirit of the original. (Rev: BL 10/1/07; SLJ 1/08)

9904 Grayson, Devin. *X-Men: Evolution: Hearing Things* (5–8). Illus. by UDON, et al. Series: X-Men Evolution. 2006, ABDO LB $21.35 (978-1-59961-053-5). In this comic-book adventure from the early years of the X-Men series, Jean Grey comes to grips with her telepathic and telekinetic powers. (Rev: SLJ 11/06)

9905 *Green Lantern* (4–10). Series: Showcase Presents. 2005, DC Comics paper $9.99 (978-1-4012-0759-5). 526pp. A collection of black-and-white reprints of the early comics about the handsome crime fighter. (Rev: SLJ 5/06)

9906 Hakamada, Mera. *Fairy Idol Kanon, Vol. 1* (2–5). Illus. by author. Series: Manga for Kids. 2009, Udon paper $7.99 (978-1-897376-89-8). 200pp. Kanon, a 4th-grader who loves to sing, meets a fairy who may make her a star in this manga for young readers. (Rev: BLO 4/30/09; LMC 10/09)

9907 Harper, Charise Mericle. *Fashion Kitty Versus the Fashion Queen* (4–7). Illus. by author. 2007, Hyperion paper $8.99 (978-0-7868-3726-7). 89pp. Superhero Fashion Kitty (Kiki Kittie's alter ego) continues to rescue victims of fashion emergencies in this funny sequel to *Fashion Kitty* (2005). (Rev: BCCB 7–8/07; SLJ 11/07)

9908 Hicks, Faith Erin. *The War at Ellsmere* (5–8). Illus. by author. 2008, SLG paper $12.95 (978-1-59362-140-7). 156pp. The war is between wealthy snobs and a scholarship student at a classy boarding school, with a legendary unicorn thrown into this readable mix. (Rev: BL 3/1/09)

9909 Holm, Jennifer. *Skater Girl* (3–5). Illus. by Matthew Holm. Series: Babymouse. 2007, Random

LB $12.99 (978-0-375-93989-1); paper $5.99 (978-0-375-83989-4). 96pp. Babymouse is good at skating but does she have the determination to make it big on the ice? This 7th installment in the series will also attract reluctant readers. (Rev: BL 9/1/07; HB 11/07)

9910 Holm, Jennifer, and Matthew Holm. *Babymouse: Monster Mash* (4–6). Illus. by Jennifer Holm. 2008, Random LB $11.99 (978-0-375-93789-7); paper $5.99 (978-0-375-84387-7). 96pp. Orange replaces pink as the dominant color in this Halloween-themed installment in the series about the young mouse. (Rev: BLO 7/22/08; HB 9/08)

9911 Holm, Jennifer, and Matthew Holm. *Babymouse: Our Hero* (4–6). Illus. 2005, Random LB $12.99 (978-0-375-93230-4); paper $5.95 (978-0-375-83230-7). 96pp. Babymouse dreads competing in her class's annual dodgeball tournament, but when her best friend is threatened she surprises herself and saves the day for her team. (Rev: BL 12/1/05; SLJ 3/06)

9912 Holm, Jennifer, and Matthew Holm. *Babymouse: Queen of the World* (4–6). Illus. 2005, Random LB $12.99 (978-0-375-93229-8); paper $5.95 (978-0-375-83229-1). 96pp. Babymouse learns some important lessons about the true meaning of friendship after she slights Wilson Weasel to win an invitation to Felicia Furrypaws' slumber party. (Rev: BL 12/1/05; SLJ 3/06)

9913 Holm, Jennifer, and Matthew Holm. *Babymouse: The Musical* (4–6). Illus. by Jennifer Holm. 2009, Random LB $11.99 (978-0-375-93791-0); paper $5.99 (978-0-375-84388-4). 96pp. It's school musical time, and — despite her shortcomings on stage — Babymouse tries out for a role on the urging of a new student, British hedgehog Henry Higgins. (Rev: BL 3/1/09)

9914 Huey, Debbie. *Bumperboy and the Loud, Loud Mountain* (2–4). 2006, AdHouse paper $8.95 (978-0-9766610-1-6). 128pp. Bumperboy and his faithful canine sidekick try to unravel the mysteries surrounding the disappearance of the Grums and an endangered talking mountain called Jumbra; the second installment in a graphic-novel series. (Rev: BL 8/06)

9915 Hugo, Victor. *The Hunchback of Notre Dame* (5–8). Illus. by Penko Gelev. Series: Graphic Classics. 2007, Barron's $15.99 (978-0-7641-5979-4). 48pp. The dramatic artwork will draw readers into this story; information on author Victor Hugo gives background and historical context. (Rev: SLJ 5/07)

9916 Hunter, Erin, and Dan Jolley. *The Lost Warrior, Vol. 1* (4–6). Illus. by James L. Barry. Series: Warriors. 2007, paper $6.99 (978-0-06-124020-1). 96pp. Graystripe resents his capture and domestication in this adaptation of the author's series of novels. Also use *Warrior's Refuge, The Rise of Scourge,* and *Escape from the Forest,* in the Warriors: Tigerstar and Sasha series (all 2007). (Rev: LMC 11/07; SLJ 7/07)

9917 Ikezawa, Satomi. *Guru Guru Pon-Chan, Vol. 1* (5–12). Trans. from Japanese by Douglas Varenas. Illus. by author. 2005, Del Rey paper $10.95 (978-0-345-48095-8). 171pp. In this whimsical shape-changing story, Ponta, a Labrador retriever puppy, nibbles on a newly invented "chit-chat" bone and turns into a human girl who comically retains doggy behavior. (Rev: SLJ 11/05)

9918 Ikumi, Mia. *Tokyo Mew Mew a la Mode, Vol. 1* (5–8). Trans. from Japanese by Yoohae Yang. Illus. by author. 2005, TokyoPop paper $9.99 (978-1-59532-789-5). 197pp. In the opening volume of the Tokyo Mew Mew a la Mode series, 12-year-old Berry Shirayuki is shanghaied into a team of girl superheroes and soon finds herself doing battle with dragons and the evil Saint Rose Crusaders. (Rev: SLJ 11/05)

9919 Irwin, Jane, and Jeff Berndt. *Vogelein: Clockwork Faerie* (5–12). Illus. 2003, Fiery Studios paper $12.95 (978-0-9743110-0-5). 168pp. A beautiful 17th-century mechanical fairy who is immortal but depends on others to wind her up stars in this graphic novel. (Rev: BL 11/1/03)

9920 Johns, Geoff, et al. *Teen Titans: The Future Is Now* (5–8). Illus. Series: Teen Titans. 2005, DC Comics paper $9.99 (978-1-4012-0475-4). 224pp. In volume four of the series, the title characters return from a mission into the future to learn that Robin's father died while they were away. (Rev: BL 3/15/06)

9921 Jolley, Dan. *The Hero Twins: Against the Lords of Death* (3–5). Illus. by David Witt. Series: Graphic Myths and Legends. 2008, Lerner LB $26.60 (978-0-8225-7495-8). 48pp. An action-packed myth about two Mayan twins who anger the Lords of Death. (Rev: BLO 3/3/08; SLJ 7/08) [741.5]

9922 Jolley, Dan. *The Time Travel Trap* (4–8). Illus. by Matt Wendt. Series: Twisted Journeys. 2008, Lerner LB $27.93 (978-0-7613-9472-3); paper $7.95 (978-0-8225-8874-0). 112pp. Readers can choose which way the plot will go in this time-travel adventure story. (Rev: SLJ 5/08)

9923 Kibuishi, Kazu, ed. *Flight Explorer, Vol. 1* (4–6). Illus. by Kazu Kibuishi. 2008, Villard paper $10.00 (978-0-345-50313-8). 112pp. A collection of 10 pieces of graphic fiction that showcases the genre's variety of artistic styles and subject and story strategies. (Rev: BL 3/15/08; SLJ 5/08)

9924 Kibuishi, Kazu. *The Stonekeeper* (4–7). Illus. by author. Series: Amulet. 2008, Scholastic $21.99 (978-0-439-84680-6); paper $9.99 (978-0-439-84681-3). 190pp. Emily's father is killed in a car crash and her mother swallowed by a monster after opening a doorway to another world in this first volume in the series. (Rev: BL 12/1/07; LMC 1/08; SLJ 1/08)

9925 Kobayashi, Makoto. *Planet of the Cats* (5–8). Series: What's Michael? 2006, Dark Horse paper $9.95 (978-1-59307-525-5). 104pp. In this 11th, concluding volume of the graphic novel series first published in Japan, Hanako, a human exobiologist, and her spaceship crew find themselves stranded on a planet ruled by house cats. (Rev: BL 9/1/06)

9926 Kobayashi, Makoto. *Sleepless Nights* (5–8). Illus. Series: What's Michael? 2005, Dark Horse paper $8.95 (978-1-59307-337-4). 88pp. Volume ten of the continuing adventures of the house cat who has been described as "Japan's version of Garfield, Heathcliff, and Krazy Kat all rolled into one." (Rev: BL 9/1/05)

9927 Kochalka, James. *Johnny Boo: The Best Little Ghost in the World!* (K–3). Illus. by author. 2008, Top Shelf paper $9.95 (978-1-60309-013-1). 40pp. Johnny is a good little ghost and proud of his "boo" but this doesn't stop him being afraid of the Ice Cream Monster. (Rev: BL 3/15/08; LMC 5/09)

9928 Krosoczka, Jarrett J. *Lunch Lady and the Cyborg Substitute* (2–4). Illus. by author. 2009, Knopf LB $11.99 (978-0-375-94683-7); paper $5.99 (978-0-375-84683-0). 96pp. Lunch Lady, an undercover crime fighter, with her assistant Betty and three students investigates a cyborg plot to replace teachers with robots. (Rev: BL 3/1/09)

9929 Lawrie, Robin, and Chris Lawrie. *Cheat Challenge* (2–6). Illus. by Robin Lawrie. Series: Ridge Riders. 2007, Stone Arch LB $21.26 (978-1-59889-347-2). 32pp. Should Slam reveal the location of a secret mountain-bike racecourse to his fellow Ridge Riders? Another action-packed installment in the series that emphasizes good character and also includes *Fear 3.1, Snow Bored,* and *White Lightning* (all 2007). (Rev: LMC 10/07; SLJ 9/07)

9930 Lee, Stan. *The Fantastic Four, Vol. 1* (4–12). Illus. by Jack Kirby. 2009, Marvel paper $24.99 (978-0-7851-3710-8). 272pp. This volume collects the first 10 stories about the four who returned to Earth with superhuman abilities after being exposed to cosmic rays. (Rev: BLO 4/30/09)

9931 Lobdell, Scott. *The Ocean of Osyria* (4–6). Illus. by Lea Hernandez. 2005, Papercutz paper $7.95 (978-1-59707-001-0). 96pp. Joe and Frank Hardy appear in a fast-paced graphic novel full of high-tech features — the first in a new series — and attempt to rescue their best friend, who has been implicated in an important theft. (Rev: BL 5/15/05)

9932 Loux, Matthew. *Salt Water Taffy: The Seaside Adventures of Jack and Benny* (2–4). Illus. by author. 2008, Oni paper $5.95 (978-1-932664-94-2). 96pp. Brothers Jack, 11, and Benny, 8, are dreading a vacation on the coast of Maine but soon find lots of exciting adventures there. (Rev: BL 7/08; SLJ 11/08)

9933 Lowry, Shannon, and Suzette Haden Elgin, adapts. *Murder and Mystery* (4–8). Illus. by Mike Vosburg and Dan Spiegle. Series: Bank Street Graphic Novels. 2007, World Almanac LB $29.27 (978-0-8368-7928-5). 56pp. Well-drawn graphic versions *The Hound of the Baskervilles, Macbeth,* and *The Legend of Sleepy Hollow* are included here. (Rev: SLJ 7/07)

9934 Mack, Stan, and Susan Champlin. *Road to Revolution!* (4–6). Illus. by Stan Mack. Series: The Cartoon Chronicles of America. 2009, Bloomsbury $16.99 (978-1-59990-013-1); paper $9.99 (978-1-59990-371-2). 128pp. In 1775, Penny and Nick help the revolutionary cause and meet many important personalities, such as Samuel Adams and Paul Revere. (Rev: BL 6/1–15/09; SLJ 7/09)

9935 McKeever, Sean. *The Loyalty Thing* (5–8). Illus. by Takeshi Miyazawa and Norman Lee. Series: Mary Jane. 2006, ABDO LB $21.35 (978-1-59961-037-5). All about Spider-Man's girlfriend before Spidey enters her life. (Rev: SLJ 5/07)

9936 McKeever, Sean. *Marvel Adventures Spider-Man: Power Struggle* (4–6). Illus. by Patrick Scherberger. 2006, Marvel paper $6.99 (978-0-7851-1903-6). A Spider-Man for modern readers, well-drawn and lots of fun for fans of superheroes. (Rev: SLJ 7/06)

9937 McKeever, Sean. *The Money Thing* (5–8). Illus. by Takeshi Miyazawa and Norman Lee. Series: Mary Jane. 2006, ABDO LB $21.35 (978-1-59961-038-2). All about Spider-Man's girlfriend before Spidey enters her life and written in a contemporary style, this will appeal to girls who want the other side of the story. (Rev: SLJ 5/07)

9938 Maeda, Shunshin. *Ninja Baseball Kyuma, Vol. 1* (2–4). Illus. by author. 2009, Udon paper $7.99 (978-1-897376-86-7). 200pp. Kyuma, a ninja who has been living alone on a mountain with his dog, finds himself drawn suddenly into the world of baseball, which he totally misunderstands; an action-filled manga. (Rev: BLO 3/11/09)

9939 Martin, Ann M., and Raina Telgemeier. *Kristy's Great Idea* (4–6). Illus. by Raina Telgemeier. Series: Baby-Sitters Club. 2006, Scholastic paper $16.99 (978-0-439-80241-3). 192pp. The first volume in the popular Baby-Sitters Club series returns in graphic-novel format. Also in this series: *The Truth About Stacey* (2006). (Rev: BL 3/15/06; SLJ 7/06)

9940 Masters, Anthony. *Joker* (2–4). Illus. by Michael Reid. Series: Graphic Trax. 2006, Stone Arch LB $21.26 (978-1-59889-024-2). 66pp. In this easy-to-read graphic novel, Mel's magic performances in the classroom have fallen flat, but the boy comes to the rescue when his dad — a bank manager — is seized by would-be robbers. (Rev: SLJ 9/06)

9941 Mazan, and Cecile Chicault. *Tales from the Brothers Grimm* (3–5). Trans. by Joe Johnson. Illus. Series: Classics Illustrated Deluxe. 2008, Papercutz LB $17.95 (978-1-59707-101-7); paper $13.95 (978-1-59707-100-0). 130pp. "Hansel and Gretel," "The Valiant Little Tailor," "Learning to Shudder," and "The Devil and the Three Golden Hairs" are the four tales included in this comic-book adaptation. (Rev: BLO 7/30/08; LMC 11/08)

9942 Melville, Herman. *Moby Dick* (5–8). Illus. by Penko Gelev. Series: Graphic Classics. 2007, Barron's $15.99 (978-0-7641-5977-0). 48pp. The dramatic artwork will draw readers into this story; information on author Herman Melville gives background and historical context. (Rev: SLJ 5/07)

9943 Miller, Frank. *Batman: Year One* (4–8). Illus. by David Mazzucchelli and Richmond Lewis. 2007, DC Comics paper $19.99 (978-1-4012-0752-6). 96pp. This collection of four comic originally produced in 1988 emphasizes Batman's dark early days and the shady characters he had to deal with. (Rev: SLJ 5/07)

9944 Misako Rocks!. *Biker Girl* (5–8). Illus. 2006, Hyperion paper $7.99 (978-0-7868-3676-5). 112pp. Aki, a shy, bookish girl, is transformed into a super-hero after finding a discarded bicycle in her grand-father's garage. (Rev: BL 3/15/06; SLJ 9/06)

9945 Morse, Scott. *Magic Pickle* (2–4). Illus. by author. 2008, Scholastic paper $9.99 (978-0-439-87995-8). 64pp. A superhero pickle — Weapon Kosher — explodes into grade-schooler Jojo's life. Will she become the pickle's sidekick and enjoy more wacky adventures? (Rev: BL 3/15/08; SLJ 7/08)

9946 Nagda, Ann Whitehead. *The Perfect Cat-Sitter* (3–5). Illus. by Stephanie Roth. 2007, Holiday $15.95 (978-0-8234-2112-1). 112pp. Susan faces many challenges as she pet-sits for Rana and her family while they are in India. (Rev: BCCB 1/08; BL 12/1/07; SLJ 4/08)

9947 Nykko. *The Shadow Spies*. Bk. 2 (4–8). Illus. by Bannister. Series: The ElseWhere Chronicles. 2009, Lerner LB $27.93 (978-0-7613-4460-5); paper $6.95 (978-0-7613-3964-9). 48pp. Max, Theo, Noah, and Rebecca enter a strange world called ElseWhere and must evade the Shadow Spies to get back home. (Rev: LMC 10/09; SLJ 5/09)

9948 O' Donnell, Liam. *Soccer Sabotage* (4–7). Illus. by Mike Deas. Series: Graphic Guide Adven-ture. 2009, Orca paper $9.95 (978-1-55143-884-9). 56pp. Why is their soccer team experiencing so many problems in the national under-18 tourna-ment? Nadia and Devin investigate in this mystery full of soccer tips. (Rev: BL 3/1/09)

9949 O'Brien, Anne S. *The Legend of Hong Kil Dong: The Robin Hood of Korea* (3–5). 2006, Charlesbridge $14.95 (978-1-58089-302-2). 48pp. In graphic novel format, this is a Korean tale — per-haps the first novel written in the Korean alphabet — that features a strong character seeking to undo injustices. (Rev: BL 7/06; SLJ 9/06)

9950 O'Donnell, Liam. *Blackbeard's Sword: The Pirate King of the Carolinas* (3–5). Illus. by Mike Spoor. Series: Graphic Flash. 2007, Stone Arch LB $23.93 (978-1-59889-309-0). 48pp. History and fic-tion combine in this graphic story of a boy who wrongly admires Blackbeard. (Rev: LMC 10/07; SLJ 8/07)

9951 O'Donnell, Liam. *Max Finder Mystery: Col-lected Casebook, Vol. 1* (4–7). Illus. by Michael Cho. 2009, Owlkids paper $9.95 (978-2-8957-9116-4). 96pp. First published in *Owl Magazine*, this graphic novel collection includes 10 mysteries star-ring 7th-graders Max Finder and Alison Santos that invite the reader to help solve the case — answers and puzzles are included. Also use *Max Finder Mystery: Collected Casebook* Vols. 2 and 3 (both 2009). (Rev: BL 7/09)

9952 O'Donnell, Liam. *Ramp Rats* (4–6). Illus. by Mike Deas. Series: Graphic Guide Adventure. 2008, Orca paper $9.95 (978-1-55143-880-1). 60pp. This graphic novel about Bounce, an avid skateboarder, also features bullies and a motorcycle gang as well as skateboarding tips. (Rev: BL 9/15/08)

9953 O'Donnell, Liam. *Wild Ride* (4–6). Illus. by Mike Deas. Series: Graphic Guide Adventure. 2007, Orca paper $8.95 (978-1-55143-756-9). 64pp. Reluctant readers will enjoy this adventure in which three young people must rely on their survival skills after their plane crashes in the Canadian woods. (Rev: BL 1/1–15/08; LMC 3/08; SLJ 7/08; VOYA 2/08)

9954 Orme, David. *Ice Caves of Pluto* (2–4). Illus. by Peter Richardson. Series: Billy Blaster. 2009, Stone Arch LB $22.65 (978-1-4342-1275-7). 40pp. Billy and Wu Hoo travel to icy Pluto in this sleek, manga-style story that relies more on art than on dialogue. Also use *Mind Thief* (2009). (Rev: LMC 10/09; SLJ 5/09)

9955 Patterson, James, and Leopold Gout. *Alien Hunter* (5–8). Illus. by Klaus Lyngeled. 2008, Little, Brown paper $9.99 (978-0-316-00425-1). 128pp. This action-packed graphic novel follows the exploits of Daniel, an orphaned alien who hunts evil extraterrestrials on Earth. (Rev: BL 10/1/08; SLJ 11/08; VOYA 6/08)

9956 Peters, Stephanie. *Rapunzel* (2–4). Illus. by Jef-frey Stewart Timmins. Series: Graphic Spin. 2009, Stone Arch LB $16.99 (978-1-4342-1194-1). 40pp. This graphic-novel adaptation offers arresting art-work. (Rev: BL 3/1/09)

9957 Petrucha, Stefan. *Beowulf* (4–10). Illus. by Kody Chamberlain. 2007, HarperTrophy paper $8.99 (978-0-06-134390-2). A graphic novel ver-sion of the epic story. (Rev: SLJ 1/08; VOYA 2/08)

9958 Petrucha, Stefan. *Nancy Drew: The Demon of River Heights* (4–9). Series: Nancy Drew, Girl Detective. 2005, Papercutz $12.95 (978-1-59707-004-1). The familiar heroine returns in graphic-novel format with this story in which Nancy, Bess, George discover the secret behind a legendary mon-ster. (Rev: SLJ 8/05)

9959 Plessix, Michel. *The Wind in the Willows*. Rev. ed. (4–7). Illus. by author. Series: Classics Illustrat-ed Deluxe. 2008, Papercutz $17.95 (978-1-59707-095-9); paper $13.95 (978-1-59707-096-6). 144pp. The classic animal story, presented in a graphic for-mat with beautiful illustrations. (Rev: BL 3/18/08)

9960 Poe, Marshall. *A House Divided* (4–6). Illus. by Leland Purvis. Series: Turning Points. 2009, Aladdin paper $8.99 (978-1-4169-5057-8). 128pp. Black-and-white art illustrates the story of brothers Owen and Amos Bennington, who choose different directions after their abolitionist parents are mur-dered in 1856, one opting for peaceful action and the other for more aggressive means. (Rev: BLO 2/9/09; SLJ 3/09)

9961 Poe, Marshall. *Sons of Liberty* (3–7). Illus. by Leland Purvis. Series: Turning Points. 2008, Simon & Schuster paper $7.99 (978-1-4169-5067-7). 120pp. Young Nathaniel joins the cause of the American Revolution and even meets Samuel Adams and Paul Revere as he fights for the young nation. (Rev: LMC 1/09; SLJ 7/08)

9962 Poon, Janice. *Claire and the Water Wish* (2–4). Illus. by author. 2009, Kids Can $15.95 (978-1-55453-381-7); paper $7.95 (978-1-55453-382-4).

120pp. Mystery, environmental concerns, and photography are interwoven in this graphic novel about Claire and her new friends Jet and Sky, who investigate toxic waste in a lake; includes craft ideas. (Rev: BL 4/15/09; SLJ 9/09)

9963 Raicht, Mike. *Spider-Man: Kraven the Hunter* (5–8). Illus. by Jamal Igle, et al. Series: Spider-Man. 2006, ABDO LB $21.35 (978-1-59961-009-2). Spider-Man once again does battle with Kraven the Hunter, one of his oldest enemies. (Rev: SLJ 11/06)

9964 Reit, Seymour, adapt. *Great Heroes* (4–6). Illus. by Ernie Colon. 2007, World Almanac LB $29.27 (978-0-8368-7925-4). 56pp. Stories of King Arthur, Don Quixote, and Sherlock Holmes are presented here in condensed, graphic-novel form to appeal to reluctant readers and comic-book fans. (Rev: SLJ 7/07)

9965 Reit, Seymour. *Science Fiction and Fantasy* (4–6). Illus. by Ernie Colon. Series: Bank Street Graphic Novels. 2007, World Almanac LB $29.27 (978-0-8368-7929-2). 56pp. *Frankenstein*, *The War of the Worlds*, and *20,000 Leagues Under the Sea* are presented here in condensed, graphic-novel form to appeal to reluctant readers and comic-book fans. (Rev: SLJ 7/07)

9966 Reit, Seymour, adapt. *Travel and Adventure* (4–8). Illus. by Ernie Colon and Richard Rockwell. Series: Bank Street Graphic Novels. 2007, World Almanac LB $29.27 (978-0-8368-7930-8). 56pp. *The Travels of Marco Polo*, *Moby-Dick*, and *Gulliver's Travels* are transformed into graphic novels. (Rev: SLJ 7/07)

9967 Renier, Aaron. *Spiral Bound: Top Secret Summer* (4–7). Illus. 2005, Top Shelf paper $14.95 (978-1-891830-50-1). 180pp. This delightful graphic novel chronicles the summer adventures of the animal residents of the Town, a community with a monster in its pond. (Rev: BL 11/1/05)

9968 Reynolds, Aaron. *Creepy Crawly Crime* (3–5). Illus. by Neil Numberman. 2009, Holt $16.95 (978-0-8050-8242-5). 96pp. Crime fighter Joey Fly and his sidekick Sammy Stingtail investigate the case of a missing diamond pencil box in this hardboiled graphic novel. (Rev: BCCB 5/09; BL 3/1/09)

9969 Robbins, Trina. *The Time Team* (3–6). Illus. by Anne Timmons. Series: Go Girl! 2004, Dark Horse paper $5.95 (978-1-59307-230-8). 96pp. Three high school girls find themselves stuck in the days of the dinosaurs. (Rev: BL 1/1–15/05)

9970 Robinson, Fiona. *The 3-2-3 Detective Agency: The Disappearance of Dave Warthog* (2–4). Illus. by author. 2009, Abrams $17.95 (978-0-8109-8489-9); paper $9.95 (978-0-8109-7094-6). 80pp. An entertaining ensemble of animal detectives investigate disappearances in Whiska City. (Rev: BL 7/09; SLJ 9/09)

9971 Rodi, Rob. *Crossovers* (5–12). Illus. 2003, CrossGeneration paper $15.95 (978-1-931484-85-5). 160pp. This graphic novel is an entertaining look at a suburban family whose members possess a unique power. (Rev: BL 2/1/04)

9972 Rosenstiehl, Agnes. *Silly Lilly* (PS). Illus. by author. 2008, Raw Junior/TOON $12.95 (978-0-

9799238-1-4). 36pp. For beginning readers, this graphic novel follows bright and imaginative young Lilly as she moves through familiar seasonal activities from spring through winter and back again. (Rev: BL 3/15/08; HB 7/08; SLJ 5/08)

9973 Ross, Stewart. *Instruments of Death* (3–6). Illus. by Inklink. 2007, DK $14.99 (978-0-7566-2566-5); paper $3.99 (978-0-7566-2565-8). 48pp. Eleven-year-old Shen is called to the emperor's court and encounters a mystery in this story set in ancient China. The graphic-novel format will interest young readers. (Rev: SLJ 5/07)

9974 Ross, Stewart. *The Price of Victory* (3–6). Illus. by Inklink. 2007, DK $14.99 (978-0-7566-2568-9); paper $3.99 (978-0-7566-2567-2). 48pp. Eleven-year-old Pylades tries to find out who is trying to keep his brother from competing in the Olympics in this story set in ancient Greece. (Rev: SLJ 5/07)

9975 Ross, Stewart. *The Terror Trail* (3–6). Illus. by Inklink. 2007, DK $14.99 (978-0-7566-2570-2); paper $3.99 (978-0-7566-2569-6). 48pp. Sabina and Publius, two children living in North Africa in A.D. 145, fear for their father, who is nearly condemned to death in the Colosseum. (Rev: SLJ 5/07)

9976 Runton, Andy. *Flying Lessons* (3–5). Illus. Series: Owly. 2005, Top Shelf paper $10.00 (978-1-891830-76-1). 140pp. A flying squirrel at first resists Owly's overtures of friendship but later offers to teach the young bird to fly. Also use *A Time to Be Brave* (2007). (Rev: BL 3/15/06)

9977 Russell, P. Craig. *The Birthday of the Infanta: Fairy Tales of Oscar Wilde, Vol. 3* (5–8). Illus. 1998, NBM $15.95 (978-1-56163-213-8). A graphic novel version of Wilde's fairy tale about the misshapen dwarf who dies of a broken heart. (Rev: BL 4/1/99)

9978 Sava, Scott Christian. *Hyperactive* (2–6). Illus. by Joseph Bergin. 2008, IDW paper $12.99 (978-1-60010-313-1). 112pp. A zippy, funny story about Joey Johnson, whose innate speediness accelerates to superhero proportions and brings him joy and angst. (Rev: BL 3/1/09)

9979 Scieszka, Jon. *Nightmare on Joe's Street* (2–4). Ed. by Zachary Rau. Illus. by Peter K. Hirsch. Series: Time Warp Trio. 2006, paper $6.99 (978-0-06-111639-1). 96pp. In the opening volume of this graphic-novel adaptation of the Time Warp Trio television series, Joe and Sam transport Frankenstein's monster back in time so that he can reconcile his differences with his creator, Mary Shelley. (Rev: BL 10/1/06; SLJ 1/07)

9980 Sewell, Anna. *Anna Sewell's Black Beauty: The Graphic Novel* (4–6). Ed. and illus. by June Brigman and Roy Richardson. Series: Puffin Graphics. 2005, Puffin $10.99 (978-0-14-240408-9). 176pp. A graphic-novel version of the classic Victorian story about an impressive horse's complex life. (Rev: BL 5/1/05) [741.5]

9981 Sfar, Joann, and Lewis Trondheim. *Zenith: Back in Style, Vol. 3* (5–9). Trans. from French by Joe Johnson. Illus. by Boulet. Series: Dungeon. 2009, NBM paper $14.95 (978-1-56163-550-4). A story in an animal-inhabited fantasy land based on

Dungeons and Dragons and full of romance, danger, and humor. (Rev: SLJ 7/09)

9982 Shanower, Eric. *Adventures in Oz* (4–7). Illus. by author. 2007, IDW $75.00 (978-1-60010-071-0); paper $39.99 (978-1-933239-61-3). 256pp. Dorothy and her friends from Oz return in this beautifully drawn collection of five graphic novel adventures. (Rev: BL 3/15/07; SLJ 3/07; VOYA 4/07)

9983 *Showcase Presents the House of Mystery, Vol. 1* (5–9). 2006, DC Comics paper $16.99 (978-1-4012-0786-1). 552pp. A collection of relatively tame horror comics that first appeared in the 1960s, in black and white. (Rev: SLJ 7/06)

9984 Slade, Christian. *Korgi*. Bk. 1 (2–8). Illus. by author. 2007, Top Shelf paper $10.00 (978-1-891830-90-7). 84pp. A young girl and her dog have adventures in the woods of Korgi in this beautifully drawn, almost wordless book that features a fairy people and beasts including giant spiders. (Rev: LMC 1/08; SLJ 3/08)

9985 Smith, Jeff. *Eyes of the Storm, Vol. 3* (4–8). Illus. by author. Series: Bone. 2006, Scholastic $19.99 (978-0-439-70625-4); paper $9.99 (978-0-439-70638-4). 192pp. The final book in the first Bone trilogy, this comic-book fantasy has funny moments, suspense and dream sequences that fans will love. (Rev: SLJ 7/06)

9986 Smith, Jeff. *Old Man's Cave* (5–12). Illus. by author. Series: Bone. 2007, Scholastic $18.99 (978-0-439-70628-5); paper $9.99 (978-0-439-70635-3). 128pp. Episode six of this series that combines goofy-looking characters with dramatic fantasy plots finds Phoney Bone and Thorn in grave danger. (Rev: BL 11/1/07)

9987 Soo, Kean. *Jellaby* (4–7). Illus. by author. 2008, Hyperion $18.99 (978-1-4231-0337-0); paper $9.99 (978-1-4231-0303-5). 160pp. A gentle purple monster changes the lives of 10-year-old Portia and her friend Jason. (Rev: BL 3/15/08; SLJ 1/08)

9988 Steinberg, D. J. *Game On!* (3–5). Illus. by Brian Smith. 2009, Grosset paper $5.99 (978-0-448-44700-1). 96pp. Loud Boy and his friends must stop an evil plot to turn all the children in the world into a video game. (Rev: BL 6/1–15/09)

9989 Steinberg, D. J. *Sound Off! The Adventures of Daniel Boom aka Loud Boy* (3–5). Illus. by Brian Smith. 2008, Grosset paper $5.99 (978-0-448-44698-1). 96pp. This well-paced title with nice tension and great puns follows Daniel, an almost-10-year-old with a voice that shatters glass, to a special school where his "problem" is unveiled as a super-power. (Rev: BL 3/15/08; SLJ 11/08)

9990 Stevenson, Robert Louis. *Kidnapped* (4–8). Illus. by Penko Gelev. Series: Graphic Classics. 2007, Barron's LB $15.99 (978-0-7641-5980-0); paper $8.99 (978-0-7641-3494-4). 48pp. The dramatic artwork will draw readers into this story; information on Stevenson gives background and historical context. (Rev: SLJ 11/07)

9991 Stine, R. L. *Terror Trips* (3–7). Adapted by Jill Thompson, Jamie Tolagson, & Amy Kim Thompson. Illus. by Jill Thompson, et al. Series: Goosebumps Graphix. 2007, Scholastic $16.99 (978-0-

439-85777-2); paper $8.99 (978-0-439-85780-2). 139pp. *One Day at Horrorland, A Shocker on Shock Street,* and *Deep Trouble,* all originally full-length Goosebumps novels, are presented here as action-packed black-and-white graphic novels. (Rev: SLJ 5/07)

9992 Storrie, Paul D. *Nightmare on Zombie Island* (4–8). Illus. by David Witt. Series: Twisted Journeys. 2008, Lerner LB $27.93 (978-0-8225-6198-9); paper $7.95 (978-0-8225-6200-9). 112pp. Readers can choose which way the plot will go in this horror story. (Rev: SLJ 5/08)

9993 Taniguchi, Tomoko. *Call Me Princess* (5–8). Trans. from Japanese by Mutsumi Masuda and C. B. Cebulski. Illus. by author. 2003, CPM Manga paper $9.99 (978-1-58664-898-5). This graphic novel, set in Japan, centers on the young heroine's romantic attachments but gets a "G" rating. (Rev: SLJ 3/04)

9994 Tatsuyama, Sayuri. *Happy Happy Clover, Vol. 1* (3–6). Illus. by author. 2009, VIZ Media paper $7.99 (978-1-4215-2656-0). 200pp. Clover and her young rabbit friends explore Crescent Forest and the world outside it in this manga offering. (Rev: BL 3/1/09)

9995 Team, Marathon. *The O. P.* (3–5). Illus. 2006, Papercutz paper $7.95 (978-1-59707-043-0). 96pp. Based on the Cartoon Network's "Totally Spies" series, this slight but enjoyable graphic novel features teen girls who spy for the World Organization of Human Protection. (Rev: BL 1/1–15/07)

9996 *Teen Titans: Jam Packed Action!* (4–8). 2005, DC Comics paper $7.99 (978-1-4012-0902-5). 96pp. Two exciting technology-oriented stories are drawn from the Cartoon Network show. (Rev: SLJ 5/06)

9997 Telgemeier, Raina. *Claudia and Mean Janine* (3–5). Illus. by author. Series: Baby-Sitters Club. 2008, Scholastic paper $8.99 (978-0-439-88517-1). 176pp. A graphic-novel adaptation of the book about two different sisters and their way of coping with their grandmother after she has a stroke. (Rev: BL 3/1/09)

9998 Telgemeier, Raina. *Mary Anne Saves the Day* (4–6). Illus. by author. Series: Baby-sitters' Club. 2007, Scholastic paper $8.99 (978-0-439-88516-4). 158pp. Twelve-year-old Mary Anne copes with feuding club members feud as well as an overly strict father while she manages to overcome shyness and make a new friend. (Rev: BL 11/1/07)

9999 Tolkien, J. R. R. *The Hobbit; or, There and Back Again* (5–10). Adapted by Charles Dixon. Illus. 1990, Eclipse Books paper $12.95 (978-0-345-36858-4). The classic story of Bilbo Baggins and his companions is introduced to reluctant readers in this full-color graphic novel. (Rev: BL 9/1/91)

10000 Trondheim, Lewis. *Mister O* (4–8). Illus. by author. 2004, NBM $13.95 (978-1-56163-382-1). 32pp. Mister O, portrayed in wordless rectangular cartoons, is a round caricature who — à la Wile E. Coyote — can't seem conquer a chasm, no matter how many successful crossings he views. (Rev: SLJ 9/04)

10001 Trondheim, Lewis. *Tiny Tyrant* (4–7). Illus. by Fabrice Parme. 2007, Roaring Brook paper $12.95 (978-1-59643-094-5). 128pp. Ethelbert, the diminutive and willful 6-year-old child-king of Portocristo, is used to getting his own way in this series of funny episodes. (Rev: BL 3/15/07; SLJ 9/07)

10002 Verne, Jules. *Journey to the Center of the Earth* (4–8). Illus. by Penko Gelev. Series: Graphic Classics. 2007, Barron's LB $15.99 (978-0-7641-5982-4); paper $8.99 (978-0-7641-3495-1). 48pp. The dramatic artwork will draw readers into this story; information on Verne gives background and historical context. (Rev: SLJ 11/07)

10003 Watts, Irene N. *Good-Bye Marianne* (3–7). Illus. by Kathryn E. Shoemaker. 2008, Tundra paper $12.95 (978-0-88776-830-9). 128pp. Marianne, an 11-year-old Jewish girl first seen in *Remember Me* (2000), deals with various problems as the Nazis take over in 1937 Berlin in this affecting graphic novel. (Rev: BLO 9/24/08)

10004 Wilson, Bob. *Fearless Dave* (2–6). Illus. by author. 2006, Frances Lincoln $15.95 (978-1-84507-496-8). This is an enjoyably silly story about a reluctant knight named Dave whose mother succeeds in bringing him glory — and the princess. (Rev: SLJ 12/06)

10005 Wolfram, Amy. *Teen Titans: Year One* (5–8). Illus. by Karl Kerschl. 2008, DC Comics paper $14.99 (978-1-4012-1927-7). 144pp. A collection of six comic book stories following five young friends (Robin, Wonder Girl, Kid Flash, Aqualad, and Speedy) as they join forces to defeat evil. (Rev: BLO 1/7/09)

10006 Wood, Don. *Into the Volcano* (4–7). Illus. by author. 2008, Scholastic $18.99 (978-0-439-72671-9). 176pp. An action-packed graphic-novel thriller in which two brothers, Duffy and Sumo, find themselves inside an erupting volcano. (Rev: BCCB 11/08; BL 11/15/08; HB 9/08; LMC 1/09; SLJ 9/08)

10007 Zirkel, Huddleston. *A Bit Haywire* (4–7). Illus. 2006, Viper paper $11.95 (978-0-977788-35-4). 64pp. Owen has many extraordinary powers, but he's having trouble figuring out how to control them. (Rev: BL 3/15/07)

10008 Zornow, Jeff. *The Legend of Sleepy Hollow* (5–7). Illus. by author. Series: Graphic Planet: Graphic Horror. 2008, ABDO LB $18.95 (978-1-60270-060-4). 32pp. A graphic adaptation of the classic story with satisfyingly creepy illustrations. (Rev: BL 3/15/08; SLJ 5/08)

Growing into Maturity

Family Problems

10009 Adler, C. S. *The Silver Coach* (4–6). 1988, Avon paper $2.50 (978-0-380-75498-4). 112pp. Chris and her sister adjust to their parents' imminent divorce during a summer with their grandmother. A reissue.

10010 Amato, Mary. *The Naked Mole Rat Letters* (4–7). 2005, Holiday $16.95 (978-0-8234-1927-2).

266pp. Through emails and diary entries, readers learn about Frankie's fear that her father is becoming involved in a new romance. (Rev: BL 6/1–15/05; SLJ 8/05)

10011 Angle, Kimberly Greene. *Hummingbird* (4–6). 2008, Farrar $16.95 (978-0-374-33376-8). 256pp. On a Georgia watermelon farm, 12-year-old March Anne must learn new skills and face much sadness when her grandmother becomes seriously ill. (Rev: BL 7/08; SLJ 9/08)

10012 Baptiste, Tracey. *Angel's Grace* (5–8). Illus. 2005, Simon & Schuster $15.95 (978-0-689-86773-6). 176pp. Thirteen-year-old Grace, who has always felt different, embarks on a search for the man she believes is her biological father. (Rev: BL 2/1/05; SLJ 3/05)

10013 Birdseye, Tom. *Just Call Me Stupid* (4–6). 1993, Holiday House $16.95 (978-0-8234-1045-3). 128pp. Patrick's reading problems are complicated by an unfortunate home situation and his feelings of unworthiness. (Rev: BL 1/15/94; SLJ 10/93)

10014 Brown, Susan Taylor. *Hugging the Rock* (5–8). 2006, Tricycle $15.95 (978-1-58246-180-9). 171pp. In this poignant novel told in free-verse poetry, Rachel describes the difficulties she and her dad have in coping after her mother's departure. (Rev: SLJ 9/06)

10015 Bryant, Ann. *You Can't Fall for Your Stepsister* (4–7). Series: Step-Chain. 2003, Lobster paper $3.95 (978-1-894222-77-8). 190pp. Ollie, 13, thinks he may be falling in love with his stepsister Frankie, but she ends up becoming his new best friend. (Rev: SLJ 5/04)

10016 Bunting, Eve. *The Summer of Riley* (4–6). 2001, HarperCollins LB $16.89 (978-0-06-029142-6). 176pp. The acquisition of a dog helps William to overcome his distress over his parents' separation and grandfather's death, but then the dog gets in trouble with the law. (Rev: BL 7/01; HBG 10/01; SLJ 6/01)

10017 Butler, Dori. *Yes, I Know the Monkey Man* (5–7). 2009, Peachtree $16.95 (978-1-56145-479-2). 208pp. This tense sequel to *Do You Know the Monkey Man?* (2005) flips the narrative to T.J., the discovered twin, as she struggles to connect with her recently found mom and sister and deal with her father's deception. (Rev: BLO 6/16/09; LMC 10/09; SLJ 7/09)

10018 Cardenas, Teresa. *Letters to My Mother* (5–8). Trans. by David Unger. 2006, Groundwood paper $6.95 (978-0-88899-721-0). 104pp. In unhappy letters to her dead mother, a 10-year-old Cuban girl describes cruelty and prejudice at the hands of her relatives. (Rev: BL 5/1/06; SLJ 8/06)

10019 Cheaney, J. B. *The Middle of Somewhere* (5–8). 2007, Knopf $15.99 (978-0-375-83790-6). 256pp. Put in charge of her learning disabled brother while her mother recovers from knee surgery, 12-year-old Ronnie Sparks comes under even greater pressure when she and her brother accompany their grandfather on a trip to Kansas. (Rev: BL 3/15/07; SLJ 7/07)

10020 Clifford, Eth. *The Remembering Box* (4–6). Illus. 1985, Morrow paper $4.99 (978-0-688-11777-1). 64pp. Joshua enjoys a special relationship with his grandmother, who shortly before her death gives him a "remembering box" in which she places a girlhood picture of herself. (Rev: BCCB 12/85; BL 12/1/85; HB 3/86)

10021 Crist-Evans, Craig. *North of Everything* (4–6). 2004, Candlewick $14.99 (978-0-7636-2098-1). 80pp. Told from the viewpoint of a young boy, this spare — but moving — novel tells of the joys and tragedies that a family experiences after its move from Miami to a farm in Vermont. (Rev: BL 1/1–15/05; SLJ 11/04)

10022 Danziger, Paula. *Amber Brown Wants Extra Credit* (3–5). Illus. 1996, Penguin $16.99 (978-0-399-22900-8). 112pp. Troubled by her parents' divorce, Amber begins having problems with her schoolwork. (Rev: BCCB 10/96; BL 6/1–15/96; SLJ 8/96)

10023 Danziger, Paula. *Forever Amber Brown* (2–4). Illus. 1996, Penguin $15.99 (978-0-399-22932-9). 101pp. Amber's divorced mother is being courted by Max, and the young girl is concerned. (Rev: BL 11/15/96; SLJ 2/97)

10024 Day, Karen. *Tall Tales* (5–8). 2007, Random $15.99 (978-0-375-83773-9). 240pp. As she starts school in yet another new town, 12-year-old Meg conceals her father's alcoholism and abuse, afraid it will frighten off potential friends. (Rev: BL 4/1/07; SLJ 6/07)

10025 Doren, Marion. *Nell of Blue Harbor* (4–6). 1990, Harcourt $15.95 (978-0-15-256889-4). 160pp. From a commune in Vermont, 11-year-old Nell finds it difficult to adjust to life in Maine. (Rev: BCCB 1/91; BL 9/1/90; SLJ 11/90)

10026 Dowell, Frances O'Roark. *Chicken Boy* (4–7). 2005, Simon & Schuster $15.95 (978-0-689-85816-1). 208pp. A new friend called Henry brings some comfort into Tobin's sad life. (Rev: BL 5/15/05*; SLJ 7/05*)

10027 Enderle, Dotti. *Man in the Moon* (4–6). Illus. by Kristina Swarner. 2008, Delacorte $14.99 (978-0-385-73566-7). 152pp. In 1961, a mysterious man arrives at the Texas farm where Janine is dreading a summer stuck with her sick brother and teaches them a lot about life; a satisfying novel with a tightly woven plot and realistic characters. (Rev: BCCB 10/08; LMC 8/08; SLJ 9/08)

10028 Ferber, Brenda. *Julia's Kitchen* (5–8). 2006, Farrar $16.00 (978-0-374-39932-0). 160pp. Eleven-year-old Cara Segal's faith is tested when her mother and sister die in a house fire while Cara is sleeping over at a friend's home. (Rev: BL 2/1/06; SLJ 4/06)

10029 Fletcher, Susan. *The Stuttgart Nanny Mafia* (4–6). 1991, Macmillan LB $14.95 (978-0-689-31709-5). 160pp. When her mother marries a dentist, Aurora realizes that her life is about to be "taken over." (Rev: BCCB 9/91; BL 12/15/91; SLJ 10/91)

10030 Fogelin, Adrian. *Anna Casey's Place in the World* (4–6). 2001, Peachtree $14.95 (978-1-56145-249-1). 207pp. Twelve-year-old orphan Anna must adjust to her new foster home and begin to make friends. (Rev: BL 10/15/01; HBG 3/02; SLJ 12/01)

10031 Gallagher, Mary Collins. *Ginny Morris and Dad's New Girlfriend* (3–5). Illus. by Whitney Martin. 2006, Magination $14.95 (978-1-59147-386-2); paper $9.95 (978-1-59147-387-9). 64pp. Ginny is distressed to discover that her divorced father has a girlfriend in this story written to help children dealing with divorce. (Rev: SLJ 2/07)

10032 Geisert, Bonnie. *Lessons* (4–6). 2005, Houghton $15.00 (978-0-618-47899-6). 192pp. In 1950s South Dakota, 10-year-old Rachel realizes that her new baby brother is making her father sad; eventually she finds out about the baby who died and did not receive a Christian burial. (Rev: BL 5/15/05; SLJ 5/05)

10033 Gingras, Charlotte. *Emily's Piano* (4–6). Illus. by Stephane Jorisch. 2005, Firefly $18.95 (978-1-55037-913-6); paper $7.95 (978-1-55037-912-9). 64pp. Shaken by the breakup of her parents' marriage, Emily remembers the piano as a symbol of happiness and tracks it down. (Rev: BL 1/1–15/06; SLJ 5/06)

10034 Greene, Stephanie. *The Lucky Ones* (5–8). 2008, Greenwillow $16.99 (978-0-06-156586-1). 288pp. Twelve-year-old Cecile wants things the way they were before her parents began fighting and her sister became interested in boys in this coming-of-age novel set during a summer vacation on an island. (Rev: BL 10/1/08; SLJ 11/08)

10035 Gregory, Nan. *I'll Sing You One-O* (5–8). 2006, Clarion $16.00 (978-0-618-60708-2). 220pp. Twelve-year-old Gemma is overwhelmed when relatives — including a twin brother — turn up to take her from the foster home she's come to love, and she becomes convinced that an angel will save the day. (Rev: BL 8/06; SLJ 10/06*)

10036 Grimes, Nikki. *The Road to Paris* (4–7). 2006, Putnam $15.99 (978-0-399-24537-4). 160pp. Half-white and half-black, 9-year-old Paris suddenly finds herself separated from her older brother Malcolm and living with a foster family in a mostly white neighborhood. Coretta Scott King Author Honor Book, 2007. (Rev: BL 8/06; SLJ 12/06) ∩

10037 Harness, Cheryl. *Just for You to Know* (5–8). 2006, HarperCollins $17.99 (978-0-06-078313-6). 308pp. Life is turned upside down for 13-year-old Carmen Cathcart, an aspiring artist, when her mother dies during childbirth. (Rev: SLJ 9/06)

10038 Heneghan, James, and Norma Charles. *Bank Job* (5–7). 2009, Orca paper $9.95 (978-1-55143-855-9). 165pp. A gripping read about three foster children who will resort to robbery to stay together. (Rev: BL 5/15/09)

10039 Henkes, Kevin. *Two Under Par* (4–6). Illus. by author. 1987, Greenwillow $19.99 (978-0-688-06708-3). 128pp. Wedge doesn't like his new stepfather — the miniature golf king! — and he's doubly unhappy with the prospect of a new baby. (Rev: BL 6/1/87; HB 7/87; SLJ 6–7/87)

10040 Hest, Amy. *Remembering Mrs. Rossi* (3–5). Illus. by Heather Maione. 2007, Candlewick $14.99

(978-0-7636-2163-6). 192pp. The sudden death of 8-year-old Annie's mother, a sixth-grade teacher, shocks those left behind, and while Annie and her father move toward healing, they take comfort in a scrapbook created by her mother's class. (Rev: BL 1/1–15/07)

10041 Holmes, Elizabeth. *Tracktown Summer* (5–8). 2009, Dutton $16.99 (978-0-525-47946-8). 256pp. Spending summer with his newly separated and remote father, 12-year-old Jake turns to a 14-year-old neighbor called Adrian for company and eventually discovers the reasons for his strange behavior — he is protecting his mentally ill father. (Rev: BCCB 7–8/09; BL 5/15/09; SLJ 7/09; VOYA 8/09)

10042 Kaye, Marilyn. *Happily Ever After* (4–6). 1992, Avon paper $3.50 (978-0-380-76555-3). 116pp. When two friends become stepsisters, adjustment problems begin. (Rev: SLJ 4/92)

10043 Kinsey-Warnock, Natalie. *Gifts from the Sea* (2–5). 2003, Random $14.95 (978-0-375-82257-5). 128pp. In this historical novel set in Maine, 12-year-old Aquila finds comfort after her mother's death in caring for a baby she rescues from a shipwreck. (Rev: BL 6/1–15/03; HBG 10/03; SLJ 6/03)

10044 Klise, Kate. *Deliver Us from Normal* (5–8). 2005, Scholastic $16.95 (978-0-439-52322-6). 240pp. Charles Harrisong, 11, is embarrassed by his abnormal family life in Normal, Illinois, and is horrified when his parents decide to move them all to a houseboat off the Alabama coast. (Rev: BL 3/1/05; SLJ 5/05)

10045 Krishnaswami, Uma. *Naming Maya* (5–8). 2004, Farrar $16.00 (978-0-374-35485-5). 192pp. On a trip to India with her mother, 12-year-old Maya learns some important lessons about herself and the real reasons for the breakup of her parents' marriage. (Rev: BL 4/1/04; HB 7/04; SLJ 6/04; VOYA 6/04)

10046 Leal, Ann Haywood. *Also Known as Harper* (4–6). 2009, Holt $16.95 (978-0-8050-8881-6). 256pp. Harper has problems — her alcoholic father has left the family, her mother is struggling to make ends meet, and they face eviction — but the poems she writes and some new friends help her to cope. (Rev: BL 3/1/09; SLJ 6/09)

10047 Lindbergh, Anne. *Nobody's Orphan* (4–6). 1983, Avon paper $2.95 (978-0-380-70395-1). Martha believes that she is adopted, though she has no proof.

10048 Loftis, Chris. *The Boy Who Sat by the Window* (3–6). Illus. by Catharine Gallagher. 1997, New Horizon paper $12.95 (978-0-88282-147-4). 52pp. Using free verse, the author tells the story of a boy who has been randomly shot while riding his bike to school. (Rev: BL 6/1–15/97; SLJ 8/97)

10049 Love, D. Anne. *Semiprecious* (4–6). 2006, Simon & Schuster $16.95 (978-0-689-85638-9). 304pp. Garnet and her sister Opal are left at an aunt's house in small-town Oklahoma while their mother goes off in pursuit of stardom in this novel set in the 1960s. (Rev: BL 7/06; SLJ 9/06)

10050 Lowery, Linda. *Laurie Tells* (4–6). 1994, Carolrhoda LB $19.95 (978-0-87614-790-0). 40pp. Her mother ignores 11-year-old Laurie when she says she has been sexually abused by her father. (Rev: BL 6/1–15/94; SLJ 7/94)

10051 Lupica, Mike. *Hot Hand* (4–6). Series: Comeback Kids. 2007, Philomel $9.99 (978-0-399-24714-9). 165pp. Ten-year-old Billy and his younger brother Ben have a lot to cope with: their parents' separation, their mother's frequent absence, Billy's friction with his father — a demanding basketball coach, and Ben's unappreciated passion for the piano. (Rev: SLJ 10/07)

10052 McKinnon, Hannah Roberts. *Franny Parker* (5–8). 2009, Farrar $16.00 (978-0-374-32469-8). 160pp. Animal-loving Franny, 12, has been expecting another long hot Oklahoma summer with the usual activities, but then a boy and his mother move in next door and she learns about a different kind of life. (Rev: BCCB 9/09; BL 4/1/09; SLJ 7/09)

10053 MacLachlan, Patricia. *Edward's Eyes* (3–5). 2007, Atheneum $15.99 (978-1-4169-2743-3). 128pp. When Jake's beloved brother, Edward, dies in an accident, their parents donate Edward's eyes and organs to other children. (Rev: BL 9/1/07; SLJ 10/07)

10054 Madden, Kerry. *Gentle's Holler* (5–8). Series: Maggie Valley. 2005, Viking $16.99 (978-0-670-05998-0). 144pp. Livy Two, part of a large, poor family living in the North Carolina mountains, learns a lesson when her father is injured. (Rev: BL 3/1/05; SLJ 6/05)

10055 Madden, Kerry. *Louisiana's Song* (5–8). Series: Maggie Valley. 2007, Viking $16.99 (978-0-670-06153-2). 256pp. Their father is home from the hospital but cannot work, so Livy Two and her nine siblings do everything they can to support their family in this sequel to *Gentle's Holler* (2005) set in North Carolina in 1963. (Rev: BL 6/1–15/07; SLJ 8/07)

10056 Martine, Carmela A. *Rosa, Sola* (4–6). 2005, Candlewick $15.99 (978-0-7636-2395-1). 256pp. Rosa is bereft when the baby brother she's dreamed about is stillborn. (Rev: BCCB 1/06; BL 12/1/05*; HBG 4/06; LMC 11/05; SLJ 10/05)

10057 Mead, Alice. *Madame Squidley and Beanie* (4–7). 2004, Farrar $16.00 (978-0-374-34688-1). 144pp. Ten-year-old Beanie's mother has chronic fatigue syndrome and her illness is affecting the 5th-grader's life. (Rev: BL 4/15/04; SLJ 6/04)

10058 Monthei, Betty. *Looking for Normal* (5–8). 2005, HarperCollins LB $16.89 (978-0-06-072506-8). 192pp. Annie, 12, and her younger brother are sent to live with their grandparents after their father kills their mother and then himself; unfortunately, life does not improve as they must cope with Grandma's drinking and abuse and Grandpa's indifference. (Rev: BL 6/1–15/05; SLJ 4/05)

10059 O'Connor, Barbara. *How to Steal a Dog* (4–6). 2007, Farrar $16.00 (978-0-374-33497-0). 176pp. Desperate to restore some sense of order to her life, in tatters since her father left the family, young Georgina decides to steal a dog and collect a reward. (Rev: BL 3/15/07)

10060 Olson, Gretchen. *Call Me Hope* (4–7). 2007, Little, Brown $15.99 (978-0-316-01236-2). 288pp. Beaten down by her mother's verbal abuse, 11-year-old Hope screws up the courage to confront her mother and tell her how badly she has been hurt by the name calling. (Rev: BL 3/15/07; SLJ 5/07)

10061 Paratore, Coleen Murtagh. *Sunny Holiday* (3–6). 2009, Scholastic $15.99 (978-0-545-07579-4). 176pp. Fourth-grader Sunny, who misses her imprisoned father and worries about her always-busy mother, is nevertheless a great optimist and invents one holiday a month to brighten her difficult life. (Rev: BL 1/1–15/09; SLJ 2/09)

10062 Park, Barbara. *Don't Make Me Smile* (4–6). 1981, Avon paper $2.95 (978-0-380-61994-8). Charles refuses to face the fact of his parents' divorce.

10063 Porter, Pamela. *Sky* (3–5). Illus. by Mary Jane Gerber. 2004, Groundwood $15.95 (978-0-88899-566-7). 83pp. Georgia, an 11-year-old Native American girl, finds comfort in a foal named Sky after a series of traumas including the deaths of her parents, a narrow escape from a burst dam, and an uncomfortable stay in a shelter where she and her grandparents experience prejudice. (Rev: BCCB 12/04; HB 1/05; SLJ 4/05)

10064 Russo, Marisabina. *A Portrait of Pia* (5–8). 2007, Harcourt $17.00 (978-0-15-205577-6). 240pp. Overwhelmed by her brother's schizophrenia and her mother's new boyfriend, 12-year-old Pia, already a talented artist, travels to Italy to meet her long-absent father and learns how to love her family despite its flaws. (Rev: BL 4/1/07; SLJ 8/07)

10065 Sachs, Marilyn. *Fran Ellen's House* (4–6). 1989, Avon paper $2.75 (978-0-380-70583-2). Although her family is back together, Fran Ellen's baby sister won't talk to her and their house is in a shambles. A sequel to: *The Bears' House* (1987). (Rev: BCCB 11/87; BL 11/1/87; SLJ 10/87)

10066 Seagraves, Donny Bailey. *Gone from These Woods* (4–7). 2009, Delacorte $15.99 (978-0-385-73629-9). 192pp. With help from a school counselor, Daniel — whose father is an abusive alcoholic — tries to come to terms with the hunting accident in which he shot and killed his beloved uncle. (Rev: BCCB 9/09; BLO 5/27/09; SLJ 9/09)

10067 Sheinmel, Courtney. *My So-Called Family* (5–8). 2008, Simon & Schuster $15.99 (978-1-4169-5785-0). 194pp. Leah, 13, discovers that she shares the same sperm donor father as a half-sister and three half-brothers. (Rev: BCCB 10/08; BL 11/15/08; SLJ 12/08)

10068 Shyer, Marlene Fanta. *Fleabiscuit Sings!* (3–6). 2005, Marshall Cavendish $15.95 (978-0-7614-5213-3). 150pp. Twelve-year-old Nicky discovers that Fleabiscuit, the dog he walks for Mr. Muffin, can sing and adds the pooch to his family's subway performances. (Rev: BCCB 5/05; HB 8–9/05; SLJ 5/05)

10069 Siebold, Jan. *Rope Burn* (4–6). Illus. 1998, Whitman $13.95 (978-0-8075-7109-5). 82pp. To fulfill a school writing assignment, 11-year-old Richard writes about the terrible effects his parents' divorce has had on him, his difficulties making new friends, and his problems communicating with his mother. (Rev: BCCB 6/98; BL 6/1–15/98; SLJ 6/98)

10070 Strauss, Linda Leopold. *Really, Truly, Everything's Fine* (5–8). 2004, Marshall Cavendish $15.95 (978-0-7614-5163-1). 160pp. Life changes dramatically for 14-year-old Jill Rider when her father is arrested for jewelry theft. (Rev: BL 5/15/04; SLJ 7/04)

10071 Trueit, Trudi. *Julep O'Toole: Miss Independent* (4–6). Illus. 2006, Dutton $15.99 (978-0-525-47637-5). 160pp. Eleven-year-old Julep and her mother have differing views on Julep's abilities to make her own decisions; a sequel to *Julep O'Toole: Confessions of a Middle Child* (2005). (Rev: BL 4/15/06; SLJ 3/06)

10072 Villareal, Ray. *My Father, the Angel of Death* (5–8). 2006, Piñata paper $9.95 (978-1-55885-466-6). 192pp. Newly relocated to Texas and unhappy with his home life, Jesse Baron wonders what life would be like if his dad were not the well-known wrestler called the Angel of Death; suitable for reluctant readers. (Rev: SLJ 10/06)

10073 Ware, Cheryl. *Catty-Cornered* (4–6). Illus. by Paul Yalowitz. 1998, Orchard LB $16.99 (978-0-531-33067-8). 106pp. A smart, curious, and funny girl keeps a journal of the two months she had to spend with her grandmother in a trailer park. (Rev: BL 4/1/98; HBG 10/98; SLJ 3/98)

10074 Weeks, Sarah. *Jumping the Scratch* (4–6). 2006, HarperCollins $15.99 (978-0-06-054109-5). 176pp. Burdened with a dark secret and in shock after some radical changes in his home life, Jamie Reardon focuses his attention on helping his recently injured aunt to recover her short-term memory. (Rev: BL 2/1/06; SLJ 5/06) ∩

10075 Wenberg, Michael. *Seattle Blues* (5–8). 2009, WestSide $16.95 (978-1-934813-04-1). 236pp. When unhappy 13-year-old Maya, spending a reluctant summer with her grandmother in Seattle, finds a musical instrument hidden in the attic she also find the key to growing into a happier person. (Rev: BLO 1/14/09; SLJ 7/09)

10076 Willner-Pardo, Gina. *Spider Storch's Carpool Catastrophe* (2–4). Illus. by Nick Sharratt. 1997, Whitman LB $11.95 (978-0-8075-7575-8); paper $3.95 (978-0-8075-7576-5). 60pp. Joey, nicknamed Spider, is afraid that his mother's friendship with Mrs. Brennerman will mean that he will have to get involved with her unpopular daughter. (Rev: HBG 3/98; SLJ 11/97)

10077 Zimmer, Tracie Vaughn. *42 Miles* (4–6). Illus. by Elaine Clayton. 2008, Clarion $16.00 (978-0-618-61867-5). 80pp. Nearly 13, JoEllen seeks to integrate the two halves of her life — her weekday life in the city with her mother, who calls her Ellen, and her weekends in the country with her father, who calls her Joey. (Rev: BCCB 6/08; BL 4/1/08; SLJ 4/08)

10078 Zimmer, Tracie Vaughn. *Sketches from a Spy Tree* (3–5). Illus. by Andrew Glass. 2005, Clarion $16.00 (978-0-618-23479-0). 64pp. In a series of poems, a young girl with an identical twin who doesn't always share her views recounts her family's attempts to regain its footing after a devastating divorce. (Rev: BL 8/05; SLJ 8/05)

Personal Problems

10079 Adler, C. S. *Willie, the Frog Prince* (4–7). 1994, Clarion $15.00 (978-0-395-65615-0). 163pp. Willie's inability to accept responsibility almost causes the loss of his dog, Booboo. (Rev: BL 4/15/94; SLJ 6/94)

10080 Applegate, Katherine. *Home of the Brave* (5–8). 2007, Feiwel & Friends $16.95 (978-0-312-36765-7). 256pp. Young refugee Kek, who barely escaped death in Sudan, where his brother and father were murdered, finds a new home — and culture shock — in Minnesota. (Rev: BCCB 2/08; BL 7/07; HB 11/07; SLJ 10/07) ⌒

10081 Atkinson, Elizabeth. *From Alice to Zen and Everyone in Between* (5–7). 2008, Carolrhoda $16.95 (978-0-8225-7271-8). 248pp. Alice moves to a new suburb with her dad and quickly becomes friends with Zen, but when school starts she realizes he's part of the wrong crowd. (Rev: BL 5/1/08; SLJ 9/08)

10082 Auch, Mary Jane. *Seven Long Years Until College* (4–7). 1991, Holiday $13.95 (978-0-8234-0901-3). 160pp. Natalie runs away from home to join her older sister at college. (Rev: BCCB 1/92; SLJ 10/91)

10083 Banks, Kate. *Lenny's Space* (4–6). 2007, Farrar $16.00 (978-0-374-34575-4). 160pp. Lenny, a very smart but uncontrolled 9-year-old, learns about friendship and managing his emotions when he makes friends with a boy who has leukemia. (Rev: BCCB 11/07; BL 10/1/07; HB 1/08; SLJ 11/07)

10084 Bartek, Mary. *Funerals and Fly Fishing* (4–7). 2004, Holt $16.95 (978-0-8050-7409-3). 160pp. A visit to the grandfather he has never met gives Brad Stanislawski new confidence to deal with the classmates at his new school. (Rev: SLJ 8/04)

10085 Baskin, Nora Raleigh. *Anything But Typical* (4–7). 2009, Simon & Schuster $15.99 (978-1-4169-6378-3). 208pp. This deftly told story centers on Jason, an autistic 6th-grader who can create dynamic stories and relationships on paper but is painfully at a loss in real social situations. (Rev: BCCB 4/09; BL 2/1/09; HB 5/09; SLJ 3/09) ⌒

10086 Benjamin, Carol Lea. *The Wicked Stepdog* (4–7). Illus. by author. 1982, Avon paper $2.50 (978-0-380-70089-9). Louise is in the midst of puberty problems and her father's remarriage.

10087 Betancourt, Jeanne. *Kate's Turn* (5–8). 1992, Scholastic $13.95 (978-0-590-43103-3). This story of the young ballerina Kate, who decides the price of fame is too high, shows the grueling, often painful life of a dancer. (Rev: BL 1/1/92; SLJ 2/92)

10088 Birdseye, Tom. *Tarantula Shoes* (3–6). 1995, Holiday House $16.95 (978-0-8234-1179-5); Puffin paper $5.99 (978-0-14-037955-6). 96pp. With the help of a new friend and his pet tarantula, Ryan is able to buy the basketball shoes of his dreams. (Rev: BL 4/15/95; SLJ 5/95)

10089 Blume, Judy. *Then Again, Maybe I Won't* (5–8). 1971, Dell paper $4.99 (978-0-440-48659-6). Thirteen-year-old Tony faces many problems when his family relocates to suburban Long Island.

10090 Bonners, Susan. *Edwina Victorious* (3–5). Illus. by author. 2000, Farrar $16.00 (978-0-374-31968-7). 131pp. A charming story about a girl who forges her great-grandaunt's signature on letters to the mayor to try to win much-needed reforms. (Rev: BCCB 10/00; BL 9/1/03; HBG 3/01; SLJ 10/00)

10091 Bradley, Kimberly Brubaker. *Leap of Faith* (4–7). 2007, Dial $16.99 (978-0-8037-3127-1). 192pp. Abigail finds herself attracted to the new ideas she's learning at the Catholic school where she ended up after being expelled from public school. (Rev: BCCB 9/07; BL 7/07; SLJ 8/07)

10092 Buck, Pearl. *The Big Wave* (4–6). 1973, HarperCollins LB $16.89 (978-0-381-99923-0); paper $4.99 (978-0-06-440171-5). 88pp. The loss of family and home in a tidal wave reveals the courage of a little Japanese boy.

10093 Bulion, Leslie. *Uncharted Waters* (4–8). 2006, Peachtree $14.95 (978-1-56145-365-8). 185pp. Jonah's summer of self-discovery following a dismal school year includes a heroic rescue at sea and excelling at his true talent. (Rev: SLJ 6/06)

10094 Bulla, Clyde Robert. *The Paint Brush Kid* (2–4). Illus. by Ellen Beier. 1999, Random LB $11.99 (978-0-679-99282-0); paper $3.99 (978-0-679-89282-3). 64pp. In this beginning chapter book, the pictures Gregory has painted on a house depicting his uncle's life in Mexico are going to be destroyed because the house is slated for demolition. (Rev: HBG 10/99; SLJ 8/99)

10095 Bulla, Clyde Robert. *Shoeshine Girl* (3–5). Illus. by Leigh Grant. 1975, HarperCollins LB $17.89 (978-0-690-04830-8); paper $4.99 (978-0-06-440228-6). 80pp. A somewhat indolent 10-year-old girl matures during a summer working for Al at his shoeshine stand.

10096 Bunting, Eve. *Doll Baby* (5–10). Illus. by Catherine Stock. 2000, Clarion $15.00 (978-0-395-93094-6). 48pp. A simple, direct narrative in which 15-year-old Ellie explains how being pregnant and having a baby radically changed her life. (Rev: BL 11/1/00; HB 9/00; HBG 3/01; SLJ 10/00)

10097 Bunting, Eve. *Your Move* (2–5). Illus. by James Ransome. 1998, Harcourt $16.00 (978-0-15-200181-0). 32pp. A 10-year-old boy and his young brother are caught up in the violence that accompanies the rivalry between street gangs. (Rev: BCCB 6/98; BL 2/15/98; HBG 10/98; SLJ 5/98)

10098 Burch, Robert. *Queenie Peavy* (5–7). 1987, Penguin paper $5.99 (978-0-14-032305-4). Queenie, whose father is in prison, is growing up a defiant, disobedient girl in rural Georgia in the 1930s.

10099 Caldwell, V. M. *The Ocean Within* (5–7). 1999, Milkweed paper $6.95 (978-1-57131-624-0). 273pp. Elizabeth, who is on her third set of foster parents since she was orphaned five years before, has built walls of silence around herself that are impossible to penetrate. (Rev: BCCB 1/00; BL 9/1/99; HBG 3/00; SLJ 11/99; VOYA 4/00)

10100 Caldwell, V. M. *Runt* (5–7). 2006, Milkweed $16.95 (978-1-57131-662-2); paper $6.95 (978-1-57131-661-5). 196pp. Runt, a 13-year-old who is trying to cope with his mother's death and his new living arrangements, becomes close to Mitch, who is dying of cancer. (Rev: SLJ 7/06)

10101 Cameron, Ann. *Colibri* (5–8). 2003, Farrar $17.00 (978-0-374-31519-1). 240pp. Twelve-year-old Rosa, who was kidnapped from her Mayan village when she was four, seeks to escape from the abusive "uncle" who is exploiting her. (Rev: BCCB 10/03; BL 10/1/03*; HB 9/03; HBG 4/04; SLJ 10/03*)

10102 Cameron, Ann. *Gloria's Way* (2–4). 2000, Farrar $15.00 (978-0-374-32670-8). 112pp. In this easy chapter book, readers meet African American Gloria and, in six short episodes, learn about her problems with friendships and family. (Rev: BCCB 2/00; BL 2/15/00; HB 3/00; HBG 10/00; SLJ 3/00)

10103 Caseley, Judith. *Praying to A. L.* (5–8). 2000, Greenwillow $15.95 (978-0-688-15934-4). 192pp. After her father dies, 12-year-old Sierra transfers all her love to a portrait of Abraham Lincoln given to her by her father. (Rev: BL 5/15/00; HBG 10/00; SLJ 6/00)

10104 Cleary, Beverly. *Dear Mr. Henshaw* (4–7). Illus. by Paul Zelinsky. 1983, Morrow LB $16.89 (978-0-688-02406 2). 144pp. A Newbery Medal winner (1984) about a boy who pours out his problems in letters to a writer he greatly admires.

10105 Clements, Andrew. *The Jacket* (3–6). Illus. by Dan Gonzalez. 2002, Simon & Schuster $12.95 (978-0-689-82595-8). 80pp. This story about a sixth-grade boy examining race relations and facing his own prejudices is sure to prompt discussion. (Rev: BCCB 3/02; BL 3/1/02; HBG 10/02; SLJ 3/02)

10106 Collard, Sneed B., III. *Dog Sense* (5–8). 2005, Peachtree $14.95 (978-1-56145-351-1). 192pp. Unhappy after moving from sunny California to a small town in Montana, 13-year-old Guy Martinez finds solace in time spent with his dog, Streak, and a newfound friend named Luke. (Rev: BL 10/15/05; SLJ 11/05)

10107 Comerford, Lynda B. *Rissa Bartholomew's Declaration of Independence* (3–7). 2009, Scholastic $16.99 (978-0-545-05058-6). 320pp. Sixth-grader Clarissa is at a new school with a body and an internal guidance system that seem different moment by moment in this book about friendship and change. (Rev: BCCB 6/09; BL 5/15/09; SLJ 6/09)

10108 Conford, Ellen. *Hail, Hail Camp Timberwood* (5–7). Illus. by Gail Owens. 1978, Little, Brown $14.95 (978-0-316-15291-4). Thirteen-year-old Melanie's first summer at camp.

10109 Conly, Jane L. *Crazy Lady!* (5–8). 1993, HarperCollins LB $18.89 (978-0-06-021360-2). 196pp. In a city slum, Vernon forms a friendship with an eccentric woman and helps her care for her disabled teenage son. (Rev: BCCB 7–8/93; BL 5/15/93*; SLJ 4/93*)

10110 Conrad, Pam. *Staying Nine* (4–6). Illus. by Mike Wimmer. 1988, HarperCollins paper $4.99 (978-0-06-440377-1). 80pp. A private few days in the life of a young girl who doesn't want to be ten. (Rev: BCCB 10/88; BL 11/15/88; SLJ 12/88)

10111 Conway, Celeste. *The Goodbye Time* (4–6). 2008, Delacorte $15.99 (978-0-385-73555-1). 112pp. Fifth-grader Anna struggles to cope with her brother's departure for college, problems with her best friend Katy, and her own insecurities. (Rev: BCCB 1/09; LMC 3/09; SLJ 2/09)

10112 Coolidge, Susan. *What Katy Did* (4–6). 1988, Buccaneer LB $19.95 (978-0-89966-585-6). Tomboy Katy Carr overcomes a tragic accident in this classic story.

10113 Cooper, Ilene. *Absolutely Lucy* (2–4). Illus. Series: Read to Reading. 2000, Golden LB $10.99 (978-0-307-48502-1); paper $3.99 (978-0-307-26502-9). 76pp. An easy chapter book about a boy whose beagle puppy helps him conquer his shyness. (Rev: BCCB 5/00; BL 3/15/00; SLJ 3/01)

10114 Cooper, Ilene. *The Annoying Team* (2–4). Illus. by Colin Paine. Series: Road to Reading. 2002, Random LB $11.99 (978-0-307-46512-2); paper $3.99 (978-0-307-26512-8). 80pp. In this beginning chapter book, Tim tries a new approach to combat the bullying of Big Jon Ferguson. (Rev: BL 6/1–15/02; HBG 10/02)

10115 Cornwell, Nicki. *Christophe's Story* (2–4). Illus. by Karin Littlewood. 2007, Frances Lincoln $14.95 (978-1-84507-765-5). 96pp. Cristophe, a Rwandan refugee living in England, tells his new classmates about his family's escape, including the death of his baby brother. (Rev: BL 12/15/07)

10116 Cosby, Bill. *My Big Lie* (2–4). Illus. 1999, Scholastic $15.95 (978-0-590-52160-4); paper $3.99 (978-0-590-52161-1). 40pp. Late for dinner because of a baseball game, Little Bill tells a lie to protect himself and only gets into worse trouble. (Rev: BL 10/15/99; HBG 10/99; SLJ 8/99)

10117 Cox, Judy. *Mean, Mean Maureen Green* (2–5). Illus. 1999, Holiday House $15.95 (978-0-8234-1502-1). 88pp. Lilley is a fearful person who dreads going to school because of a mean neighborhood dog, a school bully, and her new bike without training wheels. (Rev: BCCB 2/00; BL 12/1/99; HBG 10/00; SLJ 3/00)

10118 Crilley, Mark. *Spring* (4–7). Illus. Series: Miki Falls. 2007, HarperTempest paper $8.99 (978-0-06-084616-9). 176pp. In this manga-style romance novel, high school senior Miki is determined to break through the defenses of the gorgeous but secretive new boy called Hiro. (Rev: BL 3/15/07; SLJ 7/07)

10119 Crowe, Carole. *Groover's Heart* (4–6). 2001, Boyds Mills $15.95 (978-1-56397-953-8). 144pp. Orphan Charlotte, age 11, has trouble adjusting to the ways of her guardian, wealthy Aunt Viola. (Rev: BL 4/15/01; HBG 10/01; SLJ 4/01)

10120 Curtis, Christopher Paul. *Bud, Not Buddy* (4–6). 1999, Delacorte $15.95 (978-0-385-32306-2). 272pp. In this Newbery Medal winner set in Michigan during the Great Depression, 10-year-old Bud, on the run from his orphanage and his latest foster parents, is determined to find his father. (Rev: BCCB 11/99; BL 9/1/99; HB 11/99; HBG 3/00; SLJ 9/99)

10121 Curtis, Sandra R. *Gabriel's Ark* (2–5). Illus. 1998, Alef Design Group paper $16.95 (978-1-881283-22-5). 64pp. Gabe, who was born disabled, celebrates his bar mitzvah in his own way, thanks to a supportive family and an understanding rabbi. (Rev: BL 10/1/98; SLJ 1/99)

10122 Davis, Katie. *The Curse of Addy McMahon* (4–6). Illus. 2008, Greenwillow $16.99 (978-0-06-128711-4). 256pp. Sixth-grader Addy fears she is living under a family curse — her father has died, her mother's boyfriend is moving in, she has upset her best friend — and she describes these calamities in an accessible comic strip/diary "autobiogra-strip." (Rev: BL 7/08; SLJ 7/08)

10123 Dee, Barbara. *Just Another Day in My Insanely Real Life* (4–7). 2006, Simon & Schuster $15.95 (978-1-4169-0861-6). 256pp. Cassie must deal with the fallout from her parents' divorce, with her irresponsible older sister and demanding little brother, and with her former best friends in this novel about an all-too-real situation. (Rev: BL 5/15/06; SLJ 8/06)

10124 Dee, Barbara. *Solving Zoe* (4–7). 2009, Simon & Schuster $15.99 (978-1-4169-6128-4). 240pp. Zoe drifts in a sea of bright students and fading friends until her talent for codes and puzzles unlocks her new direction. (Rev: BCCB 6/09; BL 6/1–15/09; SLJ 6/09)

10125 DeGross, Monalisa. *Donavan's Double Trouble* (2–4). Illus. by Amy Bates. 2008, HarperCollins $15.99 (978-0-06-077293-2). 192pp. Fourth-grader Donavan, last seen in *Donavan's Word Jar* (1994), adjusts to his amputee uncle's disability and overcomes his difficulties at school with the help of his supportive African American family. (Rev: BL 12/15/07; SLJ 4/08)

10126 de Guzman, Michael. *Finding Stinko* (5–8). 2007, Farrar $16.00 (978-0-374-32305-9). 144pp. On the run from his latest and worst set of foster parents, Newboy, an elective mute, finds new voice with a ventriloquist's dummy; a compelling book of survival on the streets. (Rev: BL 4/15/07; SLJ 6/07)

10127 DeKeyser, Stacy. *Jump the Cracks* (5–8). 2008, Flux paper $9.95 (978-0-7387-1274-1). 216pp. Victoria, 15, sees a little boy being mistreated at a train station and ends up taking him to Georgia — an originally compassionate act that she soon finds will have huge complications. (Rev: BL 3/1/08; SLJ 9/08)

10128 Deriso, Christine Hurley. *Do-Over* (5–8). 2006, Delacorte LB $17.99 (978-0-385-90350-9). 183pp. Between the recent death of her mother and the move to a new school, 7th-grader Elsa is having a hard time of it, but things look up when her mother mysteriously appears one night and grants her do-over power. (Rev: SLJ 8/06)

10129 Deriso, Christine Hurley. *Talia Talk* (4–6). 2008, Delacorte $15.99 (978-0-385-73620-6). 192pp. Eleven-year-old Talia is coping with friend-ship problems and her mother's new romance, but she's still unhappy that her talk show host mother told stories about her on the air. (Rev: BCCB 2/09; SLJ 12/08)

10130 DiCamillo, Kate. *Because of Winn-Dixie* (4–6). 2000, Candlewick $15.99 (978-0-7636-0776-0). 184pp. In this Newbery Honor book, lonely 10-year-old India Opal Buloni adopts a stray dog, named Winn-Dixie, who changes her life. (Rev: BCCB 6/00; BL 5/1/00; HB 7/00; HBG 10/00; SLJ 6/00)

10131 DiCamillo, Kate. *The Tiger Rising* (4–6). 2001, Candlewick $12.99 (978-0-7636-0911-5). 128pp. This novel of grieving, friendship, and animal love involves Rob whose mother has just died, an outsider named Sistine with whom he becomes friends, and a caged tiger. (Rev: HB 5/01; HBG 10/01; SLJ 3/01)

10132 Donofrio, Beverly. *Thank You, Lucky Stars* (4–6). 2008, Random $16.99 (978-0-375-83964-1). 240pp. Early in 5th grade, Ally, abandoned by her friend Betsy, develops a surprising alliance with new girl Tina in this novel full of dance situations and awakening recognition of how to cope with social and family situations. (Rev: BCCB 1/08; BL 1/1–15/08; HB 5/08; SLJ 5/08)

10133 Dorman, N. B. *Petey and Miss Magic* (3–5). 1993, Shoe String LB $16.00 (978-0-208-02345-2). 99pp. A lonely boy who longs for a pet finds a worm that he begins to care for. (Rev: SLJ 3/93)

10134 Dreyer, Ellen. *Speechless in New York: Going to New York* (5–8). Series: Going To. 2000, Four Corners paper $7.95 (978-1-893577-01-5). 96pp. Jessie is beset with personal problems when she flies to New York from Minnesota with the Prairie Youth Chorale. (Rev: SLJ 3/00)

10135 Dunnion, Kristyn. *Missing Matthew* (4–6). 2004, Red Deer paper $7.95 (978-0-88995-278-2). 112pp. The three girls in the Rebel Rescue Squad decide to investigate the disappearance of 10-year-old Matthew, and instead of a kidnapping they find a sad boy who has run away from home. (Rev: BL 3/1/04; SLJ 5/04)

10136 Ellis, Sarah. *Pick-Up Sticks* (5–8). 1992, Macmillan LB $15.00 (978-0-689-50550-8). A disgruntled teen learns a lesson in life after being sent to live with relatives. (Rev: BL 1/15/92; SLJ 3/92*)

10137 Emery, Joanna. *Brothers of the Falls* (4–6). Illus. by Dave Erickson. 2004, Silver Moon LB $14.95 (978-1-893110-37-3). 92pp. Irish orphan James, 13, arrives in America alone and must find shelter and money to help him search for the brother who was left behind. (Rev: SLJ 8/04)

10138 English, Karen. *Birthday Blues* (2–4). Illus. by Laura Freeman. Series: Nikki and Deja. 2009, Clarion $15.00 (978-0-618-97787-1). 96pp. Deja, an African American girl, wonders whether her father will come to her eighth birthday party — and whether her classmates will go to a competing event. (Rev: BCCB 4/09; BL 2/1/09; SLJ 1/09)

10139 Evangelista, Beth. *Gifted* (5–8). 2005, Walker $16.95 (978-0-8027-8994-5). 192pp. George R. Clark is gifted and colossally unpopular with most of his classmates, so he is uneasy about going on his 8th-grade science field trip without his principal-father to protect him from the bullies; funny and real. (Rev: BL 12/15/05*; HBG 4/06; LMC 11/05; SLJ 1/06; VOYA 10/05)

10140 Evans, Douglas. *So What Do You Do?* (5–8). 1997, Front St. $14.95 (978-1-886910-20-1). Two middle-schoolers help their beloved former teacher who has become a homeless drunk. (Rev: BCCB 3/98; BL 11/1/97; HBG 3/98; SLJ 1/98; VOYA 2/98)

10141 Evans, Mari. *Dear Corinne, Tell Somebody! A Book About Secrets* (3–7). 1999, Just Us Bks. $12.95 (978-0-940975-81-1). 48pp. A book of letters in which Corinne's friends try to get her to seek help for her problem, which is later revealed as child abuse. (Rev: HBG 3/00; SLJ 12/99)

10142 Fagan, Cary. *The Market Wedding* (2–5). Illus. by Regolo Ricci. 2000, Tundra $16.95 (978-0-88776-492-9). The guests that Minnie and Morris invite to their wedding are so in awe of the luxurious trappings that they are afraid to attend. (Rev: BCCB 10/00; BL 12/1/00; HBG 3/01; SLJ 3/01)

10143 Flake, Sharon G. *A Freak Like Me* (5–9). 1999, Hyperion paper $5.99 (978-0-7868-1307-0). In her inner-city middle school, Maleeka Madison is picked on by classmates because she is poorly dressed, darker than the others, and gets good grades. (Rev: BL 9/1/98; SLJ 11/98)

10144 Fletcher, Ralph J. *Spider Boy* (5–8). 1997, Houghton $16.00 (978-0-395-77606-3). Bobby — nicknamed Spider Boy because he knows so much about spiders — has trouble adjusting to his new life in the town of New Paltz, New York. (Rev: BCCB 4/97; BL 6/1–15/97; HB 7/97; SLJ 7/97)

10145 Fogelin, Adrian. *The Sorta Sisters* (5–8). Illus. by author. 2007, Peachtree $14.95 (978-1-56145-424-2). 240pp. Anna, a foster child who lives in Tallahassee, Florida, corresponds with Mica, who lives with her alcoholic father on a boat in the Florida Keys, and their friendship brings them both solace. (Rev: BL 1/1–15/08; SLJ 12/07)

10146 Fox, Paula. *Monkey Island* (5–8). 1991, Watts LB $16.99 (978-0-531-08562-2). 160pp. A homeless, abandoned 11-year-old boy in New York City contracts pneumonia and is cared for by a homeless African American teenager and retired teacher, who share their place in the park with him. (Rev: BCCB 10/91*; BL 9/1/91*; HB 9/91*; SLJ 8/91)

10147 Fox, Paula. *Western Wind* (5–9). 1993, Orchard LB $17.99 (978-0-531-08652-0). At first resentful of being sent to spend a summer with her grandmother on a Maine island, Elizabeth gradually adjusts and learns a great deal about herself. (Rev: BCCB 9/93; BL 10/15/93; SLJ 12/93*; VOYA 12/93)

10148 Frasier, Debra. *Miss Alaineus: A Vocabulary Disaster* (3–5). Illus. 2000, Harcourt $16.00 (978-0-15-202163-4). 32pp. Fifth-grader Sage mistakes the word *miscellaneous* for *Miss Alaineus* but turns this embarrassment into a triumph. (Rev: BL 9/15/00; HBG 3/01; SLJ 9/00)

10149 Freeman, Martha. *The Trouble with Cats* (2–4). 2000, Holiday House $15.95 (978-0-8234-

1479-6). 76pp. A beginning chapter book about Holly, who is adjusting to a new life in San Francisco with a new stepfather and a new school situation. (Rev: BCCB 4/00; BL 3/15/00; HBG 10/00; SLJ 7/00)

10150 Friedman, Aileen. *A Cloak for the Dreamer* (3–5). Illus. by Kim Howard. 1995, Scholastic $16.95 (978-0-590-48987-4). 15pp. Misha sets out to find his fortune in an amazing cloak designed by his father and brothers. (Rev: BL 2/1/95; SLJ 4/95)

10151 Friedman, Laurie. *In Business with Mallory* (2–4). Illus. by Barbara Pollak. 2006, Carolrhoda LB $15.95 (978-1-57505-925-9). 159pp. Mallory comes up with a scheme to earn the money she needs to buy a coveted purse, then isn't sure if that's the wisest use of her cash. (Rev: SLJ 6/06)

10152 Friesen, Gayle. *Men of Stone* (5–8). 2000, Kids Can $16.95 (978-1-55074-781-2). 216pp. While Ben Conrad traces his own family roots, he confronts a local bully in this story of a boy's journey to maturity. (Rev: HBG 3/01; SLJ 10/00; VOYA 2/01)

10153 Gardner, Graham. *Inventing Elliot* (5–9). 2004, Dial $16.99 (978-0-8037-2964-3). 192pp. Despite efforts to avoid bullies at his new high school, 14-year-old Elliot Sutton finds himself embroiled with the Guardians, a group that metes out punishment to those it deems "losers." (Rev: BL 5/15/04; SLJ 3/04; VOYA 4/04)

10154 Gephart, Donna. *As If Being 12 3/4 Isn't Bad Enough, My Mother Is Running for President!* (4–6). 2008, Delacorte $15.99 (978-0-385-73481-3). 224pp. Her mom is running for president and now Vanessa must deal with real fears as well as the typical problems of 7th grade. (Rev: BL 2/15/08; SLJ 2/08)

10155 Gifaldi, David. *Toby Scudder, Ultimate Warrior* (4–6). 1993, Clarion $15.00 (978-0-395-66400-1). 201pp. A new teacher helps overweight Toby find the self-esteem he lacks. (Rev: BCCB 11/93; BL 10/15/93; SLJ 10/93*)

10156 Gilbert, Barbara Snow. *Stone Water* (5–9). 1996, Front St. $15.95 (978-1-886910-11-9). Fourteen-year-old Grant must decide if he will honor his ailing grandfather's wish to help him commit suicide. (Rev: BL 12/15/96; SLJ 12/96*; VOYA 4/97)

10157 Golding, Theresa Martin. *Kat's Surrender* (5–8). 1999, Boyds Mills $16.95 (978-1-56397-755-8). 179pp. Thirteen-year-old Kat misses her deceased mother terribly, but she tries to hide it in her friendships for an old man and a wacky girl. (Rev: BL 10/15/99; HBG 3/00; SLJ 11/99; VOYA 4/00)

10158 Gordon, Amy. *The Gorillas of Gill Park* (4–7). Illus. 2003, Holiday $16.95 (978-0-8234-1751-3). 256pp. Shy, lonely Willie comes into his own when he spends the summer with his eccentric Aunt Bridget and meets her zany neighbors. (Rev: BL 6/1–15/03; HBG 10/03; SLJ 5/03)

10159 Gordon, Amy. *The Secret Life of a Boarding School Brat* (5–7). 2004, Holiday House $16.95 (978-0-8234-1779-7). 252pp. Lydia, already unhappy about her parents' divorce and her grandmother's death, becomes even more miserable at her new boarding school and chronicles her woes in her diary. (Rev: HB 7/04; SLJ 8/04)

10160 Gorman, Carol. *Games: A Tale of Two Bullies* (4–7). 2007, HarperCollins $16.99 (978-0-06-057027-9). 288pp. Instead of suspending Mick and Boot for fighting, their principal requires them to play board games together; after a rocky start punctuated with petty crimes, the boys explore a hidden tunnel together, discovering that they both cope with alcoholic, abusive fathers. (Rev: BL 1/1–15/07; SLJ 1/07)

10161 Gosselin, Kim. *Smoking Stinks!!* (2–4). Illus. by Thom Buttner. 1997, JayJo $16.95 (978-0-9639449-5-5). When Maddie's grandfather comes to school to tell her class why he smokes, he agrees that smoking stinks. (Rev: BL 4/1/98; SLJ 1/98)

10162 Grant, Vicki. *Nine Doors* (5–9). Series: Orca Currents. 2009, Orca $16.95 (978-1-55469-074-9); paper $9.95 (978-1-55469-073-2). 96pp. Emery lets his friend talk him into pranks that escalate to an uncomfortable level in this fast-paced book for reluctant readers. (Rev: BLO 5/27/09; SLJ 8/09)

10163 Grant, Vicki. *Pigboy* (5–9). Series: Orca Currents. 2006, Orca $14.95 (978-1-55143-666-1); paper $8.95 (978-1-5314-3643-8). 101pp. Certain that his classmates' teasing will reach a new high, Dan Hogg dreads the field trip to a pig farm, but he deals well with the challenges that await him as he faces off with an escaped convict; suitable for reluctant readers and gripping enough for others. (Rev: SLJ 12/06)

10164 Gray, Dianne E. *Holding Up the Earth* (5–8). 2000, Houghton $15.00 (978-0-618-00703-5). 224pp. Sarah, a foster child now living on a Nebraska farm, does some research and uncovers stories of the many generations of women who preceded her on the farm and their struggles and problems. (Rev: BL 1/1–15/01; HB 9/00; HBG 3/01; SLJ 10/00)

10165 Grindley, Sally. *Bravo, Max!* (3–5). Illus. by Tony Ross. 2007, Simon & Schuster $15.99 (978-1-4169-0393-2). 160pp. In his continuing correspondence with his favorite author, 11-year-old Max — first seen in *Dear Max* (2006) — writes about his dislike of his mother's boyfriend, the play Max has written that parallels events in his life, and the joys and agonies of growing up. (Rev: BL 3/15/07)

10166 Groth, B. L., and Thomas Wray, eds. *Home Is Where We Live* (3–5). Illus. 1995, Cornerstone paper $7.95 (978-0-940895-34-8). 32pp. A simple story told in photos and narrative of a homeless child in a Chicago shelter. (Rev: BL 10/15/95; SLJ 12/95)

10167 Grove, Vicki. *Reaching Dustin* (5–8). 1998, Putnam paper $6.99 (978-0-698-11839-3). As part of a 6th-grade assignment, Carly must get to know Dustin Groat, the class outcast, and as she learns more about him and his family, she realizes that her attitudes toward him in the past have helped create his problems. (Rev: BCCB 3/98; BL 5/1/98; SLJ 5/98)

10168 Guest, Elissa Haden. *Iris and Walter* (1–3). Illus. 2000, Harcourt $14.00 (978-0-15-202122-1). 44pp. It takes time, but gradually Iris comes to enjoy living in the country far from the city activities she loved, in this beginning chapter book. (Rev: BCCB 12/00*; BL 10/15/00; HBG 3/01; SLJ 11/00)

10169 Gugler, Laurel Dee. *A Piece of Forever* (3–6). 2009, Lorimer paper $8.95 (978-1-55277-026-9). 120pp. In the mid-1950s as a Veterans Day ceremony approaches, Rose struggles with her Mennonite family's pacifist stance. (Rev: BLO 4/23/09)

10170 Haas, Jessie. *Will You, Won't You?* (5–8). 2000, Greenwillow LB $15.89 (978-0-06-029197-6). 192pp. Mad (short for Madison) is a shy middle-schooler who comes out of her shell during a summer she spends with her wise grandmother in the country. (Rev: BCCB 10/00; BL 2/1/01; HBG 3/01; SLJ 10/00)

10171 Hahn, Mary D. *Anna on the Farm* (3–5). Illus. 2001, Clarion $15.00 (978-0-618-03605-9). 152pp. When 9-year-old Anna arrives at her aunt and uncle's farm for a week, she finds they have taken in an orphan named Theodore, and a hearty rivalry begins. (Rev: BL 2/15/01; HB 5/01; HBG 10/01; SLJ 3/01)

10172 Hamilton, Virginia. *Drylongso* (3–5). Illus. by Jerry Pinkney. 1992, Harcourt $18.95 (978-0-15-224241-1). 64pp. During a great duststorm on the prairie in 1975, a tall boy appears who helps Lindy and her family find water. (Rev: BCCB 10/92*; BL 7/92*; HB 9/92; SLJ 1/93)

10173 Harper, Charise Mericle. *Still Just Grace* (2–4). Illus. by author. 2007, Houghton $15.00 (978-0-618-64643-2). 160pp. Still searching for her own identity, 3rd-grader Grace (last seen in *Just Grace*, 2007)deals with a variety of problems in this appealing novel presented in a format that will appeal to beginning chapter-book readers. (Rev: BL 9/15/07; SLJ 10/07) ∩

10174 Harrah, Madge. *The Nobody Club* (4–6). 1989, Avon paper $2.50 (978-0-380-75631-5). 166pp. Three misunderstood girls form a club to help solve one another's problems. (Rev: SLJ 8/89)

10175 Hartling, Peter. *Ben Loves Anna* (4–6). Trans. by J. H. Auerbach. Illus. by Ellen Weinstein. 1990, Overlook $12.95 (978-0-87951-401-3). 96pp. The feelings of a lovestruck 10-year-old boy are captured by one of Germany's most distinguished children's writers. (Rev: BCCB 4/91; BL 6/15/91; SLJ 5/91)

10176 Hatton, Caroline. *Vero and Philippe* (3–5). Illus. by Preston McDaniels. 2001, Front St. $14.95 (978-0-8126-2940-8). 120pp. Nine-year-old Vero and her family, Vietnamese immigrants to France, move from the country into the city, an adjustment made more difficult for Vero when her beloved nanny is fired. (Rev: BCCB 3/02; HBG 3/02; SLJ 12/01)

10177 Henderson, Aileen K. *Treasure of Panther Peak* (4–7). Illus. 1998, Milkweed paper $6.95 (978-1-57131-619-6). 184pp. Twelve-year-old Ellie Williams gradually adjusts to her new home when her mother, fleeing an abusive husband, moves to Big Bend National Park to teach in a one-room school. (Rev: BL 12/1/98; HBG 3/99; VOYA 8/99)

10178 Henkes, Kevin. *Sun and Spoon* (3–5). 1997, Greenwillow $19.99 (978-0-688-15232-1). 144pp. Spoon takes his dead grandmother's solitaire cards as a memento, but later he regrets his action. (Rev: BL 8/97; HB 9/97; HBG 3/98; SLJ 7/97*)

10179 Henson, Heather. *Here's How I See It, Here's How It Is* (5–7). 2009, Atheneum $16.99 (978-1-4169-4901-5). 272pp. Twelve-year-old Junebug is a budding actress working at her parents' summer stock theater but suddenly circumstances change and she faces a number of problems including her parents' separation and a boy with Asperger's syndrome. (Rev: BCCB 6/09; BL 4/1/09; SLJ 6/09)

10180 Hershey, Mary. *My Big Sister Is So Bossy She Says You Can't Read This Book* (4–6). 2005, Random LB $17.99 (978-0-385-90917-4). 176pp. A realistic story about the various problems 10-year-old Effie faces at school and at home: her grandfather has died, her father is in prison, her best friend has moved away, and her older sister has stolen the Angel Scout funds. A sequel is *Ten Lucky Things That Have Happened to Me Since I Almost Got Hit by Lightning* (2008). (Rev: BL 6/1–15/05; SLJ 6/05)

10181 High, Linda O. *The Summer of the Great Divide* (5–8). 1996, Holiday $15.95 (978-0-8234-1228-0). With the political events of 1969 as a backdrop, 13-year-old Wheezie sorts herself out at her relatives' farm. (Rev: BCCB 7–8/96; BL 6/1–15/96; SLJ 4/96)

10182 Holden, Dwight. *Grand-Gran's Best Trick* (3–5). Illus. by Michael Chesworth. 1989, Brunner paper $8.95 (978-0-945354-16-1). 48pp. A young girl faces the sad experience of her beloved grandfather's death. (Rev: BL 12/1/89)

10183 Holmes, Elizabeth. *Pretty Is* (4–6). 2007, Dutton $16.99 (978-0-525-47813-3). 216pp. Erin must deal with a mean former friend and an unconventional older sister as she waits for the summer before sixth grade to end. (Rev: BCCB 7–8/07; SLJ 7/07)

10184 Holmes, Sara. *Letters from Rapunzel* (5–8). 2007, HarperCollins $15.99 (978-0-06-078073-9). 184pp. In letters to an unknown correspondent, Cadence — who calls herself Rapunzel — describes her father's depression and her sense of being alone. (Rev: SLJ 2/07)

10185 Horrocks, Anita. *Almost Eden* (5–8). 2006, Tundra paper $9.95 (978-0-88776-742-5). 288pp. Elsie is a Mennonite girl who must deal with her mother's depression, the onset of puberty, and religious doubts in this story set in Canada in the 1960s. (Rev: BL 5/15/06)

10186 Horvath, Penny. *Everything on a Waffle* (5–7). 2001, Farrar $16.00 (978-0-374-32236-6). 160pp. Eleven-year-old Primrose Squarp does not believe her parents drowned during a storm. In the meantime she is moved from pillar to post, ending up as a foster child to an elderly couple. Newbery Honor Book, 2002. (Rev: BCCB 3/01*; BL 2/15/01; HB 5/01*; HBG 10/01; SLJ 4/01; VOYA 6/01)

10187 Horvath, Polly. *The Vacation* (5–7). 2005, Farrar $16.00 (978-0-374-30870-4). 197pp. When his parents go to Africa as missionaries, 12-year-old

Henry is taken on an eye-opening, cross-country trip by his eccentric maiden aunts, Magnolia and Pigg; comedy and weirdness ensue. (Rev: BCCB 10/05; BL 6/05; HB 7/05; SLJ 8/05*)

10188 Jarrow, Gail. *Beyond the Magic Sphere* (4–6). 1994, Harcourt $15.95 (978-0-15-200193-3). 192pp. S. B.'s only ray of hope during the summer she is spending with her unsympathetic cousin is meeting Cally, who plays a strange fantasy game. (Rev: BL 10/15/94; SLJ 11/94)

10189 Johnson, Emily Rhoads. *Write Me If You Dare!* (4–6). 2000, Front St. $15.95 (978-0-8126-2944-6). 208pp. While coping with her mother's death and her father's new girlfriend, 11-year-old Maddie decides that her pen pal is really a ghost. (Rev: BCCB 12/00; BL 11/1/00; HB 1/01; HBG 3/01; SLJ 11/00)

10190 Joosse, Barbara M. *Anna and the Cat Lady* (3–6). Illus. by Gretchen Will Mayo. 1992, HarperCollins LB $13.89 (978-0-06-020243-9). 176pp. Two third-graders rescue a kitten and meet an elderly eccentric woman who they later realize needs their help to survive. (Rev: BCCB 2/92; BL 1/1/92; SLJ 3/92)

10191 Jukes, Mavis. *Smoke* (4–6). 2009, Farrar $16.95 (978-0-374-37085-5). 176pp. Twelve-year-old Colt struggles with his parents' divorce, a move to California, his mother's new boyfriend, and finally the disappearance of his cat Smoke; he sets off to find the missing cat. (Rev: BCCB 4/09; BL 4/1/09; HB 3/09)

10192 Kane, Kim. *Pip: The Story of Olive* (5–8). 2009, Random $15.99 (978-0-385-75171-1). 256pp. When her friend Mathilda drops her, lonely Olive suddenly finds she has a twin sister called Pip, who is bright and adventurous as Olive is pale and retiring; with Pip beside her, Olive decides to look for the father she never met. (Rev: BCCB 7–8/09; SLJ 7/09)

10193 Kaye, Marilyn. *Real Heroes* (5–7). 1993, Avon paper $3.50 (978-0-380-72283-9). 144pp. Kevin finds he is in the middle of a situation involving quarrels between parents and between best friends, and a controversy about a teacher who is HIV positive. (Rev: BCCB 5/93; BL 4/1/93)

10194 Keene, Carolyn. *Love Times Three* (5–8). Series: River Heights. 1991, Pocket paper $3.50 (978-0-671-96703-1). 156pp. Nikki has a crush on Tim, but Brittany wants him too. (Rev: BL 12/15/89)

10195 Kerr, Dan. *Candy on the Edge* (5–8). 2002, Coteau paper $8.95 (978-1-55050-189-6). 137pp. Candy, an 8th grader, finds herself drawn into a world of crime as she makes new friends and falls for Ramon. (Rev: SLJ 5/02)

10196 Kerz, Anna. *The Mealworm Diaries* (3–5). 2009, Orca paper $9.95 (978-1-55143-982-2). 176pp. Jeremy, still upset about his father's death, has trouble adjusting to his new school in Toronto, especially his difficult science-fair partner Aaron. (Rev: BL 4/15/09)

10197 Khan, Rukhsana. *Wanting Mor* (5–8). 2009, Greenwood $17.95 (978-0-88899-858-3). 192pp. This is a harrowing tale about a young Afghani girl,

Jameela, who faces abuse, abandonment, and an orphanage after the death of her mother; based on a true story. (Rev: BCCB 9/09; BL 4/1/09; HB 7/09)

10198 Killien, Christi. *Artie's Brief: The Whole Truth, and Nothing But* (5–7). 1989, Avon paper $2.95 (978-0-380-71108-6). 112pp. Sixth-grader Artie deals with the suicide of his older brother. (Rev: BL 5/15/89)

10199 Kimmel, Elizabeth C. *Lily B. on the Brink of Love* (5–8). 2005, HarperCollins LB $16.89 (978-0-06-075543-0). 224pp. In this charming sequel to *Lily B. on the Brink of Cool* (2003), the title character, an aspiring writer and advice columnist for her school paper, needs counsel herself when she falls in love. (Rev: BL 10/1/05; SLJ 7/05)

10200 Kimmel, Elizabeth C. *Spin the Bottle* (5–7). 2008, Dial $16.99 (978-0-8037-3191-2). 240pp. Phoebe gets a small part in a middle-school play and must deal with spin-the-bottle games, the popular crowd, and changing friendships. (Rev: BL 5/1/08; SLJ 6/08)

10201 Kimmel, Haven. *Kaline Klattermaster's Tree House* (3–5). Illus. by Peter Brown. 2007, Atheneum $15.99 (978-1-4169-5207-7). 150pp. Third-grader Kaline is easily distracted and finds that his imaginary world — especially a tree house where he pretends he has two older brothers — helps him deal with everyday problems including his father's disappearance and bullies at school. (Rev: BCCB 4/08; BL 12/15/07)

10202 Klass, Sheila S. *Little Women Next Door* (3–6). 2000, Holiday House $15.95 (978-0-8234-1472-7). 144pp. Lonely 11-year-old Susan Wilson's life changes when a group experimenting with communal life moves into the neighborhood. (Rev: HBG 3/01; SLJ 11/00)

10203 Klass, Sheila S. *The Uncivil War* (4–6). 1998, Holiday House $15.95 (978-0-8234-1329-4). 162pp. After she is taunted by the class bully, middle schooler Asa decides to mend her ways and, among other things, lose weight. (Rev: HBG 10/98; SLJ 4/98)

10204 Kline, Suzy. *Mary Marony and the Chocolate Surprise* (2–4). Illus. 1995, Penguin $15.99 (978-0-399-22829-2). 86pp. Mary Marony cheats to become a contest winner and later wonders if it was worth it. (Rev: BL 12/1/95; SLJ 12/95)

10205 Konigsburg, E. L. *Altogether, One at a Time* (4–6). Illus. by Gail E. Haley. 1971, Macmillan paper $4.99 (978-0-689-71290-6). 88pp. Four short stories by the Newbery Medal-winning writer, each of which explores the theme that compromise is often necessary to appreciate life fully.

10206 Korman, Gordon. *Liar, Liar, Pants on Fire* (2–4). Illus. by JoAnn Adinolfi. 1997, Scholastic $14.95 (978-0-590-27142-4). 84pp. Third-grader Zoe lies so much that no one believes her when she tells the truth. (Rev: HBG 3/98; SLJ 9/97)

10207 Kornblatt, Marc. *Izzy's Place* (4–7). 2003, Simon & Schuster $16.95 (978-0-689-84639-7). 28pp. Summer with his grandmother proves more rewarding than 10-year-old Henry anticipated as he

makes friends and gains a new outlook on life. (Rev: BL 6/1–15/03; HBG 10/03; SLJ 7/03)

10208 Koss, Amy Goldman. *The Girls* (5–9). 2000, Dial $17.99 (978-0-8037-2494-5). 128pp. In chapters narrated by different protagonists, this book tells of Maya who has been dropped for no apparent reason from a clique of five popular girls in the middle school she attends. (Rev: BCCB 6/00; BL 8/00; HB 7/00; HBG 10/00; SLJ 6/00)

10209 Krumgold, Joseph. *Onion John* (5–8). Illus. by Symeon Shimin. 1959, HarperCollins LB $17.89 (978-0-690-04698-4); paper $5.99 (978-0-06-440144-9). 248pp. A Newbery Medal winner (1960) about a boy's friendship with an old man. Also use the Newbery winner . . . *And Now Miguel* (1954).

10210 Lawson, Julie. *Turns on a Dime* (5–8). 1999, Stoddart paper $7.95 (978-0-7737-5942-8). In this sequel to *Goldstone* (1998), set in British Columbia, 11-year-old Jo faces many new situations, including finding a boyfriend, discovering that she is adopted, and learning that her beloved babysitter is pregnant. (Rev: SLJ 6/99)

10211 Lemieux, Michele. *Stormy Night* (4–8). Illus. by author. 1999, Kids Can $15.95 (978-1-55074-692-1). 240pp. A long picture book in which a young girl who can't sleep ponders questions that are common to preteen girls. (Rev: BL 12/1/99; HBG 3/00; SLJ 12/99)

10212 Lester, Alison. *The Quicksand Pony* (5–8). 1998, Houghton $15.00 (978-0-395-93749-5). In this novel set in Australia, 17-year-old Joycie fakes a drowning and seeks a new life in the bush with her infant son, but two young girls stumble on the truth nine years later. (Rev: BCCB 10/98; BL 12/15/98; HB 1/99; HBG 3/99; SLJ 10/98; VOYA 2/99)

10213 Levy, Elizabeth. *Cheater, Cheater* (5–8). 1994, Scholastic paper $3.50 (978-0-590-45866-5). Lucy Lovello has been labeled a cheater and even her teachers don't trust her. When she finds her best friend cheating, she faces a moral dilemma. (Rev: BL 10/1/93; SLJ 10/93; VOYA 12/93)

10214 Lewis, Beverly. *Catch a Falling Star* (5–8). Series: Summerhill Secrets. 1995, Bethany paper $5.99 (978-1-55661-478-1). 144pp. An Amish boy faces excommunication when he begins paying too much attention to a non-Amish girl. (Rev: BL 3/15/96)

10215 Lewis, Beverly. *Night of the Fireflies* (5–8). Series: Summerhill Secrets. 1995, Bethany House paper $5.99 (978-1-55661-479-8). In this sequel to *Catch a Falling Star* (1995), Levi, an Amish boy, tries to save his young sister, who has been struck by a car. (Rev: BL 3/15/96)

10216 Lewis, Maggie. *Morgy Makes His Move* (3–5). Illus. 1999, Houghton $15.00 (978-0-395-92284-2). 80pp. A pleasant novel that tells of third-grader Morgan and his adjustment to his new home in Massachusetts, which involves coping with a bully named Ferguson. (Rev: BCCB 10/99; BL 12/15/99; HBG 3/00; SLJ 11/99)

10217 Little, Jean. *Birdie for Now* (3–5). Illus. 2002, Orca paper $5.95 (978-1-55143-203-8). 160pp. Troubled, hyperactive Dickon moves to a new home and finds joy and self-knowledge when he gets the opportunity to train an abused dog. (Rev: BL 11/1/02; SLJ 12/02)

10218 Liu, Cynthea. *Paris Pan Takes the Dare* (5–7). 2009, Putnam $16.99 (978-0-399-25043-9). 256pp. New girl Paris Pan, a 12-year-old Chinese American, is pleased to be asked a clique but distressed when she hears about The Dare. (Rev: BLO 5/27/09; SLJ 8/09)

10219 Look, Lenore. *Alvin Ho: Allergic to Girls, School, and Other Scary Things* (2–4). Illus. by LeUyen Pham. 2008, Random $15.99 (978-0-375-83914-6). 160pp. Chinese American Alvin Ho, a timid second-grader who becomes mute when he arrives at school, survives a number of challenges at home and at school. (Rev: BL 7/08; SLJ 8/08)

10220 Lopez, Diana. *Confetti Girl* (4–7). 2009, Little, Brown $15.99 (978-0-316-02955-1). 208pp. Sixth-grader Lina Flores, living in Texas, struggles to cope with her mother's death, her best friend's problems, her schoolwork, and typical middle-school friendship and romantic challenges; this coming-of-age story is sprinkled with Spanish phrases. (Rev: BL 5/15/09; SLJ 7/09)

10221 Love, D. Anne. *My Lone Star Summer* (4–6). 1996, Holiday House $15.95 (978-0-8234-1235-8). 192pp. Jill experiences the first problems of adolescence when she spends her 12th summer visiting her grandmother's ranch. (Rev: BCCB 7–8/96; BL 5/1/96; SLJ 3/96)

10222 Ludwig, Trudy. *Sorry!* (2–5). Illus. by Maurie J. Manning. 2006, Tricycle $15.95 (978-1-58246-173-1). Jack learns about insincere apologies when he makes friends with the popular Charlie; appended are an author's note, discussion questions, and "Apology Dos and Don'ts." (Rev: SLJ 12/06)

10223 McClintock, Norah. *Back* (5–8). 2009, Orca LB $16.95 (978-1-55143-991-4); paper $9.95 (978-1-55143-989-1). The compelling story of Jojo, who returns from prison to an unwelcoming community. (Rev: BL 4/15/09)

10224 McGhee, Alison. *Julia Gillian: (And the Quest for Joy)* (4–5). Illus. by Drazen Kozjan. 2009, Scholastic $16.99 (978-0-525-03350-3). 320pp. Julia is beset with an assortment of problems in this funny and spirited look at a 5th-grader's life at home and at school. (Rev: HB 5/09; SLJ 7/09)

10225 McKay, Hilary. *Indigo's Star* (5–8). 2004, Simon & Schuster $15.95 (978-0-689-86563-3). 272pp. In this sequel to *Saffy's Angel* (2002), Saffy's younger siblings — 12-year-old Indigo and 8-year-old Rose — take a stand against school bullies with the help of a lonely young American called Tom. (Rev: BL 9/15/04; SLJ 9/04*)

10226 McKenna, Colleen O'Shaughnessy. *Fifth Grade: Here Comes Trouble* (4–6). 1991, Scholastic paper $3.25 (978-0-590-41734-1). 128pp. Collette feels insecure when her rich friend invites her to her first boy-girl party. (Rev: BCCB 10/89; SLJ 9/89)

10227 MacLachlan, Patricia. *The Facts and Fictions of Minna Pratt* (5–7). 1988, HarperCollins paper $6.99 (978-0-06-440265-1). 144pp. A budding young cellist on the verge of adolescence experi-

ences her first boyfriend. (Rev: BCCB 4/88; BL 6/15/88; SLJ 6–7/88)

10228 MacLachlan, Patricia. *Unclaimed Treasures* (5–8). 1984, HarperCollins paper $6.99 (978-0-06-440189-0). 128pp. A romantic story of a young girl finding herself.

10229 MacLean, Christine Cole. *Mary Margaret, Center Stage* (3–5). Illus. by Vicky Lowe. 2006, Dutton $15.99 (978-0-525-47597-2). 176pp. Longtime teacher's pet Mary Margaret is jealous when a new girl joins her fourth-grade class and begins to steal the spotlight. (Rev: BL 2/1/06; SLJ 6/06)

10230 Marino, Nan. *Neil Armstrong Is My Uncle and Other Lies Muscle Man McGinty Told Me* (3–6). 2009, Roaring Brook $16.95 (978-1-59643-499-8). 160pp. In 1969, a scornful 10-year-old Tammy takes out her anger at life on a boastful foster child called Douglas (aka Muscle Man McGinty). (Rev: BCCB 7–8/09; BL 4/15/09; LMC 10/09; SLJ 6/09)

10231 Martinez, Claudia Guadalupe. *The Smell of Old Lady Perfume* (4–6). 2008, Cinco Puntos $15.95 (978-1-933693-18-7). 256pp. Already stressed by problems at school, sixth-grader Chela is overwhelmed when her father suffers a stroke and her grandmother (she of the old lady perfume) comes to stay. (Rev: BL 9/1/08; SLJ 9/08)

10232 May, Eleanor. *Ty's Triple Trouble* (2–4). Illus. by Amy Wummer. Series: Social Studies Connects. 2007, Kane paper $4.99 (978-1-57565-237-5). 32pp. A cheerful yet cautionary tale about what happens when Ty takes on too much at once, this story encourages readers to consider volunteering. (Rev: SLJ 6/07)

10233 Miles, Miska. *Annie and the Old One* (2–5). Illus. by Peter Parnall. 1972, Little, Brown $16.95 (978-0-316-57117-3); paper $7.95 (978-0-316-57120-3). Annie, a young Navajo girl, realizes her wonderful grandmother is dying and tries to put off the inevitable.

10234 Miles, Miska. *Gertrude's Pocket* (3–5). Illus. by Emily Arnold McCully. 1984, Peter Smith $15.75 (978-0-8446-6164-3). A reissue of a 1970 title in which Gertrude's tormentor gets his comeuppance in a story about poor folk in Appalachia.

10235 Mills, Claudia. *Cally's Enterprise* (4–6). 1989, Avon paper $2.75 (978-0-380-70693-8). 128pp. Cally, the daughter of overachievers, breaks her foot and can't go to ballet and gym, and to her surprise learns that she likes being a businesswoman when her friend Chuck gets her to sell magazines. (Rev: BCCB 4/88; BL 6/1/88; SLJ 5/88)

10236 Mills, Claudia. *Makeovers by Marcia* (4–7). Series: West Creek Middle School. 2005, Farrar $16.00 (978-0-374-34654-6). 160pp. Marcia learns that beauty is more than skin deep — and that there are more important things than the school dance — when she gives makeovers to the women in a nursing home. (Rev: BL 3/1/05; SLJ 2/05)

10237 Mills, Claudia. *Perfectly Chelsea* (3–5). Illus. by Jacqueline Rogers. 2004, Farrar $16.00 (978-0-374-31244-2). 128pp. Perfectionist fourth-grader Chelsea must question her own behavior in this story in which religion plays a large role. (Rev: BL 2/1/04; HB 5/04; SLJ 5/04)

10238 Mills, Lauren. *The Rag Coat* (3–5). Illus. 1991, Little, Brown $16.95 (978-0-316-57407-5). 32pp. A picture book that celebrates Appalachia. (Rev: BCCB 1/92; BL 10/15/91; HB 11/91; SLJ 11/91*)

10239 Morgan, Nicola. *Chicken Friend* (5–7). 2005, Candlewick $15.99 (978-0-7636-2735-5). 160pp. When her family moves to the country, Becca tries too hard to be cool and winds up in trouble in this story told from a believable pre-teen point of view. (Rev: BL 3/1/05; SLJ 4/05)

10240 Morris, Kimberly. *Just for Now: Kids and the People of the Court* (K–4). Illus. by Tony Sansevero. 2007, Child Advocates $16.95 (978-0-9754953-9-1). 48pp. Rachel and her little brother, Gilbert, arrive at a foster home trying to sort through why their mother abandoned them. Then they encounter a runaway dog in need of a caring home and realize that the dog's situation mirrors their own. (Rev: SLJ 6/07)

10241 Myracle, Lauren. *Eleven* (4–7). 2004, Dutton $16.99 (978-0-525-47165-3). 208pp. Covering Winnie's life from her 11th birthday to her 12th, this novel reveals typical friendship and family tensions. (Rev: BL 4/15/04; SLJ 2/04)

10242 Nagda, Ann Whitehead. *Tarantula Power!* (2–4). Illus. by Stephanie Roth. 2007, Holiday $15.95 (978-0-8234-1991-3). 96pp. With the help of schoolmates and a pet tarantula, a 4th-grader helps a younger student overcome being bullied. (Rev: BL 7/07; LMC 11/07; SLJ 6/07)

10243 Neri, G. *Chess Rumble* (5–8). Illus. by Jesse Joshua Watson. 2007, Lee & Low $18.95 (978-1-58430-279-7). 64pp. Marcus learns to channel his anger — over his sister's death and his father's absence — into chess, and tells about it in free verse. (Rev: BL 1/1–15/08; SLJ 11/07)

10244 Nielsen, Susin. *Word Nerd* (4–8). 2008, Tundra $18.95 (978-0-88776-875-0). 256pp. Twelve-year-old Ambrose, tired of moving and suffering bullies, makes friends with a 25-year-old ex-con neighbor who introduces him to Scrabble and broadens his horizons. (Rev: BCCB 9/08; BLO 12/30/08; SLJ 12/08)

10245 Olmstead, Kathleen, retel. *Anne of Green Gables* (3–4). Illus. by Lucy Corvino. 2005, Sterling $5.95 (978-1-4027-1130-5). 153pp. A pared-down version of the well-loved story for younger readers, with black-and-white illustrations and a large typeface. (Rev: SLJ 7/05)

10246 Parkinson, Siobhan. *Second Fiddle* (4–7). 2007, Roaring Brook $16.95 (978-1-59643-122-5). 192pp. Mags and Gillian attempt to track down Gillian's father in the hopes that he will help finance her education at a music school in England. (Rev: BCCB 6/07; BL 2/15/07; HB 3/07; SLJ 6/07)

10247 Paterson, Katherine. *The Great Gilly Hopkins* (4–6). 1978, HarperCollins LB $17.89 (978-0-690-03838-5); paper $5.99 (978-0-06-440201-9). 192pp. Precocious Gilly bounces from one foster home to another.

10248 Patron, Susan. *The Higher Power of Lucky* (4–6). Illus. by Matt Phelan. 2006, Simon & Schuster $16.95 (978-1-4169-0194-5). 144pp. In a tiny California hamlet called Hard Pan, 10-year-old Lucky feels constantly uncertain about her life and seeks a "higher power" that will bring her some peace. Newbery Medal, 2007. (Rev: BL 12/1/06; SLJ 12/06) ∩

10249 Paulsen, Gary. *The Amazing Life of Birds: (The Twenty-Day Puberty Journal of Duane Homer Leech)* (5–7). 2006, Random $13.95 (978-0-385-74660-1). 84pp. Having a bad time with the onset of puberty and its accompanying embarrassments — amusingly confided in his journal — 12-year-old Duane identifies with a baby bird developing in a nest outside his window. (Rev: SLJ 10/06)

10250 Paulsen, Gary. *Brian's Return* (5–8). 1999, Delacorte $15.95 (978-0-385-32500-4). 117pp. Brian, the hero of *Brian's Winter,* becomes so disheartened with life at school away from the wilderness that he decides to leave society behind forever. (Rev: BL 2/1/99; HB 1/99; HBG 10/99; SLJ 2/99)

10251 Paulsen, Gary. *The Cookcamp* (5–7). 1991, Orchard paper $15.95 (978-0-531-05927-2). 128pp. After a 5-year-old boy discovers his mother is having an affair, he is sent off to northern Minnesota in this World War II story. (Rev: BCCB 3/91; BL 3/1/91; HB 3/91; SLJ 2/91*)

10252 Pearce, Jacqueline. *Dog House Blues* (4–6). 2005, Orca paper $6.95 (978-1-55143-360-8). 150pp. Dog-loving Erika, tired of being teased and bullied by a former friend, learns how to stand up for herself. (Rev: SLJ 4/06)

10253 Peterseil, Tehila. *The Safe Place* (5–8). 1996, Pitspopany $16.95 (978-0-943706-71-9); paper $12.95 (978-0-943706-72-6). 136pp. A moving story of an Israeli girl and the problems she faces at school because of a learning disability. (Rev: SLJ 12/96)

10254 Philbrick, Rodman. *The Fire Pony* (5–8). 1996, Scholastic paper $14.95 (978-0-590-55251-6). Rescued from a foster home by his half-brother Joe, Roy hopes that life will be better on the ranch where Joe finds work. (Rev: BCCB 7–8/96; BL 5/1/96; HB 7/96; SLJ 9/96; VOYA 10/96)

10255 Pitchford, Dean. *Captain Nobody* (4–6). 2009, Putnam $16.99 (978-0-399-25034-7). 192pp. Newt is a quiet 10-year-old boy who struggles while his football-playing older brother enjoys popularity until tragedy strikes and Newt finds a unique way to contribute to society and hopefully help his brother. (Rev: BL 7/09) ∩

10256 Polikoff, Barbara Garland. *Why Does the Coqui Sing?* (5–8). 2004, Holiday $16.95 (978-0-8234-1817-6). 213pp. Thirteen-year-old Luz and her brother Rome have trouble adjusting when they move from Chicago to Puerto Rico with their mother and stepfather. (Rev: BL 5/15/04; SLJ 6/04)

10257 Porter, Tracey. *A Dance of Sisters* (5–8). 2002, HarperCollins LB $17.89 (978-0-06-029239-3). 288pp. When a young ballet dancer's dreams are dashed, she is comforted by her sister. (Rev: BCCB 1/03; BL 2/15/03; HBG 3/03; SLJ 1/03)

10258 Richardson, Judith B. *David's Landing* (4–6). Illus. by Molly Bang. 1984, Woods Hole $10.95 (978-0-9611374-1-0). 150pp. A boy troubled by his parents' divorce is healed in this old-fashioned story of life in a small town. (Rev: BL 8/85; HB 9/85)

10259 Roberts, Marion. *Sunny Side Up* (5–8). Illus. 2009, Random $15.99 (978-0-385-73672-5). 224pp. An 11-year-old Australian girl struggles to balance a complex set of relationships that include divorced parents with newly emerging families, a long-lost grandmother and a best friend whose sudden interest in a boy threatens their pizza delivery business. (Rev: BCCB 2/09; BL 1/1–15/09; SLJ 2/09)

10260 Rodowsky, Colby. *The Next-Door Dogs* (2–4). Illus. by Amy June Bates. 2005, Farrar $15.00 (978-0-374-36410-6). 112pp. Sara overcomes her fear of dogs in order to help her new next-door neighbor. (Rev: BL 3/1/05; SLJ 6/05)

10261 Rosen, Michael. *Michael Rosen's Sad Book* (2–4). Illus. by Quentin Blake. 2005, Candlewick $16.99 (978-0-7636-2597-9). 32pp. An honest and very moving look at the author's grief over the death of his son. (Rev: BL 5/15/05; SLJ 3/05)

10262 Rottman, S. L. *Hero* (5–8). 1997, Peachtree $14.95 (978-1-56145-159-3). When his home life becomes unbearable, Sean is sent to Carbondale Ranch, where his sense of self-worth gradually grows. (Rev: BL 12/1/97; HBG 3/98; SLJ 12/97; VOYA 12/97)

10263 Roy, James. *Max Quigley: Technically Not a Bully* (4–7). Illus. by author. 2009, Houghton $12.95 (978-0-547-15263-9). 208pp. Max Quigley is a bully, although he doesn't see himself this way, and he is forced to spend time with smart but nerdy classmate Triffin in hopes that each will learn from the other. (Rev: BCCB 6/09; BL 3/15/09; HB 5/09)

10264 Ryan, Mary C. *The Voice from the Mendelsohns' Maple* (5–7). Illus. by Irena Roman. 1990, Little, Brown $13.95 (978-0-316-76360-8). 132pp. Penny tries to cope with many problems, including finding out the identity of the woman who is hiding in the neighbor's maple tree. (Rev: SLJ 12/89)

10265 Rylant, Cynthia. *Missing May* (5–8). 1992, Orchard LB $15.99 (978-0-531-08596-7). 96pp. Caring about each other is the tender message in this story of 12-year-old Summer, who, along with her uncle, must cope with the death of her beloved aunt. Newbery Medal winner, 1993. (Rev: BCCB 3/92*; BL 2/15/92*; HB 3/92; SLJ 3/92*)

10266 Sachar, Louis. *Marvin Redpost: Why Pick on Me?* (2–4). Illus. by Barbara Sullivan. 1993, Random LB $11.99 (978-0-679-91947-6); paper $3.99 (978-0-679-81947-9). 40pp. Marvin becomes a social outcast after he is wrongfully accused of picking his nose. (Rev: BCCB 2/93; BL 5/1/93)

10267 Santucci, Barbara. *Loon Summer* (1–4). Illus. by Andrea Shine. 2001, Eerdmans $16.00 (978-0-8028-5182-6). Rainie has fun at the lake with her newly separated father and, although she wishes her mother were there, she learns to accept that things have changed. (Rev: SLJ 8/01)

10268 Say, Allen. *The Sign Painter* (5–9). Illus. 2000, Houghton $17.00 (978-0-395-97974-7). 32pp. An Asian American youth who wants to be a serious artist gets a job painting signboards scattered through the desert. (Rev: BL 10/1/00; IIB 9/00; HBG 3/01; SLJ 9/00)

10269 Schumacher, Julie. *The Book of One Hundred Truths* (5–8). 2006, Delacorte $15.95 (978-0-385-73290-1). 192pp. While spending the summer with her grandparents at the Jersey shore, 12-year-old Thea finds herself baby-sitting her younger cousin Jocelyn and struggling to keep private the truths she is listing in her diary. (Rev: BL 11/1/06)

10270 Shreve, Susan. *Jonah, the Whale* (4–6). 1998, Scholastic $14.95 (978-0-590-37133-9). 128pp. After his family moves to New Haven, Connecticut, overweight 11-year-old Jonah finds friendship with another outsider, the sassy Blister, and achieves fulfillment by fantasizing that he is a famous TV personality. (Rev: BCCB 4/98; BL 5/1/98; HBG 10/98; SLJ 4/98)

10271 Shreve, Susan. *Kiss Me Tomorrow* (5–8). 2006, Scholastic $16.99 (978-0-439-68047-9). 160pp. Alyssa (aka Blister) is not having a good 7th grade; she feels abandoned by best friend Jonah although she's quick to help him when he's in trouble; she is unhappy about her mother's new boyfriend; and she worries about everything else from clothes to sex. (Rev: BL 9/15/06; SLJ 10/06)

10272 Shura, Mary Francis. *The Search for Grissi* (4–6). Illus. by Ted Lewin. 1987, Avon paper $3.50 (978-0-380-70305-0). Eleven-year-old Peter has difficulty adjusting to life in Peoria until his little sister involves him in a search for her lost cat. (Rev: BCCB 7–8/85; BL 3/15/85; SLJ 5/85)

10273 Shura, Mary Francis. *The Sunday Doll* (5–7). 1988, Avon paper $2.95 (978-0-380-70618-1). 112pp. Thirteen-year-old Emmy is miffed when the family won't tell her what has happened to upset her older sister Jayne, until she learns that Jayne's boyfriend has committed suicide. (Rev: BCCB 7–8/88; BL 7/88; SLJ 8/88)

10274 Siebold, Jan. *Doing Time Online* (3–5). 2002, Whitman $14.99 (978-0-8075-5959-8). 96pp. Young Mitch learns an important lesson through his community-service e-mail correspondence with the elderly Wootie. (Rev: BL 5/15/02; HBG 10/02; SLJ 3/02)

10275 Siebold, Jan. *My Nights at the Improv* (4–8). 2005, Whitman $14.95 (978-0-8075-5630-6). 98pp. Lizzie, a shy 8th-grader whose father died two years before, learns how to speak out by eavesdropping on an improvisational theater class, in the process also learning about bullying Vanessa. (Rev: BCCB 7–8/05; SLJ 11/05)

10276 Silverman. *Mirror Mirror: Twisted Tales* (5–8). 2002, Scholastic paper $15.95 (978-0-439-29593-2). 192pp. Disturbing stories serve as metaphors for the problems of drug use, divorce, homelessness, and other ills. (Rev: BL 9/1/02; HBG 10/02; SLJ 8/02; VOYA 6/02)

10277 Skinner, Daphne. *Almost Invisible Irene* (1–3). Illus. by Jerry Smath. Series: Science Solves It! 2003, Kane paper $4.99 (978-1-57565-129-3). 32pp. Little Irene is very, very shy, so she applies the lessons she's learned about animal camouflage to avoid unwanted attention by blending in with her surroundings. (Rev: SLJ 1/04)

10278 Slepian, Jan. *The Broccoli Tapes* (5–8). 1989, Scholastic paper $3.50 (978-0-590-43473-7). Sara uses tapes during her stay in Hawaii to keep up with her class oral history project. (Rev: BCCB 4/89; BL 4/15/89; SLJ 4/89; VOYA 6/89)

10279 Smith, Doris Buchanan. *A Taste of Blackberries* (4–6). Illus. by Charles Robinson. 1973, HarperCollins LB $16.89 (978-0-690-80512-3); paper $4.99 (978-0-06-440238-5). 64pp. Young Jamie dies unexpectedly of a bee sting, and his friends adjust to this loss.

10280 Smith, Robert K. *Jelly Belly* (4–6). Illus. by Bob Jones. 1982, Dell paper $4.50 (978-0-440-44207-3). 160pp. A boy is sent to a weight-loss camp by his parents.

10281 Smith, Yeardley. *I, Lorelei* (5–8). 2009, HarperCollins $16.99 (978-0-06-149344-7). 352pp. In diary entries addresses to her dead cat, 11-year old Lorelei talks about her parents' failing marriage, her friends at her private school in Washington, D.C., a cute boy named Bo, and her efforts to land a role in the school play. (Rev: BL 1/1–15/09; SLJ 3/09)

10282 Sonenklar, Carol. *Mighty Boy* (3–6). 1999, Orchard LB $16.99 (978-0-531-33203-0). 128pp. Transplanted to New York City, lonely 9-year-old Howard Weinstein retreats into a fantasy world when the class bully harasses him. (Rev: BCCB 1/00; BL 10/15/99; HBG 3/00; SLJ 10/99)

10283 Sonenklar, Carol. *My Own Worst Enemy* (5–8). 1999, Holiday $15.95 (978-0-8234-1456-7). In this first-person narrative, Eve Belkin finds there is a price to pay when she outdoes herself to be popular in her new school. (Rev: BL 5/15/99; HBG 9/99; SLJ 8/99; VOYA 10/99)

10284 Soto, Gary. *Mercy on These Teenage Chimps* (5–8). 2007, Harcourt $16.00 (978-0-15-206022-0). 147pp. Friends Ronnie Gonzalez and Joey Rios have just turned 13 and are wrestling with physical and emotional changes. (Rev: BL 12/1/06; SLJ 2/07)

10285 Soto, Gary. *The Pool Party* (4–7). Illus. by Robert Casilla. 1992, Delacorte $13.95 (978-0-385-30890-8). 112pp. Rudy, part of a Mexican American family, has growing-up problems. (Rev: SLJ 6/93)

10286 Spinelli, Jerry. *Wringer* (4–7). 1997, HarperCollins LB $17.89 (978-0-06-024914-4). 192pp. A sensitive boy must participate in the massacre of thousands of pigeons released at an annual fair. (Rev: BL 9/1/97*; HB 9/97; HBG 3/98; SLJ 9/97*)

10287 Spurr, Elizabeth. *Lupe and Me* (3–4). Illus. by Enrique O. Sánchez. 1995, Harcourt $13.00 (978-0-15-200522-1). 40pp. Susan is upset when her mother's housekeeper, 16-year-old Lupe, has to return to Mexico because she is an illegal alien. (Rev: BL 6/1–15/95; SLJ 6/95)

10288 Stevenson, Robin. *Impossible Things* (5–7). 2008, Orca paper $8.95 (978-1-55143-736-1). 185pp. Cassidy befriends a new girl in town who claims to have magical powers in the hopes that she can become magical too and overpower mean girls and bullies. (Rev: BL 4/15/08; SLJ 8/08)

10289 Stewart, Jennifer J. *The Bean King's Daughter* (5–7). 2002, Holiday $15.95 (978-0-8234-1644-8). 138pp. Phoebe, a 12-year-old heiress, reluctantly learns about herself and her young stepmother while at an Arizona ranch. (Rev: BL 9/1/02; HBG 10/02; SLJ 7/02)

10290 Stiles, Martha Bennett. *Sarah the Dragon Lady* (4–6). 1986, Avon paper $2.75 (978-0-380-70471-2). 96pp. Sarah tries to adjust to life in a small Kentucky town and face the fact of trouble in her parents' marriage. (Rev: BCCB 2/87; BL 1/1/87; SLJ 12/86)

10291 Stinson, Kathy. *King of the Castle* (3–4). Illus. by Kasia Charko. 2001, Second Story paper $5.95 (978-1-896764-35-1). 61pp. Watching his grandson at his studies inspires school custodian Mr. Elliott to learn to read himself. (Rev: SLJ 8/01)

10292 Stone, Phoebe. *Deep Down Popular* (4–6). 2008, Scholastic $16.99 (978-0-439-80245-1). 176pp. When Conrad hurts his leg and starts wearing a brace, his popularity wanes and tomboy Jessie Lou, who has a major crush on him, finds herself forming a real friendship with him. (Rev: BL 3/15/08*; LMC 3/08; SLJ 3/08)

10293 Strasser, Todd. *CON-fidence* (5–8). 2002, Holiday $16.95 (978-0-8234-1394-2). 176pp. Shy Lauren falls under the spell of the dazzling Celeste, failing to perceive Celeste's underlying motives. (Rev: BCCB 2/03; BL 4/15/03; HBG 10/03; SLJ 1/03; VOYA 4/03)

10294 Swallow, Pamela C. *It Only Looks Easy* (4–7). 2003, Millbrook $15.95 (978-0-7613-1790-6). 176pp. Kat's problems start when her dog is hit by a car and she "borrows" a bicycle to get to the vet only to have it stolen from her. (Rev: BL 4/15/03; HBG 10/03; SLJ 4/03)

10295 Tabor, Nancy María Grande. *Bottles Break* (1–4). Illus. by author. 1999, Charlesbridge LB $15.95 (978-0-88106-317-2); paper $6.95 (978-0-88106-318-9). A young narrator, the child of an alcoholic mother, tells about his fears, confusion, and low self-esteem and about the help he receives from an understanding teacher. (Rev: HBG 10/99; SLJ 5/99)

10296 Tamar, Erika. *Katherine's Story* (4–6). Series: The Girls of Lighthouse Lane. 2004, HarperCollins LB $13.89 (978-0-06-054342-6). 165pp. Twelve-year-old Kat's artistic ambitions are stymied in this novel set in the early 20th century and the first in a series based on Thomas Kinkade's paintings. (Rev: SLJ 4/04)

10297 Testa, Maria. *Nine Candles* (3–5). Illus. 1996, Carolrhoda LB $19.93 (978-0-87614-940-9). 32pp. Raymond is looking forward to visiting his mother, who is in prison. (Rev: BCCB 9/96; BL 7/96; SLJ 9/96)

10298 Testa, Maria. *Someplace to Go* (3–5). Illus. 1996, Whitman LB $16.99 (978-0-8075-7524-6). 32pp. Unlike his classmates, Davey has no home to return to after school. (Rev: BCCB 3/96; BL 4/15/96; SLJ 5/96)

10299 Timberlake, Amy. *That Girl Lucy Moon* (5–8). 2006, Hyperion $15.99 (978-0-7868-5298-7). 294pp. When her mother takes off on an extended photography assignment, Lucy Moon is left without her biggest ally in her campaigns for animal rights, social justice, and, now, for the liberation of a sledding hill. (Rev: SLJ 9/06)

10300 Tolan, Stephanie. *Wishworks Inc* (3–5). Illus. by Amy June Bates. 2009, Scholastic $15.99 (978-0-545-03154-7). 160pp. A bullied 3rd-grader named Max, struggling to adjust to his parents' divorce and a new school, finally gets a dog but it's not quite the dog he had imagined in his daydreams. (Rev: BL 4/1/09; HB 9/09; SLJ 7/09)

10301 Tolliver, Ruby C. *I Love You, Daisy Phew* (4–6). 1994, Hendrick-Long LB $12.95 (978-0-937460-86-3). 168pp. Blake finds an unusual pet in a goat named Daisy Phew when the troubled boy goes to live with his grandfather in Texas. (Rev: BL 1/15/95)

10302 Toten, Teresa. *The Onlyhouse* (5–8). 1996, Red Deer paper $7.95 (978-0-88995-137-2). Eleven-year-old Lucija, whose family was originally from Croatia, relocates to a new house in suburban Toronto after several years in a dense downtown neighborhood with a large immigrant population, and must adjust to a new school, peer pressures, and bullies. (Rev: SLJ 7/96)

10303 Vail, Rachel. *Daring to Be Abigail* (4–6). 1996, Orchard LB $16.99 (978-0-531-08867-8). 144pp. At summer camp, Abigail deliberately misbehaves so she won't be considered an outsider by the in-crowd. (Rev: BCCB 2/96; BL 3/1/96; HB 5/96; SLJ 3/96*)

10304 Vail, Rachel. *Ever After* (5–9). 1994, Orchard LB $16.99 (978-0-531-08688-9). Fourteen-year-old Molly is trying to act maturely but always seems to mess things up. (Rev: BCCB 4/94; BL 3/1/94; HB 5/94, 7/94; SLJ 5/94*; VOYA 6/94)

10305 Wagner, Jane. *J.T.* (4–6). Photos by Gordon Parks. 1972, Dell paper $4.99 (978-0-440-44275-2). 128pp. J. T. Gamble lives in Harlem, and his most prized possessions are a tiny portable radio and a stray cat, for whom he has made a home.

10306 Wainwright, Richard M. *Mountains to Climb* (3–5). Illus. by Jack Crompton. 1991, Family Life $18.00 (978-0-9619566-3-9). 56pp. During his two-year stay in the United States, a young Ecuadoran boy gradually wins his classmates' acceptance. (Rev: BL 12/15/91; SLJ 1/92)

10307 Walpole, Peter. *The Healer of Harrow Point* (4–7). 2000, Hampton Roads paper $11.95 (978-1-57174-167-7). 131pp. A novel of love and compassion about a boy who is promised a hunting trip for his twelfth birthday but wonders if he can kill a deer, particularly after seeing one killed by poachers and after meeting Emma, who can heal animals with her touch. (Rev: SLJ 10/00)

10308 Walter, Mildred P. *Justin and the Best Biscuits in the World* (3–5). Illus. by Catherine Stock. 1986, Lothrop $16.99 (978-0-688-06645-1); Knopf paper $3.25 (978-0-679-80346-1). 128pp. Justin thinks some things as "women's work" until his grandfather shows him differently. (Rev: BCCB 12/86; BL 10/15/86; SLJ 11/86)

10309 Wetter, Bruce. *The Boy with the Lampshade on His Head* (5–8). 2004, Simon & Schuster $16.95 (978-0-689-85032-5). 304pp. Painfully shy, 11-year-old Stanley Krakow maintains a low profile but a rich inner life until he makes friends with an abused girl and finds the inner strength to be a real hero. (Rev: BL 5/1/04; SLJ 8/04)

10310 Williams, Laura E. *Slant* (5–8). 2008, Milkweed $16.95 (978-1-57131-681-3); paper $6.95 (978-1-57131-682-0). 160pp. Lauren, an 8th-grader and Korean American adoptee, wants to have surgery to make her eyes more Western in this compelling story of identity, culture, and belonging. (Rev: BLO 1/13/09; SLJ 12/08)

10311 Willner-Pardo, Gina. *Jumping into Nothing* (3–5). Illus. 1999, Clarion $14.00 (978-0-395-84130-3). 64pp. Sophie is afraid to jump off the high board at the local pool, but gradually she overcomes her fear. (Rev: BCCB 4/99; BL 3/15/99; HB 5/99; HBG 10/99; SLJ 5/99)

10312 Wilson, Johnniece M. *Poor Girl* (5–7). 1992, Scholastic $13.95 (978-0-590-44732-4). 176pp. A first-person story about Miranda, who spends the summer trying to earn money for contact lenses before the fall. (Rev: BCCB 4/92; BL 8/92; SLJ 4/92)

10313 Wilson, Johnniece M. *Robin on His Own* (4–6). 1992, Scholastic paper $2.95 (978-0-590-41809-6). 144pp. Watusi the cat comforts a young black boy when his mother dies. (Rev: BL 10/15/90; SLJ 1/91)

10314 Wojciechowska, Maia. *Shadow of a Bull* (5–8). Illus. by Alvin Smith. 1964, Macmillan $16.95 (978-0-689-30042-4). 160pp. Manolo, surviving son of a great bullfighter, has his own "moment of truth" when he faces his first bull. Newbery Medal winner, 1965.

10315 Wolfson, Jill. *Home, and Other Big, Fat Lies* (5–7). 2006, Holt $16.95 (978-0-8050-7670-7). 281pp. Shuttled through the foster care system for much of her life, 11-year-old Whitney isn't expecting much out of her latest stop with a family in remote northern California, but her interest in nature — and some new friendships — open her eyes to the importance of fighting for what you believe in. (Rev: SLJ 12/06)

10316 Wolfson, Jill. *What I Call Life* (5–8). 2005, Holt $16.95 (978-0-8050-7669-1). 272pp. Five young girls — all refugees from troubled families — find friendship and strength during their stay in a group home run by a wise Knitting Lady. (Rev: BCCB 9/05; BL 11/1/05; HBG 4/06; LMC 5/06; SLJ 9/05; VOYA 12/05)

10317 Woodruff, Elvira. *The Secret Funeral of Slim Jim the Snake* (4–5). 1993, Holiday House $16.95 (978-0-8234-1014-9). 144pp. Nick lives over a funeral home and faces some problems with humorous solutions. (Rev: SLJ 3/93)

10318 Wright, Betty R. *The Summer of Mrs. Mac-Gregor* (5–8). 1986, Holiday $15.95 (978-0-8234-0628-9). 160pp. Meeting an exotic teenager who calls herself Mrs. Lillina MacGregor helps Linda solve her problem of jealousy toward her older sister. (Rev: BCCB 12/86; BL 11/1/86; SLJ 11/86; VOYA 4/87)

10319 Wright, Betty R. *The Wish Master* (3–6). 2000, Holiday House $15.95 (978-0-8234-1611-0). 112pp. Transported to his grandparents' home in Wisconsin for the summer, unhappy Corby wishes on a pile of rocks known as the Wish Master for a way to go home. (Rev: BCCB 1/01; BL 11/1/00; HBG 10/01; SLJ 12/00)

10320 Young, Ronder T. *Moving Mama to Town* (5–8). 1997, Orchard LB $18.99 (978-0-531-33025-8). Although his father is a gambler and a failure, Fred never loses faith in him in this story of a boy who must help support his family although he's only 13. (Rev: BL 6/1–15/97; HB 7/97; SLJ 6/97)

10321 Zinnen, Linda. *The Truth About Rats, Rules, and Seventh Grade* (5–7). 2001, HarperCollins LB $15.89 (978-0-06-028800-6). 160pp. Larch, who faces multiple problems at home and at school, tries to live her life by a set of unemotional rules, but a friendly stray dog and the discovery of the truth about her father's death make these rules hard to keep. (Rev: BCCB 6/01; BL 4/1/01*; HBG 10/01; SLJ 2/01)

Physical and Emotional Problems

10322 Abbott, Deborah, and Henry Kisor. *One TV Blasting and a Pig Outdoors* (3–5). Illus. 1994, Whitman LB $16.99 (978-0-8075-6075-4). 40pp. A book that describes what it's like to live in a household where the father is deaf. (Rev: BL 9/15/94; SLJ 12/94)

10323 Auch, Mary Jane. *One-Handed Catch* (4–6). 2006, Holt $16.95 (978-0-8050-7900-5). 256pp. In this inspiring novel set just after World War II, 11-year-old Norm strives to live a normal life after he loses a hand in an accident, succeeding not only in music and art but also baseball. (Rev: BL 10/1/06; SLJ 11/06)

10324 Betancourt, Jeanne. *My Name Is Brain/Brian* (4–6). 1993, Scholastic $14.95 (978-0-590-44921-2). 176pp. Brian, a sixth-grader who is dyslexic, matures and changes his attitudes toward his friends and teachers. (Rev: BCCB 4/93; BL 4/1/93; SLJ 4/93)

10325 Blue, Rose. *Me and Einstein: Breaking Through the Reading Barrier* (4–6). Illus. by Peggy Luks. 1984, Human Sciences $16.95 (978-0-87705-388-0); paper $10.95 (978-0-89885-185-4). Bobby, a dyslexic youngster, tries to hide the fact that he can't read.

10326 Blume, Judy. *Deenie* (5–8). 1982, Dell paper $5.50 (978-0-440-93259-8). 192pp. Instead of becoming a model, Deenie must cope with scoliosis and wearing a back brace.

10327 Brooks, Bruce. *Vanishing* (5–8). 1999, HarperCollins LB $14.89 (978-0-06-028237-0). A challenging novel about a hospitalized girl who gives up eating so she can't be sent home to her dysfunctional family, and the boy she meets who is in remission from a fatal disease. (Rev: BL 5/15/99; HB 5/99; HBG 10/99; SLJ 6/99; VOYA 10/99)

10328 Butts, Nancy. *Cheshire Moon* (5–7). 1996, Front St. $14.95 (978-1-886910-08-9). A friendless deaf girl grieves for a cousin who has drowned at sea in this novel in an island setting. (Rev: BL 10/15/96; SLJ 11/96; VOYA 4/97)

10329 Byars, Betsy. *The Summer of the Swans* (5–7). Illus. by Ted Coconis. 1970, Puffin paper $5.99 (978-0-14-031420-5). 144pp. The story of a 14-year-old named Sara — moody, unpredictable, and on the brink of womanhood — and how her life changes when her younger, mentally retarded brother disappears. Newbery Medal winner, 1971.

10330 Carter, Anne Laurel. *In the Clear* (4–7). 2001, Orca paper $6.95 (978-1-55143-192-5). 133pp. A 12-year-old Canadian polio survivor in the 1950s works through her fears and struggles to recapture her lost childhood. (Rev: BL 11/15/01; SLJ 1/02)

10331 Cunningham, Julia. *Burnish Me Bright* (4–6). 1980, Peter Smith $18.75 (978-0-8446-6252-7). An imaginative mute boy named Auguste is scorned by the inhabitants of the French village where he lives.

10332 Deans, Sis. *Rainy* (4–6). 2005, Holt $16.95 (978-0-8050-7831-2). 208pp. Rainy, an energetic 10-year-old girl with attention deficit hyperactivity disorder whose parents reject medication, has trouble at summer camp. (Rev: BL 8/05; SLJ 10/05; VOYA 10/05)

10333 Denenberg, Barry. *Mirror, Mirror on the Wall: The Diary of Bess Brennan* (4–8). Series: Dear America. 2002, Scholastic paper $10.95 (978-0-439-19446-4). 144pp. When she comes home at weekends, 12-year-old Bess, who has lost her sight, shares her new life and school experiences with her twin sister, in this novel set in the Depression that includes many details of how the blind cope. (Rev: BL 10/1/02; HBG 3/03; SLJ 10/02)

10334 Farnes, Catherine. *Snow* (5–9). 1999, Bob Jones Univ. $6.49 (978-1-57924-199-5). 158pp. A thoughtful novel about an albino girl's problems being accepted, even among students who profess to have Christian charity. (Rev: BL 7/99)

10335 Galante, Cecilia. *Hershey Herself* (5–8). 2008, Aladdin paper $5.99 (978-1-4169-5463-7). 336pp. While living at a shelter for battered women with her mother and younger sister, Hershey discovers real friends and a real talent. (Rev: BL 5/15/08)

10336 Gantos, Jack. *I Am Not Joey Pigza* (5–8). 2007, Farrar $16.00 (978-0-374-39941-2). 224pp. Joey's father returns to the Pigza family with lottery winnings, a new name, and promises of a new future based on a diner. (Rev: BL 8/07; SLJ 9/07) ∩

10337 Gantos, Jack. *Joey Pigza Loses Control* (4–7). 2000, Farrar $16.00 (978-0-374-39989-4). 208pp. Joey, a hyperactive kid, tries to please his father but goes haywire when his father destroys his medication in this Newbery Honor Book. (Rev: BCCB 9/00*; BL 9/1/00*; HB 9/00; HBG 3/01; SLJ 9/00; VOYA 2/01)

10338 Gantos, Jack. *Joey Pigza Swallowed the Key* (4–8). 1998, Farrar $16.00 (978-0-374-33664-6). Joey, who suffers from attention deficit disorder, causes so much trouble that he is sent to a special education center, where he learns to cope with his problem. (Rev: BCCB 11/98; BL 12/15/98; HB 11/98; HBG 3/99; SLJ 12/98*; VOYA 2/99)

10339 Gantos, Jack. *What Would Joey Do?* (5–8). 2002, Farrar $16.00 (978-0-374-39986-3). 240pp. Hyperactive Joey is nearly overwhelmed by the antics of his parents, his dying grandmother, and the needs of his blind homeschool partner, but manages to cope in his own unusual way in this final installment in the Joey Pigza trilogy. (Rev: BCCB 11/02; BL 10/1/02*; HB 11/02; HBG 3/03; SLJ 9/02*; VOYA 12/02)

10340 Garfield, James B. *Follow My Leader* (4–6). Illus. 1994, Puffin paper $5.99 (978-0-14-036485-9). 192pp. With the aid of friends and a guide dog, an 11-year-old boy resumes his life.

10341 Gould, Marilyn. *Golden Daffodils* (5–7). 1991, Allied Crafts paper $10.95 (978-0-9632305-1-5). 17pp. Janis adjusts to her handicap resulting from cerebral palsy.

10342 Gould, Marilyn. *The Twelfth of June* (5–8). 1994, Allied Crafts LB $12.95 (978-0-9632305-4-6). Janis, who suffers from cerebral palsy, is suffering the first pangs of adolescence and is still fighting the battle to be treated like other girls her age, in this sequel to *Golden Daffodils* (1982). (Rev: SLJ 11/86; VOYA 12/86)

10343 Graff, Lisa. *The Thing About Georgie* (3–5). 2007, HarperCollins $15.99 (978-0-06-087589-3). 224pp. Nine-year-old Georgie's school and family problems, compounded by his dwarfism, are sensitively explored in this upbeat, often funny novel. (Rev: BL 1/1–15/07; SLJ 2/07)

10344 Graff, Lisa. *Umbrella Summer* (4–6). 2009, HarperCollins $15.99 (978-0-06-143187-6). 240pp. It takes time and friends to help 9-year-old Annie get over her brother's death and stop seeing danger around every corner. (Rev: BCCB 7–8/09; BL 8/09; HB 7/09; SLJ 6/09)

10345 Haddix, Margaret P. *Because of Anya* (3–6). 2002, Simon & Schuster $15.95 (978-0-689-38298-7). 128pp. Anya's friend Keely rallies round when Anya must wear a wig because of her alopecia. (Rev: SLJ 11/02)

10346 Hartry, Nancy. *Watching Jimmy* (5–8). 2009, Tundra $16.95 (978-0-88776-871-2). 144pp. Carolyn saw it happen and she keeps her mouth shut until she just can't keep quiet anymore. (Rev: BL 6/1–15/09; SLJ 6/09)

10347 Howe, James. *A Night Without Stars* (5–7). 1983, Avon paper $2.95 (978-0-380-69877-6). 192pp. A novel about a young girl's hospitalization and serious operation.

10348 Jung, Reinhardt. *Dreaming in Black and White* (5–8). Trans. from German by Anthea Bell. 2003, Penguin $15.99 (978-0-8037-2811-0). 112pp. A boy with disabilities has waking dreams in which he travels back to Nazi Germany and suffers at the hands of his classmates, teachers, and eventually his father, in this compelling novel translated from German. (Rev: BCCB 9/03; BL 5/15/03; HB 9/03*; HBG 4/04; SLJ 8/03)

10349 Kachur, Wanda G. *The Nautilus* (5–7). 1997, Peytral paper $7.95 (978-0-9644271-5-0). 171pp. A compassionate novel about a girl's rehabilitation after receiving spinal cord injuries in an automobile accident. (Rev: SLJ 9/97)

10350 Kelley, Ann. *Inchworm* (5–8). 2009, Luath paper $12.95 (978-1-906307-62-2). 203pp. Recovering from a heart and lung transplant, 12-yera-old Gussie is living in London and missing Cornwall, worrying about her parents' divorce, and hoping to live to the age of 22. (Rev: SLJ 4/09; VOYA 4/09)

10351 Kwasney, Michelle D. *Itch* (5–8). 2008, Holt $16.95 (978-0-8050-8083-4). 256pp. When Itch and her grandmother move from Florida to Ohio, Itch makes friends with a popular girl who has a sad secret. (Rev: BL 4/15/08; SLJ 9/08)

10352 Lachtman, Ofelia Dumas. *Leticia's Secret* (5–8). 1997, Arte Publico $14.95 (978-1-55885-205-1); paper $7.95 (978-1-55885-209-9). Rosario, from a Mexican American family, shares many adventures with her cousin, the pretty Leticia, and is devastated to learn that she has a fatal disease. (Rev: SLJ 1/98)

10353 Levine, Edna S. *Lisa and Her Soundless World* (3–5). Illus. by Gloria Kamen. 1984, Human Sciences $18.95 (978-0-87705-104-6); paper $10.95 (978-0-89885-204-2). The plight of a deaf girl is explored in this gripping, realistic story of Lisa and her problems.

10354 Little, Jean. *From Anna* (4–6). Illus. by Joan Sandin. 1972, HarperCollins paper $5.99 (978-0-06-440044-2). 208pp. Anna's family emigrates to Canada to escape Nazi persecution, and this opens up a new world and a wonderful change for the partially sighted girl.

10355 McDaniel, Lurlene. *To Live Again* (5–9). 2001, Bantam paper $4.99 (978-0-553-57151-6). 152pp. After three years of remission from leukemia, 16-year-old Dawn suffers a stroke that produces a terrible bout of depression. (Rev: BL 3/1/01)

10356 McDonald, Megan. *Judy Moody Gets Famous* (2–4). Illus. by Peter Reynolds. 2001, Candlewick $15.99 (978-0-7636-0849-1). 126pp. In this beginning chapter book, Judy Moody is plagued by jealousy until she manages to become famous anonymously and finds she enjoys it. (Rev: HB 9/01; HBG 3/02; SLJ 10/01)

10357 MacKall, Dandi Daley. *Larger-Than-Life Lara* (4–6). 2006, Dutton $16.99 (978-0-525-47726-6). 192pp. Ten-year-old Laney uses the writing skills she has learned to recount fat Lara's arrival at school and her amazing ability to shrug off slights. (Rev: BL 8/06; SLJ 9/06)

10358 McMahon, Patricia. *Summer Tunes: A Martha's Vineyard Vacation* (3–6). Photos by Peter Simon. 1996, Boyds Mills $16.95 (978-1-56397-572-1). 47pp. A photo-essay about Conor, a 10-year-old physically handicapped boy, and his family, who go to Martha's Vineyard for a vacation. (Rev: SLJ 10/96)

10359 Marino, Jan. *Eighty-Eight Steps to September* (5–7). 1989, Avon paper $2.95 (978-0-380-71001-0). 162pp. Amy and Robbie have the usual sibling rivalry, until Robbie develops leukemia. (Rev: BCCB 5/89; BL 8/89)

10360 Matlin, Marlee, and Doug Cooney. *Nobody's Perfect* (4–6). 2006, Simon & Schuster $15.95 (978-0-689-86986-0). 240pp. Fourth-grader Megan, who is deaf, has a hard time understanding why the new girl at school seems unfriendly in this sequel to *Deaf Child Crossing* (2002). (Rev: BL 7/06; SLJ 8/06)

10361 Nails, Jennifer. *Next to Mexico* (4–6). 2008, Houghton $16.00 (978-0-618-96635-6). 235pp. Both new to Tucson's Susan B. Anthony Middle School, Lylice and Mexico (newly arrived from Nogales, a talented artist, and a diabetic) form a fragile friendship. (Rev: BCCB 12/08; SLJ 12/08; VOYA 10/08)

10362 Nicholls, Sally. *Ways to Live Forever* (3–7). 2008, Scholastic $16.99 (978-0-545-06948-9). 224pp. Eleven-year-old Sam tells a poignant first-person story of his losing struggle with leukemia. (Rev: BCCB 11/08; BL 11/15/08; HB 9/09;1/09; SLJ 11/08)

10363 Polacco, Patricia. *The Lemonade Club* (2–4). Illus. by author. 2007, Philomel $16.99 (978-0-399-24540-4). 48pp. In 5th grade, Traci discovers that both her best friend and her teacher have cancer; based on a true story. (Rev: BL 10/1/07; LMC 11/07; SLJ 10/07)

10364 Riskind, Mary. *Apple Is My Sign* (5–6). 1995, Houghton paper $6.95 (978-0-395-65747-8). 160pp. A deaf and mute boy is sent to a special school in the early 1900s.

10365 Seidler, Tor. *The Silent Spillbills* (5–8). 1998, HarperCollins LB $14.89 (978-0-06-205181-3). 224pp. Katrina faces problems trying to overcome her stuttering but stands up to her tyrannical grandfather to help save from extinction a rare bird known as the silent spillbill. (Rev: BCCB 1/99; BL 12/15/98; HBG 3/99; SLJ 4/99)

10366 Shyer, Marlene Fanta. *Welcome Home, Jellybean* (5–8). 1978, Macmillan paper $4.99 (978-0-689-71213-5). 160pp. Twelve-year-old Neil encounters a near-tragic situation when his older retarded sister comes home to stay.

10367 Snyder, Zilpha Keatley. *The Witches of Worm* (5–8). Illus. by Alton Raible. 1972, Dell paper $5.50 (978-0-440-49727-1). 192pp. A deeply disturbed girl believes that her selfish and destructive acts are caused by bewitchment.

10368 Strachan, Ian. *The Flawed Glass* (5–8). 1990, Little, Brown $14.95 (978-0-316-81813-1). 208pp. Physically disabled Shona makes friends with an American boy on an island off the Scottish coast. (Rev: BCCB 11/90; BL 12/1/90; SLJ 1/91)

10369 Striegel, Jana. *Homeroom Exercise* (4–7). 2002, Holiday $16.95 (978-0-8234-1579-3). 192pp. A 12-year-old who dreams of becoming a professional dancer is diagnosed with juvenile rheumatoid arthritis. (Rev: BL 3/1/02; HBG 10/02; SLJ 6/02; VOYA 8/02)

10370 Testa, Maria. *Thumbs Up, Rico!* (3–4). Illus. 1994, Whitman LB $14.95 (978-0-8075-7906-0). 40pp. Rico, a boy with Down's syndrome, tells about his trials and triumphs in this simple chapter book. (Rev: BL 4/15/94; SLJ 7/94)

10371 Wanous, Suzanne. *Sara's Secret* (2–4). Illus. by Shelly O. Haas. 1995, Carolrhoda LB $14.95 (978-0-87614-856-3). 40pp. Sara's secret is that she has a brother who is a victim of cerebral palsy and is mentally retarded. (Rev: BL 7/95; SLJ 8/95)

10372 Warner, Sally. *This Isn't About the Money* (4–6). 2002, Viking $15.99 (978-0-670-03574-8). 224pp. Twelve-year-old Janey, disfigured in the car crash that killed her parents, tries to adjust to her new life in Arizona with her grandfather and great-aunt. (Rev: BCCB 12/02; BL 9/1/02; HBG 3/03; SLJ 9/02)

10373 Welch, Sheila K. *Don't Call Me Marda* (4–6). Illus. 1991, Our Child Pr. $16.95 (978-0-9611872-3-1); paper $12.95 (978-0-9611872-4-8). 138pp. Marsha is disappointed when the girl her parents adopt is mentally handicapped. (Rev: SLJ 3/91)

10374 Whelan, Gloria. *Hannah* (3–5). Illus. by Leslie Bowman. 1991, Knopf LB $11.99 (978-0-679-91397-9). 42pp. In northern Michigan in 1887, 9-year-old Hannah is encouraged by the new teacher to attend school despite her blindness. (Rev: BCCB 6/91; BL 3/1/91; HB 5/91; SLJ 6/91)

10375 Wright, Betty R. *Rosie and the Dance of the Dinosaurs* (4–6). 1989, Holiday House $15.95 (978-0-8234-0782-8). 112pp. Rosie, who has only nine fingers, is worried about the piano recital in which she must perform. (Rev: BCCB 2/90; BL 11/15/89; HB 3/90)

10376 Zimmer, Tracie Vaughn. *Reaching for the Sun* (5–8). 2007, Bloomsbury $14.95 (978-1-59990-037-7). 192pp. Seventh-grader Josie faces daunting troubles: school, loneliness, cerebral palsy, and her rural area's development; a new, science-loving neighbor becomes a friend and Josie redefines her relationship with her mother in this appealing verse novel. (Rev: BL 1/1–15/07; SLJ 3/07)

Historical Fiction and Foreign Lands

General and Miscellaneous

10377 Bell, Helen. *Idjhil: And the Land Cried for Its Lost Soul* (3–6). Illus. by author. 2003, Cygnet paper $11.95 (978-1-876268-90-9). 40pp. The life of Idjhil, a happy aboriginal boy in Western Australia, is turned upside down when he is forcibly removed from his family and relocated by the government. (Rev: SLJ 10/03)

10378 Belpre, Pura. *Firefly Summer* (5–8). 1996, Piñata paper $9.95 (978-1-55885-180-1). This gentle novel depicts family and community life in rural Puerto Rico at the turn of the 20th century as experienced by young Teresa Rodrigo, who has just completed 7th grade. (Rev: SLJ 2/97; VOYA 4/97)

10379 Broome, Errol. *Gracie and the Emperor* (4–6). 2005, Annick $18.95 (978-1-55037-891-7); paper

$7.95 (978-1-55037-890-0). 123pp. Life changes dramatically for 11-year-old Gracie when Napoleon Bonaparte is exiled to the island of St. Helena, where the girl lives with her widowed father. (Rev: SLJ 12/05)

10380 Campbell, Nicola I. *Shi-shi-etko* (2–4). Illus. by Kim LaFave. 2005, Groundwood $16.95 (978-0-88899-659-6). 32pp. A young Canadian Indian girl savors the final few days before she is to be sent away to residential school, far from her family. (Rev: BL 11/1/05; SLJ 11/05)

10381 Carmi, Daniella. *Samir and Yonatan* (4–8). Trans. from Hebrew by Yael Lotan. 2000, Scholastic paper $15.95 (978-0-439-13504-7). 192pp. Samir, a young Palestinian, is sent to a Jewish hospital for surgery and there he meets some Jewish contemporaries. (Rev: BCCB 4/00; BL 2/1/00; HBG 10/00; SLJ 3/00; VOYA 6/00)

10382 Caswell, Maryanne. *Pioneer Girl* (5–8). Illus. by Lindsay Grater. 2001, Tundra $16.95 (978-0-88776-550-6). 82pp. In letters to her grandmother, a 14-year-old girl describes the hardships and interesting experiences of her journey from Ontario to the prairies in the late 1880s. (Rev: HBG 10/01; SLJ 10/01)

10383 Crook, Connie Brummel. *The Hungry Year* (5–8). 2001, Stoddart paper $7.95 (978-0-7737-6206-0). 190pp. Twelve-year-old Kate must care for her brothers and handle the household chores during a severe Canadian winter in the late 1700s. (Rev: BL 1/1–15/02; SLJ 11/01)

10384 Crook, Connie Brummel. *The Perilous Year* (5–7). 2003, Fitzhenry & Whiteside paper $8.95 (978-1-55041-818-7). 197pp. In this fast-paced sequel to *The Hungry Year* (2001), 11-year-old twins Alex and Ryan face constant challenges and adventures — including more encounters with pirates — in 18th-century Canada. (Rev: SLJ 3/04)

10385 Crosbie, Duncan. *Life on a Famine Ship: A Journal of the Irish Famine, 1845–1850* (4–6). Illus. by Brian Lee and Peter Bull Studios. 2006, Barron's $16.99 (978-0-7641-6004-2). 25pp. Informative and illustrative flaps and pop-ups of the ship add to 9-year-old Michael's account of flight from Ireland and a long and dangerous journey to the United States. (Rev: SLJ 12/06)

10386 Curtis, Chara M. *No One Walks on My Father's Moon* (4–8). Illus. 1996, Voyage LB $16.95 (978-0-9649454-1-8). A Turkish boy is accused of blasphemy when he states that a man has walked on the moon. (Rev: BL 11/15/96)

10387 D'Adamo, Francesco. *Iqbal: A Novel* (4–7). 2003, Simon & Schuster $15.95 (978-0-689-85445-3). 128pp. The sad story of the death of Iqbal, the young child labor activist, is brought to life through the fictional narrative of a young Pakistani girl who worked with him in the carpet factories. (Rev: BL 11/1/03; HB 11/03; HBG 4/04; SLJ 11/03)

10388 Danticat, Edwidge. *Anacaona, Golden Flower: Haiti, 1490* (5–8). Series: Royal Diaries. 2005, Scholastic $10.95 (978-0-439-49906-4). 208pp. In 15th-century Haiti, Anacaona, a girl of royal her-

itage, records her people's struggles against the Spanish explorers. (Rev: BL 5/15/05)

10389 Downie, Mary Alice, and John Downie. *Danger in Disguise* (5–8). Series: On Time's Wing. 2001, Roussan paper $6.95 (978-1-896184-72-2). 170pp. Young Jamie, a Scot raised in Normandy in secrecy, is scooped up to serve in the British navy and sent to Quebec to fight the French in this complex tale of adventure and intrigue set in the mid-18th century. (Rev: SLJ 5/01)

10390 Dowswell, Paul. *Prison Ship: Adventures of a Young Sailor* (5–9). 2006, Bloomsbury $16.95 (978-1-58234-676-2). 313pp. In this action-packed sequel to *Powder Monkey* set at the beginning of the 19th century, 13-year-old English sailor Sam Witchall is falsely convicted of theft and sent off to prison in Australia, where he escapes into the Outback. (Rev: SLJ 12/06)

10391 Eboch, Chris. *The Well of Sacrifice* (5–8). Illus. 1999, Houghton $16.00 (978-0-395-90374-2). In this novel set during Mayan times, Eveningstar Macaw sets out to avenge the death of her older brother, Smoke Shell. (Rev: BL 4/1/99; HBG 10/99; SLJ 5/99; VOYA 2/00)

10392 Ellis, Deborah. *Mud City* (4–7). Series: Breadwinner Trilogy. 2003, Douglas & McIntyre $15.95 (978-0-88899-518-6). 164pp. Feisty Afghan refugee Shauzia sets off on her own, dreaming of a life of freedom in France and prepared to dress as a boy and beg, but circumstances force her back to the camp on the Pakistan border in this final novel in the trilogy. (Rev: BL 11/15/03; HBG 4/04; SLJ 11/03)

10393 Fitz-Gibbon, Sally. *Lizzie's Storm* (3–5). Illus. by Muriel Wood. Series: New Beginnings. 2004, Fitzhenry & Whiteside $14.95 (978-1-55041-793-7); paper $7.95 (978-1-55041-795-1). 67pp. Orphaned in 1931 at the age of 10, Lizzie leaves London to live with relatives on the challenging Canadian prairie and shows her mettle when a dangerous dust storm hits the farm. (Rev: BL 9/1/04; SLJ 10/04)

10394 Gantos, Jack. *Jack's New Power: Stories from a Caribbean Year* (5–8). 1995, Farrar $16.00 (978-0-374-33657-8); paper $5.95 (978-0-374-43715-2). 214pp. Eight stories about the interesting people Jack meets when his family moves to the Caribbean. A sequel to *Heads or Tails* (1994). (Rev: BCCB 12/95; BL 12/1/95; SLJ 11/95*)

10395 Goldring, Ann. *Spitfire* (4–6). 2002, Raincoast paper $6.95 (978-1-55192-490-8). 160pp. A Canadian girl is determined to compete in a boys-only soapbox derby in this novel set in 1943. (Rev: BL 5/15/02; SLJ 4/02)

10396 Gray, Elizabeth Janet. *Adam of the Road* (5–8). Illus. by Robert Lawson. 1942, Puffin paper $7.99 (978-0-14-032464-8). 320pp. Adventures of a 13th-century minstrel boy. Newbery Medal winner, 1943.

10397 Gregory, Kristiana. *Catherine: The Great Journey* (4–7). Series: Royal Diaries. 2005, Scholastic $10.99 (978-0-439-25385-7). 169pp. The imagined diary of Catherine the Great's teenage years and her engagement to the Grand Duke of Russia;

plenty of historical background gives readers a sense of Catherine's times. (Rev: SLJ 5/06)

10398 Hammer, Loretta J., and Gail L. Karwoski. *The Tree That Owns Itself: And Other Adventure Tales from Out of the Past* (3–6). Illus. by James Watling. 1996, Peachtree paper $8.95 (978-1-56145-120-3). 149pp. In these 12 stories, famous characters associated with the history of Georgia come to life and interact with fictitious young heroes and heroines. (Rev: SLJ 7/96)

10399 Harrison, Troon. *A Bushel of Light* (5–8). 2001, Stoddart paper $7.95 (978-0-7737-6140-7). 244pp. Fourteen-year-old orphan Maggie juggles her need to search for her twin sister and her responsibilities for 4-year-old Lizzy, in this novel set in Canada in the early 1900s. (Rev: SLJ 10/01)

10400 Hartnett, Sonya. *The Silver Donkey* (5–8). Illus. by Don Powers. 2006, Candlewick $15.99 (978-0-7636-2937-3). 272pp. Two young French children find and help a wounded World War I soldier in the woods near their home, and as he heals he tells them stories about the tiny silver donkey he carries with him. (Rev: BL 11/15/06; SLJ 12/06)

10401 Haworth-Attard, Barbara. *Home Child* (5–8). 1996, Roussan paper $6.95 (978-1-896184-18-0). Set in Canada during the early 1900s, this is the story of 13-year-old Arthur Fellowes, a London orphan who is treated like an outcast when he joins the Wilson family as a home child (that is, a cheap farm laborer). (Rev: VOYA 8/97)

10402 Holeman, Linda. *Promise Song* (5–8). 1997, Tundra paper $6.95 (978-0-88776-387-8). In 1900, Rosetta, an English orphan who has been sent to Canada, becomes an indentured servant. (Rev: BL 6/1–15/97; SLJ 10/97)

10403 Ibbotson, Eva. *Journey to the River Sea* (5–8). 2002, Dutton $17.99 (978-0-525-46739-7). 336pp. Orphaned Maia journeys from 1910 London to live with relatives in Brazil in this complex story that involves an unwelcoming family, a beloved governess, a child actor, a runaway, and the wonders of Brazil, all presented with a mix of drama and humor. (Rev: BCCB 4/02; BL 12/15/01; HB 1/02; HBG 10/02; SLJ 1/02*; VOYA 12/01)

10404 Jocelyn, Marthe. *Mable Riley: A Reliable Record of Humdrum, Peril, and Romance* (5–10). Illus. 2004, Candlewick $15.99 (978-0-7636-2120-9). 288pp. This is a charming, humorous diary set in 1901 by a 14-year-old girl who accompanies her sister when she becomes a teacher in Stratford, Ontario. (Rev: BL 3/1/04; HB 5/04; SLJ 3/04; VOYA 6/04)

10405 Kirkpatrick, Katherine. *Escape Across the Wide Sea* (4–6). 2004, Holiday House $17.95 (978-0-8234-1854-1). 210pp. This gripping novel follows 9-year-old Daniel and his Huguenot family as they flee religious persecution in their native France and find themselves on a slave ship to the New World. (Rev: BL 1/1–15/05; SLJ 11/04)

10406 Laird, Elizabeth. *Oranges in No Man's Land* (3–6). 2008, Haymarket paper $9.95 (978-1-931859-56-1). 10pp. During the Lebanese civil war 30 years ago, 10-year-old Ayesha crosses the violent city of Beirut to find a doctor to save her grandmother's life. (Rev: BLO 12/30/08)

10407 Lawson, Julie. *Goldstone* (5–8). 1998, Stoddart paper $7.95 (978-0-7737-5891-9). Karin, a 13-year-old Swedish Canadian girl, lives with her family in a mountainous town in British Columbia in 1910 when heavy winter snows bring avalanches that cause death and destruction. (Rev: BL 7/97; SLJ 5/98)

10408 Lawson, Sue. *Ferret Boy* (4–6). Illus. by Annie Mertzlin. Series: Takeaways. 2003, Lothian paper $8.95 (978-0-7344-0465-7). 256pp. Josh Trimble faces unexpected challenges when, in a hasty moment, he agrees to race his beloved pet ferret in a derby. (Rev: SLJ 8/03)

10409 Levine, Anna. *Running on Eggs* (5–9). 1999, Front St. $15.95 (978-0-8126-2875-3). 136pp. The story of two girls — one Jewish and the other Palestinian — and a friendship that withstands cultural and political differences. (Rev: BCCB 11/99; BL 1/1–15/00; HBG 3/00; SLJ 12/99; VOYA 2/00)

10410 Logan, Claudia. *The 5,000-Year-Old Puzzle: Solving a Mystery of Ancient Egypt* (3–5). Illus. by Melissa Sweet. 2002, Farrar $17.00 (978-0-374-32335-6). 48pp. Part fact and part fiction, this picture book for older children takes readers along on an actual 1924 expedition to uncover tombs from the days of ancient Egypt. (Rev: BL 4/15/02; HBG 10/02; SLJ 6/02)

10411 Major, Kevin. *Ann and Seamus* (5–9). Illus. by David Blackwood. 2003, Groundwood $16.95 (978-0-88899-561-2). 128pp. Based on an early 19th-century shipwreck off the coast of Newfoundland, this historical novel in verse chronicles the romance that develops between 17-year-old Ann Harvey and the Irish teenager she rescues from the ship. (Rev: BL 3/1/04; HB 3/04; SLJ 2/04; VOYA 4/04)

10412 Mallam, Sally. *Dende Maro: The Golden Prince* (2–4). Illus. by author. 2009, Hoopoe $17.99 (978-1-933779-48-5). 40pp. This title offers an original creation myth in which a golden prince teaches the ancients how to live. (Rev: BL 6/1–15/09; LMC 8/09; SLJ 6/09)

10413 Michelson, Richard. *Tuttle's Red Barn: The Story of America's Oldest Family Farm* (1–3). Illus. by Mary Azarian. 2007, Putnam $16.99 (978-0-399-24354-7). 40pp. Michelson chronicles the history of the farm that has been in the Tuttle family for 12 generations. (Rev: BL 10/1/07; HB 1/08; LMC 11/07; SLJ 10/07) [975.1]

10414 Miles, Victoria. *Magnifico* (4–6). 2006, Fitzhenry & Whiteside $15.95 (978-1-55041-960-3). 262pp. Mariangela Benitti must endure teasing and torturous practice to master the accordion, an instrument foisted upon her by her immigrant Italian family, in this story set in Canada in 1939. (Rev: BL 7/06; SLJ 7/06)

10415 Nunes, Susan. *To Find the Way* (4–6). Illus. by Cissy Gray. 1992, Univ. of Hawaii $12.95 (978-0-8248-1376-5). 48pp. A picture story of the amazing voyage by the ancient Polynesians from Tahiti to Hawaii, seen through a child's eyes. (Rev: BL 1/15/93)

10416 Platt, Richard. *Roman Diary: The Journal of Iliona of Mytilini, Who Was Captured and Sold As a Slave in Rome, AD 107* (3–6). Illus. by David Parkins. 2009, Candlewick $18.99 (978-0-7636-3480-3). 64pp. In A.D. 107, Iliona and her brother Apollo are captured by pirates and become Roman slaves; Iliona leads a relatively easy life that she documents carefully in her diary. This oversized picture book includes useful back matter. (Rev: BLO 5/27/09; SLJ 6/09)

10417 Polisar, Barry Louis. *Stolen Man: The Story of the Amistad Rebellion* (3–5). 2006, Rainbow Morning Music paper $7.95 (978-0-938663-50-8). 7.95pp. An account of the *Amistad* slave rebellion of 1839 from the perspective of a slave named Sengbe Pieh (later known at Joseph Cinque). (Rev: BL 2/1/07)

10418 Reynolds, Susan. *The First Marathon: The Legend of Pheidippides* (2–4). Illus. by Daniel Minter. 2006, Albert Whitman $16.95 (978-0-8075-0867-1). 32pp. The role of long-distance runner Pheidippides in the important Battle of Marathon is told in a dramatic, fictionalized text with large illustrations and an informative afterword. (Rev: BL 2/15/06; SLJ 3/06)

10419 Russell, Christopher. *Dogboy* (4–6). 2006, Greenwillow $15.99 (978-0-06-084116-4). 272pp. Twelve-year-old Brind, who was raised with dogs and now is renowned for his talent as a kennel boy, faces many challenges and finds a new friend, Aurelie, in this novel set amid the Hundred Years War between France and England. (Rev: BL 4/15/06; SLJ 8/06; VOYA 8/06)

10420 Schwartz, Virginia Frances. *Messenger* (5–9). 2002, Holiday $17.95 (978-0-8234-1716-2). 277pp. This story of the hardships and joys of a Croatian family living in Ontario's mining towns in the 1920s and 1930s is based on the lives of the author's mother and grandmother. (Rev: HBG 3/03; SLJ 11/02; VOYA 12/02)

10421 Shulevitz, Uri. *The Travels of Benjamin of Tudela: Through Three Continents in the Twelfth Century* (4–7). Illus. 2005, Farrar $17.00 (978-0-374-37754-0). 48pp. Based on Benjamin's diaries, this picture book, which is incredibly detailed in both illustrations and text, tells of his perilous journey through parts of Europe, the Mediterranean, and the Middle East. (Rev: BL 3/15/05*; SLJ 4/05)

10422 Skrypuch, Marsha Forchuk. *Aram's Choice* (3–5). Illus. by Muriel Wood. 2006, Fitzhenry & Whiteside $14.95 (978-1-55041-352-6); paper $8.95 (978-1-55041-354-0). 72pp. Aram, a 12-year-old refugee from the Armenian genocide in Turkey in the early 1900s, travels with other orphans to a new home in Canada; based on truth, this compelling story contains many interesting facts and a historical note follows the text. (Rev: BL 8/06; SLJ 9/06)

10423 Skrypuch, Marsha Forchuk. *Call Me Aram* (3–5). Illus. by Muriel Wood. Series: New Beginnings. 2009, Fitzhenry & Whiteside $16.95 (978-1-55455-000-5); paper $10.95 (978-1-55455-001-). 88pp. This short novel about an Armenian orphan in Canada who grapples with losing his identity in a

new country is a sequel to *Aram's Choice* (2006). (Rev: BLO 6/16/09)

10424 Southern, Randy. *Ruled Out* (3–5). 2000, Bethany House paper $5.99 (978-1-56179-884-1). 112pp. In this story with a biblical basis, Ethan and his family remain faithful to the god of Moses when others have begun to worship the golden calf. (Rev: SLJ 2/01)

10425 Steer, Dugald, ed. *Pirateology: The Sea Journal of Captain William Lubber* (4–7). Illus. by Yvonne Gilbert. 2006, Candlewick $19.99 (978-0-7636-3143-7). 32pp. An authentic-looking large-format scrapbook chronicling the pirate-chasing adventures of a sea captain of old, complete with treasure maps and a working compass. (Rev: BL 7/06; SLJ 12/06)

10426 Taylor, Joanne. *There You Are: A Novel* (4–7). 2004, Tundra paper $8.95 (978-0-88776-658-9). 199pp. On post-World War II Cape Breton Island, 12-year-old Jeannie lives in a remote community and longs for a friend. (Rev: SLJ 11/04)

10427 Trottier, Maxine. *A Circle of Silver* (5–8). 2000, Stoddart paper $7.95 (978-0-7737-6055-4). 216pp. Set in the 1760s, this is the story of 13-year-old John MacNeil who is sent to Canada by his father to toughen him up. (Rev: SLJ 9/00)

10428 Valgardson, W. D. *Sarah and the People of Sand River* (3–5). Illus. by Ian Wallace. 1996, Douglas & McIntyre $16.95 (978-0-88899-255-0). 56pp. An Icelandic family, now relocated in Manitoba, Canada, is helped by Cree Indians. (Rev: BCCB 12/96; BL 11/1/96*; SLJ 12/96) [398.2]

10429 Ware, Jim. *Crazy Jacob* (3–5). Series: KidWitness Tales. 2000, Bethany House paper $5.99 (978-1-56179-885-8). 115pp. Based on a Bible story, this novel features Crazy Jacob whose demons are cast out by Jesus and turned into swine. (Rev: SLJ 2/01)

10430 Williams, Karen Lynn, and Khadra Mohammed. *Four Feet, Two Sandals* (1–3). Illus. by Doug Chayka. 2007, Eerdmans $17.00 (978-0-8028-5296-0). 32pp. Two 10-year-olds in a refugee camp on the Afghanistan-Pakistan border become friends when they discover that between them they own a beautiful pair of sandals. (Rev: BL 9/15/07; LMC 1/08; SLJ 10/07)

Prehistory

10431 Caselli, Giovanni. *An Ice Age Hunter* (3–5). 1992, Bedrick LB $12.95 (978-0-87226-103-7). 30pp. The story of a year in the life of an ice-age family as experienced by a young girl. (Rev: SLJ 7/92)

10432 Craig, Ruth. *Malu's Wolf* (4–6). 1995, Orchard LB $16.99 (978-0-531-08784-8). 192pp. Set in Stone Age Europe, this novel tells how Malu domesticated a wolf cub named Kono. (Rev: BL 12/15/95; SLJ 10/95)

10433 Denzel, Justin. *Boy of the Painted Cave* (5–7). 1988, Putnam $17.99 (978-0-399-21559-9). 160pp. The story of a boy who longs to be a cave artist, set in Cro Magnon times. (Rev: BL 11/1/88; SLJ 11/88)

10434 Ross, Stewart. *Curse of the Crocodile God* (3–6). Illus. by Inklink. 2007, DK $14.99 (978-0-7566-2564-1); paper $3.99 (978-0-7566-2563-4). 48pp. Two thirteen-year-olds in ancient Egypt solve a murder mystery in this story that will get children interested in studying this time period. (Rev: SLJ 5/07)

Africa

10435 Asare, Meshack. *Sosu's Call* (1–4). Illus. by author. 2002, Kane $15.95 (978-1-929132-21-8). 37pp. Sosu, an African boy who is rejected by the villagers because he cannot walk, saves them from a terrible storm with the help of his dog. (Rev: BCCB 5/02; HBG 10/02; SLJ 6/02)

10436 Burns, Khephra. *Mansa Musa: The Lion of Mali* (4–7). Illus. by Diane Dillon and Leo Dillon. 2001, Harcourt $18.00 (978-0-15-200375-3). 56pp. Lavish illustrations complement this handsome, challenging book about Mansa Musa's journey from a rural village boyhood to becoming the king of Mali. (Rev: BL 12/1/01; HB 11/01; HBG 3/02; SLJ 10/01)

10437 Ellis, Deborah. *The Heaven Shop* (5–8). 2004, Fitzhenry & Whiteside $16.95 (978-1-55041-908-5). 192pp. The AIDS epidemic has a devastating impact on the family of Binti, a 13-year-old Malawi girl. (Rev: BL 9/1/04; SLJ 10/04)

10438 Ellis, Veronica F. *Afro-Bets First Book About Africa* (2–5). Illus. by George Ford. 1990, Just Us Bks. LB $13.95 (978-0-940975-12-5); paper $6.95 (978-0-940975-03-3). 32pp. A classroom of African Americans learns about the history and culture of Africa. (Rev: BL 3/1/90*; SLJ 5/90)

10439 Farmer, Nancy. *Clever Ali* (2–4). Illus. by Gail de Marcken. 2006, Scholastic $17.99 (978-0-439-37014-1). 40pp. This beautifully written and illustrated picture book for older children, based on a true story of medieval Egypt, features 7-year-old Ali, who must find a way to outwit an evil sultan. (Rev: BL 10/1/06; SLJ 10/06)

10440 Farmer, Nancy. *Do You Know Me?* (4–6). Illus. by Shelley Jackson. 1993, Orchard LB $16.99 (978-0-531-08624-7). 112pp. There are culture clashes (many amusing) when 9-year-old Tapiwa's uncle comes from rural Mozambique to live with her family in the city. (Rev: BL 4/1/93; SLJ 4/93)

10441 Gregory, Kristiana. *Cleopatra VII: Daughter of the Nile* (5–8). Series: Royal Diaries. 1999, Scholastic paper $10.95 (978-0-590-81975-6). 224pp. This mock-diary recounts various events in the life of 12-year-old Cleopatra who, even at that age, was involved in palace intrigue. (Rev: BL 1/1–15/00; HBG 3/00; SLJ 10/99)

10442 Grifalconi, Ann. *The Village That Vanished* (2–5). Illus. by Kadir Nelson. 2002, Dial $16.99 (978-0-8037-2623-9). 40pp. African villagers escape slavers by dismantling their village piece by piece. (Rev: BCCB 11/02; BL 9/15/02; HB 9/02; HBG 3/03; SLJ 12/02)

10443 Havill, Juanita. *Sato and the Elephants* (2–4). Illus. by Jean Tseng and Mou-Sien Tseng. 1993, Lothrop LB $14.89 (978-0-688-11156-4). 32pp. A young ivory carver realizes that animals must be killed to supply him with material and therefore decides to try working in stone the next time. (Rev: BL 10/15/93; SLJ 4/94)

10444 Hawes, Louise. *Muti's Necklace: The Oldest Story in the World* (2–4). Illus. by Rebecca Guay. 2006, Houghton $16.00 (978-0-618-53583-5). 32pp. In ancient Egypt, servant Muti risks everything to retrieve her treasured necklace and receives a proposal of marriage from the pharaoh in return; based on an ancient Egyptian story. (Rev: BL 7/06; SLJ 6/06)

10445 Kurtz, Jane. *The Storyteller's Beads* (5–8). Illus. 1998, Harcourt $15.00 (978-0-15-201074-4). Two Ethiopian refugees, one a girl from a traditional Ethiopian culture and the other a blind Jewish girl, overcome generations of prejudice against Jews when they face common danger as they flee war and famine during the 1980s. (Rev: BCCB 9/98; BL 5/1/98; HBG 10/98; SLJ 7/98; VOYA 10/98)

10446 Lattimore, Deborah N. *The Winged Cat: A Tale of Ancient Egypt* (3–6). Illus. 1992, Harper-Collins $15.00 (978-0-06-023635-9). 32pp. A serving girl witnesses the killing of the sacred cat Bast in this handsomely illustrated tale of ancient Egypt. (Rev: BL 9/1/92; SLJ 4/92)

10447 Levitin, Sonia. *Dream Freedom* (5–9). 2000, Harcourt $17.00 (978-0-15-202404-8). 288pp. A novel that graphically portrays the plight of Sudanese slaves, juxtaposed with the story of an American 5th-grade class that joins the fight to free them. (Rev: BL 11/1/00; HBG 3/01; SLJ 10/00; VOYA 12/00)

10448 McCall Smith, Alexander. *Akimbo and the Elephants* (3–5). Illus. by LeUyen Pham. 2005, Bloomsbury $9.95 (978-1-58234-686-1). 80pp. Ten-year-old Akimbo, who lives with his ranger father on an African game preserve, helps to track down poachers who are killing full-grown elephants for their ivory tusks. Also use *Akimbo and the Lions* (2005), in which he adopts a lion cub. (Rev: BL 9/1/05; SLJ 11/05)

10449 McCaughrean, Geraldine. *Casting the Gods Adrift; A Tale of Ancient Egypt* (5–8). Illus. by Patricia D. Ludlow. 2003, Cricket $15.95 (978-0-8126-2684-1). 112pp. History and fiction are intertwined in this well-illustrated, suspenseful novel about two boys who are content to be taken in by the Pharoah Akhenaten, and a father enraged by the Pharaoh's refusal to worship the traditional Egyptian gods. (Rev: BCCB 10/03; BL 10/15/03; HBG 4/04; SLJ 8/03)

10450 McKissack, Patricia C. *Nzingha: Warrior Queen of Matamba* (5–8). Illus. Series: Royal Diaries. 2000, Scholastic paper $10.95 (978-0-439-11210-9). 144pp. Based on fact, this is the story of 17th-century African queen Nzingha who, in present-day Angola, resisted the Portuguese colonizers and slave traders. (Rev: BL 11/1/00; HBG 3/01; SLJ 12/00)

10451 Mankell, Henning. *Secrets in the Fire* (4–8). 2003, Annick $14.95 (978-1-55037-801-6); paper

$7.95 (978-1-55037-800-9). 176pp. This is the true story of Sofia, a courageous Mozambican girl who lost both legs — and her sister — when a landmine exploded. (Rev: BL 12/15/03*; SLJ 5/04)

10452 Marie, D. *Tears for Ashan* (3–6). Illus. by Norman Childers. 1989, Creative $12.95 (978-0-9621681-0-9). 32pp. Set in Africa years ago. Kumasi sees his best friend taken captive by slave traders. (Rev: BL 12/1/89)

10453 Marsden, Carolyn, and Philip Matzigkeit. *Sahwira: An African Friendship* (5–8). 2009, Candlewick $15.99 (978-0-7636-3575-6). 208pp. In Rhodesia in the late 1960s, Evan, son of a white American teacher, and Blessing, son of a Shona pastor, find their friendship is challenged by the political and racial tensions that surround them. (Rev: BCCB 7–8/09; BL 4/15/09; SLJ 5/09; VOYA 6/09)

10454 Marston, Elsa. *The Ugly Goddess* (5–8). 2002, Cricket $16.95 (978-0-8126-2667-4). 224pp. In 523 B.C. Egypt, a 14-year-old Egyptian princess, a young Greek soldier who is in love with her, and an Egyptian boy become embroiled in a mystery adventure that blends fact, fiction, and fantasy. (Rev: BL 1/1–15/03; HBG 3/03; SLJ 12/02)

10455 Michael, Jan. *City Boy* (5–8). 2009, Clarion $16.00 (978-0-547-22310-0). 192pp. In Malawi, after his parents' deaths from AIDS Sam must swap his urban environment for his aunt's one-room hut. (Rev: BL 5/1/09; HB 9/09)

10456 Milway, Katie Smith. *One Hen: How One Small Loan Made a Big Difference* (2–5). Illus. by Eugenie Fernandes. 2008, Kids Can $18.95 (978-1-55453-028-1). 32pp. In a village in rural Ghana where microlending is being introduced, young Kojo gets enough money to buy a hen; the eggs from the hen give him enough money to buy another and he eventually creates a large enterprise and is able in turn to help others. (Rev: BCCB 3/08; BL 6/1–15/08; LMC 5/08; SLJ 5/08)

10457 Mwangi, Meja. *The Mzungu Boy* (5–8). 2005, Groundwood $15.95 (978-0-88899-653-4). 160pp. In 1950s Kenya, a 12-year-old Kenyan boy becomes friendly with the white landowner's son despite both families' disapproval. (Rev: BL 8/05; SLJ 11/05)

10458 Naidoo, Beverley. *No Turning Back* (5–9). 1997, HarperCollins $15.89 (978-0-06-027506-8). Jaabu, a homeless African boy, looks for shelter in contemporary Johannesburg. (Rev: BCCB 2/97; BL 12/15/96*; HB 3/97; SLJ 2/97; VOYA 10/97)

10459 Platt, Richard. *Egyptian Diary: The Journal of Nakht* (4–6). Illus. by David Parkins. 2005, Candlewick $17.99 (978-0-7636-2756-0). 64pp. Nakht, a 9-year-old Egyptian boy training to become a scribe like his father, records in his journal observations about life in ancient Memphis, giving readers a good idea of Egyptian culture that is bolstered by the back matter. (Rev: BL 11/15/05; SLJ 2/06)

10460 Ross, Stewart. *Egypt in Spectacular Cross-Section* (2–4). Illus. by Stephen Biesty. 2005, Scholastic $18.99 (978-0-439-74537-6). 32pp. Illustrator Biesty's detailed cross-sections provide lots of ways to inform readers of interesting facts within

the framework of Ross's story about a trip down the Nile family wedding in the Egypt of Ramses II. (Rev: BL 9/1/05; SLJ 9/05) [932]

10461 Turner, Ann. *Maïa of Thebes: 1463 B.C.* (4–6). Series: Life and Times. 2005, Scholastic $10.95 (978-0-439-65223-0). 160pp. In the time of Queen Hatshepsut, 13-year-old Maïa finds her life in danger. (Rev: BL 6/1–15/05)

10462 Watson, Pete. *The Heart of the Lion* (3–5). Illus. by Mary Watson. 2005, Shenanigan $15.95 (978-0-9726614-1-6). 32pp. A young American boy visits a West African village, meets a new friend, and learns about the region's distinctive culture. (Rev: BL 8/05; SLJ 10/05)

10463 Welch, Leona N. *Kai: The Lost Statue* (3–6). Illus. Series: Girlhood Journeys. 1997, Simon & Schuster paper $5.99 (978-0-689-81571-3). 72pp. In this historical novel set in southwestern Nigeria, Kai encounters problems when she becomes an apprentice to a sculptor. (Rev: BL 4/1/98; SLJ 4/98)

10464 Whelan, Gloria. *Yatandou* (2–4). Illus. by Peter Sylvada. Series: Tales of the World. 2007, Sleeping Bear $17.95 (978-1-58536-211-0). 32pp. This story follows 8-year-old Yatandou as she tries to help others in her traditional West African village. (Rev: BL 10/1/07; SLJ 10/07)

10465 Williams, Mary. *Brothers in Hope: The Story of the Lost Boys of Sudan* (3–5). Illus. by R. Gregory Christie. 2005, Lee & Low $17.95 (978-1-58430-232-2). 40pp. Garang, a Sudanese boy, flees to Ethiopia and then Kenya, where he finds a home in a refugee camp and hopes to find a way to get to America; this first-person account includes evocative paintings. (Rev: BL 5/1/05; SLJ 6/05)

10466 Yohalem, Eve. *Escape Under the Forever Sky* (5–8). 2009, Chronicle $16.99 (978-0-8118-6653-8). 228pp. Lucy, 13-year-old daughter of the U.S. ambassador to Ethiopia, sneaks out of the house and is kidnapped; her survival skills help her when she manages to escape. (Rev: BL 5/1/09; SLJ 5/09)

Asia

10467 Alexander, Lloyd. *Dream-of-Jade: The Emperor's Cat* (3–5). Illus. by D. Brent Burkett. 2005, Cricket $16.95 (978-0-8126-2736-7). 48pp. Dream-of-Jade, a talking cat, develops a close friendship with a lonely Chinese emperor. (Rev: BL 9/15/05; HBG 4/06; SLJ 11/05)

10468 Atkins, Jeannine. *Aani and the Tree Huggers* (2–5). Illus. by Venantius J. Pinto. 1995, Lee & Low $15.95 (978-1-880000-24-3). In this tale set in India, a village woman tries to save a tree from big-city developers by throwing her arms around it. (Rev: SLJ 12/95)

10469 Balgassi, Haemi. *Peacebound Trains* (3–5). Illus. by Chris K. Soentpiet. 1996, Clarion $15.00 (978-0-395-72093-6). 47pp. Sumi's grandmother tells about the perilous journey she took to escape the Communists during the Korean War. (Rev: BCCB 10/96; BL 9/15/96; SLJ 1/97)

10470 Bouchard, David. *Buddha in the Garden* (4–6). Illus. by Zhong-Yang Huang. 2001, Raincoast

$14.95 (978-1-55192-452-6). 32pp. An abandoned baby raised in a monastery learns to tend the garden in this quiet introduction to Buddhism illustrated with evocative water colors. (Rev: BL 1/1–15/02; SLJ 12/01)

10471 Chrisman, Arthur B. *Shen of the Sea* (4–6). Illus. by Else Hasselriis. 1968, Dutton $16.99 (978-0-525-39244-6). 224pp. These engaging short stories of Chinese life received the Newbery Award, 1926.

10472 Coatsworth, Elizabeth. *The Cat Who Went to Heaven* (4–6). Illus. by Lynd Ward. 1990, Simon & Schuster LB $17.00 (978-0-02-719710-5). 72pp. A charming legend of a Japanese artist, his cat, and a Buddhist miracle. Newbery Medal winner, 1931.

10473 Conlogue, Ray. *Shen and the Treasure Fleet* (5–8). 2007, Annick $21.95 (978-1-55451-104-4); paper $11.95 (978-1-55451-103-7). 256pp. Shen and his sister Chang try to free their mother and learn their father's fate while at sea with Zheng He's "treasure fleet" in early 15th-century China. (Rev: BL 11/15/07)

10474 Ellis, Deborah. *The Breadwinner* (5–7). 2001, Groundwood $15.95 (978-0-88899-419-6). 170pp. In Kabul under the strict rule of the Taliban, Parvana dresses as a boy so she can work to feed the remaining women in her family. (Rev: BL 3/1/01; HBG 10/01; SLJ 7/01; VOYA 6/01)

10475 Fleischman, Sid. *The White Elephant* (3–5). Illus. by Robert McGuire. 2006, Greenwillow $15.99 (978-0-06-113136-3). 112pp. Run Run, a young elephant trainer, angers Prince Noi and as a punishment is given a white elephant that he must care for but cannot put to work because of its rarity. (Rev: BL 9/1/06; SLJ 10/06)

10476 Glass, Tom. *Even a Little Is Something: Stories of Nong* (4–6). Illus. by Elena Gerard. 1997, Linnet LB $19.50 (978-0-208-02457-2). 119pp. Accurately depicts the daily struggle of peasants living hand-to-mouth in northeastern Thailand. (Rev: HBG 3/98; SLJ 2/98)

10477 Ho, Minfong. *The Clay Marble* (5–9). 1991, Houghton $12.00 (978-0-395-77155-6). After fleeing from her Cambodian home in the early 1980s, 12-year-old Dara is separated from her family during an attack on a refugee camp on the Thailand border. (Rev: BL 11/15/91; SLJ 10/91)

10478 Hollyer, Belinda. *River Song* (5–8). 2008, Holiday $16.95 (978-0-8234-2149-7). 164pp. Set in New Zealand, this story of a half-Maori girl torn between two cultures is infused with magical elements from Maori legend. (Rev: BL 5/1/08; SLJ 6/08)

10479 Hong, Chen Jiang. *Little Eagle* (3–5). Trans. by Claudia Zoe Bedrick. Illus. by author. 2007, Enchanted Lion $16.95 (978-1-59270-071-4). 36pp. In 15th-century China a kung fu master takes in an orphaned boy and trains him as his disciple, calling him "Little Eagle." (Rev: BL 11/1/07; LMC 1/08; SLJ 11/07)

10480 Hoobler, Dorothy, and Thomas Hoobler. *The Sword That Cut the Burning Grass* (5–8). Series: The Samurai Mysteries. 2005, Philomel $10.99

(978-0-399-24272-4). 224pp. In this fourth book about the aspiring young samurai, Seikei tackles a challenging task involving the teenage emperor. (Rev: BL 5/1/05; SLJ 10/05)

10481 Huynh, Quang Nhuong. *The Land I Lost: Adventures of a Boy in Vietnam* (5–8). Illus. by Mai Vo-Dinh. 1990, HarperCollins $15.89 (978-0-397-32448-4); paper $5.99 (978-0-06-440183-8). 128pp. The story of a boy's growing up in rural Vietnam before the war.

10482 Kamal, Aleph. *The Bird Who Was an Elephant* (3–5). Illus. by Frane Lessac. 1990, HarperCollins LB $14.89 (978-0-397-32446-0). 32pp. The story of what a bird sees as it flies over an Indian village. (Rev: BCCB 7–8/90; BL 4/15/90; SLJ 8/90)

10483 Keido, Ippo, retel. *The Butterfly's Dream: Children's Stories from China* (3–6). Illus. by Kazuko Stone. 2003, Tuttle $15.95 (978-0-8048-3480-3). This richly illustrated collection features a number of stories, linked by the flight of a butterfly, based on the ancient Chinese Chuang-Tzu. (Rev: HBG 4/04; SLJ 1/04)

10484 Lasky, Kathryn. *Jahanara: Princess of Princesses* (4–8). Series: Royal Diaries. 2002, Scholastic paper $10.95 (978-0-439-22350-8). 192pp. Princess Jaharana, the daughter of Shah Jahan (who built the Taj Mahal) writes detailed diary accounts of her 17th-century life, with rich descriptions of her surroundings, palace intrigues, and dealing with her family. (Rev: BL 1/1–15/03; HBG 3/03; SLJ 1/03)

10485 Lattimore, Deborah N. *Fool and the Phoenix: A Tale of Ancient Japan* (3–6). Illus. 1997, HarperCollins LB $14.89 (978-0-06-026211-2). 40pp. Hideo, a mute, falls in love with the phoenix bird of Japan and catches her in a net. (Rev: BL 8/97; HBG 3/98; SLJ 9/97)

10486 Louis, Catherine. *Liu and the Bird: A Journey in Chinese Calligraphy* (2–4). Trans. by Sibylle Kazeroid. Illus. by Feng Xiao Min. 2006, North-South $16.95 (978-0-7358-2050-0). 40pp. A young Chinese girl draws for her grandfather the things she saw on her journey to visit him in this introduction to calligraphic symbols. (Rev: BL 4/15/06; SLJ 4/06)

10487 Marsden, Carolyn, and Thay Phap Niem. *The Buddha's Diamonds* (3–5). 2008, Candlewick $14.99 (978-0-7636-3380-6). 112pp. Ten-year-old Vietnamese Tinh struggles to help his family after a cyclone devastates his small fishing village; includes Buddhist concepts, a glossary, and endnotes. (Rev: BL 3/15/08; LMC 3/08; SLJ 6/08)

10488 Neuberger, Anne E. *The Girl-Son* (3–6). Illus. 1994, Carolrhoda LB $21.27 (978-0-87614-846-4). 132pp. Based on fact, this is the story of a Korean girl born in 1896 and her fight for women's rights. (Rev: BCCB 2/95; BL 1/1/95; SLJ 2/95)

10489 Neville, Emily C. *The China Year* (5–8). 1991, HarperCollins $15.95 (978-0-06-024383-8). Henri, 14, has left his New York City home, school, and friends to go to Peking University for a year with his father. (Rev: BL 5/1/91; SLJ 5/91)

10490 Niemann, Christoph. *The Pet Dragon: A Story About Adventure, Friendship, and Chinese Charac-*

ters (1–4). Illus. by author. 2008, Greenwillow $16.99 (978-0-06-157776-5). 32pp. An excellent way to introduce Chinese language and characters, this is a story about a young girl, Lin, and her escapee dragon. (Rev: BL 9/1/08; SLJ 9/08)

10491 Noyes, Deborah. *When I Met the Wolf Girls* (3–5). Illus. by August Hall. 2007, Houghton $17.00 (978-0-618-60567-5). 40pp. An orphan girl named Bulu narrates this story, based on truth, about two young girls raised by wolves and their difficulties adapting to life at an Indian orphanage. (Rev: BL 3/15/07)

10492 Park, Linda Sue. *The Kite Fighters* (4–6). 2000, Clarion $15.00 (978-0-395-94041-9). 144pp. Contests involving kite flying are the subject of this exciting novel set in 15th-century Korea. (Rev: BCCB 6/00; BL 4/1/00; HB 5/00; HBG 10/00; SLJ 6/00)

10493 Park, Linda Sue. *Seesaw Girl* (4–7). Illus. 1999, Clarion $14.00 (978-0-395-91514-1). 90pp. In 17th-century Korea, 12-year-old Jade Blossom wanders away from her aristocratic palace and discovers the reality and poverty of the world outside. (Rev: BCCB 12/99; BL 9/1/99; HBG 3/00; SLJ 9/99)

10494 Park, Linda Sue. *A Single Shard* (4–8). 2001, Clarion $15.00 (978-0-395-97827-6). 152pp. This Newbery Medal winner describes a Korean boy's journey through unknown territory to deliver two valuable pots. (Rev: BCCB 3/01; BL 4/1/01*; HBG 10/01; SLJ 5/01*)

10495 Park, Linda Sue. *When My Name Was Keoko* (5–9). 2002, Clarion $16.00 (978-0-618-13335-2). 208pp. A young brother and sister tell, in first-person accounts, what life was like during the Japanese occupation of Korea. (Rev: BCCB 5/02; BL 3/1/02; HB 5/02; HBG 10/02; SLJ 4/02)

10496 Paterson, Kathrine. *The Master Puppeteer* (4–7). Illus. by Haru Wells. 1989, HarperCollins paper $5.99 (978-0-06-440281-1). 192pp. Feudal Japan is the setting for this story about a young apprentice puppeteer and his search for a mysterious bandit.

10497 Paterson, Katherine. *Of Nightingales That Weep* (4–7). Illus. by Haru Wells. 1974, Harper-Collins paper $6.99 (978-0-06-440282-8). 192pp. A story set in feudal Japan tells of Takiko, a samurai's daughter, who is sent to the royal court when her mother remarries.

10498 Paterson, Katherine. *The Sign of the Chrysanthemum* (5–7). Illus. by Peter Landa. 1973, Harper-Collins LB $14.89 (978-0-690-04913-8); paper $5.99 (978-0-06-440232-3). 128pp. At the death of his mother, a young boy sets out to find his samurai father in 12th-century Japan.

10499 Place, François. *The Old Man Mad About Drawing* (5–8). Trans. by William Rodarmor. Illus. 2003, Godine $19.95 (978-1-56792-260-8). 128pp. In 19th-century Edo (now Tokyo), Tojiro, a 9-year-old orphan who sells rice cakes, becomes the assistant to a famous old artist. (Rev: BL 3/15/04*; HB 3/04; SLJ 5/04)

10500 Russell, Ching Yeung. *Child Bride* (4–7). Illus. 1999, Boyds Mills $15.95 (978-1-56397-748-0). 133pp. Set in China in the early 1940s, this is the story of 11-year-old Ying, her arranged marriage, and an understanding bridegroom who allows her to go home to her ailing grandmother. (Rev: BL 3/1/99; HBG 10/99; SLJ 4/99)

10501 Russell, Ching Yeung. *Lichee Tree* (4–7). 1997, Boyds Mills $15.95 (978-1-56397-629-2). 182pp. Growing up in China during the 1940s, Ying dreams of selling lichee nuts and visiting Canton. (Rev: BCCB 4/97; BL 3/15/97; SLJ 6/97)

10502 Say, Allen. *Erika-San* (2–5). Illus. by author. 2009, Houghton $17.00 (978-0-618-88933-4). 32pp. As a little girl, Erika was enchanted by a painting of a Japanese tea house, and when she grows up she finally finds the place of her dreams far from the madding crowd on a remote island in Japan. (Rev: BL 12/1/08; HB 1/09; LMC 10/09; SLJ 12/08)

10503 Say, Allen. *Kamishibai Man* (1–3). Illus. 2005, Houghton $17.00 (978-0-618-47954-2). 32pp. An elderly Japanese man who once made the rounds selling candy and telling stories to children revisits the magic of a bygone era. (Rev: BCCB 11/05; BL 9/15/05*; HB 11/05; HBG 4/06; LMC 3/06; SLJ 10/05*)

10504 Shea, Pegi Deitz. *The Carpet Boy's Gift* (2–5). Illus. by Leane Morin. 2003, Tilbury House $16.95 (978-0-88448-248-2). 40pp. This beautifully illustrated fictional picture-book tale of a young Pakistani boy working under dreadful conditions was inspired by the murder of 12-year-old activist Iqbal Masih. (Rev: BL 1/1–15/04; SLJ 2/04)

10505 Spivak, Dawnine. *Grass Sandals: The Travels of Basho* (3–5). Illus. by Demi. 1997, Simon & Schuster $16.00 (978-0-689-80776-3). 40pp. An outstanding picture book about the 17th-century poet and his travels around Japan. (Rev: BCCB 7–8/97; BL 5/1/97*; HBG 3/98; SLJ 4/97) [895.6]

10506 Sreenivasan, Jyotsna. *Aruna's Journeys* (4–7). Illus. 1997, Smooth Stone paper $6.95 (978-0-9619401-7-1). 136pp. Aruna denies her Indian heritage until she spends a summer in Bangalore, India. (Rev: BL 7/97)

10507 Tenzing, Norbu. *Himalaya* (3–5). Trans. from French by Shelley Tanaka. Illus. by author. 2002, Groundwood $16.95 (978-0-88899-480-6). A gripping saga, beautifully illustrated, about the Dolpo people of Nepal, their grueling treks through the mountains, and the transfer of leadership. (Rev: HBG 3/03; SLJ 1/03)

10508 Tenzing, Norbu, and Stephane Frattini. *Secret of the Snow Leopard* (3–5). Trans. from French by Shelley Tanaka. Illus. by Tenzing Norbu. 2004, Groundwood $16.95 (978-0-88899-544-5). In beautifully illustrated Nepal, young Tsering defies his stepfather and travels through a dangerous pass where his father lost his life; there he encounters a snow leopard and must draw on his inner strength. (Rev: SLJ 8/04)

10509 Vejjajiva, Jane. *The Happiness of Kati* (4–7). Trans. by Prudence Borthwick. 2006, Simon & Schuster $15.95 (978-1-4169-1788-5). 144pp. Nine-year-old Kati's mother is dying and the identity of her father is a mystery in this story set in Thailand. (Rev: BL 5/15/06; SLJ 6/06)

10510 Whelan, Gloria. *Goodbye, Vietnam* (5–8). 1992, Turtleback paper $11.65 (978-0-606-05848-3). 144pp. Young Mai and her family escape from Vietnam to Hong Kong, suffering through a difficult boat journey; originally published in 1992. (Rev: BL 4/15/06; HB 1/93; SLJ 9/92)

10511 Whitesel, Cheryl Aylward. *Blue Fingers: A Ninja's Tale* (5–8). 2004, Clarion $15.00 (978-0-618-38139-5). 256pp. In 16th-century Japan, 12-year-old Koji is trained to become a ninja warrior. (Rev: BL 3/15/04; SLJ 3/04)

10512 Whitesel, Cheryl Aylward. *Rebel: A Tibetan Odyssey* (5–8). 2000, HarperCollins $16.99 (978-0-688-16735-6). 190pp. In Tibet about a century ago, a young boy named Thunder is sent to live with his uncle, an important lama in a Buddhist monastery. (Rev: BCCB 5/00; BL 4/15/00; HBG 3/01; SLJ 7/00)

10513 Wu, Priscilla. *The Abacus Contest: Stories from Taiwan and China* (5–8). Illus. 1996, Fulcrum $15.95 (978-1-55591-243-7). Six simple short stories explore life in a Taiwanese city. (Rev: BL 7/96; SLJ 6/96)

10514 Yep, Laurence. *Lady of Ch'iao Kuo: Warrior of the South* (5–8). Illus. Series: Royal Diaries. 2001, Scholastic $10.95 (978-0-439-16483-2). 300pp. In this volume of the Royal Diaries series, the teenage Princess Redbird of the Hsien tribe must use her diplomatic skills to save the lives of both her own people and Chinese colonists in the 6th century A.D. Historical notes add background information. (Rev: BL 11/1/01)

10515 Young, Ed. *Beyond the Great Mountains: A Visual Poem About China* (4–6). Illus. 2005, Chronicle $17.95 (978-0-8118-4343-0). 36pp. The vastness and beauty of China are celebrated in an appealing but challenging blend of simple poetry and paper collage artwork. (Rev: BL 11/1/05; SLJ 10/05)

10516 Yue, Guo, and Clare Farrow. *Little Leap Forward: A Boy in Beijing* (3–6). Illus. by Helen Cann. 2008, Barefoot Books $16.99 (978-1-84686-114-7). 126pp. A caged bird teaches 8-year-old Leap Forward about freedom in this moving story set during the 1960s Cultural Revolution in China; based on the author's childhood. (Rev: BL 8/08; HB 9/08)

Europe

10517 Anholt, Laurence. *Leonardo and the Flying Boy* (2–4). Illus. 2000, Barron's $15.99 (978-0-7641-5225-2). 32pp. A fictionalized account of da Vinci's life and accomplishments as reflected in anecdotes about his young apprentices. (Rev: BL 1/1–15/01; SLJ 2/01)

10518 Armstrong, Alan. *Raleigh's Page* (5–7). Illus. by Tim Jessell. 2007, Random $16.99 (978-0-375-83319-9). 336pp. As page to Walter Raleigh, 11-year-old Andrew learns about court life, becomes embroiled in intrigues, and has adventures that

include visiting the New World. (Rev: BL 8/07; HB 11/07; LMC 11/07; SLJ 11/07)

10519 Attema, Martha. *Daughter of Light* (3–5). Illus. 2001, Orca paper $4.99 (978-1-55143-179-6). 138pp. In this affecting novel, which takes place in the Nazi-occupied Netherlands during World War II, a 9-year-old girl braves German soldiers and risks her freedom to help her pregnant mother. (Rev: BL 2/1/02; SLJ 12/01)

10520 Balit, Christina. *Escape from Pompeii* (1–4). Illus. by author. 2003, Holt $17.95 (978-0-8050-7324-9). This fictionalized account of the fall of the Italian city of Pompeii tells of a young boy and girl who manage to flee to the sea before the eruption of Mount Vesuvius totally destroys the city. (Rev: HBG 4/04; SLJ 11/03)

10521 Banks, Lynne Reid. *Tiger, Tiger* (5–8). 2005, Delacorte LB $17.99 (978-0-385-90264-9). 256pp. Two tiger cubs arrive in Rome destined for different fates; Brute is trained to be a killer of men in the Colosseum while Boots becomes a pet for the caesar's daughter, a decision with dangerous consequences. (Rev: BL 5/15/05; SLJ 6/05)

10522 Bawden, Nina. *The Real Plato Jones* (5–8). 1993, Clarion $15.00 (978-0-395-66972-3). British teen Plato Jones and his mother return to Greece for his grandfather's funeral, where Plato discovers that his grandfather may have been a coward and traitor while serving in the Greek Resistance. (Rev: BCCB 11/93; BL 10/15/93; SLJ 11/93*)

10523 Bradley, Kimberly Brubaker. *The Lacemaker and the Princess* (4–8). 2007, Simon & Schuster $16.99 (978-1-4169-1920-9). 208pp. As the French Revolution gathers strength, a young lace maker becomes the companion of Princess Marie-Thérèse, daughter of Marie Antoinette and King Louis XVI, and witness the growing social unrest. (Rev: BL 4/15/07; SLJ 7/07)

10524 Casanova, Mary. *The Klipfish Code* (4–7). 2007, Houghton $16.00 (978-0-618-88393-6). 240pp. Marit and her brother Lars struggle under the restrictions of Nazi-occupied Norway in this action- and suspense-filled novel. (Rev: BL 10/15/07; SLJ 10/07)

10525 Celenza, Anna Harwell. *The Farewell Symphony* (2–4). Illus. by JoAnn E. Kitchel. 2000, Charlesbridge LB $19.95 (978-1-57091-406-5). A fictional version of the story behind Haydn's "Farewell Symphony" and the effect it had on Prince Nicholas, the composer's sponsor. (Rev: HBG 3/01; SLJ 7/00)

10526 Clements, Bruce. *A Chapel of Thieves* (4–6). 2002, Farrar $16.00 (978-0-374-37701-4). 224pp. In this sequel to *I Tell a Lie Every So Often* (1974), Henry, an adventurous 15-year-old, journeys across the Atlantic to Paris in 1849 to rescue his older brother from a gang of thieves. (Rev: BCCB 4/02; BL 3/15/02; HBG 10/02; SLJ 5/02)

10527 Comora, Madeleine. *Rembrandt and Titus: Artist and Son* (4–6). Illus. by Thomas Locker. 2005, Fulcrum $17.95 (978-1-55591-490-5). 32pp. Titus, son of Dutch artist Rembrandt, describes his father's life and vision; the full-page illustrations are based on Rembrandt's paintings or etchings. (Rev: BL 9/1/05; SLJ 10/05)

10528 Coville, Bruce. *Hans Brinker* (3–5). Illus. by Laurel Long. 2007, Dial $16.99 (978-0-8037-2868-4). 32pp. A picture-book version of the story about the courageous and generous Dutch boy and his ice-skating race. (Rev: BL 9/15/07; HB 11/07; SLJ 2/08)

10529 Creech, Sharon. *The Castle Corona* (4–7). Illus. by David Diaz. 2007, HarperCollins $18.99 (978-0-06-084621-3). 336pp. This lively and entertaining fairy tale set in medieval Italy follows a pair of orphaned peasant children named Pia and Enzio who become tasters for the royal family of Castle Corona. (Rev: BL 9/1/07; SLJ 10/07) ☊

10530 Debon, Nicolas. *A Brave Soldier* (2–5). Illus. 2002, Groundwood $15.95 (978-0-88899-481-3). 32pp. This picture book for older children, narrated by a young Canadian soldier, introduces readers to the trenches of World War I. (Rev: BL 11/1/02; HBG 3/03; SLJ 2/03)

10531 de Cervantes, Miguel, and Martin Jenkins. *Don Quixote* (5–8). Illus. by Chris Riddell. 2009, Candlewick $27.99 (978-0-7636-4081-1). 352pp. Suitably lighthearted, this is a faithful and nicely illustrated retelling of the story of Don Quixote and his exploits. (Rev: BL 4/15/09)

10532 DeJong, Meindert. *Wheel on the School* (4–7). Illus. by Maurice Sendak. 1954, HarperCollins LB $18.89 (978-0-06-021586-6); paper $6.95 (978-0-06-440021-3). 256pp. The storks are brought back to their island by the schoolchildren in a Dutch village. Newbery Medal winner, 1955.

10533 Deverell, Catherine. *Stradivari's Singing Violin* (3–5). Illus. by Andrea Shine. 1992, Carolrhoda LB $13.95 (978-0-87614-732-0). 48pp. A fictional account of the historical figure behind what is perhaps the world's best-known musical instrument. (Rev: BL 2/15/93)

10534 Eisner, Will. *The Last Knight: An Introduction to Don Quixote by Miguel de Cervantes* (4–8). Illus. 2000, NBM $15.95 (978-1-56163-251-0). 32pp. Using an engaging text and a comic book format, this is a fine retelling of Cervantes' classic. (Rev: BL 6/1–15/00; HBG 10/00; SLJ 7/00)

10535 Ellis, Deborah. *A Company of Fools* (5–8). 2002, Fitzhenry & Whiteside $15.95 (978-1-55041-719-7). 180pp. Quiet Henri and free-spirited Micah try to cheer the people of a France devastated by the Black Death of 1348 by singing. (Rev: BCCB 1/03; BL 1/1–15/03; HB 1/03; HBG 3/03; VOYA 2/03)

10536 Fagan, Cary. *Daughter of the Great Zandini* (3–5). Illus. by Cybele Young. 2001, Tundra LB $16.95 (978-0-88776-534-6). 57pp. The Great Zandini's son has been groomed to follow in his father's magician footsteps, but it is Fanny, the neglected daughter, who is the success in this story set in 19th-century Paris. (Rev: HBG 3/02; SLJ 4/02)

10537 Ford, Michael. *Birth of a Warrior* (5–8). 2008, Bloomsbury $16.99 (978-0-8027-9794-0). 256pp. Lysander's Spartan heritage is in conflict with his fondness for the Helot villages with whom he grew

up in this exciting, sometimes violent, sequel to *The Fire of Ares* (2008). (Rev: BLO 12/18/08; SLJ 2/09)

10538 Ford, Michael. *The Fire of Ares* (4–6). Series: Spartan Quest. 2008, Walker $16.95 (978-0-8027-9744-5). 250pp. In ancient Sparta, a young slave called Lysander is rescued by a man who recognizes Lysander's amulet as once belonging to his son. (Rev: BL 4/1/08; LMC 8/08; SLJ 4/08)

10539 French, Jackie. *Rover* (5–8). 2007, HarperCollins $17.99 (978-0-06-085078-4). 304pp. When Vikings raid Hekja's Scottish village, she and her puppy are taken to Greenland, where she's enslaved to Freydis, Leif Erikson's sister; Hekja's dog can spot icebergs, and the two accompany Freydis on her voyage to North America in this compelling, historically accurate story. (Rev: BL 1/1–15/07; SLJ 6/07)

10540 Gilman, Laura Anne. *Grail Quest: The Camelot Spell* (5–8). Series: Grail Quest. 2006, HarperCollins LB $14.89 (978-0-06-077280-2). 304pp. On the eve of King Arthur's quest for the Holy Grail, three young teens of different backgrounds — Gerard, Newt, and Ailias — must reverse a spell crippling all adults. (Rev: BL 2/1/06; SLJ 6/06)

10541 Gilson, Jamie. *Stink Alley* (4–7). 2002, HarperCollins LB $15.89 (978-0-06-029217-1). 192pp. Twelve-year-old orphan Lizzy Tinker, a Separatist who fled England with her family for Holland in 1608, is befriended by the boy who would one day be known as Rembrandt. (Rev: BCCB 9/02; BL 4/15/02; HB 9/02; HBG 3/03; SLJ 7/02)

10542 Glaser, Linda. *Bridge to America* (3–5). 2005, Houghton $16.00 (978-0-618-56301-2). 208pp. Fivel, a young Jew from Poland, describes his life in the shtetl, the agonizing wait for money to fund his family's journey to join his father in the United States, and the difficulties in adjusting when he arrives. (Rev: BL 8/05; SLJ 11/05)

10543 Glatshteyn, Yankev. *Emil and Karl* (5–8). Ed. by Jeffrey Shandler. 2006, Roaring Brook $16.95 (978-1-59643-119-5). 208pp. Two 9-year-old friends — one Jewish, one Aryan — try to elude the Nazis on the streets of Vienna shortly after Germany's invasion; a fast-paced, moving story initially published in 1940. (Rev: BL 4/15/06; SLJ 6/06*; VOYA 4/06)

10544 Gordon, Sharon. *Greece* (2–4). Illus. Series: Discovering Cultures. 2003, Benchmark LB $25.64 (978-0-7614-1718-7). 48pp. This well-illustrated overview of Greece and its people includes the usual information offered for this age group, plus some less well-known details. (Rev: SLJ 4/04) [949.5]

10545 Greene, Jacqueline D. *Marie: Summer in the Country* (3–6). Illus. Series: Girlhood Journeys. 1997, Simon & Schuster paper $5.99 (978-0-689-81562-1). 72pp. In this historical novel set in France, Marie plots to save her country cousin from being sent away to work as a servant. (Rev: BL 4/1/98; SLJ 4/98)

10546 Greene, Jacqueline D. *One Foot Ashore* (4–6). 1994, Walker $16.95 (978-0-8027-8281-6). 208pp. To escape servitude in Brazil, Maria stows away on a boat bound for Amsterdam, where she finds work in the home of Rembrandt. (Rev: BCCB 6/94; BL 4/1/94; HB 7/94; SLJ 6/94)

10547 Gregory, Kristiana. *Eleanor: Crown Jewel of Aquitaine* (3–6). Series: Royal Diaries. 2002, Scholastic $10.95 (978-0-439-16484-9). 192pp. Eleanor's fictional diary details her daily life in the 12th century — as a child and later as a queen — giving readers a good sense of her times. (Rev: BL 2/1/03; HBG 3/03; SLJ 1/03)

10548 Holub, Josef. *The Robber and Me* (5–8). Trans. from German by Elizabeth D. Crawford. 1997, Holt $16.95 (978-0-8050-5591-7). On his way to live with his uncle, an orphan is helped by a mysterious stranger and he must later make a decision about whether to stand up to his uncle and the town authorities to clear the name of this man in this novel set in 19th-century Germany. (Rev: SLJ 12/97*)

10549 Hugo, Victor. *The Hunchback of Notre Dame* (4–6). Retold by Tim Wynne-Jones. Illus. by Bill Slavin. 1997, Orchard $15.95 (978-0-531-30055-8). This abridgement of the Hugo classic captures the spirit of Paris in the Middle Ages and Quasimodo's love for Esmeralda. (Rev: HBG 3/98; SLJ 4/98)

10550 Ibbotson, Eva. *The Star of Kazan* (4–8). Illus. by Kevin Hawkes. 2004, Dutton $16.99 (978-0-525-47347-3). 336pp. Set in the Austro-Hungarian empire, this richly detailed and very readable novel tells the story of 12-year-old Annika, who gets a rude awakening when her aristocratic mother whisks her away from her adoptive family. (Rev: BL 10/15/04*; SLJ 10/04*)

10551 Jacobson, Rick. *The Mona Lisa Caper* (2–4). Illus. 2005, Tundra $15.95 (978-0-88776-726-5). 24pp. This fact-based tale chronicles the 1911 theft of Leonardo da Vinci's *Mona Lisa* from the Louvre in Paris. (Rev: BL 7/05; SLJ 8/05)

10552 Johnston, Tony. *The Harmonica* (3–6). Illus. by Ron Mazellan. 2004, Charlesbridge $15.95 (978-1-57091-547-5). 32pp. This moving tale of a young Jewish boy who plays his harmonica for the concentration camp commandant is based on truth. (Rev: BL 1/1–15/04; SLJ 5/04)

10553 Jones, Terry. *The Lady and the Squire* (5–7). Illus. 2001, Pavilion $22.95 (978-1-86205-417-2). 304pp. A beautiful aristocrat joins Tom and Ann as they make their way through a war-torn countryside to the papal court at Avignon. (Rev: BL 2/15/01; SLJ 3/01)

10554 Juster, Norton. *Alberic the Wise* (4–8). Illus. by Leonard Baskin. 1992, Picture Book $16.95 (978-0-88708-243-6). 32pp. In this picture book set in the Renaissance, Alberic becomes an apprentice to a stained-glass maker. (Rev: BCCB 2/93; BL 1/15/93; SLJ 3/93)

10555 Kacer, Kathy. *The Night Spies* (4–7). 2003, Second Story paper $5.95 (978-1-896764-70-2). 197pp. Hiding from the Nazis, Gabi and her family can leave their cramped quarters only at night, but Gabi and her cousin Max manage to help the partisans. (Rev: BL 1/1–15/04; SLJ 3/04)

10556 Kanefield, Teri. *Rivka's Way* (4–8). 2001, Front St. $15.95 (978-0-8126-2870-8). 144pp. Daily life inside and outside the Prague ghetto in 1778 is explored in this novel about an unconventional Jewish girl, 15-year-old Rivka Liebermann. (Rev: BCCB 3/02; BL 4/1/01; HBG 10/01; SLJ 3/01; VOYA 10/01)

10557 Kelly, Eric P. *The Trumpeter of Krakow* (5–9). Illus. by Janina Domanska. 1966, Macmillan $17.95 (978-0-02-750140-7); paper $4.99 (978-0-689-71571-6). 224pp. Mystery surrounds a precious jewel and the youthful patriot who stands watch over it in a church tower in this novel of 15th-century Poland. Newbery Medal winner, 1929.

10558 Kimmel, Elizabeth C. *Before Columbus: The Leif Eriksson Expedition: A True Adventure* (3–6). Series: Landmark Books. 2003, Random $14.95 (978-0-375-81347-4). 112pp. Kimmel extrapolates from the little that is known about Eriksson's life and adventures to create a portrait of a bold Viking explorer. (Rev: BL 7/03; HBG 4/04; SLJ 10/03) [970.01]

10559 Kimmel, Eric A. *Count Silvernose: A Story from Italy* (3–6). Illus. by Omar Rayyan. 1996, Holiday House $15.95 (978-0-8234-1216-7). 30pp. Set in the late Renaissance, this adventure story tells how Assunta sets out to find her sisters, who have been abducted by Count Silvernose. (Rev: BCCB 7–8/96; BL 3/15/96*; HB 7/96; SLJ 3/96)

10560 Kingfisher, Rupert. *Madame Pamplemousse and Her Incredible Edibles* (4–6). Illus. by Sue Hellard. 2008, Bloomsbury $15.99 (978-1-59990-306-4). 144pp. In this foodfest of a novel, a young Parisian girl named Madeleine is sent by her restaurateur Uncle Lard to spy on Madame Pamplemousse and discover her culinary secrets. (Rev: BLO 8/28/08; LMC 1/09)

10561 Knight, Joan MacPhail. *Charlotte in Giverny* (4–6). Illus. 2000, Chronicle $15.95 (978-0-8118-2383-8). 64pp. In this novel set in France in the 1890s a young American girl gets to know many of the American artists who are studying with Monet at Giverny and even meets the reclusive painter himself. (Rev: BL 7/00; HBG 10/00; SLJ 6/00)

10562 Knight, Joan MacPhail. *Charlotte in Paris* (3–6). Illus. by Melissa Sweet. 2003, Chronicle $16.95 (978-0-8118-3766-8). It's 1893, and Charlotte — of *Charlotte in Giverny* (2000) — is now living in Paris and details in her journal all the places she goes and the people she meets. (Rev: HBG 4/04; SLJ 1/04)

10563 Lasky, Kathryn. *Broken Song* (5–8). 2005, Viking $15.99 (978-0-670-05931-7). 160pp. Reuven Bloom, a 15-year-old Jew and promising violinist, escapes from late 19th-century Russia with his baby sister, the only surviving member of his family. (Rev: BL 1/1–15/05; SLJ 3/05)

10564 Lasky, Kathryn. *Dancing Through Fire* (4–7). Series: Portraits. 2005, Scholastic paper $9.99 (978-0-439-71009-1). 160pp. The Franco-Prussian War interrupts the dreams of 13-year-old Sylvie, a student at the Paris Opera Ballet in the 1870s. (Rev: BCCB 1/06; BL 12/1/05; SLJ 11/05)

10565 Lasky, Kathryn. *Marie Antoinette: Princess of Versailles* (5–8). Series: Royal Diaries. 2000, Scholastic paper $10.95 (978-0-439-07666-1). 240pp. This fictional diary covers two years in the life of Marie Antoinette, beginning in 1769 when the 13-year-old was preparing for her fateful marriage. (Rev: BL 4/15/00; HBG 10/00; SLJ 5/00; VOYA 6/00)

10566 Lasky, Kathryn. *Mary, Queen of Scots: Queen Without a Country* (5–8). Illus. Series: Royal Diaries. 2002, Scholastic paper $10.95 (978-0-439-19404-4). 224pp. Part of the Royal Diary series, this is a fictional diary of the year 1553, when Mary was betrothed to the son of King Henry II of France. (Rev: BL 5/15/02; HBG 10/02; SLJ 6/02)

10567 Lawrence, Caroline. *The Charioteer of Delphi* (5–8). Series: Roman Mysteries. 2007, Roaring Brook $16.95 (978-1-59643-085-3). 224pp. Flavia, Jonathan, Nubia, and Lupus find themselves involved in chariot racing in Rome. (Rev: BL 8/07)

10568 Lawrence, Caroline. *Gladiators from Capua* (5–8). Series: Roman Mysteries. 2005, Roaring Brook $16.95 (978-1-59643-074-7). 198pp. In their search for Jonathan, who may be alive after all, Flavia, Lupus, and Nubia venture into the coliseum and witness gladiator fights. (Rev: BL 12/1/05; SLJ 2/06)

10569 Lewis, J. Patrick. *The Stolen Smile* (3–6). Illus. by Gary Kelley. 2004, Creative Editions $17.95 (978-1-56846-192-2). 40pp. Vincenzo Peruggia tells the story, based on real events, of his theft of the Mona Lisa from the Louvre in 1911. (Rev: SLJ 1/05)

10570 Littlesugar, Amy. *Willy and Max: A Holocaust Story* (2–4). Illus. by William Low. 2006, Philomel $15.99 (978-0-399-23483-5). 40pp. When the Nazis invade Belgium, Jewish boy Max and his family must flee, leaving a precious painting with the gentile family of Max's friend Willy; many years later, the painting — which was taken by the Nazis — is returned to Max's son in America; an author's note discusses the wholesale theft of artworks by the Germans. (Rev: BL 1/1–15/06; SLJ 3/06)

10571 McDonough, Yona Zeldis. *The Doll with the Yellow Star* (3–5). Illus. by Kimberly B. Root. 2005, Holt $16.95 (978-0-8050-6337-0). 64pp. Claudine, an 8-year-old Jewish girl living in France during the Nazi occupation, is sent to safety in America. (Rev: BL 9/1/05; SLJ 10/05)

10572 Meyer, Carolyn. *Anastasia: The Last Grand Duchess, Russia, 1914* (4–8). Series: Royal Diaries. 2000, Scholastic paper $10.95 (978-0-439-12908-4). 224pp. Anastasia's fictional diary begins when she is 12 in 1914 and ends with her captivity in 1918. (Rev: HBG 10/01; SLJ 10/00; VOYA 4/01)

10573 Mitchell, Jack. *The Roman Conspiracy* (5–9). 2005, Tundra paper $8.95 (978-0-88776-713-5). 164pp. In this compelling historical thriller set in the Roman Empire, young Aulus Spurinna travels to Rome in a desperate attempt to protect his homeland of Etruria from military pillagers. (Rev: SLJ 11/05)

10574 Morpurgo, Michael. *The Amazing Story of Adolphus Tips* (4–7). 2006, Scholastic $16.99 (978-

0-439-79661-3). 128pp. This is the story of Lily, a 12-year-old British girl who struggles with anger as her father is sent to war in 1943 and her family is relocated to make room for Allied rehearsals of the Normandy invasion. (Rev: BL 4/15/06; SLJ 8/06)

10575 Morpurgo, Michael. *Toro! Toro!* (4–6). Illus. by Michael Foreman. 2004, Collins paper $7.95 (978-0-00-710718-6). 128pp. During the Spanish Civil War, young Antonio bonds with a bull calf born on the family farm but must let it go when the Nationalists attack their village. (Rev: BL 2/15/04; SLJ 5/04)

10576 Morpurgo, Michael. *War Horse* (5–8). 2007, Scholastic $16.99 (978-0-439-79663-7). 176pp. This gripping tale of World War I and all its horrors is told from the point of view of Joey, an English farm horse that's been drafted for service on the battlefront. (Rev: BL 4/1/07)

10577 Morrison, Taylor. *The Neptune Fountain: The Apprenticeship of a Renaissance Sculptor* (3–6). Illus. 1997, Holiday House LB $15.95 (978-0-8234-1293-8). 32pp. The creation of a marble sculpture is described in this novel about an apprentice to a famous sculptor in 17th-century Rome. (Rev: BL 6/1–15/97; SLJ 6/97)

10578 Moss, Marissa. *Galen: My Life in Imperial Rome* (3–6). Illus. 2002, Harcourt $15.00 (978-0-15-216535-2). 48pp. Historically accurate details about life in the house of Roman Emperor Augustus are revealed through the eyes of a fictitious Greek slave in a gripping text accompanied by maps, glossary, and captioned illustrations. (Rev: BL 12/15/02; HBG 3/03; SLJ 10/02)

10579 Napoli, Donna Jo. *Fire in the Hills* (5–8). 2006, Dutton $16.99 (978-0-525-47751-8). 256pp. In this fact-based sequel to *Stones in Water* (1997), 14-year-old Roberto returns to Italy after escaping from a Nazi prison camp and joins the resistance movement. (Rev: BL 9/1/06; SLJ 9/06)

10580 Pausewang, Gudrun. *Dark Hours* (5–8). Trans. from German by John Brownjohn. 2006, Annick $21.95 (978-1-55451-042-9). 208pp. In Germany during the closing days of World War II, Gisela and her younger siblings become trapped in an air raid shelter after being separated from their mother and grandmother. (Rev: BL 11/1/06; SLJ 2/07)

10581 Pernoud, Regine. *A Day with a Miller* (4–7). Trans. by Dominique Clift. Illus. by Giorgio Bacchin. 1997, Runestone LB $22.60 (978-0-8225-1914-0). 48pp. A description of the life of a miller and his family in the 12th century and how hydraulic energy was being introduced at that time. (Rev: HBG 3/98; SLJ 3/98)

10582 Rappaport, Doreen. *The Secret Seder* (2–4). Illus. by Emily Arnold McCully. 2005, Hyperion $16.99 (978-0-7868-0777-2). 40pp. Young Jacques attends a secret seder in Nazi-occupied France. (Rev: BL 1/1–15/05; SLJ 2/05)

10583 Riordan, James. *Escape from War* (4–6). 2005, Kingfisher paper $6.95 (978-0-7534-5794-8). 192pp. Parallel, intersecting stories present an English boy called Frank and a German Jewish refugee called Hannah and their experiences in the English countryside during World War II. (Rev: BL 5/15/05)

10584 Robertson, Bruce. *Marguerite Makes a Book* (3–6). 1999, Getty Museum $19.95 (978-0-89236-372-8). 48pp. A stunning picture book for older readers, set in 15th-century Paris, in which young Marguerite takes over her father's book-painting craft when the old man become too infirm to work. (Rev: BL 11/15/99; HBG 3/00; SLJ 1/00)

10585 Rosen, Sidney, and Dorothy S. Rosen. *The Magician's Apprentice* (5–8). 1994, Carolrhoda LB $19.95 (978-0-87614-809-9). An orphan in a French abbey in the Middle Ages is accused of having a heretical document in his possession and is sent to spy on Roger Bacon, the English scientist. (Rev: BL 5/1/94; SLJ 6/94)

10586 Roy, Jennifer. *Yellow Star* (5–8). 2006, Marshall Cavendish $16.95 (978-0-7614-5277-5). 256pp. The fictionalized story, told in first-person free-verse chapters introduced by historical notes, of the author's aunt Syvia, a Holocaust survivor who spent much of her childhood in the grim Lodz ghetto. (Rev: BL 4/15/06; SLJ 7/06*; VOYA 6/06) ☊

10587 Rubalcaba, Jill. *The Wadjet Eye* (5–8). 2000, Clarion $15.00 (978-0-395-68942-4). 128pp. After mummifying his dead mother, Damon sets off to find his father and is later hired by Cleopatra as a spy in this action-filled novel set in the Roman Empire of 45 B.C. (Rev: BL 5/15/00; HBG 10/00; SLJ 6/00; VOYA 6/00)

10588 Russell, Christopher. *Hunted* (5–8). 2007, HarperCollins $15.99 (978-0-06-084119-5). 254pp. Set in the Middle Ages, this is the exciting tale of two teens who run away after being falsely accused of bringing the Black Death to the manor in which they work. (Rev: SLJ 6/07)

10589 Schwartz, Ellen. *Jesse's Star* (2–5). Illus. 2000, Orca paper $4.99 (978-1-55143-143-7). 108pp. Jesse travels back in time and becomes his great-great-grandfather, a Jewish boy growing up in Russia, reliving his part in helping villagers and himself escape the pogroms and make their way to Canada. (Rev: BL 7/00; SLJ 11/00)

10590 Scott, Elaine. *Secrets of the Cirque Medrano* (5–8). 2008, Charlesbridge $15.95 (978-1-57091-712-7). 216pp. In Montmartre, Paris, in 1904, 14-year-old Brigitte works in her aunt's cafe and meets the young artist Pablo Picasso and the circus performers who posed for his painting *Family of Saltambiques*. (Rev: BL 1/1–15/08; LMC 10/08; SLJ 3/08)

10591 Seredy, Kate. *The Good Master* (4–6). Illus. by author. 1986, Puffin paper $5.99 (978-0-14-030133-5). 196pp. Warm and humorous story of a city girl on her uncle's farm in prewar Hungary.

10592 Skurzynski, Gloria. *The Minstrel in the Tower* (3–4). Illus. by Julek Heller. 1988, Random paper $3.99 (978-0-394-89598-7). 64pp. Alice and Roger search for their uncle after their father has been killed in the Crusades, in this story of life in the Middle Ages. (Rev: BCCB 7–8/88; BL 7/88)

10593 Smith, Roland. *Elephant Run* (5–8). 2007, Hyperion $15.99 (978-1-4231-0402-5). 320pp. During World War II, 14-year-old Nick is sent to his father's plantation in Burma to escape the London Blitz but ends up running from cruel Japanese occupiers in this suspenseful historical novel. (Rev: BL 2/15/08; SLJ 1/08)

10594 Spring, Debbie. *The Righteous Smuggler* (4–6). Series: Holocaust Remembrance. 2006, Second Story paper $5.95 (978-1-896764-97-9). 160pp. Hendrik, the 12-year-old son of a Dutch fisherman, helps his father to smuggle Jews out of the country after Germany invades the Netherlands. (Rev: BL 1/1–15/06; SLJ 4/06)

10595 Stuchner, Joan Betty. *Honey Cake* (3–5). Illus. by Cynthia Nugent. 2008, Random $11.99 (978-0-375-85189-6). 112pp. David, a 10-year-old Jewish boy living in Copenhagen, Denmark, becomes involved in the Resistance during World War II. (Rev: BL 7/08)

10596 Toksvig, Sandi. *Hitler's Canary* (5–8). 2007, Roaring Brook $16.95 (978-1-59643-247-5). 191pp. A Danish family decides to risk everything in order to help Jews escape the Nazis. (Rev: BL 1/1–15/07; SLJ 4/07)

10597 Trottier, Maxine. *The Paint Box* (2–4). Illus. by Stella East. 2003, Fitzhenry & Whiteside $16.95 (978-1-55041-804-0). A compelling fictional story about Marietta, daughter of Tintoretto and talented artist herself, with beautiful illustrations and background information on the era. (Rev: BL 5/15/2003; SLJ 5/03)

10598 Visconti, Guido. *The Genius of Leonardo* (3–6). Trans. by Mark Roberts. Illus. 2000, Barefoot Books $16.99 (978-1-84148-301-6). 40pp. Using many quotes from the writings of Leonardo da Vinci, this novel tries to re-create this great man's in the eyes of his servant, Giacomo. (Rev: BCCB 10/00; BL 9/15/00; HBG 10/01; SLJ 9/00)

10599 Wild, Margaret. *Let the Celebrations Begin!* (3–6). Illus. by Julie Vivas. 1991, Watts LB $16.99 (978-0-531-08537-0). 32pp. A picture book for older children about a group of Polish women in the Belsen death camp who organized a party for the surviving children after liberation. (Rev: BCCB 9/91; BL 8/91; SLJ 7/91)

10600 Williams, Laura E. *The Spider's Web* (5–7). Illus. 1999, Milkweed paper $6.95 (978-1-57131-622-6). 134pp. Lexi, a modern German girl, joins a racist skinhead organization and discovers the consequences of irrational hatred — from her own actions and from speaking with an older woman who was once a member of Hitler's Youth. (Rev: BL 6/1–15/99; HBG 10/99)

10601 Wilson, John. *Flames of the Tiger* (5–8). 2003, Kids Can $16.95 (978-1-55337-618-7). 176pp. The horrors of World War II are seen through the eyes of 17-year-old Dieter, who with his younger sister is fleeing his native Germany as the war nears an end. (Rev: SLJ 1/04; VOYA 6/04) [813]

10602 Winter, Jonah. *The 39 Apartments of Ludwig van Beethoven* (3–5). Illus. by Barry Blitt. 2006, Random $15.95 (978-0-375-83602-2). 40pp. A funny "mockumentary" about Beethoven's constant moving from one apartment to another — along with his five legless pianos — and the putative reasons for these moves. (Rev: BL 8/06; SLJ 10/06)

Great Britain and Ireland

10603 Avi. *Crispin: At the Edge of the World* (5–8). 2006, Hyperion $16.99 (978-0-7868-5152-2). 240pp. In this compelling sequel to *Crispin: The Cross of Lead*, Bear, who Crispin now regards as a father, is seriously wounded and they make friends with a disfigured girl named Troth; Crispin now finds himself making decisions for the three. (Rev: BCCB 1/07; BL 9/15/06*; HB 9/06; HBG 4/07; LMC 1/07; SLJ 10/06*; VOYA 10/06) ∩

10604 Avi. *Crispin: The Cross of Lead* (5–8). 2002, Hyperion paper $6.99 (978-0-7868-1658-3). 320pp. Thirteen-year-old orphan Crispin seeks protection from a juggler named Bear in this complex novel set in medieval England. Newbery Medal. (Rev: BL 5/15/02; HB 9/02; HBG 3/03; SLJ 6/02*)

10605 Barrie, J. M. *Peter Pan* (5–8). Illus. 1995, NAL paper $4.95 (978-0-451-52088-3). The classic tale of the boy who wouldn't grow up and of his adventures with the Darling children. (Rev: BL 12/15/87)

10606 Blackwood, Gary L. *Shakespeare Stealer* (5–8). 1998, NAL $16.99 (978-0-525-45863-0). A 14-year-old apprentice at the Globe Theater is sent by a rival theater company to steal Shakespeare's plays. (Rev: BL 6/1–15/98; HB 7/98; HBG 10/98; SLJ 6/98; VOYA 8/98)

10607 Blackwood, Gary L. *Shakespeare's Spy* (5–8). 2003, Dutton $16.99 (978-0-525-47145-5). 280pp. Romance and intrigue are at hand as Widge continues his career at the Globe Theatre in this sequel to *The Shakespeare Stealer* (1998) and *Shakespeare's Scribe* (2000). (Rev: BL 9/1/03; HB 11/03; HBG 4/04; SLJ 10/03)

10608 Bowler, Tim. *Playing Dead* (5–8). 2009, Philomel $16.99 (978-0-399-25186-3). 240pp. Full of British slang and violence, this speedily paced thriller features 14-year-old Blade, a street kid with an instinct for survival amid a culture of gangs. (Rev: BL 5/1/09; HB 5/09; LMC 10/09; VOYA 6/09)

10609 Bunting, Eve. *Walking to School* (2–4). Illus. by Michael Dooling. 2008, Clarion $16.00 (978-0-618-26144-4). 32pp. A Catholic girl passing through a Protestant neighborhood in Northern Ireland experiences both heckling and an enriching moment with a Protestant girl; an author's note provides context. (Rev: BL 9/1/08; SLJ 9/08)

10610 Carroll, Lewis. *Alice's Adventures in Wonderland* (5–12). Illus. by Iassen Ghiuselev. 2003, Simply Read $29.95 (978-1-894965-00-2). 136pp. Interesting illustrations by Ghiuselev that interpret incidents and characters in a different way highlight this new edition of an old classic. (Rev: BL 2/1/04; SLJ 6/04)

10611 Chaucer, Geoffrey. *Canterbury Tales* (4–8). Adapted by Barbara Cohen. Illus. by Trina S. Hyman. 1988, Lothrop $26.99 (978-0-688-06201-9). 96pp. Several of the popular stories are retold with handsome illustrations by Trina Schart Hyman. (Rev: BL 9/1/88; SLJ 8/88)

10612 Chaucer, Geoffrey. *The Canterbury Tales* (5–9). Adapted by Geraldine McCaughrean. Illus. 1985, Checkerboard $14.95 (978-1-56288-259-4). An adaptation for young readers of 13 tales that still keep the flavor and spirit of the originals. (Rev: SLJ 2/86) [826]

10613 Cooper, Susan. *Victory* (4–7). 2006, Simon & Schuster $16.95 (978-1-4169-1477-8). 208pp. Homesick Molly finds her fate is intertwined with that of Sam, a child sailor of the 19th century who fought in the Battle of Trafalgar; chapters alternate between the present and the past. (Rev: BL 5/1/06; LMC 11/06; SLJ 7/06)

10614 Cottrell Boyce, Frank. *Framed* (4–7). 2006, HarperCollins $16.99 (978-0-06-073402-2). 320pp. Life changes dramatically for 9-year-old Dylan Hughes and his quiet Welsh village when priceless art from London's National Gallery is temporarily stored in a nearby quarry. (Rev: BL 9/1/06; SLJ 8/06*) ∩

10615 Cushman, Karen. *Matilda Bone* (4–8). 2000, Clarion $15.00 (978-0-395-88156-9). 176pp. Set in the 14th century, this novel describes the development of Matilda, 13, who serves as an assistant to the local bone setter in exchange for food and shelter. (Rev: BCCB 12/00; BL 8/00; HB 11/00; HBG 3/01; SLJ 9/00*; VOYA 12/00)

10616 De Angeli, Marguerite. *The Door in the Wall* (5–7). Illus. by author. 1990, Dell paper $5.50 (978-0-440-40283-1). Crippled Robin proves his courage in plague-ridden 19th-century London. Newbery Medal winner, 1950.

10617 Dhami, Narinder. *Bhangra Babes* (5–8). Series: Babes. 2006, Delacorte $14.95 (978-0-385-73318-2). 192pp. Their troublesome auntie's marriage plans go awry in this funny, engaging final volume of the trilogy about the Bindi sisters who are adapting their Indian heritage to life in England. (Rev: BL 4/15/06; SLJ 6/06)

10618 Doherty, Berlie. *Street Child* (5–7). 1994, Orchard LB $18.99 (978-0-531-08714-5). 160pp. The story of a street urchin in Victorian London who is forced to work on a river barge until he escapes. (Rev: BCCB 11/94; BL 9/1/94; SLJ 10/94)

10619 Dowswell, Paul. *Powder Monkey: Adventures of a Young Sailor* (5–9). 2005, Bloomsbury $16.95 (978-1-58234-675-5). 276pp. In this stirring historical novel set in the opening years of the 19th century, 13-year-old Sam Witchall begins his career at sea as a "powder monkey," assisting the gun crews on a warship. (Rev: SLJ 11/05; VOYA 10/05)

10620 Duey, Kathleen. *Lara and the Gray Mare* (4–6). Series: Hoofbeats. 2005, Dutton paper $4.99 (978-0-14-240230-6). 128pp. In medieval Ireland, 9-year-old Lara cares for her beloved gray mare as the animal suffers through a difficult pregnancy. (Rev: BL 2/1/05)

10621 Finney, Patricia. *Feud* (4–7). Series: Lady Grace Mysteries. 2006, Delacorte $7.95 (978-0-385-73323-6); paper $9.99 (978-0-385-90342-4). 208pp. Lady Grace, maid of honor to Queen Elizabeth I, attempts to unravel the mystery surrounding the poisoning of another maid of honor. (Rev: BL 10/15/06)

10622 Flegg, Aubrey. *Katie's War* (5–8). 2000, O'Brien paper $7.95 (978-0-86278-525-3). 192pp. Set during Ireland's fight for independence from England, this story shows a girl torn between two sides when her father wants peace and her brother is preparing to use force. (Rev: BL 12/1/00)

10623 Geary, Rick. *Great Expectations*. Rev. ed. (4–7). Illus. by author. Series: Classics Illustrated. 2008, Papercutz $9.95 (978-1-59707-097-3). 56pp. The Dickens classic is retold in graphic novel format with illustrations that highlight the key parts of the story. (Rev: BL 3/15/08)

10624 Graber, Janet. *The White Witch* (5–8). 2009, Roaring Brook $16.95 (978-1-59643-337-3). 160pp. Set in 17th-century England, and with period prose that some may find challenging, this is a suspenseful story about 14-year-old Gwendoline's trials when the Great Plague breaks out. (Rev: BL 4/15/09; LMC 10/09; SLJ 7/09; VOYA 6/09)

10625 Grant, K. M. *Green Jasper* (5–9). Series: The de Granville Trilogy. 2006, Walker $16.95 (978-0-8027-8073-7). 249pp. Will and Gavin, introduced in *Blood Red Horse* (2005), come home from the crusade to find England in chaos and Gavin's beloved Ellie abducted by Constable de Scabious; a multilayered medieval adventure story. (Rev: SLJ 6/06; VOYA 8/06)

10626 Graves, Robert. *An Ancient Castle* (4–6). Illus. by Elizabeth Graves. 1991, Michael Kesend paper $10.95 (978-0-935576-33-7). 72pp. A novel of heroes, villains, and buried treasures set in pre–World War I Britain.

10627 Griffin, Margot. *Dancing for Danger: A Meggy Tale* (4–6). Illus. 2001, Stoddart $6.95 (978-0-7737-6136-0). 112pp. Meggy shows real bravery when her forbidden "hedge school" is under threat in 19th-century Ireland. (Rev: BL 6/1–15/01; SLJ 2/02)

10628 Harrison, Cora. *The Famine Secret* (5–7). Illus. by Orla Roche. Series: Drumshee Timeline. 1998, Irish American paper $6.95 (978-0-86327-649-1). 128pp. In 1847 the four McMahon children are orphaned and sent to an Irish workhouse, but their determination prevails and they are soon plotting to regain their home. (Rev: SLJ 12/98)

10629 Harrison, Cora. *The Secret of Drumshee Castle* (5–7). Illus. by Orla Roche. Series: Drumshee Timeline. 1998, Irish American paper $6.95 (978-0-86327-632-3). 128pp. Grace Barry, the orphaned heiress to a castle in Ireland during Elizabethan times, flees to England to escape threats by her acquisitive guardians. (Rev: SLJ 12/98)

10630 Harrison, Cora. *The Secret of the Seven Crosses* (4–7). Illus. 1998, Wolfhound paper $6.95 (978-0-86327-616-3). 128pp. In medieval Ireland, three youngsters hope to find hidden treasure by examining sources in their monastery library. Preceded by *Nauala and Her Secret Wolf* and followed by *The Secret of Drumshee Castle*. (Rev: BL 12/15/98)

10631 Heneghan, James. *Safe House* (5–8). 2006, Orca paper $7.95 (978-1-55143-640-1). 160pp.

Twelve-year-old Liam Fogarty is forced to go on the run after he sees the face of one of the gunmen who killed his mother and father in their Belfast home. (Rev: BL 11/1/06; SLJ 1/07)

10632 Hinton, Nigel. *Time Bomb* (5–8). 2006, Tricycle $15.95 (978-1-58246-186-1). 284pp. Coming of age in post-World War II London, four 12-year-old friends who have lost their trust in adults discover an unexploded German bomb and set in motion a chain of events. (Rev: SLJ 12/06)

10633 Holmes, Victoria. *The Horse from the Sea* (5–8). 2005, HarperCollins LB $16.89 (978-0-06-052029-8). 320pp. In 1588, Nora, an Irish girl, defies the English and helps a young Spanish sailor and a beautiful stallion, survivors of a shipwreck. (Rev: BL 5/15/05; SLJ 8/05)

10634 Hooper, Mary. *At the Sign of the Sugared Plum* (5–8). 2003, Bloomsbury $16.95 (978-1-58234-849-0). 167pp. The horrors of the bubonic plague and the squalor of 17th-century London are brought to life in this story of Hannah and her sister Sarah, owner of a sweetmeats shop. (Rev: BL 9/15/03; HBG 4/04; SLJ 8/03; VOYA 10/03)

10635 Kirwan, Anna. *Victoria: May Blossom of Britannia* (5–8). Series: Royal Diaries. 2001, Scholastic paper $10.95 (978-0-439-21598-5). 224pp. Young Victoria's fictional diary describes her overregimented life at the ages of 10 and 11; background material adds some historical context to this account of the girl who grew up to rule England. (Rev: BL 12/1/01; HBG 10/02; SLJ 1/02; VOYA 2/02)

10636 Knight, Joan MacPhail. *Charlotte in London* (2–5). Illus. by Melissa Sweet. 2008, Chronicle $16.99 (978-0-8118-5635-5). 52pp. Charlotte is in London in this installment in the series that began with *Charlotte in Giverny* (2000) and with her friend Lizzy visits many landmarks and meets interesting artists and writers, all recorded in her diary. (Rev: BL 3/15/09; SLJ 3/09)

10637 Lasky, Kathryn. *Elizabeth I: Red Rose of the House of Tudor* (4–7). Series: Royal Diaries. 1999, Scholastic paper $10.95 (978-0-590-68484-2). 192pp. Told in diary form, this is a fictionalized account of Elizabeth I's childhood after her mother was killed and she lived with her father, Henry VIII, and Catherine Parr. (Rev: BCCB 12/99; BL 9/15/99; HBG 3/00; SLJ 10/99)

10638 Lawrence, Iain. *The Smugglers* (5–8). 1999, Delacorte $15.95 (978-0-385-32663-6). 178pp. In this continuation of *The Wreckers*, 16-year-old John Spencer faces more adventures aboard the *Dragon*, where he faces powerful enemies and must bring the ship safely to port. (Rev: BCCB 7–8/99; BL 4/1/99*; HB 5/99; HBG 10/99; SLJ 6/99)

10639 Lawrence, Iain. *The Wreckers* (5–8). 1998, Bantam paper $5.50 (978-0-440-41545-9). In this historical novel, young John Spencer narrowly escapes with his life after the ship on which he is traveling is wrecked off the Cornish coast, lured to its destruction by a gang seeking to plunder its cargo. (Rev: BCCB 6/98; BL 6/1–15/98; HB 7/98*; HBG 10/98; SLJ 6/98; VOYA 2/99)

10640 Love, D. Anne. *The Puppeteer's Apprentice* (3–6). 2003, Simon & Schuster $16.95 (978-0-689-84424-9). 192pp. In medieval England, an orphan girl called Mouse runs away to become a puppeteer's apprentice. (Rev: BL 3/15/03; HBG 10/03; SLJ 5/03)

10641 MacDonald, George. *Sir Gibbie* (4–6). 1987, Sunrise $35.00 (978-0-940652-55-2). The story of a Scottish waif and the triumph of love over hardship.

10642 McKenzie, Nancy. *Guinevere's Gift* (5–8). 2008, Knopf $15.99 (978-0-375-84345-7). 256pp. As a young orphan, the plucky Guinevere lives with her aunt, Queen Alyse, and involves herself in castle intrigue, coming to realize that her destiny may be closer to prophecy than she thought. (Rev: BL 6/1–15/08; SLJ 4/08)

10643 Mayer, Marianna. *Sir Walter Scott's Ivanhoe* (4–6). Illus. by John Rush. 2004, Chronicle $17.95 (978-1-58717-248-9). 56pp. An attractive, large-format adaptation of the classic romantic adventure, with rich illustrations. (Rev: BL 2/1/05; SLJ 1/05)

10644 Merrill, Linda, and Sarah Ridley. *The Princess and the Peacocks: Or, The Story of the Room* (4–6). Illus. by Tennessee Dixon. 1993, Hyperion LB $15.49 (978-1-56282-328-3). 32pp. For older readers, this fictionalized account tells how the painter Whistler decorated his famous Peacock Room. (Rev: BL 6/1–15/93; SLJ 8/93)

10645 Morris, Gerald. *The Adventures of Sir Givret the Short* (3–5). Illus. by Aaron Renier. Series: Knights' Tales. 2008, Houghton $15.00 (978-0-618-77715-0). 112pp. This entertaining medieval tale follows Sir Givret who is short on height but long on wily ways as he helps a brother knight rescue his fair maiden. (Rev: BL 2/1/09; SLJ 1/09)

10646 Morris, Gerald. *The Ballad of Sir Dinadan* (5–9). 2003, Houghton $16.00 (978-0-618-19099-7). 256pp. An amusing retelling from Arthurian legend that features the younger brother of Sir Tristram as a music lover and reluctant knight. (Rev: BL 5/1/03; HB 5/03; HBG 10/03; SLJ 4/03*; VOYA 6/03)

10647 Morris, Gerald. *The Quest of the Fair Unknown* (5–8). 2006, Houghton $16.00 (978-0-618-63152-0). 272pp. To fulfill the deathbed plea of his mother, Beaufils sets off to find his long-absent father, a knight in the court of King Arthur. (Rev: BL 10/15/06; SLJ 11/06)

10648 Morris, Gerald. *The Squire, His Knight, and His Lady* (5–9). 1999, Houghton $16.00 (978-0-395-91211-9). 240pp. This is a retelling, from the perspective of a knight's squire, of the classic story of Sir Gawain and the Green Knight. (Rev: BL 5/1/99; HBG 10/99; SLJ 5/99; VOYA 8/99)

10649 Morris, Gerald. *The Squire's Tale* (5–9). 1998, Houghton $16.00 (978-0-395-86959-8). The peaceful existence of 14-year-old Terence is shattered when he becomes the squire of Sir Gawain and becomes involved in a series of quests. (Rev: BL 4/15/98; HB 7/98; SLJ 7/98; VOYA 8/98)

10650 Newbery, Linda. *At the Firefly Gate* (5–8). 2007, Random $15.99 (978-0-385-75113-1). 160pp. Henry befriends a neighbor who was once engaged to another Henry, a Royal Air Force pilot who failed to return from a mission in World War II. When Henry begins to see a mysterious figure at his gate and reenacts the pilot's final flight on a simulator, the war seems not so long ago. (Rev: BCCB 4/07; BL 2/15/07; HB 3/07; SLJ 3/07)

10651 O'Brien, Patrick. *The Making of a Knight: How Sir James Earned His Armor* (3–6). Illus. 1998, Charlesbridge $15.95 (978-0-88106-354-7); paper $6.95 (978-0-88106-355-4). 32pp. This novel traces the studies, training, and experiences of young James and his journey from page to squire and finally to knight in medieval England. (Rev: BL 8/98; HBG 3/99; SLJ 9/98)

10652 Osborne, Mary Pope. *Kate and the Beanstalk* (PS–3). Illus. by Giselle Potter. 2000, Atheneum $16.00 (978-0-689-82550-7). 40pp. Kate, the daughter of a knight killed by the giant, is the heroine of this delightful version of Jack and the Beanstalk. (Rev: BCCB 1/01; BL 11/15/00*; HBG 3/01; SLJ 10/00) [398.2]

10653 Parker, Marjorie Hodgson. *David and the Mighty Eighth* (4–7). Illus. by Mark Postlethwaite. 2007, Bright Sky $17.95 (978-1-931721-93-6). 176pp. David is sent to stay on his grandparents' farm in rural England and there befriends an American soldier stationed with the U.S. Eighth Air Force in this novel set in 1944. (Rev: BL 12/15/07)

10654 Priestley, Chris. *The White Rider* (5–8). 2005, Corgi paper $8.99 (978-0-440-86608-4). 192pp. In this riveting sequel to *Death and the Arrow*, 16-year-old Tom Marlowe is swept up in a series of intrigues in early 18th-century London. (Rev: BL 10/15/05)

10655 Rogers, Gregory. *The Boy, the Bear, the Baron, the Bard* (K–2). Illus. by author. 2004, Roaring Brook $15.95 (978-1-59643-009-9). 32pp. A young boy finds himself transported to Elizabethan England and has many adventures, including encounters with Shakespeare and the Queen, in this wordless picture book. (Rev: BL 10/1/04; LMC 3/05; SLJ 12/04*)

10656 Schmidt, Gary D. *Anson's Way* (5–9). 1999, Houghton $16.00 (978-0-395-91529-5). During the reign of George II, Anson begins his proud career in the British army as part of the forces occupying Ireland, then becomes disillusioned as he develops a growing respect and concern for the Irish. (Rev: BL 4/1/99*; HBG 10/99; SLJ 4/99; VOYA 8/99)

10657 Snicket, Lemony. *The Austere Academy* (4–6). Illus. Series: Unfortunate Events. 2000, HarperCollins LB $14.89 (978-0-06-028884-6). 240pp. The Baudelaire orphans endure horrible hardships when they enroll as students at Prufrock Academy, where their only friends — the Quagmire orphans — are kidnapped by wicked Count Olaf. (Rev: BL 10/15/00)

10658 Thomas, Jane Resh. *The Counterfeit Princess* (5–8). 2005, Clarion $15.00 (978-0-395-93870-6). 198pp. Iris, a young English girl with an uncanny resemblance to Princess Elizabeth (soon to be Elizabeth I), finds herself embroiled in intrigue in this novel set in the 16th century. (Rev: BL 11/15/05; SLJ 10/05)

10659 Toews, Marj. *Black-and-White Blanche* (1–3). Illus. by Dianna Bonder. 2006, Fitzhenry & Whiteside $16.95 (978-1-55005-132-2). The Witherspoons, a Victorian family that rigidly adheres to the social ban on colored clothing, are forced to relax their standards when the family's youngest member insists on wearing pink. (Rev: SLJ 8/06)

10660 Vogiel, Eva. *Friend or Foe?* (5–8). 2001, Judaica $19.95 (978-1-880582-66-4). 269pp. In this novel set in London during 1948, the girls of the Migdal Binoh School for Orthodox Jewish girls notice strange happenings when the Campbell family moves next door. (Rev: BL 4/1/01)

10661 Wiley, Melissa. *Beyond the Heather Hills* (3–5). Illus. by Renee Graef. Series: Martha Years. 2003, HarperCollins paper $6.99 (978-0-06-440715-1). 208pp. Set in 18th-century Scotland, this fourth volume continues the series on Laura Ingalls Wilder's great-grandmother. Here, she leaves home at age 10 to live with her married older sister. (Rev: BL 5/15/03; HBG 10/03)

10662 Williams, Marcia. *Archie's War* (3–6). Illus. by author. 2007, Candlewick $17.99 (978-0-7636-3532-9). 48pp. World War I comes to dramatic life in a British boy's scrapbook of cartoon drawings, news items, letters, and so forth spanning the years from 1914 to the end of the war. (Rev: BCCB 2/08; LMC 5/08*; SLJ 3/08; VOYA 2/08)

10663 Williams, Marcia. *Chaucer's Canterbury Tales* (4–8). Illus. 2007, Candlewick $16.99 (978-0-7636-3197-0). 45pp. The exploits of Chaucer's pilgrims are recounted in age-appropriate double-page spreads that are alive with action and humor; the illustrations help to define the more difficult words. (Rev: BL 2/15/07; HB 3/07; LMC 8/07; SLJ 3/07*)

10664 Woodruff, Elvira. *Fearless* (5–8). 2008, Scholastic $16.99 (978-0-439-67703-5). 208pp. Young brothers Digory and Cubby are befriended by Henry Winstanley, the builder of a unusual lighthouse on the Cornish coast, in this intriguing and action-packed story, set in 1703, about bravery and sacrifice. (Rev: BL 5/1/08; LMC 5/08; SLJ 4/08)

10665 Woodruff, Elvira. *The Ravenmaster's Secret* (4–7). 2003, Scholastic $15.95 (978-0-439-28133-1). 225pp. Eleven-year-old Forrest becomes embroiled in dangerous intrigue in this story set inside the Tower of London in the early 18th century, with a glossary and historical notes appended. (Rev: BL 1/1–15/04; SLJ 1/04; VOYA 4/04)

10666 Zucker, Jonny. *The Bombed House* (5–8). Illus. by Paul Savage. Series: Keystone Books. 2006, Stone Arch LB $21.26 (978-1-59889-092-1). 33pp. This fast-paced story, which will attract reluctant readers, features brothers Ned and Harry Jennings, who find a German soldier hiding in London during World War II. (Rev: SLJ 1/07)

Latin America and Caribbean

10667 Cohn, Diana. *Dream Carver* (3–6). Illus. by Amy Córdova. 2002, Chronicle $15.95 (978-0-8118-1244-3). 32pp. A simple story based on the career of the artist Manuel Jimenez, about a young sculptor who carves small wooden animals but dreams of creating big, colorful animals. (Rev: BCCB 10/02; BL 6/1–15/02; HBG 10/02; SLJ 7/02)

10668 Ellis, Deborah. *Sacred Leaf: The Cocalero Novels* (5–8). Series: The Cocalera Novels. 2007, Groundwood $16.95 (978-0-88899-751-7). 208pp. Twelve-year-old Diego is living with a family of poor Bolivian coca farmers when their crop is destroyed by soldiers and they join a national protest. (Rev: BL 1/1–15/08; SLJ 12/07)

10669 Lattimore, Deborah N. *The Flame of Peace: A Tale of the Aztecs* (4–6). Illus. 1987, HarperCollins paper $7.95 (978-0-06-443272-6). 48pp. Details about Aztec life are compiled in this folklorelike story. (Rev: BL 11/15/87; SLJ 11/87)

10670 Mordecai, Martin. *Blue Mountain Trouble* (5–8). 2009, Scholastic $16.99 (978-0-545-04156-0). 336pp. A strange goat appears to 11-year-old twins Pollyread and Jackson, who live high in the Blue Mountains of Jamaica, and coincidentally there is a series of strange events. (Rev: BL 4/15/09; HB 5/09; SLJ 7/09)

10671 Ramírez, Antonio. *Napí* (PS–2). Illus. by Domi. 2004, Groundwood $15.95 (978-0-88899-610-7). 32pp. This is a very visual portrayal of the importance of nature and colors in the life and dreams of a young Indian girl living in a Mexican village. (Rev: BL 11/15/04; SLJ 9/04)

10672 Ramírez, Antonio. *Napí Goes to the Mountain* (1–3). Trans. from Spanish by Elisa Amado. Illus. by Domi. 2006, Groundwood $18.95 (978-0-88899-713-5). A young Mexican girl and her younger brother go upriver into the jungle in search of their father, and during the course of their search are transformed into deer and meet a series of folkloric creatures; a sequel to *Napí* (2004). (Rev: SLJ 2/07)

10673 Rohmer, Harriet. *Uncle Nacho's Hat* (3–6). Illus. by Mira Reisberg. 1993, Children's Book Pr. $15.95 (978-0-89239-043-4); paper $7.95 (978-0-89239-112-7). 32pp. This bilingual book tells a Nicaraguan tale about how hard it is to break habits. A reissue.

10674 Skarmeta, Antonio. *The Composition* (3–5). Trans. by Elisa Amado. Illus. 2000, Douglas & McIntyre $14.95 (978-0-88899-390-8). 32pp. Set in a police state in Latin America, this picture book tells of a young boy who is under pressure from the police to betray his parents. (Rev: BL 5/1/00; HB 9/00; HBG 10/00; SLJ 8/00)

10675 Stanley, Diane. *Elena* (3–5). Illus. 1996, Hyperion LB $14.49 (978-0-7868-2211-9). 56pp. A daughter recalls the life of her Mexican mother, who defied authority and took her family on a dangerous journey to the United States. (Rev: BCCB 3/96; BL 4/1/96; SLJ 6/96)

10676 Yolen, Jane. *Encounter* (2–5). Illus. by David Shannon. 1992, Harcourt $16.00 (978-0-15-225962-4). 32pp. From the viewpoint of a Taino Indian boy, this picture book tells of the first meeting between Native Americans and Columbus. (Rev: BCCB 5/92; BL 3/1/92; SLJ 5/92)

United States

NATIVE AMERICANS

10677 Armstrong, Nancy M. *Navajo Long Walk* (4–7). Illus. 1994, Roberts Rinehart $8.95 (978-1-879373-56-3). 120pp. The story of the Long Walk of the Navajo in 1864 and their confinement in an internment camp are vividly told. (Rev: BL 10/1/94; SLJ 1/95)

10678 Bird, E. J. *The Rainmakers* (4–6). Illus. 1993, Carolrhoda LB $15.95 (978-0-87614-748-1). 120pp. This novel about a young Indian boy and his pet bear is centered around the life of the Anasazi Indians, who disappeared from the Southwest around A.D. 1300. (Rev: BL 6/1–15/93)

10679 Browne, Vee. *The Stone Cutter and the Navajo Maiden: Tsé Yitsidí dóó Ch'ikééh Bitsédaashjéé'* (K–3). Trans. from Navajo by Lorraine Begay Manavi. Illus. by Johnson Yazzie. 2008, Salina Bookshelf $17.95 (978-1-893354-92-0). This tale of a motherless girl's quest to find someone who can repair her grinding stone is presented in both English and Navajo. (Rev: SLJ 9/08)

10680 Bruchac, Joseph. *A Boy Called Slow: The True Story of Sitting Bull* (5–8). Illus. by Rocco Baviera. 1995, Putnam $17.99 (978-0-399-22692-2). 32pp. The story of the boyhood of Sitting Bull, who, because of his sluggishness, had been called Slow. (Rev: BCCB 4/95; BL 3/15/95; HB 9/95; SLJ 10/95)

10681 Bruchac, Joseph. *Crazy Horse's Vision* (2–4). Illus. by S. D. Nelson. 2000, Lee & Low $16.95 (978-1-880000-94-6). 40pp. This is the story of how a young Native American boy, nicknamed Curly, gained the name Crazy Horse and became a leader of the Lakota. (Rev: BCCB 9/00; BL 5/15/00; HB 7/00; HBG 10/00; SLJ 7/00)

10682 Bruchac, Joseph. *The Journal of Jesse Smoke: The Trail of Tears, 1838* (5–8). Illus. Series: My Name Is America. 2001, Scholastic paper $10.95 (978-0-439-12197-2). 206pp. Jesse, a 16-year-old Cherokee, chronicles in his diary the tribe's forced journey to Oklahoma and tries to understand the reasons behind this cruel action. (Rev: BL 7/01; HBG 10/01; SLJ 7/01; VOYA 8/01)

10683 Bruchac, Marge. *Malian's Song* (2–4). Illus. by William Maughan. 2006, Vermont Folklife Center $16.95 (978-0-916718-26-8). 32pp. Malian, a young Abenaki girl, tells how she fled to safety while her father died defending the family's home in 1759; the story of this British raid was passed from generation to generation. This text includes Abenaki words as well as details of Abenaki life. (Rev: BL 8/06; SLJ 1/07)

10684 Bunting, Eve. *Cheyenne Again* (3–5). Illus. by Irving Toddy. 1995, Clarion $16.00 (978-0-395-70364-9). 32pp. In the 1880s, a young Cheyenne boy is taken from the reservation and sent to a white boarding school. (Rev: BCCB 9/95; BL 8/95; SLJ 12/95)

10685 Burks, Brian. *Runs with Horses* (5–9). 1995, Harcourt paper $6.00 (978-0-15-200994-6). An adventure story set in 1886 in which 16-year-old Runs with Horses completes his Apache warrior training by performing feats of endurance, survival, and daring, and partly as a result of information he gathers during raids, his tribe realizes that they can no longer continue to resist the white man. (Rev: BL 11/1/95; SLJ 11/95; VOYA 2/96)

10686 Campbell, Nicola I. *Shin-chi's Canoe* (3–5). Illus. by Kim LaFave. 2008, Groundwood $18.95 (978-0-88899-857-6). 40pp. A Native American brother and sister are forced into a church boarding school and forbidden to speak to each other. (Rev: BLO 12/30/08; SLJ 3/09)

10687 Cooper, James Fenimore. *Last of the Mohicans* (3–5). Adapted by Les Martin. Illus. by Shannon Stirnweis. Series: Step-Up Classics. 1993, Random paper $3.99 (978-0-679-84706-9). 96pp. A simplified version of the Cooper classic that illuminates details and abridges the plot for young readers. (Rev: SLJ 10/93)

10688 Driving Hawk Sneve, Virginia. *Lana's Lakota Moons* (5–8). 2008, Univ. of Nebraska paper $12.95 (978-0-8032-6028-3). 112pp. Lori and Lana, Lakotas whose lives are a combination of Native American tradition and modern American culture, have disturbing premonitions about the future that sadly come true in this thoughtful, moving story. (Rev: BL 5/1/08)

10689 Erdrich, Louise. *The Game of Silence* (5–8). 2005, HarperCollins LB $16.89 (978-0-06-029790-9). 272pp. As 9-year-old Omakayas is coming of age, the intrusion of the European settlers increasingly impacts the Ojibwe lifestyle in this sequel to *The Birchbark House* (1999). (Rev: BL 5/15/05*; SLJ 7/05)

10690 Erdrich, Louise. *The Porcupine Year* (4–7). Illus. by author. 2008, HarperCollins $15.99 (978-0-06-029787-9). 208pp. In this sequel to *The Birchbark House* (1999) and *The Game of Silence* (2005), Omakayas is now 12 and the family is traveling north, looking for a new home far from the intruding white settlers. (Rev: BL 6/1–15/08; SLJ 9/08)

10691 Grutman, Jewel, and Gay Matthaei. *The Ledgerbook of Thomas Blue Eagle* (4–8). Illus. by Adam Cvijanovic. 1994, Thomasson-Grant $17.95 (978-1-56566-063-2). 72pp. A young Native American boy attends a white man's school but tries to retain his own identity and culture in this story that takes place in the West 100 years ago. (Rev: SLJ 12/94)

10692 Hudson, Jan. *Sweetgrass* (5–8). 1989, Scholastic paper $3.99 (978-0-590-43486-7). 160pp. A description of the culture of the Dakota Indians in the 1830s. (Rev: BCCB 4/89; BL 4/1/89; SLJ 4/89)

10693 Hunter, Sara H. *The Unbreakable Code* (2–4). Illus. by Julia Miner. 1996, Northland LB $15.95 (978-0-87358-638-2). A Navajo man reassures his grandson that he will adjust successfully to a move off the reservation with his mother and new stepfather. (Rev: SLJ 8/96)

10694 Kittredge, Frances. *Neeluk: An Eskimo Boy in the Days of the Whaling Ships* (3–5). Illus. by Howard Rock. 2001, Alaska Northwest paper

$18.95 (978-0-88240-545-2). 88pp. Illustrations by an Inupiat artist combine with simple stories to present the Inupiat way of life in the late 1800s. (Rev: BL 8/01; HBG 3/02; SLJ 1/02)

10695 Lunge-Larsen, Lise, and Margi Preus. *The Legend of the Lady Slipper: An Ojibwe Tale* (PS–3). Illus. by Andrea Arroyo. 1999, Houghton $15.00 (978-0-395-90512-8). 32pp. An Ojibwa tale about how a young girl's moccasins are turned into the plant known as lady slippers, as a reward for her saving her village from a plague. (Rev: BCCB 7–8/99; BL 4/15/99; HBG 10/99; SLJ 5/99) [398.2]

10696 Maher, Ramona. *Alice Yazzie's Year* (3–6). Illus. by Shonto Begay. 2004, Tricycle $15.95 (978-1-58246-080-2). 40pp. Reissued with new illustrations, this picture book written in verse chronicles a year in the life of an 11-year-old Navajo girl. (Rev: BL 8/03; HBG 4/04; SLJ 11/03)

10697 Marchand, Peter. *What Good Is a Cactus?* (3–5). Illus. by Craig Brown. 1994, Roberts Rinehart paper $7.95 (978-1-879373-83-9). Through talking to a wise Native American and observing nature, a scientist realizes the importance of all living things and the role each plays. (Rev: SLJ 11/94)

10698 Matthaei, Gay, and Jewel Grutman. *The Sketchbook of Thomas Blue Eagle* (4–7). Illus. 2001, Chronicle $16.95 (978-0-88182-908-2). 64pp. Through drawings and narration, the Lakota artist Thomas Blue Eagle tells how he joined Buffalo Bill's show, traveled to Europe, and made enough money to marry. (Rev: BCCB 5/01; BL 4/1/01)

10699 Messinger, Carla. *When the Shadbush Blooms* (K–5). Illus. by David Kanietakeron Fadden. 2007, Tricycle $15.95 (978-1-58246-192-2). Traditional Sister and Contemporary Sister describe their Lenni Lenape family traditions in this effective book with endnotes and a pronunciation guide. (Rev: SLJ 11/07)

10700 O'Dell, Scott, and Elizabeth Hall. *Thunder Rolling in the Mountains* (5–9). 1992, Dell paper $5.50 (978-0-440-40879-6). From the viewpoint of Chief Joseph's daughter, this historical novel concerns the forced removal of the Nez Perce from their homeland in 1877. (Rev: BL 6/15/92*; SLJ 8/92)

10701 Osborne, Mary Pope. *Standing in the Light: The Captive Diary of Catharine Carey Logan* (3–6). Illus. Series: Dear America. 1998, Scholastic $10.95 (978-0-590-13462-0). 192pp. After 13-year-old Caty and her younger brother are captured by Lenape Indians in rural Pennsylvania in 1763, they gradually learn to appreciate the values in this foreign culture. (Rev: BL 10/15/98; HBG 3/99; SLJ 1/99)

10702 Raczek, Linda. *Rainy's Powwow* (3–5). Illus. by Gary Bennett. 1999, Northland $15.95 (978-0-87358-686-3). 32pp. Lorraine is seeking to develop her own special dance at the powwow, when an eagle feather changes her hopes. (Rev: BL 4/1/99; HBG 10/99; SLJ 6/99)

10703 Roop, Peter. *The Buffalo Jump* (2–4). Illus. by Bill Farnsworth. 1996, Northland LB $14.95 (978-0-87358-616-0). Little Blaze, a Native American boy, saves his older brother's life during a buffalo hunt. (Rev: SLJ 2/97)

10704 Schwartz, Virginia Frances. *Initiation* (5–8). Illus. 2003, Fitzhenry & Whiteside $15.95 (978-1-55005-053-0). 268pp. Kwakiuti Indian twins Nana and Nanolatch prepare to face the responsibilities of adulthood in this story set on the West Coast of North America in the 15th century. (Rev: SLJ 3/04) [813]

10705 Shaw, Janet. *Meet Kaya: An American Girl* (3–5). Illus. by Bill Farnsworth. 2002, Pleasant $12.95 (978-1-58485-424-1); paper $6.95 (978-1-58485-423-4). 70pp. Nine-year-old Kaya is distracted from babysitting by a riding challenge and the other children of the Nez Perce tribe won't let her forget it, in this tale that includes many historical details. Also use *Kaya's Escape! A Survival Story* (2002). (Rev: BL 1/1–15/03; HBG 3/03)

10706 Smith, Patricia Clark. *Weetamoo: Heart of the Pocassets, Massachusetts — Rhode Island, 1653* (5–8). Illus. Series: Royal Diaries. 2003, Scholastic $10.95 (978-0-439-12910-7). 208pp. Weetamoo prepares to succeed her father as leader of the tribe and describes relationships with the European settlers and how daily life changes with the seasons. (Rev: BL 12/15/03; HBG 4/04; SLJ 1/04)

10707 Sneve, Virginia Driving Hawk. *Bad River Boys: A Meeting of the Lakota Sioux with Lewis and Clark* (2–4). Illus. by Bill Farnsworth. 2005, Holiday $16.95 (978-0-8234-1856-5). 32pp. Based on an entry from William Clark's journal, this fictional story tells of an encounter between three Lakota boys and members of Lewis and Clark's Corps of Discovery expedition. (Rev: BL 11/15/05; SLJ 11/05)

10708 Tapahonso, Luci. *Songs of Shiprock Fair* (2–4). Illus. by Anthony Chee Emerson. 1999, Kiva $15.95 (978-1-885772-11-4). This is the story of the oldest fair in the Navajo Nation at Shiprock, New Mexico, as seen through the eyes of a little girl who experiences it from the early preparations to the ceremonial dances on the last night. (Rev: HBG 3/00; SLJ 4/00)

10709 Vick, Helen H. *Shadow* (5–7). Series: Courage of the Stone. 1998, Roberts Rinehart $15.95 (978-1-57098-218-7); paper $9.95 (978-1-57098-195-1). 122pp. Shadow, an independent Pueblo Indian girl in pre-Columbian Arizona, leaves her home to rescue her father. (Rev: SLJ 10/98)

10710 Von Ahnen, Katherine. *Heart of Naosaqua* (4–6). Illus. 1996, Roberts Rinehart paper $9.95 (978-1-57098-010-7). 160pp. In 1823, Naosaqua and her people, the Mesquakie Indians, must find a new home. (Rev: BL 7/96)

10711 Wyss, Thelma Hatch. *Bear Dancer: The Story of a Ute Girl* (4–7). 2005, Simon & Schuster $15.95 (978-1-4169-0285-0). 192pp. In this fact-based historical novel, life is turned upside down for Elk Girl, a member of the Tabaguache Ute, when she is kidnapped by a rival tribe. (Rev: BL 10/15/05; SLJ 10/05)

COLONIAL PERIOD

10712 Atkins, Jeannine. *Anne Hutchinson's Way* (2–4). Illus. by Michael Dooling. 2007, Farrar $17.00 (978-0-374-30365-5). 32pp. Through the eyes of young Susanna, who has 10 older siblings, readers learn about Massachusetts in 1634 and the issue of religious freedom; based on the story of Anne Hutchinson, Susanna's mother, who was banished for her renegade beliefs. (Rev: BL 7/07; SLJ 8/07)

10713 Borden, Louise. *Sleds on Boston Common: A Story of the American Revolution* (3–5). Illus. 2000, Simon & Schuster $17.00 (978-0-689-82812-6). 40pp. Just before the Revolution, 9-year-old Henry Price and his brothers confront British soldiers on Boston Common and ask them to move so they can use the sled runs. (Rev: BCCB 7–8/00; BL 7/00; HB 11/00; HBG 3/01; SLJ 12/00)

10714 Bulla, Clyde Robert. *A Lion to Guard Us* (3–6). Illus. by Michele Chessare. 1981, Harper-Collins paper $4.99 (978-0-06-440333-7). 128pp. Three motherless children sail for America to be united with their father in the Jamestown, Virginia, colony.

10715 Butler, Amy. *Virginia Bound* (4–7). 2003, Clarion $15.00 (978-0-618-24752-3). 192pp. Thirteen-year-old Rob is kidnapped in London and shipped to Virginia as an indentured servant to work on a tobacco farm in 1627. (Rev: BL 3/1/03; HBG 10/03; SLJ 6/03)

10716 Carbone, Elisa. *Blood on the River: James Town, 1607* (5–8). 2006, Viking $16.99 (978-0-670-06060-3). 256pp. As a page for Captain John Smith in the Jamestown Colony, 11-year-old Samuel Collier experiences firsthand the hardships and adventures that confront the settlers; a powerful, historically detailed novel. (Rev: BL 4/15/06; LMC 1/07; SLJ 7/06*)

10717 Cocca-Leffler, Maryann. *Spotlight on Stacey* (2–4). Illus. by author. Series: Social Studies Connects. 2007, Kane paper $4.99 (978-1-57565-236-8). 32pp. A thoughtful aunt and a trip to a colonial village help Stacey prepare for a role in a play. Readers will learn facts about colonial times from Stacey's research. (Rev: SLJ 6/07)

10718 Collier, James Lincoln. *The Corn Raid: A Story of the Jamestown Settlement* (5–9). 2000, Jamestown paper $5.95 (978-0-8092-0619-3). 142pp. History and fiction mix in this adventure tale set in the Jamestown settlement and featuring a 12-year-old indentured servant and his cruel master. (Rev: SLJ 4/00)

10719 Couvillon, Alice, and Elizabeth Moore. *Evangeline for Children* (3–5). Illus. by Alison Davis Lyne. 2002, Pelican $15.95 (978-1-56554-709-4). 32pp. In this picture book for older children, the story of Evangeline and her love for Gabriel in colonial Louisiana is retold. (Rev: BL 6/1–15/02; HBG 10/02; SLJ 7/02)

10720 Dalgliesh, Alice. *Courage of Sarah Noble* (3–5). Illus. by Leonard Weisgard. 1954, Macmillan $15.99 (978-0-684-18830-0); paper $4.99 (978-0-689-71540-2). 64pp. The true story of a brave little girl who in 1707 went with her father into the wilds of Connecticut.

10721 Dell, Pamela. *Giles and Metacom: A Story of Plimoth and the Wampanoag* (4–6). Series: Scrapbooks of America. 2002, Tradition LB $28.50 (978-1-59187-012-8). 47pp. Eleven-year-old Giles becomes friends with an Indian boy whom he suspects of stealing. (Rev: SLJ 5/03)

10722 Duble, Kathleen Benner. *Quest* (5–8). 2008, Simon & Schuster $16.99 (978-1-4169-3386-1). 256pp. Through the thoughts of four characters, two of them on Henry Hudson's ship *Discovery*, readers will learn of the significance of the voyage to find the Northwest Passage and why it failed. (Rev: BL 4/15/08; SLJ 8/08)

10723 Durrant, Lynda. *The Beaded Moccasins: The Story of Mary Campbell* (5–9). 1998, Clarion $15.00 (978-0-395-85398-6). Told in the first person, this is a fictionalized account of the true story of 12-year-old Mary Campbell who was captured by the Delaware Indians in 1759. (Rev: BCCB 5/98; BL 3/15/98; HBG 10/98; SLJ 6/98; VOYA 12/98)

10724 Edmonds, Walter. *The Matchlock Gun* (5–7). Illus. by Paul Lantz. 1941, Putnam $16.99 (978-0-399-21911-5). 64pp. Exciting, true story of a courageous boy who protected his mother and sister from the Indians of the Hudson Valley. Newbery Medal winner, 1942.

10725 Field, Rachel. *Calico Bush* (5–7). Illus. by Allen Louis. 1987, Macmillan $17.95 (978-0-02-734610-7). 224pp. This 1932 Newbery Honor Book is an adventure story of a French girl "loaned" to a family of American pioneers in Maine in the 1740s.

10726 Grote, JoAnn A. *Queen Anne's War* (5–8). Series: The American Adventure. 1998, Chelsea LB $15.95 (978-0-7910-5045-3). During Queen Anne's War in 1710, Will Smith's family becomes involved in the attempt to drive the French out of New England, but 11-year-old Will is preoccupied with a jealous classmate. (Rev: HBG 3/99; SLJ 1/99)

10727 Hermes, Patricia. *Salem Witch* (5–8). Series: My Side of the Story. 2006, Kingfisher paper $7.95 (978-0-7534-5991-1). 172pp. Two teenage friends develop different views during the witch trials in 17th-century Salem, and readers can flip the book to read each person's opinion. (Rev: SLJ 2/07)

10728 Hermes, Patricia. *Season of Promise* (3–6). Series: My America, Elizabeth's Jamestown Colony Diary. 2002, Scholastic $10.95 (978-0-439-38898-6). 108pp. In 1611, ten-year-old Elizabeth continues to describe life in Jamestown as her twin brother Caleb returns, her father plans to remarry, and there is food to eat, although the colonial leaders are strict. (Rev: HBG 3/03; SLJ 2/03)

10729 Howard, Ginger. *William's House* (K–3). Illus. by Larry Day. 2001, Millbrook LB $22.90 (978-0-7613-1674-9). 32pp. An informative story that describes how a colonist built a house like the one he left behind in England and gradually had to change and modify it to adjust to a new climate and environment. (Rev: BL 3/15/01*; HBG 10/01; SLJ 3/01)

10730 Hurst, Carol Otis, and Rebecca Otis. *A Killing in Plymouth Colony* (5–7). 2003, Houghton $15.00 (978-0-618-27597-7). 160pp. John Bradford, the son of the governor of Plymouth Colony, has always struggled to gain his father's approval and feels an affinity toward an outcast who is accused of murder. (Rev: BL 12/1/03; HBG 4/04; SLJ 10/03)

10731 Jaspersohn, William. *The Scrimshaw Ring* (2–4). Illus. by Vernon Thornblad. 2002, Vermont Folklife Center $15.95 (978-0-916718-19-0). 32pp. In this book set in 1710 New England and based on reality, an amazing thing happens to young William Bateman — one of the pirates plundering his home gives the boy a ring that is then passed down the generations. (Rev: BL 11/15/02; SLJ 12/02)

10732 Karr, Kathleen. *Worlds Apart* (4–7). 2005, Marshall Cavendish $15.95 (978-0-7614-5195-2). 196pp. In 1670 South Carolina, Christopher — a teenage settler — and Sewee Indian Asha-po become friends. (Rev: BCCB 5/05; SLJ 5/05)

10733 Karwoski, Gail L. *Surviving Jamestown: The Adventures of Young Sam Collier* (5–7). Illus. by Paul Casale. 2001, Peachtree $14.95 (978-1-56145-239-2); paper $8.95 (978-1-56145-245-3). 198pp. Full of facts, this novel tells the story of a 12-year-old English boy who sails in 1606 for the colony of Virginia, with details of the struggles the colonists faced. (Rev: HBG 10/01; SLJ 8/01; VOYA 8/01)

10734 Ketchum, Liza. *Where the Great Hawk Flies* (4–7). 2005, Clarion $16.00 (978-0-618-40085-0). 272pp. The Coombs family and the Tuckers have trouble getting along — even the young boys — because Mrs. Tucker is a Pequot Indian and the Coombs suffered mightily during an Indian raid seven years before. (Rev: BCCB 12/05; BL 9/15/05*; HB 1/06; LMC 1/06; SLJ 1/06; VOYA 4/06)

10735 Kimmel, Eric A. *Blackbeard's Last Fight* (2–4). Illus. by Leonard Everett Fisher. 2006, Farrar $17.00 (978-0-374-30780-6). 32pp. In the early 18th century, cabin boy Jeremy Hobbs hears conflicting reports about Blackbeard the pirate and witnesses his capture and execution; vivid paintings (avoiding the final scene) add to the exciting story. (Rev: BL 3/1/06; SLJ 5/06)

10736 Lasky, Kathryn. *A Journey to the New World: The Diary of Remember Patience Whipple* (4–7). Series: Dear America. 1996, Scholastic paper $10.95 (978-0-590-50214-6). 144pp. Using diary entries as a format, this is the story of 12-year-old Mem Whipple, her journey on the *Mayflower*, and her first year in the New World. (Rev: BCCB 10/96; HB 9/96; SLJ 8/96; VOYA 10/96)

10737 Littlesugar, Amy. *The Spinner's Daughter* (3–5). Illus. 1994, Pippin LB $14.95 (978-0-945912-22-4). 32pp. In her strict Puritan community in Connecticut, Elspeth is considered sinful because she has a cornhusk doll. (Rev: BL 9/1/94; SLJ 9/94)

10738 Ovecka, Janice. *Cave of Falling Water* (4–8). Illus. by David K. Fadden. 1992, New England Pr. paper $10.95 (978-0-933050-98-3). 116pp. A cave in the hills of Vermont plays a part in the lives of three girls, one an Indian and one white, both from colonial times, and the last, a contemporary adolescent. (Rev: BL 5/1/93)

10739 Rinaldi, Ann. *The Journal of Jasper Jonathan Pierce: A Pilgrim Boy, Plymouth, 1620* (4–8). 2000, Scholastic paper $10.95 (978-0-590-51078-3). 155pp. This fictionalized account of the Pilgrims in journal format follows the adventures of a 14-year-old indentured servant aboard the *Mayflower* and during his first year in the New World. (Rev: BL 2/15/00; HBG 10/00; SLJ 7/00)

10740 Schwabach, Karen. *A Pickpocket's Tale* (5–8). 2006, Random LB $17.99 (978-0-375-93379-0). 240pp. After being caught picking pockets on the streets of London in 1730, 10-year-old orphan Molly is exiled to America where she learns many new things from the Jewish family to which she is indentured. (Rev: BL 11/15/06; SLJ 11/06)

10741 Sheely, Robert. *In the Hands of the Enemy* (4–6). Illus. by John Martin. Series: Adventures in America. 2003, Silver Moon LB $14.95 (978-1-893110-31-1). 75pp. In this suspenseful tale, 14-year-old John becomes lost after wandering away from Plymouth Colony only months after arriving from England on the *Mayflower*; he is rescued by a Nauset Indian boy, who resists his initial impulse to kill John in revenge for his father's murder by the English. (Rev: HBG 10/03; SLJ 9/03)

10742 Stainer, M. L. *The Lyon's Cub* (5–9). Illus. 1998, Chicken Soup Pr. LB $9.95 (978-0-9646904-5-5); paper $6.95 (978-0-9646904-6-2). This novel, a continuation of *The Lyon's Roar* (1997), tells what happened to the settlers of the lost colony of Roanoke and their life with peaceful Indian tribes. Continued in *The Lyon's Pride* (1998). (Rev: SLJ 8/98)

10743 Strickland, Brad. *The Guns of Tortuga* (5–8). 2003, Simon & Schuster paper $4.99 (978-0-689-85297-8). 160pp. Young Davy helps the crew of the *Aurora* defeat a band of pirates in this sequel to *Mutiny!* (Rev: BL 2/1/03; SLJ 3/03)

10744 Strohmeier, Lenice. *Mingo* (2–4). Illus. by Bill Farnsworth. 2003, Marshall Cavendish $16.95 (978-0-7614-5111-2). 32pp. The importance of freedom is the main theme in this poignant story of the close relationship between young Olivia and the elderly Robin Mingo, a family slave; historical details about 18th-century Massachusetts are interwoven throughout the picture book. (Rev: BL 6/1–15/03; HBG 10/03; SLJ 6/03)

10745 Tripp, Valerie. *Changes for Felicity: A Winter Story* (2–5). Illus. by Dan Andreasen. Series: American Girl. 1992, Pleasant $12.95 (978-1-56247-038-8); paper $6.95 (978-1-56247-037-1). 34pp. In this story of a girl who lives in colonial Williamsburg, the father of her best friend is jailed as a Loyalist. Also use: *Felicity Saves the Day: A Summer Story;* and *Happy Birthday, Felicity* (both 1992). (Rev: BL 5/1/92)

10746 Tripp, Valerie. *Felicity Learns a Lesson: A School Story* (3–5). Illus. by Dan Andreasen. Series: American Girl. 1991, Pleasant paper $6.95 (978-1-56247-007-4). 69pp. Felicity learns to control her temper in this story set in colonial Williamsburg. (Rev: BL 1/1/91; SLJ 1/92)

10747 Tripp, Valerie. *Felicity's Surprise: A Christmas Story* (3–5). Illus. by Dan Andreasen. Series: American Girl. 1991, Pleasant paper $6.95 (978-1-56247-010-4). 69pp. The family must depend more on Felicity when her mother is ill, in this story of colonial Williamsburg. (Rev: BL 1/1/91; SLJ 1/92)

10748 Troeger, Virginia B. *Secret Along the St. Mary's* (3–5). Illus. by Michael-Che Swisher. Series: Mysteries in Time. 2003, Silver Moon LB $14.95 (978-1-893110-35-9). 92pp. Motherless 12-year-old Susannah, who must keep house for her father and brother in 17th-century Maryland, faces tough choices — some involving indentured servitude — in this story that interweaves historical fact. (Rev: SLJ 3/04)

10749 Wisler, G. Clifton. *This New Land* (5–9). 1987, Walker LB $14.85 (978-0-8027-6727-1). Twelve-year-old Richard and his family begin a new life in Plymouth, Massachusetts, in 1620. (Rev: BL 3/15/88; SLJ 11/87)

THE REVOLUTION

10750 Alsheimer, Jeanette E., and Patricia J. Friedle. *The Trouble with Tea* (5–8). 2002, Pentland $15.95 (978-1-57197-299-6). 208pp. When Patience visits her friend Anne in Boston in 1773, she witnesses many of the events that led to the American Revolution. (Rev: BL 6/1–15/02)

10751 Armstrong, Jennifer. *Thomas Jefferson: Letters from a Philadelphia Bookworm* (5–8). Illus. Series: Dear Mr. President. 2001, Winslow $8.95 (978-1-890817-30-5). 128pp. Twelve-year-old Amelia and President Jefferson discuss the events of the times in a continuing exchange of letters. (Rev: BL 5/15/01; HBG 10/01; SLJ 6/01; VOYA 8/01)

10752 Avi. *The Fighting Ground* (5–9). Illus. by Ellen Thompson. 1984, HarperCollins LB $16.89 (978-0-397-32074-5); paper $5.99 (978-0-06-440185-2). 160pp. Thirteen-year-old Jonathan marches off to fight the British. (Rev: BL 4/87)

10753 Banim, Lisa. *Drums at Saratoga* (3–5). Series: Stories of the States. 1993, Silver Moon LB $14.95 (978-1-881889-20-5). 58pp. Young Nathaniel Phillips and a black servant are captured by the American forces during the Revolutionary War. (Rev: SLJ 10/93)

10754 Banim, Lisa. *The Hessian's Secret Diary* (3–5). Illus. 1997, Silver Moon LB $14.95 (978-1-881889-86-1). 80pp. In 1776, a young Brooklyn resident helps a wounded Hessian soldier, even though this endangers her family's safety. (Rev: BL 5/1/97; SLJ 4/97)

10755 Banim, Lisa. *A Spy in the King's Colony* (3–5). Illus. by Tatyana Yuditskaya. Series: Mysteries in Time. 1994, Silver Moon $14.95 (978-1-881889-54-0). 76pp. In 1775, 11-year-old Emily Parker is living in British-occupied Boston, where spies for both sides abound. (Rev: SLJ 7/94)

10756 Bartoletti, Susan C. *The Flag Maker* (1–4). Illus. by Claire A. Nivola. 2004, Houghton $16.00 (978-0-618-26757-6). 32pp. In this story of the British attack on Fort McHenry, Bartoletti focuses on the 13-year-old girl who helped her mother sew the garrison's huge American flag. (Rev: BL 3/1/04*; HB 5/04; SLJ 4/04)

10757 Berleth, Richard. *Samuel's Choice* (4–6). Illus. by James Watling. 1990, Whitman LB $16.99 (978-0-8075-7218-4). 40pp. Samuel, 14, is a young black slave in Brooklyn who plays a heroic role in the Battle of Long Island during the American Revolution. (Rev: BCCB 1/91; BL 1/1/91; SLJ 4/91)

10758 Bruchac, Joseph. *The Arrow over the Door* (4–7). Illus. 1998, Dial $15.99 (978-0-8037-2078-7). 96pp. Two boys, one a Quaker and the other a Native American, share the narration of this story that takes place immediately before the Battle of Saratoga in 1777. (Rev: BCCB 4/98; BL 2/15/98; HBG 10/98; SLJ 4/98)

10759 DeFelice, Cynthia. *The Ghost of Poplar Point* (4–6). 2007, Farrar $16.00 (978-0-374-32540-4). 192pp. Allie, 12, and her friend Dub learn about a 1770s massacre in this fourth ghost story in the series. (Rev: BL 9/15/07; SLJ 10/07)

10760 Dell, Pamela. *Freedom's Light: A Story About Paul Revere's Midnight Ride* (4–6). Series: Scrapbooks of America. 2002, Tradition LB $28.50 (978-1-59187-016-6). 47pp. Fact and fiction are interwoven in this story of 12-year-old Mary Cates, a polisher in Revere's silver shop who becomes a spy when she discovers that a coworker is plotting against Revere. (Rev: SLJ 5/03)

10761 Demas, Corinne. *If Ever I Return Again* (5–8). 2000, HarperCollins LB $15.89 (978-0-06-028718-4). 224pp. Twelve-year-old Celia describes life aboard a whaling ship in letters home to her cousin. (Rev: BCCB 6/00; BL 4/1/00; HBG 10/00; SLJ 8/00)

10762 Duey, Kathleen. *Silence and Lily: 1773* (3–6). Series: Hoofbeats. 2007, Dutton $15.99 (978-0-525-47852-2); paper $paperback,.00 (978-0-14-240909-1). 160pp. With war on the horizon and constant chores at home, Silence longs to spend time with her beloved horse Lily. (Rev: SLJ 10/1/07)

10763 Durrant, Lynda. *Betsy Zane, the Rose of Fort Henry* (5–8). 2000, Clarion $15.00 (978-0-395-97899-3). 176pp. Toward the end of the Revolutionary War, Betsy sets out alone from Philadelphia to rejoin her five brothers in western Virginia. (Rev: BCCB 10/00; BL 9/15/00; HBG 3/01; SLJ 4/01)

10764 Elliott, L. M. *Give Me Liberty* (5–8). 2006, HarperCollins $16.99 (978-0-06-074421-2). 384pp. Nathaniel Dunn, a 13-year-old indentured servant in colonial Virginia, is taken under the wing of an elderly schoolmaster and watches as the revolutionary movement grows and affects his own behavior. (Rev: BL 10/1/06; SLJ 9/06)

10765 Fleming, Candace. *The Hatmaker's Sign: A Story by Benjamin Franklin* (3–5). Illus. by Robert Andrew Parker. 1998, Orchard $15.95 (978-0-531-30075-6). 40pp. When Jefferson complains to Dr. Franklin about the mutilation of his Declaration of Independence by Congress, the good doctor tells him a comforting parable. (Rev: BL 2/15/98; HB 3/98; HBG 10/98; SLJ 4/98)

10766 Fritz, Jean. *George Washington's Breakfast* (3–5). Illus. by Paul Galdone. 1998, Penguin paper $6.99 (978-0-698-11611-5). 43pp. George W. Allen knows all there is to know about our first president — except what he had for breakfast.

10767 Goodman, Joan E. *Hope's Crossing* (5–8). 1998, Houghton $16.00 (978-0-395-86195-0). 160pp. Kidnapped by British loyalists during the Revolution, Hope must try to escape and find her way home. (Rev: BCCB 7–8/98; BL 6/1–15/98; HBG 10/98; SLJ 5/98; VOYA 8/98)

10768 Gregory, Kristiana. *Five Smooth Stones: Hope's Diary* (3–5). Series: My America. 2001, Scholastic $10.95 (978-0-439-14827-6). 112pp. Set in 1776 Philadelphia and told in diary format, this novel tells of a 9-year-old girl and her family's problems at the beginning of the Revolutionary War. (Rev: BL 1/1–15/01; HBG 10/01)

10769 Gregory, Kristiana. *We Are Patriots: Hope's Revolutionary War Diary, Book Two* (2–4). Series: My America. 2002, Scholastic $10.95 (978-0-439-21039-3); paper $4.99 (978-0-439-36906-0). 108pp. Ten-year-old Hope tells her diary the details of the war raging around Philadelphia in 1777. (Rev: HBG 10/02; SLJ 8/02)

10770 Jones, Elizabeth McDonald. *Peril at King's Creek: A Felicity Mystery* (3–5). Series: American Girl Mysteries. 2006, Pleasant paper $6.95 (978-1-59369-101-1). 168pp. Spending the summer of 1776 at her family's Virginia plantation, Felicity hears reports that British troops are raiding the farms of patriots and becomes suspicious of a visitor who shows a lot of interest in her horse. (Rev: BL 6/1–15/06; SLJ 4/06)

10771 Kirkpatrick, Katherine. *Redcoats and Petticoats* (3–5). Illus. by Ronald Himler. 1999, Holiday House $16.95 (978-0-8234-1416-1). 32pp. When 13-year-old Thomas Strong is sent on some unusual errands, he is unaware at first that he is part of a spy network conveying messages to the forces of George Washington during the Revolutionary War. (Rev: BL 3/1/99; HBG 10/99; SLJ 4/99)

10772 Moore, Ruth Nulton. *Distant Thunder* (5–8). Illus. by Allan Eitzen. 1991, Herald paper $6.99 (978-0-8361-3557-2). 160pp. During the Revolution, when wounded Americans are sent to Pennsylvania to recover, young Kate experiences the horrors of war. (Rev: BCCB 1/92; SLJ 1/92)

10773 Noble, Trinka Hakes. *The Scarlet Stockings Spy* (2–4). Illus. by Robert Papp. 2004, Sleeping Bear $16.95 (978-1-58536-230-1). 48pp. Maddy Rose, a young seamstress in revolutionary-era Philadelphia, devises a clever signaling system to keep patriot forces informed about what ships are docked in the city's harbor. (Rev: BL 2/1/05)

10774 Nordan, Robert. *The Secret Road* (5–9). 2001, Holiday $16.95 (978-0-8234-1543-4). 144pp. Young Laura helps an escaped slave on a long and suspenseful journey to freedom by posing as her sister. (Rev: BL 9/15/01; HBG 3/02; SLJ 10/01; VOYA 12/01)

10775 Roop, Peter, and Connie Roop. *An Eye for an Eye: A Story of the Revolutionary War* (5–9). 2000, Jamestown paper $5.95 (978-0-8092-0628-5). 168pp. During the Revolutionary War, Samantha, disguised as boy, sets out to save her brother who is being held prisoner on a British ship. (Rev: BCCB 7–8/00; SLJ 4/00)

10776 Schurfranz, Vivian. *A Message for General Washington* (3–4). Illus. by John F. Martin. Series: Stories of the States. 1998, Silver Moon LB $14.95 (978-1-881889-89-2). 92pp. Hannah, age 12, undertakes a perilous journey from Yorktown to Williamsburg, where she delivers a message to General Washington. (Rev: HBG 10/98; SLJ 11/98)

10777 Sheinkin, Steve. *King George: What Was His Problem? Everything Your Schoolbooks Didn't Tell You About the American Revolution* (4–7). Illus. by Tim Robinson. 2008, Roaring Brook $19.95 (978-1-59643-319-9). 192pp. First published as *The American Revolution* (2005), this is a breezy and often funny collection of stories that history students will remember. (Rev: BL 8/08) [973.3]

10778 Sweetzer, Anna Leah. *Treason Stops at Oyster Bay* (4–6). Illus. 1999, Silver Moon LB $14.95 (978-1-893110-03-8). 96pp. Sally is attracted to Colonel Simcoe, a British officer billeted in her family's house on Long Island, and must decide if she should pass on vital information she has overheard to her brother who is a Patriot spy. (Rev: BL 8/99; HBG 3/00)

10779 Tripp, Valerie. *Very Funny, Elizabeth!* (3–5). Illus. by Dan Andreasen. Series: American Girl. 2005, American Girl paper $6.95 (978-1-59369-061-8). 81pp. Ten-year-old Elizabeth Cole and her friend Felicity, who are growing up in Revolutionary-era Williamsburg, enjoy teasing Elizabeth's older sister Annabelle in this volume that provides historical detail. (Rev: SLJ 3/06)

10780 Walker, Sally M. *The 18 Penny Goose* (2–4). Illus. by Ellen Beier. Series: I Can Read. 1998, HarperCollins LB $15.89 (978-0-06-027557-0). 64pp. In this easy reader based on fact, a little girl is afraid that the British army raiders will eat her pet goose during the Revolutionary War. (Rev: BL 2/1/98; HB 5/98; HBG 10/98; SLJ 3/98)

10781 Waters, John F. *Night Raiders Along the Cape* (3–5). Illus. 1998, Silver Moon LB $14.95 (978-1-881889-85-4). 96pp. Asa rows from his island home to warn the mainlanders of a British plot in this novel set in Massachusetts during the American Revolution. (Rev: BL 2/15/98; HBG 10/98; SLJ 7/98)

THE YOUNG NATION, 1789–1861

10782 Arbuckle, Scott. *Zeb, the Cow's on the Roof Again! And Other Tales of Early Texas Dwellings* (3–7). Illus. by author. 1996, Eakin $15.95 (978-1-57168-102-7). 128pp. Four youngsters tell about their dwellings in stories that take place at various times in Texas history. (Rev: SLJ 4/97)

10783 Barker, M. P. *A Difficult Boy* (5–9). 2008, Holiday $16.95 (978-0-8234-2086-5). 304pp. Indentured to a shopkeeper against his will, Ethan befriends young Daniel, a young Irishman, and the two find friendship and a joint love of horses in this story set in 1839 Massachusetts. (Rev: BL 4/15/08; SLJ 5/08)

10784 Blos, Joan W. *Letters from the Corrugated Castle: A Novel of Gold Rush California, 1850–1852* (4–8). 2007, Simon & Schuster $17.99 (978-0-689-87077-4). 320pp. Reunited with a mother long believed to be dead, 13-year-old Eldora must learn to adjust to living a life of comfort in San Francisco; newspaper articles and her correspondence with Luke, who hopes to find a fortune, reveal much about life during the Gold Rush. (Rev: BL 4/15/07; SLJ 6/07)

10785 Broyles, Anne. *Priscilla and the Hollyhocks* (2–4). Illus. by Anna Alter. 2008, Charlesbridge $15.95 (978-1-57091-675-5). 32pp. A hollyhock patch is a source of comfort for a young slave girl separated from her mother; she has hollyhock seeds in her pocket when she is later purchased by a Cherokee family, and it is on the Trail of Tears that she finds her freedom and can eventually plant her own patch. (Rev: BL 2/1/08; LMC 10/08; SLJ 3/08)

10786 Carrick, Carol. *Stay Away from Simon!* (4–6). Illus. by Donald Carrick. 1985, Houghton paper $6.95 (978-0-89919-849-1). 64pp. Mentally handicapped Simon has a reputation of being dangerous, but Lucy discovers he also has a generous heart in this story set in Martha's Vineyard in the 1830s. (Rev: BCCB 11/85; BL 8/85; SLJ 4/85)

10787 Crook, Connie Brummel. *Laura Secord's Brave Walk* (2–5). Illus. by June Lawrason. 2001, Second Story $14.95 (978-1-896764-34-4). During the War of 1812, Laura Secord hears American soldiers' plans to attack at Beavers Dam, and sets off on a dangerous journey to warn the British in this novel with realistic battlefield illustrations. (Rev: SLJ 7/01)

10788 Dahlberg, Maurine F. *The Story of Jonas* (4–7). 2007, Farrar $16.00 (978-0-374-37264-4). 148pp. In the mid-1800s, Jonas, a 13-year-old slave, is sent on an expedition to find gold in the Kansas Territory and realizes that freedom is not beyond his grasp. (Rev: BL 4/07; SLJ 4/07)

10789 DeFelice, Cynthia. *Bringing Ezra Back* (4–6). 2006, Farrar $16.00 (978-0-374-39939-9). 160pp. In this sequel to *Weasel* (1990), 12-year-old Nathan travels from Ohio to Pennsylvania in 1840 in an attempt to locate and help Ezra, the man grievously injured by Weasel. (Rev: BL 8/06; SLJ 9/06)

10790 Donaldson, Joan. *A Pebble and a Pen* (5–8). 2000, Holiday $15.95 (978-0-8234-1500-7). 176pp. In 1853, to avoid an arranged marriage, 14-year-old Matty runs away to study penmanship at Mr. Spencer's famous Ohio school. (Rev: BCCB 12/00; BL 1/1–15/01; HBG 10/01; SLJ 12/00; VOYA 2/01)

10791 Duble, Kathleen Benner. *Hearts of Iron* (5–8). 2006, Simon & Schuster $15.95 (978-1-4169-0850-0). 256pp. In a Connecticut iron-working community in the early 19th century, two young lovers rebel against their families' plans for their future. (Rev: BL 9/15/06; SLJ 11/06)

10792 Duey, Kathleen, and Karen A. Bale. *Cave-In: St. Claire, Pennsylvania, 1859* (4–6). Series: Sur-

vival! 1998, Simon & Schuster paper $3.99 (978-0-689-82350-3). 158pp. In this survival story set in the coal mines of Pennsylvania during 1859, two boys and their landlady's daughter are trapped underground in a mine after a cave-in. (Rev: SLJ 2/99)

10793 Duey, Kathleen, and Karen A. Bale. *Hurricane: Open Seas, 1844* (5–7). Series: Survival! 1999, Simon & Schuster paper $4.50 (978-0-689-82544-6). 169pp. This exciting sea story, set in 1844, tells of two youngsters who are on a whaler when a killer hurricane strikes. (Rev: SLJ 8/99)

10794 Garland, Sherry. *In the Shadow of the Alamo* (5–8). Series: Great Episodes. 2001, Harcourt $17.00 (978-0-15-201744-6). 282pp. Fifteen-year-old Lorenzo Bonifacio, a conscript in the Mexican army of Santa Ana, describes the harsh life of the soldiers and the family members who follow them on the trek to Texas and the battle of the Alamo. (Rev: BCCB 1/02; BL 10/15/01; HB 11/01; HBG 3/02; SLJ 12/01; VOYA 10/01)

10795 Giblin, James Cross. *The Boy Who Saved Cleveland* (3–6). Illus. by Michael Dooling. 2006, Holt $15.95 (978-0-8050-7355-3). 64pp. This fact-based story recounts the trials of 10-year-old Seth Doan who helped to nurse early settlers of Cleveland, Ohio, through a malaria outbreak in the late 18th century. (Rev: BL 4/15/06; SLJ 5/06)

10796 Givens, Steven J. *Levi Dust: A Tale from the Kerry Patch* (2–4). 1997, New Canaan paper $4.95 (978-1-889658-07-0). 56pp. Ten-year-old twins get lost on the streets of St. Louis in the 1850s and are brought home by a kindly bell ringer. (Rev: BL 2/1/98)

10797 Greenwood, Barbara. *The Last Safe House: A Story of the Underground Railroad* (3–6). Illus. by Heather Collins. 1998, Kids Can $16.95 (978-1-55074-507-8); paper $10.95 (978-1-55074-509-2). 119pp. Using a Canadian family's participation in the Underground Railroad in 1856 as a framework, this book supplies good background on the railroad's organization, accomplishments, and the fight against slavery. (Rev: HBG 3/99; SLJ 1/99)

10798 Guccione, Leslie D. *Come Morning* (4–7). 1995, Carolrhoda LB $19.15 (978-0-87614-892-1). 120pp. A young boy takes over his father's duties as a conductor on the Underground Railroad. (Rev: BCCB 1/96; HB 11/95; SLJ 11/95)

10799 Hegamin, Tonya Cherie. *Most Loved in All the World* (K–2). Illus. by Cozbi A. Cabrera. 2009, Houghton $17.00 (978-0-618-41903-6). 40pp. Text, quilt art, and primitive paintings tell the story of a slave mother who selflessly pieces together a quilt to guide the people who will help her smuggle her daughter to freedom on the Underground Railroad. (Rev: BCCB 1/09; BL 2/1/09; LMC 10/09; SLJ 1/09)

10800 Helgerson, Joseph. *Crows and Cards* (4–7). Illus. by Peter De Seve. 2009, Houghton $16.00 (978-0-618-88395-0). 352pp. In the mid-19th century, 12-year-old Zeb is sent off to become a tanner but on the riverboat to St. Louis meets a gambler who offers a more enticing life. (Rev: BL 4/15/09; HB 5/09; LMC 10/09; SLJ 8/09)

10801 Hill, Donna. *Shipwreck Season* (5–8). 1998, Clarion $16.00 (978-0-395-86614-6). 215pp. In the 1800s, 16-year-old Daniel joins a crew of seamen who patrol America's eastern coastline, rescuing people and cargo from shipwrecks. (Rev: BCCB 7–8/98; BL 6/1–15/98; HBG 3/99; SLJ 6/98)

10802 Hilts, Len. *Timmy O'Dowd and the Big Ditch: A Story of the Glory Days on the Old Erie Canal* (5–7). 1988, Harcourt $13.95 (978-0-15-200606-8). 91pp. Timmy and his cousin Dennis don't get along, but when the canals threaten to flood, they realize each other's strengths and stamina. (Rev: BCCB 12/88; BL 10/1/88; SLJ 12/88)

10803 Houston, Gloria. *Bright Freedom's Song: A Story of the Underground Railroad* (4–7). 1998, Harcourt $17.00 (978-0-15-201812-2). 145pp. A tense, dramatic story about a girl who helps her parents operate a North Carolina station on the Underground Railroad. (Rev: BCCB 1/99; BL 11/1/98; HBG 3/99; SLJ 12/98; VOYA 2/99)

10804 Howard, Ellen. *The Log Cabin Wedding* (2–4). Illus. by Ronald Himler. 2006, Holiday $15.95 (978-0-8234-1989-0). 48pp. Elvirey is upset when her widowed father falls in love with the Widow Aiken in this chapter-book sequel to the picture books *Log Cabin Quilt* (1996), *The Log Cabin Christmas* (2000), and *The Log Cabin Church* (2002). (Rev: BL 9/15/06; SLJ 12/06)

10805 Hurst, Carol Otis. *Through the Lock* (5–8). 2001, Houghton $15.00 (978-0-618-03036-1). 172pp. In this novel set in Connecticut in the first half of the 19th century, a young orphan named Etta shares many adventures with a boy who lives in an abandoned cabin by a canal. (Rev: BCCB 3/01; BL 4/1/01; HB 3/01; HBG 10/01; SLJ 3/01; VOYA 4/01)

10806 Jakes, John. *Susanna of the Alamo: A True Story* (3–5). Illus. by Paul Bacon. 1986, Harcourt $13.95 (978-0-15-200592-4); paper $7.00 (978-0-15-200595-5). 32pp. Only women, children, and slaves were spared by the Mexicans at the battle of the Alamo in 1836, and one, Susanna Dickinson, was spared to inform Sam Houston of the outcome. (Rev: BCCB 6/86; BL 6/15/86; SLJ 8/86)

10807 Johnson, Lois W. *Midnight Rescue* (4–6). 1996, Bethany House paper $5.99 (978-1-55661-353-1). 160pp. Twelve-year-old Libby, a riverboat captain's daughter, becomes involved with the Underground Railroad and an escaped slave. (Rev: BL 1/1–15/97)

10808 Ketchum, Liza. *Orphan Journey Home* (5–7). Illus. 2000, Avon $15.99 (978-0-380-97811-3). 162pp. When their parents die in southern Illinois in 1828, Jesse and her three siblings must find their way to their grandmother in eastern Kentucky. (Rev: BCCB 6/00; BL 6/1–15/00; HBG 10/00; SLJ 8/00)

10809 Killcoyne, Hope Lourie. *The Lost Village of Central Park* (3–5). Illus. by Mary Lee Majno. Series: Mysteries in Time. 1999, Silver Moon LB $14.95 (978-1-893110-02-1). 89pp. An exciting story about life in Seneca Village, an African American settlement in 19th-century New York City, and the slave catchers that terrorized its people. (Rev: HBG 10/00; SLJ 2/00)

10810 Kohl, Susan. *The Ghost of Gracie Mansion* (3–5). Illus. by Ned Butterfield. Series: Mysteries in Time. 1999, Silver Moon LB $14.95 (978-1-893110-04-5). 96pp. When the Gracie family move to their new mansion in northern Manhattan in 1803, they encounter a mystery concerning disappearing objects. (Rev: SLJ 2/00)

10811 Kroll, Steven. *John Quincy Adams: Letters from a Southern Planter's Son* (4–6). Illus. Series: Dear Mr. President. 2001, Winslow $9.95 (978-1-890817-93-0). 122pp. A fictional correspondence between a young boy and President John Quincy Adams details historical events and gives insight into Adams's character and concerns. (Rev: BL 1/1–15/02; HBG 3/02; SLJ 12/01)

10812 Lunn, Janet. *Laura Secord: A Story of Courage* (3–6). Illus. by Maxwell Newhouse. 2002, Tundra $16.95 (978-0-88776-538-4). Lunn's text and the accompanying illustrations give drama to the story of Secord's trek to warn the British during the War of 1812. (Rev: HB 3/02; HBG 10/02; SLJ 4/02)

10813 McGill, Alice. *Way Up and Over Everything* (2–5). Illus. by Jude Daly. 2008, Houghton $16.00 (978-0-618-38796-0). 32pp. Five recently arrived slaves simply disappear up into the air in this folktale set in the mid-19th century. (Rev: BCCB 7/08; BL 2/1/08; HB 7/08; SLJ 9/08) [398.2]

10814 McKissack, Patricia C. *A Picture of Freedom: The Diary of Clotee, a Slave Girl* (4–6). 1997, Scholastic $9.95 (978-0-614-25386-3). 208pp. Using a diary format, this novel describes the life of slaves on a Southern plantation as seen through the eyes of a young slave girl. (Rev: BL 4/15/97; SLJ 9/97)

10815 McKissack, Patricia C., and Fredrick McKissack. *Let My People Go* (5–8). Illus. 1998, Simon & Schuster $20.00 (978-0-689-80856-2). This novel set in the early 19th century combines Bible stories and the hardships endured by slaves as told by Price Jefferson, a former slave who is now an abolitionist living in South Carolina. (Rev: BCCB 12/98; BL 10/1/98; HBG 3/99; SLJ 11/98)

10816 Mazer, Harry. *My Brother Abe: Sally Lincoln's Story* (4–6). 2009, Simon & Schuster $15.99 (978-1-4169-3884-2). 208pp. Mazer expands the facts we know about Lincoln's sister Sally into a story about the family's hard-scrabble life in the early 19th-century Midwest. (Rev: BCCB 2/09; BL 1/1–15/09; LMC 5/09; SLJ 2/09)

10817 Minahan, John A. *Abigail's Drum* (2–5). Illus. 1995, Pippin $15.95 (978-0-945912-25-5). 64pp. During the War of 1812, Rebecca and Abigail try to save their father, who has been captured by the British. (Rev: BCCB 2/96; BL 2/15/96; SLJ 2/96)

10818 Monjo, F. N. *The Drinking Gourd* (2–4). Illus. by Fred Brenner. 1970, HarperCollins LB $16.89 (978-0-06-024330-2); paper $3.99 (978-0-06-444042-4). 64pp. A New England white boy helps a black family escape on the Underground Railroad.

10819 Paterson, Katherine. *Jip: His Story* (5–9). 1998, Puffin paper $6.99 (978-0-14-038674-5). Jip, a foundling boy in Vermont of the 1850s, wonders about his origins, particularly after he finds he is being watched by a mysterious stranger. (Rev: BCCB 12/96; BL 9/1/96*; HB 11/96; SLJ 10/96*; VOYA 4/97)

10820 Rappaport, Doreen. *Freedom River* (3–5). Illus. 2000, Hyperion $14.99 (978-0-7868-0350-7). 32pp. Based on fact, this is a picture book for older readers that tells how John Parker, an ex-slave, helped a family to escape from Kentucky via the Underground Railroad. (Rev: BL 10/1/00; HBG 3/01; SLJ 10/00)

10821 Raven, Margot Theis. *Night Boat to Freedom* (1–3). Illus. by E. B. Lewis. 2006, Farrar $16.00 (978-0-374-31266-4). 40pp. Twelve-year-old Christmas John, urged on by Granny Judith, helps dozens of slaves escape to freedom, but when she tells the boy that he, too, must flee, he refuses to go without her; text and illustrations blend to make this a touching story. (Rev: BCCB 12/06; BL 10/15/06; SLJ 11/06)

10822 Rinaldi, Ann. *The Blue Door* (5–8). Series: Quilt. 1996, Scholastic paper $15.95 (978-0-590-46051-4). In this final volume of the Quilt trilogy — following *A Stitch in Time* (1994) and *Broken Days* — Amanda is forced to take a mill job in Lowell, Massachusetts, after an adventurous trip north from her South Carolina home. (Rev: BL 11/1/96; VOYA 2/97)

10823 Rinaldi, Ann. *The Ever-After Bird* (5–8). 2007, Harcourt $17.00 (978-0-15-202620-2). 240pp. CeCe travels with her uncle, an abolitionist and ornithologist, to Georgia to search for a rare bird and help slaves get to the Underground Railroad. (Rev: BL 11/1/07; LMC 1/08; SLJ 12/07)

10824 Sanchez, Anita. *The Invasion of Sandy Bay* (5–8). 2008, Boyds Mills $16.95 (978-1-59078-560-7). 152pp. Twelve-year-old Lemuel attempts to save his little fishing village during the War of 1812 when he spots a British warship in the harbor; with extensive historical endnotes. (Rev: BL 10/1/08; LMC 1/02; VOYA 10/08)

10825 Schneider, Mical. *Annie Quinn in America* (5–9). 2001, Carolrhoda LB $15.95 (978-1-57505-510-7). 252pp. In 1847, young Annie and her brother travel from Ireland, a land ravaged by the potato famine, to America, a land fraught with dangers of its own. (Rev: BL 11/15/01; HBG 3/02; SLJ 9/01)

10826 Schwartz, Virginia Frances. *Send One Angel Down* (5–8). 2000, Holiday $16.95 (978-0-8234-1484-0). 163pp. This is the story of a young slave girl, Eliza, the skills she learns on the plantation, and how this knowledge helps her when she gains freedom. (Rev: BL 6/1–15/00; HB 7/00; HBG 10/00; SLJ 8/00)

10827 Siegelson, Kim L. *Escape South* (2–4). Illus. by Shelley Jackson. Series: Road to Reading. 2000, Golden $10.99 (978-0-307-46504-7). This easy chapter book tells, in fictionalized form, how some runaway slaves were given shelter and land by the Seminole Indians in Florida and later left for land out west. (Rev: BL 2/15/01; HBG 3/01)

10828 Siegelson, Kim L. *In the Time of the Drums* (2–5). Illus. by Brian Pinkney. 1999, Hyperion LB $16.49 (978-0-7686-2386-4). 32pp. Told from the standpoint of a young African American, this is the legend of the slave rebellion at Ibo's Landing in South Carolina's Sea Islands. (Rev: BL 4/1/99)

10829 Stowe, Cynthia M. *The Second Escape of Arthur Cooper* (5–7). 2000, Marshall Cavendish LB $14.95 (978-0-7614-5069-6). 112pp. Based on a true story, this novel tells of Arthur Cooper, an escaped slave, and the Quakers on Nantucket Island who saved him from slave catchers in 1822. (Rev: BL 8/00; HBG 3/01; SLJ 10/00)

10830 Thomas, Velma M. *Lest We Forget: The Passage from Africa to Slavery and Emancipation* (5–8). Illus. 1997, Crown $29.95 (978-0-609-60030-6). An interactive book about slavery based on material from the Black Holocaust Museum. (Rev: BL 12/15/97) [973.6]

10831 Tingle, Tim. *Crossing Bok Chitto* (2–4). Illus. by Jeanne Rorex Bridges. 2006, Cinco Puntos $17.95 (978-0-938317-77-7). 40pp. Martha Tom, a young Choctaw girl in 1800s Mississippi, befriends a slave boy and his family and leads them to freedom when they face a crisis. (Rev: BCCB 7–8/06; BL 4/15/06*; LMC 11/06)

10832 Trottier, Maxine. *Under a Shooting Star* (5–8). Series: The Circle of Silver Chronicles. 2002, Stoddart paper $7.95 (978-0-7737-6228-2). 212pp. During the War of 1812, a 15-year-old boy who is half English and half Oneida Indian struggles with conflicting loyalties as he tries to protect the two American girls he is escorting. (Rev: SLJ 5/02)

10833 Turner, Glennette Tilley. *Running for Our Lives* (5–7). Illus. 1994, Holiday $16.95 (978-0-8234-1121-4). 198pp. A thoroughly researched novel about a boy and his family who escape slavery in the 1850s and traveled on the Underground Railroad to Canada. (Rev: BCCB 6/94; BL 6/1–15/94; SLJ 4/94)

10834 Wait, Lea. *Finest Kind* (4–7). 2006, Simon & Schuster $16.95 (978-1-4169-0952-1). 256pp. When his family falls on hard times and is forced to move from Boston to Maine in the 1830s, 12-year-old Jake Webber finds himself shouldering new responsibilities, including looking after his disabled younger brother. (Rev: BL 10/15/06; SLJ 11/06)

10835 Wait, Lea. *Seaward Born* (4–7). 2003, Simon & Schuster $16.95 (978-0-689-84719-6). 160pp. Michael, a young slave, makes a dangerous journey to Canada and freedom in this dramatic historical novel. (Rev: BL 2/15/03; HBG 10/03; SLJ 1/03)

10836 Wall, Bill. *The Cove of Cork* (5–9). 1999, Irish American paper $7.95 (978-0-85635-225-6). In this novel, the third in a trilogy revolving around the War of 1812, an Irish lad, the first mate of the American schooner *Shenandoah*, sees action in a battle against a British vessel and eventually wins the hand of the granddaughter of a shipbuilding magnate. (Rev: SLJ 7/99)

10837 Wanttaja, Ronald. *The Key to Honor* (5–9). 1996, Royal Fireworks paper $9.99 (978-0-88092-270-8). During the War of 1812, midshipman Nate Lawton has doubts about his courage in battle and worries about his father, who has been taken prisoner by the British. (Rev: VOYA 8/96)

10838 West, Tracey. *Mr. Peale's Bones* (4–6). Series: Stories of the States. 1994, Silver Moon LB $14.95 (978-1-881889-50-2). 63pp. In this novel, set in upstate New York in 1801, Will and his estranged father find a new bond when they help Charles Willson Peale and his excavation of mammoth bones. (Rev: SLJ 7/94)

10839 Whelan, Gloria. *Farewell to the Island* (5–8). 1998, HarperCollins $16.95 (978-0-06-027751-2). In this sequel to *Once on This Island*, Mary leaves her Michigan home after the War of 1812 and travels to England where she falls in love with Lord Lindsay. (Rev: BL 12/1/98; HBG 3/99; SLJ 1/99)

10840 Whelan, Gloria. *Friend on Freedom River* (3–5). Illus. by Gijsbert van Frankenhuyzen. 2005, Sleeping Bear $16.95 (978-1-58536-222-6). In 1850, on a cold December night on the Detroit River, young Louis is asked to ferry runaway slaves to Canada. (Rev: BL 5/15/04; SLJ 6/05)

10841 Whelan, Gloria. *Once on This Island* (4–7). 1995, HarperCollins LB $14.89 (978-0-06-026249-5). 224pp. In 1812, Mary and her older brother and sister must tend the family farm on Mackinac Island when their father goes off to war. (Rev: BCCB 11/95; BL 10/1/95; SLJ 11/95; VOYA 2/96)

10842 Wiley, Melissa. *On Tide Mill Lane* (4–8). Illus. 2001, HarperCollins $16.95 (978-0-06-027013-1). 208pp. Charlotte experiences a number of household crises in Roxbury, Massachusetts, where she lives with her blacksmith father at the time of the War of 1812. (Rev: BL 2/15/01; HBG 10/01)

10843 Woods, Brenda. *My Name Is Sally Little Song* (4–7). 2006, Putnam $15.99 (978-0-399-24312-7). 176pp. Eleven-year-old Sally, a slave on a Georgia plantation at the beginning of the 19th century, escapes with her family and heads south to seek refuge with the Seminole Indians. (Rev: BCCB 11/06; BL 8/06; HBG 4/07; SLJ 9/06)

10844 Woodson, Jacqueline. *Show Way* (3–5). Illus. by Hudson Talbott. 2005, Putnam $16.99 (978-0-399-23749-2). 48pp. Woodson looks back in her own family history to tell the story of seven generations of women who pass down secret "Show Way" quilt patterns and a tradition of fighting for freedom. Newbery Honor Book, 2006. (Rev: BCCB 1/06; BL 9/15/05*; HB 11/05; HBG 4/06; SLJ 11/05*)

10845 Wright, Courtni C. *Journey to Freedom: A Story of the Underground Railroad* (3–5). Illus. by Griffith Gershom. 1994, Holiday House LB $17.95 (978-0-8234-1096-5). 28pp. A picture book that tells of 8-year-old Joshua and his flight to freedom on the Underground Railroad. (Rev: BL 11/15/94; SLJ 1/95)

10846 Wyeth, Sharon Dennis. *Flying Free: Corey's Underground Railroad Diary* (2–4). Illus. Series: My America. 2002, Scholastic $10.95 (978-0-439-24443-5). 112pp. In diary form, this novel traces the travels of Corey, a black boy, and his family to freedom in Canada via the Underground Railroad. (Rev: BL 6/1–15/02; HBG 10/02; SLJ 8/02)

PIONEERS AND WESTWARD EXPANSION

10847 Altman, Linda J. *The Legend of Freedom Hill* (2–4). Illus. by Cornelius Van Wright and Ying-Hwa Hu. 2000, Lee & Low $15.95 (978-1-58430-003-8). 32pp. Set in Gold Rush California, this novel tells how Rosabel, the daughter of a runaway slave, and her Jewish friend Sophia pan enough gold to buy the freedom of Rosabel's mother. (Rev: BL 11/1/00; HBG 3/01; SLJ 8/00)

10848 Anderson, Joan. *Pioneer Children of Appalachia* (4–6). Illus. 1986, Houghton paper $7.95 (978-0-395-54792-2). The Davis family is shown in everyday life in Appalachia of the early 1800s. (Rev: BCCB 12/86; BL 11/1/86; SLJ 10/86)

10849 Applegate, Stan. *The Devil's Highway* (5–8). Illus. by James Watling. 1998, Peachtree paper $8.95 (978-1-56145-184-5). 148pp. In this adventure novel set in the early 1800s, 14-year-old Zeb and his horse, Christmas, set out on the bandit-infested Natchez Trail to search for the boy's grandfather. (Rev: SLJ 2/99)

10850 Bailer, Darice. *The Last Rail* (3–5). Illus. by Bill Farnsworth. Series: Odyssey. 1996, Smithsonian Institution $14.95 (978-1-56899-362-1); paper $6.95 (978-1-56899-363-8). 32pp. Using a fictional format, this book tells about a young girl who witnesses the building of the first transcontinental railroad. (Rev: BL 10/15/96)

10851 Bauer, Marion Dane. *Land of the Buffalo Bones: The Diary of Mary Elizabeth Rodgers, an English Girl in Minnesota* (4–8). Series: Dear America. 2003, Scholastic $12.95 (978-0-439-22027-9). 224pp. Based on real-life events, Polly Rodgers's diary reveals the hardships endured by a group of English settlers who arrived in Minnesota in 1873. (Rev: BL 5/15/03; HBG 10/03; SLJ 9/01)

10852 Benner, J. A. *Uncle Comanche* (5–8). 1996, Texas Christian Univ. paper $12.95 (978-0-87565-152-1). Based on fact, this is the story of the adventures of 12-year-old Sul Ross, who runs away from home in pre-Civil War Texas and is pursued by a family friend nicknamed Uncle Comanche. (Rev: VOYA 10/96)

10853 Blakeslee, Ann R. *A Different Kind of Hero* (5–7). 1997, Marshall Cavendish $14.95 (978-0-7614-5000-9). 144pp. In 1881 Colorado, Renny is criticized for befriending and helping a Chinese boy new to town. (Rev: BL 9/1/97; HBG 3/98; SLJ 1/98)

10854 Byars, Betsy. *Trouble River* (3–6). Illus. by Rocco Negri. 1989, Puffin paper $4.99 (978-0-14-034243-7). 160pp. Dewey uses his canoe to escape Indians.

10855 Chrismer, Melanie. *Phoebe Clappsaddle for Sheriff* (1–3). Illus. by Virginia M. Roeder. 2003, Pelican $15.95 (978-1-58980-127-1). In this rollicking tale set in the early years of Texas's statehood, diminutive Phoebe Clappsaddle fills in as sheriff when she's selected by the governor to meet the stagecoach carrying the town's new schoolteacher. (Rev: HBG 4/04; SLJ 1/04)

10856 Collier, James Lincoln. *Wild Boy* (5–8). 2002, Marshall Cavendish $15.95 (978-0-7614-5126-6). 160pp. After knocking his father out during an argument, 12-year-old Jesse runs away from his frontier home to live in the mountains, where he has many adventures, learns many skills, and reflects on his own characteristics before finally deciding to return home in this story that appears to be set in the 19th century. (Rev: BL 11/1/02; HBG 10/03; SLJ 11/02)

10857 Couloumbis, Audrey. *The Misadventures of Maude March, or, Trouble Rides a Fast Horse* (5–8). 2005, Random LB $17.99 (978-0-375-93245-8). 291pp. When their aunt and sole guardian is killed, Maude and Sallie March rebel against their new foster family and set off on their own in this rollicking tale of the Old West. (Rev: SLJ 9/05)

10858 Cushman, Karen. *The Ballad of Lucy Whipple* (5–8). 1996, Clarion $16.00 (978-0-395-72806-2). 208pp. Lucy hates being stuck in the California wilderness with an overbearing mother who runs a boarding house. (Rev: BCCB 9/96; BL 8/96*; HB 9/96; SLJ 8/96*; VOYA 12/96)

10859 Durrant, Lynda. *The Sun, the Rain, and the Apple Seed: A Novel of Johnny Appleseed's Life* (5–8). 2003, Clarion $15.00 (978-0-618-23487-5). 200pp. This fictionalized biography of John Chapman's life focuses on his eccentricities. (Rev: BL 5/15/03; HBG 10/03; SLJ 5/03)

10860 Ferris, Jean. *Much Ado About Grubstake* (5–8). 2006, Harcourt $17.00 (978-0-15-205706-0). 265pp. Sixteen-year-old Arley, owner of her family's mine and boarding house in 1888 Grubstake, Colorado, becomes suspicious when a stranger takes an unusual interest in the rundown mining town; adventure, romance, and humor are combined in this mystery. (Rev: BL 8/06; SLJ 11/06)

10861 Finley, Mary Peace. *Meadow Lark* (5–8). Series: Santa Fe Trail trilogy. 2003, Filter $15.95 (978-0-86541-070-1). 208pp. In this sequel to *Soaring Eagle* (1993) and *White Grizzly* (2000) set in 1845, Teresita Montoya, 13, has various adventures on the Santa Fe Trail as she searches for her older brother and for a new life for herself. (Rev: BL 12/1/03; HBG 4/04; SLJ 2/04)

10862 Finley, Mary Peace. *White Grizzly* (5–9). 2000, Filter $15.95 (978-0-86541-053-4); paper $8.95 (978-0-86541-058-9). 215pp. Fifteen-year-old Julio sets out on an arduous journey along the Santa Fe Trail to discover his true identity. (Rev: BL 12/1/00; HBG 10/01; SLJ 1/01; VOYA 2/01)

10863 Fleischman, Paul. *The Borning Room* (5–8). 1991, HarperCollins paper $4.99 (978-0-06-447099-5). 80pp. Georgina remembers important turning points in her life and the role played by the room set aside for giving birth and dying in her grandfather's house in 19th-century rural Ohio. (Rev: BCCB 9/91; BL 10/1/91*; HB 11/91*; SLJ 9/91*)

10864 Fleischman, Sid. *Bandit's Moon* (3–6). Illus. 1998, Greenwillow $17.99 (978-0-688-15830-9). 144pp. Based partly on fact, this is a humorous adventure story about Annyrose, a young girl who,

disguised as a boy, joins a band of Mexican bandits led by Wakeen, the notorious robber. (Rev: BCCB 11/98; BL 10/1/98*; HB 11/98; HBG 3/99; SLJ 9/98)

10865 Fleischman, Sid. *Jim Ugly* (4–6). Illus. by Joseph A. Smith. 1992, Greenwillow $17.99 (978-0-688-10886-1). 144pp. In the time of the Old West, Jake — accompanied by his dad's mongrel dog — sets off in search of his missing father. (Rev: BCCB 3/92*; BL 5/15/92; SLJ 4/92)

10866 Garland, Sherry. *Valley of the Moon: The Diary of Rosalia de Milagros* (5–8). Illus. 2001, Scholastic paper $10.95 (978-0-439-08820-6). 224pp. Rosalia, a 13-year-old orphan, keeps a diary about working on a California ranch in 1846. (Rev: BL 4/1/01; HBG 3/02; SLJ 4/01; VOYA 8/01)

10867 Glass, Andrew. *A Right Fine Life: Kit Carson on the Santa Fe Trail* (3–5). Illus. 1997, Holiday House LB $16.95 (978-0-8234-1326-3). 48pp. This tall tale tells about 16-year-old Kit Carson's first journey west and his many adventures along the way. (Rev: BL 2/1/98; HBG 3/98; SLJ 2/98)

10868 Glaze, Lynn. *Seasons of the Trail* (4–6). Illus. by Matthew Archambault. 2000, Silver Moon LB $14.95 (978-1-893110-20-5). 92pp. To avoid the oncoming Civil War, 14-year-old Lucy Scott and her family leave their home in Missouri and journey to California by covered wagon. (Rev: HBG 3/01; SLJ 1/01)

10869 Gregory, Kristiana. *Across the Wide and Lonesome Prairie: The Oregon Trail Diary of Hattie Campbell* (4–7). Illus. Series: Dear America. 1997, Scholastic paper $10.95 (978-0-590-22651-6). 149pp. In a diary format, this novel chronicles the hardships that pioneers endured during a trip west on the Oregon Trail. (Rev: SLJ 3/97)

10870 Gregory, Kristiana. *My Darlin' Clementine* (4–7). 2009, Holiday $16.95 (978-0-8234-2198-5). 208pp. Based on the traditional folk song, this is the story of 16-year-old Clementine, who in Idaho Territory in the late 1860s has to deal with family problems including her father's gambling and drinking while still hoping to become a doctor. (Rev: BL 4/15/09; SLJ 5/09; VOYA 6/09)

10871 Gregory, Kristiana. *Seeds of Hope: The Gold Rush Diary of Susanna Fairchild* (4–8). 2001, Scholastic paper $10.95 (978-0-590-51157-5). 182pp. After Susanna's mother dies in 1849, the 14-year-old takes over her journal and describes the hardships she and her sisters face when their father decides to move the family to California in search of gold. (Rev: BL 9/1/01; HBG 10/01; SLJ 7/01; VOYA 10/01)

10872 Hahn, Mary D. *The Gentleman Outlaw and Me — Eli: A Story of the Old West* (5–8). 1996, Clarion $16.00 (978-0-395-73083-6). 224pp. In frontier days, Eliza, masquerading as a boy, travels west in search of her father. (Rev: BCCB 4/96; BL 4/1/96; HB 9/96; SLJ 5/96; VOYA 6/96)

10873 Hart, Alison. *Anna's Blizzard* (3–5). Illus. by Paul Bachem. 2005, Peachtree $12.95 (978-1-56145-349-8). 141pp. Twelve-year-old Anna Vail loves life on the prairie although she lacks confidence at school, but when a blizzard traps children in the schoolhouse, it's Anna and her faithful pony who guide them all to safety. (Rev: SLJ 10/05)

10874 Heisel, Sharon E. *Precious Gold, Precious Jade* (5–8). 2000, Holiday $16.95 (978-0-8234-1432-1). 185pp. At the end of the Gold Rush in southern Oregon, two sisters create hostilities when they befriend a Chinese family that has moved to town. (Rev: BCCB 4/00; HBG 10/00; SLJ 4/00)

10875 Helldorfer, M. C. *Hog Music* (K–4). Illus. by S. D. Schindler. 2000, Viking $15.99 (978-0-670-87182-7). Set in the first half of the 19th century, this book chronicles the routes and vehicles involved in transporting a hat from the east to Illinois. (Rev: BCCB 9/00; HBG 10/00; SLJ 5/00)

10876 Henry, Joanne L. *A Clearing in the Forest: A Story About a Real Settler Boy* (3–5). Illus. by Charles Robinson. 1992, Macmillan $14.95 (978-0-02-743671-6). 44pp. Action highlights this historical novel about growing up in Indianapolis in the 1830s. (Rev: BCCB 6/92; BL 3/1/92; SLJ 3/92)

10877 Hermes, Patricia. *A Perfect Place: Joshua's Oregon Trail Diary* (3–5). Series: My America. 2002, Scholastic $10.95 (978-0-439-19999-5). 112pp. In this sequel to *Westward to Home* (2000), 9-year-old Joshua records the difficult conditions in the Willamette Valley as winter closes in. (Rev: BL 1/1–15/03; HBG 3/03; SLJ 11/02)

10878 Hoff, Carol. *Johnny Texas* (4–6). Illus. by Bob Meyers. 1992, Hendrick-Long paper $13.95 (978-0-937460-81-8). 160pp. Texas history is interwoven into this story of a pioneer German family. A reissue.

10879 Holland, Isabelle. *The Journey Home* (4–6). 1990, Scholastic $13.95 (978-0-590-43110-1). 192pp. Two orphaned girls start life anew in the second half of the 19th century when they are adopted by a couple in Kansas. (Rev: BCCB 12/90; SLJ 12/90)

10880 Holland, Isabelle. *The Promised Land* (5–8). 1996, Scholastic paper $15.95 (978-0-590-47176-3). Orphaned Maggie and Annie, who have been happily living with the Russell family on the Kansas frontier for three years, are visited by an uncle who wants them to come home with him to Catholicism and their Irish heritage in New York City. A sequel to *The Journey Home.* (Rev: BL 4/15/96; SLJ 8/96; VOYA 6/96)

10881 Holling, Holling C. *Tree in the Trail* (4–7). Illus. by author. 1942, Houghton $20.00 (978-0-395-18228-4); paper $11.95 (978-0-395-54534-8). 64pp. The history of the Santa Fe Trail, described through the life of a cottonwood tree, a 200-year-old landmark to travelers and a symbol of peace to the Indians.

10882 Holm, Jennifer. *Boston Jane: An Adventure* (5–8). 2001, HarperCollins LB $17.89 (978-0-06-028739-9). 288pp. A well-bred young woman faces hardships as she searches the 19th-century Washington Territory for her lost fiancé. (Rev: BL 9/1/01; HB 9/01; HBG 3/02; SLJ 8/01)

10883 Holm, Jennifer. *Boston Jane: The Claim* (5–8). 2004, HarperCollins $15.99 (978-0-06-029045-0).

240pp. In the third installment in Jane's story, an old rival named Sally and a former suitor cause difficulties for Jane. (Rev: BL 3/1/04; SLJ 5/04; VOYA 4/04)

10884 Holm, Jennifer. *Boston Jane: Wilderness Days* (5–8). 2002, HarperCollins LB $18.89 (978-0-06-029044-3). 256pp. Jane's continued adventures in 1854 Washington Territory include helping to stop a murderer and adjusting to the hardships of pioneer life. (Rev: BL 9/1/02; HB 9/02; HBG 3/03; SLJ 10/02)

10885 Hooks, William H. *Pioneer Cat* (2–4). Illus. by Charles Robinson. 1988, Random paper $3.99 (978-0-394-82038-5). 64pp. Kate smuggles a cat aboard the prairie schooner as the family heads west on the Oregon Trail. (Rev: BCCB 12/88; BL 1/15/89; SLJ 3/89)

10886 Hopkinson, Deborah. *Cabin in the Snow* (2–4). Series: Prairie Skies. 2002, Simon & Schuster paper $3.99 (978-0-689-84351-8). 80pp. Charlie must care for his pregnant mother while his father is away in this story set in Kansas during the free-state movement. (Rev: BL 12/15/02; HBG 3/03; SLJ 1/03)

10887 Hopkinson, Deborah. *Our Kansas Home* (3–5). Illus. by Patrick Faricy. Series: Prairie Skies. 2003, Simon & Schuster paper $3.99 (978-0-689-84353-2). 80pp. In this final volume in the trilogy, Charlie and his father tangle with pro-slavery ruffians and Charlie helps a runaway slave. (Rev: BL 3/1/03; HBG 10/03; SLJ 3/03)

10888 Hopkinson, Deborah. *Sailing for Gold* (2–4). Illus. by Bill Farnsworth. Series: Ready-for-Chapters. 2004, Simon & Schuster paper $3.99 (978-0-689-86031-7). 64pp. The first installment in an exciting and information-packed trilogy about orphan David Hill, 11, who sets off from Seattle for the Klondike in search of his uncle. (Rev: BL 1/1–15/04; SLJ 7/04)

10889 Karr, Kathleen. *Exiled: Memoirs of a Camel* (4–8). 2004, Marshall Cavendish $15.95 (978-0-7614-5164-8). 240pp. This fascinating story of the U.S. Camel Corps is told from the viewpoint of Ali, an Egyptian camel drafted for service in this short-lived branch of the United States Army. (Rev: BL 5/1/04; SLJ 5/04)

10890 Karr, Kathleen. *Oregon Sweet Oregon* (5–8). Series: Petticoat Party. 1997, HarperCollins LB $14.89 (978-0-06-027234-0). This novel, set in Oregon City, Oregon, from 1846 through 1848, recounts the adventures of 13-year-old Phoebe Brown and her family when they stake a land claim along the Willamette River. (Rev: BL 7/97; SLJ 7/98)

10891 Karwoski, Gail L. *Seaman: The Dog Who Explored the West with Lewis and Clark* (4–8). 1999, Peachtree paper $8.95 (978-1-56145-190-6). This historical novel dramatizes the story of Seaman, the Newfoundland dog that accompanied Lewis and Clark on their expedition. (Rev: BL 8/99; HBG 10/03; SLJ 10/99)

10892 Kent, Deborah. *Blackwater Creek* (4–6). Series: Saddles, Stars, and Stripes. 2005, Kingfisher $8.95 (978-0-7534-5885-3). 152pp. In 1849 California, Hungarian immigrant Erika looks after horses for a local rancher while her brother and father search for gold. (Rev: SLJ 3/06)

10893 Kent, Deborah. *Riding the Pony Express* (3–7). Series: Saddles, Stars, and Stripes. 2006, Kingfisher $8.95 (978-0-7534-6001-6). 149pp. Despite the fact that her father has died and her brother is accused of robbery, 15-year-old Lexie has no intention of being shipped back East and, disguising herself as a boy, sets off on her own along the Pony Express trail to prove her brother innocent. (Rev: SLJ 8/06)

10894 Kent, Peter. *Quest for the West: In Search of Gold* (3–6). Illus. 1997, Millbrook LB $21.40 (978-0-7613-0302-2). 32pp. The Hornik family leave their Czech homeland in 1849 to find a new life in the United States in this novel with excellent pen-and-ink and watercolor illustrations. (Rev: BL 12/1/97; SLJ 6/98)

10895 Kerr, Rita. *Texas Footprints* (4–7). Illus. 1988, Eakin $13.95 (978-0-89015-676-6). 80pp. A tale of the author's great-great-grandparents who went to Texas in 1823. (Rev: BL 3/1/89)

10896 Kimmel, Elizabeth C. *The Adventures of Young Buffalo Bill: In the Eye of the Storm* (3–7). Series: Adventures of Young Buffalo Bill. 2003, HarperCollins LB $16.89 (978-0-06-029116-7). 144pp. At the age of nine, young Bill must look after the Kansas homestead in his father's absence and feels resentment against these heavy duties. (Rev: BL 1/1–15/03; HBG 10/03; SLJ 2/03)

10897 Kramer, Sydelle. *Wagon Train* (2–4). Illus. by Deborah Kogan Ray. Series: All Aboard Reading. 1997, Penguin paper $3.99 (978-0-448-41334-1). 48pp. This easy-to-read book follows a family as it crosses the United States wagon in 1848. (Rev: BL 2/1/98)

10898 Laurgaard, Rachel K. *Patty Reed's Doll: The Story of the Donner Party* (3–6). Illus. by Elizabeth Michaels. 1989, Tomato Enterprises paper $9.95 (978-0-9617357-2-2). 144pp. A fantasy seen through the eyes of a doll about a survivor of the Donner Party. A reissue. (Rev: SLJ 11/89)

10899 Lawlor, Laurie. *Addie Across the Prairie* (3–5). Illus. 1986, Pocket paper $3.99 (978-0-671-70147-5). 128pp. Nine-year-old Addie learns about sod houses and curious Indians as her family travels cross-country to the Dakota Territory. (Rev: BL 8/86; SLJ 10/86)

10900 Lawlor, Laurie. *Gold in the Hills* (4–6). 1995, Walker $15.95 (978-0-8027-8371-4). 152pp. When their father sets out to find gold, Hattie and her brother must stay with bitter, tyrannical cousin Tirzah in this novel set in Colorado during frontier days. (Rev: BCCB 7–8/95; BL 6/1–15/95; SLJ 8/95)

10901 Lawlor, Laurie. *The School at Crooked Creek* (2–5). Illus. by Ronald Himler. 2004, Holiday House $15.95 (978-0-8234-1812-1). 83pp. Lawlor paints an engaging portrait of life on the frontier in this story of 6-year-old Beansie, who lives with his family in a one-room cabin in 1820s Indiana and hates the idea of going to school. (Rev: BL 4/15/04)

10902 Leland, Dorothy K. *Sallie Fox: The Story of a Pioneer Girl* (4–6). 1995, Tomato Enterprises paper $9.95 (978-0-9617357-6-0). 115pp. A fictionalized account of the trek of 12-year-old Sallie Fox by wagon train with her family from Iowa to California in the mid 1800s. (Rev: SLJ 2/96)

10903 Levine, Ellen. *The Journal of Jedediah Barstow: An Emigrant on the Oregon Trail* (4–7). Series: My Name Is America. 2002, Scholastic $10.95 (978-0-439-06310-4). 176pp. Jedediah continues his mother's journal about their experiences on the Oregon Trail after she and the rest of his family are drowned while crossing a river. (Rev: BL 2/15/03; HBG 10/03; SLJ 11/02)

10904 Levitin, Sonia. *Clem's Chances* (4–7). 2001, Scholastic paper $17.95 (978-0-439-29314-3). 200pp. Fourteen-year-old Clem becomes acquainted with the hardships and rewards of frontier life when he travels to California to find his father in 1860. (Rev: BL 9/15/01; HB 11/01; HBG 3/02; SLJ 10/01)

10905 Love, D. Anne. *Bess's Log Cabin Quilt* (2–5). Illus. by Ronald Himler. 1995, Holiday House $15.95 (978-0-8234-1178-8). 72pp. In frontier Oregon, Bess hopes that by winning a quilt contest she can help ease her family's financial problems. (Rev: BCCB 6/95; BL 2/15/95; SLJ 6/95)

10906 Luger, Harriett M. *The Last Stronghold: A Story of the Modoc Indian War, 1872–1873* (5–8). 1995, Linnet paper $17.50 (978-0-208-02403-9). The Modoc Indian War of 1872–1873 is re-created in this story involving three young people: Charka, a Modoc youth; Ned, a frontier boy; and Yankel, a Russian Jew who has been tricked into joining the army. (Rev: VOYA 6/96)

10907 MacBride, Roger L. *In the Land of the Big Red Apple* (3–7). Illus. by David Gilleece. 1995, HarperCollins LB $15.89 (978-0-06-024964-9). 352pp. In the mid-1890s, the farm at Rocky Ridge, where Rose Wilder Lane is growing up, gradually prospers. (Rev: BL 5/15/95; SLJ 9/95)

10908 MacBride, Roger L. *Little Farm in the Ozarks* (3–6). Illus. 1994, HarperCollins paper $7.99 (978-0-06-440510-2). 304pp. Based on the journals of Rose Wilder Lane, this novel tells about the Wilder family's first spring and summer in Mansfield, Missouri. (Rev: BL 5/1/94)

10909 MacBride, Roger L. *Little House on Rocky Edge* (3–7). Illus. by David Gilleece. 1993, HarperCollins paper $7.99 (978-0-06-440478-5). 304pp. This reworking of Laura Ingalls Wilder's material tells the story from Rose's perspective of the Wilder family's move from South Dakota to Missouri. This is the first part of a projected five-part series. (Rev: BL 6/1–15/93)

10910 MacBride, Roger L. *New Dawn on Rocky Ridge* (4–7). Illus. Series: Rocky Ridge. 1997, HarperCollins paper $7.99 (978-0-06-440581-2). 320pp. This part of the Wilder family story covers 1900–1903 and focuses on Rose's difficult early teen years. (Rev: BL 11/1/97; HBG 3/98; SLJ 2/98)

10911 McDonald, Brix. *Riding on the Wind* (5–10). 1998, Avenue paper $5.95 (978-0-9661306-0-7). 243pp. In frontier Wyoming during the early 1860s, 15-year-old Carrie Sutton is determined to become a rider in the Pony Express after her family's ranch has been chosen as a relay station. (Rev: SLJ 1/99)

10912 McKissack, Patricia C. *Run Away Home* (4–7). 1997, Scholastic paper $14.95 (978-0-590-46751-3). 176pp. In 1888 rural Alabama, a young African American girl helps shelter a fugitive Apache boy. (Rev: BL 10/1/97; HB 11/97; HBG 3/98; SLJ 11/97)

10913 MacLachlan, Patricia. *Grandfather's Dance* (4–6). Series: Sarah Plain and Tall. 2006, HarperCollins $14.99 (978-0-06-027560-0). 96pp. At Anna's wedding, Cassie, the fourth-grade daughter of Sarah (of *Sarah Plain and Tall*), mulls over her bonds with the rest of the family in this closing installment in the series. (Rev: BL 7/06; SLJ 11/06)

10914 MacLachlan, Patricia. *Sarah, Plain and Tall* (3–5). Illus. by Marcia Sewall. 1985, HarperCollins LB $16.89 (978-0-06-024102-5); paper $5.99 (978-0-06-440205-7). 64pp. Two children wait on the prairie for the arrival of their new stepmother, who has answered their father's ad for a wife. Newbery Medal winner, 1986. (Rev: BCCB 5/85; BL 5/1/89; SLJ 5/85)

10915 McMullan, Kate. *As Far as I Can See: Meg's Prairie Diary* (2–4). Series: My America. 2002, Scholastic $10.95 (978-0-439-42517-9). 112pp. City girl Meg describes her new life in Kansas, where she and her brother have been sent to avoid a cholera epidemic in 1856, and writes about the help she gives to a runaway slave. (Rev: BL 10/1/02; HBG 3/03; SLJ 8/02)

10916 McMullan, Kate. *A Fine Start: Meg's Prairie Diary* (4–6). Series: My America. 2003, Scholastic LB $12.95 (978-0-439-37061-5). 106pp. In this fictional diary, 9-year-old Meg recounts the hardships her family endures on the prairies of the Kansas Territory. (Rev: HBG 4/04; SLJ 1/04)

10917 Mercati, Cynthia. *Wagons Ho! A Diary of the Oregon Trail* (3–5). Illus. 2000, Perfection Learning $16.95 (978-0-7807-9011-7). 56pp. A simple read in diary form about young Lisa and her adventures in a Conestoga wagon heading west with her family in 1849. (Rev: BL 10/15/00)

10918 Milligan, Bryce. *With the Wind, Kevin Dolan: A Novel of Ireland and Texas* (5–7). Illus. 1987, Corona paper $7.95 (978-0-931722-45-5). 194pp. The story of Kevin and Tom, brothers who leave the famine in Ireland in the 1830s and head for America. (Rev: BL 8/87; SLJ 9/87)

10919 Moeri, Louise. *Save Queen of Sheba* (5–7). 1990, Avon paper $3.50 (978-0-380-71154-3). 112pp. Young David survives a wagon train massacre and must take care of his young sister. (Rev: BL 9/1/02; HB 9/02; HBG 3/03; SLJ 9/02)

10920 Myers, Laurie. *Lewis and Clark and Me: A Dog's Tale* (3–6). Illus. by Michael Dooling. 2002, Holt $16.95 (978-0-8050-6368-4). 64pp. The Lewis and Clark expedition told from the point of view of Seaman, Lewis's Newfoundland dog, with excerpts from Lewis's journal, illustrations and a map of the route. (Rev: BL 9/1/02; HB 9/02; HBG 3/03; SLJ 9/02)

10921 Nixon, Joan Lowery. *In the Face of Danger* (5–8). 1996, Bantam paper $4.99 (978-0-440-

22705-2). Megan fears she will bring bad luck to her adoptive family in this story set in the prairies of Kansas. This is the third part of the Orphan Train Quartet. (Rev: SLJ 12/88; VOYA 12/88)

10922 Oatman, Eric. *Cowboys on the Western Trail: The Cattle Drive Adventures of Josh McNabb and Davy Bartlett* (4–7). Illus. Series: I Am America. 2004, National Geographic paper $6.99 (978-0-7922-6553-5). 40pp. The excitement of a cattle drive is shown in the journals and letters of two young teen boys in this blend of fact and fiction set in 1887 and presented in an appealing magazine format. (Rev: BL 5/15/04)

10923 O'Dell, Scott. *Streams to the River, River to the Sea: A Novel of Sacagawea* (5–9). 1986, Houghton $16.00 (978-0-395-40430-0). 191pp. A fictionalized portrait of the real-life Indian woman who traveled west with Lewis and Clark on their famous journey. (Rev: BL 3/15/86; HB 9/86; SLJ 5/86; VOYA 6/86)

10924 Olson, Tod. *How to Get Rich on the Oregon Trail: My Adventures Among Cows, Crooks, and Heroes on the Road to Fame and Fortune* (4–8). Illus. by Scott Allred. 2009, National Geographic $16.95 (978-1-4263-0412-5). 48pp. In his journal, 15-year-old Will Reed records the events of his family's 1852 journey to Oregon. (Rev: BCCB 5/09; BL 3/1/09; SLJ 5/09)

10925 Paulsen, Gary. *The Legend of Bass Reeves* (5–8). 2006, Random $15.95 (978-0-385-74661-8). 160pp. This fictionalized biography profiles the little-known life and career of Bass Reeves, the former slave who became one of the West's most effective lawmen. (Rev: BCCB 10/06; BL 6/1–15/06; HBG 10/07; SLJ 8/06)

10926 Pearsall, Shelley. *Crooked River* (4–6). 2005, Knopf LB $17.99 (978-0-375-92389-0). 256pp. In early-19th-century Ohio, 13-year-old Rebecca learns about truth and justice as she watches the plight of a Native American accused of killing a trapper. (Rev: BL 5/15/05)

10927 Philbrick, Rodman. *The Journal of Douglas Allen Deeds: The Donner Party Expedition* (5–7). Series: My Name Is America. 2001, Scholastic paper $10.95 (978-0-439-21600-5). 160pp. A fictional account of the Donner Party's hardships as written in a 15-year-old orphaned boy's journal. (Rev: BL 1/1–15/02; HBG 3/02; SLJ 12/01)

10928 Pryor, Bonnie. *Luke: 1849 — On the Golden Trail* (3–6). Illus. 1999, Morrow $15.00 (978-0-688-15670-1). 160pp. Luke's pioneer family has such misfortune farming that the boy decides to leave and accompany his wealthy uncle to Boston. (Rev: BL 8/99; HBG 10/99; SLJ 8/99)

10929 Rinaldi, Ann. *The Second Bend in the River* (5–9). 1997, Scholastic paper $15.95 (978-0-590-74258-0). In Ohio in 1798, 7-year-old Rebecca begins a long-lasting friendship with the Shawnee chief Tecumseh that eventually leads to a marriage proposal. (Rev: BCCB 3/97; BL 2/15/97; HBG 3/98; SLJ 6/97)

10930 Schultz, Jan Neubert. *Battle Cry* (5–9). 2006, Carolrhoda LB $15.95 (978-1-57505-928-0). 240pp.

Native American Chaska and white settler Johnny are drawn into the bloody 1862 Dakota Conflict in this dramatic tale. (Rev: SLJ 7/06)

10931 Schultz, Jan Neubert. *Horse Sense* (5–7). 2001, Carolrhoda LB $15.95 (978-1-57505-998-3); paper $6.95 (978-1-57505-999-0). 180pp. Fourteen-year-old Will and his father do not get along, but they join a posse tracking dangerous outlaws in this adventure based on a true story. (Rev: BL 8/01; HBG 3/02; VOYA 12/01)

10932 Scillian, Devin. *Pappy's Handkerchief* (2–4). Illus. by Chris Ellison. Series: Tales of Young Americans. 2007, Sleeping Bear $17.95 (978-1-58536-316-2). 32pp. Moses, a young African American boy from Baltimore, must take on a lot of responsibility after a series of accidents befall his family during the Oklahoma Land Run. (Rev: BL 10/1/07; SLJ 1/08)

10933 Seeley, Debra. *Grasslands* (5–8). 2002, Holiday $16.95 (978-0-8234-1731-5). 128pp. The hard life on the prairie disappoints a 13-year-old newcomer from Virginia until he has the chance to ride as a cowboy in this novel set in the late 19th century. (Rev: BL 11/1/02; HBG 3/03; SLJ 1/03*; VOYA 12/02)

10934 Shaw, Janet. *Happy Birthday Kirsten!* (3–5). Illus. 1987, Pleasant $12.95 (978-0-937295-88-5); paper $6.95 (978-0-937295-33-5). 72pp. It is 1854 in Minnesota and Kirsten looks forward to the gift of a day off from household chores. Also use: *Changes for Kirsten; Kirsten Saves the Day* (both 1988). (Rev: BL 4/1/88)

10935 Shaw, Janet. *Kirsten Learns a Lesson: A School Story* (3–5). Illus. 1986, Pleasant LB $12.95 (978-0-937295-82-3); paper $6.95 (978-0-937295-10-6). 72pp. Kirsten, a young immigrant girl, lives with her Swedish family in 1854 Minnesota. Others in this series are: *Kirsten's Surprise: A Christmas Story; Meet Kirsten: An American Girl* (both 1986). (Rev: BL 12/1/86)

10936 Sommerdorf, Norma. *Red River Girl* (4–7). 2006, Holiday $16.95 (978-0-8234-1903-6). 216pp. In 1846 after her Ojibwa mother dies, 12-year-old Metis girl Josette starts a journal that documents her family's journey by wagon train from Canada to St. Paul, Minnesota, where they settle and she becomes a teacher. (Rev: BL 11/15/06; SLJ 12/06)

10937 Stevens, Carla. *Trouble for Lucy* (4–6). Illus. by Ronald Himler. 1979, Houghton paper $5.95 (978-0-89919-523-0). 80pp. Lucy's pup Finn causes trouble during a wagon trip to the Oregon Territory.

10938 Thomas, Joyce C. *I Have Heard of a Land* (3–6). Illus. by Floyd Cooper. 1998, HarperCollins LB $14.89 (978-0-06-023478-2). 32pp. This tribute to the pioneer spirit tells, through the eyes of a black woman, what it was like to come to the untamed frontier, build a home, and put down roots. (Rev: BCCB 6/98; BL 2/15/98*; HBG 10/98; SLJ 7/98)

10939 Tripp, Valerie. *Happy Birthday, Josefina! A Springtime Story* (3–5). Series: American Girls. 1998, Pleasant $12.95 (978-1-56247-588-8); paper $6.95 (978-1-56247-587-1). 68pp. In the New Mexico of 1824, Josefina discovers she can become a

healer after she cures a friend bitten by a rattlesnake. (Rev: BL 8/98; HBG 3/99)

10940 Tripp, Valerie. *Josefina Saves the Day: A Summer Story* (3–5). Illus. Series: American Girls. 1998, Pleasant $12.95 (978-1-56247-590-1); paper $6.95 (978-1-56247-589-5). 68pp. A heavily illustrated novel, set in the New Mexico of 1824, in which young Josefina's father must decide whether or not to trust an American trader. (Rev: BL 8/98; HBG 3/99)

10941 Tripp, Valerie. *Meet Josefina: An American Girl* (3–5). Illus. Series: American Girls. 1997, Pleasant paper $6.95 (978-1-56247-515-4). 85pp. In this story set in 1824 on a Mexican ranch in what is now New Mexico, the young heroine helps manage the ranch after her mother's death. Also use *Josefina Learns a Lesson: A School Story* (1997). (Rev: BL 10/1/97; HBG 3/98; SLJ 12/97)

10942 Welch, Catherine A. *Clouds of Terror* (2–4). Illus. by Laurie K. Johnson. 1994, Carolrhoda LB $23.93 (978-0-87614-771-9). 48pp. The harm caused by hordes of grasshoppers is depicted in this story set on a Minnesota farm during the 1870s. (Rev: BL 9/15/94; SLJ 8/94)

10943 Whelan, Gloria. *Miranda's Last Stand* (4–7). 1999, HarperCollins LB $14.89 (978-0-06-028252-3). 128pp. After her husband was killed at Little Big Horn, Miranda's mother can't bear to be around Indians, including Sitting Bull, who works with her at Buffalo Bill's Wild West Show. (Rev: BL 11/1/99; HBG 3/00; SLJ 11/99)

10944 Whelan, Gloria. *Next Spring an Oriole* (2–4). Illus. 1987, Random LB $6.99 (978-0-394-99125-2); paper $3.99 (978-0-394-89125-5). 64pp. The story of 10-year-old Libby who journeys to Michigan from Virginia in a covered wagon with her family in 1837. (Rev: BCCB 10/87; BL 10/1/87)

10945 Whelan, Gloria. *Return to the Island* (4–7). 2000, HarperCollins LB $15.89 (978-0-06-028254-7). 192pp. In the early 19th century on Mackinac Island, Mary must decide between two men who love her: White Hawk, an orphan raised by a white family, and James, an English painter. (Rev: BL 1/1–15/01; HBG 3/01; SLJ 12/00)

10946 Wilder, Laura Ingalls. *The Long Winter* (5–8). Illus. 1953, HarperCollins LB $17.89 (978-0-06-026461-1). Number six in the Little House books. In this one, the Ingalls face a terrible winter with only seed grain for food.

10947 Wilkes, Maria D. *Little Clearing in the Woods* (3–6). Illus. by Dan Andreasen. Series: The Caroline Years. 1998, HarperCollins LB $15.89 (978-0-06-026998-2). 315pp. Caroline Quiner (the mother of Laura Ingalls Wilder) and her family move to a small cabin in the woods, where her widowed mother takes a job cooking for neighborhood laborers. (Rev: HBG 10/98; SLJ 10/98)

10948 Wilkes, Maria D. *Little House in Brookfield* (3–6). Illus. by Dan Andreasen. Series: The Brookfield Years. 1996, HarperCollins paper $6.99 (978-0-06-440610-9). 298pp. This spinoff from the *Little House* books tells of the childhood in Brookfield, Wisconsin, of Caroline Quiner, who much later would become the mother of Laura Ingalls Wilder. (Rev: SLJ 8/96)

10949 Wisler, G. Clifton. *All for Texas: A Story of Texas Liberation* (4–8). 2000, Jamestown paper $5.95 (978-0-8092-0629-2). 140pp. A thirteen-year-old boy tells about moving west with his family in 1838 to Texas, where his father has been promised land if he will fight against Mexico. (Rev: BCCB 7–8/00; SLJ 8/00)

10950 Yep, Laurence. *The Journal of Wong Ming-Chung* (4–7). Illus. 2000, Scholastic paper $10.95 (978-0-590-38607-4). 224pp. Told in diary format beginning in October 1851, this is the story of a Chinese boy nicknamed Runt who travels from his native country to join an uncle in the gold mining fields of America. (Rev: BL 4/1/00; HBG 10/00; SLJ 4/00; VOYA 6/00)

10951 Young, Judy. *Minnow and Rose* (3–5). Illus. by Bill Farnsworth. Series: Tales of Young Americans. 2009, Sleeping Bear $17.95 (978-1-58536-421-3). 40pp. In the mid-1800s, Rose, who is traveling west with her family, meets a Native American girl named Minnow and the two learn about each other's lives. (Rev: BL 3/1/09)

THE CIVIL WAR

10952 Avi. *Iron Thunder* (5–8). 2007, Hyperion $14.99 (978-1-4231-0446-9). 224pp. Tom, a 13-year-old naval yard worker and later crew member, describes the construction of the *Monitor,* the perilous voyage to the Union blockade, and the ensuing battle with the *Merrimac*; period photographs and newspaper headlines add historic context. (Rev: BL 8/07; LMC 11/07; SLJ 9/07)

10953 Brill, Marlene T. *Diary of a Drummer Boy* (4–7). 1998, Millbrook LB $23.90 (978-0-7613-0118-9). 48pp. Using a diary format, this novel tells of a 12-year-old's experiences as a drummer in the Union Army during the Civil War. (Rev: BL 3/1/98; HBG 10/98; SLJ 5/98)

10954 Crist-Evans, Craig. *Moon over Tennessee: A Boy's Civil War Journal* (4–7). 1999, Houghton $15.00 (978-0-395-91208-9). 64pp. In free-verse diary entries, 13-year-old Crist-Evans reports on the Civil War from his vantage point in a camp behind the front lines. (Rev: BCCB 6/99; BL 5/15/99; HBG 10/99; SLJ 8/99; VOYA 10/99)

10955 Denslow, Sharon Phillips. *All Their Names Were Courage* (4–6). 2003, HarperCollins LB $15.99 (978-0-06-623810-4). 144pp. Eleven-year-old Sallie Burd writes to her soldier brother about her quest to learn about the horses of Union and Confederate generals. (Rev: BL 8/03; HBG 4/04; SLJ 10/03)

10956 Donahue, John. *An Island Far from Home* (4–7). 1994, Carolrhoda LB $15.95 (978-0-87614-859-4). 180pp. Joshua, a Union supporter, forms an unusual friendship through corresponding with a young Southern soldier who is a prisoner of war. (Rev: BCCB 2/95; BL 2/15/95; SLJ 2/95)

10957 Durrant, Lynda. *My Last Skirt* (5–8). 2006, Clarion $16.00 (978-0-618-57490-2). 208pp. After migrating from Ireland to America, Jennie Hodgers,

who prefers wearing pants to skirts, adopts the persona of Albert Cashier and joins the Union army in this novel based on a true story. (Rev: BL 2/15/06; SLJ 4/06*)

10958 Ernst, Kathleen. *Hearts of Stone* (5–8). 2006, Dutton $16.99 (978-0-525-47686-3). 256pp. Fifteen-year-old Hannah and her three younger siblings struggle to survive after they're orphaned in Civil War Tennessee. (Rev: BL 11/1/06; SLJ 12/06)

10959 Ernst, Kathleen. *Retreat from Gettysburg* (5–8). Illus. 2000, White Mane LB $17.95 (978-1-57249-187-8). 142pp. When a doctor orders 14-year-old Chig and his mother to care for a wounded Confederate soldier, the boy finds it hard to be kind to a man who belongs to the side that killed his father and brothers. (Rev: BL 9/15/00; HBG 10/01; SLJ 12/00)

10960 Fleischner, Jennifer. *Nobody's Boy* (5–8). Illus. 2006, Missouri Historical Society $12.95 (978-1-883982-58-4). 96pp. George's mother buys freedom for herself and her son; she goes on to work for Mrs. Lincoln in the White House while George chooses the more dangerous avenue of helping slaves find freedom. (Rev: BL 2/1/07)

10961 Garrity, Jennifer Johnson. *The Bushwhacker: A Civil War Adventure* (5–8). Illus. by Paul Bachem. 1999, Peachtree paper $8.95 (978-1-56145-201-9). 196pp. The clash of divided loyalties is the main conflict in this story of a boy torn between his Unionist feelings and the friendship he feels towards his protector, a Confederate sympathizer. (Rev: SLJ 4/00)

10962 Hart, Alison. *Fires of Jubilee* (5–7). 2003, Simon & Schuster paper $4.99 (978-0-689-85528-3). 192pp. Abby, 13, is suddenly a free person when the Civil War ends and finally able to search for her mother, who left long before. (Rev: BL 11/1/03; SLJ 3/04)

10963 Hawk, Fran. *The Story of the H. L. Hunley and Queenie's Coin* (3–5). Illus. by Dan Nance. 2004, Sleeping Bear $16.95 (978-1-58536-218-9). 40pp. This story of the ill-fated Confederate submarine *H. L. Hunley* focuses on the lucky coin given to its developer by his fiancee. (Rev: BL 1/1–15/05; SLJ 5/05)

10964 Hopkinson, Deborah. *Billy and the Rebel* (1–3). Illus. by Brian Floca. Series: Ready-to-Read. 2005, Simon & Schuster $14.95 (978-0-689-83964-1). 48pp. A young boy and his mother give sanctuary to a Confederate deserter at their farm near Gettysburg in this story based on a real incident. (Rev: BL 2/1/05; SLJ 4/05)

10965 Hopkinson, Deborah. *From Slave to Soldier: Based on a True Civil War Story* (2–4). Illus. by Brian Floca. Series: Ready-to-Read. 2005, Simon & Schuster $14.95 (978-0-689-83965-8). 48pp. Inspired by real events, this book for beginning readers chronicles the experiences of a slave boy who runs off to join the Union army and works as a mule driver; an afterword adds context. (Rev: BL 1/1–15/06; SLJ 10/05)

10966 Hughes, Pat. *Seeing the Elephant: A Story of the Civil War* (2–4). Illus. by Ken Stark. 2007, Farrar $16.00 (978-0-374-38024-3). A 10-year-old boy, who longs to fight for the Union with his older brothers, learns about war when he meets a captured Confederate soldier. (Rev: SLJ 11/07)

10967 Hurst, Carol Otis. *Torchlight* (4–7). 2006, Houghton $16.00 (978-0-618-27601-1). 160pp. As tension mounts between the Yankee and Irish immigrant settlers in a Massachusetts town in 1864, Charlotte and Maggie struggle to maintain their friendship. (Rev: BL 12/1/06; SLJ 1/07)

10968 Keehn, Sally M. *Anna Sunday* (4–8). 2002, Putnam $18.99 (978-0-399-23875-8). 272pp. In 1863, 12-year-old Anna travels with her younger brother from Pennsylvania to Virginia to find her wounded father. (Rev: BCCB 9/02; BL 6/1–15/02; HBG 10/02; SLJ 6/02; VOYA 8/02)

10969 Kent, Deborah. *Chance of a Lifetime* (4–6). Series: Saddles, Stars, and Stripes. 2005, Kingfisher $8.95 (978-0-7534-5884-6). 173pp. In 1849, 14-year-old Jacquetta May Logan enlists the help of a slave girl to hide her family's Morgan horses from advancing Union forces. (Rev: SLJ 3/06)

10970 Love, D. Anne. *Three Against the Tide* (5–8). 1998, Holiday $15.95 (978-0-8234-1400-0). 162pp. In this Civil War novel, 12-year-old Confederate Susanna Simons must care for her two younger brothers when Yankee troops invade South Carolina. (Rev: BL 12/1/98; HBG 10/99; SLJ 1/99)

10971 Lyons, Mary E., and Muriel M. Branch. *Dear Ellen Bee: A Civil War Scrapbook of Two Union Spies* (5–8). Illus. 2000, Atheneum $17.00 (978-0-689-82379-4). 161pp. Set in Richmond, Virginia, before and during the Civil War, this novel, based on fact, tells how a strong-willed lady and her emancipated slave get involved in a spying adventure. (Rev: BCCB 10/00; BL 11/1/00; HBG 3/01; SLJ 10/00; VOYA 2/01)

10972 McGowen, Tom. *Jesse Bowman: A Union Boy's War Story* (5–8). Series: Historical Fiction Adventure. 2008, Enslow LB $20.95 (978-0-7660-2929-3). 160pp. The story of a young soldier who is horrified by the brutality of the Civil War. (Rev: BL 4/15/08; SLJ 7/08)

10973 McMullan, Margaret. *How I Found the Strong: A Civil War Story* (5–9). 2004, Houghton $15.00 (978-0-618-35008-7). The Civil War changes the way a boy looks at life when it takes away his father and brother and comes close to his Mississippi home. (Rev: BL 2/15/04; SLJ 4/04; VOYA 6/04)

10974 Noble, Trinka Hakes. *The Last Brother: A Civil War Tale* (2–4). Illus. by Robert Papp. 2006, Sleeping Bear $17.95 (978-1-58536-253-0). 48pp. Eleven-year-old Gabe, who has lost two brothers in battle, joins the Union Army with older brother Davy and learns to be a bugler. (Rev: BL 9/1/06; SLJ 12/06)

10975 Owens, L. L. *The Code of the Drum* (3–6). Illus. by Margaret Sanfilippo. Series: Cover-to-Cover Books. 2000, Perfection Learning $16.95 (978-0-7807-9654-6); paper $8.95 (978-0-7891-5310-4). 54pp. When his father is killed in the Civil War, 12-year-old Jacob McCoy joins his dad's

Union regiment as a drummer boy. (Rev: SLJ 12/00)

10976 Paulsen, Gary. *Soldier's Heart* (5–8). 1998, Delacorte $15.95 (978-0-385-32498-4). 144pp. A powerful novel about the agony of the Civil War, based on the real-life experiences of a Union soldier who was only 15 when he went to war. (Rev: BCCB 9/98; BL 6/1–15/98*; HB 11/98; HBG 3/99; SLJ 9/98; VOYA 10/98)

10977 Philbrick, Rodman. *The Mostly True Adventures of Homer P. Figg* (4–7). 2009, Scholastic $16.99 (978-0-439-66818-7). 224pp. There's comedy in the midst of war and innocence in the midst of knavery as Homer runs away from from his evil uncle and has many adventures while seeking to save the brother forced to join the Union Army. (Rev: BCCB 1/09; BL 1/1–15/09; HB 1/09; SLJ 1/09) ⌒

10978 Pinkney, Andrea D. *Abraham Lincoln: Letters from a Slave Girl* (4–7). Illus. Series: Dear Mr. President. 2001, Winslow $8.95 (978-1-890817-60-2). 136pp. Twelve-year-old Lettie Tucker, a slave, exchanges thought-provoking letters with President Abraham Lincoln in this story set in the 1860s packed with interesting illustrations. (Rev: BCCB 2/02; BL 9/1/01; HBG 3/02; SLJ 9/01)

10979 Polacco, Patricia. *Pink and Say* (K–5). Illus. 1994, Penguin $16.99 (978-0-399-22671-7). 32pp. Based on a true incident during the Civil War, this book tells of the friendship of two Union soldiers: Say, a white man who is rescued by a black man, Pinkus, known as Pink. (Rev: BCCB 9/94; BL 9/1/94; HB 11/94; SLJ 10/94*)

10980 Porter, Connie. *Addy Learns a Lesson* (3–6). Illus. by Melodye Rosales. Series: American Girls. 1993, Pleasant $12.95 (978-1-56247-078-4); paper $6.95 (978-1-56247-077-7). 70pp. In the year 1864, young Addy and her mother try to escape slavery by fleeing to the North after her father is sold again and they are separated. (Rev: BL 8/93; SLJ 1/94)

10981 Porter, Connie. *Addy Saves the Day: A Summer Story* (2–4). Illus. by Bradford Brown. 1994, Pleasant paper $6.95 (978-1-56247-083-8). 59pp. In this novel set in Philadelphia in 1864, Addy, a former slave, and her family try to make money to search for relatives lost in the Civil War. Also use *Happy Birthday, Addy!* (1994). (Rev: BL 11/1/94; SLJ 11/94)

10982 Pryor, Bonnie. *Joseph's Choice — 1861* (3–5). Illus. Series: American Adventures. 2000, HarperCollins LB $14.89 (978-0-06-029226-3). 176pp. At the beginning of the Civil War in a small Kentucky town, young Joseph realizes that he must take sides. (Rev: BL 12/15/00; HBG 10/01; SLJ 10/00)

10983 Rappaport, Doreen. *Freedom Ship* (2–4). Illus. by Curtis James. 2006, Hyperion $15.99 (978-0-7868-0645-4). 40pp. Slaves seize control of a Confederate steamship and turn it over to Union forces in this fictionalized version of a real event that is followed by a fascinating historical note. (Rev: BL 10/1/06; SLJ 11/06)

10984 Rinaldi, Ann. *Juliet's Moon* (5–8). Series: Great Episodes. 2008, Harcourt paper $17.00 (978-

0-15-206170-8). 256pp. Juliet's home and family are destroyed by the Civil War, and she and her brother, Seth, must fight and even kill to survive in this novel, which is loosely based on actual events. (Rev: BL 4/15/08)

10985 Rinaldi, Ann. *My Vicksburg* (5–8). 2009, Harcourt $16.00 (978-0-15-206624-6). 160pp. In 1863 Vicksburg, Mississippi, families choose to live in caves for safety and 13-year-old Claire Louise worries about the members of her family serving on different sides of the war. (Rev: BL 4/15/09; SLJ 7/09; VOYA 8/09)

10986 Spain, Susan Rosson. *The Deep Cut* (5–8). 2006, Marshall Cavendish $16.99 (978-0-7614-5316-1). 224pp. Thirteen-year-old Lonzo, often considered "slow," finally gains the respect of his father for his actions during the hostilities. (Rev: BL 12/1/06*; SLJ 12/06)

10987 Stolz, Mary. *A Ballad of the Civil War* (4–6). Illus. 1997, HarperCollins LB $13.89 (978-0-06-027363-7). 64pp. Based on a Civil War ballad, this is the story of two Southern brothers who enlist on opposite sides. (Rev: BL 10/1/97; SLJ 2/98)

10988 Thomas, Carroll. *Blue Creek Farm* (4–8). 2001, Smith & Kraus paper $9.95 (978-1-57525-243-8). 185pp. In Kansas of the 1860s, Matty Trescott and her father manage a farm and feel the effects of the Civil War. (Rev: BL 4/1/01; VOYA 6/01)

10989 Turner, Ann. *Drummer Boy: Marching to the Civil War* (3–5). Illus. by Mark Hess. 1998, HarperCollins LB $17.89 (978-0-06-027697-3). 32pp. In this first-person account, a 13-year-old runs away from home to become a drummer boy during the Civil War and later encounters the reality of war and death. (Rev: BCCB 11/98; BL 9/15/98; HBG 3/99; SLJ 11/98)

10990 Wells, Rosemary. *Lincoln and His Boys* (3–5). Illus. by P. J. Lynch. 2009, Candlewick $16.99 (978-0-7636-3723-1). 96pp. Inspired by an essay written by Lincoln's son Willie, Wells presents three vignettes about the president and his two younger sons in the White House during the Civil War years. (Rev: BCCB 1/09; BL 1/1–15/09; LMC 5/09; SLJ 1/09)

10991 Winnick, Karen B. *Cassie's Sweet Berry Pie* (1–3). Illus. 2005, Boyds Mills $16.95 (978-1-56397-984-2). 32pp. When Yankee soldiers are approaching, Cassie must think quickly to protect her younger siblings in this story of the Civil War. (Rev: BL 2/15/05; SLJ 3/05)

RECONSTRUCTION TO WORLD WAR II, 1865–1941

10992 Adler, Susan S. *Meet Samantha: An American Girl* (3–5). Illus. 1986, Pleasant LB $12.95 (978-0-937295-80-9); paper $6.95 (978-0-937295-04-5). 72pp. Samantha is an orphan living with her wealthy grandmother in the America of 1904. Two others in the series are: *Samantha Learns a Lesson; Samantha's Surprise* (both 1986). (Rev: BL 12/1/86)

10993 Alter, Judith. *Luke and the Van Zandt County War* (5–9). Illus. 1984, Texas Christian Univ.

$14.95 (978-0-912646-88-6). 132pp. Life in Reconstruction Texas as seen through the eyes of two 14-year-olds. (Rev: SLJ 3/85)

10994 Arato, Rona. *Ice Cream Town* (5–8). Illus. 2007, Fitzhenry & Whiteside paper $11.95 (978-1-55041-591-9). 186pp. Ten-year-old Sammy Levin, a recent Jewish immigrant from Poland, finds it tough to adjust to his new life on the streets of New York City's Lower East Side in the early 1900s. (Rev: BL 4/1/07; SLJ 6/07)

10995 Armstrong, Jennifer. *Theodore Roosevelt: Letters from a Young Coal Miner* (3–6). Illus. Series: Dear Mr. President. 2000, Winslow $8.95 (978-1-890817-27-5). 128pp. Using fictional letters between a 13-year-old Pennsylvania coal miner and Teddy Roosevelt, this book introduces the hardships of a miner's life as well as the character and administration of President Roosevelt. (Rev: BL 3/1/01; HBG 10/01)

10996 Atwell, Debby. *Pearl* (K–3). Illus. 2001, Houghton $16.00 (978-0-395-88416-4). 32pp. Pearl, a woman in her 90s, covers a substantial part of American history in her reminiscences, which stretch from her grandfather's encounter with George Washington through World Wars I and II and her hope that her great-granddaughter might someday go to the moon. (Rev: BCCB 4/01; BL 5/1/01; HBG 10/01; SLJ 6/01)

10997 Avi. *Abigail Takes the Wheel* (2–4). Illus. by Don Bolognese. Series: I Can Read. 1999, HarperCollins LB $17.89 (978-0-06-027663-8). 64pp. In this easily read story set in the 1880s, young Abigail steers a freight boat up the Hudson after the mate gets sick. (Rev: BCCB 6/99; BL 4/1/99; HB 3/99; HBG 10/99; SLJ 5/99)

10998 Avi. *The Secret School* (3–6). 2001, Harcourt $16.00 (978-0-15-216375-4). 153pp. Rather than risking her future education, 14-year-old Ida Bidson takes over as teacher and runs a secret school when the one-room schoolhouse in their mountain district is suddenly closed in 1925. (Rev: BCCB 10/01; HB 11/01; HBG 3/02; SLJ 9/01)

10999 Avi. *Silent Movie* (K–3). Illus. by C. B. Mordan. 2003, Simon & Schuster $16.95 (978-0-689-84145-3). 48pp. In black-and-white silent-movie format, this is the story of an immigrant mother and son arriving in America in the early 20th century, the difficulties they have finding Papa, and the near-miraculous reunion. (Rev: BL 3/1/03*; HB 3/03; HBG 10/03; SLJ 3/03)

11000 Bader, Bonnie. *East Side Story* (3–5). Series: Stories of the States. 1993, Silver Moon LB $14.95 (978-1-881889-22-9). 72pp. The story of an 11-year-old Jewish immigrant girl and her sister, both of whom work in the Triangle Shirtwaist Factory in New York City during the early 1900s. (Rev: SLJ 2/94)

11001 Baier, Joan Foley. *Luvella's Promise* (3–5). 1999, Writers Club paper $9.95 (978-1-893652-04-0). 83pp. Luvella is growing up with her family in a logging town in Pennsylvania in 1905 when typhoid fever strikes. (Rev: SLJ 11/99)

11002 Barasch, Lynne. *Radio Rescue* (2–5). Illus. 2000, Farrar $16.00 (978-0-374-36166-2). 40pp. Based on fact, this novel set in New York in 1923 tells how a young amateur radio operator saved Florida hurricane victims by picking up their distress signals. (Rev: BCCB 7–8/00; BL 9/15/00; HB 9/00; HBG 3/01; SLJ 10/00)

11003 Beard, Darleen Bailey. *The Babbs Switch Story* (5–8). 2002, Farrar $16.00 (978-0-374-30475-1). 176pp. A young girl saves her sister from a fire on Christmas Eve in 1924 in this fictional account of a real event. (Rev: BL 3/15/02; HBG 10/02; SLJ 3/02; VOYA 4/02)

11004 Birney, Betty. *The Seven Wonders of Sassafras Springs* (3–6). Illus. by Matt Phelan. 2005, Simon & Schuster $16.95 (978-0-689-87136-8). 224pp. It's 1923 and Eben McAllister longs to travel but first he must meet his father's challenge to find the hidden wonders in his small farming community. (Rev: BL 9/1/05; SLJ 8/05)

11005 Blackwood, Gary L. *Moonshine* (5–8). 1999, Marshall Cavendish $14.95 (978-0-7614-5056-6). 158pp. Thirteen-year-old Thad, growing up with his mother in rural Mississippi during the Depression, makes a little extra money by running an illegal still that produces moonshine for the locals. (Rev: BCCB 11/99; BL 9/1/99; HBG 3/00; SLJ 10/99)

11006 Blakeslee, Ann R. *Summer Battles* (5–8). 2000, Marshall Cavendish $14.95 (978-0-7614-5064-1). 127pp. The story of Kath, age 11, growing up in a small town in Indiana in 1926 and of her father, a preacher, who is attacked for opposing the Ku Klux Klan. (Rev: BCCB 3/00; BL 4/1/00; HBG 10/00; SLJ 4/00)

11007 Boling, Katharine. *January 1905* (4–7). 2004, Harcourt $16.00 (978-0-15-205119-8). 160pp. In alternating voices, 11-year-old mill worker Pauline and her deformed, stay-at-home twin sister Arlene describe the harsh circumstances of their early 20th-century life. (Rev: BL 5/15/04; HB 7/04; SLJ 7/04)

11008 Bornstein, Ruth. *Butterflies and Lizards, Beryl and Me* (5–7). 2002, Marshall Cavendish LB $14.95 (978-0-7614-5118-1). 160pp. Eleven-year-old Charley befriends an odd woman named Beryl while her mother works hard to make it through the Great Depression. (Rev: BL 5/15/02; HBG 10/02; SLJ 5/02)

11009 Burandt, Harriet, and Shelley Dale. *Tales from the Homeplace: Adventures of a Texas Farm Girl* (4–8). 1997, Holt $15.95 (978-0-8050-5075-2). A family story that takes place on a Texas cotton farm during the Depression and features spunky 12-year-old heroine Irene and her six brothers and sisters. (Rev: BCCB 7–8/97; HB 5/97; SLJ 4/97*; VOYA 12/97)

11010 Burleigh, Robert. *Into the Air: The Story of the Wright Brothers' First Flight* (5–8). Illus. by Bill Wylie. Series: American Heroes. 2002, Harcourt paper $6.00 (978-0-15-216803-2). A high-interest, comic-book presentation of the first flight with fictionalized dialogue. (Rev: HBG 3/03; SLJ 9/02)

11011 Byars, Betsy. *Keeper of the Doves* (5–8). 2002, Viking $14.99 (978-0-670-03576-2). 112pp. Young

Amie McBee is a thoughtful child who loves to write and — unlike her older twin sisters — has the sensitivity to see the softer side of the mysterious Polish immigrant who lives on their estate and keeps doves in this story set at the turn of the 20th century and presented in 26 short, alphabetical chapters. (Rev: BCCB 1/03; BL 10/1/02*; HB 9/02*; HBG 3/03; SLJ 10/02)

11012 Carter, Alden R. *Crescent Moon* (5–8). 1999, Holiday $16.95 (978-0-8234-1521-2). 153pp. In the early part of the 20th century, Jeremy joins Great-Uncle Mac on a log drive where they become friends with a Native American and his daughter and, through them, experience the shame of racial prejudice. (Rev: BCCB 1/00; BL 2/15/00; HB 3/00; HBG 10/00; SLJ 3/00; VOYA 6/00)

11013 Celenza, Anna Harwell. *Gershwin's Rhapsody in Blue* (2–4). Illus. by JoAnn E. Kitchel. 2006, Charlesbridge $19.95 (978-1-57091-556-7). 32pp. The story of Gershwin's struggle to produce a concerto in a few short weeks in 1924 is accompanied by CD of the resulting classic. (Rev: BL 11/1/06; SLJ 7/06)

11014 Clark, Clara Gillow. *Hattie on Her Way* (4–7). Series: Hattie. 2005, Candlewick $15.99 (978-0-7636-2286-2). 208pp. The sequel to *Hill Hawk Hattie* (2003) finds Hattie living with her grandmother after her mother's death and seeking to solve a family mystery. (Rev: BL 3/1/05; SLJ 3/05)

11015 Crisp, Marty. *White Star: A Dog on the Titanic* (4–6). 2004, Holiday House $16.95 (978-0-8234-1598-4). 150pp. Sam Harris, a 12-year-old passenger on the *Titanic,* offers to help care for the dogs in the ship's kennel and develops a strong relationship with an Irish setter named Star; back matter gives historical detail on the disaster. (Rev: BL 5/15/04; SLJ 6/04)

11016 Cross, Gillian. *The Great American Elephant Chase* (5–8). 1993, Holiday $17.95 (978-0-8234-1016-3). In 1881, Tad, 15, and young friend Cissie attempt to get to Nebraska with her showman father's elephant, pursued by two unsavory characters who claim they have bought the animal. (Rev: BCCB 6/93; BL 3/15/93*; SLJ 5/93*; VOYA 10/93)

11017 Cummings, Priscilla. *Saving Grace* (4–7). 2003, Dutton $17.99 (978-0-525-47123-3). 192pp. Eleven-year-old Grace faces a tough dilemma when a wealthy family offers to adopt her while her own family is suffering grinding poverty and illness during the Depression. (Rev: BCCB 9/03; BL 5/15/03; HBG 10/03; SLJ 6/03; VOYA 10/03)

11018 Currier, Katrina Saltonstall. *Kai's Journey to Gold Mountain* (4–7). Illus. by Gabhor Utomo. 2005, Angel Island $16.95 (978-0-9667352-7-7); paper $10.95 (978-0-9667352-4-6). 44pp. Based on the experiences of a Chinese immigrant to the United States in the 1930s, this troubling tale describes the internment of 12-year-old Kai on Angel Island in San Francisco Bay. (Rev: BL 2/15/05*)

11019 Cushman, Karen. *Rodzina* (5–9). 2003, Clarion $16.00 (978-0-618-13351-2). 224pp. On an orphan train going from Chicago to California in 1881, plucky Rodzina worries about her fate and aims to find a better life than some of the other children on the train. (Rev: BCCB 3/03; BL 3/1/03*; HB 5/03; HBG 10/03; SLJ 4/03*)

11020 Danneberg, Julie. *Family Reminders* (4–6). Illus. by John Shelley. 2009, Charlesbridge $14.95 (978-1-58089-320-6). 112pp. In an 1890s gold-mining town in Colorado, 10-year-old Mary's life is turned upside down when her father is injured and the family suddenly faces financial hardship. (Rev: BLO 6/19/09; HB 7/09)

11021 De Angeli, Marguerite. *Copper-Toed Boots* (3–6). Illus. by author. 1996, Wayne State Univ. paper $18.95 (978-0-8143-2654-1). 96pp. American family life in the early 20th century.

11022 DeClements, Barthe. *The Bite of the Gold Bug: A Story of the Alaskan Gold Rush* (3–6). Illus. by Dan Andreasen. Series: Once upon America. 1994, Puffin paper $4.99 (978-0-14-036081-3). 64pp. The story of 12-year-old Bucky who spends six months in the gold fields with his father and uncle. (Rev: BCCB 5/92; BL 5/15/92; SLJ 8/92)

11023 Dell, Pamela. *Liam's Watch: A Strange Story of the Great Chicago Fire* (4–6). Series: Scrapbooks of America. 2002, Tradition LB $28.50 (978-1-59187-014-2). 47pp. Twelve-year-old Liam and his family must flee their home during the Great Chicago Fire of 1871; background historical information is provided in boxed notes and a timeline. (Rev: SLJ 5/03)

11024 Dotty, Kathryn Adams. *Wild Orphan* (5–8). 2006, Edinborough $14.95 (978-1-889020-20-4). 144pp. In the Midwest in the 1920s, Lizbeth's friendship with an independent-minded orphan named Georgiana gives her courage. (Rev: BL 6/1–15/06)

11025 Dudley, David L. *The Bicycle Man* (5–8). 2005, Clarion $16.00 (978-0-618-54233-8). 256pp. In this poignant portrait of African American life in the rural South during the late 1920s, 12-year-old Carissa develops a mutually beneficial relationship with Bailey, an elderly jack-of-all-trades to whom she and her mother offer a home. (Rev: BL 11/15/05; SLJ 11/05)

11026 Durbin, William. *El Lector* (4–6). 2006, Random $15.95 (978-0-385-74651-9). 160pp. Thirteen-year-old Bella dreams of one day becoming a *lector* like her grandfather, who reads books and newspapers to workers in a Florida cigar factory. (Rev: BL 2/1/06; SLJ 2/06)

11027 Easton, Richard. *A Real American* (4–7). 2002, Clarion $15.00 (978-0-618-03339-3). 160pp. Against his father's wishes, 11-year-old Nathan befriends Arturo, the son of Italian immigrants newly arrived in a Pennsylvania coal-mining town. (Rev: BCCB 9/02; BL 5/15/02; SLJ 3/02)

11028 Erickson, John R. *Moonshiner's Gold* (5–9). 2001, Viking $15.99 (978-0-670-03502-1). 176pp. Fourteen-year-old Riley becomes embroiled in exciting intrigue involving moonshiners and corruption in this novel set in Texas in the 1920s. (Rev: HBG 3/02; SLJ 8/01; VOYA 10/01)

11029 Fisher, Leonard E. *The Jetty Chronicles* (5–9). Illus. 1997, Marshall Cavendish $15.95 (978-0-7614-5017-7). A series of vignettes based on fact about the unusual people the author met while growing up in Sea Gate, New York, at a time when the United States was drifting into World War II. (Rev: BL 10/15/97; HBG 3/98; SLJ 12/97; VOYA 2/98)

11030 Franklin, Kristine L. *Grape Thief* (5–9). 2003, Candlewick $16.99 (978-0-7636-1325-9). 304pp. In 1925 Washington State, a boy of Croatian heritage tries to find a way to stay in school even though his family is in financial difficulty. (Rev: BL 10/1/03; SLJ 9/03)

11031 Fuqua, Jonathon. *Darby* (4–7). 2002, Candlewick $15.99 (978-0-7636-1417-1). 256pp. A 9-year-old white girl, Darby, and her family become the target of KKK violence after she protests the killing of a black sharecropper's son in 1926 South Carolina. (Rev: BCCB 7–8/02; BL 3/15/02; HB 3/02; HBG 10/02; SLJ 3/02; VOYA 4/02)

11032 Giff, Patricia Reilly. *Water Street* (5–8). 2006, Random $15.95 (978-0-385-73068-6). 176pp. In this poignant sequel to *Nory Ryan's Song* (2000) and *Maggie's Door* (2003), set in late 19th-century Brooklyn and told from alternating points of view, 13-year-old Bird Ryan and her new upstairs neighbor Thomas develop a close friendship. (Rev: BCCB 1/07; BL 8/06; HB 9/06; HBG 4/07; LMC 1/07; SLJ 9/06) ⌒

11033 Goodman, Susan. *Hazelle Boxberg* (2–4). Illus. by Doris Ettlinger. 2004, Simon & Schuster LB $11.89 (978-0-689-84983-1). 64pp. The moving story, based on truth, of 11-year-old Hazelle's trip to Texas by orphan train and her escape from the family that chooses her from a lineup at the Masonic Hall. (Rev: BL 3/1/04)

11034 Granfield, Linda. *97 Orchard Street, New York: Stories of Immigrant Life* (3–6). Photos by Arlene Alda. 2001, Tundra paper $15.00 (978-0-88776-580-3). 55pp. A detailed and appealing look at the immigrant experience through the stories of families who lived in the building that is now the Lower East Side Tenement Museum, with black-and-white photographs. (Rev: SLJ 12/01) [305.9]

11035 Gray, Dianne E. *Together Apart* (5–9). 2002, Houghton $16.00 (978-0-618-18721-8). 208pp. After surviving the blizzard of 1888, Isaac and Hannah discover their love for each other while working for feminist publisher Eliza Moore. (Rev: BCCB 11/02; BL 9/15/02; HB 11/02; HBG 3/03; SLJ 12/02; VOYA 2/03)

11036 Greenwood, Barbara. *Factory Girl* (5–8). Illus. 2007, Kids Can $18.95 (978-1-55337-648-4); paper $12.95 (978-1-55337-649-1). 136pp. A story about 12-year-old Emily, who in the early 20th century must take a job in a sweatshop and suffer intolerable conditions, is accompanied by historic photographs of children at work and details of key events on the road to reform. (Rev: BL 2/15/07; LMC 8/07; SLJ 5/07)

11037 Gregory, Kristiana. *Earthquake at Dawn* (5–9). Series: Great Episodes. 2003, Harcourt paper

$6.99 (978-0-15-204681-1). Based on actual letters and photographs, this historical novel depicts the devastating 1906 San Francisco earthquake. (Rev: BL 4/15/92; SLJ 8/92)

11038 Gregory, Kristiana. *Orphan Runaways* (5–7). 1998, Scholastic paper $15.95 (978-0-590-60366-9). 160pp. Two brothers run away from a San Francisco orphanage in 1879 to look for an uncle in the gold fields. (Rev: BCCB 3/98; BL 2/15/98; HBG 10/98; SLJ 3/98)

11039 Gundisch, Karin. *How I Became an American* (4–8). Trans. by James Skofield. 2001, Cricket $15.95 (978-0-8126-4875-1). 128pp. This is the story of Johann, a young German immigrant, who arrives in an Ohio steel town in the early 20th century. (Rev: BL 11/15/01; HBG 3/02; SLJ 12/01; VOYA 4/02)

11040 Gutman, Dan. *Race for the Sky: The Kitty Hawk Diaries of Johnny Moore* (4–7). 2003, Simon & Schuster $15.95 (978-0-689-84554-3). 178pp. Fact and fiction are interwoven in this diary by 14-year-old John Moore, recording his firsthand observations of the Wright brothers' progress. (Rev: BL 1/1–15/04; SLJ 1/04)

11041 Haas, Jessie. *Chase* (5–9). 2007, HarperCollins $16.99 (978-0-06-112850-9). 256pp. In mid-19th-century Pennsylvania, Phin Chase witnesses a murder and flees, pursued by a stranger and a horse that seems to have tracking abilities. (Rev: BL 2/1/07; SLJ 4/07)

11042 Haddix, Margaret P. *Uprising* (5–8). 2007, Simon & Schuster $16.99 (978-1-4169-1171-5). 352pp. Three very different young girls — 15-year-old Italian immigrant Bella, Russian Jewish immigrant Yetta, and privileged Jane — give their perspective of the strike that occurred 13 months before the Triangle Shirtwaist Fire in 1911, protesting working conditions in the garment industry. (Rev: BL 9/15/07; SLJ 9/07)

11043 Hahn, Mary D. *Anna All Year Round* (3–5). Illus. 1999, Clarion $15.00 (978-0-395-86975-8). 144pp. Using an early 1900s urban setting, this warm family story tells about German immigrants and their children adjusting to America. (Rev: BCCB 6/99; BL 3/15/99; HB 7/99; HBG 10/99; SLJ 5/99)

11044 Hall, Donald. *The Milkman's Boy* (3–5). Illus. 1997, Walker LB $16.85 (978-0-8027-8465-0). 32pp. Around the time of World War I, Paul's father, a milkman, does not believe in the necessity of pasteurization. (Rev: BL 9/1/97; HBG 3/98; SLJ 9/97)

11045 Hansen, Joyce. *I Thought My Soul Would Rise and Fly: The Diary of Patsy, a Freed Girl* (4–8). Series: Dear America. 1997, Scholastic paper $10.95 (978-0-590-84913-5). 208pp. In this novel in the form of a diary, a freed slave girl wonders what to do with her life after leaving the plantation. (Rev: BL 12/15/97; HBG 3/98; SLJ 11/97)

11046 Harper, Jo, and Josephine Harper. *Finding Daddy: A Story of the Great Depression* (1–3). Illus. by Ron Mazellan. 2005, Turtle Bks. $16.95 (978-1-890515-31-7). 42pp. Young Bonnie is bereft when

her father must leave home to find work, and she sets out to find him; a timeline, glossary, and song lyrics provide more information about the Great Depression. (Rev: SLJ 9/05)

11047 Harris, Carol Flynn. *A Place for Joey* (4–8). 2001, Boyds Mills $15.95 (978-1-56397-108-2). 90pp. Twelve-year-old Joey, an Italian immigrant living in Boston in the early 20th century, learns an important lesson through a heroic act. (Rev: BL 9/1/01; HBG 3/02; SLJ 9/01; VOYA 10/01)

11048 Hesse, Karen. *Letters from Rifka* (4–8). 1992, Holt $16.95 (978-0-8050-1964-3). In letters back to Russia, Rifka, 12, recounts her long journey to the United States in 1919, starting with the dangerous escape over the border. (Rev: BCCB 10/92; BL 7/92; HB 9/92*; SLJ 8/92*)

11049 Hesse, Karen. *A Time of Angels* (5–8). 1995, Hyperion LB $16.49 (978-0-7868-2072-6). As influenza sweeps her city in 1918, killing thousands, Hannah tries to escape its ravages by moving to Vermont, where an old farmer helps her. (Rev: BCCB 1/96; BL 12/1/95; SLJ 12/95)

11050 Hill, Kirkpatrick. *Dancing at the Odinochka* (4–7). 2005, Simon & Schuster $15.95 (978-0-689-87388-1). 272pp. An atmospheric life of Erinia — daughter of a Russian father and Athabascan mother — growing up in the 1860s in what is now Alaska. (Rev: BL 8/05; SLJ 8/05)

11051 Hoberman, Mary Ann. *Strawberry Hill* (3–5). Illus. by Wendy A. Halperin. 2009, Little, Brown $15.99 (978-0-316-04136-2). 240pp. When she moves to Strawberry Hill during the Depression, 10-year-old Allie finds no berries, but she does find friendship. (Rev: BL 6/1–15/09; SLJ 7/09)

11052 Holland, Isabelle. *Paperboy* (4–6). 1999, Holiday House $16.95 (978-0-8234-1422-2). 137pp. Growing up in a New York City slum in 1881, 12-year-old Kevin O'Donnell helps out his family by getting a job as a messenger for the owner of the *New York Chronicle*. (Rev: BCCB 10/99; HBG 3/00; SLJ 9/99)

11053 Hoobler, Dorothy, and Thomas Hoobler. *The First Decade: Curtain Going Up* (4–6). Illus. Series: Century Kids. 2000, Millbrook LB $22.90 (978-0-7613-1600-8). 160pp. Presents the first decade of the 20th century in the life of the Aldriches, a theatrical family living in Maine. (Rev: BCCB 7–8/00; BL 5/1/00; HBG 10/00; SLJ 7/00)

11054 Hoobler, Dorothy, and Thomas Hoobler. *The Second Decade: Voyages* (4–6). Illus. Series: Century Kids. 2000, Millbrook LB $22.90 (978-0-7613-1601-5). 160pp. In the second decade of the 20th century, Peggy Aldrich and her sister photograph the factory workers in Lowell, Massachusetts, explore issues involving child labor and women's suffrage, and feel the effects of the sinking of the *Titanic*. (Rev: BCCB 7–8/00; BL 5/1/00; HBG 10/00; SLJ 7/00)

11055 Hopkinson, Deborah. *Sky Boys: How They Built the Empire State Building* (2–4). Illus. by James Ransome. 2006, Random $16.95 (978-0-375-83610-7). 48pp. A young boy and his unemployed father watch as daring workers defy gravity in the construction of New York City's Empire State Building; dramatic illustrations highlight the heights. (Rev: BL 12/1/05; SLJ 2/06)

11056 Hulme, Joy N. *Climbing the Rainbow* (4–6). 2004, HarperCollins LB $16.89 (978-0-06-054304-4). 224pp. In 1911, 10-year-old Dora's large family moves to New Mexico; there Dora faces various challenges, including starting school and the death of a friend. (Rev: BL 1/1–15/04; SLJ 2/04)

11057 Hulme, Joy N. *Through the Open Door* (4–6). 2000, HarperCollins $14.95 (978-0-380-97870-0). 162pp. Told by 9-year-old Dora Cookson, this is an appealing story of a Mormon family and their move from Utah to homestead in New Mexico in 1910. (Rev: BCCB 6/00; HBG 3/01; SLJ 8/00)

11058 Hurst, Carol Otis. *You Come to Yokum* (3–5). Illus. by Life Kay. 2005, Houghton $15.00 (978-0-618-55122-4). 144pp. The Carlyle family's move to rural western Massachusetts does nothing to dampen Mrs. Carlyle's enthusiastic — and sometimes embarrassing — support for the women's suffrage movement. (Rev: BL 9/1/05; SLJ 1/06)

11059 Hurwitz, Johanna. *Faraway Summer* (5–7). Illus. by Mary Azarian. 1998, Morrow $14.95 (978-0-688-15334-2). 112pp. In 1910, a Jewish orphan who lives in a tenement in New York City is thrilled at the thought of spending two weeks on a farm in Vermont, thanks to the Fresh Air Fund. (Rev: BL 3/1/98; HB 7/98; HBG 10/98; SLJ 5/98)

11060 Hyatt, Patricia Rusch. *Coast to Coast with Alice* (3–6). Illus. 1995, Carolrhoda LB $21.27 (978-0-87614-789-4). 72pp. A fictionalized account of the first automobile cross-country trip by a woman in 1909. (Rev: BCCB 9/95; BL 7/95; HB 11/95; SLJ 8/95)

11061 Jackson, Alison. *Rainmaker* (5–8). 2005, Boyds Mills $16.95 (978-1-59078-309-2). 192pp. The farmers in Pidge Martin's town hire a rainmaker in the hopes that she will save their crops in this story set in 1939 Florida. (Rev: BL 3/15/05; SLJ 4/05)

11062 Jaspersohn, William. *The Two Brothers* (2–4). Illus. Series: Family Heritage. 2000, Vermont Folklife Center $14.95 (978-0-916718-16-9). 32pp. Based on a true story, this novel tells of two German brothers who immigrated separately to the United States in the 1880s and were miraculously reunited. (Rev: BL 11/1/00; SLJ 9/00)

11063 Jocelyn, Marthe. *Earthly Astonishments* (4–8). 2000, Tundra paper $7.95 (978-0-88776-628-2). 179pp. The setting is New York City in the 1880s and the novel involves a girl who is only 22 inches tall and her career in a glorified freak show. (Rev: BCCB 2/00; HBG 10/00; SLJ 4/00)

11064 Jocelyn, Marthe. *How It Happened in Peach Hill* (5–9). 2007, Random $15.99 (978-0-375-83701-2). 232pp. Fifteen-year-old Annie, who does research for her "clairvoyant" mother mainly by pretending she is stupid, longs for a normal life in this compelling novel set in the 1920s. (Rev: BL 1/1–15/07; SLJ 4/07*)

11065 Jorgensen, Norman. *In Flanders Fields* (4–7). Illus. by Brian Harrison-Lever. 2002, Fremantle Arts Centre $22.95 (978-1-86368-369-2). During a Christmas Day ceasefire in the World War I trenches, a soldier rescues a trapped robin. (Rev: SLJ 2/03)

11066 Kalman, Esther. *Tchaikovsky Discovers America* (3–5). Illus. by Laura Fernandez and Rick Jacobson. 1995, Orchard $14.98 (978-0-531-06894-6). 32pp. Through a diary kept by 11-year-old Eugenia, the reader learns about Tchaikovsky's trip to the United States in 1891. (Rev: BL 3/15/95; HB 1/95, 5/95; SLJ 4/95)

11067 Kelly, Jacqueline. *The Evolution of Calpurnia Tate* (4–7). 2009, Holt $16.95 (978-0-8050-8841-0). 352pp. In Texas at the turn of the 20th century, 11-year-old Calpurnia, the only daughter among seven children, has an independent streak and an interest in natural science that she shares with her grandfather. (Rev: BL 5/1/09; HB 9/09; LMC 10/09; SLJ 5/09; VOYA 4/09) ∩

11068 Kirwan, Anna. *Of Flowers and Shadows* (4–6). Series: Portraits. 2005, Scholastic $9.99 (978-0-439-71010-7). 182pp. This appealing fictional tale, inspired by Winslow Homer's "Girl and Laurel" painting, tells how Aurelia, an orphan and servant for a family in Townsend, Massachusetts, came to pose for the artist. (Rev: BL 11/15/05; SLJ 11/05)

11069 Klass, Sheila S. *A Shooting Star: A Novel About Annie Oakley* (4–8). 1996, Holiday $15.95 (978-0-8234-1279-2). A fictionalized biography of the woman who rose from poverty to become a famous show-business sharpshooter. (Rev: BL 12/15/96; SLJ 5/97)

11070 Koller, Jackie F. *Nothing to Fear* (5–7). 1991, Harcourt $14.95 (978-0-15-200544-3); paper $8.00 (978-0-15-257582-3). 288pp. Danny Garvey is a first-generation Catholic Irish American growing up in New York City in the 1930s. (Rev: BCCB 3/91; BL 3/1/91; SLJ 5/91)

11071 Kudlinski, Kathleen V. *Shannon: The Schoolmarm Mysteries, San Francisco, 1880* (3–5). Illus. by Bill Farnsworth. Series: Girlhood Journeys. 1997, Simon & Schuster paper $5.99 (978-0-689-81561-4). 71pp. This mystery features Shannon O'Brien, a recent Irish immigrant living in San Francisco in 1880. (Rev: SLJ 4/98)

11072 Kudlinski, Kathleen V. *Shannon, Lost and Found: San Francisco, 1880* (4–6). Illus. 1997, Simon & Schuster paper $5.99 (978-0-689-80988-0). 72pp. In 1880, Shannon and her friend Mi Ling become involved in collecting books for the new San Francisco Public Library. (Rev: BCCB 11/96; BL 5/1/97)

11073 Lasky, Kathryn. *Dreams in the Golden Country: The Diary of Zipporah Feldman, a Jewish Immigrant Girl* (4–8). 1998, Scholastic paper $10.95 (978-0-590-02973-5). Twelve-year-old Zipporah Feldman, a Jewish immigrant from Russia, keeps a diary about her life with her family on New York's Lower East Side around 1910. (Rev: BL 4/1/98; HBG 9/98; SLJ 5/98)

11074 Lasky, Kathryn. *A Time for Courage: The Suffragette Diary of Kathleen Bowen, Washington, DC, 1917* (4–6). Series: Dear America. 2002, Scholastic

$10.95 (978-0-590-51141-4). 217pp. Thirteen-year-old Kat records her increasing interest in politics and her activities supporting the women's suffrage movement. (Rev: HBG 10/02; SLJ 8/02)

11075 Lenski, Lois. *Strawberry Girl* (4–6). Illus. by author. 1945, HarperCollins LB $18.89 (978-0-397-30110-2); paper $5.99 (978-0-06-440585-0). 192pp. Lively adventures of a little girl, full of the flavor of the Florida lake country. Newbery Medal winner, 1946.

11076 Levine, Kristin. *The Best Bad Luck I Ever Had* (5–8). 2009, Putnam $16.99 (978-0-399-25090-3). 272pp. In early-20th-century small-town Alabama, 12-year-old Dit is surprised that the new postmaster is African American and disappointed that his daughter is unskilled in baseball, hunting, and fishing; as Emma and Dit become friends they have to deal with racism and injustice. (Rev: BCCB 4/09; BL 11/15/08; HB 5/09; LMC 3/09; SLJ 1/09)

11077 Lewis, Zoe. *Keisha Discovers Harlem* (3–5). Illus. by Dan Burr and Rich Grot. Series: Magic Attic Club. 1999, Magic Attic LB $17.40 (978-1-57513-144-3). 74pp. Keisha puts on a flapper costume and finds herself transported to New York City during the Harlem Renaissance. (Rev: SLJ 4/99)

11078 Littlefield, Holly. *Fire at the Triangle Factory* (4–6). Illus. 1996, Carolrhoda LB $23.93 (978-0-87614-868-6); paper $5.95 (978-0-87614-970-6). 48pp. Two young workers — Jewish Minnie and Catholic Tessa — work at the Triangle Shirtwaist Company at the time of the fire of 1911. (Rev: BL 8/96; SLJ 10/96)

11079 Love, D. Anne. *I Remember the Alamo* (4–6). 2000, Holiday House $15.95 (978-0-8234-1426-0). 156pp. The McCann family moves to San Antonio and becomes embroiled in the battle of the Alamo and its aftermath in this historical novel. (Rev: BL 1/1–15/00; HB 3/00; HBG 3/00; SLJ 1/00)

11080 Love, D. Anne. *A Year Without Rain* (4–6). 2000, Holiday House $15.95 (978-0-8234-1488-8). 118pp. Set in the late 19th century, this novel tells how Rachel, who lives on the Dakota prairie, tries to thwart her father's plans to remarry. (Rev: BCCB 7–8/00; BL 4/1/00; HB 7/00; HBG 10/00; SLJ 9/00)

11081 MacKall, Dandi Daley. *Rudy Rides the Rails: A Depression Era Story* (3–5). Illus. by Chris Ellison. 2007, Sleeping Bear $17.95 (978-1-58536-286-8). 40pp. Powerful illustrations bring to life this story of a Depression-era teen who hops freight trains in search of work. (Rev: BL 5/1/07; SLJ 6/07)

11082 McKay, Sharon E. *Charlie Wilcox* (5–8). 2000, Stoddart paper $7.95 (978-0-7737-6093-6). 221pp. This is the story of a 14-year-old Canadian boy who becomes involved in the trench warfare in France during World War I. (Rev: SLJ 11/00)

11083 McKissack, Patricia C. *Color Me Dark: The Diary of Nellie Lee Love, the Great Migration North* (4–6). Series: Dear America. 2000, Scholastic $10.95 (978 0-590-51159-9). 224pp. Told in diary form, this is the fictional story of African American Nellie Lee Love, whose family moves from Tennessee to Chicago in 1919 and encounters prejudice,

corruption, and race riots. (Rev: BL 2/15/00; HBG 10/00; SLJ 7/00)

11084 McMullan, Margaret. *When I Crossed No-Bob* (5–8). 2007, Houghton $16.00 (978-0-618-71715-6). 216pp. Addy O'Donnell, 12, manages to separate herself from her violent and racist family in this novel about post-Civil War Mississippi and the beginnings of the Ku Klux Klan. (Rev: BL 10/1/07; HB 1/08; SLJ 11/07)

11085 Matas, Carol. *Rosie in New York City: Gotcha!* (3–6). 2003, Simon & Schuster paper $4.99 (978-0-689-85714-0). 124pp. In early-20th-century New York City, 11-year-old Rosie takes a factory job when her mother falls ill. (Rev: BL 5/15/03; SLJ 8/03)

11086 Mattern, Joanne. *Coming to America: The Story of Immigration* (4–8). Illus. by Margaret Sanfilippo. 2000, Perfection Learning $17.95 (978-0-7807-9715-4); paper $8.95 (978-0-7891-2851-5). 64pp. A fictional presentation centering on the Martini family and their journey from Italy at the turn of the 20th century to find a new home in America. (Rev: HBG 3/01; SLJ 2/01)

11087 Meltzer, Milton. *Tough Times* (5–8). 2007, Clarion $16.00 (978-0-618-87445-3). 176pp. With detailed historical background, this novel describes the struggles and despair experienced by high school senior Joey Singer and his family as the Depression deepens. (Rev: BL 9/1/07; SLJ 12/07)

11088 Mitchell, Margaree King. *Uncle Jed's Barber Shop* (2–5). Illus. by James Ransome. 1993, Simon & Schuster $16.00 (978-0-671-76969-7); paper $6.99 (978-0-689-81913-1). 40pp. Uncle Jed, an African American barber in the 1920s, hopes to open his own shop, but his generosity always prevents him from saving enough money. (Rev: BCCB 9/93; BL 9/1/93; HB 11/93; SLJ 10/93)

11089 Moss, Jenny. *Winnie's War* (5–8). 2009, Walker $16.99 (978-0-8027-9819-0). 224pp. In 1918 Texas Winnie, 12, must deal with her difficult grandmother, her troubled mother, her overworked father, her two little sisters, and now an epidemic of flu. (Rev: BCCB 2/09; BLO 12/9/08)

11090 Moss, Marissa. *Rose's Journal: The Story of a Girl in the Great Depression* (3–5). Illus. by author. Series: Young American Voices. 2001, Harcourt $15.00 (978-0-15-202423-9). 56pp. In her pink-lined journal, young Rose records the hardships her family faces during the dust storms of 1935 Kansas and details outside events such as the Hauptmann trial. (Rev: HBG 3/02; SLJ 12/01)

11091 Myers, Anna. *Hoggee* (5–7). 2004, Walker $16.95 (978-0-8027-8926-6). 182pp. Despite all his own problems, 14-year-old mule driver Howard decides to do what he can to help a deaf mute girl in this novel set in 19th-century New York State. (Rev: SLJ 11/04)

11092 Oneal, Zibby. *A Long Way to Go* (3–5). Illus. by Michael Dooling. 1992, Puffin paper $4.99 (978-0-14-032950-6). 64pp. Lila's life changes when her grandmother is jailed for fighting for women's rights in 1917 America. (Rev: BCCB 9/90; BL 3/1/90; HB 7/90; SLJ 9/90)

11093 Paterson, Katherine. *Bread and Roses, Too* (5–8). 2006, Clarion $16.00 (978-0-618-65479-6). 288pp. Jake and Rosa, children from different backgrounds, suffer from the effects of the textile workers' strike in early 20th-century Massachusetts. (Rev: BCCB 3/07; BL 8/06; HB 9/06; HBG 4/07; LMC 1/07; SLJ 9/06; VOYA 12/06) ∩

11094 Paterson, Katherine. *Preacher's Boy* (5–8). 1999, Clarion $15.00 (978-0-395-83897-6). In small-town Vermont in 1899, a time of new ideas and technological change, Robbie, the restless, imaginative, questioning son of a preacher, causes unforeseen trouble when he plans his own kidnapping for profit. (Rev: BCCB 10/99; BL 8/99; HB 9/99; HBG 3/00; SLJ 8/99)

11095 Peck, Richard. *Fair Weather* (4–6). 2001, Dial $16.99 (978-0-8037-2516-4). 160pp. A 13-year-old Illinois farm girl and her family take an exciting trip to the 1893 World's Columbian Exposition in Chicago. (Rev: BCCB 10/01; BL 9/1/01; HB 11/01*; HBG 3/02; SLJ 9/01*)

11096 Peck, Richard. *Here Lies the Librarian* (5–8). 2006, Dial $16.99 (978-0-8037-3080-9). 208pp. Four young female librarians arrive in a small town in Indiana in 1914 and inspire 14-year-old Peewee McGrath to consider her future in different ways. (Rev: BL 3/1/06; SLJ 4/06*; VOYA 2/06)

11097 Peck, Robert Newton. *Arly* (5–8). 1989, Walker $16.95 (978-0-8027-6856-8). A teacher changes the life of a young boy in a migrant camp in Florida in 1927. (Rev: BL 7/89; VOYA 8/89)

11098 Porter, Tracey. *Billy Creekmore* (5–7). 2007, HarperCollins $16.99 (978-0-06-077570-4). 320pp. From a grim orphanage to the mines of West Virginia and on to a life in the circus, 10-year-old Billy describes in picaresque style the difficult life of the young and poor in the early 20th century. (Rev: BL 4/15/07; SLJ 7/07)

11099 Porter, Tracey. *Treasures in the Dust* (5–7). 1997, HarperCollins LB $14.89 (978-0-06-027564-8). 160pp. With alternating points of view, two girls from poor families in Oklahoma's Dust Bowl tell their stories. (Rev: BL 8/97; HB 9/97; HBG 3/98; SLJ 12/97*; VOYA 10/98)

11100 Rabe, Berniece. *Hiding Mr. McMulty* (5–8). 1997, Harcourt $18.00 (978-0-15-201330-1). This novel, set in southeast Missouri in 1937, tells a story of race and class conflicts as experienced by 11-year-old Rass. (Rev: BL 10/15/97; HBG 3/98; SLJ 12/97; VOYA 2/98)

11101 Ransom, Candice F. *Fire in the Sky* (3–5). Illus. 1997, Carolrhoda LB $19.93 (978-0-87614-867-9). 72pp. In the late 1930s in New Jersey, Stenny becomes involved in the flight of the dirigible *Hindenburg* and the rescue operation after it burns. (Rev: BL 5/1/97; SLJ 8/97)

11102 Ransom, Candice F. *Jimmy Crack Corn* (3–5). Illus. 1994, Carolrhoda LB $19.95 (978-0-87614-786-3). 56pp. The beginning of the Great Depression as seen through the experiences of a farm family sinking into poverty with no hope for the future. (Rev: BCCB 6/94; BL 7/94; SLJ 6/94)

11103 Ray, Delia. *Ghost Girl: A Blue Ridge Mountain Story* (5–8). 2003, Clarion $16.00 (978-0-618-33377-6). 224pp. In rural Virginia during the Depression, young April longs to go to the new school built by President Hoover and learn to read, but her family circumstances do not make this easy. (Rev: BCCB 11/03; BL 11/15/03; HB 1/04*; HBG 4/04; SLJ 11/03*)

11104 Reich, Susanna. *Penelope Bailey Takes the Stage* (4–7). 2006, Marshall Cavendish $16.95 (978-0-7614-5287-4). 208pp. A frustrated Penny takes a role in the school play against the wishes of her aunt in this novel set in Victorian San Francisco. (Rev: BL 5/15/06; SLJ 5/06)

11105 Robinet, Harriette G. *Forty Acres and Maybe a Mule* (4–7). 1998, Simon & Schuster $16.00 (978-0-689-82078-6). 144pp. After the Civil War, Gideon and other freed slaves begin working the 40 acres of land each has been promised in spite of the opposition of white settlers. (Rev: BL 1/1–15/99; HBG 3/99; SLJ 11/98)

11106 Rogers, Lisa Waller. *Get Along, Little Dogies: The Chisholm Trail Diary of Hallie Lou Wells: South Texas, 1878* (4–7). 2001, Texas Tech Univ. $14.50 (978-0-89672-446-4); paper $8.95 (978-0-89672-448-8). 174pp. Feisty 14-year-old Hallie Lou records in her diary the details and dangers of a cattle drive from Texas to Kansas. (Rev: HBG 10/01; SLJ 7/01)

11107 Rubright, Lynn. *Mama's Window* (4–6). Illus. by Patricia C. McKissack. 2005, Lee & Low $16.95 (978-1-57480-160-6). 96pp. Sugar, an 11-year-old African American orphan living with his uncle on the Mississippi Delta, fights to ensure that his late mother's dream of a stained-glass window for the local church becomes a reality. (Rev: BL 7/05; SLJ 8/05)

11108 Ryan, Pam Muñoz. *Esperanza Rising* (5–8). 2000, Scholastic paper $17.99 (978-0-439-12041-8). 272pp. During the Great Depression, poverty forces Esperanza and her mother to leave Mexico and seek work in an agricultural labor camp in California. (Rev: BCCB 12/00; BL 12/1/00; HB 1/01; HBG 3/01; SLJ 10/00; VOYA 12/00)

11109 Sandin, Joan. *The Long Way Westward* (2–4). Illus. 1989, HarperCollins paper $3.99 (978-0-06-444198-8). 64pp. In this continuation of *A Long Way to a New Land* (1981), the immigrant Swedish family continues its journey to Minnesota. (Rev: BCCB 11/89; BL 9/15/89; HB 9/89; SLJ 9/89)

11110 Schwabach, Karen. *The Hope Chest* (4–6). 2008, Random $16.99 (978-0-375-84095-1). 274pp. Eleven-year-old Violet runs away from home and joins the fight for the women's rights in the 1920s. (Rev: HB 3/08; LMC 3/08; SLJ 3/08)

11111 Sherman, Eileen B. *Independence Avenue* (5–9). 1990, Jewish Publication Soc. $14.95 (978-0-8276-0367-7). This story of Russian Jews who immigrate to Texas in 1907 has a resourceful, engaging hero, an unusual setting, and plenty of action. (Rev: BL 2/15/91; SLJ 1/91)

11112 Stroud, Bettye. *Dance Y'All* (2–4). Illus. by Cornelius Van Wright and Ying-Hwa Hu. 2001,

Marshall Cavendish $15.95 (978-0-7614-5065-8). With some help, Jack Henry overcomes his fear of the snake in the barn in this novel set at the beginning of the 20th century. (Rev: HBG 3/02; SLJ 11/01)

11113 Tate, Eleanora. *Celeste's Harlem Renaissance* (4–7). 2007, Little, Brown $15.99 (978-0-316-52394-3). 288pp. In the early 1920s Celeste arrives in New York from North Carolina and discovers that her aunt is not the famous singer and dancer she was told but that the lively spirit of the Harlem Renaissance brings her rewards. (Rev: BL 2/1/07; SLJ 5/07)

11114 Tolliver, Ruby C. *Boomer's Kids* (4–6). Illus. by Lyle Miller. 1992, Hendrick-Long paper $10.95 (978-0-88577-722-8). 128pp. Teenagers Andy and Ellie are tired of moving, as the family follows their father, a "boomer" in the oil fields in 1901. (Rev: BL 8/92)

11115 Tripp, Valerie. *Changes for Kit: A Winter Story* (3–5). Illus. by Walter Rane. Series: American Girl. 2001, Pleasant $12.95 (978-1-58485-027-4); paper $6.95 (978-1-58485-026-7). 70pp. A section of historical facts and photographs follows the story of Kit seeking clothing donations for children at the local soup kitchen and learning to cope with her grumpy uncle during the Depression. (Rev: BL 12/1/01; HBG 3/02)

11116 Tripp, Valerie. *Changes for Samantha: A Winter Story* (3–5). Illus. by Robert Grace and Nancy Niles. 1988, Pleasant LB $12.95 (978-0-937295-95-3); paper $6.95 (978-0-937295-47-2). 72pp. Wealthy New Yorker Samantha now lives with her aunt and uncle in a series that takes place in 1904 and includes: *Happy Birthday Samantha* (1987); *Samantha Saves the Day* (1988). (Rev: BL 1/1/89; SLJ 2/89)

11117 Tripp, Valerie. *Happy Birthday, Kit! A Springtime Story, 1934* (3–5). Illus. Series: American Girl. 2001, Pleasant $12.95 (978-1-58485-023-6); paper $6.95 (978-1-58485-022-9). 70pp. Kit greets her Aunt Millie's arrival with mixed emotions. (Rev: BL 8/01; HBG 3/02)

11118 Tripp, Valerie. *Kit Learns a Lesson: A School Story* (3–5). Illus. 2000, Pleasant $12.95 (978-1-58485-121-9). 67pp. As the Great Depression grows more serious, it affects all facets of Kit Kittredge's life including her family and school. (Rev: BL 9/1/00; HBG 3/01; SLJ 12/00)

11119 Tripp, Valerie. *Kit Saves the Day: A Summer Story, 1934* (3–5). Illus. Series: American Girl. 2001, Pleasant $12.95 (978-1-58485-025-0); paper $6.95 (978-1-58485-024-3). 68pp. Kit discovers that a hobo's life isn't as much fun as she first thought. (Rev: BL 8/01; HBG 3/02)

11120 Tripp, Valerie. *Meet Kit: An American Girl* (3–5). Illus. by Walter Rane. Series: American Girls. 2000, Pleasant $12.95 (978-1-58485-017-5). 70pp. In 1934, Kit Kittredge and her family feel the effects of the Great Depression when her father loses his job and her mother takes in boarders. (Rev: BL 9/1/00; HBG 3/01; SLJ 12/00)

11121 Tubb, Kristin O'Donnell. *Autumn Winifred Oliver Does Things Different* (4–6). 2008, Delacorte $15.99 (978-0-385-73569-8). 224pp. In the Great Smoky Mountains during the Depression, 11-year-old Autumn and her grandfather try to stop the government from destroying their mountain home. (Rev: BL 11/15/08; LMC 3/09; SLJ 1/09)

11122 Tucker, Terry Ward. *Moonlight and Mill Whistles* (5–7). 1998, Summerhouse $15.00 (978-1-887714-32-7). 120pp. Thirteen-year-old Tommy is unaware how his life will change after he meets a gypsy girl named Rhona in this novel set in an early 1900s South Carolina cotton mill town. (Rev: BL 3/1/99; SLJ 5/99)

11123 Vander Zee, Ruth. *Mississippi Morning* (3–6). Illus. by Floyd Cooper. 2004, Eerdmans $16.00 (978-0-8028-5211-3). A picture-book story of a 12-year-old boy in 1933 Mississippi who must come to terms with the racism that is all around him, even in his father. (Rev: BL 10/15/04*; SLJ 9/04)

11124 Waldman, Neil. *Say-Hey and the Babe: Two Mostly True Baseball Stories* (4–6). Illus. by author. 2006, Holiday $16.95 (978-0-8234-1857-2). 40pp. Two stories based on fact link a baseball autographed by Babe Ruth and subsequently lost with a stickball player's discovery in a sewer grate 14 years later; sidebars add lots of baseball lore and separate fact from fiction. (Rev: BL 5/15/06; SLJ 7/06)

11125 Waldman, Neil. *They Came from the Bronx: How the Buffalo Were Saved from Extinction* (2–5). Illus. by author. 2001, Boyds Mills $16.95 (978-1-56397-891-3). A Comanche grandmother and grandson await a small herd of buffalo in a story based on efforts to return bison to the plains in 1907. (Rev: HBG 10/02; SLJ 9/01)

11126 Warner, Sally. *Finding Hattie* (5–8). 2001, HarperCollins $15.95 (978-0-06-028464-0). 234pp. Hattie Knowlton's 1882 journal describes Miss Bulkey's school in Tarrytown, New York, and the people she meets there, including her sophisticated, shallow but popular cousin Sophie. (Rev: BCCB 6/01; BL 2/1/01; HB 5/01; HBG 10/01; SLJ 2/01; VOYA 8/01)

11127 Wax, Wendy. *Empire Dreams* (3–6). Illus. by Todd Doney. Series: Adventures in America. 2000, Silver Moon LB $14.95 (978-1-893110-19-9). 91pp. Eleven-year-old Julie, growing up in New York during the construction of the Empire State Building, secretly takes a job to help out her family after her father becomes unemployed. (Rev: HBG 3/01; SLJ 3/01)

11128 Wells, Rosemary, and Tom Wells. *The House in the Mail* (2–5). Illus. by Dan Andreasen. 2002, Viking $16.99 (978-0-670-03545-8). 32pp. A scrapbook-style accounting by a 12-year-old girl of her family's mail-order home in 1927 Kentucky. (Rev: BCCB 2/02; BL 3/1/02; HBG 10/02; SLJ 3/02)

11129 West, Tracey. *Fire in the Valley* (3–5). Illus. Series: Stories of the States. 1993, Silver Moon LB $14.95 (978-1-881889-32-8). 80pp. Eleven-year-old Sarah becomes involved in mob violence concerning water rights in this novel set in 1905 California. (Rev: SLJ 12/93)

11130 Whelan, Gloria. *The Locked Garden* (3–6). 2009, HarperCollins $15.99 (978-0-06-079094-3). 176pp. At the turn of the 20th century, after their mother's death, Verna and her sister Carlie move with their doctor father to a mental asylum in northern Michigan, where prejudices persist. (Rev: BL 4/15/09; SLJ 7/09)

11131 Winthrop, Elizabeth. *Franklin Delano Roosevelt: Letters from a Mill Town Girl* (5–7). Illus. Series: Dear Mr. President. 2001, Winslow $9.95 (978-1-890817-61-9). 128pp. Fictional letters between Franklin Delano Roosevelt and a 12-year-old girl illustrate living conditions and government policy during the Depression. (Rev: BL 2/1/02; HBG 3/02; SLJ 12/01)

11132 Wolfert, Adrienne. *Making Tracks* (5–7). Illus. Series: Adventures in America. 2000, Silver Moon LB $14.95 (978-1-893110-16-8). 96pp. In this novel set in the Depression, young Henry leaves his foster home to ride the rails to Chicago to find his father. (Rev: BL 7/00; HBG 3/01; SLJ 11/00)

11133 Wyatt, Leslie J. *Poor Is Just a Starting Place* (5–8). 2005, Holiday $16.95 (978-0-8234-1884-8). 196pp. In rural Kentucky during the Great Depression, 12-year-old Artie longs for a different life. (Rev: BL 6/1–15/05; SLJ 7/05)

11134 Wyss, Thelma Hatch. *A Tale of Gold* (4–6). 2007, Simon & Schuster $15.99 (978-1-4169-4212-2). 160pp. In the late 1890s, a 14-year-old orphan named James sets out from San Francisco heading for the gold fields of Alaska, meeting many interesting characters on the exciting journey. (Rev: BL 10/15/07; SLJ 10/07)

11135 Yep, Laurence. *The Earth Dragon Awakes: The San Francisco Earthquake of 1906* (3–5). 2006, HarperCollins $14.99 (978-0-06-027524-2). 128pp. Best friends Henry and Ching, both fans of "penny dreadful" adventure novels, live through the earthquake and realize that their fathers are heroes. (Rev: BL 3/1/06; SLJ 5/06)

11136 Yolen, Jane. *Tea with an Old Dragon: A Story of Sophia Smith, Founder of Smith College* (2–4). Illus. by Monica Vachula. 1998, Boyds Mills $15.95 (978-1-56397-657-5). In this historical story set in a 19th-century New England town, a little girl becomes friends with Miss Sophy Smith, the founder of Smith College. (Rev: HBG 3/99; SLJ 10/98)

WORLD WAR II AND AFTER

11137 Adler, David A. *Don't Talk to Me About the War* (4–7). 2008, Viking $15.99 (978-0-670-06307-9). 176pp. Tommy tries hard to ignore the problems overseas and at home in this novel set in the Bronx in 1940. (Rev: BL 4/15/08; SLJ 3/08)

11138 Avi. *Who Was That Masked Man, Anyway?* (5–7). 1992, Orchard LB $17.99 (978-0-531-08607-0). 176pp. In a story told through dialogue, 6th-grader Frankie lives through World War II by immersing himself in his beloved radio serials.

(Rev: BCCB 10/92*; BL 8/92*; HB 3/93; SLJ 10/92*)

11139 Bishop, Claire Huchet. *Twenty and Ten* (4–6). Illus. by William Pene du Bois. 1984, Peter Smith $21.25 (978-0-8446-6168-1); Puffin paper $5.99 (978-0-14-031076-4). A nun and 20 French children hide ten young refugees from the Nazis.

11140 Blume, Lesley M. M. *The Rising Star of Rusty Nail* (4–6). 2007, Knopf $15.99 (978-0-375-83524-7). 288pp. Set in a small Minnesota town in 1953, this is the story of Franny, a musically talented 10-year-old who tries to get a Russian immigrant (suspected of being a Communist spy) to become her piano teacher. (Rev: BL 6/1–15/07*; LMC 10/07; SLJ 7/07)

11141 Borden, Louise. *Across the Blue Pacific* (3–5). Illus. by Robert Andrew Parker. 2006, Houghton $17.00 (978-0-618-33922-8). 48pp. In this poignant fictional memoir, a woman recalls her concern as a fourth grader for the welfare of a neighbor who served on a submarine in the Pacific during World War II; watercolor paintings evoke the mood and time period. (Rev: BCCB 6/06; BL 4/1/06*; HB 5/06; HBG 10/06; LMC 1/07; SLJ 5/06)

11142 Bryant, Jen. *Kaleidoscope Eyes* (5–7). 2009, Knopf $15.99 (978-0-375-84048-7). 272pp. In 1968 New Jersey, 13-year-old Lyza and her friends search for buried treasure; a compelling free-verse novel that conveys the tensions of the time. (Rev: BL 4/15/09; LMC 8/09; SLJ 6/09; VOYA 6/09)

11143 Buckey, Sarah Masters. *The Light in the Cellar* (3–6). 2007, Pleasant $10.95 (978-1-59369-159-2); paper $6.95 (978-1-59369-158-5). 158pp. Set in the United States during World War II, this story follows Molly and her friend, Emily, as they try to solve the mystery of the disappearance of the town's sugar, which is prized because of rationing (includes historical background information and photographs at the end). (Rev: BL 5/1/07; SLJ 5/07)

11144 Buckvar, Felice. *Dangerous Dream* (4–6). Ed. by Myrna Kemnitz. 1998, Royal Fireworks paper $9.99 (978-0-88092-277-7). 123pp. A 13-year-old Holocaust survivor is suspicious of the man who claims to be her father. (Rev: SLJ 4/99)

11145 Coerr, Eleanor. *Mieko and the Fifth Treasure* (4–7). 2003, Puffin paper $5.99 (978-0-698-11990-1). 78pp. A Japanese girl believes that she will never draw again after she is injured during the atomic bomb attack on Nagasaki. (Rev: BCCB 4/93; BL 4/1/93*; SLJ 7/93)

11146 Coleman, Evelyn. *Freedom Train* (5–8). 2008, Simon & Schuster $15.99 (978-1-4169-5211-4). 160pp. Clyde, who comes from a poor white family, stands up for himself by refusing to join his father in harassing a black family in this story set in 1947 Atlanta. (Rev: BL 2/1/08)

11147 Copeland, Cynthia. *Elin's Island* (5–7). 2003, Millbrook LB $22.90 (978-0-7613-2522-2). 144pp. Raised since infancy by lighthouse keepers, 13-year-old Elin is left on her own to tend the house and light on an eventful night in 1941. (Rev: BL 3/15/03; HBG 10/03; SLJ 7/03)

11148 Crum, Shutta. *Spitting Image* (5–8). 2003, Clarion $15.00 (978-0-618-23477-6). 224pp. Jessie has a busy summer in 1967 in her Kentucky hometown, tackling family problems and dealing with well-meaning volunteers and reporters who view them as "rural poor." (Rev: BL 3/1/03; HBG 10/03; SLJ 4/03*)

11149 Deedy, Carmen A. *The Yellow Star: The Legend of King Christian X of Denmark* (3–5). 2000, Peachtree $16.95 (978-1-56145-208-8). Although in real life it did not happen, this picture book tells how the King of Denmark wore a Jewish star in World War II to show Hitler that in his country there are only Danes. (Rev: BCCB 11/00; BL 7/00; HBG 3/01; SLJ 9/00)

11150 Dowell, Frances O'Roark. *Shooting the Moon* (4–8). 2008, Atheneum $16.99 (978-1-4169-2690-0). 176pp. Jamie is surprised when her military father is not pleased about her big brother volunteering to go to Vietnam, until TJ sends home increasingly disturbing photographs of the war. (Rev: BL 3/15/08; SLJ 5/08)

11151 Elmer, Robert. *Into the Flames* (5–7). Series: Young Underground. 1995, Bethany paper $5.99 (978-1-55661-376-0). 144pp. Danish twins are captured by the Gestapo while trying to rescue their uncle during World War II. (Rev: BL 5/15/95; SLJ 8/95)

11152 Ferrari, Michael. *Born to Fly* (4–6). 2009, Delacorte $15.99 (978-0-385-73715-9). 224pp. On Bird's 11th birthday the Japanese attack Pearl Harbor and her whole life changes; her pilot father joins the Air Force and her friendship with a Japanese American boy named Kenji brings new complications in this action-packed novel. (Rev: BL 5/15/09; SLJ 9/09)

11153 Flood, Pansie Hart. *Sylvia and Miz Lula Maye* (3–5). Illus. by Felicia Marshall. 2002, Carolrhoda $15.95 (978-0-87614-204-2). 120pp. A 10-year-old African American girl and her 100-year-old neighbor form an unlikely friendship in this novel set in 1970s South Carolina. (Rev: BL 2/15/02; HBG 10/02; SLJ 4/02)

11154 Giff, Patricia Reilly. *Lily's Crossing* (5–8). 1997, Delacorte $15.95 (978-0-385-32142-6). During World War II, motherless Lily loses her father when he is sent to fight in France but becomes friendly with Albert, an orphaned Hungarian refugee. (Rev: BCCB 4/97; BL 2/1/97; HB 3/97; SLJ 2/97)

11155 Giff, Patricia Reilly. *Willow Run* (4–6). 2005, Random $15.95 (978-0-385-73067-9). 176pp. Life changes dramatically for 11-year-old Meggie Dillon when her immediate family moves to Michigan so that her father can work in a airplane factory in World War II. (Rev: BCCB 12/05; BL 7/05*; HB 9/05; HBG 4/06; LMC 1/06; SLJ 9/05; VOYA 2/06) ∩

11156 Going, K. L. *The Liberation of Gabriel King* (4–6). 2005, Penguin $15.99 (978-0-399-23991-5). 160pp. Ten-year-old Gabriel, a small and fearful white boy in 1976 Georgia, and his assertive African American friend Frita agree to tackle

Gabe's (and her) fears and find themselves strong enough to withstand racist attacks. (Rev: BL 5/15/05; SLJ 6/05)

11157 Graff, Nancy P. *Taking Wing* (5–8). 2005, Clarion $15.00 (978-0-618-53591-0). 224pp. A multilayered story set in 1942 Vermont and featuring 13-year-old Gus, who, over the course of the book, learns about prejudice, and about killing and death. (Rev: BL 5/15/05*; SLJ 5/05)

11158 Griffis, Molly Levite. *The Feester Filibuster* (4–8). 2002, Eakin $17.95 (978-1-57168-541-4); paper $8.95 (978-1-57168-694-7). 224pp. John Allen Feester is determined to show he's not a spy in this sequel to *The Rachel Resistance* (2001). (Rev: BL 11/1/02; HBG 10/01)

11159 Gwaltney, Doris. *Homefront* (5–8). 2006, Simon & Schuster $15.95 (978-0-689-86842-9). 320pp. A young girl must cope with the diverse effects of World War II on her Virginia farming family. (Rev: BCCB 10/06; BL 7/06; SLJ 7/06*)

11160 Hahn, Mary D. *Stepping on the Cracks* (5–8). 1991, Houghton $16.00 (978-0-395-58507-8); Avon paper $5.99 (978-0-380-71900-6). 218pp. The compelling story of a 6th-grade girl during World War II and her difficult decision whether to help a pacifist deserter. (Rev: BCCB 12/91*; BL 10/15/91*; HB 11/91; SLJ 12/91*)

11161 Harrar, George. *The Wonder Kid* (4–7). Illus. by Anthony Winiarski. 2006, Houghton $16.00 (978-0-618-56317-3). 245pp. As a kid growing up in the 1950s, Jesse contracts polio and with the encouragement of a friend passes the time creating a comic strip hero called the Wonder Kid. (Rev: SLJ 3/07)

11162 Herman, Charlotte. *My Chocolate Year: A Novel with 12 Recipes to Make Your World a Little Sweeter* (3–5). Illus. by LeUyen Pham. 2008, Simon & Schuster $15.99 (978-1-4169-3341-0). 176pp. This portrait of a Jewish family in post-World War II Chicago features Dorrie, a 5th-grader with culinary ambitions and worries about relatives abroad; recipes are sprinkled throughout. (Rev: BLO 7/29/08; SLJ 2/08)

11163 Hoestlandt, Jo. *Star of Fear, Star of Hope* (2–4). Trans. by Mark Polizzotti. Illus. by Johanna Kang. 1995, Walker LB $16.85 (978-0-8027-8374-5). 32pp. In World War II–occupied France, Helen witnesses the growing persecution of her Jewish friend Lydia. (Rev: BCCB 6/95; BL 5/1/95; HB 9/95; SLJ 8/95)

11164 Holm, Jennifer. *Penny from Heaven* (5–8). 2006, Random $15.95 (978-0-375-83687-9). 288pp. Set in 1953, this is the story of how 12-year-old Penny gets to know her late father's lively Italian American family and comes to understand the circumstances surrounding her father's death. Newbery Honor Book, 2007. (Rev: BL 4/15/06; HB 3/07; SLJ 7/06)

11165 Hoobler, Dorothy, and Thomas Hoobler. *The 1940s: Secrets* (3–6). Illus. Series: Century Kids. 2001, Millbrook LB $22.90 (978-0-7613-1604-6). 176pp. The story of various branches of the Aldrich family and their contributions to the home front during World War II. (Rev: BL 4/1/01; HBG 10/01; SLJ 5/01)

11166 Hostetter, Joyce Moyer. *Blue* (4–7). 2006, Boyds Mills $16.95 (978-1-59078-389-4). 200pp. When her father leaves for World War II, Ann Fay, the oldest of four children, struggles to keep up with the chores in their North Carolina home until polio strikes the community. (Rev: BL 2/15/06; SLJ 6/06)

11167 Judge, Lita. *One Thousand Tracings: Healing the Wounds of World War II* (3–6). Illus. by author. 2007, Hyperion $15.99 (978-1-4231-0008-9). 40pp. Set in postwar America, this is a beautifully illustrated story of a little girl in the Midwest who helps her mother prepare care packages to be sent to Europeans who lack many basic necessities, including clothing and shoes. (Rev: BL 5/15/07; SLJ 7/07)

11168 Kadohata, Cynthia. *Weedflower* (5–8). 2006, Simon & Schuster $16.95 (978-0-689-86574-9). 260pp. Sumiko and her Japanese American family are moved from their California flower farm to an internment camp in Arizona after the attack on Pearl Harbor; there she grows a garden and befriends a local Mojave boy. (Rev: BL 4/15/06*; HB 7/06; SLJ 7/06*) ∩

11169 Kerley, Barbara. *Greetings from Planet Earth* (4–6). 2007, Scholastic $16.99 (978-0-439-80203-1). 246pp. In 1977, as he considers a class project on space exploration, 12-year-old Theo is more preoccupied with family questions — why can he never discuss his father, who never returned from Vietnam? (Rev: BL 4/15/07)

11170 Klages, Ellen. *The Green Glass Sea* (4–7). 2006, Viking $16.99 (978-0-670-06134-1). 272pp. In 1943, talented 10-year-old Dewey goes to live with her father at the Los Alamos compound, a tense place where she initially has trouble making friends. (Rev: BL 11/15/06; SLJ 11/06) ∩

11171 Klages, Ellen. *White Sands, Red Menace* (5–8). 2008, Viking $16.99 (978-0-670-06235-5). 320pp. In this riveting sequel to *The Green Glass Sea* (2006), Dewey's father has died and she is living near Los Alamos with her friend Suze, whose father is working on a new rocket for the space race. (Rev: BL 8/08)

11172 Kochenderfer, Lee. *The Victory Garden* (4–6). 2002, Delacorte $14.95 (978-0-385-32788-6). 166pp. Eleven-year-old Teresa writes to her pilot brother and helps her father tend a victory garden in this tale set in Kansas in 1943. (Rev: BCCB 3/02; BL 3/1/02; HBG 10/02; SLJ 1/02)

11173 Kogawa, Joy. *Naomi's Tree* (3–5). Illus. by Ruth Ohi. 2009, Fitzhenry & Whiteside $19.95 (978-1-55455-055-5). 32pp. Interned in Canada during World War II, Naomi clings to memories of the cherry tree planted by her Japanese grandparents, and of her mother who cannot return from Japan. (Rev: BL 5/1/09)

11174 Kudlinski, Kathleen V. *Pearl Harbor Is Burning! The Story of World War II* (4–6). Illus. by Ronald Himler. 1993, Puffin paper $5.99 (978-0-14-034509-4). 64pp. Historical events are brought into perspective in a fictional framework as Frank, a newcomer to Hawaii, must learn to adjust to island living. (Rev: BCCB 10/91; BL 11/15/91; SLJ 2/92)

11175 Lawrence, Iain. *Gemini Summer* (4–7). 2006, Delacorte $15.95 (978-0-385-73089-1). 224pp. In the mid-1960s, soon after Danny's brother Beau dies in an accident, a stray dog appears and adopts Danny; Danny becomes devoted to the dog and, because he sees much of Beau in Rocket, he and Rocket set off for Cape Canaveral to realize Beau's dream of seeing the Gemini mission. (Rev: BL 12/15/06; SLJ 11/06)

11176 Lemna, Don. *When the Sergeant Came Marching Home* (4–7). Illus. by Matt Colins. 2008, Holiday $16.95 (978-0-8234-2083-4). 224pp. Set in the 1940s, this novel of a family that moves to a farm in Montana paints a realistic picture of the hardships and joys of rural life at that time. (Rev: BL 4/15/08; SLJ 7/08)

11177 Levine, Ellen. *Catch a Tiger by the Toe* (5–8). 2005, Viking $15.99 (978-0-670-88461-2). 208pp. Jamie's world is turned upside down when her father is put in jail for refusing to reveal the names of other Communists to the House Un-American Activities Committee. (Rev: BL 3/15/05*; SLJ 6/05)

11178 Levitin, Sonia. *Journey to America* (5–8). Illus. by Charles Robinson. 1970, Macmillan paper $4.99 (978-0-689-71130-5). 160pp. A Jewish mother and her three daughters flee Nazi Germany in 1938 and undertake a long and difficult journey to join their father in America. (Rev: BL 9/1/93)

11179 Lowry, Lois. *Number the Stars* (5–7). 1989, Houghton $16.00 (978-0-395-51060-5); Dell paper $5.99 (978-0-440-40327-2). 160pp. The story of war-torn Denmark and best friends Annemarie Johansen and Ellen Rosen. Newbery Medal winner, 1990. (Rev: BCCB 3/89; BL 3/1/89; SLJ 3/89)

11180 McDowell, Marilyn Taylor. *Carolina Harmony* (4–7). 2009, Delacorte $16.99 (978-0-385-73590-2). 336pp. In 1964 in the Blue Ridge Mountains, 10-year-old runaway orphan Carolina begins to recover from the traumas she has experienced. (Rev: BL 2/1/09; SLJ 8/09)

11181 McKissack, Patricia C. *Abby Takes a Stand* (2–4). Illus. by Gordon C. James. Series: Scraps of Time. 2005, Viking $14.99 (978-0-670-06011-5). 112pp. Grandma Gee, an African American, tells her granddaughters about her humiliation when refused entry to a department store restaurant in 1960 and about her efforts to support the civil rights movement. (Rev: BL 5/15/05)

11182 McKissack, Patricia C. *Away West* (3–6). Illus. by Gordon C. James. Series: Scraps of Time. 2006, Viking $14.99 (978-0-670-06012-2). 112pp. In this second volume in the series, the Webster children learn the story of Everett Turner, who works in a livery stable after the Civil War and dreams of living in the African American town of Nicodemus, Kansas. (Rev: BL 4/15/06; SLJ 5/06)

11183 McSwigan, Marie. *Snow Treasure* (4–7). Illus. by Andre Le Blanc. 1986, Scholastic paper $4.99 (978-0-590-42537-7). 156pp. Children smuggle gold out of occupied Norway on their sleds.

11184 Madden, Kerry. *Jessie's Mountain* (5–8). Series: Maggie Valley. 2008, Viking $16.99 (978-0-670-06154-9). 256pp. Livy Two and her family are still struggling to make it in this final installment in the series, but they start to turn things around using their love of music. (Rev: BL 2/8/08; SLJ 3/08)

11185 Maguire, Gregory. *The Good Liar* (4–6). 1999, Clarion $15.00 (978-0-395-90697-2). 129pp. A first-person novel about a boy growing up in occupied France during World War II and the deception involved when his parents hide a Jewish woman and her daughter. (Rev: BCCB 3/99; BL 4/15/99*; HB 7/99; HBG 10/99; SLJ 5/99)

11186 Mathews, Ellie. *The Linden Tree* (4–6). 2007, Milkweed $16.95 (978-1-57131-673-8); paper $6.95 (978-1-57131-674-5). 170pp. After her mother's sudden death, 9-year-old Katy Sue must cope with her grief, added responsibilities on the family farm, and the arrival of her mother's sister, Aunt Katherine. (Rev: BCCB 9/07; BL 5/1/07; LMC 10/07; SLJ 9/07)

11187 Mercer, Peggy. *There Come a Soldier* (2–4). Illus. by Ron Mazellan. 2007, Handprint $17.95 (978-1-59354-192-7). 40pp. Memories of his youth on a Georgia farm sustain a World War II paratrooper in this picture-book story based on her father's experiences. (Rev: BL 11/15/07; SLJ 11/07)

11188 Mori, Hana. *Jirohattan* (3–6). Trans. from Japanese by Tamiko Kurosaki and Elizabeth Crowe. Illus. by Elizabeth Crowe. 1993, Bess paper $6.95 (978-1-880188-69-9). 76pp. In this tale set in World War II Japan, a slow-witted boy named Jirohattan helps others but is unable to comprehend death. (Rev: BCCB 2/94; SLJ 5/94)

11189 Moses, Shelia P. *Sallie Gal and the Wall-a-kee Man* (2–4). Illus. by Niki Daly. 2007, Scholastic $15.99 (978-0-439-90890-0). 152pp. African American Sallie Mae, almost 9, lives in a hardscrabble sharecropping community in North Carolina in the 1970s and longs to have new hair ribbons. (Rev: BCCB 2/08; BL 10/1/07; HB 9/07; LMC 1/08; SLJ 9/07)

11190 Myers, Walter Dean. *The Journal of Scott Pendleton Collins: A World War II Soldier* (5–9). Illus. Series: My Name Is America. 1999, Scholastic paper $10.95 (978-0-439-05013-5). Through a series of letters, readers get to know 17-year-old Collins, an American soldier who participates in the D-Day invasion of Europe. (Rev: BL 6/1–15/99; HBG 10/99; SLJ 7/99)

11191 Myers, Walter Dean. *Patrol: An American Soldier in Vietnam* (4–8). Illus. by Ann Grifalconi. 2002, HarperCollins LB $17.89 (978-0-06-028364-3). 40pp. A penetrating picture book for older readers told in narrative verse from the perspective of a teenage soldier in Vietnam. (Rev: BL 3/15/02; HB 7/02; HBG 10/02; SLJ 5/02)

11192 Parkhurst, Liz. *Under One Flag: A Year at Rohwer* (3–5). Illus. by Tom Clifton. 2005, August House $16.95 (978 0 87483-759-9). 32pp. A young Japanese American intern and the son of the camp administrator become friends during World War II. (Rev: BL 5/15/05; SLJ 4/05)

11193 Peck, Richard. *On the Wings of Heroes* (4–6). 2007, Dial $16.99 (978-0-8037-3081-6). 148pp. Life before and during World War II is presented from the perspective of Davy Bowman, who lives in small-town America and has an older brother in the Air Force. (Rev: BL 12/1/06; SLJ 4/07*; VOYA 4/07)

11194 Pérez, L. King. *Remember as You Pass Me By* (5–8). 2007, Milkweed $16.95 (978-1-57131-677-6); paper $6.95 (978-1-57131-678-3). 224pp. In 1950s Texas racial tensions come between 12-year-old Silvy Lane and her black friend Mabelee. (Rev: LMC 1/08; SLJ 11/07)

11195 Radin, Ruth Yaffe. *Escape to the Forest: Based on a True Story of the Holocaust* (4–6). Illus. by Janet Hamlin. 2000, HarperCollins LB $13.89 (978-0-06-028521-0). 80pp. A realistic story of a Jewish girl named Sarah and her part in resistance against the Nazis during World War II. (Rev: BCCB 3/00; HBG 10/00; SLJ 3/00)

11196 Ray, Delia. *Singing Hands* (4–7). 2006, Clarion $16.00 (978-0-618-65762-9). 256pp. Gussie's parents are deaf, which means she can be even more mischievous than the average child in this book set in the 1940s American South. (Rev: BL 5/1/06; SLJ 7/06)

11197 Rodman, Mary Ann. *Jimmy's Stars* (5–8). 2008, Farrar $16.95 (978-0-374-33703-2). 272pp. Ellie's beloved brother Jimmy's deferments run out and he is sent off to fight in World War II; when news arrives that he has been killed, Ellie finds it almost impossible to believe. (Rev: BL 4/1/08; SLJ 6/08)

11198 Rodman, Mary Ann. *Yankee Girl* (4–8). 2004, Farrar $17.00 (978-0-374-38661-0). 224pp. In 1964, Alice's family moves from Chicago to Mississippi and 6th-grader Alice must cope not only with the stress of a new school but also with her ambivalence about the only black girl in her class; newspaper headlines introducing each chapter keep the racial violence of the time in the reader's mind. (Rev: BL 3/1/04; SLJ 4/04)

11199 Rogers, Kenny, and Donald Davenport. *Christmas in Canaan* (5–8). 2002, HarperCollins $15.99 (978-0-06-000746-1). 336pp. In 1960s Texas, after a black boy and a white boy fight on the school bus, the adults decree that the two boys must spend time together, and a difficult start ends in the boys becoming fast friends when they help a wounded dog. (Rev: BL 11/1/02; HBG 3/03; SLJ 10/02; VOYA 4/03)

11200 Salisbury, Graham. *House of the Red Fish* (5–8). 2006, Random $16.95 (978-0-385-73121-8). 160pp. After his father is sent to an internment camp, Japanese American teen Tomi rallies the community to help raise his father's sunken fishing boat in this inspiring sequel to *Under the Blood-Red Sun* (2005). (Rev: BL 4/15/06; LMC 10/06; SLJ 8/06)

11201 Say, Allen. *Music for Alice* (4–7). Illus. 2004, Houghton $17.00 (978-0-618-31118-7). 32pp. Based on a real story, this is the moving portrait of a Japanese American couple who make the best of the challenges forced upon them during World War II. (Rev: BL 2/1/04; HB 5/04; SLJ 4/04)

11202 Shemin, Margaretha. *The Little Riders* (4–6). Illus. by Peter Spier. 1988, Morrow paper $5.99 (978-0-688-12499-1). 80pp. An 11-year-old girl is trapped in German-occupied Netherlands during World War II. A reissue.

11203 Smith, D. James. *The Boys of San Joaquin* (5–8). 2005, Simon & Schuster $15.95 (978-0-689-87606-6). 240pp. An episodic tale set in the 1950s, in which 12-year-old Paolo describes events of his life and a mystery involving a half-eaten $20 bill. (Rev: BL 3/1/05; SLJ 1/05)

11204 Smith, D. James. *Probably the World's Best Story About a Dog and the Girl Who Loved Me* (5–8). 2006, Simon & Schuster $15.95 (978-1-4169-0542-4). 240pp. In 1951 California, 12-year-old Paolo's beloved dog Rufus is dognapped and he enlists the help of his younger brother and a deaf cousin to unravel the mystery while also coping with a new paper route and a budding romance; this sequel to *The Boys of San Joaquin* (2004) introduces a sign language word with each chapter. (Rev: BL 9/1/06; SLJ 8/06)

11205 Smith, Icy. *Mei Ling in China City* (3–5). Illus. by Gayle Garner Roski. 2008, East West Discovery $18.95 (978-0-9701654-8-0). In 1942 Los Angeles, Mei Ling describes life in China City and the family's efforts to raise funds for people back home, and details her efforts to stay in touch with her friend Yayeko, a Japanese friend who has been interned. (Rev: LMC 11/08; SLJ 5/08)

11206 Sullivan, Jacqueline Levering. *Annie's War* (4–7). 2007, Eerdmans $15.00 (978-0-8028-5325-7). 190pp. In 1946, 10-year-old Annie is having a hard time coping with her father's MIA status and her 19-year-old uncle's emotional problems, and she finds some comfort in imagined conversations with President Truman. (Rev: BL 8/07; SLJ 9/07)

11207 Taylor, Marilyn. *Faraway Home* (5–8). 2000, O'Brien paper $7.95 (978-0-86278-643-4). 221pp. Taken from his Austrian homeland by the Kindertransport, 13-year-old Karl is sent to County Down in Ireland where he endures the hardship of country life and the hostility of the locals. (Rev: BL 3/1/01)

11208 Testa, Maria. *Almost Forever* (2–5). 2003, Candlewick $14.99 (978-0-7636-1996-1). 80pp. In free verse, a first grader describes her feelings during the year her father spends as a doctor in the Vietnam War. (Rev: BL 9/1/03; SLJ 10/03)

11209 Tripp, Valerie. *Brave Emily* (2–4). Illus. by Nick Backes. 2006, Pleasant $12.95 (978-1-59369-211-7); paper $6.95 (978-1-59369-210-0). 78pp. Sent to live with an American family to escape the bombing of London in World War II, shy third grader Emily has trouble adjusting to the dramatic changes in her life. (Rev: BL 11/1/06; SLJ 2/07)

11210 Tripp, Valerie. *Meet Molly: An American Girl* (3–5). Illus. by C. F. Payne. 1986, Pleasant LB $12.95 (978-0-937295-81-6); paper $6.95 (978-0-937295-07-6). 72pp. Molly is growing up without a father during World War II in America. Others in the series are: *Molly Learns a Lesson* (1986); *Molly's Surprise* (1986); *Molly Saves the Day* (1988); *Happy Birthday, Molly!* (1987); *Changes for Molly* (1988). (Rev: BL 12/1/86)

11211 Uchida, Yoshiko. *The Bracelet* (1–5). Illus. by Joanna Yardley. 1993, Penguin $16.99 (978-0-399-22503-1). 32pp. Emi, a Japanese American girl, is confused and frightened when she is interned in a prison camp during World War II. (Rev: BCCB 9/93; BL 9/15/93; HB 11/93; SLJ 12/93)

11212 Vander Els, Betty. *The Bombers' Moon* (5–7). 1992, Farrar paper $4.50 (978-0-374-30877-3). 168pp. Missionary children Ruth and Simeon are evacuated to escape the Japanese invasion of China; they will not see their parents for four years. A sequel is *Leaving Point* (1987). (Rev: BCCB 9/85; BL 11/1/85; HB 9/85)

11213 Waters, Zack C. *Blood Moon Rider* (5–8). 2006, Pineapple $13.95 (978-1-56164-350-9). 126pp. Abandoned by his stepmother after his father is killed in World War II, 14-year-old Harley Wallace survives an eventful journey to the home of a grandfather he's never met and there finds more excitement waiting. (Rev: SLJ 8/06)

11214 Watts, Irene. *Good-bye Marianne: A Story of Growing Up in Nazi Germany* (5–8). 1998, Tundra paper $7.95 (978-0-88776-445-5). In this autobiographical novel, 11-year-old Marianne Kohn is Jewish and experiencing Nazi persecution in 1938 Berlin when her parents decide to sent her to Britain as part of the Kindertransport rescue operation. (Rev: BCCB 7–8/98; BL 8/98; SLJ 8/98)

11215 Watts, Irene N. *Finding Sophie: A Search for Belonging in Postwar Britain* (5–8). 2002, Tundra paper $6.95 (978-0-88776-613-8). 144pp. In this sequel to *Remember Me* (2000), World War II has ended and 13-year-old Sophie waits anxiously to hear news of her Jewish family in Germany, at the same time hoping she will not have to leave her happy life in London. (Rev: BL 1/1–15/03; SLJ 3/03; VOYA 8/03)

11216 Watts, Irene N. *Remember Me: A Search for Refuge in Wartime Britain* (5–8). 2000, Tundra paper $7.95 (978-0-88776-519-3). 176pp. A heart-tugging story of an 11-year-old Jewish girl who, at the beginning of World War II, is transported from her home in Berlin to live in a Welsh mining town where she knows no one and speaks no English. (Rev: BL 12/1/00; SLJ 1/01; VOYA 2/01)

11217 Weatherford, Carole Boston. *Freedom on the Menu: The Greensboro Sit-ins* (1–3). Illus. by Jerome Lararrigue. 2005, Dial $16.99 (978-0-8037-2860-8). 32pp. Seen through the eyes of a young African American girl, this is the story of the 1960 lunch counter sit-ins in North Carolina. (Rev: BL 2/1/05; SLJ 4/05)

11218 Weston, Elise. *The Coastwatcher* (5–8). 2005, Peachtree $14.95 (978-1-56145-350-4). 160pp. Vacationing on the South Carolina coast with his family in 1943, 11-year-old Hugh sees some signs that Germans are nearby and is determined to convince the doubting adults that he is right. (Rev: BL 11/1/05; SLJ 3/06)

11219 White, Ruth. *Little Audrey* (5–8). 2008, Farrar $16.00 (978-0-374-34580-8). 160pp. Using the voice of her older sister, the author describes their family life in the late 1940s; 11-year-old Audrey must cope with her own physical problems, her father's drinking, her mother's emotional absence, and her three needy little sisters. (Rev: BL 9/1/08*; SLJ 9/08*; VOYA 8/08)

11220 White, Ruth. *Way Down Deep* (4–7). 2007, Farrar $16.00 (978-0-374-38251-3). 197pp. In 1944 West Virginia, the arrival of a new family in a town called Way Down Deep suddenly raises questions about the origins of Ruby June, a foundling who has lived there for 10 years. (Rev: BL 3/1/07; SLJ 4/07)

11221 Whittenberg, Allison. *Hollywood and Maine* (5–8). 2009, Delacorte $15.99 (978-0-385-73671-8). 176pp. When her jailbird uncle shows up to displace her from her attic bedroom, 14-year-old Maine Upshaw puts her energy into winning a beauty contest and steps on a lot of toes in this sequel to *Sweet Thang* (2006) set in the 1970s. (Rev: BCCB 3/09; BL 2/1/09; SLJ 2/09)

11222 Williams, Laura E. *Behind the Bedroom Wall* (5–8). Illus. 1996, Milkweed paper $6.95 (978-1-57131-606-6). Korinna, a young Nazi, discovers that her parents are hiding a Jewish couple in wartime Germany. (Rev: BL 8/96; SLJ 9/96)

11223 Winkler, Allan M. *Cassie's War* (4–6). 1994, Royal Fireworks paper $9.99 (978-0-88092-106-0). 94pp. Cassie is growing up in California during World War II, which brings internment to her Japanese American friend and death to her soldier father. (Rev: BL 2/1/95)

11224 Woods, Brenda. *The Red Rose Box* (5–8). 2002, Putnam $16.99 (978-0-399-23702-7). 144pp. In 1953, Leah, a southern black girl, and her family travel to Los Angeles where they find a different culture and more progressive attitudes. (Rev: BCCB 7–8/02; BL 6/1–15/02; HBG 10/02; SLJ 6/02; VOYA 6/02)

11225 Woodworth, Chris. *Georgie's Moon* (5–8). 2006, Farrar $16.00 (978-0-374-33306-5). 176pp. Seventh-grader Georgie Collins lives her life waiting for her father to return from Vietnam, and is unable to accept his death at first. (Rev: BL 3/1/06; SLJ 4/06)

11226 Yep, Laurence. *Hiroshima* (4–7). 1995, Scholastic paper $9.95 (978-0-590-20832-1). 64pp. A powerful work of fiction that explores the bombing of Hiroshima in 1945 and its aftermath. (Rev: BCCB 6/95; BL 3/15/95*; HB 9/95; SLJ 5/95)

11227 Ylvisaker, Anne. *Little Klein* (3–6). 2007, Candlewick $15.99 (978-0-7636-3359-2). 186pp. In the Midwest in the mid-20th century, 9-year-old Harold Klein is younger, smaller, and frailer than his rambunctious brothers but he's tough underneath and with his adopted dog he can be very effective. (Rev: BCCB 3/08; SLJ 1/08; VOYA 2/08)

11228 Zeinert, Karen. *To Touch the Stars: A Story of World War II* (5–8). Series: Jamestown's American Portraits. 2000, Jamestown paper $5.95 (978-0-8092-0630-8). 126pp. Eighteen-year-old Liz Erickson, who loves to fly airplanes, longs for independence while she investigates possible sabotage in the Women's Airforce Service pilots program. (Rev: SLJ 9/00)

Holidays and Holy Days

11229 Alcott, Louisa May. *An Old Fashioned Thanksgiving* (4–5). Illus. by Jody Wheeler. 1990, Applewood paper $5.95 (978-1-55709-135-2). 40pp. The happenings in a New Hampshire farm family in the 1820s, first published in 1881. (Rev: BL 10/1/89; SLJ 10/89)

11230 Axelrod, Amy. *Pigs Go to Market: Halloween Fun with Math and Shopping* (2–4). Illus. by Sharon McGinley-Nally. 1997, Simon & Schuster paper $14.00 (978-0-689-81069-5). At Halloween, the Pig family eats all the candy before the guests arrive. (Rev: HBG 3/98; SLJ 9/97)

11231 Bauer, Caroline Feller, ed. *Halloween: Stories and Poems* (3–6). Illus. by Peter Sís. 1989, HarperCollins LB $14.89 (978-0-397-32301-2). 96pp. An anthology with spooky happenings for reading on Halloween, although not directly related to the holiday. (Rev: BL 9/1/89; SLJ 10/89)

11232 Burton, Tim. *The Nightmare Before Christmas* (3–5). Illus. 1993, Hyperion $15.95 (978-1-56282-411-2). 40pp. Based on the movie of the same name, this book tells of Jack Skellington's diabolical decision to trade places with Santa. (Rev: BL 10/1/93)

11233 Caudill, Rebecca. *A Certain Small Shepherd* (3–6). Illus. by William Pene du Bois. 1997, Holt paper $6.95 (978-0-8050-5392-0). A mute boy gets an opportunity to play one of the shepherds in a Christmas pageant.

11234 Chaikin, Miriam. *Alexandra's Scroll: The Story of the First Hanukkah* (4–6). Illus. by Stephen Fieser. 2002, Holt $18.95 (978-0-8050-6384-4). 113pp. Alexandra and her family are caught up in the tumultuous events that lead to the first Hanukkah in this brightly illustrated historical novel. (Rev: BL 9/1/02; HB 9/02; HBG 3/03; SLJ 10/02)

11235 Chaikin, Miriam. *Angel Secrets: Stories Based on Jewish Legend* (4–6). Illus. by Leonid Gore. 2005, Holt $18.95 (978-0-8050-7150-4). 80pp. In this collection of six short stories based on Jewish folklore, angels do God's work on Earth as well as in Heaven. (Rev: BL 10/1/05; SLJ 9/05) [296.3]

11236 *A Christmas Treasury: Very Merry Stories and Poems* (2–5). Illus. by Kevin Hawkes. 2001, HarperCollins LB $16.89 (978-0-688-12040-5). 48pp. This combination of Christmas stories, carols, and poems is enhanced by Hawkes's detailed, full-color art. (Rev: BL 9/1/01; HBG 3/02; SLJ 10/01)

11237 Codell, Esmé Raji. *Hanukkah, Shmanukkah!* (3–5). Illus. by LeUyen Pham. 2005, Hyperion $16.99 (978-0-7868-5197-3). 48pp. Dickens's *A Christmas Carol* is retold as a Hanukkah tale full of humor and Yiddish phrases; a glossary is provided. (Rev: BL 9/1/05)

11238 Evans, Richard Paul. *The Christmas Candle* (3–6). Illus. by Jacob Collins. 2007, Simon & Schuster $9.99 (978-1-4169-5047-9). 32pp. A magical candle he buys on Christmas morning allows Thomas to see strangers in a new, charitable light. (Rev: BL 9/15/07)

11239 Fireside, Bryna J. *Private Joel and the Sewell Mountain Seder* (2–4). Illus. by Shawn Costello. 2008, Lerner $16.95 (978-0-8225-7240-4); paper $6.95 (978-0-8225-9050-7). 48pp. A group of Jewish soldiers cobble together a seder meal during the Civil War; based on a true story. (Rev: BL 4/1/08; LMC 8/08; SLJ 6/08)

11240 Funke, Cornelia. *When Santa Fell to Earth* (3–5). 2006, Scholastic $15.99 (978-0-439-78204-3). 176pp. With the help of his new friends Charlotte and Ben, a good Santa must try to save Christmas from the evil schemes of Gerold Geronimus Goblynch. (Rev: BL 11/15/06; SLJ 10/06)

11241 Gerstein, Mordicai. *The White Ram: A Story of Abraham and Isaac* (3–5). 2006, Holiday $16.95 (978-0-8234-1897-8). 32pp. This beautifully illustrated retelling of the Old Testament story of Abraham and Isaac focuses on the white ram that ultimately takes the place of Isaac on the sacrificial altar. (Rev: BL 10/1/06; SLJ 9/06*)

11242 Henry, O. *The Gift of the Magi* (5–8). Illus. by Carol Heyer. 1994, Ideals $14.95 (978-1-57102-003-1). 32pp. The classic story of unselfish love at Christmas gets some handsome illustrations. Another fine edition is illustrated by Kevin King (1988, Simon & Schuster). (Rev: BL 8/94)

11243 Jacobs, Laurie A. *A Box of Candles* (2–4). Illus. by Shelly Schonebaum Ephraim. 2005, Boyds Mills $17.95 (978-1-59078-169-2). 40pp. Given a silver candlestick and a year's worth of candles for her birthday, 7-year-old Ruthie faithfully observes Shabbat and other Jewish holidays as she struggles to adjust to changes in her family life. (Rev: BL 10/15/05; SLJ 9/05)

11244 Kimmel, Eric A. *The Spotted Pony: A Collection of Hanukkah Stories* (3–6). Illus. by Leonard Everett Fisher. 1992, Holiday House $15.95 (978-0-8234-0936-5). 70pp. A collection of wonderfully earthy and joyous Jewish folktales. (Rev: BL 11/15/92)

11245 Kline, Suzy. *Horrible Harry and the Holidaze* (2–3). Illus. by Frank Remkiewicz. 2003, Penguin $13.99 (978-0-670-03642-4). 64pp. Horrible Harry's 3rd-grade class learns about five winter holidays — Three Kings' Day, Korean New Year, Kwanzaa, Hanukkah, and Christmas — while Harry worries about his grandfather's move to a nursing home. (Rev: BL 9/1/03; HBG 4/04; SLJ 10/03)

11246 Koller, Jackie F. *The Promise* (3–6). Illus. 1999, Knopf LB $17.99 (978-0-679-98484-9). 80pp. When Matt goes out with his dog one Christmas to feed suet to the birds, they are chased by a bear. (Rev: BL 9/1/99)

11247 Krosoczka, Jarrett J. *Annie Was Warned* (PS–3). Illus. by author. 2003, Knopf LB $17.99 (978-0-375-91567-3). By turns suspenseful and amusing, this engaging story tells what happens when Annie, acting on a dare, disregards her parents' warnings and visits a creepy neighborhood mansion on Halloween night. (Rev: HBG 4/04; SLJ 9/03)

11248 Lewis, Beverly. *The Crazy Christmas Angel Mystery* (2–4). Series: Cul-de-Sac Kids. 1995, Bethany House paper $3.99 (978-1-55661-627-3). 62pp. Eric is convinced that his strange new neighbor is dancing with angels in this holiday mystery story. (Rev: BL 9/15/95)

11249 Low, Alice. *The Witch Who Was Afraid of Witches* (2–4). Illus. Series: I Can Read. 1999, HarperCollins LB $14.89 (978-0-06-028306-3). 48pp. In this easy chapter book, Wendy, a witch who doubts her own powers, gains confidence one Halloween night. (Rev: BL 9/1/99; HBG 3/00; SLJ 12/99)

11250 McDonald, Megan. *Judy Moody and Stink: The Holly Joliday* (2–4). Illus. by Peter H. Reynolds. 2007, Candlewick $14.99 (978-0-7636-3237-3). 96pp. Judy Moody uses toilet paper for her lengthy Christmas list but Stink's request is simple — snow. (Rev: BL 11/15/07; HB 11/07)

11251 Maguire, Gregory. *Five Alien Elves* (3–5). Illus. by Elaine Clayton. 1998, Clarion $15.00 (978-0-395-83894-5). 176pp. On Christmas Eve, five space aliens kidnap the town mayor, and two rival clubs — the Copycats and the Tattletales — join forces to rescue him. (Rev: HBG 3/99; SLJ 10/98)

11252 Marunas, Nathaniel. *Manga Claus: The Blade of Kringle* (5–8). Illus. by Erik Craddock. 2006, Penguin $12.99 (978-1-59514-134-7). 80pp. In this graphic novel Christmas tale, a disgruntled elf triggers a series of events that wrecks Santa's North Pole workshop and threatens to ruin Christmas for millions of children around the world. (Rev: BL 10/15/06; SLJ 10/06)

11253 Mass, Wendy. *11 Birthdays* (4–6). 2009, Scholastic $16.99 (978-0-545-05239-9). 272pp. Born on the same day and friends for their first nine years, Amanda and Leo fell out on their 10th birthday, but their 11th birthday brings a strange time loop, making them relive the day over and over. (Rev: BCCB 2/09; BL 12/15/08)

11254 Matthews, Caitlin. *While the Bear Sleeps: Winter Tales and Traditions* (4–6). Illus. 1999, Barefoot Books $19.95 (978-1-902283-81-4). 80pp. A satisfying anthology of tales about winter holidays and customs, including Hanukkah, Kwanzaa, Christmas, and Twelfth Night, tied together by a story involving a little girl and her guide, a bear. (Rev: BL 11/15/99; SLJ 10/99)

11255 O'Connell, Rebecca. *Penina Levine Is a Potato Pancake* (3–5). Illus. by Majella Lue Sue. 2008, Roaring Brook $16.95 (978-1-59643-213-0). 144pp. Penina is not looking forward to Hanukkah — her best friend will be in Aruba, her favorite teacher is moving away, and Penina will have to deal with her pesky younger sister Mimsy. (Rev: BLO 10/7/08; SLJ 12/08)

11256 Osborne, Mary Pope. *Christmas in Camelot* (2–5). Series: Magic Tree House. 2001, Random LB $13.99 (978-0-375-91373-0). 116pp. Stalwart Jack and Annie time-travel to Camelot and must solve riddles to break the spell of the evil Mordred and save the knights of the Round Table. (Rev: BL 12/15/01; HBG 3/02; SLJ 10/01)

11257 Papineau, Lucie. *Christmas Eve Magic* (2–5). Trans. from French by Brigitte Shapiro. Illus. by Stéphane Poulin. 2006, Kids Can $16.95 (978-1-55337-953-9). In this story inspired by Dickens's *A Christmas Carol*, animals take the leading roles, led by a greedy pig called Barton. (Rev: SLJ 10/06)

11258 Penn, Malka. *The Hanukkah Ghosts* (3–5). 1995, Holiday House $14.95 (978-0-8234-1145-0). 88pp. Susan — who is living with an elderly aunt on an English moor during Hanukkah — is visited by children who lived there during World War II. (Rev: BL 9/15/95)

11259 Pirotta, Saviour, retel. *Joy to the World: Christmas Stories from Around the World* (3–4). Illus. by Sheila Moxley. 1998, HarperCollins $15.95 (978-0-06-027902-8). 44pp. This book retells five Christmas stories, one each from Syria, Malta, Mexico, Ghana, and Russia. (Rev: HBG 10/99; SLJ 10/98) [398.2]

11260 Polacco, Patricia. *Christmas Tapestry* (3–6). Illus. 2002, Penguin $16.99 (978-0-399-23955-7). 160pp. In this heartwarming Christmas story, a boy and his father use a tapestry to cover a hole in a church wall, only to find that the fabric has special meaning to a Jewish couple. (Rev: BCCB 10/02; BL 9/1/02; HBG 3/03; SLJ 10/02)

11261 Pollock, Beth. *Harley's Gift* (3–5). Series: Streetlights. 2008, James Lorimer paper $7.95 (978-1-55028-992-3). 123pp. In Toronto, 11-year-old Harley anticipates Christmas and her father's once-a-year visit with some trepidation. (Rev: BL 5/15/08)

11262 Robinson, Barbara. *The Best Christmas Pageant Ever* (4–6). Illus. by Judith G. Brown. 1972, HarperCollins LB $16.89 (978-0-06-025044-7); paper $5.99 (978-0-06-440275-0). 96pp. When a family of unrestrained children takes over the church Christmas pageant, the results are hilarious.

11263 Ross, Richard. *Arctic Airlift* (1–3). Illus. 2005, Blue Fox $17.00 (978-0-9763119-0-4). 40pp. Santa's workshop is threatened by a flood, and young ham radio operator Robert picks up the distress call. (Rev: BL 10/15/05; SLJ 10/05)

11264 Russell, Ching Yeung. *Moon Festival* (3–5). Illus. by Christopher Zhong-Yuan. 1997, Boyds Mills $15.95 (978-1-56397-596-7). 32pp. Ying and her friends celebrate the summer Moon Festival in many ways, including making paper lanterns. (Rev: BL 9/15/97; HBG 3/98)

11265 Rylant, Cynthia. *Children of Christmas: Stories for the Season* (4–6). Illus. by S. D. Schindler. 1987, Orchard paper $6.95 (978-0-531-07042-0). 48pp. Six quiet stories about the emotions of Christmas. (Rev: BCCB 10/87; BL 9/1/87)

11266 Sawyer, Ruth. *The Wee Christmas Cabin of Carn-na-ween* (3–5). Illus. by Max Grafe. 2005, Candlewick $14.99 (978-0-7636-2553-5). 40pp. Life holds little hope for Oona, who was abandoned by tinkers as a baby and has spent her life caring for others, until she pays a Christmas visit to the Gentle People of Carn-na-ween. (Rev: BL 11/15/05; SLJ 10/05)

11267 *A Simply Wonderful Christmas: A Literary Advent Calendar* (3–6). Illus. by Silke Leffler. 2006, North-South $25.00 (978-0-7358-2100-2). 133pp. Arranged like an advent calendar, this collection of stories and poems contains a special literary treat for each night in December leading up to Christmas. (Rev: SLJ 10/06)

11268 Snow, Alan. *How Santa Really Works* (2–4). 2004, Simon & Schuster $15.95 (978-0-689-85817-8). 48pp. Is there a Santa? The answers in this picture book may be implausible but they will keep young readers highly entertained. (Rev: BL 11/15/04; SLJ 10/04)

11269 Spinelli, Eileen. *The Perfect Thanksgiving* (PS–2). Illus. by JoAnn Adinolfi. 2003, Holt $15.95 (978-0-8050-6531-2). Rhyming text and lively illustrations enhance this amusing comparison of the very different Thanksgiving experiences of two families. (Rev: HBG 4/04; SLJ 9/03)

11270 Steinhofel, Andreas. *An Elk Dropped In* (2–4). Illus. by Kerstin Meyer. 2006, Boyds Mills $16.95 (978-1-932425-80-2). 79pp. In a German village, an elk named Mr. Moose takes Santa's sleigh out for a practice run and ends up crashing into Billy Wagner's house, where they happily care for him until he recuperates. (Rev: BL 11/15/06; SLJ 10/06)

11271 Thompson, Lauren. *A Christmas Gift for Mama* (3–5). Illus. by Jim Burke. 2003, Scholastic $16.95 (978-0-590-30725-3). 48pp. Inspired by O. Henry's "The Gift of the Magi," this holiday tale tells how Grace trades a treasured belonging to buy a matching figurine for her mother's collection, only to find that her mother disposed of the figurine to buy Grace a gift. (Rev: BL 9/1/03; HBG 4/04; SLJ 10/03)

11272 Thury, Fredrick H. *The Last Straw* (2–3). Illus. 1999, Charlesbridge $15.95 (978-0-88106-152-9). 32pp. An ailing, aged camel is too proud to refuse to carry any of the gifts, regardless of their weight, to the child in Bethlehem. (Rev: BL 9/1/99; HBG 3/00; SLJ 10/99)

11273 Trondheim, Lewis. *Happy Halloween, Li'l Santa* (1–3). Illus. by Thierry Robin. 2003, NBM $14.95 (978-1-56163-361-6). 48pp. Li'l Santa is pitted against loggers who seem determined to cut down his forest of Christmas trees in this graphic novel. (Rev: BL 11/15/03; HBG 4/04)

11274 Van Leeuwen, Jean. *The Great Christmas Kidnapping Caper* (3–5). Illus. by Steven Kellogg. 1975, Dial $12.95 (978-0-685-01454-7). 144pp. A group of mice who live in a dollhouse at Macy's solve the mystery of the disappearance of Santa Claus.

11275 Wallace, Ian. *The Man Who Walked the Earth* (3–5). Illus. by author. 2003, Groundwood $16.95 (978-0-88899-545-2). On a prairie farm in the 1930s, a mother, daughter, and son wait for the return of their long-absent husband and father — and on Christmas Day a mysterious stranger arrives. (Rev: HBG 4/04; SLJ 10/03)

11276 Weatherford, Carole Boston. *Juneteenth Jamboree* (2–4). Illus. by Yvonne Buchanan. 1995, Lee & Low $15.95 (978-1-880000-18-2). Two youngsters, new to Texas, celebrate Juneteenth, which commemorates the day Texas slaves learned that the Emancipation Proclamation freed them. (Rev: SLJ 1/96)

11277 Wiggin, Kate Douglas. *The Birds' Christmas Carol* (3–5). Illus. by Jessie Gillespie. 1941, Houghton $9.95 (978-0-395-07205-9). A beautiful edition of a story first published in 1888. (Rev: HBG 3/98)

11278 Zalben, Jane Breskin. *The Magic Menorah: A Modern Chanukah Tale* (3–5). Illus. by Donna Diamond. 2001, Simon & Schuster $15.00 (978-0-689-82606-1). 56pp. Twelve-year-old Stanley dreads Hanukkah — lots of annoying relatives arrive and his grandfather always looks sad — but this year a strange man appears from a menorah Stanley finds in the attic and grants him three wishes. (Rev: HBG 3/02; SLJ 10/01)

Humorous Stories

11279 Agee, Jon. *Nothing* (K–3). Illus. by author. 2007, Hyperion $16.99 (978-0-7868-3694-9). 32pp. The customer is always right, so when a rich woman wants to buy "nothing" Otis the shopkeeper complies. (Rev: BL 9/1/07; SLJ 8/07)

11280 Ahlberg, Allan. *The Children Who Smelled a Rat* (2–4). Illus. by Katharine McEwen. 2005, Candlewick $15.99 (978-0-7636-2870-3). 80pp. In this action-packed tale about the Gaskitt family, twins Gus and Gloria try to figure out what caused their teacher's weird behavior, taxi driver Mom finds strange packages, and Dad chases after the baby's runaway shopping cart. (Rev: BCCB 11/05; BL 11/1/05; HBG 4/06; LMC 1/06; SLJ 10/05*)

11281 Amato, Mary. *Drooling and Dangerous: The Riot Brothers Return!* (3–5). Illus. by Ethan Long. Series: The Riot Brothers. 2006, Holiday $16.95 (978-0-8234-1986-9). 177pp. Wilbur and Orville Riot return for more zany adventures — as spies, as movie stars, and as school principals. (Rev: BL 5/15/06; HBG 10/06; SLJ 10/06)

11282 Amato, Mary. *Stinky and Successful: The Riot Brothers Never Stop* (2–5). Illus. by Ethan Long. 2007, Holiday House $16.95 (978-0-8234-2100-8). 150pp. Wilbur and Orville turn into helpful knights, tease their mother, and take up science in this imaginative, humorous, and fast-paced book. (Rev: SLJ 10/07)

11283 Anderson, M. T. *The Clue of the Linoleum Lederhosen: M. T. Anderson's Thrilling Tales* (4–7). Illus. by Kurt Cyrus. 2006, Harcourt $15.00 (978-0-15-205352-9). 256pp. Jasper Dash, Boy Technonaut, Katie, and Lily are caught up in an exciting mystery at Moose Tongue Lodge in this zany sequel to *Whales on Stilts* (2005). (Rev: BCCB 7–8/06; BL 5/1/06*; HB 5/06; HBG 10/06; SLJ 6/06; VOYA 6/06) ∩

11284 Applegate, Katherine. *Don't Swap Your Sweater for a Dog* (1–2). Illus. by Brian Biggs. Series: Roscoe Riley Rules. 2008, HarperCollins $14.99 (978-0-06-114886-6). 79pp. First-grader Roscoe figures a way to enter a pet contest even though he doesn't have a pet in this humorous early chapter book, the third in a series that also includes *Never Glue Your Friends to Chairs* (2008) and *Don't Tap-Dance on Your Teacher* (2009). (Rev: LMC 3/09; SLJ 9/08)

11285 Ardagh, Philip. *Dreadful Acts* (4–7). Illus. by David Roberts. Series: Eddie Dickens. 2003, Holt $14.95 (978-0-8050-7155-9). 144pp. This zany sequel to *A House Called Awful End* (2002) throws more wild adventures at 12-year-old Eddie Dickens. (Rev: BL 4/15/03; HBG 10/03; SLJ 5/03)

11286 Ardagh, Philip. *Terrible Times* (4–7). Illus. by David Roberts. 2003, Holt $12.95 (978-0-8050-7156-6). 160pp. Young Eddie Dickens sails for America and encounters all sorts of zany situations in this last installment in the trilogy set in Victorian England. (Rev: BL 2/1/04; SLJ 12/03)

11287 Asch, Frank. *Gravity Buster: Journal #2 of a Cardboard Genius* (3–5). Illus. by author. Series: Cardboard Genius. 2007, Kids Can $14.95 (978-1-55453-068-7); paper $5.95 (978-1-55453-069-4). 143pp. Alex describes the inventive contraptions that he and his little brother, Jonathan, build to aid in their imaginative play in this sequel to *Star Jumper*. (Rev: SLJ 5/07)

11288 Asch, Frank. *Star Jumper: Journal of a Cardboard Genius* (3–5). 2006, Kids Can $14.95 (978-1-55337-886-0); paper $5.95 (978-1-55337-887-7). 128pp. Intending to escape his little brother, Alex goes about building a spaceship and a duplicator, with some unintended consequences. (Rev: BL 7/06; HBG 10/06; LMC 1/07; SLJ 6/06)

11289 Atwater, Richard, and Florence Atwater. *Mr. Popper's Penguins* (4–6). Illus. by Robert Lawson. 1938, Little, Brown $16.95 (978-0-316-05842-1). 144pp. Mr. Popper has to get a penguin from the zoo to keep his homesick penguin company; soon there are 12.

11290 Auch, Mary Jane. *I Was a Third Grade Bodyguard* (1–3). Illus. by Herm Auch. 2003, Holiday House $15.95 (978-0-8234-1775-9). 73pp. When third grader Brian volunteers to look after the class chicken during Christmas vacation, the responsibility for watching the bird falls mainly on Arful, Brian's dog. (Rev: HBG 4/04; SLJ 12/03)

11291 Auch, Mary Jane. *I Was a Third Grade Science Project* (2–4). Illus. by Herm Auch. 1998, Holiday House $15.95 (978-0-8234-1357-7). 94pp. Brian tries to hypnotize his dog into believing he's a cat, but the spell works on one of Brian's classmates instead. (Rev: BL 3/15/98; HBG 10/98; SLJ 5/98)

11292 Babbitt, Natalie. *Jack Plank Tells Tales* (2–6). 2007, Scholastic $15.95 (978-0-545-00496-1). 128pp. Jack, an unsuccessful pirate, searches for a more suitable profession and describes his quest using entertaining, fantastic tales. By the author of *Tuck Everlasting*. (Rev: SLJ 5/07)

11293 Banscherus, J. *Detective's Duel* (3–6). Trans. from German by Daniel C. Baron. Illus. by Ralf Butschkow. Series: Klooz. 2007, Stone Arch LB $22.60 (978-1-59889-339-7). 65pp. Klooz's monopoly on detective work is threatened when another boy, King, begins solving mysteries the high-tech way. (Rev: LMC 10/07; SLJ 7/07)

11294 Banscherus, J. *The Great Snake Swindle. Bk. 1* (3–6). Trans. from German by Daniel C. Baron. Illus. by Ralf Butschkow. Series: Klooz. 2007, Stone Arch LB $22.60 (978-1-59889-340-3). 67pp. Sean is scamming his classmates by selling them "magic" balls, but Klooz uncovers his trickery and gets his friends their money back. (Rev: SLJ 7/07)

11295 Barrows, Anne. *Ivy + Bean Break the Fossil Record* (1–3). Illus. by Sophie Blackall. 2007, Chronicle $14.95 (978-0-8118-5683-6). 132pp. In this hilarious book, all the 2nd-graders are trying to set different new world records, and Ivy and Bean decide to dig in Bean's backyard in hopes of becoming the youngest people ever to find dinosaur bones. (Rev: BL 7/07; SLJ 7/07)

11296 Barry, Dave, and Ridley Pearson. *Science Fair: A Story of Mystery, Danger, International Suspense, and a Very Nervous Frog* (5–8). 2008, Hyperion $18.99 (978-1-4231-1324-9). 400pp. Inept secret agents from Krpshtskan plan to use American middle-school students to build secret weapons in their science fair projects. (Rev: BL 12/15/08; SLJ 3/09; VOYA 12/08) ⌒

11297 Basye, Dale E. *Heck: Where the Bad Kids Go* (3–6). 2008, Random $16.99 (978-0-375-84075-3). 304pp. When they die in a freak accident, outgoing 13-year-old Marlo and her timid younger brother Milton find themselves in Heck, a kind of reform school in limbo from which they long to escape; this humorous tale has its dark side but is full of word-play and classical allusions. (Rev: BL 6/1–15/08; SLJ 9/08)

11298 Bateman, Teresa. *The Ring of Truth* (3–6). Illus. by Omar Rayyan. 1997, Holiday House $16.95 (978-0-8234-1255-6). 32pp. In this picture book with an Irish flavor, a famous fibber, who is also a car salesman, is denied the right to lie. (Rev: BCCB 5/97; BL 7/97; SLJ 5/97)

11299 Beard, Darleen Bailey. *The Flimflam Man* (2–4). Illus. 1998, Farrar $15.00 (978-0-374-32346-2). 96pp. On a hot day in 1950, an advance man for a circus begins selling tickets for future performances, but some townspeople think that he is a fraud. (Rev: BCCB 5/98; BL 2/15/98; HB 3/98; HBG 10/98; SLJ 3/98)

11300 Benton, Jim. *Attack of the 50-Foot Cupid* (2–4). Illus. Series: Franny K. Stein, Mad Scientist. 2004, Simon & Schuster $14.95 (978-0-689-86292-2). 112pp. Franny's new lab assistant turns out to be a fairly inept mongrel who succeeds in unleashing a giant, arrow-shooting Cupid in this humorous beginning chapter book. Also use *The Invisible Fran* (2004). (Rev: BL 3/1/04; SLJ 5/04)

11301 Benton, Jim. *The Fran That Time Forgot* (2–4). Illus. by author. Series: Franny K. Stein, Mad Scientist. 2005, Simon & Schuster $14.95 (978-0-

689-86294-6). 102pp. Franny travels back in time in an attempt to change her middle name (Kissypie) in this half-funny, half-scary story. (Rev: SLJ 8/05)

11302 Benton, Jim. *Frantastic Voyage* (2–4). Illus. Series: Franny K. Stein, Mad Scientist. 2005, Simon & Schuster $14.95 (978-1-4169-0229-4). 112pp. When her canine assistant swallows a tiny doomsday device, girl scientist Franny shrinks herself so she can go and retrieve it; gross scenes will attract reluctant readers to this beginning chapter book with black-and-white cartoons. (Rev: BL 1/1–15/06; SLJ 4/06)

11303 Birdseye, Tom. *I'm Going to Be Famous* (4–6). 1986, Holiday House $16.95 (978-0-8234-0630-2). 144pp. Fifth-grader Arlo Moore is going to break the Guinness Book of World Records' time for eating bananas. (Rev: BCCB 1/87; BL 12/1/86)

11304 Birney, Betty. *Trouble According to Humphrey* (2–4). 2007, Putnam $14.99 (978-0-399-24505-3). 176pp. Humphrey the class hamster describes his concerns about Paul's grades, Mandy's family's financial problems, and other woes in this third, funny installment in the series. (Rev: BL 1/1–15/07; SLJ 2/07)

11305 Birney, Betty. *The World According to Humphrey* (2–5). 2004, Penguin $14.99 (978-0-399-24198-7). 144pp. Humphrey the hamster has a very varied and mostly enjoyable life as the class pet, but he worries about his future at the hands of Mrs. Brisbane. (Rev: BL 3/1/04; SLJ 4/04)

11306 Bliss, Corinne D. *Electra and the Charlotte Russe* (2–4). Illus. by Michael Garland. 1997, Boyds Mills $14.95 (978-1-56397-436-6). When she trips and upsets the cream on the pastries she is taking home, Electra tries to reshape them with her tongue. (Rev: HBG 3/98; SLJ 10/97)

11307 Blume, Judy. *Freckle Juice* (2–5). Illus. by Sonia O. Lisker. 1971, Macmillan $15.00 (978-0-02-711690-8); Dell paper $4.50 (978-0-440-42813-8). 40pp. A gullible second-grader pays 50 cents for a recipe to grow freckles.

11308 Blume, Judy. *Starring Sally J. Freedman as Herself* (4–7). 1977, Dell paper $5.99 (978-0-440-48253-6). 296pp. A story of a 5th-grader's adventures in New Jersey and Florida in the late 1940s.

11309 Bond, Michael. *Paddington Takes the Test* (3–5). Illus. 2002, Houghton $15.00 (978-0-618-18384-5). 144pp. This new edition of a 1980 release about the ever-popular bear sports a new jacket illustration and a larger typeface. (Rev: BL 3/15/02; HBG 10/02)

11310 Boniface, William. *The Return of Meteor Boy?* (4–6). Illus. by Stephen Gilpin. Series: The Extraordinary Adventures of Ordinary Boy. 2007, HarperCollins $16.99 (978-0-06-077467-7). 344pp. Ordinary Boy, the only person in Superopolis without superpowers, suspects that the Amazing Indestructo may have had something to do with Meteor Boy's disappearance in this second book in the series. (Rev: SLJ 8/07)

11311 Bragg, Georgia. *Matisse on the Loose* (4–6). 2009, Delacorte $16.99 (978-0-385-73570-4). 160pp. A boy who makes copies of famous masterpieces replaces one of the masterworks in a museum with one of his own. (Rev: BL 6/1–15/09; SLJ 7/09)

11312 Brockmeier, Kevin. *Grooves: A Kind of Mystery* (4–7). 2006, HarperCollins LB $17.89 (978-0-06-073692-7). 208pp. In this funny mystery with science fiction overtones, unprepossessing 7th-grader Dwayne Ruggles finds out that the sounds coming from his blue jeans are really cries for help from imprisoned factory workers. (Rev: BL 2/1/06; SLJ 3/06)

11313 Brooke, William J. *A Is for AARRGH!* (5–8). 1999, HarperCollins LB $14.89 (978-0-06-023394-5). 160pp. A humorous story about a prehistoric boy, Mog, and his amazing discoveries about language and communication. (Rev: BCCB 11/99; BL 10/15/99; HB 9/99; HBG 3/00; SLJ 9/99)

11314 Bunting, Eve. *Nasty, Stinky Sneakers* (4–6). Illus. 1994, HarperCollins LB $15.89 (978-0-06-024237-4). 128pp. Colin thinks his sneakers are so smelly that they will win a prize, and then they suddenly disappear. (Rev: BL 5/1/94; SLJ 6/94)

11315 Butterworth, Oliver. *The Enormous Egg* (3–6). Illus. by Louis Darling. 1995, Houghton $9.00 (978-0-395-73249-6). The story of a boy whose hen lays a large egg, which hatches a triceratops!

11316 Byars, Betsy. *Bingo Brown's Guide to Romance* (5–8). 2000, Puffin paper $5.99 (978-0-14-036080-6). Romance, confusion, and comedy occur when Bingo Brown meets his true love in the produce section of the grocery store. (Rev: BL 4/1/92; SLJ 4/92)

11317 Byars, Betsy. *The Cybil War* (4–6). Illus. by Gail Owens. 1981, Puffin paper $5.99 (978-0-14-034356-4). 144pp. A humorous story about the relationship between two boys and a girl, Cybil.

11318 Byars, Betsy. *Me Tarzan* (3–5). 2000, HarperCollins LB $15.89 (978-0-06-028707-8). 96pp. Dorothy's Tarzan yell is so effective that she wins the part of Tarzan in the school play, and also finds that animals respond to her call. (Rev: BCCB 6/00; BL 3/15/00; HB 5/00; HBG 10/00; SLJ 7/00)

11319 Byars, Betsy. *The Seven Treasure Hunts* (3–5). Illus. by Jennifer Barrett. 1992, HarperCollins paper $4.99 (978-0-06-440435-8). 80pp. Readers giggle and guess their way through the story of Jackson and friend Goat who are into treasure hunts. (Rev: BCCB 4/91; BL 3/15/91; HB 7/91; SLJ 6/91)

11320 Cabot, Meg. *Princess in Waiting* (5–7). Series: Princess Diaries. 2003, HarperCollins $16.99 (978-0-06-009607-6). 240pp. Princess Mia gets in a royal mess when her duties interfere with her love life. (Rev: BL 5/15/03; HBG 10/03; SLJ 5/03; VOYA 6/03)

11321 Callen, Larry. *Who Kidnapped the Sheriff? Tales from Tickfaw* (4–6). Illus. by Stephen Gammell. 1985, Little, Brown $14.95 (978-0-316-12499-7). 176pp. The small town of Tickfaw has lots of characters, who are introduced in these related short stories. (Rev: BL 6/1/85; HB 5/85; SLJ 8/85)

11322 Calmenson, Stephanie, and Joanna Cole. *Gator Halloween* (2–4). Illus. 1999, Morrow LB $14.89 (978-0-688-14785-3). 64pp. Amy and Allie's plan to win the best Halloween costume prize gets sidetracked when they try to find a lost pet. (Rev: BL 9/1/99; HBG 3/00; SLJ 9/99)

11323 Calmenson, Stephanie, and Joanna Cole. *Get Well, Gators!* (2–4). Illus. Series: Gator Girls. 1998, Morrow LB $15.89 (978-0-688-14787-7). 64pp. When Allie, who was to sing a duet with Amy at the Swamp Town fair, comes down with swamp flu, Amy is afraid to sing solo in this simple, humorous story. (Rev: BL 11/15/98; HBG 3/99; SLJ 10/98)

11324 Child, Lauren. *Clarice Bean, Don't Look Now* (2–5). 2007, Candlewick $15.99 (978-0-7636-3536-7). 252pp. Clarice Bean's problems justify her constant worrying: the ceiling falls, her best friend is moving, and a new student arrives arrives from Sweden. (Rev: SLJ 10/07)

11325 Child, Lauren. *Clarice Bean Spells Trouble* (3–5). 2005, Candlewick $15.99 (978-0-7636-2813-0). 192pp. Vowing to be more like Ruby Redfort, a character in books and a TV series, Clarice Bean tries to prepare for an upcoming spelling bee while also vying for a leading part in a school production of *The Sound of Music*. (Rev: BL 9/1/05; SLJ 8/05)

11326 Cibos, Lindsay, and Jared Hodges. *Peach Fuzz, Vol. 1* (3–5). Illus. by authors. 2005, TokyoPop paper $9.99 (978-1-59532-599-0). The story of a girl and her pet ferret, told from both pet's and owner's point of view. (Rev: SLJ 7/05)

11327 Cleary, Beverly. *Ellen Tebbits* (3–5). Illus. by Louis Darling. 1951, Morrow $15.89 (978-0-688-31264-0); Avon paper $5.99 (978-0-380-70913-7). 160pp. Eight-year-old Ellen has braces on her teeth, takes ballet lessons, and, worst of all, wears long woolen underwear.

11328 Cleary, Beverly. *Emily's Runaway Imagination* (3–6). Illus. by Beth Krush and Joe Krush. 1961, Avon paper $5.99 (978-0-380-70923-6). 224pp. Emily's imagination helps get a library for Pitchfork, Oregon, in the 1920s.

11329 Cleary, Beverly. *Henry Huggins* (3–5). Illus. by Louis Darling. 1950, Avon paper $5.99 (978-0-380-70912-0). 160pp. Henry is a small boy with a knack for creating hilarious situations. Others in the series: *Henry and Beezus* (1952); *Henry and Ribsy* (1954); *Henry and the Paper Route* (1957); *Henry and the Clubhouse* (1962). (Rev: HBG 10/01)

11330 Cleary, Beverly. *Otis Spofford* (3–6). Illus. by Louis Darling. 1953, Avon paper $5.99 (978-0-380-70919-9). 192pp. This story of Otis stirring up a little excitement at school is full of humor.

11331 Clifford, Eth. *Harvey's Horrible Snake Disaster* (3–5). 1984, Houghton $15.00 (978-0-395-35378-3). 128pp. Harvey tries to disguise the fact that he is petrified of snakes.

11332 Collins, Ross. *Medusa Jones* (4–7). Illus. by author. 2008, Scholastic $16.99 (978-0-439-90100-0). 135pp. Yes, Medusa does have snakes for hair, and her friend Mino is half bull; they are part of the outcast group at school, where Theseus and his friends push them around. A trip to Mount Olympus changes all that, since the students must pull together. (Rev: BL 12/1/07; LMC 3/08; SLJ 1/08)

11333 Cooney, Doug. *The Beloved Dearly* (4–6). Illus. by Tony DiTerlizzi. 2002, Simon & Schuster LB $16.00 (978-0-689-83127-0). 192pp. A 12-year-old goes into the pet funeral business in this humorous and inventive novel aimed at a middle-grade audience. (Rev: BCCB 5/02; BL 1/1–15/02; HBG 10/02; SLJ 1/02)

11334 Cowell, Cressida. *How to Cheat a Dragon's Curse: The Heroic Misadventures of Hiccup the Viking* (3–5). Illus. by author. Series: Hiccup. 2007, Little, Brown $10.99 (978-0-316-11425-7). 244pp. Another zany Hiccup adventure finds our hero on a quest to find the Vegetable That No One Dares Name, a task that involves evading Norbert the Nutjob and training a dragon. Entertaining illustrations add to the fun. (Rev: SLJ 5/07)

11335 Cox, Judy. *Third Grade Pet* (2–3). Illus. 1998, Holiday House $15.95 (978-0-8234-1379-9). 93pp. In this easy chapter book, Rosemary takes her class's pet rat home to save him from the class bully and has problems keeping him hidden and safe. (Rev: BCCB 2/99; BL 12/15/98; HBG 3/99; SLJ 2/99)

11336 Cox, Judy. *Weird Stories from the Lonesome Cafe* (2–5). Illus. 2000, Harcourt $15.00 (978-0-15-202134-4). 80pp. An easy chapter book in which Sam and his uncle open a roadside cafe to which celebrities come incognito. (Rev: BCCB 4/00; BL 4/15/00; HBG 10/00; SLJ 6/00)

11337 Danziger, Paula. *Amber Brown Goes Fourth* (2–4). Illus. 1995, Penguin $16.99 (978-0-399-22849-0). 112pp. Amber Brown, a fourth-grader unsure of herself, doesn't know how to react to her divorced mother's new boyfriend. (Rev: BCCB 11/95; BL 10/15/95; HB 11/95; SLJ 10/95*)

11338 Danziger, Paula. *Amber Brown Is Feeling Blue* (3–5). Illus. 1998, Penguin $16.99 (978-0-399-23179-7). 32pp. Amber's humorous adventures continue when her divorced mother takes a new boyfriend, her father returns from Paris, and a new girl in her class also has a color-name, Kelly Green. (Rev: BL 12/1/98; SLJ 11/98)

11339 Danziger, Paula. *Amber Brown Is Not a Crayon* (2–4). Illus. by Tony Ross. 1994, Penguin $16.99 (978-0-399-22509-3). 80pp. Amber Brown's close friendship with Justin Daniels will end soon because Justin's family is moving. (Rev: BCCB 6/94; BL 4/15/94; HB 7/94; SLJ 5/94*)

11340 Danziger, Paula. *Amber Brown Sees Red* (2–4). Illus. 1997, Penguin $15.99 (978-0-399-22901-5). 120pp. Amber Brown is now in the fourth grade and is increasingly upset with her parents' custody battles involving her. (Rev: BL 5/15/97; SLJ 7/97)

11341 Danziger, Paula. *I, Amber Brown* (3–6). Illus. by Tony Ross. 1999, Penguin $14.99 (978-0-399-23180-3). 140pp. Amber Brown, daughter of divorced parents, gets her ears pierced when she is with her father, in spite of her mother's objections. (Rev: BL 10/15/99; HBG 3/00; SLJ 11/99)

11342 Danziger, Paula. *You Can't Eat Your Chicken Pox, Amber Brown* (2–4). Illus. by Tony Ross. 1995, Penguin $15.99 (978-0-399-22702-8). 112pp.

Amber visits London with her aunt while her parents are getting a divorce. A sequel to *Amber Brown Is Not a Crayon* (1994). (Rev: BCCB 4/95; BL 3/15/95; SLJ 6/95*)

11343 Derby, Kenneth. *The Top 10 Ways to Ruin the First Day of 5th Grade* (4–6). 2004, Holiday House $16.95 (978-0-8234-1851-0). 164pp. Fifth-grader Tony Madison, a big fan of David Letterman's late-night TV show, indulges in increasingly outrageous stunts in an effort to appear on the show. (Rev: BL 2/1/05; SLJ 1/05)

11344 du Bois, William Pene. *Twenty-One Balloons* (4–6). Illus. by author. 1947, Puffin paper $6.99 (978-0-14-032097-8). 184pp. Truth and fiction are combined in the adventures of a professor who sails around the world in a balloon. Newbery Medal winner, 1948.

11345 Durand, Hallie. *Dessert First* (2–4). Illus. by Christine Davenier. 2009, Atheneum $14.99 (978-1-4169-6385-1). 160pp. Eight-year-old Dessert, whose teacher urges students to march to their own drummers, tries to persuade her parents to start dinner with dessert. (Rev: BCCB 9/09; BLO 5/28/09; LMC 8/09; SLJ 7/09)

11346 Elliott, David. *Evangeline Mudd and the Great Mink Escapade* (3–5). 2006, Candlewick $15.99 (978-0-7636-2295-4). 192pp. Evangeline Mudd, enthusiastic warrior for animal rights, sets out to free a number of minks before they are turned into ballet costumes. (Rev: BL 2/15/06; SLJ 3/06)

11347 Evans, Douglas. *Math Rashes and Other Classroom Tales* (2–4). Illus. 2000, Front St. $15.95 (978-1-886910-66-9). 112pp. Wacky third-grade experiences are the subject of this collection of original short stories. (Rev: BL 12/15/00; HBG 3/01; SLJ 11/00)

11348 Feiffer, Jules. *The Man in the Ceiling* (5–7). Illus. 1993, HarperCollins paper $9.99 (978-0-06-205907-9). 192pp. Jimmy turns to cartooning in an effort to gain some recognition in a family that is intent on ignoring him. (Rev: BCCB 12/93; BL 11/15/93; SLJ 2/94*)

11349 Ferguson, Alane. *The Practical Joke War* (3–6). 1993, Avon paper $3.50 (978-0-380-71721-7). 160pp. All-out war is declared when the Dillon children — lovers of practical jokes — are left to themselves one summer. (Rev: BCCB 7–8/91; BL 4/1/91; SLJ 6/91)

11350 Fine, Anne. *The Return of the Killer Cat* (3–5). Illus. by Steve Cox. 2007, Farrar $16.00 (978-0-374-36248-5). 74pp. In this sequel to *The Diary of a Killer Cat* (2006), Tuffy plans to do as he pleases while his family vacations, but his hopes are dashed when he learns that the vicar is coming to cat-sit him. (Rev: BL 3/15/07; SLJ 2/07)

11351 Fleischman, Paul. *The Dunderheads* (3–5). Illus. by David Roberts. 2009, Candlewick $16.99 (978-0-7636-2498-9). 56pp. Miss Breakbone keeps an electric chair in the classroom and the students plan to overthrow the throne. (Rev: BCCB 7–8/09; BL 6/1–15/09; HB 7/09; SLJ 6/09)

11352 Fleischman, Sid. *Chancy and the Grand Rascal* (5–7). Illus. by Eric Von Schmidt. 1966, Little,

Brown $14.95 (978-0-316-28575-9); paper $4.95 (978-0-316-26012-1). 190pp. The boy and his uncle, the grand rascal, combine hard work and quick wits to outsmart a scoundrel, hoodwink a miser, and capture a band of outlaws.

11353 Fleischman, Sid. *The Ghost on Saturday Night* (3–5). Illus. by Eric Von Schmidt. 1974, Little, Brown $14.95 (978-0-316-28583-4). 64pp. Ten-year-old Opie's efforts to raise money for a saddle involve him in a ghost-raising session and the recovery of money stolen from a bank.

11354 Fleischman, Sid. *McBroom Tells the Truth* (3–5). Illus. by Walter Lorraine. 1981, Little, Brown $12.45 (978-0-316-28550-6). 48pp. A tall tale about a New England farmer named McBroom. Also use: *McBroom and the Great Race* (1980). (Rev: SLJ 1/05)

11355 Fleischman, Sid. *Mr. Mysterious and Company* (3–5). Illus. by Eric Von Schmidt. 1997, Greenwillow $15.00 (978-0-688-14921-5). A traveling magic show during the 1880s makes for an entertaining family story that is also an excellent historical novel.

11356 Foley, June. *Susanna Siegelbaum Gives Up Guys* (5–8). 1992, Scholastic paper $3.25 (978-0-590-43700-4). 160pp. Susanna, a flirt, makes a bet that she can give up guys for three months. (Rev: SLJ 8/91)

11357 Fowler, Susi G. *Albertina, the Animals, and Me* (3–5). Illus. 2000, Greenwillow LB $14.89 (978-0-06-029160-0). 96pp. A humorous story of two friends, Molly and Albertina, who try various schemes to get their parents to allow them to have pets. (Rev: BL 12/15/00; HBG 3/01; SLJ 12/00)

11358 Freeman, Martha. *The Polyester Grandpa* (4–5). 1998, Holiday House $15.95 (978-0-8234-1398-0). 145pp. Grandma turns up with a new husband — brash, uncouth Jimmy Barkenfalt — and 10-year-old Morgan Knight's family has a fit. (Rev: BCCB 1/99; BL 12/1/98; HBG 3/99; SLJ 12/98)

11359 Gannett, Ruth. *My Father's Dragon* (4–6). Illus. by author. 1986, Knopf paper $4.99 (978-0-394-89048-7). 88pp. Hilarious adventures of Elmer Elevator. Also use: *The Dragons of Blueland* (1963); *Elmer and the Dragon* (1987).

11360 Gardiner, John Reynolds. *Top Secret* (4–6). Illus. by Marc Simont. 1995, Little, Brown paper $4.95 (978-0-316-30363-7). 129pp. Allen is convinced he can solve the world's hunger problem, and when no one believes him he goes to the president of the United States. (Rev: BCCB 11/85; BL 1/15/86; SLJ 11/85)

11361 Gauthier, Gail. *A Girl, a Boy, and a Monster Cat* (3–4). Illus. by Joe Cepeda. 2007, Putnam $14.99 (978-0-399-24689-0). 83pp. Despite their differences, Brandon and Hannah enjoy playing together after school, spying on Hannah's cat, and avoiding the crazy chihuahua next door. (Rev: BCCB 10/07; HB 7/07; SLJ 8/07)

11362 Geras, Adele. *The Fabulous Fantoras: Book One: Family Files* (4–6). 1998, Avon $14.00 (978-0-380-97547-1). 144pp. The antics of an eccentric English family, in which each member has a special

zany talent, are recorded by the family cat, Ozymandias, or Ozzy for short. (Rev: BL 11/1/98; HBG 3/99; SLJ 1/99)

11363 Getz, David. *Almost Famous* (3–5). Illus. 1994, Holt paper $5.95 (978-0-8050-3464-6). 182pp. Overbearing Maxine knows she's destined to be an inventor, but for now, she has to team up with Toni the troublemaker for an invention contest partner. (Rev: BL 12/15/92*; SLJ 2/93)

11364 Gifford, Peggy. *Moxy Maxwell Does Not Love Writing Thank-you Notes* (2–4). Illus. by Valorie Fisher. 2008, Random $12.99 (978-0-375-84270-2). 176pp. Ten-year-old Moxy knows she has to write these 12 thank-you notes but will she ever actually get around to it? (Rev: BL 9/1/08; HB 9/08; SLJ 8/08)

11365 Gleitzman, Morris. *Toad Away* (4–6). 2006, Random $14.95 (978-0-375-82766-2). 208pp. Limpy, the Australian cane toad, journeys to the Amazon in his quest to find a way to peacefully coexist with humans. (Rev: BL 2/15/06; SLJ 4/06)

11366 Gleitzman, Morris. *Toad Rage* (3–6). 2004, Random $14.95 (978-0-375-82762-4). 176pp. A plucky Australian cane toad sets out to stop the carnage of his fellow amphibians on the roads. (Rev: BL 3/1/04; SLJ 4/04)

11367 Gondosch, Linda. *The Monsters of Marble Avenue* (2–4). Illus. by Cat B. Smith. 1988, Little, Brown $10.95 (978-0-316-31991-1). 64pp. Luke learns the meaning of "the show must go on" when the puppets for his upcoming show are given away by mistake. (Rev: BL 4/1/87; SLJ 8/88)

11368 Gorman, Carol. *Lizard Flanagan, Supermodel?? *(4–7). 1998, HarperCollins $14.95 (978-0-06-024868-0). 160pp. Sixth-grader Lizard Flanagan will do anything to make enough money to go by bus from her home in Iowa to a game in Wrigley Field, but is entering a local fashion show for teens going too far? (Rev: BL 11/15/98; HBG 3/99; SLJ 10/98)

11369 Gormley, Beatrice. *The Magic Mean Machine* (4–6). Illus. by Emily Arnold McCully. 1989, Avon paper $2.95 (978-0-380-75519-6). 128pp. Marvin invents a special machine to ensure that friend Alison will beat bully Spencer at chess. (Rev: BL 7/89)

11370 Goscinny, René. *Nicholas,* (4–6). Trans. from French by Anthea Bell. Illus. by Jean-Jacques Sempé. 2005, Phaidon $19.95 (978-0-7148-4529-6). 128pp. Nicholas, a mischievous schoolboy, and his friends get into one scrape after another in this collection of tales by the author of the *Asterix* comics. (Rev: SLJ 10/05)

11371 Goscinny, René. *Nicholas on Vacation* (2–5). Trans. from French by Anthea Bell. Illus. by Jean-Jacques Sempé. 2006, Phaidon $19.95 (978-0-7148-4678-1). 126pp. Follow Nicholas on his summer vacation as he travels to the beach with his parents and goes to a camp to stay overnight for the first time. *Nicholas and the Gang* (2007) is the fourth book about the boy who attracts trouble wherever he goes. (Rev: SLJ 3/07)

11372 Greenburg, Dan. *Tell a Lie and Your Butt Will Grow* (2–4). Illus. by Jack E. Davis. Series: Zack

Files. 2002, Grosset paper $4.99 (978-0-448-42682-2). 58pp. Andrew, Zack's less-than-truthful partner on a science fair project, discovers to his dismay that his backside is getting bigger with every fib he tells. (Rev: SLJ 4/03)

11373 Hagerup, Klaus. *Markus and Diana* (4–6). Trans. from Norwegian by Tara Chace. 2006, Front St. $17.95 (978-1-932425-59-8). 188pp. Markus, a Norwegian sixth grader, strikes up a correspondence with a beautiful soap-opera actress by pretending to be a mountain-climbing millionaire, but things threaten to get out of control when she insists on meeting him in person. (Rev: SLJ 12/06)

11374 Hamilton, Richard. *Cal and the Amazing Anti-Gravity Machine* (3–5). 2006, Bloomsbury paper $5.95 (978-1-58234-714-1). 128pp. In this funny chapter book for new readers, 10-year-old Cal — accompanied by his talking dog Frankie — investigates his neighbor's newly developed antigravity machine with unsettling results. (Rev: BL 4/15/06; SLJ 7/06)

11375 Hannan, Peter. *Goofballs in Paradise. Bk. #2* (2–4). Illus. by author. Series: Super Goofballs. 2007, HarperCollins $15.99 (978-0-06-085214-6); paper $4.99 (978-0-06-085213-9). 162pp. The Goofballs defend everyone's right to be goofy by defeating Mondo Grumpo while at a tropical resort. (Rev: SLJ 6/07)

11376 Hannan, Peter. *That Stinking Feeling. Bk. #1* (2–4). Illus. by author. Series: Super Goofballs. 2007, HarperCollins $15.99 (978-0-06-085212-2); paper $4.99 (978-0-06-085211-5). 145pp. Amazing Techno Dude and his grandmother, Bodacious Backwoods Woman, round up a group of goofball superhero friends to fight the evil Queen Smellina and Fabian the Flatulent Fiend. (Rev: SLJ 6/07)

11377 Harper, Charise Mericle. *Just Grace* (2–4). Illus. 2007, Houghton $15.00 (978-0-618-64642-5). 144pp. Just Grace (misnamed by her teacher to set her apart from the other three Graces in her class) deals successfully with the usual third-grade problems in this funny chapter book, but her well-intentioned efforts to find a neighbor's cat go awry. (Rev: BL 3/1/07*)

11378 Hayes, Daniel. *Eye of the Beholder* (5–8). 1992, Fawcett paper $6.99 (978-0-449-00235-3). Tyler and Lymie are in trouble again when they fake some works of a famous sculptor. (Rev: BL 2/1/93; SLJ 12/92)

11379 Heide, Florence Parry. *The Shrinking of Treehorn* (2–5). Illus. by Edward Gorey. 1971, Holiday House LB $16.95 (978-0-8234-0189-5); paper $6.95 (978-0-8234-0975-4). 64pp. Treehorn has a special talent — he can become smaller by the moment — but nobody notices. A sequel is: *The Adventures of Treehorn* (1983).

11380 Hermes, Patricia. *Kevin Corbett Eats Flies* (4–6). Illus. 1986, Harcourt $13.95 (978-0-15-242290-5). 160pp. Kevin and his father move around whenever the mood strikes; now Kevin doesn't want to move anymore and thinks that if his father fell in love, he wouldn't want to either. (Rev: BCCB 9/86; BL 8/86; SLJ 5/86)

11381 Hite, Sid. *Those Darn Dithers* (5–8). 1996, Holt $15.95 (978-0-8050-3838-5). A humorous novel about the dithering Dithers with adventures involving Porcellina the dancing pig and an eccentric who drifts out to sea on a rubber raft. (Rev: BL 12/15/96; SLJ 12/96; VOYA 10/97)

11382 Horvath, Polly. *The Trolls* (3–6). Illus. by Wendy A. Halperin. 1999, Farrar $16.00 (978-0-364-37787-1). 144pp. Aunt Sally spins some fanciful tales when she entertains two nieces and a nephew left in her care. (Rev: BL 3/1/99*; SLJ 4/99)

11383 Horvath, Polly. *When the Circus Came to Town* (5–8). 1996, FSG paper $5.95 (978-0-374-48367-8). 144pp. Opinion is sharply divided in Ivy's town when a circus troupe decides to relocate there. (Rev: BCCB 12/96; BL 11/15/96; SLJ 12/96*)

11384 Howe, Deborah, and James Howe. *Bunnicula: A Rabbit Tale of Mystery* (4–6). Illus. by Alan Daniel. 1979, Macmillan LB $16.00 (978-0-689-30700-3); Avon paper $3.99 (978-0-380-51094-8). 112pp. A dog named Harold tells the story of a rabbit many believe to be a vampire. Two sequels by James Howe are: *Howliday Inn* (1982); *The Celery Stalks at Midnight* (1983).

11385 Howe, James. *Bunnicula Meets Edgar Allan Crow* (4–7). Illus. by Eric Fortune. 2006, Simon & Schuster $15.95 (978-1-4169-1458-7). 138pp. When world-famous author M. T. Graves and his pet, Edgar Allan Crow, come to stay with the Monroe family, Bunnicula the vampire bunny suspects that the household guests are up to no good. (Rev: BL 1/1–15/07; SLJ 2/07)

11386 Howe, James. *Bunnicula Strikes Again!* (3–6). 1999, Simon & Schuster $15.00 (978-0-689-81463-1). 128pp. In this sequel to *Bunnicula*, the fanged rabbit, who needs a diet of carrot juice, is again pursued by Chester, who is afraid other vegetables might be endangered. (Rev: BL 10/1/99; HBG 3/00; SLJ 12/99)

11387 Howe, James. *Howie Monroe and the Doghouse of Doom* (3–5). Illus. by Brett Helquist. 2002, Simon & Schuster $9.95 (978-0-689-83951-1). 96pp. Puppy Howie is self-congratulatory about his literary creation, a funny parody of Harry Potter. (Rev: BL 10/1/02; HBG 3/03)

11388 Howe, James. *The New Nick Kramer or My Life as a Baby-Sitter* (5–9). 1995, Hyperion LB $14.49 (978-0-7868-2053-5). Nick and rival Mitch make an unusual bet on who will win the affections of newcomer Jennifer. (Rev: BL 12/15/95; SLJ 1/96)

11389 Howe, James. *Nighty-Nightmare* (3–6). Illus. by Leslie Morrill. 1987, Macmillan $15.00 (978-0-689-31207-6); Avon paper $3.99 (978-0-380-70490-3). 128pp. Harold the canine and friends set out on a camping trip. (Rev: BCCB 4/87; BL 3/1/87; SLJ 4/87)

11390 Ives, David. *Monsieur Eek* (4–7). 2001, HarperCollins LB $15.89 (978-0-06-029530-1). 192pp. Thirteen-year-old Emmaline defends a monkey against criminal charges in the not-quite-right town of MacOongafoondsen, population 21. (Rev: BL 6/1–15/01; HBG 3/02; SLJ 6/01)

11391 Jennings, Richard W. *Ferret Island* (5–7). 2007, Houghton $16.00 (978-0-618-80632-4). 240pp. Will and a huge, friendly ferret named Jim are on the run from a ferret gang that has been trained to attack McDonald's restaurants. (Rev: BCCB 5/07; BL 7/07; HB 5/07; SLJ 5/07)

11392 Jennings, Richard W. *My Life of Crime* (4–8). 2002, Houghton $15.00 (978-0-618-21433-4). 160pp. Nothing goes right when 6th-grader Fowler decides to "rescue" a caged parrot. (Rev: BL 1/1–15/03; HBG 3/03; VOYA 2/03)

11393 Keehn, Sally M. *Magpie Gabbard and the Quest for the Buried Moon* (5–8). 2007, Philomel $16.99 (978-0-399-24340-0). 206pp. Thirteen-year-old Magpie Gabbard must fulfill a prophecy and put aside her cussedness in order to save the moon in this exuberant and complex tall tale. (Rev: BL 4/15/07; SLJ 2/07)

11394 Kerrin, Jessica Scott. *Martin Bridge Sound the Alarm!* (2–4). Illus. by Joseph Kelly. Series: Martin Bridge. 2007, Kids Can $14.95 (978-1-55337-976-8); paper $4.95 (978-1-55337-977-5). 110pp. What kid wouldn't like to be locked in a toy store? When this really happens to Martin and his friend, Martin comes up with an ingenious plan to call for help. (Rev: SLJ 5/07)

11395 Kidd, Ronald. *Sammy Carducci's Guide to Women* (5–7). 1995, Dramatic Publg. $6.25 (978-0-87129-522-4). 112pp. A somewhat sexist 6th grader discovers that, where women are concerned, perhaps he is not as irresistible as he thinks he is. (Rev: BCCB 1/92; BL 1/1/92; SLJ 1/92)

11396 Kinney, Jeff. *Diary of a Wimpy Kid: The Last Straw* (5–8). Illus. by author. 2009, Abrams $12.95 (978-0-8109-7068-7). 224pp. Middle-school not-jock Greg Heffley keeps a diary in which he details his angst about his troublesome brothers, his demanding father, and other aspects of life. (Rev: BL 2/1/09; SLJ 4/09) ∩

11397 Kinney, Jeff. *Rodrick Rules* (5–8). Illus. by author. 2008, Abrams $12.95 (978-0-8109-9473-7). 224pp. Twelve-year-old Greg Heffley of *Diary of a Wimpy Kid* (2007) will make readers laugh again with this diary that recounts his struggles at home and at school, particularly those involving his annoying older brother Rodrick. (Rev: BL 2/1/08; SLJ 3/08)

11398 Kline, Suzy. *Orp Goes to the Hoop* (5–7). 1993, Avon paper $3.50 (978-0-380-71829-0). 109pp. Seventh-grader Orp gets a chance to play a big part in the basketball team's big game. (Rev: BCCB 7–8/91; BL 7/91; SLJ 7/91)

11399 Klise, Kate. *Regarding the Bathrooms: A Privy to the Past* (4–6). Illus. by M. Sarah Klise. Series: Regarding the . . . 2006, Harcourt $15.00 (978-0-15-205164-8). 160pp. The principal of Geyser Creek Middle School grows increasingly frustrated as unexpected events delay progress on the school's bathroom remodeling project in this multilayered, funny story involving a dollop of Roman/bathroom history and told through letters, memos, newspaper articles, and police reports. (Rev: BL 9/1/06; SLJ 8/06)

11400 Klise, Kate. *Regarding the Bees: A Lesson in Letters, on Honey, Dating and Other Sticky Subjects* (4–6). Illus. by M. Sarah Klise. 2007, Harcourt $15.00 (978-0-15-205711-4). 144pp. Now in 7th grade, the students at Geyser Creek Middle School must prepare for the Basic Education Evaluation (BEE) standardized test through corresponding via fax and letter with fountain designer Florence Waters. (Rev: BL 11/1/07; SLJ 9/07)

11401 Klise, Kate. *Regarding the Fountain: A Tale, in Letters, of Liars and Leaks* (4–6). Illus. 1998, Avon $16.99 (978-0-380-97538-9). 144pp. Dry Creek's school needs a new water fountain, causing a flurry of letters, memos, and other communications involving the school and fountain designer, Florence Waters. (Rev: BL 8/98; HB 5/98; HBG 10/98; SLJ 6/98)

11402 Klise, Kate. *Regarding the Trees: A Splintered Saga Rooted in Secrets* (4–6). Illus. by M. Sarah Klise. 2005, Harcourt $15.00 (978-0-15-205163-1). 160pp. In a scrapbook format using letters, news articles, and illustrations, this is the funny, pun-filled, and complex story of a dispute over trimming the trees at the middle school and a community's various interests. (Rev: BL 11/1/05; SLJ 11/05)

11403 Korman, Gordon. *Maxx Comedy: The Funniest Kid in America* (4–6). 2003, Hyperion $15.99 (978-0-7868-0746-8). 160pp. The joke-filled story of Max Carmody's quest to be the funniest kind in America also resonates with themes of friendship and loyalty. (Rev: BL 6/1–15/03; HBG 10/03; SLJ 9/03)

11404 Kurzweil, Allen. *Leon and the Champion Chip* (3–6). Illus. by Bret Bertholf. 2005, Greenwillow $15.99 (978-0-06-053933-7). 336pp. Leon Zeisel starts fifth grade, plans revenge on bully Henry Lumpkin, and discovers to his amazement that his science class will spend a semester researching the potato chip, his favorite snack food; a funny sequel to *Leon and the Spitting Image* (2003). (Rev: BL 11/1/05; SLJ 3/06)

11405 Laden, Nina. *Romeow and Drooliet* (2–6). Illus. by author. 2005, Chronicle $16.95 (978-0-8118-3973-0). Romance is surely doomed when cat Romeow and dog Drooliet fall for each other. (Rev: SLJ 6/05)

11406 Lawson, Robert. *Ben and Me* (5–8). Illus. by author. 1939, Little, Brown $16.95 (978-0-316-51732-4); paper $5.99 (978-0-316-51730-0). The events of Benjamin Franklin's life, as told by his good mouse Amos, who lived in his old fur cap.

11407 Lawson, Robert. *Captain Kidd's Cat* (3–5). Illus. by author. 1984, Little, Brown paper $7.95 (978-0-316-51735-5). A narrative recount by McDermot, faithful cat of Captain William Kidd.

11408 Lawson, Robert. *Mr. Revere and I* (5–8). Illus. by author. 1953, Little, Brown paper $6.99 (978-0-316-51729-4). 152pp. A delightful account of certain episodes in Revere's life, as revealed by his horse Scheherazade. (Rev: SLJ 1/05)

11409 Levoy, Myron. *The Magic Hat of Mortimer Wintergreen* (4–6). 1988, HarperCollins $11.95 (978-0-06-023841-4). 224pp. Joshua and Amy escape from creepy Aunt Vootch with a magician and search for their grandparents. (Rev: BL 2/15/88; SLJ 3/88)

11410 Lewis, Cynthia C. *Dilly's Summer Camp Diary* (3–5). Illus. by author. 1999, Millbrook LB $19.90 (978-0-7613-1416-5). Told in diary form, this is the humorous story of Dilly's three weeks at summer camp with all its delights and trials. (Rev: HBG 10/99; SLJ 6/99)

11411 Lindgren, Astrid. *Pippi Longstocking* (4–6). Trans. by Florence Lamborn. Illus. by Louis Glanzman. 1950, Puffin paper $5.99 (978-0-14-030957-7). 158pp. A little Swedish tomboy who has a monkey and a horse for companions. Also use: *Pippi Goes on Board* (1957); *Pippi in the South Seas* (1959).

11412 Lowry, Lois. *Anastasia, Absolutely* (4–6). Series: Anastasia Krupnik. 1995, Houghton $16.00 (978-0-395-74521-2); Bantam paper $3.99 (978-0-440-41222-9). 176pp. Anastasia absentmindedly throws a bag filled with her dog's poop into a mailbox and incurs an investigation by the police. (Rev: BCCB 9/95; BL 10/1/95; HB 11/95; SLJ 10/95)

11413 Lowry, Lois. *Anastasia at This Address* (5–9). 1991, Houghton $16.00 (978-0-395-56263-5); Dell paper $4.50 (978-0-440-40652-5). The irrepressible Anastasia answers a personal ad, using her mother's picture instead of her own, with typically hilarious results. (Rev: BCCB 3/91; BL 4/1/91; SLJ 8/91)

11414 Lowry, Lois. *Anastasia on Her Own* (5–7). Illus. 1985, Houghton $16.00 (978-0-395-38133-5); Dell paper $4.50 (978-0-440-40291-6). 131pp. Seventh-grader Anastasia Krupnik must face both domestic crisis and romance. Another chapter in Anastasia's busy life is recounted in *Anastasia Has the Answers* (1986). (Rev: BL 5/15/85; HB 9/85; SLJ 8/85)

11415 Lowry, Lois. *Anastasia's Chosen Career* (5–7). 1987, Houghton $16.00 (978-0-395-42506-0); Bantam paper $4.50 (978-0-440-40100-1). Thirteen-year-old Anastasia gets some surprises when she begs to go to charm school to change her freaky looks. Anastasia's baby brother is featured in *All About Sam* (1988). (Rev: BCCB 9/87; BL 9/1/87; SLJ 9/87)

11416 Lowry, Lois. *Attaboy, Sam!* (2–5). Illus. by Diane deGroat. 1992, Houghton $16.00 (978-0-395-61588-1). 116pp. Anastasia Krupnik's little brother, Sam, decides to make perfume for his mother's birthday. (Rev: BCCB 4/92; BL 2/15/92*; HB 7/92*; SLJ 5/92*)

11417 Lowry, Lois. *See You Around, Sam!* (3–6). Illus. by Diane deGroat. 1996, Houghton $15.00 (978-0-395-81664-6). 144pp. Sam decides to run away to Alaska because his mother won't let him wear his plastic fangs. (Rev: BCCB 11/96; BL 10/1/96*; HB 9/96; SLJ 10/96*)

11418 Lowry, Lois. *Switcharound* (5–7). 1985, Houghton $16.00 (978-0-395-39536-3). Caroline and her nemesis brother J.P. must spend the summer with their divorced father's new family in Des Moines. A sequel to *The One Hundredth Thing About Caroline* (1983). (Rev: BCCB 1/86; BL 10/1/85; HB 1/86)

11419 Lowry, Lois. *The Willoughbys* (4–6). Illus. by author. 2008, Houghton $16.00 (978-0-618-97974-5). 176pp. The dreadful Willoughby parents take off on vacation and try to sell the house in their absence, leaving their four children — who are in the care of a much-despised nanny — plotting to become "deserving orphans." (Rev: BL 2/15/08; HB 3/08; SLJ 4/08; VOYA 8/08) ⌒

11420 Lowry, Lois. *Zooman Sam* (3–5). Illus. 1999, Houghton $16.00 (978-0-395-97393-6). 160pp. Sam Krupnick is in seventh heaven when he learns to read in his nursery school. (Rev: BCCB 9/99; BL 7/99; HB 9/99; HBG 3/00; SLJ 9/99)

11421 Lubar, David. *Punished!* (4–7). 2006, Darby Creek $15.95 (978-1-58196-042-6). 96pp. Thanks to a curse, Logan becomes a non-stop punster and must uncover oxymorons, anagrams, and palindromes to break the spell. (Rev: BL 5/1/06; SLJ 5/06*)

11422 McCloskey, Robert. *Homer Price* (3–6). Illus. by author. 1943, Puffin paper $6.99 (978-0-14-030927-0). 160pp. Popular and preposterous adventures of a Midwestern boy. Continued in: *Centerburg Tales* (1951).

11423 MacDonald, Amy. *No More Nice* (4–7). Illus. 1996, Orchard LB $15.99 (978-0-531-08892-0). 128pp. A humorous story about a spring vacation spent by a boy with his eccentric great-aunt and -uncle. (Rev: BCCB 10/96; BL 9/1/96; SLJ 9/96)

11424 McDonald, Megan. *Judy Moody Predicts the Future* (2–4). Illus. by Peter H. Reynolds. Series: Judy Moody. 2003, Candlewick $15.99 (978-0-7636-1792-9). 160pp. Eight-year-old Judy Moody is convinced that she has newfound psychic abilities when she slips on the mood ring from the cereal box. (Rev: BL 9/15/03; HBG 4/04; SLJ 11/03)

11425 McDonald, Megan. *Stink and the Incredible Super-Galactic Jawbreaker* (2–4). Illus. by Peter H. Reynolds. Series: Stink. 2006, Candlewick $12.99 (978-0-7636-2158-2). 128pp. When he discovers that a letter of complaint can yield free candy, Stink — Judy Moody's younger brother — embarks on a letter-writing campaign. (Rev: BL 4/15/06; SLJ 7/06)

11426 Mackay, Claire, sel. *Laughs* (5–8). 1997, Tundra paper $6.95 (978-0-88776-393-9). An anthology of humorous stories (and some poems) by several well-known Canadian writers. (Rev: SLJ 9/97)

11427 McKenna, Colleen O'Shaughnessy. *Mother Murphy* (5–7). 1993, Scholastic paper $2.95 (978-0-590-44856-7). 160pp. With her mother confined to bed, 12-year-old Collette volunteers as mother-for-a-day with disasterous and funny results. (Rev: BCCB 2/92; BL 2/1/92; SLJ 2/92)

11428 MacLachlan, Patricia. *Arthur, for the Very First Time* (4–6). Illus. by Lloyd Bloom. 1980, HarperCollins paper $4.99 (978-0-06-440288-0). 128pp. Arthur spends a summer on the farm of his aunt and uncle.

11429 McMahen, Chris. *Tabloidology* (4–6). 2009, Orca paper $9.95 (978-1-55469-009-1). 176pp. It's either close the school newspaper or hire loose cannon Trixie Wilder as a writer. What's a boy to do? (Rev: BL 6/1–15/09)

11430 Manes, Stephen. *Chocolate-Covered Ants* (4–6). 1993, Scholastic paper $3.99 (978-0-590-40961-2). 128pp. Max bets his brother that people do eat chocolate-covered ants. (Rev: BCCB 12/92; BL 9/1/90; SLJ 12/90)

11431 Manes, Stephen. *Make Four Million Dollars by Next Thursday!* (3–6). Illus. by George Ulrich. 1996, Bantam paper $4.50 (978-0-440-41370-7). 112pp. Would-be millionaire Jazon Nozzle finds a book that tells him how to do it. (Rev: BCCB 2/91; BL 2/15/91; SLJ 6/91)

11432 Mason, Simon. *The Quigleys in a Spin* (3–5). Illus. by Helen Stephens. 2006, Random $14.95 (978-0-385-75098-1). 192pp. Lucy painting her sleeping dad's toenails and having a dreadful birthday party are only two of the funny episodes in this British chapter book. (Rev: BL 1/1–15/06; SLJ 4/06)

11433 Meacham, Margaret. *A Fairy's Guide to Understanding Humans* (5–8). 2007, Holiday $16.95 (978-0-8234-2078-0). 192pp. Morgan's unreliable fairy godmother tries to improve 14-year-old Morgan's life after her move to a new house and new school in this sequel to *A Mid-Semester Night's Dream* (2004). (Rev: BL 2/1/08; SLJ 2/08)

11434 Mills, Claudia. *Alex Ryan, Stop That!* (4–7). Series: West Creek Middle School. 2003, Farrar $16.00 (978-0-374-34655-3). 160pp. All Alex's efforts to attract classmate Marcia go awry in this humorous account of 7th-grade and son-father relations. (Rev: BL 4/1/03; HBG 10/03; SLJ 4/03)

11435 Montgomery, Claire, and Monte Montgomery. *Hubert Invents the Wheel* (4–7). Illus. by Jeff Shelly. 2005, Walker $16.95 (978-0-8027-8990-7). 184pp. Hubert, a struggling 15-year-old inventor in ancient Sumeria, finally finds success when he invents the wheel, but things quickly spin out of control. (Rev: SLJ 11/05)

11436 Morgan, Christopher. *Pirates Drive Buses* (2–4). 2008, Roaring Brook $14.95 (978-1-59643-313-7). 80pp. This zany seagoing adventure opens with brother Bill and sister Heidi on their way to school when they meet their pirate friend and are persuaded to join him on a search for his ship. (Rev: BL 3/1/08; LMC 3/08; SLJ 5/08)

11437 Mulford, Philippa Greene. *Making Room for Katherine* (5–9). 1994, Macmillan $14.95 (978-0-02-767652-5). A 16-year-old is recovering from her father's death when a 13-year-old cousin arrives from Paris to visit for the summer. (Rev: BL 4/15/94; SLJ 5/94; VOYA 8/94)

11438 Naylor, Phyllis Reynolds. *Alice in April* (5–8). 1993, Dell paper $4.50 (978-0-440-91032-9). Alice is back, this time caught between her desire to be a perfect housekeeper and her fascination with her developing body. (Rev: BL 3/1/93; SLJ 6/93)

11439 Naylor, Phyllis Reynolds. *Alice the Brave* (5–7). 1995, Simon & Schuster paper $4.99 (978-0-689-80598-1). 131pp. Alice conquers her fear of deep water and also feels the pangs of growing up in this amusing continuation of a popular series. (Rev: BCCB 4/95; BL 5/1/95; HB 7/95; SLJ 5/95)

11440 Naylor, Phyllis Reynolds. *All But Alice* (5–8). 1992, Macmillan $15.95 (978-0-689-31773-6). 128pp. Alice, now a 7th grader and still motherless, deals with the challenges of friendship and popularity. (Rev: BCCB 5/92; BL 3/1/92; HB 7/92; SLJ 5/92*)

11441 Naylor, Phyllis Reynolds. *Boys Against Girls* (4–6). 1994, Delacorte $14.95 (978-0-385-32081-8). 147pp. Boys and girls try to trick each other into believing that a strange monster exists, and maybe they are right. (Rev: BCCB 11/94; BL 9/1/94; SLJ 11/94)

11442 Naylor, Phyllis Reynolds. *Boys Rock!* (4–6). 2005, Delacorte $15.95 (978-0-385-73140-9). 144pp. To earn extra reading credits over the summer, the Hatford brothers decide to publish a newspaper, an undertaking that becomes even more complicated when they reluctantly ask the Malloy sisters to join them. (Rev: BL 10/1/05; SLJ 1/06)

11443 Naylor, Phyllis Reynolds. *Reluctantly Alice* (5–8). 1991, Macmillan $16.00 (978-0-689-31681-4). 192pp. Alice's life in the 7th grade seems full of embarrassment. (Rev: BCCB 4/91*; BL 2/1/91; HB 7/91; SLJ 3/91*)

11444 Naylor, Phyllis Reynolds. *Who Won the War?* (4–7). 2006, Delacorte LB $17.99 (978-0-385-90172-7). 160pp. In the last weeks before they return to Ohio (and the last volume in the series), the Malloy sisters mount a last-ditch campaign to prove their superiority over the Hatford boys. (Rev: BL 11/1/06; SLJ 9/06)

11445 Ogden, Charles. *Pet's Revenge* (4–6). Illus. by Rick Carton. Series: Edgar and Ellen. 2006, Simon & Schuster $9.95 (978-1-4169-1408-2). 192pp. Edgar has to act by himself to save their house when Ellen undergoes a character change and endorses a neat, tidy life. (Rev: BL 5/15/06)

11446 O'Malley, Kevin. *Captain Raptor and the Moon Mystery* (K–4). Illus. by Patrick O'Brien. 2005, Walker $16.95 (978-0-8027-8935-8). Captain Raptor and his dinosaur crew blast into space to investigate the landing of a UFO — carrying alien humans — on one of Jurassica's moons. (Rev: BCCB 4/05; SLJ 4/05)

11447 Park, Barbara. *Buddies* (5–8). 1986, Avon paper $2.95 (978-0-380-69992-6). 144pp. Dinah's dreams of being popular at camp are dashed in this humorous novel because she is forever being accompanied by Fern, the camp nerd. (Rev: BCCB 5/85; BL 4/15/85; SLJ 5/85)

11448 Park, Barbara. *Junie B. Jones and a Little Monkey Business* (2–3). Illus. by Denise Brunkus. 1993, Random paper $3.99 (978-0-679-83886-9). 46pp. Junie is amazed to learn that her new brother is a monkey after grandmother declares, "He's the cutest monkey I've ever seen!" (Rev: BL 3/1/93)

11449 Park, Barbara. *Junie B. Jones and the Stupid Smelly Bus* (2–3). Illus. by Denise Brunkus. 1992, Random $11.99 (978-0-679-92642-9); paper $3.99

(978-0-679-82642-2). 70pp. Junie B. is a cross between Lily Tomlin's Edith Ann and Eloise in this funny story of a youngster on her way to kindergarten. (Rev: BL 12/1/92; SLJ 11/92)

11450 Park, Barbara. *Junie B. Jones Is a Beauty Shop Guy* (2–3). 1998, Random LB $11.99 (978-0-679-98939-4); paper $3.99 (978-0-679-88931-1). 67pp. Junie B. Jones believes she has a calling to become a barber and, after practicing on various stuffed animals, decides to move on to a human subject — herself. (Rev: BL 11/15/98; SLJ 12/98)

11451 Park, Barbara. *Junie B. Jones Smells Something Fishy* (2–4). Illus. 1998, Random paper $3.99 (978-0-679-89130-7). 67pp. When all her plans to take a pet to school fail, a disappointed Junie brings a fish stick instead and wins a prize for the most well-behaved pet. (Rev: BL 3/15/99)

11452 Park, Barbara. *The Kid in the Red Jacket* (4–6). 1988, Knopf paper $3.99 (978-0-394-80571-9). 128pp. Ten-year-old Howard is having some trouble adjusting to life in Massachusetts when his family moves from Arizona. (Rev: BCCB 3/87; BL 2/15/87; SLJ 3/87)

11453 Park, Barbara. *Operation: Dump the Chump* (3–6). Illus. by Robert Sauber. 1989, Knopf paper $4.99 (978-0-394-82592-2). 128pp. Oscar Winkle devises a plan to get rid of his young brother.

11454 Paulsen, Gary. *Lawn Boy* (5–8). 2007, Random $12.99 (978-0-385-74686-1). 96pp. Given his late grandfather's somewhat battered riding mower as a gift, a 12-year-old entrepreneur launches a phenomenally successful lawn care business in this zany, tongue-in-cheek story. (Rev: BL 4/15/07; HB 7/07; SLJ 6/07)

11455 Peck, Robert Newton. *Higbee's Halloween* (5–7). 1990, Walker LB $14.85 (978-0-8027-6969-5). 101pp. Higbee decides something must be done about the unruly Striker children. (Rev: SLJ 10/90)

11456 Pennypacker, Sara. *The Talented Clementine* (2–4). Illus. by Marla Frazee. 2007, Hyperion $14.99 (978-0-7868-3870-7). 144pp. Third-grader Clementine views the forthcoming talent show with nothing but dread in this funny chapter book. (Rev: BL 3/15/07) ∩

11457 Petty, J. T. *Clemency Pogue: Fairy Killer* (3–6). Illus. by Will Davis. 2005, Simon & Schuster $9.95 (978-0-689-87236-5). 125pp. A satirical tale in which Clemency is inadvertently responsible for killing six innocent fairies and must set things right. (Rev: SLJ 4/05)

11458 Petty, J. T. *The Squampkin Patch: A Nasselrogt Adventure* (4–7). Illus. by David Michael Friend. 2006, Simon & Schuster $15.95 (978-1-4169-0274-4). 251pp. A funny, far-fetched fantasy about two children who escape hard labor at the zipper factory/orphanage (their parents are tied up in tanning beds) and find themselves pursued by squampkins — pumpkin-like creatures — that are out for blood. (Rev: SLJ 7/06)

11459 Pilkey, Dav. *The Adventures of Captain Underpants* (2–4). Illus. 1997, Scholastic $16.99 (978-0-590-84627-1). 128pp. A superhero spoof in which two boys capture their principal and turn him

into Captain Underpants. (Rev: BL 7/97; HBG 3/98; SLJ 12/97)

11460 Pilkey, Dav. *The Adventures of Super Diaper Baby* (2–5). Illus. by author. 2002, Scholastic paper $5.99 (978-0-439-37606-8). 125pp. As a penance for bad behavior, Harold and George are ordered to tackle the topic of good citizenship and instead invent a diaper-clad superhero. (Rev: HBG 10/02; SLJ 6/02)

11461 Pilkey, Dav. *Captain Underpants and the Attack of the Talking Toilets* (3–5). Illus. 1999, Scholastic $16.99 (978-0-590-63136-5). 144pp. George, Harold, and their school principal, who is also Captain Underpants, get involved in an army of teacher-eating toilets led by supercommode Turbo Toilet 2000. (Rev: BCCB 5/99; BL 5/1/99; HBG 10/99; SLJ 6/99)

11462 Pilkey, Dav. *Captain Underpants and the Invasion of the Incredibly Naughty Cafeteria Ladies from Outer Space (and the Subsequent Assault of the Equally Evil Lunchroom Zombie Nerds)* (4–6). Illus. 1999, Scholastic $16.99 (978-0-439-04995-5). 144pp. Another wacky adventure featuring fourth-graders George and Harold, their principal who becomes Captain Underpants, and a threat from outer space. (Rev: BL 9/15/99; HBG 3/00; SLJ 11/99)

11463 Pilkey, Dav. *Captain Underpants and the Perilous Plot of Professor Poopypants* (3–5). Illus. 2000, Scholastic $16.95 (978-0-439-04997-9). 160pp. Captain Underpants, aka Mr. Krupp, an elementary school principal, and students George and Harold combat a mad scientific genius, Pippy Pee-pee Poopypants. (Rev: BL 2/15/00; HBG 10/00; SLJ 5/00)

11464 Pilkey, Dav. *Captain Underpants and the Preposterous Plight of the Purple Potty People* (2–5). Illus. by author. 2006, Scholastic $16.99 (978-0-439-37613-6); paper $4.99 (978-0-439-37614-3). 175pp. George and Harold find themselves in an alternate universe inhabited by evil versions of themselves. (Rev: SLJ 12/06)

11465 Pilkey, Dav. *Captain Underpants and the Wrath of the Wicked Wedgie Woman* (3–6). Illus. 2001, Scholastic $16.99 (978-0-439-04999-3); paper $5.99 (978-0-439-05000-5). 176pp. George and Harold of Captain Underpants fame create a comic book about their teacher, Mrs. Ribble, whom they dub Wicked Wedgie Woman. (Rev: BL 1/1–15/02; HBG 3/02)

11466 Pinkwater, Daniel. *The Artsy Smartsy Club* (4–6). Illus. by Jill Pinkwater. 2005, HarperCollins LB $16.89 (978-0-06-053558-2). 176pp. Chalk sidewalk portraits of Henrietta (the giant chicken of *The Hoboken Chicken Emergency* [1977]) prompt a group of friends to investigate, leading them to an exploration of art in general and entertaining efforts to start up a new art festival. (Rev: BL 5/1/05; SLJ 5/05)

11467 Poploff, Michelle. *Busy O'Brien and the Great Bubble Gum Blowout* (3–5). Illus. by Abby Carter. 1990, Walker LB $13.85 (978-0-8027-6984-8). 80pp. Ten-year-old Busy O'Brien wishes she had more time to spend with her mom so she devises a plan. (Rev: BL 12/15/90; SLJ 10/90)

11468 Pryor, Bonnie. *Vinegar Pancakes and Vanishing Cream* (2–4). Illus. by Gail Owens. 1987, Morrow $16.00 (978-0-688-06728-1). 128pp. The ups and downs of life for Martin Elwood Snodgrass, who has too-successful older siblings and a too-cute baby brother. (Rev: BL 6/15/87; SLJ 6–7/87)

11469 Raskin, Ellen. *The Mysterious Disappearance of Leon (I Mean Noel)* (4–6). Illus. by author. 1989, Puffin paper $5.99 (978-0-14-032945-2). 160pp. Humorous saga of Mrs. Carillon's search for her husband Leon (or Noel), who is the joint heir to a soup fortune.

11470 Rees, Douglas. *Uncle Pirate* (2–4). Illus. by Tony Auth. 2008, Simon & Schuster $15.99 (978-1-4169-4762-2). 100pp. Fourth-grader Wilson's life changes for the better when his wicked pirate uncle comes to live with him and reorganizes his poorly run, dangerous school in shocking, amusing ways. (Rev: BCCB 9/08; SLJ 2/09)

11471 Riddell, Chris. *Ottoline Goes to School* (3–6). Illus. by author. 2009, HarperCollins $10.99 (978-0-06-144900-0). 176pp. Ottoline and her doggy best friend Mr. Monroe attend the Alice B. Smith School for the Differently Gifted, where Ottoline does not initially excel; the combination of chapter-book text and graphic novel illustrations is effective. (Rev: SLJ 7/09)

11472 Riddleburger, Sam. *The Qwikpick Adventure Society* (3–6). 2007, Dial $16.99 (978-0-8037-3178-3). 127pp. Lyle, Marilla, and Dave are fascinated by the "poop fountain" at the nearby water treatment plant and record their visit there in a scrapbook. (Rev: BCCB 7–8/07; SLJ 7/07)

11473 Robertson, Keith. *Henry Reed, Inc.* (5–7). Illus. by Robert McCloskey. 1989, Puffin paper $6.99 (978-0-14-034144-7). 240pp. Told deadpan in diary form, this story of Henry's enterprising summer in New Jersey presents one of the most amusing boys since Tom and Huck. Others in the series *Henry Reed's Journey* (1963); *Henry Reed's Baby-Sitting Service* (1966); *Henry Reed's Big Show* (1970).

11474 Robinson, Barbara. *The Best School Year Ever* (3–5). 1994, HarperCollins LB $16.89 (978-0-06-023043-2). 128pp. Beth has to write a complimentary composition about a classmate who appears to have no redeeming qualities. (Rev: BL 10/15/94; HB 11/94; SLJ 10/94)

11475 Robinson, Barbara. *My Brother Louis Measures Worms and Other Louis Stories* (3–6). 1988, HarperCollins LB $15.89 (978-0-06-025083-6); paper $4.95 (978-0-06-440362-7). 160pp. Events in ten stories of the wild Lawson family. (Rev: BCCB 12/88; BL 11/1/88; SLJ 12/88)

11476 Rockwell, Thomas. *How to Eat Fried Worms* (4–6). Illus. by Emily Arnold McCully. 1973, Watts LB $29.00 (978-0-531-02631-1); Dell paper $4.99 (978-0-440-44545-6). 128pp. In this very humorous story, Billy takes on a bet — he will eat 15 worms in 15 days. His family and friends help devise ways to cook them.

11477 Rodgers, Mary. *Freaky Friday* (4–7). 1972, HarperCollins LB $16.89 (978-0-06-025049-2); paper $5.99 (978-0-06-440046-6). 156pp. Thirteen-year-old Annabel learns some valuable lessons during the day she becomes her mother. Two sequels are *A Billion for Boris* (1974) and *Summer Switch* (1982). (Rev: BL 4/15/89)

11478 Roos, Stephen. *Twelve-Year-Old Vows Revenge After Being Dumped by Extraterrestrial on First Date* (5–6). Illus. 1991, Dell paper $3.25 (978-0-440-40465-1). 119pp. The rivalry between two girls reaches such a point that they take the matter to court. (Rev: BL 5/15/90; SLJ 7/90)

11479 Root, Phyllis. *Aunt Nancy and the Bothersome Visitors* (1–4). Illus. by David Parkins. Series: Aunt Nancy. 2007, Candlewick $16.99 (978-0-7636-3074-4). 57pp. Old Man Trouble, Cousin Lazybones, Old Woeful, and Mister Death visit Aunt Nancy, but she doesn't let any of them get the better of her in this collection of tall tales. (Rev: BCCB 10/07; HB 9/07; LMC 11/07; SLJ 8/07)

11480 Rumble, Chris. *Moby Stink* (3–5). Illus. by author. Series: The Adventures of Uncle Stinky. 2005, Tricycle paper $5.95 (978-1-58246-145-8). 89pp. After landing a huge catfish in his hometown's annual fishing derby, Uncle Stinky frees the creature, infuriating celebrity angler Barry Cooter, who then plots to destroy the town and everyone in it; a wacky, pun-filled tall tale. (Rev: SLJ 1/06)

11481 Ryan, Mary C. *My Friend, O'Connell* (3–5). Illus. by Patrick Chapin. 1991, Avon paper $2.95 (978-0-380-76145-6). 104pp. In this humorous story, Bradley and friend O'Connell get involved in such situations as running a golf tournament and organizing a school cafeteria boycott. (Rev: BL 6/15/91)

11482 Sachar, Louis. *Marvin Redpost: Is He a Girl?* (2–4). Illus. by Barbara Sullivan. 1993, Random LB $11.99 (978-0-679-91948-3); paper $3.99 (978-0-679-81948-6). 74pp. Marvin wonders if he is turning into a girl because he seems to be developing feminine interests. (Rev: BCCB 6/94; BL 11/15/93)

11483 Sachar, Louis. *Sideways Arithmetic from Wayside School* (4–8). Series: Wayside School. 1992, Scholastic paper $4.99 (978-0-590-45726-2). 89pp. Sue learns a new kind of math and encounters some humorous brainteasers when she transfers to Wayside School. (Rev: BL 12/15/89)

11484 Sandburg, Carl. *Never Kick a Slipper at the Moon* (1–3). Illus. by Rosanne Litzinger. 2008, Holiday $16.95 (978-0-8234-2160-2). 32pp. This humorous Rootabaga story explains exactly why you should not kick slippers at the moon. (Rev: BLO 7/30/08)

11485 Scieszka, Jon. *Squids Will Be Squids: Fresh Morals, Beastly Fables* (2–6). Illus. by Lane Smith. 1998, Viking $17.99 (978-0-670-88135-2). 48pp. This book by the author of the *Stinky Cheese Man* presents 18 contemporary, goofy fables, each with a silly moral attached. (Rev: BCCB 11/98; BL 9/15/98; HB 11/98; HBG 3/99; SLJ 10/98)

11486 Scrimger, Richard. *Noses Are Red* (4–7). 2002, Tundra paper $7.95 (978-0-88776-590-2). 208pp.

Norbert, the alien who likes to live in Alan's nose, works to Alan's benefit once again when Alan and a friend meet a variety of perils on a camping trip. (Rev: BL 1/1–15/03; HBG 3/03; SLJ 12/02; VOYA 2/03)

11487 Scrimger, Richard. *The Way to Schenectady* (4–6). Illus. 1999, Tundra paper $5.95 (978-0-88776-427-1). 168pp. A girl who is traveling from Ontario to Massachusetts with her family takes pity on a homeless man and hides him in the back of the van. (Rev: BL 5/1/99; SLJ 6/99)

11488 Scroggs, Kirk. *Dracula vs. Grampa at the Monster Truck Spectacular* (2–5). Illus. by author. Series: Wiley and Grampa's Creature Features. 2006, Little, Brown paper $2.99 (978-0-316-05941-1). 106pp. Grampa provokes Gramma's ire when he takes grandson Wiley to Colonel Dracula's Monster Truck Spectacular on Halloween night; an exciting evening that includes a strong tornado. Also use *Grampa's Zombie BBQ* (2006). (Rev: SLJ 10/06)

11489 Seuling, Barbara. *Oh No, It's Robert* (2–4). Illus. 1999, Front St. $14.95 (978-0-8126-2934-7). 128pp. Robert is anxious to excel at something, but things always go wrong, especially when he lets the class hamster loose in his living room. (Rev: BL 7/99; HBG 10/99; SLJ 7/99)

11490 Seuling, Barbara. *Robert and the Weird and Wacky Facts* (2–4). Illus. by Paul Brewer. 2002, Cricket $15.95 (978-0-8126-2653-7). 120pp. Robert believes that he has developed magical powers and can make his wishes come true in this humorous addition to an appealing series. (Rev: BL 4/1/02; HB 7/02; HBG 10/02; SLJ 7/02)

11491 Seuling, Barbara. *Robert Goes to Camp* (2–4). Illus. by Paul Brewer. 2007, Cricket $16.95 (978-0-8126-2753-4). 112pp. Robert becomes friends with a troublemaker at day camp. (Rev: SLJ 10/07)

11492 Sherman, Deborah. *The Triple Chocolate Brownie Genius* (4–6). 2007, Fitzhenry & Whiteside $10.95 (978-1-55455-035-7). 151pp. When Michael, 13, goes from being a popular class clown to a super smart student, he and his friends discover that a computer chip in the homemade brownies Michael ate has caused the change, which they humorously struggle to reverse. (Rev: BL 12/1/07; SLJ 1/08)

11493 Shipton, Paul. *The Pig Who Saved the World: By Gryllus the Pig* (5–8). 2007, Candlewick $15.99 (978-0-7636-3446-9). 272pp. In this sequel to *The Pig Scrolls* (2005), Gryllus the pig and his mythological friends — including the young poet Homer — are searching for Circe, the sorceress who can make Gryllus human again. (Rev: BL 10/1/07; SLJ 11/07)

11494 Smallcomb, Pam. *The Last Burp of Mac McGerp* (3–5). Illus. by Lizzy Bromley. 2003, Bloomsbury $15.95 (978-1-58234-856-8). 120pp. No one can belch quite like fifth-grader Mac, but his hopes of entering the National Burping Competition are threatened by a strict new school principal. (Rev: BL 2/15/04; HBG 4/04; SLJ 9/03)

11495 Snicket, Lemony. *The Bad Beginning* (4–7). Illus. Series: A Series of Unfortunate Events. 1999, HarperCollins $12.99 (978-0-06-440766-3). 192pp.

A humorous story about the ill-fated Beaudelaire orphans and the creepy, wicked villains they never seem to avoid. (Rev: BL 12/1/99; HBG 3/00; SLJ 11/99)

11496 Snicket, Lemony. *The Carnivorous Carnival* (4–8). Illus. by Brett Helquist. Series: A Series of Unfortunate Events. 2002, HarperCollins LB $15.89 (978-0-06-029640-7). 304pp. The Baudelaire orphans pose as carnival freaks in the ninth volume of this unhappily-ever-after series. (Rev: BL 12/15/02; HBG 3/03; SLJ 1/03)

11497 Snicket, Lemony. *The End* (5–8). Illus. by Brett Helquist. Series: A Series of Unfortunate Events. 2006, HarperCollins $12.99 (978-0-06-441016-8). 357pp. The Baudelaire orphans find themselves stranded on an island with none other than the villainous Count Olaf; will this be the last installment in the series? (Rev: BL 10/15/06)

11498 Snicket, Lemony. *The Wide Window* (4–7). Illus. Series: A Series of Unfortunate Events. 2000, HarperCollins LB $15.89 (978-0-06-028314-8). 128pp. The three Baudelaire children have a new guardian, timid cousin Josephine, but they are pursued by former keeper Count Olaf. (Rev: BL 2/1/00; HBG 10/00; SLJ 1/00)

11499 Sonnenblick, Jordan. *Dodger for President* (4–6). 2009, Feiwel & Friends $16.99 (978-0-312-37794-6). 176pp. Dodger, the zany blue chimp only visible to Willie and Lizzie, does what he can to support Willie's run for class president with Lizzie as his running mate. (Rev: BL 4/15/09; VOYA 10/09)

11500 Soto, Gary. *Summer on Wheels* (5–8). 1995, Scholastic paper $13.95 (978-0-590-48365-0). 144pp. In this sequel to *Crazy Weekend* (1994), Hector and Mando take a bike ride from their barrio home in Los Angeles to Santa Monica. (Rev: BL 1/15/95; SLJ 4/95; VOYA 4/95)

11501 Spiegelman, Art, and Francoise Mouly, eds. *Little Lit: It Was a Dark and Silly Night* (2–5). Illus. Series: Little Lit. 2003, HarperCollins $19.99 (978-0-06-028628-6). 48pp. Fifteen authors and artists each offer a cartoon story that begins with the line "It was a dark and silly night. . . . " (Rev: HBG 4/04; SLJ 9/03)

11502 Spinelli, Jerry. *The Bathwater Gang* (2–4). Illus. by Meredith Johnson. 1990, Little, Brown $10.95 (978-0-316-80720-3). 59pp. Bertie is bored, so she forms a Girls Only gang, and the boys retaliate. (Rev: BCCB 9/90; BL 6/15/90; SLJ 5/90)

11503 Spinelli, Jerry. *The Library Card* (4–8). 1997, Scholastic paper $15.95 (978-0-590-46731-5). Four humorous, poignant stories about how books changed the lives of several youngsters. (Rev: BCCB 3/97; BL 2/1/97; HB 3/97; SLJ 3/97; VOYA 10/97)

11504 Spinelli, Jerry. *Tooter Pepperday* (3–5). Illus. 1995, Random LB $11.99 (978-0-679-94702-8); paper $3.99 (978-0-679-84702-1). 85pp. Tooter has some hilarious adventures while adjusting to life on a farm far from her beloved city. (Rev: BCCB 6/95; BL 5/1/95; HB 9/95; SLJ 7/95)

11505 Standford, Natalie. *Blonde at Heart* (5–8). Series: Elle Woods. 2006, Hyperion $4.99 (978-0-7868-3843-1). 240pp. How Elle Woods, the central character of the 2001 movie *Legally Blonde*, became a blond bombshell in her effort to attract the attention of her crush. (Rev: BL 7/06; SLJ 5/06)

11506 Stanley, George E. *Hershell Cobwell and the Miraculous Tattoo* (4–8). 1991, Avon paper $2.95 (978-0-380-75897-5). 128pp. A junior high boy decides to gain popularity by getting a tattoo. (Rev: BL 3/15/91)

11507 Steig, Jeanne. *Tales from Gizzard's Grill* (3–6). Illus. by Sandy Turner. 2004, HarperCollins LB $17.89 (978-0-06-000960-1). 72pp. Arresting verses with a tall-tale flair portray the many different characters found in the Old West town of Fiasco. (Rev: HB 5/04; SLJ 6/04)

11508 Steiner, Barbara. *Oliver Dibbs to the Rescue!* (4–6). Illus. 1985, Avon paper $2.50 (978-0-380-70465-1). 96pp. To save threatened wildlife, Oliver paints his dog Dolby as a tiger and exhibits him in a shopping mall. When Dolby "escapes," Oliver lands in the police station. Also use: *Oliver Dibbs and the Dinosaur Cause* (1986). (Rev: BL 12/1/85; SLJ 3/86)

11509 Tacang, Brian. *Bully-Be-Gone* (3–6). Series: The Misadventures of Millicent Madding. 2006, HarperCollins $16.99 (978-0-06-073911-9). 216pp. Twelve-year-old Millicent Madding, an inventor with an uneven level of success, comes up with a fragrance that's designed to repel bullies; full of alliteration and wacky characters. (Rev: SLJ 1/06)

11510 Tayleur, Karen. *Excuses! Survive and Succeed with David Mortimore Baxter* (3–6). Illus. by Brann Garvey. 2006, Stone Arch LB $23.93 (978-1-59889-073-0). 71pp. David is good avoiding work and shares all his excuses for getting out of homework, chores, eating veggies, and more in this hilarious story. (Rev: SLJ 3/07)

11511 Tayleur, Karen. *Secrets! The Secret Life of David Mortimore Baxter* (3–6). Illus. by Brann Garvey. 2006, Stone Arch LB $23.93 (978-1-59889-077-8). 82pp. When a well-known wrestler acknowledges Davey as a trustworthy friend on national TV, Davey gets lots more attention and confidences than he needs. (Rev: SLJ 3/07)

11512 Thompson, Colin. *The Floods: Good Neighbors* (3–6). Illus. by Crab Scrambly. 2008, HarperCollins $15.99 (978-0-06-113196-7). 224pp. The Floods, a family of weird-looking witches and wizards — except for the very normal Betty, are usually easy-going but the behavior of their neighbors, the Dents, pushes them over the edge. (Rev: BL 5/15/08)

11513 Timberlake, Amy. *The Dirty Cowboy* (K–4). Illus. by Adam Rex. 2003, Farrar $16.00 (978-0-374-31791-1). A filthy cowboy is so transformed by his annual bath that his dog, assigned to guard his clothes while he bathed, doesn't recognize him and refuses to surrender the cowpoke's duds. (Rev: SLJ 9/03)

11514 Trahey, Jane. *The Clovis Caper* (5–8). 1990, Avon paper $2.95 (978-0-380-75914-9). 138pp.

Martin is so upset at leaving his dog, Clovis, when going to England that Aunt Hortense plots to smuggle the dog out of the country. (Rev: BL 7/90)

11515 Trine, Greg. *The Fake Cape Caper* (2–5). Illus. by Rhode Montijo. Series: Melvin Beederman, Superhero Series. 2007, Holt $16.95 (978-0-8050-8158-9); paper $5.99 (978-0-8050-8159-6). 144pp. Melvin Breederman, superhero in charge of Los Angeles, attends the Superhero's Convention in Las Vegas, leaving his young sidekick to keep Los Angeles safe from evil bad guys and bullies. (Rev: SLJ 11/07)

11516 Trine, Greg. *Melvin Beederman, Superhero: The Curse of the Bologna Sandwich* (2–4). Illus. by Rhode Montijo. Series: Melvin Beederman, Superhero. 2006, Holt $15.95 (978-0-8050-7928-9); paper $5.99 (978-0-8050-7836-7). 138pp. Hapless superhero Melvin is almost defeated by his love for bologna in this installment in the laugh-out-loud series. The adventures continue in *Melvin Beederman, Superhero: The Revenge of the McNasty Brothers* (2005). (Rev: SLJ 5/06)

11517 Trueit, Trudi. *No Girls Allowed (Dogs Okay)* (2–5). Illus. by Jim Paillot. Series: Secrets of a Lab Rat. 2009, Aladdin $14.99 (978-1-4169-7592-2). 128pp. Nine-year-old bad boy Scab McNally wants a puppy and decides to sell his "sister-repellent" to raise the necessary funds. (Rev: BCCB 3/09; BL 4/1/09; SLJ 3/09) ∩

11518 Tulloch, Richard. *Weird Stuff* (5–8). Illus. by Shane Nagle. 2006, Walker $16.95 (978-0-8027-8058-4). 195pp. A borrowed pen gives school soccer star Brian Hobble amazing new writing abilities, but they're limited to a single genre — romantic fiction. (Rev: SLJ 8/06)

11519 Uderzo, Albert. *Asterix and Son* (4–8). Trans. by Anthea Bell and Derek Hockridge. Illus. 2002, Orion paper $9.95 (978-0-7528-4775-7). 48pp. In comic-book format, this is the entertaining story of French heroes Asterix and Obelix and how they became guardians of a kidnapped baby. Also use *Asterix and the Black Gold* (2002) and *Asterix and the Great Divide* (2002). (Rev: BL 4/15/02)

11520 Uderzo, Albert. *Asterix and the Actress* (4–7). Trans. by Anthea Bell and Derek Hockridge. Illus. 2001, Sterling $12.95 (978-0-7528-4657-6). 48pp. These pun-filled, graphic novel exploits of Asterix the Gaul include a boisterous shared birthday with the rotund Obelix and a daring rescue of prisoners in a Roman jail. (Rev: BL 8/01)

11521 Van Draanen, Wendelin. *Shredderman: Secret Identity* (3–5). Illus. by Brian Biggs. 2004, Knopf $12.95 (978-0-375-82351-0). 144pp. To get the best of a school bully called Bubba, brainy but somewhat nerdy fifth-grader Nolan makes Bubba the "star" of a Web site. (Rev: BL 2/1/04*; SLJ 5/04)

11522 Wallace, Bill. *Ferret in the Bedroom, Lizards in the Fridge* (4–6). 1986, Holiday House $16.95 (978-0-8234-0600-5). 144pp. Liz would certainly win the sixth-grade presidency if it weren't that her zoology teacher-father keeps so many unusual animals around the house and scares away her friends. (Rev: BCCB 7–8/86; BL 6/15/86)

11523 Wardlaw, Lee. *101 Ways to Bug Your Parents* (3–6). 1996, Dial $17.99 (978-0-8037-1901-9). 208pp. Sneeze Wyatt uses a summer session at school to compile a book on how to annoy parents. (Rev: BCCB 11/96; BL 10/1/96; SLJ 10/96)

11524 Ware, Cheryl. *Venola in Love* (4–7). Illus. by Kristin Sorra. 2000, Orchard LB $16.99 (978-0-531-33306-8). 160pp. Told through diary entries, e-mail messages, and class notes, this humorous novel tells how 7th-grader Venola discovers the problems of falling in love. (Rev: BCCB 10/00; HBG 10/01; SLJ 10/00)

11525 Weeks, Sarah. *Oggie Cooder* (3–5). 2008, Scholastic $16.99 (978-0-439-92791-8). 168pp. Fourth-grader Oggie Cooder's talent for nibbling on slices of cheese until they form the outlines of the states wins the formerly unpopular boy celebrity and some new friends. (Rev: BCCB 2/08; BL 1/1–15/08; SLJ 3/08) ∩

11526 Weeks, Sarah. *Regular Guy* (4–6). 1999, HarperCollins LB $14.89 (978-0-06-028368-1). 128pp. In this humorous book, Guy is so unhappy with the wild behavior of his hippy parents that he tries to switch them for another pair. (Rev: BCCB 7–8/99; BL 9/1/99; HB 5/99; HBG 10/99; SLJ 6/99)

11527 Whitehouse, Howard. *The Island of Mad Scientists: Being an Excursion to the Wilds of Scotland, Involving Many Marvels of Experimental Invention, Pirates, a Heroic Cat, a Mechanical Man and a Monkey* (4–7). Illus. by Bill Slavin. Series: The Mad Misadventures of Emmaline and Rubberbones. 2008, Kids Can $17.95 (978-1-55453-236-0); paper $7.95 (978-1-55453-237-7). 262pp. The third and final installment in this fast-paced series involves more running from villains, crazy characters, and many comic moments, as the group tries to reach Urrgghh. (Rev: SLJ 2/09)

11528 Wight, Eric. *Frankie Pickle and the Closet of Doom* (2–4). Illus. by author. 2009, Simon & Schuster $12.99 (978-1-4169-6484-1). 96pp. Frankie Pickle is blessed with a vivid imagination and an outstandingly messy room in this combination chapter book/graphic novel. (Rev: LMC 10/09; SLJ 7/09)

11529 Wisniewski, David. *The Secret Knowledge of Grown-ups* (3–5). Illus. 1998, Lothrop LB $17.89 (978-0-688-15340-3). 48pp. A zany book that explores the truth behind such parental directives as "Drink your milk" and "Don't bite your fingernails." (Rev: BCCB 7–8/98; BL 3/1/98; HBG 10/98; SLJ 3/98)

11530 Wynne-Jones, Tim. *Ned Mouse Breaks Away* (2–4). Illus. by Dusan Petricic. 2003, Groundwood $14.95 (978-0-88899-474-5). 68pp. Ned Mouse attempts an ingenious escape from prison in this surreally funny story. (Rev: SLJ 4/03)

11531 Yee, Lisa. *Stanford Wong Flunks Big-Time* (4–7). 2005, Scholastic $16.99 (978-0-439-62247-9). 256pp. In this rollicking sequel to *Millicent Min, Girl Genius*, Stanford Wong is upset when his parents hire Millicent, his arch-nemesis, to tutor him in English. (Rev: BL 11/15/05; SLJ 12/05)

11532 Young, Steve. *Winchell Mink: The Misadventure Begins* (4–6). 2004, HarperCollins LB $16.89 (978-0-06-053500-1). 135pp. Changes in font, musical notes, and asides and commentary add to the humor and liveliness of this fast-paced story involving bullies, time travel, and an 11-year-old boy exchanging bodies with his pet turtle, Hannibal. (Rev: BCCB 9/04; SLJ 6/04)

School Stories

11533 Amato, Mary. *Please Write in This Book* (2–5). Illus. by Eric Brace. 2006, Holiday House $16.95 (978-0-8234-1932-6). 97pp. A teacher's effort to get children writing is only successful after hurtful slurs and rivalries run their course. (Rev: BCCB 3/07; BL 12/15/06; HBG 4/07; SLJ 4/07)

11534 Asch, Frank. *Hands Around Lincoln School* (4–6). 1994, Scholastic $13.95 (978-0-590-44149-0). 217pp. Amy, a sixth-grader, decides to start a Save the Earth Club in her school to fight pollution and help save the environment. (Rev: BL 1/15/94; SLJ 3/94)

11535 Bagert, Brod. *Hormone Jungle: Coming of Age in Middle School* (5–8). Illus. 2006, Maupin House $23.95 (978-0-929895-87-1). 121pp. The scrapbook of Christina Curtis's middle-school years tells the story of the poetry war that erupted in sixth grade and of the changing relationships between the young people as they learned more about each other. (Rev: SLJ 6/06)

11536 Bauer, Marion Dane. *The Double-Digit Club* (3–5). 2004, Holiday House $15.95 (978-0-8234-1805-3). 118pp. Nine-year-old Sarah is devastated when her best friend Paige, now 10, abandons her to join the exclusive Double-Digit Club. (Rev: BL 3/15/04; SLJ 4/04)

11537 Beam, Matt. *Can You Spell Revolution?* (5–8). 2008, Dutton $17.99 (978-0-525-47998-7). 208pp. New student Clouds McFadden brings together four unlikely classmates to overthrow the lousy administration at Laverton Middle School, using strategies gleaned from history. (Rev: BL 12/1/08; SLJ 1/09)

11538 Bell, Alison. *Zibby Payne and the Drama Trauma* (4–6). Series: Zibby Payne. 2007, Lobster paper $6.95 (978-1-897073-47-6). 94pp. Zibby is excited to win a part in the school musical until she learns she has to kiss a boy in this second book in the series. (Rev: SLJ 7/07)

11539 Benjamin, Saragail Katzman. *My Dog Ate It* (4–6). 1994, Holiday House $14.95 (978-0-8234-1047-7). 166pp. Danny dislikes homework so much that he decides to go on strike, but his teacher comes up with a novel solution. (Rev: SLJ 5/94)

11540 Birdseye, Tom. *Attack of the Mutant Underwear* (3–6). 2003, Holiday House $16.95 (978-0-8234-1689-9). 199pp. Dreams of past underwear-related humiliation haunt Cody Lee Carson as he prepares to begin fifth grade in a new town; his entertaining diary recounts his progress. (Rev: BL 1/1–15/04; HBG 4/04; SLJ 1/04)

11541 Bowe, Julie. *My Last Best Friend* (3–4). 2007, Harcourt $16.00 (978-0-15-205777-0). 146pp. Despite the best efforts of a mean girl named Jenna, Ida seeks out a new friend to get her through fourth grade. (Rev: SLJ 5/07)

11542 Bulion, Leslie. *The Trouble with Rules* (3–5). 2008, Peachtree $14.95 (978-1-56145-440-2). 137pp. Fourth grade brings new rules — boys and girls can't be friends anymore — but Nadie's got a few ideas of her own. (Rev: LMC 8/08; SLJ 9/08)

11543 Buzzeo, Toni. *Our Librarian Won't Tell Us Anything!* (2–5). Illus. by Sachiko Yoshikawa. 2006, Upstart $17.95 (978-1-932146-73-8). Robert, a new student at Liberty Elementary, discovers that the conventional wisdom is awry and the librarian is in fact very helpful. (Rev: SLJ 2/07)

11544 Byars, Betsy. *The 18th Emergency* (4–6). Illus. by Robert Grossman. 1981, Puffin paper $4.99 (978-0-14-031451-9). 128pp. A young boy, nicknamed Mousi, incurs the wrath of the school bully and awaits his inevitable punishment with fear.

11545 Cameron, Ann. *Gloria Rising* (2–4). Illus. by Lis Toft. 2002, Farrar $15.00 (978-0-374-32675-3). 112pp. A young African American girl named Gloria stars in this easy chapter book involving an inspiring woman astronaut and an intimidating fourth-grade teacher. (Rev: BCCB 4/02; BL 2/15/02; HBG 10/02; SLJ 3/02)

11546 Catalanotto, Peter, and Pamela Schembri. *The Secret Lunch Special* (1–3). Illus. by Peter Catalanotto. Series: Second Grade Friends. 2006, Holt $15.95 (978-0-8050-7838-1). 64pp. Misunderstanding a classmate's remarks, young Emily — new to coping with second grade — worries about the consequences of leaving her lunch bag on the school bus. (Rev: BL 9/1/06; SLJ 9/06)

11547 Cheng, Andrea. *Where the Steps Were* (2–5). Illus. by author. 2008, Boyds Mills $16.95 (978-1-932425-88-8). 144pp. Five multicultural students in Miss D.'s 3rd-grade class speak of their dreams and their sadness that their inner-city Cincinnati school is being demolished. (Rev: BL 3/1/08; HB 5/08; SLJ 5/08)

11548 Cleary, Beverly. *Mitch and Amy* (3–5). Illus. by Bob Marstall. 1991, Morrow $16.99 (978-0-688-10806-9); Avon paper $5.99 (978-0-380-70925-0). 224pp. Twins Mitch and Amy squabble their way through fourth grade.

11549 Clements, Andrew. *Extra Credit* (4–7). Illus. by Mark Elliot. 2009, Atheneum $16.99 (978-1-4169-4929-9). 192pp. Abby, 11, becomes pen pals with a student in Afghanistan. (Rev: BCCB 9/09; BL 6/1–15/09; HB 7/09)

11550 Clements, Andrew. *Frindle* (3–6). Illus. 1996, Simon & Schuster $15.00 (978-0-689-80669-8). 105pp. Nick's desire to get even with a teacher gets out of hand. (Rev: BL 9/1/96; HB 11/96; SLJ 9/96)

11551 Clements, Andrew. *Jake Drake, Class Clown* (2–5). Illus. by Dolores Avendano. 2002, Simon & Schuster $15.00 (978-0-689-83921-4). 72pp. Jake is determined to make the new student teacher crack a smile. (Rev: HBG 10/02; SLJ 7/02)

11552 Clements, Andrew. *Jake Drake, Teacher's Pet* (3–5). Illus. by Dolores Avendano. 2001, Simon & Schuster $15.00 (978-0-689-83919-1). 80pp. In this beginning chapter book, Jake Drake faces the worst day of his life — the day he becomes the teacher's pet. (Rev: BL 1/1–15/02; HBG 10/02; SLJ 4/02)

11553 Clements, Andrew. *The Janitor's Boy* (3–7). 2000, Simon & Schuster $15.00 (978-0-689-81818-9). 144pp. Jack Rankin is ashamed that his father is the janitor in the middle school that he is attending. Once his classmates find out about his father, the teasing begins. (Rev: BCCB 9/00; BL 3/1/00; HB 7/00; HBG 10/00; SLJ 5/00)

11554 Clements, Andrew. *The Landry News* (3–7). Illus. 1999, Simon & Schuster $15.00 (978-0-689-81817-2). 128pp. When Cara's editorial about a lazy teacher causes him to lose his job, issues of responsibility and freedom of the press emerge. (Rev: BCCB 6/99; BL 6/1–15/99; HB 7/99; HBG 10/99; SLJ 7/99)

11555 Clements, Andrew. *Lost and Found* (3–6). Illus. by Mark Elliot. 2008, Atheneum $16.99 (978-1-4169-0985-9). 176pp. Jay and Ray, 12-year-old twins who would prefer to be seen as individuals, move to a new school and get a chance to experiment with taking turns to attend as a single student. (Rev: BL 8/08; HB 9/08) ∩

11556 Clements, Andrew. *Lunch Money* (4–6). Illus. by Brian Selznick. 2005, Simon & Schuster $15.95 (978-0-689-86683-8). 222pp. Greg comes up with a great idea to make money but runs into setbacks when the school bans his product and another student develops a competing one. (Rev: SLJ 8/05)

11557 Clements, Andrew. *No Talking* (3–6). Illus. by Mark Elliott. 2007, Simon & Schuster $15.99 (978-1-4169-0983-5). 160pp. The teachers find it quite unsettling when a boisterous 5th-grade decides to practice silence. (Rev: BCCB 10/07; BL 9/15/07; SLJ 9/07) ∩

11558 Clements, Andrew. *The Report Card* (4–7). 2004, Simon & Schuster $15.95 (978-0-689-84515-4). 176pp. Nora, a bright 5th-grader, deliberately gets low grades in a bid to boost her friend Stephen's self-esteem, but her plans backfire. (Rev: BL 2/15/04; SLJ 3/04)

11559 Cohen, Barbara. *Two Hundred Thirteen Valentines* (3–5). Illus. by Wil Clay. 1993, Holt paper $4.95 (978-0-8050-2627-6). 55pp. Two African American children who transfer to a school for the gifted must rethink their attitudes. (Rev: BCCB 1/92; BL 9/1/91; HB 3/92; SLJ 11/91)

11560 Copeland, Cynthia L. *Dilly for President* (3–5). Illus. by author. 2006, Millbrook paper $6.95 (978-0-7613-2442-3). 64pp. In her diary, Dilly describes her classmates and teachers as she enters fourth grade and decides to run for class president. (Rev: SLJ 4/06)

11561 Cox, Judy. *Cool Cat, School Cat* (2–4). Illus. by Blanche Sims. 2002, Holiday House $15.95 (978-0-8234-1714-8). 96pp. Young Gus is extremely forgetful and puts a stray cat in danger of being fumigated. (Rev: BCCB 2/03; HBG 3/03; SLJ 9/02)

11562 Creech, Sharon. *Hate That Cat* (3–6). 2008, HarperCollins $15.99 (978-0-06-143092-3). 176pp. In this sequel to *Love That Dog* (2001), Jack is in 5th grade, still writing poetry, and resisting the idea of a pet to replace his beloved dog. (Rev: BL 8/08; HB 11/08) ∩

11563 Crew, Gary. *Troy Thompson's Excellent Poetry Book* (4–7). Illus. by Craig Smith. 2003, Kane $14.95 (978-1-929132-52-2). Troy Thompson, an 11-year-old Australian boy, uses different forms of poetry to express his feelings about various elements of his life, participating in a yearlong literature assignment and, we learn at the end, winning the grand prize. (Rev: SLJ 1/04)

11564 Daly, Niki. *Bettina Valentino and the Picasso Club* (4–6). Illus. by author. 2009, Farrar $16.00 (978-0-374-30753-0). 112pp. Bettina Valentino is in 5th grade and bowled over by the new art teacher, who needs support when Maxine's parents criticize his teaching; readers learn about various artists and movements. (Rev: BL 3/15/09)

11565 DeClements, Barthe. *Liar, Liar* (4–6). 1998, Marshall Cavendish $14.95 (978-0-7614-5021-4). 144pp. Sixth-grader Gretchen finds her secure and happy social and school life ends when newcomer Marybelle begins her scheming ways. (Rev: BCCB 7–8/98; BL 8/98; HB 7/98; HBG 10/98)

11566 DeClements, Barthe. *Nothing's Fair in Fifth Grade* (4–6). 1981, Puffin paper $5.99 (978-0-14-034443-1). 144pp. Overweight Elsie steals lunch money to feed her habits. A sequel is: *Seventeen and In-Between* (1984).

11567 DeClements, Barthe. *Sixth Grade Can Really Kill You* (4–6). 1995, Puffin paper $5.99 (978-0-14-037130-7). 146pp. "Bad Helen" acts up to cover her embarrassment about her reading problem in this portrayal of life for a learning-disabled child. (Rev: BCCB 12/85; BL 11/1/85; SLJ 11/85)

11568 DeLaCroix, Alice. *The Hero of the Third Grade* (2–4). Illus. by Cynthia Fisher. 2002, Holiday House $15.95 (978-0-8234-1745-2). 96pp. Randall, a third-grader, is miserable — his parents have split up, he's moved with his mom to a new town, the kids don't like him — until he remembers the example of the Scarlet Pimpernel and decides to devote himself to helping others. (Rev: BL 1/1–15/03; HBG 3/03; SLJ 12/02)

11569 Delton, Judy. *Kitty from the Start* (4–6). 1987, Houghton $16.00 (978-0-395-42847-4). 141pp. The story of Kitty, a Catholic girl growing up in the 1940s, and her life in third grade. (Rev: BL 4/1/87; HB 5/87; SLJ 5/87)

11570 DiPucchio, Kelly. *Grace for President* (1–3). Illus. by LeUyen Pham. 2008, Hyperion $15.99 (978-0-7868-3919-3). 40pp. African American Grace runs for president of the elementary school in this appealing novel that explains much about the American election process. (Rev: BL 2/15/08; SLJ 2/08)

11571 DiSalvo, DyAnne. *The Sloppy Copy Slipup* (3–5). Illus. 2006, Holiday $16.95 (978-0-8234-1947-0). 103pp. Brian Higman complains that he can't find anything interesting to write about, but

his teacher and classmates show him that the stuff of his everyday life provides plenty of inspiration. (Rev: BL 3/1/06; SLJ 5/06)

11572 Dowell, Frances O'Roark. *Phineas L. MacGuire . . . Blasts Off!* (2–5). Illus. Series: From the Highly Scientific Notebooks of Phineas L. MacGuire. 2008, Atheneum $16.99 (978-1-4169-2689-). 208pp. Phineas gets a job dog-walking to earn money for Space Camp, and decides to investigate the properties of slobber. (Rev: BLO 7/31/08)

11573 Dowell, Frances O'Roark. *Phineas L. MacGuire . . . Erupts! The First Experiment* (3–5). Illus. by Preston McDaniels. Series: From the Highly Selective Notebooks of Phineas L. MacGuire. 2006, Simon & Schuster $15.95 (978-1-4169-0195-2). 176pp. Science fair success seems unlikely when Phineas L. MacGuire is paired with the obnoxious new kid to work on a fourth-grade science project. (Rev: BL 6/1–15/06; SLJ 6/06)

11574 Edwards, Michelle. *Stinky Stern Forever* (1–3). Illus. Series: Jackson Friends. 2005, Harcourt $14.00 (978-0-15-216389-1). 56pp. Pa Lia Vang and her second-grade classmates have complex reactions when the class bully dies in an accident. (Rev: BL 9/1/05; SLJ 10/05*)

11575 Fitzgerald, Dawn. *Soccer Chick Rules* (5–8). 2006, Roaring Brook $16.95 (978-1-59643-137-9). 160pp. When her school's sports program is threatened, Tess Munro, a talented 13-year-old soccer player, joins the campaign to win approval for the school levy. (Rev: BL 9/1/06; SLJ 10/06)

11576 Floca, Brian. *The Frightful Story of Harry Walfish* (2–4). Illus. 1997, Orchard LB $16.99 (978-0-531-33008-1). 32pp. When Ms. Leonard-Brakhurst's class misbehaves at the natural-history museum, she tells them a cautionary tale that quiets them down. (Rev: BL 4/1/97; SLJ 3/97)

11577 Flood, Pansie Hart. *Tiger Turcotte Takes on the Know-It-All* (2–4). Illus. by Amy Wummer. 2005, Carolrhoda LB $19.93 (978-1-57505-814-6); paper $6.95 (978-1-57505-900-6). 71pp. A beginning chapter book about a second-grade boy-girl rivalry. (Rev: SLJ 7/05)

11578 Frank, Lucy. *The Homeschool Liberation League* (5–8). 2009, Dial $16.99 (978-0-8037-3230-8). 288pp. Eighth-grader Katya is disappointed when home schooling does not turn out to give her the freedom she desires, and she sets out — with the help of a cute violin player named Milo — to change this. (Rev: BCCB 9/09; BLO 5/27/09; HB 9/09; SLJ 8/09)

11579 Fredericks, Mariah. *In the Cards: Love* (5–8). Illus. 2007, Simon & Schuster $15.99 (978-0-689-87654-7). 288pp. Three eighth-grade girls in Manhattan use tarot cards to discover whether Anna will succeed in turning her crush on Declan into a romance; likable, believable characters populate this funny novel. (Rev: BL 1/1–15/07; SLJ 4/07)

11580 Freeman, Martha. *Fourth Grade Weirdo* (3–5). 1999, Holiday House $15.95 (978-0-8234-1460-4). 147pp. Even though Dexter thinks he is the weirdest kid in Mr. Dizwinkle's fourth-grade class, he is able to catch the thief whose robberies have cast suspicions on his teacher. (Rev: HBG 3/00; SLJ 1/00)

11581 Friedman, Laurie. *Back to School, Mallory* (2–4). Illus. by Tamara Schmitz. 2004, Carolrhoda LB $15.95 (978-1-57505-658-6). 176pp. Mallory, 8, is at a new school and, if that isn't bad enough, her mother is the music teacher in this beginning chapter book with appealing illustrations. (Rev: SLJ 8/04)

11582 Gallagher, Diana G. *Guilty! The Complicated Life of Claudia Cristina Cortez* (4–7). Illus. by Brann Garvey. Series: Claudia Cristina Cortez. 2008, Stone Arch LB $23.93 (978-1-59889-838-5); paper $5.95 (978-1-59889-881-1). 81pp. Claudia and are friend Monica are accused of stealing $10 in this novel that will attract reluctant readers. Also use *Whatever!* (2008), in which the girls in Claudia's club must decide whether a boy can join and *Camp Can't* (2008), about Claudia's efforts to become a junior counselor. (Rev: SLJ 1/08)

11583 Gallagher, Diana G. *Vote! The Complicated Life of Claudia Cristina Cortez* (5–7). Illus. by Brann Garvey. Series: Claudia Cristina Cortez. 2008, Stone Arch LB $23.93 (978-1-4342-0770-8); paper $5.95 (978-1-4342-0866-8). 88pp. Claudia and her classmates deal with the ups and downs of a class election in this visually appealing story for reluctant readers that includes a discussion guide and Internet links. (Rev: LMC 5/09; SLJ 2/09)

11584 German, Carol. *A Midsummer Night's Dork* (4–7). 2004, HarperCollins $15.99 (978-0-06-050718-3). 224pp. In this sequel to *Dork on the Run* (2002), 6th-grader Jerry's class puts on an Elizabethan fair and Jerry has to stand up to another bully, even if it means making a fool of himself. (Rev: BL 2/1/04; SLJ 3/04)

11585 Giblin, James Cross. *Did Fleming Rescue Churchill?* (3–5). Illus. by Erik Brooks. 2008, Holt $16.95 (978-0-8050-8183-1). 80pp. Jason, a 5th-grade report writer, discovers the pleasures of research as he investigates a possible connection between Alexander Fleming and Winston Churchill. (Rev: BL 3/15/08; LMC 3/08; SLJ 4/08)

11586 Giff, Patricia Reilly. *Fourth Grade Celebrity* (3–5). Illus. by Leslie Morrill. 1989, Bantam paper $4.50 (978-0-440-42676-9). 128pp. Casey decides that she wants to become famous, and she does, in a most surprising way. Two sequels are: *The Girl Who Knew It All* (1979); *The Winter Worm Business* (1981).

11587 Giff, Patricia Reilly. *Look Out, Washington, D.C.!* (2–4). Illus. 1995, Dell paper $3.99 (978-0-440-40934-2). 118pp. A series of setbacks dull Emily's enthusiasm for the field trip the Polk Street School class is taking to Washington, D.C. (Rev: BCCB 7–8/95; BL 6/1–15/95; SLJ 10/95)

11588 Gilson, Jamie. *Bug in a Rug* (2–4). Illus. 1998, Clarion $15.00 (978-0-395-86616-0). 69pp. In this easily read chapter book, the reader follows Richard through a day in the second grade, including the embarrassment of having to wear purple pants — a gift from his visiting Aunt Nannie. (Rev: BL 4/15/98; HBG 10/98; SLJ 6/98)

11589 Gilson, Jamie. *Gotcha!* (2–4). Illus. by Amy Wummer. 2006, Clarion $15.00 (978-0-618-54356-4). 68pp. Information on spiders is interwoven into a story about second-grader Richard and his relationship with a bully named Patrick; an easy, humorous chapter book with line drawings. (Rev: BL 4/1/06; SLJ 4/06)

11590 Gilson, Jamie. *It Goes Eeeeeeeeeeeee!* (2–4). Illus. by Diane deGroat. 1994, Clarion $15.00 (978-0-395-67063-7). 68pp. Patrick, a conceited new boy in school, is put in his place when he spreads misinformation about bats in class and is corrected by Dawn Marie. (Rev: BCCB 5/94; BL 4/1/94; SLJ 6/94)

11591 Graff, Lisa. *The Life and Crimes of Bernetta Wallflower* (4–6). 2008, HarperCollins $15.99 (978-0-06-087592-3). 256pp. The curious and very original Bernetta loses her scholarship when she is falsely accused of cheating, and is willing to try almost anything in order to raise $9,000 so she can return to her school. (Rev: BL 3/1/08; SLJ 2/08)

11592 Greene, Stephanie. *Owen Foote, Second Grade Strongman* (2–3). Illus. 1996, Clarion $15.00 (978-0-395-72098-1). 96pp. When Owen openly criticizes the school nurse, Mrs. Jackson, he gets into trouble with the principal and his parents. (Rev: BCCB 3/96; BL 4/15/96; HB 5/96; SLJ 4/96)

11593 Gutman, Dan. *The Homework Machine* (4–6). 2006, Simon & Schuster $15.95 (978-0-689-87678-3). 160pp. A magical homework machine creates an unlikely alliance between a fifth-grade computer geek, a teacher's pet, the class clown, and a slacker. (Rev: BCCB 3/06; BL 2/1/06*; HBG 10/06; LMC 10/06; SLJ 4/06*)

11594 Gutman, Dan. *Return of the Homework Machine* (4–6). Series: Homework Machine. 2009, Simon & Schuster $15.99 (978-1-4169-5416-). 176pp. The four characters from *The Homework Machine* (2006) are now in 6th grade and on the track of the computer chip that powered their device. (Rev: BL 4/15/09; SLJ 7/09)

11595 Herrera, Juan Felipe. *The Upside Down Boy / El niño de cabeza* (2–5). Illus. by Elizabeth Gomez. 2000, Children's Book Pr. $15.95 (978-0-89239-162-2). 31pp. Juanito, a young Hispanic American, is afraid that he won't fit into his new Anglo school, but he is pleasantly surprised. (Rev: BCCB 4/00; HB 9/00; HBG 10/00; SLJ 3/00)

11596 Herrick, Steven. *Naked Bunyip Dancing* (2–5). Illus. by Beth Norling. 2008, Front St. $16.95 (978-1-59078-499-0). In humorous free verse, this novel follows a class of Australian 11- and 12-year-olds as they interreact with their new hippie teacher. (Rev: BCCB 5/08; BL 4/15/08; HB 5/08; LMC 5/08; SLJ 4/08)

11597 Hill, Kirkpatrick. *The Year of Miss Agnes* (4–6). 2000, Simon & Schuster $16.00 (978-0-689-82933-8). 128pp. Set in northern Canada, this is a gentle story about a schoolteacher named Miss Agnes and the changes she makes in her pupils during the year she teaches in a one-room schoolhouse. (Rev: BCCB 11/00; BL 10/15/00; HB 11/00; HBG 3/01; SLJ 9/00)

11598 Hoffman, Mary. *Encore, Grace!* (2–5). Illus. by June Allen. 2003, Penguin $14.99 (978-0-8037-2951-3). 112pp. Grace deals with a class play and difficult friends and family in this chapter book with occasional illustrations. (Rev: BL 12/1/03; HBG 4/04; SLJ 12/03)

11599 Holmes, Barbara W. *Charlotte Shakespeare and Annie the Great* (4–6). Illus. by John Himmelman. 1989, HarperCollins $12.95 (978-0-06-022614-5); paper $3.95 (978-0-06-440385-6). 126pp. Charlotte writes a Halloween school play and gets jealous because of all the attention the leading lady receives. (Rev: BCCB 11/89; BL 11/15/89; SLJ 11/89)

11600 Honeycutt, Natalie. *The All New Jonah Twist* (4–6). Illus. 1987, Avon paper $3.50 (978-0-380-70317-3). 128pp. Jonah is determined to change his image at the start of third grade — he'll no longer be inattentive in class, and he'll prove himself responsible enough for a pet. A sequel is: *The Best-Laid Plans of Jonah Twist* (1988). (Rev: BL 5/15/86; SLJ 8/86)

11601 Honeycutt, Natalie. *Invisible Lissa* (4–6). Illus. 1986, Avon paper $2.75 (978-0-380-70120-9). 192pp. Lissa challenges the student power structure in her fifth-grade class. (Rev: BCCB 7–8/85; BL 4/1/85; SLJ 8/85)

11602 Hughes, Dean. *Re-Elect Nutty!* (4–6). 1995, Simon & Schuster $14.00 (978-0-671-31862-8). 122pp. In this humorous novel, Nutty decides to run for reelection even though he was considered the worst student council president his school has ever had. (Rev: BL 5/1/95; SLJ 6/95)

11603 Hurwitz, Johanna. *Class President* (3–5). Illus. by Sheila Hamanaka. 1990, Morrow $15.99 (978-0-688-09114-9); Scholastic paper $4.50 (978-0-590-44064-6). 160pp. Julio works to get his friend elected class president, but discovers that he's the one with leadership qualities. (Rev: BCCB 5/90; BL 4/1/90; HB 7/90; SLJ 5/90)

11604 Jacobson, Jennifer. *Andy Shane and the Very Bossy Dolores Starbuckle* (1–3). Illus. by Abby Carter. 2005, Candlewick $15.99 (978-0-7636-1940-4). 64pp. A bully is making life at school miserable for Andy Shane until his Granny Webb pays a visit to the classroom. (Rev: BL 7/05; SLJ 8/05*)

11605 Jacobson, Jennifer. *Winnie at Her Best* (2–4). Illus. by Alissa Imre Geis. 2006, Houghton $16.00 (978-0-618-47277-2). 112pp. Winnie must choose between helping out a young friend in need or pursuing her newfound interest in art. (Rev: BL 8/06; SLJ 9/06)

11606 Kinney, Jeff. *Diary of a Wimpy Kid* (5–8). 2007, Abrams $14.95 (978-0-8109-9313-6). 224pp. Greg Heffley writes in his very funny journal about the highlights — and the frequent low moments — of his first year in middle school. (Rev: BL 4/1/07; SLJ 4/07; VOYA 4/07)

11607 Kline, Suzy. *Horrible Harry at Halloween* (2–3). Illus. 2000, Viking $14.99 (978-0-670-88864-1). 38pp. At Halloween, Harry must solve the mystery of a stolen party costume in this story about Class 3B. (Rev: BL 9/15/00; HBG 3/01; SLJ 9/00)

11608 Kline, Suzy. *Horrible Harry Cracks the Code* (2–4). Illus. by Frank Remkiewicz. 2007, Viking $13.99 (978-0-670-06200-3). 66pp. Readers will unwittingly learn a math lesson as they read about how Harry, a 3rd-grader, tries to figure out a number code used to award daily prizes. (Rev: BL 5/1/07)

11609 Kline, Suzy. *Horrible Harry Moves Up to Third Grade* (2–3). Illus. 1998, Viking $14.99 (978-0-670-87873-4). 128pp. During a third-grade field trip to an underground mine, Harry has to conquer his fears and also find his nemesis, Sidney, who suddenly disappears. (Rev: BL 10/15/98; HBG 3/99; SLJ 9/98)

11610 Knudson, Mike, and Steve Wilkinson. *Raymond and Graham Rule the School* (2–4). Illus. by Stacy Curtis. 2008, Viking $14.99 (978-0-670-01101-8). 136pp. A funny, feel-good ride through 4th grade as two buddies who expected to revel in being the oldest kids in the school find themselves thwarted at every turn. (Rev: SLJ 9/08)

11611 Korman, Gordon. *The 6th Grade Nickname Game* (4–6). 1998, Hyperion LB $15.49 (978-0-7868-2382-6). 160pp. Typical problems encountered in the sixth grade are faced by Wiley and Jeff along with the anxiety of mounting a campaign to save the substitute teacher, Mr. Hughes. (Rev: BL 10/15/98)

11612 Korman, Gordon. *The Zucchini Warriors* (4–6). 1991, Scholastic paper $4.50 (978-0-590-44174-2). 208pp. The boys at a Canadian boarding school have a wild and woolly adventure. (Rev: BL 1/1/89; SLJ 9/88)

11613 Langston, Laura. *The Trouble with Cupid* (4–8). 2008, Fitzhenry & Whiteside paper $11.95 (978-1-55455-059-3). 251pp. Eighth-grader Erin is asked to train the school's mascot for a dog food contest and finds the job more complicated and educational than she had expected; the gorgeous Zach Cameron is going to help, though. (Rev: SLJ 2/09; VOYA 6/08)

11614 LeBlanc, Louise. *Maddie's Big Test* (2–4). Illus. by Marie-Louise Gay. 2007, Formac paper $4.95 (978-0-8878-0714-5). 64pp. Maddie, who's much more interested in becoming a star than in math, is so nervous about her test that she decides to cheat. (Rev: BL 4/1/07)

11615 Levy, Elizabeth. *Keep Ms. Sugarman in the Fourth Grade* (3–5). 1991, HarperCollins LB $14.89 (978-0-06-020427-3). 96pp. Smart-alecky and disruptive Jackie meets her match in Ms. Sugarman, a gifted teacher. (Rev: BL 12/1/91; SLJ 1/92)

11616 Lewis, Beverly. *Frog Power* (2–5). Illus. 1995, Bethany House paper $3.99 (978-1-55661-645-7). 80pp. Stacy, who is afraid of frogs, is dismayed when she learns that Jason has brought his pet frog to school. (Rev: BL 10/1/95)

11617 Lindberg, Becky T. *Thomas Tuttle, Just in Time* (2–4). Illus. 1994, Whitman LB $14.99 (978-0-8075-7898-8). 112pp. Thomas, a third-grader, might do a little better if he would only get organized. (Rev: BL 11/15/94; SLJ 10/94)

11618 Lovelace, Maud H. *Betsy-Tacy* (3–4). Illus. by Lois Lenski. 1940, HarperCollins paper $5.99 (978-0-06-440096-1). 113pp. Two 5-year-olds are inseparable at school and at play. One of a popular series. Five sequels are: *Betsy-Tacy and Tib* (1941); *Betsy and Tacy Go over the Big Hill* (1942); *Betsy and Tacy Go Downtown* (1943); *Heaven to Betsy* (1945); *Betsy in Spite of Herself* (1946).

11619 Lowry, Lois. *Gooney Bird and the Room Mother* (2–4). Illus. by Middy Thomas. Series: Gooney Bird. 2005, Houghton $15.00 (978-0-618-53230-8). 80pp. Gooney Bird brings in a secret room mother and saves the class Thanksgiving pageant in this sequel to *Gooney Bird Greene*. (Rev: BL 3/1/05; SLJ 5/05)

11620 Lowry, Lois. *Gooney Bird Greene* (2–5). Illus. by Middy Thomas. 2002, Houghton $15.00 (978-0-618-23848-4). 96pp. Gooney Bird is a colorful character: a new second-grader who has a fondness for dressing outrageously and telling fanciful stories. (Rev: BCCB 10/02; BL 9/1/02; HB 9/02; HBG 3/03; SLJ 11/02)

11621 Lowry, Lois. *Gooney the Fabulous* (2–4). Illus. by Middy Thomas. 2007, Houghton $15.00 (978-0-618-76691-8). 96pp. In this third outing, second-grader Gooney Bird Green leads her classmates in writing their own fables after Miss Pidgeon reads them an Aesop's tale. (Rev: BL 1/1–15/07)

11622 Luddy, Karon. *Spelldown: The Big-Time Dreams of a Small-Town Word Whiz* (5–8). 2007, Simon & Schuster $15.99 (978-1-4169-1610-9). 211pp. Mentored by her Latin teacher, 13-year-old Karlene manages to win the spelling championship in her rural South Carolina county and moves on to competitions at the state and national levels. (Rev: BL 1/1–15/07; LMC 8/07; SLJ 2/07)

11623 Lurie, Jon. *Allison's Story: A Book About Homeschooling* (2–4). Illus. by Rebecca Dallinger. 1996, Lerner $21.27 (978-0-8225-2579-0). 40pp. A photo-essay about an 8-year-old's experiences with home schooling. (Rev: BL 11/1/96; SLJ 12/96) [649]

11624 MacDonald, Amy. *No More Nasty* (3–6). Illus. by Cat B. Smith. 2001, Farrar $16.00 (978-0-374-35529-6). 176pp. Eleven-year-old Simon is put in a difficult situation when his great-aunt becomes his substitute teacher. (Rev: BL 9/1/01; HB 11/01; HBG 3/02; SLJ 9/01)

11625 MacDonald, Maryann. *Secondhand Star* (2–5). Illus. by Eileen Christelow. 1994, Hyperion $11.95 (978-1-56282-616-1). 64pp. Francie, who is cast as Toto in the school production of "The Wizard of Oz," becomes a last-minute replacement for an ill Dorothy. (Rev: BL 7/94; SLJ 7/94)

11626 McDonald, Megan. *Judy Moody* (2–4). Illus. 2000, Candlewick $15.99 (978-0-7636-0685-5). 196pp. A beginning chapter book about Judy Moody, a third-grader, and her everyday trials and tribulations. (Rev: BCCB 5/00; BL 7/00; HBG 10/00; SLJ 7/00)

11627 McDonald, Megan. *Judy Moody Goes to College* (2–4). Illus. by Peter H. Reynolds. 2008, Candlewick $15.99 (978-0-7636-2833-8). 144pp. When third-grader Judy visits a local college to meet her new math tutor she becomes immersed in a new way of thinking. (Rev: BL 9/1/08) 🎧

11628 McDonald, Megan. *Judy Moody Saves the World!* (2–5). Illus. by Peter Reynolds. 2002, Candlewick $15.99 (978-0-7636-1446-1). 160pp. Third-grader Judy is busy saving the world with a recycling project in this third installment in the series in which she stars. (Rev: BL 9/1/02; HBG 3/03)

11629 McDonald, Megan. *Stink and the World's Worst Super-Stinky Sneakers* (2–4). Illus. by Peter H. Reynolds. 2007, Candlewick $12.99 (978-0-7636-2834-5). 144pp. Stink, who got his name as a baby, had been intent on winning the smelly sneaker contest but is willing to give up this chance to become one of the judges instead. (Rev: BL 4/15/07)

11630 McKenna, Colleen O'Shaughnessy. *Live from the Fifth Grade* (4–6). Illus. 1994, Scholastic $13.95 (978-0-590-46684-4). 145pp. Practical joker Roger Friday becomes serious when a friendly custodian at his school is accused of theft. (Rev: BL 11/15/94; SLJ 10/94)

11631 McKenna, Colleen O'Shaughnessy. *Third Grade Stinks!* (2–4). Illus. by Stephanie Roth. 2001, Holiday House $15.95 (978-0-8234-1595-3). 99pp. Gordie is really disappointed when he learns he has to share his third-grade locker with show-off Lucy and concocts a plan to stink her out. (Rev: BCCB 11/01; BL 12/15/01; HBG 10/02; SLJ 11/01)

11632 Maguire, Gregory. *One Final Firecracker* (4–7). Illus. by Elaine Clayton. Series: The Hamlet Chronicles. 2005, Clarion $17.00 (978-0-618-27480-2). 226pp. In the final pun-filled installment in the series, the rival Tattletales and Copycats must cooperate to defend the class and the soon-to-be-wed Miss Earth from myriad threats. (Rev: SLJ 5/05)

11633 Maguire, Gregory. *Three Rotten Eggs* (3–7). Illus. by Elaine Clayton. Series: Hamlet Chronicles. 2002, Clarion $16.00 (978-0-618-09655-8). 192pp. The boys are in competition with the girls in Miss Earth's annual spring egg hunt until a swaggering bully named Thud Tweed joins their class. (Rev: BL 4/1/02; HBG 10/02; SLJ 3/02)

11634 Marsden, Carolyn. *The Gold-Threaded Dress* (3–5). 2002, Candlewick $13.99 (978-0-7636-1569-7). 73pp. Fourth-grader Oy is torn between her desire to make friends and her classmates' interest in her precious Thai dress. (Rev: BCCB 6/02; BL 5/1/02*; HBG 3/03; SLJ 4/02)

11635 Marsden, Carolyn. *The Quail Club* (3–5). 2006, Candlewick $15.99 (978-0-7636-2635-8). 144pp. Thai American fifth-grader Oy faces a cultural dilemma when her school schedules a talent show: honor her heritage with a traditional Thai dance or succumb to her classmate's demand that Oy join her in an American dance; a sequel to *The Gold-Threaded Dress* (2002). (Rev: BL 3/1/06; SLJ 4/06)

11636 Martin, Ann M. *Belle Teal* (4–6). 2001, Scholastic $16.95 (978-0-439-09823-6). 224pp. Fifth-grader Belle befriends the only black student in her class in this story about the early days of desegregation. (Rev: BCCB 2/02; BL 10/1/01; HB 1/02; HBG 3/02; SLJ 9/01)

11637 Matson, Nancy. *The Boy Trap* (4–6). Illus. 1999, Front St. $14.95 (978-0-8126-2663-6). 112pp. Emma decides that by entering the best project in her fifth-grade class's science fair, she will be able to prove that girls are better than boys. (Rev: BL 1/1–15/00; HBG 10/00; SLJ 11/99)

11638 Mills, Claudia. *Being Teddy Roosevelt* (3–5). Illus. by R. W. Alley. 2007, Farrar $16.00 (978-0-374-30657-1). 96pp. In this funny school story, fourth-grader Riley, assigned to research and depict Theodore Roosevelt, employs some of T.R.'s enterprising zeal to obtain an unaffordable saxophone to play in the school band. (Rev: BL 1/1–15/07; SLJ 3/07)

11639 Mills, Claudia. *7 x 9 = Trouble!* (2–4). Illus. by G. Brian Karas. 2002, Farrar $15.00 (978-0-374-36746-6). 112pp. Third-grader Wilson loves the class pet, a hamster, and his best friend, Josh, but he has terrible problems with math, particularly the 12 times tables. (Rev: BL 4/1/02; HB 3/02; HBG 10/02; SLJ 4/02)

11640 Morgenstern, Susie. *A Book of Coupons* (4–6). Illus. 2001, Viking $13.99 (978-0-670-89970-8). 64pp. An elderly teacher rewards his fifth-grade class with books of coupons that are redeemable for such treats as dancing in class, and not going to the blackboard when summoned. (Rev: BL 4/1/01; HB 5/01; HBG 10/01; SLJ 5/01)

11641 Moss, Marissa. *Amelia's Book of Notes and Note Passing* (3–5). Series: Amelia. 2006, Simon & Schuster $9.95 (978-0-689-87446-8). 80pp. Amelia's world is jarred off-orbit when a new girl joins her class at school and Amelia starts receiving hateful anonymous notes. (Rev: BL 5/1/06)

11642 Moss, Marissa. *Amelia's Most Unforgettable Embarrassing Moments* (3–5). Illus. by author. 2005, Simon & Schuster $9.95 (978-0-689-87041-5). Faced with a three-day class field trip, Amelia worries about whether her bedtime apparel will pass muster; her older sister's presence as a teaching aide adds to her angst but ends up helping her realize she's not alone in her fears. (Rev: SLJ 11/05)

11643 Moss, Marissa. *Amelia's Science Fair Disaster* (4–6). Illus. by author. Series: Amelia's Notebook: Life in Middle School. 2008, Simon & Schuster $9.99 (978-1-4169-6494-0). 80pp. Amelia gets stuck with dreadful partners for a 7th-grade science project. (Rev: BLO 1/13/09)

11644 Moss, Marissa. *Amelia's 6th-Grade Notebook* (4–6). Illus. 2005, Simon & Schuster $10.95 (978-0-689-87040-8). 80pp. Entering middle school, Amelia has to deal with the presence of her older sister and a really mean English teacher. (Rev: BL 7/05; SLJ 10/05)

11645 Moss, Marissa. *Vote 4 Amelia* (4–7). Illus. by author. 2007, Simon & Schuster $9.99 (978-1-4169-2789-1). 80pp. Amelia is running for secretary and

her friend Carly for president; they didn't expect the campaign to be so intense and Amelia's diary entries are — as always — humorous and revealing. (Rev: SLJ 9/07)

11646 Naylor, Phyllis Reynolds. *Alice in Blunderland* (3–7). 2003, Simon & Schuster $15.95 (978-0-689-84397-6). 200pp. Fourth-grader Alice is well-intentioned but blunder-prone in this second of three prequels to the Alice books. (Rev: HBG 4/04; SLJ 9/03)

11647 Naylor, Phyllis Reynolds. *Starting with Alice* (3–8). 2002, Simon & Schuster $15.95 (978-0-689-84395-2). 192pp. In this prequel, Alice (first seen in *The Agony of Alice* in 1985) is in third grade in a new school in Maryland, initially has trouble finding friends, and still misses her dead mother. (Rev: BCCB 11/02; BL 11/15/02; HB 9/02; HBG 3/03; SLJ 9/02)

11648 Papademetriou, Lisa. *Sixth-Grade: Glommers, Norks, and Me* (4–6). 2005, Hyperion $14.99 (978-0-7868-5169-0). 224pp. Allie must contend with squabbling friends and likes to invent new words to do so in this enjoyable look at life in middle school. (Rev: BL 3/15/05; SLJ 5/05)

11649 Park, Barbara. *Junie B., First Grader: Cheater Pants* (1–2). 2003, Random LB $13.99 (978-0-375-92301-2). 96pp. Junie B. is back again, and she's learning some tough lessons about cheating at school. (Rev: BL 9/15/03; HBG 4/04; SLJ 9/03)

11650 Park, Barbara. *Junie B., First Grader: Toothless Wonder* (2–4). Illus. by Denise Brunkus. 2002, Random LB $13.99 (978-0-375-90295-6). 96pp. Junie B. is losing her first tooth and decides to look into the existence of the tooth fairy, which she rather doubts. (Rev: BL 11/1/02; HBG 3/03; SLJ 12/02)

11651 Park, Barbara. *Junie B. Jones and her Big Fat Mouth* (2–4). Illus. by Denise Brunkus. 1993, Random $11.99 (978-0-679-94407-2); paper $3.99 (978-0-679-84407-5). 72pp. In this hilarious story of kindergartner Junie B. Jones, the little girl has trouble with the Pledge of Allegiance, keeping quiet in class, and deciding what to be on Job Day. (Rev: BL 11/15/93)

11652 Park, Barbara. *Junie B. Jones and the Yucky Blucky Fruitcake* (2–4). Illus. by Denise Brunkus. Series: Junie B. Jones. 1995, Random paper $3.99 (978-0-679-86694-7). 71pp. A young kindergartner tells about her many troubles at school, where she is always a loser. (Rev: BL 12/15/95)

11653 Pearsall, Shelley. *All of the Above* (5–8). 2006, Little, Brown $15.99 (978-0-316-11524-7). 242pp. In this inspiring, fact-based novel, a 7th-grade math teacher challenges his students to build the world's largest tetrahedron and ends up involving the whole community; alternating chapters are narrated by the teacher and four of the students. (Rev: BL 9/1/06; SLJ 9/06)

11654 Proimos, James. *Cowboy Boy* (3–6). Illus. 2003, Scholastic $14.95 (978-0-439-41681-8). 96pp. Cartoon art adds to the fun as sixth grader Ricky Smootz transforms himself into Cowboy Boy to foil a persistent bully. (Rev: BL 9/1/03; HBG 4/04; SLJ 11/03)

11655 Sachar, Louis. *Marvin Redpost: Class President* (2–4). Illus. 1999, Random LB $11.99 (978-0-679-98999-8); paper $3.99 (978-0-679-88999-1). 80pp. In this beginning chapter book, Marvin's third-grade class has a surprise visit from the president of the United States. (Rev: BCCB 4/99; BL 4/15/99; HBG 10/99; SLJ 6/99)

11656 Sachar, Louis. *Wayside School Is Falling Down* (3–6). Illus. by Joel Schick. 1989, Lothrop $15.99 (978-0-688-07868-3); Avon paper $5.99 (978-0-380-75484-7). 192pp. Episodes with the children who inhabit the world's wackiest elementary school. (Rev: BL 5/1/89; SLJ 5/89)

11657 Sand-Eveland, Cyndi. *Dear Toni* (3–6). Illus. by author. 2008, Tundra $12.95 (978-0-88776-876-7). 129pp. At her new school, 6th-grader Gene initially finds it difficult to write a journal that will not be read for 40 years, but she soon enjoys recording her new and sometimes dramatic life. (Rev: SLJ 2/09)

11658 Schwartz, Virginia Frances. *The 4 Kids in 5E and 1 Crazy Year* (3–5). 2006, Holiday $16.95 (978-0-8234-1946-3). 261pp. A fifth-grade ESL teacher helps each of her four students find themselves through reading and writing; the story is told through the students' journal entries. (Rev: BL 12/1/06; SLJ 11/06)

11659 Selzer, Adam. *I Put a Spell on You: From the Files of Chrissie Woodward, Spelling Bee Detective* (5–7). 2008, Delacorte $15.99 (978-0-385-73504-9). 247pp. Ambitious adults may be planning to fix the spelling bee at the Gordon Liddy Community School, and sleuth Chrissie Woodward is determined to find out what's going on. (Rev: BCCB 9/08; HB 9/08; SLJ 11/08)

11660 Seuling, Barbara. *Robert and the Back-to-School Special* (2–4). Illus. by Paul Brewer. 2002, Cricket $15.95 (978-0-8126-2662-9). 112pp. Insecure third-grader Robert thinks his classmates are mocking him because of the length of his hair, but his brother's efforts to fix it don't make things any better. (Rev: BL 1/1–15/03; HB 1/03; HBG 3/03; SLJ 1/03)

11661 Seuling, Barbara. *Robert and the Practical Jokes* (2–4). Illus. by Paul Brewer. 2006, Cricket $15.95 (978-0-8126-2741-1). 136pp. In addition to getting in trouble at school and being fooled into eating a worm, Robert attends a wedding and learns to dance. (Rev: BL 5/1/06; SLJ 3/06)

11662 Seuling, Barbara. *Robert Takes a Stand* (2–4). Illus. by Paul Brewer. 2004, Cricket $15.95 (978-0-8126-2712-1). 176pp. Third-grader Robert tackles a variety of topics — class politics, animal rights, and caring for a new puppy — in this appealing book for beginning readers. Also use *Robert Finds a Way* (2005). (Rev: BL 4/1/04; HB 7/04; SLJ 4/04)

11663 Sharmat, Marjorie W. *Getting Something on Maggie Marmelstein* (3–5). Illus. by Ben Shecter. 1971, HarperCollins LB $16.89 (978-0-06-025552-7). 110pp. When Thad's mortal enemy, Maggie, sees him cooking and begins teasing him, Thad

must find some way of blackmailing her into silence. Two sequels are: *Maggie Marmelstein for President* (1975); *Mysteriously Yours, Maggie Marmelstein* (1982).

11664 Sonnenblick, Jordan. *Zen and the Art of Faking It* (5–8). 2007, Scholastic $16.99 (978-0-439-83707-1). 264pp. Adopted from China as a child and tired of moving to new schools, 8th-grader San Lee decides to play the role of a Zen master when he arrives in Pennsylvania. (Rev: BL 10/1/07; HB 11/07; LMC 1/08; SLJ 10/07)

11665 Spinelli, Jerry. *Loser* (3–6). 2002, HarperCollins LB $16.89 (978-0-06-000483-5). 224pp. Donald Zinkoff, labeled a "loser" by his classmates, is nonetheless happy and secure, unconcerned about what others think of him. (Rev: BCCB 5/02; BL 5/15/02; HB 7/02; HBG 10/02; SLJ 5/02)

11666 Walker, Kate. *I Hate Books!* (2–4). Illus. by David Cox. 2007, Cricket $16.95 (978-0-8126-2745-8). 88pp. Hamish is so skilled at telling stories that his teachers are slow to realize he has not learned to read. (Rev: BL 3/15/07)

11667 Walters, Eric. *Special Edward* (5–8). 2009, Orca $16.95 (978-1-55469-096-1); paper $9.95 (978-1-55469-092-3). 108pp. Eddy, a lazy sophomore, figures that if he can get himself into special ed class, he won't have to work so hard. (Rev: BL 5/15/09)

11668 Warner, Sally. *Super Emma* (2–3). Illus. by Jamie Harper. 2006, Viking $14.99 (978-0-670-06140-2). 90pp. When Emma rescues EllRay from the clutches of a school bully, the reactions of her classmates — including EllRay — are not at all what she expected. (Rev: SLJ 10/06)

11669 Weissman, Elissa Brent. *Standing for Socks* (3–6). 2009, Simon & Schuster $15.99 (978-1-4169-4801-8). 220pp. Fara enjoyed wearing mismatched socks to school in 5th grade, but as she enters 6th grade and runs for class president she wants to be recognized for other achievements. (Rev: BCCB 4/09; BL 3/15/09; SLJ 4/09)

11670 Weissman, Elissa Brent. *The Trouble with Mark Hopper* (4–6). 2009, Dutton $16.99 (978-0-525-42067-5). 240pp. Two boys with the same name, in the same middle school, even looking much alike — confusion and competition reign at first. (Rev: BCCB 9/09; BLO 5/28/09; SLJ 8/09)

11671 Wilkowski, Sue. *The Bad Luck Chair* (3–5). Illus. by CB Decker. 2007, Dutton $15.99 (978-0-525-47794-5). 124pp. Can Addy overcome the misfortune that comes from sitting in her fourth-grade classroom's "bad luck" chair? (Rev: BCCB 10/07; SLJ 7/07)

11672 Willner-Pardo, Gina. *Spider Storch's Music Mess* (2–3). Illus. by Nick Sharratt. 1998, Whitman LB $11.95 (978-0-8075-7583-3); paper $3.95 (978-0-8075-7584-0). 76pp. In this easy chapter book, Spider tries to get out of music class, but when he succeeds in getting bounced, he finds he misses it. (Rev: HBG 3/99; SLJ 3/99)

11673 Willner-Pardo, Gina. *Spider Storch's Teacher Torture* (2–4). Illus. 1997, Whitman LB $11.95 (978-0-8075-7577-2); paper $3.95 (978-0-8075-

7578-9). 60pp. Spider Storch thinks up some wild schemes to prevent his beloved teacher from retiring. (Rev: BL 1/1–15/98; HBG 3/98; SLJ 11/97)

11674 Winerip, Michael. *Adam Canfield of the Slash* (4–7). 2005, Candlewick $15.99 (978-0-7636-2340-1). 336pp. As editors of the *Slash*, the Harris Elementary/Middle School student newspaper, Adam and Jennifer chase scoops and tackle ethical questions. (Rev: BL 5/1/05; SLJ 3/05)

11675 Winkler, Henry, and Lin Oliver. *My Secret Life as a Ping-Pong Wizard* (3–5). Illus. Series: Hank Zipzer. 2005, Grosset $13.99 (978-0-448-43877-1); paper $4.99 (978-0-448-43749-1). 158pp. When his fifth-grade classmates begin to get serious about sports, dedicated underachiever Hank Zipzer takes up ping-pong and discovers, much to his surprise, that sports can be fun. (Rev: BL 1/1–15/06)

11676 Zollman, Pam. *Don't Bug Me!* (4–6). 2001, Holiday House $15.95 (978-0-8234-1584-7). 134pp. Megan, a sixth-grader, aims to complete her bug project despite her pesky, interfering brother and her annoying classmate Charlie. (Rev: BL 7/01; HBG 3/02; SLJ 10/01)

Science Fiction

11677 Anderson, Kevin J., and Ralph McQuarrie. *Stars Wars: Jabba's Palace Pop-Up Book* (2–4). Illus. 1996, Little, Brown $19.45 (978-0-316-53513-7). 14pp. A pop-up book using sound and pictures to illustrate parts of the *Star Wars* films. (Rev: BL 12/15/96)

11678 Applegate, K. A. *Animorphs #1: The Invasion* (5–8). 1996, Scholastic paper $4.99 (978-0-590-62977-5). Jake, an average suburban kid, is confronted one night by a creature from space who teaches him how to morph into the forms of other creatures. (Rev: VOYA 12/96)

11679 Asimov, Janet. *Norby and the Terrified Taxi* (4–8). 1997, Walker $15.95 (978-0-8027-8642-5). Norby, the bungling robot, is kidnapped, and while trying to find him, Jeff and his friends stumble on a plot by Garc the Great to take over the Federation. This is one of a large series of Norby books suitable for middle school readers. (Rev: BL 1/1–15/98; SLJ 12/97)

11680 Asimov, Janet. *The Package in Hyperspace* (5–7). Illus. 1988, Walker LB $14.85 (978-0-8027-6823-0). 84pp. Two space-wrecked children must fend for themselves as they try to reach Merkina. (Rev: BL 1/1/89; SLJ 11/88)

11681 Asimov, Janet, and Isaac Asimov. *Norby and the Invaders* (5–8). 1985, Walker LB $10.85 (978-0-8027-6607-6). Jeff and his unusual robot Norby travel to a planet to help one of Norby's ancestors. Part of a series that includes *Norby's Other Secret*. (Rev: BL 3/1/86; SLJ 2/86)

11682 Asimov, Janet, and Isaac Asimov. *Norby and the Oldest Dragon* (3–5). 1990, Walker LB $15.85 (978-0-8027-6910-7). 110pp. When Jeff visits the planet Jamyn, he finds that a mysterious vapor surrounds him and other residents. (Rev: SLJ 7/90)

11683 Asimov, Janet, and Isaac Asimov. *Norby and Yobo's Great Adventure* (5–8). 1989, Walker LB $13.85 (978-0-8027-6894-0). Norby the robot time-travels to help Admiral Yobo of Mars to trace his family roots. Part of a series that also includes *Norby Down to Earth*. (Rev: BL 10/15/89)

11684 Asimov, Janet, and Isaac Asimov. *Norby Finds a Villain* (4–8). 1987, Walker LB $13.85 (978-0-8027-6711-0). 102pp. Norby the robot and his human friends set out to free Pera, who has been robot-napped by the traitor Ing, in this sixth book of the Norby series. Also use *Norby and the Queen's Necklace* (1986). (Rev: BL 1/1/88; SLJ 11/87)

11685 Asimov, Janet, and Isaac Asimov. *Norby, the Mixed-up Robot* (4–6). 1984, Walker LB $10.85 (978-0-8027-6496-6). 96pp. Jeff, his brother Fargo, and a robot named Norby combat Ing the Ingrate. A sequel is: *Norby's Other Secret* (1984).

11686 Bawden, Nina. *Off the Road* (5–9). 1998, Clarion $16.00 (978-0-395-91321-5). In this science fiction novel set in a time when the elderly are exterminated, 11-year-old Tom follows his grandfather to the "savage jungle" Outside the Wall, where the old man hopes to escape his fate, and discovers a different kind of society. (Rev: BCCB 10/98; BL 9/15/98; HBG 10/99; SLJ 11/98)

11687 Brennan, Herbie. *Zartog's Remote* (3–5). Illus. by Neal Layton. 2001, Carolrhoda LB $14.95 (978-1-57505-507-7). 96pp. A fearful 8-year-old alien named Zartog and a feisty 8-year-old girl named Rachel band together when Zartog loses the remote control for his spaceship. (Rev: HBG 10/01; SLJ 4/01)

11688 Butts, Nancy. *The Door in the Lake* (5–8). 1997, Front St. $17.95 (978-1-886910-27-0). Twenty-seven months after being abducted by aliens, Joey returns home to find that everything has changed while he has remained the same. (Rev: BCCB 7–8/98; BL 5/15/98; HBG 10/98; SLJ 6/98; VOYA 10/98)

11689 Byars, Betsy. *The Computer Nut* (4–6). 1984, Puffin paper $5.99 (978-0-14-032086-2). 144pp. Through her computer, Kate encounters an extraterrestrial being.

11690 Cameron, Eleanor. *Mr. Bass's Planetoid* (4–6). Illus. by Louis Darling. 1958, Little, Brown $14.95 (978-0-316-12525-3). A further story about the Mushroom Planet, Mr. Bass, and two young heroes. Also use: *Stowaway to the Mushroom Planet* (1956).

11691 Cameron, Eleanor. *The Wonderful Flight to the Mushroom Planet* (4–6). Illus. by Robert Henneberger. 1988, Little, Brown paper $7.95 (978-0-316-12540-6). Science fiction combined with magic in the story of two boys who take off on a spaceship with a magical man named Tyco Bass.

11692 Carman, Patrick. *Atherton: The House of Power* (5–8). 2007, Little, Brown $16.99 (978-0-316-16670-6). 352pp. Atherton is a socially divided world under threat and 12-year-old Edgar has a book that contains key secrets. (Rev: BL 5/15/07; LMC 11/07; SLJ 6/07) 🎧

11693 Clayton, Emma. *The Roar* (5–8). 2009, Scholastic $17.99 (978-0-439-92593-8). 496pp. This fast-paced science fiction novel revolves around twins from a society ruined by plagues and chemicals and under the control of an evil government bent on selecting (through arcade games) and training unsuspecting youth for an army. (Rev: BCCB 5/09; LMC 5/09; SLJ 5/09) 🎧

11694 Cole, Steve. *Riddle of the Raptors* (3–5). Illus. by Charlie Fowkes. Series: Astrosaurs. 2006, Simon & Schuster paper $4.99 (978-0-689-87841-1). 126pp. In the opening installment of this humorous science fiction series, Teggs, an Earth-orbiting dinosaur, and his crew of astrosaurs, set out to rescue a couple of their plant-eating athletes who were taken captive by meat-eating velociraptors. (Rev: SLJ 8/06)

11695 Cooper, Clare. *Ashar of Qarius* (5–8). 1990, Harcourt $14.95 (978-0-15-200409-5). A teenage girl, two children, and their pets are left alone in a space dome and must find a way to survive. (Rev: BL 5/15/90; SLJ 7/90)

11696 Cousins, Steven. *Frankenbug* (4–6). 2000, Holiday House $15.95 (978-0-8234-1496-3). 151pp. Adam gets revenge on the bully, Jeb, by creating a super bug by sewing together parts of insects he has bought through a mail-order catalog and, then, frightening his tormentor. (Rev: HBG 10/01; SLJ 3/01)

11697 Cowley, Joy. *Starbright and the Dream Eater* (5–8). 2000, HarperCollins LB $14.89 (978-0-06-028420-6). 144pp. A child born to a mentally disabled teenage mother and named Starbright is destined to save the earth from the Dream Eater. (Rev: BCCB 7–8/00; BL 4/15/00; HBG 10/00; SLJ 6/00)

11698 Craig, Joe. *Jimmy Coates: Assassin?* (4–7). 2005, HarperCollins LB $16.89 (978-0-06-077264-2). 224pp. Thirty-five percent human and 65 percent technologically engineered assassin, 11-year-old Jimmy Coates faces external dangers and internal struggles, all with action, suspense, and humor. (Rev: BL 5/1/05; SLJ 6/05)

11699 Craig, Joe. *Jimmy Coates: Target* (5–8). 2007, HarperCollins $16.99 (978-0-06-077266-6). 272pp. Jimmy Coates, mostly robot but part human, chooses his human side and ends up on the run from the government that wants him assassinated. (Rev: BL 6/1–15/07)

11700 Crilley, Mark. *Akiko: The Training Master* (3–6). Illus. by author. Series: Akiko. 2005, Delacorte $9.95 (978-0-385-73043-3). 207pp. Fifth-grader Akiko is in outer space at the Intergalactic Space Patrollers Training Camp in this latest installment in the humorous, lively series. (Rev: SLJ 7/05)

11701 Daley, Michael J. *Rat Trap* (4–6). 2008, Holiday $16.95 (978-0-8234-2093-3). 212pp. In this sequel to *Space Station Rat* (2005), Jeff and his genetically engineered friend Rat face the evil Dr. Vivexian. (Rev: BL 9/1/08)

11702 Daley, Michael J. *Shanghaied to the Moon* (5–8). 2007, Putnam $16.99 (978-0-399-24619-7). 256pp. In the year 2165, 13-year-old Stewart Hale wants above all to become a space pilot like his mother was before she died in a crash; when his father refuses to help him, he runs away and finds himself on a secret mission to the moon. (Rev: BL 5/1/07; SLJ 5/07)

11703 Doyle, Debra, and James D. MacDonald. *Groogleman* (5–8). 1996, Harcourt $15.00 (978-0-15-200235-0). In this novel set in the future, 13-year-old Dan is immune to the plague that is devastating the countryside and sets out with friend Leesie to help tend the sick. (Rev: BCCB 12/96; SLJ 12/96; VOYA 6/97)

11704 Dunkle, Clare B. *The Sky Inside* (4–8). 2008, Atheneum $16.99 (978-1-4169-2422-7). 240pp. Martin discovers the terrible truth about his flawless, enclosed suburb when he gathers the courage to venture outside it. (Rev: BL 5/15/08; SLJ 5/08)

11705 Dunkle, Clare B. *The Walls Have Eyes* (5–8). 2009, Atheneum $16.99 (978-1-4169-5379-1). 240pp. Martin continues his life-threatening adventures as he faces the controlling forces of his society in this sci-fi sequel to *The Sky Inside* (2008). (Rev: BL 7/09)

11706 DuPrau, Jeanne. *The City of Ember* (5–7). Series: Books of Ember. 2003, Random LB $17.99 (978-0-375-92274-9). 288pp. Lina and Doon work to find a way out of their isolated and decaying city, where the population is beginning to panic. (Rev: BL 4/15/03; HB 5/03; HBG 10/03; SLJ 5/03; VOYA 6/03)

11707 Enthoven, Sam. *Tim, Defender of the Earth* (5–8). 2008, Penguin $19.99 (978-1-59514-184-2). 288pp. Tim, a huge, T. rex-type fighting monster, breaks out of his underground lab to save London and the world from a crazy scientist — with the help of 14-year-old Anna and her friend Chris. (Rev: BL 1/1–15/08; SLJ 3/08)

11708 Etra, Jonathan, and Stephanie Spinner. *Aliens for Breakfast* (3–5). Illus. 1988, Random paper $3.99 (978-0-394-82093-4). 64pp. Richard meets an alien who needs help to find a secret weapon. (Rev: BCCB 12/88; BL 1/15/89; SLJ 3/89)

11709 Evans, Douglas. *The Classroom at the End of the Hall* (2–4). Illus. 1996, Front St. $14.95 (978-1-886910-07-2). 128pp. Typical third-graders have some atypical adventures in these 11 stories. (Rev: BCCB 9/96; BL 8/96; SLJ 10/96)

11710 Fields, Bryan W. *Lunchbox and the Aliens* (3–6). Illus. by Kevan Atteberry. 2006, Holt $16.95 (978-0-8050-7995-1). 185pp. Two dimwitted aliens — Frazz and Grunfloz — kidnap Lunchbox the basset hound and program him to convert garbage into food; a funny, complex story. (Rev: SLJ 10/06)

11711 Follett, Ken. *The Power Twins* (4–8). 1991, Scholastic paper $2.75 (978-0-590-42507-0). 90pp. Three youngsters travel to a planet where large, gentle worms live. (Rev: SLJ 1/91)

11712 Gaiman, Neil, and Michael Reaves. *InterWorld* (5–8). 2007, Eos $16.99 (978-0-06-123896-3). 256pp. Joey, 16, discovers that he can walk into alternate dimensions where he finds other versions of himself and is recruited into an army of Joeys that battles Lord Dogknife and Lady Indigo, two evil magicians. (Rev: BL 9/1/07; SLJ 11/07) 🎧

11713 Gilden, Mel. *Outer Space and All That Junk* (5–7). Illus. 1989, HarperCollins LB $12.89 (978-0-397-32307-4). 176pp. Myron's uncle is collecting junk, which he believes will help aliens return to their home in outer space. (Rev: BL 12/1/89; SLJ 12/89)

11714 Gormley, Beatrice. *Paul's Volcano* (4–6). Illus. 1988, Avon paper $2.50 (978-0-380-70562-7). 143pp. Adam and new kid Paul tangle over a science-fair volcano model that seems to have a mind of its own. (Rev: BL 5/15/87; SLJ 3/87)

11715 Gormley, Beatrice. *Wanted: UFO* (3–6). Illus. by Emily Arnold McCully. 1992, Avon paper $2.99 (978-0-380-71313-4). 128pp. Elise and Nick discover two aliens in the backyard. (Rev: BCCB 6/90; BL 7/90; SLJ 7/90)

11716 Greer, Gery, and Bob Ruddick. *Max and Me and the Wild West* (4–6). 1988, Harcourt $12.95 (978-0-15-253136-2). 138pp. Professor Flybender's time machine once more lands Steve and Max in the middle of an adventure — this time in 1882 Arizona Territory. (Rev: BL 2/15/88)

11717 Guibert, Emmanuel. *Sardine in Outer Space* (3–5). Trans. by Sasha Watson. Illus. by Joann Sfar. Series: Sardine in Outer Space. 2006, Roaring Brook paper $12.95 (978-1-59643-126-3). 128pp. In this comic book space fantasy, an import from France, a young girl named Sardine enlists the help of her cousin and uncle to foil the villainous plans of Supermuscleman. (Rev: BL 3/15/06; SLJ 7/06)

11718 Guibert, Emmanuel. *Sardine in Outer Space 2* (4–6). Illus. by Joann Sfar. Series: Sardine in Outer Space. 2006, Roaring Brook paper $12.95 (978-1-59643-127-0). 128pp. In the second volume of this graphic novel series, the redheaded Sardine and her fellow space pirates duel once again with the villainous — but slow-witted — Supermuscleman. (Rev: BL 9/1/06; SLJ 11/06)

11719 Guibert, Emmanuel, and Joann Sfar. *Sardine in Outer Space 3* (5–8). Trans. by Elisabeth Brizzi. Illus. 2007, Roaring Brook paper $12.95 (978-1-59643-128-7). 112pp. Sardine and her space-pirate friends tackle Supermuscleman among others in this series of zany adventures. Also use *Sardine in Outer Space 4* (2007). (Rev: BL 3/15/07; SLJ 7/07)

11720 Haarsma, P. J. *Betrayal on Orbis 2* (5–8). Series: The Softwire. 2008, Candlewick $16.99 (978-0-7636-2710-2). 304pp. This sequel to *Virus on Orbis I* finds JT and his friends enslaved to aquatic aliens called Samirans on a wormhole ring. (Rev: BL 5/15/08; SLJ 7/08)

11721 Haddix, Margaret P. *Among the Barons* (5–8). 2003, Simon & Schuster $16.95 (978-0-689-83906-1). 182pp. Luke, a third child who has been living underground in this two-child society, comes close to exposure in this exciting installment in the series that began with *Among the Hidden* (1998). (Rev: BL 5/15/03; HBG 10/03; SLJ 6/03; VOYA 8/03)

11722 Haddix, Margaret P. *Among the Betrayed* (5–9). 2002, Simon & Schuster $16.95 (978-0-689-83905-4). 160pp. In this third novel in the series that started with *Among the Hidden* (1998), illegal third child Nina faces danger and difficult decisions. (Rev: BCCB 10/02; HBG 10/02; SLJ 6/02; VOYA 6/02)

11723 Haddix, Margaret P. *Among the Enemy* (5–8). Series: Shadow Children. 2005, Simon & Schuster $15.95 (978-0-689-85796-6). 224pp. Matthias, one of the third children illegal in his society, is mistakenly welcomed into the Population Police; there he is confused by divided loyalties. (Rev: BL 6/1–15/05; SLJ 6/05)

11724 Haddix, Margaret P. *Among the Free* (5–8). Series: Shadow Children. 2006, Simon & Schuster $16.95 (978-0-689-85798-0). 208pp. Illegal third child Luke inadvertently sets off an uprising that leads to the overthrow of his country's oppressive government. (Rev: BL 6/1–15/06; SLJ 8/06)

11725 Haddix, Margaret P. *Among the Hidden* (5–8). 1998, Simon & Schuster $16.95 (978-0-689-81700-7). 154pp. In a society where only two children are allowed per family, Luke, the third, endures a secret life hidden from authorities. (Rev: HBG 3/99; SLJ 9/98; VOYA 10/98)

11726 Haddix, Margaret P. *Among the Impostors* (5–7). 2001, Simon & Schuster $16.00 (978-0-689-83904-7). 172pp. As a third child in a society that allows only two per family, Luke has assumed a new identity and at age 12 enrolls in a nightmarish boarding school. (Rev: BCCB 9/01; BL 4/15/01; HBG 10/01; SLJ 7/01; VOYA 8/01)

11727 Haddix, Margaret P. *Double Identity* (5–8). 2005, Simon & Schuster $15.95 (978-0-689-87374-4). 224pp. In this science fiction page-turner, 12-year-old Bethany Cole, left with her aunt after her mother suffers a nervous breakdown, uncovers some shocking family secrets. (Rev: BL 10/1/05; SLJ 11/05; VOYA 10/05)

11728 Heath, Jack. *The Lab* (5–8). 2008, Scholastic $17.99 (978-0-545-06860-4). 352pp. This action-packed thriller features a teen known as Agent Six of Hearts who was created in a lab using a variety of genes and works for an underground organization called The Deck. (Rev: BCCB 12/08; BL 12/1/08; LMC 1/09; SLJ 2/09)

11729 Heintze, Ty. *Valley of the Eels* (5–8). 1993, Eakin $15.95 (978-0-89015-904-0). A dolphin leads two boys to an underwater station where friendly aliens are cultivating trees to replant on their own planet. (Rev: BL 3/1/94)

11730 Hill, William. *The Magic Bicycle* (5–8). 1998, Otter Creek paper $13.95 (978-1-890611-00-2). 326pp. For helping an alien escape, Danny receives a magical bicycle that is capable of transporting him through time and space. (Rev: BL 1/1–15/98; SLJ 3/98)

11731 Hobbs, Will. *Go Big or Go Home* (5–8). 2008, HarperCollins $15.99 (978-0-06-074141-9). 192pp. A meteorite crashes into Brady's bedroom in South Dakota, and Brady soon finds that something in the space debris has changed him. (Rev: BL 4/1/08; HB 5/08; SLJ 4/08)

11732 Holt, K. A. *Mike Stellar: Nerves of Steel* (4–7). 2009, Random $15.99 (978-0-375-84556-7). 272pp. Mike's world is turned upside down when his parents make him move to Mars, and he discovers that they are part of a secret plot. (Rev: BLO 7/6/09)

11733 Johansen, K. V. *The Cassandra Virus* (5–8). 2006, Orca paper $7.95 (978-1-55143-497-1). 153pp. Computer geek Jordan designs a powerful computer program that takes on a life of its own, spreading via the Internet to other computers and taking control of their operations. (Rev: SLJ 11/06; VOYA 8/06)

11734 Kahn, Sharon. *Kacy and the Space Shuttle Secret: A Space Adventure for Young Readers* (4–6). Illus. by Mark Mitchell. 1996, Eakin $16.95 (978-1-57168-025-9). 128pp. An exciting science fiction adventure in which a young would-be scientist helps launch a space shuttle. (Rev: SLJ 4/96)

11735 Key, Alexander. *The Forgotten Door* (5–7). 1986, Scholastic paper $4.99 (978-0-590-43130-9). 144pp. When little Jon falls to earth from another planet, he encounters suspicion and hostility as well as sympathy. A reissue.

11736 Lee, Tanith. *Indigara* (4–7). 2007, Penguin $11.99 (978-0-14-240922-0). 192pp. Jet and her dog Otis encounter mindless celebrities in the underworld of Planet Obelisk in this humorous meeting of science fiction and pop culture. (Rev: BL 12/15/07; SLJ 12/07)

11737 Lennon, Joan. *Questors* (5–8). 2007, Simon & Schuster $16.99 (978-1-4169-3658-9). 359pp. When an energy leak threatens the existence of three separate worlds, three youthful half siblings — Bryn, Madlen, and Cam — find they bear a heavy responsibility. (Rev: BL 8/07; HB 1/08; LMC 1/08; SLJ 12/07)

11738 Lisle, Janet T. *Angela's Aliens* (4–6). Series: Unknown. 1996, Orchard LB $15.99 (978-0-531-08891-3). 128pp. Angela is abducted by mysterious aliens in the fourth and final volume of the Unknown series. (Rev: BL 11/1/96; SLJ 11/96)

11739 Lowenstein, Sallie. *Evan's Voice* (5–8). Illus. 1998, Lion Stone paper $15.00 (978-0-9658486-1-9). 187pp. Teenager Jake cares for his catatonic younger brother while seeking civilization's last chance for survival in an area known as the Dead Zone. (Rev: BL 3/1/99; VOYA 6/99)

11740 Lowenstein, Sallie. *Focus* (5–9). Illus. 2001, Lion Stone paper $15.00 (978-0-9658486-3-3). 284pp. The Haldrans leave their planet and relocate to Miners World, where humans live, in order to save their son from discrimination because of his creative intelligence. (Rev: BL 4/15/01; SLJ 8/01; VOYA 8/01)

11741 Luzzatto, Caroline. *Interplanetary Avenger* (4–6). 2005, Holiday House $16.95 (978-0-8234-1933-3). 120pp. Transported to a school on another planet after he opens a mysterious package, middle-schooler Sam must chase after a shape-shifting ne'er-do-well who is threatening Earth; full of gross humor and zany situations. (Rev: SLJ 12/05)

11742 Mackel, Kathy. *Alien in a Bottle* (4–8). 2004, HarperCollins LB $16.89 (978-0-06-029282-9). 208pp. An entertaining and action-packed novel in which 8th-grader Sean Winger, an aspiring glass-blower, mistakes an alien space ship for an ornate glass bottle and becomes swept up in intergalactic intrigue. (Rev: BL 5/1/04; SLJ 4/04)

11743 McKinty, Adrian. *The Lighthouse Land* (5–8). 2006, Abrams $16.95 (978-0-8109-5480-9). 388pp. In this first installment in an action-packed science fiction series, Jamie (a 13-year-old who is mute after losing his left arm to bone cancer) and his mother move to an Irish island, where he and a new friend discover an artifact that transports them to a far-off planet in time to help a girl named Wish-away. (Rev: BL 11/15/06; SLJ 1/07)

11744 McNamee, Eoin. *The Frost Child* (5–8). Illus. by Jon Goodell. Series: The Navigator. 2009, Random $15.99 (978-0-385-73563-6). 352pp. In this action-packed concluding volume to the trilogy the Navigator must once again rally the Resistors to battle against the Harsh. (Rev: BLO 4/24/09; SLJ 10/09)

11745 McNamee, Eoin. *The Navigator: Chosen to Save the World* (5–8). 2007, Random $15.99 (978-0-375-83910-8). 352pp. Owen finds himself suddenly in a different world where he and a girl named Cati must battle the Harsh, evil beings who freeze all that they touch and have set time running backward. (Rev: BL 12/1/06; SLJ 3/07)

11746 Meacham, Margaret. *Quiet! You're Invisible* (3–5). 2001, Holiday House $15.95 (978-0-8234-1651-6). 80pp. Fifth-grader Hoby is visited by a boy from the future and must outsmart the middle-school bully to retrieve a stolen part from his new friend's space cruiser. (Rev: BL 1/1–15/02; HBG 3/02; SLJ 11/01)

11747 Miller, Wiley. *The Extraordinary Adventures of Ordinary Basil: The Impossible Flight to Helios* (3–5). 2006, Scholastic $14.99 (978-0-439-85665-2). 128pp. When a man appears outside bored Basil's window in a floating balloon, he hops in and goes on an adventure to Helios, a secret city in the sky where he has exciting adventures in this well-illustrated book set in the late 19th century. (Rev: BL 2/15/07; SLJ 2/07)

11748 Nelson, Peter. *Herbert's Wormhole* (4–6). Illus. by Rohitash Rao. 2009, HarperCollins paper $12.99 (978-0-06-168868-3). 256pp. Superkids venture into the near future for some supremely silly fun. (Rev: BL 6/1–15/09)

11749 Philbrick, Rodman. *REM World* (4–6). 2000, Scholastic $16.95 (978-0-439-08362-1). 192pp. Ten-year-old Arthur gets stuck in the REM world when he tries to use a REM sleep machine to lose weight. (Rev: BCCB 6/00; BL 5/1/00; HBG 10/00; SLJ 5/00)

11750 Pierce, Tamora. *Street Magic* (5–9). Series: The Circle Opens. 2001, Scholastic paper $16.95 (978-0-590-39628-8). 304pp. Briar, a 14-year-old former gang member, finds he is again caught between warring gangs when he helps a female street urchin in this futuristic novel. (Rev: BL

4/15/01; HB 3/01; HBG 10/01; SLJ 7/01; VOYA 4/01)

11751 Powell, J. *Big Brother at School* (5–8). Illus. by Paul Savage. Series: Keystone Books. 2006, Stone Arch LB $21.26 (978-1-59889-091-4). 33pp. At a school where cameras watch students' every move, Lee becomes convinced that the principal and a visiting doctor are aliens and takes step to save his fellow students from abduction. (Rev: SLJ 1/07)

11752 Reeve, Philip. *Larklight, or, The Revenge of the White Spiders!, or, To Saturn's Rings and Back!* (5–8). Illus. by David Wyatt. 2006, Bloomsbury $16.95 (978-1-59990-020-9). 384pp. Art and Myrtle Mumby, who live with their father in a Victorian mansion orbiting the earth, become embroiled in a plot to destroy the solar system; a science fiction romp with a touch of romance and a dollop of Victorian manners. (Rev: BCCB 2/07; BL 10/1/06; HB 11/06; HBG 4/07; LMC 1/07; SLJ 11/06*; VOYA 12/06)

11753 Reeve, Philip. *Mothstorm* (5–8). Illus. by David Wyatt. 2008, Bloomsbury $16.99 (978-1-59990-303-3). 320pp. All is calm and all is bright as the Mumbys gather to celebrate Christmas but new threats soon arise, involving a cloud of giant moths and an evil Shaper. (Rev: BLO 4/9/09; HB 1/09; SLJ 12/08)

11754 Reeve, Philip. *Starcross* (5–8). Illus. by David Wyatt. 2007, Bloomsbury $16.95 (978-1-59990-121-3). 320pp. Starcross is the name of the asteroid belt hotel where Art, Myrtle, and their mother go for a holiday that turns into a strange journey through time; the sequel to *Larklight* (2006). (Rev: BL 11/1/07; HB 1/08; SLJ 12/07)

11755 Regan, Dian C. *Princess Nevermore* (5–7). 1995, Scholastic $14.95 (978-0-590-47582-2). 232pp. A princess from another world gets her wish to visit Earth, where she is befriended by two teenagers, Sarah and Adam. (Rev: BCCB 11/95; SLJ 9/95)

11756 Reisman, Michael. *Simon Bloom, the Gravity Keeper* (4–7). 2008, Dutton $15.99 (978-0-525-47922-2). 256pp. When a book teaches 11-year-old Simon how to control gravity, velocity, friction, and other physical properties; magic, adventure, and suspense ensue. (Rev: BL 3/1/08; SLJ 4/08)

11757 Reisman, Michael. *Simon Bloom, The Octopus Effect* (4–6). 2009, Dutton $16.99 (978-0-525-42082-8). 304pp. Twelve-year-old Simon, fortified by octopus DNA and with the help of friends, fights to squash the evil Sirabetta's plans for world domination in this sequel to *Simon Bloom, the Gravity Keeper*. (Rev: BLO 1/7/09; LMC 5/09) ∩

11758 Rex, Adam. *The True Meaning of Smekday* (5–8). 2007, Hyperion $16.99 (978-0-7868-4900-0). 432pp. Gratuity (called Tip) resents having to write an essay about the day aliens took over America in this funny and visually engaging story. (Rev: BL 10/1/07; HB 11/07; LMC 1/08; SLJ 11/07)

11759 Schmid, Susan Maupin. *Lost Time* (5–8). 2008, Philomel $16.99 (978-0-399-24460-5). 176pp. On the sparsely populated planet Lindos, Violynne searches for her lost parents while living

with her aunt Madelyn. (Rev: BL 5/15/08; SLJ 9/08)

11760 Schooley, Bob, and Mark McCorkle. *Liar of Kudzu* (4–6). 2007, Simon & Schuster $15.99 (978-1-4169-1488-4). 183pp. Pete (who is known as Liar), Justine, and Bobby Ray discover a crashed UFO that holds information about the future and must decide what to do. (Rev: SLJ 5/07)

11761 Scieszka, Jon. *See You Later, Gladiator* (4–6). Illus. 2000, Viking $14.99 (978-0-670-89340-9). 80pp. The three members of the Time Warp Trio travel back to ancient Rome, where they attend gladiator school and fight in the Colosseum in this hilarious spoof. (Rev: BL 1/1–15/01; HBG 3/01; SLJ 11/00)

11762 Scrimger, Richard. *A Nose for Adventure* (3–6). 2001, Tundra paper $6.95 (978-0-88776-499-8). 184pp. After meeting on a plane to New York City, 13-year-old Alan and sassy, wheelchair-bound Frieda get involved in a smuggling plot at the airport and encounter Norbert, a small alien from Jupiter. (Rev: BL 2/15/01)

11763 Scrimger, Richard. *The Nose from Jupiter* (5–8). 1998, Tundra paper $5.95 (978-0-88776-428-8). Alan doesn't mind that Norbert, an alien from Jupiter, is living in his nose, but Norbert's outspoken remarks often get Alan into trouble. Also use *The Boy from Earth* (2004). (Rev: BL 7/98)

11764 Service, Pamela F. *Stinker from Space* (3–6). 1988, Macmillan $12.95 (978-0-684-18910-9); Fawcett paper $5.50 (978-0-449-70330-4). 96pp. When his spaceship crashes to earth, Tsyng Tyr from the Sylon Confederacy takes over the body of a skunk. (Rev: BL 3/1/88; HB 9/88)

11765 Simmons, Michael. *Alien Feast* (5–8). Illus. by George O'Connor. Series: Chronicles of the First Invasion. 2009, Roaring Brook $15.95 (978-1-59643-281-9). 240pp. Aliens have invaded Earth in 2017 and 12-year-old William, who has already faced many adversities in his life, joins up with his friend Sophie and Uncle Maynard to try to rescue Sophie's parents; humor, action, and science fiction conventions add to the drama. (Rev: BCCB 7–8/08; BL 5/15/09; HB 5/09; LMC 5/08; SLJ 8/08)

11766 Simons, Jamie, and E. W. Scollon. *Goners: The Hunt Is On* (4–7). Illus. 1998, Avon paper $3.99 (978-0-380-79730-1). 150pp. Four alien teens from the planet Roma time-travel to Monticello to fetch Thomas Jefferson. (Rev: BL 5/15/98)

11767 Skurzynski, Gloria. *The Choice* (5–8). Series: The Virtual War Chronologs. 2006, Simon & Schuster $16.95 (978-0-689-84267-2). 228pp. In the fast-paced concluding installment in the series, 16-year-old Corgan has a final confrontation with the murderous Brigand. (Rev: SLJ 10/06)

11768 Slote, Alfred. *My Robot Buddy* (5–8). Illus. 1986, HarperCollins $12.95 (978-0-397-31641-0). An easily read novel about Danny and the robot that is created for him. (Rev: BL 11/1/87)

11769 Stevenson, Robert Louis. *The Strange Case of Dr. Jekyll and Mr. Hyde* (5–8). Illus. Series: Whole Story. 2003, Barnes & Noble paper $3.95 (978-1-59308-054-9). 112pp. Using lively ink-and-watercolor illustrations, this book offers the complete text of the classic in an attractive format. (Rev: BL 5/1/00; HBG 10/00)

11770 Thompson, Kate. *Fourth World* (5–8). Series: Missing Link. 2005, Bloomsbury $16.95 (978-1-58234-650-2). 320pp. Christie and his older step-brother Danny go from Ireland to Scotland, where they discover strange developments at Fourth World, the compound where Danny's scientist mother lives and works, in this first volume of a trilogy. (Rev: BL 5/15/05; SLJ 10/05)

11771 Voake, Steve. *The Web of Fire* (5–8). Illus. by Mark Watkinson. 2007, Bloomsbury $17.95 (978-1-58234-737-0). 318pp. Sam and Skipper are back with new adventures and gadgetry in this fast-paced sequel to *The Dreamwalker's Child* (2006). (Rev: SLJ 6/07)

11772 Walsh, Jill Paton. *The Green Book* (4–7). Illus. by Lloyd Bloom. 1982, Farrar paper $4.95 (978-0-374-42802-0). 80pp. The exodus of a group of Britons from dying Earth to another planet.

11773 Wells, H. G. *The Time Machine* (3–5). Adapted by Les Martin. Illus. by John Edens. 1990, Random paper $3.99 (978-0-679-80371-3). 93pp. A clever adaptation of a classic science fiction story about a time traveler and his friends. (Rev: SLJ 4/91)

11774 Whitman, John. *Star Wars: The Death Star* (2–5). Illus. by Barbara Gibson. 1997, Little, Brown $15.95 (978-0-316-93592-0). 12pp. Action-packed science fiction is featured in this pop-up book. Also use *Millennium Falcon* (1997). (Rev: BL 12/15/97)

11775 Yolen, Jane, et al., eds. *Spaceships and Spells* (5–9). 1987, HarperCollins $12.95 (978-0-06-026796-4). A collection of 13 original tales, mostly science fiction but also some fantasy. (Rev: BL 1/15/88; SLJ 11/87)

11776 Zakour, John. *Baxter Moon: Galactic Scout* (4–7). 2008, Brown Barn paper $8.95 (978-0-9768126-9-2). 208pp. Baxter and his crew travel through space to rescue an Aquarian ship from robotic aliens in this entertaining romp. (Rev: BL 5/15/08; SLJ 6/08)

Short Stories and Anthologies

11777 Asher, Sandy, and David L. Harrison, eds. *Dude! Stories and Stuff for Boys* (4–7). 2006, Dutton $17.99 (978-0-525-47684-9). 224pp. Selections for boys — poems, short stories, and other works — offer diverse experiences; authors include Sneed B. Collard III, Clyde Robert Bulla, Jane Yolen, and Ron Koertge. (Rev: BL 7/06; HBG 4/07; LMC 1/07; SLJ 8/06; VOYA 12/06)

11778 Avi, sel. *Best Shorts: Favorite Short Stories for Sharing* (5–9). Ed. by Carolyn Shute. Illus. by Chris Raschka. 2006, Houghton $16.95 (978-0-618-47603-9). 397pp. The 24 short stories in this anthology provide a sampling of some of the best writing in a wide variety of genres. (Rev: SLJ 10/06)

11779 *The Big Book of Horror: 21 Tales to Make You Tremble* (5–7). Illus. by Pedro Rodriguez. 2007, Sterling $12.95 (978-1-4027-3860-9). 112pp. This collection of 21 horror tales includes stories by Edgar Allan Poe, Charles Dickens, Robert Louis Stevenson, and H. P. Lovecraft. (Rev: BL 3/15/07; SLJ 7/07)

11780 Bruchac, Joseph, et al. *Lay-ups and Long Shots* (4–6). 2008, Darby Creek $15.95 (978-1-58196-078-5). 112pp. A collection of nine short stories featuring a wide range of sports and appealing young people who play them. (Rev: BL 9/15/08)

11781 Canfield, Jack, et al., eds. *Chicken Soup for the Kid's Soul: 101 Stories of Courage, Hope and Laughter* (4–7). 1998, Health Communications paper $14.95 (978-1-55874-609-1). 396pp. A collection of inspiring true stories, some by well-known people, but mostly by children who sent them to the editors. (Rev: BL 9/1/98; HBG 3/99) [158.1]

11782 Canfield, Jack, et al., eds. *Chicken Soup for the Preteen Soul: 101 Stories of Changes, Choices and Growing Up for Kids Ages 9–13* (5–7). Illus. 2000, Health Communications $24.00 (978-1-55874-801-9); paper $14.95 (978-1-55874-800-2). 386pp. The usual mix of verse and prose written by and for preteens, with the aim of offering inspiration, comfort, and practical advice. (Rev: HBG 10/01; SLJ 4/01) [158.1]

11783 Carus, Marianne, ed. *Fire and Wings: Dragon Tales from East and West* (3–6). Illus. by Nilesh Mistry. 2002, Cricket $17.95 (978-0-8126-2664-3). 146pp. A collection of 15 stories, most of which have appeared in *Cricket* magazine, about all kinds of dragons, by authors including Jane Yolen, Patricia MacLachlan, Eric A. Kimmel, Vida Chu, and E. Nesbit. (Rev: HBG 3/03; SLJ 12/02)

11784 Crebbin, June, ed. *Horse Tales* (4–7). Illus. by Inga Moore. 2005, Candlewick $18.99 (978-0-7636-2657-0). 152pp. Diverse short stories about horses, with color illustrations. (Rev: BL 9/1/05; SLJ 8/05)

11785 Davis, Donald. *Mama Learns to Drive and Other Stories: Stories of Love, Humor, and Wisdom* (4–7). 2005, August House $17.95 (978-0-87483-745-2). 119pp. Brief, slow-paced short stories based on his mother, who grew up in the Smoky Mountains in the 1930s, are mixed with tales about the author's own youth in the 1950s. (Rev: BL 8/05; SLJ 10/05)

11786 Editors of McSweeney's. *Noisy Outlaws, Unfriendly Blobs, and Some Other Things* (4–7). Illus. 2005, McSweeney's $22.00 (978-1-932416-35-0). 208pp. Kid-friendly stories by well-known authors including Nick Hornby, Neil Gaiman, and Jon Scieskza. (Rev: BL 9/1/05)

11787 Evans, Douglas. *Mouth Moths: More Classroom Tales* (2–4). Illus. by Larry Di Fiori. 2006, Front St. $15.95 (978-1-932425-23-9). 112pp. The short stories in this collection showcase eccentric students in a third grade classroom. (Rev: BL 11/1/06; SLJ 11/06)

11788 Gac-Artigas, Alejandro. *Off to Catch the Sun* (5–8). 2001, Ediciones Nuevo Espacio paper $11.95

(978-1-930879-28-7). 148pp. Thirteen-year-old author Gac-Artigas explores serious issues through poetry, essays, and short stories. (Rev: BL 1/1–15/02)

11789 Hart, Sue. *Tales of the Full Moon* (2–4). Illus. by Chris Harvey. 2006, Fulcrum $16.95 (978-1-55591-582-7). 93pp. Facts about African animals are interwoven into folktale-like stories told by Spinosa the spider. (Rev: BL 7/06)

11790 Hearne, Betsy. *Hauntings and Other Tales of Danger, Love, and Sometimes Loss* (5–8). 2007, Greenwillow $15.99 (978-0-06-123910-6). 224pp. A collection of 15 eerie stories set in the past (mostly in Ireland), in the present (mostly America), and in the hereafter (mostly Heaven and Hell). (Rev: BL 8/07; LMC 10/07; SLJ 11/07)

11791 Highlights for Children, eds. *Ashanti Festival* (3–5). 1996, Boyds Mills paper $3.95 (978-1-56397-608-7). 96pp. Sixteen excellent short stories taken from the pages of *Highlights for Children*. (Rev: SLJ 1/97)

11792 Hoffman, Mary. *The Barefoot Book of Brother and Sister Tales* (2–5). Illus. 2000, Barefoot Books $19.99 (978-1-84148-029-9). 63pp. An anthology of uplifting original stories about children who suffer hardships resulting from such problems as cruel queens, witches, and stepmothers. (Rev: BL 11/15/00; HBG 3/01; SLJ 1/01)

11793 Hollander, John, ed. *O. Henry* (5–8). Illus. by Miles Hyman. 2006, Sterling $14.95 (978-1-4027-0988-3). 80pp. A collection of seven O. Henry short stories, including "The Gift of the Magi," with helpful introductions before each story. (Rev: BL 4/15/06; SLJ 5/06)

11794 Holt, Kimberly Willis. *Part of Me: Stories of a Louisiana Family* (5–8). 2006, Holt $16.95 (978-0-8050-6360-8). 224pp. Reading is the thread that links this collection of short stories that spans four generations of a Louisiana family, from 1939 to the early 21st century. (Rev: BL 9/1/06; SLJ 9/06)

11795 Jocelyn, Marthe, sel. *Secrets* (5–8). 2005, Tundra paper $8.95 (978-0-88776-723-4). 175pp. A collection of 12 short stories that reveal the importance of secrets. (Rev: SLJ 2/06)

11796 Kantor, Susan, ed. *One-Hundred-and-One African-American Read-Aloud Stories* (3–8). 1998, Black Dog & Leventhal $12.98 (978-1-57912-039-9). 416pp. This book includes folktales, excerpts from novels, biographies, and history books, plus a sampling of songs, poetry, and chants all about African Americans and their heritage. (Rev: SLJ 6/99)

11797 Lubar, David. *The Battle of the Red Hot Pepper Weenies and Other Warped and Creepy Tales* (4–7). 2009, Tor $15.95 (978-0-7653-2099-5). 192pp. A collection of 35 varied short stories with something for everyone — humor, horror, science fiction, suspense. (Rev: BLO 3/5/09; SLJ 5/09)

11798 Lubar, David. *Invasion of the Road Weenies and Other Warped and Creepy Tales* (4–7). 2005, Tor $16.95 (978-0-7653-1447-5). 192pp. Entertaining stories about how things don't always work out how you hope or expect; suitable for reluctant readers. (Rev: BL 8/05; SLJ 9/05; VOYA 10/05)

11799 McCall Smith, Alexander. *The Perfect Hamburger and Other Delicious Stories* (3–5). Illus. by Laura Rankin. 2007, Bloomsbury $15.95 (978-1-59990-134-3). 288pp. Three entertaining stories revolving around food and children's creative efforts to solve problems were previously published in Britain. (Rev: BL 10/15/07; LMC 1/08; SLJ 10/07)

11800 Maccaulay, David. *Black and White* (2–6). Illus. 1990, Houghton $17.00 (978-0-395-52151-9). 32pp. With thought-provoking illustrations, four short stories are presented. Caldecott Medal winner, 1991. (Rev: BCCB 5/90; BL 4/1/90*; HB 9/90)

11801 McKissack, Patricia C. *Porch Lies: Tales of Slicksters, Tricksters, and Other Wily Characters* (3–5). Illus. by Andre Carrilho. 2006, Random $18.95 (978-0-375-83619-0). 160pp. Ten funny and spooky original stories full of bad characters are based on stories McKissack heard on her grandparents' porch. (Rev: BCCB 10/06; BL 5/15/06; HB 9/06; HBG 4/07; LMC 1/07; SLJ 9/06)

11802 Martin, Ann M., and David Levithan, eds. *Friends: Stories About New Friends, Old Friends, and Unexpectedly True Friends* (4–6). 2005, Scholastic $16.95 (978-0-439-72991-8). 208pp. The many faces of friendship are reflected in this collection of short stories by such well-known authors as Meg Cabot, Pam Muñoz Ryan, and Brian Selznick. (Rev: BL 11/15/05; SLJ 1/06)

11803 Mazer, Anne, ed. *America Street: A Multicultural Anthology of Stories* (5–8). 1993, Persea paper $7.95 (978-0-89255-191-0). Fourteen short stories about growing up in America's diverse society by Robert Cormier, Langston Hughes, Grace Paley, Gary Soto, and others. (Rev: BCCB 11/93; BL 9/1/93; SLJ 11/93; VOYA 12/93)

11804 Morpurgo, Michael, comp. *The Kingfisher Book of Great Boy Stories: A Treasury of Classics from Children's Literature* (4–8). Illus. 2000, Kingfisher $19.95 (978-0-7534-5320-9). 160pp. An attractively illustrated collection of stories from authors including Carlo Collodi, Roald Dahl, Ted Hughes, C. S. Lewis, A. A. Milne, Donald Sobol, and Mark Twain. (Rev: HBG 10/01; SLJ 4/01)

11805 Oldfield, Jenny, comp. *The Kingfisher Book of Horse and Pony Stories* (4–7). Illus. 2005, Kingfisher $16.95 (978-0-7534-5850-1). 127pp. The special relationship between horses and humans is celebrated in this collection of 12 contemporary, fantasy, and historical short stories. (Rev: SLJ 12/05)

11806 Olson, Arielle North, and Howard Schwartz. *More Bones: Scary Stories from Around the World* (4–7). Illus. by E. M. Gist. 2008, Viking $15.99 (978-0-670-06339-0). 176pp. This collection of 22 retellings of scary stories from around the world features witches and wizards, corpses and ghosts, and lots of unexpected twists. (Rev: BL 10/1/08; SLJ 9/08)

11807 Paulsen, Gary, ed. *Shelf Life: Stories by the Book* (4–7). 2003, Simon & Schuster $16.95 (978-0-689-84180-4). 192pp. Books are the stars of these 10 stories by well-known authors that show that reading can change lives. (Rev: BL 8/03; HBG 4/04; SLJ 8/03; VOYA 8/03)

11808 Peck, Richard. *Past Perfect, Present Tense* (5–12). 2004, Dial $16.99 (978-0-8037-2998-8). 192pp. This anthology includes 11 previously published stories and two new ones, with comments on each story's inspiration and tips on writing fiction. (Rev: BL 4/1/04; HB 3/04; SLJ 4/04; VOYA 6/04)

11809 Sandberg, Rosemary, ed. *Great Girl Stories: A Treasury of Classics from Children's Literature* (4–6). Illus. 1999, Kingfisher $18.95 (978-0-7534-5207-3). 160pp. A lavish gift book containing excerpts from 16 stories with central girl characters, including *Heidi, Anne of Green Gables,* and *The Great Gilly Hopkins.* (Rev: BL 10/15/99; HBG 3/00; SLJ 12/99)

11810 Schulman, Janet, sel. *You Read to Me and I'll Read to You: 20th-Century Stories to Share* (K–3). 2001, Knopf $34.95 (978-0-375-81083-1). 250pp. A selection of stories for beginning readers by authors including Judy Blume, Roald Dahl, Astrid Lindgren, Louis Sachar, and Wiliam Steig. (Rev: HBG 3/02; SLJ 12/01)

11811 Spiegelman, Art, and Francoise Mouly, eds. *Little Lit: Strange Stories for Strange Kids* (4–9). Illus. 2001, HarperCollins paper $19.95 (978-0-06-028626-2). 64pp. This collection of offbeat, imaginative, graphic stories includes something for everyone, from humor to fantasy to horror, from Maurice Sendak to David Sedaris. (Rev: BL 12/15/01; HB 1/02; HBG 3/02; SLJ 3/02)

11812 *Sports Shorts* (4–7). 2005, Darby Creek $15.99 (978-1-58196-040-2). 128pp. Eight writers contribute "semi-autobiographical" tales about their sporting achievements at school, many humorously revealing failings rather than triumphs. (Rev: BL 9/1/05; SLJ 11/05)

Sports Stories

11813 Adler, David A. *Mama Played Baseball* (K–3). Illus. by Chris O'Leary. 2003, Harcourt $16.00 (978-0-15-202196-2). Amy and her mother grow closer when Mama starts playing in the first women's pro baseball league during the early 1940s. (Rev: HBG 10/03; SLJ 4/03)

11814 Alvord, Douglas. *Sarah's Boat: A Young Girl Learns the Art of Sailing* (3–6). Illus. 1994, Tilbury House $16.95 (978-0-88448-117-1). 44pp. Sarah learns how to sail from her grandfather and enters her *Bluejay* sloop in the Labor Day race. (Rev: BL 7/94)

11815 Auch, Mary Jane. *Angel and Me and the Bayside Bombers* (2–4). Illus. by Cat B. Smith. 1989, Little, Brown $9.95 (978-0-316-05914-5); paper $2.95 (978-0-316-05915-2). 60pp. A poor soccer player, Brian bribes his way onto the team. (Rev: BL 1/15/90; HB 3/90; SLJ 3/90)

11816 Barwin, Steven. *Icebreaker* (4–8). Series: Sports Stories. 2007, Lorimer paper $7.95 (978-1-55028-950-3). 128pp. Hockey fans will love this book featuring Greg, a junior high school hockey player whose year gets complicated when his stepsister tries out for the team. (Rev: SLJ 7/07)

11817 Barwin, Steven, and Gabriel David Tick. *Slam Dunk* (5–7). Series: Sports Stories. 1999, Orca paper $5.50 (978-1-55028-598-7). 88pp. An easy read about a junior high basketball team in Canada that goes coed and the problems that result. (Rev: SLJ 1/00)

11818 Bates, Cynthia. *Shooting Star* (4–6). Series: Sports Stories. 2001, Lorimer paper $5.50 (978-1-55028-726-4). 102pp. Eight-grader Quyen Ha, who was a basketball star at her middle school, has some reservations about her decision to join a bantam team in this novel set in Canada that has information on Vietnamese family life. (Rev: SLJ 1/02)

11819 Bildner, Phil. *The Greatest Game Ever Played* (1–3). Illus. by Zachary Pullen. 2006, Putnam $16.99 (978-0-399-24171-0). 40pp. The legendary 1958 NFL championship game between the New York Giants and the Baltimore Colts comes to life in this appealing story about a father and son struggling to adjust to the loss of their hometown baseball team. (Rev: BL 9/1/06; SLJ 8/06)

11820 Bledsoe, Lucy Jane. *The Big Bike Race* (2–4). 1995, Holiday House $15.95 (978-0-8234-1206-8). 80pp. Though disappointed that he did not receive the bike of his dreams for his birthday, Ernie trains for the Citywide Cup race. (Rev: BCCB 12/95; BL 10/1/95; SLJ 11/95)

11821 Bledsoe, Lucy Jane. *Hoop Girlz* (5–7). 2002, Holiday $16.95 (978-0-8234-1691-2). 128pp. When 11-year-old River is denied a place on the girls' basketball team, she forms her own team, with her brother as the coach. (Rev: BL 9/1/02; HBG 10/03; SLJ 12/02)

11822 Bo, Ben. *The Edge* (5–8). 1999, Lerner LB $14.95 (978-0-8225-3307-8). 139pp. Conflicted Declan is sent to a rehabilitation program in Canada's Glacier National Park, where he learns to snowboard and is drawn into a duel with the local champion. (Rev: BCCB 1/00; BL 10/15/99; HBG 3/00; SLJ 1/00; VOYA 4/00)

11823 Bowen, Fred. *The Final Cut* (4–7). Illus. by Ann Barrow. Series: AllStar Sport Story. 1999, Peachtree paper $4.95 (978-1-56145-192-0). 102pp. A fast-paced novel about four friends and their efforts to make the junior high school basketball team. (Rev: SLJ 7/99)

11824 Bowen, Fred. *Full Court Fever* (3–6). Illus. by Ann Barrow. Series: AllStar Sport Story. 1998, Peachtree paper $4.95 (978-1-56145-160-9). 103pp. Michael and the rest of the seventh-grade basketball team are fearful about the coming match against the eighth graders. (Rev: SLJ 12/98)

11825 Bowen, Fred. *On the Line* (4–7). Illus. by Ann Barrow. 1999, Peachtree paper $4.95 (978-1-56145-199-9). 103pp. A young boy learns about self-image and open-mindedness while trying to improve his foul shots in this novel about an 8th grader and his basketball skills. (Rev: SLJ 4/00)

11826 Bowen, Fred. *Playoff Dreams* (3–5). Illus. 1997, Peachtree paper $4.95 (978-1-56145-155-5).

112pp. When Brendan begins to feel that he is the only salvation open to his baseball team, Uncle Jack steps in with some good advice. (Rev: BL 11/1/97; SLJ 3/98)

11827 Bowen, Fred. *T.J.'s Secret Pitch* (3–5). Illus. by Jim Thorpe. Series: AllStar Sport Story. 1996, Peachtree paper $4.95 (978-1-56145-119-7). 104pp. A young Little Leaguer copies the famous pitch of the legendary Truett "Rip" Sewell and achieves fame. (Rev: SLJ 7/96)

11828 Bowen, Fred. *Winners Take All* (3–7). Illus. by Paul Casale. 2000, Peachtree paper $4.95 (978-1-56145-229-3). 104pp. Twelve-year-old Kyle eventually confesses to faking a catch in this story that includes discussion of Christy Mathewson, a pro pitcher in the early 1900s who was admired for his sportsmanship. (Rev: SLJ 4/01)

11829 Brooks, Bruce. *Dooby* (5–8). Series: Wolfbay Wings. 1998, HarperCollins LB $14.89 (978-0-06-027898-4); paper $4.50 (978-0-06-440708-3). Dooby sulks when he is not made captain of his Peewee hockey team, but is completely humiliated to learn he has lost out to a girl. Also recommended in this series is *Reed* (1998). (Rev: HBG 3/99; SLJ 2/99)

11830 Brooks, Bruce. *Prince* (5–8). Series: Wolfbay Wings. 1998, HarperCollins paper $4.50 (978-0-06-440600-0). 122pp. Prince, the only African American boy on the Wolfbay Wings hockey team, is pressured by his middle school coach to switch to basketball. (Rev: HBG 10/98; SLJ 6/98)

11831 Brooks, Bruce. *Reed* (5–8). Series: Wolfbay Wings. 1998, HarperCollins LB $14.89 (978-0-06-028055-0). 128pp. Reed, a member of the Wolfbay Wings hockey team, is considered a "puck-hog" and must learn to be more of a team player. (Rev: HBG 3/99; SLJ 2/99)

11832 Brooks, Bruce. *Shark* (5–8). Series: Wolfbay Wings. 1998, HarperCollins LB $14.89 (978-0-06-027570-9); paper $4.50 (978-0-06-440681-9). In spite of being fat, slow, and confused, Shark becomes a valuable player on the Wolfbay Wings hockey team. (Rev: HBG 10/98; SLJ 6/98)

11833 Bruchac, Joseph. *The Warriors* (5–8). 2003, Darby Creek $15.95 (978-1-58196-002-0). 192pp. Jake Forrest, a Native American teenager and lacrosse whiz, leaves the reservation to attend a private school and encounters many new situations, including a different attitude toward sports. (Rev: BL 12/1/03; HBG 10/01; SLJ 10/03)

11834 Bunting, Eve. *Snowboarding on Monster Mountain* (4–6). Illus. by Karen Ritz. 2003, Cricket $15.95 (978-0-8126-2704-6). 80pp. Facing her fear of heights and her worries about new girl Izzy, 11-year-old Callie agrees to go snowboarding with her best friend Jen. (Rev: BL 1/1–15/04; HBG 4/04; SLJ 1/04)

11835 Butcher, Kristin. *Cairo Kelly and the Man* (4–8). 2002, Orca paper $6.95 (978-1-55143-211-3). 176pp. When Midge discovers that his baseball team's umpire, Hal Mann, is illiterate, Midge and his friend Kelly set out to solve the problem. (Rev: BL 9/1/02; VOYA 4/03)

11836 Butler, Dori. *Sliding into Home* (5–8). 2003, Peachtree $14.95 (978-1-56145-222-4). 192pp. Joelle, 13, refuses to acccpt a ban on girls playing baseball when she moves to a small town in Iowa. (Rev: BL 5/1/03; HBG 10/03; SLJ 1/04)

11837 Christopher, Matt. *Baseball Turnaround* (4–6). 1977, Little, Brown paper $4.50 (978-0-316-14264-9). 160pp. After Sandy has had a brush with the law, he tries to keep this part of his past a secret from his teammates. (Rev: BL 6/1–15/97; SLJ 8/97)

11838 Christopher, Matt. *The Comeback Challenge* (4–6). Illus. 1996, Little, Brown paper $4.50 (978-0-316-14152-9). 160pp. Twelve-year-old Mark has problems with Vince, the captain of his soccer team. (Rev: BL 1/1–15/96; SLJ 1/96)

11839 Christopher, Matt. *Dirt Bike Racer* (3–5). Illus. by Barry Bomzer. 1986, Little, Brown paper $4.50 (978-0-316-14053-9). Ron finds a bike at the bottom of a lake and begins dirt bike racing. Another sports story from the same author is: *Dirt Bike Runaway* (1989).

11840 Christopher, Matt. *The Dog That Pitched a No-Hitter* (2–4). Illus. by Daniel Vasconcellos. 1993, Little, Brown paper $3.95 (978-0-316-14103-1). 42pp. Mike's dog Harry has powers of ESP and helps Mike with his pitching game. (Rev: BL 5/15/88; SLJ 8/88)

11841 Christopher, Matt. *The Hit-Away Kid* (2–5). Illus. 1988, Little, Brown paper $4.50 (978-0-316-14007-2). 55pp. Barry McGee, left fielder for the Peach Street Mudders, learns a lesson in sportsmanship and telling the truth. Two other baseball stories are: *Supercharged Infield* (1985); *The Spy on Third Base* (1988). (Rev: BCCB 5/88; BL 4/1/88; SLJ 5/88)

11842 Christopher, Matt. *Mountain Bike Mania* (5–7). 1998, Little, Brown paper $4.50 (978-0-316-14292-2). 160pp. Will is at loose ends with no after-school activities until he becomes involved in a mountain bike club. (Rev: BL 2/1/99; HBG 10/99; SLJ 3/99)

11843 Christopher, Matt. *Penalty Shot* (3–5). Illus. 1997, Little, Brown paper $3.95 (978-0-316-14190-1). 134pp. Kevin is thrown off the hockey team for bad grades but is determined to get back on. (Rev: BL 1/1–15/97; SLJ 2/97)

11844 Christopher, Matt. *Prime-Time Pitcher* (4–7). 1998, Little, Brown paper $4.50 (978-0-316-14213-7). 138pp. Koby Caplin becomes arrogant about his winning streak on the baseball team and soon loses games because of his lack of teamwork. (Rev: HBG 3/99; SLJ 12/98)

11845 Christopher, Matt. *Red-Hot Hightops* (4–6). Illus. 1992, Little, Brown paper $4.50 (978-0-316-14089-8). 128pp. Shyness prevents Kelly from showing off her basketball skills or speaking to a boy she likes until she finds a pair of red sneakers in her locker. (Rev: BL 1/15/88)

11846 Christopher, Matt. *Return of the Home Run Kid* (4–7). Illus. by Paul Casale. 1994, Little, Brown paper $4.50 (978-0-316-14273-1). 176pp. In this sequel to *The Kid Who Only Hit Homers* (1972), Sylvester learns to be more aggressive on the field but gets criticism from his friends. (Rev: BL 4/15/92; SLJ 5/92)

11847 Christopher, Matt. *Snowboard Maverick* (4–7). 1997, Little, Brown paper $4.50 (978-0-316-14203-8). 152pp. Dennis overcomes his fears and begins snowboarding. (Rev: BL 4/1/98; HBG 3/98; SLJ 3/98)

11848 Christopher, Matt. *Soccer Halfback* (4–6). Illus. by Larry Johnson. 1985, Little, Brown paper $4.50 (978-0-316-13981-6). Everyone wants Jabber to play football, but his favorite sport is soccer.

11849 Clare, Cassandra. *Toby Wheeler: Eighth-Grade Bench Warmer* (5–8). 2007, Delacorte $14.99 (978-0-385-73390-8). 208pp. Toby, an 8th-grader, joins the basketball team to be closer to his best friend but find himself stuck on the bench, the 12th man. (Rev: BL 9/1/07; SLJ 9/07)

11850 Clippinger, Carol. *Open Court* (5–8). 2007, Knopf $15.99 (978-0-375-84049-4). 262pp. Thirteen-year-old Holloway ("Hall") is only 13 but must deal with the pressures of competitive tennis as well as everyday stresses of being a teenager. (Rev: SLJ 7/07)

11851 Cohen, Barbara. *Thank You, Jackie Robinson* (4–6). Illus. by Richard Cuffari. 1989, Scholastic paper $3.99 (978-0-590-42378-6). A memoir written by Sam about his friendship with an old man and his devotion as a boy to the Brooklyn Dodgers and Ebbets Field.

11852 Corbett, Sue. *Free Baseball* (4–7). 2006, Dutton $15.99 (978-0-525-47120-2). 152pp. An endearing 11-year-old called Felix, who loves baseball and is annoyed that his mother won't tell him more about his Cuban outfielder father, is thrilled when he gets the chance to be batboy for a minor league Florida team. (Rev: BCCB 2/06; SLJ 2/06; VOYA 4/06)

11853 Coy, John. *Around the World* (1–4). Illus. by Antonio Reonegro and Tom Lynch. 2005, Lee & Low $17.95 (978-1-58430-244-5). A fast-paced game of basketball moves from one location to another around the world; the art adds to the energy. (Rev: SLJ 1/06)

11854 Coy, John. *Strong to the Hoop* (2–5). Illus. 1999, Lee & Low $16.95 (978-1-880000-80-9). 32pp. In this basketball story, 10-year-old James is drafted to play with the older kids when one of their teammates hurts his ankle. (Rev: BL 12/15/99; HBG 10/00; SLJ 10/99)

11855 Coy, John. *Top of the Order* (4–6). 2009, Feiwel & Friends $16.99 (978-0-312-37329-0). 96pp. Four fifth-grade boys, plus one girl, each have problems but share a love of baseball in this action-packed novel. (Rev: BCCB 4/09; BL 3/1/09; SLJ 3/09)

11856 Drumtra, Stacy. *Face-Off* (4–8). 1992, Avon paper $3.50 (978-0-380-76863-9). 118pp. T.J. and his twin Brad become rivals for friends and for status on the hockey team. (Rev: BL 4/1/93; SLJ 1/05; VOYA 8/93)

11857 Durant, Alan, sel. *Sports Stories* (5–9). Illus. by David Kearney. Series: Story Library. 2000, Kingfisher $14.95 (978-0-7534-5322-3). 221pp. A collection of 21 previously published short stories by well-known authors dealing with a variety of sports. (Rev: HBG 10/01; SLJ 11/00)

11858 Fitzgerald, Dawn. *Getting in the Game* (4–7). 2005, Roaring Brook $15.95 (978-1-59643-044-0). 136pp. In first-person narrative, Joanna Giordano describes her difficult experiences as the only girl on a 7th-grade ice hockey team that doesn't want her, plus her problems with peers, parents, and ailing grandfather. (Rev: BCCB 9/05; BL 3/1/05; SLJ 7/05; VOYA 6/05)

11859 Forsyth, C. A. *Power Hitter* (4–6). Series: Sports Stories. 2001, Lorimer paper $5.50 (978-1-55028-732-5). 86pp. A 13-year-old boy goes to visit relatives in Winnipeg for a summer full of baseball, unaware that his parents are divorcing and his mother is ill. (Rev: SLJ 1/02)

11860 Garza, Xavier. *Lucha Libre: The Man in the Silver Mask: A Bilingual Cuento* (2–5). Trans. by Luis Humberto Crosthwaite. Illus. by author. 2005, Cinco Puntos $17.95 (978-0-938317-92-0). Young Carlitos goes to a professional wrestling match ("lucha libre") in Mexico City and is thrilled by the sight of his favorite masked wrestler; can it be someone Carlitos knows? (Rev: SLJ 10/05)

11861 Gratz, Alan. *The Brooklyn Nine* (5–8). 2009, Dial $16.99 (978-0-8037-3224-7). 320pp. This saga, told in nine stories or "innings," follows nine generations of a German immigrant family with links to both baseball and Brooklyn. (Rev: BCCB 4/09; BL 2/1/09; HB 3/09; LMC 5/09; SLJ 3/09)

11862 Green, Tim. *Football Champ* (4–8). 2009, HarperCollins $16.99 (978-0-06-162689-0). 288pp. Twelve-year-old Troy, who has an amazing ability to predict football plays, is accused of cheating in this exciting sequel to *Football Genius* (2007). (Rev: BL 9/15/09; SLJ 7/09)

11863 Green, Tim. *Football Genius* (5–8). 2007, HarperCollins $16.99 (978-0-06-112270-5). 256pp. Troy's football skills are ignored until a linebacker for the Atlanta Falcons sees his ability to predict upcoming plays and uses him as the team's secret weapon. (Rev: BL 5/1/07; SLJ 7/07)

11864 Gutman, Dan. *Coach Hyatt Is a Riot!* (3–5). Illus. by Jim Paillot. Series: My Weird School Daze. 2009, HarperCollins LB $15.89 (978-0-06-155408-7); paper $3.99 (978-0-06-155406-3). 106pp. This humorous beginning chapter book about A.J. and his less-than-ideal Pee Wee Football team will appeal to reluctant readers. (Rev: SLJ 6/09)

11865 Hale, Daniel J., and Matthew LaBrot. *Red Card* (4–7). Series: Zeke Armstrong Mystery. 2002, Top paper $8.95 (978-1-929976-15-7). 170pp. Someone is trying to kill the soccer coach, and young Zeke sets out to discover who and why. (Rev: SLJ 12/02; VOYA 12/02)

11866 Hall, Donald. *When Willard Met Babe Ruth* (4–6). Illus. by Barry Moser. 1996, Harcourt $16.00 (978-0-15-200273-2). 48pp. A young New Hampshire farm boy and his father have a chance meeting with Babe Ruth. (Rev: BCCB 6/96; BL 3/15/96*; HB 9/96; SLJ 5/96)

11867 Harkrader, L. D. *Airball: My Life in Briefs* (4–7). 2005, Roaring Brook $15.95 (978-1-59643-060-0). 208pp. Kirby's middle school basketball team begins to improve when their coach — whom Kirby secretly believes is his father — insists the boys practice in their underwear. (Rev: BL 9/1/05; SLJ 11/05; VOYA 10/05)

11868 Haven, Paul. *Two Hot Dogs with Everything* (4–7). Illus. by Tim Jessell. 2006, Random LB $17.99 (978-0-375-83349-6). 320pp. Danny, 11, follows many superstitious rituals each time the Sluggers play, but his efforts seem to have no effect until he chews some 108-year-old gum that belonged to the team's founder. (Rev: BL 4/1/06)

11869 Heymsfeld, Carla. *Coaching Ms. Parker* (3–5). Illus. by Jane O'Connor. 1992, Macmillan LB $13.00 (978-0-02-743715-7). 96pp. Fourth-graders face the challenge of teaching Ms. Parker baseball in time for the faculty versus sixth-grade game. (Rev: BCCB 6/92; BL 6/15/92; SLJ 7/92)

11870 Hicks, Betty. *Scaredy-Cat Catcher* (2–4). Illus. by Adam McCauley. Series: Gym Shorts. 2009, Roaring Brook $16.95 (978-1-59643-246-8). 64pp. After breaking his arm while playing catcher, and developing an unfortunate retreating reflex, Rocky gets help from his friends and his dog and makes a comeback. (Rev: SLJ 4/09)

11871 Hirschfeld, Robert. *Goalkeeper in Charge* (5–7). Series: Christopher Sports. 2002, Little, Brown paper $4.50 (978-0-316-07548-0). 144pp. Seventh-grader Tina works to overcome her shyness on and off the soccer field. (Rev: BL 9/1/02; HBG 3/03)

11872 Holohan, Maureen. *Catch Shorty by Rosie* (4–8). Series: The Broadway Ballplayers. 1999, Broadway Ballplayers paper $6.95 (978-0-9659091-6-7). 160pp. Sixth-grader Rosie Jones devotes her time to organizing an all-girls football league while coping with a series of minor personal problems at home and school. (Rev: SLJ 3/00)

11873 Hurwitz, Johanna. *Baseball Fever* (3–6). Illus. by Ray Cruz. 1981, Morrow paper $3.95 (978-0-688-10495-5). 128pp. Mr. Feldman loathes baseball, but his son Ezra loves it.

11874 Isadora, Rachel. *Luke Goes to Bat* (PS–2). Illus. 2005, Penguin $15.99 (978-0-399-23604-4). 32pp. In this appealing tale set in 1950s Brooklyn, Luke, a young African American boy who idolizes Jackie Robinson, longs for a chance to play stickball with the older boys in his neighborhood; when he finally gets his chance at bat, he strikes out but realizes that the keys to success are determination and persistence. (Rev: BL 2/1/05; SLJ 2/05)

11875 Jennings, Patrick. *Out Standing in My Field* (3–5). 2005, Scholastic $16.95 (978-0-439-46581-6). 176pp. Ty, a not-so-talented baseball player, has a revealing conversation with his sister while Ty's team loses yet another game. (Rev: BL 3/15/05; SLJ 4/05)

11876 Johnson, Scott. *Safe at Second* (5–8). 2001, Penguin paper $7.99 (978-0-698-11877-5). The story of the friendship between Paulie and Todd, their love of baseball, and what happens after Todd

is hit during a game and loses an eye. (Rev: BL 6/1–15/99; SLJ 7/99; VOYA 8/99)

11877 Joosse, Barbara M. *The Losers Fight Back* (3–6). Illus. 1994, Clarion $15.00 (978-0-395-62335-0). 128pp. When the Bruisers, a losing soccer team, bribe Chuckie to join them, they find that he takes over their games. (Rev: BL 9/15/94; SLJ 11/94)

11878 King, Donna. *Double Twist* (5–8). 2007, Kingfisher paper $5.95 (978-0-7534-6023-8). 144pp. When her ice-dancing partner injures his knee, 12-year-old Laura Lee scrambles to replace him just one month before the Junior Grand Prix. (Rev: BL 1/1–15/07)

11879 King, Donna. *Game, Set, and Match* (4–6). 2007, Kingfisher paper $5.95 (978-0-7534-6022-1). Match 136pp. Carrie's summer at a Florida tennis camp is a time for her to prove her independence and her talent at the sport. (Rev: SLJ 5/07)

11880 Knudson, R. R. *Rinehart Lifts* (4–6). 1982, Avon paper $1.95 (978-0-380-57059-1). 88pp. A failure at all sports, Rinehart finds he can excel in weight lifting.

11881 Kroll, Steven. *New Kid in Town* (2–4). Illus. 1992, Avon paper $3.50 (978-0-380-76407-5). 80pp. Phil finally makes the Raymondtown Rockets baseball team, only to find his happiness threatened because his father may be transferred. (Rev: BL 3/15/92)

11882 Levy, Elizabeth. *Tackling Dad* (5–8). 2005, HarperCollins LB $16.89 (978-0-06-000050-9). 144pp. Cassie, 13, has won a place on the football team but her father won't sign the consent form. (Rev: BL 9/1/05; SLJ 8/05)

11883 Lupica, Mike. *The Big Field* (5–8). 2008, Philomel $17.99 (978-0-399-24625-8). 240pp. Fourteen-year-old Hutch and his team are going to the Florida State finals, but Hutch's happiness is marred by troubled relationships with his father and a new, difficult teammate. (Rev: BL 12/1/07; SLJ 2/08)

11884 Lupica, Mike. *Summer Ball* (5–8). 2007, Philomel $17.99 (978-0-399-24487-2). 256pp. Even though his coach offers little encouragement, Danny Walker's determination helps him lead his summer basketball team to victory. (Rev: BL 4/15/07; SLJ 6/07)

11885 Lupica, Mike. *Two-Minute Drill* (4–6). Series: Comeback Kids. 2007, Philomel $9.99 (978-0-399-24715-6). 180pp. Scott Parry, the worst player on the 6th-grade football team finds an unusual way to help his team. (Rev: SLJ 10/07)

11886 McEwan, Jamie. *Rufus the Scrub Does Not Wear a Tutu* (2–3). Illus. by John Margeson. 2007, Darby Creek $14.95 (978-1-58196-060-0). 64pp. Rufus takes up ballet and must deal with teasing — until his newfound coordination helps him on the football field. A sequel to *Willy the Scrub* and *Whitewater Scrubs*. (Rev: SLJ 6/07)

11887 McKissack, Patricia C. *The Home-Run King* (3–6). Illus. by Gordon C. James. Series: Scraps of Time. 2008, Viking $14.99 (978-0-670-01085-1). 96pp. The Webster cousins learn about about baseball's segregated past when Grandma Gee tells them a story set in 1937 about the Nashville "chitlin' circuit," which provided homes for traveling Negro League players. (Rev: BL 2/1/09; HB 1/09)

11888 Maddox, Jake. *Diving Off the Edge* (4–7). Illus. by Sean Tiffany. Series: Jake Maddox Sports Fiction. 2009, Stone Arch $17.99 (978-1-4342-1205-4). 72pp. A fast-paced story about swimming, peer pressure, and friendship. (Rev: BLO 3/19/09)

11889 Maddox, Jake. *Full Court Dreams* (4–7). Illus. by Tuesday Mourning. Series: Impact. 2008, Stone Arch LB $16.95 (978-1-4342-0469-1). 63pp. Megan is determined to make the basketball team this year and gives the tryouts her all; for reluctant readers. (Rev: BL 4/1/08)

11890 Maddox, Jake. *Paintball Blast* (4–6). Illus. by Sean Tiffany. Series: Impact Books — A Jake Maddox Sports Story. 2007, Stone Arch LB $22.60 (978-1-59889-322-9). 65pp. Paintball experts Max and Tyler are suspicious about the constant wins registered by a new player named Ryan. Could he be cheating? Reluctant readers enjoy this series, which also includes *Speedway Switch* (2007). (Rev: SLJ 11/07)

11891 Maddox, Jake, and Eric Stevens. *Karate Countdown* (4–7). Illus. by Sean Tiffany. Series: Jake Maddox Sports Fiction. 2009, Stone Arch $17.99 (978-1-4342-1200-9). 72pp. Karate helps Kenny to defuse his anger over his mother's death. (Rev: BLO 3/19/09)

11892 Maifair, Linda Lee. *Batter Up, Bailey Benson!* (3–5). 1997, Zondervan paper $3.99 (978-0-310-20705-4). 64pp. Bailey faces jealousy problems when she finds that she is on a different baseball team than her friend Nicole. (Rev: BL 3/15/97)

11893 Maifair, Linda Lee. *Go Figure, Gabriella Grant!* (3–5). 1997, Zondervan paper $3.99 (978-0-310-20702-3). 64pp. Gabriella has problems budgeting her time when she takes up figure skating. (Rev: BL 3/15/97)

11894 Mantell, Paul. *Stealing Home* (3–6). Series: Matt Christopher. 2004, Little, Brown paper $4.50 (978-0-316-60742-1). 135pp. Seventh grader Joey Gallagher enjoys being a baseball star and is not pleased at first to discover the exchange student visiting from Nicaragua, Jesus, also has real talent. (Rev: SLJ 11/04)

11895 Mazer, Abby. *The Amazing Days of Abby Hayes* (3–6). 2000, Scholastic paper $4.99 (978-0-439-14977-8). 144pp. Told in prose, journal entries, and drawings, this is the story of Abby Hayes, who tries without much success to shine at soccer. (Rev: BL 8/00)

11896 Mills, Claudia. *Gus and Grandpa at Basketball* (2–4). Illus. by Catherine Stock. 2001, Farrar $14.00 (978-0-374-32818-4). 48pp. In this seventh book in the series, Grandpa helps Gus overcome his anxiety about playing basketball in front of a crowd. (Rev: BL 11/15/01; HB 11/01; HBG 3/02; SLJ 9/01)

11897 Myers, Walter Dean. *Me, Mop, and the Moondance Kid* (5–7). Illus. 1988, Dell paper $4.99 (978-0-440-40396-8). 128pp. The efforts of T.J. and Moondance to get their friend Mop adopted. (Rev: BCCB 12/88; BL 2/1/89; SLJ 1/88)

11898 Nicholson, Lorna Schultz. *Roughing* (5–8). 2005, Lorimer paper $5.50 (978-1-55028-858-2). 108pp. This story set in a hockey camp in Calgary, Alberta, features Josh, a boy with type 1 diabetes; Peter, a native Canadian; and Peter, a bully who plans to teach Peter a lesson. (Rev: BL 5/15/05; SLJ 9/05)

11899 Nicholson, Lorna Schultz. *Too Many Men* (4–8). Series: Sports Stories. 2007, Lorimer paper $7.95 (978-1-55028-948-0). 128pp. Hockey player Sam juggles his busy home life with hockey practice as starting goalie. (Rev: SLJ 7/07)

11900 Nitz, Kristin Wolden. *Defending Irene* (5–7). 2004, Peachtree $14.95 (978-1-56145-309-2). 185pp. When her family moves to Italy for a year, 13-year-old Irene is determined to continue playing soccer, even if it's on the boys' team. (Rev: SLJ 9/04)

11901 Park, Linda Sue. *Keeping Score* (4–7). 2008, Clarion $16.00 (978-0-618-92799-9). 208pp. In 1951 fireman Jim teaches Brooklyn Dodgers fan Maggie, 9, how to score a game and the two remain friends even when Jim is sent to Korea; when Jim is horribly injured, Maggie is determined to help. (Rev: BL 2/1/08; SLJ 3/08)

11902 Patneaude, David. *Haunting at Home Plate* (4–7). 2000, Albert Whitman LB $15.99 (978-0-8075-3181-5). Twelve-year-old Nelson is amazed when mysterious instructions are left on the playing field in this baseball novel about a losing team that suddenly seems to be getting help from a ghost. (Rev: BCCB 11/00; BL 9/1/00; HBG 3/01; SLJ 9/00)

11903 Peers, Judi. *Shark Attack* (5–7). Series: Sports Stories. 1999, Orca paper $6.50 (978-1-55028-620-5). 74pp. An easily read story set in Canada, in which a young baseball player wants to impress his father but doesn't think he can ever reach his older brother's record. (Rev: SLJ 1/00)

11904 Preller, James. *Six Innings* (5–8). 2008, Feiwel & Friends $16.95 (978-0-312-36763-3). 160pp. Six innings of a Little League game reveal much about the game's young players and about the young announcer, a player side-lined by cancer. (Rev: BL 4/1/08; SLJ 4/08)

11905 Priebe, Val. *Running Rivals* (4–8). Illus. by Tuesday Mourning. Series: Impact Books: A Jake Maddox Sports Story. 2008, Stone Arch LB $17.95 (978-1-4342-0874-3); paper $5.99 (978-1-4342-0778-4). 72pp. Amy, an African American girl who lives for her running, suffers an injury and faces two months without practice. (Rev: SLJ 3/09)

11906 Richardson, Charisse K. *The Real Lucky Charm* (3–5). 2005, Dial $16.99 (978-0-8037-3105-9); paper $4.99 (978-0-14-240431-7). 96pp. Ten-year-old Mia attributes her basketball skill to the new charm for her bracelet, and is happy to play on the team with her twin brother Marcus; but when she loses the charm her confidence evaporates. (Rev: BL 9/1/05; SLJ 10/05)

11907 Ritter, John H. *The Boy Who Saved Baseball* (5–7). 2003, Putnam $17.99 (978-0-399-23622-8). 224pp. A small town depends on its baseball team to rescue it from big developers. (Rev: BL 5/1/03*; HBG 4/04; SLJ 6/03; VOYA 8/03)

11908 Ritter, John H. *Choosing Up Sides* (5–9). 1998, Putnam $18.99 (978-0-399-23185-8). 176pp. Jake is a great southpaw in baseball, but his preacher father forbids the boy to use his left hand for pitching as it is the instrument of Satan. (Rev: BCCB 6/98; BL 5/1/98; HBG 10/98; SLJ 6/98; VOYA 12/98)

11909 Roberts, Ken. *Thumb on a Diamond* (3–5). Illus. by Leanne Franson. 2006, Groundwood $15.95 (978-0-88899-629-9); paper $6.95 (978-0-88899-705-0). 128pp. The children of a remote fishing village on the coast of British Columbia form a baseball team and enter a regional tournament as part of their scheme to visit a big city. (Rev: BL 6/1–15/06; SLJ 8/06)

11910 Roberts, Kristi. *My Thirteenth Season* (5–8). 2005, Holt $15.95 (978-0-8050-7495-6). 144pp. When Fran, whose mother has recently died, tries to play baseball for the boys' team in her new town, she is in for a world of trouble. (Rev: BL 3/15/05*; SLJ 3/05)

11911 Rodriguez, Alex. *Out of the Ballpark* (2–4). Illus. by Frank Morrison. 2007, HarperCollins $16.99 (978-0-06-115194-1). 32pp. The Yankees player draws on his childhood experiences in this story of a determined young athlete who succeeds through hard work. (Rev: BL 3/15/07)

11912 Rud, Jeff. *In the Paint* (5–8). 2005, Orca paper $7.95 (978-1-55143-337-0). 128pp. Matt is glad to make the basketball team but soon finds there are pressures he would prefer to avoid. (Rev: BL 7/05)

11913 Scaletta, Kurtis. *Mudville* (4–8). 2009, Knopf $15.99 (978-0-375-85579-5). 272pp. It has been raining in Moundville (aka Mudville) for 22 years, but with the arrival of a foster child named Sturgis the sun suddenly reappears and allows baseball and the interrupted game against Sinister Bend to resume. (Rev: BL 3/1/09; SLJ 3/09)

11914 Schnur, Steven. *The Koufax Dilemma* (4–6). Illus. 1997, Morrow $15.00 (978-0-688-14221-6). 192pp. Danny faces problems because of his parents' divorce and the fact that his mother won't let him play baseball in the big game on Passover. (Rev: BCCB 5/97; BL 3/15/97; SLJ 5/97)

11915 Scudamore, Beverly. *Misconduct* (4–6). Series: Sports Stories. 2005, Lorimer paper $5.50 (978-1-55028-854-4). 107pp. Matthew is influenced by a new kid on his hockey team and must figure out if the friendship is worth his integrity. (Rev: SLJ 8/05)

11916 Shannon, David. *How Georgie Radbourn Saved Baseball* (1–5). Illus. 1994, Scholastic $14.95 (978-0-590-47410-8). 32pp. A rich and powerful wheeler-dealer decides to ban baseball, and it's up to young Georgie Radbourn to save it. (Rev: BL 1/15/94; SLJ 4/94*)

11917 Slote, Alfred. *Finding Buck McHenry* (4–6). 1991, HarperCollins LB $15.89 (978-0-06-021653-5). 256pp. Is Jason's baseball coach really the for-

mer great player he sees on a baseball card? (Rev: BCCB 5/91; BL 3/15/91; SLJ 5/91)

11918 Sullivan, Ann. *Molly Maguire: Wide Receiver* (4–6). 1992, Avon paper $2.99 (978-0-380-76114-2). 104pp. Molly wants to show a certain bully that she can play football, with the help of her next-door neighbor, who played for Notre Dame. (Rev: BL 10/1/92)

11919 Swan, Bill. *The Enforcer* (5–8). Series: Canadian Sports Stories. 2008, James Lorimer $8.95 (978-1-55028-981-7); paper $8.95 (978-1-55028-979-4). 136pp. Hockey is the focus in this book about Jake, a boy with three grandfathers who all intrude into his life in different ways. (Rev: BL 6/1–15/08)

11920 Telander, Rick. *String Music* (4–6). 2002, Cricket $15.95 (978-0-8126-2647-6). 144pp. Robbie, a fifth-grader with plenty of problems, runs away to the big city, sneaks into a basketball game, and meets basketball's greatest player. (Rev: BCCB 7–8/02; BL 5/1/02)

11921 Temple, Bob. *Free Climb* (4–8). Illus. by Sean Tiffany. Series: Impact Books: A Jake Maddox Sports Story. 2008, Stone Arch LB $22.60 (978-1-4342-0784-5); paper $5.99 (978-1-4342-0880-4). 72pp. Fourteen-year-old Amir is convinced to abandon climbing buildings and spend his time at the gym instead. (Rev: SLJ 3/09)

11922 Tocher, Timothy. *Bill Pennant, Babe Ruth, and Me* (5–9). 2009, Cricket $16.95 (978-0-8126-2755-8). 184pp. In 1920, 16-year-old Hank Cobb is put in charge of the Giants' mascot, a Mexican wildcat, and then must keep an eye on the Yankees' new player called Babe Ruth. (Rev: LMC 8/09; SLJ 6/09)

11923 Trembath, Don. *Frog Face and the Three Boys* (4–7). Series: Black Belt. 2001, Orca paper $6.95 (978-1-55143-165-9). 157pp. Three very different 7th-graders are enrolled in a karate class to teach them discipline. (Rev: BL 3/1/01; SLJ 9/01; VOYA 8/02)

11924 Wallace, Bill. *Never Say Quit* (5–7). 1993, Holiday $16.95 (978-0-8234-1013-2). 212pp. A group of misfits who don't make the soccer team decide to form one of their own. (Rev: BL 4/15/93)

11925 Wallace, Rich. *Dunk Under Pressure* (4–6). Series: Winning Season. 2006, Viking $14.99 (978-0-670-06095-5). 119pp. Sixth-grader Dunk (Cornell Duncan), free-throw star, learns about being a team player. (Rev: SLJ 6/06)

11926 Wallace, Rich. *Southpaw* (4–6). Series: Winning Season. 2006, Viking $14.99 (978-0-670-06053-5). 128pp. Jimmy Fleming, who has moved to Hudson City with his recently divorced father, joins his school's baseball team and manages to win the acceptance of his teammates after a shaky start. (Rev: BL 2/15/06; SLJ 3/06; VOYA 2/06)

11927 Walter, Mildred P. *Suitcase* (3–6). 1999, Lothrop $16.99 (978-0-688-16547-5). 112pp. Xander, a tall African American boy with great artistic talent, disappoints his father when he proves to be inept at basketball, but regains his affection as a star pitcher on the baseball team. (Rev: BCCB 10/99; BL 9/15/99; HB 11/99; HBG 3/00; SLJ 9/99)

11928 Walters, Eric. *Full Court Press* (3–5). 2001, Orca paper $5.95 (978-1-55143-169-7). 152pp. Though only in the third grade, Nick and Kia decide to try out for the fifth-grade basketball team. (Rev: BL 4/1/01)

11929 Walters, Eric. *Long Shot* (2–5). Illus. by John Mantha. 2002, Orca paper $5.95 (978-1-55143-216-8). 140pp. The new coach of Nick and Kia's basketball team is so unpleasant that all the players walk out. (Rev: SLJ 7/02)

11930 Walters, Eric. *Three on Three* (3–5). Illus. 2000, Orca paper $4.99 (978-1-55143-170-3). 122pp. Third-graders Nick and Kia, excellent basketball players, get the best player in school to join them for a 3-on-3 tournament, but unforeseen problems arise. (Rev: BCCB 6/00; BL 6/1–15/00)

11931 Weatherford, Carole Boston. *Champions on the Bench: The Cannon Street YMCA All-Stars* (2–4). Illus. by Leonard Jenkins. 2007, Dial $16.99 (978-0-8037-2987-2). 32pp. In 1955 South Carolina, 61 white Little League teams refuse to play against an African American team. (Rev: BL 2/1/07; SLJ 1/07)

11932 Webster-Doyle, Terrence. *Breaking the Chains of the Ancient Warrior: Tests of Wisdom for Young Martial Artists* (5–8). Illus. 1995, Martial Arts for Peace paper $14.95 (978-0-942941-32-6). A collection of inspirational stories, karate parables, and tests that promote ethical behavior, with accompanying follow-up questions and a message for adult readers. (Rev: SLJ 1/96)

11933 Wolff, Virginia E. *Bat 6* (5–9). 1998, Scholastic paper $16.95 (978-0-590-89799-0). 240pp. In this novel narrated by the members of the opposing teams, a Japanese American girl just out of an internment camp meets a bitter girl whose father was killed at Pearl Harbor, and the two become rivals in baseball. (Rev: BCCB 6/98; BL 5/1/98*; HBG 10/98; SLJ 5/98; VOYA 6/98)

11934 Wooldridge, Frosty. *Strike Three! Take Your Base* (5–9). Illus. by Pietri Freeman. 2001, Brookfield Reader $16.95 (978-1-930093-01-0); paper $6.95 (978-1-930093-07-2). 160pp. Baseball provides the setting as two brothers deal individually with the sudden death of their umpire father. (Rev: SLJ 3/02)

11935 Zirpoli, Jane. *Roots in the Outfield* (5–7). 1988, Houghton $16.00 (978-0-395-45184-7). 133pp. Josh spends a summer with his newly married father in Wisconsin and discovers some baseball memorabilia that help him overcome his own fears and ineptness in right field. (Rev: BL 4/1/88; SLJ 5/88)

Fairy Tales

11936 Abeya, Elisabet. *Hansel and Gretel / Hansel y Gretel* (K–3). Illus. by Cristina Losantos. 2005, Chronicle $14.95 (978-0-8118-4793-3); paper $6.95 (978-0-8118-4794-0). 32pp. An entertaining, bilingual (Spanish and English) retelling of the classic fairy tale with ink-and-watercolor illustrations. (Rev: BL 8/05; HBG 4/06; SLJ 10/05) [398.2]

11937 Ahlberg, Allan. *Previously* (PS–2). Illus. by Bruce Ingman. 2007, Candlewick $16.99 (978-0-7636-3542-8). For children who already know their fairy tales, this is an entertaining cumulative story in reverse involving Goldilocks, Cinderella, Jack and the beanstalk, the gingerbread man, and so forth. (Rev: BCCB 11/07; LMC 1/08; SLJ 11/07) [398.2]

11938 Alley, Zoe B. *There's a Wolf at the Door* (K–3). Illus. by R. W. Alley. 2008, Roaring Brook $19.95 (978-1-59643-275-8). 32pp. A well-dressed Wolf moves from one bad situation to another in this humorous, oversize collection of five traditional tales. (Rev: BL 9/1/08; HB 11/08; SLJ 9/08) [398.2]

11939 Andersen, Hans Christian. *Andersen's Fairy Tales* (3–5). Trans. by Anthea Bell. Illus. by Silke Leffler. 2007, North-South $19.95 (978-0-7358-2141-5). 96pp. A handsome, large-format collection of 13 Andersen tales. (Rev: BL 10/15/07; SLJ 12/07) [398.2]

11940 Andersen, Hans Christian. *For Sure! For Sure!* (1–4). Trans. from German by Mus White. Illus. by Stefan Czernecki. 2004, August House $16.95 (978-0-87483-742-1). Andersen's tale about a chicken who views herself as more beautiful with one less feather and how the story is amplified as it spreads across the town. (Rev: SLJ 11/04) [398.2]

11941 Andersen, Hans Christian. *The Little Match Girl* (4–6). Illus. by Blair Lent. 1975, Houghton paper $1.95 (978-0-685-02294-8). The touching story of the lonely, shivering little match girl who sees visions in the flames of the matches she cannot sell. [398.2]

11942 Andersen, Hans Christian. *The Little Match Girl* (2–4). Illus. by Kveta Pacovska. 2005, Putnam $18.99 (978-0-698-40027-6). 32pp. Avant-garde illustrations enliven this retelling of Andersen's beloved fairy tale. (Rev: BL 10/1/05; SLJ 11/05) [398.2]

11943 Andersen, Hans Christian. *Little Mermaids and Ugly Ducklings: Favorite Fairy Tales by Hans Christian Andersen* (4–6). Illus. by Gennady Spirin. 2001, Chronicle $15.95 (978-0-8118-3320-2). 59pp. Handsome, imaginative illustrations of differing styles and sizes enhance six well-known tales. (Rev: BL 12/1/01; HBG 3/02) [398.2]

11944 Andersen, Hans Christian. *The Princess and the Pea* (PS). Illus. by Rachel Isadora. 2007, Putnam $16.99 (978-0-399-24611-1). 32pp. The classic tale is relocated to a beautifully illustrated East Africa. (Rev: BL 4/15/07) [398.2]

11945 Andersen, Hans Christian. *Stories from Hans Christian Andersen* (2–4). Retold by Andrew Matthews. Illus. by Alan Snow. 1993, Orchard $18.95 (978-0-531-05463-5). 96pp. Eleven popular Andersen fairy tales, like *The Steadfast Tin Soldier* and *The Little Mermaid*, are retold in a simplified, conversational manner. (Rev: SLJ 12/93) [398.2]

11946 Andersen, Hans Christian. *Thumbelina* (PS–2). Retold and illus. by Brian Pinkney. 2003, Greenwillow LB $17.89 (978-0-688-17477-4). Pinkney's picture-book retelling is faithful to the original and features interesting artwork that differs from his usual style. (Rev: HBG 4/04; SLJ 9/03) [398.2]

11947 Andersen, Hans Christian. *The Top and the Ball* (K–2). Illus. by Elisabeth Nyman. 1992, Ideals LB $15.00 (978-0-8249-8583-7). 32pp. In the 19th century, a wooden top loves a ball in a boy's toy box. (Rev: BL 10/15/92) [398.2]

11948 Andersen, Hans Christian. *The Ugly Duckling* (K–3). Illus. by Pirkko Vainio. 2009, North-South $16.95 (978-0-7358-2226-9). 32pp. This beautifully illustrated, simple retelling was first published in Switzerland. (Rev: BLO 4/24/09; SLJ 6/09) [398.2]

11949 Andersen, Hans Christian. *The Ugly Duckling* (PS–1). Illus. by Rachel Isadora. 2009, Putnam $16.99 (978-0-399-25029-3). 32pp. Set in Africa, this gentle retelling has the ugly duckling turning into a black swan. (Rev: BL 5/1/09; SLJ 6/09) [398.2]

11950 Andersen, Hans Christian. *The Ugly Duckling* (K–4). Illus. by Steve Johnson and Lou Fancher. 2008, Candlewick $16.99 (978-0-7636-2159-9). Illustrated with elegant paint-and-collage artwork, this is a worthy retelling of the classic story. (Rev: BCCB 3/08; HB 1/08; SLJ 1/08) [398.2]

11951 Balcells, Jacqueline. *The Enchanted Raisin* (3–6). Trans. by Elizabeth G. Miller. Illus. 1989, Latin American Literary Review Pr. paper $11.00 (978-0-935480-38-2). 103pp. Ten contemporary fairy stories by a noted Chilean writer for children. (Rev: BL 12/1/89) [398.2]

11952 Bar-El, Dan. *Such a Prince* (K–2). Illus. by John Manders. 2007, Clarion $16.00 (978-0-618-71468-1). 32pp. A funny fractured version of a French fairy tale, "Three May Peaches," in which an aging fairy called Libby Gaborchik helps a love-starved Princess Vera. (Rev: SLJ 1/08) [398.2]

11953 Batt, Tanya. *The Princess and the White Bear King* (1–3). Illus. by Nicoletta Ceccoli. 2004, Barefoot Books $16.99 (978-1-84148-339-9). 40pp. Borrowing from three traditional folktales, Batt has created a charming story about a beautiful young princess who is kidnapped by a white bear and taken to his stately palace. (Rev: BL 11/1/04; SLJ 1/05) [398.2]

11954 Batt, Tanya Robyn. *The Faerie's Gift* (K–3). Illus. by Nicoletta Ceccoli. 2003, Barefoot Books $16.99 (978-1-84148-998-8). 32pp. A fairy offers a woodcutter one wish, and the wish he makes pleases everyone in his family. (Rev: BL 2/15/03; HBG 10/03; SLJ 6/03) [398.2]

11955 Bazilian, Barbara. *The Red Shoes* (K–2). Illus. 1997, Whispering Coyote $10.95 (978-1-879085-56-5). 40pp. This attractive retelling of Andersen's story has been changed to make it less preachy and gory. (Rev: BL 11/1/97; HBG 3/98; SLJ 10/97) [398.2]

11956 Bell, Anthea. *The Porridge Pot* (K–2). Illus. by Claudia Carls. 2007, Penguin $16.99 (978-0-698-40073-3). 32pp. Eye-catching, detailed illustrations combining sculpture and painting illuminate this folktale about a poor little girl who loses her parents and her shoe in the woods but finds a prince. (Rev: BL 9/1/07; SLJ 11/07) [398.2]

11957 Birdseye, Tom. *Look Out, Jack! The Giant Is Back!* (K–3). Illus. by Will Hillenbrand. 2001, Holiday House $16.95 (978-0-8234-1450-5). 32pp. The giant of "Jack and the Beanstalk" fame has a big brother who wants revenge — and Jack narrowly escapes him in this colorful picture book. (Rev: BCCB 10/01; BL 9/1/01; HBG 3/02; SLJ 10/01) [398.2]

11958 Blackaby, Susan, retel. *The Little Mermaid* (K–2). Illus. by Charlene DeLage. Series: Read-It! Readers Fairy Tales. 2004, Picture Window LB $19.93 (978-1-4048-0221-6). 32pp. In this attractive retelling for beginning readers of Hans Christian Andersen's classic story, a beautiful mermaid longs to become human so that she can win the heart of a handsome prince. (Rev: SLJ 1/04) [398.2]

11959 Blackaby, Susan, retel. *The Princess and the Pea* (K–2). Illus. by Charlene DeLage. Series: Read-It! Readers Fairy Tales. 2004, Picture Window LB $19.93 (978-1-4048-0223-0). 32pp. In this beautifully illustrated adaptation for beginning readers of Hans Christian Andersen's classic fairy tale, an unlikely looking young woman claims to be a princess and proves she is when a tiny pea under a pile of 20 mattresses keeps her from a good night's sleep. (Rev: SLJ 1/04) [398.2]

11960 Boada, Francesc. *Cinderella / Cenicienta* (PS–1). Illus. by Monse Fransoy. Series: Bilingual Editions. 2001, Chronicle paper $6.95 (978-0-8118-3090-4). 32pp. A bilingual version full of humor that stays close to the original tale. (Rev: BL 7/01; HBG 10/01) [398.2]

11961 Bofill, Francesc. *Rapunzel* (K–3). Illus. by Joma. 2006, Chronicle $14.95 (978-0-8118-5059-9); paper $6.95 (978-0-8118-5060-5). 32pp. A nicely illustrated bilingual retelling of the classic tale, with enjoyable twists. (Rev: BL 3/1/06; SLJ 6/06) [398.2]

11962 Bradman, Tony. *Mr. Wolf Bounces Back* (2–4). Illus. by Sarah Warburton. 2009, Stone Arch LB $23.99 (978-1-4342-1306-8). 56pp. Bradman tells the story of Granny and the wolf after the well-known episode; Granny is lonely and the big bad wolf has become a father and needs a different kind of job. (Rev: LMC 10/09; SLJ 6/09) [398.2]

11963 Brett, Jan, retel. *Beauty and the Beast* (PS–3). Illus. 1989, Houghton $16.00 (978-0-89919-497-4). 32pp. A smooth, brief retelling of the old classic. (Rev: BCCB 12/89; BL 10/1/89; SLJ 11/89) [398.2]

11964 Child, Lauren. *The Princess and the Pea* (K–3). Illus. by Polly Borland. 2006, Hyperion $16.99 (978-0-7868-3886-8). 40pp. The queen puts a potential bride for her son to the pea-under-the-mattress test in this fractured fairy tale. (Rev: BL 2/15/06; SLJ 3/06*) [398.2]

11965 Claflin, Willy. *The Uglified Ducky: A Maynard Moose Tale* (K–3). Illus. by James Stimson. 2008, August House $18.95 (978-0-87483-858-9). 32pp. Andersen's tale about an ugly duckling is moved to northern Maine where a moose grows up as a member of a duck "fambly"; a humorous read with an accompanying CD. (Rev: LMC 3/09; SLJ 9/08) [398.2]

11966 Collodi, Carlo. *Pinocchio* (3–5). Illus. by Robert Ingpen. 2005, Purple Bear $19.95 (978-1-933327-00-6). 136pp. A handsome, large-format version of the classic tale about the puppet who wants to become a real boy. (Rev: BL 11/15/05; SLJ 12/05) [398.2]

11967 Coombs, Kate. *The Runaway Princess* (4–7). 2006, Farrar $17.00 (978-0-374-35546-3). 288pp. In this entertaining takeoff on traditional fairy tales, 15-year-old Princess Meg, angry over being sequestered while princes from far and wide compete for her hand in marriage, escapes and takes matters into her own hands. (Rev: BL 9/1/06; SLJ 9/06) [398.2]

11968 Copper, Melinda. *Snow White* (K–2). Illus. 2005, Dutton $16.99 (978-0-525-47474-6). 40pp. Animals play the leading roles in this beautifully illustrated version of the classic fairy tale from the Brothers Grimm. (Rev: BL 8/05; SLJ 11/05) [398.2]

11969 Craft, K. Y. *Cinderella* (2–4). Illus. 2000, North-South LB $15.88 (978-1-58717-005-8). 32pp. An exquisite version of Cinderella based on the Lang and Rackham text and accompanied by wonderful oil-over-watercolor paintings. (Rev: BCCB 11/00; BL 11/1/00*; HBG 3/01; SLJ 11/00) [398.2]

11970 Craft, Mahlon F. *Sleeping Beauty* (2–4). Illus. by Kinuko Craft. 2002, North-South LB $16.50 (978-1-58717-121-5). 32pp. A beautifully illustrated retelling of the traditional fairy tale. (Rev: BCCB 1/03; BL 9/15/02; HBG 3/03; SLJ 10/02) [398.2]

11971 Datlow, Ellen, and Terri Windling, eds. *Troll's-Eye View: A Book of Villainous Tales* (5–8). 2009, Viking $16.99 (978-0-670-06141-9). 176pp. The villains in fairy tales get a chance to tell their stories in this collection of varied, original tales and poems by authors including Neil Gaiman, Garth Nix, and Jane Yolen. (Rev: BCCB 7–8/09; BL 3/1/09; SLJ 4/09) [398.2]

11972 de Hann, Linda, and Stern Nijland. *King and King* (PS–2). Illus. 2002, Tricycle $15.99 (978-1-58246-061-1). 32pp. When his mother the queen wants him to marry, a prince falls in love with another prince, and they marry and live happily ever after in this alternative fairy tale. (Rev: BL 7/02; HB 7/02; HBG 10/02; SLJ 3/02) [398.2]

11973 de la Paz, Myrna J. *Abadeha: The Philippine Cinderella* (K–3). Illus. by Youshan Tang. 2001, Shen's $16.95 (978-1-885008-17-6). 32pp. A Philippine version of the Cinderella story in which Abadeha is helped by kindly spirits and wins the prince by removing a ring that is stuck on his finger. (Rev: BL 7/01; HBG 3/02; SLJ 12/01) [398.2]

11974 Delessert, Etienne. *The Seven Dwarfs* (3–4). Illus. 2001, Creative Editions LB $17.95 (978-1-56846-139-7). 32pp. One of Snow White's dwarfs, Stephane, recounts the princess's story in this imaginative take on the fairy tale. (Rev: BL 1/1–15/02; HB 1/02; HBG 3/02) [398.2]

11975 Demi. *The Emperor's New Clothes* (PS–3). Illus. 2000, Simon & Schuster $19.95 (978-0-689-83068-6). 42pp. Employing a Chinese motif in the illustrations, this is a new, interesting, multicultural retelling of the Andersen tale. (Rev: BL 6/1–15/00; HB 5/00; HBG 10/00; SLJ 6/00) [398.2]

11976 Doyle, Malachy. *The Barefoot Book of Fairy Tales* (K–3). Illus. by Nicoletta Ceccoli. 2005, Barefoot Books $19.99 (978-1-84148-798-4). 160pp. Twelve fairy tales from around the world are collected in this quirky and accessible anthology. (Rev: BL 12/1/05; SLJ 2/06) [398.2]

11977 Edens, Cooper, ed. *Princess Stories: A Classic Illustrated Edition* (2–4). Series: Classics Illustrated Editions. 2004, Chronicle $19.95 (978-0-8118-4032-3). 136pp. Familiar stories — by Hans Christian Andersen, the Grimm brothers, and Charles Perrault, among others — of princesses pursuing romantic aspirations are paired with vintage images. (Rev: BL 10/15/04; SLJ 1/05) [398.2]

11978 Eilenberg, Max. *Beauty and the Beast* (2–4). Illus. by Angela Barrett. 2006, Candlewick $17.99 (978-0-7636-3160-4). 64pp. A wonderful retelling of the classic tale of Beauty and the Beast, set in the nineteenth century and accompanied by lovely, expressive watercolor illustrations. (Rev: BL 12/1/06; SLJ 12/06*) [398.2]

11979 Ensor, Barbara. *Cinderella (As If You Didn't Already Know the Story)* (3–6). Illus. 2006, Random $12.95 (978-0-375-83620-6). 109pp. Cinderella and her prince end up living happily ever after in this retelling, each finding a fulfilling career; Cinderella's letters to her deceased mother tell part of the story. (Rev: SLJ 7/06) [398.2]

11980 Ensor, Barbara. *Thumbelina, Tiny Runaway Bride* (2–5). Illus. by author. 2008, Random $12.99 (978-0-375-83960-3). 160pp. The story of Thumbelina is reimagined in this early chapter book. (Rev: BL 7/08; LMC 8/08; SLJ 11/08) [398.2]

11981 Escardo i Bas, Merce. *The Three Little Pigs / Los tres cerditos* (K–2). Illus. by Pere Joan. 2006, Chronicle $14.95 (978-0-8118-5063-6). 24pp. The familiar story is told in both English and Spanish, with comic-book style illustrations. (Rev: BL 5/1/06; SLJ 6/06) [398.2]

11982 Ferris, Jean. *Once Upon a Marigold* (5–8). 2002, Harcourt $17.00 (978-0-15-216791-2). 272pp. Christian falls in love with Princess Marigold and wins her heart through his bravery in this fairy tale full of fun. (Rev: BCCB 2/03; BL 9/15/02; HB 9/02; HBG 3/03; SLJ 11/02; VOYA 12/02) [398.2]

11983 Ferris, Jean. *Twice Upon a Marigold: Part Comedy, Part Tragedy, Part Two* (5–8). 2008, Harcourt $17.00 (978-0-15-206382-5). 304pp. Queen Marigold and King Christian, introduced in *Once upon a Marigold*, are now married and Queen Olympia, who fell into a river at the end of the first book, is now dried off and back to her wicked ways. (Rev: BL 4/15/08; SLJ 6/08) [398.2]

11984 Fleischman, Paul. *Glass Slipper, Gold Sandal* (K–2). Illus. by Julie Paschkis. 2007, Holt $16.95 (978-0-8050-7953-1). 32pp. Fleischman interweaves elements of a number of cultures in this unusual and beautifully illustrated retelling of Cinderella. (Rev: BCCB 11/07; BL 11/15/07; HB 1/08; LMC 11/07; SLJ 9/07) [398.2]

11985 Foreman, Michael, retel. *Classic Fairy Tales* (PS–3). Illus. by Michael Foreman. 2006, Sterling LB $12.95 (978-1-4027-2865-5). 176pp. These beautifully illustrated retellings of 14 classic fairy tales reduce the violence level and will suit a younger, more sensitive audience. (Rev: SLJ 4/06) [398.2]

11986 Garland, Michael. *King Puck* (K–3). Illus. by author. 2007, HarperCollins $16.99 (978-0-06-084809-5). Father Seamus is lonely on his mountaintop with only one book, so the fairies give the gift of speech to his goat, who goes on to win the grand prize at the fair — king for a day plus the granting of a wish; and the goat asks for books. (Rev: SLJ 2/07) [398.2]

11987 Geras, Adele. *Sleeping Beauty* (2–4). Illus. by Christian Birmingham. 2004, Scholastic $18.95 (978-0-439-58180-6). 64pp. Black-and-white illustrations and a number of beautiful pastels enhance this retelling. (Rev: BL 5/1/04; SLJ 8/04) [398.2]

11988 Goode, Diane. *The Dinosaur's New Clothes* (PS–1). Illus. 1999, Scholastic $15.95 (978-0-590-38360-8). 40pp. This variation on the Andersen tale is set in the Palace of Versailles and features dinosaurs as characters. (Rev: BCCB 12/99; BL 11/15/99; HBG 3/00; SLJ 9/99) [398.2]

11989 Gordon, David. *Hansel and Diesel* (PS–K). 2006, HarperCollins $16.99 (978-0-06-058122-0). 32pp. Hansel and Diesel are two little trucks facing the Wicked Winch in this strikingly illustrated twist on the well-known fairy tale. (Rev: BL 5/1/06; SLJ 7/06) [398.2]

11990 Gray, Margaret. *The Ugly Princess and the Wise Fool* (3–6). Illus. by Randy Cecil. 2002, Holt $15.95 (978-0-8050-6847-4). 176pp. There's a happy ending to this tale despite the fact that the princess is ugly and wisdom has been banned from the land. (Rev: BCCB 12/02; BL 11/15/02; HBG 3/03; SLJ 10/02) [398.2]

11991 Grimm, Jacob, and Wilhelm Grimm. *Rapunzel* (K–3). Trans. by Anthea Bell. Illus. by Dorothee Duntze. 2005, North-South $16.95 (978-0-7358-2013-5). 32pp. Sunny artwork gives this large-format retelling a more lighthearted feel than usual. (Rev: BL 12/1/05; SLJ 11/05) [398.2]

11992 Grimm Brothers. *The Frog Prince* (1–2). Adapted by Sindy McKay. Illus. by George Ulrich. Series: We Both Read. 1998, Treasure Bay $7.99 (978-1-891327-02-5). This fairy tale is retold twice — with an adult's and a child's vocabulary. (Rev: SLJ 12/98) [398.2]

11993 Gustafson, Scott, sel. *Classic Fairy Tales* (PS–6). Illus. by Scott Gustafson. 2003, Greenwich Workshop $19.95 (978-0-86713-089-8). 144pp. Scott Gustafson's breathtaking artwork highlights these retellings of 10 classic fairy tales, including "Snow White," "Puss in Boots," and "Hansel and Gretel." (Rev: BL 1/1–15/04; SLJ 12/03) [398.2]

11994 Hale, Bruce. *Snoring Beauty* (PS–2). Illus. by Howard Fine. 2008, Harcourt $16.00 (978-0-15-216314-3). 44pp. Full of wordplay and fun, this retelling of "Sleeping Beauty" features Princess Margarine and her parents King Gluteus and Queen Esophagus. (Rev: BL 5/15/08; LMC 11/08; SLJ 6/08) [398.2]

11995 Haylesworth, Jim, retel. *Goldilocks and the Three Bears* (PS–2). Illus. by Barbara McClintock. 2003, Scholastic $16.95 (978-0-439-39545-8). A handsome retelling with traditional illustrations and language that will appeal nonetheless to today's readers. (Rev: HB 11/03; HBG 4/04; SLJ 10/03) [398.2]

11996 Helmer, Marilyn. *Three Teeny Tiny Tales* (K–2). Illus. by Veselina Tomova. Series: Once-Upon-a-Time. 2001, Kids Can $10.95 (978-1-55074-841-3). 32pp. "The Elves and the Shoemaker," "The Gingerbread Man," and "Thumbelina" are retold in picture-book format. (Rev: BL 7/01; HBG 3/02; SLJ 6/01) [398.2]

11997 Hoberman, Mary Ann. *You Read to Me, I'll Read to You: Very Short Fairy Tales to Read Together* (2–4). Illus. by Michael Emberly. 2004, Little, Brown $16.95 (978-0-316-14611-1). 32pp. Designed for two voices, this picture book features retellings of eight popular fairy tales. (Rev: BL 7/04; HB 5/04; SLJ 5/04) [398.2]

11998 Hopkins, Jackie Mims. *The Horned Toad Prince* (PS–2). Illus. by Michael Austin. 2000, Peachtree $15.95 (978-1-56145-195-1). 32pp. This breezy update of the fairy tale is set in the Southwest and features a frog who demands that the heroine feed him chili. (Rev: BCCB 7–8/00; BL 5/15/00; HBG 10/00; SLJ 4/00) [398.2]

11999 Impey, Rose. *Read Me a Fairy Tale: A Child's Book of Classic Fairy Tales* (3–6). Illus. by Ian Beck. 1993, Scholastic $16.95 (978-0-590-49431-1). 128pp. A collection of 14 favorite fairy tales told in an informal style. (Rev: BL 1/15/94; SLJ 2/94) [398.2]

12000 Isadora, Rachel. *The Fisherman and His Wife* (PS–1). Illus. by author. 2008, Putnam $16.99 (978-0-399-24771-2). 32pp. The traditional Grimm story is set in Africa in this beautifully illustrated volume. (Rev: BL 4/1/08; HB 3/08; LMC 10/08; SLJ 3/08) [398.2]

12001 Isadora, Rachel. *Hansel and Gretel* (PS–2). Illus. by author. 2009, Putnam $16.99 (978-0-399-25028-6). 32pp. The story of the two innocent children and the wicked witch is moved to an African setting and illustrated with traditional Kente patterns. (Rev: BL 1/1–15/09; SLJ 4/09) [398.2]

12002 Jackson, Ellen. *Cinder Edna* (PS–3). Illus. by Kevin O'Malley. 1994, Lothrop $17.99 (978-0-688-12322-2). 32pp. Whereas Cinderella is a passive wimp, Cinder Edna is a spirited girl who mows lawns to make money so she can attend the ball. In this book, the two stories are told side by side. (Rev: BL 3/15/94; SLJ 4/94) [398.2]

12003 Jolley, Dan. *Pigling: A Cinderella Story* (3–6). Illus. by Anne Timmons. Series: Graphic Myths and Legends. 2008, Lerner LB $27.93 (978-0-8225-7174-2). 48pp. This brightly illustrated graphic novel tells the story of how Pear Blossom, a Korean Cinderella, eases her sorrow and overcomes her cruel stepmother and stepsister for a happy-ever-after ending. (Rev: BL 9/15/08; LMC 1/09) [398.2]

12004 Kellogg, Steven. *The Pied Piper's Magic* (K–1). 2009, Dial $16.99 (978-0-8037-2818-9). 40pp. Based loosely on the well-known Pied Piper story, this version tells the story of Peterkin whose magic pipe allows him to conjure up words and objects and then transform them — so that troublesome "rats" become "stars," for example. (Rev: BCCB 7–8/09; BL 1/1–15/09; SLJ 5/09) [398.2]

12005 Ketteman, Helen. *Waynetta and the Cornstalk: A Texas Fairy Tale* (K–3). Illus. by Diane Greenseid. 2007, Albert Whitman $16.95 (978-0-8075-8687-7). In this fractured version of "Jack and the Beanstalk" set in Texas, life on the ranch changes for the better when cowgirl Waynetta plants some magic corn and scales a huge cornstalk to find a gigantic ranch inhabited by a giant. (Rev: SLJ 4/07) [398.2]

12006 Kimmel, Eric A. *The Fisherman and the Turtle* (K–2). Illus. by Martha Aviles. 2008, Marshall Cavendish $16.99 (978-0-7614-5387-1). 32pp. A fisherman granted a wish by a green sea turtle finds his greedy wife disagreeing with his choice in this adaptation of "The Fisherman and His Wife," a Grimm tale set in ancient Mexico. (Rev: BL 4/1/08; LMC 10/08; SLJ 5/08) [398.2]

12007 Kroll, Steven. *Queen of the May* (PS–3). Illus. by Patience Brewster. 1993, Holiday House LB $15.95 (978-0-8234-1004-0). 32pp. Sylvie becomes Queen of the May in spite of her meddling stepmother and stepsister. (Rev: BL 4/1/93; SLJ 7/93) [398.2]

12008 Lach, William, ed. *Fairyland: In Art and Poetry* (3–7). Illus. by Richard Doyle. 2002, Holt $17.95 (978-0-8050-7006-4). 40pp. Illustrations from Richard Doyle's classic *In Fairyland* (1870) are paired with selections from writers including Shakespeare, de la Mare, Langston Hughes, and Laura Ingalls Wilder in a handsome volume suited to browsing. (Rev: HBG 10/02; SLJ 7/02) [398.2]

12009 Lang, Andrew, ed. *Blue Fairy Book* (4–6). 1965, Dover paper $10.95 (978-0-486-21437-5). 390pp. A fine edition of this classic collection. There are 11 other "color" Fairy Books. Some are: *Green Fairy Book* (1965); *Yellow Fairy Book* (1966); *Grey Fairy Book; Orange Fairy Book; Red Fairy Book* (all 1968). [398.2]

12010 Langton, Jane. *The Queen's Necklace: A Swedish Folktale* (3–5). Illus. by Ilse Plume. 1994, Hyperion LB $16.49 (978-0-7868-2007-8). 40pp. When a queen gives away pearls to help the poor, her cruel king demands her life. (Rev: BL 10/1/94; SLJ 10/94) [398.2]

12011 LaRochelle, David. *The End* (PS–3). Illus. by Richard Egielski. 2007, Scholastic $16.99 (978-0-439-64011-4). From the beginning — "And they all lived happily ever after" — to the final "Once upon a time" this zany fairy tale keeps up its topsy-turvy nature. (Rev: BL 1/1–15/07; HB 5/07; HBG 10/07; LMC 5/07; SLJ 4/07*) [398.2]

12012 Levine, Gail C. *Cinderellis and the Glass Hill* (4–6). Illus. 2000, HarperCollins LB $14.89 (978-0-06-028337-7). 96pp. This humorous variation on the Cinderella story has as its central character a boy named Ellis who is ignored by his older brothers but eventually wins the princess Marigold. (Rev: BL 1/1–15/00; HBG 10/00) [398.2]

12013 Levine, Gail C. *Ella Enchanted* (5–8). 1997, HarperCollins LB $17.89 (978-0-06-027511-2). 240pp. A spirited, cleverly plotted retelling of the Cinderella story in which Ella is finally paired with the Prince Charmant. (Rev: BCCB 5/97; BL 4/15/97*; HB 5/97; SLJ 4/97*; VOYA 8/97) [398.2]

12014 Levine, Gail C. *The Princess Test* (3–6). Illus. 1999, HarperCollins LB $8.89 (978-0-06-028063-5). 80pp. In this variation on *The Princess and the Pea*, a blacksmith's daughter turns out to be more sensitive than a princess. (Rev: BL 4/15/99) [398.2]

12015 Lewis, Naomi, retel. *Elf Hill: Tales from Hans Christian Andersen* (K–3). Illus. by Emma Chichester Clark. 1999, Star Bright $20.95 (978-1-887734-70-7). 68pp. A straightforward retelling of nine tales from the familiar "The Princess and the Pea" to the unfamiliar "The Money-Box Pig." (Rev: SLJ 1/00) [398.2]

12016 Lewis, Naomi, and Hans Christian Andersen. *The Snow Queen* (2–4). Illus. by Christian Birmingham. 2008, Candlewick $16.99 (978-0-7636-3229-8). 64pp. Word and image work together to retell this Andersen fairy tale that features a surprisingly warm and lovely Snow Queen. (Rev: BCCB 2/09; BLO 1/13/09; HB 1/09; SLJ 2/09) [398.2]

12017 Lin, Grace. *The Red Thread: An Adoption Fairy Tale* (K–3). Illus. by author. 2007, Albert Whitman $16.95 (978-0-8075-6922-1). 32pp. Lin interweaves a fairy tale based on a traditional Chinese belief with a story about a contemporary adopted child. (Rev: BL 10/15/07; SLJ 9/07) [398.2]

12018 Ljungkvist, Laura. *Snow White and the Seven Dwarfs* (PS–2). Illus. 2003, Abrams $14.95 (978-0-8109-4241-7). 38pp. Snow White gets a contemporary look in this beautifully illustrated simple retelling. (Rev: BL 4/15/03; HBG 10/03; SLJ 7/03) [398.2]

12019 Long, Laurel, and Jacqueline Ogburn, retels. *The Lady and the Lion: A Brothers Grimm Tale* (2–4). Illus. by Laurel Long. 2003, Dial $16.99 (978-0-8037-2651-2). Lush oil paintings decorate this romantic adaptation of a Grimm story about a lion who turns into a price at night. (Rev: BL 1/1/04; HBG 4/04; SLJ 2/04) [398.2]

12020 Lorenz, Albert. *Jack and the Beanstalk: How a Small Fellow Solved a Big Problem* (PS–3). Illus. 2002, Abrams $16.95 (978-0-8109-1160-4). 40pp. Realistic, highly detailed illustrations emphasize the importance of size and Jack's inventiveness. (Rev: BL 10/1/02; HBG 3/03; SLJ 10/02) [398.2]

12021 Lowell, Susan. *Cindy Ellen: A Wild Western Cinderella* (K–3). Illus. by Jane Manning. 2000, HarperCollins LB $17.89 (978-0-06-027447-4). 40pp. This version of the Cinderella story features a mean stepmother, a godmother with a six-gun, and a cowboy hero named Joe Prince. (Rev: BCCB 9/00; BL 5/15/00; HBG 10/00) [398.2]

12022 McClintock, Barbara. *Cinderella* (K–3). Illus. 2005, Scholastic $15.99 (978-0-439-56145-7). 32pp. This beautifully illustrated adaptation of the classic Cinderella fairy tale is set in the Paris of Louis XIV. (Rev: BL 1/1–15/06; SLJ 10/05*) [398.2]

12023 MacDonald, George. *The Golden Key* (2–6). Illus. by Maurice Sendak. 1993, Farrar paper $6.95 (978-0-374-42590-6). 96pp. In this classic fairy tale, two young people search for a keyhole where their golden key will fit. [398.2]

12024 MacDonald, George. *The Light Princess* (1–6). Adapted by Robin McKinley. Illus. by Katie T. Treherne. 1988, Harcourt $13.95 (978-0-15-245300-8). 44pp. A prince breaks the spell of a princess who has been deprived of gravity. (Rev: BL 7/88) [398.2] ∩

12025 MacDonald, Margaret Read. *The Great Smelly, Slobbery, Small-Toothed Dog* (PS–2). Illus. by Julie Paschkis. 2007, Random $16.95 (978-0-87483-808-

4). 32pp. A big, slobbery dog saves a rich man from a thief and chooses as his reward the rich man's daughter in this variant of "Beauty and the Beast." (Rev: BL 11/1/07; LMC 1/08; SLJ 12/07) [398.2]

12026 MacDonald, Margaret Read. *The Old Woman Who Lived in a Vinegar Bottle: A British Fairy Tale* (PS–2). Illus. by Nancy D. Fowlkes. 1995, August House $15.95 (978-0-87483-415-4). 32pp. In this English folktale, a fairy discovers that there is no pleasing some people when she supplies better housing for an old woman who had been living in a vinegar bottle. (Rev: BL 10/1/95; SLJ 1/96) [398.2]

12027 McDonald, Megan. *The Hinky-Pink: An Old Tale* (K–3). Illus. by Brian Floca. 2008, Atheneum $16.99 (978-0-689-87588-5). 48pp. In Florence long ago, Anabel must produce a princess gown in a week, which she could do very well thank you were it not for the little sprite who drives her to distraction. (Rev: BCCB 11/08; BL 9/15/08; HB 11/08; LMC 11/08; SLJ 8/08) [398.2]

12028 Marcantonio, Patricia Santos. *Red Ridin' in the Hood, and Other Cuentos* (3–5). Illus. by Renato Alarcão. 2005, Farrar $16.00 (978-0-374-36241-6). 208pp. Traditional fairy tales are turned inside-out and given Latino flair. (Rev: BL 3/15/05; SLJ 4/05) [398.2]

12029 Martin, Rafe. *The Storytelling Princess* (PS–3). Illus. by Kimberly B. Root. 2001, Penguin $16.99 (978-0-399-22924-4). 32pp. A prince and princess who have both refused arranged marriages find their respective criteria are met in each other. (Rev: BCCB 7–8/01; BL 7/01; HBG 3/02; SLJ 9/01) [398.2]

12030 Matthews, Caitlin. *The Barefoot Book of Princesses* (4–6). Illus. 1998, Barefoot Books $19.99 (978-1-901223-74-3). 64pp. In a collection of fairy tales from around the world, the reader meets a number of princesses (some familiar, such as Sleeping Beauty, others not) and their challenging situations. (Rev: BL 11/15/98; SLJ 11/98) [398.2]

12031 Mayer, Marianna. *Beauty and the Beast* (3–5). Illus. by author. 1987, Simon & Schuster paper $6.95 (978-0-689-71151-0). 48pp. A fine retelling made memorable by dazzling pictures. Another version is: *Beauty and the Beast* by Deborah Apy, illus. by Michael Hague (1995, Henry Holt). [398.2]

12032 Melmed, Laura K. *The Rainbabies* (PS–2). Illus. by Jim LaMarche. 1992, Lothrop LB $16.89 (978-0-688-10756-7). 32pp. An elderly couple care for 12 teeny babies they find in the grass. (Rev: BL 11/1/92; HB 3/93; SLJ 12/92) [398.2]

12033 Mitchell, Stephen. *Iron Hans: A Grimms' Fairy Tale* (1–3). Illus. by Matt Tavares. 2007, Candlewick $16.99 (978-0-7636-2160-5). 40pp. In this retelling of a Grimm tale, a young prince comes to the aid of a wild giant man (Iron Hans) only to disappoint the giant and be sent out into the world where he saves the kingdom and regains the support of the giant. (Rev: BL 12/15/07; LMC 1/08; SLJ 11/07) [398.2]

12034 Mitchell, Stephen. *The Tinderbox* (2–4). Illus. by Bagram Ibatoulline. 2007, Candlewick $17.99 (978-0-7636-2078-3). 48pp. A soldier, after both gaining and losing riches, uses a magic tinderbox to summon three huge-eyed dogs, secretly court a princess, and, ultimately, escape death; this rich retelling is enhanced by Ibatoulline's ink illustrations that portray the period setting, people, and creatures. (Rev: BL 1/1–15/07) [398.2]

12035 Morpurgo, Michael. *Gentle Giant* (K–3). Illus. by Michael Foreman. 2004, Collins $16.95 (978-0-00-711064-3). 32pp. A lonely giant finds acceptance when he saves the village of Ballyloch from ecological disaster. (Rev: BL 4/15/04; SLJ 5/04) [398.2]

12036 Moses, Will. *Hansel and Gretel: A Retelling from the Original Tale by the Brothers Grimm* (K–3). Illus. 2006, Philomel $16.99 (978-0-399-24234-2). 40pp. Moses adheres to the darker side of the Grimm story, adding detailed and lush folk-art illustrations. (Rev: BL 2/1/06; SLJ 3/06) [398.2]

12037 Murphy, Shirley Rousseau. *Wind Child* (K–4). Illus. by Leo and Diane Dillon. 1999, HarperCollins LB $15.89 (978-0-06-024904-5). 40pp. A romantic fairy tale about a lonely girl whose extraordinary weaving skills attract a prince who falls in love with her. (Rev: BL 6/1–15/99; HBG 10/99; SLJ 4/99) [398.2]

12038 Nesbit, E. *Jack and the Beanstalk* (K–3). Illus. by Matt Tavares. 2006, Candlewick $16.99 (978-0-7636-2124-7). 48pp. Large illustrations with eye-catching perspectives illustrate this retelling that features a lazy, clumsy Jack who succeeds in the end. (Rev: BL 9/15/06; SLJ 11/06*) [398.2]

12039 Nesbit, Edith. *Melisande* (K–3). Illus. by P. J. Lynch. 1989, Harcourt $13.95 (978-0-15-253164-5). 48pp. The fairies take their revenge when a royal family excludes them from the daughter's christening party. (Rev: BL 10/1/89*; HB 11/89; SLJ 1/90) [398.2]

12040 Nikly, Michelle. *The Perfume of Memory* (3–7). Illus. by Jean Claverie. 1999, Scholastic $16.95 (978-0-439-08206-8). In this fairy tale, a young child uses various perfumes to restore the memory of the queen. (Rev: HBG 3/00; SLJ 11/99) [398.2]

12041 Ogburn, Jacqueline. *The Magic Nesting Doll* (PS–3). Illus. by Laurel Long. 2000, Dial $17.99 (978-0-8037-2414-3). 32pp. An original fairy tale set in Russia about a girl who inherits a set of nesting dolls with magical powers. (Rev: BL 9/15/00; HBG 3/01; SLJ 12/00) [398.2]

12042 O'Neal, Shaquille. *Shaq and the Beanstalk: And Other Very Tall Tales* (K–4). Illus. by Shane W. Evans. 1999, Scholastic $15.95 (978-0-590-91823-7). 80pp. A collection of fractured fairy tales that feature Shaq O'Neal and such characters as the Big Bad Wolf, the three bears, and a hen that lays golden basketballs. (Rev: HBG 10/00; SLJ 2/00) [398.2]

12043 Osborne, Mary Pope. *Sleeping Bobby* (PS–2). Illus. by Giselle Potter. 2005, Simon & Schuster $16.95 (978-0-689-87668-4). 40pp. In this gender-swapping adaptation of "Sleeping Beauty," a handsome prince is awakened from a deep slumber by the spell-breaking kiss of a lovely princess. (Rev: BL 1/1–15/06; SLJ 10/05) [398.2]

12044 Paul, Ann Whitford. *Tortuga in Trouble* (PS–1). Illus. by Ethan Long. 2009, Holiday $16.95 (978-0-8234-2180-0). 32pp. Tortuga the turtle's friends Conejo, Culebra, and Iguana save the day in this version of "Little Red Riding Hood" laced with Spanish words. (Rev: BCCB 3/09; BL 5/1/09; HB 3/09; LMC 10/09; SLJ 2/09) [398.2]

12045 Pearce, Philippa. *The Squirrel Wife* (K–3). Illus. by Wayne Anderson. 2007, Candlewick $16.99 (978-0-7636-3551-0). 32pp. When Jack rescues a small green man in the forest, he is rewarded with a baby squirrel who transforms into a human female and becomes his wife, much to the disapproval of his jealous older brother who tries to ruin his happiness. (Rev: BL 11/15/07; LMC 5/08; SLJ 1/08) [398.2]

12046 Perrault, Charles. *The Complete Fairy Tales of Charles Perrault* (4–6). Trans. by Neil Philip and Nicoletta Simborowski. Illus. by Sally Holmes. 1993, Clarion $28.00 (978-0-395-57002-9). 156pp. Eleven tales by Perrault, newly translated and illustrated with watercolors and printed with fine historical notes. (Rev: BL 11/1/93; SLJ 9/93) [398]

12047 Perrault, Charles. *Perrault's Fairy Tales* (4–6). Illus. by Gustave Dore. 1969, Dover paper $10.95 (978-0-486-22311-7). 117pp. A classic edition with illustrations by the French master. [398.2]

12048 Perrault, Charles. *Puss in Boots* (K–3). Illus. by Paul Galdone. 1983, Houghton paper $7.95 (978-0-89919-192-8). 32pp. A recommended version of this favorite French tale, now available with an audio version. [398.2]

12049 Perrault, Charles. *Puss in Boots* (K–4). Illus. by Fred Marcellino. 1990, Farrar $16.00 (978-0-374-36160-0). 32pp. A handsomely illustrated version of this classic tale. (Rev: BCCB 12/90; BL 12/1/90*; HB 3/91*; SLJ 1/91) [398.2]

12050 Pienkowski, Jan. *The Fairy Tales* (K–3). Trans. by David Walser. Illus. by author. 2006, Viking $19.99 (978-0-670-06189-1). 192pp. This handsome collection includes four of the genre's best-known stories — "Cinderella," "Hansel and Gretel," "Sleeping Beauty," and "Snow White" — translated from German and illustrated with dramatic silhouettes filled with color. (Rev: BL 11/1/06; SLJ 11/06) [398.2]

12051 Pinkney, Jerry. *Little Red Riding Hood* (PS). Illus. by author. 2007, Little, Brown $16.99 (978-0-316-01355-0). 40pp. A retelling of how Red survives her encounter with the wolf, with old-fashioned watercolor renderings. (Rev: BL 9/1/07; HB 11/07; LMC 3/08; SLJ 10/07) [398.2]

12052 Pinkney, Jerry. *The Nightingale* (K–4). Illus. 2002, Penguin $16.99 (978-0-8037-2426-6). 40pp. The familiar fairy tale of a king and a nightingale with a magical voice is transplanted to Morocco and accompanied by beautiful illustrations. (Rev: BCCB 11/02; BL 9/1/02) [398.2]

12053 Pinkney, Jerry. *The Ugly Duckling* (PS–3). 1999, Morrow LB $17.89 (978-0-688-15933-7). 40pp. Gorgeous double-page spreads are used in

this handsome retelling of Hans Christian Andersen's classic story. Caldecott Honor Book, 2000. (Rev: BCCB 3/99; BL 3/1/99*; HB 5/99; HBG 10/99; SLJ 5/99) [398.2]

12054 Pirotta, Saviour. *The Golden Slipper: An Ancient Egyptian Fairy Tale and Cinderella* (3–5). Illus. by Alan Marks. Series: Once Upon a World. 2008, Black Rabbit LB $22.95 (978-1-59771-077-0). 32pp. An Egyptian Cinderella tale, featuring a Greek slave girl called Rhodopis, is followed by a traditional version. (Rev: BL 4/1/08) [398.2]

12055 Pirotta, Saviour. *The McElderry Book of Grimm's Fairy Tales* (K–3). Illus. by Emma Chichester Clark. 2006, Simon & Schuster $19.95 (978-1-4169-1798-4). 128pp. Ten classic Grimm tales are retold in appealing text and illustrations. (Rev: BL 11/1/06; SLJ 11/06) [398.2]

12056 Poole, Amy Lowry. *The Pea Blossom* (K–2). Illus. 2005, Holiday House $16.95 (978-0-8234-1864-0). 32pp. A watercolor picture book, set in China, retelling the Hans Christian Andersen tale of a pea that helps a sick little girl. (Rev: BL 3/1/05; SLJ 3/05) [398.2]

12057 Prokofiev, Sergei. *The Love for Three Oranges* (2–4). Illus. by Elzbieta Gaudasinska. Series: Musical Stories. 2006, Pumpkin House $16.95 (978-0-9646010-3-1). 40pp. The fairy-tale story, based on the libretto for Prokofiev's opera, of a prince who is cursed to fall in love with three oranges and must steal them from a faraway castle, in the process finding his true love. (Rev: BL 11/15/06; SLJ 10/06) [398.2]

12058 Puttapipat, Niroot. *Musicians of Bremen* (PS–2). Illus. 2005, Candlewick $15.99 (978-0-7636-2758-4). 32pp. The focus is on music in this retelling that features realistic animals who end up not in Bremen but happily ensconced in a comfortable cottage. (Rev: BL 11/15/05; SLJ 12/05) [398.2]

12059 Pyle, Howard. *The Swan Maiden* (K–3). Illus. by Robert Sauber. 1994, Holiday House LB $15.95 (978-0-8234-1088-0). 28pp. In this fairy tale, one of the king's sons discovers that a swan maiden is stealing pears from his father's pear tree. (Rev: BL 10/15/94; SLJ 1/95) [398.2]

12060 Pyle, Howard. *The Wonder Clock: Or Four and Twenty Marvelous Tales* (4–6). Illus. by author. 1915, Dover paper $10.95 (978-0-486-21446-7). 319pp. Tales for each hour of the day, told by figures on a clock. [398.2]

12061 Rae, Jennifer. *Dog Tales* (1–3). Illus. by Rose Cowles. 1999, Tricycle $14.95 (978-1-58246-011-6). 28pp. Six fractured fairy tales are told using dogs as characters. One example is "The Doberman's New Clothes." (Rev: HBG 10/00; SLJ 12/99) [398.2]

12062 Reinhart, Matthew. *Cinderella: A Pop-Up Fairy Tale* (K–2). Illus. Series: Classic Collectible Pop-Up. 2005, Simon & Schuster $24.95 (978-1-4169-0501-1). 12pp. Inventive paper engineering makes this Cinderella memorable. (Rev: BL 11/1/05) [398.2]

12063 Roberts, Lynn. *Little Red: A Fizzingly Good Yarn* (2–4). Illus. by David Roberts. 2005, Abrams

$16.95 (978-0-8109-5783-1). 32pp. In this variation on the story of Little Red Riding Hood, the heroine is replaced by a little boy named Thomas who tricks the wolf into gulping down a ginger ale and belching up the boy's recently devoured grandmother. (Rev: BL 10/15/05; SLJ 11/05) [398.2]

12064 Roberts, Lynn, retel. *Rapunzel: A Groovy Fairy Tale* (PS–2). Illus. by David Roberts. 2003, Abrams $16.95 (978-0-8109-4242-4). In this retelling set in the 1970s, Rapunzel is locked away in an apartment building by her evil aunt, who chops off Rapunzel's long hair when she discovers the girl is sneaking time with a rock singer. (Rev: HBG 4/04; SLJ 11/03) [398.2]

12065 Ros, Roser. *Musicians of Bremen / Los musicos de Bremner* (2–4). Illus. by Pep Montserrat. 2005, Chronicle $14.95 (978-0-8118-4795-7); paper $6.95 (978-0-8118-4796-4). 32pp. This strikingly illustrated bilingual adaptation of the Grimm tale — in which four aging animals, cast out by their owners, travel to Bremen to join the city band — uses European Spanish. (Rev: BL 11/1/05; SLJ 10/05) [398.2]

12066 Ruskin, John. *The King of the Golden River* (3–5). Illus. by Iassen Ghiuselev. 2005, Simply Read $19.95 (978-1-894965-16-3). 64pp. In this brightly illustrated adaptation of Ruskin's fairy tale, Gluck, a kindhearted lad of 12, is badly treated by his older siblings Hans and Schwartz who are eventually undone by their greed and misanthropy. (Rev: BL 12/1/05) [398.2]

12067 Russell, P. Craig. *The Fairy Tales of Oscar Wilde: The Devoted Friend, The Nightingale and the Rose* (5–8). Illus. by author. 2004, NBM $15.95 (978-1-56163-391-3). 32pp. Two of Oscar Wilde's fairy tales — "The Devoted Friend" and "The Nightingale and the Rose" — are presented in a rich, picture-book-size graphic novel format. (Rev: BL 8/04; SLJ 11/04) [398.2]

12068 Rylant, Cynthia. *Hansel and Gretel* (K–2). Illus. by Jen Corace. 2008, Hyperion $16.99 (978-1-4231-1186-3). 40pp. With illustrations that extend the text, this retelling of the classic story emphasizes the children's domestic problems. (Rev: BCCB 11/08; BL 8/08; HB 11/08; SLJ 9/08) [398.2]

12069 Sanderson, Ruth. *Cinderella* (PS–3). Illus. 2002, Little, Brown $15.95 (978-0-316-77965-4). 32pp. An exquisitely produced version of the Cinderella story with detailed illustrations and an elegant text. (Rev: BL 4/15/02*; HBG 10/02; SLJ 6/02) [398.2]

12070 San José, Christine. *The Emperor's New Clothes* (PS–3). Illus. by Anastassija Archipowa. 1998, Boyds Mills $15.95 (978-1-56397-699-5). 32pp. A new version of Andersen's familiar story in a large-format picture book with graceful watercolor pictures. (Rev: BL 4/1/98; HBG 10/98; SLJ 4/98) [398.2]

12071 San José, Christine. *The Little Match Girl* (PS–3). Illus. by Kestutis Kasparavicius. 2002, Boyds Mills $15.95 (978-1-59078-000-8). 32pp. Lovely illustrations accompany this retelling of the sad story in which the little girl dies. (Rev: BL 10/1/02; HBG 3/03; SLJ 10/02) [398.2]

12072 San José, Christine, retel. *Six Swans: A Folktale* (1–4). Illus. by Jes Cole. 2006, Boyds Mills $16.95 (978-1-59078-056-5). Full-page illustrations offering changing perspectives add to the appeal of this retelling, which the princess herself narrates, of the story of the six brothers who have been changed into swans. (Rev: SLJ 12/06) [398.2]

12073 San José, Christine. *Sleeping Beauty* (K–3). Illus. by Dominic Catalano. 1997, Boyds Mills $14.95 (978-1-56397-636-0). 32pp. Dormouse characters are used in this successful retelling of the traditional fairy tale. (Rev: BL 10/15/97; HBG 3/98; SLJ 9/97) [398.2]

12074 San Souci, Robert D. *Cendrillon: A Caribbean Cinderella* (PS–3). Illus. by Brian Pinkney. 1998, Simon & Schuster $16.00 (978-0-689-80668-1). 40pp. An enchanting new version of the Cinderella story that is based on a French Creole tale and uses Martinique as its setting. (Rev: BCCB 1/99; BL 10/15/98; HB 11/98; HBG 3/99; SLJ 9/98) [398.2]

12075 San Souci, Robert D. *Cinderella Skeleton* (3–5). Illus. by David Catrow. 2000, Harcourt $16.00 (978-0-15-202003-3). 32pp. A macabre variation on the Cinderella story in which the heroine is a stick-figure skeleton who lives in Boneyard Acres and falls in love with Prince Charnel. (Rev: BCCB 10/00; BL 9/1/00; HB 9/00; HBG 3/01; SLJ 9/00) [398.2]

12076 San Souci, Robert D., retel. *The White Cat: An Old French Fairy Tale* (3–4). Illus. by Gennady Spirin. 1990, Orchard LB $17.99 (978-0-531-08409-0). 32pp. The retelling of the story of three princes who vie for their father's kingdom. (Rev: BCCB 11/90; BL 9/1/90; HB 11/90; SLJ 10/90) [398.2]

12077 Sauvant, Henriette. *Rapunzel and Other Magic Fairy Tales* (4–7). Trans. by Anthea Bell. Illus. by author. 2008, Egmont $15.95 (978-1-4052-2702-5). 160pp. Retellings of fourteen fairy tales, many of them by the Grimm brothers, and some of them grim or even grisly, accompanied by lush illustrations. (Rev: BL 5/1/08; SLJ 7/08) [398.2]

12078 Schlitz, Laura Amy. *The Bearskinner: A Tale of the Brothers Grimm* (3–5). Illus. by Max Grafe. 2007, Candlewick $16.99 (978-0-7636-2730-0). 40pp. This retelling features a destitute soldier who makes a deal with the devil — if he can live for seven years without bathing or grooming while wearing a bearskin, he will be rich; if he fails, he forfeits his soul. (Rev: BCCB 12/07; BL 11/15/07; HB 1/08; LMC 1/08; SLJ 12/07) [398.2]

12079 Scieszka, Jon. *The Frog Prince Continued* (1–4). Illus. by Steve Johnson. 1991, Viking $15.99 (978-0-670-83421-1). 32pp. After the princess and the former frog are married, he still keeps hopping about and wonders if he should change back into a frog. (Rev: BCCB 5/91; BL 6/1/91; HB 7/91; SLJ 5/91) [398.2]

12080 Scott-Mitchell, Clare. *Cinderella* (PS–2). Illus. by Gordon Fitchett. 2001, Penguin $16.99 (978-0-8037-2577-5). 32pp. In this fresh version of Cinderella all the characters are animals, including the heroine, who is a black-and white cat. (Rev: BL 1/1–15/01; SLJ 2/01) [398.2]

12081 Setterington, Ken, retel. *Clever Katarina: A Tale in Six Parts* (2–6). Illus. by Nelly Hofer and Ernst Hofer. 2006, Tundra $17.95 (978-0-88776-764-7). 40pp. The artwork shines in this retelling of a Grimm fairy tale originally called "The Peasant's Clever Daughter," in which a beautiful peasant girl called Katarina must solve a riddle to win the king's hand and save her father from being cast into prison. (Rev: SLJ 12/06) [398.2]

12082 Setterington, Ken. *Hans Christian Andersen's The Snow Queen* (3–5). Illus. by Nelly Hofer and Ernst Hofer. 2000, Tundra $16.95 (978-0-88776-497-4). 48pp. A secular retelling of the Andersen story illustrated with old-fashioned black-and-white silhouettes. (Rev: BL 12/15/00; HBG 10/01; SLJ 3/01) [398.2]

12083 Shepard, Aaron. *One-Eye! Two-Eyes! Three-Eyes! A Very Grimm Fairy Tale* (K–2). Illus. by Gary Clement. 2006, Atheneum $16.95 (978-0-689-86740-8). 32pp. A girl with two eyes is the butt of much derision from her one-eyed and three-eyed sisters. (Rev: BL 1/1–15/07; SLJ 1/07) [398.2]

12084 Sierra, Judy. *The Gift of the Crocodile* (PS–3). Illus. by Reynold Ruffins. 2000, Simon & Schuster $17.00 (978-0-689-82188-2). 40pp. This is an exotic version of Cinderella, set in the Spice Islands, with a river crocodile serving as Grandmother Crocodile, the fairy godmother. (Rev: BCCB 12/00; BL 1/1–15/01; HB 1/01; HBG 3/01; SLJ 11/00) [398.2]

12085 Smith, Scudder, retel. *Jack and the Beanstalk* (PS–2). Illus. by Felipe López Salán. 2006, Purple Bear $15.95 (978-1-933327-11-2). This retelling of the classic fairy tale is fairly faithful to the original but a bit kinder and gentler in tone. (Rev: SLJ 8/06) [398.2]

12086 Snyder, Laurel. *Up and Down the Scratchy Mountains* (3–5). Illus. 2008, Random $16.99 (978-0-375-84719-6). 256pp. In the land of Bewilderness, a young milkmaid named Lucy and a prince named Wynston go in search of Lucy's missing mother. (Rev: BL 9/15/08; HB 1/09; SLJ 9/08) [398.2]

12087 Stanley, Diane. *Goldie and the Three Bears* (PS–1). Illus. by author. 2003, HarperCollins LB $17.89 (978-0-06-000009-7). Goldie has been looking high and low for a friend "to love with all her heart;" her quest ends when she goes snooping around in the home of the Three Bears. (Rev: HB 9/03; HBG 4/04; SLJ 11/03) [398.2]

12088 Steig, Jeanne. *A Handful of Beans* (PS–3). Illus. by William Steig. 1998, HarperCollins $21.99 (978-0-06-205162-2). 144pp. Six favorite fairy tales, including Rumpelstiltskin, Hansel and Gretel, and Jack and the Beanstalk, are informally retold with cartoon-style drawings. (Rev: BL 11/15/98*; HB 1/99; HBG 3/99; SLJ 12/98) [398.2]

12089 Stewig, John W. *Whuppity Stoorie* (2–4). Illus. by Preston McDaniels. 2004, Holiday House $16.95 (978-0-8234-1749-0). 32pp. This picture-book story of a young widow who foils a fairy's attempts to steal her son is set in Scotland, with suitable dialect and illustrations. (Rev: BL 2/15/04; SLJ 3/04) [398.2]

12090 Storace, Patricia. *Sugar Cane: A Caribbean Rapunzel* (K–3). Illus. by Raúl Colón. 2007, Hyperion $16.99 (978-0-7868-0791-8). 48pp. Filled with striking illustrations and beautifully descriptive language, this Rapunzel is set on a Caribbean island full of magic. (Rev: BCCB 10/07; BL 7/07; LMC 10/07; SLJ 7/07) [398.2]

12091 Thomas, Joyce Carol. *The Gospel Cinderella* (PS–2). Illus. by David Diaz. 2004, HarperCollins $15.99 (978-0-06-025387-5). 40pp. In this retelling, the daughter of Queen Mother Rhythm falls into the clutches of Cruel Crooked Foster Mother and can only be saved by her talent as a gospel singer. (Rev: BL 2/15/04; SLJ 5/04) [398.2]

12092 Thurber, James. *Many Moons* (2–4). Illus. by Marc Simont. 1990, Harcourt $14.95 (978-0-15-251872-1). 48pp. A sick princess asks her father for the moon to help her get better. The original edition, illustrated by Louis Slobodkin, was the 1944 Caldecott Medal winner. (Rev: BL 9/15/90; HB 1/90*; SLJ 1/91) [398.2]

12093 Tym, Kate. *Princess Stories from Around the World* (3–5). Illus. by Sophy Williams. 2008, Trafalgar paper $13.95 (978-1-84365-100-0). 64pp. An appealing, large-format collection of traditional tales about princesses of all kinds, told in an up-to-date conversational style with vivid illustrations. (Rev: BLO 7/30/08) [398.2]

12094 Vande Velde, Vivian. *The Rumpelstiltskin Problem* (4–6). 2000, Houghton $15.00 (978-0-618-05523-4). 116pp. After a criticism of the logic behind this famous fairy tale, the author presents six new versions of the tale that, supposedly, make more sense. (Rev: BCCB 2/01; HBG 3/01; SLJ 11/00) [398.2]

12095 Waters, Fiona. *The Emperor and the Nightingale* (PS–3). Illus. by Paul Birkbeck. 2000, Bloomsbury $19.95 (978-0-7475-3559-1). 32pp. A fine retelling of this classic fairy tale with lavish illustrations and sensitive language. (Rev: BL 11/15/00; SLJ 1/01) [398.2]

12096 Wegman, William. *Cinderella* (PS–2). Illus. 1993, Hyperion $16.95 (978-1-56282-348-1). 38pp. The characters in this reworking of the Cinderella story are all dogs, but the story remains the same. (Rev: BCCB 7–8/93; BL 5/15/93; SLJ 4/93) [398.2]

12097 Wenzel, David, and Doug Wheeler. *Fairy Tales of the Brothers Grimm* (4–6). Illus. 1995, NBM $15.95 (978-1-56163-130-8). 48pp. Using a comic book format, some of the best-known tales of the Grimm Brothers are retold, with an emphasis on story-telling pictures. (Rev: BL 4/15/96) [398.2]

12098 Whipple, Laura. *If the Shoe Fits* (5–8). Illus. by Laura Beingessner. 2002, Simon & Schuster $17.95 (978-0-689-84070-8). 80pp. A handsome retelling of the Cinderella story using blank verse. (Rev: BCCB 3/02; BL 5/1/02; HBG 10/02; SLJ 8/02) [398.2]

12099 Wilcox, Leah. *Falling for Rapunzel* (PS–2). Illus. by Lydia Monks. 2003, Penguin $14.99 (978-

0-399-23794-2). In this hilarious variation, Rapunzel misinterprets the prince's pleas, throwing down socks instead of lock, her maid instead of her braid. (Rev: BL 12/1/03; HB 11/03; HBG 4/04; SLJ 12/03) [398.2]

12100 *The Wild Swans* (4–6). Retold by Ken Setterington. Illus. by Ernst Hofer and Nelly Hofer. 2003, Tundra $17.95 (978-0-88776-615-2). 40pp. The story of how Elise saves her brothers from being turned into swans is presented in clear, flowing text and intricate cut-paper art. (Rev: BL 11/15/03; HBG 4/04; SLJ 12/03) [398.2]

12101 Wilde, Oscar. *The Happy Prince* (3–5). Illus. by Robin Muller. 2002, Stoddart $15.95 (978-0-7737-3218-6). 24pp. Wilde's unusual fairy tale in which a swallow and a statue make sacrifices for each other is retold with effective illustrations. (Rev: BL 3/15/02) [398.2]

12102 Willard, Nancy. *Cinderella's Dress* (K–2). Illus. by Jane Dyer. 2003, Scholastic $16.95 (978-0-590-56927-9). With the help of two magpies, a ring hammered from fairy gold, and her fairy godmother, Cinderella finally makes it to the ball despite the best efforts of the horrible stepsisters. (Rev: HBG 4/04; SLJ 11/03) [398.2]

12103 Willard, Nancy. *The Flying Bed* (2–4). Illus. by John Thompson. 2007, Scholastic $16.99 (978-0-590-25610-0). A Florentine baker's business booms after he buys a very special bed, but his greed jeopardizes his luck. (Rev: BCCB 5/07; BL 1/1/07; LMC 8/07; SLJ 4/07) [398.2]

12104 Williams, Brenda. *The Real Princess: A Mathemagical Tale* (K–2). Illus. by Sophie Fatus. 2008, Barefoot Books $16.99 (978-1-905236-88-6). 40pp. The story of the princess who felt the pea through the mattress is retold with many opportunities for counting. (Rev: BL 5/15/08; LMC 10/08; SLJ 6/08) [398.2]

12105 Wisnewski, Andrea, retel. *Little Red Riding Hood* (PS–3). Illus. by Andrea Wisnewski. 2007, Godine $18.95 (978-1-56792-303-2). Detailed painted prints give this retelling of the fairy tale a classic look. (Rev: SLJ 6/07) [398.2]

12106 Wood, Audrey. *Heckedy Peg* (PS–2). Illus. by Don Wood. 1987, Harcourt $16.00 (978-0-15-233678-3); paper $7.00 (978-0-15-233679-0). 32pp. Mother promises gifts to her seven children, all named for days of the week, taken from a 16th-century game still played in England. (Rev: BCCB 12/87; BL 9/15/87; SLJ 11/87) [398.2]

12107 Young, Ed. *Hook* (PS–1). Illus. by author. 2009, Roaring Brook $17.95 (978-1-59643-363-2). 32pp. This variation of the Ugly Duckling features a fear-of-flying eaglet hatched by a mother hen. (Rev: BCCB 9/09; BL 6/1–15/09; HB 5/09; LMC 8/09; SLJ 6/09) [398.2]

12108 Young, Ed. *Lon Po Po: A Red-Riding-Hood Story from China* (2–4). Illus. 1989, Penguin $16.99 (978-0-399-21619-0). 32pp. In this variation of the Red Riding Hood story, Mother visits Grandmother, leaving her three children in danger from a marauding wolf. Caldecott Medal winner, 1990. (Rev: BCCB 11/89*; BL 11/15/89; HB 1/90*; SLJ 12/89*) [398.2] ∩

12109 Zalben, Jane Breskin. *Hey, Mama Goose* (PS–K). Illus. by Emilie Chollat. 2005, Dutton $15.99 (978-0-525-47097-7). 32pp. Mama Goose, real estate agent, brokers deals in which familiar fairy-tale characters exchange dwellings with one another. (Rev: BL 2/15/05; SLJ 2/05) [398.2]

Folklore

General

12110 Ada, Alma Flor, and F. Isabel Campoy. *Tales Our Abuelitas Told: A Hispanic Folktale Collection* (3–5). Illus. by Felipe Davalos. 2006, Simon & Schuster $19.95 (978-0-689-82583-5). 128pp. The 12 folk tales in this collection have their roots in Hispanic culture but touch on universal themes; interesting notes add relevance. (Rev: BL 9/1/06; SLJ 9/06) [398.2]

12111 Adler, Naomi. *The Barefoot Book of Animal Tales* (2–4). Illus. by Amanda Hall. 2002, Barefoot Books $19.99 (978-1-84148-941-4). 80pp. Lovely, vivid illustrations brighten retellings of nine animal tales, including a Native American story and the German classic about the Bremen musicians. (Rev: BL 1/1–15/03; HBG 3/03; SLJ 6/03) [398.2]

12112 Adler, Naomi. *Play Me a Story: Nine Tales About Musical Instruments* (3–6). Illus. 1998, Millbrook LB $23.40 (978-0-7613-0401-2). 80pp. Beginning with the tale of the Pied Piper of Hamelin, this book contains nine stories about musical instruments from different countries, including a Native American story and a myth from ancient Greece. (Rev: BL 7/98; HBG 10/98; SLJ 4/98) [398]

12113 Andrews, Jan. *Out of the Everywhere: Tales for a New World* (2–6). Illus. by Simon Ng. 2001, Groundwood $19.95 (978-0-88899-402-8). 95pp. Andrews retells stories, setting them in the New World and showing their relevance to immigrants or people seeking new situations. (Rev: HB 9/01; HBG 3/02; SLJ 9/01) [813]

12114 Batt, Tanya. *The Fabrics of Fairytale: Stories Spun from Far and Wide* (4–6). Illus. 2000, Barefoot Books $19.99 (978-1-84148-061-9). 80pp. This book contains seven retold folktales, each related to a different kind of fabric or an article of clothing, like silk brocade, a patchwork coat, or a feather cloak. Patchwork illustrations are reminiscent of a story quilt. (Rev: BL 11/15/00; HBG 10/01; SLJ 11/00) [398.23]

12115 Batt, Tanya Robyn. *A Child's Book of Faeries* (3–5). Illus. by Gail Newey. 2002, Barefoot Books $19.99 (978-1-84148-954-4). 64pp. Four stories, with snippets of poetry and folklore, introduce the magical world of fairies and leprechauns. (Rev: BL 12/15/02; HBG 3/03; SLJ 1/03) [398.21]

12116 Beeler, Selby B. *Throw Your Tooth on the Roof: Tooth Traditions from Around the World* (PS–3). Illus. by G. Brian Karas. 1998, Houghton $16.00 (978-0-395-89108-7). 32pp. As well as some basic facts about teeth, this book outlines lost-tooth traditions from around the world, each of which makes placing the tooth under a pillow to get money from the tooth fairy seem very tame. (Rev: BCCB 11/98; BL 7/98; HBG 3/99; SLJ 9/98) [398]

12117 Bini, Renata, retel. *A World Treasury of Myths, Legends, and Folktales: Stories from Six Continents* (3–6). Trans. from Italian by Alexandra Bonfante-Warren. Illus. by Mikhail Fiodorov. 2000, Abrams $24.95 (978-0-8109-4554-8). 126pp. These brief retellings of tales from around the world cover many cultures and times; about one-quarter are from Native American sources. (Rev: BL 1/1–15/01; HBG 3/01; SLJ 12/00) [398.2]

12118 Blackstone, Stella. *Storytime: First Tales for Sharing* (PS–K). Illus. by Anne Wilson. 2005, Barefoot Books $19.99 (978-1-84148-345-0). 96pp. Seven familiar tales — including such classics as "Goldilocks and the Three Bears" and "The Gingerbread Man" — are faithfully retold and accompanied by attractive collage and acrylic illustrations. (Rev: BL 1/1–15/06; SLJ 11/05) [398.2]

12119 Borlenghi, Patricia. *Chaucer the Cat and the Animal Pilgrims* (3–6). Illus. by Giles Greenfield. 2000, Bloomsbury $22.95 (978-0-7475-4491-3). 77pp. A group of animal pilgrims from around the world led by Chaucer the Cat from London tell folk tales on their way to honor Saint Francis at Assisi. (Rev: SLJ 1/01) [398.2]

12120 Brill, Marlene T. *Tooth Tales from Around the World* (K–2). Illus. by Katya Krenina. 1998, Charlesbridge LB $15.95 (978-0-88106-398-1);

paper $6.95 (978-0-88106-399-8). 32pp. An outline of the many traditions and beliefs from around the world concerning lost teeth. For example, ancient Egyptians threw their teeth to the sun in the belief that the sun made teeth strong. (Rev: BL 7/98; HBG 10/98) [398]

12121 Caduto, Michael J. *Earth Tales from Around the World* (5–8). Illus. 1997, Fulcrum paper $17.95 (978-1-55591-968-9). 192pp. This collection of 48 folktales from around the world emphasizes respect for the natural world. (Rev: BL 4/1/98; SLJ 5/98; VOYA 4/98) [398.27]

12122 Cecil, Laura. *Cunning Cat Stories* (K–2). Illus. by Emma Chichester Clark. 2003, Pavilion $19.95 (978-1-86205-376-2); paper $.00 (978-1-84365-023-2). 80pp. Three feline-themed folk tales — "Puss in Boots," "Sir Pussycat," and "The White Cat" — are retold in this attractively illustrated collection. (Rev: BL 6/1–15/04; SLJ 5/04)

12123 Climo, Shirley. *King of the Birds* (PS–3). Illus. by Ruth Heller. 1991, HarperCollins paper $5.95 (978-0-06-443273-3). 32pp. The long-ago legend of how the birds chose a king. (Rev: BL 2/15/88; SLJ 8/88) [398.2]

12124 Cooling, Wendy. *Farmyard Tales from Far and Wide* (PS–2). Illus. by Rosslyn Moran. 1998, Barefoot Books $15.95 (978-1-901223-38-5). 48pp. Each of these seven folktales deals with common farmyard animals and comes from the folklore of a different country. (Rev: BL 11/1/98; SLJ 11/98) [398.2]

12125 Czarnota, Lorna MacDonald. *Medieval Tales That Kids Can Read and Tell* (3–6). Series: World Folktale Collections. 2000, August House $21.95 (978-0-87483-589-2); paper $12.95 (978-0-87483-588-5). 96pp. This collection of folk tales suitable for children to tell features such characters as Robin Hood, William Tell, Robert Bruce, Joan of Arc, and Beowulf. (Rev: HBG 10/00; SLJ 2/01) [398.2]

12126 dePaola, Tomie, ed. *Tomie dePaola's Favorite Nursery Tales* (PS–3). Illus. by Tomie dePaola. 1986, Penguin $25.99 (978-0-399-21319-9). 128pp. The artist's favorite childhood remembrances in an attractive package. (Rev: BCCB 2/87; BL 11/1/86; SLJ 1/87) [398.2]

12127 DeSpain, Pleasant. *Tales of Cats* (3–5). Illus. by Don Bell. Series: The Books of Nine Lives. 2003, August House $14.95 (978-0-87483-713-1). 80pp. Nine folktales about cats from diverse cultures may appeal in particular to reluctant readers. (Rev: HBG 4/04; SLJ 1/04) [398.2]

12128 DeSpain, Pleasant. *Tales of Enchantment* (3–5). Illus. by Don Bell. Series: The Books of Nine Lives. 2003, August House $14.95 (978-0-87483-711-7). 80pp. This collection of nine folk tales offers stories of fantasy and the supernatural from cultures around the world. (Rev: HBG 4/04; SLJ 1/04) [398.2]

12129 DeSpain, Pleasant. *Tales of Nonsense and Tomfoolery* (3–5). Illus. Series: Books of Nine Lives. 2001, August House paper $3.99 (978-0-87483-645-5). 80pp. A collection of tales from

around the world that specialize in nonsense. (Rev: BL 7/01) [398.2]

12130 DeSpain, Pleasant. *Tales of Tricksters* (3–5). Illus. Series: Books of Nine Lives. 2001, August House paper $3.99 (978-0-87483-644-8). 80pp. A collection of tales from around the world that specialize in tricksters. (Rev: BL 7/01) [398.2]

12131 DeSpain, Pleasant. *Tales of Wisdom and Justice* (3–5). Illus. Series: Books of Nine Lives. 2001, August House paper $3.99 (978-0-87483-646-2). 80pp. A collection of tales from around the world that specialize in wise decisions. (Rev: BL 7/01) [398.2]

12132 DeSpain, Pleasant. *Tales to Frighten and Delight* (3–5). Illus. by Don Bell. Series: The Books of Nine Lives. 2003, August House $14.95 (978-0-87483-712-4). 80pp. Nine spine-chilling folktales are collected from cultures around the world. (Rev: HBG 4/04; SLJ 1/04) [398.27]

12133 DeSpain, Pleasant, retel. *Thirty-Three Multicultural Tales to Tell* (3–7). Illus. by Joe Shlichta. Series: American Folklore and Storytelling. 1993, August House paper $15.00 (978-0-87483-266-2). 126pp. An interesting international collection of folktales that span a number of subjects and moods. (Rev: SLJ 6/94) [398.2]

12134 Dijkstra, Lida. *Little Mouse* (PS–K). Illus. by Lida Grobler. 2004, Front St. $15.95 (978-1-932425-06-2). 32pp. A retelling of a traditional tale in which a little mouse, accompanied by her adoptive hermit father, searches for "the strongest being on earth" to be her mate. (Rev: BL 1/1–15/05; SLJ 2/05) [398.2]

12135 Emberley, Rebecca, and Ed Emberley. *Chicken Little* (PS–K). Illus. by Rebecca Emberley. 2009, Roaring Brook $16.95 (978-1-59643-464-6). 32pp. Bright, colorful collage illustrations full of fun enhance this lively retelling. (Rev: BL 5/1/09; HB 5/09; SLJ 5/09) [398.2]

12136 Evetts-Secker, Josephine. *The Barefoot Book of Father and Son Tales* (3–6). Illus. 1999, Barefoot Books $19.95 (978-1-902283-32-6). 80pp. Father-son relationships are explored in this collection of folktales that includes the Daedalus-Icarus myth. (Rev: BL 4/1/99; SLJ 6/99) [398.27]

12137 Evetts-Secker, Josephine. *The Barefoot Book of Mother and Son Tales* (3–6). 1999, Barefoot Books $19.95 (978-1-902283-05-0). 80pp. Using colorful illustrations and a choice of tales from the world's folklore, this collection explores mother-son relationships. (Rev: BL 4/1/99; SLJ 6/99) [398.27]

12138 Forest, Heather. *Wisdom Tales from Around the World* (4–7). 1996, August House $27.95 (978-0-87483-478-9); paper $19.95 (978-0-87483-479-6). 160pp. Fifty fables, folktales, and myths from around the world. (Rev: BCCB 2/97; BL 3/1/97; SLJ 4/97) [398.2]

12139 Forest, Heather. *Wonder Tales from Around the World* (4–6). Illus. 1995, August House paper $16.95 (978-0-87483-422-2). 160pp. A collection of 27 traditional stories, some familiar and others never anthologized before. (Rev: BL 11/15/95; SLJ 4/96) [398.2]

12140 Gibbons, Gail. *Behold . . . the Dragons!* (K–3). Illus. 1999, Morrow LB $17.89 (978-0-688-15527-8). 32pp. Drawing on the world's folklore, this book follows dragons through different cultures and times. (Rev: BL 5/1/99; HBG 10/99; SLJ 4/99) [398]

12141 Gilchrist, Cherry. *A Calendar of Festivals* (3–7). Illus. 1998, Barefoot Books $18.95 (978-1-901223-68-2). 80pp. This anthology includes folktales and stories for many of the major holidays celebrated annually around the world. (Rev: BL 9/15/98; SLJ 12/98) [394.2]

12142 Gilchrist, Cherry. *Stories from the Silk Road* (3–7). Illus. 1999, Barefoot Books $19.95 (978-1-902283-25-8). 80pp. Seven exotic folktales represent the culture and history of the countries along the fabled Silk Road that stretched from China to Persia. (Rev: BL 9/15/99; SLJ 11/99) [398.27]

12143 Gilchrist, Cherry. *Sun-Day, Moon-Day: How the Week Was Made* (3–5). Illus. by Amanda Hall. 1998, Barefoot Books $18.95 (978-1-901223-63-7). 80pp. Each day of the week is highlighted, with background information and a tale from Greek, Norse, Roman, Babylonian, and other folklore traditions. (Rev: SLJ 9/98) [398.2]

12144 Hamilton, Martha, and Mitch Weiss. *How and Why Stories: World Tales Kids Can Read and Tell* (5–10). Illus. 1999, August House $21.95 (978-0-87483-562-5); paper $12.95 (978-0-87483-561-8). 96pp. This excellent collection of 25 pourquoi (how and why) stories from around the world also contains a useful introduction on folklore, plus tips on delivering each of the tales. (Rev: BL 5/15/00; HBG 3/00; SLJ 1/00) [398.2]

12145 Hamilton, Martha, and Mitch Weiss. *Noodlehead Stories: World Tales Kids Can Read and Tell* (3–5). Illus. 2000, August House $21.95 (978-0-87483-584-7); paper $12.95 (978-0-87483-585-4). 96pp. Includes 23 humorous stories from around the world, with tips on effective delivery and general storytelling advice. (Rev: BL 2/15/01; HBG 10/01; SLJ 1/01) [389.2]

12146 Hamilton, Virginia. *A Ring of Tricksters: Animal Tales from North America, the West Indies, and Africa* (3–6). Illus. by Barry Moser. 1997, Scholastic $22.95 (978-0-590-47374-3). 112pp. This is a stunning collection of trickster tales, many from Africa and others that were adapted by slaves to reflect conditions in the West Indies and the United States. (Rev: BL 1/1–15/98; HBG 3/98; SLJ 11/97) [398.2]

12147 Hartman, Bob. *The Lion Storyteller Book of Animal Tales* (K–3). Illus. by Susie Poole. 2004, Lion paper $13.95 (978-0-7459-4838-6). 116pp. A diverse and entertaining collection of more than 30 tales to do with animals. (Rev: SLJ 8/04) [398.2]

12148 Henderson, Kathy. *Lugalbanda: The Boy Who Got Caught Up in a War* (2–4). Illus. by Jane Ray. 2006, Candlewick $16.99 (978-0-7636-2782-9). 80pp. This retelling of an ancient Sumerian legend recounts how a young prince named Lugalbanda receives the strength he needs for war. (Rev: BL 5/1/06; SLJ 4/06*) [398.2]

12149 Hoffman, Mary. *A Twist in the Tail: Animal Stories from Around the World* (K–3). Illus. by Jan Ormerod. 1998, Holt $18.95 (978-0-8050-5945-8). 68pp. Ten lively folktales about animals from such places as India, China, Malaysia, and Nigeria are included in this anthology. (Rev: BL 11/15/98; SLJ 11/98) [398.245]

12150 Hutchinson, Duane. *The Gunny Wolf and Other Fairy Tales* (4–6). Illus. 1993, Foundation paper $6.95 (978-0-934988-29-2). 88pp. A total of seven folktales, including Tom Thumb and The Six Swans, are included in this collection. (Rev: BL 5/15/93) [398.2]

12151 Jaffe, Nina, and Steve Zeitlin. *The Cow of No Color: Riddle Stories and Justice Tales from Around the World* (5–8). Illus. 1998, Holt $17.00 (978-0-8050-3736-4). 160pp. A collection of folktales from around the world that deal with the theme of justice. (Rev: BCCB 12/98; BL 11/1/98; HBG 3/99; SLJ 12/98) [398.2]

12152 Jones, Christianne C. *Chicken Little* (K–1). Illus. by Kyle Hermanson. Series: Read-It! Readers/FolkTales. 2005, Picture Window LB $19.93 (978-1-4048-0972-7). 32pp. The familiar story is retold for beginning readers, with colorful illustrations. (Rev: SLJ 7/05) [398.2]

12153 Kampen, Vlasta van, ed. *Bear Tales: Three Treasured Stories* (PS–1). Illus. 2000, Annick LB $18.95 (978-1-55037-619-7); paper $6.95 (978-1-55037-618-0). 40pp. Three bear stories are retold here, one from Czech sources, one from Russian, and one from Native American folklore. (Rev: BL 6/1–15/00; HBG 10/00; SLJ 10/00) [398.2]

12154 Ketteman, Helen. *Armadilly Chili* (K–3). Trans. and illus. by Will Terry. 2004, Whitman $16.95 (978-0-8075-0457-4). 32pp. This charming retelling of the Little Red Hen story is transposed to the American Southwest. (Rev: BL 6/1–15/04; SLJ 5/04) [398.2]

12155 Krishnaswami, Uma. *Stories of the Flood* (4–6). Illus. 1994, Roberts Rinehart $15.95 (978-1-57098-007-7). 41pp. In a picture-book format, nine flood myths from such places as ancient Sumeria and Hawaii are retold. (Rev: BL 2/1/95; SLJ 2/95) [291.13]

12156 Laird, Elizabeth. *Beautiful Bananas* (PS–2). Illus. by Liz Pichon. 2004, Peachtree $15.95 (978-1-56145-305-4). 32pp. In this charming circular folktale, young Beatrice sets off for her grandfather's house with a bunch of bananas balanced on her head; various encounters with animals along the way cause substitutions for the bananas. (Rev: BL 5/1/04; SLJ 4/04) [398.2]

12157 Lansky, Bruce, sel. *Girls to the Rescue: Tales of Clever, Courageous Girls from Around the World* (3–6). 1995, Meadowbrook paper $3.95 (978-0-88166-215-3). 100pp. A collection of stories about resourceful young women, many of which originated in the world's folklore. (Rev: SLJ 12/95) [398.2]

12158 Lansky, Bruce, ed. *Girls to the Rescue Book 2: Tales of Clever, Courageous Girls from Around the World* (3–6). 1996, Meadowbrook LB $3.95 (978-0-671-57375-1). 103pp. In each of the folktales gathered from around the world, young women must rely on their ingenuity to overcome obstacles. (Rev: SLJ 2/97) [398.2]

12159 Lunge-Larsen, Lise. *The Hidden Folk: Stories of Fairies, Gnomes, Selkies, and Other Secret Beings* (3–5). Illus. by Beth Krommes. 2004, Houghton $18.00 (978-0-618-17495-9). 80pp. Drawing on the folkloric traditions of northern Europe, Lunge-Larsen offers up eight tales about magical beings. (Rev: BL 9/1/04) [398.2]

12160 Lupton, Hugh, ed. *The Songs of Birds: Stories and Poems from Many Cultures* (4–7). Illus. 2000, Barefoot Books $19.95 (978-1-84148-045-9). 80pp. A beautifully illustrated collection of stories (mostly creation myths) and poems about birds culled from a wide range of cultures. (Rev: BL 3/15/00; SLJ 9/00) [808.819]

12161 Lupton, Hugh. *The Story Tree: Tales to Read About* (PS–2). Illus. by Sophie Fatus. 2001, Barefoot Books $18.99 (978-1-84148-312-2). 64pp. This volume includes seven folktales from around the world, including favorites such as "The Three Billy Goats Gruff" and "The Magic Porridge Pot." (Rev: BL 10/1/01; HBG 3/02; SLJ 11/01) [398.2]

12162 Lupton, Hugh, retel. *Tales of Wisdom and Wonder* (2–6). Illus. by Niamh Sharkey. 1998, Barefoot Books $18.95 (978-1-901223-09-5). 64pp. Seven traditional stories from different cultures, such as Haitian, Cree, West African, Russian, and Irish, are retold in this anthology. (Rev: SLJ 10/98) [398.2]

12163 McBratney, Sam. *One Voice, Please: Favorite Read-Aloud Stories* (2–4). Illus. by Russell Ayto. 2008, Candlewick $15.99 (978-0-7636-3479-7). 176pp. A collection of more than 50 short, traditional stories that are suitable for reading aloud. (Rev: BL 4/1/08; HB 5/08; SLJ 8/08) [398.2]

12164 MacDonald, Margaret Read, comp. *Earth Care: World Folktales to Talk About* (3–7). 1999, Linnet LB $26.50 (978-0-208-02416-9); paper $17.50 (978-0-208-02426-8). 161pp. These 41 folk stories from 30 countries deal with humans and their relationship to nature. (Rev: BL 1/1–15/00; HBG 3/00; SLJ 4/00) [398.2]

12165 MacDonald, Margaret Read. *Peace Tales: World Folktales to Talk About* (5–7). Illus. 1992, Shoe String LB $25.00 (978-0-208-02328-5); paper $17.50 (978-0-208-02329-2). 114pp. Stories and proverbs directed toward achieving world peace. (Rev: BL 6/15/92; SLJ 10/92) [398.2]

12166 Maddern, Eric. *The Cow on the Roof* (PS). Illus. by Paul Hess. 2006, Frances Lincoln $15.95 (978-1-84507-374-9). Convinced that he does the lion's share of work, a farmer switches jobs for a day with his wife, only to learn that her chores are not nearly as easy as he had imagined; a traditional tale reset in Wales. (Rev: SLJ 10/06) [398.2]

12167 Mama, Raouf. *The Barefoot Book of Tropical Tales* (3–5). Illus. 2000, Barefoot Books $19.95 (978-1-902283-21-0). 64pp. Backed up by extensive source notes, this book contains eight folktales that come from either African or Afro-Caribbean traditions. (Rev: BL 4/1/00; SLJ 9/00) [398.2]

12168 Matthews, Andrew. *Marduk the Mighty and Other Stories of Creation* (4–6). Illus. by Sheila Moxley. 1997, Millbrook LB $22.40 (978-0-7613-0204-9). 96pp. A collection of 24 creation stories, beginning with Genesis and ending with a Norse myth about the fall of the gods. (Rev: BCCB 6/97; BL 6/1–15/97; SLJ 7/97) [291.1]

12169 Matthews, Caitlin. *Fireside Stories: Tales for a Winter's Eve* (K–3). Illus. by Helen Cann. 2007, Barefoot Books $19.99 (978-1-84686-065-2). 96pp. Winter-themed folk tales from Austria, Russia, Canada, and the Czech Republic are among those included here. (Rev: BL 12/1/07; LMC 1/08; SLJ 2/08) [398.2]

12170 Matthews, John. *The Barefoot Book of Knights* (4–7). Illus. by Giovanni Manna. 2002, Barefoot Books $19.99 (978-1-84148-064-0). 80pp. This book contains retellings of seven tales of knights and chivalry from countries around the world. (Rev: BCCB 9/02; BL 4/15/02; HBG 10/02; SLJ 6/02) [398.2]

12171 Matthews, John. *Giants, Ghosts and Goblins* (4–6). Illus. 1999, Barefoot Books $19.95 (978-1-902283-27-2). 80pp. Nine stories of ghosts, some of them friendly, from such faraway places as Australia. (Rev: BL 10/15/99; SLJ 10/99) [398.2]

12172 Matthews, John, and Caitlin Matthews. *The Wizard King and Other Spellbinding Tales* (3–6). Illus. 1998, Barefoot Books $18.95 (978-1-901223-84-2). 80pp. An interesting collection of nine folk and fairy stories from around the world that feature dragons, monsters, spells, and wizards. (Rev: BL 10/15/98; SLJ 12/98) [398.2]

12173 Milord, Susan. *Bird Tales from Near and Far* (1–5). Illus. 1999, Williamson $12.95 (978-1-885593-18-4). 96pp. From many cultures, this collection of folktales about a variety of birds also contains factual information, projects, and crafts. (Rev: BL 2/15/99; SLJ 11/98) [398.2]

12174 Milord, Susan. *Tales Alive! Ten Multicultural Folktales with Activities* (4–6). Illus. 1995, Williamson paper $14.25 (978-0-913589-79-3). 128pp. This book contains 19 folktales plus such related material as riddles, puzzles, and craft projects. (Rev: BL 4/15/95; SLJ 3/95) [398.2]

12175 Milord, Susan, retel. *Tales of the Shimmering Sky: Ten Global Folktales with Activities* (3–6). Illus. by JoAnn E. Kitchel. Series: A Williamson Tales Alive! Book. 1996, Williamson paper $14.25 (978-1-885593-01-6). 128pp. Ten folktales from different cultures explore such topics as the sky, wind, seasons, colors, and the weather, with additional background material and many suggested projects. (Rev: SLJ 2/97) [398.2]

12176 Mutén, Burleigh. *Grandfather Mountain: Stories of Gods and Heroes from Many Cultures* (4–7). Retold by Burleigh Muten. Illus. by Siân Bailey. 2004, Barefoot Books $19.99 (978-1-84148-789-2). 80pp. Strong male protagonists are featured in folktales from England, Greece, Ireland, Japan, Mexico, New Zealand, Nigeria, and the Seneca Indians. (Rev: BL 11/15/04; SLJ 1/05) [398.2]

12177 Mutén, Burleigh. *Grandmothers' Stories: Wise Woman Tales from Many Cultures* (3–5). Illus. 1999, Barefoot Books $19.99 (978-1-902283-24-1). 80pp. An anthology of folktales from around the world that portray older women in a favorable light. (Rev: BL 11/15/99; SLJ 3/00) [398.27]

12178 Norman, Howard. *Between Heaven and Earth: Bird Tales from Around the World* (3–7). Illus. by Leo Dillon and Diane Dillon. 2004, Harcourt $22.00 (978-0-15-201982-2). 96pp. Five beautifully illustrated bird-themed folktales hail from Africa, Australia, China, Norway, and Sri Lanka. (Rev: BL 11/1/04) [398.2]

12179 Oliver, Narelle. *Mermaids Most Amazing* (2–4). Illus. 2005, Penguin $15.99 (978-0-399-24288-5). 32pp. The origins of folklore and mythology about mermaids are briefly explored in this attractive import from Australia. (Rev: BL 2/1/05; SLJ 2/05) [398.21]

12180 Oram, Hiawyn. *Not-So-Grizzly Bear Stories* (3–4). 1998, Little Tiger $16.95 (978-1-888444-41-4). 96pp. An exciting retelling of ten folktales about bears from around the world. (Rev: BL 3/1/99; HBG 3/99; SLJ 4/99) [398.24]

12181 Osborne, Mary Pope, ed. *Mermaid Tales from Around the World* (3–6). Illus. by Troy Howell. 1993, Scholastic $16.95 (978-0-590-44377-7). 96pp. Twelve stories about mermaids collected from the world's folklore. (Rev: BCCB 2/94; BL 10/15/93; SLJ 11/93) [398.21]

12182 Pearson, Maggie. *The Fox and the Rooster and Other Tales* (K–3). Illus. by Joanne Moss. 1997, Little Tiger $14.95 (978-1-888444-17-9). 77pp. Fourteen countries — e.g., Norway, Japan, and Ireland — are represented in this collection of folktales. (Rev: BCCB 3/98; BL 2/15/98; HBG 10/98) [398.2]

12183 Pearson, Maggie. *The Headless Horseman and Other Ghoulish Tales* (4–7). Illus. 2001, Interlink $18.95 (978-1-56656-377-2). 96pp. From Bluebeard to Baba Yaga and Ichabod Crane, this is a collection of 14 tales about eerie beings. (Rev: BL 3/1/01; HBG 10/01; SLJ 1/01) [398.2]

12184 Peters, Andrew F. *Strange and Spooky Stories* (3–6). Illus. 1997, Millbrook LB $23.90 (978-0-7613-0321-3). 80pp. Nine unusual but appealing tales from North America, the British Isles, Central Europe, and the Czech Republic. (Rev: BL 2/1/98; HBG 3/98) [398.2]

12185 Phelps, Ethel Johnston. *Tatterhood and Other Tales* (3–6). Illus. by Pamela Baldwin-Ford. 1978, Feminist paper $9.95 (978-0-912670-50-8). 192pp. Tales in which women play a vital and decisive role. [398.2]

12186 Pringle, Laurence. *Imagine a Dragon* (2–4). Illus. by Eujin Kim Neilan. 2008, Boyds Mills $16.95 (978-1-56397-328-4). 32pp. Pringle explores the history of dragons east and west — from those that tangled with St. George and to legends of Norway, Egypt, and the Far East. (Rev: BL 3/1/08; LMC 3/08; SLJ 7/08) [398.24]

12187 Rosen, Michael J. *How the Animals Got Their Colors* (5–8). Illus. by John Clementson. 1992, Har-court $14.95 (978-0-15-236783-1). 48pp. Tales from around the world that explain such things as a leopard's spots and the green on a frog's back. (Rev: BCCB 7–8/92; BL 6/15/92; SLJ 9/91) [398.2]

12188 Rossel, Seymour. *Sefer Ha-Aggadah: The Book of Legends for Young Readers* (4–7). Illus. by Judy Dick. 1996, UAHC paper $14.00 (978-0-8074-0603-8). 67pp. A collection of legends based on stories about the Jewish people from the Old Testament. (Rev: SLJ 3/97) [398.2]

12189 Shah, Idries. *The Man and the Fox* (K–3). Illus. by Sally Mallam. 2006, Hoopoe Bks. $18.00 (978-1-883536-43-5); paper $7.99 (978-1-883536-60-2). A clever fox outwits a man's plot to capture him. (Rev: SLJ 12/06) [398.2]

12190 Shannon, George. *Rabbit's Gift* (PS–1). Illus. by Laura Dronzek. 2007, Harcourt $16.00 (978-0-15-206073-2). 32pp. Rabbit, Donkey, Goat, and Deer all show compassion for one another during a winter storm and share the last turnip in this ancient folktale with a theme common to many cultures. (Rev: BCCB 12/07; BL 11/1/07; SLJ 12/07) [398.2]

12191 Shannon, George. *Stories to Solve: Folktales from Around the World* (4–6). Illus. by Peter Sís. 1985, Morrow paper $4.95 (978-0-688-10496-2). 56pp. Fourteen stories combine puzzles and folklore asking readers how the problem was figured out or the mystery solved. (Rev: BL 12/1/85; HB 9/85; SLJ 9/85) [398.2]

12192 Sherman, Josepha. *Magic Hoofbeats: Horse Tales from Many Lands* (2–4). Illus. by Linda Wingerter. 2004, Barefoot Books $19.99 (978-1-84148-091-6). 80pp. Horses with magical abilities are the focus of these brief folktales. (Rev: BL 11/1/04; SLJ 2/05) [398.2]

12193 Sherman, Josepha. *Merlin's Kin: World Tales of the Heroic Magician* (5–8). 1998, August House paper $11.95 (978-0-87483-519-9). A splendid international collection of folktales that feature magicians, sorcerers, shamans, healers, and wizards. (Rev: BL 4/15/99; SLJ 3/99; VOYA 12/98) [398.21]

12194 Sherman, Josepha. *Told Tales: Nine Folktales from Around the World* (4–6). Illus. 1995, Silver Moon LB $14.95 (978-1-881889-64-9). 80pp. A general introduction for beginning storytellers that uses a question-and-answer technique and supplies nine folktales from around the world. (Rev: BL 2/1/96; SLJ 1/96) [398.2]

12195 Sierra, Judy. *Can You Guess My Name? Traditional Tales Around the World* (3–5). Illus. by Stefano Vitale. 2002, Clarion $21.00 (978-0-618-13328-4). 128pp. In this handsome volume with lengthy endnotes, Sierra has collected 15 folktales from all corners of the world that are variants of five favorite stories. (Rev: BL 11/15/02; HB 1/03*; HBG 3/03; SLJ 11/02*) [398.2]

12196 Sierra, Judy, ed. *Nursery Tales Around the World* (4–6). Illus. by Stefano Vitale. 1996, Clarion $20.00 (978-0-395-67894-7). 114pp. This fascinating work retells folktales with similar themes as they exist in different cultures. (Rev: BCCB 2/96; BL 3/1/96; HB 5/96; SLJ 4/96) [398.2]

12197 Sierra, Judy. *Silly and Sillier: Read-Aloud Tales from Around the World* (PS–2). Illus. by Valeri Gorbachev. 2002, Knopf $19.95 (978-0-375-80609-4). 96pp. These 20 folktales from around the world and the wonderful illustrations that accompany them are sure to bring smiles to young readers' faces. (Rev: BL 12/15/02; HBG 3/03; SLJ 11/02) [398.2]

12198 Singh, Rina, and Debbie Lush. *Moon Tales: Myths of the Moon from Around the World* (3–6). 2000, Bloomsbury $22.95 (978-0-7475-4112-7). 77pp. A stylish retelling of folk tales from around the world dealing with the moon and its powers. (Rev: SLJ 3/01) [398.2]

12199 Spencer, Ann. *Song of the Sea: Myths, Tales, and Folklore* (4–6). Illus. 2001, Tundra paper $17.95 (978-0-88776-487-5). 208pp. A handsome and varied collection of sea-related lore from around the world. (Rev: BL 8/01; SLJ 7/01) [398.23]

12200 Spiegelman, Art. *Little Lit: Folklore and Fairy Tale Funnies* (4–9). Illus. 2000, HarperCollins $19.95 (978-0-06-028624-8). 64pp. In this presentation in graphic novel format, 15 different artists create brilliant variations on standard fairy and folk tales. (Rev: BL 1/1–15/01*; HB 9/00; HBG 3/01; SLJ 12/00) [398.2]

12201 Thompson, Stith, ed. *One Hundred Favorite Folktales* (5–8). Illus. by Franz Altschuler. 1968, Indiana Univ. $39.95 (978-0-253-15940-3); paper $19.95 (978-0-253-20172-0). 456pp. A selection from an international store of folktales. [398.2]

12202 Van Kampen, Vlasta. *A Drop of Gold* (PS–2). Illus. 2001, Annick LB $18.95 (978-1-55037-677-7); paper $7.95 (978-1-55037-676-0). 32pp. Spirited artwork illustrates this pourquoi tale of how Mother Nature and her helpers colored the world's birds. (Rev: BL 2/1/02; HBG 3/02; SLJ 1/02) [813]

12203 Villaseñor, Victor. *Little Crow to the Rescue / El cuervito al rescate* (PS–3). Trans. by Elizabeth Cummins Munoz. Illus. by Felipe Ugalde Alcántara. 2005, Arte Publico $15.95 (978-1-55885-430-7). 32pp. In Spanish and English, this is a pourquoi tale about the reasons for crows' disdain for humans. (Rev: BL 10/1/05; SLJ 2/06) [398.2]

12204 Vogel, Carole G. *Legends of Landforms: Native American Lore and the Geology of the Land* (4–6). Illus. 1999, Millbrook LB $27.90 (978-0-7613-0272-8). 96pp. This book contains 14 legends about such geological formations as the Grand Canyon and Martha's Vineyard, with scientific background material on each. (Rev: BL 11/15/99; HBG 10/00; SLJ 1/00) [398.2]

12205 Waldherr, Kris. *Sacred Animals* (3–6). Illus. 2001, HarperCollins LB $16.89 (978-0-688-16380-8). 48pp. Animal folklore and legends from around the world are organized in four sections — earth, water, fire, and air animals — and surrounded with wonderful illustrations and borders. (Rev: BL 10/1/01; HBG 3/02; SLJ 11/01) [398.2]

12206 Walker, Barbara K., ed. *A Treasury of Turkish Folktales for Children* (4–7). 1988, Shoe String LB $25.00 (978-0-208-02206-6). 155pp. A witty collec-tion interspersed with riddles. (Rev: BL 10/15/88; SLJ 10/88) [398.2]

12207 Walker, Richard. *The Barefoot Book of Pirates* (4–6). Illus. 1998, Barefoot Books $19.99 (978-1-901223-79-8). 64pp. Pirates and robbers from folklore, including Robin Hood and Pirate Grace, are included in this entertaining collection of folktales from around the world. (Rev: BL 11/15/98; SLJ 9/98) [398.2]

12208 Walker, Richard. *The Barefoot Book of Trickster Tales* (3–6). Illus. 1998, Barefoot Books $18.95 (978-1-902283-08-1). 80pp. A collection of trickster tales from around the world, including an Anansi story, a Jack tale, a Brer Rabbit adventure, and a Red Riding Hood story from Bengal. (Rev: BL 1/1–15/99; SLJ 11/98) [398]

12209 *Wicked Wolf Stories* (K–2). Retold by Laura Cecil. Illus. by Emma Chichester Clark. 2003, Pavilion $19.95 (978-1-86205-460-8); paper $10.95 (978-1-84365-018-8). 80pp. Three popular children's stories featuring wolves are featured in this attractive volume. (Rev: BL 6/1–15/04)

12210 Willey, Margaret. *Clever Beatrice and the Best Little Pony* (K–2). Illus. by Heather Solomon. 2004, Simon & Schuster $16.95 (978-0-689-85339-5). 40pp. Beatrice triumphs over the lutin, a leprechaun-like being, who seems to be riding her pony at night. (Rev: BL 2/1/05; SLJ 11/04) [398.2]

12211 Yolen, Jane. *Meow: Cat Stories from Around the World* (1–3). Illus. by Hala Wittwer. 2005, HarperCollins $16.99 (978-0-06-029161-7). 40pp. Ten beautifully illustrated cat stories look at cat — and human — behavior around the world. (Rev: BL 8/05; SLJ 8/05) [398.24]

12212 Yolen, Jane, ed. *Mightier than the Sword: World Folktales for Strong Boys* (4–8). Illus. by Raúl Colón. 2003, Harcourt $20.00 (978-0-15-216391-4). 128pp. Yolen has collected stories from countries including Afghanistan, Angola, and China that portray intelligence as an invaluable asset. (Rev: BL 4/1/03; HB 5/03; HBG 10/03; SLJ 5/03) [398.2]

12213 Yolen, Jane, ed. *Not One Damsel in Distress: World Folktales for Strong Girls* (3–6). Illus. 2000, Harcourt $21.00 (978-0-15-202047-7). 112pp. A collection of folktales from such different locales as Argentina, Romania, and Germany in which girls face obstacles difficult to surmount. (Rev: BCCB 4/00; BL 3/1/00; HBG 10/00; SLJ 7/00) [398.22]

12214 Yolen, Jane. *Once Upon a Bedtime Story* (K–3). Illus. by Ruth T. Councell. 1997, Boyds Mills $17.95 (978-1-57397-484-4). 96pp. This is a charming collection of 16 folktales, fairy tales, and fables, chiefly from Europe. (Rev: BL 11/15/97; SLJ 9/97) [398.2]

12215 Young, Richard A., and Judy Dockery Young, eds. *Stories from the Days of Christopher Columbus: A Multicultural Collection for Young Readers* (5–9). 1992, August House paper $8.95 (978-0-87483-198-6). An anthology of stories translated from a variety of languages, including Italian, Spanish, Portuguese, and Aztec. (Rev: BL 9/15/92; SLJ 7/92) [398.2]

Africa

12216 Aardema, Verna, retel. *Bringing the Rain to Kapiti Plain: A Nandi Tale* (PS–2). Illus. by Beatriz Vidal. 1981, Puffin paper $7.99 (978-0-14-054616-3). 32pp. A rhyming book on how the rain was brought to an African plain. [398.2]

12217 Aardema, Verna. *The Lonely Lioness and the Ostrich Chicks* (PS–2). Illus. by Yumi Heo. 1996, Knopf LB $18.99 (978-0-679-96934-1). 32pp. In this Masai story, a lonely lioness is determined to raise an ostrich's four chicks. (Rev: BCCB 2/97; BL 11/15/96; SLJ 12/96*) [398.2]

12218 Aardema, Verna. *Rabbit Makes a Monkey of Lion* (K–1). Illus. by Jerry Pinkney. 1989, Puffin paper $6.99 (978-0-14-054593-7). 32pp. A Swahili tale of a wily little rabbit outwitting the big brawny lion. (Rev: BL 3/1/89; HB 5/89; SLJ 6/89) [398.2]

12219 Aardema, Verna. *Sebgugugu the Glutton: A Bantu Tale from Rwanda, Africa* (4–6). Illus. by Nancy L. Clouse. 1993, Africa World $14.95 (978-0-86543-377-9). 32pp. In this Rwandian folktale, a foolish man loses everything because of his greed. (Rev: BL 4/1/93; SLJ 6/93) [398.2]

12220 Aardema, Verna, ed. *Why Mosquitoes Buzz in People's Ears: A West African Tale* (K–3). Illus. by Leo Dillon and Diane Dillon. 1992, Puffin paper $7.99 (978-0-14-054905-8). 32pp. Bold, stylized paintings illustrate this tale of a mosquito who tells a whopping lie, thus setting off a chain of events. Caldecott Medal winner, 1976. [398.2]

12221 Ahmed, Said Salah. *The Lion's Share / Qayb Libaax: A Somali Folktale* (PS–2). Illus. by Kelly Dupre. 2006, Minnesota Humanities Commission $15.95 (978-1-931016-12-4); paper $7.95 (978-1-931016-13-1). 32pp. After cooperating to kill a camel, the hungry animals must divide the loot, but as always the "lion's share is not fair." (Rev: BL 1/1–15/07; SLJ 1/07) [398.2]

12222 Anderson, David A. *The Origin of Life on Earth: An African Creation Myth* (2–6). Illus. by Kathleen A. Wilson. 1991, Sights LB $18.95 (978-0-9629978-5-3). This African myth tells how earthly creatures were formed and how the world began spinning. (Rev: SLJ 7/92) [398.2]

12223 Araujo, Frank P. *The Perfect Orange: A Tale from Ethiopia* (K–3). Illus. by Xiao Jun Li. Series: Toucan Tales. 1994, Rayve $17.95 (978-1-877810-94-7). In this Ethiopian folktale, a simple girl impresses a king with her generosity, and he rewards her with gold and jewels. (Rev: SLJ 3/95) [398.2]

12224 Arkhurst, Joyce Cooper. *The Adventures of Spider: West African Folktales* (4–7). Illus. by Jerry Pinkney. 1992, Little, Brown paper $8.99 (978-0-316-05107-1). Six humorous stories featuring the crafty spider. [398.2]

12225 Ashabranner, Brent, and Russell Davis. *The Lion's Whiskers and Other Ethiopian Tales* (4–7). Illus. 1997, Linnet LB $19.95 (978-0-208-02429-9). 96pp. A classic collection of 16 Ethiopian folktales

originally published in 1995. (Rev: BL 10/1/97; SLJ 5/97*) [398.2]

12226 Barbosa, Rogerio Andrade. *African Animal Tales* (4–6). Trans. by Feliz Guthrie. Illus. by Cica Fittipaldi. 1993, Volcano $17.95 (978-0-912078-96-0). 63pp. Weak, small animals outwit stronger animals in this collection of ten African folktales. (Rev: BL 2/15/94) [398.2]

12227 Bryan, Ashley. *Beat the Story-Drum, Pum-Pum* (K–4). Illus. by author. 1987, Macmillan paper $8.95 (978-0-689-71107-7). 80pp. A retelling of five Nigerian folktales. [398.2]

12228 Bryan, Ashley. *Beautiful Blackbird* (K–2). Illus. 2003, Simon & Schuster $16.95 (978-0-689-84731-8). 40pp. Bold collages illustrate the Zambian tale of Blackbird, who is the envy of all the brightly colored birds in Africa and generously agrees to share his blackening potion, so that all the birds can be black and beautiful. (Rev: BCCB 2/03; BL 1/1–15/03; HB 3/03*; HBG 10/03; SLJ 1/03) [398.2]

12229 Bryan, Ashley. *The Night Has Ears: African Proverbs* (K–3). Illus. 1999, Simon & Schuster $16.00 (978-0-689-82427-2). 32pp. Presenting one proverb per page, this is a collection of 26 aphorisms from various African tribes. (Rev: BL 9/15/99; HBG 3/00; SLJ 1/00) [398.9]

12230 Courlander, Harold, and George Herzog. *The Cow-Tail Switch: And Other West African Stories* (4–6). Illus. by Madye Lee Chastain. 1988, Holt paper $9.95 (978-0-8050-0298-0). 160pp. Originally published in 1947, this is a fine collection of folktales about foolish and wise men and animals. [398.2]

12231 Cummings, Pat. *Ananse and the Lizard* (PS–3). Illus. 2002, Holt $16.95 (978-0-8050-6476-6). 40pp. The trickster spider meets his match when a cunning lizard wins the competition for the hand of the chief's daughter. (Rev: BL 11/1/02; HBG 3/03; SLJ 10/02) [398.2]

12232 Dee, Ruby. *Two Ways to Count to Ten: A Liberian Folktale* (PS–1). Illus. by Susan Meddaugh. 1990, Holt paper $6.95 (978-0-8050-1314-6). 32pp. The antelope outsmarts them all when the king advertises for a successor. (Rev: BL 7/88; SLJ 6–7/88) [398.2]

12233 Diakité, Baba Wague, retel. *The Hatseller and the Monkeys* (K–3). Illus. by Baba Wague Diakité. 1999, Scholastic $17.99 (978-0-590-96069-4). This is an interesting West African version of the traditional tale about a peddler whose hats are stolen by a group of monkeys. (Rev: BCCB 2/99; HB 5/99; HBG 10/99; SLJ 2/99) [398.2]

12234 Diakité, Baba Wague. *The Hunterman and the Crocodile: A West African Folktale* (K–3). Illus. 1997, Scholastic $16.95 (978-0-590-89828-7). 32pp. A West African folktale about the Hunterman who runs afoul of Bamba the Crocodile and is helped by Rabbit. (Rev: BCCB 2/97; BL 3/15/97; SLJ 3/97) [398.2]

12235 Diakité, Baba Wague. *The Magic Gourd* (2–4). Illus. 2003, Scholastic $16.95 (978-0-439-43960-2). 32pp. A retelling of a folktale from Mali about a rabbit who, when his magic gourd is stolen, receives a magic rock to help recover it. (Rev: BCCB 3/03; BL 2/15/03; HBG 10/03; SLJ 2/03) [398.2]

12236 Echewa, T. Obinkaram. *The Magic Tree: A Folktale from Nigeria* (PS–3). Illus. by E. B. Lewis. 1999, Morrow LB $15.89 (978-0-688-16232-0). 32pp. In this Nigerian folktale, a young outsider gains power and prestige when a magic udara tree gives him fruit and obeys his commands. (Rev: BCCB 4/99; BL 6/1–15/99*; HBG 10/99; SLJ 8/99) [398.2]

12237 Eisner, Will. *Sundiata: A Legend of Africa* (5–8). Illus. 2003, NBM $15.95 (978-1-56163-332-6). 32pp. A retelling, in comic book style, of an African folktale about a lame prince who conquers an evil king. (Rev: BL 2/1/03; HBG 10/03; SLJ 2/03) [398.2]

12238 Gershator, Phillis. *Only One Cowry* (K–3). Illus. by David Soman. 2000, Orchard LB $17.99 (978-0-531-33288-7). 32pp. This African folktale in picture-book format tells about tricksters, weddings, and dowries and employs collages made of cut and torn paper to illustrate its events. (Rev: BCCB 1/01; BL 10/15/00; HBG 3/01; SLJ 9/00) [398.2]

12239 Gershator, Phillis. *Zzzng! Zzzng! Zzzng! A Yoruba Tale* (PS–1). Illus. by Theresa Smith. 1998, Orchard LB $16.99 (978-0-531-08873-9). 32pp. In this Yoruba folktale from Nigeria, Mosquito faces rejection when he tries to marry above his station and takes out his anger by buzzing and biting. (Rev: BCCB 10/98; BL 8/98; HBG 3/99; SLJ 10/98) [398.2]

12240 Greaves, Nick. *When Hippo Was Hairy: And Other Tales from Africa* (4–8). Illus. 1988, Barron's paper $11.95 (978-0-8120-4548-2). 144pp. Thirty-one traditional African tales, a combination of folklore and fact. (Rev: BL 2/15/89; SLJ 2/89) [398.2]

12241 Green, Roger L. *Tales of Ancient Egypt* (5–9). 1972, Penguin paper $4.99 (978-0-14-036716-4). A collection of folktales from ancient Egypt including one about the source of the Nile. [398]

12242 Grifalconi, Ann. *The Village of Round and Square Houses* (PS–2). Illus. by author. 1986, Little, Brown $16.95 (978-0-316-32862-3). 32pp. This blend of fiction, anthropology, and folklore centers around the central African remote village of Tos. (Rev: BCCB 6/86; BL 6/15/86; SLJ 8/86) [398.2]

12243 Haley, Gail E. *A Story, a Story* (1–4). Illus. by author. 1970, Macmillan LB $17.00 (978-0-689-20511-8); paper $5.99 (978-0-689-71201-2). 36pp. How African "spider stories" began is traced back to the time when Ananse, the Spider Man, made a bargain with the Sky God. Caldecott Medal winner, 1971. [398.2]

12244 Hull, Robert, retel. *Egyptian Stories* (4–6). Illus. by Noel Bateman and Barbara Loftus. Series: Tales from Around the World. 1994, Thomson Learning LB $24.26 (978-1-56847-155-6). 48pp. Introduces seven traditional tales, including a creation story, as well as life in ancient Egypt. (Rev: SLJ 8/94) [398.2]

12245 Janisch, Heinz. *The Fire: An Ethiopian Folk Tale* (PS–2). Trans. by Shelley Tanaka. Illus. by Fabricio Vandenbroeck. 2002, Groundwood $15.95 (978-0-88899-450-9). 32pp. A slave must spend the night on a snow-capped mountain peak with no clothes or shelter to win his freedom in this Ethiopian folktale with evocative double-page paintings. (Rev: BL 12/15/02; HBG 3/03; SLJ 2/03) [398.2]

12246 Kimmel, Eric A. *Anansi and the Magic Stick* (PS–2). Illus. by Janet Stevens. 2001, Holiday House $16.95 (978-0-8234-1443-7). 32pp. Things don't go as Anansi the tricky spider plans when he steals a magic stick to do his work for him. (Rev: BCCB 12/01; BL 9/15/01; HBG 3/02; SLJ 9/01) [398.2]

12247 Kimmel, Eric A. *Anansi and the Moss-Covered Rock* (PS–3). Illus. by Janet Stevens. 1988, Holiday House LB $16.95 (978-0-8234-0689-0); paper $6.95 (978-0-8234-0798-9). 32pp. Anansi the trickster discovers a magic rock that knocks animals out, and then he steals their food. (Rev: BCCB 10/88; BL 10/1/88; SLJ 11/88) [398.2]

12248 Kimmel, Eric A. *Anansi and the Talking Melon* (PS–3). Illus. by Janet Stevens. 1994, Holiday House LB $16.95 (978-0-8234-1104-7). 32pp. Hiding inside a melon, Anansi the Spider tricks all the animals into believing that the melon can speak in this African folktale. (Rev: BCCB 6/94; BL 2/15/94; SLJ 3/94*) [398.2]

12249 Kimmel, Eric A. *Anansi Goes Fishing* (K–3). Illus. by Janet Stevens. 1992, Holiday House LB $16.95 (978-0-8234-0918-1). 32pp. Lazy but lovable trickster Anansi is outwitted by the clever turtle in this contemporary rendition of an old tale. (Rev: BL 3/15/92; SLJ 5/92) [398.2]

12250 Kimmel, Eric A. *Anansi's Party Time* (PS–2). Illus. by Janet Stevens. 2008, Holiday $16.95 (978-0-8234-1922-7). 32pp. Turtle gets his revenge on the trickster spider Anansi in this humorous folktale. (Rev: BL 9/15/08; LMC 5/09; SLJ 9/08) [398.2]

12251 Kimmel, Eric A. *Rimonah of the Flashing Sword: A North African Tale* (K–3). Illus. by Omar Rayyan. 1995, Holiday House LB $15.95 (978-0-8234-1093-4). 32pp. An Egyptian folktale that is a variation on the Snow White story about a princess fleeing the wrath of a wicked stepmother. (Rev: BL 3/1/95; SLJ 3/95) [398.2]

12252 Knutson, Barbara. *How the Guinea Fowl Got Her Spots: A Swahili Tale of Friendship* (PS–2). Illus. 1990, Carolrhoda LB $15.95 (978-0-87614-416-9). 24pp. Cow returns a favor given by Nganga the Guinea Fowl by giving her spots that can help her hide from enemies. (Rev: BCCB 7–8/90*; BL 6/15/90; HB 9/90; SLJ 9/90) [398.2]

12253 Lake, Mary D., retel. *The Royal Drum: An Ashanti Tale* (K–2). Illus. by Carol O'Malia. 1996, Mondo $14.95 (978-1-57255-140-4). Using a rebus approach, this tale from Ghana tells how Anansi the spider gets all of the animals to participate in making a drum for Lion the king. (Rev: SLJ 11/96) [398.2]

12254 Lilly, Melinda. *Kwian and the Lazy Sun: African Tales and Myths* (K–3). Series: African Tales and Myths. 1998, Rourke LB $26.60 (978-1-57103-243-0). In this South African tale, a young girl figures out how to get the sun and the moon into the sky. Also use from the same series and author *Tamba and the Chief: A Tenne Tale* and *Warrior Son of a Warrior Son: A Masai Tale* (both 1998). (Rev: SLJ 4/99) [398.2]

12255 Lilly, Melinda, retel. *Spider and His Son Find Wisdom: An Akan Tale* (2–4). Illus. by Charles Reasoner. Series: African Tales and Myths. 1998, Rourke LB $19.95 (978-1-57103-244-7). 31pp. The spider, Anansi, tries to retrieve all the good advice he has given to unappreciative villagers in this Akan tale told in a picture-book format. (Rev: SLJ 3/99) [398.2]

12256 Lilly, Melinda, retel. *Wanyana and Matchmaker Frog: A Bagandan Tale* (2–4). Illus. by Charles Reasoner. Series: African Tales and Myths. 1998, Rourke LB $19.95 (978-1-57103-247-8). 31pp. To repay a kindness he received when in distress, a frog gives a young girl good advice in choosing a husband in this African folk tale. (Rev: SLJ 3/99) [398.2]

12257 Lilly, Melinda, retel. *Zimani's Drum: A Malawian Tale* (2–4). Illus. by Charles Reasoner. Series: African Tales and Myths. 1998, Rourke LB $19.95 (978-1-57103-248-5). 31pp. Blind Zimani rescues his brother and two sisters from the clutches of Mkango the Lion. (Rev: SLJ 3/99) [398.2]

12258 Linn, Dennis, et al. *What Is My Song?* (2–4). Illus. by Francisco Miranda. 2005, Paulist Press $16.95 (978-0-8091-6722-7). 32pp. In this adaptation of an African folktale, a boy strives to live up to what he believes to be his God-given purpose in life. (Rev: BL 12/1/04)

12259 Lottridge, Celia B., retel. *The Name of the Tree* (K–5). Illus. by Ian Wallace. 1990, Macmillan $16.00 (978-0-689-50490-7). This Bantu tale begins with hungry animals finding a tree laden with every fruit imaginable. (Rev: BCCB 4/90; SLJ 3/90) [398.2]

12260 McDermott, Gerald. *Anansi, the Spider: A Tale from the Ashanti* (K–3). Illus. by author. 1972, Holt LB $16.95 (978-0-8050-0310-9); paper $6.95 (978-0-8050-0311-6). 48pp. Because Anansi and his sons quarrel, the moon remains in the sky. [398.2]

12261 McDermott, Gerald. *Zomo the Rabbit: A Trickster Tale from West Africa* (PS–3). Illus. 1992, Harcourt $14.95 (978-0-15-299967-4). 32pp. An enduring Nigerian tale of a trickster who is cunning but not always wise. (Rev: BCCB 9/92*; BL 9/15/92*; SLJ 11/92*) [398.2]

12262 McIntosh, Gavin. *Hausaland Tales from the Nigerian Marketplace* (4–9). Illus. 2002, Linnet $22.50 (978-0-208-02523-4). 98pp. This collection of 12 Nigerian folktales skillfully interweaves details of contemporary Hausa society. (Rev: HBG 3/03; SLJ 11/02) [398.2]

12263 Mama, Raouf, retel. *Why Goats Smell Bad and Other Stories from Benin* (4–8). Illus. 1998, Linnet LB $21.50 (978-0-208-02469-5). A delightful collection of 20 folktales from the Fon culture of Benin, handsomely illustrated with woodcuts. (Rev: BCCB 5/98; BL 2/15/98; HBG 9/98; SLJ 4/98) [398.2]

12264 Medearis, Angela Shelf. *The Singing Man* (PS–3). Illus. by Terea D. Shaffer. 1994, Holiday House LB $17.95 (978-0-8234-1103-0). 36pp. Banzar is scorned in his Nigerian village because he wants to become a musician, but eventually he returns to his home in triumph. (Rev: BL 7/94; SLJ 9/94) [398.2]

12265 Mollel, Tololwa M. *Ananse's Feast: An Ashanti Tale* (K–3). Illus. by Andrew Glass. 1997, Clarion $16.00 (978-0-395-67402-4). 32pp. Akye the turtle gets revenge on Ananse the spider in this gentle Ashanti tale. (Rev: BL 4/15/97; SLJ 5/97) [398.2]

12266 Mollel, Tololwa M. *Kitoto the Mighty* (K–3). Illus. by Kristi Frost. 1998, Stoddart $14.95 (978-0-7737-3019-9). An African folktale about Kitoto, a mouse who sets out to find a force strong enough to protect him from a hawk. (Rev: BCCB 11/98; SLJ 2/99) [398.2]

12267 Mollel, Tololwa M. *Subira Subira* (PS–2). Illus. by Linda Saport. 2000, Clarion $15.00 (978-0-395-91809-8). 32pp. A Tanzanian folktale in which a brave young girl named Tatu is given advice by a spirit woman on how to control her difficult younger brother. (Rev: BCCB 5/00; BL 2/15/00; HBG 10/00; SLJ 4/00) [398.22]

12268 Mollel, Tololwa M. *To Dinner, for Dinner* (PS–3). Illus. by Synthia Saint James. 2000, Holiday House $16.95 (978-0-8234-1527-4). 32pp. Based on a Tanzanian story, this tale tells of a rabbit, Juhudi, and his tricks to keep from becoming Leopard's dinner. (Rev: BL 9/1/00; HBG 10/01; SLJ 8/00) [398.2]

12269 Olaleye, Isaac. *In the Rainfield: Who Is the Greatest?* (K–3). Illus. by Ann Grifalconi. 2000, Scholastic $16.95 (978-0-590-48363-6). 32pp. In this folktale from Nigeria, three elements — Wind, Fire, and Rain — compete to see which is greatest. (Rev: BCCB 2/00; BL 2/15/00; HBG 10/00; SLJ 4/00) [398.2]

12270 Oram, Hiawyn, retel. *Counting Leopard's Spots: Animal Stories from Africa* (K–4). Illus. by Tim Warnes. 1998, Little Tiger $16.95 (978-1-888444-31-5). 96pp. A handsome book that contains a variety of tales from Africa, including cautionary, pourquoi, and trickster stories. (Rev: BL 8/98; HBG 10/98; SLJ 12/98) [398.2]

12271 Paye, Won-Ldy, and Margaret H. Lippert. *Head, Body, Legs: A Story from Liberia* (PS–2). Illus. by Julie Paschkis. 2002, Holt $16.95 (978-0-8050-6570-1). 32pp. This amusing tale from Liberia about disjointed body parts teaches the value of cooperation. (Rev: BL 8/02; HB 5/02; HBG 10/02; SLJ 4/02) [398.2]

12272 Paye, Won-Ldy, and Margaret H. Lippert, retels. *Mrs. Chicken and the Hungry Crocodile* (PS–3). Illus. by Julie Paschkis. 2003, Holt $16.95 (978-0-8050-7047-7). Mrs. Chicken manages to survive a difficult encounter with a crocodile in this newly illustrated folktale from the Dan people of Liberia that appeared in *Why Leopard Has Spots* (Fulcrum, 1998). (Rev: HB 5/03; HBG 10/03; SLJ 7/03) [398.2]

12273 Paye, Won-Ldy, and Margaret H. Lippert, retels. *The Talking Vegetables* (K–4). Illus. by Julie Paschkis. 2006, Holt $16.95 (978-0-8050-7742-1). In this spirited retelling of a Liberian folk tale, Spider is lazy and chooses not to join with his neighbors in planting a field of vegetables, so when he tries to pick some for his own use the vegetables turn him away. (Rev: SLJ 11/06) [398.2]

12274 Seeger, Pete, and Paul Dubois Jacobs. *Abiyoyo Returns* (1–3). Illus. by Michael Hays. 2001, Simon & Schuster $17.00 (978-0-689-83271-0). 40pp. The giant Abiyoyo returns to help the villagers build a dam in this sequel to Seeger's 1986 retelling of a South African folktale. (Rev: BCCB 11/01; BL 11/15/01; HB 11/01; HBG 3/02; SLJ 11/01) [398.2]

12275 Steptoe, John. *Mufaro's Beautiful Daughters: An African Tale* (PS–2). Illus. by author. 1987, Lothrop LB $17.89 (978-0-688-04046-8). 32pp. Two sisters of opposite natures vie for the hand of the king. (Rev: BCCB 4/87; BL 4/15/87; SLJ 6–7/87) [398.2]

12276 Tchana, Katrin. *Sense Pass King: A Story from Cameroon* (PS–2). Illus. by Trina S. Hyman. 2002, Holiday House $16.95 (978-0-8234-1577-9). 32pp. Sense Pass King is the name that a child prodigy acquires when she succeeds in discrediting the stupid king and becomes leader of her people. (Rev: BL 11/1/02; HB 11/02; HBG 3/03; SLJ 9/02) [398.2]

12277 Tchana, Katrin. *The Serpent Slayer and Other Stories of Strong Women* (4–7). Illus. 2000, Little, Brown $21.95 (978-0-316-38701-9). 128pp. A collection of 18 folktales from around the world featuring brave, creative, and strong women and girls. (Rev: BCCB 11/00*; BL 12/15/00; HB 11/00; HBG 3/01; SLJ 11/00) [398.2]

12278 Washington, Donna L. *A Pride of African Tales* (2–5). Illus. by James Ransome. 2004, HarperCollins $16.99 (978-0-06-024929-8). 80pp. These effective retellings introduce African trickster, pourquoi, and other tales from varied cultures. (Rev: BL 3/15/04; SLJ 8/04) [398.2]

12279 Wisniewski, David. *Sundiata: Lion King of Mali* (K–5). Illus. 1992, Houghton $17.00 (978-0-395-61302-3). 32pp. The dying king gives his kingdom to a sickly prince who cannot walk or speak, but in time, he becomes a great and brave leader. (Rev: BL 12/1/92*; HB 3/93; SLJ 10/92*) [398.2]

12280 Yohannes, Gebregeorgis. *Silly Mammo: An Ethiopian Tale* (PS). Illus. by Bogale Belachew. 2002, African Sun paper $10.00 (978-1-883701-04-8). 32pp. A contemporary Ethiopian village is the setting for this traditional tale in which a hapless lad gets everything wrong until he kisses a fair lady. (Rev: BL 10/1/02; SLJ 2/03) [398.2]

Asia

General and Miscellaneous

12281 Berger, Barbara Helen. *All the Way to Lhasa: A Tale from Tibet* (PS–2). Illus. 2002, Penguin $17.99 (978-0-399-23387-6). 32pp. Courage and perseverance win over headlong speed in this tale of two young men journeying to the holy city of Lhasa, with illustrations that contain many Tibetan Buddhist touches. (Rev: BL 10/1/02; HBG 3/03; SLJ 9/02) [398.2]

12282 Chodzin, Sherab, and Alexandra Kohn. *The Wisdom of the Crows and Other Buddhist Tales* (3–5). Illus. 1998, Tricycle $17.95 (978-1-883672-68-3). 80pp. This collection of Asian folktales illustrated with clear watercolors represents various facets of Buddhist thought and beliefs. (Rev: BL 6/1–15/98; SLJ 04/98) [294]

12283 Climo, Shirley. *The Korean Cinderella* (K–3). Illus. by Ruth Heller. 1993, HarperCollins $17.99 (978-0-06-020432-7). 48pp. After Pear Blossom's mother dies and her father remarries, she is mistreated by her stepmother and stepsister. (Rev: BCCB 6/93; BL 5/1/93; SLJ 8/93) [398.2]

12284 Conger, David, et al., retels. *Asian Children's Favorite Stories: A Treasury of Folktales from China, Japan, Korea, India, the Philippines, Thailand, Indonesia and Malaysia* (K–4). Illus. by Patrick Yee. 2006, Tuttle $24.95 (978-0-8048-3669-2). 112pp. A collection of 13 tales from different Asian countries including "The Lucky Farmer Becomes King" and "The Crane's Gratitude." (Rev: SLJ 3/07) [398.2]

12285 Davison, Katherine. *Moon Magic: Stories from Asia* (3–5). Illus. 1994, Carolrhoda LB $19.95 (978-0-87614-751-1). 56pp. A retelling of four Asian myths that deal with the moon and its phases. (Rev: BL 5/15/94; SLJ 6/94) [398.2]

12286 Froese, Deborah. *The Wise Washerman: A Folktale from Burma* (K–3). Illus. by Wang Kui. 1996, Hyperion LB $15.49 (978-0-7868-2232-4). A jealous neighbor tries to get an industrious washerwoman into trouble in this Burmese folktale. (Rev: BCCB 12/96; SLJ 1/97) [398.2]

12287 Garland, Sherry. *Children of the Dragon: Selected Tales from Vietnam* (3–5). Illus. 2001, Harcourt $18.00 (978-0-15-224200-8). 64pp. Six tales from Vietnam are introduced by material on the land, its history, and folk traditions. (Rev: BL 7/01; HBG 3/02; SLJ 10/01*) [398.2]

12288 Ginsburg, Mirra. *The Chinese Mirror* (1–3). Illus. by Margot Zemach. 1991, Harcourt paper $6.00 (978-0-15-217508-5). 26pp. An old folktale from Korea tells of a man who brings home a mirror — unknown to his fellow villagers — from a trip to China. (Rev: BCCB 5/88; BL 4/15/88; SLJ 4/88) [398.2]

12289 Han, Suzanne C. *The Rabbit's Tail: A Story from Korea* (K–3). Illus. by Richard Wehrman. 1999, Holt $15.95 (978-0-8050-4580-2). 32pp. A charming folktale in which Tiger, through a series of misunderstandings, becomes involved with a rabbit that loses its tail. (Rev: BCCB 6/99; BL 2/15/99; HBG 10/99; SLJ 3/99) [398.2]

12290 Heo, Yumi. *The Green Frogs* (K–3). Illus. 1996, Houghton $17.00 (978-0-395-68378-1). 32pp. Two disobedient frogs decide to honor their mother's last wish in this Korean folktale. (Rev: BCCB 10/96; BL 7/96; HB 11/96) [398.2]

12291 Holt, Daniel D., sel. *Tigers, Frogs, and Rice Cakes: A Book of Korean Proverbs* (2–4). Illus. by Soma Han Stickler. 1999, Shen's $15.95 (978-1-885008-10-7). Each of the 20 Korean proverbs included are given in both English and Korean, with explanations. (Rev: BCCB 5/99; HBG 10/99; SLJ 6/99) [398.2]

12292 McClure, Gillian. *The Land of the Dragon King and Other Korean Stories* (3–5). Illus. by author. 2008, Frances Lincoln $19.95 (978-1-84507-805-8). 64pp. A collection of nine varied folktales from Korea — fables and pourquoi and trickster tales — with handsome Korean-inspired illustrations. (Rev: BLO 1/13/09; SLJ 12/08) [398.2]

12293 Otsuka, Yuzo. *Suho's White Horse: A Mongolian Legend* (PS–3). Trans. by Richard McNamara. Illus. by Suekichi Akaba. 2007, R.I.C. $17.95 (978-1-74126-021-2). 48pp. The sad legend of the invention of the Mongolian fiddle, in which a young shepherd boy's champion horse is seized by an evil ruler. (Rev: BL 4/1/07) [398.2]

12294 Park, Janie Jaehyun. *The Love of Two Stars: A Korean Legend* (K–2). Illus. 2005, Groundwood $16.95 (978-0-88899-672-5). 32pp. An accessible retelling of the Korean folktale in which two lovers, punished for neglecting their work, win support from the birds when they cannot reunite. (Rev: BL 10/15/05; SLJ 11/05) [398.2]

12295 Park, Janie Jaehyun. *The Tiger and the Dried Persimmon* (K–3). Illus. 2002, Groundwood $15.95 (978-0-88899-485-1). 32pp. Vibrant artwork accompanies this version of a comic Korean folktale about a tiger who misinterprets a woman's words to her child and ends up terrified of persimmons. (Rev: BL 12/15/02; HBG 3/03) [398.2]

12296 Rose, Naomi. *Tibetan Tales for Little Buddhas* (PS–2). Trans. by Pasang Tenzin. Illus. by author. 2003, Clear Light $16.95 (978-1-57416-081-9). 63pp. Three traditional folktales are retold in this charming bilingual (English and Tibetan) picture book. (Rev: BL 12/15/04; SLJ 3/05) [398.2]

12297 San Souci, Daniel. *In the Moonlight Mist: A Korean Tale* (PS–3). Illus. by Eujin Kim Neilan. 1999, Boyds Mills $16.95 (978-1-56397-754-1). 32pp. In this Korean tale, a poor woodcutter saves a deer and, as a reward, is granted his wish to have a wife who loves him. (Rev: BCCB 4/99; BL 3/1/99; HBG 10/99; SLJ 4/99) [398.2]

12298 San Souci, Daniel, retel. *The Rabbit and the Dragon King: Based on a Korean Folk Tale* (1–4). Illus. by Eujin Kim Neilan. 2002, Boyds Mills $17.95 (978-1-56397-880-7). San Souci retells with humor and drama the story of the king who rules the ocean, who in this case is convinced that eating a rabbit's heart will cure his ills. (Rev: SLJ 11/02) [398.2]

12299 Seros, Kathleen, adapt. *Sun and Moon: Fairy Tales from Korea* (2–5). Illus. by Norman Sibley and Robert Krause. 1983, Hollym $18.50 (978-0-

930878-25-2). 61pp. A collection of seven stories from Korea. [398.2]

12300 Shah, Idries. *The Man with Bad Manners* (K–3). Illus. by Rose Mary Santiago. 2003, Hoopoe $18.00 (978-1-883536-30-5). Colorful and simple illustrations lighten this retelling of an Afghani folktale about conflict resolution, now set in the present. (Rev: SLJ 4/04) [398.2]

China

12301 Bedard, Michael, ed. *The Painted Wall and Other Strange Tales* (4–7). 2003, Tundra $16.95 (978-0-88776-652-7). 120pp. Chinese folktales collected centuries ago are full of action and the supernatural. (Rev: BL 1/1–15/04; SLJ 1/04) [398.2]

12302 Bouchard, David. *The Great Race* (3–6). Illus. by Zhong-Yang Huang. 1997, Millbrook LB $21.40 (978-0-7613-0305-3). 32pp. This folktale tells that the order of the animals in the Chinese zodiac was determined by a great race. (Rev: BL 2/1/98; HBG 3/98; SLJ 1/98) [398.2]

12303 Carpenter, F. R. *Tales of a Chinese Grandmother* (5–7). Illus. by Malthe Hasselriis. 1973, Amereon LB $24.95 (978-0-89190-481-6); Tuttle paper $8.95 (978-0-8048-1042-5). 293pp. A boy and a girl listen to 30 classic Chinese tales. [398.2]

12304 Casanova, Mary. *The Hunter* (PS–3). Illus. by Ed Young. 2000, Simon & Schuster $16.95 (978-0-689-82906-2). 32pp. This is a Chinese tale of a simple hunter who is granted the ability to understand the language of animals. He bravely tells his people that a great flood is coming and that he has learned of it from the animals, but he is turned to stone for divulging his secret ability. (Rev: BCCB 11/00*; BL 5/15/00; HBG 10/01; SLJ 8/00) [398.2]

12305 Chen, Debby. *Monkey King Wreaks Havoc in Heaven* (4–6). Illus. by Wenhai Ma. 2001, Pan Asian $16.95 (978-1-57227-068-8). 36pp. A retelling of a Chinese tale about the sly Monkey King. (Rev: BL 10/15/01) [398.2]

12306 Chin, Yin-lien C., ed. *Traditional Chinese Folktales* (5–8). Illus. by Lu Wang. 1989, East Gate $44.95 (978-0-87332-507-3). 180pp. This is a collection of 12 Chinese folktales that express a variety of themes and genres from faithful lovers to trickster tales. (Rev: SLJ 8/89) [398.2]

12307 Compestine, Ying Chang. *The Real Story of Stone Soup* (PS–2). Illus. by Stephanie Jorisch. 2007, Dutton $16.99 (978-0-525-47493-7). 32pp. An officious, lazy fisherman gets his comeuppance when his young assistants convince him that the flavor in the soup comes from carefully chosen stones, while the pictures show the truth. (Rev: BL 1/1–15/07; SLJ 1/07) [398.2]

12308 Demi. *The Dragon's Tale and Other Animal Fables of the Chinese Zodiac* (3–6). Illus. 1996, Holt $18.95 (978-0-8050-3446-2). 26pp. A collection of 12 fables that involve the animals in the Chinese zodiac. (Rev: BCCB 1/97; BL 9/15/96; SLJ 10/96) [398.2]

12309 Demi. *The Empty Pot* (K–2). Illus. by author. 1990, Holt $16.95 (978-0-8050-1217-0). 32pp.

Young Ping finds out that honesty pays when the emperor gives seeds to each child in the kingdom to produce the best flower. (Rev: BL 4/1/90; HB 5/90; SLJ 7/90) [398.2]

12310 Demi. *The Greatest Treasure* (PS–3). Illus. 1998, Scholastic $16.95 (978-0-590-31339-1). 32pp. In this retelling of a traditional Chinese folktale, poor peasant Li receives a gift of money from his rich neighbor and his lifestyle changes as he begins to worry about how to care for his newfound wealth. (Rev: BL 8/98*; HBG 3/99; SLJ 9/98) [398.2]

12311 Han, Carolyn. *Why Snails Have Shells: Minority and Han Folktales from China* (4–6). Trans. by Jay Han. Illus. 1994, Univ. of Hawaii $7.95 (978-0-8248-1505-9). 73pp. Attractive paintings accompany this splendid collection of 20 folktales from China. (Rev: BL 8/94; SLJ 2/05) [398.2]

12312 Heyer, Marilee. *The Weaving of a Dream: A Chinese Folktale* (3–5). Illus. by author. 1989, Puffin paper $7.99 (978-0-14-050528-3). 32pp. The third of an old widow's sons retrieves her precious brocade, from whence steps the Red Fairy, and all three live happily ever after. (Rev: BL 4/15/86; SLJ 4/86) [398.2]

12313 Hong, Chen Jiang. *The Magic Horse of Han Gan* (PS–2). Trans. by Claudia Zoe Bedrick. Illus. 2006, Enchanted Lion $16.95 (978-1-59270-063-9). 38pp. This attractive picture book recounts the moving and dramatic legend of a magical horse created by 9th-century Chinese artist Han Gan. (Rev: BL 11/1/06; SLJ 12/06*) [398.2]

12314 Hong, Lily T. *Two of Everything: A Chinese Folktale* (K–3). Illus. 1993, Whitman LB $16.95 (978-0-8075-8157-5). 32pp. Elderly Mr. Haktak finds a magical brass pot in his garden. (Rev: BL 3/15/93*; HB 7/93*; SLJ 6/93*) [398.2]

12315 Kimmel, Eric A. *The Rooster's Antlers: A Story of the Chinese Zodiac* (PS–3). Illus. by Yong-Sheng Xuan. 1999, Holiday House $16.95 (978-0-8234-1385-0). This Chinese folktale tells how Rooster gets his revenge when he isn't chosen by the emperor to be part of the Chinese calendar. (Rev: BCCB 10/99; BL 12/15/99; HBG 3/00; SLJ 10/99) [398.2]

12316 Kimmel, Eric A. *Ten Suns: A Chinese Legend* (K–3). Illus. by YongSheng Xuan. 1998, Holiday House $15.95 (978-0-8234-1317-1). 32pp. When the ten sons (suns) of Di Jun decide that they will no longer make their solitary journeys across the sky each day but instead walk together, their father is afraid the combined heat will destroy the earth. (Rev: BCCB 6/98; BL 5/1/98; HBG 10/98; SLJ 5/98) [398.2]

12317 Krasno, Rena, and Yeng-Fong Chiang. *Cloud Weavers: Ancient Chinese Legends* (2–6). 2003, Pacific View $22.95 (978-1-881896-26-5). 96pp. Nearly two dozen Chinese stories — legends, tales from Chinese history, and stories from Chinese literature — are introduced with background information and accompanied by Chinese posters from the early 20th century. (Rev: BL 7/03; SLJ 8/03) [398.2]

12318 Lee, Jeanne. *The Song of Mu Lan* (5–8). Illus. 1995, Front St. $17.95 (978-1-886910-00-3). 32pp. Mu Lan disguises herself as a boy and joins the emperor's army in this traditional Chinese tale. (Rev: BL 11/15/95; SLJ 12/95) [398.2]

12319 Louie, Ai-Ling, retel. *Yeh-Shen: A Cinderella Story from China* (2–6). Illus. by Ed Young. 1982, Penguin $16.99 (978-0-399-20900-0). 32pp. A Chinese story about a poor girl living with her cruel stepmother and stepsisters. [398.2]

12320 Mahy, Margaret. *The Seven Chinese Brothers* (K–3). Illus. by Jean Tseng. 1992, Scholastic paper $6.99 (978-0-590-42057-0). 40pp. Each of seven Chinese brothers has an amazing gift, used to help one another. (Rev: BCCB 7–8/90; BL 4/1/90; HB 7/90; SLJ 3/90*) [398.2]

12321 Mosel, Arlene. *Tikki Tikki Tembo* (K–2). Illus. by Blair Lent. 1968, Holt $16.95 (978-0-8050-0662-9). 32pp. Explains why the Chinese no longer honor their firstborn with an unusually long name. [398.2]

12322 Poole, Amy Lowry. *How the Rooster Got His Crown* (K–3). Illus. 1999, Holiday House $15.95 (978-0-8234-1389-8). 32pp. A little rooster persuades a sun to leave its cave and is rewarded with a crown in this Chinese pourquoi tale. (Rev: BL 4/15/99; HB 5/99; HBG 10/99; SLJ 5/99) [398.2]

12323 Sanfield, Steve. *Just Rewards, or Who Is That Man in the Moon and What's He Doing Up There Anyway?* (PS–3). Illus. by Emily Lisker. 1996, Orchard LB $15.99 (978-0-531-08885-2). 32pp. The origin of the belief that there is a man in the moon is retold in this Chinese folktale. (Rev: BL 10/1/96; HB 11/96; SLJ 9/96*) [398.2]

12324 Shepard, Aaron. *Lady White Snake: A Tale from Chinese Opera* (4–6). Illus. by Song Nan Zhang. 2001, Pan Asian $16.95 (978-1-57227-072-5). 30pp. A lavishly illustrated story from Chinese opera about a snake that turns into a beautiful woman. (Rev: BL 10/15/01; SLJ 3/02) [398.2]

12325 Storrie, Paul D. *Yu the Great: Conquering the Flood* (4–7). Illus. by Sandy Carruthers. Series: Graphic Myths and Legends. 2007, Lerner LB $26.60 (978-0-8225-3088-6). 48pp. In this graphic novel adaptation of an ancient Chinese folk tale, the emperor Shun asks Yu to save China and its people from the floods that are ravaging the land. (Rev: BL 3/15/07; SLJ 5/07) [398.2]

12326 Te Loo, Sanne. *Ping-Li's Kite* (PS–1). Illus. 2002, Front St. $15.95 (978-1-886910-75-1). 32pp. A young Chinese boy angers the Emperor of the Sky when he flies an undecorated kite in this book based on a Chinese folktale. (Rev: BL 8/02; HBG 10/02; SLJ 5/02) [398.2]

12327 Tseng, Grace. *White Tiger, Blue Serpent* (K–3). Illus. by Jean Tseng and Mou-Sien Tseng. 1999, Lothrop $16.00 (978-0-688-12515-8). 32pp. A Chinese folktale in which a young peasant, Kai, faces many dangers while journeying to the palace of the goddess Qin to retrieve a silk brocade. (Rev: BL 8/99; HBG 10/99; SLJ 7/99) [398.2]

12328 Wang, Rosalind C. *The Treasure Chest: A Chinese Tale* (PS–3). Illus. by Will Hillenbrand. 1995, Holiday House LB $15.95 (978-0-8234-1114-

6). 32pp. In this Chinese tale, a humble peasant gets help from the Ocean King to fight an evil despot. (Rev: BL 6/1–15/95; SLJ 6/95) [398.2]

12329 Xuan, Yong-Sheng. *The Dragon Lover and Other Chinese Proverbs* (K–3). 1999, Shen's $16.95 (978-1-885008-11-4). 32pp. Illustrated with Chinese paper cuts, this lovely book contains the stories behind five well-known Chinese proverbs. (Rev: BCCB 7–8/99; BL 5/15/99; HBG 10/99; SLJ 8/99) [398.2]

12330 Ye, Ting-xing. *Three Monks, No Water* (K–3). Illus. by Harvey Chan. 1997, Annick LB $16.95 (978-1-55037-443-8); paper $6.95 (978-1-55037-442-1). 32pp. This story supposedly explains the origin of the Chinese expression "Three monks, no water," which is used when children try to avoid chores. (Rev: BL 2/1/98; SLJ 12/97) [398.2]

12331 Yip, Mingmei. *Chinese Children's Favorite Stories* (3–5). Illus. 2004, Tuttle $18.95 (978-0-8048-3589-3). 96pp. Thirteen varied stories introduce readers to traditional Chinese characters — dragons, emperors, scholars, and so forth. (Rev: BL 2/1/05; SLJ 3/05) [398.2]

12332 Yolen, Jane. *The Emperor and the Kite* (K–3). Illus. by Ed Young. 1988, Penguin $16.99 (978-0-399-21499-8). 32pp. Oriental-like paper cuts illustrate this Chinese legend about the unshakable loyalty of the emperor's smallest daughter. First published in 1967. [398.2]

12333 Young, Ed. *The Sons of the Dragon King: A Chinese Legend* (3–5). Illus. 2004, Simon & Schuster $16.95 (978-0-689-85184-1). 32pp. This beautifully illustrated Chinese folktale about the Dragon King and his nine sons recounts how the king comes to accept and take advantage of his sons' unique talents and abilities. (Rev: BL 5/15/04; SLJ 6/04) [398.2]

India

12334 Arenson, Roberta. *Manu and the Talking Fish* (PS–3). Illus. 2000, Barefoot Books $15.95 (978-1-84148-032-9). 32pp. This Indian variation on the Noah story tells of Manu, a prince, who rescues a fish. When the fish grows up, he warns Manu of an impending flood that will destroy the world. (Rev: BL 4/1/00; SLJ 6/00) [398.2]

12335 Bateson-Hill, Margaret. *Chanda and the Mirror of Moonlight* (3–4). Illus. by Karin Littlewood. 2001, Zero to Ten $17.95 (978-1-84089-217-8). An evil stepmother tries to trick the prince into marrying her daughter instead of Chanda, but the mirror reveals the truth. (Rev: SLJ 5/02) [398.2]

12336 Beach, Milo Cleveland. *The Adventures of Rama* (4–6). Illus. 1983, Smithsonian Institution $15.00 (978-0-934686-51-8). 64pp. Tales from the Hindu epic Ramayana. (Rev: SLJ 2/05) [398.2]

12337 Birch, David. *The King's Chessboard* (3–5). Illus. by Devis Grebu. 1988, Puffin paper $6.99 (978-0-14-054880-8). 32pp. A wise man outsmarts a vain king when he is offered a reward. (Rev: BL 5/15/88; SLJ 4/88) [398.2]

12338 Conover, Sarah, ed. *Kindness: A Treasury of Buddhist Wisdom for Children and Parents* (4–7). Illus. 2001, Eastern Washington Univ. paper $19.95 (978-0-910055-67-3). 164pp. Thirty-one stories related to Buddhism, including Jataka tales about the Buddha's incarnations, have been effectively translated and adapted for this anthology. (Rev: BL 2/15/01; SLJ 3/01) [294.3]

12339 Demi. *One Grain of Rice* (3–6). Illus. 1997, Scholastic $19.95 (978-0-590-93998-0). 40pp. Rani outwits the rajah to gain food for her people in this Indian folktale. (Rev: BCCB 2/97; BL 3/1/97*; SLJ 3/97*) [398.2]

12340 Ernst, Judith, retel. *The Golden Goose King: A Tale Told by the Buddha* (3–6). Illus. by Judith Ernst. 1995, Parvardigar $19.95 (978-0-9644362-0-6). A Jataka tale about a queen who captures the Golden Goose King, who is actually Buddha. (Rev: BL 9/1/95; SLJ 9/95) [398.2]

12341 French, Fiona, retel. *Jamil's Clever Cat: A Folk Tale from Bengal* (PS–2). Illus. by Fiona French and Dick Newby. 1999, Star Bright $13.95 (978-1-887734-72-1). In this tale from Bengal, a cat helps his master gain riches and a bride. (Rev: SLJ 3/00) [398.2]

12342 Fusek-Peters, Andrew. *The Tiger and the Wise Man* (PS–2). Illus. by Diana Mayo. 2005, Child's Play paper $7.99 (978-1-904550-07-5). 32pp. In this brightly illustrated retelling of a traditional Indian folktale, a wise man may have to pay a very high price for foolishly releasing a vicious tiger from its cage. (Rev: BL 8/05; SLJ 6/05) [398.2]

12343 Galdone, Paul. *The Monkey and the Crocodile: A Jataka Tale from India* (K–3). Illus. by author. 1969, Houghton paper $6.95 (978-0-89919-524-7). 32pp. A crocodile decides he will catch a monkey. [398.2]

12344 Hamilton, Martha, and Mitch Weiss. *The Ghost Catcher* (PS–2). Illus. by Kristen Balouch. 2008, August House $16.95 (978-0-87483-835-0). 32pp. A barber's generosity to his poorer clients enrages his wife, and he cleverly tricks a ghost into providing him with riches; a traditional tale from Bengal. (Rev: BCCB 9/08; BL 5/15/08; LMC 8/08; SLJ 6/08) [398.2]

12345 Jaffrey, Madhur. *Seasons of Splendor: Tales, Myths, and Legends from India* (5–8). Illus. by Michael Foreman. 1985, Puffin paper $7.95 (978-0-317-62172-3). 128pp. Folktales and family stories as well as accounts of Rama and Krishna. (Rev: BCCB 1/86; BL 1/15/86) [398.2]

12346 Jendresen, Erik, and Joshua M. Greene, retels. *Hanuman: Based on Valmiki's Ramayana* (3–6). Illus. by Li Ming. 1998, Tricycle $15.95 (978-1-883672-78-2). A retelling of the section of the Ramayana in which the monkey clan under Hanuman helps Rama rescue his wife Sita. (Rev: BCCB 3/99; HBG 10/99; SLJ 11/98) [398.2]

12347 Lee, Jeanne. *I Once Was a Monkey: Stories Buddha Told* (2–4). Illus. 1999, Farrar $16.00 (978-0-374-33548-9). 40pp. This handsome volume contains six *Jatakas* or birth stories from the Buddhist faith. (Rev: BCCB 4/99; BL 3/15/99; HBG 10/99; SLJ 3/99) [294.3]

12348 Martin, Rafe. *The Brave Little Parrot* (K–3). Illus. by Susan Gaber. 1998, Penguin $16.99 (978-0-399-22825-4). 32pp. As a reward for trying to put out a forest fire, a little parrot is given colored plumage in this Indian jataka tale. (Rev: BCCB 3/98; BL 2/15/98; SLJ 5/98) [298.2]

12349 Martin, Rafe. *Foolish Rabbit's Big Mistake* (PS–2). Illus. by Ed Young. 1985, Penguin $17.99 (978-0-399-21178-2). 32pp. A tale from India reminiscent of Chicken Little, about a little rabbit who fears the end of the world and tells everyone that the earth is breaking up. A Jataka tale. (Rev: BCCB 12/85; BL 12/15/85; HB 3/86; SLJ 2/05) [398.2]

12350 Moseley, James. *The Ninth Jewel of the Mughal Crown: The Birbal Tales from the Oral Traditions of India* (3–6). Illus. 2001, Summerwind $24.95 (978-0-9704447-1-4). 154pp. A collection of stories from India that involve the 14th-century Emperor Akbar and his clever and amusing adviser Birbal. (Rev: BL 7/01; SLJ 10/01) [398.2]

12351 Nanji, Shenaaz. *Indian Tales: A Barefoot Collection* (4–6). Illus. by Christopher Corr. 2007, Barefoot Books $19.99 (978-1-84686-083-6). 96pp. A colorful introduction to Indian folklore, with a tale from each of eight different states preceded by background information that adds context. (Rev: BCCB 12/07; BL 11/15/07; LMC 1/08; SLJ 1/08) [398.2]

12352 Rao, Sandhya, retel. *And Land Was Born* (1–4). Illus. by Uma Krishnaswami. Series: Visual Expressions. 1999, Banyan Tree $19.99 (81-86895-13-2). A delightful creation story from central India that tells how a tortoise helps produce land in a world where only water existed. (Rev: SLJ 7/99) [398.2]

12353 Shepard, Aaron, retel. *Savitri: A Tale of Ancient India* (3–6). Illus. by Vera Rosenberry. 1992, Whitman LB $16.95 (978-0-8075-7251-1). 40pp. In picture-book format, the retelling of India's epic poem, the Mahabharata. (Rev: BCCB 3/92; BL 3/15/92; SLJ 5/92) [398.2]

12354 Young, Ed. *Seven Blind Mice* (PS–3). Illus. 1992, Penguin $17.99 (978-0-399-22261-0). 44pp. A stunning picture book illustrating a version of the old Indian folktale about seven blind men and one elephant. (Rev: BCCB 3/92*; BL 4/1/92*; HB 3/92; SLJ 4/92) [398.2]

Japan

12355 Edmonds, I. G. *Ooka the Wise: Tales of Old Japan* (3–6). Illus. by Sanae Yamazaki. 1994, Linnet LB $16.00 (978-0-208-02379-7). 96pp. A collection of 17 Japanese folktales featuring the legendary judge Ooka Tadasuke, who is devoted to the cause of justice. (Rev: BL 5/15/94) [398.2]

12356 Hedlund, Irene. *Mighty Mountain and the Three Strong Women* (PS–3). Trans. by Judith Elkin. Illus. 1990, Volcano $14.95 (978-0-912078-86-1). 32pp. A sumo wrestler meets three women who surpass him in strength. (Rev: BL 6/1/90; SLJ 10/90) [398.2]

12357 Hodges, Margaret, adapt. *The Boy Who Drew Cats* (K–3). Illus. by Aki Sogabe. 2002, Holiday House $16.95 (978-0-8234-1594-6). 32pp. A young boy's obsession with drawing cats everywhere he goes eventually changes his life in this tale of the supernatural. (Rev: BCCB 4/02; BL 6/1–15/02; HB 5/02; HBG 10/02; SLJ 3/02) [398.2]

12358 Kimmel, Eric A. *The Greatest of All: A Japanese Folktale* (PS–3). Illus. by Giora Carmi. 1991, Holiday House LB $17.95 (978-0-8234-0885-6). 32pp. The father of Chuko Mouse is not happy when she tells him she wants to marry a humble, but handsome, field mouse. (Rev: BL 10/15/91; SLJ 10/91) [398.2]

12359 Kimmel, Eric A. *Three Samurai Cats: A Story from Japan* (PS–2). Illus. by Mordicai Gerstein. 2003, Holiday House $16.95 (978-0-8234-1742-1). 32pp. In this colorful adaptation of a Japanese folktale, a feudal lord seeks help from a trio of samurai cats to rid his castle of a bothersome rat. (Rev: BL 4/15/03; HB 7/03; HBG 10/03; SLJ 6/03) [398.2]

12360 Krensky, Stephen. *Bokuden and the Bully: A Japanese Folktale* (2–5). Illus. by Cheryl Kirk Noll. Series: On My Own Folklore. 2008, Millbrook LB $25.26 (978-0-8225-7547-4). 48pp. In 16th-century Japan and nobleman who is talented with the sword unmans a bullying warrior. (Rev: SLJ 3/09) [398.2]

12361 McCarthy, Ralph F. *The Inch-High Samurai* (K–3). Illus. by Shiro Kasamatsu. 1993, Kodansha $19.95 (4-7700-1758-8). 48pp. Pint-sized Inchy Bo performs some mighty deeds, including fighting an ogre, in this Japanese folktale. (Rev: BL 12/15/93; SLJ 2/94) [398.2]

12362 McCarthy, Ralph F. *The Moon Princess* (3–6). Illus. by Kancho Oda. Series: Children's Classics. 1993, Kodansha $19.95 (4-7700-1756-1). 48pp. Retellings in verse of three Japanese folktales, one about a virtuous old man and his dog, another a Tom Thumb–like character, and another, the title story, about a couple who find a tiny girl inside a bamboo. (Rev: SLJ 2/94) [398.2]

12363 McDermott, Gerald. *The Stonecutter: A Japanese Folk Tale* (K–3). Illus. by author. 1975, Puffin paper $6.99 (978-0-14-050289-3). 32pp. The familiar tale of the stonecutter who kept demanding greater power is brilliantly illustrated with colorful, stylized collage paintings. [398.2]

12364 Merrill, Jean. *The Girl Who Loved Caterpillars: A Twelfth-Century Tale from Japan* (5–8). Illus. by Floyd Cooper. 1992, Putnam $16.99 (978-0-399-21871-2). 32pp. The story of a young Izumi who has no interest in lute playing or writing poetry but is fascinated with "creepy crawlies" instead. (Rev: BCCB 11/92; BL 9/1/92*; SLJ 9/92) [398.2]

12365 Myers, Tim, retel. *The Furry-Legged Teapot* (1–4). Illus. by Robert McGuire. 2007, Marshall Cavendish $16.99 (978-0-7614-5295-9). Yoshi the tanuki changes himself into a teapot but cannot change back until he is saved by the emperor's grandson. By the author of *Tanuki's Gift: A Japanese Tale*. (Rev: SLJ 5/07)

12366 Myers, Tim. *The Outfoxed Fox* (1–3). Illus. by Ariel Ya-Wen Pang. 2007, Marshall Cavendish $16.99 (978-0-7614-5356-7). In this traditional Japanese play or kyogen, an old fox rejects a young fox's idea and lives to regret it. (Rev: LMC 1/08; SLJ 11/07)

12367 Myers, Tim. *Tanuki's Gift: A Japanese Tale* (K–3). Illus. by Robert Roth. 2003, Marshall Cavendish $16.95 (978-0-7614-5101-3). 32pp. A Japanese folktale of a fond relationship between a Buddhist priest and a magical creature called a tanuki. (Rev: BL 3/15/03; HBG 10/03; SLJ 7/03) [398.2]

12368 Sakade, Florence, ed. *Japanese Children's Favorite Stories* (2–4). Illus. by Yoshio Kurosaki. 1958, Tuttle $16.95 (978-0-8048-0284-0). 120pp. Twenty folktales traditionally told to Japanese children. [398.2]

12369 Schroeder, Alan. *The Tale of Willie Monroe* (1–3). Illus. by Andrew Glass. 1999, Clarion $15.00 (978-0-395-69852-5). 32pp. An adaptation of the Japanese folktale that uses a hillbilly hero instead of a Japanese wrestler. (Rev: BCCB 6/99; BL 4/15/99; HB 3/99; HBG 10/99; SLJ 6/99) [398.2]

12370 Snyder, Dianne. *The Boy of the Three-Year Nap* (K–3). Illus. by Allen Say. 1988, Houghton $16.95 (978-0-395-44090-2). 32pp. In this Japanese folktale adaptation, Taro, who does nothing but eat and sleep, schemes to marry his rich neighbor's daughter. (Rev: BCCB 4/88; BL 4/1/88; HB 5/88) [398.2]

12371 Wada, Stephanie. *Momotaro and the Island of Ogres* (2–4). Illus. by Kano Naganobu. 2005, George Braziller $21.95 (978-0-8076-1552-2). 398pp. Silk handscrolls from the 19th century illustrate this retelling of the Japanese legend about a child, born from a peach, who succeeds in defeating threatening ogres. (Rev: BL 5/15/05) [398.2]

12372 Williams, Carol Ann. *Tsubu the Little Snail* (K–3). Illus. by Tatsuro Kiuchi. 1995, Simon & Schuster $15.00 (978-0-671-87167-3). 24pp. Love transforms a snail into a handsome young man in this Japanese folktale. (Rev: BL 6/1–15/95) [398.2]

Southeast Asia

12373 Climo, Shirley. *Tuko and the Birds: A Tale from the Philippines* (1–3). Illus. by Francisco Mora. 2008, Holt $16.95 (978-0-8050-6559-6). 40pp. The birds of Mount Pinatubo are fed up with the noise created by a gecko named Tuko and look for ways to get rid of him; lush illustrations and Filipino words add to this lively folktale. (Rev: BL 4/15/08; HB 5/08; LMC 8/08; SLJ 5/08) [398.2]

12374 Coburn, Jewell Reinhart, and Tzexa Cherta Lee, adapt. *Jouanah: A Hmong Cinderella* (K–3). Illus. by Anne S. O'Brien. 1996, Shen's $15.95 (978-1-885008-01-5). This version of the Cinderella story from the Hmong of Southeast Asia takes place in a peasant village. (Rev: BCCB 12/96; SLJ 3/97) [398.2]

12375 Day, Nancy Raines. *Piecing Earth and Sky Together* (2–4). Illus. by Genna Panzarella. 2001, Shen's $17.95 (978-1-885008-19-0). 32pp. In this creation story from Laos with beautiful illustrations, two heavenly brothers set out to create the sky and the earth. (Rev: BL 4/1/02; HBG 10/02; SLJ 7/02) [398.2]

12376 Ha, Song. *Indebted as Lord Chom / No Nhu Chua Chom: The Legend of the Forbidden Street* (1–4). Trans. from Vietnamese by William Smith. Illus. by Ly Thu Ha. 2006, East West Discovery $16.95 (978-0-9701654-6-6). 32pp. This engaging Vietnamese folk tale, presented in both English and Vietnamese, explains the origins of two Hanoi street names. (Rev: SLJ 1/07) [398.2]

12377 Lee, Jeanne, retel. *Toad Is the Uncle of Heaven: A Vietnamese Folk Tale* (4–7). Illus. by Jeanne Lee. 1985, Holt paper $6.95 (978-0-8050-1147-0). 32pp. This book tells the story of Toad who collects companions on his way to see the King of Heaven, who makes it rain. (Rev: BL 11/1/85; HB 3/86) [398.2]

12378 MacDonald, Margaret Read, retel. *The Girl Who Wore Too Much: A Folktale from Thailand* (PS–3). Illus. by Yvonne Davis. 1998, August House $15.95 (978-0-87483-503-8). In this updated folktale from Thailand, a young girl learns the value of simplicity when she wears all her beautiful dresses to a dance and is so weighted down she can't keep up with her friends. (Rev: HBG 10/98; SLJ 6/98) [398.2]

12379 MacDonald, Margaret Read. *Go to Sleep, Gecko! A Balinese Folktale* (PS–2). Illus. by Geraldo Valério. 2006, August House $16.95 (978-0-87483-780-3). Gecko complains repeatedly to Elephant, the village chief, that fireflies are keeping him awake at night, but realizes eventually that it's all part of the natural order. (Rev: SLJ 10/06) [398.2]

12380 Mason, Victor, and Gillian Beal, retels. *Balinese Children's Favorite Stories* (1–4). Illus. by Trina Bohan-Tyrie. 2001, Tuttle $16.95 (962-593-440-5). 96pp. Eleven tales from Bali, many of which are about animals, are paired with varied illustrations including detailed Balinese costumes. (Rev: SLJ 5/02) [398.2]

12381 Meeker, Clare Hodgson. *A Tale of Two Rice Birds: A Folktale from Thailand* (4–8). Illus. by Christine Lamb. 1994, Sasquatch $14.95 (978-1-57061-008-0). 32pp. Two rice birds are reincarnated as a princess and a farmer's son in this Thai folktale. (Rev: BL 1/15/95; SLJ 11/94) [398.2]

12382 Quoc, Minh. *Tam and Cam / Tam Cam: The Ancient Vietnamese Cinderella Story* (1–4). Trans. from Vietnamese by William Smith. Illus. by Mai Long. 2006, East West Discovery $16.95 (978-0-9701654-4-2). 32pp. Reminiscent of the Cinderella story, this Vietnamese folk tale, offered here in both English and Vietnamese, features a young girl who is mistreated by her stepsister and stepmother but eventually wins the heart of the king. (Rev: SLJ 1/07) [398.2]

12383 Quoc, Tran. *The Tet Pole / Su Tich Cay Neu Ngay Tet: The Story of the Tet Festival* (1–4). Trans. from Vietnamese by William Smith. Illus. by Nguyen Bich. 2006, East West Discovery $16.95

(978-0-9701654-5-9). 32pp. In this charming bilingual Vietnamese folk tale that explains the origins of the Tet festival, Buddha helps a group of poor farmers outwit the demons that have seized control of their fields. (Rev: SLJ 1/07) [398.2]

12384 Scott, Nathan Kumar. *Mangoes and Bananas* (2–4). Illus. by T. Balaji. 2006, Tara $14.95 (81-86211-06-3). 32pp. In this retelling of an Indonesian folk tale, clever deer Kanchil and a greedy monkey called Monyet plant a fruit garden together on the agreement that they will share equally; an endnote describes the methods used to create the textile-based illustrations. (Rev: BL 4/1/06; SLJ 6/06) [398.2]

12385 Scott, Nathan Kumar. *The Sacred Banana Leaf* (2–4). Illus. by Radhashyam Raut. 2008, Tara $16.95 (978-8-1862-1128-1). 32pp. A clever mouse deer trickster named Kanchil falls into a pit and must find a way to persuade other animals to help him out; a beautifully illustrated tale from Indonesia. (Rev: BL 5/15/08; SLJ 6/08) [398.2]

12386 Souhami, Jessica. *No Dinner! The Story of the Old Woman and the Pumpkin* (PS–1). Illus. 2000, Marshall Cavendish $15.95 (978-0-7614-5059-7). 32pp. In this South Asian folktale, Grandma outwits a wolf, a tiger, and a bear on her way to and from visiting her granddaughter in the forest. (Rev: BCCB 3/00; BL 3/1/00; HBG 10/00; SLJ 4/00) [823.914]

12387 Sugiura, Kuniko, ed. *Indonesian Fables of Feats and Fortunes* (K–6). Trans. by Matthew Galgani. Illus. by Koji Honda. 2007, Heian $16.95 (978-0-89346-950-4). 32pp. Three traditional Indonesian stories, accompanied by illustrations on every page, tell of animals and people overcoming difficulty. (Rev: SLJ 8/07)

12388 Sugiura, Kuniko. *Indonesian Tales of Treasures and Brides* (K–6). Trans. by Matthew Galgani. Illus. by Koji Honda. Series: Asian Folktales Retold. 2007, Heian $16.95 (978-0-89346-951-1). 32pp. Three traditional Indonesian stories, accompanied by illustrations on every page, tell of brides and grooms and their fortunes. (Rev: SLJ 8/07)

12389 Vuong, Lynette Dyer. *The Brocaded Slipper and Other Vietnamese Tales* (5–7). Illus. by Vo-Dinh Mai. 1982, HarperCollins paper $4.95 (978-0-06-440440-2). 96pp. Five Vietnamese fairy tales, some of which are similar to our own. [398.2]

12390 Weitzman, David. *Rama and Sita: A Tale from Ancient Java* (1–3). Illus. 2002, Godine $19.95 (978-1-56792-151-9). 32pp. A retelling of the story *The Ramayana*, in the style of Javanese shadow puppetry. (Rev: BL 2/15/03; HBG 10/03; SLJ 6/03) [398.2]

12391 Xiong, Blia. *Nine-in-One, Grr! Grr!* (3–6). Adapted by Cathy Spagnoli. Illus. by Nancy Hom. 1993, Children's Book Pr. $14.95 (978-0-89239-048-9); paper $7.95 (978-0-89239-110-3). 32pp. In this folktale from Laos, Bird comes up with a trick to prevent the earth from being overpopulated with tigers. A reissue. [398.2]

Australia and the Pacific Islands

12392 Galdone, Paul. *The Turtle and the Monkey: A Philippine Tale* (K–2). Illus. by author. 1990, Houghton paper $7.95 (978-0-395-54425-9). 32pp. Turtle asks monkey to help him save a banana tree. [398.2]

12393 Gittins, Anne. *Tales from the South Pacific Islands* (4–6). Illus. by Frank Rocca. 1977, Stemmer $12.95 (978-0-916144-02-9). 96pp. Twenty-two folktales from such places as Fiji and Samoa in which the sea and its creatures play prominent roles. [398.3]

12394 Morin, Paul. *Animal Dreaming: An Aboriginal Dreamtime Story* (3–6). Illus. by author. 1998, Harcourt $16.00 (978-0-15-200054-7). A folktale from Australia that tells how three animals — a kangaroo, a turtle, and an emu — try to bring peace to a warring world. (Rev: HBG 10/98; SLJ 3/98) [398.2]

12395 Romulo, Liana. *Filipino Children's Favorite Stories* (3–6). Illus. 2001, Periplus $16.95 (962-593-765-X). 96pp. This is an engaging collection of 14 traditional myths and folktales from the Philippines. (Rev: BL 4/1/01; HBG 3/02; SLJ 11/01) [398.2]

12396 Wolkstein, Diane. *Sun Mother Wakes the World: An Australian Creation Story* (PS–2). Illus. by Bronwyn Bancroft. 2004, HarperCollins $17.99 (978-0-688-13915-5). 32pp. This colorfully illustrated retelling of an aboriginal folktale offers an appealing explanation of the Earth's creation. (Rev: BL 4/15/04; SLJ 4/04) [398.2]

Europe

Central and Eastern Europe

12397 Brett, Jan. *The Mitten* (PS–2). Illus. 1990, Penguin $16.99 (978-0-399-21920-7). In this Ukrainian folktale, Nicki loses in the snow one of the mittens that his grandmother knit him. (Rev: BCCB 12/89; BL 9/15/89*; HB 11/89; SLJ 11/89) [398.2]

12398 Gorbachev, Valeri. *Fool of the World and the Flying Ship* (1–3). Illus. by author. 1998, Star Bright $15.95 (978-1-887734-19-6). 40pp. A new adaptation of the Ukrainian tale about a tsar who promises his daughter in marriage to the man who brings him a flying ship. (Rev: SLJ 4/99) [398.2]

12399 Hasler, Eveline. *A Tale of Two Brothers* (K–3). Trans. by Marianne Martens. Illus. by Kathi Bhend. 2006, North-South $16.95 (978-0-7358-2102-6). 40pp. Hunchbacked brothers Morris and Boris have opposite outlooks on life, and Morris is rewarded for his sunny good nature and enjoyment of all around him. (Rev: BL 9/1/06; SLJ 9/06) [398.2]

12400 Hogrogian, Nonny. *One Fine Day* (K–3). Illus. by author. 1971, Macmillan $16.00 (978-0-02-744000-3); paper $5.99 (978-0-02-043620-1). 32pp. Based on an Armenian folktale, this cumulative story is ideal for reading aloud. Caldecott Medal winner, 1972. [398.2]

12401 Keding, Dan. *Stories of Hope and Spirit: Folktales from Eastern Europe* (3–6). Illus. 2004, August House $18.95 (978-0-87483-727-8). 77pp. A collection of stories that show the diversity of Eastern Europe and entertain while providing life lessons. (Rev: SLJ 7/05) [398.2]

12402 Kimmel, Eric A. *The Castle of Cats: A Story from Ukraine* (PS–2). Retold by Eric A. Kimmel. Illus. by Katya Krenina. 2004, Holiday House $16.95 (978-0-8234-1565-6). 32pp. A farmer tests the mettle of his three sons by sending them on a mission in this story based on a Latvian folktale. (Rev: BL 10/15/04; SLJ 11/04)

12403 Kimmel, Eric A. *Sirko and the Wolf* (K–3). Illus. by Robert Sauber. 1997, Holiday House LB $15.95 (978-0-8234-1257-0). 32pp. When a dog grows too old to be useful, he strikes a bargain with a wolf in this Ukrainian folktale. (Rev: BL 9/15/97; HBG 3/98; SLJ 11/97) [398.2]

12404 Larson, Jean Russell. *The Fish Bride and Other Gypsy Tales* (4–6). Illus. 2000, Linnet $22.50 (978-0-208-02474-9). 90pp. Sixteen tales of romance, adventure, and humor from the rich traditions of Rom or Gypsies are attractively retold in this entertaining collection. (Rev: BL 11/1/00; HB 11/00; HBG 3/01; SLJ 9/00) [398.2]

12405 Marshall, Bonnie C., retel. *Tales from the Heart of the Balkans* (3–5). Illus. Series: World Folklore. 2001, Libraries Unlimited $29.00 (978-1-56308-870-4). 166pp. Marshall retells folk and fairy tales from the region, preceded by historical and cultural information. (Rev: SLJ 2/02) [398.2]

12406 Molnar, Irma. *One-Time Dog Market at Buda and Other Hungarian Folktales* (5–8). Illus. by Georgeta-Elena Enesel. 2001, Linnet $25.00 (978-0-208-02505-0). 160pp. A collection of 23 clever, thought-provoking Hungarian folktales for older readers. (Rev: BL 1/1–15/02; HBG 3/02; SLJ 2/02) [398.2]

12407 Philip, Neil. *Noah and the Devil* (PS–3). Illus. by Isabelle Brent. 2001, Clarion $16.00 (978-0-618-11754-3). 32pp. The devil makes trouble aboard the ark in this retelling of the Bible story. (Rev: BL 10/1/01; HBG 3/02; SLJ 8/01) [398.2]

12408 Rascol, Sabina I. *The Impudent Rooster* (PS–2). Illus. by Holly Berry. 2004, Dutton $16.99 (978-0-525-47179-0). 32pp. A rooster foils the attempts of a greedy nobleman to steal a coin-filled purse intended for the rooster's master in this adaptation of a Romanian folktale. (Rev: BL 2/15/04; HB 5/04; SLJ 4/04) [398.2]

12409 San Souci, Robert D., retel. *A Weave of Words* (2–5). Illus. by Raúl Colón. 1998, Orchard LB $17.99 (978-0-531-33053-1). In this Armenian tale, an imprisoned king uses his weaving skills to communicate with his wife. (Rev: BCCB 4/98; HBG 10/98; SLJ 3/98) [398.2]

12410 Tresselt, Alvin, ed. *The Mitten* (K–2). Illus. by Yaroslava Mills. 1964, Lothrop LB $16.89 (978-0-688-51053-4); paper $6.99 (978-0-688-09238-2). 30pp. An old Ukrainian folktale about a little boy and his lost mitten. [398.2]

12411 Weber, Ilse. *Mendel Rosenbusch: Tales for Jewish Children* (3–6). Trans. from German by Ruth Fisher and Hans Fisher. 2001, Herodias $14.00 (978-1-928746-19-5). 102pp. A collection of Czech tales about a poor but wise man who lives behind a synagogue and is visited one night by an angel who gives him a gift — the ability to become invisible. (Rev: HBG 3/02; SLJ 11/01) [398.2]

France

12412 Brown, Marcia. *Stone Soup* (1–4). Illus. by author. 1979, Macmillan $16.00 (978-0-684-92296-6); paper $5.99 (978-0-689-71103-9). 48pp. An old French tale about three soldiers who make soup from stones. [398.2]

12413 DeFelice, Cynthia, and Mary DeMarsh. *Three Perfect Peaches* (K–2). Illus. by Irene Trivas. 1995, Orchard LB $16.99 (978-0-531-08722-0). 32pp. In this French folktale, a young farmboy claims the hand of a princess he helped save from death. (Rev: BCCB 4/95; BL 1/15/95; SLJ 4/95) [398.2]

12414 Forest, Heather. *Stone Soup* (PS–3). Illus. by Susan Gaber. 1998, August House $15.95 (978-0-87483-498-7). 32pp. Using a contemporary village as its setting, this is a handsome retelling of the ancient tale that originated in France and, in a different version, Sweden. (Rev: BL 9/1/98; HBG 10/98; SLJ 5/98) [398.2]

12415 Gershator, David, and Phyllis Gershator. *Kallaloo! A Caribbean Tale* (PS–3). Illus. by Diane Greenseid. 2005, Marshall Cavendish $16.95 (978-0-7614-5110-5). A hungry grandmother decides to make soup from a shell, and the curious neighbors contribute various ingredients in this West Indian version of "Stone Soup." (Rev: SLJ 6/05) [398.2]

12416 Huck, Charlotte. *Toads and Diamonds* (K–3). Illus. by Anita Lobel. 1996, Greenwillow $15.89 (978-0-688-13681-9). 32pp. A downtrodden girl is rewarded for her kindness in this retelling of a folktale. (Rev: BCCB 1/97; BL 11/1/96*; HB 11/96; SLJ 9/96) [398.2]

12417 Kimmel, Eric A. *Three Sacks of Truth: A Story from France* (PS–3). Illus. by Robert Rayevsky. 1993, Holiday House LB $15.95 (978-0-8234-0921-1). 32pp. In this French folktale, a king promises his daughter to the man who can bring him the perfect peach. (Rev: BCCB 7–8/93; BL 4/15/93; SLJ 7/93) [398.2]

12418 McGovern, Ann, adapt. *Stone Soup* (PS–1). Illus. by Winslow Pels. 1986, Scholastic paper $3.99 (978-0-590-41602-3). 32pp. The old story of the young man who asks for food and is refused by the old woman, then he asks her for a stone. (Rev: BCCB 2/87; BL 10/15/86; SLJ 11/86) [398.2]

12419 Muth, Jon J. *Stone Soup* (K–2). Illus. 2003, Scholastic $17.99 (978-0-439-33909-4). 32pp. In this version of the traditional tale, Buddhist monks want Chinese villagers to learn the joy of sharing, and as contributions come into the soup pot and the mix richens, so do the colors of the lush illustrations. (Rev: BCCB 3/03; BL 1/1–15/03; HB 3/03; HBG 10/03; SLJ 3/03) [398.2]

12420 Pullman, Philip. *Puss in Boots: The Adventures of That Most Enterprising Feline* (PS–3). Illus. by Ian Beck. 2001, Knopf $16.95 (978-0-375-81354-2). 32pp. Pullman's version adds a few new characters and a couple of mysteries to be solved. (Rev: BCCB 5/02; BL 7/01; HBG 3/02; SLJ 8/01) [398.2]

12421 Seeger, Pete, and Paul Dubois Jacobs. *Some Friends to Feed: The Story of Stone Soup* (K–2). Illus. by Michael Hays. 2005, Putnam $16.99 (978-0-399-24017-1). 48pp. This nicely illustrated retelling of the classic story of a hungry soldier and the children who come to his aid is packaged with an audio CD and musical notation. (Rev: BL 9/1/05; SLJ 10/05) [398.2]

12422 Watts, Bernadette. *The Rich Man and the Shoemaker: A Fable by La Fontaine* (2–4). Illus. 2002, North-South LB $16.50 (978-0-7358-4676-0). 32pp. A Renaissance setting graces this tale of the shoemaker who returns a bribe when the gold causes him anxiety. (Rev: BL 10/1/02; HBG 3/03) [398.2]

Germany

12423 Andreasen, Dan. *Rose Red and the Bear Prince* (PS–1). Illus. 2000, HarperCollins LB $16.89 (978-0-06-027967-7). 40pp. In this version of the Brothers Grimm tale, Rose Red helps a wandering bear to break the enchantment that has turned him from a prince to this animal. (Rev: BL 1/1–15/00; HBG 10/00; SLJ 2/00) [398.2]

12424 Artell, Mike. *Petite Rouge: A Cajun Red Riding Hood* (PS–2). Illus. by Jim Harris. 2001, Dial $16.99 (978-0-8037-2514-0). 32pp. The wolf becomes an alligator and the little girl a duck in this Louisiana version of the classic tale. (Rev: BL 7/01; HBG 10/01; SLJ 6/01) [398.2]

12425 Bateman, Teresa. *The Princesses Have a Ball* (K–3). Illus. by Lynne W. Cravath. 2002, Whitman $16.95 (978-0-8075-6626-8). 32pp. A suspicious king asks detectives to find out what his girls are up to, but a cobbler finds the answer first and advises the young ladies to reveal their athletic skills in this basketball version of "The Twelve Dancing Princesses." (Rev: BL 11/1/02; HB 1/03; HBG 3/03; SLJ 12/02) [398.2]

12426 Cech, John. *The Twelve Dancing Princesses* (PS–2). Illus. by Lucy Corvino. 2009, Sterling $14.95 (978-1-4027-4435-8). 28pp. A lushly illustrated retelling of the story about the princesses who mysteriously manage to wear out their shoes every night. (Rev: BL 3/15/09; SLJ 7/09) [398]

12427 Daly, Niki. *Pretty Salma: Little Red Riding Hood Story from Africa* (PS–2). Illus. 2007, Clarion $16.00 (978-0-618-72345-4). 32pp. In Ghana, pretty Salma disobeys her grandmother and talks to a strange Mr. Dog, who takes her clothes and tricks Granny into thinking he's Salma. (Rev: BL 2/1/07) [398.2]

12428 de la Mare, Walter. *The Turnip* (1–4). Illus. by Kevin Hawkes. 1992, Godine $18.95 (978-0-87923-934-3). 32pp. Based on a Grimm brothers tale, the

story of a good but poor man with an enormous turnip and his greedy, rich half-brother. (Rev: BL 11/15/92; HB 1/93; SLJ 12/92) [398.2]

12429 Eisner, Will. *The Princess and the Frog: By the Grimm Brothers* (4–7). Illus. 1999, NBM $15.95 (978-1-56163-244-2). 32pp. A retelling of the familiar fairy tale in graphic novel style. (Rev: BL 12/15/99; HBG 3/00) [398.2]

12430 Evetts-Secker, Josephine. *Little Red Riding Hood* (PS–2). Illus. by Nicoletta Ceccoli. 2004, Barefoot Books $16.99 (978-1-84148-621-5). 32pp. Nicoletta Ceccoli's stunning artwork enlivens this child-friendly retelling. (Rev: BL 3/15/04; SLJ 8/04) [389.2]

12431 Foreman, Michael. *Rock-A-Doodle-Do!* (K–2). Illus. 2000, Andersen $16.95 (978-0-86264-951-7). 32pp. This entertaining version of *The Bremen Town Musicians* takes place in the American Southwest in the 1950s. (Rev: BL 3/1/01)

12432 Grimm Brothers. *The Complete Grimm's Fairy Tales* (4–6). Illus. by Josef Scharl. 1974, Pantheon paper $18.00 (978-0-394-70930-7). Based on Margaret Hunt's translation, this has become the standard edition of these perennial favorites. [398.2]

12433 Grimm Brothers. *The Elves and the Shoemaker* (PS–K). Retold and illus. by Paul Galdone. 1984, Houghton paper $6.95 (978-0-89919-422-6). 32pp. A poor shoemaker is visited by elves at night. [398.2]

12434 Grimm Brothers. *Household Stories of the Brothers Grimm* (4–7). Illus. by Walter Crane. 1963, Dover paper $9.95 (978-0-486-21080-3). 269pp. First published in the United States in 1883. [398.2]

12435 Grimm Brothers. *Little Red Riding Hood / Caperucita roja: A Bilingual Book* (K–2). Trans. by James Surges. Illus. by Pau Estrada. 1999, Chronicle $12.95 (978-0-8118-2561-0); paper $6.95 (978-0-8118-2562-7). A bilingual version of the favorite folktale with charming yet scary illustrations. (Rev: SLJ 2/00) [398.2]

12436 Grimm Brothers. *Rumpelstiltskin* (PS–1). Illus. by Paul Galdone. 1985, Houghton $16.00 (978-0-89919-266-6); paper $7.95 (978-0-395-52599-9). 32pp. Bold drawings highlight this straightfoward version of the little man who spins straw into gold. Another fine edition is: Illus. by John Wallner (1984, Prentice). (Rev: BL 6/1/ 5; SLJ 8/85) [398.2]

12437 Grimm Brothers. *Rumpelstiltskin* (PS–2). Retold by Paul O. Zelinsky. Illus. by Paul Zelinsky. 1986, Dutton $16.99 (978-0-525-44265-3). 40pp. Closeups and much detail in the illustrations highlight the retelling of this old favorite. (Rev: BCCB 10/86; BL 9/1/86; SLJ 10/86) [398.2]

12438 Grimm Brothers. *The Shoemaker and the Elves* (K–2). Retold and illus. by Ilse Plume. 1991, Harcourt $14.95 (978-0-15-274050-4). This folktale is relocated to Renaissance Italy, but the plot is the same except that the elves now number four. (Rev: SLJ 1/92) [398.2]

12439 Grimm Brothers. *The Three Feathers* (5–8). Illus. by Eleonore Schmid. 1984, Creative Editions LB $13.95 (978-0-87191-941-0). 32pp. A version for older readers that is faithful to the original. [398.2]

12440 Grimm Brothers. *The Three Languages* (3–5). Illus. by Ivan Chermayeff. 1984, Creative Ed. LB $13.95 (978-0-87191-940-3). 32pp. The tale of the seemingly foolish son who ends up as Pope of Rome. [398.2]

12441 Grimm Brothers. *The Water of Life: A Tale from the Brothers Grimm* (PS–3). Retold by Barbara Rogasky. Illus. by Trina S. Hyman. 1986, Holiday House LB $16.95 (978-0-8234-0552-7). 40pp. Three brothers journey to find the water of life for their ailing father. (Rev: BCCB 11/86; BL 9/15/86; HB 3/87) [398.2]

12442 Hamilton, Virginia. *The Girl Who Spun Gold* (PS–3). Illus. by Leo Dillon and Diane Dillon. 2000, Scholastic $17.95 (978-0-590-47378-1). 40pp. Stunning illustrations and stirring prose mark this outstanding retelling of the Rumpelstiltskin folktale using a West Indian setting. (Rev: BCCB 12/00; BL 8/00*; HB 9/00; HBG 3/01; SLJ 9/00) [398.2]

12443 Hodges, Margaret. *The Hero of Bremen* (3–6). Illus. by Charles Mikolaycak. 1993, Holiday House LB $17.95 (978-0-8234-0934-1). 32pp. In this German folktale, a disabled cobbler is helped by the ghost of Roland, the legendary knight who saved the city of Bremen centuries before. (Rev: BCCB 10/93; BL 10/15/93; HB 11/93; SLJ 10/93) [398.2]

12444 Jackson, Bobby L., retel. *Little Red Ronnika* (1–4). Illus. by Rhonda Mitchell. 1998, Multicultural Publns. LB $16.95 (978-1-884242-80-9). 32pp. In this version of Little Red Riding Hood, the characters are all African Americans. Granny is a hip senior and the wolf is a rapper. (Rev: SLJ 1/99) [398.2]

12445 Kimmel, Eric A. *The Goose Girl: A Story from the Brothers Grimm* (4–6). Illus. by Robert Sauber. 1995, Holiday House LB $15.95 (978-0-8234-1074-3). 32pp. A retelling of the Brothers Grimm tale of the young princess who is cheated out of her birthright by a greedy serving girl. (Rev: BL 10/15/95; SLJ 10/95) [398.2]

12446 Kimmel, Eric A. *Iron John* (K–4). Illus. by Trina S. Hyman. 1994, Holiday House LB $17.95 (978-0-8234-1073-6). 32pp. An adaptation of a Grimm tale about Prince Walter, who meets Iron John in the forest and breaks a spell that has been cast over him. (Rev: BCCB 12/94; BL 11/1/94; SLJ 12/94) [398.2]

12447 Kimmel, Eric A. *Seven at One Blow: A Tale from the Brothers Grimm* (PS–1). Illus. by Megan Lloyd. 1998, Holiday House $16.95 (978-0-8234-1383-6). 32pp. After amazing himself by killing seven flies on his jelly sandwich with one blow, a little tailor sets out to seek his fortune in this tale from the Brothers Grimm. (Rev: BL 11/15/98; HB 1/99; HBG 3/99; SLJ 12/98) [398.2]

12448 McDermott, Denis. *The Golden Goose* (PS–2). Illus. 2000, HarperCollins LB $15.89 (978-0-688-11403-9). 32pp. In this version of the Grimm Brothers tale, young Hans is rewarded for helping a troll by the gift of a talking golden goose. (Rev: BL 5/15/00; HBG 10/00; SLJ 7/00) [398.2]

12449 Marshall, James, retel. *Hansel and Gretel* (K–3). Illus. 1990, Puffin paper $7.99 (978-0-14-050836-9). A retelling of the famous story with innovative, often humorous, illustrations. (Rev: SLJ 12/90*) [398.2]

12450 Norling, Beth. *Sister Night and Sister Day* (PS–2). Illus. 2001, Allen & Unwin $14.95 (978-1-86448-863-0). 32pp. There are quite different outcomes when twin sisters Ruby and Rose go to work for Mother Earth, in this retelling of a Grimm tale. (Rev: BL 8/01; SLJ 6/01) [398.2]

12451 Orgel, Doris. *The Bremen Town Musicians and Other Animal Tales from Grimm* (PS–2). Illus. by Bert Kitchen. 2004, Roaring Brook $18.95 (978-1-59643-040-2). 48pp. Six animal-themed fairy tales from the brothers Grimm are accompanied by arresting illustrations. (Rev: BL 1/1–15/05) [398.2]

12452 Orgel, Doris. *Doctor All-Knowing* (PS–2). Illus. by Alexandra Boiger. 2008, Atheneum $16.99 (978-1-4169-1246-0). 40pp. A retelling of a tale about a poor man who seeks to make a better life for himself and his daughter, and succeeds more through luck than good judgment. (Rev: BL 9/1/08) [398.2]

12453 Osborne, Mary Pope. *The Brave Little Seamstress* (K–3). Illus. by Giselle Potter. 2002, Atheneum $16.00 (978-0-689-84486-7). 40pp. A clever retelling of "The Brave Little Tailor" folktale using a saucy young girl as its heroine. (Rev: BCCB 5/02; BL 4/1/02; HBG 10/02; SLJ 4/02) [398.2]

12454 Price, Kathy. *The Bourbon Street Musicians* (4–6). Illus. by Andrew Glass. 2002, Clarion $16.00 (978-0-618-04076-6). 40pp. A retelling of "The Bremen Town Musicians" moved to New Orleans and with a Cajun beat. (Rev: BL 6/1–15/02; HBG 10/02; SLJ 5/02) [398.2]

12455 Shulman, Janet. *The Nutcracker* (K–5). Illus. by Renee Graef. 1999, HarperCollins $19.99 (978-0-06-027814-4). 48pp. An adaptation of Hoffman's story *The Nutcracker and the Mouse King,* with a CD consisting of the narration and some excerpts from the Tchaikovsky ballet. (Rev: BL 9/1/99; HBG 3/00; SLJ 10/99)

12456 Sweet, Melissa. *Carmine: A Little More Red* (PS–2). Illus. by author. 2005, Houghton $16.00 (978-0-618-38794-6). A fresh and amusing take on the tale of Little Red Riding Hood, told in the form of a sophisticated alphabet book that highlights a different word in the alphabet on each page. (Rev: SLJ 8/05*) [398.2]

12457 Wallace, Ian. *Hansel and Gretel* (2–4). Illus. 1996, Douglas & McIntyre $14.95 (978-0-88899-212-3). 32pp. A scary retelling in a contemporary setting of the famous Grimms folktale. (Rev: BL 6/1–15/96; SLJ 5/96) [398.2]

12458 Wolkstein, Diane, retel. *The Glass Mountain* (K–4). Illus. by Louisa Bauer. 1999, Morrow LB $15.89 (978-0-688-14848-5). A lesser-known Grimm Brothers tale in which a young girl is held prisoner in an underground cave by an unpleasant old man named Old Rinkrank. (Rev: BCCB 3/99; HBG 10/99; SLJ 7/99) [398.2]

12459 Zelinsky, Paul. *Rapunzel* (3–5). Illus. 1997, Dutton $17.99 (978-0-525-45607-0). 48pp. Rich oil paintings illustrate this tale of the enduring power of love. Caldecott Medal winner, 1998. (Rev: BL 11/15/97*; HBG 3/98; SLJ 11/97*) [398.2]

Great Britain and Ireland

12460 Artell, Mike. *Three Little Cajun Pigs* (K–3). Illus. by Jim Harris. 2006, Dial $16.99 (978-0-8037-2815-8). The classic tale is given a funny Cajun spin when a hungry gator fills in for the big, bad wolf. (Rev: HBG 4/07; SLJ 12/06) [398.2]

12461 Asch, Frank. *Ziggy Piggy and the Three Little Pigs* (PS–1). Illus. 1998, Kids Can $14.95 (978-1-55074-515-3). 32pp. A variation on the story of the three little pigs in which a fourth little pig, Ziggy, rescues his brothers from the wolf and takes them to a raft he made from driftwood. (Rev: BL 11/15/98; HB 11/98; HBG 3/99) [398.2]

12462 Aylesworth, Jim. *The Gingerbread Man* (PS–2). Illus. by Barbara McClintock. 1998, Scholastic $16.95 (978-0-590-97219-2). 32pp. A traditional retelling of the old folktale about the cheerful elderly couple who created a gingerbread man who comes to life and leads them a merry chase. (Rev: BL 4/1/98; HBG 10/98; SLJ 4/98) [398.21]

12463 Barton, Byron. *The Little Red Hen* (PS–2). Illus. 1993, HarperCollins LB $17.89 (978-0-06-021676-4). 32pp. A new interpretation of this favorite story of the industrious hen, with appealing illustrations. (Rev: BL 5/1/93; SLJ 7/93) [398.2]

12464 Barton, Byron. *The Three Bears* (PS). Illus. 1991, HarperCollins LB $17.89 (978-0-06-020424-2). 32pp. For the very young, this is a retelling of the story of Goldilocks and the Three Bears. (Rev: BL 1/1/91; SLJ 11/91) [398.2]

12465 Behan, Brendan. *The King of Ireland's Son* (3–5). Illus. by P. J. Lynch. 1997, Orchard $16.95 (978-0-531-09549-2). 32pp. A rich retelling of the Irish folktale about three princes who set out to find the origin of the heavenly music that is heard in their land. (Rev: BCCB 4/97; BL 4/15/97; SLJ 6/97) [398.2]

12466 Beneduce, Ann Keay. *Jack and the Beanstalk* (1–3). Illus. by Gennady Spirin. 1999, Penguin $17.99 (978-0-399-23118-6). 32pp. An expanded version of the classic tale, based on a Victorian retelling, in which a fairy figures prominently as Jack's helper. (Rev: BCCB 12/99; BL 11/1/99; HBG 3/00; SLJ 11/99) [398.2]

12467 Bofill, Francesc. *Jack and the Beanstalk / Juan y los frijoles magicos* (2–4). 1998, Chronicle $13.95 (978-0-8118-2062-2). 32pp. Using an easy English/Spanish text, this is an attractive retelling of the classic folktale. (Rev: BL 11/15/98; SLJ 8/98) [398.2]

12468 Brett, Jan. *Gingerbread Baby* (PS–3). Illus. 1999, Penguin $16.99 (978-0-399-23444-6). 32pp. In this updated version of the old tale, Gingerbread Baby escapes and wreaks havoc in the Swiss village where he had been baked. (Rev: BL 11/15/99; HBG 3/00; SLJ 11/99)

12469 Brett, Jan. *The Three Snow Bears* (1–3). Illus. by author. 2007, Putnam $16.99 (978-0-399-24792-7). 32pp. In the cold north, an Inuit girl called Alooki loses her sled dogs and comes across an empty igloo in this re-imagining of "Goldilocks and the Three Bears." (Rev: BL 9/15/07; LMC 11/07; SLJ 12/07) [398.2] ∩

12470 Brown, Marcia. *Dick Whittington and His Cat* (K–3). Illus. by author. 1988, Macmillan $16.00 (978-0-684-18998-7). 32pp. A reissue of a Caldecott Honor Book published in 1950 about the boy who went to London to seek his fortune. [398.2]

12471 Buehner, Caralyn. *Goldilocks and the Three Bears* (PS–1). Illus. by Mark Buehner. 2007, Dial $16.99 (978-0-8037-2939-1). Three well-behaved bears live in a lovely little log cabin in the woods that a boisterous rope-jumping Goldilocks invades in their absence. (Rev: BL 3/1/07; SLJ 4/07) [398.2]

12472 Burns, Batt. *The King with Horse's Ears and Other Irish Folktales* (3–6). Illus. by Igor Oleynikov. Series: Folktales of the World. 2009, Sterling $14.95 (978-1-4027-3772-5). 96pp. Thirteen Irish tales feature warriors, heroes, fairies, and leprechauns; includes Gaelic words and Celtic-style illustrations. (Rev: BL 3/1/09; SLJ 3/09) [398.2]

12473 Carpenter, Stephen. *The Three Billy Goats Gruff* (PS). Illus. Series: Harper Growing Tree. 1998, HarperCollins $9.99 (978-0-694-01033-2). 24pp. For the very young, this is a simple but accurate retelling of the old English folktale using double-page pictures. (Rev: BL 5/15/98; HBG 10/98; SLJ 7/98) [398.2]

12474 Cech, John. *Jack and the Beanstalk* (1–3). Illus. by Robert MacKenzie. 2008, Sterling $14.95 (978-1-4027-3064-1). 32pp. Yet another variation on the Jack-and-the-beanstalk story with a funny ending and endnotes trace the story's themes to tales throughout history. (Rev: BL 3/15/08; SLJ 5/08) [398.2]

12475 Christelow, Eileen. *Where's the Big Bad Wolf?* (PS–1). Illus. 2002, Clarion $16.00 (978-0-618-18194-0). 32pp. This humorous retelling of the classic tale — featuring cartoon illustrations and dialogue balloons — is written as a mystery, featuring Detective Doggedly in search of BBW (Big Bad Wolf). (Rev: BL 10/15/02; HBG 3/03; SLJ 9/02)

12476 Ciddor, Anna. *Night of the Fifth Moon* (5–8). 2008, Allen & Unwin paper $9.95 (978-1-74114-814-5). 243pp. Set in ancient Ireland and filled with beautiful imagery, this engaging novel tells the story of Ket who must leave his family and struggle for the chance to become a druid. (Rev: SLJ 5/09; VOYA 10/08)

12477 Collins, Sheila Hebert. *Jolie Blonde and the Three Heberts: A Cajun Twist to an Old Tale* (K–4). Illus. by Patrick Soper. 1999, Pelican $15.95 (978-1-56554-324-9). In this Cajun version of Goldilocks, the heroine is Jolie Blonde and the bears are three humans named Hebert whose gumbo is eaten while they are away. (Rev: HBG 10/99; SLJ 6/99) [398.2]

12478 Collins, Sheila Hebert, retel. *Les Trois Cochons* (2–5). Illus. by Patrick Soper. 1999, Pelican $15.95 (978-1-56554-325-6). A Cajun rendering of the

"Three Little Pigs" that contains a number of Cajun phases that are fun but can be confusing. (Rev: SLJ 4/00) [398.2]

12479 Cooper, Susan, retel. *The Silver Cow: A Welsh Tale* (K–4). Illus. by Warwick Hutton. 1991, Simon & Schuster paper $5.99 (978-0-689-71512-9). 32pp. A greedy farmer inherits a silver cow from his son, who received it for his harp playing. [398.2]

12480 Davis, Donald. *The Pig Who Went Home on Sunday: An Appalachian Folktale* (K–4). Illus. by Jennifer Mazzucco. 2004, August House $16.95 (978-0-87483-571-7). In this Appalachian variation of "The Three Little Pigs," only one youngster heeds his mother's advice and survives to come home at the weekend. (Rev: SLJ 8/04) [398.2]

12481 dePaola, Tomie, retel. *Fin M'Coul: The Giant of Knockmany Hill* (PS–3). Illus. by Tomie dePaola. 1981, Holiday House LB $16.95 (978-0-8234-0384-4); paper $6.95 (978-0-8234-0385-1). 32pp. Fin's wife saves him from the most feared giant in Ireland. [398.2]

12482 dePaola, Tomie. *Jamie O'Rourke and the Big Potato: An Irish Folktale* (PS–3). Illus. 1992, Penguin $16.99 (978-0-399-22257-3). 32pp. Lazy Jamie gets a seed from a leprechaun and produces an enormous potato. (Rev: BL 2/15/92; SLJ 4/92) [398.2]

12483 Doyle, Malachy. *Tales from Old Ireland* (3–6). Illus. 2000, Barefoot Books $19.99 (978-1-902283-97-5). 96pp. A heady collection of traditional Irish tales that includes the familiar "Children of Lir" and "The Soul Cages." (Rev: BL 11/15/00; HB 3/01; HBG 10/01; SLJ 11/00) [398.2]

12484 Ernst, Lisa Campbell. *The Gingerbread Girl* (PS–2). 2006, Dutton $16.99 (978-0-525-47667-2). 32pp. In this whimsical twist on the story of the Gingerbread Boy, his sister proves much more resourceful than her ill-fated sibling. (Rev: BL 9/1/06; SLJ 11/06) [398.2]

12485 Escott, John, retel. *The Little Red Hen* (PS–K). Illus. by Annie West. 2003, Gingham Dog $15.95 (978-1-57768-492-3). 32pp. A retelling of the story of the Little Red Hen and her unhelpful friends. (Rev: HBG 4/04; SLJ 4/04) [398.2]

12486 Finch, Mary. *The Little Red Hen and the Ear of Wheat* (PS–K). Illus. by Elisabeth Bell. Series: A Barefoot Beginner Book. 1999, Barefoot Books $15.95 (978-1-902283-47-0). A retelling of the famous folktale about the little red hen who can't find helpers to prepare a loaf of bread. (Rev: SLJ 5/99) [398.2]

12487 Forest, Heather, retel. *The Little Red Hen: An Old Fable* (PS–2). Illus. by Susan Gaber. 2006, August House $16.95 (978-0-87483-795-7). A charming, rhyming version of the classic story featuring a black-and-white cat, a Corgi with a blanket, and a literary mouse as the hen's friends. (Rev: SLJ 11/06) [398.2]

12488 Forest, Heather. *The Woman Who Flummoxed the Fairies: An Old Tale from Scotland* (K–3). Illus. by Susan Gaber. 1990, Harcourt $14.95 (978-0-15-299150-0). In this retelling of a tale from Scotland,

the fairies kidnap a baker so she will make cakes only for them. (Rev: BL 4/1/90; SLJ 6/90) [398.2]

12489 Galdone, Paul. *The Gingerbread Boy* (PS–1). Illus. by author. 1983, Houghton $16.00 (978-0-395-28799-6); paper $6.95 (978-0-89919-163-8). 40pp. Humorous and vigorous illustrations enhance this favorite folktale of the adventures of a runaway gingerbread boy. [398.2]

12490 Galdone, Paul. *Henny Penny* (K–2). Illus. by author. 1979, Houghton $16.00 (978-0-395-28800-9); paper $6.95 (978-0-89919-225-3). 32pp. A retelling of the favorite cumulative folktale of the hen who thought the sky was falling. [398.2]

12491 Galdone, Paul. *The Little Red Hen* (K–2). Illus. by author. 1979, Houghton $15.00 (978-0-395-28803-0); paper $5.95 (978-0-89919-349-6). A little hen works for her lazy housemates in this reworking of the old tale. Another fine edition is: *The Little Red Hen: An Old Story,* illus. by Margot Zemach (1983, Farrar). [398.2]

12492 Galdone, Paul. *The Three Bears* (K–2). Illus. by author. 1979, Houghton $16.00 (978-0-395-28811-5); paper $6.95 (978-0-89919-401-1). 32pp. The illustrations for this familiar story are large, colorful, and humorous; excellent to use with a group. [398.2]

12493 Galdone, Paul. *The Three Little Pigs* (PS–1). Illus. by author. 1979, Houghton $16.00 (978-0-395-28813-9). The old folktale told in verse. Another recommended edition is: Illus. by Erik Blegvad (1980, Macmillan). [398.2]

12494 Green, Roger L. *Adventures of Robin Hood* (5–9). 1994, Knopf $15.00 (978-0-679-43636-2); Puffin paper $4.99 (978-0-14-036700-3). The exploits of this folk hero are retold in this reissue of a classic version. [398]

12495 Greene, Ellin. *The Little Golden Lamb* (PS–2). Illus. by Rosanne Litzinger. 2000, Clarion $15.00 (978-0-395-71526-0). 32pp. Anyone who touches the lamb with a golden fleece becomes stuck to it in this amusing folktale. (Rev: BCCB 5/00; BL 3/15/00; HB 5/00; HBG 10/00; SLJ 6/00) [398.22]

12496 Gross, Gwen, ed. *Knights of the Round Table* (2–5). Illus. by Norman Green. 1992, Random paper $3.99 (978-0-394-84579-8). 112pp. A retelling of many of the most popular Arthurian legends. (Rev: BCCB 9/85; SLJ 2/86) [398.2]

12497 Harris, Jim, retel. *The Three Little Dinosaurs* (K–3). Illus. by Jim Harris. 1999, Pelican $15.95 (978-1-56554-371-3). In this version the three little pigs folktale, three young brachiosaurs build different homes to withstand the big bad Tyrannosaurus rex. (Rev: HBG 3/00; SLJ 2/00) [398.2]

12498 Hassett, John, and Ann Hassett. *Can't Catch Me* (PS–2). Illus. by John Hassett. 2006, Houghton $16.00 (978-0-618-70490-3). 32pp. In this lively adaptation of "The Gingerbread Man," an ice cube escapes from the freezer and makes a dash for the sea. (Rev: SLJ 10/06) [398.2]

12499 Hewitt, Kathryn, adapt. *The Three Sillies* (K–3). Illus. by Kathryn Hewitt. 1989, Harcourt paper $3.95 (978-0-15-286856-7). A suitor sets out to find three sillier people than his betrothed's family. (Rev: BCCB 5/86; BL 4/1/86; SLJ 5/86) [398.2]

12500 Heyer, Carol, retel. *Robin Hood* (2–4). Illus. by Carol Heyer. 1993, Ideals LB $15.00 (978-0-8249-8648-3). This handsome book retells the most famous of Robin Hood's exploits, culminating in the King's pardon. (Rev: SLJ 11/93) [398.2]

12501 Hodges, Margaret. *Dick Whittington and His Cat* (PS–2). Illus. by Melisande Potter. 2006, Holiday $16.95 (978-0-8234-1987-6). 32pp. Retells the British legend of the orphan who became Lord Mayor of London. (Rev: BL 5/1/06; SLJ 5/06) [398.2]

12502 Hodges, Margaret, retel. *The Kitchen Knight: A Tale of King Arthur* (3–6). Illus. by Trina S. Hyman. 1990, Holiday House LB $17.95 (978-0-8234-0787-3). A lavishly illustrated version of the story of the king who hides his identity to work in the kitchen at King Arthur's court. (Rev: BCCB 11/90*; HB 3/91; SLJ 1/91) [398.2]

12503 Hodges, Margaret. *St. George and the Dragon: A Golden Legend* (2–5). Illus. by Trina S. Hyman. 1984, Little, Brown $16.95 (978-0-316-36789-9). A reworking of the English tale as it appeared in Edmund Spenser's Fairie Queen. Caldecott Medal winner, 1985. [398.2]

12504 Hodges, Margaret. *Up the Chimney* (K–2). Illus. by Amanda Harvey. 1998, Holiday House $15.95 (978-0-8234-1354-6). 32pp. When a girl goes out to seek her fortune, she is helped by all the objects and animals she has helped in the past, but when her uncharitable, cruel sister goes out, her fate is different. (Rev: BCCB 12/98; BL 11/15/98; HBG 3/99; SLJ 1/99) [398.2]

12505 Huck, Charlotte. *The Black Bull of Norroway* (2–4). Illus. by Anita Lobel. 2001, Greenwillow LB $15.89 (978-0-688-16901-5). 40pp. A Scottish beauty-and-the-beast tale, richly illustrated and accompanied by a discussion of the story's origins and variants. (Rev: BCCB 5/01; BL 9/15/01; HB 5/01; HBG 10/01; SLJ 6/01) [398.2]

12506 Jacobs, Joseph. *Celtic Fairy Tales* (3–6). Illus. by John D. Batten. 1968, Peter Smith $24.00 (978-0-8446-2302-3); Dover paper $7.95 (978-0-486-21826-7). 267pp. A classic collection. Followed by: *More Celtic Fairy Tales* (1969, Dover paper). [398.2]

12507 Jacobs, Joseph. *English Fairy Tales* (3–6). Illus. by John D. Batten. 1969, Peter Smith $23.75 (978-0-8446-2303-0); Dover paper $10.95 (978-0-486-21818-2). A standard collection by a master storyteller. [398.2]

12508 Jones, Carol. *The Gingerbread Man* (PS–K). Illus. 2002, Houghton $16.00 (978-0-618-18822-2). 32pp. In this spirited retelling, it is nursery rhyme characters who chase the gingerbread boy. (Rev: BL 2/15/02; HBG 10/02; SLJ 4/02) [398.2]

12509 Ketteman, Helen. *The Three Little Gators* (PS–2). Illus. by Will Terry. 2009, Albert Whitman $16.99 (978-0-8075-7824-7). 32pp. Three young alligators build their houses with rocks, sticks, and sand, respectively, in this entertaining version of the

"Three Little Pigs" set in Texas. (Rev: BLO 4/24/09; LMC 10/09; SLJ 6/09)

12510 Kilgannon, Eily. *Folktales of the Yeats Country* (5–8). Illus. 1990, Mercier paper $10.95 (978-0-85342-861-9). Seventeen folktales that originate in County Sligo in Ireland. (Rev: BL 8/90; SLJ 2/91) [398.2]

12511 Kimmel, Eric A. *The Gingerbread Man* (PS–K). Illus. by Megan Lloyd. 1993, Holiday House LB $16.95 (978-0-8234-0824-5). 32pp. This is a modern version of a classic tale about the cookie that says he can't be caught. (Rev: BL 3/15/93; SLJ 6/93*) [398.2]

12512 Kimmel, Eric A. *The Old Woman and Her Pig* (PS–3). Illus. by Giora Carmi. 1992, Holiday House LB $17.95 (978-0-8234-0970-9). 32pp. An excellent retelling of the classic British folktale. (Rev: BL 1/1/93; SLJ 10/92) [398.2]

12513 Kimmel, Eric A. *The Three Little Tamales* (K–3). Illus. by Valeria Docampo. 2009, Marshall Cavendish $17.99 (978-0-7614-5519-6). 32pp. Three little tamales flee for their lives and build houses made of different materials in this fractured "Three Little Pigs" set in the Southwest. (Rev: BL 3/15/09; LMC 8/09; SLJ 6/09) [398.2]

12514 Krull, Kathleen, ed. *A Pot o' Gold: A Treasury of Irish Stories, Poetry, Folklore and (of Course) Blarney* (4–8). Illus. by David McPhail. 2004, Hyperion $16.99 (978-0-7868-0625-6). 192pp. This is a comprehensive collection — including riddles, blessing, and battle cries — with attractive and appropriate illustrations. (Rev: BL 2/15/04; SLJ 3/04) [820.8]

12515 Leavy, Una. *Irish Fairy Tales and Legends* (4–8). Illus. 1997, Roberts Rinehart $18.95 (978-1-57098-177-7). An attractive book that contains 10 Irish legends, some going back 2,000 years. (Rev: BL 2/1/98; HBG 10/98; SLJ 2/98) [398.2]

12516 Light, Steve. *Puss in Boots* (PS–2). Illus. 2002, Abrams $14.95 (978-0-8109-4368-1). 24pp. Collages illustrate this faithful version of a favorite folktale. (Rev: BCCB 5/02; BL 4/15/02; HBG 10/02; SLJ 4/02) [398.2]

12517 Lowell, Susan. *Dusty Locks and the Three Bears* (PS–1). Illus. by Randy Cecil. 2001, Holt $15.95 (978-0-8050-5862-8). 32pp. A western version of Goldilocks starring a bad-tempered, ill-mannered runaway. (Rev: BCCB 7–8/01; BL 7/01; HB 7/01; HBG 10/01; SLJ 7/01) [398.2]

12518 Lupton, Hugh. *Pirican Pic and Pirican Mor* (2–4). Illus. by Yumi Heo. 2003, Barefoot Books $16.99 (978-1-84148-070-1). 40pp. A humorous cumulative Celtic folktale recounts the conflict between Pirican Pic and Pirican Mor over the latter's theft of the former's hard-won walnuts. (Rev: BL 4/1/03; HB 7/03; HBG 10/03; SLJ 5/03) [398.2]

12519 MacDonald, Margaret Read. *Slop! A Welsh Folktale* (K–2). Illus. by Yvonne Davis. 1997, Fulcrum $15.95 (978-1-55591-352-6). 24pp. In this Welsh folktale, fairies become annoyed when their neighbor continually empties his slop bucket on top of their cottage. (Rev: BL 11/1/97; HBG 3/98; SLJ 11/97) [398.2]

12520 MacDonald, Margaret Read. *Teeny Weeny Bop* (K–2). Illus. by Diane Greenseid. 2006, Albert Whitman $16.95 (978-0-8075-7992-3). 32pp. When Teeny Weeny Bop makes a series of bad decisions, she ends up with a slug as a pet in this silly story that incorporates folkloric features. (Rev: BL 5/15/06; SLJ 8/06) [398.2]

12521 McGovern, Ann. *Too Much Noise* (K–3). Illus. by Simms Taback. 1967, Houghton $16.00 (978-0-395-18110-2); paper $6.95 (978-0-395-62985-7). 48pp. An old man follows the advice of the village wise man when he complains that his house is too noisy. [398.2]

12522 McKay, Sindy, adapt. *Jack and the Beanstalk* (1–2). Illus. by Lydia Halverson. Series: We Both Read. 1998, Treasure Bay $7.99 (978-1-891327-00-1). This traditional English folktale is told twice — with an adult's and a child's vocabulary. (Rev: SLJ 12/98) [398.2]

12523 Malory, Thomas. *Merlin and Making of the King* (4–6). Retold by Margaret Hodges. Illus. by Trina S. Hyman. 2004, Holiday House $16.95 (978-0-8234-1647-9). 40pp. The Arthurian tales of the "Sword in the Stone," "Excalibur," and "The Lady of the Lake" are simply told and beautifully illustrated with rich medieval effects. (Rev: BL 9/15/04; SLJ 9/04*) [398.2]

12524 Matthews, Caitlin, retel. *Celtic Memories* (1–6). Illus. by Olwyn Whelan. 2003, Barefoot Books $19.99 (978-1-84148-097-8). 80pp. The Celts of Ireland, Wales, Scotland, and Brittany are the source of this well-illustrated collection of folklore, songs, blessings, and poems, which includes informative notes and pronunciation guides. (Rev: BL 1/1–15/04; HBG 4/04; SLJ 3/04) [398.2]

12525 Milligan, Bryce. *Brigid's Cloak: An Ancient Irish Story* (1–3). Illus. by Helen Cann. 2002, Eerdmans $16.00 (978-0-8028-5224-3). 32pp. This book with Celtic and early Christian undertones tells the story of Saint Brigid, who is transported to Jerusalem in a vision and helps care for the baby Jesus. (Rev: BL 10/15/02; HBG 3/03; SLJ 2/03) [398.2]

12526 Milligan, Bryce. *The Prince of Ireland and the Three Magic Stallions* (1–3). Illus. by Preston McDaniels. 2003, Holiday House $16.95 (978-0-8234-1573-1). 32pp. An Irish folktale in which a story saves the lives of the storyteller and his friends. (Rev: BL 3/15/03*; HBG 10/03; SLJ 6/03) [398.2]

12527 Morris, Gerald. *The Adventures of Sir Lancelot the Great* (3–5). Illus. by Aaron Renier. Series: The Knights' Tales. 2008, Houghton $15.00 (978-0-618-77714-3). 96pp. The brave knight's courageous side is emphasized in this collection of episodes full of humor. (Rev: BCCB 5/08; BL 6/1–15/08; LMC 1/09; SLJ 6/08) [398.2]

12528 Murphy, Jim. *Fergus and the Night-Demon: An Irish Ghost Story* (1–3). Illus. by John Manders. 2006, Clarion $16.00 (978-0-618-33955-6). 32pp. Out for a night of fun, Fergus O'Mara, a lazy young Irishman, encounters the towering Night-Demon and must try to talk himself out of deep trouble. (Rev: BL 9/1/06; SLJ 8/06)

12529 Perkins, John. *Perceval: King Arthur's Knight of the Holy Grail* (4–7). Illus. by Gennady Spirin. 2007, Marshall Cavendish $16.99 (978-0-7614-5339-0). 38pp. A traditional tale of the flawed Perceval, whose decision to follow King Arthur causes his mother to die of a broken heart. Beautiful illustrations make this book lovely to read. (Rev: LMC 10/07; SLJ 7/07)

12530 Pinkney, Jerry. *The Little Red Hen* (PS–K). Illus. 2006, Dial $16.99 (978-0-8037-2935-3). 32pp. Pinkney's colorful artwork breathes new life into the classic tale. (Rev: BL 3/1/06; SLJ 5/06*) [398.2]

12531 Pyle, Howard. *The Story of the Grail and the Passing of Arthur* (5–8). Illus. by author. 1985, Macmillan paper $12.95 (978-0-486-27361-7). 340pp. The last title of a four-volume King Arthur series, first published in 1910. (Rev: BL 12/15/85) [398.2]

12532 Rosales, Melodye. *Leola and the Honeybears: An African-American Retelling of Goldilocks and the Three Bears* (PS–1). Illus. 1999, Scholastic $15.95 (978-0-590-38358-5). 38pp. The changes in the text of this classic tale are minor, but the paintings are outstanding in this version of Goldilocks in which the heroine is an African American. (Rev: BCCB 10/99; BL 11/1/99; HBG 3/00; SLJ 11/99) [398.22]

12533 Rumford, James, retel. *Beowulf: A Hero's Tale Retold* (5–8). Illus. by James Rumford. 2007, Houghton $17.00 (978-0-618-75637-7). Beautifully illustrated, this is a simplified retelling of the ancient tale about the warrior who defeats the monster Grendel. (Rev: BCCB 11/07; BL 8/07; HB 7/07; SLJ 8/07) [398.2]

12534 Ryan, Patrick. *Shakespeare's Storybook: Folk Tales That Inspired the Bard* (3–5). Illus. by James Mayhew. 2001, Barefoot Books $19.99 (978-1-84148-307-8). 80pp. A retelling of seven folk tales that may have served as the inspiration for works by Shakespeare. (Rev: BL 11/15/01; HBG 3/02; SLJ 1/02) [822.3]

12535 San Souci, Robert D. *Brave Margaret: An Irish Adventure* (1–4). Illus. by Sally Wern Comport. 1999, Simon & Schuster $17.00 (978-0-689-81072-5). 40pp. An intrepid girl survives a shipwreck, challenges a giant, and saves her boyfriend in this adaptation of an Irish folktale. (Rev: BCCB 5/99; BL 3/1/99; HBG 10/99; SLJ 9/99) [398.2]

12536 Scieszka, Jon. *The True Story of the Three Little Pigs: By A. Wolf* (PS–2). Illus. 1989, Viking $16.99 (978-0-670-82759-6). 32pp. A hip and funny version, from the wolf's point of view. (Rev: BCCB 9/89*; BL 9/1/89; HB 1/90; SLJ 10/89) [398.2]

12537 Shepard, Aaron. *King o' the Cats* (1–3). Illus. by Kristin Sorra. 2004, Simon & Schuster $16.95 (978-0-689-82082-3). 32pp. Newly hired church sexton Peter Black, burdened by a reputation for telling tall tales, has difficulty getting anyone to believe accounts of his encounters with a strange group of cats. (Rev: BL 10/15/04; SLJ 8/04) [398.2]

12538 Shulman, Lisa. *The Matzo Ball Boy* (PS–1). Illus. by Rosanne Litzinger. 2005, Dutton $15.99 (978-0-525-47169-1). 32pp. A grandmother preparing chicken soup for the Passover Seder creates a matzo ball boy who jumps from the soup and takes off to see the world in this appealing variation of the Gingerbread Boy. (Rev: BL 2/1/05; SLJ 3/05) [398.2]

12539 Singer, Marilyn. *The Maiden on the Moor* (1–3). Illus. by Troy Howell. 1995, Morrow LB $14.93 (978-0-688-08765-4). 40pp. In this English ballad, two shepherd brothers discover a young woman lying unconscious and must decide if they should care for her. (Rev: BL 4/15/95; SLJ 4/95) [398.2]

12540 *Sir Gawain and the Green Knight* (4–7). Retold by Michael Morpurgo. Illus. by Michael Foreman. 2005, Candlewick $18.99 (978-0-7636-2519-1). 112pp. Morpurgo retells in contemporary prose the story of the Green Knight's challenge to the court of King Arthur. (Rev: BL 11/1/04*; SLJ 10/04)

12541 Souhami, Jessica. *Mrs. McCool and the Giant Cuhullin: An Irish Tale* (K–3). Illus. 2002, Holt $16.95 (978-0-8050-6852-8). 32pp. A giant of Irish lore, Cuhullin, goes in search of another, Finn McCool, to see who is strongest, but Finn's wife turns out to be strongest of all. (Rev: BL 2/15/02; HB 5/02*; HBG 10/02; SLJ 3/02) [398.2]

12542 Spirin, Gennady. *Goldilocks and the Three Bears* (PS–2). Illus. by author. 2009, Marshall Cavendish $17.99 (978-0-7614-5596-7). 32pp. A simple retelling with lush, detailed illustrations. (Rev: BLO 3/18/09; SLJ 3/09) [398.2]

12543 Squires, Janet. *The Gingerbread Cowboy* (PS–K). Illus. by Holly Berry. 2006, HarperCollins $17.99 (978-0-06-077863-7). 32pp. The familiar tale of the runaway gingerbread boy is given a lively, western twist. (Rev: BL 4/15/06; SLJ 8/06) [398.21]

12544 Sturges, Philemon. *The Little Red Hen (Makes a Pizza)* (PS–2). Illus. by Amy Ward. 1999, Dutton $15.99 (978-0-525-45953-8). 32pp. In this variation on the classic folktale, the industrious Little Red Hen makes pizza instead of bread. (Rev: BCCB 2/00; BL 11/15/99; HBG 3/00; SLJ 12/99*) [398.2]

12545 Sutcliff, Rosemary, retel. *Beowulf* (5–8). Illus. by Charles Keeping. 1984, Smith $24.50 (978-0-8446-6165-0). This is a reissue of the Anglo-Saxon tale published originally in 1962. Also use the King Arthur story, *The Sword and the Circle* (1981, Dutton). [398.2]

12546 Szobody, Michelle. *Beowulf, Book 1: Grendel the Ghastly* (3–6). Illus. by Justin Gerard. 2007, Portland Studios $17.95 (978-0-9797183-0-4). 32pp. This picture-book presentation of one of Beowulf's adventures makes it accessible to younger readers. (Rev: BL 12/1/07; SLJ 7/08) [398.2]

12547 Talbott, Hudson. *Lancelot* (5–7). Illus. 1999, Morrow LB $15.89 (978-0-688-14833-1). 40pp. A retelling of the life of Lancelot, from his rescue as a child by the Lady of the Lake to his love for Guinevere, marriage to Elaine, and fathering of Galahad. (Rev: BL 9/1/99; HBG 3/00; SLJ 10/99) [398.2]

12548 Vivian, French. *Henny Penny* (PS–2). Illus. by Sophie Windham. 2006, Bloomsbury $16.95 (978-1-58234-706-6). 32pp. On their way to tell the king that the sky is falling, Henny Penny and her feathered friends fall into the clutches of Foxy Loxy. (Rev: BL 8/06; SLJ 7/06) [398.2]

12549 Wahl, Jan. *Little Johnny Buttermilk* (PS–1). Illus. by Jennifer Mazzucco. 1999, August House $15.95 (978-0-87483-559-5). 32pp. An English tale about Little Johnny and how he escapes from a witch after being captured on his way to market. (Rev: BL 12/15/99; HBG 3/00; SLJ 2/00) [398.2]

12550 Whatley, Bruce. *Wait! No Paint!* (K–2). Illus. 2001, HarperCollins LB $16.89 (978-0-06-028271-4). 32pp. It's the illustrator himself who threatens the fate of the three little pigs and the big bad wolf in this colorful and inventive retelling. (Rev: BL 8/01; HB 9/01; HBG 3/02; SLJ 7/01) [398.2]

12551 Wiesner, David. *The Three Pigs* (K–6). Illus. by author. 2001, Clarion $16.00 (978-0-618-00701-1). This is a fresh twist on the familiar tale, with excellent and inventive illustrations, that has a bewildered wolf searching for pigs that have been blown into a fantasy universe until they return and set the world to rights. Caldecott Medal winner, 2002. (Rev: BCCB 5/01; BL 5/15/01*; HB 5/01*; HBG 10/01; SLJ 4/01*) [398.2]

12552 Zemach, Harve. *Duffy and the Devil: A Cornish Tale Retold* (1–3). Illus. by Margot Zemach. 1973, Farrar $17.00 (978-0-374-31887-1); paper $6.95 (978-0-374-41897-7). 40pp. A variant of "Rumpelstiltskin," this folktale is told with humor and verve and boldly illustrated. Caldecott Medal winner, 1974. [398.2]

Greece and Italy

12553 Aesop. *The Aesop for Children* (3–5). Illus. by Milo Winter. 1984, Checkerboard $12.95 (978-1-56288-039-2); paper $5.99 (978-0-590-47977-6). This edition, reissued with the original artwork, includes 126 tales. [398.2]

12554 Aesop. *Fables of Aesop* (4–6). Illus. by David Levine. 1984, Harvard Common $13.95 (978-0-87645-074-1); paper $8.95 (978-0-87645-116-8). 108pp. One of many recommended editions of this classic. [398.2]

12555 Aesop. *The Tortoise and the Hare: An Aesop Fable* (PS–K). Illus. by Janet Stevens. 1984, Holiday House LB $16.95 (978-0-8234-0510-7); paper $6.95 (978-0-8234-0564-0). 32pp. An updated, charming retelling of the classic fable. [398.2]

12556 Ash, Russell, and Bernard A. Higton, eds. *Aesop's Fables* (3–6). Illus. 1991, Chronicle $17.95 (978-0-87701-780-6). 95pp. More than 50 fables reprinted and illustrated with artists from the past. (Rev: SLJ 3/91) [398.2]

12557 Brown, Stephanie Gwyn. *Professor Aesop's the Crow and the Pitcher* (K–4). Illus. by author. 2003, Tricycle $15.95 (978-1-58246-087-1). A clever crow, temporarily foiled in his attempts to drink from a pitcher, comes up with an ingenious solution. (Rev: HBG 10/03; SLJ 9/03) [398.2]

12558 Carle, Eric. *The Rabbit and the Turtle* (K–3). Illus. by author. 2008, Scholastic $16.99 (978-0-545-00541-8). 32pp. A collection of Aesop fables, many previously published by Carle, are redesigned here, each ending with the moral. (Rev: BL 6/1–15/08; LMC 10/08) [398.2]

12559 Cech, John. *Aesop's Fables* (1–4). Illus. by Martin Jarrie. 2009, Sterling $16.95 (978-1-4027-5298-8). 40pp. A collection of 36 of the lesser-known Aesop tales. (Rev: BLO 4/13/09; SLJ 7/09) [398.2]

12560 Corwin, Oliver J. *Hare and Tortoise Race to the Moon* (K–3). Illus. 2002, Abrams $14.95 (978-0-8109-0566-5). 40pp. In this modern twist on Aesop's classic, Tortoise and Hare race to the moon in rocket ships. (Rev: BL 10/15/02; HBG 3/03; SLJ 11/02) [398.2]

12561 dePaola, Tomie. *Days of the Blackbird: A Tale of Northern Italy* (K–3). Illus. 1997, Penguin $16.99 (978-0-399-22929-9). 32pp. An Italian tale about a faithful bird that stays through the winter to sing for an ailing duke. (Rev: BL 3/15/97; HB 3/97; SLJ 3/97*)

12562 dePaola, Tomie. *The Mysterious Giant of Barletta: An Italian Folktale* (K–3). Illus. by author. 1988, Harcourt paper $6.00 (978-0-15-256349-3). 32pp. A statue of an old lady saves the town from marauders. [398.2]

12563 dePaola, Tomie. *Strega Nona* (PS–2). Illus. by author. 1979, Simon & Schuster paper $6.95 (978-0-671-66606-4). 32pp. The old Italian folktale retold. Also use: *Big Anthony and the Magic Ring* (1979) and *Strega Nona's Magic Lessons* (1982). [398.2]

12564 dePaola, Tomie. *Strega Nona: Her Story* (PS–3). Illus. 1996, Penguin $16.99 (978-0-399-22818-6). 32pp. This book supplies background information on the birth and youth of Nona and how she became the village strega. (Rev: BL 9/15/96; HB 11/96; SLJ 10/96) [398.2]

12565 Downard, Barry, retel. *The Race of the Century* (PS–5). Illus. by reteller. 2008, Simon & Schuster $15.99 (978-1-4169-2509-5). A funny retelling of the race between the tortoise and the hare, in which it is a big media event. (Rev: BCCB 1/08; LMC 3/08; SLJ 2/08) [398.24]

12566 Egielski, Richard. *Saint Francis and the Wolf* (PS–2). Illus. 2005, HarperCollins $15.99 (978-0-06-623870-8). 40pp. St. Francis communicates with a wolf that has been terrorizing an Italian town and strikes a compromise that satisfies all parties. (Rev: BL 10/1/05*; SLJ 10/05) [398.2]

12567 Forest, Heather. *The Contest Between the Sun and the Wind* (K–3). Illus. by Susan Gaber. 2008, August House $16.95 (978-0-87483-832-9). 32pp. This Aesop fable retells the story of how the wind and the sun battle to make a man take off his coat. (Rev: BL 3/15/08; SLJ 4/08) [398.2]

12568 Fox, Paula. *Amzat and His Brothers: Three Italian Tales* (3–5). Illus. by Emily Arnold McCully. 1993, Orchard $16.95 (978-0-531-05462-8). 80pp. Tales retold from a grandfather who lived in a small Italian village. (Rev: BCCB 3/93*; BL 3/15/93; HB 7/93; SLJ 7/93) [398.2]

12569 Gal, Laszlo, and Raffaella Gal. *The Parrot* (K–3). Illus. 1997, Douglas & McIntyre $16.95 (978-0-88899-287-1). 32pp. In this Italian folktale, a prince assumes the identity of a parrot to help a princess. (Rev: BL 9/15/97; SLJ 10/97) [398.2]

12570 Hamilton, Martha, and Mitch Weiss. *Priceless Gifts* (K–2). Illus. by John Kanzler. 2007, August House $16.95 (978-0-87483-788-9). 32pp. A Genoese merchant sails to the Spice Islands to trade his goods, receiving a rich reward for bringing cats to a rat-infested island; his jealous competitor seeks the same fortune, with less favorable results. (Rev: BL 6/1–15/07) [398.2]

12571 Hennessy, B. G., reteller. *The Boy Who Cried Wolf* (PS–1). Illus. by Boris Kulikov. 2006, Simon & Schuster $15.95 (978-0-689-87433-8). 40pp. The fable about the shepherd boy who cried wolf is given vivid new life in this beautifully illustrated, funny picture book. (Rev: BL 2/1/06; SLJ 3/06*) [398.2]

12572 Herman, Gail, retel. *The Lion and the Mouse* (1). Illus. by Lisa McCue. Series: Early Step into Reading. 1998, Random paper $3.99 (978-0-679-88674-7). 32pp. The classic Aesop fable is retold dramatically in a simple text suitable for beginning readers. (Rev: BL 11/1/98; SLJ 2/99) [398.2]

12573 Jones, Carol. *The Hare and the Tortoise* (K–3). Illus. 1996, Houghton $13.95 (978-0-395-81368-3). 32pp. Peepholes and detailed illustrations are used in this retelling of the famous Aesop fable. (Rev: BL 9/1/96; SLJ 9/96) [398.24]

12574 Langton, Jane. *Saint Francis and the Wolf* (PS–1). Illus. by Ilse Plume. 2007, Godine $16.95 (978-1-56792-320-9). 32pp. A brief retelling of the legend of Francis of Assisi and the wolf that was plaguing Gubbio. (Rev: BL 10/1/07; SLJ 12/07) [398.2]

12575 Lowell, Susan. *The Tortoise and the Jackrabbit* (PS–2). Illus. by Jim Harris. 1994, Northland LB $15.95 (978-0-87358-586-6). 32pp. This favorite Aesop fable is retold with the tortoise an aged grandmother and the hare a conceited egocentric. (Rev: BL 1/15/95; HB 3/05; SLJ 2/95)

12576 Lynch, Tom, adapt. *Fables from Aesop* (3–5). Illus. by Tom Lynch. 2000, Viking $15.99 (978-0-670-88948-8). A striking presentation of 13 of the most famous fables from Aesop. (Rev: HBG 10/01; SLJ 10/00) [398.2]

12577 McClintock, Barbara. *Animal Fables from Aesop* (4–6). Illus. 1991, Godine $18.95 (978-0-87923-913-8). 48pp. The text is an expansion of nine fables complete with dialogue and dramatic situations. (Rev: BCCB 1/92; BL 1/1/92; HB 1/92; SLJ 1/92) [398.2]

12578 Morpurgo, Michael. *The McElderry Book of Aesop's Fables* (PS–2). Illus. by Emma Chichester Clark. 2005, Simon & Schuster $19.95 (978-1-4169-0290-4). 96pp. Twenty-one classic fables are retold in conversational style with humorous watercolors. (Rev: BL 5/1/05; SLJ 6/05) [398.2]

12579 Morrison, Toni, and Slade Morrison. *The Ant or the Grasshopper?* (K–5). Illus. by Pascal LeMaitre. Series: Who's Got Game? 2003, Scribner $16.95 (978-0-7432-2247-1). Kid A, an ant, and his close grasshopper buddy Foxy G decide the time for summer fun has passed and begin to prepare for the coming of winter. (Rev: BL 5/15/03; HBG 10/03; SLJ 9/03) [741.5]

12580 Pinkney, Jerry. *Aesop's Fables* (2–4). Illus. 2000, North-South $19.95 (978-1-58717-000-3). 96pp. A first-rate collection of 60 of Aesop's tales retold and illustrated by this acclaimed artist. (Rev: BCCB 12/00; BL 12/15/00*; HB 1/01; HBG 3/01; SLJ 10/00) [398.24]

12581 Poole, Amy Lowry. *The Ant and the Grasshopper* (PS–1). Illus. 2000, Holiday House $17.95 (978-0-8234-1477-2). 32pp. This version of Aesop's fable is transported to China, and the ink and gouache illustrations on rice paper impart a quaint Oriental look. (Rev: BCCB 12/00; BL 8/00; HBG 3/01; SLJ 9/00) [398.24]

12582 Repchuk, Caroline. *The Race* (K–3). Illus. by Alison Jay. 2002, Chronicle $15.95 (978-0-8118-3500-8). 24pp. This update has the hare and the tortoise racing around the world. (Rev: BL 4/15/02; HBG 10/02; SLJ 7/02) [398.24]

12583 Santangelo, Colony Elliot. *Brother Wolf of Gubbio: A Legend of Saint Francis* (K–3). Illus. 2000, Handprint $15.95 (978-1-929766-07-9). 32pp. In this old Italian tale, Saint Francis tames a wolf that has been terrorizing a village. (Rev: BCCB 1/01; BL 1/1–15/01; HBG 3/01; SLJ 2/01) [398.2]

12584 Sneed, Brad, retel. *Aesop's Fables* (2–5). Illus. by Brad Sneed. 2003, Dial $16.99 (978-0-8037-2751-9). Contemporary language is used in these lighthearted retellings of 15 tales, with eye-catching illustrations. (Rev: HBG 4/04; SLJ 11/03) [398.2]

12585 Sogabe, Aki, retel. *Aesop's Fox* (K–3). Illus. by Aki Sogabe. 1999, Harcourt $16.00 (978-0-15-201671-5). Several of Aesop's fables involving the fox are interwoven into a single narrative with striking pictures. (Rev: BCCB 11/99; HBG 3/00; SLJ 12/99) [398.2]

12586 Valeri, Maria Eulalia. *The Hare and the Tortoise / La liebre y la tortuga* (4–6). Illus. by Max. 2006, Chronicle $14.95 (978-0-8118-5057-5); paper $6.95 (978-0-8118-5058-2). 32pp. A bilingual retelling of the classic fable. (Rev: BL 9/1/06; SLJ 10/06) [398.2]

12587 Ward, Helen. *The Hare and the Tortoise* (PS–3). Illus. 1999, Millbrook LB $23.90 (978-0-7613-1318-2). 40pp. A witty, straightforward retelling of the fable, illustrated with outstanding watercolor paintings. (Rev: BCCB 6/99; BL 5/15/99*; HBG 10/99; SLJ 7/99) [398.24]

12588 Ward, Helen. *Unwitting Wisdom: An Anthology of Aesop's Fables* (2–5). Illus. 2004, Chronicle $18.95 (978-0-8118-4450-5). 64pp. Arresting ink-and-watercolor illustrations accompany well-worded retellings of a dozen Aesop tales. (Rev: BL 9/15/04; SLJ 10/04) [398.2]

12589 Watts, Bernadette. *The Town Mouse and the Country Mouse: An Aesop Fable* (PS–2). Illus. 1998, North-South LB $15.88 (978-1-55858-988-9). 28pp. A delightful version of the old Aesop fable about two mice that visit each other and discover that home is best. (Rev: BL 11/15/98; HBG 3/99; SLJ 3/99) [398.2]

12590 Wormell, Christopher. *Mice, Morals and Monkey Business: Lively Lessons from Aesop's Fables* (K–3). Illus. 2005, Running Pr. $18.95 (978-0-7624-2404-7). 64pp. The moral messages contained in some of Aesop's most memorable fables are highlighted in striking woodcut illustrations; concise versions of the stories are given at the back of the book. (Rev: BL 9/15/05; SLJ 11/05*) [395]

Russia

12591 Arnold, Katya, retel. *That Apple Is Mine!* (PS–1). Illus. by Katya Arnold. 2000, Holiday House $15.95 (978-0-8234-1629-5). In this Russian folktale, Bear teaches the animals to share when they all want the same apple. (Rev: HB 1/01; HBG 3/01; SLJ 12/00) [398.2]

12592 Davis, Aubrey. *The Enormous Potato* (PS–1). Illus. by Dusan Petricic. 1998, Kids Can $14.95 (978-1-55074-386-9). 32pp. This variation on the Russian tale about a turnip uses a gigantic potato that again requires the help of everyone, including a tiny mouse, to get it out of the ground. (Rev: BCCB 10/98; BL 11/1/98; HBG 3/99; SLJ 11/98) [398.2]

12593 De Regniers, Beatrice S. *Little Sister and the Month Brothers* (K–3). Illus. by Margot Tomes. 1976, Houghton $8.95 (978-0-8164-3147-2). 48pp. A delightful retelling of an old Slavic tale reminiscent of the Cinderella theme. [398.2]

12594 Ginsburg, Mirra. *Good Morning, Chick* (PS–K). Illus. by Byron Barton. 1980, Morrow paper $6.99 (978-0-688-08741-8). 32pp. A Russian folktale about a chick who must learn his identity. [398.2]

12595 Hester, Denia Lewis. *Grandma Lena's Big Ol' Turnip* (K–2). Illus. by Jackie Urbanovic. 2005, Whitman $16.95 (978-0-8075-3027-6). 32pp. It takes a whole family to pull up the giant turnip in Grandma Lena's garden, but the reward afterward is home-cooked soul food in this story based on Alexei Tolstoy's "The Turnip." (Rev: BL 3/15/05; SLJ 5/05)

12596 Hoffman, Mary. *Clever Katya: A Fairy Tale from Old Russia* (K–3). Illus. by Marie Cameron. 1998, Barefoot Books $15.95 (978-1-901223-64-4). 32pp. In this Russian folktale, 7-year-old Katya so impresses the czar with her intelligence that he asks her to visit him in his palace. (Rev: BL 10/1/98; SLJ 10/98) [398.2]

12597 Hogrogian, Nonny. *The Contest* (3–5). Illus. by author. 1976, Greenwillow $18.89 (978-0-688-84042-6). 32pp. Adaptation of the folktale about two robbers who discover that they are engaged to the same girl. [398.2]

12598 Jackson, Ellen. *The Impossible Riddle* (K–3). Illus. by Alison Winfield. 1995, Whispering Coyote $14.95 (978-1-879085-93-0). 32pp. In this Russian folktale, a czar hopes to prevent his daughter's marriage by demanding that prospective suitors answer an impossible riddle. (Rev: BL 1/1–15/96) [398.2]

12599 Kimmel, Eric A. *Baba Yaga: A Russian Folktale* (K–3). Illus. by Megan Lloyd. 1991, Holiday House LB $16.95 (978-0-8234-0854-2). 32pp. A traditional Russian folktale about Marina, whose wicked stepmother sends her to the forest witch. (Rev: BL 5/1/91; SLJ 6/91) [398.2]

12600 Kimmel, Eric A. *Bearhead: A Russian Folktale* (K–3). Illus. by Charles Mikolaycak. 1991, Holiday House LB $16.95 (978-0-8234-0902-0). 32pp. A peasant woman finds an odd-looking foundling with the body of a human and the head of a bear. (Rev: BCCB 12/91; BL 9/1/91; SLJ 10/91) [398.2]

12601 Kimmel, Eric A. *The Birds' Gift: A Ukrainian Easter Story* (PS–3). Illus. by Katya Krenina. 1999, Holiday House $16.95 (978-0-8234-1384-3). 34pp. After saving a group of birds, on Easter morning townspeople find beautifully decorated eggs left behind as gifts. (Rev: BL 4/15/99; HBG 10/99; SLJ 6/99) [398.2]

12602 Kimmel, Eric A. *I Know Not What, I Know Not Where: A Russian Tale* (4–6). Illus. by Robert Sauber. 1994, Holiday House LB $16.95 (978-0-8234-1020-0). 64pp. In this Russian fairy tale, a hunter is rewarded for saving an enchanted dove's life by getting help to perform tasks demanded by the czar. (Rev: BCCB 7–8/94; BL 3/1/94; SLJ 6/94) [398.2]

12603 Kimmel, Eric A. *One Eye, Two Eyes, Three Eyes: A Hutzul Tale* (PS–3). Illus. by Dirk Zimmer. 1996, Holiday House LB $15.95 (978-0-8234-1183-2). 32pp. A traveler unwittingly bargains away his daughter in this Ukrainian tale. (Rev: BL 11/1/96; SLJ 1/97) [398.2]

12604 Langton, Jane. *Salt: From a Russian Folktale* (K–3). Trans. by Alice Plume. Illus. by Ilse Plume. 1992, Hyperion $14.95 (978-1-56282-178-4). 48pp. A Russian folktale about three brothers who go to sea to seek their fortunes. (Rev: BCCB 1/93; BL 10/15/92; SLJ 12/92) [398.2]

12605 McCaughrean, Geraldine. *Grandma Chickenlegs* (K–3). Illus. by Moira Kemp. 1999, Carolrhoda $15.95 (978-1-57505-415-5). 32pp. In this classic Russian folktale, young Tatia is sent to the witch's house to borrow a needle and is soon a prisoner of the horrible Baba Yaga. (Rev: BL 10/15/99; HBG 3/00; SLJ 1/00) [398.2]

12606 Martin, Rafe. *The Twelve Months* (2–4). Illus. by Vladyana Langer Krykorka. 2001, Stoddart $15.95 (978-0-7737-3249-0). 32pp. In this Russian variation on the Cinderella story, 12 men, representing the 12 months, help the poor young heroine supply the exotic gifts that her mean aunt and cousin demand. (Rev: BL 4/15/01; SLJ 11/01) [398.2]

12607 Mayer, Marianna. *Baba Yaga and Vasilisa the Brave* (PS–3). Illus. by Kinuko Craft. 1994, Morrow $17.99 (978-0-688-08500-1). 40pp. Vasilisa survives both the schemes of her wicked stepmother and a visit to the witch Baba Yaga and finally marries the czar. (Rev: BL 6/1–15/94; SLJ 7/94*) [398.2]

12608 Pogorelsky, Antony, and Elizabeth James. *The Little Black Hen* (1–3). Retold by Elizabeth James. Illus. by Gennady Spirin. 2003, Simply Read $16.95 (978-1-894965-03-3). 32pp. This fable, written for Alexei Tolstoi by his uncle, recounts the story of Alyosha, a Russian boy who is granted one wish but is almost undone by his greed and arrogance. (Rev: BL 9/15/03; SLJ 12/03) [398.2]

12609 Prokofiev, Sergei. *Peter and the Wolf* (4–8). Adapted by Miguelanxo Prado. Illus. by author. 1998, NBM $15.95 (978-1-56163-200-8). 22pp. A somber version of the Russian folktale filled with menacing situations and scary settings. (Rev: HBG 10/98; SLJ 6/98) [398.2]

12610 Radunsky, Vladimir. *The Mighty Asparagus* (4–7). Illus. 2004, Harcourt $16.00 (978-0-15-216743-1). 34pp. In this entertaining version of the Russian folktale "The Enormous Turnip" with eye-catching illustrations full of artistic allusions, a gigantic stalk of asparagus sprouts in the courtyard of an Italian king. (Rev: BL 5/15/04; SLJ 7/04) [398.2]

12611 Ransome, Arthur. *The Fool of the World and the Flying Ship* (1–4). Illus. by Uri Shulevitz. 1968, Farrar $16.00 (978-0-374-32442-1); paper $6.95 (978-0-374-42438-1). 48pp. Colorful, panoramic scenes extend this retelling of a popular Russian folktale about a simple peasant boy who acquires a flying ship. Caldecott Medal winner, 1969. [398.2]

12612 Ransome, Arthur. *Little Daughter of the Snow* (K–3). Ed. by Shena Guild. Illus. by Tom Bower. 2005, Frances Lincoln $15.95 (978-1-84507-297-1). 32pp. An enchanting adaptation of Ransome's telling of a traditional Russian tale about a childless couple who create a snow girl who magically comes to life. (Rev: BL 12/1/05; SLJ 1/06) [398.2]

12613 Reyher, Becky. *My Mother Is the Most Beautiful Woman in the World* (2–5). Illus. by Ruth Gannett. 1945, Lothrop LB $16.93 (978-0-688-51251-4). 40pp. A girl tries to find her mother in this Russian setting. [398.2]

12614 Robbins, Ruth. *Baboushka and the Three Kings* (2–4). Illus. by Nicholas Sidjakov. 1960, Houghton $16.00 (978-0-395-27673-0); paper $6.95 (978-0-395-42647-0). 32pp. The Russian legend of the old woman who refused to follow the three kings in search of the Holy Child. Caldecott Medal winner, 1961. [398.2]

12615 Spirin, Gennady. *The Tale of the Firebird* (K–3). Trans. by Tatiana Popova. Illus. 2002, Penguin $16.99 (978-0-399-23584-9). 32pp. The tsar's youngest son survives a number of tests before finding the firebird and winning the love of the beautiful Yelena in this lush picture book that melds three traditional Russian tales. (Rev: BCCB 11/02; BL 11/15/02; HBG 3/03; SLJ 9/02) [398.2]

12616 Stihler, Ch rie B. *The Giant Cabbage: An Alaska Folktale* (PS–2). Illus. by Jeremiah Trammell. 2003, Sasquatch paper $9.95 (978-1-57061-357-9). In this Alaskan variation on a traditional Russian folktale, Moose enlists the help of a band of animals to get his giant cabbage to the fair for judging. (Rev: SLJ 8/03) [398.2]

12617 Tolstoy, Aleksei. *The Gigantic Turnip* (PS–2). Illus. by Niamh Sharkey. Series: Barefoot Beginner. 2000, Barefoot Books $15.95 (978-1-902283-12-8). 40pp. A rather complicated retelling of the popular Russian folktale about a husband and wife who need help to uproot a huge turnip. (Rev: BCCB 7–8/99; SLJ 4/99) [398.2]

12618 Yolen, Jane. *The Firebird* (PS–3). Illus. by Vladimir Vagin. 2002, HarperCollins LB $17.89 (978-0-06-028539-5). 32pp. An effective retelling of the Russian story that combines elements from the original story with the ballet version. (Rev: BCCB 7–8/02; BL 6/1–15/02; HBG 10/02; SLJ 6/02) [398.2]

12619 Zunshine, Tatiana, retel. *A Little Story About a Big Turnip* (PS–1). Illus. by Evgeny Antonenkov. 2004, Pumpkin House $15.95 (978-0-9646010-0-0). A simple retelling of the Russian folktale, in which it takes the combined strength of grandfather, grandmother, granddaughter, dog, cat, and mouse to pull the turnip out of the ground. (Rev: SLJ 11/04) [398.2]

Scandinavia

12620 Asbjornsen, Peter C. *The Three Billy Goats Gruff* (PS–2). Retold by Glen Rounds. Illus. 1993, Holiday House LB $15.95 (978-0-8234-1015-6). 32pp. This veteran illustrator noted for animal drawings illustrates and retells this famous Norweigan folktale. (Rev: BL 4/15/93; HB 7/93; SLJ 6/93*) [398.2]

12621 Asbjornsen, Peter C., and Jörgen Moe. *Norwegian Folk Tales* (3–6). Illus. by Erik Werenskiold and Theodor Kittelsen. 1978, Pantheon paper $14.00 (978-0-394-71054-9). This edition retains the original illustrations from the 1845 edition. [398.2]

12622 Brett, Jan. *Who's That Knocking on Christmas Eve?* (K–2). Illus. 2002, Penguin $16.99 (978-0-399-23873-4). 32pp. A beautifully illustrated folktale of a Christmas Eve feast nearly ruined by hungry trolls. (Rev: BCCB 10/02; BL 9/1/02; HBG 3/03; SLJ 10/02)

12623 Coville, Bruce. *Thor's Wedding Day* (4–7). 2005, Harcourt $15.00 (978-0-15-201455-1). 128pp. A hilarious retelling of an ancient Norse poem, in which Thor's goat boy describes how he helped Thor to retrieve his stolen magic hammer. (Rev: BL 8/05) [398.2]

12624 Del Negro, Janice M. *Willa and the Wind* (1–3). Illus. by Heather Solomon. 2005, Marshall Cavendish $16.95 (978-0-7614-5232-4). 40pp. In this adaptation of an old Norwegian folktale adorned with airy, swirling illustrations, courageous Willa confronts the North Wind and a wicked innkeeper. (Rev: BL 9/1/05; SLJ 12/05) [398.2]

12625 Finch, Mary, retel. *The Three Billy Goats Gruff* (PS). Illus. by Roberta Arenson. 2001, Barefoot Books LB $15.99 (978-1-84148-349-8). A gentler version of the tale for this young age group, with colorful goats and a singing troll. (Rev: HBG 3/02; SLJ 11/01) [398.2]

12626 Galdone, Paul. *The Three Billy Goats Gruff* (PS–3). Illus. by author. 1973, Houghton $16.00 (978-0-395-28812-2). 32pp. A troll meets his match. (Rev: SLJ 3/05) [398.2]

12627 Hassett, John, and Ann Hassett. *The Three Silly Girls Grubb* (PS–1). Illus. 2002, Houghton $15.00 (978-0-618-14183-8). 32pp. The three Grubb girls must get past Ugly-Boy Bobby in this goofy version of "The Three Billy Goats Gruff." (Rev: BCCB 11/02; BL 9/15/02; HB 9/02; HBG 3/03; SLJ 11/02*) [398.2]

12628 Kimmel, Eric A. *Boots and His Brothers: A Norwegian Tale* (PS–3). Illus. by Kimberly B. Root. 1992, Holiday House LB $14.95 (978-0-8234-0886-3). 32pp. In this Norwegian folktale, three brothers set out to seek their fortunes, but only the youngest, Boots, succeeds. (Rev: BCCB 3/92; BL 3/1/92) [398.2]

12629 Kimmel, Eric A. *Easy Work! An Old Tale* (PS–3). Illus. by Andrew Glass. 1998, Holiday House $17.95 (978-0-8234-1349-2). 32pp. In this variation on the classic Norwegian folktale, farmer McTeague and his wife decide to exchange roles for a day, with disastrous results. (Rev: BL 4/15/98; HBG 10/98; SLJ 6/98) [398.2]

12630 Kimmel, Eric A. *The Three Cabritos* (PS–1). Illus. by Stephen Gilpin. 2007, Marshall Cavendish $16.99 (978-0-7614-5343-7). 32pp. Three goats must cross a bridge into Mexico when they encounter a legendary monster in this lighthearted retelling of "The Three Billy Goats Gruff." (Rev: BCCB 5/07; BL 7/07; SLJ 5/07) [398.2]

12631 Lunge-Larsen, Lise. *The Troll with No Heart in His Body* (2–4). Illus. 1999, Houghton $18.00 (978-0-395-91371-0). 96pp. A collection of nine Norwegian folktales, including "Three Billy Goats Gruff." (Rev: BCCB 1/00; BL 9/1/99; HB 11/99; HBG 3/00; SLJ 11/99) [398.2]

12632 MacDonald, Margaret Read. *Fat Cat* (PS–3). Illus. by Julie Paschkis. 2001, August House $15.95 (978-0-87483-616-5). 32pp. Brilliant illustrations and rhythmic prose are featured in this Danish folktale about a cat that gobbles up anyone who calls him fat, and the cunning mouse that saves them all. (Rev: BL 11/15/01; HBG 3/02; SLJ 1/02) [398.2]

12633 Maddern, Eric. *Nail Soup* (K–3). Illus. by Paul Hess. 2007, Frances Lincoln $15.95 (978-1-84507-479-1). A Swedish variant of the traditional "Stone Soup," in which a Traveller seeking shelter offers to make a housewife a soup. (Rev: BCCB 1/08; SLJ 4/08) [398.2]

12634 Salley, Coleen. *Who's That Tripping over My Bridge?* (K–2). Illus. by Amy Jackson Dixon. 2002, Pelican $15.95 (978-1-56554-890-9). In this retelling of the Norwegian tale, the three Gruff goats live north of Baton Rouge and must cross a bridge guarded by a troll in order to reach the green grasses on the other side. (Rev: HBG 10/02; SLJ 5/02) [398.2]

12635 Youngquist, Catherine Valente. *The Three Billygoats Gruff and Mean Calypso Joe* (K–3). Illus. by Kristin Sorra. 2002, Simon & Schuster $16.00 (978-0-689-82824-9). 32pp. The classic story of the three billy goats gets a Caribbean twist, complete with a troll named Calypso Joe. (Rev: BL 8/02; HBG 10/02; SLJ 11/02) [398.2]

Spain and Portugal

12636 Ada, Alma Flor. *The Three Golden Oranges* (K–3). Illus. by Reg Cartwright. 1999, Simon & Schuster $16.00 (978-0-689-80775-6). 32pp. A retelling of the Spanish folktale about the three princes who want wives, and to get them must bring three oranges to a wise old woman. (Rev: BCCB 7–8/99; BL 5/15/99; HBG 10/99; SLJ 7/99) [398.2]

12637 Araujo, Frank P. *Nekane, the Lamina and the Bear: A Tale of the Basque Pyrenees* (K–2). Illus. by Xiao Jun Li. 1993, Rayve $16.95 (978-1-877810-01-5). 32pp. In this Basque version of the standard fairy tale, Red Riding Hood becomes Nekane, who is stopped by a forest spirit on her way to her uncle's home. (Rev: BCCB 3/94; BL 2/1/94; SLJ 5/94) [398.2]

12638 Hall, Amanda. *Prince of the Birds* (PS–2). Illus. 2005, Frances Lincoln $15.95 (978-1-84507-102-8). 32pp. A classic love story, set in southern Spain, in which a prince and a princess, each imprisoned in a tower, find each other with the aid of birds. (Rev: BL 5/1/05) [398.2]

12639 Kimmel, Eric A. *Bernal and Florinda: A Spanish Tale* (K–3). Illus. by Robert Rayevsky. 1994, Holiday House LB $15.95 (978-0-8234-1089-7). 32pp. A comic fairy tale about two Spanish lovers who are united in marriage despite the objections of the bride's father. (Rev: BCCB 9/94; BL 9/15/94; SLJ 11/94) [398.2]

12640 Kimmel, Eric A. *Squash It! A True and Ridiculous Tale* (3–5). Illus. by Robert Rayevsky. 1997, Holiday House LB $15.95 (978-0-8234-1299-0). 32pp. The Spanish tale of the king who adopted a louse as his favorite pet. (Rev: BL 6/1–15/97; HB 7/97; SLJ 7/97) [398.2]

12641 Montejo, Victor. *White Flower: A Maya Princess* (K–3). Illus. by Rafael Yockteng. 2005, Groundwood $16.95 (978-0-88899-599-5). 36pp. In this reinterpretation of a Spanish folk tale, White Flower, daughter of a Mayan king, uses her magical powers to help a young nobleman and win his heart. (Rev: BL 12/1/05; SLJ 1/06) [398.2]

12642 Robbins, Sandra. *The Firefly Star: A Hispanic Folk Tale* (PS–3). Illus. by Iku Oseki. 1995, See-More's Workshop paper $6.95 (978-1-882601-23-3). 32pp. In this Spanish folktale, the important holiday Three Kings' Day almost doesn't take place until a mouse and a ladybug intervene. (Rev: BL 12/1/95; SLJ 2/96) [398.2]

12643 Sierra, Judy. *The Beautiful Butterfly: A Folktale from Spain* (K–3). Illus. by Victoria Chess. 2000, Clarion $15.00 (978-0-395-90015-4). 32pp. This popular Spanish folktale ends happily when the fish that had swallowed Butterfly's new husband — a mouse — spits him out, thus reuniting the happy pair. (Rev: BCCB 5/00; BL 3/15/00; HBG 10/00; SLJ 8/00) [398.2]

Jewish Folklore

12644 Aroner, Miriam. *The Kingdom of Singing Birds* (K–5). Illus. by Shelly O. Haas. 1993, Kar-Ben $13.95 (978-0-929371-43-6); paper $5.95 (978-0-929371-44-3). In this Jewish folktale, a rabbi tells a king that the only way to get his birds to sing is to set them free. (Rev: SLJ 9/93) [398.2]

12645 Blades, Ann. *Too Small* (K–2). Illus. by author. 2000, Groundwood $15.95 (978-0-88899-400-4). A variation on the traditional Yiddish tale about a house that becomes crowded when a lot of friends and animals are invited in. (Rev: HBG 3/01; SLJ 10/00) [398.2]

12646 Clement, Gary. *Just Stay Put: A Chelm Story* (K–4). Illus. 1996, Douglas & McIntyre $14.95 (978-0-88899-239-0). 32pp. A resident of Chelm, Poland, mistakes his hometown for Warsaw. (Rev: BL 9/15/96; SLJ 6/96) [398.2]

12647 Davis, Aubrey. *Bone Button Borscht* (K–3). Illus. by Dusan Petricic. 1997, Kids Can $15.95 (978-1-55074-224-4). 32pp. An Eastern European version of *Stone Soup*, in which a beggar persuades the synagogue caretaker to let him make borscht from his coat buttons. (Rev: BL 11/1/97; SLJ 11/97) [398.2]

12648 Geras, Adele. *My Grandmother's Stories: A Collection of Jewish Folk Tales* (1–5). Illus. by Anita Lobel. 2003, Knopf LB $21.99 (978-0-375-92285-5). 96pp. In this beautifully illustrated collection, each of 10 stories is introduced by a young girl's question to her grandmother. (Rev: HBG 4/04; SLJ 8/03) [398.2]

12649 Gershator, Phillis, and Alexa Ginsburg. *Wise . . . and Not So Wise: Ten Tales from the Rabbis* (3–6). Series: New Children's Titles. 2004, Jewish Publication Soc. $15.95 (978-0-8276-0755-2). 120pp. Ten stories drawn from traditional Jewish sources present interesting situations and are followed by questions that will provoke thoughtful analysis of their meaning and relevance today. (Rev: BL 10/1/04; SLJ 1/05) [296.1]

12650 Gerstein, Mordicai. *The Shadow of a Flying Bird: A Legend from the Kurdistani Jews* (1–5). Illus. 1994, Hyperion LB $16.49 (978-0-7868-2012-2). 32pp. God comes to earth to claim the life of his faithful servant Moses in this Jewish folktale. (Rev: BL 10/1/94; SLJ 9/94) [398.2]

12651 Gilman, Phoebe. *Something from Nothing* (PS–3). Illus. 1993, Scholastic $16.95 (978-0-590-47280-7). 32pp. This folktale tells how a frugal grandfather recycles the material from a jacket to ever smaller objects, ending with the covering for a button. (Rev: BCCB 2/94; BL 9/1/93; HB 11/93; SLJ 1/94) [398.2]

12652 Icenoggle, Jodi. `Til the Cows Come Home* (K–4). Illus. by Normand Chartier. 2004, Boyds Mills $15.95 (978-1-56397-987-3). The Jewish folktale "The Button Story," newly set in the American West, follows a piece of leather over the years as it becomes a pair of chaps, then a pair of gloves, and finally a button. (Rev: SLJ 3/04)

12653 Jaffe, Nina. *Tales for the Seventh Day: A Collection of Sabbath Stories* (3–7). Illus. by Kelly Stribling Sutherland. 2000, Scholastic $15.95 (978-0-590-12054-8). 73pp. A collection of Jewish tales that honor the traditions and the celebration of the Sabbath. (Rev: BL 12/15/00; HBG 3/01; SLJ 11/00) [398.2]

12654 Jaffe, Nina. *The Way Meat Loves Salt: A Cinderella Tale from the Jewish Tradition* (PS–2). Illus. by Louise August. 1998, Holt $15.95 (978-0-8050-4384-6). A Yiddish folktale that combines King Lear with Cinderella and casts Elijah the Prophet in the role of fairy godmother. (Rev: BCCB 11/98; BL 10/1/98; HB 9/98; HBG 3/99; SLJ 9/98) [398.2]

12655 Kimmel, Eric A. *The Adventures of Hershel of Ostropol* (K–4). Illus. by Trina S. Hyman. 1995, Holiday House $16.95 (978-0-8234-1210-5). 64pp. Ten Jewish folktales that use as a locale a village community in the Ukraine during the 19th century. (Rev: BL 10/15/95; SLJ 11/95) [398.2]

12656 Kimmel, Eric A. *Gershon's Monster* (2–4). Illus. by Jon J. Muth. 2000, Scholastic $17.99 (978-0-439-10839-3). 32pp. Based on an early Hasidic legend, this is the story of Gershon and how his sins catch up with him. (Rev: BCCB 10/00; BL 10/1/00; HB 9/00; HBG 3/01; SLJ 9/00) [398.2]

12657 Kimmel, Eric A. *The Jar of Fools: Eight Hanukkah Stories from Chelm* (PS–3). Illus. by Mordicai Gerstein. 2000, Holiday House $18.95 (978-0-8234-1463-5). 56pp. This collection of eight stories — some original plus some traditional Fools of Chelm tales — is filled with silliness and slapstick. (Rev: BL 9/1/00; HB 9/00; HBG 3/01)

12658 Kimmel, Eric A. *Onions and Garlic* (PS–3). Illus. by Katya Arnold. 1996, Holiday House $15.95 (978-0-8234-1222-8). 32pp. In this Hebrew folktale, young Getzel is able to use a sackful of onions to obtain a fortune in diamonds. (Rev: BCCB 6/96; BL 4/1/96; SLJ 7/96) [398.2]

12659 Kushner, Lawrence, and Gary Schmidt. *In God's Hands* (1–3). Illus. by Matthew J. Baek. 2005, Jewish Lights $16.99 (978-1-58023-224-1). 32pp. Jacob, a rich man who believes he is following a divine mandate, bakes loaves of bread and takes them to the synagogue where they are gratefully retrieved by David, a man so poor he can't afford to feed his family. (Rev: BL 10/1/05*; SLJ 10/05) [398.2]

12660 Oberman, Sheldon. *Solomon and the Ant* (5–8). 2006, Boyds Mills $19.95 (978-1-59078-307-8). 168pp. Nearly 50 traditional Jewish stories are arranged chronologically and accompanied by notes and commentary. (Rev: BL 2/1/06; SLJ 3/06) [398.2]

12661 Patterson, Jose. *Angels, Prophets, Rabbis and Kings: From the Stories of the Jewish People* (3–6). Illus. by Claire Bushe. 1991, Bedrick LB $24.95 (978-0-87226-912-5). 144pp. A treasure chest of stories and parables. (Rev: BL 9/15/91; SLJ 8/91) [398.2]

12662 Philip, Neil. *The Pirate Princess and Other Fairy Tales* (4–6). Illus. by Mark Weber. 2005, Scholastic $19.99 (978-0-590-10855-3). 96pp. A large, handsome collection of seven compelling fairy tales/parables written by Nahman ben Simha, a 19th-century Hasidic rabbi — tales that cover themes of true love, adventure, fortune, and health and happiness. (Rev: BL 1/1–15/06; SLJ 3/06) [398.2]

12663 Podwal, Mark. *Golem: A Giant Made of Mud* (K–4). Illus. 1995, Greenwillow LB $14.93 (978-0-688-13812-7). 32pp. A collection of stories about the mysterious shape-changing creature that is associated with Prague. (Rev: BL 10/1/95; SLJ 11/95) [398.2]

12664 Prose, Francine. *The Angel's Mistake: Stories of Chelm* (PS–4). Illus. by Mark Podwal. 1997, Greenwillow $14.89 (978-0-688-14906-2). 24pp. A series of anecdotes about the city of Chelm — where fools reside — its creation and eventual destruction. (Rev: BCCB 7–8/97; BL 3/1/97; HB 7/97; SLJ 4/97) [398.2]

12665 Prose, Francine. *You Never Know: A Legend of the Lamed-vavniks* (K–4). Illus. by Mark Podwal. 1998, Greenwillow LB $14.89 (978-0-688-15807-1). 24pp. Gradually the town of Plotchnik realizes that poor Schmuel the Shoemaker is one of God's holy Lamed-vavniks — 36 righteous people living in secret throughout the world. (Rev: BCCB 7–8/98; BL 6/1–15/98; HBG 10/98; SLJ 8/98) [398.2]

12666 Rogasky, Barbara. *Dybbuk: A Version* (4–6). Illus. by Leonard Everett Fisher. 2005, Holiday $16.95 (978-0-8234-1616-5). 64pp. In this dark tale based on Jewish folklore, a girl is possessed by the spirit of the boy she was destined to marry. (Rev: BL 10/15/05; SLJ 12/05) [398.2]

12667 Rogasky, Barbara. *The Golem* (4–6). Illus. by Trina S. Hyman. 1996, Holiday House $18.95 (978-0-8234-0964-8). 96pp. The story of the giant monster of the 16th century and its use to help protect the Jewish people in Prague from persecution. (Rev: BCCB 9/96; BL 10/1/96*; HB 1/96; SLJ 10/96) [398.2]

12668 Roth, Rita. *The Power of Song and Other Sephardic Tales* (3–5). Illus. by Alexa Ginsburg. 2007, Jewish Publication Soc. $16.00 (978-0-8276-0844-3). 150pp. An anthology of 13 tales of the Sephardic Jews who lived on the Iberian Peninsula; each story concludes with cultural commentary. (Rev: BL 10/1/07) [389.2]

12669 Rothenberg, Joan. *Yettele's Feathers* (PS–3). Illus. 1995, Hyperion LB $15.49 (978-0-7868-2081-8). 40pp. A rabbi makes Yettele realize how harmful her gossiping can be. (Rev: BL 5/1/95; SLJ 4/95) [398.2]

12670 Schram, Peninnah, retel. *The Magic Pomegranate* (K–2). Illus. by Melanie Hall. 2007, Millbrook LB $25.26 (978-0-8225-6742-4). 48pp. A retelling of a well known story from the Jewish literature involves three brothers who bring healing gifts to a dying princess and ends happily ever after. (Rev: SLJ 10/07) [398.2]

12671 Schram, Peninnah. *Ten Classic Jewish Children's Stories* (3–6). Illus. 1998, Pitspopany $16.95 (978-0-943706-96-2). 48pp. A volume that contains the retelling of ten traditional Jewish tales — many that illustrate situations in the Torah — with questions to reflect on the lessons taught. (Rev: BL 11/15/98; SLJ 3/99) [296.1]

12672 Schwartz, Howard. *Before You Were Born* (PS–2). Illus. by Kristina Swarner. 2005, Roaring Brook $16.95 (978-1-59643-028-0). 32pp. From Jewish legend, this is the story of the angel Lailah, who guides the human soul. (Rev: BL 5/15/05; SLJ 4/05) [398.2089]

12673 Schwartz, Howard, ed. *A Journey to Paradise: And Other Jewish Tales* (1–4). Illus. by Giora Carmi. 2000, Pitspopany $16.95 (978-0-943706-21-4); paper $9.95 (978-0-943706-16-0). 48pp. A collection of eight Jewish folktales that revolve around mystery, magic, and life after death. (Rev: BL 4/15/00; HBG 10/00; SLJ 6/00) [296.1]

12674 Sherman, Josepha. *Rachel the Clever and Other Jewish Folktales* (4–6). Illus. 1993, August House paper $10.95 (978-0-87483-307-2). 176pp. Jewish tales gathered from many lands. (Rev: BL 3/15/93) [398.2]

12675 Shollar, Leah. *A Thread of Kindness: A Tzedaka Story* (2–4). Illus. by Shoshana Mekibel. 2000, Hachai $10.95 (978-1-929628-01-8). 32pp. This traditional tale tells of a poor but virtuous farmer who gains wealth through his kindness to others. (Rev: BL 10/1/00; HBG 10/01; SLJ 1/01) [398.2]

12676 Souhami, Jessica. *The Little, Little House* (PS–2). Illus. 2006, Frances Lincoln $15.95 (978-1-84507-108-0). 32pp. Collage artwork breathes new life into the classic rabbinical fable about a poor man who looks for a way to make his family's crowded dwelling more comfortable. (Rev: BL 2/1/06; SLJ 3/06) [309.2]

12677 Stampler, Ann R. *Shlemazel and the Remarkable Spoon of Pohost* (PS–2). Illus. by Jacqueline M. Cohen. 2006, Clarion $16.00 (978-0-618-36959-1). 40pp. In this adaptation of a traditional Yiddish folk tale, the shtetl's miller uses trickery to transform lazy Shlemazel into a hardworking member of the community. (Rev: BL 6/1–15/06; SLJ 7/06) [398.2]

12678 Stampler, Ann R. *Something for Nothing* (1–3). Illus. by Jacqueline M. Cohen. 2003, Clarion $15.00 (978-0-618-15982-6). 32pp. A clever dog devises a scheme to free his life of three pesky cats in this Jewish folktale. (Rev: BL 5/15/03 ; HBG 10/03; SLJ 4/03) [398.2]

12679 Taback, Simms. *Joseph Had a Little Overcoat* (PS–2). Illus. 1999, Viking $16.99 (978-0-670-87855-0). 40pp. The many uses of a piece of cloth — from an overcoat to only enough material to cover a button — are the subject of this picture book based on an old Yiddish song. The mixed-media and collage illustrations are warm and lively. Caldecott Medal, 2000. (Rev: BCCB 3/00; BL 1/1–15/00; HBG 3/00; SLJ 1/00) [398.2]

12680 Taback, Simms. *Kibitzers and Fools: Tales My Zayda Told Me* (K–3). Illus. by author. 2005, Viking $16.99 (978-0-670-05955-3). 48pp. Set in the shtetls of Eastern Europe during the late 19th and early 20th centuries, these 13 tales, each of which spotlights a word or two in Yiddish, offer valuable life lessons. (Rev: BL 10/15/05; SLJ 10/05) [398.2]

12681 Tarbescu, Edith. *The Boy Who Stuck Out His Tongue: A Yiddish Folktale* (PS–1). Illus. by Judith C. Mills. 2000, Barefoot Books $15.99 (978-1-84148-067-1). 32pp. A disobedient son sticks out his tongue and it freezes to a cold iron fence. All the villagers try to free him in this Jewish folktale. (Rev: BCCB 11/00; BL 5/15/00; HBG 3/01; SLJ 9/00) [398.2]

12682 Uhlberg, Myron. *Lemuel the Fool* (PS–3). Illus. by Sonja Lamut. 2001, Peachtree $15.95 (978-1-56145-220-0). 32pp. In this Yiddish folktale, a dreamer sets out to see the world but, because he is walking in a circle, finds himself back home. (Rev: BL 4/15/01; HBG 10/01; SLJ 8/01) [398.2]

12683 Ungar, Richard. *Even Higher* (PS–2). Illus. by author. 2007, Tundra $18.95 (978-0-88776-758-6). 32pp. An adaptation of a Eastern European Jewish folktale in which young Reuven he discovers that the rabbi has indeed ascended "even higher" than heaven by secretly cutting wood for a poor widow. (Rev: BL 9/1/07; SLJ 9/07) [398.2]

12684 Waldman, Debby. *A Sack Full of Feathers* (PS–2). Illus. by Cindy Revell. 2006, Orca $17.95 (978-1-55143-332-5). 32pp. In this vividly portrayed retelling of a Jewish folktale, Yankel learns about the dangers of spreading hurtful gossip. (Rev: BL 10/15/06; SLJ 2/07) [398.2]

12685 Wisniewski, David. *Golem* (3–6). Illus. 1996, Clarion $17.00 (978-0-395-72618-1). 30pp. The terrifying story of the golem, who was created by Rabbi Loew in the 16th century to help protect his people in the Prague ghetto. Caldecott Medal winner, 1997. (Rev: BCCB 9/96; BL 10/1/96*; SLJ 10/96) [398.2]

12686 Zalben, Jane Breskin. *Light* (PS–2). Illus. by author. 2007, Dutton $17.99 (978-0-525-47827-0). 40pp. The importance of light is emphasized in this traditional Jewish story about repairing a broken world. (Rev: BL 10/1/07; LMC 11/07; SLJ 9/07) [398.2]

12687 Zemach, Margot. *It Could Always Be Worse: A Yiddish Folktale* (K–3). Illus. by author. 1976, Scholastic paper $4.95 (978-0-374-43636-0). 32pp. A Yiddish version of an old tale with colorful, humorous illustrations. [398.2]

Middle East

12688 dePaola, Tomie. *The Legend of the Persian Carpet* (K–3). Illus. by Claire Ewart. 1993, Penguin $16.99 (978-0-399-22415-7). 32pp. When his prize diamond is stolen and shattered, a Persian king finds solace in a beautiful new carpet woven for him. (Rev: BL 10/1/93; SLJ 1/94) [398.2]

12689 Ganeri, Anita. *Islamic Stories* (1–6). Illus. by Rebecca Wallis. Series: Traditional Religious Tales. 2006, Picture Window LB $26.60 (978-1-4048-1313-7). 32pp. Most of the Islamic stories in this collection recount incidents from the life of Muhammad, but they also touch on Abraham, Hagar, Ishmael, and Moses. (Rev: SLJ 4/06) [297.1]

12690 Hickox, Rebecca. *The Golden Sandal: A Middle Eastern Cinderella Story* (K–3). Illus. by Will Hillenbrand. 1998, Holiday House $17.95 (978-0-8234-1331-7). 32pp. A vivid retelling with atmospheric illustrations of an Iraqi folktale that is a variation of the Cinderella story. (Rev: BCCB 6/98; BL 4/1/98; HB 3/98; HBG 10/98; SLJ 4/98) [398.2]

12691 Hofmeyr, Dianne. *The Star-Bearer: A Creation Myth from Ancient Egypt* (3–5). Illus. by Judy Daly. 2001, Farrar $16.00 (978-0-374-37481-5). 32pp. In this picture book for older readers, a creation myth from Egypt is retold in which the god of rain and dew and the god of air emerge from a lotus bud. (Rev: BCCB 3/01; BL 2/15/01) [299]

12692 Johnson-Davies, Denys. *Goha the Wise Fool* (2–4). Illus. by Hany El Saed Ahmed and Hag Hamdy Mohamed Fattouh. 2005, Philomel $16.99 (978-0-399-24222-9). 40pp. Traditional tapestries illustrate a collection of memorable tales about a Middle Eastern trickster-fool called Goha. (Rev: BL 6/1–15/05*; HB 9/05) [398.2]

12693 Kherdian, David. *The Golden Bracelet* (K–4). Illus. by Nonny Hogrogian. 1998, Holiday House $16.95 (978-0-8234-1362-1). 32pp. An Armenian story about a prince who uses his skill as a weaver to send a message to his wife when he is held prisoner by an evil sorcerer. (Rev: BL 6/1–15/98; HBG 10/98; SLJ 8/98) [398.2]

12694 Kimmel, Eric A. *The Tale of Aladdin and the Wonderful Lamp: A Story from the Arabian Nights* (PS–3). Illus. by Ju-Hong Chen. 1992, Holiday House LB $14.95 (978-0-8234-0938-9). 32pp. A humorous retelling of the famous story. (Rev: BL 11/1/92; SLJ 12/92) [398.2]

12695 Kimmel, Eric A. *The Three Princes* (K–3). Illus. by Leonard Everett Fisher. 1994, Holiday House LB $16.95 (978-0-8234-1115-3). 30pp. A beautiful princess shows great wisdom in choosing her husband from the three noble cousins who are her suitors in this Middle Eastern folktale. (Rev: BCCB 4/94; BL 3/1/94*; SLJ 3/94) [398.2]

12696 Lang, Andrew. *The Arabian Nights Entertainments* (5–9). Illus. 1969, Dover paper $12.95 (978-0-486-22289-9). Aladdin and Sinbad are only two of the characters in these 26 tales of Arabia and the East. (Rev: BL 9/1/89) [398.2]

12697 L'Homme, Erik. *Tales of a Lost Kingdom: A Journey into Northwest Pakistan* (3–5). Trans. by Claudia Zoe Bedrick. Illus. by François Place. 2007, Enchanted Lion $17.95 (978-1-59270-072-1). 48pp. Three folk tales from Pakistan, each ending with a question and a moral. (Rev: BL 1/1–15/08; SLJ 12/07) [398.209549]

12698 MacDonald, Margaret Read. *Tunjur! Tunjur! Tunjur! A Palestinian Folktale* (PS–2). Illus. by Alik Arzoumanian. 2006, Marshall Cavendish $16.95 (978-0-7614-5225-6). 32pp. A woman's prayers for a child to love are rewarded with the arrival of a little cooking pot with unfortunate larcenous tendencies. (Rev: BL 3/1/06; SLJ 4/06) [398.2]

12699 Mitchell, Stephen. *Genies, Meanies, and Magic Rings: Three Tales from the Arabian Nights* (3–5). Illus. by Tom Pohrt. 2007, Walker $16.95 (978-0-8027-9639-4). 192pp. Mitchell retells "Ali Baba and the 40 Thieves," "Abu Keer and Abu Seer," and "Aladdin and the Magic Lamp." (Rev: BCCB 10/07; BL 10/1/07; HB 9/07; SLJ 10/07) [398.2]

12700 Oppenheim, Shulamith Levey. *Iblis* (1–4). Illus. by Ed Young. 1994, Harcourt $15.95 (978-0-15-238016-8). 32pp. In this Islamic version of Adam and Eve's expulsion from Eden, the devil is called Iblis. (Rev: BCCB 4/94; BL 3/15/94; SLJ 4/94) [297]

12701 Philip, Neil. *The Arabian Nights* (4–6). Illus. by Sheila Moxley. 1994, Orchard $19.95 (978-0-531-06868-7). 160pp. With lovely paintings and colorful prose, this is an excellent retelling of 16 of the Arabian Nights stories, including Ali Baba, Scheherazade, and Aladdin. (Rev: BL 12/15/94; HB 5/94; SLJ 12/94*) [398.2]

12702 Pullman, Philip. *Aladdin and the Enchanted Lamp* (3–5). Illus. by Sophy Williams. 2005, Scholastic $16.95 (978-0-439-69255-7). 64pp. An exotic presentation, full of wit and dramatic art. (Rev: BL 5/1/05) [398.22]

12703 Riordan, James. *The Seven Voyages of Sinbad the Sailor* (4–6). Illus. by Shelley Fowles. 2008, Frances Lincoln $18.95 (978-1-84507-531-6). 64pp. A lively retelling of Sinbad's voyages using contemporary language and with detailed maps on the endpapers. (Rev: BLO 7/30/08; LMC 1/09; SLJ 8/08) [398.2]

12704 Shah, Idries. *The Boy Without a Name* (PS–2). Illus. by Mona Caron. 2000, Hoopoe $17.00 (978-1-883536-20-6). 32pp. Based on an Islamic story, this folktale tells of a boy who visits a wise man to get a name. (Rev: BL 12/1/00; SLJ 2/01) [398.22]

12705 Shah, Idries. *The Clever Boy and the Terrible, Dangerous Animal* (1–4). Illus. by Rose Mary Santiago. 2000, Hoopoe $17.00 (978-1-883536-18-3). In this Middle Eastern folktale, a young boy quiets some villagers by explaining that the animal they fear is really just a melon. (Rev: SLJ 12/00) [398.2]

12706 Shah, Idries. *Fatima the Spinner and the Tent* (PS–2). Illus. by Natasha Delmar. 2006, Hoopoe $18.00 (978-1-883536-42-8); paper $7.99 (978-1-883536-61-9). 32pp. Fatima, daughter of a well-to-do spinner, suffers a series of tragedies that turn out to have taught her useful skills in this retelling of an 18th-century Turkish tale. (Rev: BL 9/15/06; SLJ 11/06) [398.2]

12707 Shah, Idries. *The Lion Who Saw Himself in the Water* (PS–2). Illus. by Ingrid Rodriguez. 1998, Hoopoe $17.00 (978-1-883536-12-1). 32pp. In this Sufi tale from Islam, a lion is so frightened by his reflection in the water that he can't drink from the pool until a friendly butterfly helps him conquer his fear. (Rev: BL 10/1/98; SLJ 12/98) [398.24]

12708 Shah, Idries. *The Magic Horse* (3–5). Illus. by Julie Freeman. 1998, Hoopoe $17.00 (978-1-883536-11-4). 34pp. This picture-book version of a Muslim Sufi tale involves two brothers and their separate quests. (Rev: SLJ 2/99) [398.2]

12709 Shah, Idries. *Neem the Half-Boy* (PS–2). Illus. by Midori Mori and Robert Revels. 1998, Hoopoe $17.00 (978-1-883536-10-7). 32pp. In this story based on an ancient Sufi tale from Islam, Neem remains a half-boy until he successfully confronts a dragon in his lair. (Rev: BL 10/1/98; SLJ 1/99) [398.22]

12710 Smith, Chris. *One City, Two Brothers* (K–3). Illus. by Aurelia Fronty. 2007, Barefoot Books $16.99 (978-1-84686-042-3). 32pp. Introduced by King Solomon, this story about the founding of Jerusalem features two caring brothers who try to make sure each has enough grain. (Rev: BL 10/1/07; LMC 1/08; SLJ 12/07) [398.20933]

12711 Vallverdu, Josep. *Aladdin and the Magic Lamp / Aldino y la lampara maravillosa* (4–6). Illus. by Pep Montserrat. 2006, Chronicle $14.95 (978-0-8118-5061-2); paper $6.95 (978-0-8118-5062-9). 32pp. An attractive bilingual retelling. (Rev: BL 9/1/06; SLJ 10/06) [398.22]

12712 Wolfson, Margaret Olivia. *The Patient Stone: A Persian Love Story* (3–7). Illus. by Juan Caneba Clavero. 2001, Barefoot Books $16.99 (978-1-84148-085-5). 32pp. This retelling of the story of Fatima, who after many trials earns the love of a prince thanks to a magic stone, is accompanied by beautiful watercolors and handsome borders, as well as an author's note that explains some of the symbolism. (Rev: BL 9/15/01; HBG 3/02; SLJ 2/02) [398.2]

12713 Young, Ed. *What About Me?* (K–3). Illus. 2002, Penguin $16.99 (978-0-399-23624-2). 40pp. A colorful cumulative tale of Sufi origin about a boy who must provide the grand master with a carpet before he will give the youngster the gift of knowledge. (Rev: BCCB 7–8/02; BL 5/1/02*; HB 7/02; HBG 10/02; SLJ 6/02) [398.2]

12714 Zeman, Ludmila. *Sindbad: From the Tales of the Thousand and One Nights* (3–5). Illus. 1999, Tundra $17.95 (978-0-88776-460-8). 32pp. Using extraordinary illustrations, the author-artist tells the stories of two of the famous voyages of Sinbad, one involving a giant whale and the other featuring a huge bird. (Rev: BL 1/1–15/00*; SLJ 1/00) [813.54]

12715 Zeman, Ludmila. *Sindbad in the Land of Giants* (PS–3). Illus. 2001, Tundra $17.95 (978-0-88776-461-5). 32pp. Sindbad's cunning and courage are tested in this beautifully illustrated adventure. (Rev: BL 8/01; HBG 10/01; SLJ 8/01) [398.2]

12716 Zeman, Ludmila, retel. *Sindbad's Secret: From The Tales of the Thousand and One Nights* (2–5). Illus. by Ludmila Zeman. 2003, Tundra $17.95 (978-0-88776-462-2). Sindbad recounts two wondrous escapes and his discovery of the ultimate treasure is this last volume of Zeman's trilogy. (Rev: HBG 10/03; SLJ 3/03) [813.54]

North America

Canada

12717 Carrier, Roch, retel. *The Flying Canoe* (3–6). Trans. from French by Sheila Fischman. Illus. by Sheldon Cohen. 2004, Tundra $15.95 (978-0-88776-636-7). On a New Year's Eve in the mid-19th century, 11-year-old Baptiste and his homesick lumberjack friends are transported home by magical canoe; a French Canadian folktale. (Rev: SLJ 4/05) [398.2]

12718 Johnson, Emily Pauline. *The Lost Island* (2–4). Illus. by Atanas Matsoureff. 2005, Simply Read $16.95 (978-1-894965-07-1). 40pp. In this retelling of an Indian folktale, an elderly man tells of his search for a mysterious lost island said to hold the bravery of a once-powerful leader of the Squamish. (Rev: BL 1/1–15/05) [398.2]

12719 Jorisch, Stephane, adapt. *As for the Princess? A Folktale from Quebec* (K–3). Illus. by Stephane Jorisch. 2001, Annick LB $19.95 (978-1-55037-695-1); paper $7.95 (978-1-55037-694-4). A not-very-bright young man finally gets his revenge against a beautiful but light-fingered princess. (Rev: HBG 3/02; SLJ 3/02) [398.2]

Inuit

12720 Hall, Amanda. *The Stolen Sun: A Story of Native Alaska* (PS–3). Illus. 2002, Eerdmans $17.00 (978-0-8028-5225-0). 32pp. A Native Alaskan tale with folkloric flavor about the creation of the world and its inhabitants. (Rev: BL 2/15/02; HBG 10/02; SLJ 9/02) [398.2]

12721 Houston, James. *Tikta'liktak: An Eskimo Legend* (4–6). Illus. by author. 1990, Harcourt paper $10.00 (978-0-15-287748-4). 63pp. Legend of a young Inuit hunter who is carried out to sea on a drifting ice floe with only his bow and arrows and a harpoon. Also use: *The White Archer: An Eskimo Legend* (1990). [398.2]

12722 Murphy, Claire R. *Caribou Girl* (K–3). Illus. by Linda Russell. 1998, Roberts Rinehart $16.95 (978-1-57098-145-6). A young Inuit changes into a caribou to bring the herd to her starving people. (Rev: HBG 10/98; SLJ 7/98) [398.2]

Native Americans

12723 Ata, Te. *Baby Rattlesnake* (PS–K). Adapted by Lynn Moroney. Illus. by Veg Reisberg. 1990, Children's Book Pr. $14.95 (978-0-89239-049-6). 32pp. A baby rattlesnake doesn't know how to behave when he is given a rattle before reaching maturity. (Rev: BL 3/1/90; SLJ 4/90) [398.2]

12724 Bierhorst, John, ed. *The People with Five Fingers: A Native Californian Creation Tale* (K–3). Illus. by Robert Andrew Parker. 2000, Marshall Cavendish $15.95 (978-0-7614-5058-0). 32pp. A Native American creation tale about how Coyote put the animals to work to prepare for the arrival of humans in the world. (Rev: BCCB 3/00; BL 4/1/00; HBG 10/00; SLJ 6/00) [398.2]

12725 Bierhorst, John. *The Woman Who Fell from the Sky: The Iroquois Story of Creation* (K–4). Illus. by Robert Andrew Parker. 1993, Morrow LB $14.89 (978-0-688-10681-2). 32pp. Sky Woman, with the help of her two sons, creates the earth. (Rev: BCCB 5/93; BL 3/15/93; HB 5/93; SLJ 4/93) [398.2]

12726 Bruchac, James, and Joseph Bruchac, retels. *The Girl Who Helped Thunder and Other Native American Folktales* (3–6). Illus. by Stefano Vitale. 2008, Sterling $14.95 (978-1-4027-3263-8). 96pp. Arranged geographically, this anthology includes stories from diverse peoples, with background information that provides historical and cultural context. (Rev: BCCB 1/09; HB 1/09; LMC 5/09; SLJ 12/08) [398.2]

12727 Bruchac, Joseph. *Dog People: Native Dog Stories* (3–6). Illus. by Murv Jacob. 1995, Fulcrum $14.95 (978-1-55591-228-4). 63pp. This book contains five very readable stories about the Abenaki Indian children and their dogs. (Rev: SLJ 1/96) [398.2]

12728 Bruchac, Joseph. *Native American Animal Stories* (5–8). Illus. 1992, Fulcrum paper $12.95 (978-1-55591-127-0). Animal stories from various Native American tribes, for reading aloud and storytelling. (Rev: BL 9/1/92; SLJ 11/92) [398.2]

12729 Bruchac, Joseph. *Native Plant Stories* (4–8). Illus. 1995, Fulcrum paper $12.95 (978-1-55591-212-3). 128pp. A collection of stories about plants that come from various Native American cultures in North and Central America. (Rev: BL 9/1/95) [398.24]

12730 Bruchac, Joseph, and James Bruchac. *How Chipmunk Got His Stripes: A Tale of Bragging and Teasing* (1–3). Illus. by Ariane Dewey and Jose Aruego. 2001, Dial $16.99 (978-0-8037-2404-4). 32pp. In this Native American story, squirrel is punished for teasing Big Bear by having the now-familiar chipmunk stripe placed on his back. (Rev: BCCB 3/01; BL 2/1/01; HBG 10/01; SLJ 2/01) [398.24]

12731 Bruchac, Joseph, and James Bruchac. *When the Chenoo Howls* (3–6). Illus. 1998, Walker $16.95 (978-0-8027-8638-8). 128pp. This anthology consists of 12 scary stories from the Northeast woodland Native Americans — most of them traditional folktales together with a few original stories that incorporate legendary characters. (Rev: BCCB 9/98; BL 8/98; HBG 3/99; SLJ 12/98) [398.2]

12732 Bushyhead, Robert H. *Yonder Mountain: A Cherokee Legend* (PS–3). Illus. by Kristina Rodanas. 2002, Marshall Cavendish $16.95 (978-0-7614-5113-6). 32pp. In this Cherokee folktale, an old chief tests three young men to determine who will be his successor. (Rev: BL 2/15/03; HBG 10/03; SLJ 12/02) [398.2]

12733 Charles, Veronika M., retel. *Maiden of the Mist: A Legend of Niagara Falls* (1–3). Illus. by Veronika M. Charles. 2001, Stoddart $13.95 (978-0-7737-3297-1); paper $6.95 (978-0-7737-6207-7). A

beautifully illustrated story of the maiden who sacrifices herself to the Thunder God in order to save her people from illness. (Rev: SLJ 1/02) [398.2]

12734 Cohen, Caron L. *The Mud Pony: A Traditional Skidi Pawnee Tale* (K–3). Illus. by Shonto Begay. 1988, Scholastic $15.95 (978-0-590-41525-5). 32pp. The moving story of a boy too poor to have a pony of his own who grows up to become chief of his people. (Rev: BCCB 12/88; BL 12/1/88; SLJ 1/89) [398.2]

12735 Connolly, James E. *Why the Possum's Tail Is Bare: And Other North American Indian Nature Tales* (4–7). Illus. 1992, Stemmer $15.95 (978-0-88045-069-0); paper $7.95 (978-0-88045-107-9). 64pp. Nature and folklore are combined in 13 Native American animal tales. (Rev: BL 9/1/85; SLJ 10/85) [398.2]

12736 Crook, Connie Brummel. *Maple Moon* (K–4). Illus. by Scott Cameron. 1998, Stoddart $15.95 (978-0-7737-3017-5). 32pp. A crippled young Mississauga boy accidentally discovers tree sap as a source of food for his people in this adaptation of two Native American folktales. (Rev: BL 4/15/98; SLJ 4/98) [398.2]

12737 Curry, Jane Louise. *Hold Up the Sky and Other Native American Tales from Texas and the Southern Plains* (3–7). Illus. 2003, Simon & Schuster $17.95 (978-0-689-85287-9). 176pp. These varied folktales offer a mix of adventure, pourquoi stories, and humor and are accompanied by brief supplementary information about the 14 tribes from which they originated. (Rev: BL 4/1/03; HBG 10/03; SLJ 10/03) [398.2]

12738 De Montano, Marty Kreipe. *Coyote in Love with a Star* (PS–3). Illus. by Tom Coffin. 1998, Abbeville $14.95 (978-0-7892-0162-1). 31pp. In this updated pourquoi tale that explains why coyotes howl at the moon, Coyote travels to New York City and there falls in love with a star. (Rev: BL 12/1/98; HB 3/99; HBG 3/99; SLJ 2/99) [398.2]

12739 Dengler, Marianna. *The Worry Stone* (3–5). Illus. by Sibyl G. Gerig. 1996, Northland LB $15.95 (978-0-87358-642-9). 34pp. When her grandfather dies, Amanda finds that she gets comfort from rubbing a stone that the old man had given to her. (Rev: BL 12/15/96; SLJ 1/97) [398.2]

12740 dePaola, Tomie, retel. *The Legend of the Bluebonnet: An Old Tale of Texas* (K–3). Illus. by Tomie dePaola. 1983, Penguin $16.99 (978-0-399-20937-6). 32pp. This book retells the Comanche Indian story of the origin of the Texas bluebonnet flower. [398.2]

12741 Dominic, Gloria, adapt. *Brave Bear and the Ghosts: A Sioux Legend* (2–4). Illus. by Charles Reasoner. Series: Native American Lore and Legends. 1996, Rourke LB $19.95 (978-0-86593-429-0). 47pp. A charming trickster tale with a surprise ending from the Sioux. Also use *Coyote and the Grasshoppers: A Pomo Legend* and *Song of the Hermit Thrush: An Iroquois Legend* (both 1996). (Rev: SLJ 3/97) [398.2]

12742 Duvall, Deborah L. *The Opossum's Tale: A Grandmother Story* (PS–2). Illus. by Murv Jacob.

2005, Univ. of New Mexico $15.95 (978-0-8263-3694-1). 32pp. Based on Cherokee folklore, this richly illustrated picture book tells how the opossum got its distinctive hairless tail. (Rev: BL 3/15/06; SLJ 2/06) [398.2]

12743 Dwyer, Mindy, retel. *Coyote in Love* (PS–3). Illus. by Mindy Dwyer. 1997, Alaska Northwest $15.95 (978-0-88240-485-1). This Native American tale of how Crater Lake was formed tells of Coyote's unrequited love for a star. (Rev: SLJ 7/97) [398.2]

12744 Esbensen, Barbara J. *Ladder to the Sky: How the Gift of Healing Came to the Ojibway Nation* (K–3). Illus. by Helen K. Davie. 1989, Little, Brown $15.95 (978-0-316-24952-2). 32pp. Although the Ojibwa (Chippewa) lost their direct connection to the Great Spirit, they were granted healing powers. (Rev: BCCB 2/90; BL 11/1/89; SLJ 10/89) [398.2]

12745 Goble, Paul. *Crow Chief: A Plains Indian Story* (K–3). Illus. by author. 1992, Orchard LB $17.99 (978-0-531-08547-9). 32pp. This Plains Indian legend explains why crows have black feathers. (Rev: BCCB 4/92; BL 2/15/92; HB 3/92; SLJ 3/92) [398.2]

12746 Goble, Paul. *The Great Race: Of the Birds and Animals* (K–3). Illus. by author. 1991, Simon & Schuster paper $5.99 (978-0-689-71452-8). 32pp. The story of the great race between the animals and humans in which the people won and now have responsibility to care for animals. (Rev: BCCB 9/85; BL 9/15/85; SLJ 9/85) [398.2]

12747 Goble, Paul. *Iktomi and the Berries: A Plains Indian Story* (K–2). Illus. by author. 1992, Orchard paper $6.95 (978-0-531-07029-1). 32pp. A witty folktale about a disreputable hero. (Rev: BCCB 12/89*; BL 9/15/89; HB 11/89; SLJ 9/89*) [398.2]

12748 Goble, Paul. *Iktomi and the Boulder: A Plains Indian Story* (3–5). Illus. by author. 1988, Orchard $16.95 (978-0-531-05760-5); paper $6.95 (978-0-531-07023-9). 32pp. Iktomi, a trickster, is the hero of many humorous adventures in these Sioux tales. (Rev: BCCB 7–8/88; BL 8/88; HB 9/88) [398.2]

12749 Goble, Paul. *Iktomi and the Buffalo Skull: A Plains Indian Story* (K–3). Illus. by author. 1996, Orchard paper $5.95 (978-0-531-07077-2). 32pp. Iktomi the trickster tries to impress girls but ends up with his head stuck in a buffalo skull. (Rev: BL 2/1/91; HB 5/91; SLJ 3/91) [398.2]

12750 Goble, Paul. *Iktomi and the Coyote: A Plains Indian Story* (3–5). Illus. by author. 1998, Orchard LB $17.99 (978-0-531-33108-8). Iktomi, a trickster, thinks he has found himself a meal of prairie dog, but he is outwitted by a clever coyote. (Rev: BCCB 1/99; HBG 3/99; SLJ 11/98) [398.2]

12751 Goble, Paul. *The Legend of the White Buffalo Woman* (4–8). Illus. 1998, National Geographic $16.95 (978-0-7922-7074-4). In this picture book for older readers recounting a Lakata Indian tale, an earth woman and an eagle mate after a great flood to produce a new people. (Rev: BL 3/15/98; HBG 10/98; SLJ 5/98) [398.2]

12752 Goble, Paul. *Mystic Horse* (2–3). 2003, Harper-Collins $17.99 (978-0-06-029813-5). 40pp. Inspired by a Pawnee folktale, this is a mystical story of a boy and a magical horse. (Rev: BL 7/03; HB 5/03; HBG 10/03; SLJ 5/03) [398.2]

12753 Goble, Paul. *Remaking the Earth: A Creation Story from the Great Plains of North America* (3–6). Illus. 1996, Orchard LB $16.99 (978-0-531-08874-6). 32pp. In this creation myth, Earth Maker re-creates the land after a destructive flood. (Rev: BL 9/15/96; SLJ 10/96) [398.2]

12754 Goble, Paul, retel. *Star Boy* (2–4). 1991, Simon & Schuster paper $5.99 (978-0-689-71499-3). 32pp. A legend on how Star Boy was able to rid himself of a disfiguring scar. [398.2]

12755 Highwater, Jamake. *Anpao: An American Indian Odyssey* (5–8). Illus. by Fritz Scholder. 1993, HarperCollins paper $8.99 (978-0-06-440437-2). 256pp. A young hero encounters great danger on his way to meet his father, the Sun, in this dramatic American Indian folktale. [398.2]

12756 Hillerman, Tony, ed. *The Boy Who Made Dragonfly: A Zuni Myth* (5–7). Illus. by Laszlo Kubinyi. 1986, Univ. of New Mexico paper $11.95 (978-0-8263-0910-5). 85pp. A Zuni boy and his little sister are left behind by their tribe and survive hunger and deprivation through the intervention of the Cornstalk Being. [398.2]

12757 Jones, Jennifer B. *Heetunka's Harvest: A Tale of the Plains Indians* (K–3). Illus. by Shannon Keegan. 1995, Roberts Rinehart $15.95 (978-1-879373-17-4). 32pp. Nature takes revenge on a thieving Dakota Indian woman who steals from Heetunka the bean mouse. (Rev: BL 1/1/95; SLJ 4/95) [398.2]

12758 *Kokopelli, Drum in Belly* (3–5). Trans. and illus. by Gail E. Haley. 2003, Filter $12.95 (978-0-86541-069-5). Rich illustrations enhance this telling of the Native American legend of Kokopelli the Cicada. (Rev: BL 10/15/03; HBG 4/04; SLJ 2/04)

12759 Larrabee, Lisa. *Grandmother Five Baskets* (2–4). Illus. by Lori Sawyer. 1993, Harbinger paper $9.95 (978-0-943173-90-0). 60pp. Using five baskets that have been made by a Poarch Creek Indian woman as a metaphor, different stages of life are explained. (Rev: SLJ 3/94)

12760 Lavitt, Edward, and Robert E. McDowell. *Nihancan's Feast of Beaver: Animal Tales of the North American Indians* (2–6). Illus. by Bunny P. Huffman. 1990, Museum of New Mexico paper $12.95 (978-0-89013-211-1). 120pp. This handsome book contains 36 tales from nine different cultural areas in North America. (Rev: BL 3/1/91) [398.2]

12761 Lind, Michael. *Bluebonnet Girl* (K–3). Illus. by Kate Kiesler. 2003, Holt $16.95 (978-0-8050-6573-2). 40pp. A Comanche legend telling why bluebonnets bloom in Texas. (Rev: BL 3/15/03; HBG 4/04; SLJ 4/03) [398.2]

12762 Luenn, Nancy. *The Miser on the Mountain: A Nisqually Legend of Mount Rainier* (3–6). Illus. by Pierr Morgan. 1997, Sasquatch $15.95 (978-1-57061-082-0). 32pp. An Indian legend set on Ta-co-bet, or Mount Rainier, in which greed leads to a man's downfall. (Rev: BL 9/15/97; HBG 3/98; SLJ 1/98) [398.2]

12763 McDermott, Gerald. *Coyote: A Trickster Tale from the American Southwest* (PS–K). Illus. 1994, Harcourt $15.00 (978-0-15-220724-3). 32pp. Obnoxious Coyote has a comedown when he tries to fly with the crows. (Rev: BCCB 11/94; BL 8/94*; SLJ 11/94) [398.2]

12764 McDermott, Gerald. *Raven: A Trickster Tale from the Pacific Northwest* (K–4). Illus. by author. 1993, Harcourt $16.00 (978-0-15-265661-4). 32pp. A traditional tale told by the tribes of the area, illustrated by a Caldecott Medal winner. (Rev: BCCB 6/93*; BL 3/1/93*; HB 7/93*; SLJ 5/93*) [398]

12765 Malotki, Ekkehart, comp. *The Magic Hummingbird: A Hopi Folktale* (2–4). Illus. by Michael Lacapa. 1996, Kiva $15.95 (978-1-885772-04-6). In this Hopi tale, a boy makes a toy hummingbird that comes to life and helps end a drought by taking the boy and his sister to the fertility god. (Rev: SLJ 11/96) [398.2]

12766 Martin, Rafe. *The Rough-Face Girl* (1–4). Illus. by David Shannon. 1992, Penguin LB $16.99 (978-0-399-21859-0). 32pp. This variation on the Cinderella tale takes place in an Algonquin village on the shores of Lake Ontario. (Rev: BL 4/15/92; HB 7/92; SLJ 5/92) [398.2]

12767 Martin, Rafe. *The World Before This One* (5–8). Illus. by Calvin Nichols. 2002, Scholastic paper $16.95 (978-0-590-37976-2). 208pp. Crow, a Seneca Indian, comes upon a storytelling stone that tells him about the origins of the earth in this series of stories. (Rev: BL 2/15/03; HBG 3/03; SLJ 12/02; VOYA 2/03) [398.2]

12768 Max, Jill, ed. *Spider Spins a Story: Fourteen Legends from Native America* (3–6). Illus. 1997, Northland $16.95 (978-0-87358-611-5). 72pp. Spider plays a prominent role in these folktales, illustrated by six Native American artists. (Rev: BL 12/15/97; HBG 10/98; SLJ 1/98) [398.2]

12769 Mayo, Gretchen Will, retel. *Big Trouble for Tricky Rabbit!* (2–4). Illus. by Gretchen Will Mayo. Series: Native American Trickster Tales. 1994, Walker LB $13.85 (978-0-8027-8276-2). 38pp. Using simple vocabulary and short sentences, the author retells five trickster tales from Native American folklore, all involving Rabbit. (Rev: BCCB 6/94; SLJ 7/94) [398.2]

12770 Mayo, Gretchen Will. *Earthmaker's Tales: North American Indian Stories About Earth Happenings* (4–6). Illus. 1989, Walker LB $13.85 (978-0-8027-6840-7). 96pp. Legends that center on the earth itself. (Rev: BL 3/1/89) [398.2]

12771 Mayo, Gretchen Will. *Here Comes Tricky Rabbit!* (2–4). Illus. Series: Native American Trickster Tales. 1994, Walker LB $13.85 (978-0-8027-8274-8). 48pp. These five folktales reveal Rabbit to be a wily trickster. (Rev: BCCB 6/94; BL 8/94; SLJ 7/94) [398.2]

12772 Mayo, Gretchen Will, retel. *Meet Tricky Coyote!* (2–5). Illus. by Gretchen Will Mayo. Series: Native American Trickster Tales. 1993, Walker LB $13.85 (978-0-8027-8199-4). 36pp. A retelling of some short, humorous Native American stories about the clever trickster coyote. Companion volumes are *That Tricky Coyote!* and *Magical Tales from Many Lands* (both 1993). (Rev: SLJ 9/93) [398.2]

12773 Mayo, Gretchen Will. *Star Tales: North American Indian Stories About the Stars* (4–7). Illus. by author. 1987, Walker LB $13.85 (978-0-8027-6673-1). 96pp. Fourteen tales, each introduced by a one-page commentary on a constellation. (Rev: BL 6/15/87; SLJ 5/87) [398.2]

12774 Mayo, Gretchen Will. *That Tricky Coyote!* (PS–3). Illus. 1993, Walker LB $13.85 (978-0-8027-8201-4). 32pp. Five short stories from different tribes that deal with the escapades of the trickster Coyote. (Rev: BL 9/1/93; SLJ 9/93) [398.2]

12775 Medicine Crow, Joseph. *Brave Wolf and the Thunderbird* (PS–3). Illus. by Linda R. Martin. 1998, Abbeville $14.95 (978-0-7892-0160-7). 31pp. Written and illustrated by Native Americans, this is the traditional tale of the kidnapping of Brave Wolf by Thunderbird to assist in the rescue of Thunderbird's chicks from a sea monster. (Rev: BL 12/1/98; HBG 3/99; SLJ 4/99) [398.2]

12776 Nelson, S. D. *Gift Horse: A Lakota Story* (PS–3). Illus. 1999, Abrams $14.95 (978-0-8109-4127-4). 40pp. Flying Cloud earns his status as a Lakota warrior when he joins a raiding party to return horses stolen by Crow enemies. (Rev: BL 12/1/99; HBG 3/00; SLJ 11/99) [978]

12777 Pollock, Penny. *The Turkey Girl: A Zuni Cinderella Story* (4–6). Illus. by Ed Young. 1996, Little, Brown $16.95 (978-0-316-71314-6). 32pp. In this Zuni folktale, Turkey Girl's magical transformation ends in disaster when she forgets her promise to return to her flock of birds. (Rev: BCCB 4/96; BL 4/15/96; HB 5/96; SLJ 5/96) [398.2]

12778 Powell, Patricia Hruby. *Ch'at Tó Yinílo' / Frog Brings Rain* (K–3). Ed. by Jessie Ruffenach. Trans. from Navajo by Peter A. Thomas. Illus. by Kendrick Benally. 2006, Salina Bookshelf $17.95 (978-1-893354-08-1). A bilingual retelling of a Navajo story about a frog that helps douse a fire and save the First People. (Rev: SLJ 7/06) [398.2]

12779 Powell, Patricia Hruby. *Zinnia: How the Corn Was Saved* (1–5). Trans. by Peter A. Thomas. Illus. by Kendrick Benally. 2004, Salina Bookshelf $17.95 (978-1-893354-38-8). This authentic retelling, in both Navajo and English, of a folktale about a knowledgeable Spider Woman is notable for its illustrations. (Rev: SLJ 6/04) [398.2]

12780 Raczek, Linda. *Stories from Native North America* (2–4). Illus. by Richard Hook. Series: Multicultural Stories. 2000, Raintree LB $27.12 (978-0-7398-1336-2). 48pp. A fine collection of Native American folktales that represents many geographical locations. (Rev: HBG 10/00; SLJ 11/00) [398.2]

12781 Riordan, James. *The Songs My Paddle Sings* (2–5). Illus. 1998, Pavilion paper $16.95 (978-1-86205-076-1). 128pp. An anthology of 20 legends from various Native American peoples, including creation stories, hero legends, and cautionary tales. (Rev: BL 3/15/98; SLJ 5/98) [398.2]

12782 Rodanas, Kristina, adapt. *The Dragonfly's Tale* (PS–3). Illus. 1992, Houghton $17.00 (978-0-395-57003-6). 28pp. The Ashiwi's waste of food causes the Corn Maiden to bring famine to the village, but a boy and his sister find a way to harvest a successful crop. (Rev: BCCB 6/92; BL 4/1/92; SLJ 7/92) [398.2]

12783 Runningwolf, Michael. *On the Trail of Elder Brother* (3–6). Illus. 2000, Persea $17.95 (978-0-89255-248-1). 128pp. Sixteen tales including creation myths and pourquoi stories are included in this collection of Micmac folktales about Glous'gap, called Elder Brother, the embodiment of the Great Spirit. (Rev: BCCB 6/00; BL 7/00; HBG 10/00) [398.2]

12784 San Souci, Robert D. *Two Bear Cubs* (K–4). Illus. by Daniel San Souci. 1997, Yosemite $14.95 (978-0-939666-87-4). Two bear cubs fall asleep on a rock that grows into a mountain in this Native American folktale that explains the rock formation known as El Capitan in Yosemite National Park. (Rev: BCCB 3/98; BL 1/1–15/98; SLJ 4/98) [398.2]

12785 Shenandoah, Joanne, and Douglas M. George-Kanentiio. *Skywoman: Legends of the Iroquois* (4–8). Illus. 1998, Clear Light $14.95 (978-0-940666-99-3). Good writing and effective artwork are combined in this retelling of nine traditional Iroquois tales, including a series of creation stories. (Rev: HBG 10/99; SLJ 2/99) [398.2]

12786 Steptoe, John, retel. *The Story of Jumping Mouse: A Native American Legend* (1–4). 1984, Morrow paper $6.99 (978-0-688-08740-1). 40pp. The legend of the mouse who, because of good acts, is transformed into an eagle. [398.2]

12787 Stevens, Janet. *Coyote Steals the Blanket: A Ute Tale* (4–6). Illus. 1993, Holiday House LB $17.95 (978-0-8234-0996-9). 32pp. In this amusing legend, a rock chases a coyote after the animal steals a blanket that had covered it. (Rev: BCCB 5/93*; BL 4/1/93; SLJ 6/93) [398.2]

12788 Stevens, Janet. *Old Bag of Bones: A Coyote Tale* (K–4). Illus. 1996, Holiday House LB $16.95 (978-0-8234-1215-0). 32pp. Coyote, who resents growing old, persuades Young Buffalo to share his youth with him in this Shoshone tale. (Rev: BCCB 5/96; BL 5/1/96; HB 7/96; SLJ 5/96*) [398.24]

12789 Swamp, Chief Jake. *Giving Thanks: A Native American Good Morning Message* (PS–1). Illus. by Erwin Printup. 1995, Lee & Low $15.95 (978-1-880000-15-1). 24pp. A Mohawk chieftain gives thanks for Mother Earth and the universe that surrounds her. (Rev: BL 10/15/95; SLJ 11/95) [299]

12790 *Tatanka and the Lakota People: A Creation Story* (1–4). Illus. by Donald F. Montileaux. 2006, South Dakota State Historical Soc. $16.95 (978-0-9749195-8-4). This creation story tells how the Lakota people were tricked into leaving their Underworld with promises of easy living; English and Lakota words are side by side and the illustrations draw on traditional art. (Rev: SLJ 2/07) [398.2]

12791 Taylor, C. J. *All the Stars in the Sky: Native Stories from the Heavens* (2–4). Illus. by author.

2006, Tundra $17.95 (978-0-88776-759-3). 40pp. A collection of seven diverse stories about the night sky from various Native American groups. (Rev: BL 12/1/06) [398.2]

12792 Taylor, C. J. *How We Saw the World: Nine Native Stories of the Way Things Began* (4–6). Illus. 1993, Tundra $17.99 (978-0-88776-302-1). 32pp. These nine stories from various tribes explain the origin of several animals, like horses, and geographical landmarks, like Niagara Falls. (Rev: BL 11/1/93; SLJ 2/94) [398.3]

12793 Taylor, C. J. *The Secret of the White Buffalo* (K–3). Illus. 1993, Tundra paper $13.95 (978-0-88776-321-2). 24pp. Two Native American scouts encounter a beautiful woman when they set out to track buffalo in this Oglala Indian folktale. (Rev: BL 1/1/94) [398.2]

12794 Tingle, Tim. *When Turtle Grew Feathers: A Folktale from the Choctaw Nation* (PS–2). Illus. by Stacey Schuett. 2007, August House $16.95 (978-0-87483-777-3). A rhyming version of a Native American take on the tortoise-and-the-hare legend, with lively illustrations. (Rev: SLJ 5/07)

12795 Van Laan, Nancy. *In a Circle Long Ago: A Treasury of Native Lore from North America* (3–5). Illus. 1995, Knopf LB $21.99 (978-0-679-95807-9). 128pp. Nature is explored in 25 geographically arranged tales, with an introduction to their cultural origins. (Rev: BL 11/15/95; SLJ 11/95) [392.2]

12796 Waboose, Jan B. *SkySisters* (PS–2). Illus. by Brian Deines. 2000, Kids Can $15.95 (978-1-55074-697-6). 32pp. Two Ojibwaa sisters encounter three guardian spirits — a rabbit, a deer, and a coyote — as they venture out one night to see the Northern Lights. (Rev: BL 11/15/00; HBG 3/01; SLJ 1/01) [398.2]

12797 Webster, M. L., retel. *On the Trail Made of Dawn: Native American Creation Stories* (4–9). 2001, Linnet LB $19.50 (978-0-208-02497-8). 69pp. The author retells 13 creation stories and places them in cultural context. (Rev: HBG 3/02; SLJ 12/01) [398.2]

12798 Wolfson, Evelyn. *Inuit Mythology* (5–9). Illus. by William Sauts Bock. Series: Mythology. 2001, Enslow LB $26.60 (978-0-7660-1559-3). 128pp. Seven tales from Inuit folklore are accompanied by information on the history and culture of the Inuit peoples. (Rev: BL 4/15/02; HBG 3/02; SLJ 3/02) [398.2]

12799 Wood, Audrey. *The Rainbow Bridge: Inspired by a Chumash Tale* (1–4). Illus. by Robert Florczak. 1995, Harcourt $16.00 (978-0-15-265475-7). 32pp. In this Chumash tale, earth goddess Hutash turns some of her people into dolphins to save them from drowning. (Rev: BCCB 12/95; BL 12/1/95; SLJ 10/95) [398.24]

12800 Young, Richard, and Judy D. Young, eds. *Race with Buffalo: And Other Native American Stories for Young Readers* (3–7). Illus. by Wendell E. Hall. 1994, August House $19.95 (978-0-87483-343-0); paper $9.95 (978-0-87483-342-3). 175pp. This collection of 32 American Indian folktales includes such genres as creation and trickster stories. (Rev: SLJ 8/94) [398.2]

United States

12801 Anaya, Rudolfo. *My Land Sings: Stories from the Rio Grande* (5–9). 1999, Morrow $17.00 (978-0-688-15078-5). A magical collection of 10 stories, set mostly in New Mexico, that deal with Mexican and Native American folklore. (Rev: BL 8/99; HBG 10/00; SLJ 9/99) [398.2]

12802 Birdseye, Tom. *Soap! Soap! Don't Forget the Soap! An Appalachian Folktale* (3–6). Illus. by Andrew Glass. 1993, Holiday House LB $16.95 (978-0-8234-1005-7). 32pp. An adaptation of a familiar story about a forgetful hero sent to the store by his mother. (Rev: BCCB 6/93; BL 3/15/93; HB 5/93) [398.2]

12803 Blair, Eric. *Paul Bunyan* (K–1). Illus. by Micah Chambers-Coldberg. Series: Read-It! Readers Tall Tales. 2005, Picture Window LB $19.93 (978-1-4048-0976-5). 32pp. The familiar tall tale is retold for beginning readers, with colorful illustrations. (Rev: SLJ 7/05) [398.2]

12804 Brimner, Larry Dane, retel. *Captain Stormalong* (PS–2). Illus. by Chi Chung. Series: Imagination Series: Tall Tales. 2004, Compass Point LB $26.60 (978-0-7565-0601-8). 32pp. Captain Stormalong, a larger-than-life character who first appeared in an old sea chantey, springs to life again in this spirited retelling of some of his most audacious adventures. (Rev: SLJ 7/04) [398.2]

12805 Brown, Marcia. *Backbone of the King: The Story of Paka'a and His Son Ku* (5–7). Illus. by author. 1984, Univ. of Hawaii $19.00 (978-0-8248-0963-8). 180pp. A reissue of the book based on a Hawaiian legend of a boy who wants to help his exiled father. [398.2]

12806 Cohen, Daniel. *Railway Ghosts and Highway Horrors* (3–5). Illus. by Stephen Marchesi. 1993, Scholastic paper $2.95 (978-0-590-45423-0). 112pp. Phantom hitchhikers and accident victims fill this anthology of American and British travelers' lore. (Rev: BL 11/15/91) [133.1]

12807 Davis, Aubrey. *Sody Salleratus* (PS–2). Illus. by Alan Daniel and Lea Daniel. 1998, Kids Can $14.95 (978-1-55074-281-7). 32pp. In this American folktale, a wise squirrel solves the problem of having a bear in town that delights in eating everyone. (Rev: BL 3/15/98; HBG 10/98; SLJ 4/98) [398.2]

12808 Davis, David. *Texas Zeke and the Longhorn* (PS–3). Illus. by Alan Fearl Stacy. 2006, Pelican $15.95 (978-1-58980-348-0). Set in Texas, this version of "The Old Woman and Her Pig" features Old Zeke, who buys a longhorn steer that refuses to be corralled and must turn to a parade of others for help. (Rev: SLJ 9/06) [398.2]

12809 Davis, Donald. *Jack and the Animals* (PS–2). Illus. by Kitty Harvill. 1995, August House $15.95 (978-0-87483-413-0). 32pp. Jack and a group of unhappy animals outwit a gang of robbers in this Appalachian tale. (Rev: BL 10/1/95; SLJ 1/96)

12810 dePaola, Tomie. *Tomie dePaola's Front Porch Tales and North Country Whoppers* (2–5). Illus. by author. 2007, Putnam $17.99 (978-0-399-24754-5). 64pp. Arranged by season, this is a humorous collection of original jokes, tall tales, stories, and short quips inspired by 35 years living in New England. (Rev: BCCB 12/07; BL 11/1/07; SLJ 11/07) [398.2]

12811 DeSpain, Pleasant. *Sweet Land of Story: Thirty-Six American Tales to Tell* (4–6). Illus. 2000, August House $19.95 (978-0-87483-569-4). 176pp. This anthology of 36 American folktales ranges from tall tales and Native American stories to Jack tales and traditional ghost stories. (Rev: BL 12/15/00; HBG 10/01; SLJ 12/00) [398.2]

12812 Doucet, Sharon Arms. *Lapin Plays Possum: Trickster Tales from the Louisiana Bayou* (4–6). Illus. by Scott Cook. 2002, Farrar $18.10 (978-0-374-34328-6). 64pp. This is a well-illustrated collection of three tales about the trickster rabbit from Cajun country told with many humorous bayou phrases. (Rev: BL 4/15/02; HB 5/02; HBG 10/02; SLJ 4/02) [398.2]

12813 Doucet, Sharon Arms. *Why Lapin's Ears Are Long and Other Tales from the Louisiana Bayou* (4–6). Illus. by David Catrow. 1997, Orchard LB $19.99 (978-0-531-33041-8). 64pp. Three entertaining folktales from Cajun country that feature the trickster rabbit. (Rev: BL 8/97; HB 9/97; HBG 3/98; SLJ 9/97) [398.2]

12814 Galdone, Joanna. *The Tailypo: A Ghost Story* (1–3). Illus. by Paul Galdone. 1984, Houghton paper $7.95 (978-0-395-30084-8). In this ghostly story, a mysterious creature returns to retrieve his tail, cut off by an old man. [398.2]

12815 Hamilton, Martha, and Mitch Weiss. *The Hidden Feast: A Folktale from the American South* (PS–2). Illus. by Don Tate. 2006, August House $16.95 (978-0-87483-758-2). 32pp. Rooster learns an important lesson when he rejects what he believes is cornbread at a party. (Rev: BL 3/1/06; SLJ 4/06) [398.2]

12816 Hamilton, Virginia. *Bruh Rabbit and the Tar Baby Girl* (K–4). Illus. by James Ransome. 2003, Scholastic $16.95 (978-0-590-47376-7). Rich watercolors and the Gullah dialect make this an appealing retelling of the familiar story. (Rev: HBG 4/04; SLJ 11/03) [398.2]

12817 Hamilton, Virginia. *Her Stories: African American Folktales, Fairy Tales, and True Tales* (5–8). Illus. 1995, Scholastic paper $22.95 (978-0-590-47370-5). Nineteen tales about African American females are retold in the wonderful style of Virginia Hamilton. (Rev: BL 11/1/95*; SLJ 11/95*) [398.2]

12818 Hamilton, Virginia. *The People Could Fly: American Black Folk Tales* (4–9). Illus. by Leo Dillon and Diane Dillon. 1985, Knopf LB $18.99 (978-0-394-96925-1); paper $13.00 (978-0-679-84336-8). 192pp. A retelling of 24 folktales — some little known, others familiar, such as Tar Baby. (Rev: BCCB 7–8/85; BL 7/85; SLJ 11/85) [398.2]

12819 Harper, Wilhelmina, retel. *The Gunniwolf* (PS–1). Illus. by Barbara Upton. 2003, Dutton

$15.99 (978-0-525-46785-4). Harper's classic tale of the Little Girl who disregards warnings and encounters the not-so-fearsome Gunniwolf appears with new illustrations and a woodland setting. (Rev: HBG 10/03; SLJ 9/03) [398.2]

12820 Harris, Jim. *Jack and the Giant: A Story Full of Beans* (K–4). Illus. 1997, Northland LB $15.95 (978-0-87358-680-1). 32pp. This version of "Jack and the Beanstalk" had Jack living on a ranch in Arizona with his mother, Annie Okey-Dokey. (Rev: BL 2/1/98; HBG 3/98; SLJ 2/98) [398.2]

12821 Harris, Joel Chandler. *Jump! The Adventures of Brer Rabbit* (3–5). Adapted by Van Dyke Parks and Malcolm Jones. Illus. by Barry Moser. 1986, Harcourt $15.95 (978-0-15-241350-7); paper $7.00 (978-0-15-201493-3). 40pp. An edition with tracings of the stories' roots in oral tradition. (Rev: BCCB 11/86; BL 1/1/87; SLJ 11/86) [398.2]

12822 Hayes, Joe. *El Cucuy! A Bogeyman Cuento in English and Spanish* (K–4). Illus. by Honorio Robledo. 2001, Cinco Puntos $15.95 (978-0-938317-54-8). 32pp. A southwestern bogeyman comes down from his mountain to carry off bad children. (Rev: BL 7/01; HBG 10/01; SLJ 7/01) [398.2]

12823 Hayes, Joe. *Little Gold Star / Estrellita de oro: A Cinderella Cuento* (PS–3). Illus. by Gloria Osuna Perez and Lucía Angela Pérez. 2000, Cinco Puntos $15.95 (978-0-938317-49-4). 32pp. Told in English and Spanish, this is an interesting version of the Cinderella story that is popular in the mountain communities of New Mexico. (Rev: BCCB 7–8/00; BL 5/15/00; HBG 10/00; SLJ 6/00) [398.2]

12824 Hayes, Joe. *Pajaro Verde / The Green Bird* (2–4). Illus. by Antonio Castro L. 2002, Cinco Puntos $16.95 (978-0-938317-65-4). 40pp. A young woman marries a bird to save him from evil in this New Mexican folktale, told in both Spanish and English, filled with magic and monsters. (Rev: BL 10/15/02; HBG 3/03) [398.2]

12825 Hayward, Linda. *All Stuck Up* (1–3). Illus. by Normand Chartier. 1990, Random paper $3.99 (978-0-679-80216-7). 32pp. The tar baby story featuring Brer Rabbit is retold. (Rev: BCCB 7–8/92; BL 6/1/90; SLJ 8/90) [398.2]

12826 Hicks, Ray, and Lynn Salsi. *The Jack Tales* (3–5). Illus. 2000, Callaway $24.95 (978-0-935112-58-0). 40pp. Two different versions of each of three plucky Jack tales are effectively presented in print and on a CD. (Rev: BL 11/15/00*; HBG 3/01; SLJ 11/00) [398.2]

12827 Hunt, Angela E. *The Tale of Three Trees: A Traditional Folktale* (K–2). Illus. by Tim Jonke. 1989, Lion $14.99 (978-0-7459-1743-6). 32pp. A folktale about three trees — a manger for the Christ child, a fishing boat that carries Jesus, and timbers that become the cross. (Rev: BL 11/1/89) [398.2]

12828 Hurston, Zora Neale. *Lies and Other Tall Tales* (PS–2). Illus. by Christopher Myers. 2005, HarperCollins $15.99 (978-0-06-000655-6). 40pp. Imaginative illustrations enhance the irreverence of these tall tales collected by Hurston in the 1930s. (Rev: BL 9/15/05*; SLJ 11/05) [398.2]

12829 Hurston, Zora Neale. *The Six Fools* (PS–2). Ed. by Joyce Carol Thomas. Illus. by Ann Tanksley. 2006, HarperCollins $15.99 (978-0-06-000646-4). 40pp. In this story drawn from the collection of folk tales collected by Zora Neale Hurston during the 1930s, a young groom-to-be travels the world in search of fools as big as his fiancee and her parents. (Rev: BL 2/1/06; SLJ 1/06*) [398.2]

12830 Hurston, Zora Neale, and Joyce Carol Thomas. *The Three Witches* (2–4). Illus. by Faith Ringgold. 2006, HarperCollins $15.99 (978-0-06-000649-5). 32pp. In this adaptation of an African American tale first collected by Zora Neale Hurston, two young siblings escape the clutches of three witches with a little help from their grandmother, three hound dogs, and a snake. (Rev: BL 6/1–15/06; SLJ 8/06) [398.2]

12831 Jacobs, Jimmy. *Moonlight Through the Pines: Tales from Georgia Evenings* (5–7). Illus. 2000, Franklin-Sarrett paper $11.95 (978-0-9637477-3-0). 115pp. A collection of humorous reminiscences, family stories, tall tales, and other examples of folklore, all from the South. (Rev: BL 8/00) [398.2]

12832 Keats, Ezra Jack. *John Henry: An American Legend* (1–3). Illus. by author. 1965, Knopf paper $5.99 (978-0-394-89052-4). 32pp. Large, bold figures capture the spirit of the hero who died with a hammer in his hand. [398.2]

12833 Kellogg, Steven. *Paul Bunyan* (K–4). Illus. by author. 1984, Morrow $17.89 (978-0-688-03850-2); paper $6.99 (978-0-688-05800-5). 40pp. Several stories about Paul and the blue ox Babe, all wittily illustrated. (Rev: BL 2/1/04) [398.2]

12834 Kellogg, Steven, retel. *Pecos Bill* (K–3). Illus. by Steven Kellogg. 1986, Scholastic paper $6.99 (978-0-688-09924-4). 32pp. Humor permeates these tall tales of the American folk hero. (Rev: BCCB 11/86; BL 9/1/86; SLJ 9/86) [398.2]

12835 Kellogg, Steven. *Sally Ann Thunder Ann Whirlwind Crockett* (PS–3). Illus. 1995, Morrow $16.89 (978-0-688-14043-4). 48pp. A humorous look at the life of Davy Crockett's wife and her equally amazing exploits. (Rev: BCCB 9/95; BL 8/95; SLJ 10/95) [398.2]

12836 Kidd, Ronald, ed. *On Top of Old Smoky: A Collection of Songs and Stories from Appalachia* (4–6). Illus. by Linda Anderson. 1992, Ideals $13.95 (978-0-8249-8569-1). 38pp. A handsome collection of songs and stories from Appalachia with distinctive illustrations. (Rev: BL 12/1/92; SLJ 4/05) [782]

12837 Kimmel, Eric A. *The Frog Princess: A Tlingit Legend from Alaska* (PS–2). Illus. by Rosanne Litzinger. 2006, Holiday $16.95 (978-0-8234-1618-9). 32pp. A beautiful girl falls in love with and marries a frog, much to the dismay of her Tlingit family. (Rev: BL 5/1/06; SLJ 6/06) [398.2]

12838 Kimmel, Eric A. *The Runaway Tortilla* (K–2). Illus. by Randy Cecil. 2000, Winslow $16.95 (978-1-890817-18-3). A silly tortilla runs away but is finally caught and eaten by Señor Coyote. (Rev: BCCB 12/00; HBG 10/01; SLJ 10/00) [398.2]

12839 Krensky, Stephen. *John Henry* (2–4). Illus. by Mark Oldroyd. Series: On Your Own Folklore.

2006, Lerner $25.26 (978-1-57505-887-0). 48pp. Tall tales chronicle some of the amazing feats attributed to John Henry in American railroading folklore. (Rev: BL 9/1/06; SLJ 8/06) [398.2]

12840 Krensky, Stephen, adapt. *Paul Bunyan* (1–4). Illus. by Craig Orback. Series: On My Own Folklore. 2006, Millbrook LB $25.26 (978-1-57505-888-7). 48pp. For beginning readers, this is an introduction to lumberjack Paul Bunyan and his amazing feats. Also use *Pecos Bill* (2006). (Rev: SLJ 8/06) [398.2]

12841 Liddell, Janice. *Imani and the Flying Africans* (2–5). Illus. by Linda Nickens. 1994, Africa World $14.95 (978-0-86543-365-6); paper $6.95 (978-0-86543-366-3). After hearing about the Flying Africans, who could rise into the air and escape slavery, young Imani dreams that he is captured by kidnappers and uses the same method to achieve freedom. (Rev: SLJ 11/94) [398.2]

12842 Lyons, Mary. *Roy Makes a Car* (PS–2). Illus. by Terry Widener. 2005, Simon & Schuster $16.95 (978-0-689-84640-3). 32pp. A tall tale about auto mechanic Roy's designn for an accident-proof car, based on a folktale collected by Zora Neale Hurston in the 1930s. (Rev: BL 2/1/05; SLJ 2/05) [398.2]

12843 McDermott, Gerald. *Pig-Boy: A Trickster Tale from Hawai'i* (K–1). Illus. by author. 2009, Harcourt $16.00 (978-0-15-216590-1). 32pp. A naughty Pig-Boy uses his grandmother's magic to shapeshift and evade the annoyed King and Pele, the goddess of fire, in this story based on Hawaiian myth. (Rev: BCCB 5/09; BL 5/15/09; HB 7/09; SLJ 7/09) [398.2]

12844 McGill, Alice. *Sure as Sunrise: Stories of Bruh Rabbit and His Walkin' Talkin' Friends* (PS–3). Illus. by Don Tate. 2004, Houghton $17.00 (978-0-618-21196-8). 48pp. Characterful illustrations accompany these five trickster tales that McGill learned when she was growing up in an African American community in North Carolina. (Rev: BL 4/15/04*; SLJ 6/04) [398.2]

12845 Medearis, Angela Shelf. *Tailypo: A Newfangled Tall Tale* (K–3). Illus. by Sterling Brown. 1996, Holiday House LB $15.95 (978-0-8234-1249-5). 32pp. A variation on the folktale about a monster that leaves its tail behind in the cabin of an African American boy. (Rev: BL 11/1/96; SLJ 1/97) [398.2]

12846 Miller, Bobbi. *One Fine Trade* (PS–2). Illus. by Will Hillenbrand. 2009, Holiday $16.95 (978-0-8234-1836-7). 32pp. Based on a folk song, this is a cumulative tale about a peddler seeking a dress for his daughter's wedding. (Rev: BCCB 5/09; BLO 5/27/09; SLJ 3/09) [398.2]

12847 Nordenstrom, Michael. *Pele and the Rivers of Fire* (2–4). Illus. 2002, Bess $10.95 (978-1-57306-079-0). 32pp. The power of Pele, the Hawaiian volcano goddess, is brought to life by spectacular, vivid paintings accompanied by a simple retelling of Pele's move to Hawaii from Tahiti and her battles with her sister. (Rev: BL 12/1/02; HBG 3/03; SLJ 1/03) [299]

12848 Philip, Neil, ed. *Stockings of Buttermilk: American Folktales* (4–5). Illus. 1999, Clarion $20.00 (978-0-395-84980-4). 124pp. A collection of 18 folktales that had their roots in Europe (e.g., "Jack and the Beanstalk") but were changed when imported into America — often by African American storytellers. (Rev: BL 9/1/99; HB 11/99; HBG 3/00; SLJ 10/99) [398.2]

12849 Quattlebaum, Mary. *Sparks Fly High: The Legend of Dancing Point* (PS–2). Illus. by Leonid Gore. 2006, Farrar $16.00 (978-0-374-34452-8). 40pp. In this spirited retelling of a Virginia folktale, Colonel Lightfoot competes with the devil in a dance contest. (Rev: BL 10/15/06; SLJ 12/06) [398.2]

12850 Reneaux, J. J. *Haunted Bayou: And Other Cajun Ghost Stories* (4–8). 1994, August House paper $9.95 (978-0-87483-385-0). 158pp. Thirteen scary, entertaining folktales from Cajun country are retold effectively. (Rev: SLJ 12/94) [398.2]

12851 Reneaux, J. J. *Why Alligator Hates Dog* (1–3). Illus. by Donnie Lee Green. 1995, August House $15.95 (978-0-87483-412-3). 32pp. Dog loves to torment Alligator, but the wily reptile plots his revenge. (Rev: BL 10/15/95; SLJ 1/96) [398.3]

12852 Rounds, Glen. *Ol' Paul, the Mighty Logger* (3–6). Illus. by author. 1976, Holiday House paper $5.95 (978-0-8234-0713-2). 96pp. An account of the incredible exploits of one of our national folk heroes. [398.2]

12853 San Souci, Robert D. *Little Pierre: A Cajun Story from Louisiana* (1–4). Illus. by David Catrow. 2003, Harcourt $16.00 (978-0-15-202482-6). Drawn from Cajun folklore, this variation on the Tom Thumb theme tells how Pierre, dwarfed by his four older brothers, saves the day and rescues his fumbling brothers and the comely Marie-Louise from the Swamp Ogre. (Rev: HBG 4/04; SLJ 1/04) [398.2]

12854 San Souci, Robert D. *The Secret of the Stones* (2–4). Illus. by James Ransome. 1999, Penguin $16.99 (978-0-8037-1640-7). 40pp. In this folktale with roots in both Arkansas and Zaire, a childless couple tries to rescue two orphans who have been turned into pebbles. (Rev: BCCB 1/00; BL 1/1–15/00; HBG 3/00; SLJ 2/00) [398.2]

12855 San Souci, Robert D., retel. *Sister Tricksters: Rollicking Tales of Clever Females* (3–6). Illus. by Daniel San Souci. 2006, August House $19.95 (978-0-87483-791-9). 69pp. Molly Cottontail, Miz Grasshopper, and Miz Goose are among the characters in this collection of retold tales about memorable female tricksters. (Rev: SLJ 9/06*) [398.2]

12856 Schwartz, Alvin. *More Scary Stories to Tell in the Dark* (4–7). Illus. by Stephen Gammell. 1984, HarperCollins LB $16.89 (978-0-397-32082-0); paper $5.99 (978-0-06-440177-7). 128pp. Brief tales from folk stories and hearsay with a scary bent. [398.2]

12857 Schwartz, Alvin, ed. *Scary Stories to Tell in the Dark* (3–8). Illus. by Stephen Gammell. 1981, HarperCollins LB $16.89 (978-0-397-31927-5); paper $5.99 (978-0-06-440170-8). 128pp. Ghost stories collected from American folklore. [398.2]

12858 Stevens, Janet. *Tops and Bottoms* (PS–2). Illus. 1995, Harcourt $16.00 (978-0-15-292851-3). 32pp. An African American folktale about how Hare takes unfair advantage of Bear in a garden project. (Rev: BCCB 4/95; BL 3/15/95*; HB 5/95; SLJ 5/95) [398.2]

12859 Willey, Margaret. *Clever Beatrice* (PS–3). Illus. by Heather Solomon. 2001, Simon & Schuster $16.00 (978-0-689-83254-3). 40pp. A tall tale from the wilds of Michigan in which a little girl named Beatrice outwits a rich giant. (Rev: BL 7/01; HB 11/01*; HBG 3/02; SLJ 10/01) [398.2]

12860 Wooldridge, Connie N. *Wicked Jack* (K–3). Illus. by Will Hillenbrand. 1995, Holiday House LB $16.95 (978-0-8234-1101-6). 32pp. A retelling of the Southern tale about a mean blacksmith who outwits the Devil and his young sons. (Rev: BCCB 12/95; BL 11/1/95; SLJ 12/95*) [398.2]

South and Central America

Mexico and Other Central American Lands

12861 Bierhorst, John. *Doctor Coyote: A Native American Aesop's Fables* (3–5). Illus. by Wendy Watson. 1987, Macmillan LB $15.95 (978-0-02-709780-1). 48pp. Aesop's fables as they were translated into Spanish in the New World. (Rev: BCCB 3/87; BL 3/15/87; SLJ 5/87) [398.2]

12862 Climo, Shirley, retel. *The Little Red Ant and the Great Big Crumb* (PS–2). Illus. by Francisco Mora. 1995, Clarion $16.00 (978-0-395-70732-6). 39pp. A tiny ant seeks help in vain from other animals to move a heavy crumb in this Mexican tale. (Rev: SLJ 11/95) [398.2]

12863 Coburn, Jewell Reinhart. *Domitila: A Cinderella Tale from the Mexican Tradition* (3–5). Illus. 2000, Shen's $16.95 (978-1-885008-13-8). 32pp. This variation on the story of Cinderella comes from the folklore of Hidalgo, Mexico. (Rev: BL 5/15/00; HBG 10/00; SLJ 7/00) [398.2]

12864 Czernecki, Stefan, and Timothy Rhodes. *The Sleeping Bread* (1–3). Illus. by Stefan Czernecki. 1992, Hyperion $14.95 (978-1-56282-183-8). 40pp. In this Central American folktale, the tears of a beggar who is driven out of town change the village's bread when they are added to the dough. (Rev: BCCB 9/92; BL 4/15/92; SLJ 8/92) [398.2]

12865 dePaola, Tomie. *The Legend of the Poinsettia* (K–4). Illus. 1994, Penguin LB $16.99 (978-0-399-21692-3). 32pp. Lucinda is unhappy because she has ruined the blanket that was intended for use in a Christmas procession. (Rev: BL 8/94; HB 11/94; SLJ 4/05) [398.2]

12866 de Sauza, James. *Brother Anansi and the Cattle Ranch / El Hermano Anansi y el Rancho de Ganada* (3–6). Adapted by Harriet Rohmer. Illus. by Stephen Von Mason. 1989, Children's Book Pr. $14.95 (978-0-89239-044-1). 32pp. A bilingual retelling of the ancient folktale about the trickster spider, now transplanted to Nicaragua. Two others in this dual-language series are: *Mr. Sugar Came to Town/La Visita del Señor Azucar* (1989); *Uncle Nacho's Hat/El Sombrero de Tio Nacho* (1989). (Rev: BL 11/15/89) [398.2]

12867 Ehlert, Lois. *Cuckoo / Cucu* (PS–2). Trans. by Gloria de Aragon Andujar. Illus. 1997, Harcourt $16.00 (978-0-15-200274-9). 40pp. In this Mayan tale, Cuckoo saves the annual harvest of seeds on which the other birds live during the winter. (Rev: BCCB 6/97; BL 4/1/97*; HBG 3/98; SLJ 3/97) [398.2]

12868 Endredy, James. *The Journey of Tunuri and the Blue Deer: A Huichol Indian Story* (1–4). 2003, Bear & Company $15.95 (978-1-59143-016-2). 32pp. Based on a traditional folk tale, this gentle story highlighted by traditional yarn art tells how an enchanted deer leads a young Huichol boy on a magical journey to meet the spirits of nature. (Rev: BL 12/1/03; SLJ 1/04) [398.2]

12869 Gerson, Mary-Joan. *Fiesta Feminina: Celebrating Women in Mexican Folktales* (4–8). Illus. 2001, Barefoot Books $19.99 (978-1-84148-365-8). 64pp. This volume includes eight tales from Mexican folklore about strong and magical women, presented with bold illustrations, a pronunciation guide, and a glossary. (Rev: BL 9/15/01; HBG 3/02; SLJ 10/01) [398.2]

12870 Harper, Jo. *The Legend of Mexicatl* (K–3). Illus. by Robert Casilla. 1998, Turtle $15.95 (978-1-890515-05-8). 32pp. A handsome retelling of the Mexican legend about the teenage boy who is destined to lead his people out of the desert. (Rev: BL 4/15/98) [398.2]

12871 Kimmel, Eric A. *Cactus Soup* (1–3). Trans. and illus. by Phil Huling. 2004, Marshall Cavendish $16.95 (978-0-7614-5155-6). 32pp. "Stone Soup" meets chiles and beans in this Mexico-based variant involving hungry revolutionary forces. (Rev: BL 9/15/04*; SLJ 10/04) [398.2]

12872 Kimmel, Eric A. *Montezuma and the Fall of the Aztecs* (2–5). Illus. by Daniel San Souci. 2000, Holiday House $16.95 (978-0-8234-1452-9). 32pp. After introducing the history and culture of the Aztecs, this picture book covers the reign of Montezuma, the coming of Cortes, and the Aztec leader's defeat. (Rev: BL 1/1–15/00; HBG 10/00; SLJ 3/00) [972]

12873 Kimmel, Eric A. *The Two Mountains: An Aztec Legend* (3–5). Illus. 2000, Holiday House $16.95 (978-0-8234-1504-5). 32pp. This Aztec legend tells how two young lovers are transformed into the two mountains that overlook the Valley of Mexico. (Rev: BL 5/15/00; HBG 10/00; SLJ 4/00) [398.2]

12874 Love, Hallie N., and Bonni Larson, retels. *Watakame's Journey: The Story of the Great Flood and the New World: A Huichol Indian Tale* (2–6). Illus. 1999, Clear Light $14.95 (978-1-56416-029-4). 84pp. This is a Mexican version of the Noah story featuring a young boy who is selected by the goddess of all growing things to build a boat to withstand the coming flood. (Rev: SLJ 12/99) [398.2]

12875 Lowery, Linda, and Richard Keep. *The Choco-late Tree: A Mayan Folktale* (PS–3). Illus. by Janice L. Porter. 2008, Lerner LB $25.26 (978-0-8225-7545-0). 48pp. This delicious beginning chapter book features lively words and attractive illustrations that tell the Mayan story of how humans got chocolate. (Rev: BL 9/15/08) [398.2]

12876 MacDonald, Margaret Read. *Conejito: A Folk-tale from Panama* (K–3). Illus. by Geraldo Vaério. 2006, August House $16.95 (978-0-87483-779-7). 32pp. In this rhyming folktale from Panama, Cone-jito, a little rabbit, sets off to visit his aunt and along the way cleverly manages to escape the clutches of three fearsome predators. Conejito's song is included, tempting young children to sing along. (Rev: BL 3/15/06; SLJ 4/06) [398.2]

12877 Madrigal, Antonio H. *The Eagle and the Rain-bow: Timeless Tales from México* (4–7). Illus. by Tomie dePaola. 1997, Fulcrum $15.95 (978-1-55591-317-5). 56pp. A collection of wise, wonder-ful, but little-known folktales from Mexico. (Rev: BL 7/97; HBG 4/04) [398.2]

12878 Marcos, Subcomandante. *The Story of Colors / La Historia de los Colores: A Folktale from the Jungles of Chiapas* (K–4). Trans. by Anne Bar Din. Illus. by Domitila Domínguez. 1999, Cinco Puntos $15.95 (978-0-938317-45-6). This folktale told in both Spanish and English explains the origins of the colors in the world and how the macaw got its bright plumage. (Rev: HBG 10/99; SLJ 5/99) [398.2]

12879 Menchú, Rigoberta, and Dante Liano. *The Honey Jar* (4–6). Trans. by David Unger. Illus. by Domi. 2006, Groundwood $18.95 (978-0-88899-670-1). 64pp. Menchú, winner of the Nobel Peace Prize, recounts Guatemalan folktales she learned as a child; illustrations reflect the text in folk-art style. (Rev: BL 3/15/06; SLJ 6/06) [398.2]

12880 Montejo, Victor, retel. *Popol Vuh: A Sacred Book of the Maya* (5–8). Trans. by David Under. Illus. by Luis Garay. 1999, Groundwood $19.95 (978-0-88899-334-2). 85pp. A creation story from the Mayans in a beautifully designed book that fea-tures gods, giants, mortals, and animals. (Rev: HBG 3/00; SLJ 12/99) [398.2]

12881 Mora, Pat. *The Night the Moon Fell* (PS–K). Illus. by Domi. 2000, Douglas & McIntyre $16.95 (978-0-88899-398-4). 32pp. A Mayan myth about how Luna, the moon, is shattered when she falls from the sky and how she gathers strength to repair herself and return to her home. (Rev: BL 9/1/00; HBG 3/01; SLJ 11/00) [398.2]

12882 Mora, Pat. *The Race of Toad and Deer* (PS–1). Illus. by Domi. 2001, Groundwood $15.95 (978-0-88899-434-9). 32pp. This is a newly illustrated and rewritten version of the Mayan take on the tortoise and the hare, first published in 1995. (Rev: BCCB 12/01; BL 12/15/01; HBG 3/02) [398.2]

12883 Ober, Hal. *How Music Came to the World: An Ancient Mexican Myth* (1–4). Illus. by Carol Ober. 1994, Houghton $17.00 (978-0-395-67523-6). 32pp. How music came to the world is the subject of this folktale dating to pre-Columbian times. (Rev: BL 3/15/94; SLJ 10/94) [398.2]

12884 Philip, Neil, ed. *Horse Hooves and Chicken Feet: Mexican Folktales* (4–8). Illus. by Jacqueline Main. 2003, Clarion $19.00 (978-0-618-19463-6). 83pp. Bright folk-art illustrations accompany 14 stories that feature humor and the importance of the Catholic church. (Rev: BL 10/15/03; HBG 4/04; SLJ 9/03) [398.2]

12885 Rockwell, Anne. *The Boy Who Wouldn't Obey* (2–4). Illus. 2000, Greenwillow $17.99 (978-0-688-14881-2). 24pp. In this Mayan legend a young boy steals the tools of Chac, the god of the sky, but doesn't know how to control them. (Rev: BCCB 7–8/00; BL 5/15/00; HBG 10/00; SLJ 6/00) [398.2]

Puerto Rico and Other Caribbean Islands

12886 Breinburg, Petronella. *Stories from the Carib-bean* (2–4). Illus. by Syrah Arnold and Tina Barber. Series: Multicultural Stories. 2000, Raintree LB $27.12 (978-0-7398-1334-8). 48pp. Ghost stories, creation fables, and animal stories are included in this interesting anthology. (Rev: HBG 10/00; SLJ 11/00) [398.2]

12887 Deedy, Carmen A. *Martina the Beautiful Cockroach* (K–3). Illus. by Michael Austin. 2007, Peachtree $16.95 (978-1-56145-399-3). 32pp. A surprise ends this rollicking story of how Martina, a lovely cockroach, chooses a husband; an adaptation of a Cuban folktale. (Rev: BL 10/1/07; LMC 1/08; SLJ 10/07) [398.2] ∩

12888 Gershator, Phillis. *Tukama Tootles the Flute* (PS–3). Illus. by Synthia Saint James. 1994, Orchard LB $16.99 (978-0-531-08661-2). 32pp. A flute-playing youngster uses his music to escape the clutches of a giant in this folktale from the Virgin Islands. (Rev: BCCB 4/94; BL 5/1/94; HB 5/94; SLJ 4/94) [398.2]

12889 Hallworth, Grace. *Sing Me a Story: Song and Dance Stories from the Caribbean* (K–3). Illus. by John Clementson. 2002, August House $19.95 (978-0-87483-672-1). 48pp. Caribbean folktales that involve song are accompanied by music and lyrics as well as lively and evocative collage borders. (Rev: BL 11/1/02; HBG 3/03; SLJ 9/02) [398.2]

12890 Hayes, Joe, retel. *Baila, Nana, Baila/Dance, Nana, Dance: Cuban Folktales in English and Spanish* (3–6). Illus. by Mauricio Trenard Sayago. 2008, Cinco Puntos $20.95 (978-1-933693-17-0). 128pp. Thirteen diverse, bilingual folk tales from Cuba have elements of stories from Spain, Africa, and the Caribbean. (Rev: BCCB 1/09; LMC 5/09; SLJ 2/09) [398.2]

12891 Izcoa, Carmen Rivera, adapt. *Mediopollito / Half-a-Chick* (K–3). Illus. by Nívea O. Montáñez. 1996, Ediciones Huracan $10.50 (978-0-929157-43-6). A Puerto Rican folktale about a bird that punish-es the king for being mean and selfish. (Rev: BL 2/1/04; SLJ 11/97) [398.2]

12892 Jaffe, Nina. *The Golden Flower: A Taino Myth from Puerto Rico* (K–3). Illus. by Enrique O. Sánchez. 1996, Simon & Schuster $16.95 (978-0-

689-80469-4). 32pp. The creation of the island of Puerto Rico is told in this Taino myth about a magical pumpkin. (Rev: BCCB 6/96; BL 6/1–15/96; SLJ 7/96) [398.2]

12893 Keens-Douglas, Richard. *Mama God, Papa God: A Caribbean Tale* (K–2). Illus. by Stefan Czernecki. 1999, Crocodile LB $15.95 (978-1-56656-307-9). A Caribbean Island folktale attractively illustrated that tells a creation story centering around Mama God and Papa God and how they created diversity in the people that they made. (Rev: HBG 10/99; SLJ 7/99) [398.2]

12894 Linzer, Lila. *Once Upon an Island* (2–5). 1999, Front St. $15.95 (978-1-886910-10-2). 76pp. Four tales about animals (including bees, goats, and doves) from the island of St. Croix are retold in a dialect that captures the lilting rhythms of West Indian English. (Rev: HBG 10/99; SLJ 4/99) [398.2]

12895 MacDonald, Amy. *Please, Malese!* (K–3). Illus. by Emily Lisker. 2002, Farrar $16.00 (978-0-374-36000-9). 32pp. This variation of a Haitian folktale tells the story of wily Malese, a trickster who can convince the villagers of anything. (Rev: BL 8/02; HB 9/02; HBG 3/03; SLJ 9/02) [398.2]

12896 Moreton, Daniel. *La Cucaracha Martina: A Caribbean Folktale* (PS–2). Illus. 1997, Turtle $14.95 (978-1-890515-03-4). 32pp. A refined cockroach finally finds her mate, a handsome cricket, in this Caribbean folktale. (Rev: BL 1/1–15/98; SLJ 11/97) [398.2]

12897 San Souci, Robert D. *The Faithful Friend* (K–4). Illus. by Brian Pinkney. 1995, Simon & Schuster paper $16.00 (978-0-02-786131-0). 40pp. On the island of Martinique, Hippolyte tries to save his friend's wedding from destruction by the bride's evil uncle. (Rev: BCCB 9/95; BL 4/15/95*; HB 9/95; SLJ 6/95) [398.2]

South America

12898 Aldana, Patricia, ed. *Jade and Iron: Latin American Tales from Two Cultures* (5–8). Trans. by Hugh Hazelton. Illus. 1996, Douglas & McIntyre $18.95 (978-0-88899-256-7). 64pp. Fourteen folktales on a variety of subjects and from many regions in Latin America are retold in this large-format picture book. (Rev: BCCB 1/97; BL 12/1/96) [398.2]

12899 Delacre, Lulu, retel. *Golden Tales: Myths, Legends, and Folktales from Latin America* (4–8). Illus. 1996, Scholastic paper $18.95 (978-0-590-48186-1). Twelve important Latin American folktales from before and after the time of Columbus are featured. (Rev: BL 12/15/96; SLJ 9/96) [398.2]

12900 DeSpain, Pleasant. *The Dancing Turtle: A Folktale from Brazil* (K–3). Illus. by David Boston. 1998, August House $15.95 (978-0-87483-502-1). 32pp. Through trickery, wily Turtle escapes from her human captors in this Brazilian folktale set in a tropical rain forest. (Rev: BL 5/1/98; HBG 10/98; SLJ 5/98) [398.2]

12901 Ehlert, Lois. *Moon Rope: A Peruvian Folktale* (4–8). Illus. 1992, Harcourt $17.00 (978-0-15-255343-2). 40pp. In both English and Spanish, this is the story of Fox, who wants to go to the moon and persuades his friend Mole to go along. (Rev: BCCB 12/92; BL 10/15/92*; HB 11/92; SLJ 10/92*) [398.2]

12902 Knutson, Barbara. *Love and Roast Chicken: A Trickster Tale from the Andes Mountains* (PS–2). Illus. Series: Carolrhoda Picture Books. 2004, Carolrhoda $16.95 (978-1-57505-657-9). 32pp. A tiny guinea pig outwits both a fox and a farmer in this trickster tale set in the Andes. (Rev: BL 9/15/04; SLJ 11/04) [398.2]

12903 McDermott, Gerald. *Jabuti the Tortoise: A Trickster Tale from the Amazon* (K–2). Illus. 2001, Harcourt $16.00 (978-0-15-200496-5). 32pp. A brilliantly colorful retelling of the story of Jabuti, a tortoise who is tricked by a jealous vulture, who in turn is punished as the other birds gain colors and songs. (Rev: BL 9/15/01; HBG 3/02; SLJ 9/01) [398.2]

12904 MacDonald, Margaret Read, retel. *A Hen, a Chick and a String Guitar* (PS). Illus. by Sophie Fatus. 2005, Barefoot Books $17.99 (978-1-84148-796-0). An entertaining, musical, and instructive cumulative tale with Chilean origins in which a child's collection of animals grows until he has 16, plus a string guitar; a CD is included. (Rev: BCCB 5/05; SLJ 5/05) [398.2]

12905 Munduruku, Daniel. *Tales of the Amazon: How the Munduruku Indians Live* (5–8). Trans. by Jane Springer. Illus. by Laurabeatriz. 2000, Groundwood $18.95 (978-0-88899-392-2). 56pp. This is an interesting view of the life of the human inhabitants of the Amazon rain forest with material on lifestyles, houses, languages, myths, and marriage. (Rev: BL 9/1/03; HBG 3/01; SLJ 9/00) [981]

12906 Olaondo, Susana. *Julieta, ?Que Plantaste? / Julieta, What Did You Plant?* (K–2). Illus. 2001, Alfaguara paper $9.95 (9974-671-00-0). 32pp. This folktale about industrious Julieta the armadillo and the indolent but clever fox who tries to outwit her is sprinkled with Uruguayan phrases and accompanied by cartoonlike illustrations. (Rev: BL 12/15/01) [398.2]

12907 Pitcher, Caroline. *Mariana and the Merchild: A Folk Tale from Chile* (PS–3). Illus. by Jackie Morris. 2000, Eerdmans $17.00 (978-0-8028-5204-5). 32pp. In this Chilean folktale, Mariana, who lives alone on the beach, raises an infant mermaid until she is old enough to survive in the sea. (Rev: BL 3/1/00; HBG 10/00; SLJ 5/00) [398.2]

12908 Weiss, Jacqueline Shachter. *Young Brer Rabbit: And Other Trickster Tales from the Americas* (4–6). Illus. 1985, Stemmer $14.95 (978-0-88045-037-9); paper $9.95 (978-0-88045-138-3). 80pp. Fifteen stories translated from Spanish, French, and Portuguese. (Rev: BCCB 1/86; BL 3/1/86; SLJ 1/86) [398.2]

Mythology

General and Miscellaneous

12909 Baynes, Pauline. *Questionable Creatures: A Bestiary* (4–6). 2006, Eerdmans $18.00 (978-0-8028-5284-7). 48pp. A great introduction to the mythical animals and creatures that were thought to have existed in medieval times such as unicorns, satyrs, and the phoenix. (Rev: BL 11/15/06; SLJ 4/07) [398.24]

12910 Boughn, Michael. *Into the World of the Dead: Astonishing Adventures in the Underworld* (5–8). Illus. 2006, Annick LB $24.95 (978-1-55037-959-4); paper $12.95 (978-1-55037-958-7). 56pp. This illustrated collection of myths and legends from diverse cultures includes a variety of gods, monsters, and heroes who survived travels to the Underworld. (Rev: SLJ 1/07) [398.2]

12911 Dalal, Anita. *Myths of Oceania* (5–8). Series: Mythic World. 2002, Raintree LB $27.12 (978-0-7398-4978-1). 48pp. Information about Oceania and its people is included as well as 10 myths about the sea, fishing, and other unique aspects of island living. (Rev: BL 7/02; HBG 10/02) [398.3]

12912 Dalal, Anita. *Myths of Russia and the Slavs* (5–8). Series: Mythic World. 2002, Raintree LB $27.12 (978-0-7398-4979-8). 48pp. This lavishly illustrated, oversize volume contains 10 myths from Eastern Europe as well as material on the society that created them. (Rev: BL 7/02; HBG 10/02; SLJ 5/02) [398.2]

12913 Daning, Tom. *Mesoamerican Mythology: Quetzalcoatl* (3–6). Illus. 2006, Rosen LB $22.50 (978-1-4042-3401-7). 24pp. A graphic-novel version of the myth about the gods Quetzalcoatl and Tezcatlipoca and how they put their differences aside to defeat the demon caiman of the sea, resulting in the creation of the land and sky. (Rev: SLJ 3/07) [398.2]

12914 Demi. *The Girl Who Drew a Phoenix* (1–3). Illus. by author. 2008, Simon & Schuster $21.99 (978-1-4169-5347-0). 40pp. A girl's persistent efforts to evoke the spirit of the mythical phoenix bird in her drawings eventually meet with success; graceful illustrations with foldouts. (Rev: BL 8/08; LMC 1/09; SLJ 9/08)

12915 Edwards, Katie. *Myths and Monsters: Secrets Revealed* (K–5). Illus. by Simon Mendez. 2004, Charlesbridge LB $16.95 (978-1-57091-581-9); paper $6.95 (978-1-57091-582-6). 29pp. Introduces 10 mythical creatures and shows the real animals on which these "monsters" may have been based. (Rev: SLJ 2/05) [398.24]

12916 Fisher, Leonard Everett. *The Gods and Goddesses of Ancient China* (2–5). 2003, Holiday House $16.95 (978-0-8234-1694-3). 36pp. This colorful picture book introduces 17 deities found in the myths of ancient China and includes a pronunciation guide, glossary, and map. (Rev: BL 7/03; HBG 4/04; SLJ 10/03) [299]

12917 Fisher, Leonard Everett. *Gods and Goddesses of the Ancient Maya* (4–7). Illus. 1999, Holiday $16.95 (978-0-8234-1427-7). 36pp. This book provides a fascinating introduction to Mayan mythology by describing 10 gods and two goddesses. (Rev: BL 2/1/00; HBG 3/00; SLJ 12/99) [299]

12918 Gibbons, Gail. *Behold . . . the Unicorns!* (2–4). Illus. 2001, HarperCollins LB $15.89 (978-0-688-17958-8). 32pp. This handsomely designed book introduces the unicorn and all the myths and symbolism that surround one-horned beasts. (Rev: BCCB 12/01; BL 12/1/01; HBG 3/02; SLJ 12/01) [398.24]

12919 Green, Jen. *Myths of China and Japan* (5–8). Series: Mythic World. 2002, Raintree LB $27.12 (978-0-7398-4977-4). 48pp. This handsome, oversize book explores the ancient mythology of China and Japan and, in addition to the retelling of 10 myths, contains information on the societies that created them. (Rev: BL 7/02; HBG 10/02) [398.2]

12920 Harris, Geraldine. *Gods and Pharaohs from Egyptian Mythology* (5–8). Illus. by David O'Connor and John Sibbick. 1992, Bedrick LB $24.95

(978-0-87226-907-1). 132pp. A collection of myths and legends from ancient Egypt. [398.2]

12921 January, Brendan. *The New York Public Library Amazing Mythology: A Book of Answers for Kids* (5–8). Illus. 2000, Wiley paper $14.95 (978-0-471-33205-3). 169pp. This compendium of information covers Middle Eastern, African, Mediterranean, Asian, Pacific, Northern European, and North and Central American mythology. (Rev: BL 11/1/00; SLJ 9/00) [291.1]

12922 Limke, Jeff. *Isis and Osiris: To the Ends of the Earth* (4–6). Illus. Series: Graphic Myths and Legends. 2006, Lerner $26.60 (978-0-8225-3086-2). 48pp. The lives of ancient Egyptian deities Isis and Osiris are chronicled in graphic-novel format. (Rev: BL 10/15/06; SLJ 11/06) [398.2]

12923 Lorenz, Albert, and Joy Schleh. *The Trojan Horse* (3–5). Illus. 2006, Abrams $17.95 (978-0-8109-5986-6). 40pp. Learn all about the Trojan War in this humorous, visual approach to the Trojan War that offers conversational text, cartoon panels, and cross-sections of the Greek ships, the Trojan horse, and the city of Troy. (Rev: BL 11/15/06; SLJ 11/06) [398.2]

12924 Lupton, Hugh, and Daniel Morden. *The Adventures of Odysseus* (3–5). Illus. by Christina Balit. 2006, Barefoot Books $19.99 (978-1-84148-800-4). 128pp. A large-format picture-book retelling of Homer's classic story, with bright, attractive illustrations and fast-paced, sometimes challenging text. (Rev: BL 12/1/06; SLJ 11/06*) [398.20938]

12925 Marshall, James Vance. *Stories from the Billabong* (3–5). Illus. by Francis Firebrace. 2009, Frances Lincoln $19.95 (978-1-84507-704-4). 64pp. A collection of 10 aboriginal stories about creation and nature, with distinctive illustrations. (Rev: BLO 3/24/09; SLJ 5/09) [398.2]

12926 Mutén, Burleigh, retel. *The Lady of Ten Thousand Names: Goddess Stories from Many Cultures* (4–7). Illus. by Helen Cann. 2001, Barefoot Books $19.99 (978-1-84148-048-0). 79pp. Eight myths that feature goddesses from cultures around the world are retold in this appealing volume. (Rev: HBG 3/02; SLJ 11/01) [291.2]

12927 Penner, Lucille R. *Dragons* (3–5). Trans. and illus. by Peter David Scott. 2004, Random LB $11.99 (978-0-307-46417-0); paper $3.99 (978-0-307-26417-6). 48pp. The dragon's role in the mythologies and cultures of many nations and peoples are explored here. (Rev: BL 8/04) [398.24]

12928 Philip, Neil. *The Illustrated Book of Myths: Tales and Legends of the World* (5–8). Illus. by Nilesh Mistry. 1995, DK paper $19.99 (978-0-7894-0202-8). 192pp. Ancient myths from both the Old World and the New World have been collected under such headings as creation, destruction, and fertility. (Rev: BL 12/1/95; SLJ 12/95; VOYA 4/96) [291.1]

12929 Schomp, Virginia. *The Ancient Egyptians* (5–7). Series: Myths of the World. 2007, Marshall Cavendish LB $22.95 (978-0-7614-2549-6). 96pp. Schomp provides background information on the myths of ancient Egypt and retells several of the

best-known ones; full-color illustrations add to the appeal. (Rev: LMC 3/08; SLJ 1/08)

12930 Schomp, Virginia. *The Native Americans* (5–7). Series: Myths of the World. 2007, Marshall Cavendish LB $22.95 (978-0-7614-2550-2). 96pp. Schomp provides background information on the myths of the Native Americans and retells several of the best-known ones; full-color illustrations add to the appeal. (Rev: LMC 3/08; SLJ 1/08)

12931 Sherman, Pat. *The Sun's Daughter* (2–4). Illus. by R. Gregory Christie. 2005, Clarion $16.00 (978-0-618-32430-9). 32pp. The harvest is explained through a story based on Iroquois myths. (Rev: BL 3/15/05; SLJ 6/05) [398.2]

12932 Storrie, Paul D. *Beowulf: Monster Slayer: A British Legend* (4–7). Illus. by Ron Randall. Series: Graphic Myths and Legends. 2007, Lerner LB $26.60 (978-0-8225-6757-8). 48pp. An introduction to the ancient legend, carefully presented to preserve the tone of the original story. (Rev: BL 9/07; SLJ 11/07)

12933 Tchana, Katrin. *Changing Woman and Her Sisters* (5–8). Illus. by Trina S. Hyman. 2006, Holiday $18.95 (978-0-8234-1999-9). 80pp. An illustrated collection of traditional stories about 10 goddesses from a variety of lesser-known cultures, including Celtic, ancient Mayan, Shinto, Buddhist, and Navajo. (Rev: BCCB 9/06; BL 6/1–15/06; HB 7/06; HBG 10/06; LMC 1/07; SLJ 8/06) [398.2]

12934 Thomson, Ruth. *Myths* (2–6). Illus. Series: A First Look at Art. 2005, Chelsea Clubhouse $23.00 (978-0-7910-8316-1). 32pp. A look at the portrayal of mythological beings and stories in artwork from around the world. Also use *Weather* (2005). (Rev: SLJ 11/05) [398.2]

12935 West, David. *Mesoamerican Myths* (5–9). Illus. by Mike Taylor. Series: Graphic Mythology. 2006, Rosen LB $29.25 (978-1-4042-0802-5). 48pp. Presented in graphic novel format are three tales from the mythology of Mexico and Central America — two creation stories and a hero tale. (Rev: SLJ 9/06) [398.2]

Classical

12936 Bateman, Teresa. *Damon, Pythias, and the Test of Friendship* (PS–3). Illus. by Layne Johnson. 2009, Albert Whitman $16.99 (978-0-8075-1445-0). 32pp. A handsome retelling of the legend about Damon's amazing trust in his friend Pythias. (Rev: BL 5/1/09; SLJ 6/09) [398.20938]

12937 Burleigh, Robert. *Pandora* (3–6). Illus. by Raúl Colón. 2002, Harcourt $17.00 (978-0-15-202178-8). 32pp. A handsome retelling of the Greek myth about Pandora, her longings to open the box, and the terror it produced when she did. (Rev: BCCB 5/02; BL 6/1–15/02; HBG 10/02; SLJ 5/02) [398.2]

12938 Byrd, Robert. *The Hero and the Minotaur: The Fantastic Adventures of Theseus* (2–4). 2005, Dutton $17.99 (978-0-525-47391-6). 40pp. Byrd succeeds in retelling the complex adventures of Theseus in child-friendly narrative and compelling, detailed illustrations. (Rev: BL 7/05; SLJ 8/05*) [398.2]

12939 Catran, Ken. *Voyage with Jason* (5–8). 2003, Lothian paper $10.95 (978-0-7344-0151-9). 208pp. A new twist on the story of Jason and the Argonauts, narrated by a youth who is part of the eventful three-year quest for the Golden Fleece and concentrating on character as well as adventure. (Rev: SLJ 4/04) [398.2]

12940 Clayton, Sally Pomme. *Persephone* (2–4). Illus. by Virginia Lee. 2009, Eerdmans $18.00 (978-0-8028-5349-3). 26pp. This retelling of the story of the girl who is taken to the Underworld by Hades follows the traditional line and is enhanced by graceful artwork with a classical flavor. (Rev: BL 3/15/09; SLJ 5/09) [398.2]

12941 Climo, Shirley. *Atalanta's Race: A Greek Myth* (3–5). Illus. by Alexander Koshkin. 1995, Clarion $16.00 (978-0-395-67322-5). 32pp. A retelling of the Greek myth about Atalanta, who, abandoned at birth, becomes the world's fastest runner. (Rev: BCCB 6/95; BL 4/15/95; SLJ 4/95*) [398.21]

12942 Curlee, Lynn. *Mythological Creatures: A Classical Bestiary* (4–8). Illus. by author. 2008, Atheneum $17.99 (978-1-4169-1453-2). 40pp. A beautiful book with dreamy color illustrations of creatures that roam through classical mythology, such as gryphons, the Minotaur, Cerberus, and centaurs; each illustration is accompanied by comments about the creature's part in mythology. (Rev: BL 4/1/08; SLJ 5/08) [292.2]

12943 Cuyler, Margery. *Roadsigns: A Harey Race with a Tortoise* (PS–1). Illus. by Steve Haskamp. 2000, Winslow $15.95 (978-1-890817-23-7). 40pp. The Aesop fable of the race between the tortoise and the hare is cleverly retold using road signs and bright, cartoonlike illustrations. (Rev: BL 12/1/00; HBG 3/01; SLJ 9/00) [398.2]

12944 D'Aulaire, Ingri, and Edgar D'Aulaire. *D'Aulaire's Book of Greek Myths* (3–6). Illus. by authors. 1962, Dell paper $18.95 (978-0-440-40694-5). Full-color pictures highlight these brief stories, which are excellent for first readers in mythology. [398.2]

12945 Demi. *King Midas* (2–4). Illus. 2002, Simon & Schuster $19.95 (978-0-689-83297-0). 48pp. Rich illustrations accompany this retelling of the King Midas tale for younger readers. (Rev: BL 3/15/02; HB 5/02; HBG 10/02; SLJ 5/02) [398.2]

12946 Fisher, Leonard Everett. *Cyclops* (1–6). Illus. 1991, Holiday House paper $5.95 (978-0-8234-1062-0). 32pp. The retelling of this classical tale inspires pity and terror in the reader. (Rev: BCCB 12/91; BL 1/1/91*; SLJ 1/92) [398.2]

12947 Fisher, Leonard Everett. *Theseus and the Minotaur* (3–6). Illus. by author. 1988, Holiday House paper $5.95 (978-0-8234-0954-9). 32pp. The story of the birth of Theseus, his adventures, and his killing of the Minotaur. (Rev: BCCB 10/88; BL 10/15/88; SLJ 10/88) [398.2]

12948 Fontes, Justine, and Ron Fontes. *Demeter and Persephone: Spring Held Hostage: A Greek Myth* (1–3). Illus. by Steve Kurth and Barbara Schulz. Series: Graphic Myths and Legends. 2007, Lerner LB $26.60 (978-0-8225-5966-5). 48pp. The myth of Persephone retold in graphic-novel format to reach a wider audience, with imaginative illustrations. (Rev: SLJ 5/07)

12949 Green, Jen. *Myths of Ancient Greece* (5–8). Illus. Series: Mythic World. 2001, Raintree LB $27.12 (978-0-7398-3191-5). 48pp. This volume for older readers separates myth from reality about ancient Greece. (Rev: BL 3/1/02; HBG 3/02; SLJ 12/01) [398.2]

12950 Harris, John. *Strong Stuff: Herakles and His Labors* (4–7). Illus. by Gary Baseman. 2005, Getty $16.95 (978-0-89236-784-9). 32pp. A lively, tongue-in-cheek account of the 12 labors of ancient Greece's mythical strongman, Herakles (known to the ancient Romans as Hercules). (Rev: BL 11/15/05; SLJ 11/05) [398.2]

12951 Hawthorne, Nathaniel. *Wonder Book and Tanglewood Tales* (5–7). 1972, Ohio State Univ. $72.95 (978-0-8142-0158-9). 476pp. This is a highly original retelling of the Greek myths, originally published in 1853. (Rev: BL 2/15/04; SLJ 4/04) [398.2]

12952 Homer. *The Odyssey* (3–5). Adapted by Adrian Mitchell. Illus. by Stuart Robertson. 2000, DK $14.99 (978-0-7894-5455-3). 64pp. A handsomely illustrated version of the Odyssey that covers all the major plot developments and the journeys of Odysseus. (Rev: BL 9/1/03; HBG 4/04; SLJ 9/00) [398.2]

12953 Kimmel, Eric A. *The McElderry Book of Greek Myths* (K–3). Illus. by Pep Montserrat. 2008, Simon & Schuster $21.99 (978-1-4169-1534-8). 112pp. Simple, clear language, classically inspired computer-generated art, and lots of action are features of theses retellings of stories about such characters as Midas, Icarus, Theseus, and Narcissus. (Rev: BL 1/1–15/08; SLJ 3/08) [398.2]

12954 Low, Alice. *The Macmillan Book of Greek Gods and Heroes* (4–6). Illus. by Arvis Stewart. 1985, Macmillan LB $18.00 (978-0-02-761390-2). 192pp. Well-known myths and legends from ancient Greece in a large-format edition. (Rev: BCCB 11/85; BL 11/15/85; SLJ 1/86) [398.2]

12955 McCarty, Nick, retel. *The Iliad* (4–8). Illus. by Victor G. Ambrus. 2000, Kingfisher paper $15.95 (978-0-7534-5321-6). 95pp. This account of the Trojan War uses an exciting text and action-packed illustrations. (Rev: SLJ 1/01) [398.2]

12956 Mayer, Marianna. *Pegasus* (3–6). Illus. by Kinuko Craft. 1998, Morrow $16.99 (978-0-688-13382-5). 40pp. A retelling of the Greek myth about the winged horse Pegasus and how it helped Bellerophon kill Chimera the monster. (Rev: BL 3/15/98; HBG 10/98; SLJ 4/98) [398.2]

12957 Morley, Jacqueline, retel. *Greek Myths* (3–6). Illus. by Giovanni Caselli. 1998, Bedrick $22.50 (978-0-87226-560-8). 96pp. Beginning with the rise of the Titans and ending with Odysseus's wanderings, the myths in this book include those involving

Prometheus, Arachne, Psyche, the Minotaur, and Apollo. (Rev: HBG 10/98; SLJ 7/98) [398.2]

12958 Myers, Christopher. *Wings* (PS–4). Illus. 2000, Scholastic $16.95 (978-0-590-03377-0). 40pp. In this modern retelling of the Icarus myth, a young boy who can fly nearly crashes, not because he flies too close to the sun but because repressive adults and bullying kids in the schoolyard try to break his spirit. (Rev: BCCB 12/00; BL 5/15/00; HBG 3/01; SLJ 10/00)

12959 *Odysseus* (4–8). Retold by Geraldine McCaughrean. 2004, Cricket $15.95 (978-0-8126-2721-3). 128pp. Homer's dramatic story is retold in rhythmic prose. (Rev: BL 12/15/04; SLJ 12/04)

12960 Osborne, Mary Pope. *Favorite Greek Myths* (3–6). Illus. by Troy Howell. 1989, Scholastic paper $19.95 (978-0-590-41338-1). 96pp. This large-format book contains 13 of the best-known stories from classical mythology. (Rev: BL 8/89) [398.2]

12961 Oyibo, Papa. *Big Brother, Little Sister* (PS–3). Illus. by John Clementson. 2000, Barefoot Books $15.95 (978-1-84148-117-3). 40pp. The Aesop fable about the lion and the mouse is retold using an elephant instead of a lion. (Rev: BL 4/1/00; SLJ 8/00)

12962 Philip, Neil, retel. *The Adventures of Odysseus* (3–6). Illus. by Peter Malone. 1997, Orchard $17.95 (978-0-531-30000-8). 72pp. A fine retelling of the epic journey home by Odysseus and his encounters with such creatures as Cyclops, Circe, and the Sirens. (Rev: SLJ 5/97*) [292.1]

12963 Pickels, Dwayne E. *Roman Myths, Heroes, and Legends* (5–8). Series: Costume, Tradition, and Culture: Reflecting on the Past. 1998, Chelsea $28.00 (978-0-7910-5164-1). Using double-page spreads and old collectors' cards as illustrations, this work retells the major Roman myths and introduces their important characters. (Rev: BL 3/15/99; HBG 10/99) [398.2]

12964 Richards, Jean. *The First Olympic Games: A Gruesome Greek Myth with a Happy Ending* (2–4). Illus. 2000, Millbrook LB $23.90 (978-0-7613-1311-3). 32pp. The story of Pelops, who was killed and eaten by his father, Tantalus, restored to life by the gods, and later created the first Olympic Games. (Rev: BCCB 11/00; BL 10/15/00; HBG 10/01; SLJ 11/00) [398.2]

12965 Schomp, Virginia. *The Ancient Greeks* (5–7). Series: Myths of the World. 2007, Marshall Cavendish LB $22.95 (978-0-7614-2547-2). 96pp. Schomp provides background information on the myths of ancient Greece and retells several of the best-known ones; full-color illustrations add to the appeal. (Rev: LMC 3/08; SLJ 1/08)

12966 Schulte, Mary. *The Minotaur* (4–6). Series: Monsters. 2008, Gale LB $26.20 (978-0-7377-3590-

1). 48pp. Schulte tells the story of the Minotaur and Theseus's decision to venture into the Labyrinth to slay this half-man half-bull, and then discusses the Minotaur's appearances in popular culture. (Rev: SLJ 12/08) [398]

12967 Shone, Rob. *Greek Myths* (5–9). Illus. by author. Series: Graphic Mythology. 2006, Rosen LB $29.25 (978-1-4042-0801-8). 48pp. "Jason and the Golden Fleece," "Icarus," and "The Labors of Hercules" are the three tales presented here in graphic novel format. (Rev: SLJ 9/06) [292.1]

12968 Stewig, John W. *King Midas* (K–3). Illus. by Omar Rayyan. 1999, Holiday House $17.95 (978-0-8234-1423-9). 32pp. Filled with illustrations containing comic details, this is a fine retelling of the tale about the greedy king who turned his daughter into gold. (Rev: BCCB 3/99; BL 2/15/99; HBG 10/99; SLJ 3/99) [398.2]

12969 Wilbur, Helen L. *Z Is for Zeus: A Greek Mythology Alphabet* (3–6). Illus. by Victor Juhasz. 2008, Sleeping Bear $17.95 (978-1-58536-341-4). 32pp. An appealing alphabetical introduction to classic Greek stories and heroes, with poetic text and detailed illustrations. (Rev: BLO 2/8/08; LMC 10/08; SLJ 10/08) [292.1]

12970 Woff, Richard. *A Pocket Dictionary of Greek and Roman Gods and Goddesses* (4–8). 2003, Getty $9.95 (978-0-89236-706-1). 48pp. Varied reproductions from the British Museum add visual appeal to this brief who's who. (Rev: SLJ 2/04) [292.2]

Scandinavian

12971 Fisher, Leonard Everett. *Gods and Goddesses of the Ancient Norse* (K–4). Illus. 2002, Holiday House $16.95 (978-0-8234-1569-4). 40pp. An introduction to 15 ancient Norse gods and goddesses, with a pronunciation guide and a family tree. (Rev: BCCB 6/02; BL 3/1/02; HBG 10/02; SLJ 3/02) [293]

12972 Lunge-Larsen, Lise, retel. *The Adventures of Thor the Thunder God* (3–6). Illus. by Jim Madsen. 2007, Houghton $19.95 (978-0-618-47301-4). 76pp. Stories of Thor ("protector and defender of civilization"), his family members, and his fellow gods fill the pages of this heavily illustrated volume. (Rev: SLJ 7/07)

12973 Schomp, Virginia. *The Norsemen* (5–7). Series: Myths of the World. 2007, Marshall Cavendish LB $22.95 (978-0-7614-2548-9). 96pp. Schomp provides background information on the myths of Scandinavia and retells several of the best-known ones; full-color illustrations add to the appeal. (Rev: LMC 3/08; SLJ 1/08)

Poetry

General

12974 Adoff, Arnold. *Touch the Poem* (PS–3). Illus. by Lisa Desimini. 2000, Scholastic $16.95 (978-0-590-47970-7). 32pp. Common childhood experiences like walking on a beach or feeling the fuzz on a peach are explored in this collection of original poems illustrated with photographs. (Rev: BCCB 2/00; BL 3/15/00; HBG 10/00; SLJ 6/00) [811]

12975 Adoff, Jaime. *Small Fry* (1–3). Illus. by Mike Reed. 2008, Dutton $16.99 (978-0-525-46935-3). 32pp. This collection of 19 poems explores the pros and cons of being short. (Rev: BCCB 11/08; BL 11/15/08; LMC 1/09; SLJ 11/08) [811]

12976 Agard, John. *Half-Caste and Other Poems* (4–7). 2005, Hodder $16.99 (978-0-340-89382-1). 80pp. Guyana-born Agard offers a collection of his saucy, Caribbean-flavored poetry dealing with topics such as tolerance and diversity that young people will recognize. (Rev: BL 10/15/05; HB 1/06; HBG 4/06; SLJ 1/06; VOYA 2/06) [811]

12977 Alarcón, Francisco X. *Poems to Dream Together / Poemas para soñar juntos* (3–5). Illus. by Paula Barragán. 2005, Lee & Low $16.95 (978-1-58430-233-9). 32pp. A collection of short, bilingual poems about aspirations. (Rev: BL 7/05; HBG 10/05; LMC 1/06; SLJ 10/05) [811]

12978 Anaya, Rudolfo. *Elegy on the Death of Cesar Chavez* (4–7). Illus. 2000, Cinco Puntos $16.95 (978-0-938317-51-7). 32pp. This is an elegiac poem that celebrates the life, work, and struggle of the respected labor leader. (Rev: BL 12/15/00; HBG 3/01; SLJ 1/01) [811]

12979 Andrews, Sylvia. *Dancing in My Bones* (PS). Illus. by Ellen Mueller. 2001, HarperCollins $10.99 (978-0-694-01316-6). 24pp. A multicultural cast of kids dance their way through a park, adding lines to a rhyme along the way. (Rev: BL 11/1/01; HBG 3/02; SLJ 12/01) [811]

12980 Appelt, Kathi. *My Father's House* (PS–2). Illus. by Raúl Colón. 2007, Viking $16.99 (978-0-670-03669-1). 32pp. Through verse and colorfully rendered illustrations, this book expresses thanks to the Creator for the Earth's beauty and diversity. (Rev: BL 5/15/07; SLJ 8/07) [811]

12981 Archer, Peggy. *From Dawn to Dreams: Poems for Busy Babies* (PS). Illus. by Hanako Wakiyama. 2007, Candlewick $15.99 (978-0-7636-2467-5). Beautiful illustrations of adorable babies accompany poems about little ones' daily routines. (Rev: SLJ 7/07)

12982 Argueta, Jorge. *A Movie in My Pillow / Una pelicula en mi almohada* (4–8). Illus. by Elizabeth Gomez. 2001, Children's $15.95 (978-0-89239-165-3). 32pp. The author remembers in poetry his family's immigration to the United States from El Salvador, with each poem accompanied by the translation and rich illustrations. (Rev: BL 10/1/01; HBG 10/01; SLJ 5/01*) [861]

12983 Argueta, Jorge. *Sopa de frijoles / Bean Soup: Un poema para cocinar / A Cooking Poem* (1–3). Illus. by Rafael Yockteng. 2009, Groundwood $18.95 (978-0-88899-881-1). 32pp. In Spanish and English this is a free-verse recipe for bean soup. (Rev: BL 3/15/09; SLJ 4/09) [861]

12984 Argueta, Jorge. *Talking with Mother Earth / Hablando con Madre Tierra: Poems / Poemas* (3–8). Illus. by Lucía Angela Pérez. 2006, Groundwood $15.95 (978-0-88899-626-8). Beautiful bilingual poems give voice to a young Central American Indian's feelings of kinship with nature. (Rev: HBG 4/07; LMC 1/07; SLJ 10/06) [811]

12985 Attenborough, Liz, ed. *Poetry by Heart: A Child's Book of Poems to Remember* (3–5). Illus. 2001, Scholastic $17.95 (978-0-439-29657-1). 128pp. An eclectic, enchanting collection of poetry for younger readers. (Rev: BL 1/1–15/02; HBG 10/02; SLJ 2/02) [811.54]

12986 Bagert, Brod. *Shout! Little Poems That Roar* (K–2). Illus. by Sachiko Yoshikawa. 2007, Dial $16.99 (978-0-8037-2972-8). This appealing collection of 21 energetic rhyming poems celebrates the wonders — and occasional disappointments — of childhood. (Rev: BL 2/1/07; SLJ 2/07) [811]

12987 Barbe, Walter B., sel. *A School Year of Poems: 180 Favorites from Highlights* (K–3). Illus. by Dennis Hockerman. 2005, Boyds Mills paper $11.95 (978-1-59078-395-5). 116pp. The poems in this anthology are divided into nine child-friendly categories, including animals, weather, and holidays. (Rev: SLJ 10/05) [811]

12988 Bauer, Caroline Feller, ed. *Rainy Day: Stories and Poems* (3–5). Illus. by Michele Chessare. 1986, HarperCollins LB $15.89 (978-0-397-32105-6). 96pp. Poems and stories from mostly well-known children's poets such as John Ciardi and Langston Hughes. Also use: *Snowy Day: Stories and Poems* (1986). (Rev: BCCB 9/86; BL 7/86; SLJ 9/86)

12989 Bauer, Marion Dane. *Love Song for a Baby* (PS–K). Illus. by Dan Andreasen. 2002, Simon & Schuster $15.95 (978-0-689-82268-1). 40pp. A tender poem about parents' love for their growing baby, with excellent oil paintings and rhyming text. (Rev: BL 9/1/02; HBG 3/03; SLJ 8/02) [811]

12990 Baylor, Byrd. *The Way to Start a Day* (3–5). Illus. by Peter Parnall. 1978, Macmillan $16.00 (978-0-684-15651-4); paper $5.99 (978-0-689-71054-4). 32pp. A poetic tribute to the many ways people have greeted a new day.

12991 Becker, Helaine. *Mama Likes to Mambo* (K–2). Illus. by John Beder. 2002, Stoddart $15.95 (978-0-7737-3316-9). 32pp. A collection of amusing, attractively illustrated poems of differing lengths on varied subjects. (Rev: BL 9/15/02; HBG 10/02; SLJ 5/02) [811]

12992 Bennett, Jill, ed. *A Cup of Starshine: Poems and Pictures for Young Children* (PS–1). Illus. by Graham Percy. 1991, Harcourt $16.95 (978-0-15-220982-7). 64pp. These include the traditional rhymes with modern verse and full-color drawings. (Rev: BL 10/15/91; SLJ 12/91) [811]

12993 Bernier-Grand, Carmen. *Cesar: ¡Sí, Se Puede! Yes, We Can!* (3–6). Illus. by David Diaz. 2004, Marshall Cavendish $16.95 (978-0-7614-5172-3). 48pp. A series of 19 free-verse poems chronicles the life of Cesar Chavez, from his migrant worker childhood to his leadership in the struggle for farm workers' rights. (Rev: BL 10/15/04; SLJ 10/04) [811]

12994 Berry, James, ed. *Around the World in Eighty Poems* (3–5). Illus. by Katherine Lucas. 2002, Chronicle $19.95 (978-0-8118-3506-0). 96pp. A collection of poems from countries around the world, illustrated with paintings. (Rev: BCCB 1/03; BL 7/02; HBG 3/03; SLJ 4/03) [808.81]

12995 Berry, James, ed. *Classic Poems to Read Aloud* (4–8). Illus. 1995, Kingfisher $18.95 (978-1-85697-987-0). 256pp. Jamaican writer Berry has collected old favorites, mostly British, along with new voices usually excluded from the literary canon. (Rev: BL 5/1/95; SLJ 5/95) [811]

12996 Blake, Quentin. *All Join In* (PS–2). Illus. 1991, Little, Brown $14.95 (978-0-316-09934-9). 32pp. The theme of cooperation is explored in six bright poems. (Rev: BCCB 5/91; BL 4/15/91; SLJ 7/91) [821]

12997 Borden, Louise. *America Is . . .* (2–4). Illus. by Stacey Schuett. 2002, Simon & Schuster $16.95 (978-0-689-83900-9). 40pp. This patriotic poem for younger readers examines life in America through many prisms. (Rev: BL 8/02; HBG 10/02; SLJ 6/02) [811]

12998 Brand, Dionne. *Earth Magic* (4–7). Illus. by Eugenie Fernandes. 2006, Kids Can $14.95 (978-1-55337-706-1). 32pp. In her first collection of poetry for young people, Brand writes about life in Trinidad, the island of her birth. (Rev: BL 4/1/06; SLJ 7/06) [811]

12999 Brewton, Sara, et al., eds. *Of Quarks, Quasars and Other Quirks: Quizzical Poems for the Supersonic Age* (5–8). Illus. by Quentin Blake. 1977, HarperCollins LB $13.89 (978-0-690-04885-8). 128pp. Contemporary poems that poke fun at such modern innovations as transplants and water beds.

13000 Brown, Calef. *Soup for Breakfast* (PS–2). Illus. by author. 2008, Houghton $16.00 (978-0-618-91641-2). 32pp. A collection of playful poetry about food. (Rev: BL 11/15/08; HB 3/09; SLJ 2/09) [811]

13001 Brown, Margaret Wise. *Give Yourself to the Rain: Poems for the Very Young* (PS–1). Illus. by Teri L. Weidner. 2002, Simon & Schuster $16.95 (978-0-689-83344-1). 32pp. A collection of 24 previously unpublished poems for young readers, illustrated in beautiful warm pastels. (Rev: BL 2/15/02; HBG 10/02; SLJ 3/02) [811]

13002 Bryan, Ashley. *Sing to the Sun: Poems and Pictures* (K–8). Illus. 1996, HarperCollins paper $7.99 (978-0-06-443437-9). Short poems with a Caribbean lilt. (Rev: BCCB 10/92; BL 10/15/92; HB 3/93; SLJ 10/92) [811.54]

13003 Bunting, Eve. *Sing a Song of Piglets: A Calendar in Verse* (PS–1). Illus. by Emily Arnold McCully. 2002, Clarion $16.00 (978-0-618-01137-7). 32pp. Readers follow a pair of piglets through the year, with lively watercolors that match the bounciness of the simple rhymes. (Rev: BL 11/15/02; HBG 3/03; SLJ 8/02) [811]

13004 Burkholder, Kelly. *Poetry* (2–5). Series: Artistic Adventures. 2001, Rourke LB $23.93 (978-1-57103-354-3). 24pp. This book explains the basic elements of poetry like rhythm, rhyme, and repetition, introduces different types of poems, and gives advice on how to write your own poetry. (Rev: SLJ 2/01) [811]

13005 Carlson, Lori M. *Sol a Sol* (2–5). Illus. by Emily Lisker. 1998, Holt $17.00 (978-0-8050-4373-0). A bilingual anthology of poems that describe the daily activities of a Hispanic family. (Rev: BCCB 5/98; BL 4/1/98; HB 5/98; HBG 10/98; SLJ 3/98) [808]

13006 Carney, Mary Lou, ed. *Absolutely Angels: Poems for Children and Other Believers* (PS–3). Illus. by Viqui Maggio. 1998, Boyds Mills $14.95 (978-1-56397-708-4). A collection of poems, mostly by contemporary poets, about the role of angels as protectors and helpers. (Rev: BL 11/1/98; HBG 3/99; SLJ 11/98) [808.81]

13007 Chorao, Kay, ed. *Rhymes Round the World* (PS–2). Illus. by Kay Chorao. 2009, Dutton $16.99 (978-0-525-47875-1). 40pp. Forty light poems and songs, many of them familiar, take children on a world tour. (Rev: BL 3/1/09; SLJ 2/09) [821]

13008 Cleary, Brian P. *Rainbow Soup: Adventures in Poetry* (3–6). Illus. by Neal Layton. 2004, Carolrhoda $16.95 (978-1-57505-597-8). 96pp. In multiple poetry forms, Cleary celebrates various aspects of children's everyday lives, including school, sports, and food. (Rev: BL 4/1/04; SLJ 6/04) [808.1]

13009 Cooling, Wendy. *Come to the Great World: Poems from Around the Globe* (PS–3). Illus. by Sheila Moxley. 2004, Holiday House $16.95 (978-0-8234-1822-0). 32pp. Diverse poems about children and the issues that affect them are illustrated with colorful paintings. (Rev: BL 3/15/04; SLJ 4/04) [811]

13010 Cooney, Barbara, retel. *Chanticleer and the Fox* (1–4). Illus. by Barbara Cooney. 1958, HarperCollins LB $17.89 (978-0-690-18562-1); paper $3.95 (978-0-690-04318-1). 36pp. Chaucer's Nun's Priest Tale retold by the illustrator. Caldecott Medal winner, 1959.

13011 Creech, Sharon. *Who's That Baby? New-Baby Songs* (PS–2). Illus. by David Diaz. 2005, HarperCollins $15.99 (978-0-06-052939-0). 32pp. In this collection of short poems and songs, Creech chronicles the early days of a newborn baby and its interaction with the world around it. (Rev: BL 8/05) [811]

13012 Dahl, Roald. *Vile Verses* (5–8). Illus. 2005, Viking $25.00 (978-0-670-06042-9). 192pp. New illustrations adorn the poems in this aptly titled collection. (Rev: BL 11/1/05; SLJ 11/05*) [811]

13013 Dawes, Kwame Senu Neville. *I Saw Your Face* (3–5). Illus. by Tom Feelings. 2005, Dial $16.99 (978-0-8037-1894-4). 32pp. Sketches of black faces around the world are paired with evocative poetry celebrating their global reach. (Rev: BL 2/1/05; SLJ 3/05) [811]

13014 De Regniers, Beatrice S., ed. *Sing a Song of Popcorn: Every Child's Book of Poems* (PS–6). Illus. by Marcia Brown. 1988, Scholastic $18.95 (978-0-590-43974-9). 160pp. A treasure from highly regarded poets, with exciting artwork. (Rev: BCCB 10/88; BL 8/88; SLJ 8/88)

13015 Di Pasquale, Emanuel. *Cartwheel to the Moon: My Sicilian Childhood* (3–6). Illus. by K. Dyble Thompson. 2003, Cricket $16.95 (978-0-8126-2679-7). 64pp. Di Pasquale's poems paint a vivid word picture of his chidhood in Sicily during the 1940s and 1950s. (Rev: BL 4/1/03; HBG 10/03; SLJ 7/03) [811]

13016 Dotlich, Rebecca. *Lemonade Sun and Other Summer Poems* (PS–3). Illus. by Jan S. Gilchrist. 1998, Boyds Mills paper $15.95 (978-1-56397-660-5). 32pp. This book of poems shows children in everyday situations and depicts their sense of wonder. (Rev: BL 2/15/98; HBG 10/98; SLJ 3/98) [811]

13017 Dotlich, Rebecca Kai. *In the Spin of Things: Poetry of Motion* (2–5). Illus. by Karen M. Dugan. 2003, Boyds Mills $16.95 (978-1-56397-145-7).

32pp. Everyday items whirl into motion in this collection of free-form poems. (Rev: BL 4/1/03; HBG 10/03; SLJ 3/03) [811]

13018 Dotlich, Rebecca Kai. *Over in the Pink House* (PS–2). Illus. by Melanie Hall. 2004, Boyds Mills $15.95 (978-1-59078-027-5). 32pp. Rhythm and sound trump meaning in this collection of rhyming verses. (Rev: BL 5/1/04; SLJ 4/04) [796.2]

13019 Dotlich, Rebecca Kai. *When Riddles Come Rumbling: Poems to Ponder* (2–5). Illus. 2001, Boyds Mills $16.95 (978-1-56397-846-3). 32pp. Short, rhythmic poems along with picture clues form riddles about everyday objects. (Rev: BL 11/1/01; HBG 3/02; SLJ 10/01) [811]

13020 *Dream Makers: Young People Share Their Hopes and Aspirations* (3–6). Illus. by Neil Waldman. 2003, Boyds Mills $15.95 (978-1-59078-178-4). 32pp. The dreams and aspirations of 42 American boys and girls are collected in this attractive large-format volume of rhyming and free verse marking the 150th anniversary of the Children's Aid Society. (Rev: BL 9/1/03; HBG 4/04; SLJ 12/03) [811]

13021 *Drift Upon a Dream: Poems for Sleepy Babies* (PS–1). Illus. by Melanie Williamson. 2004, Charlesbridge paper $6.95 (978-1-57091-578-9). 32pp. This anthology of 21 bedtime poems includes selections by Tennyson, Lee Bennett Hopkins, Eve Merriam, Eleanor Farjeon, and by Foster himself. (Rev: BL 9/1/04) [811]

13022 Eastwick, Ivy O. *I Asked a Tiger to Tea* (2–6). Illus. by Melanie Hall. 2002, Boyds Mills $15.95 (978-1-56397-515-8). 32pp. This is a richly illustrated, lyrical collection of poems about nature and childhood. (Rev: BL 12/15/02; HBG 3/03; SLJ 11/02) [811.54]

13023 Eastwick, Ivy O. *Some Folks Like Cats and Other Poems* (1–3). Ed. by Walter B. Barbe. Illus. by Mary Kurnich Maass. 2002, Boyds Mills $15.95 (978-1-56397-450-2). 28pp. A collection of 20 of the author's poems that deal with such subjects as sunflowers, leaves, rain, and small animals. (Rev: BL 4/15/02; HBG 10/02; SLJ 7/02) [811.54]

13024 Eccleshare, Julia, ed. *First Poems* (PS–3). Illus. by Selina Young. 1994, Bedrick $16.95 (978-0-87226-373-4). 64pp. A collection of happy, often humorous poems, including a number of old favorites and several by contemporary poets. (Rev: BL 7/94; SLJ 8/94) [821]

13025 Esbensen, Barbara J. *Who Shrank My Grandmother's House? Poems of Discovery* (1–3). Illus. by Eric Beddows. 1992, HarperCollins $15.00 (978-0-06-021827-0). 48pp. This book presents a celebration of everything in a collection of 23 poems. (Rev: BCCB 4/92; BL 6/1/92; HB 5/92; SLJ 4/92*) [811]

13026 Evans, Dilys, ed. *Monster Soup and Other Spooky Poems* (PS–1). Illus. by Jacqueline Rogers. 1992, Scholastic $14.95 (978-0-590-45208-3). 40pp. Watercolor paintings illustrate 16 poems that monster fans are sure to love. (Rev: BL 8/92; SLJ 10/92) [811]

13027 Ferris, Helen, ed. *Favorite Poems Old and New* (4–6). Illus. by Leonard Weisgard. 1957, Doubleday $24.95 (978-0-385-07696-8). 598pp. A book brimming with all kinds of poetry — lyrics, rhymes, doggerel, songs. (Rev: HB 5/04)

13028 Field, Eugene. *Wynken, Blynken, and Nod: A Dutch Lullaby* (PS–1). Illus. by Giselle Potter. 2008, Random $16.99 (978-0-375-84196-5). 40pp. A large-format, dreamy interpretation of the classic bedtime poem. (Rev: BL 5/15/08; HB 5/07; SLJ 7/08) [811]

13029 Fisher, Aileen. *I Heard a Bluebird Sing* (2–5). Illus. by Jennifer Emery. 2002, Boyds Mills $18.95 (978-1-56397-191-4). 64pp. The 41 poems included in this anthology were selected by children around the United States; they are preceded by excerpts from an article by Fisher and by introductions to the thematically organized sections. (Rev: BL 11/15/02; HBG 3/03; SLJ 10/02) [811.54]

13030 Fisher, Aileen. *Sing of the Earth and Sky: Poems About Our Planet and the Wonders Beyond* (2–4). Illus. 2001, Boyds Mills $15.95 (978-1-56397-802-9). 48pp. A collection of short original poems that are divided into four subjects: earth, sun, moon, and stars. (Rev: BL 3/15/01; HBG 10/01) [811]

13031 Fleischman, Paul. *Big Talk: Poems for Four Voices* (4–7). Illus. 2000, Candlewick $17.99 (978-0-7636-0636-7). 48pp. This collection of spirited, evocative poems for four voices to read aloud covers a variety of topics. (Rev: BCCB 4/00; BL 6/1–15/00; HB 5/00; HBG 10/00; SLJ 6/00) [811]

13032 Fletcher, Ralph. *Buried Alive: The Elements of Love* (5–8). 1996, Simon & Schuster $14.00 (978-0-689-80593-6). A series of free-verse poems that explore various aspects of love — puppy and otherwise. (Rev: BCCB 6/96; BL 5/1/96; SLJ 5/96; VOYA 10/96) [811]

13033 Fletcher, Ralph. *Have You Been to the Beach Lately? Poems* (4–7). Photos by Andrea Sperling. 2001, Scholastic paper $15.95 (978-0-531-30330-6). 48pp. More than 30 chatty poems, illustrated with black-and-white photographs, are written from the perspective of a smart and funny 11-year-old. (Rev: HBG 10/01; SLJ 8/01) [811]

13034 Fletcher, Ralph. *Moving Day* (3–6). Illus. by Jennifer Emery. 2006, Boyds Mills $17.95 (978-1-59078-339-9). Free-verse poems give voice to the feelings of a 12-year-old who is leaving behind the only world he's known and moving to a new and unfamiliar place. (Rev: SLJ 12/06*) [811]

13035 Fletcher, Ralph. *Relatively Speaking: Poems About Family* (5–7). Illus. 1999, Orchard LB $15.99 (978-0-531-33141-5). 48pp. From an 11-year-old boy's point of view, these original poems explore relationships as family members go through periods of change. (Rev: BCCB 5/99; BL 7/99; HBG 10/99; SLJ 4/99) [811]

13036 Fletcher, Ralph. *A Writing Kind of Day* (3–5). Illus. by April Ward. 2005, Boyds Mills $17.95 (978-1-59078-276-7); paper $9.95 (978-1-59078-353-5). 32pp. A collection of 27 poems by a young author who isn't afraid to write about the everyday and even the silly. (Rev: BL 3/15/05; SLJ 4/05) [811]

13037 Franco, Betsy. *Counting Our Way to the 100th Day! 100 Poems and 100 Pictures to Celebrate the 100th Day of School* (K–2). Illus. by Steven Salerno. 2004, Simon & Schuster $15.95 (978-0-689-84793-6). 48pp. Many of the 100 poems in this stylishly illustrated collection focus on the number "100" and will help students count down the first 100 days of school. (Rev: BL 8/04; SLJ 7/04) [811]

13038 Franco, Betsy. *Messing Around on the Monkey Bars and Other School Poems for Two Voices* (2–4). Illus. by Jessie Hartland. 2009, Candlewick $17.99 (978-0-7636-3174-1). 48pp. Nineteen lively school-themed poems are suitable for two or more voices. (Rev: BCCB 5/09; BL 5/15/09; HB 7/09; LMC 10/09; SLJ 11/09) [811]

13039 Frank, John. *Keepers: Treasure-Hunt Poems* (2–5). Illus. 2008, Roaring Brook $17.95 (978-1-59643-197-3). 64pp. Short poems focus on treasures of all kinds — sea glass, baseball cards, pottery jars, and so forth. (Rev: BL 3/15/08; SLJ 6/08) [811]

13040 Frost, Helen. *Spinning Through the Universe: A Novel in Poems from Room 214* (5–7). 2004, Farrar $16.00 (978-0-374-37159-3). 112pp. A variety of poetic forms — including haiku, tercelle, sonnet, pantoun, and tanka — are used in these diverse and compelling poems about the lives of a fifth-grade teacher and her students. (Rev: BL 4/1/04; SLJ 4/04) [811]

13041 George, Kristine O'Connell. *Fold Me a Poem* (1–3). Illus. by Lauren Stringer. 2005, Harcourt $16.00 (978-0-15-202501-4). 56pp. A boy creates origami animals and then uses them for imaginative play in this book of 32 poems. (Rev: BL 3/15/05; SLJ 3/05) [811]

13042 George, Kristine O'Connell. *Swimming Upstream: Middle School Poems* (5–8). Illus. by Debbie Tilley. 2002, Clarion $14.00 (978-0-618-15250-6). 80pp. Brief poems describe how one girl navigates the rapids of middle school, discussing everything from school lunches and lockers to making friends and relationships with boys. (Rev: BL 1/1–15/03; HB 1/03; HBG 3/03; SLJ 9/02) [811]

13043 George, Kristine O'Connell. *Toasting Marshmallows: Camping Poems* (K–4). Illus. by Kate Kiesler. 2001, Clarion $16.00 (978-0-618-04597-6). 48pp. Thirty simple poems clearly depict a family camping trip, from the details of pitching a tent to the wonders of the natural world, with attractive and varied artwork. (Rev: HBG 10/01; SLJ 7/01*) [811]

13044 Gilchrist, Jan Spivey. *My America* (K–2). Illus. by Ashley Bryan. 2007, HarperCollins $16.99 (978-0-06-079104-9). 40pp. Celebrates the diversity of America in its landscape, animal life, and people. (Rev: BL 4/15/07) [813]

13045 Gillooly, Eileen, ed. *Rudyard Kipling* (4–8). Illus. by Jim Sharpe. 2000, Sterling $14.95 (978-0-8069-4484-5). 48pp. This book contains complete poems or excerpts from 28 poems by this well-liked writer including "If" and "The Ballad of East and West." (Rev: HBG 3/01; SLJ 5/00) [821]

13046 Graham, Joan B. *Flicker Flash* (3–6). Illus. 1999, Houghton $16.00 (978-0-395-90501-2). 32pp. A collection of verses in geometric forms associated with light, among them a camera, a firefly, a lightbulb, and fireworks. (Rev: BL 1/1–15/00; HBG 3/00; SLJ 12/99*) [811]

13047 *Grandad's Tree: Poems About Families* (2–4). Illus. by Julia Cairns. 2003, Barefoot Books $16.99 (978-1-84148-541-6). 32pp. Twenty poems complemented by watercolor illustrations explore various aspects of family life; poets featured include Eloise Greenfield, Judith Viorst, Christina Rossetti, and Carl Sandburg. (Rev: BL 4/1/03; HBG 10/03) [811.008]

13048 Grandits, John. *Blue Lipstick: Concrete Poems* (5–9). Illus. by author. 2007, Clarion $15.00 (978-0-618-56860-4); paper $5.95 (978-0-618-85132-4). A visually entertaining collection of poems about Jessie, a 9th-grader whose main concerns are clothes, friends, and conflicts with her parents. (Rev: SLJ 7/07) [811]

13049 Greenberg, David T. *The Book of Boys (for Girls) and The Book of Girls (for Boys)* (K–3). Illus. by Joy Allen. 2005, Little, Brown $15.99 (978-0-316-36210-8). 32pp. Rhyming text presents opposing points of view from the two genders on a variety of everyday issues. (Rev: BL 5/15/05) [811]

13050 Greenberg, Jan, ed. *Heart to Heart: New Poems Inspired by Twentieth-Century American Art* (5–10). Illus. 2001, Abrams $19.95 (978-0-8109-4386-5). 80pp. This book contains specially commissioned poems from well-known writers to accompany some of the finest artworks of the 20th century. (Rev: BL 3/15/01*; HBG 10/01; SLJ 4/01*; VOYA 8/01) [811]

13051 Greenfield, Eloise. *Under the Sunday Tree* (2–5). Illus. by Amos Ferguson. 1988, HarperCollins paper $10.99 (978-0-06-443257-3). 48pp. Poems of life in the Bahamas. (Rev: BCCB 12/88; HB 11/88)

13052 Greenfield, Eloise. *When the Horses Ride By: Children in the Times of War* (2–4). Illus. by Jan Spivey Gilchrist. 2006, Lee & Low $17.95 (978-1-58430-249-0). 40pp. The poems in this collection celebrate the resiliency of children and their ability to rise above the horrors of war and conflict around the world. (Rev: BL 6/1–15/06; SLJ 9/06) [811]

13053 Grimes, Nikki. *A Dime a Dozen* (5–8). Illus. 1998, Dial $17.99 (978-0-8037-2227-9). 56pp. Through a series of original poems, the writer explores her childhood: its happy moments, its painful memories — including divorce, foster homes, and parents with drinking and gambling problems — and her search for herself as a teenager. (Rev: BL 12/1/98; HBG 3/99; SLJ 11/98; VOYA 4/99) [811]

13054 Grimes, Nikki. *Oh, Brother!* (2–4). Illus. by Mike Benny. 2008, Greenwillow $16.99 (978-0-688-17294-7). 32pp. In this collection of poems about a multicultural family, Xavier struggles to adjust to his new, younger stepbrother, Chris. (Rev: BL 12/1/07; SLJ 2/08) [811]

13055 Grimes, Nikki. *A Pocketful of Poems* (K–3). Illus. by Javaka Steptoe. 2001, Clarion $15.00 (978-0-618-93868-1). 32pp. Poems by a young African American girl named Tiana about urban topics —

pigeons, baseball, the moon — are presented in double-page spreads, each traditional poem facing a haiku. (Rev: BL 2/15/01*) [811]

13056 Grimes, Nikki. *Shoe Magic* (2–5). Illus. by Terry Widener. 2000, Orchard LB $17.99 (978-0-531-33286-3). 32pp. In this collection of poems about different kinds of shoes, each shoe embodies a young person's pride in accomplishment and hope for the future. (Rev: BL 9/15/00; HBG 3/01; SLJ 10/00) [811]

13057 Grimes, Nikki. *Tai Chi Morning: Snapshots of China* (4–8). Illus. by Ed Young. 2004, Cricket $15.95 (978-0-8126-2707-7). 64pp. Grimes's journal in verse describes her impressions on a tour of China. (Rev: BL 3/1/04; SLJ 5/04) [811]

13058 Grimes, Nikki. *What Is Goodbye?* (4–8). Illus. by Raúl Colón. 2004, Hyperion $15.99 (978-0-7868-0778-9). 64pp. A brother and sister mourn the death of their older brother in poems in alternating voices. (Rev: BL 5/1/04; SLJ 6/04) [811]

13059 Gunning, Monica. *America, My New Home* (2–5). Illus. by Ken Condon. 2004, Boyds Mills $16.95 (978-1-59078-057-2). In a series of poems, a young Jamaican girl, newly arrived in the United States, tells about her initial reactions to life in America and her homesickness for her native Caribbean island. (Rev: BL 8/05) [811]

13060 Gunning, Monica. *Under the Breadfruit Tree* (3–6). Illus. 1998, Boyds Mills $15.95 (978-1-56397-539-4). 48pp. These 38 poems describe the Caribbean peoples and their culture from the standpoint of a young Jamaican girl. (Rev: BL 2/15/98; HB 7/04; HBG 10/98; SLJ 4/98) [811]

13061 Hague, Michael, sel. *The Book of Fairy Poetry* (K–5). Illus. by Michael Hague. 2004, HarperCollins $19.99 (978-0-688-14004-5). 156pp. An oversize collection of varied works by poets including Walter de la Mare, Sir Walter Scott, Annie R. Rentoul, and Shakespeare. (Rev: SLJ 5/05) [811]

13062 Hale, Glorya, ed. *An Illustrated Treasury of Read-Aloud Poems for Young People: More Than 100 of the World's Best-Loved Poems for Parent and Child to Share* (2–6). Illus. 2003, Black Dog & Leventhal $14.95 (978-1-57912-289-8). 192pp. This thematically organized anthology of poetry — perfect for reading aloud — contains more than 100 poems from such well-known American and English poets as Maya Angelou, Robert Frost, Rudyard Kipling, Henry Wadsworth Longfellow, and William Wordsworth. (Rev: HBG 4/04; SLJ 11/03) [821.008]

13063 Hall, Donald. *The Man Who Lived Alone* (4–7). Illus. 1998, Godine paper $11.95 (978-1-56792-050-5). 36pp. A narrative poem concerning a man who ran away from abuse to see the world and returns in later life.

13064 Hall, Donald, ed. *The Oxford Illustrated Book of American Children's Poems* (PS–4). Illus. 1999, Oxford $25.00 (978-0-19-512373-9). 93pp. From classics like *A Visit from St. Nicholas* to works by Robert Frost, Shel Silverstein, Nikki Giovanni, Karla Kuskin, and others, this is an attractive anthology, perfect for reading aloud. (Rev: BL 1/1–15/00; HBG 3/00; SLJ 1/00) [811]

13065 Harley, Avis. *Fly with Poetry: An ABC of Poetry* (3–5). Illus. by author. 2000, Boyds Mills $13.95 (978-1-56397-798-5). 48pp. A collection of 27 original short poems, generally one for each letter of the alphabet (Y leaves space to write one's own poem). (Rev: SLJ 9/00) [811]

13066 Harrison, David L. *The Alligator in the Closet: And Other Poems Around the House* (2–4). Illus. by Jane Kendall. 2003, Boyds Mills $16.95 (978-1-56397-944-6). 48pp. Common childhood experiences in the home are the focus of these short and accessible poems. (Rev: BL 4/1/03) [811]

13067 Harrison, David L. *Pirates* (3–6). Illus. by Dan Burr. 2008, Boyds Mills $17.95 (978-1-59078-455-6). A realistic look, in poetry, at the lives of pirates; lush paintings accompany the 20 poems. (Rev: BCCB 9/08; SLJ 6/09) [811]

13068 Harrison, David L. *The Purchase of Small Secrets* (3–5). Illus. by Meryl Henderson. 1998, Boyds Mills $14.95 (978-1-56397-054-2). 48pp. This introspective collection of poems touches upon some of the landmark occasions in a boy's journey to maturity, such as fistfights, flirting, and shooting a gun. (Rev: HBG 3/99; SLJ 11/98) [811]

13069 Harrison, David L. *Vacation: We're Going to the Ocean* (2–4). Illus. by Rob Shepperson. 2009, Boyds Mills $16.95 (978-1-59078-568-3). 64pp. A boy narrates in verse the ups and downs of a family visit to the beach. (Rev: BL 5/1/09; SLJ 6/09) [811]

13070 Harrison, Michael, and Christopher Stuart-Clark, comps. *The Oxford Treasury of Time Poems* (4–9). 1999, Oxford LB $25.00 (1-19-276175-7). 155pp. From John Milton and William Blake to W. H. Auden and Sylvia Plath, this anthology contains poetry and thoughts about time. (Rev: SLJ 7/99) [811]

13071 Hayford, James. *Knee-Deep in Blazing Snow: Growing Up in Vermont* (4–7). Illus. by Michael McCurdy. 2005, Boyds Mills $17.95 (978-1-59078-338-2). 64pp. Hayford's simple, quiet poems evoke a simpler country life. (Rev: BL 1/1–15/06; SLJ 11/05) [811]

13072 Heard, Georgia, ed. *Falling down the Page: A Book of List Poems* (3–6). 2009, Roaring Brook $16.95 (978-1-59643-220-8). 48pp. This handsomely designed volume presents 45 list poems by contemporary authors including Jane Yolen, Lee Bennett Hopkins, and Eileen Spinelli. (Rev: BCCB 5/09; BL 3/1/09; SLJ 4/09) [811]

13073 High, Linda Oatman. *A Humble Life: Plain Poems* (2–4). Illus. by Bill Farnsworth. 2001, Eerdmans $17.00 (978-0-8028-5207-6). 40pp. Graceful poems and evocative paintings depict a year in a Mennonite and Amish county in Pennsylvania. (Rev: BL 12/15/01; HBG 3/02; SLJ 10/01) [811]

13074 Hittleman, Carol G., and Daniel R. Hittleman, eds. *A Grand Celebration: Grandparents in Poetry* (3–7). Illus. by Kay Life. 2002, Boyds Mills $16.95 (978-1-56397-901-9). 32pp. This anthology of 26 poems about grandparents represents a variety of cultures, levels of activity, and ages. (Rev: BL 4/1/02; HBG 10/02; SLJ 6/02) [808.819]

13075 Hoberman, Mary Ann. *You Read to Me, I'll Read to You: Very Short Scary Tales to Read Together* (PS–2). Illus. by Michael Emberley. 2007, Little, Brown $16.99 (978-0-316-01733-6). 32pp. Not-very-scary poems for two voices feature a variety of monsters and ghouls. (Rev: BL 5/1/07; SLJ 9/07) [811.54]

13076 Hoberman, Mary Ann. *You Read to Me, I'll Read to You: Very Short Stories to Read Together* (2–3). Illus. by Michael Emberley. 2001, Little, Brown $15.95 (978-0-316-36350-1). 32pp. A collection of short poems designed to be spoken aloud by two readers. (Rev: BL 8/01; HB 11/01; HBG 3/02; SLJ 8/01*) [811.54]

13077 Hollander, John, ed. *American Poetry* (4–10). Illus. by Sally Wern Comport. Series: Poetry for Young People. 2004, Sterling $14.95 (978-1-4027-0517-5). 48pp. A colorful celebration of American life, containing 26 poems by well-known poets including Robert Frost, Walt Whitman, Maya Angelou, and Langston Hughes. (Rev: SLJ 8/04) [811]

13078 Hollyer, Belinda, ed. *The Kingfisher Book of Family Poems* (3–5). Illus. by Holly Swain. 2003, Kingfisher $18.95 (978-0-7534-5557-9). 224pp. Poems in this large and varied anthology touch on all aspects of family life and emotions. (Rev: BL 5/1/03; HBG 10/03; SLJ 7/03) [821.008]

13079 Hollyer, Belinda, sel. *She's All That! Poems About Girls* (4–7). Illus. by Susan Hellard. 2006, Kingfisher $14.95 (978-0-7534-5852-5). 128pp. Poems celebrate today's diverse girls and their interests and concerns, with breezy, hip illustrations. (Rev: SLJ 7/06) [811]

13080 Hooper, Patricia. *Where Do You Sleep, Little One?* (PS–K). Illus. by John Winch. 2001, Holiday House $16.95 (978-0-8234-1668-4). 32pp. Animals answer the title's question in verse, and gather around a manger to see a sleeping child in this book that features beautiful collage illustrations. (Rev: BL 9/1/01; HBG 3/02; SLJ 9/01) [811]

13081 Hopkins, Lee Bennett, ed. *America at War: Poems Selected by Lee Bennett Hopkins* (5–8). Illus. by Stephen Alcorn. 2008, Simon & Schuster $21.99 (978-1-4169-1832-5). 96pp. A collection of 50-plus poems about American wars from the Revolutionary War to the conflict in Iraq, many centered on the pain felt by soldiers and their families. (Rev: BL 3/1/08; SLJ 3/08) [811]

13082 Hopkins, Lee Bennett, ed. *Behind the Museum Door* (K–3). Illus. by Stacey Dressen-McQueen. 2007, Abrams $16.95 (978-0-8109-1204-5). 32pp. The poems in this anthology celebrate the sights and sensations found within the walls of a museum. (Rev: BL 4/1/07) [811]

13083 Hopkins, Lee Bennett. *City I Love* (2–4). Illus. by Marcellus Hall. 2009, Abrams $16.95 (978-0-8109-8327-4). 32pp. Eighteen poems celebrate the urban wonders of cities around the world. (Rev: BL 3/15/09; SLJ 3/09) [811]

13084 Hopkins, Lee Bennett, ed. *Days to Celebrate: A Full Year of Poetry, People, Holidays, History, Fascinating Facts, and More* (4–7). Illus. by

Stephen Alcorn. 2005, Greenwillow LB $19.89 (978-0-06-000766-9). 112pp. A wide-ranging collection organized by month, each introduced by a calendar page that highlights important dates. (Rev: BL 1/1–15/05; SLJ 1/05) [811]

13085 Hopkins, Lee Bennett, ed. *Good Books, Good Times* (K–3). Illus. by Harvey Stevenson. 1990, HarperCollins LB $16.89 (978-0-06-022528-5). 32pp. Fourteen short poems celebrate book reading. (Rev: BL 11/15/90; HB 1/91; SLJ 10/90*) [811]

13086 Hopkins, Lee Bennett, ed. *Got Geography!* (4–7). Illus. by Philip Stanton. 2006, Greenwillow LB $17.89 (978-0-06-055602-0). 32pp. Poems celebrate the joys of travel and the maps that guide the way. (Rev: BL 2/1/06; SLJ 5/06) [811]

13087 Hopkins, Lee Bennett, ed. *Hamsters, Shells, and Spelling Bees: School Poems* (PS–3). Illus. by Sachiko Yoshikawa. Series: I Can Read! 2008, HarperCollins $16.99 (978-0-06-074112-9). 48pp. Suitable for beginning readers, these poems about school life were written by well-known poets such as Jane Yolen and Alice Schertle and feature a variety of formats. (Rev: BL 6/1–15/08; SLJ 8/08) [811]

13088 Hopkins, Lee Bennett, ed. *Hand in Hand* (5–8). 1994, Simon & Schuster $21.95 (978-0-671-73315-5). An overview of the history of American poetry, with an interesting selection of poems arranged chronologically. (Rev: BCCB 1/95; BL 1/1/95; SLJ 12/94; VOYA 4/95) [811]

13089 Hopkins, Lee Bennett, ed. *Incredible Inventions* (1–4). Illus. by Julia Sarcone-Roach. 2009, Greenwillow $17.99 (978-0-06-087245-8). 32pp. A collection of 16 diverse poems celebrating inventions from blue jeans to Band-Aids, fig newtons to roller coasters. (Rev: BL 12/1/08; SLJ 2/09) [600]

13090 Hopkins, Lee Bennett, ed. *Lives: Poems About Famous Americans* (3–6). Illus. 1999, HarperCollins $17.99 (978-0-06-027767-3). 40pp. Fourteen poems — 12 new to this collection — celebrate the lives of such famous Americans as Sacagawea, Thomas Edison, Eleanor Roosevelt, and Rosa Parks. (Rev: BL 3/15/99; HBG 10/99; SLJ 6/99) [811.008]

13091 Hopkins, Lee Bennett, sel. *My America: A Poetry Atlas of the United States* (3–8). Illus. by Stephen Alcorn. 2000, Simon & Schuster $19.95 (978-0-689-81247-7). 83pp. Seven regions of the United states including Washington, D.C., are explored in this anthology of 51 poems by 40 different poets. (Rev: BCCB 10/00; BL 9/1/03; HBG 3/01; SLJ 9/00) [811]

13092 Hopkins, Lee Bennett, ed. *Oh, No! Where Are My Pants?* (PS–2). Illus. by Wolf Erlbruch. 2005, HarperCollins LB $17.89 (978-0-688-17861-1). 32pp. Simple works by well-known poets about the impact of everyday disasters are paired with lovely illustrations. (Rev: BL 2/15/05; SLJ 2/05) [811]

13093 Hopkins, Lee Bennett, ed. *Surprises* (K–4). Illus. by Megan Lloyd. 1984, HarperCollins paper $3.99 (978-0-06-444105-6). 64pp. A collection of simple poems for beginning readers.

13094 Hopkins, Lee Bennett, ed. *Wonderful Words: Poems About Reading, Writing, Speaking, and Listening* (3–6). Illus. by Karen Barbour. 2004, Simon

& Schuster $16.95 (978-0-689-83588-9). 32pp. This colorfully illustrated collection of poems celebrates the wonders of language. (Rev: BL 2/1/04; SLJ 3/04) [811]

13095 Hubbell, Patricia. *City Kids* (PS–1). Illus. by Teresa Flavin. 2001, Marshall Cavendish $15.95 (978-0-7614-5079-5). 32pp. Simple poems and cheery pictures show kids engaged in such big-city activities as playing stickball, skipping rope, and stretching up like a skyscraper. (Rev: BL 3/1/01; HBG 10/01) [811]

13096 Hughes, Ted. *Collected Poems for Children* (4–8). Illus. by Raymond Briggs. 2007, Farrar $18.00 (978-0-374-31429-3). 272pp. A nicely illustrated collection of 250 British-flavored children's poems by the late Hughes, some funny, some serious, some even scary. (Rev: BL 2/15/07; HB 7/07; LMC 11/07; SLJ 3/07) [811]

13097 Iyengar, Malathi Michelle. *Tan to Tamarind: Poems About the Color Brown* (K–3). Illus. by Jamel Akib. 2009, Children's Book Pr. $16.95 (978-0-89239-227-8). 32pp. A poetic celebration of the color brown — in skin tones, foods, nature — with an emphasis on the beauty of diversity. (Rev: BL 3/15/09; SLJ 5/09) [811]

13098 Janeczko, Paul B., ed. *Dirty Laundry Pile* (3–6). 2001, HarperCollins LB $16.89 (978-0-688-16252-8). 40pp. An anthology of 27 poems told from the standpoint of an object or an animal such as a seashell, a cat, and a tree. (Rev: BL 4/15/01*; HB 7/01*; HBG 10/01; SLJ 8/01) [811]

13099 Janeczko, Paul B., sel. *Hey, You! Poems to Skyscrapers, Mosquitoes, and Other Fun Things* (1–4). 2007, HarperCollins $15.99 (978-0-06-052347-3). 40pp. These short poems — which include works by Ogden Nash, Nikki Grimes, Douglas Florian — directly address a diverse range of animals, inanimate objects, and concepts, from the lowly dust mite to black holes. (Rev: BL 4/15/07) [811]

13100 Janeczko, Paul B., ed. *A Kick in the Head: An Everyday Guide to Poetic Forms* (4–6). Illus. by Chris Raschka. 2005, Candlewick $17.99 (978-0-7636-0662-6). 64pp. Twenty-nine different types of poems (sonnets, ballads, haiku, etc.) are introduced; some funny, some sad, some silly, but all engaging and accompanied by beautiful collages. (Rev: BL 3/15/05; SLJ 3/05) [811.008]

13101 Janeczko, Paul B. *The Place My Words Are Looking For: What Poets Say About and Through Their Work* (4–9). Illus. 1990, Macmillan $17.95 (978-0-02-747671-2). 128pp. A collection of works by some of the best contemporary poets. (Rev: BCCB 7–8/90; BL 5/1/90; HB 5/90*; SLJ 5/90; VOYA 6/90) [811]

13102 Janeczko, Paul B., ed. *Stone Bench in an Empty Park* (5–12). Illus. 2000, Orchard LB $16.99 (978-0-531-33259-7). 40pp. An inspired collection of haiku from a variety of poets, illustrated with stunning black-and-white photographs. (Rev: BCCB 6/00; BL 3/15/00*; HB 3/00; HBG 10/00; SLJ 3/00) [811]

13103 Johnson, Dave, ed. *Movin': Teen Poets Take Voice* (5–10). Illus. by Chris Raschka. 2000, Orchard $15.95 (978-0-531-30258-3); paper $6.95 (978-0-531-07171-7). 52pp. An anthology of poems by teens who participated in New York Public Library workshops or submitted their work via the Web. (Rev: BL 3/15/00; HBG 10/00; SLJ 5/00; VOYA 6/00) [811]

13104 Johnston, Tony. *The Ancestors Are Singing* (4–8). Illus. by Karen Barbour. 2003, Farrar $16.00 (978-0-374-30347-1). 64pp. Mexico's geography, history, and culture are portrayed in poems full of vivid images. (Rev: BL 4/1/03; HBG 10/03; SLJ 4/03; VOYA 10/03) [811]

13105 Johnston, Tony. *My Mexico / México Mío* (K–3). Illus. by F. John Sierra. 1996, Penguin $16.99 (978-0-399-22275-7). 36pp. Mexican scenes are presented in double-page spreads with 18 poems in both English and Spanish. (Rev: BCCB 7–8/96; HB 5/96; SLJ 4/96) [811]

13106 Johnston, Tony. *Voice from Afar: Poems of Peace* (3–6). Illus. by Susan Guevara. 2008, Holiday House $16.95 (978-0-8234-2012-4). 32pp. Using diverse poetic forms, Johnston reflects on war and peace. (Rev: BL 12/15/08; SLJ 12/08) [811]

13107 Katz, Bobbi. *Once Around the Sun* (K–2). Illus. by LeUyen Pham. 2006, Harcourt $16.00 (978-0-15-216397-6). 40pp. Simple, happy poems celebrate the highlights of each month in an urban neighborhood. (Rev: BL 4/15/06; SLJ 5/06) [811]

13108 Katz, Bobbi, ed. *Pocket Poems* (PS–1). Illus. by Marylin Hafner. 2004, Dutton $15.99 (978-0-525-47172-1). 32pp. This collection of playful short poems is organized into chronological periods throughout the day. Also use *More Pocket Poems* (2009). (Rev: BL 2/1/04; SLJ 2/04) [811]

13109 Katz, Bobbi. *Trailblazers: Poems of Exploration* (3–8). Illus. by Carin Berger. 2007, Harper-Collins $18.99 (978-0-688-16533-8). 208pp. Poems about 120 explorers throughout the world and across the ages will arouse new interest in these figures. (Rev: SLJ 7/07)

13110 Katz, Susan. *Mrs. Brown on Exhibit and Other Museum Poems* (2–4). Illus. by R. W. Alley. 2002, Simon & Schuster $16.95 (978-0-689-82970-3). 40pp. A collection of poems about Mrs. Brown's class field trips to museums and the many discoveries they find there. (Rev: BL 6/1–15/02; HBG 3/03; SLJ 8/02) [811]

13111 Kennedy, Caroline, ed. *A Family of Poems: My Favorite Poetry for Children* (4–7). Illus. by Jon J. Muth. 2005, Hyperion $19.95 (978-0-7868-5111-9). 144pp. This collection of poems for children includes a number of Kennedy family favorites. (Rev: BL 10/15/05; SLJ 12/05*) [811]

13112 Kennedy, X. J., and Dorothy M. Kennedy, eds. *Talking Like the Rain: A First Book of Poems* (PS–3). Illus. by Jane Dyer. 1992, Little, Brown $19.95 (978-0-316-48889-1). 96pp. This is a cheerful collection of 100 well-illustrated poems in a variety of subjects and moods. (Rev: BCCB 7–8/92; BL 3/15/92; HB 7/92; SLJ 6/92) [821]

13113 Kipling, Rudyard. *If: A Father's Advice to His Son* (4–6). Photos by Charles R. Smith Jr. 2007, Simon & Schuster $14.99 (978-0-689-87799-5). Kipling's classic poem is given new life in this attractive volume full of photographs of boys and young men competing in a wide array of athletic events. (Rev: SLJ 2/07) [811]

13114 Lansky, Bruce, ed. *No More Homework! No More Tests! Kids' Favorite Funny School Poems* (2–6). Illus. 1997, Meadowbrook LB $8.00 (978-0-671-57702-5). 80pp. Humorous, often outrageous, poems that deal with real and fantastic school situations. (Rev: BL 9/15/97) [811]

13115 Larios, Julie. *Imaginary Menagerie: A Book of Curious Creatures* (K–3). Illus. by Julie Paschkis. 2008, Harcourt $16.00 (978-0-15-206325-2). 32pp. Gargoyles, trolls, dragons, and centaurs are among the creatures in these short, rhythmic poems accompanied by folk paintings that extend the words. (Rev: BL 3/15/08; SLJ 6/08) [811]

13116 Lawson, JonArno. *Black Stars in a White Night Sky* (4–7). Illus. by Sherwin Tjia. 2008, Boyds Mills $16.95 (978-1-59078-521-8). 118pp. An eclectic collection of poems — some silly, some serious, and all full of unusual turns of phrase and wordplay. (Rev: BL 2/15/08; SLJ 4/08) [811]

13117 Lee, Claudia M., ed. *Messengers of Rain and Other Poems from Latin America* (2–6). Illus. by Rafael Yockteng. 2002, Groundwood $18.95 (978-0-88899-470-7). 80pp. An anthology of more than 60 poems on a wide range of topics, translated from Spanish, by well-known and less-familiar writers. (Rev: SLJ 1/03) [811]

13118 Lesynski, Loris. *Dirty Dog Boogie* (2–5). Illus. by author. 1999, Annick LB $16.95 (978-1-55037-572-5); paper $6.95 (978-1-55037-573-2). 32pp. A joyous collection of poems that are filled with musical rhythms and quirky language. (Rev: HBG 10/99; SLJ 7/99) [811]

13119 Lesynski, Loris. *Zigzag: Zoems for Zindergarten* (PS–K). Illus. by author. 2004, Annick LB $19.95 (978-1-55037-875-7); paper $8.95 (978-1-55037-882-5). 32pp. Great for reading aloud, thse poems feature nonsense verse and bouncy rhythms. (Rev: BL 12/1/04; SLJ 1/05) [811]

13120 Levin, Jonathan, ed. *Walt Whitman: Poetry for Young People* (5–9). Illus. 1997, Sterling $14.95 (978-0-8069-9530-4). After a brief biographical sketch, this volume contains 26 poems and excerpts from longer poems, each introduced with an analysis. (Rev: HBG 3/98; SLJ 11/97) [811]

13121 Lewis, Claudia. *Long Ago in Oregon* (3–7). Illus. by Joel Fontaine. 1987, HarperCollins $11.95 (978-0-06-023839-1). 64pp. Short poems that recall the nostalgia of childhood in Oregon in the early 1900s. (Rev: BCCB 5/87; BL 7/87; SLJ 9/87)

13122 Lewis, J. Patrick. *Blackbeard: The Pirate King* (3–5). 2006, National Geographic $16.95 (978-0-7922-5585-7). 26pp. Poems about the infamous pirate are accompanied by diverse artwork. (Rev: BL 5/1/06; SLJ 12/06) [811]

13123 Lewis, J. Patrick. *Heroes and She-roes: Poems of Amazing and Everyday Heroes* (4–7). Illus. by

Jim Cooke. 2005, Dial $16.99 (978-0-8037-2925-4). 40pp. Helen Keller, Rosa Parks, and Gandhi are among the courageous individuals featured in this collection of poems. (Rev: BL 1/1–15/05; SLJ 3/05) [811]

13124 Lewis, J. Patrick. *Please Bury Me in the Library* (2–4). Illus. by Kyle M. Stone. 2005, Harcourt $16.00 (978-0-15-216387-7). 32pp. Sixteen original poems celebrate the joys of reading. (Rev: BL 2/15/05; SLJ 6/05) [811]

13125 Lewis, J. Patrick. *The Underwear Salesman: And Other Jobs for Better or Verse* (2–5). Illus. by Serge Bloch. 2009, Atheneum $16.99 (978-0-689-85325-8). 64pp. Nearly 50 poems full of wordplay look at a variety of occupations. (Rev: BL 3/1/09; SLJ 4/09) [811]

13126 Lewis, J. Patrick. *Vherses: A Celebration of Outstanding Women* (4–7). Illus. by Mark Summers. 2005, Creative $18.95 (978-1-56846-185-4). 32pp. The accomplishments of 14 notable and diverse women — including Emily Dickinson, Georgia O'Keeffe, and Venus and Serena Williams — are celebrated in an appealing blend of poetry and art. (Rev: BL 12/15/05) [811]

13127 Lewis, J. Patrick. *A World of Wonders: Geographic Travels in Verse and Rhyme* (3–5). Illus. by Alison Jay. 2002, Dial $16.99 (978-0-8037-2579-9). 40pp. Geographic terminology and facts are skillfully woven into verse in this attractive volume that touches on topics including seas, deserts, the poles, and the equator. (Rev: BL 3/15/02; HB 3/02; HBG 10/02; SLJ 4/02) [811]

13128 Lewis, J. Patrick. *The World's Greatest Poems* (1–4). Illus. by Keith Graves. 2008, Chronicle $16.99 (978-0-8118-5130-5). 33pp. Twenty-five nicely illustrated, diverse poems celebrate achievements documented in the *Guinness Book of Record,* chosen for their quirky content. (Rev: HB 7/08; SLJ 4/08)

13129 Lewis, J. Patrick, and Rebecca Kai Dotlich. *Castles: Old Stone Poems* (4–7). Illus. by Dan Burr. 2006, Boyds Mills $18.95 (978-1-59078-380-1). 48pp. The poems in this attractive collection celebrate castles of past and present. (Rev: BL 10/1/06; SLJ 10/06) [811]

13130 Lewis, J. Patrick, and Paul B. Janeczko. *Birds on a Wire* (2–4). Illus. by Gary Lippincott. 2008, Boyds Mills $17.95 (978-1-59078-383-2). 32pp. Realistic illustrations accompany this renga, a Japanese form of poetry in which one author writes a three-line verse and a second author writes the two lines following. (Rev: BCCB 9/08; BL 8/08; LMC 1/09) [811]

13131 Lillegard, Dee. *Go!* (PS). Illus. 2006, Knopf $14.95 (978-0-375-82387-9). 32pp. The short rhyming poems in this collection celebrate motion and things that move, ranging from skateboards and lawnmowers to garbage trucks and school buses. (Rev: BL 11/1/06; SLJ 12/06) [811]

13132 Lindbergh, Reeve. *On Morning Wings* (PS–1). Illus. by Holly Meade. 2002, Candlewick $15.99 (978-0-7636-1106-4). 32pp. A poem, based on Psalm 139 and illustrated in watercolors, thanking God for His loving care. (Rev: BL 9/15/02; HBG 3/03; SLJ 12/02)

13133 Little, Jean. *I Gave My Mom a Castle* (4–7). Illus. by Kady M. Denton. 2004, Orca paper $7.95 (978-1-55143-253-3). 80pp. Gifts — expected and unexpected, rewarding and trying — are the theme of this diverse collection of prose poems. (Rev: BL 3/1/04; SLJ 4/04) [811]

13134 Longfellow, Henry Wadsworth. *The Children's Hour* (K–2). Illus. by Glenna Lang. 1993, Godine $17.95 (978-0-87923-971-8). 32pp. The classic poem is illustrated with paintings depicting Longfellow spending time with his children. (Rev: BL 11/15/93) [811]

13135 Longfellow, Henry Wadsworth. *The Children's Own Longfellow* (5–8). Illus. 1908, Houghton $20.00 (978-0-395-06889-2). 109pp. Eight selections from the best-known and best-loved of Longfellow's poems. (Rev: BL 2/15/04*; SLJ 3/04)

13136 Longfellow, Henry Wadsworth. *Hiawatha and Megissogwon* (4–7). Illus. by Jeffrey Thompson. 2001, National Geographic $16.95 (978-0-7922-6676-1). 32pp. Artwork with an authentic Native American feel illustrates Hiawatha's exciting adventures in the "Pearl-Feather" section of Longfellow's epic poem. (Rev: BCCB 3/02; BL 11/15/01; HBG 3/02; SLJ 9/01) [811]

13137 Longfellow, Henry Wadsworth. *The Midnight Ride of Paul Revere* (2–4). Illus. by Christopher Bing. 2001, Handprint $17.95 (978-1-929766-13-0). 40pp. Bing's design juxtaposes historical objects, watercolors, and scratchboard work to great effect in this rendering of Longfellow's famous poem that also includes maps and notes. (Rev: BCCB 2/02; BL 12/15/01; HB 3/02; HBG 10/02; SLJ 12/01*) [811]

13138 Longfellow, Henry Wadsworth. *Paul Revere's Ride* (2–5). Illus. by Monica Vachula. 2003, Boyds Mills $16.95 (978-1-56397-799-2). 32pp. Longfellow's famous poem, with attractive illustrations that show background scenery. (Rev: BL 2/1/03; HBG 10/03; SLJ 5/03) [811]

13139 Longfellow, Henry Wadsworth. *Paul Revere's Ride: The Landlord's Tale* (2–5). Illus. by Charles Santore. 2003, HarperCollins LB $17.89 (978-0-06-623747-3). 40pp. The poem about Revere's famous ride is accompanied here by dramatic illustrations that convey a sense of urgency. (Rev: BL 2/1/03; HBG 10/03; SLJ 3/03) [811]

13140 McCord, David. *All Day Long: Fifty Rhymes of the Never Was and Always Is* (4–7). Illus. by Henry B. Kane. 1975, Little, Brown paper $6.95 (978-0-316-55532-6). A collection of poems on a variety of subjects, chiefly times that are important in childhood.

13141 McCord, David. *One at a Time: His Collected Poems for the Young* (3–8). Illus. by Henry B. Kane. 1986, Little, Brown $18.95 (978-0-316-55516-6). All seven of the poet's anthologies in one handsome volume.

13142 McGough, Roger, sel. *The Kingfisher Book of Funny Poems* (4–7). Illus. by Caroline Holden. 2002, Kingfisher $19.00 (978-0-7534-5480-0).

256pp. An anthology of poems arranged by theme that includes many by familiar names such as Ogden Nash, Lewis Carroll, and Shel Silverstein. (Rev: SLJ 6/02) [811]

13143 Martin, Bill, Jr., and Michael Sampson, eds. *The Bill Martin Jr. Big Book of Poetry* (PS–3). Illus. 2008, Simon & Schuster $21.00 (978-1-4169-3971-9). 176pp. This good-looking collection contains nearly 200 illustrated poems from mainly well-known poets. (Rev: BL 11/15/08; HB 1/09; LMC 3/09; SLJ 12/08) [811]

13144 Marzollo, Jean. *I Love You: A Rebus Poem* (PS). Illus. by Suse MacDonald. 2000, Scholastic paper $7.95 (978-0-590-37656-3). 40pp. A rebus puzzle book is used to present a series of simple poems about loving one another. (Rev: BL 12/15/99; HBG 10/00; SLJ 2/00) [811.54]

13145 Mavor, Salley, ed. *You and Me: Poems of Friendship* (PS–3). Illus. 1997, Orchard LB $17.99 (978-0-531-33045-6). 32pp. An anthology of 19 enjoyable poems that celebrate the joys and problems that come with friendships. (Rev: BL 7/97; HBG 3/98; SLJ 9/97) [811]

13146 Maynard, John, ed. *Alfred, Lord Tennyson* (5–8). Illus. by Allen Garns. Series: Poetry for Young People. 2004, Sterling $14.95 (978-0-8069-6612-0). 48pp. This large-format introduction to Tennyson's works includes an informative profile of the poet, selections accompanied by notes, and rich illustrations. (Rev: BL 2/15/04) [821]

13147 Maynard, John, ed. *Poetry for Young People: William Blake* (4–6). Illus. by Alessandra Cimatoribus. 2007, Sterling $14.95 (978-0-8069-3647-5). 48pp. A selection of Blake's poems follow a brief biography and a review of his literary importance. (Rev: BL 4/1/07) [811]

13148 Medina, Jane. *The Dream on Blanca's Wall / El sueño pegado en la pared de Blanca: Poems in English and Spanish / Poemas en ingles y espanol* (4–6). Illus. by Robert Casilla. 2004, Boyds Mills $16.95 (978-1-56397-740-4); paper $9.95 (978-1-59078-264-4). 48pp. Sixth-grader Blanca has wanted to be a teacher since the second grade; poems in English and Spanish describe her dreams and the looming personal and economic challenges. (Rev: SLJ 4/04) [811]

13149 Medina, Jane. *My Name Is Jorge: On Both Sides of the River* (3–7). Illus. by Fabricio Vandenbroeck. 1999, Boyds Mills $15.95 (978-1-56397-811-1). 48pp. An immigrant boy from Mexico describes his experiences in a series of 27 poems in English and Spanish. (Rev: HBG 3/00; SLJ 2/00) [811]

13150 Medina, Tony. *Love to Langston* (3–6). Illus. by R. Gregory Christie. 2002, Lee & Low $16.95 (978-1-58430-041-0). A celebration in poetry of the life and work of poet Langston Hughes, with biographical notes appended. (Rev: BCCB 3/02; BL 2/15/02; HBG 10/02; SLJ 3/02) [811]

13151 Micklos, John, ed. *Daddy Poems* (3–5). Illus. 2000, Boyds Mills $15.95 (978-1-56397-735-0). 32pp. This anthology of poems about dads and how they interact with their children contains the work of both well-known and less-well-known poets. (Rev: BL 8/00; HBG 10/00; SLJ 10/00) [811]

13152 Micklos, John, comp. *Grandparent Poems* (K–4). Illus. by Layne Johnson. 2004, Boyds Mills $15.95 (978-1-56397-900-2). 32pp. A collection of more than 20 poems by contemporary poets about grandparents and the special relationships between generations. (Rev: SLJ 3/04) [811]

13153 Micklos, John, ed. *Mommy Poems* (K–3). Illus. by Lori McElrath-Eslick. 2001, Boyds Mills $16.95 (978-1-56397-849-4); paper $9.95 (978-1-56397-908-8). 32pp. An anthology of 18 poems about mothers by such writers as Gary Soto and Nikki Giovanni. (Rev: BL 3/15/01; HBG 10/01) [811]

13154 Micklos, John, Jr. *No Boys Allowed: Poems About Brothers and Sisters* (PS–3). Illus. by Kathleen O'Malley. 2006, Boyds Mills $15.95 (978-1-59078-051-0). 31pp. A collection of poems that address with love and humor the sometimes-tricky relationship between brothers and sisters. (Rev: SLJ 5/06) [811]

13155 Miller, Kate. *Poems in Black and White* (4–7). Illus. 2007, Boyds Mills $17.95 (978-1-59078-412-9). 40pp. The poems and striking artwork in this slim volume explore images in black and white. (Rev: BL 4/1/07; SLJ 5/07) [811]

13156 Mitchell, Stephen. *The Wishing Bone and Other Poems* (3–6). Illus. by Tom Pohrt. 2003, Candlewick $16.99 (978-0-7636-1118-7). 56pp. Whimsical illustrations accompany these humorous and thought-provoking poems. (Rev: BL 4/1/03; HB 7/03; HBG 10/03; SLJ 5/03) [811]

13157 Moore, Lilian. *Beware, Take Care: Fun and Spooky Poems* (PS–1). Illus. by Howard Fine. 2006, Holt $16.95 (978-0-8050-6917-4). 32pp. Fifteen creepy poems about ghosts and monsters were first published more than 30 years ago. (Rev: BL 9/1/06; SLJ 10/06) [811]

13158 Mora, Pat. *Confetti* (1–4). Illus. by Enrique O. Sánchez. 1996, Lee & Low $15.95 (978-1-880000-25-0). 32pp. A series of poems that mingle Spanish expressions with basic English. (Rev: BL 11/15/96; SLJ 11/96) [811]

13159 Mora, Pat. *Join Hands* (K–3). Illus. by George Ancona. 2008, Charlesbridge $15.95 (978-1-58089-202-5); paper $6.95 (978-1-58089-203-2). 32pp. Celebrating creativity, this imaginative poem uses the Malaysian *pantoum* format and is illustrated with photographs of children in action. (Rev: BLO 7/30/08) [811]

13160 Mora, Pat, ed. *Love to Mama: A Tribute to Mothers* (PS–4). Illus. by Paula Barragán. 2001, Lee & Low $16.95 (978-1-58430-019-9). 32pp. A celebration of Latina mothers and grandmothers that ends with a glossary and notes about the poets. (Rev: BL 5/1/01; HB 7/01; HBG 10/01; SLJ 4/01*) [811]

13161 Mora, Pat. *Yum! Mmmm! Que rico!* (1–4). Illus. by Rafael Lopez. 2007, Lee & Low $16.95 (978-1-58430-271-1). 48pp. Haiku poems introduce readers to foods native to the Americas including blueberry, papaya, vanilla, and corn. (Rev: BCCB 12/07; BL 12/1/07; LMC 1/08; SLJ 9/07) [811]

13162 Mordhorst, Heidi. *Squeeze: Poems from a Juicy Universe* (2–4). Illus. by Jesse Torrey. 2005, Boyds Mills $16.95 (978-1-59078-292-7). 32pp. Twenty-four free-form poems and color photographs celebrates the experiences that are the essence of childhood. (Rev: BL 10/15/05; SLJ 3/06) [811]

13163 Morgenstern, Constance. *Waking Day* (4–7). Illus. 2006, North Word $17.95 (978-1-55971-919-3). 32pp. In a picture book for older readers, Morgenstern melds Impressionist works with lines from her own poetry. (Rev: BL 2/15/06) [811]

13164 Morninghouse, Sundaira. *Nightfeathers* (PS–K). Illus. by Jody Kim. 1990, Open Hand $9.95 (978-0-940880-27-6); paper $4.95 (978-0-940880-28-3). 32pp. In 24 short poems, a typical day in the life of an African American child is portrayed. (Rev: BL 6/1/90) [811]

13165 Morris, Jackie, comp. *The Barefoot Book of Classic Poems* (3–9). Illus. by Jackie Morris. 2006, Barefoot Books $19.99 (978-1-905236-56-5). 128pp. A handsomely illustrated anthology of nearly 75 classic poems, with works by such well-known writers as Robert Frost, John Donne, Robert Louis Stevenson, and William Wordsworth. (Rev: SLJ 1/07) [811]

13166 Morrison, Lillian. *Way to Go! Sports Poems* (4–8). Illus. by Susan Spellman. 2001, Boyds Mills $16.95 (978-1-56397-961-3). 48pp. Sport lovers will appreciate this collection of poems full of rhythm and life, with vibrant illustrations. (Rev: HBG 3/02; SLJ 10/01) [811]

13167 Moss, Jeff. *Bone Poems* (3–5). Illus. by Tom Leigh. 1997, Workman $14.95 (978-0-7611-0884-9). 78pp. A group of rhymes that explore facts about dinosaurs and make paleontology fun. (Rev: HBG 3/98; SLJ 12/97*) [811]

13168 Moss, Jeff. *The Butterfly Jar* (2–5). Illus. by Chris L. Demarest. 1989, Bantam $17.95 (978-0-553-05704-1). 128pp. Upbeat poetry, including the silly and the serious. (Rev: BL 2/1/90; SLJ 7/90) [811]

13169 Mozelle, Shirley. *The Kitchen Talks* (PS–2). Illus. by Petra Mathers. 2006, Holt $15.95 (978-0-8050-7143-6). 32pp. This collection of short poems — often involving riddles — reveals the innermost thoughts of inanimate objects from the kitchen. (Rev: BL 3/15/06; SLJ 4/06) [811]

13170 Mullins, Tom, ed. *Running Lightly . . . : Poems for Young People* (4–9). 1998, Mercier paper $12.95 (978-1-85342-193-8). A charming collection of old songs and ballads, nonsense rhymes, and lyrics. (Rev: BL 5/15/98; SLJ 7/98) [811]

13171 Myers, Walter Dean. *Blues Journey* (5–8). Illus. by Christopher Myers. 2003, Holiday $18.95 (978-0-8234-1613-4). 48pp. Poems reflecting the soulfulness of blues music, accompanied by illustrations. (Rev: BL 2/15/03; HB 5/03; HBG 10/03; SLJ 4/03*; VOYA 4/03) [811]

13172 Myers, Walter Dean. *Jazz* (3–5). Illus. by Christopher Myers. 2006, Holiday $18.95 (978-0-8234-1545-8). 48pp. This vibrant blend of poetry and artwork celebrates jazz and the musicians who

helped to shape this uniquely American brand of music. (Rev: BCCB 2/07; BL 9/1/06; HBG 4/07; SLJ 9/06) [811]

13173 New, William. *The Year I Was Grounded* (4–7). Illus. by Robert Kakegamic. 2009, Tradewind paper $12.95 (978-1-896580-35-7). 104pp. Stuck at home, Geordie finds plenty of time to write in his journal, recording events and thoughts in a variety of poetic forms. (Rev: BL 5/1/09; SLJ 7/09) [811]

13174 Nicholls, Judith, ed. *Someone I Like: Poems About People* (3–5). Illus. 2000, Barefoot Books $16.95 (978-1-84148-004-6). 40pp. This anthology of 26 poems explores children's feelings for family members and friends. (Rev: BL 4/1/00; SLJ 7/00) [808.819]

13175 Norman, Lissette. *My Feet Are Laughing* (K–3). Illus. by Frank Morrison. 2006, Farrar $16.00 (978-0-374-35096-3). 32pp. In this collection of 16 energetic free-verse poems with evocative illustrations, a young Dominican American girl describes her family and life in New York City's Harlem. (Rev: BL 4/1/06; SLJ 5/06) [811]

13176 *Once Upon a Poem: Favorite Poems That Tell Stories* (4–7). Illus. 2004, Scholastic $18.95 (978-0-439-65108-0). 128pp. This appealing collection of 15 narrative poems includes offerings from Lewis Carroll, Longfellow, C. S. Lewis, Roald Dahl, Edward Lear, and Robert Service. (Rev: BL 1/1–15/05; SLJ 1/05) [811]

13177 O'Neill, Mary. *Hailstones and Halibut Bones* (PS–3). Illus. by Leonard Weisgard. 1973, Doubleday paper $8.95 (978-0-385-41078-6). Imaginative poems about color. (Rev: BL 3/1/04)

13178 Paraskevas, Betty. *Junior Kroll* (2–4). Illus. by Michael Paraskevas. 1993, Harcourt $13.95 (978-0-15-241497-9). Fifteen poems about a mischievous boy and his adventures. (Rev: BCCB 5/93; BL 3/1/04; SLJ 6/93) [822]

13179 Park, Linda Sue. *Tap Dancing on the Roof: Sijo (Poems)* (3–6). Illus. by Istvan Banyai. 2007, Clarion $16.00 (978-0-618-23483-7). 48pp. Using a traditional form of poetry from Korea, *sijo*, Park presents images of everyday experiences such as lunchtime and school while also encouraging readers to experiment with their own *sijo*. (Rev: BCCB 11/07; BL 12/1/07; HB 1/08; SLJ 11/07) [811]

13180 Paschen, Elise, ed. *Poetry Speaks to Children* (3–5). Illus. 2005, Sourcebooks $19.95 (978-1-4022-0329-9). 112pp. A broad selection of poems (nearly 100) representing many genres and poets, with an accompanying CD. (Rev: BL 12/15/05; SLJ 1/06) [811]

13181 Pearson, Susan, ed. *The Drowsy Hours: Poems for Bedtime* (PS–1). Illus. by Peter Malone. 2002, HarperCollins LB $16.89 (978-0-06-029421-2). 40pp. This thoughtful anthology captures the bedtime mood perfectly, but will be appreciated any time of the day. (Rev: BL 10/15/02; HBG 10/02; SLJ 6/02) [811.008]

13182 Perdomo, Willie. *Visiting Langston* (2–4). Illus. by Bryan Collier. 2002, Holt $15.95 (978-0-8050-6744-6). A young girl anticipates in poetry a visit to poet Langston Hughes's house in Harlem.

(Rev: BCCB 3/02; BL 2/15/02; HBG 10/02; SLJ 4/02) [811]

13183 Philip, Neil, ed. *The Fish Is Me: Bathtime Rhymes* (PS). Illus. by Claire Henley. 2002, Clarion $16.00 (978-0-618-15939-0). 28pp. These 18 rhymes are drawn from poets from several countries, and will immediately appeal to children, whether they enjoy baths or not. (Rev: BL 11/1/02; HBG 3/03; SLJ 8/02) [811.008]

13184 Philip, Neil, ed. *Hot Potato: Mealtime Rhymes* (PS–1). Illus. by Claire Henley. 2004, Clarion $16.00 (978-0-618-31554-3). 32pp. The bouncy rhyming poems in this vividly illustrated picture-book collection focus on the sounds and rhythms of eating. (Rev: BL 4/15/04; SLJ 5/04) [811]

13185 Philip, Neil, ed. *Songs Are Thoughts: Poems of the Inuit* (K–4). Illus. by Maryclare Foa. 1995, Orchard $15.95 (978-0-531-06893-9). 32pp. Short Inuit poems are featured in double-page spreads, each containing a poem and an illustration. (Rev: BCCB 5/95; BL 4/15/95; SLJ 4/95) [897]

13186 Podwal, Mark. *Jerusalem Sky: Stars, Crosses, and Crescents* (3–5). Illus. 2005, Doubleday $15.95 (978-0-385-74689-2). 32pp. In poems and paintings, Podwal celebrates the power and majesty of Jerusalem, a city sacred to three religions: Christianity, Islam, and Judaism. (Rev: BL 10/1/05*; SLJ 9/05) [811]

13187 Pomerantz, Charlotte. *Thunderboom! Poems for Everyone* (PS–2). Illus. by Rob Shepperson. 2006, Front St. $17.95 (978-1-932425-40-6). 48pp. There's something for everyone in this diverse collection of poems ranging from boisterous to playful to quiet. (Rev: BL 4/1/06; SLJ 5/06) [811]

13188 Prelutsky, Jack. *Be Glad Your Nose Is on Your Face and Other Poems* (K–5). Illus. by Brandon Dorman. 2008, Greenwillow $22.99 (978-0-06-157653-9). 208pp. More than 100 poems by the first Children's Poet Laureate are collected in this brightly illustrated volume. (Rev: BLO 3/5/09; SLJ 3/09) [811]

13189 Prelutsky, Jack. *The Frogs Wore Red Suspenders* (PS–3). Illus. by Petra Mathers. 2002, Greenwillow LB $17.89 (978-0-688-16720-2). 64pp. Splendid illustrations accompany whimsical rhymes in this charming book for preschoolers and young readers. (Rev: BCCB 3/02; BL 3/15/02; HB 3/02; HBG 10/02; SLJ 2/02*) [811]

13190 Prelutsky, Jack. *Me I Am!* (PS–2). Illus. by Christine Davenier. 2007, Farrar $16.00 (978-0-374-34902-8). 32pp. Prelutsky's previously published poem about individuality and diversity is shown in dynamic illustrations of three different children. (Rev: BL 4/1/07) [811]

13191 Prelutsky, Jack. *Monday's Troll* (4–6). Illus. by Peter Sís. 1996, Greenwillow $15.89 (978-0-688-14373-2). 40pp. Seventeen original poems that deal with supernatural beings like witches, trolls, wizards, and ogres. (Rev: BCCB 3/96; BL 4/15/96; HB 5/96; SLJ 4/96*) [811]

13192 Prelutsky, Jack. *Nightmares: Poems to Trouble Your Sleep* (5–8). Illus. by Arnold Lobel. 1976, Greenwillow LB $17.89 (978-0-688-84053-2).

38pp. Shuddery, macabre poems that will frighten but amuse a young audience. A sequel is *The Headless Horseman Rides Tonight: More Poems to Trouble Your Sleep* (1980).

13193 Prelutsky, Jack. *A Pizza the Size of the Sun* (3–6). Illus. by James Stevenson. 1996, Greenwillow $19.89 (978-0-688-13236-1). 160pp. Humorous, imaginative light verses explore a variety of subjects. (Rev: BCCB 9/96; BL 9/15/96*; HB 9/96; SLJ 9/96*) [811]

13194 Prelutsky, Jack, ed. *The Random House Book of Poetry for Children* (2–6). Illus. by Arnold Lobel. 1983, Random LB $21.99 (978-0-394-95010-5). 248pp. Old standbys and new gems are included in this fine anthology of 572 poems.

13195 Prelutsky, Jack, ed. *Read a Rhyme, Write a Rhyme* (3–5). Illus. by Meilo So. 2005, Knopf $16.95 (978-0-375-82286-5). 32pp. Organized in themes — dogs, bugs, birthdays, and so forth — this anthology groups poems on spreads and on each encourages readers to finish an uncompleted "poem-start." (Rev: BL 11/15/05; SLJ 11/05) [811]

13196 Prelutsky, Jack. *Scranimals* (2–4). Illus. by Peter Sís. 2002, HarperCollins LB $18.89 (978-0-688-17820-8). 48pp. The imaginary animals that inhabit Scranimal Island (the "Ban` anconda" and the "Orangutangerine," for example) are described in fanciful verse and art. (Rev: BCCB 10/02; BL 9/15/02; HB 1/03; HBG 3/03; SLJ 9/02*) [811]

13197 Prelutsky, Jack. *The Swamps of Sleethe: Poems from Beyond the Solar System* (3–5). Illus. by Jimmy Pickering. 2009, Knopf $16.99 (978-0-375-84674-8). 40pp. An entertaining collection of poems full of wordplay and grisly, fascinating horror, with suitably macabre illustrations. (Rev: BL 3/1/09; HB 5/09; SLJ 3/09) [811]

13198 Prelutsky, Jack, ed. *The 20th Century Children's Poetry Treasury* (3–5). Illus. 1999, Random $19.95 (978-0-679-89314-1). 96pp. On each of the illustrated two-page spreads, there are four to six poems on a single theme, for a total of more than 200 poems by 137 poets. (Rev: BL 12/15/99; HBG 3/00; SLJ 12/99*) [811]

13199 Quattlebaum, Mary. *Family Reunion* (2–3). Illus. by Andrea Shine. 2004, Eerdmans $16.00 (978-0-8028-5237-3). 32pp. Ten-year-old Jodie's summer trip to a family reunion is engagingly portrayed in this collection of varied short poems. (Rev: BL 4/1/04; SLJ 6/04) [811]

13200 Rogasky, Barbara, ed. *Leaf by Leaf: Autumn Poems* (5–8). Illus. by Marc Tauss. 2001, Scholastic paper $16.95 (978-0-590-25347-5). 40pp. Verses by poets including Shelley, Yeats, and Whitman accompany stunning autumnal photographs. (Rev: BL 7/01; HBG 3/02; SLJ 9/01*) [811.008]

13201 Rosen, Michael. *The Best of Michael Rosen* (3–5). Illus. by Quentin Blake. 1995, Wetlands paper $16.95 (978-1-57143-046-5). 136pp. Sixty-five insightful, often lighthearted poems by the popular English poet. (Rev: BL 2/1/96; SLJ 5/05) [808.81]

13202 Rosen, Michael, ed. *Poems for the Very Young* (PS–2). Illus. by Bob Graham. 1993, Kingfisher

$17.95 (978-1-85697-908-5). 80pp. A delightful collection of rhymes for young children, chiefly from American and British sources and illustrated with charming cartoonlike drawings. (Rev: BL 1/1/94*; SLJ 1/94) [821]

13203 Rossetti, Christina. *Sing Song: A Nursery Rhyme Book* (K–3). Illus. by Arthur Hughes. 1969, Dover paper $7.95 (978-0-486-22107-6). 130pp. Many of the poems are about small creatures and familiar objects and have a singing quality that young children enjoy.

13204 Rosten, Norman. *A City Is* (PS–2). Illus. by Melanie Hope Greenberg. 2004, Holt $16.95 (978-0-8050-6793-4). 32pp. Varied short poems in free verse evoke both the hustle and bustle and the quiet moments of life in a city, many of them specifically about New York. (Rev: BL 3/1/04; SLJ 4/04) [811]

13205 Rowden, Justine. *Paint Me a Poem: Poems Inspired by Masterpieces of Art* (4–7). Illus. 2005, Boyds Mills $16.95 (978-1-59078-289-7). 32pp. Each of the 14 poems in this collection is inspired by a famous painting from the National Gallery of Art. (Rev: BL 11/1/05; SLJ 10/05) [811.54]

13206 Ruddell, Deborah. *A Whiff of Pine, a Hint of Skunk: A Forest of Poems* (1–3). Illus. by Joan Rankin. 2009, Simon & Schuster $16.99 (978-1-4169-4211-5). 40pp. Poetry and facts are interwoven in this whimsical look at the lives of plants and animals in a forest. (Rev: BCCB 3/09; BL 3/15/09; LMC 8/09; SLJ 4/09*) [811]

13207 Rylant, Cynthia. *Baby Face: A Book of Love for Baby* (PS). Illus. by Diane Goode. 2008, Simon & Schuster $16.99 (978-1-4169-4909-1). 40pp. Six little poems highlight various activities of a multicultural group of babies. (Rev: BL 3/1/08; SLJ 8/08) [811]

13208 Rylant, Cynthia. *The Stars Will Still Shine* (PS–1). Illus. by Tiphanie Beeke. 2005, HarperCollins $16.99 (978-0-06-054639-7). 40pp. In rhyming text, the author celebrates the continuity of life and such constants as the sky, stars, birds, and church bells. (Rev: BL 10/15/05; SLJ 10/05) [811]

13209 Schertle, Alice. *Button Up!* (PS–2). Illus. by Petra Mathers. 2009, Harcourt $16.00 (978-0-15-205050-4). 40pp. Articles of clothing describe their roles and characteristics in verse accompanied by humorous illustrations. (Rev: BCCB 6/09; BL 5/15/09; HB 5/09; SLJ 5/09) [811]

13210 Schertle, Alice. *Keepers* (1–4). Illus. by Ted Rand. 1996, Lothrop LB $15.89 (978-0-688-11635-4). 32pp. A collection of original poems in which everyday objects become transformed through one's imagination. (Rev: BL 10/15/96; SLJ 12/96) [811]

13211 Schertle, Alice. *Teddy Bear, Teddy Bear* (PS–2). Illus. by Linda Hill Griffith. 2003, HarperCollins LB $16.89 (978-0-688-16871-1). Subjects dear to children are presented in bouncy poems. (Rev: HBG 10/03; SLJ 7/03) [811]

13212 Schertle, Alice. *When the Moon Is High* (PS). Illus. by Julia Noonan. 2003, HarperCollins LB $16.89 (978-0-688-15144-7). When baby can't fall asleep, Daddy decides to take a moonlight stroll with the child in his arms and on their way they

encounter a number of nighttime creatures. (Rev: HBG 10/03; SLJ 7/03) [811]

13213 Schmidt, Gary D., ed. *Robert Frost* (5–7). Illus. by Henri Sorensen. Series: Poetry for Young People. 1994, Sterling $14.95 (978-0-8069-0633-1). 48pp. An anthology of 25 poems suitable for young people, with watercolor illustrations that picture the New England landscape that Frost loved. (Rev: BL 12/1/94; SLJ 2/95) [811]

13214 Schoonmaker, Frances, ed. *Edna St. Vincent Millay* (3–7). Illus. Series: Poetry for Young People. 2000, Sterling $14.95 (978-0-8069-5928-3). 48pp. A representative collection of Millay's poetry illustrated with evocative watercolors. (Rev: BL 3/15/00; HBG 10/00; SLJ 2/00) [811]

13215 Schoonmaker, Frances, ed. *Henry Wadsworth Longfellow* (4–8). Illus. Series: Poetry for Young People. 1999, Sterling $14.95 (978-0-8069-9417-8). A generous, carefully selected presentation of Longfellow's poetry illustrated by full-color paintings and accompanied by biographical notes. (Rev: BL 3/15/99; HBG 9/99; SLJ 3/99) [811]

13216 Shields, Carol Diggory. *BrainJuice: American History Fresh Squeezed!* (4–8). Illus. by Richard Thompson. 2002, Handprint $14.95 (978-1-929766-62-8). 80pp. A timeline runs across the tops of these pages of poems about events in American history. (Rev: HBG 3/03; SLJ 1/03) [811]

13217 Sidman, Joyce. *Eureka! Poems About Inventors* (4–6). Illus. by K. Bennett Chavez. 2002, Millbrook LB $24.90 (978-0-7613-1665-7). 48pp. Sidman celebrates the lives and inventions of people throughout history in a chronological collection of free-verse poetry. (Rev: BL 10/15/02; HBG 3/03; SLJ 1/03) [811.54]

13218 Sidman, Joyce. *This Is Just to Say: Poems of Apology and Forgiveness* (4–7). Illus. by Pamela Zagarenski. 2007, Houghton $16.00 (978-0-618-61680-0). 48pp. Poems of all kinds written by a fictional 6th-grade class to say "sorry" are paired with responses from the recipients. (Rev: BL 5/15/07; SLJ 5/07) [811]

13219 Siebert, Diane. *Heartland* (K–4). Illus. by Wendell Minor. 1989, HarperCollins paper $6.99 (978-0-06-443287-0). 32pp. A lyrical celebration of the Midwest. (Rev: BL 3/1/89; SLJ 5/89)

13220 Siebert, Diane. *Motorcycle Song* (K–4). Illus. 2002, HarperCollins LB $16.89 (978-0-06-028733-7). 32pp. Invigorating poetry and energetic artwork capture the thrill of a motorcycle ride. (Rev: BL 2/1/02; HBG 10/02; SLJ 4/02) [793.73]

13221 Siebert, Diane. *Tour America: A Journey Through Poems and Art* (4–7). 2006, Chronicle $17.95 (978-0-8118-5056-8). 64pp. Natural and manmade sights across America are celebrated in this appealing collection of poetry and art. (Rev: BL 6/1–15/06; SLJ 6/06*) [811]

13222 Silverstein, Shel. *Falling Up* (3–6). Illus. 1996, HarperCollins LB $19.89 (978-0-06-024803-1). 176pp. More than 150 delightful original poems that amuse and amaze. (Rev: BCCB 6/96; BL 7/96*; HB 9/96; SLJ 7/96) [811]

13223 Simon, Seymour, ed. *Star Walk* (4–8). Illus. 1995, Morrow LB $14.93 (978-0-688-11887-7). 32pp. Simple poems and outstanding photographs create an impressive introduction to stars and outer space. (Rev: BL 3/1/95; SLJ 4/95) [811]

13224 Singer, Marilyn. *All We Needed to Say: Poems About School from Tanya and Sophie* (PS–3). Illus. by Lorna Clark. 1996, Simon & Schuster $15.00 (978-0-689-80667-4). 28pp. Two girls compare their school experiences in a series of short monologues. (Rev: BCCB 9/96; BL 8/96; SLJ 9/96) [811]

13225 Singer, Marilyn. *Central Heating: Poems About Fire and Warmth* (3–5). Illus. by Meilo So. 2005, Knopf LB $17.99 (978-0-375-82912-3). 48pp. From the warmth of chili peppers and roasted marshmallows to the heat of electricity and bombs, Singer explores the properties of fire. (Rev: BL 12/1/04; SLJ 1/05*) [811]

13226 Smith, Hope Anita. *Keeping the Night Watch* (5–8). Illus. by E. B. Lewis. 2008, Holt $18.95 (978-0-8050-7202-0). 80pp. In this equally poetic and well-illustrated sequel to *The Way a Door Closes* (2003), 13-year-old C.J.'s father is back home but the family's foundation remains shaky at first. Coretta Scott King Author Honor Book, 2009. (Rev: BL 3/15/08; SLJ 6/08) [811]

13227 Smith, William Jay, comp. *Up the Hill and Down: Poems for the Very Young* (PS–2). Illus. by Allan Eitzen. 2003, Boyds Mills $16.95 (978-1-56397-028-3). 32pp. Robert Louis Stevenson, Aileen Fisher, and Marchette Chute are among the writers represented in this collection of nearly 30 poems. (Rev: HBG 4/04; SLJ 11/03) [811]

13228 *Songs, Seas, and Green Peas: Poems for Anywhere* (K–4). Series: Poetry Parade. 2000, Heinemann LB $21.36 (978-1-57572-400-3). 32pp. A collection of poems by both well-known and obscure poets that contains no particular theme or subjects. Also use *Wishes, Wings, and Other Things: Poems for Anytime* (2000). (Rev: HBG 3/01; SLJ 2/01) [811]

13229 Soto, Gary. *Canto Familiar* (4–6). Illus. 1995, Harcourt $18.00 (978-0-15-200067-7). 88pp. Simple poems, many involving Mexican Americans, celebrate experiences at school, home, and in the street. A companion to *Neighborhood Odes* (1992). (Rev: BL 10/1/95; SLJ 12/95*) [811]

13230 Soto, Gary. *Fearless Fernie: Hanging Out with Fernie and Me* (4–6). Illus. by Regan Dunnick. 2002, Penguin $14.99 (978-0-399-23615-0). 64pp. Older readers are invited into the mind and life of an unnamed middle-school boy in this exceptional collection of poems. (Rev: BL 3/15/02; HB 7/02; HBG 10/02; SLJ 3/02*) [811]

13231 Soto, Gary. *Neighborhood Odes* (4–6). Illus. by David Diaz. 1992, Harcourt $15.95 (978-0-15-256879-5). 80pp. Unrhymed verses celebrate such items in a Mexican-American neighborhood as pinatas, weddings, libraries, and tennis shoes. (Rev: BL 6/15/92; HB 5/92*; SLJ 5/92) [811]

13232 Spinelli, Eileen. *Tea Party Today: Poems to Sip and Savor* (1–3). Illus. by Karen M. Dugan. 1999, Boyds Mills $15.95 (978-1-56397-662-9).

32pp. Tea and teatime inspired this group of poems about the ceremony and the emotions it evokes. (Rev: BL 4/1/99; HBG 10/99; SLJ 4/99) [811.54]

13233 Stavans, Ilan, ed. *Wachale! Poetry and Prose About Growing Up Latino in America* (5–8). 2001, Cricket $16.95 (978-0-8126-4750-1). 160pp. A bilingual anthology about Latino experiences, both in the past and in the present. (Rev: BCCB 2/02; BL 2/1/02; HBG 10/02; SLJ 2/02; VOYA 6/02) [810.8]

13234 Steig, Jeanne. *Alpha Beta Chowder* (5–8). Illus. 1992, HarperCollins LB $14.89 (978-0-06-205007-6). A collection of nonsense verses celebrating the joy of words — their sound and meaning — with each verse playing with a letter of the alphabet. (Rev: BL 11/15/92; SLJ 12/92) [811]

13235 Stevenson, James. *Candy Corn* (2–5). Illus. 1999, Greenwillow $16.99 (978-0-688-15837-8). 56pp. Humorous recollections and details of ordinary life are the subjects of this delightful book of poems illustrated with ink-and-watercolor pictures. (Rev: BCCB 5/99; BL 3/15/99*; HB 7/99; HBG 10/99; SLJ 5/99) [811]

13236 Stevenson, James. *Cornflakes: Poems* (3–5). Illus. 2000, Greenwillow $16.99 (978-0-688-16718-9). 48pp. An eclectic collection of short verses on many subjects, illustrated with bright, clear, ink-and-watercolor pictures. (Rev: BL 3/15/00; HB 7/00; HBG 10/00; SLJ 6/00) [811]

13237 Stevenson, Robert Louis. *Block City* (PS). Illus. by Daniel Kirk. 2005, Simon & Schuster $14.95 (978-0-689-86964-8). 32pp. Stevenson's 1883 poem gets new life in a picture book that shows the joys of building — and then destroying — towers of building blocks. (Rev: BL 6/1–15/05) [811]

13238 Stevenson, Robert Louis. *A Child's Garden of Verses* (K–4). Illus. 1989, Chronicle $17.95 (978-0-87701-608-3). 121pp. A handsome edition of the old favorite, using some 100 19th-century illustrations. (Rev: BL 11/1/89*; SLJ 2/90) [821]

13239 Stevenson, Robert Louis. *Poetry for Young People: Robert Louis Stevenson* (3–5). Illus. Series: Poetry for Young People. 2000, Sterling $14.95 (978-0-8069-4956-7). 48pp. Chosen mainly from *A Child's Garden of Verses,* this is a representative collection of Stevenson's work for children preceded by a biographical note. (Rev: BL 3/15/00; HBG 10/00; SLJ 7/00) [821]

13240 Stockland, Patricia M., comp. *Cobwebs, Chatters, and Chills: A Collection of Scary Poems* (3–6). Illus. by Sara Rojo Perez. Series: The Poet's Toolbox. 2004, Compass Point LB $23.93 (978-0-7565-0565-3). 32pp. An illustrated anthology of poems by well-known writers that demonstrate poetic forms and concepts. (Rev: SLJ 6/04) [811]

13241 Stockland, Patricia M., comp. *The Free and the Brave: A Collection of Poems About the United States* (3–6). Illus. by Sara Rojo Perez. Series: The Poet's Toolbox. 2004, Compass Point LB $23.93 (978-0-7565-0563-9). 32pp. Patriotic poetry by authors ranging from Carl Sandburg to Ogden Nash is illustrated with cartoon art and used to demonstrate poetic concepts. (Rev: SLJ 6/04) [811]

13242 Sturges, Philemon. *Down to the Sea in Ships* (3–5). Illus. by Giles Laroche. 2005, Penguin $16.99 (978-0-399-23464-4). 32pp. Birch canoes, Viking ships, cod schooners, and modern ferries are among the vessels depicted in stunning illustrations and varied verses. (Rev: BL 5/15/05; SLJ 6/05) [811]

13243 Swados, Elizabeth. *Hey You! C'mere: A Poetry Slam* (2–5). Illus. by Joe Cepeda. 2002, Scholastic $16.95 (978-0-439-09257-9). 47pp. A collection of poems, presented by a group of urban children, that reflect their everyday concerns. (Rev: BL 4/15/02; HBG 10/02; SLJ 4/02) [811]

13244 Swenson, May. *The Complete Poems to Solve* (5–8). Illus. by Christy Hale. 1993, Macmillan $13.95 (978-0-02-788725-9). 128pp. From simple riddles to more complex questions, each of these poems contains a puzzle. (Rev: HB 3/93; SLJ 5/93) [811]

13245 Szekeres, Cyndy, ed. *A Small Child's Book of Cozy Poems* (PS). Illus. 1999, Scholastic $6.95 (978-0-590-38364-6). 32pp. From Mother Goose to nonsense verse, this is a sweet collection of rhymes for the very young. (Rev: BL 2/1/99; HBG 10/99; SLJ 4/99) [811.008]

13246 Taberski, Sharon, ed. *Morning, Noon, and Night: Poems to Fill Your Day* (PS–3). Illus. by Nancy Doniger. 1996, Mondo $14.95 (978-1-57255-128-2). 32pp. The day's activities are traced in 29 poems by well-known writers. (Rev: BL 12/15/96; SLJ 5/96) [811]

13247 Tadjo, Veronique, ed. *Talking Drums: A Selection of Poems from Africa South of the Sahara* (4–8). Illus. by Veronique Tadjo. 2004, Bloomsbury $15.95 (978-1-58234-813-1). 96pp. Arranged by theme, these 75 poems — traditional and contemporary — cover a broad range of topics. (Rev: BL 3/1/04; SLJ 4/04; VOYA 4/04) [811]

13248 Temperley, Howard. *In the Days of Dinosaurs: A Rhyming Romp Through Dino History* (3–5). Illus. by Michael Kline. 2004, Williamson paper $12.95 (978-0-8249-8662-9). 61pp. Nearly 40 humorous and fact-filled poems describe specific dinosaurs and reflect on dinosaur-related issues. (Rev: SLJ 3/05) [811]

13249 Tennyson, Alfred Lord. *The Lady of Shalott* (5–7). Illus. by Genevieve Cote. 2005, Kids Can $16.95 (978-1-55337-874-7). 48pp. The setting of Tennyson's "The Lady of Shalott" is moved from the England of King Arthur to the streets of an early 20th-century city in this beautifully illustrated adaptation. (Rev: BL 10/1/05; SLJ 12/05) [821]

13250 Thaler, Mike. *Pig Little* (PS–1). Illus. by Paige Miglio. 2006, Holt $16.95 (978-0-8050-6977-8). A little pig describes all the fun of a day at the beach with his mommy. (Rev: SLJ 7/06) [811]

13251 Vecchione, Patrice, ed. *Whisper and Shout: Poems to Memorize* (4–6). 2002, Cricket $16.95 (978-0-8126-2656-8). 144pp. An anthology of 55 accessible poems (many by contemporaries) with a lengthy introduction on poetry and a closing section on resources and biographies. (Rev: BL 4/15/02; HBG 10/02; SLJ 5/02) [811]

13252 Vestergaard, Hope. *I Don't Want to Clean My Room: A Mess of Poems About Chores* (PS–2). Illus. by Carol Koeller. 2007, Dutton $16.99 (978-0-525-47776-1). Simple, upbeat poems feature children helping out around the house and finding satisfaction in doing a good job. (Rev: SLJ 7/07)

13253 Viorst, Judith. *If I Were in Charge of the World and Other Worries: Poems for Children and Their Parents* (5–8). Illus. 1984, Macmillan paper $5.99 (978-0-689-70770-4). Easily read poems focus on topics familiar to young people. [811]

13254 Walker, Rob D. *Mama Says: A Book of Love for Mothers and Sons* (PS–3). Illus. by Leo and Diane Dillon. 2009, Scholastic $16.99 (978-0-439-93208-0). 32pp. In 12 languages — including Hebrew, Arabic, Cherokee, Russian, and English — this is a celebration of the ways in which mothers guide their children. (Rev: BL 4/15/09; SLJ 5/09) [811]

13255 Wallace, Daisy, ed. *Ghost Poems* (4–7). Illus. by Tomie dePaola. 1979, Holiday paper $4.95 (978-0-8234-0849-8). 32pp. New and old poems to delight and frighten young readers.

13256 Wallace, Daisy, ed. *Witch Poems* (3–6). Illus. by Trina S. Hyman. 1976, Holiday House LB $14.95 (978-0-8234-0281-6); paper $4.95 (978-0-8234-0850-4). 32pp. Eighteen poems chosen from several different sources on a wide variety of witches.

13257 Waters, Fiona, comp. *Dark as a Midnight Dream: Poetry Collection 2* (5–8). Illus. by Zara Slattery. 1999, Evans Brothers $24.95 (978-0-237-51845-5). 286pp. An extensive anthology of poetry arranged by subjects such as "Mythical Creatures" and "City Life" that features such writers as Robert Browning, William Shakespeare, William Butler Yeats, William Wordsworth, Langston Hughes, and Carl Sandburg. (Rev: SLJ 11/99) [811]

13258 Weatherford, Carole Boston. *Birmingham, 1963* (3–6). Illus. 2007, Boyds Mills $17.95 (978-1-59078-440-2). 32pp. An anonymous fictional 10-year-old tells, in free verse, the story of the Ku Klux Klan church bombing in 1963 that killed four young girls. (Rev: BL 9/15/07; LMC 10/07; SLJ 12/07) [811]

13259 Weatherford, Carole Boston. *Sidewalk Chalk: Poems of the City* (3–6). Illus. by Dimitrea Tokunbo. 2001, Boyds Mills $15.95 (978-1-56397-084-9). 32pp. Poems about the pleasures of urban life are accompanied by colorful full-page illustrations. (Rev: BL 9/15/01; HBG 3/02; SLJ 1/02) [811]

13260 Weisburd, Stefi. *Barefoot: Poems for Naked Feet* (K–3). Illus. by Lori McElrath-Eslick. 2008, Boyds Mills $16.95 (978-1-59078-306-1). 32pp. The pleasures and perils of bare feet are explored in 27 poems and watercolor illustrations. (Rev: BL 2/15/08; LMC 3/08; SLJ 8/08) [811]

13261 Whipple, Laura. *Eric Carle's Dragons Dragons and Other Creatures That Never Were* (2–6). Illus. by Eric Carle. 1991, Penguin $21.99 (978-0-399-22105-7). 69pp. This is a collection of poems about dragons and other mythological creatures illustrated by Eric Carle. (Rev: BCCB 12/91; BL 11/1/91; HB 11/91; SLJ 10/91) [811]

13262 Whitman, Walt. *Nothing but Miracles* (K–2). Illus. by Susan L. Roth. 2003, National Geographic $15.95 (978-0-7922-6143-8). A joyful cat family, shown in naive collages, illustrates the words to Whitman's poem from *Leaves of Grass*. (Rev: HBG 4/04; SLJ 1/04) [811.3]

13263 Whitman, Walt. *When I Heard the Learn'd Astronomer* (K–3). Illus. by Loren Long. 2004, Simon & Schuster $16.95 (978-0-689-86397-4). 32pp. A young boy's growing appreciation of the universe around him is shown in vivid acrylic artwork and the Whitman verse. (Rev: BL 11/15/04*) [811]

13264 Wilbur, Richard. *Runaway Opposites* (4–6). Illus. by Henrik Drescher. 1995, Harcourt $15.00 (978-0-15-258722-2). 32pp. An intriguing, involved book of poems that deal with synonyms and antonyms. (Rev: BCCB 4/95; BL 4/15/95; SLJ 5/95) [811]

13265 Willard, Nancy. *A Visit to William Blake's Inn: Poems for Innocent and Experienced Travelers* (2–5). Illus. by Alice Provensen and Martin Provensen. 1981, Harcourt $16.00 (978-0-15-293822-2); paper $7.00 (978-0-15-293823-9). 44pp. A collection of poems that won the Newbery Award, 1982.

13266 Wilson, Edwin Graves, ed. *Maya Angelou* (4–10). Illus. by Jerome Lagarrigue. Series: Poetry for Young People. 2007, Sterling $14.95 (978-1-4027-2023-9). 48pp. Twenty-five carefully selected poems — with commentary, footnotes, and illustrations — are introduced by information on Angelou's life and influences. (Rev: SLJ 10/07*) [811]

13267 Winnick, Karen B. *A Year Goes Round: Poems for the Months* (K–2). Illus. by author. 2001, Boyds Mills $15.95 (978-1-56397-898-2). A look at the months of the year in short, simple poems about children's activities. (Rev: HBG 3/02; SLJ 11/01) [811]

13268 Winters, Kay. *Voices of Ancient Egypt* (3–6). Illus. by Barry Moser. 2003, National Geographic $16.95 (978-0-7922-7560-2). 32pp. Two-page spreads introduce ancient Egyptian workers — among them a scribe, a pyramid builder, and a herdsman — who describe their lives in first-person free verse. (Rev: BL 9/15/03; HBG 4/04; SLJ 9/03) [932]

13269 Wong, Janet S. *Knock on Wood: Poems About Superstitions* (2–5). Illus. by Julie Paschkis. 2003, Simon & Schuster $17.95 (978-0-689-85512-2). 40pp. Vampires, ghosts, broken mirrors, and black cats are just some of the topics of these aptly illustrated poems about potential bad luck. (Rev: BL 11/15/03; HB 9/03; HBG 4/04; SLJ 12/03)

13270 Wong, Janet S. *Twist: Yoga Poems* (3–5). Illus. by Julie Paschkis. 2007, Simon & Schuster $17.99 (978-0-689-87394-2). 32pp. Short, accessible poems, each focusing on a familiar pose, consider both physical and philosophical aspects of yoga, while illustrations feature multiethnic practitioners and colorful borders of animals and plants. (Rev: BL 1/1–15/07) [811]

13271 Worth, Valerie. *Peacock and Other Poems* (3–6). Illus. by Natalie Babbitt. 2002, Farrar $15.00 (978-0-374-35766-5). 48pp. A posthumously published collection of 26 poems in the author's signature style, beautifully illustrated with detailed pencil drawings. (Rev: BCCB 6/02; BL 8/02; HB 7/02*; HBG 10/02; SLJ 5/02) [811]

13272 Worthen, Tom, ed. *Broken Hearts . . . Healing: Young Poets Speak Out on Divorce* (5–9). Illus. by Kyle Hernandez. Series: Young Poets Speak Out. 2001, Poet Tree $26.95 (978-1-58876-150-7); paper $14.95 (978-1-58876-151-4). 234pp. This large selection of poems written by their peers about divorce, family breakups, and blended families will resonate with young readers. (Rev: SLJ 9/01; VOYA 10/01) [811]

13273 Xinran Xue. *Motherbridge of Love* (PS–2). Illus. by Josee Masse. 2007, Barefoot Books $16.99 (978-1-84686-047-8). 32pp. The illustrations for this lyrical poem directed at an adopted girl show a happy girl with Chinese features and her birth mother and adoptive mother. (Rev: BL 10/15/07; LMC 3/08; SLJ 1/08) [895.1]

13274 Yolen, Jane. *O Jerusalem* (4–6). Illus. by John Thompson. 1996, Scholastic $15.95 (978-0-590-48426-8). A group of original poems that explore the importance of Jerusalem in Judaism, Christianity, and Islam. (Rev: BL 2/1/96*; SLJ 3/96*) [811]

13275 Yolen, Jane. *Sacred Places* (5–9). Illus. 1996, Harcourt $16.00 (978-0-15-269953-6). An international collection of informational poems about the places sacred to various faiths. (Rev: BCCB 12/00; BL 10/1/96; SLJ 3/96) [811]

13276 Yolen, Jane, and Andrew F. Peters, eds. *Here's a Little Poem* (PS). Illus. by Polly Dunbar. 2007, Candlewick $21.99 (978-0-7636-3141-3). 112pp. This appealing anthology of more than 60 diverse poems includes works by Jack Prelutsky, Langston Hughes, Rosemary Wells, Gertrude Stein, A. A. Milne, Robert Louis Stevenson. (Rev: BL 4/1/07) [811]

13277 Yolen, Jane, and Heidi Stemple. *Dear Mother, Dear Daughter* (3–5). Illus. 2001, Boyds Mills $15.95 (978-1-56397-886-9). 32pp. Using simple verses this book consists of double-page spreads; on one side is a letter from a daughter to her mother, on the other the reply. (Rev: BL 3/15/01; HBG 10/01) [811]

13278 Zimmer, Tracie Vaughn. *Steady Hands: Poems About Work* (4–7). Illus. by Megan Halsey. 2009, Clarion $16.00 (978-0-618-90351-1). 48pp. Short poems celebrate a variety of contemporary occupations from bakers to surgeons to dog walkers. (Rev: BL 1/1–15/09; SLJ 4/09) [811]

African American Poetry

13279 Adedjouma, Davida, ed. *The Palm of My Heart: Poetry by African American Children* (1–4). Illus. by R. Gregory Christie. 1996, Lee & Low $15.95 (978-1-880000-41-0). 32pp. Twenty poems by African American children about the beauty and joy of being black. (Rev: BCCB 12/96; BL 2/15/97; SLJ 1/97) [811]

13280 Boling, Katharine. *New Year Be Coming! A Gullah Year* (K–3). Illus. by Daniel Minter. 2002, Whitman $16.99 (978-0-8075-5590-3). 32pp. These twelve poems — one for each month of the year — are written in the unique Gullah dialect of a group of African Americans living on the coast of South Carolina and Georgia. (Rev: BCCB 1/03; BL 11/15/02; HB 11/02; HBG 3/03; SLJ 9/02) [811]

13281 Brooks, Gwendolyn. *Bronzeville Boys and Girls* (K–4). Illus. by Faith Ringgold. 2007, Harper-Collins $16.99 (978-0-06-029505-9). 41pp. This newly illustrated collection of poems by Pulitzer Prize-winner Gwendolyn Brooks, originally published in 1956, celebrates the universal joys of childhood. (Rev: BL 2/1/07; SLJ 2/07) [811]

13282 Burleigh, Robert. *Langston's Train Ride* (3–6). Trans. and illus. by Leonard Jenkins. 2004, Scholastic LB $16.99 (978-0-439-35239-0). 32pp. Langston Hughes's well-known poem "The Negro Speaks of Rivers," written when he was only 18, is beautifully complemented by the collage artwork. (Rev: BL 9/15/04) [811]

13283 Clifton, Lucille. *Everett Anderson's Goodbye* (K–2). Illus. by Ann Grifalconi. 1983, Holt paper $5.95 (978-0-8050-0800-5). 32pp. Poems about a young African American boy. (Rev: BL 3/1/04)

13284 Forman, Ruth. *Young Cornrows Callin Out the Moon* (PS). Illus. by Cbabi Bayoc. 2007, Children's Book Pr. $16.95 (978-0-89239-218-6). 32pp. A happy poem about summer life among the brownstones of South Philadelphia. (Rev: BL 2/1/07) [811]

13285 Giovanni, Nikki, ed. *Hip Hop Speaks to Children: A Celebration of Poetry with a Beat* (3–5). Illus. by Kristen Balouch. 2008, Sourcebooks $19.99 (978-1-4022-1048-8). 72pp. Fifty-one poems — by authors including Langston Hughes, Gwendolyn Brooks, Eloise Greenfield, Tupac Shakur, and Queen Latifah — provide a historical collage of African American poetry in print and voice; accompanying CD. (Rev: BL 9/15/08) [811]

13286 Giovanni, Nikki. *Knoxville, Tennessee* (PS–3). Illus. by Larry Johnson. 1994, Scholastic $14.95 (978-0-590-47074-2). 32pp. Nikki Giovanni re-creates the summers she spent growing up in Knoxville and the simple pleasures she enjoyed. (Rev: BCCB 7–8/94; BL 2/15/94; HB 9/94; SLJ 4/94) [811]

13287 Giovanni, Nikki. *The Sun Is So Quiet* (K–2). Illus. by Ashley Bryan. 1996, Holt $14.95 (978-0-8050-4119-4). 32pp. Thirteen poems that depict everyday occurrences, with illustrations that feature African American children in many cultures. (Rev: BL 10/15/96; SLJ 1/97) [811]

13288 Greenfield, Eloise. *Honey, I Love* (PS–2). Illus. by Jan S. Gilchrist. 2003, HarperCollins LB $18.89 (978-0-06-009124-8). 32pp. An illustrated collection of poems about the loves of a young African American girl (such as her mother, car rides, swimming), first published in 1978. (Rev: BL 2/15/03; HBG 10/03; SLJ 2/03) [811.54]

13289 Greenfield, Eloise. *Honey, I Love, and Other Love Poems* (2–4). Illus. by Diane Dillon and Leo Dillon. 1978, HarperCollins $16.99 (978-0-690-01334-4); paper $6.99 (978-0-06-443097-5). 48pp. Sixteen poems on family love and friendship as experienced by an African American girl.

13290 Greenfield, Eloise. *Nathaniel Talking* (2–5). Illus. by Jan S. Gilchrist. 1988, Writers & Readers $12.95 (978-0-86316-200-8). 32pp. Simple poems on an African American's recollection of childhood. (Rev: BL 12/15/89; HB 9/90; SLJ 8/89) [811]

13291 Grimes, Nikki. *Danitra Brown Leaves Town* (PS–3). Illus. by Floyd Cooper. 2002, HarperCollins LB $16.89 (978-0-688-13156-2). 32pp. Best friends Danitra and Zuri describe their very different summer experiences through letters in this book of free-verse poems. (Rev: BCCB 4/02; BL 2/15/02; HBG 10/02; SLJ 2/02) [811]

13292 Grimes, Nikki. *My Man Blue* (2–5). Illus. by Jerome Lagarrigue. 1999, Dial $16.99 (978-0-8037-2326-9). 32pp. In a series of lyrical poems, Damon describes being a child in Harlem and his friendship for an older man, Blue, whose son was killed on the streets. (Rev: BL 10/15/99; HBG 10/99; SLJ 5/99) [811]

13293 Grimes, Nikki. *Stepping Out with Grandma Mac* (4–7). Illus. 2001, Orchard paper $16.95 (978-0-531-30320-7). 48pp. A loving 10-year-old girl describes a very independent grandmother. (Rev: BL 5/15/01*; HBG 10/01; SLJ 7/01) [811.54]

13294 Grimes, Nikki. *Thanks a Million* (1–3). Illus. by Cozbi A. Cabrera. 2006, Greenwillow $16.99 (978-0-688-17292-3). 32pp. Poetry in various forms celebrates the joys of showing gratitude for everyday kindnesses and pleasures. (Rev: BL 3/15/06; SLJ 3/06) [811]

13295 Grimes, Nikki. *When Daddy Prays* (PS–K). Illus. by Tim Ladwig. 2002, Eerdmans $16.00 (978-0-8028-5152-9). 32pp. An African American child's impressions of his father's reliance on faith during everyday activities such as gardening, attending a baseball game, and celebrating the New Year. (Rev: BL 3/1/02; HBG 10/02; SLJ 4/02) [811.54]

13296 Hudson, Wade, ed. *Pass It On: African-American Poetry for Children* (PS–3). Illus. by Floyd Cooper. 1993, Scholastic $15.95 (978-0-590-45770-5). 32pp. A fine anthology with contributions by such writers as Langston Hughes and Gwendolyn Brooks. (Rev: BL 1/15/93*) [811]

13297 Hughes, Langston. *My People* (PS–3). Illus. by Charles R. Smith Jr. 2009, Atheneum $17.99 (978-1-4169-3540-7). 40pp. With striking sepia portraits of African Americans of all ages, Smith brings new life to Hughes's brief poem. (Rev: BL 2/1/09; LMC 5/09; SLJ 2/09) [811]

13298 Hughes, Langston. *The Negro Speaks of Rivers* (K–3). Illus. by E. B. Lewis. 2009, Disney $16.99 (978-0-7868-1867-9). 32pp. The classic poem about the link between waterways and African American experience is beautifully illustrated. (Rev: BL 11/15/08; LMC 5/09; SLJ 2/09) [811]

13299 *In Daddy's Arms I Am Tall: African Americans Celebrating Fathers* (3–5). Illus. by Javaka

Steptoe. 1997, Lee & Low $15.95 (978-1-880000-31-1). 32pp. An impressively illustrated book of poems about African American fathers and their many roles. (Rev: BL 2/15/98*; HB 5/05; HBG 3/98; SLJ 2/98) [811]

13300 Johnson, Dinah. *Hair Dance!* (K–3). Illus. 2007, Holt $16.95 (978-0-8050-6523-7). 32pp. Color photographs and rhythmic verses celebrate African American hair in diverse styles. (Rev: BCCB 12/07; BL 12/15/07; SLJ 11/07) [811]

13301 Lewis, J. Patrick. *Freedom Like Sunlight: Praisesongs for Black Americans* (5–12). Illus. 2000, Creative $17.95 (978-1-56846-163-2). 40pp. This collection of original poems pays tribute to such important African Americans as Sojourner Truth, Arthur Ashe, Rosa Parks, Marian Anderson, Malcolm X, and Langston Hughes. (Rev: BL 9/15/00*; HBG 3/01; SLJ 12/00) [811]

13302 Medina, Tony. *DeShawn Days* (2–5). Illus. by R. Gregory Christie. 2001, Lee & Low $16.95 (978-1-58430-022-9). DeShawn is a young African American boy who describes in verse his home in the projects, the constant sound of sirens, the grim news on TV, his friends, and the music they enjoy. (Rev: HBG 10/01; SLJ 7/01*) [811]

13303 Muse, Daphne, ed. *The Entrance Place of Wonders: Poems of the Harlem Renaissance* (3–5). Illus. by Charlotte Riley-Webb. 2006, Abrams $16.95 (978-0-8109-5997-2). 32pp. Lively oil paintings illustrate this collection of 20 child-friendly poems from the Harlem Renaissance. (Rev: BL 2/1/06; SLJ 3/06) [811]

13304 Myers, Walter Dean. *Angel to Angel: A Mother's Gift of Love* (4–8). Illus. 1998, HarperCollins LB $15.89 (978-0-06-027722-2). 40pp. A photo/poetry montage with 10 distinctly styled poems and photographs focusing on African American mothers and children, and reflecting the relationship between words and pictures. (Rev: BL 2/15/98; HBG 10/98; SLJ 6/98) [811]

13305 Nikola-Lisa, W. *Bein' with You This Way* (PS–2). Illus. by Michael Bryant. 1994, Lee & Low $15.95 (978-1-880000-05-2). 32pp. A rap poem led by an African American girl talks about racial tolerance. (Rev: BL 7/94; SLJ 7/94) [811]

13306 Richards, Beah E. *Keep Climbing, Girls* (K–3). Illus. by R. Gregory Christie. 2006, Simon & Schuster $15.95 (978-1-4169-0264-5). 32pp. "Keep climbing" is the recommendation for girls in this beautifully illustrated poem written by the late African American actress. (Rev: BL 2/1/06; SLJ 2/06*) [811]

13307 Shange, Ntozake. *Ellington Was Not a Street* (3–5). Illus. by Kadir Nelson. 2004, Simon & Schuster $15.95 (978-0-689-82884-3). 40pp. Adapted from Shange's poem "Mood Indigo," this richly illustrated picture book for older readers celebrates his childhood home and the many African American intellectuals and artists who visited. (Rev: BL 2/15/04; SLJ 1/04) [811]

13308 Smith, Hope Anita. *The Way a Door Closes* (5–8). Illus. by Shane W. Evans. 2003, Holt $18.95 (978-0-8050-6477-3). 64pp. A series of poems con-

vey the feelings of a 13-year-old African American boy whose warm, loving home is destroyed when his father loses his job. (Rev: BL 5/1/03; HBG 10/03; SLJ 5/03*) [811]

13309 Thomas, Joyce Carol. *The Blacker the Berry* (PS–2). Illus. by Floyd Cooper. 2008, HarperCollins $16.99 (978-0-06-025375-2). 32pp. The many skin shades of an African heritage are celebrated in this collection of poems. (Rev: BCCB 7–8/08; BL 5/15/08; HB 8–9/08; SLJ 8/08) [811]

13310 Troupe, Quincy. *Little Stevie Wonder* (2–4). Illus. by Lisa Cohen. 2005, Houghton $18.00 (978-0-618-34060-6). 32pp. Vibrant illustrations highlight this free-verse account of Stevie Wonder's childhood and early success. (Rev: BL 2/1/05; SLJ 6/05) [811]

13311 Woodson, Jacqueline. *Locomotion* (3–6). 2003, Penguin $15.99 (978-0-399-23115-5). 128pp. A young boy whose parents have died and whose sister is in a different foster home expresses his grief through poetry. (Rev: BCCB 3/03; BL 2/15/03; HB 3/03*; HBG 10/03; SLJ 1/03) [811]

Animals

13312 Alonzo, Sandra. *Gallop-o-Gallop* (1–4). Illus. by Kelly Murphy. 2007, Dial $16.99 (978-0-8037-2967-4). All sorts of horses — tame and wild, working in rodeos, farms, and ranches —are represented in this collection of poems accompanied by beautiful artwork. (Rev: SLJ 6/07)

13313 Andreae, Giles. *Rumble in the Jungle* (PS). Illus. by David Wojtowycz. 1997, Little Tiger $14.95 (978-1-888444-08-7). A collection of poems about the animals that a small group of ants encounter as they march through the jungle. (Rev: HBG 3/98; SLJ 11/97) [811]

13314 Carryl, Charles Edward. *The Camel's Lament* (K–3). Illus. by Charles Santore. 2004, Random LB $18.99 (978-0-375-91426-3). 32pp. Stunning watercolors breathe new life into Edward Carryl Charles's poem about the lowly camel. (Rev: BL 7/04; SLJ 10/04*) [811]

13315 Chernaik, Judith, ed. *Carnival of the Animals: Poems Inspired by Saint-Saëns' Music* (K–3). Illus. by Satoshi Kitamura. 2006, Candlewick $16.99 (978-0-7636-2960-1). 32pp. In this brightly illustrated title, which is bundled with an audio CD, poets offer their profiles of animal characters portrayed musically in the Saint-Saëns classic. (Rev: BCCB 5/06; BL 3/15/06*; HBG 10/06; LMC 10/06; SLJ 4/06) [811]

13316 Crawley, Dave. *Dog Poems* (PS–2). Illus. by Tamara Petrosino. 2007, Boyds Mills $16.95 (978-1-59078-454-9). 32pp. Lighthearted rhyming poems look at dogs and their relations with humans. (Rev: BCCB 10/07; BL 9/1/07; SLJ 8/07) [811]

13317 De Vos, Philip. *Carnival of the Animals* (1–4). Illus. by Piet Grobler. 2000, Front St. $16.95 (978-1-886910-47-8). 38pp. Surreal paintings accompany clever verses to bring to life the Saint-Saens musical fantasy. (Rev: BL 8/00; HBG 10/00; SLJ 7/00) [821]

13318 Elliott, David. *On the Farm* (PS–2). Illus. by Holly Meade. 2008, Candlewick $16.99 (978-0-7636-3322-6). 32pp. The animals of an appealing farmyard are celebrated in verse and woodblock and watercolor illustrations. (Rev: BCCB 3/08; BL 5/15/08; HB 3/08; SLJ 2/08) [636]

13319 Fleischman, Paul. *I Am Phoenix: Poems for Two Voices* (4–9). Illus. 1985, HarperCollins paper $5.99 (978-0-06-446092-7). A group of love poems about birds that are designed to be read by two voices or groups of voices. (Rev: BL 12/1/85) [811]

13320 Fleischman, Paul. *Joyful Noise: Poems for Two Voices* (3–6). Illus. by Eric Beddows. 1988, HarperCollins LB $16.89 (978-0-06-021853-9); paper $5.99 (978-0-06-446093-4). 64pp. Poems for reading aloud that explore the lives of insects. Newbery Medal winner, 1989. (Rev: BL 2/15/88; HB 5/88; SLJ 2/88)

13321 Florian, Douglas. *Bow Wow Meow Meow* (PS–2). Illus. 2003, Harcourt $17.00 (978-0-15-216395-2). 56pp. A collection of offbeat poems about cats and dogs, accompanied by watercolor illustrations. (Rev: BL 2/1/03*; HB 5/03; HBG 10/03; SLJ 5/03) [811]

13322 Florian, Douglas. *Dinothesaurus: Prehistoric Poems and Paintings* (K–3). Illus. by author. 2009, Atheneum $17.99 (978-1-4169-7978-4). 56pp. Twenty humorous poems provide puns and facts about dinosaurs in this accessible book with collage art and a pronunciation guide. (Rev: BCCB 2/09; BL 3/1/09; HB 3/09; SLJ 5/09) [811]

13323 Florian, Douglas. *Insectlopedia* (3–5). Illus. 1998, Harcourt $16.00 (978-0-15-201306-6). 56pp. A well-designed book of poems about insects and spiders. (Rev: BCCB 7–8/98; BL 3/15/98; SLJ 4/98) [811]

13324 Florian, Douglas. *Lizards, Frogs, and Polliwogs* (3–5). Illus. 2001, Harcourt $16.00 (978-0-15-202591-5). 48pp. Playful poetry and imaginative artwork are combined in this book of short original poems about a variety of reptiles and amphibians. (Rev: BL 3/15/01*; HB 5/01; HBG 10/01) [811]

13325 Florian, Douglas. *Mammalabilia* (2–4). Illus. 2000, Harcourt $16.00 (978-0-15-202167-2). 48pp. Twenty-one short, clever rhymes and inventive illustrations examine various members of the animal kingdom. (Rev: BCCB 3/00; BL 3/15/00; HB 3/00; HBG 10/00; SLJ 4/00) [811]

13326 Florian, Douglas. *Omnibeasts: Animal Poems and Paintings* (1–4). 2004, Harcourt $18.00 (978-0-15-205038-2). 96pp. Entertaining wordplay and inventive shapes add to this inviting collection of poems and art about animals. (Rev: BL 10/15/04; SLJ 10/04) [811]

13327 Florian, Douglas. *Zoo's Who: Poems and Paintings* (K–3). Illus. 2005, Harcourt $17.00 (978-0-15-204639-2). 56pp. Clever, brief verses about all sorts of animals (not just the ones found in zoos) are accompanied by unusual art. (Rev: BL 3/15/05; SLJ 4/05) [811]

13328 Franco, Betsy. *A Curious Collection of Cats* (PS–3). Illus. by Michael Wertz. 2009, Tricycle $16.99 (978-1-58246-248-6). 32pp. Thirty-four concrete poems celebrate cats' essential catness. (Rev: BCCB 7–8/09; BL 3/15/09; HB 5/09; SLJ 4/09) [811]

13329 Frost, Robert. *The Runaway* (PS–2). Illus. by Glenna Lang. 1998, Godine $17.95 (978-1-56792-006-2). 32pp. Lovely illustrations accompany this poem about a colt's reaction to the first snowfall. (Rev: BL 3/1/99; HBG 3/99; SLJ 3/99) [811]

13330 George, Kristine O'Connell. *Little Dog and Duncan* (PS–2). Illus. by June Otani. 2002, Clarion $14.00 (978-0-618-11758-1). 38pp. Preschoolers and beginning readers alike will enjoy the gentle poetry and charming watercolors in this story of two dogs having a sleepover. (Rev: BL 3/1/02; HB 7/02*; HBG 10/02; SLJ 3/02*) [811]

13331 George, Kristine O'Connell. *Little Dog Poems* (PS–K). Illus. by June Otani. 1999, Clarion $13.00 (978-0-395-82266-1). 40pp. Charming watercolors illustrate these simple, original poems about a little girl and her beloved dog. (Rev: BL 3/15/99; HB 3/99; HBG 10/99; SLJ 5/99) [811]

13332 Ghigna, Charles. *Animal Tracks: Wild Poems to Read Aloud* (K–3). Illus. by John Speirs. 2004, Abrams $14.95 (978-0-8109-4841-9). 38pp. Animals occupy center stage in this collection of 32 brief, illustrated poems, many of which will generate a laugh. (Rev: BL 5/1/04; SLJ 4/04) [811]

13333 Gottfried, Maya. *Good Dog* (K–3). Illus. by Robert Rahway Zakanitch. 2005, Knopf LB $17.99 (978-0-375-93049-2). Free-verse poems express the thoughts of a variety of canine personalities and their views of their human companions. (Rev: SLJ 4/05) [811]

13334 Harley, Avis. *African Acrostics: A Word in Edgewise* (4–7). Illus. by Deborah Noyes. 2009, Candlewick $17.99 (978-0-7636-3621-0). 40pp. Poems featuring acrostic puzzles are paired with photographs of animals in Africa. (Rev: BL 7/09; SLJ 6/09) [811.6]

13335 Harley, Avis. *The Monarch's Progress: Poems with Wings* (3–5). Illus. by author. 2008, Boyds Mills $16.95 (978-1-59078-558-4). 32pp. Eighteen diverse poems celebrating butterflies — monarchs in particular —are accompanied by detailed drawings and factual notes. (Rev: BL 2/15/08; SLJ 8/08) [811]

13336 Harley, Avis. *Sea Stars* (1–5). Photos by Margaret Butschler. 2006, Boyds Mills $16.95 (978-1-59078-429-7). 35pp. Short poems of varied constructions and close-up color photographs introduce a number of sea creatures. (Rev: SLJ 10/06) [811]

13337 Hoberman, Mary Ann. *A Fine Fat Pig* (K–5). Illus. by Malcah Zeldis. 1991, HarperCollins $14.95 (978-0-06-022425-7). These 14 poems deal with animals, their characteristics, and habits. (Rev: HB 5/91; SLJ 4/91) [811]

13338 Hollander, John, ed. *Animal Poems* (5–7). Illus. by Simona Mulazzani. Series: Poetry for Young People. 2005, Sterling $14.95 (978-1-4027-0926-5). 48pp. A collection of classic poems (by such poets as Blake, Frost, Melville, and Yeats) accompanied by artwork and explanatory notes. (Rev: BL 4/1/05; SLJ 3/05) [808.81]

13339 Howitt, Mary. *The Spider and the Fly* (2–5). Illus. by Tony DiTerlizzi. 2002, Simon & Schuster $16.95 (978-0-689-85289-3). 40pp. Outstanding monochrome artwork brings new life to the classic poem. Caldecott Honor Book, 2003. (Rev: BCCB 11/02; BL 10/1/02; HBG 3/03; SLJ 9/02*) [811]

13340 Hubbell, Patricia. *Earthmates* (K–4). Illus. by Jean Cassels. 2000, Marshall Cavendish $15.95 (978-0-7614-5062-7). 32pp. A collection of impressive poems about such animals as a lion, rat, frog, bat, and deer. (Rev: BL 3/15/00; HBG 10/00; SLJ 3/00) [811]

13341 Jackson, Rob. *Animal Mischief* (2–4). Illus. by Laura Jacobsen. 2006, Boyds Mills $15.95 (978-1-59078-254-5). 32pp. The oddities of animal behavior and appearance are celebrated from a biologist's point of view in this collection of 18 amusing poems. (Rev: BL 4/1/06; SLJ 5/06) [811]

13342 Johnston, Tony. *Cat, What Is That?* (1–4). Illus. by Wendell Minor. 2001, HarperCollins LB $16.89 (978-0-06-027743-7). 32pp. Abstract verses and detailed, realistic illustrations bring to life cats of all kinds in a variety of typical feline activities. (Rev: BL 10/1/01; HBG 3/02; SLJ 9/01)

13343 Johnston, Tony. *Gopher Up Your Sleeve* (PS–3). Illus. by Trip Park. 2002, Rising Moon $15.95 (978-0-87358-794-5). Humorous poems about animals are accompanied by fanciful illustrations. (Rev: HBG 10/02; SLJ 11/02) [811]

13344 Kiesler, Kate. *Wings on the Wind: Bird Poems* (PS–2). Illus. 2002, Clarion $14.00 (978-0-618-13333-8). 32pp. Vivid oil paintings are used to illustrate this collection of poems about birds by such writers as Edward Lear, Carl Sandburg, and Margaret Wise Brown. (Rev: BL 4/15/02; HBG 10/02; SLJ 4/02) [811.008]

13345 Kirk, Daniel. *Cat Power!* (1–4). Illus. by author. 2007, Hyperion $18.99 (978-1-4231-0081-2). 48pp. Eighteen poems celebrate all things feline — even the litter box; a CD of songs is included in this companion to *Dogs Rule!* (2003). (Rev: SLJ 11/07) [811]

13346 Kumin, Maxine. *Mites to Mastodons: A Book of Animal Poems* (2–4). Illus. by Pamela Zagarenski. 2006, Houghton $16.00 (978-0-618-50753-5). 32pp. Animals large and small are celebrated in poems that both appeal and convey information; the whimsical collage illustrations add another dimension. (Rev: BL 10/1/06; SLJ 10/06) [811]

13347 Kuskin, Karla. *Toots the Cat* (PS–2). Illus. by Lisze Bechtold. 2005, Holt $16.95 (978-0-8050-6841-2). 32pp. Poems celebrate the life and adventures of Toots, an independent-minded cat. (Rev: BL 9/1/05; SLJ 1/06) [811.54]

13348 Larios, Julie. *Yellow Elephant: A Bright Bestiary* (K–3). Illus. by Julie Paschkis. 2006, Harcourt $16.00 (978-0-15-205422-9). 32pp. Using vivid, folk-art illustrations of animals and nature, this collection of poems looks at colors and animals. (Rev:

BCCB 5/06; BL 3/15/06*; HBG 10/06; LMC 11/06; SLJ 4/06) [811]

13349 Levy, Constance. *I'm Going to Pet a Worm Today and Other Poems* (3–5). Illus. by Ronald Himler. 1991, Macmillan $14.00 (978-0-689-50535-5). 48pp. This book of original poems celebrates such creatures of nature as spiders, worms, and beetles. (Rev: BCCB 2/92*; BL 11/15/92; SLJ 10/91) [811]

13350 Livingston, Myra Cohn, ed. *If You Ever Meet a Whale* (1–4). Illus. by Leonard Everett Fisher. 1992, Holiday House LB $14.95 (978-0-8234-0940-2). 32pp. Seventeen whale poems with full-color paintings. (Rev: BL 11/15/92) [811]

13351 Luján, Jorge. *Rooster / Gallo* (PS–1). Illus. by Manuel Monroy. 2004, Groundwood $14.95 (978-0-88899-558-2). 24pp. Brief poetic text celebrates the rooster and its relationship to the cycle of day and night. (Rev: BL 5/15/04; HB 3/04; SLJ 9/04) [811]

13352 MacLachlan, Patricia, and Emily MacLachlan Charest. *Once I Ate a Pie* (2–4). Illus. by Katy Schneider. 2006, HarperCollins $17.99 (978-0-06-073531-9). 40pp. An appealing bunch of dogs reveal in poems things they love and various doggy characteristics. (Rev: BL 5/1/06; SLJ 5/06) [811.54]

13353 Maddox, Marjorie. *A Crossing of Zebras: Animal Packs in Poetry* (2–5). Illus. by Philip Huber. 2008, Boyds Mills (978-1-59078-510-2). 32pp. Fourteen brief poems about animals use alliteration and inventive collective nouns, such as "a rumba of rattlesnakes." (Rev: LMC 3/08; SLJ 7/08) [811]

13354 Nichol, Barbara. *Biscuits in the Cupboard* (K–4). Illus. by Philippe Beha. 1998, Stoddart $12.95 (978-0-7737-3025-0). 32pp. A delightful collection of poems about dogs, written entirely from their point of view. (Rev: BL 3/1/04; SLJ 3/98) [808]

13355 Pearson, Susan. *Squeal and Squawk: Barnyard Talk* (K–3). Illus. by David Slonim. 2004, Marshall Cavendish $16.95 (978-0-7614-5160-0). 31pp. Humorous illustrations enhance poems about barnyard animals, from a lovelorn rooster to flying pigs. (Rev: SLJ 6/04) [811]

13356 Pearson, Susan. *Who Swallowed Harold?* (K–4). Illus. by David Slonim. 2005, Marshall Cavendish $16.95 (978-0-7614-5193-8). 31pp. Eighteen humorous poems look at children's relationships with their pets. (Rev: BL 2/1/04*; SLJ 4/05) [811]

13357 Polisar, Barry L. *Insect Soup: Bug Poems* (K–4). Illus. by David Clark. 1999, Rainbow $14.95 (978-0-938663-22-5). Fifteen original poems about insects that are sometimes humorous, sometimes gross, and sometimes amazing. (Rev: SLJ 8/99) [811]

13358 Prelutsky, Jack, ed. *The Beauty of the Beast: Poems from the Animal Kingdom* (3–7). Illus. by Meilo So. 1997, Knopf $25.00 (978-0-679-87058-6). 101pp. A wonderful, beautifully illustrated collection of more than 200 animal poems by 20th-century writers whose works are arranged by animal genus. (Rev: BL 9/15/97; HBG 3/98; SLJ 1/98*) [811]

13359 Prelutsky, Jack. *If Not for the Cat* (PS–3). Illus. by Ted Rand. 2004, Greenwillow LB $17.89 (978-0-06-059678-1). 40pp. Seventeen haiku poems explore life from the vantage point of various animals. (Rev: BL 10/1/04; SLJ 10/04) [811]

13360 Prelutsky, Jack. *Tyrannosaurus Was a Beast* (2–5). Illus. by Arnold Lobel. 1988, Morrow paper $6.99 (978-0-688-11569-2). 32pp. Poems and watercolor portraits bring dinosaurs to life. (Rev: BCCB 9/88; BL 8/88; HB 9/88)

13361 Prevert, Jacques. *How to Paint the Portrait of a Bird* (K–3). Trans. and illus. by Mordicai Gerstein. 2007, Roaring Brook $14.95 (978-1-59643-215-4). 40pp. A beautifully illustrated and translated version of French surrealist Prévert's poem, featuring a boy who follows directions that start with painting a cage with an open door for the bird to fly in, then erasing the cage and replacing it with a forest. (Rev: BCCB 2/08; BL 11/15/07; HB 1/08; LMC 11/07; SLJ 1/08) [841]

13362 Rosen, Michael J. *The Cuckoo's Haiku: And Other Birding Poems* (3–6). Illus. by Stan Fellows. 2009, Candlewick $17.99 (978-0-7636-3049-2). Haiku poems and lovely watercolors introduce 24 familiar North American birds. (Rev: BCCB 3/09; SLJ 4/09; VOYA 8/09) [811]

13363 Ruddell, Deborah. *Today at the Bluebird Cafe: A Branchful of Birds* (1–3). Illus. by Joan Rankin. 2007, Simon & Schuster $15.99 (978-0-689-87153-5). 40pp. Paired with light-filled watercolors, these playful poems combine imaginative anthropomorphizing with facts about birds. (Rev: BL 1/1–15/07; SLJ 2/07*) [811]

13364 Ryder, Joanne. *Toad by the Road: A Year in the Life of These Amazing Amphibians* (2–4). Illus. by Maggie Kneen. 2007, Holt $16.95 (978-0-8050-7354-6). 32pp. This collection of poems chronicles a year in the life of a toad. (Rev: BL 4/1/07; SLJ 4/07) [811]

13365 Schmidt, Amy. *Loose Leashes* (K–2). Illus. by Ron Schmidt. 2009, Random $16.99 (978-0-375-85641-9). 40pp. A variety of dogs — portrayed in poses that complement the poems — express their individual aspirations, complaints, and opinions in verse. (Rev: BL 1/1–15/09; SLJ 2/09) [811]

13366 Sidman, Joyce. *Meow Ruff: A Story in Concrete Poetry* (1–3). Illus. by Michelle Berg. 2006, Houghton $16.00 (978-0-618-44894-4). 32pp. Recounted in concrete — or visual — poetry, this simple tale with creative graphics tells how a friendship develops between a cat and dog seeking shelter from a storm. (Rev: BCCB 5/06; BL 3/15/06*; HB 5/06; HBG 10/06; SLJ 7/06) [811]

13367 Sierra, Judy. *Antarctic Antics: A Book of Penguin Poems* (PS–2). Illus. by Jose Aruego and Ariane Dewey. 1998, Harcourt $16.00 (978-0-15-201006-5). 32pp. Thirteen poems of varying length and accompanying pictures describe the behavior and play of baby penguins in their Antarctic home. (Rev: BL 5/1/98; HBG 10/98; SLJ 5/98) [811]

13368 Singer, Marilyn. *The Company of Crows: A Book of Poems* (2–4). Illus. by Linda Saport. 2002, Clarion $16.00 (978-0-618-08340-4). 48pp. The intelligent crow is presented in poems written from the viewpoint of onlookers, including children, a farmer, and other animals. (Rev: BL 11/15/02; HBG 3/03; SLJ 11/02) [811]

13369 Singer, Marilyn. *Fireflies at Midnight* (2–4). Illus. by Ken Robbins. 2003, Simon & Schuster $16.95 (978-0-689-82492-0). 32pp. Computer-enhanced photograph collages illustrate verses about animals and their behavior on a summer day. (Rev: BL 4/1/03; HBG 10/03; SLJ 5/03) [811]

13370 Sklansky, Amy E. *From the Doghouse: Poems to Chew On* (1–4). Illus. 2002, Holt $17.95 (978-0-8050-6673-9). 44pp. A delightful collection of poems from the canine perspective about things dogs like — walks in the park and car rides, for example — and things dogs don't like — such as fleas and baths. (Rev: HBG 3/03; SLJ 8/02) [811]

13371 Spinelli, Eileen. *Song for the Whooping Crane* (PS–3). Illus. by Elsa Warnick. 2000, Eerdmans $16.00 (978-0-8028-5172-7). 32pp. A poem that celebrates the endangered whooping crane, its beauty, and its life cycle. (Rev: BL 10/1/00; HBG 3/01; SLJ 3/01) [811]

13372 Stockland, Patricia M., ed. *Fur, Fangs, and Footprints: A Collection of Animal Poems* (3–6). Illus. by Sara Rojo Perez. Series: Poet's Toolbox. 2004, Compass Point LB $23.93 (978-0-7565-0562-2). 32pp. Poems about animals by a selection of writers introduce various poetry concepts. (Rev: BL 4/1/04) [808.81]

13373 Tiller, Ruth. *Cats Vanish Slowly* (K–3). Illus. by Laura L. Seeley. 1995, Peachtree $16.95 (978-1-56145-106-7). 32pp. Twelve poems about the cats (including B.P., for "bad penny") that are found on the farm of the author's grandmother. (Rev: BL 1/1–15/96; SLJ 1/96) [811]

13374 Whipple, Laura, ed. *Eric Carle's Animals Animals* (PS–3). Illus. by Eric Carle. 1989, Penguin $22.99 (978-0-399-21744-9). Eric Carle's collages illustrate various writers' poems, each dealing with an animal. (Rev: BCCB 10/89*; BL 9/1/89*; HB 11/89; SLJ 11/89) [811]

13375 Worth, Valerie. *Animal Poems* (4–7). Illus. 2007, Farrar $17.00 (978-0-374-38057-1). 48pp. A diverse, sometimes challenging collection of poems highlighting animals' individual characteristics. (Rev: BL 4/1/07; SLJ 4/07*) [811]

13376 Yang, Huan. *Homes* (PS–K). Illus. by Hsiao-yen Huang. 2005, Heryin $13.99 (978-0-9762056-3-0). 32pp. A brief, gentle poem about nature and the homes of diverse animals ends with a final spread of parents and children in a comfortable, sunlit home. (Rev: BL 12/1/05) [895.1]

13377 Yolen, Jane. *Count Me a Rhyme: Animal Poems by the Numbers* (3–5). Illus. by Jason Stemple. 2006, Boyds Mills $17.95 (978-1-59078-345-0). 32pp. Poet mother and photographer son team up to create this attractive combination of counting book (nonet, novena, IX, and so forth) and nature study. (Rev: BL 4/1/06; SLJ 4/06) [811]

13378 Yolen, Jane. *Fine Feathered Friends: Poems for Young People to Perform* (3–6). Illus. by Jason Stemple. 2004, Boyds Mills $17.95 (978-1-59078-

193-7). 32pp. Poetry and photographs combine to convey striking images of individual species of birds. (Rev: BL 11/1/04; SLJ 12/04) [811]

13379 Yolen, Jane. *A Mirror to Nature: Poems About Reflection* (2–5). Illus. by Jason Stemple. 2009, Boyds Mills $17.95 (978-1-59078-624-6). 32pp. Eye-catching photographs of animals and their reflections are accompanied by short verses. (Rev: BL 3/15/09; SLJ 6/09) [811]

13380 Yolen, Jane. *Wild Wings: Poems for Young People* (3–6). Illus. by Jason Stemple. 2002, Boyds Mills $19.95 (978-1-56397-904-0). 32pp. Unusual photographs accompany beautiful poems about birds. (Rev: BL 5/15/02; HBG 10/02; SLJ 6/02) [811.54]

13381 Ziefert, Harriet, and Fred Ehrlich. *A Bunny Is Funny: And So Is This Book!* (PS–3). Illus. by Todd McKie. 2008, Blue Apple $16.95 (978-1-934706-03-9). Short poems celebrate key characteristics of 19 different animals. (Rev: LMC 10/08; SLJ 7/08) [811]

Haiku

13382 Clements, Andrew. *Dogku* (2–4). Illus. by Tim Bowers. 2007, Simon & Schuster $16.99 (978-0-689-85823-9). 32pp. Told in haiku form, this is an entertaining story about a stray dog adapting to family life. (Rev: BL 5/1/07; LMC 10/07; SLJ 7/07) [811]

13383 Donegan, Patricia. *Haiku: Asian Arts and Crafts for Creative Kids* (4–8). Illus. 2004, Tuttle $14.95 (978-0-8048-3501-5). 64pp. Haiku advice and exercises follow an introduction to the verse form. (Rev: BL 3/15/04; SLJ 8/04) [372.6]

13384 *In the Eyes of the Cat: Japanese Poetry for All Seasons* (PS–3). Trans. by Tze-si Huang. Illus. by Demi. 1994, Holt paper $6.95 (978-0-8050-3383-0). 80pp. These short Japanese poems, known as haiku, use words and images appreciated by young readers. (Rev: BCCB 5/92; BL 4/15/92; SLJ 5/92) [895.6]

13385 Issa, Kobayashi. *Today and Today* (K–3). Illus. by G. Brian Karas. 2007, Scholastic $16.99 (978-0-439-59078-5). 40pp. Issa's haiku are woven together to create a poetic tapestry chronicling a year in the life of a family. (Rev: BL 4/1/07) [895.6]

13386 Janeczko, Paul B., and J. Patrick Lewis. *Wing Nuts: Screwy Haiku* (2–4). Illus. by Tricia Tusa. 2006, Little, Brown $14.99 (978-0-316-60731-5). 32pp. This picture book introduces readers to *senryu*, a poetic form similar to haiku but generally humorous and focused more on people than nature. (Rev: BL 3/15/06; SLJ 5/06) [811]

13387 Yolen, Jane. *Least Things: Poems About Small Natures* (K–5). Photos by Jason Stemple. 2003, Boyds Mills $17.95 (978-1-59078-098-5). 32pp. The wonders of nature are celebrated in this appealing blend of haikus by Jane Yolen and vibrant color photographs by her son, Jason Stemple. (Rev: HBG 4/04; SLJ 10/03) [811]

Holidays

13388 Cunningham, Julia. *The Stable Rat and Other Christmas Poems* (3–6). Illus. by Anita Lobel. 2001, Greenwillow LB $15.89 (978-0-688-17800-0). 24pp. These interconnected poems portray Christmas from the viewpoint of the animal and other observers, with vivid artwork. (Rev: BCCB 11/01; BL 9/15/01; HB 11/01; HBG 3/02; SLJ 10/01) [811]

13389 Fisher, Aileen. *Do Rabbits Have Christmas?* (PS–2). Illus. by Sarah Fox-Davies. 2007, Holt $16.95 (978-0-8050-7491-8). 32pp. Fifteen short poems accompanied by appealing illustrations describe the joys of the season. (Rev: BL 10/15/07; HB 11/07) [811]

13390 Ghigna, Charles, and Debra Ghigna. *Christmas Is Coming* (PS–3). Illus. by Mary O'Keefe. 2000, Charlesbridge $15.95 (978-0-88106-113-0). 32pp. A number of Christmas preparations, like selecting a tree and baking cookies, are depicted in these 27 original poems with expressive illustrations. (Rev: BL 9/1/00; HBG 3/01) [811]

13391 Grimes, Nikki. *At Jerusalem's Gate: Poems of Easter* (5–8). Illus. by David Frampton. 2005, Eerdmans $20.00 (978-0-8028-5183-3). 48pp. More than 20 poems are introduced by thoughtful paragraphs and enhanced by handsome illustrations. (Rev: BL 2/15/05; SLJ 3/05) [232.96]

13392 Harrison, Michael, and Christopher Stuart-Clark, eds. *Bright Star Shining: Poems for Christmas* (3–8). Illus. 1998, Eerdmans $15.00 (978-0-8028-5177-2). 48pp. Illustrated by three different artists, this is a fine collection of 32 Christmas poems. (Rev: BL 9/1/98; HBG 3/99) [808.81]

13393 Hopkins, Lee Bennett, ed. *Christmas Presents: Holiday Poetry* (K–3). Illus. by Melanie W. Hall. Series: An I Can Read Book. 2004, HarperCollins LB $16.89 (978-0-06-008055-6). 32pp. Twelve Christmas poems explore all aspects of the holiday and demonstrate different styles and devices. (Rev: BL 8/04; SLJ 10/04) [811]

13394 Hopkins, Lee Bennett, sel. *Halloween Howls: Holiday Poetry* (K–3). Illus. by Stacey Schuett. 2005, HarperCollins $15.99 (978-0-06-008060-0). 32pp. A dozen previously published poems celebrate the sights, sounds, and smells of Halloween; suitable for beginning readers. (Rev: SLJ 10/05) [811]

13395 Horton, Joan. *Halloween Hoots and Howls* (2–5). Illus. 1999, Holt $15.95 (978-0-8050-5805-5). 32pp. A collection of amusing — sometimes wacky — poems about Halloween. (Rev: BCCB 9/99; BL 9/1/99; HBG 3/00; SLJ 10/99) [811]

13396 Johnston, Tony. *Noel* (K–4). Illus. by Cheng-Khee Chee. 2005, Carolrhoda LB $15.95 (978-1-57505-752-1). A church bell's chimes summon humans and animals to worship on Christmas Eve in this lyrical poem accompanied by beautiful impressionistic watercolors. (Rev: SLJ 10/05) [811]

13397 Koontz, Dean. *Every Day's a Holiday: Amusing Rhymes for Happy Times* (3–6). Illus. by Phil

Parks. 2003, HarperCollins LB $18.89 (978-0-06-008585-8). 144pp. Each of the 64 poems in this collection celebrates a special day on the calendar — holidays and other landmark days, such as the beginning of autumn and the shortest day of the year. (Rev: HBG 4/04; SLJ 10/03) [811]

13398 Lansky, Bruce, et al. *Happy Birthday to Me! Kids Pick the Funniest Birthday Poems* (2–5). Illus. by Jack Lindstrom. 1998, Meadowbrook $8.95 (978-0-671-57703-2). 27pp. Nine poets are represented in this joyous collection of 21 poems that celebrate birthdays. (Rev: SLJ 5/98) [811]

13399 Livingston, Myra Cohn, ed. *Celebrations* (1–4). Illus. by Leonard Everett Fisher. 1985, Holiday House LB $16.95 (978-0-8234-0550-3); paper $6.95 (978-0-8234-0654-8). 32pp. A handsome book of verse illustrating 16 celebrations, such as Valentine's Day, birthdays, and Easter. (Rev: BCCB 4/85; BL 4/1/85; HB 5/85)

13400 Livingston, Myra Cohn, ed. *Christmas Poems* (PS–3). Illus. by Trina S. Hyman. 1984, Holiday House LB $16.95 (978-0-8234-0508-4). 32pp. A collection of 18 poems, half of which were commissioned for the volume.

13401 Livingston, Myra Cohn, ed. *Poems for Jewish Holidays* (K–6). Illus. by Lloyd Bloom. 1986, Holiday House LB $15.95 (978-0-8234-0606-7). 32pp. Poems that contain the essence of major Jewish holidays. (Rev: BCCB 2/87; BL 11/1/86; HB 1/87)

13402 Livingston, Myra Cohn, ed. *Valentine Poems* (3–6). Illus. 1987, Holiday House LB $16.95 (978-0-8234-0587-9). 32pp. Sprightly poems from established names and modern ones, too. (Rev: BL 1/15/87; SLJ 12/86)

13403 Moore, Clement C. *The Night Before Christmas* (PS–2). Illus. by Richard J. Watson. 2006, HarperCollins $16.99 (978-0-06-075741-0). 40pp. Moore's classic poem features a high-tech sleigh complete with a fully equipped cockpit, multicultural elves, and dynamic, realistic art. (Rev: BL 9/15/06; SLJ 10/06) [811]

13404 Moore, Clement C. *The Night Before Christmas* (PS–2). Illus. by Will Moses. 2006, Philomel $16.99 (978-0-399-23745-4). 40pp. Folk artist Will Moses portrays the traditional poem in nostalgic paintings full of welcoming houses lit by candles. (Rev: BL 9/15/06; SLJ 10/06) [811]

13405 Moore, Clement C. *The Night Before Christmas* (PS–2). Illus. by Gennady Spirin. 2006, Marshall Cavendish $16.99 (978-0-7614-5298-0). 32pp. Spirin's interpretation of the poem is set in a quaint European village of days gone by, with illustrations full of contrasting light. (Rev: BL 9/15/06; SLJ 10/06) [811]

13406 Moore, Clement C. *The Night Before Christmas* (PS–1). Illus. by Cheryl Harness. 1990, Random $8.99 (978-0-394-82698-1). 40pp. A traditional treatment of the classic holiday poem. (Rev: BL 11/1/90; HB 11/90) [811]

13407 Moore, Clement C. *The Night Before Christmas* (PS–2). Illus. by Jan Brett. 1998, Penguin LB $16.99 (978-0-399-23190-2). This version of the classic Christmas poem contains illustrations of a Victorian house, an old-world Santa, and two stowaway elves. (Rev: HBG 3/99; SLJ 10/98) [811]

13408 Moore, Clement C. *The Night Before Christmas* (PS–1). Ed. by Cooper Edens and Harold Darling. Illus. 1998, Chronicle $16.95 (978-0-8118-1712-7). 44pp. This new edition of the classic poem uses illustrations that originally appeared between 1890 and 1928. (Rev: BL 10/1/98; HBG 3/99; SLJ 10/98) [811]

13409 Moore, Clement C. *The Night Before Christmas* (PS–2). Illus. by Tasha Tudor. 1999, Little, Brown $14.95 (978-0-316-85579-2). Wild and domestic animals on a Vermont farm form an important part of the illustrations in this version of the classic poem. (Rev: HBG 3/00; SLJ 10/99) [811]

13410 Moore, Clement C. *The Night Before Christmas* (PS–3). Illus. by Bruce Whatley. 1999, HarperCollins LB $16.89 (978-0-06-028380-3). 40pp. The pictures in this attractive edition of the favorite poem depict events from the father's point of view. (Rev: BL 9/1/99*; HBG 3/00; SLJ 10/99) [811]

13411 Moore, Clement C. *The Night Before Christmas* (PS–3). Illus. by Tomie dePaola. 1980, Holiday House LB $16.95 (978-0-8234-0414-8); paper $6.95 (978-0-8234-0417-9). 32pp. A lovely edition of this popular and loved Christmas poem. Another edition is: Illus. by Anita Lobel (Knopf 1996).

13412 Moore, Clement C. *The Night Before Christmas* (K–3). Illus. by Lisbeth Zwerger. 2005, Penguin $15.99 (978-0-698-40030-6). 32pp. The immortal Christmas poem is given new life in the dream-like blue and green artwork accented by the red suit. (Rev: BL 10/15/05; SLJ 10/05) [811]

13413 Moore, Clement C. *The Night Before Christmas: Or, a Visit of St. Nicholas* (PS–3). Illus. 1989, Penguin $19.99 (978-0-399-21614-5). 32pp. This handsomely produced edition of the famous poem was illustrated years ago by a now-forgotten artist. (Rev: BL 9/15/89) [811]

13414 Moore, Clement C. *The Teddy Bears' Night Before Christmas* (PS–K). Illus. by Monica Stevenson. 1999, Scholastic $12.95 (978-0-590-03243-8). 40pp. Photographs of stuffed animals in snowy scenes illustrate this version of the classic rhyme. (Rev: BL 9/1/99; HBG 3/00; SLJ 10/99) [811]

13415 Moore, Clement C. *'Twas the Night Before Christmas; or, Account of a Visit from St. Nicholas* (PS–2). Illus. by Matt Tavares. 2002, Candlewick $16.00 (978-0-7636-1585-7). 32pp. The classic, original version of the poem, accompanied by old-fashioned artwork. (Rev: BL 9/1/02; HBG 3/03) [811]

13416 Prelutsky, Jack. *It's Christmas!* (PS–1). Illus. by Marylin Hafner. Series: I Can Read. 2008, Greenwillow $16.99 (978-0-06-053706-7). 48pp. For beginning readers, this is a collection of happy verses about various aspects of Christmas. (Rev: BL 12/1/08; HB 11/08) [811]

13417 Prelutsky, Jack. *It's Valentine's Day* (1–4). Illus. by Yossi Abolafia. 1985, Scholastic paper $2.50 (978-0-590-40979-7). 48pp. Bright, humorous poems in celebration of love and Valentine's Day.

13418 *A Small Treasury of Easter: Poems and Prayers* (K–4). Illus. by Susan Spellman. 1997, Boyds Mills $8.95 (978-1-56397-647-6). 32pp. An illustrated collection of secular and religious Easter poems, divided into two parts: "A Time to Play" and "A Time to Pray." (Rev: SLJ 7/97) [811]

13419 Snell, Gordon. *'Twas the Day After Christmas* (PS–2). Illus. by Sean Delonas. 2003, HarperCollins LB $16.89 (978-0-06-028953-9). This amusing variation on Clement C. Moore's holiday poem paints a portrait of the somewhat messy day after Christmas from the viewpoint of a tiny mouse. (Rev: HBG 4/04; SLJ 10/03) [811]

13420 Whitehead, Jenny. *Holiday Stew: A Kid's Portion of Holiday and Seasonal Poems* (K–3). Illus. by author. 2007, Holt $17.95 (978-0-8050-7715-5). 64pp. Holidays big and small are celebrated in these 78 child-centered poems. (Rev: BL 5/15/07; SLJ 5/07) [811]

Humorous Poetry

13421 Agee, Jon. *Orangutan Tongs* (1–4). Illus. by author. 2009, Hyperion $16.99 (978-1-4231-0315-8). 32pp. Full of elaborate tongue twisters, this is a collection of funny verses. (Rev: BCCB 4/09; BL 3/1/09; HB 3/09; LMC 5/09; SLJ 3/09) [818]

13422 Aylesworth, Jim. *The Burger and the Hot Dog* (K–3). Illus. by Stephen Gammell. 2001, Simon & Schuster $16.95 (978-0-689-83897-2). 32pp. A collection of funny poems about anthropomorphic foods with effective, messy illustrations. (Rev: BCCB 12/01; BL 10/1/01; HBG 3/02; SLJ 1/02) [811]

13423 Bagert, Brod. *Giant Children* (K–3). Illus. by Tedd Arnold. 2002, Dial $16.99 (978-0-8037-2556-0). 32pp. Side-splitting artwork is the perfect accompaniment to this eclectic collection of poems for young readers. (Rev: BL 8/02; HBG 3/03; SLJ 8/02) [811]

13424 Bagert, Brod. *School Fever* (1–3). Illus. by Robert Neubecker. 2008, Dial $16.99 (978-0-8037-3201-8). 40pp. Quirky first-person poems chronicle a boy's school day, from morning "fever" to bullies to his crush on his teacher. (Rev: BL 8/08; LMC 11/08; SLJ 7/08) [811]

13425 Billings, John. *My Pet Crocodile and Other Slightly Outrageous Verse* (PS–3). Illus. by Janette Todd. 1993, Chokecherry $16.95 (978-1-884035-55-5). 128pp. Humorous poems on such subjects as bungee jumping, nose picking, and bubble gum. (Rev: BL 1/1/94) [811]

13426 Brown, Calef. *Dutch Sneakers and Flea Keepers: 14 More Stories* (3–5). Illus. 2000, Houghton $16.00 (978-0-618-05183-0). 32pp. A collection of original poems that introduce the reader to several odd and eccentric characters, such as the Flea Keepers, who train fleas for cash. (Rev: BCCB 7–8/00; BL 4/1/00; HBG 10/00; SLJ 4/00) [811.54]

13427 Brown, Calef. *Flamingos on the Roof* (3–5). Illus. 2006, Houghton $16.00 (978-0-618-56298-5).

64pp. A delightful collection of nonsense poems accompanied by funky illustrations. (Rev: BL 4/15/06; SLJ 7/06) [811]

13428 Bush, Timothy. *Ferocious Girls, Steamroller Boys, and Other Poems in Between* (1–4). Illus. by author. 2000, Orchard LB $17.99 (978-0-531-33250-4). A funny book that uses seven poems to explore unusual boys and girls and their strange behavior. (Rev: HBG 10/00; SLJ 7/00) [811]

13429 Carroll, Lewis. *Jabberwocky* (3–5). Illus. by Christopher Myers. 2007, Hyperion $15.99 (978-1-4231-0372-1). 32pp. Vibrant artwork supports a reinterpretation of the classic nonsense poem set on a contemporary basketball court. (Rev: BL 9/1/07; LMC 11/07; SLJ 8/07) [821]

13430 Ciardi, John. *You Read to Me, I'll Read to You* (4–6). Illus. by Edward Gorey. 1987, HarperCollins paper $7.99 (978-0-06-446060-6). 64pp. A collection of original verse for both adults and children.

13431 Cole, William, ed. *Poem Stew* (2–6). Illus. by Karen Ann Weinhaus. 1981, HarperCollins $7.66 (978-0-397-31963-3). 96pp. A collection of 57 witty poems about food.

13432 Cox, Kenyon. *Mixed Beasts* (3–5). Illus. by Wallace Edwards. 2005, Kids Can $17.95 (978-1-55337-796-2). Nonsense poems about beasts such as the kangarooster and bumblebeaver are accompanied by full-page, detailed illustrations. (Rev: SLJ 1/06) [811]

13433 Dakos, Kalli. *The Bug in Teacher's Coffee: And Other School Poems* (K–2). Illus. by Mike Reed. Series: An I Can Read Book. 1999, HarperCollins LB $16.89 (978-0-06-027940-0). 38pp. For beginning readers, a book of humorous poetry with zany illustrations that use everyday objects found in a school. (Rev: HBG 3/00; SLJ 12/99) [811]

13434 Florian, Douglas. *Bing Bang Boing* (4–6). Illus. 1994, Harcourt $16.00 (978-0-15-233770-4). 144pp. A lighthearted, imaginative collection of short, humorous verses. (Rev: BCCB 11/94; BL 12/1/94; SLJ 11/94) [811]

13435 Florian, Douglas. *Laugh-Eteria* (3–5). Illus. 1999, Harcourt $17.00 (978-0-15-202084-2). 158pp. A collection of 150 original, humorous poems that will appeal to a child's sometimes gross sense of humor. (Rev: BCCB 4/99; BL 3/15/99; HBG 10/99; SLJ 6/99) [811]

13436 Grandits, John. *Technically, It's Not My Fault: Concrete Poems* (4–6). Illus. by author. 2004, Clarion paper $5.95 (978-0-618-50361-2). Eleven-year-old Robert's unique — and sometimes gross — vision of the world around him is expressed in arresting poetry with an inventive presentation. (Rev: BL 12/15/04; SLJ 4/05) [811]

13437 Greenberg, David. *Don't Forget Your Etiquette! The Essential Guide to Misbehavior* (1–3). Illus. by Nadine Bernard Westcott. 2006, Farrar $16.00 (978-0-374-34990-5). 40pp. In humorous poems, "Miss Information" dispenses advice that turns proper etiquette on its head. (Rev: BL 10/1/06; SLJ 10/06) [811]

13438 Greenfield, Eloise. *Brothers and Sisters: Family Poems* (1–4). Illus. by Jan Spivey Gilchrist.

2009, HarperCollins $17.99 (978-0-06-056284-7). 32pp. This collection of 25 short poems chronicles the pleasures and perils of life with siblings; illustrations feature African American characters in watercolor-and-ink. (Rev: BL 2/1/09; HB 3/09; SLJ 1/09) [811]

13439 Greenfield, Eloise. *I Can Draw a Weeposaur and Other Dinosaurs* (K–3). Illus. by Jan S. Gilchrist. 2001, Greenwillow LB $14.89 (978-0-688-17635-8). 31pp. A group of poems about fanciful, imaginary dinosaurs along with drawings of them by the girl who dreamed them up. (Rev: HBG 10/01; SLJ 3/01) [811]

13440 Grimes, Nikki. *Is It Far to Zanzibar? Poems About Tanzania* (PS–3). Illus. by Betsy Lewin. 2000, Lothrop LB $15.89 (978-0-688-13158-6). 32pp. A series of rhyming, singsong verses that fancifully describe life in Tanzania. (Rev: BL 3/15/00; HBG 10/00; SLJ 5/00) [811]

13441 Horton, Joan. *Hippopotamus Stew: And Other Silly Animal Poems* (PS–2). Illus. by JoAnn Adinolfi. 2006, Holt $16.95 (978-0-8050-7350-8). 32pp. A menagerie of wacky animals — and humans — is introduced in this collection of 21 nonsense poems illustrated with lively, funny collages. (Rev: BL 2/1/06; SLJ 3/06) [811]

13442 Horton, Joan. *I Brought My Rat for Show-and-Tell* (1–3). Trans. and illus. by Melanie Siegel. Series: All Aboard Poetry Reader. 2004, Penguin LB $3.99 (978-0-448-43364-6). 48pp. The eye-catching cartoon illustrations and nonsensical rhyming poems in this collection will appeal to beginning readers. (Rev: BL 8/04; SLJ 10/04) [811]

13443 Janeczko, Paul B., ed. *A Poke in the I: A Collection of Concrete Poems* (3–8). Illus. by Chris Raschka. 2001, Candlewick $15.99 (978-0-7636-0661-9). 36pp. A collection of original humorous poems each of which takes a different shape on the page, for example, the poem about a popsicle is on a stick. (Rev: BL 3/15/01*; HB 7/01*; HBG 10/01) [811.008]

13444 Katz, Alan. *Oops!* (2–5). Illus. by Edward Koren. 2008, Simon & Schuster $17.99 (978-1-4169-0204-1). 144pp. A collection of 100 little rhyming poems that employ wordplay, puns, and pure nonsense. (Rev: BL 3/1/08; SLJ 4/08) [811]

13445 Kennedy, X. J. *Uncle Switch: Loony Limericks* (1–3). Illus. by John O'Brien. 1997, Simon & Schuster $15.00 (978-0-689-80967-5). 32pp. Twenty-two funny limericks involving the dimwitted Uncle Switch. (Rev: BCCB 4/97; BL 5/1/97; SLJ 4/97) [811]

13446 Korman, Gordon, and Bernice Korman. *The D-Poems of Jeremy Bloom: A Collection of Poems About School, Homework, and Life (Sort Of)* (4–6). 1992, Scholastic paper $3.50 (978-0-590-44819-2). 98pp. The engaging and funny poems of rambunctious sixth-grader Jeremy Bloom. (Rev: BL 1/15/93; SLJ 2/93) [811]

13447 Lansky, Bruce, ed. *A Bad Case of the Giggles: Kids' Favorite Funny Poems* (2–5). Illus. by Stephen Carpenter. 1994, Meadowbrook $14.00 (978-0-88166-213-9). 132pp. A great collection of humorous poems that includes puns, tongue twisters, and parodies, many by well-known writers. (Rev: BL 11/15/94; SLJ 2/95) [811]

13448 Lansky, Bruce, ed. *Miles of Smiles: Kids Pick the Funniest Poems, Book 3* (2–6). Illus. by Stephen Carpenter. 1998, Meadowbrook $16.00 (978-0-88166-313-6). 115pp. A collection of 72 humorous poems some of them earthy in content and dealing with subjects such as underwear and bathroom humor. (Rev: HBG 3/99; SLJ 11/98) [811]

13449 Lansky, Bruce, ed. *Rolling in the Aisles: A Collection of Laugh-Out-Loud Poems* (3–6). Illus. by Stephen Carpenter. 2004, Meadowbrook $17.00 (978-0-88166-473-7). 115pp. Organized by kid-friendly topics, these poems — many by familiar authors and selected by young readers — are accompanied by large cartoons. (Rev: SLJ 1/05) [811]

13450 Lear, Edward. *Complete Nonsense Book of Edward Lear* (4–6). Illus. by author. 1951, Dover paper $11.95 (978-0-486-20167-2). 287pp. Verse, prose, drawings, alphabets, and other amusing absurdities.

13451 Lear, Edward. *The Owl and the Pussycat* (5–10). Illus. by Stephane Jorisch. Series: Visions in Poetry. 2007, Kids Can $16.95 (978-1-55337-828-0); paper $9.95 (978-1-55453-232-2). A charmingly illustrated version of Lear's classic poem using watercolor and ink. (Rev: SLJ 1/08)

13452 Lear, Edward. *The Owl and the Pussycat* (PS–1). Illus. by Jan Brett. 1991, Penguin $16.99 (978-0-399-21925-2). 32pp. Beautiful double-page spreads enhance the enchantment of this retelling. (Rev: BL 3/1/91*; SLJ 2/91*) [821]

13453 Lear, Edward. *The Owl and the Pussycat* (PS–1). Illus. by James Marshall. 1998, HarperCollins LB $15.89 (978-0-06-205011-3). 32pp. Fresh and funny artwork from James Marshall highlight this edition of the classic nonsense poem. (Rev: BL 2/1/99; HB 3/99; HBG 10/99; SLJ 12/98) [821]

13454 Lear, Edward. *The Owl and the Pussycat* (PS–4). Illus. by Anne Mortimer. 2006, HarperCollins $15.99 (978-0-06-027228-9). The beloved old rhyme, illustrated in a lush, lovely style. (Rev: SLJ 7/06) [811]

13455 Lear, Edward. *Poetry for Young People* (3–5). Ed. by Edward Mendelson. Illus. by Huliska-Beit Laura. 2002, Sterling $14.95 (978-0-8069-3077-0). 48pp. An introduction to the limericks and poetry of Edward Lear. (Rev: BL 3/1/02; HBG 10/02) [821]

13456 Lear, Edward. *The Quangle Wangle's Hat* (PS–2). Illus. by Louise Voce. 2005, Candlewick $15.99 (978-0-7636-1289-4). 32pp. The Quangle Wangle, all alone in his tree, is glad when his giant hat becomes home to other animals as fanciful as he. (Rev: BL 3/1/05; SLJ 1/05) [811]

13457 Lesynski, Loris. *Nothing Beats a Pizza* (3–6). Illus. by author. 2001, Annick LB $18.95 (978-1-55037-701-9); paper $7.95 (978-1-55037-700-2). 32pp. Lesynski's verses take a humorous approach to the serious topic of pizza. (Rev: HBG 3/02; SLJ 2/02) [811]

13458 Lewis, J. Patrick. *Once Upon a Tomb: Gravely Humorous Verses* (2–4). Illus. by Simon Bartram. 2006, Candlewick $16.99 (978-0-7636-1837-7). 32pp. This collection of amusing epitaphs marks the passing of such diverse individuals as an underwear salesman, dairy farmer, schoolteacher, food critic, and fortune teller. (Rev: BL 8/06; SLJ 8/06) [811]

13459 Lewis, J. Patrick. *Tulip at the Bat* (K–3). Illus. by Amiko Hirao. 2007, Little, Brown $16.99 (978-0-316-61280-7). 32pp. The Boston Beasts are up against the New York Pets in this silly, pun-filled World Series championship game. (Rev: BL 4/1/07) [811]

13460 McGough, Roger, ed. *Wicked Poems* (4–8). Illus. by Neal Layton. 2005, Bloomsbury paper $15.00 (978-0-7475-6195-8). 198pp. Misbehavior of varying degrees is displayed in this varied collection of poems accompanied by cartoons. (Rev: SLJ 1/05) [811]

13461 Mendelson, Edward, ed. *Poetry for Young People: Lewis Carroll* (3–5). Illus. 2001, Sterling $14.95 (978-0-8069-5541-4). 48pp. The poetry that is scattered throughout Lewis Carroll's books is collected here, including some of his nonsense creations like *Jabberwocky*. (Rev: BL 3/1/01; HBG 10/01; SLJ 3/01) [821]

13462 Morrison, Lillian. *I Scream, You Scream: A Feast of Food Rhymes* (3–5). Illus. 1997, August House $12.95 (978-0-87483-495-6). 96pp. Food is the subject of this humorous collection of rhymes, autograph-book verses, tongue twisters, and jokes. (Rev: BL 11/15/97; HBG 3/98; SLJ 11/97) [811]

13463 Nash, Ogden. *The Adventures of Isabel* (PS–2). Illus. by Bridget S. Taylor. 2008, Sourcebooks $16.95 (978-1-4022-1027-3). 32pp. With large bright watercolors, Taylor illustrates the Nash poem about a brave girl who takes on all scary challenges; an accompanying CD offers an audio of Nash reading the verses. (Rev: BL 6/1–15/08; SLJ 6/08) [811.54]

13464 Nesbitt, Kenn. *My Hippo Has the Hiccups: And Other Poems I Totally Made Up* (2–5). Illus. by Ethan Long. 2009, Sourcebooks $17.99 (978-1-4022-1809-5). 172pp. This fun and wacky collection of 100 poems (39 read by the author on the included CD) entertains with its unusual subjects such as angry stew vegetable and pink-headed zebras. (Rev: LMC 10/09; SLJ 5/09) [811]

13465 Opie, Iona, and Peter Opie, eds. *I Saw Esau: The Schoolchild's Pocket Book* (2–5). Illus. by Maurice Sendak. 1992, Candlewick $19.99 (978-1-56402-046-8). 160pp. Schoolyard folk rhymes that are absurd, fierce, vulgar, and compelling. (Rev: BCCB 5/92*; BL 4/15/92*; SLJ 6/92*) [811]

13466 Paraskevas, Betty. *Junior Kroll and Company* (K–3). Illus. by Michael Paraskevas. 1994, Harcourt $13.95 (978-0-15-292855-1). 40pp. A mischievous, shrewd toddler has a series of adventures, like learning to waltz with Cousin Blanche. (Rev: BL 4/15/94; SLJ 5/94) [811]

13467 Perry, Andrea. *Here's What You Do When You Can't Find Your Shoe: Ingenious Inventions for Pesky Problems* (3–5). Illus. by Alan Snow. 2003, Simon & Schuster $16.95 (978-0-689-83067-9). 40pp. Humorous poems imagine the invention of such child-friendly innovations as a spray that will empty the family shopping cart of offensive vegetables and a leaf-eater to help with raking. (Rev: BL 4/1/03; HBG 10/03; SLJ 5/03) [811]

13468 Perry, Andrea. *The Snack Smasher: And Other Reasons Why It's Not My Fault* (2–5). Illus. by Alan Snow. 2007, Simon & Schuster $16.99 (978-0-689-85469-9). 33pp. These humorous poems provide whimsical explanations for some of life's most puzzling mysteries. (Rev: SLJ 2/07) [811]

13469 Phinn, Gervase. *What I Like! Poems for the Very Young* (PS–K). Illus. by Jane Eccles. 2005, Child's Play paper $7.99 (978-1-904550-12-9). 32pp. A lively collection of amusing rhymes and illustrations about subjects close to young children's hearts. (Rev: BL 5/1/05) [811]

13470 Prelutsky, Jack. *Awful Ogre Running Wild* (K–3). Illus. by Paul Zelinsky. 2008, Greenwillow $17.99 (978-0-06-623866-1). 40pp. The Awful Ogre rides again as he sets out on his summer vacation in this new volume of 17 humorous first-person poems illustrated with chaotic good cheer. (Rev: BL 9/1/08) [811]

13471 Prelutsky, Jack. *Awful Ogre's Awful Day* (PS–3). Illus. by Paul Zelinsky. 2001, Greenwillow LB $16.89 (978-0-688-07779-2). 40pp. Humorous poems look at an ogre's daily routine — from breakfast to bedtime — with amusing illustrations. (Rev: BCCB 9/01; BL 10/15/01; HB 9/01; HBG 3/02; SLJ 9/01*) [811.54]

13472 Prelutsky, Jack. *Behold the Bold Umbrellaphant and Other Poems* (3–5). Illus. by Carin Berger. 2006, Greenwillow LB $17.89 (978-0-06-054318-1). 32pp. Combinations of animals and objects — alarmadillo, spatuloon, panthermometer, tubaboon, to name just a few — star in these 17 silly poems. (Rev: BL 9/1/06; SLJ 10/06*) [811]

13473 Prelutsky, Jack. *In Aunt Giraffe's Green Garden* (PS–3). Illus. by Petra Mathers. 2007, Greenwillow $16.99 (978-0-06-623868-5). 32pp. Silly poetry and clever illustrations highlight this book about animal friends vacationing in various U.S. locations. (Rev: BL 7/07; SLJ 8/07) [811] ∩

13474 Prelutsky, Jack. *It's Raining Pigs and Noodles* (PS–3). Illus. by James Stevenson. 2000, Greenwillow LB $18.89 (978-0-06-029195-2). 160pp. There are more than 100 nonsense rhymes in this delightful collection; scribbly drawings carry on the humor. (Rev: BCCB 10/00; BL 11/1/00; HBG 3/01; SLJ 11/00) [811]

13475 Prelutsky, Jack. *My Dog May Be a Genius* (2–5). Illus. by James Stevenson. 2008, Greenwillow $18.99 (978-0-06-623862-3). 160pp. A collection of well-crafted silly poetry accompanied by cartoon illustrations. (Rev: BL 3/1/08; HB 3/08; LMC 11/08; SLJ 2/08) [811] ∩

13476 Prelutsky, Jack. *The New Kid on the Block: Poems* (3–6). Illus. by James Stevenson. 1984, Greenwillow $18.89 (978-0-688-02272-3). 160pp. A collection of over 100 humorous poems by this prolific master.

13477 Prelutsky, Jack. *Ride a Purple Pelican* (PS–2). Illus. by Garth Williams. 1986, Greenwillow $18.99 (978-0-688-04031-4). 64pp. New verses that sound like old favorites. (Rev: BL 10/1/86; HB 1/87; SLJ 11/86)

13478 Prelutsky, Jack. *Something Big Has Been Here* (4–6). Illus. by James Stevenson. 1990, Greenwillow $17.99 (978-0-688-06434-1). 160pp. A bountiful collection of witty poems. (Rev: BCCB 12/90; BL 9/1/90*; HB 11/90*; SLJ 10/90*) [811]

13479 Prelutsky, Jack. *What a Day It Was at School!* (K–2). Illus. by Doug Cushman. 2006, Greenwillow $16.99 (978-0-06-082335-1). 40pp. This collection of poems — some fantastical and some realistic but all humorous — celebrates the school experience. (Rev: BL 8/06; SLJ 7/06) [811]

13480 Proimos, James. *If I Were in Charge the Rules Would Be Different* (3–5). Illus. 2002, Scholastic $16.95 (978-0-439-20864-2). 80pp. Playful poems about childhood, with humorous illustrations. (Rev: BL 5/15/02; HBG 10/02; SLJ 3/02) [811]

13481 Rash, Andy. *The Robots Are Coming* (2–5). Illus. 2000, Scholastic $15.95 (978-0-439-06306-7). 40pp. This collection of 16 original poems includes as subjects an abominable snowman, a werewolf, and the Loch Ness Monster. (Rev: BCCB 12/00; BL 11/15/00; HBG 3/01; SLJ 11/00) [811]

13482 Rex, Adam. *Frankenstein Makes a Sandwich* (2–5). Illus. by author. 2006, Harcourt $16.00 (978-0-15-205766-4). 40pp. Laugh-out-loud poems reveal untold episodes in the lives of some favorite monsters. (Rev: SLJ 9/06*) [811]

13483 Shapiro, Karen Jo. *Because I Could Not Stop My Bike-and Other Poems* (3–6). Illus. by Matt Faulkner. 2003, Charlesbridge LB $15.95 (978-1-58089-035-9). 32pp. With apologies to the authors, Shapiro borrows rhymes and meters from 26 classic poems and transforms them for today's young readers. (Rev: HBG 4/04; SLJ 8/03) [811]

13484 Shields, Carol Diggory. *Almost Late to School and More School Poems* (1–3). Illus. by Paul Meisel. 2003, Penguin $15.99 (978-0-525-45743-5). 32pp. Humorous poems and vivid cartoon illustrations highlight a variety of elementary-school experiences. (Rev: BL 8/03; HBG 4/04; SLJ 8/03) [811]

13485 Silverstein, Shel. *Runny Babbit: A Billy Sook* (2–4). Illus. 2005, HarperCollins LB $18.89 (978-0-06-028404-6). 96pp. Runny Babbit and friends including Toe Jurtle and Goctor Doose feature in clever spoonerist poems. (Rev: BL 5/1/05; SLJ 4/05) [811]

13486 Silverstein, Shel. *Where the Sidewalk Ends* (3–6). Illus. by author. 1974, HarperCollins LB $19.89 (978-0-06-025668-5). 176pp. The author explores various facets and interests of children, with appropriate cartoonlike drawings. Also use: *A Light in the Attic* (1981). [811]

13487 Smith, William J. *Laughing Time: Collected Nonsense* (3–5). Illus. by Fernando Krahn. 1990, Farrar paper $3.50 (978-0-374-44315-3). 176pp. New poems have been added to this satisfyingly silly collection. Revision of the 1980 edition. (Rev: BL 2/15/90; SLJ 3/91) [811]

13488 Soto, Gary. *Worlds Apart: Traveling with Fernie and Me* (4–6). Illus. by Greg Clarke. 2005, Penguin $15.99 (978-0-399-24218-2). 64pp. Fernie and his best friend go on a globe-trotting adventure in this book composed of poems illustrated in black and white. (Rev: BL 3/15/05; SLJ 3/05) [811]

13489 Steinberg, David. *Grasshopper Pie and Other Poems* (K–2). Illus. by Adrian C. Sinnott. Series: All Aboard Poetry Reader. 2004, Grosset paper $3.99 (978-0-448-43347-9). 48pp. Nonsense poetry with bouncy illustrations is full of arresting rhymes. (Rev: BL 7/04; SLJ 10/04) [811]

13490 Stockland, Patricia M., ed. *Recess, Rhyme, and Reason: A Collection of Poems About School* (3–6). Illus. by Sara Rojo Perez. 2004, Compass Point LB $23.93 (978-0-7565-0564-6). 32pp. This lighthearted anthology of poems about school is designed to entertain and to educate young readers about different poetry concepts. (Rev: BL 4/1/04; SLJ 6/04) [808.81]

13491 Tripp, Wallace, ed. *A Great Big Ugly Man Came Up and Tied His Horse to Me: A Book of Nonsense Verse* (K–3). Illus. by Wallace Tripp. 1974, Little, Brown LB $14.95 (978-0-316-85280-7). 48pp. The hilarious drawings that accompany this selection of nonsense verses make this an especially entertaining book.

13492 Turner, Steve. *Dad, You're Not Funny and Other Poems* (3–5). Illus. by David Mostyn. 2000, Lion $16.95 (978-0-7459-4024-3). 96pp. A collection of humorous light verse from this well-known English writer. (Rev: BL 9/15/03; HBG 4/04; SLJ 11/00) [821]

13493 Weinstock, Robert. *Food Hates You, Too* (1–3). Illus. by author. 2009, Hyperion $15.99 (978-1-4231-1391-1). 32pp. Nineteen funny poems present a different perspective on the topic of food. (Rev: BCCB 1/09; BL 1/1–15/09; LMC 5/09; SLJ 1/09) [808.1]

13494 Westcott, Nadine Bernard. *The Lady with the Alligator Purse* (PS–1). Illus. by author. 1988, Little, Brown paper $4.95 (978-0-316-93136-6). The lady with the alligator purse chooses pizza instead of penicillin in this jump-rope rhyme. (Rev: BL 3/15/88; HB 5/88; HBG 4/04)

13495 Whitehead, Jenny. *Lunch Box Mail and Other Poems* (2–4). Illus. 2001, Holt $16.95 (978-0-8050-6259-5). 48pp. Everyday life and experiences are captured in this collection of poems that emphasizes the humorous side of life. (Rev: BL 4/1/01; HBG 3/02; SLJ 10/01) [811]

13496 Wilson, Karma. *What's the Weather Inside?* (2–5). Illus. by Barry Blitt. 2009, Simon & Schuster $17.99 (978-1-4169-0092-4). 170pp. A humorous collection of more than 100 poems full of wordplay that focus mainly on a child's world. (Rev: BCCB 5/09; SLJ 7/09) [811]

Native Americans

13497 Bruchac, Joseph, and Jonathan London. *Thirteen Moons on Turtle's Back: A Native American Year of Moons* (1–5). Illus. by Thomas Locker. 1997, Putnam paper $6.99 (978-0-399-22141-5). 32pp. For each of the 13 moon cycles in a year, this book contains a poem and an oil painting illustrating it. (Rev: BL 3/1/92; SLJ 7/92) [811.54]

13498 Longfellow, Henry Wadsworth. *The Song of Hiawatha* (3–10). Illus. by Margaret Early. 2003, Handprint $16.95 (978-1-59354-002-9). A beautifully illustrated edition of the epic poem that traces the eventful life of the Native American leader. (Rev: HBG 4/04; SLJ 1/04) [811]

13499 Sneve, Virginia Driving Hawk, ed. *Dancing Teepees: Poems of American Indian Youth* (3–8). Illus. by Stephen Gammell. 1989, Holiday House LB $17.95 (978-0-8234-0724-8); paper $8.95 (978-0-8234-0879-5). 32pp. A collection of traditional tribal prayers, songs, and short poems. (Rev: BCCB 5/89; BL 5/15/89; SLJ 6/89)

Nature and the Seasons

13500 Alarcón, Francisco X. *Angels Ride Bikes and Other Fall Poems: Los Angeles Andan en Bicicleta y Otros Poems de Otono* (K–3). Illus. by Maya Christina Gonzalez. 1999, Children's Book Pr. $15.95 (978-0-89239-160-8). 32pp. Twenty poems written in English and Spanish tell about the fall season in Los Angeles. (Rev: BL 12/1/99; HBG 3/00; SLJ 10/99) [811.54]

13501 Alarcón, Francisco X. *Iguanas in the Snow and Other Winter Poems / Iguanas en la Nieve y Otros Poemas de Invierno* (1–3). Illus. by Maya Christina Gonzalez. 2001, Children's Book Pr. $15.95 (978-0-89239-168-4). 32pp. A collection of poems about the beauty of winter in northern California, in Spanish and English. (Rev: BL 10/1/01; HBG 3/02; SLJ 8/01) [811]

13502 Baird, Audrey B. *A Cold Snap! Frosty Poems* (2–5). Illus. by Patrick O'Brien. 2002, Boyds Mills $15.95 (978-1-56397-633-9). 32pp. Effective poems and illustrations capture winter's chill. (Rev: BL 9/15/02; HBG 3/03; SLJ 12/02) [811.54]

13503 Baird, Audrey B. *Storm Coming!* (2–4). Illus. by Patrick O'Brien. 2001, Boyds Mills $15.95 (978-1-56397-887-6). 32pp. Twenty-two original poems explore the nature and effects of storms from many points of view. (Rev: BL 3/15/01; HBG 10/01) [811]

13504 Bishop, Rudine Sims, comp. *Wonders: The Best Children's Poems of Effie Lee Newsome* (K–3). Illus. by Lois Mailou Jones. 1999, Boyds Mills paper $8.95 (978-1-56397-825-8). 40pp. A collection of original nature poems by Effie Lee Newsome that were published 60 years ago and were long out of print. (Rev: BCCB 2/00; HBG 3/00; SLJ 4/00) [811]

13505 Buchanan, Ken, and Debby Buchanan. *It Rained on the Desert Today* (2–4). Illus. by Libba Tracy. 1994, Northland LB $14.95 (978-0-87358-575-0). 32pp. A rainstorm in the desert is evoked in free verse and evocative watercolors. (Rev: BL 10/15/94; SLJ 8/94) [811]

13506 Cameron, Eileen. *Canyon* (3–5). Illus. by Michael Collier. 2002, Mikaya $16.95 (978-1-931414-03-6). 32pp. Water flows from mountains to rivers to a canyon in this poetic book illustrated with striking photographs of nature. (Rev: BL 5/15/02; HBG 10/02; SLJ 5/02) [811]

13507 Cyrus, Kurt. *Oddhopper Opera: A Bug's Garden of Verses* (3–5). Illus. 2001, Harcourt $16.00 (978-0-15-202205-1). 32pp. A variety of garden creatures are featured in both the art and the poems in this original collection. (Rev: BL 3/15/01; HBG 10/01) [811]

13508 Esbensen, Barbara J. *Swing Around the Sun* (K–3). Illus. 2003, Carolrhoda LB $16.95 (978-0-87614-143-4). 48pp. The seasons are the focus of this collection that is illustrated by four well-known artists. (Rev: HBG 10/03; SLJ 3/03) [811]

13509 Florian, Douglas. *Autumnblings: Poems and Paintings* (2–5). Illus. by author. 2003, Greenwillow LB $17.89 (978-0-06-009279-5). 48pp. Rhyming verse, creative word play, and lovely illustrations bring autumn to life. (Rev: HB 11/03; HBG 4/04; SLJ 10/03) [811]

13510 Florian, Douglas. *Comets, Stars, the Moon and Mars* (3–5). Illus. 2007, Harcourt $16.00 (978-0-15-205372-7). 56pp. Large-format, double-page spreads combine mixed-media illustrations with lyrical poems about celestial bodies. (Rev: BL 4/1/07) [811]

13511 Florian, Douglas. *Handsprings* (K–3). Illus. 2006, Greenwillow $15.99 (978-0-06-009280-1). 48pp. Florian follows *Winter Eyes* (1999), *Summersaults* (2002), and *Autumnblings* (2003) with a volume of breezy poems about the joys of spring. (Rev: BL 3/15/06; SLJ 4/06) [811]

13512 Florian, Douglas. *Summersaults* (K–4). Illus. 2002, HarperCollins LB $17.89 (978-0-06-029268-3). 48pp. The freedom and beauty of summer are evoked in this collection of short, rhymed poems with playful pictures. (Rev: BCCB 5/02; BL 4/1/02; HB 7/02; HBG 10/02; SLJ 5/02*)

13513 Florian, Douglas. *Winter Eyes* (K–4). Illus. 1999, Greenwillow $16.99 (978-0-688-16458-4). 48pp. A series of short, quiet poems that show the effects of winter on a small child. (Rev: BCCB 11/99; BL 11/1/99; HB 11/99; HBG 3/00; SLJ 9/99) [811.54]

13514 Geis, Jacqueline. *Where the Buffalo Roam* (PS–3). Illus. 1992, Ideals LB $14.00 (978-0-8249-8584-4). 32pp. With illustrations and verses to the familiar cowboy tune, the American Southwest is celebrated. (Rev: BL 11/15/92; SLJ 1/93) [811]

13515 George, Kristine O'Connell. *The Great Frog Race and Other Poems* (4–6). Illus. by Kate Kiesler. 1997, Clarion $16.00 (978-0-395-77607-0). 40pp. A richly atmospheric picture book that captures some of the outdoor activities of children, including watching captured frogs race. (Rev: BCCB 6/97; BL 3/15/97*; SLJ 4/97*) [811]

13516 George, Kristine O'Connell. *Old Elm Speaks: Tree Poems* (2–6). Illus. by Kate Kiesler. 1998, Clarion $16.00 (978-0-395-87611-4). 48pp. A collection of original poems that celebrates every wonderful aspect of trees. (Rev: BL 9/1/98*; HBG 3/99; SLJ 9/98) [811]

13517 Harrison, David L. *Wild Country* (4–6). Illus. 1999, Boyds Mills $14.95 (978-1-56397-784-8). 48pp. A collection of original nature poems that celebrates such natural wonders as butterflies, mountains, and forests. (Rev: BL 11/15/99; HBG 3/00; SLJ 12/99) [811]

13518 Havill, Juanita. *I Heard It from Alice Zucchini: Poems About the Garden* (K–3). Illus. by Christine Davenier. 2006, Chronicle $15.95 (978-0-8118-3962-4). 32pp. The science and magic of gardening are celebrated in this collection of poems illustrated with pen-and-ink and watercolor sketches. (Rev: BL 4/1/06; SLJ 4/06*) [811]

13519 Hazeltine, Alice I., and Elva Smith, eds. *The Year Around: Poems for Children* (4–6). Illus. by Paula Hutchison. 1973, Ayer $15.00 (978-0-8369-6403-5). A collection of seasonal poems.

13520 Highwater, Jamake. *Songs for the Seasons* (PS–4). Illus. by Sandra Speidel. 1995, Lothrop LB $14.93 (978-0-688-10659-1). 32pp. A gentle look at the changes that occur with plants and animals during the cycle of the four seasons. (Rev: BL 4/15/95; SLJ 4/95) [811]

13521 Hines, Anna Grossnickle. *Winter Lights: A Season in Poems and Quilts* (1–3). Illus. 2005, Greenwillow $16.99 (978-0-06-000817-8). 32pp. The lights and warmth of various winter holidays are celebrated in a collection of poems and quilts. (Rev: BL 9/1/05*; SLJ 10/05*) [811]

13522 Hopkins, Lee Bennett. *Sky Magic* (1–3). Illus. by Mariusz Stawarski. 2009, Dutton $17.99 (978-0-525-47862-1). 32pp. Fourteen poems — from writers including Carl Sandburg, Alice Schertle, and Ashley Bryan — celebrate various features of the sky and are accompanied by dreamy illustrations. (Rev: HB 7/09; SLJ 6/09) [811]

13523 Hopkins, Lee Bennett, ed. *Small Talk: A Book of Short Poems* (2–4). Illus. by Susan Gaber. 1995, Harcourt $14.00 (978-0-15-276577-4). 48pp. Short poems by distinguished authors are arranged according to seasonal changes. (Rev: BCCB 5/95; BL 8/95; HB 5/95; SLJ 5/95*) [811]

13524 Hubbell, Patricia. *Black Earth, Gold Sun* (2–6). 2001, Marshall Cavendish $15.95 (978-0-7614-5090-0). 32pp. Watercolor illustrations echo the sentiments of these poems about the delights of a garden. (Rev: BL 9/15/01; HBG 3/02; SLJ 11/01) [811.54]

13525 Hundal, Nancy. *Prairie Summer* (3–5). Illus. 1999, Fitzhenry & Whiteside $16.95 (978-1-55041-403-5). 32pp. A poem, illustrated with impressionistic paintings, that depicts life on the prairie. (Rev: BL 11/1/99) [813.54]

13526 Katz, Susan. *Looking for Jaguar: And Other Rain Forest Poems* (2–4). Illus. by Lee Christiansen. 2005, Greenwillow LB $16.89 (978-0-06-029793-0). 40pp. Nineteen poems introduce the flora and fauna of the world's rain forests; supplementary features include an essay about the importance of these habitats and a compilation of relevant facts and figures. (Rev: BL 2/15/05; SLJ 3/05) [811]

13527 Lewis, J. Patrick. *Earth and Us — Continuous: Nature's Past and Future* (K–3). Illus. by Christopher Canyon. Series: Sharing Nature with Children. 2001, Dawn $16.95 (978-1-58469-024-5); paper $7.95 (978-1-58469-023-8). 32pp. A book of attractively illustrated poems about the wonders of the earth and our responsibility to care for it. (Rev: BL 9/1/01; HBG 3/02) [550]

13528 Livingston, Myra Cohn. *Calendar* (PS–K). Illus. by Will Hillenbrand. 2007, Holiday $16.95 (978-0-8234-1725-4). 32pp. This simple poem, colorfully illustrated with mixed-media artwork, highlights the special features of the months of the year. (Rev: BL 4/1/07) [811.54]

13529 Livingston, Myra Cohn. *A Circle of Seasons* (3–5). Illus. by Leonard Everett Fisher. 1982, Holiday House paper $5.95 (978-0-8234-0656-2). 32pp. A group of poems that brings the seasons to life.

13530 Livingston, Myra Cohn. *Up in the Air* (3–5). Illus. by Leonard Everett Fisher. 1989, Holiday House LB $14.95 (978-0-8234-0736-1). 32pp. A celebration of flight begins as an airliner takes off. (Rev: BCCB 5/89; BL 5/15/89)

13531 Luján, Jorge. *Colors! Colores!* (K–3). Trans. by John Oliver Simon. Illus. by Piet Grobler. 2008, Groundwood $17.95 (978-0-88899-863-7). 24pp. This bilingual book celebrating color offers short free-verse poems in English and Spanish illustrated with playful watercolors. (Rev: BLO 2/9/09; LMC 8/09; SLJ 5/08) [811]

13532 Merriam, Eve. *The Singing Green: New and Selected Poems for All Seasons* (3–7). Illus. by Kathleen C. Howell. 1992, Morrow $14.00 (978-0-688-11025-3). 112pp. The wordplay romps and frolics in this celebration of sun, trees, and the child in us all. (Rev: BCCB 2/93; BL 12/1/92; HB 1/93; SLJ 12/92) [811]

13533 Mora, Pat. *The Desert Is My Mother / El Desierto Es Mi Madre* (PS–3). Illus. by Daniel Lechon. 1994, Arte Publico $14.95 (978-1-55885-121-4). 32pp. In this bilingual book of poems, everyday life in the desert is seen through the eyes of a child. (Rev: BL 1/15/95) [811]

13534 Nicholls, Judith, comp. *The Sun in Me: Poems About the Planet* (1–4). Illus. by Beth Krommes. 2003, Barefoot Books $16.99 (978-1-84148-058-9). 40pp. An anthology of poems from different places and times that celebrate nature. (Rev: HBG 10/03; SLJ 3/03) [811]

13535 Paolilli, Paul, and Dan Brewer. *Silver Seeds* (K–2). Illus. by Lou Fancher and Steve Johnson. 2001, Viking $15.99 (978-0-670-88941-9). 32pp. In each of these 15 nature poems the first letters of each line spell out the name of the poem. (Rev: BL 12/15/00; HBG 10/01) [811.6]

13536 Peters, Lisa Westberg. *Earthshake: Poems from the Ground Up* (2–4). Illus. by Cathie Felstead. 2003, HarperCollins LB $17.89 (978-0-06-029266-9). 32pp. Twenty-two poems exploring various aspects of earth science — including fossils, tectonic plates, lava, and strata — are accompanied by relevant collages in this large-format book. (Rev: BL 11/15/03; HBG 4/04; SLJ 9/03) [811]

13537 Powell, Consie. *Amazing Apples* (PS–4). Illus. by author. 2003, Whitman LB $16.99 (978-0-8075-0399-7). Simple acrostic poems follow an apple orchard through the seasons. (Rev: HBG 4/04; SLJ 10/03) [811]

13538 Prelutsky, Jack. *Dog Days: Rhymes Around the Year* (PS–K). Illus. by Dyanna Wolcott. 1999, Knopf LB $16.00 (978-0-375-80104-4). 32pp. In these 12 original poems, one for each month, a dog reveals his favorite activities in each season. (Rev: BL 11/1/99) [811]

13539 Prelutsky, Jack. *It's Snowing! It's Snowing! Winter Poems* (K–3). Illus. by Yossi Abolafia. Series: I Can Read. 2006, HarperCollins $15.99 (978-0-06-053715-9). 48pp. Sixteen loosely connected, easily read poems celebrate the joys of winter. (Rev: BL 1/1–15/06; SLJ 7/06) [811]

13540 Rickey, Ann Heiskell. *Bugs and Critters I Have Known* (3–6). Illus. by Ardeane Heiskell Smith. 1998, Old Canyon $12.95 (978-0-9667834-1-4). 93pp. Illustrated with pen-and-ink drawings, this humorous collection of original poems deals mainly with insects. (Rev: SLJ 6/99) [811]

13541 Roemer, Heidi. *Come to My Party: And Other Shape Poems* (PS–3). Trans. and illus. by Hideko Takahashi. 2004, Holt $17.95 (978-0-8050-6620-3). 32pp. Organized by season, this collection of brief poems explores common experiences and introduces interesting sounds and shapes. (Rev: BL 6/1–15/04; HB 5/04; SLJ 5/04) [811]

13542 Rogasky, Barbara. *Winter Poems* (3–6). Illus. by Trina S. Hyman. 1994, Scholastic $15.95 (978-0-590-42872-9). 40pp. An anthology of poems that deal with winter around the world and activities associated with it. (Rev: BCCB 1/95; BL 9/15/94; HB 11/94; SLJ 10/94*) [811]

13543 Shakespeare, William. *Winter Song: A Poem by William Shakespeare* (K–4). Illus. by Melanie Hall. 2006, Boyds Mills $15.95 (978-1-59078-275-0). Wintry illustrations depict an Elizabethan scene as the backdrop for the poem that appears at the conclusion of his play, *Love's Labor's Lost*. (Rev: SLJ 11/06) [821.3]

13544 Shannon, George. *Busy in the Garden* (PS–2). Illus. by Sam Williams. 2006, Greenwillow $15.99 (978-0-06-000464-4). 40pp. This collection of 24 lively poems celebrates the joys — and headaches — of a backyard garden. (Rev: BL 1/1–15/06; SLJ 2/06) [811]

13545 Sidman, Joyce. *Butterfly Eyes and Other Secrets of the Meadow* (3–5). Illus. by Beth Krommes. 2006, Houghton $16.00 (978-0-618-56313-5). 48pp. The diversity of life in and around a country meadow is celebrated in poems that include both scientific facts and riddles. (Rev: BL 10/1/06; SLJ 10/06*) [811]

13546 Sidman, Joyce. *Just Us Two: Poems About Animal Dads* (1–4). Illus. by Susan Swan. 2000, Millbrook LB $22.90 (978-0-7613-1563-6). Using double-page illustrations, this book of 11 original poems is about different fathers in the animal world. (Rev: HBG 3/01; SLJ 12/00) [811]

13547 Sidman, Joyce. *Red Sings from Treetops: A Year in Colors* (PS–1). Illus. by Pamela Zagarenski. 2009, Houghton $16.00 (978-0-547-01494-4). 32pp. The seasons are defined by their colors in evocative text and illustrations. (Rev: BCCB 3/09; BL 5/1/09; HB 3/09; SLJ 4/09) [811]

13548 Sidman, Joyce. *Song of the Waterboatman and Other Pond Poems* (3–5). Illus. by Becky Prange. 2005, Houghton $16.00 (978-0-618-13547-9). 32pp. Poems that teach about the ecology of a pond are accompanied by woodcut illustrations. Caldecott Honor Book, 2006. (Rev: BL 3/15/05) [811]

13549 Siegen-Smith, Nikki, ed. *Sea Dream: Poems from Under the Waves* (2–5). Illus. by Joel Stewart. 2002, Barefoot Books $16.99 (978-1-84148-905-6). 40pp. An absorbing anthology of 26 poems about sea creatures both real and imagined. (Rev: BL 10/15/02; HBG 3/03; SLJ 12/02) [808.81]

13550 Spinelli, Eileen. *Polar Bear, Arctic Hare: Poems of the Frozen North* (PS–2). Illus. by Eugenie Fernandes. 2007, Boyds Mills $16.95 (978-1-59078-344-3). 48pp. Twenty-four poems about the animals of the Arctic are paired with large acrylic paintings. (Rev: BL 4/15/07) [811]

13551 Stevenson, Robert Louis. *The Moon* (PS–1). Illus. by Tracey Campbell Pearson. 2006, Farrar $16.00 (978-0-374-35046-8). 40pp. Stevenson's poem "The Moon" becomes a story of a boy and his father viewing the moon and nocturnal animals on a private nighttime boat trip. (Rev: BL 7/06; HBG 4/07; SLJ 9/06*) [821]

13552 Thomas, Patricia. *Nature's Paintbox: A Seasonal Gallery of Art and Verse* (2–4). Illus. by Craig Orback. 2007, Lerner $16.95 (978-0-8225-6807-0). 32pp. Verses about the seasons are paired with illustrations in different media — pen and ink for winter, pastel chalk for spring, watercolors for summer, and oils for fall. (Rev: BL 10/15/07; LMC 1/08; SLJ 11/07) [811]

13553 Updike, John. *A Child's Calendar* (3–5). Illus. by Trina S. Hyman. 1999, Holiday House $16.95 (978-0-8234-1445-1). 32pp. Updike has written a poem for each month, depicting seasonal activities of a multiracial family in rural New Hampshire. Caldecott Honor Book, 2000. (Rev: BCCB 3/00; BL 9/1/99; HBG 3/00; SLJ 9/99) [811]

13554 Van Wassenhove, Sue. *The Seldom-Ever-Shady Glades* (3–5). Illus. by author. 2008, Boyds Mills $17.95 (978-1-59078-352-8). 32pp. Poems and quilted illustrations express delight in the natural world in this tour of the diversity of the Everglades. (Rev: BL 2/15/08; LMC 3/08*; SLJ 5/08) [811]

13555 Walker, Alice. *There Is a Flower at the Tip of My Nose Smelling Me* (K–3). Illus. by Stefano

Vitale. 2006, HarperCollins $16.99 (978-0-06-057080-4). 32pp. Brief poems celebrate the interconnectedness between nature and humanity. (Rev: BL 4/1/06; SLJ 5/06) [811]

13556 Whipple, Laura, comp. *A Snowflake Fell: Poems About Winter* (PS–3). Illus. by Hatsuki Hori. 2003, Barefoot Books $16.99 (978-1-84148-033-6). 40pp. Beautifully illustrated, this anthology includes diverse poems about winter by poets including Douglas Florian, Nancy Wood, James Whitcomb Riley, and Marilyn Singer. (Rev: HBG 4/04; SLJ 11/03) [811]

13557 Windham, Sophie. *The Mermaid and Other Sea Poems* (3–5). Illus. 1996, Scholastic $16.95 (978-0-590-20898-7). 32pp. Sea creatures from mermaids to fish are featured in 18 poems by well-known writers. (Rev: BL 2/1/96; SLJ 5/96) [821]

13558 Yang-Huan. *Where Is Spring?* (PS–K). Illus. by H. Y. Huang and A. Yang. 2007, Heryin $15.95 (978-0-9762-0568-5). Sweet illustrations accompany a Chinese poet's interpretation of the joys of the season. (Rev: SLJ 8/07)

13559 Yolen, Jane. *Color Me a Rhyme: Nature Poems for Young People* (4–6). Illus. 2000, Boyds Mills $19.95 (978-1-56397-892-0). 32pp. Using related photos as illustrations, these poems each evoke a particular color in nature. (Rev: BL 10/15/00*; HBG 3/01; SLJ 12/00) [811.54]

13560 Yolen, Jane, sel. *Once Upon Ice: And Other Frozen Poems* (4–8). 1997, Boyds Mills $19.95 (978-1-56397-408-3). A collection of 17 poems inspired by photographs of ice formations, which are also included. (Rev: BL 2/1/97; SLJ 3/97) [811]

13561 Yolen, Jane. *Shape Me a Rhyme: Nature's Forms in Poetry* (3–6). Photos by Jason Stemple. 2007, Boyds Mills $17.95 (978-1-59078-450-1). 32pp. Words and photographs work together in this collection of verses about shapes in nature. (Rev: SLJ 11/07) [811]

13562 Yolen, Jane. *Snow, Snow: Winter Poems for Children* (2–5). Illus. by Jason Stemple. 1998, Boyds Mills $16.95 (978-1-56397-721-3). 32pp. Inspired by photographs of snow scenes, these original poems depict occurrences and express various moods involving winter landscapes and activities. (Rev: BCCB 10/98; BL 11/15/98; HBG 3/99; SLJ 12/98) [811.5]

Sports

13563 Fehler, Gene. *Change-Up: Baseball Poems* (3–5). Illus. by Donald Wu. 2009, Clarion $16.00 (978-0-618-71962-4). 48pp. Poems about baseball chronicle anticipation of the oncoming season and the following dreams and successes. (Rev: BCCB 3/09; BL 3/15/09) [811]

13564 Gutman, Dan. *Casey Back at Bat* (2–4). Illus. by Steve Johnson. 2007, HarperCollins $16.99 (978-0-06-056025-6). 32pp. Gutman playfully extends Thayer's classic poem as Casey wallops the baseball around the world and back in time, bump-ing against the poor Leaning Tower of Pisa and knocking the nose off the Sphinx; glowing, textured illustrations borrowed from 19th-century art extend the fun. (Rev: BL 1/1–15/07; SLJ 1/07*) [811]

13565 Hopkins, Lee Bennett, ed. *Extra Innings: Baseball Poems* (4–6). Illus. by Scott Medlock. 1993, Harcourt $16.00 (978-0-15-226833-6). 48pp. Nineteen poems about baseball. (Rev: BL 3/15/93; SLJ 4/93) [811]

13566 Hopkins, Lee Bennett, ed. *Opening Days: Sports Poems* (3–6). Illus. by Scott Medlock. 1996, Harcourt $16.00 (978-0-15-200270-1). 48pp. There are 18 poems in this collection dealing with a variety of sports, each accompanied by a full-page painting. (Rev: BL 2/15/96; HB 5/96; SLJ 5/96) [811]

13567 Hopkins, Lee Bennett, ed. *Sports! Sports! Sports! A Poetry Collection* (1–3). Illus. by Brian Floca. 1999, HarperCollins LB $15.89 (978-0-06-027801-4). 48pp. The thrills and excitement of sports activities are captured in this collection of poems by several authors, including the editor. (Rev: BCCB 2/99; BL 4/1/99; HB 1/99; HBG 10/99; SLJ 3/99) [811]

13568 Korman, Gordon, and Bernice Korman. *The Last-Place Sports Poems of Jeremy Bloom: A Collection of Poems About Winning, Losing, and Being a Good Sport (Sometimes)* (3–6). 1996, Scholastic paper $3.99 (978-0-590-25516-5). 92pp. A book that explores the world of sports by using different kinds of poetry, from haiku to narrative verse. (Rev: SLJ 4/97) [811]

13569 Maddox, Marjorie. *Rules of the Game: Baseball Poems* (5–8). Illus. by John Sandford. 2009, Boyds Mills $16.95 (978-1-59078-603-1). 32pp. Maddox celebrates the game of baseball in this collection of more than 40 brief poems with titles such as "View from the Dugout" and "Sacrifice Bunt." (Rev: BL 4/15/09; SLJ 5/09) [811]

13570 Morrison, Lillian, ed. *At the Crack of the Bat* (4–6). Illus. by Steve Cieslawski. 1992, Little, Brown LB $15.49 (978-1-56282-177-7). 64pp. Full-color paintings add to the hero-loving glory of this all-American sport. (Rev: BCCB 5/92; BL 8/92; SLJ 6/92) [811]

13571 Prelutsky, Jack. *Good Sports: Rhymes About Running, Jumping, Throwing, and More* (K–5). Illus. by Chris Raschka. 2007, Knopf $16.99 (978-0-375-83700-5). The rhyming poems in this collection celebrate the excitement of participating in a wide variety of sports and other physical activities. (Rev: BL 3/1/07*; SLJ 2/07) [811]

13572 Smith, Charles R. *Diamond Life: Baseball Sights, Sounds, and Swings* (1–4). Illus. 2004, Scholastic $15.95 (978-0-439-43180-4). 32pp. Brightly illustrated, the poems — some of them cleverly shaped — in this collection celebrate baseball and its players. (Rev: BL 3/1/04; SLJ 3/04) [796.357]

13573 Smith, Charles R. *Hoop Kings* (4–7). Illus. 2004, Candlewick $14.99 (978-0-7636-1423-2). 40pp. This celebration of basketball, presented in a blend of rap-style poetry with eye-catching photographs, focuses on 12 of the biggest stars. (Rev: BL 2/15/04; SLJ 3/04) [811]

13574 Thayer, Ernest L. *Casey at the Bat* (5–10). Illus. by Joe Morse. Series: Visions in Poetry. 2006, Kids Can $16.95 (978-1-55337-827-3). The famous poem is reimagined in a contemporary setting, with a multicultural crowd and modern technology grounding the poem in the here-and-now. (Rev: SLJ 6/06) [811]

13575 Thayer, Ernest L. *Casey at the Bat* (2–6). Illus. by LeRoy Neiman. 2002, HarperCollins $19.95 (978-0-06-009068-5). 96pp. The famous baseball poem, illustrated in a bold, striking manner; with an introduction by Jose Torre. (Rev: BCCB 1/01*; BL 9/1/02) [811]

13576 Thayer, Ernest L. *Casey at the Bat: A Ballad of the Republic Sung in the Year 1888* (4–8). Illus. by C. F. Payne. 2003, Simon & Schuster $16.95 (978-0-689-85494-1). 40pp. An impossibly muscular Casey is the star of this version of the classic baseball poem. (Rev: BCCB 1/01*; BL 2/1/03; HBG 10/03; SLJ 3/03*) [811]

13577 Thayer, Ernest L. *Casey at the Bat: A Ballad of the Republic Sung in the Year 1888* (K–3). Illus. by Christopher Bing. 2000, Handprint $17.95 (978-1-929766-00-0). 32pp. Fictional clippings and scratchboard engravings are used as illustrations to give an actual-event atmosphere to this poem about Casey's terrible defeat at bat. Caldecott Honor Book, 2001. (Rev: BCCB 1/01*; BL 2/15/01; HB 3/01; HBG 10/01; SLJ 1/01) [811.5]

Plays

General

13578 Birch, Beverley. *Shakespeare's Tales* (5–8). Illus. by Stephen Lambert. 2002, Hodder $22.95 (978-0-340-79725-9). 126pp. This appealing and accessible large-format book introduces modern teens to the plots and language of four Shakespeare plays — *Hamlet, Othello, Antony and Cleopatra*, and *The Tempest*. (Rev: BL 1/1–15/03; SLJ 4/03) [823.914]

13579 Bruchac, Joseph. *Pushing Up the Sky: Seven Native American Plays for Children* (2–6). Illus. 2000, Dial $21.99 (978-0-8037-2168-5). 96pp. Several folktales from Native American cultures are adapted into simple plays that are easily produced. (Rev: BCCB 2/00; BL 3/1/00; HBG 10/00; SLJ 3/00) [812]

13580 Burkholder, Kelly. *Plays* (2–5). Series: Artistic Adventures. 2001, Rourke LB $23.93 (978-1-57103-357-4). 24pp. Details on putting on a play are given including material on writing scripts, costumes, props, characters, and using voice and movement. (Rev: SLJ 2/01) [792]

13581 Butterfield, Moira. *Hansel and Gretel* (2–4). Photos by Trever Clifford. Illus. by Frances Cony. Series: Playtales. 1997, Heinemann $19.92 (978-1-57572-648-9). 24pp. Contains the script of a play based on this folktale plus direction on how to stage it, from casting and making props to the actual performance. Also use *Sleeping Beauty* (1997). (Rev: BL 4/1/04; HB 3/04; HBG 3/98; SLJ 2/98) [809]

13582 Butterfield, Moira. *Little Red Riding Hood* (2–4). Photos by Trever Clifford. Illus. by Frances Cony. Series: Playtales. 1997, Heinemann $19.92 (978-1-57572-650-2). 24pp. Provides a script based on this fairy tale, as well as a list of parts, directions for production of the play, and instructions for making costumes and sets. Also use *Puss-in-Boots* (1997). (Rev: HBG 3/98; SLJ 3/98) [809]

13583 Chanda, Justin, ed. *Acting Out* (4–8). 2008, Atheneum $16.99 (978-1-4169-6213-7). 192pp. Young people challenge authority in these one-act plays written by six Newbery Medal winners. (Rev: BL 6/1–15/08) [812]

13584 Fredericks, Anthony D. *Tadpole Tales and Other Totally Terrific Treats for Readers Theatre* (4–8). 1997, Libraries Unlimited paper $23.00 (978-1-56308-547-5). 139pp. A delightful collection of scripts for young performers that are spin-offs from folktales, fables, and nursery rhymes. (Rev: BL 3/1/98) [372.67]

13585 Gerke, Pamela. *Multicultural Plays for Children Grades K–3* (K–3). 1996, Smith & Kraus paper $19.95 (978-1-57525-005-2). 159pp. Ten entertaining plays, each of which deals with a different racial group. Also use volume 2 (1996), which contains ten plays for grades four to six. (Rev: BL 12/1/96; SLJ 9/96) [812]

13586 Jennings, Coleman A., and Aurand Harris, eds. *Plays Children Love: A Treasury of Contemporary and Classic Plays for Children, Vol. II* (5–8). Illus. by Susan Swan. 1988, St. Martin's $19.95 (978-0-312-01490-2). 512pp. A group of 20 plays requiring royalties based on such stories as *Charlotte's Web, The Wizard of Oz,* and *The Wind in the Willows*. [812]

13587 Kahle, Peter V. T. *Shakespeare's The Tempest: A Prose Narrative* (5–8). Illus. by Barbara Nickerson. 1999, Seventy Fourth Street $22.95 (978-0-9655702-2-0). 96pp. An illustrated retelling of Shakespeare's play that uses much of its dialogue. (Rev: SLJ 1/00) [822.3]

13588 Kamerman, Sylvia, ed. *The Big Book of Large-Cast Plays: 27 One-Act Plays for Young Actors* (5–10). 1994, Plays $12.95 (978-0-8238-0302-6). Thirty short plays on varied subjects, arranged according to audience appeal. (Rev: BL 3/15/95) [812]

13589 Kamerman, Sylvia, ed. *Great American Events on Stage: 15 Plays to Celebrate America's Past* (5–8). 1996, Plays paper $15.95 (978-0-8238-0305-7). A collection of short plays, each of which revolves around a single incident or individual important in U.S. history. (Rev: SLJ 5/97) [812]

13590 Kamerman, Sylvia E., ed. *Thirty Plays from Favorite Stories: Royalty-Free Dramatizations of Myths, Folktales, and Legends from Around the World* (2–4). 1997, Plays paper $15.95 (978-0-8238-0306-4). 291pp. Thirty short plays based loosely on folktales from around the world. (Rev: SLJ 12/97) [809]

13591 Kohl, MaryAnn F. *Making Make-Believe: Fun Props, Costumes, and Creative Play Ideas* (PS–4). 1999, Gryphon paper $14.95 (978-0-87659-198-7). 191pp. Using simple materials, this book supplies ideas for creating 138 different make-believe situations or plays. (Rev: SLJ 10/99) [809]

13592 McCullough, L. E. *"Now I Get It!": 12 Ten-Minute Classroom Drama Skits for Science, Math, Language, and Social Studies, Vol. I* (4–6). Series: Now I Get It! 2001, Smith & Kraus $11.95 (978-1-57525-161-5). 136pp. In addition to these 12 curriculum-related skits, there are before and after activities, discussion questions, and staging suggestions. Also use *"Now Get It Right!" Volume II* (2001). (Rev: BL 2/1/01) [812]

13593 McCullough, L. E. *Plays from Fairy Tales: Grades K–3* (1–3). 1998, Smith & Kraus $14.95 (978-1-57525-109-7). 192pp. Using well-known fairy tales as a basis, this collection of original plays includes recommendations for casting, costumes, sets, and related material. (Rev: BL 9/15/98; SLJ 8/98) [812]

13594 McCullough, L. E. *Plays from Mythology: Grades 4–6* (4–6). 1998, Smith & Kraus $14.95 (978-1-57525-110-3). 192pp. This is a collection of original plays based on important world myths such as the stories of Midas and Gilgamesh, with accompanying detailed notes and production tips. (Rev: BL 9/15/98; SLJ 7/98) [812]

13595 McCullough, L. E. *Plays of America from American Folklore for Children Grades K–6* (3–6). Series: Young Actors. 1996, Smith & Kraus paper $14.95 (978-1-57525-038-0). 161pp. A collection of 15 plays from American folklore and history that represent many cultural backgrounds. (Rev: SLJ 8/96) [808.82]

13596 McCullough, L. E. *Plays of the Wild West* (3–7). 1997, Smith & Kraus paper $14.95 (978-1-57525-105-9). 224pp. Both serious and slapstick views of the Wild West are reflected in these 12 plays, mostly musicals. A companion volume is *Plays of the Wild West: Grades K–3* (1997). (Rev: BL 11/1/97; SLJ 1/98) [812]

13597 MacDonald, Margaret Read. *The Skit Book: 101 Skits from Kids* (3–6). Illus. by Marie-Louise Scull. 1990, Shoe String LB $25.00 (978-0-208-02258-5); paper $18.00 (978-0-208-02283-7). 160pp. Funny, silly skits from kids that kids will like. (Rev: BL 6/1/90; SLJ 6/90) [812]

13598 McKeown, Adam. *Julius Caesar* (5–8). Illus. by Janet Hamlin. Series: Young Reader's Shakespeare. 2008, Sterling $14.95 (978-1-4027-3579-0). 80pp. An accessible retelling to assist students of the play, with engaging illustrations and a tone that

is respectful to the original. (Rev: BL 5/15/08; SLJ 6/08) [813.6]

13599 Miller, Helen L. *First Plays for Children* (3–7). 1985, Plays paper $12.95 (978-0-8238-0268-5). 295pp. A useful collection of nonroyalty plays.

13600 Nolan, Paul T. *Folk Tale Plays Round the World: A Collection of Royalty-Free, One-Act Plays About Lands Far and Near* (4–7). 1982, Plays paper $15.00 (978-0-8238-0253-1). Johnny Appleseed and Robin Hood are heroes featured in two of the 17 plays in this collection.

13601 Schlitz, Laura Amy. *Good Masters! Sweet Ladies!* (5–8). Illus. by Robert Byrd. 2007, Candlewick $19.99 (978-0-7636-1578-9). 72pp. Providing a glimpse into medieval life, a series of interconnected monologues and dialogues feature 23 young people in medieval England and convey information about society at the time. Newbery Medal, 2008. (Rev: BL 8/07*; HB 11/07; LMC 11/07; SLJ 8/07) [812.6] ∩

13602 Shakespeare, William. *William Shakespeare* (5–7). Ed. by David Scott Kastan and Marina Kastan. Illus. Series: Poetry for Young People. 2000, Sterling $14.95 (978-0-8069-4344-2). 48pp. In a large format illustrated by paintings, this volume contains three sonnets and 23 short excerpts from the plays of William Shakespeare. (Rev: BL 1/1–15/01; HBG 3/01; SLJ 1/01) [821]

13603 Shepard, Aaron. *Stories on Stage: Children's Plays for Reader's Theater (or Readers Theatre) with 15 Play Scripts from 15 Authors.* 2nd ed. (1–6). 2005, Shepard paper $15.00 (978-0-938497-22-6). 160pp. The 15 story scripts in this collection represent the work of 15 popular writers including Roald Dahl, Louis Sachar, and Harold Courlander. (Rev: SLJ 2/06) [812.5408]

13604 Slaight, Craig, and Jack Sharrar, eds. *Great Scenes and Monologues for Children* (5–8). Series: Young Actors. 1993, Smith & Kraus paper $12.95 (978-1-880399-15-6). Includes selections from children's novels and fairy tales, as well as adult drama and short stories. (Rev: BL 10/1/93; SLJ 11/93) [808.82]

13605 Stevens, Chambers. *Magnificent Monologues for Kids* (4–8). Ed. by Renee Rolle-Whatley. 1999, Sandcastle paper $13.95 (978-1-883995-08-9). A collection of 51 monologues — some best for girls, others for boys — representing different situations and emotions. (Rev: BL 4/1/99; SLJ 8/99) [808.82]

13606 Trimble, Marcia. *Malinda Martha Meets Mariposa: A Star Is Born* (2–4). Illus. by John Lund. 1999, Images LB $15.95 (978-1-891577-57-4). 32pp. Malinda Martha conjures an unusual play presenting the four stages in the development of the Monarch butterfly with costumed children as cast members. (Rev: SLJ 9/99) [812]

13607 Van Steenwyk, Elizabeth. *One Fine Day: A Radio Play* (3–5). Illus. by Bill Farnsworth. 2003, Eerdmans $16.00 (978-0-8028-5234-2). 32pp. A fictional conversation between Orville and Wilbur Wright during their first flight is presented in the form of a radio play. (Rev: BL 1/1–15/03; HBG 10/03; SLJ 4/03)

13608 Vigil, Angel. *¡Teatro! Hispanic Plays for Young People* (4–8). Illus. 1996, Teacher Ideas paper $25.00 (978-1-56308-371-6). 220pp. This collection contains 14 English-language scripts that integrate elements of the Hispanic traditions of the Southwest. (Rev: BL 3/1/97; VOYA 6/97) [812]

Shakespeare

13609 Birch, Beverley, retel. *Shakespeare's Stories: Comedies* (5–9). Illus. 1990, Bedrick paper $6.95 (978-0-87226-225-6). This is the first of three volumes that retell in attractive, straightforward prose the most popular of his plays. The others are *Shakespeare's Stories: Histories* and *Shakespeare's Stories: Tragedies* (both 1988). (Rev: BL 2/15/89; SLJ 2/89) [813]

13610 Burdett, Lois. *Hamlet for Kids* (2–4). Series: Shakespeare Can Be Fun! 2000, Firefly LB $19.95 (978-1-55209-522-5); paper $9.95 (978-1-55209-530-0). 64pp. A retelling of *Hamlet* in rhymed couplets with illustrations by the author's students, ages seven to 12. (Rev: HBG 3/01; SLJ 8/00) [822]

13611 Conner, Dan, adapt. *William Shakespeare's A Midsummer Night's Dream* (5–9). Illus. by Rod Espinosa. Series: Graphic Shakespeare. 2008, ABDO LB $19.95 (978-1-60270-191-5). 48pp. An entertaining graphic version of *A Midsummer Night's Dream,* using dialogue from the play and featuring commentary on its plot, characters, themes, and other aspects. (Rev: SLJ 1/09)

13612 Coville, Bruce. *William Shakespeare's Hamlet* (4–8). Illus. by Leonid Gore. 2004, Dial $18.99 (978-0-8037-2708-3). 40pp. This masterful prose retelling makes the famous play accessible to young people. (Rev: BL 5/15/04; SLJ 2/04) [822.3]

13613 Coville, Bruce. *William Shakespeare's Macbeth* (4–8). Illus. 1997, Dial $18.99 (978-0-8037-1899-9). Using a picture-book format, the story of Macbeth is retold with emphasis on the supernatural aspects. (Rev: BL 11/1/97; HBG 3/98; SLJ 12/97) [822.3]

13614 Coville, Bruce. *William Shakespeare's Romeo and Juliet* (4–6). 1999, Dial $17.99 (978-0-8037-2462-4). 40pp. A successful retelling of the Shakespearean tragedy with lushly romantic illustrations. (Rev: BL 12/1/99; HBG 3/00; SLJ 1/00) [822.3]

13615 Coville, Bruce. *William Shakespeare's The Winter's Tale* (4–7). Illus. by LeUyen Pham. 2007, Dial $16.99 (978-0-8037-2709-0). 40pp. An illustrated prose retelling of the classic tale of jealousy and renewal. (Rev: BL 11/1/07; SLJ 12/07) [822.3]

13616 Coville, Bruce. *William Shakespeare's Twelfth Night* (3–6). Illus. by Tim Raglin. 2003, Dial $16.99 (978-0-8037-2318-4). 40pp. Coville provides an easy-reading version of the humorous play, accompanied by appealing ink drawings. (Rev: BL 1/1–15/03; HBG 10/03; SLJ 3/03) [822]

13617 Davidson, Rebecca Piatt. *All the World's a Stage* (K–3). Illus. by Anita Lobel. 2003, Greenwillow LB $16.89 (978-0-06-029627-8). This introduction to Shakespeare and nine of his best-known plays takes the form of an extended rhyming poem and action-packed illustrations. (Rev: HBG 10/03; SLJ 5/03) [822.3]

13618 Dunn, Rebecca, adapt. *William Shakespeare's Hamlet* (5–9). Illus. by Ben Dunn. Series: Graphic Shakespeare. 2008, ABDO LB $19.95 (978-1-60270-188-5). 48pp. An entertaining graphic version of *Hamlet,* using dialogue from the play and featuring commentary on its plot, characters, themes, and other aspects. (Rev: SLJ 1/09)

13619 Farrens, Brian, adapt. *William Shakespeare's King Lear* (5–9). Illus. by Ben Dunn. Series: Graphic Shakespeare. 2008, ABDO LB $19.95 (978-1-60270-189-2). 48pp. An entertaining graphic version of *King Lear,* using dialogue from the play and featuring commentary on its plot, characters, themes, and other aspects. (Rev: SLJ 1/09)

13620 Kindermann, Barbara. *William Shakespeare's Romeo and Juliet* (4–7). Trans. by J. Alison James. Illus. by Christa Unzner. 2006, North-South $17.95 (978-0-7358-2090-6). 36pp. This well-phrased prose retelling of the ill-fated romance is enhanced by the Renaissance-style illustrations. (Rev: BL 8/06; SLJ 12/06)

13621 McKeown, Adam, retel. *Macbeth* (5–10). Illus. by Lynne Cannoy. Series: The Young Reader's Shakespeare. 2005, Sterling $14.95 (978-1-4027-1116-9). 96pp. This conversational prose retelling includes an introduction to the play and incorporates many of the important poetic passages. (Rev: BL 3/1/05; SLJ 5/05) [822.3]

13622 McKeown, Adam. *Romeo and Juliet: Young Reader's Shakespeare* (5–10). Illus. by Peter Fiore. 2004, Sterling $14.95 (978-1-4027-0004-0). 96pp. Faithful to the original, this retelling uses finely crafted prose and interweaves many of the best-known poetic stanzas. (Rev: BL 8/04; SLJ 10/04) [822.3]

Biography

Adventurers and Explorers

Collective

13623 Clements, Gillian. *The Picture History of Great Explorers* (2–4). Illus. 2005, Frances Lincoln $19.95 (978-1-84507-075-5). 96pp. A comprehensive and very visual guide, suitable for browsers, to explorers from prehistory through space travel. (Rev: BL 1/1–15/06) [920]

13624 Fritz, Jean. *Around the World in a Hundred Years: From Henry the Navigator to Magellan* (4–6). Illus. 1994, Penguin paper $8.99 (978-0-698-11638-2). 128pp. A history of exploration and explorers, from 1421 to 1522, in a series of short biographies. (Rev: BCCB 6/94; BL 5/15/94; HB 7/94; SLJ 8/94) [920]

13625 Gifford, Clive. *10 Explorers Who Changed the World* (5–8). Illus. by David Cousens. 2008, Kingfisher $14.95 (978-0-7534-6103-7). 64pp. Marco Polo, Magellan, and Roald Amundsen are among the explorers briefly profiled in this bright volume with cartoon illustrations and a strong sense of adventure. (Rev: BL 12/1/08; SLJ 2/09) [920]

13626 Gogerly, Liz. *Amundsen and Scott's Race to the South Pole* (4–6). Series: Great Journeys Across Earth. 2007, Heinemann LB $31.43 (978-1-4034-9753-6); paper $8.99 (978-1-4034-9761-1). 48pp. Useful for reports, this volume is a colorful introduction to the men who raced to the South Pole. (Rev: LMC 1/08; SLJ 4/08) [920]

13627 Gueldenpfennig, Sonia. *Spectacular Women in Space* (4–6). Series: The Women's Hall of Fame. 2005, Second Story paper $7.95 (978-1-896764-88-7). 111pp. After a history of women's achievements in the field of space exploration, this volume profiles 10 women who made significant contributions. (Rev: SLJ 4/05) [920]

13628 Hacker, Carlotta. *Explorers* (3–6). Series: Women in Profile. 1998, Crabtree LB $22.60 (978-0-7787-0004-3). 48pp. Six famous female explorers are featured, with profiles on about a dozen more. (Rev: SLJ 9/98) [920]

13629 Jones, Charlotte F. *Westward Ho! Explorers of the American West* (5–8). Illus. 2005, Holiday $22.95 (978-0-8234-1586-1). 233pp. Intriguing narrative describes the lives and adventures of 11 explorers, including Zebulon Pike and John Wesley Powell. (Rev: BL 5/1/05; SLJ 8/05) [920]

13630 Kerr, Jim. *Hillary and Norgay's Mount Everest Adventure* (4–6). Series: Great Journeys Across Earth. 2007, Heinemann LB $31.43 (978-1-4034-9755-0); paper $8.99 (978-1-4034-9763-5). 48pp. Useful for reports, this volume is a colorful introduction to expedition, the men who conquered the mountain, and the science used. (Rev: LMC 1/08; SLJ 4/08) [920]

13631 Kimmel, Elizabeth C. *The Look-It-Up-Book of Explorers* (5–9). Illus. 2004, Random LB $17.99 (978-0-375-92478-1); paper $10.99 (978-0-375-82478-4). 128pp. Chronologically arranged spreads introduce explorers from Leif Eriksson to Robert Ballard, with maps, illustrations, and historical context. (Rev: SLJ 1/05) [920]

13632 McLean, Jacqueline. *Women of Adventure* (5–9). Series: Profiles. 2003, Oliver LB $19.95 (978-1-881508-73-1). 160pp. Seven 19th- and 20th-century women with diverse interests who broke social barriers by exploring far from home are profiled here, with biographical information, photographs, and maps. (Rev: BCCB 5/03; HBG 10/03; SLJ 7/03; VOYA 8/03) [910]

13633 McLean, Jacqueline. *Women with Wings* (4–7). Illus. Series: Profiles. 2001, Oliver $19.95 (978-1-881508-70-0). 160pp. An absorbing account of the achievements of women pilots, including Bessie Coleman, Amelia Earhart, and Anne Morrow Lindbergh. (Rev: BL 5/15/01; HBG 10/01; SLJ 10/01) [629.13]

13634 McLoone, Margo. *Women Explorers of the Mountains: Nina Mazuchelli, Fanny Bullock Workman, Mary Vaux Walcott, Gertrude Benham, Junko Tabei* (3–6). Illus. Series: Capstone Short Biographies. 1999, Capstone LB $23.93 (978-0-7368-0311-3). 48pp. This book profiles five adventurous female mountaineers and includes information on their achievements as well as maps and photos. (Rev: BL 3/1/00) [920]

13635 Maynard, Christopher. *Pirates! Raiders of the High Seas* (2–4). Illus. Series: Eyewitness Reader. 1998, DK $12.99 (978-0-7894-3768-6); paper $3.99 (978-0-7894-3443-2). 48pp. Double-page spreads are used to outline the lives and ways of a number of pirates, such as Henry Morgan, Billy the Kidd, and Blackbeard. (Rev: BL 3/1/99; HBG 10/99) [920]

13636 Rooney, Frances. *Extraordinary Women Explorers* (5–8). Illus. Series: Women's Hall of Fame. 2005, Second Story paper $7.95 (978-1-896764-98-6). 118pp. Women endowed with curiosity and courage are celebrated in this text-dense volume. (Rev: BL 3/1/06; SLJ 12/05) [910]

13637 St. George, Judith. *So You Want to Be an Explorer?* (2–4). Illus. by David Small. 2005, Philomel $16.99 (978-0-399-23868-0). 56pp. This lighthearted overview of explorers celebrates the accomplishments of diverse figures and distinguishes between "good" and "bad" explorers according to their treatment of native peoples. (Rev: BL 9/15/05; SLJ 9/05) [910]

13638 Sharp, Anne Wallace. *Daring Pirate Women* (5–8). Series: Biography. 2002, Lerner LB $27.93 (978-0-8225-0031-5). 112pp. Profiles are given of notorious and ruthless female pirates such as Anne Bonny, Mary Read, and Grace O'Malley. (Rev: BL 6/1–15/02; HBG 10/02; SLJ 8/02) [920]

13639 Thompson, Gare. *Roald Amundsen and Robert Scott Race to the South Pole* (2–4). Illus. Series: National Geographic History Chapters. 2007, National Geographic LB $17.90 (978-1-4263-0187-2). 48pp. Featuring simple text and many illustrations, this volume tells the compelling story of the competition between the two explorers. (Rev: BL 10/15/07; SLJ 1/08) [919.8]

13640 Twist, Clint. *Magellan and da Gama: To the Far East and Beyond* (4–7). Illus. Series: Beyond the Horizons. 1994, Raintree LB $24.26 (978-0-8114-7254-8). 48pp. Describes the period in which these two explorers lived, as well as their voyages and accomplishments. (Rev: BL 8/94) [920]

13641 Weatherly, Myra. *Women Pirates: Eight Stories of Adventure* (4–7). Illus. 1998, Morgan Reynolds LB $21.95 (978-1-883846-24-4). 112pp. These stories of eight women pirates from the 17th and 18th centuries — including Grace O'Malley, Maria Cobham, and Rachel Wall — are enlivened by period prints and portraits and good maps. (Rev: BCCB 4/98; BL 4/15/98; HBG 3/99; SLJ 7/98; VOYA 10/98) [920]

13642 Yolen, Jane. *Sea Queens: Women Pirates Around the World* (4–7). Illus. by Christine Joy Pratt. 2008, Charlesbridge $18.95 (978-1-58089-131-8). 32pp. Yolen introduces 12 women pirates — from Artemisia in the 5th century B.C. to Madame Ching in the 19th century and including the well-known Anne Bonny. (Rev: BL 6/1–15/08; SLJ 7/08) [920]

Individual

ANZA, JUAN BAUTISTA DE

13643 Bankston, John. *Juan Bautista de Anza* (5–7). Series: Latinos in American History. 2003, Mitchell Lane LB $29.95 (978-1-58415-196-8). 48pp. The biography of the Spanish explorer of the American Southwest who was a governor of New Mexico in the late 18th century. (Rev: BL 1/1–15/04) [921]

ARMSTRONG, NEIL

13644 Byers, Ann. *Neil Armstrong: The First Man on the Moon* (4–7). Illus. Series: The Library of Astronaut Biographies. 2004, Rosen LB $29.25 (978-0-8239-4461-3). 112pp. A lively overview focusing mainly on Armstrong's education and training. (Rev: SLJ 1/05) [921]

13645 Zemlicka, Shannon. *Neil Armstrong* (2–5). Illus. Series: History Maker Bios. 2002, Lerner LB $26.60 (978-0-8225-0395-8). 48pp. A simple, absorbing account of the life of the first man to reach the moon, with helpful sidebars that amplify material in the text. (Rev: HBG 3/03; SLJ 12/02) [921]

BALBOA, VASCO NUNEZ DE

13646 Otfinoski, Steven. *Vasco Nunez de Balboa: Explorer of the Pacific* (5–8). Series: Great Explorations. 2004, Benchmark LB $29.93 (978-0-7614-1609-8). 79pp. After material on Balboa's early life, Otfinoski looks at the Spanish explorer's trip to the Pacific. (Rev: SLJ 3/05) [921]

BLANCHARD, JEAN-PIERRE

13647 Wallner, Alexandra. *The First Air Voyage in the United States: The Story of Jean-Pierre Blanchard* (K–4). Illus. 1996, Holiday House $15.95 (978-0-8234-1224-2). 32pp. The story of the man who participated in 1793 in the first air flight in the United States. (Rev: BCCB 5/96; BL 5/15/96; SLJ 6/96) [921]

BOONE, DANIEL

13648 Armentrout, David, and Patricia Armentrout. *Daniel Boone* (2–4). Series: Discover Someone Who Made a Difference. 2001, Rourke LB $14.95 (978-1-58952-052-3). 24pp. As well as a life of this famous outdoorsman, this biography explains how he has influenced our lives today. (Rev: BCCB 3/02; BL 1/1–15/02; SLJ 3/02) [921]

13649 Calvert, Patricia. *Daniel Boone: Beyond the Mountains* (5–8). Series: Great Explorations. 2001, Marshall Cavendish LB $29.93 (978-0-7614-1243-4). 79pp. An attractive biography of the American pioneer who explored the Cumberland Gap region and helped settlers in the Kentucky region. (Rev: BCCB 3/02; BL 4/1/02; HBG 3/02; SLJ 3/02) [921]

13650 Kozar, Richard. *Daniel Boone and the Exploration of the Frontier* (4–6). Series: Explorers of

New Worlds. 2000, Chelsea LB $25.00 (978-0-7910-5510-6). 63pp. Using a variety of illustrations and a crisp text, this book gives good information about Daniel Boone and the forces that inspired him to explore the frontier. (Rev: HBG 10/00; SLJ 7/00) [921]

13651 McCarthy, Pat. *Daniel Boone* (5–8). Series: Historical American Biographies. 2000, Enslow LB $26.60 (978-0-7660-1256-1). 128pp. A well-organized and thoroughly documented biography of the legendary pioneer and hero of the American Revolution who died in 1820. (Rev: BL 1/1–15/00; HBG 10/00; SLJ 5/00) [921]

13652 Riehecky, Janet. *Daniel Boone* (3–6). Series: Raintree Biographies. 2003, Raintree LB $25.69 (978-0-7398-5672-7). 32pp. A simple biography of the pioneer's life and achievements, with sidebar features containing primary and background material. (Rev: BCCB 3/02; HBG 3/03; SLJ 3/03) [921]

13653 Spradlin, Michael P. *Daniel Boone's Great Escape* (K–2). Illus. by Ard Hoyt. 2008, Walker $16.95 (978-0-8027-9581-6). 32pp. Spradin focuses on a time when Boone was captured by Shawnee warriors. (Rev: BL 7/08; LMC 8/08; SLJ 7/08) [976.9]

BROADWICK, GEORGIA "TINY"

13654 Roberson, Elizabeth Whitley. *Tiny Broadwick: The First Lady of Parachuting* (4–8). Illus. 2001, Pelican paper $9.95 (978-1-56554-780-3). 112pp. Less than 5 feet tall, "Tiny" Broadwick joined a hot-air balloon act as a teenager and became the first woman to jump with a parachute. (Rev: BL 7/01) [797.5]

BURTON, RICHARD FRANCIS

13655 Young, Serinity. *Richard Francis Burton: Explorer, Scholar, Spy* (5–9). Series: Great Explorations. 2006, Benchmark LB $32.79 (978-0-7614-2222-8). 80pp. This biography chronicles the English adventurer's explorations in Africa, the Middle East, South Asia, and South America and looks at his interest in the cultures of the people he encountered there. (Rev: SLJ 1/07) [921]

BYRD, ADMIRAL RICHARD EVELYN

13656 Burleigh, Robert. *Black Whiteness: Admiral Byrd Alone in the Antarctic* (4–8). Illus. by Walter L. Krudop. 1998, Simon & Schuster $16.95 (978-0-689-81299-6). 40pp. An outstanding picture biography, with generous quotations from Byrd's diary that describe his great endurance and his lonely vigil in a small underground structure in the Antarctic. (Rev: BL 1/1–15/98*; HB 3/98; HBG 10/98; SLJ 3/98) [921]

CABEZA DE VACA, ALVAR NUNEZ

13657 Menard, Valerie. *Alvar Nunez Cabeza de Vaca* (5–7). Series: Latinos in American History. 2002, Mitchell Lane LB $29.95 (978-1-58415-153-1). 48pp. A biography of the 16th-century Spanish nobleman who lived with Native Americans for eight years and who claimed Florida, Louisiana, and Texas for Spain. (Rev: BL 2/15/03; HBG 10/03) [921]

13658 Waldman, Stuart. *We Asked for Nothing: The Remarkable Journey of Cabeza de Vaca* (5–8). Illus. by Tom McNeely. Series: A Great Explorers Book. 2003, Mikaya $19.95 (978-1-931414-07-4). 46pp. Drawing on the writings of Cabeza de Vaca, Waldman tells the riveting story of the Spaniard's eight years in 16th-century Texas and Mexico. (Rev: SLJ 2/04) [921]

CABOT, JOHN

13659 Doak, Robin. *Cabot: John Cabot and the Journey to North America* (4–6). Series: Exploring the World. 2003, Compass Point LB $23.93 (978-0-7565-0420-5). 48pp. Chronicles his 1497 voyage, with material on his early life and with rich historical context, including the impact of these foreigners' arrival on the native inhabitants. (Rev: SLJ 12/03) [921]

13660 Shields, Charles J. *John Cabot and the Rediscovery of North America* (4–8). Series: Explorers of New Worlds. 2001, Chelsea $25.00 (978-0-7910-6438-2); paper $25.00 (978-0-7910-6439-9). 63pp. An absorbing biography that focuses on Cabot's expeditions at the end of the 15th century in search of a passage to Asia. (Rev: SLJ 3/02) [921]

CARSON, KIT

13661 Boraas, Tracey. *Kit Carson: Mountain Man* (4–6). Series: Let Freedom Ring. 2002, Capstone LB $23.93 (978-0-7368-1349-5). 48pp. An absorbing account of the life and exploits of the legendary trapper and scout. (Rev: HBG 3/03; SLJ 2/03) [921]

CARTIER, JACQUES

13662 Blashfield, Jean F. *Cartier: Jacques Cartier in Search of the Northwest Passage* (4–6). Series: Exploring the World. 2001, Compass Point LB $23.93 (978-0-7565-0122-8). 48pp. The story of Cartier's efforts to find a route to China, with color reproductions of maps, paintings, and prints, and information on his contemporaries. (Rev: SLJ 1/02) [921]

CHAMPLAIN, SAMUEL DE

13663 Faber, Harold. *Samuel de Champlain: Explorer of Canada* (5–8). Series: Great Explorations. 2004, Benchmark LB $29.93 (978-0-7614-1608-1). 80pp. Drawing on Champlain's own accounts, this well-illustrated volume examines his voyages to Canada and achievements as governor of New France. (Rev: SLJ 3/05) [921]

13664 Moore, Christopher. *Champlain* (4–6). Illus. by Francis Back. 2004, Tundra $18.95 (978-0-88776-657-2). 56pp. This attractive, revised edition chronicles the French explorer's early-17th-century journeys in eastern Canada and places his importance in historical context. (Rev: BL 10/15/04; SLJ 11/04) [921]

13665 Sherman, Josepha. *Samuel de Champlain: Explorer of the Great Lakes Region and Founder of Quebec* (4–7). Series: The Library of Explorers and Exploration. 2003, Rosen LB $33.25 (978-0-8239-3629-8). 112pp. In addition to covering Champlain's life, this volume places his explorations in historical context and gives interesting information on the fur trade and relations with Native Americans. (Rev: SLJ 9/03) [971.01]

COCHRAN, JACQUELINE

13666 Smith, Elizabeth Simpson. *Coming Out Right: The Story of Jacqueline Cochran, the First Woman Aviator to Break the Sound Barrier* (5–8). Illus. 1991, Walker LB $15.85 (978-0-8027-6989-3). 114pp. From her impoverished childhood to her triumphs in the air and later, this is the story of a female aviation pioneer. (Rev: BL 4/15/91; SLJ 5/91) [921]

COLEMAN, BESSIE

13667 Borden, Louise, and Mary Kay Kroeger. *Fly High! The Story of Bessie Coleman* (1–4). Illus. by Teresa Flavin. 2001, Simon & Schuster $16.00 (978-0-689-82457-9). 40pp. A highly illustrated, short biography of airplane pilot Bessie Coleman, who in 1921 became the first African American to get a pilot's license. (Rev: BCCB 2/01; BL 2/15/01; HBG 10/01; SLJ 1/01) [921]

13668 Braun, Eric. *Bessie Coleman* (K–2). Series: First Biographies. 2005, Capstone LB $17.26 (978-0-7368-4229-7). 24pp. With its simple sentences and clear black-and-white photographs, this profile of the first African American woman to earn a pilot's license gives basic, introductory information. (Rev: SLJ 2/06) [921]

13669 Fisher, Lillian M. *Brave Bessie: Flying Free* (4–7). Illus. 1995, Hendrick-Long $16.95 (978-0-937460-94-8). 88pp. This biography tells of the struggles of Bessie Coleman, who became the first African American aviatrix in the United States. (Rev: BL 2/15/96; SLJ 2/96) [921]

13670 Grimes, Nikki. *Talkin' About Bessie: The Story of Aviator Elizabeth Coleman* (2–5). Illus. by E. B. Lewis. 2002, Scholastic $16.95 (978-0-439-35243-7). 48pp. In this unusual biography, Grimes uses the voices of friends and relatives at Coleman's funeral to tell the story of her love of flying and her achievements as the first African American woman flyer. (Rev: BL 11/15/02; HB 1/03*; HBG 3/03; SLJ 10/02) [629.13]

13671 Hart, Philip S. *Up In the Air: The Story of Bessie Coleman* (5–8). 1996, Carolrhoda LB $16.95 (978-0-87614-949-2). 80pp. Forced by restrictions in the United States to get her training in France in the 1920s, Coleman became the first African American female airplane pilot. (Rev: BL 8/96; SLJ 8/96) [921]

13672 Plantz, Connie. *Bessie Coleman: First Black Woman Pilot* (4–8). 2001, Enslow LB $26.60 (978-

0-7660-1545-6). 128pp. This is a readable biography that breathes life into Coleman's childhood, training as a pilot, and tragic death. (Rev: HBG 3/02; SLJ 1/02) [921]

COLUMBUS, CHRISTOPHER

13673 Adler, David A. *A Picture Book of Christopher Columbus* (K–3). Illus. by John Wallner. Series: Picture Book Biographies. 1991, Holiday House LB $16.95 (978-0-8234-0857-3); paper $6.95 (978-0-8234-0949-5). 32pp. The life of this famous explorer is described in simple text and many illustrations. (Rev: BL 6/1/91; SLJ 5/91) [921]

13674 Bailey, Gerry, and Karen Foster. *Columbus's Chart* (3–5). Illus. by Leighton Noyes and Karen Radford. Series: Stories of Great People. 2008, Crabtree LB $29.27 (978-0-7787-3686-8); paper $9.95 (978-0-7787-3708-7). 40pp. At an antique market, fictitious characters Digby Platt and his older sister Hannah find a chart belonging to Columbus and learn lots of facts about the man and his explorations. (Rev: LMC 11/08; SLJ 7/08) [921]

13675 Clare, John D., ed. *The Voyages of Christopher Columbus* (5–8). Illus. Series: Living History. 1992, Harcourt $16.95 (978-0-15-200507-8). 64pp. Using actors and backdrops of the period, this account reconstructs each of Columbus's New World voyages. (Rev: SLJ 11/92) [921]

13676 Fritz, Jean. *Where Do You Think You're Going, Christopher Columbus?* (3–5). Illus. by Margot Tomes. 1980, Penguin $18.99 (978-0-399-20723-5); paper $6.99 (978-0-698-11580-4). 80pp. A fresh, interesting account of Columbus and his voyages. [921]

13677 Molzahn, Arlene Bourgeois. *Christopher Columbus: Famous Explorer* (3–5). Illus. Series: Explorers! 2003, Enslow LB $23.93 (978-0-7660-2066-5). 48pp. Arresting illustrations and well-written text make this an appealing volume. (Rev: HBG 10/03; SLJ 8/03) [921]

13678 Pelta, Kathy. *Discovering Christopher Columbus: How History Is Invented* (5–7). Illus. 1991, Lerner LB $23.93 (978-0-8225-4899-7). 112pp. After telling what we know about Columbus, the author examines how myths and legends about him have grown over the years. (Rev: BL 10/1/91) [921]

COOK, CAPTAIN JAMES

13679 Bingham, Jane. *Captain Cook's Pacific Explorations* (4–6). Series: Great Journeys Across Earth. 2007, Heinemann LB $31.43 (978-1-4034-9756-7); paper $8.99 (978-1-4034-9764-2). 48pp. Useful for reports, this volume is a colorful introduction to the 18th-century expeditions of Captain Cook and explains the science involved. (Rev: LMC 1/08; SLJ 4/08) [921]

13680 Meltzer, Milton. *Captain James Cook: Three Times Around the World* (5–8). Series: Great Explorations. 2001, Marshall Cavendish LB $28.50 (978-0-7614-1240-3). 80pp. Using both text and illustrations, this is a fine biography of the English mariner and explorer who, among other feats, explored the west coast of North America. (Rev: BL 4/1/02; HBG 3/02) [921]

CORONADO, FRANCISCO VASQUEZ DE

13681 Doak, Robin. *Coronado: Francisco Vásquez de Coronado Explores the Southwest* (4–6). Series: Exploring the World. 2001, Compass Point LB $23.93 (978-0-7565-0123-5). 48pp. The story of Coronado's quest for gold in the Southwest, with color reproductions of maps, paintings, and prints, and information on his contemporaries. (Rev: SLJ 1/02) [921]

CORTES, HERNAN

13682 West, David, and Jackie Gaff. *Hernan Cortes: The Life of a Spanish Conquistador* (4–6). Illus. by Jim Eldridge. Series: Rosen's Graphic Nonfiction. 2005, Rosen LB $29.25 (978-1-4042-0244-3). 48pp. The story of the explorer's life in a comic-book format. (Rev: BL 3/15/05) [921]

CROCKETT, DAVY

13683 Adler, David A. *A Picture Book of Davy Crockett* (K–3). Illus. by John Wallner. Series: Picture Book Biographies. 1996, Holiday House $16.95 (978-0-8234-1212-9). 32pp. With simple, brief text and many illustrations, this is a beginning biography of a frontier hero. (Rev: BL 4/15/96; SLJ 5/96) [921]

13684 Alphin, Elaine M. *Davy Crockett* (2–4). Illus. Series: History Maker Bios. 2002, Lerner LB $26.60 (978-0-8225-0393-4). 48pp. Legend and fact are clearly separated in this biography that looks mainly at Crockett's career. (Rev: HBG 3/03; SLJ 12/02) [921]

13685 Feeney, Kathy. *Davy Crockett* (2–4). Series: Photo-Illustrated Biographies. 2002, Capstone LB $22.60 (978-0-7368-1110-1). 24pp. Crockett's life and contributions to the exploration of the West are presented, with care to distinguish between fact and legend. (Rev: SLJ 7/02) [921]

13686 Krensky, Stephen. *Davy Crockett: A Life on the Frontier* (1–3). Illus. by Debra Bandelin and Bob Dacey. Series: Ready-to-Read Stories of Famous Americans. 2004, Simon & Schuster paper $3.99 (978-0-689-85944-1). 48pp. Krensky provides both legend and fact in this engaging biography of the frontiersman. (Rev: BL 12/1/04; SLJ 3/05) [921]

DA GAMA, VASCO

13687 Calvert, Patricia. *Vasco da Gama: So Strong a Spirit* (5–8). Series: Great Explorations. 2004, Benchmark LB $29.93 (978-0-7614-1611-1). 96pp. After material on da Gama's early life, Calvert looks at the 15th-century Portuguese explorer's voyages. (Rev: SLJ 3/05) [921]

13688 Draper, Allison Stark. *Vasco da Gama: The Portuguese Quest for a Sea Route from Europe to India* (5–8). Illus. Series: Library of Explorers and Exploration. 2003, Rosen LB $33.25 (978-0-8239-

3632-8). 112pp. Da Gama's achievements and brutal behavior are given equal exposure in this well-illustrated volume. (Rev: BL 6/1–15/03) [910]

13689 Kratoville, Betty Lou. *Vasco da Gama* (4–7). Series: Trade Route Explorers. 2000, High Noon paper $17.00 (978-1-57128-168-5). 44pp. The story of the famous explorer who rounded the Cape of Good Hope and visited India, told in a simple, interesting account. (Rev: SLJ 3/01) [921]

DE SOTO, HERNANDO

13690 Stein, R. Conrad. *Hernando De Soto: A Life of Adventure* (4–6). Illus. Series: A Proud Heritage: The Hispanic Library. 2005, Child's World LB $28.50 (978-1-59296-385-0). 40pp. The story of the Spaniard's life and explorations in the New World. [921]

13691 Whiting, Jim. *Hernando de Soto* (5–7). Series: Latinos in American History. 2002, Mitchell Lane LB $29.95 (978-1-58415-147-0). 48pp. A simple biography of the Spanish explorer who discovered the Mississippi River in the 16th century while traveling through what is now the southern United States. (Rev: BL 2/15/03; HBG 10/03; SLJ 6/03) [921]

DRAKE, SIR FRANCIS

13692 Gallagher, Jim. *Sir Francis Drake and the Foundation of a World Empire* (4–8). Series: Explorers of New Worlds. 2000, Chelsea $31.00 (978-0-7910-5950-0); paper $25.00 (978-0-7910-6160-2). 63pp. This appealing and readable biography of Sir Francis Drake presents his life from childhood and details his major accomplishments, with photographs, sidebar features, documents, and maps. (Rev: HBG 10/01; SLJ 4/01) [921]

13693 Rice, Earle, Jr. *Sir Francis Drake: Navigator and Pirate* (5–8). Series: Great Explorations. 2002, Benchmark LB $29.93 (978-0-7614-1483-4). 76pp. A profile of the 16th-century British explorer who circumnavigated the globe and fought the Spanish Armada, with maps, timeline, and reproductions. (Rev: HBG 10/03; SLJ 6/03) [942.05]

EARHART, AMELIA

13694 Adler, David A. *A Picture Book of Amelia Earhart* (1–3). Illus. by Jeff Fisher. Series: Picture Book Biographies. 1998, Holiday House $17.95 (978-0-8234-1315-7). 32pp. Single- and double-page illustrations are used in this interesting biography that highlights Amelia Earhart's unusual childhood. (Rev: BL 4/15/98; HBG 10/98; SLJ 4/98) [921]

13695 Brown, Jonatha A. *Amelia Earhart* (2–4). Illus. Series: People We Should Know. 2005, Gareth Stevens LB $21.00 (978-0-8368-4465-8). 24pp. An easy-to-read basic biography of the famous pilot, with photographs. (Rev: BL 3/1/05) [629.13]

13696 Bull, Angela. *Flying Ace: The Story of Amelia Earhart* (2–4). Illus. by Chris Forsey. Series: Eyewitness Reader. 2000, DK $14.99 (978-0-7894-

5436-2); paper $3.99 (978-0-7894-5435-5). 48pp. An interesting biography for beginning readers that reveals many details of Earhart's life and speculates on the cause of her disappearance. (Rev: HBG 10/00; SLJ 7/00) [921]

13697 Feinstein, Stephen. *Read About Amelia Earhart* (2–4). Series: I Like Biographies! 2006, Enslow LB $21.26 (978-0-7660-2582-0). 24pp. For early researchers, this is an introductory biography that includes information on Earhart's youth and her work during World War I. (Rev: SLJ 4/06) [921]

13698 Lakin, Patricia. *Amelia Earhart: More Than a Flier* (2–3). Illus. by Alan Daniel and Lea Daniel. Series: Childhood of Famous Americans. 2003, Simon & Schuster paper $3.99 (978-0-689-85575-7). 46pp. A simple, colorful account of Earhart's childhood, love for adventure, and achievements as a woman aviator. (Rev: HBG 10/03; SLJ 10/03) [921]

13699 Landsman, Susan. *What Happened to Amelia Earhart?* (3–5). Illus. 1991, Avon paper $3.50 (978-0-380-76221-7). 96pp. While giving background information on Amelia Earhart, this book focuses on her disappearance. (Rev: BL 9/15/91) [921]

13700 Lauber, Patricia. *Lost Star: The Story of Amelia Earhart* (5–7). Illus. 1988, Scholastic paper $4.50 (978-0-590-41159-2). 96pp. A candid biography of the famed lost aviator. (Rev: BL 10/1/88; SLJ 12/88) [921]

13701 Mara, Wil. *Amelia Earhart* (K–2). Series: Rookie Biographies. 2002, Children's Book Pr. LB $20.50 (978-0-516-22522-7); paper $4.95 (978-0-516-27338-9). 32pp. For beginning readers, this is a simple introduction to the famed aviatrix. (Rev: SLJ 12/02) [921]

13702 Micklos, John, Jr. *Unsolved: What Really Happened to Amelia Earhart?* (4–8). 2006, Enslow LB $31.93 (978-0-7660-2365-9). 144pp. The mystery of Earhart's last flight makes this a compelling read, even for researchers, and it provides what they need in terms of information about her childhood and motivations, photographs, maps, and so forth. (Rev: SLJ 7/07) [921]

13703 Sloate, Susan. *Amelia Earhart: Challenging the Skies* (5–8). Illus. 1990, Fawcett paper $6.99 (978-0-449-90396-4). 128pp. The aviator's life story is told along with an examination of all the theories concerning her disappearance. (Rev: SLJ 6/90) [921]

13704 Tanaka, Shelley. *Amelia Earhart: The Legend of the Lost Aviator* (2–4). Illus. by David Craig. 2008, Abrams $18.95 (978-0-8109-7095-3). 48pp. With archival photographs and original art, this picture-book biography for older readers tells the story of Amelia's life and love of planes. (Rev: BCCB 9/08; BL 6/1–15/08; SLJ 11/08) [921]

ERIKSSON, LEIF

13705 Klingel, Cynthia, and Robert B. Noyed. *Leif Eriksson: Norwegian Explorer* (3–5). Series: Spirit of America: Our People. 2002, Child's World LB $27.07 (978-1-56766-163-7). 32pp. Eriksson's story

is placed in the context of Viking exploration, settlement, society, and family life. (Rev: SLJ 12/02)

EXQUEMELIN

13706 Exquemelin, A. O. *Exquemelin and the Pirates of the Caribbean* (5–8). Ed. by Jane Shuter. Illus. Series: History Eyewitness. 1995, Raintree LB $24.26 (978-0-8114-8282-0). 48pp. An edited version of the exciting journal of the 17th-century Frenchman who joined a pirate gang as a barber-surgeon. (Rev: BL 4/15/95) [921]

FREMONT, JOHN C.

13707 Faber, Harold. *John Charles Fremont: Pathfinder to the West* (5–8). Series: Great Explorations. 2002, Benchmark LB $29.93 (978-0-7614-1481-0). 79pp. A profile of the 19th-century explorer who helped open the American West to settlers, with maps, timeline, and reproductions. (Rev: HBG 10/03; SLJ 6/03) [979]

GAGARIN, YURI

13708 Feldman, Heather. *Yuri Gagarin: The First Man in Space* (2–3). Series: Space Firsts. 2003, Rosen LB $21.25 (978-0-8239-6245-7). 24pp. This brief biography includes information on the cosmonaut's early life, training, and first, pioneering flight into space. (Rev: SLJ 11/03) [629.45]

GRISSOM, GUS

13709 Bredeson, Carmen. *Gus Grissom: A Space Biography* (3–7). Illus. Series: Space Biography. 1998, Enslow LB $23.93 (978-0-89490-974-0). 48pp. Using large color pictures and a simple text, this book traces the exciting career of this space pioneer and his many contributions to the NASA space program. (Rev: BL 4/1/98; HBG 10/98; SLJ 5/98) [629.45]

HENRY THE NAVIGATOR

13710 Gallagher, Aileen. *Prince Henry the Navigator: Pioneer of Modern Exploration* (5–8). Illus. Series: Library of Explorers and Exploration. 2003, Rosen LB $33.25 (978-0-8239-3621-2). 112pp. During the 15th century, Prince Henry of Portugal spurred others to seek a route to India, claim new territory, and spread Christianity. (Rev: BL 6/1–15/03) [946.9]

HENSON, MATTHEW

13711 Armentrout, David, and Patricia Armentrout. *Matthew Henson* (1–3). Illus. Series: Discover a Life of an American Legend. 2003, Rourke LB $20.64 (978-1-58952-658-7). 24pp. An introduction to the life and achievements of the African American polar explorer. (Rev: BL 2/1/04; SLJ 3/04) [919.8]

13712 Ferris, Jeri. *Arctic Explorer: The Story of Matthew Henson* (3–6). Illus. 1989, Carolrhoda LB

$24.50 (978-0-87614-370-4). 80pp. Robert Peary described his African American assistant as "a most nearly indispensable man." (Rev: BL 6/1/89; HB 7/89)

13713 Hoena, B. A. *Matthew Henson: Arctic Adventurer* (4–7). Illus. by Phil Miller. Series: Graphic Biographies. 2005, Capstone LB $26.60 (978-0-7368-4634-9). 32pp. The life of the African American explorer is presented in speedy, user-friendly, classic comic book format. (Rev: BL 11/1/05) [910]

13714 Johnson, Dolores. *Onward: A Photobiography of African-American Polar Explorer Matthew Henson* (5–8). Illus. Series: National Geographic Photobiography. 2005, National Geographic LB $27.90 (978-0-7922-7915-0). 64pp. The extraordinary life and achievements of African American explorer Matthew Henson are beautifully documented in this volume that also discusses the racism that Henson faced. (Rev: BCCB 5/06; BL 12/15/05*; HB 5/06; HBG 10/06; LMC 8/06; SLJ 3/06*; VOYA 6/06) [910]

13715 Weatherford, Carole Boston. *I, Matthew Henson: Polar Explorer* (2–5). Illus. by Eric Velasquez. 2007, Walker $16.95 (978-0-8027-9688-3). 32pp. This first-person poetic narrative traces the explorer's life from the age of 13 and reveals his many talents and his determination in the face of considerable challenges. (Rev: BL 2/1/08; HB 3/08; LMC 5/08; SLJ 1/08*) [921]

13716 Weidt, Maryann N. *Matthew Henson* (2–4). Illus. Series: History Maker Bios. 2002, Lerner LB $26.60 (978-0-8225-0397-2). 48pp. Henson's explorations are the main focus of this biography that touches on his youth. (Rev: SLJ 12/02) [921]

HEYERDAHL, THOR

13717 Malam, John. *Thor Heyerdahl* (1–4). Series: Tell Me About. 1999, Carolrhoda LB $19.93 (978-1-57505-364-6). 24pp. A lively biography of the fearless voyager who set out in a balsa-wood raft, the *Kon Tiki*, to explore the Pacific Ocean. (Rev: HBG 10/99; SLJ 8/99) [921]

HILLARY, SIR EDMUND

13718 Brennan, Kristine. *Sir Edmund Hillary: Modern-Day Explorer* (4–8). Series: Explorers of New Worlds. 2000, Chelsea $25.00 (978-0-7910-5953-1); paper $25.00 (978-0-7910-6163-3). 63pp. An appealing overview of the life and accomplishments of the mountaineer and explorer, with photographs and maps. (Rev: SLJ 4/01) [796.52]

13719 Coburn, Broughton. *Triumph on Everest: A Photobiography of Sir Edmund Hillary* (5–8). 2000, National Geographic $17.95 (978-0-7922-7114-7). 64pp. Using many quotations and excellent photographs, this work records the lifetime accomplishments of one of the first men to reach the top of Mount Everest. (Rev: BCCB 9/00; HBG 3/01; SLJ 10/00) [921]

13720 Elish, Dan. *Edmund Hillary: First to the Top* (5–9). Series: Great Explorations. 2006, Benchmark LB $32.79 (978-0-7614-2224-2). 80pp. This biogra-

phy focuses on the New Zealand mountain climber's 1953 conquest of Mount Everest and includes coverage of Sherpa Tenzing Norgay. (Rev: SLJ 1/07) [921]

13721 Stewart, Whitney. *Sir Edmund Hillary: To Everest and Beyond* (5–8). Photos by Anne B. Keiser. Illus. Series: Newsmakers. 1996, Lerner LB $30.35 (978-0-8225-4927-7). 128pp. The life of this famous mountain climber is presented with interesting details about his other interests, including bee keeping, conservation, and helping the Sherpa people. (Rev: SLJ 9/96) [921]

HUDSON, HENRY

13722 Doak, Robin. *Hudson: Henry Hudson Searches for a Passage to Asia* (4–6). Series: Exploring the World. 2003, Compass Point LB $23.93 (978-0-7565-0422-9). 48pp. Traces the four voyages of English-born explorer Henry Hudson in search of a short navigable route from Europe to the Far East. (Rev: LMC 11/03; SLJ 12/03) [921]

13723 Goodman, Joan E. *Beyond the Sea of Ice: The Voyages of Henry Hudson* (3–6). Illus. Series: Great Explorers Books. 1999, Mikaya $19.95 (978-0-9650493-8-2). 48pp. This biography focuses on Hudson's four voyages of exploration. (Rev: BL 11/1/99; HBG 3/00; SLJ 3/00) [921]

13724 Saffer, Barbara. *Henry Hudson: Ill-Fated Explorer of North America's Coast* (4–8). Series: Explorers of New Worlds. 2001, Chelsea $25.00 (978-0-7910-6436-8); paper $25.00 (978-0-7910-6437-5). 63pp. This absorbing biography focuses on Hudson's early 17th-century expeditions from England in search of a sea route to the Far East. (Rev: HBG 10/02; SLJ 3/02) [921]

JEMISON, MAE

13725 Braun, Eric. *Mae Jemison* (K–2). Series: First Biographies. 2005, Capstone LB $17.26 (978-0-7368-4231-0). 24pp. With its simple sentences and clear black-and-white photographs, this profile of the first African American woman to become an astronaut gives basic, introductory information. (Rev: SLJ 2/06) [921]

13726 Burby, Liza N. *Mae Jemison: The First African American Woman Astronaut* (1–3). Series: Making Their Mark: Women in Science and Medicine. 1997, Rosen LB $18.75 (978-0-8239-5027-0). 24pp. A short, clearly written biography of this space pioneer for beginning readers. (Rev: SLJ 7/98) [921]

13727 Feinstein, Stephen. *Mae Jemison* (1–4). Series: African-American Heroes. 2007, Enslow LB $21.26 (978-0-7660-2762-6). 24pp. A basic and straightforward look at the life of the African-American astronaut, with photographs. (Rev: SLJ 8/07)

13728 Kraske, Robert. *Mae Jemison: Space Pioneer* (1–3). Series: Fact Finders Biographies. 2006, Capstone LB $22.60 (978-0-7368-6420-6). 32pp. Large, easy-to-read print recounts the life of the first African American astronaut from her childhood through her resignation from NASA in 1994. (Rev: SLJ 1/07) [921]

13729 Naden, Corinne J., and Rose Blue. *Mae Jemison: Out of This World* (2–5). Illus. Series: Gateway. 2003, Millbrook LB $23.90 (978-0-7613-2570-3). 48pp. The life story of the first African American woman in space. (Rev: BL 2/15/03; HBG 10/03) [629.45]

13730 Raum, Elizabeth. *Mae Jemison* (3–5). Illus. Series: American Lives. 2005, Heinemann LB $18.75 (978-1-4034-6942-7). 32pp. This is a brief but thorough and easily understood of the first African American woman to become an astronaut. (Rev: BL 2/15/06) [921]

13731 Streissguth, Thomas. *Mae Jemison* (2–4). Illus. Series: Explore Space! 2003, Capstone LB $22.60 (978-0-7368-1626-7). 24pp. A slim, basic biography of the first African American woman to travel in space. (Rev: HBG 10/03; SLJ 3/04) [921]

LA SALLE, CAVELIER DE

13732 Faber, Harold. *La Salle: Down the Mississippi* (5–8). Series: Great Explorations. 2001, Marshall Cavendish LB $29.93 (978-0-7614-1239-7). 80pp. The exciting story of the French explorer who traveled down the Mississippi River to the Gulf of Mexico and named the region Louisiana. (Rev: BL 4/1/02; HBG 3/02; SLJ 3/02) [921]

13733 Goodman, Joan Elizabeth. *Despite All Obstacles: La Salle and the Conquest of the Mississippi* (3–6). Illus. by Tom McNeely. Series: Great Explorers. 2001, Mikaya $19.95 (978-1-931414-01-2). 48pp. Journal entries, excerpts from letters, a map, and attractive illustrations enhance this life of explorer Rene-Robert Cavalier, Sieur de La Salle. (Rev: BL 1/1–15/02; HBG 10/02; SLJ 4/02) [973.2]

LAW, RUTH

13734 Brown, Don. *Ruth Law Thrills a Nation* (1–3). Illus. 1993, Ticknor $17.00 (978-0-395-66404-9). 32pp. A simple biography about the woman flier who broke a nonstop cross-country record. (Rev: BL 8/93) [921]

LEWIS AND CLARK

13735 Adler, David A. *A Picture Book of Lewis and Clark* (2–4). Illus. by Ronald Himler. Series: Picture Book Biographies. 2003, Holiday House $16.95 (978-0-8234-1735-3). 32pp. Biographical information about the two explorers and information on the expedition itself are found in this accessible book. (Rev: BL 2/15/03; HBG 10/03; SLJ 3/03) [917.804]

13736 Kroll, Steven. *Lewis and Clark: Explorers of the American West* (1–5). Illus. by Richard Williams. 1994, Holiday House LB $17.95 (978-0-8234-1034-7). 32pp. An appealing picture book that dramatically describes the famous journey of Lewis and Clark. (Rev: BCCB 11/94; BL 11/1/94; SLJ 9/94) [921]

13737 Streissguth, Thomas. *Lewis and Clark: Explorers of the Northwest* (4–9). Series: Historical American Biographies. 1998, Enslow LB $26.60 (978-0-7660-1016-1). 128pp. The story of the two intrepid explorers who made their way overland to the Pacific Ocean. (Rev: BL 8/98) [921]

LIVINGSTONE, DAVID

13738 Otfinoski, Steven. *David Livingstone: Deep in the Heart of Africa* (5–9). Series: Great Explorations. 2006, Benchmark LB $32.79 (978-0-7614-2226-6). 79pp. This biography focuses on the three decades during which the Scottish-born adventurer explored central Africa. (Rev: SLJ 1/07) [921]

LUCID, SHANNON

13739 Bredeson, Carmen. *Shannon Lucid* (4–6). Illus. 1998, Millbrook LB $20.90 (978-0-7613-0406-7). 48pp. A biography of America's most experienced astronaut who spent 188 days on *Mir* and later joked that she hadn't showered for six months. (Rev: BL 1/1–15/99; HBG 3/99; SLJ 1/99) [921]

MCAULIFFE, CHRISTA

13740 Naden, Corinne J., and Rose Blue. *Christa McAuliffe: Teacher in Space* (3–5). Illus. Series: Gateway Biographies. 1991, Millbrook LB $23.90 (978-1-56294-046-1). 48pp. Personal anecdotes about America's "first private citizen in space" are crisscrossed with space program information. (Rev: BL 1/1/92; SLJ 1/92) [921]

MCNAIR, RONALD

13741 Naden, Corinne J. *Ronald McNair* (5–8). Illus. Series: Black Americans of Achievement. 1991, Chelsea LB $21.95 (978-0-7910-1133-1). 109pp. An inspirational biography of the second African American astronaut, a victim of the *Challenger* disaster. (Rev: BL 4/1/91; SLJ 3/91) [921]

MAGELLAN, FERDINAND

13742 Burgan, Michael. *Magellan: Ferdinand Magellan and the First Trip Around the World* (4–6). Series: Exploring the World. 2001, Compass Point LB $23.93 (978-0-7565-0125-9). 48pp. An encompassing look at Magellan's achievements with excellent illustrations, a timeline, and Web site information. (Rev: SLJ 1/02) [921]

13743 Burnett, Betty. *Ferdinand Magellan: The First Voyage Around the World* (4–7). Series: The Library of Explorers and Exploration. 2003, Rosen LB $33.25 (978-0-8239-3617-5). 112pp. In addition to covering Magellan's life, this volume places his 16th-century voyage in historical context and gives interesting information on the funding of such expeditions and life at sea. (Rev: SLJ 9/03) [910]

13744 Gallagher, Jim. *Ferdinand Magellan and the First Voyage Around the World* (4–6). Series: Explorers of New Worlds. 2000, Chelsea LB $31.00 (978-0-7910-5508-3). 63pp. With well-chosen illustrations and a lively text, this book re-creates the historic voyages of Magellan, the first man to circle the globe. (Rev: HBG 10/00; SLJ 7/00) [921]

13745 Levinson, Nancy S. *Magellan and the First Voyage Around the World* (5–8). Illus. 2001, Clarion $19.00 (978-0-395-98773-5). 144pp. A straightforward biography of Magellan, with information on his times and insightful analysis of his character. (Rev: BCCB 2/02; BL 2/1/02; HB 1/02; HBG 3/02; SLJ 1/02) [910.92]

13746 Meltzer, Milton. *Ferdinand Magellan: First to Sail Around the World* (5–8). Illus. Series: Great Explorations. 2001, Benchmark LB $29.93 (978-0-7614-1238-0). 80pp. An encompassing look at Magellan's achievements is complemented by excellent illustrations, a timeline, and Web site information. (Rev: BL 1/1–15/02; HBG 3/02; SLJ 3/02) [910]

13747 Molzahn, Arlene Bourgeois. *Ferdinand Magellan: First Explorer Around the World* (3–5). Series: Explorers! 2003, Enslow LB $23.93 (978-0-7660-2068-9). 48pp. Illustrations and maps enhance this account of Magellan's life and travels. (Rev: HBG 10/03; SLJ 9/03) [921]

13748 Waldman, Stuart. *Magellan's World* (4–7). Illus. by Gregory Manchess. Series: Great Explorers. 2007, Mikaya $22.95 (978-1-931414-19-7). 48pp. "Magellan was driven to ever-greater extremes of brilliance, courage, brutality and madness as he sailed around the world," states this book, which offers an unvarnished portrait of the explorer as well as beautiful illustrations and maps. (Rev: BL 11/1/07) [921]

MALLORY, GEORGE

13749 Salkeld, Audrey. *Mystery on Everest: A Photobiography of George Mallory* (5–8). Illus. Series: Photobiography. 2000, National Geographic $17.95 (978-0-7922-7222-9). 64pp. The life of the famous English mountain climber George Mallory, who died in 1924 in a climbing accident on Mount Everest, written by a member of the team that discovered his body in 1999. (Rev: BCCB 9/00; BL 11/1/00; HBG 3/01; SLJ 11/00) [921]

MARKHAM, BERYL

13750 Bowen, Andy Russell. *Flying Against the Wind: A Story About Beryl Markham* (3–6). Illus. 1998, Carolrhoda LB $22.60 (978-1-57505-081-2). 64pp. From her childhood in East Africa to her solo transatlantic flight in 1936, this is a thrilling biography of the English aviator. (Rev: BL 10/15/98; HBG 10/98; SLJ 8/98) [921]

13751 Markham, Beryl. *The Good Lion* (K–3). Illus. by Don Brown. 2005, Houghton $16.00 (978-0-618-56306-7). 32pp. In this excerpt from her autobiography, author/pilot/adventurer Markham recalls how as a girl she was attacked by a supposedly tame lion on an East African farm. (Rev: BL 9/15/05; SLJ 10/05) [921]

OCHOA, ELLEN

13752 Iverson, Teresa. *Ellen Ochoa* (4–8). Series: Hispanic-American Biographies. 2005, Raintree LB $32.86 (978-1-4109-1299-2). 64pp. The personal

and professional life of the first Hispanic American woman astronaut. (Rev: SLJ 1/06) [921]

13753 Johnston, Lissa. *Ellen Ochoa: Pioneering Astronaut* (2–4). Illus. Series: Fact Finders Biographies: Great Hispanics. 2006, Capstone LB $23.93 (978-0-7368-5438-2). 32pp. A brief profile of the life and career of America's first Hispanic woman to travel into space; NASA and personal photographs are included, along with timelines and research resources. (Rev: BL 4/1/06) [921]

13754 Latham, Donna. *Ellen Ochoa: Reach for the Stars!* (2–4). Series: Defining Moments. 2005, Bearport LB $25.27 (978-1-59716-076-6). 32pp. A clearly written account of Ochoa's life, with information on her childhood and education. (Rev: SLJ 2/06) [921]

13755 Paige, Joy. *Ellen Ochoa: The First Hispanic Woman in Space* (4–7). Illus. Series: The Library of Astronaut Biographies. 2004, Rosen LB $29.25 (978-0-8239-4457-6). 112pp. A lively overview focusing mainly on Ochoa's education and training. (Rev: SLJ 1/05) [921]

OTERO, KATHERINE STINSON

13756 Petrick, Neila Skinner. *Katherine Stinson Otero: High Flyer* (K–3). Illus. by Daggi Wallace. 2006, Pelican $15.95 (978-1-58980-368-8). 32pp. The story of one of the first American women pilots, with information about her world travels and plenty of illustrations. (Rev: SLJ 6/06) [921]

PATCH, SAM

13757 Cummins, Julie. *Sam Patch: Daredevil Jumper* (2–4). Illus. by Michael Allen Austin. 2009, Holiday $16.95 (978-0-8234-1741-4). 32pp. Sam Patch, who was born in the early 19th century, is remembered for his amazing jumping stunts; a leap into Genesee Falls in 1929 proved his undoing. (Rev: BLO 4/29/09; SLJ 3/09) [921]

PEARY, ROBERT E.

13758 Calvert, Patricia. *Robert E. Peary: To the Top of the World* (5–8). Series: Great Explorations. 2001, Marshall Cavendish LB $29.93 (978-0-7614-1242-7). 80pp. The exciting story of the Arctic explorer who, after several attempts, reached the North Pole in 1909. (Rev: BL 4/1/02; HBG 3/02; SLJ 3/02) [921]

PIKE, ZEBULON

13759 Calvert, Patricia. *Zebulon Pike: Lost in the Rockies* (5–8). Series: Great Explorations. 2004, Benchmark LB $29.93 (978-0-7614-1612-8). 96pp. Presents the life and career of the army officer who explored the West and Southwest. (Rev: SLJ 3/05) [921]

13760 Witteman, Barbara. *Zebulon Pike: Soldier and Explorer* (4–6). Series: Let Freedom Ring. 2002, Capstone LB $23.93 (978-0-7368-1351-8). 48pp. An absorbing account of the life and exploits of the explorer who discovered Pikes Peak. (Rev: HBG 3/03; SLJ 2/03) [921]

POLO, MARCO

13761 Demi. *Marco Polo* (4–7). Illus. by author. 2008, Marshall Cavendish $19.99 (978-0-7614-5433-5). 64pp. A visually impressive picture-book biography of the explorer who made an incredible journey from Europe to China taking nearly a quarter of a century; with a double-page map. (Rev: BL 10/1/08; LMC 3/09; SLJ 9/08) [910.4]

13762 Otfinoski, Steven. *Marco Polo: To China and Back* (4–8). Series: Great Explorations. 2002, Benchmark LB $29.93 (978-0-7614-1480-3). 77pp. Readable text accompanied by many illustrations and sidebar features traces Polo's life and adventures. (Rev: HBG 10/03; SLJ 5/03) [915.04]

13763 Senker, Cath. *Marco Polo's Travels on Asia's Silk Road* (4–6). Series: Great Journeys Across Earth. 2007, Heinemann LB $31.43 (978-1-4034-9751-2); paper $8.99 (978-1-4034-9759-8). 48pp. Useful for reports, this volume is a colorful introduction to Marco Polo's amazing adventures. (Rev: LMC 1/08; SLJ 4/08) [921]

13764 Smalley, Roger. *The Adventures of Marco Polo* (4–6). Illus. by Brian Bascle. Series: Graphic Library. 2005, Capstone LB $26.60 (978-0-7368-3830-6). 32pp. This story of the explorer's life is presented in comic-book format. (Rev: BL 3/15/05) [921]

PONCE DE LEON, JUAN

13765 Dolan, Sean. *Juan Ponce de León* (5–9). Series: Hispanics of Achievement. 1995, Chelsea LB $14.95 (978-0-7910-2023-4). 112pp. The story of the Spanish explorer who after accompanying Columbus on his second voyage set out on his own and eventually became the discoverer of Florida. (Rev: BL 10/15/95) [921]

13766 Harmon, Dan. *Juan Ponce de León and the Search for the Fountain of Youth* (4–6). Series: Explorers of New Worlds. 2000, Chelsea LB $31.00 (978-0-7910-5517-5). 63pp. As well as the life of Ponce de Leon and his exploits, this book gives good background information on the social and political forces that inspired him. (Rev: HBG 10/00; SLJ 7/00) [921]

13767 Otfinoski, Steven. *Juan Ponce de Leon: Discoverer of Florida* (5–8). Series: Great Explorations. 2004, Benchmark LB $29.93 (978-0-7614-1610-4). 76pp. A well-illustrated account of the explorer's life and discoveries, dismissing the idea that he was really searching for the fountain of youth. (Rev: SLJ 3/05) [921]

13768 Whiting, Jim. *Juan Ponce de Leon* (5–7). Series: Latinos in American History. 2002, Mitchell Lane LB $29.95 (978-1-58415-149-4). 48pp. This is the story of the man who is credited with discovering Florida in 1513 while searching for the fountain of youth. (Rev: BL 2/15/03; HBG 10/03; SLJ 6/03) [921]

13769 Worth, Richard. *Ponce de Leon and the Age of Spanish Exploration in World History* (5–9). Series: In World History. 2003, Enslow LB $26.60 (978-0-7660-1940-9). 112pp. As well as a biography of this great adventurer from Spain, this book describes the work of other Spanish explorers in the Americas. (Rev: BL 11/15/03; HBG 4/04) [921]

POWELL, JOHN WESLEY

13770 Bruns, Roger. *John Wesley Powell: Explorer of the Grand Canyon* (5–8). Illus. Series: Historical American Biographies. 1997, Enslow LB $26.60 (978-0-89490-783-8). 128pp. This biography tells about Powell's youth, education, and Civil War days, as well as his many expeditions and research activities. (Rev: SLJ 10/97) [921]

13771 Ray, Deborah Kogan. *Down the Colorado: John Wesley Powell, the One-Armed Explorer* (3–5). Illus. by author. 2007, Farrar $17.00 (978-0-374-31838-3). 48pp. Primary source material as well as beautiful color illustrations help make this biography of the famous naturalist worth reading. (Rev: BL 6/1–15/07; HB 1/08; SLJ 12/07) [921]

13772 Ross, Michael E. *Exploring the Earth with John Wesley Powell* (3–5). Series: Naturalist's Apprentice. 2000, Carolrhoda $19.93 (978-1-57505-254-0). 48pp. This biography of the noted explorer, geologist, and naturalist covers his important expeditions into the Grand Canyon and the Colorado plateau region. (Rev: BL 4/15/00; SLJ 8/00) [921]

QUIMBY, HARRIET

13773 Moss, Marissa. *Brave Harriet* (2–4). Illus. by C. F. Payne. 2001, Harcourt $17.00 (978-0-15-202380-5). 32pp. A picture book for older readers telling in first person the story of Harriet Quimby, the first woman to fly solo across the English Channel. (Rev: BL 7/01; HBG 3/02; SLJ 9/01) [629.1]

RALEIGH, SIR WALTER

13774 Korman, Susan. *Sir Walter Raleigh: English Explorer and Author* (4–6). Series: Colonial Leaders. 2001, Chelsea LB $27.50 (978-0-7910-5969-2); paper $27.50 (978-0-7910-6126-8). 80pp. Korman gives readers a good overview of the many sides of Raleigh, covering his roles as soldier, scientist, and courtier as well as his efforts to colonize Virginia. (Rev: SLJ 7/01) [942.05]

RAMON, ILAN

13775 Sofer, Barbara. *Ilan Ramon: Israel's Space Hero* (4–8). 2004, Lerner LB $16.95 (978-1-58013-115-5); paper $6.95 (978-1-58013-116-2). 63pp. The story of the first Israeli astronaut, from his early life and schooling to his selection for the crew of the ill-fated Columbia space shuttle that broke apart on re-entry in 2003. (Rev: SLJ 6/04) [921]

RIDE, SALLY

13776 Hurwitz, Jane, and Sue Hurwitz. *Sally Ride: Shooting for the Stars* (5–8). 1989, Ballantine paper $6.99 (978-0-449-90394-0). 128pp. An interestingly written account in paperback format of the female space pioneer. (Rev: BL 12/15/89; SLJ 2/90; VOYA 2/90) [921]

13777 Wade, Linda R. *Sally Ride: The Story of the First American Female in Space* (4–5). Series: Unlocking the Secrets of Science. 2002, Mitchell Lane LB $25.70 (978-1-58415-139-5). 56pp. Profiles the first American woman to travel in space. (Rev: HBG 10/03)

SCOTT, BLANCHE STUART

13778 Cummins, Julie. *Tomboy of the Air: Daredevil Pilot Blanche Stuart Scott* (3–6). Illus. 2001, HarperCollins LB $17.89 (978-0-06-029243-0). 80pp. Scott was a daredevil from childhood, graduating from driving cars to stunt-flying, and was the first American woman flyer. (Rev: BL 5/15/01; HB 5/01; HBG 3/02; SLJ 6/01*) [629.13]

SELKIRK, ALEXANDER

13779 Kraske, Robert. *Marooned: The Strange but True Adventures of Alexander Selkirk, the Real Robinson Crusoe* (5–8). Illus. by Robert Andrew Parker. 2005, Clarion $15.00 (978-0-618-56843-7). 128pp. The adventurous life of Alexander Selkirk, the Scottish navigator who served as the model for Daniel Defoe's *Robinson Crusoe*. (Rev: BL 11/15/05; SLJ 12/05) [996.1]

SHACKLETON, SIR ERNEST

13780 Calvert, Patricia. *Sir Ernest Shackleton: By Endurance We Conquer* (4–8). Series: Great Explorations. 2002, Benchmark LB $29.93 (978-0-7614-1485-8). 80pp. Readable text accompanied by many illustrations and sidebar features traces Shackleton's life and adventures. (Rev: HBG 10/03; SLJ 5/03) [919.8904]

13781 Kostyal, K. M. *Trial by Ice: A Photobiography of Sir Ernest Shackleton* (4–8). Illus. 1999, National Geographic $17.95 (978-0-7922-7393-6). 64pp. A biography that details the life of Sir Ernest Shackleton, his 1915 Antarctic expedition, and the survival of the explorers aboard the *Endurance*. (Rev: BCCB 12/99; BL 12/1/99; HBG 3/00; SLJ 3/00) [921]

13782 Marcovitz, Hal. *Sir Ernest Shackleton and the Struggle Against Antarctica* (4–6). Illus. Series: Explorers of New Worlds. 2001, Chelsea LB $25.00 (978-0-7910-6424-5). 63pp. Photographs from Shackleton's last expedition and quotations from his own writings add interest to this exploration of his motivations and his voyages. (Rev: HBG 10/02; SLJ 4/02)

SHEPARD, ALAN

13783 Orr, Tamra. *Alan Shepard: The First American in Space* (4–7). Illus. Series: The Library of Astronaut Biographies. 2004, Rosen LB $29.25 (978-0-8239-4455-2). 112pp. A lively overview focusing mainly on Shepard's education and training. (Rev: SLJ 1/05) [921]

SMITH, JEDEDIAH

13784 Nelson, Sharlene, and Ted Nelson. *Jedediah Smith* (3–6). Series: Watts Library. 2004, Scholastic LB $25.50 (978-0-531-12287-7). 64pp. Jedediah Smith's explorations of the American West are covered here with many illustrations, maps, a timeline, and other helpful features. (Rev: BL 6/1–15/04) [921]

SMITH, JOHN

13785 Doak, Robin. *Smith: John Smith and the Settlement of Jamestown* (4–6). Series: Exploring the World. 2003, Compass Point LB $23.93 (978-0-7565-0423-6). 48pp. Examines the important role played by John Smith in opening North America to European settlement. (Rev: SLJ 12/03) [921]

13786 Schanzer, Rosalyn. *John Smith Escapes Again!* (4–6). 2006, National Geographic $16.95 (978-0-7922-5930-5). 64pp. While the accuracy of Smith's writings, used as the basis for Schanzer's account, is controversial (and examined in an author's note), this volume's stellar design and compelling writing combine to illuminate a poorly understood figure in the history of colonial America. (Rev: BL 1/1–15/07; SLJ 11/06) [921]

WHITMAN, NARCISSA

13787 Harness, Cheryl. *The Tragic Tale of Narcissa Whitman and a Faithful History of the Oregon Trail* (4–7). Illus. 2006, National Geographic $16.95 (978-0-7922-5920-6). 144pp. A biography of Narcissa Whitman, the first woman to cross the Rockies on the perilous Oregon Trail in order to bring her Christian beliefs to the Indians of that area. (Rev: BL 12/1/06) [917.804]

Artists, Composers, Entertainers, and Writers

Collective

13788 Ball, Heather. *Magnificent Women in Music* (4–7). Series: The Women's Hall of Fame. 2006, Second Story paper $7.95 (978-1-897187-02-9). 108pp. Ten women from different times and with different musical gifts are profiled here, including Clara Schumann, Marian Anderson, and k.d. lang. (Rev: SLJ 7/06) [920]

13789 Benedict, Kitty, and Karen Covington. *The Literary Crowd: Writers, Critics, Scholars, Wits* (5–9). Series: Remarkable Women. 2000, Raintree LB $32.82 (978-0-8172-5732-3). 80pp. Profiles of 150 women writers and others associated with the literary world, including Virginia Woolf, Jane Austen, and Maya Angelou. (Rev: SLJ 8/00) [920]

13790 Bostrom, Kathleen Long. *Winning Authors: Profiles of the Newbery Medalists* (5–10). Series: Popular Authors. 2003, Libraries Unlimited $52.00 (978-1-56308-877-3). 338pp. Report writers will find useful information on the authors who won this prestigious award, including quotations and material on experiences that relate to the winning books. (Rev: SLJ 6/04; VOYA 6/04) [920]

13791 Bredeson, Carmen. *American Writers of the 20th Century* (5–8). Illus. 1996, Enslow LB $20.95 (978-0-89490-704-3). 104pp. Ten writers for adults, including Toni Morrison and F. Scott Fitzgerald, are introduced in brief profiles. (Rev: BL 6/1–15/96; SLJ 9/96) [920]

13792 Covington, Karen. *Creators: Artists, Designers, Craftswomen* (5–9). Series: Remarkable Women. 2000, Raintree LB $32.85 (978-0-8172-5725-5). 80pp. Mary Cassatt, Georgia O'Keefe, Frido Kahlo, and Beatrix Potter are four of the 150 female artists celebrated in this collective biography. (Rev: BL 6/1–15/00; SLJ 8/00) [920]

13793 Cummins, Julie. *Women Daredevils: Thrills, Chills, and Frills* (3–6). Illus. by Cheryl Harness. 2008, Dutton $17.99 (978-0-525-47948-2). 48pp. Cummins chronicles the daring feats of 14 women

in the late 18th and early 19th centuries — a human canonball, a bareback rider, wing walkers, and so forth — providing historical context and a full-page portrait of each fearless performer. (Rev: BCCB 2/08; BL 11/15/07; SLJ 1/08) [920]

13794 Curry, Barbara K., and James Michael Brodie. *Sweet Words So Brave: The Story of African American Literature* (5–8). Illus. 1996, Zino $24.95 (978-1-55933-179-1). 64pp. An outline of African American literature, from slave narratives to the great writers of today, such as Nikki Giovanni and Toni Morrison. (Rev: BL 2/15/97*; SLJ 4/97) [810.9]

13795 Datnow, Claire. *American Science Fiction and Fantasy Writers* (5–8). Illus. Series: Collective Biographies. 1999, Enslow LB $26.60 (978-0-7660-1090-1). 128pp. Science fiction and fantasy writers profiled in this book include Asimov, Heinlein, Bradbury, Anderson, Norton, L'Engle, and Le Guin. (Rev: BL 4/15/99; VOYA 6/99) [920]

13796 Dillon, Leo, and Diane Dillon. *Jazz on a Saturday Night* (1–3). Illus. by Leo Dillon. 2007, Scholastic $16.99 (978-0-590-47893-9). 40pp. This engaging picture-book collective biography sets up a clever mythical jam session that brings together jazz greats; with accompanying CD. (Rev: BL 9/15/07; LMC 10/07; SLJ 9/07) [920]

13797 Ford, Carin T. *Legends of American Dance and Choreography* (5–7). Series: Collective Biographies. 2000, Enslow LB $26.60 (978-0-7660-1378-0). 128pp. This collective work presents 10 short biographies of such dance luminaries as George Balanchine and Martha Graham. (Rev: BL 6/1–15/00; HBG 10/00; SLJ 7/00) [920]

13798 Gaines, Ann Graham. *American Photographers: Capturing the Image* (4–7). Series: Collective Biographies. 2002, Enslow LB $26.60 (978-0-7660-1833-4). 112pp. The lives and contributions of 10 well-known photographers are presented with photographs and a brief history of photography. (Rev: HBG 10/02; SLJ 10/02) [921]

13799 George-Warren, Holly. *Honky-Tonk Heroes and Hillbilly Angels: The Pioneers of Country and Western Music* (4–6). Illus. by Laura Levine. 2006, Houghton $16.00 (978-0-618-19100-0). 32pp. Loretta Lynn, Gene Autry, Patsy Cline, and the Carter family are just some of the artists covered in short biographies. (Rev: BL 6/1–15/06; SLJ 6/06) [920]

13800 Gourse, Leslie. *Sophisticated Ladies: The Great Women of Jazz* (5–8). Illus. by Martin French. 2007, Dutton $19.99 (978-0-525-47198-1). 64pp. Profiles 14 female jazz singers, with full-color portraits, biographical details, and comments on vocal style and importance. (Rev: BL 12/15/06; SLJ 5/07) [920]

13801 Govenar, Alan. *Extraordinary Ordinary People: Five American Masters of Traditional Arts* (5–8). 2006, Candlewick $19.99 (978-0-7636-2047-9). 96pp. Five American artists, recipients of National Endowment for the Arts fellowships, who practice unique — but traditional — art forms are profiled here. (Rev: BL 9/1/06; SLJ 8/06*) [920]

13802 Hacker, Carlotta. *Great African Americans in Jazz* (3–5). Series: Outstanding African Americans. 1997, Crabtree LB $22.60 (978-0-86505-804-0). 64pp. Seven portraits of great African American jazz musicians are given, among them Louis Armstrong, Duke Ellington, Billie Holiday, and Bessie Smith, plus seven other brief profiles. (Rev: BL 9/15/97) [920]

13803 Hasday, Judy. *Extraordinary People in the Movies* (5–9). Series: Extraordinary People. 2003, Children's LB $40.00 (978-0-516-22348-3); paper $16.95 (978-0-516-27857-5). 288pp. Brief biographies of individuals associated with the movie business are arranged chronologically by date of birth and interspersed with short essays on related topics. (Rev: SLJ 7/03) [791.43]

13804 Hill, Christine M. *Ten Terrific Authors for Teens* (5–7). Series: Collective Biographies. 2000, Enslow LB $26.60 (978-0-7660-1380-3). 112pp. Among the authors profiled are Judy Blume, Virginia Hamilton, Julius Lester, Lois Lowry, Katherine Paterson, Gary Soto, and Lawrence Yep. (Rev: BL 9/15/00; HBG 10/01; SLJ 12/00; VOYA 8/01) [920]

13805 Holme, Merilyn, and Bridget McKenzie. *Expressionists* (5–9). Series: Artists in Profile. 2002, Heinemann LB $28.50 (978-1-58810-647-6). 64pp. Introduces the movement and gives biographical information on the major artists and their key works, with reproductions and photographs. Also use *Impressionists* and *Pop Artists* (both 2002). (Rev: HBG 3/03; SLJ 3/03) [759.06]

13806 Hunter, Shaun. *Visual and Performing Artists* (3–6). Series: Women in Profile. 1999, Crabtree LB $8.95 (978-0-7787-0035-7); paper $22.60 (978-0-7787-0013-5). 48pp. This salute to women in show business features six profiles of important performing artists and brief entries for 15 more. (Rev: BL 9/15/99; SLJ 8/99) [920]

13807 Ishizuka, Kathy. *Asian American Authors* (5–9). Series: Collective Biographies. 2000, Enslow LB $26.60 (978-0-7660-1376-6). 128pp. Writers for children (including Laurence Yep) and for adults (such as Amy Tan) are included in this collective biography of 10 Asian American writers. (Rev: HBG 10/01; SLJ 3/01) [920]

13808 Krull, Kathleen. *Lives of the Artists: Masterpieces, Messes (and What the Neighbors Thought)* (4–6). Illus. by Kathryn Hewitt. 1995, Harcourt $20.00 (978-0-15-200103-2). 96pp. Nineteen thumbnail sketches on such artists as van Gogh, O'Keeffe, and Warhol. (Rev: BCCB 11/95; BL 11/1/95; SLJ 10/95) [920]

13809 Krull, Kathleen. *Lives of the Musicians: Good Times, Bad Times (And What the Neighbors Thought)* (5–8). Illus. 1993, Harcourt $20.00 (978-0-15-248010-3). 96pp. Biographies of 16 musical giants, from Vivaldi, Mozart, and Beethoven to Gershwin, Joplin, and Woody Guthrie. (Rev: BL 4/1/93*; SLJ 5/93*) [920]

13810 Krull, Kathleen. *Lives of the Writers: Comedies, Tragedies (and What the Neighbors Thought)* (3–6). Illus. by Kathryn Hewitt. 1994, Harcourt $20.00 (978-0-15-248009-7). 96pp. Twenty profiles of authors, some well known, like E. B. White and Shakespeare, and others more obscure. (Rev: BCCB 10/94; BL 9/15/94; SLJ 10/94*) [920]

13811 Marcus, Leonard. *A Caldecott Celebration: Seven Artists and Their Paths to the Caldecott Medal* (3–8). Illus. 2008, Walker $19.95 (978-0-8027-9703-2). 56pp. An updated version of the 1998 edition, this volume features seven Caldecott-winning artists (one for each decade of the award), introducing their prize-winning books and supplying background information on each. The artists are Sendak, McCloskey, Marcia Brown, Steig, Van Allsburg, Wiesner, and now Gerstein. (Rev: HB 11/08; LMC 5/08; SLJ 4/08) [920]

13812 Marcus, Leonard. *Pass It Down: Five Picture-Book Families Make Their Mark* (5–8). 2007, Walker $19.95 (978-0-8027-9600-4). 56pp. Multigenerational families of picture book authors/illustrators are featured here: Donald Crews, Ann Jonas, and Nina Crews; Clement, Edith, and Thacher Hurd; Walter Dean and Christopher Myers; Jerry and Brian Pinkney; and Harlow, Anne, and Lizzy Rockwell. (Rev: BL 12/15/06; SLJ 1/07) [920]

13813 Marquez, Heron. *Latin Sensations* (5–9). 2001, Lerner LB $27.93 (978-0-8225-4993-2); paper $7.95 (978-0-8225-9695-0). 112pp. A collective biography that features profiles of Selena, Ricky Martin, Jennifer Lopez, Marc Anthony, and Enrique Iglesias. (Rev: HBG 10/01; SLJ 3/01) [920]

13814 Nobleman, Marc Tyler. *Boys of Steel: The Creators of Superman* (1–3). Illus. by Ross MacDonald. 2008, Knopf $16.99 (978-0-375-83802-6). 40pp. With evocative illustrations by MacDonald, Nobleman introduces Joe Shuster and Jerry Siegel, the creators of Superman, and describes their long-running dispute with DC Comics. (Rev: BCCB 10/08; BL 6/1–15/08; HB 7/08; LMC 11/08) [920]

13815 Rediger, Pat. *Great African Americans in Entertainment* (4–6). Illus. Series: Outstanding African Americans. 1996, Crabtree LB $22.60 (978-

0-86505-799-9). 64pp. Bill Cosby, Spike Lee, and Whoopi Goldberg are three of the 13 African Americans profiled. (Rev: BL 9/15/96) [920]

13816 Rediger, Pat. *Great African Americans in Literature* (4–6). Illus. Series: Outstanding African Americans. 1996, Crabtree LB $22.60 (978-0-86505-802-6). 64pp. Some of the 13 African Americans profiled are Maya Angelou, Toni Morrison, James Baldwin, and Alex Haley. (Rev: BL 9/15/96; SLJ 8/96) [920]

13817 Rubin, Susan G. *The Yellow House: Vincent van Gogh and Paul Gauguin Side by Side* (K–3). Illus. by Joseph A. Smith. 2001, Abrams $17.95 (978-0-8109-4588-3). 40pp. Juxtaposed illustrations introduce the works of Vincent van Gogh and Paul Gauguin who, for a short time in 1888, lived and worked together in a studio in the south of France. (Rev: BL 11/15/01; HBG 3/02; SLJ 1/02) [759.4]

13818 Shone, Rob. *War Correspondents* (4–6). Illus. by Chris Forsey. Series: Graphic Careers. 2009, Rosen LB $21.95 (978-1-4042-1449-1). 48pp. Ernie Pyle and Sydney Schanberg are two of the correspondents profiled in this volume that combines a text section with comic-book-style pages. (Rev: BL 1/1–15/09) [070.4]

13819 Strickland, Michael R. *African-American Poets* (5–10). Illus. Series: Collective Biographies. 1996, Enslow LB $26.60 (978-0-89490-774-6). 112pp. The lives and works of 10 prominent African American poets from Phillis Wheatley to Rita Dove are covered, with quotations from their works and a single full-length poem from each. (Rev: BL 2/15/97; SLJ 1/97) [920]

13820 Tate, Eleanora. *African American Musicians* (4–7). Series: Black Stars. 2000, Wiley $24.95 (978-0-471-25356-3). 170pp. This collective biography highlights both past and present contributions to different kinds of music by several African Americans. (Rev: BL 7/00; HBG 3/01; SLJ 7/00) [920]

13821 Wilkinson, Brenda. *African American Women Writers* (4–7). Illus. Series: Black Stars. 1999, Wiley $22.95 (978-0-471-17580-3). 166pp. Arranged chronologically, this collective biography contains short profiles of more than 20 important female African American writers. (Rev: BL 2/15/00; HBG 10/00; SLJ 2/00) [910]

Artists and Architects

ADAMS, ANSEL

13822 Dunlap, Julie. *Eye on the Wild: A Story About Ansel Adams* (3–6). Illus. Series: Creative Minds. 1995, Carolrhoda LB $21.27 (978-0-87614-944-7). 64pp. A brief biography about the great nature photographer Ansel Adams. (Rev: BL 10/15/95; SLJ 12/95) [921]

ALBERS, JOSEF

13823 Wing, Natasha. *An Eye for Color: The Story of Josef Albers* (3–6). Illus. by Julia Breckenreid.

2009, Holt $16.99 (978-0-8050-8072-8). 40pp. Artist Josef Alber's early life is mentioned, but this book concentrates on his well-known color theory and includes pages dedicated to his color experiments, a glossary, a color wheel, and several projects. (Rev: BL 7/09; SLJ 9/09) [921]

ARCIMBOLDO, GIUSEPPE

13824 Strand, Claudia. *Hello, Fruit Face! The Paintings of Giuseppe Arcimboldo* (3–5). Trans. by Michele A. Schons. Illus. 1999, Prestel $14.95 (3-7913-2084-X). 30pp. This is a well-illustrated biography of Arcimboldo, a 16th-century Italian artist who was noted for using everyday objects such as fruits and flowers and arranging them to present a human portrait. (Rev: BL 9/15/99; SLJ 1/00) [921]

AUDUBON, JOHN JAMES

13825 Armstrong, Jennifer. *Audubon: Painter of Birds in the Wild Frontier* (2–4). Illus. by Jos. A. Smith. 2003, Abrams $17.95 (978-0-8109-4238-7). 38pp. An excellent introduction to the early life of naturalist-painter John James Audubon, this large-format picture book recounts many of the artist's experiences on the American frontier, including his meeting with the legendary Daniel Boone. (Rev: BL 4/1/03; HBG 10/03; SLJ 5/03) [598]

13826 Burleigh, Robert. *Into the Woods: John James Audubon Lives His Dream* (2–5). Illus. by Wendell Minor. 2003, Simon & Schuster $16.95 (978-0-689-83040-2). 40pp. Charming watercolors and selections of Audubon's own detailed drawings combine with simple, poetic text and quotes from Audubon's journals to give a good picture of the bird-lover who rejected urban life. (Rev: BL 1/1–15/03; HBG 10/03; SLJ 2/03) [921]

13827 Davies, Jacqueline. *The Boy Who Drew Birds: A Story of John James Audubon* (2–4). Illus. by Melissa Sweet. 2004, Houghton $16.00 (978-0-618-24343-3). 32pp. This engaging biography focuses on Audubon's early enthusiasm for birds and his decision to band them to trace their movements. (Rev: BL 11/1/04) [598]

13828 Roop, Peter, and Connie Roop, eds. *Capturing Nature* (5–7). Illus. by Rick Farley. 1993, Walker LB $17.85 (978-0-8027-8205-2). 48pp. Audubon's prints and original paintings and excerpts from his journals are combined to produce a stunning biography. (Rev: BCCB 12/93; BL 12/15/93; SLJ 1/94) [921]

BENTLEY, SNOWFLAKE

13829 Martin, Jacqueline B. *Snowflake Bentley* (K–3). Illus. by Mary Azarian. 1998, Houghton $17.00 (978-0-395-86162-2). 32pp. As a child Bentley was so obsessed with snow that he devoted his attention to photographing snow crystals and, now nicknamed Snowflake, gained a reputation as a nature photographer. Caldecott Medal, 1999. (Rev: BCCB 12/98; BL 10/1/98*; HB 9/98; HBG 3/99; SLJ 9/98) [921]

BOTTICELLI, SANDRO

13830 Connolly, Sean. *Botticelli* (4–8). Illus. Series: Lives of the Artists. 2005, World Almanac LB $31.00 (978-0-8368-5648-4). 48pp. A tall, slender volume full of facts about Botticelli's life and times, with many color reproductions. (Rev: BL 6/1–15/04; SLJ 3/05) [921]

BOURKE-WHITE, MARGARET

13831 Welch, Catherine A. *Margaret Bourke-White* (2–4). Illus. 1997, Carolrhoda LB $23.93 (978-0-87614-890-7). 56pp. The life of this outstanding photographer reveals the excitement and danger involved in her work. (Rev: BL 9/1/97; HBG 3/98; SLJ 8/97) [921]

13832 Welch, Catherine A. *Margaret Bourke-White: Racing with a Dream* (4–8). Illus. 1998, Carolrhoda LB $30.35 (978-1-57505-049-2). 104pp. A fine biography of the important photographer whose subjects included skyscrapers, the Depression, Buchenwald, and South African miners. (Rev: BL 10/1/98; HBG 3/99; SLJ 7/98) [921]

BRADY, MATHEW

13833 Pflueger, Lynda. *Mathew Brady* (5–8). Series: Historical American Biographies. 2001, Enslow LB $26.60 (978-0-7660-1444-2). 128pp. A biography of the photographer known primarily for his coverage of the Civil War, illustrated with many of his works. (Rev: BL 1/1–15/02; HBG 10/01; SLJ 9/01; VOYA 2/02) [921]

BRUEGEL, PIETER

13834 Malam, John. *Pieter Bruegel* (2–4). Series: Tell Me About. 1999, Carolrhoda LB $19.93 (978-1-57505-366-0). 24pp. The author explores Bruegel's life and times as well as his ideas and masterpieces. (Rev: HBG 10/99; SLJ 7/99) [921]

13835 Woodhouse, Jane. *Pieter Bruegel* (3–4). Series: The Life and Work Of. 2000, Heinemann LB $21.36 (978-1-57572-344-0). 32pp. This biography of the Flemish painter includes many examples of his paintings of earthy peasants and their surroundings. (Rev: BL 10/15/00; HBG 10/01; SLJ 2/01) [921]

BRYAN, ASHLEY

13836 Bryan, Ashley. *Words to My Life's Song* (3–7). Illus. by author. 2009, Atheneum $18.99 (978-1-4169-0541-7). 64pp. An inspirational autobiography by the famous children's illustrator, tracing Bryan's life from his Depression childhood to an island in Maine, with lots of illustrations plus a visual tour of his studio. (Rev: BCCB 1/09; BL 12/15/08; SLJ 2/09) [818]

CALDECOTT, RANDOLPH

13837 Hegel, Claudette. *Randolph Caldecott: An Illustrated Life* (5–9). Series: Avisson Young Adult. 2004, Avisson $27.50 (978-1-888105-60-5). 176pp.

Many of Caldecott's drawings are included in this account of the artist's life and work, with coverage of the children's award named in his honor. (Rev: BL 10/1/04; SLJ 11/04) [741.6]

CALDER, ALEXANDER

13838 Stone, Tanya L. *Sandy's Circus: A Story About Alexander Calder* (1–3). Illus. by Boris Kulikov. 2008, Viking $16.99 (978-0-670-06268-3). 40pp. In this picture-book biography, Stone tells the story of the young Calder's interest in wire sculptures and circus structures that preceded his famous mobiles. (Rev: BCCB 9/08; BL 6/1–15/08; HB 9/08; SLJ 9/08) [921]

CARLE, ERIC

13839 Carle, Eric. *Flora and Tiger: 19 Very Short Stories from My Life* (4–8). Illus. 1997, Putnam $17.99 (978-0-399-23203-9). 64pp. An autobiography of the famous picture-book artist who was born in Germany but who has lived in the United States since 1952. (Rev: BL 12/15/97; HBG 3/98; SLJ 2/98) [921]

CARR, EMILY

13840 Bogart, Jo Ellen. *Emily Carr: At the Edge of the World* (4–8). Illus. by Maxwell Newhouse. 2003, Tundra $18.95 (978-0-88776-640-4). 40pp. This picture book for older readers presents the life and work of the Canadian artist and writer who became famous for her depictions of the native peoples of the Pacific Coast. (Rev: BL 11/1/03; HBG 4/04; SLJ 12/03) [759.11]

13841 Debon, Nicolas. *Four Pictures by Emily Carr* (5–9). Illus. 2003, Douglas & McIntyre $15.95 (978-0-88899-532-2). 32pp. This small comic-book biography uses four of Carr's paintings to introduce chapters that trace the Canadian artist's life and interest in Native Americans. (Rev: BL 12/1/03; HB 1/04; HBG 3/02; SLJ 11/03) [759.11]

13842 Griek, Susan Vande. *The Art Room* (PS–3). Illus. by Pascal Milelli. 2002, Groundwood $15.95 (978-0-88899-449-3). 24pp. This biography of the West Coast Canadian artist concentrates on her teaching of young students and the inspiration she gave them. (Rev: BL 4/1/02; HBG 10/02; SLJ 6/02) [921]

CASSATT, MARY

13843 Ferrara, Cos. *Mary Cassatt: The Life and Art of a Genteel Rebel* (5–8). Illus. Series: Girls Explore, Reach for the Stars. 2005, Girls Explore $20.00 (978-0-9749456-3-7). 101pp. Cassatt's art, shown in small full-color reproductions, is introduced in this biography that also discusses her independence and feminist views. (Rev: BL 2/15/05) [921]

13844 Giesecke, Ernestine. *Mary Cassatt* (3–5). Illus. Series: Life and Work Of. 1999, Heinemann LB $21.36 (978-1-57572-955-8). 32pp. This biography of the famous American artist who lived and worked in Paris is complemented by many examples of her work. (Rev: BL 2/1/00; SLJ 1/00) [921]

13845 Harris, Lois V. *Mary Cassatt: Impressionist Painter* (2–4). Illus. 2007, Pelican $15.95 (978-1-58980-452-4). 32pp. American Impressionist Cassatt is the subject of this simple biography containing basic and personal facts about her life and work along with a generous number of reproductions. (Rev: BL 11/1/07; SLJ 12/07) [921]

13846 Hoena, Blake A. *Mary Cassatt* (2–4). Series: Masterpieces: Artists and Their Works. 2003, Capstone LB $22.60 (978-0-7368-2229-9). 24pp. A small-format introductory biography of the artist featuring simple text and color reproductions, with emphasis on Cassatt's association with the Impressionists and how she faced prejudice because of her gender. (Rev: SLJ 3/04) [921]

13847 O'Connor, Jane. *Mary Cassatt: Family Pictures* (3–4). Illus. by Jennifer Kalis. Series: Smart and Art. 2003, Grosset paper $5.99 (978-0-448-43152-9). 32pp. Presented as a school report, this is a simple but appealing overview of the artist's life. (Rev: HBG 10/03; SLJ 7/03) [921]

13848 Streissguth, Thomas. *Mary Cassatt* (4–8). Series: Trailblazers. 1999, Lerner LB $27.93 (978-1-57505-291-5). 112pp. Full-color illustrations enhance this biography of the American painter who was associated with the Impressionists and spent most of her adult life in France. (Rev: BL 5/1/99; HBG 10/99; SLJ 9/99) [921]

CATLIN, GEORGE

13849 Plain, Nancy. *The Man Who Painted Indians: George Catlin* (3–6). Series: Biographies. 1996, Benchmark LB $21.36 (978-0-7614-0486-6). 48pp. The story of the artist, born in 1796, who left his law career to live in the American wilderness and paint its people and places. (Rev: SLJ 2/97) [921]

CÉZANNE, PAUL

13850 Burleigh, Robert. *Paul Cézanne: A Painter's Journey* (4–7). Illus. 2006, Abrams $17.95 (978-0-8109-5784-8). 32pp. A lavishly illustrated and thoughtfully written profile of Cézanne's life and art. (Rev: BL 2/15/06; SLJ 3/06) [759.4]

13851 Connolly, Sean. *Paul Cézanne* (3–4). Series: The Life and Work Of. 1999, Heinemann LB $21.36 (978-1-57572-957-2). 32pp. Covers the life and work of this famous Impressionist painter. (Rev: BL 2/15/00; SLJ 1/00) [921]

13852 Sellier, Marie. *Cézanne from A to Z* (4–8). Trans. from French by Claudia Zoe Bedrick. Illus. Series: Artists from A to Z. 1996, Bedrick LB $14.95 (978-0-87226-476-2). 59pp. An imaginative, well-executed account of the life and works of Cézanne, enhanced by reproductions of many of his paintings. (Rev: SLJ 5/96) [921]

13853 Tracy, Kathleen. *Paul Cézanne* (4–7). Series: Art Profiles for Kids. 2007, Mitchell Lane LB $29.95 (978-1-58415-565-2). 48pp. Suitable for both research and browsing, this examination of the artist's life and times includes many reproductions

and interesting sidebars. (Rev: LMC 1/08; SLJ 12/07) [921]

13854 Venezia, Mike. *Paul Cézanne* (4–6). Series: Getting to Know. 1998, Children's Book Pr. LB $28.00 (978-0-516-20762-9). 32pp. Along with an easy-to-read text and full-color reproductions, this introduction to the life and art of Cézanne includes many amusing cartoon illustrations. (Rev: BL 8/98; HBG 10/98) [921]

CHAGALL, MARC

13855 Hopler, Brigitta. *Marc Chagall: Life Is a Dream* (4–7). Trans. by Catherine McCreadie. Illus. Series: Adventures in Art. 1999, Prestel $14.95 (978-3-7913-1986-5). 30pp. This biography of the surrealist painter not only relates the artist's life story but also encourages the reader to discover the meanings behind the images. (Rev: BL 2/1/99; SLJ 2/99) [921]

13856 Landmann, Bimba. *I Am Marc Chagall* (2–4). Illus. 2006, Eerdmans $18.00 (978-0-8028-5305-9). 40pp. Loosely inspired by Chagall's *My Life*, this first-person narrative describes Chagall's life from childhood through emigration to the United States and features painterly illustrations. (Rev: BL 1/1–15/06; SLJ 4/06) [921]

13857 Lemke, Elisabeth, and Thomas David. *Marc Chagall: What Colour Is Paradise?* (4–8). Illus. Series: Adventures in Art. 2001, Prestel $14.95 (978-3-7913-2393-0). 28pp. Using Chagall's biographical paintings as a focus, this innovative biography tells of his life, career, and work. (Rev: BL 1/1–15/01; SLJ 4/01) [921]

13858 Markel, Michelle. *Dreamer from the Village: The Story of Marc Chagall* (K–3). Illus. by Emily Lisker. 2005, Holt $16.95 (978-0-8050-6373-8). 40pp. This excellent profile traces the artist's life and career and introduces the importance of his work; browsers may find this more useful than report writers. (Rev: BL 8/05; SLJ 9/05) [709]

13859 Mason, Antony. *Marc Chagall* (4–8). Illus. Series: Lives of the Artists. 2005, World Almanac LB $31.00 (978-0-8368-5649-1). 48pp. A tall, slender volume full of facts about Chagall's life and times, with many color reproductions. (Rev: BL 6/1–15/04; SLJ 3/05) [921]

13860 Venezia, Mike. *Marc Chagall* (2–4). Series: Getting to Know. 2000, Children's Book Pr. LB $28.00 (978-0-516-21055-1). 32pp. A biography of the innovative 20th-century painter told with an easy-to-read text, full-color reproductions, and amusing cartoons. (Rev: BL 5/15/00) [921]

COROT, JEAN CAMILLE

13861 Larroche, Caroline. *Corot from A to Z* (5–8). Trans. from French by Claudia Zoe Bedrick. Series: Artists from A to Z. 1996, Bedrick LB $14.95 (978-0-87226-477-9). 60pp. Although the text is somewhat confusing, the strength of this account of Corot's life and work is the full-color reproductions of his work. (Rev: SLJ 1/97) [921]

DA VINCI, LEONARDO

13862 Barretta, Gene. *Neo Leo: The Ageless Ideas of Leonardo da Vinci* (1–3). Illus. by author. 2009, Holt $16.99 (978-0-8050-8703-1). 40pp. A visually appealing book that juxtaposes Leonardo da Vinci's original plans for several inventions with the modern end-result. (Rev: BL 7/09; SLJ 8/09) [609.2]

13863 Byrd, Robert. *Leonardo, Beautiful Dreamer* (4–6). Illus. by author. 2003, Penguin $17.99 (978-0-525-47033-5). 40pp. This large-format overview of da Vinci's life and work is beautifully illustrated and packed with information that is presented in varied and appropriate styles. (Rev: BL 8/03; HB 9/03; HBG 4/04; SLJ 9/03) [921]

13864 Connolly, Sean. *Leonardo da Vinci* (3–4). Series: The Life and Work Of. 1999, Heinemann LB $21.36 (978-1-57572-954-1). 32pp. This book explores the life and accomplishments of Leonardo da Vinci and tells how events influenced his masterpieces. (Rev: BL 2/15/00; SLJ 1/00) [921]

13865 Hart, Tony. *Leonardo da Vinci* (3–5). Illus. by Susan Hellard. Series: Famous Children. 1994, Barron's paper $7.99 (978-0-8120-1828-8). 24pp. This biography focuses on the childhood of Leonardo and how his genius was shown at an early age. (Rev: SLJ 8/94) [921]

13866 Herbert, Janis. *Leonardo da Vinci for Kids: His Life and Ideas* (4–8). Illus. 1998, Chicago Review paper $16.95 (978-1-55652-298-7). 101pp. This biography of Leonardo da Vinci contains background information on history, art techniques, science, and philosophy. (Rev: BL 3/1/99; SLJ 4/99) [921]

13867 Krull, Kathleen. *Leonardo da Vinci* (5–8). Illus. by Boris Kulikov. Series: Giants of Science. 2005, Viking $15.99 (978-0-670-05920-1). 128pp. The less attractive features of da Vinci's times are covered here, along with the artist's childhood and adolescence and his development into both an artist and a scientist, drawing connections between the two disciplines and incorporating much from da Vinci's notebooks. (Rev: BL 9/1/05; SLJ 10/05*) [921]

13868 Kuhne, Heinz. *Leonardo da Vinci: Dreams, Schemes, and Flying Machines* (4–8). Illus. Series: Adventures in Art. 2000, Prestel $14.95 (978-3-7913-2166-0). 32pp. This well-illustrated biography covers da Vinci's accomplishments as a scientist, engineer, inventor, and artist. (Rev: BL 7/00) [921]

13869 Malam, John. *Leonardo da Vinci* (2–4). Series: Tell Me About. 1999, Carolrhoda LB $19.93 (978-1-57505-367-7). 24pp. A biography that gives details on da Vinci's life and accomplishments as well as material on the period in which he lived. (Rev: HBG 10/99; SLJ 7/99) [921]

13870 Mason, Antony. *Leonardo da Vinci* (4–8). Illus. 1994, Barron's paper $8.99 (978-0-8120-1997-1). 32pp. A brief biography that chronicles the achievements of this multifaceted genius and supplies pictures of some of his great triumphs. (Rev: BL 12/1/94) [921]

13871 O'Connor, Barbara. *Leonardo da Vinci: Renaissance Genius* (5–8). Series: Trailblazer Biogra-

phies. 2002, Carolrhoda LB $27.93 (978-0-87614-467-1). 112pp. An excellent biography that details Leonardo's life from childhood, discusses some of his famous paintings, and looks at his inventions and experiments. (Rev: BL 3/15/03; HBG 3/03; SLJ 11/02; VOYA 8/03) [921]

13872 Reed, Jennifer B. *Leonardo da Vinci: Genius of Art and Science* (4–7). Illus. Series: Great Minds of Science. 2005, Enslow LB $26.60 (978-0-7660-2500-4). 128pp. Reed describes da Vinci's wide-ranging achievements — showing, for example, his urban planning ideas, his design for a flying machine, and his anatomical drawings — and emphasizes his originality and creativity. (Rev: SLJ 6/05) [921]

13873 Venezia, Mike. *Da Vinci* (2–5). Illus. by author. Series: Getting to Know. 1989, Children's Book Pr. LB $28.00 (978-0-516-02275-8). 32pp. Using text, cartoons, and the artist's paintings, this is an introduction to the life and work of Leonardo da Vinci. (Rev: SLJ 3/90) [921]

DALI, SALVADOR

13874 Anderson, Robert. *Salvador Dali* (5–8). Illus. Series: Artists in Their Time. 2002, Watts LB $24.00 (978-0-531-12231-0). 48pp. This volume presents Dali's life and influence with many illustrations, news clippings, and useful information. (Rev: BL 10/15/02) [709]

DEGAS, EDGAR

13875 Venezia, Mike. *Edgar Degas* (2–4). Illus. Series: Getting to Know. 2000, Children's Book Pr. LB $28.00 (978-0-516-21593-8); paper $6.95 (978-0-516-27172-9). 32pp. An easy-to-read text, several reproductions, and humorous cartoons are used to introduce the life and works of this French master. (Rev: BL 9/15/00) [921]

DE KOONING, WILLEM

13876 Hawes, Louise. *Willem de Kooning: The Life of an Artist* (4–6). Series: Artist Biographies. 2002, Enslow LB $23.93 (978-0-7660-1884-6). 48pp. Covers de Kooning's life from youth, his artistic techniques and work habits, and the impact of his lifestyle. (Rev: HBG 10/03; SLJ 3/03) [921]

DELACROIX, EUGENE

13877 Venezia, Mike. *Eugene Delacroix* (1–3). Illus. Series: Getting to Know the World's Greatest Artists. 2003, Children's Pr. LB $28.00 (978-0-516-22576-0); paper $6.95 (978-0-516-26976-4). 32pp. An easy-to-read text and humorous cartoons are used to introduce this famous French artist and his work. [921]

DESJARLAIT, PATRICK

13878 Williams, Neva. *Patrick DesJarlait: Conversations with a Native American Artist* (5–7). Illus. 1994, Lerner LB $22.60 (978-0-8225-3151-7).

56pp. A beautifully illustrated biography of the Native American artist who worked at the Red Lake Indian Reservation in Minnesota. (Rev: BL 1/1/95; SLJ 1/95) [921]

DISNEY, WALT

13879 Ford, Barbara. *Walt Disney* (4–8). Illus. 1989, Walker LB $17.00 (978-0-8027-6865-0). 160pp. The story of Disney's youth and his struggle to fulfill his dreams. (Rev: BL 5/15/89) [791.430924]

13880 Selden, Bernice. *The Story of Walt Disney, Maker of Magical Worlds* (4–6). Illus. Series: Yearling Biographies. 1989, Dell paper $4.50 (978-0-440-40240-4). 92pp. A balanced account of the genius who established the art of animation in Hollywood. (Rev: BL 3/15/90; SLJ 4/90) [921]

EL GRECO

13881 Venezia, Mike. *El Greco* (2–4). Series: Getting to Know. 1997, Children's Book Pr. LB $28.00 (978-0-516-20586-1). 32pp. This appealing introduction to El Greco and his works contains several color reproductions plus the author's playful cartoons. (Rev: BL 10/15/97; HBG 3/98) [921]

ELLABBAD, MOHIEDDIN

13882 Ellabbad, Mohieddin. *The Illustrator's Notebook* (5–10). Trans. from French by Sarah Quinn. Illus. by author. 2006, Groundwood $16.95 (978-0-88899-700-5). 30pp. In this fascinating journal printed from right to left, Egyptian-born illustrator Ellabbad reflects on the influences that led him to a life in art and offers valuable insights into Arabic cultural sensibilities. (Rev: SLJ 8/06) [921]

GÁG, WANDA

13883 Ray, Deborah Kogan. *Wanda Gág: The Girl Who Lived to Draw* (2–4). Illus. by author. 2008, Viking $16.99 (978-0-670-06292-8). 40pp. Covering the life of the creator of *Millions of Cats* from her childhood in Bohemia, Ray emphasizes Gág's lifelong interest in art and includes many quotations. (Rev: BCCB 12/08; BL 12/15/08; LMC 11/08; SLJ 10/08) [921]

GAUDI, ANTONI

13884 Rodriguez, Rachel. *Building on Nature: The Life of Antoni Gaudi* (1–3). Illus. by Julie Paschkis. 2009, Holt $16.99 (978-0-8050-8745-1). 32pp. Full of poetic language and rich images, this is an appealing profile of the innovative Catalonian architect. (Rev: BL 6/1–15/09; LMC 10/09) [921]

GAUGUIN, PAUL

13885 Anderson, Robert. *Paul Gauguin* (4–8). Series: Artists in Their Time. 2003, Watts LB $24.00 (978-0-531-12239-6); paper $6.95 (978-0-531-16647-5). 46pp. An interesting life of Gauguin, with reproductions of his works and of those of fellow painters,

with a timeline that adds historical context. (Rev: SLJ 6/03) [759.4]

GEHRY, FRANK

13886 Bodden, Valerie. *Frank Gehry* (4–7). Series: Xtraordinary Artists. 2008, Creative Education LB $32.80 (978-1-58341-662-4). 48pp. Bodden provides an interesting overview of the architect's life with well-chosen illustrations. (Rev: LMC 8/09; SLJ 4/09) [921]

GIACOMETTI, ALBERTO

13887 Gaff, Jackie. *Alberto Giacometti* (5–8). Series: Artists in Their Time. 2002, Watts LB $24.00 (978-0-531-12224-2); paper $6.95 (978-0-531-16617-8). 48pp. The life of this Italian artist noted for his elongated sculptures is re-created with comments on his social period and reproductions of his work. (Rev: BL 10/15/02) [921]

GIOTTO

13888 Venezia, Mike. *Giotto* (2–4). Series: Getting to Know. 2000, Children's Book Pr. LB $22.00 (978-0-516-21592-1). 32pp. The story of the Florentine Renaissance artist and architect who influenced all of European painting is told in text, reproductions, and witty cartoons. (Rev: BL 5/15/00) [921]

GOYA, FRANCISCO

13889 Venezia, Mike. *Francisco Goya* (2–5). Illus. Series: Getting to Know. 1991, Children's Book Pr. LB $28.00 (978-0-516-02292-5). 32pp. This is an introduction to the life and work of the great Spanish portrait artist who was also a bitter social satirist. (Rev: BL 8/91; SLJ 12/91) [921]

HOKUSAI, KATSUSHIKA

13890 Ray, Deborah Kogan. *Hokusai* (2–4). Illus. 2001, Farrar $18.00 (978-0-374-33263-1). 40pp. Covers the life of Japanese artist Hokusai from birth, with excellent descriptions of life in late 18th- and 19th-century Japan. (Rev: BL 11/1/01; HBG 3/02; SLJ 12/01*) [796.92]

HOMER, WINSLOW

13891 *Winslow Homer* (1–3). Illus. by Mike Venezia. Series: Getting to Know the World's Greatest Artists. 2004, Scholastic LB $6.95 (978-0-516-26979-5). 32pp. This beautifully illustrated biography chronicles the life and work of the late-19th-century American artist. (Rev: BL 6/1–15/04) [921]

HOPPER, EDWARD

13892 Foa, Emma. *Edward Hopper* (4–8). Series: Artists in Their Time. 2003, Watts LB $24.00 (978-0-531-12240-2); paper $6.95 (978-0-531-16641-3). 46pp. An interesting life of Hopper, with reproductions of his works and of those of fellow painters, and a timeline that adds historical context. (Rev: SLJ 6/03) [759.13]

13893 Lyons, Deborah. *Edward Hopper: Summer at the Seaside* (4–8). Series: Adventures in Art. 2003, Prestel $14.95 (978-3-7913-2737-2). 30pp. The story of the American painter who died in 1967, with a good analysis of many of his important works. (Rev: BL 11/15/03; SLJ 9/03) [921]

13894 Rubin, Susan G. *Edward Hopper: Painter of Light and Shadow* (5–8). Illus. 2007, Abrams $18.95 (978-0-8109-9347-1). 48pp. Along with a life of the painter, Rubin provides good reproductions of his work plus discussion of his themes, images, and technique. (Rev: BL 9/1/07; SLJ 10/07) [921]

13895 Spangenburg, Ray, and Kit Moser. *Edward Hopper: The Life of an Artist* (3–5). Series: Artist Biographies. 2002, Enslow LB $23.93 (978-0-7660-1881-5). 48pp. A look at the life and work of the artist and his realistic paintings. (Rev: HBG 10/03; SLJ 4/03) [921]

JACKSON, WILLIAM HENRY

13896 Lawlor, Laurie. *Window on the West: The Frontier Photography of William Henry Jackson* (5–8). 1999, Holiday $18.95 (978-0-8234-1380-5). 132pp. In addition to tracing the life of this famous photographer who captured the life and spirit of frontier America, this account covers the history and development of the West and pioneer life. (Rev: BL 2/15/00; HB 3/00; HBG 10/00; SLJ 3/00; VOYA 12/00) [921]

KAHLO, FRIDA

13897 Frazier, Nancy. *Frida Kahlo: Mysterious Painter* (5–7). Illus. Series: Library of Famous Women. 1993, Rosen $24.95 (978-1-56711-012-8). 64pp. A biography of this enigmatic artist with examples of her work. (Rev: BL 2/15/93) [921]

13898 Frith, Margaret. *Frida Kahlo: The Artist Who Painted Herself* (3–5). Illus. by Tomie dePaola. Series: Smart About Art. 2003, Grosset paper $5.99 (978-0-448-42677-8). 32pp. This picture-book biography presents the life of the Mexican artist as seen through the eyes of a young girl who is researching her for a school report. (Rev: HB 11/03; HBG 4/04; SLJ 11/03) [921]

13899 Garza, Hedda. *Frida Kahlo* (5–9). Series: Hispanics of Achievement. 1994, Chelsea LB $21.95 (978-0-7910-1698-5); paper $9.95 (978-0-7910-1699-2). 119pp. Known once only as the wife of Diego Rivera, this painter, who lived most of her life in Mexico, is now considered a great artist. (Rev: BL 3/1/94) [921]

13900 Guzmán, Lila, and Rick Guzmán. *Frida Kahlo: Painting Her Life* (3–5). Series: Famous Latinos. 2006, Enslow LB $22.60 (978-0-7660-2643-8). 32pp. A brief, accessible portrait of the Mexican artist, chronicling her personal life and artistic accomplishments in text for young readers that will also suit older reluctant readers. (Rev: BL 10/15/06; SLJ 2/07) [759.972]

13901 Holzhey, Magdalena. *Frida Kahlo: The Artist in the Blue House* (4–8). Series: Adventures in Art. 2003, Prestel $14.95 (978-3-7913-2863-8). 30pp. A colorful introduction to this Mexican painter with an interesting analysis of individual paintings. (Rev: BL 11/15/03; SLJ 9/03) [921]

13902 Laidlaw, Jill A. *Frida Kahlo* (5–8). Series: Artists in Their Time. 2003, Watts LB $24.00 (978-0-531-12236-5); paper $6.95 (978-0-531-16642-0). 46pp. An interesting life of Kahlo, with reproductions of her works and a timeline and informative sidebars that add historical context. (Rev: SLJ 6/03) [759]

13903 Venezia, Mike. *Frida Kahlo* (2–4). Series: Getting to Know. 1999, Children's Book Pr. LB $28.00 (978-0-516-20975-3). 32pp. A brief biography of Kahlo that includes many reproductions of her works and some humorous cartoons about her by the author. (Rev: BL 9/15/99) [921]

13904 Winter, Jonah. *Frida* (PS–3). Illus. by Ana Juan. 2002, Scholastic $16.95 (978-0-590-20320-3). 32pp. An inspirational biography of Mexican artist Frida Kahlo. (Rev: BCCB 2/02; BL 3/1/02; HB 3/02; HBG 10/02; SLJ 3/02) [759.9]

13905 Woronoff, Kristen. *Frida Kahlo: Mexican Painter* (3–5). Series: Famous Women Juniors. 2002, Gale LB $23.70 (978-1-56711-594-9). 32pp. This account focuses on Kahlo's youth and the events that led to her life as an artist. (Rev: SLJ 9/02) [921]

KEATS, EZRA JACK

13906 Engel, Dean, and Florence B. Freedman. *Ezra Jack Keats: A Biography with Illustrations* (3–6). Illus. 1995, Silver Moon $24.95 (978-1-881889-65-6). 96pp. Using first-hand sources, including interviews, this is the story of the artist/author best known for *The Snowy Day*. (Rev: BCCB 9/95; BL 4/15/95; HB 5/95, 9/95; SLJ 6/95) [921]

KIRBY, JACK

13907 Hamilton, Sue. *Jack Kirby* (4–8). Illus. Series: Comic Book Creators. 2007, ABDO LB $16.95 (978-1-59928-298-5). 32pp. A biography of comic book legend Kirby, with information on his childhood, early career, and work on comics such as the *Incredible Hulk* and *Captain America*. (Rev: BL 5/1/07; SLJ 8/07) [921]

KLEE, PAUL

13908 Connolly, Sean. *Paul Klee* (3–4). Series: The Life and Work Of. 1999, Heinemann LB $21.36 (978-1-57572-952-7). 32pp. An illustrated introduction to the life and work of the Swiss abstract painter. (Rev: BL 2/15/00) [921]

13909 Laidlaw, Jill A. *Paul Klee* (5–8). Series: Artists in Their Time. 2002, Watts LB $24.00 (978-0-531-12230-3). 46pp. Photographs, reproductions, maps, and a timeline that links world events with events in the artist's life make this suitable both for browsing and report writing. (Rev: BL 10/15/02; SLJ 1/03) [921]

13910 Venezia, Mike. *Paul Klee* (2–5). Illus. Series: Getting to Know. 1991, Children's Book Pr. LB $28.00 (978-0-516-02294-9). 32pp. An informal, simple biography of this Swiss artist, as well as many examples of his work and comments on his style. (Rev: BL 1/15/92) [921]

KURELEK, WILLIAM

13911 Kurelek, William. *A Prairie Boy's Summer* (3–5). Illus. by author. 1975, Tundra paper $10.99 (978-0-88776-116-4). 48pp. Each of this Canadian artist's paintings depicts a farm activity, which the accompanying text describes in this companion piece to the author's earlier *A Prairie Boy's Winter* (1984). [921]

LANGE, DOROTHEA

13912 Venezia, Mike. *Dorothea Lange* (2–4). Illus. Series: Getting to Know. 2000, Children's Book Pr. LB $28.00 (978-0-516-22026-0); paper $6.95 (978-0-516-27171-2). 32pp. A biography — enriched with amusing cartoons — of the famous American photographer noted mainly for her haunting pictures of migrant workers and victims of the Great Depression. (Rev: BL 9/15/00) [921]

LAWRENCE, JACOB

13913 Duggleby, John. *Story Painter: The Life of Jacob Lawrence* (5–8). Illus. 1998, Chronicle $16.95 (978-0-8118-2082-0). 64pp. Using 50 color reproductions, this biography of the great African American illustrator and painter tells how he moved to Harlem in the 1930s and developed his own techniques and style. (Rev: BCCB 1/99; BL 10/15/98; HB 3/99; HBG 3/99; SLJ 12/98) [921]

13914 Leach, Deba Foxley. *I See You I See Myself: The Young Life of Jacob Lawrence* (5–9). Illus. by Jacob Lawrence. 2002, Phillips Collection $20.00 (978-0-943044-26-2). 64pp. A look at the early life and work of the African American artist, with information on his paintings as a teen. (Rev: SLJ 12/02) [759.13]

13915 Venezia, Mike. *Jacob Lawrence* (2–4). Illus. by author. Series: Getting to Know. 1999, Children's Book Pr. LB $28.00 (978-0-516-21012-4). 32pp. A fine introduction to the life and work of this contemporary African American artist that focuses on the aspects of his life that affected his art. (Rev: SLJ 5/00) [921]

LEE, STAN

13916 Hamilton, Sue. *Stan Lee* (3–5). Illus. Series: Comic Book Creators. 2007, ABDO LB $16.95 (978-1-59928-301-2). 32pp. Comics fans will enjoy this introduction to part of the team behind Spider-Man, the X-Men, the Hulk, and other superheroes. Vintage strips are included. (Rev: SLJ 8/07)

13917 Miller, Raymond H. *Stan Lee: Creator of Spider-Man* (4–8). Series: Inventors and Creators. 2006, Gale LB $26.20 (978-0-7377-3447-8). 48pp. Superhero fans will enjoy this biography of the man behind Spider-Man and other comic-book characters. (Rev: SLJ 6/06) [921]

LEWIN, TED

13918 Lewin, Ted. *Touch and Go: Travels of a Children's Book Illustrator* (4–6). Illus. 1999, Lothrop $15.00 (978-0-688-14109-7). 80pp. The famous children's book illustrator tells how he has gathered material for his work from around the world and describes his adventures along the way. (Rev: BL 4/15/99; SLJ 7/99) [921]

LEWIS, MAUD

13919 Bogart, Jo Ellen. *Capturing Joy: The Story of Maud Lewis* (3–6). Illus. by Mark Lang. 2002, Tundra $16.95 (978-0-88776-568-1). 32pp. The story of the life and work of the Canadian artist who used a folk-art style. (Rev: BL 6/1–15/02; HBG 10/02; SLJ 7/02) [921]

LIN, MAYA

13920 Ling, Bettina. *Maya Lin* (5–7). Illus. Series: Contemporary Asian Americans. 1997, Raintree LB $17.98 (978-0-8172-3992-3). 48pp. A profile of the Asian American architect and an introduction to many of her projects, including the Vietnam War Memorial in Washington, D.C. (Rev: BL 5/1/97) [921]

MARTINEZ, MARIA

13921 Morris, Juddi. *Tending the Fire: The Story of Maria Martinez* (5–8). 1997, Northland paper $6.95 (978-0-87358-654-2). 120pp. The life story of New Mexico's most famous potter, who was born in an Indian pueblo in 1887. (Rev: BL 12/1/97; HBG 3/98; SLJ 12/97) [921]

MATISSE, HENRI

13922 Anholt, Laurence. *Matisse: The King of Color* (1–3). Illus. by author. Series: Anholt's Artists. 2007, Barron's $14.99 (978-0-7641-6047-9). 32pp. This colorful picture book tells the story behind Matisse's creation — when he is in his 80s — of stained glass windows for a nunnery chapel. (Rev: BL 11/15/07; SLJ 2/08) [921]

13923 Hollein, Max, and Nina Hollein. *Matisse: Cut-Out Fun with Matisse* (4–8). Series: Adventures in Art. 2003, Prestel $14.95 (978-3-7913-2858-4). 30pp. This large-formatted book that originated in Germany, successfully introduces the life and work of the great French master. (Rev: BL 11/15/03; HBG 3/02; SLJ 8/01) [921]

13924 Sturm, Ellen. *Matisse* (2–4). Series: Masterpieces: Artists and Their Works. 2003, Capstone LB $22.60 (978-0-7368-2227-5). 24pp. A small-format introductory biography of the artist featuring simple text and color reproductions and including material on his early life, training, and influences. (Rev: SLJ 3/04) [921]

13925 Venezia, Mike. *Henri Matisse* (2–4). Illus. Series: Getting to Know. 1997, Children's Book Pr. LB $28.00 (978-0-516-20311-9). 32pp. A light but realistic overview of Matisse and his work, with many color reproductions, clever cartoon illustrations, and an interesting story line. (Rev: BL 7/97) [921]

13926 Welton, Jude. *Henri Matisse* (5–8). Series: Artists in Their Time. 2002, Watts LB $24.00 (978-0-531-12228-0); paper $6.95 (978-0-531-16621-5). 48pp. The artistic and social periods during which Matisse worked are re-created along with a biography and several color examples of his work. (Rev: BL 10/15/02; SLJ 1/03) [921]

MICHELANGELO

13927 *Michelangelo* (5–8). Series: The Lives of the Artists. 2004, World Almanac LB $31.00 (978-0-8368-5600-2). 48pp. A tall, slender volume full of facts about Michelangelo's life and times, with many color reproductions. (Rev: SLJ 8/04) [921]

13928 Tames, Richard. *Michelangelo Buonarroti* (3–4). Series: The Life and Work Of. 2000, Heinemann LB $21.36 (978-1-57572-343-3). 32pp. A brief biography of Michelangelo that gives examples of some of his finest works, including the Sistine Chapel. (Rev: BL 10/15/00; HBG 10/01; SLJ 2/01) [921]

13929 Whiting, Jim. *Michelangelo* (4–7). Series: Art Profiles for Kids. 2007, Mitchell Lane LB $29.95 (978-1-58415-562-1). 48pp. Suitable for both research and browsing, this examination of the artist's life and times includes many reproductions and interesting sidebars. (Rev: LMC 1/08; SLJ 12/07) [921]

MILLER, TOM

13930 Miller, Tom, and Camay C. Murphy. *Can a Coal Scuttle Fly?* (2–5). Illus. 1996, Maryland Historical Soc. $14.00 (978-0-938420-55-2). 32pp. Baltimore artist Tom Miller tells about his life and the great joy that can be found in art. (Rev: BL 10/15/96) [921]

MONET, CLAUDE

13931 Connolly, Sean. *Claude Monet* (3–4). Series: The Life and Work Of. 1999, Heinemann LB $21.36 (978-1-57572-956-5). 32pp. This is a simple introduction to the life and works of Monet, with photos showing him at different stages in his career. (Rev: BL 2/15/00; SLJ 1/00) [921]

13932 Connolly, Sean. *Claude Monet* (4–8). Illus. Series: Lives of the Artists. 2005, World Almanac LB $31.00 (978-0-8368-5650-7). 48pp. A tall, slender volume full of facts about Monet's life and times, with many color reproductions. (Rev: BL 6/1–15/04; SLJ 3/05) [921]

13933 Hodge, Susie. *Claude Monet* (5–8). Illus. Series: Artists in Their Time. 2002, Watts LB $24.00 (978-0-531-12226-6). 46pp. Photographs, reproductions, maps, and a timeline that links world events with events in the artist's life make this suitable both for browsing and report writing. (Rev: SLJ 1/03) [921]

13934 Kelley, True. *Claude Monet: Sunshine and Waterlilies* (2–4). Illus. Series: Smart About Art. 2001, Penguin paper $5.99 (978-0-448-42522-1). 32pp. An interesting overview of Claude Monet's life and work, presented in the Smart About Art school-report format with cartoon drawings. (Rev: BL 11/1/01; HBG 3/02; SLJ 11/01) [759.4]

13935 Koja, Stephan, and Katja Miksovsky. *Claude Monet: The Magician of Color* (3–7). Trans. by Andrea Belloli. Illus. Series: Adventures in Art. 1997, Prestel $14.95 (978-3-7913-1812-7). 32pp. A straightforward biography of Monet that is enlivened by drawings, paintings, and photos. (Rev: SLJ 1/98) [921]

13936 Malam, John. *Claude Monet* (2–4). Series: Tell Me About. 1998, Carolrhoda LB $19.93 (978-1-57505-250-2). 24pp. Numerous color reproductions and a simple text are used to bring to life the artist Monet and his career. (Rev: HBG 3/99; SLJ 1/99) [921]

13937 Venezia, Mike. *Monet* (2–5). Illus. Series: Getting to Know. 1990, Children's Book Pr. LB $28.00 (978-0-516-02276-5). 32pp. Using many paintings by Monet, this book introduces the reader to Impressionism. (Rev: SLJ 11/90) [921]

13938 Whiting, Jim. *Claude Monet* (4–7). Series: Art Profiles for Kids. 2007, Mitchell Lane LB $29.95 (978-1-58415-563-8). 48pp. Suitable for both research and browsing, this examination of the artist's life and times includes many reproductions and interesting sidebars. (Rev: LMC 1/08; SLJ 12/07) [921]

MOORE, HENRY

13939 Connolly, Sean. *Henry Moore* (3–5). Illus. Series: Life and Work Of. 1999, Heinemann LB $21.36 (978-1-57572-953-4). 32pp. Color photos show examples of Moore's work while black-and-white photos document his life in this biography of the famous English sculptor. (Rev: BL 2/1/00; SLJ 1/00) [921]

13940 Gardner, Jane M. *Henry Moore: From Bones and Stones to Sketches and Sculptures* (2–4). Illus. 1993, Macmillan $15.95 (978-0-02-735812-4). 32pp. A simple biography told mainly through photographs of the great British 20th-century sculptor, Henry Moore. (Rev: BCCB 4/93; BL 4/15/93; HB 7/93; SLJ 6/93) [921]

MORGAN, JULIA

13941 Mannis, Celeste Davidson. *Julia Morgan Built a Castle* (2–4). Illus. by Miles Hyman. 2006, Viking $17.99 (978-0-670-05964-5). 40pp. This intriguing large-format biography covers the life of Julia Morgan, who grew up in the late 19th century, achieved many "firsts" for women in the field, and designed many impressive buildings — including William

Randolph Hearst's huge castle at San Simeon. (Rev: BL 11/15/06; SLJ 11/06) [921]

MOSES, GRANDMA

13942 Wallner, Alexandra. *Grandma Moses* (PS–3). Illus. 2004, Holiday House $16.95 (978-0-8234-1538-0). 32pp. Moses did not become an active artist until late in life; this picture book illustrated in a style reminiscent of the artist's primitives also describes her early years. (Rev: BL 3/1/04; HB 7/04; SLJ 5/04) [759.13]

MOUNT, WILLIAM SIDNEY

13943 Howard, Nancy S. *William Sidney Mount: Painter of Rural America* (4–7). Illus. 1994, Sterling $14.95 (978-1-871922-75-2). 48pp. An interactive book that explores the work and paintings of the 19th-century American painter William Sidney Mount. (Rev: BL 1/15/95) [921]

NAST, THOMAS

13944 Pflueger, Lynda. *Thomas Nast: Political Cartoonist* (5–8). Series: Historical American Biographies. 2000, Enslow LB $26.60 (978-0-7660-1251-6). 128pp. An informative, entertaining, and well-written biography of this influential political cartoonist and critic. (Rev: BL 9/15/00; HBG 10/01; SLJ 11/00) [921]

OBATA, CHIURA

13945 Ross, Michael E. *Nature Art with Chiura Obata* (3–6). Series: Naturalist's Apprentice. 2000, Lerner $19.95 (978-1-57505-378-3). 48pp. From his childhood in Japan to his move to the U.S. in 1903 to his death in 1975, this is the story of the great painter who used Japanese painting techniques to depict the American landscape. (Rev: BCCB 3/00; BL 2/1/00; HBG 10/00; SLJ 4/00) [921]

O'KEEFFE, GEORGIA

13946 Bryant, Jen. *Georgia's Bones* (2–4). Illus. by Bethanne Andersen. 2005, Eerdmans $16.00 (978-0-8028-5217-5). 32pp. This beautifully illustrated book introduces readers to Georgia O'Keeffe's life and preoccupation with shapes and structures. (Rev: BL 2/15/05; SLJ 4/05) [921]
13947 Kucharczyk, Emily Rose. *Georgia O'Keeffe: Desert Painter* (3–5). Series: Famous Women Juniors. 2002, Gale LB $23.70 (978-1-56711-592-5). 32pp. This account focuses on the artist's youth and the events that led to her life as an artist. (Rev: SLJ 9/02) [921]
13948 Lowery, Linda. *Georgia O'Keeffe* (2–4). Illus. 1996, Carolrhoda LB $23.93 (978-0-87614-860-0); paper $5.95 (978-0-87614-898-3). 48pp. A simple account of the life and work of this amazing painter of the Southwest. (Rev: BL 9/1/96; SLJ 8/96) [921]
13949 Rodríguez, Rachel Victoria. *Through Georgia's Eyes* (K–3). Illus. by Julie Paschkis. 2006, Holt $16.95 (978-0-8050-7740-7). 32pp. O'Keeffe's

life — including her childhood — and work are presented in compelling text and vibrant illustrations. (Rev: BCCB 4/06; BL 2/15/06*; HB 5/06; HBG 10/06; LMC 10/06; SLJ 3/06) [921]
13950 Spangenburg, Ray, and Kit Moser. *Georgia O'Keeffe: The Life of an Artist* (2–4). Illus. Series: Artist Biographies. 2002, Enslow LB $23.93 (978-0-7660-1882-2). 48pp. This informative profile of American painter Georgia O'Keeffe includes a timeline, glossary, list of Web sites, and full-color reproductions of selected O'Keeffe paintings. (Rev: BL 4/1/03; HBG 10/03) [759.13]
13951 Winter, Jeanette. *My Name Is Georgia* (2–4). Illus. 1998, Harcourt $17.00 (978-0-15-201649-4). 48pp. Told from the artist's point of view, this is a quiet but intense look at the life and work of Georgia O'Keeffe. (Rev: BCCB 11/98; BL 10/15/98*; HB 9/98; HBG 3/99; SLJ 12/98) [921]

PARKS, GORDON

13952 Parr, Ann. *Gordon Parks: No Excuses* (3–5). Illus. by Kathryn Breidenthal. 2006, Pelican $15.95 (978-1-58980-411-1). 32pp. African American photographer Parks's camera work takes center stage in this brief, large-format biography. (Rev: BL 7/06; SLJ 6/06) [770.92]

PEET, BILL

13953 Peet, Bill. *Bill Peet: An Autobiography* (2–5). Illus. 1989, Houghton $22.00 (978-0-395-50932-6). 192pp. The autobiography of the author/illustrator who worked at the Disney Studio for many years. (Rev: BL 7/89; HB 7/89*; SLJ 7/89) [921]

PEI, I. M.

13954 Englar, Mary. *I. M. Pei* (3–5). Illus. Series: Asian-American Biographies. 2005, Raintree LB $32.86 (978-1-4109-1056-1). 64pp. Profiles the life and career of the Chinese American architect who designed many notable structures, with sidebars that add historical context. (Rev: BL 10/15/05; SLJ 3/06) [921]

PICASSO, PABLO

13955 Gogerly, Liz. *Pablo Picasso: Master of Modern Art* (3–5). 2004, Raintree LB $29.93 (978-0-7398-6628-3). 48pp. Picasso's youth, education, and artistic evolution are strong features of this biography that includes photographs, quotations, and a timeline. (Rev: SLJ 1/05) [921]
13956 Hodge, Susie, and Pablo Picasso. *Pablo Picasso* (4–8). Series: Lives of the Artists. 2004, Gareth Stevens LB $11.95 (978-0-8368-5606-4). 48pp. Works by the young Picasso are a feature of this well illustrated profile. (Rev: BL 6/1–15/04) [921]
13957 Lowery, Linda. *Pablo Picasso* (2–3). Illus. by Janice L. Porter. Series: On My Own Biography. 1999, Lerner $23.93 (978-1-57505-331-8); paper $5.95 (978-1-57505-370-7). 48pp. An easy-to-read biography that touches on Picasso's different paint-

ing periods, his personal life, and his great originality. (Rev: BL 2/1/00; HBG 3/00; SLJ 2/00) [921]

13958 Meadows, Matthew. *Pablo Picasso* (5–7). Illus. Series: Art for Young People. 1996, Sterling $14.95 (978-0-8069-6160-6). 32pp. In double-page spreads, presents the life and work of this multitalented Spanish artist. (Rev: BL 2/1/97; HB 5/96; SLJ 3/97) [921]

13959 Pfleger, Susanne. *A Day with Picasso* (4–7). Series: Adventures in Art. 2000, Prestel $14.95 (978-3-7913-2165-3). 30pp. An introduction to the life and work of Picasso, including many full-color reproductions. (Rev: BL 2/15/00; SLJ 2/00) [921]

13960 *Picasso: Soul on Fire* (4–7). Trans. by Rick Jacobson. Illus. by Rick Jacobson and Laura Fernandez. 2004, Tundra $15.95 (978-0-88776-599-5). 32pp. Oil paintings of the Spanish-born artist, along with reproductions of some of his best-known pieces, introduce his work and brief facts about his life. (Rev: BL 11/1/04) [921]

13961 Scarborough, Kate. *Pablo Picasso* (5–8). Series: Artists in Their Time. 2002, Watts LB $24.00 (978-0-531-12229-7); paper $6.95 (978-0-531-16622-2). 48pp. This biography of the 20th century's most famous artist is accompanied by material on the social conditions of his time. (Rev: BL 10/15/02; SLJ 1/03) [921]

13962 Selfridge, John W. *Pablo Picasso* (5–9). Series: Hispanics of Achievement. 1993, Chelsea LB $32.00 (978-0-7910-1777-7). 111pp. A colorful biography of this great Spanish painter, who lived most of his life as a political exile in France, with some examples of his enormous output. (Rev: BL 3/1/94) [9212]

13963 Venezia, Mike. *Picasso* (PS–4). Illus. 1988, Children's Book Pr. LB $28.00 (978-0-516-02271-0); paper $6.95 (978-0-516-42271-8). 32pp. Amusing facts are tucked in with information about the artist and his work. (Rev: BL 10/1/88; SLJ 9/88)

13964 Wallis, Jeremy. *Pablo Picasso* (5–8). Series: Creative Lives. 2001, Heinemann LB $27.07 (978-1-58810-206-5). 64pp. Picasso's eccentricities are highlighted in this volume that covers his life, his family, and his work. (Rev: HBG 10/02; SLJ 3/02) [921]

PIPPIN, HORACE

13965 Venezia, Mike. *Horace Pippin* (3–5). Illus. by author. Series: Getting to Know the World's Greatest Artists. 2007, Children's Pr. LB $28.00 (978-0-531-18527-8). 32pp. Simply written but packed with information, this is an attractive profile of the African American artist known for his naive paintings of life during slavery and segregation. (Rev: SLJ 2/08)

POLITI, LEO

13966 Stalcup, Ann. *Leo Politi: Artist of the Angels* (4–9). Illus. by Leo Politi. 2004, Silver Moon $24.95 (978-1-893110-38-0). 104pp. The life of the American-born man who spent his formative years in Italy and returned as an adult to make his home in Los Angeles and portray the ethnic communities there in his books for children. (Rev: SLJ 4/05) [921]

POLLOCK, JACKSON

13967 Bennett, Leonie. *Jackson Pollock* (1–3). Illus. Series: Life and Work. 2005, Heinemann LB $22.79 (978-1-4034-5073-9). 32pp. The life and work of the artist, with photographs of both. (Rev: BL 3/15/05) [921]

13968 Oliver, Clare. *Jackson Pollock* (5–8). Series: Artists in Their Time. 2003, Watts LB $24.00 (978-0-531-12237-2). 46pp. An interesting life of Pollock, with reproductions of his works and of those of fellow painters, and a timeline that adds historical context. (Rev: SLJ 5/03) [759]

REAM, VINNIE

13969 Fitzgerald, Dawn. *Vinnie and Abraham* (2–4). Illus. by Catherine Stock. 2007, Charlesbridge paper $7.95 (978-1-5709-1644-1). 32pp. This charmingly illustrated picture-book biography illuminates the life of Vinnie Ream, who was not only one of the U.S. Postal Service's first female workers but was also a talented artist and did a life-size sculpture of President Lincoln. (Rev: BL 1/1–15/07) [921]

REMBERT, WINFRED

13970 Rembert, Winfred. *Don't Hold Me Back: My Life and Art* (4–7). Illus. 2003, Cricket $19.95 (978-0-8126-2703-9). 40pp. Rembert reflects on his life in the South as a sharecropper's son — picking cotton, dealing with racism, the civil rights movement — and displays his evocative works of art with comments on their creation. (Rev: BL 11/1/03*; HBG 4/04; SLJ 12/03*) [759.1]

REMBRANDT VAN RIJN

13971 De Bie, Ceciel, and Martijn Leenen. *Rembrandt: See and Do Children's Book* (3–7). Illus. 2001, Getty $19.95 (978-0-89236-621-7). 64pp. An effectively organized biography is combined with activities that encourage children to look closely at the art. (Rev: HBG 3/02; SLJ 4/02) [921]

13972 Mason, Antony. *Rembrandt* (4–8). Illus. Series: Lives of the Artists. 2005, World Almanac LB $31.00 (978-0-8368-5651-4). 48pp. A tall, slender volume full of facts about Rembrandt's life and times, with many color reproductions. (Rev: BL 6/1–15/04; SLJ 3/05) [921]

13973 Mis, Melody S. *Rembrandt* (3–5). Illus. Series: Meet the Artist. 2007, Rosen LB $15.95 (978-1-4042-3840-4). 24pp. With at least one captioned reproduction on every spread, this is a basic biography of the artist and his career. (Rev: BL 11/1/07; SLJ 1/08) [921]

13974 Niz, Xavier. *Rembrandt* (2–4). Series: Masterpieces: Artists and Their Works. 2003, Capstone LB $22.60 (978-0-7368-2230-5). 24pp. An introductory biography of the 17th-century artist, including material on his childhood and early training plus discussion of his techniques. (Rev: SLJ 3/04) [921]

13975 Venezia, Mike. *Rembrandt* (PS–4). Illus. 1988, Children's Book Pr. LB $28.00 (978-0-516-02272-7); paper $6.95 (978-0-516-42272-5). 32pp. Learning about art and great artists can be fun. (Rev: BL 10/1/88; SLJ 9/88)

REMINGTON, FREDERIC

13976 Giesecke, Ernestine. *Frederic Remington* (3–4). Series: The Life and Work Of. 1999, Heinemann LB $21.36 (978-1-57572-951-0). 32pp. This account of Remington's life and career as a painter, illustrator, and sculptor of the American West includes many illustrations of his works and photos of the artist and his world. (Rev: BL 2/15/00; SLJ 1/00) [921]

RENOIR, PIERRE-AUGUSTE

13977 Parsons, Tom. *Pierre Auguste Renoir* (5–7). Illus. Series: Art for Young People. 1996, Sterling $14.95 (978-0-8069-6162-0). 32pp. The life and work of this prolific French artist are examined in a series of double-page spreads. (Rev: BL 2/1/97; SLJ 3/97) [921]

13978 Somervill, Barbara. *Pierre-Auguste Renoir* (5–8). Illus. Series: Art Profiles for Kids. 2007, Mitchell Lane LB $29.95 (978-1-58415-566-9). 48pp. A brief introduction to the artist's life and work and the times in which he lived, with reproductions of his art. (Rev: BL 1/1–15/08; LMC 1/08; SLJ 12/07) [921]

13979 Venezia, Mike. *Pierre Auguste Renoir* (2–4). Illus. Series: Getting to Know. 1996, Children's Book Pr. LB $28.00 (978-0-516-02225-3). 32pp. This biography includes examples of Renoir's paintings and an introduction to Impressionism. (Rev: BL 9/15/96; SLJ 12/96) [921]

RINGGOLD, FAITH

13980 Venezia, Mike. *Faith Ringgold* (3–5). Illus. by author. Series: Getting to Know the World's Greatest Artists. 2007, Children's Pr. LB $28.00 (978-0-531-18526-1). 32pp. Simply written but packed with information, this is an attractive profile of the African American artist known for her children's books and story quilts. (Rev: SLJ 2/08)

RIVERA, DIEGO

13981 Bankston, John. *Diego Rivera* (5–7). Series: Latinos in American History. 2003, Mitchell Lane LB $29.95 (978-1-58415-208-8). 48pp. A biography of the famous 20th-century Mexican artist who is best known for his murals with political overtones. (Rev: BL 1/1–15/04; HBG 4/04; SLJ 2/04) [921]

13982 Cockcroft, James D. *Diego Rivera* (5–9). Series: Hispanics of Achievement. 1991, Chelsea LB $21.95 (978-0-7910-1252-9). 119pp. The life of this Mexican artist and activist, with several illustrations. (Rev: BL 11/1/91; SLJ 1/92) [921]

13983 Guzmán, Lila, and Rick Guzmán. *Diego Rivera: Artist of Mexico* (3–4). Series: Famous Latinos. 2006, Enslow LB $22.60 (978-0-7660-2641-4). 32pp. The Mexican artist's life is described in easy-to-understand language, focusing in particular on his vibrantly colored murals. (Rev: SLJ 2/07) [921]

13984 Kent, Deborah. *Diego Rivera: Painting Mexico* (3–6). Series: A Proud Heritage. 2005, Child's World LB $28.50 (978-1-59296-384-3). 40pp. Covers Rivera's childhood and education, discussing in age-appropriate language his four marriages and how his communist leanings are reflected in his paintings. (Rev: SLJ 6/05) [921]

ROCKWELL, NORMAN

13985 Gherman, Beverly. *Norman Rockwell: Storyteller with a Brush* (4–7). Illus. 2000, Simon & Schuster $19.95 (978-0-689-82001-4). 58pp. An appealing biography of this New England artist who reflected mid-20th-century American life and values in his many paintings. (Rev: BCCB 7–8/00; BL 2/15/00; HB 3/00; HBG 10/00; SLJ 2/00) [921]

13986 Roy, Jennifer, and Gregory Roy. *Norman Rockwell: The Life of an Artist* (4–6). Series: Artist Biographies. 2002, Enslow LB $23.93 (978-0-7660-1883-9). 48pp. Rockwell's early interest in art and his popularity are highlighted in this account of his life and work. (Rev: HBG 10/03; SLJ 3/03) [921]

13987 Venezia, Mike. *Norman Rockwell* (2–4). Series: Getting to Know. 2000, Children's Book Pr. LB $28.00 (978-0-516-21594-5). 32pp. The popular American artist is introduced with many full color reproductions, a lively text, and some amusing cartoons. (Rev: BL 1/1–15/01) [921]

RODIN, AUGUSTE

13988 Tames, Richard. *Auguste Rodin* (3–4). Series: The Life and Work Of. 2000, Heinemann LB $21.36 (978-1-57572-342-6). 32pp. This book chronicles the life and work of Rodin and includes material on the events that influenced his growth and development as an artist. (Rev: BL 10/15/00; HBG 10/01) [921]

ROUSSEAU, HENRI

13989 Pfleger, Susanne. *Henri Rousseau: A Jungle Expedition* (4–7). Trans. by Catherine McCreadie. Illus. Series: Adventures in Art. 1999, Prestel $14.95 (978-3-7913-1987-2). 28pp. The story of Henri Rousseau and the art that evolved from his visits to a botanical garden. (Rev: BL 2/1/99; SLJ 2/99) [921]

13990 Venezia, Mike. *Henri Rousseau* (2–4). Series: Getting to Know the World's Greatest Artists. 2002, Children's Book Pr. LB $28.00 (978-0-516-22495-4); paper $6.95 (978-0-516-26998-6). 32pp. An easy-to-read text and humorous cartoons are used to introduce this famous French artist and his work. (Rev: BL 4/1/02) [921]

SARGENT, JOHN SINGER

13991 Kreiter, Eshel, and Marc Zabludoff. *John Singer Sargent: The Life of an Artist* (2–4). Illus. Series: Artist Biographies. 2002, Enslow LB $23.93 (978-0-7660-1879-2). 48pp. This concise, well-illustrated introduction to the life and work of the American painter includes a glossary, timeline, and list of Web sites. (Rev: BL 4/1/03; HBG 10/03) [759.13]

SCHULZ, CHARLES

13992 Marvis, Barbara. *Charles Schulz: The Story of the Peanuts Gang* (4–8). Illus. Series: Robbie Reader. 2004, Mitchell Lane LB $25.70 (978-1-58415-289-7). 32pp. This photo-filled biography traces Schulz's life and his love of cartoons; it is especially suitable for reluctant readers. (Rev: BL 9/1/05)

13993 Whiting, Jim. *Charles Schulz* (3–4). Series: Real-Life Reader Biographies. 2002, Mitchell Lane LB $15.95 (978-1-58415-131-9). 32pp. A simple retelling of the life of the talented storyteller and cartoonist who created the comic strip "Peanuts." (Rev: BL 9/15/02; SLJ 4/03) [921]

13994 Woods, Mae. *Charles Schulz* (2–4). Series: Children's Authors. 2000, ABDO LB $21.35 (978-1-57765-425-4). 24pp. An attractive, brief biography of the creator of Peanuts and the gang. (Rev: HBG 3/01; SLJ 1/01) [921]

SEURAT, GEORGES

13995 Burleigh, Robert. *Seurat and la Grande Jatte: Connecting the Dots* (3–6). 2004, Abrams $17.95 (978-0-8109-4811-2). 32pp. The well-known painting of "La Grande Jatte" serves as an introduction to Seurat's work and time in this oversized picture book for older readers. (Rev: BL 6/1–15/04; SLJ 6/04) [759.4]

SIMMONS, PHILIP

13996 Lyons, Mary E. *Catching the Fire: Philip Simmons, Blacksmith* (4–8). 1997, Houghton $17.00 (978-0-395-72033-2). 48pp. A biography of the contemporary African American craftsman and artist from Charleston, South Carolina, with extensive quotations from personal interviews. (Rev: BL 9/1/97; HBG 3/98; SLJ 9/97) [921]

SIMON, JOE

13997 Hamilton, Sue. *Joe Simon* (3–5). Illus. Series: Comic Book Creators. 2007, ABDO LB $16.95 (978-1-59928-300-5). 32pp. Comics fans will enjoy this introduction to part of the team behind Captain America and other superheroes. Vintage strips are included. (Rev: SLJ 8/07)

THIEBAUD, WAYNE

13998 Rubin, Susan G. *Delicious: The Life and Art of Wayne Thiebaud* (5–8). Illus. 2007, Chronicle $15.95 (978-0-8118-5168-8). 108pp. Paintings (by Thiebaud, of course) of gum balls and cupcakes on the cover of this nicely designed volume draw readers in to the story of a man who paints "happy pictures." (Rev: BL 2/15/08; SLJ 3/08) [921]

TITIAN

13999 Venezia, Mike. *Titian* (1–3). Illus. Series: Getting to Know the World's Greatest Artists. 2003, Children's Pr. LB $28.00 (978-0-516-22575-3); paper $6.95 (978-0-516-26975-7). 32pp. An easy-to-read text and humorous cartoons are used to introduce this famous Italian artist and his work. [921]

TOULOUSE-LAUTREC, HENRI

14000 Burleigh, Robert. *Toulouse-Lautrec: The Moulin Rouge and the City of Light* (3–5). Illus. 2005, Abrams $17.95 (978-0-8109-5867-8). 32pp. A biography of the French artist, with plenty of colorful reproductions of his work and information about the Paris of his day. (Rev: BL 3/1/05; SLJ 5/05) [921]

TURNER, JOSEPH

14001 Woodhouse, Jane. *Joseph Turner* (3–4). Series: The Life and Work Of. 2000, Heinemann LB $21.36 (978-1-57572-345-7). 32pp. The life and works of this English painter noted chiefly for his luminous seascapes are covered in this brief, well-illustrated biography. (Rev: BL 10/15/00; HBG 10/01) [921]

VAN GOGH, VINCENT

14002 Bodden, Valerie. *Vincent van Gogh* (4–7). Series: Xtraordinary Artists. 2008, Creative Education LB $32.80 (978-1-58341-663-1). 48pp. Bodden provides an interesting overview of the artist's life with well-chosen illustrations and excerpts from his own writing. (Rev: LMC 8/09; SLJ 4/09) [921]

14003 Bucks, Brad, and Joan Holub. *Vincent van Gogh: Sunflowers and Swirly Stars* (2–4). Series: Smart About Art. 2001, Grosset $5.99 (978-0-448-42521-4). 32pp. Using lively cartoon drawings and reproductions of the artist's works, the life and output of van Gogh are introduced through the eyes of a young student. (Rev: BL 1/1–15/02; HBG 3/02) [921]

14004 Connolly, Sean. *Vincent van Gogh* (3–4). Series: The Life and Work Of. 1999, Heinemann LB $21.36 (978-1-57572-958-9). 32pp. A biography of Vincent van Gogh, encompassing his work as well as the people and events that influenced him most. (Rev: BL 2/15/00) [921]

14005 Green, Jen. *Vincent van Gogh* (5–8). Series: Artists in Their Time. 2002, Watts LB $24.00 (978-0-531-12238-9). 48pp. The life and times of this 20th-century artistic genius are covered, with a number of reproductions of his paintings. (Rev: BL 10/15/02) [921]

14006 Lucas, Eileen. *Vincent van Gogh* (2–4). Illus. 1997, Carolrhoda LB $23.93 (978-1-57505-038-6). 56pp. A simple biography that captures the life and anxieties of the artist, with a good commentary on his work. (Rev: BCCB 9/96; BL 9/1/97; HBG 3/98; SLJ 9/97) [921]

14007 Malam, John. *Vincent van Gogh* (K–3). Series: Tell Me About. 1998, Carolrhoda LB $19.93 (978-1-57505-249-6). 24pp. This brief account that describes van Gogh's troubled life is illustrated with photographs and reproductions of his paintings. (Rev: HBG 3/99; SLJ 3/99) [921]

VELAZQUEZ, DIEGO

14008 *Diego Velazquez* (1–3). Illus. by Mike Venezia. Series: Getting to Know the World's Greatest Artists. 2004, Scholastic LB $6.95 (978-0-516-26980-1). 32pp. Full-color reproductions and cartoons add to the basic information about the life of the17th-century Spanish painter. (Rev: BL 6/1–15/04) [921]

VERMEER, JOHANNES

14009 Mis, Melody S. *Vermeer* (2–4). Series: Meet the Artist. 2007, Rosen LB $15.95 (978-1-4042-3843-5). 24pp. Vermeer's life and work are covered in this clear, well-designed volume. (Rev: BL 10/15/07) [921]

14010 Venezia, Mike. *Johannes Vermeer* (2–4). Series: Getting to Know the World's Greatest Artists. 2002, Children's Book Pr. LB $28.00 (978-0-516-22282-0); paper $6.95 (978-0-516-26999-3). 32pp. The life and work of this Dutch master are presented with a simple text and many cartoons. (Rev: BL 4/1/02) [921]

WALDMAN, NEIL

14011 Waldman, Neil. *Out of the Shadows: An Artist's Journey* (5–8). Illus. 2006, Boyds Mills $21.95 (978-1-59078-411-2). 144pp. In this candid memoir, Waldman describes how his challenging childhood experiences influenced him as an artist. (Rev: BL 4/15/06; SLJ 5/06) [741.6]

WANG YANI

14012 Zhensun, Zheng, and Alice Low. *A Young Painter: The Life and Paintings of Wang Yani — China's Extraordinary Young Artist* (5–8). 1991, Scholastic paper $17.95 (978-0-590-44906-9). 80pp. The story of a self-taught prodigy whose paintings are highly regarded in China. Includes many examples of her unique work, based on the traditional Chinese style. (Rev: BCCB 9/91; BL 10/1/91*; SLJ 8/91) [921]

WARHOL, ANDY

14013 Bolton, Linda. *Andy Warhol* (5–8). Series: Artists in Their Time. 2002, Watts LB $24.00 (978-0-531-12225-9); paper $6.95 (978-0-531-16618-5). 48pp. This biography includes material on the social period in which Warhol worked. (Rev: BL 10/15/02) [921]

14014 Ford, Carin T. *Andy Warhol: The Life of an Artist* (3–5). Series: Artist Biographies. 2002, Enslow LB $23.93 (978-0-7660-1880-8). 48pp. Warhol's personal life is covered in this brief biography that also introduces his famous works. (Rev: HBG 10/03; SLJ 4/03) [921]

14015 Rubin, Susan G. *Andy Warhol: Pop Art Painter* (4–7). Illus. 2006, Abrams $18.95 (978-0-8109-5477-9). 48pp. This picture-book biography chronicles Warhol's life and career, focusing in particular on his art and his childhood in Pittsburgh; there are many reproductions plus a timeline and a glossary. (Rev: BL 11/1/06; SLJ 11/06) [700]

14016 Venezia, Mike. *Andy Warhol* (2–4). Illus. Series: Getting to Know. 1996, Children's Book Pr. LB $28.00 (978-0-516-20053-8). 32pp. An appealing introduction to this pop artist's life and work, with many fine art reproductions. (Rev: BL 12/15/96; HB 5/96) [921]

14017 Warhola, James. *Uncle Andy's: A Faabbbulous Visit with Andy Warhol* (K–3). Illus. 2003, Penguin $16.99 (978-0-399-23869-7). 32pp. A young boy (the author as a child) enjoys visiting his eccentric artist uncle, Andy Warhol, and is inspired by his work. (Rev: BL 2/15/03; HB 3/03; HBG 10/03; SLJ 4/03) [921]

WEST, BENJAMIN

14018 Brenner, Barbara. *The Boy Who Loved to Draw: Benjamin West* (1–3). Illus. by Olivier Dunrea. 1999, Houghton $15.00 (978-0-395-85080-0). 48pp. A portrait of the colonial painter whose talent was so great that his parents sent him to Philadelphia to study with an artist at age 9. (Rev: BL 9/15/99; HB 9/99; HBG 3/00; SLJ 10/99) [921]

WOOD, GRANT

14019 Duggleby, John. *Artist in Overalls: The Life of Grant Wood* (4–8). 1996, Chronicle $15.95 (978-0-8118-1242-9). 48pp. The life of this American artist tells of his difficult struggle with poverty and his great attachment to the Midwest. (Rev: BCCB 6/96; BL 4/15/96; HB 7/96; SLJ 5/96) [921]

WOOD, MICHELE

14020 Igus, Toyomi. *Going Back Home: An Artist Returns to the South* (4–8). Illus. 1996, Children's $16.95 (978-0-89239-137-0). 32pp. The author recreates the family history and life of the African American illustrator Michele Wood. (Rev: BCCB 12/96; BL 9/15/96; SLJ 7/97) [921]

WRIGHT, FRANK LLOYD

14021 Davis, Frances A. *Frank Lloyd Wright: Maverick Architect* (5–9). Illus. 1996, Lerner LB $30.35 (978-0-8225-4953-6). 128pp. A well-documented life of this influential 20th-century architect, with many black-and-white photographs of his most important buildings. (Rev: BL 1/1–15/97; SLJ 1/97) [921]

14022 Mayo, Gretchen Will. *Frank Lloyd Wright* (5–8). Scrics: Trailblazers of the Modern World. 2004, World Almanac LB $31.00 (978-0-8368-5101-4). 48pp. Report writers will find useful information on Wright's life, achievements, and lasting contributions. (Rev: SLJ 7/04) [921]

14023 Middleton, Haydn. *Frank Lloyd Wright* (5–8). Series: Creative Lives. 2001, Heinemann LB $27.07 (978-1-58810-203-4). 64pp. An attractive look at the architect's life and career with illustrations and a useful timeline. (Rev: HBG 10/02; SLJ 3/02) [921]

14024 Thorne-Thomsen, Kathleen. *Frank Lloyd Wright for Kids* (4–6). Illus. 1994, Chicago Review paper $14.95 (978-1-55652-207-9). 144pp. In addition to providing a life of this famous architect, this book contains many projects related to his work and a recipe for his favorite breakfast. (Rev: BL 4/15/94; SLJ 7/94) [921]

ZHANG, ANGE

14025 Zhang, Ange. *Red Land, Yellow River: A Story from the Cultural Revolution* (5–8). 2004, Groundwood $16.95 (978-0-88899-489-9). 56pp. In this compelling autobiography, artist Ange Zhang tells how he came of age during one of the most turbulent periods in modern Chinese history — the Cultural Revolution of the late 1960s. (Rev: BL 12/1/04*; SLJ 12/04) [921]

Composers

BACH, JOHANN SEBASTIAN

14026 Lynch, Wendy. *Bach* (K–3). Series: Lives and Times. 2000, Heinemann LB $19.92 (978-1-57572-214-6). 24pp. A brief account of the highlights of Bach's life illustrated with drawings and photographs. (Rev: SLJ 9/00) [921]

14027 Venezia, Mike. *Johann Sebastian Bach* (2–4). Series: Getting to Know. 1998, Children's Book Pr. LB $27.00 (978-0-516-20760-5). 32pp. A mix of historic prints and clever cartoon drawings help bring this prolific composer to life. (Rev: BL 5/15/98; HBG 10/98) [921]

14028 Winter, Jeanette. *Sebastian: A Book About Bach* (2–4). Illus. 1999, Harcourt $16.00 (978-0-15-200629-7). 40pp. A simple picture book that explores Bach's life, music, and times. (Rev: BCCB 5/99; BL 4/1/99*; HB 7/99; HBG 10/99; SLJ 4/99) [921]

BEETHOVEN, LUDWIG VAN

14029 Balcavage, Dynise. *Ludwig Van Beethoven: Composer* (4–8). Series: Great Achievers: Lives of the Physically Challenged. 1997, Chelsea LB $21.95 (978-0-7910-2082-1). 119pp. This is an information-rich account of the composer's public and private life, with good coverage of his compositions. (Rev: SLJ 7/97) [921]

14030 Venezia, Mike. *Ludwig Van Beethoven* (2–4). Illus. Series: Getting to Know. 1996, Children's Book Pr. LB $27.00 (978-0-516-04542-9). 32pp. An informal portrait of Beethoven and an introduction to his music. (Rev: BL 9/15/96) [921]

14031 Viegas, Jennifer. *Beethoven's World* (5–8). Series: Music Throughout History. 2007, Rosen LB $29.25 (978-1-4042-0724-0). 64pp. Six biographical chapters cover the composer's early life, family, personal life, musical training, compositions, and influences, with photographs of key people and places. (Rev: SLJ 1/08)

BERLIN, IRVING

14032 Furstinger, Nancy. *Say It with Music: The Story of Irving Berlin* (5–9). Illus. Series: Masters of Music. 2003, Morgan Reynolds LB $23.95 (978-1-931798-12-9). 128pp. Well-researched and very readable, this account traces Berlin's life from Russia to the United States and his popular and lasting success as a songwriter. (Rev: BL 6/1–15/03; HBG 4/04; SLJ 10/03) [780.92]

14033 Streissguth, Thomas. *Say It with Music: A Story About Irving Berlin* (3–5). Illus. 1994, Carolrhoda LB $22.60 (978-0-87614-810-5). 64pp. This biography of the great American songwriter concentrates on his first 30 years, from childhood in Russia to success on Broadway. (Rev: BL 5/1/94; SLJ 8/94) [921]

BERLIOZ, HECTOR

14034 Whiting, Jim. *The Life and Times of Hector Berlioz* (5–7). Series: Masters of Music: The World's Greatest Composers. 2004, Mitchell Lane LB $20.95 (978-1-58415-259-0). 48pp. A brief biography of the talented and troubled creator of the *Symphonie fantastique*. (Rev: SLJ 2/05) [921]

BERNSTEIN, LEONARD

14035 Blashfield, Jean F. *Leonard Bernstein: Composer and Conductor* (4–7). Series: Ferguson Career Biographies. 2001, Ferguson LB $25.00 (978-0-89434-337-7). 127pp. Numerous black-and-white photographs accompany the easily read text in this interesting account of Bernstein's life and career. (Rev: SLJ 7/01) [780]

14036 Hurwitz, Johanna. *Leonard Bernstein: A Passion for Music* (4–8). Illus. by Sonia O. Lisker. 1993, Jewish Publication Soc. $14.95 (978-0-8276-0501-5). 80pp. The career of this amazing conductor and composer who was also a gifted pianist and teacher. (Rev: BL 2/15/94; SLJ 12/93) [921]

14037 Venezia, Mike. *Leonard Bernstein* (2–4). Series: Getting to Know. 1997, Children's Book Pr. LB $27.00 (978-0-516-20492-5). 32pp. A brief profile of this great American composer, who also excelled as a conductor and pianist. (Rev: BL 10/15/97; HBG 3/98) [921]

CHOPIN, FREDERIC

14038 Dineen, Jacqueline. *Frederic Chopin* (K–3). Series: Tell Me About. 1998, Carolrhoda LB $19.93 (978-1-57505-248-9). 24pp. A short chapterless book on the life and accomplishments of the Polish pianist and composer who died prematurely of tuberculosis. (Rev: HBG 3/99; SLJ 3/99) [921]

14039 Malaspina, Ann. *Chopin's World* (5–8). Series: Music Throughout History. 2007, Rosen LB $29.25 (978-1-4042-0723-3). 64pp. Six biographical chapters cover the composer's early life, family, personal life, musical training, compositions, and influences, with photographs of key people and places. (Rev: SLJ 1/08)

COLTRANE, JOHN

14040 Weatherford, Carole Boston. *Before John Was a Jazz Giant: A Song of John Coltrane* (K–3). Illus. by Sean Qualls. 2008, Holt $16.95 (978-0-8050-7994-4). 32pp. Coltrane's intense interest in sound and music as a young boy is the focus of this biography. (Rev: BCCB 4/08; BL 2/1/08; HB 5/08; LMC 8/08; SLJ 4/08) [921]

FOSTER, STEPHEN

14041 Pancella, Peggy. *Stephen Foster: The Man Behind Our Best-Loved Songs* (1–3). Series: Lives and Times. 2005, Heinemann LB $24.21 (978-1-4034-6748-5). 32pp. Profiles the composer's life and examines the qualities that made his songs so popular with Americans. (Rev: SLJ 2/06) [921]

GERSHWIN, GEORGE

14042 Mitchell, Barbara. *America, I Hear You: A Story About George Gershwin* (3–5). Illus. 1987, Carolrhoda LB $19.93 (978-0-87614-309-4). 64pp. The life, times, and career of one of America's great musicians. (Rev: BCCB 11/87; BL 10/1/87; SLJ 12/87)

14043 Reef, Catherine. *George Gershwin: American Composer* (5–8). Illus. Series: Masters of Music. 2000, Morgan Reynolds LB $23.95 (978-1-883846-58-9). 112pp. This biography traces the life one of America's great composers, giving insight into his personality, family, and times. (Rev: BL 2/15/00; HBG 10/00; SLJ 3/00) [921]

14044 Venezia, Mike. *George Gershwin* (2–4). Illus. by author. Series: Getting to Know. 1994, Children's Book Pr. LB $27.00 (978-0-516-04536-8). 32pp. A breezy retelling of the life and times of this multitalented American composer of both classical and popular music. (Rev: SLJ 4/95) [921]

14045 Whiting, Jim. *The Life and Times of George Gershwin* (4–6). Series: Masters of Music: The World's Greatest Composers. 2004, Mitchell Lane LB $20.95 (978-1-58415-279-8). 48pp. The challenges that Gershwin faced in both his personal and professional lives are discussed and placed in historical perspective. (Rev: SLJ 5/05) [921]

GUIDO, D'AREZZO

14046 Roth, Susan L. *Do Re Mi: If You Can Read Music, Thank Guido d'Arezzo* (K–5). Illus. by author. 2007, Houghton $17.00 (978-0-618-46572-9). 40pp. This colorful fictionalized biography of Guido d'Arezzo focuses on the 11th-century Italian monk's development of a musical notation system. (Rev: BL 12/1/06; SLJ 2/07) [921]

GUTHRIE, WOODY

14047 Coombs, Karen Mueller. *Woody Guthrie: America's Folksinger* (4–6). Series: Trailblazer Biographies. 2002, Carolrhoda LB $27.93 (978-1-57505-464-3). 120pp. A balanced look at the life of the singer/songwriter who died in 1967. (Rev: HBG 10/02; SLJ 7/02) [921]

HANDEL, GEORGE FRIDERIC

14048 Anderson, M. T. *Handel, Who Knew What He Liked* (3–6). Illus. by Kevin Hawkes. 2001, Candlewick $16.99 (978-0-7636-1046-3). 48pp. Here's an irreverent large-format account of the interesting life of composer Handel, including lively anecdotes and detailed, dramatic illustrations that give a flavor of the time with a dollop of humor. (Rev: BCCB 1/02; BL 12/15/01; HB 11/01*; HBG 3/02; SLJ 12/01*)

14049 Lee, Lavina. *Handel's World* (5–8). Series: Music Throughout History. 2007, Rosen LB $29.25 (978-1-4042-0726-4). 64pp. Six biographical chapters cover the composer's early life, family, personal life, musical training, compositions, and influences, with photographs of key people and places. (Rev: LMC 1/08; SLJ 1/08)

HAYDN, FRANZ JOSEPH

14050 Norton, James R. *Haydn's World* (5–8). Series: Music Throughout History. 2007, Rosen LB $29.25 (978-1-4042-0727-1). 64pp. Six biographical chapters cover the composer's early life, family, personal life, musical training, compositions, and influences, with photographs of key people and places. (Rev: SLJ 1/08)

IVES, CHARLES

14051 Gerstein, Mordicai. *What Charlie Heard* (3–5). Illus. 2002, Farrar $17.00 (978-0-374-38292-6). 40pp. This picture-book biography focuses on the American composer Charles Ives and his childhood influences. (Rev: BCCB 4/02; BL 4/1/02; HB 5/02*; HBG 10/02; SLJ 3/02) [921]

JONES, QUINCY

14052 Kavanaugh, Lee H. *Quincy Jones: Musician, Composer, Producer* (5–8). 1998, Enslow LB $20.95 (978-0-89490-814-9). 128pp. This biography describes Quincy Jones's 50-year career in music and how he overcame poverty, racism, and health problems to become a musical director, composer, producer, arranger, and driving force behind many award-winning recordings. (Rev: VOYA 8/98) [921]

JOPLIN, SCOTT

14053 Bankston, John. *The Life and Times of Scott Joplin* (5–7). Series: Masters of Music: The World's Greatest Composers. 2004, Mitchell Lane LB $20.95 (978-1-58415-270-5). 48pp. Joplin's career as a ragtime piano player and composer is documented, with coverage of his African American heritage. (Rev: SLJ 2/05) [921]

14054 Gillis, Jennifer Blizin. *Scott Joplin: The King of Ragtime* (2–4). Illus. Series: Lives and Times. 2005, Heinemann LB $16.95 (978-1-4034-6789-8). 32pp. Brief, large text and illustrations cover Joplin's childhood, musical career, death, and later popularity. (Rev: BL 11/1/05) [921]

14055 Mitchell, Barbara. *Raggin': A Story About Scott Joplin* (3–5). Illus. 1987, Carolrhoda LB $22.60 (978-0-87614-310-0); paper $6.95 (978-0-87614-589-0). 64pp. The story of a great American musician whose genius was not recognized until after his death. (Rev: BL 10/1/87; SLJ 12/87)

MESSIAEN, OLIVIER

14056 Bryant, Jen. *Music for the End of Time* (4–7). Illus. by Beth Peck. 2005, Eerdmans $17.00 (978-0-8028-5229-8). 32pp. This fictionalized picture-book biography tells how French soldier Olivier Messiaen composed and performed music while in a German prison camp during World War II. (Rev: BL 9/1/05; SLJ 12/05) [921]

MOZART, WOLFGANG AMADEUS

14057 Allman, Barbara. *Musical Genius: A Story About Wolfgang Amadeus Mozart* (3–5). Illus. by Janet Hamlin. Series: Creative Minds Biographies. 2004, Carolrhoda LB $22.60 (978-1-57505-604-3); paper $6.95 (978-1-57505-637-1). 64pp. An accessible introduction to Mozart that starts with his childhood. (Rev: SLJ 8/04) [921]

14058 Ekker, Ernst A. *Wolfgang Amadeus Mozart: A Musical Picture Book* (3–6). Illus. by Doris Eisenburger. 2006, North-South $20.00 (978-0-7358-2056-2). 32pp. A musical CD accompanies this biography that covers the composer's life and career and adds personal details. (Rev: SLJ 5/06) [921]

14059 Lynch, Wendy. *Mozart* (K–3). Series: Lives and Times. 2000, Heinemann LB $19.92 (978-1-57572-219-1). 24pp. After a brief biography of Mozart, there is a section on how young readers can learn more about him. (Rev: SLJ 9/00) [921]

14060 Malam, John. *Wolfgang Amadeus Mozart* (2–4). Series: Tell Me About. 1998, Carolrhoda LB $19.93 (978-1-57505-247-2). 24pp. Illustrations include period paintings of Mozart's family, musical scores, and outdoor scenes of Salzburg and Vienna, in this life of Mozart told simply for young readers. (Rev: HBG 3/99; SLJ 1/99) [921]

14061 Riggs, Kate. *Wolfgang Amadeus Mozart* (4–7). Series: Xtraordinary Artists. 2008, Creative Education LB $32.80 (978-1-58341-664-8). 48pp. Bodden provides an interesting overview of the composer's

life with well-chosen illustrations and excerpts from his own writing. (Rev: LMC 8/09; SLJ 4/09) [921]

14062 Ross, Stewart. *Wolfgang Amadeus Mozart: Musical Genius* (3–5). Series: Famous Lives. 2004, Raintree LB $29.93 (978-0-7398-6627-6). 48pp. A simple, lively, and well-illustrated biography that chronicles Mozart's major works. (Rev: SLJ 1/05) [921]

14063 Sís, Peter. *Play, Mozart, Play!* (K–3). Illus. 2006, Greenwillow $16.99 (978-0-06-112181-4). 32pp. This beautifully illustrated picture-book biography with a simple text focuses on the musical prodigy's childhood. (Rev: BL 3/15/06; SLJ 5/06*) [780.92]

14064 Stanley, Diane. *Mozart: The Wonder Child* (3–5). Illus. by author. 2009, Collins $17.99 (978-0-06-072674-4). 48pp. A puppet play forms the framework for this account of Mozart's often difficult life and early acceptance as an accomplished composer. (Rev: BCCB 2/09; BL 12/15/08; SLJ 2/09) [921]

14065 Weeks, Marcus. *Mozart: The Boy Who Changed the World with His Music* (5–8). Series: World History Biographies. 2007, National Geographic $17.95 (978-1-4263-0002-8). 64pp. An attractive, well-organized life of the young composer, with details of his music lessons and instruments, his first job, and his later financial worries. (Rev: SLJ 6/07) [921]

SAINT-GEORGE, JOSEPH BOLOGNE

14066 Brewster, Hugh. *The Other Mozart: The Life of the Famous Chevalier de Saint-George* (4–6). Illus. by Eric Velasquez. 2006, Abrams $18.95 (978-0-8109-5720-6). 32pp. A captivating picture-book biography of Joseph Bologne Saint-George, a famous 18th-century composer who was the son of a white plantation owner in Guadeloupe and a black slave. (Rev: BL 2/1/07) [921]

SATIE, ERIK

14067 Anderson, M. T. *Strange Mr. Satie* (1–3). Illus. by Petra Mathers. 2003, Penguin $16.99 (978-0-670-03637-0). 32pp. The offbeat life and unusual music of French composer Erik Satie are explored in this engaging picture-book biography. (Rev: BL 11/1/03; HB 9/03; HBG 4/04; SLJ 10/03)

SCHUBERT, FRANZ PETER

14068 Bankston, John. *The Life and Times of Franz Peter Schubert* (4–6). Series: Masters of Music. 2003, Mitchell Lane $29.95 (978-1-58415-177-7). 48pp. Bankston examines the short but prolific life and career of the 19th-century Austrian composer and includes interesting sidebars that add context. (Rev: SLJ 2/04) [921]

SOUSA, JOHN PHILIP

14069 Gillis, Jennifer Blizin. *John Philip Sousa: The King of March Music* (1–3). Series: Lives and Times. 2005, Heinemann LB $24.21 (978-1-4034-

6751-5). 32pp. The youth and adult accomplishments of the composer of marches are covered in this interesting volume. (Rev: SLJ 2/06) [921]

STRAVINSKY, IGOR

14070 Venezia, Mike. *Igor Stravinsky* (2–4). Illus. Series: Getting to Know. 1996, Children's Book Pr. LB $27.00 (978-0-516-20054-5). 32pp. The life of this great 20th-century composer and his work are briefly presented, with many illustrations. (Rev: BCCB 7–8/96; BL 12/15/96) [921]

TCHAIKOVSKY, PETER

14071 Venezia, Mike. *Peter Tchaikovsky* (2–4). Illus. by author. Series: Getting to Know. 1994, Children's Book Pr. LB $27.00 (978-0-516-04537-5). 32pp. An introduction to the life, times, and music of this Russian composer, in a visually pleasing format. (Rev: SLJ 4/95) [921]

VERDI, GIUSEPPE

14072 Whiting, Jim. *The Life and Times of Giuseppe Verdi* (4–6). Series: Masters of Music: The World's Greatest Composers. 2004, Mitchell Lane LB $20.95 (978-1-58415-281-1). 48pp. The challenges that Verdi faced in both his personal and professional lives are discussed and placed in historical perspective. (Rev: SLJ 5/05) [921]

VIVALDI, ANTONIO

14073 Shefelman, Janice. *I, Vivaldi* (2–5). Illus. by Tom Shefelman. 2008, Eerdmans $18.00 (978-0-8028-5318-9). 32pp. A charming, first-person account of Vivaldi's childhood and the tensions between his love of music and his mother's determination that he become a priest. (Rev: HB 1/08; LMC 10/08; SLJ 3/08) [921]

Entertainers

ABDUL, PAULA

14074 Zannos, Susan. *Paula Abdul* (4–8). Series: Real-Life Reader Biographies. 1999, Mitchell Lane LB $15.95 (978-1-883845-74-2). A brief biography of this choreographer and recording artist that recounts her many problems, including a struggle with bulimia and a series of failed marriages. (Rev: BL 6/1–15/99) [921]

AGUILERA, CHRISTINA

14075 Granados, Christine. *Christina Aguilera* (3–4). Series: Real-Life Reader Biographies. 2000, Mitchell Lane LB $15.95 (978-1-58415-044-2). 32pp. The story of the little girl with the big voice who started out as a member of the *New Mickey Mouse Club*. (Rev: BL 11/15/00) [921]

AILEY, ALVIN

14076 Cruz, Barbara C. *Alvin Ailey: Celebrating African-American Culture in Dance* (5–9). Series: African-American Biographies. 2004, Enslow LB $26.60 (978-0-7660-2293-5). 112pp. Ailey's life and contributions to dance are detailed, including a chapter on the classic "Revelations" and information on his contemporaries. (Rev: SLJ 1/05) [921]

ANDERSON, MARIAN

14077 Ferris, Jeri. *What I Had Was Singing: The Story of Marian Anderson* (3–6). Illus. 1994, Carolrhoda LB $27.93 (978-0-87614-818-1); paper $8.95 (978-0-87614-634-7). 96pp. The story of this African American contralto's struggles and triumphs, including her appearances at the Lincoln Memorial in 1939 and the Metropolitan Opera in the 1950s. (Rev: BL 7/94) [921]

14078 Freedman, Russell. *The Voice That Challenged a Nation: Marian Anderson and the Struggle for Equal Rights* (4–8). 2004, Houghton $18.00 (978-0-618-15976-5). 128pp. Beautifully illustrated with period photographs, this picture-book biography of the African American vocalist describes her life and the events leading up to her historic concert at the Lincoln Memorial. Newbery Honor Book, 2005. (Rev: BL 6/1–15/04; HB 5/04; SLJ 7/04) [921]

14079 Livingston, Myra Cohn. *Keep on Singing: A Ballad of Marian Anderson* (K–3). Illus. by Samuel Byrd. 1994, Holiday House LB $15.95 (978-0-8234-1098-9). 32pp. In a narrative poem, the life and career of Marian Anderson is celebrated. (Rev: BL 11/1/94; SLJ 3/95) [921]

14080 McKissack, Patricia C., and Fredrick McKissack. *Marian Anderson: A Great Singer*. Rev. ed. (2–4). Illus. Series: Great African Americans. 2001, Enslow LB $18.60 (978-0-89490-303-8). 32pp. A biography of the great American concert singer, the first African American to sing with the Metropolitan Opera in New York City. (Rev: SLJ 11/91) [921]

14081 Ryan, Pam Muñoz. *When Marian Sang: The True Recital of Marian Anderson* (K–3). Illus. by Brian Selznick. 2002, Scholastic $17.99 (978-0-439-26967-4). 40pp. This large-format picture-book biography presents Anderson's life in glowing words and pictures and interweaves the spirituals that Anderson sang. (Rev: BL 11/15/02; HB 11/02; HBG 3/03; SLJ 11/02*) [782.1]

ARMSTRONG, LOUIS

14082 Kimmel, Eric A. *A Horn for Louis* (2–4). Illus. by James Bernardin. Series: Stepping Stones. 2005, Random $11.95 (978-0-375-83252-9). 96pp. This beginning chapter book tells the story of how jazz musician Louis Armstrong got his first cornet and evokes New Orleans in the early 1900s. (Rev: BL 2/1/06; SLJ 2/06) [921]

14083 McKissack, Patricia C., and Fredrick McKissack. *Louis Armstrong: Jazz Musician*. Rev. ed. (2–4). Illus. Series: Great African Americans. 2001, Enslow LB $18.60 (978-0-89490-307-6). 32pp. A simple biography of this well-loved American musician. (Rev: BL 1/1/92; SLJ 2/92) [921]

14084 Old, Wendie. *Louis Armstrong: King of Jazz* (5–9). Series: African-American Biographies. 1998, Enslow LB $26.60 (978-0-89490-997-9). The life and accomplishments of the legendary jazz trumpeter know as Satchmo who lived from 1900 to 1971. (Rev: BL 11/15/98; SLJ 11/98) [921]

14085 Orgill, Roxane. *If I Only Had a Horn* (PS–3). Illus. by Leonard Jenkins. 1997, Houghton $16.00 (978-0-395-75919-6); paper $6.95 (978-0-618-25076-9). 32pp. A biography of jazz musician Louis Armstrong, with colorful illustrations. (Rev: BL 2/15/03) [921]

ASTAIRE, FRED AND ADELE

14086 Orgill, Roxane. *Footwork: The Story of Fred and Adele Astaire* (3–5). Illus. by Stephane Jorisch. 2007, Candlewick $17.99 (978-0-7636-2121-6). 48pp. This account follows Fred and his older sister Adele as they leave Nebraska at a young age to attend school in New York and go on to become a successful vaudeville act and find success on Broadway. (Rev: BCCB 1/08; BL 11/1/07; LMC 1/08; SLJ 12/07) [793]

BALANCHINE, GEORGE

14087 Kristy, Davida. *George Balanchine: American Ballet Master* (5–9). Illus. Series: Biographies. 1996, Lerner LB $27.93 (978-0-8225-4951-2). 128pp. The story of the Russian émigré choreographer and how he changed the world of American ballet. (Rev: BL 9/1/96; SLJ 8/96) [921]

BALL, LUCILLE

14088 Krohn, Katherine E. *Lucille Ball: Pioneer of Comedy* (4–6). Illus. Series: Achievers. 1992, Lerner LB $18.60 (978-0-8225-0543-3). 64pp. A biography that tries to capture the hilarity that was the "I Love Lucy" show. (Rev: BL 6/15/92; SLJ 7/92) [921]

BANKS, TYRA

14089 Levin, Pam. *Tyra Banks* (5–8). Illus. Series: Black Americans of Achievement. 1999, Chelsea $30.00 (978-0-7910-5195-5); paper $30.00 (978-0-7910-4964-8). 104pp. This is the story of an "ugly duckling" who was awkward and uncoordinated as a child but who later became a supermodel. (Rev: BL 2/15/00; HBG 3/00) [921]

BARNUM, P. T.

14090 Fleming, Alice. *P. T. Barnum: The World's Greatest Showman* (5–8). 1993, Walker LB $15.85 (978-0-8027-8235-9). A look at the circus owner's childhood and various successful entrepreneurial ventures. (Rev: BL 1/15/94; SLJ 12/93; VOYA 2/94) [921]

14091 Fleming, Candace. *The Great and Only Barnum: The Tremendous, Stupendous Life of Show-*

man *P. T. Barnum* (4–8). Illus. by Ray Fenwick. 2009, Random $18.99 (978-0-375-84197-2). 160pp. The story of Barnum's rags-to-success life providing entertainment to the public, with frank discussion of some of his methods and personality defects. (Rev: BL 6/1–15/09; HB 9/09) [921]

14092 Warrick, Karen Clemens. *P. T. Barnum: Genius of the Three-Ring Circus* (5–8). Series: Historical American Biographies. 2001, Enslow LB $26.60 (978-0-7660-1447-3). 112pp. The story of the showman and creator of "The Greatest Show on Earth" who presented such attractions as General Tom Thumb and Jenny Lind. (Rev: BL 4/15/01; HBG 10/01; SLJ 7/01) [921]

BARR, ROSEANNE

14093 Gaines, Ann. *Roseanne: Entertainer* (5–8). Series: Overcoming Adversity. 1999, Chelsea LB $21.95 (978-0-7910-4706-4); paper $8.95 (978-0-7910-4707-1). The story of how this overweight housewife made difficult decisions and many sacrifices to achieve her goal of becoming successful not just in show business, but also in the difficult field of comedy, and later as a TV personality. (Rev: VOYA 8/98) [921]

BARRYMORE, DREW

14094 Zannos, Susan. *Drew Barrymore* (3–4). Series: Real-Life Reader Biographies. 2000, Mitchell Lane LB $15.95 (978-1-58415-035-0). 32pp. The ups and downs in the career and life of the actress who starred in such films as *E. T.* as a child are touched on in this brief biography. (Rev: BL 11/15/00) [921]

BATES, CLAYTON "PEG LEG"

14095 Barasch, Lynne. *Knockin' on Wood: Starring Peg Leg Bates* (2–3). 2004, Lee & Low $16.95 (978-1-58430-170-7). 32pp. In the early 20th century, African American Clayton "Peg Leg" Bates found fame as a dancer despite losing a leg in a childhood accident and despite his race. (Rev: BL 6/1–15/04; SLJ 6/04) [792.7]

BEATLES (MUSICAL GROUP)

14096 Roberts, Jeremy. *The Beatles* (5–8). Series: Biography. 2001, Lerner LB $27.93 (978-0-8225-4998-7). This is the story of the Beatles, from Liverpool to international stardom and eventual separation. (Rev: BL 4/1/02; HBG 10/02) [921]

14097 Venezia, Mike. *The Beatles* (2–4). Illus. Series: Getting to Know. 1997, Children's Book Pr. LB $27.00 (978-0-516-20310-2). 32pp. Color photos, humorous cartoons, and a clever text are used to re-create the fabulous careers of these boys from Liverpool. (Rev: BL 5/15/97) [920]

14098 Woog, Adam. *The Beatles* (4–8). Series: Importance Of. 1997, Lucent LB $28.70 (978-1-56006-088-8). 128pp. Outlines the lives and careers of these four Liverpool natives and their many achievements. (Rev: BL 10/15/97; SLJ 12/97) [921]

BLACK, JACK

14099 Mitchell, Susan K. *Jack Black* (3–6). Series: Today's Superstars. Entertainment. 2008, Gareth Stevens LB $24.00 (978-0-8368-9237-6). 32pp. This brief profile is mostly about Black's professional life with a few personal details, plus Web sites and DVDs for more information. (Rev: SLJ 2/09) [921]

BLACK, SHIRLEY TEMPLE

14100 Bankston, John. *Shirley Temple: Child Star* (4–6). Series: A Blue Banner Biography. 2003, Mitchell Lane LB $25.70 (978-1-58415-172-2). 32pp. This brief biography of Shirley Temple Black focuses primarily on her years as one of America's most popular child stars but also touches on key events in her adult life, including her involvement in Republican politics and her appointment as U.S. ambassador to Ghana. (Rev: SLJ 11/03) [791.43]

BLADES, RUBEN

14101 Cruz, Barbara C. *Ruben Blades: Salsa Singer and Social Activist* (4–9). Series: Hispanic Biographies. 1997, Enslow LB $26.60 (978-0-89490-893-4). The inspiring story of the Panama-born musician and his involvement in social activism and politics. (Rev: HBG 3/98; SLJ 1/98; VOYA 2/98) [921]

14102 Marton, Betty A. *Rubén Blades* (5–9). Series: Hispanics of Achievement. 1992, Chelsea LB $32.00 (978-0-7910-1235-2). The story of the Panamanian salsa singer who is also a poet and activist. (Rev: BL 10/1/92; SLJ 11/92) [921]

BOONE, JOHN WILLIAM

14103 Harrah, Madge. *Blind Boone* (5–8). Illus. 2003, Carolrhoda LB $30.60 (978-1-57505-057-7). 112pp. The son of a runaway slave, Boone became blind as an infant but soon revealed a musical talent and went on to become a composer and concert pianist. (Rev: BL 12/1/03; HBG 3/02; SLJ 10/01) [781.64]

BRANDY (SINGER)

14104 Hayes, Donna. *Brandy* (3–4). Series: Real-Life Reader Biographies. 1999, Mitchell Lane LB $15.95 (978-1-883845-93-3). 32pp. A simple biography of this successful African American singer. (Rev: BL 10/15/99) [921]

14105 Newman, Michael. *Brandy* (5–8). Series: Galaxy of Superstars. 2000, Chelsea $25.00 (978-0-7910-5781-0). 64pp. A biography of the famous singer and star of *Moesha*. (Rev: BL 12/15/00; HBG 10/01) [921]

BROOKS, GARTH

14106 Powell, Phelan. *Garth Brooks: Award-Winning Country Music Star* (4–7). Series: Real-Life Reader Biographies. 1999, Mitchell Lane LB $15.95 (978-1-58415-004-6). 32pp. A biography of the award-winning country music star and how he got there. (Rev: SLJ 1/00)

BULLOCK, SANDRA

14107 Hill, Anne E. *Sandra Bullock* (5–8). Series: People in the News. 2000, Lucent LB $27.45 (978-1-56006-711-5). 96pp. Quotations from Bullock and others expand this biography and explain how and why she has gained prominence as a Hollywood actress. (Rev: BL 9/15/00) [921]

14108 Zannos, Susan. *Sandra Bullock* (3–4). Series: Real-Life Reader Biographies. 2000, Mitchell Lane LB $24.95 (978-1-58415-027-5). 32pp. A simple biography of the movie actress that stresses her hard work and determination. (Rev: BL 11/15/00; SLJ 1/01) [921]

BURKE, CHRIS

14109 Geraghty, Helen M. *Chris Burke* (5–9). Series: Great Achievers: Lives of the Physically Challenged. 1994, Chelsea LB $19.95 (978-0-7910-2081-4). This biography of the star of TV's *Life Goes On* looks at Burke's family life and career success despite Down's syndrome. (Rev: BL 10/15/94) [921]

CARREY, JIM

14110 Wukovits, John. *Jim Carrey* (5–9). Series: People in the News. 1999, Lucent LB $28.70 (978-1-56006-561-6). From his boyhood in Canada to stardom in such movies as *The Truman Show*, this biography reveals Carrey's efforts to become a multidimensional actor. (Rev: BL 8/99; HBG 3/00) [921]

CASALS, PABLO

14111 Garza, Hedda. *Pablo Casals* (5–9). Series: Hispanics of Achievement. 1993, Chelsea LB $21.95 (978-0-7910-1237-6). The story of the legendary Spanish cellist and his exile from his homeland during Franco's regime. (Rev: BL 4/1/93; SLJ 7/93; VOYA 8/93) [921]

CHAPLIN, CHARLIE

14112 Turk, Ruth. *Charlie Chaplin: Genius of the Silent Screen* (5–9). 2000, Lerner LB $30.35 (978-0-8225-4957-4). 112pp. A competent overview of this great movie maker's life from his childhood in England to his exile in Switzerland. (Rev: BL 2/15/00; HBG 10/00; SLJ 4/00) [921]

CHARLES, RAY

14113 Turk, Ruth. *Ray Charles: Soul Man* (5–8). Illus. Series: Newsmakers. 1996, Lerner LB $30.35 (978-0-8225-4928-4). 112pp. A candid biography of the great blind entertainer that includes compelling details about his childhood. (Rev: SLJ 8/96) [921]

CISNEROS, EVELYN

14114 Krohn, Katherine. *Evelyn Cisneros: Prima Ballerina* (1–3). Series: Fact Finders, Biographies, Great Hispanics. 2006, Capstone LB $23.93 (978-0-7368-6416-9). 32pp. Large, easy-to-read print recounts the life of the Mexican American ballerina from childhood until her retirement from the San Francisco Ballet. (Rev: SLJ 1/07) [921]

COSBY, BILL

14115 Haskins, James. *Bill Cosby: America's Most Famous Father* (5–7). Illus. 1988, Walker LB $17.00 (978-0-8027-6786-8). 128pp. The childhood and career of this famous entertainer. (Rev: BL 6/1/88) [921]

CRUZ, CELIA

14116 Chambers, Veronica. *Celia Cruz, Queen of Salsa* (2–4). Illus. by Julie Maren. 2005, Dial $16.99 (978-0-8037-2970-4). 40pp. From her childhood in Cuba to her status as a global superstar, this is the story of the salsa singer, with a discography and glossary of Spanish words. (Rev: BL 5/15/05) [921]

CYRUS, MILEY

14117 Magid, Jennifer. *Miley Cyrus/Hannah Montana* (3–6). Series: Today's Superstars. Entertainment. 2008, Gareth Stevens LB $24.00 (978-0-8368-9236-9). 32pp. Miley Cyrus's biography is mostly about her professional life with a few personal details such as her education and friend issues. (Rev: SLJ 2/09) [921]

DAMON, MATT

14118 Greene, Meg. *Matt Damon* (5–8). Series: Galaxy of Superstars. 2000, Chelsea $25.00 (978-0-7910-5779-7). 64pp. An entertaining biography of the actor who gained star status as the cowriter and lead actor in *Good Will Hunting*. (Rev: BL 12/15/00; HBG 10/01) [921]

DAVIS, MILES

14119 Dell, Pamela. *Miles Davis: Jazz Master* (5–8). Series: Journey to Freedom. 2005, Child's World LB $28.50 (978-1-59296-232-7). 40pp. An easy-to-read biography that deals frankly with the trumpeter's addiction to heroin and his difficult personality. (Rev: SLJ 8/05) [921]

DICAPRIO, LEONARDO

14120 Stauffer, Stacey. *Leonardo DiCaprio* (5–8). Illus. Series: Galaxy of Superstars. 1999, Chelsea $25.00 (978-0-7910-5151-1); paper $25.00 (978-0-7910-5326-3). 63pp. The story of this young actor's life, with special attention to his role in *Titanic*. (Rev: BL 4/15/99; HBG 10/99; SLJ 5/99) [921]

DION, CELINE

14121 Cole, Melanie. *Celine Dion* (3–6). Series: Real-Life Reader Biographies. 1998, Mitchell Lane LB $15.95 (978-1-883845-76-6). 32pp. This overview of the life of singer Celine Dion uses many quotes and sidebar facts. (Rev: SLJ 2/99) [921]

14122 Lutz, Norma Jean. *Celine Dion* (5–8). Series: Galaxy of Superstars. 2000, Chelsea $25.00 (978-0-7910-5777-3). 64pp. The story of the amazing career of this French Canadian singer and how she gained worldwide popularity. (Rev: BL 10/15/00; HBG 10/01) [921]

DOMINGO, PLÁCIDO

14123 Stefoff, Rebecca. *Plácido Domingo* (5–9). Series: Hispanics of Achievement. 1992, Chelsea LB $14.95 (978-0-7910-1563-6). The story of the amazing Spanish-born tenor and his sensational international career, with some information on his private life. (Rev: BL 12/1/92; SLJ 1/93) [921]

DUFF, HILARY

14124 Kjelle, Marylou Morano. *Hilary Duff: Actress and Singer* (2–4). Illus. Series: Robbie Reader. 2004, Mitchell Lane LB $25.70 (978-1-58415-295-8). 32pp. This photo-filled biography traces the life of Hilary Duff and is especially suitable for reluctant readers. [921]

DUNCAN, ISADORA

14125 O'Connor, Barbara. *Barefoot Dancer: The Story of Isadora Duncan* (5–7). Illus. 1994, Carolrhoda LB $27.93 (978-0-87614-807-5). 96pp. The story of this eccentric individualist who influenced and liberated a generation of dancers. (Rev: BCCB 10/94; BL 7/94) [921]

DUNHAM, KATHERINE

14126 O'Connor, Barbara. *Katherine Dunham: Pioneer of Black Dance* (5–8). Illus. 2000, Carolrhoda LB $30.35 (978-1-57505-353-0). 104pp. A fine biography of the African American choreographer who used her study of anthropology to create works for her own dance company and for stage and screen productions. (Rev: BL 5/15/00; HBG 10/00; SLJ 7/00; VOYA 2/01) [921]

EFRON, ZAC

14127 Keedle, Jayne. *Zac Efron* (3–6). Series: Today's Superstars. Entertainment. 2008, Gareth Stevens LB $24.00 (978-0-8368-9239-0). 32pp. This brief profile is mostly about Efron's professional life with a few personal details, plus Web sites and DVDs for more information. (Rev: SLJ 2/09) [921]

ELLINGTON, DUKE

14128 Pinkney, Andrea D. *Duke Ellington: The Piano Prince and His Orchestra* (K–3). Illus. by Brian Pinkney. 1998, Hyperion $15.95 (978-0-

7868-0178-7). The story of the jazz great and his wonderful music, with vivid illustrations. (Rev: BL 2/15/03; HBG 9/98; SLJ 5/98) [781.65]

ESTEFAN, GLORIA

14129 Benson, Michael. *Gloria Estefan* (4–6). Series: A&E Biography. 2000, Lerner LB $27.93 (978-0-8225-4982-6). 112pp. A candid look at a singer who is also a devoted wife and mother, a humanitarian, and an outstanding performer. (Rev: BL 6/1–15/00; HBG 10/00) [921]

14130 Boulais, Sue. *Gloria Estefan* (3–4). Series: Real-Life Reader Biographies. 1998, Mitchell Lane LB $15.95 (978-1-883845-62-9). 32pp. The story of this music star, born in Cuba, and the accident in 1990 that almost ended her career. (Rev: BL 10/15/98; HBG 10/98) [921]

14131 Gonzales, Doreen. *Gloria Estefan: Singer and Entertainer* (5–9). Series: Hispanic Biographies. 1998, Enslow LB $26.60 (978-0-89490-890-3). This story of the singer who started with the Miami Sound Machine and then branched out as a soloist also reveals her devotion to her family and many social causes. (Rev: HBG 3/99; SLJ 10/98; VOYA 10/98) [921]

14132 Rodriguez, Janel. *Gloria Estefan* (4–8). Illus. Series: Contemporary Hispanic Americans. 1995, Raintree LB $24.26 (978-0-8172-3982-4). A fine biography of this Cuban American entertainer who, at the height of her career, overcame severe medical problems and remained a star singer. (Rev: BL 3/15/96; SLJ 1/96) [921]

14133 Shirley, David. *Gloria Estefan* (4–7). Illus. Series: Hispanics of Achievement. 1994, Chelsea LB $15.95 (978-0-7910-2114-9); paper $7.65 (978-0-7910-2117-0). 80pp. A nicely illustrated biography of the Cuban-born rock star. (Rev: BL 11/15/94; SLJ 10/94) [921]

14134 Stefoff, Rebecca. *Gloria Estefan* (5–9). Series: Hispanics of Achievement. 1991, Chelsea LB $21.95 (978-0-7910-1244-4). The story of the singer who broke her back in a 1990 accident but bounced back to success. (Rev: BL 8/91; SLJ 12/91) [782.42164]

14135 Strazzabosco, Jeanne M. *Learning About Determination from the Life of Gloria Estefan* (2–5). Illus. Series: A Character Building Book. 1996, Rosen LB $18.75 (978-0-8239-2416-5). 24pp. The life story of this important entertainer, emphasizing that her success came from the determination to overcome obstacles. (Rev: BL 10/15/96; SLJ 12/96) [921]

FERRERA, AMERICA

14136 Anderson, Sheila. *America Ferrera: Latina Superstar* (5–8). Illus. 2009, Enslow LB $23.93 (978-0-7660-3210-1). 48pp. A celebrity biography of a Latina role model. (Rev: BL 6/1–15/09) [791.4302]

FITZGERALD, ELLA

14137 Pinkney, Andrea D. *Ella Fitzgerald: The Tale of a Vocal Virtuosa* (3–5). Illus. by Brian Pinkney. 2002, Hyperion $16.99 (978-0-7868-0568-6). 32pp. A picture-book biography told by Scat Cat Monroe with a lengthy text about the singer's life and the thrill of witnessing one of her performances. (Rev: BL 4/1/02; HBG 10/02; SLJ 5/02) [921]

FONDA, JANE

14138 Shorto, Russell. *Jane Fonda: Political Activist* (4–6). Series: New Directions. 1991, Houghton paper $5.70 (978-0-395-63564-3). 101pp. Covers Jane Fonda's public and private life, her acting career, and her devotion to a number of causes. (Rev: SLJ 10/91) [921]

GELLAR, SARAH MICHELLE

14139 Powell, Phelan. *Sarah Michelle Gellar* (3–4). Series: Real-Life Reader Biographies. 2000, Mitchell Lane LB $15.95 (978-1-58415-034-3). 32pp. This short biography tells the story of the popular star of *Buffy the Vampire Slayer,* who began acting at age 4. (Rev: BL 11/15/00) [921]

GILLESPIE, DIZZY

14140 Winter, Jonah. *Dizzy* (2–4). Illus. by Sean Qualls. 2006, Scholastic $16.99 (978-0-439-50737-0). 48pp. This compelling account of trumpeter Dizzy Gillespie's life and career is enhanced by vivid, eye-catching illustrations. (Rev: BL 11/1/06*; SLJ 10/06*) [921]

GOLDBERG, WHOOPI

14141 Katz, Sandor. *Whoopi Goldberg: Performer with a Heart* (5–8). Series: Junior Black Americans of Achievement. 1996, Chelsea $18.65 (978-0-7910-2396-9). A look at Whoopi Goldberg's life and career, focusing on how she feels about her profession and the causes she believes in. (Rev: BL 10/15/96; SLJ 1/97) [921]

GOULD, GLENN

14142 Konieczny, Vladimir. *Struggling for Perfection: The Story of Glenn Gould* (3–5). Illus. by Chrissie Wysotski. Series: Stories of Canada. 2004, Napoleon $16.95 (978-0-929141-13-8). 96pp. The Canadian-born pianist's talents and eccentricities are all discussed in this entertaining volume. (Rev: BL 7/04; SLJ 9/04) [786.2]

GRAHAM, MARTHA

14143 Freedman, Russell. *Martha Graham: A Dancer's Life* (4–8). 1998, Clarion $19.00 (978-0-395-74655-4). Martha Graham's amazing talents, driving force, and complex personality are well depicted in this handsomely illustrated biography. (Rev: BCCB 6/98; BL 4/1/98; SLJ 5/98; VOYA 8/98) [921]

GRANT, AMY

14144 Italia, Bob. *Amy Grant: From Gospel to Pop* (4–6). Illus. Series: Leading Lady. 1992, ABDO LB $22.78 (978-1-56239-145-4). 32pp. An engaging biography with high-low interest. (Rev: BL 2/1/93; SLJ 4/93) [921]

HANSON (MUSICAL GROUP)

14145 Powell, Phelan. *Hanson* (5–8). Series: Galaxy of Superstars. 1999, Chelsea $25.00 (978-0-7910-5148-1); paper $25.00 (978-0-7910-5325-6). 63pp. An attractive volume with information on the three-brother singing group that hails from Tulsa, Oklahoma. (Rev: BL 4/15/98; HBG 10/99) [921]

HART, MELISSA JOAN

14146 Gaines, Ann Graham. *Melissa Joan Hart* (3–4). Series: Real-Life Reader Biographies. 2000, Mitchell Lane LB $15.95 (978-1-58415-036-7). 32pp. A simple profile of the TV actress best known for her roles as Clarissa and Sabrina. (Rev: BL 11/15/00) [921]

HENSON, JIM

14147 Durrett, Deanne. *Jim Henson* (2–5). Illus. Series: Inventors and Creators. 2002, Gale LB $23.70 (978-0-7377-0996-4). 48pp. This look at the life of the Muppets creator includes lots of details on the popular characters. (Rev: BL 11/1/02) [791.5]

HEWITT, JENNIFER LOVE

14148 Severs, Vesta-Nadine. *Jennifer Love Hewitt* (3–4). Series: Real-Life Reader Biographies. 2000, Mitchell Lane LB $24.95 (978-1-58415-032-9). 32pp. The story of the popular actress who has been a professional since doing Barbie commercials for Mattel as a preteen. (Rev: BL 11/15/00) [921]

HILL, FAITH

14149 Hinman, Bonnie. *Faith Hill* (5–9). 2001, Chelsea $25.00 (978-0-7910-6471-9). 64pp. A look at the life and career of the country music star, with information on Nashville's Grand Ole Opry. (Rev: HBG 10/02; SLJ 4/02) [921]

HILL, LAURYN

14150 Greene, Meg. *Lauryn Hill* (5–8). Series: Galaxy of Superstars. 1999, Chelsea $25.00 (978-0-7910-5495-6). 64pp. A biography of the music superstar who won five Grammy Awards for her breakout solo album. (Rev: BL 3/15/00; HBG 10/00) [921]

HINES, GREGORY

14151 DeAngelis, Gina. *Gregory Hines* (4–7). Illus. Series: Black Americans of Achievement. 1999, Chelsea $30.00 (978-0-7910-5197-9); paper $9.95 (978-0-7910-5198-6). 99pp. Though he is known primarily as a dancer, this biography of Gregory Hines points out his many other talents, including acting. (Rev: BL 2/15/00; HBG 3/00) [921]

HOLMES, KATIE

14152 Boulais, Sue. *Katie Holmes* (3–4). Series: Real-Life Reader Biographies. 2000, Mitchell Lane LB $15.95 (978-1-58415-038-1). 32pp. A brief biography of the young actress who wisely completed high school before accepting the role in *Dawson's Creek* that made her famous. (Rev: BL 11/15/00) [921]

HOUDINI, HARRY

14153 Adler, David A., and Michael S. Adler. *A Picture Book of Harry Houdini* (K–2). Illus. by Matt Collins. Series: Picture Book Biographies. 2009, Holiday $17.95 (978-0-8234-2059-9). 32pp. Paintings of Houdini's performances enliven information about his life and career choice. (Rev: BL 7/09) [921]

14154 Cox, Clinton. *Houdini: Master of Illusion* (5–9). Illus. 2001, Scholastic paper $16.95 (978-0-590-94960-6). 208pp. A fast-paced account of the life of the world-famous magician from childhood on, with eight pages of photographs and reproductions. (Rev: BL 11/15/01; HB 1/02; HBG 3/02; SLJ 12/01; VOYA 2/02) [793.8]

14155 Fleischman, Sid. *Escape! The Story of the Great Houdini* (4–8). 2006, HarperCollins $18.99 (978-0-06-085694-6). 210pp. A lively and entertaining biography by a great writer and professional magician, who reveals just enough of the magic behind the tricks; includes many photographs. (Rev: SLJ 8/06*; VOYA 6/06) [921]

14156 Lalicki, Tom. *Spellbinder: The Life of Harry Houdini* (5–8). Illus. 2000, Holiday $18.95 (978-0-8234-1499-4). 88pp. A biography of Elrich Weiss, aka Harry Houdini, and his career as a magician and escape artist. (Rev: BCCB 3/01; BL 9/1/00; HBG 3/01; SLJ 9/00; VOYA 12/00) [921]

14157 MacLeod, Elizabeth. *Harry Houdini: A Magical Life* (4–6). Illus. 2005, Kids Can $14.95 (978-1-55337-769-6); paper $6.95 (978-1-55337-770-2). 32pp. This concise biography separates fact from fiction in describing Houdini's life and feats. (Rev: BL 10/15/05; SLJ 4/06) [793.8]

HOUSTON, WHITNEY

14158 Cox, Ted. *Whitney Houston: Singer Actress* (5–8). Illus. Series: Black Americans of Achievement. 1997, Chelsea LB $30.00 (978-0-7910-4455-1); paper $8.95 (978-0-7910-4456-8). A readable biography that shows Whitney Houston growing up in New Jersey, the major influences in her life, her rise to fame, marriage, and philanthropic endeavors. (Rev: BL 8/98; HBG 10/98) [921]

IGLESIAS, ENRIQUE

14159 Granados, Christine. *Enrique Iglesias* (3–4). Series: Real-Life Reader Biographies. 2000, Mitchell Lane LB $15.95 (978-1-58415-045-9). 32pp. A profile of the son of singer Julio Iglesias and how he started out in show business as Enrique Martinez because he wanted to gain recognition based not his father's name but on his own ability. (Rev: BL 11/15/00) [921]

JACKSON, JANET

14160 Dyson, Cindy. *Janet Jackson* (4–7). Series: Black Americans of Achievement. 2000, Chelsea $32.00 (978-0-7910-5283-9). 109pp. The life story of the popular singer and the ups and downs of her career. (Rev: BL 6/1–15/00; HBG 10/00) [921]

JACKSON, MICHAEL

14161 Graves, Karen Marie. *Michael Jackson* (5–8). Series: People in the News. 2001, Lucent LB $35.15 (978-1-56006-707-8). The unusual life of this show business legend is outlined in text and photographs. (Rev: BL 4/1/02) [921]

14162 Nicholson, Lois. *Michael Jackson* (4–8). Illus. Series: Black Americans of Achievement. 1994, Chelsea paper $8.95 (978-0-7910-1930-6). 104pp. A biography of the pop star that examines his loneliness and his family ties, and touches on the allegations against him of sexual abuse. (Rev: BL 10/15/94; SLJ 10/94) [921]

JACKSON, SAMUEL L.

14163 Dils, Tracey E. *Samuel L. Jackson* (4–7). Series: Black Americans of Achievement. 2000, Chelsea $30.00 (978-0-7910-5281-5). 104pp. The life story of the African American actor who has portrayed diverse characters in films including *Pulp Fiction* and *A Time to Kill*. (Rev: BL 6/1–15/00; HBG 10/00) [921]

JAY-Z

14164 Heos, Bridget. *Jay-Z* (5–8). Illus. 2009, Rosen LB $26.50 (978-1-4358-5052-1). 48pp. Hip hop biography; timeline, discography and glossary. (Rev: BL 6/1–15/09) [782]

JONAS BROTHERS

14165 Janic, Susan. *Jonas Brothers Forever: The Unofficial Story of Kevin, Joe and Nick* (5–8). Illus. 2009, ECW paper $14.95 (978-1-55022-851-9). 158pp. A well-designed profile of the popular trio, with plenty of photographs. (Rev: BLO 3/24/09) [782.42166092]

JULIA, RAUL

14166 Perez, Frank, and Ann Well. *Raul Julia* (4–8). Illus. Series: Contemporary Hispanic Americans. 1995, Raintree LB $28.80 (978-0-8172-3984-8). 48pp. The story of the brilliant stage and film actor who gained fame in *The Addams Family* and on *Sesame Street*. This biography was written before his untimely death. (Rev: BL 3/15/96; SLJ 1/96) [921]

KEATON, BUSTER

14167 Brighton, Catherine. *Keep Your Eye on the Kid: The Early Years of Buster Keaton* (3–5). Illus. by author. 2008, Roaring Brook $16.95 (978-1-59643-158-4). 32pp. A first-person account of the comedian's youth, covering his role in his parents' vaudeville act and his introduction to silent films. (Rev: BCCB 5/08; BL 4/15/08; HB 5/08; LMC 5/08; SLJ 4/08) [921]

KELLY, EMMETT, SR.

14168 Wilkerson, J. L. *Sad-Face Clown: Emmett Kelly* (5–8). Illus. Series: The Great Heartlanders. 2004, Acorn paper $9.95 (978-0-9664470-9-5). 118pp. The story of Emmett Kelly, Sr., who — as Weary Willie — became possibly the world's most famous circus clown. (Rev: SLJ 4/04) [791.3]

KISS (ROCK GROUP)

14169 Weintraub, Aileen. *KISS: I Wanna Rock and Roll All Night* (5–8). Illus. Series: Rebels of Rock. 2009, Enslow LB $23.95 (978-0-7660-3027-5). 112pp. An accessible account of the flamboyant rock group's ascent to stardom and subsequent revivals. (Rev: BL 4/1/09) [921]

LATIFAH, QUEEN

14170 Bloom, Sara R. *Queen Latifah* (4–7). Series: Black Americans of Achievement. 2001, Chelsea $30.00 (978-0-7910-6287-6). Numerous photographs add interest to this biography of the amazing singer-actress and her rise to fame. (Rev: BL 4/1/02; HBG 10/02; SLJ 6/02) [921]

14171 Ruth, Amy. *Queen Latifah* (5–8). Series: A&E Biography. 2000, Lerner LB $27.93 (978-0-8225-4988-8). 112pp. The story of the female rap singer who used her positive attitudes, hard work, and determination to get ahead. (Rev: BL 3/1/01; HBG 10/01) [921]

LEE, BRUCE

14172 Mochizuki, Ken. *Be Water, My Friend: The Early Years of Bruce Lee* (2–4). Illus. by Dom Lee. 2006, Lee & Low $16.95 (978-1-58430-265-0). 32pp. This picture-book biography focuses on the actor's childhood in Hong Kong and his early interest in martial arts. (Rev: BL 9/1/06; SLJ 11/06) [921]

14173 Tagliaferro, Linda. *Bruce Lee* (5–10). Series: A&E Biography. 2000, Lerner LB $27.93 (978-0-8225-4948-2); paper $7.95 (978-0-8225-9688-2). 112pp. This colorful biography of the famous action star is filled with information about him, his films, and his family. (Rev: HBG 10/00; SLJ 5/00) [921]

LEE, SPIKE

14174 Shields, Charles J. *Spike Lee* (5–7). Illus. 2002, Chelsea $30.00 (978-0-7910-6715-4). 112pp. This look at Spike Lee's career, working methods, and importance includes both strengths and weaknesses and includes many photographs and quotations. (Rev: BL 11/1/02; HBG 3/03) [791.43]

LENNON, JOHN

14175 Gogerly, Liz. *John Lennon* (4–6). Series: Famous Lives. 2003, Raintree LB $27.12 (978-0-7398-5522-5). 48pp. The story of the legendary member of the Beatles and how he influenced young people to cherish peace and love. (Rev: BL 2/15/03; HBG 10/03) [921]

LIMÓN, JOSÉ

14176 Reich, Susanna. *José! Born to Dance: The Story of José Limón* (2–4). Illus. by Raúl Colón. 2005, Simon & Schuster $16.95 (978-0-689-86576-3). 32pp. This biography of the Mexican-born dancer and choreographer emphasizes how the music and events of his childhood impacted his later career. (Rev: BCCB 9/05; BL 8/05*; HBG 4/06; LMC 1/06; SLJ 10/05) [921]

LOMAX, JOHN AVERY

14177 Hopkinson, Deborah. *Home on the Range: John A. Lomax and His Cowboy Songs* (1–3). Illus. by S. D. Schindler. 2009, Putnam $16.99 (978-0-399-23996-0). 40pp. A picture-book profile of the man who loved cowboy songs and became a musicologist, collecting, documenting, and recording folk songs. (Rev: BCCB 1/09; BL 1/1–15/09; HB 1/09; LMC 5/09; SLJ 1/09) [921]

LOPEZ, JENNIFER

14178 Hill, Anne E. *Jennifer Lopez* (5–8). Series: Galaxy of Superstars. 2000, Chelsea $25.00 (978-0-7910-5775-9). 64pp. This book chronicles the career of the young Latina star who is a fine singer and actress. (Rev: BL 10/15/00; HBG 10/01) [921]

14179 Menard, Valerie. *Jennifer Lopez* (3–4). Series: Real-Life Reader Biographies. 2000, Mitchell Lane LB $15.95 (978-1-58415-025-1). 32pp. This popular singer-actress got her big break when she played another young singer, Selena. (Rev: BL 11/15/00) [921]

LUCAS, GEORGE

14180 Rau, Dana Meachen, and Christopher Rau. *George Lucas: Creator of Star Wars* (5–8). Series: Book Report Biographies. 1999, Watts LB $22.00 (978-0-531-11457-5). 112pp. An entertaining look at the popular filmmaker's life and accomplishments, illustrated with black-and-white photographs. (Rev: HBG 10/99; SLJ 7/99) [921]

14181 Shields, Charles J. *George Lucas* (5–7). Illus. Series: Behind the Camera. 2002, Chelsea $30.00 (978-0-7910-6712-3). 112pp. A profile of the famous filmmaker, with information on his strengths and weaknesses, his working methods, and his importance to the American film industry, backed up by many photographs and quotations. (Rev: BL 11/1/02; HBG 3/03) [791.43]

14182 White, Dana. *George Lucas* (5–8). Series: A&E Biography. 1999, Lerner LB $27.93 (978-0-8225-4975-8); paper $7.95 (978-0-8225-9684-4). 128pp. This book covers the childhood and early career of this filmmaker but concentrates on his masterpiece, the creation of the *Star Wars* saga. (Rev: HBG 3/00; SLJ 3/00) [921]

MCGREGOR, EWAN

14183 Jones, Veda Boyd. *Ewan McGregor* (5–8). Series: Galaxy of Superstars. 1999, Chelsea $25.00 (978-0-7910-5501-4). 64pp. A well-illustrated biography of the Scottish-born actor in the *Star Wars* prequels. (Rev: BL 3/15/00; HBG 10/00) [921]

MARLEY, BOB

14184 Medina, Tony. *I and I: Bob Marley* (4–8). Illus. by Jesse Joshua Watson. 2009, Lee & Low $19.95 (978-1-60060-257-3). 48pp. A picture book biography done in verse profiles the musician who put reggae into the spotlight. (Rev: BL 6/1–15/09; SLJ 6/09) [782]

MARSALIS, WYNTON

14185 Ellis, Veronica F. *Wynton Marsalis* (4–6). Illus. Series: Contemporary African Americans. 1997, Raintree LB $24.26 (978-0-8172-3998-5). 48pp. A fine biography of this Grammy award–winning musician who is equally at home with jazz and classical music. (Rev: BL 5/15/97; SLJ 2/98) [921]

MARTIN, RICKY

14186 Menard, Valerie. *Ricky Martin* (3–4). Series: Real-Life Reader Biographies. 1999, Mitchell Lane LB $15.95 (978-1-58415-059-6). 32pp. Black-and-white photos illustrate this easily read biography of the Puerto Rican singing sensation. (Rev: BL 11/15/99) [921]

MILANO, ALYSSA

14187 Bankston, John. *Alyssa Milano* (3–4). Series: Real-Life Reader Biographies. 2000, Mitchell Lane LB $15.95 (978-1-58415-040-4). 32pp. The life story of the young actress who grew up on TV's *Who's the Boss* and went on to star in *Charmed*. (Rev: BL 11/15/00) [921]

MILLER, NORMA

14188 Govenar, Alan, ed. *Stompin' at the Savoy: The Story of Norma Miller* (5–8). Illus. by Martin French. 2006, Candlewick $16.99 (978-0-7636-2244-2). 56pp. The energy of Norma Miller, who was still going strong in her early 80s, infuses the pages of this brief biography, made up largely of excerpts from interviews with the legendary African American swing dancer. (Rev: BL 2/1/06; SLJ 3/06) [792.8]

MONK, THELONIOUS

14189 Raschka, Chris. *Mysterious Thelonious* (3–7). Illus. 1997, Orchard LB $14.99 (978-0-531-33057-9). 32pp. In a lively mixture of color and motion, this book presents an unusual handling of an unusual subject, a tribute to jazz musician Thelonious Monk. (Rev: BL 11/1/97; HBG 3/98; SLJ 9/97*) [921]

MORENO, RITA

14190 Suntree, Susan. *Rita Moreno* (5–9). Series: Hispanics of Achievement. 1992, Chelsea LB $21.95 (978-0-7910-1247-5). A biography of the Puerto Rican entertainer and her successes on stage and screen. (Rev: BL 2/1/93) [921]

NEW KIDS ON THE BLOCK (MUSICAL GROUP)

14191 McGibbon, Robin. *New Kids on the Block: The Whole Story* (5–8). Illus. 1990, Avon paper $6.95 (978-0-380-76344-3). 120pp. Stories about members of this band have been collected from a variety of sources, including the members themselves. (Rev: BL 10/1/90) [921]

NORRIS, CHUCK

14192 Cole, Melanie. *Chuck Norris* (3–6). Series: Real-Life Reader Biographies. 1998, Mitchell Lane LB $15.95 (978-1-883845-91-9). 32pp. This action star of movies and television is a martial arts guru and claims Native American ancestry. (Rev: SLJ 2/99) [921]

NUREYEV, RUDOLF

14193 Maybarduk, Linda. *The Dancer Who Flew: A Memoir of Rudolf Nureyev* (5–9). Illus. 1999, Tundra $18.95 (978-0-88776-415-8). 188pp. The author, a friend and colleague of Nureyev, not only gives a straightforward biography of the dancer but also tells many backstage stories and introduces his most important roles. (Rev: BL 1/1–15/00; HBG 3/00; SLJ 2/00; VOYA 4/00) [921]

OAKLEY, ANNIE

14194 Dadey, Debbie. *Shooting Star: Annie Oakley, the Legend* (K–3). Illus. by Scott Goto. 1997, Walker LB $16.85 (978-0-8027-8485-8). 32pp. Fact and fiction mingle in this tall tale about the famous Western sharp shooter. (Rev: BCCB 6/97; BL 3/15/97; HB 5/97; SLJ 4/97*) [921]

14195 Feinstein, Stephen. *Read About Annie Oakley* (2–4). Series: I Like Biographies. 2006, Enslow $21.26 (978-0-7660-2583-7). 24pp. The fascinating life of the sharpshooter is told in simple text and photographs and illustrations. (Rev: BL 7/06; SLJ 4/06) [799.3]

14196 Flynn, Jean. *Annie Oakley: Legendary Sharpshooter* (4–9). Series: Historical American Biographies. 1998, Enslow LB $26.60 (978-0-7660-1012-3). Using a concise text, fact boxes, and a chronology, this is the story of the star attraction of Buffalo Bill's Wild West Show. (Rev: BL 8/98; SLJ 8/98) [921]

14197 Krensky, Stephen. *Shooting for the Moon: The Amazing Life and Times of Annie Oakley* (1–4). Illus. by Bernie Fuchs. 2001, Farrar $17.00 (978-0-374-36843-2). 32pp. A combination of simple, concise text and skillful oil paintings convey the life of Annie Oakley, from her childhood to her fame for her shooting skills. (Rev: BL 9/15/01; HBG 3/02; SLJ 9/01) [799.3]

14198 Landau, Elaine. *Annie Oakley: Wild West Sharpshooter* (3–6). Series: Best of the West Biographies. 2004, Enslow LB $23.93 (978-0-7660-2205-8). 48pp. Period photographs add to this engaging account of Oakley's personal and professional life that will appeal to reluctant readers. (Rev: SLJ 8/04) [921]

14199 Macy, Sue. *Bull's-Eye: A Photobiography of Annie Oakley* (5–8). Illus. 2001, National Geographic $17.95 (978-0-7922-7008-9). 64pp. This book separates fact from fiction in the life of Phoebe Ann Moses Butler, who came to be known as Annie Oakley. (Rev: BL 11/15/01; HBG 3/02; SLJ 10/01; VOYA 4/02) [799.3]

14200 Whiting, Jim. *Annie Oakley* (2–4). Series: A Robbie Reader: What's So Great About? 2006, Mitchell Lane LB $25.70 (978-1-58415-477-8). 32pp. With large text and lots of white space, this introductory biography chronicles the life of the female sharpshooter who became a star attraction with Buffalo Bill's Wild West show. (Rev: SLJ 1/07) [921]

14201 Wukovits, John. *Annie Oakley* (4–8). Series: Legends of the West. 1997, Chelsea LB $18.65 (978-0-7910-3906-9). A profile of the famous sharpshooter and her career with Buffalo Bill's Wide West Show. (Rev: SLJ 10/97) [921]

O'DONNELL, ROSIE

14202 Granados, Christine. *Rosie O'Donnell* (3–4). Series: Real-Life Reader Biographies. 1999, Mitchell Lane LB $15.95 (978-1-883845-98-8). 32pp. The story of the comedienne, actress, and talk-show host who has used her success to give to others. (Rev: BL 10/15/99) [921]

14203 Kallen, Stuart A. *Rosie O'Donnell* (4–8). Series: People in the News. 1999, Lucent LB $27.45 (978-1-56006-546-3). An interesting, well-researched biography of this popular actress, comedienne, and talk-show host, covering her personal and professional life. (Rev: BL 8/99; HBG 3/00) [921]

14204 Krohn, Katherine E. *Rosie O'Donnell* (4–8). Series: A&E Biography. 1998, Lerner LB $27.93 (978-0-8225-4939-0). A breezy look at O'Donnell's rise from stand-up comic to TV fame with glimpses into her personal life, her mother's death when she was a child, and her fulfilling adoption of two children. (Rev: HBG 3/99; SLJ 2/99) [921]

14205 Stone, Tanya L. *Rosie O'Donnell: America's Favorite Grown-Up Kid* (4–7). Illus. 2000, Millbrook LB $23.90 (978-0-7613-1724-1). 48pp. A well-designed, chatty biography of the popular talk-show host and comedienne. (Rev: BL 12/15/00; HBG 3/01) [792.7]

OLMOS, EDWARD JAMES

14206 Carrillo, Louis. *Edward James Olmos* (4–8). Illus. Series: Contemporary Hispanic Americans. 1997, Raintree LB $17.98 (978-0-8172-3989-3). 48pp. Along with a timeline and glossary, this account traces the life of this contemporary human rights activist and actor. (Rev: BL 4/15/97) [921]

OZAWA, SEIJI

14207 Tan, Sheri. *Seiji Ozawa* (5–7). Illus. Series: Contemporary Asian Americans. 1997, Raintree LB $17.98 (978-0-8172-3993-0). 48pp. A profile of the Asian American musician who has been the chief conductor of the Boston Symphony for more than 20 years. (Rev: BL 5/1/97; SLJ 9/97) [921]

PAUL, LES

14208 Wyckoff, Edwin Brit. *Electric Guitar Man: The Genius of Les Paul* (3–6). Illus. Series: Genius at Work! Great Inventor Biographies. 2008, Enslow LB $16.95 (978-0-7660-2847-0). 32pp. A lively account of the life and work of the musician who invented an early electric guitar and electronic recording devices. (Rev: BL 9/15/08) [921]

PAVLOVA, ANNA

14209 Allman, Barbara. *Dance of the Swan: A Story About Anna Pavlova* (3–6). Illus. by Shelly O. Haas. Series: Creative Minds Biographies. 2001, Carolrhoda LB $21.27 (978-1-57505-463-6). 64pp. Allman presents Pavlova's life from childhood and discusses her love of nature and of children as well as her commitment to ballet. (Rev: HBG 10/01; SLJ 7/01) [792.8]

PRESLEY, ELVIS

14210 Krohn, Katherine E. *Elvis Presley: The King* (5–7). Illus. 1994, Lerner LB $18.60 (978-0-8225-2877-7). 64pp. A somewhat sanitized biography of Elvis Presley that highlights important events in his career. (Rev: BL 7/94; SLJ 7/94) [921]

PRINZE, FREDDIE, JR.

14211 Wilson, Wayne. *Freddie Prinze, Jr.* (3–4). Series: Real-Life Reader Biographies. 2000, Mitchell Lane LB $15.95 (978-1-58415-063-3). 32pp. The story of the talented performer and actor whose famous father died before he could get to know him. (Rev: BL 11/15/00) [921]

PUENTE, TITO

14212 Olmstead, Mary. *Tito Puente* (4–7). Illus. Series: Hispanic-American Biographies. 2004, Raintree LB $32.86 (978-1-4109-0713-4). 64pp. A concise account of the life and career of Tito Puente, the popular American bandleader and percussionist who in the 1950s was nicknamed the Mambo King. (Rev: BL 2/1/05; SLJ 8/05) [784.4]

QUINN, ANTHONY

14213 Amdur, Melissa. *Anthony Quinn* (5–9). Series: Hispanics of Achievement. 1993, Chelsea LB $19.95 (978-0-7910-1251-2). The life of this Mexican American actor is told with many interesting asides concerning his career and black-and-white stills from his movies. (Rev: BL 9/15/93) [921]

REESE, DELLA

14214 Dean, Tanya. *Della Reese* (4–7). Series: Black Americans of Achievement. 2001, Chelsea $30.00 (978-0-7910-6291-3). The life and career of this show business giant are outlined with special coverage on her recent successes in television. (Rev: BL 4/1/02) [921]

REEVE, CHRISTOPHER

14215 Apte, Sunita. *Christopher Reeve: Don't Lose Hope!* (3–4). Series: Defining Moments. 2005, Bearport LB $25.27 (978-1-59716-074-2). 32pp. This easy-to-read biography looks at Reeve's childhood as well as his achievements and the challenges he faced. (Rev: SLJ 1/06) [921]

RIMES, LEANN

14216 Zymet, Cathy Alter. *LeAnn Rimes* (5–8). Series: Galaxy of Superstars. 1999, Chelsea $25.00 (978-0-7910-5152-8); paper $25.00 (978-0-7910-5327-0). 63pp. This book covers the rise to stardom and the career of this country-western singer who hails from Jackson, Mississippi. (Rev: BL 4/15/98; HBG 10/99) [921]

ROBERTS, JULIA

14217 Wilson, Wayne. *Julia Roberts* (3–4). Series: Real-Life Reader Biographies. 2000, Mitchell Lane LB $15.95 (978-1-58415-028-2). 32pp. A simple biography with plenty of pictures of the actress whose career took off after her performance in *Pretty Woman*. (Rev: BL 11/15/00; SLJ 1/01) [921]

ROBESON, PAUL

14218 Greenfield, Eloise. *Paul Robeson*. Rev. ed. (2–5). Illus. by George Ford. 2009, Lee & Low $18.95 (978-1-60060-256-6); paper $9.95 (978-1-60060-262-7). 40pp. This updated biography chronicles the civil rights work of the activist, actor, and singer during the McCarthy era. (Rev: SLJ 6/09) [921]

14219 McKissack, Patricia C., and Fredrick McKissack. *Paul Robeson: A Voice to Remember.* Rev. ed. (2–5). Series: Great African Americans. 2001, Enslow LB $18.60 (978-0-7660-1674-3). 32pp. Presents Robeson's personal and professional life and the hardships he faced because of his race and beliefs. (Rev: HBG 10/01; SLJ 8/01) [921]

14220 Wright, David K. *Paul Robeson: Actor, Singer, Political Activist* (5–9). Illus. Series: African-American Biographies. 1998, Enslow LB $26.60 (978-0-89490-944-3). 128pp. This book details Robeson's personal and professional life and the hardships he faced because of his race and beliefs. (Rev: BL 11/15/98; SLJ 11/98) [921]

ROBINSON, BILL "BOJANGLES"

14221 Dillon, Leo, and Diane Dillon. *Rap a Tap Tap: Here's Bojangles — Think of That!* (PS–2). Illus. 2002, Scholastic $16.99 (978-0-590-47883-0). 32pp. A brilliantly illustrated picture book about legendary tap artist Bill "Bojangles" Robinson. (Rev: BL 10/15/02; HBG 3/03; SLJ 9/02) [792.7]

ROCK, CHRIS

14222 Blue, Rose, and Corinne J. Naden. *Chris Rock* (4–7). Series: Black Americans of Achievement. 2000, Chelsea $30.00 (978-0-7910-5277-8). 104pp. The story of the comedian and actor who began his career on *Saturday Night Live* and is noted for his acerbic wit. (Rev: BL 6/1–15/00; HBG 10/00) [921]

14223 Gorman, Jacqueline Laks. *Chris Rock* (3–6). Series: Today's Superstars. Entertainment. 2008, Gareth Stevens LB $24.00 (978-0-8368-9235-2). 32pp. This brief profile is mostly about Chris Rock's professional life with a few personal details, plus Web sites and DVDs for more information. (Rev: SLJ 2/09) [921]

RODRIGUEZ, ROBERT

14224 Marvis, Barbara. *Robert Rodriguez* (5–10). Series: A Real-Life Reader Biography. 1997, Mitchell Lane LB $15.95 (978-1-883845-48-3). This simple, attractive biography of the successful movie maker focuses on his problems growing up in a large family and clinging to his career dreams. (Rev: BL 6/1–15/98; HBG 3/98; SLJ 2/98) [921]

ROGERS, WILL

14225 Bennett, Cathereen L. *Will Rogers: Quotable Cowboy* (4–6). Illus. 1995, Lerner LB $19.95 (978-0-8225-3155-5). 96pp. The exciting life of Will Rogers — noted actor, writer, humorist, and humanitarian. (Rev: BL 3/1/96; SLJ 12/95) [921]

14226 Dadey, Debbie. *Will Rogers: Larger than Life* (K–3). Illus. by Scott Goto. 1999, Walker LB $16.85 (978-0-8027-8682-1). 32pp. A picture-book introduction to the laconic, humble entertainer who displayed a unique sense of humor. (Rev: BL 4/1/99; HBG 10/99; SLJ 9/99)

14227 Donovan, Sandy. *Will Rogers: Cowboy, Comedian, and Commentator* (4–8). Series: Signature

Lives. 2007, Compass Point LB $31.93 (978-0-7565-2542-9). 112pp. This detailed biography of Will Rogers will be useful for report writers. (Rev: SLJ 6/07) [921]

14228 Keating, Frank. *Will Rogers* (K–3). Illus. by Mike Wimmer. 2002, Harcourt $17.00 (978-0-15-202405-5). 32pp. A beautifully illustrated profile of the humorist and newspaper columnist who lived from 1879 to 1935, written by Oklahoma governor Frank Keating. (Rev: BL 9/15/02; HBG 3/03; SLJ 11/02) [792.7]

RONSTADT, LINDA

14229 Amdur, Melissa. *Linda Ronstadt* (5–9). Series: Hispanics of Achievement. 1993, Chelsea LB $14.95 (978-0-7910-1781-4). This biography of the popular Mexican American singer describes her roots and pride in her Hispanic heritage. (Rev: BL 9/15/93; SLJ 10/93) [921]

RUSSELL, KERI

14230 Hasday, Judy. *Keri Russell* (3–4). Series: Real-Life Reader Biographies. 2000, Mitchell Lane LB $15.95 (978-1-58415-033-6). 32pp. An easily read biography of the young actress who plays Felicity. (Rev: BL 11/15/00) [921]

RYDER, WINONA

14231 Menard, Valerie. *Winona Ryder* (3–4). Series: Real-Life Reader Biographies. 2000, Mitchell Lane LB $15.95 (978-1-58415-039-8). 32pp. A simple biography of the talented actress who appeared in 23 movies before her 30th birthday. (Rev: BL 11/15/00) [921]

SANDLER, ADAM

14232 Seldman, David. *Adam Sandler* (5–8). Series: Galaxy of Superstars. 2000, Chelsea $25.00 (978-0-7910-5773-5). 64pp. An entertaining biography of the actor and comedian who gained notoriety from his roles in *The Waterboy* and *Big Daddy*. (Rev: BL 12/15/00; HBG 10/01) [921]

SARALEGUI, CRISTINA

14233 Menard, Valerie. *Cristina Saralegui* (3–4). Illus. Series: Real-Life Reader Biographies. 1998, Mitchell Lane LB $15.95 (978-1-883845-60-5). 32pp. A Cuban refugee, Cristina is an Emmy Award-winning talk show host who is known as the Spanish-language Oprah Winfrey. (Rev: BL 10/15/98; HBG 10/98) [921]

SCHUMANN, CLARA

14234 Allman, Barbara. *Her Piano Sang: A Story About Clara Schumann* (4–7). Illus. 1996, Carolrhoda LB $25.55 (978-1-57505-012-6). 64pp. The story of this groundbreaking composer and pianist who also championed her husband's music. (Rev: BL 1/1–15/97; SLJ 1/97) [921]

14235 Reich, Susanna. *Clara Schumann: Piano Virtuoso* (5–8). 1999, Houghton $18.00 (978-0-395-89119-3). 128pp. A thorough, well-researched biography of this amazing pianist and composer that describes her life as a child prodigy, her marriage to Robert Schumann, and her life promoting his music after his death. (Rev: BL 8/99; HB 3/99; HBG 10/99; SLJ 4/99*; VOYA 4/00) [921]

SELENA (SINGER)

14236 Marvis, Barbara. *Selena* (5–10). Series: A Real-Life Reader Biography. 1997, Mitchell Lane LB $15.95 (978-1-883845-47-6). A simple, attractive biography of the singer, her supportive family, and her tragic death. (Rev: BL 6/1–15/98; HBG 3/98; SLJ 2/98) [921]

14237 Romero, Maritza. *Selena Perez: Queen of Tejano Music* (2–3). Series: Great Hispanics of Our Time. 1998, Rosen LB $18.75 (978-0-8239-5086-7). 24pp. Double-page spreads are used to tell the story of this popular Tejano singer and her tragic, premature death. (Rev: SLJ 9/98) [921]

SIEGEL, SIENA CHERSON

14238 Siegel, Siena Cherson. *To Dance: A Ballerina's Graphic Novel* (5–8). Illus. by Mark Siegel. 2006, Simon & Schuster $17.95 (978-0-689-86747-7). 64pp. In graphic novel format, Siegel tells the story of her dance career, from her introduction to ballet at the age of 6 to her stage debut with the New York City Ballet. Sibert Honor Book, 2007. (Rev: BCCB 1/07; BL 9/1/06; LMC 1/07; SLJ 11/06*; VOYA 4/07) [921]

SILVERSTONE, ALICIA

14239 Powell, Phelan. *Alicia Silverstone* (3–4). Series: Real-Life Reader Biographies. 2000, Mitchell Lane LB $15.95 (978-1-58415-037-4). 32pp. The life story of this popular young actress who began modeling at age 6 and had been in several movies by the time she turned 20. (Rev: BL 11/15/00) [921]

SMITH, BESSIE

14240 Manera, Alexandria. *Bessie Smith* (2–5). Series: African-American Biographies. 2003, Raintree LB $28.56 (978-0-7398-6875-1). 64pp. A simple profile of the singer, with interesting sidebars and good archival photographs that convey a sense of the time in which she lived. (Rev: HBG 4/04; SLJ 11/03) [921]

SMITS, JIMMY

14241 Cole, Melanie. *Jimmy Smits* (3–4). Illus. Series: Real-Life Reader Biographies. 1998, Mitchell Lane LB $24.95 (978-1-883845-59-9). 32pp. The story of the Latin American actor from New York who starred in such TV shows as *L.A. Law* and *NYPD Blue*. (Rev: BL 10/15/98; HBG 10/98) [921]

SPEARS, BRITNEY

14242 Gaines, Ann Graham. *Britney Spears* (3–4). Series: Real-Life Reader Biographies. 1999, Mitchell Lane LB $15.95 (978-1-58415-060-2). 32pp. This is a simple biography of the singer who is a former Mouseketeer and who once shared the stage with 'N Sync. (Rev: BL 11/15/99) [921]

14243 Lutz, Norma Jean. *Britney Spears* (5–8). Series: Galaxy of Superstars. 1999, Chelsea $25.00 (978-0-7910-5499-4). 64pp. A profile of the popular entertainer, telling how her childhood influenced her career path. (Rev: BL 3/15/00; HBG 10/00) [921]

SPICE GIRLS (MUSICAL GROUP)

14244 Shore, Nancy. *Spice Girls* (5–8). Series: Galaxy of Superstars. 1999, Chelsea $25.00 (978-0-7910-5149-8); paper $25.00 (978-0-7910-5328-7). 63pp. Biographies of members of the popular singing group that took first Britain and then the world by storm. (Rev: BL 4/15/98; HBG 10/99; SLJ 5/99) [921]

SPIELBERG, STEVEN

14245 Edge, Laura B. *Steven Spielberg: Director of Blockbuster Films* (5–8). Illus. Series: People to Know Today. 2008, Enslow LB $23.95 (978-0-7660-2888-3). 128pp. With many photographs and lists of print and Web resources, this profile provides up-to-date information on the filmmaker's career, personal life, work ethic, and storytelling skills. (Rev: BL 6/1–15/08) [921]

14246 Schoell, William. *Magic Man: The Life and Films of Steven Spielberg* (4–7). Illus. 1998, Tudor $18.95 (978-0-936389-57-8). 128pp. This biography of Spielberg concentrates on how he produces the astonishing special effects for his movies. (Rev: BL 5/15/98; SLJ 2/99) [921]

SUPREMES (MUSICAL GROUP)

14247 Rivera, Ursula. *The Supremes* (4–8). Illus. Series: Rock and Roll Hall of Famers. 2002, Rosen LB $29.25 (978-0-8239-3527-7). 112pp. The Supremes' rise to stardom — and eventual fall from fame without leader Diana Ross — is chronicled here with photographs, glossary, discography, and bibliography. (Rev: BL 10/1/02; SLJ 5/02) [782.421644]

TALLCHIEF, MARIA

14248 Tallchief, Maria, and Rosemary Wells. *Tallchief: America's Prima Ballerina* (3–5). 1999, Viking $16.99 (978-0-670-88756-9). 32pp. An autobiography of New York City Ballet's former star who began taking dance lessons while growing up on an Osage Indian reservation in Oklahoma. (Rev: BL 11/1/99*; HBG 3/00; SLJ 11/99) [921]

TATUM, ART

14249 Parker, Robert Andrew. *Piano Starts Here: The Young Art Tatum* (2–4). Illus. by author. 2008,

Random $16.99 (978-0-375-83965-8). 32pp. Tatum's youth is well covered in this profile of the jazz pianist who was nearly blind. (Rev: BL 2/1/08; SLJ 2/08) [921]

TWAIN, SHANIA

14250 Gallagher, Jim. *Shania Twain: Grammy Award-Winning Singer* (4–7). Series: Real-Life Reader Biographies. 1999, Mitchell Lane LB $15.95 (978-1-58415-000-8). 32pp. The story of the entertainer who was adopted into the Ojibwa tribe, began singing in bars at age eight, and went on to marry producer Mutt Lange. (Rev: SLJ 1/00) [921]

TYLER, LIV

14251 Boulais, Sue. *Liv Tyler* (3–4). Series: Real-Life Reader Biographies. 2000, Mitchell Lane LB $15.95 (978-1-58415-041-1). 32pp. This is the story of the talented model and actress who didn't learn until her teens that her father was Aerosmith's Steven Tyler. (Rev: BL 11/15/00) [921]

VON TRAPP, MARIA

14252 Ransom, Candice F. *Maria von Trapp: Beyond the Sound of Music* (4–6). Illus. Series: Trailblazer Biographies. 2002, Carolrhoda LB $25.26 (978-1-57505-444-5). 112pp. A portrait of Maria von Trapp, based on her own writings, that describes her life in war-torn Austria and move to a ski lodge in Vermont. (Rev: BL 3/1/02; HBG 10/02; SLJ 5/02) [782.42]

WASHINGTON, DENZEL

14253 Simmons, Alex. *Denzel Washington* (4–6). Illus. Series: Contemporary African Americans. 1997, Raintree LB $24.26 (978-0-8172-3986-2). 48pp. In this biography of actor Denzel Washington, he claims that his mother and the Boys Club saved him from a life of crime. (Rev: BL 5/15/97; SLJ 2/98) [921]

WHITE, DIANA

14254 White, Diana. *Ballerina Dreams* (1–3). Illus. by Jacqueline Rogers. Series: Hello Reader! 1998, Scholastic paper $3.99 (978-0-590-37233-6). This easy chapter book is the autobiography of a ballerina with the New York City Ballet that contains a description of how she overcame many problems to achieve her goals. (Rev: SLJ 3/99) [921]

WILLIAMS, ROBIN

14255 Zannos, Susan. *Robin Williams* (3–4). Series: Real-Life Reader Biographies. 2000, Mitchell Lane LB $15.95 (978-1-58415-029-9). 32pp. From playing Mork the alien on TV to winning an Oscar for his film work, this is a brief biography of the famous comedian and actor. (Rev: BL 11/15/00) [921]

WILLIAMS, VANESSA

14256 Boulais, Sue. *Vanessa Williams* (4–8). Series: Real-Life Reader Biographies. 1999, Mitchell Lane LB $15.95 (978-1-883845-75-9). The life story of the African American who lost her title of Miss America in 1983 but rebounded with a brilliant career in show business. (Rev: BL 6/1–15/99) [921]

WINFREY, OPRAH

14257 Feinstein, Stephen. *Oprah Winfrey* (1–4). Series: African-American Heroes. 2007, Enslow LB $21.26 (978-0-7660-2764-0). 24pp. A basic and straightforward look at the life of the very successful talk-show host, with photographs. (Rev: SLJ 8/07)

14258 Krohn, Katherine. *Oprah Winfrey* (5–8). Series: Biography. 2001, Lerner LB $27.93 (978-0-8225-4999-4). The media genius and talk-show hostess is profiled in an interesting text with many photographs. (Rev: BL 4/1/02; HBG 10/02) [921]

14259 Nicholson, Lois. *Oprah Winfrey: Talking with America* (5–8). Series: Junior Black Americans of Achievement. 1997, Chelsea LB $28.00 (978-0-7910-2390-7); paper $4.95 (978-0-7910-4460-5). A biography that skims the life of this personality, with material on her difficult childhood, sexual abuse, college experiences, early career, weight problems, and success on television. (Rev: SLJ 8/97) [921]

14260 Stone, Tanya L. *Oprah Winfrey: Success with an Open Heart* (4–7). Illus. Series: Gateway Biographies. 2001, Millbrook LB $23.90 (978-0-7613-1814-9). 48pp. Oprah's story, with concise text and excellent photographs, will attract and inspire young readers. (Rev: BL 6/1–15/01; HBG 10/01) [791.45]

14261 Westen, Robin. *Oprah Winfrey: "I Don't Believe in Failure"* (5–8). Series: African-American Biography Library. 2005, Enslow LB $31.93 (978-0-7660-2462-5). 128pp. Winfrey's phenomenal rise to success in the worlds of business and entertainment is placed in social context. (Rev: SLJ 11/05; VOYA 6/06) [921]

WONG, ANNA MAY

14262 Yoo, Paula. *Shining Star: The Anna May Wong Story* (4–6). Illus. by Lin Wang. 2009, Lee & Low $17.95 (978-1-60060-259-7). 32pp. Profile of a pioneer who broke the Asian barriers in the American film industry. (Rev: BL 6/1–15/09; SLJ 7/09) [791.4302]

Writers

AARDEMA, VERNA

14263 Aardema, Verna. *A Bookworm Who Hatched* (2–5). Illus. by Dede Smith. Series: Meet the Author. 1993, Richard C. Owen $14.95 (978-1-878450-39-5). 32pp. In this autobiographical account, the noted author reveals stories about her life, writing techniques, and how she interacts with her reading audience. (Rev: BL 9/1/93; HB 9/93) [921]

ADA, ALMA FLOR

14264 Parker-Rock, Michelle. *Alma Flor Ada: An Author Kids Love* (3–5). Series: Authors Kids Love. 2008, Enslow LB $23.93 (978-0-7660-2760-2). 48pp. A brief biography of the Cuban author with information on her childhood, direct quotations, photographs, and Ada's advice on how to become a writer. (Rev: SLJ 11/08)

ADLER, DAVID A.

14265 Adler, David A. *My Writing Day* (3–5). Series: Meet the Author. 1999, Richard C. Owen LB $14.95 (978-1-57274-326-7). 32pp. The creator of the Cam Jansen mysteries tells a little about his life, writing career, and workday. (Rev: BL 9/15/99; HBG 3/00; SLJ 11/99) [921]

ALCOTT, LOUISA MAY

14266 Aller, Susan Bivin. *Beyond Little Women: A Story About Louisa May Alcott* (3–5). Illus. by Qi Z. Wang. Series: Creative Minds Biographies. 2004, Carolrhoda LB $22.60 (978-1-57505-602-9); paper $6.95 (978-1-57505-636-4). 64pp. An engaging account of Alcott's life from childhood and of the responsibilities she bore as the principal money earner in the family. (Rev: SLJ 8/04) [921]

14267 McDonough, Yona Zeldis. *Louisa: The Life of Louisa May Alcott* (2–4). Illus. by Bethanne Andersen. 2009, Holt $17.99 (978-0-8050-8192-3). 48pp. The author of *Little Women* felt a strong need to support herself and her family, and worked as a nurse during the Civil War before her writing brought her security. (Rev: BL 6/1–15/09; HB 9/09) [921]

14268 Ruth, Amy. *Louisa May Alcott* (4–7). Series: A&E Biography. 1999, Lerner LB $27.93 (978-0-8225-4938-3). 128pp. A clear, readable life of the author who wrote from personal experience about family life at the time of the Civil War and later. (Rev: BL 3/15/00; HBG 3/99; SLJ 1/99) [921]

14269 Silverthorne, Elizabeth. *Louisa May Alcott* (4–7). Illus. Series: Who Wrote That? 2002, Chelsea $30.00 (978-0-7910-6721-5). 112pp. A look at the life and works of author Louisa May Alcott, with particular emphasis on how her family influenced her work. (Rev: BL 10/15/02; HBG 3/03; SLJ 10/02) [813]

14270 Warrick, Karen Clemens. *Louisa May Alcott: Author of Little Women* (5–8). Series: Historical American Biographies. 2000, Enslow LB $26.60 (978-0-7660-1254-7). 128pp. Using many direct quotations from Alcott, along with fact boxes, maps, a chronology, and chapter notes, this is an interesting biography of the prolific writer from Pennsylvania. (Rev: BL 3/15/00; HBG 10/00) [921]

ALEICHEM, SHOLOM

14271 Silverman, Erica. *Sholom's Treasure: How Sholom Aleichem Became a Writer* (K–3). Illus. by Mordicai Gerstein. 2005, Farrar $16.00 (978-0-374-38055-7). 40pp. A child-friendly biography of the Yiddish author, emphasizing his difficult youth in a Russian shtetl and his enduring love of stories and fun. (Rev: BL 2/1/05; SLJ 4/05) [921]

ALLENDE, ISABEL

14272 Benatar, Raquel. *Isabel Allende: Recuerdos para un cento / Memories for a Story* (3–5). Trans. by Patricia Petersen. Illus. by Fernando Molinari. 2004, Piñata $15.95 (978-1-55885-379-9). A bilingual picture-book biography that emphasizes the importance of Allende's unusual childhood. (Rev: SLJ 9/04) [921]

ANDERSEN, HANS CHRISTIAN

14273 Burch, Joann J. *A Fairy-Tale Life: A Story About Hans Christian Andersen* (3–5). Illus. 1994, Carolrhoda LB $21.27 (978-0-87614-829-7). 64pp. A biography that concentrates on Andersen's childhood and his development as a writer. (Rev: BL 9/1/94) [921]

14274 Hesse, Karen. *The Young Hans Christian Andersen* (3–5). Illus. by Erik Blegvad. 2005, Scholastic $16.99 (978-0-439-67990-9). 48pp. This biography focuses on the Danish storyteller's troubled childhood and how it is reflected in some of his memorable fairy tales. (Rev: BL 11/1/05; SLJ 10/05*) [921]

14275 Varmer, Hjordis. *Hans Christian Andersen: His Fairy Tale Life* (4–7). Trans. by Tina Nunnally. Illus. by Lilian Bregger. 2005, Groundwood $19.95 (978-0-88899-670-1). 112pp. This large-format, lively biography presents the Danish storyteller's single-minded struggle to rise above adversity. (Rev: BL 11/1/05; SLJ 6/06) [839.81]

14276 Yolen, Jane. *The Perfect Wizard: Hans Christian Andersen* (1–3). Illus. by Dennis Nolan. 2005, Dutton $16.99 (978-0-525-46955-1). 40pp. This biography focuses on Andersen's youth, looking in particular at incidents from his childhood that were later incorporated into his fairy tales. (Rev: BL 2/1/05; SLJ 3/05) [921]

ANGELOU, MAYA

14277 Cuffie, Terrasita A. *Maya Angelou* (4–8). Series: The Importance Of. 1999, Lucent LB $27.45 (978-1-56006-532-6). 80pp. A biography that traces Maya Angelou's life from her childhood exposure to poverty and bigotry in the rural South to her eventual fame as a writer. (Rev: BL 9/15/99; SLJ 11/99) [921]

14278 King, Sarah E. *Maya Angelou Greeting the Morning* (3–5). Illus. Series: Gateway Biographies. 1994, Millbrook LB $23.90 (978-1-56294-431-5). 48pp. The inspiring story of the great African American writer and the terrible difficulties she has overcome. (Rev: BL 8/94; SLJ 4/94) [921]

14279 Kirkpatrick, Patricia. *Maya Angelou* (5–9). Illus. by John Thompson. Series: Voices in Poetry. 2003, Creative LB $19.95 (978-1-58341-281-7). 48pp. This picture-book biography introduces readers to Angelou's poetry and life from childhood. (Rev: BL 12/1/03; SLJ 12/03) [811]

14280 Raatma, Lucia. *Maya Angelou: Author and Documentary Filmmaker* (4–8). Series: Ferguson Career Biographies. 2001, Ferguson LB $25.00 (978-0-89434-336-0). 127pp. As well as a life of Maya Angelou, this book includes information on how to become a writer, filmmaker, and director. (Rev: SLJ 2/01) [921]

ASCH, FRANK

14281 Asch, Frank. *One Man Show* (1–4). Photos by Jan Asch. Illus. Series: Meet the Author. 1997, Richard C. Owen $14.95 (978-1-57274-095-2). 32pp. In this autobiography, author Asch introduces himself and his family, interests, and writing techniques. (Rev: HBG 3/98; SLJ 9/97) [921]

ASIMOV, ISAAC

14282 Boerst, William J. *Isaac Asimov: Writer of the Future* (5–9). Illus. 1998, Morgan Reynolds LB $23.95 (978-1-883846-32-9). 112pp. An engaging biography of the amazingly prolific author and scientist who was considered a misfit in his youth. (Rev: BL 12/1/98; SLJ 1/99) [921]

14283 Judson, Karen. *Isaac Asimov: Master of Science Fiction* (5–9). Illus. 1998, Enslow LB $26.60 (978-0-7660-1031-4). 112pp. A biography of Asimov that includes two chapters particularly helpful to researchers: on his importance as a writer of science fiction and on his work in other genres. (Rev: BL 12/1/98; HBG 3/99; SLJ 2/99) [921]

AUSTEN, JANE

14284 Ruth, Amy. *Jane Austen* (5–8). Series: A&E Biography. 2001, Lerner LB $27.93 (978-0-8225-4992-5). This is the intriguing story of Jane Austen, who lived a quiet, obscure life yet produced some of the world's greatest novels. (Rev: BL 6/1–15/01; HBG 10/01; SLJ 11/01) [921]

AVI

14285 Markham, Lois. *Avi* (5–8). 1996, Learning Works paper $7.99 (978-0-88160-280-7). This profile of the gifted writer recounts his triumph over dysgraphia, a learning disability that makes writing difficult, and explores his creative process and the major themes of his work. (Rev: BL 4/1/96; SLJ 8/96) [921]

14286 Sommers, Michael A. *Avi* (5–8). Series: The Library of Author Biographies. 2004, Rosen LB $27.95 (978-0-8239-4522-1). 112pp. Covers Avi's life and career as a YA author, with analysis of his work, an interview, and lists of works and awards. (Rev: SLJ 1/05) [921]

BAUM, L. FRANK

14287 Krull, Kathleen. *The Road to Oz: Twists, Turns, Bumps, and Triumphs in the Life of L. Frank Baum* (2–5). Illus. by Kevin Hawkes. 2008, Knopf $17.99 (978-0-375-83216-1). 48pp. In this picture-book biography readers learn about Baum's life and career as well as gaining insight into the characters and themes of *The Wizard of Oz*. (Rev: BCCB 10/08; BL 6/1–15/08; HB 9/08; LMC 11/08; SLJ 9/08) [813]

BLUME, JUDY

14288 Nault, Jennifer. *Judy Blume* (2–4). Series: My Favorite Writer. 2004, Weigl LB $18.20 (978-1-59036-025-5). 32pp. This attractively illustrated biography of Judy Blume is particularly suitable for report writers. (Rev: BL 4/1/04; SLJ 10/04) [813]

14289 Wheeler, Jill C. *Judy Blume* (2–4). Series: Children's Authors. 2005, ABDO LB $21.35 (978-1-59197-604-2). 24pp. After introducing some of Blume's works, Wheeler discusses the author's childhood, influences on her work, and her determination to write about topics of real concern to children. (Rev: BL 4/1/04; SLJ 4/05) [921]

BORGES, JORGE LUÍS

14290 Lennon, Adrian. *Jorge Luís Borges* (5–9). Series: Hispanics of Achievement. 1991, Chelsea LB $19.95 (978-0-7910-1236-9). A simple account that describes the life and work of one of South America's great contemporary writers. (Rev: BL 3/15/92; SLJ 7/92) [921]

BRIDWELL, NORMAN

14291 Wheeler, Jill C. *Norman Bridwell* (2–4). Series: Children's Authors. 2005, ABDO LB $21.35 (978-1-59197-605-9). 24pp. After introducing some of Bridwell's works, Wheeler discusses the author's childhood, influences on his work, and his recognition of the limitations of Clifford the Big Red Dog. (Rev: SLJ 4/05) [921]

BRONTË FAMILY

14292 Kenyon, Karen Smith. *The Brontë Family: Passionate Literary Geniuses* (5–9). Series: Lerner Biographies. 2002, Lerner LB $30.35 (978-0-8225-0071-1). 128pp. An absorbing introduction to the individual members of this literary family, with many illustrations and quotations from letters. (Rev: HBG 3/03; SLJ 1/03; VOYA 2/03) [921]

BRUCHAC, JOSEPH

14293 Bruchac, Joseph. *Seeing the Circle* (3–5). Series: Meet the Author. 1999, Richard C. Owen LB $14.95 (978-1-57274-327-4). 32pp. Bruchac's account of his life includes his work as a children's author, focusing on Native American fiction and outstanding retellings of folklore and history. (Rev: BL 9/15/99; HBG 3/00; SLJ 11/99) [921]

BUCK, PEARL S.

14294 Mitchell, Barbara. *Between Two Worlds: A Story About Pearl Buck* (3–6). Illus. by Karen Ritz. 1988, Carolrhoda LB $22.60 (978-0-87614-332-2). 56pp. The life of this child of American missionaries in China, who grew up to become a famous novelist. (Rev: BL 3/1/89; SLJ 2/89) [921]

BUNTING, EVE

14295 Bunting, Eve. *Once Upon a Time* (2–5). Illus. 1995, Richard C. Owen $14.95 (978-1-878450-59-3). 32pp. An autobiography of the prolific writer of children's books, who spent her childhood in Ireland. (Rev: BCCB 7–8/95; BL 8/95; HB 7/95) [921]

14296 McGinty, Alice B. *Meet Eve Bunting* (2–4). Illus. Series: About the Author. 2003, Rosen LB $21.25 (978-0-8239-6411-6). 24pp. Readers learn about Bunting's youth and later life and how and why she started writing for children, with excerpts from her books, reprints from covers, photographs, and other illustrations. (Rev: BL 6/1–15/03; SLJ 3/03) [921]

BURNETT, FRANCES HODGSON

14297 Carpenter, Angelica S., and Jean Shirley. *Frances Hodgson Burnett: Beyond the Secret Garden* (4–8). Illus. 1990, Lerner LB $27.93 (978-0-8225-4905-5). 128pp. A glimpse into the private life of the woman who wrote *The Secret Garden*. (Rev: BCCB 12/90; BL 1/1/91; SLJ 3/91*) [921]

BURROUGHS, EDGAR RICE

14298 Boerst, William J. *Edgar Rice Burroughs: Creator of Tarzan* (5–8). Illus. Series: World Writers. 2000, Morgan Reynolds LB $23.95 (978-1-883846-56-5). 112pp. A concise biography of the prolific author who created Tarzan and was a pioneer of the science fiction genre. (Rev: BL 7/00; HBG 3/01; SLJ 1/01) [921]

BYARS, BETSY

14299 Byars, Betsy. *The Moon and I* (4–7). Illus. 1996, Morrow paper $5.99 (978-0-688-13704-5). 96pp. A memoir from this well-known children's author, which gives her the opportunity to tell how she likes both writing and snakes. (Rev: BCCB 3/92*; BL 5/15/92; SLJ 4/92) [921]

14300 Cammarano, Rita. *Betsy Byars* (4–7). Series: Who Wrote That? 2002, Chelsea $30.00 (978-0-7910-6720-8). 106pp. A profile in text and pictures of one of America's best-loved authors and winner of the Newbery and other prizes. (Rev: BL 10/15/02; HBG 3/03) [921]

CAEDMON

14301 Ashby, Ruth. *Caedmon's Song* (1–3). Illus. by Bill Slavin. 2006, Eerdmans $16.00 (978-0-8028-5241-0). 32pp. This picture-book biography introduces young readers to Caedmon, the 7th-century English cowherd who is said to be that country's first poet. (Rev: HBG 10/06; SLJ 3/06) [921]

CATHER, WILLA

14302 Streissguth, Thomas. *Writer of the Plains: A Story About Willa Cather* (4–7). Illus. 1997, Carolrhoda LB $22.60 (978-1-57505-015-7). 64pp. A simple introduction to the works of Willa Cather and the places where she lived and wrote. (Rev: BL 6/1–15/97; SLJ 10/97) [921]

CERVANTES, MIGUEL DE

14303 Goldberg, Jake. *Miguel de Cervantes* (5–9). Series: Hispanics of Achievement. 1993, Chelsea LB $21.95 (978-0-7910-1238-3). The absorbing story of the Spanish writer whose life rivaled that of his adventurous hero, Don Quixote. (Rev: BL 9/15/93) [921]

CHERRY, LYNNE

14304 Cherry, Lynne. *Making a Difference in the World* (3–5). Series: Meet the Author. 2000, Richard C. Owen $14.95 (978-1-57274-373-1). 32pp. This noted author and illustrator of children's picture books talks about her life and how, when, and why she works. (Rev: BL 7/00; HBG 3/01; SLJ 12/00) [921]

CHRISTIE, AGATHA

14305 Dommermuth-Costa, Carol. *Agatha Christie: Writer of Mystery* (5–9). Series: Biographies. 1997, Lerner LB $30.35 (978-0-8225-4954-3). A biography of the "First Lady of Crime," with material on her personal life, including her two marriages. (Rev: SLJ 8/97; VOYA 4/98)

CISNEROS, SANDRA

14306 Mirriam-Goldberg, Caryn. *Sandra Cisneros: Latina Writer and Activist* (5–8). Illus. Series: Hispanic Biographies. 1998, Enslow LB $19.95 (978-0-7760-1045-8). A biography, enlivened with many quotations, of the woman who received Cs and Ds in school and later became a first-rate author and leading Hispanic American activist. (Rev: BL 1/1–15/99; VOYA 10/99) [921]

CLEARY, BEVERLY

14307 Ring, Susan. *Beverly Cleary* (2–4). Series: My Favorite Writer. 2003, Weigl LB $16.95 (978-1-59036-030-9). 32pp. This attractively illustrated biography is particularly suitable for report writers. (Rev: HBG 3/03)

COVILLE, BRUCE

14308 Parker-Rock, Michelle. *Bruce Coville: An Author Kids Love* (3–5). Series: Authors Kids Love. 2008, Enslow LB $23.93 (978-0-7600-2755-8). 48pp. An engaging biography of the popular author, focusing on his writing and his childhood experiences. (Rev: SLJ 9/08) [921]

CRANE, STEPHEN

14309 Kepnes, Caroline. *Stephen Crane* (5–8). Series: Classic Storytellers. 2004, Mitchell Lane LB $29.95 (978-1-58415-272-9). 48pp. An introduction to Crane's life, work, and legacy, with background information on relevant historical, cultural, and economic factors. (Rev: BL 1/05; SLJ 1/05) [921]

CRUTCHER, CHRIS

14310 Summers, Michael A. *Chris Crutcher* (5–8). Series: The Library of Author Biographies. 2005, Rosen LB $27.95 (978-1-4042-0325-9). 112pp. An interview with Crutcher is an interesting addition to this description of the author's life — including his experiences as a novelist, educator, therapist, and child protection advocate — and his works for children. (Rev: SLJ 9/05) [921]

CURTIS, CHRISTOPHER PAUL

14311 Gaines, Ann. *Christopher Paul Curtis* (3–6). Series: Real-Life Reader Biographies. 2001, Mitchell Lane LB $15.95 (978-1-58415-076-3). 32pp. The fascinating story of the determination that took African American Curtis from writing in a journal during breaks on a car assembly line to winning notable awards. (Rev: SLJ 9/01) [813]

DAHL, ROALD

14312 Cooling, Wendy. *D Is for Dahl: A Gloriumptious A–Z Guide to the World of Roald Dahl* (5–8). Illus. by Quentin Blake. 2005, Viking $15.99 (978-0-670-06023-8). 160pp. For Dahl fans, this is an alphabetically arranged collection of trivia about his life and writings. (Rev: BL 8/05; SLJ 10/05) [823]

14313 Craats, Rennay. *Roald Dahl* (2–4). Series: My Favorite Writer. 2003, Weigl LB $18.20 (978-1-59036-029-3). 32pp. This attractively illustrated biography of Roald Dahl is particularly suitable for report writers. (Rev: SLJ 10/04)

14314 Powling, Chris. *Roald Dahl* (2–3). Series: Tell Me About. 1998, Carolrhoda $19.93 (978-1-57505-274-8). 24pp. Using many full-color photographs, this book traces the important events in Dahl's professional life, with emphasis on the use of imagination in writing. (Rev: BCCB 1/99; HBG 3/99; SLJ 1/99) [921]

14315 Shields, Charles J. *Roald Dahl* (4–7). Series: Who Wrote That? 2002, Chelsea $30.00 (978-0-7910-6722-2). 106pp. A brief biography of the master of whimsical stories that involve such strange elements as secretive chocolate factories and giant peaches. (Rev: BL 10/15/02; HBG 3/03) [921]

DANZIGER, PAULA

14316 Reed, Jennifer B. *Paula Danziger: Voice of Teen Troubles* (5–8). Series: Authors Teens Love. 2006, Enslow LB $31.93 (978-0-7660-2444-1).

104pp. This profile of the popular author includes interviews in which she discusses her dysfunctional family and her struggles with depression and bulimia. (Rev: BL 9/15/06) [921]

DEPAOLA, TOMIE

14317 Braun, Eric. *Tomie dePaola* (K–2). Series: First Biographies. 2004, Capstone LB $17.26 (978-0-7368-3641-8). 24pp. Very basic information on the author/illustrator's life and work for beginning readers and report writers, with photographs and a timeline. (Rev: SLJ 7/05) [921]

14318 dePaola, Tomie. *Christmas Remembered* (5–8). 2006, Putnam $19.99 (978-0-399-24622-7). 96pp. Folk artist dePaola recalls some of the most memorable Christmases from his past. (Rev: BL 10/1/06; SLJ 10/06) [813]

14319 dePaola, Tomie. *Here We All Are* (2–5). Illus. Series: 26 Fairmount Avenue. 2000, Penguin $13.99 (978-0-399-23496-5). 80pp. A short chapter book that continues Tomie dePaola's *26 Fairmount Avenue* memoir when, as a 5-year-old, he gets a new baby sister. (Rev: BCCB 9/00; BL 5/1/00; HB 5/00; HBG 10/00; SLJ 6/00) [921]

14320 dePaola, Tomie. *I'm Still Scared: The War Years* (2–4). Illus. Series: 26 Fairmount Avenue. 2006, Putnam $13.99 (978-0-399-24502-2). 80pp. DePaola recalls the fears and uncertainties of children growing up in America during World War II in this installment of his autobiographical series. (Rev: BL 4/15/06; SLJ 11/06) [813.54]

14321 dePaola, Tomie. *On My Way* (2–4). Illus. Series: 26 Fairmount Avenue. 2001, Penguin $13.99 (978-0-399-23583-2). 32pp. A continuation of dePaola's remembrances of his childhood that includes a visit to the 1940 World's Fair. (Rev: BCCB 3/01; BL 12/15/00; HB 3/01; HBG 10/01; SLJ 2/01)

14322 dePaola, Tomie. *Things Will Never Be the Same* (2–4). Illus. Series: 26 Fairmount Avenue. 2003, Penguin $13.99 (978-0-399-23982-3). 80pp. DePaola's autobiography, with his own drawings, continues through 1941, when he turned 7, and details his everyday life until the morning of December 7, when everything changed. (Rev: BCCB 3/03; BL 3/1/03; HBG 10/03; SLJ 5/03) [813.54]

14323 dePaola, Tomie. *26 Fairmount Avenue* (3–5). Illus. Series: 26 Fairmount Avenue. 1999, Penguin paper $13.99 (978-0-399-23246-6). 64pp. A charming memoir of his childhood by the famous children's writer. Newbery Honor Book, 2000. (Rev: BCCB 6/99; BL 8/99; HB 5/99; HBG 10/99; SLJ 6/99) [813]

14324 dePaola, Tomie. *What a Year!* (2–4). Illus. Series: 26 Fairmount Avenue. 2002, Penguin $13.99 (978-0-399-23797-3). 80pp. DePaola's memoirs continues here, taking readers into the life of 6-year-old Tomie from the beginning of 1st grade to New Year's Eve in 1940. (Rev: BCCB 3/02; BL 3/1/02; HB 3/02; HBG 10/02; SLJ 3/02) [813.54]

14325 dePaola, Tomie. *Why? The War Years: A 26 Fairmount Avenue Book* (2–4). Illus. Series: 26

Fairmount Avenue. 2007, Putnam $14.99 (978-0-399-24692-0). 80pp. Continuing his autobiographical series, dePaola includes many child-appealing vignettes, but focuses on the impact of World War II, concluding with his much-loved cousin's death. (Rev: BL 1/1–15/07) [921]

DICKENS, CHARLES

14326 Collins, David R. *Tales for Hard Times: A Story About Charles Dickens* (4–8). Illus. by David Mataya. Series: Creative Minds. 1991, Carolrhoda LB $22.60 (978-0-87614-433-6). 64pp. The life of Charles Dickens, including his poverty-ridden childhood. (Rev: SLJ 3/91) [921]

14327 Rosen, Michael. *Dickens: His Work and His World* (4–7). Illus. by Robert Ingpen. 2005, Candlewick $19.99 (978-0-7636-2752-2). 96pp. Before reviewing Dickens's major works, Rosen discusses the author's difficult childhood and the social conditions of his times. (Rev: BCCB 3/06; BL 9/15/05*; HBG 4/06; LMC 3/06; SLJ 11/05*) [921]

DORRIS, MICHAEL

14328 Weil, Ann. *Michael Dorris* (4–7). Illus. Series: Contemporary Native Americans. 1997, Raintree LB $17.98 (978-0-8172-3994-7). 48pp. The life story of the late Native American writer and teacher and his crusade to fight alcohol abuse. (Rev: BL 6/1–15/97) [921]

DOYLE, SIR ARTHUR CONAN

14329 Adams, Cynthia. *The Mysterious Case of Sir Arthur Conan Doyle* (5–8). Illus. Series: World Writers. 1999, Morgan Reynolds LB $21.95 (978-1-883846-34-3). This book traces the life of Sir Arthur Conan Doyle from his Scottish boyhood and failed medical practice to success as a writer and creator of Sherlock Holmes. (Rev: BL 3/1/99; SLJ 9/99; VOYA 10/99) [921]

EHLERT, LOIS

14330 Ehlert, Lois. *Under My Nose* (3–5). Illus. 1996, Richard C. Owen $14.95 (978-1-57274-027-3). 32pp. A simple autobiography of this artist whose children's books are widely read. (Rev: BL 9/1/96; HB 9/96; SLJ 12/96) [921]

FITZGERALD, F. SCOTT

14331 Bankston, John. *F. Scott Fitzgerald* (5–8). Series: Classic Storytellers. 2004, Mitchell Lane LB $29.95 (978-1-58415-249-1). 48pp. An introduction to Fitzgerald's life, work, and legacy, with background information on relevant historical, cultural, and economic factors. (Rev: BL 1/05; SLJ 1/05) [921]

14332 Stewart, Gail B. *F. Scott Fitzgerald* (4–8). Series: The Importance Of. 1999, Lucent LB $27.45 (978-1-56006-541-8). 112pp. The story of the famous Jazz Age author whose enduring works

reflect American life in his era. (Rev: BL 9/15/99) [921]

FLEISCHMAN, SID

14333 Freedman, Jeri. *Sid Fleischman* (5–9). Series: The Library of Author Biographies. 2004, Rosen LB $27.95 (978-0-8239-4019-6). 112pp. Traces the popular, Newbery-winning author's life and looks at his works, writing process, and inspirations, concluding with an interview and reference material. (Rev: SLJ 9/04) [921]

14334 Parker-Rock, Michelle. *Sid Fleischman: An Author Kids Love* (3–5). Series: Authors Kids Love. 2008, Enslow LB $23.93 (978-0-7660-2757-2). 48pp. A brief biography of the popular author with information on his youth, direct quotations, photographs, and Fleischman's tips on how to become a writer. (Rev: SLJ 11/08) [921]

FLETCHER, RALPH

14335 Fletcher, Ralph. *Marshfield Dreams: When I Was a Kid* (3–5). 2005, Holt $16.95 (978-0-8050-7242-6). 192pp. Children's author Fletcher recalls growing up in coastal Massachusetts as the oldest of nine siblings. (Rev: BL 10/1/05; SLJ 9/05; VOYA 8/05) [921]

FOX, PAULA

14336 Daniel, Susanna. *Paula Fox* (5–8). Series: The Library of Author Biographies. 2004, Rosen LB $27.95 (978-0-8239-4525-2). 112pp. Covers Fox's life and career, with analysis of her work and its themes, an interview, and lists of works and awards. (Rev: SLJ 1/05) [921]

FRITZ, JEAN

14337 Fritz, Jean. *Surprising Myself* (2–5). Illus. by Andrea F. Pfleger. Series: Meet the Author. 1993, Richard C. Owen $14.95 (978-1-878450-37-1). 32pp. As well as telling the reader about her life, Fritz explains how she does research for her many historical biographies. (Rev: BL 9/1/93; HB 9/93) [921]

FROST, ROBERT

14338 Wooten, Sara McIntosh. *Robert Frost: The Life of America's Poet* (5–8). Series: People to Know Today. 2006, Enslow LB $31.93 (978-0-7660-2627-8). 128pp. A fine introduction to the New England poet whose poetry is loved by young people and adults, with information on his difficult childhood and continuing struggles with depression and financial woes. (Rev: SLJ 1/07) [921]

GANTOS, JACK

14339 Parker-Rock, Michelle. *Jack Gantos: An Author Kids Love* (3–5). Series: Authors Kids Love. 2008, Enslow LB $23.93 (978-0-7600-2756-5). 48pp. An engaging biography of the creator of Joey

Pigza and Rotten Ralph, focusing on his writing (he began keeping a journal in 6th grade) and his childhood experiences. (Rev: BL 4/1/08; LMC 3/08; SLJ 9/08) [921]

GEISEL, THEODOR

14340 Carlson, Cheryl. *Dr. Seuss* (K–2). Series: First Biographies. 2004, Capstone LB $17.26 (978-0-7368-3639-5). 24pp. Very basic information on the author's life and work for beginning readers and report writers, with photographs and a timeline. (Rev: SLJ 7/05) [921]

14341 Dean, Tanya. *Theodor Geisel (Dr. Seuss)* (4–7). Illus. Series: Who Wrote That? 2002, Chelsea $30.00 (978-0-7910-6724-6). 112pp. A look at the life and works of the author and illustrator known as Dr. Seuss. (Rev: BL 10/15/02; HBG 3/03) [813]

14342 Foran, Jill. *Dr. Seuss* (2–4). Series: My Favorite Writer. 2003, Weigl LB $16.95 (978-1-59036-028-6). 32pp. This attractively illustrated biography of Theodor Geisel is particularly suitable for report writers. (Rev: SLJ 10/04)

14343 Krull, Kathleen. *The Boy on Fairfield Street: How Ted Geisel Grew Up to Become Dr. Seuss* (3–5). Illus. by Steve Johnson and Lou Fancher. 2004, Random $16.95 (978-0-375-82298-8). 42pp. Concentrating on Geisel's youth, this picture-book biography includes examples of his work. (Rev: BL 2/1/04; SLJ 1/04) [813]

14344 Lynch, Wendy. *Dr. Seuss* (1–4). Series: Lives and Times. 2000, Heinemann LB $19.92 (978-1-57572-216-0). 24pp. A simple biography of Theodor Geisel's alter ego with original drafts of artwork and many photographs. (Rev: HBG 3/01; SLJ 8/00) [921]

14345 Weidt, Maryann N. *Oh, the Places He Went: A Story About Dr. Seuss* (3–6). Illus. by Kerry Maguire. Series: Creative Minds Biographies. 1994, Carolrhoda LB $22.60 (978-0-87614-823-5); paper $6.95 (978-0-87614-627-9). 64pp. The life story of the famous children's author that tells of his many hardships and of some of his most important books. (Rev: BCCB 2/95; SLJ 1/95) [921]

14346 Woods, Mae. *Dr. Seuss* (2–4). Illus. Series: Children's Authors. 2000, ABDO $21.35 (978-1-57765-110-9). This book discusses the life and career on Theodor Geisel, better known as Dr. Seuss. (Rev: HBG 3/01; SLJ 1/01) [921]

GEORGE, JEAN CRAIGHEAD

14347 Cary, Alice. *Jean Craighead George* (4–6). Illus. 1996, Learning Works paper $7.99 (978-0-88160-283-8). 136pp. A lively re-creation of the life of this renowned nature writer and Newbery Award winner. (Rev: BL 11/15/96; SLJ 9/96) [921]

GIFF, PATRICIA REILLY

14348 Giff, Patricia Reilly. *Don't Tell the Girls: A Family Memoir* (4–7). Illus. 2005, Holiday $16.95 (978-0-8234-1813-8). 144pp. The author tells of the search for her family's roots that led her to Ireland. (Rev: BL 3/1/05; SLJ 7/05) [813]

GOBLE, PAUL

14349 Goble, Paul. *Hau Kola Hello Friend* (2–4). Illus. by Gerry Perrin. Series: Meet the Author. 1994, Richard C. Owen $14.95 (978-1-878450-44-9). 32pp. This dedicated author, who has specialized in Native American folk material, tells about his life and writing. (Rev: BL 8/94; SLJ 8/94) [921]

GRIMM BROTHERS

14350 Hettinga, Donald R. *The Brothers Grimm: Two Lives, One Legacy* (5–8). Illus. 2001, Clarion $22.00 (978-0-618-05599-9). 192pp. An interesting biography that places the brothers' lives in the context of their time and discusses their skills as lexicographers and scholars. (Rev: BL 7/01; HB 1/02; HBG 3/02; SLJ 10/01) [430]

HALE, BRUCE

14351 Parker-Rock, Michelle. *Bruce Hale: An Author Kids Love* (3–5). Series: Authors Kids Love. 2008, Enslow LB $23.93 (978-0-7660-2758-9). 48pp. A brief biography of the popular author with information on his youth, direct quotations, photographs, and Hale's advice on how to become a writer. (Rev: SLJ 11/08) [921]

HANDLER, DANIEL

14352 Haugen, Hayley Mitchell. *Daniel Handler: The Real Lemony Snicket* (3–6). Illus. Series: Inventors and Creators. 2005, Gale LB $26.20 (978-0-7377-3117-0). 48pp. The author of the popular A Series of Unfortunate Events books is profiled (and pictured), with discussion of his books. (Rev: SLJ 8/05) [921]

HELLER, RUTH

14353 Heller, Ruth. *Fine Lines* (3–5). Illus. 1996, Richard C. Owen $14.95 (978-1-878450-76-0). 32pp. In this autobiography, the author tells about her childhood, training, writing, and artwork. (Rev: BL 9/1/96; HB 9/96; SLJ 1/97) [921]

HENRY, MARGUERITE

14354 Collins, David R. *Write a Book for Me: The Story of Marguerite Henry* (4–6). Illus. 1999, Morgan Reynolds $23.95 (978-1-883846-39-8). 112pp. A straightforward biography of Marguerite Henry, the great writer of horse stories. (Rev: BL 3/15/99; SLJ 9/99) [921]

HINTON, S. E.

14355 Kjelle, Marylou Morano. *S. E. Hinton: Author of The Outsiders* (5–8). Series: Authors Teens Love. 2007, Enslow LB $31.93 (978-0-7660-2720-6). 112pp. A life of the author of the well-known novel, with an "In Her Own Words" section that researchers will find useful. (Rev: SLJ 11/07) [921]

HOMER

14356 Tracy, Kathleen. *The Life and Times of Homer* (5–8). Series: Biography from Ancient Civilizations: Legends, Folklore, and Stories of Ancient Worlds. 2004, Mitchell Lane LB $29.95 (978-1-58415-260-6). 48pp. Drawing on ancient legends, this is a profile of ancient Greek poet and storyteller Homer. (Rev: BL 10/15/04; SLJ 12/04)

HOPKINS, LEE BENNETT

14357 Hopkins, Lee Bennett. *The Writing Bug* (2–5). Illus. by Diane Rubinger. Series: Meet the Author. 1993, Richard C. Owen $14.95 (978-1-878450-38-8). 32pp. The acclaimed poet, author, and anthologist tells about his life and the experiences that inspire him to write. (Rev: BL 9/1/93; HB 9/93) [921]

14358 Strong, Amy. *Lee Bennett Hopkins: A Children's Poet* (5–8). Series: Great Life Stories. 2003, Watts LB $30.50 (978-0-531-12315-7). 111pp. An inspiring biography that chronicles Hopkins's early struggles and his love for his work. (Rev: SLJ 2/04) [921]

HOWE, JAMES

14359 Howe, James. *Playing with Words* (1–4). Photos by Michael Craine. Series: Meet the Author. 1994, Richard C. Owen $14.95 (978-1-878450-40-1). 32pp. People who love this author's zany mysteries will enjoy reading about how he writes, gets his inspiration, and spends a typical day. (Rev: BL 8/94; SLJ 8/94) [921]

HUGHES, LANGSTON

14360 Bryant, Philip S. *Langston Hughes* (2–5). Series: African-American Biographies. 2003, Raintree LB $28.56 (978-0-7398-6871-3). 64pp. This basic biography profiles Hughes's life and achievements and places them in historical context. (Rev: SLJ 11/03) [921]

14361 Cooper, Floyd. *Coming Home: From the Life of Langston Hughes* (3–6). Illus. 1994, Penguin $16.99 (978-0-399-22682-3). 32pp. A sensitive retelling of Langston Hughes's unhappy childhood and his search for a permanent home. (Rev: BCCB 1/95; BL 10/1/94; HB 9/94; SLJ 11/94) [921]

14362 McKissack, Patricia C., and Fredrick McKissack. *Langston Hughes: Great American Poet*. Rev. ed. (2–4). Series: Great African Americans. 2002, Enslow LB $18.60 (978-0-7660-1695-8). 32pp. An interesting biography of the African American author noted for both his poetry and fiction and for his role in the Harlem Renaissance. (Rev: BL 7/02; HBG 10/02) [921]

HURSTON, ZORA NEALE

14363 Bryant, Philip S. *Zora Neale Hurston* (2–5). Series: African-American Biographies. 2003, Raintree LB $28.56 (978-0-7398-6872-0). 64pp. A simple profile of the author, with interesting sidebars and good archival photographs that convey a sense of the time in which she lived. (Rev: HBG 4/04; SLJ 11/03) [921]

14364 Calvert, Roz. *Zora Neale Hurston* (5–8). Illus. Series: Black Americans of Achievement. 1993, Chelsea LB $15.95 (978-0-7910-1766-1). 80pp. A lively account of the life of the famous writer and folklorist. (Rev: BL 5/1/93; SLJ 6/93) [921]

14365 McKissack, Patricia C., and Fredrick McKissack. *Zora Neale Hurston: Writer and Storyteller*. Rev. ed. (2–4). Series: Great African Americans. 2002, Enslow LB $18.60 (978-0-7660-1694-1). 32pp. A simple biography of the African American writer who is currently enjoying a revival of interest because of her excellent novels. (Rev: BL 7/02; HBG 3/03) [921]

IRVING, WASHINGTON

14366 Collins, David R. *Washington Irving: Storyteller for a New Nation* (4–8). Illus. Series: World Writers. 2000, Morgan Reynolds LB $23.95 (978-1-883846-50-3). 112pp. This biography introduces the globetrotting American writer and gives details of his work and personality. (Rev: BL 4/1/00; HBG 3/00; SLJ 5/00; VOYA 6/01) [921]

14367 Harness, Cheryl. *The Literary Adventures of Washington Irving* (2–5). Illus. by author. 2008, National Geographic $17.95 (978-1-4263-0438-5). 48pp. An engaging picture-book account of Irving's life, work, and times with attention-grabbing artwork. (Rev: BL 1/1–15/09; SLJ 3/09) [921]

ISSA

14368 Gollub, Matthew. *Cool Melons Turn to Frogs! The Life and Poems of Issa* (3–5). Illus. by Kazuko Stone. 1998, Lee & Low $16.95 (978-1-880000-71-7). 32pp. Using lovely Japanese-like paintings and fine calligraphy, the life of Issa, the famous haiku poet is traced with many examples of his work. (Rev: BCCB 2/99; BL 12/1/98; HB 11/98; HBG 3/99; SLJ 11/98) [921]

JUANA INES DE LA CRUZ, SISTER

14369 Martinez, Elizabeth C. *Sor Juana: A Trailblazing Thinker* (3–6). Illus. Series: Hispanic Heritage. 1994, Millbrook LB $23.90 (978-1-56294-406-3). 32pp. The story of the 17th-century Mexican-born poet who is considered the finest writer of Mexico's colonial period. (Rev: BL 6/1–15/94; SLJ 4/94) [921]

14370 Mora, Pat. *A Library for Juana: The World of Sor Juana Ines* (1–3). Illus. by Beatriz Vidal. 2002, Knopf $15.95 (978-0-375-80643-8). 40pp. This is an absorbing account of the inspiring life of Sor Juana Ines, a child prodigy born in Mexico in the 17th century who became a nun and internationally known scholar and poet. (Rev: BL 11/15/02; HB 11/02; HBG 3/03; SLJ 11/02) [861]

KEHRET, PEG

14371 Kehret, Peg. *Five Pages a Day: A Writer's Journey* (4–7). 2002, Albert Whitman LB $15.99 (978-0-8075-8650-1). 192pp. Aspiring young writers will particularly enjoy Kehret's account of her writing life, from starting a newspaper about the neighborhood dogs to entering writing contests to her career as an author of children's books. (Rev: BL 12/15/02; HBG 3/03; SLJ 9/02) [813]

KING, STEPHEN

14372 Wilson, Suzan. *Stephen King* (4–6). Series: People to Know. 2000, Enslow LB $26.60 (978-0-7660-1233-2). 128pp. A well-documented, thorough account of the life of this former high-school teacher who became a best-selling writer of suspense and horror novels. (Rev: BL 1/1–15/00; HBG 10/00; SLJ 5/00) [921]

KUSKIN, KARLA

14373 Kuskin, Karla. *Thoughts, Pictures, and Words* (2–5). Illus. Series: Meet the Author. 1995, Richard C. Owen $14.95 (978-1-878450-41-8). 32pp. This renowned writer discusses her prose, poetry, and illustrations, and discusses how she approaches writing. (Rev: BCCB 7–8/95; BL 8/95; HB 7/95; SLJ 9/95) [921]

LESTER, HELEN

14374 Lester, Helen. *Author: A True Story* (2–4). Illus. 1997, Houghton $14.00 (978-0-395-82744-4). 32pp. A delightful autobiography illustrated with her own cartoons. (Rev: BCCB 4/97; BL 3/15/97; HB 5/97; SLJ 5/97*) [921]

LEVINE, GAIL CARSON

14375 McGinty, Alice B. *Meet Gail Carson Levine* (2–4). Series: About the Author. 2003, Rosen LB $18.75 (978-0-8239-6409-3). 24pp. Sample passages, book covers, childhood photographs, and an interview make this an appealing, easy-to-read profile of Levine and her writing career. (Rev: BL 6/1–15/03; SLJ 5/03) [921]

LEWIS, C. S.

14376 Parker, Vic. *C. S. Lewis* (4–7). Series: Writers Uncovered. 2006, Heinemann LB $23.00 (978-1-4034-7336-3). 48pp. In addition to providing biographical information on Lewis, Parker looks at his books, especially the Narnia series, giving plot outlines and discussing the stories and themes. (Rev: BL 8/06) [921]

LOCKER, THOMAS

14377 Locker, Thomas. *The Man Who Paints* (3–5). Series: Meet the Author. 1999, Richard C. Owen LB $14.95 (978-1-57274-328-1). 32pp. An autobiography of the artist and author of children's books noted for such nature stories as *Where the River Begins* and *The Land of Grey Wolf*. (Rev: BL 9/15/99; HBG 3/00; SLJ 11/99) [921]

LONDON, JACK

14378 Bankston, John. *Jack London* (4–7). Illus. Series: Classic Storytellers. 2005, Mitchell Lane LB $29.95 (978-1-58415-263-7). 48pp. An introduction to London's life, work, and legacy, with background information on relevant historical, cultural, and economic factors. (Rev: BL 1/05) [921]

14379 Streissguth, Thomas. *Jack London* (4–7). Series: A&E Biography. 2000, Lucent LB $27.93 (978-0-8225-4987-1). 112pp. The story of an adventurer and author who battled personal hardships and wrote eloquently about nature and survival. (Rev: BL 12/15/00; HBG 3/01; SLJ 3/01) [921]

LOVECRAFT, H. P.

14380 Schoell, William. *H. P. Lovecraft: Master of Weird Fiction* (5–8). Illus. 2003, Morgan Reynolds LB $23.95 (978-1-931798-15-0). 128pp. Lovecraft, known for his stories of horror and the supernatural, was born into privilege that ended with his parents' early deaths; his works only received real acclaim after his death. (Rev: BL 9/15/03; HBG 4/04; SLJ 12/03) [813]

LOWRY, LOIS

14381 Lowry, Lois. *Looking Back: A Book of Memories* (4–8). Illus. 1998, Houghton $17.00 (978-0-395-89543-6). 192pp. This autobiographical work centers around a series of photographs and the author's comments on each. (Rev: BL 11/1/98; HB 1/99; HBG 3/99; SLJ 9/98; VOYA 4/99) [921]

14382 Markham, Lois. *Lois Lowry* (5–8). Series: Meet the Author. 1995, Learning Works paper $7.99 (978-0-88160-278-4). This biography of the Newbery Medal–winning author tells how she became a writer and looks at the personal experiences that are reflected in her books. (Rev: SLJ 1/96) [921]

LYON, GEORGE ELLA

14383 Lyon, George E. *A Wordful Child* (3–5). Illus. 1996, Richard C. Owen $14.95 (978-1-57274-016-7). 32pp. The author tells about her life and the stories she heard as a child that influenced her work. (Rev: BL 9/1/96; HB 9/96; SLJ 1/97) [921]

MCKISSACK, PATRICIA

14384 McKissack, Patricia C. *Can You Imagine?* (2–5). Illus. Series: Meet the Author. 1997, Richard C. Owen $14.95 (978-1-878450-61-6). 32pp. An autobiographical account of this fantasy writer in which she tells of the importance of imagination in her life. (Rev: BL 6/1–15/97; HBG 3/98; SLJ 9/97) [921]

MAGEE, JOHN

14385 Granfield, Linda. *High Flight: A Story of World War II* (5–7). Illus. 1999, Tundra $15.95 (978-0-88776-469-1). 32pp. The moving story of John Magee, a young Canadian Air Force pilot who was killed in World War II and who is best known for writing the poem "High Flight." (Rev: BCCB 12/99; BL 1/1–15/00; HBG 3/00; SLJ 2/00) [921]

MAHY, MARGARET

14386 Mahy, Margaret. *My Mysterious World* (2–5). Illus. Series: Meet the Author. 1995, Richard C. Owen $14.95 (978-1-878450-58-6). 32pp. The New Zealand writer describes her many interests and how she approaches writing. (Rev: BCCB 7–8/95; BL 8/95; HB 7/95; SLJ 9/95) [921]

MÁRQUEZ, GABRIEL GARCÍA

14387 Brown, Monica. *My Name Is Gabito: The Life of Gabriel García Márquez* (2–4). Illus. by Raúl Colón. 2007, Northland/Rising Moon $15.95 (978-0-87358-934-5). 32pp. A picture-book biography of the Colombian author covering his youth and explaining his use of magical realism. (Rev: BL 2/1/08; SLJ 3/08*) [863]

MARTÍ, JOSÉ J.

14388 West, Alan. *José Martí: Man of Poetry, Soldier of Freedom* (5–8). Illus. Series: Hispanic Heritage. 1994, Millbrook LB $23.90 (978-1-56294-408-7). 32pp. The life story of the famous 19th-century Cuban poet, with excerpts from his work in both Spanish and English. (Rev: SLJ 1/95) [921]

MARTIN, RAFE

14389 Martin, Rafe. *A Storyteller's Story* (3–6). Illus. by Jill Krementz. Series: Meet the Author. 1992, Owen $14.95 (978-0-913461-03-7). 32pp. The author takes readers to his home to meet family and friends. (Rev: BCCB 9/92; BL 8/92; SLJ 8/92) [921]

MISTRAL, GABRIELA

14390 Brown, Monica. *My Name Is Gabriela / Me llamo Gabriela: The Life of Gabriela Mistral / La vida de Gabriela Mistral* (K–2). Illus. by John Parra. 2005, Luna Rising $15.95 (978-0-87358-859-1). 32pp. Lyrical first-person text tells the story of the life and writing career of Nobel Prize–winning Chilean poet Gabriela Mistral. (Rev: SLJ 2/06*) [921]

MONTGOMERY, LUCY MAUD

14391 MacLeod, Elizabeth. *Lucy Maud Montgomery: A Writer's Life* (3–5). Illus. 2001, Kids Can LB $14.95 (978-1-55074-487-3). 32pp. Both black-and-white and color illustrations are used to enhance this biography of one of Canada's most famous writers. (Rev: BL 4/1/01; HBG 10/01; SLJ 4/01) [921]

14392 Wallner, Alexandra. *Lucy Maud Montgomery: The Author of Anne of Green Gables* (1–3). 2006, Holiday $16.95 (978-0-8234-1549-6). 32pp. A picture-book life of the author, from her childhood on Prince Edward Island to her marriage to a minister and her success with *Anne*. (Rev: BL 9/15/06; SLJ 12/06) [921]

MORRISON, TONI

14393 Haskins, James. *Toni Morrison: The Magic of Words* (4–6). Illus. Series: Gateway Biographies. 2001, Millbrook $23.90 (978-0-7613-1806-4). 48pp. Young readers may not be familiar with Morrison's work, but will still enjoy this clearly presented photo-essay introducing her life from childhood, her work, and her support for other writers. (Rev: BL 6/1–15/01; HBG 10/01; SLJ 5/01) [813.5]

14394 Patrick-Wexler, Diane. *Toni Morrison* (4–6). Illus. Series: Contemporary African Americans. 1997, Raintree LB $17.98 (978-0-8172-3987-9). 48pp. A fine biography of this influential writer, who has won both the Nobel and Pulitzer prizes. (Rev: BL 5/15/97; SLJ 2/98) [921]

NAYLOR, PHYLLIS REYNOLDS

14395 Naylor, Phyllis Reynolds. *How I Came to Be a Writer*. Rev. ed. (4–9). 2001, Simon & Schuster paper $4.99 (978-0-689-83887-3). 139pp. Naylor describes the joys and difficulties of life as a writer and includes excerpts of her work in this autobiographical account. (Rev: SLJ 5/01) [921]

NERUDA, PABLO

14396 DeLano, Poli. *When I Was a Boy Neruda Called Me Policarpo* (4–6). Trans. by Sean Higgins. Illus. by Manuel Monroy. 2006, Groundwood $15.95 (978-0-88899-726-5). 96pp. The author presents his childhood memories of Chilean poet Pablo Neruda along with a number of Neruda's poems. (Rev: BL 7/06; SLJ 5/06) [861]

14397 Ray, Deborah Kogan. *To Go Singing Through the World: The Childhood of Pablo Neruda* (3–5). Illus. 2006, Farrar $17.00 (978-0-374-37627-7). 40pp. A picture-book biography of poet Pablo Neruda, describing his childhood in a Chilean rain forest town and how it shaped his views and writings. (Rev: BL 11/15/06; SLJ 11/06) [921]

NIXON, JOAN LOWERY

14398 Wade, Mary Dodson. *Joan Lowery Nixon: Masterful Mystery Writer* (5–8). Series: Authors Teens Love. 2004, Enslow LB $26.60 (978-0-7660-2194-5). 128pp. Examines Nixon's life, writings, and her focus on girls of character and strength. (Rev: SLJ 11/04) [921]

PAREDES, AMERICO

14399 Murcia, Rebecca Thatcher. *Americo Paredes* (5–7). Series: Latinos in American History. 2003, Mitchell Lane LB $29.95 (978-1-58415-207-1). 48pp. The story of the Mexican American author, folklorist, and professor at the University of Texas in Austin who is also famous for establishing a center for intercultural studies. (Rev: BL 1/1–15/04) [921]

PATERSON, KATHERINE

14400 Cary, Alice. *Katherine Paterson* (5–8). Illus. Series: Meet the Author. 1997, Learning Works paper $7.99 (978-0-88160-281-4). 136pp. A biography of the two-time Newbery winner, with many quotations from interviews and autobiographical essays. (Rev: BL 5/1/97; SLJ 7/97) [921]

14401 Kjelle, Marylou Morano. *Katherine Paterson* (4–7). Illus. Series: Classic Storytellers. 2004, Mitchell Lane LB $29.95 (978-1-58415-268-2). 48pp. Examines the life and times of the award-winning children's author, including her work as a missionary in Japan and how religious faith informs her writing. (Rev: BL 1/1–15/05; SLJ 3/05) [921]

14402 McGinty, Alice B. *Katherine Paterson* (5–8). Series: The Library of Author Biographies. 2005, Rosen LB $27.95 (978-1-4042-0328-0). 112pp. An interview with Paterson is an interesting addition to this description of the author's life and works for children. (Rev: SLJ 9/05) [921]

PAULSEN, GARY

14403 Gaines, Ann. *Gary Paulsen* (3–6). Series: Real-Life Reader Biographies. 2001, Mitchell Lane LB $15.95 (978-1-58415-077-0). 32pp. Gaines presents Paulsen's difficult childhood, his love of reading, and his fascination with sled dogs and adventure. (Rev: SLJ 9/01) [813]

14404 Paterra, Elizabeth. *Gary Paulsen* (4–7). Series: Who Wrote That? 2002, Chelsea $30.00 (978-0-7910-6723-9). 106pp. A profile of the prolific author (of almost 200 books) who is best known for his young adult outdoor survival stories. (Rev: BL 10/15/02; HBG 3/03) [921]

14405 Paulsen, Gary. *Caught by the Sea* (5–8). 2001, Delacorte $15.95 (978-0-385-32645-2). 104pp. The author describes his ongoing love of the sea and the adventures he's had, some funny, some scary. (Rev: BL 9/15/01; HBG 3/02; SLJ 10/01; VOYA 12/01) [818]

14406 Peters, Stephanie True. *Gary Paulsen* (4–8). Illus. 1999, Learning Works paper $7.99 (978-0-88160-324-8). 111pp. A straightforward biography of the outdoorsman and author that tells about his books, his interests, his alcoholism, and his continuing health problems. (Rev: BL 6/1–15/99; SLJ 6/99) [921]

PINKWATER, DANIEL

14407 McGinty, Alice B. *Meet Daniel Pinkwater* (2–4). Illus. Series: About the Author. 2003, Rosen LB $21.25 (978-0-8239-6406-2). 24pp. Readers learn about Pinkwater's youth and later life, his varied interests, how and why he started writing for children, and how he uses his own childhood experiences in his books. (Rev: SLJ 3/03) [921]

POE, EDGAR ALLAN

14408 Frisch, Aaron. *Edgar Allan Poe* (5–9). Photos by Tina Mucci. Illus. by Gary Kelley. Series: Voices in Poetry. 2005, Creative Education LB $31.35 (978-1-58341-344-9). 45pp. A brief biography that adds atmospheric paintings and photographs to a chronological narrative and excerpts from Poe's works. (Rev: SLJ 3/06) [921]

14409 Kent, Zachary. *Edgar Allan Poe* (5–8). Series: Historical American Biographies. 2001, Enslow LB $26.60 (978-0-7660-1600-2). An informative, well-presented biography of this writer whose unique stories changed the history of American literature. (Rev: BL 1/1–15/02; HBG 3/02; SLJ 9/01) [921]

14410 Lange, Karen E. *Nevermore: A Photobiography of Edgar Allan Poe* (5–8). Illus. 2009, National Geographic $17.95 (978-1-4263-0398-2). 64pp. This readable photo-biography offers an overview of the writer's work and life starting with his difficult childhood and covering his struggles as an adult. (Rev: BCCB 5/09; BL 4/1/09; SLJ 4/09) [921]

14411 Streissguth, Thomas. *Edgar Allan Poe* (5–8). Series: A&E Biography. 2001, Lerner LB $27.93 (978-0-8225-4991-8). The tortured life of this early master of the short story is brought to life in an interesting text and many black-and-white illustrations. (Rev: BL 6/1–15/01; HBG 10/01; SLJ 8/01) [921]

POTTER, BEATRIX

14412 Collins, David R. *The Country Artist: A Story About Beatrix Potter* (3–5). Illus. by Karen Ritz. 1989, Carolrhoda LB $22.60 (978-0-87614-344-5); paper $6.95 (978-0-87614-509-8). 56pp. The story of the creator of Peter Rabbit and other famous creatures. (Rev: BL 5/1/89) [921]

14413 Malam, John. *Beatrix Potter* (1–4). Series: Tell Me About. 1998, Carolrhoda LB $19.93 (978-1-57505-275-5). 24pp. A brief biography of this writer and artist that covers the basics of her life and gives examples of her enchanting work. (Rev: BCCB 1/99; HBG 3/99; SLJ 2/99) [921]

14414 Wallner, Alexandra. *Beatrix Potter* (K–3). Illus. 1995, Holiday House LB $16.95 (978-0-8234-1181-8). 32pp. A fascinating account of the life of this children's book author who was also an expert on mushrooms and an early conservationist. (Rev: BL 9/1/95; SLJ 10/95) [921]

14415 Winter, Jeanette. *Beatrix: Various Episodes from the Life of Beatrix Potter* (PS–2). Illus. 2003, Farrar $15.00 (978-0-374-30655-7). 64pp. Excerpts from Potter's writings are incorporated in this small-format biography that looks mainly at her life as a child and young woman. (Rev: BL 3/1/03; HB 5/03; HBG 10/03; SLJ 3/03) [823]

PRINGLE, LAURENCE

14416 Pringle, Laurence. *Nature! Wild and Wonderful* (2–5). Illus. Series: Meet the Author. 1997, Richard C. Owen $14.95 (978-1-57274-071-6). 32pp. An autobiographical account of this writer of more than 80 books that tells how he became interested in nature study and in writing about it. (Rev: BL 6/1–15/97; HBG 3/98; SLJ 9/97) [921]

PYLE, ERNIE

14417 O'Connor, Barbara. *The Soldiers' Voice: The Story of Ernie Pyle* (4–7). Illus. 1996, Carolrhoda LB $30.35 (978-0-87614-942-3). 80pp. The story of the renowned World War II correspondent who died in the South Pacific while covering the war. (Rev: BCCB 10/96; BL 9/1/96; SLJ 8/96) [921]

QUAN, ELIZABETH

14418 Quan, Elizabeth. *Once Upon a Full Moon* (3–5). Illus. by author. 2007, Tundra $19.95 (978-0-88776-813-2). 48pp. Beautifully written from a child's point of view, this memoir traces the Chinese Canadian author's journey as a young girl in the late 1920s to visit her grandmother in China. (Rev: BL 7/07; SLJ 10/07) [915.104]

RAWLINGS, MARJORIE KINNAN

14419 Cook, Judy, and Laura Lee Smith. *Natural Writer: A Story About Marjorie Kinnan Rawlings* (4–6). Illus. by Laurie Harden. Series: Creative Minds Biographies. 2001, Carolrhoda LB $22.60 (978-1-57505-468-1). 64pp. This easily read biography with full-page illustrations tells the life story of the author of *The Yearling*. (Rev: HBG 10/01; SLJ 8/01) [921]

REY, MARGRET AND H. A.

14420 Borden, Louise. *The Journey That Saved Curious George: The True Wartime Escape of Margret and H. A. Rey* (3–6). Illus. by Allan Drummond. 2005, Houghton $17.00 (978-0-618-33924-2). 80pp. This handsome large-format volume chronicles the escape from Nazism of Margret and H. A. Rey, the creators of the Curious George books for children. (Rev: BL 10/15/05; SLJ 10/05) [813]

RIVERA, TOMAS

14421 Medina, Jane. *Tomas Rivera* (1–2). Illus. by Edward Martinez. Series: Green Light Reader, Level 2. 2004, Harcourt LB $12.95 (978-0-15-205145-7). 24pp. Medina recounts a life-changing experience from the childhood of Mexican American writer/educator Tomas Rivera. (Rev: BL 7/04) [921]

RODRIGUEZ, LUIS

14422 Schwartz, Michael. *Luis Rodriguez* (4–8). Illus. Series: Contemporary Hispanic Americans. 1997, Raintree LB $17.98 (978-0-8172-3990-9). 48pp. The life of this contemporary Hispanic American who went from gang leader and drug addict to writer, journalist, publisher, speaker, and youth activist. (Rev: BL 4/15/97; SLJ 6/97) [921]

ROWLING, J. K.

14423 Gaines, Ann. *J. K. Rowling* (3–6). 2001, Mitchell Lane LB $15.95 (978-1-58415-078-7). 32pp. Gaines chronicles Rowling's struggles as a single mother seeking a publisher before *Harry*'s success. (Rev: BCCB 2/02; SLJ 9/01) [813]

14424 Harmin, Karen Leigh. *J. K. Rowling: Author of Harry Potter* (4–7). Series: People to Know Today. 2006, Enslow LB $31.93 (978-0-7660-1850-1). 128pp. An attractive and accessible biography of the creator of the wildly popular series, with details of her youth, career, and the impact success has had on her life; plus information on aspects of British life that will interest young readers. (Rev: BL 11/1/06) [921]

RUMI

14425 Demi. *Rumi: Whirling Dervish* (5–8). Illus. by author. 2009, Marshall Cavendish $19.99 (978-0-7614-5527-1). 48pp. This picture-book profile of the 13th-century mystical poet, whose full name was Jal?l al-D?n R?m?, Maulana, is enhanced by the rich illustrations. (Rev: BL 4/15/09; LMC 10/09; SLJ 6/09) [891]

RYLANT, CYNTHIA

14426 Rylant, Cynthia. *Best Wishes* (3–6). Illus. by Carlo Ontal. 1992, Owen $14.95 (978-1-878450-20-3). 32pp. The author takes her readers to her home in Ohio, then travels back to her childhood in West Virginia. (Rev: BCCB 9/92; BL 8/92; SLJ 8/92) [921]

SACHAR, LOUIS

14427 Greene, Meg. *Louis Sachar* (5–9). Series: The Library of Author Biographies. 2004, Rosen LB $26.50 (978-0-8239-4017-2). 112pp. Traces the popular, Newbery-winning author's life and looks at his works, writing process, and inspirations, concluding with an interview and reference material. (Rev: SLJ 9/04) [921]

SANDBURG, CARL

14428 Meltzer, Milton. *Carl Sandburg: A Biography* (5–10). Illus. 1999, Millbrook LB $31.90 (978-0-7613-1364-9). 144pp. The story of a literary giant who, in addition to his poetry, is noted for nonfiction works including a biography of Abraham Lincoln. (Rev: BL 12/15/99; HBG 10/00; VOYA 6/00) [921]

14429 Mitchell, Barbara. *"Good Morning Mr. President": A Story About Carl Sandburg* (3–6). 1988, Carolrhoda LB $19.93 (978-0-87614-329-2). 56pp. The story of Sandburg's growing up and the experiences that were later reflected in his poetry. (Rev: BL 3/1/89; SLJ 2/89) [921]

SANDOZ, MARI

14430 Wilkerson, J. L. *Scribe of the Great Plains: Mari Sandoz* (3–5). Illus. 1999, Acorn $8.95 (978-0-9664470-0-2). 144pp. This biography of the author who wrote about the history of the Great Plains describes in detail her childhood struggle to survive the hardships of pioneer life. (Rev: BL 2/1/99; SLJ 3/99) [921]

SENDAK, MAURICE

14431 Braun, Eric. *Maurice Sendak* (K–2). Series: First Biographies. 2004, Capstone LB $17.26 (978-0-7368-3640-1). 24pp. Very basic information on the author/illustrator's life and work for beginning readers and report writers, with photographs and a timeline. (Rev: SLJ 7/05) [921]

SHAKESPEARE, WILLIAM

14432 Aliki. *William Shakespeare and the Globe* (4–7). Illus. 1999, HarperCollins LB $18.89 (978-0-06-027821-2). 48pp. Shakespeare and Elizabethan England come to life in this detailed picture book that uses many quotations from his plays and also tells of the rebuilding of the Globe theater. (Rev: BCCB 4/99; BL 6/1–15/99*; HB 5/99; HBG 10/99; SLJ 5/99) [921]

14433 Bailey, Gerry, and Karen Foster. *Shakespeare's Quill* (3–5). Illus. by Leighton Noyes and Karen Radford. Series: Stories of Great People. 2008, Crabtree LB $29.27 (978-0-7787-3691-2); paper $9.95 (978-0-7787-3713-1). 40pp. Digby Platt and his older sister Hannah learn lots of facts about the man and his writing. (Rev: SLJ 7/08) [921]

14434 Dommermuth-Costa, Carol. *William Shakespeare* (5–8). Series: Biography. 2001, Lerner LB $27.93 (978-0-8225-4996-3). A readable, well-illustrated biography of the Bard of Avon with material on many of his plays. (Rev: BL 4/1/02; HBG 10/02; SLJ 3/02) [921]

14435 Fandel, Jennifer. *William Shakespeare* (5–9). Photos by Marcel Imsand. Series: Voices in Poetry. 2003, Creative Editions LB $19.95 (978-1-58341-283-1). 45pp. A brief and appealing introduction to Shakespeare's life and work, with examples of his poems, excerpts from his plays, and illustrations. (Rev: SLJ 12/03) [822.3]

14436 Hilliam, David. *William Shakespeare: England's Greatest Playwright and Poet* (5–8). Illus. Series: Rulers, Scholars, and Artists of the Renaissance. 2005, Rosen LB $33.25 (978-1-4042-0318-1). 112pp. Information on Shakespeare's life and on the theater scene in 16th-century London is interwoven with quotes from the plays and poems. (Rev: BL 8/05) [822.3]

14437 Nettleton, Pamela Hill. *William Shakespeare: Playwright and Poet* (5–9). Series: Signature Lives. 2005, Compass Point $34.60 (978-0-7565-0816-6). 112pp. Nettleton places facts about Shakespeare's

life within the context of everyday life of the time, with details about the theater and publishing. (Rev: SLJ 6/05) [921]

14438 Thrasher, Thomas. *The Importance of William Shakespeare* (4–8). Series: The Importance Of. 1998, Lucent LB $27.45 (978-1-56006-374-2). This work discusses Shakespeare and his contribution to world culture. (Rev: BL 12/15/98; VOYA 6/99) [921]

SHARMAT, MARJORIE WEINMAN

14439 Wheeler, Jill C. *Marjorie Weinman Sharmat* (2–4). Series: Children's Authors. 2005, ABDO LB $21.35 (978-1-59197-608-0). 24pp. After introducing some of Sharmat's works, Wheeler discusses the author's childhood and influences on her work. (Rev: SLJ 4/05) [921]

SHELLEY, MARY WOLLSTONECRAFT

14440 Darrow, Sharon. *Through the Tempests Dark and Wild: A Story of Mary Shelley, Creator of Frankenstein* (4–7). Illus. by Angela Barren. 2003, Candlewick $16.99 (978-0-7636-0835-4). 40pp. The dramatic story of Mary Shelley's troubled youth is told in this beautifully illustrated, fictionalized picture-book biography. (Rev: BL 6/1–15/03; HBG 10/03; SLJ 6/03) [823]

SILVERSTEIN, SHEL

14441 Ward, S. *Meet Shel Silverstein* (2–3). Series: About the Author. 2001, Rosen LB $18.75 (978-0-8239-5709-5). 24pp. This introduction to the author of "The Giving Tree" describes his life and work. (Rev: SLJ 6/01) [921]

SIMON, SEYMOUR

14442 Simon, Seymour. *From Paper Airplanes to Outer Space* (3–5). Series: Meet the Author. 2000, Richard C. Owen $14.95 (978-1-57274-374-8). 32pp. A noted writer of science books for young people talks about his life and how he writes. (Rev: BL 7/00; HBG 3/01; SLJ 12/00) [921]

SPINELLI, JERRY

14443 McGinty, Alice B. *Meet Jerry Spinelli* (2–4). Illus. Series: About the Author. 2003, Rosen LB $21.25 (978-0-8239-6408-6). 24pp. Readers learn about Spinelli's youth and later life, his varied interests, how and why he started writing for children, and how he uses his own childhood experiences in his books. (Rev: SLJ 3/03) [921]

14444 Seidman, David. *Jerry Spinelli* (5–9). Series: The Library of Author Biographies. 2004, Rosen LB $27.95 (978-0-8239-4016-5). 112pp. Traces the popular, Newbery-winning author's life and looks at his works, writing process, and inspirations, concluding with an interview and reference material. (Rev: SLJ 9/04) [921]

14445 Spinelli, Jerry. *Knots in My Yo-Yo String: The Autobiography of a Kid* (5–8). 1998, Knopf paper

$10.95 (978-0-679-88791-1). A frank, delightful memoir of growing up in Norristown, Pennsylvania, during the 1950s by the renowned Newbery Medal–winning writer of fiction for young people. (Rev: BCCB 7–8/98; BL 5/1/98; HBG 10/98; SLJ 6/98; VOYA 12/98) [921]

STEIN, GERTRUDE

14446 Winter, Jonah. *Gertrude Is Gertrude Is Gertrude Is Gertrude* (2–4). Illus. by Calef Brown. 2009, Atheneum $16.99 (978-1-4169-4088-3). 40pp. An engaging picture-book introduction to the world of writer Gertrude Stein, as she hosts a tea party for Picasso, Matisse, Hemingway, and other artists and writers; the illustrations extend the text and add to the lively atmosphere. (Rev: BCCB 1/09; BL 1/1–15/09; SLJ 2/09) [921]

STEINBECK, JOHN

14447 Tracy, Kathleen. *John Steinbeck* (5–8). Series: Classic Storytellers. 2004, Mitchell Lane LB $29.95 (978-1-58415-271-2). 48pp. An introduction to Steinbeck's life, work, and legacy, with background information on relevant historical, cultural, and economic factors. (Rev: BL 1/05; SLJ 1/05) [921]

STEVENSON, ROBERT LOUIS

14448 Carpenter, Angelica S., and Jean Shirley. *Robert Louis Stevenson: Finding Treasure Island* (5–8). Illus. 1997, Lerner LB $27.93 (978-0-8225-4955-0). A lively biography of this great writer, who was a disappointment to his family because he did not become a minister. (Rev: BL 11/15/97; HBG 3/98; SLJ 12/97) [921]

STINE, R. L.

14449 Cohen, Joel H. *R. L. Stine* (5–8). Series: People in the News. 2000, Lucent LB $28.70 (978-1-56006-608-8). 96pp. This well-documented biography, illustrated with several black-and-white photographs, tells the story of an author who enjoys scaring his readers. (Rev: BL 6/1–15/00; HBG 10/00; SLJ 8/00) [921]

14450 Parker-Rock, Michelle. *R. L. Stine: Creator of Creepy and Spooky Stories* (5–8). Series: Authors Teens Love. 2005, Enslow LB $26.60 (978-0-7660-2445-8). 104pp. Stine's writing career is the main focus of this biography that includes an interview. (Rev: SLJ 1/06) [921]

STOWE, HARRIET BEECHER

14451 Adler, David A. *A Picture Book of Harriet Beecher Stowe* (2–4). Illus. by Colin Bootman. Series: Picture Book Biographies. 2003, Holiday House $16.95 (978-0-8234-1646-2). 32pp. This picture-book biography uses realistic oil paintings to reinforce the information about this inspiring woman and the injustices of slavery. (Rev: BL 6/1–15/03; HBG 10/03; SLJ 5/03) [921]

14452 Bland, Celia. *Harriet Beecher Stowe: Antislavery Author* (3–5). Illus. Series: Junior World Biographies. 1993, Chelsea LB $15.95 (978-0-7910-1773-9). 79pp. The story of the renowned writer and her courageous stand against slavery. (Rev: SLJ 10/93) [921]

14453 Fritz, Jean. *Harriet Beecher Stowe and the Beecher Preachers* (5–9). 1994, Putnam $15.99 (978-0-399-22666-3). In addition to covering *Uncle Tom's Cabin*, this biography gives a full account of Harriet Beecher's private life, marriage, and extended family. (Rev: BCCB 10/94; BL 8/94; HB 9/94; SLJ 9/94*; VOYA 8/94) [921]

14454 Gelletly, LeeAnne. *Harriet Beecher Stowe: Author of Uncle Tom's Cabin* (3–6). 2001, Chelsea LB $25.00 (978-0-7910-6009-4). 80pp. Easy-to-read information on Stowe's life and work is accompanied by illustrations and sidebars that profile some of her contemporaries, including Harriet Tubman and William Lloyd Garrison. (Rev: SLJ 10/01) [921]

14455 Griskey, Michèle. *Harriet Beecher Stowe* (5–7). Series: Classic Storytellers. 2005, Mitchell Lane LB $29.95 (978-1-58415-375-7). 48pp. Good historical and social context makes clear the importance of Stowe's achievements. (Rev: SLJ 11/05) [921]

TAYLOR, MILDRED

14456 Houghton, Gillian. *Mildred Taylor* (5–8). Series: The Library of Author Biographies. 2005, Rosen LB $27.95 (978-1-4042-0330-3). 112pp. An interview with Taylor is an interesting addition to this description of the African American author's life and writings. (Rev: SLJ 9/05) [921]

THOMAS, DYLAN

14457 Thomas, Dylan. *A Child's Christmas in Wales* (3–6). Illus. by Chris Raschka. 2004, Candlewick $17.99 (978-0-7636-2161-2). 32pp. This new edition of Thomas's memoir, first published in 1985, of childhood Christmases in Wales features striking artwork in ink and gouache. (Rev: BL 10/1/04; SLJ 10/04) [821]

THOREAU, HENRY DAVID

14458 Burleigh, Robert. *A Man Named Thoreau* (4–6). Illus. 1985, Macmillan $15.00 (978-0-689-31122-2). 48pp. A profile of the 19th-century thinker in prose that makes him available to the younger grades. (Rev: BCCB 12/85; BL 3/15/86; SLJ 1/86) [921]

14459 Thoreau, Henry David. *Henry David's House* (2–4). Ed. by Steven Schnur. Illus. by Peter M. Fiore. 2002, Charlesbridge $16.95 (978-0-88106-116-1). 32pp. Using Thoreau's words, this picture book describes the construction of his cottage in the woods near Walden Pond. (Rev: BL 4/1/02; HBG 10/02; SLJ 5/02) [921]

TOLKIEN, J. R. R.

14460 Lynch, Doris. *J. R. R. Tolkien* (5–8). Illus. 2003, Watts LB $30.50 (978-0-531-12253-2). 128pp. An attractive biography that reveals how much the author of *The Lord of the Rings* was influenced by his surroundings and experiences. (Rev: BL 12/15/03; SLJ 7/04) [828]

TWAIN, MARK

14461 Aller, Susan Bivin. *Mark Twain* (5–8). Series: A&E Biography. 2001, Lerner LB $27.93 (978-0-8225-4994-9). The colorful life of one of America's favorite authors is re-created in accessible text, black-and-white photographs, and such additions as interesting sidebars and extensive reading lists. (Rev: BL 6/1–15/01; HBG 10/01) [921]

14462 Anderson, William. *River Boy: The Story of Mark Twain* (1–4). Illus. by Dan Andreasen. 2003, HarperCollins LB $17.89 (978-0-06-028401-5). The importance of the Mississippi in Twain's youth is highlighted in this account that includes coverage of his leaving school at the age of 12, working on a steamboat, searching for gold, and his career as a writer and humorist. (Rev: BL 4/15/03; HBG 10/03; SLJ 3/03) [921]

14463 Armentrout, David, and Patricia Armentrout. *Mark Twain* (1–3). Series: Discover the Life of an American Legend. 2004, Rourke LB $14.95 (978-1-58952-660-0). 24pp. An introductory biography that includes period photographs and other illustrations plus a glossary and pronunciation guide. (Rev: SLJ 3/04) [818]

14464 Brown, Don. *American Boy: The Adventures of Mark Twain* (2–6). Illus. by author. 2003, Houghton $16.00 (978-0-618-17997-8). Presented with wit and visual appeal, this biography focuses on Samuel Clemens's youth. (Rev: HBG 4/04; SLJ 9/03) [921]

14465 Collins, David R. *Mark T-W-A-I-N! A Story About Samuel Clemens* (3–5). Illus. by Vicky Carey. 1994, Carolrhoda LB $22.60 (978-0-87614-801-3). 64pp. Beginning with his boyhood in Hannibal, Missouri, through his many jobs as a youth, to his distinguished career as a writer, this is a lively biography of Clemens. (Rev: BL 3/1/94; SLJ 3/94) [921]

14466 Cox, Clinton. *Mark Twain: America's Humorist, Dreamer, Prophet* (5–9). 1995, Scholastic paper $14.95 (978-0-590-45642-5). A biography that includes a discussion of Twain's views on race and how they changed. (Rev: BL 9/15/95; SLJ 9/95; VOYA 12/95) [921]

14467 Fleischman, Sid. *The Trouble Begins at 8: A Life of Mark Twain in the Wild, Wild West* (5–8). Illus. 2008, Greenwillow $18.99 (978-0-06-134431-2). 196pp. This is a spirited account of Twain's adventurous early years and how they formed the foundation for his writing. (Rev: BL 6/1–15/08; SLJ 7/08) [921]

14468 Goldsmith, Howard. *Mark Twain at Work!* (PS–2). Illus. by Frank Habbas. Series: Childhood of Famous Americans. 2003, Simon & Schuster paper $3.99 (978-0-689-85399-9). 31pp. A blend of fact and fiction, this profile of Mark Twain's child-hood focuses on a real-life fence-painting scam from Twain's youth that was later incorporated into *Tom Sawyer,* one of his most popular novels. (Rev: HBG 10/03; SLJ 8/03)

14469 Lasky, Kathryn. *A Brilliant Streak: The Making of Mark Twain* (4–7). Illus. by Barry Moser. 1998, Harcourt $18.00 (978-0-15-252110-3). 48pp. Using many quotations and anecdotes from the author's work, this nicely illustrated biography of Mark Twain concentrates on his first 30 years when he was a steamboat pilot, prospector, reporter, and budding writer. (Rev: BCCB 7–8/98; BL 4/1/98; HB 5/98; HBG 10/98; SLJ 4/98) [921]

14470 MacLeod, Elizabeth. *Mark Twain: An American Star* (3–5). Series: Snapshots: Images of People and Places in History. 2008, Kids Can $14.95 (978-1-55337-908-9); paper $6.95 (978-1-55337-909-6). 32pp. This large-format introduction to Twain's life features spreads with text and a quotation on the left and a collage of images on the right. (Rev: BL 4/15/08; SLJ 5/08) [818]

14471 Pflueger, Lynda. *Mark Twain* (5–8). Series: Historical American Biographies. 1999, Enslow LB $26.60 (978-0-7660-1093-2). A balanced, well-documented biography that includes chapter notes, a bibliography, glossary, and some period black-and-white illustrations. (Rev: BL 1/1–15/00; HBG 3/00; SLJ 1/00) [921]

14472 Rasmussen, R. Kent. *Mark Twain for Kids: His Life and Times, 21 Activities* (4–7). Illus. Series: For Kids. 2004, Chicago Review paper $14.95 (978-1-55652-527-8). 160pp. An engaging biography that reveals interesting details of Twain's life and shows how many of the episodes in his books were based on his own experiences. (Rev: BL 9/15/04; SLJ 9/04) [921]

14473 Sherman, Josepha. *Mark Twain* (4–6). Series: Classic Storytellers. 2005, Mitchell Lane LB $29.95 (978-1-58415-374-0). 48pp. In addition to recounting Twain's life and career as an author, this volume touches on the pressing social issues of the day. (Rev: SLJ 2/06) [921]

VERNE, JULES

14474 Schoell, William. *Remarkable Journeys: The Story of Jules Verne* (4–8). Series: World Writers. 2002, Morgan Reynolds LB $23.95 (978-1-883846-92-3). 112pp. Writing was not Verne's first love, as Schoell explains in this accessible biography. (Rev: BL 6/1–15/02; HBG 10/02; SLJ 9/02) [843.8]

14475 Streissguth, Thomas. *Science Fiction Pioneer: A Story About Jules Verne* (3–6). Illus. by Ralph L. Ramstad. 2000, Carolrhoda LB $22.60 (978-1-57505-440-7). 64pp. This biography traces the life and career of this novelist and how he used his interest and knowledge of science in his works. (Rev: HBG 3/01; SLJ 10/00) [921]

14476 Teeters, Peggy. *Jules Verne: The Man Who Invented Tomorrow* (5–7). Illus. 1993, Walker LB $14.85 (978-0-8027-8191-8). 128pp. The life of the famous writer of science fiction, including his childhood in France. (Rev: BL 3/15/93; SLJ 5/93) [921]

WARNER, GERTRUDE CHANDLER

14477 Ellsworth, Mary Ellen. *Gertrude Chandler Warner and the Boxcar Children* (3–5). Illus. 1997, Whitman LB $15.99 (978-0-8075-2837-2). 61pp. The life story of the author who created the Boxcar Children and lived her entire life in Connecticut. (Rev: BL 8/97; HB 7/97; SLJ 7/97) [921]

14478 Wheeler, Jill C. *Gertrude Chandler Warner* (2–4). Series: Children's Authors. 2005, ABDO LB $21.35 (978-1-59197-609-7). 24pp. After introducing some of Warner's works, Wheeler discusses the author's childhood and influences on her work. (Rev: SLJ 4/05) [921]

WELLS, H. G.

14479 Boerst, William J. *Time Machine: The Story of H. G. Wells* (5–8). Illus. Series: World Writers. 1999, Morgan Reynolds LB $23.95 (978-1-883846-40-4). 112pp. The story of the intriguing English author, including material on his childhood, romances, political views, and literary works. (Rev: BL 1/1–15/00; HBG 3/00) [921]

WHEATLEY, PHILLIS

14480 Gregson, Susan R. *Phillis Wheatley* (4–6). Illus. Series: Let Freedom Ring. 2001, Capstone LB $23.93 (978-0-7368-1033-3). 48pp. Wheatley's early life, education, marriage, and writing career are placed in historical context and accompanied by excerpts of her poems. (Rev: HBG 3/02; SLJ 7/02)

14481 Kent, Deborah. *Phillis Wheatley: First Published African-American Poet* (4–7). Series: Our People. 2003, The Child's World LB $27.07 (978-1-59296-009-5). 32pp. The life of the 18th-century poet is outlined in this well-illustrated work that features large type and includes historical background. (Rev: SLJ 4/04) [921]

14482 McLendon, Jacquelyn. *Phillis Wheatley: A Revolutionary Poet* (4–7). Series: Library of American Lives and Times. 2003, Rosen LB $34.60 (978-0-8239-5750-7). 112pp. Kidnapped into slavery from Senegal, Phillis Wheatley became a major voice in the American literary scene. (Rev: BL 6/1–15/03; SLJ 5/03) [921]

14483 Salisbury, Cynthia. *Phillis Wheatley: Legendary African-American Poet* (5–8). Series: Historical American Biographies. 2001, Enslow LB $26.60 (978-0-7660-1394-0). The life story of the first important African American poet, who was brought to America as a slave and bought by a Quaker family who allowed her to develop her talents. (Rev: BL 3/1/01; HBG 10/01; SLJ 7/01) [921]

14484 Weidt, Maryann N. *Revolutionary Poet: A Story About Phillis Wheatley* (3–6). Illus. Series: Creative Minds. 1997, Carolrhoda LB $22.60 (978-1-57505-037-9); paper $6.95 (978-1-57505-059-1). 64pp. The story of the poetry-writing slave girl who was the first African American to have a book published. (Rev: BL 2/15/98; HBG 3/98) [921]

WHITE, E. B.

14485 Bernard, Catherine. *E. B. White: Spinner of Webs and Tales* (5–8). Series: Authors Teens Love. 2005, Enslow LB $26.60 (978-0-7660-2350-5). 104pp. An introductory chapter that gives a good overview of White's life is followed by chapters that delve into more detail plus a timeline and an excerpt from a 1969 interview that adds a more personal dimension. (Rev: BCCB 12/05; SLJ 10/05) [921]

14486 Collins, David R. *To the Point: A Story About E. B. White* (3–5). Illus. by Amy Johnson. 1989, Carolrhoda LB $22.60 (978-0-87614-345-2); paper $6.95 (978-0-87614-508-1). 56pp. The story of a writer who made a great impact on children's reading. (Rev: BL 5/1/89) [921]

14487 Craats, Rennay. *E. B. White* (2–4). Series: My Favorite Writer. 2004, Weigl LB $16.95 (978-1-59036-026-2). 32pp. This attractively illustrated profile of the life and career of the author of classics including *Stuart Little* is particularly suitable for report writers. (Rev: BL 4/1/04; HBG 3/03) [818]

14488 Murcia, Rebecca Thatcher. *E. B. White* (5–8). Series: Classic Storytellers. 2004, Mitchell Lane LB $29.95 (978-1-58415-273-6). 48pp. An introduction to White's life, work, and legacy, with background information on relevant historical, cultural, and economic factors. (Rev: BL 1/05; SLJ 1/05) [921]

WHITMAN, WALT

14489 Kerley, Barbara. *Walt Whitman: Words for America* (4–8). Illus. by Brian Selznick. 2004, Scholastic $16.95 (978-0-439-35791-3). 56pp. Whitman's experiences during the Civil War, including his service as a nurse to injured and dying soldiers, are highlighted in this picture-book biography. (Rev: BL 11/15/04; SLJ 11/04) [811]

WIESEL, ELIE

14490 Pariser, Michael. *Elie Wiesel: Bearing Witness* (4–6). Illus. Series: Gateway Biographies. 1994, Millbrook LB $20.90 (978-1-56294-419-3). 48pp. A slim biography of the Nobel Prize winner, who at age 15 was sent to Auschwitz. (Rev: SLJ 4/95) [921]

WILDER, LAURA INGALLS

14491 Anderson, William. *Laura's Album: A Remembrance Scrapbook of Laura Ingalls Wilder* (3–6). Illus. 1998, HarperCollins $21.99 (978-0-06-027842-7). 80pp. This is a loving scrapbook of photos, early writings, letters, and drawings by the author of the Little House series. (Rev: BL 1/1–15/99; HBG 10/99) [921]

14492 Anderson, William. *Pioneer Girl: The Story of Laura Ingalls Wilder* (2–4). Illus. by Dan Andreasen. 1998, HarperCollins LB $15.89 (978-0-06-027244-9). This biography of the author covers the significant events in her life. (Rev: HBG 10/98; SLJ 3/98) [921]

14493 Armentrout, David, and Patricia Armentrout. *Laura Ingalls Wilder* (1–3). Illus. Series: Discover a Life of an American Legend. 2003, Rourke LB $14.95 (978-1-58952-663-1). 24pp. Young fans of Wilder will enjoy this brief, photo-filled profile. (Rev: BL 2/1/04) [921]

14494 Berne, Emma Carlson. *Laura Ingalls Wilder* (5–8). Illus. Series: Essential Lives. 2007, ABDO LB $22.95 (978-1-59928-843-7). 112pp. The life of the author of the beloved Little House books, with an emphasis on the hard realities that she faced both as a pioneer child and as an adult during the Great Depression. (Rev: BL 2/1/08; SLJ 3/08) [813]

14495 Giff, Patricia Reilly. *Laura Ingalls Wilder: Growing Up in the Little House* (3–6). Illus. by Eileen McKeating. 1988, Puffin paper $4.99 (978-0-14-032074-9). 64pp. Stories of growing up in the Big Woods of Wisconsin, long, long ago. (Rev: BCCB 9/87; BL 8/87; SLJ 4/87) [921]

14496 Strudwick, Leslie. *Laura Ingalls Wilder* (2–4). Series: My Favorite Writer. 2003, Weigl LB $18.20 (978-1-59036-027-9). 32pp. This attractively illustrated biography is particularly suitable for report writers. (Rev: SLJ 10/04)

14497 Wadsworth, Ginger. *Laura Ingalls Wilder: Storyteller of the Prairie* (5–8). Series: Biography. 1997, Lerner LB $27.93 (978-0-8225-4950-5). A solid, readable biography of this author that clarifies the chronology in the Little House books. (Rev: BL 3/1/97; SLJ 4/97) [921]

14498 Wallner, Alexandra. *Laura Ingalls Wilder* (K–3). Illus. 1997, Holiday House LB $15.95 (978-0-8234-1314-0). 32pp. A concise biography that traces Wilder's life from childhoood to her emergence as a juvenile book author. (Rev: BL 10/1/97; HBG 3/98; SLJ 11/97) [921]

14499 Wilder, Laura Ingalls. *A Little House Traveler: Writings from Laura Ingalls Wilder's Journeys Across America* (5–8). 2006, HarperCollins $16.99 (978-0-06-072491-7). 352pp. Three of Wilder's diaries — one never before published — chronicle the Little House author's travels with her husband Almanzo and daughter Rose. (Rev: BL 12/15/05; VOYA 4/06) [813]

14500 Woods, Mae. *Laura Ingalls Wilder* (2–3). Series: Children's Authors. 2000, ABDO LB $21.35 (978-1-57765-113-0). 24pp. Eight double-page chapters cover Wilder's life from her birth in 1867 to her death in 1957. (Rev: HBG 3/01; SLJ 3/01) [921]

WILLIAMS, WILLIAM CARLOS

14501 Berry, S. L. *William Carlos Williams* (5–9). Illus. by Yan Nascimbene. Series: Voices in Poetry. 2003, Creative LB $19.95 (978-1-58341-284-8). 48pp. This picture-book biography introduces readers to Williams's poetry and life from childhood. (Rev: BL 12/1/03; HBG 4/04) [808]

14502 Bryant, Jen. *A River of Words: The Story of William Carlos Williams* (2–5). Illus. by Melissa Sweet. 2008, Eerdmans $17.00 (978-0-8028-5302-8). 34pp. This picture-book biography neatly integrates the life story of the doctor poet with excerpts of his poems and mixed-media artwork. Caldecott Honor Book, 2009. (Rev: BL 8/08; LMC 3/09; SLJ 9/08) [921]

WONG, JANET S.

14503 Wong, Janet S. *Before It Wriggles Away* (3–5). Illus. Series: Meet the Authors. 2007, Richard C. Owen LB $14.95 (978-1-57274-861-3). 32pp. Introduces the life and work of the children's poet, with her advice on writing. (Rev: BL 6/1–15/07) [921]

WOODSON, JACQUELINE

14504 Hinton, KaaVonia. *Jacqueline Woodson* (5–8). Illus. Series: Classic Storytellers. 2008, Mitchell Lane LB $20.95 (978-1-58415-533-1). 48pp. The story of Woodson's life, from her childhood in the 1960s to her adulthood — including her lesbian relationship — with photographs and discussions of her work. (Rev: BL 3/3/08; SLJ 8/08) [921]

YEP, LAURENCE

14505 McGinty, Alice B. *Meet Laurence Yep* (2–3). Series: About the Author. 2003, Rosen LB $21.25 (978-0-8239-6410-9). 24pp. Sample passages, book covers, childhood photographs, and an interview make this an appealing, easy-to-read profile of the Asian American writer and his career. (Rev: SLJ 5/03) [921]

YOLEN, JANE

14506 McGinty, Alice B. *Meet Jane Yolen* (2–4). Illus. Series: About the Author. 2003, Rosen LB $21.25 (978-0-8239-6407-9). 24pp. Readers learn about Yolen's youth and later life and how and why she started writing for children, with excerpts from her books and reprints of covers. (Rev: SLJ 3/03) [921]

14507 Yolen, Jane. *A Letter from Phoenix Farm* (3–6). Illus. by Jason Stemple. 1992, Owen $14.95 (978-1-878450-36-4). 32pp. Spending a day with this writer of children's books. (Rev: BCCB 9/92; BL 8/92; SLJ 8/92) [921]

ZINDEL, PAUL

14508 Daniel, Susanna. *Paul Zindel* (5–8). Series: The Library of Author Biographies. 2004, Rosen LB $27.95 (978-0-8239-4524-5). 112pp. Covers Zindel's career as a YA author, with analysis of his work, an interview, and lists of works and awards. (Rev: SLJ 1/05) [921]

Contemporary and Historical Americans

Collective

14509 Adams, Simon. *The Presidents of the United States* (3–7). 2001, Two-Can $16.95 (978-1-58728-093-1); paper $9.95 (978-1-58728-092-4). 96pp. Double-page spreads give basic information on each president, with interesting anecdotes, timelines, full-color portraits, reproductions, and a carefully chosen quotation. (Rev: SLJ 7/01) [973.0099]

14510 Adler, David A. *Enemies of Slavery* (3–6). Illus. by Donald A. Smith. 2004, Holiday House $16.95 (978-0-8234-1596-0). 32pp. Fourteen Americans who played important roles in the fight against slavery are briefly introduced, with relevant quotations, in this picture book for older children. (Rev: BL 10/1/04; SLJ 3/05) [326.8]

14511 Adler, David A. *Heroes for Civil Rights* (3–5). Illus. by Bill Farnsworth. 2008, Holiday $16.95 (978-0-8234-2008-7). 32pp. Ralph Abernathy, Fannie Lou Hamer, Martin Luther King Jr., and Thurgood Marshall are among the activists profiled in this attractive volume. (Rev: BL 2/1/08; LMC 3/08; SLJ 1/08) [920]

14512 Adler, David A. *Heroes of the Revolution* (1–4). Illus. by Donald A. Smith. 2003, Holiday House $16.95 (978-0-8234-1471-0). 32pp. Among the 12 men and women profiled here are Crispus Attucks, Deborah Sampson, Molly Pitcher, Ethan Allen, and Thomas Jefferson; each entry includes an illustration, birth and death dates, and the person's contributions to the Revolutionary War. (Rev: HBG 4/04; SLJ 11/03) [920]

14513 Ashby, Ruth. *Extraordinary People* (5–8). Series: Civil War Chronicles. 2002, Smart Apple LB $28.50 (978-1-58340-182-8). 48pp. Key military and civilian figures from both North and South are profiled. (Rev: HBG 3/03; SLJ 2/03; VOYA 4/03) [973.7]

14514 Barber, James, and Amy Pastan. *Presidents and First Ladies* (4–8). Illus. 2002, DK paper $12.99 (978-0-7894-8453-6). 96pp. For each presi-

dent and his First Lady, there are biographies, a list of key events, and a box highlighting an important event during that administration, plus plenty of color illustrations. (Rev: BL 4/1/02; HBG 10/02; SLJ 5/02) [920]

14515 Bausum, Ann. *Our Country's First Ladies* (4–8). 2007, National Geographic $19.95 (978-1-4263-0006-6). 128pp. These profiles of America's first ladies provide material for report writers and enough interest for browsers. (Rev: SLJ 1/07) [920]

14516 Bausum, Ann. *Our Country's Presidents* (4–7). Illus. 2009, National Geographic $24.95 (978-1-4263-0375-3). Full of interesting facts, quotations, and illustrations, this new edition includes information on Barack Obama as well as expanded coverage of George W. Bush's presidency, plus four new essays and an introduction by Obama. (Rev: BL 3/15/09; SLJ 3/09) [973]

14517 Beiden, Tonya. *Portraits of African-American Heroes* (3–5). Illus. by Ansel Pitcairn. 2004, Dutton $18.99 (978-0-525-47043-4). 96pp. Profiles of figures including Dizzy Gillespie and Gwendolyn Brooks use personal memoirs to draw the reader in. (Rev: BL 3/15/04; SLJ 1/04) [920]

14518 Bowdish, Lynea. *With Courage: Seven Women Who Changed America* (4–6). Illus. 2004, Mondo paper $6.95 (978-1-59336-280-5). 48pp. Rachel Carson, Condoleezza Rice, and Maya Lin are among the seven women profiled for their achievements in mainly male-dominated fields. (Rev: BL 3/1/04; SLJ 7/04) [920]

14519 Brooks, Philip. *Extraordinary Jewish Americans* (5–9). Series: Extraordinary People. 1998, Children's LB $40.00 (978-0-516-20609-7). 288pp. In chronological order, this book presents brief biographical sketches of 60 prominent Jews from a wide variety of fields including science, business, sports, the arts, entertainment, and politics. (Rev: HBG 3/99; SLJ 10/98; VOYA 6/99) [920]

14520 Bruning, John Robert. *Elusive Glory: African-American Heroes of World War II* (5–8). Illus. Series: Avisson Young Adult. 2001, Avisson paper

$19.95 (978-1-888105-48-3). 144pp. The true stories of African American servicemen, including six Tuskegee Airmen, who served the United States during World War II. (Rev: BL 1/1–15/02; SLJ 4/02) [940.54]

14521 Buller, Jon, et al. *Smart About the Presidents* (4–7). Illus. by authors. Series: Smart About History. 2004, Penguin paper $5.99 (978-0-448-43372-1). 64pp. Pertinent facts about each president are conveyed in an informative, accessible style. (Rev: BL 9/1/04; SLJ 4/05) [920]

14522 Burgan, Michael. *Great Women of the American Revolution* (4–6). Series: We the People. 2005, Compass Point LB $26.60 (978-0-7565-0838-8). 48pp. Women's exploits and achievements during the Revolutionary War are placed in historical context. (Rev: SLJ 6/05) [920]

14523 Caravantes, Peggy. *Petticoat Spies: Six Women Spies of the Civil War* (5–8). Illus. 2002, Morgan Reynolds LB $23.95 (978-1-883846-88-6). 112pp. An exciting volume about six women who spied for the Union and Confederacy during the Civil War, with photographs, source notes, a glossary, and a bibliography. (Rev: BL 3/15/02; HBG 10/02; SLJ 8/02) [973.7]

14524 Cheney, Lynne. *A Is for Abigail: An Almanac of Amazing American Women* (2–4). Illus. by Robin P. Glasser. 2003, Simon & Schuster $16.95 (978-0-689-85819-2). 48pp. Cheney celebrates the contributions of American women in all walks of life, from athletes and performers to inventors and scientists. (Rev: BL 2/1/04; HBG 4/04; SLJ 9/03) [973]

14525 Clinton, Catherine. *When Harriet Met Sojourner* (K–3). Illus. by Shane W. Evans. 2007, HarperCollins $16.99 (978-0-06-050425-0). 32pp. In alternating double-page spreads, Clinton presents the often-difficult lives of Harriet Tubman and Sojourner Truth, ending with a hypothetical meeting between the two in 1864. (Rev: BCCB 2/08; BL 10/15/07; SLJ 4/08) [920]

14526 Cook, Michelle, ed. *Our Children Can Soar: A Celebration of Rosa, Barack, and the Pioneers of Change* (PS–3). Illus. by Cozbi A. Cabrera. 2009, Bloomsbury $16.99 (978-1-59990-418-4). 32pp. With art by 13 well-known children's book illustrators, this well-presented book profiles 11 key African Americans and their importance in bringing equality. (Rev: BL 4/15/09; SLJ 5/09) [920]

14527 Cox, Clinton. *African American Teachers* (4–7). Series: Black Stars. 2000, Wiley $22.95 (978-0-471-24649-7). 172pp. A collection of short profiles of important African American teachers who have inspired their students and championed the cause of education. (Rev: BL 7/00; HBG 3/01; SLJ 7/00) [920]

14528 Davidson, Sue. *Getting the Real Story: Nellie Bly and Ida B. Wells* (4–6). 1992, Seal paper $8.95 (978-1-878067-16-6). 152pp. The story of two gallant women news reporters, both of whom fought for justice and against corruption. (Rev: SLJ 7/92) [920]

14529 Delano, Marfé Ferguson. *American Heroes* (5–8). Illus. 2005, National Geographic LB $45.90 (978-0-7922-7215-1). 192pp. Fifty men and women whose heroism has helped to shape America are profiled in this attractive large-format volume. (Rev: BL 12/1/05; SLJ 2/06) [920.073]

14530 Delisle, Jim. *Kidstories: Biographies of 20 Young People You'd Like to Know* (PS–3). Illus. 1991, Free Spirit paper $10.95 (978-0-915793-34-1). 168pp. This collection of short biographies tells about young people from different life-styles and locales. (Rev: BCCB 1/92; BL 12/15/91; SLJ 1/92) [920]

14531 Doherty, Kieran. *Explorers, Missionaries, and Trappers: Trailblazers of the West* (5–8). Series: Shaping America. 2000, Oliver LB $22.95 (978-1-881508-52-6). 176pp. Nine important pioneers of the American West are profiled including a Spanish conquistador, two Spanish priests, John Sutter, Marcus and Narcissa Whitman, and Brigham Young. (Rev: HBG 10/00; SLJ 5/00) [920]

14532 Doherty, Kieran. *Voyageurs, Lumberjacks, and Farmers: Pioneers of the Midwest* (5–8). Series: Shaping America. 2004, Oliver LB $22.95 (978-1-881508-54-0). 176pp. The lives and accomplishments of eight individuals — including Antoine Cadillac, Jean du Sable, and Josiah and Abigail Snelling — who played key roles in the settlement of the Midwest are placed in historical context, with discussion of the plight of Native Americans in the region. (Rev: SLJ 9/04) [920]

14533 Drucker, Malka. *Portraits of Jewish American Heroes* (3–6). Illus. by Elizabeth Rosen. 2008, Dutton $21.99 (978-0-525-47771-6). 96pp. Twenty contemporary and historical Jewish Americans from many walks of life — including such figures as Albert Einstein, Ruth Bader Ginsburg, Steven Spielberg, Levi Strauss, and Daniel Pearl — are presented in brief but imaginatively presented profiles. (Rev: BL 7/08; SLJ 9/08) [973]

14534 Fleischman, John. *Black and White Airmen: Their True History* (5–8). Illus. 2007, Houghton $20.00 (978-0-618-56297-8). 160pp. At a reunion decades later, white bomber pilot Herb Heilbrun and Tuskegee Airman John Leahr discover how much of World War II they shared although separated by segregation. (Rev: BL 2/1/07) [920]

14535 Fradin, Dennis Brindell. *The Founders: The 39 Stories Behind the U.S. Constitution* (4–7). Illus. by Michael McCurdy. 2005, Walker $22.95 (978-0-8027-8972-3). 176pp. The 39 men who signed the Constitution are profiled in brief chapters that include information on their home states. (Rev: BL 10/15/05; SLJ 9/05) [973.3]

14536 Furbee, Mary Rodd. *Outrageous Women of Civil War Times* (3–6). Series: Outrageous Women. 2003, Jossey-Bass paper $12.95 (978-0-471-22926-1). 124pp. This fascinating collective biography profiles a number of women — some outrageous, others not — who played important roles during the Civil War era; sidebars, photographs, prints, and paintings add appeal. (Rev: BL 10/1/03) [920]

14537 Furbee, Mary Rodd. *Outrageous Women of Colonial America* (3–6). Illus. Series: Outrageous Women. 2001, Wiley paper $12.95 (978-0-471-

38299-7). 120pp. Fourteen women are profiled here, in sections on New England, the middle colonies, and the South. (Rev: BL 5/15/01) [920]

14538 Gormley, Beatrice. *First Ladies: Women Who Called the White House Home* (4–6). Illus. 1997, Scholastic paper $7.99 (978-0-590-25518-9). 96pp. A collection of short profiles of U.S. presidents' wives, from Martha Washington to Hillary Clinton. (Rev: BL 3/15/97) [920]

14539 Green, Carl R. *The Younger Brothers* (4–6). Illus. Series: Outlaws and Lawmen. 1995, Enslow LB $21.26 (978-0-89490-592-6). 48pp. The story of the interesting characters who were involved with Jesse James in the old West. (Rev: SLJ 9/95) [920]

14540 Green, Carl R., and William R. Sanford. *Confederate Generals of the Civil War* (5–8). Illus. Series: Collective Biographies. 1998, Enslow LB $26.60 (978-0-7660-1029-1). 112pp. After a brief introduction to the Civil War, this book highlights the careers of 10 Southern generals and their contributions to the Confederate cause. (Rev: BL 8/98) [920]

14541 Green, Carl R., and William R. Sanford. *Union Generals of the Civil War* (5–8). Illus. 1998, Enslow LB $26.60 (978-0-7660-1028-4). 112pp. Using period photographs and prints plus a concise text, this book outlines the careers of 10 Union generals and supplies background material on the Civil War, including charts and maps. (Rev: BL 8/98) [920]

14542 Hacker, Carlotta. *Great African Americans in History* (5–8). Series: Outstanding African Americans. 1997, Crabtree LB $22.60 (978-0-86505-805-7); paper $8.95 (978-0-86505-819-4). There are profiles of 13 great African Americans in American history, including Frederick Douglass, Harriet Tubman, W. E. B. Du Bois, Mary McLeod Bethune, and George Washington Carver. (Rev: BL 9/15/97; SLJ 1/98) [920]

14543 Harmon, Rod. *American Civil Rights Leaders* (5–7). Series: Collective Biographies. 2000, Enslow LB $26.60 (978-0-7660-1381-0). 104pp. This collective biography profiles 10 individuals who are currently or once were active in the civil rights movement in the United States. (Rev: BL 12/15/00; HBG 10/01) [920]

14544 Harness, Cheryl. *Rabble Rousers: 20 Women Who Made a Difference* (3–6). Illus. 2003, Dutton $17.99 (978-0-525-47035-9). 64pp. Girls especially will be drawn to these inspiring two-page accounts of feminists ranging from the famous, such as Susan B. Anthony, to less-known figures, including Ann Lee, founder of the Shaker movement, all presented with handsome sepia portraits, timelines, and addresses of relevant organizations. (Rev: BL 1/1–15/03; HBG 10/03; SLJ 1/03) [305.42]

14545 Harness, Cheryl. *Remember the Ladies* (4–7). Illus. 2001, HarperCollins $16.99 (978-0-688-17017-2). 64pp. Brief profiles of 100 important American women are each accompanied by a portrait. (Rev: BL 4/15/01; HBG 10/01; SLJ 2/01) [920]

14546 Harris, Laurie L., ed. *Biography for Beginners: Presidents of the United States* (3–6). Series: Biog-

raphy for Beginners. 1998, Omnigraphics LB $50.00 (978-0-7808-0262-9). 467pp. A fine introduction to the lives and accomplishments of each of our presidents, ending with Clinton. (Rev: SLJ 11/98) [920]

14547 Hart, Philip S. *Flying Free: America's First Black Aviators* (5–9). 1992, Lerner LB $22.60 (978-0-8225-1598-2). The contributions of African Americans who succeeded against great odds to become aerial performers, combat pilots, and aviation instructors. (Rev: BL 10/15/92; SLJ 1/93) [629.13]

14548 Haskins, James. *One More River to Cross: The Stories of Twelve Black Americans* (4–8). Illus. 1992, Scholastic $13.95 (978-0-590-42896-5). 160pp. Eight men and four women who defied the odds to achieve prominence in their fields are introduced, including Ralph Bunche, Shirley Chisholm, and Ron McNair. (Rev: BCCB 4/92; BL 2/1/92; SLJ 4/92) [920]

14549 Hoose, Phillip. *We Were There, Too! Young People in U.S. History* (5–8). Illus. 2001, Farrar $28.00 (978-0-374-38252-0). 276pp. Hoose tells the stories of dozens of young people who contributed to the making of America — some famous but many who will be new to readers. (Rev: BCCB 10/01; BL 8/01; HB 9/01*; HBG 3/02; SLJ 8/01*) [973]

14550 Hudson, Wade, and Valerie Wesley Wilson. *Afro-Bets Book of Black Heroes from A to Z: An Introduction to Important Black Achievers* (4–7). Illus. 1988, Just Us Bks. paper $7.95 (978-0-940975-02-6). 64pp. Forty-nine African American men and women of outstanding accomplishment. (Rev: BL 1/1/89; SLJ 12/88) [920]

14551 Hughes, Chris. *The Constitutional Convention* (5–9). Series: People at the Center Of. 2005, Gale LB $24.95 (978-1-56711-918-3). 48pp. After an overview of the convention, this volume provides biographical information on key figures including George Washington, Benjamin Franklin, James Madison, and Alexander Hamilton. (Rev: SLJ 6/05) [920]

14552 Igus, Toyomi, ed. *Great Women in the Struggle* (3–6). Illus. Series: Book of Black Heroes. 1992, Just Us Bks. LB $17.95 (978-0-940975-27-9); paper $10.95 (978-0-940975-26-2). 107pp. More than 80 contemporary African American women are profiled. (Rev: SLJ 8/92) [920]

14553 Keenan, Sheila. *Scholastic Encyclopedia of Women in United States History* (4–9). 1996, Scholastic paper $17.95 (978-0-590-22792-6). More than 200 brief biographies of American women representing a variety of professions and accomplishments, organized into six chronologically arranged chapters. (Rev: SLJ 2/97) [920]

14554 Kimmel, Elizabeth C. *Ladies First: 40 Daring American Women Who Were Second to None* (4–7). 2006, National Geographic $18.95 (978-0-7922-5393-8). 192pp. From well-known women such as Sacagawea and Helen Keller to racing driver Shirley Muldowney and rabbi Sally Priesand, this is a well-written and informative resource. (Rev: SLJ 10/06; VOYA 8/06) [920]

14555 King, David C. *First Facts About American Heroes* (3–6). Illus. 1995, Blackbirch LB $36.20 (978-1-56711-165-1). 112pp. The lives and accomplishments of 42 famous Americans are presented, each with a full-page photograph or painting and a single page of facts. (Rev: SLJ 2/96) [920]

14556 Knapp, Ron. *American Generals of World War II* (5–8). Series: Collective Biographies. 1998, Enslow LB $26.60 (978-0-7660-1024-6). 128pp. The 10 U.S. generals profiled here are Henry Arnold, Omar Bradley, Dwight Eisenhower, Curtis LeMay, Douglas MacArthur, George Marshall, George Patton, Matthew Ridgway, Holland Smith, and Joseph Stilwell. (Rev: SLJ 9/98) [920]

14557 Kramer, Barbara. *Trailblazing American Women* (5–7). Series: Collective Biographies. 2000, Enslow LB $26.60 (978-0-7660-1377-3). 112pp. This collection of biographies profiles women who dared to branch out into new fields and break new ground. (Rev: BL 9/15/00; HBG 10/01; SLJ 12/00) [920]

14558 Krohn, Katherine. *Women of the Wild West* (4–6). Series: A&E Biography. 2000, Lerner LB $27.93 (978-0-8225-4980-2). 112pp. Among its several profiles, this book examines the lives of some infamous women of the Wild West: Calamity Jane, Belle Starr, Pearl Hart, and Annie Oakley. (Rev: BL 6/1–15/00; HBG 3/01; SLJ 9/00) [920]

14559 Krull, Kathleen. *Lives of the Presidents: Fame, Shame (and What the Neighbors Thought)* (4–8). Illus. by Kathryn Hewitt. 1998, Harcourt $20.00 (978-0-15-200808-6). 96pp. An entertaining collective biography that stresses the human side of U.S. presidents, with interesting, insightful tidbits and details that bring the presidents to life. (Rev: BL 8/98; HB 11/98; HBG 3/99; SLJ 9/98) [920]

14560 Lindop, Edmund. *Dwight D. Eisenhower, John F. Kennedy, Lyndon B. Johnson* (4–7). Illus. Series: Presidents Who Dared. 1996, Twenty-First Century LB $23.90 (978-0-8050-3404-2). 64pp. The highlights of these three administrations are presented, preceded by an introduction to the American presidency. (Rev: BL 4/15/96; SLJ 6/96) [920]

14561 Lindop, Edmund. *George Washington, Thomas Jefferson, Andrew Jackson* (4–7). Illus. Series: Presidents Who Dared. 1995, Twenty-First Century LB $23.90 (978-0-8050-3401-1). 64pp. After a general introduction on the duties of the president, brief biographies of three are given, with emphasis on their accomplishments in office. (Rev: BL 1/1–15/96; SLJ 11/95) [920]

14562 Lindop, Edmund. *James K. Polk, Abraham Lincoln, Theodore Roosevelt* (4–7). Illus. Series: Presidents Who Dared. 1995, Twenty-First Century LB $23.90 (978-0-8050-3402-8). 64pp. Highlights and evaluations of the presidencies of Polk, Lincoln, and Theodore Roosevelt. (Rev: BL 1/1–15/96; SLJ 11/95) [920]

14563 Lindop, Edmund. *Richard M. Nixon, Jimmy Carter, Ronald Reagan* (4–8). Series: Presidents Who Dared. 1996, Twenty-First Century LB $23.90 (978-0-8050-3405-9). This account traces salient events in each of these presidents' terms, for example: Nixon and Watergate and relations with China; Carter and ending the war between Egypt and Israel; and Reagan and his arms agreement with the Soviet Union. (Rev: BL 4/15/96; SLJ 6/96) [920]

14564 Lindop, Edmund. *Woodrow Wilson, Franklin D. Roosevelt, Harry S. Truman* (5–8). Illus. Series: Presidents Who Dared. 1995, Twenty-First Century LB $23.90 (978-0-8050-3403-5). 64pp. After an overview of the presidency and brief profiles of these men, this account looks at daring decisions they made as presidents. (Rev: BL 1/1–15/96; SLJ 11/95; VOYA 6/96) [920]

14565 Lynne, Douglas. *Contemporary United States: 1968 to the Present* (5–8). Illus. Series: Presidents of the United States. 2007, Weigl LB $20.35 (978-1-59036-753-7). 48pp. The lives and times of recent U.S. presidents — from Nixon to George W. Bush — are covered in this eighth volume in the series. (Rev: BL 10/15/07) [973.92092]

14566 Marvis, Barbara. *Famous People of Asian Ancestry, Vol. 4* (4–7). Illus. Series: Contemporary American Success Stories. 1994, Mitchell Lane paper $10.95 (978-1-883845-09-4). 96pp. A collective biography of Asian Americans, including actor Dustin Nguyen, novelist Amy Tan, and businessman Rocky Aoki. Also use volumes 1 through 3 (2nd ed., 1997). (Rev: BL 10/1/94; SLJ 11/94) [920]

14567 Marvis, Barbara. *Famous People of Hispanic Heritage, Vol. 4* (4–9). Illus. Series: Contemporary American Success Stories. 1996, Mitchell Lane paper $12.95 (978-1-883845-29-2). The lives of two Hispanic men and two women who have succeeded in their careers are presented in an easy-to-read style. Other volumes in this series by the same author are available. (Rev: BL 12/15/96; SLJ 1/97; VOYA 2/97) [920]

14568 Masters, Nancy Robinson. *Extraordinary Patriots of the United States of America: Colonial Times to Pre-Civil War* (5–8). Series: Extraordinary People. 2005, Children's Pr. LB $40.00 (978-0-516-24404-4). 288pp. Interesting 3- to 5-page profiles are arranged chronologically by year of birth. (Rev: SLJ 2/06) [920]

14569 Meisner, James, and Amy Ruth. *American Revolutionaries and Founders of the Nation* (5–7). Series: Collective Biographies. 1999, Enslow LB $26.60 (978-0-7660-1115-1). 112pp. Ten brief biographies of prominent leaders of the American Revolution, each with a black-and-white portrait. (Rev: BL 9/15/99) [920]

14570 Morin, Isobel V. *Women Chosen for Public Office* (5–7). Illus. 1995, Oliver LB $19.95 (978-1-881508-20-5). 160pp. Nine biographies of women who are involved in the federal government from the superintendent of army nurses to Supreme Court Justice Ruth Bader Ginsburg. (Rev: BL 5/1/95; SLJ 6/95) [920]

14571 Morris, Juddi. *At Home with the Presidents* (4–8). 1999, Wiley paper $13.95 (978-0-471-25300-6). 172pp. In three to five pages each, this account profiles the presidents of the United States from Washington through Clinton. (Rev: SLJ 3/00) [920]

14572 Munson, Sammye. *Today's Tejano Heroes* (5–8). Illus. 2000, Eakin $13.95 (978-1-57168-328-1). 80pp. In alphabetical order, this volume introduces 16 important 20th-century Mexican Americans who have contributed to the history and culture of Texas, including Vikki Carr, Attorney General Dan Morales, and federal judge Hilda Tagle. (Rev: BL 2/1/01) [920]

14573 O'Connor, Jane. *If the Walls Could Talk: Family Life at the White House* (4–7). Illus. by Gary Hovland. 2004, Simon & Schuster $16.95 (978-0-689-86863-4). 48pp. This inside view of family life within the White House — with caricatures and interesting trivia — is similar to Judith St. George's *So You Want to Be President* (Putnam, 2000). (Rev: BL 8/04; SLJ 9/04)

14574 Pelz, Ruth. *Black Heroes of the Wild West* (3–5). Illus. by Leandro Della Piana. 1989, Open Hand $12.95 (978-0-940880-25-2); paper $6.95 (978-0-940880-26-9). 56pp. The stories of five black men and four black women who contributed to the history of the Old West. (Rev: BL 6/1/90) [920]

14575 Pelz, Ruth. *Women of the Wild West: Biographies from Many Cultures* (3–5). Illus. 1995, Open Hand paper $6.95 (978-0-940880-50-4). 64pp. The biographies of eight women — e.g., Sacajawea and ex-slave Biddy Mason — who played important roles in the history of the American West. (Rev: BL 3/1/95) [921]

14576 Pinkney, Andrea D. *Let It Shine: Stories of Black Women Freedom Fighters* (5–8). Illus. 2000, Harcourt $20.00 (978-0-15-201005-8). 120pp. This work contains chatty profiles of 10 important African American women, including Sojourner Truth, Rosa Parks, and Shirley Chisholm. (Rev: BCCB 11/00; BL 11/15/00; HB 11/00; HBG 3/01; SLJ 10/00; VOYA 12/00) [921]

14577 *Presidents of the United States* (3–6). Illus. Series: Time for Kids. 2006, HarperCollins $17.99 (978-0-06-081554-7). 70pp. Following a discussion of the three branches of government, this browsable volume covers the presidents in chronological order, giving basic personal information and a portrait, political cartoons, notable quotations, and so forth; several presidents are selected for more in-depth information. (Rev: SLJ 10/06) [920]

14578 Raatma, Lucia. *Great Women of the Civil War* (4–6). Series: We the People. 2005, Compass Point LB $26.60 (978-0-7565-0839-5). 48pp. Women's exploits and achievements during the Civil War are placed in historical context. (Rev: BL 5/15/04; HBG 3/98; SLJ 6/05) [920]

14579 Rappaport, Doreen. *In the Promised Land: Lives of Jewish Americans* (4–7). Illus. by Cornelius Van Wright. 2005, HarperCollins LB $16.89 (978-0-06-059395-7). 32pp. A look at the lives and diverse accomplishments of 13 notable Jewish Americans, including Asser Levy, Harry Houdini, Jonas Salk, and Steven Spielberg. (Rev: BL 1/1–15/05; SLJ 5/05) [920]

14580 Rappaport, Doreen. *We Are the Many: A Picture Book of American Indians* (K–3). Illus. by Cornelius Van Wright and Ying-Hwa Hu. 2002, HarperCollins LB $17.89 (978-0-06-001139-0). 32pp. A collection of 13 brief biographies of Native Americans from different tribes, including Tisquantum (Squanto), Jim Thorpe, and Maria Tallchief. (Rev: BL 10/15/02; HBG 3/03; SLJ 9/02) [970.004]

14581 Roop, Connie, and Peter Roop. *Tales of Famous Americans* (3–5). Illus. by Charlie Powell. 2007, Scholastic $17.99 (978-0-439-64116-6). 112pp. With caricatures and anecdotes from their childhoods, this volume introduces figures ranging from George Washington and Pocahontas to Mia Hamm and Yo-Yo Ma. (Rev: BL 11/15/07; SLJ 2/08) [920]

14582 Sullivan, Otha R. *African American Millionaires* (5–10). Series: Black Stars. 2004, Wiley $24.95 (978-0-471-46928-5). 158pp. Tyra Banks and Oprah Winfrey are included here, but so are many names that may be unfamiliar to readers, such as William Alexander Leidesdorff and Annie Turnbo Malone. (Rev: SLJ 5/05) [920]

14583 Thomson, Sarah L. *What Presidents Are Made Of* (2–4). Illus. by Hanoch Piven. 2004, Simon & Schuster $15.95 (978-0-689-86880-1). 40pp. Collage caricatures and brief text give wry and unusual portraits of 17 of America's presidents and their outstanding characteristics or interests. (Rev: BL 8/04; SLJ 8/04) [973]

14584 Wheeler, Jill C. *America's Leaders* (4–7). Series: War on Terrorism. 2002, ABDO LB $25.65 (978-1-57765-661-6). 48pp. This book contains brief profiles of important American figures in the war against terrorism such as President Bush, Colin Powell, John Ashcroft, and Rudy Giuliani. (Rev: BL 5/15/02; HBG 10/02) [920]

African Americans

ALLEN, RICHARD

14585 Klots, Steve. *Richard Allen* (5–8). Illus. Series: Black Americans of Achievement. 1990, Chelsea LB $19.95 (978-1-55546-570-4). 112pp. Born a slave in 1780, this convert to Christianity founded the first African American Methodist Church. (Rev: SLJ 2/91) [921]

BALL, CHARLES

14586 Shuter, Jane, ed. *Charles Ball and American Slavery* (5–8). Illus. Series: History Eyewitness. 1995, Raintree LB $24.26 (978-0-8114-8281-3). 48pp. This autobiographical account in simple language brings the horrors of slavery to life, with period prints and maps. (Rev: BL 4/15/95; SLJ 5/95) [975]

BETHUNE, MARY MCLEOD

14587 Kelso, Richard. *Building a Dream: Mary Bethune's School* (2–4). Illus. by Debbe Heller.

Series: Stories of America. 1993, Raintree LB $27.12 (978-0-8114-7217-3). 46pp. The story of Mary Bethune and how she realized her dream of building a school for poor African American children. (Rev: SLJ 7/93) [921]

14588 McKissack, Patricia C., and Fredrick McKissack. *Mary McLeod Bethune: A Great Teacher*. Rev. ed. (2–4). Series: Great African Americans. 2001, Enslow LB $18.60 (978-0-7660-1680-4). 32pp. An updated biography of the former slave who dedicated her life to the education of African Americans, with new illustrations. (Rev: HBG 3/02; SLJ 5/02) [921]

14589 Meltzer, Milton. *Mary McLeod Bethune: Voice of Black Hope* (4–7). Illus. 1988, Puffin paper $4.99 (978-0-14-032219-4). 64pp. An effective profile of the African American educator. (Rev: BCCB 5/87; BL 3/15/87; SLJ 3/87) [370.0924]

14590 Somervill, Barbara. *Mary McLeod Bethune: African-American Educator* (4–7). Series: Our People. 2003, The Child's World LB $27.07 (978-1-59296-008-8). 32pp. A profile of the African American educator and leader, with sidebars that add historical context. (Rev: SLJ 4/04) [921]

BROWN, AUNT CLARA

14591 Lowery, Linda. *Aunt Clara Brown: Official Pioneer* (2–4). Illus. by Janice L. Porter. Series: On My Own Biography. 1999, Carolrhoda LB $14.95 (978-1-57505-045-4). 48pp. The inspiring story of a freed slave who used the wealth she accumulated in Colorado to help other freed blacks after the Civil War. (Rev: BCCB 12/99; HBG 3/00; SLJ 11/99*) [921]

BUNCHE, RALPH J.

14592 McKissack, Patricia C., and Fredrick McKissack. *Ralph J. Bunche: Peacemaker*. Rev. ed. (2–4). Series: Great African Americans. 2002, Enslow LB $18.60 (978-0-7660-1701-6). 32pp. The inspiring story of the African American diplomat who was active in UN affairs and won the Nobel Peace Prize in 1950. (Rev: BL 7/02; HBG 10/02) [921]

CARMICHAEL, STOKELY

14593 Cwiklik, Robert. *Stokely Carmichael and Black Power* (4–6). Illus. Series: Gateway Civil Rights. 1993, Millbrook LB $23.90 (978-1-56294-276-2). 32pp. The life of the controversial civil rights leader who coined the term "black power." (Rev: BCCB 5/93; BL 8/93) [921]

CARY, MARY ANN SHADD

14594 Ferris, Jeri Chase. *Demanding Justice: A Story About Mary Ann Shadd Cary* (2–4). Illus. by Kimanne Smith. Series: Creative Minds Biographies. 2003, Carolrhoda LB $22.60 (978-1-57505-177-2); paper $6.95 (978-0-87614-928-7). 64pp. Cary was a free black woman who worked as a teacher and lawyer during the 18th century and

sought to improve the lives of other African Americans. (Rev: HBG 10/03; SLJ 8/03) [921]

DOUGLASS, FREDERICK

14595 Adler, David A. *A Picture Book of Frederick Douglass* (K–3). Illus. by Samuel Byrd. Series: Headliners. 1993, Holiday House LB $16.95 (978-0-8234-1002-6). 32pp. A simple life story of the famous African American abolitionist who died in 1895. (Rev: BL 4/1/93; SLJ 8/93) [921]

14596 Lutz, Norma Jean. *Frederick Douglass: Abolitionist and Author* (3–5). Illus. 2001, Chelsea $25.00 (978-0-7910-6003-2); paper $8.95 (978-0-7910-6141-1). This brief introduction to the life of the abolitionist includes material on his youth and education. (Rev: BL 5/1/01) [972.81]

14597 McKissack, Patricia C., and Fredrick McKissack. *Frederick Douglass: Leader Against Slavery*. Rev. ed. (2–4). Illus. Series: Great African Americans. 2002, Enslow LB $18.60 (978-0-7660-1696-5). 32pp. An updated version of a previously released biography about the slave-turned-abolitionist, which includes archival photographs and Web site information. (Rev: BL 2/15/02; SLJ 5/02) [973.8]

14598 Marlowe, Sam. *Learning About Dedication from the Life of Frederick Douglass* (2–5). Illus. Series: A Character Building Book. 1996, Rosen LB $17.25 (978-0-8239-2425-7). 24pp. Both slavery and the life of the man who fought against it are covered in this short book. (Rev: BL 10/15/96; SLJ 1/97) [921]

14599 Schomp, Virginia. *He Fought for Freedom: Frederick Douglass* (3–6). Illus. Series: Biographies. 1996, Benchmark LB $21.36 (978-0-7614-0488-0). 48pp. A brief but thorough account of the former slave who led the antislavery movement, with quotes from his autobiography. (Rev: HB 11/96; SLJ 2/97) [921]

14600 Schuman, Michael A. *Frederick Douglass: "Truth Is of No Color"* (4–8). Illus. 2009, Enslow LB $23.95 (978-0-7660-3025-1). 128pp. This biography tracks the famous abolitionist's life from his childhood escape from slavery into his adult years. (Rev: BL 6/1–15/09) [973.8]

14601 Slade, Suzanne. *Frederick Douglass: Writer, Speaker, and Opponent of Slavery* (K–3). Illus. by Robert McGuire. Series: Biographies. 2007, Picture Window LB $23.93 (978-1-4048-3102-5). 24pp. Beginning readers will benefit from this simple biography of the outspoken abolitionist, with color illustrations. (Rev: SLJ 8/07)

DU BOIS, W. E. B.

14602 Cavan, Seamus. *W. E. B. Du Bois and Racial Relations* (3–5). Illus. Series: Gateway Civil Rights. 1993, Millbrook LB $20.90 (978-1-56294-288-5). 32pp. The story of the life and contributions of this great African American civil rights leader and author who died in 1963. (Rev: BL 10/1/93; SLJ 10/93) [921]

EVERS, MEDGAR

14603 St. Lawrence, Genevieve. *Medgar Evers* (3–5). Illus. Series: African-American Biographies. 2003, Raintree LB $28.56 (978-0-7398-7028-0). 64pp. An account of the short life of the civil rights leader who was assassinated at the age of 37. (Rev: BL 1/1–15/04; HBG 4/04) [921]

FARMER, JAMES

14604 Jakoubek, Robert E. *James Farmer and the Freedom Rides* (3–5). Illus. Series: Gateway Civil Rights. 1994, Millbrook LB $20.90 (978-1-56294-381-3). 32pp. The story of the Freedom Riders and their leader, James Farmer, who dedicated his life to the struggle for civil rights. (Rev: BL 4/15/94; SLJ 6/94) [921]

FORTEN, JAMES

14605 Figley, Marty Rhodes. *Prisoner for Liberty* (2–4). Illus. by Craig Orback. Series: On My Own History. 2008, Lerner LB $25.26 (978-0-8225-7280-0); paper $6.95 (978-0-8225-9022-4). 48pp. For early readers, this is the story of a 15-year-old African American, James Forten, who in the Revolutionary War rejected the chance to escape imprisonment because he was helping a white friend; Forten's later contributions are covered in an Afterword. (Rev: BL 1/1–15/08; SLJ 8/08) [921]

14606 Krebs, Laurie. *A Day in the Life of a Colonial Sailmaker* (2–3). Series: The Library of Living and Working in Colonial Times. 2004, Rosen LB $19.95 (978-0-8239-6231-0). 24pp. Fact and fiction are interwoven as James Forten, an African American living in Philadelphia who became a wealthy man through his innovative sails, goes about his daily business. (Rev: BL 9/1/04) [921]

HAMER, FANNIE LOU

14607 Donovan, Sandy. *Fannie Lou Hamer* (3–5). Illus. Series: African-American Biographies. 2003, Raintree LB $28.56 (978-0-7398-7030-3). 64pp. The life of the woman, the youngest of 20 children of a Mississippi sharecropper, who become a civil rights activist. (Rev: BL 1/1–15/04) [921]

14608 Fiorelli, June Estep. *Fannie Lou Hamer: A Voice for Freedom* (5–10). Series: Avisson Young Adult. 2005, Avisson paper $19.95 (978-1-888105-62-9). 117pp. Hamer's life, including her youth, are described and placed in the context of events in the United States at the time. (Rev: SLJ 2/06) [921]

HILL, ANITA

14609 Italia, Bob. *Anita Hill: Speaking Out Against Harassment* (4–6). Illus. Series: Everyone Contributes. 1993, ABDO LB $20.95 (978-1-56239-259-8). 32pp. This biography concentrates on the Clarence Thomas hearings and Anita Hill's role in them. (Rev: BL 12/1/93; SLJ 1/94) [921]

JACKSON, JESSE

14610 Mis, Melody S. *Meet Jesse Jackson* (2–4). Illus. Series: Civil Rights Leaders. 2008, Rosen $15.95 (978-1-4042-4212-8). 24pp. Jackson's life and accomplishments are placed in the larger context of the civil rights movement. (Rev: BL 6/1–15/08) [921]

14611 Steffens, Bradley, and Dan Wood. *Jesse Jackson* (5–8). Series: People in the News. 2000, Lucent LB $32.45 (978-1-56006-631-6). 126pp. This well-documented look at the life of the religious and civil rights leader gives interesting information on the events and people who influenced him. (Rev: BL 6/1–15/00; HBG 10/00) [921]

JACOBS, HARRIET A.

14612 Fleischner, Jennifer. *I Was Born a Slave: The Story of Harriet Jacobs* (4–8). Illus. 1997, Millbrook LB $26.90 (978-0-7613-0111-0). The turbulent life of Harriet Jacobs, who was born into slavery and lived for many years as a fugitive before winning her freedom and becoming an abolitionist. (Rev: BL 9/15/97; HBG 3/98; SLJ 1/98) [921]

JORDAN, BARBARA

14613 Patrick-Wexler, Diane. *Barbara Jordan* (4–6). Illus. Series: Contemporary African Americans. 1995, Raintree LB $17.98 (978-0-8172-3976-3). 48pp. The story of the famous African American congresswoman from childhood through her later career as an educator. (Rev: BL 2/15/96; SLJ 4/96) [921]

KING, CORETTA SCOTT

14614 Bankston, John. *Coretta Scott King and the Story Behind the Coretta Scott King Award* (4–8). Series: Great Achievement Awards. 2003, Mitchell Lane LB $29.95 (978-1-58415-202-6). 48pp. The story of the widow of Martin Luther King, Jr., her continuing fight for civil rights, and the children's book prize named after her are covered in this biography. (Rev: BL 10/15/03; SLJ 10/03) [921]

14615 Mattern, Joanne. *Coretta Scott King: Civil Rights Activist* (1–3). Illus. Series: Women Who Shaped History. 2003, Rosen LB $19.95 (978-0-8239-6504-5). 24pp. The life of Coretta Scott King, for new readers. (Rev: BL 2/15/03) [323]

14616 Rhodes, Lisa R. *Coretta Scott King* (5–8). Illus. Series: Black Americans of Achievement. 1999, Chelsea $30.00 (978-0-7910-4690-6); paper $6.65 (978-0-7910-4691-3). This biography of Coretta Scott King describes her childhood, education, marriage, participation in the civil rights movement, and her work since her husband's assassination. (Rev: BL 8/98; HBG 10/98; SLJ 8/98) [323.092]

14617 Shange, Ntozake. *Coretta Scott* (K–3). Illus. by Kadir Nelson. 2009, Amistad $17.99 (978-0-06-125364-5). 32pp. This artful biography blends simple elegant verse with glowing illustrations to highlight Coretta Scott's life from her childhood days to her civil rights work with her husband, Martin Luther King, Jr. (Rev: BCCB 2/09; BL 1/1–15/09; LMC 10/09; SLJ 1/09) [921]

KING, MARTIN LUTHER, JR.

14618 Adler, David A. *Dr. Martin Luther King, Jr.* (1–3). Illus. by Colin Bootman. Series: Holiday House Reader. 2001, Holiday House $15.95 (978-0-8234-1572-4). 48pp. A brief account of King's life, achievements, and legacy that will also appeal to older children who are having difficulties reading. (Rev: BL 7/01; SLJ 6/01) [323]

14619 Adler, David A. *A Picture Book of Martin Luther King, Jr.* (PS–2). Illus. by Robert Casilla. Series: Picture Book Biographies. 1989, Holiday House LB $17.95 (978-0-8234-0770-5); paper $6.95 (978-0-8234-0847-4). 32pp. The life of the civil rights leader is presented in picture-book format. (Rev: BCCB 2/90; BL 11/1/89; SLJ 9/89) [921]

14620 Brown, Jonatha A. *Martin Luther King Jr.* (2–4). Illus. Series: People We Should Know. 2005, Gareth Stevens LB $21.00 (978-0-8368-4467-2). 24pp. For beginning readers, a simple explanation of King's importance with attractive layout and historical and contemporary photographs. [921]

14621 Darby, Jean. *Martin Luther King, Jr.* (4–8). Illus. Series: Lerner Biographies. 1990, Lerner LB $27.93 (978-0-8225-4902-4). 144pp. An in-depth look at King's life and the civil rights movement. (Rev: BL 7/90; SLJ 11/90) [921]

14622 Farris, Christine King. *March On!* (2–5). Illus. by London Ladd. 2008, Scholastic $17.99 (978-0-545-03537-8). 32pp. A compelling picture book by Martin Luther King Jr.'s older sister, highlighting their childhood together and the 1963 March on Washington. (Rev: BL 8/08) [323.092] ∩

14623 Farris, Christine King. *My Brother Martin* (K–3). Illus. by Chris Soentpiet. 2003, Simon & Schuster $17.95 (978-0-689-84387-7). 40pp. A fond biography of Dr. Martin Luther King, Jr., by his older sister. (Rev: BL 2/15/03; HB 3/03; HBG 10/03; SLJ 2/03) [323]

14624 Haskins, James. *I Have a Dream* (4–6). Illus. 1992, Millbrook LB $29.90 (978-1-56294-087-4). 112p. A well-researched biography, supported by excerpts from King's writings and speeches. (Rev: BL 2/15/93) [921]

14625 January, Brendan. *Martin Luther King Jr.: Minister and Civil Rights Activist* (4–8). Series: Ferguson Career Biographies. 2001, Ferguson LB $25.00 (978-0-89434-342-1). 127pp. This concise account focuses on King's career as a minister as well as his work as an advocate of civil rights and includes a section on training for the ministry. (Rev: SLJ 4/01) [921]

14626 Leslie, Tonya. *Martin Luther King, Jr.: A Life of Fairness* (1–3). Illus. by Tina Walski. Series: Blastoff! Readers: People of Character. 2007, Children's Pr. LB $20.00 (978-0-531-14712-2). 24pp. For beginning readers, this is a simple account of King's life and importance. (Rev: SLJ 1/08) [021]

14627 Lowery, Linda. *Martin Luther King Day* (2–4). Illus. by Hetty Mitchell. 2003, Turtleback LB $17.15 (978-0-87614-299-8). 56pp. Presents the origins of the holiday and discusses the key points of Dr. King's life. (Rev: BL 4/1/87; SLJ 6–7/87) [921]

14628 McKissack, Patricia C., and Fredrick McKissack. *Martin Luther King, Jr.: Man of Peace* Rev. ed. (2–4). Series: Great African Americans. 2001, Enslow LB $18.60 (978-0-7660-1678-1). 32pp. A newly illustrated edition of this title that includes information on King's early life. (Rev: HBG 3/02; SLJ 5/02) [921]

14629 McLeese, Don. *Martin Luther King, Jr.* (2–5). Series: Equal Rights Leaders. 2002, Rourke LB $20.64 (978-1-58952-286-2). 24pp. Simple text and well-chosen illustrations tell the story of King's life, with good coverage of his youth and education. (Rev: SLJ 1/03) [323]

14630 Marzollo, Jean. *Happy Birthday, Martin Luther King* (PS–3). Illus. by Brian Pinkney. 1992, Scholastic $16.95 (978-0-590-44065-3). 32pp. The focus is on King's ability to bring people together in this simple biography. (Rev: BL 12/15/92; SLJ 3/93) [921]

14631 Myers, Walter Dean. *I've Seen the Promised Land: The Life of Dr. Martin Luther King, Jr.* (1–4). Illus. by Leonard Jenkins. 2004, HarperCollins LB $17.89 (978-0-06-027704-8). A moving and well-illustrated picture-book biography that covers King's political and private lives. (Rev: SLJ 4/04) [921]

14632 Pastan, Amy. *Martin Luther King, Jr.* (5–10). Illus. Series: DK Biography. 2004, DK LB $14.99 (978-0-7566-0491-2); paper $4.99 (978-0-7566-0342-7). 128pp. A heavily illustrated, attractive biography of King that offers broad historical background. (Rev: BL 6/1–15/04) [921]

14633 Patrick, Denise Lewis. *A Lesson for Martin Luther King Jr.* (K–2). Illus. by Rodney S. Pate. Series: Childhood of Famous Americans. 2003, Simon & Schuster paper $3.99 (978-0-689-85397-5). 32pp. A childhood event that helped Martin Luther King Jr. to define his mission in life is the focus of this slim volume. (Rev: HBG 4/04; SLJ 2/04) [921]

14634 Rappaport, Doreen. *Martin's Big Words* (PS–4). Illus. by Bryan Collier. 2007, Hyperion paper $6.99 (978-1-4231-0635-7). 32pp. This picture-book biography interweaves King's own words and a simple narrative to create an inspiring portrait of the man. A paperback edition of the 2001 book that won the 2002 Caldecott Medal. (Rev: BL 10/1/01*; HB 1/02; SLJ 10/01) [921]

14635 Roop, Peter, and Connie Roop. *Martin Luther King, Jr.* (2–3). Series: Lives and Times. 1997, Heinemann $19.92 (978-1-57572-560-4). 24pp. A simple picture-book biography that gives a very brief introduction to the life and contributions of Martin Luther King, Jr. (Rev: BL 3/15/98; HB 5/97; SLJ 6/98) [921]

14636 Schuman, Michael A. *Martin Luther King, Jr.: Leader for Civil Rights* (5–8). Series: African-American Biographies. 1996, Enslow LB $26.60 (978-0-89490-687-9). A straightforward biography that covers the important events in King's life. (Rev: SLJ 12/96) [921]

14637 Strazzabosco, Jeanne M. *Learning About Dignity from the Life of Martin Luther King, Jr.* (2–5). Illus. Series: A Character Building Book. 1996, Rosen $18.75 (978-0-8239-2415-8). 24pp. This brief biography describes King's many virtues, above all his innate dignity. (Rev: BL 10/15/96; SLJ 12/96) [921]

LAW, WESTLEY WALLACE

14638 Haskins, James. *Delivering Justice: W. W. Law and the Fight for Civil Rights* (2–4). Illus. by Benny Andrews. 2005, Candlewick $16.99 (978-0-7636-2592-4). 32pp. A picture-book biography of Westley Wallace Law that chronicles the mail carrier's campaign to win equal treatment for African Americans in his hometown of Savannah, Georgia. (Rev: BL 9/15/05) [921]

LEWIS, JOHN

14639 Haskins, James, and Kathleen Benson. *John Lewis in the Lead: A Story of the Civil Rights Movement* (3–5). Illus. by Benny Andrews. 2006, Lee & Low $17.95 (978-1-58430-250-6). 40pp. This picture-book biography for older readers covers Lewis's civil rights activism, including his role in "Bloody Sunday" in Selma, Alabama, and his political career. (Rev: BL 10/1/06; SLJ 12/06) [921]

LYON, MARITCHA REYMOND

14640 Bolden, Tonya. *Maritcha: A Nineteenth-Century American Girl* (4–7). Illus. 2005, Abrams $17.95 (978-0-8109-5045-0). 48pp. Drawing on primary sources, Bolden tells the story of Maritcha Remond Lyon, a free black girl who succeeded in her fight to attend an all-white high school in Rhode Island in the mid-19th century. Coretta Scott King Illustrator Award and Author Honor Book, 2006. (Rev: BL 2/1/05*; SLJ 2/05) [921]

MALCOLM X

14641 Adoff, Arnold. *Malcolm X.* Rev. ed. (3–6). Illus. 2000, HarperCollins paper $4.99 (978-0-06-442118-8). 64pp. This clearly written biography reflects the intense drama of the African American leader's life and death. (Rev: BL 2/15/00) [921]

14642 Benson, Michael. *Malcolm X* (5–8). Series: Biography. 2001, Lerner LB $27.93 (978-0-8225-5025-9). An accessible text and many photographs are used to enliven this biography of the African American civil rights leader who was assassinated in 1965. (Rev: BL 4/1/02; HBG 3/02; SLJ 3/02) [921]

14643 Graves, Renee. *Malcolm X* (3–5). Series: Cornerstones of Freedom. 2003, Children's Pr. LB $26.00 (978-0-516-24224-8). 48pp. A vivid, well-written life of the African American leader. (Rev: SLJ 2/04) [921]

MARSHALL, THURGOOD

14644 Adler, David A. *A Picture Book of Thurgood Marshall* (3–4). Illus. by Robert Casilla. Series: Picture Book Biographies. 1997, Holiday House LB $16.95 (978-0-8234-1308-9). 32pp. The life of this Supreme Court justice is well re-created in simple language that chronicles his battles against segregation and discrimination. (Rev: BL 11/15/97; HBG 3/98; SLJ 1/98) [921]

14645 Frost, Helen. *Thurgood Marshall* (K–2). Illus. Series: Famous Americans. 2003, Capstone LB $17.26 (978-0-7368-1643-4). 24pp. This brief biography of Thurgood Marshall introduces young readers to the life and career of the African American attorney who helped bring an end to school segregation and was later appointed to the U.S. Supreme Court. (Rev: HBG 10/03; SLJ 11/03) [347.73]

14646 Kallen, Stuart A. *Thurgood Marshall: A Dream of Justice for All* (3–5). Illus. Series: I Have a Dream. 1993, ABDO LB $22.78 (978-1-56239-258-1). 40pp. The story of the first African American to serve on the Supreme Court and his contributions to the struggle for civil rights. (Rev: BL 2/1/94) [921]

14647 Taylor-Butler, Christine. *Thurgood Marshall* (1–2). Series: Rookie Biographies. 2006, Children's Pr. LB $20.50 (978-0-516-25015-1); paper $4.95 (978-0-516-27099-9). 32pp. For beginning readers, this is a simple introduction to the life of the African American jurist from his childhood in Baltimore to his appointment to the U.S. Supreme Court. (Rev: SLJ 9/06) [921]

MASON, BIDDY

14648 Ferris, Jeri Chase. *With Open Hands: A Story About Biddy Mason* (4–6). Illus. by Ralph L. Ramstad. 1999, Carolrhoda LB $22.60 (978-1-57505-330-1). 64pp. The inspiring story of the woman, born a slave, who accompanied her Mormon master and his family to Utah where she later became a midwife, a wealthy landowner, and a philanthropist. (Rev: BL 2/1/99; HBG 10/99; SLJ 5/99) [921]

14649 Williams, Jean Kinney. *Bridget "Biddy" Mason: From Slave to Businesswoman* (4–6). Illus. Series: Signature Lives: American Frontier Era. 2005, Compass Point $34.60 (978-0-7565-1001-5). 112pp. A life of Bridget "Biddy" Mason, who was born a slave in 1818, traveled west with her Mormon master, gained her freedom, and died in 1891 as one of the richest women in Los Angeles. (Rev: BL 10/15/05; SLJ 3/06; VOYA 6/06) [921]

MEREDITH, JAMES

14650 Elish, Dan. *James Meredith and School Desegregation* (3–5). Illus. Series: Gateway Civil Rights. 1994, Millbrook LB $22.90 (978-1-56294-379-0). 32pp. The biography of the young African American man who was a pioneer in integrating institutions of higher education in Mississippi. (Rev: BL 4/15/94; SLJ 5/94) [921]

PARKS, ROSA

14651 Adler, David A. *A Picture Book of Rosa Parks* (2–4). Illus. by Robert Casilla. Series: Picture Book Biographies. 1993, Holiday House LB $16.95 (978-0-8234-1041-5). 30pp. The life story of the civil rights leader who refused to give up her bus seat to a white passenger. (Rev: BL 10/15/93; SLJ 12/93) [921]

14652 Collard, Sneed B., III. *Rosa Parks: The Courage to Make a Difference* (3–5). Series: American Heroes. 2006, Benchmark LB $28.50 (978-0-7614-2163-4). 40pp. Parks's life and contributions are clearly described in large typeface and illustrations. (Rev: SLJ 3/07) [921]

14653 Davis, Kenneth C. *Don't Know Much About Rosa Parks* (4–7). Illus. by Sergio Martinez. Series: Don't Know Much About. 2005, HarperCollins paper $4.99 (978-0-06-442126-3). 128pp. A question-and-answer format, interesting sidebars, and news photographs enliven this profile of Parks, which emphasizes her long-term commitment to civil rights. (Rev: BL 2/1/05) [323]

14654 Dubois, Muriel L. *Rosa Parks* (2–4). Illus. Series: Photo-Illustrated Biographies. 2003, Capstone LB $22.60 (978-0-7368-1607-6). 24pp. A useful introduction to Rosa Parks and her pivotal role in the American civil rights movement. (Rev: HBG 10/03; SLJ 1/04)

14655 Dubowski, Cathy E. *Rosa Parks: Don't Give In!* (2–4). Series: Defining Moments. 2005, Bearport LB $25.27 (978-1-59716-078-0). 32pp. A clearly written account of Parks's life and contribution to the civil rights movement. (Rev: SLJ 2/06) [921]

14656 Fine, Edith Hope. *Rosa Parks: Meet a Civil Rights Hero* (3–4). Illus. Series: Meeting Famous People. 2004, Enslow LB $22.60 (978-0-7660-2099-3). 32pp. The story of Rosa Parks and her role in the struggle for civil rights is recounted in this brief but effective biography. (Rev: BL 2/15/04) [323]

14657 Giovanni, Nikki. *Rosa* (3–5). Illus. by Bryan Collier. 2005, Holt $16.95 (978-0-8050-7106-1). 40pp. This compelling picture-book biography brings Rosa and her reluctance to accept the status quo into new focus. Caldecott Honor Book, 2006. (Rev: BL 6/1–15/05) [323]

14658 Greenfield, Eloise. *Rosa Parks* (2–4). Illus. by Eric Marlow. 1996, HarperCollins paper $4.25 (978-0-06-442025-9). 40pp. A convincing sketch of the woman whose brave stand precipitated the Montgomery bus strike and her ensuing involvement with the civil rights struggle. [921]

14659 Holland, Gini. *Rosa Parks* (2–4). Illus. by David Price. Series: First Biographies. 1997, Raintree LB $25.69 (978-0-8172-4451-4). 32pp. A simple account of Rosa Parks's life, covering her childhood, civil rights work, imprisonment, and release. (Rev: SLJ 2/98) [921]

14660 McLeese, Don. *Rosa Parks* (2–5). Series: Equal Rights Leaders. 2002, Rourke LB $20.64 (978-1-58952-287-9). 24pp. Simple text and well-chosen illustrations tell the story of Parks's life,

with good coverage of her youth and education. (Rev: SLJ 1/03) [323]

14661 Ringgold, Faith. *If a Bus Could Talk: The Story of Rosa Parks* (K–4). Illus. 1999, Simon & Schuster $16.00 (978-0-689-81892-9). 32pp. A picture-book biography that combines elements of fantasy with the true story of Rosa Parks, often called the mother of the Civil Rights movement. (Rev: BCCB 1/00; BL 1/1–15/00; HBG 3/00; SLJ 1/00) [921]

14662 Schraff, Anne. *Rosa Parks: "Tired of Giving In"* (4–8). Series: African-American Biography Library. 2005, Enslow LB $31.93 (978-0-7660-2463-2). 128pp. An accessible profile of Parks and her importance. (Rev: SLJ 10/05) [921]

QUARLLS, CAROLINE

14663 Pferdehirt, Julia. *Caroline Quarlls and the Underground Railroad* (3–6). Illus. Series: Badger Biographies. 2008, Wisconsin Historical Soc. paper $12.95 (978-0-87020-388-6). 110pp. The exciting story of the 16-year-old slave's escape from Missouri and long, difficult journey to freedom in Canada. (Rev: BLO 6/17/08) [921]

RANDOLPH, A. PHILIP

14664 Cwiklik, Robert. *A. Philip Randolph and the Labor Movement* (3–5). Series: Gateway Civil Rights. 1993, Millbrook LB $20.90 (978-1-56294-326-4). 32pp. The story of the African American who organized the sleeping-car porters into a union and later directed a march on Washington, D.C., in 1941, to protest unfair labor practices. (Rev: BL 10/1/93; SLJ 10/93) [921]

14665 Hanley, Sally. *A. Philip Randolph* (5–9). 1988, Chelsea LB $19.95 (978-1-55546-607-7); paper $8.95 (978-0-7910-0222-3). 112pp. A life of the African American labor leader who founded the Brotherhood of Sleeping Car Porters. (Rev: BL 10/1/88; VOYA 2/89) [921]

RUSTIN, BAYARD

14666 Brimner, Larry Dane. *We Are One: The Story of Bayard Rustin* (5–8). Illus. 2007, Boyds Mills $17.95 (978-1-59078-498-3). 48pp. With lively text, photographs, quotations, and song lyrics, Brimner explains Bayard Rustin's importance in the struggle for civil rights. (Rev: BL 9/1/07; SLJ 11/07) [921]

SMALLS, ROBERT

14667 Halfmann, Janet. *Seven Miles to Freedom: The Robert Smalls Story* (3–5). Illus. by Duane Smith. 2008, Lee & Low $17.95 (978-1-60060-232-0). 32pp. This biography of the slave who stole a Confederate ship and went on to serve in the U.S. Congress tells the story of his escape to the North. (Rev: BL 6/1–15/08; LMC 1/09; SLJ 7/08) [921]

14668 Kennedy, Robert F., Jr. *Robert Smalls: The Boat Thief* (3–6). Illus. by Patrick Faricy. Series: American Heroes. 2008, Hyperion $16.99 (978-1-4231-0802-3). 48pp. The inspiring life of the slave who at the age of 24 masterminded the theft of a Confederate ship and its delivery to the Federal Navy, an event that was only the beginning of a long and influential political career. (Rev: BL 6/1–15/08) [921]

TAYLOR, SUSIE KING

14669 Jordan, Denise M. *Susie King Taylor: Destined to Be Free* (3–5). Illus. by Higgins Bond. 1994, Just Us Bks. paper $5.00 (978-0-940975-50-7). 42pp. The story of the freed slave who, after the Civil War, became a teacher of African American children and adults and wrote an account of her life. (Rev: SLJ 7/95) [921]

TERRELL, MARY CHURCH

14670 Fradin, Dennis Brindell, and Judith B. Fradin. *Fight On! Mary Church Terrell's Battle for Integration* (5–9). Illus. 2003, Clarion $18.00 (978-0-618-13349-9). 192pp. Terrell's efforts to end discrimination are detailed in a readable, large-format biography that includes primary sources and lots of illustrations. (Rev: BL 6/1–15/03; HB 7/03; HBG 10/03; SLJ 5/03*; VOYA 6/03) [323]
14671 Lommel, Cookie. *Mary Church Terrell: Speaking Out for Civil Rights* (4–7). Series: African-American Biographies. 2003, Enslow LB $26.60 (978-0-7660-2116-7). 112pp. This interesting account of Terrell's life and her passion for education and activism contains many black-and-white photographs. (Rev: HBG 4/04; SLJ 10/03) [323]
14672 McKissack, Patricia C., and Fredrick McKissack. *Mary Church Terrell: Leader for Equality*. Rev. ed. (2–4). Illus. Series: Great African Americans. 2002, Enslow LB $18.60 (978-0-7660-1697-2). 32pp. An updated version of a previously released biography about the 19th-century activist, including archival photographs and Web site information. (Rev: BL 2/15/02; HBG 10/02; SLJ 5/02) [323]
14673 Swain, Gwenyth. *Civil Rights Pioneer: A Story About Mary Church Terrell* (3–6). Illus. 1999, Lerner $22.60 (978-1-57505-355-4). 64pp. A straightforward biography of the well-educated African American woman who devoted her life to fighting for civil rights. (Rev: BL 1/1–15/00; HBG 3/00; SLJ 2/00) [921]

THURMAN, HOWARD

14674 Issa, Kai Jackson. *Howard Thurman's Great Hope* (3–5). Illus. by Arthur L. Dawson. 2008, Lee & Low $16.95 (978-1-60060-249-8). 32pp. Issa describes the struggles and triumphs of this influential minister and civil rights leader. (Rev: BL 11/15/08; LMC 3/09; SLJ 9/08) [921]

TILLAGE, LEON

14675 Tillage, Leon W. *Leon's Story* (4–9). Illus. 1997, Farrar $15.00 (978-0-374-34379-8). An autobiographical account of growing up African American and poor in the segregated South and of

participating in the civil rights movement. (Rev: BL 10/1/97*; HB 11/97; HBG 3/98; SLJ 12/97) [975.6]

TRUTH, SOJOURNER

14676 Adler, David A. *A Picture Book of Sojourner Truth* (2–4). Illus. by Gershom Griffith. Series: Picture Book Biographies. 1994, Holiday House LB $16.95 (978-0-8234-1072-9). In an easily read format, the life and works of Sojourner Truth are introduced. (Rev: SLJ 6/94) [921]
14677 Bernard, Catherine. *Sojourner Truth: Abolitionist and Women's Rights Activist* (5–8). Series: Historical American Biographies. 2001, Enslow LB $26.60 (978-0-7660-1257-8). 112pp. The life story of the freed slave who traveled throughout the North preaching emancipation and women's rights before the Civil War. (Rev: BL 4/15/01; HBG 10/01) [921]
14678 Butler, Mary G. *Sojourner Truth: From Slave to Activist for Freedom* (4–8). Series: Library of American Lives and Times. 2003, Rosen LB $34.60 (978-0-8239-5736-1). 112pp. A forerunner of the modern civil rights movement, Sojourner Truth rose from slavery to become a crusader for good race relations and women's rights. (Rev: BL 6/1–15/03; SLJ 5/03; VOYA 6/03) [921]
14679 Ferris, Jeri. *Walking the Road to Freedom: A Story About Sojourner Truth* (3–6). Illus. 1988, Carolrhoda LB $21.27 (978-0-87614-318-6); Lerner paper $22.60 (978-0-87614-505-0). 64pp. The story of the woman born into slavery who vowed to travel the land singing of its evils. (Rev: BL 3/1/88; SLJ 3/88)
14680 McKissack, Patricia C., and Fredrick McKissack. *Sojourner Truth: A Voice for Freedom*. Rev. ed. (2–4). Series: Great African Americans. 2002, Enslow LB $18.60 (978-0-7660-1693-4). 32pp. A simple biography of the black American evangelist and reformer who gained fame as a preacher and fighter for women's suffrage. (Rev: BL 7/02) [921]
14681 Mattern, Joanne. *Sojourner Truth: Early Abolitionist* (1–3). Illus. Series: Women Who Shaped History. 2003, Rosen LB $19.95 (978-0-8239-6502-1). 24pp. The life of Sojourner Truth, for new readers. (Rev: BL 2/15/03) [305.5]
14682 Merchant, Peter. *Sojourner Truth: Path to Glory* (3–5). Illus. by Julia Denos. 2007, Simon & Schuster LB $11.89 (978-0-689-87208-2); paper $3.99 (978-0-689-87207-5). 48pp. A biography of the famous abolitionist, accompanied by striking line drawings. (Rev: SLJ 5/07)
14683 Rockwell, Anne. *Only Passing Through* (4–8). Illus. 2000, Knopf $16.95 (978-0-679-89186-4). 32pp. A moving picture-book biography of Sojourner Truth, who was a pioneer in the struggle for racial equality and devoted her life to the abolitionist movement. (Rev: BCCB 1/01; BL 11/15/00; HB 11/00; HBG 3/01; SLJ 12/00) [921]
14684 Roop, Peter, and Connie Roop. *Sojourner Truth* (3–5). Illus. Series: In Their Own Words. 2003, Scholastic paper $4.99 (978-0-439-26323-8). 128pp. A simply written account of the former slave who became an abolitionist, drawing from Truth's own words. (Rev: BL 2/15/03; SLJ 7/03) [305.5]

TUBMAN, HARRIET

14685 Adler, David A. *A Picture Book of Harriet Tubman* (2–4). Illus. by Samuel Byrd. Series: Picture Book Biographies. 1992, Holiday House LB $16.95 (978-0-8234-0926-6). 32pp. Easy-to-read text describes the life of this famous American who helped slaves gain freedom. (Rev: BCCB 7–8/92; BL 6/15/92; SLJ 6/92) [921]

14686 Ferris, Jeri. *Go Free or Die: A Story About Harriet Tubman* (3–6). Illus. 1988, Carolrhoda LB $22.60 (978-0-87614-317-9); Lerner paper $6.95 (978-0-87614-504-3). 64pp. The story of the former slave and her fight to rid the country of slavery. (Rev: BL 3/1/88; SLJ 3/88) [921]

14687 Gayle, Sharon. *Harriet Tubman and the Freedom Train* (1–3). Illus. by Felicia Marshall. Series: Ready-to-Read Stories of Famous Americans. 2003, Simon & Schuster paper $3.99 (978-0-689-85480-4). 32pp. A fictionalized account of the former slave's efforts to free others. (Rev: BL 2/15/03; HBG 10/03; SLJ 3/03) [973.7]

14688 Klingel, Cynthia. *Harriet Tubman: Abolitionist and Underground Railroad Conductor* (3–6). Series: Our People. 2003, Child's World LB $27.07 (978-1-59296-004-0). 32pp. An interesting profile of Tubman and her anti-slavery activities. (Rev: BL 1/1–15/04; SLJ 4/04)

14689 Mortensen, Lori. *Harriet Tubman: Hero of the Underground Railroad* (K–3). Illus. by Frances Moore. 2007, Picture Window LB $23.93 (978-1-4048-3103-2). 24pp. A simple biography of the slave rescuer, beginning with her childhood and accompanied by illustrations. (Rev: SLJ 8/07)

14690 Mosher, Kiki. *Learning About Bravery from the Life of Harriet Tubman* (2–5). Illus. Series: A Character Building Book. 1996, Rosen LB $18.75 (978-0-8239-2424-0). 24pp. This short biography shows how the element of courage was paramount in the life of this leader of the Underground Railroad. (Rev: BL 10/15/96; SLJ 1/97) [921]

14691 Rowley, John. *Harriet Tubman* (2–3). Illus. Series: Lives and Times. 1997, Heinemann $19.92 (978-1-57572-558-1). 24pp. A simple picture-book biography that talks about slavery and tells of the life, courage, and endurance of this leader on the Underground Railroad. (Rev: BL 3/15/98; SLJ 6/98) [921]

14692 Schraff, Anne. *Harriet Tubman: Moses of the Underground Railroad* (4–8). Series: African-American Biographies. 2001, Enslow LB $26.60 (978-0-7660-1548-7). 128pp. This is an absorbing account of the life of the Underground Railroad leader that covers her work as a nurse, a scout, and a spy. (Rev: HBG 3/02; SLJ 10/01) [921]

14693 Taylor, M. W. *Harriet Tubman* (5–8). Illus. Series: Black Americans of Achievement. 1990, Chelsea LB $30.00 (978-1-55546-612-1). 111pp. The story of the famous conductor on the Underground Railroad. (Rev: SLJ 1/91) [921]

14694 Troy, Don. *Harriet Ross Tubman* (4–6). Series: Journey to Freedom. 1999, Child's World LB $28.50 (978-1-56766-568-0). 40pp. The life of a gallant, energetic former slave and abolitionist who is best remembered for her work with the Underground Railroad. (Rev: BL 7/99; HBG 10/99; SLJ 7/99) [921]

14695 Turner, Glennette Tilley. *An Apple for Harriet Tubman* (K–2). Illus. by Susan Ketter. 2006, Albert Whitman $15.95 (978-0-8075-0395-9). 32pp. This picture book poignantly re-creates unhappy incidents from Harriet Tubman's childhood as a slave. (Rev: BL 8/06; SLJ 10/06) [921]

14696 Weatherford, Carole Boston. *Moses: When Harriet Tubman Led Her People to Freedom* (1–3). Illus. by Kadir Nelson. 2006, Hyperion $15.99 (978-0-7868-5175-1). 48pp. Harriet Tubman's first trip north and her determination to return south to rescue others are celebrated in this moving blend of free verse and beautiful art. Caldecott Honor Book, 2007. (Rev: BL 8/06; SLJ 10/06*) [921]

WALKER, MAGGIE

14697 Branch, Muriel M., and Dorothy M. Rice. *Pennies to Dollars: The Story of Maggie Lena Walker* (4–8). 1997, Linnet LB $19.50 (978-0-208-02453-4); paper $13.95 (978-0-208-02455-8). Maggie Walker, the daughter of a former slave, helped African Americans through her financial schemes, including the founding of the Penny Savings Bank. (Rev: BL 11/1/97; SLJ 10/97) [921]

WASHINGTON, BOOKER T.

14698 Amper, Thomas. *Booker T. Washington* (2–5). Illus. 1998, Carolrhoda $23.93 (978-1-57505-094-2). 48pp. The inspiring story of the young Booker T. Washington and his determination to receive an education in spite of his race and his extreme poverty. (Rev: BL 11/15/98; HBG 3/99; SLJ 11/98) [921]

14699 Braun, Eric. *Booker T. Washington: Great American Educator* (2–6). Illus. by Cynthia Martin. Series: Graphic Library, Graphic Biographies. 2005, Capstone LB $26.60 (978-0-7368-4630-1). 32pp. This graphic-novel biography profiles the life and career of the noted African American educator and author. (Rev: SLJ 3/06) [921]

14700 Brimner, Larry Dane. *Booker T. Washington: Getting into the Schoolhouse* (2–4). Series: American Heroes. 2008, Marshall Cavendish $20.95 (978-0-7614-3063-6). 42pp. With sections on "Important Dates" and "Words to Know," this brief biography traces Washington's life from slavery to his work as an educator. (Rev: SLJ 3/09) [921]

14701 McKissack, Patricia C., and Fredrick McKissack. *Booker T. Washington: Leader and Educator*. Rev. ed. (2–4). Illus. Series: Great African Americans. 2001, Enslow LB $18.60 (978-0-7660-1679-8). 32pp. Updated artwork gives this previously published biography of former slave and educator Booker T. Washington a new look. (Rev: BL 1/1–15/02; HBG 3/02) [370]

WATTS, J. C.

14702 Lutz, Norma Jean. *J. C. Watts* (4–7). Series: Black Americans of Achievement. 2000, Chelsea

$30.00 (978-0-7910-5338-6). 110pp. The story of a former Oklahoma University football player who entered politics and was first elected to the House of Representatives in 1994. (Rev: BL 6/1–15/00; HBG 10/00) [921]

WELLS-BARNETT, IDA B.

14703 Dray, Philip. *Yours for Justice, Ida B. Wells: The Daring Life of a Crusading Journalist* (2–4). Illus. by Stephen Alcorn. 2008, Peachtree $18.95 (978-1-56145-417-4). 48pp. A thorough picture-book biography of the black civil rights crusader and journalist who fought to end lynching. (Rev: BL 2/1/08; LMC 3/08; SLJ 4/08) [921]

14704 Fradin, Dennis Brindell, and Judith B. Fradin. *Ida B. Wells: Mother of the Civil Rights Movement* (5–10). 2000, Clarion $19.00 (978-0-395-89898-7). 178pp. An inspiring biography of the African American who was born a slave and went on to become a school teacher, journalist, and an activist who fought for black women's right to vote and helped found the NAACP. (Rev: BL 2/15/00; HB 5/00; HBG 10/00; SLJ 4/00*) [921]

14705 Freedman, Suzanne. *Ida B. Wells-Barnett and the Anti-Lynching Crusade* (3–5). Illus. Series: Gateway Civil Rights. 1994, Millbrook LB $20.90 (978-1-56294-377-6). 32pp. The biography of the African American journalist who fought for civil rights and justice in the South. (Rev: BL 4/15/94; SLJ 5/94) [921]

14706 McKissack, Patricia C., and Fredrick McKissack. *Ida B. Wells-Barnett: A Voice Against Violence*. Rev. ed. (2–4). Illus. Series: Great African Americans. 2001, Enslow LB $18.60 (978-0-89490-301-4). 32pp. A simple biography of the founder of the NAACP. (Rev: SLJ 11/91) [921]

14707 Myers, Walter Dean. *Ida B. Wells: Let the Truth Be Told* (2–4). Illus. by Bonnie Christensen. 2008, Collins $16.99 (978-0-06-027705-5). 40pp. An inspirational picture-book profile of the human rights activist who was born into slavery. (Rev: BCCB 11/08; BL 11/15/08; HB 1/08; SLJ 11/08) [921]

14708 Welch, Catherine A. *Ida B. Wells-Barnett: Powerhouse with a Pen* (5–8). Illus. Series: Trailblazer Biographies. 2000, Carolrhoda LB $30.35 (978-1-57505-352-3). 104pp. This book introduces Wells-Barnett, who was born a slave and became a powerful journalist and activist as well as a spokesperson for all African Americans. (Rev: BL 6/1–15/00; HBG 10/00; SLJ 7/00; VOYA 2/01) [921]

WHITE, WALTER

14709 Jakoubek, Robert E. *Walter White and the Power of Organized Protest* (3–5). Illus. Series: Gateway Civil Rights. 1994, Millbrook LB $23.90 (978-1-56294-378-3). 32pp. Background material on the NAACP is given through the life story of one of its leaders, Walter White. (Rev: BL 4/15/94; SLJ 6/94) [921]

WILLIAMS, J. W.

14710 Barbour, Karen. *Mr. Williams* (K–3). Illus. 2005, Holt $16.95 (978-0-8050-6773-6). 32pp. An African American farmer's matter-of-fact recollections of his childhood in Louisiana in the 1930s and 1940s are enhanced by the compelling illustrations. (Rev: BL 9/1/05; SLJ 8/05*) [973]

WOODSON, CARTER G.

14711 Haskins, James, and Kathleen Benson. *Carter G. Woodson: The Man Who Put "Black" in American History* (4–6). Illus. 2000, Millbrook LB $24.90 (978-0-7613-1264-2). 48pp. This biography examines the obstacles and triumphs experienced by the man who created the Association for the Study of Negro Life and History in 1915 and Negro History Week in 1926. (Rev: BL 4/1/00; HBG 10/00; SLJ 7/00) [921]

14712 McKissack, Patricia C., and Fredrick McKissack. *Carter G. Woodson: The Father of Black History*. Rev. ed. (2–4). Series: Great African Americans. 2002, Enslow LB $18.60 (978-0-7660-1698-9). 32pp. A beginning chapter book that covers the life of the black historian who founded the Association for the Study of Negro Life and History in 1915 and began its *Journal of Negro History*. (Rev: BL 7/02) [921]

YORK (C. 1775–1815)

14713 Pringle, Laurence. *American Slave, American Hero: York of the Lewis and Clark Expedition* (3–5). Illus. by Cornelius Wright. 2006, Boyds Mills $17.95 (978-1-59078-282-8). 32pp. This is a careful, well-illustrated picture-book biography of York, the slave who was part of the famous expedition, drawing largely on historical journals. (Rev: BL 11/1/06; SLJ 1/07) [917.8]

Hispanic Americans

ANTONNETTY, EVELINA LOPEZ

14714 Mohr, Nicholasa. *All for the Better: A Story of El Barrio* (2–5). Illus. by Rudy Gutierrez. 1993, Raintree LB $27.12 (978-0-8114-7220-3). 56pp. The story of Evelina Lopez Antonnetty and the difference she made in Spanish Harlem, New York. (Rev: BCCB 7–8/93; SLJ 5/93) [921]

CHAVEZ, CESAR

14715 Apte, Sunita. *Cesar Chavez: We Can Do It!* (3–4). Series: Defining Moments. 2005, Bearport LB $25.27 (978-1-59716-073-5). 32pp. An easy-to-read biography with plenty of photographs, this covers Chavez's childhood as well as his achievements. (Rev: SLJ 1/06) [921]

14716 Braun, Eric. *Cesar Chavez: Fighting for Farmworkers* (2–6). Illus. by Harry Roland, et al. Series: Graphic Library, Graphic Biographies. 2005, Capstone LB $26.60 (978-0-7368-4631-8). 32pp. A graphic-novel biography that introduces the life of the Mexican American labor leader; includes highlighted quotations from primary sources. (Rev: SLJ 3/06) [921]

14717 Brown, Jonatha A. *Cesar Chavez* (5–8). Series: Trailblazers of the Modern World. 2004, World Almanac LB $31.00 (978-0-8368-5097-0). 48pp. Report writers will find lots of suitable information in this work that covers Chavez's life and accomplishments. (Rev: SLJ 7/04) [921]

14718 Collins, David R. *Farmworker's Friend: The Story of Cesar Chavez* (3–5). Illus. 1996, Carolrhoda LB $23.93 (978-0-87614-982-9). 80pp. The story of this champion of poor farm workers is retold from a variety of original sources. (Rev: BL 12/15/96) [921]

14719 Griswold del Castillo, Richard. *César Chávez: The Struggle for Justice / La lucha por la justicia* (2–4). Illus. by Anthony Accardo. 2002, Arte Publico $15.95 (978-1-55885-324-9). 32pp. Bilingual text and full-page paintings bring Mexican American labor leader César Chávez to life. (Rev: BL 12/15/02) [331.88]

14720 Guzmán, Lila, and Rick Guzmán. *César Chávez: Fighting for Fairness* (3–4). Series: Famous Latinos. 2006, Enslow LB $22.60 (978-0-7660-2370-3). 32pp. A look at Chavez's early life and his peaceful fight for better conditions for migrant workers, with an attractive layout and many photographs. (Rev: SLJ 3/07) [921]

14721 Krull, Kathleen. *Harvesting Hope: The Story of Cesar Chavez* (2–4). Illus. by Yuri Morales. 2003, Harcourt $17.00 (978-0-15-201437-7). 48pp. This inspiring picture-book biography chronicles Chavez's rise from the ranks of migrant workers to a leadership position in the American labor movement. (Rev: BL 6/1–15/03; HB 7/03; HBG 10/03; SLJ 6/03) [921]

14722 McLeese, Don. *Cesar E. Chavez* (2–5). 2002, Rourke LB $14.95 (978-1-58952-285-5). 24pp. Simple text and well-chosen illustrations tell the story of Chavez's life, with good coverage of his youth, education, and early years working in the fields. (Rev: SLJ 1/03) [331.88]

14723 Tracy, Kathleen. *Cesar Chavez* (5–7). Series: Latinos in American History. 2003, Mitchell Lane LB $29.95 (978-1-58415-224-8). 48pp. This biography covers the life and accomplishments of the Mexican American labor leader who founded the United Farm Workers. (Rev: BL 1/1–15/04) [921]

14724 Wadsworth, Ginger. *Cesar Chavez* (2–4). Illus. by Mark Schroder. Series: On My Own Biography. 2005, Lerner LB $25.26 (978-1-57505-652-4); paper $5.95 (978-1-57505-764-4). 48pp. Chavez's own story and the plight of migrant farm workers are intertwined in this picture-book biography. (Rev: BL 5/1/05) [921]

14725 Zannos, Susan. *Cesar Chavez* (3–6). Series: Real-Life Reader Biographies. 1998, Mitchell Lane LB $15.95 (978-1-883845-71-1). 32pp. A life of this inspired Latino labor leader whose hard work

and accomplishments are still influential. (Rev: SLJ 2/99) [921]

CISNEROS, HENRY

14726 Martinez, Elizabeth C. *Henry Cisneros: Mexican-American Leader* (3–6). Illus. Series: Hispanic Heritage. 1993, Millbrook LB $23.90 (978-1-56294-368-4). 32pp. A biography of the Mexican American who was once a mayor and is still an important politician. (Rev: BL 11/15/93) [921]

DE ZAVALA, LORENZO

14727 Tracy, Kathleen. *Lorenzo de Zavala* (5–7). Series: Latinos in American History. 2002, Mitchell Lane LB $29.95 (978-1-58415-154-8). 48pp. The biography of the 19th-century Mexican who became vice president of the Republic of Texas and was one of the signers of its constitution. (Rev: BL 2/15/03; HBG 10/03) [921]

GAC-ARTIGAS, ALEJANDRO

14728 Gac-Artigas, Alejandro. *Yo, Alejandro* (5–7). 2000, Ediciones Nuevo Espacio paper $11.95 (978-1-930879-21-8). 106pp. This is a collection of personal essays written by the author before his 12th birthday about his life in Puerto Rico, the state of Georgia, and later New York City. (Rev: BL 3/1/01) [921]

GALAN, NELY

14729 Rodriguez, Janel. *Nely Galan* (4–8). Illus. Series: Contemporary Hispanic Americans. 1997, Raintree LB $17.98 (978-0-8172-3991-6). 48pp. The life of this contemporary Hispanic American who, as a Hollywood producer, is responsible for developing TV and video projects for other Hispanic Americans. (Rev: BL 4/15/97) [921]

HUERTA, DOLORES

14730 Gillis, Jennifer Blizin. *Dolores Huerta* (3–6). Series: American Lives. 2005, Heinemann LB $26.79 (978-1-4034-6980-9). 32pp. Using large type and simple text, this volume describes the Mexican American labor leader's efforts to improve working conditions for farm workers. (Rev: SLJ 4/06) [921]

14731 Murcia, Rebecca Thatcher. *Dolores Huerta* (5–7). Series: Latinos in American History. 2002, Mitchell Lane LB $29.95 (978-1-58415-155-5). 48pp. The story of the gallant woman who worked along with Cesar Chavez to protect the rights of farm workers. (Rev: BL 2/15/03; HBG 10/03) [921]

14732 Perez, Frank. *Dolores Huerta* (4–8). Illus. Series: Contemporary Hispanic Americans. 1995, Raintree LB $28.80 (978-0-8172-3981-7). The accomplishments of Dolores Huerta, a Hispanic American who cofounded the United Farm Workers, are described in this informative biography. (Rev: BL 3/15/96) [921]

IDAR, JOVITA

14733 Gibson, Karen Bush. *Jovita Idar* (5–7). Series: Latinos in American History. 2002, Mitchell Lane LB $29.95 (978-1-58415-151-7). 48pp. The inspiring story of the Latin American woman who started San Antonio's first free kindergarten and who founded the League of Mexican American women in 1911 to educate poor children. (Rev: BL 2/15/03; HBG 10/03) [921]

MARÍN, LUIS MUÑOZ

14734 Bernier-Grand, Carmen. *Poet and Politician of Puerto Rico: Don Luis Muñoz Marín* (5–8). 1995, Orchard LB $16.99 (978-0-531-08737-4). This story of the life of the man who helped make Puerto Rico a commonwealth also includes a history of the island. (Rev: BL 5/15/95; SLJ 4/95) [921]

MORENO, LUISA

14735 Moore, Heidi. *Luisa Moreno* (3–6). Series: American Lives. 2005, Heinemann LB $26.79 (978-1-4034-6978-6). 32pp. Using large type and simple text, this volume describes the Guatemalan American social activist's fight to improve working conditions for factory workers, particularly those from Latin America. (Rev: SLJ 4/06) [921]

SERRA, JUNÍPERO

14736 Dolan, Sean. *Junípero Serra* (5–9). Series: Hispanics of Achievement. 1991, Chelsea LB $21.95 (978-0-7910-1255-0). The story of the devoted Spanish Franciscan missionary who was responsible for founding the famous missions on the coast of California. (Rev: BL 11/1/91; SLJ 2/92) [921]

14737 Whiting, Jim. *Junípero José Serra* (5–7). Series: Latinos in American History. 2003, Mitchell Lane LB $29.95 (978-1-58415-187-6). 48pp. Profiles the monk who was responsible for founding nine California missions and converting thousands of Native Americans to Christianity. (Rev: BL 1/1–15/04; SLJ 3/00) [921]

TENAYUCA, EMMA

14738 Tafolla, Carmen, and Sharyll Tenayuca. *That's Not Fair! / ¡No es justo!* (2–4). Illus. by Terry Ybanez. 2008, Wings $17.95 (978-0-916727-33-8). 40pp. A bilingual picture-book biography of Mexican American labor activist Emma Tenayuca, who worked to improve the lot of factory and farm workers in Texas in the 1920s and 1930s. (Rev: BL 7/08; SLJ 3/09) [921]

VALLEJO, MARIANO GUADALUPE

14739 Tracy, Kathleen. *Mariano Guadalupe Vallejo* (5–7). Series: Latinos in American History. 2002, Mitchell Lane LB $29.95 (978-1-58415-152-4). 48pp. The story of the 19th-century military man who supported the U.S. annexation of California

and later served in the state's first Senate. (Rev: BL 2/15/03; HBG 10/03) [921]

Historical Figures and Important Contemporary Americans

ADAMS, SAMUEL

14740 Adler, David A., and Michael S. Adler. *A Picture Book of Samuel Adams* (1–3). Illus. by Ronald Himler. Series: A Picture Book of. 2005, Holiday House $16.95 (978-0-8234-1846-6). 32pp. Historical details are woven into the succinct information on Adams's youth and achievements as an adult. (Rev: BL 6/1–15/05; SLJ 6/05) [973.3]

14741 Burgan, Michael. *Samuel Adams: Patriot and Statesman* (4–7). Illus. Series: Signature Lives (Revolutionary War Era). 2005, Compass Point LB $34.60 (978-0-7565-0823-4). 48pp. Profiles the man who played a key role in the tax rebellion and Boston Tea Party. (Rev: BL 4/1/05) [921]

14742 Doeden, Matt. *Samuel Adams: Patriot and Statesman* (4–6). Illus. by Tod Smith, et al. Series: Graphic Biographies. 2006, Capstone LB $25.26 (978-0-7368-6500-5). 32pp. This graphic-novel treatment of the story of Samuel Adams, a key figure in the Revolutionary War, will be useful to report-writers and reluctant readers. (Rev: SLJ 5/07)

14743 Fradin, Dennis Brindell. *Samuel Adams: The Father of American Independence* (5–9). Illus. 1998, Houghton $20.00 (978-0-395-82510-5). An attractive biography of the amazing Sam Adams, whom Jefferson called "the Man of the Revolution." (Rev: BCCB 7–8/98; BL 7/98; SLJ 7/98; VOYA 2/99) [921]

14744 Fritz, Jean. *Why Don't You Get a Horse, Sam Adams?* (3–5). Illus. by Trina S. Hyman. 1974, Penguin paper $6.99 (978-0-698-11416-6). 48pp. How Sam Adams was finally persuaded to ride a horse is told in this humorous re-creation of Revolutionary times. [921]

ALBRIGHT, MADELEINE

14745 Blue, Rose, and Corinne J. Naden. *Madeleine Albright: U.S. Secretary of State* (3–5). Illus. 1998, Blackbirch LB $26.20 (978-1-56711-253-5). 64pp. The rise of this secretary of state is traced, along with a description of the job, the responsibilities, and its history. (Rev: BL 12/1/98; HBG 3/99) [921]

14746 Byman, Jeremy. *Madam Secretary: The Story of Madeleine Albright* (5–9). Series: Notable Americans. 1997, Morgan Reynolds LB $21.95 (978-1-883846-23-5). 96pp. The emphasis in this biography is on Albright's public life, first as adviser to various political figures, then as ambassador to the United Nations, and finally as secretary of state. (Rev: BL 12/15/97; SLJ 4/98; VOYA 6/98) [921]

14747 Maass, Robert. *UN Ambassador: A Behind-the-Scenes Look at Madeleine Albright's World* (3–5). Illus. 1995, Walker LB $17.85 (978-0-8027-8356-1). 48pp. A biography of Madeleine Albright, who, at the time of writing, was U.S. ambassador to the United Nations. (Rev: BL 11/15/95; SLJ 11/95) [921]

ALLEN, ETHAN

14748 Aronson, Virginia. *Ethan Allen: Revolutionary Hero* (4–6). 2000, Chelsea LB $27.50 (978-0-7910-5974-6); paper $27.50 (978-0-7910-6132-9). 80pp. This introduction to the life of Ethan Allen presents both his triumphs and his failings. (Rev: SLJ 7/01) [973.3]

14749 Haugen, Brenda. *Ethan Allen: Green Mountain Rebel* (4–7). Illus. Series: Signature Lives (Revolutionary War Era). 2005, Compass Point LB $34.60 (978-0-7565-0824-1). 48pp. Traces the life of the man who, along with Benedict Arnold, led the Green Mountain Boys in capturing Fort Ticonderoga from the British. (Rev: BL 4/1/05; SLJ 8/05) [921]

14750 Raabe, Emily. *Ethan Allen: The Green Mountain Boys and Vermont's Path to Statehood* (4–7). Series: Library of American Lives and Times. 2001, Rosen LB $34.60 (978-0-8239-5722-4). 112pp. Extraordinary illustrations and fine text tell the story of the controversial founder of Vermont who led the Green Mountain Boys in the capture of Fort Ticonderoga and Crown Point. (Rev: BL 10/15/01) [921]

ARNOLD, BENEDICT

14751 Dell, Pamela. *Benedict Arnold: From Patriot to Traitor* (4–7). Illus. Series: Signature Lives (Revolutionary War Era). 2005, Compass Point LB $34.60 (978-0-7565-0825-8). 48pp. A well-designed and informative profile of the man who betrayed his country. (Rev: BL 4/1/05) [921]

14752 Gaines, Ann Graham. *Benedict Arnold: Patriot or Traitor?* (5–8). Series: Historical American Biographies. 2001, Enslow LB $26.60 (978-0-7660-1393-3). 112pp. Many facets of the character of this controversial American are examined in this well-illustrated volume. (Rev: BL 4/15/01; HBG 10/01; SLJ 6/01) [921]

14753 Gregson, Susan R. *Benedict Arnold* (5–6). Series: Let Freedom Ring. 2001, Capstone LB $23.93 (978-0-7368-1032-6). 48pp. An introduction to Arnold's life and contributions, with discussion of the reasons why he became a traitor. (Rev: HBG 3/02; SLJ 4/02) [921]

14754 King, David C. *Benedict Arnold and the American Revolution* (5–9). Series: Notorious Americans and Their Times. 1998, Blackbirch LB $28.70 (978-1-56711-221-4). Benedict Arnold's life and military accomplishments are placed in the context of the period in which he lived and the conflicts he faced. (Rev: BL 12/15/98; HBG 3/99; SLJ 12/98) [921]

14755 Powell, Walter L. *Benedict Arnold: Revolutionary War Hero and Traitor* (5–8). Series: Library of American Lives and Times. 2004, Rosen LB $34.60 (978-0-8239-6627-1). 112pp. The life of Benedict Arnold, the American patriot who switched his allegiance to the British cause. (Rev: SLJ 7/04) [921]

14756 Sonneborn, Liz. *Benedict Arnold: Hero and Traitor* (4–8). Series: Leaders of the American Revolution. 2005, Chelsea House LB $30.00 (978-0-7910-8617-9). 130pp. An even-handed introduction to Arnold's life, presented chronologically with occasional factboxes; suitable for report writers. (Rev: SLJ 1/06) [921]

AUSTIN, STEPHEN F.

14757 Haley, James L. *Stephen F. Austin and the Founding of Texas* (5–8). Series: The Library of American Lives and Times. 2003, Rosen LB $34.60 (978-0-8239-5738-5). 112pp. A concise biography of the pioneer who became one of the founders of Texas. (Rev: SLJ 5/03) [976.4]

BATES, MARTIN VAN BUREN

14758 Andreasen, Dan. *The Giant of Seville: A "Tall" Tale Based on a True Story* (PS–2). Illus. 2007, Abrams $16.95 (978-0-8109-0988-5). 32pp. As a retired circus performer, Martin Van Buren Bates, nearly 8 feet tall, wanted a quiet place to live, and the residents of Seville, Ohio, were determined to give him just that. (Rev: BL 2/1/07) [921]

BEAN, JUDGE ROY

14759 Green, Carl R., and William R. Sanford. *Judge Roy Bean* (4–6). Illus. Series: Outlaws and Lawmen. 1995, Enslow LB $21.26 (978-0-89490-591-9). 48pp. A biography of this colorful, many-sided character from the old Wild West. (Rev: SLJ 9/95) [921]

BECKWOURTH, JAMES

14760 Gregson, Susan R. *James Beckwourth: Mountaineer, Scout, and Pioneer* (5–8). Series: Signature Lives. 2005, Compass Point LB $34.60 (978-0-7565-1000-8). 112pp. Beckwourth was one of the first African Americans to play a role in the exploration of the West. (Rev: SLJ 2/06) [921]

BILLY THE KID

14761 Bruns, Roger. *Billy the Kid* (5–8). Series: Historical American Biographies. 2000, Enslow LB $26.60 (978-0-7660-1091-8). A well-researched and thoroughly documented biography of America's famous outlaw. (Rev: BL 1/1–15/00; HBG 10/00; SLJ 5/00) [921]

14762 Green, Carl R., and William R. Sanford. *Billy the Kid* (3–5). Illus. 2008, Enslow LB $17.95 (978-0-7660-3173-9). 48pp. A revised edition of the life story of the outlaw William H. Bonney, who lived from 1859 to 1881. (Rev: BL 1/1–15/09) [921]

BLY, NELLIE

14763 Butcher, Nancy. *It Can't Be Done, Nellie Bly! A Reporter's Race Around the World* (2–5). Illus. by Jen L. Singh. 2003, Peachtree $12.95 (978-1-56145-289-7). The story of reporter Nellie Bly's attempt to beat the round-the-world journey of Jules Verne's fictional Phineas Fogg. (Rev: BL 3/1/04; HBG 4/04; SLJ 6/04) [921]

14764 Fredeen, Charles. *Nellie Bly: Daredevil Reporter* (5–9). Series: Lerner Biographies. 2000, Lerner LB $25.26 (978-0-8225-4956-7). 112pp. The story of the daring reporter who traveled around the world in 72 days and was a champion of the women's suffrage movement. (Rev: HBG 10/00; SLJ 3/00) [921]

14765 Kendall, Martha E. *Nellie Bly: Reporter for the World* (3–5). Illus. Series: Gateway Biographies. 1992, Millbrook LB $21.90 (978-1-56294-061-4); paper $4.80 (978-0-395-64538-3). 48pp. The life story of the famous woman journalist whose real name was Elizabeth Seaman. (Rev: BL 8/92; SLJ 11/92) [921]

14766 Krensky, Stephen. *Nellie Bly: A Name to Be Reckoned With* (3–4). Illus. by Rebecca Guay. Series: Milestone. 2003, Simon & Schuster paper $3.99 (978-0-689-85573-3). 80pp. This is an appealing biography of the pioneering woman journalist who made a 72-day trip around the world, with lots of vivid illustrations. (Rev: BL 6/1–15/03; HBG 4/04) [921]

BOOTH, EDWIN AND JOHN WILKES

14767 Giblin, James Cross. *Good Brother, Bad Brother: The Story of Edwin Booth and John Wilkes Booth* (5–8). Illus. 2005, Clarion $22.00 (978-0-618-09642-8). 256pp. In a compelling and highly readable narrative, Giblin reveals the alcoholism and depression that plagued the theatrical Booth family, the disagreement between the two brothers over the Civil War, and the effects of the assassination on Edwin's later life. (Rev: BL 5/1/05*; SLJ 5/05) [921]

BOWIE, JIM

14768 Edmondson, J. R. *Jim Bowie: Frontier Legend, Alamo Hero* (4–7). Series: Library of American Lives and Times. 2003, Rosen LB $34.60 (978-0-8239-5734-7). 112pp. As well as being a rogue, slave trader, and murderer, Jim Bowie was also a hero of the famous battle of the Alamo. (Rev: BL 6/1–15/03; SLJ 7/03) [921]

14769 Gaines, Ann Graham. *Jim Bowie* (5–8). Series: Historical American Biographies. 2000, Enslow LB $26.60 (978-0-7660-1253-0). A well-documented biography of Jim Bowie, a hero of the revolution in Texas who was best known for fighting in the battle of the Alamo. (Rev: BL 1/1–15/00; HBG 10/00; SLJ 5/00) [921]

BRADFORD, WILLIAM

14770 Doherty, Kieran. *William Bradford: Rock of Plymouth* (5–9). 1999, Twenty-First Century LB $24.90 (978-0-7613-1304-5). 192pp. Using Bradford's own writings and other contemporary accounts as sources, this is an objective biography of the man who was the governor of the Plymouth Plantation. (Rev: BL 12/1/99; HBG 3/00; SLJ 1/00) [921]

BRADLEY, BILL

14771 Andryszewski, Tricia. *Bill Bradley: Scholar, Athlete, Statesman* (4–6). Illus. Series: Gateway Biographies. 1999, Millbrook LB $21.90 (978-0-7613-1669-5). 48pp. Using material from Bill Bradley's autobiography, this account describes the life and struggles of the famous basketball star turned successful politician. (Rev: BL 11/15/99; HBG 3/00) [921]

14772 Buckley, James, Jr. *Bill Bradley* (5–8). Illus. Series: Basketball Hall of Famers. 2002, Rosen LB $29.25 (978-0-8239-3479-9). 112pp. An easy-to-read, detailed biography of the former athlete, with plenty of photographs. (Rev: BL 9/1/02) [921]

BRANDEIS, LOUIS

14773 Freedman, Suzanne. *Louis Brandeis* (4–9). Illus. Series: Justices of the Supreme Court. 1996, Enslow LB $26.60 (978-0-89490-678-7). A biography of the great justice who advocated many public causes and was known as the "people's attorney." (Rev: BL 8/96; SLJ 11/96) [921]

BROWN, JOHN

14774 Brackett, Virginia. *John Brown: Abolitionist* (3–5). Series: Famous Figures of the Civil War Era. 2001, Chelsea LB $25.00 (978-0-7910-6408-5). Told with many color illustrations and a vivid text, this is the story of the obsessive abolitionist who was hanged for treason in 1859. (Rev: BL 4/1/02; HBG 10/02; SLJ 5/02) [921]

14775 Streissguth, Thomas. *John Brown* (2–4). Illus. by Ralph L. Ramstad. Series: On My Own Biography. 1999, Carolrhoda LB $23.93 (978-1-57505-334-9). 48pp. This is a fine life story of the abolitionist, his beliefs and actions, plus a good look at the dispute over slavery before the Civil War. (Rev: HBG 3/00; SLJ 11/99) [921]

BURR, AARON

14776 Ingram, Scott. *Aaron Burr and the Young Nation* (5–8). Series: Major World Leaders. 2002, Chelsea $28.70 (978-1-56711-250-4). 112pp. The story of the controversial political leader who killed Alexander Hamilton in a duel and later was tried and found guilty of treason. (Rev: BL 1/1–15/03; SLJ 10/02) [921]

14777 Melton, Buckner F. *Aaron Burr: The Rise and Fall of an American Politician* (5–8). Series: Library of American Lives and Times. 2004, Rosen LB $34.60 (978-0-8239-6626-4). 112pp. This engaging biography chronicles the rise and fall of the Revolutionary War hero who was later branded a traitor. (Rev: SLJ 7/04) [921]

CAPONE, AL

14778 King, David C. *Al Capone and the Roaring Twenties* (5–9). Illus. Series: Notorious Americans and Their Times. 1998, Blackbirch LB $28.70 (978-1-56711-218-4). 80pp. In this biography of the gangster, the reader also gets information on the Jazz Age, the Ku Klux Klan, and other personalities of the time, such as Earhart and Lindbergh. (Rev: BL 12/15/98; HBG 3/99; SLJ 12/98) [921]

CASSIDY, BUTCH

14779 Green, Carl R., and William R. Sanford. *Butch Cassidy* (4–8). Series: Outlaws and Lawmen of the Wild West. 1995, Enslow LB $21.26 (978-0-89490-587-2). 48pp. The Wild West is re-created in this brief account of the life of this colorful outlaw, whose death remains a mystery. (Rev: BL 6/1–15/95; SLJ 7/95) [921]

14780 Wukovits, John F. *Butch Cassidy* (4–7). Series: Legends of the West. 1997, Chelsea $18.65 (978-0-7910-3857-4). 64pp. This biography of Robert Leroy Parker, who is better known as Butch Cassidy, emphasizes the fact that he was a ruthless criminal and not the idealized character of the movies. (Rev: HBG 3/98; SLJ 4/98) [921]

CHAMBERLAIN, JOSHUA LAWRENCE

14781 Kennedy, Robert F., Jr. *Joshua Chamberlain and the American Civil War* (3–5). Illus. by Nikita Andreev. 2007, Hyperion $16.99 (978-1-4231-0771-2). 48pp. Joshua Chamberlain served as a Union general during the Civil War, leading his soldiers to battle at Gettysburg and playing a key role at Appomattox. (Rev: BL 12/15/07; LMC 3/08; SLJ 1/08) [921]

CHAPMAN, JOHN

14782 Aliki. *The Story of Johnny Appleseed* (K–3). Illus. by author. 1971, Simon & Schuster paper $5.95 (978-0-671-66746-7). A picture story of the man who wandered through the Midwest spreading love and apple seeds.

14783 Hodges, Margaret. *The True Tale of Johnny Appleseed* (K–3). Illus. by Kimberly B. Root. 1997, Holiday House LB $16.95 (978-0-8234-1282-2). 32pp. A biography that tells about John Chapman's childhood in Massachusetts and his relocation in the West, where he was noted for planting and caring for apple trees. (Rev: BL 7/97; SLJ 9/97) [921]

14784 Kellogg, Steven. *Johnny Appleseed* (2–4). Illus. by author. 1988, Morrow $17.89 (978-0-688-06418-1). 48pp. The story of the famed John Chapman, who traveled the country in the 1700s spreading good cheer and apple seeds. (Rev: BCCB 11/88; BL 9/1/88; SLJ 10/88)

14785 Moses, Will. *Johnny Appleseed: The Story of a Legend* (4–6). Illus. 2001, Penguin $17.99 (978-0-399-23153-7). 32pp. This account of the life of Johnny Appleseed is enhanced by the author's folk-art paintings. (Rev: BL 9/1/01; HBG 3/02; SLJ 9/01) [634]

14786 Warrick, Karen Clemens. *John Chapman: The Legendary Johnny Appleseed* (5–8). Series: Historical American Biographies. 2001, Enslow LB $26.60 (978-0-7660-1443-5). 112pp. An engrossing, nicely illustrated portrait of the man who wandered the

Midwest promoting apple cultivation. (Rev: BL 4/15/01; HBG 10/01; SLJ 4/01) [921]

14787 Yolen, Jane. *Johnny Appleseed: The Legend and the Truth* (K–3). Illus. by Jim Burke. 2008, HarperCollins $16.99 (978-0-06-059135-9). 32pp. Yolen looks at both fact and fiction about Appleseed's life and travels in this appealing picture-book biography. (Rev: BL 6/1–15/08; SLJ 10/08) [921]

CHAPMAN, OSCAR

14788 Hopkinson, Deborah. *Sweet Land of Liberty* (3–7). Illus. by Leonard Jenkins. 2007, Peachtree $16.95 (978-1-56145-395-5). 32pp. With bold illustrations, this volume traces the life of Oscar Chapman, a white government official who spent much of his life fighting injustice, most notably finding a public venue for singer Marian Anderson after she was denied the right to perform in Constitution Hall. (Rev: BL 4/15/07) [921]

CODY, BUFFALO BILL

14789 Shields, Charles J. *Buffalo Bill Cody* (3–6). Series: Famous Figures of the American Frontier. 2001, Chelsea LB $25.00 (978-0-7910-6497-9); paper $8.95 (978-0-7910-6498-6). 64pp. An appealing account of Cody's life with black-and-white and full-color illustrations and handy fact boxes. (Rev: SLJ 3/02) [921]

14790 Spies, Karen B. *Buffalo Bill Cody: Western Legend* (5–8). Series: Historical American Biographies. 1998, Enslow LB $26.60 (978-0-7660-1015-4). An in-depth look at this legendary frontiersman and the Wild West show he founded. (Rev: BL 3/15/98; SLJ 5/98) [921]

COFFIN, LEVI

14791 Swain, Gwenyth. *President of the Underground Railroad: A Story About Levi Coffin* (3–6). Illus. by Ralph L. Ramstad. Series: Creative Minds Biographies. 2001, Carolrhoda LB $22.60 (978-1-57505-551-0); paper $6.95 (978-1-57505-552-7). 64pp. This is a readable account of the life of Levi Coffin, a Quaker from North Carolina who devoted time and money to helping slaves escape to freedom. (Rev: HBG 10/01; SLJ 7/01) [973.7]

COUP, W. C.

14792 Covert, Ralph, and G. Riley Mills. *Sawdust and Spangles: The Amazing Life of W.C. Coup* (K–3). Illus. by Giselle Potter. 2007, Abrams $20.95 (978-0-8109-9351-8). 32pp. Coup ran away from home to join the circus at a young age and went on to be come a colleague of P. T. Barnum and creator of the New York Aquarium. (Rev: BLO 1/15/08; LMC 1/08) [921] ∩

CUSTER, GEORGE ARMSTRONG

14793 Anderson, Paul Christopher. *George Armstrong Custer: The Indian Wars and the Battle of the Little Big Horn* (4–8). Series: The Library of

American Lives and Times. 2004, Rosen LB $34.60 (978-0-8239-6631-8). 112pp. The importance of understanding history is emphasized in this balanced and well-illustrated look at Custer's life and stance at Little Big Horn. (Rev: SLJ 7/04) [920]

14794 Kent, Zachary. *George Armstrong Custer* (5–8). Series: Historical American Biographies. 2000, Enslow LB $26.60 (978-0-7660-1255-4). Using extensive chapter notes, a glossary, bibliography, and index, this is a well-documented and objective assessment of Custer's life and deeds. (Rev: BL 1/1–15/00; HBG 10/00) [921]

DAVIS, JEFFERSON

14795 Burch, Joann J. *Jefferson Davis: President of the Confederacy* (5–8). Series: Historical American Biographies. 1998, Enslow LB $26.60 (978-0-7660-1064-2). Using personal documents and well-chosen illustrations, this lively biography describes Jefferson Davis's life as well as the causes and major events of the Civil War. (Rev: BL 10/15/98; SLJ 1/99) [921]

14796 Frazier, Joey. *Jefferson Davis: Confederate President* (3–5). Illus. 2001, Chelsea $25.00 (978-0-7910-6006-3); paper $25.00 (978-0-7910-6144-2). 80pp. A brief biography that covers Davis's life, with information on his education, his rise to become president of the Confederacy, and the problems of his administration. (Rev: BL 5/1/01; SLJ 9/01) [973.7]

DOUGLAS, STEPHEN

14797 Bonner, Mike. *Stephen Douglas: Champion of the Union* (3–5). Series: Famous Figures of the Civil War Era. 2001, Chelsea LB $25.00 (978-0-7910-6402-3). The story of the American politician named the "Little Giant" who engaged in a famous series of debates with Lincoln but later became his staunch supporter. (Rev: BL 4/1/02; HBG 10/02; SLJ 5/02) [921]

EARP, WYATT

14798 Green, Carl R., and William R. Sanford. *Wyatt Earp*. Rev. ed. (4–8). Illus. Series: Outlaws and Lawmen of the Wild West. 2008, Enslow LB $23.93 (978-0-89490-367-0). 48pp. With maps and authentic illustrations, this biography tells the story of the deputy marshal who tried to clean up Tombstone, Arizona. (Rev: BL 10/1/92; SLJ 11/92) [921]

14799 Staeger, Rob. *Wyatt Earp* (3–6). Series: Famous Figures of the American Frontier. 2001, Chelsea LB $25.00 (978-0-7910-6485-6); paper $8.95 (978-0-7910-6486-3). 64pp. An appealing biography of the famous gunfighter, with black-and-white and full-color illustrations and handy fact boxes. (Rev: HBG 10/02; SLJ 3/02) [921]

EDWARDS, JONATHAN

14800 Lutz, Norma Jean. *Jonathan Edwards: Colonial Religious Leader* (5–7). Series: Colonial Leaders. 2001, Chelsea $27.50 (978-0-7910-5961-6).

80pp. The life of Edwards, a leader in the Great Awakening spiritual movement and preacher among Native American tribes, is presented here with discussion of his contributions and his failings. (Rev: SLJ 5/01) [921]

FARRAGUT, DAVID

14801 Adelson, Bruce. *David Farragut: Union Admiral* (3–5). Series: Famous Figures of the Civil War Era. 2001, Chelsea LB $25.00 (978-0-7910-6416-0). The story of the American admiral who served in the War of 1812 and the Mexican War, and gained fame as a blockade runner during the Civil War. (Rev: BL 4/1/02) [921]

14802 Stein, R. Conrad. *David Farragut: First Admiral of the U.S. Navy* (3–6). Series: A Proud Heritage. 2005, Child's World LB $28.50 (978-1-59296-383-6). 40pp. Covers Farragut joining the navy at the age of 10 and his rise to become an admiral. (Rev: SLJ 6/05) [921]

FRANKLIN, BENJAMIN

14803 Adler, David A. *B. Franklin, Printer* (4–8). Illus. 2001, Holiday $19.95 (978-0-8234-1675-2). 128pp. Quotations, anecdotes, and wonderful illustrations round out this excellent volume about the life and accomplishments of Benjamin Franklin. (Rev: BCCB 2/02; BL 1/1–15/02; HBG 10/02; SLJ 2/02*; VOYA 4/02) [973.3]

14804 Adler, David A. *A Picture Book of Benjamin Franklin* (K–3). Illus. by John Wallner and Alexandra Wallner. Series: Picture Book Biographies. 1990, Holiday House LB $16.95 (978-0-8234-0792-7); paper $13.90 (978-0-8234-0882-5). 32pp. Glimpses of personality and family are interwoven in this simple biography. (Rev: BL 4/15/90; HB 5/90; SLJ 5/90) [921]

14805 Ashby, Ruth. *The Amazing Mr. Franklin: Or the Boy Who Read Everything* (3–5). Illus. by Michael Montgomery. 2004, Peachtree $12.95 (978-1-56145-306-1). 144pp. Readers will learn about Franklin's youth as well as his later accomplishments in this attractive, small-format volume. (Rev: BL 7/04; SLJ 11/04) [973.3]

14806 Barretta, Gene. *Now and Ben: The Modern Inventions of Benjamin Franklin* (2–4). 2006, Holt $16.95 (978-0-8050-7917-3). 40pp. Franklin's many interests and inventions are the focus of this reader-friendly overview with appealing illustrations. (Rev: BL 3/1/06; SLJ 3/06) [609]

14807 Collard, Sneed B., III. *Benjamin Franklin: The Man Who Could Do Just About Anything* (3–5). Series: American Heroes. 2006, Benchmark LB $28.50 (978-0-7614-2161-0). 40pp. An excellent introductory biography of Franklin, covering his many talents and including attractive well-chosen illustrations and easy-to-read text. (Rev: SLJ 3/07) [921]

14808 Ford, Carin T. *Benjamin Franklin: Inventor and Patriot* (1–3). Illus. Series: Famous Inventors. 2003, Enslow LB $22.60 (978-0-7660-1859-4). 32pp. For young report writers, this volume presents the salient facts about Franklin in an attractive and accessible manner. (Rev: HBG 10/03; SLJ 1/04) [921]

14809 Foster, Leila M. *Benjamin Franklin: Founding Father and Inventor* (5–8). Series: Historical American Biographies. 1997, Enslow LB $26.60 (978-0-89490-784-5). An admiring biography that describes Franklin's many talents — as a printer, businessman, scientist, inventor, and statesman. (Rev: SLJ 11/97) [921]

14810 Fradin, Dennis Brindell. *Who Was Ben Franklin?* (3–5). Illus. by John O'Brien. 2002, Penguin paper $4.99 (978-0-448-42495-8). 112pp. This book traces the fascinating, eclectic life and varied careers of Benjamin Franklin. (Rev: BL 3/1/02; HBG 10/02; SLJ 3/02) [973.3]

14811 Harness, Cheryl. *The Remarkable Benjamin Franklin* (2–5). 2005, National Geographic $17.95 (978-0-7922-7882-5). 48pp. An appealing profile that combines interesting text with striking illustrations full of details, quotations, and a timeline. (Rev: BCCB 4/06; BL 3/1/06*; HB 3/06; HBG 10/06; LMC 3/06; SLJ 11/05) [921]

14812 Krensky, Stephen. *Ben Franklin and His First Kite* (1–3). Illus. by Bert Dodson. Series: Childhood of Famous Americans. 2002, Simon & Schuster paper $3.99 (978-0-689-84984-8). 31pp. The story of young Franklin's first experiment with a kite is told for beginning readers. (Rev: HBG 3/03; SLJ 10/02) [921]

14813 McCurdy, Michael. *So Said Ben* (3–5). Illus. by author. 2007, Creative Editions LB $17.95 (978-1-56846-147-2). 32pp. Quotations from Ben Franklin are illustrated with humorous woodcut illustrations. (Rev: BL 12/1/07; LMC 5/08; SLJ 1/08) [921]

14814 Nettleton, Pamela Hill. *Benjamin Franklin: Writer, Inventor, Statesman* (K–3). Illus. by Jeff Yesh. Series: Biographies. 2003, Picture Window LB $25.26 (978-1-4048-0186-8). 24pp. A brightly illustrated profile that is suitable for beginning readers. (Rev: SLJ 4/04) [921]

14815 Quackenbush, Robert. *Benjamin Franklin and His Friends* (2–3). Illus. 1991, Pippin $14.95 (978-0-945912-14-9). 40pp. A friend is described in each chapter, emphasizing the influence on Franklin's life. (Rev: BL 12/1/91; SLJ 11/91) [921]

14816 Riley, John. *Benjamin Franklin: A Photo Biography* (1–3). Series: First Biographies. 2000, Morgan Reynolds LB $16.95 (978-1-883846-64-0). 24pp. A very simple biography of Franklin for beginning readers that has a full-page illustration opposite each page of text. (Rev: HBG 10/00; SLJ 8/00) [921]

14817 Rushby, Pamela. *Ben Franklin: Printer, Author, Inventor, Politician* (2–4). Series: National Geographic History Chapters. 2007, National Geographic LB $17.90 (978-1-4263-0191-9). 40pp. Simple sentences, with photographs and drawings, tell the story of Franklin's youth and later accomplishments; a "How to Write an A+ Report" section gives useful advice. (Rev: LMC 1/08*; SLJ 1/08) [921]

14818 Schanzer, Rosalyn. *How Ben Franklin Stole the Lightning* (2–4). Illus. by author. 2003, HarperCollins LB $17.89 (978-0-688-16994-7). A lively account of Franklin's role as an inventor, with a focus on his flying a kite during a rainstorm. (Rev: BCCB 3/03; HBG 10/03; SLJ 1/03) [530]

14819 Sherrow, Victoria. *Benjamin Franklin* (3–4). Series: History Maker Bios. 2002, Lerner LB $26.60 (978-0-8225-0198-5). 48pp. The life of this multitalented genius of the colonial period is presented in a simple text with many illustrations. (Rev: BL 6/1–15/02; HBG 3/03) [921]

14820 Streissguth, Thomas. *Benjamin Franklin* (4–6). Series: Just the Facts Biographies. 2005, Lerner LB $27.93 (978-0-8225-2210-2). 112pp. This attractive and informative biography covers Franklin's youth and education as well as his later life, with interesting factboxes. (Rev: SLJ 2/05) [921]

14821 Streissguth, Thomas. *Benjamin Franklin* (5–8). Series: A&E Biography. 2001, Lerner LB $27.93 (978-0-8225-4997-0). A readable biography of the many-faceted genius of the newly formed United States. (Rev: BL 4/1/02; HBG 10/02) [921]

14822 Van Vleet, Carmella. *Amazing Ben Franklin Inventions You Can Build Yourself* (4–8). Illus. 2007, Nomad paper $14.95 (978-0-9771294-7-8). 120pp. Activities — making invisible ink, wave bottles, kites, and so forth — and the accompanying narrative bring Franklin's inquisitive nature to light. (Rev: LMC 1/08; SLJ 11/07) [921]

GALLAUDET, THOMAS

14823 Bowen, Andy Russell. *A World of Knowing: A Story About Thomas Hopkins Gallaudet* (3–5). Illus. Series: Creative Minds Biographies. 1995, Carolrhoda LB $22.60 (978-0-87614-871-6). 64pp. The story of the man who empathized with deaf persons and developed sign language to enable them to communicate with others. (Rev: BL 1/1–15/96; SLJ 1/96) [921]

GANCI, PETER J.

14824 Ganci, Chris. *Chief: The Life of Peter J. Ganci, a New York Firefighter* (3–5). Illus. 2003, Scholastic $16.95 (978-0-439-44386-9). 40pp. This loving portrait of a New York City firefighter who lost his life on September 11, 2001, was written by his son and is dedicated to firefighters around the world. (Rev: BL 4/15/03; HBG 10/03; SLJ 4/03) [921]

GEE, MAGGIE

14825 Moss, Marissa. *Sky High: The True Story of Maggie Gee* (3–5). Illus. by Carl Angel. 2009, Tricycle $16.99 (978-1-58246-280-6). 32pp. Born with a love of flying, Maggie Gee becomes one of World War II's WASP corps of female pilots; prejudice (she is Asian American) is a side issue. (Rev: BL 6/1–15/09) [921]

GLENN, JOHN

14826 Hilliard, Richard. *Godspeed, John Glenn* (1–3). 2006, Boyds Mills $16.95 (978-1-59078-384-9). 32pp. This picture-book biography offers a brief overview of the astronaut's life but focuses primarily on his first space voyage in the *Friendship 7* capsule. (Rev: BL 10/1/06; SLJ 10/06) [921]

14827 Holden, Henry M. *Trailblazing Astronaut John Glenn* (4–6). Illus. Series: Space Flight Adventures and Disasters. 2004, Enslow LB $25.26 (978-0-7660-5166-9). 48pp. Supported by Web sites, this is an account of the life of the astronaut who went into space twice, decades apart. [921]

14828 Mitchell, Don. *Liftoff: A Photobiography of John Glenn* (4–6). 2006, National Geographic $17.95 (978-0-7922-5899-5). 64pp. This photo-filled biography offers a brief overview of the former astronaut's life and many accomplishments. (Rev: BL 8/06) [629.45]

14829 Streissguth, Thomas. *John Glenn* (2–4). Illus. Series: Explore Space! 2003, Capstone LB $22.60 (978-0-7368-1625-0). 24pp. A slim, basic profile of the first American to orbit the earth, who went on to be a United States Senator. (Rev: HBG 10/03; SLJ 3/04) [921]

14830 Streissguth, Thomas. *John Glenn* (5–8). Series: A&E Biography. 1999, Lerner LB $25.26 (978-0-8225-4947-5); paper $7.95 (978-0-8225-9685-1). 112pp. This account of John Glenn's life includes childhood influences, his career with NASA, and his political life as a senator. (Rev: HBG 3/00; SLJ 3/00) [921]

14831 Vogt, Gregory L. *John Glenn's Return to Space* (4–7). Illus. 2000, Twenty-First Century LB $24.90 (978-0-7613-1614-5). 72pp. As well as describing John Glenn's two space flights on the *Mercury* capsule and later the *Discovery,* this biography gives information on astronauts' training and equipment. (Rev: BL 9/15/00; HBG 10/01; SLJ 1/01) [921]

GORE, AL

14832 Italia, Bob. *Al Gore: The Vice President of the United States* (4–6). Illus. Series: All the President's Men and Women. 1993, ABDO LB $21.95 (978-1-56239-253-6). 32pp. This biography of Gore covers his personality and interests, as well as his public life. (Rev: SLJ 3/94) [921]

14833 Stefoff, Rebecca. *Al Gore: Vice President* (3–5). Illus. Series: Gateway Biographies. 1994, Millbrook LB $23.90 (978-1-56294-433-9). 48pp. The life story of the vice president and his climb to high political office. (Rev: BL 8/94; SLJ 4/94) [921]

GREENE, NATHANAEL

14834 Mierka, Gregg A. *Nathanael Greene: The General Who Saved the Revolution* (5–8). Illus. Series: Forgotten Heroes of the American Revolution. 2006, OTTN LB $23.95 (978-1-59556-012-4). 88pp. Employing primary and previously unpublished sources, Mierka's lively text examines Greene's pivotal role as quartermaster general and southern commander in Washington's Revolutionary army. (Rev: BL 1/1–15/07) [973.3]

HALE, NATHAN

14835 Krizner, L. J., and Lisa Sita. *Nathan Hale: Patriot and Martyr of the American Revolution* (4–7). Series: Library of American Lives and Times. 2001, Rosen $31.95 (978-0-8239-5724-8). 112pp. Nathan Hale, executed by the British in 1776, represented the life-and-death issues fought for in the Revolution and became a symbol of courage and patriotism. (Rev: BL 10/15/01) [921]

14836 Tracy, Kathleen. *The Life and Times of Nathan Hale* (5–8). Illus. Series: Profiles in American History. 2007, Mitchell Lane LB $19.95 (978-1-58415-447-1). 48pp. This is an appealing life of Nathan Hale, from his childhood through his execution by the British. (Rev: SLJ 7/07) [921]

14837 Zemlicka, Shannon. *Nathan Hale: Patriot Spy* (2–4). Illus. by Craig Orback. Series: On My Own Biography. 2002, Carolrhoda LB $23.93 (978-0-87614-597-5); paper $5.95 (978-0-87614-905-8). 48pp. For beginning readers, this is an absorbing life of the Revolutionary War hero who was executed for spying. (Rev: HBG 3/03; SLJ 12/02) [973.3]

HAMILTON, ALEXANDER

14838 DeCarolis, Lisa. *Alexander Hamilton: Federalist and Founding Father* (4–7). Series: Library of American Lives and Times. 2003, Rosen LB $31.95 (978-0-8239-5735-4). 112pp. The story of the military hero of the American Revolution who was the first secretary of the treasury and helped write the Federalist Papers. (Rev: BL 6/1–15/03; SLJ 4/03) [921]

14839 Haugen, Brenda. *Alexander Hamilton: Founding Father and Statesman* (4–7). Illus. Series: Signature Lives (Revolutionary War Era). 2005, Compass Point LB $34.60 (978-0-7565-0827-2). 48pp. Traces the life of the man who became the first secretary of the treasury. (Rev: BL 4/1/05; SLJ 8/05) [921]

14840 Kallen, Stuart A. *Alexander Hamilton* (4–6). Series: Founding Fathers. 2001, ABDO LB $25.65 (978-1-57765-006-5). 64pp. A lively biography of the first secretary of the U.S. Treasury that covers his underprivileged early life and details his importance in the creation of the United States. (Rev: HBG 3/02; SLJ 1/02) [921]

HANCOCK, JOHN

14841 Adler, David A., and Michael S. Adler. *A Picture Book of John Hancock* (2–4). Illus. by Ronald Himler. 2007, Holiday $16.95 (978-0-8234-2005-6). 32pp. This well-illustrated biography of Hancock focuses on his importance to the American Revolution (includes notes, timeline, bibliography and Web sites). (Rev: BL 5/1/07; SLJ 7/07) [921]

14842 Fritz, Jean. *Will You Sign Here, John Hancock?* (3–5). Illus. by Trina S. Hyman. 1997, Penguin paper $5.99 (978-0-698-11440-1). 48pp. Under the sprightly title is a delightful, well-researched biography of this signer of the Declaration of Independence.

14843 Kjelle, Marylou Morano. *The Life and Times of John Hancock* (5–8). Illus. Series: Profiles in American History. 2007, Mitchell Lane LB $19.95 (978-1-58415-443-3). 48pp. Little-known facts about John Hancock's life make this well-organized biography an interesting read. (Rev: SLJ 7/07) [921]

14844 Ransom, Candice F. *John Hancock* (3–4). Illus. Series: History Maker Bios. 2004, Lerner LB $26.60 (978-0-8225-1547-0). 48pp. A simple biography, useful for report writers, with information about Hancock's youth and good photographs and illustrations. (Rev: SLJ 1/05) [921]

HAYSLIP, LE LY

14845 Englar, Mary. *Le Ly Hayslip* (5–8). Series: Asian-American Biographies. 2005, Raintree LB $23.00 (978-1-4109-1055-4). 64pp. An interesting profile of the Vietnamese-born woman who started the East Meets West Foundation. (Rev: SLJ 3/06) [921]

HENRY, PATRICK

14846 Adler, David A. *A Picture Book of Patrick Henry* (K–3). Illus. by John Wallner and Alexandra Wallner. Series: Picture Book Biographies. 1995, Holiday House LB $15.95 (978-0-8234-1187-0). 32pp. The story of the famous patriot who served five terms as governor of Virginia. (Rev: BL 9/15/95; SLJ 12/95) [921]

14847 Kukla, Amy, and Jon Kukla. *Patrick Henry: Voice of the Revolution* (4–7). Illus. Series: Library of American Lives and Times. 2001, Rosen $31.95 (978-0-8239-5725-5). 112pp. Detailed text, a variety of illustrations, and a timeline give readers a good understanding of Henry's importance. (Rev: BL 10/15/01) [973.3]

HERSHEY, MILTON S.

14848 Burford, Betty. *Chocolate by Hershey: A Story About Milton S. Hershey* (3–6). Illus. by Loren Chantland. Series: Creative Minds. 1994, Carolrhoda LB $22.60 (978-0-87614-830-3); paper $6.95 (978-0-87614-641-5). 64pp. An engrossing biography of the candy-making entrepreneur and his many philanthropies. (Rev: SLJ 1/95) [921]

HESCHEL, ABRAHAM JOSHUA

14849 Rose, Or. *Abraham Joshua Heschel* (4–8). Illus. 2003, Jewish Publication Soc. paper $9.95 (978-0-8276-0758-3). 72pp. A portrait of the rabbi and teacher who was born in Poland, emigrated to the United States, and became a leader in the civil rights movement. (Rev: BL 6/1–15/03; HBG 10/01) [921]

HICKOK, WILD BILL

14850 Green, Carl R., and William R. Sanford. *Wild Bill Hickok*. Rev. ed. (4–8). Illus. Series: Outlaws and Lawmen of the Wild West. 2008, Enslow LB $23.93 (978-0-89490-366-3). 48pp. The life story of the famous frontier marshal in Kansas is retold in text and pictures. (Rev: BL 7/92; SLJ 8/92) [921]

14851 Rosa, Joseph G. *Wild Bill Hickok: Sharpshooter and U.S. Marshal of the Wild West* (4–8). Series: The Library of American Lives and Times. 2004, Rosen LB $34.60 (978-0-8239-6632-5). 112pp. The importance of understanding history is emphasized in this balanced and well-illustrated look at Hickok's life. (Rev: SLJ 7/04) [921]

HOLLIDAY, DOC

14852 Green, Carl R., and William R. Sanford. *Doc Holliday* (5–8). Series: Outlaws and Lawmen of the Wild West. 1995, Enslow LB $21.26 (978-0-89490-589-6). The life and exploits of this colorful western hero are reproduced with the help of photographs and maps. (Rev: BL 6/1–15/95) [921]

HOOVER, J. EDGAR

14853 Cunningham, Kevin. *J. Edgar Hoover: Controversial FBI Director* (5–8). Series: Signature Lives. 2005, Compass Point LB $34.60 (978-0-7565-0997-2). 112pp. This introduction to Hoover's career provides limited personal details, concentrating instead on his political ambitions and tendency to ignore ethical standards. (Rev: SLJ 1/06) [921]

14854 Streissguth, Thomas. *J. Edgar Hoover: Powerful FBI Director* (5–8). Series: Historical American Biographies. 2002, Enslow LB $26.60 (978-0-7660-1623-1). 128pp. Streissguth looks at Hoover's life from youth, his personality, and his work as head of the FBI, and explores the areas in which his influence was felt, including civil rights and politics. (Rev: HBG 10/02; SLJ 8/02) [363.25092]

HOUSTON, SAM

14855 Boraas, Tracey. *Sam Houston: Soldier and Statesman* (3–5). Illus. Series: Let Freedom Ring. 2002, Capstone LB $23.93 (978-0-7368-1350-1). 48pp. A thorough look at the life and multiple careers of Sam Houston, who led the fight to wrest Texas from Mexican control. (Rev: HBG 3/03; SLJ 4/03)

14856 Caravantes, Peggy. *An American in Texas: The Story of Sam Houston* (5–8). Series: Founders of the Republic. 2003, Morgan Reynolds LB $23.95 (978-1-931798-19-8). 144pp. A portrait of the colorful general who became the first president of the Republic of Texas. (Rev: SLJ 5/04) [921]

14857 Harkins, Susan Sales, and William H. Harkins. *Sam Houston* (2–4). Series: A Robbie Reader: What's So Great About? 2006, Mitchell Lane LB $25.70 (978-1-58415-482-2). 32pp. A life of the Virginia native who led the fight for Texas's independence and was elected its first president after it became a republic. (Rev: SLJ 1/07) [921]

14858 Wade, Mary D. *I Am Houston* (3–5). Illus. 1993, Colophon $13.95 (978-1-882539-05-5); paper $7.95 (978-1-882539-06-2). 64pp. The biography of the soldier and politician who has become one of Texas's favorite heroes. (Rev: BL 4/15/93) [921]

14859 Woodward, Walter M. *Sam Houston: For Texas and the Union* (5–8). Series: The Library of American Lives and Times. 2003, Rosen LB $34.60 (978-0-8239-5739-2). 112pp. A concise biography of the man credited with gaining Texas's independence. (Rev: SLJ 5/03) [976.4]

JACKSON, STONEWALL

14860 Pflueger, Lynda. *Stonewall Jackson: Confederate General* (5–8). Illus. Series: Historical American Biographies. 1997, Enslow LB $26.60 (978-0-89490-781-4). This sympathetic biography of Jackson, who favored neither slavery nor secession but became a Confederate general in the Civil War, provides good material on his personal life and beliefs, quoting generously from firsthand sources. (Rev: BL 10/1/97) [921]

JAMES, JESSE

14861 Bruns, Roger. *Jesse James: Legendary Outlaw* (5–8). Series: Historical American Biographies. 1998, Enslow LB $26.60 (978-0-7660-1055-0). Using fact boxes, maps, a chronology, and chapter notes as well as an interesting text and black-and-white photographs, this book gives a fine biography of Jesse James and his exploits. (Rev: BL 10/15/98; SLJ 8/98) [921]

14862 Green, Carl R., and William R. Sanford. *Jesse James*. Rev. ed. (4–8). Illus. Series: Outlaws and Lawmen of the Wild West. 2008, Enslow LB $23.93 (978-0-89490-365-6). 48pp. This easy-to-read text portrays the legendary gunman as both outlaw and hero. (Rev: BL 3/1/92; SLJ 5/92) [921]

14863 Wukovits, John F. *Jesse James* (5–8). Illus. Series: Legends of the West. 1996, Chelsea $18.65 (978-0-7910-3876-5). 60pp. An action-packed biography that tries to probe the complex nature of the famous Western outlaw. (Rev: SLJ 4/97) [921]

JAY, JOHN

14864 Kallen, Stuart A. *John Jay* (4–6). Series: Founding Fathers. 2001, ABDO LB $25.65 (978-1-57765-013-3). 64pp. A lively biography of the first chief justice of the Supreme Court that covers his life and details his importance in the creation of the United States. (Rev: SLJ 1/02) [921]

JOHNSTON, JOSEPH E.

14865 Ditchfield, Christin. *Joseph E. Johnston: Confederate General* (3–5). Series: Famous Figures of the Civil War Era. 2001, Chelsea LB $25.00 (978-0-7910-6412-2). The story of the Confederate general who commanded forces during the Civil War and later served a term in the U.S. House of Representatives. (Rev: BL 4/1/02) [921]

JONES, JOHN PAUL

14866 Bradford, James C. *John Paul Jones and the American Navy* (4–7). Series: Library of American Lives and Times. 2001, Rosen $34.60 (978-0-8239-5726-2). 112pp. This attractively designed volume combines the life story of the naval hero of the American Revolution with a history of the birth and growth of the American navy. (Rev: BL 10/15/01) [921]

14867 Cooper, Michael L. *Hero of the High Seas: John Paul Jones* (4–7). 2006, National Geographic $21.95 (978-0-7922-5547-5). 128pp. This biography focuses on the Scottish immigrant's naval heroics during the American Revolution and includes a detailed timeline and a useful listing of "Words and Expressions from the Days of Sailing Ships." (Rev: BL 6/1–15/06; SLJ 9/06) [973.3]

14868 Lutz, Norma Jean. *John Paul Jones: Father of the U.S. Navy* (3–6). Series: Revolutionary War Leaders. 2000, Chelsea LB $31.00 (978-0-7910-5359-1). 80pp. From his boyhood in Scotland to his death at age 45, this is the biography of a hero of the Revolutionary War. (Rev: HBG 10/00; SLJ 5/00) [921]

14869 Riley, John. *John Paul Jones: A Photo Biography* (1–3). Series: First Biographies. 2000, Morgan Reynolds LB $16.95 (978-1-883846-63-3). 24pp. A heavily illustrated simple biography for beginning readers of the Revolutionary War hero. (Rev: HBG 10/00; SLJ 8/00) [921]

14870 Tibbitts, Alison Davis. *John Paul Jones: Father of the American Navy* (5–8). Series: Historical American Biographies. 2002, Enslow LB $26.60 (978-0-7660-1448-0). The life of the American naval officer noted for his role in the Revolution and for the statement, "I have not yet begun to fight." (Rev: BL 4/1/02; HBG 10/02; SLJ 5/02) [921]

KANDER, LIZZIE

14871 Kann, Bob. *A Recipe for Success: Lizzie Kander and Her Cookbook* (5–8). Illus. Series: Badger Biographies. 2006, Wisconsin Historical Soc. paper $12.95 (978-0-87020-373-2). 144pp. Lizzie Kander was a social reformer in the mid-19th century, responsible among other things for a successful cookbook that benefited the Milwaukee Settlement House; in addition to a profile of Kander, this volume offers interesting information on the time she lived in. (Rev: BL 2/15/07) [921]

KENNEDY, ROBERT F.

14872 Koestler-Grack, Rachel A. *The Assassination of Robert F. Kennedy* (5–8). Series: American Moments. 2005, ABDO LB $25.65 (978-1-59197-931-9). 48pp. Kennedy's assassination is placed in historical context, with a brief biography and discussion of the aftermath of this tragedy. (Rev: SLJ 11/05) [921]

KEY, FRANCIS SCOTT

14873 Gregson, Susan R. *Francis Scott Key: Patriotic Poet* (3–5). Illus. Series: Let Freedom Ring. 2003, Capstone LB $23.93 (978-0-7368-1554-3). 48pp. Chronicles the life of the lawyer and poet who wrote the words that were eventually to become the lyrics of America's national anthem. (Rev: HBG 10/03; SLJ 9/03)

14874 Kjelle, Marylou Morano. *Francis Scott Key* (1–4). Series: A Robbie Reader, What's So Great About? 2006, Mitchell Lane LB $25.70 (978-1-58415-474-7). 32pp. This brief biography covers the life of the man who wrote "The Star-Spangled Banner." (Rev: SLJ 11/06) [921]

KOREMATSU, FRED

14875 Chin, Steven A. *When Justice Failed: The Fred Korematsu Story* (3–6). Illus. by David Tamura. 1993, Raintree LB $28.55 (978-0-8114-7236-4). 105pp. The biography of the Japanese American whose rights were continually violated during World War II. (Rev: SLJ 7/93) [921]

LEE, ROBERT E.

14876 Adler, David A. *A Picture Book of Robert E. Lee* (3–4). Illus. by Alexandra Wallner and John Wallner. Series: Picture Book Biographies. 1994, Holiday House LB $16.95 (978-0-8234-1111-5). Using a story format, this simple account covers the highlights of Lee's life and military career. (Rev: SLJ 5/94) [921]

14877 Anderson, Paul Christopher. *Robert E. Lee: Legendary Commander of the Confederacy* (4–7). Series: Library of American Lives and Times. 2003, Rosen LB $34.60 (978-0-8239-5748-4). 112pp. Extensive original sources are used to re-create the life of this Confederate general and the times in which he lived. (Rev: BL 6/1–15/03) [921]

14878 Kerby, Mona. *Robert E. Lee: Southern Hero of the Civil War* (5–8). Illus. Series: Historical American Biographies. 1997, Enslow LB $26.60 (978-0-89490-782-1). 128pp. This thorough, sympathetic biography of Lee points out that he did not approve of slavery or the South's secession from the Union. (Rev: BL 10/1/97; SLJ 9/97) [921]

LIEBERMAN, JOSEPH

14879 Feinberg, Barbara S. *Joseph Lieberman: Keeping the Faith* (4–6). Illus. 2001, Millbrook LB $23.90 (978-0-7613-2303-7). 48pp. This profile of the first Jewish candidate for the vice presidency of the United States includes photographs, a timeline, and a bibliography. (Rev: BL 9/15/01; HBG 3/02) [973.929]

LINCOLN, THOMAS AND WILLIAM WALLACE

14880 Rabin, Staton. *Mr. Lincoln's Boys: Being the Mostly True Adventures of Abraham Lincoln's Troublemaking Sons Tad and Willie* (2–4). Illus. by

Bagram Ibatoulline. 2008, Viking $16.99 (978-0-670-06169-3). 40pp. With only a little embellishment, Rabin presents the antics of Lincoln's two young sons during their days in the White House; Ibatoulline's detailed illustrations add historical atmosphere. (Rev: BL 7/08; LMC 1/09; SLJ 9/08) [973.7092]

MACARTHUR, DOUGLAS

14881 Fox, Mary V. *Douglas MacArthur* (4–8). Series: The Importance Of. 1999, Lucent LB $27.45 (978-1-56006-545-6). 96pp. The story of one of the nation's most prominent generals, whose unorthodox actions made him a controversial figure. (Rev: BL 9/15/99) [921]

14882 Gaines, Ann Graham. *Douglas MacArthur: Brilliant General, Controversial Leader* (5–8). Series: Historical American Biographies. 2001, Enslow LB $26.60 (978-0-7660-1445-9). 112pp. Using many black-and-white photographs as illustrations, this account gives a well-rounded, unbiased picture of this controversial general. (Rev: BL 4/15/01; HBG 10/01; SLJ 6/01) [921]

14883 Haugen, Brenda. *Douglas MacArthur: America's General* (5–8). Series: Signature Lives. 2005, Compass Point LB $34.60 (978-0-7565-0994-1). 112pp. This introduction to MacArthur's career provides limited personal details but concentrates instead on his leadership abilities and military achievements. (Rev: SLJ 1/06) [921]

MCCAIN, JOHN

14884 Feinberg, Barbara S. *John McCain: Serving His Country* (4–7). Illus. Series: Gateway. 2000, Millbrook LB $23.90 (978-0-7613-1974-0). 48pp. A biography of the senator that tells about his youth and later political career but concentrates on his stint in the navy and his imprisonment during the Vietnam War. (Rev: BL 3/1/01; HBG 10/01) [921]

14885 Wells, Catherine. *John McCain* (5–8). Illus. Series: Political Profiles. 2008, Morgan Reynolds LB $27.95 (978-1-59935-046-2). 112pp. Beginning with his early years and ending just before his nomination as a presidential candidate, this book examines McCain's life as well as his public and military service. (Rev: BL 5/15/08; SLJ 1/08) [921]

MCCLELLAN, GEORGE

14886 Kelley, Brent. *George McClellan: Union General* (3–5). Series: Famous Figures of the Civil War Era. 2001, Chelsea LB $25.00 (978-0-7910-6404-7). The life of this important Union army leader, who was removed from his command by Lincoln, is re-created in pictures and text. (Rev: BL 4/1/02; SLJ 5/02) [921]

MARION, FRANCIS

14887 Towles, Louis P. *Francis Marion: The Swamp Fox of the American Revolution* (4–7). Series: Library of American Lives and Times. 2001, Rosen LB $34.60 (978-0-8239-5728-6). The life of the

Revolutionary War hero known as the Swamp Fox because of his stealthy retreats into the swamp lands. (Rev: BL 1/1–15/02) [921]

MEADE, GEORGE GORDON

14888 Adelson, Bruce. *George Gordon Meade: Union General* (3–5). Series: Famous Figures of the Civil War Era. 2001, Chelsea LB $25.00 (978-0-7910-6410-8). The story of the Civil War general who fought in battles including Bull Run, Antietam, Chancellorsville, and Gettysburg. (Rev: BL 4/1/02; HBG 10/02) [921]

MORRIS, GOUVERNOR

14889 Crompton, Samuel Willard. *Gouverneur Morris: Creating a Nation* (5–8). Series: America's Founding Fathers. 2004, Enslow LB $26.60 (978-0-7660-2213-3). 128pp. An introduction to the life and legacy of Gouvernor Morris, who helped to edit the final draft of the Declaration of Independence. (Rev: SLJ 7/04) [973.4]

NEWTON, JOHN

14890 Granfield, Linda. *Amazing Grace: The Story of the Hymn* (4–8). Illus. 1997, Tundra $15.95 (978-0-88776-389-2). The life story of John Newton, a sea captain in the slave trade who later rejected slavery, became a minister, and wrote several hymns, including "Amazing Grace." (Rev: SLJ 8/97) [921]

OGLETHORPE, JAMES

14891 Lommel, Cookie. *James Oglethorpe: Humanitarian and Soldier* (4–6). Series: Colonial Leaders. 2001, Chelsea LB $27.50 (978-0-7910-5963-0); paper $27.50 (978-0-7910-6120-6). 80pp. Oglethorpe, the English founder and first governor of the colony of Georgia, was active in a number of areas including prison reform, the guarantee of religious freedom, and relations with Native Americans. (Rev: HBG 10/01; SLJ 7/01) [975.8]

OLMSTED, FREDERICK LAW

14892 Dunlap, Julie. *Parks for the People: A Story About Frederick Law Olmsted* (3–6). Illus. by Susan F. Lieber. Series: Creative Minds Biographies. 1994, Carolrhoda LB $22.60 (978-0-87614-824-2). 63pp. The life story of America's first landscape architect, his masterpiece — Central Park in New York City — and how he tried to save Yosemite from commercial exploitation. (Rev: SLJ 2/95) [921]

14893 Wishinsky, Frieda. *The Man Who Made Parks: The Story of Parkbuilder Frederick Law Olmsted* (2–4). Illus. by Song Nan Zhang. 1999, Tundra $15.95 (978-0-88776-435-6). A short, illustrated biography of the man who created and designed some of the most beautiful parks in America, including Central Park in New York City. (Rev: BL 8/99; HBG 10/99; SLJ 10/99) [921]

PAINE, THOMAS

14894 Burgan, Michael. *Thomas Paine: Great Writer of the Revolution* (4–7). Illus. Series: Signature Lives (Revolutionary War Era). 2005, Compass Point LB $34.60 (978-0-7565-0830-2). 48pp. A well-designed profile of the revolutionary thinker. (Rev: BL 4/1/05) [921]

14895 McCarthy, Pat. *Thomas Paine: Revolutionary Patriot and Writer* (5–8). Series: Historical American Biographies. 2001, Enslow LB $26.60 (978-0-7660-1446-6). 112pp. A balanced, well-researched biography of the American political theorist and writer who created controversy throughout his lifetime. (Rev: BL 4/15/01; HBG 10/01) [921]

14896 McCartin, Brian. *Thomas Paine: Common Sense and Revolutionary Pamphleteering* (4–7). Series: Library of American Lives and Times. 2001, Rosen $34.60 (978-0-8239-5729-3). 112pp. The story of the British-born colonialist who heard the cries for liberty around him and whose writings set the stage for the Declaration of Independence. (Rev: BL 10/15/01) [921]

14897 Waxman, Laura Hamilton. *Uncommon Revolutionary: A Story About Thomas Paine* (3–5). Illus. by Craig Orback. Series: Creative Minds Biographies. 2003, Carolrhoda LB $22.60 (978-1-57505-180-2). 64pp. An illustrated biography of the Revolutionary War pamphleteer who supported the cause of American independence. (Rev: HBG 4/04; SLJ 5/04) [921]

PARKHURST, CHARLEY

14898 Kay, Verla. *Rough, Tough Charley* (K–3). Illus. by Adam Gustavson. 2007, Tricycle $15.95 (978-1-58246-184-7). 32pp. The life of Charley Parkhurst, a female stagecoach driver who dressed as a man and whose sex was only revealed after her death. (Rev: BL 6/1–15/07; SLJ 8/07) [921]

PATTON, GEORGE S., JR.

14899 Sutcliffe, Jane. *George S. Patton Jr.* (2–5). Illus. Series: History Maker Bios. 2005, Lerner LB $26.60 (978-0-8225-2436-6); paper $6.95 (978-0-8225-5461-5). 48pp. The life and times of the general, with plenty of information for report writers; includes photographs, drawings, and Web sites. (Rev: SLJ 8/05) [921]

PEARY, MARIE AHNIGHITO

14900 Kirkpatrick, Katherine. *The Snow Baby: The Arctic Childhood of Robert E. Peary's Daring Daughter* (5–8). Illus. 2007, Holiday $16.95 (978-0-8234-1973-9). 48pp. This engaging account of a child growing up partly among the Inuit and partly in her mother's nice home in the United States is based on the autobiography, published in 1934, of Marie Ahnighito Peary, daughter of explorer Robert E. Peary, who was born north of the Arctic Circle in 1893. (Rev: BL 4/15/07; SLJ 3/07) [921]

PENN, WILLIAM

14901 Kroll, Steven. *William Penn: Founder of Pennsylvania* (3–5). Illus. 2000, Holiday House $16.95 (978-0-8234-1439-0). 29pp. This picture book on the life of William Penn discusses his conversion to the Quaker faith and the land grant that was given him in the New World. (Rev: BL 2/15/00; HBG 10/00; SLJ 4/00) [974.8]

PINKERTON, ALLAN

14902 Green, Carl R., and William R. Sanford. *Allan Pinkerton* (4–8). Illus. Series: Outlaws and Lawmen of the Wild West. 1995, Enslow LB $16.95 (978-0-89490-590-2). 48pp. A profile of the Scottish immigrant who organized Pinkerton's National Detective Agency, whose specialty was antiunion actions. (Rev: BL 11/15/95) [921]

14903 Josephson, Judith P. *Allan Pinkerton: The Original Private Eye* (5–8). Illus. Series: Lerner Biographies. 1996, Lerner $17.21 (978-0-8225-4923-9). 128pp. The story of the famed criminal-catcher who founded the world-famous detective agency. (Rev: BL 10/15/96; SLJ 10/96) [921]

PITCHER, MOLLY

14904 Rockwell, Anne. *They Called Her Molly Pitcher* (3–5). Illus. by Cynthia von Buhler. 2002, Knopf $15.95 (978-0-679-89187-1). 32pp. The story of the gallant Revolutionary War heroine who offered water to soldiers during the Battle of Monmouth and fired her husband's canon after he was shot. (Rev: BCCB 6/02; BL 4/15/02; HB 5/02; HBG 10/02; SLJ 6/02) [921]

POWELL, COLIN

14905 Blue, Rose, and Corinne J. Naden. *Colin Powell: Straight to the Top*. Rev. ed. (4–8). Series: Gateway Biographies. 1997, Millbrook LB $23.90 (978-0-7613-0256-8); paper $9.95 (978-0-7613-0242-1). A balanced biography of Colin Powell that focuses on his adult life and his stint as chairman of the Joint Chiefs of Staff. (Rev: BL 9/15/97; SLJ 1/98) [921]

14906 Feinstein, Stephen. *Colin Powell* (1–4). Series: African-American Heroes. 2007, Enslow LB $21.26 (978-0-7660-2761-9). 24pp. An easy-to-read account of the African American's life and career, with photographs. (Rev: SLJ 8/07)

14907 Finlayson, Reggie. *Colin Powell* (5–8). Series: A&E Biography. 2003, Lerner LB $27.93 (978-0-8225-4966-6); paper $7.95 (978-0-8225-9698-1). 112pp. Documents Powell's rise through the military and transition into the political and diplomatic world. (Rev: BL 1/1–15/04; HBG 4/04) [921]

14908 Finlayson, Reggie. *Colin Powell: People's Hero* (5–8). Series: Achievers Biographies. 1997, Lerner LB $25.55 (978-0-8225-2891-3). From his birth in Harlem to his distinguished military career, this is a fine biography of Colin Powell. (Rev: SLJ 4/97; VOYA 6/97) [921]

14909 Patrick-Wexler, Diane. *Colin Powell* (4–6). Illus. Series: Contemporary African Americans. 1995, Raintree LB $25.69 (978-0-8172-3977-0). 48pp. A simple biography of the man who grew up in the Bronx and rose to be a four-star general and chairman of the Joint Chiefs of Staff. (Rev: BL 2/15/96; SLJ 1/96) [921]

14910 Senna, Carl. *Colin Powell: A Man of War and Peace* (4–8). Illus. 1992, Walker LB $16.85 (978-0-8027-8181-9). 192pp. The life of the general who became the first African American chairman of the Joint Chiefs of Staff. (Rev: BL 3/15/93) [921]

14911 Shichtman, Sandra H. *Colin Powell: "Have a Vision. Be Demanding."* (5–8). Series: African-American Biography Library. 2005, Enslow LB $31.93 (978-0-7660-2464-9). 128pp. Sandra H. Shichtman profiles former Secretary of State Colin Powell in this title from the African-American Biography Library series. (Rev: SLJ 11/05) [921]

14912 Strazzabosco, Jeanne M. *Learning About Responsibility from the Life of Colin Powell* (2–4). Illus. Series: A Character Building Book. 1996, Rosen LB $15.93 (978-0-8239-2414-1). 24pp. This biography emphasizes the many important responsibilities that Colin Powell faced in his various positions in the U.S. government. (Rev: SLJ 5/97) [921]

PRINTZ, MICHAEL

14913 Bankston, John. *Michael L. Printz and the Story of the Michael L. Printz Award* (4–8). Illus. Series: Great Achievement Awards. 2003, Mitchell Lane LB $19.95 (978-1-58415-182-1). 48pp. Printz's career as a high school librarian is highlighted in this account of his establishment of the well-known award for YA literature, which includes a list of prize winners. (Rev: BL 10/15/03; SLJ 10/03) [020]

REVERE, PAUL

14914 Adler, David A. *A Picture Book of Paul Revere* (K–3). Illus. Series: Picture Book Biographies. 1995, Holiday House LB $16.95 (978-0-8234-1144-3). 42pp. A simple biography of this Revolutionary War hero, with an emphasis on colorful illustrations. (Rev: BL 3/15/95; SLJ 4/95) [921]

14915 Ford, Carin T. *Paul Revere: Patriot* (2–4). Series: Heroes of American History. 2003, Enslow LB $22.60 (978-0-7660-2001-6). 32pp. A concise introduction to Revere and his midnight ride, with full-color reproductions. (Rev: HBG 10/03; SLJ 6/03) [921]

14916 Giblin, James Cross. *The Many Rides of Paul Revere* (4–7). Illus. 2007, Scholastic $17.99 (978-0-439-57290-3). 96pp. This well-illustrated, large-format book provides lots of often overlooked information on Paul Revere, covering his childhood, training, career, and role in the American Revolution. (Rev: BL 9/1/07; SLJ 11/07) [973.3]

14917 Randolph, Ryan P. *Paul Revere and the Minutemen of the American Revolution* (4–7). Series: Library of American Lives and Times. 2001, Rosen $34.60 (978-0-8239-5727-9). 112pp. Fairly large type and many illustrations bring to life Paul Revere, a businessman and family man but also a soldier and spy, and the group of patriots known as the Minutemen. (Rev: BL 10/15/01) [921]

14918 Sutcliffe, Jane. *Paul Revere* (3–4). Series: History Maker Bios. 2002, Lerner LB $26.60 (978-0-8225-0195-4). 48pp. This basic biography describes the life of this patriot who fought in the Revolutionary War and also worked as a silversmith, dentist, coppersmith, and printer. (Rev: BL 6/1–15/02; HBG 3/03) [921]

14919 Tieck, Sarah. *Paul Revere* (K–3). Series: First Biographies. 2006, ABDO LB $25.65 (978-1-59679-787-1). 32pp. A beginner's profile of Paul Revere and his contributions to American history, with lots of illustrations, a large typeface, and highlighted words that appear in the glossary. (Rev: SLJ 3/07) [921]

14920 Winter, Jonah. *Paul Revere and the Bell Ringers* (K–2). Illus. by Bert Dodson. 2003, Simon & Schuster paper $3.99 (978-0-689-85635-8). 32pp. This brief profile focuses on a childhood experience that helped to instill a sense of responsibility. (Rev: HBG 4/04; SLJ 2/04) [921]

ROGERS, ROBERT

14921 Quasha, Jennifer. *Robert Rogers: Rogers' Rangers and the French and Indian War* (4–7). Series: Library of American Lives and Times. 2001, Rosen $34.60 (978-0-8239-5731-6). 112pp. A beautifully illustrated biography of Major Robert Rogers, who recruited companies of soldiers known as Rogers' Rangers to fight for the British in the French and Indian War. (Rev: BL 10/15/01) [921]

ROSS, BETSY

14922 Duden, Jane. *Betsy Ross* (4–6). Illus. Series: Let Freedom Ring. 2001, Capstone LB $23.93 (978-0-7368-1036-4). 48pp. Ross's early life, her work as an upholsterer, and the famous sewing of the flag are placed in historical context. (Rev: HBG 3/02; SLJ 7/02) [921]

14923 Harkins, Susan Sales, and William H. Harkins. *The Life and Times of Betsy Ross* (5–8). Illus. Series: Profiles in American History. 2007, Mitchell Lane LB $19.95 (978-1-58415-446-4). 48pp. This profile provides a balanced account of what is known about the life of Betsy Ross and her role, if any, in creating the American flag. (Rev: SLJ 7/07) [921]

14924 Miller, Susan Martins. *Betsy Ross: American Patriot* (3–6). Series: Revolutionary War Leaders. 2000, Chelsea LB $31.00 (978-0-7910-5360-7). 80pp. The story of the Quaker seamstress who went on to create the most recognized symbol of the United States. (Rev: HBG 10/00; SLJ 5/00) [921]

14925 Randolph, Ryan P. *Betsy Ross: The American Flag and Life in a Young America* (4–7). Series: Library of American Lives and Times. 2001, Rosen $34.60 (978-0-8239-5730-9). This contemporary of George Washington was supposedly the seamstress of the American flag. (Rev: BL 1/1–15/02) [921]

14926 St. George, Judith. *Betsy Ross: Patriot of Philadelphia* (3–6). Illus. 1997, Holt $15.95 (978-0-8050-5439-2). 118pp. A biography of Betsy Ross that tells of her childhood as a Quaker in Philadelphia as well as the meeting with George Washington that led to making our first flag. (Rev: BL 1/1–15/98; SLJ 2/98) [921]

14927 Wallner, Alexandra. *Betsy Ross* (K–3). Illus. 1994, Holiday House LB $16.95 (978-0-8234-1071-2). 32pp. A biography of the famous seamstress who advised General Washington on the nature of the nation's first flag and ran the family business until her death in 1836. (Rev: BCCB 3/94; BL 2/15/94; SLJ 4/94) [921]

SAMPSON, DEBORAH

14928 McGovern, Ann. *The Secret Soldier: The Story of Deborah Sampson* (4–6). Illus. by Ann Grifalconi. 1987, Macmillan paper $4.99 (978-0-590-43052-4). 64pp. The story of the woman who disguised herself as a man and joined the Continental army. A reissue.

SCHWARZENEGGER, ARNOLD

14929 Sexton, Colleen. *Arnold Schwarzenegger* (5–8). Series: A&E Biography. 2004, Lerner LB $29.27 (978-0-8225-1634-7). 112pp. This even-handed profile, with many photographs and quotations, covers Schwarzenegger's life from his childhood in Austria to his election as governor of California and appends a list of his films. (Rev: BL 11/1/04) [921]

SEWARD, WILLIAM HENRY

14930 Burgan, Michael. *William Henry Seward: Senator and Statesman* (3–5). Series: Famous Figures of the Civil War Era. 2001, Chelsea LB $25.00 (978-0-7910-6418-4). A clear and concise biography of the man who was secretary of state during the Civil War and who later negotiated the purchase of Alaska from Russia. (Rev: BL 4/1/02; HBG 10/02) [921]

SHERBURNE, ANDREW

14931 Sherburne, Andrew. *The Memoirs of Andrew Sherburne: Patriot and Privateer of the American Revolution* (5–8). Ed. by Karen Zeinert. Illus. 1993, Linnet LB $17.50 (978-0-208-02354-4). This excerpt from Sherburne's autobiography of the war years describes his early life at sea and his capture and imprisonment by the British. (Rev: BL 5/15/93; SLJ 7/93) [921]

SHERIDAN, PHILIP

14932 Balcavage, Dynise. *Philip Sheridan: Union General* (3–5). Series: Famous Figures of the Civil War Era. 2001, Chelsea LB $25.00 (978-0-7910-6406-1). About 20 full-color illustrations are used with a simple text to tell the story of the Civil War army commander who forced Lee's surrender at Appomattox. (Rev: BL 4/1/02) [921]

SHREVE, HENRY MILLER

14933 McCall, Edith. *Mississippi Steamboatman: The Story of Henry Miller Shreve* (5–8). Illus. 1986, Walker $11.95 (978-0-8027-6597-0). The story of Henry Shreve, whose freight and passenger boats helped open up the Midwest. (Rev: SLJ 3/86; VOYA 4/86) [921]

STANTON, EDWIN

14934 Allison, Amy. *Edwin Stanton: Union War Secretary* (3–5). Series: Famous Figures of the Civil War Era. 2001, Chelsea LB $25.00 (978-0-7910-6420-7). The fascinating story of the lawyer and public official who was secretary of war during the Civil War and whose feud with President Johnson was legendary. (Rev: BL 4/1/02) [921]

STUART, JEB

14935 Greene, Meg. *James Ewell Brown Stuart: Confederate General* (3–5). Series: Famous Figures of the Civil War Era. 2001, Chelsea LB $25.00 (978-0-7910-6414-6). Known as Jeb Stuart, this distinguished Confederate army leader was killed in 1864 at Spotsylvania Courthouse. (Rev: BL 4/1/02; HBG 10/02) [921]

14936 Pflueger, Lynda. *Jeb Stuart: Confederate Cavalry General* (5–8). Series: Historical American Biographies. 1998, Enslow LB $20.95 (978-0-7660-1013-0). The life of the brilliant general who had successes at the battles of Bull Run, Antietam, and Fredericksburg, but who committed a tactical error at Gettysburg. (Rev: BL 8/98; SLJ 8/98) [921]

STUYVESANT, PETER

14937 Krizner, L. J., and Lisa Sita. *Peter Stuyvesant: New Amsterdam, and the Origins of New York* (4–7). Series: Library of American Lives and Times. 2001, Rosen LB $34.60 (978-0-8239-5732-3). 112pp. The story of New Amsterdam's best-known leader and how the Dutch presence in America influenced our culture for years to come. (Rev: BL 10/15/01; SLJ 7/01*) [921]

SUTTER, JOHN

14938 Engstrand, Iris, and Ken Owens. *John Sutter: Sutter's Fort and the California Gold Rush* (4–8). Series: The Library of American Lives and Times. 2004, Rosen LB $34.60 (978-0-8239-6630-1). 112pp. The importance of understanding history is emphasized in this balanced and well-illustrated look at Sutter's life. (Rev: SLJ 7/04) [921]

THOMAS, DAVE

14939 Kramer, Barbara. *Dave Thomas: Honesty Pays* (3–5). Illus. 2005, Enslow LB $23.93 (978-0-7660-2375-8). 48pp. An interesting profile of Thomas, the founder of Wendy's, who was adopted at birth and has worked to improve the lives of others. (Rev: BL 4/1/05) [338.7]

TWEED, WILLIAM "BOSS"

14940 Johnson, Suzan. *Boss Tweed and Tammany Hall* (5–8). Series: Major World Leaders. 2002, Chelsea LB $27.44 (978-1-56711-224-5). 112pp. The amazing life of the corrupt New York politician who defrauded the city of more than $30 million and whose life ended in prison. (Rev: BL 1/1–15/03) [921]

WEBSTER, DANIEL

14941 Harvey, Bonnie Carman. *Daniel Webster* (5–8). Series: Historical American Biographies. 2001, Enslow LB $26.60 (978-0-7660-1392-6). An engrossing biography of the American statesman, lawyer, and orator who fought to save the Union. (Rev: BL 1/1–15/02; HBG 3/02; SLJ 12/01) [921]

WILSON, BILL

14942 White, Tom. *Bill W., a Different Kind of Hero* (4–7). Illus. 2003, Boyds Mills $16.95 (978-1-59078-067-1). 64pp. The founder of Alcoholics Anonymous is the subject of this biography that describes his long battle with addiction. (Rev: BL 4/15/03; HBG 10/03; SLJ 2/03) [362.292]

YOUNG, BRIGHAM

14943 Gunderson, Cory. *Brigham Young: Pioneer and Prophet* (3–5). Illus. Series: Let Freedom Ring. 2002, Capstone LB $23.93 (978-0-7368-1346-4). 48pp. With good illustrations, this profile of Young's controversial life includes solid information and historical context. (Rev: HBG 3/03; SLJ 4/03) [921]

Native Americans

BLACK ELK

14944 Shaw, Maura D. *Black Elk: Native American Man of Spirit* (4–6). Series: Spiritual Biographies for Young Readers. 2004, SkyLight Paths $12.99 (978-1-59473-043-6). 32pp. The violent aspects of the life of the thoughtful Lakota Sioux warrior named Black Elk are in contrast to his conviction that humans must learn to love and respect the earth and all living things. (Rev: BL 12/15/04)

CAMPBELL, BEN NIGHTHORSE

14945 Henry, Christopher. *Ben Nighthorse Campbell: Cheyenne Chief and U.S. Senator* (5–8). Illus. Series: North American Indians of Achievement. 1994, Chelsea $19.95 (978-0-7919-2046-6). The story of the Cheyenne leader who gained prominence not only among his own people but also in the U.S. Congress. (Rev: BL 6/1–15/93) [921]

CHIPETA

14946 Krudwig, Vickie Leigh. *Searching for Chipeta: The Story of a Ute and Her People* (4–7). 2004, Fulcrum paper $12.95 (978-1-55591-466-0). 128pp. In the second half of the 19th century, Chipeta and her Ute husband worked tirelessly — but ultimately unsuccessfully — to forge an agreement with the U.S. government that would allow the tribe to remain in its traditional homeland. (Rev: BL 9/1/04) [921]

CRAZY HORSE (SIOUX CHIEF)

14947 Birchfield, D. L. *Crazy Horse* (3–6). Series: Raintree Biographies. 2003, Raintree LB $25.69 (978-0-7398-5673-4). 32pp. A simple biography of the Sioux chief's life and achievements, with sidebar features containing primary and background material. (Rev: HBG 3/03; SLJ 3/03) [978]

14948 Brennan, Kristine. *Crazy Horse* (4–7). Series: Famous Figures of the American Frontier. 2001, Chelsea $25.00 (978-0-7910-6493-1); paper $25.00 (978-0-7910-6494-8). 64pp. Report writers will find this a useful source of information on this Native American leader's adult life and achievements in battle. (Rev: HBG 10/02; SLJ 4/02) [921]

14949 Brimner, Larry Dane. *Chief Crazy Horse: Following a Vision* (2–4). Series: American Heroes. 2008, Marshall Cavendish $20.95 (978-0-7614-3061-2). 42pp. With sections on "Important Dates" and "Words to Know," this brief biography introduces the warrior chief of the Oglala tribe of the Sioux nation. (Rev: SLJ 3/09) [921]

14950 Cunningham, Chet. *Chief Crazy Horse* (4–6). Series: A&E Biography. 2000, Lerner LB $27.93 (978-0-8225-4978-9). 112pp. This biography relates the life of the military leader of the Lakota Indians and tells how he became known for his bravery and ferocity in battle. (Rev: BL 6/1–15/00; HBG 3/01; SLJ 9/00) [921]

14951 Haugen, Brenda. *Crazy Horse: Sioux Warrior* (5–8). Series: Signature Lives. 2005, Compass Point LB $34.60 (978-0-7565-0999-6). 112pp. Crazy Horse's life and efforts to save his native lands and way of life are documented here. (Rev: SLJ 2/06) [921]

CROW, JOSEPH MEDICINE

14952 Medicine Crow, Joseph. *Counting Coup: Becoming a Crow Chief on the Reservation and Beyond* (5–8). Illus. 2006, National Geographic LB $23.90 (978-0-7922-8328-7); paper $6.95 (978-0-7922-7297-7). 128pp. The memoirs of a Crow chief who was educated in mission and boarding schools and went on to fight in World War II. (Rev: BCCB 5/06; BL 4/15/06; LMC 11/06; SLJ 7/06) [967.62]

GERONIMO

14953 Feinstein, Stephen. *Read About Geronimo* (2–4). Series: I Like Biographies! 2006, Enslow LB $21.26 (978-0-7660-2598-1). 24pp. This brief, introductory biography of Geronimo offers an overview of Apache life and the achievements of one of its greatest chiefs. (Rev: SLJ 4/06) [921]

14954 Haugen, Brenda. *Geronimo: Apache Warrior* (5–8). Series: Signature Lives. 2005, Compass Point LB $34.60 (978-0-7565-1002-2). 112pp. Geronimo's unsuccessful efforts to secure freedom for his people are documented in this attractive book. (Rev: SLJ 2/06) [921]

14955 Hermann, Spring. *Geronimo: Apache Freedom Fighter* (4–6). Illus. Series: Native American Biographies. 1997, Enslow LB $26.60 (978-0-89490-864-4). 128pp. The story of the great Apache chieftain who led his people first against the Mexicans and then against the Americans. (Rev: BL 4/15/97; SLJ 6/97) [921]

14956 Thompson, Bill, and Dorcas Thompson. *Geronimo* (4–7). Series: Famous Figures of the American Frontier. 2001, Chelsea $25.00 (978-0-7910-6491-7); paper $8.95 (978-0-7910-6492-4). 64pp. A balanced biography of the Apache leader that report writers will find a useful resource. (Rev: HBG 10/02; SLJ 4/02) [921]

14957 Welch, Catherine A. *Geronimo* (3–5). Illus. Series: History Maker Bios. 2004, Lerner LB $26.60 (978-0-8225-0698-0). 47pp. A well-illustrated profile of the Apache chief who fought strongly against attempts to confine his people to reservations. (Rev: SLJ 4/04) [921]

HARRIS, LA DONNA

14958 Schwartz, Michael. *La Donna Harris* (4–7). Illus. Series: Contemporary Native Americans. 1997, Raintree LB $17.98 (978-0-8172-3995-4). 48pp. The life story and accomplishments of this Native American, who has openly championed her people's rights before the Senate. (Rev: BL 6/1–15/97) [921]

HAYES, IRA

14959 Nelson, S. D. *Quiet Hero* (3–5). 2006, Lee & Low $16.95 (978-1-58430-263-6). 32pp. Traces the short life of Ira Hayes, a shy Native American who was one of the marines shown raising the flag at Iwo Jima but, despite his acclaim as a hero, slid into depression on his return home. (Rev: BL 9/15/06; SLJ 9/06) [921]

JOSEPH, CHIEF

14960 Klingel, Cynthia, and Robert B. Noyed. *Chief Joseph: Chief of the Nez Perce* (3–6). Illus. Series: Our People. 2002, Child's World LB $27.07 (978-1-56766-165-1). 32pp. This is an attractive, brief introduction to the leader of the Nez Perce Indians. (Rev: BL 1/1–15/03; SLJ 2/03) [979.004]

14961 Sutcliffe, Jane. *Chief Joseph* (3–5). Illus. Series: History Maker Bios. 2004, Lerner LB $26.60 (978-0-8225-0696-6). 48pp. Focuses on the famed Nez Perce chief who fought fiercely against European settlers' encroachment on his people's land. (Rev: SLJ 4/04) [921]

KA'IULANI, PRINCESS

14962 Linnea, Sharon. *Princess Ka'iulani: Hope of a Nation, Heart of a People* (5–8). 1999, Eerdmans $18.00 (978-0-8028-5145-1). The story of the Hawaiian princess who tried to prevent the annexation of her country by the United States and of her untimely death at age 22. (Rev: BL 7/99; SLJ 6/99; VOYA 10/99) [921]

14963 Stanley, Fay. *The Last Princess: The Story of Princess Ka'iulani of Hawaii* (4–6). Illus. by Diane Stanley. 1991, Macmillan LB $18.00 (978-0-02-786785-5). 40pp. The ill-fated princess who never achieved her goal of being queen of Hawaii. (Rev: BL 3/15/91*) [921]

LADUKE, WINONA

14964 Silverstone, Michael. *Winona LaDuke: Restoring Land and Culture in Native America* (5–8). Series: Women Changing the World. 2001, Feminist $19.95 (978-1-55861-260-0). 112pp. A candidate for the vice presidency under Ralph Nader in 2000, this author and environmental and Native American rights activist lives on a reservation in Minnesota, where she is dedicated to restoring the land and the culture. (Rev: BL 12/15/01; HBG 10/02) [921]

LILIUOKALANI, QUEEN

14965 Guzzetti, Paula. *The Last Hawaiian Queen: Liliuokalani* (3–5). Illus. Series: Biographies. 1996, Benchmark LB $21.36 (978-0-7614-0490-3). 48pp. A history of Hawaii with special emphasis on the life of its last queen, the fascinating Liliuokalani. (Rev: SLJ 3/97) [921]

LOYIE, LARRY

14966 Loyie, Larry, and Constance Brissenden. *As Long as the Rivers Flow* (3–6). Illus. by Heather D. Holmlund. 2003, Douglas & McIntyre $16.95 (978-0-88899-473-8). 40pp. Loyie describes the summer he was 10, living happily among his extended Cree family in the wilds of Alberta but dreading the impending threat of government-enforced boarding school. (Rev: BL 4/15/03; SLJ 10/03) [971.23]

MANKILLER, WILMA

14967 Glassman, Bruce. *Wilma Mankiller: Chief of the Cherokee Nation* (5–7). Illus. Series: Library of Famous Women. 1992, Blackbirch $24.94 (978-1-56711-032-6). 64pp. This is an inspiring biography of the amazing woman who led her Cherokee Indians through difficult crises. (Rev: BL 6/1/92; SLJ 4/92) [921]

14968 Lowery, Linda. *Wilma Mankiller* (2–4). Illus. 1996, Carolrhoda LB $23.93 (978-0-87614-880-8); paper $5.95 (978-0-87614-953-9). 56pp. The great hardships that were faced by the Native American woman are the focus of this inspiring, simple biography. (Rev: BCCB 9/96; BL 9/1/96; SLJ 9/96) [921]

MONTEZUMA, CARLOS

14969 Capaldi, Gina. *A Boy Named Beckoning: A True Story of Dr. Carlos Montezuma, Native American Hero* (2–4). Illus. by author. 2008, Carolrhoda $16.95 (978-0-8225-7644-0). 32pp. Capaldi traces the life of the Yavapai Indian who was captured as a child but grew up to become a doctor and activist for his people. (Rev: BL 3/15/08; LMC 10/08; SLJ 3/08) [921]

OSCEOLA

14970 Koestler-Grack, Rachel A. *Osceola: 1804–1838* (3–6). Illus. Series: American Indian Biographies. 2003, Capstone LB $23.93 (978-0-7368-1211-5). 32pp. In addition to covering Osceola's leadership against American forces, this concise volume looks at his childhood and the Seminole culture. (Rev: HBG 3/03; SLJ 4/03) [921]

PARKER, CHIEF QUANAH

14971 Zemlicka, Shannon. *Quanah Parker* (3–5). Illus. Series: History Maker Bios. 2004, Lerner LB $26.60 (978-0-8225-0724-6). 48pp. Quanah Parker, the last chief of the Comanche, is profiled in this well-illustrated entry that highlights the losses suffered by the Native Americans. (Rev: SLJ 4/04) [921]

PARKER, ELY

14972 Van Steenwyk, Elizabeth. *Seneca Chief, Army General: A Story About Ely Parker* (4–6). Illus. by Karen Ritz. Series: Creative Minds Biographies. 2000, Carolrhoda LB $22.60 (978-1-57505-431-5). 64pp. The story of the Native American who was appointed by Ulysses Grant as Commissioner of Indian Affairs, the first Native American to hold that post. (Rev: HBG 3/01; SLJ 2/01) [921]

PHILIP (SACHEM OF THE WAMPANOAGS)

14973 Averill, Esther. *King Philip: The Indian Chief* (5–8). Illus. by Vera Belsky. 1993, Shoe String LB $20.00 (978-0-208-02357-5). 148pp. The story of the Wampanoag chief who befriended the Pilgrims and later waged war against the settlers. (Rev: BL 7/93) [921]

PICOTTE, SUSAN LAFLESCHE

14974 Ferris, Jeri. *Native American Doctor: The Story of Susan LaFlesche Picotte* (4–6). Illus. 1991, Carolrhoda LB $27.93 (978-0-87614-443-5). The story of the first Native American woman to earn a medical degree. (Rev: BCCB 12/91; BL 1/1/91; HB 1/92) [921]

14975 Wilkerson, J. L. *A Doctor to Her People: Dr. Susan LaFlesche Picotte* (4–6). Illus. 1999, Acorn paper $9.95 (978-0-9664470-2-6). 100pp. Many maps, drawings, and photographs enhance this biography of Susan LaFlesche Picotte, the first female Native American doctor. (Rev: BL 6/1–15/99; SLJ 12/99) [921]

POCAHONTAS

14976 Brimner, Larry Dane. *Pocahontas: Bridging Two Worlds* (2–4). Series: American Heroes. 2008, Marshall Cavendish $20.95 (978-0-7614-3065-0). 42pp. With sections on "Important Dates" and "Words to Know," this brief biography traces the life of the Native American woman who helped the Virginia settlers. (Rev: SLJ 3/09) [921]

14977 Nettleton, Pamela Hill. *Pocahontas: Peacemaker and Friend to the Colonists* (K–3). Illus. by Jeff Yesh. 2003, Picture Window LB $25.26 (978-1-4048-0187-5). 24pp. A brightly illustrated profile that is suitable for beginning readers. (Rev: SLJ 4/04) [921]

14978 Raatma, Lucia. *Pocahontas* (1–5). 2001, Compass Point LB $21.26 (978-0-7565-0115-0). 32pp. An accessible and attractive book that is careful to distinguish facts from legends. (Rev: SLJ 1/02) [921]

14979 Sullivan, George. *Pocahontas* (3–5). Series: In Their Own Words. 2002, Scholastic $12.95 (978-0-439-32668-1); paper $4.99 (978-0-439-16585-3). 128pp. After explaining the difference between primary and secondary sources, the author re-creates the life of Pocahontas by quoting from original documents. (Rev: BL 8/02; HBG 10/02; SLJ 11/02) [921]

14980 Zemlicka, Shannon. *Pocahontas* (2–3). Illus. by Jeni Reeves. Series: On My Own Biography. 2002, Carolrhoda LB $23.93 (978-0-87614-598-2); paper $5.95 (978-0-87614-906-5). 48pp. This biography for beginning readers covers the Powhatan Indian's birth, contacts with English settlers, family life, and death, and points out what information is reliable and where exaggeration may occur. (Rev: SLJ 1/03) [921]

SACAGAWEA

14981 Adler, David A. *A Picture Book of Sacagawea* (1–4). Illus. by Dan Brown. Series: Picture Book. 2000, Holiday House $16.95 (978-0-8234-1485-7). 32pp. The important known facts about Sacagawea, from her birth to the silver dollar in her image, are recounted in this competent biography. (Rev: BL 6/1–15/00; HBG 10/00; SLJ 6/00) [921]

14982 Collard, Sneed B., III. *Sacagawea: Brave Shoshone Girl* (2–4). Illus. Series: American Heroes. 2006, Marshall Cavendish LB $28.50 (978-0-7614-2166-5). 48pp. Archival images add to this life of the Shoshone Indian, which looks at her early life as well as her experiences on the Lewis and Clark expedition. (Rev: BL 1/1–15/07; SLJ 3/07) [921]

14983 DeKeyser, Stacy. *Sacagawea* (3–6). Series: Watts Library. 2004, Scholastic LB $25.50 (978-0-531-12290-7). 64pp. The story of Sacagawea and her journeys with Lewis and Clark's Corps of Discovery is recounted with many illustrations, maps, a timeline, and other helpful features. (Rev: BL 6/1–15/04) [978.004]

14984 Erdrich, Lise. *Sacagawea* (2–6). 2003, Carolrhoda $16.95 (978-0-87614-646-0). 40pp. This large-format biography of Sacagawea, which features full-page oil paintings, stays close to historical facts as it traces the story of the Shoshone woman who traveled with Lewis and Clark. (Rev: BL 9/1/03; HBG 4/04; SLJ 10/03) [921]

14985 Marcovitz, Hal. *Sacagawea: Guide for the Lewis and Clark Expedition* (4–6). Illus. Series: Explorers of New Worlds. 2000, Chelsea LB $25.00 (978-0-7910-5959-3); paper $25.00 (978-0-7910-6169-5). 63pp. In addition to the usual information on Sacagawea's life, this biography discusses why she has remained such an inspiration. (Rev: SLJ 4/01) [921]

14986 Rowland, Della. *The Story of Sacajawea: Guide to Lewis and Clark* (4–6). Illus. by Richard Leonard. 1989, Dell paper $3.99 (978-0-440-40215-2). 96pp. In brief text, this account tells of the courage and daring of the Shoshone woman who guided Lewis and Clark. (Rev: BCCB 9/89; BL 12/15/89; SLJ 12/89) [921]

14987 St. George, Judith. *Sacagawea* (4–6). 1997, Penguin $16.99 (978-0-399-23161-2). 128pp. A sympathetic account of the life of this Shoshone Indian woman and her exciting adventures while helping in the Lewis and Clark expedition. (Rev: BL 8/97; HBG 3/98; SLJ 3/98) [921]

14988 White, Alana J. *Sacagawea: Westward with Lewis and Clark* (4–8). Series: Native American Biographies. 1997, Enslow LB $26.60 (978-0-89490-867-5). A well-written account of this gallant woman's life, accompanied by a reading list, chapter notes, and a chronology. (Rev: BL 4/15/97; SLJ 8/97; VOYA 8/97) [921]

SEQUOYAH

14989 Basel, Roberta. *Sequoyah: Inventor of Written Cherokee* (5–8). Series: Signature Lives. 2007, Compass Point LB $31.93 (978-0-7565-1887-5). 112pp. A life of the Cherokee leader whose efforts to transcribe spoken Cherokee into a written language were not greatly appreciated; this volume will be useful for report writers. (Rev: SLJ 7/07) [921]

14990 Fitterer, C. Ann. *Sequoyah: Native American Scholar* (2–4). Series: Spirit of America: Our People. 2002, Child's World LB $27.07 (978-1-56766-167-5). 32pp. A concise introduction to the life of the Cherokee Indian who invented an alphabet for their language. (Rev: SLJ 12/02) [921]

14991 Klausner, Janet. *Sequoyah's Gift: A Portrait of the Cherokee Leader* (4–7). Illus. 1993, HarperCollins LB $16.89 (978-0-06-021236-0). 128pp. The life of this Cherokee leader is retold, with material on his invention of a written alphabet and his behavior during the Trail of Tears journey. (Rev: BL 9/1/93; HB 9/93; SLJ 11/93) [921]

14992 Rumford, James. *Sequoyah: The Cherokee Man Who Gave His People Writing* (1–3). Trans. by Anna Sixkiller Huckaby. Illus. 2004, Houghton $16.00 (978-0-618-36947-8). 32pp. Cherokee translations appear below the English text in this tall slim volume on Sequoyah. (Rev: BL 10/15/04; SLJ 8/04) [921]

SITTING BULL (SIOUX CHIEF)

14993 Aller, Susan Bivin. *Sitting Bull* (3–5). Illus. Series: History Maker Bios. 2004, Lerner LB $26.60 (978-0-8225-0700-0). 47pp. The valiant Sioux chief's life is detailed in this well-illustrated biography that highlights the losses suffered by the Native Americans. (Rev: SLJ 4/04) [921]

14994 Marcovitz, Hal. *Sitting Bull* (3–6). Series: Famous Figures of the American Frontier. 2001, Chelsea LB $25.00 (978-0-7910-6487-0); paper $8.95 (978-0-7910-6488-7). 64pp. The Sioux chief's efforts to improve relations between the Native Americans and the European newcomers are emphasized in this appealing biography. (Rev: SLJ 3/02) [921]

14995 Schleichert, Elizabeth. *Sitting Bull: Sioux Leader* (4–6). Illus. Series: Native American Biographies. 1997, Enslow LB $26.60 (978-0-89490-868-2). 112pp. As well as describing the life of this great leader who fought to save the lands occupied by the Sioux, there is information on the life and culture of the Sioux. (Rev: BL 4/15/97; SLJ 6/97) [921]

SQUANTO

14996 Bulla, Clyde Robert. *Squanto, Friend of the Pilgrims* (3–6). Illus. by Peter Burchard. 1990, Scholastic paper $5.99 (978-0-590-44055-4). 112pp. The story of the first Native American to reach Europe.

14997 Kessel, Joyce K. *Squanto and the First Thanksgiving* (2–3). Illus. by Lisa Donze. 1983, Carolrhoda LB $21.27 (978-0-87614-199-1); paper $5.95 (978-0-87614-452-7). 48pp. An easily read story of a Native American sold into slavery but eventually freed close to the Plymouth Colony.

TECUMSEH

14998 Koestler-Grack, Rachel A. *Tecumseh: 1768–1813* (3–6). Illus. Series: American Indian Biographies. 2003, Capstone LB $23.93 (978-0-7368-1212-2). 32pp. In addition to covering Tecumseh's efforts to bring together the Native American tribes, this concise volume looks at his childhood and the Shawnee culture. (Rev: HBG 3/03; SLJ 4/03) [921]

WALKING COYOTE

14999 Bruchac, Joseph. *Buffalo Song* (1–3). Illus. by Bill Farnsworth. 2008, Lee & Low $17.95 (978-1-58430-280-3). 40pp. Bruchac tells the story of a Salish Indian, Walking Coyote, who worked to save the buffalo from extinction. (Rev: BL 4/1/08; LMC 11/08; SLJ 6/08) [305.897]

WEBER, EDNAH NEW RIDER

15000 Weber, EdNah New Rider. *Rattlesnake Mesa: Stories from a Native American Childhood* (4–8). 2004, Lee & Low $18.95 (978-1-58430-231-5). In this poignant memoir, Weber tells of her life as a student at a government-run boarding school for Native Americans during the 1920s. (Rev: BL 12/15/04; SLJ 12/04) [921]

WINNEMUCCA, SARAH

15001 Morrow, Mary Frances. *Sarah Winnemucca* (3–5). Illus. by Ken Bronikowski. Series: American Indian Stories. 1990, Raintree paper $4.95 (978-0-8114-4095-0). 32pp. The life story of the Paiute woman who stood for Native American rights and education. (Rev: SLJ 10/90) [921]

Presidents

ADAMS, JOHN

15002 Behrman, Carol H. *John Adams* (5–8). Illus. Series: Presidential Leaders. 2003, Lerner LB $29.27 (978-0-8225-0820-5). 112pp. This biography provides lots of details and illustrations, covering Adams's life and career. (Rev: BL 1/1–15/04) [973.4]

15003 Feinberg, Barbara S. *John Adams* (5–8). Illus. Series: Encyclopedia of Presidents. 2003, Children's Pr. LB $34.00 (978-0-516-22680-4). 128pp. An informative and appealing account of Adams's life and achievements, with glossary, timeline, and lists of books and Web sites. (Rev: BL 1/1–15/04) [973.4]

15004 Feinstein, Stephen. *John Adams* (5–9). 2002, Enslow LB $25.26 (978-0-7660-5001-3). 48pp. A well-written and accessible overview of Adams's life and contributions that is extended by a number of recommended Web sites. (Rev: SLJ 6/02) [921]

15005 Harness, Cheryl. *The Revolutionary John Adams* (3–6). Illus. 2002, National Geographic $17.95 (978-0-7922-6970-0). 48pp. Ample quotes, appealing illustrations, and a timeline enhance this biography of America's somewhat neglected second president. (Rev: BL 12/1/02; HBG 3/03; SLJ 2/03) [973.3]

15006 Welsbacher, Anne. *John Adams* (K–2). Series: United States Presidents. 1999, ABDO LB $22.78 (978-1-56239-738-8). 32pp. For beginning readers, this simple biography of John Adams gives an overview of his life and administration with a section on important facts and statistics. (Rev: HBG 10/99; SLJ 7/99) [921]

ADAMS, JOHN AND ABIGAIL

15007 Ashby, Ruth. *John and Abigail Adams* (5–8). Illus. Series: Presidents and First Ladies. 2005, Gareth Stevens LB $31.00 (978-0-8368-5755-9). 48pp. An accessible, balanced, and attractive discussion of the Adamses and the contributions each made to their joint lives. (Rev: BL 3/1/05) [921]

ADAMS, JOHN QUINCY

15008 Feinstein, Stephen. *John Quincy Adams* (5–9). 2002, Enslow LB $25.26 (978-0-7660-5002-0).

48pp. Adams's early and later life are covered in this concise biography that includes several pages of annotated Web site recommendations. (Rev: HBG 10/02; SLJ 10/02) [921]

15009 McCollum, Sean. *John Quincy Adams* (4–6). Illus. Series: Encyclopedia of Presidents. 2003, Children's Pr. LB $34.00 (978-0-516-22867-9). 110pp. An updated profile that looks at Adams's life and contributions, providing many illustrations and sidebars. (Rev: SLJ 1/04) [921]

15010 Venezia, Mike. *John Quincy Adams: Sixth President* (1–3). Illus. by author. Series: Getting to Know the U.S. Presidents. 2004, Children's Pr. LB $28.00 (978-0-516-22611-8); paper $7.95 (978-0-516-27480-5). 32pp. This unusual biography takes a light-hearted approach to the key details of the president's life, adding comic-book-style graphics and dialogue bubbles to the large type. (Rev: BL 4/1/04; HBG 4/04; SLJ 4/05) [921]

15011 Walker, Jane C. *John Quincy Adams* (4–6). Series: United States Presidents. 2000, Enslow LB $26.60 (978-0-7660-1161-8). 128pp. A well-organized profile of the man who was a Revolutionary War leader, vice president, and was elected president in 1824. (Rev: BL 10/15/00; HBG 3/01) [921]

ARTHUR, CHESTER A.

15012 Young, Jeff C. *Chester A. Arthur* (4–7). Series: Presidents. 2002, Enslow LB $25.26 (978-0-7660-5077-8). 48pp. As well as an overview of the life and accomplishments of Chester A. Arthur, this book gives a pre-evaluated listing of Web sites where more material can be found. (Rev: BL 12/15/02) [921]

BUCHANAN, JAMES

15013 Young, Jeff C. *James Buchanan* (4–7). Series: Presidents. 2003, Enslow LB $25.26 (978-0-7660-5101-0). 48pp. The story of the fifteenth president who had an extensive political career before becoming president. (Rev: BL 6/1–15/03; HBG 10/03) [921]

BUSH, GEORGE W.

15014 Burgan, Michael. *George W. Bush: Our Forty-Third President* (3–5). Illus. Series: Our Presidents. 2005, Child's World LB $28.50 (978-1-59296-494-9). 48pp. With much material on the war on terrorism, this volume covers Bush's life from childhood through the 2004 elections. [921]

15015 Cohen, Daniel. *George W. Bush: The Family Business* (4–6). Illus. 2000, Millbrook $23.90 (978-0-7613-1851-4). 48pp. This slim biography ends before the 2000 election that resulted in Bush winning the presidency, but gives valuable information about his youth and family. (Rev: BL 5/1/00; HBG 10/00) [921]

15016 Jones, Veda Boyd. *George W. Bush* (5–8). Illus. Series: Modern World Leaders. 2006, Chelsea House $30.00 (978-0-7910-9217-0). 128pp. This biography traces Bush's life and political career

from his 1946 birth in New Haven, Connecticut, through the first five years of his presidency. (Rev: BL 10/15/06) [973.9]

15017 Kachurek, Sandra J. *George W. Bush* (4–7). Series: United States Presidents. 2004, Enslow LB $26.60 (978-0-7660-2040-5). 128pp. A balanced and well-documented profile with plenty of photographs plus lists of Web sites and places to visit. (Rev: BL 9/15/04) [921]

15018 Marquez, Heron. *George W. Bush* (5–8). Illus. Series: Presidential Leaders. 2006, Lerner LB $29.27 (978-0-8225-1507-4). 112pp. A balanced profile that examines Bush's childhood and adolescence as well as his accomplishments and the controversies surrounding some of his decisions. (Rev: BL 10/15/06) [921]

15019 Ryan, Patrick. *George W. Bush* (1–3). Illus. Series: United States Presidents. 2001, ABDO LB $22.78 (978-1-57765-302-8). 32pp. Report writers will find the basic information they need on Bush's life, with many clear photographs in both color and black and white. (Rev: HBG 10/01; SLJ 9/01) [921]

15020 Thompson, Bill, and Dorcas Thompson. *George W. Bush* (4–8). Illus. Series: Childhoods of the Presidents. 2003, Mason Crest $17.95 (978-1-59084-281-2). 48pp. Bush's privileged childhood and education, his role as eldest son, and the death of his sister from leukemia are covered in an interesting narrative that highlights his character. (Rev: BL 6/1–15/03; SLJ 2/03) [973.931]

15021 Wheeler, Jill C. *George W. Bush* (4–7). Series: War on Terrorism. 2002, ABDO LB $25.65 (978-1-57765-662-3). 48pp. A brief profile of President Bush with particular emphasis on his war on terrorism. (Rev: BL 5/15/02; HBG 10/02) [921]

15022 Wukovits, John F. *George W. Bush* (5–8). Series: People in the News. 2000, Lucent LB $32.45 (978-1-56006-693-4). 96pp. Published before the 2000 election, this biography uses extensive quotations from Mr. Bush, his friends, and critics. (Rev: BL 9/15/00; HBG 3/01; SLJ 10/00) [921]

CARTER, JIMMY

15023 Kent, Deborah. *Jimmy Carter* (4–7). Illus. Series: Encyclopedia of Presidents — Second Series. 2005, Children's Pr. LB $34.00 (978-0-516-22975-1). 112pp. Updated from the 1989 volume, this new, redesigned edition covers the former president's life and career and adds information about his recent work. (Rev: BL 6/1–15/05) [973.926]

15024 O'Shei, Tim. *Jimmy Carter* (5–9). 2002, Enslow LB $25.26 (978-0-7660-5051-8). 48pp. This introduction to Carter's life, including his childhood, and his contributions contains a long list of recommended Web sites that extend the printed material. (Rev: HBG 10/02; SLJ 6/02) [921]

15025 Richman, Daniel A. *James E. Carter* (5–8). Series: Presidents of the United States. 1989, GEC LB $21.27 (978-0-944483-24-4). 121pp. The story of this former U.S. president, his political career, family, and present charitable activities. (Rev: SLJ 9/89) [921]

15026 Santella, Andrew. *James Earl Carter Jr.* (4–7). Series: Profiles of the Presidents. 2002, Compass Point LB $26.60 (978-0-7565-0283-6). 64pp. A straightforward profile that touches on Carter's southern roots, his successes and failures as president, and his subsequent work in the fields of human rights and democracy. (Rev: SLJ 1/03) [921]

15027 Slavin, Ed. *Jimmy Carter* (4–8). Illus. 1989, Chelsea LB $19.95 (978-1-55546-828-6). 112pp. Introducing the 39th president of the United States. (Rev: BL 7/89) [921]

15028 Smith, Betsy. *Jimmy Carter, President* (5–7). Illus. 1986, Walker LB $13.85 (978-0-8027-6652-6). 128pp. A profile of Jimmy Carter and his one-term presidency. (Rev: BL 2/15/87; SLJ 12/86) [921]

CLINTON, BILL

15029 Cwiklik, Robert. *Bill Clinton: President of the 90's.* Rev. ed. (4–8). Series: Gateway Biographies. 1997, Millbrook $22.90 (978-0-7613-0129-5); paper $8.95 (978-0-7613-0146-2). A readable biography that concentrates on Clinton's career as governor of Arkansas and his early years as president. (Rev: BL 9/15/97; SLJ 7/97) [921]

15030 Heinrichs, Ann. *William Jefferson Clinton* (4–8). Series: Profiles of the Presidents. 2002, Compass Point LB $26.60 (978-0-7565-0207-2). 64pp. This absorbing account of Clinton's life and career covers both the good and bad sides of his presidency and includes a discussion of Hillary's role. (Rev: SLJ 6/02) [921]

15031 Marcovitz, Hal. *Bill Clinton* (4–8). Illus. Series: Childhoods of the Presidents. 2003, Mason Crest LB $17.95 (978-1-59084-273-7). 48pp. This brief, well-illustrated overview of Clinton's childhood and adolescence looks in particular at his relationships with family members, his support for civil rights, and his popularity. (Rev: BL 6/1–15/03; SLJ 2/03) [973.929]

COOLIDGE, CALVIN

15032 Joseph, Paul. *Calvin Coolidge* (2–5). Illus. Series: United States Presidents. 1999, ABDO LB $22.78 (978-1-57765-237-3). 32pp. In this biography of Coolidge, there are chapters on youth, marriage, early career, presidential issues, and final years. (Rev: HBG 3/00; SLJ 12/99) [921]

EISENHOWER, DWIGHT D.

15033 Adler, David A. *A Picture Book of Dwight David Eisenhower* (1–3). Illus. Series: Picture Book Biographies. 2002, Holiday House $16.95 (978-0-8234-1702-5). 32pp. Traces the life of the 34th president, Dwight D. Eisenhower, from his childhood in Kansas to his death in 1969. (Rev: BL 10/15/02; HBG 3/03; SLJ 10/02) [921]

15034 Alphin, Elaine M., and Arthur B. Alphin. *Dwight D. Eisenhower* (3–4). Illus. Series: History Maker Bios. 2004, Lerner LB $26.60 (978-0-8225-1544-9). 48pp. A simple biography, useful for report writers, with information about Eisenhower's youth and good photographs and illustrations. (Rev: SLJ 1/05) [921]

15035 Deitch, Kenneth, and Joanne B. Weisman. *Dwight D. Eisenhower: Man of Many Hats* (5–7). Illus. by Jay Connolly. 1990, Discovery LB $14.95 (978-1-878668-02-8). 48pp. Each stage of Eisenhower's multifaceted career is represented. (Rev: SLJ 2/91) [921]

15036 Raatma, Lucia. *Dwight D. Eisenhower* (4–7). Series: Profiles of the Presidents. 2002, Compass Point LB $26.60 (978-0-7565-0279-9). 64pp. A straightforward account that focuses on Eisenhower's military career and successes in World War II. (Rev: SLJ 1/03) [921]

15037 Van Steenwyk, Elizabeth. *Dwight David Eisenhower, President* (5–8). Illus. 1987, Walker LB $13.85 (978-0-8027-6671-7). 128pp. The focus is on the career of this war-hero president. (Rev: BL 5/15/87) [921]

FILLMORE, MILLARD

15038 Gottfried, Ted. *Millard Fillmore* (4–7). Series: Presidents and Their Times. 2007, Marshall Cavendish LB $22.95 (978-0-7614-2431-4). 96pp. A clear and thorough life of the president, describing his early years, presidential career, and later life, with discussion of important events that took place during his life. (Rev: SLJ 1/08)

GARFIELD, JAMES A.

15039 Young, Jeff C. *James A. Garfield* (4–7). Series: Presidents. 2003, Enslow LB $25.26 (978-0-7660-5100-3). 48pp. The story of the twentieth president of the U.S. who served as a major general during the Civil War and was assassinated while he was still in office. (Rev: BL 6/1–15/03) [921]

GRANT, ULYSSES S.

15040 Alter, Judy. *Ulysses S. Grant* (5–9). 2002, Enslow LB $25.26 (978-0-7660-5014-3). 48pp. Grant's early and later life are covered in this concise and balanced biography that includes several pages of annotated Web site recommendations. (Rev: SLJ 10/02) [921]

15041 Sapp, Richard. *Ulysses S. Grant and the Road to Appomattox* (5–8). Series: In the Footsteps of American Heroes. 2006, World Almanac LB $34.00 (978-0-8368-6431-1). 64pp. This life of Grant includes information on historical sites in sidebar features. (Rev: SLJ 9/06) [921]

HARDING, WARREN G.

15042 Joseph, Paul. *Warren G. Harding* (2–5). Illus. Series: United States Presidents. 1999, ABDO LB $22.78 (978-1-57765-234-2). 32pp. In addition to Harding's life story, this account includes a section on little-known facts and two pages of vital statistics. (Rev: HBG 3/00; SLJ 12/99) [921]

HARRISON, WILLIAM HENRY

15043 Gaines, Ann Graham. *William Henry Harrison: Our Ninth President* (4–6). Series: Spirit of America: Our Presidents. 2001, Child's World LB $28.50 (978-1-56766-848-3). 48pp. A well-illustrated and appealing biography that discusses influences that shaped Harrison's policies and looks at his legacy. (Rev: SLJ 12/01) [920]

15044 Venezia, Mike. *William Henry Harrison* (3–4). Illus. Series: Getting to Know the U.S. Presidents. 2005, Children's Pr. LB $28.00 (978-0-516-22614-9); paper $7.95 (978-0-516-27483-6). 32pp. A light-hearted approach to the key details of Harrison's life, adding comic-book-style graphics and dialogue bubbles to the large-type text. [921]

HOOVER, HERBERT

15045 Hilton, Suzanne. *The World of Young Herbert Hoover* (4–8). Illus. 1987, Walker LB $13.85 (978-0-8027-6709-7). This brief biography takes Hoover through his college years and gives some indication of events to follow. (Rev: SLJ 1/88) [921]

15046 Holford, David M. *Herbert Hoover* (5–8). Series: United States Presidents. 1999, Enslow LB $26.60 (978-0-7660-1035-2). 128pp. An insightful look at the president who was orphaned as a child and gained a reputation for being rigid and insensitive. (Rev: SLJ 1/00) [921]

15047 Ruth, Amy. *Herbert Hoover* (5–8). Series: Presidential Leaders. 2004, Lerner LB $29.27 (978-0-8225-0821-2). 112pp. Quotations, photographs, and informative sidebars add to the engaging text about Hoover's life and times. (Rev: SLJ 1/05) [921]

JACKSON, ANDREW

15048 Behrman, Carol H. *Andrew Jackson* (5–8). Series: Presidential Leaders. 2002, Lerner LB $29.27 (978-0-8225-0093-3). 111pp. Jackson's life and character are brought to life in this narrative that points out his failings as well as his achievements. (Rev: HBG 3/03; SLJ 1/03) [921]

15049 Feinstein, Stephen. *Andrew Jackson* (5–9). 2002, Enslow LB $25.26 (978-0-7660-5003-7). 48pp. A well-written and accessible overview of Jackson's life and contributions that is extended by a number of recommended Web sites. (Rev: SLJ 6/02; VOYA 8/02) [921]

15050 Venezia, Mike. *Andrew Jackson: Seventh President, 1829–1837* (3–4). Illus. Series: Getting to Know the U.S. Presidents. 2005, Children's Pr. LB $28.00 (978-0-516-22612-5); paper $7.95 (978-0-516-27481-2). 32pp. A light-hearted approach to the key details of Jackson's life, adding comic-book-style graphics and dialogue bubbles to the large-type text. [921]

JEFFERSON, THOMAS

15051 Adler, David A. *A Picture Book of Thomas Jefferson* (K–3). Illus. by John Wallner and Alexandra Wallner. Series: Picture Book Biographies. 1990, Holiday House LB $16.95 (978-0-8234-0791-0); paper $6.95 (978-0-8234-0881-8). 32pp. Basic facts and personal glimpses make up this simple biography of the third U.S. president. (Rev: BL 4/15/90; SLJ 5/90) [921]

15052 Aldridge, Rebecca. *Thomas Jefferson* (5–6). Series: Let Freedom Ring. 2001, Capstone LB $23.93 (978-0-7368-1035-7). 48pp. An introduction to the life and work of Jefferson that touches on his attachment to Sally Hemmings. (Rev: HBG 3/02; SLJ 4/02) [921]

15053 Davis, Kenneth C. *Don't Know Much About Thomas Jefferson* (4–7). Illus. by Rob Shepperson. Series: Don't Know Much About. 2005, HarperTrophy paper $4.99 (978-0-06-442128-7). 128pp. Jefferson's many accomplishments and contributions are presented in a question-and-answer format amplified by sidebar features, maps, and quotations that add context. (Rev: BL 2/1/05; SLJ 5/05) [921]

15054 Ferris, Jeri. *Thomas Jefferson: Father of Liberty* (5–8). 1998, Lerner LB $30.35 (978-1-57505-009-6). This readable biography covers both the public and the private sides of Jefferson's life, with details on his personality and his family. (Rev: BL 3/1/99; HBG 3/99; SLJ 12/98) [921]

15055 Ford, Carin T. *Thomas Jefferson: The Third President* (2–4). Illus. Series: Heroes of American History. 2003, Enslow LB $22.60 (978-0-7660-1861-7). 32pp. Jefferson's life and achievements are covered here, as are questions about his ownership of slaves. (Rev: HBG 10/03; SLJ 9/03) [921]

15056 Giblin, James Cross. *Thomas Jefferson: A Picture Book Biography* (4–6). Illus. by Michael Dooling. 1994, Scholastic $16.95 (978-0-590-44838-3). 48pp. This handsome, historically accurate biography of Thomas Jefferson covers his presidency and his accomplishments. (Rev: BCCB 10/94; BL 10/15/94; SLJ 9/94) [921]

15057 Gomez, Rebecca. *Thomas Jefferson* (2–3). Illus. Series: First Biographies. 2003, ABDO LB $22.78 (978-1-57765-947-1). 32pp. For young report writers, this is a simple account of Jefferson's major accomplishments. (Rev: HBG 4/04; SLJ 9/03) [921]

15058 Harness, Cheryl. *Thomas Jefferson* (4–7). Illus. 2004, National Geographic $17.95 (978-0-7922-6496-5). 48pp. Harness paints a personal portrait of Jefferson and his various roles in this picture book, enhanced by maps and eye-catching illustrations. (Rev: BL 2/1/04; SLJ 2/04) [973.4]

15059 Leslie, Tonya. *Thomas Jefferson: A Life of Patriotism* (1–3). Illus. by Tina Walski. Series: Blastoff! Readers. People of Character. 2007, Children's Pr. LB $20.00 (978-0-531-14715-3). 24pp. For beginning readers, this is a simple account of Jefferson's life and goals. (Rev: SLJ 1/08) [921]

15060 Nardo, Don. *Thomas Jefferson* (3–6). Series: Encyclopedia of Presidents. 2003, Children's Pr. LB $34.00 (978-0-516-22768-9). 110pp. A well-designed biography with maps, drawings, facts, a timeline, and other features that will be useful for report writers. (Rev: SLJ 4/04) [921]

15061 Old, Wendie. *Thomas Jefferson* (5–8). Series: United States Presidents. 1997, Enslow LB $26.60 (978-0-89490-837-8). An account of the life and career of the multifaceted Jefferson. (Rev: BL 2/1/98; HBG 3/98; SLJ 3/98) [921]

15062 Reiter, Chris. *Thomas Jefferson* (4–7). Illus. Series: MyReportLinks.com. 2002, Enslow LB $25.26 (978-0-7660-5071-6). 48pp. A concise biography suitable for students doing reports that provides extensive Web links for further research and uses Web site images among the many illustrations. (Rev: BL 9/1/02; HBG 3/03) [973.4]

15063 Sherrow, Victoria. *Thomas Jefferson* (3–4). Illus. Series: History Maker Bios. 2002, Lerner LB $26.60 (978-0-8225-0197-8). 48pp. A heavily illustrated story of the multitalented man who was also an important president. (Rev: BL 6/1–15/02) [973.4]

15064 Venezia, Mike. *Thomas Jefferson* (3–4). Illus. Series: Getting to Know the U.S. Presidents. 2004, Children's Pr. LB $28.00 (978-0-516-22608-8); paper $7.95 (978-0-516-27477-5). 32pp. A lighthearted approach to the key details of Jefferson's life, adding comic-book-style graphics and dialogue bubbles to the large-type text. [921]

JOHNSON, ANDREW

15065 Alter, Judy. *Andrew Johnson* (5–8). 2002, Enslow LB $25.26 (978-0-7660-5007-5). 48pp. This overview of Johnson's life and career contains a listing of about 30 Web sites that will extend the information contained in the book. (Rev: SLJ 6/02) [921]

15066 Stevens, Rita. *Andrew Johnson: 17th President of the United States* (5–7). Illus. 1989, Garrett LB $21.27 (978-0-944483-16-9). 122pp. Story of the man who became president on Lincoln's assassination. (Rev: BL 5/1/89) [973.810924]

JOHNSON, LYNDON B.

15067 Colbert, Nancy A. *Great Society: The Story of Lyndon Baines Johnson* (4–8). Illus. 2002, Morgan Reynolds LB $23.95 (978-1-883846-84-8). 144pp. A solid, readable life of the hardworking president that presents fairly both his virtues and defects. (Rev: BL 4/15/02; HBG 3/03; SLJ 8/02) [921]

15068 Falkof, Lucille. *Lyndon B. Johnson: 36th President of the United States* (5–8). Illus. 1989, Garrett LB $21.27 (978-0-944483-20-6). An informative biography that covers both the public and private life of this president. (Rev: BL 5/1/89; SLJ 8/89) [921]

15069 Levy, Debbie. *Lyndon B. Johnson* (5–9). Series: Presidential Leaders. 2003, Lerner LB $29.27 (978-0-8225-0097-1). 112pp. A look at the fascinating personal and political life of the president known for his support for civil rights and for increasing the U.S. involvement in Vietnam. (Rev: HBG 10/03; SLJ 2/03) [921]

KENNEDY, JOHN F.

15070 Adler, David A. *A Picture Book of John F. Kennedy* (2–4). Illus. by Robert Casilla. Series: Picture Book Biographies. 1991, Holiday House LB $16.95 (978-0-8234-0884-9). A straightforward account in an attractive format that provides basic information about President John F. Kennedy. (Rev: SLJ 12/91) [921]

15071 Anderson, Catherine Corley. *John F. Kennedy* (5–8). Series: Presidential Leaders. 2004, Lerner LB $29.27 (978-0-8225-0812-0). 112pp. Quotations, photographs, and informative sidebars add to the engaging text about Kennedy's life and times. (Rev: SLJ 1/05) [921]

15072 Heiligman, Deborah. *High Hopes: A Photobiography of John F. Kennedy* (4–6). Ed. by Nancy Feresten. 2003, National Geographic $17.95 (978-0-7922-6141-4). 64pp. This lavishly illustrated biography looks at Kennedy's achievements and his assassination. (Rev: BL 11/15/03; HBG 4/04; SLJ 4/04) [921]

15073 Hodge, Marie. *John F. Kennedy: Voice of Hope* (5–8). Series: Sterling Biographies. 2007, Sterling $12.95 (978-1-4027-4749-6); paper $5.95 (978-1-4027-3232-4). 124pp. This generally admiring, well-illustrated profile covers Kennedy's life from childhood. (Rev: SLJ 5/07) [921]

15074 Jones, Veda Boyd. *John F. Kennedy* (1–2). Series: Rookie Biographies. 2006, Children's Pr. LB $20.50 (978-0-516-25038-0); paper $4.95 (978-0-516-29797-2). 32pp. For beginning readers, this is a simple introduction to the life of the president. (Rev: SLJ 9/06) [921]

15075 Kaplan, Howard S. *John F. Kennedy* (5–10). Illus. Series: DK Biography. 2004, DK paper $4.99 (978-0-7566-0340-3). 128pp. A heavily illustrated, attractive biography of Kennedy that offers broad historical background. (Rev: BL 6/1–15/04) [921]

15076 Schultz, Randy. *John F. Kennedy* (4–7). Illus. Series: MyReportLinks.com. 2002, Enslow LB $25.26 (978-0-7660-5012-9). 48pp. A basic, illustrated account of Kennedy's life and accomplishments that provides extensive Web links for students to do further research. (Rev: BL 9/1/02) [973.922]

15077 Time For Kids Eds., and Ritu Upadhyay. *John F. Kennedy: The Making of a Leader* (3–5). Series: Time for Kids Biographies. 2005, HarperCollins $15.99 (978-0-06-057603-5); paper $3.99 (978-0-06-057602-8). 44pp. Attractive photo-filled pages describe Kennedy's childhood, education, and later life, with interesting sidebar features on topics including Jackie's redecoration of the White House. (Rev: SLJ 2/05) [921]

15078 Todd, Anne. *John F. Kennedy: A Life of Citizenship* (1–3). Illus. by Tina Walski. Series: Blastoff! Readers: People of Character. 2007, Children's Pr. LB $20.00 (978-0-531-14709-2). 24pp. For beginning readers, this is a simple account of Kennedy's life and goals, mentioning the Peace Corps. (Rev: SLJ 1/08)

LINCOLN, ABRAHAM

15079 *Abraham Lincoln: Defender of the Union* (4–6). Series: The Civil War. 2005, Cobblestone $17.95 (978-0-8126-7902-1). 47pp. This solid profile with excellent illustrations covers Lincoln's childhood, courtship of Mary Todd, family life, political career, and presidency. (Rev: HBG 10/06; SLJ 3/06) [921]

15080 Adler, David A. *A Picture Book of Abraham Lincoln* (PS–3). Illus. by John Wallner and Alexandra Wallner. 1989, Holiday House LB $17.95 (978-0-8234-0731-6); paper $6.95 (978-0-8234-0801-6). 32pp. The life of perhaps our most famous president told in a profusely illustrated format. (Rev: BL 6/1/89; SLJ 5/89)

15081 *The Assassination of Abraham Lincoln* (3–6). Illus. by Otha Zachariah Edward Lohse. Series: Graphic Library/Graphic History. 2005, Capstone LB $26.60 (978-0-7368-3831-3). 32pp. This graphic "novel" — factual, but embellished — about the fateful event will appeal to reluctant readers. (Rev: SLJ 7/05) [921]

15082 Aylesworth, Jim. *Our Abe Lincoln* (PS–2). Illus. by Barbara McClintock. 2009, Scholastic $16.99 (978-0-439-92548-8). 40pp. To the tune of "The Old Gray Mare," 12 verses recount key information about Lincoln. (Rev: BCCB 1/09; BL 12/1/08; HB 5/09; SLJ 12/08) [973.7092]

15083 Brenner, Martha. *Abe Lincoln's Hat* (1–3). Illus. by Donald Cook. 1994, Random paper $3.99 (978-0-679-84977-3). 48pp. A simple biography of Lincoln that makes him a believable person through the retelling of simple anecdotes. (Rev: BL 9/15/94; SLJ 11/94) [921]

15084 Bryant, Jen. *Abe's Fish: A Boyhood Tale of Abraham Lincoln* (2–4). Illus. by Amy June Bates. 2009, Sterling $15.95 (978-1-4027-6252-9). 40pp. Inspired by few lines in an 1890 biography, this engaging story follows 6-year-old Abe as he presents a fish he has caught to a tired soldier who leaves him pondering the word "freedom." (Rev: BL 1/1–15/09; SLJ 4/09) [921]

15085 Burgan, Michael. *The Assassination of Abraham Lincoln* (3–6). Illus. Series: We the People. 2004, Compass Point LB $26.60 (978-0-7565-0678-0). 48pp. A well-illustrated, concise introduction to Lincoln's untimely death. [921]

15086 Burke, Rick. *Abraham Lincoln* (1–4). Series: American Lives. 2003, Heinemann LB $24.22 (978-1-4034-0155-7). 32pp. This easy-to-understand biography discusses Lincoln's youth and achievements, and includes plentiful, interesting illustrations. (Rev: HBG 10/03; SLJ 7/03) [921]

15087 Burleigh, Robert. *Abraham Lincoln Comes Home* (2–4). Illus. by Wendell Minor. 2008, Holt $16.95 (978-0-8050-7529-1). 40pp. This volume beautifully integrates history with the story of a little boy watching and waiting for Lincoln's funeral train. (Rev: BL 9/15/08; LMC 3/09) [921]

15088 Collard, Sneed B., III. *Abraham Lincoln: A Courageous Leader* (3–5). Series: American Heroes. 2006, Benchmark $28.50 (978-0-7614-2162-7). 40pp. A basic biography of the sixteenth president, featuring interesting facts about his life and career presented in large typeface with large illustrations. (Rev: SLJ 3/07) [921]

15089 Davis, Kenneth C. *Don't Know Much About Abraham Lincoln* (4–8). Illus. by Rob Shepperson. Series: Don't Know Much About. 2004, HarperCollins LB $15.89 (978-0-06-028820-4). 142pp. A question-and-answer format gives easy access to key details about Lincoln's life. (Rev: BL 2/1/05; SLJ 2/04) [921]

15090 Fontes, Justine, and Ron Fontes. *Abraham Lincoln: Lawyer, Leader, Legend* (2–4). Illus. Series: Dorling Kindersley Readers. 2001, DK $14.99 (978-0-7894-7376-9); paper $3.99 (978-0-7894-7375-2). 48pp. An accessible introduction to Lincoln's life with many facts, illustrations, and maps. (Rev: BCCB 2/02; HBG 10/01; SLJ 8/01) [921]

15091 Ford, Carin T. *Abraham Lincoln: The 16th President* (2–4). Illus. Series: Heroes of American History. 2003, Enslow LB $22.60 (978-0-7660-2000-9). 32pp. A well-illustrated and well-written biography that covers Lincoln's flaws as well as his great achievements. (Rev: HBG 10/03; SLJ 9/03) [921]

15092 Freedman, Russell. *Lincoln: A Photobiography* (4–8). Illus. 1987, Houghton $20.00 (978-0-89919-380-9); paper $9.95 (978-0-395-51848-9). 160pp. A no-nonsense, unromanticized look at this beloved president. Newbery Medal winner, 1988. (Rev: BL 12/15/87; SLJ 12/87) [921]

15093 Gross, Ruth Belov. *True Stories About Abraham Lincoln* (2–5). Illus. by Jill Kastner. 1991, Scholastic paper $2.50 (978-0-590-43879-7). 48pp. This is a collection of anecdotes about Lincoln. Originally published in 1973. (Rev: BCCB 3/90; BL 3/1/90; SLJ 4/90) [921]

15094 Harness, Cheryl. *Abe Lincoln Goes to Washington, 1837–1865* (1–4). Illus. 1997, National Geographic $18.00 (978-0-7922-3736-5). 48pp. In this sequel to *Young Abe Lincoln* (1996), Lincoln's life from his arrival in Springfield, Illinois, to his assassination is covered. (Rev: BL 1/1–15/97; SLJ 3/97*) [921]

15095 Harness, Cheryl. *Young Abe Lincoln* (1–4). Illus. 1996, National Geographic $15.95 (978-0-7922-2713-7). 32pp. A picture book that traces Lincoln's early life until he leaves for Springfield, Illinois. (Rev: BL 9/1/96; SLJ 6/96) [921]

15096 Herbert, Janis. *Abraham Lincoln for Kids: His Life and Times with 21 Activities* (4–8). Illus. 2007, Chicago Review paper $14.95 (978-1-55652-656-5). 154pp. With many quotations, illustrations, and sidebars, this volume covers Lincoln's life, beliefs, and contributions and includes activities (such as drawing a cartoon and learning Morse code). (Rev: SLJ 10/07) [921]

15097 Holzer, Harold. *The President Is Shot! The Assassination of Abraham Lincoln* (5–8). Illus. 2004, Boyds Mills $17.95 (978-1-56397-985-9). 144pp. A riveting account of Lincoln's assassination, with archival illustrations and historical context. (Rev: BL 3/1/04*; SLJ 2/04) [973.7]

15098 Jackson, Ellen. *Abe Lincoln Loved Animals* (1–3). Illus. by Doris Ettlinger. 2008, Albert Whitman $16.99 (978-0-8075-0123-8). 32pp. This picture book tells a series of stories about Lincoln the animal lover from the time he was a boy until the time he established the presidential tradition of pardoning a turkey on Thanksgiving. (Rev: BL 9/15/08) [973.7092]

15099 Judson, Karen. *Abraham Lincoln* (4–6). Series: United States Presidents. 1998, Enslow LB $26.60 (978-0-89490-939-9). 128pp. Original source documents and a chronology are included in this insightful biography of a great president. (Rev: BL 12/15/98; HBG 3/99) [921]

15100 Mara, Wil. *Abraham Lincoln* (1–2). Illus. Series: Rookie Biographies. 2002, Children's Book Pr. LB $20.50 (978-0-516-22518-0); paper $4.95 (978-0-516-27334-1). 31pp. A simple account of Lincoln's life for beginning readers. (Rev: BCCB 2/02; SLJ 1/03) [921]

15101 Mosher, Kiki. *Learning About Honesty from the Life of Abraham Lincoln* (2–5). Illus. Series: A Character Building Book. 1996, Rosen LB $18.75 (978-0-8239-2420-2). 24pp. A brief biography of Lincoln that emphasizes his belief in honesty and truth. (Rev: BL 10/15/96; SLJ 12/96) [921]

15102 Rappaport, Doreen. *Abe's Honest Words: The Life of Abraham Lincoln* (2–4). Illus. by Kadir Nelson. 2008, Hyperion $16.99 (978-1-4231-0408-7). 40pp. Lincoln's own words are combined with Rappaport's free verse and Nelson's powerful art to form an elegant portrait of the president's life and beliefs. (Rev: BCCB 10/08; BL 6/1–15/08; HB 11/08; LMC 1/09; SLJ 10/08) [921]

15103 Roberts, Jeremy. *Abraham Lincoln* (5–7). Series: Presidential Leaders. 2003, Lerner LB $29.27 (978-0-8225-0817-5). 112pp. From childhood through assassination, this is a thorough, well-illustrated, and well-organized account of Lincoln's life. (Rev: SLJ 2/04) [921]

15104 St. George, Judith. *Stand Tall, Abe Lincoln* (2–4). Illus. by Matt Faulkner. 2007, Philomel $16.99 (978-0-399-24174-1). 48pp. An appealing look at Lincoln's childhood, showing him working on the family farm and developing a love for reading and learning. (Rev: BL 10/1/07; SLJ 11/07) [921]

15105 Schott, Jane A. *Abraham Lincoln* (3–4). Series: History Maker Bios. 2002, Lerner LB $26.60 (978-0-8225-0196-1). 48pp. Using many true stories, historical photography, and other artwork, this lively biography describes Lincoln's journey from log cabin to the White House. (Rev: BCCB 2/02; BL 6/1–15/02) [921]

15106 Sloate, Susan. *Abraham Lincoln: The Freedom President* (5–8). 1989, Ballantine paper $15.00 (978-0-449-90375-9). An accessible account of the president who led his country through division back to unity. (Rev: BL 12/15/89) [921]

15107 Stone, Tanya L. *Abraham Lincoln* (5–10). Illus. Series: DK Biography. 2005, DK $14.99 (978-0-7566-0833-0); paper $4.99 (978-0-7566-0834-7). 128pp. A heavily illustrated, attractive biography of Lincoln that offers broad historical background. (Rev: BL 6/1–15/04) [921]

15108 Sullivan, George. *Abraham Lincoln* (3–5). Illus. Series: In Their Own Words. 2001, Scholastic $12.95 (978-0-439-14750-7); paper $4.99 (978-0-439-09554-9). 128pp. Using speeches, letters, and other primary sources, this is an entertaining, appealing biography of Lincoln. (Rev: BCCB 2/02; BL 4/1/01; HBG 10/01; SLJ 4/01) [921]

15109 Sullivan, George. *Picturing Lincoln: Famous Photographs That Popularized the President* (5–8). Illus. 2000, Clarion $16.00 (978-0-395-91682-7). 88pp. Using five images of Lincoln taken between 1846 and 1864, this book gives historical and biographical information on each and tells how they have been used for posters, button, ribbons, postage stamps, and currency. (Rev: BL 2/1/01; HB 3/01; HBG 10/01; SLJ 3/01) [921]

15110 Thomson, Sarah L. *What Lincoln Said* (K–3). Illus. by James Ransome. 2009, Collins LB $18.89 (978-0-06-084820-0). 32pp. This picture-book biography traces Lincoln's life from childhood through signing the Emancipation Proclamation, providing direct quotations throughout. (Rev: BL 9/15/08) [921]

15111 Van Steenwyk, Elizabeth. *When Abraham Talked to the Trees* (K–3). Illus. by Bill Farnsworth. 2000, Eerdmans $16.00 (978-0-8028-5191-8). 32pp. A picture book that tells of Lincoln's youth, his many outdoor activities, and the books he read. (Rev: BL 10/1/00; HBG 3/01; SLJ 12/00) [921]

15112 Waldman, Neil. *Voyages: Reminiscences of Young Abe Lincoln* (5–8). Illus. by author. 2009, Boyds Mills $16.95 (978-1-59078-471-6). 32pp. Blending fiction and nonfiction, these anecdotes about the life of the young Lincoln include direct quotations in a contrasting color. (Rev: BL 3/15/09; SLJ 4/09) [921]

15113 Winters, Kay. *Abe Lincoln: The Boy Who Loved Books* (K–2). Illus. by Nancy Carpenter. 2003, Simon & Schuster $16.95 (978-0-689-82554-5). 40pp. Simple language and detailed illustrations describe Lincoln's childhood and young adult years, with a focus on his love of reading. (Rev: BL 1/1–15/03; HBG 10/03; SLJ 1/03) [973.7]

MADISON, JAMES

15114 Elish, Dan. *James Madison* (4–7). Series: Presidents and Their Times. 2007, Marshall Cavendish LB $22.95 (978-0-7614-2432-1). 96pp. A clear and thorough profile of the president, describing his early years, presidential career, and later life, with discussion of important events that took place during his life. (Rev: LMC 5/08; SLJ 1/08)

15115 Kent, Zachary. *James Madison: Creating a Nation* (5–8). Series: America's Founding Fathers. 2004, Enslow LB $26.60 (978-0-7660-2180-8). 128pp. This profile of Madison focuses largely on his public life from the period leading up to the American Revolution through his presidency. (Rev: BL 6/1–15/04) [921]

15116 Malone, Mary. *James Madison* (4–6). Illus. 1997, Enslow LB $26.60 (978-0-89490-834-7).

128pp. This interesting, well-researched biography of James Madison focuses on his presidency. (Rev: BL 9/15/97; HBG 3/98; SLJ 9/97) [921]

15117 Quackenbush, Robert. *James Madison and Dolley Madison and Their Times* (3–6). Illus. 1992, Pippin $14.95 (978-0-945912-18-7). 40pp. A fact-filled short biography of James and Dolley Madison with many interesting bits about their personal lives. (Rev: BL 1/15/93; SLJ 1/93) [921]

15118 Santella, Andrew. *James Madison* (3–5). Series: Profiles of the Presidents. 2002, Compass Point LB $26.60 (978-0-7565-0252-2). 64pp. Madison's adult years are the focus of this volume that includes a brief chapter on his youth. (Rev: SLJ 4/03) [921]

15119 Venezia, Mike. *James Madison* (3–4). Illus. Series: Getting to Know the U.S. Presidents. 2004, Children's Pr. LB $28.00 (978-0-516-22609-5); paper $7.95 (978-0-516-27478-2). 32pp. A light-hearted approach to the key details of Madison's life, adding comic-book-style graphics and dialogue bubbles to the large-type text. [921]

MADISON, JAMES AND DOLLEY

15120 Adler, David A., and Michael S. Adler. *A Picture Book of Dolley and James Madison* (K–3). Illus. by Ronald Himler. 2009, Holiday $17.95 (978-0-8234-2009-4). 32pp. A thorough picture-book biography of the 4th president and his wife, with illustrations that extend the text. (Rev: BLO 5/15/09; SLJ 3/09) [021]

15121 Ashby, Ruth. *James and Dolley Madison* (5–8). Illus. Series: Presidents and First Ladies. 2005, Gareth Stevens LB $31.00 (978-0-8368-5757-3). 48pp. An accessible, balanced, and attractive discussion of the Madisons and the contributions each made to their joint lives. (Rev: BL 3/1/05; SLJ 8/05) [921]

MONROE, JAMES

15122 Old, Wendie. *James Monroe* (4–6). Series: United States Presidents. 1998, Enslow LB $26.60 (978-0-89490-941-2). 128pp. Profiles the fifth president, who is noted for drafting the doctrine that barred European intervention in the New World. (Rev: BL 12/15/98; HBG 3/99) [921]

15123 Teitelbaum, Michael. *James Monroe* (3–5). Series: Profiles of the Presidents. 2002, Compass Point LB $26.60 (978-0-7565-0253-9). 64pp. Monroe's adult years are the focus of this volume that includes a brief chapter on his youth. (Rev: SLJ 4/03) [921]

15124 Venezia, Mike. *James Monroe* (3–4). Illus. Series: Getting to Know the U.S. Presidents. 2004, Children's Pr. LB $28.00 (978-0-516-22610-1); paper $7.95 (978-0-516-27479-9). 32pp. A light-hearted approach to the key details of Monroe's life, adding comic-book-style graphics and dialogue bubbles to the large-type text. [921]

15125 Welsbacher, Anne. *James Monroe* (K–2). Series: United States Presidents. 1999, ABDO LB $22.78 (978-1-56239-810-1). 32pp. A biography for beginning readers that gives basic facts about Monroe and the meaning of the doctrine that bears his name. (Rev: HBG 10/99; SLJ 7/99) [921]

NIXON, RICHARD M.

15126 Aronson, Billy. *Richard M. Nixon* (5–8). Illus. Series: Presidents and Their Times. 2007, Marshall Cavendish LB $22.95 (978-0-7614-2428-4). 96pp. This biography of the 37th president covers his childhood, his candidacy, and his accomplishments in office, as well as his downfall and impeachment. (Rev: BL 10/15/07; SLJ 1/08) [921]

15127 Joseph, Paul. *Richard Nixon* (K–2). Series: United States Presidents. 1999, ABDO LB $22.78 (978-1-56239-746-3). 32pp. For beginning readers, this is an overview of Nixon's life and accomplishments with a double-page spread of important facts and statistics. (Rev: HBG 10/99; SLJ 7/99) [921]

15128 Marquez, Heron. *Richard M. Nixon* (5–7). Series: Presidential Leaders. 2003, Lerner LB $29.27 (978-0-8225-0098-8). 112pp. The Vietnam War, relations with China, and Watergate all feature prominently in this look at Nixon's private and public life. (Rev: BL 4/15/03; HBG 10/03; SLJ 2/03) [921]

OBAMA, BARACK

15129 Feinstein, Stephen. *Barack Obama* (1–3). Illus. Series: African-American Heroes. 2008, Enslow LB $15.95 (978-0-7660-2893-7). 24pp. This slender biography for young readers chronicles the president's life from childhood with a timeline, reading list, and photographs. (Rev: BL 3/15/08) [921]

15130 Obama, Barack. *Change Has Come: An Artist Celebrates Our American Spirit* (1–6). Illus. by Kadir Nelson. 2009, Simon & Schuster $12.99 (978-1-4169-8955-4). 64pp. With compelling images, Nelson celebrates Obama's election. (Rev: LMC 8/09; SLJ 3/09) [921]

15131 Schuman, Michael A. *Barack Obama: "We Are One People"* (5–8). Illus. Series: African-American Biography Library. 2008, Enslow LB $23.95 (978-0-7660-2891-3). 128pp. Opening with Obama's speech at the 2004 Democratic Convention, this biography goes on to cover his life chronologically from childhood through running for president. (Rev: BL 6/1–15/08) [328.730]

15132 Wheeler, Jill C. *Barack Obama* (1–4). Illus. Series: United States Presidents. 2009, ABDO LB $18.95 (978-1-60453-481-8). 40pp. This accessible profile is arranged chronologically and includes a timeline, photographs, a useful "Did You Know?" page of facts, and an overview of the U.S. government and the role of the president. (Rev: BL 3/15/09) [921]

PIERCE, FRANKLIN

15133 Brown, Fern G. *Franklin Pierce* (5–8). Series: Presidents of the United States. 1989, GEC LB $21.27 (978-0-944483-25-1). 121pp. The story of

Pierce, his political life and presidency, plus material on his personal life. (Rev: SLJ 9/89) [921]

POLK, JAMES K.

15134 Tibbitts, Alison Davis. *James K. Polk* (4–6). Series: United States Presidents. 1999, Enslow LB $26.60 (978-0-7660-1037-6). 128pp. The story of the 11th president of the United States, whose term encompassed the 1846–1848 war with Mexico, which brought California and New Mexico into the union. (Rev: BL 9/15/99; HBG 10/99) [921]

15135 Venezia, Mike. *James K. Polk: Eleventh President, 1845–1849* (3–4). Illus. Series: Getting to Know the U.S. Presidents. 2005, Children's Pr. LB $28.00 (978-0-516-22616-3); paper $7.95 (978-0-516-27485-0). 32pp. A light-hearted approach to the key details of Polk's life, adding comic-book-style graphics and dialogue bubbles to the large-type text. [921]

REAGAN, RONALD

15136 Hinkle, Donald Henry. *Ronald Reagan* (4–7). Series: Presidents. 2003, Enslow LB $25.26 (978-0-7660-5112-6). 48pp. The life story of the fortieth president with material on the successes and failures of his two terms. (Rev: BL 6/1–15/03; HBG 10/03) [921]

15137 Robbins, Neal. *Ronald W. Reagan: 40th President of the United States* (K–2). Illus. Series: Presidents of the United States. 1990, Garrett LB $21.27 (978-0-944483-66-4). 124pp. The life of Ronald Reagan is presented. (Rev: BL 8/90) [921]

15138 Sullivan, George. *Ronald Reagan* (5–8). Illus. 1991, Simon & Schuster $14.98 (978-0-671-74537-0). 142pp. This revised edition adds new material on Reagan's second term. (Rev: BL 1/15/92) [921]

ROOSEVELT, FRANKLIN D.

15139 Allport, Alan. *Franklin Delano Roosevelt* (5–7). Series: Great American Presidents. 2003, Chelsea House LB $30.00 (978-0-7910-7598-2). 102pp. A concise life of the longest-serving president in U.S. history, from his childhood through his years in the White House, with a foreword by Walter Cronkite. (Rev: SLJ 4/04) [921]

15140 Bardhan-Quallen, Sudipta. *Franklin Delano Roosevelt: A National Hero* (5–8). Series: Sterling Biographies. 2007, Sterling $12.95 (978-1-4027-4747-2); paper $5.95 (978-1-4027-3545-5). 124pp. The author emphasizes the contrast between Roosevelt's privileged background and his concern about social injustice. (Rev: SLJ 5/07) [921]

15141 Burgan, Michael. *Franklin D. Roosevelt* (4–8). Series: Profiles of the Presidents. 2002, Compass Point LB $26.60 (978-0-7565-0203-4). 64pp. An absorbing introduction to Roosevelt's life and career, with details of his youth and education and the role that his illness played in shaping his character. (Rev: SLJ 6/02) [973.917092]

15142 Freedman, Russell. *Franklin Delano Roosevelt* (5–8). Illus. 1990, Houghton $20.00 (978-0-89919-

379-3). 200pp. A carefully researched and well-illustrated account of the man and the times. (Rev: HB 3/90; SLJ 12/90*) [921]

15143 Greenblatt, Miriam. *Franklin D. Roosevelt: 32nd President of the United States* (5–8). Illus. 1989, Garrett LB $21.27 (978-0-944483-06-0). A clearly written, objective biography of the man who guided the country through World War II, with information on his family life. (Rev: BL 5/1/89; SLJ 8/89) [921]

15144 Haugen, Brenda. *Franklin Delano Roosevelt: The New Deal President* (4–8). Series: Signature Lives. 2006, Compass Point LB $34.60 (978-0-7565-1586-7). 112pp. Slim but fact-filled, this is a useful biography for report writers, with excerpts from speeches and writings and full discussion of key events in Roosevelt's life. (Rev: SLJ 9/06) [921]

15145 Knapp, Ron. *Franklin D. Roosevelt* (5–9). 2002, Enslow LB $25.26 (978-0-7660-5009-9). 48pp. A listing of recommended Web sites extends the contents of this introduction to Roosevelt's life and presidency. (Rev: HBG 10/02; SLJ 6/02) [921]

15146 Morris, Jeffrey. *The FDR Way* (5–8). Illus. Series: Great Presidential Decisions. 1996, Lerner LB $23.93 (978-0-8225-2929-3). A straightforward, incisive analysis of far-reaching, often painful decisions that FDR made, and an assessment of their consequences. (Rev: BL 3/15/96) [921]

15147 St. George, Judith. *Make Your Mark, Franklin Roosevelt* (2–5). Illus. by Britt Spencer. Series: Turning Point. 2007, Philomel $16.99 (978-0-399-24175-8). 48pp. Focuses on the president's childhood and his decision as a teenager to move beyond his life of privilege and devote himself to public service. (Rev: BL 11/15/06; SLJ 2/07*) [921]

15148 Van Steenwyk, Elizabeth. *First Dog Fala* (PS–3). Illus. by Michael G. Montgomery. 2008, Peachtree $16.95 (978-1-56145-411-2). 32pp. Meet Fala, the black Scottish terrier who won the hearts of President Franklin Roosevelt and the American people; illustrated with paintings that give us a terrier's-eye view of the FDR White House. (Rev: BL 10/1/08; LMC 3/08) [973.917]

ROOSEVELT, FRANKLIN D. AND ELEANOR

15149 Ashby, Ruth. *Franklin and Eleanor Roosevelt* (5–8). Illus. Series: Presidents and First Ladies. 2005, Gareth Stevens LB $31.00 (978-0-8368-5758-0). 48pp. An accessible, balanced, and attractive discussion of the Roosevelts and the contributions each made to their joint lives. (Rev: BL 3/1/05) [921]

ROOSEVELT, THEODORE

15150 Brown, Don. *Teedie: The Story of Young Teddy Roosevelt* (1–3). Illus. by author. 2009, Houghton $16.00 (978-0-618-17999-2). 32pp. The story of the president's sickly childhood and how he overcame them to become a man of many, including athletic, interests. (Rev: BL 4/1/09; HB 5/09; SLJ 4/09) [921]

15151 Elish, Dan. *Theodore Roosevelt* (4–7). Series: Presidents and Their Times. 2007, Marshall Cavendish LB $22.95 (978-0-7614-2429-1). 96pp. A clear and thorough profile of the president, describing his early years, presidential career, and later life, with discussion of important events that took place during his life. (Rev: SLJ 1/08)

15152 Harness, Cheryl. *Young Teddy Roosevelt* (3–5). Illus. 1998, National Geographic $17.95 (978-0-7922-7094-2). 48pp. Illustrated with lavish watercolors, this picture-book biography tells of Roosevelt's sickly childhood and ends with him becoming president of the United States. (Rev: BCCB 4/98; BL 3/15/98; HBG 10/98) [921]

15153 Keating, Frank. *Theodore* (2–6). Illus. by Mike Wimmer. 2006, Simon & Schuster $16.95 (978-0-689-86532-9). 32pp. This attractive and compelling biography of Theodore Roosevelt examines all aspects of his life and emphasizes his loves of nature, reading, and hard work. (Rev: SLJ 3/06*) [921]

15154 Kelley, Alison Turnbull. *Theodore Roosevelt* (5–7). Series: Great American Presidents. 2003, Chelsea House LB $30.00 (978-0-7910-7606-4). 102pp. An illustrated profile of the 26th president, from his childhood through his public life and legacy. (Rev: SLJ 4/04) [921]

15155 Kraft, Betsy Harvey. *Theodore Roosevelt: Champion of the American Spirit* (5–9). Illus. 2003, Clarion $19.00 (978-0-618-14264-4). 180pp. The determination that carried Roosevelt through a difficult childhood and drove his successful career is emphasized in this engrossing biography of his life and survey of his diverse accomplishments. (Rev: BL 10/15/03; HB 11/03; HBG 4/04; SLJ 12/03*; VOYA 10/03) [973.9]

15156 Roosevelt, Theodore. *My Tour of Europe: By Teddy Roosevelt, Age 10* (1–3). Ed. by Ellen Jackson. Illus. by Catherine Brighton. 2003, Millbrook LB $23.90 (978-0-7613-2516-1). 32pp. This collection of excerpts from Teddy Roosevelt's boyhood journal describes the 10-year-old future president's experiences on a family trip to Europe. (Rev: BL 4/15/03; HBG 10/03; SLJ 6/03) [973.91]

15157 St. George, Judith. *You're on Your Way, Teddy Roosevelt!* (2–4). Illus. by Matt Faulkner. Series: Turning Point Book. 2004, Philomel $16.99 (978-0-399-23888-8). 48pp. Teddy Roosevelt's childhood is the focus of this picture-book biography that looks at his love for animals and his victory over asthma, which paved the way for his success as both an athlete and a student. (Rev: BL 11/1/04; SLJ 10/04) [921]

15158 Schuman, Michael A. *Theodore Roosevelt* (5–8). Series: United States Presidents. 1997, Enslow LB $26.60 (978-0-89490-836-1). An objective biography of the life of this active president whose life spanned both the Civil War and World War I, with good background information. (Rev: BL 2/1/98; HBG 3/98; SLJ 2/98) [921]

15159 Time For Kids Eds., and Lisa DeMauro. *Theodore Roosevelt: The Adventurous President* (3–5). Series: Time for Kids Biographies. 2005, HarperCollins $15.99 (978-0-06-057606-6); paper $3.99 (978-0-06-057604-2). 44pp. Attractive photo-filled pages describe Roosevelt's childhood, education, love for nature, and later life, with interesting sidebar features on topics ranging from the Teddy bear and Mount Rushmore to his "Big Stick" policy. (Rev: BL 3/15/04; SLJ 2/05) [921]

TAYLOR, ZACHARY

15160 Brunelli, Carol. *Zachary Taylor: Our Twelfth President* (4–6). Series: Spirit of America: Our Presidents. 2001, Child's World $28.50 (978-1-56766-836-0). 48pp. A well-illustrated and appealing biography that discusses influences that shaped Taylor's policies and looks at his legacy. (Rev: SLJ 12/01) [921]

15161 Collins, David R. *Zachary Taylor: 12th President of the United States* (5–7). Illus. 1989, Garrett LB $21.27 (978-0-944483-17-6). 121pp. Tells the life story of a military man elected president in 1848. (Rev: BL 5/1/89) [921]

15162 Venezia, Mike. *Zachary Taylor: Twelfth President, 1849–1850* (3–4). Illus. Series: Getting to Know the U.S. Presidents. 2005, Children's Pr. LB $28.00 (978-0-516-22617-0); paper $7.95 (978-0-516-27486-7). 32pp. A light-hearted approach to the key details of Taylor's life, adding comic-book-style graphics and dialogue bubbles to the large-type text. [921]

TRUMAN, HARRY S

15163 Cannarella, Deborah. *Harry S. Truman* (3–5). Series: Profiles of the Presidents. 2002, Compass Point LB $26.60 (978-0-7565-0278-2). 64pp. Truman's adult years are the focus of this volume that includes a brief chapter on his youth. (Rev: SLJ 4/03) [921]

15164 Joseph, Paul. *Harry S. Truman* (2–5). Illus. Series: United States Presidents. 1999, ABDO LB $22.78 (978-1-56239-743-2). 32pp. A good biography of Truman that also contains a section on trivia, a map, and two pages of vital statistics. (Rev: HBG 3/00; SLJ 12/99) [921]

15165 Lazo, Caroline. *Harry S Truman* (5–7). Illus. Series: Presidential Leaders. 2003, Lerner LB $29.27 (978-0-8225-0096-4). 112pp. Truman's youth, education, family life, and career are all covered in this concise biography full of photographs. (Rev: BL 4/15/03; HBG 10/03) [973.918]

TYLER, JOHN

15166 Ochester, Betsy. *John Tyler* (4–6). Illus. Series: Encyclopedia of Presidents. 2003, Children's Pr. LB $34.00 (978-0-516-22850-1). 110pp. An updated profile that looks at Tyler's life and contributions, providing many illustrations and sidebars. (Rev: SLJ 1/04) [921]

15167 Venezia, Mike. *John Tyler* (3–5). Illus. by author. Series: Getting to Know the U.S. Presidents. 2005, Children's Pr. LB $28.00 (978-0-516-22615-6). 32pp. A lighthearted introduction to the 10th president, with plenty of visual information. (Rev: SLJ 7/05) [921]

VAN BUREN, MARTIN

15168 Doak, Robin. *Martin Van Buren* (4–7). 2003, Compass Point LB $26.60 (978-0-7565-0256-0). 64pp. Van Buren's strengths and weakness receive equal weight in this balanced and readable biography that covers his life from a young age. (Rev: SLJ 11/03) [973.5]

15169 Ellis, Rafaela. *Martin Van Buren: 8th President of the United States* (5–7). Illus. 1989, Garrett LB $21.27 (978-0-944483-12-1). 120pp. The story of a New York governor who became president. (Rev: BL 5/1/89) [921]

15170 Favor, Lesli J. *Martin Van Buren* (3–6). Series: Encyclopedia of Presidents. 2003, Children's Pr. LB $34.00 (978-0-516-22770-2). 110pp. A concise illustrated biography of the eighth president of the United States, with plenty of illustrations and sidebars. (Rev: SLJ 4/04) [921]

15171 Venezia, Mike. *Martin Van Buren: Eighth President 1837–1841* (3–4). Illus. Series: Getting to Know the U.S. Presidents. 2005, Children's Pr. LB $28.00 (978-0-516-22613-2); paper $7.95 (978-0-516-27482-9). 32pp. A light-hearted approach to the key details of Van Buren's life, adding comic-book-style graphics and dialogue bubbles to the large-type text. [921]

WASHINGTON, GEORGE

15172 Adler, David A. *George Washington: An Illustrated Biography* (5–7). 2004, Holiday House $24.95 (978-0-8234-1838-1). 288pp. Adler presents a balanced and well-researched biography of Washington, giving details of his character as well as information on key events of his time. (Rev: BL 9/15/04; SLJ 12/04) [973.4]

15173 Adler, David A. *A Picture Book of George Washington* (PS–3). Illus. by John Wallner and Alexandra Wallner. 1989, Holiday House LB $17.95 (978-0-8234-0732-3); paper $6.95 (978-0-8234-0800-9). 32pp. A picture biography of America's first president for young readers. (Rev: BL 6/1/89; SLJ 5/89)

15174 Adler, David A. *President George Washington* (1–3). Illus. by John Wallner. Series: Holiday House Reader. 2005, Holiday $14.95 (978-0-8234-1604-2). 32pp. For beginning readers, this picture-book biography that gives a brief overview of Washington's youth and adult accomplishments uses short sentences, large typeface, and lots of white space. (Rev: BL 9/15/05; SLJ 11/05) [921]

15175 Armentrout, David, and Patricia Armentrout. *George Washington* (1–3). Series: Discover the Life of an American Legend. 2004, Rourke LB $20.64 (978-1-58952-662-4). 24pp. An introductory book about the first U.S. president, including a glossary and chronology. (Rev: SLJ 3/04) [973.4]

15176 Burke, Rick. *George Washington* (1–4). Series: American Lives. 2003, Heinemann LB $24.22 (978-1-4034-0158-8). 32pp. Easy to read, this richly

illustrated biography covers Washington's life from childhood. (Rev: HBG 10/03; SLJ 7/03) [921]

15177 Chandra, Deborah, and Madeleine Comora. *George Washington's Teeth* (K–3). Illus. by Brock Cole. 2003, Farrar $16.00 (978-0-374-32534-3). 40pp. George Washington's dental problems are examined in lively, witty verses perfectly paired with sprightly watercolors. (Rev: BCCB 2/03; BL 1/1–15/03; HB 3/03*; HBG 10/03; SLJ 1/03) [973.4]

15178 Collier, James Lincoln. *The George Washington You Never Knew* (4–6). Illus. by Greg Copeland. Series: You Never Knew. 2003, Children's Pr. LB $25.50 (978-0-516-24343-6). 80pp. In an accessible style, Collier reveals the inner man behind the legend, combining historical facts and debunking myths while providing a solid account of the early days of the United States. (Rev: SLJ 1/04) [921]

15179 Falkof, Lucille. *George Washington: 1st President of the United States* (5–8). Illus. 1989, Garrett LB $21.27 (978-0-944483-19-0). An objective, readable portrait of the life and times of our first president. (Rev: BL 5/1/89; SLJ 8/89) [921]

15180 Ford, Carin T. *George Washington: The First President* (2–4). Series: Heroes of American History. 2003, Enslow LB $22.60 (978-0-7660-1999-7). 32pp. A concise introduction to the military and political leader. (Rev: HBG 10/03; SLJ 6/03) [921]

15181 Harness, Cheryl. *George Washington* (3–5). Illus. 2000, National Geographic $17.95 (978-0-7922-7096-6). 48pp. A heavily illustrated, large-format biography that covers the important events in Washington's life and describes his personality. (Rev: BL 3/1/00; HBG 10/00; SLJ 4/00) [921]

15182 Hilton, Suzanne. *The World of Young George Washington* (5–8). 1987, Walker $12.95 (978-0-8027-6657-1). Washington as a youth plus detailed information on life in pre-Revolutionary America. (Rev: SLJ 4/87) [921]

15183 Hort, Lenny. *George Washington* (5–10). Illus. Series: DK Biography. 2005, DK $14.99 (978-0-7566-0832-3); paper $4.99 (978-0-7566-0835-4). 128pp. A heavily illustrated, attractive biography of the man born in Virginia. (Rev: BL 6/1–15/04) [921]

15184 Jurmain, Suzanne Tripp. *George Did It* (2–4). Illus. by Larry Day. 2005, Dutton $16.99 (978-0-525-47560-6). 40pp. George Washington's reluctance to take on the responsibilities of the presidency is depicted in lively text and cartoon drawings. (Rev: BL 12/15/05*; SLJ 12/05*) [921]

15185 McNeese, Tim. *George Washington: America's Leader in War and Peace* (4–8). Series: Leaders of the American Revolution. 2005, Chelsea House LB $30.00 (978-0-7910-8619-3). 140pp. An even-handed introduction to Washington's life and contributions, presented chronologically with occasional factboxes; suitable for report writers. (Rev: SLJ 1/06) [921]

15186 Mara, Wil. *George Washington* (K–4). Illus. 2002, Children's Book Pr. LB $20.50 (978-0-516-22519-7); paper $4.95 (978-0-516-27335-8). 32pp.

A simple account of Washington's life for beginning readers. (Rev: SLJ 1/03) [921]

15187 Miller, Brandon M. *George Washington for Kids: His Life and Times with 21 Activities* (3–6). Illus. 2007, Chicago Review $14.95 (978-1-55652-655-8). 130pp. This absorbing biography offers an unusual amount of information on Washington's personality plus varied activities. (Rev: BL 7/07; SLJ 10/07) [921]

15188 Mosher, Kiki. *Learning About Leadership from the Life of George Washington* (2–5). Illus. Series: A Character Building Book. 1996, Rosen LB $21.25 (978-0-8239-2421-9). 24pp. A brief biography of Washington that emphasizes his leadership qualities. (Rev: BL 10/15/96; SLJ 12/96) [921]

15189 Nettleton, Pamela Hill. *George Washington: Farmer, Soldier, President* (K–3). Illus. by Jeff Yesh. Series: Biographies. 2003, Picture Window LB $25.26 (978-1-4048-0184-4). 24pp. A brightly illustrated profile that is suitable for beginning readers. (Rev: SLJ 4/04) [921]

15190 Old, Wendie. *George Washington* (5–8). Illus. Series: United States Presidents. 1997, Enslow LB $26.60 (978-0-89490-832-3). Washington's personal life and political career are dealt with equally in this thoughtful biography. (Rev: BL 9/15/97; SLJ 12/97) [921]

15191 Ransom, Candice F. *George Washington* (3–4). Series: History Maker Bios. 2002, Lerner LB $26.60 (978-0-8225-0374-3). 48pp. An introductory biography of the man who was chosen to lead the army and then the country during and after the American Revolution. (Rev: BL 6/1–15/02) [921]

15192 Roberts, Jeremy. *George Washington* (5–7). Series: Presidential Leaders. 2003, Lerner LB $29.27 (978-0-8225-0818-2). 112pp. This engaging biography chronicles the life and achievements of America's first president and dispels some widely believed myths. (Rev: SLJ 2/04) [921]

15193 Rockwell, Anne. *Big George: How a Shy Boy Became President Washington* (K–3). Illus. by Matt Phelan. 2009, Houghton $17.00 (978-0-15-216583-3). 48pp. Washington is portrayed as a studious, shy boy with a respect for honor who becomes a soldier because he feels it is his duty; his bravery and leadership led to his role as the first president. (Rev: BCCB 2/09; BL 1/1–15/09; HB 3/09; SLJ 2/09) [921]

15194 St. George, Judith. *Take The Lead George Washington* (2–4). Illus. by Daniel Powers. Series: Turning Points. 2005, Penguin $16.99 (978-0-399-23887-1). 48pp. Washington's first job — as a surveyor, at the age of 16 — is the turning point in this picture-book profile of his transition from childhood to adult. (Rev: BL 12/1/04; SLJ 1/05) [921]

15195 Thomas, Peggy. *Farmer George Plants a Nation* (3–5). Illus. by Layne Johnson. 2008, Boyds Mills $17.95 (978-1-59078-460-0). 32pp. Thomas looks at George Washington's role as a farmer and how his efforts in this area paralleled his work for the new nation. (Rev: BL 2/15/08; LMC 3/08; SLJ 3/08) [921]

WILSON, WOODROW

15196 Collins, David R. *Woodrow Wilson: 28th President of the United States* (5–8). Illus. 1989, Garrett LB $21.27 (978-0-944483-18-3). 121pp. A compact biography of a Nobel Peace Prize–winning president. (Rev: BL 5/1/89; SLJ 8/89) [921]

15197 Randolph, Sallie. *Woodrow Wilson, President* (5–9). Series: Presidential Biography. 1992, Walker LB $15.85 (978-0-8027-8144-4). Offers a concise overview of Wilson's tragic personal and political struggles, his achievements, and his place in history. (Rev: BL 12/15/91; SLJ 3/92) [921]

15198 Schraff, Anne. *Woodrow Wilson* (5–8). Series: United States Presidents. 1998, Enslow LB $26.60 (978-0-89490-936-8). 112pp. The story of the brilliant 28th president, his initial opposition to entering World War I, the defeat of his proposals concerning the League of Nations, and the stroke he suffered. (Rev: SLJ 9/98) [921]

WILSON, WOODROW AND EDITH

15199 Ashby, Ruth. *Woodrow and Edith Wilson* (5–8). Illus. Series: Presidents and First Ladies. 2005, Gareth Stevens LB $31.00 (978-0-8368-5759-7). 48pp. An accessible, balanced, and attractive discussion of the Wilsons and the contributions each made to their joint lives. (Rev: BL 3/1/05; SLJ 8/05) [921]

First Ladies and Other Women

ADAMS, ABIGAIL

15200 Ching, Jacqueline. *Abigail Adams: A Revolutionary Woman* (4–7). Series: Library of American Lives and Times. 2001, Rosen $34.60 (978-0-8239-5723-1). 112pp. This biography of Abigail Adams stresses the fact that her husband, John Adams, relied heavily on her advice and that her vision of equality and justice inspired the early consideration of women's rights. (Rev: BCCB 4/01; BL 10/15/01) [921]

15201 Ferris, Jeri Chase. *Remember the Ladies: A Story About Abigail Adams* (3–5). Illus. by Ellen Beier. Series: Creative Minds Biographies. 2000, Carolrhoda LB $22.60 (978-1-57505-292-2). 64pp. A biography of this early first lady that relies heavily on original sources including the writings of Abigail Adams. (Rev: HBG 3/01; SLJ 1/01) [921]

15202 McCarthy, Pat. *Abigail Adams: First Lady and Patriot* (5–8). Series: Historical American Biographies. 2002, Enslow LB $26.60 (978-0-7660-1618-7). The life story of the prolific letter-writer who was wife of the second president of the United States, John Adams. (Rev: BCCB 4/01; BL 4/1/02; HBG 10/02; SLJ 7/02) [921]

15203 Wallner, Alexandra. *Abigail Adams* (K–3). Illus. 2001, Holiday House $16.95 (978-0-8234-1442-0). 32pp. A picture-book biography that examines the life of Abigail Adams, the wife of a president, the mother of another, and a champion of women's rights. (Rev: BL 3/15/01; HB 7/01; HBG 10/01) [921]

ADDAMS, JANE

15204 Armentrout, David, and Patricia Armentrout. *Jane Addams* (2–4). Series: Discover Someone Who Made a Difference. 2001, Rourke LB $14.95 (978-1-58952-054-7). A beginning biography of the famous American social worker who won a Nobel Peace Prize. (Rev: BL 1/1–15/02; SLJ 3/02) [921]

15205 Caravantes, Peggy. *Waging Peace: The Story of Jane Addams* (5–8). 2004, Morgan Reynolds LB $23.95 (978-1-931798-40-2). 144pp. Covers Addams's life and achievements, with good material on her youth and the lessons she learned from her Quaker father. (Rev: SLJ 2/05) [921]

15206 Harvey, Bonnie Carman. *Jane Addams: Nobel Prize Winner and Founder of Hull House* (5–8). Illus. Series: Historic American Biographies. 1999, Enslow LB $26.60 (978-0-7660-1094-9). 128pp. This biography of the Nobel Peace Prize winner and founder of Hull House traces her life and her outstanding achievements as a social worker. (Rev: BL 11/1/99; HBG 3/00; SLJ 11/99) [921]

15207 McPherson, Stephanie S. *Peace and Bread: The Story of Jane Addams* (5–8). 1993, Carolrhoda LB $27.93 (978-0-87614-792-4). An introduction to Jane Addams's work among the poor of Chicago and her leadership in international organizations on behalf of world peace. (Rev: BL 1/15/94; SLJ 2/94) [921]

ANTHONY, SUSAN B.

15208 Hopkinson, Deborah. *Susan B. Anthony: Fighter for Women's Rights* (2–4). Illus. by Amy Bates. Series: Ready to Read: Stories of America. 2005, Simon & Schuster paper $3.99 (978-0-689-86909-9). 32pp. This brief biography focuses on Anthony's lifelong fight for women's rights. (Rev: BL 2/1/06; SLJ 5/06) [305.42]

15209 Klingel, Cynthia, and Robert B. Noyed. *Susan B. Anthony: Reformer* (3–6). Illus. 2002, Child's World LB $27.07 (978-1-56766-171-2). 32pp. An attractive, brief introduction to the life of Susan B. Anthony. (Rev: BL 1/1–15/03) [305.42]

15210 Levin, Pamela. *Susan B. Anthony: Fighter for Women's Rights* (3–5). Illus. Series: Junior World Biographies. 1993, Chelsea LB $28.00 (978-0-7910-1762-3). 79pp. An informative, interesting biography of the great fighter for social causes, including women's right to vote. (Rev: SLJ 10/93) [921]

15211 McLeese, Don. *Susan B. Anthony* (2–5). Series: Equal Rights Leaders. 2002, Rourke LB $20.64 (978-1-58952-284-8). 24pp. Simple text and well-chosen illustrations tell the story of Anthony's life, with good coverage of her youth and education. (Rev: SLJ 1/03) [324.6]

15212 Mosher, Kiki. *Learning About Fairness from the Life of Susan B. Anthony* (2–5). Illus. Series: A Character Building Book. 1996, Rosen LB $18.75 (978-0-8239-2422-6). 24pp. The spirit of fairness

and justice is shown in the life of this leader for women's rights. (Rev: BL 10/15/96; SLJ 12/96) [921]

15213 Orr, Tamra. *The Life and Times of Susan B. Anthony* (5–8). Illus. Series: Profiles in American History. 2007, Mitchell Lane LB $19.95 (978-1-58415-445-7). 48pp. This biography of Anthony traces her life and work in the women's rights movement and contains supplemental facts that will interest readers. (Rev: SLJ 7/07) [921]

15214 Parker, Barbara Keevil. *Susan B. Anthony: Daring to Vote* (4–6). Illus. Series: Gateway Biographies. 1998, Millbrook LB $20.90 (978-0-7613-0358-9). 48pp. This interesting biography of this early abolitionist and fighter in the suffrage movement also contains brief biographies of other early feminists. (Rev: BL 6/1–15/98; HBG 10/98; SLJ 7/98) [921]

15215 Roop, Peter, and Connie Roop. *Susan B. Anthony* (2–3). Series: Lives and Times. 1997, Heinemann $19.92 (978-1-57572-563-5). 24pp. A simple picture-book biography that gives a short introduction to the life and times of this fighter for women's rights. (Rev: BL 3/15/98) [921]

15216 Slade, Suzanne. *Susan B. Anthony: Fighter for Freedom and Equality* (2–4). Illus. by Craig Orback. 2007, Picture Window $17.95 (978-1-4048-3104-9). 24pp. An age-appropriate profile that covers Anthony's life from childhood. (Rev: BL 6/1–15/07; SLJ 8/07) [921]

15217 Weidt, Maryann N. *Fighting for Equal Rights: A Story About Susan B. Anthony* (3–5). Illus. by Amanda Sartor. Series: Creative Minds Biographies. 2003, Carolrhoda LB $22.60 (978-1-57505-181-9). 64pp. A straightforward account of the life of the women's rights campaigner, starting with her childhood and schooling, and of the time in which she lived. (Rev: HBG 4/04; SLJ 3/04) [921]

BANNAKY, MOLLY

15218 McGill, Alice. *Molly Bannaky* (PS–4). Illus. by Chris K. Soentpiet. 1999, Houghton $17.00 (978-0-395-72287-9). 32pp. This is the amazing story of white colonialist Molly Bannaky, who dared to buy and marry a slave and eventually became the grandmother of Benjamin Banneker, the famous African American astronomer and mathematician. (Rev: BCCB 10/99; BL 9/15/99; HBG 3/00; SLJ 10/99) [921]

BARTON, CLARA

15219 Dubowski, Cathy E. *Clara Barton: I Want to Help!* (3–5). Illus. Series: Defining Moments. 2005, Bearport LB $25.27 (978-1-59716-075-9). 32pp. This inspiring biography of Clara Barton tells how she overcame her shyness to nurse the wounded on bloody Civil War battlefields and later established the American Red Cross. (Rev: BL 10/15/05; SLJ 2/06) [921]

15220 Francis, Dorothy. *Clara Barton: Founder of the American Red Cross* (4–6). Series: Gateway Greens. 2002, Millbrook LB $23.90 (978-0-7613-

2621-2). 48pp. The story of the Red Cross founder who obtained and distributed supplies for the wounded during the Civil War. (Rev: BL 7/02; HBG 3/03) [921]

15221 Hamilton, Leni. *Clara Barton* (5–10). Illus. 1987, Chelsea LB $19.95 (978-1-55546-641-1). The story of the Civil War nurse and how she prepared for the founding of the American Red Cross. (Rev: BL 11/1/87) [921]

15222 Koestler-Grack, Rachel A. *The Story of Clara Barton* (4–7). Illus. Series: Breakthrough Biographies. 2004, Chelsea House LB $23.00 (978-0-7910-7312-4). 32pp. From her childhood and early career to her founding of the American Red Cross, this profile gives personal details and historical context. (Rev: BL 3/1/04; SLJ 9/04) [361.763]

15223 Rose, Mary Catherine. *Clara Barton: Soldier of Mercy* (3–5). Illus. 1991, Chelsea LB $12.95 (978-0-7910-1403-5). A simply written account of this courageous nurse who founded the Red Cross.

15224 Somervill, Barbara. *Clara Barton: Founder of the American Red Cross* (5–8). Illus. Series: Signature Lives: Civil War Era. 2007, Compass Point LB $23.95 (978-0-7565-1888-2). 112pp. Chronicles the life of Clara Barton and provides information on the time in which she worked. (Rev: BL 6/1–15/07) [921]

15225 Whitelaw, Nancy. *Clara Barton: Civil War Nurse* (5–9). Series: Historical American Biographies. 1997, Enslow LB $26.60 (978-0-89490-778-4). Using material from her diaries and published books, this biography relates Barton's life story and amazing accomplishments. (Rev: BL 3/15/98; SLJ 2/98) [921]

BRIDGMAN, LAURA DEWEY

15226 Alexander, Sally Hobart, and Robert Alexander. *She Touched the World: Laura Bridgman, Deaf-Blind Pioneer* (5–8). Illus. 2008, Clarion $18.00 (978-0-618-85299-4). 96pp. A little-known pioneer in the education of the deaf-blind, Bridgman (two generations older than Helen Keller) is an important figure, and this book ably introduces her to young readers. (Rev: BL 3/1/08; SLJ 3/08) [921]

15227 Hunter, Edith Fisher. *Child of the Silent Night* (3–5). Illus. 1963, Houghton $16.00 (978-0-395-06835-9). 128pp. The story of a blind-deaf child who paved the way for the successes of Helen Keller.

BUSH, LAURA WELCH

15228 Gormley, Beatrice. *Laura Bush: America's First Lady* (5–8). Illus. 2003, Simon & Schuster paper $4.99 (978-0-689-85366-1). 112pp. A chronological account of Laura Bush's life, with information on her childhood as well as her later public life. (Rev: BL 3/1/03; HBG 10/03; SLJ 5/03) [973.931]

15229 Stone, Tanya L. *Laura Welch Bush* (4–6). Illus. 2001, Millbrook LB $23.90 (978-0-7613-2304-4). 48pp. A biography of President George W. Bush's wife, with photographs and "fun facts." (Rev: BL 9/15/01; HBG 3/02; SLJ 9/01) [973.931]

CATT, CARRIE CHAPMAN

15230 Somervill, Barbara. *Votes for Women! The Story of Carrie Chapman Catt* (5–8). Illus. 2002, Morgan Reynolds LB $23.95 (978-1-883846-96-1). 128pp. This is the story of Carrie Chapman Catt, who devoted her early life to the quest for women's right to vote and later turned her energies to helping Jewish refugees. (Rev: BL 11/15/02; HBG 3/03; SLJ 1/03; VOYA 2/03) [324.6]

CHILD, LYDIA MARIA

15231 Stux, Erica. *Writing for Freedom: A Story About Lydia Maria Child* (3–5). Illus. Series: Creative Minds Biographies. 2000, Carolrhoda $22.60 (978-1-57505-439-1). A biography of the poet who was also an abolitionist and courageously fought against slavery. (Rev: HBG 10/01; SLJ 1/01) [921]

CLINTON, HILLARY RODHAM

15232 Guernsey, JoAnn B. *Hillary Rodham Clinton* (5–8). Illus. 2005, Lerner LB $29.27 (978-0-8225-2372-7); paper $7.95 (978-0-8225-9613-4). 112pp. Traces Clinton's life from childhood, and covers the trials of her husband's second term in office in some detail. (Rev: BL 6/1–15/05; SLJ 7/05) [921]

15233 Levert, Suzanne. *Hillary Rodham Clinton: First Lady* (3–5). Illus. Series: Gateway Biographies. 1994, Millbrook paper $8.95 (978-1-56294-726-2). 48pp. A biography of the First Lady that ends in 1993. (Rev: BL 7/94) [921]

15234 Wells, Catherine. *Hillary Clinton* (5–8). Illus. Series: Political Profiles. 2007, Morgan Reynolds LB $27.95 (978-1-59935-047-9). 144pp. Readers will learn of the former First Lady and presidential hopeful's life and achievements from this positive portrait. (Rev: BL 11/15/07) [921]

CRANDALL, PRUDENCE

15235 Jurmain, Suzanne. *The Forbidden Schoolhouse: The True and Dramatic Story of Prudence Crandall and Her Students* (5–8). Illus. 2005, Houghton $19.00 (978-0-618-47302-1). 160pp. The inspiring story of Prudence Crandall, who in the 1830s risked ostracism — and worse — from the townspeople of Canterbury, Connecticut, when she opens her academy to young African American women. (Rev: BCCB 11/05; BL 10/1/05*; HB 11/05; HBG 4/06; LMC 8/05; SLJ 11/05) [370]

15236 Lucas, Eileen. *Prudence Crandall: Teacher for Equal Rights* (1–3). Illus. by Kimanne Smith. 2001, Carolrhoda LB $21.27 (978-1-57505-480-3). 48pp. A biography for beginning readers of Crandall, a Quaker teacher who struggled to run a school for African American students in the 1830s. (Rev: HBG 3/02; SLJ 1/02) [921]

DAY, DOROTHY

15237 Shaw, Maura D. *Dorothy Day: A Catholic Life of Action* (3–6). Illus. by Stephen Marchesi. Series: Spiritual Biographies for Young Readers. 2004,

SkyLight Paths $12.99 (978-1-59473-011-5). 32pp. Roman Catholic journalist/social activist Dorothy Day worked to help the homeless and hungry. (Rev: BL 10/1/04) [921]

DIX, DOROTHEA

15238 Herstek, Amy Paulson. *Dorothea Dix* (5–8). Series: Historical American Biographies. 2001, Enslow LB $26.60 (978-0-7660-1258-5). The life of this militant reformer who fought for more humane treatment of the insane. (Rev: BL 1/1–15/02; HBG 3/02; SLJ 1/02) [921]

DOLE, ELIZABETH

15239 Lucas, Eileen. *Elizabeth Dole: A Leader in Washington* (4–6). Illus. Series: Gateway Biographies. 1998, Millbrook LB $23.90 (978-0-7613-0203-2). 48pp. This book takes the reader from Elizabeth Dole's childhood in North Carolina through her career in government and public service. (Rev: BL 6/1–15/98; HBG 10/98; SLJ 6/98) [921]

EDMONDS, EMMA

15240 Reit, Seymour. *Behind Rebel Lines: The Incredible Story of Emma Edmonds, Civil War Spy* (5–8). 1988, Harcourt $12.95 (978-0-15-200416-3); paper $6.00 (978-0-15-200424-8). 144pp. The remarkable Canadian-born spy who helped to defend the Union in the Civil War. (Rev: BL 3/1/88; SLJ 3/88) [973.785]

FEINSTEIN, DIANNE

15241 McElroy, Lisa. *Meet My Grandmother: She's a United States Senator* (2–4). Series: Grandmothers at Work. 2000, Millbrook LB $22.90 (978-0-7613-1721-0). 32pp. Dianne Feinstein, once mayor of San Francisco and now a U.S. senator, as seen through the eyes of her 6-year-old granddaughter. (Rev: BL 3/15/00; HBG 10/00; SLJ 1/01) [921]

GORE, TIPPER

15242 Guernsey, JoAnn B. *Tipper Gore: Voice for the Voiceless* (4–6). Illus. 1994, Lerner LB $21.27 (978-0-8225-2876-0); paper $6.95 (978-0-8225-9651-6). 64pp. This biography of the vice president's wife reveals her to be an independent, determined woman who champions a number of worthy causes. (Rev: BL 9/15/94; SLJ 7/94) [921]

GRAHAM, KATHARINE

15243 Mattern, Joanne. *Katharine Graham and 20th Century American Journalism* (1–4). Series: Women Who Shaped History. 2003, Rosen LB $19.95 (978-0-8239-6500-7). 24pp. The story of the woman who ran the *Washington Post* after her husband's death and who helped uncover the Watergate scandal. (Rev: BL 2/15/03; SLJ 5/03) [921]

GRIMKE, SARAH AND ANGELINA

15244 McPherson, Stephanie S. *Sisters Against Slavery: A Story About Sarah and Angelina Grimke* (4–7). Illus. by Karen Ritz. Series: Creative Minds Biographies. 1999, Carolrhoda LB $21.27 (978-1-57505-361-5). 64pp. The story of the remarkable Grimke sisters from South Carolina who fought against slavery and later became suffragettes. (Rev: BCCB 1/00; HBG 3/00; SLJ 12/99) [921]

HOOVER, LOU

15245 Colbert, Nancy A. *Lou Hoover: The Duty to Serve* (5–8). Illus. 1997, Morgan Reynolds LB $21.95 (978-1-883846-22-0). President Hoover's wife was a most interesting person, who, among other accomplishments, was the first woman to get a degree in geology in this country, was the translator — with her husband — of a 16th-century Latin mining text, was an advocate of physical education for women, and was fluent in seven languages, including Chinese. (Rev: BL 2/15/98; HBG 3/98; SLJ 3/98) [973.91]

HUTCHINSON, ANNE

15246 Ilgenfritz, Elizabeth. *Anne Hutchinson* (5–8). Illus. Series: American Women of Achievement. 1990, Chelsea LB $19.95 (978-1-55546-660-2). 111pp. The story of the woman in pre-Revolutionary days who stood trial to defend religious liberty. (Rev: SLJ 4/91) [921]

15247 Mangal, Melina. *Anne Hutchinson: Religious Reformer* (4–6). Series: Let Freedom Ring. 2004, Capstone LB $23.93 (978-0-7368-2454-5). 48pp. Hutchinson was a religious liberal whose outspoken opinions resulted in her banishment from the Massachusetts Bay Colony; she later helped to found the colony of Rhode Island. (Rev: SLJ 8/04) [921]

INGLES, MARY DRAPER

15248 Furbee, Mary Rodd. *Shawnee Captive: The Story of Mary Draper Ingles* (5–8). Illus. 2001, Morgan Reynolds LB $23.95 (978-1-883846-69-5). 112pp. The tragic and exciting story of a pioneer woman captured by Shawnee Indians, her daring escape, and her long and difficult journey home. (Rev: BL 5/15/01; HBG 10/01; SLJ 6/01) [975.5]

JOHNSON, LADY BIRD

15249 Appelt, Kathi. *Miss Lady Bird's Wildflowers: How a First Lady Changed America* (1–3). Illus. by Joy Fisher Hein. 2005, HarperCollins LB $17.89 (978-0-06-001108-6). 40pp. Lady Bird Johnson's lifelong passion for flowers and her campaign as First Lady to beautify the nation's highways and cities by planting wildflowers are at the center of this volume. (Rev: BL 2/15/05) [973.923]

KELLER, HELEN

15250 Adler, David A. *Helen Keller* (1–2). Illus. by John C. Wallner. Series: Holiday House Reader.

2003, Holiday House $14.95 (978-0-8234-1606-6). 32pp. Written in simple language that is well suited for early readers, this biography covers Keller's youth and her work as an adult. (Rev: BL 7/03; HBG 4/04; SLJ 11/03) [921]

15251 Adler, David A. *A Picture Book of Helen Keller* (2–4). Illus. by John Wallner and Alexandra Wallner. Series: Picture Book Biographies. 1990, Holiday House LB $16.95 (978-0-8234-0818-4); paper $6.95 (978-0-8234-0950-1). 32pp. This account focuses on Keller's personality, stamina, and accomplishments. (Rev: BL 12/15/90; SLJ 11/90) [921]

15252 Garrett, Leslie. *Helen Keller: Biography* (5–10). Series: DK Biography. 2004, DK paper $5.99 (978-0-7566-0339-7). 128pp. Keller's struggles to conquer her physical disabilities and her worldwide recognition as a political activist and public speaker are covered in the usual rich DK format. (Rev: BL 6/1–15/04) [921]

15253 Graff, Stewart, and Polly Graff. *Helen Keller: Toward the Light* (3–5). Illus. 1992, Chelsea LB $28.00 (978-0-7910-1412-7). 80pp. A simply written biography of the woman who overcame the handicaps of blindness and deafness.

15254 Kent, Deborah. *Helen Keller: Author and Advocate for the Disabled* (3–6). Series: Our People. 2003, Child's World LB $27.07 (978-1-59296-005-7). 32pp. Report writers will find solid material in this biography that includes "Interesting Facts" sidebars. (Rev: BL 1/1–15/04; SLJ 4/04) [921]

15255 Lakin, Patricia. *Helen Keller and the Big Storm* (1–2). Illus. by Diana Magnuson. Series: Childhood of Famous Americans. 2002, Simon & Schuster paper $3.99 (978-0-689-84104-0). 30pp. An anecdote about her teacher rescuing Helen when she is caught in a tree during a storm serves to introduce beginning readers to Helen's character and problems. (Rev: HBG 10/02; SLJ 7/02) [921]

15256 Lawlor, Laurie. *Helen Keller: Rebellious Spirit* (4–8). Illus. 2001, Holiday $22.95 (978-0-8234-1588-5). 161pp. This account puts Keller's life in the context of her time and looks at the opinions and beliefs that made her a "rebellious spirit," with photographs, quotations, a bibliography, and the manual alphabet. (Rev: BL 9/1/01; HB 9/01; HBG 3/02; SLJ 9/01*; VOYA 2/02) [362.4]

15257 MacLeod, Elizabeth. *Helen Keller: A Determined Life* (3–5). Illus. Series: Snapshots: Images of People and Places in History. 2004, Kids Can $14.95 (978-1-55337-508-1). 32pp. Attractive double-page spreads with well-positioned and interesting text make this profile inviting for browsers. (Rev: BL 3/1/04; SLJ 5/04) [921]

15258 Shichtman, Sandra H. *Helen Keller: Out of a Dark and Silent World* (4–6). Series: Gateway Greens. 2002, Millbrook LB $23.90 (978-0-7613-2550-5). 48pp. The inspiring story of the woman who overcame multiple handicaps to become a role model for others. (Rev: BL 7/02; HBG 3/03) [921]

15259 Sullivan, George. *Helen Keller* (3–5). Illus. 2001, Scholastic $12.95 (978-0-439-14751-4); paper $4.50 (978-0-439-59555-1). 128pp. Using

excerpts from her biographical works, the author presents an interesting picture of Keller, her problems, and her life. (Rev: BL 4/1/01; HBG 10/01) [921]

15260 Sullivan, George. *Helen Keller: Her Life in Pictures* (4–6). Illus. 2007, Scholastic $17.99 (978-0-439-91815-2). 80pp. This photo-biography spans the life of Keller from infancy to her 80s with black-and-white photographs, simbraille (a print representation of braille characters), and informative back matter. (Rev: BCCB 12/07; BL 11/15/07; LMC 5/08; SLJ 3/08) [921]

15261 Sutcliffe, Jane. *Helen Keller* (2–4). Illus. by Elaine Verstraete. Series: On My Own Biography. 2002, Carolrhoda LB $23.93 (978-0-87614-600-2); paper $5.95 (978-0-87614-903-4). 48pp. For beginning readers, this is an appealing introduction to Keller's life. (Rev: HBG 3/03; SLJ 12/02) [921]

KELLEY, FLORENCE

15262 Saller, Carol. *Florence Kelley* (2–4). Illus. by Ken Green. Series: On My Own Biography. 1997, Carolrhoda LB $19.93 (978-1-57505-016-4). 48pp. The story of the labor leader and her fight against child labor. (Rev: BCCB 7–8/97; BL 6/1–15/97; SLJ 11/97) [921]

LINCOLN, MARY TODD

15263 Hull, Mary. *Mary Todd Lincoln* (5–8). Series: Historical American Biographies. 2000, Enslow LB $26.60 (978-0-7660-1252-3). This biography faithfully records the tragic life of Lincoln's widow, whose emotional health declined after the deaths of her son and her husband. (Rev: BL 1/1–15/00; HBG 10/00; SLJ 5/00) [921]

LOCKWOOD, BELVA

15264 Bardhan-Quallen, Sudipta. *Ballots for Belva: The True Story of a Woman's Race for the Presidency* (1–3). Illus. by Courtney A. Martin. 2008, Abrams $16.95 (978-0-8109-7110-3). 32pp. Belva Lockwood was the first woman lawyer to appear before the Supreme Court, and ran for president in 1884. (Rev: BL 11/15/08; LMC 5/09; SLJ 9/08) [921]

15265 Norgren, Jill. *Belva Lockwood: Equal Rights Pioneer* (5–8). Illus. Series: Trailblazer Biographies. 2008, Twenty-First Century $31.93 (978-0-8225-9068-2). 112pp. Norgren introduces the 19th-century woman who worked for the rights of Native Americans and for equal voting rights for all. (Rev: BL 1/1–15/09; SLJ 11/08) [340.092]

LONGWORTH, ALICE ROOSEVELT

15266 Kerley, Barbara. *What to Do About Alice? How Alice Roosevelt Broke the Rules, Charmed the World, and Drove Her Father Teddy Crazy!* (K–3). Illus. by Edwin Fotheringham. 2008, Scholastic $16.99 (978-0-439-92231-9). 48pp. An entertaining biography of the very original and lively Alice Roosevelt, daughter of president Theodore, with engaging digital art. (Rev: BL 1/1–15/08; SLJ 3/08) [973.9092]

LYON, MARY

15267 Rosen, Dorothy S. *A Fire in Her Bones: The Story of Mary Lyon* (5–7). Illus. 1995, Carolrhoda LB $30.35 (978-0-87614-840-2). 88pp. A biography of the woman who defied social barriers and founded Mount Holyoke Female Seminary, now known as Mount Holyoke College. (Rev: BL 6/1–15/95; SLJ 4/95) [921]

MADISON, DOLLEY

15268 Brown, Don. *Dolley Madison Saves George Washington* (1–3). Illus. by author. 2007, Houghton $16.00 (978-0-618-41199-3). 32pp. A lively biography of Dolley Madison, farm girl turned first lady, who saved George Washington's portrait in 1814 when the British attacked the White House. (Rev: BCCB 11/07; BL 9/1/07; SLJ 9/07) [921]

15269 Klingel, Cynthia, and Robert B. Noyed. *Dolley Madison: First Lady* (2–4). Illus. Series: Spirit of America: Our People. 2002, Child's World LB $27.07 (978-1-56766-170-5). 32pp. A solid introduction to the life of Dolley Madison and her skill as a hostess. (Rev: SLJ 1/03) [921]

15270 Patrick, Jean L. S. *Dolley Madison* (3–4). Illus. Series: History Maker Bios. 2002, Lerner LB $26.60 (978-0-8225-0194-7). 48pp. Using both cartoons and regular illustrations, this is a biography of the brave and gracious first lady who became a famous hostess. (Rev: BL 6/1–15/02; HBG 3/03) [921]

15271 Pflueger, Lynda. *Dolley Madison: Courageous First Lady* (5–8). Series: Historical American Biographies. 1999, Enslow LB $26.60 (978-0-7660-1092-5). An interesting biography of the woman who defined the role of First Lady and who was known for her political acumen and diplomatic and social skills as well as her patriotism and her ability to inspire others. (Rev: SLJ 1/99) [921]

15272 Weatherly, Myra. *Dolley Madison: America's First Lady* (5–8). Illus. Series: Founders of the Republic. 2002, Morgan Reynolds LB $23.95 (978-1-883846-95-4). 128pp. This portrait of Dolley Madison conveys her popularity and courage, with reproductions of period paintings, prints, and maps. (Rev: BL 11/1/02; HBG 3/03; SLJ 3/03) [973.5]

MORRIS, ESTHER

15273 White, Linda Arms. *I Could Do That! Esther Morris Gets Women the Vote* (2–4). Illus. by Nancy Carpenter. 2005, Farrar $16.00 (978-0-374-33527-4). 40pp. The story of Esther Morris, the little-known suffragist who led a successful campaign to win the vote for women in the Wyoming Territory. (Rev: BL 9/15/05*; SLJ 9/05) [324.6]

NATION, CARRY A.

15274 Harvey, Bonnie Carman. *Carry A. Nation: Saloon Smasher and Prohibitionist* (5–8). Series:

Historical American Biographies. 2002, Enslow LB $26.60 (978-0-7660-1907-2). 128pp. A lively and balanced biography of the prohibitionist who fought alcohol with violence. (Rev: HBG 3/03; SLJ 1/03) [921]

OBAMA, MICHELLE

15275 Brophy, David Bergen. *Michelle Obama: Meet the First Lady* (4–8). 2008, Collins $16.99 (978-0-06-177991-6); HarperCollins paper $6.99 (978-0-06-177990-9). 128pp. A chronological look at Obama's life from childhood, incorporating many quotations but few photographs. (Rev: BL 3/1/09) [328]

15276 Colbert, David. *Michelle Obama: An American Story* (5–8). Illus. 2009, Houghton $16.00 (978-0-547-24941-4); paper $6.99 (978-0-547-24770-0). 160pp. This profile looks mainly at Obama's ancestry and her childhood and early married life. (Rev: BL 3/1/09) [921]

15277 Wheeler, Jill C. *Michelle Obama* (2–4). Illus. 2009, ABDO LB $24.21 (978-1-60453-633-1). 32pp. This introduction to the first lady highlights her childhood and early adult years. (Rev: BL 6/1–15/09) [973.932092]

OBAMA, SASHA

15278 Snyder, Gail. *Sasha* (3–5). Illus. 2009, Mason Crest LB $19.95 (978-1-4222-1480-0). 64pp. A biography of Sasha Obama, the daughter of the president, laced with political background. (Rev: BL 6/1–15/09; SLJ 7/09) [973.932092]

O'CONNOR, SANDRA DAY

15279 McElroy, Lisa. *Meet My Grandmother: She's a Supreme Court Justice* (2–4). Illus. Series: Grandmothers at Work. 1999, Millbrook LB $22.90 (978-0-7613-1566-7). 32pp. An affectionate portrait of a woman who is both a Supreme Court justice and a beloved grandmother. (Rev: BL 1/1–15/00; HBG 3/00; SLJ 12/99) [921]

15280 McElroy, Lisa. *Sandra Day O'Connor: Supreme Court Justice* (4–6). Series: Gateway Biographies. 2003, Millbrook LB $23.90 (978-0-7613-2502-4). 48pp. Published before O'Connor announced her plans to retire, this biography chronicles her life and legal career in concise, lively text with many photographs and quotations. (Rev: HBG 4/04; SLJ 1/04) [921]

15281 O'Connor, Sandra Day. *Chico: A True Story from the Childhood of the First Woman Supreme Court Justice* (1–3). Illus. by Dan Andreasen. 2005, Dutton $16.99 (978-0-525-47452-4). 32pp. Former Supreme Court justice O'Connor gives a good sense of her youth in Arizona in this story about coming across a rattlesnake when riding on her horse Chico as a 6-year-old. (Rev: BL 10/1/05; SLJ 9/05) [921]

15282 Williams, Jean Kinney. *Sandra Day O'Connor: Lawyer and Supreme Court Justice* (4–6). Series: Ferguson Career Biographies. 2001, Ferguson LB $25.00 (978-0-89434-355-1). 127pp. The story of O'Connor's life from childhood plus information on the confirmation process for Supreme Court appointees and on how to become a lawyer or judge. (Rev: SLJ 5/01) [921]

PELOSI, NANCY

15283 Shichtman, Sandra H. *Nancy Pelosi* (5–8). Series: Political Profiles. 2007, Morgan Reynolds LB $27.95 (978-1-59935-049-3). 112pp. An admiring portrait of this important political figure, with photographs. (Rev: BL 11/15/07; SLJ 1/08) [328.7]

RANKIN, JEANNETTE

15284 Marx, Trish. *Jeannette Rankin: First Lady of Congress* (3–5). Illus. by Dan Andreasen. 2006, Simon & Schuster $18.95 (978-0-689-86290-8). 48pp. This biography uses clear and simple text to chronicle the life and times of the first woman elected to the U.S. House of Representatives. (Rev: BL 1/1–15/06; SLJ 2/06) [921]

RICE, CONDOLEEZZA

15285 Cunningham, Kevin. *Condoleezza Rice* (2–4). Illus. Series: Journey to Freedom. 2009, Child's World LB $28.50 (978-1-60253-120-8). 32pp. Cunningham looks at Rice's life and accomplishments in the areas of music, education, and politics. (Rev: BL 3/15/09) [921]

15286 Ditchfield, Christin. *Condoleezza Rice: America's Leading Stateswoman*. Rev. ed. (5–8). Series: Great Life Stories. 2006, Watts LB $30.50 (978-0-531-13874-8). 111pp. An updated version of the 2003 biography, adding information on Rice's role as secretary of state and the continuing events in Iraq. (Rev: SLJ 2/07) [921]

15287 Ryan, Bernard. *Condoleezza Rice: National Security Advisor and Musician* (5–8). 2003, Ferguson LB $25.00 (978-0-8160-5480-0). 155pp. Rice's life and career are detailed, up to the invasion of Iraq. (Rev: SLJ 5/04) [921]

15288 Wade, Mary Dodson. *Condoleezza Rice: Being the Best* (4–7). Illus. 2003, Millbrook LB $23.90 (978-0-7613-2619-9). 48pp. An interesting profile with a focus on Rice's talented youth and southern upbringing. (Rev: BL 3/1/03; HBG 10/03; SLJ 4/03) [355]

ROOSEVELT, ELEANOR

15289 Adler, David A. *A Picture Book of Eleanor Roosevelt* (K–3). Illus. by Robert Casilla. Series: Picture Book Biographies. 1991, Holiday House LB $16.95 (978-0-8234-0856-6). 32pp. The life of this well-known First Lady is described in simple text and many illustrations. (Rev: BCCB 4/91; BL 6/1/91; SLJ 5/91) [921]

15290 Brown, Jonatha A. *Eleanor Roosevelt* (2–4). Illus. Series: People We Should Know. 2005, Gareth Stevens LB $21.00 (978-0-8368-4468-9). 24pp. For beginning readers, a simple explanation of Eleanor Roosevelt's importance with an attrac-

tive layout and historical and contemporary photographs. [921]

15291 Cooney, Barbara. *Eleanor* (K–3). Illus. 1996, Viking $15.99 (978-0-670-86159-0). 40pp. A picture-book biography that supplies details on Eleanor Roosevelt's life, particularly her lonely childhood. (Rev: BCCB 11/96; BL 9/15/96*; HB 9/96; SLJ 9/96*) [921]

15292 Feinberg, Barbara S. *Eleanor Roosevelt: A Very Special Lady* (3–5). Illus. Series: Gateway. 2003, Millbrook LB $23.90 (978-0-7613-2623-6). 48pp. A biography of the First Lady, with photographs, a timeline, and a list of relevant Web sites. (Rev: BL 2/1/03; HBG 10/03; SLJ 4/03) [973.917]

15293 Freedman, Russell. *Eleanor Roosevelt: A Life of Discovery* (5–9). 1993, Clarion $17.95 (978-0-89919-862-0). This admiring photobiography captures Roosevelt's public role and personal sadness. (Rev: BL 7/93*; SLJ 8/93*; VOYA 2/94) [921]

15294 Jacobson, Ryan. *Eleanor Roosevelt: First Lady of the World* (2–6). Illus. by Gordon Purcell and Barbara Schulz. Series: Graphic Library, Graphic Biographies. 2005, Capstone LB $26.60 (978-0-7368-4969-2). 32pp. This graphic-novel biography introduces Roosevelt's life and discusses her active support of her husband's domestic programs and her increased involvement in foreign affairs after her husband's death. (Rev: SLJ 3/06) [921]

15295 Jones, Victoria Garrett. *Eleanor Roosevelt: A Courageous Spirit* (5–8). Series: Sterling Biographies. 2007, Sterling $12.95 (978-1-4027-4746-5); paper $5.95 (978-1-4027-3371-0). 124pp. This well-illustrated profile covers Eleanor Roosevelt's life from childhood and discusses her contributions as First Lady, a position she transformed. (Rev: SLJ 5/07) [921]

15296 Koestler-Grack, Rachel A. *The Story of Eleanor Roosevelt* (4–7). Illus. Series: Breakthrough Biographies. 2004, Chelsea House LB $23.00 (978-0-7910-7313-1). 32pp. This brief biography covers Roosevelt's early years as well as her later contributions to her country and to the world. (Rev: BL 3/1/04) [973917]

15297 Lassieur, Allison. *Eleanor Roosevelt: Activist for Social Change* (5–8). Series: Great Life Stories. 2006, Children's Pr. LB $30.50 (978-0-531-13871-7). 112pp. This biography of Eleanor Roosevelt focuses on the first lady's personal life and on her social activism while in the White House and later as an envoy to the United Nations. (Rev: SLJ 2/07) [921]

15298 MacLeod, Elizabeth. *Eleanor Roosevelt: An Inspiring Life* (4–6). 2006, Kids Can $14.95 (978-1-55337-778-8); paper $6.95 (978-1-55337-811-2). 32pp. Traces the first lady's life from her difficult childhood to the humanitarian work that she pursued after the death of her husband, with many quotations and period photographs. (Rev: SLJ 11/06) [921]

15299 Mattern, Joanne. *Eleanor Roosevelt: More than a First Lady* (1–4). Series: Women Who Shaped History. 2003, Rosen LB $19.95 (978-0-8239-6501-4). 24pp. Through classic photographs and an accessible text, readers will learn about the amazing woman who changed the role of the first lady and had a great influence on world affairs. (Rev: BL 2/15/03) [921]

15300 Rosenberg, Pam. *Eleanor Roosevelt: First Lady, Humanitarian, and World Citizen* (3–6). Series: Our People. 2003, Child's World LB $27.07 (978-1-59296-001-9). 32pp. An accessible life of Roosevelt, emphasizing her contributions to society. (Rev: BL 1/1–15/04)

15301 Somervill, Barbara. *Eleanor Roosevelt: First Lady of the World* (5–8). Illus. Series: Signature Lives: Modern America. 2005, Compass Point $34.60 (978-0-7565-0992-7). 112pp. An appealing biography that traces the First Lady's life and focuses on her tireless efforts to make life better for America's disadvantaged minorities. (Rev: BL 10/15/05) [973.917]

15302 Weidt, Maryann N. *Stateswoman to the World: A Story About Eleanor Roosevelt* (4–6). Illus. by Lydia M. Anderson. 1991, Carolrhoda LB $21.27 (978-0-87614-663-7). 64pp. A frank biography of the First Lady so admired and respected throughout the world. (Rev: BL 12/15/91; SLJ 12/91) [921]

15303 Westervelt, Virginia Veeder. *Here Comes Eleanor: A New Biography of Eleanor Roosevelt for Young People* (5–8). Series: Avisson Young Adult. 1999, Avisson paper $16.00 (978-1-888105-33-9). 142pp. A clear account of the life of Eleanor Roosevelt that gives a fine assessment of her many contributions to humankind. (Rev: BL 2/15/99; SLJ 7/99; VOYA 10/99) [921]

15304 Winget, Mary. *Eleanor Roosevelt* (5–8). Series: A&E Biography. 2000, Lerner LB $27.93 (978-0-8225-4985-7). 112pp. Growing up in a troubled but loving family, Eleanor Roosevelt showed that an ordinary woman can achieve greatness. (Rev: BL 3/1/01; HBG 10/01) [921]

SHAW, ANNA HOWARD

15305 Brown, Don. *A Voice from the Wilderness: The Story of Anna Howard Shaw* (1–3). Illus. 2001, Houghton $16.00 (978-0-618-08362-6). 32pp. This is the story of Anna Howard Shaw, who came to America in the mid-19th century and overcame adversity to become a teacher and champion of women's suffrage. (Rev: BL 9/15/01; HB 11/01; HBG 3/02; SLJ 9/01) [324.6]

SMITH, MARGARET CHASE

15306 Plourde, Lynn. *Margaret Chase Smith: A Woman for President* (3–5). Illus. by David McPhail. 2008, Charlesbridge $16.95 (978-1-58089-234-6); paper $7.95 (978-1-58089-235-3). 32pp. Smith, the first woman candidate for president from a major U.S. political party, lived to be 97; this is a chronological account of her life and career in politics. (Rev: BL 4/15/08; LMC 10/08; SLJ 4/08) [921]

STANTON, ELIZABETH CADY

15307 Fritz, Jean. *You Want Women to Vote, Lizzie Stanton?* (4–7). Illus. 1995, Putnam $18.99 (978-0-399-22786-8). 96pp. An exciting, witty re-creation of the life of Elizabeth Cady Stanton, fighter for women's rights, including suffrage. (Rev: BCCB 10/95; BL 8/95*; SLJ 9/95*) [921]

15308 Loos, Pamela. *Elizabeth Cady Stanton* (5–8). Illus. Series: Women of Achievement. 2000, Chelsea $30.00 (978-0-7910-5293-8). 120pp. Drawing largely on Stanton's autobiography, this is the life story of the well-known suffragist of the 19th century. (Rev: BL 2/15/01; HBG 10/01) [921]

15309 Miller, Connie Colwell. *Elizabeth Cady Stanton: Women's Rights Pioneer* (2–6). Illus. by Cynthia Martin. Series: Graphic Library, Graphic Biographies. 2005, Capstone LB $26.60 (978-0-7368-4971-5). 32pp. This graphic-novel biography covers Stanton's role in the women's rights movement and provides links to related online resources. (Rev: SLJ 3/06) [921]

15310 Salisbury, Cynthia. *Elizabeth Cady Stanton: Leader of the Fight for Women's Rights* (5–8). Series: Historical American Biographies. 2002, Enslow LB $26.60 (978-0-7660-1616-3). The life of the fighter for women's suffrage and the organizer of the first women's rights convention. (Rev: BL 4/1/02; HBG 10/02; SLJ 5/02) [921]

15311 Stone, Tanya L. *Elizabeth Leads the Way: Elizabeth Cady Stanton and the Right to Vote* (1–3). Illus. by Rebecca Gibbon. 2008, Holt $16.95 (978-0-8050-7903-6). 32pp. This brief biography introduces young readers to Stanton's fight for women's rights, focusing more on her beliefs than on historical events. (Rev: BL 4/15/08; HB 5/08; LMC 8/08; SLJ 5/08) [921]

15312 Swain, Gwenyth. *The Road to Seneca Falls* (3–6). Illus. Series: Creative Minds. 1996, Carolrhoda LB $22.60 (978-0-87614-947-8); paper $6.95 (978-1-57505-025-6). 64pp. This biography of Elizabeth Cady Stanton chronicles the birth of the women's rights movement. (Rev: BL 2/15/97; SLJ 3/97) [921]

STEINEM, GLORIA

15313 Hoff, Mary. *Gloria Steinem: The Women's Movement* (4–6). Illus. Series: New Directions. 1991, Millbrook LB $21.90 (978-1-878841-19-3). 96pp. The life story of this journalist who questioned women's roles in modern society. (Rev: SLJ 4/91) [921]

15314 Lazo, Caroline. *Gloria Steinem: Feminist Extraordinaire* (5–7). Illus. Series: Lerner Biographies. 1998, Lerner LB $27.93 (978-0-8225-4934-5). 128pp. The story of Steinem, who overcame a troubled childhood to become a great humanitarian, writer, and leader of the feminist movement. (Rev: BL 7/98; SLJ 7/98) [921]

STINSON, KATHERINE

15315 Winegarten, Debra L. *Katherine Stinson: The Flying Schoolgirl* (4–7). 2001, Eakin $26.95 (978-1-57168-459-2). 115pp. An absorbing introduction to Stinson's accomplishments, which include a whole series of "firsts," that interweaves fiction and fact. (Rev: HBG 10/01; SLJ 6/01) [629.13092]

STONE, LUCY

15316 McPherson, Stephanie S. *I Speak for the Women: A Story About Lucy Stone* (4–6). Illus. by Brian Liedahl. Series: Creative Minds. 1992, Carolrhoda LB $19.95 (978-0-87614-740-5). 64pp. The life of a dedicated abolitionist and champion of women's rights in 19th-century America. (Rev: BCCB 3/93; BL 3/15/93; SLJ 2/93) [921]

SULLIVAN, ANNIE

15317 Delano, Marfé Ferguson. *Helen's Eyes: A Photobiography of Annie Sullivan, Helen Keller's Teacher* (4–7). Illus. 2008, National Geographic $17.95 (978-1-4263-0209-1). 64pp. Full of photographs, this attractive, oversize book tells the story of Sullivan's often-sad life. (Rev: BL 6/1–15/08; SLJ 9/08) [921]

TIENDA, MARTA

15318 O'Connell, Diane. *People Person: The Story of Sociologist Marta Tienda* (5–8). Series: Women's Adventures in Science. 2005, Watts LB $31.50 (978-0-531-16781-6). 108pp. An informative and accessible profile of sociologist Marta Tienda and her work to create opportunities for people around the world. (Rev: SLJ 12/05) [921]

WALTERS, BARBARA

15319 Remstein, Henna. *Barbara Walters* (5–8). 1998, Chelsea $21.95 (978-0-7910-4716-3); paper $9.95 (978-0-7910-4717-0). The life story of Barbara Walters, who broke many barriers for women in the communications field and has become an icon in the field of journalism. (Rev: HBG 3/99; VOYA 4/99) [921]

WASHINGTON, MARTHA

15320 McPherson, Stephanie S. *Martha Washington: First Lady* (4–6). Illus. Series: Historical American Biographies. 1998, Enslow LB $26.60 (978-0-7660-1017-8). 128pp. Using many period paintings and contemporary photos, this book traces the life of Martha Washington, her two marriages, and her private and public lives. (Rev: BL 1/1–15/99; SLJ 1/99) [921]

15321 Raatma, Lucia. *First of First Ladies: Martha Washington* (2–4). Illus. 2009, Compass Point LB $26.65 (978-0-7565-4125-5). 48pp. This title introduces the first lady as a young widow with two children at the time of her marriage to George Washington. (Rev: BL 6/1–15/09) [973.4]

WASHINGTON, MARY BALL

15322 Fritz, Jean. *George Washington's Mother* (2–3). Illus. by DyAnne Disalvo-Ryan. 1992, Penguin paper $3.99 (978-0-448-40384-7). 48pp. A simple biography of Mary Ball Washington, the mother of the first president. (Rev: BL 10/1/92; SLJ 10/92) [921]

WONG, LI KENG

15323 Wong, Li Keng. *Good Fortune: My Journey to Gold Mountain* (4–7). 2006, Peachtree $14.95 (978-1-56145-367-2). 144pp. Wong, who migrated to the United States from China with her mother and sister in 1933, writes about the challenges of adjusting to a new culture. (Rev: BL 3/1/06; SLJ 7/06) [979.4]

WOODHULL, VICTORIA

15324 Krull, Kathleen. *A Woman for President: The Story of Victoria Woodhull* (3–5). Illus. by Jane Dyer. 2004, Walker $16.95 (978-0-8027-8908-2). Woodhull's fascinating life included working as a spiritualist and financial adviser, amassing wealth, starting a newspaper, and running for president. (Rev: SLJ 9/04) [921]

Scientists, Inventors, Naturalists, and Business Figures

Collective

15325 Aaseng, Nathan. *Business Builders in Computers* (5–8). Series: Business Builders. 2000, Oliver LB $22.95 (978-1-881508-57-1). 160pp. Bill Gates, Steve Jobs of Apple, and Steve Case of AOL are among the individuals profiled in this interesting volume on the growth of the computer industry. (Rev: BL 2/1/01; HBG 10/01; SLJ 5/01) [338.4]

15326 Aaseng, Nathan. *Business Builders in Fast Food* (5–8). Series: Business Builders. 2001, Oliver $22.95 (978-1-881508-58-8). 160pp. An interesting look at the creators of fast food empires such as McDonald's and Wendy's. (Rev: BL 9/15/01; HBG 10/01; SLJ 9/01) [381]

15327 Aaseng, Nathan. *Business Builders in Oil* (5–8). Series: Business Builders. 2000, Oliver LB $22.95 (978-1-881508-56-4). 160pp. This lively introduction to the oil industry provides profiles of key individuals such as John D. Rockefeller, Andrew Mellon, and J. Paul Getty. (Rev: BL 2/1/01; HBG 10/01; SLJ 5/01) [338.2]

15328 Aaseng, Nathan. *Construction: Building the Impossible* (5–9). Illus. 2000, Oliver LB $21.95 (978-1-881508-59-5). 144pp. This book profiles eight famous builders — from Imhotep, who built the first stone pyramids in Egypt, to Frank Crowe, the visionary behind the Hoover Dam. (Rev: BL 5/1/00; HBG 10/00; SLJ 10/00) [920]

15329 Bankston, John. *Francis Crick and James Watson: Pioneers in DNA Research* (5–7). Series: Unlocking the Secrets of Science. 2002, Mitchell Lane LB $17.95 (978-1-58415-122-7). 56pp. An accessible account of the discovery of the structure of DNA and the lives of the two scientists involved. (Rev: HBG 10/03; SLJ 1/03) [576.5]

15330 Barton, Chris. *The Day-Glo Brothers: The True Story of Bob and Joe Switzer's Bright Ideas and Brand-New Colors* (2–5). Illus. by Tony Persiani. 2009, Charlesbridge $18.95 (978-1-57091-673-1). 44pp. The story of the two inventive brothers who created glow-in-the-dark paint colors. (Rev: BL 6/1–15/09) [535]

15331 Camp, Carole Ann. *American Astronomers: Searchers and Wonderers* (5–8). Series: Collective Biographies. 1996, Enslow LB $26.60 (978-0-89490-631-2). This volume presents brief profiles of important astronomers including Maria Mitchell, Edwin Hubble, and Carl Sagan. (Rev: BL 4/15/96; SLJ 5/96) [920]

15332 Camp, Carole Ann. *American Women Inventors* (5–10). Illus. Series: Collective Biographies. 2004, Enslow LB $26.60 (978-0-7660-1913-3). 104pp. A collective biography of 10 important American female inventors, their lives, and their discoveries. (Rev: BL 3/1/04) [920]

15333 Cox, Clinton. *African American Healers* (4–7). Illus. Series: Black Stars. 1999, Wiley $24.95 (978-0-471-24650-3). 164pp. Using entries of two to three pages each, this work profiles more than 20 African Americans who have achieved prominence in medicine and related areas. (Rev: BL 2/15/00; HBG 10/00; SLJ 2/00) [910]

15334 DeAngelis, Gina. *Science and Medicine* (5–9). Series: Female Firsts in Their Fields. 1999, Chelsea $28.00 (978-0-7910-5143-6). 64pp. The six women profiled here are Elizabeth Blackwell, Clara Barton, Marie Curie, Margaret Mead, Rachel Carson, and Antonia Novello. (Rev: BL 5/15/99; HBG 10/99; SLJ 9/99; VOYA 8/99) [920]

15335 Fortey, Jacqueline. *Great Scientists* (5–8). Illus. Series: Eyewitness. 2007, DK $15.99 (978-0-7566-2974-8). 72pp. From Aristotle to Stephen Hawking, this volume offers brief introductions to 30 great scientists, discussing their accomplishments and providing personal information, a timeline, and a few photographs with captions adding historical details. (Rev: BL 9/1/07) [500]

15336 French, Laura. *Internet Pioneers: The Cyber Elite* (5–9). Series: Collective Biographies. 2001, Enslow LB $26.60 (978-0-7660-1540-1). 112pp. French tells the stories of 10 Internet innovators — including Andrew Grove, Bill Gates, Larry Ellison, and Jeff Bezos — detailing their successes and revealing their very different backgrounds. (Rev: HBG 3/02; SLJ 9/01) [920]

15337 Hacker, Carlotta. *Scientists* (3–6). Series: Women in Profile. 1998, Crabtree LB $22.60 (978-0-7787-0006-7). 48pp. This collection focuses on six female scientists, with about a dozen shorter sketches of others. (Rev: SLJ 9/98) [920]

15338 Hansen, Ole Steen. *The Wright Brothers and Other Pioneers of Flight* (4–7). Series: The Story of Flight. 2003, Crabtree $25.27 (978-0-7787-1200-8). 32pp. In text and pictures, this book introduces the pioneers of flight, with a concentration on the Wright brothers. (Rev: BL 10/15/03) [921]

15339 Harris, Laurie L., ed. *Biography Today: Profiles of People of Interest to Young Readers* (4–7). Illus. Series: Scientists and Inventors. 1996, Omnigraphics LB $39.00 (978-0-7808-0068-7). 194pp. Profiles of 14 important contemporaries including Carl Sagan and Jane Goodall are accompanied by those of some lesser-known figures, such as geneticist and AIDS fighter Mathilde Krim. (Rev: SLJ 2/97) [920]

15340 Hudson, Wade. *Book of Black Heroes: Scientists, Healers and Inventors* (5–8). Illus. 2002, Just Us Bks. $9.95 (978-0-940975-97-2). 70pp. One historic or present-day African American figure is presented on each page of this collective biography of doctors, engineers, and inventors. (Rev: BL 2/15/03) [925]

15341 Hunter, Shaun. *Leaders in Medicine* (3–6). Illus. Series: Women in Profile. 1999, Crabtree LB $22.60 (978-0-7787-0010-4); paper $8.95 (978-0-7787-0032-6). 48pp. Maria Montessori, Helen Taussig, and Elisabeth Kubler-Ross are among the women featured in this collective biography that contains six long profiles and 15 thumbnail sketches of famous women involved in medicine. (Rev: BL 9/15/99; SLJ 8/99) [920]

15342 Jeffrey, Laura S. *Great American Businesswomen* (4–7). Illus. 1996, Enslow LB $26.60 (978-0-89490-706-7). 112pp. Profiles of 10 successful American businesswomen, including Maggie L. Walker and Katharine Graham. (Rev: BL 9/1/96; SLJ 9/96) [920]

15343 Jones, Lynda. *Great Black Heroes: Five Brilliant Scientists* (2–3). Illus. by Ron Garnett. Series: Hello Reader! 2000, Scholastic paper $3.99 (978-0-590-48031-4). 48pp. This easy-to-read book profiles five African American scientists, among them Ernest Just, a marine biologist, and Percy Lavon Julian, a chemist. (Rev: BL 7/00; SLJ 8/00) [920]

15344 Kang, Zhu. *Science and Scientists* (3–5). Illus. by Hong Tao and Feng Congying. Series: True Stories from Ancient China. 2005, Long River $9.95 (978-1-59265-038-5). 48pp. Profiles the lives and accomplishments of four ancient Chinese scientists — Zhang Heng, Zu Chongzhi, Yi Xing, and Xu Xiake. (Rev: BL 12/1/05) [509.22]

15345 Kent, Jacqueline C. *Women in Medicine* (4–6). Series: Profiles. 1998, Oliver LB $19.95 (978-1-881508-46-5). 160pp. A collective biography of eight American women pioneers in medicine,

including Elizabeth Blackwell, May Edward Chinn, and Dorothy Lavinia Brown. (Rev: SLJ 10/98) [920]

15346 Kimmel, Elizabeth C. *Dinosaur Bone War: Cope and Marsh's Fossil Feud* (4–7). Illus. 2006, Random $11.99 (978-0-375-91349-5); paper $5.99 (978-0-375-81349-8). 128pp. The story of American fossil hunters Edward Cope and Othniel Charles Marsh and the bitter rivalry that led to many dinosaur fossil discoveries and spurred the development of paleontology as a science. (Rev: BL 12/1/06) [560.92]

15347 Kirsh, Shannon, and Florence Kirsh. *Fabulous Female Physicians* (4–8). 2002, Second Story paper $7.95 (978-1-896764-43-6). 100pp. Using short chapters and black-and-white photographs, this account profiles 10 mostly unknown female doctors and their accomplishments. (Rev: BL 6/1–15/02; VOYA 8/02) [921]

15348 Lomask, Milton. *Great Lives: Invention and Technology* (5–8). Series: Invention and Technology. 1991, Scribner $23.00 (978-0-684-19106-5). Profiles of great names in invention and technology around the world. (Rev: BL 11/1/91; SLJ 1/92) [920]

15349 McClure, Judy. *Healers and Researchers: Physicians, Biologists, Social Scientists* (5–9). Series: Remarkable Women. 2000, Raintree LB $32.85 (978-0-8172-5734-7). 80pp. This book profiles 150 women from the scientific community including Barbara McClintock, Anna Freud, Jocelyn Elders, and Sushila Nyir. (Rev: SLJ 8/00) [920]

15350 McCutcheon, Marc. *The Kid Who Named Pluto and the Stories of Other Extraordinary Young People in Science* (3–6). Illus. by Jon Cannell. 2004, Chronicle $15.95 (978-0-8118-3770-5). 85pp. A collection of profiles of nine young people who made significant contributions to science while they still were young. (Rev: BL 4/1/04; SLJ 6/04) [920]

15351 Mayberry, Jodine. *Business Leaders Who Built Financial Empires* (5–8). Illus. Series: 20 Events. 1995, Raintree LB $27.12 (978-0-8114-4934-2). 48pp. The biographies of 19 financial wizards and entrepreneurs, beginning with Levi Strauss and Andrew Carnegie and ending with Steven Jobs and Anita Roddick. (Rev: SLJ 7/95) [920]

15352 Mulcahy, Robert. *Medical Technology: Inventing the Instruments* (5–8). Illus. Series: Innovators. 1997, Oliver LB $21.95 (978-1-881508-34-2). 144pp. Seven short biographies of scientists who were responsible for such inventions as the X-ray, stethoscope, thermometer, and electrocardiograph. (Rev: BCCB 7–8/97; SLJ 7/97) [920]

15353 Polking, Kirk. *Oceanographers and Explorers of the Sea* (5–9). Series: Collective Biographies. 1999, Enslow LB $20.95 (978-0-7660-1113-7). 128pp. Profiles 10 scientists and adventurers who have devoted their lives to the oceans, marine life, and ocean-related pursuits, including Maurice Ewing, who mapped the ocean floor, and Robert Ballard, discoverer of the *Titanic*. (Rev: BL 8/99; SLJ 9/99) [920]

15354 Richie, Jason. *Space Flight: Crossing the Last Frontier* (5–9). Illus. Series: Innovators. 2002, Oliver LB $21.95 (978-1-881508-77-9). 144pp. Biographies of seven men who were instrumental in the development of space flight — including Robert Goddard, Wernher von Braun, and Sergei Korolev — are arranged in chronological order. (Rev: HBG 3/03; LMC 5/03; SLJ 4/03) [629.4]

15355 Sherman, Josepha. *Jerry Yang and David Filo: Chief Yahoos of Yahoo* (5–8). Series: Techies. 2001, Millbrook LB $23.90 (978-0-7613-1961-0). This is the story of the creators of Yahoo!, the world's most heavily trafficked Web site. (Rev: BL 4/1/02; HBG 3/02; SLJ 12/01) [921]

15356 Stanley, Phyllis M. *American Environmental Heroes* (4–7). Illus. 1996, Enslow LB $26.60 (978-0-89490-630-5). 128pp. John Muir, Barry Commoner, Sylvia Earle, and seven other environmentalists are profiled. (Rev: BL 9/1/96; SLJ 7/96) [920]

15357 Sullivan, Otha R. *African American Inventors* (5–8). Ed. by Jim Haskins. Illus. Series: Black Stars. 1998, Wiley $24.95 (978-0-471-14804-3). Among the African American inventors profiled in two- and three-page spreads are Benjamin Banneker, Madam C. J. Walker, and Dr. Charles Drew, whose research laid the basis for blood donation. (Rev: BL 7/98; SLJ 6/98) [920]

15358 Thimmesh, Catherine. *The Sky's the Limit: Stories of Discovery by Women and Girls* (5–7). Illus. by Melissa Sweet. 2002, Houghton $16.00 (978-0-618-07698-7). 80pp. Details discoveries in the sciences, all made by women and girls. A sequel to *Girls Think of Everything* (2000). (Rev: BL 3/1/02; HB 5/02; HBG 10/02; SLJ 5/02; VOYA 6/02) [500]

15359 VanCleave, Janice. *Janice VanCleave's Scientists Through the Ages* (4–7). Illus. 2003, Wiley paper $12.95 (978-0-471-25222-1). 128pp. A collective biography profiling 25 scientists, with explanations of each one's important work and a relevant experiment for the reader to perform. (Rev: BL 12/1/03) [509]

15360 White, Casey. *Sergey Brin and Larry Page: The Founders of Google* (5–9). Illus. Series: Internet Career Biographies. 2006, Rosen LB $31.95 (978-1-4042-0716-5). 112pp. The interesting story of the two Stanford graduates who created a company that added a new word to our vocabulary. (Rev: LMC 8/07; SLJ 5/07) [920]

15361 Wilkinson, Philip, and Michael Pollard. *Scientists Who Changed the World* (3–5). Illus. by Robert Ingpen. Series: Turning Points. 1994, Chelsea LB $21.95 (978-0-7910-2763-9). 93pp. Twenty brief biographies of scientists, including Galileo, Marie Curie, DNA decoders, and the first men on the moon. (Rev: BL 12/1/94) [920]

Individual

ALVAREZ, LUIS

15362 Allison, Amy. *Luis Alvarez and the Development of the Bubble Chamber* (5–8). Series: Unlocking the Secrets of Science. 2002, Mitchell Lane LB $25.70 (978-1-58415-140-1). 48pp. Alvarez was a scientist of wide-ranging interests who won a Nobel Prize for developing a bubble chamber to track atomic particles. (Rev: HBG 3/03; SLJ 2/03; VOYA 6/03) [921]

ANDREESSEN, MARC

15363 Ehrenhaft, Daniel. *Marc Andreessen: Web Warrior* (5–8). Illus. Series: The Techies. 2001, Twenty-First Century LB $23.90 (978-0-7613-1964-1). 80pp. This biography introduces Marc Andreessen, who coauthored the Web-browsing software Mosaic, cofounded the firm Netscape, and was a multimillionaire at age 24. (Rev: BL 3/15/01; HBG 10/01; SLJ 7/01; VOYA 8/01) [921]

ANDREWS, ROY CHAPMAN

15364 Bausum, Ann. *Dragon Bones and Dinosaur Eggs: A Photobiography of Explorer Roy Chapman Andrews* (5–8). Illus. 2000, National Geographic $17.95 (978-0-7922-7123-9). 48pp. A biography of the famous paleontologist who made several important dinosaur discoveries in central Asia and later became director of the American Museum of Natural History in New York City. (Rev: BCCB 5/00*; BL 3/15/00; HBG 10/00; SLJ 3/00) [921]

ANNING, MARY

15365 Anholt, Laurence. *Stone Girl, Bone Girl: The Story of Mary Anning* (K–3). Illus. by Sheila Moxley. 1999, Orchard $15.95 (978-0-531-30148-7). 32pp. The story of the 12-year-old British fossil hunter who discovered the skeleton of a huge sea creature, 165 million years old, in the limestone cliffs near Lyme Regis, Dorset. (Rev: BCCB 2/99; BL 2/1/99*; HBG 10/99; SLJ 5/99) [921]

15366 Atkins, Jeannine. *Mary Anning and the Sea Dragon* (K–4). Illus. by Michael Dooling. 1999, Farrar $16.00 (978-0-374-34840-3). 32pp. A picture book that tells of the exciting life of fossil hunter Mary Anning and her discoveries. (Rev: BL 9/1/99; HBG 3/00; SLJ 10/99) [560]

15367 Brighton, Catherine. *The Fossil Girl: Mary Anning's Dinosaur Discovery* (2–4). Illus. by author. 1999, Millbrook LB $22.90 (978-0-7613-1468-4). Born in 1799, Mary Anning was the amazing youngster who discovered and studied fossils, including an enormous creature embedded in rock that she found close to her English coastal home. (Rev: HBG 10/99; SLJ 5/99) [921]

15368 Goodhue, Thomas. *Curious Bones: Mary Anning and the Birth of Paleontology* (5–8). Illus. 2002, Morgan Reynolds LB $23.95 (978-1-883846-93-0). 112pp. A readable biography of the groundbreaking female paleontologist (1799–1847) that places her achievements in historical context, with a glossary, bibliography, and timeline. (Rev: BL 7/02; HBG 3/03; SLJ 9/02) [560.92]

15369 Walker, Sally M. *Mary Anning: Fossil Hunter* (2–3). Series: On My Own. 2000, Carolrhoda LB $23.93 (978-1-57505-425-4). 48pp. Using many original documents as sources, this simple biography tells the life story of Mary Anning, who hunted for fossils on the cliffs of Lyme Regis in England. (Rev: BL 8/00; HBG 3/01; SLJ 12/00) [921]

ARCHIMEDES

15370 Gow, Mary. *Archimedes: Mathematical Genius of the Ancient World* (5–8). Illus. Series: Great Minds of Science. 2005, Enslow LB $26.60 (978-0-7660-2502-8). 128pp. Archimedes' mathematical discoveries are explained and placed in social, scientific, and cultural context. (Rev: SLJ 12/05) [921]

AVERY, OSWALD

15371 Severs, Vesta-Nadine, and Jim Whiting. *Oswald Avery and the Story of DNA* (4–7). Series: Unlocking the Secrets of Science. 2002, Mitchell Lane LB $25.70 (978-1-58415-110-4). 48pp. The importance of Avery's early research is reinforced by a description of DNA evidence being used to free wrongly accused prisoners. (Rev: HBG 10/02; SLJ 6/02) [579.3092]

BAIRD, JOHN LOGIE

15372 Reid, Struan. *John Logie Baird* (4–6). Series: Groundbreakers. 2000, Heinemann LB $25.64 (978-1-57572-372-3). 48pp. The ground-breaking inventor of television is featured in this biography that tells of his poor health and his many setbacks. (Rev: HBG 3/01; SLJ 3/01) [921]

BANNEKER, BENJAMIN

15373 Blue, Rose, and Corinne J. Naden. *Benjamin Banneker: Mathematician and Stargazer* (4–6). Illus. Series: Gateway Biographies. 2001, Millbrook LB $23.90 (978-0-7613-1805-7). 48pp. An informative introduction to Banneker's life and achievements as America's "first major black man of science." (Rev: HBG 3/02; SLJ 9/01) [921]

15374 Conley, Kevin. *Benjamin Banneker* (5–9). Illus. 1989, Chelsea LB $30.00 (978-1-55546-573-5). Banneker was a remarkable 18th-century African American who excelled in mathematics and science. (Rev: BL 1/1/90; SLJ 5/90; VOYA 4/90) [921]

15375 Ferris, Jeri. *What Are You Figuring Now? A Story About Benjamin Banneker* (3–6). Illus. 1988, Lerner LB $21.27 (978-0-87614-331-5); Carolrhoda paper $22.60 (978-0-87614-521-0). 56pp. The life of this African American who was a math whiz. (Rev: BL 1/1/89; SLJ 2/89)

BARNARD, CHRISTIAAN

15376 Bankston, John. *Christiaan Barnard and the Story of the First Successful Heart Transplant* (4–5). Series: Unlocking the Secrets of Science. 2002, Mitchell Lane LB $25.70 (978-1-58415-120-3). 48pp. A concise but complete look with interesting anecdotal information at the life of the courageous doctor who performed the first successful heart transplant. (Rev: BL 8/02; SLJ 10/02) [921]

BARTRAM, WILLIAM

15377 Ray, Deborah Kogan. *The Flower Hunter: William Bartram, America's First Naturalist* (3–5). Illus. 2004, Farrar $17.00 (978-0-374-34589-1). 40pp. This brief but information-packed biography of Bartram tells how a childhood interest in his father's botanical studies grew into a full-time occupation as America's first naturalist. (Rev: BL 4/15/04; SLJ 5/04) [580]

BELL, ALEXANDER GRAHAM

15378 Bankston, John. *Alexander Graham Bell and the Story of the Telephone* (5–8). Illus. Series: Uncharted, Unexplored, and Unexplained. 2004, Mitchell Lane LB $29.95 (978-1-58415-243-9). 48pp. As a teacher of the deaf and son of a deaf mother, Bell had a special interest in finding new and better ways to communicate. (Rev: BL 10/15/04) [921]

15379 Berger, Melvin, and Gilda Berger. *Did You Invent the Phone Alone, Alexander Graham Bell?* (3–4). Illus. by Brandon Dorman. Series: Science SuperGiants. 2007, Scholastic paper $4.99 (978-0-439-83381-3). 48pp. "Who made the first telephone call?" "When did telephone service start in the United States?" Using a question-and-answer format, this profile provides biographical and basic scientific information. (Rev: SLJ 2/08) [921]

15380 Carson, Mary Kay. *Alexander Graham Bell: Giving Voice to the World* (5–8). Series: Sterling Biographies. 2007, Sterling LB $12.95 (978-1-4027-4951-3); paper $5.95 (978-1-4027-3230-0). 124pp. Covers Bell's childhood and his lifelong commitment to improving communication. (Rev: SLJ 10/07) [921]

15381 Gaines, Ann. *Alexander Graham Bell* (2–3). Series: Discover the Life of an Inventor. 2001, Rourke LB $20.64 (978-1-58952-117-9). 24pp. Besides a life of this great inventor, this book describes the science behind the telephone. (Rev: BL 10/15/01; SLJ 1/02) [921]

15382 Garmon, Anita. *Alexander Graham Bell Invents* (2–4). Series: National Geographic History Chapters. 2007, National Geographic LB $17.90 (978-1-4263-0189-6). 40pp. Simple sentences, with photographs and drawings, tell the story of Bell's younger life and later accomplishments; a "How to Write an A+ Report" section gives useful advice. (Rev: LMC 1/08*; SLJ 1/08) [921]

15383 MacLeod, Elizabeth. *Alexander Graham Bell: An Inventive Life* (4–6). Illus. 1999, Kids Can

$12.95 (978-1-55074-456-9); paper $5.95 (978-1-55074-458-3). 32pp. A series of double-page spreads cover Bell's invention of the telephone, his experiments building airplanes, and summers spent with his family on Cape Breton Island. (Rev: BL 4/15/99; HBG 10/99; SLJ 5/99) [921]

15384 Matthews, Tom L. *Always Inventing: A Photobiography of Alexander Graham Bell* (3–6). Illus. 1999, National Geographic $16.99 (978-0-7922-7391-2). 64pp. A large-format book filled with period photographs tells about the inventor of the telephone and his many other interests and contributions. (Rev: BL 6/1–15/99; HB 7/99; HBG 10/99; SLJ 3/99) [921]

15385 Pollard, Michael. *Alexander Graham Bell: Father of Modern Communication* (5–7). Series: Giants of Science. 2000, Blackbirch LB $27.44 (978-1-56711-334-1). 64pp. Known primarily for the invention of the telephone, Bell also invented the first hydrofoil, an air-conditioning system, and an early fax machine. (Rev: BL 1/1–15/01; HBG 3/01) [921]

15386 Reid, Struan. *Alexander Graham Bell* (4–6). Series: Groundbreakers. 2000, Heinemann LB $25.64 (978-1-57572-366-2). 48pp. This biography of Bell covers the invention of the telephone plus other innovations he pioneered and his important work with the deaf. (Rev: SLJ 3/01) [921]

15387 Sherrow, Victoria. *Alexander Graham Bell* (1–3). Illus. by Elaine Verstraete. Series: On My Own Biography. 2001, Carolrhoda LB $21.27 (978-1-57505-460-5); paper $5.95 (978-1-57505-533-6). 48pp. Bell's early working years and growing interest in inventions are the focus of this biography that will suit reluctant and beginning readers, with an afterword that covers his personal life and later career. (Rev: HBG 3/02; SLJ 1/02) [921]

15388 Williams, Brian. *Bell and the Science of the Telephone* (4–6). Illus. by David Antram. Series: The Explosion Zone. 2006, Barron's $12.99 (978-0-7641-5972-5). 32pp. This biography focuses on Bell's invention of the telephone and its impact but also touches on the related topics of Morse code, telephone exchanges, and tuning forks. (Rev: SLJ 11/06) [921]

BENZ, KARL

15389 Bankston, John. *Karl Benz and the Single Cylinder Engine* (5–8). Illus. Series: Uncharted, Unexplored, and Unexplained. 2004, Mitchell Lane LB $29.95 (978-1-58415-244-6). 48pp. The first person to build a three-wheeled automobile, Benz went on to design many more-sophisticated cars. (Rev: BL 10/15/04) [921]

BERNERS-LEE, TIM

15390 Gaines, Ann. *Tim Berners-Lee and the Development of the World Wide Web* (4–7). Series: Unlocking the Secrets of Science. 2001, Mitchell Lane LB $25.70 (978-1-58415-096-1). 48pp. A profile of the man who created the user-friendly way of accessing much of the information on the Internet. (Rev: HBG 10/02; SLJ 2/02) [921]

15391 Stewart, Melissa. *Tim Berners-Lee: Inventor of the World Wide Web* (4–7). Series: Ferguson Career Biographies. 2001, Ferguson LB $25.00 (978-0-89434-367-4). 127pp. Young readers will be fascinated by the details of Berners-Lee's life and career and the accompanying information on the skills needed to become a computer programmer. (Rev: SLJ 10/01) [921]

BEZOS, JEFF

15392 Garty, Judy. *Jeff Bezos* (5–8). Illus. Series: Internet Biographies. 2003, Enslow LB $23.93 (978-0-7660-1972-0). 48pp. A reader-friendly biography of the creator of Amazon.com, with plenty of information on his youth. (Rev: BL 3/15/03; HBG 10/03) [380.1]

15393 Sherman, Josepha. *Jeff Bezos: King of Amazon* (5–8). Illus. 2001, Twenty-First Century LB $23.90 (978-0-7613-1963-4). 80pp. Jeff Bezos, the genius behind Amazon.com, is introduced along with information on his struggle to found a book company on the Web. (Rev: BL 3/15/01; HBG 10/01; SLJ 7/01; VOYA 8/01) [921]

BLACKWELL, ELIZABETH

15394 Kent, Deborah. *Elizabeth Blackwell: Physician and Health* (3–6). Series: Our People. 2003, Child's World LB $27.07 (978-1-59296-002-6). 32pp. The life and career of Elizabeth Blackwell, the first woman to graduate from medical school and a pioneer in medical education for women. (Rev: SLJ 4/04) [610]

15395 Kline, Nancy. *Elizabeth Blackwell: A Doctor's Triumph* (5–9). Series: Barnard Biography. 1997, Conari paper $11.95 (978-1-57324-057-4). The story of the first woman doctor in America, with generous excerpts from her journal and letters. (Rev: BL 2/15/97; SLJ 6/97; VOYA 12/97) [921]

15396 Peck, Ira. *Elizabeth Blackwell: The First Woman Doctor* (4–5). Illus. 2000, Millbrook $23.90 (978-0-7613-1854-5). 48pp. This solid biography tells the story of the first woman to graduate from medical school in the United States and of her many accomplishments in her field. (Rev: BL 9/15/00; HBG 10/01) [921]

BRAHE, TYCHO

15397 Nardo, Don. *Tycho Brahe: Pioneer of Astronomy* (5–8). Illus. Series: Signature Lives: Scientific Revolution. 2007, Compass Point LB $23.95 (978-0-7565-3309-0). 112pp. In addition to this Danish scientist's career and discoveries, this well-designed volume explores the basics of scientific investigation and the nature of his breakthroughs. (Rev: BL 12/1/07; SLJ 1/08) [921]

BRAILLE, LOUIS

15398 Adler, David A. *A Picture Book of Louis Braille* (2–4). Illus. by John Wallner and Alexandra

Wallner. Series: Picture Book Biographies. 1997, Holiday House $16.95 (978-0-8234-1291-4). 34pp. For young readers, this is a simple, well-illustrated biography that also includes a page of the braille raised-dot alphabet and numbers. (Rev: BL 4/15/97; SLJ 6/97) [921]

15399 Bryant, Jennifer. *Louis Braille: Inventor* (5–7). Illus. 1994, Chelsea LB $21.95 (978-0-7910-2077-7). 112pp. This well-researched biography of Braille tells about the horror of his own blindness as well as the development of the alphabet that allows blind people to read. (Rev: BL 7/94; SLJ 8/94) [921]

15400 Freedman, Russell. *Out of Darkness: The Story of Louis Braille* (4–8). Illus. 1997, Clarion $16.00 (978-0-395-77516-5). The story of the blind Frenchman who, more than 170 years ago, invented a system of reading using raised dots. (Rev: BCCB 5/97; BL 3/1/97; HB 5/97; SLJ 3/97*) [686.2]

15401 O'Connor, Barbara. *The World at His Fingertips: A Story About Louis Braille* (3–5). Illus. by Rochelle Draper. Series: Creative Minds Biographies. 1997, Carolrhoda LB $22.60 (978-1-57505-052-2). 64pp. A fast-paced biography that reveals many interesting facts about this inventor of a writing system for the blind. (Rev: HBG 3/98; SLJ 10/97) [921]

15402 Woodhouse, Jayne. *Louis Braille* (2–3). Series: Lives and Times. 1997, Heinemann $19.92 (978-1-57572-559-8). 24pp. The life and contributions of this famous French blind man are told in this simple picture-book biography with a brief text. (Rev: BL 3/15/98) [921]

BROWN, BARNUM

15403 Sheldon, David. *Barnum Brown: Dinosaur Hunter* (2–4). Illus. by author. 2006, Walker $16.95 (978-0-8027-9602-8). 32pp. A compelling picture-book biography of dinosaur hunter Barnum Brown, who was fascinated by fossils from a young age and discovered a Tyrannosaurus rex in the early 20th century. (Rev: BL 12/1/06; SLJ 11/06) [560.92]

BROWN, HELEN GURLEY

15404 Falkof, Lucille. *Helen Gurley Brown: The Queen of Cosmopolitan* (5–8). Series: Wizards of Business. 1992, Garrett LB $17.26 (978-1-56074-013-1). An interesting, accessible, and inspiring biography of the magazine magnate. (Rev: BL 6/15/92; SLJ 7/92) [921]

BURROUGHS, JOHN

15405 Wadsworth, Ginger. *John Burroughs: The Sage of Slabsides* (5–8). Illus. 1997, Clarion $16.95 (978-0-395-77830-2). A biography of the American naturalist and essayist who lived in a cabin in the Catskill Mountains and wrote about his observations. (Rev: BCCB 5/97; BL 3/15/97; HB 7/97; SLJ 5/97) [508.73]

CARLSON, CHESTER

15406 Zannos, Susan. *Chester Carlson and the Development of Xerography* (4–5). Series: Unlocking the Secrets of Science. 2002, Mitchell Lane LB $25.70 (978-1-58415-117-3). 56pp. The story of the man whose determination to simplify the process of copying documents led to the invention of xerography. (Rev: BL 9/15/02; HBG 3/03; SLJ 11/02) [921]

CAROTHERS, WALLACE

15407 Gaines, Ann Graham. *Wallace Carothers and the Story of DuPont Nylon* (4–5). Series: Unlocking the Secrets of Science. 2001, Mitchell Lane LB $17.95 (978-1-58415-097-8). 56pp. This biography of the inventor of nylon includes information on his suicide. (Rev: BL 10/15/01; SLJ 11/01) [547]

CARSON, RACHEL

15408 Bruchac, Joseph. *Rachel Carson: Preserving a Sense of Wonder* (3–5). Illus. by Thomas Locker. 2004, Fulcrum $17.95 (978-1-55591-482-0). 32pp. Bruchac captures Carson's intense care for the environment and in particular her love of the sea, and includes details of her youth and of her writings. (Rev: BL 7/04; SLJ 6/04) [333.95]

15409 Ehrlich, Amy. *Rachel: The Story of Rachel Carson* (2–4). Illus. by Wendell Minor. 2003, Harcourt $17.00 (978-0-15-216227-6). 32pp. Fine illustrations enhance this picture-book biography that concentrates on Carson's environmental concerns. (Rev: BL 6/1–15/03; HBG 10/03; SLJ 5/03) [921]

15410 Kudlinski, Kathleen V. *Rachel Carson: Pioneer of Ecology* (3–6). Illus. 1988, Puffin paper $4.99 (978-0-14-032242-2). 64pp. The life of the famous nature writer and environmentalist, born in 1907. (Rev: BL 3/15/88; SLJ 8/88) [921]

15411 Landau, Elaine. *Rachel Carson and the Environmental Movement* (4–6). Series: Cornerstones of Freedom. 2004, Children's Pr. LB $26.00 (978-0-516-24232-3). 48pp. Carson's life and accomplishments are laid out in clear prose, with photographs and covers of her books. (Rev: SLJ 7/04) [921]

15412 Ransom, Candice F. *Listening to Crickets: A Story About Rachel Carson* (3–5). Illus. by Shelly O. Haas. 1993, Carolrhoda LB $22.60 (978-0-87614-727-6). 64pp. Beginning with her childhood, this account traces the life of the woman who helped make millions aware of the destruction of their environment. (Rev: BL 5/15/93; SLJ 7/93) [921]

15413 Ring, Elizabeth. *Rachel Carson: Caring for the Earth* (3–5). Illus. Series: Eyewitness Juniors. 1992, Millbrook LB $23.90 (978-1-56294-056-0). 48pp. The story of the pioneer conservationist whose book Silent Spring influenced a whole generation. (Rev: BL 8/92; SLJ 11/92) [921]

15414 Wadsworth, Ginger. *Rachel Carson: Voice for the Earth* (5–7). Illus. Series: Lerner Biographies. 1992, Lerner LB $27.93 (978-0-8225-4907-9). 128pp. The life and work of the conservationist and author, best known for *Silent Spring*. (Rev: BL 6/1/92; HB 7/92; SLJ 7/92) [921]

CARVER, GEORGE WASHINGTON

15415 Adler, David A. *A Picture Book of George Washington Carver* (2–4). Illus. by Dan Brown. Series: Picture Book Biographies. 1999, Holiday House $16.95 (978-0-8234-1429-1). A biography of this famous scientist with an emphasis on his private life and the racism he encountered. (Rev: BL 4/15/99; HBG 10/99; SLJ 5/99) [921]

15416 Bolden, Tonya. *George Washington Carver* (3–6). Illus. 2008, Abrams $18.95 (978-0-8109-9366-2). 48pp. An inviting and well-researched biography of this African American scientist, educator, and conservationist, with historical photographs and prints, reproductions of Carver's drawings, and many quotations. (Rev: BL 2/1/08; SLJ 4/08) [921]

15417 Carter, Andy, and Carol Saller. *George Washington Carver* (2–3). Series: On My Own. 2000, Carolrhoda LB $23.93 (978-1-57505-427-8); paper $5.95 (978-1-57505-458-2). 48pp. Born a slave near the end of the Civil War, Carver became famous for helping farmers grow better crops while sharing with them his love of nature. (Rev: BL 8/00; HBG 3/01) [921]

15418 Harness, Cheryl. *The Groundbreaking, Chance-Taking Life of George Washington Carver and Science and Invention in America* (4–6). Illus. by author. 2008, National Geographic $16.95 (978-1-4263-0196-4). 144pp. This lively biography, which places Carver's life and achievements in historical context, will appeal to general readers as well as to researchers. (Rev: BL 7/08; LMC 10/08; SLJ 7/08) [630.92]

15419 Krensky, Stephen. *A Man for All Seasons: The Life of George Washington Carver* (2–4). Illus. by Wil Clay. 2008, Collins $16.99 (978-0-06-027885-4). 32pp. A picture-book introduction to the life of the African American scientist, full of interesting details and with excellent paintings and a useful timeline. (Rev: BL 7/08; LMC 11/08; SLJ 6/08) [921]

15420 McKissack, Patricia C., and Fredrick McKissack. *George Washington Carver: The Peanut Scientist*. Rev. ed. (2–4). Series: Great African Americans. 2002, Enslow LB $18.60 (978-0-7660-1700-9). 32pp. Black-and-white photographs and a readable style are highlights of this biography about the famous African American botanist who was the son of slave parents. (Rev: BL 7/02) [921]

15421 MacLeod, Elizabeth. *George Washington Carver: An Innovative Life* (4–7). Illus. 2007, Kids Can $14.95 (978-1-55337-906-5); paper $6.95 (978-1-55337-907-2). 32pp. Well-organized with attractive graphics, this biography of Carver provides interesting details about his life as well as his major accomplishments. (Rev: SLJ 6/07) [921]

15422 Mitchell, Barbara. *A Pocketful of Goobers: A Story About George Washington Carver* (3–5). Illus. 1986, Carolrhoda LB $22.60 (978-0-87614-292-9); Lerner paper $6.95 (978-0-87614-474-9). 64pp. An introductory biography partly fictionalized, with

much information on Carver's research with peanuts. (Rev: BL 8/86; SLJ 9/86)

15423 Riley, John. *George Washington Carver: A Photo Biography* (1–3). Series: First Biographies. 2000, Morgan Reynolds LB $16.95 (978-1-883846-62-6). 24pp. With full-page pictures and a simple text this is a biography of the great African American scientist for beginning readers. (Rev: HBG 10/00; SLJ 8/00) [921]

CASE, STEVE

15424 Ashby, Ruth. *Steve Case: America Online Pioneer* (5–8). Series: Techies. 2002, Millbrook LB $23.90 (978-0-7613-2655-7). The story of the Honolulu native who was a leader of AOL and the driving force behind its merger with Time-Warner. (Rev: BL 4/1/02; HBG 10/02) [921]

CHIEN-SHIUNG WU

15425 Cooperman, Stephanie H. *Chien-Shiung Wu: Pioneering Physicist and Atomic Researcher* (5–8). Illus. Series: Women Hall of Famers in Mathematics and Science. 2004, Rosen LB $29.25 (978-0-8239-3875-9). 112pp. This biography describes Wu's life and achievements, explaining how she found a flaw in a widely held assumption about atoms. (Rev: BL 3/1/04; SLJ 9/04) [921]

CLARK, EUGENIE

15426 Butts, Ellen R., and Joyce R. Schwartz. *Eugenie Clark: Adventures of a Shark Scientist* (5–8). Illus. 2000, Linnet $19.50 (978-0-208-02440-4). 107pp. An interesting biography of a contemporary American scientist — an ichthyologist who has produced some startling research on sharks. (Rev: BCCB 2/00; BL 2/15/00; HBG 10/00; SLJ 7/00) [921]

15427 Ross, Michael. *Fish Watching with Eugenie Clark* (3–5). Series: Naturalist's Apprentice. 2000, Lerner LB $19.93 (978-1-57505-384-4). 48pp. This American scientist of Japanese ancestry has been fascinated by fish since childhood and has turned her interest into a groundbreaking scientific career. (Rev: BL 8/00; HBG 10/00; SLJ 7/00) [921]

COPERNICUS

15428 Andronik, Catherine M. *Copernicus: Founder of Modern Astronomy* (4–8). Illus. Series: Great Minds of Science. 2002, Enslow LB $26.60 (978-0-7660-1755-9). 112pp. This absorbing biography that covers Copernicus's youth and succeeds in explaining necessary scientific concepts also includes activities that reinforce this understanding. (Rev: HBG 10/02; SLJ 6/02) [520.92]

15429 Fradin, Dennis Brindell. *Nicolaus Copernicus: The Earth Is a Planet* (3–6). Illus. by Cynthia von Buhler. 2004, Mondo $15.95 (978-1-59336-006-1). 32pp. This succinct, illustrated profile of Polish astronomer Copernicus recounts his life and explores how he developed his theory that the planets revolve around the sun. (Rev: BL 4/1/04; SLJ 6/04) [921]

15430 Ingram, Scott. *Nicolaus Copernicus: Father of Modern Astronomy* (5–9). Series: Giants of Science. 2004, Gale LB $26.20 (978-1-56711-489-8). 64pp. Copernicus's life, the influences of the church, and his important contributions to science are presented in clear prose and historical context. (Rev: SLJ 6/05) [921]

COUSTEAU, JACQUES

15431 Bankston, John. *Jacques-Yves Cousteau: His Story Under the Sea* (4–5). Series: Unlocking the Secrets of Science. 2002, Mitchell Lane LB $17.95 (978-1-58415-112-8). 48pp. A concise look at the pioneering undersea explorer and inventor of the aqualung that opened up exploration of the ocean. (Rev: BL 8/02; HBG 3/03; SLJ 9/02) [921]

15432 Berne, Jennifer. *Manfish: The Story of Jacques Cousteau* (K–3). Illus. by Eric Puybaret. 2008, Chronicle $16.99 (978-0-8118-6063-5). 32pp. A lyrical description of the young Cousteau's love of water and how this translated into careers that involved much time underwater. (Rev: BCCB 7–8/08; BL 6/1–15/08; LMC 11/08) [921]

15433 DuTemple, Lesley A. *Jacques Cousteau* (4–6). Series: A&E Biography. 2000, Lerner LB $27.93 (978-0-8225-4979-6). 112pp. This is the story of the pioneering underwater adventurer and filmmaker who spent most of his life exploring the silent world beneath the sea. (Rev: BL 6/1–15/00; HBG 3/01; SLJ 9/00) [921]

15434 King, Roger. *Jacques Cousteau and the Undersea World* (4–6). Illus. Series: Explorers of New Worlds. 2000, Chelsea LB $25.00 (978-0-7910-5956-2); paper $25.00 (978-0-7910-6166-4). 63pp. This account of Cousteau's life starts with his childhood, and covers his creativity in designing equipment for underwater exploration as well as his other important contributions. (Rev: SLJ 4/01) [921]

15435 Yaccarino, Dan. *The Fantastic Undersea Life of Jacques Cousteau* (K–3). Illus. by author. 2009, Knopf $16.99 (978-0-375-85573-3). 40pp. Starting with Cousteau's childhood, this effective biography traces the oceanographer's love of the sea. (Rev: BCCB 3/09; BL 1/1–15/09; HB 7/09; SLJ 3/09) [921]

CRUM, GEORGE

15436 Taylor, Gaylia. *George Crum and the Saratoga Chip* (2–4). Illus. by Frank Morrison. 2006, Lee & Low $16.95 (978-1-58430-255-1). 32pp. This attractive picture book recounts how George Crum, a chef of mixed African American and Native American ancestry, invented the potato chip to please a demanding customer and eventually opened his own restaurant. (Rev: BL 4/1/06; SLJ 5/06) [921]

CURIE, MARIE

15437 Birch, Beverley. *Marie Curie: Courageous Pioneer in the Study of Radioactivity* (5–7). Illus. Series: Giants of Science. 2000, Blackbirch LB $24.95 (978-1-56711-333-4). 64pp. This biography of Marie Curie covers her youth, her struggles to get an education, her marriage, and her scientific career and accomplishments. A bilingual (English/Spanish) version is also available. (Rev: BL 1/1–15/01; HBG 3/01) [921]

15438 Graham, Ian. *Curie and the Science of Radioactivity* (4–6). Illus. by David Antram. Series: The Explosion Zone. 2006, Barron's $12.99 (978-0-7641-5973-2). 32pp. This biography of Marie Curie covers the Polish-born scientist's life and career and explains concepts related to her work, including half-life, transmutation, and the measurement of radiation; suitable for report writers despite cartoon illustrations. (Rev: SLJ 11/06) [921]

15439 Krull, Kathleen. *Marie Curie* (5–8). Illus. by Boris Kulikov. Series: Giants of Science. 2007, Viking $15.99 (978-0-670-05894-5). 128pp. This biography of the Nobel Prize-winning scientist supplies plenty of information about her family life and personality as well as her discoveries and her legacy. (Rev: BL 12/15/07; HB 11/07; SLJ 12/07) [540.92]

15440 McCormick, Lisa Wade. *Marie Curie* (1–2). Series: Rookie Biographies. 2006, Children's Pr. LB $20.50 (978-0-516-25040-3); paper $4.95 (978-0-516-21445-0). 32pp. For beginning readers, this is a simple overview of the scientist's life with emphasis on her discoveries. (Rev: SLJ 9/06) [921]

15441 MacLeod, Elizabeth. *Marie Curie* (K–3). Illus. by John Mantha. Series: Kids Can Read Alone. 2009, Kids Can $14.95 (978-1-55453-296-4); paper $3.95 (978-1-55453-297-1). 32pp. For early readers this is an interesting introduction to the Polish scientist and her importance. (Rev: BL 5/1/09) [540.92]

15442 Poynter, Margaret. *Marie Curie: Discoverer of Radium*. Rev. ed. (4–7). Illus. Series: Great Minds of Science. 2007, Enslow LB $31.93 (978-0-89490-477-6). 128pp. The life and significance of this discoverer of radium are covered, with a chapter of suggested activities. (Rev: BL 1/1/95; SLJ 10/94) [921]

15443 Wishinsky, Frieda. *Manya's Dream: A Story of Marie Curie* (2–5). 2003, Maple Tree $19.95 (978-1-894379-53-3); paper $6.95 (978-1-894379-54-0). 32pp. This inspiring biography of Polish-born scientist Marie Curie focuses principally on the facts of her life, including her childhood in Poland, studies at the Sorbonne in Paris, and rescue work during World War I. (Rev: BL 12/15/03)

15444 Yannuzzi, Della A. *New Elements: The Story of Marie Curie* (5–10). Illus. Series: Profiles in Science. 2006, Morgan Reynolds $26.95 (978-1-59935-023-3). 144pp. More about the scientist's life than about the significance of her research, this introduction will be helpful to report writers. (Rev: BL 12/1/06; SLJ 1/07) [921]

DAMADIAN, RAYMOND

15445 Kjelle, Marylou Morano. *Raymond Damadian and the Development of MRI* (5–7). Series: Unlocking the Secrets of Science. 2002, Mitchell Lane LB $25.70 (978-1-58415-141-8). 48pp. This account focuses on Damadian's scientific accomplishments. (Rev: HBG 10/03; SLJ 1/03) [921]

DARWIN, CHARLES

15446 Anderson, Margaret J. *Charles Darwin: Naturalist.* Rev. ed. (4–7). Illus. Series: Great Minds of Science. 2008, Enslow LB $31.93 (978-0-89490-476-9). 128pp. In addition to a biography of this controversial naturalist, there is a chapter on activities for the reader. (Rev: BL 1/1/95; SLJ 10/94) [921]

15447 Ashby, Ruth. *Young Charles Darwin and the Voyage of the Beagle* (4–7). Illus. by Suzanne Duranceau. 2009, Peachtree $12.95 (978-1-56145-478-5). 132pp. Focusing on Darwin's five-year voyage on the *Beagle*, this interesting biography includes many direct quotations. (Rev: BL 3/15/09; SLJ 3/09) [921]

15448 Fullick, Ann. *Charles Darwin* (4–6). Series: Groundbreakers. 2000, Heinemann LB $25.64 (978-1-57572-368-6). 48pp. This biography of the scientist who formulated the theory of evolution concentrates on his five-year voyage on the *H.M.S. Beagle.* (Rev: SLJ 2/01) [921]

15449 Gibbons, Alan. *Charles Darwin* (3–6). Illus. by Leo Brown. 2008, Kingfisher $16.95 (978-0-7534-6251-5). 64pp. A fictional cabin boy keeps a diary of Darwin's voyage aboard the *Beagle*, giving personal details as well as observations of scientific studies; an extensive later section of the book discusses the voyage, life at sea, and other facets of Darwin's life. (Rev: BL 1/1–15/09; LMC 5/09*) [921]

15450 Lasky, Kathryn. *One Beetle Too Many: The Extraordinary Adventures of Charles Darwin* (3–5). Illus. by Matthew Trueman. 2009, Candlewick $17.99 (978-0-7636-1436-2). 48pp. This large-format biography highlights Darwin's curiosity as it explores his life and work. (Rev: BCCB 2/09; BL 1/1–15/09; SLJ 1/09) [921]

15451 Lawson, Kristan. *Darwin and Evolution for Kids: His Life and Ideas with 21 Activities* (5–9). Illus. 2003, Chicago Review paper $16.95 (978-1-55652-502-5). 146pp. The naturalist's life and work are examined in clear, interesting text, with thorough coverage of his five-year research voyage on *H.M.S. Beagle* and the continuing controversy over his theories. (Rev: SLJ 4/04) [921]

15452 McGinty, Alice B. *Darwin* (1–4). Illus. by Mary Azarian. 2009, Houghton $18.00 (978-0-618-99531-8). 48pp. This appealing picture-book biography juxtaposes narrative about his life with quotations from Darwin's journals and letters. (Rev: BL 1/1–15/09; SLJ 3/09) [921]

15453 Schanzer, Rosalyn. *What Darwin Saw: The Journey that Changed the World* (3–6). Illus. by author. 2009, National Geographic $17.95 (978-1-4263-0396-8). 48pp. This brightly illustrated large-format picture book, which focuses mainly on his voyage aboard the *Beagle* and the opinions he forms then, uses many quotations from Darwin's journals, books, and letters and includes a map of the jour-

ney. (Rev: BCCB 3/09; BL 3/15/09; SLJ 3/09) [921]

15454 Senker, Cath. *Charles Darwin* (4–8). Illus. Series: Scientists Who Made History. 2002, Raintree LB $27.12 (978-0-7398-4843-2). 48pp. Darwin's life and contributions are presented in clear text and ample illustrations, with historical detail that places the information in context. (Rev: HBG 10/02; SLJ 9/02) [576.8092]

15455 Sís, Peter. *The Tree of Life: Charles Darwin* (4–7). Illus. 2003, Farrar $18.00 (978-0-374-45628-3). 44pp. Highly illustrated, this imaginative and visual biography traces Darwin's life and development as a naturalist, with a focus on his voyages on the *Beagle.* (Rev: BL 10/15/03; HB 11/03*; HBG 4/04; SLJ 10/03*) [576.8]

15456 Sproule, Anna. *Charles Darwin: Visionary Behind the Theory of Evolution* (4–7). Illus. Series: Giants of Science. 2003, Gale $26.20 (978-1-56711-655-7). 64pp. Darwin's life and accomplishments are presented in concise text. (Rev: SLJ 1/03) [921]

DEERE, JOHN

15457 Hall, Margaret. *John Deere* (2–4). Series: Lives and Times. 2004, Heinemann LB $22.79 (978-1-4034-5327-3). 32pp. Profiles the life and achievements of John Deere, a blacksmith whose invention of an improved farm plow launched the farm equipment business that still bears his name. (Rev: BL 7/04; SLJ 9/04) [921]

DE LA RENTA, OSCAR

15458 Carrillo, Louis. *Oscar de la Renta* (4–8). Illus. Series: Contemporary Hispanic Americans. 1995, Raintree LB $28.80 (978-0-8172-3980-0). This account focuses on the professional life of the renowned Hispanic American fashion designer who was born in the Dominican Republic. (Rev: BL 3/15/96; SLJ 1/96) [921]

DE PASSE, SUZANNE

15459 Mussari, Mark. *Suzanne De Passe: Motown's Boss Lady* (5–8). Illus. Series: Wizards of Business. 1992, Garrett LB $17.26 (978-1-56074-026-1). 64pp. The story of the woman who helped make Motown the great name in the music industry. (Rev: BL 6/15/92) [921]

DOMAGK, GERHARD

15460 Bankston, John. *Gerhard Domagk and the Discovery of Sulfa* (4–5). Series: Unlocking the Secrets of Science. 2002, Mitchell Lane LB $25.70 (978-1-58415-115-9). 56pp. The story of the man who discovered the antibiotic properties of sulfa but whose accomplishments were overshadowed by other advances in antibiotics. (Rev: BL 9/15/02; SLJ 11/02) [921]

DREW, CHARLES

15461 Whitehurst, Susan. *Dr. Charles Drew: Medical Pioneer* (4–6). Series: Journey to Freedom: The African American Library. 2001, Child's World LB $17.95 (978-1-56766-926-8). 40pp. An attractive biography of this pioneering American black scientist who was noted for his research in blood plasma and his work in developing the concept of the Blood Bank. (Rev: BL 12/15/01; HBG 3/02; SLJ 1/02) [921]

DYSON, ESTHER

15462 Jablonski, Carla. *Esther Dyson: Web Guru* (5–8). Series: Techies. 2002, Millbrook LB $23.90 (978-0-7613-2657-1). A leading light in the computer world, Dyson is the owner of EDventure Holdings, and is an active developer of emerging technologies and companies. (Rev: BL 4/1/02; HBG 10/02) [921]

15463 Morales, Leslie. *Esther Dyson: Internet Visionary* (5–8). Series: Internet Biographies. 2003, Enslow LB $23.93 (978-0-7660-1973-7). 48pp. Dyson, a skillful businesswoman, has played an influential role in the development of the Internet as a tool suitable for everyday use. (Rev: HBG 10/03; SLJ 10/03) [338.4]

EARLE, SYLVIA

15464 Baker, Beth. *Sylvia Earle: Guardian of the Sea* (4–7). Illus. Series: Lerner Biographies. 2000, Lerner LB $27.93 (978-0-8225-4961-1). 112pp. This is a thrilling biography of the famous underwater explorer and marine scientist who was one of the first humans to swim with whales. (Rev: BL 10/15/00; HBG 3/01; SLJ 11/00) [921]

EASTMAN, CHARLES

15465 Ross, Michael E. *Wildlife Watching with Charles Eastman* (4–6). Illus. by Laurie Caple. Series: Naturalist's Apprentice. 1997, Carolrhoda LB $14.95 (978-1-57505-004-1). 48pp. Charles Eastman, who was born in 1858 in the Dakota Nation, became a physician and later used his childhood experiences to teach children to love and respect nature. (Rev: BL 5/15/98; HBG 3/98; SLJ 3/98) [921]

EASTMAN, GEORGE

15466 Gillis, Jennifer Blizin. *George Eastman* (2–4). 2004, Heinemann LB $22.79 (978-1-4034-5326-6). 32pp. This concise biography profiles the life and work of George Eastman, whose late-19th-century introduction of the Kodak camera first made photography widely available to the public. (Rev: BL 7/04) [921]

EASTWOOD, ALICE

15467 Ross, Michael E. *Flower Watching with Alice Eastwood* (3–5). Illus. Series: Naturalist's Apprentice. 1997, Carolrhoda LB $19.93 (978-1-57505-005-8). 46pp. This account of the life of Alice Eastwood — an African American who became an expert on the wildflowers of the Rockies and the West Coast -- also gives tips to the amateur flower watcher. (Rev: BL 3/1/98; HBG 3/98; SLJ 3/98) [921]

EDISON, THOMAS ALVA

15468 Carlson, Laurie. *Thomas Edison for Kids: His Life and Ideas: 21 Activities* (4–7). Illus. 2006, Chicago Review paper $14.95 (978-1-55652-584-1). 160pp. Activities allow readers to try some of the inventor's experiments; the biography section covers Edison's personal life as well as his achievements and introduces some of his contemporaries. (Rev: BL 2/15/06; SLJ 6/06) [621.3]

15469 Dolan, Ellen M. *Thomas Alva Edison: Inventor* (5–8). Series: Historical American Biographies. 1998, Enslow LB $26.60 (978-0-7660-1014-7). Direct quotations, fact boxes, a chronology, and chapter notes make this an attractive life of the great inventor. (Rev: BL 8/98) [921]

15470 Dooling, Michael. *Young Thomas Edison* (1–3). Illus. 2005, Holiday $16.95 (978-0-8234-1868-8). 40pp. This engaging biography focuses on the inventor's youth, his hearing loss, his homeschooling, and his early experiments. (Rev: BL 1/1–15/06; SLJ 2/06*) [921]

15471 Gaines, Ann. *Thomas Edison* (2–3). Series: Discover the Life of an Inventor. 2001, Rourke LB $20.64 (978-1-58952-122-3). 24pp. A simple, introductory biography that describes Edison's life, contributions, and struggles. (Rev: BL 10/15/01; SLJ 1/02) [921]

15472 Gomez, Rebecca. *Thomas Edison* (2–3). Illus. Series: First Biographies. 2003, ABDO LB $22.78 (978-1-57765-945-7). 32pp. A brief easy-reader overview of the inventor's life and accomplishments. (Rev: HBG 4/04; SLJ 9/03) [921]

15473 Graham, Amy. *Thomas Edison: Wizard of Light and Sound* (5–8). Illus. Series: Inventors Who Changed the World. 2007, Enslow LB $24.95 (978-1-59845-052-1). 128pp. The text of this profile of Edison and his achievements is augmented by links to carefully evaluated Web sites. (Rev: SLJ 11/07) [921]

15474 Mason, Paul. *Thomas A. Edison* (4–6). Illus. Series: Scientists Who Made History. 2001, Raintree LB $27.12 (978-0-7398-4414-4). 48pp. This well-illustrated profile of Edison and his life and work will be useful for report writers. (Rev: HBG 10/02; SLJ 2/02) [921]

15475 Mitchell, Barbara. *The Wizard of Sound: A Story About Thomas Edison* (4–6). Illus. by Hetty Mitchell. Series: Creative Minds. 1991, Carolrhoda LB $22.60 (978-0-87614-445-9). 64pp. The story of how a shy, inept youngster became the inventor of wonders. (Rev: SLJ 1/92) [921]

15476 Mortensen, Lori. *Thomas Edison: Inventor, Scientist, and Genius* (K–3). Illus. by Jeffrey Thompson. Series: Biographies. 2007, Picture Window LB $23.93 (978-1-4048-3105-6). 24pp. An introduction to the inventor for beginning readers who will enjoy learning of Edison's childhood and his achievements as an adult. (Rev: SLJ 8/07)

15477 Sproule, Anna. *Thomas Edison: The World's Greatest Inventor* (5–7). Series: Giants of Science. 2000, Blackbirch paper $24.95 (978-1-56711-331-0). 64pp. A prolific inventor, Edison not only worked on the electric light bulb but also the phonograph, the movie projector, and an early answering machine. (Rev: BL 1/1–15/01; HBG 3/01; SLJ 1/01) [921]

15478 Woodside, Martin. *Thomas A. Edison: The Man Who Lit Up the World* (5–8). Series: Sterling Biographies. 2007, Sterling LB $12.95 (978-1-4027-4955-1); paper $5.95 (978-1-4027-3229-4). 124pp. A concise account of Edison's life from childhood and his many achievements in varied fields. (Rev: SLJ 10/07) [921]

EHRLICH, PAUL

15479 Zannos, Susan. *Paul Ehrlich and Modern Drug Development* (4–5). Series: Unlocking the Secrets of Science. 2002, Mitchell Lane LB $17.95 (978-1-58415-121-0). 56pp. The story of the man often called the "father of modern drug development" and his discovery of a "magic bullet." (Rev: BL 9/15/02; SLJ 3/03) [921]

EINSTEIN, ALBERT

15480 Bankston, John. *Albert Einstein and the Theory of Relativity* (5–8). Series: Unlocking the Secrets of Science. 2002, Mitchell Lane LB $25.70 (978-1-58415-137-1). 56pp. Einstein's accomplishments and the many challenges he faced are explored in concise text with many black-and-white photographs. (Rev: SLJ 2/03) [921]

15481 Berger, Melvin, and Gilda Berger. *Did It Take Creativity to Find Relativity, Albert Einstein?* (3–4). Illus. by Brandon Dorman. Series: Science Super-Giants. 2007, Scholastic paper $4.99 (978-0-439-83384-4). 48pp. "What did Einstein discover about light?" "How could scientists test Einstein's theory?" Using a question-and-answer format, this profile provides biographical and basic scientific information. (Rev: SLJ 2/08) [921]

15482 Brown, Don. *Odd Boy Out: Young Albert Einstein* (3–5). Illus. 2004, Houghton $16.00 (978-0-618-49298-5). 32pp. Einstein's awkward and unpromising youth is described in this picture-book biography that also introduces his adult achievements. (Rev: BL 9/1/04; SLJ 10/04) [921]

15483 Delano, Marfé Ferguson. *Genius: A Photobiography of Albert Einstein* (5–8). Illus. 2005, National Geographic $17.95 (978-0-7922-9544-0). 64pp. Photographs of the scientist's life, as well as brief explanations of his work, help to make the man and his theories more accessible to young readers; an oversized and engaging volume. (Rev: BL 4/1/05*; SLJ 5/05) [921]

15484 Lakin, Patricia. *Albert Einstein: Genius of the Twentieth Century* (2–4). Illus. by Alan Daniel. Series: Ready-to-Read: Stories of Famous Americans. 2005, Simon & Schuster paper $3.99 (978-0-

689-87034-7). 48pp. This effective easy-to-read biography describes Einstein's intelligence and key accomplishments. (Rev: BL 12/1/05) [921]

15485 Lassieur, Allison. *Albert Einstein: Genius of the Twentieth Century* (5–8). Series: Great Life Stories. 2005, Watts LB $30.50 (978-0-531-12401-7). 127pp. In addition to placing Einstein's life (including his childhood) and contributions in historical and social context, Lassieur explains his theories and their application. (Rev: SLJ 9/05) [921]

15486 MacDonald, Fiona. *Albert Einstein: The Genius Behind the Theory of Relativity* (5–7). Illus. Series: Giants of Science. 2000, Blackbirch LB $27.44 (978-1-56711-330-3). 64pp. As well as his childhood, education, theories, personal life, and international awards, this biography of Albert Einstein assesses his lasting contributions to physics and mathematics. (Rev: BL 1/1–15/01; HBG 3/01; SLJ 1/01) [921]

15487 MacLeod, Elizabeth. *Albert Einstein: A Life of Genius* (5–7). Illus. 2003, Kids Can $14.95 (978-1-55337-396-4); paper $6.95 (978-1-55337-397-1). 32pp. Small photographs and illustrations accompany this attractive chronological introduction to the life of Einstein that focuses on the man rather than his theories. (Rev: BL 3/1/03; HBG 10/03; SLJ 5/03) [530]

15488 McPherson, Stephanie S. *Ordinary Genius: The Story of Albert Einstein* (4–7). Illus. 1995, Carolrhoda LB $27.93 (978-0-87614-788-7). 96pp. Good historical background information is given on the life of Einstein plus a clear explanation of his discoveries. (Rev: BL 6/1–15/95; SLJ 9/95) [921]

15489 Meltzer, Milton. *Albert Einstein: A Biography* (3–5). Illus. 2008, Holiday $16.95 (978-0-8234-1966-1). 32pp. Although brief, this appealing and accessible biography presents lots of solid information on Einstein's life and achievements, including his interests outside science. (Rev: BL 2/1/08; LMC 3/08; SLJ 3/08) [921]

15490 Wyborny, Sheila. *Albert Einstein* (3–6). Series: Inventors and Creators. 2003, Gale LB $23.70 (978-0-7377-1278-0). 48pp. An interesting biography of the German-born physicist and his lasting contributions to scientific knowledge. (Rev: SLJ 6/03) [921]

ELION, GERTRUDE

15491 MacBain, Jennifer. *Gertrude Elion: Nobel Prize Winner in Physiology and Medicine* (5–8). Illus. Series: Women Hall of Famers in Mathematics and Science. 2004, Rosen LB $29.25 (978-0-8239-3876-6). 112pp. Elion, a biochemist and pharmacologist who never earned a doctorate, won a Nobel Prize for her advances in the field of chemotherapy. (Rev: BL 3/1/04; SLJ 9/04) [615]

ELLISON, LARRY

15492 Ehrenhaft, Daniel. *Larry Ellison: Sheer Nerve* (5–8). Series: Techies. 2001, Millbrook LB $23.90 (978-0-7613-1962-7). The life story of one of the world's richest men and co-founder of Oracle, the world's leading supplier of software for information management. (Rev: BL 4/1/02; HBG 3/02; SLJ 12/01) [921]

15493 Peters, Craig. *Larry Ellison: Database Genius of Oracle* (5–8). Series: Internet Biographies. 2003, Enslow LB $23.93 (978-0-7660-1974-4). 48pp. A look at the life and accomplishments of the cofounder of Oracle Corporation. (Rev: HBG 10/03; SLJ 10/03) [338.7]

ERICSSON, JOHN

15494 Wooldridge, Connie N. *Thank You Very Much, Captain Ericsson* (1–5). Illus. by Andrew Glass. 2005, Holiday House $16.95 (978-0-8234-1626-4). 32pp. The struggles of the Civil-War era inventor are presented in lighthearted text with funny cartoons. (Rev: SLJ 8/05) [921]

FANNING, SHAWN

15495 Mitten, Christopher. *Shawn Fanning: Napster and the Music Revolution* (5–8). Series: Techies. 2002, Millbrook LB $23.90 (978-0-7613-2656-4). Using many photographs and an interesting text, this is the biography of the creator of Napster, a software package for downloading music from computers. (Rev: BL 4/1/02; HBG 10/02; SLJ 6/02) [921]

FARNSWORTH, PHILO

15496 Krull, Kathleen. *The Boy Who Invented TV: The Story of Philo Farnsworth* (3–5). Illus. by Greg Couch. 2009, Knopf $16.99 (978-0-375-84561-1). 40pp. Krull recounts how the young Farnsworth conceived of the idea of television, explains the underlying scientific concepts, and in an afterword details his loss of the patent. (Rev: BL 6/1–15/09; LMC 10/09) [921]

15497 McPherson, Stephanie S. *TV's Forgotten Hero: The Story of Philo Farnsworth* (4–7). Illus. 1996, Carolrhoda LB $27.93 (978-1-57505-017-1). 96pp. The biography of the genius who invented electronic television when he was only 14. (Rev: BL 2/1/97; SLJ 2/97) [921]

15498 Roberts, Russell. *Philo T. Farnsworth; the Life of Television's Forgotten Inventor* (4–5). Series: Unlocking the Secrets of Science. 2003, Mitchell Lane LB $25.70 (978-1-58415-176-0). 48pp. This brief biography recounts the bittersweet story of Philo T. Farnsworth, whose pioneering developments in the field of television were never fully acknowledged during his lifetime. (Rev: BL 11/15/03; SLJ 9/03)

FLEMING, ALEXANDER

15499 Bankston, John. *Alexander Fleming and the Story of Penicillin* (5–8). Series: Unlocking the Secrets of Science. 2001, Mitchell Lane LB $25.70 (978-1-58415-106-7). 56pp. This absorbing biography of the Scottish Nobel Prize winner covers his personal life as well as his scientific career. (Rev: HBG 3/02; SLJ 1/02) [616.014092]

15500 Birch, Beverley. *Alexander Fleming: Pioneer with Antibiotics* (4–7). Illus. Series: Giants of Science. 2003, Gale $26.20 (978-1-56711-656-4). 64pp. Fleming's life, education, research, and discovery of penicillin are presented in concise text. (Rev: SLJ 1/03) [921]

15501 Tocci, Salvatore. *Alexander Fleming: The Man Who Discovered Penicillin* (5–8). Series: Great Minds of Science. 2002, Enslow LB $26.60 (978-0-7660-1998-0). 128pp. An absorbing account of Fleming's childhood and later life, with solid information on his contributions to medical science and his legacy. (Rev: HBG 10/02; SLJ 9/02) [921]

FORD, HENRY

15502 Bankston, John. *Henry Ford and the Assembly Line* (4–5). Series: Unlocking the Secrets of Science. 2003, Mitchell Lane LB $17.95 (978-1-58415-173-9). 48pp. This brief biography chronicles the life of Henry Ford and includes photographs and reproductions. (Rev: BL 11/15/03; SLJ 9/03)

15503 Gaines, Ann. *Henry Ford* (2–3). Illus. Series: Discover the Life of an Inventor. 2001, Rourke LB $20.64 (978-1-58952-120-9). 24pp. This biography of Ford concentrates on his influence on the automobile industry. (Rev: BL 10/15/01) [338.7]

15504 Kulling, Monica. *Eat My Dust! Henry Ford's First Race* (1–2). Series: Step into Reading. 2004, Random LB $11.99 (978-0-375-91510-9); paper $3.99 (978-0-375-81510-2). 48pp. Beginning readers, especially boys, will enjoy this dramatic account of Henry Ford's auto race victory against Alexander Winton. (Rev: BL 8/04) [338.7]

15505 McCarthy, Pat. *Henry Ford: Building Cars for Everyone* (5–8). Series: Historical American Biographies. 2002, Enslow LB $26.60 (978-0-7660-1620-0). 128pp. Ford is shown as an eccentric but successful father, engineer, and businessman, who made the automobile widely available but expected his workers to suffer difficult conditions. (Rev: HBG 3/03; SLJ 1/03) [338.76292092]

15506 Mitchell, Barbara. *We'll Race You, Henry: A Story About Henry Ford* (3–5). Illus. 1986, Carolrhoda LB $22.60 (978-0-87614-291-2); Lerner paper $6.95 (978-0-87614-471-8). 64pp. The focus is on race-car ventures in this partly fictionalized biography. (Rev: BL 8/86; SLJ 9/86) [921]

15507 Schaefer, Lola M. *Henry Ford* (K–2). Series: Famous People in Transportation. 2000, Capstone LB $17.26 (978-0-7368-0546-9). 24pp. For beginning readers, this is a biography of Henry Ford that uses double-page spreads to present important facts about his life and accomplishments. (Rev: HBG 10/00; SLJ 9/00) [921]

FOSSEY, DIAN

15508 Blue, Rose, and Corinne J. Naden. *Dian Fossey: At Home with the Giant Gorillas* (4–6). Series: Gateway Greens. 2002, Millbrook LB $23.90 (978-0-7613-2569-7). 48pp. A brief, nicely illustrated biography of the U.S.-born zoologist who studied the mountain gorilla in its natural habitat in Africa and was killed because of her efforts. (Rev: BL 7/02; HBG 3/03) [921]

15509 Gogerly, Liz. *Dian Fossey* (5–8). Illus. Series: Scientists Who Made History. 2003, Raintree LB $27.12 (978-0-7368-5225-8). 48pp. A riveting profile of the woman who became an expert on gorillas and the militant stance that may have led to her murder. (Rev: BL 3/1/03) [599.884]

15510 Matthews, Tom L. *Light Shining Through the Mist: A Photobiography of Dian Fossey* (4–6). Illus. 1998, National Geographic $17.95 (978-0-7922-7300-4). 64pp. An illustrated book relating the life and work of Dian Fossey, founder of the Karisoke Research Center in Rwanda, who studied mountain gorillas and worked to prevent poachers from killing off this endangered species. (Rev: BL 9/15/98; HB 9/98; HBG 3/99; SLJ 9/98) [921]

15511 Schott, Jane A. *Dian Fossey and the Mountain Gorillas* (2–3). Series: On My Own Biography. 2000, Carolrhoda LB $19.93 (978-1-57505-082-9). 48pp. The exciting story one of the foremost primate researchers of the 20th century, her groundbreaking work observing mountain gorillas in their native habitat, and her efforts to stop their poaching. (Rev: BL 6/1–15/00; HBG 10/00; SLJ 6/00) [921]

FRANKLIN, ROSALIND

15512 Senker, Cath. *Rosalind Franklin* (5–8). Illus. Series: Scientists Who Made History. 2003, Raintree $27.12 (978-0-7398-5226-2). 48pp. An interesting biography of the woman who never gained credit for her contributions to the discovery of the structure of DNA. (Rev: BL 3/1/03; HBG 10/03; SLJ 4/03) [572.8]

FULTON, ROBERT

15513 Bowen, Andy Russell. *A Head Full of Notions: A Story About Robert Fulton* (4–6). Illus. 1997, Carolrhoda LB $22.60 (978-0-87614-876-1); paper $6.95 (978-1-57505-026-3). 64pp. A brief biography of the life and times of the man who worked first on plans for a submarine and then on his famous steamboat. (Rev: BL 4/15/97; SLJ 3/97) [921]

15514 Flammang, James M. *Robert Fulton: Inventor and Steamboat Builder* (5–8). Illus. Series: Historical American Biographies. 1999, Enslow LB $26.60 (978-0-7660-1141-0). 128pp. Beginning with Fulton's 1807 demonstration of his steamboat, this biography moves back and forth in time to trace the complete career of this man who changed America's transportation history. (Rev: BL 11/1/99; HBG 3/00) [921]

15515 Gillis, Jennifer Blizin. *Robert Fulton* (1–4). Series: Lives and Times. 2004, Heinemann LB $22.79 (978-1-4034-5328-0). 32pp. Report writers will find useful information in this biography that has a timeline and "Fact File" boxes. (Rev: SLJ 9/04)

15516 Pierce, Morris A. *Robert Fulton and the Development of the Steamboat* (4–8). Series: Library of American Lives and Times. 2003, Rosen LB $34.60 (978-0-8239-5737-8). 112pp. The inventor of the steamboat was a man of determination and wide interests who also worked on naval weapons. (Rev: BL 6/1–15/03; SLJ 4/03) [921]

15517 Whiting, Jim. *Robert Fulton* (2–4). Series: A Robbie Reader: What's So Great About? 2006, Mitchell Lane LB $25.70 (978-1-58415-478-5). 32pp. With large text and lots of white space, this introductory biography looks at the life and career of the man responsible for developing the first commercially successful steam-powered vessel. (Rev: SLJ 1/07) [921]

GALILEO

15518 Goldsmith, Mike. *Galileo Galilei* (4–6). Illus. Series: Scientists Who Made History. 2001, Raintree LB $27.12 (978-0-7398-4416-8). 48pp. This well-illustrated profile of Galileo and his life and work will be useful for report writers. (Rev: HBG 10/02; SLJ 2/02) [921]

15519 Hightower, Paul. *Galileo: Astronomer and Physicist* (4–7). Illus. Series: Great Minds of Science. 1997, Enslow LB $26.60 (978-0-89490-787-6). 128pp. This biography not only includes material on the life and accomplishments of this courageous scientist but also contains several activities that give an understanding of his work. (Rev: BL 6/1–15/97) [921]

15520 Hilliam, Rachel. *Galileo Galilei: Father of Modern Science* (5–8). Series: Rulers, Scholars, and Artists of the Renaissance. 2005, Rosen LB $33.25 (978-1-4042-0314-3). 112pp. Ford places Galileo's life and accomplishments in the context of culture and politics of the time. (Rev: SLJ 10/05) [921]

15521 Lewis, J. Patrick. *Galileo's Universe* (3–5). Illus. by Tom Curry. 2005, Creative Editions $24.95 (978-1-56846-183-0). 18pp. This unusual pop-up biography recounts the life of Galileo in rhyming verse. (Rev: BL 12/1/05) [921]

15522 Panchyk, Richard. *Galileo for Kids: His Life and Ideas* (5–9). Illus. 2005, Chicago Review paper $16.95 (978-1-55652-566-7). 166pp. A clearly written and well-illustrated overview of Galileo's life and scientific achievements, with excerpts from Galileo's writings and suggested activities. (Rev: SLJ 9/05) [921]

15523 Sís, Peter. *Starry Messenger* (4–6). Illus. 1996, Farrar $16.00 (978-0-374-37191-3). 32pp. The world of Galileo and his amazing life and accomplishments are re-created in this unusual picture book. (Rev: BCCB 11/96; BL 10/15/96*; SLJ 10/96*) [921] ⌒

15524 Steele, Philip. *Galileo: The Genius Who Faced the Inquisition* (3–6). Series: National Geographic World History Biographies. 2005, National Geographic $17.95 (978-0-7922-3656-6). 64pp. The scientist's place in history is clearly set out in this well-designed, informative book. (Rev: SLJ 6/06) [921]

GATES, BILL

15525 Barton-Wood, Sara. *Bill Gates: Computer Legend* (4–6). Illus. Series: Famous Lives. 2001, Raintree LB $27.12 (978-0-7398-4432-8). 48pp. An introduction to the life and career of Microsoft founder Bill Gates. (Rev: BL 1/1–15/02; HBG 10/02) [338.7]

15526 Lesinski, Jeanne. *Bill Gates* (4–6). Series: A&E Biography. 2000, Lerner LB $27.93 (978-0-8225-4949-9). 112pp. The story of the man whose name has become synonymous with computers, software, and wealth. (Rev: BL 6/1–15/00; HBG 3/01; SLJ 9/00) [921]

15527 Lockwood, Brad. *Bill Gates: Profile of a Digital Entrepreneur* (5–8). 2007, Rosen LB $31.95 (978-1-4042-1906-9). 112pp. Well-written and updated, this volume on Gates focuses on his career. (Rev: LMC 1/08; SLJ 3/08)

15528 Peters, Craig. *Bill Gates* (5–8). Illus. Series: Internet Biographies. 2003, Enslow LB $23.93 (978-0-7660-1969-0). 48pp. A reader-friendly biography of the creator of Microsoft, with information on his youth as well as his successful later life. (Rev: BL 3/15/03; HBG 10/03) [338.7]

15529 Schuman, Michael A. *Bill Gates: Computer Mogul and Philanthropist* (5–8). 2007, Enslow LB $31.93 (978-0-7660-2693-3). 128pp. Gates and his wife Melinda and their far-reaching philanthropic efforts are covered in this clearly written volume. (Rev: SLJ 3/08) [921]

15530 Sherman, Josepha. *Bill Gates: Computer King* (4–6). Series: Gateway Biographies. 2000, Millbrook LB $23.90 (978-0-7613-1771-5). 48pp. This book successfully tells the story of Bill Gates's life and gives a history of Microsoft. (Rev: HBG 3/01; SLJ 11/00) [921]

15531 Woog, Adam. *Bill Gates* (4–7). Illus. Series: Famous People. 2003, Gale $26.20 (978-0-7377-1400-5). 48pp. Woog covers Gates's childhood, education, interest in computers, and career, with photographs. (Rev: BL 6/1–15/03) [338.7]

GODDARD, ROBERT

15532 Bankston, John. *Robert Goddard and the Liquid Rocket Engine* (4–7). Series: Unlocking the Secrets of Science. 2001, Mitchell Lane LB $17.95 (978-1-58415-107-4). 56pp. Bankston combines an introduction to Goddard's commitment to rocketry and his difficulty finding funding with an understandable explanation of the scientific challenges. (Rev: HBG 3/02; SLJ 2/02) [621.43]

15533 Streissguth, Thomas. *Rocket Man: The Story of Robert Goddard* (5–7). Illus. Series: Trailblazers. 1995, Carolrhoda LB $27.93 (978-0-87614-863-1). 88pp. A history of rocketry, with emphasis on the life and accomplishments of Goddard. (Rev: BL 10/15/95; SLJ 9/95) [921]

GOODALL, JANE

15534 Goodall, Jane. *My Life with the Chimpanzees* (3–6). Illus. 1992, Houghton paper $11.04 (978-0-395-61849-3). The famed zoologist talks about her life studying the chimps of Africa. (Rev: BCCB 5/88; BL 7/88; SLJ 4/88)

15535 January, Brendan. *Jane Goodall: Animal Behaviorist and Writer* (4–7). Series: Ferguson Career Biographies. 2001, Ferguson LB $25.00 (978-0-89434-370-4). 127pp. This easily read biography will appeal in particular to reluctant readers and students seeking quick information for a report. (Rev: SLJ 9/01) [921]

15536 Kittinger, Jo S. *Jane Goodall* (1–2). Series: Scholastic News Nonfiction Readers. 2005, Children's Pr. LB $20.00 (978-0-516-24940-7). 24pp. This simple, photo-filled biography for beginning readers spotlights Goodall's breakthrough work with chimpanzees. (Rev: SLJ 4/06) [921]

15537 Pratt, Paula B. *Jane Goodall* (4–8). Illus. Series: The Importance Of. 1997, Lucent LB $27.45 (978-1-56006-082-6). The story of the great naturalist who studied and protected the primates of Africa. (Rev: BL 1/1–15/97; SLJ 2/97) [921]

15538 Sean, J. A. *Jane Goodall: Naturalist* (4–6). Illus. Series: Library of Famous Women. 1993, Blackbirch LB $24.95 (978-1-56711-010-4). 64pp. An accurate, engrossing account of the life of this great naturalist, who produced landmark studies on apes and their society. (Rev: BL 11/15/93; SLJ 2/94) [921]

GUTENBERG, JOHANNES

15539 Burch, Joann J. *Fine Print: A Story About Johann Gutenberg* (3–6). Illus. by Kent A. Aldrich. 1991, Carolrhoda LB $22.60 (978-0-87614-682-8). 64pp. An account of the man who changed world history by inventing the process of printing books from movable type. (Rev: BL 1/1/92; SLJ 3/92) [686.2]

15540 Feinstein, Stephen. *Johannes Gutenberg: The Printer Who Gave Words to the World* (5–8). Illus. 2008, Enslow LB $33.27 (978-1-59845-077-4). 128pp. A history of printing from the ancient civilizations to the Renaissance is included in this book about Johannes Gutenberg's contribution of a movable metal type and printing press. (Rev: SLJ 2/09) [921]

15541 Pollard, Michael. *Johann Gutenberg: Master of Modern Printing* (5–7). Series: Giants of Science. 2001, Blackbirch LB $27.44 (978-1-56711-335-8). 64pp. Good use of illustrations and an interesting text are highlights of this life of the German printer who first used movable type. (Rev: BL 8/1/01; HBG 3/02) [921]

HAMILTON, ALICE

15542 McPherson, Stephanie S. *The Workers' Detective: A Story About Dr. Alice Hamilton* (3–6). Illus. by Janet Schulz. Series: Creative Minds. 1992, Carolrhoda LB $21.27 (978-0-87614-699-6). 64pp. Introducing the woman who studied the effects of lead and other lethal materials on workers' health and changed industrial medicine. (Rev: BL 1/15/93; SLJ 10/92) [921]

HARRISON, JOHN

15543 Borden, Louise. *Sea Clocks: The Story of Longitude* (2–4). Illus. by Erik Blegvad. 2004, Simon & Schuster $18.95 (978-0-689-84216-0). 48pp. John Harrison's struggles to promote his chronomoter — and to gain credit for its invention — are recounted in an attractive picture-book biography. (Rev: BL 12/1/03; HB 3/04; SLJ 1/04)

15544 Lasky, Kathryn. *The Man Who Made Time Travel* (3–5). Illus. by Kevin Hawkes. 2003, Farrar $17.00 (978-0-374-37488-4). 48pp. This oversize book presents the story of John Harrison, who worked for 50 years to perfect a timepiece that would track longitude in shipboard navigation. (Rev: BL 3/1/03*; SLJ 4/03) [526]

HARVEY, WILLIAM

15545 Yount, Lisa. *William Harvey: Discoverer of How Blood Circulates*. Rev. ed. (4–8). Illus. Series: Great Minds of Science. 2008, Enslow LB $31.93 (978-0-89490-481-3). 128pp. A biography of the 17th-century scientist that describes early theories about the blood system and the importance of Harvey's discoveries. (Rev: SLJ 2/95) [921]

HEWLETT, WILLIAM

15546 Tracy, Kathleen. *William Hewlett: Pioneer of the Computer Age* (5–7). Series: Unlocking the Secrets of Science. 2002, Mitchell Lane LB $25.70 (978-1-58415-142-5). 48pp. This accessible account focuses on Hewlett's scientific accomplishments and career in business. (Rev: SLJ 1/03) [921]

HILL, JULIA BUTTERFLY

15547 Fitzgerald, Dawn. *Julia Butterfly Hill: Saving the Redwoods* (4–6). Series: Gateway Greens. 2002, Millbrook LB $23.90 (978-0-7613-2654-0). 48pp. This is a handsome biography of the environmental activist who lived in a 200-foot-tall redwood named Luna from December 1997 to December 1999. (Rev: BL 7/02; HBG 3/03) [921]

HOOKE, ROBERT

15548 Gow, Mary. *Robert Hooke: Creative Genius, Scientist, Inventor* (5–9). Series: Great Minds of Science. 2006, Enslow LB $31.93 (978-0-7660-2547-9). 128pp. A biography of the 17th-century man of science and arts who made discoveries in many fields and also helped to redesign London after the fire of 1666. (Rev: SLJ 6/07) [921]

HOPPER, GRACE

15549 Mattern, Joanne. *Grace Hopper: Computer Pioneer* (1–4). Series: Women Who Shaped History. 2003, Rosen LB $19.95 (978-0-8239-6505-2). 24pp. The amazing story of the U.S. Navy rear admiral who was a pioneer software engineer and the inventor of the compiler that translates English to the language of the target computer. (Rev: BL 2/15/03; SLJ 5/03) [921]

15550 Murphy, Patricia J. *Grace Hopper: Computer Whiz* (2–4). Series: Famous Inventors. 2004, Enslow LB $22.60 (978-0-7660-2273-7). 32pp. Describes Hopper's trail-blazing achievements and pioneering work in computers. (Rev: SLJ 2/05) [921]

HOUNSFIELD, GODFREY

15551 Zannos, Susan. *Godfrey Hounsfield and the Invention of CAT Scans* (4–5). Series: Unlocking the Secrets of Science. 2002, Mitchell Lane LB $17.95 (978-1-58415-119-7). 56pp. The story of the man who realized that X-rays could be manipulated by computers and later invented the amazingly accurate diagnostic device known as the computerized axial tomography or CAT scanner. (Rev: BL 9/15/02; SLJ 1/03) [921]

HOWARD, LUKE

15552 Hannah, Julie, and Joan Holub. *The Man Who Named the Clouds* (3–5). Illus. by Paige Billin-Frye. 2006, Albert Whitman $16.99 (978-0-8075-4974-2). 40pp. This fascinating book intertwines a profile of Luke Howard, the man who classified clouds into seven types, with a contemporary boy's weather journal. (Rev: BL 8/06; SLJ 10/06) [921]

HUBBLE, EDWIN

15553 Datnow, Claire. *Edwin Hubble: Discoverer of Galaxies* (4–8). Illus. Series: Great Minds of Science. 1997, Enslow LB $26.60 (978-0-89490-934-4). 128pp. A portrait of the great astronomer, noted for his amazing scientific abilities and quirky pretentions. (Rev: BL 12/1/97; HBG 3/98; SLJ 3/98; VOYA 12/97) [921]

IVE, JONATHAN

15554 Hirschmann, Kris. *Jonathan Ive: Designer of the iPod* (5–8). Illus. Series: Innovators. 2007, Gale LB $27.45 (978-0-7377-3533-8). 48pp. Introduces the man behind this popular gadget; the inside info on Apple is also fascinating. (Rev: BL 12/15/07) [745.2092]

JACKSON, SHIRLEY ANN

15555 O'Connell, Diane. *Strong Force: The Story of Physicist Shirley Ann Jackson* (5–8). Series: Women's Adventures in Science. 2005, Watts LB $31.50 (978-0-531-16784-7). 110pp. The life and scientific career of Jackson, physicist and former chairman of the U.S. Nuclear Regulatory Commission. (Rev: SLJ 12/05) [921]

JARVIK, ROBERT

15556 Bankston, John. *Robert Jarvik and the First Artificial Heart* (4–5). Series: Unlocking the Secrets of Science. 2002, Mitchell Lane LB $25.70 (978-1-58415-116-6). 48pp. This readable biography with interesting, unexpected facts covers the life and work of the doctor who invented the first artificial heart. (Rev: BL 8/02; HBG 3/03; SLJ 10/02) [921]

JOBS, STEVE

15557 Brashares, Ann. *Steve Jobs: Thinks Different* (5–8). Series: Techies. 2001, Twenty-First Century LB $23.90 (978-0-7613-1959-7). 80pp. The life story of the amazing creator of Apple computers and his phenomenal success as a businessman and entrepreneur. (Rev: BL 3/15/01; HBG 10/01) [921]

15558 Gaines, Ann Graham. *Steve Jobs* (3–4). Series: Real-Life Reader Biographies. 2000, Mitchell Lane LB $15.95 (978-1-58415-026-8). 32pp. The story of the founder of Apple computers who, after leaving the company he built, was brought back to rescue it from mismanagement. (Rev: BL 11/15/00) [921]

KARAN, DONNA

15559 Tippins, Sherill. *Donna Karan: Designing an American Dream* (5–8). Illus. Series: Wizards of Business. 1992, Garrett LB $17.26 (978-1-56074-019-3). 64pp. Along with the life story of one of America's top fashion designers is advice for those who wish to enter the field. (Rev: BL 6/15/92) [921]

KENNY, ELIZABETH

15560 Crofford, Emily. *Healing Warrior: A Story About Sister Elizabeth Kenny* (3–6). Illus. by Steve Michaels. Series: Creative Minds. 1989, Carolrhoda LB $21.27 (978-0-87614-382-7). 64pp. The story of the Australian nurse renowned for her revolutionary therapy and rehabilitation work with polio patients. (Rev: BL 2/15/90; SLJ 3/90) [921]

KNIGHT, MARGARET

15561 Brill, Marlene T. *Margaret Knight: Girl Inventor* (2–5). Illus. by Joanne Friar. 2001, Millbrook $22.90 (978-0-7613-1756-2). 32pp. Margaret Knight was driven to invent life- and labor-saving devices by her early experiences working in a textile mill. (Rev: BL 9/15/01; HBG 3/02; SLJ 12/01) [609.2]

15562 McCully, Emily Arnold. *Marvelous Mattie: How Margaret E. Knight Became an Inventor* (K–3). Illus. 2006, Farrar $16.00 (978-0-374-34810-6). 32pp. The life of the 19th-century inventor of a machine that made paper grocery bags, among other products, and fought a court battle to get a patent. (Rev: BL 2/15/06; SLJ 2/06) [921]

KOLFF, WILLEM

15563 Tracy, Kathleen. *Willem Kolff and the Invention of the Dialysis Machine* (5–8). Illus. Series: Unlocking the Secrets of Science. 2002, Mitchell Lane LB $25.70 (978-1-58415-135-7). 48pp. Kolff invented the dialysis machine in 1942 in the Nazi-occupied Netherlands. (Rev: HBG 3/03; SLJ 12/02) [617.461059092]

LAMARR, HEDY

15564 Gaines, Ann. *Hedy Lamarr* (2–3). Illus. Series: Discover the Life of an Inventor. 2001, Rourke LB $20.64 (978-1-58952-119-3). 24pp. The little-known story of the actress Hedy Lamarr and the communications system she devised during World War II, for beginning readers. (Rev: BL 10/15/01; SLJ 1/02) [621.382]

LAVOISIER, ANTOINE

15565 Yount, Lisa. *Antoine Lavoisier: Founder of Modern Chemistry*. Rev. ed. (4–7). Illus. Series: Great Minds of Science. 2008, Enslow LB $31.93 (978-0-89490-785-2). 128pp. In addition to providing an assessment of the life and works of Lavoisier, called the Father of Chemistry, this book includes several hands-on activities that depend on an understanding of his work. (Rev: BL 6/1–15/97) [921]

LEAKEY, LOUIS AND MARY

15566 Poynter, Margaret. *The Leakeys: Uncovering the Origins of Humankind* (5–8). Illus. Series: Great Minds of Science. 1997, Enslow LB $26.60 (978-0-89490-788-3). 128pp. The story of the famous husband-and-wife team of scientists, Louis and Mary Leakey, and how they expanded our knowledge of evolution. (Rev: BL 12/1/97; HBG 3/98; SLJ 12/97) [921]

LEEUWENHOEK, ANTONI VAN

15567 Yount, Lisa. *Antoni van Leeuwenhoek: First to See Microscopic Life*. Rev. ed. (4–8). Series: Great Minds of Science. 2008, Enslow LB $31.93 (978-0-89490-680-0). 128pp. A brief biography of the Dutch maker of microscopes, who was also the first to examine closely bacteria and blood cells. (Rev: BL 10/15/96; SLJ 12/96) [921]

LEOPOLD, ALDO

15568 Lorbiecki, Marybeth. *Of Things Natural, Wild, and Free: A Story About Aldo Leopold* (4–7). Illus. 1993, Carolrhoda LB $15.95 (978-0-87614-797-9). 64pp. The story of a man who was a great hunter until he realized the importance of the balance in nature, and then turned a tract of farmland into a nature refuge. (Rev: BL 11/1/93; SLJ 11/93) [921]

15569 Yannuzzi, Della A. *Aldo Leopold: Protector of the Wild* (4–6). Series: Gateway Greens. 2002, Millbrook LB $23.90 (978-0-7613-2465-2). 48pp. An attractive biography of the U.S. environmentalist who helped create the first national wildlife area in 1924 and founded the Wilderness Society in 1935. (Rev: BL 7/02; HBG 3/03) [921]

LINNAEUS, CARL

15570 Anderson, Margaret J. *Carl Linnaeus: Father of Classification*. Rev. ed. (4–8). Series: Great Minds of Science. 2009, Enslow LB $31.93 (978-0-89490-786-9). This biography discusses the personal life of Linnaeus, including his explorations in

Lapland, but the focus is on the development of his important biological classification system. (Rev: BL 12/1/97; HBG 3/98; SLJ 9/97) [921]

MAATHAI, WANGARI

15571 Nivola, Claire A. *Planting the Trees of Kenya* (K–3). Illus. by author. 2008, Farrar $16.95 (978-0-374-39918-4). 32pp. The founder of the Green Belt Movement and first African woman to receive the Nobel Peace Prize is the focus of this simple, clear biography. (Rev: BL 2/15/08; HB 5/08; SLJ 4/08) [333.72092]

15572 Winter, Jeanette. *Wangari's Trees of Peace: A True Story from Africa* (1–3). Illus. by author. 2008, Harcourt $17.00 (978-0-15-206545-4). 32pp. Wangari Maathai, winner of the 2004 Nobel Peace Prize, grew up in Kenya, was educated in America, and returned to her country to become the founder of the Green Belt Movement. (Rev: BCCB 10/08; BL 12/15/08; LMC 1/09; SLJ 11/08) [921]

MCCLINTOCK, BARBARA

15573 Tracy, Kathleen. *Barbara McClintock: Pioneering Geneticist* (4–7). Series: Unlocking the Secrets of Science. 2001, Mitchell Lane LB $25.70 (978-1-58415-111-1). 48pp. An absorbing look at the life and research of this Nobel Prize winner. (Rev: HBG 3/02; SLJ 2/02) [921]

MALONE, ANNIE TURNBO

15574 Wilkerson, J. L. *Story of Pride, Power and Uplift: Annie T. Malone* (4–8). Illus. 2003, Acorn $9.95 (978-0-9664470-8-8). 96pp. Malone, a child of slaves, created beauty products for African American women at the turn of the 20th century and became a wealthy woman and philanthropist. (Rev: BL 3/1/03; SLJ 7/03) [646.7]

MARTINI, HELEN DELANEY

15575 Lyon, George E. *Mother to Tigers* (K–3). Illus. by Peter Catalanotto. 2003, Simon & Schuster $16.95 (978-0-689-84221-4). 32pp. A picture-book biography of the woman who looked after tiger cubs in her own home before she established a nursery at the Bronx Zoo. (Rev: BL 3/1/03; HB 5/03; HBG 10/03; SLJ 3/03) [590]

MATZELIGER, JAN

15576 Mitchell, Barbara. *Shoes for Everyone: A Story About Jan Matzeliger* (3–5). Illus. 1986, Carolrhoda LB $22.60 (978-0-87614-290-5); Lerner paper $6.95 (978-0-87614-473-2). 64pp. The life of the African American inventor who changed the industry with his shoe-lasting machine. (Rev: BCCB 7–8/86; BL 8/86; SLJ 9/86) [921]

MAYO, WILLIAM AND CHARLES

15577 Crofford, Emily. *Frontier Surgeons: A Story About the Mayo Brothers* (3–6). Illus. by Karen Ritz. Series: Creative Minds Biographies. 1989, Carolrhoda LB $21.27 (978-0-87614-381-0); paper $5.95 (978-0-87614-553-1). 56pp. The fascinating story of the brothers, William and Charles, who started what became a world-class medical facility. (Rev: BL 2/15/90; SLJ 3/90) [921]

MEAD, MARGARET

15578 Horn, Geoffrey M. *Margaret Mead* (5–8). Series: Trailblazers of the Modern World. 2004, World Almanac LB $31.00 (978-0-8368-5099-4). 48pp. Report writers will find useful information on Mead's life, achievements, and lasting contributions. (Rev: SLJ 7/04) [921]

15579 Ziesk, Edra. *Margaret Mead* (5–8). Illus. Series: American Women of Achievement. 1990, Chelsea LB $19.95 (978-1-55546-667-1). 109pp. A useful volume covering the career and personal life of this unconventional anthropologist. (Rev: BL 2/15/90; SLJ 9/90; VOYA 8/90) [921]

MENDEL, GREGOR

15580 Bankston, John. *Gregor Mendel and the Discovery of the Gene* (5–8). Illus. Series: Uncharted, Unexplored, and Unexplained. 2004, Mitchell Lane LB $29.95 (978-1-58415-266-8). 48pp. Profiles the 19th-century Austrian monk who discovered the laws of genetics. (Rev: BL 10/15/04; SLJ 12/04) [921]

15581 Bardoe, Cheryl. *Gregor Mendel: The Friar Who Grew Peas* (2–4). Illus. by Joe A. Smith. 2006, Abrams $18.95 (978-0-8109-5475-5). 32pp. A biography of the father of genetics, with child-friendly explanations of the science and accompanied by beautiful watercolors. (Rev: BL 7/06) [921]

15582 Klare, Roger. *Gregor Mendel: Father of Genetics* (5–7). Illus. Series: Great Minds of Science. 1997, Enslow LB $26.60 (978-0-89490-789-0). 128pp. The science of genetics is introduced through the life of Mendel and his experimentation with peas. (Rev: BL 12/1/97; HBG 3/98; SLJ 12/97; VOYA 12/97) [921]

MENDELEYEV, DMITRI

15583 Zannos, Susan. *Dmitri Mendeleyev and the Periodic Table* (5–8). Series: Uncharted, Unexplored, and Unexplained. 2004, Mitchell Lane LB $29.95 (978-1-58415-267-5). 48pp. This brief biography looks at the life of the inventor of the periodic table, focusing initially on his childhood and offering political context. (Rev: BL 10/15/04) [540]

MERCATOR, GERARDUS

15584 Heinrichs, Ann. *Gerardus Mercator: Father of Modern Mapmaking* (5–12). Series: Signature Lives. 2007, Compass Point LB $31.93 (978-0-7565-3312-0). 112pp. Scientific concepts are presented clearly in this profile that covers Mercator's life, with excerpts from his writing and a timeline that adds historical context. (Rev: SLJ 1/08)

MITCHELL, MARIA

15585 McPherson, Stephanie S. *Rooftop Astronomer: A Story About Maria Mitchell* (4–6). 1990, Carolrhoda LB $22.60 (978-0-87614-410-7). 64pp. The woman who became the first professional female astronomer in the United States. (Rev: BCCB 11/90; BL 11/15/90; SLJ 1/91) [921]

MORGAN, ANN

15586 Ross, Michael E. *Pond Watching with Ann Morgan* (3–5). Series: Naturalist's Apprentice. 2000, Carolrhoda $19.93 (978-1-57505-385-1). 48pp. A biography about the expert on ponds that also serves as a field guide to pond ecology. (Rev: BL 4/15/00; HBG 10/00; SLJ 7/00) [921]

MORSE, SAMUEL

15587 Hall, M. C. *Samuel Morse* (1–4). Series: Lives and Times. 2004, Heinemann LB $22.79 (978-1-4034-5329-7). 32pp. Report writers will find useful information in this biography that has a timeline and "Fact File" boxes. (Rev: SLJ 9/04) [921]

MORTON, J. STERLING

15588 Beaty, Sandy, and J. L. Wilkerson. *Champion of Arbor Day: J. Sterling Morton* (4–6). Series: The Great Heartlanders. 1999, Acorn paper $8.95 (978-0-9664470-1-9). 130pp. The story of the early conservationist who inspired Nebraskans to plant one million trees on the first Arbor Day in 1872. (Rev: SLJ 3/99) [921]

MUIR, JOHN

15589 Armentrout, David, and Patricia Armentrout. *John Muir* (2–4). Illus. 2002, Rourke LB $14.95 (978-1-58952-055-4). 24pp. A simple introduction for younger readers to the life of naturalist John Muir. (Rev: BL 1/1–15/02; SLJ 3/02) [333.7]

15590 Dunlap, Julie, and Marybeth Lorbiecki. *John Muir and the Stickeen: An Icy Adventure with a No Good Dog* (2–4). Illus. by Bill Farnsworth. 2004, T&N Children's Publishing $16.95 (978-1-55971-903-2). 32pp. Beautifully illustrated and drawing heavily on Muir's personal journals, this engaging book tells how a dog named Stickeen helped to guide the famed conservationist through a brush with death in Alaska. (Rev: BL 11/15/04) [921]

15591 Locker, Thomas. *John Muir: America's Naturalist* (2–4). 2004, Fulcrum $17.95 (978-1-55591-393-9). 32pp. This brief picture-book biography of the Scottish-born naturalist is beautifully illustrated with paintings of his beloved Yosemite. (Rev: BL 6/1–15/03; HBG 4/04; SLJ 9/03) [921]

15592 Naden, Corinne J., and Rose Blue. *John Muir: Saving the Wilderness* (3–5). Illus. Series: Gateway Biographies. 1992, Millbrook LB $23.90 (978-1-56294-110-9). 48pp. The life and work of this well-known conservationist, especially his role in founding the national parks. (Rev: BL 5/1/92; SLJ 6/92)

15593 Wadsworth, Ginger. *John Muir: Wilderness Protector* (4–6). Illus. 1992, Lerner LB $18.95 (978-0-8225-4912-3). 144pp. From his childhood in Scotland to adulthood in California, this biography focuses on why Muir became a conservationist and his efforts in this area. (Rev: SLJ 9/92) [921]

MURRAY, JOSEPH E.

15594 Mattern, Joanne. *Joseph E. Murray and the Story of the First Human Kidney Transplant* (5–8). Illus. Series: Unlocking the Secrets of Science. 2002, Mitchell Lane LB $25.70 (978-1-58415-136-4). 48pp. A look at the work of the surgeon who performed the first successful kidney transplant. (Rev: SLJ 12/02; VOYA 6/03) [617.95092]

MURRELL, MELVILLE

15595 Seymour, Tres. *Our Neighbor Is a Strange, Strange Man* (PS–3). Illus. by Walter L. Krudop. 1999, Orchard LB $16.99 (978-0-531-33107-1). 32pp. A picture-book story of Melville Murrell, who built the first human-powered airplane in 1876, years before the Wright brothers. (Rev: BCCB 2/99; BL 2/1/99; HBG 10/99; SLJ 3/99) [629.13]

NAVY, CARYN

15596 Verheyden-Hilliard, Mary Ellen. *Mathematician and Computer Scientist, Caryn Navy* (2–4). Illus. 1988, Equity paper $12.00 (978-0-932469-12-0). 32pp. Brief biography of a woman scientist who is blind. (Rev: BL 2/15/89; SLJ 1/89)

NEWTON, ISAAC

15597 Anderson, Margaret J. *Isaac Newton: The Greatest Scientist of All Time*. Rev. ed. (4–7). Illus. Series: Great Minds of Science. 2008, Enslow LB $31.93 (978-0-89490-681-7). 128pp. The life of the great English mathematician and physicist who formulated the laws of motion and gravity. (Rev: BL 10/15/96; SLJ 12/96) [921]

15598 Hollihan, Kerrie Logan. *Isaac Newton and Physics for Kids: His Life and Ideas with 21 Activities* (4–8). Illus. 2009, Chicago Review $16.95 (978-1-55652-778-4). 144pp. This well-balanced story offers a picture of the physicist's work and personal life. (Rev: BL 6/1–15/09) [530.092]

15599 Krull, Kathleen. *Isaac Newton* (5–8). Illus. by Boris Kulikov. Series: Giants of Science. 2006, Viking $15.99 (978-0-670-05921-8). 128pp. Newton's childhood and adult personality are highlighted in this readable biography that gives good explanations of his scientific theories. (Rev: BL 4/1/06; SLJ 3/06*; VOYA 6/06) [530]

15600 Mason, Paul. *Isaac Newton* (4–8). Illus. Series: Scientists Who Made History. 2002, Raintree LB $27.12 (978-0-7398-4845-6). 48pp. Newton's life and contributions are presented in clear text and ample illustrations, with historical detail that places the information in context. (Rev: HBG 10/02; SLJ 9/02) [530.092]

15601 Steele, Philip. *Isaac Newton: The Scientist Who Changed Everything* (4–7). Illus. Series: National Geographic World History Biographies. 2007, National Geographic $17.95 (978-1-4263-0114-8). 64pp. A colorful, well-designed survey of Newton's life and legacy. (Rev: BL 12/1/07; SLJ 6/07) [921]

NICE, MARGARET MORSE

15602 Dunlap, Julie. *Birds in the Bushes: A Story About Margaret Morse Nice* (3–5). Illus. by Ralph L. Ramstad. Series: Creative Minds. 1996, Carolrhoda LB $19.93 (978-1-57505-006-5). 63pp. A biography of the noted American ornithologist and conservationist who died in 1974. (Rev: SLJ 10/96) [921]

15603 Ross, Michael E. *Bird Watching with Margaret Morse Nice* (4–6). Illus. by Laurie Caple. Series: Naturalist's Apprentice. 1997, Carolrhoda LB $19.93 (978-1-57505-002-7). 48pp. At the turn of the century, Margaret Morse Nice raised her family while pursuing her hobby of bird watching. (Rev: HBG 3/98; SLJ 3/98) [921]

NOBEL, ALFRED

15604 Bankston, John. *Alfred Nobel and the Story of the Nobel Prize* (4–8). Series: Great Achievement Awards. 2003, Mitchell Lane LB $29.95 (978-1-58415-168-5). 48pp. An intriguing biography of the inventor of dynamite and the founder of the famous prizes. (Rev: BL 10/15/03; SLJ 9/03) [921]

OMIDYAR, PIERRE

15605 Viegas, Jennifer. *Pierre Omidyar: The Founder of eBay* (5–8). Illus. Series: Internet Career Biographies. 2006, Rosen LB $31.95 (978-1-4042-0715-8). 112pp. A look at the successful founder of eBay and his hopes for the future. (Rev: BL 10/15/06; SLJ 5/07) [921]

OPPENHEIMER, J. ROBERT

15606 Allman, Toney. *J. Robert Oppenheimer: Father of the Atomic Bomb* (5–9). Series: Giants of Science. 2005, Gale $26.20 (978-1-56711-889-6). 64pp. Controversial physicist Oppenheimer, who played a key role in the development of the atomic bomb, is profiled in readable text with lots of details for report writers. (Rev: SLJ 7/05) [921]

PACHCIARZ, JUDITH

15607 Verheyden-Hilliard, Mary Ellen. *Scientist and Physician, Judith Pachciarz* (2–4). Illus. 1988, Equity paper $12.00 (978-0-932469-13-7). 32pp. The story of an M.D. and microbiologist who is deaf. (Rev: BL 2/15/89; SLJ 4/89) [921]

PASTEUR, LOUIS

15608 Alphin, Elaine M. *Germ Hunter: A Story About Louis Pasteur* (3–6). Illus. by Elaine Ver-
straete. 2003, Carolrhoda LB $22.60 (978-1-57505-179-6); paper $6.95 (978-0-87614-929-4). 64pp. Pasteur's early life is covered well in this simple biography that reads more like a novel and is more suitable for reluctant readers than for report writers. (Rev: HBG 10/03; SLJ 7/03) [921]

15609 Armentrout, David, and Patricia Armentrout. *Louis Pasteur* (2–4). Series: Discover Someone Who Made a Difference. 2001, Rourke LB $14.95 (978-1-58952-056-1). This basic biography describes the life and times of Pasteur and how his accomplishments affect our lives today. (Rev: BL 1/1–15/02; SLJ 3/02) [921]

15610 Birch, Beverley. *Louis Pasteur: Father of Modern Medicine* (5–7). Series: Giants of Science. 2001, Blackbirch LB $27.44 (978-1-56711-336-5). 64pp. A readable, well-organized biography of the French chemist whose varied accomplishments include discovery of the process known now as pasteurization. (Rev: BL 8/1/01; HBG 3/02) [921]

15611 Fullick, Ann. *Louis Pasteur* (4–6). 2000, Heinemann LB $25.64 (978-1-57572-373-0). 48pp. As well as covering Pasteur's life, this book tells of the impact of his discoveries on medicine and science. (Rev: SLJ 2/01) [921]

15612 Smith, Linda W. *Louis Pasteur: Disease Fighter*. Rev. ed. (4–8). Illus. Series: Great Minds of Science. 2007, Enslow LB $31.93 (978-0-89490-790-6). 128pp. The story of the "father of microbiology," who discovered pasteurization while working on a wine problem for Napoleon. (Rev: BL 12/1/97; HBG 3/98; SLJ 12/97) [921]

PAULING, LINUS

15613 Zannos, Susan. *Linus Pauling and the Chemical Bond* (4–5). Series: Unlocking the Secrets of Science. 2003, Mitchell Lane LB $25.70 (978-1-58415-123-4). 48pp. This brief biography recounts the life and scientific achievements of American chemist Linus Pauling. (Rev: BL 11/15/03; SLJ 10/03) [921]

PAVLOV, IVAN

15614 Saunders, Barbara R. *Ivan Pavlov: Exploring the Mysteries of Behavior*. Rev. ed. (5–9). Series: Great Minds of Science. 2006, Enslow LB $31.93 (978-0-7660-2506-6). 112pp. This well-written profile chronicles Pavlov's famous experiments and discoveries and shows how his work influenced other branches of science. (Rev: SLJ 6/07) [921]

PINCHOT, GIFFORD

15615 Hines, Gary. *Midnight Forests* (3–5). Illus. by Robert Casilla. 2005, Boyds Mills $16.95 (978-1-56397-148-8). 32pp. Gifford Pinchot, an American who became secretary of agriculture in 1898 and who was responsible for saving large areas of forest in the West, is introduced in this large-format picture-book biography. (Rev: BL 5/15/05; SLJ 4/05) [333.75]

PLOTKIN, MARK

15616 Pascoe, Elaine, adapt. *Mysteries of the Rain Forest: 20th Century Medicine Man* (4–8). Series: The New Explorers. 1997, Blackbirch LB $18.95 (978-1-56711-229-0). An exploration of the life and discoveries of Mark Plotkin, an ethnobotanist fascinated by the plants and people of the Amazon. (Rev: HBG 3/98; SLJ 2/98) [921]

PULITZER, JOSEPH

15617 Zannos, Susan. *Joseph Pulitzer and the Story Behind the Pulitzer Prize* (4–8). Illus. Series: Great Achievement Awards. 2003, Mitchell Lane LB $29.95 (978-1-58415-179-1). 48pp. Pulitzer's difficulty personality and passion for journalism are highlighted in this account of his establishment of the well-known awards. (Rev: BL 10/15/03; SLJ 9/03) [070.9]

QUADRINO, JAMES

15618 Pearce, Q. L. *James Quadrino: Wildlife Protector* (4–7). Series: Young Heroes. 2006, Gale LB $23.70 (978-0-7377-3612-0). 48pp. At age 13, James Quadrino took it upon himself to save a fire-ravaged bird sanctuary by building nesting boxes. (Rev: SLJ 6/07) [921]

RICHARDS, ELLEN

15619 Vare, Ethlie A. *Adventurous Spirit: A Story About Ellen Swallow Richards* (3–6). Illus. by Jennifer Hagerman. Series: Creative Minds. 1992, Carolrhoda LB $19.93 (978-0-87614-733-7). 64pp. The life of the first woman accepted at M.I.T. (Rev: BL 1/15/93) [921]

RICHTER, CHARLES

15620 Zannos, Susan. *Charles Richter and the Story of the Richter Scale* (4–5). Series: Unlocking the Secrets of Science. 2003, Mitchell Lane LB $17.95 (978-1-58415-175-3). 48pp. This brief biography of Charles Richter chronicles the life and achievements of the American physicist and seismologist who is credited with developing the scale for measuring earthquake intensity. (Rev: BL 11/15/03; SLJ 10/03) [921]

RINGLING BROTHERS

15621 Apps, Jerry. *Tents, Tigers, and the Ringling Brothers* (3–7). Illus. Series: Badger Biographies. 2006, Wisconsin Historical Soc. paper $12.95 (978-0-87020-374-9). 114pp. The true story of how the seven Ringling Brothers followed their dreams and began their own circus, describing their day-to-day struggles to keep the business successful. (Rev: BL 2/15/07) [920]

ROBERTS, EDWARD

15622 Zannos, Susan. *Edward Roberts and the Story of the Personal Computer* (5–7). Series: Unlocking

the Secrets of Science. 2002, Mitchell Lane LB $25.70 (978-1-58415-118-0). 48pp. This accessible account focuses on Roberts's accomplishments as an electronic engineer. (Rev: HBG 10/03; SLJ 1/03) [921]

ROCKEFELLER, JOHN D.

15623 Laughlin, Rosemary. *John D. Rockefeller: Oil Baron and Philanthropist* (5–8). Illus. Series: American Business Leaders. 2001, Morgan Reynolds LB $21.95 (978-1-883846-59-6). 128pp. A biography of the determined and skilled businessman who made Standard Oil the dominant company in the oil industry and who was later noted for his philanthropy. (Rev: BL 3/1/01; HBG 10/01; SLJ 7/01) [921]

ROENTGEN, WILHELM

15624 Garcia, Kimberly. *Wilhelm Roentgen and the Discovery of X Rays* (4–5). Series: Unlocking the Secrets of Science. 2002, Mitchell Lane LB $17.95 (978-1-58415-114-2). 48pp. The story of the German physical scientist who stumbled upon X-rays while working on experiments with electricity. (Rev: BL 8/02; HBG 3/03; SLJ 10/02) [921]

ROOKS, JUNE

15625 Verheyden-Hilliard, Mary Ellen. *Scientist and Strategist, June Rooks* (2–4). Illus. 1988, Equity paper $12.00 (978-0-932469-14-4). 32pp. The story of June Rooks, an African American who battled poverty and polio to gain a degree in physics and a research analysis job in the navy. (Rev: BL 2/15/89; SLJ 1/89)

SAGAN, CARL

15626 Butts, Ellen R., and Joyce R. Schwarts. *Carl Sagan* (5–8). Series: A&E Biography. 2000, Lerner LB $27.93 (978-0-8225-4986-4). 112pp. The story of the great astronomer who interested millions in the study of the stars and the question of whether there is life elsewhere in our universe. (Rev: BL 10/15/00; HBG 3/01; SLJ 10/00) [921]

15627 Byman, Jeremy. *Carl Sagan: In Contact with the Cosmos* (5–8). Illus. Series: Great Scientists. 2000, Morgan Reynolds LB $21.95 (978-1-883846-55-8). 112pp. An informative biography of the scientist who popularized astronomy while maintaining a highly productive scholarly life. (Rev: BL 11/1/00; HBG 10/00; SLJ 8/00) [921]

SALK, JONAS

15628 Bankston, John. *Jonas Salk and the Polio Vaccine* (4–5). Series: Unlocking the Secrets of Science. 2001, Mitchell Lane LB $25.70 (978-1-58415-093-0). 56pp. A biography of the famous scientist, with photographs, a glossary, and a list of additional resources. (Rev: BL 10/15/01; SLJ 11/01) [610]

15629 Durrett, Deanne. *Jonas Salk* (2–5). Illus. Series: Inventors and Creators. 2002, Gale LB

$23.70 (978-0-7377-1277-3). 48pp. This brief biography presents Salk's life from childhood and his determination to persevere to find a cure for polio, with many photographs, a glossary, and a bibliography. (Rev: BL 11/1/02; SLJ 10/02) [610]

15630 McPherson, Stephanie S. *Jonas Salk: Conquering Polio* (5–8). Series: Lerner Biographies. 2001, Lerner LB $27.93 (978-0-8225-4964-2). 128pp. An absorbing account of Salk's life and contributions to medicine that discusses his confrontation with Sabin and the early failures of Salk's vaccine. (Rev: HBG 3/02; SLJ 4/02) [921]

15631 Tocci, Salvatore. *Jonas Salk: Creator of the Polio Vaccine* (4–7). Illus. Series: Great Minds of Science. 2003, Enslow LB $26.60 (978-0-7660-2097-9). 128pp. This book covers the life of the scientist and the importance and impact of the vaccine he developed. (Rev: BL 5/15/03; HBG 10/03) [610]

SCHALLER, GEORGE

15632 Turner, Pamela S. *A Life in the Wild: George Schaller's Struggle to Save the Last Great Beasts* (5–8). Illus. 2008, Farrar $21.95 (978-0-374-34578-5). 112pp. Turner traces the environmentalist's work to save gorillas, tigers, lions, snow leopards, and other large endangered animals. (Rev: BCCB 11/08; BL 12/1/08; SLJ 11/08) [590.92]

SILVA, MARINA

15633 Hildebrant, Ziporah. *Marina Silva: Defending Rainforest Communities in Brazil* (5–8). Series: Women Changing the World. 2001, Feminist $19.95 (978-1-55861-292-1). 112pp. Though battling a serious illness, this gallant women, once a leader of the native Amazonians, has become a leading figure in protecting the forests of Brazil. (Rev: BL 12/15/01) [921]

STEARNER, PHYLLIS

15634 Verheyden-Hilliard, Mary Ellen. *Scientist and Activist, Phyllis Stearner* (2–4). Illus. 1988, Equity paper $12.00 (978-0-932469-15-1). 32pp. A biography of an expert in radiation biology who has cerebral palsy. (Rev: BL 2/15/89; SLJ 1/89) [921]

STRAUSS, LEVI

15635 Van Steenwyk, Elizabeth. *Levi Strauss: The Blue Jeans Man* (5–9). 1988, Walker LB $14.85 (978-0-8027-6796-7). A biography of the Bavarian immigrant, Levi Strauss, who became the blue jeans king of the western world. (Rev: BL 6/15/88; SLJ 10/88; VOYA 8/88) [921]

15636 Weidt, Maryann N. *Mr. Blue Jeans: A Story About Levi Strauss* (3–5). Illus. 1990, Carolrhoda LB $22.60 (978-0-87614-421-3). 64pp. The story of the phenomenal blue jeans and of their phenomenal creator. (Rev: BL 12/1/90; SLJ 1/91) [921]

STRONG, MAURICE

15637 Westrup, Hugh. *Maurice Strong: Working for Planet Earth* (3–6). Illus. 1994, Millbrook LB $20.90 (978-1-56294-414-8). 48pp. A biography of the Canadian environmentalist who organized the Rio de Janeiro Earth Summit. (Rev: BL 12/1/94; SLJ 12/94) [921]

SUZUKI, HIROMI

15638 Barasch, Lynne. *Hiromi's Hands* (K–3). Illus. 2007, Lee & Low $17.95 (978-1-58430-275-9). 32pp. This picture-book biography of Japanese American sushi chef Hiromi Suzuki begins with the immigration of her father — also a successful sushi chef — to the United States from Japan. (Rev: BL 3/15/07) [921]

SWANSON, ANNE BARRETT

15639 Verheyden-Hilliard, Mary Ellen. *Scientist and Teacher, Anne Barrett Swanson* (2–4). Illus. 1988, Equity paper $12.00 (978-0-932469-16-8). 32pp. The story of a scientist who overcame a brittle bone condition that hampered her physical growth. (Rev: BL 2/15/89; SLJ 4/89) [921]

TAJIRI, SATOSHI

15640 Mortensen, Lori. *Satoshi Tajiri* (4–7). Illus. 2009, Gale LB $27.45 (978-0-7377-4269-5). 48pp. A brief biography of the Japanese designer known for creating Pokemon and other Nintendo games, with information on his diagnosis with Asperger's syndrome. (Rev: BLO 5/28/09; SLJ 8/09) [921]

TELLER, EDWARD

15641 Bankston, John. *Edward Teller and the Development of the Hydrogen Bomb* (5–8). Series: Unlocking the Secrets of Science. 2001, Mitchell Lane LB $25.70 (978-1-58415-108-1). 56pp. The life of the scientist born in Hungary who played a key role in the development of the H-bomb. (Rev: HBG 3/02; SLJ 1/02) [539.7092]

TESLA, NIKOLA

15642 Dommermuth-Costa, Carol. *Nikola Tesla: A Spark of Genius* (5–9). 1994, Lerner LB $27.93 (978-0-8225-4920-8). Traces the life and career of this pioneer in the field of electricity. (Rev: BL 12/15/94; SLJ 2/95) [921]

TORVALDS, LINUS

15643 Brashares, Ann. *Linus Torvalds: Software Rebel* (5–8). Series: Techies. 2001, Millbrook LB $23.90 (978-0-7613-1960-3). The story of the computer genius who created the Linux operating system. (Rev: BL 4/1/02; HBG 3/02; SLJ 12/01) [921]

TURNER, HENRY

15644 Ross, Michael E. *Bug Watching with Charles Henry Turner* (3–5). Illus. Series: Naturalist's Apprentice. 1997, Carolrhoda $19.93 (978-1-57505-003-4). 48pp. As well as providing many hints on bug watching, this book is a biography of the important African American zoologist who studied insects for many years. (Rev: BL 3/1/98; HBG 3/98; SLJ 3/98) [921]

VEDDER, AMY

15645 Ebersole, Rene. *Gorilla Mountain: The Story of Wildlife Biologist Amy Vedder* (5–8). Series: Women's Adventures in Science. 2005, Watts LB $31.50 (978-0-531-16779-3). 118pp. An informative and accessible account of Vedder's efforts to protect the endangered mountain gorillas of Rwanda. (Rev: SLJ 12/05) [921]

WAKSMAN, SELMAN

15646 Gordon, Karen. *Selman Waksman and the Discovery of Streptomycin* (4–5). Series: Unlocking the Secrets of Science. 2002, Mitchell Lane LB $25.70 (978-1-58415-138-8). 48pp. An interesting profile of the scientist who discovered streptomycin and coined the term "antibiotic." (Rev: HBG 10/03; SLJ 1/03) [921]

WALKER, MADAM C. J.

15647 Bundles, A'Lelia Perry. *Madam C. J. Walker* (5–10). Series: Black Americans of Achievement. 1993, Chelsea LB $32.00 (978-1-55546-615-2); paper $30.00 (978-0-7910-0251-3). Written by Walker's great-great-granddaughter, this volume describes the developer of a line of hair-care products whose entrepreneurial ability made her into the "foremost colored businesswoman in America." (Rev: BL 3/1/94) [921]

15648 Colman, Penny. *Madam C. J. Walker: Building a Business Empire* (3–6). Illus. 1994, Millbrook LB $20.90 (978-1-56294-338-7). 48pp. The success story of the African American woman who rose from extreme poverty to found a beauty preparation empire. (Rev: BL 6/1–15/94; SLJ 9/94) [921]

15649 McKissack, Patricia C., and Fredrick McKissack. *Madam C. J. Walker: Self-Made Millionaire*. Rev. ed. (2–4). Illus. by Michael Bryant. Series: Great African Americans. 2001, Enslow LB $18.60 (978-0-89490-311-3). 32pp. The story of the woman who built a cosmetics empire and became the first self-made African American woman millionaire. (Rev: BL 10/15/92; SLJ 12/92) [921]

15650 Nichols, Catherine. *Madame C. J. Walker* (K–2). Illus. Series: Scholastic News Nonfiction Readers: Biographies. 2005, Scholastic LB $20.00 (978-0-516-24941-4). 24pp. This brief biography chronicles the inspiring story of the pioneering African American hair-care entrepreneur; large type, simple text, and ample illustrations make this suitable for beginning readers. (Rev: BL 2/1/06; SLJ 4/06) [338.7]

WEINBERG, ROBERT A.

15651 Gaines, Ann, and Jim Whiting. *Robert A. Weinberg and the Search for the Cause of Cancer* (4–7). Series: Unlocking the Secrets of Science. 2002, Mitchell Lane LB $25.70 (978-1-58415-095-4). 48pp. The life and achievements of the scientist who specializes in the genetic causes of disease. (Rev: HBG 10/02; SLJ 6/02) [616.9940092]

WELCH, THOMAS BRAMWELL

15652 Carney, Mary Lou. *Dr. Welch and the Great Grape Story* (1–3). Illus. by Sherry Meidell. 2005, Boyds Mills $16.95 (978-1-59078-039-8). 32pp. This picture-book biography traces Thomas Bramwell Welch's efforts to find a nonalcoholic drink based on grapes. (Rev: BL 5/1/05) [921]

WHITNEY, ELI

15653 Gaines, Ann. *Eli Whitney* (2–3). Series: Discover the Life of an Inventor. 2001, Rourke LB $20.64 (978-1-58952-118-6). 24pp. The life of the inventor of the cotton gin is presented simply with material on how this invention works. (Rev: BL 10/15/01) [921]

15654 Gibson, Karen Bush. *The Life and Times of Eli Whitney* (5–8). Illus. Series: Profiles in American History. 2006, Mitchell Lane LB $20.95 (978-1-58415-434-1). 48pp. An interesting profile of the cotton gin inventor, with period reproductions and relevant sidebar features. (Rev: BL 10/15/06) [609.2]

WILLIAMS, DANIEL HALE

15655 Kaye, Judith. *The Life of Daniel Hale Williams* (5–8). Illus. Series: Pioneers in Health and Medicine. 1993, Twenty-First Century LB $16.90 (978-0-8050-2302-2). 80pp. The life story of the famous doctor who pioneered heart surgery and also helped open up the medical profession to African Americans. (Rev: SLJ 1/94) [921]

WOZNIAK, STEPHEN

15656 Gold, Rebecca. *Steve Wozniak: A Wizard Called Woz* (3–5). Illus. Series: Achievers. 1994, Lerner LB $21.27 (978-0-8225-2881-4). 72pp. The biography of the math whiz and multimillionaire who founded the Apple Computer Company. (Rev: BL 12/1/94) [921]

15657 Riddle, John, and Jim Whiting. *Stephen Wozniak and the Story of Apple Computer* (4–7). Series: Unlocking the Secrets of Science. 2001, Mitchell Lane LB $17.95 (978-1-58415-109-8). 48pp. A profile of the life and achievements of the co-founder of Apple, who is known for his philanthropy and teaching in elementary schools. (Rev: HBG 10/02; SLJ 2/02) [921]

WRIGHT, WILBUR AND ORVILLE

15658 Berger, Melvin, and Gilda Berger. *Can You Fly High, Wright Brothers?* (3–4). Illus. by Brandon

Dorman. Series: Science SuperGiants. 2007, Scholastic paper $4.99 (978-0-439-83378-3). 48pp. Using a question-and-answer format, Berger tells the story of the brothers' life and fascination with aviation. (Rev: SLJ 2/08) [921]

15659 Borden, Louise, and Trish Marx. *Touching the Sky: The Flying Adventures of Wilbur and Orville Wright* (2–4). Illus. by Peter M. Fiore. 2003, Simon & Schuster $18.95 (978-0-689-84876-6). 64pp. Wilbur and Orville are shown as celebrities in this picture book that recounts unusual appearances they made separately. (Rev: BL 9/15/03; HBG 4/04; SLJ 10/03) [921]

15660 Busby, Peter. *First to Fly* (3–5). Illus. by David Craig. 2003, Crown $19.95 (978-0-375-81287-3). 32pp. The obstacles surmounted by the Wright brothers as they took to the sky are handsomely presented in this large, richly illustrated text. (Rev: BL 1/1–15/03; HBG 10/03; SLJ 3/03) [921]

15661 Collins, Mary. *Airborne: A Photobiography of Wilbur and Orville Wright* (4–8). Illus. 2003, National Geographic $18.95 (978-0-7922-6957-1). 64pp. Sixty photographs are only the beginning of this intriguing book packed with information about the brothers and their famous flight. (Rev: BL 2/1/03*; HB 3/03; HBG 10/03; SLJ 3/03) [629.13]

15662 Dixon-Engel, Tara, and Mike Jackson. *The Wright Brothers: First in Flight* (5–8). Series: Sterling Biographies. 2007, Sterling LB $12.95 (978-1-4027-4954-4); paper $5.95 (978-1-4027-3231-7). 124pp. The brothers' early life, inspiration, and eventual success are all covered here. (Rev: SLJ 10/07) [921]

15663 Ford, Carin T. *The Wright Brothers: Heroes of Flight* (2–4). Illus. Series: Famous Inventors. 2003, Enslow LB $22.60 (978-0-7660-2002-3). 32pp. Photographs enhance this well-written account of the Wright brothers' inventive abilities. (Rev: HBG 10/03; SLJ 10/03) [921]

15664 Gaines, Ann. *Orville and Wilbur Wright* (2–3). Series: Discover the Life of an Inventor. 2001, Rourke LB $20.64 (978-1-58952-121-6). 24pp. A very simple biography of the Wright brothers with material on their struggles and an explanation of how the airplane works. (Rev: BL 10/15/01) [973]

15665 MacLeod, Elizabeth. *The Wright Brothers: A Flying Start* (3–5). Illus. 2002, Kids Can $14.95 (978-1-55074-933-5). 32pp. Using double-page spreads, with pictures on one and text on the other, this attractive biography is a fine introduction to the Wright brothers and their work. (Rev: BL 4/1/02; HBG 10/02; SLJ 7/02) [921]

15666 McPherson, Stephanie S., and Joseph Sammartino Gardner. *Wilbur and Orville Wright: Taking Flight* (4–7). Illus. Series: Trailblazer Biographies. 2003, Carolrhoda LB $30.60 (978-1-57505-443-8). 120pp. A well-written, detailed account of the Wright brothers' landmark experiments, enlivened with period photographs and other illustrations. (Rev: SLJ 4/04) [921]

15667 Old, Wendie. *The Wright Brothers* (5–8). Series: Historical American Biographies. 2000, Enslow LB $26.60 (978-0-7660-1095-6). An accurate and objective biography of the heroes of Kitty Hawk, containing chapter notes, a bibliography, and a glossary. (Rev: BL 1/1–15/00; HBG 10/00; SLJ 7/00) [921]

15668 O'Sullivan, Robyn. *The Wright Brothers Fly* (2–4). Series: National Geographic History Chapters. 2007, National Geographic LB $17.90 (978-1-4263-0188-9). 40pp. Simple sentences, with photographs and drawings, tell the story of the Wright brothers' youth and later accomplishments; a "How to Write an A+ Report" section gives useful advice. (Rev: LMC 1/08*; SLJ 1/08) [921]

15669 Reynolds, Quentin. *The Wright Brothers* (5–8). 1963, Random paper $5.99 (978-0-394-84700-9). An easily read account of the two young men and their dream of flight. [921]

15670 Sproule, Anna. *The Wright Brothers: The Birth of Modern Aviation* (5–8). Series: Giants of Science. 1999, Blackbirch LB $24.95 (978-1-56711-328-0). 64pp. This slim biography with an inviting format stresses the lasting contributions of the Wright brothers to world transportation. (Rev: HBG 10/00; SLJ 2/00) [921]

15671 Tieck, Sarah. *Wright Brothers* (K–3). Series: First Biographies. 2007, ABDO LB $25.65 (978-1-59679-790-1). 32pp. A beginner's profile of Wilbur and Orville Wright and their contributions to the development of the airplane, with lots of illustrations, a large typeface, and highlighted words that appear in the glossary. (Rev: SLJ 3/07) [921]

15672 Yolen, Jane. *My Brothers' Flying Machine: Wilbur, Orville, and Me* (3–5). Illus. by Jim Burke. 2003, Little, Brown $16.95 (978-0-316-97159-1). 32pp. The story of the Wright brothers is told in free verse by their sister Katherine, who looked after the brothers while they tended to their dream. (Rev: BL 3/1/03; HBG 10/03; SLJ 3/03) [629.13]

Sports Figures

Collective

15673 Bryant, Jill. *Amazing Women Athletes* (4–8). Illus. Series: Women's Hall of Fame. 2002, Second Story paper $7.95 (978-1-896764-44-3). 100pp. This book contains profiles of 10 distinguished women athletes including mountain climber Annie Smith Peck and tennis stars Venus and Serena Williams. (Rev: BL 6/1–15/02; SLJ 8/02) [920]

15674 Donkin, Andrew. *Going for Gold!* (2–4). Series: Eyewitness Reader. 1999, DK $14.99 (978-0-7894-4765-4); paper $3.99 (978-0-7894-4764-7). 48pp. Tennis, swimming, and the shot put are three of the sports covered in this biography of six Olympians including Jesse Owen, Shelley Mann, Mamo Wolde, and Kerri Strug. (Rev: HBG 3/00; SLJ 2/00) [920]

15675 Golenbock, Peter. *Teammates* (1–3). Illus. by Paul Bacon. 1990, Harcourt $16.00 (978-0-15-200603-7). 32pp. Segregated life in the United States of the 1940s introduces the reader to the Negro Leagues. (Rev: BCCB 4/90; BL 4/1/90; HB 5/90; SLJ 6/90) [796.357]

15676 Hall, Kirsten. *Kids in Sports: A Chapter Book* (3–6). Series: True Tales. 2004, Children's Pr. LB $22.50 (978-0-516-23733-6); paper $4.95 (978-0-516-24685-7). 48pp. True stories of young people who have excelled in the area of sports. (Rev: SLJ 1/05) [920]

15677 Hotchkiss, Ron. *The Matchless Six: The Story of Canada's First Women's Olympic Team* (5–8). Illus. 2006, Tundra $16.95 (978-0-88776-738-8). 200pp. Profiles the individual athletes and achievements of Canada's groundbreaking women's Olympic team of 1928. (Rev: BL 3/15/06; SLJ 6/06) [796.48]

15678 Kaminsky, Marty. *Uncommon Champions: Fifteen Athletes Who Battled Back* (5–8). Illus. 2000, Boyds Mills $14.95 (978-1-56397-787-9). 147pp. Profiles of 15 athletes in several different sports who have conquered such mental and physi-

cal problems as blindness and drug addiction to achieve their goals. (Rev: BCCB 1/01; BL 11/1/00; HBG 3/01; SLJ 10/00; VOYA 12/00) [921]

15679 Kelly, J. *Superstars of Women's Basketball* (4–6). Series: Female Sports Stars. 1997, Chelsea LB $18.65 (978-0-7910-4389-9). 64pp. Five outstanding female basketball stars are featured in this book, which tells about each one's rise to fame. (Rev: SLJ 4/98) [920]

15680 Krull, Kathleen. *Lives of the Athletes* (4–7). Illus. by Kathryn Hewitt. 1997, Harcourt $20.00 (978-0-15-200806-2). 96pp. A collective biography that describes the public and private lives of 20 famous athletes, including Johnny Weissmuller, Red Grange, Babe Didrikson Zaharias, Sonja Henie, and Bruce Lee. (Rev: BCCB 6/97; BL 3/15/97; HB 5/97; SLJ 5/97) [920]

15681 Lipsyte, Robert. *Heroes of Baseball: The Men Who Made It America's Favorite Game* (4–7). Illus. 2006, Simon & Schuster $19.95 (978-0-689-86741-5). 96pp. As well as introducing key players of the game, this volume presents a concise history of the sport itself. (Rev: BL 2/15/06; SLJ 4/06) [796.357]

15682 McDaniel, Melissa. *Pushing the Limits: A Chapter Book* (3–6). Series: True Tales. 2004, Children's Pr. LB $22.50 (978-0-516-23734-3); paper $4.95 (978-0-516-24688-8). 48pp. A look at athletes in the areas of marathon running, triathlons, weight lifting, and sled dog racing. (Rev: SLJ 1/05) [920]

15683 Nichols, Catherine. *Record Breakers: A Chapter Book* (3–6). Series: True Tales. 2004, Children's Pr. LB $22.50 (978-0-516-23732-9); paper $4.95 (978-0-516-24689-5). 48pp. Gertrude Ederle and Mark McGwire are two of the record-setting individuals featured in this volume. (Rev: SLJ 1/05) [921]

15684 Packard, Mary. *Beating the Odds: A Chapter Book* (3–6). Illus. Series: True Tales. 2004, Children's Pr. LB $22.50 (978-0-516-23731-2); paper $4.95 (978-0-516-24682-6). 48pp. Wilma Rudolph (polio) and Lance Armstrong (cancer) are two of the inspiring individuals featured in this volume of true tales about overcoming physical difficulties. (Rev: SLJ 1/05) [920]

15685 Piven, Hanoch. *What Athletes Are Made Of* (2–4). 2006, Simon & Schuster $16.95 (978-1-4169-1002-2). 40pp. Each of the well-known athletes in this visually interesting, offbeat book has an unusual feature to show what he or she is "made of." (Rev: BL 7/06; SLJ 8/06) [920]

15686 Rappoport, Ken. *Guts and Glory: Making It in the NBA* (4–8). 1997, Walker LB $16.85 (978-0-8027-8431-5). The 10 basketball players profiled in this book had to overcome obstacles to get to the top. (Rev: BL 8/97; SLJ 7/97) [920]

15687 Rappoport, Ken. *Ladies First: Women Athletes Who Made a Difference* (5–8). Illus. 2005, Peachtree $14.95 (978-1-56145-338-2). 160pp. Gymnast Nadia Comaneci and dogsled racer Susan Butcher are only two of the many women in diverse sports featured in this collective biography that also gives a brief history of women's participation in sports. (Rev: BL 5/1/05; SLJ 6/05) [920]

15688 Rappoport, Ken. *Profiles in Sports Courage* (4–7). 2006, Peachtree $15.95 (978-1-56145-368-9). 160pp. Twelve stories of bravery on and off the playing field (or court, ring, or track) by men and women from all types of sport and from all around the world. (Rev: BL 7/06; SLJ 6/06) [796.092]

15689 Rediger, Pat. *Great African Americans in Sports* (4–6). Illus. Series: Outstanding African Americans. 1996, Crabtree LB $22.60 (978-0-86505-801-9). 64pp. Three of the 13 sports heroes profiled are Michael Jordan, Jackie Joyner-Kersee, and Carl Lewis. (Rev: BL 9/15/96) [920]

15690 Roberts, Angela. *NASCAR's Greatest Drivers* (2–4). Illus. 2009, Random LB $11.99 (978-0-375-94813-8); paper $3.99 (978-0-375-94813-1). 48pp. A basic introduction to NASCAR opens this collective biography suitable for beginning readers. (Rev: BLO 1/7/09) [920]

15691 Rutledge, Rachel. *The Best of the Best in Figure Skating* (4–7). Series: Women of Sports. 1998, Millbrook LB $24.90 (978-0-7613-1302-1). 64pp. After a brief history of figure skating and mention of its women pioneers, this book devotes separate chapters to the sport's present-day female leaders. (Rev: BL 2/15/99; HBG 10/99) [920]

15692 Rutledge, Rachel. *The Best of the Best in Gymnastics* (5–8). Series: Women of Sports. 1999, Millbrook LB $24.90 (978-0-7613-1321-2); paper $7.95 (978-0-7613-0784-6). 64pp. After an overview of the sport and its history, the author profiles eight important contemporary female gymnasts, five of whom are American. (Rev: HBG 10/99; SLJ 7/99; VOYA 2/00) [920]

15693 Rutledge, Rachel. *The Best of the Best in Soccer* (4–7). Series: Women of Sports. 1998, Millbrook LB $24.90 (978-0-7613-1315-1). 64pp. A revised edition of the 1998 title, containing a brief history of women's soccer and profiles of the top women players of yesterday, today, and tomorrow. (Rev: BL 2/15/99; HBG 10/99) [920]

15694 Rutledge, Rachel. *The Best of the Best in Track and Field* (5–8). Series: Women of Sports. 1999,

Millbrook LB $24.90 (978-0-7613-1300-7); paper $7.95 (978-0-7613-0446-3). 64pp. A brief history of track and field is followed by profiles of eight female athletes from the United States and abroad, with material on their careers and off-the-field lives. (Rev: HBG 10/99; SLJ 7/99; VOYA 2/00) [920]

15695 Savage, Jeff. *Home Run Kings* (4–6). Illus. 1999, Raintree $22.83 (978-0-7398-0216-8); paper $6.95 (978-0-7398-0215-1). 48pp. Brief profiles are given of such home-run record setters as Babe Ruth, Roger Maris, Mark McGwire, Sammy Sosa, Hank Aaron, Mickey Mantle, and Willie Mays plus lots of World Series action. (Rev: BL 5/15/99; HBG 10/99) [920]

15696 Schilling, Vincent. *Native Athletes in Action!* (4–6). Illus. Series: Native Trailblazers. 2007, 7th Generation paper $9.95 (978-0-9779183-0-0). 125pp. This well-written collective biography profiles 13 Native American athletes from Canada and the United States — many of whom will be unfamiliar to young readers — and focuses on values that helped them succeed. (Rev: BL 9/1/07; SLJ 9/07) [920]

15697 Schnakenberg, Robert E. *Teammates: Karl Malone and John Stockton* (5–7). Illus. 1998, Millbrook LB $23.90 (978-0-7613-0300-8). 96pp. Despite very different backgrounds, these two leading players on the Utah Jazz basketball team have become close personal friends. (Rev: BL 8/98; HBG 10/98; SLJ 5/98) [920]

15698 Schwabacher, Martin. *Superstars of Women's Tennis* (4–6). Illus. Series: Female Sports Stars. 1997, Chelsea LB $28.00 (978-0-7910-4393-6). 64pp. Profiles tennis greats Billie Jean King, Chris Evert, Martina Navratilova, Steffi Graff, and Monica Seles. (Rev: SLJ 8/97) [920]

15699 Shea, Therese. *Soccer Stars* (3–5). Series: Greatest Sports Heroes. 2006, Children's Pr. $24.50 (978-0-531-12588-5). 48pp. Profiles some of today's best-known soccer players, including Freddy Adu, David Beckham, and Kristine Lilly. (Rev: BL 9/1/06) [920]

15700 Smith, Pohla. *Superstars of Women's Figure Skating* (4–6). Illus. Series: Female Sports Stars. 1997, Chelsea LB $28.00 (978-0-7910-4392-9). 64pp. A clear easy reader that includes profiles of Sonja Henie, Peggy Fleming, Dorothy Hamill, Katarina Witt, Kristi Yamaguchi, and Oksana Baiul. (Rev: SLJ 8/97) [920]

15701 Strudwick, Leslie. *Athletes* (3–6). Series: Women in Profile. 1999, Crabtree LB $22.60 (978-0-7787-0015-9); paper $8.95 (978-0-7787-0037-1). 48pp. Color photos and interesting information are included in this book that profiles six internationally known female athletes and briefly sketches an additional 12. (Rev: BL 9/15/99) [920]

15702 Ungs, Tim. *Superstars of Men's Soccer* (3–5). Series: Male Sports Stars. 1998, Chelsea LB $12.95 (978-0-7910-4588-6). 64pp. After an introduction to soccer, this collective biography profiles Pele, Franz Beckenbauer, Johann Cruyff, and Diego Maradona. (Rev: HBG 3/99; SLJ 12/98) [920]

15703 Wickham, Martha. *Superstars of Women's Track and Field* (4–6). Series: Female Sports Stars. 1997, Chelsea LB $28.00 (978-0-7910-4394-3). 64pp. This book profiles five important female track-and-field stars, with details on their careers and a good selection of action photos. (Rev: SLJ 4/98) [920]

15704 Winter, Jonah. *Beisbol! Latino Baseball Pioneers and Legends* (3–8). Illus. 2001, Lee & Low $16.95 (978-1-58430-012-0). 32pp. Sports fans will appreciate the format here, with statistics and other facts about 14 Latino baseball players presented in trading-card-style profiles. (Rev: BCCB 10/01; BL 10/1/01; HBG 10/01; SLJ 7/01) [796.357]

15705 Winter, Jonah. *Fair Ball! 14 Great Stars from Baseball's Negro Leagues* (3–5). Illus. 1999, Scholastic $15.95 (978-0-590-39464-2). 32pp. Using double-page spreads, this book profiles 14 great baseball players from the Negro Leagues, including Cool Papa Bell, Josh Gibson, and Satchel Paige. (Rev: BL 4/15/99; HBG 10/99; SLJ 3/99) [920]

15706 Woods, Bob. *Racer Girls* (2–5). Series: Girls Rock! 2006, The Child's World LB $25.64 (978-1-59296-742-1). 32pp. Profiles female racing car drivers around the world in large text and full-color photographs; suitable for browsing by beginning readers. (Rev: SLJ 4/07) [920]

Automobile Racing

EARNHARDT, DALE, JR.

15707 Stewart, Mark. *Dale Earnhardt Jr.: Driven by Destiny* (5–8). Series: Auto Racing's New Wave. 2003, Millbrook LB $22.90 (978-0-7613-2908-4). 48pp. An exciting biography of the NASCAR driver who was voted the most popular driver of 2003. (Rev: BL 6/1–15/03; HBG 10/03; SLJ 10/03) [796.72]

GORDON, JEFF

15708 Doeden, Matt. *Jeff Gordon* (3–6). Series: Stars of NASCAR. 2008, Capstone LB $22.60 (978-1-4296-1976-9). 32pp. Simple sentences, color photographs, fact boxes, and statistics make this an appealing profile of the NASCAR driver. (Rev: SLJ 12/08) [921]

15709 Gitlin, Marty. *Jeff Gordon: Racing's Brightest Star* (5–8). Illus. Series: Heroes of Racing. 2008, Enslow LB $23.95 (978-0-7660-2997-2). 128pp. For NASCAR fans, a biography that concentrates on Gordon's victories and charisma. (Rev: BL 4/1/08) [796.72]

15710 Powell, Phelan. *Jeff Gordon* (3–4). Series: Real-Life Reader Biographies. 1999, Mitchell Lane LB $15.95 (978-1-58415-005-3). 32pp. A simple biography of the race-car driving star and his climb to fame. (Rev: BL 10/15/99) [921]

JOHNSON, JIMMIE

15711 Doeden, Matt. *Jimmie Johnson* (3 6). Series: Stars of NASCAR. 2008, Capstone LB $22.60 (978-1-4296-1977-6). 32pp. Simple sentences, color photographs, fact boxes, and statistics make this an appealing profile of the NASCAR driver. (Rev: SLJ 12/08) [921]

KAHNE, KASEY

15712 Doeden, Matt. *Kasey Kahne* (3–6). Series: Stars of NASCAR. 2008, Capstone LB $22.60 (978-1-4296-1980-6). 32pp. Simple sentences, color photographs, fact boxes, and statistics make this an appealing profile of the NASCAR driver. (Rev: SLJ 12/08) [921]

LABONTE, TERRY AND BOBBY

15713 Hubbard-Brown, Janet. *The Labonte Brothers* (4–8). Series: Race Car Legends: Collector's Edition. 2005, Chelsea House LB $25.00 (978-0-7910-8767-1). 72pp. The famous brothers Terry and Bobby Labonte and their racing rivalry and successes are the focus of this readable, photo-filled volume. (Rev: SLJ 5/06) [921]

PATRICK, DANICA

15714 Mello, Tara Baukus. *Danica Patrick* (5–8). Illus. Series: Race Car Legends Collector's Edition. 2008, Chelsea House LB $25.00 (978-0-7910-9126-5). 71pp. An attractive portrait of this history-making race car driver. (Rev: BL 4/15/08) [921]

PETTY FAMILY

15715 Stewart, Mark. *The Pettys: Triumphs and Tragedies of Auto Racing's First Family* (4–8). Illus. 2001, Millbrook LB $24.90 (978-0-7613-2273-3). 64pp. Photographs, quotations, anecdotes, and informative text introduce readers to the famous Petty family and their sometimes tragic involvement in automobile racing. (Rev: BL 9/1/01; HBG 3/02) [796.72]

STEWART, TONY

15716 Leebrick, Kristal. *Tony Stewart* (4–7). Illus. Series: NASCAR Racing. 2004, Capstone LB $23.93 (978-0-7368-2425-5). 32pp. This profile of auto racing star Tony Stewart chronicles his meteoric rise from go-karts and midget racers to the top ranks of NASCAR. (Rev: BL 4/1/04) [790.72]

UNSER FAMILY

15717 Bentley, Karen. *The Unsers* (4–8). Series: Race Car Legends: Collector's Edition. 2005, Chelsea House LB $25.00 (978-0-7910-8764-0). 72pp. The famous Unser automobile racing family is the focus of this book that describes their rivalries with the Andretti family and their victories at important races including the Indianapolis 500. (Rev: SLJ 5/06) [921]

Baseball

AARON, HANK

15718 Golenbock, Peter. *Hank Aaron: Brave in Every Way* (2–4). Illus. by Paul Lee. 2001, Harcourt $16.00 (978-0-15-202093-4). 32pp. Part of this stirring biography focuses on Hank Aaron's goal of breaking Babe Ruth's batting record and the controversy it caused because he was African American. (Rev: BL 2/15/01; HBG 10/01) [921]

15719 Spencer, Lauren. *Hank Aaron* (4–7). Series: Baseball Hall of Famers. 2003, Rosen LB $29.25 (978-0-8239-3600-7). 112pp. In 1974, Hank Aaron, an African American, was crowned home run king, taking the title away from Babe Ruth. This is his story. (Rev: BL 6/1–15/03; SLJ 6/03) [921]

BELL, COOL PAPA

15720 McCormack, Shaun. *Cool Papa Bell* (4–7). Series: Baseball Hall of Famers of the Negro Leagues. 2002, Rosen LB $29.25 (978-0-8239-3474-4). 112pp. A biography of James Thomas "Cool Papa" Bell of Negro League baseball, who is said to have stolen 175 bases in one season. (Rev: BL 7/02) [921]

BONILLA, BOBBY

15721 Rappoport, Ken. *Bobby Bonilla* (5–9). 1993, Walker LB $15.85 (978-0-8027-8256-4). A biography of the baseball player who rose from poverty in the South Bronx to superstardom and multimillionaire status. (Rev: BL 5/15/93; SLJ 5/93; VOYA 8/93) [921]

CAMPANELLA, ROY

15722 Adler, David A. *Campy: The Story of Roy Campanella* (2–4). Illus. by Gordon C. James. 2007, Viking $15.99 (978-0-670-06041-2). 40pp. African American baseball player joined the Brooklyn Dodgers only a year after Jackie Robinson and was a major star until a 1958 accident left him paralyzed. (Rev: BL 2/1/07; SLJ 4/07) [921]

CLEMENTE, ROBERTO

15723 Gilbert, Tom. *Roberto Clemente* (5–8). Illus. 1991, Chelsea LB $32.00 (978-0-7910-1240-6). 112pp. The life of the first Hispanic in the Baseball Hall of Fame. (Rev: BL 8/91) [921]

15724 Kingsbury, Robert. *Roberto Clemente* (4–7). Series: Baseball Hall of Famers. 2003, Rosen LB $29.25 (978-0-8239-3602-1). 112pp. The story of the National League battling champion who faced racism and discrimination because of his Hispanic background. (Rev: BL 6/1–15/03; SLJ 6/03) [921]

15725 Marquez, Heron. *Roberto Clemente: Baseball's Humanitarian Hero* (4–7). Illus. 2005, Carolrhoda LB $30.60 (978-1-57505-767-5). 112pp. The story of the ballplayer, from his birth in Puerto Rico to his death in a plane crash, with photographs. (Rev: BL 3/15/05; SLJ 5/05) [796.357]

15726 Winter, Jonah. *Roberto Clemente: Pride of the Pittsburgh Pirates* (2–4). Illus. by Raúl Colón. 2005, Simon & Schuster $16.95 (978-0-689-85643-3). 40pp. Clemente's character, career success, and tragic death are all covered in this engaging picture-book biography. (Rev: BL 2/15/05; SLJ 5/05) [921]

DIMAGGIO, JOE

15727 Sakany, Lois. *Joe DiMaggio* (4–6). Series: Baseball Hall of Famers. 2004, Rosen LB $29.25 (978-0-8239-3779-0). 112pp. Report writers will find solid information on the life and career of the Yankees star. (Rev: SLJ 6/04) [921]

DOUTY, SHEILA CORNELL

15728 Douty, Sheila Cornell, and Judith Cohen. *You Can Be a Woman Softball Player* (3–6). Illus. 2000, Cascade Pass $13.95 (978-1-880599-47-1); paper $7.00 (978-1-880599-46-4). 40pp. This is the story of Sheila Douty, from her youth, when she was considered a "problem" child, to the 1996 Olympics, where she helped her team win a gold medal. (Rev: BL 7/00) [921]

GAGNE, ERIC

15729 Gagné, Eric, and Greg Brown. *Eric Gagne: Break Barriers* (3–6). Series: Athletes. 2004, Positively for Kids $15.95 (978-0-9634650-6-1). 48pp. A lively and attractively designed first-person account of Gagne's life and career in baseball, with lots of personal details about his childhood, family life, and sporting successes. (Rev: BL 9/1/04) [921]

GALARRAGA, ANDRES

15730 Boulais, Sue. *Andres Galarraga* (3–4). Series: Real-Life Reader Biographies. 1998, Mitchell Lane LB $15.95 (978-1-883845-61-2). 32pp. The story of a baseball hero from Caracas, Venezuela, his career in Atlanta, and his struggle with cancer. (Rev: BL 10/15/98; HBG 10/98; SLJ 12/98) [921]

GEHRIG, LOU

15731 Adler, David A. *Lou Gehrig: The Luckiest Man* (3–5). Illus. by Terry Widener. 1997, Harcourt $16.00 (978-0-15-200523-8). 32pp. An excellent biography of the "Iron Horse," the baseball legend who was a model of sportsmanship and courage. (Rev: BCCB 4/97; BL 5/15/97; HB 7/97, 9/97; SLJ 5/97) [921]

15732 Viola, Kevin. *Lou Gehrig* (4–7). Series: Sports Heroes and Legends. 2004, Lerner LB $8.95 (978-0-8225-5311-3). Starting with Gehrig's sad retirement and his "Luckiest Man" speech, this well-written and informative biography goes back to look at his life and successful career. (Rev: BL 9/1/04) [921]

GIBSON, JOSH

15733 Twemlow, Nick. *Josh Gibson* (4–7). Series: Baseball Hall of Famers of the Negro Leagues. 2002, Rosen LB $29.25 (978-0-8239-3475-1). 112pp. In addition to racial prejudice in the world of baseball, Josh Gibson suffered many personal misfortunes as this life story recounts. (Rev: BL 7/02) [921]

GREENBERG, HANK

15734 McDonough, Yona Zeldis. *Hammerin' Hank: The Life of Hank Greenberg* (K–2). Illus. by Malcah Zeldis. 2006, Walker $16.95 (978-0-8027-8997-6). 32pp. This profile of the first Jewish American baseball star discusses his parents' disapproval of his choice of career, the prejudice he faced, and the difficult decisions he had to make. (Rev: BL 3/1/06; SLJ 4/06*) [921]

IRVIN, MONTE

15735 Haegele, Katie. *Monte Irvin* (4–7). Series: Baseball Hall of Famers of the Negro Leagues. 2002, Rosen LB $29.25 (978-0-8239-3477-5). 112pp. Though recruited into the Negro leagues when he was 17, Irvin, a very talented player, was past his prime when he finally became a major leaguer. (Rev: BL 7/02) [921]

JETER, DEREK

15736 Robinson, Tom. *Derek Jeter: Captain On and Off the Field* (5–8). Series: Sports Stars with Heart. 2006, Enslow LB $31.93 (978-0-7660-2819-7). 128pp. This biography focuses primarily on Jeter's career in baseball and his work with the philanthropic Turn 2 Foundation. (Rev: BL 9/1/06) [921]

15737 Stewart, Mark. *Derek Jeter: Substance and Style* (4–6). Series: Baseball's New Wave. 1999, Millbrook LB $22.90 (978-0-7613-1516-2). 48pp. This biography that ends with the 1998 season gives a good close-up view of the star shortstop of the New York Yankees. (Rev: HBG 3/00; SLJ 2/00) [921]

15738 Thornley, Stew. *Derek Jeter* (3–6). Illus. Series: Sports Leaders. 2004, Enslow LB $26.60 (978-0-7660-2035-1). 104pp. An accessible profile of the shortstop's life and career. [921]

15739 Torres, John. *Derek Jeter* (3–4). Series: Real-Life Reader Biographies. 2000, Mitchell Lane LB $15.95 (978-1-58415-031-2). 32pp. A brief, attractive biography of the young star of the New York Yankees. (Rev: BL 11/15/00) [921]

JOHNSON, JUDY

15740 Billus, Kathleen. *Judy Johnson* (4–7). Illus. Series: Baseball Hall of Famers of the Negro Leagues. 2002, Rosen LB $29.25 (978-0-8239-3476-8). 112pp. A biography of Johnson covering his years as player, coach, manager, and scout, with black-and-white photographs, glossary, timeline, and lists of additional resources. (Rev: BL 7/02) [796.357]

JOHNSON, MAMIE "PEANUT"

15741 Green, Michelle Y. *A Strong Right Arm: The Story of Mamie "Peanut" Johnson* (4–7). 2002, Dial $15.99 (978-0-8037-2661-1). 128pp. The life story of the woman who was one of three to play professional baseball and of her career as pitcher with the Negro Leagues' Indianapolis Clowns. (Rev: BL 6/1–15/02*; HBG 3/03; SLJ 8/02; VOYA 8/02) [921]

KOUFAX, SANDY

15742 Winter, Jonah. *You Never Heard of Sandy Koufax?!* (2–4). Illus. by Andre Carrilho. 2009, Random $17.99 (978-0-375-83738-8). 40pp. A compelling picture-book biography of the Jewish player for the Dodgers. (Rev: BCCB 2/09; BL 12/15/08; HB 3/09; SLJ 2/09) [921]

LEONARD, BUCK

15743 Payment, Simone. *Buck Leonard* (4–7). Series: Baseball Hall of Famers of the Negro Leagues. 2002, Rosen LB $29.25 (978-0-8239-3473-7). 112pp. The story of one of the greatest baseball players of all time, who missed worldwide fame because of his color. (Rev: BL 7/02) [921]

MCGWIRE, MARK

15744 Dougherty, Terri. *Mark McGwire* (2–4). Series: Jam Session. 1999, ABDO LB $24.21 (978-1-57765-349-3). 32pp. A heavily illustrated biography of the amazing batter that uses quotes from friends and family. (Rev: HBG 10/99; SLJ 8/99) [921]

MANTLE, MICKEY

15745 Marlin, John. *Mickey Mantle* (4–7). Series: Sports Heroes and Legends. 2004, Lerner LB $27.93 (978-0-8225-1796-2). A concise, well-written biography that focuses on Mantle's illustrious career. (Rev: BL 9/1/04; SLJ 11/04) [921]

15746 Weinstein, Howard. *Mickey Mantle* (4–6). Series: Baseball Hall of Famers. 2004, Rosen LB $29.25 (978-0-8239-3782-0). 112pp. Report writers will find solid information on the life and career of the Yankees star. (Rev: SLJ 6/04) [921]

MITCHELL, JACKIE

15747 Moss, Marissa. *Mighty Jackie: The Strike-Out Queen* (K–3). Illus. by C. F. Payne. 2004, Simon & Schuster $16.95 (978-0-689-86329-5). Jackie's story opens with the day in 1931 when — at age 17 — she struck out both Lou Gehrig and Babe Ruth. (Rev: BL 1/1–15/04; SLJ 2/04) [921]

PAIGE, SATCHEL

15748 Adler, David A. *Satchel Paige: Don't Look Back* (K–3). Illus. by Terry Widener. Series: Paige, Satchel. 2007, Harcourt $16.00 (978-0-15-205585-1). 32pp. This picture-book biography gives a the great pitcher's early life and successful career in both the Negro leagues and the majors. (Rev: BL 1/1–15/07) [921]

15749 Cline-Ransome, Lesa. *Satchel Paige* (2–4). Illus. by James Ransome. 2000, Simon & Schuster $16.00 (978-0-689-81151-7). 40pp. The mythic hero of baseball comes to life, with all his swagger and accomplishments, in this biography. (Rev: BCCB 2/00; BL 12/15/99*; HB 3/00; HBG 10/00; SLJ 3/00) [921]

15750 McKissack, Patricia C., and Fredrick McKissack. *Satchel Paige: The Best Arm in Baseball*. Rev. ed. (2–4). Illus. by Michael D. Blegel. Series: Great African Americans. 2002, Enslow LB $18.60 (978-0-89490-317-5). 32pp. The life story of the Hall of Famer who was the first African American pitcher in the American League. (Rev: BL 10/15/92; SLJ 1/93) [921]

15751 Schmidt, Julie. *Satchel Paige* (4–7). Illus. Series: Baseball Hall of Famers of the Negro Leagues. 2002, Rosen LB $29.25 (978-0-8239-3478-2). 112pp. A biography of the famous pitcher who became the oldest rookie ever, with black-and-white photographs, glossary, timeline, and lists of additional resources. (Rev: BL 7/02; VOYA 6/02) [796.357]

PALMEIRO, RAFAEL

15752 Marvis, Barbara. *Rafael Palmeiro* (3–5). Series: Real-Life Reader Biographies. 1998, Mitchell Lane LB $15.95 (978-1-883845-49-0). 32pp. Using short chapters, black-and-white photos, and a simple vocabulary, this is the story of Rafael Palmeiro, the Cuban refugee who became first baseman for the Texas Rangers. (Rev: BL 6/1–15/98; HBG 3/98) [921]

PUCKETT, KIRBY

15753 Puckett, Kirby, and Greg Brown. *Kirby Puckett: Be the Best You Can Be* (2–4). Illus. by Tim Houle. 1993, Waldman $14.95 (978-0-931674-20-4). A picture-book autobiography of the star of the Minnesota Twins, filled with advice on how to achieve one's potential. (Rev: BL 8/93; SLJ 2/94) [921]

PUJOLS, ALBERT

15754 Buckingham, Mark. *Albert Pujols: MVP On and Off the Field* (4–7). Illus. 2007, Enslow LB $23.95 (978-0-7660-2866-1). 128pp. Presents facts on the life of the baseball legend, including his childhood in the Dominican Republic, his move to the United States, his career and accomplishments with the St. Louis Cardinals, and his family. (Rev: BL 9/1/07) [921]

RIPKEN, CAL, JR.

15755 Ripken, Cal, Jr. *The Longest Season: The Story of the Orioles' 1988 Losing Streak* (2–5). Illus. by Ron Mazellan. 2007, Philomel $16.99 (978-0-399-24492-6). 32pp. The famous ballplayer relates the story of that difficult season, and readers will learn that even top athletes experience difficult times. (Rev: SLJ 5/07)

ROBINSON, JACKIE

15756 Adler, David A. *Jackie Robinson: He Was the First* (3–5). Illus. by Robert Casilla. 1989, Holiday House LB $15.95 (978-0-8234-0734-7). 48pp. A profile of the first African American player in the major leagues. (Rev: BL 7/89) [921]

15757 Adler, David A. *A Picture Book of Jackie Robinson* (K–3). Illus. by Robert Casilla. Series: Picture Book Biographies. 1994, Holiday House LB $16.95 (978-0-8234-1122-1). 32pp. This simple biography of the baseball giant reads like a story for young children. (Rev: BL 11/15/94; SLJ 12/94) [921]

15758 Coombs, Karen Mueller. *Jackie Robinson: Baseball's Civil Rights Legend* (5–7). Illus. Series: African-American Biographies. 1997, Enslow LB $26.60 (978-0-89490-690-9). 128pp. The story of the baseball great who stood up to racism in athletics. (Rev: BL 6/1–15/97) [921]

15759 Davidson, Margaret. *The Story of Jackie Robinson: Bravest Man in Baseball* (3–7). Illus. 1988, Dell paper $3.99 (978-0-440-40019-6). 92pp. The life of the man who broke the baseball color barrier. (Rev: BL 6/1/88; SLJ 5/88)

15760 DeAngelis, Gina. *Jackie Robinson: Overcoming Adversity* (5–8). Illus. Series: Overcoming Adversity. 2000, Chelsea $30.00 (978-0-7910-5897-8). 104pp. Using a highly readable text and black-and-white photographs, this book gives a real picture of Robinson that touches on the reasons he felt extreme anger and his great determination to make a difference. (Rev: BL 2/15/01; HBG 10/01) [921]

15761 Denenberg, Barry. *Stealing Home: The Story of Jackie Robinson* (4–6). Illus. 1997, Scholastic paper $5.99 (978-0-590-42560-5). 116pp. A biography that balances Robinson's life and significance on and off the baseball diamond. (Rev: SLJ 1/91) [921]

15762 Ford, Carin T. *Jackie Robinson: Hero of Baseball* (2–4). Illus. Series: Heroes of American History. 2006, Enslow LB $22.60 (978-0-7660-2600-1). 32pp. A brief, readable account of Robinson's life and accomplishments, with information about segregation in general. (Rev: BL 2/1/06; SLJ 8/06) [921]

15763 Mara, Wil. *Jackie Robinson* (K–2). Series: Rookie Biographies. 2002, Children's Book Pr. paper $4.95 (978-0-516-27336-5). 32pp. For beginning readers, this is a simple introduction to the legendary baseball player. (Rev: SLJ 12/02) [821]

15764 O'Connor, Jim. *Jackie Robinson and the Story of All-Black Baseball* (3–5). Illus. by Jim Butcher. 1989, Random paper $3.99 (978-0-394-82456-7).

48pp. The story of Jackie Robinson and the Negro Leagues, preceding his entry into pro ball. (Rev: BCCB 9/89; BL 7/89) [921]

15765 O'Sullivan, Robyn. *Jackie Robinson Plays Ball* (2–4). Series: National Geographic History Chapters. 2007, National Geographic LB $17.90 (978-1-4263-0190-2). 40pp. Simple sentences, with photographs and drawings, tell the story of Robinson's younger life and later accomplishments; a "How to Write an A+ Report" section gives useful advice. (Rev: LMC 1/08*; SLJ 1/08) [921]

15766 Robinson, Sharon. *Promises to Keep: How Jackie Robinson Changed America* (3–7). Illus. 2004, Scholastic $16.95 (978-0-439-42592-6). 64pp. The inspiring story of Robinson's life and his struggle to break into major league baseball is told by his daughter. (Rev: BL 2/15/04*; SLJ 3/04) [796.357]

15767 Scott, Richard. *Jackie Robinson* (5–10). Illus. 1987, Chelsea LB $30.00 (978-1-55546-609-1). A well-researched biography giving good material on Robinson's life outside baseball. (Rev: BL 9/1/87; SLJ 9/87) [921]

15768 Time for Kids Editorial Staff, and Denise Lewis Patrick, eds. *Jackie Robinson: Strong Inside and Out* (2–4). Illus. Series: Time for Kids Biographies. 2005, HarperCollins $15.99 (978-0-06-057601-1); paper $3.99 (978-0-06-057600-4). 48pp. A lively overview of Robinson's life drawing on the archives of Time-Life and ending with an interview with his daughter Sharon. (Rev: BL 2/1/05) [921]

15769 Wukovits, John F. *Jackie Robinson and the Integration of Baseball* (5–8). Series: Lucent Library of Black History. 2006, Gale LB $32.45 (978-1-59018-913-9). 104pp. The social background to Robinson's achievements is well laid out in this biography suitable for report writers. (Rev: SLJ 3/07) [921]

RODRIGUEZ, ALEX

15770 Stewart, Mark. *Alex Rodriguez: Gunning for Greatness* (4–6). Series: Baseball's New Wave. 1999, Millbrook LB $22.90 (978-0-7613-1515-5). 48pp. An attractive biography with sidebars and plenty of photos on this superstar shortstop of the Seattle Mariners that ends with the 1998 season. (Rev: HBG 10/00; SLJ 2/00) [921]

RUTH, BABE

15771 Burleigh, Robert. *Home Run: The Story of Babe Ruth* (3–6). Illus. by Mike Wimmer. 1998, Harcourt $16.00 (978-0-15-200970-0). 32pp. A picture book for older readers that relates the life, career, character, and accomplishments of one of baseball's great heroes. (Rev: BCCB 9/98; BL 8/98; HBG 3/99; SLJ 8/98) [921]

15772 Kelly, David A. *Babe Ruth and the Baseball Curse* (3–5). Illus. by Tim Jessell. 2009, Random LB $11.99 (978-0-375-95603-4); paper $4.99 (978-0-375-85603-7). 112pp. In addition to covering Ruth's childhood and career, Kelly reviews the spotty achievements of the Boston Red Sox after

they traded Babe Ruth to the Yankees in 1918. (Rev: BCCB 2/09; BL 1/1–15/09) [921]

15773 Murphy, Frank. *Babe Ruth Saves Baseball!* (1–3). Illus. by Richard Walz. Series: Step into Reading. 2005, Random LB $11.99 (978-0-375-93048-5); paper $3.99 (978-0-375-83048-8). 48pp. Babe Ruth's character comes to the fore in this lively biography for beginning readers. (Rev: BL 6/1–15/05) [921]

15774 Nicholson, Lois. *Babe Ruth: Sultan of Swat* (5–8). Illus. 1995, Goodwood $17.95 (978-0-9625427-1-8). 119pp. This well-written account of the famous slugger explains his lasting influence on baseball. (Rev: SLJ 7/95) [921]

SOCKALEXIS, LOUIS

15775 Wise, Bill. *Louis Sockalexis: Native American Baseball Pioneer* (3–5). Illus. by Bill Farnsworth. 2007, Lee & Low $16.95 (978-1-58430-269-8). 32pp. Colorful illustrations evoke the turn-of-the-century time period in profile the first Native American to play baseball for a major league team. (Rev: BL 7/07; LMC 11/07; SLJ 5/07) [921]

SOSA, SAMMY

15776 Dougherty, Terri. *Sammy Sosa* (2–4). Series: Jam Session. 1999, ABDO LB $24.21 (978-1-57765-348-6). 32pp. Using quotes from friends, family, and teammates, this simple, heavily illustrated biography presents the life and accomplishments of amazing batter Sammy Sosa. (Rev: HBG 10/99; SLJ 8/99) [921]

STRAWBERRY, DARRYL

15777 Torres, John A., and Michael J. Sullivan. *Darryl Strawberry* (4–6). Illus. Series: Sports Great Books. 1990, Enslow LB $17.95 (978-0-89490-291-8). 64pp. The story of the fine but controversial baseball player, with good coverage of his childhood. (Rev: SLJ 11/90) [921]

SUZUKI, ICHIRO

15778 Leigh, David S. *Ichiro Suzuki* (4–6). 2004, Lerner LB $27.93 (978-0-8225-1792-4). 106pp. Suzuki's youth and career in Japan are covered in addition to his contributions in the U.S. major leagues. (Rev: SLJ 11/04) [921]

15779 Levin, Judith. *Ichiro Suzuki* (5–8). Illus. Series: Baseball Superstars. 2007, Chelsea House LB $30.00 (978-0-7910-9440-2). 135pp. A biography of the record-setting, award-winning Seattle Mariners player from Japan. (Rev: BL 3/18/08) [921]

15780 Stewart, Mark. *Ichiro Suzuki: Best in the West* (4–7). Illus. Series: Sports New Wave. 2002, Millbrook LB $22.90 (978-0-7613-2616-8). 48pp. A well-constructed biography of the famous Japanese Seattle Mariners player that offers information on the game itself as well as statistics, color photographs, and quotations that illustrate his achievements. (Rev: BL 9/1/02; HBG 3/03) [796.357]

WEISS, ALTA

15781 Hopkinson, Deborah. *Girl Wonder: A Baseball Story in Nine Innings* (2–4). Illus. by Terry Widener. 2003, Simon & Schuster $16.95 (978-0-689-83300-7). 40pp. Alta Weiss's inspiring story swings along in lyrical prose, relating her adventures as a teenage baseball phenomenon who pitched for a men's team in 1907 at the age of 17. (Rev: BL 1/1–15/03*; HB 3/03; HBG 10/03; SLJ 3/03)

WILLIAMS, TED

15782 McCormack, Shaun. *Ted Williams* (4–6). Series: Baseball Hall of Famers. 2004, Rosen LB $29.25 (978-0-8239-3783-7). 112pp. Report writers will find solid information on the life and career of the Boston Red Sox star. (Rev: SLJ 6/04) [921]

Basketball

ABDUL-JABBAR, KAREEM

15783 Kneib, Martha. *Kareem Abdul-Jabbar* (5–8). Series: Basketball Hall of Famers. 2002, Rosen LB $29.25 (978-0-8239-3483-6). 112pp. An in-depth look at this basketball great's life, with highlights from his childhood through his NBA career. (Rev: BL 9/1/02) [921]

ANTHONY, CARMELO

15784 Anthony, Carmelo, and Greg Brown. *Carmelo Anthony: It's Just the Beginning* (3–6). Illus. Series: Athletes. 2004, Positively for Kids $15.95 (978-0-9634650-7-8). 48pp. A lively and attractively designed first-person account of Anthony's life and career in basketball, with lots of personal details about his childhood, family life, and sporting successes. [921]

BARKLEY, CHARLES

15785 Dolan, Sean. *Charles Barkley* (5–7). Illus. Series: Basketball Legends. 1996, Chelsea LB $18.65 (978-0-7910-2433-1). 62pp. The life of this basketball superstar, with details on his record on the court. (Rev: BL 7/96) [921]

BIRD, SUE

15786 Bird, Sue, and Greg Brown. *Sue Bird: Be Yourself* (3–6). Illus. Series: Athletes. 2004, Positively for Kids $15.95 (978-0-9634650-5-4). 48pp. A lively and attractively designed first-person account of Bird's life and career in basketball, with lots of personal details about her childhood, family life, and sporting successes. [921]

BRYANT, KOBE

15787 Savage, Jeff. *Kobe Bryant: Basketball Big Shot* (4–7). Illus. Series: Sports Biography. 2000, Lerner LB $22.60 (978-0-8225-3680-2). 64pp. A very readable, attractive biography of the new NBA sensation that ends with the 1999–2000 season. (Rev: BL 1/1–15/01; HBG 10/01) [921]

15788 Schnakenberg, Robert E. *Kobe Bryant* (4–6). Illus. Series: Basketball Legends. 1998, Chelsea $12.95 (978-0-7910-5005-7). 64pp. A detailed biography of the Lakers star who became the youngest man ever to play in an NBA game. (Rev: BL 3/1/99; HBG 10/99) [921]

15789 Stewart, Mark. *Kobe Bryant: Hard to the Hoop* (4–8). Series: Basketball's New Wave. 2000, Millbrook LB $20.90 (978-0-7613-1800-2). 48pp. The life story of this basketball star who was the son of an NBA player and who became the youngest player in league history to star in the All-Star Game. (Rev: HBG 10/00; SLJ 8/00) [921]

15790 Thornley, Stew. *Super Sports Star Kobe Bryant* (2–5). Illus. Series: Super Sports Stars. 2001, Enslow LB $23.93 (978-0-7660-1514-2). 48pp. Photographs and statistics accompany text about the famous basketball player, from his childhood to his professional career with the L.A. Lakers. (Rev: BL 10/15/01; HBG 3/02) [796.323]

15791 Torres, John. *Kobe Bryant* (3–4). Series: Real-Life Reader Biographies. 2000, Mitchell Lane LB $24.95 (978-1-58415-030-5). 32pp. An easily read biography of the well-known basketball player who was a star before he graduated from high school. (Rev: BL 11/15/00) [921]

CARTER, VINCE

15792 Carter, Vince, and Greg Brown. *Vince Carter: Choose Your Course* (3–6). Series: Athletes. 2004, Positively for Kids $15.95 (978-0-9634650-2-3). 48pp. A first-person account of Carter's life and career in basketball, with lots of details about his childhood, family life, and sporting successes. (Rev: BL 9/1/04) [921]

15793 Thornley, Stew. *Super Sports Star Vince Carter* (2–5). Series: Super Sports Stars. 2002, Enslow LB $23.93 (978-0-7660-1805-1). 48pp. The life of the Toronto Raptors guard-forward is told in an account that features simple text, large type, and many color photographs. (Rev: BL 9/1/02; HBG 10/02) [921]

15794 Torres, John A. *Vince Carter: Slam Dunk Artist* (3–6). Illus. Series: Sports Leaders. 2004, Enslow LB $26.60 (978-0-7660-2173-0). 104pp. An accessible profile of the talented basketball player's life and career. [921]

COOPER, CYNTHIA

15795 Schnakenberg, Robert E. *Cynthia Cooper* (5–9). Series: Women Who Win. 2000, Chelsea $25.00 (978-0-7910-5796-4). 64pp. A biography of this basketball star that focuses on her career and game-related information. (Rev: HBG 3/01; SLJ 2/01; VOYA 4/01) [921]

DUNCAN, TIM

15796 Adams, Scan. *Tim Duncan* (4–7). Illus. Series: Sports Heroes and Legends. 2004, Lerner LB $27.93 (978-0-8225-1793-1). 106pp. A balanced, well-crafted life of the basketball star. (Rev: BL 9/1/04) [921]

15797 Byman, Jeremy. *Tim Duncan* (4–8). Illus. Series: Great Athletes. 2000, Morgan Reynolds LB $18.95 (978-1-883846-43-5). 64pp. This biography about a basketball hero who has been playing professionally for only a short time focuses on his college years, his outstanding talent, and his determination. (Rev: BL 6/1–15/00; HBG 3/01) [921]

15798 Stewart, Mark. *Tim Duncan: Tower of Power* (4–8). Series: Basketball's New Wave. 1999, Millbrook LB $22.90 (978-0-7613-1513-1). 48pp. Although this biography of basketball's rising star is brief, the information is ample and important topics are all covered. (Rev: HBG 10/00; SLJ 7/00) [921]

EWING, PATRICK

15799 Wiener, Paul. *Patrick Ewing* (4–6). Illus. Series: Basketball Legends. 1996, Chelsea LB $12.95 (978-0-7910-2434-8). 64pp. The story of this New York Knicks center and his quest for an NBA championship. (Rev: BL 7/96) [921]

GARNETT, KEVIN

15800 Stewart, Mark. *Kevin Garnett: Shake Up the Game* (4–7). Series: Sports New Wave. 2002, Millbrook LB $22.90 (978-0-7613-2615-1). 48pp. A short biography that chronicles the career of the new star of the Minnesota Timberwolves. (Rev: BL 9/1/02; HBG 10/02) [921]

15801 Thornley, Stew. *Super Sports Star Kevin Garnett* (2–5). Series: Super Sports Stars. 2001, Enslow LB $23.93 (978-0-7660-1515-9). 48pp. Garnett, a small forward for the Minnesota Timberwolves, gets an interesting profile complete with game details and statistics plus plenty of action photographs. (Rev: BL 10/15/01; HBG 3/02) [921]

HARDAWAY, PENNY

15802 Rappoport, Ken. *Super Sports Star Penny Hardaway* (2–5). Illus. Series: Super Sports Stars. 2001, Enslow LB $23.93 (978-0-7660-1516-6). 48pp. Photographs and statistics accompany text about the famous basketball player, from his childhood to his professional career. (Rev: BL 10/15/01; HBG 3/02) [796.323]

HILL, GRANT

15803 Lowenstein, Felicia. *Grant Hill* (2–5). Series: Super Sports Stars. 2001, Enslow LB $23.93 (978-0-7660-1517-3). Simple sentences and many color photographs are used in this beginning biography of the Orlando Magic forward. (Rev: BL 4/1/02; HBG 10/02) [921]

HOWARD, JUWAN

15804 Sirak, Ron. *Juwan Howard* (5–8). 1998, Chelsea LB $18.65 (978-0-7910-4575-6). A biography of one of the great basketball players of the 1990s, with good material on his early years and the influence of his grandmother. (Rev: HBG 3/99; VOYA 6/99) [921]

JAMES, LEBRON

15805 Mattern, Joanne. *LeBron James* (2–5). Series: A Robbie Reader. 2004, Mitchell Lane LB $25.70 (978-1-58415-293-4). 32pp. This photo-filled biography that presents information on James's childhood and career is especially suitable for reluctant readers. (Rev: BL 11/15/04) [921]

15806 Sandler, Michael. *LeBron James: I Love Challenges!* (3–5). Series: Defining Moments: Super Athletes. 2009, Bearport LB $25.27 (978-1-59716-856-4). 32pp. A look at key events in the life of the basketball player, with a timeline, facts, and engaging anecdotes. (Rev: SLJ 6/09) [921]

JOHNSON, MAGIC

15807 Greenberg, Keith E. *Magic Johnson: Champion with a Cause* (4–7). Illus. Series: Achievers. 1992, Lerner LB $27.15 (978-0-8225-0546-4). 64pp. The story of the gifted athlete for the L.A. Lakers, whose career was cut short when he discovered he was HIV-positive. (Rev: BL 8/92; SLJ 7/92) [921]

JORDAN, MICHAEL

15808 Berger, Phil, and John Rolfe. *Michael Jordan* (4–7). Illus. 1990, Little, Brown paper $4.95 (978-0-316-09229-6). 124pp. This account covers Jordan's childhood and his career development. (Rev: BL 12/15/90; SLJ 4/91) [921]

15809 Christopher, Matt. *On the Court with . . . Michael Jordan* (3–7). Illus. Series: Matt Christopher Sports Biography. 1996, Little, Brown paper $4.95 (978-0-316-13792-8). 144pp. The life of this pro basketball legend whose self-determination and family support helped him rise to the top. (Rev: BL 2/15/97; SLJ 6/97) [921]

15810 Cooper, Floyd. *Jump! From the Life of Michael Jordan* (K–3). 2004, Penguin $15.99 (978-0-399-24230-4). 40pp. Eye-catching illustrations and conversational text reveal the successes and challenges of Jordan's childhood and adolescence. (Rev: BL 9/1/04) [921]

KIDD, JASON

15811 Rappoport, Ken. *Jason Kidd: Leader on the Court* (3–6). Illus. Series: Sports Leaders. 2004, Enslow LB $26.60 (978-0-7660-2214-0). 104pp. An accessible profile of the basketball star's life and career. [921]

15812 Thornley, Stew. *Super Sports Star Jason Kidd* (2–5). Series: Super Sports Stars. 2002, Enslow LB $23.93 (978-0-7660-1806-8). 48pp. Complete with game statistics and sports action, this is a simple, attractive biography of the star guard of the New Jersey Nets. (Rev: BL 9/1/02; HBG 10/02) [921]

LESLIE, LISA

15813 Kelley, Brent. *Lisa Leslie* (5–9). Series: Women Who Win. 2000, Chelsea $25.00 (978-0-7910-5794-0). 64pp. This profile of a pioneer in the Women's National Basketball Association contains much game-related information. (Rev: HBG 3/01; SLJ 2/01) [921]

LIEBERMAN-CLINE, NANCY

15814 Greenberg, Doreen, and Michael Greenberg. *A Drive to Win: The Story of Nancy Lieberman-Cline* (4–8). Illus. by Phil Velikan. Series: Anything You Can Do — New Sports Heroes for Girls. 2000, Wish paper $9.95 (978-1-930546-40-0). 98pp. Based on personal interviews, this is an informative biography of the basketball star Lieberman-Cline. (Rev: SLJ 3/01; VOYA 2/01) [921]

LUCAS, JOHN

15815 Simmons, Alex. *John Lucas* (4–6). Illus. Series: Contemporary African Americans. 1995, Raintree LB $17.98 (978-0-8172-3978-7). 48pp. An inspiring story of the man who conquered drug addiction and became the first African American coach of the San Antonio Spurs. (Rev: BL 2/15/96; SLJ 4/96) [921]

MARBURY, STEPHON

15816 Plum-Ucci, Carol. *Super Sports Star Stephon Marbury* (2–5). Series: Super Sports Stars. 2002, Enslow LB $23.93 (978-0-7660-1810-5). 48pp. An exciting life story of Marbury, the black basketball player who has established a reputation as point guard for the Phoenix Suns. (Rev: BL 2/15/03; HBG 3/03) [921]

MING, YAO

15817 Clark, Travis. *Yao Ming* (5–8). Series: Modern Role Models. 2008, Mason Crest LB $22.95 (978-1-4222-0484-9). 64pp. Yao Ming's great basketball career, his generous charitable works, and his influences are examined in this book, part of a high-interest biography series that includes a section with more information on awards, events, and organizations. (Rev: SLJ 2/09) [921]

15818 Savage, Jeff. *Yao Ming* (2–4). Illus. Series: Amazing Athletes/LernerSports. 2005, Lerner LB $23.93 (978-0-8225-2432-8). 32pp. A well-illustrated introduction to the Chinese-born basketball player. [921]

15819 Young, Jeff C. *Yao Ming: Basketball's Big Man* (3–6). Illus. Series: Sports Leaders. 2005, Enslow LB $26.60 (978-0-7660-2422-9). 104pp. An accessible profile of the Chinese-born basketball player's life and career. [921]

NAISMITH, JAMES

15820 Wyckoff, Edwin Brit. *The Man Who Invented Basketball: James Naismith and His Amazing Game* (2–4). Illus. Series: Genius at Work! Great Inventor Biographies. 2007, Enslow LB $16.95 (978-0-7660-2846-3). 32pp. A compelling biography of the young Canadian who came up with the game of basketball in the late 19th century. (Rev: BL 9/1/07; LMC 11/07; SLJ 7/08) [921]

NUNEZ, TOMMY

15821 Boulais, Sue, and Barbara Marvis. *Tommy Nunez* (3–5). Illus. Series: Real-Life Reader Biographies. 1998, Mitchell Lane LB $15.95 (978-1-883845-52-0). 32pp. A simple biography that traces Nunez's life from the Phoenix barrio to a career as a referee in the National Basketball Association. (Rev: BL 6/1–15/98; HBG 3/98) [921]

OLAJUWON, HAKEEM

15822 McMane, Fred. *Hakeem Olajuwon* (5–7). Series: Basketball Legends. 1997, Chelsea LB $18.65 (978-0-7910-4385-1). 64pp. The story of this basketball star of the Houston Rockets, his boyhood in Nigeria, and his role as part of the U.S. Olympic "Dream Team." (Rev: BL 9/15/97) [921]

O'NEAL, SHAQUILLE

15823 Torres, John A. *Shaquille O'Neal: Gentle Giant* (3–6). Illus. Series: Sports Leaders. 2004, Enslow LB $26.60 (978-0-7660-2175-4). 104pp. Report writers and basketball fans will appreciate this overview of Shaq's life and career. (Rev: BL 4/1/04) [796.323]

15824 Ungs, Tim. *Shaquille O'Neal* (5–7). Illus. Series: Basketball Legends. 1996, Chelsea LB $18.65 (978-0-7910-2437-9). 64pp. An interesting portrait of the unstoppable Lakers basketball superstar. (Rev: BL 7/96) [921]

PARKER, TONY

15825 MacRae, Sloan. *Meet Tony Parker: Basketball's Famous Point Guard* (3–5). Illus. 2009, PowerKids LB $23.95 (978-1-4358-2710-3). 32pp. A straightforward sports biography of the point guard for the San Antonio Spurs. (Rev: BL 6/1–15/09) [796.323092]

PAYTON, GARY

15826 Mandell, Judith. *Super Sports Star Gary Payton* (2–5). Series: Super Sports Stars. 2001, Enslow LB $23.93 (978-0-7660-1519-7). 48pp. With large type and colorful photographs, this is an easily read biography of the black point guard of the Los Angeles Lakers. (Rev: BL 10/15/01; HBG 3/02) [921]

PIPPEN, SCOTTIE

15827 McMane, Fred. *Scottie Pippen* (5–7). Illus. Series: Basketball Legends. 1996, Chelsea LB

$12.95 (978-0-7910-2498-0). 64pp. The life of this basketball star, highlighting his special abilities and his court record. (Rev: BL 7/96) [921]

15828 Pippen, Scottie, and Greg Brown. *Reach Higher* (4–7). 1997, Taylor $14.95 (978-0-87833-981-5). 40pp. The story of the famous Chicago Bulls basketball star, who came from a family of 12 and whose original sports were baseball and football. (Rev: BL 10/1/97) [921]

RICE, GLEN

15829 Rappoport, Ken. *Super Sports Star Glen Rice* (2–5). Series: Super Sports Stars. 2002, Enslow LB $23.93 (978-0-7660-1808-2). 48pp. Large type, colorful photographs, and an appealing format highlight this simple biography of the Houston Rockets star. (Rev: BL 9/1/02; HBG 10/02) [921]

ROBINSON, DAVID

15830 Bock, Hal. *David Robinson* (5–7). Series: Basketball Legends. 1997, Chelsea LB $18.65 (978-0-7910-4387-5). 64pp. The story of this star of the San Antonio Spurs, who was a brilliant student and an officer in the U.S. Navy before turning to professional sports. (Rev: BL 9/15/97) [921]

RODMAN, DENNIS

15831 Frank, Steven. *Dennis Rodman* (4–8). Series: Basketball Legends. 1997, Chelsea LB $18.65 (978-0-7910-4388-2). 64pp. A candid look at the bad boy of basketball, his troubled youth, and rebellious attitudes. (Rev: HBG 3/98; SLJ 4/98) [921]

SPREWELL, LATRELL

15832 Pellowski, Michael J. *Super Sports Star Latrell Sprewell* (2–5). Series: Super Sports Stars. 2002, Enslow LB $23.93 (978-0-7660-1811-2). 48pp. With color photographs on each page plus a simple text, this is an exciting biography of the NBA star who plays guard and forward for the New York Knicks. (Rev: BL 9/1/02; HBG 3/03) [921]

STILES, JACKIE

15833 Stewart, Mark. *Jackie Stiles: Gym Dandy* (4–7). Illus. Series: Sports New Wave. 2002, Millbrook LB $22.90 (978-0-7613-2614-4). 48pp. A biography of the WNBA star, with information on her childhood and family, statistics, color photographs, and general material on the game itself. (Rev: BL 9/1/02; HBG 3/03) [796.323]

SWOOPES, SHERYL

15834 Schweitzer, Karen. *Sheryl Swoopes* (5–8). Series: Modern Role Models. 2008, Mason Crest LB $22.95 (978-1-4222-0491-7). 64pp. Swoopes's decision to reveal that she is gay and expose her financial problems are discussed impartially in this high-interest biography that also includes a section

with information on awards, events, and organizations. (Rev: SLJ 2/09) [921]

VAN HORN, KEITH

15835 Kelley, Brent. *Keith Van Horn* (4–6). Illus. Series: Basketball Legends. 1998, Chelsea $12.95 (978-0-7910-5009-5). 64pp. This biography stressing team spirit traces the life and career of the New Jersey Nets player who helped his team reach the playoffs for the first time in four years. (Rev: BL 3/1/99; HBG 10/99) [921]

WEBBER, CHRIS

15836 Thornley, Stew. *Chris Webber* (2–5). Series: Super Sports Stars. 2002, Enslow LB $23.93 (978-0-7660-1807-5). A simple biography with many action photographs of Webber, the NBA power forward of the Sacramento Kings. (Rev: BL 4/1/02; HBG 10/02) [921]

WEST, JERRY

15837 Ramen, Fred. *Jerry West* (5–8). Series: Basketball Hall of Famers. 2002, Rosen LB $29.25 (978-0-8239-3482-9). 112pp. Facts, stories, and full-color photographs are used to bring alive the story of this basketball great, with material on his NBA career and beyond. (Rev: BL 9/1/02) [921]

Boxing

ALI, MUHAMMAD

15838 Bolden, Tonya. *The Champ: The Story of Muhammad Ali* (2–5). Illus. by R. Gregory Christie. 2004, Knopf LB $19.99 (978-0-375-92401-9). 40pp. This engaging biography shows Ali as child, fighter, activist, and poet. (Rev: BL 11/15/04; SLJ 1/05*) [921]

15839 Feinstein, Stephen. *Muhammad Ali* (1–4). 2007, Enslow LB $21.26 (978-0-7660-2763-3). 24pp. A basic and straightforward look at the life of the famous fighter, with photographs. (Rev: SLJ 8/07)

15840 Garrett, Leslie. *The Story of Muhammad Ali* (2–4). Illus. 2002, DK $12.99 (978-0-7894-8516-8); paper $3.99 (978-0-7894-8517-5). 48pp. A chapterbook biography of Muhammad Ali, from childhood to his battle with Parkinson's disease. (Rev: BL 3/1/02; HBG 10/02; SLJ 4/02) [796.83]

15841 Smith, Charles R. *Twelve Rounds to Glory: The Story of Muhammad Ali* (5–8). Illus. by Bryan Collier. 2007, Candlewick $19.99 (978-0-7636-1692-2). 80pp. Twelve poems and dynamic mixed-media pictures illustrate the drama of Ali's victories and his life's struggles. Coretta Scott King Author Honor Book, 2008. (Rev: BL 2/1/08; SLJ 12/07) [921]

15842 Winter, Jonah. *Muhammad Ali: Champion of the World* (3–6). Illus. by François Roca. 2008, Random $16.99 (978-0-375-83622-0). 32pp. This picture-book biography emphasizes how Ali brought a new spirit to boxing and to sportsmanship. (Rev: BL 2/1/08; SLJ 1/08) [921]

CHAVEZ, JULIO CESAR

15843 Dolan, Terrance. *Julio Cesar Chavez* (5–8). Illus. Series: Hispanics of Achievement. 1994, Chelsea LB $21.95 (978-0-7910-2021-0). 128pp. A biography of the fighting boxer and his struggle to get to the top. (Rev: BL 9/15/94) [921]

DE LA HOYA, OSCAR

15844 Menard, Valerie. *Oscar De La Hoya* (3–4). Illus. Series: Real-Life Reader Biographies. 1998, Mitchell Lane LB $15.95 (978-1-883845-58-2). 24pp. The story of the amazing boxer whose father predicted he would be a champion after taking him to a gym at age six. (Rev: BL 10/15/98; HBG 10/98) [921]

LOUIS, JOE

15845 Adler, David A. *Joe Louis: America's Fighter* (2–6). Illus. by Terry Widener. 2005, Harcourt $16.00 (978-0-15-216489-8). 32pp. This picture-book biography looks at the obstacles the boxer had to overcome to become a world champion. (Rev: BCCB 12/05; BL 9/1/05; HB 1/06; HBG 4/06; LMC 3/06) [921]

Figure Skating

BOITANO, BRIAN

15846 Boitano, Brian, and Suzanne Harper. *Boitano's Edge: Inside the Real World of Figure Skating* (4–8). Illus. 1997, Simon & Schuster $25.00 (978-0-689-81915-5). In this autobiography, Boitano tells about his life, the 1988 Olympics, his training programs, touring, and preparing for competitions. (Rev: BCCB 3/98; BL 2/15/98; SLJ 4/98; VOYA 4/98) [921]

GORDEEVA, EKATERINA

15847 Shea, Pegi Deitz. *Ekatarina Gordeeva* (4–8). Series: Female Figure Skating Legends. 1999, Chelsea LB $12.95 (978-0-7910-5027-9). 64pp. Sports lovers will enjoy this look at the life of the famous skater before and after the death of her partner and husband, Sergei Grinkov. (Rev: SLJ 4/99) [921]

HUGHES, SARAH

15848 Krawiec, Richard. *Sudden Champion: The Sarah Hughes Story* (4–6). Series: Avisson Young Adult. 2002, Avisson paper $19.95 (978-1-888105-53-7). 100pp. A profile of Sarah Hughes, the figure skater who won the gold medal at the 2002 Winter Olympics in Salt Lake City. (Rev: SLJ 4/03) [921]

KERRIGAN, NANCY

15849 Edelson, Paula. *Nancy Kerrigan* (4–6). Illus. 1998, Chelsea LB $18.65 (978-0-7910-5028-6). 64pp. The triumphs and tragedies of an Olympic medal winner are outlined in this biography. (Rev: BL 3/1/99) [921]

KWAN, MICHELLE

15850 James, Laura. *Michelle Kwan: Heart of a Champion* (4–8). Illus. 1997, Scholastic paper $14.95 (978-0-590-76340-0). A highly personal account of this figure-skating champion, who describes how she succeeded in placing second at the World Championships in 1997 only one month after two falls cost her the position of U.S. women's champion, and who reveals a maturity beyond her years. (Rev: BL 11/15/97; HBG 3/98; SLJ 11/97) [921]

15851 Stewart, Mark, and Mike Kennedy. *Michelle Kwan: Quest for Gold* (4–6). Illus. 2002, Millbrook LB $24.90 (978-0-7613-2622-9). 64pp. A chronological biography of Chinese American figure skater Michelle Kwan with color photographs. (Rev: BL 3/1/02; HBG 10/02) [796.91]

WITT, KATARINA

15852 Coffey, Wayne. *Katarina Witt* (4–7). Illus. 1992, Blackbirch $16.45 (978-1-56711-001-2). 64pp. This biography highlights the 1988 Olympic Games, where this figure skater became a star. (Rev: SLJ 11/92) [921]

15853 Kelly, Evelyn B. *Katarina Witt* (4–6). Illus. 1998, Chelsea LB $18.65 (978-0-7910-5026-2). 64pp. This biography of the Olympic ice skater describes her years growing up in East Germany and her determination, in spite of her age, to compete in the 1994 Olympics. (Rev: BL 3/1/99) [921]

Football

BARBER, RONDE AND TIKI

15854 Barber, Tiki, and Ronde Barber. *By My Brother's Side* (1–3). Illus. by Barry Root. 2004, Simon & Schuster $16.95 (978-0-689-86559-6). 32pp. The NFL player twins describe their energetic youth. (Rev: BL 9/1/04; SLJ 11/05) [921]

15855 Barber, Tiki, and Ronde Barber. *Game Day* (1–3). Illus. by Barry Root. 2005, Simon & Schuster $16.95 (978-1-4169-0093-1). 32pp. The NFL's Barber twins tell a simple story about their football-playing youth and the rivalry between them. (Rev: BL 9/1/05; SLJ 1/06) [921]

15856 Barber, Tiki, and Ronde Barber. *Teammates* (1–3). Illus. by Barry Root. 2006, Simon & Schuster $16.95 (978-1-4169-2489-0). 32pp. Downcast after their football team loses a game, twin brothers Tiki and Ronde begin a morning practice routine designed to improve Tiki's ball-handling abilities; a large-format picture book illustrated with watercolor-and-gouache paintings. (Rev: BL 9/1/06; SLJ 11/06) [921]

15857 Barber, Tiki, and Paul Mantell. *Kickoff!* (4–6). 2007, Simon & Schuster $15.99 (978-1-4169-3618-3). 156pp. The Barbers reveal much about their lives in junior high and their efforts to make the football team. (Rev: BL 9/1/07; SLJ 12/07)

BRADY, TOM

15858 Gatto, Kimberly. *Tom Brady: Never-Quit Quarterback* (3–6). Illus. Series: Sports Leaders. 2005, Enslow LB $26.60 (978-0-7660-2475-5). 104pp. An accessible profile of the quarterback's life and career. [921]

15859 Stewart, Mark. *Tom Brady: Heart of the Huddle* (4–7). Series: Sports New Wave. 2003, Millbrook LB $22.90 (978-0-7613-2907-7). 48pp. The story of the popular young football player who is quarterback for the New England Patriots. (Rev: BL 6/1–15/03; HBG 10/03) [921]

CULPEPPER, DAUNTE

15860 Stewart, Mark. *Daunte Culpepper: Command and Control* (4–7). Series: Sports New Wave. 2002, Millbrook LB $22.90 (978-0-7613-2613-7). 48pp. This brief biography celebrates the career of the young African American footballer and his achievements as quarterback of the Minnesota Vikings. (Rev: BL 9/1/02; HBG 10/02) [921]

15861 Thornley, Stew. *Super Sports Star Daunte Culpepper* (2–5). Series: Super Sports Stars. 2002, Enslow LB $23.93 (978-0-7660-2051-1). 48pp. The life of Culpepper, the black quarterback of the Minnesota Vikings, is excitingly re-created with colorful photographs and interesting game statistics. (Rev: BL 2/15/03; HBG 10/03) [921]

DAVIS, TERRELL

15862 Stewart, Mark. *Terrell Davis: Toughing It Out* (4–8). Series: Football's New Wave. 1999, Millbrook LB $22.90 (978-0-7613-1514-8). 48pp. A brief biography of this football hero that uses color photographs and many fact boxes. (Rev: HBG 10/00; SLJ 7/00) [921]

ESIASON, BOOMER

15863 Esiason, Boomer. *A Boy Named Boomer* (1–2). Illus. by Jacqueline Rogers. 1995, Scholastic paper $3.99 (978-0-590-52835-1). 46pp. Boomer Esiason, a former NFL quarterback, recalls several incidents from his childhood in this easy reader. (Rev: BL 1/1–15/96; SLJ 3/96) [921]

FAVRE, BRETT

15864 Mooney, Martin. *Brett Favre* (5–7). Illus. Series: Football Legends. 1997, Chelsea LB $18.65 (978-0-7910-4396-7). 64pp. The story of the famous quarterback who took the Green Bay Packers to victory in the 1997 Super Bowl. (Rev: BL 1/1–15/98; HBG 3/98) [921]

15865 Thornley, Stew. *Super Sports Star Brett Favre* (2–5). Series: Super Sports Stars. 2002, Enslow LB $23.93 (978-0-7660-2048-1). 48pp. Using colorful photographs and exciting game details, this is the story of Brett Favre, quarterback of the Green Bay Packers. (Rev: BL 2/15/03; HBG 10/03) [921]

GONZALEZ, TONY

15866 Gonzales, Tony, and Greg Brown. *Tony Gonzalez: Catch and Connect* (3–6). Illus. Series: Athletes. 2004, Positively for Kids $15.95 (978-0-9634650-8-5). 48pp. A lively and attractively designed first-person account of Gonzalez's life and career in football, with lots of personal details about her childhood, family life, and sporting successes. [921]

JACKSON, BO

15867 Devaney, John. *Bo Jackson: A Star for All Seasons* (5–7). Illus. 1992, Walker LB $15.85 (978-0-8027-8179-6). 110pp. Biography of the Kansas City Royals baseball star, who also played pro football for the Los Angeles Raiders. (Rev: BL 2/15/89; SLJ 1/89) [921]

JOHNSON, BRAD

15868 Johnson, Brad, and Greg Brown. *Brad Johnson: Play with Passion* (3–6). Illus. Series: Athletes. 2004, Positively for Kids $15.95 (978-0-9634650-4-7). 48pp. A lively and attractively designed first-person account of Johnson's life and career in football, with lots of personal details about her childhood, family life, and sporting successes. [921]

LOMBARDI, VINCE

15869 Roensch, Greg. *Vince Lombardi* (4–7). Series: Football Hall of Famers. 2003, Rosen LB $29.25 (978-0-8239-3610-6). 112pp. A lively, detailed, and inspiring biography of the legendary coach for whom the Super Bowl trophy is named. (Rev: SLJ 4/03) [796.332]

MCNABB, DONOVAN

15870 Mattern, Joanne. *Donovan McNabb: Football Star* (2–4). Illus. Series: Robbie Reader. 2004, Mitchell Lane LB $25.70 (978-1-58415-294-1). 32pp. This photo-filled biography traces the life and career of Donovan McNabb and is especially suitable for reluctant readers. [921]

MANNING, PEYTON

15871 Stewart, Mark. *Peyton Manning: Rising Son* (4–8). Series: Football's New Wave. 2000, Millbrook LB $22.90 (978-0-7613-1517-9). 48pp. An easily read account of the professional football player's life and family, including a father who also played in the NFL. (Rev: HBG 10/00; SLJ 1/01) [921]

MOSS, RANDY

15872 Stewart, Mark. *Randy Moss: First in Flight* (4–8). Illus. Series: Football's New Wave. 2000, Millbrook LB $22.90 (978-0-7613-1518-6). The story of the footballer who came from a poor, segregated West Virginia town, was arrested as a young man, but went on to attend college and play professional football. (Rev: HBG 10/00; SLJ 1/01) [921]

15873 Thornley, Stew. *Super Sports Star Randy Moss* (2–5). Series: Super Sports Stars. 2002, Enslow LB $23.93 (978-0-7660-2049-8). 48pp. An easily read biography of the black wide receiver of the Minnesota Vikings. (Rev: BL 2/15/03; HBG 10/03) [921]

TARKENTON, FRAN

15874 Hulm, David. *Fran Tarkenton* (4–7). Series: Football Hall of Famers. 2003, Rosen LB $29.25 (978-0-8239-3608-3). 112pp. A lively, detailed, and inspiring biography of the star of the Minnesota Vikings and the New York Giants who went on to become a successful businessman. (Rev: SLJ 4/03; VOYA 4/03) [796.332]

Tennis

ASHE, ARTHUR

15875 Cunningham, Kevin. *Arthur Ashe: Athlete and Activist* (5–8). Illus. Series: Journey to Freedom: The African American Library. 2005, Child's World LB $28.50 (978-1-59296-228-0). 40pp. Chronicles the Virginia-born athlete's rise to tennis stardom and his involvement in the fight against apartheid. (Rev: BL 2/1/05) [921]

15876 Lazo, Caroline. *Arthur Ashe* (4–7). Series: A&E Biography. 1999, Lerner $25.26 (978-0-8225-1932-4). 128pp. The inspiring story of this great African American tennis star and humanitarian is told in a clear, well-organized text with several black-and-white photographs. (Rev: BL 3/15/00) [921]

15877 Mantell, Paul. *Arthur Ashe: Young Tennis Champion* (3–5). Illus. by Meryl Henderson. Series: Childhood of Famous Americans. 2006, Simon & Schuster paper $5.99 (978-0-689-87346-1). 224pp. Ashe's childhood encounters with prejudice and his success on the tennis court are recounted in this fictionalized biography that is faithful to real events. (Rev: BL 2/1/06) [921]

FERNANDEZ, MARY JOE

15878 Cole, Melanie. *Mary Joe Fernandez* (3–4). Series: Real-Life Reader Biographies. 1998, Mitchell Lane LB $15.95 (978-1-883845-63-6). 32pp. The story of the talented and charitable tennis star who turned pro at age 14 but continued with her education. (Rev: BL 10/15/98; HBG 10/98; SLJ 12/98) [921]

GIBSON, ALTHEA

15879 Deans, Karen. *Playing to Win: The Story of Althea Gibson* (1–4). Illus. by Elbrite Brown. 2007, Holiday $16.95 (978-0-8234-1926-5). 32pp. A picture-book biography of the tennis star, emphasizing the barriers she had to overcome. (Rev: BL 9/1/07; SLJ 9/07) [921]

15880 Stauffacher, Sue. *Nothing But Trouble: The Story of Althea Gibson* (K–3). Illus. by Greg Couch. 2007, Knopf $16.99 (978-0-375-83408-0). 40pp. The story of how a "nothing but trouble" Harlem girl went on to become a world tennis star. (Rev: BL 2/1/08; HB 11/07; LMC 11/07; SLJ 9/07) [921]

SELES, MONICA

15881 Murdico, Suzanne J. *Monica Seles* (5–8). Illus. Series: Overcoming the Odds. 1998, Raintree $28.80 (978-0-8172-4128-5). The story of the great tennis player and the courtside stabbing that resulted in a trauma difficult to overcome. (Rev: HBG 9/98; VOYA 8/98) [921]

WILLIAMS, VENUS

15882 Aronson, Virginia. *Venus Williams* (5–8). Illus. Series: Galaxy of Superstars. 1999, Chelsea $25.00 (978-0-7910-5153-5); paper $25.00 (978-0-7910-5329-4). 63pp. The story of this superstar of tennis, how her father trained her, and how he made her education more important than her tennis. (Rev: BL 4/15/99; HBG 10/99; SLJ 5/99; VOYA 4/00) [921]

15883 Sandler, Michael. *Tennis: Victory for Venus Williams* (3–5). Series: Upsets and Comebacks. 2006, Bearport LB $25.27 (978-1-59716-170-1). 32pp. Venus Williams's determination to keep winning despite physical and emotional challenges is underlined here. (Rev: SLJ 7/06) [796.352]

WILLIAMS, VENUS AND SERENA

15884 Brown, Jonatha A. *Venus and Serena Williams* (2–4). Illus. Series: People We Should Know. 2005, Gareth Stevens LB $14.50 (978-0-86384-470-6). 24pp. For beginning readers, a simple account of the Williams sisters' triumphs with an attractive layout and many photographs. [921]

15885 Fillon, Mike. *Young Superstars of Tennis: The Venus and Serena Williams Story* (4–8). Series: Avisson Young Adult. 1999, Avisson LB $19.95 (978-1-888105-43-8). 144pp. This biography of the Williams sisters tells about their childhood, the influence of their father, and their determination to get to the top in tennis. (Rev: BL 12/15/99; SLJ 3/00; VOYA 4/00) [921]

15886 Stewart, Mark. *Venus and Serena Williams: Sisters in Arms* (4–7). Series: Tennis's New Wave. 2000, Millbrook LB $22.90 (978-0-7613-1803-3). 48pp. A simple biography of the amazing tennis-playing sisters with good coverage of their early lives. (Rev: HBG 3/01; SLJ 3/01) [921]

15887 Stout, Glenn. *On the Court with . . . Venus and Serena Williams* (4–6). Illus. Series: Matt Christopher Sports Bio Bookshelf. 2002, Little, Brown paper $4.95 (978-0-316-13814-7). 128pp. A biography of the tennis greats, with information on their childhoods and family (and the influential role of their father) and details of important matches. (Rev: BL 9/1/02) [796.342]

Track and Field

DEVERS, GAIL

15888 Gutman, Bill. *Gail Devers* (3–6). Illus. Series: Overcoming the Odds. 1996, Raintree LB $17.98 (978-0-8172-4122-3). 48pp. The story of this track star who was largely self-trained, her childhood in San Diego, and her participation in the 1993 World Championships. (Rev: SLJ 11/96) [921]

JONES, MARION

15889 Rutledge, Rachel. *Marion Jones: Fast and Fearless* (4–7). 2000, Millbrook LB $22.90 (978-0-7613-1870-5). 48pp. A biography of the track-and-field star of the 2000 Sydney Olympics that stresses her drive and tenacity. (Rev: HBG 3/01; SLJ 3/01) [921]

LEWIS, RAY

15890 Cooper, John. *Rapid Ray: The Story of Ray Lewis* (5–9). 2002, Tundra paper $8.95 (978-0-88776-612-1). 144pp. An absorbing profile of the Canadian-born black athlete (and train porter) who won a bronze medal in the 1932 Olympics and the racial hurdles he had to overcome. (Rev: SLJ 6/03) [796.42]

O'BRIEN, DAN

15891 Gutman, Bill. *Dan O'Brien* (5–8). Series: Overcoming the Odds. 1998, Raintree $28.80 (978-0-8172-4129-2). A biography of this great decathlete that describes his struggles to overcome attention-deficit hyperactivity disorder as well as various injuries. (Rev: HBG 9/98; VOYA 8/98) [921]

OWENS, JESSE

15892 Adler, David A. *A Picture Book of Jesse Owens* (K–3). Illus. by Robert Casilla. Series: Picture Book Biographies. 1992, Holiday House LB $16.95 (978-0-8234-0966-2); paper $6.95 (978-0-8234-1066-8). 32pp. Relying heavily on illustrations to supply details, this is an introduction to the famous track-and-field star. (Rev: BL 11/15/92; SLJ 12/92) [921]

15893 Israel, Elaine. *Jesse Owens: Running into History* (2–5). Illus. Series: Time for Kids Biographies. 2008, HarperCollins LB $15.99 (978-0-06-057621-9); paper $3.99 (978-0-06-057620-2). 48pp. Follows this runner's life story from Alabama sharecropper family to Olympic champion and later life. (Rev: BLO 3/3/08) [921]

15894 McKissack, Patricia C., and Fredrick McKissack. *Jesse Owens: Olympic Star*. Rev. ed. (2–5). Series: Great African Americans. 2001, Enslow LB $18.60 (978-0-7660-1681-1). 32pp. This is an updated version of the 1992 book about the African American athlete whose four medals in the 1936 Olympics displeased Hitler, with factual updates, improved illustrations, and lists of print and Internet resources. (Rev: HBG 10/01; SLJ 8/01) [921]

15895 Streissguth, Thomas. *Jesse Owens* (4–6). Illus. Series: A&E Biography. 1999, Lerner $25.26 (978-0-8225-4940-6). 112pp. A biography of the remarkable African American athlete who won four gold medals at the 1936 Summer Olympics in Berlin. (Rev: BL 2/15/00; HBG 3/00) [921]

15896 Sutcliffe, Jane. *Jesse Owens* (2–3). Series: On My Own. 2000, Carolrhoda LB $23.93 (978-1-57505-451-3); paper $5.95 (978-1-57505-487-2). 48pp. A simple biography of the athlete who overcame sickness, poverty, and discrimination to become a gold medal winner in Berlin in 1936. (Rev: BL 8/00; HBG 10/01) [921]

RUDOLPH, WILMA

15897 Braun, Eric. *Wilma Rudolph* (K–2). Series: First Biographies. 2005, Capstone LB $17.26 (978-0-7368-4234-1). 24pp. With its simple sentences and clear black-and-white photographs, this profile of the first African American woman to win three gold medals at a single Olympic Games gives basic, introductory information. (Rev: SLJ 2/06) [921]

15898 Harper, Jo. *Wilma Rudolph: Olympic Runner* (3–6). Illus. by Meryl Henderson. Series: Childhood of Famous Americans. 2004, Simon & Schuster paper $4.99 (978-0-689-85873-4). 192pp. A moving, fictionalized account of Rudolph's triumph over polio, prejudice, and poverty. (Rev: BL 5/15/04)

15899 Krull, Kathleen. *Wilma Unlimited: How Wilma Rudolph Became the World's Fastest Woman* (2–5). Illus. by David Diaz. 1996, Harcourt $16.00 (978-0-15-201267-0). 48pp. A biography of the amazing Wilma Rudolph, who overcame incredible obstacles to become a track star. (Rev: BL 5/1/96*; HB 9/96; SLJ 6/96*) [921]

15900 Ruth, Amy. *Wilma Rudolph* (4–6). Series: A&E Biography. 2000, Lerner LB $27.93 (978-0-8225-4976-5). 112pp. The inspiring story of the African American athlete who overcame polio and won three gold medals in Olympic track-and-field events in 1960. (Rev: BL 6/1–15/00; HBG 10/00) [921]

15901 Sherrow, Victoria. *Wilma Rudolph* (2–3). Illus. by Larry Johnson. Series: On My Own Biography. 2000, Lerner LB $23.93 (978-1-57505-246-5); paper $5.95 (978-1-57505-442-1). 48pp. The story of how a young girl whose legs were thin and crooked from polio grew up to win Olympic gold medals for running is told with simplicity and dignity. (Rev: BL 2/15/00; HBG 10/00; SLJ 2/00) [921]

15902 Sherrow, Victoria. *Wilma Rudolph: Olympic Champion* (4–6). Illus. Series: Junior World Biographies. 1995, Chelsea LB $15.95 (978-0-7910-2290-0). 79pp. The life of this great track star and of the poverty, bad health, and emotional challenges she faced and overcame in her desire to succeed. (Rev: BCCB 4/96; SLJ 8/95) [921]

THORPE, JIM

15903 Brown, Don. *Bright Path: Young Jim Thorpe* (K–3). Illus. by author. 2006, Roaring Brook $17.95 (978-1-59643-041-9). 40pp. The importance of athletics in Thorpe's unhappy childhood is emphasized in this nicely illustrated biography. (Rev: SLJ 11/06) [921]

15904 Bruchac, Joseph. *Jim Thorpe: Original All-American* (5–8). 2006, Dial $16.99 (978-0-8037-3118-9). 208pp. Using the first person, this biography chronicles the Native American's youth, his amazing sporting abilities, and his quiet determination to overcome barriers. (Rev: BL 6/1–15/06; SLJ 8/06) [921]

15905 Bruchac, Joseph. *Jim Thorpe's Bright Path* (2–3). Trans. and illus. by S. D. Nelson. 2004, Lee & Low $17.95 (978-1-58430-166-0). 40pp. This inspiring profile of Jim Thorpe focuses on the future Olympic champion's childhood, tracing his life from birth in a log cabin to the start of his scholastic football career at Carlisle Indian School in Pennsylvania. (Rev: BL 8/04; SLJ 6/04) [921]

15906 Long, Barbara. *Jim Thorpe: Legendary Athlete* (5–7). Illus. Series: Native American Biographies. 1997, Enslow LB $20.95 (978-0-89490-865-1). 128pp. The story of the amazing Native American athlete whose career had tremendous highs and lows. (Rev: BL 6/1–15/97) [921]

Miscellaneous Sports

ADU, FREDDY

15907 Murcia, Rebecca Thatcher. *Freddy Adu: Young Soccer Superstar* (3–5). Illus. Series: A Robbie Reader. 2005, Mitchell Lane $25.70 (978-1-58415-385-6). 32pp. A brief, photo-filled biography of the young Ghanaian-born soccer phenomenon. (Rev: BL 10/15/05; SLJ 10/05) [921]

ARMSTRONG, LANCE

15908 Armstrong, Kristin. *Lance Armstrong: The Race of His Life* (2–3). Illus. Series: All Aboard Reading. 2000, Penguin paper $3.99 (978-0-448-42407-1). 48pp. A book for beginning readers that tells about this famous cyclist, his many triumphs, and his battle with cancer — written by his wife. (Rev: BL 12/1/00; HBG 3/01) [921]

15909 Benson, Michael. *Lance Armstrong: Cyclist* (5–8). Series: Ferguson Career Biographies. 2003, Ferguson LB $25.00 (978-0-8160-5479-4). 139pp. Traces the inspiring life of the great bicycle-racer through his fifth Tour de France win, with an emphasis on his perseverance and optimism. (Rev: SLJ 5/04) [796.6]

15910 Donovan, Sandy. *Lance Armstrong* (2–4). Illus. Series: Amazing Athletes. 2005, Lerner LB $23.93 (978-0-8225-3691-8). 32pp. Armstrong's cycling career is the focus of this easy-reading biography that also touches on his childhood. (Rev: BL 2/15/05; SLJ 3/05) [921]

15911 Garcia, Kimberly. *Lance Armstrong* (3–4). Series: Real-Life Reader Biographies. 2002, Mitchell Lane LB $15.95 (978-1-58415-125-8). 32pp. Using a conversational style and black-and-white photographs, this is a biography of the Tour de France-winning cyclist who overcame cancer. (Rev: BL 9/15/02; SLJ 12/02) [921]

ATLAS, CHARLES

15912 McCarthy, Meghan. *Strong Man: The Story of Charles Atlas* (1–3). Illus. by author. 2007, Knopf $15.99 (978-0-375-82940-6). 40pp. This biography of the legendary fitness pioneer is entertaining and well-illustrated; the author is careful to stick with known facts about the subject's often-embellished life. (Rev: BCCB 7–8/07; BL 6/1–15/07; HB 9/07; SLJ 7/07) [921]

BASS, TOM

15913 Wilkerson, J. L. *From Slave to World-Class Horseman: Tom Bass* (4–8). 2000, Acorn paper $9.95 (978-0-9664470-3-3). 135pp. A fast-paced narrative about the man who was born a slave and later became such a renowned horseman that he performed for Queen Victoria. (Rev: SLJ 4/00) [921]

BECKHAM, DAVID

15914 Savage, Jeff. *David Beckham* (3–5). Illus. Series: Amazing Athletes. 2008, Lerner LB $23.93 (978-0-8225-8834-4); paper $6.95 (978-0-8225-8975-4). 32pp. A brief overview of the life of the British soccer star who came to the United States to play for Los Angeles Galaxy. (Rev: BL 6/1–15/08) [921]

BLAIR, BONNIE

15915 Blair, Bonnie, and Greg Brown. *A Winning Edge* (3–5). Illus. 1996, Taylor $14.95 (978-0-87833-931-0). 40pp. The autobiography of the Olympic medal-winning speed skater, with insights into her life off the ice. (Rev: BL 5/15/96) [921]

BUTCHER, SUSAN

15916 Dolan, Ellen M. *Susan Butcher and the Iditarod Trail* (5–7). Illus. 1993, Walker LB $15.85 (978-0-8027-8212-0). 112pp. This book gives the history of the Iditarod sled dog race and tells the story of Susan Butcher, who first entered the race in 1978. (Rev: BL 4/1/93; SLJ 4/93) [921]

DIMAS, TRENT

15917 Menard, Valerie, and Sue Boulais. *Trent Dimas* (3–5). Series: Real-Life Reader Biographies. 1998, Mitchell Lane LB $15.95 (978-1-883845-50-6). 32pp. The story of a young gymnast who saw his dreams come true when he took the gold medal in the 1992 Olympics. (Rev: BL 6/1–15/98; HBG 3/98; SLJ 4/98) [921]

EDERLE, GERTRUDE

15918 Adler, David A. *America's Champion Swimmer: Gertrude Ederle* (2–4). Illus. by Terry Widener. 2000, Harcourt $16.00 (978-0-15-201969-3). 32pp. A simple biography of the amazing athlete who was the first woman to swim across the English Channel. (Rev: BCCB 4/00; BL 3/15/00*; HB 5/00; HBG 10/00; SLJ 6/00) [921]

EL CHINO

15919 Say, Allen. *El Chino* (3–6). Illus. 1990, Houghton $17.00 (978-0-395-52023-9). 32pp. The first-person narrative of a Chinese American civil engineer who becomes a matador. (Rev: BCCB 9/90*; BL 9/1/90*; HB 1/91; SLJ 11/90) [921]

HAMILTON, BETHANY

15920 Sandler, Michael. *Bethany Hamilton: Follow Your Dreams!* (3–6). Series: Defining Moments, Overcoming Challenges. 2006, Bearport LB $25.27 (978-1-59716-270-8). 32pp. Surfer Bethany Hamilton lost her left arm in a shark attack when she was only 13; she was back on her surfboard only weeks after the attack and has since worked to raise funds for victims of disasters. (Rev: SLJ 1/07) [921]

HAMM, MIA

15921 Rutledge, Rachel. *Mia Hamm: Striking Superstar* (3–6). Series: Soccer's New Wave. 2000, Millbrook LB $22.90 (978-0-7613-1802-6). 48pp. A fully rounded biography of the soccer star who was a member of the 1991 and 1999 Gold Medal World Cup Soccer teams. (Rev: HBG 10/00; SLJ 7/00) [921]

15922 Torres, John. *Mia Hamm* (3–4). Series: Real-Life Reader Biographies. 1999, Mitchell Lane LB $15.95 (978-1-883845-94-0). 32pp. An inspiring biography of this great female soccer player and how she succeeded through spirit and determination. (Rev: BL 10/15/99) [921]

15923 Zarzycki, Daryl. *Mia Hamm* (2–5). Series: Robbie Reader. 2004, Mitchell Lane LB $25.70 (978-1-58415-286-6). 32pp. This photo-filled biography that presents information on Hamm's childhood and career is especially suitable for reluctant readers. (Rev: BL 11/15/04) [921]

HOGAN, HULK

15924 Zannos, Susan. *Hollywood Hulk Hogan: The Story of Terry Bollea* (3–4). Series: Real-Life Reader Biographies. 1999, Mitchell Lane LB $15.95 (978-1-58415-021-3). 32pp. A simple biography about this world-famous wrestler and how he devotes time and money to charities that help sick children. (Rev: BL 10/15/99) [921]

JOHNSON, DWAYNE ("THE ROCK")

15925 Kjelle, Marylou Morano. *Dwayne "The Rock" Johnson* (1–3). Illus. Series: Robbie Reader Contemporary Biography. 2009, Mitchell Lane LB $17.95 (978-1-58415-722-9). 32pp. For beginning readers, this is an appealing biography of the wrestler/actor. (Rev: BLO 5/27/09) [921]

15926 Ross, Dan. *The Story of the Wrestler They Call "The Rock"* (4–7). Series: Pro Wrestling Legends. 2000, Chelsea $25.00 (978-0-7910-5831-2). 64pp. This is the story of the third-generation wrestler known as "The Rock." (Rev: BL 10/15/00; HBG 3/01) [796.8]

KAHANAMOKU, DUKE

15927 Crowe, Ellie. *Surfer of the Century: The Life of Duke Kahanamoku* (4–7). Illus. by Richard Waldrep. 2007, Lee & Low $18.95 (978-1-58430-276-6). 48pp. A wonderfully illustrated picture-book biography of Duke Kahanamoku, an Olympic Gold Medal swimmer and well-known surfer from Hawaii who was born in 1890. (Rev: BL 9/1/07; SLJ 10/07) [921]

KELLERMAN, ANNETTE

15928 Corey, Shana. *Mermaid Queen: The Spectacular True Story of Annette Kellerman, Who Swam Her Way to Fame, Fortune, and Swimsuit History* (3–6). Illus. by Edwin Fotheringham. 2009, Scholastic $17.99 (978-0-439-69835-1). 48pp. The title tells the story of this splashy biography. (Rev: BL 6/1–15/09; SLJ 3/09) [797.2]

KRONE, JULIE

15929 Gutman, Bill. *Julie Krone* (3–6). Illus. Series: Overcoming the Odds. 1996, Raintree LB $17.98 (978-0-8172-4121-6). 48pp. An absorbing biography of this female jockey, her participation in more than 16,000 races, and the 1993 accident that left her seriously injured. (Rev: SLJ 2/97) [921]

LEE, SAMMY

15930 Yoo, Paula. *Sixteen Years in Sixteen Seconds: The Sammy Lee Story* (2–4). Illus. by Dom Lee. 2005, Lee & Low $16.95 (978-1-58430-247-6). 32pp. All about the Korean American Olympic diver, who in 1948 defied prejudice and family expectations to become the first Asian American to win a gold medal. (Rev: BL 3/15/05; SLJ 4/05) [797.2]

LEMIEUX, MARIO

15931 Rossiter, Sean. *Mario Lemieux* (4–8). Illus. Series: Hockey Heroes. 2001, Sterling $12.95 (978-

1-55054-870-9). 64pp. A detailed look at the career of Pittsburgh Penguin Mario Lemieux. (Rev: BL 2/15/02) [796.962]

15932 Stewart, Mark. *Mario Lemieux: Own the Ice* (5–8). Illus. 2002, Millbrook LB $24.90 (978-0-7613-2555-0); paper $8.95 (978-0-7613-1687-9). 64pp. A readable biography of the ice hockey star, with photographs, statistics, and information about the athlete's personal life and work ethic. (Rev: BL 9/15/02; HBG 3/03) [796.962]

MOCEANU, DOMINIQUE

15933 Durrett, Deanne. *Dominique Moceanu* (5–8). Series: People in the News. 1999, Lucent LB $32.45 (978-1-56006-099-4). 111pp. Drawing heavily on Moceanu's autobiography, this is the life story of the phenomenal gymnast, with behind-the scenes glimpses of competitions, training, scoring, and routines. (Rev: HBG 3/00; SLJ 8/99) [921]

15934 Quiner, Krista. *Dominique Moceanu: A Gymnastics Sensation* (4–7). Illus. 1997, Bradford paper $12.95 (978-0-9643460-3-1). 191pp. The story of the United States' youngest gold medal winner in gymnastics, with a special 24-page insert of photographs. (Rev: SLJ 3/97) [921]

MONPLAISIR, SHARON

15935 Greenberg, Doreen, and Michael Greenberg. *Sword of a Champion: The Story of Sharon Monplaisir* (4–8). Illus. by Phil Velikan. Series: Anything You Can Do — New Sports Heroes for Girls. 2000, Wish paper $9.95 (978-1-930546-39-4). 81pp. The life story of the timid, shy high schooler who found her place in fencing via a coach who encouraged her to develop her natural talents. (Rev: SLJ 3/01; VOYA 2/01) [796.8]

MURPHY, ISAAC

15936 Trollinger, Patsi B. *Perfect Timing: How Issac Murphy Became One of the World's Greatest Jockeys* (1–3). Illus. by Jerome Lagarrigue. 2006, Viking $15.99 (978-0-670-06083-2). 32pp. This attractive picture-book biography describes how Isaac Murphy, the Kentucky-born grandson of slaves, became one of horse racing's most illustrious jockeys, riding to victory in three Kentucky Derbys. (Rev: BL 9/1/06; SLJ 12/06) [798.40092]

NASH, KEVIN

15937 Mudge, Jacqueline. *Kevin Nash* (4–7). Series: Pro Wrestling Legends. 2000, Chelsea paper $25.00 (978-0-7910-5828-2). 64pp. This is the biography of the wrestler known as "Diesel." (Rev: BL 10/15/00; HBG 3/01) [921]

PAK, SE RI

15938 Stewart, Mark. *Se Ri Pak: Driven to Win* (4–8). Series: Golf's New Wave. 2000, Millbrook LB $22.90 (978-0-7613-1519-3). 48pp. The story of the South Korean who won the Ladies Professional Golf Association Championship in 1998. (Rev: HBG 10/00; SLJ 8/00) [921]

PELE (SOCCER PLAYER)

15939 Brown, Monica. *Pele, King of Soccer / Pele, el rey del futbol* (1–3). Illus. by Rudy Gutierrez. 2009, HarperCollins $17.99 (978-0-06-122779-0). 40pp. A bilingual (English/Spanish) profile of the Brazilian soccer player's life, with energetic illustrations. (Rev: BL 11/15/08; SLJ 4/09) [921]

15940 Cline-Ransome, Lesa. *Young Pele: Soccer's First Star* (K–3). Illus. by James Ransome. 2007, Random $16.99 (978-0-375-83599-5). 40pp. A picture-book biography of the Brazilian-born soccer star who learned to play barefoot using a ball made from a sock full of rags. (Rev: BCCB 3/08; BL 9/1/07; HB 11/07; LMC 11/07; SLJ 8/07) [921]

PHELPS, MICHAEL

15941 Goldish, Meish. *Michael Phelps: Anything Is Possible* (2–4). Illus. Series: Defining Moments: Super Athletes. 2009, Bearport LB $18.95 (978-1-59716-855-7). 32pp. A basic introduction to the Olympic swimmer's life. (Rev: BL 4/1/09; SLJ 6/09) [921]

15942 Phelps, Michael. *How to Train with a T. Rex and Win 8 Gold Medals* (PS–2). Illus. by Ward Jenkins. 2009, Simon & Schuster $17.99 (978-1-4169-8669-0). 32pp. Olympian Michael Phelps explains his rigorous training routines in an appealing and understandable manner. (Rev: BCCB 9/09; BLO 6/19/09) [921]

15943 Zuehlke, Jeffrey. *Michael Phelps* (2–4). Illus. Series: Amazing Athletes/LernerSports. 2005, Lerner LB $23.93 (978-0-8225-2431-1). 32pp. A well-illustrated introduction to the Olympic swimmer. [921]

RIDDLES, LIBBY

15944 Riddles, Libby. *Storm Run: The Story of the First Woman to Win the Iditarod Sled Dog Race* (2–5). Illus. by Shannon Cartwright. 2002, Sasquatch $16.95 (978-1-57061-298-5). 48pp. Initially published in 1986, this first-person account of training and racing in the Iditarod, written by the first woman ever to win it, is bolstered by fresh illustrations. (Rev: BL 3/1/02; HBG 10/02) [798.8]

ROSENFELD, FANNY BOBBIE

15945 Dublin, Anne. *Bobbie Rosenfeld: The Olympian Who Could Do Everything* (5–8). 2004, Second Story paper $11.95 (978-1-896764-82-5). 120pp. Fanny Bobbie Rosenfeld migrated from the Ukraine to Canada in 1905, became an outstanding athlete excelling in many sports, and led the Canadian women's relay team to an Olympic gold in 1928. (Rev: BL 9/1/04) [921]

TAYLOR, MARSHALL

15946 Brill, Marlene T. *Marshall "Major" Taylor: World Champion Bicyclist, 1899–1901* (5–8). Illus. Series: Trailblazer Biographies. 2007, Lerner LB $31.93 (978-0-8225-6610-6). 112pp. An inspiring profile of the first African American world cycling champion and his struggles with racism. (Rev: BL 9/1/07) [921]

15947 Cline-Ransome, Lesa. *Major Taylor, Champion Cyclist* (2–4). Illus. by James Ransome. 2004, Simon & Schuster $16.95 (978-0-689-83159-1). 40pp. Prejudice is a theme throughout this biography of the African American cyclist who won the world championship in 1899. (Rev: BL 2/15/04; SLJ 2/04) [796.2]

THOMPSON, JENNY

15948 Greenberg, Doreen, and Michael Greenberg. *Fast Lane to Victory: The Story of Jenny Thompson* (3–6). Illus. by Phil Velikan. Series: Anything You Can Do — New Sports Heroes for Girls. 2001, Wish paper $9.95 (978-1-930546-38-7). 141pp. Swimmer Jenny Thompson's determination to excel and the highlights of her career are presented here. (Rev: SLJ 8/01) [797.21]

TREVINO, LEE

15949 Gilbert, Thomas. *Lee Trevino* (5–9). Series: Hispanics of Achievement. 1991, Chelsea LB $19.95 (978-0-7910-1256-7). The story of one of golf's all-time greats to 1990. (Rev: BL 3/15/92) [796.352]

VENTURA, JESSE

15950 Greenberg, Keith E. *Jesse Ventura* (5–8). Illus. Series: A&E Biography. 1999, Lerner LB $27.93 (978-0-8225-4977-2); paper $7.95 (978-0-8225-9680-6). 112pp. A look at this larger-than-life pop culture hero who has been an actor, a professional wrestler, a Navy SEAL, and the governor of Minnesota. (Rev: BL 3/1/00; HBG 3/00; SLJ 2/00) [921]

15951 Uschan, Michael V. *Jesse Ventura* (5–8). Series: People in the News. 2001, Lucent LB $35.15 (978-1-56006-777-1). From a career in wrestling to a state governorship, this is the story of the amazing Jesse Ventura. (Rev: BL 4/1/02) [921]

WHITE, SHAUN

15952 Doeden, Matt. *Shaun White* (2–4). Series: Amazing Athletes. 2006, Lerner LB $23.93 (978-0-8225-6840-7). 32pp. At the age of 19, snowboarder White won a gold medal at the 2006 Olympics. (Rev: SLJ 1/07) [921]

15953 Schweitzer, Karen. *Shaun White* (5–8). Series: Modern Role Models. 2008, Mason Crest LB $22.95 (978-1-4222-0493-1). 64pp. Shaun White's story of how he became the best snowboarder and skateboarder is detailed in this book, a high-interest biography that includes additional information on awards, events, and organizations. (Rev: SLJ 2/09; VOYA 8/09) [921]

WICKENHEISER, HAYLEY

15954 Etue, Elizabeth. *Hayley Wickenheiser: Born to Play* (4–7). Illus. 2005, Kids Can paper $6.95 (978-1-55337-791-7). 40pp. The story of Canadian-born Wickenheiser, a member of Canada's gold medal-winning women's ice hockey team at the Salt Lake City Olympics, who went on to become the first woman to play professional hockey. (Rev: BL 9/1/05) [921]

WIE, MICHELLE

15955 Wheeler, Jill C. *Michelle Wie* (3–5). Illus. Series: Awesome Athletes. 2007, ABDO LB $15.95 (978-1-59928-309-8). 32pp. This brief profile tells the story of golfer Michelle Wie, who became a pro golfer before her 16th birthday. (Rev: BL 5/15/07) [921]

WINKFIELD, JIMMY

15956 Hubbard, Crystal. *The Last Black King of the Kentucky Derby* (2–4). Illus. by Robert McGuire. 2008, Lee & Low $17.95 (978-1-58430-274-2). 40pp. This picture book profiles the life of Jimmy "Wink" Winkfield, a 19th-century African American jockey who overcame discrimination and won the Derby. (Rev: BL 9/1/08) [921]

WOODS, TIGER

15957 Boyd, Aaron. *Tiger Woods* (5–10). 1997, Morgan Reynolds LB $18.95 (978-1-883846-19-0). A brief, straightforward biography of this amazing golfer who was a young prodigy. (Rev: BL 5/1/97; HBG 3/98; SLJ 8/97; VOYA 10/97) [921]

15958 Brown, Jonatha A. *Tiger Woods* (2–4). Illus. Series: People We Should Know. 2005, Gareth Stevens LB $21.00 (978-0-8368-4313-2). 24pp. For beginning readers, a simple account of Woods's life and triumphs, with an attractive layout and many photographs. [921]

15959 Christopher, Matt. *On the Course with . . . Tiger Woods* (3–5). Illus. 1998, Little, Brown paper $4.50 (978-0-316-13445-3). 128pp. A brief biography of Tiger Woods, including a short history of golf and its rules. (Rev: BL 7/98) [921]

15960 Collins, David R. *Tiger Woods: Golf Superstar* (K–3). Illus. by Larry Nolte. 1999, Pelican $15.95 (978-1-56554-321-8). This simple biography stresses the determination and hard work that made Tiger Woods the golf star that the world admires. (Rev: SLJ 6/99) [921]

15961 Collins, David R. *Tiger Woods, Golfing Champion* (5–8). Illus. by Larry Nolte. 1999, Pelican $14.95 (978-1-56554-322-5). 88pp. A chronologically arranged book ending in 1999 that reveals Tiger Woods's determination and love of the game. (Rev: SLJ 1/00) [921]

15962 Roberts, Jeremy. *Tiger Woods* (5–8). Series: Biography. 2002, Lerner LB $27.93 (978-0-8225-

0030-8). The story of the likable wonder boy of golf is told in text and pictures. (Rev: BL 4/1/02; HBG 10/02) [921]

15963 Savage, Jeff. *Tiger Woods: King of the Course* (4–5). Illus. 1998, Lerner LB $14.95 (978-0-8225-3655-0). 64pp. Lavish color photographs illustrate this biography of Tiger Woods, which includes his family background, his training, style, and tournament action. (Rev: BL 7/98; HBG 10/98; SLJ 6/98) [921]

15964 Sirimarco, Elizabeth. *Tiger Woods* (3–6). Series: Sports Heroes. 2000, Capstone LB $23.93 (978-0-7368-0581-0). 48pp. This brief biography focuses on Woods's athletic development from childhood and the key accomplishments in his career, with plenty of photographs and statistics. (Rev: SLJ 5/01) [921]

ZAHARIAS, BABE DIDRIKSON

15965 Sutcliffe, Jane. *Babe Didrikson Zaharias: All-Around Athlete* (2–3). Series: On My Own Biography. 2000, Carolrhoda LB $23.93 (978-1-57505-421-6). 48pp. A simple biography of one of the greatest athletes of the 20th century, winner of three medals in track and field at the 1932 Olympics. (Rev: BL 6/1–15/00; HBG 10/00; SLJ 6/00) [921]

15966 Wakeman, Nancy. *Babe Didrikson Zaharias: Driven to Win* (4–7). Illus. Series: Biography. 2000, Lerner LB $27.93 (978-0-8225-4917-8). 112pp. The account focuses on this sportswoman's professional career and her strong personality plus her accomplishments in track and field, basketball, and baseball. (Rev: BL 6/1–15/00; HBG 10/00; SLJ 7/00; VOYA 12/00) [921]

World Figures

Collective

15967 Aaseng, Nathan. *The Peace Seekers: The Nobel Peace Prize* (5–8). Illus. 1987, Lerner paper $7.95 (978-0-8225-9604-2). 80pp. Martin Luther King, Jr., and Lech Walesa are among those whose lives and works are introduced. (Rev: BL 2/1/88) [327.1720922]

15968 Avakian, Monique. *Reformers: Activists, Educators, Religious Leaders* (5–9). Series: Remarkable Women. 2000, Raintree LB $32.85 (978-0-8172-5733-0). 80pp. This book contains 150 profiles of woman who, throughout history and from many cultures, have fought for human rights, including Harriet Tubman, Mother Teresa, and Dolores Huerta. (Rev: SLJ 8/00) [920]

15969 Bardhan-Quallen, Sudipta. *The Mexican-American War* (5–9). Series: People at the Center Of. 2005, Gale LB $24.95 (978-1-56711-927-5). 48pp. After an overview of the war, this volume provides biographical information on key figures including James K. Polk, Abraham Lincoln, Santa Anna, and Zachary Taylor. (Rev: SLJ 6/05) [920]

15970 Billinghurst, Jane. *Growing Up Royal: Life in the Shadow of the British Throne* (4–7). Illus. 2001, Annick $22.95 (978-1-55037-623-4); paper $12.95 (978-1-55037-622-7). 176pp. A look at what it's like to be young and royal, with a focus on the lives of today's British royalty, with color photographs and interesting anecdotes. (Rev: BL 9/1/01; HBG 3/02; SLJ 11/01; VOYA 4/02) [971.082]

15971 Blue, Rose, and Corinne J. Naden. *People of Peace* (4–7). Illus. 1994, Millbrook LB $26.90 (978-1-56294-409-4). 80pp. Brief biographies of 10 people in modern history who have made great sacrifices for world peace, including Mohandas Gandhi and Desmond Tutu. (Rev: BL 12/15/94; SLJ 2/95) [920]

15972 Chin-Lee, Cynthia. *Akira to Zoltan: Twenty-Six Men Who Changed the World* (3–5). Illus. by Megan Halsey. 2006, Charlesbridge $15.95 (978-1-57091-579-6). 32pp. A companion to *Amelia to Zora: Twenty-Six Women Who Changed the World* (2005), this volume spotlights the accomplishments of 26 men who have made significant contributions in diverse walks of life, including the arts, sciences, politics, and sports. (Rev: BL 6/1–15/06; SLJ 7/06) [920.7109]

15973 Chin-Lee, Cynthia. *Amelia to Zora: Twenty-Six Women Who Changed the World* (4–7). Illus. 2005, Charlesbridge $15.95 (978-1-57091-522-2). 32pp. Brief information on 26 remarkable and varied women (scientists, artists, athletes, inventors) along with beautiful artwork and quotations from the subjects. (Rev: BL 4/1/05*; SLJ 4/05) [920.72]

15974 Cotter, Charis. *Kids Who Rule: The Remarkable Lives of Five Child Monarchs* (5–8). Illus. 2007, Annick $24.95 (978-1-55451-062-7); paper $14.95 (978-1-55451-061-0). 120pp. King Tutankhamen, Mary Queen of Scots, Queen Christina of Sweden, Emperor Puyi of China, and the fourteenth Dalai Lama are the young rulers included in this interesting book that provides historical context. (Rev: BL 12/15/07) [920.0068]

15975 Gifford, Clive. *10 Kings and Queens Who Changed the World* (4–8). Illus. by David Cousens. 2009, Kingfisher $14.99 (978-0-7534-6252-2). 64pp. Collective biography of royalty across the ages. (Rev: BL 6/1–15/09; SLJ 7/09) [929.7]

15976 Hacker, Carlotta. *Humanitarians* (3–6). Illus. Series: Women in Profile. 1999, Crabtree LB $22.60 (978-0-7787-0011-1); paper $8.95 (978-0-7787-0033-3). 48pp. Six major profiles and 15 brief biographies of female humanitarians, including Helen Keller and Mother Teresa, are included in this informative title. (Rev: BL 9/15/99; SLJ 8/99) [920]

15977 Hacker, Carlotta. *Nobel Prize Winners* (3–6). Illus. Series: Women in Profile. 1998, Crabtree LB $22.60 (978-0-7787-0007-4); paper $8.95 (978-0-7787-0029-6). 48pp. In addition to biographies of six female Nobel Prize winners, including Barbara McClintock, Toni Morrison, Marie Curie, and

Nadine Gordimer, this collection contains short profiles of dozens of other notables, such as Mother Teresa and Jane Addams. (Rev: BL 9/1/98; SLJ 9/98) [920]

15978 Hacker, Carlotta. *Rebels* (3–6). Series: Women in Profile. 1999, Crabtree LB $22.60 (978-0-7787-0014-2); paper $8.95 (978-0-7787-0036-4). 48pp. This work provides six major profiles and 15 brief sketches about women who, throughout history, have challenged the status quo. (Rev: BL 9/15/99; SLJ 8/99) [920]

15979 Haskins, James. *African Heroes* (5–8). Series: Black Stars. 2005, Wiley $24.95 (978-0-471-46672-7). 163pp. Profiles 27 important Africans, both contemporary and from the past, in entries of varying length. (Rev: SLJ 7/05) [920]

15980 Hazell, Rebecca. *The Barefoot Book of Heroic Children* (4–7). Illus. 2000, Barefoot Books $19.95 (978-1-902283-23-4). 96pp. This book presents the lives of 12 heroic children from different times and places, among them Anne Frank, Fanny Mendelssohn, Annie Sullivan, and Iqbal Masih. (Rev: BL 4/15/00) [920]

15981 Hazell, Rebecca. *Heroes: Great Men Through the Ages* (5–8). Illus. 1997, Abbeville $19.95 (978-0-7892-0289-5). A collection of 12 biographies, from Socrates to Martin Luther King, Jr., and including Shakespeare, Mohandas Gandhi, Leonardo da Vinci, and Jorge Louis Borges. (Rev: SLJ 6/97) [920]

15982 Hazell, Rebecca. *Heroines: Great Women Through the Ages* (5–8). Illus. 1996, Abbeville $19.95 (978-0-7892-0210-9). This is a collective biography of 12 great women spanning the period from ancient Greece to modern times, including Sacagawea, Madame Sun Yat-Sen, Frida Kahlo, Joan of Arc, Harriet Tubman, and Marie Curie. (Rev: SLJ 12/96) [920]

15983 Hughes, Susan. *No Girls Allowed: Tales of Daring Women Dressed as Men for Love, Freedom and Adventure* (4–6). Illus. by Willow Dawson. 2008, Kids Can $16.95 (978-1-55453-177-6); paper $8.95 (978-1-55453-178-3). 80pp. Seven women — starting with Egypt's Hatshepsut — who adopted male identities for a variety of reasons are introduced in graphic novel format. (Rev: BLO 7/29/08; LMC 11/08; SLJ 9/08) [920]

15984 Humphrey, Sandra McLeod. *Dare to Dream! 25 Extraordinary Lives* (4–7). 2005, Prometheus paper $15.98 (978-1-59102-280-0). 115pp. Twenty-five individuals — including artists, athletes, politicians, and scientists — who overcame obstacles to achieve greatness are profiled, with information on childhood and adult life. (Rev: BL 3/1/05; SLJ 6/05) [920]

15985 Hunter, Ryan Ann. *In Disguise: Stories of Real Women Spies* (5–8). Illus. 2004, Beyond Words paper $9.95 (978-1-58270-095-3). 133pp. Profiles 26 women who risked their lives to spy for causes in which they believed, from 1640 to the Cold War. (Rev: SLJ 8/04) [920]

15986 Krull, Kathleen. *Lives of Extraordinary Women: Rulers, Rebels (and What the Neighbors Thought)* (5–8). Illus. Series: Extraordinary Lives. 2000, Harcourt $20.00 (978-0-15-200807-9). 96pp. Short biographies of women who affected the course of history, from Cleopatra to contemporary Burma's Aung San Suu Kyi. (Rev: BCCB 9/00; BL 9/1/00; HB 11/00; HBG 3/01; SLJ 9/00; VOYA 6/01) [920]

15987 Lace, William W. *Leaders and Generals* (5–10). Series: American War. 2000, Lucent LB $28.70 (978-1-56006-664-4). 112pp. The following World War II leaders are profiled: Erwin Rommel, Georgi Zhukov, Erich von Manstein, Yamamoto Isoroku, Douglas MacArthur, Chester Nimitz, Dwight Eisenhower, and Bernard Law Montgomery. (Rev: BL 4/15/00; HBG 10/00; SLJ 6/00) [920]

15988 Leon, Vicki. *Outrageous Women of Ancient Times* (4–7). Illus. Series: Outrageous Women. 1997, Wiley paper $12.95 (978-0-471-17006-8). 128pp. Fifteen unusual women from ancient civilizations in Asia, Europe, and Africa are profiled, among them warriors, philosophers, empresses, artists, and professional poisoners, and including Cleopatra and Sappho. (Rev: BL 11/1/97; SLJ 12/97) [920]

15989 Leon, Vicki. *Outrageous Women of the Middle Ages* (4–7). Illus. Series: Outrageous Women. 1998, Wiley paper $12.95 (978-0-471-17004-4). 128pp. Using a witty writing style and modern comparisons, this fascinating book profiles a diverse group of amazing women who lived from the 6th through the 14th centuries in Europe, Asia, and Africa. (Rev: BL 4/15/98; SLJ 8/98) [920]

15990 McLuskey, Krista. *Entrepreneurs* (3–6). Series: Women in Profile. 1999, Crabtree LB $22.60 (978-0-7787-0012-8); paper $8.95 (978-0-7787-0034-0). 48pp. Six female entrepreneurs, including Oprah Winfrey, are profiled here, with brief sketches of 15 more. (Rev: BL 9/15/99) [920]

15991 Marzollo, Jean. *My First Book of Biographies: Great Men and Women Every Child Should Know* (2–4). Illus. by Irene Trivas. 1994, Scholastic $14.95 (978-0-590-45014-0). 80pp. Brief profiles of 45 famous people whom youngsters have heard about, from Cleopatra to Beatrix Potter. (Rev: BL 12/1/94; HB 5/04; SLJ 9/94) [920]

15992 Meltzer, Milton. *Ten Kings and the Worlds They Ruled* (5–8). Illus. by Bethanne Andersen. 2002, Scholastic paper $21.95 (978-0-439-31293-6). 144pp. Ten kings from around the world and across the ages are discussed in this attractive book that includes impressive portraits and other illustrations. Also use *Ten Queens* (1998). (Rev: BCCB 9/02; BL 7/02; HBG 10/02; SLJ 10/02*) [920.02]

15993 Norris, Kathleen. *The Holy Twins: Benedict and Scholastica* (K–3). Illus. by Tomie dePaola. 2001, Penguin $18.99 (978-0-399-23424-8). 32pp. The abbot who became Saint Benedict and founded the Benedictine order is much better known than his twin sister Saint Scholastica, but the story of both siblings' lives is told here with illustrations that evoke Italy in the sixth century. (Rev: BCCB 7–8/01; BL 10/1/01; HBG 3/02; SLJ 9/01) [271]

15994 Parker, Janice. *Political Leaders* (3–6). Illus. 1998, Crabtree LB $22.60 (978-0-7787-0008-1). 48pp. As well as detailed sketches of Corazon Aquino, Benazir Bhutto, Indira Gandhi, Golda Meir, Margaret Thatcher, and Eva Peron, this book contains shorter profiles of other important female political leaders. (Rev: BL 9/1/98) [920]

15995 Pollard, Michael. *People Who Care* (4–6). Series: Pioneers in History. 1992, Garrett LB $19.93 (978-1-56074-035-3). 48pp. Nineteen individuals who devoted their lives to helping others are profiled in this book. People who participated in revolutions are covered in *Revolutionary Power* (1992) and great philosophers in *Thinkers* (1992). (Rev: SLJ 9/92) [920]

15996 Sanderson, Ruth. *More Saints: Lives and Illuminations* (4–7). Illus. 2007, Eerdmans $20.00 (978-0-8028-5272-4). 40pp. A sequel to *Saints: Lives and Illuminations* (2003), this volume adds profiles of 36 saints, this time of the second millennium. (Rev: BL 2/1/07) [270]

15997 Sanderson, Ruth. *Saints: Lives and Illuminations* (4–6). Illus. 2003, Eerdmans $20.00 (978-0-8028-5220-5). 40pp. The lives and deaths of 40 saints, accompanied by painted portraits. (Rev: BL 2/1/03; HBG 10/03; SLJ 5/03) [270]

15998 Shaw, Maura D. *Ten Amazing People: And How They Changed the World* (4–7). Illus. 2002, SkyLight Paths $17.95 (978-1-893361-47-8). 48pp. Shaw presents 10 well-illustrated biographies of 20th-century religious figures, each with timelines, a quotation, and a glossary, and an emphasis on the individual's beliefs. (Rev: BL 10/1/02; HBG 3/03; SLJ 12/02) [200]

15999 Sullivan, George. *In the Line of Fire* (3–6). Illus. 1996, Scholastic paper $3.99 (978-0-590-48294-3). 118pp. From the American Revolution through World War II, the stories of eight female spies are retold. (Rev: BL 6/1–15/96) [920]

16000 Thimmesh, Catherine. *Madam President: The Extraordinary, True (and Evolving) Story of Women in Politics*. Rev. ed. (4–7). Illus. by Douglas B. Jones. 2008, Houghton $17.00 (978-0-618-39666-5); paper $8.95 (978-0-618-97143-5). 80pp. This update includes profiles of more than 20 women who have been influential in the political arena, including Margaret Chase Smith, Sirimavo Bandaranaike, Margaret Thatcher, Nancy Pelosi, Hillary Clinton, and Condoleezza Rice. (Rev: BL 10/1/04*; SLJ 5/08) [920]

16001 Wales, Dirk. *Twice a Hero: Polish American Heroes of the American Revolution* (3–5). Illus. by Lynn Ihsen Peterson. 2007, Great Plains $18.95 (978-0-963245-94-6). 32pp. Profiles two Polish-born heroes — Thaddeus Kosciuszko and Casimir Pulaski — who helped Americans to defeat the British during the Revolutionary War; an accompanying DVD expands the briefer information on Pulaski. (Rev: BL 4/15/07) [920]

16002 Wilkinson, Philip, and Jacqueline Dineen. *People Who Changed the World* (3–5). Illus. by Robert Ingpen. Series: Turning Points. 1994, Chelsea LB $21.95 (978-0-7910-2764-6). 93pp. Includes brief biographies of religious leaders, philosophers, and explorers like Pericles, Jesus Christ, Karl Marx, and Martin Luther King, Jr. Also use *Statesmen Who Changed the World* (1994). (Rev: BL 12/15/94) [920]

16003 Wilkinson, Philip, and Michael Pollard. *Generals Who Changed the World* (4–6). Illus. by Robert Ingpen. Series: Turning Points. 1994, Chelsea LB $12.95 (978-0-7910-2761-5). 93pp. A profile of 20 important military men and how their accomplishments changed the course of history. (Rev: SLJ 11/94) [920]

16004 Zalben, Jane Breskin. *Paths to Peace: People Who Changed the World* (4–7). Illus. 2006, Dutton $18.99 (978-0-525-47734-1). 48pp. Zalben profiles 16 individuals who have devoted much of their lives to the goal of making peace a reality. (Rev: BL 1/1–15/06; SLJ 2/06) [920]

Individual

ALEXANDER THE GREAT

16005 Adams, Simon. *Alexander: The Boy Soldier Who Conquered the World* (5–7). Series: National Geographic World History Biographies. 2005, National Geographic LB $27.90 (978-0-7922-3661-0). 64pp. An attractive, well-illustrated account of Alexander's life and accomplishments, with references to his less-appealing characteristics. (Rev: HBG 4/06; SLJ 9/05) [921]

16006 Greenblatt, Miriam. *Alexander the Great and Ancient Greece* (5–8). Illus. Series: Rulers and Their Times. 1999, Marshall Cavendish LB $29.93 (978-0-7614-0913-7). 80pp. The first part of this biography introduces Alexander the Great and his accomplishments and the second tells about daily life in ancient Greece. (Rev: BL 1/1–15/00; HBG 10/00; SLJ 2/00) [921]

16007 McGowen, Tom. *Alexander the Great: Conqueror of the Ancient World* (5–8). Series: Rulers of the Ancient World. 2006, Enslow LB $27.93 (978-0-7660-2560-8). 160pp. Excellent for report writers, this biography covers Alexander the Great's life and distinguishes between fact and legend. (Rev: BL 6/1–15/06; SLJ 6/06) [921]

16008 Saunders, Nicholas. *The Life of Alexander the Great* (5–8). Illus. Series: Stories from History. 2006, School Specialty $9.95 (978-0-7696-4713-5); paper $6.95 (978-0-7696-4694-7). 48pp. Full-color illustrations and graphic-novel format make this engaging biography — which covers the bond between Alexander and his horse as well as his relationship with Hephaestion — attractive to reluctant readers. (Rev: SLJ 1/07) [921]

16009 Shecter, Vicky Alvear. *Alexander the Great Rocks the World* (5–8). Illus. by Terry Naughton. 2006, Darby Creek $18.95 (978-1-58196-045-7). 128pp. Shecter employs an irreverent, kid-appealing tone to accurately present Alexander's amazing travels; cartoons, historical depictions, detailed notes, and resources round out the volume. (Rev: BL 1/1–15/07; SLJ 12/06) [921]

ANIELEWICZ, MORDECHAI

16010 Callahan, Kerry P. *Mordechai Anielewicz: Hero of the Warsaw Uprising* (5–8). Series: Holocaust Biographies. 2001, Rosen LB $31.95 (978-0-8239-3377-8). 112pp. The story of Anielewicz and other members of the Jewish resistance in the Warsaw ghetto is told in gripping text accompanied by black-and-white photographs. (Rev: BL 10/15/01) [921]

ARAFAT, YASIR

16011 Headlam, George. *Yasser Arafat* (5–8). Series: A&E Biography. 2003, Lerner LB $29.27 (978-0-8225-5004-4); paper $7.95 (978-0-8225-9902-9). 112pp. The story of the Palestinian leader, his rise to power, and his current status. (Rev: BL 1/1–15/04; HBG 4/04; SLJ 2/04)

16012 Williams, Colleen Madonna Flood. *Yasir Arafat* (5–8). Illus. 2002, Chelsea $30.00 (978-0-7910-6941-7); paper $30.00 (978-0-7910-7186-1). 112pp. The controversial PLO leader is shown as a man of conviction who struggles to balance the desires of his people and of the rest of the world. (Rev: BL 1/1–15/03; HBG 3/03; SLJ 2/03) [956.9405]

ARISTOTLE

16013 Anderson, Margaret J., and Karen F. Stephenson. *Aristotle: Philosopher and Scientist* (5–8). Series: Great Minds of Science. 2004, Enslow LB $26.60 (978-0-7660-2096-2). 112pp. Aristotle's life, times, and contributions to philosophy and science are examined in concise text. (Rev: SLJ 7/04) [921]

ATTILA THE HUN

16014 Price, Sean Stewart. *Attila the Hun: Leader of the Barbarian Hordes* (5–8). Illus. Series: Wicked History. 2009, Scholastic LB $30.00 (978-0-531-21801-3); paper $5.95 (978-0-531-20737-6). 128pp. This compelling, well-designed biography provides lots of historical context. (Rev: BL 4/15/09; VOYA 6/09) [936]

BEGIN, MENACHEM

16015 Brackett, Virginia. *Menachem Begin* (5–8). Series: Major World Leaders. 2002, Chelsea $30.00 (978-0-7910-6946-2). 104pp. The life of the important Israeli prime minister who was in office when peace was declared between Israel and Egypt. (Rev: BL 1/1–15/03; SLJ 2/03) [921]

BHATT, ELA

16016 Sreenivasan, Jyotsna. *Ela Bhatt: Uniting Women in India* (5–8). Illus. Series: Women Changing the World. 2000, Feminist $19.95 (978-1-55861-229-7). 112pp. Inspired by Gandhi, this Indian lawyer founded an organization to help and protect the lives of her country's poorest women and organized a labor union for them. (Rev: BL 9/15/00; HBG 3/01; SLJ 12/00) [921]

BIN LADEN, OSAMA

16017 Louis, Nancy. *Osama bin Laden* (4–7). Series: War on Terrorism. 2002, ABDO LB $25.65 (978-1-57765-663-0). 48pp. A brief biography of the terrorist leader told through a matter-of-fact text and many color photographs. (Rev: BL 5/15/02; HBG 10/02) [921]

16018 Woolf, Alex. *Osama Bin Laden* (5–8). Series: A&E Biography. 2003, Lerner LB $29.27 (978-0-8225-5003-7); paper $7.95 (978-0-8225-9900-5). 112pp. The story of the leader of the Al Qaeda terrorist movement and his family background in Saudi Arabia. (Rev: BL 1/1–15/04; HBG 4/04; SLJ 2/04) [921]

BLAIR, TONY

16019 Wilson, Wayne, and Jim Whiting. *Tony Blair* (3–6). 2002, Mitchell Lane LB $15.95 (978-1-58415-143-2). 32pp. Blair's colorful youth — as mild rebel and as aspiring rock singer — will draw readers into the story of his later achievements that puts an emphasis on his support of the United States. (Rev: SLJ 12/02) [921]

BLOOMER, ELIZABETH

16020 Reed, Jennifer B. *Elizabeth Bloomer: Child Labor Activist* (4–8). Series: Young Heroes. 2006, Gale LB $23.70 (978-0-7377-3615-1). 48pp. Bloomer became an activist against child labor when she was in middle school and learned about Iqbal Masih, a Pakistani boy sold into slavery. (Rev: SLJ 5/07) [921]

BONETTA, SARAH FORBES

16021 Myers, Walter Dean. *At Her Majesty's Request: An African Princess in Victorian England* (5–8). Illus. 1999, Scholastic paper $17.95 (978-0-590-48669-9). The intriguing story of the African princess who at age 7 was saved from becoming a sacrifice and was sent to England, where she became the ward of Queen Victoria. (Rev: BCCB 2/99; BL 4/1/99; HBG 10/99; SLJ 1/99; VOYA 4/99) [921]

BRESNICK-PERRY, ROSLYN

16022 Bresnick-Perry, Roslyn. *Leaving for America* (K–3). Illus. by Mira Reisberg. 1992, Children's Book Pr. $14.95 (978-0-89239-105-9). 32pp. Remembrances by the author, who left Russia in 1929 as a young child. (Rev: BCCB 2/93; BL 1/15/93; SLJ 2/93) [947]

BUDDHA

16023 Gedney, Mona. *The Life and Times of Buddha* (5–7). Series: Biography from Ancient Civilizations: Legends, Folklore, and Stories of Ancient Worlds. 2005, Mitchell Lane LB $29.95 (978-1-58415-342-9). 48pp. Gedney recounts what is known of the life of Siddartha Gautama, whose search for a better way of living led to the founding of Buddhism. (Rev: SLJ 9/05) [921]

16024 Stewart, Whitney. *Becoming Buddha: The Story of Siddhartha* (3–5). Illus. by Sally Rippin. 2005, Lothian $16.95 (978-0-89346-946-7). 32pp. A picture-book biography of Buddha that chronicles Prince Siddhartha's lifelong search for enlightenment. (Rev: BL 10/1/05; SLJ 11/05) [921]

CAESAR, JULIUS

16025 Galford, Ellen. *Julius Caesar: The Boy Who Conquered an Empire* (5–8). Series: World History Biographies. 2007, National Geographic $17.95 (978-1-4263-0064-6). 64pp. A brief but well-organized biography of Caesar, covering his childhood, adolescence, marriage, military career, rise to power, and murder, and offering pertinent historical context. (Rev: SLJ 6/07) [921]

16026 Saunders, Nicholas. *The Life of Julius Caesar* (5–8). Illus. Series: Stories from History. 2006, School Specialty $9.95 (978-0-7696-4717-3); paper $6.95 (978-0-7696-4697-8). 48pp. Full-color illustrations and graphic-novel format make this engaging biography attractive to reluctant readers. (Rev: SLJ 1/07) [921]

CAROLINE, PRINCESS OF MONACO

16027 Wheeler, Jill C. *Princess Caroline of Monaco* (4–6). Illus. Series: Leading Ladies. 1992, ABDO LB $20.95 (978-1-56239-117-1). 32pp. A simple biography of the princess who is the daughter of the late Grace Kelly. (Rev: BL 2/1/93; SLJ 3/93) [921]

CASTRO, FIDEL

16028 Platt, Richard. *Fidel Castro: From Guerrilla to World Statesman* (5–7). Series: Twentieth-Century History Makers. 2003, Raintree LB $32.85 (978-0-7398-6141-7). 112pp. Platt traces Castro's life from childhood through today, presenting opposing opinions of his achievements in a chapter called "Hero or Monster?" (Rev: HBG 4/04; SLJ 9/03) [973.9106]

16029 Press, Petra. *Fidel Castro: An Unauthorized Biography* (5–7). Series: Heinemann Profiles. 2000, Heinemann LB $24.22 (978-1-57572-497-3). 56pp. An interesting introduction to the life of Cuba's dictator, with photographs that show urban and rural Cuba. (Rev: SLJ 6/01) [972.91064092]

CHAMPOLLION, JEAN-FRANCOIS

16030 Rumford, James. *Seeker of Knowledge: The Man Who Deciphered Egyptian Hieroglyphs* (3–5). Illus. 2000, Houghton $16.00 (978-0-395-97934-1). 32pp. The story of Jean-Francois Champollion, who studied the Rosetta Stone and found the key to understanding Egyptian hieroglyphs. (Rev: BCCB 4/00; BL 4/15/00; HBG 10/00; SLJ 5/00) [493]

CHORN-POND, ARN

16031 Lord, Michelle. *A Song for Cambodia* (3–5). Illus. by Shino Arihara. 2008, Lee & Low $16.95 (978-1-60060-139-2). 32pp. When the Khmer Rouge took over his village in 1975, Arn Chorn was taken from his family and sent to a work camp; there he learned to play the khim, and his love of music supported him through many challenges he faced before being adopted and brought to the United States. (Rev: BL 4/1/08; LMC 10/08; SLJ 4/08) [921]

CHRISTOPHER, SAINT

16032 dePaola, Tomie. *Christopher: The Holy Giant* (K–3). Illus. 1994, Holiday House LB $17.95 (978-0-8234-0862-7). 32pp. The story of Saint Christopher and how Jesus gave him that name for his good works. (Rev: BL 5/1/94; HB 5/94; SLJ 3/94*) [398.22]

CHURCHILL, SIR WINSTON

16033 Ashworth, Leon. *Winston Churchill* (5–8). Illus. Series: British History Makers. 2002, Cherrytree $17.95 (978-1-84234-072-1). 32pp. A balanced look at the life and career of the British statesman, with a useful timeline and excellent illustrations. (Rev: SLJ 8/02) [941.082092]

16034 Binns, Tristan Boyer. *Winston Churchill* (5–8). Series: Great Life Stories. 2004, Watts LB $30.50 (978-0-531-12361-4). 127pp. The complex life of Churchill is well portrayed in this biography that covers his youth and career, triumphs and losses, and many and varied interests. (Rev: SLJ 3/05) [921]

16035 Haugen, Brenda. *Winston Churchill: British Soldier, Writer, Statesman* (4–8). 2006, Compass Point LB $34.60 (978-0-7565-1582-9). 112pp. Slim but fact-filled, this is a useful biography for report writers, with excerpts from speeches and writings and full discussion of key events in Churchill's life. (Rev: SLJ 9/06) [921]

16036 Severance, John B. *Winston Churchill: Soldier, Statesman, Artist* (5–8). Illus. 1996, Clarion $19.00 (978-0-395-69853-2). A well-organized, clearly written account of the life and works of Britain's great statesman. (Rev: BL 4/15/96; HB 7/96; SLJ 4/96*; VOYA 6/96) [941.084]

CID, EL

16037 Koslow, Philip. *El Cid* (5–8). Illus. Series: Hispanics of Achievement. 1993, Chelsea LB $21.95 (978-0-7910-1239-0). 112pp. The story of Spain's national hero, who gained fame fighting the Moors. (Rev: BL 9/15/93) [921]

CLEOPATRA

16038 Streissguth, Thomas. *Queen Cleopatra* (4–7). Series: A&E Biography. 2000, Lerner LB $27.93 (978-0-8225-4946-8). 112pp. The story of Cleopatra and her impact on world history. (Rev: BL 3/15/00; HBG 10/00; SLJ 5/00) [921]

COLUMBA, SAINT

16039 Brown, Don. *Across a Dark and Wild Sea* (K–4). Illus. 2002, Millbrook LB $22.90 (978-0-7613-2415-7). 32pp. The story of the 6th-century Irish monk and scholar Columcille, or Saint Columba, who founded a monastery on the Scottish island of Iona. (Rev: BCCB 5/02; BL 4/1/02*; HB 5/02; HBG 10/02; SLJ 5/02) [921]

CONFUCIUS

16040 Freedman, Russell. *Confucius: The Golden Rule* (4–8). Illus. by Frederic Clement. 2002, Scholastic paper $17.99 (978-0-439-13957-1). 48pp. This absorbing account of the life and philosophy of Confucius gives new insight into the character of the man who had so much influence on China. (Rev: BL 10/1/02*; HB 1/03; HBG 3/03; SLJ 9/02*) [181]

CUNXIN, LI

16041 Cunxin, Li. *Dancing to Freedom: The True Story of Mao's Last Dancer* (2–4). Illus. by Anne Spudvilas. 2008, Walker $16.95 (978-0-8027-9777-3). 40pp. The author recalls his difficult early life in rural China, his rigorous training as a ballet dancer, and his defection to the West. (Rev: BCCB 9/08; BL 6/1–15/08; LMC 5/08; SLJ 6/08) [921]

CYR, LOUIS

16042 Debon, Nicolas. *The Strongest Man in the World: Louis Cyr* (2–4). Illus. 2007, Groundwood $17.95 (978-0-88899-731-9). 36pp. The exploits of circus strongman Cyr, a Canadian who amazed audiences in America and Europe at the end of the 19th century, are shown in this visual biography. (Rev: BL 4/1/07) [921]

DALAI LAMA

16043 Demi. *The Dalai Lama* (3–6). Illus. by author. 1998, Holt $17.95 (978-0-8050-5443-9). This biography of the contemporary, now-exiled, Dalai Lama also supplies details of his functions, mission, and responsibilities. (Rev: BCCB 4/98; HB 3/98; HBG 10/98; SLJ 3/98) [921]

16044 Gibb, Chris. *The Dalai Lama* (4–6). Series: Famous Lives. 2003, Raintree LB $27.12 (978-0-7398-5520-1). 48pp. The story of Tibet's exiled political and spiritual leader and of his teachings of peace and civil disobedience. (Rev: BL 2/15/03; HBG 10/03; SLJ 5/03) [921]

16045 Kimmel, Elizabeth C. *Boy on the Lion Throne: The Childhood of the 14th Dalai Lama* (5–8). 2009, Roaring Brook $18.95 (978-1-59643-394-6). 160pp. The compelling and wide-ranging story of the childhood of the current Dalai Lama, who was born Lhamo Thondup in 1935. (Rev: BCCB 6/09; SLJ 6/09) [921]

16046 Stewart, Whitney. *The 14th Dalai Lama: Spiritual Leader of Tibet* (5–8). Series: Newsmakers. 1996, Lerner LB $30.35 (978-0-8225-4926-0). As well as describing the life and spiritual beliefs of the 14th Dalai Lama, this account describes the political situation in Tibet at the time. (Rev: SLJ 6/96; VOYA 10/96) [921]

DE PORTOLA, GASPAR

16047 Whiting, Jim. *Gaspar de Portola* (5–7). Series: Latinos in American History. 2002, Mitchell Lane LB $29.95 (978-1-58415-148-7). 48pp. The story of the Latino governor of "Las Californias" from 1768 to 1770 who was responsible for expelling Jesuits from the area. (Rev: BL 2/15/03; HBG 10/03) [921]

DIANA, PRINCESS OF WALES

16048 Brennan, Kristine. *Diana, Princess of Wales* (5–8). Series: Women of Achievement. 1998, Chelsea $32.00 (978-0-7910-4714-9); paper $30.00 (978-0-7910-4715-6). This book covers the facts about Diana's life, disappointing marriage, struggle for happiness, and untimely death. (Rev: HBG 3/99; VOYA 4/99) [921]

16049 Licata, Renora. *Princess Diana: Royal Ambassador* (4–6). Illus. Series: The Library of Famous Women. 1993, Blackbirch LB $26.19 (978-1-56711-013-5). 64pp. Princess Diana comes alive in this account that covers her celebrity status and her public service work. (Rev: BL 6/1–15/93; SLJ 8/93) [921]

16050 Oleksy, Walter. *Princess Diana* (5–8). Series: People in the News. 2001, Lucent LB $27.45 (978-1-56006-579-1). A well-documented life of this tragic, troubled princess, with many quotations and black-and-white photographs. (Rev: BCCB 10/98; BL 4/1/02; HBG 3/01) [921]

16051 Wood, Richard. *Diana: The People's Princess* (4–7). Illus. 1998, Raintree paper $7.95 (978-0-8172-7849-6). 48pp. A biography that reveals some personal information about this multifaceted woman and details the many causes she supported. (Rev: BL 7/98; HBG 10/98; SLJ 8/98) [921]

ELIZABETH I, QUEEN OF ENGLAND

16052 Adams, Simon. *Elizabeth I: The Outcast Who Became England's Queen* (3–6). Series: National Geographic World History Biographies. 2005, National Geographic $17.95 (978-0-7922-3649-8). 64pp. The queen's life and accomplishments are placed in historical context in this well-designed, informative book. (Rev: HBG 10/06; SLJ 6/06) [921]

16053 Brassey, Richard. *Elizabeth I* (3–5). Series: Brilliant Brits. 2006, Orion paper $8.99 (978-1-84255-233-9). 24pp. The queen up-close and personal, with lots of illustrations in comic-book style and an emphasis on the quirks and the drama of the royal family and their times. (Rev: BL 7/06) [921]

16054 Havelin, Kate. *Elizabeth I* (5–8). Series: Biography. 2002, Lerner LB $27.93 (978-0-8225-0029-

2). 112pp. The story of one of the most powerful queens in history and how she learned, at an early age, the politics of survival. (Rev: BCCB 12/99; BL 6/1–15/02; HBG 10/02; SLJ 7/02) [921]

16055 Stanley, Diane, and Peter Vennema. *Good Queen Bess: The Story of Elizabeth of England* (4–6). Illus. 1990, Macmillan LB $16.95 (978-0-02-786810-4). 40pp. An excellent biography of Elizabeth I, with emphasis on understanding the reasons for her actions in the context of the time. (Rev: BCCB 10/90; BL 9/1/90*; HB 1/91*; SLJ 12/90) [921]

16056 Thomas, Jane Resh. *Behind the Mask: The Life of Queen Elizabeth I* (5–8). Illus. 1998, Clarion $20.00 (978-0-395-69120-5). 196pp. A behind-the-scenes look at the long-ruled queen, discussing her childhood, how she overcame opposition to become queen, and her subsequent manipulation of people, the court, and foreigners to attain greatness. (Rev: BL 12/15/98; HB 1/99; HBG 3/99; SLJ 12/98*; VOYA 4/99) [921]

ELIZABETH II, QUEEN OF ENGLAND

16057 Barton-Wood, Sara. *Queen Elizabeth II: Monarch of Our Times* (4–6). Illus. Series: Famous Lives. 2001, Raintree LB $27.12 (978-0-7398-4430-4). 48pp. An affectionate look at the life of Queen Elizabeth II, from childhood through her Golden Jubilee. (Rev: BL 1/1–15/02; HBG 10/02; SLJ 3/02) [941.085]

FOX, VICENTE

16058 Paprocki, Sherry Beck. *Vicente Fox* (5–8). Series: Major World Leaders. 2002, Chelsea $30.00 (978-0-7910-6944-8). 104pp. The story of the man who became president of Mexico in July 2000, the first opposition candidate to gain presidential office in more than 70 years. (Rev: BL 1/1–15/03) [921]

FRANCIS OF ASSISI, SAINT

16059 dePaola, Tomie. *Francis: The Poor Man of Assisi* (4–7). Illus. by author. 1982, Holiday $18.95 (978-0-8234-0435-3); paper $9.95 (978-0-8234-0812-2). 48pp. A simple retelling of the life of St. Francis with fine pictures by dePaola. [921]

16060 Kennedy, Robert F., Jr. *Saint Francis of Assisi: A Life of Joy* (2–4). Illus. by Dennis Nolan. 2005, Hyperion $18.99 (978-0-7868-1875-4). 31pp. Environmental activist Robert F. Kennedy Jr. chronicles the life of Saint Francis of Assisi, his patron saint. (Rev: BL 2/15/05; SLJ 5/05) [921]

16061 Wildsmith, Brian. *Saint Francis* (1–3). Illus. 1996, Eerdmans $20.00 (978-0-8028-5123-9). 36pp. A large-size picture book that tells the story of St. Francis as a first-person narrative with a biographical note following the story. (Rev: BCCB 7–8/96; BL 1/1–15/96; SLJ 2/96) [921]

FRANK, ANNE

16062 Adler, David A. *A Picture Book of Anne Frank* (2–4). Illus. by Karen Ritz. 1993, Holiday House LB $16.95 (978-0-8234-1003-3). 32pp. A simple biography for young readers. (Rev: BCCB 3/93; BL 3/1/93; SLJ 5/93) [921]

16063 Alagna, Magdalena. *Anne Frank: Young Voice of the Holocaust* (5–8). Series: Holocaust Biographies. 2001, Rosen LB $26.50 (978-0-8239-3373-0). 112pp. This book describes Anne's childhood, her time spent in hiding, her diary, and her life in the concentration camps. (Rev: BL 10/15/01) [921]

16064 Colbert, David. *Anne Frank* (5–8). Illus. Series: 10 Days That Shook Your World. 2008, Aladdin paper $6.99 (978-1-4169-6445-2). 160pp. Interweaving fact and fiction, Colbert describes 10 important days in Anne Frank's life — from the Netherlands' surrender to March 1945, when Anne is moved to a new camp full of disease. (Rev: BLO 12/8/08) [921]

16065 Frank, Anne. *Anne Frank: The Diary of a Young Girl* (5–8). 1967, Pocket paper $3.95 (978-0-685-05466-6). 312pp. The moving diary of a young Jewish girl hiding from the Nazis in World War II Amsterdam. [921]

16066 Gold, Alison L. *Memories of Anne Frank: Reflections of a Childhood Friend* (4–8). Illus. 1997, Scholastic paper $16.95 (978-0-590-90722-4). Anne Frank's story as told through recollections of her best friend in Amsterdam, Hannah Goslar, a survivor of the Holocaust. (Rev: BL 9/1/97; HBG 3/98; SLJ 11/97) [921]

16067 Hermann, Spring. *Anne Frank: Hope in the Shadows of the Holocaust* (5–7). Series: Holocaust Heroes and Nazi Criminals. 2005, Enslow LB $27.93 (978-0-7660-2531-8). 160pp. The story of Anne Frank before, during, and after the two years she and her family hid from the Nazis. (Rev: SLJ 11/05) [921]

16068 Hurwitz, Johanna. *Anne Frank: Life in Hiding* (4–7). Illus. by Vera Rosenberry. 1989, Jewish Publication Soc. $13.95 (978-0-8276-0311-0). 64pp. This biography describes Anne's life in hiding. (Rev: BL 4/15/89) [921]

GANDHI, MAHATMA

16069 Barraclough, John. *Mohandas Gandhi* (2–3). Illus. Series: Lives and Times. 1997, Heinemann $19.92 (978-1-57572-561-1). 24pp. A simple picture-book biography that tells of Gandhi's work in South Africa and his struggle against British rule in India. (Rev: BL 3/15/98) [921]

16070 Claybourne, Anna. *Gandhi* (4–6). Series: Famous Lives. 2003, Raintree LB $27.12 (978-0-7398-5521-8). 48pp. A brief biography of the Indian leader, his triumphs and hardships, and the story of the nonviolent movement he led. (Rev: BCCB 12/01; BL 2/15/03; HBG 10/03; SLJ 5/03) [921]

16071 Demi. *Gandhi* (3–6). Illus. 2001, Simon & Schuster $19.95 (978-0-689-84149-1). 40pp. A moving look at a remarkable man that brings to life his character and the time in which he lived. (Rev: BCCB 12/01; BL 6/1–15/01; HB 9/01; HBG 3/02; SLJ 8/01) [954.03]

16072 Martin, Christopher. *Mohandas Gandhi* (4–7). Series: A&E Biography. 2000, Lucent LB $27.93

(978-0-8225-4984-0). 112pp. The story of the man who sought to unite and free his people not through violence but by prayer, civil disobedience, and communication. (Rev: BL 12/15/00; HBG 3/01; SLJ 1/01) [921]

16073 Shaw, Maura D. *Gandhi: India's Great Soul* (3–6). Illus. by Stephen Marchesi. Series: Spiritual Biographies for Young Readers. 2004, SkyLight Paths $12.95 (978-1-893361-91-1). 32pp. An overview of Gandhi's life and beliefs is followed by discussion of how his ideals remain relevant and achievable. (Rev: BL 2/15/04; SLJ 9/04) [921]

16074 Wilkinson, Philip. *Gandhi: The Young Protestor Who Founded a Nation* (4–7). Illus. Series: World History Biographies. 2005, National Geographic LB $27.90 (978-0-7922-3648-1). 64pp. Gandhi's character shines through the straightforward text and interesting anecdotes in this biography that gives historical context plus maps and photographs. (Rev: BL 6/1–15/05) [954.03]

GENGHIS KHAN

16075 Goldberg, Enid A., and Norman Itzkowitz. *Genghis Khan: 13th-Century Mongolian Tyrant* (5–7). Illus. Series: Wicked History. 2007, Scholastic LB $30.00 (978-0-531-12596-0). 128pp. The bloody deeds of the tyrant are emphasized (this is the Wicked History series, after all), but readers will also learn about ancient Mongolia and its people as well as the few positive results of Genghis Khan's rule. (Rev: BL 12/15/07; LMC 1/08; SLJ 1/08) [921]

16076 Greenblatt, Miriam. *Genghis Khan and the Mongol Empire* (5–8). Series: Rulers and Their Times. 2001, Marshall Cavendish LB $29.93 (978-0-7614-1027-0). This handsomely illustrated book presents, in three parts, a life of Genghis Khan, a section on society during his reign, and a selection of documents of the time. (Rev: BL 1/1–15/02; HBG 3/02; SLJ 2/02) [947]

GROSS, ELLY BERKOVITS

16077 Gross, Elly Berkovits. *Elly: My True Story of the Holocaust* (4–7). Illus. 2009, Scholastic $14.99 (978-0-545-07494-0). 128pp. A memoir of a woman recalling her experiences as a teenager in a concentration camp and later as a factory slave laborer. (Rev: BL 6/1–15/09) [940.53]

HALILBEGOVICH, NADJA

16078 Halilbegovich, Nadja. *My Childhood Under Fire: A Sarajevo Diary* (4–7). 2006, Kids Can $14.95 (978-1-55337-797-9). 120pp. As a 12-year-old, Halilbegovich kept a diary that reveals the frightening details of her life during the Balkans war. (Rev: BL 5/15/06; SLJ 6/06) [949.703]

HANH, THICH NHAT

16079 Shaw, Maura D. *Thich Nhat Hanh: Buddhism in Action* (4–6). Illus. by Stephen Marchesi. Series: Spiritual Biographies for Young Readers. 2004,

SkyLight Paths $12.95 (978-1-893361-87-4). 32pp. This brief biography of the Vietnamese Buddhist monk touches lightly on his anti-war activism; it offers an introduction to the benefits of peace and tranquility. (Rev: BL 2/1/04; SLJ 9/04) [294.3]

HANNIBAL

16080 Warrick, Karen Clemens. *Hannibal: Great General of the Ancient World* (5–8). Series: Rulers of the Ancient World. 2006, Enslow LB $27.93 (978-0-7660-2564-6). 160pp. The story of Hannibal's life and successes against the Romans are placed in historical context, with details of important battles as well as insight into his character. (Rev: SLJ 6/06) [921]

HATSHEPSUT

16081 Galford, Ellen. *Hatshepsut: The Princess Who Grew Up to Be King* (4–6). Illus. Series: World History Biographies. 2005, National Geographic $17.95 (978-0-7922-3645-0). 64pp. A life of Hatshepsut, who ruled Egypt about 3,500 years ago, with well-chosen illustrations, interesting sidebars, and clear distinctions between fact and surmise. (Rev: BL 7/05; SLJ 9/05) [921]

HILDEGARD, SAINT

16082 Winter, Jonah. *The Secret World of Hildegard* (1–4). Illus. by Jeanette Winter. 2007, Scholastic $16.99 (978-0-439-50739-4). 64pp. This is an interesting introduction to the life and work of Hildegard of Bingen, the medieval mystic, with a focus on her childhood. (Rev: BCCB 10/07; BL 10/1/07; HB 9/07; SLJ 10/07) [921]

HITLER, ADOLF

16083 Ayer, Eleanor. *Adolf Hitler* (4–8). Illus. Series: The Importance Of. 1996, Lucent LB $27.45 (978-1-56006-072-7). 128pp. This study of Hitler's rise and impact on Germany and the world includes analyses of the dictator's mental state, leadership qualities, and personality traits. (Rev: BL 3/15/96; SLJ 1/96) [921]

HODGMAN, ANN

16084 Hodgman, Ann. *The House of a Million Pets* (3–6). Illus. by Eugene Yelchin. 2007, Holt $16.95 (978-0-8050-7974-6). 272pp. This memoir chronicles the author's ongoing menagerie of animals ranging from hedgehogs and rabbits to owls and a bulbul, and is frank about the deaths as well as the happier experiences. (Rev: BCCB 11/07; BL 9/1/07; HB 1/08; SLJ 12/07) [636.088]

HONG, CHEN JIANG

16085 Hong, Chen Jiang. *Mao and Me* (4–8). Trans. by Claudia Zoe Bedrick. Illus. by author. 2008, Enchanted Lion $19.95 (978-1-59270-079-0). 96pp. A picture-book memoir about growing up during the Chinese Cultural Revolution, contrasting the personal with the political in often harrowing detail. (Rev: BL 12/15/08; SLJ 2/09) [951.05]

HUSSEIN, SADDAM

16086 Anderson, Dale. *Saddam Hussein* (5–8). Series: A&E Biography. 2003, Lerner LB $29.27 (978-0-8225-5005-1); paper $7.95 (978-0-8225-9901-2). 112pp. This biography of the Iraqi despot tells his story up to the decision that led to the American invasion. (Rev: BL 1/1–15/04; HBG 4/04; SLJ 2/04) [921]

16087 Shields, Charles J. *Saddam Hussein* (5–8). Illus. Series: Major World Leaders. 2002, Chelsea $30.00 (978-0-7910-6943-1). 112pp. An account of the Iraqi leader's regime, with information on the Iran-Iraq and Persian Gulf wars and on United Nations sanctions and weapons inspections. (Rev: BL 2/1/03; HBG 3/03; SLJ 4/03) [956.7044]

HYPATIA

16088 Love, D. Anne. *Of Numbers and Stars: The Story of Hypatia* (1–3). Illus. by Pam Paparone. 2006, Holiday $16.95 (978-0-8234-1621-9). 32pp. This picture-book biography of Hypatia profiles the life of the female scholar and philosopher whose father's devotion opened up to her worlds that were forbidden to most women. (Rev: BL 4/15/06; SLJ 5/06) [510]

JESUS CHRIST

16089 Demi. *Jesus* (3–5). Illus. 2005, Simon & Schuster $19.95 (978-0-689-86905-1). 48pp. Striking illustrations illustrate this life of Jesus, told chronologically in the tone of the King James version of the Bible. (Rev: BL 10/1/05; SLJ 10/05) [921]

JOAN OF ARC

16090 Bunson, Margaret, and Matthew Bunson. *St. Joan of Arc* (4–6). Illus. Series: Saints You Should Know. 1992, Sunday Visitor paper $5.95 (978-0-87973-558-6). 56pp. A clear, unsentimental portrait of the saint who lost her life trying to save her country. (Rev: BL 1/1/93) [921]

16091 Corey, Shana. *Joan of Arc* (2–3). Illus. by Dan Andreasen. Series: Step into Reading. 2003, Random paper $3.99 (978-0-375-80620-9). 48pp. The dramatic story of Joan of Arc is presented in picture-book form for beginning readers. (Rev: BL 7/03; HBG 4/04) [921]

16092 Hodges, Margaret. *Joan of Arc: The Lily Maid* (2–4). Illus. by Robert Rayevsky. 1999, Holiday House $16.95 (978-0-8234-1424-6). A simple, understandable account of the life of Joan of Arc and her devotion and bravery. (Rev: BL 11/1/99*; HBG 3/00; SLJ 9/99) [921]

16093 Lee, William W. *Joan of Arc and the Hundred Years' War in World History* (5–9). Series: In World History. 2003, Enslow LB $26.60 (978-0-7660-1938-6). 128pp. This combination of biogra-

phy and history tells the story of Joan of Arc and gives details on the long conflict between France and England. (Rev: BL 6/1–15/03; HBG 10/03; SLJ 9/03) [921]

16094 Poole, Josephine. *Joan of Arc* (K–3). Illus. by Angela Barrett. 1998, Knopf LB $19.99 (978-0-679-99041-3). 32pp. A lovely picture book that highlights the life of Joan of Arc, with emphasis on her courage and sense of purpose. (Rev: BCCB 9/98; BL 8/98*; HBG 3/99; SLJ 9/98) [921]

16095 Roberts, Jeremy. *Saint Joan of Arc* (4–6). Series: A&E Biography. 2000, Lerner LB $25.26 (978-0-8225-4981-9). 112pp. The story of a young woman whose honesty, devotion, and courage inspired an army, a king, and eventually a country to follow her. (Rev: BL 6/1–15/00; HBG 10/00) [921]

16096 Stanley, Diane. *Joan of Arc* (4–8). Illus. 1998, Morrow $16.89 (978-0-688-14330-5). Using glorious illustrations, this picture book for older readers gives a detailed history of the life and times of Joan of Arc. (Rev: BCCB 9/98; BL 8/98; HB 9/98*; HBG 3/99; SLJ 9/98) [921]

16097 Tompert, Ann. *Joan of Arc: Heroine of France* (1–4). Illus. by Michael Garland. 2003, Boyds Mills $15.95 (978-1-59078-009-1). 32pp. This solid account puts the events in Joan's life in clear historical context. (Rev: BL 3/1/03; HBG 10/03; SLJ 3/03) [944]

16098 Yeatts, Tabatha. *Joan of Arc: Heavenly Warrior* (4–7). Illus. Series: Sterling Biographies. 2009, Sterling $12.95 (978-1-4027-6542-1); paper $5.95 (978-1-4027-5662-7). 124pp. An accessible biography with many illustrations, maps, a timeline, and useful sources. (Rev: BL 2/1/09) [921]

JOHN PAUL II, POPE

16099 Mohan, Claire J. *The Young Life of Pope John Paul II* (4–6). Illus. 1995, Young Sparrow $14.95 (978-0-943135-11-3); paper $7.99 (978-0-943135-12-0). 64pp. The story of Pope John Paul II when he was Karol Wojtyla growing up in Poland. (Rev: BL 9/1/95; SLJ 11/95) [921]

JUAREZ, BENITO

16100 Palacios, Argentina. *Viva Mexico! A Story of Benito Juarez and Cinco de Mayo* (2–4). Illus. by Howard Berelson. 1993, Raintree LB $17.98 (978-0-8114-7214-2). 32pp. For very young readers, this is a simple biography of the man often referred to as the architect of modern Mexico. (Rev: BL 5/15/93; SLJ 7/93) [921]

KOLBE, SAINT MAXIMILIAN

16101 Mohan, Claire J. *Saint Maximilian Kolbe: The Story of the Two Crowns* (4–8). Illus. 1999, Young Sparrow paper $8.95 (978-0-9621500-3-6). 72pp. The story of a Polish Catholic monk who took the place of a fellow prisoner who was condemned to die at Auschwitz. (Rev: BL 2/1/00) [921]

KOLLEK, TEDDY

16102 Rabinovich, Abraham. *Teddy Kollek: Builder of Jerusalem* (5–8). Illus. 1996, Jewish Publication Soc. $14.95 (978-0-8276-0559-6); paper $9.95 (978-0-8276-0561-9). The story of the former mayor of Jerusalem, who supervised the city's unification after the Six Days War in 1967. (Rev: BL 5/15/96) [921]

KORCZAK, JANUSZ

16103 Adler, David A. *A Hero and the Holocaust: The Story of Janusz Korczak and His Children* (3–5). Illus. by Bill Farnsworth. 2002, Holiday House $16.95 (978-0-8234-1548-9). 32pp. The story of Janusz Korczak's efforts to care for young Jewish children in the Warsaw ghetto and on the trip to the Treblinka death camp, presented in memorable illustrations and a simple text, accompanied by quotes from his diary. (Rev: BL 12/1/02; HBG 3/03; SLJ 3/03) [943.8]

16104 Spielman, Gloria. *Janusz Korczak's Children* (1–3). Illus. by Matthew Archambault. 2007, Lerner $17.95 (978-1-58013-255-8); Kar-Ben paper $7.95 (978-0-8225-7050-9). 40pp. Spielman tells the story of the Polish doctor who refused to abandon the Jewish orphans he looked after and accompanied them to the death camp at Treblinka. (Rev: BL 10/15/07; LMC 1/08; SLJ 10/07) [921]

KOSSMAN, NINA

16105 Kossman, Nina. *Behind the Border* (5–7). 1994, Lothrop $14.00 (978-0-688-13494-5). 128pp. This book contains 12 episodes about the author's childhood in Communist Russia before emigrating to the United States. (Rev: BCCB 10/94; BL 8/94; SLJ 10/94) [921]

LAFAYETTE, MARQUIS DE

16106 Fritz, Jean. *Why Not, Lafayette?* (5–8). Illus. 1999, Putnam $17.99 (978-0-399-23411-8). Using plenty of quotations, interesting anecdotes, and dry humor, this is a fine biography of General Lafayette, the French-born hero of the American Revolution. (Rev: BCCB 12/99; BL 9/15/99; HB 11/99; HBG 3/00; SLJ 12/99) [921]

16107 Payan, Gregory. *Marquis de Lafayette: French Hero of the American Revolution* (4–7). Illus. Series: Library of American Lives and Times. 2001, Rosen $34.60 (978-0-8239-5733-0). 112pp. Payan introduces the French general who assisted the American cause, with illustrations, maps, and other aids to understanding his times. (Rev: BL 10/15/01) [944.04]

LAMBKE, BRYAN

16108 Lambke, Bryan, and Tom Lambke. *I Just Am: A Story of Down Syndrome Awareness and Tolerance* (4–10). 2006, Five Star $14.99 (978-1-58985-020-0). 86pp. In this compelling photoessay, a young adult with Down syndrome — with some help from his father — explains what it's like to live with this disability. (Rev: SLJ 10/06) [921]

LAO TZU

16109 Demi. *The Legend of Lao Tzu and the Tao Te Ching* (4–7). Illus. by author. 2007, Simon & Schuster $21.99 (978-1-4169-1206-4). 48pp. A well-designed introduction to the legendary Chinese religious figure Lao Tzu, with 20 verses from the book of wisdom associated with him. (Rev: BL 5/15/07; HB 7/07; LMC 11/07; SLJ 5/07) [921]

LEKUTON, JOSEPH LEMASOLAI

16110 Lekuton, Joseph Lemasolai. *Facing the Lion: Growing Up Maasai on the African Savanna* (5–12). 2003, National Geographic $15.95 (978-0-7922-5125-5). 144pp. Lekuton, a member of a nomadic Masai tribe and now a teacher in Virginia, remembers his youth in Kenya. (Rev: BCCB 5/06; BL 9/15/03; HBG 4/04; LMC 11/06; SLJ 10/03*) [967.62]

MACHIAVELLI, NICCOLÒ

16111 Ford, Nick. *Niccolò Machiavelli: Florentine Statesman, Playwright, and Poet* (5–8). Series: Rulers, Scholars, and Artists of the Renaissance. 2005, Rosen LB $33.25 (978-1-4042-0316-7). 112pp. Ford places Machiavelli's life and accomplishments in the context of culture and politics of the time. (Rev: SLJ 10/05) [921]

MANDELA, NELSON

16112 Connolly, Sean. *Nelson Mandela: An Unauthorized Biography* (5–7). 2000, Heinemann LB $24.22 (978-1-57572-225-2). 56pp. An appealing biography that contains good background material on South Africa, past and present. (Rev: SLJ 1/01) [921]

16113 Finlayson, Reggie. *Nelson Mandela* (4–8). Illus. Series: A&E Biography. 1999, Lerner LB $27.93 (978-0-8225-4936-9). 112pp. An overview that concentrates on Mandela's childhood, his training as a lawyer, and his rise through the ranks of the African National Congress, with only brief coverage of his imprisonment, release, and presidency. (Rev: BL 2/15/00; HBG 3/99; SLJ 2/99) [921]

16114 Holland, Gini. *Nelson Mandela* (2–4). Illus. by Mike White. Series: First Biographies. 1997, Raintree LB $25.69 (978-0-8172-4454-5). 32pp. A simple retelling of Nelson Mandela's life from his childhood as the son of a black chieftain to his release from prison in 1990 and resumption of his political career. (Rev: SLJ 2/98) [921]

16115 Kramer, Ann. *Mandela: The Rebel Who Led His Nation to Freedom* (4–6). Series: National Geographic World History Biographies. 2005, National Geographic $17.95 (978-0-7922-3658-0). 64pp. Mandela's life and accomplishments are placed in the context of the changing political climate in South Africa. (Rev: SLJ 10/05) [921]

16116 Roberts, Jack L. *Nelson Mandela: Determined to Be Free* (2–4). Illus. Series: Gateway Biographies. 1995, Millbrook LB $23.90 (978-1-56294-558-9). 48pp. A short, direct biography illustrated by numerous photographs. (Rev: BL 5/1/95) [921]

16117 Strazzabosco, Jeanne M. *Learning About Forgiveness from the Life of Nelson Mandela* (2–5). Illus. Series: A Character Building Book. 1996, Rosen LB $21.25 (978-0-8239-2413-4). 24pp. Covers, in a small-format book, the life of this South African hero and politician who fought successfully against apartheid. (Rev: BL 10/15/96; SLJ 11/96) [921]

MARSHAL, WILLIAM

16118 Weatherly, Myra. *William Marshal: Medieval England's Greatest Knight* (5–8). Illus. 2001, Morgan Reynolds LB $23.95 (978-1-883846-48-0). 112pp. The story of the brave medieval English knight whose accomplishments numbered fighting in tournaments, traveling to the Holy Land, helping to draw up the Magna Carta, and serving as regent when Henry III was a child. (Rev: BCCB 3/01; BL 1/1–15/01; HBG 10/01; SLJ 3/01) [921]

MEDICI, LORENZO DE

16119 Hancock, Lee. *Lorenzo De' Medici: Florence's Great Leader and Patron of the Arts* (5–8). Series: Rulers, Scholars, and Artists of the Renaissance. 2005, Rosen LB $33.25 (978-1-4042-0315-0). 112pp. Hancock places de Medici's life and accomplishments in the context of culture and politics of the time. (Rev: SLJ 10/05) [921]

MENCHU, RIGOBERTA

16120 Menchú, Rigoberta, and Dante Liano. *The Girl from Chimel* (4–7). Trans. by David Unger. Illus. by Domi. 2005, Groundwood $16.95 (978-0-88899-666-4). 56pp. Rigoberta Menchu, winner of the 1992 Nobel Peace Prize and Maya activist, tells about growing up in the Guatemalan Indian village of Chimel. (Rev: BL 11/1/05; SLJ 2/06) [868]

MILLMAN, ISAAC

16121 Millman, Isaac. *Hidden Child* (4–7). Illus. 2005, Farrar $18.00 (978-0-374-33071-2). 80pp. The author relates his experiences as a child in World War II, when he was hidden in various homes in France to save him from the Nazis. (Rev: BL 6/1–15/05*; SLJ 9/05) [921]

MOHAPATRA, JYOTIRMAYEE

16122 Woog, Adam. *Jyotirmayee Mohapatra: Advocate for India's Young Women* (4–8). Illus. Series: Young Heroes. 2006, Gale LB $27.45 (978-0-7377-3611-3). 48pp. From a village in rural India, Mohapatra became worried at a young age about the challenges facing girls and young women; she went on to found the network of Meena Clubs for which

she received the prestigious Youth Action Network award. (Rev: BL 1/1–15/07; SLJ 4/07) [921]

MONTESSORI, MARIA

16123 Shephard, Marie T. *Maria Montessori: Teacher of Teachers* (5–7). Illus. 1996, Lerner LB $30.35 (978-0-8225-4952-9). 128pp. A biography of the Italian educator and her unusual teaching methods for the young. (Rev: BL 8/96; SLJ 9/96) [921]

MUGABE, ROBERT

16124 Worth, Richard. *Robert Mugabe of Zimbabwe* (5–8). Illus. Series: In Focus Biographies. 1990, Silver Burdett LB $13.95 (978-0-671-68987-2); paper $7.95 (978-0-671-70684-5). 111pp. Tells the story of Zimbabwe's first prime minister, along with a history of this emerging country. (Rev: SLJ 2/91) [921]

MUHAMMAD

16125 Demi. *Muhammad* (4–7). Illus. 2003, Simon & Schuster $19.95 (978-0-689-85264-0). 48pp. This readable account of the life of the founding prophet of Islam is accompanied by quotations from the Koran and intricate illustrations. (Rev: BL 6/1–15/03*; HB 7/03; HBG 4/04; SLJ 8/03) [297.6]

NAKAHAMA, MANJIRO

16126 Blumberg, Rhoda. *Shipwrecked! The True Adventures of a Japanese Boy* (5–9). Illus. 2001, HarperCollins $16.95 (978-0-688-17484-2). 80pp. The story of a shipwrecked Japanese boy who was adopted by an American sea captain, brought to Massachusetts for an education, and became the first Japanese person to live in the United States. (Rev: BCCB 3/01; BL 2/1/01*; HB 3/01; HBG 10/01; SLJ 2/01) [921]

16127 McCully, Emily Arnold. *Manjiro: The Boy Who Risked His Life for Two Countries* (2–5). Illus. by author. 2008, Farrar $16.95 (978-0-374-34792-5). 40pp. A large-format picture-book biography of the 14-year-old Japanese castaway who was rescued by an American and was influential in acquainting Japan with the outside world. (Rev: BL 9/1/08; HB 11/08) [921]

NAPOLEON I

16128 Burleigh, Robert. *Napoleon: The Story of the Little Corporal* (5–8). Illus. 2007, Abrams $18.95 (978-0-8109-1378-3). 48pp. This informative and attractive biography of Napoleon from his childhood through his final defeat and exile uses an accessible, conversational style. (Rev: BL 6/1–15/07; SLJ 7/07) [921]

NEZAHUALCOYOTL

16129 Serrano, Francisco. *The Poet King of Tezcoco: A Great Leader of Ancient Mexico* (5–8). Trans. by Trudy Balch. Illus. by Pablo Serrano. 2007, Groundwood $18.95 (978-0-88899-787-6). 48pp. This picture book for older readers introduces the life of Nezahualcoyotl, a 15th-century Toltec royal and poet who brought much advancement to his kingdom. (Rev: BL 6/1–15/07; SLJ 12/07) [972]

NIGHTINGALE, FLORENCE

16130 Adler, David A. *A Picture Book of Florence Nightingale* (K–3). Illus. by John Wallner. Series: Picture Book Biographies. 1992, Holiday House LB $16.95 (978-0-8234-0965-5). 32pp. Through simple text and illustrations that supply details of time and place, the life of this gallant nurse is introduced. (Rev: BL 11/15/92; SLJ 10/92) [921]

16131 Armentrout, David, and Patricia Armentrout. *Florence Nightingale* (2–4). Illus. Series: People Who Made a Difference. 2001, Rourke LB $20.64 (978-1-58952-053-0). 24pp. A simple introduction for younger readers to the life of nursing pioneer Florence Nightingale. (Rev: BL 1/1–15/02; SLJ 3/02) [610.73]

16132 Barnham, Kay. *Florence Nightingale* (4–6). Series: Famous Lives. 2003, Raintree LB $27.12 (978-0-7398-5523-2). 48pp. The inspirational story of the gallant nurse who treated the wounded soldiers on the front lines during the Crimean War. (Rev: BL 2/15/03; HBG 10/03; SLJ 7/03) [921]

16133 Tieck, Sarah. *Florence Nightingale* (K–3). Series: First Biographies. 2006, ABDO LB $25.65 (978-1-59679-786-4). 32pp. A brief biography that introduces the life and work of the famous nurse in clear text and many photographs and reproductions. (Rev: SLJ 3/07) [921]

PAHLAVI, MOHAMMED REZA

16134 Barth, Linda. *Mohammed Reza Pahlavi* (5–8). Series: Major World Leaders. 2002, Chelsea $30.00 (978-0-7910-6948-6). 104pp. An engrossing biography of the last Shah of Iran, who ruled during a tumultuous time in the region. (Rev: BL 1/1–15/03) [921]

PATRICK, SAINT

16135 dePaola, Tomie. *Patrick: Patron Saint of Ireland* (PS–3). Illus. 1992, Holiday House LB $17.95 (978-0-8234-0924-2). 32pp. Simple text and glowing pictures portray the life of Ireland's saint. (Rev: BCCB 4/92; BL 3/15/92; HB 9/92; SLJ 5/92) [921]

PETER THE GREAT

16136 Greenblatt, Miriam. *Peter the Great and Tsarist Russia* (5–8). Illus. Series: Rulers and Their Times. 1999, Marshall Cavendish LB $29.93 (978-0-7614-0914-4). 80pp. A biography of the czar who westernized Russia is followed by a section on daily life during his reign. (Rev: BL 1/1–15/00; HBG 10/00; SLJ 2/00) [921]

PETIT, PHILIPPE

16137 Gerstein, Mordicai. *The Man Who Walked Between the Towers* (PS–3). Illus. by author. 2007, Square Fish paper $6.99 (978-0-312-36878-4). 40pp. This beautifully illustrated book vividly captures the day in 1974 when French aerialist Philippe Petit performed tricks on a high wire strung between the twin towers of New York City's World Trade Center. A paperback edition of the 2003 publication that won the 2004 Caldecott Medal. (Rev: BL 11/1/03; HB 11/03; HBG 4/04; SLJ 11/03) [791.3]

PULASKI, CASIMIR

16138 Collins, David R. *Casimir Pulaski: Soldier on Horseback* (4–8). Illus. 1995, Pelican $14.95 (978-1-56554-082-8). A smoothly written biography of the Polish patriot who, though he could scarcely speak English, became an important figure helping the colonists during the Revolutionary War. (Rev: BL 2/15/96) [921]

PUTIN, VLADIMIR

16139 Shields, Charles J. *Vladimir Putin* (5–8). Illus. Series: Major World Leaders. 2002, Chelsea $30.00 (978-0-7910-6945-5). 112pp. Putin's family life, ambitions to be a spy, and accession to power are all covered in this fine biography. (Rev: BL 2/1/03; HBG 3/03; SLJ 3/03) [947.086]

RINGELBLUM, EMMANUEL

16140 Beyer, Mark. *Emmanuel Ringelblum: Historian of the Warsaw Ghetto* (5–8). Illus. Series: Holocaust Biographies. 2001, Rosen LB $31.95 (978-0-8239-3375-4). 112pp. This true story of a man who recorded events in the Warsaw Ghetto during the Holocaust includes black-and-white photographs. (Rev: BL 10/15/01) [940.53]

SADAT, ANWAR

16141 Kras, Sara Louise. *Anwar Sadat* (5–8). Series: Major World Leaders. 2002, Chelsea $30.00 (978-0-7910-6949-3). 112pp. An absorbing account of the life of the famous Egyptian leader who shared the 1978 Nobel Peace Prize with Israeli Prime Minister Menachem Begin. (Rev: BL 1/1–15/03; HBG 3/03) [921]

SANTA ANNA, ANTONIO LOPEZ DE

16142 Bankston, John. *Antonio López de Santa Anna* (5–7). Series: Latinos in American History. 2003, Mitchell Lane LB $29.95 (978-1-58415-209-5). 48pp. A biography of the Mexican general, president, and statesman who is best known for his part in the Battle of the Alamo. (Rev: BL 1/1–15/04; HBG 4/04; SLJ 2/04) [921]

SCHLIEMANN, HEINRICH

16143 Schlitz, Laura Amy. *The Hero Schliemann: The Dreamer Who Dug for Troy* (4–6). Illus. by

Robert Byrd. 2006, Candlewick $17.99 (978-0-7636-2283-1). 72pp. This frank biography of Heinrich Schliemann reveals the flaws in the man who excavated Troy. (Rev: SLJ 9/06) [921]

SIEGAL, ARANKA

16144 Siegal, Aranka. *Memories of Babi* (4–7). 2008, Farrar $16.00 (978-0-374-39978-8). 128pp. The author recalls her pleasant, simple life as a child in Hungary and her closeness to her Jewish grandmother in the years preceding those covered in *Upon the Head of a Goat* (1981). (Rev: BL 12/15/07; HB 9/08) [947.7]

SOCRATES

16145 Dell, Pamela. *Socrates: Ancient Greek in Search of Truth* (5–8). Illus. Series: Signature Lives. 2006, Compass Point LB $34.60 (978-0-7565-1874-5). 112pp. A solid profile of the Greek philosopher that underlines his importance and provides insight into life in ancient Athens. (Rev: BL 10/15/06) [183]

16146 Usher, M. D. *Wise Guy: The Life and Philosophy of Socrates* (2–4). Illus. by William Bramhall. 2005, Farrar $16.00 (978-0-374-31249-7). 40pp. This is a useful but not altogether successful effort to combine a life of Socrates, including his childhood, and a discussion of his philosophical beliefs. (Rev: BL 1/1–15/06; SLJ 1/06) [921]

SOYER, ALEXIS

16147 Arnold, Ann. *The Adventurous Chef: Alexis Soyer* (3–6). Illus. 2002, Farrar $17.00 (978-0-374-31665-5). 40pp. A fascinating, well-illustrated biography that introduces a famous 19th-century chef and innovator who cooked for the rich but also strove to improve nutrition for the poor, the hungry, and the military. (Rev: BL 12/15/02; HB 11/02; HBG 3/03; SLJ 10/02) [641.5]

STEINER, MATTHEW

16148 Warren, Andrea. *Escape from Saigon: How a Vietnam War Orphan Became an American Boy* (5–12). Illus. 2004, Farrar $17.00 (978-0-374-32224-3). 128pp. An inspiring account of a young Amerasian war orphan's long journey from Vietnam to a new and successful life in the United States; Long was part of the 1975 Operation Babylift and took the name of Matt Steiner when he was adopted by an American family. (Rev: BL 6/1–15/04*; SLJ 10/04) [959.704]

SU, DONGPO

16149 Demi. *Su Dongpo: Chinese Genius* (2–4). Illus. 2006, Lee & Low $24.00 (978-1-58430-256-8). 56pp. This picture-book biography chronicles the life and accomplishments of Su Dongpo (also known as Su Shi), a Chinese poet and statesman in the 11th century. (Rev: BL 11/1/06; SLJ 11/06) [921]

SUGIHARA, CHIUNE

16150 Gold, Alison L. *A Special Fate: Chiune Sugihara: Hero of the Holocaust* (5–10). 2000, Scholastic paper $15.95 (978-0-590-39525-0). 176pp. The life story of the Japanese diplomat who saved thousands of Jewish lives during the Holocaust while he was stationed in Lithuania. (Rev: BCCB 5/00; BL 4/1/00; HB 5/00; HBG 10/00; SLJ 5/00; VOYA 6/00) [921]

SUZUKI, SHINICHI

16151 Collins, David R. *Dr. Shinichi Suzuki: Teaching Music from the Heart* (4–8). 2001, Morgan Reynolds LB $23.95 (978-1-883846-49-7). 112pp. This account covers Suzuki's childhood, his interest in music, and his development of a successful method of teaching music, especially the violin, to young children. (Rev: BL 12/15/01; HBG 3/02; SLJ 4/02; VOYA 10/03) [780]

TAMANG, JHALAK MAN

16152 Miller, Raymond H. *Jhalak Man Tamang: Slave Labor Whistleblower* (4–7). Series: Young Heroes. 2006, Gale LB $23.70 (978-0-7377-3616-8). 48pp. This biography chronicles the life of Tamang, who was able to escape a life as a child weaving carpets in Nepal and bring to light the abuses of the industry. (Rev: SLJ 6/07) [921]

TENZING NORGAY

16153 Burleigh, Robert. *Tiger of the Snows: Tenzing Norgay: The Boy Whose Dream Was Everest* (4–6). Illus. by Ed Young. 2006, Simon & Schuster $16.95 (978-0-689-83042-6). 40pp. This picture-book biography of Tenzing Norgay uses beautiful illustrations and poetry to tell the story of the Sherpa guide who conquered Mount Everest in 1953 with Sir Edmund Hillary. (Rev: BL 6/1–15/06; SLJ 6/06) [921]

TERESA, MOTHER

16154 Barraclough, John. *Mother Teresa* (2–3). Series: Lives and Times. 1997, Heinemann $19.92 (978-1-57572-562-8). 24pp. A simple picture-book biography that gives a very brief introduction to the life and contributions of Mother Teresa. (Rev: BL 3/15/98) [921]

16155 Demi. *Mother Teresa* (3–5). Illus. 2005, Simon & Schuster $19.95 (978-0-689-86407-0). 40pp. This informative picture-book biography looks at the nun's life, mission, and religious devotion. (Rev: BL 1/1–15/05; SLJ 2/05) [291]

16156 Dils, Tracey E. *Mother Teresa* (4–8). Series: Women of Achievement. 2001, Chelsea $30.00 (978-0-7910-5887-9). 112pp. An absorbing account of the humanitarian's life from her childhood in Albania through her early years in India and her international work with the Missionaries of Charity. (Rev: HBG 3/02; SLJ 11/01) [921]

16157 Ganeri, Anita. *Mother Teresa's Alms Bowl* (2–4). Illus. by Leighton Noyes. Series: Stories of

Great People. 2008, Crabtree LB $29.27 (978-0-7787-3690-5); paper $9.95 (978-0-7787-3712-4). 40pp. A fictional story is used as the framework for solid information about the nun and her work. (Rev: BL 4/1/08; SLJ 7/08) [921]

16158 Jacobs, William J. *Mother Teresa: Helping the Poor* (3–5). Illus. Series: Gateway Biographies. 1991, Millbrook LB $23.90 (978-1-56294-020-1). 48pp. An admiring portrait of this woman of compassion and peace, including an overview of her work with the poor. (Rev: BL 1/1/92; SLJ 1/92) [921]

16159 Johnson, Linda C. *Mother Teresa: Protector of the Sick* (5–8). Illus. Series: Library of Famous Women. 1991, Blackbirch $24.95 (978-1-56711-034-0). 64pp. Tracing Mother Teresa's life from her childhood in Yugoslavia to her renowned efforts to aid the sick around the world. (Rev: BL 3/15/93) [921]

16160 Mohan, Claire J. *The Young Life of Mother Teresa of Calcutta* (4–6). Illus. by Jane Robbins. 1996, Young Sparrow $14.95 (978-0-943135-26-7); paper $7.99 (978-0-943135-25-0). 64pp. This biography concentrates on Mother Teresa's life from when she was called to serve God at age 12 to her leaving the convent to go to Calcutta. (Rev: SLJ 1/97) [921]

16161 Morgan, Nina. *Mother Teresa: Saint of the Poor* (4–7). Illus. 1998, Raintree paper $7.95 (978-0-8172-7848-9). 48pp. A biography of the nun whose work with the poor of India made her an international celebrity and earned her a Nobel Peace Prize. (Rev: BL 7/98; HBG 10/98; SLJ 7/98) [921]

16162 Ransom, Candice F. *Mother Teresa* (1–3). Illus. by Elaine Verstraete. Series: On My Own Biography. 2001, Carolrhoda LB $23.93 (978-1-57505-441-4). 48pp. Mother Teresa's life from childhood and devotion to charitable work are presented in easy-reading text and full-page, realistic art. (Rev: HBG 10/01; SLJ 7/01) [921]

16163 Rice, Tanya. *Mother Teresa* (5–8). Illus. Series: The Life and Times Of. 1999, Chelsea LB $12.95 (978-0-7910-4637-1). A straightforward account of the life of Mother Teresa, from her birth in Albania to devout Catholic parents and her religious calling as a child, to her work in India and her commitment to helping the poor, to the winning of the Nobel Peace Prize, and her death. (Rev: SLJ 8/98) [921]

16164 Tilton, Rafael. *Mother Teresa* (4–8). Series: The Importance Of. 2000, Lucent LB $27.45 (978-1-56006-565-4). This thoroughly researched account describes the life of Mother Teresa and gives an honest appraisal of her importance. (Rev: BL 1/1–15/00; HBG 9/00) [921]

16165 Weiss, Ellen. *Mother Teresa: A Life of Kindness* (1–3). Illus. by Tina Walski. Series: Blastoff! Readers: People of Character. 2007, Children's Pr. LB $20.00 (978-0-531-14714-6). 24pp. For beginning readers, this is a simple account of Mother Teresa's life and work for the poor. (Rev: SLJ 1/08) [921]

THERESE OF LISIEUX, SAINT

16166 Driscoll, Chris. *God's Little Flower: The Story of St. Therese of Lisieux* (PS–3). Illus. by Patrick Kelley. 2001, Ambassador $13.95 (978-1-929039-05-0). 32pp. A simple, illustrated story of the little girl who became a saint. (Rev: BL 10/1/01; HBG 10/01) [270]

TOUSSAINT L'OUVERTURE, FRANÇOIS-DOMINIQUE

16167 Rockwell, Anne. *Open the Door to Liberty: A Biography of Toussaint L' Ouverture* (5–8). Illus. by R. Gregory Christie. 2009, Houghton $18.00 (978-0-618-60570-5). 80pp. A well-written and well-researched biography of the freed slave who led a rebellion against the French in 1793 on what is now known as Haiti. (Rev: BL 2/1/09; SLJ 3/09) [921]

TRYSZYNSKA, LUBA

16168 Tryszynska-Frederick, Luba. *Luba: The Angel of Bergen-Belsen* (3–6). Illus. by Ann Marshall. 2004, Tricycle $17.99 (978-1-58246-098-7). 48pp. The true story of Luba Tryszynska, a Polish Jew who sheltered and fed more than 50 Dutch Jewish children she found abandoned near her Bergen-Belsen barracks, is recounted in simple, moving prose and accompanied by factual front and back matter. (Rev: BL 11/1/03; HBG 4/04; SLJ 12/03)

TUTANKHAMEN, KING

16169 Hawass, Zahi. *Tutankhamun: The Mystery of the Boy King* (4–7). Illus. 2005, National Geographic $17.95 (978-0-7922-8354-6). 64pp. The director of excavations at key Egyptian archaeological sites offers a fascinating account of the life, death, and burial of King Tut and of new revelations about his fate. (Rev: BL 11/1/05; SLJ 10/05*) [932]

16170 Sabuda, Robert. *Tutankhamen's Gift* (K–4). Illus. 1994, Atheneum $17.00 (978-0-689-31818-4). 32pp. A fictionalized account of the boyhood of Tutankhamen and how he became pharaoh at an early age. (Rev: BL 4/15/94; SLJ 5/94) [921]

16171 Stewart, David. *You Wouldn't Want to Be Tutankhamen! A Mummy Who Really Got Meddled With* (3–6). Illus. by David Antram. Series: You Wouldn't Want to . . . 2007, Watts LB $28.50 (978-0-531-18725-8); paper $9.95 (978-0-531-18924-5). 32pp. An entertaining look at the boy king and the problems he faced. Cartoons keep the tone light. (Rev: SLJ 8/07)

VILLA, PANCHO

16172 O'Brien, Steven. *Pancho Villa* (5–9). Series: Hispanics of Achievement. 1994, Chelsea LB $21.95 (978-0-7910-1257-4). The life and accomplishments of this Mexican freedom fighter. (Rev: BL 9/15/94; VOYA 8/94) [921]

WALLENBERG, RAOUL

16173 Linnea, Sharon. *Raoul Wallenberg: The Man Who Stopped Death* (5–7). Illus. 1993, Jewish Publication Soc. paper $9.95 (978-0-8276-0448-3). 120pp. This Swedish architect saved thousands of Jews in Hungary from the Nazi Holocaust. (Rev: BL 6/1–15/93) [940]

16174 McArthur, Debra. *Raoul Wallenberg: Rescuing Thousands from the Nazis' Grasp* (5–7). Series: Holocaust Heroes and Nazi Criminals. 2005, Enslow LB $27.93 (978-0-7660-2530-1). 160pp. A well-documented profile of the courageous Swedish diplomat who saved thousands of Hungarian Jews and disappeared after the end of the war. (Rev: SLJ 11/05) [921]

WEISSBERGER, ELA

16175 Rubin, Susan G., and Ela Weissberger. *The Cat with the Yellow Star: Coming of Age in Terezin* (3–6). 2006, Holiday House $16.95 (978-0-8234-1831-2). 40pp. A survivor of the Terezin death camp recalls her time there as a child, especially playing the role of a cat in the opera Brundibar; photographs and other features help young children to understand what happened at the camp. (Rev: SLJ 6/06*) [940.53]

WIESENTHAL, SIMON

16176 Rubin, Susan G. *The Anne Frank Case: Simon Wiesenthal's Search for the Truth* (4–7). Illus. by Bill Farnsworth. 2009, Holiday $18.95 (978-0-8234-2109-1). 40pp. This profile of the Nazi hunter and his career starts with an account of Holocaust deniers prompting Wiesenthal to search for the Gestapo officer who arrested Anne Frank's family. (Rev: BCCB 4/09; BL 3/1/09; SLJ 3/09) [921]

WILLIAM, PRINCE

16177 Dougherty, Terri. *Prince William* (5–8). Series: People in the News. 2001, Lucent LB $32.45 (978-1-56006-982-9). Using many quotes, good photographs, and an interesting text, this is a biography of the royal Prince Charming. (Rev: BL 4/1/02) [921]

16178 Landau, Elaine. *Prince William: W.O.W., William of Wales* (4–6). Illus. Series: Gateway Biographies. 2002, Millbrook LB $23.90 (978-0-7613-2120-0). 48pp. A competent biography that explores the life of the very popular prince and his family through text and many color photographs. (Rev: BL 4/15/02; HBG 10/02) [921]

16179 Wyborny, Sheila. *Prince William* (4–7). Illus. Series: Famous People. 2003, Gale $26.20 (978-0-7377-1401-2). 48pp. An interesting biography of the young prince that covers his mother's death and the difficulties of living in the limelight, with lots of color photographs. (Rev: BL 6/1–15/03) [941.085]

XIAOPING, DENG

16180 Stewart, Whitney. *Deng Xiaoping: Leader in a Changing China* (4–7). Series: Lerner Biographies. 2001, Lerner LB $30.35 (978-0-8225-4962-8). 128pp. An accessible biography of the most powerful man in China from the 1970s until his death, with details of how his reputation was tarnished by the Tiananmen Square massacre. (Rev: BL 9/15/01; HBG 10/01; SLJ 7/01) [921]

YEBOAH, EMMANUEL OFOSU

16181 Currie-Mcghee, Leanne K. *Emmanuel Ofosu Yeboah: Champion for Ghana's Disabled* (4–7). Series: Young Heroes. 2006, Gale LB $23.70 (978-0-7377-3614-4). 48pp. The inspiring story of a disabled Ghanaian who fought for equal rights in a culture that discriminated against the physically challenged. (Rev: SLJ 6/07)

ZHENG HE

16182 Zhang, Hao Yu, and Song Nan Zhang. *The Great Voyages of Zheng He* (4–6). Illus. by Song Nan Zhang. 2005, Pan Asian $16.95 (978-1-57227-088-6). 32pp. The voyages of discovery of Zheng He, a Chinese explorer in the early 1400s, are described in this large-format, richly illustrated volume. (Rev: BL 10/15/05; SLJ 11/05) [910.92]

The Arts and Language

Art and Architecture

General and Miscellaneous

16183 *A Is for Artist* (PS–1). Illus. 1997, Getty Museum $16.95 (978-0-89236-377-3). 60pp. Using an alphabetical approach, this book introduces 26 glorious paintings from the Getty Museum. (Rev: BL 10/15/97; HBG 3/98) [708.194]

16184 Agee, Jon, et al. *Why Did the Chicken Cross the Road?* (1–4). Illus. 2006, Dial $16.99 (978-0-8037-3094-6). Why did the chicken cross the road? Fourteen artists — including Chris Raschka, Mo Willems, and Jerry Pinkney — answer the question. (Rev: BCCB 11/06; BL 10/1/06; HBG 4/07; LMC 3/07; SLJ 10/06*) [741.5]

16185 Ajmera, Maya, and John D. Ivanko. *To Be an Artist* (K–3). Illus. 2004, Charlesbridge $15.95 (978-1-57091-503-1). 32pp. This photo-filled excursion shows young people in countries around the world participating in various artistic activities; a map pinpoints their locations. (Rev: BL 3/1/04; SLJ 3/04) [700]

16186 Alcraft, Rob. *Zoom City* (3–6). Illus. by Jonathan Adams. 1998, Heinemann LB $17.95 (978-1-57572-717-2). 32pp. Using strange camera angles and perspectives, this view of city life includes full-page photos of a traffic jam, underground life, a harbor, a skyscraper, parks, and a stadium. (Rev: HBG 10/99; SLJ 3/99) [725]

16187 Ancona, George. *Murals: Walls That Sing* (5–8). Illus. 2003, Marshall Cavendish $17.95 (978-0-7614-5131-0). 48pp. A photoessay showing murals stretching back from today's urban frescos to the cave paintings of Lascaux. (Rev: BL 4/15/03; HBG 4/04; SLJ 5/03) [751.7]

16188 Andrews-Goebel, Nancy. *The Pot That Juan Built* (2–4). Illus. by David Diaz. 2002, Lee & Low $16.95 (978-1-58430-038-0). 32pp. This almost-multimedia introduction to the work of Mexican potter Juan Quezada allows the reader to choose between rhyme, prose, illustration, and photography

that all describe facets of the artist's life and work. (Rev: BL 9/15/02; HBG 3/03; SLJ 9/02*) [738]

16189 *Artist to Artist: 23 Major Illustrators Talk to Children About Their Art* (5–8). Illus. 2007, Philomel $30.00 (978-0-399-24600-5). 64pp. More than 20 children's book illustrators (including Quentin Blake, Leo Lionni, and Tomie dePaola) contribute creative self-portraits and insightful thoughts to this beautiful gatefolded book. (Rev: BL 11/1/07; SLJ 10/07) [741.6]

16190 Barber, Nicola. *Islamic Art and Culture* (5–8). Illus. Series: World Art and Culture. 2005, Raintree LB $32.86 (978-1-4109-1105-6). 56pp. High-quality color photographs document the architecture, sculpture, painting, pottery, music, dance, and other art forms found in the Islamic world from early times to the present. (Rev: BL 4/1/04)

16191 Bingham, Jane. *Illusion Art* (3–6). Illus. Series: Art off the Wall. 2006, Heinemann LB $32.86 (978-1-4034-8290-7). 56pp. The optical illusion on the cover of this book will draw in young artists who would like to create similar works. Professional artists and their techniques are featured. (Rev: SLJ 5/07)

16192 Bingham, Jane. *Indian Art and Culture* (5–8). Illus. Series: World Art and Culture. 2004, Raintree LB $29.99 (978-0-7398-6607-8). 56pp. High-quality color photographs document the architecture, sculpture, painting, pottery, music, dance, and other art forms found in India from early times to the present. Also use *Aboriginal Art and Culture* (2004). (Rev: BL 4/1/04; SLJ 2/04) [709]

16193 Bingham, Jane. *Science and Technology* (4–7). Series: Through Artists' Eyes. 2006, Raintree LB $32.86 (978-1-4109-2241-0). 56pp. A brief but interesting exploration of the ways in which artists have documented the progress of science and technology over the years. Also use *Landscape and the Environment* and *Society and Class* (both 2006). (Rev: SLJ 1/07)

16194 Bingham, Jane. *War and Conflict* (3–5). Illus. Series: Through Artists' Eyes. 2006, Raintree LB

$23.00 (978-1-4109-2236-6). 56pp. This title examines works of art — fine art but also cartoons, posters, films, stories, plays, and poems — that explore themes of war and conflict. (Rev: BL 8/06; SLJ 1/07) [700]

16195 Björk, Christina. *Linnea in Monet's Garden* (1–4). Trans. by Joan Sandin. Illus. by Lena Anderson. 1987, Farrar $13.00 (9-129-58314-4). 56pp. Linnea, a young French girl, learns about flowers, the painter Monet, and Impressionism from her friend Mr. Bloom. (Rev: BL 12/1/87)

16196 Blake, Quentin. *Tell Me a Picture* (K–6). Illus. by author. 2003, Millbrook LB $29.90 (978-0-7613-2748-6). 128pp. Adapted from an exhibit at London's National Gallery, this book contains 26 pictures — some from picture books and others from British art galleries — and guidance for finding the story in each. (Rev: HB 7/03; HBG 10/03; SLJ 10/03)

16197 Blanquet, Claire-Helene. *Miró: Earth and Sky* (5–7). Trans. from French by John Goodman. Illus. Series: Art for Children. 1994, Chelsea LB $15.95 (978-0-7910-2813-1). 59pp. Using a conversational style and some fictitious characters, the life and works of the famous 20th-century French painter Miró are introduced. (Rev: SLJ 12/94) [709]

16198 Blizzard, Gladys S. *Come Look with Me: Enjoying Art with Children* (1–4). Illus. 1991, Thomasson-Grant $15.95 (978-0-934738-76-7). 32pp. Readers are urged to examine 12 paintings of children by famous artists. (Rev: BCCB 5/91; BL 6/1/91) [750.1]

16199 Blizzard, Gladys S. *Come Look with Me: Exploring Landscape Art with Children* (1–4). Illus. 1992, Thomasson-Grant $15.95 (978-0-934738-95-8). 32pp. For primary-grade youngsters, this is an introduction to different styles of landscape painting as seen through the work of 12 important artists. (Rev: BL 3/1/92; HB 9/92) [758.1]

16200 Blizzard, Gladys S. *Come Look with Me: World of Play* (1–4). Illus. 1993, Thomasson-Grant $15.95 (978-1-56566-031-1). 32pp. This art appreciation book reproduces 11 paintings and one sculpture that depict various ways in which children play. (Rev: BL 9/1/93) [701.1]

16201 Bos, Samone. *Super Structures* (5–8). Illus. by Alessandro Rabatti. 2008, DK $19.99 (978-0-7566-4088-0). 80pp. Captivating photographs, illustrations, and diagrams enhance the text in this fascinating survey of buildings and structures across history. (Rev: BL 12/1/08; SLJ 3/09) [720]

16202 Brewster, Hugh. *Carnation, Lily, Lily, Rose: The Story of a Painting* (3–5). Illus. by John Singer Sargent. 2007, Kids Can $17.95 (978-1-55453-137-0). 48pp. Kate, an English girl who hopes to be a model for John Singer Sargent's painting *Carnation, Lily, Lily, Rose,* is disappointed when he chooses other children, then relieved when she realizes the difficulty of being an artist's model in this fictionalized story illustrated with photographs and reproductions of Sargent's work and drawing on primary sources. (Rev: BL 11/1/07; LMC 1/08; SLJ 1/08) [813]

16203 Browne, Anthony. *The Shape Game* (K–4). Illus. by author. 2003, Farrar $16.00 (978-0-374-36764-0). 32pp. Browne's inventive account of a visit to an art museum offers plenty of humor and facts about art. (Rev: HB 9/03; HBG 4/04; SLJ 9/03) [708]

16204 Capek, Michael. *Artistic Trickery: The Tradition of Trompe l'Oeil Art* (5–8). Illus. 1995, Lerner LB $22.60 (978-0-8225-2064-1). 64pp. The art of creating images so perfect that the viewer thinks they are real is introduced, with many historical and contemporary examples. (Rev: BCCB 7–8/95; BL 6/1–15/95; SLJ 7/95) [758]

16205 Capek, Michael. *Murals: Cave, Cathedral, to Street* (5–8). Illus. 1996, Lerner LB $28.80 (978-0-8225-2065-8). 80pp. A history of mural painting, from cave painting to such modern masters as Diego Rivera. (Rev: BL 6/1–15/96; SLJ 10/96; VOYA 10/96) [751.7]

16206 Carter, David A. *600 Black Spots: A Pop-up Book for Children of All Ages* (3–6). Illus. by author. 2007, Simon & Schuster $19.99 (978-1-4169-4092-0). 24pp. More suitable for display than circulation, this marvel of paper engineering stimulates its audience with colorful abstract paper sculptures, each spread containing a challenge to find a given number of black spots. (Rev: BL 11/1/07; SLJ 1/08) [735]

16207 Chaplik, Dorothy. *Latin American Arts and Cultures* (5–8). Illus. 2001, Davis $26.95 (978-0-87192-547-3). 128pp. An encompassing look at Latin American art, architecture, and culture, from pre-Columbian to present-day, complete with pronunciation guide and captioned reproductions or photographs on each page. (Rev: BL 11/1/01) [700.9]

16208 Chapman, Caroline. *Battles and Weapons: Exploring History Through Art* (4–9). Series: Picture That! 2007, Two-Can $19.95 (978-1-58728-588-2). 64pp. A look at how weapons and war have been depicted in artwork beginning in ancient times and ending in the 1950s. (Rev: SLJ 8/07)

16209 Coyne, Jennifer Tarr. *Come Look with Me: Discovering Women Artists for Children* (4–7). Illus. Series: Come Look with Me. 2005, Lickle $15.95 (978-1-890674-08-3). 32pp. Beautifully reproduced examples of works by women artists are paired with brief biographical information and questions that direct the reader's attention to different aspects of art. (Rev: BL 5/1/05; SLJ 6/05) [709]

16210 Cressy, Judith. *Can You Find It?* (2–5). Illus. 2002, Abrams $15.95 (978-0-8109-3279-1). 48pp. Readers are challenged to search for details (bows, cats, flowers, and other items) within artwork from New York City's Metropolitan Museum of Art. (Rev: BL 2/15/03; HBG 3/03; SLJ 1/03) [759]

16211 Cressy, Judith. *Can You Find It, Too? Search and Discover More Than 150 Details in 20 Works of Art* (2–5). 2004, Abrams $15.95 (978-0-8109-5046-7). 40pp. This sequel to *Can You Find It?* (2003) invites readers to search for features of 20 pieces of art. (Rev: BL 11/1/04) [750]

16212 Delafosse, Claude. *Animals* (PS–2). Illus. by Tony Ross. Series: First Discovery Art. 1995, Scholastic $11.95 (978-0-590-55202-8). 26pp. Youngsters are introduced to art through a series of laminated pages that alternate with transparencies and give the impression of change and motion. (Rev: BL 1/1–15/96; SLJ 1/96) [701]

16213 Delafosse, Claude. *Landscapes* (4–7). Illus. Series: First Discovery Art. 1996, Scholastic $11.95 (978-0-590-50216-0). 24pp. The art and techniques of landscape painting are introduced, with many examples from the masters in various historical periods. (Rev: BL 6/1–15/96; SLJ 7/96) [750]

16214 Delafosse, Claude. *Paintings* (4–7). Illus. Series: First Discovery Art. 1996, Scholastic $11.95 (978-0-590-55201-1). 28pp. A general introduction to painting, with many reproductions and lessons in art appreciation. (Rev: BL 6/1–15/96; SLJ 7/96) [750]

16215 Delafosse, Claude. *Portraits* (PS–2). Illus. by Tony Ross. Series: First Discovery Art. 1995, Scholastic $11.95 (978-0-590-55200-4). 26pp. Objects gain new dimensions when seen through transparencies in this introduction to art appreciation. (Rev: BL 1/1–15/96; SLJ 1/96) [701]

16216 Desnoëttes, Caroline. *Look Closer: Art Masterpieces Through the Ages* (3–6). 2006, Walker $18.95 (978-0-8027-9614-1). Readers' attention to the diverse masterpieces is focused through the innovative use of flaps that ask questions, offer information, and pinpoint areas of interest. (Rev: SLJ 12/06) [759]

16217 D'Harcourt, Claire. *Art Up Close: From Ancient to Modern* (3–5). 2003, Chronicle $19.95 (2-02-059694-6). 63pp. Readers are challenged to find details in 23 representative works that span the history of art; the second part of this oversize book with flaps provides information on the works and artists. (Rev: HBG 4/04; SLJ 12/03) [709]

16218 D'Harcourt, Claire. *Masterpieces Up Close: Western Painting from the 14th to 20th Centuries* (4–8). Trans. from French by Shoshanna Kirk. Series: Up Close. 2006, Chronicle $22.95 (978-0-8118-5403-0). 63pp. An oversize volume that challenges readers to analyze major works of Western art. (Rev: SLJ 7/06) [759]

16219 Domeniconi, David. *M Is for Masterpiece: An Art Alphabet* (4–6). Illus. by Will Bullas. 2006, Sleeping Bear $17.95 (978-1-58536-276-9). 32pp. An A-to-Z look at the world of art, covering everything from famous artists and artwork to different art styles and the various tools needed. (Rev: BL 12/1/06; SLJ 11/06) [700]

16220 Finley, Carol. *Aboriginal Art of Australia: Exploring Cultural Traditions* (5–9). Series: Art Around the World. 1999, Lerner LB $23.93 (978-0-8225-2076-4). 56pp. The author covers aboriginal art, aboriginal beliefs, and the contemporary works that reflect the Australian natives' struggle for equality. (Rev: HBG 3/00; SLJ 11/99) [701]

16221 Fisanick, Christina, ed. *Eco-Architecture* (5–10). Series: Opposing Viewpoints. 2008, Gale $36.20 (978-0-7377-3996-1); paper $24.95 (978-0-

7377-3997-8). 234pp. This is a wide-ranging discussion of green building techniques and the benefits to the environment. (Rev: SLJ 11/08) [720]

16222 Forward, Toby. *Shakespeare's Globe: An Interactive Pop-up Theatre* (5–8). Illus. by Juan Wijngaard. 2005, Candlewick $19.99 (978-0-7636-2694-5). 14pp. A large-format pop-up model of the Globe Theatre, with narrative by a Shakespeare colleague and scenes from Shakespeare's plays. (Rev: BL 5/1/05; SLJ 11/05) [792]

16223 Gibbons, Gail. *The Art Box* (PS–3). Illus. 1998, Holiday House $16.95 (978-0-8234-1386-7). 32pp. In a series of brightly colored illustrations, the author displays the various tools and supplies that an artist uses. (Rev: BL 9/15/98; HBG 3/99; SLJ 12/98) [702]

16224 Goldberg, Dana, ed. *On My Block: Stories and Paintings by Fifteen Artists* (1–5). 2007, Children's Book Pr. $16.95 (978-0-89239-220-9). 32pp. A visually engaging array of artwork by diverse artists that offer readers a specific sense of place. (Rev: SLJ 12/07) [704]

16225 Gonyea, Mark. *Another Book About Design: Complicated Doesn't Make It Bad* (3–5). Illus. by author. 2007, Holt $19.95 (978-0-8050-7576-2). 64pp. Foreground and background, positive and negative space, and repetitive use of shapes are among the design concepts introduced here, with each principle progressing toward a finished picture. (Rev: BCCB 10/07; BL 7/07; SLJ 9/07) [745.5]

16226 Gonyea, Mark. *A Book About Design: Complicated Doesn't Make It Good* (3–5). Illus. 2005, Hyperion $18.95 (978-0-7868-7575-7). 144pp. A stylish but challenging introduction to the principles of graphic design, covering topics including shape, color, and contrast and providing plenty of illustrations to help young artists see what good design looks like. (Rev: BL 5/1/05; SLJ 7/05) [745.4]

16227 Harris, Nathaniel. *Mosaics* (4–6). Illus. 2008, PowerKids LB $18.95 (978-1-4042-4438-2). 32pp. This broad introduction defines mosaics and discusses how they are made, then looks at some individual mosaics and provides four craft ideas. (Rev: BL 12/15/08; SLJ 7/09) [738.5]

16228 Harris, Nathaniel. *Wall Paintings* (4–8). Series: Stories in Art. 2008, Rosen LB $25.25 (978-1-4042-4440-5). 30pp. What are wall paintings? How are they made? After a discussion of mural history and techniques, the author looks at outstanding examples and presents three visually engaging projects with clear directions and interesting stories. (Rev: LMC 8/09; SLJ 7/09) [751.7]

16229 Henry, Sandi. *Making Amazing Art: 40 Activities Using the 7 Elements of Art Design* (2–5). Illus. by Sarah Cole. Series: Kids Can. 2007, Williamson $16.99 (978-0-8249-6794-9); paper $12.99 (978-0-8249-6795-6). 128pp. This title takes one artistic concept (shape, texture, color, for example) at at time and teams it with projects that clarify and extend the concept. (Rev: SLJ 12/07) [745.5]

16230 Heslewood, Juliet. *The History of Western Painting: A Young Person's Guide* (5–9). Illus. 1995, Raintree LB $25.68 (978-0-8172-4000-4).

64pp. Beginning with cave paintings, this large-format book gives a cursory overview of Western painting, with several pages devoted to contemporary artists and movements. (Rev: BL 1/1–15/96; SLJ 12/95) [759]

16231 Heslewood, Juliet. *The History of Western Sculpture* (5–9). Illus. 1995, Raintree LB $25.68 (978-0-8172-4001-1). 64pp. This oversize, heavily illustrated book traces the history of Western sculpture from the ancient Greeks to contemporary masters. (Rev: BL 1/1–15/96; SLJ 12/95) [730]

16232 Hibbert, Clare. *Chinese Art and Culture* (5–8). Illus. Series: World Art and Culture. 2005, Raintree LB $29.99 (978-1-4109-1107-0). 56pp. High-quality color photographs document the architecture, sculpture, painting, pottery, music, dance, and other art forms found in China from early times to the present. (Rev: BL 4/1/04)

16233 *The History of Printmaking* (3–6). Illus. Series: Voyages of Discovery. 1996, Scholastic $19.95 (978-0-590-47649-2). 48pp. Overlays and foldouts are used to present a history of prints and print images, including computer images. (Rev: BL 12/15/97) [769]

16234 Hosack, Karen. *Animals* (2–4). Series: How Artists View. 2004, Heinemann LB $24.22 (978-1-4034-4850-7). 32pp. Animals are the subject of this interesting volume in a series that looks at the ways in which artists view and depict various themes. Also in this series are *Nature*, *Families*, *Weather*, *Food*, and *Homes* (all 2004). (Rev: BL 12/1/04) [704.9]

16235 Hosack, Karen. *Paintings* (4–8). Series: What Is Art? 2008, Raintree LB $27.50 (978-1-4109-3162-7). 32pp. This is an attractive introduction to paintings of many styles, asking readers to consider composition, audience, symbolism, and so forth. (Rev: SLJ 3/09) [750]

16236 Jakab, Cheryl. *Clay* (3–6). Illus. Series: Artists at Work. 2007, Smart Apple LB $27.10 (978-1-58340-775-2). 32pp. Readers will learn how artists work in clay and view some of the pieces they have made — both historical and contemporary. Also in this series, use *Metals, Stone,* and *Wood* (2007). (Rev: SLJ 5/07)

16237 Jockel, Nils. *Bruegel's Tower of Babel: The Builder with the Red Hat* (4–7). Illus. Series: Adventures in Art. 1998, Prestel $14.95 (978-3-7913-1941-4). 30pp. A detailed analysis of Pieter Bruegel's surreal masterpiece, using one of the characters in the painting to supply a point of view and an examination of the meaning of its contents. (Rev: BL 8/98; SLJ 8/98) [759.9493]

16238 Johmann, Carol A. *Skyscrapers!* (3–6). Illus. by Michael Kline. Series: Kaleidoscope Kids. 2001, Williamson paper $14.25 (978-1-885593-50-4). 96pp. Cartoonlike drawings and black-and-white photographs are including in this appealing and informative look at skyscrapers, their history, and the structural and design challenges they pose, which also includes a a number of related activities. (Rev: BL 12/15/01; SLJ 3/02) [720]

16239 Kalman, Bobbie. *The Victorian Home* (3–5). Illus. by Barbara Bedell. Series: Historic Communities. 1997, Crabtree LB $25.27 (978-0-86505-431-8); paper $7.95 (978-0-86505-461-5). 32pp. Examines 19th-century homes, their exteriors, interior rooms, and furnishings. (Rev: SLJ 7/97) [690]

16240 Khanduri, Kamini. *Japanese Art and Culture* (5–8). Illus. Series: World Art and Culture. 2004, Raintree LB $29.99 (978-0-7398-6609-2). 56pp. High-quality color photographs document the architecture, sculpture, painting, pottery, music, dance, and other art forms found in Japan from early times to the present. (Rev: BL 4/1/04)

16241 King, Penny, and Clare Roundhill. *Animals* (2–4). Illus. Series: Artists' Workshop. 1996, Crabtree paper $8.95 (978-0-86505-861-3). 32pp. Readers learn how animals are depicted in art, examine six appropriate art works, and are given tips on how to create their own pictures. Also use *Landscapes, Portraits,* and *Stories* (all 1996). (Rev: SLJ 1/97) [709]

16242 King, Penny, and Clare Roundhill. *Myths and Legends* (3–6). Illus. by Lindy Norton. Series: Artists' Workshop. 1997, Crabtree LB $22.60 (978-0-86505-855-2); paper $8.95 (978-0-86505-865-1). 32pp. This book presents famous paintings from the 15th through the 20th century that depict mythological figures and scenes from around the world, as well as works on similar subjects by children. (Rev: HBG 3/98; SLJ 4/98) [750]

16243 King, Penny, and Clare Roundhill. *Sports and Games* (3–6). Illus. by Lindy Norton. Series: Artists' Workshop. 1997, Crabtree LB $22.60 (978-0-86505-854-5). 32pp. Famous works of art from ancient times to the present are combined with children's art to show how various sports such as swimming, sailing, wrestling, and childhood games have been depicted. (Rev: HBG 3/98; SLJ 4/98) [750]

16244 Knapp, Ruthie, and Janice Lehmberg. *Impressionist Art* (5–9). Illus. Series: Off the Wall Museum Guides for Kids. 1999, Davis paper $9.95 (978-0-87192-385-1). 72pp. This pocket-size guide supplies an overview of Impressionism and brief introductions to major artists, including Sisley and Monet. (Rev: BL 1/1–15/99) [709.03]

16245 Knapp, Ruthie, and Janice Lehmberg. *Modern Art* (5–9). Series: Off the Wall Museum Guides for Kids. 2001, Davis paper $9.95 (978-0-87192-458-2). 72pp. A lively and colorful survey of 20th-century art including examples from expressionists, cubists, surrealists, and pop artists. (Rev: BL 8/1/01) [709]

16246 Kutschbach, Doris. *The Blue Rider: The Yellow Cow Sees the World in Blue* (3–7). Trans. by Andrea Belloli. Illus. Series: Adventures in Art. 1997, Prestel $14.95 (3-7913-1811-X). 35pp. This art appreciation volume explores a group of painters — including Klee and Kandinsky — who freed color and form from reality. (Rev: SLJ 1/98) [709]

16247 Lach, William. *Can You Hear It?* (K–3). Illus. 2007, Abrams $18.95 (978-0-8109-5721-3). 32pp. A handsome picture book in which reproductions of artistic masterpieces are paired with classical music selections on the accompanying CD; author Lach suggests connections and focal points and provides information on the artists, composers, and musical instruments. (Rev: BL 3/15/07) [780]

16248 Lane, Kimberly. *Come Look with Me: Asian Art* (3–7). Illus. by author. 2008, Charlesbridge $15.95 (978-1-890674-19-9). 32pp. Lane introduces readers to a wide variety of Asian works of art, prefacing each with pertinent questions. (Rev: BLO 6/17/08; SLJ 8/08) [709.5]

16249 Lane, Kimberly. *Come Look with Me: Latin American Art* (4–8). Illus. Series: Come Look with Me. 2007, Charlesbridge $15.95 (978-1-890674-20-5). 32pp. An oversize introduction to Latin American art over the last two centuries, with color reproductions and information on the artists' lives and techniques. (Rev: BL 8/07; LMC 1/08; SLJ 8/07) [709.8]

16250 Loumaye, Jacqueline. *Chagall: My Sad and Joyous Village* (4–8). Trans. from French by John Goodman. Illus. by Veronique Boiry. Series: Art for Children. 1994, Chelsea LB $25.00 (978-0-7910-2807-0). 57pp. A youngster learns about Chagall and his paintings from a violinist who grew up in the artist's home town in Russia. (Rev: SLJ 8/94) [709]

16251 Loumaye, Jacqueline. *Degas: The Painted Gesture* (4–8). Trans. from French by John Goodman. Illus. by Nadine Massart. Series: Art for Children. 1994, Chelsea LB $25.00 (978-0-7910-2809-4). 57pp. Using a series of workshops for children at the Orsay Museum (Paris) as a focus, the life and works of Degas are introduced. (Rev: SLJ 8/94) [709]

16252 Loumaye, Jacqueline. *Van Gogh: The Touch of Yellow* (4–8). Trans. from French by John Goodman. Illus. by Claudine Roucha. Series: Art for Children. 1994, Chelsea LB $31.00 (978-0-7910-2817-9). 57pp. Two youngsters visit the museums in Amsterdam to learn about van Gogh, his tragic life, and his paintings. (Rev: SLJ 8/94) [709]

16253 MacDonald, Fiona. *Design* (3–5). Illus. Series: Culture Encyclopedia. 2002, Mason Crest LB $18.95 (978-1-59084-476-2). 40pp. The importance of design in such areas as fashion, food, technology, and architecture is discussed in this introduction to style around the world. (Rev: SLJ 3/03)

16254 Mallat, Kathy, and Bruce McMillan. *The Picture That Mom Drew* (2–4). Illus. 1997, Walker LB $15.85 (978-0-8027-8618-0). 24pp. Using "The House That Jack Built" as a framework, the materials and techniques used by an artist are introduced. (Rev: BL 1/1–15/97*; SLJ 4/97) [741.2]

16255 Mark, Jan. *The Museum Book: A Guide to Strange and Wonderful Collections* (3–5). Illus. by Richard Holland. 2007, Candlewick $18.99 (978-0-7636-3370-7). 56pp. This wide-ranging volume introduces the history of museums and the various kinds of collections — whether scientific, historical, or art-based — found around the world, with interesting information on holy relics and other artifacts and on fakes and mistakes. (Rev: BCCB 12/07; BL 11/1/07; HB 1/08; SLJ 1/08) [069]

16256 Mason, Antony. *Art* (3–5). Illus. Series: Culture Encyclopedia. 2002, Mason Crest LB $18.95 (978-1-59084-475-5). 40pp. An introduction to art over the centuries that looks at all kinds of drawing, painting, sculpture, photography, commercial art, and so forth. (Rev: SLJ 3/03)

16257 Micklethwait, Lucy. *A Child's Book of Art: Great Pictures, First Words* (1–4). Illus. 1993, DK $19.99 (978-1-56458-203-4). 64pp. Combines a word book with art appreciation by showing how common concepts like work and numbers are shown in great works of art. (Rev: BL 1/15/94; SLJ 2/94) [701]

16258 Niepold, Mil, and Jean-Yves Verdu. *Oooh! Matisse* (2–4). Illus. by Mil Niepold. 2007, Tricycle $14.95 (978-1-58246-227-1). 48pp. Using bold, colorful shapes from portions of Matisse's works, the reader is challenged to a visual guessing game and is prompted to look at art from different perspective before the painting is revealed in its entirety. (Rev: BL 11/1/07; SLJ 11/07) [759.4]

16259 Nilsen, Anna. *Art Auction Mystery* (5–8). Illus. 2005, Kingfisher $16.95 (978-0-7534-5842-6). 48pp. Wannabe art sleuths are challenged to find forgeries hidden in a selection of world-famous paintings. (Rev: BL 11/1/05; SLJ 1/06; VOYA 12/05) [759]

16260 Nilsen, Anna. *Art Fraud Detective* (4–6). Illus. 2000, Kingfisher $15.95 (978-0-7534-5308-7). 48pp. The reader becomes an art forgery detective in this oversize book that compares originals and forgeries of works by such artists as da Vinci, Picasso, and van Gogh. (Rev: BL 10/15/00; HBG 10/01; SLJ 12/00) [751.5]

16261 Nilsen, Anna. *The Great Art Scandal: Solve the Crime, Save the Show!* (4–9). Illus. 2003, Kingfisher $16.95 (978-0-7534-5587-6). 48pp. Readers must solve a mystery involving an art exhibition in this comic-book-format work that introduces many famous paintings and artists. (Rev: SLJ 3/04) [759.06]

16262 Presilla, Maricel E. *Mola: Cuna Life Stories and Art* (5–7). Illus. 1996, Holt $17.95 (978-0-8050-3801-9). 32pp. An examination of the life and art of the Cuna Indians, who live on islands off the coast of Panama. (Rev: BCCB 1/97; BL 10/1/96; SLJ 10/96) [305.48]

16263 Raczka, Bob. *Art Is . . .* (K–5). 2003, Millbrook LB $22.90 (978-0-7613-2874-2). 32pp. An excellent introductory guide to art and its appreciation, this attractive title exposes readers to images of 26 famous works of art, each of which is accompanied by explanatory text discussing the art's significance and quality. (Rev: HBG 10/03; SLJ 10/03)

16264 Raczka, Bob. *Artful Reading* (1–4). Illus. by author. 2007, Millbrook LB $25.26 (978-0-8225-6754-7). 32pp. These 23 artistic studies of a variety of subjects reading books proves yet again that one picture is worth a thousand words; the artists include Degas, Rossetti, and Picasso. (Rev: SLJ 10/07) [700.4557]

16265 Raczka, Bob. *Here's Looking at Me: How Artists See Themselves* (3–5). 2006, Lerner LB

$23.93 (978-0-7613-3404-0). 32pp. Self-portraits of important artists throughout the ages, with an emphasis on form and technique. (Rev: BL 5/1/06; SLJ 6/06) [760]

16266 Raczka, Bob. *No One Saw: Ordinary Things Through the Eyes of an Artist* (PS–3). Illus. 2002, Millbrook LB $23.90 (978-0-7613-2370-9). 32pp. Simple verse introduces young readers to the singular viewpoints of modern artists including Georgia O'Keeffe and Vincent van Gogh. (Rev: BL 1/1–15/02; HBG 10/02; SLJ 1/02) [759.06]

16267 Raczka, Bob. *Unlikely Pairs: Fun with Famous Works of Art* (4–10). 2005, Millbrook LB $23.93 (978-0-7613-2936-7); paper $9.95 (978-0-7613-2378-5). 32pp. Raczka pairs famous works from different eras and styles (Rodin's "The Thinker" appears to be considering a move on Klee's chessboard, for example); a closing catalog offers factual information. (Rev: SLJ 12/05) [750]

16268 Raczka, Bob. *Where in the World? Around the Globe in 13 Works of Art* (5–8). Illus. Series: Art Adventures. 2007, Lerner LB $23.93 (978-0-8225-6371-6). 32pp. Full-page reproductions and lively text introduce 13 famous works of art, with information on the artist. (Rev: BL 6/1–15/07; SLJ 8/07) [709]

16269 Raimondo, Joyce. *Express Yourself!* (3–5). Illus. Series: Art Explorers. 2005, Watson-Guptill $12.95 (978-0-8230-2506-0). 48pp. Introduces readers to the work of six expressionist painters — Edvard Munch, Vincent van Gogh, Ernest Ludwig Kirchner, Vasily Kandinsky, Willem de Kooning, and Jackson Pollack — and examines a representative work and outlines projects that further illuminate each artist's style. (Rev: BL 11/1/05; SLJ 2/06) [372.5]

16270 Raimondo, Joyce. *Imagine That! Activities and Adventures in Surrealism* (4–6). Series: New Children's: Art Explorers. 2004, Watson-Guptill $12.95 (978-0-8230-2502-2). 48pp. This engaging volume encourages readers to try their hands at projects that incorporate elements of surrealism. (Rev: BL 12/1/04; SLJ 9/04) [709]

16271 Raimondo, Joyce. *Picture This! Activities and Adventures in Impressionism* (1–5). Illus. 2004, Watson-Guptill $12.95 (978-0-8230-2503-9). 48pp. Monet, Pissarro, and Degas are among the artists used to demonstrate the techniques of Impressionism in this volume faturing discussion and step-by-step activities. (Rev: SLJ 1/05) [701]

16272 Renshaw, Amanda. *The Art Book for Children: Book Two* (3–6). Illus. 2007, Phaidon $19.95 (978-0-7148-4706-1). 80pp. This volume contains beautifully reproduced works from a variety of time periods and poses questions that encourage close examination. (Rev: BL 11/1/07; SLJ 2/08) [701]

16273 Richards, Julie. *Stadiums and Domes* (4–6). Illus. Series: Smart Structures. 2003, Smart Apple LB $24.25 (978-1-58340-349-5). 32pp. An overview of the use of the dome in construction, from Roman times to the present, with helpful photographs and diagrams. (Rev: SLJ 3/04) [721]

16274 Richmond, Robin. *Children in Art: The Story in a Picture* (4–6). Illus. by author. 1992, Ideals LB $16.00 (978-0-8249-8588-2). 48pp. Children are introduced to art by the use of pictures with children as subjects. (Rev: BL 12/15/92; SLJ 2/93) [750]

16275 Roalf, Peggy. *Dogs* (5–8). Illus. Series: Looking at Paintings. 1993, Hyperion paper $6.95 (978-1-56282-530-0). 48pp. Various ways that dogs have been represented in paintings are reproduced, with explanations, in this attractive book on art appreciation. (Rev: BL 2/15/94; SLJ 2/94) [758.3]

16276 Rohmer, Harriet, ed. *Just Like Me: Stories and Self-Portraits by Fourteen Artists* (3–6). Illus. 1997, Children's Book Pr. $15.95 (978-0-89239-149-3). 32pp. In double-page spreads, 14 artists, all of whom have produced books for children, talk about themselves and their inspirations. (Rev: BL 9/1/97; HBG 3/98; SLJ 12/97) [704.9]

16277 Rolling, James Haywood, Jr. *Come Look with Me: Discovering African American Art for Children* (K–5). Series: Come Look with Me. 2005, Lickle $15.95 (978-1-890674-07-6). 32pp. Twelve examples of African American art, by artists including Romare Bearden and Jacob Lawrence, are paired with background information and questions that encourage young readers to examine the art. (Rev: SLJ 6/05)

16278 Rubin, Susan G. *Degas and the Dance: The Painter and the Petits Rats, Perfecting Their Art* (3–5). Illus. 2002, Abrams $17.95 (978-0-8109-0567-2). 32pp. This volume, with excellent reproductions of preliminary sketches as well as finished works, will attract budding artists and budding ballet dancers; the "petits rats" are young dancers who posed for the painter. (Rev: BL 12/1/02; HBG 3/03; SLJ 12/02) [759.4]

16279 Rubin, Susan G. *There Goes the Neighborhood: Ten Buildings People Loved to Hate* (4–7). 2001, Holiday $18.95 (978-0-8234-1435-2). 96pp. Many buildings create an uproar from their earliest design but later become nostalgic favorites, among them the Eiffel Tower and Guggenheim Museum, which are profiled here in an absorbing, colorful account that discusses materials and methods of construction. (Rev: BCCB 9/01; BL 8/01; HBG 3/02; SLJ 9/01; VOYA 10/01) [720]

16280 Ruggi, Gilda Williams. *The Art Book for Children* (2–4). Illus. 2005, Phaidon $19.95 (978-0-7148-4511-1). 72pp. Art critic Ruggi introduces young readers to classic and contemporary works of art and encourages critical thinking and creating connections to children's own experiences. (Rev: BL 11/1/05) [701]

16281 Salvi, Francesco. *The Impressionists*. Rev. ed. (5–8). Illus. by L. R. Galante. Series: Art Masters. 2008, Oliver LB $24.95 (978-1-934545-03-4). 64pp. A look at the work of the main artists contributing to this movement: Manet, Monet, Renoir, Degas, Cezanne, Pissaro, Sisley, Morisot, Cassatt, Guillaumin, and Caillebotte; the appealing design will please report writers. (Rev: BL 4/15/08) [759.054]

16282 Sayre, Henry M. *Cave Paintings to Picasso: The Inside Scoop on 50 Famous Masterpieces* (3–7). Illus. 2004, Chronicle Bks. $22.95 (978-0-8118-3767-5). 96pp. This short but impressive historical overview chronicles the evolution of the visual arts from prehistoric cave paintings to the 1960s, presenting 50 major works and including historical context and information on the artist. (Rev: BL 11/1/04; SLJ 10/04) [709]

16283 Schulte, Jessica. *Can You Find It Outside?* (2–4). Illus. 2005, Abrams $10.95 (978-0-8109-5795-4). 32pp. Rhyming text provides clues to help readers find details in these paintings from the collections of New York's Metropolitan Museum of Art. (Rev: BL 11/1/05; SLJ 12/05) [759]

16284 Sellier, Marie. *Matisse from A to Z* (3–7). Trans. from French by Claudia Zoe Bedrick. Illus. 1995, Bedrick LB $14.95 (978-0-87226-475-5). 59pp. The subjects used by Matisse in his paintings and events in his life feature in this unusual alphabet book containing many reproductions of his work. (Rev: SLJ 12/95) [759.4]

16285 Shofner, Shawndra. *Sydney Opera House* (3–6). Series: Modern Wonders of the World. 2006, Creative Editions LB $18.95 (978-1-58341-442-2). 32pp. The story of the construction and current uses of the eye-catching Opera House on Sydney's harbor, completed in 1973. (Rev: BL 10/15/06) [725]

16286 Slaymaker, Melissa Eskridge. *Bottle Houses: The Creative World of Grandma Prisbrey* (1–3). Illus. by Julie Paschkis. 2004, Holt $16.95 (978-0-8050-7131-3). 32pp. Grandma Prisbrey's offbeat creations open young readers' eyes to artistic possibilities. (Rev: BL 3/1/04; HB 7/04; SLJ 9/04) [745]

16287 Sousa, Jean. *Faces, Places, and Inner Spaces* (5–8). Illus. 2006, Abrams $18.95 (978-0-8109-5966-8). 48pp. The director of interpretive exhibitions and family programs at the Art Institute of Chicago introduces a variety of works — portraits, landscapes, and abstract pieces — and asks questions that stimulate analysis. (Rev: BL 5/15/06; SLJ 7/06) [701]

16288 Spilsbury, Richard. *Comics and Graphic Novels* (3–6). Illus. Series: Art off the Wall. 2006, Heinemann LB $32.86 (978-1-4034-8286-0). 56pp. The anime-like cover of this book will draw in young artists who would like to create similar works. Professional artists and their techniques are featured. (Rev: SLJ 5/07)

16289 Swain, Sally. *Once Upon a Picture* (1–5). Illus. by author. 2005, Allen & Unwin $16.95 (978-1-74114-001-9). Four world-famous paintings are used as the departure point for storytelling and additional paintings. (Rev: SLJ 2/06) [759]

16290 Terzian, Alexandra M. *The Kids' Multicultural Art Book: Art and Craft Experiences from Around the World* (3–6). Illus. 1993, Williamson paper $12.95 (978-0-913589-72-4). 160pp. Using a walking tour across the continents as a framework, this book introduces the cultures of many areas in Africa, Asia, and Central America, with a section on the Indians of North America. (Rev: BL 9/1/93; SLJ 8/93) [745]

16291 Thomson, Ruth. *Creatures* (2–5). Illus. Series: First Look at Art. 2004, Chelsea House LB $23.00 (978-0-7910-7945-4). 32pp. Readers are introduced to the elements of art through a variety of works depicting animals and imaginary creatures. Also use *Portraits* (2004). (Rev: BL 5/1/04; SLJ 9/04) [750]

16292 Thomson, Ruth. *Places* (3–6). Illus. Series: A First Look at Art. 2004, Chelsea Clubhouse LB $23.00 (978-0-7910-7947-8). 32pp. Using famous works representing various styles as examples, this book looks at the depiction of landscapes and other places and includes creative activities. Also use *Families* (2004) and *Celebrations* (2005). (Rev: SLJ 9/04) [704.9]

16293 Van Gogh, Vincent. *Vincent's Colors: Words and Pictures by Vincent van Gogh* (1–3). Ed. by William Lach. 2005, Chronicle $14.95 (978-0-8118-5099-5). 48pp. An excellent introduction to the Dutch artist's works, this attractive volume couples key paintings with excerpts from letters Vincent wrote to his brother Theo. (Rev: BL 11/1/05*; HBG 4/06; SLJ 11/05) [759.9]

16294 Vogel, Jennifer. *A Library Story: Building a New Central Library* (4–7). 2006, Lerner $26.60 (978-0-8225-5916-0). 64pp. The construction of the new central library in Minneapolis is the topic of this lively, well-illustrated book that looks at the reasons for the building, architectural and engineering concerns, and artistic choices that were made. (Rev: BL 8/06; SLJ 9/06) [727]

16295 Voss, Gisela. *Museum Colors* (PS–1). Illus. 1994, Museum of Fine Arts, Boston $14.00 (978-0-87846-369-5). 20pp. Works of art are used to point out different colors in this board book. Also use *Museum Numbers* and *Museum Shapes* (both 1994). (Rev: BL 5/1/94; SLJ 8/94) [701.8]

16296 Wallace, Nancy Elizabeth, and Linda K. Friedlaender. *Look! Look! Look!* (K–3). 2006, Marshall Cavendish $16.95 (978-0-7614-5282-9). 40pp. Three mice are so inspired by a beautiful postcard that they learn to make their own pictures; followed by instructions on making a self-portrait postcard. (Rev: BL 5/1/06; SLJ 3/06)

16297 Wenzel, Angela. *Edgar Degas: Dance Like a Butterfly* (4–6). Trans. from German by Rosie Jackson. Series: Adventures in Art. 2002, Prestel $14.95 (3-7913-2736-4). 28pp. Degas's ballet paintings are presented in a way that encourages readers to appreciate movement, light, and color. (Rev: HBG 3/03; SLJ 11/02)

16298 Wenzel, Angela. *Rene Magritte: Now You See It — Now You Don't* (4–7). Illus. Series: Adventures in Art. 1998, Prestel $14.95 (978-3-7913-1873-8). 30pp. An examination of some of the works of Belgian surrealist Rene Magritte. (Rev: BL 8/98; SLJ 8/98) [759.949]

16299 White, Matt. *Cameras on the Battlefield: Photos of War* (5–7). Series: High Five Reading. 2002, Capstone LB $23.93 (978-0-7368-4004-0). 64pp. For reluctant readers, this is an appealing look at photographs of war, both those that celebrate war and those that document its horrors. (Rev: SLJ 8/02) [779.9355]

16300 Wolfe, Gillian. *Look! Body Language in Art* (3–5). 2004, Lincoln $16.95 (978-1-84507-034-2). 40pp. In this excellent introduction to art appreciation, Wolfe asks readers — incorporating activity ideas and leading questions — to observe the body language depicted in paintings by artists including Vincent van Gogh and Pablo Picasso. (Rev: BL 11/1/04) [758.9]

16301 Wolfe, Gillian. *Look! Seeing the Light in Art* (3–5). Illus. 2007, Frances Lincoln $16.95 (978-1-84507-467-8). 48pp. Well-known works of art are presented for readers to observe, focusing on the artist's use of light. (Rev: BL 12/15/07) [750]

16302 Zaunders, Bo. *Gargoyles, Girders, and Glass Houses* (3–6). Illus. by Roxie Munro. 2004, Penguin $17.99 (978-0-525-47284-1). 48pp. Among the architects profiled in this large-format overview of major design and engineering feats are Gustave Eiffel, Antoni Gaudi, and the Roeblings. (Rev: BL 11/1/04; SLJ 12/04) [720.9]

Africa

16303 Finley, Carol. *The Art of African Masks: Exploring Cultural Traditions* (5–9). Series: Art Around the World. 1999, Lerner LB $23.93 (978-0-8225-2078-8). 64pp. This account on African mask making past and present focuses on the western Sudan, the Guinea Coast, and Central Africa. (Rev: HBG 10/99; SLJ 11/99) [745.5]

16304 Stelzig, Christine. *Can You Spot the Leopard? African Masks* (3–6). Trans. from German by Fiona Elliot. Series: Adventures in Art. 1997, Prestel $14.95 (3-7913-1874-8). 28pp. An appealing book that pictures over 30 masks from different African peoples and explains where each came from, how it was made, and its significance. (Rev: SLJ 6/98) [750]

The Ancient World

16305 Chrisp, Peter. *Ancient Rome* (4–8). Series: History in Art. 2004, Raintree LB $29.93 (978-1-4109-0520-8). 48pp. A look at what art can reveal about the culture and technology of a society. (Rev: SLJ 4/05) [709]

16306 Hinshaw, Kelly Campbell. *Ancient Egypt* (1–3). Series: Art Across the Ages. 2007, Chronicle $14.95 (978-0-8118-5668-3); paper $4.95 (978-0-8118-5669-0). 32pp. Simple text and clear photographs introduce the art treasures of ancient Egypt to beginning and reluctant readers. (Rev: LMC 5/08; SLJ 11/07)

16307 Hinshaw, Kelly Campbell. *The Art of Ancient Mexico* (2–4). Illus. Series: Art Across the Ages. 2007, Chronicle $14.95 (978-0-8118-5670-6); paper $4.95 (978-0-8118-5671-3). 32pp. This beautifully illustrated introduction to the art of ancient Mexico

has simple text that is suitable for beginning readers. (Rev: BL 10/15/07; SLJ 11/07) [704.03]

16308 Hodge, Susie. *Prehistoric Art* (3–6). Series: Art in History. 1997, Heinemann LB $24.22 (978-1-57572-553-6). 32pp. This book focuses on the materials and methods used by prehistoric people to create art objects in such areas as the Pacific, Africa, and North and South America. (Rev: SLJ 4/98) [930]

16309 Knapp, Ruthie, and Janice Lehmberg. *Egyptian Art* (5–9). Illus. Series: Off the Wall Museum Guides for Kids. 1999, Davis paper $9.95 (978-0-87192-384-4). 72pp. This pocket-size art appreciation book discusses mummies, sculpture, hieroglyphs, and other artifacts from Egyptian art. (Rev: BL 1/1–15/99) [709.32]

16310 Knapp, Ruthie, and Janice Lehmberg. *Greek and Roman Art* (5–9). Series: Off the Wall Museum Guides for Kids. 2001, Davis paper $9.95 (978-0-87192-549-7). 72pp. Using many photographs, this account highlights a number of art objects, explains relevant terms associated with them, describes their uses, and gives details on Greek and Roman culture. (Rev: BL 8/1/01) [936]

16311 Langley, Andrew. *Ancient Greece* (4–8). Series: History in Art. 2004, Raintree LB $29.93 (978-1-4109-0517-8). 48pp. A look at what art can reveal about the culture and technology of a society. (Rev: SLJ 4/05) [709]

16312 Mann, Elizabeth. *The Parthenon: The Height of Greek Civilization* (4–7). Illus. by Yuan Lee. 2006, Mikaya $22.95 (978-1-931414-15-9). 48pp. The engineering feats involved in the construction of the Parthenon are placed in historical and cultural context; includes a foldout spread, a useful map, and many illustrations. (Rev: BL 12/1/06; SLJ 3/07) [938.5]

16313 Shuter, Jane. *Ancient Chinese Art* (4–6). Illus. Series: Art in History. 2001, Heinemann LB $24.22 (978-1-58810-090-0). 32pp. Painting, calligraphy, bronzes, terracotta, and lacquer and jade are among the art forms featured. (Rev: HB 5/03; HBG 3/02; SLJ 12/01)

16314 Whiting, Jim. *Threat to Ancient Egyptian Treasures* (3–5). Series: A Robbie Reader. On the Verge of Extinction: Crisis in the Environment. 2007, Mitchell Lane LB $25.70 (978-1-58415-588-1). 32pp. Whiting discusses the threats to important archaeological sites in Egypt; a "What You Can Do" section will help emerging activists. (Rev: LMC 1/08; SLJ 11/07) [932]

Native American Arts and Crafts

16315 Finley, Carol. *Art of the Far North: Inuit Sculpture, Drawing, and Printmaking* (4–6). Illus. Series: Art Around the World. 1998, Lerner LB $22.60 (978-0-8225-2075-7). 56pp. Inuit art from 1950 to the present is the focus of this heavily illustrated book containing a lengthy chapter on the influence of myths and legends. (Rev: BL 11/15/98; HBG 10/99; SLJ 1/99) [704.03]

16316 January, Brendan. *Native American Art and Culture* (5–8). Series: World Art and Culture. 2005, Raintree LB $32.86 (978-1-4109-1108-7). 56pp. Pottery, textiles, carving, painting, textiles, and architecture are all discussed, along with body art, ceremonies, songs, and dances; many color photographs are included and a list of museums is appended. (Rev: BL 4/1/04; SLJ 6/05)

16317 Keams, Geri. *Snail Girl Brings Water: A Navajo Story* (2–4). Illus. by Richard Ziehler-Martin. 1998, Rising Moon $15.95 (978-0-87358-662-7). 32pp. A retelling of the Navajo myth that relates how slow-moving Snail Girl was able to bring water to the Earth's surface. (Rev: BL 11/15/98; HBG 10/99; SLJ 5/99) [398.2]

16318 Press, Petra. *Native American Art* (4–6). Illus. Series: Art in History. 2001, Heinemann LB $24.22 (978-1-58810-092-4). 32pp. Rock art, stone sculpture, sand painting, textiles, and basketry are among the kinds of art featured here. (Rev: HBG 3/02; SLJ 12/01)

Middle Ages and the Renaissance

16319 Barter, James. *A Renaissance Painter's Studio* (5–9). Series: The Working Life. 2003, Gale LB $29.95 (978-1-59018-178-2). 112pp. An exploration of daily life for a painter at a time when art was growing in social importance. (Rev: HBG 10/03; SLJ 5/03) [759.5]

16320 Fritz, Jean. *Leonardo's Horse* (4–7). Illus. by Hudson Talbott. 2001, Putnam $18.99 (978-0-399-23576-4). 40pp. The story of a Leonardo da Vinci sculpture that was begun in 1493 and finally completed — thanks to the efforts of Charles Dent — in 1999, along with biographical information about da Vinci and examples of his work. (Rev: BCCB 10/01; BL 10/15/01; HB 9/01; HBG 3/02; SLJ 9/01) [730]

16321 Gunderson, Jessica. *Gothic Art* (5–10). Series: Movements in Art. 2008, Creative Education $32.80 (978-1-58341-610-5). 48pp. With good reproductions and clear historical context, Gunderson looks at the era of Gothic art. Also use *Realism* and *Romanticism* (both 2008). (Rev: SLJ 12/08) [709.02]

16322 Macaulay, David. *Building the Book Cathedral* (5–9). 1999, Houghton $29.95 (978-0-395-92147-0). 112pp. The author retells the fascinating story behind the creation of the original *Cathedral* book 25 years ago and adds numerous changes as he leads a tour of the cathedral, such as alterations in scale and page placement. (Rev: BCCB 12/99; BL 11/15/99; HB 9/99; SLJ 9/99) [726]

16323 Macaulay, David. *Castle* (5–8). Illus. by author. 1977, Houghton $20.00 (978-0-395-25784-5); paper $9.95 (978-0-395-32920-7). 80pp. Another of the author's brilliant, detailed works, this one on the planning and building of a Welsh castle. [940.1]

16324 Raczka, Bob. *The Vermeer Interviews: Conversations with Seven Works of Art* (3–7). 2009, Millbrook LB $25.26 (978-0-8225-9402-4). 32pp. Raczka uses an interview format here, talking directly to the subjects of seven important Vermeer works and learning about their lives and times. (Rev: LMC 8/09; SLJ 5/09; VOYA 4/09) [759.9492]

16325 Ross, Stewart. *Art and Architecture* (5–8). Series: Medieval Realms. 2004, Gale LB $29.95 (978-1-59018-534-6). 48pp. Romanesque, Gothic, Moorish, and Islamic art and architecture are covered in this well-organized and well-illustrated volume that includes discussions of houses of the poor as well as castles, manors, monasteries, and cathedrals. (Rev: SLJ 3/05) [720]

United States

16326 Albert, Michael. *An Artist's America* (3–8). 2008, Holt $17.95 (978-0-8050-7857-2). Pop artist Albert uses recycled materials to create collages interpreting a number of historic events and trends. (Rev: SLJ 4/08) [709.2]

16327 Arbogast, Joan Marie. *Buildings in Disguise: Architecture That Looks Like Animals, Food, and Other Things* (4–7). 2004, Boyds Mills $16.95 (978-1-59078-099-2). 48pp. Buildings in the shapes of milk bottles, elephants, wigwams, and baskets are among the wonders shown in many period and contemporary photographs. (Rev: BL 11/1/04; SLJ 1/05) [720]

16328 Baverstock, Alison. *Joseph Cornell: Secrets in a Box* (3–6). Illus. Series: Prestel Adventures in Art. 2003, Prestel $14.95 (3-7913-2928-6). 30pp. The collage boxes of artist Joseph Cornell are explored in detail in this richly illustrated book, which also shows readers how they can make similar creations of their own. (Rev: BL 11/1/03) [709.2]

16329 Butler, Jerry. *A Drawing in the Sand: A Story of African American Art* (4–7). Illus. 1999, Zino $24.95 (978-1-55933-216-3). 64pp. This oversize book contains two narratives; the first is a history of African American art and artists, the second, an autobiography of Jerry Butler, the African American artist. (Rev: BL 2/15/99*) [704.03]

16330 Cummings, Pat. *Talking with Artists, Vol. 3* (4–8). Series: Talking with Artists. 1999, Clarion $22.00 (978-0-395-89132-2). 96pp. This is the third volume of interviews with children's artists and includes Peter Sís, Betsy Lewin, and Paul O. Zelinsky, with examples of their works. (Rev: BCCB 4/99; BL 3/15/99; HB 5/99; HBG 10/99; SLJ 4/99) [741.6]

16331 Curlee, Lynn. *Skyscraper* (4–7). Illus. 2007, Simon & Schuster $17.99 (978-0-689-84489-8). 48pp. Accompanied by striking acrylic paintings, Curlee's detailed narrative explores the architectural history and engineering of skyscrapers. (Rev: BL 1/1–15/07; SLJ 3/07) [720]

16332 Degezelle, Terri. *The U.S. Capitol* (K–2). Series: American Symbols. 2003, Capstone LB

$21.26 (978-0-7368-2294-7). 24pp. A well-illustrated profile of the U.S. Capitol, from the initial design contest to the numerous changes and expansions made to the building over the years. (Rev: SLJ 4/04) [975.3]

16333 Esterman, M. M. *A Fish That's a Box: Folk Art from the National Museum of American Art, Smithsonian Institution* (4–6). Illus. 1990, Great Ocean $12.95 (978-0-915556-21-2). 32pp. An eye-pleasing introduction to American folk art. (Rev: BCCB 2/91; BL 12/15/90; SLJ 3/91) [745]

16334 Glenn, Patricia Brown. *Under Every Roof: A Kid's Style and Field Guide to the Architecture of American Houses* (5–8). 1993, Preservation $16.95 (978-0-89133-214-5). 112pp. An introduction to the history and styles of architecture of American homes, with a look at more than 70 houses. (Rev: BL 7/94; SLJ 6/94) [728]

16335 Howard, Nancy S. *Jacob Lawrence: American Scenes, American Struggles* (4–7). Illus. 1996, Davis $14.95 (978-0-87192-302-8). 48pp. The narrative paintings of this contemporary African American artist are featured, with several suggested follow-up activities. (Rev: BL 11/1/96) [759.13]

16336 Knapp, Ruthie, and Janice Lehmberg. *American Art* (5–9). Series: Off the Wall Museum Guides for Kids. 1999, Davis paper $9.95 (978-0-87192-386-8). 72pp. An informal pocket-size art appreciation book that features portraits from several centuries of American art, plus various artifacts and furniture. (Rev: BL 1/1–15/99) [709.73]

16337 Leach, Deba Foxley. *Grant Wood: The Artist in the Hayloft* (2–4). Illus. by Grant Wood. Series: Adventures in Art. 2005, Prestel $14.95 (3-7913-3401-8). 30pp. Large, color reproductions of Wood's works are accompanied by brief text that will engage readers' attention plus biographical information. (Rev: BL 11/1/05) [745.13]

16338 Macaulay, David. *Mill* (5–8). Illus. by author. 1983, Houghton $19.00 (978-0-395-34830-7); paper $9.95 (978-0-395-52019-2). 128pp. Rhode Island textile mills of the 19th century are described in text and excellent drawings. [690]

16339 Morrison, Taylor. *The Buffalo Nickel* (2–4). Illus. 2002, Houghton $16.00 (978-0-618-10855-8). 32pp. The story of the artist who designed the buffalo nickel, with information about coin production. (Rev: BL 5/15/02; HBG 10/02; SLJ 4/02) [730]

16340 Murray, Julie. *Gateway Arch* (2–3). Illus. Series: All Aboard America. 2003, ABDO LB $21.35 (978-1-57765-671-5). 24pp. This photo-filled book takes young readers on a tour of St. Louis's Gateway Arch, constructed to memorialize the Missouri city's role as a gateway to the West. (Rev: HBG 10/03; SLJ 11/03) [725]

16341 Murray, Julie. *Mount Rushmore* (2–3). Illus. Series: All Aboard America. 2003, ABDO LB $21.35 (978-1-57765-667-8). 24pp. A brief overview of the creation of the giant presidential profiles carved into the mountain. (Rev: HBG 10/03; SLJ 11/03) [978.3]

16342 Nikola-Lisa, W. *The Year with Grandma Moses* (2–5). Illus. 2000, Holt $20.00 (978-0-8050-6243-4). 32pp. The seasons as they are experienced in rural America are chronicled in 13 paintings by Grandma Moses; the narrative, some of it drawn from the artist's memoir, describes seasonal activities. (Rev: BCCB 11/00; BL 10/15/00; HBG 3/01; SLJ 10/00) [759.13]

16343 Pascoe, Elaine, ed. *The Pentagon* (4–7). Series: Super Structures of the World. 2003, Gale LB $24.95 (978-1-56711-867-4). 48pp. An architectural tour of the Pentagon, headquarters of the U.S. Department of Defense. (Rev: SLJ 4/04) [355.6]

16344 Seltzer, Isadore. *The House I Live In: At Home in America* (2–5). Illus. by author. 1992, Macmillan $14.95 (978-0-02-781801-7). 32pp. Describes 12 American house designs, from log cabins to apartment buildings. (Rev: BCCB 4/92; BL 3/15/92; SLJ 5/92) [728]

16345 Spilsbury, Richard. *Pop Art* (5–8). Illus. Series: Art on the Wall. 2008, Heinemann LB $23.00 (978-1-4329-1368-7). 48pp. An introduction to the pop art movement and its key figures. (Rev: BL 1/1–15/09; SLJ 4/09) [709.04]

16346 Weaver, Janice. *Building America* (5–8). Illus. by Bonnie Shemie. 2002, Tundra $17.95 (978-0-88776-606-0). 56pp. This brief history of architecture in America, from the 17th century to today, features detailed renderings, an illustrated timeline, and a useful glossary. (Rev: HBG 3/03; SLJ 5/03) [721]

Communication

General and Miscellaneous

16347 Platt, Richard. *Communication from Hieroglyphs to Hyperlinks* (4–6). Illus. Series: Kingfisher Knowledge. 2004, Kingfisher $11.95 (978-0-7534-5769-6). 64pp. Tracing the development of communication from early days to modern high-tech media, this colorful overview will attract browsers and reluctant older readers. (Rev: BL 9/1/04; SLJ 11/04) [302.2]

Codes and Ciphers

16348 Dickson, Louise. *Lu and Clancy's Secret Languages* (1–4). Illus. by Pat Cupples. 2001, Kids Can $14.95 (978-1-55337-025-3); paper $6.95 (978-1-55074-695-2). 40pp. Dog detectives Lu and Clancy hone their knowledge of language (Pig Latin, pictograms, invisible ink, and so forth). Also use *Lu and Clancy's Spy Stuff* (2001). (Rev: HBG 10/01; SLJ 8/01) [652.8]

Flags

16349 Ayer, Eleanor. *Our Flag* (4–6). Illus. Series: I Know America. 1992, Millbrook paper $9.95 (978-1-878841-86-5). 48pp. This volume gives a colorfully illustrated introduction to the U.S. flag, its parts, and their meaning. (Rev: BL 5/15/92) [929.9]

16350 Ferry, Joseph. *The American Flag* (5–7). Series: American Symbols and Their Meanings. 2002, Mason Crest LB $18.95 (978-1-59084-026-9). 48pp. Designs that preceded the familiar flag accompany material on Betsy Ross and Francis Scott Key, illustrations of important flag raisings, and discussion of proper use and treatment of the flag, all in a package that will appeal to reluctant readers. (Rev: SLJ 4/02) [929.9]

16351 Radlauer, Ruth. *Honor the Flag: A Guide to Its Care and Display* (4–7). Illus. by J. J. Smith-Moore. 1992, Forest LB $14.95 (978-1-878363-61-9). 48pp. Lots of information about the American flag and its care. (Rev: BL 10/15/92) [929.92]

16352 Rollo, Vera F. *The American Flag* (3–6). Illus. by Alvin C. Jasper. 1990, Maryland $12.95 (978-0-917882-28-9). 78pp. The history of the U.S. flag plus myths that have grown up about its origins. (Rev: BL 6/1/90) [929.9]

16353 Ryan, Pam Muñoz. *The Flag We Love* (2–4). Illus. by Ralph Masiello. 1996, Charlesbridge $16.95 (978-0-88106-845-0). 32pp. The origins of the American flag, its history, and its uses are described in this colorful picture book. (Rev: BL 1/1–15/96; SLJ 5/96) [929.9]

16354 Smith, Whitney. *Flag Lore of All Nations* (4–6). Illus. 2001, Millbrook $29.90 (978-0-7613-1753-1). 112pp. One hundred and ninety-one flags are represented in this book. (Rev: BL 9/1/01; SLJ 9/01) [929.9]

16355 Spencer, Eve. *A Flag for Our Country* (K–3). Illus. by Mike Eagle. Series: Stories of America. 1993, Raintree LB $17.98 (978-0-8114-7211-1). 32pp. The story of how Betsy Ross made the first American flag. (Rev: SLJ 5/93) [929.9]

16356 Williams, Earl P. *What You Should Know About the American Flag* (4–8). Illus. 1989, Thomas paper $5.95 (978-0-939631-10-0). 68pp. A comprehensive guide to facts and legends, history and traditions concerning the U.S. flag. (Rev: BL 11/15/87) [929.9]

Language and Languages

16357 Beinstein, Phoebe. *Dora's Book of Words / Libro de Palabras de Dora* (PS–2). Trans. by Argentina Palacios Ziegler. Illus. by Thompson

Bros. 2003, Simon & Schuster $10.95 (978-0-689-85626-6). 16pp. Dora the Explorer looks at some everyday words loved by children in a format that allows the reader to switch from English to Spanish by pulling on a tab. (Rev: SLJ 3/03)

16358 Burns, Peggy. *Writing* (3–5). Illus. Series: Stepping Through History. 1995, Raintree LB $5.00 (978-1-56847-341-3). 32pp. A history of writing from ancient forms like hieroglyphics to the many languages of today. (Rev: BL 7/95) [411]

16359 Cooper, Kay. *Why Do You Speak as You Do? A Guide to World Languages* (5–8). Illus. by Brandon Kruse. 1992, Children's LB $14.85 (978-0-8027-8165-9). 66pp. A simple yet lively presentation of linguistics. (Rev: BCCB 2/93; BL 1/15/93) [400]

16360 Dubosarsky, Ursula. *The Word Snoop* (5–8). Illus. by Tohby Riddle. 2009, Dial $16.99 (978-0-8037-3406-7). 272pp. The character Word Snoop introduces readers to many aspects, old and new, some amazing, of the English language and includes puzzles, secret codes, and humor. (Rev: BLO 6/23/09; HB 9/09) [400]

16361 Elya, Susan Middleton. *Say Hola to Spanish* (PS–4). Illus. by Loretta Lopez. 1996, Lee & Low $15.95 (978-1-880000-29-8). 32pp. More than 70 common Spanish words are introduced in delightful rhymes with pencil illustrations. (Rev: BL 5/1/96; SLJ 6/96) [468.1]

16362 Evans, Lezlie. *Can You Greet the Whole Wide World? 12 Common Phrases in 12 Different Languages* (K–3). Illus. by Denis Roche. 2006, Houghton $16.00 (978-0-618-56327-2). 32pp. A new school year gives a little kitten a chance to greet others in 12 languages, including Arabic, Hindi, Japanese, and Zulu. (Rev: BL 5/1/06; SLJ 6/06) [395.4]

16363 Fine, Edith Hope. *Cryptomania! Teleporting into Greek and Latin with the CryptoKids* (4–6). Illus. by Kim Doner. 2004, Tricycle $15.95 (978-1-58246-062-8). 44pp. Zander and his friends teleport to various places and times, amassing information on Greek and Latin words for a vocabulary assignment; with extensive index/glossary. (Rev: SLJ 11/04)

16364 Goldstein, Peggy. *Long Is a Dragon: Chinese Writing for Children* (2–5). Illus. 1991, China Books $17.95 (978-1-881896-01-2). 32pp. This introduction to Chinese writing gives a brief history and 75 simple characters, including the numbers 1 to 12. (Rev: BCCB 5/91; BL 6/1/91; SLJ 7/91) [495.1]

16365 Guy, Ginger F. *My School / Mi escuela* (PS–1). Illus. by Vivi Escriva. 2006, HarperCollins $12.99 (978-0-06-079101-8). 24pp. An attractive introduction to school vocabulary in English and Spanish. (Rev: BL 8/06; SLJ 6/06) [372.21]

16366 Johnson, Stephen T. *Alphabet City* (4–7). Illus. 1995, Viking $16.99 (978-0-670-85631-2). 32pp. A sophisticated alphabet book that consists of a series of paintings, each of which represents a letter. (Rev: BCCB 11/95; BL 1/1–15/96; HB 11/95; SLJ 1/96*) [421]

16367 Kenny, Chantal Lacourciere. *The Kids Can Press French and English Phrase Book* (1–4). Illus. by Linda Hendry. 1999, Kids Can $12.95 (978-1-55074-477-4). 40pp. The daily life of an 8-year-old girl is illustrated with drawings and the actions are described in both French and English phrases. A companion book is *The Kids Can Press Spanish and English Phrase Book* (1999). (Rev: SLJ 10/99) [407]

16368 Klingel, Cynthia. *You Let the Cat Out of the Bag!* (K–3). Illus. by Mernie Gallagher-Cole. Series: Sayings and Phrases. 2007, Child's World LB $22.79 (978-1-59296-903-6). 32pp. This is an entertaining look at common idioms, playfully pairing a literal illustration of the phrase with its actual meaning and background explanation. (Rev: BL 11/15/07; LMC 3/08; SLJ 4/08) [428]

16369 O'Reilly, Gillian. *Slangalicious: Where We Got That Crazy Lingo* (4–6). Illus. by Krista Johnston. 2004, Annick $24.95 (978-1-55037-765-1); paper $12.95 (978-1-55037-764-4). 88pp. Two computer characters with their own Slangalicious Web site feature in the fictional story that serves as a framework for this entertaining overview of slang. (Rev: BL 12/15/04; SLJ 1/05)

16370 Park, Linda Sue, and Julia Durango. *Yum! Yuck! A Foldout Book of People Sounds* (PS–3). Illus. by Sue Ramá. 2005, Charlesbridge $9.95 (978-1-57091-659-5). 36pp. The different noises that people of different cultures make to express themselves are paired with illustrations of children from around the world. (Rev: SLJ 8/05) [418]

16371 Prap, Lila. *Animals Speak* (PS–2). Illus. 2006, North-South $15.95 (978-0-7358-2058-6). 40pp. More than 40 languages are included in this multilingual guide to the pronunciation of animal sounds in countries around the world. (Rev: BL 3/1/06; SLJ 5/06)

16372 Stojic, Manya. *Hello World! Greetings in 42 Languages Around the Globe!* (K–2). Illus. 2002, Scholastic $14.95 (978-0-439-36202-3). 40pp. Readers learn how to pronounce 42 words for hello, each introduced by a simple, bold painting of a child from the country and the name of the language concerned. (Rev: BL 12/1/02; HBG 3/03; SLJ 12/02) [413]

16373 Takahashi, Peter X. *Jimi's Book of Japanese: A Motivating Method to Learn Japanese* (3–6). Illus. by Yumie Toka. 2002, PB&J paper $18.95 (978-0-9723247-0-0). 72pp. A book featuring the Japanese characters (*kana*) and how to write them, for beginning speakers and writers of the language. (Rev: BL 2/15/03) [495.6]

16374 *To Swim in Our Own Pond: A Book of Vietnamese Proverbs* (3–6). Trans. from Vietnamese by Ngoc-Dung Tran. Illus. by Xuan-Quang Dang. 1998, Shen's $16.95 (978-1-885008-08-4). 32pp. This collection of 22 Vietnamese proverbs also contains the best Western equivalents plus a series of delightful paintings. (Rev: SLJ 3/99) [398]

16375 Vinton, Ken. *Alphabetic Antics: Hundreds of Activities to Challenge and Enrich Letter Learners of All Ages* (5–8). Illus. 1996, Free Spirit paper

$19.95 (978-1-57542-008-0). 144pp. For each letter of the alphabet, there is a history, how it appears in different alphabets, important words that begin with the letter, a quotation from someone whose name starts with it, and a number of interesting related projects. (Rev: SLJ 1/97) [411]

16376 Young, Ed. *Voices of the Heart* (4–8). Illus. 1997, Scholastic paper $17.95 (978-0-590-50199-6). 32pp. In this sumptuous picture book, the author lists and explains 26 Chinese characters, each of which expresses a different emotion. (Rev: BCCB 4/97; BL 4/15/97; HB 5/97; SLJ 6/97) [179]

Reading, Speaking, and Writing

Books, Printing, Libraries, and Schools

16377 Armstrong, Thomas. *You're Smarter Than You Think: A Kid's Guide to Multiple Intelligences* (5–8). 2003, Free Spirit paper $15.95 (978-1-57542-113-1). 192pp. Eight different intelligences are defined in understandable terms, with quizzes that help readers investigate their own strengths. (Rev: BL 4/15/03; SLJ 6/03; VOYA 6/03) [153.9]

16378 Asimov, Isaac. *Science Fiction: Vision of Tomorrow?* (3–5). Illus. Series: Isaac Asimov's 21st Century Library of the Universe. 2004, Gareth Stevens LB $26.00 (978-0-8368-3952-4). 32pp. A revised, well-illustrated edition of a previously published book, this discusses the major themes found in science fiction, looking also at real developments that were predicted in advance. (Rev: SLJ 3/05) [500]

16379 Botzakis, Stergios. *Pretty in Print: Questioning Magazines* (4–7). Illus. Series: Fact Finders. Media Literacy. 2006, Capstone LB $22.60 (978-0-7368-6764-1). 32pp. This book explores how magazines capture readers' attention, why they need to do so, and the influences they may have on society; it includes colorful graphics and interesting sidebars. (Rev: SLJ 6/07) [050]

16380 Brown, Don. *Kid Blink Beats the World* (2–5). Illus. by author. 2004, Roaring Brook $16.95 (978-1-59643-003-7). 32pp. Young newspaper vendors' 1899 rebellion against William Randolph Hearst and Joseph Pulitzer is described in this arresting picture book for older children. (Rev: BL 9/15/04) [331]

16381 Davidson, Tish. *School Conflict* (4–8). Series: Life Balance. 2003, Watts LB $20.50 (978-0-531-12251-8); paper $6.95 (978-0-531-15571-4). 80pp. This book examines the various conflicts, including violence, that exist in public education today and how these affect the lives and mental health of students. (Rev: BL 10/15/03; SLJ 3/04) [370]

16382 *Dear Author: Students Write About the Books That Changed Their Lives* (5–9). 1995, Conari paper $9.95 (978-1-57324-003-1). 150pp. A collection of young adults' letters to authors, both dead and alive, expressing, with wit and honesty, how the authors' books have affected them. (Rev: BL 1/1–15/96; SLJ 11/95) [028.5]

16383 Farrell, Juliana, and Beth Mayall. *Middle School: The Real Deal* (5–7). Illus. 2001, HarperCollins paper $7.99 (978-0-380-81313-1). 144pp. Advice on coping with school work, teachers, and social life is presented in an appealing format. (Rev: BL 6/1–15/01; VOYA 8/01) [373.18]

16384 Forget, Thomas. *The Creation of Captain America* (4–6). Illus. Series: Action Heroes. 2006, Rosen LB $21.95 (978-1-4042-0766-0). 48pp. A look at Captain America, one of Marvel's most famous superheroes and an American icon, and how he was created. (Rev: SLJ 3/07) [741.5]

16385 Fowler, Allan. *The Dewey Decimal System* (3–5). Illus. 1996, Children's Book Pr. LB $25.00 (978-0-516-20132-0). 47pp. An explanation of the Dewey Decimal System, using clear text and many examples. (Rev: BL 2/1/97; SLJ 4/97) [025.4]

16386 Funk, Gary. *A Balancing Act: Sports and Education* (5–8). Illus. Series: Sports Issues. 1995, Lerner LB $28.75 (978-0-8225-3301-6). 95pp. A frank, thorough discussion of the many issues involved in sports and their place in educational institutions. (Rev: BL 1/1–15/96; SLJ 9/95) [796.04]

16387 Gibbons, Gail. *Check It Out: The Book About Libraries* (K–3). Illus. 1985, Harcourt paper $6.00 (978-0-15-216401-0). 32pp. An overview of what the library is and how it functions in picture-book format that is lively enough for older readers. (Rev: BCCB 9/85; BL 10/1/85; HB 11/85)

16388 Gorman, Jacqueline Laks. *The Library* (K–2). Illus. Series: I Like to Visit. 2005, Weekly Reader LB $21.00 (978-0-8368-4452-8). 24pp. A simple photoessay that shows what to expect on a visit to the library. Others in this series include *The Museum*, *The Aquarium*, and *The Playground* (all 2005). (Rev: BL 4/1/05) [027]

16389 Hauser, Jill F. *Wow! I'm Reading! Fun Activities to Make Reading Happen* (PS–3). Illus. by Stan Jaskiel. Series: A Williamson Little Hands Book. 2000, Williamson paper $12.95 (978-1-885593-41-2). 141pp. A collection of activities designed to smooth the path to reading, with references to recommended picture books and bright black-and-white cartoons. (Rev: SLJ 4/01) [372.41]

16390 Hayward, Linda. *I Am a Book* (1–3). Illus. by Carol Nicklaus. Series: Silly Millies. 2005, Lerner LB $17.90 (978-0-7613-2905-3); paper $4.99 (978-0-7613-1826-2). 32pp. In easy-to-understand text with whimsical illustrations, a book explains how it was made. (Rev: BL 1/1–15/06; SLJ 10/05) [002]

16391 Heiligman, Deborah. *The New York Public Library Kid's Guide to Research* (5–8). Illus. by David Cain. 1998, Scholastic paper $14.95 (978-0-590-30715-4). 134pp. A fine introduction to research techniques including material on taking notes, using print and nonprint resources, conducting interviews and surveys, searching the Internet, and locating toll-free numbers. (Rev: HBG 3/99; SLJ 2/99) [808.023]

16392 Knowlton, Jack. *Books and Libraries* (2–5). Illus. by Harriett Barton. 1991, HarperCollins LB $14.89 (978-0-06-021610-8). 48pp. The history of books and libraries is traced from cave paintings to the present. (Rev: BCCB 3/91; BL 4/1/91; SLJ 4/91) [002]

16393 Koscielniak, Bruce. *Johann Gutenberg and the Amazing Printing Press* (2–5). 2003, Houghton $16.00 (978-0-618-26351-6). 40pp. This history of early book making traces the evolution of the process from the Chinese development of paper up to Johann Gutenberg's 15th-century invention of the printing press. (Rev: BL 7/03; HBG 4/04; SLJ 9/03) [686.2]

16394 Krensky, Stephen. *Comic Book Century: The History of American Comic Books* (5–8). Illus. Series: People's History. 2007, Lerner LB $30.60 (978-0-8225-6654-0). 112pp. The history of comics is presented as a part of America's history in this illustration- and photo-filled volume. (Rev: BL 10/1/07; LMC 1/08; SLJ 11/07) [741.5]

16395 McElroy, Lisa, and Abigail Jane Cobb. *Meet My Grandmother: She's a Children's Book Author* (1–4). Photos by Joel Benjamin. 2001, Millbrook LB $22.90 (978-0-7613-1972-6). 31pp. Nine-year-old Vicki Cobb describes her grandmother's work and how books are created and published. (Rev: HBG 3/02; SLJ 8/01) [509.2]

16396 Marshall, Pam. *From Idea to Book* (PS–2). Series: Start to Finish. 2004, Lerner LB $18.60 (978-0-8225-1385-8). 24pp. The basics of book development are laid out in simple terms for young readers. (Rev: BL 6/1–15/04; SLJ 9/04) [002]

16397 Nathan, Amy. *Surviving Homework: Tips from Teens* (5–8). Illus. 1997, Millbrook LB $24.90 (978-1-56294-185-7). 80pp. Using answers on questionnaires given to high school juniors and seniors, this book supplies many useful study tips and suggestions on how to organize one's time. (Rev: BL 6/1–15/97; SLJ 7/97) [372.12]

16398 Pfeffer, Susan Beth. *Who Were They Really? The True Stories Behind Famous Characters* (3–6). Illus. 1999, Millbrook LB $24.90 (978-0-7613-0405-0). 72pp. This book explores the real people behind such fictional characters as Alice in Wonderland, the Lost Boys of Peter Pan, and Christopher Robin. (Rev: BL 12/15/99; HBG 10/00; SLJ 12/99) [820.9]

16399 Pickering, Marianne. *Lessons for Life: Education and Learning* (5–8). Series: Our Human Family. 1995, Blackbirch LB $27.45 (978-1-56711-127-9). 80pp. A look at educational practices around the world that shows great similarities regardless of the culture. (Rev: SLJ 1/96) [370]

16400 Raatma, Lucia. *Libraries* (2–4). Series: True Books. 1998, Children's Book Pr. LB $25.00 (978-0-516-20672-1). 47pp. From the clay tablets of Mesopotamia to the specialized multimedia centers of today, this account traces the history and functions of the world's libraries. (Rev: HBG 10/98; SLJ 9/98) [027]

16401 Radabaugh, Melinda. *Going to the Library* (PS–1). Series: First Time. 2003, Heinemann LB $18.50 (978-1-4034-0230-1). 24pp. A reassuring, simple introduction to a library and its contents. (Rev: HBG 10/03; SLJ 6/03) [027]

16402 Ruurs, Margriet. *My Librarian Is a Camel: How Books are Brought to Children Around the World* (3–5). Illus. 2005, Boyds Mills $16.95 (978-1-59078-093-0). 32pp. Boats, camels, bicycles, wheelbarrows — this is a look at the unusual means librarians employ to get books to readers in remote areas of the world. (Rev: BL 7/05; SLJ 8/05) [027.4]

16403 Sawa, Maureen. *The Library Book: The Story of Libraries from Camels to Computers* (3–5). Illus. by Bill Slavin. 2006, Tundra $18.95 (978-0-88776-698-5). 72pp. This appealing study of libraries and their widespread impact traces their history from the ancient Library of Alexandria to electronic texts available from digital archives. (Rev: SLJ 12/06) [027]

16404 Schneider, Meg. *Help! My Teacher Hates Me* (5–8). 1994, Workman paper $7.95 (978-1-56305-492-1). 288pp. Helpful hints for developing a positive attitude in school. (Rev: BL 3/15/95) [371.8]

16405 *Scholastic Explains Reading Homework: Everything Children (and Parents) Need to Survive 2nd and 3rd Grade* (2–3). Series: Scholastic Explains Homework. 1998, Scholastic $14.95 (978-0-590-39755-1); paper $6.95 (978-0-590-39758-2). 64pp. Using a variety of learning approaches, this book helps primary-grade students develop reading comprehension. (Rev: SLJ 12/98) [372.4]

16406 Senisi, Ellen B. *Reading Grows* (PS–K). Photos by author. 1999, Whitman LB $16.99 (978-0-8075-6898-9). 32pp. Colorful photographs show children reacting to books, from babies looking at board books to older children reading alone or with others. (Rev: HBG 10/99; SLJ 8/99) [790.1]

16407 Shea, Kitty. *Out and About at the Public Library* (1–3). Illus. by Zachary Trover. 2005, Picture Window LB $26.60 (978-1-4048-1150-8). 24pp. This attractive title takes readers on a field trip to a public library, where they learn about everything from checking out books to using the computer catalog and consulting the reference department. (Rev: SLJ 2/06) [027.4]

16408 Somervill, Barbara. *The History of the Library* (3–6). Series: Our Changing World: The Timeline Library. 2006, The Child's World LB $27.07 (978-1-59296-438-3). 32pp. An exploration of how books have been made and stored from ancient times to today, with a peek at future developments. (Rev: SLJ 7/06) [027.009]

16409 Stevens, Janet. *From Pictures to Words: A Book About Making a Book* (2–4). Illus. 1995, Holiday House LB $16.95 (978-0-8234-1154-2). 42pp. This manual for youngsters who want to create their own picture books deals with such topics as setting, plot, and characterization. (Rev: BCCB 6/95; BL 4/15/95; SLJ 7/95*) [741.6]

16410 Swain, Gwenyth. *Bookworks: Making Books by Hand* (4–7). Illus. 1995, Carolrhoda LB $22.60 (978-0-87614-858-7). 64pp. After a brief history of books and printing, this account gives directions for making paper and various kinds of books. (Rev: BL 7/95; SLJ 8/95*) [745.5]

16411 Teitelbaum, Michael. *Making Comic Books* (2–5). Illus. by Howard Bender and David Tanguay. Series: Boys Rock! 2006, The Child's World LB $25.64 (978-1-59296-733-9). 32pp. Follows a comic book's creation from script through storyboard through illustration and lettering; a good choice for beginning and reluctant readers (girls as well as boys). (Rev: SLJ 2/07) [741.5]

16412 Wu, Dana Y. *Our Libraries* (2–4). Series: I Know America. 2001, Millbrook LB $24.90 (978-0-7613-1856-9). 48pp. The Dewey decimal system, the Library of Congress, Banned Books Week, and even MARC records are among the topics covered in this comprehensive overview of libraries. (Rev: HBG 10/01; SLJ 7/01) [027.073]

16413 Zeman, Anne, and Kate Kelly. *Everything You Need to Know About American History Homework: A Desk Reference for Students and Parents* (4–6). Illus. Series: Scholastic Homework Reference. 1994, Scholastic $18.95 (978-0-590-49362-8). 136pp. This book helps youngsters understand concepts in American history and how to apply them while doing homework assignments. Also use *Everything You Need to Know About Math Homework* and *Everything You Need to Know About Science Homework* (both 1994). (Rev: SLJ 1/95) [372.13]

Signs and Symbols

16414 Ault, Kelly. *Let's Sign! Every Baby's Guide to Communicating with Grownups* (PS). Illus. by Leo Landry. 2005, Houghton $17.00 (978-0-618-50774-0). 77pp. Simple stories about mealtime, playtime, and bedtime are accompanied by attractive illustrations and depictions of signs used for key words. (Rev: SLJ 12/05) [419]

16415 Bateman, Teresa. *Red, White, Blue and Uncle Who? The Stories Behind Some of America's Patriotic Symbols* (3–6). Illus. by John O'Brien. 2001, Holiday House $16.95 (978-0-8234-1285-3). 64pp. The meaning of patriotic symbols such as Uncle Sam, war memorials, and Mount Rushmore is explained with surprising detail in simple, appealing, and often humorous terms, enhanced by sprightly line drawings. (Rev: BL 12/15/01; HBG 10/02; SLJ 11/01) [929.9]

16416 Gryski, Camilla. *Hands On, Thumbs Up: Secret Handshakes, Fingerprints, Sign Languages and More Handy Ways to Have Fun with Hands* (3–6). Illus. by Pat Cupples. 1991, Addison-Wesley paper $8.95 (978-0-201-56756-4). 112pp. All about the human hand — facts, trivia, superstitions, jokes, and more. (Rev: BL 12/15/91) [611.97]

16417 Heller, Lora. *Sign Language for Kids: A Fun and Easy Guide to American Sign Language* (4–6). 2004, Sterling $14.95 (978-1-4027-0672-1). 96pp. Color photographs and clear directions make this an excellent introduction to sign language. (Rev: BL 9/15/04) [419]

16418 Jango-Cohen, Judith. *The Bald Eagle* (K–2). Series: Pull Ahead Books. 2003, Lerner LB $22.60 (978-0-8225-3645-1); paper $5.95 (978-0-8225-

4750-1). 32pp. For beginning report writers, this is a simple, well-illustrated look at the eagle and its choice as a national symbol. (Rev: SLJ 1/04) [929.9]

16419 Jeffrey, Laura S. *All About Braille: Reading by Touch* (2–4). Illus. Series: Transportation and Communication. 2004, Enslow LB $23.93 (978-0-7660-2184-6). 48pp. A simple, easy-to-read overview of the invention of the Braille system and how it changed the lives of blind people, with true stories. [411]

16420 Kubler, Annie. *My First Signs* (PS). Illus. 2005, Child's Play $6.99 (978-1-904550-39-6). 12pp. An introduction to American Sign Language, for both hearing and deaf children. (Rev: BL 5/15/05) [302.2]

16421 Lowenstein, Felicia. *All About Sign Language: Talking With Your Hands* (2–4). Illus. Series: Transportation and Communication. 2004, Enslow LB $23.93 (978-0-7660-2028-3). 48pp. A simple, easy-to-read overview of the history of sign language and how it changed the lives of deaf people, with true stories. (Rev: SLJ 12/04) [419]

16422 Mignon, Philippe. *Labyrinths: Can You Escape from the 26 Letters of the Alphabet?* (2–5). Illus. 2002, Firefly $14.95 (978-1-55297-559-6); paper $9.95 (978-1-55297-579-4). 64pp. A complex and attractive combination of alphabet book, mazes, poetry, and intriguing tidbits both ancient and modern. (Rev: BL 1/1–15/03; HBG 3/03; SLJ 12/02) [843]

16423 Milich, Zoran. *City Signs* (PS–K). Illus. 2002, Kids Can $15.95 (978-1-55337-003-1). 32pp. A photographic look at worded signs that will leave preschoolers proud of their "reading" skills. (Rev: BL 10/15/02; HB 1/03; HBG 3/03) [659.13]

16424 Petelinsek, Kathleen, and E. Russell Primm. *At School / En la escuela* (K–2). Illus. by Kathleen Petelinsek. Series: Talking Hands. 2006, The Child's World LB $21.36 (978-1-59296-450-5). 24pp. Students demonstrate simple school-related words using American Sign Language; the text is in both English and Spanish. (Rev: SLJ 6/06) [419]

16425 Searcy, John. *Signs in Our World: Spot the Signs All Around You!* (PS–2). Illus. 2006, DK $15.99 (978-0-7566-1834-6); paper $5.99 (978-0-7566-1827-8). 32pp. A colorful introduction to a wide variety of signs — some wordless — found across America and in some foreign countries. (Rev: BL 4/15/06) [302.2]

16426 Votry, Kim, and Curt Waller. *Baby's First Signs* (PS–2). Illus. 2001, Gallaudet Univ. $6.95 (978-1-56368-114-1). 16pp. Basic words are introduced in sign language, showing a child signing and clear directions for signing the word yourself. Also use *More Baby's First Signs* (2001). (Rev: SLJ 2/02) [419]

16427 Warner, Penny. *Signing Fun: American Sign Language Vocabulary, Phrases, Games and Activities* (4–8). Illus. by Paula Gray. 2006, Gallaudet Univ. paper $19.95 (978-1-56368-292-6). 218pp. This fun-filled introduction to American Sign Language introduces the basic vocabulary of ASL and offers a wide selection of related games and puzzles. (Rev: SLJ 12/06) [419]

16428 Woods, Mary B., and Michael Woods. *Ancient Communication: From Grunts to Graffiti* (5–8). Series: Ancient Technologies. 2000, Runestone LB $25.26 (978-0-8225-2996-5). 88pp. Beginning with cave paintings and hieroglyphics and ending with modern alphabets and universal languages, this account of the history of communication emphasizes ancient cultures. (Rev: BL 9/15/00; HBG 3/01; SLJ 1/01) [652]

16429 Yanuck, Debbie L. *Uncle Sam* (K–2). Series: American Symbols. 2003, Capstone LB $21.26 (978-0-7368-2295-4). 24pp. An introduction to Uncle Sam, the bearded symbol of the United States who grew from a political cartoon to an image known around the world. (Rev: SLJ 4/04) [398.2]

Words and Grammar

16430 Agee, Jon. *Smart Feller Fart Smeller* (2–4). Illus. 2006, Hyperion $14.95 (978-0-7868-3692-5). 64pp. Black-and-white cartoons illustrate this celebration of spoonerisms, such as the one about the smart student who "burned a lunch." (Rev: BCCB 6/06; BL 3/15/06; HB 5/06; HBG 10/06; LMC 11/06; SLJ 5/06) [793.734]

16431 Alda, Arlene. *Did You Say Pears?* (K–3). Illus. 2006, Tundra $16.95 (978-0-88776-739-5). 32pp. Fun with homonyms and homophones is provided in minimal text and eye-catching photographs. (Rev: BL 3/1/06; HBG 10/06; LMC 10/06; SLJ 6/06) [428.1]

16432 Bailey, LaWanda. *Miss Myrtle Frag, the Grammar Nag* (5–9). Illus. by Brian Strassburg. 2000, Absey paper $13.95 (978-1-888842-19-7). 84pp. A clever book that explains key grammar rules through a series of witty letters from Miss Myrtle Frag. (Rev: SLJ 2/01) [415]

16433 Baker, Rosalie. *In a Word: 750 Words and Their Fascinating Stories and Origins* (4–8). Illus. by Tom Lopes. 2003, Cobblestone $17.95 (978-0-8126-2710-7). 250pp. Useful for reference, this guide to the origins and meanings of words and phrases is drawn from a monthly column in *Cobblestone.* (Rev: BL 2/15/04; SLJ 4/04) [422]

16434 Barretta, Gene. *Dear Deer* (K–3). Illus. by Gene Baretta. 2007, Holt $16.95 (978-0-8050-8104-6). 32pp. An entertaining introduction to homophones, featuring Aunt Ant, a moose who loves mousse, and so forth. (Rev: BL 9/15/07; LMC 1/08) [423]

16435 Brennan-Nelson, Denise. *My Daddy Likes to Say* (2–4). Illus. by Jane Monroe Donovan. 2009, Sleeping Bear $15.95 (978-1-58536-432-9). 32pp. Common figures of speech — "cool as a cucumber," "the buck stops here" — are illustrated with humor. (Rev: BLO 4/14/09; SLJ 6/09) [398.9]

16436 Brennan-Nelson, Denise. *My Momma Likes to Say* (2–4). Illus. by Jane Monroe Donovan. 2003, Sleeping Bear $15.95 (978-1-58536-106-9). 32pp. Illustrations and rhymes expand on the meanings of such phrases as "money doesn't grow on trees" and

"cat got your tongue?" (Rev: BL 7/03; SLJ 9/03) [398.9]

16437 Cleary, Brian P. *Dearly, Nearly, Insincerely: What Is an Adverb?* (2–4). Illus. by Brian Gable. Series: Words Are CATegorical. 2003, Carolrhoda LB $14.95 (978-0-87614-924-9). 32pp. Energetic illustrations accompany a bouncy rhyming text that introduces adverbs of all kinds. Also use *Lazily, Crazily, Just a Bit Nasally* (2003). (Rev: HBG 10/03; SLJ 3/03) [428.1]

16438 Cleary, Brian P. *Hairy, Scary, Ordinary: What Is an Adjective?* (PS–3). Illus. by Jenya Prosmitsky. 2000, Lerner $14.95 (978-1-57505-401-8). 32pp. A playful rhyming text helps to explain what an adjective is and how it functions. (Rev: BL 6/1–15/00; HBG 10/00; SLJ 7/00) [428.2]

16439 Cleary, Brian P. *How Much Can a Bare Bear Bear? What Are Homonyms and Homophones?* (2–5). Illus. by Brian Gable. Series: Words Are CATegorical. 2005, Millbrook LB $15.95 (978-1-57505-824-5). Rhyming wordplay introduces readers to homonyms and homophones. (Rev: SLJ 11/05) [428.1]

16440 Cleary, Brian P. *I and You and Don't Forget Who: What Is a Pronoun?* (2–4). Illus. by Brian Gable. Series: Words Are CATegorical. 2004, Carolrhoda $15.95 (978-1-57505-596-1). 32pp. This clever blend of rhyming text and cartoon drawings makes its lessons about pronouns easy to digest. (Rev: BL 5/1/04; SLJ 7/04) [428.2]

16441 Cleary, Brian P. *A Mink, a Fink, a Skating Rink: What Is a Noun?* (2–4). Illus. by Jenya Prosmitsky. Series: Words Are CATegorical. 1999, Carolrhoda LB $14.95 (978-1-57505-402-5). 32pp. Humorous rhymes and illustrations are used to introduce various kinds of nouns. Also use *A Lime, a Mime, a Pool of Slime* (2006). (Rev: HBG 3/00; SLJ 11/99) [415]

16442 Cleary, Brian P. *Pitch and Throw, Grasp and Know: What Is a Synonym?* (2–4). Illus. by Brian Gable. Series: Words Are CATegorical. 2005, Carolrhoda $15.95 (978-1-57505-796-5). 32pp. Bright cartoon illustrations of humorous situations introduce synonyms. Also use *Stroll and Walk, Babble and Talk* (2009). (Rev: BL 2/1/05; SLJ 3/05) [428.1]

16443 Cleary, Brian P. *Rhyme and PUNishment: Adventures in Wordplay* (2–5). Illus. by J. P. Sandy. 2006, Millbrook LB $15.95 (978-1-57505-849-8). 48pp. Puns — some of them quite sophisticated — are delivered inside brief poems accompanied by cartoonish illustrations. (Rev: SLJ 6/06) [811]

16444 Cleary, Brian P. *Stop and Go, Yes and No: What Is an Antonym?* (K–3). Illus. by Brian Gable. Series: Words Are CATegorical. 2006, Millbrook LB $15.95 (978-1-57505-860-3). Simple and not-so-simple antonyms — from "front and back" to "excite and soothe" — are accompanied by amusing drawings; Cleary also explains the use of prefixes such as "un" and "im." Also use *Straight and Curvy, Meek and Nervy* (2009). (Rev: SLJ 6/06) [428.1]

16445 Cleary, Brian P. *To Root, to Toot, to Parachute: What Is a Verb?* (K–3). Illus. by Jenya Prosmitsky. 2001, Carolrhoda $14.95 (978-1-57505-403-2). 32pp. A delightful, lively introduction to verbs with action-packed illustrations. (Rev: BL 4/15/01; HBG 10/01; SLJ 7/01) [428.2]

16446 Cleary, Brian P. *Under, Over, By the Clover: What Is a Preposition?* (2–4). Illus. by Brian Gable. 2002, Carolrhoda $14.95 (978-1-57505-524-4). 32pp. A pack of crazy-colored cartoonlike animals and rhyming text teach younger readers all about prepositions. (Rev: BL 3/1/02; HBG 10/02; SLJ 6/02) [428.2]

16447 Coffelt, Nancy. *Big, Bigger, Biggest!* (PS–2). Illus. by author. 2009, Holt $16.95 (978-0-8050-8089-6). 32pp. Synonyms, antonyms, and comparisons are introduced by competitive animals. (Rev: BL 3/1/09; SLJ 3/09) [423]

16448 Cooper, Barbara. *Alan Apostrophe* (2–4). Illus. by Maggie Raynor. Series: Meet the Puncs: A Remarkable Punctuation Family. 2005, Gareth Stevens LB $24.00 (978-0-8368-4223-4). 32pp. Alan Apostrophe, captain of a fishing boat, wears an eye patch in the shape of an apostrophe and his speech, with many dropped letters, involves much use of the punctuation for which he is named. Also in this series from Britain: *Christopher Comma* and *Emma Exclamation Point* (both 2005). (Rev: SLJ 4/05)

16449 Dahl, Michael. *If You Were a Noun* (1–3). Illus. by Sara Gray. Series: Word Fun. 2006, Picture Window LB $26.60 (978-1-4048-1355-7). 24pp. An attractive and accessible introduction to nouns and their roles in speech. Also use *If You Were a Verb* and *If You Were an Adverb* (2006). (Rev: SLJ 9/06) [428.1]

16450 Dahl, Michael. *If You Were an Adjective* (1–3). Illus. by Sara Gray. Series: If You Were. 2006, Picture Window LB $26.60 (978-1-4048-1356-4). 24pp. A picture-book format is used to introduce young readers to adjectives and the role they play in English grammar and sentence structure. (Rev: BL 4/1/06; SLJ 9/06) [428.1]

16451 Edwards, Wallace. *Monkey Business* (4–8). Illus. 2004, Kids Can $16.95 (978-1-55337-462-6). 32pp. Whimsical artwork introduces such common idioms as "opening a can of worms" and "a bull in a china shop"; readers will also enjoy looking for hidden monkeys. (Rev: BL 11/1/04; SLJ 9/04*) [423]

16452 *Flip-a-Word: Pig Wig* (K–2). Illus. by Yukiko Kido. 2006, Blue Apple $12.95 (978-1-59354-175-0); paper $5.95 (978-1-59354-178-1). Bright, colorful pictures introduce three-letter words containing the letter combinations of "at," "ig," and "ug." Also use *Flip-a-Word: Snake Cake* (2006). (Rev: SLJ 11/06)

16453 Hambleton, Laura, and Sedat Turhan. *Monkey Business: Fun with Idioms* (K–3). Illus. by Herve Tullet. Series: Milet Wordwise. 2007, Milet paper $5.99 (978-1-840594-99-7). 28pp. Illustrations provide literal interpretations of such idioms as "monkey business," "I'll give you a hand," and "barking up the wrong tree." (Rev: BL 4/15/07) [440]

16454 Hambleton, Laura, and Sedat Turhan. *Strawberry Bullfrog: Fun with Compound Words* (K–2). Illus. by Sally Hagin. Series: Milet Wordwise. 2007, Milet paper $8.95 (978-1-84059-500-0). The words "honeymoon," "copycat," "cowboy," and "strawberry," along with others, inspire interesting illustrations in this introduction to compound words. (Rev: SLJ 5/07)

16455 Hambleton, Laura, and Sedat Turhan. *Telling Tails: Fun with Homonyms* (K–2). Illus. by Laura Hambleton. Series: Wordwise. 2007, Milet paper $8.95 (978-1-84059-498-0). Sound-alike words with different meanings inspire interesting illustrations in this introduction that includes explanations of the jokes. (Rev: SLJ 5/07)

16456 Hamilton, Fran Santoro. *Hands-On English* (4–8). Illus. 1998, Portico paper $9.95 (978-0-9664867-0-4). 150pp. A user-friendly volume that takes a visual approach to illustrate sentence patterns, such as using icons to represent the eight parts of speech, with clear, interesting explanations. Also included are irregular verbs, using modifiers, spelling rules, punctuation and capitalization, homonyms, and how to make outlines. (Rev: SLJ 2/99; VOYA 4/99) [415]

16457 Heinrichs, Ann. *Similes and Metaphors* (3–6). Series: The Magic of Language. 2005, The Child's World LB $27.07 (978-1-59296-434-5). 32pp. Advice on using similes and metaphors to brighten sentences is accompanied by attractive graphics and photographs. Also use *Spelling Rules* and *Synonyms and Antonyms* (both 2005). (Rev: SLJ 12/05) [808]

16458 Heller, Ruth. *Behind the Mask: A Book About Prepositions* (2–4). Illus. 1995, Penguin $18.99 (978-0-448-41123-1). 48pp. Using rhymes, a variety of prepositions are introduced and used. (Rev: BL 12/15/95) [428.2]

16459 Heller, Ruth. *Up, Up and Away: A Book About Adverbs* (2–5). Illus. 1991, Penguin paper $7.99 (978-0-698-11663-4). 32pp. In color drawings and catchy rhymes, Heller explains how adverbs answer precisely the questions of how, how often, when, and where. Also use by Heller: *A Cache of Jewels and Other Collective Nouns* (on collective nouns) and *Kites Sail High* (on verbs) (both 1998). (Rev: BCCB 1/92; BL 1/15/92; SLJ 2/92) [418]

16460 Klingel, Cynthia. *Go Fly a Kite! (And Other Sayings We Don't Really Mean)* (2–5). Illus. by Mernie Gallagher-Cole. Series: Sayings and Phrases. 2007, The Child's World LB $22.79 (978-1-59296-904-3). 24pp. Introduces more than 20 common idioms and their meanings, with colorful illustrations. Also use *Ack! There's a Bug in My Ear! (And Other Sayings That Just Aren't True)* and *You're Clean as a Whistle! (And Other Silly Sayings)* (2007). (Rev: LMC 3/08; SLJ 4/08) [428]

16461 Kompelien, Tracy. *The Castle Is Cold, Ancient and Old!* (2–5). Series: Synonyms. 2007, ABDO LB $19.93 (978-1-59928-728-7). 24pp. Using plenty of examples, this book introduces readers to synonyms with text and photographs. Also use *Ella Is Right, Smart and Bright!* and *Why Are You Sad and Blue?* (Rev: SLJ 8/07)

16462 Lederer, Richard. *The Circus of Words: Acrobatic Anagrams, Parading Palindromes, Wonderful Words on a Wire, and More Lively Letter Play* (5–8). Illus. by Dave Morice. 2001, Chicago Review paper $12.95 (978-1-55652-380-9). 143pp. Lovers of words will find lots of entertainment in this selection of challenging exercises. (Rev: SLJ 8/01) [428.1]

16463 Leedy, Loreen, and Pat Street. *There's a Frog in My Throat: 440 Animal Sayings a Little Bird Told Me* (2–5). Illus. by Loreen Leedy. 2003, Holiday House $16.95 (978-0-8234-1774-2). 32pp. An amusing romp through animal-related expressions such as "social butterfly" and "barrel of monkeys." (Rev: BL 3/15/03*; HB 5/03; HBG 10/03; SLJ 4/03) [428.1]

16464 McKerns, Dorothy, and Leslie Motchkavitz. *The Kid's Guide to Good Grammar* (3–7). 1998, Lowell House paper $8.95 (978-1-56565-697-0). 96pp. An entertaining guide that combines information on grammar, spelling, parts of speech, common errors, and vocabulary, with related craft projects, puzzles, and games. (Rev: SLJ 4/99) [425]

16465 Oelschlager, Vanita. *Birds of a Feather: A Book of Idioms and Silly Pictures* (K–3). Illus. by Robin Hegan. 2009, Vanita $17.95 (978-0-9800162-8-4). 32pp. Idioms are explained through humorous illustrations, brief paragraphs, and in-depth explanations at the end of the book for older readers. (Rev: BL 7/09) [428.24]

16466 Pulver, Robin. *Nouns and Verbs Have a Field Day* (K–3). Illus. by Lynn Rowe Reed. 2006, Holiday $16.95 (978-0-8234-1982-1). 32pp. A companion to *Punctuation Takes a Vacation* (2003), this zany volume features a field day in which verbs and nouns refuse to cooperate with each other. (Rev: BL 4/1/06; SLJ 3/06)

16467 Pulver, Robin. *Punctuation Takes a Vacation* (1–3). Illus. by Lynn Rowe Reed. 2003, Holiday House $17.95 (978-0-8234-1687-5). 32pp. Punctuation marks take offense at a teacher's comment and disappear, leaving children unable to write properly. (Rev: BL 3/1/03; HB 5/03; HBG 10/03; SLJ 4/03)

16468 Rayevsky, Kim. *Antonyms, Synonyms and Homonyms* (1–3). Illus. by Robert Rayevsky. 2006, Holiday $16.95 (978-0-8234-1889-3). 32pp. Learn all about antonyms, synonyms, and homonyms with this funny book about an alien trying to make some sense out of life on Earth. (Rev: BL 12/1/06; SLJ 1/07) [428.1]

16469 Root, Betty. *My First Dictionary* (PS–2). Illus. by Jonathan Langley. Series: My First Reference. 1993, DK $17.99 (978-1-56458-277-5). 96pp. Definitions and illustrations are given for 1,000 words commonly used by children plus an appended collection of word games. (Rev: SLJ 1/94) [423]

16470 Scarry, Richard. *Richard Scarry's Best Word Book Ever* (PS–2). Illus. by author. 1963, Western $13.99 (978-0-307-15510-8). 72pp. A diverse, unorthodox picture dictionary for children who like lots of little pictures.

16471 Shields, Carol Diggory. *English, Fresh Squeezed! 40 Thirst-for-Knowledge-Quenching Poems* (4–7). Illus. by Tony Ross. Series: BrainJuice. 2005, Handprint $14.95 (978-1-59354-053-1). 80pp. A humorous, rhyming look at annoying grammatical and other rules of language, with appealing illustrations and useful mnemonic devices. (Rev: BL 2/15/04; HB 5/04; SLJ 5/05)

16472 Shiffman, Lena. *My First Book of Words: 1,000 Words Every Child Should Know* (PS). Illus. by author. 1992, Scholastic $13.95 (978-0-590-45142-0). 62pp. Through a series of illustrations, many objects, actions, and emotions are identified in this basic word book. (Rev: SLJ 3/92)

16473 Swanson, Diane. *A Crash of Rhinos, A Party of Jays* (K–2). Illus. by Mariko Ando Spencer. 2006, Annick $19.95 (978-1-55451-048-1); paper $8.95 (978-1-55451-047-4). 24pp. Introduces collective nouns for groups of animals, including the well-known (a pride of lions) and the obscure (a bouquet of pheasants), and provides interesting facts and eye-catching illustrations. (Rev: BL 1/1–15/07) [591]

16474 Terban, Marvin. *Building Your Vocabulary* (4–8). Illus. Series: Scholastic Guides. 2002, Scholastic paper $12.95 (978-0-439-28561-2). 188pp. In addition to techniques for increasing vocabulary, Terban discusses etymology and how to use a dictionary and thesaurus, giving clear, often entertaining examples throughout. (Rev: SLJ 8/02) [428.1]

16475 Terban, Marvin. *Checking Your Grammar* (5–8). Series: Scholastic Guides. 1993, Scholastic paper $10.95 (978-0-590-49454-0). 144pp. An attractive, witty guide to effective writing of all sorts of letters, book reports, essays, and reviews. (Rev: BL 10/1/93; SLJ 2/94) [428.2]

16476 Terban, Marvin. *The Dove Dove: Funny Homograph Riddles* (4–7). Illus. by Tom Huffman. 1988, Houghton paper $7.95 (978-0-89919-810-1). 64pp. Making homographs less puzzling. Also use *Mad as a Wet Hen! And Other Funny Idioms* (1987). (Rev: BL 1/1/89) [818.5402]

16477 Terban, Marvin. *Guppies in Tuxedos: Funny Eponyms* (3–6). Illus. by Giulio Maestro. 1988, Houghton paper $7.95 (978-0-89919-770-8). 64pp. Telling the story behind 100 eponyms arranged by categories. (Rev: BL 7/88; SLJ 8/88)

16478 Terban, Marvin. *Punching the Clock: Funny Action Idioms* (3–6). Illus. by Tom Huffman. 1990, Houghton paper $7.95 (978-0-89919-865-1). 64pp. Such expressions as "playing possum" and "batting a thousand" are among the nearly 100 explained and illustrated with amusing drawings. (Rev: BL 6/15/90; SLJ 7/90) [428.1]

16479 Terban, Marvin. *Punctuation Power: Punctuation and How to Use It* (4–9). Illus. by Eric Brace. 2000, Scholastic paper $12.95 (978-0-590-38673-9). 96pp. After a description of each punctuation mark and its uses, this account covers topics including bibliographies, quotations, play scripts, and sentences, and the kinds of punctuation they require. (Rev: SLJ 7/00) [410]

16480 Thomson, Ruth. *A First Thesaurus* (K–3). Illus. 2003, Thameside LB $28.50 (978-1-931983-

08-2). 64pp. Pictures and words are combined to introduce youngsters to the thesaurus; children are encouraged to select alternative words from the illustrated choices provided. Also use *A First Word Bank* (2003). (Rev: BL 12/1/02) [423]

16481 *Tiny the Mouse Dictionary for 1-year-olds* (PS). Series: Tiny the Mouse. 1999, Sterling $4.95 (978-0-8069-5932-0). 11pp. In this board book, a familiar object is pictured and on the verso four related items are also shown. There are also Tiny the Mouse Dictionaries for 2-, 3-, and 4-year-olds in this series. (Rev: SLJ 9/99)

16482 Truss, Lynne. *Eats, Shoots, and Leaves: Why, Commas Really Do Make a Difference* (2–4). Illus. by Bonnie Timmons. 2006, Putnam $15.99 (978-0-399-24491-9). 32pp. The scope of Truss's bestseller for adults is narrowed to the role of the comma in this effective picture book full of funny examples of its misuse — "Eat here and get gas," for example. (Rev: BL 9/1/06; SLJ 8/06) [428.2]

16483 Truss, Lynne. *The Girl's Like Spaghetti: Why, You Can't Manage Without Apostrophes!* (2–4). Illus. by Bonnie Timmons. 2007, Putnam $16.99 (978-0-399-24706-4). 32pp. Amusing cartoons help teach important lessons about the use of apostrophes. (Rev: BL 7/07; SLJ 7/07) [428.2]

16484 Van Allsburg, Chris. *The Z Was Zapped: A Play in Twenty-Six Acts* (3–8). Illus. 1987, Houghton $18.95 (978-0-395-44612-6). 56pp. The 26 acts turn out to be a new way to introduce the alphabet. (Rev: BL 11/1/87; SLJ 11/87)

16485 Verdick, Elizabeth. *Words Are Not for Hurting* (PS). Illus. by Marieka Heinlen. 2004, Free Spirit $11.95 (978-1-57542-156-8). 24pp. Verdick urges children to consider the power of the words they use and to assess their capacity to reassure or to wound. (Rev: BL 10/15/04; SLJ 11/04) [177]

16486 Wilbur, Richard. *Opposites* (5–7). Illus. by author. 1991, Harcourt $11.95 (978-0-15-258720-8). 39pp. Through verses and cartoonlike illustrations, antonyms are given for a series of words. [811.52]

16487 Wittels, Harriet, and Joan Greisman. *A First Thesaurus* (4–6). Illus. 1985, Western paper $8.99 (978-0-307-15835-2). 144pp. Simple entry words are in boldface with synonyms and antonyms for more than 2,000 words. (Rev: BL 11/1/85; SLJ 2/86)

16488 Ziefert, Harriet. *Baby Buggy, Buggy Baby* (PS–2). Illus. by Richard Brown. Series: Word Play Flap Book. 1997, Houghton $10.95 (978-0-395-85161-6). 8pp. Using flaps, this word book shows how phrases change meaning if one reverses the word order. Homonyms are introduced in *Night, Knight* (1997). (Rev: BCCB 4/97; SLJ 7/97)

Writing and Speaking

16489 Adler, Bill, ed. *Kids' Letters to Harry Potter* (3–6). 2001, Carroll & Graf $18.00 (978-0-7867-0890-1). 200pp. Fans of the Harry Potter novels share thoughts on the books and characters through letters to the boy wizard. (Rev: BL 11/1/01; SLJ 11/01) [826]

16490 Asher, Sandy. *Where Do You Get Your Ideas? Helping Young Writers Begin* (5–7). Illus. 1987, Walker LB $13.85 (978-0-8027-6691-5). 96pp. Keeping a journal and other interesting ideas for would-be journalists. (Rev: BCCB 12/87; BL 9/15/87; SLJ 9/87) [808.02]

16491 Bailly, Sharon. *Pass It On!* (3–5). Illus. 1995, Millbrook LB $23.40 (978-1-56294-588-6). 64pp. Hints on how to perk up the writing and sending of notes, including secret codes. (Rev: BL 2/1/96; SLJ 2/96) [652]

16492 Bauer, Marion Dane. *What's Your Story? A Young Person's Guide to Writing Fiction* (5–10). 1992, Clarion paper $7.95 (978-0-395-57780-6). 144pp. An award-winning writer gives advice to young authors, including suggestions for planning, writing, and revising. (Rev: BL 4/15/92; SLJ 6/92*) [808.3]

16493 Bauer, Marion Dane. *A Writer's Story: From Life to Fiction* (5–8). 1995, Clarion $14.95 (978-0-395-72094-3); paper $6.95 (978-0-395-75053-7). 144pp. Readers and aspiring writers will enjoy this famous author's explanations of how she draws on her own experiences to develop her works. (Rev: BL 9/15/95; SLJ 10/95; VOYA 2/96) [813]

16494 Bentley, Nancy, and Donna Guthrie. *Writing Mysteries, Movies, Monster Stories, and More* (5–8). Illus. 2001, Millbrook LB $24.90 (978-0-7613-1452-3). 80pp. This book gives solid information on all kinds of fictional writing, including novels, short stories, fantasy, science fiction, humor, and even movie scripts. (Rev: BL 3/15/01; HBG 10/01; SLJ 4/01; VOYA 8/01) [808]

16495 Betz, Adrienne, comp. *Scholastic Treasury of Quotations for Children* (4–8). 1998, Scholastic paper $16.95 (978-0-590-27146-2). 254pp. From Socrates to Bill Clinton, this is a useful compendium of quotations arranged under 75 subjects. (Rev: SLJ 2/99) [080]

16496 Bullard, Lisa. *You Can Write a Story! A Story-Writing Recipe for Kids* (2–4). Illus. by Deborah Haley Melmon. 2007, Two-Can $16.95 (978-1-58128-587-5). 48pp. The basic ingredients for a good story can be flavored in any way an author/cook can imagine, counsels this entertaining book that makes composition fun. (Rev: SLJ 5/07)

16497 Burkholder, Kelly. *Pen Pals* (2–5). Series: Artistic Adventures. 2001, Rourke LB $23.93 (978-1-57103-353-6). 24pp. This title tells how and why one wants to communicate with others through regular mail and e-mail, with a section on safety tips involving the computer. (Rev: SLJ 2/01) [808]

16498 Burkholder, Kelly. *Stories* (2–5). Series: Artistic Adventures. 2001, Rourke LB $23.93 (978-1-57103-356-7). 24pp. This book introduces different types of writing — descriptive, persuasive, expository, and narrative — with ideas on expressing oneself through writing plus material on editing and revising. (Rev: SLJ 2/01) [808]

16499 Burns, Peggy. *News* (3–5). Illus. Series: Stepping Through History. 1995, Thomson Learning LB

$5.00 (978-1-56847-342-0). 32pp. A history of journalism and the distribution of news from ancient times to the present. (Rev: BL 7/95) [070.4]

16500 Christelow, Eileen. *What Do Authors Do?* (3–5). Illus. 1995, Clarion $16.00 (978-0-395-71124-8). 32pp. Using cartoonlike drawings, the process of writing a book is traced using the experiences of two imaginary authors. (Rev: BCCB 11/95; BL 9/15/95; HB 11/95; SLJ 12/95*) [808.06]

16501 Cibula, Matt. *How to Be the Greatest Writer in the World* (4–8). Illus. by Brian Strassburg. 1999, Zino $11.95 (978-1-55933-276-7). 92pp. A spiral-bound book that presents 88 interesting and engaging exercises to help youngsters who feel they have nothing to write about. (Rev: SLJ 2/00) [808]

16502 Donoughue, Carol. *The Story of Writing* (4–7). Illus. 2007, Firefly $19.95 (978-1-55407-306-1). 48pp. From early alphabets through tablets and scrolls, illuminated manuscripts, and the printing press, this is an appealing introduction to the development of writing. (Rev: BL 1/1–15/08) [411.09]

16503 Dubrovin, Vivian. *Storytelling Adventures: Stories Kids Can Tell* (4–7). Illus. by Bobbi Shupe. 1997, Storycraft paper $14.95 (978-0-9638339-2-1). 64pp. This book not only includes a selection of stories to tell but also suggests appropriate props to use, with directions on how to make them. (Rev: SLJ 5/97) [808.5]

16504 Dubrovin, Vivian. *Storytelling for the Fun of It* (4–8). Illus. by Bobbi Shupe. 1994, Storycraft paper $16.95 (978-0-9638339-0-7). 160pp. This useful guide is divided into three parts that give general information, where and what kinds of stories to tell, and how to learn and perform them. (Rev: SLJ 4/94) [808.5]

16505 Farrell, Tish. *Write Your Own Fantasy Story* (4–8). Series: Write Your Own. 2006, Compass Point LB $33.26 (978-0-7565-1639-0). 64pp. Covering characters, viewpoint, plot, and speech, this is a helpful guide to writing fantasy literature. Also use *Write Your Own Mystery Story* and *Write Your Own Science Fiction Story* (both 2006). (Rev: SLJ 8/06) [808.3]

16506 Fletcher, Ralph. *How to Write Your Life Story* (5–8). 2007, HarperCollins $15.99 (978-0-06-050770-1); paper $5.99 (978-0-06-050769-5). 128pp. Writing exercises and examples will help readers to get started on autobiographies or memoirs. (Rev: BL 10/1/07; SLJ 11/07) [808]

16507 Fletcher, Ralph. *How Writers Work: Finding a Process That Works for You* (4–8). 2000, HarperTrophy paper $4.99 (978-0-380-79702-8). 114pp. Using a conversational style, the author explains the process of writing with material on brainstorming, rough drafts, revising, proofreading, and publishing. (Rev: SLJ 12/00) [808]

16508 Fletcher, Ralph. *Poetry Matters: Writing a Poem from the Inside Out* (4–7). 2002, HarperTrophy paper $5.99 (978-0-380-79703-5). 128pp. A how-to book for young poets, with ideas on how to make images and "music" with words. (Rev: BL 5/15/02; HBG 10/02; SLJ 2/02*) [808.1]

16509 Gaines, Ann Graham. *Don't Steal Copyrighted Stuff!* (5–10). Illus. 2008, Enslow LB $28.95 (978-0-7660-2861-6). 192pp. Students who don't see the harm in cutting and pasting from the Internet will discover that plagiarism can ruin reputations and careers; the story of a writer who got caught brings this truth home, and there are plenty of practical tips on keeping one's work original. (Rev: BL 4/1/08; LMC 3/08) [808]

16510 Gibbons, Gail. *Deadline! From News to Newspaper* (K–3). 1987, HarperCollins LB $17.89 (978-0-690-04602-1). 32pp. With a small-town newspaper as a backdrop, readers can follow the workings of the press. (Rev: BL 6/15/87; HB 5/87; SLJ 6–7/87)

16511 Gilbert, Sara. *Write Your Own Article: Newspaper, Magazine, Online* (4–8). Series: Write Your Own. 2008, Compass Point LB $33.26 (978-0-7565-3855-2). 64pp. A practical guide to selecting a story, interview techniques, choosing viewpoint, developing a story, remaining objective, and so forth, with excerpts as examples. (Rev: SLJ 3/09) [808]

16512 Graham, Paula W. *Speaking of Journals: Children's Book Writers Talk About Their Diaries, Notebooks and Sketchbooks* (5–8). Illus. 1999, Boyds Mills paper $14.95 (978-1-56397-741-1). 226pp. A book that discusses the how-tos and the rewards of keeping a personal journal, and features interviews with 27 writers including Jim Arnosky, Pam Conrad, and Jean George. (Rev: BL 3/1/99; SLJ 5/99; VOYA 2/00) [818]

16513 Guthrie, Donna, and Nancy Bentley. *The Young Journalist's Book: How to Write and Produce Your Own Newspaper* (4–7). Illus. 1998, Millbrook $24.40 (978-0-7613-0360-2). 64pp. The authors explain what a journalist does and, in addition to explaining the parts of a newspaper, tells how to start one. (Rev: BL 3/1/99; HBG 3/99; SLJ 12/98) [070.1]

16514 Hambleton, Vicki, and Cathleen Greenwood. *So, You Wanna Be a Writer? How to Write, Get Published, and Maybe Even Make It Big!* (5–9). Illus. by Laura Eldridge and Corey Mistretta. Series: So, You Wanna Be. 2001, Beyond Words paper $8.95 (978-1-58270-043-4). 160pp. Practical advice is offered in straightforward text with lots of examples, sample letters, interviews with published writers, details of writing contests, and lists of magazines that accept submissions from young writers. (Rev: SLJ 10/01; VOYA 2/02) [808]

16515 Hamilton, John. *You Write It! Horror* (4–7). Illus. Series: You Write It! 2009, ABDO LB $17.95 (978-1-60453-506-8). 32pp. Tips for budding horror writers cover inspiration, good work habits, effective plots, and how to get published. (Rev: BL 4/1/09) [808.3]

16516 Hamilton, Martha, and Mitch Weiss. *Stories in My Pocket: Tales Kids Can Tell* (4–7). Illus. 1997, Fulcrum paper $15.95 (978-1-55591-957-3). 184pp. This handbook of storytelling for young storytellers includes 30 tales to begin with. (Rev: BL 1/1–15/97) [372.6]

16517 Holbrook, Sara. *Wham! It's a Poetry Jam: Discovering Performance Poetry* (2–5). 2002, Boyds Mills paper $9.95 (978-1-59078-011-4). 55pp. Holbrook includes some of her poems in this guide to performing poetry — how to move, project your voice, express emotion, and so forth. (Rev: HBG 10/02; SLJ 5/02)

16518 Hudson, Wade. *Powerful Words: More Than 200 Years of Extraordinary Writing by African Americans* (5–9). Illus. by Sean Qualls. 2004, Scholastic $19.95 (978-0-439-40969-8). 192pp. Excerpts from the writings and speeches of both well-known and less-familiar African Americans are accompanied by notes on the context and the writer. (Rev: BL 2/15/04; SLJ 2/04) [081]

16519 Hulme, Joy N., and Donna Guthrie. *How to Write, Recite, and Delight in All Kinds of Poetry* (3–6). 1996, Millbrook LB $24.90 (978-1-56294-576-3). 96pp. Using examples of poetry written by grade school children, this book introduces different types of poetry and gives help in writing and reciting poems. (Rev: SLJ 12/96) [811]

16520 James, Elizabeth, and Carol Barkin. *How to Write Super School Reports*. Rev. ed. (4–9). Series: A School Survival Guide Book. 1998, Lothrop $15.00 (978-0-688-16132-3). 90pp. This research guide takes readers through the steps involved in writing a research paper with material on choosing a topic, finding facts, using a library, organizing notes, and putting the report together. (Rev: HBG 3/99; SLJ 2/99) [808.023]

16521 Janeczko, Paul B. *How to Write Poetry* (4–8). Series: Scholastic Guides. 1999, Scholastic paper $12.95 (978-0-590-10077-9). 128pp. An enthusiastic, clearly written how-to manual that uses many examples from well-known poems. (Rev: BL 3/15/99; HBG 10/99; SLJ 7/99; VOYA 8/99) [808.1]

16522 Janeczko, Paul B., comp. *Poetry from A to Z: A Guide for Young Writers* (4–8). Illus. Series: Net-Guide. 1994, Simon & Schuster $16.95 (978-0-02-747672-9). 176pp. This book of 72 poems, alphabetized by topic, gives examples to get young writers started, and the 23 poets represented give advice on how to become a better poet. (Rev: BCCB 3/95; BL 12/15/94; VOYA 5/95) [808.1]

16523 Leedy, Loreen. *Look at My Book: How Kids Can Write and Illustrate Terrific Books* (K–3). Illus. 2004, Holiday House $16.95 (978-0-8234-1590-8). 32pp. This picture book covers all aspects of publishing a work, from initial concept through writing, revision, and selecting design and binding. (Rev: BL 2/15/04; SLJ 4/04) [808]

16524 Leedy, Loreen. *Messages in the Mailbox: How to Write a Letter* (2–4). Illus. 1991, Holiday House LB $16.95 (978-0-8234-0889-4). 32pp. In this cheery guide, an alligator teacher shows the class of children and animals how to write a letter. (Rev: BCCB 12/91; BL 1/1/91; SLJ 9/91*) [295.4]

16525 Levine, Gail C. *Writing Magic: Creating Stories That Fly* (5–10). 2006, HarperCollins $16.99 (978-0-06-051961-2); paper $5.99 (978-0-06-051960-5). 167pp. Well-known author Levine provides upbeat, practical tips on such topics as finding story ideas, character and plot development, and investigating the possibility of publication. (Rev: BL 12/15/06; SLJ 2/07*) [808.3]

16526 Loewen, Nancy. *Words, Wit, and Wonder: Writing Your Own Poem* (2–4). Illus. by Christopher Lyles. 2008, Picture Window LB $17.99 (978-1-4048-5344-7). 32pp. This primer provides aspiring poets with 12 useful tools. (Rev: BL 4/1/09; SLJ 6/09) [808.1]

16527 Nobleman, Marc Tyler. *Extraordinary E-Mails, Letters, and Resumes* (5–8). Illus. by Kevin Pope. Series: F. W. Prep. 2005, Watts LB $31.00 (978-0-531-16759-5). 128pp. Advice for students who want to write effective e-mails, letters, and resumés, with an explanation of the importance of communicating clearly. (Rev: SLJ 1/06) [808]

16528 Otfinoski, Steven. *Extraordinary Short Story Writing* (5–8). Illus. by Kevin Pope. Series: F. W. Prep. 2005, Watts LB $31.00 (978-0-531-16760-1). 128pp. Tips and activities reinforce the information on writing different types of stories, choosing ideas, and using available resources effectively; a sample short story offers step-by-step guidance. (Rev: SLJ 2/06) [808]

16529 Otfinoski, Steven. *Speaking Up, Speaking Out: A Kid's Guide to Making Speeches, Oral Reports, and Conversation* (5–8). Illus. 1996, Millbrook LB $24.90 (978-1-56294-345-5). 80pp. All kinds of public-speaking situations are introduced, with suggestions on how to be a success at each. (Rev: BL 1/1–15/97; SLJ 1/97) [808.5]

16530 Prelutsky, Jack. *Pizza, Pigs, and Poetry: How to Write a Poem* (4–6). 2008, Greenwillow paper $5.99 (978-0-06-143448-8). 208pp. An appealing blend of writing tips, examples of the author's own efforts, anecdotes about his life, and a selection of "poemstarts." (Rev: BCCB 6/08; BL 5/1/08; SLJ 6/08) [811]

16531 Rivera, Sheila. *The Media War* (5–8). Illus. Series: World in Conflict. 2004, ABDO LB $25.65 (978-1-59197-418-5). 48pp. A brief overview of American journalism's impact on war from the Civil War to the U.S. invasion of Afghanistan. (Rev: BL 4/1/04) [070.1]

16532 Rosinsky, Natalie M. *Write Your Own Biography* (4–8). Series: Write Your Own. 2007, Compass Point LB $31.93 (978-0-7565-3366-3). 64pp. A helpful guide to writing a biography with excerpts from published works and writing exercises. (Rev: SLJ 12/07) [808]

16533 Roy, Jennifer. *You Can Write a Story or Narrative* (4–8). Illus. Series: You Can Write! 2003, Enslow LB $22.60 (978-0-7660-2085-6). 64pp. Sound advice for plotting and writing a wide array of different narratives, including adventure, history, fantasy, and folklore. (Rev: SLJ 1/04; VOYA 4/04) [808]

16534 *Scholastic Explains Writing Homework: Everything Children (and Parents) Need to Survive 2nd and 3rd Grade* (2–3). Series: Scholastic Explains Homework. 1998, Scholastic $14.95 (978-0-590-39756-8). 64pp. This book helps children and parents understand such writing concepts as characters, reviews, and basic grammar. (Rev: SLJ 12/98) [808]

16535 Somervill, Barbara. *Backstage at a Newscast* (5–8). Illus. Series: Backstage Pass. 2003, Children's LB $24.50 (978-0-516-24326-9); paper $6.95 (978-0-516-24388-7). 48pp. Somerville provides information on how a newscast is created, along with guidance on careers in journalism. (Rev: BL 5/1/03) [070.1]

16536 Trueit, Trudi. *Keeping a Journal* (4–8). Illus. 2004, Watts LB $20.50 (978-0-531-12262-4). 80pp. Trueit encourages readers to keep journals, offering tips on getting started, writing prompts and exercises, a calendar of ideas, and alternatives for those who don't enjoy writing, such as scrapbooks and drawing. (Rev: BL 10/15/03; SLJ 3/05) [808]

16537 Veljkovic, Peggy, and Arthur Schwartz, eds. *Writing from the Heart: Young People Share Their Wisdom* (5–9). 2001, Templeton Foundation paper $12.95 (978-1-890151-48-5). 189pp. A collection of the best essays by young people that have been sub-

mitted to the Laws of Life program since it began in 1987. (Rev: SLJ 6/01) [170]

16538 Vinton, Ken. *Alphabet Antics: Hundreds of Activities to Challenge and Enrich Letter Learners of All Ages* (5–8). Illus. by author. 1996, Free Spirit paper $19.95 (978-0-915793-98-3). 135pp. For each letter of the alphabet, there is a history, how it appears in different alphabets, important words that begin with that letter, a quotation from someone whose name starts with it, and a number of interesting related projects. (Rev: SLJ 1/97) [411]

16539 Wong, Janet S. *You Have to Write* (2–4). Illus. by Teresa Flavin. 2002, Simon & Schuster $17.00 (978-0-689-83409-7). 40pp. Wong uses poetic text and a photo album approach to spur young people to think about writing assignments in new ways. (Rev: BL 7/02; HBG 3/03; SLJ 7/02) [811]

16540 Young, Sue. *Writing with Style* (5–8). Series: Scholastic Guides. 1997, Scholastic $12.95 (978-0-590-50977-0). 144pp. A guide for the novice writer, with chapters on planning, presenting, and publishing one's work. (Rev: BL 3/1/97; SLJ 5/97) [372.6]

Music

General

16541 Aliki. *Ah, Music!* (1–3). Illus. 2003, Harper-Collins LB $17.89 (978-0-06-028727-6). 48pp. Rhythm, harmony, melody, jazz, instruments, and a brief history are among the many aspects of music that Aliki manages to cover in this slim volume. (Rev: BL 6/1–15/03; HB 5/03; HBG 10/03; SLJ 5/03) [780]

16542 Allen, Patrick. *Europe* (4–6). Series: World of Music. 2007, Heinemann LB $31.43 (978-1-4034-9890-8). 48pp. With photographs and discussion of famous players and current styles, this volume offers a broad overview of the music, instruments, and folk traditions of Europe. (Rev: LMC 5/08; SLJ 3/08)

16543 Ayazi-Hashjin, Sherry. *Rap and Hip Hop: The Voice of a Generation* (4–7). Illus. Series: Library of African American Arts and Culture. 1999, Rosen LB $26.50 (978-0-8239-1855-3). 62pp. This account traces the history of rap and hip hop music from their origins in spirituals, jazz, blues, and story-telling traditions; it also gives some information on musicians. (Rev: BL 2/15/00; SLJ 1/00) [782.4]

16544 Barnes, Deb. *Inside a Rock Band* (2–4). Series: Girls Rock! 2006, Child's World $25.64 (978-1-59296-745-2). 32pp. An inside look at what it's like to be in a professional band. (Rev: BL 11/15/06; SLJ 4/07) [781.66]

16545 Bertholf, Bret. *The Long Gone Lonesome History of Country Music* (5–8). Illus. 2007, Little, Brown $18.99 (978-0-316-52393-6). 64pp. A chatty survey of country music, discussing its roots and early instruments, tracing the evolution to today's sounds, and introducing some of its greatest performers. (Rev: BL 4/1/07; SLJ 4/07*) [781.642]

16546 Bryan, Ashley. *Let It Shine: Three Favorite Spirituals* (PS–5). Illus. by author. 2007, Simon & Schuster $16.99 (978-0-689-84732-5). This large-format, beautifully illustrated volume showcases three familiar spirituals: "This Little Light of Mine," "He's Got the Whole World in His Hands," and "When the Saints Go Marching In." (Rev: BL 11/15/06; SLJ 1/07*)

16547 Cefrey, Holly. *Backstage at a Music Video* (5–8). Illus. Series: Backstage Pass. 2003, Children's paper $6.95 (978-0-516-24386-3). 48pp. The history of music videos is coupled with information on how they are financed and produced, along with guidance on careers in the music business. (Rev: BL 5/1/03) [791.45]

16548 Celenza, Anna Harwell. *Pictures at an Exhibition* (K–4). Illus. by JoAnn E. Kitchel. 2003, Charlesbridge LB $19.95 (978-1-57091-492-8). 32pp. Drawing on primary-source documents, Celenza has created an arresting account of the friendship that was the catalyst for Mussorgsky's famous piece. (Rev: HBG 4/04; SLJ 4/03)

16549 Cornish, Melanie J. *The History of Hip Hop* (4–7). Illus. 2009, Crabtree LB $19.95 (978-0-7787-3820-6); paper $8.95 (978-0-7787-3841-1). 32pp. A single house party in 1973 started Hip Hop and it bopped on from there. (Rev: BL 6/1–15/09) [782.42164909]

16550 Corr, Christopher. *Whole World* (PS). Illus. 2007, Barefoot Books $16.99 (978-1-846860-43-0). 32pp. This illustrated version of the classic spiritual (with a sing-along CD) shows children around the world enjoying nature and makes a clear plea for environmental protection. (Rev: BL 4/15/07) [782.42]

16551 Ench, Rick, and Jay Cravath. *North American Indian Music* (5–7). Illus. Series: Watts Library: Indians of the Americas. 2002, Watts LB $25.50 (978-0-531-11772-9); paper $8.95 (978-0-531-16230-9). 64pp. This title looks at the importance of music in the rituals of North American Indian tribes and describes the forms of beat, rhythm, and melody, with illustrations, a glossary, bibliography, and timeline. (Rev: BL 7/02) [782.62]

16552 Garty, Judy. *Techniques of Marching Bands* (5–8). Series: Let's Go Team. 2003, Mason Crest LB $19.95 (978-1-59084-538-7). 64pp. The slim volume supplies a look at the functions of a marching band, how they operate, and the joys of playing in one. (Rev: BL 10/15/03; SLJ 11/03) [785.06]

16553 Gatti, Anne, retel. *The Magic Flute* (4–8). Illus. by Peter Malone. 1997, Chronicle $17.95 (978-0-8118-1003-6). 40pp. An elegant retelling of the Mozart opera, with each scene given a full-color painting and a page of text. The accompanying CD has 16 selections coded to each page. (Rev: SLJ 1/98*) [782.1]

16554 George-Warren, Holly. *Shake, Rattle and Roll: The Founders of Rock and Roll* (4–7). 2001, Houghton $16.00 (978-0-618-05540-1). 32pp. After an informative introduction on the history of rock and roll, there is a series of one-page biographies of famous personalities. (Rev: BL 3/1/01; HBG 10/01; SLJ 5/01*) [781.66]

16555 Greene, Ellin. *Mother's Song: A Lullaby* (PS). Illus. by Elizabeth Sayles. 2008, Clarion $17.00 (978-0-395-71527-7). 32pp. A celebration of a mother's love for her child, with pastel illustrations featuring fairies and a woodland landscape plus original music. (Rev: BL 7/08; SLJ 4/08) [782.42]

16556 Handyside, Christopher. *Country* (5–9). Series: A History of American Music. 2006, Heinemann LB $31.43 (978-1-4034-8151-1). 48pp. This history of country music traces the genre from its hillbilly roots to the present and introduces some of its most influential figures, including the Carter family, Johnny Cash, Loretta Lynn, and John Denver. (Rev: SLJ 9/06) [781.642]

16557 Hannah, Johnny. *Hot Jazz Special* (4–6). Illus. 2005, Candlewick $16.99 (978-0-7636-2308-1). 40pp. This brightly illustrated volume with a fold-out poster celebrates the contributions of jazz players including Louis Armstrong, Duke Ellington, Billie Holliday, Jelly Roll Morton, and Django Reinhardt. (Rev: BL 7/05; SLJ 3/05)

16558 Husain, Shahrukh. *The Barefoot Book of Stories from the Opera* (4–6). Illus. 1999, Barefoot Books $19.95 (978-1-902283-28-9). 80pp. The plots of seven operas that would appeal to children because of their familiar stories (e.g., *La Cenerentola, Hansel and Gretel, The Magic Flute*) are retold with many illustrations. (Rev: BL 11/1/99; SLJ 10/99) [782.1]

16559 Igus, Toyomi. *I See the Rhythm* (5–8). Illus. 1998, Children's $15.95 (978-0-89239-151-6). 32pp. Using a timeline to set the social context, this title traces African American contributions to such musical forms as the blues, big band, jazz, bebop, gospel, and rock. (Rev: BCCB 7–8/98; BL 2/15/98; SLJ 6/98) [780]

16560 Joel, Billy. *New York State of Mind* (PS–2). Illus. by Izak. 2005, Scholastic $16.99 (978-0-439-55382-7). 32pp. Using Billy Joel's song as the framework, Izak portrays the essence of New York City through a dog's Christmas visit. (Rev: BL 11/15/05) [782.42164]

16561 Lee, Jeanne. *Jam! The Story of Jazz Music* (4–7). Illus. Series: Library of African American Arts and Culture. 1999, Rosen LB $26.50 (978-0-8239-1852-2). 62pp. This book tells about the African American musicians who were responsible for the early development of jazz and blues. (Rev: BL 2/15/00; SLJ 1/00) [781.65]

16562 Nelson, Kadir. *He's Got the Whole World in His Hands* (PS–3). Illus. 2005, Dial $16.99 (978-0-8037-2850-9). 32pp. An African American boy savors life with his family and the wonders of the world around him in this picture-book interpretation of the popular spiritual. (Rev: BL 10/1/05*; HBG 4/06; SLJ 9/05)

16563 Olson-Brown, Ellen. *Hush Little Digger* (PS–K). Illus. by Lee White. 2006, Tricycle $12.95 (978-1-58246-160-1). 28pp. This twist on the popular lullaby "Hush Little Baby" features a father promising his son increasingly large pieces of equipment. (Rev: BL 4/1/06; SLJ 6/06) [782.42]

16564 Pinkney, Gloria Jean. *Music from Our Lord's Holy Heaven* (2–4). Illus. by Jerry Pinkney, et al. 2005, HarperCollins LB $18.89 (978-0-06-000769-0). 48pp. Children's author Pinkney pairs the lyrics of African American spirituals with relevant psalms in this beautifully illustrated picture book that comes bundled with an audio CD. (Rev: BL 10/1/05; SLJ 12/05) [264]

16565 Richer, Linda A., and Anita Stoltzfus Breckbill, eds. *Chatter with the Angels: An Illustrated Songbook for Children* (2–6). Illus. 2000, GIA $29.95 (978-1-57999-082-4). 90pp. An outstanding songbook containing 90 selections of Christian music from different countries and cultures that are printed with piano and guitar arrangements. (Rev: BL 10/1/00; HBG 3/01) [782.25]

16566 Rowe, Julian. *Music* (4–7). Illus. Series: Science Encounters. 1997, Rigby paper $25.55 (978-1-57572-091-3). 32pp. This book shows how scientific principles are used in music, musical instruments, hearing, and recording devices. (Rev: SLJ 10/97) [780]

16567 Saint-Saens, Camille. *Carnival of the Animals* (PS–2). Illus. by Sue Williams. 1999, Holt $19.95 (978-0-8050-6180-2). 45pp. This book gives a one-page explanation of each part of this piece by Saint-Saens; the accompanying CD contains the music. (Rev: SLJ 1/00) [780]

16568 Schaefer, A. R. *Forming a Band* (5–8). Illus. Series: Rock Music Library. 2003, Capstone LB $23.93 (978-0-7368-2146-9). 32pp. A hip and practical guide suitable for reluctant readers. Also use *Booking a First Gig* (2003). (Rev: BL 12/1/03) [784.100]

16569 Solway, Andrew. *Africa* (4–6). Series: World of Music. 2007, Heinemann LB $31.43 (978-1-4034-9891-5). 48pp. With photographs and discussion of famous players, this volume offers a broad overview of the music, instruments, and folk traditions of Africa. (Rev: LMC 5/08; SLJ 3/08)

16570 Solway, Andrew. *Latin America and the Caribbean* (4–6). Series: World of Music. 2007, Heinemann LB $31.43 (978-1-4034-9889-2). 48pp. With photographs and discussion of famous players and blending of Amerindian, African, and European influences, this volume offers a broad overview of the music, instruments, and traditions of Latin America and the Caribbean. (Rev: SLJ 3/08)

16571 *This Little Light of Mine* (PS–2). Illus. by E. B. Lewis. 2005, Simon & Schuster $16.95 (978-0-689-83179-9). 32pp. The words of this familiar African American spiritual spring to life in the vibrant illustrations as a boy moves through his community, sharing experiences. (Rev: BL 2/1/05; SLJ 3/05) [782.25]

16572 Underwood, Deborah. *Australia, Hawaii, and the Pacific* (4–6). Series: World of Music. 2007, Heinemann LB $31.43 (978-1-4034-9894-6). 48pp. With photographs and discussion of famous players, this volume offers a broad overview of the music, instruments, and traditions of Australia. (Rev: LMC 5/08; SLJ 3/08)

Ballads and Folk Songs

16573 Arnold, Tedd. *Catalina Magdalena Hoopensteiner Wallendiner Hogan Logan Bogan Was Her Name* (PS–2). Illus. by author. 2004, Scholastic $10.95 (978-0-590-10994-9). 40pp. A classic camp song serves as inspiration for an unlikely heroine. (Rev: SLJ 8/04) [782.421]

16574 Boynton, Sandra. *Dog Train* (PS–2). Illus. by author. 2005, Workman $17.95 (978-0-7611-3966-9). 64pp. A collection of songs with a distinct rock 'n' roll feel, this book provides spreads for songs that are included on the accompanying CD. (Rev: SLJ 3/06) [782.4]

16575 Burke, Bobby, and Horace Gerlach. *Daddy's Little Girl* (PS–2). Illus. by Maggie Kneen. 2004, HarperCollins $14.99 (978-0-06-028722-1). 32pp. The 1950s song "Daddy's Little Girl" becomes a book starring a family of rabbits. (Rev: SLJ 5/04) [782.4]

16576 Cabrera, Jane. *Old MacDonald Had a Farm* (PS). Illus. by author. 2008, Holiday $16.95 (978-0-8234-2141-1). 32pp. A farmer and his animals have fun in this version of the song that ends with the arrival of a human baby. (Rev: BL 3/15/08; SLJ 3/08) [782.42]

16577 Catalano, Dominic. *Frog Went A-Courting: A Musical Play in Six Acts* (PS–1). Illus. 1998, Boyds Mills $15.95 (978-1-56397-637-7). 32pp. This charming adaptation of the folk song includes stunning paintings and charcoal drawings. (Rev: BL 10/15/98; HBG 3/99; SLJ 10/98) [782.42]

16578 Clarke, Gus. *E I E I O: The Story of Old MacDonald Who Had a Farm* (PS–K). Illus. 1993, Lothrop $14.00 (978-0-688-12215-7). 32pp. With cartoonlike illustrations, this is an old favorite folk song with a surprise ending. (Rev: BL 5/1/93) [782.42]

16579 Cony, Frances, and Iain Smyth. *Old MacDonald Had a Farm* (PS–K). Illus. 1999, Orchard $10.95 (978-0-531-30129-6). 12pp. A pop-up version of the familiar song, with chickens moving their heads in time to the music. (Rev: BL 12/15/99; SLJ 6/99) [784.4]

16580 Emberley, Rebecca, and Adrian Emberley. *There Was an Old Monster* (PS–K). Illus. by Rebecca Emberley. 2009, Scholastic $16.99 (978-0-545-10145-5). 32pp. A monster swallows more and bigger creatures until he's ready to explode in this twist on the classic cumulative song. (Rev: BL 6/1–15/09; SLJ 6/09) [782.42]

16581 Emmett, Jonathan. *She'll Be Coming 'Round the Mountain* (PS–K). Illus. 2007, Simon & Schuster $16.99 (978-1-4169-3652-7). 32pp. A lively cowgirl dressed in pink pajamas and a huge green hat stars in this rollicking expanded version of the classic song. (Rev: BL 4/1/07; SLJ 3/07) [782.42]

16582 Farjeon, Eleanor. *Morning Has Broken* (PS–3). Illus. by Tim Ladwig. 1996, Eerdmans $15.00 (978-0-8028-5127-7); paper $8.00 (978-0-8028-5132-1). 32pp. An illustrated version of the hymn that was once recorded by Cat Stevens. (Rev: BL 10/1/96; SLJ 12/96) [782]

16583 Handyside, Christopher. *Folk* (5–9). 2006, Heinemann LB $31.43 (978-1-4034-8150-4). 48pp. This attractive volume traces the evolution of American folk music from its post-Civil War roots to its influence on the contemporary music scene and introduces some of its most influential figures, including Leadbelly, Woody Guthrie, Joan Baez, and Bob Dylan. (Rev: SLJ 9/06) [781.62]

16584 *Here We Go Round the Mulberry Bush* (PS–K). Illus. by Sophie Fatus. 2007, Barefoot Books $16.99 (978-1-84686-035-5). An illustrated version of the familiar nursery song, with a discussion of the song's history, the sheet music, and directions for a dance to go along with it. (Rev: BL 6/1–15/07; SLJ 6/07) [782.42]

16585 Langstaff, John. *Frog Went A-Courtin'* (K–3). Illus. by Feodor Rojankovsky. 1955, Harcourt $14.95 (978-0-15-230214-6); paper $7.00 (978-0-15-633900-1). 32pp. A rollicking folk song with matching illustrations. Caldecott Medal winner, 1956.

16586 McGill, Alice. *In the Hollow of Your Hand: Slave Lullabies* (5–7). Illus. 2000, Houghton $18.00 (978-0-395-85755-7). 40pp. Family life in the days of slavery is revealed in this moving collection of 13 folk lullabies; a CD of the songs is also included. (Rev: BCCB 1/01; BL 11/15/00; HBG 3/01; SLJ 12/00) [811.008]

16587 McNeil, Keith, and Rusty McNeil. *Colonial and Revolution Songbook: With Historical Commentary* (4–7). 1996, WEM Records paper $11.95 (978-1-878360-08-3). 71pp. This songbook contains 39 traditional songs from the 17th century through the War of 1812, with brief historical comments for each. (Rev: SLJ 12/96) [973]

16588 Mattox, Cheryl W., ed. *Shake It to the One That You Love the Best: Play Songs and Lullabies from Black Musical Traditions* (PS–6). Illus. by Varnette P. Honeywood. 1990, Warren-Mattox paper $7.95 (978-0-9623381-0-6). 56pp. Music and lyrics for 16 songs and ten lullabies. (Rev: BL 12/1/90*) [781.62]

16589 Mitchell, Susan K. *The Rainforest Grew All Around* (PS–3). Illus. by Connie McLennan. 2007, Dell $15.95 (978-0-9768823-6-7). 32pp. Adapting the familiar "The Green Grass Grew All Around," this brightly illustrated book introduces young children to a wide variety of rain forest animals and plants. (Rev: BL 6/1–15/07; SLJ 8/07) [578.734]

16590 Nic Leodhas, Sorche. *Always Room for One More* (K–3). Illus. by Nonny Hogrogian. 1965, Holt $14.95 (978-0-8050-0331-4); paper $5.95 (978-0-8050-0330-7). 32pp. From the Scottish folk song about Machie MacLachlan, who had so many people into his house that it burst. Caldecott Medal winner, 1966.

16591 O'Neal, Debbie Trafton. *Twinkle, Twinkle, Little Star* (PS). Illus. by Benrei Huang. Series: Sing-It. 2003, Augsburg $8.99 (978-0-8066-4350-2). 32pp. This beautifully illustrated book celebrates the familiar children's song and even adds a new verse written by the author. (Rev: HBG 10/03; SLJ 9/03)

16592 Penner, Fred. *The Cat Came Back* (PS–2). Illus. by Renee Reichert. 2005, Roaring Brook $15.95 (978-1-59643-030-3). 32pp. Excellent artwork elevates the humor of the traditional song about a man determined to rid himself of a pesky cat. (Rev: BL 11/1/05; SLJ 10/05) [782.4]

16593 Pinkney, Brian. *Hush, Little Baby* (PS). Illus. 2006, Greenwillow $15.99 (978-0-06-055993-9). 32pp. Mama has gone off for the day and it is up to Papa and older brother to look after the little girl; set in an African American family in the early 1900s. (Rev: BL 2/1/06; SLJ 3/06) [782.42125]

16594 Raffi. *This Little Light of Mine* (PS–3). Illus. by Stacey Schuett. Series: Raffi Songs to Read. 2004, Knopf LB $17.99 (978-0-375-92871-0). 32pp. This book-CD package uses the framework of children preparing for a performance of the song, and uses a variety of lights effectively. (Rev: SLJ 7/04) [782.42]

16595 *Rock-a-Bye Baby: Lullabies for Bedtime* (PS–2). Illus. by Margaret Walty. 1998, Barefoot Books $14.95 (978-1-902283-03-6). 40pp. This is a charming collection of 16 bedtime songs including "Twinkle, Twinkle, Little Star." (Rev: BL 12/15/98; SLJ 1/99) [781.5]

16596 Sayre, April P. *Hush, Little Puppy* (PS). Illus. by Susan Winter. 2007, Holt $15.95 (978-0-8050-7102-3). 32pp. This gentle picture book captures the joyful friendship of a boy and his puppy as the boy uses his own version of "Hush Little Baby" at bedtime. (Rev: BL 6/1–15/07; SLJ 8/07) [782.42]

16597 Schwartz, Amy. *Old MacDonald* (PS–1). Illus. 1999, Scholastic $15.95 (978-0-590-46189-4). 32pp. Double-page spreads and wonderful paintings breathe new life into this humorous traditional song. (Rev: BL 5/15/99; HB 3/99; HBG 10/99; SLJ 6/99) [782.42162]

16598 Shulman, Lisa. *Old MacDonald Had a Woodshop* (PS–2). Illus. by Ashley Wolff. 2002, Penguin $17.99 (978-0-399-23596-2). 32pp. Old MacDonald, a female sheep, shares her woodshop with the other farm animals in this entertaining version of the familiar song. (Rev: BL 9/15/02; HB 9/02; HBG 3/03; SLJ 9/02*) [784.4]

16599 Silverman, Jerry. *Children's Songs* (4–6). Illus. 1993, Chelsea paper $13.25 (978-0-7910-1847-7). 64pp. This collection of 31 African American songs includes church songs, slave songs, and folk songs. (Rev: BL 2/15/94; SLJ 12/93) [782]

16600 Silverman, Jerry. *Singing Our Way West: Songs and Stories of America's Westward Expansion* (4–6). Illus. 1998, Millbrook LB $27.40 (978-0-7613-0417-3). 96pp. Twelve stories and folk songs associated with specific events in the settling of the West, including the railroad, the Erie Canal, and the Chisholm and Oregon Trails. (Rev: BL 12/1/98; HBG 3/99; SLJ 6/99) [782.4]

16601 Siomades, Lorianne. *The Itsy Bitsy Spider* (PS). Illus. 1999, Boyds Mills $9.95 (978-1-56397-727-5). 24pp. The spider, in this version of the catchy rhyme and song, carries an umbrella and waves a flashlight. (Rev: BL 3/1/99; HBG 10/99; SLJ 4/99)

16602 Trapani, Iza. *Froggie Went A-Courtin'* (PS–3). Illus. by author. 2002, Charlesbridge LB $15.95 (978-1-58089-028-1). 32pp. A new, humorous version of the song about Froggie's constant rejections. (Rev: HBG 3/03; SLJ 7/02) [784]

16603 Trapani, Iza. *The Itsy Bitsy Spider* (K–1). Illus. 1993, Whispering Coyote $16.95 (978-1-879085-77-0). 32pp. Building on the popular song, this book continues the adventures of the tiny spider. (Rev: BL 3/1/93)

16604 Trapani, Iza. *Row Row Row Your Boat* (PS–1). Illus. by author. 1999, Whispering Coyote $15.95 (978-1-58089-022-9). 32pp. The traditional song is reprinted with additional verses and pictures that depict a bear family on a boat excursion. (Rev: HBG 3/00; SLJ 11/99) [782]

16605 Tyler, Gillian. *Froggy Went a-Courtin'* (PS–2). Illus. 2005, Candlewick $15.99 (978-0-7636-2306-7). 32pp. Eyecatching watercolor-and-ink artwork highlights this adaptation of the familiar folk song about the unlikely romantic relationship between a frog and a mouse. (Rev: BL 1/1–15/05; SLJ 1/05) [782.4]

16606 Voake, Charlotte. *Tweedle-Dee-Dee* (PS–2). Illus. by author. 2008, Candlewick $16.99 (978-0-7636-3797-2). 32pp. A picture-book version of the folk song "The Green Grass Grew All Around," with appealing illustrations of nature, simple text, plus the music and lyrics. (Rev: BL 6/1–15/08; SLJ 6/08) [782.42]

16607 Wells, Rosemary. *Old MacDonald* (PS). Illus. by author. Series: Bunny Reads Back. 1998, Scholastic $6.99 (978-0-590-76985-3). 18pp. A board-book version of the traditional song, featuring a rabbit in overalls as Old MacDonald. (Rev: HBG 10/98; SLJ 10/98) [782]

16608 Westcott, Nadine Bernard. *I Know an Old Lady Who Swallowed a Fly* (2–4). Illus. by author. 1980, Little, Brown paper $6.95 (978-0-316-93127-4). 32pp. A newly illustrated edition of this outrageously funny song.

16609 Westcott, Nadine Bernard. *I've Been Working on the Railroad* (PS–1). Illus. 1996, Hyperion LB $14.49 (978-0-7868-2041-2). 32pp. This familiar folk song is seen through the eyes of a small boy who, with his dog, have adventures on a train. (Rev: BL 4/1/96; SLJ 6/96) [782]

16610 Yarrow, Peter. *Sleepytime Songs* (PS–2). Illus. by Terry Widener. 2008, Sterling $16.95 (978-1-4027-5962-8). 48pp. A collection of bedtime songs, with a CD, from Peter of Peter, Paul and Mary. (Rev: BL 1/1–15/09; SLJ 2/09) [782.42162]

16611 Yarrow, Peter, and Lenny Lipton. *Puff, the Magic Dragon* (PS–2). Illus. by Eric Puybaret. 2007, Sterling $16.95 (978-1-4027-4782-3). 24pp. The classic 1960s song about a friendly dragon is expanded in this picture book with accompanying four-song CD featuring Yarrow (of Peter, Paul, and Mary) and his daughter. (Rev: BL 9/15/07; SLJ 8/07) [782.42]

16612 Yolen, Jane. *Apple for the Teacher: Thirty Songs for Singing While You Work* (4–7). Illus. 2005, Abrams $24.95 (978-0-8109-4825-9). 160pp. This collection of work songs, compiled by Yolen and featuring music arrangements by her son Adam Stemple, celebrates 30 diverse occupations from astronaut to weaver. (Rev: BL 10/1/05; SLJ 10/05) [782.42]

Holidays

16613 Boys Choir of Harlem Staff. *O Holy Night: Christmas with the Boys Choir of Harlem* (PS–3). Illus. by Faith Ringgold. 2004, HarperCollins LB $19.89 (978-0-06-051819-6). 40pp. Rich illustrations of an African American holy family and onlookers of all races accompany the words to five Christmas carols, which are featured on the CD. (Rev: BL 9/1/04; SLJ 10/04)

16614 Brebeuf, Jean de. *The Huron Carol* (PS–2). Trans. by Jesse Edgar Middleton. Illus. by Ian Wallace. 2006, Groundwood $16.95 (978-0-88899-711-1). 32pp. Wallace illustrates in watercolor the 17th-century Christmas carol that sets the Nativity in Huron culture. (Rev: BL 10/15/06; SLJ 10/06) [782.28]

16615 Conahan, Carolyn. *The Twelve Days of Christmas Dogs* (K–3). Illus. 2005, Dutton $15.99 (978-0-525-47486-9). 32pp. A rambunctious parody involving a lot of dogs and one intrusive cat. (Rev: BL 10/15/05; SLJ 10/05)

16616 Delacre, Lulu. *Las Navidades: Popular Christmas Songs from Latin America* (K–4). Illus. 1990, Scholastic $13.95 (978-0-590-43548-2). 32pp. Christmas traditions of Latin America through seasonal songs. (Rev: BL 11/15/90) [782.42]

16617 Feliciano, Jose. *Feliz Navidad: Two Stories Celebrating Christmas* (PS–K). Illus. by David Diaz. 2003, Scholastic $15.95 (978-0-439-51717-1). 28pp. The lyrics of Feliciano's popular Christmas song are presented in Spanish and English, with beautiful illustrations of Puerto Rican and traditional American festivities. (Rev: HBG 4/04; SLJ 10/03) [782]

16618 Freeman, Martha. *Who Is Stealing the 12 Days of Christmas?* (4–6). 2003, Holiday House $16.95 (978-0-8234-1788-9). 200pp. When Christmas displays at the 12 houses on Chickadee Court — each

decorated for a different stanza of "The 12 Days of Christmas" — begin disappearing, Alex Parakeet and his best friend Yasmeen try to find out who — or what — is responsible. (Rev: HB 11/03; HBG 4/04; SLJ 10/03)

16619 *The Glorious Christmas Songbook* (3–7). Illus. 1999, Chronicle $18.95 (978-0-8118-2204-6). 77pp. A collection of traditional and modern Christmas carols and songs, with charming period illustrations and a few bars of the music. (Rev: BL 9/1/99; HBG 3/00; SLJ 10/99) [782.42172]

16620 Granfield, Linda. *Silent Night: The Song from Heaven* (2–4). Illus. by Nelly Hofer and Ernst Hofer. 1997, Tundra $15.95 (978-0-88776-395-3). 24pp. The story of the writing and first performance of this hymn, as experienced by two children who are helping in the church in Obendorf, Austria, where it was written in 1818. (Rev: HBG 3/98; SLJ 10/97)

16621 Katz, Alan. *Where Did They Hide My Presents? Silly Dilly Christmas Songs* (2–5). Illus. by David Catrow. 2005, Simon & Schuster $15.95 (978-0-689-86214-4). New lyrics for familiar songs celebrate the silly side of Christmas. (Rev: SLJ 10/05) [782.42]

16622 McCullough, L. E. *Stories of the Songs of Christmas* (3–5). Illus. by Irene Kelly. 1997, Smith & Kraus paper $19.95 (978-1-57525-116-5). 149pp. Background material on such Christmas carols and songs as "Silent Night," "Jingle Bells," and "The Twelve Days of Christmas." (Rev: SLJ 10/97) [782]

16623 McGinley, Sharon. *The Friendly Beasts* (PS–K). Illus. 2000, Greenwillow $15.95 (978-0-688-17421-7). 24pp. This joyful picture book illustrates the text of the carol "The Friendly Beasts," which describes the roles played by several different animals during the Nativity. (Rev: BCCB 11/00; BL 9/15/00; HBG 10/01) [782.28]

16624 Neale, John M. *Good King Wenceslas* (PS–2). Illus. by Tim Ladwig. 2005, Eerdmans $16.00 (978-0-8028-5209-0). 32pp. The words of the familiar Christmas carol and oversize double-spread, expressive artwork combine to celebrate the story of King Wenceslas, a 10th-century Bohemian monarch. (Rev: BL 10/15/05; SLJ 10/05) [782.28]

16625 Orozco, Jose-Luis. *Fiestas: A Year of Latin American Songs of Celebration* (2–4). Illus. by Elisa Kleven. 2002, Dutton $17.99 (978-0-525-45937-8). 56pp. Orozco presents 21 songs in Spanish and English, with music,. (Rev: BL 9/15/02; HBG 3/03) [782.42]

16626 Spirin, Gennady. *We Three Kings* (K–3). Illus. by author. 2007, Atheneum $16.99 (978-0-689-82114-1). 32pp. In a Renaissance-reminiscent style, Spirin richly illustrates verses and choruses to the well-known Christmas carol "We Three Kings." (Rev: BL 11/1/07) [782.42]

16627 Stevens, Jan R. *Twelve Lizards Leaping: A New Twelve Days of Christmas* (PS–3). Illus. by Christine Mau. 1999, Rising Moon $14.95 (978-0-87358-744-0). 32pp. A southwestern version of the standard Christmas carol with music, lyrics, and vivid paintings. (Rev: HBG 3/00; SLJ 10/99) [782]

16628 Sturges, Philemon. *The Twelve Days of Christmas: A Pinata for the Pinon Tree* (K–2). Illus. by Ashley Wolff. 2007, Little, Brown $16.99 (978-0-316-82323-4). 40pp. Southwestern images (coyotes yowling, skinks a-skulking) replace the familiar partridges and lords a leaping in this fractured Christmas song. (Rev: BL 9/15/07)

16629 *The Twelve Days of Christmas* (PS–3). Illus. by Vladimir Vagin. 1999, HarperCollins LB $15.89 (978-0-06-028399-5). 32pp. A finely illustrated version of this carol that evokes allusions to both Russian folklore and New England landscapes. (Rev: BL 1/1–15/00; HBG 3/00) [782.42]

16630 Tyrrell, Frances. *Woodland Christmas: Twelve Days of Christmas in the North Woods* (PS–2). Illus. 1996, Scholastic $15.95 (978-0-590-86367-4). 32pp. Woodland creatures portray the "true love's" gifts on each of the 12 days of Christmas. (Rev: BL 9/1/96) [782]

Musical Instruments

16631 Aylmore, Angela. *Banging* (PS–K). Illus. Series: Making Music. 2005, Raintree LB $20.64 (978-1-4109-1604-4). 24pp. Children show how to use a variety of instruments including drums and Indonesian gongs in this brightly illustrated volume; companion volumes are *Blowing*, *Plucking*, and *Shaking* (all 2005). (Rev: SLJ 1/06) [786.819]

16632 Barber, Nicola. *Should I Play the Flute?* (3–5). Illus. Series: Learning Musical Instruments. 2006, Heinemann LB $28.21 (978-1-4034-8187-0). 32pp. Chapters answer such questions as "How does a flute make its sound?", "What types of music can you play on a flute?", and "How would I learn to play the flute?" Also use *Should I Play the Piano?* (2006). (Rev: SLJ 2/07) [788.3]

16633 Crask, Tom. *Should I Play the Drums?* (3–5). Illus. Series: Learning Musical Instruments. 2006, Heinemann LB $28.21 (978-1-4034-8186-3). 32pp. Answering the title question, this well-organized and attractive volume gives the history of the drums, discusses how their sound is produced, and names famous drum players and drum recordings. Also use *Should I Play the Guitar?* and *Should I Play the Violin?* (both 2006). (Rev: SLJ 2/07) [786.9]

16634 Day, Eileen M. *I'm Good at Making Music* (PS–1). Series: I'm Good At. 2003, Heinemann LB $18.50 (978-1-4034-0900-3). 24pp. A beginning look at making music on such simple instruments as the triangle, kazoo, and drum. (Rev: HBG 4/04; SLJ 4/04) [780]

16635 Dunleavy, Deborah. *The Kids Can Press Jumbo Book of Music* (2–6). Illus. by Louise Phillips. Series: A Kids Can Press Jumbo Book. 2001, Kids Can paper $14.95 (978-1-55074-723-2). 208pp. Instructions for making a variety of musical instruments from everyday materials are accompanied by suggestions of appropriate music and groupings of instruments. (Rev: SLJ 4/01) [780]

16636 Ganeri, Anita. *The Young Person's Guide to the Orchestra: Benjamin Britten's Composition on CD* (4–6). Illus. 1996, Harcourt $25.00 (978-0-15-201304-2). 64pp. The text explains and illustrates the various instruments of the orchestra, with an accompanying CD of Britten's music. (Rev: BL 10/1/96; SLJ 10/96) [784.2]

16637 Hayes, Ann. *Meet the Marching Smithereens* (K–3). Illus. by Karmen Thompson. 1995, Harcourt $15.00 (978-0-15-253158-4). 32pp. Several musical instruments are introduced through a description of an animal marching band called the Smithereens. (Rev: BCCB 6/95; BL 7/95; SLJ 5/95) [784.3]

16638 Helsby, Genevieve. *Those Amazing Musical Instruments!* (4–9). Illus. 2007, Sourcebooks $19.95 (978-1-4022-0825-6). 176pp. A CD-ROM is included with this engaging and comprehensive guide to orchestral instruments. (Rev: SLJ 3/08) [784.3]

16639 Hooper, Maureen Brett. *Highlights Fun to Play Recorder Book: Learn with Easy Steps and Familiar Songs* (2–6). Illus. by Judith Hunt. 2001, Boyds Mills $14.95 (978-1-56397-965-1). 49pp. Basic instructions for playing the recorder are accompanied by suitable songs that increase in difficulty as the reader progresses through the book. (Rev: SLJ 6/01) [784]

16640 Koscielniak, Bruce. *The Story of the Incredible Orchestra* (K–4). Illus. 2000, Houghton $16.00 (978-0-395-96052-3). 40pp. This account traces the growth of the orchestra and the development of modern musical instruments and also comments on the work of several composers. (Rev: BCCB 6/00; BL 4/15/00; HBG 10/00; SLJ 6/00) [784.2]

16641 Levine, Robert. *The Story of the Orchestra* (5–7). Illus. by Meredith Hamilton. 2001, Black Dog & Leventhal $19.98 (978-1-57912-148-8). 96pp. Orchestra Bob introduces young readers to orchestra history, famous conductors and their eras, and instruments, in a guided tour that includes amusing cartoons, illustrations, and links to selections on the accompanying CD. (Rev: BL 12/15/01; SLJ 9/01) [784.2]

16642 Lynch, Wendy. *Brass* (2–4). Series: Musical Instruments. 2001, Heinemann LB $21.36 (978-1-58810-233-1). 32pp. A look at the brass family of instruments in words and pictures, with material on the trumpet, tuba, and trombone. (Rev: BL 1/1–15/02; HBG 3/02) [788]

16643 Lynch, Wendy. *Keyboards* (2–4). Illus. Series: Musical Instruments. 2001, Heinemann LB $21.36 (978-1-58810-234-8). 32pp. Lynch introduces younger readers to keyboard instruments, how they work and how they sound, with back matter that includes a glossary and a bibliography. Also use *Percussion* (2001). (Rev: BL 1/1–15/02; HBG 3/02) [786]

16644 Lynch, Wendy. *Strings* (2–4). Series: Musical Instruments. 2001, Heinemann LB $21.36 (978-1-58810-236-2). 32pp. All the stringed instruments of an orchestra are described in text and pictures with an activity based on creating the simulated sound of stringed instruments. (Rev: BL 1/1–15/02; HBG 3/02) [787]

16645 Lynch, Wendy. *Woodwind* (2–4). Series: Musical Instruments. 2001, Heinemann LB $21.36 (978-1-58810-237-9). 32pp. All the woodwinds — including the clarinet, bassoon, and saxophone — are pictured and described, and common household objects are used to simulate their sounds. (Rev: BL 1/1–15/02; HBG 3/02) [788]

16646 Moss, Lloyd. *Zin! Zin! Zin! A Violin* (1–3). Illus. by Marjorie Priceman. 1995, Simon & Schuster $16.00 (978-0-671-88239-6). 28pp. Ten instruments of the orchestra are introduced in rhyming couplets. (Rev: BL 5/15/95; SLJ 5/95*)

16647 Rubin, Mark. *The Orchestra* (2–4). Illus. by Alan Daniel. 1992, Firefly paper $8.95 (978-0-920668-99-3). 48pp. After a general introduction to music, this book introduces each of the instruments of the orchestra. (Rev: SLJ 6/92) [781.91]

16648 Sabbeth, Alex. *Rubber-Band Banjos and a Java Jive Bass: Projects and Activities on the Science of Music and Sound* (4–7). Illus. 1997, Wiley paper $12.95 (978-0-471-15675-8). 112pp. Describes the basic elements of music while giving directions for making a variety of homemade instruments. (Rev: BL 3/15/97; SLJ 6/97) [781]

16649 Thyacott, Louise. *Musical Instruments* (5–7). Illus. Series: Traditions Around the World. 1995, Thomson Learning LB $24.26 (978-1-56847-228-7). 48pp. A continent-by-continent survey of the many kinds of musical instruments found in various cultures. (Rev: BCCB 11/94; BL 9/15/95) [784.3]

16650 Wiseman, Ann Sayre, and John Langstaff. *Making Music: How to Create and Play 70 Homemade Musical Instruments* (3–5). Illus. by Ann Sayre Wiseman. 2003, Storey Kids paper $9.95 (978-1-58017-512-8). 96pp. Spoons, forks, and flowerpots are among the household items that become musical instruments in this illustrated "how-to" book. (Rev: SLJ 3/04) [784.192]

National Anthems and Patriotic Songs

16651 Bates, Katharine Lee. *America the Beautiful* (K–3). Illus. by Wendell Minor. 2003, Penguin $18.99 (978-0-399-23885-7). 32pp. Paintings on double-page spreads illustrate the verses of this poem, spanning events in the history of the country. (Rev: HBG 10/03; SLJ 7/03) [811]

16652 Berlin, Irving. *God Bless America* (PS). Illus. by Lynn Munsinger. 2002, HarperCollins $15.99 (978-0-06-009788-2). 32pp. The Irving Berlin classic song set to illustration, depicting a family of bears traveling across America. (Rev: BL 8/02; HBG 3/03) [782.421599]

16653 Bowdish, Lynea. *Francis Scott Key and "The Star Spangled Banner"* (K–3). Illus. by Harry Burman. 2002, Mondo $15.95 (978-1-59034-195-7). 32pp. A large-format book for younger readers about Francis Scott Key's penning of the national

anthem in 1814. (Rev: BL 12/15/02; HBG 3/03) [973.5]

16654 Cohan, George M. *You're a Grand Old Flag* (PS–1). Illus. by Warren Kimble. 2007, Walker $16.95 (978-0-8027-9575-5). Images of flags and scenes from the American countryside by artist Warren Kimble illustrate the lyrics to the classic tune. (Rev: SLJ 6/07)

16655 Johnson, James W. *Lift Every Voice and Sing* (PS–3). Illus. by Bryan Collier. 2007, HarperCollins $16.99 (978-0-06-054147-7). 32pp. The well-known song now recognized as the "African American National Hymn" is personally interpreted through collage and watercolor pictures subtly illustrating African American history. (Rev: BL 11/1/07; SLJ 12/07) [782.42]

16656 Johnson, James W. *Lift Ev'ry Voice and Sing* (PS–4). Illus. by Jan S. Gilchrist. 1995, Scholastic $14.95 (978-0-590-46982-1). 32pp. Using the lyrics of this beautiful anthem as a framework, the history and culture of African Americans are traced in touching illustrations. (Rev: BL 2/15/95*; SLJ 2/95) [782]

16657 Sonneborn, Liz. *The Star-Spangled Banner: The Story Behind Our National Anthem* (3–5). Illus. Series: America in Words and Song. 2004, Chelsea House LB $23.00 (978-0-7910-7337-7). 32pp. This slim volume covers the history of the national anthem and the changes it has undergone over the years. Also use *America the Beautiful: The Story Behind Our National Hymn* (2004). (Rev: BL 4/1/04; HBG 4/04) [929.9]

16658 Yanuck, Debbie L. *The Star-Spangled Banner* (K–2). Series: American Symbols. 2003, Capstone LB $21.26 (978-0-7368-2293-0). 24pp. An account of the events that inspired Francis Scott Key to write the poem that — more than 100 years later — became the lyrics to the national anthem of the United States. (Rev: SLJ 4/04) [782.42]

Singing Games and Songs

16659 Amery, Heather, comp. *The Usborne Children's Songbook* (PS–3). Illus. by Stephen Cartwright. 1998, Usborne paper $10.95 (978-0-7460-2981-7). 64pp. A collection of 35 traditional songs (e.g., "Twinkle, twinkle, little star") with musical arrangements and chords for a variety of different instruments. (Rev: SLJ 2/99) [782]

16660 Barnwell, Ysaye M. *We Are One* (PS–2). Illus. by Brian Pinkney. 2008, Harcourt $17.95 (978-0-15-205735-0). 32pp. A song celebrating community, friendship, and peace is illustrated in exuberant scenes and accompanied by a music CD. (Rev: BL 3/1/08; LMC 11/08; SLJ 3/08) [782.42]

16661 Boynton, Sandra. *Philadelphia Chickens* (PS–5). Illus. by author. 2002, Workman $16.95 (978-0-7611-2636-2). 64pp. A cast of animal characters bounce through pages of lyrics and musical notations, while the songs are performed on the accompanying CD by celebrities including Meryl

Streep and Natasha Richardson. (Rev: SLJ 3/03) [782.1]

16662 Cabrera, Jane. *If You're Happy and You Know It!* (PS). Illus. 2005, Holiday House $16.95 (978-0-8234-1881-7). 32pp. Readers clap their hands and stamp their feet along with a cast of assorted animals. (Rev: BL 2/15/05; SLJ 3/05) [782.42]

16663 Carle, Eric. *Today Is Monday* (PS–K). Illus. 1992, Penguin $16.99 (978-0-399-21966-5). 32pp. A picture book that bursts with food, animals, and energy, and also includes music and lyrics, so everyone can sing along. (Rev: BL 1/1/93*; SLJ 4/93) [782]

16664 *De Colores: Bright with Colors* (PS–3). Illus. by David Diaz. 2008, Marshall Cavendish $16.99 (978-0-7614-5431-1). 32pp. A visually pleasing illustration of the first two verses of the Spanish folk song. (Rev: BL 3/1/08; SLJ 5/08) [782.42]

16665 Delacre, Lulu, ed. *Arroz con Leche: Popular Songs and Rhymes from Latin America* (PS–1). Trans. by Elena Paz. Illus. by Lulu Delacre. 1989, Scholastic paper $5.99 (978-0-590-41886-7). 32pp. A bilingual collection of folk rhymes, chants, and fingerplays. (Rev: BCCB 5/89)

16666 DiPucchio, Kelly. *Sipping Spiders Through a Straw: Campfire Songs for Monsters* (3–5). Illus. by Gris Grimly. 2008, Scholastic $15.99 (978-0-439-58401-2). 40pp. A collection of 18 classic songs that have been reworded to enhance their gross-out quotient. (Rev: BL 5/1/08; SLJ 6/08) [782.42]

16667 Emberley, Barbara. *Drummer Hoff* (K–3). Illus. by Ed Emberley. 1967, Simon & Schuster $16.00 (978-0-671-66248-6); paper $5.95 (978-0-671-66245-5). 32pp. The classic song about the assembling of a cannon. Caldecott Medal winner, 1968.

16668 *The Farmer in the Dell* (PS). Illus. by Ilse Plume. 2004, Godine $17.95 (978-1-56792-270-7). 28pp. The familiar song is set in Pennsylvania Dutch countryside. (Rev: BL 9/15/04) [782.4]

16669 *For Our Children: A Book to Benefit the Pediatric AIDS Foundation* (PS–3). Illus. 1991, Disney LB $16.89 (978-1-56282-112-8). 72pp. An album of 20 songs by Carol King, Little Richard, and other artists. (Rev: BL 10/1/91; SLJ 10/91) [782.42]

16670 Hinojosa, Tish. *Cada Nino / Every Child: A Bilingual Songbook for Kids* (3–6). Illus. by Lucía Angela Pérez. 2002, Cinco Puntos $18.95 (978-0-938317-60-9). 56pp. This is a charming bilingual songbook, with music, presenting 11 traditional and original songs that celebrate the simple things in life. (Rev: BL 6/1–15/02; HBG 10/02) [782.42]

16671 Hoberman, Mary Ann, adapt. *Mary Had a Little Lamb* (PS–2). Illus. by Nadine Bernard Westcott. Series: Sing-Along Stories. 2003, Little, Brown $15.95 (978-0-316-60687-5). 32pp. Young readers will enjoy this extended version of the popular children's song about Mary and her little lamb that recounts what happens after the lamb gets to school. (Rev: HBG 4/04; SLJ 12/03) [782.42164]

16672 Hort, Lenny. *The Seals on the Bus* (PS–1). Illus. by G. Brian Karas. 2000, Holt $15.95 (978-0-8050-5952-6). 32pp. This variation on the song "The Wheels on the Bus" tells of a series of wild

animals who find their way onto a city bus. (Rev: BCCB 5/00; BL 4/1/00; HB 5/00; HBG 10/00; SLJ 5/00) [782.4]

16673 Johnson, Paul B. *Little Bunny Foo Foo* (PS–1). Illus. 2004, Scholastic $15.95 (978-0-439-37301-2). 32pp. In a lively adaptation full of eye-catching vehicles, the Good Fairy describes the transgressions of naughty bunny Foo Foo; music, lyrics, and suggested movements are included. (Rev: BL 1/1–15/04; SLJ 4/04)

16674 Kanzler, John. *The Big Rock Candy Mountain* (PS–2). Illus. by author. 2004, Mondo $15.95 (978-1-59336-062-7). 24pp. The folk song becomes a lively picture book as a family goes camping, boating, square dancing, and meets up with interesting creatures including some musical bears; lyrics and music are appended. (Rev: SLJ 5/04) [782.42]

16675 Karas, G. Brian. *I Know an Old Lady* (PS–1). Illus. 1995, Scholastic $14.95 (978-0-590-46575-5). 32pp. An uproarious version of the traditional cumulative nonsense rhyme. (Rev: BCCB 2/95; BL 1/15/95*; SLJ 3/95) [782]

16676 Katz, Alan. *Are You Quite Polite?* (K–3). Illus. by David Catrow. 2006, Simon & Schuster $15.95 (978-0-689-86970-9). 32pp. Silly verses set to familiar tunes focus on poor behavior (lateness, bad table manners, nose-picking, and so forth), enhanced by suitably lively cartoon art. (Rev: BL 11/15/06; SLJ 10/06) [782.42]

16677 Katz, Alan. *Going, Going, Gone!* (K–4). Illus. by David Catrow. 2009, Simon & Schuster $16.99 (978-1-4169-0696-4). 32pp. A humorous collection of familiar tunes with new, sporty lyrics — "On Top of the Bleachers" for example. (Rev: BL 1/1–15/09; SLJ 2/09) [782.42]

16678 Katz, Alan. *Take Me out of the Bathtub and Other Silly Dilly Songs* (PS–1). Illus. by David Catrow. 2001, Simon & Schuster $15.00 (978-0-689-82903-1). 32pp. Amusing adaptations of a number of familiar songs are accompanied by equally silly illustrations. (Rev: BL 7/01; HBG 10/01; SLJ 4/01) [782.4216]

16679 Kennedy, Jimmy. *The Teddy Bears' Picnic* (PS–1). Illus. by Michael Hague. 1995, Holt paper $6.95 (978-0-8050-5349-4). 32pp. A large format and drawings complement this popular song about teddy bears gathering for a picnic. (Rev: BL 4/15/92; SLJ 6/92) [782]

16680 *Knick Knack Paddy Whack* (PS). Illus. by Christiane Engel. 2008, Barefoot Books $16.99 (978-1-84686-144-4). 24pp. The classic counting song is presented in a tropical setting with a multicultural, musical cast of characters. (Rev: BL 4/1/08; SLJ 5/08) [782.42]

16681 Langstaff, Nancy, and John Langstaff. *Sally Go Round the Moon* (K–4). Illus. by Jan Pienkowski. 1986, Revels paper $14.95 (978-0-9640836-3-9). 127pp. A collection of folk songs and singing games originally published in 1970.

16682 Lessac, Frane. *Camp Granada: Sing-Along Camp Songs* (2–5). Illus. 2003, Holt $18.95 (978-0-8050-6683-8). 48pp. Colorful, humorous illustrations and a brief story about camp activities form a backdrop for the lyrics to 34 camp songs. (Rev: BL 3/1/03; HBG 10/03; SLJ 6/03) [782.42164]

16683 Loesser, Frank. *I Love You! A Bushel and a Peck* (PS). Illus. by Rosemary Wells. 2004, Harper-Collins LB $16.89 (978-0-06-028550-0). 32pp. Loesser's song from *Guys and Dolls* forms the framework for this charming story of a budding romance between two flirtatious ducklings. (Rev: BL 11/15/04; SLJ 2/05) [782.42]

16684 MacDonald, Margaret Read, and Winifred Jaeger. *The Round Book: Rounds Kids Love to Sing* (4–6). Illus. 1999, Linnet $22.50 (978-0-208-02441-1); paper $16.50 (978-0-208-02472-5). 124pp. A paperback containing 80 songs designed to be sung as rounds. (Rev: BL 9/1/99; HBG 10/99; SLJ 7/99) [782.42]

16685 Miller, J. Philip, and Sheppard M. Greene. *We All Sing with the Same Voice* (PS–K). Illus. by Paul Meisel. 2001, HarperCollins $16.99 (978-0-06-027475-7). 32pp. This book-and-CD set features the Sesame Street song about understanding one another's cultures and the similarities of children all over the world. (Rev: HBG 10/01; SLJ 2/01) [784]

16686 Moore, Mary-Alice. *The Wheels on the School Bus* (K–2). Illus. by Laura Huliska-Beith. 2006, HarperCollins $15.99 (978-0-06-059427-5). 32pp. In this adaptation of the popular song, the action is focused on a bus full of students — and also commuting teachers — as it makes its way to school. (Rev: BL 8/06; SLJ 8/06) [782.42]

16687 Moreillon, Judi. *Sing Down the Rain* (2–5). Illus. by Michael Chiago. 1997, Kiva $14.95 (978-1-885772-07-7). 32pp. This choral reading in eight parts celebrates the Saguaro Wine Ceremony of the Tohono O'odham tribe of the Sonoran desert. (Rev: SLJ 1/98) [811]

16688 Newcome, Zita. *Head, Shoulders, Knees, and Toes and Other Action Rhymes* (PS). Illus. 2002, Candlewick $15.99 (978-0-7636-1899-5). 64pp. Familiar songs and rhymes, with illustrations of children performing movements to accompany them. (Rev: BL 9/15/02; HBG 3/03; SLJ 10/02) [398.8]

16689 O'Brien, John. *The Farmer in the Dell* (PS–1). Illus. 2000, Boyds Mills $14.95 (978-1-56397-775-6). 40pp. Hilarious illustrations give new life to this favorite song. (Rev: BL 11/1/00; HBG 3/01; SLJ 9/00) [782.42]

16690 Raven, Margot Theis. *Happy Birthday to You! The Mystery Behind the Most Famous Song in the World* (2–5). Illus. by Chris Soentpiet. 2008, Sleeping Bear $17.95 (978-1-58536-169-4). 32pp. The real story of how "Happy Birthday to You" became the American birthday song. (Rev: BLO 10/7/08; LMC 5/09; SLJ 12/08) [782.42]

16691 Rounds, Glen, ed. *I Know an Old Lady Who Swallowed a Fly* (PS–3). Illus. by Glen Rounds. 1990, Holiday House LB $17.95 (978-0-8234-0814-6). 32pp. This humorous folk song is cleverly illustrated with mottled colors. (Rev: BCCB 9/90; BL 5/15/90; SLJ 8/90) [782]

16692 Rueda, Claudia. *Let's Play in the Forest While the Wolf Is Not Around* (PS). Illus. 2006, Scholastic $16.99 (978-0-439-82323-4). 32pp. The animals of the forest come out to play unaware that the wolf is in fact getting dressed and is hungry — all shown in facing pages — but it turns out that he's just hungry for pancakes; this song is based on a traditional one and the music is appended. (Rev: BL 11/15/06; SLJ 10/06) [782.42]

16693 Salas, Laura Purdie. *From Beginning to End: A Song About Life Cycles* (PS–K). Illus. by Viviana Garofoli. Series: Science Songs. 2008, Picture Window LB $25.32 (978-1-4048-5293-8). 24pp. This sing-along book pairs scientific facts about living things with familiar tunes such as "Are You Sleeping?" to help children retain information. Also use *Home on the Earth: A Song About Earth's Layers* and *Move It! Work It! A Song About Simple Machines*. (Rev: SLJ 5/09) [571.8]

16694 Sloat, Teri. *There Was an Old Lady Who Swallowed a Trout!* (PS–1). Illus. by Reynold Ruffins. 1998, Holt $15.95 (978-0-8050-4294-8). 32pp. Set in the Pacific Northwest, this variation on the popular cumulative rhyme has the old lady swallowing a trout, salmon, otter, seal, porpoise, walrus, and even a whale. (Rev: BL 11/15/98*; HBG 3/99; SLJ 11/98) [782]

16695 Sloat, Teri. *There Was an Old Man Who Painted the Sky* (PS–2). Illus. by Stefano Vitale. 2009, Holt $16.95 (978-0-8050-6751-4). 32pp. Adapting "The Old Woman Who Swallowed a Fly" Sloat tells the story of a prehistoric man whose cave painting is later discovered by a Spanish girl. (Rev: BL 5/15/09; LMC 10/09; SLJ 9/09) [782.42]

16696 Staines, Bill. *All God's Critters* (PS–1). Illus. by Kadir Nelson. 2009, Simon & Schuster $16.99 (978-0-689-86959-4). 36pp. A rollicking song performed by an exuberant cast of animals, some singing low, some singing high. (Rev: BCCB 2/09; BL 12/15/08; SLJ 1/09) [782.42]

16697 Trapani, Iza, retel. *How Much Is That Doggie in the Window?* (PS–3). Score and lyrics by Bob Merrill. Illus. by Iza Trapani. 1997, Whispering Coyote $15.95 (978-1-879085-74-9). 32pp. This expanded version of the once-popular song tells about a little boy who wants a spotted puppy in a pet shop but can't afford to buy it. (Rev: HBG 3/98; SLJ 3/98) [782]

16698 Wallner, Alexandra. *The Farmer in the Dell* (PS). Illus. 1998, Holiday House $15.95 (978-0-8234-1382-9). 32pp. An illustrated version of this favorite children's song, including the music and complete lyrics. (Rev: BL 9/1/98; HBG 3/99; SLJ 11/98) [782.4216]

16699 Weiss, George D., and Bob Thiele. *What a Wonderful World* (PS–3). Illus. by Ashley Bryan. 1995, Simon & Schuster LB $16.00 (978-0-689-80087-0). 32pp. Children use a puppet stage to introduce this song. (Rev: BL 5/15/95; SLJ 5/95)

16700 Zelinsky, Paul, adapt. *The Wheels on the Bus* (PS–1). Illus. 1990, Dutton paper $20.99 (978-0-525-44644-6). 16pp. A pop-up edition with pull tabs of the familiar song. (Rev: BCCB 10/90; SLJ 10/90) [784]

Performing Arts

Circuses, Fairs, and Parades

16701 Schubert, Leda. *Ballet of the Elephants* (K–3). Illus. by Robert Andrew Parker. 2006, Roaring Brook $17.95 (978-1-59643-075-4). 32pp. The fascinating story of the collaboration of circus owner John Ringling North, choreographer George Balanchine, and composer Igor Stravinsky to create a ballet featuring 50 elephants with ballerinas on their backs; vivid illustrations accompany the text and the author's note at the end includes a few black-and-white photographs of the performance. (Rev: BL 4/1/06; SLJ 4/06) [796.8]

Dance

16702 Augustyn, Frank, and Shelley Tanaka. *Footnotes: Dancing the World's Best-Loved Ballets* (5–8). Illus. 2001, Millbrook LB $24.90 (978-0-7613-2323-5). 96pp. A readable account that introduces ballet from a backstage perspective, with material on how it feels to be a dancer in a large ballet company. (Rev: BL 4/15/01; HBG 10/01; SLJ 6/01*; VOYA 8/01) [792.8]

16703 Barber, Antonia. *Shoes of Satin, Ribbons of Silk: Tales from the Ballet* (4–6). Illus. 1995, Kingfisher $18.95 (978-1-85697-693-0). 96pp. In dramatic retellings, the stories of nine ballets (several less well known) are presented. (Rev: BL 11/15/95; SLJ 1/96) [792.8]

16704 Bray-Moffatt, Naia. *Ballet School* (K–3). Illus. 2003, DK $12.99 (978-0-7894-9228-9). 48pp. Ample illustrations grace this friendly, large-format introduction to ballet and its techniques, methods of instruction, costumes, and performances. (Rev: BL 4/15/03; HBG 10/03; SLJ 9/03) [792.8]

16705 Castle, Kate. *Ballet* (4–6). Illus. 1996, Kingfisher $16.95 (978-0-7534-5001-7). 64pp. A well-

illustrated introduction to the world of ballet, with material on the composer, choreographer, designer, famous dancers, and stories of well-known ballets. (Rev: SLJ 12/96) [792.8]

16706 Castle, Kate. *My First Ballet Book* (K–3). 2006, Kingfisher $9.95 (978-0-7534-6026-9). 48pp. The fundamentals of ballet — from basic positions to arabesques, jumps, and pas de deux — are shown in color photographs of ethnically diverse children, accompanied by concise text. (Rev: SLJ 12/06) [792.8]

16707 Collins, Pat Lowery. *I Am a Dancer* (PS–2). Illus. by Mark Graham. 2008, Lerner LB $22.60 (978-0-8225-6369-3). 32pp. Illustrations of children in motion accompany free-verse poetry about the many ways one can dance. (Rev: BL 6/1–15/08; SLJ 6/08) [792.62]

16708 Cooper, Elisha. *Dance!* (2–4). Illus. 2001, Greenwillow $16.99 (978-0-06-029418-2). 32pp. This is a very visual introduction to the world of dance, with feathery watercolor illustrations and minimal text. (Rev: BL 9/15/01; HB 11/01; HBG 3/02; SLJ 9/01) [793.8]

16709 Dillman, Lisa. *Ballet* (4–7). Illus. Series: Get Going! Hobbies. 2005, Heinemann LB $27.79 (978-1-4034-6115-5). 32pp. A photo-filled introduction to ballet, with historical information plus basic positions and steps and exercises to help would-be dancers get in shape; also use *Tap Dancing* (2005). (Rev: BL 11/1/05; SLJ 3/06) [792.8]

16710 Elliott, Donald. *Frogs and Ballet* (4–6). Illus. by Clinton Arrowood. 1979, Harvard Common paper $8.95 (978-0-87645-119-9). 80pp. Familiar ballet steps and how they are woven into the classical ballet.

16711 Friedman, Lise. *First Lessons in Ballet* (3–5). Illus. 1999, Workman paper $8.95 (978-0-7611-1352-2). 64pp. Illustrated with photographs, this book for beginning ballet students explains techniques, positions, exercises, and more. (Rev: BL 2/15/00; SLJ 4/00) [792.8]

16712 Frith, Margaret. *Hooray for Ballet!* (2–4). Illus. by Amanda Haley. Series: Smart About the Arts. 2003, Grosset paper $5.99 (978-0-448-42884-0). 32pp. With plenty of interesting detail, Elizabeth relates the story of her visit to Lincoln Center to see *Swan Lake*. (Rev: HBG 10/03; SLJ 9/03) [792.8]

16713 Geras, Adele. *Sleeping Beauty* (3–5). Illus. Series: The Magic of Ballet. 2001, David & Charles $10.95 (978-1-86233-246-1). 26pp. The story of Sleeping Beauty is told from the perspective of four characters. Also use *Swan Lake* (2001). (Rev: BCCB 1/03; BL 7/01; SLJ 11/01) [823.914]

16714 Geras, Adele. *Time for Ballet* (PS–2). Illus. by Shelagh McNicholas. 2004, Dial $16.99 (978-0-8037-2978-0). 32pp. Soft watercolors illustrate the tale of Tilly, an aspiring dancer, as she and the other members of her ballet class prepare for a recital. (Rev: BL 2/1/04*; SLJ 2/04)

16715 Gladstone, Valerie. *A Young Dancer: The Life of an Ailey Student* (1–4). Illus. by Jose Ivey. 2009, Holt $18.95 (978-0-8050-8233-3). 48pp. This photoessay shows the dedication of Iman, a 13-year-old African American dancer, as she attends academic classes, music lessons, and long dance practices. (Rev: BCCB 5/09; BL 2/1/09; SLJ 6/09) [792.8]

16716 Hayden, Melissa, ed. *The Nutcracker Ballet* (K–4). Illus. by Stephen T. Johnson. 1992, Andrews McMeel $14.95 (978-0-8362-4501-1). 32pp. This retelling is based on Balanchine's version of the ballet. (Rev: BL 2/1/93) [792]

16717 Hayward, Linda. *A Day in the Life of a Dancer* (PS–K). Series: Dorling Kindersley Readers: Jobs People Do. 2001, DK paper $3.99 (978-0-7894-7369-1). 32pp. Using a very limited vocabulary and simple sentences, this beginning reader explores the everyday life of a ballet dancer. (Rev: BL 8/1/01; HBG 10/01) [792.8]

16718 Hoffmann, E. T. A. *The Nutcracker* (PS). Illus. by Thea Kliros. 2003, HarperCollins $5.99 (978-0-06-052745-7). 22pp. A simplified, attractively illustrated version of the story behind Tchaikovsky's world-famous ballet. (Rev: SLJ 10/03)

16719 Jeffers, Susan. *The Nutcracker* (K–2). Illus. by author. 2007, HarperCollins $16.99 (978-0-06-074386-4). 32pp. The traditional ballet story is set in the Victorian era and features rich illustrations. (Rev: BL 9/15/07; HB 11/07)

16720 Johnson, Anne E. *Jazz Tap: From African Drums to American Feet* (4–7). Series: The Library of African American Arts and Culture. 1999, Rosen LB $27.95 (978-0-8239-1856-0). 64pp. This book traces the history of jazz tap from a variety of African dances to its emergence in the 1920s and its later development in night clubs, on Broadway, and in movies. (Rev: SLJ 1/00) [793.3]

16721 Keeler, Patricia, and Julio Leitao. *Drumbeat in Our Feet* (3–5). Illus. by Patricia Keeler. 2006, Lee & Low $16.95 (978-1-58430-264-3). 32pp. Information on — and illustrations of — traditional African dances are paired with pictures of young Americans learning these dances at a studio in Harlem. (Rev: BL 11/1/06; SLJ 12/06) [793.3]

16722 Pavlova, Anna. *I Dreamed I Was a Ballerina* (3–5). Illus. by Edgar Degas. 2001, Simon & Schuster $16.00 (978-0-689-84676-2). 32pp. Beautiful Degas illustrations accompany the true story, in her own words, of Pavlova's inspiring first visit to a ballet and her subsequent rise to fame. (Rev: BL 12/1/01; HBG 3/02; SLJ 11/01) [792.8]

16723 Riordan, James. *Favorite Stories of the Ballet* (4–6). Illus. by Victor G. Ambrus. 1993, Checkerboard $14.95 (978-1-56288-252-5). These ballet stories include *The Nutcracker, Swan Lake, Sleeping Beauty,* and *Cinderella.*

16724 Schorer, Suki, and School of American Ballet. *Put Your Best Foot Forward: A Young Dancer's Guide to Life* (4–8). Photos by Chris Carroll. Illus. by Donna Ingemanson. 2005, Workman $9.95 (978-0-7611-3795-5). 96pp. Practical tips are combined with artistic advice in this helpful guide for young ballet dancers, written by a former principal dancer. (Rev: SLJ 3/06) [792.8]

16725 *Step-by-Step Ballet Class: The Official Illustrated Guide* (4–6). Illus. 1994, Contemporary paper $14.95 (978-0-8092-3499-8). 144pp. This guide developed by the Royal Academy of Dancing in England gives material for various levels of development, including positions, movements, and advice on appearance. (Rev: BL 12/1/94) [792.8]

16726 Thompson, Lauren. *Ballerina Dreams* (K–2). Illus. 2007, Feiwel & Friends $16.95 (978-0-312-37029-9). 40pp. Five little girls with cerebral palsy and other muscular disorders, through hard work and the help of a dancer/physical therapist, realize their dreams of performing in a ballet recital in this true story documented with photographs. (Rev: BL 11/1/07; SLJ 9/07) [618.92]

16727 Tythacott, Louise. *Dance* (5–7). Illus. Series: Traditions Around the World. 1995, Thomson Learning LB $24.26 (978-1-56847-275-1). 48pp. The ways people dance around the world and the reasons they do are presented with many color photographs. (Rev: BL 6/1–15/95; SLJ 9/95) [793.3]

16728 Wilkes, Angela. *The Best Book of Ballet* (1–4). Series: The Best Book Of. 2000, Kingfisher $12.95 (978-0-7534-5275-2). 32pp. A fine introduction to ballet that includes material on history, famous ballets, a ballet class, basic positions and steps, and what professional dancers do. (Rev: HBG 3/01; SLJ 7/00) [792.8]

16729 Yolen, Jane, and Heidi Stemple. *The Barefoot Book of Ballet Stories* (5–7). Illus. by Rebecca Guay. 2004, Barefoot Books $19.99 (978-1-84148-229-3). 96pp. The stories behind seven of the world's classic ballets — including "Cinderella," "The Nutcracker," "Coppelia," and "Sleeping Beauty" — are introduced by a general discussion of ballet as an art form and accompanied by production notes on each work. (Rev: BL 11/1/04; SLJ 12/04) [792.8]

Marionettes and Puppets

16730 Bryant, Jill, and Catherine Heard. *Making Shadow Puppets* (4–6). Series: Kids Can Do It! 2002, Kids Can $12.95 (978-1-55337-028-4); paper $5.95 (978-1-55337-029-1). 40pp. Two-dimensional puppets that can be created with easily found materials are presented with good step-by-step instructions. (Rev: BL 9/15/02; HBG 3/03; SLJ 12/02) [745.5]

16731 Renfro, Nancy. *Puppet Show Made Easy!* (3–6). Illus. 1984, Renfro $16.95 (978-0-931044-13-7). 96pp. Creating puppets and how to stage a show.

Motion Pictures, Radio, and Television

16732 Baker, Frank W. *Coming Distractions: Questioning Movies* (3–6). Illus. Series: Fact Finders: Media Literacy. 2007, Capstone LB $23.93 (978-0-7368-6766-5). 32pp. Readers are encouraged to analyze the images and messages they see projected on the big screen and to be aware of stereotypes and deliberate product placements; the dynamic format adds interest. (Rev: BL 4/1/07) [300]

16733 Fingeroth, Danny. *Backstage at an Animated Series* (4–8). Series: Backstage Pass. 2003, Children's paper $6.95 (978-0-516-24385-6). 48pp. Fingeroth explores the world of animated films, discussing their history, recent technological advances, and the mechanics of production, and suggesting ways to become involved. Also use *Backstage at a Movie Set* (2003). (Rev: SLJ 10/03) [791.43]

16734 Franks, Katie. *I Want to Be a Movie Star* (2–4). Series: Dream Jobs. 2007, Rosen LB $21.25 (978-1-4042-3619-6). 24pp. Reluctant readers will be drawn to the subject of this book and will learn about the preparation and training required to break into movie stardom. (Rev: SLJ 7/07)

16735 *The History of Moviemaking* (3–6). Illus. 1995, Scholastic $19.95 (978-0-590-47645-4). 47pp. A history of film is enlivened by transparencies, flaps, and other interactive devices. (Rev: BL 2/1/96; SLJ 5/96) [791]

16736 Horn, Geoffrey M. *Movie Animation* (4–6). Series: Making Movies. 2007, Gareth Stevens LB $24.00 (978-0-8368-6837-1). 32pp. This book provides a brief overview of the production of animated movies and gives snapshots of key figures including Walt Disney and Jayao Miyazaki. (Rev: SLJ 1/07) [791.43]

16737 Krauss, Ronnie. *Take a Look, It's in a Book: How Television Is Made at Reading Rainbow* (2–4). Illus. by Christopher Hornsby. 1997, Walker LB $16.85 (978-0-8027-8489-6). 32pp. A behind-the-scenes look at the television program *Reading Rain-*

bow and how it is put together. (Rev: BL 3/1/97; SLJ 6/97*) [791.45]

16738 Lund, Kristin. *Star Wars, Episode I: Incredible Locations* (3–6). Illus. 2000, DK $19.99 (978-0-7894-6692-1). 48pp. A visual treat that uses fold-out pages to present drawings and scenes from the movie *The Phantom Menace*. (Rev: BL 1/1–15/01; HBG 3/01) [791.43]

16739 McCarthy, Meghan. *Aliens Are Coming! The True Account of the 1938 War of the Worlds Radio Broadcast* (1–3). Illus. 2006, Knopf $16.95 (978-0-375-83518-6). 40pp. With varied artwork, this effective picture book presents the 1938 radio broadcast of *War of the Worlds* and the panic that followed in a way that will keep contemporary readers on the edge of their seats. (Rev: BL 2/1/06; SLJ 4/06*) [791.44]

16740 Miller, Marilyn. *Behind the Scenes at the TV News Studio* (PS–3). Illus. Series: Behind the Scenes. 1996, Raintree LB $21.40 (978-0-8172-4089-9). 32pp. A fascinating inside look at the inner workings of a TV news studio. (Rev: BL 4/15/96; SLJ 12/96) [070.1]

16741 Reynolds, David West. *Star Wars: Incredible Cross-Sections* (4–8). Series: Star Wars: Cross-Sections. 1998, DK $19.95 (978-1-78943-480-4). 32pp. This large-format book includes cross-sections of the TIE fighter, the X-wing fighter, the AT-AT, the Millennium Falcon, Jabba's sail barge, and the Death Star. (Rev: BL 12/15/98) [791.43]

16742 Reynolds, David West. *Star Wars: The Visual Dictionary* (4–8). 1998, DK $19.99 (978-0-7894-3481-4). 64pp. Using a large-format dictionary approach, the people, creatures, and droids of the *Star Wars* saga are presented, with large photographs of the characters and many stills from the movies. (Rev: BL 12/15/98; HBG 3/99; SLJ 2/99) [791.43]

16743 Reynolds, David West. *Star Wars Episode I: Incredible Cross-Sections: The Definitive Guide to the Craft of Star Wars Episode I* (4–8). Illus. by Hans Jenssen and Richard Chasemore. 1999, DK $19.95 (978-0-7894-3962-8). 32pp. An excellent guidebook that features cross-sections of vehicles and spacecraft featured in *Star Wars: Episode I*. (Rev: HBG 3/00; SLJ 12/99) [791]

16744 Reynolds, David West. *Star Wars Episode I: The Visual Dictionary* (4–8). Illus. 1999, DK $19.95 (978-0-7894-4701-2). 64pp. In this large-format book, a follow-up to *Star Wars: The Visual Dictionary*, the author, an archaeologist, reports on creatures and events in Episode I, using movie stills and posed photographs to explain the galaxy's history, technology, anthropology, and politics. (Rev: BL 8/99) [791.43]

16745 Spilsbury, Richard. *On the Film Set* (3–6). Illus. Series: Technology at Work. 2008, Raintree LB $19.25 (978-1-4109-3178-8). 32pp. An introduction to the myriad elements that go into making a film. (Rev: BL 12/1/08) [778.5]

16746 Wan, Guofang. *TV Takeover: Questioning Television* (4–7). Illus. Series: Fact Finders. Media Literacy. 2006, Capstone LB $22.60 (978-0-7368-

6763-4). 32pp. In alerting readers to the motivations behind those who produce television shows, this book fosters critical thinking about the mass media. (Rev: SLJ 6/07) [384.55]

Theater and Play Production

16747 Amendola, Dana. *A Day at the New Amsterdam Theatre* (4–9). Photos by Gino Domenico. 2004, Disney $24.95 (978-0-7868-5438-7). 125pp. A behind-the-scenes look at a production of a musical in the renovated theater in New York City, introducing the wide variety of individuals involved. (Rev: SLJ 1/05) [792]

16748 Bany-Winters, Lisa. *Funny Bones: Comedy Games and Activities for Kids* (3–6). Illus. 2002, Chicago Review paper $14.95 (978-1-55652-444-8). 155pp. In addition to learning games, skits, and songs, readers will find some history of comedy and will gain insight on how to use props, music, make-up, and other techniques to be funny. (Rev: SLJ 12/02) [793]

16749 Bany-Winters, Lisa. *On Stage: Theater Games and Activities for Kids* (4–7). Illus. 1997, Chicago Review paper $14.95 (978-1-55652-324-3). 160pp. This book provides a number of theater games involving improvisation, creating characters, using and becoming objects, and ideas for pantomime and puppetry. (Rev: BL 2/1/98; SLJ 3/98) [327.12]

16750 Caruso, Sandra, and Susan Kosoff. *The Young Actor's Book of Improvisation: Dramatic Situations Based on Literature: Ages 7–11* (2–6). 1998, Heinemann paper $19.95 (978-0-325-00048-0). 164pp. Describes hundreds of books, such as *Shiloh*, from which readers can create scenes and dramatic monologues. (Rev: BL 9/15/98) [792]

16751 Dabrowski, Kristen. *My Second Monologue Book: Famous and Historical People: 100 Monologues for Young Children* (2–6). Series: My First Acting. 2009, Smith & Kraus paper $11.95 (978-1-57525-601-6). 128pp. Monologues are divided into four sections, about familiar people (the doctor, for example), famous Americans, famous foreigners, and imaginary people and folk heroes. Also use *My Third Monologue Book: Places Near and Far: 102 Monologues for Young Children* (2009). (Rev: SLJ 5/09) [808.82]

16752 Dunleavy, Deborah. *The Jumbo Book of Drama* (4–8). Illus. by Jane Kurisu. 2004, Kids Can paper $14.95 (978-1-55337-008-6). 208pp. Divided into Acts, this volume covers all aspects of drama and stagecraft, from body movement to lighting and props. (Rev: BL 5/1/04; SLJ 6/04) [372.66]

16753 Friedman, Lise. *Break a Leg! The Kid's Guide to Acting and Stagecraft* (4–7). Illus. by Mary Dowdle. 2002, Workman paper $14.95 (978-0-7611-2208-1). 256pp. Some of the topics covered for young would-be actors include analyzing a script, memorizing lines, stage fright, body language, and monologues. (Rev: BL 5/1/02; HBG 10/02) [292]

16754 Jacobs, Paul Dubois, and Jennifer Swender. *Putting on a Play: Drama Activities for Kids* (3–4). Illus. by Debra Spina Dixon. 2005, Gibbs Smith paper $9.95 (978-1-58685-767-7). 64pp. An excellent introduction to staging a play — as a writer, designer, actor, or any support person — with ideas for story lines and discussion of improvising scenery from everyday materials. (Rev: SLJ 4/06) [792.02]

16755 McCullough, L. E. *Plays for Learning: Israel Reborn: Legends of the Diaspora and Israel's Modern Rebirth for Grades 4–6* (4–6). Series: Young Actors. 2001, Smith & Kraus paper $15.95 (978-1-57525-253-7). 204pp. A collection of 12 plays drawn from a variety of sources that portray the Jewish experience from the expulsion from Israel to the creation of the modern state. (Rev: SLJ 6/02)

16756 Miller, Kimberly M. *Backstage at a Play* (4–8). Series: Backstage Pass. 2003, Children's LB $24.50 (978-0-516-24327-6). 48pp. Miller explores the world of theater, discussing how they are produced and the degree of commitment necessary, and suggesting ways to become involved. (Rev: SLJ 10/03) [792]

16757 Morley, Jacqueline. *Shakespeare's Theater* (4–6). Illus. Series: Inside Story. 1995, Bedrick LB $18.95 (978-0-87226-309-3). 48pp. Details on Shakespeare's Globe Theatre and performances that took place there are preceded by a brief history of European theater. (Rev: BL 4/15/95) [792]

16758 Siberell, Anne. *Bravo! Brava! A Night at the Opera: Behind the Scenes, with Composers, Cast, and Crew* (3–6). Illus. by author. 2001, Oxford $22.95 (978-0-19-513966-2). 64pp. An excellent introduction to the many facets of opera, from its history to behind-the-scenes tasks such as makeup and set design. (Rev: BL 2/15/02; HBG 3/02; SLJ 1/02*) [782.1]

History and Geography

History and Geography in General

Miscellaneous

16759 Ajmera, Maya, and John D. Ivanko. *Back to School* (PS–3). Series: It's a Kid's World. 2001, Charlesbridge LB $15.95 (978-1-57091-383-9); paper $6.95 (978-1-57091-384-6). 32pp. This brief look at schooling around the world, with minimal text and color photographs, shows students studying in different situations, unusual methods of getting to school, and various kinds of clothing. (Rev: HBG 3/02; SLJ 6/02)

16760 Ajmera, Maya, and John D. Ivanko. *To Be a Kid* (PS–1). Illus. 1999, Charlesbridge $16.95 (978-0-88106-841-2). 32pp. Children from around the world share a community of interests involving play, families, schools, animals, and friends. (Rev: BL 2/1/99; HBG 10/99; SLJ 4/99) [305.23]

16761 Ajmera, Maya, and Anna R. Versola. *Children from Australia to Zimbabwe: A Photographic Journey Around the World* (3–6). Illus. 1997, Charlesbridge $18.95 (978-0-88106-999-0). 64pp. A photographic journey around the globe that introduces 25 countries and gives basic fact about each. (Rev: BL 1/1–15/98; HBG 3/98; SLJ 7/97) [305.23]

16762 Arnold, Caroline. *The Geography Book: Activities for Exploring, Mapping, and Enjoying Your World* (4–7). Illus. by Tina Cash-Walsh. 2001, Wiley paper $14.95 (978-0-471-41236-6). 112pp. An organized introduction to several geography concepts along with step-by-step instructions for projects and experiments. (Rev: BL 2/15/02; SLJ 3/02) [910]

16763 Burger, Leslie, and Debra L. Rahm. *Sister Cities in a World of Difference* (4–8). Illus. 1996, Lerner LB $22.60 (978-0-8225-2697-1). The pairing of cities internationally is covered with material on the results, mostly positive. (Rev: BL 9/1/96; SLJ 9/96; VOYA 4/97) [303.48]

16764 Defries, Cheryl L. *Seven Natural Wonders of the United States and Canada* (4–7). Illus. Series: Seven Wonders of the World. 2005, Enslow LB $25.26 (978-0-7660-5291-8). 48pp. This tour of seven of North America's natural wonders, including the Grand Canyon, Everglades, and Niagara Falls, is extended by constantly updated links to Web sites. (Rev: SLJ 11/05) [557]

16765 Dewey, Jennifer O. *Finding Your Way* (4–6). Illus. 2001, Millbrook LB $23.90 (978-0-7613-0956-7). 64pp. The author relates several tales that involve travel, using one's sense of direction, and becoming lost, in an absorbing text that conveys some basics of map reading. (Rev: BL 5/1/01; HBG 10/01; SLJ 7/01) [795.58]

16766 Gallimard Jeunesse, and Donald Grant. *Atlas of Islands* (PS–2). Series: First Discovery. 1999, Scholastic $12.95 (978-0-439-04402-8). 24pp. This simple book explains what islands are and covers other basic geographical terms. (Rev: BL 10/15/99; HBG 3/00) [551.4]

16767 Graham, Amy. *Seven Wonders of the Natural World* (4–7). Illus. Series: Seven Wonders of the World. 2005, Enslow LB $25.26 (978-0-7660-5290-1). 48pp. A tour of seven of the world's natural wonders, including Mount Everest, the Great Barrier Reef, and the Grand Canyon; the text is extended by constantly updated links to Web sites. (Rev: SLJ 11/05)

16768 Hollyer, Beatrice. *Wake Up, World! A Day in the Life of Children Around the World* (K–3). Illus. 1999, Holt $16.95 (978-0-8050-6293-9). A boy in Siberia and a girl in northern Brazil are two of the eight children from around the world in this introductory book on different environments. (Rev: BL 9/15/99; HBG 3/00; SLJ 12/99) [306.09]

16769 Jackson, Ellen. *It's Back to School We Go! First Day Stories from Around the World* (1–3). Illus. by Jan Davey Ellis. 2003, Millbrook LB $23.90 (978-0-7613-2562-8). 32pp. A look at the first day of school in 11 countries, with facts about food, clothes, subjects studied, and games played. (Rev: BL 8/03; HBG 4/04; SLJ 11/03) [371]

16770 Kindersley, Barnabas, and Anabel Kindersley. *Children Just Like Me: A Unique Celebration of*

Children Around the World (3–6). Illus. 1995, DK $19.99 (978-0-7894-0201-1). 79pp. An attractive book that views children around the world, arranged by continents. (Rev: BCCB 2/95; SLJ 1/96) [305]

16771 Lewis, J. Patrick. *Earth and You: A Closer View: Nature's Features* (2–4). Illus. by Christopher Canyon. 2001, Dawn $16.95 (978-1-58469-016-0); paper $7.95 (978-1-58469-015-3). The author and illustrator present a vivid and lyrical close-up look at natural features of the earth and its plants and animals, urging children to treat their environment with care. (Rev: HBG 10/01; SLJ 4/01) [508]

16772 Pascoe, Elaine, and Deborah Kops. *Scholastic Kid's Almanac for the 21st Century* (4–7). Illus. by Bob Italiano and David C. Bell. 1999, Scholastic paper $12.95 (978-0-590-30724-6). 352pp. An almanac that covers subjects including aerospace, animals, chemistry, computers, energy, geography, plants, religion, and sports. (Rev: SLJ 2/00) [900]

16773 Phillips, Dee, et al. *People of the World* (4–7). Illus. Series: Just the Facts. 2006, School Specialty paper $9.95 (978-0-7696-4257-4). 64pp. Statistics and fast facts on the countries and peoples of the world are presented on double-page spreads. (Rev: BL 4/1/06) [305.8]

16774 Reynolds, Jan. *Celebrate! Connections Among Cultures* (3–5). Illus. 2006, Lee & Low $16.95 (978-1-58430-253-7). 32pp. Sharing photographs from her travels, the author introduces readers to diverse cultures around the world and their traditions, including the Tuareg of the Sahara, Tibetans, and the Yanomami of the Amazon rain forest. (Rev: BL 3/15/06; SLJ 8/06) [394.26]

16775 Scandiffio, Laura. *Escapes!* (5–9). Illus. by Stephen MacEachern. Series: True Stories from the Edge. 2004, Annick $18.95 (978-1-55037-823-8); paper $7.95 (978-1-55037-822-1). 170pp. Ten stories of great escapes and escape attempts, from the first century B.C. to the late 1970s, with a concentration on resourcefulness and bravery. (Rev: SLJ 6/04) [904]

16776 Steele, Philip. *Wonders of the World* (4–6). Illus. 2007, Kingfisher $12.95 (978-0-7534-5979-9). 64pp. A broad overview of wonders old and new, including the seven ancient ones plus the Taj Mahal, the canals of Venice, the Empire State Building, the Sydney Opera House, the World Wide Web, and the Hubble telescope; with a foreword from UNESCO. (Rev: BL 5/1/07; LMC 11/07; SLJ 8/07) [930.1]

16777 Wojtanik, Andrew. *Afghanistan to Zimbabwe: Country Facts That Helped Me Win the National Geographic Bee* (5–12). 2005, National Geographic paper $12.95 (978-0-7922-7981-5). 384pp. Facts and figures about the world's 192 independent countries are organized into three categories: Physical, Political, and Environmental/Economic. (Rev: SLJ 10/05; VOYA 8/05) [910]

16778 Wood, Robert W. *Easy Geography Activities* (3–6). Illus. by John D. Wood. 1991, TAB $16.95 (978-0-8306-2493-5); paper $9.95 (978-0-8306-2492-8). 141pp. Helping to understand the principles and vocabulary of geography through such activities as reading road maps, making a compass,

and understanding continental drift. (Rev: BL 2/1/92) [910]

Maps and Globes

16779 Anderson, Scoular. *Space Pirates: A Map-Reading Adventure* (2–5). Illus. by author. 2004, Annick $19.95 (978-1-55037-881-8); paper $8.95 (978-1-55037-880-1). Basic map-reading skills are introduced within the framework of a space adventure. (Rev: SLJ 1/05) [793.73]

16780 *Atlas of Countries* (1–3). Illus. by Donald Grant. Series: First Discovery Atlases. 1996, Scholastic $12.95 (978-0-590-58282-7). This atlas explains maps and globes, landforms, the earth's evolution and rotation, while also supplying maps of the world's countries. (Rev: SLJ 9/96) [912]

16781 Baber, Maxwell. *Map Basics* (4–6). Illus. Series: Map Readers. 2006, Heinemann LB $27.07 (978-1-4034-6794-2). 32pp. This easy-to-understand introduction to mapping offers a brief history of cartography and examines such topics as projections, scale, keys, specialized maps, and the future of cartography; projects and a glossary round out the volume. (Rev: BL 10/15/06) [912]

16782 Berger, Melvin, and Gilda Berger. *The Whole World in Your Hands: Looking at Maps* (2–3). Illus. by Robert Quackenbush. Series: Discovery Readers. 1993, Ideals paper $4.50 (978-0-8249-8609-4). 48pp. This book for beginning readers introduces maps from simple to complex. (Rev: BCCB 4/93; BL 7/93) [912]

16783 Bramwell, Martyn. *Central and South America* (4–6). Illus. Series: World in Maps. 2000, Carolrhoda $23.93 (978-0-8225-2912-5). 48pp. This collection of maps of all the countries in Central and South America also covers population, government, languages, currency, size, and capitals. (Rev: BL 10/15/00; HBG 10/01; SLJ 1/01) [917.28]

16784 Bramwell, Martyn. *How Maps Are Made* (5–8). Illus. Series: Maps and Mapmakers. 1998, Lerner LB $22.60 (978-0-8225-2920-0). 48pp. The difficulties in representing the globe on a flat surface are explored, plus details on how maps are made — both by hand and by computer — and on the use of aerial photography in mapmaking. (Rev: BL 3/15/99; HBG 3/99; SLJ 2/99) [526]

16785 Bramwell, Martyn. *Mapping Our World* (4–8). Illus. Series: Maps and Mapmakers. 1998, Lerner LB $22.60 (978-0-8225-2924-8). This work shows how different kinds of maps can be used to illustrate topography, geology, climate, vegetation, population, geography, minerals, trade, pollution, and habitat. (Rev: BL 3/15/99; SLJ 2/99) [912]

16786 Bramwell, Martyn. *Mapping the Seas and Airways* (5–8). Series: Maps and Mapmakers. 1998, Lerner LB $22.60 (978-0-8225-2921-7). 48pp. This volume deals with special kinds of maps prepared and used by oceanographers and by airline cartographers. (Rev: BL 3/15/99; HBG 3/99) [912]

16787 Bramwell, Martyn. *Maps in Everyday Life* (5–8). Illus. Series: Maps and Mapmakers. 1998, Lerner LB $22.60 (978-0-8225-2923-1). 48pp. This book explains how different maps are used for different purposes, e.g., tourist maps and climate maps. (Rev: BL 3/15/99; HBG 3/99; SLJ 10/96) [912]

16788 Bredeson, Carmen. *Looking at Maps and Globes* (1–2). Illus. Series: Rookie Read-About Geography. 2001, Children's Book Pr. LB $20.50 (978-0-516-22351-3). 32pp. An introduction to maps and globes, along with explanations about features such as legends, scale, and the equator. (Rev: BL 11/1/01) [912]

16789 Chancellor, Deborah. *Maps and Mapping* (K–3). Series: Kingfisher Young Knowledge. 2004, Houghton $8.95 (978-0-7534-5759-7). 48pp. Attractive double-page spreads with many illustrations and diagrams present basic information on maps and mapmaking. (Rev: BL 9/1/04) [912]

16790 Gonzales, Doreen. *Up North and Down South: Using Map Directions* (3–5). Illus. Series: First Facts: Map Mania. 2007, Capstone LB $21.26 (978-1-4296-0055-2). 24pp. With photographs, drawings, breezy text introduced by a cartoon bird, and activities, this is an entertaining overview of how to read directions on maps. Also use *Are We There Yet? Using Map Scales* (2007). (Rev: SLJ 2/08) [912.01]

16791 Jackson, Kay. *Ways to Find Your Way: Types of Maps* (3–5). Illus. Series: First Facts: Map Mania. 2007, Capstone LB $21.26 (978-1-4296-0058-3). 24pp. With photographs, drawings, breezy text introduced by a cartoon bird, and activities, this is an entertaining overview of the various types of maps. (Rev: SLJ 2/08) [912.01]

16792 Johnson, Jinny. *Maps and Mapping* (2–4). Illus. Series: Inside Access. 2007, Kingfisher $9.95 (978-0-7534-6062-7). 32pp. Clear illustrations add to the usefulness of this introduction to maps that is narrated by an intrepid cartographer named Suki West. (Rev: BL 10/15/07) [912]

16793 Knowlton, Jack. *Maps and Globes* (2–4). Illus. 1985, HarperCollins paper $6.99 (978-0-06-446049-1). 48pp. This is a clear introduction to maps and globes and how to read them. (Rev: BCCB 3/86; BL 12/15/85)

16794 Mahaney, Ian F. *Climate Maps* (3–5). Series: Map It! 2006, Rosen LB $21.25 (978-1-4042-3058-3). 24pp. Readers will learn that maps can show much more than cities and roads in this introduction to climate maps. (Rev: SLJ 8/07)

16795 Mahaney, Ian F. *Road Maps* (3–5). Series: Map It! 2006, Rosen LB $21.25 (978-1-4042-3056-9). 24pp. Readers will learn about the features of road maps and how they are used. (Rev: SLJ 8/07)

16796 Oleksy, Walter. *Mapping the World* (5–7). Series: Watts Library: Geography. 2002, Watts LB $25.50 (978-0-531-12029-3); paper $8.95 (978-0-531-16636-9). 64pp. A history of how maps have been made, from the explorers, merchants, and mapmakers of old to the accurate modern products that use new technology. Also use *Mapping the Seas* and *Maps in History* (both 2002). (Rev: BL 10/15/02) [912]

16797 Ritchie, Scot. *Follow That Map! A First Book of Mapping Skills* (PS–3). Illus. by author. 2009, Kids Can $16.95 (978-1-55453-274-2). 32pp. Readers learn about maps as they follow this story about a girl and her friends searching for her missing dog and cat. (Rev: BL 3/15/09; LMC 8/09) [912.01]

16798 Robson, Pam. *Maps and Plans* (2–4). Illus. by Tony Kenyon. Series: Geography for Fun. 2001, Millbrook LB $22.90 (978-0-7613-2165-1). 32pp. This combination of maps, charts, games, and activities introduces some basic concepts in an entertaining way. (Rev: HBG 10/01; SLJ 9/01)

16799 Sammis, Fran. *Measurements* (2–5). 1997, Marshall Cavendish LB $22.79 (978-0-7614-0539-9). 32pp. Explains how geographical distances are measured and how these systems began. (Rev: BL 2/15/98; HBG 3/98) [910]

16800 Shores, Erika L. *If Maps Could Talk: Using Symbols and Keys* (3–5). Illus. Series: First Facts: Map Mania. 2007, Capstone LB $21.26 (978-1-4296-0056-9). 24pp. With photographs, drawings, breezy text introduced by a cartoon bird, and activities, this is an entertaining overview of the symbols and keys that appear on maps. (Rev: LMC 3/08; SLJ 2/08) [912.01]

16801 Smith, A. G. *Where Am I? The Story of Maps and Navigation* (4–8). Illus. 1997, Stoddart paper $13.95 (978-0-7737-5836-0). Important discoveries and innovations in the history of mapmaking are explained. (Rev: BL 9/1/97) [910]

16802 Stienecker, David L. *Maps* (2–5). Series: Discovering Geography. 1997, Marshall Cavendish LB $22.79 (978-0-7614-0538-2). 32pp. The evolution of maps is traced, and basic map-reading skills are introduced. (Rev: BL 2/15/98; HBG 3/98; SLJ 4/98) [912]

16803 Wilkinson, Philip. *The Kingfisher Student Atlas* (5–8). 2003, Kingfisher $24.95 (978-0-7534-5589-0). 128pp. An atlas of the earth, with detail on each area's physical characteristics and political boundaries and material on such problems as pollution and deforestation. An accompanying CD offers printable maps. (Rev: SLJ 4/04)

Paleontology and Dinosaurs

16804 Agenbroad, Larry D., and Lisa Nelson. *Mammoths: Ice-Age Giants* (5–8). Illus. Series: Discovery! 2002, Lerner LB $31.95 (978-0-8225-2862-3). 120pp. A detailed look at mammoths, theories on mammoth extinction, and mammoth discoveries, with sidebar features on topics such as human hunters in the Ice Age, and geologic timelines. (Rev: BL 6/1–15/02; HBG 10/02; SLJ 7/02) [569]

16805 Aliki. *Digging Up Dinosaurs* (2–4). Illus. by author. 1989, HarperCollins LB $17.89 (978-0-690-04716-5); paper $5.99 (978-0-06-445078-2). 32pp. This book answers the question "How do dinosaurs get into museums?"

16806 Aliki. *Dinosaur Bones* (PS–3). Illus. by author. 1988, HarperCollins paper $5.99 (978-0-06-445077-5). 32pp. In this book, her fourth on dinosaurs, Aliki discusses the discovery of fossils and the many theories that emerged about their meaning. (Rev: BCCB 1/88; BL 2/1/88; SLJ 4/88)

16807 Aliki. *My Visit to the Dinosaurs* (PS–3). Illus. by author. 1985, HarperCollins paper $5.99 (978-0-06-445020-1). 32pp. Revision of the 1969 book, including new material. Also use: *Dinosaurs Are Different* (1985). (Rev: BCCB 10/85; BL 9/15/85; SLJ 1/86)

16808 Andreae, Giles. *Dinosaurs Galore!* (PS–3). Illus. by David Wojtowycz. 2005, Tiger Tales $16.95 (978-1-58925-044-4). A varied group of dinosaurs introduces themselves and their characteristcs in humorous rhyming verse. (Rev: SLJ 5/05) [567.9]

16809 Armentrout, David, and Patricia Armentrout. *Dinosaurs* (PS–2). 2002, Rourke LB $19.95 (978-1-58952-342-5). 32pp. Simple definitions are given for 50 words about dinosaurs, along with a sentence that includes the word. (Rev: SLJ 3/03)

16810 Arnold, Caroline. *Giant Shark: Megalodon, Prehistoric Super Predator* (4–6). Illus. 2000, Clarion $16.00 (978-0-395-91419-9). 32pp. This book introduces the megalodon, an extinct giant shark, and explains how paleontologists have determined its characteristics and how it behaved. (Rev: BL 11/1/00; HBG 3/01; SLJ 11/00) [567]

16811 Arnold, Caroline. *Pterosaurs: Rulers of the Skies in the Dinosaur Age* (2–4). Illus. by Laurie Caple. 2004, Houghton $16.00 (978-0-618-31354-9). 40pp. The pterosaurs — reptiles with a wing span of nearly 40 feet — are introduced here, with plenty of facts and clear illustrations. (Rev: BL 12/1/04) [567.918]

16812 Arnold, Caroline. *When Mammoths Walked the Earth* (3–5). Illus. by Laurie Caple. 2002, Clarion $16.00 (978-0-618-09633-6). 40pp. An informative, well-illustrated book about key fossil discoveries and the lives of mammoths. (Rev: BL 8/02; HB 11/02; HBG 3/03; SLJ 10/02) [569]

16813 Ashby, Ruth. *Pteranodon: The Life Story of a Pterosaur* (1–3). Illus. by Phil Wilson. 2005, Abrams $14.95 (978-0-8109-5778-7). With simple text and striking images, the author presents what life might have been like for an ancient flying dinosaur. (Rev: SLJ 7/05) [567.918]

16814 Asimov, Isaac. *What Killed the Dinosaurs?* (3–5). Illus. Series: Isaac Asimov's 21st Century Library of the Universe. 2004, Gareth Stevens LB $26.00 (978-0-8368-3955-5). 32pp. A revised, well-illustrated edition of a previously published book, this discusses possible reasons for the extinction of the dinosaurs and looks at the gigantic Chicxulub crater. (Rev: SLJ 3/05) [567.9]

16815 Bailey, Jacqui. *The Day of the Dinosaurs* (3–5). Illus. by Matthew Lilly. Series: Cartoon History of the Earth. 2001, Kids Can $16.95 (978-1-55337-073-4); paper $7.95 (978-1-55337-082-6). 32pp. A comic-book-style presentation of the age of the dinosaurs. (Rev: BL 10/15/01; HBG 3/02; SLJ 1/02) [567.9]

16816 Bailey, Jacqui. *Monster Bones: The Story of a Dinosaur Fossil* (2–4). Illus. by Matthew Lilly. Series: Science Works. 2004, Picture Window LB $26.60 (978-1-4048-0565-1). 31pp. After a dramatic story that draws the reader in, Bailey explores the process of fossilization and the discovery, classification, reconstruction, and exhibit of fossils. (Rev: SLJ 8/04) [567.9]

16817 Barker, Robert T. *Dactyls! Dragons of the Air* (3–4). Illus. by Luis V. Key. Series: Step into Reading. 2005, Random LB $11.99 (978-0-375-93013-3); paper $3.99 (978-0-375-83013-6). 48pp. In conversational, easy-to-understand language, Barker discusses the pterodactyl and its characteristics and conveys the excitement he finds in paleontology. (Rev: SLJ 2/06) [567.918]

16818 Barner, Bob. *Dinosaur Bones* (PS–2). Illus. 2001, Chronicle $15.95 (978-0-8118-3158-1). 36pp. The lively cut-paper collage illustrations are the highlight of this book about dinosaurs and their bones. (Rev: BCCB 9/01; BL 11/1/01; HBG 3/02; SLJ 9/01) [567.9]

16819 Barton, Byron. *Dinosaurs, Dinosaurs* (PS–1). Illus. 1989, HarperCollins LB $17.89 (978-0-690-04768-4); paper $6.99 (978-0-06-443298-6). 40pp. Dinosaur characteristics in splashy colors. (Rev: BL 3/15/89; HB 5/89; SLJ 4/89)

16820 Benton, Michael. *Dinosaur and Other Prehistoric Animal Factfinder* (3–6). Illus. 1992, Kingfisher paper $14.95 (978-1-85697-802-6). 256pp. A quick reference source about prehistoric life, including profiles of dinosaurs and other animals. (Rev: BL 12/15/92) [560]

16821 Benton, Michael. *Dinosaurs* (3–6). Illus. 1998, Kingfisher $15.95 (978-0-7534-5131-1). 64pp. An easy-to-read account of the rise and fall of the dinosaurs, explaining why they became extinct. (Rev: BL 11/15/98; HBG 3/99; SLJ 11/98) [567.9]

16822 Berger, Melvin. *Mighty Dinosaurs* (4–8). Illus. 1990, Avon paper $2.95 (978-0-380-76052-7). 128pp. Covers various kinds of dinosaurs and includes the latest research on their extinction. (Rev: BL 12/15/90) [567.9]

16823 Bilgrami, Shaheen. *Amazing Dinosaur Discovery* (PS–3). Illus. by Mike Phillips and Phil Garner. Series: Magic Skeleton. 2002, Sterling $9.95 (978-0-8069-8591-6). 24pp. A visit to a museum introduces younger readers to dinosaurs and their skeletons in this picture book with an appealing format. (Rev: BL 8/02)

16824 Bishop, Nic. *Digging for Bird-Dinosaurs: An Expedition to Madagascar* (4–6). Illus. Series: Scientists in the Field. 2000, Houghton $16.00 (978-0-395-96056-1). 48pp. Shifting from Madagascar to a lab in New York, this account traces the work of paleontologist Cathy Forster, who is investigating the link between birds and dinosaurs. (Rev: BCCB 5/00; BL 4/15/00*; HB 5/00; HBG 10/00; SLJ 5/00) [567.9]

16825 Bishop, Roma. *My First Pop-up Book of Prehistoric Animals* (K–3). Illus. 1994, Simon & Schuster $12.95 (978-0-671-86556-6). An engaging text and a series of pop-ups introduce the world of the dinosaur to primary graders. (Rev: BL 11/15/94) [560]

16826 Bonner, Hannah. *When Bugs Were Big, Plants Were Strange, and Terrapods Stalked the Earth: A Cartoon Prehistory of Life Before Dinosaurs* (2–5). Illus. 2004, National Geographic $16.95 (978-0-7922-6326-5). 48pp. This fascinating, cartoon-filled excursion into the end of the Paleozoic period more than 250 million years ago offers a blend of natural history and humor. (Rev: BL 2/15/04*; SLJ 2/04) [565]

16827 Bonner, Hannah. *When Fish Got Feet, Sharks Got Teeth, and Bugs Began to Swarm* (3–5). Illus. by author. 2007, National Geographic $16.95 (978-1-4263-0078-3). 48pp. Explores life on Earth long before the dinosaurs arrived. (Rev: BCCB 11/07; BL 7/07; HB 1/08; LMC 1/08; SLJ 10/07) [560]

16828 Bradley, Timothy J. *Paleo Bugs: Survival of the Creepiest* (5–8). Illus. by author. 2008, Chronicle $15.99 (978-0-8118-6022-2). 47pp. The author provides information about prehistoric bugs alongside his own illustrations imagining what they might have looked like in those long-ago days. A companion to *Paleo Sharks*. (Rev: BL 5/15/08; SLJ 7/08) [565]

16829 Bradley, Timothy J. *Paleo Sharks: Survival of the Strangest* (4–7). Illus. 2007, Chronicle $15.95 (978-0-8118-4878-7). 47pp. Well-arranged double-page spreads introduce sharks of prehistoric times and examine how they compare to their modern descendants. (Rev: BL 4/1/07; SLJ 6/07) [567]

16830 Branley, Franklyn M. *What Happened to the Dinosaurs?* (1–3). Illus. by Marc Simont. 1989, HarperCollins LB $15.89 (978-0-690-04749-3). 32pp. A good discussion of what might have happened to cause the end of the dinosaurs. (Rev: BL 9/1/89; HB 11/89; SLJ 10/89) [567.9]

16831 Brett-Surman, Michael, and Thomas R. Holtz, Jr. *James Gurney: The World of Dinosaurs* (5–8). Illus. by James Gurney. 1998, GWP paper $19.95 (978-0-86713-046-1). 48pp. This story of the 15 dinosaur stamps designed for the U.S. Postal Service includes a description of each of the beasts. (Rev: SLJ 9/98) [567.9]

16832 Brewster, Hugh. *Dinosaurs in Your Backyard: The Coolest, Scariest Creatures Ever Found in the USA* (3–5). Illus. by Alan Barnard. 2009, Abrams $15.95 (978-0-8109-7099-1). 32pp. Tyrannosaurus rex, Stegosaurus, and Triceratops are only three of the prehistoric animals introduced in this attractive and informative volume. (Rev: BL 4/15/09; SLJ 6/09) [567.9097]

16833 Brown, Charlotte Lewis. *After the Dinosaurs: Mammoths and Fossil Mammals* (K–3). Illus. by Phil Wilson. Series: An I Can Read Book. 2006, HarperCollins $15.99 (978-0-06-053053-2). 32pp. Double-page spreads introduces some of the mammals — including woolly mammoths and saber-toothed tigers — that followed the dinosaurs; suitable for beginning readers, this solid volume includes a pronunciation guide. (Rev: SLJ 2/07) [569]

16834 Brown, Charlotte Lewis. *The Day the Dinosaurs Died* (1–3). Illus. by Phil Wilson. Series: I Can Read! 2006, HarperCollins $15.99 (978-0-06-000528-3). The author imagines what it would have been like when an asteroid hit the earth 65 million years ago, triggering the demise of the dinosaurs;

suitable for beginning readers. (Rev: SLJ 6/06) [567.9]

16835 Camper, Cathy. *Bugs Before Time: Prehistoric Insects and Their Relatives* (3–5). Illus. by Steve Kirk. 2002, Simon & Schuster $16.95 (978-0-689-82092-2). 40pp. An eye-catching introduction to the world of prehistoric insects and arthropods. (Rev: BL 3/15/02; HBG 10/02; SLJ 5/02) [565]

16836 Chin, Karen, and Thorn Holmes. *Dino Dung: The Scoop on Fossil Feces* (2–4). Illus. by Karen Carr. Series: Step into Reading. 2005, Random LB $11.99 (978-0-375-92702-7). 48pp. The topic of dinosaur dung makes a fine introduction to the science of paleontology for beginning readers. (Rev: BL 6/1–15/05) [567.9]

16837 Chrisp, Peter. *Dinosaur Detectives* (2–4). Illus. Series: Dorling Kindersley Readers. 2001, DK $14.99 (978-0-7894-7384-4); paper $3.99 (978-0-7894-7383-7). 48pp. Chrisp interweaves facts about dinosaurs with fictionalized first-person accounts by fossil hunters in a package that makes good browsing for beginning readers. (Rev: HBG 10/01; SLJ 9/01) [560]

16838 Christian, Spencer, and Antonia Felix. *Is There a Dinosaur in Your Backyard? The World's Most Fascinating Fossils, Rocks, and Minerals* (5–8). Series: Spencer Christian's World of Wonders. 1998, Wiley paper $12.95 (978-0-471-19616-7). In addition to discussing dinosaurs, this fascinating book introduces earth science, with interesting details about rocks, minerals, and fossils. (Rev: BL 9/1/98; SLJ 10/98) [552]

16839 Cohen, Daniel. *Allosaurus* (K–2). Illus. Series: Discovering Dinosaurs. 2003, Capstone LB $22.60 (978-0-7368-1618-2). 24pp. A slim, basic overview of the Allosaurus for the beginning reader, with suggested activities and experiments. Also use *Ankylosaurus* and *Brachiosaurus* (both 2003). (Rev: HBG 10/03; SLJ 3/04) [567.9]

16840 Cohen, Daniel. *Pteranodon* (3–4). Series: Discovering Dinosaurs. 2000, Bridgestone LB $22.60 (978-0-7368-0617-6). 24pp. A basic title that introduces this prehistoric animal. Also use *Stegosaurus* (2000). (Rev: HBG 3/01; SLJ 1/01) [567.9]

16841 Cooley, Brian, and Mary Ann Wilson. *Make-a-Saurus: My Life with Raptors and Other Dinosaurs* (4–8). Photos by Gary Campbell. 2000, Annick paper $14.95 (978-1-55037-644-9). 58pp. A two-part book giving a step-by step description of how museum-quality models of dinosaurs are made using the latest discoveries in paleontology, followed by an exploration of how these techniques can be adapted so the reader can make models at home. (Rev: HBG 3/01; SLJ 9/00) [567.9]

16842 Currie, Philip J., and Colleayn O. Mastin. *The Newest and Coolest Dinosaurs* (4–8). Illus. 1998, Grasshopper $18.95 (978-1-895910-41-4). Using double-page spreads, this useful volume introduces 15 recent finds in the world of dinosaurs. (Rev: SLJ 1/99) [560]

16843 Cutchins, Judy, and Ginny Johnston. *Giant Predators of the Ancient Seas* (4–7). Illus. Series: Southern Fossil Discoveries. 2001, Pineapple $14.95 (978-1-56164-237-3). 63pp. A look at the reptiles, fish, whales, sharks, and sea snakes that were found in the seas that once covered much of North America, as well as a discussion of the methods scientists used to reconstruct them. (Rev: HBG 3/02; SLJ 12/01) [566]

16844 Dahl, Michael. *Double Bones: The Adventure of Diplodocus* (K–3). Illus. by Garry Nichols. Series: Dinosaur World. 2005, Picture Window $25.26 (978-1-4048-0940-6). 24pp. Facts about the diplodocus appear alongside a simple story about its life in this review of what we know about the dinosaur. Also use *Long Arm: The Adventure of Brachiosaurus* and *Monster Fish: The Adventure of the Ichthyosaurs* (both 2005). (Rev: SLJ 8/05) [567.913]

16845 Dal Sasso, Cristiano. *Animals: Origins and Evolution* (4–8). Illus. Series: Beginnings — Origins and Evolution. 1995, Raintree LB $24.26 (978-0-8114-3333-4). 48pp. This well-illustrated account traces the development of animals from bacteria to the invertebrates and then fish, amphibians, reptiles, birds, and mammals. (Rev: BL 5/1/95; SLJ 6/95) [591]

16846 De Magalhaes, Roberto Carvalho. *Prehistory* (4–6). Series: Art and Civilization. 2000, Bedrick $16.95 (978-0-87226-615-5). 36pp. Using illustrations of many artifacts, this book explains daily life and culture during prehistoric times. (Rev: HBG 3/01; SLJ 1/01) [930.1]

16847 Dixon, Dougal. *Amazing Dinosaurs: More Feathers, More Claws, Big Horns, Wide Jaws! 2nd ed.* (5–7). 2007, Boyds Mills $19.95 (978-1-59078-537-9). 128pp. This carefully updated edition provides new illustrations and text reflecting recent discoveries about dinosaurs. (Rev: SLJ 3/08) [567.9]

16848 Dixon, Dougal. *Ankylosaurus and Other Mountain Dinosaurs* (K–3). Illus. by Steve Weston and James Field. Series: Dinosaur Find. 2004, Picture Window LB $25.26 (978-1-4048-0670-2). 24pp. Basic facts are presented in brief sentences, and include references to the dinosaur's habitat and comparisons to contemporary animals. Also use *Deltadromeus and Other Shoreline Dinosaurs* and *Triceratops and Other Forest Dinosaurs* (2004). (Rev: SLJ 2/05) [567.9]

16849 Dixon, Dougal. *Be a Dinosaur Detective* (1–4). Illus. 1988, Lerner paper $6.95 (978-0-8225-9538-0). 32pp. The author explains how all evidence for dinosaurs is deduced from fossils. (Rev: BL 5/1/88; SLJ 8/88)

16850 Dixon, Dougal. *Dougal Dixon's Amazing Dinosaurs* (3–6). Illus. 2000, Boyds Mills $17.95 (978-1-56397-773-2). 128pp. An attractive, informative field book that introduces groups of dinosaurs and offers solid information on their physical makeup, habits, and special characteristics. (Rev: BL 3/15/00; HBG 10/00; SLJ 5/00) [567.9]

16851 Dixon, Dougal. *Herbivores* (4–6). Illus. Series: Dinosaurs. 2001, Gareth Stevens LB $26.00 (978-0-8368-2916-7). 36pp. This account explores the world of the herbivore dinosaurs during the Mesozoic Era and discusses related modern species. Also use *Carnivores* and *In the Sky* (2001). (Rev: HBG 3/02; SLJ 3/02) [567.9]

16852 Dixon, Dougal. *The Search for Dinosaurs* (4–7). Illus. Series: Digging Up the Past. 1995, Thomson Learning LB $24.26 (978-1-56847-396-3). 48pp. A history of the various discoveries that paleontologists have made about dinosaurs and other prehistoric beasts. (Rev: SLJ 2/96) [567.9]

16853 Dixon, Dougal. *Triceratops: And Other Forest Dinosaurs* (K–2). Series: Dinosaur Find. 2005, Picture Window $25.26 (978-1-4048-0668-9). 24pp. A profile of Triceratops, a large herbivorous dinosaur, and other giant reptiles that also favored forested habitats. (Rev: BL 10/15/04)

16854 Dixon, Dougal. *Tyrannosaurus and Other Dinosaurs of North America* (2–4). Illus. by Steve Weston. Series: Dinosaur Find. 2007, Picture Window LB $25.26 (978-1-4048-2265-8). 24pp. Double-page spreads introduce the prehistoric reptiles that roamed North America with eye-catching art, brief text, and a box that looks at similar contemporary animals. (Rev: BL 3/15/07) [567.9097]

16855 Dixon, Dougal. *World of Dinosaurs and Other Prehistoric Life* (4–6). 2008, Barron's paper $9.99 (978-0-7641-4082-2). 112pp. An accessible guide to prehistoric life with colorful, useful information about each creature including pronunciation of the name and the geographic location of the fossils. (Rev: LMC 5/09*; SLJ 2/09) [567.9]

16856 Dodson, Peter. *An Alphabet of Dinosaurs* (2–4). Illus. by Wayne D. Barlowe. 1995, Scholastic $16.95 (978-0-590-46486-4). 64pp. Twenty-six kinds of dinosaurs are introduced in text and drawings in this unusual alphabet book. (Rev: BL 1/15/95; SLJ 3/95*) [567.9]

16857 Farlow, James O. *Bringing Dinosaur Bones to Life: How Do We Know What Dinosaurs Were Like?* (4–7). Illus. 2001, Watts LB $26.00 (978-0-531-11403-2). 64pp. An interesting look at the life of dinosaurs and at the methods paleontologists use to learn about the beasts, pointing out that although scientists can reconstruct animals from skeletons and fossil evidence, they must always differentiate between fact and educated guesses. (Rev: BL 12/15/01; SLJ 12/01) [567.9]

16858 Faulkner, Rebecca. *Fossils* (4–6). Series: Geology Rocks! 2007, Raintree LB $31.43 (978-1-4109-2752-1). 48pp. Plate tectonics, dinosaurs, and fossil fuels are among the topics covered in this appealing and well-organized, high-interest introduction to fossils with color photographs and a section on becoming a paleontologist. (Rev: SLJ 3/08) [560]

16859 French, Vivian. *T. Rex* (PS–2). Illus. by Alison Bartlett. 2005, Candlewick $15.99 (978-0-7636-2184-1). 32pp. During a visit to a T. rex exhibition, a boy and his grandfather discuss in engaging rhythmic rhyme what is known — and what science has yet to discover — about the prehistoric creature. (Rev: BL 12/1/04) [567.912]

16860 Gallant, Jonathan R. *The Tales Fossils Tell* (5–9). Series: The Story of Science. 2000, Benchmark LB $29.93 (978-0-7614-1153-6). 80pp. A fas-

cinating introduction to paleontology that explains how the importance of fossils was only clearly understood after the ideas of evolution and extinction were accepted. (Rev: BL 12/15/00; HBG 10/01; SLJ 2/01) [560]

16861 Gallant, Roy A. *Fossils* (3–5). Illus. Series: Kaleidoscope. 2000, Marshall Cavendish $25.64 (978-0-7614-1041-6). 48pp. Beginning with basic information on fossils that shows, for example, how a dying fish can become a fossil, this book goes on to more complex subjects related to paleontology. (Rev: BL 2/1/01; HBG 3/01; SLJ 3/01) [560]

16862 Gibbons, Gail. *Dinosaur Discoveries* (1–3). Illus. 2005, Holiday $16.95 (978-0-8234-1971-5). 32pp. Gibbons reviews dinosaur history in light of new discoveries and tells about paleontologists' ongoing efforts to learn more about these prehistoric creatures. (Rev: BL 10/1/05; SLJ 2/06) [597.9]

16863 Gibbons, Gail. *Dinosaurs* (2–4). Illus. 1987, Holiday House LB $16.95 (978-0-8234-0657-9); paper $6.95 (978-0-8234-0708-8). 32pp. Giant reptiles explained in simple terms for the young set. (Rev: BL 12/15/87; SLJ 11/87)

16864 Gibbons, Gail. *Dinosaurs!* (PS–2). Illus. by author. 2008, Holiday $16.95 (978-0-8234-2143-5). 32pp. An accessible overview of dinosaurs and how we have learned about them. (Rev: BL 8/08) [567.9]

16865 Gibbons, Gail. *Prehistoric Animals* (K–2). Illus. 1988, Holiday House LB $16.95 (978-0-8234-0707-1). 32pp. A brief overview of a subject that fascinates young readers. (Rev: BL 9/1/88; SLJ 10/88)

16866 Goldish, Meish. *The Fossil Feud: Marsh and Cope's Bone Wars* (3–5). Series: Fossil Hunters. 2006, Bearport LB $25.27 (978-1-59716-256-2). 32pp. The story of the dramatic 19th-century clash between American paleontologists Othniel Marsh and Edward Cope. (Rev: BL 10/15/06; SLJ 1/07) [560.92]

16867 Gray, Samantha, and Sarah Walker, eds. *Dinosaur* (3–5). Illus. Series: Eye Wonder. 2001, DK paper $9.99 (978-0-7894-7851-1). 48pp. Model dinosaurs show how the massive beasts moved, hunted, and lived; theories about their demise are also included. (Rev: BL 12/1/01; HBG 3/02) [567.9]

16868 Gray, Susan H. *Apatosaurus* (3–5). Illus. Series: Exploring Dinosaurs. 2004, Child's World LB $27.07 (978-1-59296-043-9). 32pp. Following a dramatic scene, information on physical characteristics, behavior, diet, and so forth is presented along with discussion of paleontology as a science. Also use *Oviraptor* and *Iguanodon* (both 2004). (Rev: SLJ 9/04) [567.9]

16869 Gray, Susan H. *Coelophysis* (3–6). Illus. Series: Exploring Dinosaurs. 2004, Child's World LB $27.07 (978-1-59296-185-6). 32pp. This volume in the Exploring Dinosaurs series looks at the world of the coelophysis, a small but swift carnivore of the late Triassic Period; dramatic scenes draw the reader in to facts and theories about the animals. Also use *Maiasaura* (2004). (Rev: BL 5/1/04; SLJ 9/04) [507.912]

16870 Gray, Susan H. *Megalosaurus* (3–5). Illus. Series: Exploring Dinosaurs. 2004, Child's World LB $27.07 (978-1-59296-236-5). 32pp. After a fictional opening chapter, there is information the animal's characteristics and behavior plus material on its discovery. Also use *Psittacosaurus* and *Spinosaurus* (both 2004). (Rev: SLJ 2/05) [567.9]

16871 Green, Jen. *The Dinosaur Museum* (1–4). Illus. by Sebastian Quigley. 2008, National Geographic $19.95 (978-1-4263-0335-7). 20pp. Dramatic dinosaur pop-ups are paired with interactive flaps, tabs, wheels, and minibooks that convey a surprising amount of information. (Rev: BLO 12/16/08) [567.9]

16872 Halls, Kelly Milner. *Dinosaur Mummies: Beyond Bare-Bone Fossils* (4–6). Illus. by Rick Spears. Series: A Junior Library Guild Selection. 2003, Darby Creek $17.95 (978-1-58196-000-6). 48pp. This fascinating book explains how the discovery of fossilized soft-tissue remains of dinosaurs has expanded scientific knowledge about these prehistoric creatures. (Rev: BL 11/1/03; SLJ 12/03)

16873 Harrison, Carol. *Dinosaurs Everywhere!* (PS–2). Illus. by Richard Courtney. 1998, Scholastic $14.95 (978-0-590-00089-5). 40pp. An introduction to various kinds of dinosaurs, their habits, appearance, size, and behavior — all in a big, beautiful picture book. (Rev: BL 11/15/98; HBG 3/99; SLJ 1/99) [567.9]

16874 Helm, Charles. *Daniel's Dinosaurs: A True Story of Discovery* (K–3). Photos by author. Illus. by Joan Zimmer. 2004, Maple Tree $16.95 (978-1-897066-06-5); paper $6.95 (978-1-897066-07-2). 32pp. This photoessay tells the story of 8-year-old Daniel Helm's discovery of dinosaur tracks in British Columbia. (Rev: LMC 3/05; SLJ 1/05)

16875 Henry, Michel. *Raptor: The Life of a Young Deinonychus* (2–4). Illus. by Rich Penney. 2007, Abrams $15.95 (978-0-8109-5775-6). A deinonychus matures, mates, and becomes a father. Realistic drawings give readers a glimpse of what scientists think these dinosaurs might have looked like. (Rev: SLJ 5/07)

16876 Hincks, Joseph. *Dinosaur Dictionary* (4–6). 1999, Rourke LB $27.95 (978-0-86593-586-0). 96pp. A highly readable, well-illustrated dictionary that presents two or three short paragraphs about each dinosaur. (Rev: SLJ 2/00) [567.9]

16877 Holtz, Thomas R., Jr. *Dinosaurs: The Most Complete, Up-to-Date Encyclopedia for Dinosaur Lovers of All Ages* (5–12). Illus. by Luis V. Rey. 2007, Random $34.99 (978-0-375-82419-7). 428pp. Paleontologist Holtz offers a well-organized overview of dinosaurs and everything dinosaur-related in a well-illustrated volume that will be appreciated by users of many ages (those not interested in cladistics, for example, may find just the information they need on dinosaur eggs). (Rev: HB 1/08; SLJ 12/07) [567.9]

16878 Hort, Lenny. *Did Dinosaurs Eat Pizza? Mysteries Science Hasn't Solved* (PS–3). Illus. by John O'Brien. 2006, Holt $15.95 (978-0-8050-6757-6). 32pp. A lighthearted look at science's ongoing quest

to learn more about what life was like for the dinosaurs. (Rev: BL 4/1/06; SLJ 3/06) [567.9]

16879 Hughes, Monica. *Flying Giants* (K–2). Illus. Series: I Love Reading! Dino World! 2007, Bearport LB $14.97 (978-1-59716-541-9). 24pp. Beginning readers learn to recognize and pronounce the names of dinosaurs that flew; this small, square book includes colorful illustrations. (Rev: BL 10/15/07; LMC 1/08) [567.918]

16880 Jeffrey, Gary. *Elasmosaurus: The Long-Necked Swimmer* (2–4). Illus. by Terry Riley. Series: Graphic Dinosaurs. 2009, Rosen LB $25.25 (978-1-4358-2505-5). 32pp. Arresting illustrations grab the reader's interest in this introduction to this marine dinosaur. (Rev: BL 2/1/09) [567.9]

16881 Jenkins, Steve. *Prehistoric Actual Size* (1–3). Illus. 2005, Houghton $16.00 (978-0-618-53578-1). 32pp. Dramatic cut-paper artwork offers actual-size representations of anatomical features from such prehistoric creatures as the eight-foot-tall "terror bird" and the Gigantosaurus. (Rev: BCCB 10/05; BL 10/15/05*; HB 1/06; HBG 4/06; LMC 8/06; SLJ 12/05) [560]

16882 Johnson, Jinny. *Dino Wars* (3–5). Illus. 2005, Abrams $17.95 (978-0-8109-5798-5). 144pp. Dinosaurs are rated by assets including strength, armor, speed, agility, and scariness in this informative guide with a wrestling TV show feel. (Rev: BL 12/15/05; SLJ 2/06) [567.9]

16883 Johnston, Marianne. *From the Dinosaurs of the Past to the Birds of the Present* (3–5). Illus. Series: Prehistoric Animals and Their Modern-Day Relatives. 2000, Rosen LB $21.25 (978-0-8239-5204-5). 24pp. This account points out the structural similarities between dinosaurs and birds and tells why scientists think they are related. (Rev: BL 12/1/00) [567]

16884 Keiran, Monique. *Ornithomimus: Pursuing the Bird-Mimic Dinosaur* (4–6). Illus. 2002, Raincoast $26.95 (978-1-55192-348-2). 64pp. A look at the discovery of a featherless beaked fossil in Canada with discussion of fossils and evolution in general, enhanced by color photographs and paintings. (Rev: BL 12/1/02; SLJ 11/02) [567.914]

16885 Kelsey, Elin. *Finding Out About Dinosaurs* (3–5). Illus. 2000, Owl $19.95 (978-1-895688-97-9). 40pp. Questions about dinosaurs are asked on each double-page spread, and the answers reveal how paleontologists work and what they have learned about these prehistoric animals. (Rev: BL 12/1/00; HBG 3/01; SLJ 10/00) [567.9]

16886 Kerley, Barbara. *The Dinosaurs of Waterhouse Hawkins* (3–5). Illus. by Brian Selznick. 2001, Scholastic $16.95 (978-0-439-11494-3). 48pp. The true story of Waterhouse Hawkins, the 19th-century British artist who built life-sized dinosaur models; with detailed, dramatic illustrations. Caldecott Honor Book, 2002. (Rev: BCCB 10/01; BL 9/1/01; HBG 3/02; SLJ 10/01) [567.9]

16887 Krueger, Richard. *The Dinosaurs* (5–8). Illus. Series: Prehistoric North America. 1996, Millbrook LB $22.90 (978-1-56294-548-0). With plenty of color illustrations, this chatty overview tells about

North American dinosaurs. (Rev: BL 5/15/96; SLJ 4/96) [567.9]

16888 Kudlinski, Kathleen V. *Boy, Were We Wrong About Dinosaurs!* (K–3). Illus. by S. D. Schindler. 2005, Dutton $15.99 (978-0-525-46978-0). 32pp. Scientists' misconceptions about dinosaurs and other prehistoric creatures are highlighted in interesting, thought-provoking text and realistic illustrations. (Rev: BCCB 1/06; BL 12/1/05*; HB 11/05; HBG 4/06; SLJ 12/05) [567.9]

16889 Landau, Elaine. *Pterosaurs* (2–4). Illus. Series: True Book Dinosaurs. 2006, Scholastic LB $25.00 (978-0-531-16829-5). 48pp. Colorful clear illustrations add to the appeal of this fact-packed survey of pterosaurs, fossils, and dinosaur extinction. (Rev: BL 1/1–15/07) [567.918]

16890 Larson, Peter, and Kristin Donnan. *Bones Rock! Everything You Need to Know to Be a Paleontologist* (5–9). Illus. 2004, Invisible Cities paper $19.95 (978-1-931229-35-7). 204pp. A comprehensive, accessible guide to paleontology, describing how to dig for fossils, clean them, keep records, and develop and test theories, with interesting accounts of the authors' experiences. (Rev: SLJ 11/04) [560]

16891 Lauber, Patricia. *How Dinosaurs Came to Be* (4–6). Illus. 1996, Simon & Schuster $17.00 (978-0-689-80531-8). 48pp. The ancestors of dinosaurs are described in this account that traces the evolution of these giant reptiles. (Rev: BL 4/15/96; SLJ 5/96) [567.9]

16892 Lessem, Don. *Armored Dinosaurs* (2–4). Illus. by John Bindon. Series: Meet the Dinosaurs. 2004, Lerner LB $23.93 (978-0-8225-1374-2); paper $6.95 (978-0-8225-2570-7). 32pp. Facts about these dinosaurs are presented in a lively narrative that includes present-tense scenes. Also use *Giant Meat-Eating Dinosaurs* and *Horned Dinosaurs* (both 2004). (Rev: SLJ 2/05) [567.9]

16893 Lessem, Don. *Dinosaur Worlds: New Dinosaurs, New Discoveries* (5–8). Illus. 1996, Boyds Mills $19.95 (978-1-56397-597-4). 192pp. The reader visits various dinosaur digs worldwide in a review of what we know about these amazing creatures. (Rev: BL 11/15/96; SLJ 12/96*) [567.9]

16894 Lessem, Don. *The Fastest Dinosaurs* (2–4). Illus. by John Bindon. Series: Meet the Dinosaurs. 2005, Lerner LB $23.93 (978-0-8225-1422-0); paper $6.95 (978-0-8225-2620-9). 32pp. Which dinosaurs were fastest? And how did scientists find out? Conversational text tackles these questions. Also use *The Smartest Dinosaurs* and *Flying Giants of Dinosaur Time* (both 2005). (Rev: SLJ 7/05) [567.9]

16895 Lessem, Don. *Feathered Dinosaurs* (2–4). Illus. by John Bindon. Series: Meet the Dinosaurs. 2005, Lerner LB $23.93 (978-0-8225-1423-7); paper $6.95 (978-0-8225-2621-6). 32pp. Simple text and dramatic illustrations explore the link between dinosaurs and birds. (Rev: BL 6/1–15/05) [567.912]

16896 Lessem, Don. *Ornithomimids: The Fastest Dinosaur* (3–6). Illus. Series: Special Dinosaurs. 1996, Carolrhoda LB $19.95 (978-0-87614-813-6). 40pp. How the remains of these speedy dinosaurs were discovered and how our knowledge of them was collected highlight this well-illustrated volume. (Rev: BL 2/15/96; SLJ 4/96) [567.9]

16897 Lessem, Don. *Sea Giants of Dinosaur Time* (2–3). Illus. by John Bindon. Series: Meet the Dinosaurs. 2005, Lerner LB $23.93 (978-0-8225-1425-1); paper $6.95 (978-0-8225-2623-0). 32pp. The fascinating creatures that filled the prehistoric seas are the focus of this book, complete with illustrations. (Rev: SLJ 9/05) [567.9]

16898 Lessem, Don. *Seismosaurus: The Longest Dinosaur* (3–5). Illus. by Donna Braginetz. Series: Special Dinosaurs. 1996, Carolrhoda LB $19.95 (978-0-87614-987-4). 40pp. This account introduces the seismosaurus and its characteristics and explains how we have determined these facts from fossils. (Rev: SLJ 9/96) [567.9]

16899 Lessem, Don. *Troodon: The Smartest Dinosaur* (3–6). Illus. Series: Special Dinosaurs. 1996, Carolrhoda LB $14.96 (978-0-87614-798-6). 40pp. The role of paleontologists in piecing together bits of information about this dinosaur is covered, along with information on its appearance, habits, and intelligence. (Rev: BL 2/15/96; SLJ 4/96) [567.9]

16900 Lewis, Brenda Ralph. *Meat-Eating Dinosaurs* (3–5). Illus. Series: Nature's Monsters: Dinosaurs. 2006, Gareth Stevens LB $23.93 (978-0-8368-6843-2). 32pp. Scary-looking carnivorous dinosaurs roam the pages of this introduction to the meat-eaters. Simple text and brief facts make this a good choice for young readers. (Rev: SLJ 5/07)

16901 Lewis, Brenda Ralph. *Plant-Eating Dinosaurs* (3–5). Illus. Series: Nature's Monsters: Dinosaurs. 2006, Gareth Stevens LB $23.93 (978-0-8368-6844-9). 32pp. Scary-looking herbivores roam the pages of this introduction to the plant-eaters. Simple text and brief facts make this a good choice for young readers. (Rev: SLJ 5/07)

16902 Lewis, Brenda Ralph. *Prehistoric Creatures in the Sea and Sky* (3–5). Illus. Series: Nature's Monsters: Dinosaurs. 2006, Gareth Stevens LB $23.93 (978-0-8368-6845-6). 32pp. Dinosaurs that swam or flew are featured in this introduction. Simple text and brief facts make this a good choice for young readers. (Rev: SLJ 5/07)

16903 Lewis, Brenda Ralph. *Small and Deadly Dinosaurs* (3–5). Illus. Series: Nature's Monsters: Dinosaurs. 2006, Gareth Stevens LB $23.93 (978-0-8368-6846-3). 32pp. The little guys of the prehistoric world are the focus of this book, part of a series. Simple text and brief facts make this a good choice for young readers. (Rev: SLJ 5/07)

16904 Llamas, Andreu. *The Era of the Dinosaurs* (4–8). Illus. Series: Development of the Earth. 1996, Chelsea LB $17.55 (978-0-7910-3452-1). Various kinds of dinosaurs are introduced, with an emphasis on their evolution and on how geology and climate affected their development. (Rev: SLJ 7/96) [567.9]

16905 Llamas, Andreu. *The First Amphibians* (4–8). Illus. Series: Development of the Earth. 1996, Chelsea LB $17.55 (978-0-7910-3453-8). Using many color illustrations, this book begins with the earliest land vertebrates and gives clear explanations of their adaptations over time. (Rev: SLJ 7/96) [567.9]

16906 Lunis, Natalie. *A T. Rex Named Sue: Sue Hendrickson's Huge Discovery* (3–6). Illus. Series: Fossil Hunters. 2006, Bearport LB $25.27 (978-1-59716-259-3). 32pp. In 1990 Sue Hendrickson discovered a Tyrannosaurus rex skeleton in South Dakota; this is a simply written account of the discovery and the lengthy legal battle to determine custody of the dinosaur remains. (Rev: SLJ 1/07) [567.912]

16907 McMullan, Kate. *Dinosaur Hunters* (2–4). Illus. by John R. Jones. Series: Step into Reading. 2005, Random LB $11.99 (978-0-375-92450-7); paper $3.99 (978-0-375-82450-0). 48pp. A new edition of the easy reader on how fossils are found and studied, with updated text and illustrations. (Rev: BL 9/1/05) [560]

16908 Malam, John. *Dinosaur* (5–8). Illus. 2006, DK $15.99 (978-0-7566-1412-6). 70pp. Tyrannosaurus rex is the star of this attractive book that covers the dinosaur's anatomy, life cycle, and hunting techniques plus archaeological findings and the science that has allowed us to reconstruct the animal from what we know today. (Rev: SLJ 4/07) [567.9]

16909 Manning, Mick, and Brita Granström. *Dino-Dinners* (K–2). Illus. by Mick Manning. 2007, Holiday $16.95 (978-0-8234-2089-6). 32pp. What did dinosaurs eat? Ten varieties of dinosaurs describe their eating habits in this lighthearted but informative volume. (Rev: BL 9/1/07; LMC 1/08; SLJ 10/07) [567.9]

16910 Manning, Mick, and Brita Granström. *Dinomania: Things to Do with Dinosaurs* (3–5). Illus. 2002, Holiday House $16.95 (978-0-8234-1641-7). 48pp. This book consists of a series of projects related to dinosaurs, such as creating a diorama of habitats and a mobile of flying creatures. (Rev: BL 6/1–15/02; HBG 10/02; SLJ 4/02) [745.5]

16911 Manning, Phillip Lars. *Dinomummy: The Life, Death, and Discovery of Dakota, a Dinosaur from Hell Creek* (5–8). Illus. 2007, Kingfisher $18.95 (978-0-7534-6047-4). 32pp. The 2006 discovery of a hadrosaur fossil — so complete its skin was still intact — is the subject of this dramatically designed book that takes readers into the world of paleontology. (Rev: BL 3/3/08) [567.914]

16912 Markle, Sandra. *Outside and Inside Woolly Mammoths* (4–6). Illus. Series: Outside and Inside. 2007, Walker $17.95 (978-0-8027-9589-2). 40pp. Photographs and digital images add to this account of what we know about mammoths and how they compare with today's elephants. (Rev: BL 5/1/07; HB 7/07; SLJ 6/07) [569]

16913 Matthews, Rupert. *Dinosaur Families: Unearth the Secrets Behind Dinosaur Fossils* (3–6). Series: Dinosaur Dig. 2009, QEB LB $27.10 (978-1-59566-548-5). 32pp. Reluctant readers will enjoy these highly visual books that focus on various aspects of dinosaurs and dinosaur life, with "Wow!" boxes and information on fossils and digs. Also use *Dinosaur Combat, Dinosaur Food,* and *Dinosaurs in Action* (all 2009). (Rev: SLJ 6/09) [567.9]

16914 Maynard, Christopher. *The Best Book of Dinosaurs* (3–5). 1998, Kingfisher $10.95 (978-0-7534-5116-8). 33pp. A clearly written, lavishly illustrated introduction to several groups of dinosaurs, focusing on specific traits of about 20 of them. (Rev: HBG 10/98; SLJ 7/98) [567.9]

16915 Moody, Richard. *Over 65 Million Years Ago: Before the Dinosaurs Died* (4–6). Illus. Series: History Detective. 1992, Macmillan LB $20.00 (978-0-02-767270-1). 32pp. How paleontologists have found out about dinosaurs and a summary of how they lived. (Rev: SLJ 12/92) [567.92]

16916 Morrison, Taylor. *The Great Unknown* (3–5). Illus. 2001, Houghton $16.00 (978-0-395-97494-0). 32pp. An account of Peale's discovery of mastodon bones in New York state in 1799 and their assembly into a skeleton. (Rev: BCCB 7–8/01; BL 5/1/01; HBG 10/01; SLJ 5/01) [569]

16917 Most, Bernard. *How Big Were the Dinosaurs?* (PS–2). Illus. 1994, Harcourt $16.00 (978-0-15-236800-5). 32pp. The size of 20 different dinosaurs is shown by comparisons with everyday modern objects, like a school bus or a bowling alley. (Rev: BL 3/1/94; SLJ 4/94) [567.9]

16918 Most, Bernard. *Where to Look for a Dinosaur* (1–4). Illus. 1993, Harcourt $12.95 (978-0-15-295616-5). 32pp. An actual geographical guidebook pinpointing the remains of more than 25 beasts. (Rev: BL 2/15/93; SLJ 6/93) [567.9]

16919 Munro, Margaret. *The Story of Life on Earth* (3–5). Illus. 2000, Douglas & McIntyre $19.95 (978-0-88899-401-1). 32pp. This informative introduction to the evolution of life on Earth uses double-page spreads to illustrate the flora and fauna of different geological periods. (Rev: BL 11/1/00; HBG 3/01; SLJ 12/00) [560]

16920 O'Brien, Patrick. *Mammoth* (K–3). Illus. 2002, Holt $16.95 (978-0-8050-6596-1). 40pp. O'Brien interweaves historical information about mammoths with contemporary scenes of scientists excavating and identifying a skeleton, in a well-illustrated, large-format overview of these animals that touches on their modern elephant relatives. (Rev: BL 12/1/02; HBG 3/03; SLJ 11/02) [569]

16921 O'Brien, Patrick. *Megatooth* (PS–3). Illus. by author. 2001, Holt $16.95 (978-0-8050-6214-4). 32pp. O'Brien presents the theories scientists have made about the giant beast also known as the megalodon. (Rev: HBG 10/01; SLJ 6/01)

16922 Olien, Becky. *Fossils* (2–4). Series: The Bridgestone Science Library. 2001, Capstone LB $22.60 (978-0-7368-0951-1). 24pp. Fossils, famous fossil finds, and fuels made from fossils are covered in this slim volume. (Rev: HBG 3/02; SLJ 2/02)

16923 Osborne, Will, and Mary Pope Osborne. *Dinosaurs: A Nonfiction Companion to Dinosaurs Before Dark* (2–4). Illus. by Sal Murdocca. Series: Magic Tree House Research Guide. 2000, Random LB $11.99 (978-0-375-90296-3); paper $4.99 (978-0-375-80296-6). 119pp. Using a time-travel format involving two children, this book discusses the kinds of dinosaurs, their characteristics, misconceptions about them, and the other creatures that lived at the same time. (Rev: HBG 3/01; SLJ 11/00) [567.9]

16924 Padma, T. V. *The Albertosaurus Mystery: Philip Currie's Hunt in the Badlands* (3–6). Illus. Series: Fossil Hunters. 2006, Bearport LB $25.27 (978-1-59716-254-8). 32pp. Describes paleontologist Philip Currie's search for a site containing the remains of multiple dinosaurs. (Rev: SLJ 1/07) [567.912]

16925 Pascoe, Elaine, adapt. *New Dinosaurs: Skeletons in the Sand* (4–6). Illus. Series: New Explorers. 1997, Blackbirch LB $17.95 (978-1-56711-231-3). 48pp. An account of the hardships and eventual success of a group of paleontologists who went to the Sahara in 1993 to find evidence of new dinosaurs. (Rev: HBG 3/98; SLJ 2/98) [567.9]

16926 Patent, Dorothy Hinshaw. *In Search of Maiasaurs* (4–7). Series: Frozen in Time. 1998, Benchmark LB $28.50 (978-0-7614-0787-4). 64pp. This book on dinosaurs describes the find of a huge bed of bones and Jack Horner's work to retrieve the fossils and learn from them. (Rev: HBG 10/99; SLJ 3/99) [567.9]

16927 Press, Judy. *The Kids' Natural History Book: Making Dinos, Fossils, Mammoths and More* (3–5). Illus. Series: Kids Can! 2000, Williamson $12.95 (978-1-885593-24-5). 144pp. A discussion of the animal classification system and how scientists have discovered and organized information about animals, with many related craft projects. (Rev: BL 12/15/00; SLJ 1/01) [745.5]

16928 Relf, Patricia. *A Dinosaur Named Sue: The Story of the Colossal Fossil* (3–6). Illus. 2000, Scholastic $15.95 (978-0-439-09985-1). 64pp. This is the story of the largest and most complete Tyrannosaurus rex skeleton ever found, how it was transported from South Dakota to the Field Museum in Chicago, and what life was like when Sue was alive. (Rev: BL 12/1/00; HBG 3/01; SLJ 1/01) [567.912]

16929 Rey, Luis V. *Extreme Dinosaurs* (3–7). Illus. by author. 2001, Chronicle $16.95 (978-0-8118-3086-7). 62pp. Bright, lively illustrations accompany a friendly text that provides lots of information about dinosaur evolution, dinosaur species grouped by continent, and fossil discoveries. (Rev: HBG 3/02; SLJ 9/01)

16930 Ryder, Joanne. *Tyrannosaurus Time* (K–4). Illus. by Michael Rothman. 1999, Morrow $15.95 (978-0-688-13682-6). 32pp. A vivid re-creation of a day in the life of a Tyrannosaurus rex and a memorable depiction of prehistoric life in a picture-book format. (Rev: BL 9/1/99; HBG 3/00; SLJ 9/99) [567.9]

16931 Sabuda, Robert, and Matthew Reinhart. *Encyclopedia Prehistorica: Dinosaurs* (K–4). Illus. by authors. 2005, Candlewick $26.99 (978-0-7636-2228-2). Beautifully engineered fold-outs introduce a variety of dinosaurs. (Rev: SLJ 9/05)

16932 Sabuda, Robert, and Matthew Reinhart. *Sharks and Other Sea Monsters* (1–3). Series: Encyclopedia Prehistorica. 2006, Candlewick $27.99 (978-0-7636-2229-9). 12pp. Elaborate pop-ups highlight facts about sharks, megalodons, and other prehis-

toric sea predators. (Rev: BL 6/1–15/06; SLJ 7/06) [566.22]

16933 Schlein, Miriam. *Discovering Dinosaur Babies* (2–4). Illus. by Margaret Colbert. 1991, Macmillan LB $14.95 (978-0-02-778091-8). 40pp. Explaining what is known about dinosaur babies and how mothers cared for them. (Rev: BL 3/1/91; SLJ 7/91) [567.9]

16934 Schomp, Virginia. *Ceratosaurus: And Other Horned Meat-Eaters* (3–4). Illus. Series: Prehistoric World. 2005, Benchmark LB $17.95 (978-0-7614-2009-5). 32pp. Vivid illustrations and conversational text introduce the Ceratosaurus and related prehistoric horned animals. Also use *Therizinosaurus* and *Plateosaurus* (both 2005). (Rev: SLJ 3/06)

16935 Schomp, Virginia. *Iguanodon: And Other Spiky-Thumbed Plant-Eaters* (2–4). Illus. Series: Prehistoric World. 2005, Marshall Cavendish LB $17.95 (978-0-7614-2005-7). 32pp. Accessible text and eye-catching images make this an appealing introduction to this prehistoric animal's appearance, diet, habitat, and behavior. (Rev: BL 3/1/06) [567.912]

16936 Simon, Seymour. *New Questions and Answers About Dinosaurs* (2–5). Illus. by Jennifer O. Dewey. 1990, Morrow $15.93 (978-0-688-08196-6). 48pp. Using a question-and-answer approach, covers interesting facts and figures about dinosaurs. (Rev: BCCB 5/90; BL 2/15/90; HB 7/90; SLJ 5/90) [567.9]

16937 Skrepnick, Michael W. *Sinosauropteryx: Mysterious Feathered Dinosaur* (3–4). Illus. by author. Series: I Like Dinosaurs! 2005, Enslow LB $21.26 (978-0-7660-2623-0). 24pp. Introduces the Sinosauropteryx, a small, feathered, poultry-size dinosaur whose fossilized remains were found in China in the mid-1990s. (Rev: SLJ 2/06) [567.912]

16938 Sloan, Christopher. *Feathered Dinosaurs* (3–6). Illus. 2000, National Geographic $17.95 (978-0-7922-7219-9). 64pp. Using recent paleontological discoveries as its starting point, this book explores what feathered dinosaurs, the distant ancestors of modern birds, might have looked like. (Rev: BL 11/1/00; HBG 3/01; SLJ 11/00) [567.9]

16939 Sloan, Christopher. *Supercroc and the Origin of Crocodiles* (5–8). Illus. 2002, National Geographic $18.95 (978-0-7922-6691-4). 64pp. A fascinating account of the discovery in Africa of the fossil *Sarcosuchus*, or Supercroc, with additional information on paleontology and crocodile evolution. (Rev: BCCB 5/02; BL 9/15/02; HBG 10/02; SLJ 7/02*) [567.9]

16940 Stewart, David. *Dinosaurs* (K–3). Illus. by Nicholas Hewetson. Series: World of Wonder. 2008, Children's Pr. LB $29.00 (978-0-531-20450-4); paper $9.95 (978-0-531-20541-9). 32pp. An effective question-and-answer format and vibrant layouts provide basic information on dinosaurs. (Rev: BL 4/1/08; LMC 10/08; SLJ 7/08) [567.9]

16941 Thompson, Sharon E. *Death Trap: The Story of the La Brea Tar Pits* (4–8). Illus. 1995, Lerner LB $28.75 (978-0-8225-2851-7). 72pp. A history of the 40,000-year-old tar pits in Los Angeles and of the many species of prehistoric animals that were trapped in them, with color photographs. (Rev: BL 6/1–15/95; SLJ 5/95) [560]

16942 Thomson, Sarah L. *Extreme Dinosaurs!* (K–3). Illus. 2007, HarperCollins LB $16.99 (978-0-06-089971-4); paper $6.99 (978-0-06-089967-7). 48pp. Using a conversational question-and-answer format, this volume conveys solid information. (Rev: BLO 1/15/08; SLJ 3/08) [567.9]

16943 Turner, Alan. *Prehistoric Mammals* (4–6). Illus. by Mauricio Antón. 2004, National Geographic $29.95 (978-0-7922-7134-5). 192pp. Dramatic illustrations and brief text introduce prehistoric mammals that roamed the earth after the time of the dinosaurs. (Rev: BL 11/1/04; SLJ 1/05*) [569]

16944 Unwin, David. *The New Book of Dinosaurs* (3–6). Illus. 1997, Millbrook LB $23.90 (978-0-7613-0568-2); paper $9.95 (978-0-7613-0589-7). 32pp. Computer-generated illustrations bring different dinosaurs alive, with lucid accompanying text. (Rev: BL 9/15/97; SLJ 9/97) [567.9]

16945 VanCleave, Janice. *Dinosaurs for Every Kid: Easy Activities That Make Learning Science Fun* (4–7). Illus. Series: Science for Every Kid. 1994, Wiley paper $12.95 (978-0-471-30812-6). 224pp. With accompanying activities, this book explores the world of dinosaurs and how paleontology has discovered, through fossils, how they lived. (Rev: BL 4/1/94; SLJ 7/94) [567.9]

16946 Walker, Sally M. *Fossils* (2–4). Illus. Series: Early Bird Earth Science. 2006, Lerner LB $25.26 (978-0-8225-5945-0). 48pp. Walker explains how fossils are formed, where they're mostly likely to be found, and what can be learned by studying them. (Rev: SLJ 1/07) [560]

16947 Wenzel, Gregory. *Feathered Dinosaurs of China* (4–6). Illus. by author. 2004, Charlesbridge $16.95 (978-1-57091-561-1); paper $6.95 (978-1-57091-562-8). 32pp. A trip more than 100 million years back in time to study the dinosaurs of prehistoric China and their theoretical relationship to modern-day birds. (Rev: SLJ 4/04) [567.9]

16948 Wenzel, Gregory. *Giant Dinosaurs of the Jurassic* (2–5). Illus. by author. 2004, Charlesbridge $16.95 (978-1-57091-563-5); paper $6.95 (978-1-57091-564-2). 32pp. The lives of a variety of dinosaurs are shown during a typical day in the prehistoric American West. (Rev: BL 10/1/04; SLJ 7/04) [507.9]

16949 Westrup, Hugh. *The Mammals* (5–8). Illus. Series: Prehistoric North America. 1996, Millbrook LB $22.90 (978-1-56294-546-6). The woolly mammoth and saber-toothed tiger are two of the prehistoric mammals described in words and pictures. (Rev: BL 5/15/96; SLJ 4/96) [569]

16950 Wheeler, Lisa. *Mammoths on the Move* (K–2). Illus. by Kurt Cyrus. 2006, Harcourt $16.00 (978-0-15-204700-9). 32pp. A woolly mammoth migration is the subject of this rhyming book with large illustrations. (Rev: BL 5/1/06; SLJ 6/06) [569]

16951 Wilkes, Angela. *The Big Book of Dinosaurs: A First Book for Young Children* (PS–2). Illus. 1994, DK $14.99 (978-1-56458-718-3). 32pp. An oversize book that contains double-page spreads introducing a wide variety of dinosaurs, including some that are little known. (Rev: BL 11/15/94; SLJ 1/95) [567.9]

16952 Williams, Judith. *The Discovery and Mystery of a Dinosaur Named Jane* (5–7). Illus. 2007, Enslow LB $23.93 (978-0-7660-2730-5); paper $13.26 (978-0-7660-2709-1). 48pp. A straightforward account of the discovery, excavation and installation of this important fossil find. (Rev: SLJ 7/07)

16953 Worth, Bonnie. *Oh Say Can You Say Di-nosaur? All About Dinosaurs* (K–3). Illus. by Steve Haefele. Series: The Cat in the Hat's Learning Library. 1999, Random LB $11.99 (978-0-679-99114-4). 45pp. Several of Dr. Seuss's characters introduce different dinosaurs and their physical traits using illustrations and rhyming couplets. (Rev: SLJ 9/99) [567.9]

16954 Zimmerman, Howard. *Dinosaurs! The Biggest Baddest Strangest Fastest* (2–5). Illus. 2000, Simon & Schuster $17.95 (978-0-689-83276-5). 64pp. An oversize volume that is particularly noteworthy for its excellent illustrations of all sorts of dinosaurs. (Rev: BL 9/1/00; HBG 10/00; SLJ 5/00) [567.9]

16955 Zoehfeld, Kathleen W. *Did Dinosaurs Have Feathers?* (K–4). Illus. by Lucia Washburn. Series: Let's-Read-and-Find-Out Science. 2004, HarperCollins LB $16.89 (978-0-06-029027-6); paper $5.99 (978-0-06-445218-2). 33pp. Dinosaur fossils and feathers are discussed, with mention of early discoveries and of the links between dinosaurs and birds. (Rev: BL 1/1–15/04; SLJ 2/04) [568]

16956 Zoehfeld, Kathleen W. *Dinosaur Babies* (K–3). Illus. by Lucia Washburn. Series: Let's-Read-and-Find-Out. 1999, HarperCollins LB $15.89 (978-0-06-027142-8); paper $4.99 (978-0-06-445162-8). 40pp. This simple science book explains the wonders of paleontology and how scientists use fossils to find out about dinosaurs. (Rev: BL 11/15/99; HBG 3/00; SLJ 9/99) [567.9]

16957 Zoehfeld, Kathleen W. *Dinosaur Parents, Dinosaur Young: Uncovering the Mystery of Dinosaur Families* (3–6). Illus. Series: Let's-Read-and-Find-Out Science. 2001, Clarion $17.00 (978-0-395-91338-3). 60pp. This book explains what we know about dinosaur parenting and how paleontologists have arrived at this information. (Rev: BL 4/15/01) [567.9]

16958 Zoehfeld, Kathleen W. *Dinosaur Tracks* (2–4). Illus. by Lucia Washburn. Series: Let's-Read-and-Find-Out Science. 2007, HarperCollins $16.99 (978-0-06-029024-5). 40pp. A look at how dinosaur tracks are discovered and what they can tell us about the animals that made them. (Rev: BL 12/1/06) [567.9]

16959 Zoehfeld, Kathleen W. *Dinosaurs Big and Small* (PS–1). Illus. by Lucia Washburn. Series: Let's-Read-and-Find-Out Science. 2002, HarperCollins paper $5.99 (978-0-06-445182-6). 40pp. Dinosaurs are compared with buses, elephants, and other items to help children grasp their size. (Rev: BL 7/02; HBG 10/02; SLJ 7/02) [567.9]

16960 Zoehfeld, Kathleen W. *Terrible Tyrannosaurs* (PS–2). Illus. by Lucia Washburn. 2001, HarperCollins LB $15.89 (978-0-06-027934-9). 40pp. This book highlights the most familiar and most feared dinosaur and tells what we know about it from science. (Rev: BL 2/1/01; HBG 10/01) [567.912]

16961 *Atlas of People* (PS–2). Illus. Series: First Discovery. 1996, Scholastic $12.95 (978-0-590-58281-0). 24pp. A basic introduction to the various races of humankind, with attractive visuals. (Rev: BL 10/15/96; SLJ 2/97) [305.8]

16962 Bailey, Jacqui. *The Dawn of Life* (3–5). Illus. by Matthew Lilly. Series: Cartoon History of the Earth. 2001, Kids Can $16.95 (978-1-55337-072-7); paper $7.95 (978-1-55337-081-9). 32pp. The beginnings of plant and animal life on Earth, presented in a comic-book format. Also use *The Birth of the Earth, The Day of the Dinosaurs,* and *The Stick and Stone Age* (all 2001). (Rev: BL 10/15/01; HBG 3/02; SLJ 1/02) [576.83]

16963 Batten, Mary. *Anthropologist: Scientist of the People* (4–7). Illus. Series: Scientists in the Field. 2001, Houghton $16.00 (978-0-618-08368-8). 64pp. Striking photographs of a Paraguayan tribe of hunter-gatherers serve as a powerful backdrop to this explanation of the work of anthropologists. (Rev: BL 8/01; HB 1/02*; HBG 3/02; SLJ 9/01) [627]

16964 Childress, Diana. *Prehistoric People of North America* (3–5). Illus. Series: Junior Library of American Indians. 1996, Chelsea $20.75 (978-0-7910-2481-2); paper $25.00 (978-0-7910-2482-9). 80pp. The story of the people who inhabited America in prehistoric times, with material on how they survived. (Rev: BL 11/15/96; SLJ 12/96) [970.01]

16965 Corbishley, Mike. *What Do We Know About Prehistoric People?* (4–7). Illus. Series: What Do We Know About. 1996, Bedrick LB $18.95 (978-0-87226-383-3). 40pp. Using double-page spreads, this book explores the known facts about human prehistoric life around the world. (Rev: BL 6/1–15/96) [930.1]

16966 Facchini, Fiorenzo. *Humans: Origins and Evolution* (4–8). Illus. Series: Beginnings — Origins and Evolution. 1995, Raintree LB $24.26 (978-0-8114-3336-5). 48pp. Theories and facts explaining human evolution are presented in a straightforward

way, with extensive artwork and diagrams. (Rev: BL 4/15/95; SLJ 6/95) [573.2]

16967 Gallant, Roy A. *Early Humans* (5–8). Series: The Story of Science. 1999, Benchmark LB $29.93 (978-0-7614-0960-1). 80pp. Neanderthals, Homo erectus, and early hominids are covered in this work on human evolution and important anthropological finds. (Rev: BL 2/15/00; HBG 3/00; SLJ 3/00) [573.2]

16968 Garassino, Alessandro. *Life, Origins and Evolution* (5–8). Series: Beginnings — Origins and Evolution. 1995, Raintree LB $24.26 (978-0-8114-3335-8). Using informative visuals, the author presents theories concerning the beginnings of life in the world. (Rev: BL 5/1/95) [575]

16969 Goldenberg, Linda. *Little People and a Lost World: An Anthropological Mystery* (5–8). Illus. 2006, Twenty-First Century LB $29.27 (978-0-8225-5983-2). 112pp. In 2003, a team of archaeologists and anthropologists discovered the skeleton of what's believed to be a small human being who lived more than 12,000 years ago on Flores Island in Indonesia; this book looks at the controversy over the discovery and the insights it has given into early human life. (Rev: BL 12/1/06; SLJ 4/07) [569.909598]

16970 Jenkins, Steve. *Life on Earth: The Story of Evolution* (3–6). Illus. 2002, Houghton $16.00 (978-0-618-16476-9). 40pp. Superb cut-paper illustrations depict the fundamentals of evolution, touching on Darwin, natural selection, and mutation, and ending with an extraordinary timeline. (Rev: BL 12/15/02; HB 9/02*; HBG 3/03; SLJ 12/02) [576.8]

16971 Lauber, Patricia. *Who Came First? New Clues to Prehistoric Americans* (5–10). Illus. 2003, National Geographic $18.95 (978-0-7922-8228-0). 64pp. An attractive, oversized volume that encompasses anthropology, archaeology, genetics, and linguistics in its discussion of the provenance of the peoples of the Americas. (Rev: BL 7/03*; HB 7/03; HBG 10/03; SLJ 8/03*) [970.01]

16972 McCutcheon, Marc. *The Beast in You! Activities and Questions to Explore Evolution* (4–8). Illus.

by Michael Kline. Series: A Kaleidoscope Kids Book. 1999, Williamson paper $10.95 (978-1-885593-36-8). 96pp. In a humorous, creative presentation, the author shows the similarities between humans and other animals and introduces the topic of evolution, our early ancestors, and their development. (Rev: SLJ 3/00) [575]

16973 McGowen, Tom. *Giant Stones and Earth Mounds* (4–8). Illus. 2000, Millbrook LB $25.90 (978-0-7613-1372-4). 80pp. A history of the New Stone Age of about 9,000 years ago and the constructions that still exist in the United States today from that period. (Rev: BL 10/1/00; HBG 10/01; SLJ 10/00) [930.1]

16974 Martell, Hazel M. *Over 6,000 Years Ago: In the Stone Age* (3–6). Illus. by Chris Rothero. 1992, Macmillan LB $20.00 (978-0-02-762429-8). 32pp. A look at life in the Stone Age, with watercolor drawings and photos. (Rev: BL 9/15/92; SLJ 12/92) [930.12]

16975 Patent, Dorothy Hinshaw. *Mystery of the Lascaux Cave* (4–7). Series: Frozen in Time. 1998, Benchmark LB $28.50 (978-0-7614-0784-3). 64pp. As well as displaying these remarkable cave paintings, this book covers what is known or surmised about the prehistoric people who produced these artistic wonders. (Rev: HBG 10/99; SLJ 3/99) [930.12]

16976 Patent, Dorothy Hinshaw. *Secrets of the Ice Man* (4–7). Series: Frozen in Time. 1998, Benchmark LB $28.50 (978-0-7614-0782-9). 72pp. The author discusses life during the Ice Age with material from recent discoveries. (Rev: HBG 10/99; SLJ 3/99) [937]

16977 Pickering, Robert. *The People* (5–8). Illus. Series: Prehistoric North America. 1996, Millbrook LB $22.90 (978-1-56294-550-3). An account of the development of the prehistoric North American tribes that may have crossed the land bridge from Asia to the Americas. (Rev: SLJ 4/96) [973.01]

16978 Ruiz, Andres L. *Evolution* (3–5). Illus. Series: Cycles of Life. 1997, Sterling $12.95 (978-0-8069-9329-4). 32pp. A step-by-step explanation of evolution, beginning with single-cell organisms and ending with the appearance of humans. (Rev: SLJ 6/97) [575]

16979 Schertle, Alice. *We* (1–3). Illus. by Kenneth Addison. 2007, Lee & Low $16.95 (978-1-58430-060-1). 32pp. Well-illustrated and concisely written in poetic form, this introduction to human evolution and ingenuity covers human history from its beginnings in Africa to the present day. (Rev: BL 5/1/07; LMC 11/07; SLJ 5/07) [599.93]

16980 Thimmesh, Catherine. *Lucy Long Ago: Uncovering the Mystery of Where We Came From* (5–7). Illus. 2009, Houghton $18.00 (978-0-547-05199-4). 64pp. The story behind Lucy, a skeleton found in Ethiopia in 1974, who made science rethink its how humans evolved. (Rev: BCCB 7–8/09; BL 6/1–15/09; HB 7/09; SLJ 7/09) [569.9]

16981 Winston, Robert. *Evolution Revolution* (5–8). Illus. 2009, DK $16.99 (978-0-7566-4524-3). 96pp. This attractive and accessible large-format picture book looks first at creation stories and Darwin's theories before progressing to modern understanding of genetics, evolutionary biology, and the role of DNA. (Rev: BL 3/15/09; SLJ 2/09) [576.82]

Archaeology

16982 Arnold, Caroline. *Stone Age Farmers Beside the Sea: Scotland's Prehistoric Village of Skara Brae* (5–8). 1997, Clarion $16.00 (978-0-395-77601-8). A stunning volume that tells the story of the Stone Age village of Skara Brae, dating to about 3000 B.C., that was unearthed in the Orkney Islands in 1850. (Rev: BCCB 4/97; BL 4/15/97; SLJ 7/97) [930]

16983 Avi-Yonah, Michael. *Dig This! How Archaeologists Uncover Our Past* (5–8). Series: Buried Worlds. 1993, Lerner LB $28.75 (978-0-8225-3200-2). A history of the discipline of archaeology, an examination of excavating methods, and a look at several ancient civilizations. (Rev: BL 1/15/94; SLJ 2/94) [930.1]

16984 Barber, Nicola. *The Search for Lost Cities* (4–6). Illus. Series: Treasure Hunters. 1997, Raintree LB $18.98 (978-0-8172-4840-6). 46pp. Using double-page spreads for each site, this account covers such places as Troy, Knossos, Pompeii, and Angkor Wat. (Rev: BL 11/15/97; HBG 3/98; SLJ 1/98) [909]

16985 Barber, Nicola, and Anita Ganeri. *The Search for Sunken Treasure* (4–6). Series: Treasure Hunters. 1997, Raintree LB $18.98 (978-0-8172-4838-3). 46pp. This overview covers such topics as the lost treasures in sunken ships and the sacred well of Chichén Itzá, with additional material on how ancient artifacts have been recovered and what they tell us about other times. (Rev: BL 11/15/97; HBG 3/98) [930]

16986 Barnes, Trevor. *Archaeology* (4–6). Series: Kingfisher Knowledge. 2004, Houghton $11.95 (978-0-7534-5768-9). 64pp. This colorful overview of archaeological finds and techniques will attract browsers and reluctant older readers. (Rev: BL 9/1/04; SLJ 11/04) [930.1]

16987 Buell, Janct. *Greenland Mummies* (5–8). Series: Time Travelers. 1998, Twenty-First Century LB $25.90 (978-0-7613-3004-2). By examining mummified human corpses found in Greenland, archaeologists have been able to reconstruct the life and culture of Inuits who lived 500 years ago. (Rev: SLJ 10/98) [930]

16988 Buell, Janet. *Ice Maiden of the Andes* (5–8). Illus. Series: Time Travelers. 1997, Twenty-First Century paper $25.90 (978-0-8050-5185-8). The story of the discovery of the frozen body of a young Inca girl who died 500 years ago and of how forensic methods such as DNA testing have revealed insights into Inca society, its religion, and gender roles. (Rev: BL 2/1/98; SLJ 3/98) [985]

16989 *Dazzling! Jewelry of the Ancient World* (5–8). Illus. Series: Buried Worlds. 1995, Lerner LB $28.75 (978-0-8225-3203-3). 64pp. An exploration of the jewels that archaeologists have retrieved from various ancient sites. (Rev: BL 7/95; SLJ 4/95) [739.27]

16990 Dean, Arlan. *Terra-Cotta Soldiers: Army of Stone* (4–7). Illus. Series: High Interest Books: Digging Up the Past. 2005, Children's Pr. LB $24.50 (978-0-516-25124-0); paper $6.95 (978-0-516-25093-9). 40pp. For reluctant readers, this is a useful introduction to one of the world's most extraordinary archaeological finds: the 8,000 terracotta warriors of China. (Rev: BL 10/15/05; SLJ 2/06) [931]

16991 Deem, James M. *Bodies from the Ice: Melting Glaciers and the Recovery of the Past* (4–7). Illus. 2008, Houghton $17.00 (978-0-618-80045-2). 64pp. Deem explores what researchers are learning about history and culture as melting glaciers reveal the remains of previously hidden bodies. (Rev: BCCB 12/08; BL 12/1/08; HB 1/09; SLJ 12/08) [599.9]

16992 Duke, Kate. *Archaeologists Dig for Clues* (1–4). Series: Let's-Read-and-Find-Out. 1997, HarperCollins LB $15.89 (978-0-06-027057-5). 32pp. Archaeologist Sophie describes how her colleagues collect information and analyze their findings. (Rev: BL 12/1/96; SLJ 2/97*) [930]

16993 Funston, Sylvia. *Mummies* (5–7). Illus. by Joe Weissmann. Series: Strange Science. 2000, Owl $19.95 (978-1-894379-03-8); paper $9.95 (978-1-894379-04-5). 40pp. All kinds of mummified human remains are discussed, from those in ancient Egypt to the 1999 discovery of George Mallory's body on Mount Everest. (Rev: HBG 3/01; SLJ 11/00) [909]

16994 Ganeri, Anita. *The Search for Tombs* (4–6). Illus. Series: Treasure Hunters. 1997, Raintree LB $18.98 (978-0-8172-4839-0). 46pp. This fascinating account covers such burial places as the Egyptian pyramids, the royal tombs of China, and the Roman catacombs. (Rev: BL 11/15/97; HBG 3/98; SLJ 2/98) [393]

16995 Goldenstern, Joyce. *Lost Cities* (3–6). Illus. Series: Weird and Wacky Science. 1996, Enslow LB $23.93 (978-0-89490-615-2). 48pp. The history and rediscovery of such lost cities as Troy, Machu Picchu, Mohenjo-daro, and Herculaneum are covered. (Rev: SLJ 6/96) [930]

16996 Greene, Meg. *Buttons, Bones, and the Organ-Grinder's Monkey: Tales of Historical Archaeology* (5–8). Illus. 2001, Linnet LB $25.00 (978-0-208-02498-5). 117pp. This introduction to historical archaeology looks at finds at five different sites in the United States. (Rev: BL 10/1/01; HBG 10/02; SLJ 1/02; VOYA 4/02) [973]

16997 Guiberson, Brenda Z. *Mummy Mysteries: Tales from North America* (4–7). Illus. by author. Series: A Redfeather Chapter Book. 1998, Holt $15.95 (978-0-8050-5369-2). 74pp. Reading like a mystery story, this book focuses on mummies found in North America, how and where they were found, and the information they reveal. (Rev: BCCB 2/99; HBG 3/99; SLJ 12/98) [937]

16998 Halls, Kelly Milner. *Mysteries of the Mummy Kids* (4–6). Illus. 2007, Darby Creek $18.95 (978-1-58196-059-4). 72pp. Mummified children from around the world are detailed in this compelling survey of the reasons why their bodies were preserved and the ways in which they were found. (Rev: BCCB 5/07; BL 5/1/07; LMC 10/07; SLJ 7/07) [393.3]

16999 Harris, Nathaniel. *Ancient Maya: Archaeology Unlocks the Secrets of the Maya's Past* (5–8). Illus. Series: National Geographic Investigates. 2008, National Geographic $17.95 (978-1-4263-0227-5). 64pp. With photographs, illustrations, and maps, this book shows how archaeology has uncovered information about the Maya and their culture. (Rev: BL 3/3/08) [972.8]

17000 Harrison, David L. *Cave Detectives: Unraveling the Mystery of an Ice Age Cave* (4–6). Illus. by Ashley Mims. 2007, Chronicle $15.95 (978-0-8118-5006-3). 47pp. This book describes the 2001 discovery of an Ice Age cave and explains how scientists established what prehistoric species lived there. (Rev: BL 5/1/07; SLJ 8/07) [560]

17001 Hoobler, Dorothy. *Lost Civilizations* (5–7). Illus. by Thomas Hoobler. 1992, Walker LB $15.85 (978-0-8027-8153-6). 176pp. Interesting discussion of Stonehenge, the Mound Builders, and other lost ancient civilizations. (Rev: BL 5/1/92; SLJ 9/92) [930]

17002 Jameson, W. C. *Buried Treasures of the Atlantic Coast: Legends of Sunken Pirate Treas-ures, Mysterious Caches, and Jinxed Ships — From Maine to Florida* (4–8). Series: Buried Treasure. 1997, August House $11.95 (978-0-87483-484-0). An account of how buried treasures were acquired and lost and the modern efforts to locate and retrieve them. Also use *Buried Treasures of New England* (1997). (Rev: SLJ 10/97) [910.4]

17003 Knapp, Ron. *Mummies* (3–6). Illus. Series: Weird and Wacky Science. 1996, Enslow LB $23.93 (978-0-89490-618-3). 48pp. Describes how bodies have been preserved in different cultures and situations, ending with the discovery of the Ice Man in the Alps. (Rev: SLJ 6/96) [930]

17004 Kops, Deborah. *Palenque* (5–8). Illus. Series: Unearthing Ancient Worlds. 2008, Twenty-First Century LB $30.60 (978-0-8225-7504-7). 80pp. With many large photographs and interesting text, this volume traces the discovery of the ruins at Palenque in the mid-19th century and the work that has been done since then on this Mayan site. (Rev: LMC 11/08; SLJ 2/08)

17005 Lourie, Peter. *The Mystery of the Maya: Uncovering the Lost City of Palenque* (5–8). Illus. 2001, Boyds Mills $19.95 (978-1-56397-839-5). 48pp. The author relates his interesting and often exciting experiences at a dig in Mexico and describes the work of the archaeologists and the history of the site. (Rev: BL 9/15/01; HBG 3/02; SLJ 11/01) [972.75]

17006 Malam, John. *Mummies* (5–8). Illus. Series: Kingfisher Knowledge. 2003, Kingfisher $11.95 (978-0-7534-5623-1). 63pp. A highly illustrated, readable exploration of preserved bodies of all eras and areas of the world. (Rev: HBG 4/04; SLJ 12/03) [393]

17007 Markle, Sandra. *Outside and Inside Mummies* (4–6). Illus. Series: Outside and Inside. 2005, Walker $17.95 (978-0-8027-8966-2). 40pp. This photo-filled title provides an overview of what cutting-edge medical imaging technology reveals about mummies and mummification practices. (Rev: BL 9/15/05; SLJ 8/05) [393]

17008 Panchyk, Richard. *Archaeology for Kids: Uncovering the Mysteries of Our Past with 25 Activities* (5–8). Illus. 2001, Chicago Review paper $14.95 (978-1-55652-395-3). 160pp. An introduction for older readers to the history and scientific method of archaeology, full of illustrations and with interesting activities. (Rev: BL 1/1–15/02; SLJ 12/01) [930.1]

17009 Place, Robin. *Bodies from the Past* (4–7). Illus. Series: Digging Up the Past. 1995, Thomson Learning LB $24.26 (978-1-56847-397-0). 48pp. Explores the preserved remains of people around the world from burial sites in China and mummies in peat bogs to the Ice Man discovered in the Alps. (Rev: SLJ 2/96) [567.9]

17010 Reid, Struan. *The Children's Atlas of Lost Treasures* (4–7). Illus. Series: Children's Atlases. 1997, Millbrook paper $14.95 (978-0-7613-0240-7). 96pp. Using a double-page spread for each site, this book supplies a survey of the world-famous discoveries of treasures that began as religious offerings, pirate booty, and items lost in war or by natural disasters. (Rev: HBG 3/98; SLJ 3/98) [930.1]

17011 Shuter, Jane. *Ancient China* (4–6). Illus. Series: Excavating the Past. 2005, Heinemann LB $31.43 (978-1-4034-5995-4). 48pp. The work of archaeologists is clearly shown in this well-illustrated exploration of the early history of China. (Rev: SLJ 2/06) [931]

17012 Sloan, Christopher. *Bury the Dead: Tombs, Corpses, Mummies, Skeletons, and Rituals* (5–9). Illus. 2002, National Geographic $18.95 (978-0-7922-7192-5). 64pp. Young readers will be fascinated by this serious account of burial practices throughout the ages, with timelines, color photographs, diagrams, and clear descriptions of rites around the world. (Rev: BL 12/1/02; HBG 3/03; SLJ 10/02*) [393]

17013 Smith, K. C. *Exploring for Shipwrecks* (5–7). Series: Shipwrecks. 2000, Watts LB $25.50 (978-0-531-20377-4). 64pp. This book explains and explores the world of underwater archaeology, the techniques and training involved, and gives many examples from specific shipwreck studies. (Rev: BL 10/15/00) [930.1]

17014 Smith, K. C. *Shipwrecks of the Explorers* (5–7). Illus. Series: Watts Library: Shipwrecks. 2000, Watts LB $25.50 (978-0-531-20378-1). 64pp. A look at underwater archaeology tells how scientists locate shipwrecks and what the ships reveal about the explorers who sailed in them. There are

also descriptions of famous voyages including those of Columbus and Amundsen. (Rev: BL 10/15/00) [910.4]

17015 Sonneborn, Liz. *Pompeii* (5–8). Illus. Series: Unearthing Ancient Worlds. 2008, Lerner LB $30.60 (978-0-8225-7505-4). 80pp. Concentrating on the original excavation of Pompeii in the 18th century, this book explains how early archaeological digs were conducted. (Rev: BL 4/1/08; SLJ 2/08) [937]

17016 Wilcox, Charlotte. *Mummies and Their Mysteries* (5–7). Illus. 1993, Carolrhoda LB $23.93 (978-0-87614-767-2). 64pp. An account of how throughout history many civilizations and religions have attempted to preserve bodies. (Rev: BCCB 7–8/93*; BL 6/1–15/93*) [393.3]

17017 Wilcox, Charlotte. *Mummies, Bones, and Body Parts* (4–7). Illus. 2000, Lerner paper $7.95 (978-1-57505-486-5). 64pp. The study of human remains is covered, including material on how death is treated in various cultures, embalming practices, and the work of archaeologists and anthropologists. (Rev: BCCB 9/00; BL 9/1/00; HBG 10/01; SLJ 10/00) [393]

17018 Wilkinson, Philip, and Jacqueline Dineen. *The Early Inventions* (5–8). Illus. 1995, Chelsea LB $21.95 (978-0-7910-2766-0). A look at the invention of early tools and processes, mostly for human survival purposes — eating and staying warm. (Rev: SLJ 11/95; VOYA 2/96) [930]

World History

General

17019 Aaseng, Nathan. *You Are the Explorer* (4–8). Illus. Series: Great Decisions. 2000, Oliver LB $19.95 (978-1-881508-55-7). 160pp. In this interactive book about famous explorers, the reader is asked to make decisions similar to those made by real explorers such as Columbus, Cortes, Champlain, and Robert Scott. (Rev: BL 5/1/00; HBG 10/00; SLJ 9/00) [910]

17020 Andryszewski, Tricia. *Walking the Earth: The History of Human Migration* (5–9). 2006, Twenty-First Century LB $27.93 (978-0-7613-3458-3). 80pp. A thorough introduction to the movements of human population across more than 150,000 years, with many illustrations, maps, and charts. (Rev: HBG 4/07; LMC 3/07; SLJ 1/07; VOYA 12/06) [304.8]

17021 Aronson, Marc, and John W. Glenn. *The World Made New: Why the Age of Exploration Happened and How It Changed the World* (5–8). 2007, National Geographic $17.95 (978-0-7922-6454-5). 64pp. This is an enlightening and well-illustrated survey of world exploration — in particular of European expeditions to the Western Hemisphere in the 15th and 16th centuries — looking at key figures and at the lasting consequences for the people, plants, and animals. (Rev: BL 9/15/07; SLJ 8/07) [910.9]

17022 Barber, Nicola. *The Search for Gold* (4–6). Series: Treasure Hunters. 1997, Raintree LB $18.98 (978-0-8172-4837-6). 46pp. This overview covers such topics as the Spanish destruction of the Aztec and Inca cultures, the African gold trade, and the California Gold Rush. (Rev: BL 11/15/97; HBG 3/98) [900]

17023 Blackwood, Gary L. *Highwaymen* (5–8). Illus. Series: Bad Guys. 2001, Marshall Cavendish LB $29.93 (978-0-7614-1017-1). 72pp. Period artwork, photographs, and intriguing tales bring real highway robbers, and the times they lived in, to life. (Rev: BL 1/1–15/02; HBG 3/02; SLJ 1/02) [364.15]

17024 Blackwood, Gary L. *Swindlers* (5–8). Illus. Series: Bad Guys. 2001, Marshall Cavendish LB $29.93 (978-0-7614-1031-7). 72pp. The author presents famous swindlers and cheats throughout history, providing illustrations, source notes, and recommended Web sites and further reading. (Rev: BL 1/1–15/02; HBG 3/02) [364.16]

17025 Burgan, Michael. *The Spanish Conquest of America: Prehistory to 1775* (5–8). Series: Latino-American History. 2006, Chelsea House LB $35.00 (978-0-8160-6440-3). 106pp. A thorough and clear account of Spain's influence on the Americas, with discussion of individual explorers as well as the impact on native peoples and the conflicts with other colonial powers. (Rev: BL 3/15/07) [979]

17026 Chisholm, Jane. *The Usborne Book of World History Dates: The Key Events in History* (4–8). 1998, EDC paper $22.95 (978-0-7460-2318-1). 194pp. Timelines and double-page spreads with brief topical essays present a panorama of world history. (Rev: SLJ 5/99) [910]

17027 Christie, Peter. *The Curse of Akkad: Climate Upheavals That Rocked Human History* (5–8). Illus. 2008, Annick $19.95 (978-1-55451-119-8); paper $11.95 (978-1-55451-118-1). 144pp. The effects of climate change through history are described in segments of one to three pages, making this a good choice for reluctant readers. (Rev: BL 8/08) [551.609]

17028 Claybourne, Anna, and Caroline Young. *The Usborne Book of Treasure Hunting* (4–7). Illus. 1999, Usborne paper $14.95 (978-0-7460-3445-3). 79pp. In a series of short chapters, this book covers famous treasures that were buried underground, lost at sea, or existed in ancient times — with coverage of such subjects as the clay soldiers in Huang Di's tomb and the restoration of the Tudor ship *Mary Rose*. (Rev: BL 4/1/99) [622.19]

17029 Connolly, Sean. *Gender Equality* (5–8). Series: Campaigns for Change. 2005, Smart Apple LB $29.95 (978-1-58340-515-4). 48pp. An exploration of women's status and struggles to improve it throughout history; also use *The Right to Vote* (2005). (Rev: SLJ 5/06) [305.42]

17030 Deary, Terry. *The Wicked History of the World: History with the Nasty Bits Left In!* (4–7). Illus. by Martin Brown. 2006, Scholastic $10.99 (978-0-439-87786-2). 93pp. This pun-filled survey of world history, with its emphasis on the shadier side, will attract reluctant readers with sections on "Beastly Barbarians," "Rotten Rules," and "Vicious Villains." (Rev: SLJ 12/06) [909]

17031 Gelber, Carol. *Masks Tell Stories* (5–7). Illus. Series: Beyond Museum Walls. 1993, Millbrook LB $24.90 (978-1-56294-224-3). 62pp. Explores the nature, meaning, and uses of masks in different cultures at various times. (Rev: BL 8/93) [391]

17032 Gold, Susan Dudley. *Governments of the Western Hemisphere* (5–8). Illus. Series: Comparing Continents. 1997, Twenty-First Century LB $24.90 (978-0-8050-5602-0). This book examines the struggles for independence in the United States, Canada, Mexico, Central America, and South America and the different directions taken by each once independence was achieved, highlighting the diversity across the nations. (Rev: BL 2/1/98; SLJ 3/98) [320.3]

17033 Hansen, Dianne. *Agriculture* (3–5). Series: Yesterday and Today. 2005, Gale LB $23.70 (978-1-56711-827-8). 32pp. A broad overview of the history of agriculture, from the dawn of man through today, with photographs, illustrations and a timelines; suitable for browsing. (Rev: SLJ 7/05)

17034 Harper, Charise Mericle. *Flush! The Scoop on Poop Throughout the Ages* (2–4). Illus. 2007, Little, Brown $15.99 (978-0-316-01064-1). 32pp. Combining rhyming verse, sidebar facts, and bright illustrations, this paean to poop disposal will fascinate kids drawn to its mix of gross-out humor and arcane historical information. (Rev: BL 1/1–15/07; SLJ 9/06) [392.3]

17035 Harward, Barnaby. *The Best Book of Pirates* (3–5). Illus. Series: The Best Book Of. 2002, Kingfisher $12.95 (978-0-7534-5449-7). 31pp. Covers pirates through the ages with pirate flags, information on pirate ships and equipment, and a page on contemporary buccaneers. (Rev: HBG 3/03; SLJ 3/03) [910.4]

17036 Haskins, James, and Kathleen Benson. *Bound for America: The Forced Migration of Africans to the New World* (4–9). Illus. by Floyd Cooper. Series: From African Beginnings. 1999, Lothrop LB $17.89 (978-0-688-10259-3). 48pp. This stirring account traces the fate of African slaves from capture, imprisonment, and branding to the brutal conditions on slave ships and finally to the survivors' arrival in the New World. (Rev: BCCB 3/99; BL 12/15/98; HBG 10/99; SLJ 1/99*) [382]

17037 Haslam, Andrew. *Living History: The Hands-On Approach to History* (3–6). Illus. Series: Make It Work! 2001, Two-Can $29.95 (978-1-58728-381-9). 256pp. This assemblage of volumes from the Make It Work! series features activities pertaining to daily life in Old Japan, ancient Egypt, ancient

Rome, and Native American cultures, such as making togas. (Rev: BL 3/1/02; HBG 3/02) [900]

17038 Hibbert, Clare. *Real Pirates* (3–6). Illus. by John James. 2003, Enchanted Lion $15.95 (978-1-59270-018-9). 48pp. Seagoing bandits of both sexes, from Blackbeard to Anne Bonny, and details of their ships, weapons, and tactics are presented in four geographical areas. (Rev: SLJ 5/04) [910.4]

17039 Jackson, Ellen. *Turn of the Century* (3–5). Illus. by Jan Davey Ellis. 1998, Charlesbridge LB $17.95 (978-0-88106-369-1). 32pp. This book outlines life at the turn of each century from A.D. 1000 to the present, as seen through the eyes of a child in Great Britain and later in America. (Rev: BL 7/98*; HBG 3/99; SLJ 9/98) [305.2]

17040 Jedicke, Peter. *Great Inventions of the 20th Century* (5–8). Series: Scientific American. 2007, Chelsea House LB $30.00 (978-0-7910-9048-0). 72pp. With plenty of photographs and clear text, this volume — produced in association with *Scientific American* — presents inventions of the 20th century including cellophane and the microwave in chapters such as "On the Road," "At Home," and "In the Air." (Rev: SLJ 2/08)

17041 Knight, Margy B. *Talking Walls* (3–5). Illus. by Anne S. O'Brien. 1992, Tilbury House $17.95 (978-0-88448-102-7). 40pp. Prehistoric paintings on walls in Australia and notable walls from six continents introduce children to the world and its many cultures. (Rev: BL 8/92*; SLJ 9/92) [900]

17042 Knight, Margy B. *Talking Walls: The Stories Continue* (3–7). Illus. by Anne S. O'Brien. 1996, Tilbury House $17.95 (978-0-88448-164-5). Double-page spreads are used to introduce some famous walls, like the dikes in the Netherlands, Hadrian's Wall, the Belfast Peace Lines, and prayer-wheel walls in India and Tibet. (Rev: SLJ 10/96) [900]

17043 Kurlansky, Mark. *The Story of Salt* (4–6). Illus. by S. D. Schindler. 2006, Putnam $16.99 (978-0-399-23998-4). 48pp. History, science, politics, and technology come together in this story of the sought-after element, adapted from the adult version. (Rev: BL 7/06; SLJ 10/06*) [553.6]

17044 Lankford, Mary D. *Mazes Around the World* (3–5). Illus. by Karen Dugan. 2008, HarperCollins $16.99 (978-0-688-16519-2). 32pp. Lankford looks at mazes through history, including the Minotaur's labyrinth, religious labyrinths, traditional hedge mazes, and modern water and maize mazes; paintings show each maze's structure. (Rev: BL 4/1/08; LMC 11/06; SLJ 5/08) [302.2]

17045 Lassieur, Allison. *The History of Pirates: From Privateers to Outlaws* (2–4). Illus. Series: Edge Books: Real World of Pirates. 2006, Capstone LB $23.93 (978-0-7368-6423-7). 32pp. Ideal for beginning readers, this attractive title offers a brief history of pirates with eye-catching illustrations. (Rev: BL 10/15/06) [910.4]

17046 Lauber, Patricia. *What You Never Knew About Beds, Bedrooms, and Pajamas* (2–5). Illus. by John Manders. Series: Around the House History. 2006, Simon & Schuster $16.95 (978-0-689-85211-4). A light history of sleeping customs from the Stone

Age to today, with comical commentary in cartoons; suitable for browsing. (Rev: SLJ 2/07)

17047 Lendroth, Susan. *Why Explore?* (K–3). Illus. by Enrique S. Moreiro. 2005, Tricycle $15.95 (978-1-58246-150-2). An interesting overview of human exploration of all kinds over the centuries. (Rev: SLJ 1/06)

17048 Llewellyn, Claire. *Great Discoveries and Amazing Adventures: The Stories of Hidden Marvels and Lost Treasures* (4–7). Illus. 2004, Kingfisher $18.95 (978-0-7534-5783-2). 76pp. Important discoveries — and hoaxes — are described in inviting text, plus many illustrations, factoids, and a foreword by Robert Ballard. (Rev: SLJ 1/05) [509]

17049 Love, Ann, and Jane Drake. *Sweet!* (3–5). Illus. by Claudia Dávila. 2007, Tundra $19.95 (978-0-88776-752-4). 64pp. This is an appealing survey of candy from ancient history to today, with a running timeline, cartoon illustrations, and many funny and appropriate anecdotes; more suited to browsing than reports. (Rev: BL 2/1/07) [641.8]

17050 McGowen, Tom. *Assault from the Sea: Amphibious Invasions in the Twentieth Century* (5–8). Series: Military Might. 2002, Twenty-First Century LB $26.90 (978-0-7613-1811-8). 64pp. Invasions launched from the sea during World Wars I and II and the Korean War are the subject of this introduction that includes black-and-white photographs and maps. Also use *Assault from the Sky: Airborne Infantry of World War II* (2002). (Rev: HBG 10/02; SLJ 6/02) [355.460904]

17051 McLaren, Chesley, and Pamela Jaber. *When Royals Wore Ruffles: A Funny and Fashionable Alphabet!* (1–4). Illus. by Chesley McLaren. 2009, Random $16.99 (978-0-375-85166-7). A pleasing alphabetical stroll through all fashion trends from the days of Cleopatra through modern grunge. (Rev: LMC 5/09; SLJ 3/09) [391.009]

17052 Mara, Wil. *The Seven Continents* (K–2). Series: Rookie Read-About Geography. 2005, Children's Pr. LB $20.50 (978-0-516-22748-1). 31pp. A broad geographical overview of the continents, with a picture glossary to aid new readers. (Rev: SLJ 7/05)

17053 Markle, Sandra. *Rescues!* (4–7). Illus. 2006, Lerner LB $25.26 (978-0-8225-3413-6). 88pp. Markle covers rescue efforts in 11 recent disasters (2004 to 2005), giving details of technology used and providing accounts by victims, rescuers, and eyewitnesses. (Rev: BL 4/1/06*; HBG 10/06; LMC 11/06; SLJ 8/06; VOYA 6/06) [363.34]

17054 Mason, Antony. *People Around the World* (5–7). Illus. 2002, Kingfisher $24.95 (978-0-7534-5497-8). 256pp. An oversize guide to people of different cultures around the world, organized by continent, featuring hundreds of full-color photographs and illustrations, and detailing such topics as diet, language, employment, and leisure of urban and rural dwellers. (Rev: BL 5/1/03; HBG 10/03; SLJ 4/03; VOYA 6/03) [305.8]

17055 Matthews, John. *Pirates* (3–6). 2006, Simon & Schuster $19.95 (978-1-4169-2734-1). 32pp. The fold-outs, flaps, treasure maps, and other features of this fact-packed interactive book will keep browsers and researchers happy. (Rev: BL 7/06) [364.164]

17056 Millard, Anne. *A Street Through Time* (4–8). Illus. 1998, DK $17.99 (978-0-7894-3426-5). Western European history is traced in this oversize book that contains 14 views of the same riverside location at various times in history, including the Stone Age, Viking times, the Roman period, the Middle Ages, and modern times. (Rev: BL 1/1–15/99; HB 1/99; HBG 3/99; SLJ 12/98) [936]

17057 Morgan, Kate. *The Story of Things* (3–5). Illus. by Joyce A. Zarins. 1991, Walker LB $15.85 (978-0-8027-6919-0). 32pp. A history of civilization in a slim volume that will attract a child's interest. (Rev: BL 6/15/91; SLJ 7/91) [523.4]

17058 Morris, Neil. *Pirates* (4–6). Illus. Series: Amazing History. 2008, Black Rabbit LB $18.95 (978-1-59920-104-7). 32pp. Double-page spreads look at various aspects of pirates and piracy, including their vessels and equipment, famous individuals, women pirates, and modern forms of piracy. (Rev: BL 4/1/08) [910.4]

17059 O'Brien, Patrick. *Mutiny on the Bounty* (4–7). Illus. 2007, Walker $17.95 (978-0-8027-9587-8). 40pp. Clear, balanced narrative and vivid illustrations tell both sides of the story of the famous mutiny and its aftermath. (Rev: BL 1/1–15/07; SLJ 3/07) [910.4]

17060 Parks, Peggy J. *Clothing* (3–5). Series: Yesterday and Today. 2005, Gale LB $23.70 (978-1-56711-828-5). 32pp. A broad overview of the history of apparel, from the dawn of man through today, with photographs, illustrations and a timelines; suitable for browsing. Also use *Entertainment* (2005). (Rev: SLJ 7/05)

17061 Pirotta, Saviour. *Buried Treasure* (3–5). Series: Mysteries of the Past. 2001, Raintree LB $25.69 (978-0-7398-4336-9). 32pp. Egyptian tombs, burial mounds in England, pirate legends, and Nazi loot are among the topics addressed in this overview of underground lore. (Rev: HBG 3/02; SLJ 2/02)

17062 Pirotta, Saviour. *Pirates and Treasure* (4–5). Illus. Series: Remarkable World. 1995, Thomson Learning LB $24.26 (978-1-56847-366-6). 47pp. A history of piracy from the days of the Phoenicians onward, with full-color art reproductions, maps, and many sidebars. (Rev: SLJ 1/96) [910.4]

17063 Ross, Stewart. *Conquerors and Explorers* (5–7). Illus. Series: Fact or Fiction? 1996, Millbrook LB $26.90 (978-0-7613-0532-3). 48pp. The subtitle of this work is "The Greed, Cunning, and Bravery of the Travelers and Plunderers Who Opened Up the World." (Rev: BL 10/15/96; SLJ 4/97) [910]

17064 Ruggiero, Adriane. *The Ottoman Empire* (5–8). Series: Cultures of the Past. 2002, Marshall Cavendish $29.93 (978-0-7614-1494-0). 80pp. A handsome account that traces the rise and fall of the great Ottoman Empire from its beginning in the 15th century to its collapse and the formation of modern Turkey after World War I. (Rev: BL 1/1–15/03; HBG 3/03; SLJ 2/03) [956]

17065 Rumford, James. *Traveling Man: The Journey of Ibn Battuta, 1325–1354* (3–6). Illus. by author.

2001, Houghton $16.00 (978-0-618-08366-4). Rumford retells the story of the epic travels across Asia and Africa of the 14th-century explorer and scholar Ibn Battuta, with lyric text that flows through the beautiful illustrations. (Rev: HB 1/02; HBG 3/02; SLJ 10/01) [910]

17066 Rutsala, David. *The Sea Route to Asia* (4–7). Series: Exploration and Discovery. 2002, Mason Crest LB $19.95 (978-1-59084-046-7). 64pp. Rutsala presents Portuguese explorers' efforts to find a route around Africa to Asia, with information on Prince Henry the Navigator, Bartholomeu Dias, and Vasco da Gama. (Rev: SLJ 12/02) [910]

17067 Seibert, Patricia. *We Were Here: A Short History of Time Capsules* (3–6). Illus. 2002, Millbrook LB $22.90 (978-0-7613-0423-4). 48pp. A history of time capsules, including the Century Safe that was assembled in 1876 and opened in 1976. (Rev: BL 4/1/02; HBG 10/02; SLJ 3/02) [151]

17068 Shapiro, Stephen. *Battle Stations! Fortifications Through the Ages* (5–8). Illus. 2005, Annick LB $19.95 (978-1-55037-889-4); paper $7.95 (978-1-55037-888-7). 32pp. A tall, slim, and very visual overview of fortifications around the world and throughout history. (Rev: BL 9/15/05) [355.7]

17069 Sharp, S. Pearl, and Virginia Schomp. *The Slave Trade and the Middle Passage* (5–8). Series: Drama of African-American History. 2006, Benchmark LB $23.95 (978-0-7614-2176-4). 70pp. A brief overview of the triangular trade between Africa, the American colonies, and Europe, looking at conditions aboard the slave ships. (Rev: SLJ 5/07) [306.3]

17070 Stienecker, David L. *Countries* (2–5). Series: Discovering Geography. 1997, Marshall Cavendish LB $22.79 (978-0-7614-0542-9). 32pp. Basic geographical concepts are explored in a question-and-answer format. (Rev: BL 2/15/98; HBG 3/98) [910]

17071 Swain, Ruth Freeman. *Underwear: What We Wear Under There* (2–4). Illus. by John O'Brien. 2008, Holiday $16.95 (978-0-8234-1920-3). 32pp. Swain takes a humorous look at underwear developments through the ages. (Rev: BL 12/1/08; SLJ 12/08) [391.4]

17072 Swanson, Diane. *Tunnels!* (5–8). Series: True Stories from the Edge. 2003, Annick $18.95 (978-1-55037-781-1); paper $6.95 (978-1-55037-780-4). 144pp. Ten thrilling stories of tunnel escapes and escapades are accompanied by maps. (Rev: BL 4/15/03; SLJ 5/03) [624.1]

17073 Tanaka, Shelley. *Mummies: The Newest, Coolest and Creepiest from Around the World* (4–7). Illus. 2005, Abrams $16.95 (978-0-8109-5797-8). 48pp. Mummies from across history and around the world are on display in the colorful — and often graphic — pages of this fascinating book. (Rev: BL 12/1/05*; HBG 4/06; LMC 5/06; SLJ 12/05*) [393]

17074 Wells, Don. *The Spice Trade* (5–8). Illus. Series: Great Journeys. 2004, Weigl $26.00 (978-1-59036-208-2); paper $7.95 (978-1-59036-261-7). 32pp. Colorful illustrations and an attractive format will appeal to browsers seeking information about the spice trade; a useful timeline and links to Web sites are included. (Rev: BL 11/1/04)

17075 Williams, Brian. *The Modern World: From the French Revolution to the Computer Age* (5–8). Illus. by James Field. Series: Timelink. 1994, Bedrick LB $18.95 (978-0-87226-312-3). 64pp. An overview of the 200 years of world history that outlines major events, with useful timelines and maps. (Rev: SLJ 1/95) [909]

17076 Williams, Brian, and Brenda Williams. *The Age of Discovery: From the Renaissance to American Independence* (5–8). Illus. by James Field. Series: Timelink. 1994, Bedrick LB $18.95 (978-0-87226-311-6). 64pp. An overview of world history from the Renaissance through the American Revolution presented in 50-year segments. (Rev: SLJ 1/95) [909]

17077 Wilson, Janet. *Imagine That!* (4–8). Illus. by author. 2000, Stoddart $14.95 (978-0-7737-3221-6). In the form of a reminiscence by 100-year-old Auntie Violet, this is a brief history of the past century, with major events highlighted. (Rev: SLJ 11/00) [909]

17078 Worth, Richard. *The Great Empire of China and Marco Polo in World History* (5–8). Illus. Series: In World History. 2003, Enslow LB $26.60 (978-0-7660-1939-3). 112pp. Quotations from primary documents and excerpts from Polo's own writings add context to this account of his 13th-century journeys to the Far East. (Rev: SLJ 3/04) [915.04]

17079 Wyatt, Valerie. *Who Discovered America?* (4–7). Illus. by Howie Woo. 2008, Kids Can $17.95 (978-1-55453-128-8); paper $8.95 (978-1-55453-129-5). 40pp. This large-format book examines who arrived on this continent first, introducing the possible candidates and providing lots of interesting information on archaeological finds and how researchers approach this question. (Rev: BL 10/1/08; SLJ 2/09) [970.01]

Ancient History

General and Miscellaneous

17080 Anderson, Jameson. *History and Activities of Ancient China* (3–6). Illus. Series: Hands-on Ancient History. 2006, Heinemann LB $28.21 (978-1-4034-7922-8). 32pp. Social life, arts and culture, games, and holidays and celebrations are covered in this attractive and accessible volume that includes a recipe and two crafts. (Rev: HBG 4/07; SLJ 4/07) [931]

17081 Avi-Yonah, Michael. *Piece by Piece! Mosaics of the Ancient World* (5–8). Illus. Series: Buried Worlds. 1993, Lerner LB $28.75 (978-0-8225-3204-0). This book shows how and where mosaics were made in the ancient world and how, through the wonders of archaeology, they are still being uncovered today. (Rev: BL 1/15/94; SLJ 3/94) [738.5]

17082 Ball, Jacqueline, and Richard H. Levey. *Ancient China: Archaeology Unlocks the Secrets of*

China's Past (5–8). Illus. Series: National Geographic Investigates. 2006, National Geographic $17.95 (978-0-7922-7783-5). 64pp. After an introduction to China and its history, this volume looks at individual archaeological finds and at the lives revealed; vivid illustrations and good descriptions of archaeological techniques add to the value. (Rev: BL 10/15/06) [931]

17083 Barter, James. *The Ancient Persians* (5–8). Series: Lost Civilizations. 2005, Gale LB $29.95 (978-1-59018-621-3). 112pp. The lost civilization of the ancient Persians, with information about the society's people, customs, monetary system, and military, with maps and illustrations. (Rev: SLJ 6/06) [935]

17084 Bingham, Jane. *The Ancient World* (5–8). Illus. Series: A History of Fashion and Costume. 2005, Facts on File $35.00 (978-0-8160-5944-7). 64pp. A broad overview of the clothing and personal adornment worn during ancient times, with many visual aids. (Rev: SLJ 5/06) [391]

17085 Broida, Marian. *Ancient Israelites and Their Neighbors: An Activity Guide* (4–7). Illus. 2003, Chicago Review paper $16.95 (978-1-55652-457-8). 160pp. Readers will find out what life was like for the ancient Israelis, Phoenicians, and Philistines through the information and activities in this attractive book. (Rev: BL 5/15/03; SLJ 8/03) [933]

17086 Calvert, Patricia. *The Ancient Celts* (5–8). Series: People of the Ancient World. 2005, Watts LB $30.50 (978-0-531-12359-1); paper $9.95 (978-0-531-16845-5). 112pp. Introduces readers to the arts, religious beliefs, and society of the ancient Celts, with discussion of individual occupations and of the discoveries by archaeologists and anthropologists. (Rev: SLJ 9/05) [973]

17087 Carlson, Laurie. *Classical Kids: An Activity Guide to Life in Ancient Greece and Rome* (4–6). Illus. by Fran Lee. 1998, Chicago Review paper $14.95 (978-1-55652-290-1). 186pp. After background information on these two civilizations, there are many projects under such categories as eating, dressing up, and the arts. (Rev: SLJ 1/99) [930]

17088 Corbishley, Mike. *How Do We Know Where People Came From?* (5–8). Series: How Do We Know. 1995, Raintree LB $24.26 (978-0-8114-3880-3). Using double-page spreads, this book covers early cultures and touches on such subjects as early writing, Stonehenge, the Great Wall of China, the Easter Island statues, and the pyramids. (Rev: SLJ 1/96) [930]

17089 Curlee, Lynn. *Seven Wonders of the Ancient World* (3–6). Illus. 2002, Simon & Schuster $17.00 (978-0-689-83182-9). 40pp. An informative introduction for older readers to the wonders of the ancient world, with precise illustrations and thought-provoking text. (Rev: BCCB 3/02; BL 1/1–15/02; HBG 10/02; SLJ 9/02) [709]

17090 DeAngelis, Therese. *Wonders of the Ancient World* (5–8). Illus. Series: Costume, Tradition, and Culture: Reflecting on the Past. 1998, Chelsea $19.75 (978-0-7910-5170-2). 64pp. This work features, in double-page spreads, such wonders as the

Great Pyramids, Easter Island, and Stonehenge. (Rev: BL 3/15/99; HBG 10/99) [930]

17091 Gonen, Rivka. *Fired Up! Making Pottery in Ancient Times* (5–8). Illus. Series: Buried Worlds. 1993, Lerner LB $28.75 (978-0-8225-3202-6). This book explains how pottery was made in ancient times, showing examples from different cultures, and tells how archaeologists are uncovering more and more examples. (Rev: BL 1/15/94; SLJ 4/94) [738.3]

17092 Greene, Jacqueline D. *Slavery in Ancient Greece and Rome* (4–7). Series: Watts Library: History of Slavery. 2000, Watts LB $25.50 (978-0-531-11693-7). 64pp. Topics covered include the treatment of slaves in Greece and Rome, how they thrived in Greece's democracy, the slave fire brigades, battles of slave gladiators, and the attitudes toward slavery in the early Christian church. (Rev: BL 3/1/01; SLJ 3/01) [930]

17093 Hook, Jason. *Lost Cities* (3–5). Series: Mysteries of the Past. 2001, Raintree LB $25.69 (978-0-7398-4337-6). 32pp. Ur, Knossos, Babylon, and Troy are among the cities addressed in this introduction to the mysteries surrounding the sites and the efforts to uncover the truth. (Rev: HBG 3/02; SLJ 2/02)

17094 Hunter, Erica C. D., and Mike Corbishley. *First Civilizations*. Rev. ed. (5–8). Illus. Series: Cultural Atlas for Young People. 2003, Facts on File $35.00 (978-0-8160-5149-6). 96pp. Colorful topical spreads introduce readers to the culture, geography, history, and politics of Mesopotamia, Persia, and Assyria. (Rev: SLJ 1/04) [939]

17095 Jovinelly, Joann, and Jason Netelkos. *The Crafts and Culture of the Ancient Hebrews* (5–8). Illus. Series: Crafts of the Ancient World. 2002, Rosen LB $29.25 (978-0-8239-3511-6). 48pp. The crafts of the ancient Hebrews and projects related to them are used to give basic information on their history and how they lived. (Rev: BL 4/1/02) [932]

17096 Levy, Elizabeth. *Awesome Ancient Ancestors! Mound Builders, Maya, and More* (5–8). Illus. by Daniel McFeely. Series: America's Horrible Histories. 2001, Scholastic $12.95 (978-0-439-30349-1); paper $4.99 (978-0-590-10795-2). 156pp. A humorous and chatty cockroach introduces the early inhabitants of North America and Mesoamerica. (Rev: HBG 10/02; SLJ 5/02) [970.01]

17097 Linnea, Sharon. *Lost Civilizations* (4–7). Illus. by Josh Cochran. Series: Mysteries Unwrapped. 2009, Sterling paper $5.95 (978-1-4027-3984-2). 96pp. This book discusses five famous lost civilizations: Ur, the Mayan Empire, Atlantis, Pompeii, and Angkor Wat. (Rev: BL 7/09) [930]

17098 Richardson, Hazel. *Life in Ancient Africa* (4–7). Illus. Series: Peoples of the Ancient World. 2005, Crabtree LB $26.60 (978-0-7787-2043-0); paper $8.95 (978-0-7787-2073-7). 32pp. Introduces the early civilizations of Africa, examining their arts, spiritual beliefs, government, language, and technology; color photographs, sidebars, and timelines add information and appeal. (Rev: SLJ 11/05) [973]

17099 Richardson, Hazel. *Life in the Ancient Indus River Valley* (4–7). Illus. Series: Peoples of the Ancient World. 2005, Crabtree LB $26.60 (978-0-7787-2040-9); paper $8.95 (978-0-7787-2070-6). 32pp. Introduces life in the earliest urban civilization on the Indian subcontinent, examining the arts, spiritual beliefs, government, language, and technology; color photographs, sidebars, and timelines add information and appeal. (Rev: SLJ 11/05) [973]

17100 Richardson, Hazel. *Life of the Ancient Celts* (4–7). Illus. Series: Peoples of the Ancient World. 2005, Crabtree LB $26.60 (978-0-7787-2045-4); paper $8.95 (978-0-7787-2075-1). 32pp. Introduces the early Celtic civilization, examining arts, spiritual beliefs, government, language, and technology; color photographs, sidebars, and timelines add information and appeal. (Rev: SLJ 11/05) [973]

17101 Service, Pamela F. *300 B.C.* (5–8). Series: Around the World In. 2002, Benchmark $29.93 (978-0-7614-1080-5). 96pp. The author explores what was going on in Europe, Africa, Asia, and the Americas in the year 300 B.C. Also use *1200* (2002). (Rev: HBG 3/03; SLJ 2/03) [930]

17102 Smith, K. C. *Ancient Shipwrecks* (5–7). Series: Shipwrecks. 2000, Watts LB $25.50 (978-0-531-20381-1). 64pp. From the Bronze Age through the Roman Empire, this volume explores the fascinating stories behind ancient wrecks found in the Mediterranean and explored by archaeologists. (Rev: BL 10/15/00) [930]

17103 Sonneborn, Liz. *The Ancient Kushites* (5–8). Series: People of the Ancient World. 2005, Watts LB $30.50 (978-0-531-12380-5). 112pp. Explores the arts, religious beliefs, and culture of Africa's ancient Kushites, who were also known as Nubians. (Rev: SLJ 9/05) [973]

17104 Stefoff, Rebecca. *The Ancient Mediterranean* (5–8). Series: World Historical Atlases. 2004, Benchmark LB $27.07 (978-0-7614-1641-8). 48pp. Maps, text, and illustrations give a broad overview of the cultures found in the ancient Mediterranean. Also use *The Ancient Near East* and *The Asian Empires* (both 2004). (Rev: SLJ 2/05) [930]

17105 Waldman, Neil. *Masada* (4–6). Illus. 1998, Morrow $16.00 (978-0-688-14481-4). 64pp. The story of the Masada fortress, built in the first century B.C. and captured by the Romans in 72–73 A.D. Rather than surrender, the Jewish defenders committed suicide. (Rev: BCCB 10/98; BL 10/1/98; HBG 3/99; SLJ 11/98) [933]

17106 Wells, Donald. *The Silk Road* (5–8). Series: Great Journeys. 2004, Weigl LB $26.00 (978-1-59036-207-5). Colorful illustrations and an attractive format will appeal to browsers seeking information on this ancient trade route; a useful timeline and links to Web sites are included. (Rev: BL 11/1/04) [950]

17107 Wilkinson, Philip, and Jacqueline Dineen. *The Mediterranean* (4–7). Illus. by Robert Ingpen. Series: Mysterious Places. 1994, Chelsea LB $21.95 (978-0-7910-2751-6). 92pp. Ten sites around the Mediterranean are investigated, including Knossos, Rhodes, Delphi, Mistra, the Topkapi Palace, and Hagia Sophia. (Rev: BL 1/15/94; SLJ 5/94) [930.3]

17108 Woods, Michael, and Mary Woods. *Ancient Agriculture: From Foraging to Farming* (5–8). Series: Ancient Technologies. 2000, Runestone LB $25.26 (978-0-8225-2995-8). 88pp. Beginning with prehistoric food-gathering peoples, this book traces the history of plant cultivation and agriculture through each of the great ancient civilizations. (Rev: BL 8/00; HBG 10/00; SLJ 6/00) [630]

17109 Woods, Michael, and Mary Woods. *Ancient Machines from Wedges to Waterwheels* (5–8). Series: Ancient Technologies. 1999, Lerner LB $25.26 (978-0-8225-2994-1). 88pp. This heavily illustrated account describes the important machines that came into being from ancient history to the fall of the Western Roman Empire. (Rev: BL 1/1–15/00; HBG 10/00; SLJ 6/00; VOYA 6/00) [936]

17110 Woods, Michael, and Mary B. Woods. *Ancient Medicine: From Sorcery to Surgery* (5–8). Illus. Series: Ancient Technologies. 2000, Lerner LB $25.26 (978-0-8225-2992-7). 88pp. Medical practices in ancient times and cultures — the Stone Age, ancient Egypt, and early Hindu cultures, for example — are discussed in this volume. (Rev: BL 1/1–15/00; HBG 10/00; SLJ 5/00; VOYA 6/00) [610]

17111 Woods, Michael, and Mary B. Woods. *Ancient Transportation: From Camels to Canals* (5–8). Illus. Series: Ancient Technologies. 2000, Lerner LB $25.26 (978-0-8225-2993-4). 88pp. This book covers such topics related to early transportation as the first bridges and roads, early skis and sleds, primitive wagons, and the beginnings of maps. (Rev: BL 1/1–15/00; HBG 10/00; SLJ 6/00; VOYA 6/00) [629.04]

Egypt and Mesopotamia

17112 Adams, Simon. *Ancient Egypt* (4–6). Illus. Series: Kingfisher Voyages. 2006, Kingfisher $15.95 (978-0-7534-6027-6). 54pp. Viewed from the perspective of an Egyptologist named Dr. Kent Weeks, this is a tour of important sites of ancient Egypt, with discussion of the embalming and engineering practices of the time and the modern technologies that have uncovered the answers to some mysteries. (Rev: SLJ 2/07)

17113 Alcraft, Rob. *Valley of the Kings* (5–7). Series: Visiting the Past. 1999, Heinemann LB $24.22 (978-1-57572-860-5). 32pp. This account uses double-page spreads to cover topics including the history, landscape, beliefs, and daily life of the ancient Egyptians. (Rev: SLJ 3/00) [932]

17114 Aliki. *Mummies Made in Egypt* (3–5). Illus. by author. 1979, HarperCollins paper $6.99 (978-0-06-446011-8). 32pp. The burial practices and beliefs of the ancient Egyptians are explored in text and handsome illustrations.

17115 Bailey, Linda. *Adventures in Ancient Egypt* (2–5). Illus. Series: Good Times Travel Agency. 2000, Kids Can $14.95 (978-1-55074-546-7); paper $7.95 (978-1-55074-548-1). 48pp. Using an old travel guide, three children are transported to Egypt in 2500 B.C. where they become acquainted with the sights and sites as well as becoming involved in a series of adventures. (Rev: BL 1/1–15/01; HBG 3/01; SLJ 12/00) [932]

17116 Berger, Melvin, and Gilda Berger. *Mummies of the Pharaohs: Exploring the Valley of the Kings* (4–7). Illus. 2001, National Geographic $17.95 (978-0-7922-7223-6). 64pp. Beginning with King Tut's tomb and continuing through other sites, this book uses stunning photographs and a clear text to describe workings of archaeological digs that are studying Egypt's past. (Rev: BL 2/1/01) [932]

17117 Briscoe, Diana C. *King Tut: Tales from the Tomb* (3–5). Illus. Series: High Five Reading. 2002, Capstone LB $23.93 (978-0-7368-9553-8). 48pp. For reluctant readers, this is a dramatic account of the discovery of the tomb, the life and death of the young Tut, the process of mummification, and the so-called mummy's curse. (Rev: HBG 10/03; SLJ 8/03) [932]

17118 Broida, Marian. *Ancient Egyptians and Their Neighbors: An Activity Guide* (4–8). Illus. 1999, Chicago Review paper $16.95 (978-1-55652-360-1). 208pp. The lives and times of the ancient Egyptians, Nubians, Hittites, and Mesopotamians are examined using text and a series of 40 fascinating projects. (Rev: BL 3/15/00; SLJ 2/00) [939]

17119 Burgan, Michael. *The Curse of King Tut's Tomb* (3–6). Illus. by Barbara Schulz. Series: Graphic Library/Graphic History. 2004, Capstone LB $26.60 (978-0-7368-3833-7). 32pp. A graphic "novel" — factual, but embellished — about the discovery of Tut's tomb and the legendary curse associated with it; will appeal to reluctant readers. (Rev: SLJ 7/05) [973]

17120 Chapman, Gillian. *The Egyptians* (4–8). Series: Crafts from the Past. 1997, Heinemann LB $25.64 (978-1-57572-556-7). A variety of craft projects related to the ancient Egyptians are introduced and placed within their cultural context. (Rev: SLJ 4/98) [932]

17121 Chrisp, Peter. *Mesopotamia: Iraq in Ancient Times* (4–7). Illus. Series: Picturing the Past. 2004, Enchanted Lion $15.95 (978-1-59270-024-0). 32pp. History and archaeology are the highlights of this nicely illustrated overview of Mesopotamian civilization. (Rev: BL 10/15/04; SLJ 11/04) [935]

17122 Chrisp, Peter. *Pyramid* (4–8). Illus. Series: DK Experience. 2006, DK $15.99 (978-0-7566-1410-2). 67pp. Full-color illustrations, 3-D diagrams, and CT scans make this survey of the construction and importance of the Great Pyramid of Giza informative and attractive. (Rev: SLJ 11/06) [932]

17123 Clare, John D., ed. *Pyramids of Ancient Egypt* (4–6). Illus. Series: Living History. 1992, Harcourt $16.95 (978-0-15-200509-2). 64pp. Besides telling about the building of the Pyramids, this book uses human models to describe the daily life of the ancient Egyptians. (Rev: SLJ 10/92) [932]

17124 Clarke, Sue. *The Tombs of the Pharaohs: A Three-Dimensional Discovery* (2–5). Illus. 1994, Hyperion $16.95 (978-1-56282-485-3). 10pp. In this

interactive book shaped like a pyramid, pop-ups and flaps are used to introduce topics involving ancient Egypt. (Rev: BL 11/15/94) [932]

17125 Cline, Eric H., and Jill Rubalcaba. *The Ancient Egyptian World* (5–10). Series: The World in Ancient Times. 2005, Oxford LB $32.95 (978-0-19-517391-8). 190pp. An overview of ancient Egyptian history and culture, with chronologically arranged chapters covering religion, medicine, clothing, arts, and so forth and introducing key figures such as Hatshepsut, Tutankhamen, and Cleopatra. (Rev: SLJ 1/06) [932]

17126 Crosher, Judith. *Technology in the Time of Ancient Egypt* (4–8). Series: Technology in the Time Of. 1998, Raintree LB $27.12 (978-0-8172-4875-8). 48pp. Each double-page spread presents an aspect of technology in ancient Egypt in such areas as food production, transportation, and building. (Rev: HBG 10/98; SLJ 3/99) [932]

17127 Day, Nancy. *Your Travel Guide to Ancient Egypt* (4–8). Series: Passport to History. 2000, Runestone LB $26.50 (978-0-8225-3075-6). 96pp. Written in the style of a modern-day travel guide, this book on ancient Egypt covers such subjects as sites to see, food, clothing, religious beliefs, politics, and daily life. (Rev: BL 11/15/00; HBG 3/01; SLJ 5/01; VOYA 8/01) [932]

17128 Delafosse, Claude, and Philippe Biard. *Pyramids* (PS–2). Illus. by authors. Series: First Discovery. 1995, Scholastic $12.95 (978-0-590-42786-9). Describes how the pyramids of Egypt were built, as well as mummification and the seven wonders of the ancient world. (Rev: SLJ 3/96) [932]

17129 Filer, Joyce. *Pyramids* (3–8). Illus. 2006, Oxford Univ. $19.99 (978-0-19-530521-0). 48pp. A detailed introduction to the pyramids of ancient Egypt and their design, their builders, their construction, and their contents; there is also information on pyramids outside Egypt. (Rev: SLJ 7/06) [932]

17130 Fisher, Leonard Everett. *The Gods and Goddesses of Ancient Egypt* (3–5). Illus. 1997, Holiday House LB $16.95 (978-0-8234-1286-0). 32pp. With accompanying stories, this book introduces 13 Egyptian deities, including Horus and Osiris. (Rev: BL 12/1/97; HBG 3/98; SLJ 11/97) [299]

17131 George, Charles. *Pyramids* (5–9). Series: Mysterious and Unknown. 2007, Reference Point LB $24.95 (978-1-60152-027-2). 104pp. Pyramids around the world are addressed in this well-written text with color photographs; useful for reports. (Rev: SLJ 2/08)

17132 Gibbons, Gail. *Mummies, Pyramids, and Pharaohs: A Book About Ancient Egypt* (PS–2). 2004, Little, Brown $16.95 (978-0-316-30928-8). 32pp. The history and mysteries of ancient Egypt — including mummies, pharaohs, and pyramids — are explored in an engaging blend of brief, simple narrative and ink-and-watercolor artwork. (Rev: BL 6/1–15/04; SLJ 6/04) [932]

17133 Greene, Jacqueline D. *Slavery in Ancient Egypt and Mesopotamia* (4–7). Series: Watts Library: History of Slavery. 2000, Watts LB $25.50

(978-0-531-11692-0). 64pp. This unusual book covers the earliest forms of slavery, how the pharaohs used slaves to construct the pyramids, and the place of slavery in Hebrew society. (Rev: BL 3/1/01; SLJ 3/01) [930]

17134 Harris, Geraldine. *Ancient Egypt.* Rev. ed. (5–8). Illus. Series: Cultural Atlas for Young People. 2003, Facts on File $35.00 (978-0-8160-5148-9). 96pp. Colorful topical spreads introduce readers to the culture, history, and politics of ancient Egypt. (Rev: SLJ 1/04; VOYA 2/04) [932]

17135 Hart, Avery, and Paul Mantell. *Pyramids! 50 Hands-on Activities to Experience Ancient Egypt* (3–5). Illus. Series: Kaleidoscope Kids. 1997, Williamson paper $14.25 (978-1-885593-10-8). 96pp. Some of the craft projects that explore the culture of ancient Egypt are building model pyramids, writing messages in hieroglyphics, and preparing clothes, food, and games for an Egyptian costume party. (Rev: BL 11/15/97) [932]

17136 Hawass, Zahi. *Curse of the Pharaohs: My Adventures with Mummies* (4–6). 2004, National Geographic $19.95 (978-0-7922-6665-5). 160pp. Excellent photographs and detailed endmatter add to the interesting discussion of mysteries associated with the tombs of the pharaohs. (Rev: BL 6/1–15/04; SLJ 11/04)

17137 Hibbert, Clare. *Ancient Egypt* (3–6). Illus. by Adam Hook. Series: Rich and Poor in. 2005, Smart Apple LB $27.10 (978-1-58340-720-2). 32pp. Compares the everyday lives of the rich and the poor in ancient Egypt. (Rev: SLJ 5/06) [932.01]

17138 Hodge, Susie. *Ancient Egyptian Art* (3–6). Series: Art in History. 1997, Heinemann LB $24.22 (978-1-57572-550-5). 32pp. This book presents the art of ancient Egypt as a reflection of its culture in such areas as religion and science. (Rev: HBG 3/98; SLJ 4/98) [932]

17139 Honan, Linda. *Spend the Day in Ancient Egypt: Projects and Activities That Bring the Past to Life* (3–6). Illus. by Ellen Kosmer. 1999, Wiley paper $12.95 (978-0-471-29006-3). 116pp. Craft projects and other activities are used to introduce the culture and everyday of the ancient Egyptians. (Rev: SLJ 1/00) [932]

17140 Hynson, Colin. *The Building of the Great Pyramid* (5–8). Illus. Series: Stories from History. 2006, School Specialty $9.95 (978-0-7696-4708-1); paper $6.95 (978-0-7696-4692-3). 48pp. Full-color illustrations and graphic novel format make this survey of the ancient engineering feat attractive to reluctant readers. (Rev: SLJ 1/07)

17141 James, Louise. *How We Know About the Egyptians* (3–6). Series: How We Know About. 1998, Bedrick $0.00 (978-0-87226-236-2). 32pp. Using double-page spreads, this work focuses on ancient Egypt and explains the detective-like work of archaeologists and others who have increased our knowledge of this civilization. (Rev: BL 5/15/98) [932]

17142 Jovinelly, Joann, and Jason Netelkos. *The Crafts and Culture of the Ancient Egyptians* (5–8). Series: Crafts of the Ancient World. 2002, Rosen

LB $29.25 (978-0-8239-3509-3). 48pp. As well as learning about the mysteries of ancient Egypt, readers can engage in such craft projects as designing a pharaoh's headdress and necklace and re-creating an ancient marbles game. (Rev: BL 5/15/02; SLJ 6/02) [932]

17143 Kaplan, Sarah Pitt. *The Great Pyramid at Giza: Tomb of Wonders* (5–8). Series: Digging Up the Past. 2005, Children's Pr. LB $24.50 (978-0-516-25131-8); paper $6.95 (978-0-516-25095-3). 48pp. A richly illustrated survey of the important pyramid and the reasons for its creation; suitable for reluctant readers. (Rev: SLJ 2/06) [932]

17144 Kennett, David. *Pharaoh: Life and Afterlife of a God* (4–7). Illus. by author. 2008, Walker $18.95 (978-0-8027-9567-0). 48pp. This attractive book introduces readers to the elaborate burial of Seti I and in doing so also explains many aspects of life in ancient Egypt, for royalty as well as common people. (Rev: BL 5/1/08; SLJ 2/08) [932]

17145 Lace, William W. *The Curse of King Tut* (5–8). Illus. Series: Mysterious & Unknown. 2007, Reference Point LB $24.95 (978-1-60152-024-1). 104pp. Readers will learn factual information about the discovery of King Tutankhamen's tomb while searching for the truth about his "curse." (Rev: BL 10/15/07; LMC 1/08; SLJ 2/08) [932]

17146 Landau, Elaine. *The Babylonians* (4–6). Illus. Series: Cradle of Civilization. 1997, Millbrook LB $21.40 (978-0-7613-0216-2). 64pp. The history, religion, and contributions of this early civilization that invented the wheel and was the first to establish laws and government. (Rev: BL 1/1–15/98; HBG 3/98; SLJ 3/98) [935]

17147 Landau, Elaine. *The Curse of Tutankhamen* (4–6). Illus. Series: Mysteries of Science. 1996, Millbrook LB $20.90 (978-0-7613-0014-4). 48pp. The story of the discovery of King Tut's tomb and of the curse that supposedly plagued the archaeologists that were involved. (Rev: BL 10/15/96; SLJ 11/96) [931]

17148 Landau, Elaine. *The Sumerians* (4–6). Illus. Series: Cradle of Civilization. 1997, Millbrook LB $23.90 (978-0-7613-0215-5). 64pp. An overview of the Sumerians, their rulers and gods, and their contributions to science, government, and the arts. (Rev: BL 1/1–15/98; HBG 3/98; SLJ 3/98) [935]

17149 McCall, Henrietta. *Egyptian Mummies* (3–5). Illus. by David Antram. Series: Fast Forward. 2000, Watts paper $9.95 (978-0-531-16443-3). 32pp. A concise look at mummies and embalming that uses split spreads that can be opened to reveal additional information. (Rev: SLJ 6/01) [393.3]

17150 McNeill, Sarah. *Ancient Egyptian People* (4–8). Illus. Series: People and Places. 1997, Millbrook LB $21.90 (978-0-7613-0056-4). This basic introduction to the people of ancient Egypt and how they lived consists of several attractive double-page spreads and a brief text. (Rev: BL 2/15/97; SLJ 3/97) [932]

17151 McNeill, Sarah. *Ancient Egyptian Places* (4–8). Illus. Series: People and Places. 1997, Millbrook LB $21.90 (978-0-7613-0057-1). Some of the great constructions of ancient Egypt are pictured in a series of elegant double-page spreads with a simple text. (Rev: BL 2/15/97; SLJ 3/97) [932]

17152 Malam, John. *Ancient Egypt* (3–6). Illus. Series: Picturing the Past. 2004, Enchanted Lion $15.95 (978-1-59270-021-9). 32pp. Well-written two-page chapters cover geography, history, government, religion, the arts, and home life, with maps, photos and illustrations, and informative sidebars detailing sources. (Rev: SLJ 11/04) [932]

17153 Malam, John. *Ancient Egypt* (5–8). Series: Remains to Be Seen. 1998, Evans Brothers $19.95 (978-0-237-51839-4). 47pp. This introduction to ancient Egypt's culture and history is organized in double-page spreads and is noteworthy for its many sidebars, charts, and illustrations. (Rev: SLJ 9/98) [932]

17154 Malam, John. *Ancient Egyptian Jobs* (5–7). Illus. 2002, Heinemann LB $27.07 (978-1-4034-0311-7). 48pp. The daily activities of workers such as scribes, bakers, dancers, jewelers, pyramid builders, and embalmers are described in this slim volume that also offers a general introduction to ancient Egypt. (Rev: HBG 10/03; SLJ 4/03) [331.7]

17155 Malam, John. *Mesopotamia and the Fertile Crescent: 10,000 to 539 B.C.* (5–8). Series: Looking Back. 1999, Raintree $19.98 (978-0-8172-5434-6). 32pp. The story of the ancient civilizations that grew up in the rich area around the Tigris and Euphrates rivers. (Rev: BL 5/15/99; SLJ 7/99) [930]

17156 Mann, Elizabeth. *The Great Pyramid* (4–7). Illus. Series: Wonders of the World. 1996, Mikaya $19.95 (978-0-9650493-1-3). 48pp. The building of this architectural marvel is told graphically, with details on the society of ancient Egypt. (Rev: BL 2/1/97; SLJ 6/97*) [932]

17157 Manning, Mick, and Brita Granström. *Fly on the Wall: Pharaoh's Egypt* (2–4). Illus. by authors. 2006, Frances Lincoln $15.95 (978-1-84507-100-4). 37pp. Ancient Egypt's way of life — its history, culture, and mythology in particular — is shown in an appealing scrapbook format full of facts and following several characters as they go about their business. (Rev: SLJ 4/06) [932]

17158 Manning, Ruth. *Ancient Egyptian Women* (5–8). Illus. Series: People in the Past. 2002, Heinemann LB $27.07 (978-1-4034-0313-1). 48pp. A look at the life of, and options open to, women in ancient Egypt. (Rev: BL 3/1/03; SLJ 4/03) [305.42]

17159 Marston, Elsa. *The Ancient Egyptians* (5–8). Series: Cultures of the Past. 1995, Benchmark LB $29.93 (978-0-7614-0073-8). With photographs of artifacts, monuments, and historical scenes, this book tells of ancient Egyptian history and culture, the rise and fall of the dynasties, and the people's religious beliefs and practices. (Rev: SLJ 6/96) [932]

17160 Milton, Joyce. *Mummies* (2–3). Illus. by Susan Swan. 1996, Penguin paper $3.99 (978-0-448-41325-9). 48pp. The purpose and process of mummification are explained, with special reference to ancient Egypt. (Rev: BL 11/15/96; SLJ 6/97) [932]

17161 Minnis, Ivan. *You Are in Ancient Egypt* (3–6). Illus. Series: You Are There! 2004, Raintree LB $26.36 (978-1-4109-0616-8); paper $7.50 (978-1-4109-1008-0). 32pp. In present-tense narrative, Minnis introduces the sites, sounds, food, and varied living conditions of ancient Egypt. (Rev: SLJ 2/05) [932]

17162 Montavon, Jay. *The Curse of King Tut's Tomb* (3–5). Illus. 1991, Avon paper $3.50 (978-0-380-76220-0). 96pp. Tells about King Tut and the discovery of his tomb, but focuses on the supposed curse that was associated with its opening. (Rev: BL 9/15/91) [932]

17163 Nardo, Don. *Ancient Egypt* (3–6). Illus. 2002, Gale LB $23.70 (978-0-7377-0955-1). 48pp. A basic introduction to the people of ancient Egypt, nobility and peasants, and to the importance of their religious beliefs. (Rev: SLJ 9/02)

17164 Nardo, Don. *King Tut's Tomb* (3–6). Series: Wonders of the World. 2004, Gale LB $26.20 (978-0-7377-2352-6). 48pp. Nardo discusses what we know of King Tutankhamen's life and death, and describes the discovery of his tomb. (Rev: SLJ 6/05) [932]

17165 Perl, Lila. *The Ancient Egyptians* (4–7). Series: People of the Ancient World. 2004, Watts LB $30.50 (978-0-531-12345-4). 112pp. Pharaohs, mummy makers, farmers, and brewers are among the people presented in this overview of life in ancient Egypt. (Rev: SLJ 2/05) [930]

17166 Pipe, Jim. *You Wouldn't Want to Be Cleopatra! An Egyptian Ruler You'd Rather Not Be* (3–6). Illus. by David Antram. Series: You Wouldn't Want to . . . 2007, Watts LB $28.50 (978-0-531-18726-8); paper $9.95 (978-0-531-18923-6). 32pp. An entertaining look at the queen of Egypt and the problems she faced. Cartoons keep the tone light. (Rev: SLJ 8/07)

17167 Putnam, James. *The Ancient Egypt Pop-Up Book* (5–8). Illus. 2003, Universe $29.95 (978-0-7893-0985-3). Seven imaginatively designed pop-up spreads introduce ancient Egypt, including its pyramids, pharaohs, and mummies. (Rev: SLJ 3/04)

17168 Rees, Rosemary. *The Ancient Egyptians* (3–4). Illus. Series: Understanding People in the Past. 1997, Heinemann $27.07 (978-0-431-07789-5). 64pp. Photos of museum artifacts plus maps, diagrams, and drawings are used liberally to introduce such topics about the ancient Egyptians as their pharaohs, gods, history, pyramids, and mummies. (Rev: SLJ 9/97) [932]

17169 Rubalcaba, Jill. *Ancient Egypt: Archaeology Unlocks the Secrets of Egypt's Past* (3–7). 2006, National Geographic $17.95 (978-0-7922-7784-2). 64pp. This well-illustrated overview of what archaeologists have uncovered about life in ancient Egypt highlights two related events: the 1922 discovery of King Tutankhamen's tomb and the 2005 CT scan of the boy king's mummy. (Rev: SLJ 2/07) [932]

17170 Schomp, Virginia. *Ancient Mesopotamia: The Sumerians, Babylonians, and Assyrians* (5–8). Series: People of the Ancient World. 2004, Watts LB $30.50 (978-0-531-11818-4). 112pp. This fascinating volume covers the history and culture of the Sumerians, Babylonians, and Assyrians, looking at writing, warfare, and the daily life of people ranging from farmers and traders to warriors and nobles. (Rev: SLJ 3/05) [935]

17171 Shuter, Jane. *Ancient Egypt* (4–6). Series: History Beneath Your Feet. 1999, Raintree LB $27.12 (978-0-8172-5751-4). 48pp. This work on ancient Egypt covers topics including burials, pyramids, mummies, hieroglyphs, temples, tombs, and towns plus coverage on how archaeologists have accumulated these facts. (Rev: HBG 10/00; SLJ 3/00) [932]

17172 Shuter, Jane. *The Ancient Egyptians* (3–5). Series: History Starts Here! 2000, Raintree LB $25.69 (978-0-7398-1351-5). 32pp. This overview of ancient Egypt includes material on history, culture, daily life, structures, and religion. (Rev: HBG 10/00; SLJ 7/00) [932]

17173 Shuter, Jane. *Egypt* (5–10). Series: Ancient World. 1998, Raintree LB $27.12 (978-0-8172-5058-4). Ancient Egypt's mysterious hieroglyphics, treasure-filled tombs, puzzling pyramid construction, and embalming techniques, as well as its history, politics, ideas, religion, art, architecture, science, and everyday life are covered in this introductory volume. (Rev: BL 1/1–15/99; HBG 3/99; SLJ 3/99) [932]

17174 Stewart, David. *You Wouldn't Want to Be an Egyptian Mummy! Disgusting Things You'd Rather Not Know* (4–6). Illus. by David Antram. 2001, Watts LB $29.00 (978-0-531-14597-5); paper $9.95 (978-0-531-16206-4). 32pp. The symbolism of elaborate Egyptian burials and the process of mummification are explained with many illustrations and cartoon art. (Rev: SLJ 9/01)

17175 Trumble, Kelly. *The Library of Alexandria* (5–7). Illus. by Robina MacIntyre Marshall. 2003, Clarion $17.00 (978-0-395-75832-8). 72pp. An introduction to the famous library, its collection, its scholars, and its destruction by fire. (Rev: BCCB 1/04; BL 11/15/03; HBG 4/04; SLJ 1/04) [027.032]

17176 Tyldesley, Joyce. *Egypt* (5–8). Illus. Series: Insiders. 2007, Simon & Schuster $16.99 (978-1-4169-3858-3). 64pp. An introduction to ancient Egypt — the pyramids, mummies, Abu Simbel, transportation, arts and crafts, and so forth — with eye-catching illustrations. (Rev: LMC 10/07; SLJ 12/07) [932]

17177 Walker, Jane. *Ancient Egypt* (3–6). Illus. Series: 100 Things You Should Know about. 2002, Mason Crest LB $18.95 (978-1-59084-445-8). 48pp. Organized topically, this collection of 100 facts covers history, government, religion, daily life, dress, and cuisine, and will appeal to reluctant readers. (Rev: SLJ 6/03) [932]

17178 Weitzman, David. *Pharaoh's Boat* (4–7). Illus. by author. 2009, Houghton $17.00 (978-0-547-05341-7). 48pp. Weitzman recounts the fascinating discovery in 1954 of a boat in the Great Pyramid of Giza, explains its origins (it was built as a vehicle to take the Pharaoh Cheops to the afterlife), and details its restoration. (Rev: BCCB 9/09; BL 5/15/09; HB 5/09; SLJ 4/09) [932]

17179 Woods, Geraldine. *Science in Ancient Egypt* (4–8). Series: Science of the Past. 1998, Watts paper $8.95 (978-0-531-15915-6). The many contributions to science by the ancient Egyptians, including architecture, astronomy, and mathematics, are outlined in this richly illustrated volume. (Rev: BL 6/1–15/98; HBG 10/98; SLJ 6/98) [932]

Greece

17180 Bailey, Linda. *Adventures in Ancient Greece* (3–5). Illus. by Bill Slavin. Series: Good Times Travel Agency. 2002, Kids Can $14.95 (978-1-55074-534-4); paper $7.95 (978-1-55074-536-8). 48pp. Readers take a trip to ancient Greece and learn about democracy, the Olympics, everyday life, and other aspects in an appealing layout that includes cartoon panels. (Rev: BL 11/1/02; HBG 3/03) [938]

17181 Benduhn, Tea. *Ancient Greece* (1–3). Series: Life Long Ago. 2006, Weekly Reader LB $19.93 (978-0-8368-7782-3). 24pp. Plenty of facts about ancient Greece and its people's customs, beliefs, and political system. An airy design adds to the appeal. (Rev: SLJ 6/07)

17182 Broida, Marian. *Projects About Ancient Greece* (4–6). Illus. Series: Hands-on Ancient History. 2006, Benchmark LB $29.93 (978-0-7614-2259-4). 48pp. Ten projects — including Minoan bull-dancer paintings, Mycenaean writing, and black-figure pottery — are accompanied by fictionalized scenarios that add context. (Rev: SLJ 4/07) [938]

17183 Chapman, Gillian. *The Greeks* (4–7). Series: Crafts from the Past. 1998, Heinemann LB $25.64 (978-1-57572-733-2). 39pp. Double-page spreads each outline a project inspired by an art object, i.e. a Greek vase yields pâpier-maché pottery. (Rev: SLJ 2/99) [938]

17184 Clare, John D., ed. *Ancient Greece* (3–6). Illus. Series: Living History. 1994, Harcourt $16.95 (978-0-15-200516-0). 64pp. An overview of the history of ancient Greece, with emphasis on its heritage and contributions to world civilization. (Rev: BL 4/15/94; SLJ 4/94) [938]

17185 Curlee, Lynn. *Parthenon* (5–8). Illus. by author. 2004, Simon & Schuster $17.95 (978-0-689-84490-4). 40pp. A beautifully composed overview of the construction and history of the temple built by the ancient Greeks to honor the goddess Athena. (Rev: BL 9/15/04*; HB 7/04; SLJ 6/04) [726]

17186 Day, Nancy. *Your Travel Guide to Ancient Greece* (4–8). Illus. Series: Passport to History. 2000, Runestone LB $26.50 (978-0-8225-3076-3). 96pp. An outstanding introduction to ancient Greece arranged in the format of a guided tour and covering topics including geography, history, customs, and places to visit in an exciting, interesting way. (Rev: BL 10/15/00*; HBG 3/01; SLJ 2/01) [938]

17187 Hart, Avery, and Paul Mantell. *Ancient Greece! 40 Hands-On Activities to Experience This Wondrous Age* (4–7). Illus. 1999, Williamson paper $14.25 (978-1-885593-25-2). 96pp. A concise text and several craft projects introduce us to the world of ancient Greece, its geography, history, people, culture, and lasting contributions. (Rev: BL 9/15/99; SLJ 8/99) [938]

17188 Hicks, Peter. *Ancient Greece* (4–6). Series: History Beneath Your Feet. 1999, Raintree LB $27.12 (978-0-8172-5750-7). 48pp. Using pictures of artifacts, buildings, and monuments, this account uses double-page spreads to describe the work of archaeologists and what we know, from them, about life in ancient Greece. (Rev: HBG 10/00; SLJ 3/00) [938]

17189 Hodge, Susie. *Ancient Greek Art* (4–8). Series: Art in History. 1998, Heinemann LB $24.22 (978-1-57572-551-2). A solid introduction to ancient Greek art, covering painting, mosaics, pottery, architecture, and sculpture. (Rev: HBG 3/98; SLJ 5/98) [938]

17190 Hull, Robert. *Greece* (5–10). Series: Ancient World. 1998, Raintree LB $27.12 (978-0-8172-5055-3). 64pp. This brief introduction to ancient Greece touches on its religion and mythology, its great philosophers, important historical events, and its contributions to world culture. (Rev: BL 1/1–15/99; HBG 3/99) [938]

17191 Jovinelly, Joann, and Jason Netelkos. *The Crafts and Culture of the Ancient Greeks* (5–8). Series: Crafts of the Ancient World. 2002, Rosen LB $29.25 (978-0-8239-3510-9). 48pp. As well as basic information on ancient Greece, this book outlines many craft projects. (Rev: BL 5/15/02) [938]

17192 Little, Emily. *The Trojan Horse: How the Greeks Won the War* (2–4). Illus. by Mike Eagle. 1988, Random paper $3.99 (978-0-394-89674-8). 48pp. A lesson in ancient history in this account of the Trojan horse. (Rev: BCCB 1/89; BL 3/1/89; SLJ 2/89) [398.2]

17193 MacDonald, Fiona. *I Wonder Why Greeks Built Temples and Other Questions About Ancient Greece* (2–4). Illus. Series: I Wonder Why. 1997, Kingfisher $9.95 (978-0-7534-5056-7). 32pp. Each double-page spread in this book answers two or three basic questions about the ancient Greeks, how they lived, and their accomplishments. (Rev: HBG 3/98; SLJ 9/97) [938]

17194 MacDonald, Fiona. *You Wouldn't Want to Be a Slave in Ancient Greece! A Life You'd Rather Not Have* (4–6). Illus. by David Antram. Series: You Wouldn't Want To. 2001, Watts LB $29.00 (978-0-531-14600-2); paper $9.95 (978-0-531-16203-3). 32pp. The story of a woman who is kidnapped and taken to Greece as a slave serves as a good starting point to prove the premise of this book. (Rev: SLJ 9/01)

17195 McGee, Marni. *Ancient Greece: Archaeology Unlocks the Secrets of Greece's Past* (3–7). Series: National Geographic Investigates. 2006, National Geographic $17.95 (978-0-7922-7826-9). 64pp. This well-illustrated title looks at archaeologists' efforts over the years to uncover — on land and under the sea — information about life in ancient Greece. (Rev: SLJ 2/07)

17196 Malam, John. *Ancient Greece* (4–7). Series: Picturing the Past. 2004, Enchanted Lion $15.95

(978-1-59270-022-6). 32pp. This photo-filled volume uses images of ancient Greek artifacts and structures to introduce the civilization's governmental organization, religion, mythology, recreation, and theater. (Rev: BL 10/15/04; SLJ 11/04) [938]

17197 Malam, John. *Exploring Ancient Greece* (5–8). Series: Remains to Be Seen. 1999, Evans Brothers $19.95 (978-0-237-51994-0). 47pp. Particularly noteworthy in this basic account of the history of ancient Greece are the stunning photographs of temples, theaters, artifacts, and landscapes. (Rev: SLJ 1/00) [938]

17198 Martell, Hazel M. *The Myths and Civilization of the Ancient Greeks* (4–8). Illus. Series: Myths and Civilization. 1999, Bedrick $16.95 (978-0-87226-283-6). A handsome volume that combines Greek myths and legends with information about ancient Greek artifacts, culture, and history. (Rev: HBG 10/99; SLJ 3/99) [938]

17199 Middleton, Haydn. *Ancient Greek Jobs* (4–6). Series: People in the Past. 2002, Heinemann LB $27.07 (978-1-58810-638-4). 48pp. The tasks of the doctor, banker, farmer, merchant, and other professions are explained and placed in historical context. Also use *Ancient Greek Women* and *Ancient Greek Children*. (Rev: HBG 3/03; SLJ 12/02)

17200 Minnis, Ivan. *You Are in Ancient Greece* (3–6). Illus. Series: You Are There! 2004, Raintree LB $26.36 (978-1-4109-0617-5); paper $7.50 (978-1-4109-1009-7). 32pp. In present-tense narrative, Minnis introduces the sites, sounds, food, and varied living conditions of ancient Greece. (Rev: SLJ 2/05) [938]

17201 Nardo, Don. *Ancient Athens* (5–8). Illus. Series: A Travel Guide To. 2002, Gale $28.70 (978-1-59018-016-7). 112pp. This fact-filled "guidebook" introduces aspiring travelers to everyday life in ancient Athens, in addition to information on climate, geography, important sights, and so forth. (Rev: BL 1/1–15/03; SLJ 2/03) [914.75]

17202 Nardo, Don. *Ancient Greece* (4–6). Illus. Series: Life During the Great Civilizations. 2004, Gale LB $24.95 (978-1-56711-741-7). 48pp. Nardo explores day-to-day life in ancient Greece, looking at everything from clothes and jobs to social structures and religion.

17203 Nardo, Don. *Greek Temples* (5–7). Illus. Series: Famous Structures. 2002, Watts LB $25.50 (978-0-531-12035-4). 64pp. Nardo looks at the construction, elements, use, and importance of ancient Greek temples, with illustrations. (Rev: BL 9/1/02; SLJ 8/02) [726]

17204 Pipe, Jim. *Trojan Horse* (3–5). Illus. by Roger Hutchins and Donald Hartley. Series: Mystery History. 1997, Millbrook LB $23.90 (978-0-7613-0614-6). 32pp. Using games, puzzles, and hidden pictures, this simple account introduces the causes of the Trojan War, the people involved, and the ruse that ended it. (Rev: HBG 3/98; SLJ 4/98) [938]

17205 Powell, Anton. *Ancient Greece*. Rev. ed. (5–8). Illus. Series: Cultural Atlas for Young People. 2003, Facts on File $35.00 (978-0-8160-5146-5). 96pp. Colorful topical spreads introduce readers to the culture, history, and politics of ancient Greece, with information on the Olympics, daily life, and women's role. (Rev: SLJ 1/04) [938]

17206 Rees, Rosemary. *The Ancient Greeks* (3–4). Illus. Series: Understanding People in the Past. 1997, Heinemann $27.07 (978-0-431-07790-1). 64pp. Photos of museum artifacts plus maps, diagrams, and drawings are used liberally to introduce such topics about the ancient Greeks as their history, accomplishments, buildings, Olympic games, theater, family life, and trade. (Rev: SLJ 9/97) [938]

17207 Schomp, Virginia. *The Ancient Greeks* (5–8). Series: Cultures of the Past. 1995, Benchmark LB $29.93 (978-0-7614-0070-7). Using quotations from period literature and many photographs and drawings, this volume examines the history of ancient Greece, its culture, and the importance of the numerous Greek gods and goddesses. (Rev: SLJ 6/96) [938]

17208 Shuter, Jane. *The Acropolis* (5–7). Series: Visiting the Past. 1999, Heinemann LB $24.22 (978-1-57572-855-1). 32pp. As well as describing the main buildings found in ancient Greece, this account uses double-page spreads to introduce the daily life and culture of the Athenians. (Rev: SLJ 3/00) [938]

17209 Shuter, Jane. *Builders, Traders and Craftsmen* (4–5). Series: Ancient Greece. 1999, Heinemann LB $22.79 (978-1-57572-736-3). 32pp. This book covers the builders in ancient Greece who worked on the Parthenon, the craftsmen who made clothing, statues, and pottery, and the merchants who traded goods for grain. (Rev: HBG 10/99; SLJ 7/99) [938]

17210 Shuter, Jane. *Cities and Citizens* (4–5). Series: Ancient Greece. 1999, Heinemann LB $22.79 (978-1-57572-738-7). 32pp. This book on ancient Greece describes city-states and the interests and social life of citizens including theater, acting, and sports. (Rev: HBG 10/99; SLJ 7/99) [938]

17211 Shuter, Jane. *Discoveries, Inventions and Ideas* (2–5). Series: Ancient Greece. 1999, Heinemann LB $22.79 (978-1-57572-739-4). 32pp. Following a map and timeline, this book covers many Greek innovations such as the development of libraries, advances in medicine, and progress in mapmaking. (Rev: HBG 10/99; SLJ 7/99) [938]

17212 Shuter, Jane. *Farmers and Fighters* (2–5). Series: Ancient Greece. 1999, Heinemann LB $22.79 (978-1-57572-737-0). 32pp. A heavily illustrated book that describes various aspects of warfare and the weapons used plus an account of farming methods, tools, and food preparation. (Rev: HBG 10/99; SLJ 7/99) [938]

17213 Shuter, Jane. *Life in a Greek Temple* (2–4). Illus. Series: Picture the Past. 2005, Heinemann LB $26.79 (978-1-4034-6442-2). 32pp. A basic, attractive overview of Greek temples and their construction as well as the religious beliefs and practices of the ancient Greeks. (Rev: BL 9/15/05) [292.3]

17214 Shuter, Jane. *Life in a Greek Trading Port* (2–4). Illus. Series: Picture the Past. 2005, Heinemann LB $25.64 (978-1-4034-6444-6). 32pp. This title explores various aspects of everyday life in an ancient Greek port city, including housing, cuisine,

clothing, occupations, and leisure pursuits. (Rev: SLJ 11/05)

17215 Solway, Andrew. *Ancient Greece* (3–6). Illus. by Peter Connolly. Series: Ancient World. 2001, Oxford $24.99 (978-0-19-910810-7). 64pp. Exceptional artwork and detailed descriptions of life and institutions in ancient Greece. (Rev: BL 3/1/02; HBG 3/02; SLJ 2/02) [938.04]

Rome

17216 Ash, Rhiannon. *Roman Colosseum* (3–5). Illus. by Mike Bell, et al. Series: Mystery History. 1997, Millbrook LB $23.90 (978-0-7613-0613-9). 32pp. Games, puzzles, hidden pictures, and a simple text are used to introduce the Colosseum in Rome and the activities it housed. (Rev: HBG 3/98; SLJ 4/98) [937]

17217 Beller, Susan P. *Roman Legions on the March: Soldiering in the Ancient Roman Army* (5–8). 2007, Twenty-First Century LB $33.26 (978-0-8225-6781-3). 112pp. After background information on the Roman army, this volume examines the life of the soldiers and provides interesting sidebar features and photographs. (Rev: SLJ 1/08)

17218 Benduhn, Tea. *Ancient Rome* (1–3). Series: Life Long Ago. 2006, Weekly Reader LB $19.93 (978-0-8368-7783-0). 24pp. Plenty of facts about ancient Rome and its people's customs, beliefs, and political system. An airy design adds to the appeal. (Rev: SLJ 6/07)

17219 Blacklock, Dyan. *The Roman Army* (5–8). Illus. by David Kennett. 2004, Walker $17.95 (978-0-8027-8896-2). 48pp. The soldiers, weaponry, fighting techniques, and ingenuity of the Romans are detailed here in clear text and effective cartoon-style illustrations. (Rev: BL 3/1/04*; SLJ 4/04) [355]

17220 Chapman, Gillian. *The Romans* (4–7). Series: Crafts from the Past. 1998, Heinemann LB $25.64 (978-1-57572-734-9). 39pp. Using double-page spreads, this work describes Roman culture while outlining several craft projects inspired by art objects, places, or people. (Rev: HBG 10/99; SLJ 2/99) [937]

17221 Clare, John D., ed. *Classical Rome* (3–6). Illus. Series: Living History. 1993, Harcourt $17.00 (978-0-15-200513-9). 64pp. With informative text and photos showing people in period costume, this is a good introduction to ancient Rome. (Rev: BL 2/15/93) [937.06]

17222 Corbishley, Mike. *Ancient Rome*. Rev. ed. (5–8). Illus. Series: Cultural Atlas for Young People. 2003, Facts on File $35.00 (978-0-8160-5147-2). 96pp. Colorful topical spreads introduce readers to the culture, history, and politics of ancient Rome, with information on architecture and major cities of the provinces. (Rev: SLJ 1/04) [937]

17223 Curry, Jane Louise. *Brave Cloelia: Retold from the Account in the History of Early Rome by the Roman Historian Titus Livius* (2–4). Illus. by Jeff Crosby. 2004, Getty Publications $16.95 (978-0-89236-763-4). 32pp. A brave Roman girl earns the respect of the Etruscan invader in this picture book based on the writing of Livy. (Rev: BL 11/15/04; SLJ 2/05) [937]

17224 Dargie, Richard. *Ancient Rome* (3–6). Illus. Series: Picturing the Past. 2004, Enchanted Lion $15.95 (978-1-59270-023-3). 32pp. Well-written two-page chapters cover geography, history, government, religion, the arts, and home life, with maps, photos and illustrations, and informative sidebars detailing sources. (Rev: SLJ 11/04) [937]

17225 Dargie, Richard. *Rich and Poor in Ancient Rome* (3–6). Illus. by Adam Hook. 2005, Smart Apple LB $27.10 (978-1-58340-722-6). 32pp. The everyday lives of the rich and the poor in ancient Rome are compared. (Rev: SLJ 5/06) [937]

17226 Deem, James M. *Bodies from the Ash: Life and Death in Ancient Pompeii* (5–8). Illus. 2005, Houghton $17.00 (978-0-618-47308-3). 48pp. This photoessay full of vivid illustrations outlines what archaeologists have uncovered about the destruction of Pompeii when Mount Vesuvius erupted nearly 2,000 years ago. (Rev: BL 11/1/05; SLJ 12/05*) [937]

17227 DuTemple, Lesley A. *The Colosseum* (4–7). Series: Great Building Feats. 2003, Lerner LB $27.93 (978-0-8225-4693-1). Using many colorful diagrams and illustrations, this is the story of the construction of the famous colosseum in Rome. (Rev: BL 11/15/03; HBG 4/04) [937]

17228 Ganeri, Anita. *The Ancient Romans* (3–5). Series: History Starts Here! 2000, Raintree LB $25.69 (978-0-7398-1349-2). 32pp. A brief overview that introduces ancient Rome, its daily life, culture, social structure, history, and fall. (Rev: HBG 10/00; SLJ 7/00) [937]

17229 Guittard, Charles. *The Romans: Life in the Empire* (4–6). Trans. by Mary K. LaRose. Illus. by Annie-Claude Martin. Series: People of the Past. 1992, Millbrook LB $22.40 (978-1-56294-200-7). 64pp. This account presents an overview of how life was lived in the Roman Empire and gives information on such topics as history, culture, and religion. (Rev: BL 10/15/92) [937]

17230 Hanel, Rachael. *Gladiators* (5–8). Series: Fearsome Fighters. 2007, Creative Education LB $31.35 (978-1-58341-535-1). 48pp. Weapons, armor, fighting techniques, and motivation are all discussed in this description of gladiators in ancient Rome and the kinds of people who were tempted to this career. (Rev: SLJ 1/08)

17231 Hart, Avery, and Sandra Gallagher. *Ancient Rome! Exploring the Culture, People and Ideas of This Powerful Empire* (4–6). Illus. by Michael Kline. Series: A Kaleidoscope Kids Book. 2002, Williamson paper $14.25 (978-1-885593-60-3). 96pp. A fact-filled overview that introduces readers to all aspects of ancient Rome — history, legends and myths, government, transportation, wars, key individuals, and so forth — and provides activities such as building a triumphal arch. (Rev: SLJ 3/03)

17232 Hodge, Susie. *Ancient Roman Art* (4–8). Series: Art in History. 1997, Heinemann LB $24.22 (978-1-57572-552-9). 32pp. This slim, well-illus-trated volume outlines Roman contributions to architecture, sculpture, pottery, and mosaics. (Rev: SLJ 5/98) [937.6]

17233 Humphrey, Kathryn L. *Pompeii: Nightmare at Midday* (4–6). Illus. 1995, Houghton $9.28 (978-0-395-73265-6). 64pp. The destruction caused by the eruption of Mount Vesuvius in A.D. 79. (Rev: BL 4/15/90) [937]

17234 Jovinelly, Joann, and Jason Netelkos. *The Crafts and Culture of the Romans* (5–8). Series: Crafts of the Ancient World. 2002, Rosen LB $29.25 (978-0-8239-3513-0). 48pp. The daily life and contributions of the ancient Romans are covered, as well as such craft projects as designing a toga. (Rev: BL 5/15/02; SLJ 6/02) [937]

17235 Landau, Elaine. *Exploring Ancient Rome with Elaine Landau* (3–5). Illus. Series: Exploring Ancient Civilizations. 2005, Enslow LB $23.93 (978-0-7660-2337-6). 48pp. The author and her dog Max give readers a tour of ancient Rome's society, trade, engineering, architecture, religion, and food and clothing. (Rev: BL 9/1/05; SLJ 12/05) [937]

17236 MacDonald, Fiona. *Ancient Rome* (3–6). Illus. Series: 100 Things You Should Know about. 2002, Mason Crest LB $18.95 (978-1-59084-446-5). 48pp. Organized topically, this collection of 100 facts covers history, government, religion, daily life, dress, and cuisine, and will appeal to reluctant readers. (Rev: SLJ 6/03) [937]

17237 MacDonald, Fiona. *How to Be a Roman Soldier* (2–5). Illus. by Nicholas Hewetson. Series: How to Be. 2005, National Geographic $14.95 (978-0-7922-3616-0). 32pp. Soldiers' training, weapons, compensation, recreation, and home and family life are all covered in a reader-friendly, well-illustrated format. (Rev: SLJ 12/05) [355]

17238 MacDonald, Fiona. *I Wonder Why Romans Wore Togas and Other Questions About Ancient Rome* (2–4). Illus. Series: I Wonder Why. 1997, Kingfisher $11.95 (978-0-7534-5057-4). 32pp. Each double-page spread in this book answers two or three basic questions about the ancient Romans, how they lived, their empire, and their accomplishments. (Rev: HBG 3/98; SLJ 9/97) [937]

17239 Malam, John. *You Wouldn't Want to Be a Roman Gladiator! Gory Things You'd Rather Not Know* (4–6). Illus. by David Antram. Series: You Wouldn't Want To. 2001, Watts LB $29.00 (978-0-531-14598-2); paper $9.95 (978-0-531-16204-0). 32pp. Cartoon art belies the grimness of the content in this book in which readers will find plenty of hard information on how gladiators were acquired and trained, their rules of battle, and details of other savage forms of entertainment. (Rev: SLJ 9/01)

17240 Mann, Elizabeth. *The Roman Colosseum* (4–7). Illus. Series: Wonders of the World. 1998, Mikaya $19.95 (978-0-9650493-3-7). 48pp. An oversize book that is crammed with factual material on the Colosseum in Rome. (Rev: BL 12/15/98; SLJ 2/99) [937]

17241 Markel, Rita J. *Your Travel Guide to Ancient Rome* (4–6). Illus. Series: Passport to History. 2003, Lerner LB $26.60 (978-0-8225-3071-8). 96pp.

Information about ancient Rome — everything from historical anecdotes to profiles of key indviduals to details of dress and behavior — is conveyed in the style of a travel guide complete with photographs and prints. (Rev: BL 2/15/04; HBG 4/04; SLJ 4/04) [937]

17242 Martin, Michael. *Gladiators* (3–6). Series: Edge Books: Warriors of History. 2006, Capstone LB $23.93 (978-0-7368-6429-9). 32pp. This colorful introduction to gladiators examines the history of this class of professional warriors in ancient Rome, their weapons, and their way of life. (Rev: SLJ 1/07) [796.8]

17243 Minnis. *Ancient Rome* (3–6). Series: Raintree Perspectives. 2004, Raintree LB $25.70 (978-1-4109-0618-2). 32pp. Double-page spreads with plenty of illustrations and a low readling level introduce readers to ancient Rome's culture and lifestyle. (Rev: BL 12/1/04; SLJ 2/05) [937]

17244 Morley, Jacqueline. *A Roman Villa* (4–6). Illus. by John James. Series: Inside Story. 1992, Bedrick LB $18.95 (978-0-87226-360-4). 48pp. Through many double-page spreads and cutaway drawings, the interiors and exteriors of Roman villas are explored. (Rev: BL 12/15/92; SLJ 1/93) [937]

17245 Nardo, Don. *Ancient Rome* (4–6). Illus. Series: Life During the Great Civilizations. 2004, Gale LB $24.95 (978-1-56711-742-4). 48pp. Nardo explores day-to-day life in ancient Rome, looking at everything from clothes and jobs to social structures and religion.

17246 Nardo, Don. *Roman Amphitheaters* (5–7). Illus. Series: Famous Structures. 2002, Watts LB $25.50 (978-0-531-12036-1); paper $8.95 (978-0-531-16224-8). 64pp. A clear overview of the construction, elements, use, and importance of ancient Roman amphitheaters, with illustrations. (Rev: BL 9/1/02; SLJ 8/02) [725]

17247 Osborne, Mary Pope. *Pompeii: Lost and Found* (2–4). Illus. by Bonnie Christensen. 2006, Knopf $16.95 (978-0-375-82889-8). 40pp. In addition to describing the eruption of Vesuvius in A.D. 79, Osborne discusses its excavation and how archaeological discoveries allow us to imagine daily life in the city at that time. (Rev: BL 12/1/05; SLJ 1/06) [937]

17248 Osborne, Mary Pope, and Natalie Pope Boyce. *Ancient Rome and Pompeii: A Nonfiction Companion to Vacation Under the Volcano* (2–4). Illus. by Sal Murdocca. 2006, Random $4.99 (978-0-375-83220-8). 128pp. This nonfiction companion to *Vacation Under the Volcano* provides a fascinating introduction to the history and culture of ancient Rome and Pompeii. (Rev: BL 6/1–15/06) [937]

17249 Parker, Vic. *Pompeii AD 79: A City Buried by a Volcanic Eruption* (4–7). Series: When Disaster Struck. 2006, Raintree LB $32.86 (978-1-4109-2276-2). 56pp. Parker looks at Pompeii both before and after its destruction by the eruption of Mount Vesuvius, discussing the nature (and likelihood) of volcanic eruptions and what archaeologists have learned from their excavations. (Rev: SLJ 1/07) [937.7]

17250 Patent, Dorothy Hinshaw. *Lost City of Pompeii* (4–7). Series: Frozen in Time. 1999, Benchmark LB $27.07 (978-0-7614-0785-0). 64pp. The story of the ancient city of Pompeii, its destruction, and how its excavation has given us a wealth of information about ancient Rome. (Rev: BL 2/1/00; HBG 10/00; SLJ 3/00) [937]

17251 Rees, Rosemary. *The Ancient Romans* (3–6). Series: Understanding People in the Past. 1999, Heinemann LB $27.07 (978-1-57572-890-2). 64pp. Double-page spreads with illustrations of historical sites, artifacts, art, and maps help the reader envision the daily life and contributions of the ancient Romans. (Rev: BL 6/1–15/99) [937]

17252 Ridd, Stephen, ed. *Julius Caesar in Gaul and Britain* (5–8). Illus. Series: History Eyewitness. 1995, Raintree $24.26 (978-0-8114-8283-7). An edited version of Caesar's fascinating accounts of the Gallic Wars, with pictures and maps. (Rev: BL 4/15/95; SLJ 5/95) [937.05]

17253 Sheehan, Sean. *Ancient Rome* (4–6). Series: History Beneath Your Feet. 1999, Raintree LB $27.12 (978-0-8172-5752-1). 48pp. This account, which focuses on the ruins of Pompeii, re-creates the daily life of the Romans and describes how archaeologists have gathered this information. (Rev: HBG 10/00; SLJ 3/00) [937]

17254 Sheehan, Sean, and Pat Levy. *Rome* (5–10). Series: Ancient World. 1998, Raintree LB $27.12 (978-0-8172-5057-7). A brief history of Rome and the Roman Empire, including its culture, buildings, amusements, and emperors. (Rev: BL 1/1–15/99; HBG 3/99; SLJ 3/99) [937]

17255 Snedden, Robert. *Technology in the Time of Ancient Rome* (4–8). Series: Technology in the Time Of. 1998, Raintree LB $27.12 (978-0-8172-4876-5). 48pp. Weaving, food production, construction, transportation, and metalwork are covered in this discussion of Roman technology. (Rev: HBG 10/98; SLJ 3/99) [937]

17256 Solway, Andrew. *Ancient Rome* (3–6). Illus. by Peter Connolly. Series: Ancient World. 2001, Oxford $24.99 (978-0-19-910809-1). 64pp. Exceptional artwork and detailed descriptions of daily life, culture, religion, and sports in ancient Rome. (Rev: BL 3/1/02; HBG 3/02; SLJ 1/02) [937.6]

17257 Solway, Andrew. *Rome: In Spectacular Cross-Section* (4–7). Illus. by Stephen Biesty. 2003, Scholastic paper $18.95 (978-0-439-45546-6). 32pp. An inside look at life in ancient Rome, with views of a private home, the Colosseum, the docks, and a bustling festival. (Rev: BL 2/15/03; HBG 10/03; SLJ 7/03) [937]

17258 Stewart, David. *You Wouldn't Want to Be a Roman Soldier! Barbarians You'd Rather Not Meet* (3–6). Illus. by David Antram. Series: You Wouldn't Want To. 2006, Watts LB $29.00 (978-0-531-12423-9); paper $9.95 (978-0-531-12448-2). 32pp. This book banishes romantic notions about the lives of Roman soldiers, but the cartoon illustrations lighten the portrayal of harsh conditions and deadly challenges. (Rev: SLJ 9/06) [937]

17259 Stroud, Jonathan. *Ancient Rome: A Guide to the Glory of Imperial Rome* (4–7). Series: Sightseers. 2000, Kingfisher $8.95 (978-0-7534-5235-6). 30pp. This book on ancient Rome is presented like a handbook for tourists, with material on such topics as accommodations, shopping, key sites, etc. (Rev: HBG 3/01; SLJ 9/00) [937]

17260 Whittock, Martyn. *The Roman Empire* (4–6). Illus. Series: Biographical History. 1996, Bedrick $17.95 (978-0-87226-118-1). 64pp. A history of the Roman Empire, its expansion, and life in the republic are given, with many short biographies and excerpts from both primary and secondary sources. (Rev: SLJ 9/96) [937]

17261 Williams, Brian. *Ancient Roman Women* (5–8). Illus. Series: People in the Past. 2002, Heinemann LB $27.07 (978-1-58810-632-2). 48pp. A look at the life of, and options open to, women in ancient Rome. (Rev: BL 3/1/03; HBG 10/03; SLJ 4/03) [305.8]

Aztecs, Incas, and Maya

17262 Bingham, Jane. *The Aztec Empire* (5–8). Series: Time Travel Guides. 2007, Raintree LB $34.29 (978-1-4109-2730-9). 64pp. An attractive trip back in time to the Aztec Empire, providing details about daily life there — accommodation, food, shopping, and so forth — as well as the calendar and festivals. (Rev: LMC 11/07; SLJ 9/07) [972]

17263 Bingham, Jane. *The Inca Empire* (5–8). Series: Time Travel Guides. 2007, Raintree LB $34.29 (978-1-4109-2731-6). 64pp. An attractive trip back in time to the Inca Empire, providing details about daily life there — accommodation, food, shopping, and so forth. (Rev: SLJ 9/07) [985]

17264 Calvert, Patricia. *The Ancient Inca* (5–8). Series: People of the Ancient World. 2004, Watts LB $30.50 (978-0-531-12358-4). 128pp. This fascinating volume covers the history and culture of the Inca people, looking at childhood and the daily life of people ranging from farmers to priests, warriors, and emperors. (Rev: SLJ 3/05) [985]

17265 Chapman, Gillian. *The Aztecs* (4–8). Series: Crafts from the Past. 1997, Heinemann LB $25.64 (978-1-57572-555-0). A craft book with instructions for a variety of Aztec ornaments and artifacts, including textiles and statues. (Rev: SLJ 4/98) [745]

17266 Chrisp, Peter. *The Aztecs* (4–6). Series: History Beneath Your Feet. 1999, Raintree LB $27.12 (978-0-8172-5753-8). 48pp. Using authentic drawings and paintings, this account presents the daily life of the Aztecs and how archaeologists have gathered this information. (Rev: HBG 10/00; SLJ 3/00) [972]

17267 Clare, John D. *Aztec Life* (5–8). Illus. 2006, Saddleback paper $8.95 (978-1-59905-050-8). 32pp. Covers the lifestyle, culture, and traditions of the Aztecs, with quotations from poems and sayings. (Rev: SLJ 9/06) [972]

17268 Dalal, Anita. *Myths of Pre-Columbian America* (5–8). Illus. Series: Mythic World. 2002, Raintree LB $27.12 (978-0-7398-3193-9). 48pp. This

volume for older readers separates myth from reality about cultures present in America in pre-Columbian times. (Rev: BL 3/1/02; HBG 3/02; SLJ 12/01) [398.2]

17269 Day, Nancy. *Your Travel Guide to Ancient Mayan Civilization* (4–8). Series: Passport to History. 2000, Lerner LB $26.50 (978-0-8225-3077-0). 96pp. Using the format of a modern-day travel guide, this book explores the ancient Mayan cities of Uzmal, Tikal, Copan, and others to discover the lifestyles of the Maya, their food, clothes, religion, discoveries, and behavior. (Rev: BL 3/1/01; HBG 10/01; SLJ 4/01) [972]

17270 Garcia, Guy. *Spirit of the Maya: A Boy Explores His People's Mysterious Past* (4–6). Illus. 1995, Walker LB $17.85 (978-0-8027-8380-6). 48pp. A young Mayan boy discovers his heritage when he explores the ruins at Palenque and learns of the boy-king Pacal, who is buried there. (Rev: BCCB 12/95; BL 10/1/95; SLJ 1/96) [972]

17271 Gruber, Beth. *Ancient Inca: Archaeology Unlocks the Secrets of Inca's Past* (3–7). Series: National Geographic Investigates. 2006, National Geographic $17.95 (978-0-7922-7827-6). 64pp. This well-illustrated title examines how archaeologists gain knowledge about the ancient Inca civilization of pre-Columbian America, including information on pottery, textiles, and mummies. (Rev: SLJ 2/07) [985]

17272 Hull, Robert. *The Aztecs* (5–10). Series: Ancient World. 1998, Raintree LB $27.12 (978-0-8172-5056-0). 64pp. This history of the Aztecs and their culture describes their great pyramids, feathered headdresses, gods, human sacrifices, and the coming of the Spanish. (Rev: BL 1/1–15/99; HBG 3/99) [972]

17273 Hynson, Colin. *You Wouldn't Want to Be an Inca Mummy! A One-Way Journey You'd Rather Not Make* (4–6). Illus. by David Antram. Series: You Wouldn't Want to . . . Ancient Civilization. 2007, Watts LB $29.00 (978-0-531-18744-9). 32pp. Engaging facts, fast action, cartoons, and a touch of humor make for an appealing package about the culture and religion of the Inca people. (Rev: LMC 5/08; SLJ 3/08) [393]

17274 Jovinelly, Joann, and Jason Netelkos. *The Crafts and Culture of the Aztecs* (5–8). Illus. Series: Crafts of the Ancient World. 2002, Rosen LB $29.25 (978-0-8239-3512-3). 48pp. The culture of the Aztecs is covered through a discussion of their crafts and a variety of easily accomplished projects related to them. (Rev: BL 4/1/02; VOYA 6/02) [972]

17275 Kendall, Sarita. *The Incas* (5–6). Illus. Series: World of the Past. 1992, Macmillan LB $21.00 (978-0-02-750160-5). 64pp. A history of the Incas before, during, and after the Spanish conquest. (Rev: SLJ 11/92) [940.54]

17276 Lewin, Ted. *Lost City: The Discovery of Machu Picchu* (2–4). 2003, Penguin $17.99 (978-0-399-23302-9). 48pp. Striking watercolor spreads grab attention in this picture-book account of the discovery of the lost Inca city. (Rev: BL 7/03; HB 9/03; HBG 4/04; SLJ 6/03) [985]

17277 Libura, Krystyna, et al. *What the Aztecs Told Me* (4–8). Illus. 1997, Douglas & McIntyre paper $6.95 (978-0-88899-306-9). Based on an original 12-volume work written in the 16th century, this book describes the Aztec people from observation and eyewitness accounts. (Rev: BL 12/1/97; HB 11/97; HBG 3/98; SLJ 12/97) [972]

17278 Lourie, Peter. *Hidden World of the Aztec* (5–8). Illus. 2006, Boyds Mills $17.95 (978-1-59078-069-5). 45pp. This lavishly illustrated title uses modern archaeological projects to introduce the history and culture of the ancient Aztec civilization. (Rev: BL 10/15/06; SLJ 10/06) [972]

17279 Lourie, Peter. *Lost Treasure of the Inca* (4–7). Illus. 1999, Boyds Mills $18.95 (978-1-56397-743-5). 48pp. A thrilling narrative of a modern search for the gold supposedly hidden by the Incas in the Ecuadorian mountains. (Rev: BCCB 11/99; BL 10/15/99; HBG 3/00; SLJ 11/99) [986.6]

17280 MacDonald, Fiona. *How to Be an Aztec Warrior* (2–5). Illus. by David Antram and Mark Bergin. Series: How to Be. 2005, National Geographic $14.95 (978-0-7922-3617-7). 32pp. This attractive title gives readers a look at what life was like for Aztec warriors, touching on such topics as uniforms, weapons, rank, and traditions. (Rev: SLJ 12/05) [972]

17281 MacDonald, Fiona. *You Wouldn't Want to Be an Aztec Sacrifice! Gruesome Things You'd Rather Not Know* (4–6). Illus. by David Antram. Series: You Wouldn't Want To. 2001, Watts LB $29.00 (978-0-531-14602-6); paper $9.95 (978-0-531-16209-5). 32pp. The circumstances of human sacrifice — and potential ways of avoiding this fate — are discussed with some black humor. (Rev: SLJ 3/02) [972]

17282 Mann, Elizabeth. *Machu Picchu* (3–5). Illus. Series: Wonders of the World. 2000, Mikaya $19.95 (978-0-9650493-9-9). 48pp. Beginning with the discovery of Machu Picchu in 1911, this book goes back to trace its construction and history. (Rev: BL 7/00*; HBG 10/00; SLJ 6/00) [985]

17283 Mann, Elizabeth. *Tikal: The Center of the Maya World* (4–8). Illus. by Tom McNeely. Series: Wonders of the World. 2002, Mikaya $19.95 (978-1-931414-05-0). 48pp. Mann provides an overview for older readers of the Mayan city of Tikal, covering the location, the people, the architecture, the culture, and their sometimes bloodthirsty customs. (Rev: BL 12/15/02; HBG 3/03; SLJ 1/03) [972.81]

17284 Martell, Hazel M. *Civilizations of Peru, Before 1535* (5–8). Illus. Series: Looking Back. 1999, Raintree $19.98 (978-0-8172-5428-5). 63pp. This book covers the history and culture of the Inca empire that stretched far beyond the boundaries of Peru. (Rev: BL 5/15/99; SLJ 7/99) [985]

17285 Matthews, Rupert. *You Wouldn't Want to Be a Mayan Soothsayer! Fortunes You'd Rather Not Tell* (4–6). Illus. by David Antram. Series: You Wouldn't Want to . . . Ancient Civilization. 2007, Watts LB $29.00 (978-0-531-18746-3). 32pp. Engaging

facts, fast action, cartoons, and a touch of humor make for an appealing package about the culture and religion of the Mayan people. (Rev: LMC 5/08; SLJ 3/08) [299.8]

17286 Perl, Lila. *The Ancient Maya* (5–8). Series: People of the Ancient World. 2005, Watts LB $30.50 (978-0-531-12381-2); paper $9.95 (978-0-531-16848-6). 112pp. Introduces readers to the arts, religious beliefs, and society of the Maya, with discussion of individual occupations and of the discoveries by archaeologists and anthropologists. (Rev: SLJ 9/05) [973]

17287 Rees, Rosemary. *The Aztecs* (3–6). Illus. Series: Understanding People in the Past. 1999, Heinemann LB $27.07 (978-1-57572-888-9). 64pp. Topics such as Aztec history, culture, floating gardens, food, feasts, and sports are covered in a series of double-page spreads. (Rev: BL 6/1–15/99) [972]

17288 Rees, Rosemary. *The Incas* (3–6). Illus. 1999, Heinemann LB $27.07 (978-1-57572-889-6). 64pp. In addition to giving a general history of the Incas, their culture and contributions, this book describes their calendar, family life, and the Spanish conquest. (Rev: BL 6/1–15/99) [985]

17289 Sayer, Chloe. *The Incas* (5–10). Series: Ancient World. 1998, Raintree LB $27.12 (978-0-8172-5125-3). An in-depth look at Inca life, from their beautiful gold ornaments to their unique form of record keeping and impressive citadels and forts. (Rev: BL 1/1–15/99; HBG 3/99) [985]

17290 Sherrow, Victoria. *The Maya Indians* (3–5). Illus. Series: Junior Library of American Indians. 1993, Chelsea LB $25.00 (978-0-7910-1666-4). 80pp. An account of the Mayan culture, principally of the Yucatan area of Mexico and Guatemala, its destruction by the Spaniards, and the present status of the descendants. (Rev: BL 2/15/94; SLJ 2/94) [973.81]

17291 Silate, Jennifer. *The Inca Ruins of Machu Picchu* (4–6). Illus. Series: Wonders of the World. 2005, Gale LB $26.20 (978-0-7377-3068-5). 48pp. This is a useful, easy-to-read introduction to the current knowledge about the Incas and the construction of Machu Picchu, with details of contemporary cable-car access and attempts to preserve the site. (Rev: SLJ 7/06) [985]

17292 Stein, R. Conrad. *The Aztec Empire* (5–8). Series: Cultures of the Past. 1995, Benchmark LB $29.93 (978-0-7614-0072-1). The Aztecs' history, beliefs, and lifestyles are examined in this book, with quotations from original sources and many color photographs of artifacts, monuments, and historical sites. (Rev: SLJ 6/96) [972]

17293 Wyborny, Sheila. *The Aztec Empire* (4–6). Illus. Series: Life During the Great Civilizations. 2004, Gale LB $24.95 (978-1-56711-736-3). 48pp. Wyborny explores day-to-day life among the Aztecs, looking at everything from clothes and jobs to social structures, medicine, and religion. (Rev: BL 5/15/04; SLJ 8/04) [972]

Middle Ages

17294 Adkins, Jan. *What If You Met a Knight?* (3–5). Illus. 2006, Roaring Brook $16.95 (978-1-59643-148-5). 32pp. Presents a realistic view of the life of knights in the Middle Ages and of their daily responsibilities and challenges. (Rev: BL 8/06; HBG 4/07; LMC 1/07; SLJ 9/06; VOYA 2/07) [940.1088]

17295 Bruce, Julia. *Siege: Can You Capture a Castle?* (3–6). Illus. by Peter Dennis. 2009, Enslow LB $16.95 (978-0-7660-3475-4). 32pp. A castle under siege is the dramatic frame for solid information about castle design and life on both sides of the walls. (Rev: BL 4/1/09) [355.4]

17296 *Castles* (PS–3). Illus. Series: First Discovery. 1993, Scholastic $12.95 (978-0-590-46377-5). 30pp. A highly visual introduction to castles that supplies basic information with an interactive approach. (Rev: BL 10/1/93; SLJ 8/93) [940.1]

17297 Child, John, et al. *The Crusades* (4–6). Illus. Series: Biographical History. 1996, Bedrick $17.95 (978-0-87226-119-8). 64pp. Describes the nature and the causes of the various Crusades and covers important events, battles, and people. (Rev: SLJ 9/96) [940.1]

17298 Clare, John D. *Fourteenth-Century Towns* (3–6). Illus. Series: Living History. 1993, Harcourt $17.00 (978-0-15-200515-3). 64pp. Life in a medieval town is portrayed with double-page spreads and informative text. (Rev: BL 2/15/923) [307]

17299 Clare, John D., ed. *Knights in Armor* (3–6). Illus. 1992, Harcourt $17.00 (978-0-15-200508-5). 64pp. Photos of people in period costume help bring to life this historical era. (Rev: BL 12/1/92; SLJ 11/92) [940]

17300 Clements, Gillian. *Medieval Castle* (3–6). Illus. by author. Series: Building History. 2009, Sea-to-Sea LB $18.95 (978-1-59771-145-6). 32pp. Answering questions such as "Who built the castles?" and "How did soldiers defend castles?", this volume provides lots of information in the text and in the detailed drawings. (Rev: BLO 3/11/09) [909.07]

17301 Corbishley, Mike. *The Medieval World* (5–7). Illus. Series: Timelink. 1993, Bedrick LB $18.95 (978-0-87226-362-8). 64pp. Using a chronological approach, this book covers the years 450 through 1500 in Europe, Asia, Africa, and the Americas. (Rev: SLJ 8/93) [940.1]

17302 Currie, Stephen. *Miracles, Saints, and Superstition: The Medieval Mind* (5–9). 2006, Gale LB $32.45 (978-1-59018-861-3). 104pp. Describes the Middle Ages and the role of Christianity at that time. (Rev: SLJ 3/07*) [940.1]

17303 Dunn, John M. *Life During the Black Death* (5–9). Series: The Way People Live. 2000, Lucent LB $28.70 (978-1-56006-542-5). 96pp. This account traces the spread of the Black Death from Mongolia in 1320 to Western Europe and its lasting effects on history, society, and culture. (Rev: HBG 10/00; SLJ 6/00) [940]

17304 Galloway, Priscilla. *Archers, Alchemists, and 98 Other Medieval Jobs You Might Have Loved or Loathed* (4–6). Illus. by Martha Newbigging. 2003, Annick LB $24.95 (978-1-55037-811-5); paper $14.95 (978-1-55037-810-8). 96pp. One hundred medieval occupations are described in conversational style, with cartoon illustrations and informative castle-shaped sidebars. (Rev: BL 1/1–15/04; SLJ 1/04) [909.07]

17305 George, Linda S. *800* (5–8). Illus. Series: Around the World. 2003, Marshall Cavendish LB $29.93 (978-0-7614-1085-0). 96pp. This absorbing look at civilizations around the world in the year 800 includes color reproductions, photographs, a timeline, a glossary, and lists of resources. (Rev: BL 6/1–15/03; HBG 3/03) [909.07]

17306 Gravett, Christopher. *Real Knights: Over 20 True Stories of Battle and Adventure* (4–6). Illus. by John James. 2005, Enchanted Lion $15.95 (978-1-59270-034-9). 48pp. This collection of tales about real-life knights in action includes the exploits of Richard the Lionheart, El Cid, Braveheart, and some others who are less well known. (Rev: SLJ 8/06) [940.1]

17307 Hanel, Rachael. *Knights* (5–8). Series: Fearsome Fighters. 2007, Creative Education LB $31.35 (978-1-58341-536-8). 48pp. Weapons, armor, fighting techniques, and motivation are all discussed in this description of the knights of the Middle Ages and the kinds of people who were tempted to this career. (Rev: SLJ 1/08)

17308 Hart, Avery, and Paul Mantell. *Knights and Castles: 50 Hands-On Activities to Experience the Middle Ages* (3–6). Illus. 1998, Williamson paper $14.25 (978-1-885593-17-7). 96pp. Directions for making a catapult, a castle, and a knight's helmet are three of the projects in this craft book that also supplies good information about life in the Middle Ages. (Rev: BL 11/15/98; SLJ 2/99) [940.1]

17309 Haywood, John. *Medieval Europe* (5–9). Series: Time Travel Guides. 2007, Raintree LB $34.29 (978-1-4109-2909-9); paper $9.99 (978-1-4109-2915-0). 64pp. With chapter headings like "Facts," "Everyday Life," and "Things to See and Do," this volume takes an effective travel-guide approach to the Middle Ages, incorporating many visual elements. (Rev: SLJ 1/08)

17310 Hinds, Kathryn. *The Castle* (5–8). Series: Life in the Middle Ages. 2000, Marshall Cavendish LB $29.93 (978-0-7614-1007-2). 80pp. A book that explores the construction and parts of the medieval castle as well as the lifestyles of those who lived in them, from kings and knights to humble servants. (Rev: BL 3/1/01; HBG 3/01; SLJ 3/01) [940]

17311 Hinds, Kathryn. *The Church* (5–8). Series: Life in the Middle Ages. 2000, Marshall Cavendish LB $29.93 (978-0-7614-1008-9). 80pp. Explains the role of the church and the clergy in medieval life as well as giving examples of church construction. (Rev: BL 3/1/01; HBG 3/01; SLJ 3/01) [940]

17312 Hinds, Kathryn. *The City* (5–8). Illus. Series: Life in the Middle Ages. 2000, Marshall Cavendish LB $29.93 (978-0-7614-1005-8). 80pp. A beautifully designed book that describes daily life in medieval cities and explores their roles as centers of learning, commerce, worship, construction, and recreation as well as disease and disaster. (Rev: BL 2/15/01; HBG 3/01; SLJ 3/01) [940.1]

17313 Hinds, Kathryn. *The Countryside* (5–8). Illus. Series: Life in the Middle Ages. 2000, Marshall Cavendish LB $29.93 (978-0-7614-1006-5). 80pp. The author explains manorialism — a primary social structure in rural areas during the Middle Ages — and describes a medieval village, its residents, and their work and pastimes. (Rev: BL 2/15/01; HBG 3/01; SLJ 3/01) [940.1]

17314 Howe, John. *Knights* (3–6). Illus. 1995, Orchard $18.95 (978-0-531-09456-3). 16pp. Aspects of the Middle Ages — like castles, armor, and the Crusades — come alive in this pop-up book. (Rev: BL 2/1/96) [940]

17315 Kroll, Steven. *Barbarians!* (3–6). Illus. by Robert Byrd. 2009, Dutton $18.99 (978-0-525-47958-1). 48pp. Goths, Huns, Vikings, and Mongols are the main groupings of "barbarians" discussed in this informative and attractive volume. (Rev: BL 5/1/09; LMC 10/09; SLJ 8/09) [940.1]

17316 MacDonald, Fiona. *How to Be a Medieval Knight* (2–5). Illus. by Mark Bergin. Series: How to Be. 2005, National Geographic $14.95 (978-0-7922-3619-1). 32pp. Knights' training, equipment, weapons, compensation, tournaments, and peacetime occupations and family life are all covered in a reader-friendly, well-illustrated format. (Rev: SLJ 12/05) [940.1]

17317 MacDonald, Fiona. *Knights, Castles, and Warfare in the Middle Ages* (5–8). Series: World Almanac Library of the Middle Ages. 2005, World Almanac LB $31.00 (978-0-8368-5895-2). 48pp. Describes the role of knights, the equipment they used, and their lives and homes. Also use *The Plague and Medicine in the Middle Ages* (2005). (Rev: SLJ 1/06) [940.1]

17318 Marston, Elsa. *The Byzantine Empire* (5–8). Series: Cultures of the Past. 2002, Marshall Cavendish $29.93 (978-0-7614-1495-7). 80pp. Well-written text and colorful graphics present the history and culture of the surviving eastern part of the Roman Empire. (Rev: BL 1/1–15/03; HBG 3/03; SLJ 2/03) [949.5]

17319 Martin, Alex. *Knights and Castles: Exploring History Through Art* (5–8). Illus. Series: Picture That! 2004, Two-Can $19.95 (978-1-58728-441-0). 64pp. Paintings serve as the vehicle to draw students into the discussion of life in Europe during the late medieval period. (Rev: BL 11/1/04; SLJ 2/05) [940.1]

17320 Martin, Michael. *Knights* (3–6). 2006, Capstone LB $23.93 (978-0-7368-6431-2). 32pp. This colorful overview of knights examines the history, weapons, and way of life of these medieval warriors. (Rev: SLJ 1/07) [940.1]

17321 Morgan, Gwyneth. *Life in a Medieval Village* (5–7). Illus. by author. 1991, HarperCollins paper $14.95 (978-0-06-092046-3). A story of activities in a medieval village and of the church's importance in life in the Middle Ages. [306.094265]

17322 Olmon, Kyle. *Sabuda and Reinhart Present Castle: Medieval Days and Knights* (3–5). Illus. by Tracy Sabin. 2006, Scholastic $19.99 (978-0-439-54324-8). 6pp. An intriguing look at medieval times and castles featuring three-dimensional pop-up images of everything from the castle itself to drawbridges and catapults. (Rev: BL 11/15/06; SLJ 12/06) [940.1]

17323 Padrino, Mercedes. *Cities and Towns in the Middle Ages* (5–8). Series: World Almanac Library of the Middle Ages. 2005, World Almanac LB $31.00 (978-0-8368-5893-8). 48pp. A look at medieval urban living — social structure, government structure, employment, education, religion, food and clothing, and so forth. Also use *Feudalism and Village Life in the Middle Ages* (2005). (Rev: SLJ 1/06) [940.1]

17324 Pernoud, Regine. *A Day with a Noblewoman* (5–8). Trans. by Dominique Clift. Illus. Series: A Day With. 1997, Runestone LB $27.15 (978-0-8225-1916-4). After a brief introduction to the Middle Ages, this book describes a busy day in the life of Blanche, the countess of Champagne, a French widow in the 13th century. (Rev: BL 1/1–15/98; HBG 3/98; SLJ 2/98) [940.1]

17325 Pernoud, Regine. *A Day with a Stonecutter* (3–6). Illus. 1997, Runestone LB $22.60 (978-0-8225-1913-3). 48pp. Includes both an introduction to medieval society and a case study of a stonecutter who is working on a project for an abbey. (Rev: BL 11/1/97; HBG 3/98; SLJ 1/98) [731.4]

17326 Ross, Stewart. *Monarchs* (5–8). Illus. Series: Medieval Realms. 2004, Gale $29.95 (978-1-59018-535-3). 48pp. This colorfully illustrated, oversize volume explores the structure of European governments during the Middle Ages and such topics as the birth of new nations, wars, and the Crusades. (Rev: BL 10/15/04) [940.1]

17327 Scarry, Huck. *Looking into the Middle Ages* (3–6). Illus. 1985, HarperCollins $12.50 (978-0-06-025224-3). 12pp. This 12-page pop-up book literally allows readers to look into the Middle Ages — into castles, cathedrals, jousting tournaments. (Rev: BCCB 6/85; BL 9/15/85)

17328 Senker, Cath. *The Black Death 1347–1350: The Plague Spreads Across Europe* (4–7). Series: When Disaster Struck. 2006, Raintree LB $32.86 (978-1-4109-2278-6). 56pp. Documents the widespread devastation caused by the plague that spread across Europe in the mid-14th century causing an estimated 20 million deaths and discusses current medical understanding and practices. (Rev: SLJ 1/07) [614.5732]

17329 Shuter, Jane. *The Middle Ages* (3–6). Series: History Opens Windows. 1999, Heinemann LB $21.36 (978-1-57572-886-5). 32pp. This useful account of the medieval period uses double-page spreads and many illustrations to bring the social forces and events of this period to life. (Rev: SLJ 2/00) [940.1]

17330 Steele, Philip. *Castles* (5–7). Illus. 1995, Kingfisher $16.95 (978-1-85697-547-6). 64pp. In this oversized, well-designed book, castles, jousting, armor, and feast days are described. (Rev: BL 8/95; SLJ 4/95) [940.1]

17331 Steele, Philip. *A Knight's City* (1–4). Illus. 2008, Simon & Schuster $18.99 (978-1-4169-6124-6). 32pp. Pop-ups, pull-tabs, large illustrations, and clear text provide a tour of life in a medieval European castle and town. (Rev: BLO 12/16/08; SLJ 12/08) [940.1]

17332 Steele, Philip. *The Medieval World* (5–8). Illus. Series: A History of Fashion and Costume. 2005, Facts on File $35.00 (978-0-8160-5945-4). 64pp. A broad overview of the clothing and personal adornment worn during this time period, with many visual aids. (Rev: SLJ 5/06) [391]

17333 Steer, Dugald. *Knight: A Noble Guide for Young Squires* (2–6). Illus. by Milivoj Ceran and Neil Chapman. 2006, Candlewick $17.99 (978-0-7636-3062-1). This fact-filled guide to the ways of knighthood is written as though it were a letter of guidance from an imprisoned knight to his son; the delicate flaps and playing pieces for a game called "Squire Fight" will restrict this book's circulation. (Rev: SLJ 2/07) [940.1]

17334 Walker, Jane. *Knights and Castles* (3–6). Illus. Series: 100 Things You Should Know about. 2002, Mason Crest LB $18.95 (978-1-59084-450-2). 48pp. Information about daily life in the Middle Ages, tournaments, banquets, and battles will appeal to reluctant readers. (Rev: SLJ 6/03) [940.1]

17335 Woolf, Alex. *Education* (5–8). Series: Medieval Realms. 2004, Gale LB $29.95 (978-1-59018-532-2). 48pp. Discusses the forms of education available during the Middle Ages — including apprenticeships, song schools, monastic schools, universities — and who was able to enjoy them and what they learned, ending with material on the rise of humanism. (Rev: SLJ 3/05) [370]

Renaissance

17336 Claybourne, Anna. *The Renaissance* (5–9). Series: Time Travel Guides. 2007, Raintree LB $34.29 (978-1-4109-2910-5); paper $9.99 (978-1-4109-2916-7). 64pp. With chapter headings like "Facts," "Everyday Life," and "Things to See and Do," this volume takes an effective travel-guide approach to the Renaissance, incorporating many visual elements. (Rev: SLJ 1/08)

17337 Day, Nancy. *Your Travel Guide to Renaissance Europe* (4–8). Series: Passport to History. 2000, Lerner LB $26.50 (978-0-8225-3080-0). 96pp. This book uses a travel guide format to introduce the reader to the life and people of Europe from 1350 to 1550 with coverage of culture, style, inventions, religious beliefs, and scientific discoveries. (Rev: BL 3/1/01; HBG 10/01) [940.2]

17338 Hinds, Kathryn. *The City* (5–8). Illus. Series: Life in the Renaissance. 2003, Marshall Cavendish LB $29.93 (978-0-7614-1678-4). 96pp. Using London, Paris, and Florence among the examples, this entry in a four-volume series explores most aspects of daily life within the walled cities of Western Europe during the 15th and 16th centuries. Also use *The Court* (2003). (Rev: BL 2/1/04; SLJ 4/04) [940.1]

17339 Prum, Deborah Mazzotta. *Rats, Bulls, and Flying Machines: A History of Renaissance and Reformation* (4–8). Illus. Series: Core Chronicles. 1999, Core Knowledge $21.95 (978-1-890517-19-9); paper $11.95 (978-1-890517-18-2). 106pp. A handsome volume that gives a basic history of the Renaissance and Reformation and highlights the accomplishments of people such as the Medici family, Machiavelli, Michelangelo, Cervantes, Shakespeare, and Gutenberg. (Rev: BL 12/15/99) [909.08]

17340 Schomp, Virginia. *1500* (5–8). Illus. Series: Around the World. 2003, Marshall Cavendish LB $29.93 (978-0-7614-1082-9). 96pp. This absorbing look at civilizations around the world in the year 1500 includes color reproductions, photographs, a timeline, a glossary, and lists of resources. (Rev: BL 6/1–15/03; HBG 3/03) [909]

17341 Schomp, Virginia. *The Italian Renaissance* (5–8). Series: Cultures of the Past. 2002, Marshall Cavendish $29.93 (978-0-7614-1492-6). 80pp. A handsome volume that gives a balanced, well-organized account of the Italian Renaissance, its history, personalities, art, and artifacts. (Rev: BL 1/1–15/03; HBG 3/03) [940.2]

17342 Shuter, Jane. *The Renaissance* (3–6). Series: History Opens Windows. 1999, Heinemann LB $21.36 (978-1-57572-887-2). 32pp. The people, events, and social forces that produced the Renaissance are described in text and pictures. (Rev: SLJ 2/00) [940.2]

17343 Waldman, Nomi J. *The Italian Renaissance* (5–7). Series: Daily Life. 2004, Gale LB $26.20 (978-0-7377-1398-5). 48pp. In simple language, this slim volume describes Italy's rebirth, the blossoming of commerce and culture, and daily life for people of different backgrounds. (Rev: SLJ 2/05) [945]

17344 Wood, Tim. *The Renaissance* (5–8). Series: See Through History. 1993, Viking $19.99 (978-0-670-85149-2). A series of double-page spreads explore the day-to-day lives of people during the Renaissance, including Far East trade, Italian city-states, women at court, art, and technology. (Rev: BL 12/15/93; SLJ 2/94) [940.2]

World War I

17345 Burleigh, Robert. *Fly, Cher Ami, Fly!* (K–2). Illus. by Robert MacKenzie. 2008, Abrams $16.95 (978-0-8109-7097-7). 32pp. The true story of a U.S. Army Signal Corps carrier pigeon that helped to save a battalion in World War I France. (Rev: BL 9/1/08) [940.4]

17346 Clare, John D., ed. *First World War* (5–8). Illus. Series: Living History. 1995, Gulliver $16.95 (978-0-15-200087-5). 64pp. Excellent visuals and a vivid text are used in this history of World War I. (Rev: SLJ 6/95) [940.53]

17347 Conway, John Richard. *World War I* (4–6). Illus. Series: U.S. Wars. 2003, Enslow LB $25.26 (978-0-7660-5142-3). 48pp. Supported by verified and updated Web links, this is a useful overview of the main events of World War I. (Rev: HBG 4/04)

17348 Gay, Kathlyn, and Martin Gay. *World War I* (5–8). Illus. Series: Voices from the Past. 1995, Twenty-First Century LB $25.90 (978-0-8050-2848-5). 64pp. The causes, major battles, and effects of World War I are covered, with many excerpts from personal accounts. (Rev: BL 12/15/95; SLJ 2/96) [940.3]

17349 George, Linda S. *World War I* (5–8). Series: Letters from the Homefront. 2001, Benchmark LB $29.93 (978-0-7614-1096-6). 96pp. Life at the front and at home during the First World War is depicted through letters and other firsthand accounts. (Rev: BL 10/15/01; HBG 3/02) [973.9]

17350 Granfield, Linda. *Where Poppies Grow: A World War I Companion* (4–7). 2002, Stoddart $16.95 (978-0-7737-3319-0). 48pp. The horrors of war in the trenches are portrayed in this scrapbook full of photographs, propaganda, and ephemera that includes accounts of two Canadian soldiers. (Rev: BL 6/1–15/02; HBG 10/02; SLJ 7/02) [940.3]

17351 Grant, Reg. *World War I: Armistice 1918* (5–8). Series: The World Wars. 2001, Raintree LB $27.12 (978-0-7398-2753-6). 64pp. The negotiations that ended World War I are detailed here, with discussion of the failure of the League of Nations and the lead-up to World War II. (Rev: SLJ 6/01) [940.3]

17352 Hamilton, John. *Aircraft of World War I* (5–8). Illus. Series: World War I. 2003, ABDO LB $24.21 (978-1-57765-912-9). 32pp. How aircraft became a valuable military tool for the first time in World War I, and how some of the pilots became internationally famous. (Rev: SLJ 6/04) [940.4]

17353 Hamilton, John. *Battles of World War I* (5–8). Illus. Series: World War I. 2003, ABDO LB $24.21 (978-1-57765-913-6). 32pp. A review of key battles that took place during the three years before the United States entered the conflict in 1917, with information on key figures. (Rev: SLJ 6/04) [940.4]

17354 Hamilton, John. *Events Leading to World War I* (5–8). Illus. Series: World War I. 2003, ABDO LB $24.21 (978-1-57765-914-3). 32pp. An evenhanded description of events and circumstances during the years leading up to World War I in each of the countries that became involved in the conflict. (Rev: SLJ 6/04) [940.3]

17355 Hansen, Ole Steen. *Military Aircraft of WWI* (4–7). Series: The Story of Flight. 2003, Crabtree $25.27 (978-0-7787-1201-5). 32pp. This book introduces in text and pictures the aircraft used by the allies and enemies during World War I. (Rev: BL 10/15/03) [940.3]

17356 Hansen, Ole Steen. *World War I: War in the Trenches* (5–8). Series: The World Wars. 2001, Raintree LB $27.12 (978-0-7398-2752-9). 64pp. The causes of World War I are introduced, followed by information on the major battles and descriptions of the misery of life in the trenches, with plenty of photographs, reproductions, maps, sidebars, and excerpts from primary sources. (Rev: SLJ 6/01) [940.3]

17357 Innes, Stephanie, and Harry Endrulat. *A Bear in War* (2–5). Illus. by Brian Deines. 2009, Key Porter $19.95 (978-1-55470-097-4). 40pp. In World War I, Aileen sends her teddy bear to her father, who is in the trenches; narrated by the bear, the story ends with archival photographs and objects. (Rev: BL 3/1/09; SLJ 4/09) [940.3]

17358 Myers, Walter Dean, and Bill Miles. *The Harlem Hellfighters: When Pride Met Courage* (5–8). Illus. 2006, HarperCollins LB $18.89 (978-0-06-001137-6). 160pp. A tribute to the World War I heroism of the 369th Infantry Regiment, which was made up entirely of African Americans. (Rev: BL 2/1/06; SLJ 4/06) [940.4]

17359 Preston, Diana. *Remember the Lusitania!* (5–8). Illus. 2003, Walker LB $21.85 (978-0-8027-8847-4). 112pp. This gripping account of the sinking of the *Lusitania* includes many personal stories that will hold young readers' attention. (Rev: BL 4/15/03; HB 7/03; HBG 10/03; SLJ 7/03) [940.4]

17360 Ross, Stewart. *Assassination in Sarajevo: The Trigger for World War I* (4–9). Illus. by Stefan Chabluk. Series: Point of Impact. 2001, Heinemann LB $24.22 (978-1-58810-074-0). 32pp. The assassination of the Archduke of Austria, a precipitating factor in World War I, is put into context and the alliances among the world's nations at the time are clearly explained. (Rev: HBG 10/01; SLJ 7/01) [940.3]

17361 Ross, Stewart. *The Battle of the Somme* (5–8). Series: The World Wars. 2003, Raintree LB $28.56 (978-0-7398-5479-2). 64pp. An examination of the first Battle of the Somme in 1916, an all-out assault on entrenched German forces in northern France by British and French troops, and of the enormous carnage involved. (Rev: SLJ 5/04) [940.4]

17362 Ross, Stewart. *Leaders of World War I* (4–8). Illus. Series: World Wars. 2003, Raintree LB $28.56 (978-0-7398-5481-5). 64pp. Stewart presents concise details on the large cast of world and military leaders involved in this conflict. (Rev: BL 12/1/03; HBG 10/03) [023]

17363 Ross, Stewart. *The Technology of World War I* (4–8). Illus. Series: World Wars. 2003, Raintree LB $28.56 (978-0-7398-5482-2). 64pp. New technologies used during World War I included torpedoes, mines, submarines, tanks, planes with machine guns, and mustard gas; all are shown here with maps, diagrams, period reproductions, and posters. (Rev: BL 12/1/03; HBG 10/03; SLJ 7/03) [023]

World War II

17364 Adams, Simon. *World War II* (4–8). Illus. 2000, DK $15.95 (978-0-7894-3298-8). 64pp. Each double-page spread presents a different aspect of World War II, such as the Battle of Britain, military equipment, women at work, and conditions inside the Soviet Union. (Rev: BL 11/1/00) [940.53]

17365 Adler, David A. *Child of the Warsaw Ghetto* (3–6). Illus. by Karen Ritz. 1995, Holiday House LB $16.95 (978-0-8234-1160-3). 32pp. The story of the Warsaw Ghetto during World War II as seen through the eyes of a survivor. (Rev: BCCB 5/95; BL 4/1/95; SLJ 7/95) [943.8]

17366 Adler, David A. *Hiding from the Nazis* (3–5). Illus. by Karen Ritz. 1997, Holiday House LB $16.95 (978-0-8234-1288-4). 32pp. This picture book for older children tells how Lore, a young Jewish girl, is hidden and cared for by a Dutch family during World War II. (Rev: BL 11/1/97; HBG 3/98; SLJ 2/98) [940.53]

17367 Adler, David A. *Hilde and Eli: Children of the Holocaust* (3–5). Illus. by Karen Ritz. 1994, Holiday House $6.95 (978-0-8234-1091-0). 32pp. A picture book that tells the true stories of two Jewish children who were killed in the Holocaust. (Rev: BCCB 11/94; BL 9/15/94; SLJ 12/94) [940.54]

17368 Adler, David A. *We Remember the Holocaust* (4–7). 1995, Holt paper $14.95 (978-0-8050-3715-9). 147pp. Through interview excerpts, the terrible days of the Holocaust are remembered. (Rev: SLJ 12/89) [940.54]

17369 Allen, Thomas B. *Remember Pearl Harbor: American and Japanese Survivors Tell Their Stories* (5–9). Illus. 2001, National Geographic $17.95 (978-0-7922-6690-7). 64pp. First-person accounts by Japanese and American men and women give readers a close-up view of the 1941 Japanese attack on Pearl Harbor, with maps and photographs. (Rev: BL 9/1/01; HBG 3/02; SLJ 9/01*; VOYA 10/01) [940.54]

17370 Altman, Linda J. *Crimes and Criminals of the Holocaust* (5–10). Illus. Series: Holocaust in History. 2004, Enslow LB $26.60 (978-0-7660-1995-9). 104pp. This book focuses on the end of World War II and the war crimes trials in Nuremberg as well as other cases such as that of Adolf Eichmann. (Rev: BL 5/1/04) [940.53]

17371 Altman, Linda J. *The Forgotten Victims of the Holocaust* (5–10). Illus. Series: Holocaust in History. 2003, Enslow LB $26.60 (978-0-7660-1993-5). 104pp. Altman looks at populations victimized by the Nazis that are often overlooked: Poles, Russians, gypsies, homosexuals, and the disabled. Also use *The Jewish Victims of the Holocaust* (2003), which describes Hitler's genocide of the Jews. (Rev: BL 7/03; HBG 4/04; SLJ 10/03) [940.53]

17372 Altman, Linda J. *Impact of the Holocaust* (5–10). Illus. Series: Holocaust in History. 2004, Enslow LB $26.60 (978-0-7660-1996-6). 104pp. Dscusses the Holocaust's influence in the creation

of a homeland for the Jews and a Universal Declaration of Human Rights. (Rev: BL 5/1/04) [940.53]

17373 Anflick, Charles. *Resistance: Teen Partisans and Resisters Who Fought Nazi Tyranny* (5–9). Series: Teen Witnesses to the Holocaust. 1999, Rosen LB $26.50 (978-0-8239-2847-7). 64pp. This volume celebrates the teenagers who fought against the Nazis in ghettos, concentration camps, inside Germany, and in the lands that the Nazis conquered. (Rev: BL 4/15/98; VOYA 8/99) [940.54]

17374 Auerbacher, Inge. *I Am a Star: Child of the Holocaust* (5–7). Illus. 1993, Puffin paper $5.99 (978-0-14-036401-9). 80pp. The memoirs of a former child survivor of the Terezin concentration camp in Czechoslovakia. (Rev: BCCB 7–8/87; BL 6/1/87; SLJ 4/87) [940.5]

17375 Axelrod, Toby. *In the Camps: Teens Who Survived the Nazi Concentration Camps* (5–9). Series: Teen Witnesses to the Holocaust. 1999, Rosen LB $26.50 (978-0-8239-2844-6). These are the stories of teenagers who survived the death camps, their despair and sadness, and the hope they maintained despite the horror around them. (Rev: BL 7/99) [940.54]

17376 Axelrod, Toby. *Rescuers Defying the Nazis: Non-Jewish Teens Who Rescued Jews* (5–8). Series: Teen Witnesses to the Holocaust. 1999, Rosen LB $26.50 (978-0-8239-2848-4). Inspiring stories of teenage gentiles in Poland, Denmark, and Germany who risked their lives to rescue Jews from the Holocaust. (Rev: BL 7/99; SLJ 8/99) [940.54]

17377 Ayer, Eleanor. *In the Ghettos: Teens Who Survived the Ghettos of the Holocaust* (5–8). Series: Teens Witnesses to the Holocaust. 1999, Rosen LB $27.95 (978-0-8239-2845-3). The harrowing stories of courageous teenagers who survived life in the ghettos of Lodz, Theresienstadt, and Warsaw. (Rev: BL 7/99; SLJ 8/99) [940.54]

17378 Bachrach, Susan D. *Tell Them We Remember: The Story of the Holocaust* (5–9). 1994, Little, Brown $21.95 (978-0-316-69264-9). A photohistory focusing on the young who struggled through the brutality of the Holocaust following the destruction of their world of family and friends. (Rev: BL 7/94*; SLJ 11/94; VOYA 12/94) [940.54]

17379 Beller, Susan P. *Battling in the Pacific: Soldiering in World War II* (5–8). 2007, Twenty-First Century LB $33.26 (978-0-8225-6381-5). 112pp. After background information on the war, this volume examines the life of soldiers in the Pacific and provides interesting sidebar features and photographs. (Rev: SLJ 1/08)

17380 Bodden, Valerie. *The Bombing of Hiroshima and Nagasaki* (5–9). Illus. Series: Days of Change. 2007, Creative Education LB $21.95 (978-1-58341-545-0). 48pp. Survivors of the bombings in both cities recall the horrors of the attacks; a brief background on World War II will help readers to place the bombings in context. (Rev: BL 12/15/07; SLJ 3/08) [940.54]

17381 Brooks, Philip. *The Tuskegee Airmen* (3–6). Illus. Series: We the People. 2004, Compass Point LB $26.60 (978-0-7565-0683-4). 48pp. A well-illustrated, concise account of the achievements of the African American pilots who flew during World War II.

17382 Coerr, Eleanor. *Sadako* (1–5). Illus. by Ed Young. 1993, Penguin $17.99 (978-0-399-21771-5). 40pp. A picture-book version of the story of a young Japanese girl dying of leukemia as a result of the bombing of Hiroshima. (Rev: BCCB 12/93; BL 11/1/93*; SLJ 12/93*) [362.1]

17383 Cretzmeyer, Stacy. *Your Name Is Renée: Ruth Kapp Hartz's Story as a Hidden Child in Nazi-Occupied France* (5–8). 2003, Bt. Bound $22.20 (978-0-613-56879-1). 240pp. The story of a German Jewish family living in France during the Holocaust, how they survived, and how young Ruth hid in an orphanage run by Catholic nuns. (Rev: BCCB 7–8/99; SLJ 8/99) [940.54]

17384 Crewe, Sabrina, and Dale Anderson. *The Atom Bomb Project* (3–5). Series: Events That Shaped America. 2005, Gareth Stevens LB $26.00 (978-0-8368-3404-8). 32pp. A simple, straightforward account of the Manhattan Project featuring direct quotations, editorial cartoons, photographs, reproductions, and newspaper clippings. (Rev: SLJ 3/05) [355.8]

17385 Cross, Robin. *Children and War* (4–7). Illus. Series: World War II. 1994, Thomson Learning LB $24.26 (978-1-56847-180-8). 48pp. True case histories of children in various circumstances during World War II, including in a gulag, the resistance movement, and a death camp. (Rev: BL 12/15/94; SLJ 2/95) [940.53]

17386 De Capua, Sarah E. *The Tuskegee Airmen* (4–6). Series: Journey to Freedom. 2009, The Child's World LB $28.50 (978-1-60253-138-3). 32pp. The inspiring story of the World War II squadron of African American pilots. (Rev: SLJ 7/09)

17387 Devaney, John. *America Goes to War: 1941* (5–8). 1991, Walker LB $17.85 (978-0-8027-6980-0). An illustrated, datelined, day-by-day account that covers personal and public events of America's first year of World War II. (Rev: BL 10/1/91; SLJ 8/91) [940.53]

17388 Drez, Ronald J. *Remember D-Day: The Plan, the Invasion, Survivor Stories* (4–8). 2004, National Geographic $17.95 (978-0-7922-6666-2). 64pp. Filled with period photographs and personal stories, this large-format survey of the Allied invasion of Normandy focuses on the military operation and on the strategic planning that preceded it. (Rev: BL 7/04; SLJ 7/04) [940.54]

17389 Drucker, Olga L. *Kindertransport* (5–8). 1995, Holt paper $8.95 (978-0-8050-4251-1). 146pp. A true account of a Jewish girl sent from Germany to live in England until she could join her parents in New York City in 1945. (Rev: BCCB 1/93; SLJ 11/92) [940.54]

17390 Dvorson, Alexa. *The Hitler Youth: Marching Toward Madness* (5–9). Illus. Series: Teen Witnesses to the Holocaust. 1999, Rosen LB $27.95 (978-0-8239-2783-8). 64pp. This volume describes how thousands of German boys and girls joined the Hitler Youth, why they were seduced into obeying the Nazis, and how their dreams were eventually shattered. (Rev: BL 4/15/99) [943.086]

17391 Fitzgerald, Brian. *Under Fire in World War II* (4–6). Series: On the Front Line. 2005, Raintree LB $29.93 (978-1-4109-1468-2). 48pp. This is an accessible overview of the key events of World War II, with first-person accounts, photographs, fact boxes, and a timeline. (Rev: SLJ 12/05) [940.54]

17392 Fox, Anne L., and Eva Abraham-Podietz. *Ten Thousand Children: True Stories Told by Children Who Escaped the Holocaust on the Kindertransport* (5–8). Illus. 1998, Behrman paper $12.95 (978-0-87441-648-0). 128pp. The moving stories of 21 survivors who were part of the rescue operation known as the Kindertransport that took 10,000 Jewish children from Nazi-occupied Europe to freedom during late 1938 and 1939. (Rev: BL 1/1–15/99) [940.53]

17393 Friedman, Laurie. *Angel Girl* (4–6). Illus. by Ofra Amit. 2008, Carolrhoda $16.95 (978-0-8225-8739-2). 32pp. Based on a true concentration camp story, this compelling book tells how 11-year-old Herman is saved from starvation when a farm girl risks her life to throw him apples. (Rev: BCCB 1/09; BL 8/08; LMC 1/09; SLJ 8/08) [940.53]

17394 Giddens, Sandra. *Escape: Teens Who Escaped the Holocaust to Freedom* (5–9). Series: Teen Witnesses to the Holocaust. 1999, Rosen LB $27.95 (978-0-8239-2843-9). 64pp. This volume focuses on the ordeals of four Jewish teens who were able to elude the Nazis during the Holocaust. (Rev: BL 4/15/98; VOYA 8/99) [940.54]

17395 Gorman, Jacqueline Laks. *Pearl Harbor: A Primary Source History* (5–8). Illus. Series: In Their Own Words. 2009, Gareth Stevens $27.00 (978-1-4339-0047-1). 48pp. With excerpts from primary sources, narrative text, and many photographs, this is an overview of events leading up to the attack on Pearl Harbor, the attack itself, the aftermath, and its importance today, with profiles of key figures. (Rev: BL 4/1/09) [940.54]

17396 Gourley, Catherine. *Welcome to Molly's World, 1944: Growing Up in World War Two America* (3–6). Illus. Series: American Girls Collection. 1999, Pleasant $14.95 (978-1-56247-773-8). 58pp. This book focuses on the human side of World War II, employing material on a USO canteen, blackouts in the U.S., rationing, air raids in England, and V-E Day. (Rev: BL 1/1–15/00; HBG 3/00) [940.53]

17397 Hama, Larry, and Anthony Williams. *The Battle of Iwo Jima: Guerrilla Warfare in the Pacific* (5–8). Illus. Series: Graphic Battles of World War II. 2007, Rosen LB $29.25 (978-1-4042-0781-3). 48pp. After background text to provide context, this graphic novel account of the battle of Iwo Jima takes readers behind the lines on both sides of the bloody conflict. (Rev: BL 4/1/07; SLJ 7/07) [940.54]

17398 Jones, Steven L. *The Red Tails: World War II's Tuskegee Airmen* (4–8). Illus. Series: Cover-to-Cover. 2002, Perfection Learning $17.95 (978-0-7569-0251-3); paper $8.95 (978-0-7891-5487-3). 64pp. The story of the heroic African American squadron of World War II fighter pilots, their successful missions, and the prejudices they faced. (Rev: BL 5/1/02) [940.5404]

17399 Kacer, Kathy. *Hiding Edith: A Holocaust Remembrance Book for Young Readers* (4–7). Illus. 2006, Second Story $10.95 (978-1-897187-06-7). 120pp. Focusing on a young Jewish girl named Edith Schwalb, this is the story of a French couple who hid 100 Jewish refugee children during World War II with the help of their town. (Rev: BL 12/1/06; SLJ 12/06) [940.53]

17400 Kacer, Kathy. *The Underground Reporters: A True Story* (5–8). Illus. 2005, Second Story $11.95 (978-1-896764-85-6). 156pp. Based on real events, this inspiring story tells how a newspaper, published by a group of Jewish teenagers in Budejovice, Czechoslovakia, helped to lift the spirits of the Jewish community during the years of Nazi occupation. (Rev: BL 2/15/05; SLJ 8/05) [940.53]

17401 King, David C. *World War II Days: Discover the Past with Exciting Projects, Games, Activities, and Recipes* (4–6). Illus. by Cheryl K. Noll. Series: American Kids in History. 2000, Wiley paper $12.95 (978-0-471-37101-4). 100pp. Interspersed with material on the home front during World War II are easy-to-perform projects such as making a victory garden, a flashlight, a periscope, a crystal radio, and a wind vane. (Rev: SLJ 2/01) [940.54]

17402 Kodama, Tatsuharu. *Shin's Tricycle* (5–8). Trans. by Kazuko Hokumen-Jones. Illus. by Noriyuki Ando. 1995, Walker LB $16.85 (978-0-8027-8376-9). 32pp. A father recalls the life of his young son, who was killed in the bombing of Hiroshima. (Rev: BCCB 12/95; BL 9/1/95*; SLJ 12/95) [940.54]

17403 Kramer, Ann. *Women and War* (5–8). Illus. Series: World War II. 2009, Sea-to-Sea LB $18.95 (978-1-59771-142-5). 32pp. Double-page spreads look at the situation of women during World War II, whether volunteering, serving in the military, working in factories or on farms, or coping with shortages. (Rev: BL 4/1/09) [940.53]

17404 Kuhn, Betsy. *Angels of Mercy* (5–8). Illus. 1999, Simon & Schuster $18.00 (978-0-689-82044-1). 128pp. A series of narratives on courage and bravery gives us a fascinating look at the contributions of nurses in World War II. (Rev: BCCB 12/99; BL 10/15/99; HBG 3/00; SLJ 11/99; VOYA 4/00) [940.54]

17405 Kustanowitz, Esther. *The Hidden Children of the Holocaust: Teens Who Hid from the Nazis* (5–9). Series: Teen Witnesses to the Holocaust. 1999, Rosen LB $26.50 (978-0-8239-2562-9). 64pp. Many first-person narratives are used in this account of teenage Jews who hid in homes, barns, and forests or disguised themselves as non-Jews to escape the Nazis. (Rev: BL 7/99; SLJ 8/99) [940.54]

17406 Langley, Wanda. *Flying Higher: The Women Airforce Service Pilots of World War II* (5–8). Illus. 2002, Linnet $25.00 (978-0-208-02506-7). 128pp. The women who flew in World War II gained little glory for performing many vital tasks; this arresting volume focuses on the director of the service, Jacqueline Cochran, and one of the pilots. (Rev: BL

11/1/02; HBG 3/03; SLJ 8/02; VOYA 12/02) [940.54]

17407 Lawson, Don. *The French Resistance* (5–9). 1984, Messner LB $8.79 (978-0-671-50832-6). The story of the many gallant French men and women who defied death to oppose the German forces that occupied their country. [940.53]

17408 Levine, Karen. *Hana's Suitcase* (5–8). Illus. 2003, Albert Whitman $15.95 (978-0-8075-3148-8). 112pp. A Japanese curator of a Holocaust exhibit traces the owner of a suitcase and learns the story of young Hana, who died in Auschwitz. (Rev: BL 3/15/03; HB 5/03; HBG 10/03) [940.53]

17409 Levy, Pat. *Causes* (5–9). Series: The Holocaust. 2001, Raintree LB $28.54 (978-0-7398-3257-8). 64pp. Levy discusses the causes of the Holocaust, looking at historical, religious, political, social, and economic factors. Also use *The Death Camps* (2002). (Rev: HBG 10/02; SLJ 2/02; VOYA 4/02) [940.5318]

17410 Levy, Pat. *The Home Front in World War II* (5–8). Series: The World Wars. 2003, Raintree LB $28.56 (978-0-7398-6065-6). 64pp. A description of life on the home front in World War II, both in the Allied countries and the Axis countries, including the bombing, refugees, and various shortages. (Rev: SLJ 5/04) [940.53]

17411 McGowen, Tom. *Carrier War: Aircraft Carriers in World War II* (5–7). Series: Military Might. 2001, Twenty-First Century LB $26.90 (978-0-7613-1808-8). 64pp. An introduction to the importance of aircraft carriers in World War II, with coverage of Pearl Harbor and major battles in the Pacific. (Rev: HBG 10/01; SLJ 6/01) [940.54]

17412 McGowen, Tom. *Germany's Lightning War: Panzer Divisions of World War II* (5–8). Series: Military Might. 1999, Twenty-First Century LB $26.90 (978-0-7613-1511-7). 64pp. After a general history of tank warfare, this account focuses on the Germans' Panzer tank divisions and the part they played in World War II. (Rev: HBG 3/00; SLJ 9/99) [940.54]

17413 McGowen, Tom. *Sink the Bismarck: Germany's Super-Battleship of World War II* (5–8). Series: Military Might. 1999, Twenty-First Century LB $26.90 (978-0-7613-1510-0). 64pp. A history of German sea power during World War II and the many (eventually successful) British efforts to sink the *Bismarck*. (Rev: HBG 3/00; SLJ 9/99) [940.54]

17414 McNeese, Tim. *The Attack on Pearl Harbor* (5–8). Illus. Series: First Battles. 2001, Morgan Reynolds LB $23.95 (978-1-883846-78-7). 112pp. This book details the 1941 attack on Pearl Harbor and explains the conditions in Japan that led to the assault. (Rev: BL 10/1/01; HBG 3/02; SLJ 1/02; VOYA 12/01) [940.54]

17415 Maruki, Toshi. *Hiroshima No Pika* (3–6). Illus. by author. 1982, Lothrop $17.99 (978-0-688-01297-7). 48pp. The story of a seven-year-old girl and the bombing of Hiroshima in 1945.

17416 Marx, Trish. *Echoes of World War II* (5–8). Illus. 1994, Lerner LB $14.95 (978-0-8225-4898-0). 96pp. The true stories of six children around the world whose lives were changed dramatically by World War II. (Rev: BCCB 5/94; BL 9/15/94; SLJ 5/94) [940.53]

17417 Milman, Barbara. *Light in the Shadows* (5–9). Illus. 1997, Jonathan David paper $14.95 (978-0-8246-0401-1). Illustrated with powerful woodcut prints, this book tells the story of five Holocaust survivors. (Rev: BL 11/15/97) [940.53]

17418 Mochizuki, Ken. *Passage to Freedom: The Sugihara Story* (3–5). Illus. by Dom Lee. 1997, Lee & Low $15.95 (978-1-880000-49-6). 32pp. The story of Chiune Sugihara, the Japanese consul in Lithuania, and how he issued visas during the Holocaust that enabled Polish Jews to escape. (Rev: BL 5/15/97; HB 11/97; HBG 3/98; SLJ 7/97) [940.53]

17419 Nicholson, Dorinda M. *Remember World War II: Kids Who Survived Tell Their Stories* (5–8). Illus. Series: Remember. 2005, National Geographic LB $27.90 (978-0-7922-7191-8). 64pp. First-person accounts of World War II are given historical context plus illustrations, maps, and so forth; Madeleine Albright contributes an effective introduction. (Rev: BL 7/05; SLJ 8/05) [940.53]

17420 Nobleman, Marc Tyler. *The Sinking of the USS Indianapolis* (4–7). Series: We the People. 2006, Compass Point LB $26.60 (978-0-7565-2031-1). 48pp. The story of the sinking of the *USS Indianapolis,* two weeks before the end of World War II, is told in straightforward text, with photographs and useful "Did You Know?" features. (Rev: SLJ 1/07)

17421 Panchyk, Richard. *World War II for Kids: A History with 21 Activities* (5–7). Illus. 2002, Chicago Review paper $14.95 (978-1-55652-455-4). 164pp. Features on such topics as living on rations for a day, growing a victory garden, and tracking a ship's movements depict conditions in America and Europe during the war. (Rev: SLJ 12/02) [940.53]

17422 Perl, Lila, and Marion B. Lazan. *Four Perfect Pebbles: A Holocaust Story* (5–9). Illus. 1996, Greenwillow $16.99 (978-0-688-14294-0). A memoir of the horror and incredible tribulations suffered by the author's family in the detention camps and later death camps during the Holocaust. (Rev: BL 4/1/96; SLJ 5/96) [940.53]

17423 Pfeifer, Kathryn B. *The 761st Tank Battalion* (5–8). Series: African American Soldiers. 1994, Twenty-First Century LB $24.90 (978-0-8050-3057-0). The history of an outfit of African American soldiers who served with distinction during World War II but were marginalized by racism. (Rev: BL 9/1/94; SLJ 11/94) [940.54]

17424 Pringle, Laurence. *One Room School* (1–4). Illus. by Barbara Garrison. 1998, Boyds Mills $16.95 (978-1-56397-583-7). This is a memoir by the noted author in which he remembers the year 1944, when he was attending a one-room school and collecting scrap metal for the war effort. (Rev: BCCB 4/98; BL 3/1/98; HBG 10/98; SLJ 4/98) [371]

17425 Raum, Elizabeth. *World War II: An Interactive History Adventure* (3–5). Illus. 2008, Capstone LB $20.99 (978-1-4296-2344-5). 112pp. Find yourself

in the thick of World War II and choose between many available roles — an American soldier and a Dutch resistance worker, to name just two. (Rev: BL 4/1/09) [940.53]

17426 Rice, Earle, Jr. *Blitzkrieg! Hitler's Lightning War* (5–8). Illus. Series: Monumental Milestones: Great Events of Modern Times. 2008, Mitchell Lane LB $20.95 (978-1-58415-542-3). 48pp. The joint air-and-ground attacks that brought Hitler great success at the outset of World War II are the focus of this book that will interest reluctant readers. (Rev: BL 2/15/08) [940.54]

17427 Rogow, Sally M. *Faces of Courage: Young Heroes of World War II* (5–9). 2003, Granville Island $12.95 (978-1-894694-20-9). 144pp. Based on true stories, this volume presents 12 fictionalized accounts of heroic actions by teenagers under Nazi rule in Europe. (Rev: BL 10/15/03) [940.53]

17428 Rubin, Susan G. *Fireflies in the Dark: The Story of Friedl Dicker-Brandeis and the Children of Terezin* (5–10). Illus. 2000, Holiday $18.95 (978-0-8234-1461-1). 48pp. A heartbreaking picture book that reproduces some of the artwork and writings of the children imprisoned at the Terezin concentration camp, where only 100 of 15,000 children survived. (Rev: BCCB 11/00; BL 7/00*; HB 9/00; HBG 10/00; SLJ 8/00) [940.53]

17429 Rubin, Susan G. *The Flag with Fifty-Six Stars* (4–6). Illus. by Bill Farnsworth. 2005, Holiday House $16.95 (978-0-8234-1653-0). 40pp. A picture book for older readers about the prisoners at the Mauthausen concentration camp and the American flag they sewed — with six extra stars. (Rev: BL 3/15/05; SLJ 5/05) [940.53]

17430 Rubin, Susan G. *Searching for Anne Frank: Letters from Amsterdam to Iowa* (5–12). 2003, Abrams $19.95 (978-0-8109-4514-2). 144pp. A brief penpal exchange between two sisters in Iowa and Anne Frank and her sister serves as the basis for a comparison between life in America and life for Jews in Europe. (Rev: BL 11/1/03; HB 11/03; HBG 4/04; SLJ 11/03; VOYA 10/03) [940.5]

17431 Russo, Marisabina. *Always Remember Me: How One Family Survived World War II* (3–5). Illus. 2005, Simon & Schuster $16.95 (978-0-689-86920-4). 48pp. In this moving picture book for older readers, Oma shows her granddaughter family photographs and tells about her Jewish relatives' experiences in the Second World War. (Rev: BL 3/1/05; HBG 9/98; SLJ 4/05) [940.53]

17432 Santella, Andrew. *Navajo Code Talkers* (3–6). Illus. Series: We the People. 2004, Compass Point LB $26.60 (978-0-7565-0611-7). 48pp. This absorbing account of the work of the Navajo Code Talkers during World War II includes a chart of code words for the letters of the alphabet. (Rev: BL 5/1/04; SLJ 8/04) [940.54]

17433 Santella, Andrew. *Pearl Harbor* (4–6). Series: We the People. 2004, Compass Point LB $26.60 (978-0-7565-0680-3). 48pp. A well-illustrated brief discussion of the attack, the events leading up to it, and the building of the memorial. (Rev: SLJ 2/05) [940.54]

17434 Schroeder, Peter W., and Dagmar Schroeder-Hildebrand. *Six Million Paper Clips: The Making of a Children's Holocaust Memorial* (5–8). Illus. 2004, Kar-Ben $17.95 (978-1-58013-169-8); paper $7.95 (978-1-58013-176-6). 64pp. This is the story of a Tennessee school project in which students collected 11 million paper clips to help them grasp the magnitude of the Holocaust's human toll. (Rev: BL 1/1–15/05; SLJ 7/05) [940.53]

17435 Shapiro, Stephen, and Tina Forrester. *Ultra Hush-Hush: Espionage and Special Missions* (5–8). Illus. by David Craig. Series: Outwitting the Enemy. 2003, Annick LB $29.95 (978-1-55037-779-8); paper $14.95 (978-1-55037-778-1). 96pp. Undercover activities during World War II are the focus of this volume that covers such groups and missions as the Navajo Code Talkers and Britain's double agents. (Rev: BL 8/03; SLJ 5/04) [940.54]

17436 Sheehan, Sean. *The Technology of World War II* (5–8). 2003, Raintree LB $28.56 (978-0-7398-6064-9). 64pp. New technologies introduced during World War II include radar, microwave transmissions, V-1 and V-2 rockets, the jet, codes, chemical and biological weapons, and the atom bomb. (Rev: HBG 10/03; SLJ 7/03) [940.54]

17437 Shuter, Jane, ed. *Christabel Bielenberg and Nazi Germany* (5–8). Illus. Series: History Eyewitness. 1996, Raintree LB $24.26 (978-0-8114-8285-1). Using a first-person narrative as a framework, this account traces the growth, flowering, and defeat of Nazism in Germany. (Rev: BL 5/15/96; SLJ 6/96) [943.086]

17438 Stalcup, Ann. *On the Home Front: Growing Up in Wartime England* (4–6). Illus. 1998, Linnet $19.50 (978-0-208-02482-4). 103pp. Important English children's writers, including Nina Bawden and Robert Westall, share their memories of growing up in wartime England. (Rev: BCCB 9/98; BL 10/15/98; HBG 10/98) [940.54]

17439 Steele, D. Kelly. *Would You Salute? One Child's Story of the Holocaust* (3–4). Illus. by Becky Hyatt Rickenbaker. 2006, Hidden Path $22.95 (978-0-9711534-2-4). 48pp. Margot, whose mother is Christian and whose father is Jewish, faces difficult choices in Nazi Germany. (Rev: BL 7/06) [940.53]

17440 Stein, R. Conrad. *World War II in the Pacific* (4–6). Illus. Series: U.S. Wars. 2002, Enslow LB $25.26 (978-0-7660-5093-8). 48pp. Supported by verified and updated Web links, this is a useful overview of the fighting in the Pacific during World War II. Also use *World War II in Europe* (2002). (Rev: HBG 3/03)

17441 Steins, Richard. *The Allies Against the Axis: World War II (1940–1950)* (5–8). Series: First Person America. 1994, Twenty-First Century LB $20.90 (978-0-8050-2586-6). An introduction to World War II and early postwar conditions, with generous use of primary sources. (Rev: BL 5/15/94; SLJ 12/94) [940.53]

17442 Talbott, Hudson. *Forging Freedom* (4–7). Illus. 2000, Putnam $15.99 (978-0-399-23434-7). 64pp. This is the story of Jaap Penraat, a young architectural student in Amsterdam during the Nazi occupation who saved hundreds of Jews from deportation by forging papers and smuggling them out of the city. (Rev: BCCB 11/00; BL 7/00; HB 1/01; HBG 3/01; SLJ 11/00) [940.53]

17443 Tanaka, Shelley. *Attack on Pearl Harbor: The True Story of the Day America Entered World War II* (5–8). Illus. Series: I Was There. 2001, Hyperion $19.99 (978-0-7868-0736-9). 64pp. An absorbing account of Pearl Harbor that presents the real-life, and very different, experiences of four young men who were there. (Rev: BL 8/01; HBG 10/01; SLJ 11/01; VOYA 12/01) [940.54]

17444 Taylor, Theodore. *Air Raid — Pearl Harbor: The Story of December 7, 1941* (5–8). 1991, Harcourt paper $6.00 (978-0-15-201655-5). 179pp. A fine account of why the attack occurred and the effects that were felt around the world. A revised edition. (Rev: SLJ 12/91) [940.54]

17445 Tito, E. Tina. *Liberation: Teens in the Concentration Camps and the Teen Soldiers Who Liberated Them* (5–9). Illus. Series: Teen Witnesses to the Holocaust. 1999, Rosen LB $26.50 (978-0-8239-2846-0). 64pp. A harrowing account in which two teenage Nazi camp survivors and two American soldiers who were also teenagers during World War II tell their respective stories. (Rev: BL 4/15/99; VOYA 8/99) [940.53]

17446 Vander Zee, Ruth. *Erika's Story* (3–6). Illus. by Roberto Innocenti. 2003, Creative $15.95 (978-1-56846-176-2). 24pp. A Jewish woman tells how an infant was thrown by her mother from a train headed for a concentration camp. (Rev: BL 11/1/03; HBG 4/04; SLJ 12/03)

17447 van Maarsen, Jacqueline, and Carol Ann Lee. *A Friend Called Anne: One Girl's Story of War, Peace, and a Unique Friendship with Anne Frank* (5–8). 2005, Viking $15.99 (978-0-670-05958-4). 176pp. Anne Frank's ordinary life before the war, and how things changed once the Nazis arrived, told by Anne's childhood friend. (Rev: BL 4/1/05; SLJ 4/05) [940.53]

17448 Warren, Andrea. *Surviving Hitler: A Boy in the Nazi Death Camps* (5–10). Illus. 2001, HarperCollins LB $17.89 (978-0-06-029218-8). 160pp. The true story of Jack Mandelbaum, who as a teenager survived three years in Nazi death camps through a combination of luck, courage, and friendship. (Rev: BCCB 3/01; BL 1/1–15/01; HB 3/01; HBG 10/01; SLJ 3/01) [940.53]

17449 Welch, Catherine A. *Children of the Relocation Camps* (3–6). Series: Picture the American Past. 2000, Carolrhoda $22.60 (978-1-57505-350-9). 48pp. The story of the relocation of thousands of Japanese Americans after Pearl Harbor, how the children reacted, and how they built new lives within the camps. (Rev: BL 6/1–15/00; HBG 10/00; SLJ 10/00) [940.54]

17450 White, Steve. *The Battle of Midway: The Destruction of the Japanese Fleet* (5–9). Illus. by Richard Elson. Series: Graphic Battles of World War II. 2007, Rosen LB $29.25 (978-1-4042-0783-7). 48pp. Historically accurate and detailed, this graphic account will engage readers in the story of an important World War II battle. (Rev: SLJ 7/07)

17451 Whiteman, Dorit Bader. *Lonek's Journey: The True Story of a Boy's Escape to Freedom* (5–8). Illus. 2005, Star Bright $15.95 (978-1-59572-021-4). 144pp. In this gripping true story that starts in 1939, a young Jew named Lonek survives the Nazis' arrival in Poland, a slave labor camp in Siberia, and the long, perilous journey to Palestine. (Rev: BL 11/15/05*; HBG 4/06; LMC 5/06; SLJ 1/06) [940.53]

17452 Whiting, Jim. *The Story of the Holocaust* (5–7). Series: Monumental Milestones: Great Events of Modern Times. 2006, Mitchell Lane LB $29.95 (978-1-58415-400-6). 48pp. Although slim, this volume conveys a lot of information about the roots and atrocities of the Holocaust. (Rev: SLJ 5/06) [940.53]

17453 Whitman, Sylvia. *Children of the World War II Home Front* (3–6). Series: Picture the American Past. 2001, Carolrhoda LB $22.60 (978-1-57505-484-1). 48pp. The lifestyle of children in America during World War II is presented through text and historic photographs. (Rev: BL 6/1–15/01; HBG 10/01; SLJ 7/01) [940.54]

17454 Whitman, Sylvia. *Uncle Sam Wants You!* (5–7). Illus. 1993, Lerner LB $30.35 (978-0-8225-1728-3). 80pp. This work describes the experiences of the many men and women who served in the various armed forces during World War II. (Rev: BL 5/1/93) [940.54]

Modern History

17455 Burgan, Michael. *The Berlin Airlift* (4–7). Series: We the People. 2006, Compass Point LB $26.60 (978-0-7565-2024-3). 48pp. The story of the Berlin Airlift is told in straightforward text, with photographs and useful "Did You Know?" features. (Rev: SLJ 1/07) [943]

17456 Burgan, Michael. *The My Lai Massacre* (5–8). Series: We the People. 2008, Compass Point LB $26.60 (978-0-7565-3849-1). 48pp. A simple account of the massacre with large photographs, useful for young researchers and reluctant readers. (Rev: SLJ 12/08) [959.704]

17457 Englar, Mary. *The Tet Offensive* (5–8). Series: We the People. 2008, Compass Point LB $26.60 (978-0-7565-3844-6). 48pp. A simple account of the offensive with discussion of its importance and large photographs, useful for young researchers and reluctant readers. (Rev: SLJ 12/08) [959.704]

17458 Gallagher, Jim. *Causes of the Iraq War* (5–8). Illus. Series: Road to War. 2005, OTTN LB $22.95 (978-1-59556-009-4). 72pp. Explores the case put forward for the recent Iraq War, along with the views of those who oppose the conflict with good illustrations and appended material. (Rev: BL 10/15/05) [956.7044]

17459 Gunderson, Cory. *The Need for Oil* (5–8). Illus. Series: World in Conflict. 2004, ABDO LB $25.65 (978-1-59197-417-8). 48pp. This history of conflicts over oil includes useful statistics and will be helpful to students seeking information for reports or background context before the recent Iraq war. (Rev: BL 4/1/04; SLJ 3/04) [338.2]

17460 Holden, Henry M. *The Persian Gulf War* (4–8). Series: U.S. Wars. 2003, Enslow LB $25.26 (978-0-7660-5109-6). 48pp. This concise, interesting account of the conflict in the early 1990s is enhanced by Internet access to a set of monitored Web links. (Rev: HBG 10/03; SLJ 8/03) [956.7]

17461 Murdico, Suzanne J. *The Gulf War* (5–9). Illus. Series: War and Conflict in the Middle East. 2004, Rosen LB $27.95 (978-0-8239-4551-1). 64pp. Examines the 1991 war between Iraq and a coalition of nations. (Rev: BL 11/1/04) [956.7]

17462 Santella, Andrew. *The Korean War* (4–7). Series: We the People. 2006, Compass Point LB $26.60 (978-0-7565-2027-4). 48pp. A brief overview of the roots and progress of the conflict between the two parts of a divided nation. (Rev: SLJ 1/07) [951.904]

17463 Santella, Andrew. *The Persian Gulf War* (3–6). Illus. Series: We the People. 2004, Compass Point LB $26.60 (978-0-7565-0612-4). 48pp. Provides a concise description of the fall of Kuwait, the formation of the Desert Storm coalition, and the aftermath. [956.7]

17464 Schaffer, David. *The Iran-Iraq War* (5–8). Illus. Series: World History. 2002, Gale LB $32.45 (978-1-59018-184-3). 128pp. Schaffer traces the causes and progress of this long war, incorporating useful primary and secondary source material plus interesting sidebar features. (Rev: BL 5/1/03) [955.05]

17465 Smith-Llera, Danielle. *Vietnam War POWs* (5–8). Series: We the People. 2008, Compass Point LB $26.60 (978-0-7565-3846-0). 48pp. A simple discussion of the plight of prisoners of war with large photographs, useful for young researchers and reluctant readers. (Rev: SLJ 12/08) [959.704]

17466 Stanley, George E. *America and the Cold War (1949–1969)* (5–8). Illus. Series: A Primary Source History of the United States. 2005, World Almanac LB $31.00 (978-0-8368-5830-3). 48pp. A simple narrative links well-chosen primary sources documenting the key events of the Cold War. Also use *America in Today's World (1969–2004)* (2005). (Rev: BL 4/1/05)

17467 Taylor, David. *The Cold War* (5–9). Illus. Series: 20th Century Perspectives. 2001, Heinemann LB $25.64 (978-1-57572-434-8). 48pp. An easily understood account of the causes of tension between the Soviet Union and the West and the major crises of the "war." (Rev: HBG 3/02; SLJ 11/01) [909.825]

17468 Willoughby, Douglas. *The Vietnam War* (5–9). Series: 20th Century Perspectives. 2001, Heinemann LB $25.64 (978-1-57572-439-3). 48pp. An easily understood and attractive account of Vietnam's relations with China, and of French and U.S. involvement in the country's affairs. (Rev: SLJ 11/01) [959]

Geographical Regions

Africa

General

17469 Banting, Erinn. *The Nile River: The Longest River in the World* (3–6). Illus. Series: Natural Wonders. 2004, Weigl LB $18.20 (978-1-59036-269-3). 32pp. A look at the history of the Nile, the people who live on its banks, the animals and plants it supports, and the environmental threats it faces. (Rev: BL 4/1/04; HBG 3/03; SLJ 4/05)

17470 Bingham, Jane. *African Art and Culture* (5–8). Illus. Series: World Art and Culture. 2004, Raintree LB $29.99 (978-0-7398-6606-1). 56pp. The indigenous art and culture of Africa from prehistoric times to the present are beautifully captured in this handsome and comprehensive overview. (Rev: BL 4/1/04; SLJ 2/04) [709]

17471 Bowden, Rob. *Africa* (5–8). Series: Continents of the World. 2006, World Almanac LB $34.00 (978-0-8368-5910-2). 64pp. Factboxes and "In Focus" articles add to this overview of the history, geography, people, culture, and so forth of the continent of Africa. (Rev: SLJ 2/06)

17472 Bowden, Rob. *The Nile* (5–7). Series: A River Journey. 2003, Raintree LB $28.56 (978-0-7398-6072-4). 48pp. A trip down the length of East Africa's Nile, from its source to the sea, and a look at its importance to the people who live along it and the challenge of pollution, with photographs, maps, and charts. (Rev: SLJ 3/04) [916.2]

17473 Bowden, Rob. *Settlements of the Nile* (3–5). Illus. Series: Rivers Through Time. 2005, Heinemann LB $29.93 (978-1-4034-5720-2). 48pp. Traces the history and contemporary life of major settlements along the Nile, discussing environmental and other important issues.

17474 Croze, Harvey. *Africa for Kids: Exploring a Vibrant Continent* (4–7). Illus. 2006, Chicago Review paper $17.95 (978-1-55652-598-8). 176pp. Africa's diversity is highlighted in this accessible volume that covers history, nature, key individuals, and contemporary problems such as poverty, war, AIDS, and the environment; there are 19 activities. (Rev: BL 8/06) [916.22]

17475 Golding, Vivien. *Traditions from Africa* (3–6). Illus. Series: Cultural Journeys. 1999, Raintree $25.69 (978-0-8172-8382-7). 48pp. This photoessay gives a quick view of some of the cultural characteristics of various African regions. (Rev: BL 5/15/99) [306]

17476 Graf, Mike. *Africa* (K–3). Series: Continents. 2002, Capstone LB $21.26 (978-0-7368-1414-0). 24pp. With maps and full-color graphics, this is a brief introduction to the geography, history, flora, fauna, and peoples of Africa. (Rev: HBG 3/03; SLJ 4/03)

17477 Haskins, James, and Kathleen Benson. *African Beginnings* (3–7). Illus. by Floyd Cooper. 1998, Lothrop $18.99 (978-0-688-10256-2). 48pp. Eleven ancient African cultures, including the Egyptian, are described, beginning with Nubia around 3800 B.C. (Rev: BL 2/15/98; HBG 10/98; SLJ 6/98) [960]

17478 Knight, Margy B., and Mark Melnicove. *Africa Is Not a Country* (1–3). Illus. by Anne S. O'Brien. 2000, Millbrook $24.90 (978-0-7613-1266-6). 40pp. This book celebrates the diversity of the African continent by portraying children from various countries and supplying a vignette about each of them. (Rev: BL 11/15/00; HBG 3/01; SLJ 1/01) [960]

17479 Meister, Cari. *Nile River* (3–4). Series: Rivers and Lakes. 2002, ABDO LB $21.35 (978-1-57765-098-0). 24pp. A solid introduction to the Nile, its tributaries, flora and fauna, and the ways in which it has influenced human development in the area throughout history. (Rev: HBG 10/02; SLJ 7/02) [960]

17480 Pollard, Michael. *The Nile* (4–6). Series: Great Rivers. 1997, Benchmark LB $22.79 (978-0-7614-0503-0). 45pp. The story of the Nile, the lands through which it flows, its flooding, and its place in history. (Rev: HBG 3/98; SLJ 5/98) [960]

17481 Rich, Susan, et al. *Africa South of the Sahara: Understanding Geography and History Through Art* (5–9). Series: Artisans Around the World. 1999, Raintree LB $27.12 (978-0-7398-0118-5). 48pp. After a brief overview of the history and geography of southern Africa, this book presents a colorful introduction to such crafts as beadwork from Kenya, a carved wooden mask from Congo, and a wire toy from South Africa. Most will require adult help or supervision. (Rev: HBG 3/00; SLJ 1/00) [960]

17482 Sheehan, Sean. *Great African Kingdoms* (5–10). Series: Ancient World. 1998, Raintree LB $27.12 (978-0-8172-5124-6). Coverage of the great African kingdoms includes the spectacular palace of Great Zimbabwe, the majestic sculptures of Benin, and the Zulu empire's struggle for survival. (Rev: BL 1/1–15/99; HBG 3/99) [960]

17483 Weintraub, Aileen. *Discovering Africa's Land, People, and Wildlife* (5–8). Series: Continents of the World. 2004, Enslow LB $25.26 (978-0-7660-5204-8). 48pp. An introduction to the geography, history, economy, plants and animals, culture, and peoples of the continent, with discussion of the continuing need for foreign aid in many countries. (Rev: SLJ 11/04) [916]

17484 Woods, Michael, and Mary B. Woods. *Seven Natural Wonders of Africa* (5–8). Series: Seven Natural Wonders. 2009, Twenty-First Century LB $33.26 (978-0-8225-9071-2). 80pp. The Nile, Victoria Falls, Sahara Desert, Mount Kilimanjaro, Seychelles Islands, Serengeti Plain, and mountain gorillas are the seven wonders featured in this attractive volume. (Rev: BL 4/1/09; SLJ 5/09) [508.6]

Central and Eastern Africa

17485 Allen, Christina. *Hippos in the Night: Autobiographical Adventures in Africa* (4–8). Illus. by Rob Shepperson. 2003, HarperCollins LB $17.89 (978-0-688-17827-7). 144pp. An appealing account of a camping trip through Kenya and Tanzania, with details of the exciting animals and fascinating people encountered on the way. (Rev: BL 4/15/03; HBG 10/03; SLJ 4/03) [591.96]

17486 Ayodo, Awuor. *Luo* (4–7). Illus. Series: Heritage Library of African Peoples. 1995, Rosen LB $29.25 (978-0-8239-1758-7). 64pp. A portrait of the culture, history, and society of the Luo people, who lived on the shores of Lake Victoria in Kenya. (Rev: BL 3/1/96) [967.8]

17487 Bangura, Abdul Karim. *Kipsigis* (5–8). Illus. Series: Heritage Library of African Peoples. 1994, Rosen LB $29.25 (978-0-8239-1765-5). 64pp. An attractive title that deals with the history and present status of the Kipsigis people of Kenya. (Rev: SLJ 5/95) [967.62]

17488 Barber, Nicola. *Living in the African Savannah* (3–5). Illus. 2007, Raintree LB $27.50 (978-1-4109-2814-6). 32pp. Barber looks at the Maasai people and their life on the savannah, covering homes, food and clothing, school and language, music and dance, and ceremonies. (Rev: SLJ 2/08) [305.896]

17489 Bessire, Aimee, and Mark Bessire. *Sukuma* (5–8). Series: Heritage Library of African Peoples. 1997, Rosen LB $29.25 (978-0-8239-1992-5). Describes the history, culture, leaders, customs, and present situation of the Sukuma people of Tanzania. (Rev: BL 9/15/97; VOYA 12/97) [967.6]

17490 Cobb, Vicki. *This Place Is Wild: East Africa* (3–5). Illus. Series: Imagine Living Here. 1998, Walker LB $16.85 (978-0-8027-8633-3). 32pp. This slim book explores the uniqueness of East Africa, describes its unusual animal and plant life, and introduces the reader to the Masai people. (Rev: BL 4/1/98; HBG 10/98; SLJ 5/98) [599]

17491 Corona, Laurel. *Ethiopia* (5–8). Series: Modern Nations of the World. 2000, Lucent LB $29.95 (978-1-56006-823-5). 128pp. An attractive, well-organized introduction to Ethiopia that gives its history, geography, and culture plus national statistics, a chronology, and bibliographies. (Rev: BL 3/1/01) [963]

17492 Corona, Laurel. *Kenya* (5–8). Illus. Series: Modern Nations of the World. 1999, Lucent LB $27.45 (978-1-56006-590-6). 127pp. A profile of this poor African country that is a study in contrasts and cultures, with material on such subjects as geography, economics, people, and current problems. (Rev: BL 2/15/00; HBG 10/00) [967.62]

17493 Craats, Rennay. *Maasai* (4–6). Illus. Series: Indigenous Peoples. 2005, Weigl $7.95 (978-1-59036-255-6). 32pp. A fascinating and informative overview of the Maasai people, covering history, culture, language, and family life.

17494 Deady, Kathleen W. *Rwanda* (2–5). Illus. Series: Questions and Answers: Countries. 2005, Capstone LB $23.93 (978-0-7368-3759-0). 32pp. Using a question-and-answer format, simple text, large photos, and many factboxes, this is an introduction to Rwanda today, with material on history and traditional culture.

17495 DeCapua, Sarah. *Malawi in Pictures* (5–8). Illus. Series: Visual Geography. 2009, Lerner LB $31.93 (978-0-8225-1842-6). 80pp. A revised edition of this overview of Malawi's climate, history, geography, culture, education, and other aspects of life in this African nation. (Rev: BL 2/1/89) [968.97]

17496 Delzio, Suzanne. *Ethiopia* (2–3). Illus. Series: Many Cultures, One World. 2004, Capstone LB $23.93 (978-0-7368-2449-1). 32pp. A brief, accessible introduction to Ethiopia and its people, family life, customs, and legends.

17497 Diouf, Sylviane. *Kings and Queens of Central Africa* (4–7). Series: Watts Library: Africa — Kings and Queens. 2000, Watts LB $25.50 (978-0-531-20372-9). 64pp. This look at the political and social evolution of central Africa describes some of its important royalty including the 15th-century Afonso and Bolongongo, the legendary Bakuba king, with a final chapter on the region today. (Rev: BL 3/1/01) [960]

17498 Diouf, Sylviane. *Kings and Queens of East Africa* (4–7). Illus. Series: Watts Library: Africa — Kings and Queens. 2000, Watts LB $25.50 (978-0-

531-20373-6). 64pp. This book gives biographical information about royalty in East Africa and through these sketches re-creates the history of this part of Africa. (Rev: BL 2/15/01) [967.6]

17499 DiPiazza, Francesca. *Sudan in Pictures* (5–8). Illus. Series: Visual Geography. 2006, Lerner LB $31.93 (978-0-8225-1839-6). 80pp. An updated overview of history, culture, geography, economy, education, and health in this African nation. (Rev: BL 2/1/89) [962.4]

17500 Giles, Bridget. *Kenya* (4–8). Series: Nations of the World. 2001, Raintree LB $34.26 (978-0-7398-1290-7). 128pp. From snow-capped mountains to scorching deserts, this geographically and culturally diverse African nation is attractively introduced in this volume. (Rev: BL 12/15/01; HBG 3/02; SLJ 12/01) [967.62]

17501 Gish, Steven. *Ethiopia* (4–7). Illus. Series: Cultures of the World. 1996, Marshall Cavendish LB $37.07 (978-0-7614-0276-3). 128pp. After general background information on Ethiopia, such topics as lifestyles, religion, and language are discussed. (Rev: BL 8/96; SLJ 8/96) [963]

17502 Greenberg, Keith E. *Rwanda: Fierce Clashes in Central Africa* (1–4). Photos by John Isaac. Series: Children in Crisis. 1996, Blackbirch LB $23.70 (978-1-56711-185-9). 30pp. A harrowing eyewitness account in text and photos of the effects of the war in Rwanda on the lives of children in the refugee camps. (Rev: SLJ 6/97) [967]

17503 Jones, Schuyler. *Pygmies of Central Africa* (5–8). Illus. 1989, Rourke LB $16.67 (978-0-86625-268-3). 48pp. A vivid look into the lives of these fascinating people. (Rev: BL 5/15/89) [967.00496]

17504 Kairi, Wambui. *Kenya* (2–4). Series: We Come From. 2000, Raintree LB $25.69 (978-0-8172-5512-1). 32pp. A young native guide gives basic facts about Kenya, explains how to cook some delicious dishes, and makes simple toys. (Rev: BL 4/15/00; HBG 10/00) [967.62]

17505 Klyce, Katherine P., and Virginia O. McLean. *Kenya, Jambo!* (2–5). Illus. 1989, Redbird $21.95 (978-0-9606046-4-7). 36pp. In photos and simple text, a ten-year-old girl tells of her family's vacation in Kenya. (Rev: BL 12/1/89) [916]

17506 Lindblad, Lisa. *The Serengeti Migration: Africa's Animals on the Move* (3–7). Photos by Sven-Olof Lindblad. 1994, Hyperion $15.95 (978-1-56282-668-0). 40pp. A short text and stunning photos describe the annual migration of zebras and wildebeests through Tanzania and Kenya. (Rev: BCCB 5/94; BL 7/94*; SLJ 5/94) [599.73]

17507 McCollum, Sean. *Kenya* (3–5). Illus. Series: Globe-Trotters Club. 1999, Carolrhoda LB $22.60 (978-1-57505-105-5). 48pp. This book introduces Kenya, with material on its history, geography, religion, people, culture, and population. (Rev: BL 9/15/99; HBG 10/99) [967.62]

17508 McCollum, Sean. *Kenya* (1–3). Illus. Series: A Ticket To. 1999, Carolrhoda LB $22.60 (978-1-57505-130-7). 48pp. A basic introduction to this African nation that includes many color photographs. (Rev: BL 9/15/99; HBG 10/99) [967.62]

17509 McQuail, Lisa. *The Masai of Africa* (4–7). Illus. Series: First Peoples. 2001, Lerner LB $23.93 (978-0-8225-4855-3). 48pp. McQuail provides information about the Masai people, covering their history, customs, and contemporary daily life, with photographs. (Rev: BL 10/15/01; HBG 3/02; SLJ 3/02) [967.6]

17510 Nicolotti, Muriel. *Kuntai: A Masai Child* (K–3). Series: Children of the World. 2005, Gale LB $22.45 (978-1-4103-0290-8). 24pp. Using many photographs, this volume introduces the lifestyle and customs of the Masai, a nomadic people living in East Africa; suitable for browsers rather than report writers. (Rev: SLJ 10/05) [967.62]

17511 Nnoromele, Salome. *Somalia* (5–8). Series: Modern Nations of the World. 2000, Lucent LB $27.45 (978-1-56006-396-4). 112pp. An introduction to this East African country with material on its history and geography and a large section on daily life. (Rev: BL 5/15/00; HBG 10/00) [967.73]

17512 Oghojafor, Kingsley. *Uganda* (5–8). Series: Countries of the World. 2004, Gareth Stevens LB $31.00 (978-0-8368-3112-2). 96pp. Introduces readers to the African country's geography, history, people, culture, and government and also takes a look at its relations with other countries and contemporary challenges. (Rev: SLJ 8/04) [967.61]

17513 Parris, Ronald. *Rendille* (5–8). Illus. Series: Heritage Library of African Peoples. 1994, Rosen LB $29.25 (978-0-8239-1763-1). 64pp. With extensive use of black-and-white and color photographs, introduces the history and customs of the Rendille people of Kenya. (Rev: SLJ 5/95) [967.62]

17514 Pateman, Robert. *Kenya* (4–7). Illus. Series: Cultures of the World. 1993, Marshall Cavendish LB $35.64 (978-1-85435-572-0). 128pp. The background story of Kenya is revealed through color photographs and a text that also covers present concerns. (Rev: BL 8/93) [967.62]

17515 Pritchett , Bev. *Tanzania in Pictures* (5–8). Illus. Series: Visual Geography. 2007, Lerner LB $31.93 (978-0-8225-1838-9). 80pp. This revised edition contains information on history, geography, economy, religion, and culture. (Rev: BL 2/1/89) [967.8104]

17516 Schemenauer, Elma. *Somalia* (3–5). Series: Faces and Places. 2001, Child's World LB $22.79 (978-1-56766-911-4). 32pp. Basic facts about Somalia are given in a simple introduction with large type, many color photographs, and a text that emphasizes the everyday life of the people. (Rev: BL 9/15/01; HBG 3/02; SLJ 12/01) [967.73]

17517 Schemenauer, Elma. *Uganda* (3–5). Series: Countries: Faces and Places. 2003, Child's World LB $25.64 (978-1-56766-941-1). 32pp. A brief introduction to the geography, history, people, culture, and flora and fauna of this landlocked country. (Rev: SLJ 7/03) [967.61]

17518 Schemenauer, Elma. *Welcome to Somalia* (1–4). Series: Wecome to the World. 2008, The Child's World LB $27.07 (978-1-59296-976-0). 32pp. As easy introduction to Somalia and its land, people, plants and animals, and so forth, with color photographs, maps, and recipes. (Rev: LMC 10/08; SLJ 9/08) [967]

17519 Schnapper, LaDena. *Teenage Refugees from Ethiopia Speak Out* (5–10). Series: Teenage Refugees Speak Out. 1997, Rosen LB $27.95 (978-0-8239-2438-7). Ethiopian teens now living in America tell of the violence, famine, and civil war that drove them from their country and of their reception in America. (Rev: SLJ 2/98) [963]

17520 Shoveller, Herb. *Ryan and Jimmy: And the Well in Africa That Brought Them Together* (3–6). Illus. 2006, Kids Can $16.95 (978-1-55337-967-6). 55pp. In this inspiring story of one boy's efforts to make a difference in the world, readers learn about Ryan Hreljac, a Canadian boy who raised money to build a well in Africa and worked to rescue Akana Jimmy, the young Ugandan friend abducted by rebels. (Rev: SLJ 11/06) [361.7]

17521 Stewart, Judy. *A Family in Sudan* (4–6). Illus. 1988, Lerner LB $18.60 (978-0-8225-1682-8). 32pp. Customs, work, and play are covered in this look at life in this African land. (Rev: BL 8/88)

17522 Swinimer, Ciarunji C. *Pokot* (5–8). Illus. Series: Heritage Library of African Peoples. 1994, Rosen LB $29.25 (978-0-8239-1756-3). 64pp. Using a good balance of text and visuals, this account describes the history, culture, and present status of the Pokot people of Kenya. (Rev: SLJ 5/95) [967.62]

17523 Tanguay, Bridget. *Kenya* (4–7). Illus. Series: Countries of the World. 2006, National Geographic $19.95 (978-0-7922-7628-9). 64pp. An overview of Kenya with information on the country's history, land, people, government, economy and present issues; excellent color photographs and maps are included. (Rev: SLJ 3/07) [967.6]

17524 Twagilimana, Aimable. *Hutu and Tutsi* (5–9). Series: The Heritage Library of African Peoples. 1997, Rosen LB $29.25 (978-0-8239-1999-4). A large section of this book is devoted to the current struggle between the Hutu and Tutsi people of central Africa, along with chapters on art and religion. (Rev: SLJ 3/98) [967]

17525 Twagilimana, Aimable. *Teenage Refugees from Rwanda Speak Out* (5–10). Series: Teenage Refugees Speak Out. 1997, Rosen LB $27.95 (978-0-8239-2443-1). Teenage refugees from Rwanda describe the warfare between Tutsi and Hutu peoples, the terrible living conditions that forced them to leave their country, and the challenges and difficulties they have experienced in the United States. (Rev: SLJ 2/98) [967]

17526 Willis, Terri. *Democratic Republic of the Congo* (4–6). Series: Enchantment of the World. 2004, Scholastic LB $37.00 (978-0-516-24250-7). 144pp. Contemporary life, history, geography, culture are all covered in this well-illustrated and well-written volume suitable for report writers. (Rev: BL 9/1/04) [967.51]

17527 Zeleza, Tiyambe. *Maasai* (5–8). Illus. Series: Heritage Library of African Peoples. 1994, Rosen LB $29.25 (978-0-8239-1757-0). 64pp. An introduction to these people of Kenya and Tanzania,

their culture, customs, and history. (Rev: SLJ 5/95) [967.62]

17528 Zuehlke, Jeffrey. *Ethiopia in Pictures* (5–8). Illus. Series: Visual Geography. 2005, Lerner LB $31.93 (978-0-8225-1836-5). 80pp. Land, history and government, culture, education, religion, and health are covered in this revised edition. (Rev: BL 2/1/89) [963]

Northern Africa

17529 Barber, Nicola. *Living in the Sahara* (3–5). Series: World Cultures. 2007, Raintree LB $27.50 (978-1-4109-2816-0). 32pp. Barber looks at the people of the desert and various aspects of life there including homes, food and clothing, school and leisure, music and poetry, and celebrations. (Rev: SLJ 2/08) [305.89]

17530 Blauer, Ettagale, and Jason Lauré. *Morocco* (4–7). Series: Enchantment of the World. 1999, Children's LB $37.00 (978-0-516-20961-6). 144pp. In this fine introduction to Morocco topics include history, government, economics, people, religion, culture, and the arts. (Rev: BL 9/15/99) [964]

17531 Bodden, Valerie. *Suez Canal* (3–6). Series: Modern Wonders of the World. 2006, Creative Education LB $27.10 (978-1-58341-441-5). 32pp. An interesting overview of the canal's history, construction, and impact on both world commerce and politics. (Rev: SLJ 12/06) [386]

17532 Giraud, Hervé. *Leila: A Tuareg Child* (K–3). Photos by Jean-Charles Rey. 2005, Gale LB $22.45 (978-1-4103-0545-9). 24pp. Using many photographs, this volume introduces the rootless, nomadic lifestyle of a young Berber girl. (Rev: SLJ 10/05) [966.0049]

17533 Kagda, Falaq. *Algeria* (4–7). Illus. Series: Cultures of the World. 1997, Marshall Cavendish LB $37.07 (978-0-7614-0680-8). 128pp. This book on Algeria emphasizes the people and how they live. (Rev: BL 8/97) [965]

17534 Malcolm, Peter. *Libya* (4–7). Illus. 1993, Marshall Cavendish LB $35.64 (978-1-85435-573-7). 128pp. Well-chosen photographs and readable text give good background information as well as material on present problems. (Rev: BL 8/93) [961.2]

17535 Merrick, Patrick. *Morocco* (3–5). Series: Countries: Faces and Places. 2000, Child's World LB $22.79 (978-1-56766-737-0). 32pp. An oversize book filled with color illustrations that describes the history, geography, and people of Morocco. (Rev: BL 4/15/01; HBG 3/01) [964]

17536 Raskin, Lawrie, and Debora Pearson. *52 Days by Camel: My Sahara Adventure* (4–8). Illus. 1998, Annick $24.95 (978-1-55037-519-0); paper $14.95 (978-1-55037-518-3). An engaging account of a trip from Fez to Timbuktu by bus, jeep, train, truck, and camel, with details on desert life and culture. (Rev: BL 6/1–15/98; SLJ 7/98) [964]

17537 Stewart, Judy. *A Family in Morocco* (2–4). Illus. 1986, Lerner LB $18.60 (978-0-8225-1664-4). 32pp. Basic geography and the facts of daily living, focusing on one child in a family. (Rev: BL 5/15/86; SLJ 10/86)

17538 Weintraub, Aileen. *The Sahara Desert: The Biggest Desert* (3–5). Illus. Series: Great Record Breakers in Nature. 2001, Rosen $21.25 (978-0-8239-5640-1). 24pp. Informative text and dramatic full-page photographs introduce the world's biggest desert and its composition, extraordinary range of temperatures, residents, and fossil history. (Rev: BL 12/15/01; SLJ 7/01) [966]

Southern Africa

17539 Barnes-Svarney, Patricia. *Zimbabwe* (5–9). Illus. Series: Major World Nations. 1999, Chelsea LB $29.95 (978-0-7910-4753-8). A good introduction to Zimbabwe's history, geography, government, people, pastimes, economy, and culture. (Rev: SLJ 8/98) [968]

17540 Blauer, Ettagale, and Jason Lauré. *Madagascar* (4–7). Series: Enchantment of the World. 2000, Children's LB $37.00 (978-0-516-21634-8). 144pp. Madagascar, the island nation off the coast of Africa, is introduced. Topics addressed include its land and people, wildlife, history, traditions, daily life, and economy. (Rev: BL 12/15/00) [969]

17541 Brandenburg, Jim. *Sand and Fog: Adventures in Southern Africa* (5–8). Illus. 1994, Walker LB $17.85 (978-0-8027-8233-5). 44pp. A stunning photoessay about the wildlife found in Namibia. (Rev: BCCB 5/94; BL 3/1/94*; HB 5/94; SLJ 5/94) [968.1]

17542 Brownlie, Alison. *South Africa* (2–4). Illus. Series: We Come From. 2000, Raintree $25.69 (978-0-8172-5221-2). 32pp. Readers are introduced to South Africa, the homeland of this book's 7-year-old narrator, including its geography, food, weather, work, schools, and other topics. (Rev: BL 4/15/00; HBG 10/00; SLJ 10/00) [968]

17543 Dawson, Zoe. *South Africa* (K–3). Illus. Series: Postcards From. 1995, Raintree LB $22.83 (978-0-8172-4015-8). 32pp. In double-page spreads, points of interest in South Africa are described. (Rev: SLJ 3/96) [968]

17544 Diouf, Sylviane. *Kings and Queens of Southern Africa* (4–7). Illus. Series: Watts Library: Africa — Kings and Queens. 2000, Watts LB $25.50 (978-0-531-20374-3). 64pp. Through the lives of Shaka the Zulu king, Moshoeshoe of the Sotho kingdom, and others, the reader gets a good history of this region before and during the colonial period. (Rev: BL 2/15/01) [968]

17545 Flint, David. *South Africa* (5–8). Illus. Series: Modern Industrial World. 1996, Raintree $24.26 (978-0-8172-4554-2). 48pp. The present economic status of South Africa is studied through personal narratives and case studies. (Rev: BL 2/15/97; SLJ 8/97) [968]

17546 Green, Jen. *South Africa* (4–8). Series: Nations of the World. 2001, Raintree LB $34.26 (978-0-7398-1282-2). 128pp. A profile of the strongest industrial nation in Africa, with material on its geography, resources, environment, government, economy, and future. (Rev: BL 6/1–15/01; HBG 10/01) [968]

17547 Inserra, Rose, and Susan Powell. *The Kalahari* (5–8). Series: Ends of the Earth. 1997, Heinemann LB $25.45 (978-0-431-06932-6). An introduction to the history, animal and vegetable life, and future of this desert region of southern Botswana, eastern Namibia, and western South Africa. (Rev: SLJ 11/97) [968]

17548 Langley, Andrew. *Cape Town* (4–7). Illus. Series: Great Cities of the World. 2005, World Almanac LB $31.00 (978-0-8368-5045-1). 48pp. An informative and appealing overview of this major city, with material on its history, its economy, and what it's like to live there. (Rev: BL 4/15/04)

17549 Oluonye, Mary N. *Madagascar* (1–3). Series: Globe-Trotters Club. 2000, Carolrhoda LB $22.60 (978-1-57505-120-8). 48pp. From the monsoons to the comfortable dry season, this is a simple introduction to the island off the coast of Africa that is known as "a World Apart." (Rev: BL 5/15/00; HBG 10/00) [969]

17550 Oluonye, Mary N. *South Africa* (3–5). Series: Globe-Trotters Club. 1999, Carolrhoda $22.60 (978-1-57505-116-1). 48pp. Double-page spreads cover standard topics on South Africa and are enhanced with sidebars containing activities and unusual bits of information. (Rev: BL 9/15/99; HBG 3/00; SLJ 3/00) [968]

17551 Oluonye, Mary N. *South Africa* (1–3). Series: A Ticket To. 1999, Carolrhoda LB $22.60 (978-1-57505-141-3). 48pp. Following a large map of the country, this first look at South Africa introduces the land and its people, using easy-to-understand language and many color pictures. (Rev: BL 9/15/99; HBG 3/00; SLJ 3/00) [968]

17552 Parker, Linda J. *The San of Africa* (4–6). Series: First Peoples. 2002, Lerner LB $23.93 (978-0-8225-4177-6). This account describes the history and culture of this nomadic people of the Kalahari Desert. (Rev: BL 5/15/02; HBG 10/02) [968]

17553 Rogers, Barbara Radcliffe, and Stillman D. Rogers. *Zimbabwe* (4–7). Series: Enchantment of the World. 2002, Children's LB $37.00 (978-0-516-21113-8). 144pp. This troubled African land is introduced with material on topics including history, geography, people, government, and resources. (Rev: BL 5/15/02; SLJ 7/02) [968.9]

17554 Rosemarin, Ike. *South Africa* (4–7). Illus. Series: Cultures of the World. 1993, Marshall Cavendish LB $35.64 (978-1-85435-575-1). 128pp. Historical and modern concerns are covered in this look at South Africa. (Rev: BL 8/93) [968]

17555 Ryan, Patrick. *Welcome to South Africa* (1–4). Series: Welcome to the World. 2008, The Child's World LB $27.07 (978-1-59296-977-7). 32pp. As easy introduction to South Africa and its land, people, plants and animals, and so forth, with color photographs, maps, and recipes. (Rev: LMC 10/08; SLJ 9/08) [968]

17556 *South Africa in Pictures* (5–8). Illus. Series: Visual Geography. 1996, Lerner LB $25.55 (978-0-8225-1835-8). 64pp. Focusing on climate, geography, wildlife, and the history of this troubled country. (Rev: BL 8/88) [968.06]

17557 *To Everything There Is a Season* (2–4). Illus. by Jude Daly. 2006, Eerdmans $16.00 (978-0-8028-5286-1). 32pp. The familiar words from Ecclesiastes are used as the framework for a portrait of life in rural South Africa. (Rev: BL 4/15/06; SLJ 3/06) [223]

17558 Van Wyk, Gary N. *Basotho* (5–7). Illus. Series: Heritage Library of African Peoples. 1996, Rosen LB $29.25 (978-0-8239-2005-1). 63pp. Describes the Basotho people, who live in Lesotho and South Africa, with simple text on their history, religion, social organization, and customs. (Rev: BL 11/15/96; SLJ 3/97) [968]

17559 Van Wyk, Gary N., and Robert Johnson. *Shona* (5–7). Series: Heritage Library of African Peoples. 1997, Rosen LB $29.25 (978-0-8239-2011-2). 64pp. The Shona people of Zimbabwe are presented in outstanding photographs, with a text that covers their past, their culture, and their present living conditions and problems. (Rev: BL 1/1–15/98) [968]

17560 Wulfsohn, Gisèle. *A Child's Day in a South African City* (K–3). Illus. Series: A Child's Day. 2003, Marshall Cavendish $25.64 (978-0-7614-1407-0). 32pp. A black South African child's experiences in his integrated school and blended family, with explanations of his country's customs and culture. (Rev: BL 2/15/03; HBG 3/03; SLJ 2/03) [968]

17561 *Zimbabwe in Pictures* (5–8). Illus. Series: Visual Geography. 1997, Lerner LB $25.55 (978-0-8225-1825-9). 64pp. Many photographs highlight this overview of Zimbabwe's history, climate, wildlife, and culture. (Rev: BL 4/15/88) [968]

Western Africa

17562 Adeeb, Hassan, and Bonnetta Adeeb. *Nigeria: One Nation, Many Cultures* (4–8). Illus. Series: Exploring Cultures of the World. 1995, Benchmark LB $27.07 (978-0-7614-0190-2). 64pp. Opening with an account of a legendary figure, this book continues with an introduction to Nigeria that emphasizes its culture and how the people live. (Rev: SLJ 6/96) [966.9]

17563 Adeleke, Tunde. *Songhay* (5–7). Illus. Series: Heritage Library of African Peoples. 1996, Rosen LB $29.25 (978-0-8239-1986-4). 63pp. Both historical information and material on contemporary life are given in this account of the African people who live chiefly in Mali, Niger, and Benin. (Rev: BL 11/15/96) [960]

17564 Ahiagble, Gilbert Bobbo, and Louise Meyer. *Master Weaver from Ghana* (3–5). Photos by Nestor Hernandez. 1998, Open Hand $18.00 (978-0-940880-61-0). 32pp. Daily life in Ghana is explored in this book about a master weaver, Ahiagble, his techniques, craft, and the culture he represents. (Rev: SLJ 3/99) [966.7]

17565 Barnett, Jeanie M. *Ghana* (5–9). Illus. Series: Major World Nations. 1999, Chelsea LB $21.95 (978-0-7910-4739-2). Basic facts about Ghana's history, geography, politics, government, economy, natural resources, education, and people. (Rev: HBG 9/98; SLJ 8/98) [966.7]

17566 Barr, Gary E. *History and Activities of the West African Kingdoms* (3–6). Illus. Series: Hands-on Ancient History. 2006, Heinemann LB $28.21 (978-1-4034-7925-9). 32pp. Social life, arts and culture, games, and holidays and celebrations are covered in this attractive and accessible volume that includes a recipe, two crafts, and an activity (a game of Mancala). (Rev: SLJ 4/07) [966]

17567 Boateng, Faustine Ama. *Asante* (5–7). Illus. Series: Heritage Library of African Peoples. 1996, Rosen LB $29.25 (978-0-8239-1975-8). 63pp. This African people living in present-day Ghana is described, with information on history, traditions, and lifestyle. (Rev: BL 11/15/96; SLJ 3/97) [966.7]

17568 Bowden, Rob, and Roy Maconachie. *Nigeria* (5–7). Series: The Changing Face Of. 2003, Raintree LB $28.56 (978-0-7398-6829-4). 48pp. An examination of modern-day Nigeria, with a look at the nation's past difficulties and how it may benefit from its wealth of natural resources. (Rev: SLJ 4/04) [966.9]

17569 Brace, Steve. *Ghana* (4–8). Illus. Series: Economically Developing Countries. 1995, Thomson Learning LB $24.26 (978-1-56847-242-3). 48pp. Rich and poor rural and urban families are introduced in this attractive book on Ghana, its past, and its present. (Rev: SLJ 7/95) [966.7]

17570 Brook, Larry. *Daily Life in Ancient and Modern Timbuktu* (5–7). Illus. 1999, Lerner LB $25.26 (978-0-8225-3215-6). 64pp. A fascinating look at this ancient West African city that was once a center of commerce and learning. (Rev: BL 9/1/99; HBG 10/99; SLJ 7/99) [966.23]

17571 Brownlie, Alison. *Nigeria* (2–4). Series: We Come From. 2000, Raintrec LB $25.69 (978-0-8172-5513-8). 32pp. Using a native child as a guide, this introduction to Nigeria gives basic information on the country plus such specialized coverage as a trip to local markets, making a fish stew, a game of hide and seek, and several recipes. (Rev: BL 4/15/00; HBG 10/00; SLJ 10/00) [966.9]

17572 Brownlie, Alison. *West Africa* (3–5). Series: Foods and Festivals. 1999, Raintree LB $25.69 (978-0-8172-5552-7). 32pp. Recipes for festival dishes enhance this account of life in West Africa as seen through its various holidays. (Rev: BL 5/15/99; HBG 10/99; SLJ 7/99) [966]

17573 Chambers, Catherine. *West African States: 15th Century to the Colonial Era* (5–8). Series: Looking Back. 1999, Raintree $19.98 (978-0-8172-5427-8). A brief overview of the history and culture of the great empires of West Africa and how they disappeared with the arrival of the Europeans. (Rev: BL 5/15/99; VOYA 2/00) [966.2]

17574 Chicoine, Stephen D. *A Liberian Family* (3–5). Photos by Stephen Chicoine. Series: Journey Between Two Worlds. 1997, Lerner LB $22.60 (978-0-8225-3411-2); paper $8.95 (978-0-8225-0975-2). 64pp. Explains why a family was forced to leave Liberia to escape persecution. Also gives a history of this land and its people. (Rev: HBG 3/98; SLJ 2/98) [966]

17575 Chocolate, Deborah N. *Kente Colors* (PS–3). Illus. by John Ward. 1996, Walker LB $16.85 (978-0-8027-8389-9). 32pp. The history and traditions of kente cloth of Ghana are told, along with a description of its meaning and colors. (Rev: BL 2/15/96; SLJ 6/96) [391]

17576 Diouf, Sylviane. *Kings and Queens of West Africa* (4–7). Series: Watts Library: Africa — Kings and Queens. 2000, Watts LB $25.50 (978-0-531-20375-0). 64pp. Some of the royal figures covered in this historical survey of West Africa are Emperor Mansa Musa of Mali and Nsate Yalla Mbodj, queen of the Walo of Senegal. (Rev: BL 3/1/01) [960]

17577 Dubois, Muriel L. *Liberia* (2–5). Illus. Series: Questions and Answers: Countries. 2005, Capstone LB $23.93 (978-0-7368-3755-2). 32pp. Using a question-and-answer format, simple text, large photos, and many factboxes, this is an introduction to Liberia today, with material on history and traditional culture.

17578 Hamilton, Janice. *Ivory Coast in Pictures* (5–8). Illus. Series: Visual Geography. 2004, Lerner LB $31.93 (978-0-8225-1828-0). 80pp. This updated edition looks at the geography, history and government, people, cultural life, and economy of West Africa's second-richest nation. (Rev: BL 4/15/88; SLJ 11/88) [966.68]

17579 Hathaway, Jim. *Cameroon in Pictures* (5–8). Illus. Series: Visual Geography. 1992, Lerner LB $25.55 (978-0-8225-1857-0). 64pp. With numerous charts, maps, and photographs, the country of Cameroon is introduced. (Rev: BL 9/15/89) [967]

17580 Heale, Jay. *Democratic Republic of the Congo* (5–9). Series: Cultures of the World. 1998, Marshall Cavendish LB $37.07 (978-0-7614-0874-1). A history of this nation that has been stricken with civil wars and political instability, with descriptions of its history, economy, government, people, and culture. (Rev: HBG 9/99; SLJ 6/99) [967]

17581 Heinrichs, Ann. *Niger* (4–7). Series: Enchantment of the World. 2001, Children's LB $37.00 (978-0-516-21633-1). Niger, a predominately Muslim country that is one of the hottest places in the world, is described in this attractive volume with material on topics such as resources, history, and culture. (Rev: BL 1/1–15/02) [967]

17582 Hetfield, Jamie. *The Yoruba of West Africa* (PS–2). Illus. Series: Celebrating the Peoples and Civilizations of Africa. 1996, Rosen LB $19.95 (978-0-8239-2332-8). 24pp. A simple introduction to the Yoruba people of West Africa, with material on their culture, food, rituals, and lifestyle. (Rev: SLJ 11/96) [966.9]

17583 Koslow, Philip. *Dahomey: The Warrior Kings* (5–8). Illus. Series: The Kingdoms of Africa. 1996, Chelsea LB $20.85 (978-0-7910-3137-7); paper $8.95 (978-0-7910-3138-4). 63pp. A history of the West African kingdom that flourished in the 17th and 18th centuries, describing how the slave trade affected it. (Rev: SLJ 12/96) [960]

17584 Levy, Patricia. *Nigeria* (4–7). Illus. Series: Cultures of the World. 1993, Marshall Cavendish LB $35.64 (978-1-85435-574-4). 128pp. Information on history, geography, lifestyles, people, and culture. (Rev: BL 8/93) [966.9]

17585 *Liberia in Pictures* (5–8). Illus. Series: Visual Geography. 1996, Lerner LB $25.55 (978-0-8225-1837-2). 64pp. Covers climate, geography, wildlife, vegetation, and natural resources. (Rev: BL 8/88) [966.62]

17586 Murphy, Patricia J. *Nigeria* (3–5). Illus. Series: Discovering Cultures. 2004, Benchmark LB $25.64 (978-0-7614-1795-8). 48pp. An attractive introduction to Nigeria, covering land, people, daily life, education, food, and celebrations, with discussion of the relationships among the many tribes. (Rev: SLJ 6/05)

17587 Nelson, Julie. *West African Kingdoms* (3–5). Series: Ancient Civilizations. 2001, Raintree LB $22.83 (978-0-7398-3581-4). 48pp. Readers will gain an understanding of the history and culture of the ancient civilizations of Ghana, Mali, and Songhai. (Rev: SLJ 2/02)

17588 *Nigeria in Pictures* (5–8). Illus. Series: Visual Geography. 1995, Lerner LB $25.55 (978-0-8225-1826-6). 64pp. A visual focus on this African land. (Rev: BL 8/88) [966.9]

17589 Nwanunobi, C. O. *Malinke* (5–7). Illus. Series: Heritage Library of African Peoples. 1996, Rosen LB $29.25 (978-0-8239-1979-6). 63pp. Features the culture, history, and contemporary lifeways of the Malinke people, now living along the western coast of Africa. (Rev: BL 11/15/96) [966.23]

17590 Nwanunobi, C. O. *Soninke* (5–7). Illus. Series: Heritage Library of African Peoples. 1996, Rosen LB $29.25 (978-0-8239-1978-9). 63pp. A discussion of the African people found in such countries as Ghana, Mali, Nigeria, and Senegal, with material on history, customs, and present living conditions. (Rev: BL 11/15/96) [966]

17591 Oluonye, Mary N. *Nigeria* (2–4). Illus. Series: Country Explorers. 2007, Lerner LB $27.93 (978-0-8225-7131-5). 48pp. History, geography, culture, sports, animals, and so forth are covered in conversational text and color photographs. (Rev: BL 10/15/07; LMC 1/08; SLJ 12/07) [966.9]

17592 Onyefulu, Ifeoma. *Here Comes Our Bride! An African Wedding Story* (K–3). Illus. 2004, Lincoln $15.95 (978-1-84507-047-2). 32pp. A Nigerian wedding comes to life in this attractive photoessay that captures all the local traditions and rituals before, during, and after the marriage ceremony. (Rev: BL 9/1/04) [392.5]

17593 Onyefulu, Ifeoma. *Ogbo: Sharing Life in an African Village* (1–5). Illus. 1996, Harcourt $15.00 (978-0-15-200498-9). 32pp. In a Nigerian village, people in the same age group, called *ogbo,* work together for the good of the community. (Rev: BCCB 4/96; BL 4/15/96; HB 9/96; SLJ 4/96*) [306]

17594 Onyefulu, Ifeoma. *Saying Good-Bye: A Special Farewell to Mama Nkwelle* (PS–2). Illus. 2001, Millbrook $22.90 (978-0-7613-1965-8). 32pp. A young boy describes the two weeks of mourning and the traditional Nigerian village funeral that take place on his great-grandmother's death. (Rev: BL 5/1/01; HB 7/01; HBG 10/01; SLJ 7/01) [393.9]

17595 Onyefulu, Ifeoma. *Welcome Dede! An African Naming Ceremony* (K–3). Illus. 2005, Frances Lincoln paper $7.95 (978-1-84507-311-4). 32pp. A dazzling photoessay of a traditional ceremony in a Ghanaian village. (Rev: BL 2/1/05) [392.1]

17596 Parris, Ronald. *Hausa* (5–7). Illus. Series: Heritage Library of African Peoples. 1996, Rosen LB $29.25 (978-0-8239-1983-3). 63pp. A look at the Hausa people of Niger and Nigeria, with material on history and contemporary life. (Rev: BL 11/15/96) [966]

17597 Peffer-Engels, John. *The Benin Kingdom of West Africa* (K–2). Illus. Series: Celebrating the Peoples and Civilizations of Africa. 1996, Rosen LB $19.95 (978-0-8239-2334-2). 24pp. This account describes the Benin kingdom, the Edo people, how many were enslaved and taken to the United States, and their present culture and lifestyle. (Rev: SLJ 1/97) [966.9]

17598 Provencal, Francis, and Catherine McNamara. *A Child's Day in a Ghanaian City* (1–3). Series: A Child's Day. 2001, Benchmark LB $25.64 (978-0-7614-1223-6). 32pp. A 7-year-old escorts readers through a typical day in this book that ends with brief information on history, geography, people, religion, and language. (Rev: BL 11/15/01; SLJ 3/02) [966.7]

17599 Reece, Katherine. *West African Kingdoms: Empires of Gold and Trade* (3–5). Illus. Series: Ancient Civilizations. 2005, Rourke LB $20.95 (978-1-59515-508-5). 48pp. This striking photoessay introduces the culture, geography, people, language, religion, and wildlife of three ancient West African kingdoms — Ghana, Mali, and Songhai. (Rev: BL 3/15/06; SLJ 4/06) [966]

17600 Sheehan, Patricia. *Côte d'Ivoire* (5–8). 1999, Marshall Cavendish LB $37.07 (978-0-7614-0980-9). 128pp. The Ivory Coast is presented with coverage of its geography, history, government, economy, and social and cultural life. (Rev: HBG 10/00; SLJ 4/00) [966.68]

17601 Shuter, Jane. *Ancient West African Kingdoms* (3–5). Illus. Series: History Opens Windows. 2002, Heinemann LB $22.79 (978-1-4034-0255-4). 32pp. Readers will learn about government, trade, and everyday life in the kingdoms of Ghana, Mali, and Songhai. (Rev: HBG 3/03; SLJ 3/03)

17602 Streissguth, Thomas. *Senegal in Pictures* (5–8). Illus. Series: Visual Geography. 2009, Lerner LB $31.93 (978-0-8225-1827-3). 80pp. An updated look at the geography, history, culture, and economics of Senegal. (Rev: BL 4/15/89; SLJ 11/88) [966.3]

17603 Tenquist, Alasdair. *Nigeria* (5–8). Illus. Series: Economically Developing Countries. 1996, Raintree LB $24.26 (978-0-8172-4527-6). This introduction to Nigeria emphasizes present-day government and economic conditions. (Rev: BL 3/1/97; SLJ 9/97) [330.9669]

Asia

General

17604 Bowden, Rob. *Asia* (5–8). Series: Continents of the World. 2006, World Almanac LB $34.00 (978-0-8368-5911-9). 64pp. Factboxes and "In Focus" articles add to this overview of the history, geography, people, culture, and so forth of the continent of Asia. (Rev: SLJ 2/06) [915]

17605 Bramwell, Martyn. *Southern and Eastern Asia* (4–8). Illus. Series: The World in Maps. 2001, Lerner LB $23.93 (978-0-8225-2916-3). 48pp. For each country in these geographical areas, readers will find a color map, the flag, a box containing important facts, and brief discussions of geography, industry, and economy. Also use *Northern and Western Asia* (2001). (Rev: HBG 10/01; SLJ 7/01) [915]

17606 Dramer, Kim. *The Mekong River* (4–8). Series: Watts Library. 2001, Watts LB $25.50 (978-0-531-11854-2). 63pp. A fact-filled introduction to the history of the Mekong and to the landscape and industry found along it. (Rev: SLJ 5/01) [959.7]

17607 Hammond, Paula. *China and Japan* (4–8). Illus. Series: Cultures and Costumes: Symbols of Their Period. 2003, Mason Crest LB $19.95 (978-1-59084-436-6). 64pp. A detailed survey of the history of garments and accessories worn by people of all classes in these two Asian nations prior to the 20th century. (Rev: SLJ 3/04) [391]

17608 Kalz, Jill. *Mount Everest* (4–6). Illus. Series: Natural Wonders of the World. 2004, Creative Education LB $18.95 (978-1-58341-325-8). 32pp. After establishing this important mountain's location, this oversized picture book full of color photographs looks at geology, climate, wildlife, people, and other pertinent facts. (Rev: SLJ 1/05) [915.496]

17609 Kilgallon, Conor. *India and Sri Lanka* (4–8). Illus. Series: Cultures and Costumes: Symbols of Their Period. 2003, Mason Crest LB $19.95 (978-1-59084-443-4). 64pp. A look at the history of garments and accessories worn by all classes of people in India and Sri Lanka up to the end of the 19th century. (Rev: SLJ 3/04) [391]

17610 Major, John S., and Betty J. Belanus. *Caravan to America: Living Arts of the Silk Road* (5–8). Illus. 2002, Cricket $24.95 (978-0-8126-2666-7); paper $15.95 (978-0-8126-2677-3). 144pp. The traditions and skills emanating from the ancient trade routes are shown as surviving today in the work of a rug restorer in New York, an artist-monk in Los Angeles, a cook from Iran, and other examples in this fascinating approach to an interesting subject. (Rev: BL 11/1/02; HB 1/03; HBG 3/03; SLJ 2/03; VOYA 6/03) [745]

17611 Sayre, April P. *Asia* (5–8). Illus. Series: Seven Continents. 1999, Twenty-First Century LB $25.90 (978-0-7613-1368-7). 64pp. Using maps, photographs, and sidebars, this concise work discusses Asia's people, geography and geology, climate and oceans, flora and fauna. (Rev: BL 8/99; HBG 3/00) [915]

17612 Wilkinson, Philip, and Michael Pollard. *The Magical East* (4–7). Illus. by Robert Ingpen. Series: Mysterious Places. 1994, Chelsea LB $21.95 (978-0-7910-2754-7). 92pp. An oversize volume that highlights several places and cities of importance in the history of the Orient. (Rev: BL 1/15/94; SLJ 4/94) [930.1]

China

17613 Andersen, Dale. *Ancient China* (3–5). Illus. Series: History in Art. 2004, Raintree LB $29.93 (978-1-4109-0519-2). 48pp. Examples of the era's art and sculpture accompany brief accounts of successive Chinese dynasties, pointing out what art can reveal about the life of the time. (Rev: BL 2/1/05; SLJ 4/05) [709]

17614 Bailey, Linda. *Adventures in Ancient China* (3–5). Illus. by Bill Slavin. Series: Good Times Travel Agency. 2003, Kids Can $14.95 (978-1-55337-453-4). 48pp. A fictional story about three children whisked magically to ancient China runs in cartoon fashion across the tops of the pages, while a guidebook below looks at everything from farming and transportation to family life and writing. (Rev: HBG 4/04; SLJ 1/04) [931]

17615 Baldwin, Robert F. *Daily Life in Ancient and Modern Beijing* (4–7). Illus. by Ray Webb. Series: Cities Through Time. 1999, Runestone LB $25.26 (978-0-8225-3214-9). 64pp. Topics introduced in this contrast between Beijing past and present include the arts, religion, school, history, and daily life. (Rev: HBG 10/99; SLJ 7/99) [951]

17616 Barber, Nicola. *Beijing* (4–7). Illus. Series: Great Cities of the World. 2004, World Almanac LB $31.00 (978-0-8368-5028-4). 48pp. In addition to the usual information on history and people, this attractive volume describes living conditions and leisure time and provides maps and sidebars about contemporary environmental and political issues. (Rev: BL 4/15/04; SLJ 6/04) [951]

17617 Bowden, Rob. *The Yangtze* (5–7). Series: A River Journey. 2003, Raintree LB $28.56 (978-0-7398-6074-8). 48pp. A well-illustrated trip along China's Yangtze River, concentrating on mankind's influence on the river and vice versa, with photographs, maps, and charts. (Rev: SLJ 3/04) [915.1]

17618 Chan, Arlene. *Awakening the Dragon: The Dragon Boat Festival* (3–6). Illus. by Song Nan Zhang. 2004, Tundra $15.95 (978-0-88776-656-5). 24pp. Bright illustrations accompany this overview of the history and traditions associated with Chinese dragon boat races. (Rev: BL 8/04; SLJ 6/04) [394.2]

17619 Cole, Joanna. *Imperial China* (1–3). Illus. by Bruce Degen. Series: Ms. Frizzle's Adventures. 2005, Scholastic $16.95 (978-0-590-10822-5). 48pp. From Chinatown, Frizzle and friends are transported by dragon to 11th-century China in this information-packed yet appealing volume combining fact and fiction. (Rev: BL 6/1–15/05) [951]

17620 Costain, Meredith, and Paul Collins. *Welcome to China* (3–5). Illus. Series: Countries of the World. 2001, Chelsea LB $28.00 (978-0-7910-6548-8). 32pp. A very basic overview of the country with information on plants and animals, culture, sports, and schooling. (Rev: HBG 3/02; SLJ 2/02)

17621 Crane, Carol. *D Is for Dancing Dragon* (1–4). Illus. by Zong-Zhou Wang. 2006, Sleeping Bear $17.95 (978-1-58536-273-8). An A to Z journey through China's history and culture, describing various Chinese inventions, the Great Wall, the Chinese New Year, pandas, and so forth. (Rev: SLJ 3/07) [951]

17622 Deedrick, Tami. *China* (3–6). Series: Ancient Civilizations. 2001, Raintree LB $22.83 (978-0-7398-3580-7). 48pp. Deedrick covers the Song, Yuan, and Ming dynasties of the Imperial period, giving good, clear information on history, daily life, culture, and inventions. (Rev: HBG 3/02; SLJ 9/01) [951]

17623 DuTemple, Lesley A. *The Great Wall of China* (4–7). Illus. Series: Great Building Feats. 2003, Lerner LB $27.93 (978-0-8225-0377-4). 80pp. This absorbing account tells the story of the building and importance of the Great Wall of China, with a good selection of illustrations, sidebar features, and maps. (Rev: BL 1/1–15/03; HBG 10/03; SLJ 4/03*) [931]

17624 Ferroa, Peggy. *China* (4–7). Illus. Series: Cultures of the World. 1991, Marshall Cavendish LB $35.64 (978-1-85435-399-3). 128pp. Unusual facts highlight this look at China, with emphasis on culture. (Rev: BL 2/15/92; SLJ 3/92) [951]

17625 Field, Catherine. *China* (4–8). Illus. Series: Nations of the World. 2000, Raintree LB $34.26 (978-0-8172-5781-1). 128pp. This is a fine introduction to China's past and present that supplies even more interesting information through the use of sidebars. (Rev: BL 10/15/00; HBG 10/00) [951.21]

17626 Flint, David. *China* (2–4). Series: On the Map. 1994, Raintree LB $22.83 (978-0-8114-3421-8). 32pp. Alternating a page of color photos with a page of text, such topics as China's geography, education, industry, and family life are covered. (Rev: BL 2/1/94; SLJ 7/94) [951]

17627 Harkonen, Reijo. *The Children of China* (4–6). Illus. by Matti Pitkanen. Series: The World's Children. 1990, Carolrhoda LB $23.93 (978-0-87614-394-0). 40pp. A travelogue narrative with striking color photos. (Rev: BL 6/15/90; SLJ 9/90) [951]

17628 Haskins, James. *Count Your Way Through China* (3–5). Illus. 1987, Carolrhoda LB $19.93 (978-0-87614-302-5); Lerner paper $5.95 (978-0-87614-486-2). 24pp. Concepts about China are introduced with the use of numbers 1 through 10. (Rev: BL 10/15/87; SLJ 9/87)

17629 Kagda, Falaq. *Hong Kong* (5–8). Series: Cultures of the World. 1998, Marshall Cavendish LB $37.07 (978-0-7614-0692-1). 128pp. An attractive book that introduces us to Hong Kong's history and geography, its people, and their culture and lifestyles. (Rev: HBG 3/98; SLJ 6/98) [951]

17630 Lazo, Caroline. *The Terra Cotta Army of Emperor Qin* (5–8). Illus. 1993, Macmillan LB $14.95 (978-0-02-754631-6). 80pp. The story of the 7,500 terracotta figures that guard the tomb of China's first emperor. (Rev: BL 7/93; SLJ 8/93) [931]

17631 Malaspina, Ann. *The Chinese Revolution and Mao Zedong in World History* (5–8). Series: World History. 2004, Enslow LB $26.60 (978-0-7660-1935-5). 128pp. After a brief overview of Chinese history, Malaspina provides a well-researched introduction to Chinese communism under Mao Zedong, from the early days of the party in the 1920s to the post-Mao reforms. (Rev: SLJ 3/04) [951]

17632 Mann, Elizabeth. *The Great Wall: The Story of Thousands of Miles of Earth and Stone* (4–8). Illus. Series: Wonders of the World. 1997, Mikaya $19.95 (978-0-9650493-2-0). The story behind the building of this massive structure, which began as far back as 200 B.C. and involves historical battles for land and power between the Chinese and the nomadic Mongols. (Rev: BL 1/1–15/98; SLJ 12/97) [951]

17633 March, Michael. *China* (2–5). Series: Country File. 2003, Smart Apple LB $24.25 (978-1-58340-236-8). 32pp. An introductory guide to China and its people, well illustrated with maps, charts, and photographs. (Rev: SLJ 3/04) [951]

17634 Martell, Hazel M. *The Ancient Chinese* (4–6). Illus. Series: World of the Past. 1993, Macmillan LB $14.95 (978-0-02-730653-8). 64pp. A history of early China with emphasis on culture and accomplishments. (Rev: BL 8/93) [951]

17635 Marx, Trish. *Elephants and Golden Thrones: Inside China's Forbidden City* (4–7). Illus. by Ellen B. Senisi. 2008, Abrams $18.95 (978-0-8109-9485-0). 48pp. Full of photographs, this is an inside look at the sights and history of the huge palace complex. (Rev: BL 6/1–15/08; SLJ 7/08) [951]

17636 Meister, Cari. *Yangtze River* (3–4). Series: Rivers and Lakes. 2002, ABDO LB $21.35 (978-1-57765-103-1). 24pp. A solid introduction to the Yangtze, its tributaries, flora and fauna, and the ways in which it has influenced human development in the area throughout history. (Rev: HBG 10/02; SLJ 7/02)

17637 Michels, Dia L. *Visiting China* (PS). Photos by Michael J. N. Bowles. Series: Look What I See! Where Can I Be? 2003, Platypus Media $16.95 (978-1-930775-15-2). Through the eyes of an infant, readers visit China in this unusual interactive book. (Rev: SLJ 4/04) [915.104]

17638 Minnis, Ivan. *You Are in Ancient China* (3–6). Series: You Are There! 2004, Raintree LB $26.36 (978-1-4109-0619-9). 32pp. Double-page spreads with plenty of illustrations and a low reading level introduce readers to the culture and lifestyle of the Han Dynasty. (Rev: BL 12/1/04; SLJ 2/05) [931]

17639 Morley, Jacqueline. *You Wouldn't Want to Work on the Great Wall of China! Defenses You'd Rather Not Build* (3–6). Illus. by David Antram. Series: You Wouldn't Want To. 2006, Watts LB $29.00 (978-0-531-12424-6); paper $9.95 (978-0-531-12449-9). 32pp. An unflinching look at what life was like for the workers who built the Great Wall of China, with cartoon illustrations that lighten the grimness. (Rev: SLJ 9/06) [951]

17640 O'Connor, Jane. *The Emperor's Silent Army: Terracotta Warriors of Ancient China* (4–6). 2002, Viking $17.99 (978-0-670-03512-0). 48pp. The beautifully packaged story of the amazing discovery of an army of life-size terracotta soldiers in a field in China in 1974, with information about the emperor who oversaw their construction. (Rev: BL 4/15/02*; HBG 10/02; SLJ 4/02) [931]

17641 Olson, Kay Melchisedech. *China* (2–3). Illus. Series: Many Cultures, One World. 2003, Capstone LB $23.93 (978-0-7368-1531-4). 32pp. A brief, accessible introduction to China and its people, family life, customs, and legends. (Rev: BL 10/15/03; HBG 10/03; SLJ 12/03) [951]

17642 Olson, Nathan. *China* (3–4). Illus. Series: Fact Finders: Questions and Answers. 2004, Capstone LB $23.93 (978-0-7368-2687-7). 32pp. Using a question-and-answer format, this title introduces China's history, government, economy, education, culture, sports, and lifestyle. (Rev: SLJ 1/05) [951]

17643 Patent, Dorothy Hinshaw. *The Incredible Story of China's Buried Warriors* (4–7). Series: Frozen in Time. 1999, Benchmark LB $27.07 (978-0-7614-0783-6). 64pp. This book explores the mystery of the creation of China's buried warriors, the thousands of terracotta statues that belonged to the first emperor of China and were uncovered in 1974. (Rev: BL 2/1/00; HBG 10/00; SLJ 3/00) [951]

17644 Pellegrini, Nancy. *Beijing* (4–8). Photos by Adrian Cooper. Series: Global Cities. 2007, Chelsea House LB $30.00 (978-0-7910-8848-7). 61pp. With plenty of photographs and maps, this volume introduces the history of Beijing as well as its geography, people, environment, transportation, and so forth. (Rev: SLJ 7/07)

17645 Pilon, Pascal, and Elizabeth Thomas. *We Live in China* (4–7). Illus. Series: Kids Around the World. 2006, Abrams $15.95 (978-0-8109-5735-0). 48pp. Four children from different areas of China introduce their region and everyday life; the lack of an index and photo captions limit the book's usefulness for reports, but it will nevertheless serve as an attractive introduction. (Rev: BL 10/15/06; SLJ 2/07)

17646 Pollard, Michael. *The Yangtze* (5–7). Series: Great Rivers. 1997, Benchmark LB $22.79 (978-0-7614-0505-4). 45pp. Covers historical and geographical aspects of the Yangtze River and discusses current dam-building projects. (Rev: HBG 3/98; SLJ 4/98) [951]

17647 Qing, Zheng. *China* (4–7). Illus. by Tim Hutchinson. Series: Find Out About. 2007, Barron's $12.99 (978-0-7641-5952-7). 64pp. This well-organized, attractively illustrated guide looks at China's history and contemporary life, and introduces basic phrases in Mandarin. (Rev: BL 4/1/07; SLJ 2/07) [951]

17648 Riehecky, Janet. *China* (2–4). Illus. Series: Country Explorers. 2007, Lerner LB $27.93 (978-0-8225-7129-2). 48pp. Rich in photographs, maps, and illustrations and full of accessible information, this lively book looks at the geography of the land and at all aspects of life there — family life, school life, clothes, medicine, food, sports, and so forth. (Rev: LMC 1/08*; SLJ 12/07) [915.1]

17649 Roop, Peter, and Connie Roop. *China* (1–3). Series: A Visit To. 1998, Heinemann LB $21.36 (978-1-57572-123-1). 32pp. An introduction to China in double-page spreads covering the land, its history and geography, culture, language, and transportation. (Rev: SLJ 7/98) [951]

17650 Schomp, Virginia. *The Ancient Chinese* (4–7). Series: People of the Ancient World. 2004, Watts LB $30.50 (978-0-531-11817-7). 112pp. Emperors, artisans, inventors, and healers are among the people presented in this overview of life in ancient China. (Rev: SLJ 2/05) [931]

17651 Shui, Amy, and Stuart Thompson. *China* (3–5). Illus. Series: Foods and Festivals. 1999, Raintree $25.69 (978-0-8172-5757-6). 32pp. A few suitable recipes accompany descriptions of such Chinese festivals as New Year's, the Dragon-Boat festival, and the Moon festival. (Rev: BL 5/15/99; HBG 10/99) [394.1]

17652 Shuter, Jane. *Ancient China* (5–8). Series: Time Travel Guides. 2007, Raintree LB $34.29 (978-1-4109-2729-3). 64pp. An attractive trip back in time to ancient China, providing details about daily life there — accommodation, food, shopping, and so forth — and suggesting sights to see. (Rev: SLJ 9/07) [931]

17653 So, Sungwan. *In a Chinese City* (2–4). 2001, Benchmark LB $25.64 (978-0-7614-1224-3). 32pp. A 7-year-old escorts readers through a typical day in this book that ends with brief information on history, geography, people, religion, and language. (Rev: HBG 3/02; SLJ 3/02)

17654 So, Sungwan. *Shanyi Goes to China* (PS–2). Series: Children Return to Their Roots. 2006, Frances Lincoln $15.95 (978-1-84507-470-8). 32pp. A little girl named Shanyi visits China with her family, visiting relatives and learning about everything from food and famous sites to calligraphy and religious customs. (Rev: BL 10/15/06; SLJ 12/06) [951.06]

17655 Stepanchuk, Carol. *Red Eggs and Dragon Boats: Celebrating Chinese Festivals* (3–6). Illus. 1994, Pacific View $16.95 (978-1-881896-08-1). 48pp. Five traditional Chinese festivals, including the Dragon Boat Festival and Moon Festival, are introduced, with details on customs and traditions plus recipes for food. (Rev: BL 3/15/94; SLJ 4/94) [394]

17656 Teague, Ken. *Growing Up in Ancient China* (3–5). Illus. Series: Growing Up In. 1993, Troll paper $9.10 (978-0-8167-2716-2). 32pp. An introduction to life in ancient China, with information on history, customs, schooling, food, clothing, and daily activities. (Rev: BL 1/15/94) [931]

17657 Walker, Kathryn. *Shanghai* (4–7). Illus. Series: Great Cities of the World. 2005, World Almanac LB $31.00 (978-0-8368-5046-8). 48pp. An informative and appealing overview of this important Chi-

nese city, with material on its history, its economy, and what it's like to live there. (Rev: BL 4/15/04)

17658 Wang, Xiaohong. *One Year in Beijing* (1–4). Illus. by Grace Lin. 2006, China Sprout $16.95 (978-0-9747302-5-7). 32pp. Eight-year-old Ling Ling conducts readers on a tour of popular attractions in Beijing, explaining Chinese customs and traditions as she goes; the end matter adds more facts. (Rev: BL 10/15/06; SLJ 3/07)

17659 Waterlow, Julia. *China* (2–4). Series: We Come From. 1999, Raintree LB $25.69 (978-0-8172-5219-9). 32pp. As well as a little information on Chinese home life, schools, and daily activities, this short book discusses geography and weather and gives a single recipe. (Rev: HBG 3/00; SLJ 3/00) [951]

17660 Waterlow, Julia. *China* (4–7). Illus. Series: Country Insights. 1997, Raintree LB $27.12 (978-0-8172-4787-4). 48pp. Compares the social conditions — home life, employment, schooling, and recreation — in a large city and a rural village in China. (Rev: BL 7/97; SLJ 8/97) [951]

17661 Williams, Suzanne. *Made in China: Ideas and Inventions from Ancient China* (4–6). Illus. 1997, Pacific View LB $19.95 (978-1-881896-14-2). 48pp. Covers such topics as papermaking, medicine, and inventions as they were developed in ancient China. (Rev: BL 2/1/97; SLJ 7/97) [931]

17662 Zhang, Song Nan. *The Children of China* (3–6). Illus. 1996, Tundra $17.95 (978-0-88776-363-2). 32pp. Children of nomadic minorities in China (e.g., Mongolians) are highlighted in this well-illustrated account. (Rev: BL 2/1/96) [759.11]

India

17663 Apte, Sunita. *India* (3–5). Series: A True Book — Geography: Countries. 2009, Children's Pr. LB $26.00 (978-0-531-16890-5). 48pp. An attractive overview of India, covering the differences between city and rural life, weather, daily life and culture, history, and contemporary issues such as recent terrorist attacks. (Rev: SLJ 7/09) [954]

17664 Arnold, Caroline, and Madeleine Comora. *Taj Mahal* (4–7). Illus. by Rahul Bhushan. 2007, Carolrhoda LB $17.95 (978-0-7613-2609-9). A beautifully designed, oversized picture book, this volume on the Taj Mahal and the story behind its construction includes detailed paintings and a fictionalized narrative about the Mogul prince who built it in memory of his wife. (Rev: BL 6/1–15/07; SLJ 7/07)

17665 Bowden, Rob. *The Ganges* (5–7). Series: A River Journey. 2003, Raintree LB $28.56 (978-0-7398-6070-0). 48pp. A detailed look at India's most famous river, its importance to the people who live along it, and the challenge of pollution, with photographs, maps, and charts. (Rev: SLJ 3/04) [915.4]

17666 Castelain, Céline, and Aurélien Liutkus. *Asha: A Child of the Himalayas* (K–3). Series: Children of the World. 2005, Gale LB $22.45 (978-1-4103-0286-1). 24pp. Full-color photographs introduce young readers to Asha, who lives in India's mountainous state of Himachal Pradesh; suitable for browsers rather than report writers. (Rev: SLJ 10/05) [954.5203]

17667 Cumming, David. *The Ganges Delta and Its People* (5–8). Illus. Series: People and Places. 1994, Thomson Learning LB $24.26 (978-1-56847-168-6). 48pp. An introduction to the Ganges delta, the people who live there, the economy it supports, and the tragedy of its frequent flooding. (Rev: BL 10/15/94) [954]

17668 Cumming, David. *India* (2–4). Series: We Come From. 1999, Raintree LB $25.69 (978-0-8172-5213-7). 32pp. A short book that gives an introduction to daily life in India plus some material on cities, weather, land features, and a recipe. (Rev: HBG 3/00; SLJ 3/00) [954]

17669 Cumming, David. *India* (4–7). Illus. Series: Our Country. 1998, Raintree LB $27.12 (978-0-8172-4797-3). 48pp. Several young inhabitants introduce India and describe life, customs, food, and their homes. (Rev: BL 12/1/89; HBG 10/98; SLJ 3/92) [954]

17670 Dalal, Anita. *India* (4–8). Series: Nations of the World. 2001, Raintree LB $34.26 (978-0-7398-1289-1). 128pp. A fine introduction to this vast, populous country with chapters on the land and cities, past and present, the economy, arts and living, and the future. (Rev: BL 12/15/01; HBG 3/02) [954]

17671 DuTemple, Lesley A. *The Taj Mahal* (4–7). Series: Great Building Feats. 2003, Lerner LB $27.93 (978-0-8225-4694-8). 96pp. Using many illustrations, this account traces the building of the magnificent tomb that was inspired by one man's love for his wife. (Rev: BL 11/15/03) [954]

17672 Flatt, Lizann. *India* (3–5). Series: Facts About Countries. 2009, Sea-to-Sea LB $27.10 (978-1-59771-117-3). 32pp. A well-designed introduction to India with color photographs and statistics and covering geography, history, economy, education, government, culture, and current status. (Rev: SLJ 7/09) [954]

17673 Godard, Philippe. *We Live in India* (3–6). Illus. by Sophie Duffet. Series: Kids Around the World. 2006, Abrams $15.95 (978-0-8109-5736-7). 47pp. Three Indian children from different backgrounds — one Tamil, one Bengali, and one an "untouchable" Hindi — are featured in an overview suitable for browsers. (Rev: SLJ 2/07) [954.052]

17674 Goodwin, William. *India* (5–8). Series: Modern Nations of the World. 2000, Lucent LB $27.45 (978-1-56006-598-2). 112pp. An admirable introduction to India that gives material on the land and its past but concentrates on today's population, living conditions, and problems. (Rev: BL 3/15/00; HBG 10/00) [954]

17675 Green, Jen. *Mumbai* (4–8). Photos by Chris Fairclough. Series: Global Cities. 2007, Chelsea House LB $30.00 (978-0-7910-8851-7). 61pp. With plenty of photographs and maps, this overview of the city of Mumbai (formerly Bombay) provides concise information on its history, geography, people, environment, transportation, and so forth. (Rev: SLJ 7/07)

17676 Guile, Melanie. *Culture in India* (4–7). Illus. Series: Culture In. 2005, Raintree LB $25.70 (978-1-4109-1134-6). 32pp. Customs, holidays, clothing, food, and arts and crafts are well covered in this volume that also provides basic information needed for reports and interesting sidebar features on such topics as ancestor worship and celebrities. (Rev: BL 2/15/04; SLJ 5/05) [954]

17677 Haskins, James. *Count Your Way Through India* (3–5). Illus. by Liz B. Dodson. Series: Count Your Way. 1990, Carolrhoda LB $19.93 (978-0-87614-414-5). 24pp. Using a numbers approach, this book introduces the culture, climate, and people of India. (Rev: BL 4/1/91) [954]

17678 Hermes, Jules. *The Children of India* (3–6). Illus. Series: World's Children. 1994, Carolrhoda LB $23.93 (978-0-87614-759-7). 48pp. A brief look at the diversity of children and their cultures in the vast subcontinent of India. (Rev: BCCB 4/94; BL 2/1/94) [305.23]

17679 Hirst, Mike. *A Flavor of India* (3–5). Series: Foods and Festivals. 1999, Raintree LB $25.69 (978-0-8172-5551-0). 32pp. Various festivals and holidays observed in India are discussed, with four simple recipes for the dishes associated with them. (Rev: BL 5/15/99; HBG 10/99) [954]

17680 Mann, Elizabeth. *Taj Mahal* (3–6). Illus. by Alan Witschonke. Series: Wonders of the World. 2008, Mikaya $22.95 (978-1-931414-20-3). 48pp. An interesting account of the building of the Taj Mahal, the love that prompted its construction, and the care that was taken in its incredible design. (Rev: BL 11/15/08; SLJ 1/09) [954.02]

17681 Olson, Nathan. *India: A Question And Answer Book* (2–5). Illus. Series: Questions and Answers: Countries. 2005, Capstone LB $23.93 (978-0-7368-3751-4). 32pp. Using a question-and-answer format, simple text, large photos, and many factboxes, this is an introduction to India today, with material on history and traditional culture. (Rev: SLJ 6/05)

17682 Pollard, Michael. *The Ganges* (5–7). Series: Great Rivers. 1997, Benchmark LB $22.79 (978-0-7614-0504-7). 45pp. This work describes the course of the Ganges from the Himalayas to its muddy delta, covers its history, and touches on the poverty and pollution that is found around it today. (Rev: HBG 3/98; SLJ 4/98) [954]

17683 Rowe, Percy, and Patience Coster. *Delhi* (4–7). Illus. Series: Great Cities of the World. 2005, World Almanac LB $31.00 (978-0-8368-5037-6). 48pp. An informative and appealing overview of this major Indian city, with material on its history, its economy, and what it's like to live there. (Rev: BL 4/15/04)

17684 Spilsbury, Louise, and Richard Spilsbury. *Living on the Ganges River* (3–5). Illus. Series: World Cultures. 2007, Raintree LB $27.50 (978-1-4109-2820-7). 32pp. The authors look at aspects of life along the Ganges including homes, daily life, food and clothing, school and leisure, and festivals. (Rev: SLJ 2/08) [954]

17685 Spilsbury, Richard. *Settlements of the Ganges River* (3–5). Illus. Series: Rivers Through Time.

2005, Heinemann LB $31.43 (978-1-4034-6526-9). 48pp. Traces the history and contemporary life of major settlements along the Ganges, discussing environmental and other important issues.

17686 Srinivasan, Radhika, and Leslie Jermyn. *India*. 2nd ed. (4–8). Illus. Series: Cultures of the World. 2001, Benchmark LB $37.07 (978-0-7614-1354-7). 144pp. An updated edition of the 1990 title, covering the history, geography, politics, people, arts, culture, and environmental concerns of India. (Rev: HBG 3/02; SLJ 3/02) [954]

17687 Swan, Erin Pembrey. *India* (4–7). Series: Enchantment of the World. 2002, Children's LB $37.00 (978-0-516-21121-3). 144pp. This visually attractive introduction to the past and present of India includes coverage of languages, culture, the people, economy, and government. (Rev: BL 5/15/02) [954]

Japan

17688 Baines, John. *Japan* (3–5). Illus. Series: Country Facts Files. 1994, Raintree LB $27.12 (978-0-8114-1847-8). 45pp. Contemporary Japan is introduced under such headings as landscape, climate, trade, and daily life. (Rev: SLJ 10/94) [952]

17689 Barber, Nicola. *Tokyo* (4–6). Series: Great Cities of the World. 2004, World Almanac LB $31.00 (978-0-8368-5033-8). 48pp. Report writers will find useful information on the Japanese capital's history, culture, and lifestyle. (Rev: SLJ 7/04) [952]

17690 Blumberg, Rhoda. *Commodore Perry in the Land of the Shogun* (5–8). Illus. 1985, Lothrop $21.99 (978-0-688-03723-9). 128pp. Japan was a mysterious country when Perry arrived in 1853 to open its harbors to American ships. (Rev: BL 11/1/85; SLJ 10/85) [952.025]

17691 Boraas, Tracey. *Japan* (3–6). Illus. Series: Countries and Cultures. 2001, Capstone LB $25.26 (978-0-7368-0770-8). 64pp. An overview of history, geography, government, economy, and culture that will be useful for students preparing reports. (Rev: HBG 3/02; SLJ 4/02)

17692 Bornoff, Nick. *Japan* (4–7). Illus. Series: Country Insights. 1997, Raintree LB $27.12 (978-0-8172-4786-7). 48pp. This description of modern life in the city of Okazaki and in the village of Narai compares home life, employment, schooling, and recreation. (Rev: BL 7/97; SLJ 8/97) [952]

17693 Burgan, Michael. *Japan* (2–5). Illus. Series: Questions and Answers: Countries. 2004, Capstone LB $23.93 (978-0-7368-2478-1). 32pp. Using a question-and-answer format, simple text, large photos, and many factboxes, this is an introduction to Japan today, with material on history and traditional culture.

17694 Cobb, Vicki. *This Place Is Crowded: Japan* (3–5). Illus. by Barbara Lavallee. Series: Imagine Living Here. 1992, Walker LB $15.85 (978-0-8027-8146-8). 32pp. The focus is on the concept of space in this book that provides basic information about

living in a highly populated nation of islands. (Rev: BL 9/1/92; SLJ 8/92) [952.04]

17695 Costain, Meredith, and Paul Collins. *Welcome to Japan* (3–5). Illus. Series: Countries of the World. 2001, Chelsea LB $28.00 (978-0-7910-6541-9). 32pp. A basic overview that covers history, government, culture, transportation, plants and animals, sports, and schooling. (Rev: HBG 3/02; SLJ 2/02) [952]

17696 Glaser, Jason, and Don Roley. *Ninja* (3–6). Series: Edge Books: Warriors of History. 2006, Capstone LB $23.93 (978-0-7368-6432-9). 32pp. A colorfully introduction to Japan's ninja warriors, their history, weapons, and way of life. (Rev: SLJ 1/07) [355.5]

17697 Green, Jen. *Japan* (4–8). Series: Nations of the World. 2001, Raintree LB $34.26 (978-0-8172-5783-5). 128pp. An attractive, fact-filled introduction to this island nation, its rich culture, advanced technology, and wealthy economy. (Rev: BL 6/1–15/01; HBG 10/01) [952]

17698 Hanel, Rachael. *Samurai* (5–8). Series: Fearsome Fighters. 2007, Creative Education LB $31.35 (978-1-58341-538-2). 48pp. Weapons, armor, fighting techniques, and motivation are all discussed in this description of the Japanese feudal warriors and the kinds of people who were tempted to this career. (Rev: SLJ 1/08)

17699 Haskins, James. *Count Your Way Through Japan* (3–5). Illus. 1987, Carolrhoda LB $19.93 (978-0-87614-301-8); paper $5.95 (978-0-87614-485-5). 24pp. "Two chopsticks" and other numbers help to introduce the culture of Japan. (Rev: BL 10/15/87; SLJ 9/87)

17700 Leavitt, Caroline. *Samurai* (3–5). Illus. Series: Edge Books: Warriors of History. 2006, Capstone LB $23.93 (978-0-7368-6433-6). 32pp. A solid exploration of the history and traditions associated with Japan's samurai warriors, with a wealth of illustrations. (Rev: BL 10/15/06; SLJ 1/07) [952]

17701 Littlefield, Holly. *Colors of Japan* (3–4). Illus. by Helen Byers. 1997, Carolrhoda $19.93 (978-0-87614-885-3); paper $5.95 (978-1-57505-215-1). 24pp. A picture book that uses different colors to explore various aspects of Japanese culture. (Rev: HBG 3/98; SLJ 1/98) [952]

17702 MacDonald, Fiona. *How to Be a Samurai Warrior* (2–5). Illus. by John James. Series: How to Be. 2005, National Geographic $14.95 (978-0-7922-3618-4). 32pp. A glimpse of what life was like for samurai warriors, touching on such fundamentals as clothing, weapons, job requirements, family life, and pay. (Rev: SLJ 12/05) [952.02]

17703 MacMillan, Dianne. *Japanese Children's Day and the Obon Festival* (3–5). Series: Best Holiday. 1997, Enslow LB $23.93 (978-0-89490-818-7). 48pp. The origins of these closely related Japanese holidays are described, with material on how they are celebrated. (Rev: BL 12/15/97; HBG 3/98; SLJ 8/97) [952]

17704 Metcalf, Florence E. *A Peek at Japan: A Lighthearted Look at Japan's Language and Culture* (3–6). Illus. by Tomoko. 1992, Metco paper $14.95

(978-0-9631684-3-6). 136pp. After a section on Japanese language and vocabulary, this book deals with Japan's culture, games, origami, and unusual facts. (Rev: SLJ 7/92) [952]

17705 Patchett, Kaye. *The Akashi Kaikyo Bridge* (5–8). Illus. Series: Building World Landmarks. 2004, Gale LB $24.95 (978-1-4103-0140-6). 48pp. A concise account of the amazing construction of the bridge that links Shikoku and Honshu islands. (Rev: BL 4/1/04; SLJ 4/05)

17706 Phillips, Charles. *Japan* (3–6). Illus. Series: Countries of the World. 2007, National Geographic LB $27.90 (978-1-4263-0029-5). 64pp. An attractive layout and up-to-date information combine to make this an effective and interesting introduction to the country and its culture. (Rev: SLJ 8/07)

17707 Pilbeam, Mavis. *Japan Under the Shoguns, 1185–1868* (5–8). Series: Looking Back. 1999, Raintree $19.98 (978-0-8172-5431-5). A handsome, detailed overview of the shogun society of Japan from 1185 to 1868, featuring color photographs and reproductions of original art. (Rev: BL 5/15/99) [452]

17708 Poisson, Barbara Aoki. *The Ainu of Japan* (4–6). Series: First Peoples. 2002, Lerner LB $23.93 (978-0-8225-4176-9). The Ainu of Japan have shared their homeland with the Japanese for centuries and continue to retain their independent culture. (Rev: BL 5/15/02; HBG 10/02; SLJ 8/02) [952]

17709 Richardson, Hazel. *Life in Ancient Japan* (4–7). Illus. Series: Peoples of the Ancient World. 2005, Crabtree LB $26.60 (978-0-7787-2041-6); paper $8.95 (978-0-7787-2071-3). 32pp. Introduces ancient Japan's arts, spiritual beliefs, government, language, and technology; color photographs, sidebars, and timelines add information and appeal. (Rev: SLJ 11/05) [952]

17710 Say, Allen. *Tea with Milk* (4–8). Illus. 1999, Houghton LB $17.00 (978-0-395-90495-4). 32pp. A picture book about the author's mother, who was forced by her father to leave her California residence and return to the family's original home in Japan. (Rev: BCCB 6/99; BL 3/15/99*; HB 7/99; HBG 10/99; SLJ 5/99) [952]

17711 Schemenauer, Elma. *Japan* (2–3). Illus. Series: Faces and Places. 1997, Child's World LB $22.79 (978-1-56766-371-6). 32pp. A simple introduction to Japan, with many color photos and basic information on geography, history, people, and customs. (Rev: BL 2/1/98) [952]

17712 Schomp, Virginia. *Japan in the Days of the Samurai* (5–8). Illus. Series: Cultures of the Past. 2001, Marshall Cavendish LB $29.93 (978-0-7614-0304-3). 80pp. A well-illustrated look at the history of Japan, including information on such cultural topics as the tea ceremony and samurai women. (Rev: BL 2/15/02; HBG 3/02; SLJ 3/02) [952]

17713 Shelley, Rex, and Teo Chuu Yong. *Japan*. 2nd ed. (5–8). Illus. Series: Cultures of the World. 2001, Benchmark LB $37.07 (978-0-7614-1356-1). 144pp. An updated edition of the 1996 title, covering the history, geography, politics, people, arts,

culture, and environmental concerns of Japan. (Rev: HBG 3/02; SLJ 3/02) [952]

17714 Takabayashi, Mari. *I Live in Tokyo* (1–3). Illus. 2001, Houghton $16.00 (978-0-618-07702-1). 32pp. Readers learn about the customs, traditions, and everyday activities that are part of a 7-year-old Japanese girl's life. (Rev: BL 9/15/01; HB 11/01*; HBG 3/02; SLJ 10/01) [952]

17715 Turnbull, Stephen. *Real Samurai* (4–6). Illus. by James Field. 2007, Enchanted Lion $15.95 (978-1-59270-060-8). 48pp. An eye-catching volume of information about the ancient samurai covering weapons, warrior practices, codes of honor, and related subjects. (Rev: BL 6/1–15/07; SLJ 7/07) [952]

17716 Tyler, Deborah. *Japan* (3–5). Illus. Series: Discovering. 1993, Crestwood LB $13.95 (978-0-89686-773-4). 32pp. A brief introduction to modern Japan that stresses its distinctive culture and modern accomplishments. (Rev: BL 2/1/94) [952]

Other Asian Lands

17717 *Afghanistan in Pictures* (5–8). Illus. Series: Visual Geography. 1997, Lerner LB $25.55 (978-0-8225-1849-5). 64pp. Includes sections on vegetation and wildlife, minerals, cities, history, and government. (Rev: BL 5/1/89) [958.1]

17718 Alberti, Theresa. *Vietnam ABCs* (2–4). Illus. by Alex Blanks. Series: Country ABCs. 2007, Picture Window LB $26.60 (978-1-4048-2251-1). 32pp. This alphabet-book introduction to Vietnam offers basic information about the Southeast Asian country and its troubled history. (Rev: BL 3/15/07) [959.7]

17719 Ali, Sharifah Enayat. *Afghanistan*. 2nd ed. (5–9). Illus. Series: Cultures of the World. 2006, Benchmark LB $39.93 (978-0-7614-2064-4). 144pp. A revised and updated edition of the guide to Afghanistan and its history, geography, culture, and government including maps and color photographs. (Rev: SLJ 3/07) [958.1]

17720 Barber, Nicola. *Singapore* (4–7). Illus. Series: Great Cities of the World. 2005, World Almanac LB $31.00 (978-0-8368-5047-5). 48pp. An informative and appealing overview of one of the world's most famous cities, with material on its history, its economy, and what it's like to live there. (Rev: BL 4/15/04)

17721 Boraas, Tracey. *Thailand* (4–6). Series: Countries and Cultures. 2002, Capstone LB $25.26 (978-0-7368-0940-5). 64pp. The land and people of Thailand are introduced with material on climate, landforms, history, traditions, people, and even a recipe. (Rev: BL 1/1–15/03; HBG 3/03; SLJ 2/03) [959.3]

17722 Bowden, Rob. *Settlements of the Indus River* (3–5). Illus. Series: Rivers Through Time. 2005, Heinemann LB $29.93 (978-1-4034-5718-9). 48pp. Traces the history and contemporary life of major settlements along the Indus, discussing environmental and other important issues.

17723 Brace, Steve. *Bangladesh* (4–8). Illus. Series: Economically Developing Countries. 1995, Thomson Learning LB $24.26 (978-1-56847-243-0). 48pp. An overview of life in Bangladesh told in a simple, large-print text and many color photographs. (Rev: SLJ 7/95) [954.9]

17724 Brown, Don. *Far Beyond the Garden Gate: Alexandra David-Neel's Journey to Lhasa* (PS–2). Illus. 2002, Houghton $16.00 (978-0-618-08364-0). 32pp. This is the dramatic story of the long, intrepid travels of the first Western woman to visit the holy city of Lhasa (in 1924) and of her intense interest in Buddhism. (Rev: BL 10/1/02; HB 9/02; HBG 3/03; SLJ 10/02) [915.1]

17725 Burbank, Jon. *Nepal* (4–7). Illus. Series: Cultures of the World. 1991, Marshall Cavendish LB $35.64 (978-1-85435-401-3). 128pp. The emphasis is on culture as well as the basics of geography, history, government, and people. (Rev: BL 2/15/92) [954.96]

17726 Cha, Dia. *Dia's Story Cloth* (3–5). Illus. by Chue Cha and Nhia Thao Cha. 1996, Lee & Low $15.95 (978-1-880000-34-2). 32pp. The story of the author's family, who fled first from Laos and then from Thailand to settle in the United States. (Rev: BCCB 7–8/96; BL 6/1–15/96; SLJ 7/96) [973]

17727 Clifford, Mary Louise. *The Land and People of Afghanistan* (5–7). Illus. 1989, HarperCollins LB $14.89 (978-0-397-32339-5). 240pp. An introduction to past life in this central Asian country. A reissue. [958.1]

17728 De Capua, Sarah. *Korea* (3–5). Illus. Series: Discovering Cultures. 2004, Benchmark LB $25.64 (978-0-7614-1794-1). 48pp. An attractive introduction to the Korean peninsula, covering land, people, daily life, education, food, and celebrations, with discussion of the differences between North and South. (Rev: SLJ 6/05)

17729 Ericson, Alex. *Thailand* (3–5). Series: Faces and Places. 2001, Child's World LB $22.79 (978-1-56766-913-8). 32pp. This oversize volume presents basic facts on Thailand with an emphasis on the people and how they live. (Rev: BL 9/15/01; HBG 3/02) [959.3]

17730 Fiscus, James W. *America's War in Afghanistan* (5–9). Illus. Series: War and Conflict in the Middle East. 2004, Rosen LB $27.95 (978-0-8239-4552-8). 64pp. A well-organized, balanced account of the war between the United States and Afghanistan in the aftermath of the 2001 terrorist attacks on New York and Washington, D.C. (Rev: BL 11/1/04)

17731 Fordyce, Deborah. *Welcome to Afghanistan* (3–5). Series: Welcome to My Country. 2004, Gareth Stevens LB $27.00 (978-0-8368-2557-2). 48pp. Introduces readers to Afghanistan's geography, history, people, culture, family life, government, religion, and language. (Rev: SLJ 7/04) [958.1]

17732 Giraud, Hervé. *Basha: A Hmong Child* (K–3). Photos by Jean-Charles Rey. Series: Children of the World. 2005, Gale LB $22.45 (978-1-4103-0547-3). 24pp. Using many photographs, this volume introduces the lifestyle and customs of the Hmong peo-

ple who live in northern Vietnam; suitable for browsers rather than report writers. Also use *Kradji: A Child of Cambodia* (2005). (Rev: SLJ 10/05) [305.8959]

17733 Gogol, Sara. *A Mien Family* (4–7). Illus. Series: Journey Between Two Worlds. 1996, Lerner LB $22.60 (978-0-8225-3407-5); paper $8.95 (978-0-8225-9745-2). 64pp. The story of a refugee family from the mountainous area of Laos and their journey to the United States. (Rev: BL 11/15/96; SLJ 1/97) [306.85]

17734 Goodman, Jim. *Thailand* (5–9). Series: Cultures of the World. 1991, Marshall Cavendish LB $35.64 (978-1-85435-402-0). Thailand's history, land, and culture. (Rev: BL 3/15/92) [959.3]

17735 Goodman, Susan. *Chopsticks for My Noodle Soup: Eliza's Life in Malaysia* (1–3). Illus. by Michael Doolittle. 2000, Millbrook LB $21.40 (978-0-7613-1552-0). 32pp. A kindergartner from Connecticut visits a Malaysian village with her parents and comments on its daily life and customs in an account illustrated with her father's photographs. (Rev: BL 3/15/00; HBG 10/00; SLJ 5/00) [959.5]

17736 Goom, Bridget. *A Family in Singapore* (3–4). Illus. 1986, Lerner LB $18.60 (978-0-8225-1663-7). 32pp. With the focus on one child in one family, readers discover what life is like in Singapore. (Rev: BL 5/15/86; SLJ 10/86)

17737 Guile, Melanie. *Culture in Malaysia* (4–7). Illus. Series: Culture In. 2005, Raintree LB $25.70 (978-1-4109-1133-9). 32pp. Customs, holidays, clothing, food, and arts and crafts are well covered in this volume that also provides basic information needed for reports and interesting sidebar features. (Rev: SLJ 5/05)

17738 Guile, Melanie. *Culture in Vietnam* (3–5). Illus. Series: Culture In. 2005, Raintree LB $25.70 (978-1-4109-1135-3). 32pp. Vietnam's people, language, celebrations and customs are covered, with photographs and maps adding to the appeal. (Rev: BL 3/1/05; SLJ 5/05) [306]

17739 Haberle, Susan E. *North Korea* (2–5). Illus. Series: Questions and Answers: Countries. 2005, Capstone LB $23.93 (978-0-7368-3756-9). 32pp. Using a question-and-answer format, simple text, large photos, and many factboxes, this is an introduction to North Korea today, with material on history and traditional culture.

17740 Haberle, Susan E. *South Korea* (2–5). Illus. Series: Questions and Answers: Countries. 2005, Capstone LB $23.93 (978-0-7368-3761-3). 32pp. Using a question-and-answer format, simple text, large photos, and many factboxes, this is an introduction to South Korea today, with material on history and traditional culture.

17741 Hansen, Ole Steen. *Vietnam* (5–8). Illus. Series: Economically Developing Countries. 1996, Raintree LB $24.26 (978-0-8172-4526-9). 48pp. This introduction to Vietnam includes background information and material on its emerging economy. (Rev: BL 3/1/97) [959.7]

17742 Heinrichs, Ann. *Pakistan* (2–3). Series: A True Book. 2004, Children's Pr. LB $25.00 (978-0-516-

22813-6). 47pp. Geography, history, and daily life are covered in this attractive introduction to Pakistan. (Rev: SLJ 11/04) [954.9]

17743 Hill, Valerie. *Korea* (3–6). Illus. Series: Ask About Asia. 2002, Mason Crest LB $18.95 (978-1-59084-206-5). 47pp. Geography, history, culture, government, and daily life are presented in double-page spreads with plenty of photographs, reproductions, and maps. (Rev: SLJ 4/03) [951]

17744 Holmes, Jim, and Tom Morgan. *A Child's Day in a Vietnamese City* (K–3). Series: A Child's Day. 2002, Marshall Cavendish LB $25.64 (978-0-7614-1409-4). 32pp. Present-day Vietnam is introduced through the everyday experiences of a Vietnamese child. (Rev: BL 2/15/03; HBG 3/03) [959.7]

17745 Huynh, Quang Nhuong. *Water Buffalo Days* (4–6). Illus. 1997, HarperCollins LB $13.89 (978-0-06-024958-8). 128pp. This is a story of growing up in rural Vietnam in the late 1940s and of a family's water buffalo, Tank. (Rev: BL 11/15/97; SLJ 2/98*) [636.2]

17746 Jung, Sung-Hoon. *South Korea* (5–8). Series: Economically Developing Countries. 1997, Raintree LB $24.26 (978-0-8172-4530-6). This overview of economic conditions in South Korea describes the country's success with electronic exports and provides case studies of family-run companies. (Rev: BL 5/15/97) [951.95]

17747 Karkonen, Reijo. *The Children of Nepal* (4–6). Illus. by Matti Pitkanen. Series: World's Children. 1990, Carolrhoda LB $23.93 (978-0-87614-395-7). 40pp. Comments on life in Nepal, with striking color photos. (Rev: BL 6/15/90; SLJ 8/90) [954.96]

17748 Kendra, Judith. *Tibetans* (5–8). Series: Threatened Cultures. 1994, Thomson Learning LB $24.25 (978-1-56847-152-5). Discusses Tibetan culture and religion, with emphasis on the denial by China of Tibetans' rights. Follows the daily lives of two Tibetan children, one living in the country, one in the city. (Rev: BL 7/94) [951]

17749 Knox, Barbara. *Afghanistan* (2–4). Series: Many Cultures, One World. 2004, Capstone LB $23.93 (978-0-7368-2448-4). 32pp. An interesting introduction to Afghanistan, covering city and country life, family life, laws and customs, seasons, important sights, and even favorite pets. (Rev: SLJ 8/04) [958.1]

17750 Koh, Frances M. *Korean Holidays and Festivals* (2–5). Illus. by Liz B. Dodson. 1990, East-West LB $15.00 (978-0-9606090-5-5). 32pp. Nine holidays and cultural festivals that are celebrated in South Korea are described. (Rev: BL 3/1/91; SLJ 6/91) [394.25]

17751 Kummer, Patricia K. *Tibet* (4–8). Series: Enchantment of the World. 2003, Children's Pr. LB $37.00 (978-0-516-22693-4). 144pp. A visually attractive book that covers such topics as the geography, history, government, culture, and people, with a timeline, fast facts, and a recipe. (Rev: SLJ 1/04) [951]

17752 Layton, Lesley. *Singapore* (5–8). Illus. Series: Cultures of the World. 1990, Marshall Cavendish LB $35.64 (978-1-85435-295-8). 128pp. As well as history and economy, this introduction to Singapore includes coverage of lifestyles and current problems. (Rev: BL 3/1/91; SLJ 6/91) [959.57]

17753 Levy, Patricia. *Tibet* (4–7). Illus. Series: Cultures of the World. 1996, Marshall Cavendish LB $37.07 (978-0-7614-0277-0). 128pp. Tibet is introduced with general background information, followed by material on its people and their culture, festivals, and food. (Rev: BL 8/96; SLJ 9/96) [951.1]

17754 Lewin, Ted, and Betsy Lewin. *Horse Song: The Naadam of Mongolia* (2–5). Illus. by Ted Lewin. 2008, Lee & Low $19.95 (978-1-58430-277-3). 56pp. An account of the authors' trip to Mongolia, where they watched the annual horse races that are part of the Naadam celebration; a 9-year-old jockey named Tamir teaches them about the event. (Rev: BL 5/1/08; HB 7/08; LMC 10/08; SLJ 6/08) [306.0951]

17755 Lorbiecki, Marybeth. *Children of Vietnam* (4–7). Photos by Paul P. Rome. Series: The World's Children. 1997, Carolrhoda LB $28.75 (978-1-57505-034-8). 45pp. Beginning in the north and working south, this photoessay describes the people of Vietnam and the lives of their children. (Rev: HBG 3/98; SLJ 2/98) [959.7]

17756 McNair, Sylvia. *Malaysia* (4–7). Series: Enchantment of the World. 2002, Children's LB $37.00 (978-0-516-21009-4). 144pp. This Southeast Asian nation is presented in text and many color photographs that introduce its history, geography, people, culture, and present status. (Rev: BL 9/15/02) [959.505]

17757 *Malaysia in Pictures* (5–8). Illus. Series: Visual Geography. 1997, Lerner LB $25.55 (978-0-8225-1854-9). 64pp. A basic, visual overview of this nation and its people. (Rev: BL 5/1/89) [959.5]

17758 March, Michael. *Bangladesh* (3–5). Series: Facts About Countries. 2009, Sea-to-Sea LB $27.10 (978-1-59771-113-5). 32pp. A well-designed introduction to Bangladesh with color photographs and statistics and covering geography, history, economy, education, government, culture, and current status. (Rev: SLJ 7/09) [954.92]

17759 Millett, Sandra. *The Hmong of Southeast Asia* (4–6). Series: First Peoples. 2001, Lerner LB $23.93 (978-0-8225-4852-2). 48pp. This attractive introduction to the Hmong people and their native region and culture also contrasts traditional and modern lifestyles. (Rev: HBG 3/02; SLJ 3/02) [305.895]

17760 Mirpuri, Gouri, and Robert Cooper. *Indonesia*. 2nd ed. (5–8). Illus. Series: Cultures of the World. 2001, Marshall Cavendish LB $37.07 (978-0-7614-1355-4). 144pp. An encompassing look at the history, culture, society, and geography of Indonesia. (Rev: BL 3/1/02; HBG 3/02; SLJ 4/02) [959.8]

17761 Moiz, Azra. *Taiwan* (4–7). Illus. Series: Cultures of the World. 1995, Marshall Cavendish LB $37.07 (978-0-7614-0180-3). 128pp. The accomplishments, lifestyle, and religious festivals of the people of Taiwan are covered, along with its history and geography. (Rev: BL 1/1–15/96; SLJ 9/96) [957.24]

17762 Mortenson, Greg, and David Oliver Relin. *Three Cups of Tea: One Man's Journey to Change the World . . . One Child at a Time* (4–8). Illus. 2009, Dial $16.99 (978-0-8037-3392-3). 192pp. Focusing mainly on the young people, this simplified version of Mortenson's bestseller for adults describes his successes building schools in Pakistan and Afghanistan. (Rev: BL 2/1/09; SLJ 2/09) [371]

∩ **17763** Mortenson, Greg, and Susan L. Roth. *Listen to the Wind: The Story of Dr. Greg and Three Cups of Tea* (1–3). Illus. by Susan L. Roth. 2009, Dial $16.99 (978-0-8037-3058-8). 32pp. The story of Greg Mortenson's efforts to build schools in the high mountains of Pakistan is told from the point of view of the children of Korphe, who benefited from his extraordinary determination; with effective collage artwork. (Rev: BCCB 3/09; BL 1/1–15/09; LMC 5/09; SLJ 2/09) [371.0095491]

17764 Munan, Heidi. *Malaysia* (5–8). Illus. Series: Cultures of the World. 1990, Marshall Cavendish LB $35.64 (978-1-85435-296-5). 128pp. Cultural diversity and lifestyles of the people are two topics covered in this introduction to Malaysia. (Rev: BL 3/1/91) [959.5]

17765 O'Brien, Tony, and Mike Sullivan. *Afghan Dreams: Young Voices of Afghanistan* (4–9). Photos by Tony O'Brien. 2008, Bloomsbury $18.99 (978-1-59990-287-6). 74pp. This photo-essay more than 30 young Afghans illustrates their poignant situation and provides background information. (Rev: BCCB 12/08; SLJ 12/08; VOYA 12/08) [305.235092]

17766 O'Connor, Karen. *Vietnam* (3–5). Series: Globe-Trotters Club. 1999, Carolrhoda LB $22.60 (978-1-57505-117-8). 48pp. Sidebars and stunning color photos bring to life the land and people of Vietnam in an entertaining and instructive manner. (Rev: BL 11/15/99; HBG 3/00; SLJ 2/00) [959.7]

17767 O'Connor, Karen. *Vietnam* (1–3). Series: A Ticket To. 1999, Carolrhoda LB $22.60 (978-1-57505-142-0). 48pp. This first look at Vietnam introduces the land, people, culture, customs, and famous sights with a simple, large-type text, color photos, and well-organized topics. (Rev: BL 11/15/99; HBG 3/00; SLJ 2/00) [959.7]

17768 Olson, Gillia M. *Afghanistan: A Question and Answer Book* (2–5). Series: Fact Finders. 2004, Capstone LB $23.93 (978-0-7368-2685-3). 32pp. Double-page spreads use simple text, factboxes, and plenty of color photographs to answer pertinent questions about the country's history, geography, government, and culture. (Rev: BL 11/15/04; SLJ 3/05) [958.1]

17769 Orr, Tamra. *Bangladesh* (5–9). Illus. Series: Enchantment of the World Second Series. 2007, Children's Pr. LB $36.00 (978-0-516-25012-0). 144pp. Features information on the Asian nation of Bangladesh, including its culture, religion, family life, arts, and sports and looks in particular at the country's struggles with pollution, poor living and working conditions, and political instability. (Rev: BL 8/07) [954.92]

17770 Pang, Guek-Cheng. *Mongolia* (5–8). Series: Cultures of the World. 1999, Marshall Cavendish LB $37.07 (978-0-7614-0954-0). 128pp. A clear, well-illustrated introduction to this remote land that includes good background information as well as coverage of modern life. (Rev: HBG 10/99; SLJ 10/99) [957]

17771 Park, Frances, and Ginger Park. *My Freedom Trip* (K–4). Illus. by Debra R. Jenkins. 1998, Boyds Mills $16.95 (978-1-56397-468-7). 32pp. A true story about the authors' mother, Soo, and her escape with her father from North Korea on the eve of the Korean War, leaving behind a mother she would never see again. (Rev: BL 9/1/98; HBG 3/99; SLJ 1/99) [951.93]

17772 Pascoe, Elaine, ed. *Into Wild Borneo* (3–6). Series: The Jeff Corwin Experience. 2004, Gale LB $24.95 (978-1-56711-859-9). 48pp. Jeff Corwin of the Animal Planet television series interacts with elephants, apes, and much smaller creatures in Borneo. (Rev: SLJ 4/04) [591.9598]

17773 Ramulshah, Mano. *Pakistan* (3–8). Illus. 1992, Viking $22.95 (978-0-237-60193-5). 32pp. Famous landmarks, social and political life, and history are discussed. (Rev: SLJ 8/92) [954]

17774 Razzak, Shazia. *P Is for Pakistan* (2–5). Photos by Prodeepta Das. 2007, Frances Lincoln $16.95 (978-1-84507-483-8). 28pp. From A to Z, this book introduces words in English or Urdu that convey information on Pakistan's history, culture, or geography. (Rev: SLJ 3/08) [954.9]

17775 Romano, Amy. *A Historical Atlas of Afghanistan* (4–6). Illus. Series: Historical Atlases of South Asia, Central Asia and the Middle East. 2003, Rosen LB $30.60 (978-0-8239-3863-6). 64pp. This attractive profile that includes many maps and photographs traces Afghanistan's development from prehistoric times to the present. (Rev: SLJ 8/03)

17776 Roop, Peter, and Connie Roop. *Vietnam* (1–3). Series: A Visit To. 1998, Heinemann LB $21.36 (978-1-57572-120-0). 32pp. Introduces us to the land and people of Vietnam, showing how they live, work, and celebrate their festivals. (Rev: SLJ 7/98) [959.7]

17777 Rowell, Jonathan. *Malaysia* (5–8). Illus. Series: Economically Developing Countries. 1997, Raintree LB $24.26 (978-0-8172-4531-3). 48pp. The growth and development of Malaysia are traced, with material on its high-tech sector. (Rev: BL 5/15/97) [959.505]

17778 Ryan, Patrick. *Welcome to South Korea* (1–4). Series: Wecome to the World. 2008, The Child's World LB $27.07 (978-1-59296-978-4). 32pp. As easy introduction to South Korea and its land, people, plants and animals, and so forth, with color photographs, maps, and recipes. (Rev: LMC 10/08; SLJ 9/08) [951.9]

17779 Schmidt, Jeremy, and Ted Wood. *Two Lands, One Heart: An American Boy's Journey to His Mother's Vietnam* (3–5). Illus. 1995, Walker LB $16.85 (978-0-8027-8358-5). 48pp. A young boy is introduced to the culture and life of contemporary

Vietnam when he visits his mother's homeland. (Rev: BCCB 6/95; BL 5/1/95; SLJ 4/95) [915.97]

17780 Sheehan, Sean. *Cambodia* (4–7). Illus. Series: Cultures of the World. 1996, Marshall Cavendish LB $37.07 (978-0-7614-0281-7). 128pp. The troubled land of Cambodia is introduced, with emphasis on its people, their lifestyles, and culture. (Rev: BL 8/96; SLJ 9/96) [959]

17781 Sheehan, Sean, and Shahrezad Samiuddin. *Pakistan* (5–9). Illus. Series: Cultures of the World. 2004, Benchmark LB $37.07 (978-0-7614-1787-3). 144pp. Pakistan's geography, history, economy, and people are all examined, with discussion of interesting aspects of Pakistani culture. (Rev: SLJ 2/05) [954.9]

17782 Shuter, Jane. *The Indus Valley* (3–5). Illus. Series: History Opens Windows. 2002, Heinemann LB $22.79 (978-1-4034-0253-0). 32pp. An overview of government, trade, and everyday life in ancient times in the Indus Valley that is now in Pakistan and western India. (Rev: HBG 3/03; SLJ 3/03)

17783 Simpson, Judith. *Indonesia* (3–6). Illus. Series: Ask About Asia. 2002, Mason Crest LB $18.95 (978-1-59084-208-9). 47pp. Geography, history, culture, government, and daily life are presenetd in double-page spreads with plenty of photographs, reproductions, and maps. (Rev: HBG 10/03; SLJ 4/03) [959.8]

17784 *South Korea in Pictures* (5–7). Series: Visual Geography. 1997, Lerner LB $25.55 (978-0-8225-1868-6). 64pp. An introduction to South Korea that focuses on its politics and economy. (Rev: SLJ 5/90) [951.9]

17785 Stevens, Kathryn. *Afghanistan* (2–4). Series: Faces and Places. 2003, Child's World LB $22.79 (978-1-56766-181-1). 32pp. This introduction to Afghanistan covers the central Asian country's geography, history, people, culture, government, and economy. (Rev: SLJ 8/03) [958.1]

17786 Stickler, John, and Soma Han Stickler. *Land of Morning Calm: Korean Culture Then and Now* (3–5). Illus. by authors. 2003, Shen's $16.95 (978-1-885008-22-0). 32pp. An excellent introduction to Korea for young readers, this attractive book covers the history and geography of the peninsula and also examines various cultural aspects. (Rev: BL 10/15/03; SLJ 12/03)

17787 Taus-Bolstad, Stacy. *Pakistan in Pictures.* Rev. ed. (5–9). Illus. Series: Visual Geography. 2003, Lerner LB $27.93 (978-0-8225-4682-5). 80pp. This substantially revised volume covers Pakistan's history, geography, culture, and lifestyle. (Rev: SLJ 7/03) [954.9]

17788 Thomson, Ruth, and Neil Thomson. *A Family in Thailand* (4–6). Illus. 1988, Lerner LB $18.60 (978-0-8225-1684-2). 32pp. Thai children point out the characteristics of life in their country. (Rev: BL 8/88)

17789 Tull, Mary, et al. *Northern Asia* (4–7). Illus. Series: Artisans Around the World. 1990, Raintree LB $27.12 (978-0-7398-0119-2). 48pp. This book introduces Mongolia and its neighbors, with

descriptions of arts and crafts and many projects. (Rev: BL 10/15/99; HBG 3/00; SLJ 1/00) [745.5]

17790 *Vietnam in Pictures* (5–8). Illus. Series: Visual Geography. 1994, Lerner LB $25.55 (978-0-8225-1909-6). 64pp. This well-illustrated account of Vietnam covers its history, geography, people, government, and economy. (Rev: BL 11/1/94) [915.97]

17791 Wanasundera, Nanda P. *Sri Lanka* (4–7). Illus. Series: Cultures of the World. 1991, Marshall Cavendish LB $213.86 (978-1-85435-397-9). 128pp. The history, geography, and culture of Sri Lanka are introduced with an emphasis on contemporary problems. (Rev: BL 2/15/92) [954.93]

17792 Whyte, Mariam. *Bangladesh* (5–9). Series: Cultures of the World. 1998, Marshall Cavendish LB $37.07 (978-0-7614-0869-7). A sympathetic look at the history and geography of Bangladesh, with details of the country's rich background and current problems. (Rev: HBG 10/99; SLJ 6/99) [954.9]

17793 Willis, Karen. *Vietnam* (5–8). Illus. Series: Modern Nations of the World. 2000, Lucent LB $27.45 (978-1-56006-635-4). 126pp. A thorough history of Vietnam, this work also focuses on progress after the war and daily life in modern Vietnam. (Rev: BL 9/15/00; HBG 3/01) [959.7]

17794 Willis, Terri. *Vietnam* (4–7). Series: Enchantment of the World. 2002, Children's LB $37.00 (978-0-516-22150-2). 144pp. This attractive volume presents basic material on Vietnam's history, geography, and culture, with an emphasis on progress after the war. (Rev: BL 9/15/02; SLJ 12/02) [959.7]

17795 Withington, William A. *Southeast Asia* (5–8). Illus. 1988, Gateway $16.95 (978-0-934291-32-3). 160pp. Sections on lifestyle, land and climate, history and government, festivals, sports, arts, and crafts. (Rev: BL 12/1/88)

17796 Yin, Saw Myat. *Myanmar.* Rev. ed. (4–8). Illus. Series: Cultures of the World. 2001, Benchmark LB $37.07 (978-0-7614-1353-0). 144pp. An introduction to every aspect of Myanmar with useful information on daily life and phonetic pronunciations of many foreign words. Also use *Indonesia* (2001). (Rev: HBG 3/02; SLJ 4/02) [959.1]

17797 Yu, Ling. *Taiwan in Pictures* (5–8). Illus. Series: Visual Geography. 1997, Lerner LB $25.55 (978-0-8225-1865-5). 64pp. The history and geography of Taiwan are introduced, with coverage of cities, culture, religion, and economy. (Rev: BL 9/15/89) [915.1]

Australia and the Pacific Islands

17798 Alter, Judy. *Discovering Australia's Land, People, and Wildlife* (5–8). Series: Continents of the World. 2004, Enslow LB $25.26 (978-0-7660-5207-9). 48pp. An introduction to the geography, history, economy, plants and animals, culture, and people of the continent, showing the contrast between the urban centers on the coasts and the rugged interior. (Rev: SLJ 11/04) [994]

17799 Arnold, Caroline. *Easter Island: Giant Stone Statues Tell of a Rich and Tragic Past* (4–7). Illus. 2000, Clarion LB $15.00 (978-0-395-87609-1). 48pp. This chronological history of Easter Island tells how the stone statues got there and what they mean. (Rev: BCCB 4/00; BL 3/15/00; HB 5/00; HBG 10/00; SLJ 4/00) [996.1]

17800 Arnold, Caroline. *Uluru: Australia's Aboriginal Heart* (4–8). Illus. by Arthur Arnold. 2003, Clarion $16.00 (978-0-618-18181-0). 64pp. Uluru, formerly known as Ayers Rock, is a giant sandstone monolith that changes color in the setting sun and is a spiritual landmark for the native people of the central Australian desert. (Rev: BCCB 12/03; BL 12/15/03; HB 11/03; HBG 11–12/03; SLJ 1/04) [994.01]

17801 Arnold, Caroline. *A Walk on the Great Barrier Reef* (4–7). Illus. 1988, Lerner LB $25.26 (978-0-87614-285-1). 48pp. Exploring one of the great natural wonders of the world. (Rev: BL 7/88; SLJ 8/88) [574.91943]

17802 Banting, Erinn. *The Great Barrier Reef: The Largest Coral Reef in the World* (3–6). Illus. Series: Natural Wonders. 2004, Weigl LB $18.20 (978-1-59036-272-3). 32pp. A look at this giant reef, the living creatures found there, and the dangers it faces. (Rev: SLJ 4/05) [919.43]

17803 Bartlett, Anne. *The Aboriginal Peoples of Australia* (4–7). Illus. Series: First Peoples. 2001, Lerner LB $23.93 (978-0-8225-4854-6). 48pp. An introduction to the indigenous people of Australia, including their history, customs, and daily life, with photographs. (Rev: BL 10/15/01; HBG 3/02; SLJ 3/02) [994]

17804 Bingham, Jane. *Living in the Australian Outback* (3–5). Series: World Cultures. 2007, Raintree LB $27.50 (978-1-4109-2813-9). 32pp. Bingham looks at various aspects of life in the Outback — plants and animals, food, aboriginal beliefs and culture, and survival techniques. (Rev: SLJ 2/08) [305.89]

17805 Browne, Rollo. *An Aboriginal Family* (3–6). Illus. 1985, Lerner LB $18.60 (978-0-8225-1655-2). 32pp. A taste of aboriginal culture is highlighted with color photos. (Rev: BCCB 6/85; BL 6/15/85; SLJ 10/85)

17806 Coffey, Maria, and Debora Pearson. *Jungle Islands: My South Sea Adventure* (4–6). Illus. 2000, Annick LB $26.95 (978-1-55037-597-8); paper $14.95 (978-1-55037-596-1). 88pp. The waters, land, people, and history of the Solomon Islands are presented in vibrant photos and an interesting narrative. (Rev: BL 1/1–15/01; HBG 3/01; SLJ 12/00) [919.59]

17807 Darian-Smith, Kate. *Australia, Antarctica, and the Pacific* (5–8). Series: Continents of the World. 2006, World Almanac LB $34.00 (978-0-8368-5912-6). 64pp. Factboxes and "In Focus" articles add to this overview of the history, geography, people, culture, and so forth of the continents of Australia, Antarctica, and island of the Pacific. (Rev: SLJ 2/06)

17808 Darian-Smith, Kate, and David Lowe. *The Australian Outback and Its People* (4–7). Illus. Series: People and Places. 1995, Thomson Learning LB $24.26 (978-1-56847-337-6). 48pp. A well-organized guide to the Australian outback, its exploration and history, flora and fauna, mining, environmental issues, and people. (Rev: SLJ 7/95) [994]

17809 Darlington, Robert. *Australia* (4–8). Series: Nations of the World. 2001, Raintree LB $34.26 (978-0-7398-1280-8). 128pp. Australia, the world's largest island, is introduced in this attractive volume that gives material on geography, climate, terrain, history, economy, and lifestyles. (Rev: BL 6/1–15/01; HBG 10/01) [994]

17810 Fox, Mary Virginia. *Australia* (1–3). Series: Continents. 2006, Heinemann LB $21.36 (978-1-57572-449-2). 32pp. For beginning report writers, this is a survey of Australia's geography, flora, fauna, weather, and history. (Rev: SLJ 1/07) [994]

17811 Franklin, Sharon, et al. *Southwest Pacific* (4–7). Series: Artisans Around the World. 1999, Raintree LB $27.12 (978-0-7398-0120-8). 48pp. The influence of traditions and geography is shown in this survey of folk art from Australia, New Guinea, New Zealand, and Indonesia, with directions for projects such as a Maori woven band and a batik wall hanging. (Rev: BL 10/15/99; HBG 3/00; SLJ 1/00) [994]

17812 Grabowski, John. *Australia* (5–8). Series: Modern Nations of the World. 2002, Gale LB $27.45 (978-1-56006-566-1). 112pp. The continent Down Under is introduced with coverage of history, natural resources, landmarks, economy, and people. (Rev: BL 12/15/02) [994]

17813 Grupper, Jonathan. *Destination: Australia* (4–6). Illus. 2000, National Geographic $16.95 (978-0-7922-7165-9). 32pp. This stunningly illustrated introduction to Australia covers many subjects but concentrates on its unusual animals. (Rev: BL 6/1–15/00; HBG 10/00; SLJ 5/00) [591]

17814 Hermes, Jules. *The Children of Micronesia* (4–6). Illus. Series: World's Children. 1994, Carolrhoda LB $23.93 (978-0-87614-819-8). 48pp. A look at growing up in these South Pacific islands, including the Caroline, Gilbert, and Marshall island groups. (Rev: BCCB 9/94; BL 9/15/94) [996.5]

17815 Jackson, Barbara. *New Zealand* (4–8). Series: Countries of the World. 2008, National Geographic LB $27.90 (978-1-4263-0301-2). 64pp. With lots of color images, this thorough volume looks at the geography, nature, history, culture, government, and economy of New Zealand, with interesting sidebars on customs, celebrations, and so forth. (Rev: SLJ 3/09) [992]

17816 Krasno, Rena. *Kneeling Carabao and Dancing Giants: Celebrating Filipino Festivals* (4–6). Illus. by Ileana C. Lee. 1997, Pacific View $19.95 (978-1-881896-15-9). 48pp. Contains information on Filipino festivals, customs, folktales, games, and activities. (Rev: BL 12/1/97; HBG 3/98) [394]

17817 Lester, Alison. *Are We There Yet?* (2–4). Illus. 2005, Kane $15.95 (978-1-929132-73-7). 32pp. A family of five has a great time touring Australia, seeing its sights and enjoying its unique experiences over the course of six months. (Rev: BL 3/15/05; SLJ 4/05) [823.3]

17818 Lewin, Ted, and Betsy Lewin. *Top to Bottom Down Under* (2–4). Illus. 2005, HarperCollins LB $16.89 (978-0-688-14114-1). 40pp. With plenty of Australian-speak, the Lewins offer an eye-catching adventure- and animal-filled tour down under. (Rev: BL 1/1–15/05; SLJ 3/05) [919.4]

17819 Lowe, David, and Andrea Shimmen. *Australia* (4–8). Illus. Series: Modern Industrial World. 1996, Raintree LB $24.26 (978-0-8172-4553-5). Australia's economic status, living standards, educational system, and industry are covered. (Rev: BL 2/15/97) [919.4]

17820 McCollum, Sean. *Australia* (3–5). Series: Globe-Trotters Club. 1999, Carolrhoda $22.60 (978-1-57505-104-8). 48pp. Each of the colorful two-page spreads covers a different topic about Australia, including the people, major sights, and unusual animals. (Rev: BL 9/15/99; HBG 10/99; SLJ 11/99) [994]

17821 McCollum, Sean. *Australia* (1–3). Series: A Ticket To. 1999, Carolrhoda LB $22.60 (978-1-57505-129-1). 48pp. For beginning readers, this is a first look at Australia, its people, chief attractions, and landscape. (Rev: BL 9/15/99; HBG 10/99; SLJ 11/99) [994]

17822 Macdonald, Robert. *Islands of the Pacific Rim and Their People* (5–8). Illus. Series: People and Places. 1994, Thomson Learning LB $24.26 (978-1-56847-167-9). 48pp. An overview of the islands of the Pacific Ocean and their people, different environments, and economies. (Rev: BL 10/15/94; SLJ 10/94) [990]

17823 Marshall, Diana. *Aboriginal Australians* (3–5). Series: Indigenous Peoples. 2004, Weigl LB $18.20 (978-1-59036-121-4). 32pp. A fascinating and informative overview of Australia's aboriginals, covering history, culture, language, and family life. (Rev: SLJ 7/04) [305.89]

17824 Mason, Paul. *Sydney* (4–8). Photos by Rob Bowden. Series: Global Cities. 2007, Chelsea House LB $30.00 (978-0-7910-8849-4). 61pp. With plenty of photographs and maps, this volume introduces the history of Sydney, Australia, as well as its geography, people, environment, transportation, and so forth. (Rev: SLJ 7/07)

17825 Meisel, Jacqueline D. *Australia: The Land Down Under* (3–5). Illus. Series: Exploring Cultures of the World. 1997, Marshall Cavendish LB $27.07 (978-0-7614-0139-1). 64pp. A description of various aspects of life in Australia, with material on the range of races and lifestyles. (Rev: BL 7/97; SLJ 4/98) [994]

17826 NgCheong-Lum, Roseline. *Tahiti* (4–7). Illus. Series: Cultures of the World. 1997, Marshall Cavendish LB $37.07 (978-0-7614-0682-2). 128pp. Background material on history and geography is given, with information on how Tahitians live today. (Rev: BL 8/97; HBG 3/98) [919.62]

17827 Nile, Richard. *Australian Aborigines* (4–7). Illus. Series: Threatened Cultures. 1993, Raintree LB $24.26 (978-0-8114-2303-8). 48pp. The aboriginal culture of Australia is presented. (Rev: BL 8/93; SLJ 8/93) [305]

17828 Oleksy, Walter. *The Philippines* (4–7). Series: Enchantment of the World. 2000, Children's LB $37.00 (978-0-516-21010-0). 144pp. These South Pacific islands are presented with coverage of history, geography, economy, the people, current problems, culture, and recreation. (Rev: BL 7/00) [959.9]

17829 Olson, Nathan. *Australia: A Question And Answer Book* (2–5). Illus. Series: Questions and Answers: Countries. 2005, Capstone LB $23.93 (978-0-7368-3747-7). 32pp. Using a question-and-answer format, simple text, large photos, and many factboxes, this is an introduction to Australia today, with material on history and traditional culture.

17830 Pelta, Kathy. *Rediscovering Easter Island* (5–9). Series: How History Is Invented. 2001, Lerner LB $28.75 (978-0-8225-4890-4). 112pp. An assortment of illustrations, maps, and inserts add to this exploration of the mysteries of Easter Island. (Rev: BCCB 7–8/01; HBG 10/01; SLJ 2/02) [996.18]

17831 Rajendra, Vijeya, and Sundran Rajendra. *Australia* (4–7). Illus. Series: Cultures of the World. 1991, Marshall Cavendish LB $35.64 (978-1-85435-400-6). 128pp. Beyond the basics, this volume highlights contemporary problems and concerns in the Land Down Under. (Rev: BL 2/15/92; SLJ 3/92) [994]

17832 Rau, Dana Meachen. *Australia* (3–5). Series: Facts About Countries. 2009, Sea-to-Sea LB $27.10 (978-1-59771-112-8). 32pp. A well-designed introduction to Australia with color photographs and statistics and covering geography, history, economy, education, government, culture, and current status. (Rev: SLJ 7/09) [994]

17833 Schroeder, Holly. *New Zealand ABCs: A Book About the People and Places of New Zealand* (2–4). Illus. by Claudia Wolf. Series: Country ABCs. 2004, Picture Window LB $26.60 (978-1-4048-0178-3). 32pp. Young researchers will find useful facts in this alphabetically organized volume. (Rev: SLJ 8/04) [992]

17834 Shepherd, Donna Walsh. *New Zealand* (4–7). Series: Enchantment of the World. 2002, Children's LB $37.00 (978-0-516-21099-5). 144pp. Some of the subjects covered in this fine introduction to New Zealand are history, people and languages, economy, government, culture, natural resources, and climate. (Rev: BL 5/15/02; SLJ 10/02) [992]

17835 Steele, Philip. *Sydney* (4–6). Series: Great Cities of the World. 2004, World Almanac LB $31.00 (978-0-8368-5032-1). 48pp. A profile of Australia's oldest and biggest city, well illustrated with photographs. (Rev: SLJ 6/04) [994]

17836 Theunissen, Steve. *The Maori of New Zealand* (4–6). Illus. Series: First Peoples. 2002, Lerner LB $23.95 (978-0-8225-0665-2). 48pp. Full of photographs, this is a wide-ranging introduction to the history and culture of the Polynesian people who settled in New Zealand centuries before the Europeans arrived. (Rev: HBG 3/03; SLJ 6/03) [993]

17837 Tope, Lily R. *Philippines* (4–7). Illus. Series: Cultures of the World. 1991, Marshall Cavendish LB $35.64 (978-1-85435-403-7). 128pp. With emphasis on contemporary problems and concerns, the land and culture of the Philippines are introduced in text and well-chosen color photographs. (Rev: BL 2/15/92) [959.9]

17838 Turner, Kate. *Australia* (5–8). Series: Countries of the World. 2007, National Geographic LB $27.90 (978-1-4263-0055-4). 64pp. Excellent photographs and maps make this an appealing introduction to the country's history, geography, government, economy, people, culture, and nature. (Rev: SLJ 10/07) [994]

17839 Underwood, Deborah. *The Easter Island Statues* (3–6). Illus. Series: Wonders of the World. 2004, Gale LB $26.20 (978-0-7377-3065-4). 31pp. Underwood discusses the construction and symbolism of these famous statues, and includes material on the island's geography, history, and people. (Rev: SLJ 6/05) [996.1]

17840 Webster, Christine. *Polynesians* (4–6). Illus. Series: Indigenous Peoples. 2004, Weigl LB $18.20 (978-1-59036-123-8). 32pp. Historical and contemporary issues are both covered in this detailed portrait of life among the Polynesian people and how they've endured and adapted to dramatic changes in their homelands. (Rev: BL 4/1/04; SLJ 7/04) [996]

17841 Wojahn, Rebecca Hogue, and Donald Wojahn. *An Australian Outback Food Chain: A Who-Eats-What Adventure* (3–6). Illus. Series: Follow That Food Chain. 2009, Lerner LB $30.60 (978-0-8225-7499-6). 64pp. Dingos and saltwater crocodiles are among the animals introduced in this attractive "choose your own adventure" introduction to plant and animal life in the Outback. (Rev: SLJ 6/09) [577.54]

Europe

General and Miscellaneous

17842 Bramwell, Martyn. *Europe* (4–6). Illus. Series: World in Maps. 2000, Carolrhoda $23.93 (978-0-8225-2913-2). 48pp. Portrays the countries of Europe in a series of maps and accompanying text that supply information on such topics as population, government, geography, cities, and notable physical features. (Rev: BL 10/15/00; HBG 10/01; SLJ 1/01) [940]

17843 *Cyprus in Pictures* (5–8). Illus. Series: Visual Geography. 1992, Lerner LB $25.55 (978-0-8225-1910-2). 64pp. The divided island of Cyprus is introduced, with good background information and material on the standoff between Greece and Turkey up to 1992. (Rev: BL 2/1/93) [956.45]

17844 Flint, David. *Europe* (5–8). Series: Continents of the World. 2006, World Almanac LB $34.00 (978-0-8368-5913-3). 64pp. Factboxes and "In Focus" articles add to this overview of the history, geography, people, culture, and so forth of the continent of Europe. (Rev: SLJ 2/06) [940]

17845 Holmes, Mary Tavener. *My Travels with Clara* (1–3). Illus. by Jon Cannell. 2007, Getty $17.95 (978-0-89236-880-8). 33pp. A Dutch sea captain describes his travels around Europe with a rhinoceros named Clara in the mid-18th century. (Rev: BL 10/1/07; SLJ 8/07) [599.66]

17846 Pollard, Michael. *The Rhine* (5–8). Series: Great Rivers. 1997, Benchmark LB $22.79 (978-0-7614-0500-9). After explaining how the Rhine was formed, this attractive book describes its history, importance, tributaries, tourism, and present-day role. (Rev: HBG 3/98; SLJ 3/98) [943]

17847 Sheehan, Sean. *Malta* (5–9). Series: Cultures of the World. 2000, Marshall Cavendish LB $37.07 (978-0-7614-0993-9). 128pp. This work covers the culture, geography, and history of Malta with material on such subjects as government, economy, people, lifestyles, and leisure. (Rev: HBG 10/00; SLJ 11/00) [945]

Central and Eastern Europe

17848 Andryszewski, Tricia. *Kosovo: The Splintering of Yugoslavia* (5–8). Illus. Series: Headliners. 2000, Millbrook LB $25.90 (978-0-7613-1750-0). 64pp. Introduced by refugees' accounts of the horror in Kosovo, this book traces the origins of ethnic conflicts in Yugoslavia, with a concentration on events of the past 10 years. (Rev: BL 6/1–15/00; HBG 10/00; SLJ 6/00) [949.7]

17849 Barber, Nicola. *Istanbul* (3–6). Series: Great Cities of the World. 2005, World Almanac LB $31.00 (978-0-8368-5050-5). 48pp. With color photographs and informative sidebars, this volume introduces the geography, history, culture, religion, work, and recreation of the Turkish city of Istanbul. (Rev: SLJ 11/05)

17850 Bowden, Rob. *Istanbul* (4–8). Photos by Edward Parker. Series: Global Cities. 2007, Chelsea House LB $30.00 (978-0-7910-8850-0). 61pp. With plenty of photographs and maps, this volume introduces the history of Istanbul as well as its geography, people, environment, transportation, and so forth. (Rev: SLJ 7/07)

17851 Burke, Patrick. *Eastern Europe: Bulgaria, Czech Republic, Hungary, Poland, Romania, Slovakia* (5–8). Series: Country Fact Files. 1997, Raintree LB $27.12 (978-0-8172-4628-0). In chapters two to four pages long, the impact of geography on the landscape, daily life, natural resources, transportation, and other aspects of life is examined for these six countries. (Rev: SLJ 8/97) [947]

17852 Corona, Laurel. *Poland* (5–8). Illus. Series: Modern Nations of the World. 2000, Lucent LB $28.70 (978-1-56006-600-2). 126pp. A good history of Poland that also covers Polish achievements and daily life. (Rev: BL 9/15/00; HBG 3/01) [943.8]

17853 Eboch, Chris. *Turkey* (5–9). Series: Modern Nations of the World. 2003, Gale LB $29.95 (978-1-59018-122-5). 112pp. This account presents a broad spectrum of material about Turkey including history, geography, and culture. (Rev: BL 11/15/03; SLJ 6/03) [961]

17854 Englar, Mary. *Turkey* (2–5). Illus. Series: Questions and Answers: Countries. 2005, Capstone LB $23.93 (978-0-7368-3762-0). 32pp. Using a question-and-answer format, simple text, large photos, and many factboxes, this is an introduction to Turkey today, with material on history and traditional culture.

17855 Feinstein, Steve. *Turkey in Pictures* (5–8). Illus. 1989, Lerner LB $25.55 (978-0-8225-1831-0). 64pp. An overview of Turkey and its people that includes lots of images. (Rev: BL 8/88) [956.1]

17856 Harris, Pamela K., and Brad Clemmons. *Welcome to Switzerland* (1–4). Series: Wecome to the World. 2008, The Child's World LB $27.07 (978-1-59296-980-7). 32pp. As easy introduction to Switzerland and its land, people, plants and animals, and so forth, with color photographs, maps, and recipes. (Rev: SLJ 9/08) [949.4]

17857 *Hungary in Pictures* (5–8). Illus. Series: Visual Geography. 1993, Lerner LB $25.55 (978-0-8225-1883-9). 64pp. Concise text and extensive photographs introduce the land, history, and people of Hungary. (Rev: BL 12/1/93; SLJ 12/93) [943.9]

17858 Kinkade, Sheila. *Children of Slovakia* (2–5). Photos by Elaine Little. Series: The World's Children. 2001, Carolrhoda LB $23.93 (978-1-57505-446-9). 48pp. The daily lives of children in Slovakia are used to introduce the history, geography, and culture of the country, with appealing full-color illustrations, a pronunciation guide, and map. (Rev: HBG 10/01; SLJ 6/01) [943.7305]

17859 Levy, Patricia. *Switzerland* (4–6). Illus. Series: Cultures of the World. 1994, Marshall Cavendish LB $25.95 (978-1-85435-591-1). 128pp. This attractive introduction to Switzerland includes material on lifestyles, economy, geography, arts, and leisure. (Rev: SLJ 7/94) [949.4]

17860 McCollum, Sean. *Poland* (1–3). Series: A Ticket To. 1999, Carolrhoda LB $22.60 (978-1-57505-131-4). 48pp. Easy-to-understand language and a large map enhance this beginning account of the land, people, and main cultural features of Poland. (Rev: BL 9/15/99; HBG 3/00; SLJ 1/00) [943.8]

17861 McCollum, Sean. *Poland* (3–5). Series: Globe-Trotters Club. 1999, Carolrhoda LB $22.60 (978-1-57505-106-2). 48pp. After a brief history, this book focuses on modern life covering topics including religion, food, education, and family life. (Rev: BL 9/15/99; HBG 3/00; SLJ 2/00) [943.8]

17862 Milivojevic, JoAnn. *Bosnia and Herzegovina* (4–6). Series: Enchantment of the World. 2004, Scholastic LB $37.00 (978-0-516-24247-7). 144pp. Contemporary life, history, geography, culture are all covered in this well-illustrated and well-written volume suitable for report writers. (Rev: BL 9/1/04; SLJ 7/04) [949.742]

17863 Netzley, Patricia D. *Switzerland* (5–8). Series: Modern Nations of the World. 2001, Lucent LB $27.45 (978-1-56006-821-1). 112pp. Interesting sidebars, a chronology, and excellent photographs supplement informative text introducing this small country. (Rev: BL 6/1–15/01) [949.3]

17864 Orr, Tamra. *Slovenia* (5–8). Series: Enchantment of the World. 2004, Children's Pr. LB $37.00 (978-0-516-24249-1). 144pp. Introduces the history, geography, people, and culture of Slovenia, with plenty of clear photographs and an emphasis on contemporary life. (Rev: BL 9/1/04; SLJ 7/04) [949.73]

17865 Orr, Tamra. *Turkey* (5–8). Illus. Series: Enchantment of the World, Second Series. 2003, Children's LB $37.00 (978-0-516-22679-8). 144pp. A visually attractive book that covers such topics as the geography, history, government, culture, and people, with a timeline, fast facts, and a recipe. (Rev: SLJ 5/03) [915]

17866 Rogers, Lura. *Switzerland* (4–7). Series: Enchantment of the World. 2001, Children's LB $37.00 (978-0-516-21080-3). A highly visual introduction to Switzerland that covers such topics as people and languages, history, natural resources, and climate. (Rev: BL 1/1–15/02) [949.4]

17867 *Romania in Pictures* (5–8). Illus. Series: Visual Geography. 1993, Lerner LB $25.55 (978-0-8225-1894-5). 64pp. In addition to background material on history and geography, this account gives a good picture of contemporary life in Romania. (Rev: BL 9/1/93) [949.8]

17868 Sheehan, Sean. *Austria* (4–7). Illus. Series: Cultures of the World. 1992, Marshall Cavendish LB $35.64 (978-1-85435-454-9). 128pp. This introduction to Austria covers its history, lifestyles of the people, and contemporary problems. (Rev: BL 10/15/92) [943.6]

17869 Sheehan, Sean. *Turkey* (4–7). Illus. Series: Cultures of the World. 1993, Marshall Cavendish LB $35.64 (978-1-85435-576-8). 128pp. This introduction to Turkey covers history, culture, economics, and present-day concerns. (Rev: BL 8/93) [956.1]

17870 Stein, R. Conrad. *Austria* (4–7). Series: Enchantment of the World. 2000, Children's LB $37.00 (978-0-516-21049-0). 144pp. A thorough introduction to Austria with material on such subjects as history, the land, government, people, culture, cities, and daily life. (Rev: BL 1/1–15/01) [943.6]

17871 Steins, Richard. *Hungary: Crossroads of Europe* (3–5). Illus. Series: Exploring Cultures of the World. 1997, Marshall Cavendish LB $27.07 (978-0-7614-0141-4). 64pp. Current conditions in Hungary are covered, along with good background information about its people, culture, and history. (Rev: BL 7/97; SLJ 1/98) [943.9]

17872 *Switzerland in Pictures* (5–8). Series: Visual Geography. 1996, Lerner LB $25.55 (978-0-8225-1895-2). With a generous number of color pictures, this account traces the history and geography of Switzerland, with emphasis on the modern nation and its people. (Rev: BL 9/15/96; SLJ 8/98) [949.4]

17873 Willis, Terri. *Romania* (4–7). Series: Enchantment of the World. 2001, Children's LB $37.00 (978-0-516-21635-5). Packed with photographs, original maps, and browser-friendly sidebars, this is a fine introduction to Romania that explores a number of aspects of the past and present of this country. (Rev: BL 1/1–15/02) [949.8]

France

17874 Arnold, Helen. *France* (1–3). Illus. Series: Postcards From. 1995, Raintree LB $21.40 (978-0-8172-4004-2). 32pp. France is introduced through a series of postcards written by fictitious children. (Rev: SLJ 2/96) [944]

17875 Bader, Philip. *France* (3–5). Series: Dropping In On. 2001, Rourke LB $28.50 (978-1-55916-280-7). 32pp. A brief tour of France in a hot-air balloon — with stops at interesting places — that includes material on landmarks, the people, food, and growing up. (Rev: SLJ 1/01) [944]

17876 Bailey, Linda. *Adventures in the Ice Age* (3–6). Illus. by Bill Slavin. Series: Good Times Travel Agency. 2004, Kids Can paper $8.95 (978-1-55337-504-3). 48pp. In this sixth installment of the series that blends fact and fiction, the Binkerton children are whisked off to Ice Age France, where they learn facts about life at that time. (Rev: BL 11/1/04) [559.9]

17877 Boast, Clare. *France* (2–4). Series: Next Stop. 1998, Heinemann LB $19.92 (978-1-57572-565-9). 32pp. A lively introduction to France that covers its history, geography, and people. (Rev: SLJ 6/98) [944]

17878 Butler, Daphne. *France* (2–4). Illus. Series: On the Map. 1993, Raintree LB $22.83 (978-0-8114-3675-5). 32pp. An overview of life in France, with coverage of geogrphy, industry, customs, and landmarks. (Rev: BL 9/1/93) [944]

17879 Corona, Laurel. *France* (5–8). Series: Modern Nations of the World. 2002, Gale LB $29.95 (978-1-56006-760-3). 112pp. A comprehensive introduction to the land and people of France with material on history, geography, culture, and lifestyles. (Rev: BL 12/15/02) [944]

17880 Costain, Meredith, and Paul Collins. *Welcome to France* (3–5). Illus. Series: Countries of the World. 2001, Chelsea LB $28.00 (978-0-7910-6551-8). 32pp. Young Gregoire introduces daily life, schooling, sports, transport, important places, and so forth, with interesting color photographs. (Rev: HBG 3/02; SLJ 10/01) [944]

17881 Fisher, Teresa. *France* (3–6). Series: Foods and Festivals. 1999, Raintree LB $25.69 (978-0-8172-5550-3). 32pp. This book gives an overview of the celebrations and holidays of France, with material on related food crops and special dishes plus many simple recipes. (Rev: HBG 10/99; SLJ 7/99) [944]

17882 Fisher, Teresa. *France* (2–4). Series: We Come From. 1999, Raintree LB $25.69 (978-0-8172-5212-0). 32pp. This book gives a little information on daily life in France, plus some coverage of its geography, cities, and weather, and a recipe. (Rev: HBG 3/00; SLJ 3/00) [944]

17883 Fisher, Teresa. *France: City and Village Life* (4–7). Illus. Series: Country Insights. 1997, Raintree LB $27.12 (978-0-8172-4788-1). 48pp. A specific city and village are used to compare and contrast two lifestyles in contemporary France. (Rev: SLJ 8/97) [944]

17884 Gilbert, Adrian. *The French Revolution* (4–6). Series: Revolution! 1995, Thomson Learning LB $24.26 (978-1-56847-390-1). 48pp. Beginning with the execution of Louis XVI in 1793, this account moves back in time to trace the history of the French Revolution. (Rev: SLJ 2/96) [944]

17885 Gofen, Ethel C. *France* (4–7). Illus. Series: Cultures of the World. 1992, Marshall Cavendish LB $35.64 (978-1-85435-449-5). 128pp. This account provides information on the history, culture, and people of France and discusses the current problems and concerns. (Rev: BL 10/15/92) [944]

17886 Haskins, James, and Kathleen Benson. *Count Your Way Through France* (2–4). Illus. by Andrea Shine. Series: Count Your Way. 1996, Carolrhoda LB $19.93 (978-0-87614-874-7); paper $5.95 (978-0-87614-972-0). 24pp. Using the numbers 1 through 10, each page contains useful information about the history, traditions, and people of France. (Rev: BL 9/15/96; SLJ 8/96) [944]

17887 Hoban, Sarah. *Daily Life in Ancient and Modern Paris* (4–7). Illus. 2000, Runestone LB $25.26 (978-0-8225-3222-4). 64pp. This well-illustrated history of Paris is divided chronologically into seven sections, beginning with early Paris and working through the Middle Ages to World War II and the Paris of today. (Rev: BL 2/1/01; HBG 3/01; SLJ 2/01) [944]

17888 Ingham, Richard. *France* (4–8). Illus. 2000, Raintree LB $34.26 (978-0-8172-5782-8). 128pp. A fine introduction to France — its past, its present, and its people — that is particularly noteworthy for its use of graphics. (Rev: BL 10/15/00; HBG 10/00; SLJ 7/00) [944]

17889 Pipe, Jim. *You Wouldn't Want to Be an Aristocrat in the French Revolution! A Horrible Time in Paris You'd Rather Avoid* (4–6). Illus. by David Antram. Series: You Wouldn't Want to . . . History of the World. 2007, Watts LB $29.00 (978-0-531-18745-6). 32pp. Engaging facts, fast action, cartoons, and a touch of humor make for an appealing package about the French Revolution. (Rev: LMC 5/08; SLJ 3/08) [944.04]

17890 Plain, Nancy. *Louis XVI, Marie-Antoinette and the French Revolution* (5–8). Series: Rulers and Their Times. 2001, Marshall Cavendish LB $29.93 (978-0-7614-1029-4). In three well-illustrated parts, this book offers a biography of Marie Antoinette, a history of France and its people during the French Revolution, and a generous selection of original documents of the period. (Rev: BL 1/1–15/02; HBG 3/02; SLJ 3/02) [944]

17891 Powell, Jillian. *A History of France Through Art* (5–8). Illus. Series: History Through Art. 1996, Thomson Learning LB $5.00 (978-1-56847-441-0). The basic history of France is covered in 21 double-page spreads, each dealing with an important event or subject and each containing works of art and informative background text. (Rev: BL 3/1/96; SLJ 2/96) [944]

17892 Shuter, Jane, ed. *Helen Williams and the French Revolution* (5–8). Illus. Series: History Eyewitness. 1996, Raintree LB $24.26 (978-0-8114-8287-5). 48pp. An abridged, well-illustrated firsthand account describes the causes and the course of the French Revolution. (Rev: BL 5/15/96; SLJ 6/96) [944.04]

17893 Spengler, Kremena. *France* (2–5). Illus. Series: Questions and Answers: Countries. 2004, Capstone LB $23.93 (978-0-7368-2689-1). 32pp. Using a question-and-answer format, simple text, large photos, and many factboxes, this is an introduction to France today, with material on history and traditional culture.

17894 Stacey, Gill. *Paris* (4–7). Illus. 2004, World Almanac LB $31.00 (978-0-8368-5030-7). 48pp. This attractive introduction to Paris covers the French capital's history and examines some of its modern-day problems. (Rev: BL 4/15/04; SLJ 6/04) [944]

17895 Stevens, Kathryn. *France* (3–5). Series: Countries: Faces and Places. 2000, Child's World LB $22.79 (978-1-56766-714-1). 32pp. This basic introduction to France, its history, people, and culture uses simple text, color photographs on each page, and an oversize format. (Rev: BL 4/15/01; HBG 3/01) [944]

17896 Tidmarsh, Celia. *France* (3–5). Series: Facts About Countries. 2009, Sea-to-Sea LB $27.10 (978-1-59771-115-9). 32pp. A well-designed introduction to France with color photographs and statistics and covering geography, history, economy, education, government, culture, and current status. (Rev: SLJ 7/09) [944]

17897 Yuan, Margaret Speaker. *The Arc de Triomphe* (5–8). Series: Building World Landmarks. 2004, Gale LB $24.95 (978-1-4103-0138-3). 48pp. A concise account of the design and construction of this arch, which met financial, political, and technical difficulties. (Rev: SLJ 4/05)

Germany

17898 Ayer, Eleanor. *Germany: In the Heartland of Europe* (4–6). Illus. Series: Exploring Cultures of the World. 1996, Benchmark LB $27.07 (978-0-7614-0189-6). 64pp. Good background material on Germany is presented, with special emphasis on the arts, sports, leisure, holidays, and festivals. (Rev: SLJ 6/96) [943]

17899 Barber, Nicola. *Berlin* (4–7). Illus. Series: Great Cities of the World. 2005, World Almanac LB $31.00 (978-0-8368-5043-7). 48pp. An informative and appealing overview of one of the world's most famous cities, with material on its history, its economy, and what it's like to live there. (Rev: BL 4/15/04)

17900 Fuller, Barbara. *Germany* (4–7). Illus. Series: Cultures of the World. 1992, Marshall Cavendish LB $35.64 (978-1-85435-530-0). 128pp. In addition to the usual information on the history and geography of Germany, this account stresses how the people live and their traditions. (Rev: BL 1/1/93) [943]

17901 *Germany in Pictures* (5–8). Illus. Series: Visual Geography. 1994, Lerner LB $21.27 (978-0-8225-1873-0). 64pp. The new united Germany is introduced with a basic text and copious illustrations, including maps, charts, and attractive photographs. (Rev: BL 1/15/95) [943]

17902 Gray, Susan H. *Germany* (1–3). Series: A True Book. 2003, Children's Pr. LB $25.00 (978-0-516-22673-6). 48pp. A blend of easy-to-understand text and colorful illustrations make this overview suitable for beginning readers. (Rev: SLJ 10/03) [943]

17903 Haskins, James. *Count Your Way Through Germany* (2–4). Illus. by Helen Byers. Series: Count Your Way. 1990, Carolrhoda LB $19.93 (978-0-87614-407-7). The reader is introduced to Germany through numbers. (Rev: SLJ 8/90) [943]

17904 Levy, Debbie. *The Berlin Wall* (5–8). Series: Building World Landmarks. 2004, Gale LB $24.95 (978-1-4103-0137-6). 48pp. A concise account of the wall's history and its importance in the struggle between East and West; with a timeline. (Rev: SLJ 4/05)

17905 Nickles, Greg, and Niki Walker. *Germany* (4–8). Series: Nations of the World. 2001, Raintree LB $34.26 (978-0-7398-1285-3). 128pp. A profile of this now united, highly industrialized, and urbanized country, with material on its past, present, and future. (Rev: BL 6/1–15/01; HBG 10/01) [943]

17906 Russell, Henry. *Germany* (5–8). Series: Countries of the World. 2007, National Geographic LB $27.90 (978-1-4263-0059-2). 64pp. Excellent photographs and maps make this an appealing introduction to the country's history, geography, government, economy, people, culture, and nature. (Rev: SLJ 10/07) [943]

17907 Spengler, Kremena. *Germany* (2–5). Illus. Series: Questions and Answers: Countries. 2004, Capstone LB $23.93 (978-0-7368-2690-7). 32pp. Using a question-and-answer format, simple text, large photos, and many factboxes, this is an introduction to Germany today, with material on history and traditional culture.

Great Britain and Ireland

17908 Allan, Tony. *The Irish Famine: The Birth of Irish America* (4–9). Illus. by Stefan Chabluk. Series: Point of Impact. 2001, Heinemann LB $24.22 (978-1-58810-077-1). 32pp. Allan traces the causes of the crisis that started in Ireland in 1845, the subsequent wave of emigration to the United States, and the ill feelings created between Britain and Ireland. (Rev: HBG 10/01; SLJ 7/01) [941.5081]

17909 Ashby, Ruth. *Elizabethan England* (5–9). Series: Cultures of the Past. 1998, Benchmark LB $29.93 (978-0-7614-0269-5). 80pp. Ashby looks at the cultural aspects of Elizabethan England, providing material on the art and literature of the period plus coverage of daily life, religion, and major personalities. (Rev: BL 12/15/98; HBG 10/99; SLJ 2/99) [942]

17910 Ashby, Ruth. *Victorian England* (5–8). Series: Cultures of the Past. 2002, Marshall Cavendish

$29.93 (978-0-7614-1493-3). 80pp. The political, historical, and cultural aspects of life in England during the reign of Victoria are covered in this handsome volume. (Rev: BL 1/1–15/03; HBG 3/03) [942]

17911 Bean, Rachel. *United Kingdom* (4–8). Illus. Series: Countries of the World. 2007, National Geographic LB $27.90 (978-1-4263-0126-1). 64pp. This attractive volume full of photographs covers the United Kingdom's geography, history, economy, people, and so forth. (Rev: SLJ 2/08)

17912 Bell, Rachael. *Ireland* (1–3). Series: A Visit To. 1999, Heinemann LB $21.36 (978-1-57572-847-6). 32pp. Double-page spreads present information on Ireland's geography, landmarks, homes, work, food, schools, and celebrations. (Rev: HBG 10/99; SLJ 10/99) [941.5]

17913 Blashfield, Jean F. *Ireland* (4–7). Series: Enchantment of the World. 2002, Children's LB $37.00 (978-0-516-21127-5). 144pp. Using many visual aids and a lively text, this is an introduction to Ireland — the land, the people, and the culture. (Rev: BL 5/15/02; SLJ 12/02) [941.5]

17914 Boraas, Tracey. *England* (4–6). Series: Countries and Cultures. 2002, Capstone LB $25.26 (978-0-7368-0937-5). 64pp. Using devices such as timelines, maps, sidebars, and a recipe, English history, geography, and culture are introduced. (Rev: BL 1/1–15/03; HBG 3/03; SLJ 7/03) [942]

17915 Brassey, Richard, and Stewart Ross. *The Story of Ireland* (3–5). Illus. 2002, Trafalgar $19.95 (978-1-85881-848-1). 40pp. Fast-paced narrative and brief biographies tell the history of Ireland from prehistoric times. (Rev: BL 3/1/02) [941.5]

17916 Buscher, Sarah, and Bettina Ling. *Mairead Corrigan and Betty Williams: Making Peace in Northern Ireland* (5–8). Illus. 1999, Feminist $19.95 (978-1-55861-200-6); paper $9.95 (978-1-55861-201-3). 112pp. The story of the two women in Northern Ireland who won the Nobel Peace Prize for their efforts to help end the civil strife in their country. (Rev: BL 3/15/00; SLJ 2/00; VOYA 4/00) [941]

17917 Chrisp, Peter. *Welcome to the Globe! The Story of Shakespeare's Theater* (3–5). Illus. 2000, DK $12.99 (978-0-7894-6641-9); paper $3.99 (978-0-7894-6640-2). 48pp. The Globe is presented through the words of a variety of characters, real and fictitious, working there and through detailed illustrations. (Rev: HBG 3/01; SLJ 4/01) [792]

17918 Cole, Joanna. *Ms. Frizzle's Adventures: Medieval Castle* (2–5). Illus. by Bruce Degen. Series: The Magic School Bus. 2003, Scholastic $15.95 (978-0-590-10820-1). 40pp. Ms. Frizzle is on the move again in this amusing and informative large-format volume, this time traveling back in time to medieval England with her student Arnold. (Rev: BL 7/03; HBG 4/04; SLJ 7/03) [728.8]

17919 Corona, Laurel. *Scotland* (5–8). Series: Modern Nations of the World. 2000, Lucent LB $29.95 (978-1-56006-703-0). 128pp. The history, geography, and culture of Scotland are discussed along with material on daily life in modern Scotland. (Rev: BL 3/1/01) [941]

17920 Dahl, Michael. *England* (3–4). Illus. Series: Fact Finders: Questions and Answers. 2004, Capstone LB $23.93 (978-0-7368-2477-4). 32pp. Using a question-and-answer format, this title introduces England's history, government, economy, education, culture, sports, and lifestyle. (Rev: SLJ 1/05) [942]

17921 Davis, Kenneth C. *Don't Know Much About the Kings and Queens of England* (4–7). Illus. by S. D. Schindler. Series: Don't Know Much About. 2002, HarperCollins LB $15.89 (978-0-06-028612-5). 48pp. Humorous questions and answers supply information that browsers will enjoy. (Rev: HBG 10/02; SLJ 7/02) [941.0099]

17922 Dumas, Philippe. *A Farm* (3–6). Illus. 1999, Creative $29.95 (978-1-56846-169-4). 42pp. The inner workings of a 19th-century English farm are revealed in this oversize book containing extraordinary illustrations. (Rev: BL 12/1/99) [630.42]

17923 Elgin, Kathy. *Elizabethan England, Vol. 3* (5–8). Illus. Series: A History of Fashion and Costume. 2005, Facts on File $35.00 (978-0-8160-5946-1). 64pp. A broad overview of the clothing and personal adornment worn during this time period, with many visual aids. (Rev: SLJ 5/06) [391]

17924 Flint, David. *Great Britain* (5–8). Illus. Series: Modern Industrial World. 1996, Raintree LB $24.26 (978-0-8172-4555-9). Modern Great Britain is the focus of this volume, which concentrates on the economy and industrial development. (Rev: BL 2/15/96; SLJ 8/97) [330.941]

17925 Flint, David. *The United Kingdom* (3–6). Illus. Series: Country Facts Files. 1994, Raintree LB $27.12 (978-0-8114-1849-2). 48pp. A fact-filled introduction to the United Kingdom, with coverage of such topics as its economy, daily life, climate, and traditions. (Rev: BL 9/1/94; SLJ 7/94) [941]

17926 Fuller, Barbara. *Britain* (4–6). Illus. Series: Cultures of the World. 1994, Marshall Cavendish LB $25.95 (978-1-85435-587-4). 128pp. This fact-filled, heavily illustrated account gives a good overview of life in Great Britain today. (Rev: SLJ 7/94) [941.06]

17927 Gottfried, Ted. *Northern Ireland: Peace in Our Time?* (5–8). Series: Headliners. 2002, Millbrook LB $25.90 (978-0-7613-2252-8). This attractive book gives current and background information on the struggles within Northern Ireland and the causes and possible solutions. (Rev: BL 4/15/02; HBG 10/02; SLJ 3/02) [941]

17928 Greenblatt, Miriam. *Elizabeth I and Tudor England* (5–8). Series: Rulers and Their Times. 2001, Marshall Cavendish LB $29.93 (978-0-7614-1028-7). After a biography of Elizabeth I, this colorful account traces everyday life in Elizabethan times and supplies a selection of primary documents. (Rev: BL 1/1–15/02; HBG 3/02; SLJ 3/02) [942.1]

17929 Haskins, James, and Kathleen Benson. *Count Your Way Through Ireland* (2–4). Illus. by Beth Wright. Series: Count Your Way. 1996, Carolrhoda LB $19.93 (978-0-87614-872-3); paper $5.95 (978-

0-87614-974-4). 24pp. After a brief introduction, each double-page spread, numbered from 1 to 10, gives interesting facts about Ireland. (Rev: BL 9/15/96; SLJ 8/96) [941.5]

17930 Hestler, Anna. *Wales* (5–9). Illus. Series: Cultures of the World. 2001, Marshall Cavendish LB $37.07 (978-0-7614-1195-6). 128pp. Geography, history, government, arts and culture, and lifestyle are all covered in this interesting and attractive volume. (Rev: HBG 10/01; SLJ 11/01) [942.9]

17931 Hynson, Colin. *Elizabeth I and the Spanish Armada* (5–8). Illus. Series: Stories from History. 2006, School Specialty $9.95 (978-0-7696-4703-6); paper $6.95 (978-0-7696-4629-9). 48pp. A graphic novel presentation of the confrontation between England's Queen Elizabeth I and the Spanish empire, climaxing in the defeat of the Spanish Armada by the English; full-color depictions of battles, fast facts, and maps aid comprehension. (Rev: BL 10/15/06; SLJ 1/07) [942.05]

17932 Innes, Brian. *United Kingdom* (4–8). Series: Nations of the World. 2001, Raintree LB $34.26 (978-0-7398-1288-4). 128pp. An in-depth look at the nation's geography, climate. terrain, history, government, and lifestyles. (Rev: BL 12/15/01) [941]

17933 *Ireland in Pictures* (5–8). Illus. Series: Visual Geography. 1997, Lerner LB $25.55 (978-0-8225-1878-5). 64pp. Contemporary Ireland is highlighted in this illustrated account. (Rev: BL 12/1/90) [941.5]

17934 January, Brendan. *Ireland* (2–4). Series: True Books. 1999, Children's Book Pr. LB $25.00 (978-0-516-21186-2). 47pp. A large-print text and many color illustrations introduce the history, geography, people, climate, and culture of Ireland. (Rev: HBG 10/99; SLJ 10/99) [941]

17935 Killeen, Richard. *The Easter Rising* (4–6). Illus. Series: Revolution! 1995, Thomson Learning LB $24.26 (978-1-56847-391-8). 48pp. Presents, in a well-paced text, the story of the 1916 Irish Easter Rebellion, during which the Fenians fought for independence from British rule. (Rev: SLJ 2/96) [941.508]

17936 Levy, Patricia. *Ireland* (4–7). Illus. Series: Cultures of the World. 1993, Marshall Cavendish LB $25.95 (978-1-85435-580-5). 128pp. An account that traces the role of women in Irish history to the present day. (Rev: SLJ 2/94) [941]

17937 Lyons, Mary E., ed. *Feed the Children First: Irish Memories of the Great Hunger* (4–8). Illus. 2002, Simon & Schuster $17.00 (978-0-689-84226-9). 48pp. Text, full-color reproductions, and occasional photographs clearly document the suffering of ordinary people during the Irish potato famine. (Rev: BL 12/15/01; HB 3/02; HBG 10/02; SLJ 3/02*) [941.5081]

17938 McMahon, Patricia. *One Belfast Boy* (4–6). Illus. 1999, Houghton $16.00 (978-0-395-68620-1). 64pp. This photoessay tells about the daily life of an Irish Catholic boy growing up in violence-torn Northern Ireland. (Rev: BCCB 7–8/99; BL 3/15/99; HBG 10/99; SLJ 5/99) [941]

17939 McQuinn, Anna, and Colm McQuinn. *Ireland* (4–8). Series: Countries of the World. 2008, National Geographic LB $27.90 (978-1-4263-0299-2). 64pp. With lots of color images, this thorough volume looks at the geography, nature, history, culture, government, and economy of Ireland, with interesting sidebars on customs, celebrations, and so forth. (Rev: SLJ 3/09) [941.5]

17940 Malam, John. *You Wouldn't Want to Be a Victorian Mill Worker! A Grueling Job You'd Rather Not Have* (4–6). Illus. by David Antram. Series: You Wouldn't Want to . . . History of the World. 2007, Watts LB $29.00 (978-0-531-18747-0). 32pp. Engaging facts, fast action, cartoons, and a touch of humor make for an appealing package about Victorian mill workers. (Rev: LMC 5/08; SLJ 3/08) [331.7]

17941 Mitchell, Graham. *The Napoleonic Wars* (5–9). Illus. 1990, Batsford $19.95 (978-0-7134-5729-2). This British import tells about the war chiefly from the British point of view and uses many quotations from original sources. (Rev: SLJ 3/90) [944.05]

17942 *Northern Ireland in Pictures* (5–8). Series: Visual Geography. 1991, Lerner LB $25.55 (978-0-8225-1898-3). This beautiful but troubled land is introduced in text and pictures. (Rev: BL 2/15/92) [941.6]

17943 Oxlade, Chris, and Anita Ganeri. *England* (1–3). Series: A Visit To. 2003, Heinemann LB $22.79 (978-1-4034-0965-2). 32pp. Full of photographs, this is a useful and interesting overview of the country's geography, history, and culture, suitable for beginning readers. Also use *Scotland* and *Wales* (both 2003). (Rev: HBG 10/03; SLJ 7/03) [942]

17944 Ross, Michael Elsohn. *Children of Ireland* (4–6). Series: The World's Children. 2001, Carolrhoda LB $23.93 (978-1-57505-521-3). Outstanding photographs of children are used to introduce this land and the daily lives of its people. (Rev: BL 1/1–15/02; HBG 3/02) [951.5]

17945 Ross, Michael Elsohn. *Children of Northern Ireland* (2–5). Photos by Felix Rigau. Series: The World's Children. 2001, Carolrhoda LB $23.93 (978-1-57505-433-9). 48pp. This look at the daily lives of children in Northern Ireland introduces the history, geography, and culture of the country, with appealing full-color illustrations, a pronunciation guide, and map. (Rev: HBG 10/01; SLJ 6/01) [941.6]

17946 Shuter, Jane. *Carisbrooke Castle* (4–6). Series: Visiting the Past. 1999, Heinemann LB $24.22 (978-1-57572-857-5). 32pp. This book covers the history of this stronghold on the Isle of Wight, including the construction of the castle after the Norman conquest, its uses through the centuries, and its restoration in 1896. (Rev: SLJ 3/00) [942]

17947 Stacey, Gill. *London* (4–8). Series: Great Cities of the World. 2003, World Almanac LB $31.00 (978-0-8368-5022-2). 48pp. In an appealing blend of text, photographs, quotations, and sidebar features, this volume introduces readers to some of

London's history and attractions. (Rev: SLJ 1/04) [942.1]

17948 Stein, R. Conrad. *Scotland* (4–7). Series: Enchantment of the World. 2001, Children's LB $37.00 (978-0-516-21112-1). Numerous pictures, charts, maps, and drawings contribute to a fascinating portrait of Scotland's past and present. (Rev: BL 1/1–15/02) [931]

17949 *Wales in Pictures* (5–8). Illus. 1994, Lerner LB $25.55 (978-0-8225-1877-8). 64pp. Wales is introduced and material is given on history and current conditions. (Rev: BL 12/1/90) [942.9]

Greece and Italy

17950 Allard, Denise. *Greece* (K–2). Illus. Series: Postcards From. 1996, Raintree LB $22.83 (978-0-8172-4022-6). 32pp. Using a postcard format, this book supplies a brief overview of the geography, culture, and sights of Greece. (Rev: SLJ 2/97) [938]

17951 Barber, Nicola. *Rome* (4–7). Illus. Series: Great Cities of the World. 2005, World Almanac LB $31.00 (978-0-8368-5040-6). 48pp. An informative and appealing overview of one of the world's most famous cities, with material on its history, its economy, and what it's like to live there. (Rev: BL 4/15/04)

17952 Barghusen, Joan. *Daily Life in Ancient and Modern Rome* (3–6). Illus. by Ray Webb. Series: Cities Through Time. 1999, Runestone LB $25.26 (978-0-8225-3213-2). 64pp. Daily life and the culture of ancient and modern Rome are covered in double-page spreads illustrated with original drawings and photographs. (Rev: HBG 10/99; SLJ 6/99) [945]

17953 Behnke, Alison. *Italy in Pictures*. Rev. ed. (4–8). Illus. Series: Visual Geography. 2002, Lerner LB $27.93 (978-0-8225-0368-2). 80pp. An excellent introduction to Italy that includes material on geography, history, people, economy, and culture with maps, photographs, and illustrations. (Rev: HBG 3/03; SLJ 3/03) [914.5]

17954 Britton, Tamara. *Greece* (2–4). Series: Countries. 2000, ABDO LB $22.78 (978-1-57765-385-1). 40pp. A workable introduction to Greece with a focus on modern times. (Rev: HBG 10/01; SLJ 3/01) [949.5]

17955 Butler, Daphne. *Italy* (2–4). Illus. 1992, Raintree LB $22.83 (978-0-8114-3677-9). 32pp. A broad overview of Italy, described in terms of topography and lifestyle. (Rev: BL 3/15/93) [945]

17956 Cassidy, Picot. *Italy* (4–8). Series: Nations of the World. 2001, Raintree LB $34.26 (978-0-7398-1287-7). 128pp. A fine overall picture of Italy, its past, its land, its people, its culture, and present-day problems. (Rev: BL 12/15/01; HBG 3/02) [945]

17957 Costain, Meredith, and Paul Collins. *Welcome to Greece* (1–4). Illus. Series: Countries of the World. 2001, Chelsea LB $28.00 (978-0-7910-6545-7). 32pp. An attractive introduction to the land and people of Greece, with a recipe, a craft, a brief page of facts, and many illustrations. (Rev: HBG 3/02; SLJ 12/01)

17958 De Capua, Sarah E. *Italy* (2–4). Illus. Series: First Reports. 2003, Compass Point LB $22.60 (978-0-7565-0425-0). 48pp. In this attractive title from the First Reports series, author Sarah E. De Capua introduces readers to the geography, history, people, and culture of Italy. (Rev: SLJ 10/03)

17959 Dubois, Jill, and Xenia Skoura. *Greece*. 2nd ed. (5–8). Illus. Series: Cultures of the World. 2003, Benchmark LB $37.07 (978-0-7614-1499-5). 143pp. In addition to coverage of the geography, history, and economics of Greece, this volume looks at the people and the culture of this Mediterranean nation and provides recipes. (Rev: HBG 10/03; SLJ 8/03) [949.5]

17960 Ferro, Jennifer. *Italian Foods and Culture* (3–5). Series: Festive Foods and Celebrations. 1999, Rourke LB $27.93 (978-1-57103-302-4). 48pp. Saint Joseph's Day, Christmas, and the Festival of Santa Rosalia are three of the Italian celebrations that are covered in this book that also contains recipes. (Rev: SLJ 2/00) [945]

17961 *Greece in Pictures* (5–8). Illus. Series: Visual Geography. 1996, Lerner LB $25.55 (978-0-8225-1882-2). 64pp. Photographs, maps, charts, and concise text introduce the land and people of Greece. (Rev: BL 10/1/92) [949.5]

17962 Haskins, James. *Count Your Way Through Italy* (2–4). Illus. by Beth Wright. Series: Count Your Way. 1990, Carolrhoda LB $19.93 (978-0-87614-406-0). Introduces the geography and culture of Italy through numbers. (Rev: SLJ 8/90) [945]

17963 Haskins, James, and Kathleen Benson. *Count Your Way Through Greece* (2–4). Illus. by Janice L. Porter. Series: Count Your Way. 1996, Carolrhoda LB $19.93 (978-0-87614-875-4); paper $5.95 (978-0-87614-973-7). 24pp. Greece is introduced in a counting book that goes from 1 to 10. (Rev: BL 9/15/96; SLJ 8/96) [949.5]

17964 Heinrichs, Ann. *Greece* (4–7). Series: Enchantment of the World. 2002, Children's LB $37.00 (978-0-516-22271-4). 144pp. With many color illustrations, this book gives a fascinating portrait of Greece's past and present with coverage of topics including natural resources, culture, climate, and religion. (Rev: BL 9/15/02; SLJ 12/02) [949.5]

17965 Hinds, Kathryn. *Venice and Its Merchant Empire* (5–8). Illus. Series: Cultures of the Past. 2001, Marshall Cavendish LB $29.93 (978-0-7614-0305-0). 80pp. A well-illustrated overview of the history of Venice with a focus on the city's glory during the Renaissance. (Rev: BL 2/15/02; HBG 3/02) [945]

17966 Kotapish, Dawn. *Daily Life in Ancient and Modern Athens* (5–8). Illus. by Bob Moulder. Series: Cities Through Time. 2000, Runestone LB $25.26 (978-0-8225-3216-3). 64pp. Kotapish explores everyday life, government, and culture in Athens through the ages. (Rev: HBG 3/01; SLJ 5/01) [949.5]

17967 Macaulay, David. *Rome Antics* (5–8). Illus. 1997, Houghton $18.00 (978-0-395-82279-1). The reader gets a pigeon-eye view of vistas and buildings as the bird flies over Rome. (Rev: BL 9/15/97;

SLJ 11/97*) [945]

17968 Martin, Fred. *Italy* (5–8). Series: Country Studies. 1999, Heinemann LB $27.07 (978-1-57572-894-0). Using double-page spreads filled with charts, graphs, drawings, maps, and photographs, this book provides basic material about Italy with a focus on contemporary issues. (Rev: BL 8/99; SLJ 8/99) [945]

17969 Nardo, Don. *Greece* (5–8). Series: Modern Nations of the World. 2000, Lucent LB $27.45 (978-1-56006-587-6). 128pp. Although there is coverage of ancient Greece, this account stresses modern history, the people today, and current living conditions and problems. (Rev: BL 2/15/00; HBG 10/00; SLJ 6/00) [949.5]

17970 Olson, Nathan. *Italy* (2–5). Illus. Series: Questions and Answers: Countries. 2005, Capstone LB $23.93 (978-0-7368-3754-5). 32pp. Using a question-and-answer format, simple text, large photos, and many factboxes, this is an introduction to Italy today, with material on history and traditional culture.

17971 Platt, Richard. *Pompeii* (2–5). Illus. by Manuela Cappon. 2007, Kingfisher $16.95 (978-0-7534-6044-3). 48pp. The history of Pompeii, from 750 B.C. to the eruption of Vesuvius and on to the excavation of the site, is chronicled with a focus on a single house. (Rev: BL 10/15/07; LMC 1/08; SLJ 3/08) [937]

17972 Riehecky, Janet. *Greece* (1–3). Series: Countries of the World. 2000, Bridgestone LB $21.26 (978-0-7368-0628-2). 24pp. Full-page photos and current information are the highlights of this basic introduction to Greece. (Rev: HBG 3/01; SLJ 3/01) [949.5]

17973 Winter, Jane K. *Italy* (5–8). Illus. Series: Cultures of the World. 1992, Marshall Cavendish LB $35.64 (978-1-85435-453-2). 128pp. Gives geographic and historical information about Italy and tells about its people and their concerns. (Rev: BL 10/15/92) [945]

Low Countries

17974 Burgan, Michael. *Belgium* (4–7). Series: Enchantment of the World. 2000, Children's LB $37.00 (978-0-516-21006-3). 144pp. This new edition of a standard title contains up-to-date material on such topics as geography and climate, plants and animals, people and culture, the arts, and sports. (Rev: BL 7/00) [949.3]

17975 De Capua, Sarah E. *Netherlands* (2–4). Illus. Series: First Reports. 2003, Compass Point LB $22.60 (978-0-7565-0426-7). 48pp. Simple text introduces readers to basic information on the Netherlands and its geography, history, people, and culture. (Rev: SLJ 10/03)

17976 Heinrichs, Ann. *The Netherlands* (1–3). Series: A True Book. 2003, Children's Pr. LB $25.00 (978-0-516-22675-0). 48pp. A blend of easy-to-understand text and colorful illustrations make this overview suitable for beginning readers. (Rev: SLJ 10/03) [949.2]

17977 Hintz, Martin. *The Netherlands* (4–7). Series: Enchantment of the World. 1999, Children's LB $36.00 (978-0-516-21053-7). 144pp. An up-to-date, well-illustrated, and comprehensive introduction to the Netherlands. (Rev: BL 12/15/99) [949.2]

17978 Pateman, Robert. *Belgium* (4–7). Illus. Series: Cultures of the World. 1995, Marshall Cavendish LB $37.07 (978-0-7614-0176-6). 128pp. After a brief introduction to the history and geography of Belgium, this book focuses on the populace, how they live, and their major contributions to the world. (Rev: BL 1/1–15/96; SLJ 9/96) [949.3]

17979 Sheehan, Patricia. *Luxembourg* (4–7). Illus. Series: Cultures of the World. 1997, Marshall Cavendish LB $37.07 (978-0-7614-0685-3). 128pp. Includes information on this tiny European country's history, culture, and lifestyles. (Rev: BL 8/97) [914.935]

Russia and the Former Soviet States

17980 Aizpuriete, Amanda. *Latvia* (5–8). Trans. by Katarina Hartgers. Photos by Jan Willem Bultje. Series: Looking at Europe. 2006, Oliver $22.95 (978-1-881508-37-3). 48pp. This colorful volume with excellent photographs introduces readers to Latvia's geography, history, people, culture, economy, and lifestyle. (Rev: LMC 3/07; SLJ 1/07) [947.96]

17981 *Armenia* (5–8). Series: Then and Now. 1992, Lerner LB $23.93 (978-0-8225-2806-7). The story up to 1991 of the former Soviet republic that faced many internal problems after it gained independence. (Rev: BL 2/1/93; SLJ 3/93) [956.6]

17982 Arnold, Helen. *Russia* (1–3). Illus. Series: Postcards From. 1995, Raintree LB $22.83 (978-0-8172-4006-6). 32pp. In this quick overview of Russia, such topics as food, shopping, transportation, money, and language are covered. (Rev: SLJ 2/96) [947]

17983 *Azerbaijan* (5–8). Series: Then and Now. 1993, Lerner LB $23.93 (978-0-8225-2810-4). This book introduces the small republic of Azerbaijan, once the Soviet Union's most important oil producing area. (Rev: BL 2/15/93) [947]

17984 Bassis, Volodymyr. *Ukraine* (4–7). Illus. Series: Cultures of the World. 1997, Marshall Cavendish LB $37.07 (978-0-7614-0684-6). 128pp. An introduction to this former Soviet state, with emphasis on current history and culture. (Rev: BL 8/97; SLJ 10/97) [947.7]

17985 *Belarus* (5–8). Series: Then and Now. 1993, Lerner LB $23.93 (978-0-8225-2811-1). An introduction to the history and status as of 1993 of the former Soviet republic of Belarus, which borders on Ukraine. (Rev: BL 5/15/93) [947]

17986 Boast, Clare. *Russia* (2–4). Series: Next Stop. 1998, Heinemann LB $19.92 (978-1-57572-569-7). 32pp. A general introduction to Russia, its history, geography, people, and current living standards. (Rev: SLJ 6/98) [947]

17987 Bultje, Jan Willem. *Lithuania* (5–8). Trans. by Wilma Hoving. Photos by author. Series: Looking at Europe. 2006, Oliver $22.95 (978-1-881508-43-4). 48pp. This colorful volume with excellent photographs introduces readers to Lithuania's geography, history, people, culture, economy, and lifestyle. (Rev: SLJ 1/07) [947.93]

17988 Carrion, Esther. *The Empire of the Czars* (4–7). Illus. Series: World Heritage. 1994, Children's LB $15.00 (978-0-516-08319-3). 34pp. An overview of Russian history from early times to the breakup of the Soviet Union, with special material on Russia's famous sights, such as Red Square, the Kremlin, and St. Petersburg. (Rev: SLJ 5/95) [947.07]

17989 Corona, Laurel. *Ukraine* (5–8). Series: Modern Nations of the World. 2001, Lucent LB $29.95 (978-1-56006-737-5). 112pp. This well-illustrated introduction to the former Soviet republic presents material on the people, culture, economy, history, and physical features. (Rev: BL 6/1–15/01) [947]

17990 Cumming, David. *Russia* (5–8). Illus. Series: Modern Industrial World. 1994, Thomson Learning LB $24.26 (978-1-56847-240-9). 48pp. An introduction to Russia that stresses the economic upheaval caused by the breakup of the USSR. (Rev: BL 1/15/95; SLJ 3/95) [947]

17991 Dhilawala, Sakina. *Armenia* (4–7). Illus. Series: Cultures of the World. 1997, Marshall Cavendish LB $37.07 (978-0-7614-0683-9). 128pp. An introduction to this troubled land that describes how its people live, their lifestyles, and culture. (Rev: BL 8/97; HBG 3/98) [945.56]

17992 *Estonia* (5–8). 1992, Lerner LB $23.93 (978-0-8225-2803-6). Following an introduction about the fall of communism, the book provides an overview of the land and its peoples. (Rev: BL 2/1/93; SLJ 12/92) [914.7]

17993 Frost, Helen. *A Look at Russia* (K–2). Illus. Series: Our World. 2001, Capstone LB $17.26 (978-0-7368-0986-3). 24pp. Brief text and full-page color photographs give a basic introduction to Russia's land, people, and animals. (Rev: HBG 3/02; SLJ 12/01)

17994 *Georgia* (5–8). Illus. Series: Then and Now. 1994, Lerner LB $23.93 (978-0-8225-2807-4). This former Soviet republic is introduced, with information on its geography, ethnic makeup, history, economy, and future challenges. (Rev: BL 2/1/94; SLJ 3/94) [947]

17995 Haskins, James. *Count Your Way Through Russia* (3–5). Illus. 1987, Carolrhoda LB $19.93 (978-0-87614-303-2); paper $5.95 (978-0-87614-488-6). Snowshoes and folk dancers are two of the concepts used with numbers to highlight Russian culture. (Rev: BL 10/15/87; SLJ 9/87)

17996 Ilyin, Andrey. *A Child's Day in a Russian City* (1–3). Illus. Series: A Child's Day. 2001, Marshall Cavendish $25.64 (978-0-7614-1222-9). 32pp. The events in a typical day for Polina, a 7-year-old Russian girl living in St. Petersburg, with color photographs, sections on history and culture, and other background material. (Rev: BL 11/15/01; HBG 3/02; SLJ 3/02) [947.086]

17997 Kagda, Sakina. *Lithuania* (4–7). Illus. Series: Cultures of the World. 1997, Marshall Cavendish LB $37.07 (978-0-7614-0681-5). 128pp. An introduction to Lithuania, with material on geography, history, government, culture, daily life, and festivals. (Rev: BL 8/97; SLJ 10/97) [947.93]

17998 *Kazakhstan* (5–8). Series: Then and Now. 1993, Lerner LB $23.93 (978-0-8225-2815-9). An introduction to the second-largest republic in the former USSR, with information on its status as of 1993. (Rev: BL 9/1/93; SLJ 9/93) [958]

17999 Khan, Aisha. *A Historical Atlas of Kyrgyzstan* (4–6). Illus. Series: Historical Atlases of South Asia, Central Asia and the Middle East. 2004, Rosen LB $30.60 (978-0-8239-4499-6). 64pp. This attractive profile that includes many maps and photographs traces Kyrgyzstan's development from prehistoric times to the present. (Rev: SLJ 11/04)

18000 Kollár, Daniel. *Slovakia* (4–7). Series: Looking at Europe. 2006, Oliver $22.95 (978-1-881508-49-6). 48pp. This photo-filled introduction to Slovakia explores its geography, history, people, culture, cuisine, economy, transportation, tourism, and natural resources. (Rev: SLJ 12/06) [943.73]

18001 Kummer, Patricia K. *Ukraine* (4–7). Series: Enchantment of the World. 2001, Children's LB $37.00 (978-0-516-21101-5). A fine introduction to the past and present of the Ukraine with well-chosen illustrations and material on such topics as resources, daily life, landmarks, languages, and economy. (Rev: BL 1/1–15/02; SLJ 12/01) [947.7]

18002 Liberman, Sherri. *Historical Atlas of Azerbaijan* (4–6). Illus. 2004, Rosen LB $30.60 (978-0-8239-4497-2). 64pp. Liberman traces the turbulent history of Azerbaijan in this slim volume, concentrating mainly on politics and the ethnic groups that make up the population. (Rev: BL 12/1/04; SLJ 11/04) [911]

18003 *Lithuania* (5–8). Series: Then and Now. 1992, Lerner LB $23.93 (978-0-8225-2804-3). This Baltic Sea republic is described, including its history, people, and conditions in the period immediately following its independence in 1990. (Rev: BL 2/1/93) [947]

18004 *Moldova* (5–8). Series: Then and Now. 1992, Lerner LB $23.93 (978-0-8225-2809-8). The history of this small, landlocked republic, parts of which at one time or another have belonged to the Ottoman Turks, Romania, Russia, and the USSR, and which is now independent. (Rev: BL 2/1/93; SLJ 3/93) [947]

18005 Rogers, Stillman D. *Russia* (4–7). Series: Enchantment of the World. 2002, Children's LB $37.00 (978-0-516-22494-7). 144pp. This portrait of Russia in text and illustrations covers such basic subjects as history, resources, geography, people, problems, economy, and culture. (Rev: BL 9/15/02; SLJ 10/02) [947]

18006 *Russia* (5–8). Series: Then and Now. 1992, Lerner LB $23.93 (978-0-8225-2805-0). A brief history of Russia with emphasis on its status in the period immediately following the fall of the USSR in 1991. (Rev: BL 2/1/93; SLJ 12/92) [947]

18007 Sallnow, John, and Tatyana Saiko. *Russia* (5–8). Series: Country Fact Files. 1997, Raintree LB $27.12 (978-0-8172-4625-9). The impact of geography on different aspects of life in Russia, including natural resources, daily life, the landscape, and transportation, is explored. (Rev: SLJ 8/97) [947]

18008 Schomp, Virginia. *Russia: New Freedoms, New Challenges* (4–6). Illus. Series: Exploring Cultures of the World. 1996, Benchmark LB $27.07 (978-0-7614-0186-5). 64pp. As well as providing background information on Russia, this account stresses current conditions, with an emphasis on culture and the arts. (Rev: SLJ 6/96) [947]

18009 Sheehan, Patricia. *Moldova* (5–9). Series: Cultures of the World. 2000, Marshall Cavendish LB $37.07 (978-0-7614-0997-7). 128pp. This book on the former Soviet republic that borders on the Ukraine covers such topics as culture, land, people, history, resources, and government. (Rev: HBG 10/00; SLJ 11/00) [947]

18010 Spengler, Kremena. *Russia* (2–5). Illus. Series: Questions and Answers: Countries. 2004, Capstone LB $23.93 (978-0-7368-2692-1). 32pp. Using a question-and-answer format, simple text, large photos, and many factboxes, this is an introduction to Russia today, with material on history and traditional culture.

18011 Steele, Philip. *Moscow* (3–6). Series: Great Cities of the World. 2003, World Almanac LB $31.00 (978-0-8368-5024-6). 48pp. A visit to the Russian capital, well illustrated with photographs, covering the city's history, economy, and people. (Rev: SLJ 3/04) [947]

18012 *Tajikistan* (5–8). Illus. Series: Then and Now. 1993, Lerner LB $23.93 (978-0-8225-2816-6). An introduction to the land and people of this remote former Soviet republic located north of Afghanistan. (Rev: BL 10/15/93; SLJ 11/93) [958.6]

18013 *Ukraine* (5–8). Series: Then and Now. 1992, Lerner LB $23.93 (978-0-8225-2808-1). The history of this Black Sea republic and its status in the period immediately following its independence in 1991. (Rev: BCCB 3/93; BL 2/1/93; SLJ 3/93) [947]

18014 *Uzbekistan* (5–8). Series: Then and Now. 1993, Lerner LB $23.93 (978-0-8225-2812-8). A history of this Muslim republic, its economic situation, and prospects for the future as of 1993. (Rev: BL 5/15/93) [958.7]

18015 Veceric, Danica. *Slovenia* (4–7). Series: Looking at Europe. 2006, Oliver $22.95 (978-1-881508-74-8). 48pp. A tour of Slovenia, examining the country's geography, history, people, culture, cuisine, economy, transportation, tourism, and natural resources. (Rev: SLJ 12/06) [949.73]

18016 Wilson, Neil. *Russia* (4–8). Series: Nations of the World. 2001, Raintree LB $34.26 (978-0-7398-1281-5). 128pp. Colorful photographs, charts, and maps enrich chapters on Russia's past and present, land and cities, economy, art and culture, and possible future developments. (Rev: BL 6/1–15/01; HBG 10/01) [947]

Scandinavia, Iceland, Greenland, and Finland

18017 Alatalo, Jaakko. *A Child's Day in a Nordic Village* (K–3). Series: A Child's Day. 2002, Marshall Cavendish LB $25.64 (978-0-7614-1411-7). 32pp. This book takes a Scandinavian child through a typical day, showing the reader about family, friends, culture, and language. (Rev: BL 2/15/03; HBG 3/03) [948]

18018 Bailey, Linda. *Adventures with the Vikings* (3–5). Illus. by Bill Slavin. Series: Good Times Travel Agency. 2001, Kids Can $14.95 (978-1-55074-542-9); paper $7.95 (978-1-55074-544-3). 48pp. The Binkerton children travel to the age of the Vikings in this comic-book-style story that interweaves fiction and nonfiction. (Rev: BL 10/15/01; HBG 3/02; SLJ 11/01) [948]

18019 Berger, Melvin, and Gilda Berger. *The Real Vikings: Craftsmen, Traders, and Fearsome Raiders* (4–8). Illus. 2003, National Geographic $18.95 (978-0-7922-5132-3). 64pp. A highly illustrated introduction to the Vikings and their world, with information on their political and social ideals — including democracy — as well as their more fearsome and acquisitive traits. (Rev: BL 12/1/03; HBG 4/04; SLJ 1/04) [948]

18020 Blashfield, Jean F. *Norway* (4–7). Series: Enchantment of the World. 2000, Children's LB $37.00 (978-0-516-20651-6). 144pp. An introduction to Norway that covers such subjects as geography and climate, history and government, mythology and culture, and people and economy. (Rev: BL 7/00) [948.1]

18021 Boraas, Tracey. *Sweden* (4–6). Series: Countries and Cultures. 2002, Capstone LB $25.26 (978-0-7368-0939-9). 64pp. This introduction to the land and people of Sweden explores topics including history, landforms, government, economics, and traditions. (Rev: BL 1/1–15/03; HBG 3/03) [948.5]

18022 Butler, Robbie. *Sweden* (4–8). Series: Nations of the World. 2001, Raintree LB $34.26 (978-0-8172-5784-2). 128pp. Colorful maps, charts and graphs, and photographs supplement the text in this fine profile of Sweden. (Rev: BL 6/1–15/01; HBG 10/01) [948.5]

18023 Carlsson, Bo Kage. *Sweden* (5–8). Series: Modern Industrial World. 1995, Thomson Learning LB $24.26 (978-1-56847-436-6). A survey of modern Sweden and its industries, economy, resources, and people. (Rev: BL 12/15/95) [949.4]

18024 Clare, John D., ed. *The Vikings* (3–6). Illus. 1992, Harcourt $16.95 (978-0-15-200512-2). 64pp. Period costumes and period settings help to dramatize this historical era. (Rev: BL 12/1/92; SLJ 11/92) [948]

18025 Corona, Laurel. *Norway* (5–8). Series: Modern Nations of the World. 2000, Lucent LB $29.95 (978-1-56006-647-7). 128pp. Norway is introduced with coverage of history, geography, and culture plus material on everyday modern life. (Rev: BL 3/1/01) [948.1]

18026 *Denmark in Pictures* (5–8). Illus. Series: Visual Geography. 1997, Lerner LB $25.55 (978-0-

8225-1880-8). 64pp. In photographs, maps, charts, and concise text, the land of Denmark and its people are introduced. (Rev: BL 4/1/91; SLJ 7/91) [948]

18027 Dupre, Kelly. *The Raven's Gift: A True Story from Greenland* (K–3). Illus. 2001, Houghton $15.00 (978-0-618-01171-1). 32pp. An encounter with a raven inspires two men to continue their journey around Greenland, in this effectively illustrated story of an expedition taken by the author's husband. (Rev: BL 8/01; HBG 3/02; SLJ 9/01) [919.82]

18028 DuTemple, Lesley A. *Sweden* (5–8). Series: Modern Nations of the World. 2000, Lucent LB $28.70 (978-1-56006-588-3). 112pp. A general introduction to Sweden that includes its history and geography but stresses today's living conditions and the people's lifestyles. (Rev: BL 3/15/00; HBG 10/00) [948.5]

18029 Franklin, Sharon, et al. *Scandinavia* (4–7). Series: Artisans Around the World. 1999, Raintree LB $27.12 (978-0-7398-0122-2). 48pp. This book, which contains many hands-on activities, surveys Scandinavian crafts and shows how geography has influenced this area's artisans. (Rev: BL 10/15/99; HBG 3/00; SLJ 1/00) [948]

18030 Gan, Delice. *Sweden* (4–7). Illus. Series: Cultures of the World. 1992, Marshall Cavendish LB $35.64 (978-1-85435-452-5). 128pp. This introduction to Sweden gives special coverage of the people and their lifestyles. (Rev: BL 10/15/92) [948.5]

18031 Hansen, Ole Steen. *Denmark* (4–7). Series: Country Insights. 1998, Raintree LB $27.12 (978-0-8172-4794-2). 48pp. This book provides a broad description of the country — its lifestyle, culture, and traditions — and contrasts Denmark's rural and urban environments. (Rev: BL 6/1–15/98; HBG 10/98) [948]

18032 Hopkins, Andrea. *Viking Explorers and Settlers* (3–6). Illus. Series: The Viking Library. 2001, Rosen LB $21.25 (978-0-8239-5816-0). 24pp. Beginning report writers will find basic historical information with illustrations, maps, and documents in this slim volume. Also use *Viking Gods and Legends* and *Vikings: The Norse Discovery of America* (both 2002). (Rev: SLJ 6/02) [938]

18033 *Iceland in Pictures* (5–8). Illus. Series: Visual Geography. 1996, Lerner LB $25.55 (978-0-8225-1892-1). 64pp. The history, government, people, and economy of the northern republic of Iceland are covered in words and pictures. (Rev: BL 8/91) [949.12]

18034 James, Louise. *The Vikings* (3–6). Illus. Series: How We Know About. 1997, Bedrick LB $17.95 (978-0-87226-535-6). 32pp. Using both contemporary photos and many reconstructions, the everyday life of the Vikings is described, with information on how archaeologists determined these facts. (Rev: BL 12/15/97; HBG 3/98; SLJ 10/97) [948.022]

18035 Jovinelly, Joann, and Jason Netelkos. *The Crafts and Culture of the Vikings* (5–8). Series: Crafts of the Ancient World. 2002, Rosen LB $29.25 (978-0-8239-3514-7). 48pp. In addition to giving a tour of ancient Scandinavia, this book outlines such craft projects as designing a battle shield and helmet, minting coins, and playing an ancient board game. (Rev: BL 5/15/02) [948]

18036 Kagda, Sakina. *Norway* (4–7). Illus. Series: Cultures of the World. 1995, Marshall Cavendish LB $37.07 (978-0-7614-0181-0). 128pp. After general information on Norway's geography and history, this account concentrates on the Norwegian people, how they live, and their artistic accomplishments. (Rev: BL 1/1–15/96; SLJ 9/96) [948.1]

18037 Kopka, Deborah. *Norway* (1–3). Series: Globe-Trotters Club. 2000, Carolrhoda LB $22.60 (978-1-57505-123-9). 48pp. Double-page spreads with stunning photographs introduce the land and people of Norway, with material on the Vikings, fjords, and skiing. (Rev: BL 10/15/00; HBG 3/01) [948.1]

18038 Landau, Elaine. *Exploring the World of the Vikings with Elaine Landau* (3–6). Illus. Series: Exploring Ancient Civilizations with Elaine Landau. 2005, Enslow LB $23.93 (978-0-7660-2340-6). 48pp. Readers explore the time of the Vikings along with the author and her dog Max, learning about many aspects of early Norse life and culture, including housing, food, apparel, religion, occupations, and relations with the outside world. (Rev: SLJ 12/05) [948.022]

18039 Lee, Tan Chung. *Finland* (4–7). Illus. Series: Cultures of the World. 1996, Marshall Cavendish LB $37.07 (978-0-7614-0280-0). 128pp. The small country of Finland with its thousands of lakes is introduced, with emphasis on the people and how they live. (Rev: BL 8/96; SLJ 7/96) [984.97]

18040 McMillan, Bruce. *Going Fishing* (2–4). Illus. 2005, Houghton $16.00 (978-0-618-47201-7). 32pp. Photographs capture a boy and his grandfathers as they fish for cod and lumpfish in Iceland. (Rev: BL 3/1/05; SLJ 5/05) [799.16]

18041 Manning, Mick, and Brita Granström. *Viking Longship* (3–5). Illus. by Mick Manning. Series: Fly on the Wall. 2007, Frances Lincoln $15.95 (978-1-84507-465-4). 40pp. Fact and fiction are interwoven as readers learn about Viking life — shipbuilding, meals, clothing, mythology, battles, and so forth. (Rev: BL 11/15/07) [948.022]

18042 Pitkanen, Matti A. *The Grandchildren of the Vikings* (3–6). Illus. Series: World's Children. 1996, Carolrhoda LB $23.93 (978-0-87614-889-1). 47pp. A photo-essay that explores family life in five areas settled by the Vikings, including the Faeroe Islands, Iceland, Gotland, Aland, and Lofoten. (Rev: SLJ 2/97) [949]

18043 Robinson, Deborah B. *The Sami of Northern Europe* (4–6). Series: First Peoples. 2002, Lerner LB $23.93 (978-0-8225-4175-2). This book describes the life and culture of the Sami, once known as Lapps, who were once primarily reindeer herders. (Rev: BL 5/15/02; HBG 10/02; SLJ 8/02) [948]

18044 Shuter, Jane. *Life in a Viking Town* (2–4). Illus. Series: Picture the Past. 2005, Heinemann LB $25.64 (978-1-4034-6440-8). 32pp. This colorful title gives young readers a sampling of what life was like in a Viking town, covering such topics as dwellings, jobs, food, apparel, and leisure activities. (Rev: SLJ 11/05)

18045 Shuter, Jane. *Life on a Viking Ship* (2–4). Illus. Series: Picture the Past. 2005, Heinemann LB $25.64 (978-1-4034-6441-5). 32pp. This attractive title gives young readers an overview of what life was like on a Viking ship. (Rev: SLJ 11/05)

18046 *Sweden in Pictures* (5–8). Illus. Series: Visual Geography. 1993, Lerner LB $21.27 (978-0-8225-1872-3). 64pp. Gives the background geography and history of Sweden, along with contemporary material. (Rev: BL 12/1/90) [948.5]

18047 Wilcox, Jonathan. *Iceland* (4–7). Series: Cultures of the World. 1996, Marshall Cavendish LB $37.07 (978-0-7614-0279-4). The history, geography, people, and culture of this remote island republic are introduced, with many color photographs. (Rev: SLJ 7/96) [949.12]

18048 Yanuck, Debbie L. *Sweden* (2–3). Illus. Series: Many Cultures, One World. 2004, Capstone LB $23.93 (978-0-7368-2452-1). 32pp. A brief, accessible introduction to Sweden and its people, family life, customs, and legends. (Rev: SLJ 10/04)

Spain and Portugal

18049 Anderson, Wayne. *The ETA: Spain's Basque Terrorists* (4–8). Series: Inside the World's Most Infamous Terrorist Organizations. 2003, Rosen LB $27.95 (978-0-8239-3818-6). 64pp. This is the history and present status of the violent organization committed to creating an ethnic homeland separate from Spain. (Rev: BL 10/15/03; SLJ 9/03) [946]

18050 Berendes, Mary. *Welcome to Spain* (1–4). Series: Welcome to the World. 2008, The Child's World LB $27.07 (978-1-59296-979-1). 32pp. As easy introduction to Spain and its land, people, plants and animals, and so forth, with color photographs, maps, and recipes. (Rev: SLJ 9/08) [946]

18051 Blauer, Ettagale, and Jason Lauré. *Portugal* (4–7). Series: Enchantment of the World. 2002, Children's LB $37.00 (978-0-516-21109-1). 144pp. This highly visual introduction to Portugal includes accessible information on topics including history, people and language, customs, and economy. (Rev: BL 9/15/02) [946.9]

18052 Champion, Neil. *Portugal* (5–8). Illus. Series: Modern Industrial World. 1995, Thomson Learning LB $24.26 (978-1-56847-435-9). 48pp. Modern Portugal is highlighted in text and pictures, with coverage of its economy, industries, and resources. (Rev: BL 12/15/95) [946.904]

18053 Chicoine, Stephen D. *Spain: Bridge Between Continents* (3–5). Illus. Series: Exploring Cultures of the World. 1997, Marshall Cavendish LB $27.07 (978-0-7614-0143-8). 64pp. This introduction to Spain covers geography, history, the people, family life, the arts, festivals, and recreation. (Rev: BL 7/97; SLJ 1/98) [946]

18054 Goodman, Joan Elizabeth. *A Long and Uncertain Journey: The 27,000-Mile Voyage of Vasco da Gama* (4–8). Illus. by Tom McNeely. 2001, Mikaya $19.95 (978-0-9650493-7-5). 48pp. Details of Vasco da Gama's explorations and their historical context are accompanied by biographical informa-

tion, illustrations, journal entries, a map, and a timeline. (Rev: BL 9/1/01; HBG 10/01; SLJ 6/01*; VOYA 8/01) [910]

18055 Heale, Jay. *Portugal* (5–8). Illus. Series: Cultures of the World. 1995, Marshall Cavendish LB $37.07 (978-0-7614-0169-8). 128pp. Present-day conditions in Portugal are emphasized in this account, which also covers history, geography, and culture. (Rev: SLJ 11/95) [914.9]

18056 Humble, Richard, and Mark Bergin. *A 16th Century Galleon* (4–6). Illus. Series: Inside Story. 1995, Bedrick LB $18.95 (978-0-87226-372-7). 48pp. A richly illustrated volume that begins with the construction of the galleon from massive tree trunks and continues through its launching and techniques of ocean navigation. (Rev: BL 8/95) [623.8]

18057 Kohen, Elizabeth. *Spain* (4–7). Illus. Series: Cultures of the World. 1992, Marshall Cavendish LB $35.64 (978-1-85435-451-8). 128pp. With text, photographs, maps, and fact sheets, the land and people of Spain are introduced. (Rev: BL 10/15/92) [946]

18058 Mann, Kenny. *Isabel, Ferdinand and Fifteenth-Century Spain* (5–8). Series: Rulers and Their Times. 2001, Marshall Cavendish LB $29.93 (978-0-7614-1030-0). Following biographies of these great Spanish rulers, there is a section on the life and culture of their times plus a generous selection of original documents of the period. (Rev: BL 1/1–15/02; HBG 3/02; SLJ 3/02) [946]

18059 Millar, Heather. *Spain in the Age of Exploration* (5–8). Series: Cultures of the Past. 1998, Benchmark LB $29.93 (978-0-7614-0303-6). 80pp. This book covers Spanish history from the time of Columbus to about 1700, with an emphasis on art and literature plus material on daily life and major personalities. (Rev: BL 12/15/98; HBG 10/99; SLJ 2/99) [946]

18060 Miller, Arthur. *Spain* (4–6). Illus. 1989, Chelsea LB $16.95 (978-1-55546-795-1). 112pp. Culture, history, geography, and daily lifestyles are covered in this introduction. (Rev: BL 4/1/89; SLJ 5/89)

18061 *Portugal in Pictures* (5–8). Illus. Series: Visual Geography. 1996, Lerner LB $25.55 (978-0-8225-1886-0). 64pp. Current conditions and problems in Portugal are introduced along with the standard material on history, geography, and social conditions. (Rev: BL 12/15/91) [946.9]

18062 Rogers, Lura. *Spain* (4–7). Series: Enchantment of the World. 2001, Children's LB $37.00 (978-0-516-21123-7). A well-designed book that uses clear text, numerous charts, maps, drawings, and photographs to introduce a number of topics related to Spain and its people. (Rev: BL 1/1–15/02) [946]

18063 Selby, Anna. *Spain* (4–7). Illus. Series: Country Fact Files. 1994, Raintree LB $27.12 (978 0 8114-1848-5). 45pp. A well-illustrated introduction to Spain, with coverage of such subjects as current social conditions, the economy, food and farming, and the environment. (Rev: SLJ 7/94) [946]

18064 *Spain in Pictures* (5–8). Illus. Series: Visual Geography. 1995, Lerner LB $25.55 (978-0-8225-1887-7). 64pp. Modern Spain is the focus of this introduction, which includes many photographs, charts, and maps. (Rev: BL 11/15/95) [914.6]

18065 Yanuck, Debbie L. *Spain* (2–3). Illus. Series: Many Cultures, One World. 2004, Capstone LB $23.93 (978-0-7368-2451-4). 32pp. A brief, accessible introduction to Spain and its people, family life, customs, and legends.

The Middle East

General

18066 Barr, Gary E. *History and Activities of the Islamic Empire* (3–6). Illus. Series: Hands-on Ancient History. 2006, Heinemann LB $28.21 (978-1-4034-7926-6). 32pp. Social life, arts and culture, games, and holidays and celebrations are covered in this attractive and accessible volume that includes a recipe and three crafts. (Rev: SLJ 4/07) [909]

18067 Broyles, Matthew. *The Six-Day War* (5–9). Illus. Series: War and Conflict in the Middle East. 2004, Rosen LB $27.95 (978-0-8239-4549-8). 64pp. A well-organized, balanced account of the 1973 war between Israel and its Arab neighbors Egypt, Jordan, and Syria. (Rev: BL 11/1/04; SLJ 1/05)

18068 Fiscus, James W. *The Suez Crisis* (5–9). Illus. Series: War and Conflict in the Middle East. 2004, Rosen LB $27.95 (978-0-8239-4550-4). 64pp. Examines the 1956 conflict over control of the canal, involving Egypt, Israel, Britain, and France. (Rev: BL 11/1/04)

18069 Ford, Nick. *Jerusalem Under Muslim Rule in the Eleventh Century: Christian Pilgrims Under Islamic Government* (5–9). Series: The Library of the Middle Ages. 2004, Rosen LB $29.25 (978-0-8239-4216-9). 64pp. Useful for report writers, this volume looks at life in Jerusalem for people of all religions, providing details from primary sources. (Rev: SLJ 8/04) [956.94]

18070 Hancock, Lee. *Saladin and the Kingdom of Jerusalem: The Muslims Recapture the Holy Land in AD 1187* (5–9). Series: The Library of the Middle Ages. 2004, Rosen LB $29.25 (978-0-8239-4217-6). 64pp. Useful for report writers, this volume looks at life in Jerusalem under the Crusaders, providing details from primary sources. (Rev: SLJ 8/04) [956]

18071 Hilliam, Paul. *Islamic Weapons, Warfare, and Armies: Muslim Military Operations Against the Crusaders* (5–9). Series: The Library of the Middle Ages. 2004, Rosen LB $29.25 (978-0-8239-4215-2). 64pp. Useful for report writers, this volume looks at the spread of Islam and the conflicts with the Crusaders. (Rev: SLJ 8/04) [355]

18072 King, John. *Bedouin* (4–6). Illus. Series: Threatened Cultures. 1992, Raintree LB $24.26 (978-0-8114-2304-5). 48pp. This book presents the life and culture of the nomadic Bedouins. (Rev: BCCB 7–8/93; BL 8/93; SLJ 9/93) [961]

18073 Long, Cathryn J. *The Middle East in Search of Peace*. Rev. ed. (4–7). Illus. Series: Headliners. 1996, Millbrook LB $25.90 (978-0-7613-0105-9). 64pp. An objective account of the conflict between Arabs and Jews in the Middle East, with good historical information and a description of various peace plans. (Rev: SLJ 1/97) [956]

18074 Losleben, Elizabeth. *The Bedouin of the Middle East* (4–6). Series: First Peoples. 2002, Lerner LB $23.95 (978-0-8225-0663-8). 48pp. Traditional and contemporary lifestyles are included in this presentation of the Bedouin people, the territory in which they live, and their history, culture, and economy. (Rev: HBG 3/03; SLJ 2/03) [961]

18075 MacDonald, Fiona. *A 16th Century Mosque* (4–6). Illus. Series: Inside Story. 1995, Bedrick $18.95 (978-0-87226-310-9). 48pp. After a discussion of the fundamentals of the Muslim faith, this account graphically covers the construction of the Sulemaniye mosque in Constantinople in 1557. (Rev: BL 4/15/95) [297]

18076 Rivera, Sheila. *Women of the Middle East* (4–6). Series: World in Conflict. 2004, ABDO LB $25.65 (978-1-59197-415-4). 48pp. For reluctant readers, this title studies the status of contemporary women in Saudi Arabia, Afghanistan, Iran, Egypt, and Israel, looking at the role of religion, politics, and local custom in their lives. (Rev: SLJ 3/04) [305.42]

18077 Senker, Cath. *The Arab-Israeli Conflict* (5–8). Series: Questioning History. 2004, Smart Apple LB $28.50 (978-1-58340-441-6). 64pp. A clear and balanced discussion of the history and current status of relations between Arabs and Israelis, with a timeline, glossary, and detailed index. (Rev: SLJ 2/05) [956.04]

18078 Steele, Philip. *Middle East* (4–7). Series: Kingfisher Knowledge. 2006, Kingfisher LB $12.95 (978-0-7534-5984-3). 64pp. Traces the history of the region — extending from Eastern Mediterranean countries into Iraq, Iran, and Afghanistan — as well as its geography, peoples, cultures, religions, economies, and politics. (Rev: SLJ 12/06) [956]

18079 Wingate, Katherine. *The Intifadas* (5–9). Illus. Series: War and Conflict in the Middle East. 2004, Rosen LB $27.95 (978-0-8239-4546-7). 64pp. An even-handed overview of the events leading up to the Palestinian uprisings, with statistics, maps, photographs, and profiles of leaders. (Rev: BL 11/1/04) [956.95]

Egypt

18080 Bennett, Olivia. *A Family in Egypt* (3–6). Illus. 1985, Lerner LB $18.60 (978-0-8225-1652-1). 32pp. Color photos highlight the life of a family in this Middle East land. (Rev: BL 6/15/85; SLJ 10/85)

18081 Bowden, Rob, and Roy Maconachie. *Cairo* (4–7). Illus. Series: Great Cities of the World. 2005, World Almanac LB $31.00 (978-0-8368-5035-2). 48pp. An informative and appealing overview of one of the world's most famous cities, with material on its history, its economy, and what it's like to live there. (Rev: BL 4/15/04)

18082 Deady, Kathleen W. *Egypt* (1–3). Series: Countries of the World. 2000, Bridgestone LB $21.26 (978-0-7368-0626-8). 24pp. A very basic introduction to Egypt that contains current facts and full-page photos. (Rev: HBG 3/01; SLJ 3/01) [962]

18083 Draper, Allison Stark. *Historical Atlas of Egypt* (4–6). Illus. Series: Historical Atlases of South Asia, Central Asia and the Middle East. 2004, Rosen LB $30.60 (978-0-8239-4498-9). 64pp. This attractive profile that includes many maps and photographs traces Egypt's development from prehistoric times to the present.

18084 Eldash, Khaled, and Dalia Khattab. *A Child's Day in an Egyptian City* (K–3). Series: A Child's Day. 2002, Marshall Cavendish LB $25.64 (978-0-7614-1410-0). 32pp. An accessible introduction to present-day Egypt through the daily life of its children. (Rev: BL 2/15/03; HBG 3/03) [962]

18085 Flint, David. *Egypt* (2–4). Illus. Series: On the Map. 1993, Raintree LB $22.83 (978-0-8114-3420-1). 32pp. Using many color photos, this account covers briefly such topics related to Egypt as geography, religion, history, and landmarks. (Rev: BL 2/1/94) [954.9]

18086 Gutner, Howard. *Egypt* (3–5). Series: A True Book — Geography: Countries. 2009, Children's Pr. LB $26.00 (978-0-531-16889-9). 48pp. An attractive overview of Egypt, covering geography, history, culture, and pertinent statistics. (Rev: SLJ 7/09) [962]

18087 Harkonen, Reijo. *The Children of Egypt* (4–6). Illus. by Matti Pitkanen. Series: The World's Children. 1991, Carolrhoda LB $23.93 (978-0-87614-396-4). 40pp. In this profile, two of the children highlighted guide tourists to the pyramids, and another is a brickmaker. (Rev: BL 6/1/91) [962]

18088 King, David C. *Egypt: Ancient Traditions, Modern Hopes* (3–5). Illus. Series: Exploring Cultures of the World. 1997, Marshall Cavendish LB $27.07 (978-0-7614-0142-1). 64pp. Describes various aspects of life in modern Egypt, with comparisons and contrasts made to past conditions. (Rev: BL 7/97; SLJ 1/98) [932]

18089 Krebs, Laurie. *We're Sailing Down the Nile: A Journey Through Egypt* (PS–3). Illus. by Anne Wilson. 2007, Barefoot Books $16.99 (978-1-84686-040-9). Readers will learn facts about Egypt's most famous sites and about the country's ancient history and customs in this voyage down the famous river. (Rev: LMC 11/07; SLJ 7/07)

18090 Loveridge, Emma. *Egypt* (5–8). Series: Country Fact Files. 1997, Raintree LB $27.12 (978-0-8172-4626-6). This book gives standard basic information about Egypt, including its climate, landscape, trade, industry, and daily life. (Rev: SLJ 9/97) [962]

18091 Orr, Tamra. *Egyptian Islamic Jihad* (4–8). Series: Inside the World's Most Infamous Terrorist Organizations. 2003, Rosen LB $27.95 (978-0-8239-3819-3). 64pp. Dedicated to the overthrow of the secular Egyptian government, this terrorist

organization has links to the Al Qaeda terrorist network. (Rev: BL 10/15/03) [962]

18092 Parks, Peggy J. *The Aswan High Dam* (5–8). Series: Building World Landmarks. 2004, Gale LB $24.95 (978-1-56711-329-7). 48pp. This is the fascinating story of the construction of the huge dam on the Nile and the immense technical and social challenges involved. (Rev: SLJ 6/04) [627]

18093 Pateman, Robert. *Egypt* (4–7). Illus. Series: Cultures of the World. 1992, Marshall Cavendish LB $35.64 (978-1-85435-535-5). 128pp. Egypt past and present is introduced in this account that stresses how the people live. (Rev: BL 1/1/93) [962]

18094 Roop, Peter, and Connie Roop. *Egypt* (2–4). Series: A Visit To. 1998, Heinemann LB $21.36 (978-1-57572-122-4). 32pp. An attractive introduction to modern Egypt, covering its geography, history, cities, people, and culture. (Rev: SLJ 9/98) [967]

18095 Streissguth, Thomas. *Egypt* (3–5). Series: Globe-Trotters Club. 1999, Carolrhoda $22.60 (978-1-57505-110-9). 48pp. Two-page spreads present a variety of topics related to Egypt, including its geography, history, the people, religion, schools, food, and government. (Rev: BL 9/15/99; HBG 3/00; SLJ 12/99) [962]

18096 Streissguth, Thomas. *Egypt* (1–3). Series: A Ticket To. 1999, Carolrhoda LB $22.60 (978-1-57505-135-2). 48pp. This heavily illustrated first look at Egypt covers the land, its people, and its main ethnic and cultural features. (Rev: BL 9/15/99; HBG 3/00; SLJ 12/99) [962]

18097 Tenquist, Alasdair. *Egypt* (5–7). Illus. Series: Economically Developing Countries. 1995, Thomson Learning LB $24.26 (978-1-56847-385-7). 48pp. A look at present-day conditions in Egypt and its concerns and problems. (Rev: SLJ 2/96) [962]

18098 Webster, Christine. *Egypt* (2–5). Illus. Series: Questions and Answers: Countries. 2004, Capstone LB $23.93 (978-0-7368-2688-4). 32pp. Using a question-and-answer format, simple text, large photos, and many factboxes, this is an introduction to Egypt today, with material on history and traditional culture.

18099 Wilson, Neil. *Egypt* (4–8). Series: Nations of the World. 2001, Raintree LB $34.26 (978-0-7398-1283-9). 128pp. An excellent introduction to the country that housed one of the world's oldest civilizations and is currently a center of Islamic culture and religion. (Rev: BL 6/1–15/01; HBG 10/01) [962]

18100 Zuehlke, Jeffrey. *Egypt in Pictures*. Rev. ed. (4–8). Illus. Series: Visual Geography. 2002, Lerner LB $27.93 (978-0-8225-0367-5). 80pp. Covers Egypt's geography, history, people, economy, and culture with maps, photographs, and illustrations. (Rev: SLJ 3/03) [962]

Israel

18101 Boraas, Tracey. *Israel* (4–6). Series: Countries and Cultures. 2002, Capstone LB $25.26 (978-0-7368-0938-2). 64pp. This introduction to Israel includes basic material on history, wildlife, government, geography, and economics. (Rev: BL 1/1–15/03; HBG 3/03; SLJ 4/03) [956.54]

18102 Bowden, Rob. *Jerusalem* (3–6). Series: Great Cities of the World. 2005, World Almanac LB $31.00 (978-0-8368-5051-2). 48pp. With color photographs and informative sidebars, this volume introduces the geography, history, culture, religion, work, and recreation of Jerusalem. (Rev: SLJ 11/05)

18103 Dubois, Jill. *Israel* (4–7). Illus. Series: Cultures of the World. 1992, Marshall Cavendish LB $35.64 (978-1-85435-531-7). 128pp. This introduction to Israel emphasizes its culture and the lifestyles of the people. (Rev: BL 1/1/93) [956.94]

18104 Feinstein, Steve. *Israel in Pictures* (5–8). Illus. 1992, Lerner LB $25.55 (978-0-8225-1833-4). 64pp. An overview of geography, climate, wildlife, and vegetation with photographs, maps, and charts. (Rev: BL 8/88) [956.9405]

18105 Green, Jen. *Israel* (4–8). Series: Nations of the World. 2001, Raintree LB $34.26 (978-0-7398-1286-0). 128pp. A fine, attractive introduction to the land and people of Israel, the nation that was created as a homeland for the Jewish people after World War II. (Rev: BL 6/1–15/01; HBG 10/01) [956.94]

18106 Gresko, Marcia S. *Israel* (1–3). Series: Globe-Trotters Club. 2000, Carolrhoda LB $22.60 (978-1-57505-118-5). 48pp. From the rocky Negev Desert to the Sea of Galilee, the state of Israel is brought to life in this account that introduces the country through double-page spreads on a variety of subjects. (Rev: BL 5/15/00; HBG 3/01) [956.94]

18107 Grossman, Laurie M. *Children of Israel* (2–5). Photos by author. Series: The World's Children. 2001, Carolrhoda LB $23.93 (978-1-57505-448-3). 48pp. This look at the daily lives of children in Israel introduces the history, geography, and culture of the country with appealing full-color illustrations, a pronunciation guide, and map. (Rev: HBG 10/01; SLJ 6/01)

18108 Gunderson, Cory. *The Israeli-Palestinian Conflict* (4–6). Series: World in Conflict. 2004, ABDO LB $25.65 (978-1-59197-416-1). 48pp. A politically balanced introduction to the ongoing conflict between the Israelis and Palestinians, aimed at reluctant readers, with numerous photographs and maps. (Rev: SLJ 3/04) [956.04]

18109 Haskins, James. *Count Your Way Through Israel* (2–4). Illus. by Rick Handson. Series: Count Your Way. 1990, Carolrhoda LB $19.93 (978-0-87614-415-2). Using the format of counting from 1 to 10 in Hebrew, the land and people of Israel are introduced. (Rev: SLJ 2/91) [956.94]

18110 Hayhurst, Chris. *Israel's War of Independence* (5–9). Illus. Series: War and Conflict in the Middle East. 2004, Rosen LB $27.95 (978-0-8239-4548-1). 64pp. An even-handed overview of Israel's struggle for independence and the ensuing years of violence, with statistics, maps, photographs, and profiles of leaders. (Rev: BL 11/1/04; SLJ 1/05) [956.04]

18111 Kuskin, Karla. *Jerusalem, Shining Still* (3–5). Illus. by David Frampton. 1987, HarperCollins paper $5.50 (978-0-06-443243-6). 32pp. The history of Jerusalem is briefly told in lyrical prose and

touches of verse. (Rev: BL 10/1/87; HB 11/87; SLJ 11/87)

18112 Paris, Alan. *Jerusalem 3000: Kids Discover the City of Gold!* (4–6). Illus. by Peter Gandolfi. 1995, Pitspopany $16.95 (978-0-943706-59-7). 47pp. This fine introduction to Jerusalem includes material on its history as determined by archaeological research. (Rev: SLJ 12/95) [956.94]

18113 Patterson, Jose. *Israel* (3–6). Illus. Series: Country Facts Files. 1997, Raintree LB $27.12 (978-0-8172-4627-3). 45pp. This account covers modern-day Israel and its political and economic status, resources, and people. (Rev: BL 7/97) [956.94]

18114 Scharfstein, Sol. *Understanding Israel* (5–7). Illus. 1994, KTAV paper $14.95 (978-0-88125-428-0). 144pp. A heavily illustrated introduction to Israel that covers history, religion, government, culture, and current concerns. (Rev: SLJ 10/94) [956.94]

18115 Sherman, Josepha. *Your Travel Guide to Ancient Israel* (4–8). Illus. Series: Passport to History. 2003, Lerner LB $26.60 (978-0-8225-3072-5). 80pp. An illustrated visit to Israel in the time of King Solomon, with description of foods, housing, clothing, customs, and notable people of that era. (Rev: SLJ 4/04) [933]

18116 Silverman, Maida. *Israel: The Founding of a Modern Nation* (4–7). Illus. 1998, Dial LB $15.00 (978-0-8034-2136-3). 112pp. This account covers 3,000 years of Jewish history, with emphasis on recent centuries, and includes a timeline showing Israel's history from 1948 to 1998. (Rev: BL 5/1/98) [956.94]

18117 Spengler, Kremena. *Israel* (2–5). Illus. Series: Questions and Answers: Countries. 2005, Capstone LB $23.93 (978-0-7368-3753-8). 32pp. Using a question-and-answer format, simple text, large photos, and many factboxes, this is an introduction to Israel today, with material on history and traditional culture.

18118 *Three Wishes: Palestinian and Israeli Children Speak* (5–12). 2004, Groundwood $16.95 (978-0-88899-554-4). 144pp. In an evenhanded presentation that offers an introductory historical overview, 20 first-person accounts relate the experiences of Christian, Jewish, and Muslim young people during the ongoing conflict between Israelis and Palestinians. (Rev: BL 9/1/04*; SLJ 10/04) [956.04]

18119 Waldman, Neil. *The Golden City: Jerusalem's 3,000 Years* (4–6). Illus. 1995, Simon & Schuster $15.00 (978-0-689-80080-1). 32pp. Beginning with Moses, this account traces the important events in the history of Jerusalem during its 3,000-year existence. (Rev: BL 9/1/95; SLJ 11/95) [965.94]

Other Middle Eastern Lands

18120 Anderson, Laurie Halse. *Saudi Arabia* (1–3). Series: Globe-Trotters Club. 2000, Lerner LB $22.60 (978-1-57505-121-5). 48pp. An introduction to this country on the Arabian Peninsula that tells about its landmarks, ethnic groups, oil riches, ancient traditions, and modern conveniences. (Rev: BL 12/15/00; HBG 3/01; SLJ 1/01) [953]

18121 Augustin, Byron. *United Arab Emirates* (4–7). Series: Enchantment of the World. 2002, Children's LB $36.00 (978-0-516-20473-4). 144pp. This important nation is introduced with material on topics including history, natural resources, climate, and people. (Rev: BL 5/15/02; SLJ 9/02) [953]

18122 Augustin, Byron, and Jake Kubena. *Iraq* (5–8). Illus. Series: Enchantment of the World. 2006, Children's Pr. LB $37.00 (978-0-516-24852-3). 144pp. An updated version of a 1998 book on the country, with additional information on ethnic groups, the environment, and continuing violence. (Rev: SLJ 7/06) [956.7]

18123 Bader, Philip. *Iran* (3–5). Illus. Series: Dropping In On. 2001, Rourke $28.50 (978-1-55916-285-2). This brief tour of Iran via hot-air balloon includes material on geography, famous sights, and the people. (Rev: SLJ 1/01) [955]

18124 Bauer, Brandy. *Iran: A Question And Answer Book* (2–5). Illus. Series: Questions and Answers: Countries. 2005, Capstone LB $23.93 (978-0-7368-3752-1). 32pp. Using a question-and-answer format, simple text, large photos, and many factboxes, this is an introduction to Iran today, with material on history and traditional culture.

18125 Boueri, Marijean, and Jill Boutros. *Lebanon A to Z: A Middle Eastern Mosaic* (4–8). Illus. by Tatiana Sabbagh. 2006, Publishing Works $25.00 (978-0-9744803-4-3). 77pp. Eleven-year-old Kareem takes readers on a tour through the country's present and past, with an emphasis on cultural traditions and Lebanon's people. (Rev: SLJ 7/06) [956.92]

18126 Byers, Ann. *Lebanon's Hezbollah* (4–8). Series: Inside the World's Most Infamous Terrorist Organizations. 2003, Rosen LB $27.95 (978-0-8239-3821-6). 64pp. This is the story of the Lebanese terrorist organization dedicated to installing a conservative Islamic government in Lebanon and to the destruction of Israel. (Rev: BL 10/15/03; SLJ 9/03) [956.92]

18127 Cartlidge, Cherese. *Iran* (5–8). Series: Modern Nations of the World. 2002, Gale LB $29.95 (978-1-56006-971-3). 112pp. This colorful account gives a comprehensive overview of Iran, including history, geography, and culture. (Rev: BL 12/15/02; SLJ 1/03) [955]

18128 Deady, Kathleen W. *Saudi Arabia* (2–5). Illus. Series: Questions and Answers: Countries. 2005, Capstone LB $23.93 (978-0-7368-3760-6). 32pp. Using a question-and-answer format, simple text, large photos, and many factboxes, this is an introduction to Saudi Arabia today, with material on history and traditional culture. (Rev: HBG 3/02)

18129 Dutton, Roderic. *An Arab Family* (3–6). Illus. 1985, Lerner LB $18.60 (978-0-8225-1660-6). 32pp. The author focuses mainly on one family member to give fascinating details of life, noting how the discovery of oil has influenced daily activities. (Rev: BL 11/15/85)

18130 Foster, Leila M. *Oman* (4–7). Series: Enchantment of the World. 1999, Children's LB $37.00 (978-0-516-20964-7). 144pp. A fine introduction to this oil-producing country, covering topics such as history, geography, government, religion, and the economy. (Rev: BL 9/15/99) [956]

18131 Friedman, Mel. *Iraq* (3–5). Series: A True Book — Geography: Countries. 2009, Children's Pr. LB $26.00 (978-0-531-16891-2). 48pp. An attractive overview of Iraq, covering geography, history, culture, people, and the effects of war. (Rev: SLJ 7/09) [956.7]

18132 Goodwin, William. *Saudi Arabia* (5–8). Series: Modern Nations of the World. 2001, Lucent LB $29.95 (978-1-56006-763-4). 112pp. The land ruled by the Saud dynasty is presented with details on history, government, geography, resources, and world importance. (Rev: BL 6/1–15/01) [953.8]

18133 Graham, Amy. *Iran in the News: Past, Present, and Future* (5–8). Illus. Series: Middle East Nations in the News. 2006, Enslow LB $33.27 (978-1-59845-022-4). 128pp. History, culture, people, and current political issues are all covered in this readable overview of Iran that includes links to Web sites that extend the text. (Rev: BL 4/1/06; SLJ 5/06) [955]

18134 Gray, Leon. *Iran* (4–8). Illus. Series: Countries of the World. 2008, National Geographic LB $27.90 (978-1-4263-0200-8). 64pp. Useful for researchers, this book provides basic information about the country as well as data and additional facts presented in sidebars and other features. (Rev: BL 4/15/08) [955.22]

18135 Haskins, James. *Count Your Way Through the Arab World* (3–5). Illus. 1987, Carolrhoda LB $19.93 (978-0-87614-304-9); Lerner paper $5.95 (978-0-87614-487-9). 24pp. "Muslims pray to Mecca 5 times a day" and other numbers help to introduce the culture of the Arab world. (Rev: BL 10/15/87; SLJ 9/87)

18136 Haskins, James, and Kathleen Benson. *Count Your Way Through Iran* (2–4). Illus. by Farida Zaman. Series: Count Your Way. 2006, Lerner LB $19.93 (978-1-57505-881-8). 24pp. Aspects of Iranian life from 1 to 10 are accompanied by a map and various other key facts. (Rev: BL 8/06) [955]

18137 Hassig, Susan M. *Iraq* (4–7). Illus. Series: Cultures of the World. 1992, Marshall Cavendish LB $35.64 (978-1-85435-533-1). 128pp. This introduction stresses the lifestyles of the people, their religion, and culture. (Rev: BL 1/1/93) [956.7]

18138 Heinrichs, Ann. *Saudi Arabia* (4–7). Series: Enchantment of the World. 2002, Children's LB $37.00 (978-0-516-22287-5). 144pp. Topics covered in the highly visual introduction to Saudi Arabia include history, religion, language, economy, and government. (Rev: BL 9/15/02) [953.8]

18139 Hestler, Anna. *Yemen* (5–8). Series: Cultures of the World. 1999, Marshall Cavendish LB $37.07 (978-0-7614-0956-4). 128pp. A fine introduction to this country on the Gulf of Aden with good background information and an overview of modern life. (Rev: HBG 10/99; SLJ 10/99) [956]

18140 *Iran in Pictures* (5–8). Illus. Series: Visual Geography. 1992, Lerner LB $21.27 (978-0-8225-1848-8). 64pp. Basic coverage on this Middle Eastern land and its people. (Rev: BL 5/1/89) [955]

18141 Isaac, Michael. *Historical Atlas of Oman* (4–6). Illus. Series: Historical Atlases of South Asia, Central Asia and the Middle East. 2004, Rosen LB $30.60 (978-0-8239-4500-9). 64pp. This attractive profile that includes many maps and photographs traces Oman's development from prehistoric times to the present.

18142 Janin, Hunt. *Saudi Arabia* (4–7). Illus. Series: Cultures of the World. 1992, Marshall Cavendish LB $35.64 (978-1-85435-532-4). 128pp. The history, geography, economy, language, and people are discussed in this book about Saudi Arabia. (Rev: BL 1/1/93) [953.8]

18143 *Jordan in Pictures* (5–8). Illus. 1992, Lerner LB $25.55 (978-0-8225-1834-1). 64pp. Young readers learn what life is like in this Middle East land. (Rev: BL 2/1/89; SLJ 2/89) [956.9504]

18144 *Lebanon in Pictures* (5–8). Illus. Series: Visual Geography. 1992, Lerner LB $25.55 (978-0-8225-1832-7). 64pp. A country torn apart by strife is the focus of this edition. (Rev: BL 2/1/89) [956.9204]

18145 Lobaido, Anthony C., and Yumi Ng. *The Kurds of Asia* (4–6). Illus. Series: First Peoples. 2002, Lerner LB $23.95 (978-0-8225-0664-5). 48pp. Traditional and contemporary lifestyles are both included in this presentation of the Kurd people, the territory in which they live, and their history, culture, and economy. (Rev: HBG 3/03; SLJ 2/03)

18146 Malhotra, Sonali. *Welcome to Iraq* (3–5). Series: Welcome to My Country. 2004, Gareth Stevens LB $27.00 (978-0-8368-2559-6). 48pp. Introduces readers to Iraq's geography, history, people, culture, family life, government, religion, and language. (Rev: SLJ 7/04) [956.7]

18147 Marcovitz, Hal. *Kuwait* (5–8). Illus. Series: Modern Middle East Nations. 2003, Mason Crest LB $24.95 (978-1-59084-510-3). 112pp. A thorough introduction to the geography, history, and people of Kuwait, whose wealth makes it an unusual country. (Rev: BL 6/1–15/03; HBG 4/04; SLJ 10/03) [953.67]

18148 Moktefi, Mokhtar. *The Arabs in the Golden Age* (4–6). Illus. by Veronique Ageorges. 1992, Millbrook LB $22.40 (978-1-56294-201-4). 64pp. This book takes the reader back to the 8th through mid-13th centuries. (Rev: BL 10/15/92) [909]

18149 Rajendra, Vijeya, and Gisela Kaplan. *Iran* (4–7). Illus. Series: Cultures of the World. 1992, Marshall Cavendish LB $35.64 (978-1-85435-534-8). 128pp. As well as standard introductory information about Iran, this book tells about how the people live and what the country's present problems are. (Rev: BL 1/1/93) [955]

18150 Reed, Jennifer B. *The Saudi Royal Family* (5–8). Illus. Series: Major World Leaders. 2002, Chelsea $30.00 (978-0-7910-7063-5); paper $30.00 (978-0-7910-7187-8). 112pp. Saudi Arabia's ruling royal family is profiled, detailing its rise to power,

its Islamic policies, and the various individual rulers, with a look at the contrast between the family's extravagant lifestyle and its religious beliefs. (Rev: BL 1/1–15/03; SLJ 4/03) [953.8]

18151 Romano, Amy. *A Historical Atlas of the United Arab Emirates* (4–6). Illus. 2004, Rosen LB $30.60 (978-0-8239-4501-6). 64pp. A useful supplement to more detailed books on the United Arab Emirates, this title chronicles the country's history from the time of its earliest known settlements to the present. (Rev: BL 12/1/04) [911]

18152 Romano, Amy. *Historical Atlas of Yemen* (4–6). Illus. Series: Historical Atlases of South Asia, Central Asia and the Middle East. 2004, Rosen LB $30.60 (978-0-8239-4502-3). 64pp. This attractive profile that includes many maps and photographs traces Yemen's development from prehistoric times to the present.

18153 Sheehan, Sean. *Lebanon* (5–10). Series: Cultures of the World. 1996, Marshall Cavendish LB $37.07 (978-0-7614-0283-1). A lively, well-written introduction to this war-ravaged country with details on history, economy, culture, religion and foods, including a recipe for a typical dish. (Rev: SLJ 6/97) [569.2]

18154 South, Coleman. *Jordan* (5–10). Series: Cultures of the World. 1996, Marshall Cavendish LB $37.07 (978-0-7614-0287-9). Everyday life in Jordan is the focus of this book that also covers history, religion, culture, geography, festivals, and foods; a single recipe is included. (Rev: SLJ 6/97) [569.5]

18155 Spengler, Kremena. *Iraq: A Question and Answer Book* (2–5). Illus. Series: Fact Finders. 2004, Capstone LB $23.93 (978-0-7368-2691-4). 32pp. Double-page spreads use simple text, factboxes, and plenty of color photographs to answer pertinent questions about the country's history, geography, government, and culture. (Rev: BL 11/15/04; SLJ 3/05) [956.7]

18156 Stevens, Kathryn. *Welcome to Iraq* (1–3). Illus. Series: Welcome to the World. 2007, Child's World LB $18.95 (978-1-59296-916-6). 32pp. This simple book looks at life, culture, and wildlife in Iraq and covers recent events in a matter-of-fact style. (Rev: BL 10/15/07) [956.7]

18157 Van Der Gaag, Nikki, and Felicity Arbuthnot. *Baghdad* (3–6). Series: Great Cities of the World. 2005, World Almanac LB $31.00 (978-0-8368-5049-9). 48pp. With color photographs and informative sidebars, this volume introduces the geography, history, culture, religion, work, and recreation of Baghdad. (Rev: SLJ 11/05)

18158 Wills, Karen. *Jordan* (5–8). Series: Modern Nations of the World. 2001, Lucent LB $29.95 (978-1-56006-822-8). 112pp. A good profile of Jordan is presented, with basic background material and information on present conditions and the people today. (Rev: BL 6/1–15/01) [956.95]

18159 Winter, Jeanette. *The Librarian of Basra: A True Story from Iraq* (3–5). Illus. 2005, Harcourt $16.00 (978-0-15-205445-8). 32pp. This is the inspiring, true story of an Iraqi librarian's efforts to save the 30,000 books in Basra's library collection from destruction as invading forces neared the city in 2003. (Rev: BL 12/1/04; SLJ 1/05*) [020]

18160 *Yemen in Pictures* (5–8). Illus. Series: Visual Geography. 1993, Lerner LB $25.55 (978-0-8225-1911-9). 64pp. In introduction to this Muslim republic on the Gulf of Aden, with material on its economic and social conditions. (Rev: BL 12/1/93; SLJ 12/93) [953.3]

North and South America (Excluding the United States)

North and South America

18161 Alter, Judy. *Discovering North America's Land, People, and Wildlife* (5–8). Series: Continents of the World. 2004, Enslow LB $25.26 (978-0-7660-5206-2). 48pp. An introduction to the geography, history, economy, plants and animals, culture, and people of the continent, with brief coverage of the Caribbean and Central America. (Rev: SLJ 11/04) [917]

18162 Bramwell, Martyn. *North America and the Caribbean* (4–6). Series: World in Maps. 2000, Lerner LB $23.93 (978-0-8225-2911-8). 48pp. A comprehensive and well-illustrated treatment of all the countries that make up North America, from Canada to Mexico and the Caribbean islands. (Rev: BL 10/15/00; HBG 10/01) [970]

18163 Fox, Mary Virginia. *North America* (1–3). Series: Continents. 2006, Heinemann LB $21.36 (978-1-58810-001-6). 32pp. For beginning report writers, this is a survey of North America's geography, flora, fauna, weather, and history. (Rev: SLJ 1/07) [970]

18164 Franklin, Sharon, et al. *Mexico and Central America* (4–7). Illus. Series: Artisans Around the World. 1999, Raintree LB $27.12 (978-0-7398-0121-5). 48pp. This craft book, with related projects, describes the folk art of each of the countries in Central America and Mexico. (Rev: BL 10/15/99; HBG 3/00; SLJ 1/00) [745.5]

18165 Turck, Mary C. *Mexico and Central America: A Fiesta of Cultures, Crafts, and Activities for Ages 8–12* (3–6). 2004, Chicago Review paper $14.95 (978-1-55652-525-4). 160pp. Turck provides wide-ranging information on Mexico and the countries of Central America, including items on history, geography, and culture, plus recipes, crafts, and activities. (Rev: BL 8/04; SLJ 8/04) [972]

18166 Woods, Michael, and Mary B. Woods. *Seven Natural Wonders of Central and South America* (5–8). Illus. 2009, Twenty-First Century LB $33.26 (978-0-8225-9070-5). 80pp. Angel Falls, the Amazon River, the Atacama Desert, the Galápagos Islands, the Montecristo Cloud Forest, Poás Volcano, and the Andes Mountains are the seven wonders featured in this attractive volume. (Rev: BL 4/1/09; SLJ 5/09) [508.8]

Canada

18167 Beattie, Owen, and John Geiger. *Buried in Ice: The Mystery of a Lost Arctic Expedition* (4–7). Illus. by Janet Wilson. Series: Time Quest. 1993, Scholastic paper $6.95 (978-0-590-43849-0). 64pp. The story of Sir John Franklin's unsuccessful 1845 expedition from England to find the Northwest Passage. (Rev: BCCB 3/92; BL 4/1/92; SLJ 4/92*) [919.804]

18168 Bial, Raymond. *The Inuit* (5–8). Series: Lifeways. 2001, Marshall Cavendish LB $34.21 (978-0-7614-1212-0). Using clear language and many intriguing illustrations, this is a fine introduction to the Inuit that begins with a folk story on the origins of the people and continues with material on a variety of basic topics. (Rev: BL 1/1–15/02; HBG 3/02; SLJ 4/02) [979.8]

18169 Bowers, Vivien. *Crazy About Canada! Amazing Things Kids Want to Know* (4–6). Illus. by Dianne Eastman. Series: Canadian Geographic Kids. 2006, Maple Tree $28.95 (978-1-897066-47-8); paper $18.95 (978-1-897066-48-5). 96pp. Cartoon figures Vivien and Morton ask questions about various aspects of Canada (geography, history, wildlife, and so forth) in this attractive fact-filled volume. (Rev: BL 4/1/06; SLJ 8/06) [971]

18170 Bowers, Vivien. *Wow Canada! Exploring This Land from Coast to Coast to Coast* (4–6). Illus. 2000, Firefly paper $19.95 (978-1-895688-94-8). 160pp. A family travels across Canada visiting important sites and gathering material on the land and its people in this relaxed travelogue. (Rev: BL 2/15/00; HBG 10/00; SLJ 4/00) [917.104]

18171 Braun, Eric. *Canada in Pictures*. Rev. ed. (5–9). Illus. Series: Visual Geography. 2003, Lerner LB $27.93 (978-0-8225-4679-5). 80pp. An informative and interesting overview of Canada's history, geography, government, economy, and people suitable for both research and browsing. (Rev: HBG 10/03; SLJ 7/03) [971.064]

18172 Butler, Geoff. *Ode to Newfoundland* (1–6). Illus. by author. 2003, Tundra $19.95 (978-0-88776-631-2). 32pp. A picture-book celebration of Newfoundland, with historical notes, lyrics, and music appended. (Rev: HBG 4/04; SLJ 1/04) [971.8]

18173 Campbell, Kumari. *Prince Edward Island* (3–6). Illus. Series: Hello Canada. 1996, Lerner LB $19.93 (978-0-8225-2762-6). 72pp. This volume highlights Canada's island province, its inhabitants, history, famous people, and economy. (Rev: BL 4/15/96) [971.7]

18174 *Canada in Pictures* (4–6). Series: Visual Geography. 1993, Lerner LB $21.27 (978-0-8225-1870-9). 64pp. In four separate sections that explore the land, the history and government, the people, and the economy, the basic facts about Canada and Canadians are presented. (Rev: SLJ 2/90) [971]

18175 *Christmas in Canada: Christmas Around the World from World Book* (4–6). Illus. 1994, World Book $18.50 (978-0-7166-0894-3). 80pp. An overview of how several ethnic groups in Canada spend their Christmas, with asides about special rituals and traditions. (Rev: BL 12/15/94) [394.26]

18176 Cooper, Michael. *Klondike Fever: The Famous Gold Rush of 1898* (5–8). Illus. 1990, Houghton paper $6.95 (978-0-395-54784-7). 80pp. The events that turned a remote part of the Yukon into a three-ring circus of gold-hungry prospectors. (Rev: BCCB 1/90; BL 11/15/89; HB 1/90) [971.9]

18177 Corriveau, Danielle. *The Inuit of Canada* (4–6). Illus. Series: First Peoples. 2001, Lerner $23.95 (978-0-8225-4850-8). 48pp. This attractive introduction to the Inuit people and their native region and culture also contrasts traditional and modern lifestyles. (Rev: BL 2/1/02; HBG 3/02; SLJ 3/02) [979.8]

18178 Coulter, Tony. *Jacques Cartier, Samuel de Champlain, and the Explorers of Canada* (5–8). Illus. Series: World Explorers. 1993, Chelsea LB $32.00 (978-0-7910-1298-7). This book about the early exploration of Canada includes material on Cartier, Champlain, Cabot, and Hudson, among others. (Rev: BL 1/1/93) [971]

18179 Daitch, Richard W. *Northwest Territories* (3–6). Illus. Series: Hello Canada. 1996, Lerner $19.93 (978-0-8225-2761-9). 72pp. A remote northern part of Canada is featured in this book, with material on its people, history, government, and economy. (Rev: BL 4/15/96) [971.9]

18180 Ekoomiak, Normee. *Arctic Memories* (3–5). Illus. 1990, Holt paper $5.95 (978-0-8050-2347-3). 32pp. Memories of an Inuit artist who was raised in the James Bay area of Arctic Quebec. (Rev: BCCB 3/90; BL 3/1/90; HB 5/90; SLJ 4/90) [998]

18181 Grabowski, John. *Canada* (5–8). Illus. Series: Overview: Modern Nations of the World. 1997, Lucent LB $27.45 (978-1-56006-520-3). A fine introduction to Canada and its people with coverage of major cities, industry, art and culture, government, and the separatist movement in Quebec. (Rev: BL 6/1–15/98; SLJ 8/98) [971]

18182 Greenwood, Barbara. *Gold Rush Fever: A Story of the Klondike, 1898* (4–7). Illus. by Heather Collins. 2001, Kids Can $18.95 (978-1-55074-852-9); paper $12.95 (978-1-55074-850-5). 160pp. Thirteen-year-old Tim and his older brother trek to the Yukon to try to win their fortune in this account that interweaves fact and fiction, with many details about the hardships the miners faced. (Rev: BL 12/15/01; HBG 10/02; SLJ 10/01) [971.91]

18183 Hamilton, Janice. *Canada* (3–5). Illus. Series: Globe-Trotters Club. 1999, Carolrhoda LB $22.60 (978-1-57505-108-6). 48pp. A fine introduction to Canada for young readers that includes material on history, geography, culture, religion, and present-day conditions. (Rev: BL 9/15/99; HBG 10/99) [971]

18184 Hamilton, Janice. *Canada* (1–3). Illus. Series: A Ticket To. 1999, Carolrhoda LB $22.60 (978-1-57505-133-8). 48pp. A basic, well-illustrated introduction to Canada, the land and its people. (Rev: BL 9/15/99; HBG 10/99) [971]

18185 Hamilton, Janice. *Quebec* (3–6). Illus. Series: Hello Canada. 1996, Lerner LB $19.93 (978-0-8225-2766-4). 72pp. This Canadian province, currently divided about its political future, is featured, with material on its heritage, geography, and economy. (Rev: BL 4/15/96) [971.4]

18186 Hancock, Lyn. *Nunavut* (3–6). Illus. Series: Hello Canada. 1995, Lerner LB $19.93 (978-0-8225-2758-9). 76pp. Basic information is given on this Canadian territory founded in 1993 from the eastern part of the Northwest Territories. (Rev: BL 12/15/95) [971.9]

18187 Haugen, Brenda. *Canada ABCs: A Book About the People and Places of Canada* (2–4). Illus. by David Shaw. Series: Country ABCs. 2004, Picture Window LB $26.60 (978-1-4048-0285-8). 32pp. Young researchers will find useful facts in this alphabetically organized volume. (Rev: SLJ 8/04) [971]

18188 Hughes, Susan. *Let's Call It Canada: Amazing Stories of Canadian Place Names* (3–6). Illus. by Clive Dobson and Jolie Dobson. 2003, Maple Tree $26.95 (978-1-894379-49-6); paper $16.95 (978-1-894379-50-2). 96pp. A topically organized compendium of Canadian place names and the interesting stories behind them. (Rev: SLJ 7/03) [917.1]

18189 Jackson, Lawrence. *Newfoundland and Labrador* (3–6). Illus. Series: Hello Canada. 1995, Lerner LB $19.93 (978-0-8225-2757-2). 72pp. A slim volume that presents a guided tour of these regions of Canada, with coverage on history, economic development, principal cities, and important residents, past and present. (Rev: BL 12/15/95) [971.8]

18190 Jones, Charlotte F. *Yukon Gold: The Story of the Klondike Gold Rush* (4–8). 1999, Holiday $18.95 (978-0-8234-1403-1). 99pp. A solid account of the Alaska/Yukon Gold Rush that is enlivened by black-and-white photographs and intriguing asides and anecdotes. (Rev: BCCB 6/99; HB 7/99; HBG 10/99; SLJ 5/99; VOYA 12/99) [979.8]

18191 Kalman, Bobbie. *Canada: The Culture*. Rev. ed. (4–6). Series: The Lands, Peoples, and Cultures. 2001, Crabtree LB $25.27 (978-0-7787-9360-1); paper $7.95 (978-0-7787-9728-9). 32pp. This revised and updated edition includes Native, French, and English perspectives as well as discussion of refugees. Also use *Canada: The Land* and *Canada: The People* (both 2002). (Rev: SLJ 6/02)

18192 Kalman, Bobbie. *Canada Celebrates Multiculturalism* (3–5). Illus. Series: Lands, Peoples, and Cultures. 1993, Crabtree LB $25.27 (978-0-86505-220-8); paper $7.95 (978-0-86505-300-7). 32pp. Some topics covered are the beginnings of multiculturalism in Canada, religious and heritage days, cross-cultural festivals, and the traditions of various ethnic groups. (Rev: BL 2/1/94) [971]

18193 King, David C. *The Inuit* (1–4). Series: First Americans. 2007, Marshall Cavendish LB $20.95 (978-0-7614-2679-0). 48pp. An introduction to these Native Americans, covering their history, culture, beliefs, current status, and future; with an activity and a recipe. (Rev: SLJ 4/08) [971.9004]

18194 Major, Kevin. *Eh? to Zed* (2–4). Illus. 2001, Red Deer $17.95 (978-0-88995-222-5). 32pp. Canadian history and diverse culture are presented in an alphabet running from "Arctic, apple, aurora, Anik" to "Zamboni, zipper, zinc, zed." (Rev: BL 6/1–15/01; SLJ 7/01) [421.1]

18195 Marx, David F. *Canada* (1–2). Illus. Series: Rookie Readers. 2000, Children's Book Pr. paper $5.95 (978-0-516-27083-8). 32pp. This book for beginning readers gives a quick introduction to Canada, its history, people, and languages. (Rev: BL 12/1/00) [971]

18196 Newhouse, Maxwell. *The RCMP Musical Ride* (4–6). Illus. by author. 2004, Tundra $15.95 (978-0-88776-683-1). A lively, behind-the-scenes look at the horseback displays performed by the Royal Canadian Mounted Police. (Rev: SLJ 9/04) [363.2]

18197 Oberman, Sheldon. *The Shaman's Nephew: A Life in the Far North* (4–8). Illus. 2000, Stoddart $18.95 (978-0-7737-3200-1). 56pp. This first-person narrative explores Inuit art and culture as experienced by Tookoome, an Inuit artist, who reflects on the daily life, beliefs, and myths of his people as presented in his work. (Rev: BL 6/1–15/00; SLJ 7/00) [971.9]

18198 Olson, Nathan. *Canada* (3–4). Illus. Series: Fact Finders: Questions and Answers. 2004, Capstone LB $23.93 (978-0-7368-2686-0). 32pp. Using a question-and-answer format, this title introduces Canada's history, government, economy, education, culture, sports, and lifestyle. (Rev: SLJ 1/05) [971]

18199 Pang, Guek-Cheng. *Canada*. 2nd ed. (5–9). Illus. Series: Cultures of the World. 2004, Benchmark LB $37.07 (978-0-7614-1788-0). 144pp. History, geography, and culture are all covered in this useful volume that attempts to impart a comprehensive understanding of life in all parts of Canada. (Rev: SLJ 2/05) [971]

18200 Quigley, Mary. *Canada* (1–3). Illus. Series: A Visit To. 2003, Heinemann LB $22.79 (978-1-4034-0964-5). 32pp. Full of photographs, this is a useful and interesting overview of the country's geography, history, and culture, suitable for beginning readers. (Rev: HBG 10/03; SLJ 7/03) [971]

18201 Renaud, Anne. *Pier 21: Stories from Near and Far* (4–7). Illus. by Aries Cheung. Series: Canadian Immigration. 2008, Lobster $16.95 (978-1-897073-70-4). 24pp. This book is a collection of documents, memories, photographs, and illustrations relating to the site on Halifax Harbor where thousands of immigrants to Canada (in the years 1928 to 1971) started their new lives. (Rev: BL 4/15/08) [325.71]

18202 Richardson, Gillian. *Saskatchewan* (3–6). Illus. Series: Hello Canada. 1995, Lerner LB $19.93 (978-0-8225-2760-2). 72pp. This introduction to Canada's midwestern province and bread basket includes material on history, geography, resources, and famous people. (Rev: BL 12/15/95) [971.24]

18203 Robinson, Deborah B. *The Cree of North America* (4–6). Series: First Peoples. 2002, Lerner LB $23.93 (978-0-8225-4178-3). This book describes the culture and history of the Cree of North America, who are found primarily in subarctic Canada. (Rev: BL 5/15/02; HBG 10/02) [971]

18204 Rogers, Barbara Radcliffe, and Stillman D. Rogers. *Canada* (4–7). Series: Enchantment of the World. 2000, Children's LB $37.00 (978-0-516-21076-6). 144pp. This fine introduction to Canada, its land and its people, also contains coverage of its history, economy, plants and animals, languages, sports, and the arts. (Rev: BL 1/1–15/01) [971]

18205 Rowe, Percy. *Toronto* (3–6). Series: Great Cities of the World. 2003, World Almanac LB $31.00 (978-0-8368-5026-0). 48pp. Color photographs enliven this in-depth look at Canada's most populous city, with detailed information on its history, economy, and the lives of its residents. (Rev: SLJ 3/04) [971.3]

18206 Rowe, Percy, and Patience Coster. *Montreal* (3–6). Series: Great Cities of the World. 2004, World Almanac LB $31.00 (978-0-8368-5039-0). 48pp. Montreal's history, geography, and economy are described, as are shopping and leisure attractions and the life of the city. (Rev: SLJ 4/05)

18207 Strudwick, Leslie. *Inuit* (4–6). Illus. Series: Indigenous Peoples. 2004, Weigl LB $18.20 (978-1-59036-149-8). 32pp. Historical and contemporary issues are both covered in this detailed portrait of life among the Inuit. (Rev: BL 4/1/04) [971.9004]

18208 Strudwick, Leslie. *Inuit* (3–5). Series: Indigenous Peoples. 2004, Weigl LB $18.20 (978-1-59036-122-1). 32pp. A fascinating and informative overview of the Inuit people, covering history, culture, language, and family life. (Rev: SLJ 7/04) [971.9]

18209 Thompson, Alexa. *Nova Scotia* (4–8). Series: Hello Canada. 1995, Lerner LB $19.93 (978-0-8225-2759-6). Nova Scotia's history, geography, and the economy are covered, with material on the various peoples and cultures. (Rev: SLJ 3/96) [971.6]

18210 Weaver, Janice. *Mirror with a Memory: A Nation's Story in Photographs* (4–6). Illus. 2007, Tundra $29.95 (978-0-88776-747-0). 192pp. Archival photographs of Canada's national history — from the 1864 Confederation Conference to the present day — are the focus of this volume, each captioned with commentary and historical information. (Rev: BL 11/15/07; SLJ 12/07) [971]

18211 Whitcraft, Melissa. *The Niagara River* (4–8). Series: Watts Library. 2001, Watts LB $25.50 (978-0-531-11903-7). 63pp. This absorbing and readable account with maps and historical and contemporary photographs looks at the river's history, industry, and impact on the surrounding region. (Rev: SLJ 5/01) [971.3]

18212 Williams, Brian. *Canada* (3–6). Illus. Series: Countries of the World. 2007, National Geographic LB $27.90 (978-1-4263-0025-7). 64pp. An attractive layout and up-to-date information combine to make this an effective and interesting introduction to the country and its culture. (Rev: SLJ 8/07)

18213 Williams, Suzanne M. *The Inuit* (4–6). Series: Watts Library. 2003, Watts LB $25.50 (978-0-531-12172-6). 63pp. The author profiles an Inuit family in Canada's far north, showing how they combine aspects of traditional and modern life. (Rev: SLJ 5/04) [971.9]

18214 Yates, Sarah. *Alberta* (4–8). Series: Hello Canada. 1995, Lerner LB $19.93 (978-0-8225-2763-3). A colorful, slim volume that crams many facts about this western Canadian province's culture, history, geography, and resources into a few attractive pages. (Rev: BL 12/15/95; SLJ 3/96) [971.23]

Mexico

18215 Ancona, George. *The Fiestas* (3–6). Illus. Series: Viva Mexico! 2001, Marshall Cavendish LB $27.07 (978-0-7614-1327-1). 48pp. One in a series of visually exciting photoessay books for older readers about Mexican culture and traditions that also includes *The Folk Arts* and *The Foods* (both 2001). (Rev: BL 3/1/02; HBG 3/02; SLJ 2/02) [394.26972]

18216 Ancona, George. *Pablo Remembers: The Fiesta of the Day of the Dead* (3–6). Illus. 1993, Lothrop $17.99 (978-0-688-11249-3). 48pp. The customs and traditions surrounding the three-day Mexican celebration, the Fiesta of the Day of the Dead, are described in this photoessay. A Spanish-language edition is also available. (Rev: BCCB 12/93; BL 2/1/94; SLJ 12/93) [393.9]

18217 Ancona, George. *The Pinata Maker / El Piñatero* (1–3). Illus. 1994, Harcourt paper $9.00 (978-0-15-200060-8). 40pp. Many Mexican crafts, like the piñata and puppet making, are highlighted when a group of children visit an aged craftsman in this dual-language book. (Rev: BL 2/15/94; HB 7/94; SLJ 4/94) [745]

18218 Arnold, Helen. *Mexico* (1–3). Illus. Series: Postcards From. 1995, Raintree LB $15.98 (978-0-8172-4012-7). 32pp. A quick overview of Mexico is given through a series of postcards written by fictitious children. (Rev: SLJ 2/96) [972]

18219 Burr, Claudia, et al. *Broken Shields* (4–8). Illus. 1997, Douglas & McIntyre paper $6.95 (978-0-88899-304-5). 32pp. From firsthand eyewitness accounts, this is the story of the betrayal of Montezuma at the hands of the Spanish conqueror Cortez. (Rev: BL 12/1/97; HB 11/97; HBG 3/98; SLJ 1/98) [972]

18220 Burr, Claudia, et al. *When the Viceroy Came* (3–5). Illus. 1999, Groundwood $15.95 (978-0-88899-354-0). 33pp. Told from a young boy's point of view, this slice of Mexican history relates how the new Spanish viceroy came to Mexico in 1702. (Rev: BL 8/99; SLJ 8/99) [972]

18221 Conlon, Laura. *People of Mexico* (2–4). Illus. Series: South of the Border. 1994, Rourke LB $18.60 (978-1-55916-052-0). 24pp. Introduces the various peoples of Mexico and where they live in a simple text with many attractive color photos. Also use in this series *Products of Mexico, Visiting Mexico*, and *Wonders of Mexico* (all 1994). (Rev: SLJ 2/95) [972]

18222 Cory, Steve. *Daily Life in Ancient and Modern Mexico City* (3–6). Illus. by Ray Webb. Series: Cities Through Time. 1999, Runestone LB $25.26 (978-0-8225-3212-5). 64pp. Daily life in Mexico City during the time of the Aztecs and the Spanish conquest is presented, followed by information on the city today. (Rev: HBG 10/99; SLJ 6/99) [972]

18223 Flint, David. *Mexico* (2–4). Illus. Series: On the Map. 1993, Raintree LB $22.83 (978-0-8114-3419-5). 32pp. Such topics as geography, history, customs, lifestyles, and landmarks are covered in this well-illustrated introduction to Mexico. (Rev: BL 2/1/94) [972]

18224 Furlong, Kate A. *Mexico* (2–4). Series: Countries. 2000, ABDO LB $22.78 (978-1-57765-390-5). 40pp. An adequate, brief introduction to Mexico that contains excellent photographs, a timeline, and a recipe. (Rev: HBG 10/01; SLJ 3/01) [972]

18225 Gruber, Beth. *Mexico* (4–8). Series: Countries of the World. 2006, National Geographic $19.95 (978-0-7922-7629-6). 64pp. This book covers the geography, people, language, customs, and natural resources of Mexico, with plenty of graphics to add interest to the presentation. (Rev: BL 2/15/07; LMC 5/07) [917.2]

18226 Hamilton, Janice. *Mexico in Pictures*. Rev. ed. (4–8). Illus. Series: Visual Geography. 2002, Lerner LB $27.93 (978-0-8225-1960-7). 80pp. An excellent introduction to Mexico that includes material on geography, history, people, economy, and culture with maps, photographs, and illustrations. (Rev: HBG 3/03; SLJ 3/03) [972]

18227 Higginson, Mel. *Wildlife of Mexico* (2–4). Illus. Series: South of the Border. 1994, Rourke LB $18.60 (978-1-55916-055-1). 24pp. The flora and fauna of Mexico are introduced in a heavily illustrated volume with an easy-to-read text. (Rev: SLJ 2/95) [972]

18228 Hodgkins, Fran. *Mexico* (2–5). Illus. Series: Questions and Answers: Countries. 2004, Capstone LB $23.93 (978-0-7368-2479-8). 32pp. Using a question-and-answer format, simple text, large photos, and many factboxes, this is an introduction to Mexico today, with material on history and traditional culture. (Rev: SLJ 3/05)

18229 Illsley, Linda. *Mexico* (3–5). Series: Foods and Festivals. 1999, Raintree LB $25.69 (978-0-8172-5553-4). 32pp. An overview of festivals celebrated in Mexico, the special foods associated with each, and four simple recipes to prepare authentic Mexican holiday food. (Rev: BL 5/15/99; HBG 10/99; SLJ 7/99) [972]

18230 Kalman, Bobbie. *Mexico: The Culture*. Rev. ed. (4–6). Series: Lands, Peoples, and Cultures. 2008, Crabtree LB $26.60 (978-0-7787-9295-6); paper $8.95 (978-0-7787-9663-3). 32pp. This updated edition contains new photographs and statistics; it covers art, music, dance, language and literature, holidays, cooking, sports, and folklore. Also use *Mexico: The Land* and *Mexico: The People* (2008). (Rev: SLJ 2/09) [972]

18231 Kent, Deborah. *Mexico: Rich in Spirit and Tradition* (4–8). Series: Exploring Cultures of the World. 1995, Benchmark LB $27.07 (978-0-7614-0187-2). This book begins with a Mexican folktale, then gives an overview of the country's people, culture, history, and problems. (Rev: SLJ 6/96) [972]

18232 Krebs, Laurie. *Off We Go to Mexico! An Adventure in the Sun* (PS–K). Illus. by Christopher Corr. 2006, Barefoot Books $16.99 (978-1-905236-40-4). 32pp. Readers journey to Mexico, visit some ancient sites and natural wonders, have typical tourist fun, and learn Spanish vocabulary and about Mexican culture. (Rev: BL 3/1/06; SLJ 4/06) [972]

18233 Landau, Elaine. *Mexico* (3–4). Illus. Series: A True Book. 2008, Children's Pr. LB $26.00 (978-0-531-16853-0); paper $6.95 (978-0-531-20727-7). 48pp. A succinct overview of the history, geography and culture of Mexico. (Rev: LMC 10/08; SLJ 9/08) [972]

18234 Laufer, Peter. *Made in Mexico* (K–4). Illus. by Susan L. Roth. 2000, National Geographic $16.95 (978-0-7922-7118-5). A beautifully illustrated book that describes the guitar-making business that flourishes in the remote village of Paracho in Mexico. (Rev: HBG 10/00; SLJ 4/00) [972]

18235 Lewington, Anna. *Mexico* (5–8). Illus. Series: Economically Developing Countries. 1996, Raintree LB $24.26 (978-0-8172-4528-3). A fine general profile of Mexico that includes jobs, industries, and other economic indicators. (Rev: BL 3/15/97; SLJ 2/97) [330.972]

18236 Lewis, Elizabeth. *Mexican Art and Culture* (5–8). Illus. Series: World Art and Culture. 2004, Raintree LB $29.99 (978-0-7398-6610-8). 56pp. The indigenous art and culture of Mexico from prehistoric times to the present are beautifully captured in this handsome and comprehensive overview. (Rev: BL 4/1/04; SLJ 2/04) [709]

18237 Lewis, Thomas P. *Hill of Fire* (1–3). Illus. by Joan Sandin. 1971, HarperCollins LB $17.89 (978-0-06-023804-9); paper $3.99 (978-0-06-444040-0). 64pp. The eruption of the volcano Paricutin and its effect on the lives of the people. [972]

18238 MacMillan, Dianne. *Mexican Independence Day and Cinco de Mayo* (3–5). Series: Best Holiday. 1997, Enslow LB $23.93 (978-0-89490-816-3). 48pp. The history of Mexico is interwoven in the description of these related holidays, with material on how they are celebrated. (Rev: BL 12/15/97; HBG 3/98; SLJ 8/97) [972]

18239 Marquez, Heron. *Destination Veracruz* (5–8). Series: Port Cities of North America. 1998, Lerner LB $23.93 (978-0-8225-2791-6). A description of this port city on the Gulf of Mexico that reviews its history, everyday life, the effects of development on the environment, and the city's economy, including the impact of NAFTA and a discussion of international trade, economic systems, and free trade. (Rev: HBG 3/99; SLJ 3/99) [972]

18240 Milord, Susan. *Mexico! 50 Activities to Experience Mexico Past and Present* (3–7). Series: A Kaleidoscope Kids Book. 1999, Williamson paper $14.25 (978-1-885593-22-1). 96pp. The author presents a survey of Mexican history and culture from ancient history through the Spanish conquest to the present day, followed by craft projects that include a piñata, a skull for Day of the Dead, and recipes for salsa, tortillas, and hot chocolate. (Rev: SLJ 5/99) [972]

18241 Olawsky, Lynn A. *Colors of Mexico* (2–5). Illus. by Janice L. Porter. Series: Colors of the World. 1997, Carolrhoda LB $19.93 (978-0-87614-886-0); paper $5.95 (978-1-57505-216-8). 24pp. Ten different colors are used to introduce facts about Mexico, its history, geography, traditions, and people. (Rev: HBG 3/98; SLJ 10/97) [972]

18242 Reilly, Mary J. *Mexico* (5–8). Illus. Series: Cultures of the World. 1991, Marshall Cavendish LB $35.64 (978-1-85435-385-6). 128pp. This account emphasizes the geography, history, economy, and lifestyles of the Mexican people. (Rev: BL 4/1/91) [972]

18243 Rosenblum, Morris. *Heroes of Mexico* (5–8). 1972, Fleet $9.50 (978-0-8303-0082-2). A collected group of profiles of people important in the history of Mexico. (Rev: BL 6/87) [972]

18244 Sanna, Ellyn. *Mexico: Facts and Figures* (5–8). Series: Mexico: Our Southern Neighbor. 2002, Mason Crest LB $19.95 (978-1-59084-088-7). 64pp. An introduction to Mexico and its states, with material on history, people and culture today, and issues of importance such as poverty. Also use *The Geography of Mexico*, *The Economy of Mexico*, and *The Government of Mexico*. (Rev: SLJ 12/02) [972]

18245 Staub, Frank. *The Children of the Sierra Madre* (3–6). Illus. Series: The World's Children. 1996, Carolrhoda LB $14.96 (978-0-87614-943-0); paper $7.95 (978-0-87614-967-6). 48pp. The young people of the Sierra Madre and their social conditions are discussed, with additional historical information. (Rev: BL 10/1/96; SLJ 8/96) [972]

18246 Staub, Frank. *Children of Yucatan* (3–6). Illus. Series: The World's Children. 1996, Carolrhoda LB $23.93 (978-0-87614-984-3). 48pp. The daily activities and social conditions of children in this remote part of Mexico are featured, along with good background information. (Rev: BCCB 11/96; BL 10/1/96; SLJ 10/96) [972]

18247 Streissguth, Thomas. *Mexico* (2–4). Illus. Series: Country Explorers. 2007, Lerner LB $27.93 (978-0-8225-7130-8). 48pp. Rich in photographs, maps, and illustrations and full of accessible information, this lively book looks at the geography of the land and at all aspects of life there — family life, school life, clothes, medicine, food, sports, and so forth. (Rev: LMC 1/08*; SLJ 12/07) [972]

18248 Wolf, Bernard. *Beneath the Stone: A Mexican Zapotec Tale* (4–6). Illus. 1994, Orchard LB $17.99 (978-0-531-08685-8). 48pp. In photos and text, several months in the life of a Zapotec Indian family in Mexico are followed, with descriptions of their holidays and family business. (Rev: BL 3/15/94; SLJ 8/94) [972]

Other Central American Lands

18249 Deady, Kathleen W. *El Salvador* (2–5). Illus. Series: Questions and Answers: Countries. 2005, Capstone LB $23.93 (978-0-7368-3750-7). 32pp. Using a question-and-answer format, simple text, large photos, and many factboxes, this is an introduction to El Salvador today, with material on history and traditional culture.

18250 Freedman, Russell. *In the Days of the Vaqueros: America's First True Cowboys* (5–9). Illus. 2001, Clarion $18.00 (978-0-395-96788-1). 70pp. Vivid artwork complements this history of the earliest cowboys, the Central American vaqueros who first rode the range in the late 15th century. (Rev: BL 11/15/01*; HB 1/02; HBG 3/02; SLJ 9/01) [636.2]

18251 Gaines, Ann. *The Panama Canal in American History* (4–8). Series: In American History. 1999, Enslow LB $26.60 (978-0-7660-1216-5). This is a carefully researched history of the building of the Panama Canal, including a review of events before U.S. involvement, how the United States established the country of Panama and gained control of the Canal Zone, details of the many difficulties encountered, and a description of how the canal locks operate. (Rev: BL 3/1/99; HBG 10/99; SLJ 8/99) [972.87]

18252 Grandell, Rachel. *Hands of the Maya: Villagers at Work and Play* (K–3). Illus. 2002, Holt $16.95 (978-0-8050-6687-6). 32pp. This photoessay takes readers through a day in a Mayan town and shows typical activities and recreations. (Rev: BL 5/1/02; HB 9/02; HBG 3/03; SLJ 8/02) [972.83]

18253 Hassig, Susan M. *Panama* (4–7). Illus. Series: Cultures of the World. 1996, Marshall Cavendish LB $37.07 (978-0-7614-0278-7). 128pp. The troubled history of Panama is covered, with material on geography and the lifestyle and culture of its people. (Rev: BL 8/96) [972.87]

18254 Haverstock, Nathan A. *Nicaragua in Pictures* (5–8). Illus. 1993, Lerner LB $25.55 (978-0-8225-1817-4). 64pp. A visit to this controversial country is highlighted by color photographs and clear text. (Rev: BL 10/15/87) [972.85]

18255 *Honduras in Pictures* (4–7). Illus. Series: Visual Geography. 1994, Lerner LB $25.55 (978-0-8225-1804-4). 64pp. Chapters focus on history, culture, education, people, geography, and lifestyles. (Rev: BL 8/87)

18256 Jermyn, Leslie. *Belize* (5–9). Series: Cultures of the World. 2001, Marshall Cavendish LB $37.07 (978-0-7614-1190-1). 128pp. Geography, history, government, arts and culture, and lifestyle are all covered in this interesting and attractive volume. (Rev: HBG 10/01; SLJ 11/01) [972.82]

18257 Lindop, Edmund. *Panama and the United States: Divided by the Canal* (5–8). Illus. 1997, Twenty-First Century LB $23.40 (978-0-8050-4768-4). A history of United States-Panama relations, from the building of the canal to the present. (Rev: BL 8/97; SLJ 7/97) [327.7307287]

18258 McGaffey, Leta. *Honduras* (5–9). Series: Cultures of the World. 1999, Marshall Cavendish LB $37.07 (978-0-7614-0955-7). 128pp. After background material on the history and geography of Honduras, this book focuses on modern times and such topics as the economy, population, religion, holidays, and recreation. (Rev: HBG 10/99; SLJ 11/99) [972.8]

18259 McNeese, Tim. *The Panama Canal* (5–8). Illus. Series: Building History. 1997, Lucent LB $28.70 (978-1-56006-425-1). 96pp. A description of the building of the Panama Canal that also supplies valuable insights into the economic and social conditions of the times. (Rev: BL 8/97; HBG 3/98; SLJ 7/97) [386]

18260 Malone, Michael. *A Guatemalan Family* (4–7). Illus. Series: Journey Between Two Worlds. 1996, Lerner paper $8.95 (978-0-8225-9742-1). 64pp. The story of a refugee family from Guatemala and of its resettlement in the United States. (Rev: BL 11/15/96; SLJ 1/97) [975.9]

18261 Mann, Elizabeth. *The Panama Canal* (4–6). Illus. Series: Wonders of the World. 1998, Mikaya $19.95 (978-0-9650493-4-4). 48pp. The story of the construction of the Panama Canal from the failed French attempt by Ferdinand de Lesseps to the American success and opening in 1914. (Rev: BL 2/1/99; SLJ 12/98) [972.87]

18262 Markun, Patricia M. *It's Panama's Canal!* (5–9). Illus. 1999, Linnet LB $22.50 (978-0-208-02499-2). 103pp. This account gives a good background history of the canal plus current information on Panama's control of the zone and its plans for successful management. (Rev: BL 1/1–15/00; HBG 3/00) [972.87]

18263 Morrison, Marion. *Nicaragua* (4–7). Series: Enchantment of the World. 2002, Children's LB $37.00 (978-0-516-20963-0). 144pp. Such topics as geography, history, people, language, economy, and government are covered in this introduction to Nicaragua. (Rev: BL 5/15/02) [972.8]

18264 *Panama in Pictures* (4–7). Illus. Series: Visual Geography. 1996, Lerner LB $25.55 (978-0-8225-1818-1). 64pp. The life and culture, history, and geography of the people of Panama. (Rev: BL 8/87) [972.87]

18265 Pascoe, Elaine, ed. *Into Wild Panama* (3–6). Series: The Jeff Corwin Experience. 2004, Gale LB $24.95 (978-1-56711-856-8). 48pp. Jeff Corwin of TV's Animal Planet series explores the jungles of Panama, where he encounters such creatures as a frog-eating bat. (Rev: SLJ 4/04) [591.9]

18266 Shields, Charles J. *Belize* (5–7). Illus. Series: Discovering Central America. 2002, Mason Crest LB $19.95 (978-1-59084-092-4). 64pp. Students needing facts about Belize will find everything here: geography, history, people, and culture, all backed up by maps, photographs, a timeline, and even recipes. (Rev: BL 1/1–15/03) [972.82]

18267 Shields, Charles J. *Central America: Facts and Figures* (5–7). Illus. Series: Discovering Central America. 2002, Mason Crest LB $19.95 (978-1-59084-099-3). 64pp. This look at Central America as a whole covers history, geography, inhabitants, and cultures. (Rev: BL 1/1–15/03) [972.8]

18268 Silverstone, Michael. *Rigoberta Menchu: Defending Human Rights in Guatemala* (5–8). Illus. 1999, Feminist paper $9.95 (978-1-55861-199-3). 112pp. In addition to a biography of Nobel Peace Prize winner Rigoberta Menchu, this account presents Guatemala, its civil war, and the efforts to end it. (Rev: BL 3/15/00) [972.81]

18269 Staub, Frank. *Children of Belize* (3–6). Series: The World's Children. 1997, Carolrhoda $23.93 (978-1-57505-039-3). 45pp. The reader meets a variety of children from this small Central American country with a unique history and a population of remarkable diversity. (Rev: BL 3/15/98; SLJ 3/98) [972.82]

18270 West, Tracey. *Costa Rica* (3–5). Series: Globe-Trotters Club. 1999, Carolrhoda $22.60 (978-1-57505-109-3). 48pp. The land of Costa Rica is given a colorful introduction in this informal treatment, which covers the basic topics, with an emphasis on contemporary life. (Rev: BL 9/15/99; HBG 3/00; SLJ 2/00) [972.8]

18271 West, Tracey. *Costa Rica* (1–3). Series: A Ticket To. 1999, Carolrhoda LB $22.60 (978-1-57505-134-5). 48pp. This beginning glimpse of Costa Rica introduces the country's landscape and its main ethnic and cultural features, using plenty of pictures and a simple text. (Rev: BL 9/15/99; HBG 3/00; SLJ 1/00) [972]

Puerto Rico and Other Caribbean Islands

18272 Ada, Alma Flor. *Under the Royal Palms: A Childhood in Cuba* (3–6). Illus. 1998, Simon & Schuster $15.00 (978-0-689-80631-5). 96pp. The story of a little girl growing up in a small town in Cuba is presented in a series of short vignettes. (Rev: BL 11/15/98; HBG 3/99; SLJ 12/98) [813]

18273 Ancona, George. *Cuban Kids* (3–5). Illus. 2000, Marshall Cavendish $15.95 (978-0-7614-5077-1). 40pp. This photoessay gives a fine picture of contemporary Cuba as seen through the eyes and actions of the country's children at work and at play. (Rev: BL 12/15/00; HBG 3/01; SLJ 1/01) [972.91]

18274 Bernier-Grand, Carmen. *Shake It, Morena?* (3–5). Illus. by Lulu Delacre. 2002, Millbrook LB $24.90 (978-0-7613-1910-8). 48pp. This is a collection of games, songs, riddles, and counting rhymes from Puerto Rico with explanations of origins and cultural backgrounds. (Rev: BL 4/15/02; HBG 10/02) [972.9]

18275 Capek, Michael. *Jamaica* (3–5). Series: Globe-Trotters Club. 1999, Carolrhoda $22.60 (978-1-57505-112-3). 48pp. Using two-page spreads, this breezy account provides a broad introduction to Jamaica, with many colorful photos, fact boxes, and sidebars. (Rev: BL 9/15/99; HBG 3/00) [972.92]

18276 Capek, Michael. *Jamaica* (1–3). Series: A Ticket To. 1999, Carolrhoda LB $22.60 (978-1-57505-137-6). 48pp. Color photos and a simple, concise text enhance this first look at Jamaica, which gives basic information about the people and their land. (Rev: BL 9/15/99; HBG 3/00) [972.92]

18277 Dubois, Muriel L. *Cuba* (2–5). Illus. Series: Questions and Answers: Countries. 2005, Capstone LB $23.93 (978-0-7368-3749-1). 32pp. Using a question-and-answer format, simple text, large photos, and many factboxes, this is an introduction to

Cuba today, with material on history and traditional culture.

18278 Englar, Mary. *Dominican Republic* (2–3). Illus. Series: Many Cultures, One World. 2004, Capstone LB $23.93 (978-0-7368-2453-8). 32pp. A brief, accessible introduction to the Dominican Republic and its people, family life, customs, and legends.

18279 Furlong, Kate A. *Haiti* (3–5). Illus. Series: The Countries. 2003, ABDO LB $22.78 (978-1-57765-841-2). 40pp. Full-color photographs add to this well-written introduction to Haiti. (Rev: HBG 10/03; SLJ 10/03) [972.94]

18280 Graves, Kerry A. *Haiti* (4–6). Illus. Series: Countries and Cultures. 2002, Capstone LB $25.26 (978-0-7368-1078-4). 64pp. An introduction to Haiti's geography, history, and culture, with maps, timelines, and other aids. (Rev: BL 5/15/02; HBG 3/03) [972.94]

18281 Green, Jen. *Jamaica* (4–8). Series: Countries of the World. 2008, National Geographic LB $27.90 (978-1-4263-0300-5). 64pp. With lots of color images, this thorough volume looks at the geography, nature, history, culture, government, and economy of Jamaica, with interesting sidebars on customs, celebrations, and so forth. (Rev: SLJ 3/09) [972.92]

18282 Greenberg, Keith E. *A Haitian Family* (4–7). Illus. Series: Journey Between Two Worlds. 1998, Lerner LB $22.60 (978-0-8225-3410-5). 56pp. The story of the Beaubrun family, the political oppression they suffered in Haiti, and their eventual journey to freedom in the United States. (Rev: BL 3/1/98; HBG 10/98) [305.9]

18283 Haverstock, Nathan A. *Cuba in Pictures* (5–8). Illus. Series: Visual Geography. 1997, Lerner LB $25.55 (978-0-8225-1811-2). 64pp. A look at America's island neighbor, with color photographs. Also use *Dominican Republic in Pictures* (1997). (Rev: BL 10/15/87) [972.91064]

18284 Hernandez, Romel. *Caribbean Islands: Facts and Figures* (4–6). Illus. 2009, Mason Crest $21.95 (978-1-4222-0622-5). 64pp. This introductory volume to an 11-title series gives an overview of the islands of the Caribbean and their history, geography, economies, people, and cities. (Rev: BLO 3/11/09) [972.9]

18285 Hernandez, Romel. *Trinidad and Tobago* (4–6). Series: Discovering the Caribbean. 2003, Mason Crest LB $19.95 (978-1-59084-304-8). 63pp. An appealing look at the geography, history, plants and animals, economy, and people of these Caribbean islands, with lots of photographs plus recipes and report ideas. (Rev: SLJ 10/03) [972.983]

18286 Illsley, Linda. *The Caribbean* (3–5). Illus. Series: Foods and Festivals. 1999, Raintree $25.69 (978-0-8172-5758-3). 32pp. Because the Caribbean Islands contain a diverse population, the festivals vary from Hindu and Christian holidays to the special children's carnival in Trinidad and Tobago. (Rev: BL 5/15/99; HBG 10/99) [394.1]

18287 *Jamaica in Pictures* (5–8). Illus. Series: Visual Geography. 1997, Lerner LB $25.55 (978-0-8225-

1814-3). 64pp. Color photographs highlight this visit to a popular and beautiful island. (Rev: BL 10/15/87) [972.92]

18288 McCarthy, Pat. *The Dominican Republic* (5–8). Illus. Series: Top Ten Countries of Recent Immigrants. 2004, Enslow LB $25.26 (978-0-7660-5179-9). 48pp. Information on the Dominican Republic — culture, history, climate, and people — accompanies an explanation of the reasons for migration to the United States and discussion of the contributions of this community; supported by Web links. (Rev: SLJ 3/05) [304]

18289 Marquez, Heron. *Destination San Juan* (5–8). Series: Port Cities of North America. 1998, Lerner LB $23.93 (978-0-8225-2792-3). 80pp. A matter-of-fact introduction to San Juan that describes the city, people, economy, and port activities. (Rev: HBG 3/99; SLJ 3/99) [972.95]

18290 Marx, Trish. *Reaching for the Sun: Kids in Cuba* (3–6). Photos by Cindy Karp. 2003, Millbrook LB $25.90 (978-0-7613-2261-0). 48pp. This attractive photoessay documents a Los Angeles children's arts group's month-long visit to Cuba and the personal interaction between visitors and hosts. (Rev: BL 4/15/03; HBG 10/03; SLJ 7/03) [972.9106]

18291 Milivojevic, JoAnn. *Puerto Rico* (1–3). Series: Globe-Trotters Club. 2000, Carolrhoda LB $22.60 (978-1-57505-119-2). 48pp. A simple look at the land and people of Puerto Rico, including natural wonders and such attractions as the Arecibo Observatory, home of the world's largest telescope. (Rev: BL 5/15/00; HBG 10/00; SLJ 9/00) [972.95]

18292 Milivojevic, JoAnn. *Puerto Rico* (2–3). Series: A Ticket To. 2000, Lerner LB $22.60 (978-1-57505-144-4). 48pp. A simple introduction to Puerto Rico that covers basic history, geography, and society. (Rev: HBG 10/00; SLJ 9/00) [972.9]

18293 Morrison, Marion. *Cuba* (4–7). Illus. Series: Country Insights. 1998, Raintree LB $27.12 (978-0-8172-4796-6). 48pp. An introduction to contemporary life in Cuba, showing the contrast between life in a big city (Havana) and in a country village. (Rev: BL 5/1/98; HBG 10/98) [972.91]

18294 Orr, Tamra. *Barbados* (3–5). Series: Discovering the Caribbean. 2003, Mason Crest LB $19.95 (978-1-59084-306-2). 63pp. Introduces readers to the geography, history, people, culture, and attractions of Barbados, with recipes and projects. (Rev: HBG 4/04; SLJ 1/04) [972.981]

18295 Orr, Tamra. *Windward Islands* (4–6). Illus. Series: Discovering the Caribbean. 2003, Mason Crest LB $19.95 (978-1-59084-305-5). 63pp. An appealing look at the geography, history, plants and animals, economy, and people of these Caribbean islands, with lots of photographs plus recipes and report ideas. (Rev: HBG 4/04; SLJ 10/03) [972.984]

18296 Petersen, Christine, and David Petersen. *Cuba* (3–5). Illus. Series: True Books — Geography. 2001, Children's Book Pr. paper $6.95 (978-0-516-27358-7). 48pp. A colorful overview of Cuba's history and geography, with a positive slant on Castro's influence. (Rev: BL 2/1/02) [972.91]

18297 *Puerto Rico in Pictures* (4–7). Illus. Series: Visual Geography. 1995, Lerner LB $25.55 (978-0-8225-1821-1). 64pp. Everyday life, history, culture, and geography are introduced. (Rev: BL 8/87) [972.95]

18298 Ross, Michael Elsohn. *Children of Puerto Rico* (4–6). Series: The World's Children. 2001, Carolrhoda LB $23.93 (978-1-57505-522-0). This handsome volume filled with color photographs of Puerto Rican children describes the daily life of their island home. (Rev: BL 1/1–15/02; HBG 3/02; SLJ 2/02) [972.95]

18299 Schreier, Alta. *Cuba* (2–4). Series: A Visit To. 2000, Heinemann LB $21.36 (978-1-57572-380-8). 32pp. An introductory overview of the island nation today, with information on geography, people and culture, language, schools, and transportation presented in large photographs and simple text. (Rev: HBG 10/01; SLJ 4/01) [972.9]

18300 Sheehan, Sean. *Jamaica* (5–8). Illus. Series: Cultures of the World. 1993, Marshall Cavendish LB $25.95 (978-1-85435-581-2). 128pp. This informative account describes many facets of Jamaican life, including history, religion, and reggae music. (Rev: SLJ 2/94) [972.92]

18301 Staub, Frank. *Children of Cuba* (3–6). Illus. Series: World's Children. 1996, Carolrhoda LB $23.93 (978-0-87614-989-8). 48pp. Interesting background information on Cuba is introduced through the experiences of several children. (Rev: BL 12/1/96; SLJ 2/97) [972.91]

18302 Staub, Frank. *Children of Dominica* (4–6). Illus. Series: World's Children. 1998, Lerner $23.93 (978-1-57505-217-5). 48pp. This book introduces the people of Dominica, part of the Lesser Antilles, and tells how they live, their history, and the role of children in their culture. (Rev: BL 4/1/99; SLJ 3/99) [972.9841]

18303 Telemaque, Eleanor Wong. *Haiti Through Its Holidays* (4–5). Illus. by Earl Hill. 1980, Blyden Pr. $8.50 (978-0-685-00779-2). 64pp. An introduction to Haiti through its holidays and customs surrounding them.

18304 Temple, Bob. *Dominican Republic* (3–5). Series: Discovering the Caribbean. 2003, Mason Crest LB $19.95 (978-1-59084-301-7). 63pp. Introduces readers to the geography, history, people, culture, and attractions of the Dominican Republic, with a focus on music, plus recipes and projects. (Rev: SLJ 1/04) [972.93]

18305 Tuck, Jay, and Norma C. Vergara. *Heroes of Puerto Rico* (5–8). 1969, Fleet $9.50 (978-0-8303-0070-9). A series of profiles of famous Puerto Ricans. (Rev: BL 6/87) [972.9]

18306 Will, Emily Wade. *Haiti* (5–8). Series: Modern Nations of the World. 2001, Lucent LB $29.95 (978-1-56006-761-0). 112pp. The history, geography, and culture of this island country are presented with colorful prose and pictures plus unusual facts contained in sidebars. (Rev: BL 6/1–15/01) [972.94]

18307 Williams, Colleen Madonna Flood. *The Bahamas* (4–6). Series: Discovering the Caribbean. 2003, Mason Crest LB $19.95 (978-1-59084-296-6).

63pp. An appealing look at the geography, history, plants and animals, economy, and people of the Bahamas, with lots of photographs plus recipes and report ideas. (Rev: HBG 4/04; SLJ 10/03) [972.96]

South America

18308 Allen, Nancy Kelly. *On the Banks of the Amazon / En las orillas del Amazonas* (K–2). Trans. by Eida de la Vega. Illus. by Elizabeth Driessen. 2003, Raven Tree LB $16.95 (978-0-9720192-7-9). 31pp. A lively bilingual introduction to the animals of the Amazon rain forest, featuring two wildlife photographers. (Rev: HBG 4/04; SLJ 12/03) [981]

18309 *Argentina in Pictures* (5–8). Illus. Series: Visual Geography. 1994, Lerner LB $25.55 (978-0-8225-1807-5). 64pp. An overview of climate, wildlife, cities, vegetation, and mineral resources. (Rev: BL 4/15/88; SLJ 5/88) [982]

18310 Augustin, Byron. *Bolivia* (4–7). Series: Enchantment of the World. 2001, Children's LB $37.00 (978-0-516-21050-6). With each page containing a color illustration, this attractive book introduces the land and people, economy, culture, and natural resources of Bolivia. (Rev: BL 1/1–15/02) [984]

18311 Bauer, Brandy. *Brazil* (2–5). Illus. Series: Questions and Answers: Countries. 2004, Capstone LB $23.93 (978-0-7368-2481-1). 32pp. Using a question-and-answer format, simple text, large photos, and many factboxes, this is an introduction to Brazil today, with material on history and traditional culture.

18312 Beirne, Barbara. *Children of the Ecuadorean Highlands* (3–6). Illus. Series: The World's Children. 1996, Carolrhoda LB $23.93 (978-1-57505-000-3). 48pp. Historical and geographical materials are included in this story about young people in Equador. (Rev: BL 10/1/96; SLJ 11/96) [972]

18313 Boraas, Tracey. *Colombia* (4–6). Illus. Series: Countries and Cultures. 2002, Capstone LB $25.26 (978-0-7368-1076-0). 64pp. An introduction to Colombia that covers many topics including geography, history, and culture, with maps, timelines, and other aids. (Rev: BL 5/15/02; HBG 3/03) [986.1]

18314 *Colombia in Pictures* (5–8). Illus. Series: Visual Geography. 1996, Lerner LB $25.55 (978-0-8225-1810-5). 64pp. Many photographs highlight this visit to a South American nation. (Rev: BL 10/15/87) [986.1]

18315 Corona, Laurel. *Brazil* (5–8). Series: Modern Nations of the World. 1999, Lucent LB $27.45 (978-1-56006-621-7). 128pp. A lively account of Brazil's history, geography, famous people, and conditions today. (Rev: BL 2/15/00; HBG 10/00) [981]

18316 Corona, Laurel. *Peru* (5–8). Series: Modern Nations of the World. 2001, Lucent LB $28.70 (978-1-56006-862-4). 112pp. Detailed sidebars, a chronology, and national statistics supplement the general information presented in this colorful introduction to Peru. (Rev: BL 6/1–15/01) [985]

18317 Dalal, Anita. *Argentina* (4–8). Series: Nations of the World. 2001, Raintree LB $34.26 (978-0-

7398-1279-2). 128pp. A colorful, interesting introduction to Argentina that covers its land and cities, history, culture, present economic conditions, and possible future developments. (Rev: BL 6/1–15/01; HBG 10/01) [982]

18318 Dalal, Anita. *Brazil* (4–8). Series: Nations of the World. 2001, Raintree LB $34.26 (978-0-7398-1284-6). 128pp. A profile of the home of Carnival, the Amazon, and Pele with material attractively presented on its past and present, its people, and its culture. (Rev: BL 6/1–15/01; HBG 10/01) [981]

18319 Deckker, Zilah. *Brazil* (4–8). Series: Countries of the World. 2008, National Geographic LB $27.90 (978-1-4263-0298-5). 64pp. With lots of color images, this thorough volume looks at the geography, nature, history, culture, government, and economy of Brazil, with interesting sidebars on customs, celebrations, and so forth. (Rev: SLJ 3/09) [981]

18320 Dubois, Jill. *Colombia* (5–8). Illus. Series: Cultures of the World. 1991, Marshall Cavendish LB $35.64 (978-1-85435-384-9). 128pp. Background information on Colombia is given as well as coverage of contemporary concerns. (Rev: BL 4/1/91) [986.1]

18321 Dubois, Muriel L. *Peru* (2–5). Illus. Series: Questions and Answers: Countries. 2005, Capstone LB $23.93 (978-0-7368-3758-3). 32pp. Using a question-and-answer format, simple text, large photos, and many factboxes, this is an introduction to Peru today, with material on history and traditional culture.

18322 Eagen, James. *The Aymara of South America* (4–6). Series: First Peoples. 2002, Lerner LB $23.93 (978-0-8225-4174-5). This volume describes the history and present status of the Aymara, who live in the high plains of Peru and Bolivia, where they are known for domesticating the potato. (Rev: BL 5/15/02; HBG 10/02) [985]

18323 Fajardo, Dara Andrea. *A Child's Day in a Peruvian City* (K–3). Series: A Child's Day. 2002, Marshall Cavendish LB $15.95 (978-0-7614-1408-7). 32pp. The reader meets a Peruvian child and learns about culture, work, and play in modern Peru. (Rev: BL 2/15/03; HBG 3/03; SLJ 12/02) [985]

18324 Falconer, Kieran. *Peru* (4–7). Illus. Series: Cultures of the World. 1995, Marshall Cavendish LB $37.07 (978-0-7614-0179-7). 128pp. The focus of this book is on the people of Peru, their lifestyles, artistic endeavors, religion, and leisure activities. (Rev: BL 1/1–15/96; SLJ 4/96) [985]

18325 Ferro, Jennifer. *Brazilian Foods and Culture* (3–5). Series: Festive Foods and Celebrations. 1999, Rourke LB $27.93 (978-1-57103-301-7). 48pp. Information on Brazilian history and culture are featured along with a number of recipes and explanations for such celebrations as Carnival, Iemanj, and Saint John's Day. (Rev: SLJ 2/00) [981]

18326 Fitzpatrick, Anne. *Amazon River* (4–6). Illus. Series: Natural Wonders of the World. 2004, Creative Education LB $27.10 (978-1-58341-322-7). 32pp. After establishing this important river's location, this oversized picture book full of color photographs looks at geology, climate, wildlife, people, and other pertinent facts. (Rev: SLJ 1/05) [918.1]

18327 Foley, Erin. *Ecuador* (5–8). Illus. Series: Cultures of the World. 1995, Marshall Cavendish LB $37.07 (978-0-7614-0173-5). 128pp. This book supplies good background material on Ecuador but is strongest in describing contemporary conditions. (Rev: SLJ 11/95) [980]

18328 Gofen, Ethel C. *Cultures of the World: Argentina* (5–8). Illus. Series: Cultures of the World. 1991, Marshall Cavendish LB $19.95 (978-1-85435-380-1). 128pp. This book provides standard information on history and geography and tells about the contemporary lifestyles of the people. (Rev: BL 4/1/91) [962]

18329 *Guyana in Pictures* (5–8). Illus. Series: Visual Geography. 1997, Lerner LB $25.55 (978-0-8225-1815-0). 64pp. History, climate, wildlife, and major cities are covered in this overview. (Rev: BL 4/15/88) [988.1]

18330 Haskins, James, and Kathleen Benson. *Count Your Way Through Brazil* (2–4). Illus. by Liz B. Dodson. Series: Count Your Way. 1996, Carolrhoda LB $19.93 (978-0-87614-873-0); paper $5.95 (978-0-87614-971-3). 24pp. Facts about Brazil are introduced in a counting book that goes from 1 to 10. (Rev: BL 9/15/96; SLJ 8/96) [981]

18331 Haverstock, Nathan A. *Brazil in Pictures* (4–7). Illus. Series: Visual Geography. 1997, Lerner LB $25.55 (978-0-8225-1802-0). 64pp. Current data on the political scene, plus chapters on history, people, and culture in this revised text. Also use *Chile in Pictures* (1988). (Rev: BL 8/87)

18332 Haverstock, Nathan A. *Paraguay in Pictures* (5–8). Illus. Series: Visual Geography. 1995, Lerner LB $25.55 (978-0-8225-1819-8). 64pp. This overview of Paraguay includes its history to 1987 and possible future developments. (Rev: BL 4/15/88) [989.2]

18333 Hermes, Jules. *The Children of Bolivia* (3–5). Illus. Series: World's Children. 1996, Carolrhoda LB $23.93 (978-0-87614-935-5). 47pp. By focusing on children in the country and in cities, the two distinct native cultures of Bolivia are explored. (Rev: SLJ 5/96) [984]

18334 Jermyn, Leslie. *Paraguay* (5–8). 1999, Marshall Cavendish LB $37.07 (978-0-7614-0979-3). 128pp. This book about Paraguay covers history, geography, government, and economy as well as such social and cultural topics as religion, the arts, food, and recreation. (Rev: HBG 10/00; SLJ 4/00) [989]

18335 Jones, Helga. *Venezuela* (1–3). Series: Globe-Trotters Club. 2000, Carolrhoda LB $22.60 (978-1-57505-122-2). 48pp. Some of the topics covered in this simple introduction to Venezuela are the land, people, culture, rain forests, and Angel Falls, the highest waterfall in the world. (Rev: BL 5/15/00; HBG 10/00) [987]

18336 Krebs, Laurie. *Up and Down the Andes: A Peruvian Festival Tale* (K–3). Illus. by Aurelia Fronty. 2008, Barefoot Books $16.99 (978-1-84686-203-8). 32pp. A traditional Peruvian festival is described in simple rhymes and attractive acrylic paintings. (Rev: BL 12/15/08; LMC 5/09) [394.26598]

18337 Lewington, Anna. *What Do We Know About the Amazonian Indians?* (4–6). Illus. by Ian Thompson. Series: What Do We Know About. 1993, Bedrick paper $8.95 (978-0-87226-262-1). 43pp. Double-page spreads are used to introduce the history, lives, and cultures of the Indians of the Amazon River. (Rev: SLJ 3/94) [981.1]

18338 Lichtenberg, Andre. *Brazil* (2–4). Illus. 2000, Raintree $25.69 (978-0-8172-5514-5). 32pp. A young Brazilian boy introduces the reader to his homeland, its geography, food, customs, schools, and everyday life. (Rev: BL 4/15/00; HBG 10/00) [981]

18339 Lourie, Peter. *Tierra del Fuego: A Journey to the End of the Earth* (2–5). Illus. 2002, Boyds Mills $19.95 (978-1-56397-973-6). 48pp. A fascinating first-person look at Tierra del Fuego, the southernmost island off the coast of South America, including its discovery and the fate of its native peoples. (Rev: BL 10/15/02; HBG 3/03; SLJ 9/02) [918.276]

18340 McNair, Sylvia. *Chile* (4–7). Series: Enchantment of the World. 2000, Children's LB $37.00 (978-0-516-21007-0). 144pp. This attractive new edition of an old title includes material on Chile's land and people, history and government, economics and landmarks, daily life, and sports. (Rev: BL 7/00) [983]

18341 Morrison, Marion. *Brazil* (4–7). Illus. Series: Country Insights. 1997, Raintree LB $27.12 (978-0-8172-4785-0). 48pp. Compares the home life, employment, schooling, and recreation in a large city and in a small village in Brazil. (Rev: BL 7/97; SLJ 8/97) [918.1]

18342 Morrison, Marion. *Ecuador* (4–7). Series: Enchantment of the World. 2000, Children's LB $37.00 (978-0-516-21544-0). 144pp. This book examines the geography and climate of Ecuador, its history, government, language, economy, and people. (Rev: BL 1/1–15/01) [986]

18343 Morrison, Marion. *Guyana* (5–8). Illus. Series: Enchantment of the World, Second Series. 2003, Children's LB $37.00 (978-0-516-22377-3). 144pp. A visually attractive book that covers such topics as the geography, history, government, culture, and people with a timeline, fast facts, and a recipe. (Rev: SLJ 5/03) [966.7]

18344 Morrison, Marion. *Indians of the Andes* (4–6). Illus. 1987, Rourke LB $16.67 (978-0-86625-260-7). 48pp. With attractive design and numerous color photos, the Indians of the Andes are introduced to young readers. (Rev: BL 1/15/88)

18345 Morrison, Marion. *Rio de Janeiro* (4–6). Series: Great Cities of the World. 2004, World Almanac LB $31.00 (978-0-8368-5031-4). 48pp. Report writers will find useful information on Rio's history, culture, and lifestyle. Also use *Buenos Aires* (2004). (Rev: SLJ 7/04) [981]

18346 Nesbitt, Kris. *My Amazon River Day* (2–5). Illus. 2000, Shedd Aquarium $23.95 (978-0-9701035-0-5). 48pp. This book chronicles everyday life on the banks of the Amazon River in Peru for

Patricia, her family, and her friends. (Rev: BL 10/15/00) [577.098]

18347 Parker, Edward. *Peru* (5–8). Illus. 1996, Raintree LB $24.26 (978-0-8172-4525-2). After a general introduction to Peru, this account discusses such current economic indicators as the job market, industry, and agriculture. (Rev: BL 3/15/97; SLJ 2/97) [985]

18348 Pateman, Robert. *Bolivia* (4–7). Illus. Series: Cultures of the World. 1995, Marshall Cavendish LB $37.07 (978-0-7614-0178-0). 128pp. The people of Bolivia, how they live, and their traditions are some of the topics covered in this general introduction. (Rev: BL 1/1–15/96; SLJ 4/96) [984]

18349 *Peru in Pictures* (5–8). Illus. Series: Visual Geography. 1997, Lerner LB $25.55 (978-0-8225-1820-4). 64pp. An introduction to this South American land, highlighted by color photographs. (Rev: BL 10/15/87) [985]

18350 Pollard, Michael. *The Amazon* (4–6). Series: Great Rivers. 1997, Benchmark LB $22.79 (978-0-7614-0501-6). 45pp. The story of the river that rises in the Andes of Peru and flows for almost 4,000 miles to the Atlantic. (Rev: HBG 3/98; SLJ 5/98) [981]

18351 Rawlins, Carol B. *The Orinoco River* (4–7). Illus. Series: World of Water. 1999, Watts LB $25.50 (978-0-531-11740-8). 64pp. An introduction to this important Venezuelan river, with material on its history and current status and the areas through which it passes. (Rev: BL 1/1–15/00) [987.06]

18352 Richard, Christopher. *Brazil* (5–8). Illus. Series: Cultures of the World. 1991, Marshall Cavendish LB $35.64 (978-1-85435-382-5). 128pp. Brazil is introduced with information on such topics as history, economics, people, and modern problems. (Rev: BL 4/1/91) [981]

18353 Robinson, Roger. *Brazil* (5–8). Series: Country Studies. 1999, Heinemann LB $27.07 (978-1-57572-892-6). Using colorful charts, graphs, drawings, maps, and photographs in double-page spreads, this book provides basic information about Brazil, with emphasis on regional contrasts and contemporary issues, such as population changes and the growth of agribusiness. (Rev: BL 8/99; SLJ 8/99) [981]

18354 St. John, Jetty. *A Family in Chile* (2–4). Illus. 1986, Lerner LB $18.60 (978-0-8225-1667-5). 32pp. Focusing on one child in a Chilean family, the reader learns of life in this South American land. (Rev: BL 5/15/86; SLJ 10/86)

18355 Spengler, Kremena. *Chile* (2–5). Illus. Series: Questions and Answers: Countries. 2005, Capstone LB $23.93 (978-0-7368-3748-4). 32pp. Using a question-and-answer format, simple text, large photos, and many factboxes, this is an introduction to Chile today, with material on history and traditional culture.

18356 Tagliaferro, Linda. *Galapagos Islands: Nature's Delicate Balance at Risk* (4–8). Illus. 2001, Lerner LB $27.93 (978-0-8225-0648-5). 88pp. This is a detailed but accessible introduction to the history, geology, wildlife, and ecology of the Galapagos

Islands, with maps and photographs. (Rev: BL 9/15/01; HBG 3/02; SLJ 11/01; VOYA 12/01) [561.9866]

18357 Tahan, Raya. *The Yanomami of South America* (4–6). Illus. Series: First Peoples. 2001, Lerner $23.93 (978-0-8225-4851-5). 48pp. This attractive introduction to the Yanomami people and their native region and culture also contrasts traditional and modern lifestyles. (Rev: BL 2/1/02; HBG 3/02; SLJ 3/02) [981.004]

18358 *Venezuela in Pictures* (4–7). Illus. Series: Visual Geography. 1993, Lerner LB $21.27 (978-0-8225-1824-2). 64pp. The land, people, and government of this oil-rich country are explored in maps, text, and photographs. (Rev: BL 1/1/88) [987]

18359 Walters, Tara. *Brazil* (3–4). Illus. Series: A True Book. 2008, Children's Pr. LB $26.00 (978-0-531-16851-6); paper $6.95 (978-0-531-20725-3). 48pp. A succinct overview of the history, geography, and culture of Brazil. (Rev: LMC 10/08; SLJ 9/08) [981]

18360 Watson, Galadriel. *The Amazon Rain Forest: The Largest Rain Forest in the World* (3–6). Illus. Series: Natural Wonders. 2004, Weigl LB $18.20 (978-1-59036-270-9). 32pp. A look at the history of the rain forest, the people who live there, the animals and plants it supports, and the environmental threats it faces. (Rev: SLJ 4/05)

18361 Webster, Christine. *Yanomami* (3–5). Series: Indigenous Peoples. 2004, Weigl LB $18.20 (978-1-59036-124-5). 32pp. A fascinating and informative overview of the Yanomami people of the Amazon River basin, covering history, culture, language, and family life. (Rev: SLJ 7/04) [981.0]

18362 Winter, Jane K. *Chile* (5–8). Illus. Series: Cultures of the World. 1991, Marshall Cavendish LB $35.64 (978-1-85435-383-2). 128pp. The geography, history, government, and economy of Chile are some of the topics covered in this fine introduction. (Rev: BL 4/1/91) [983]

18363 Winter, Jane K. *Venezuela* (5–8). Illus. Series: Cultures of the World. 1991, Marshall Cavendish LB $35.64 (978-1-85435-386-3). 128pp. In detailed text and color photographs, the land, people, and contemporary problems and concerns of Venezuela are introduced. (Rev: BL 4/1/91) [987]

Polar Regions

18364 Alexander, Bryan, and Cherry Alexander. *An Eskimo Family* (3–6). Illus. 1985, Lerner LB $18.60 (978-0-8225-1656-9). 32pp. Young readers get a taste of life in the far north in this look at an Eskimo family. (Rev: BL 6/15/85; SLJ 10/85)

18365 Alexander, Bryan, and Cherry Alexander. *Journey into the Arctic* (1–5). Photos by authors. 2003, Oxford LB $25.00 (978-0-19-522004-9). 48pp. A fascinating tour of Arctic regions takes readers from a village in Greenland through Arctic Canada and Siberia to the North Pole. (Rev: HBG 4/04; SLJ 1/04)

18366 Bagley, Katie. *Antarctica* (K–3). Series: Continents. 2002, Capstone LB $21.26 (978-0-7368-1415-7). 24pp. A brief introduction to the geography, history, flora (mostly lichens and moss), and fauna of Antarctica. (Rev: HBG 3/03; SLJ 4/03)

18367 Benduhn, Tea. *Living in Polar Regions* (3–4). Series: Life on the Edge. 2007, Gareth Stevens LB $19.93 (978-0-8368-8343-5). 24pp. After an introduction to the polar regions and the climate of these areas, Benduhn looks at the people who live there, the life they lead, and the problems they face. (Rev: LMC 1/08; SLJ 12/07) [910.911]

18368 Bledsoe, Lucy Jane. *How to Survive in Antarctica* (5–8). 2006, Holiday $16.95 (978-0-8234-1890-9). 102pp. An account of the author's trips to Antarctica, filled with interesting facts about the frigid land — from wildlife notes to survival tips — plus photographs by the author. (Rev: BCCB 10/06; BL 7/06; HBG 4/07; SLJ 8/06; VOYA 8/06) [919.8]

18369 Bocknek, Jonathan. *Antarctica: The Last Wilderness* (5–8). Series: Understanding Global Issues. 2003, Smart Apple $19.95 (978-1-58340-356-3). 56pp. This nicely illustrated book introduces Antarctica with material on climate, animals, exploration, and possible future developments. (Rev: BL 11/15/03; HB 9/01; HBG 3/02; SLJ 12/03) [998.9]

18370 Bredeson, Carmen. *After the Last Dog Died: The True-Life, Hair-Raising Adventures of Douglas Mawson and his 1911–1914 Antarctic Expedition* (5–8). Illus. 2003, National Geographic $18.95 (978-0-7922-6140-7). 64pp. This enthralling story of courage in the face of starvation and harsh conditions draws on primary materials including the writings of expedition leader Mawson himself. (Rev: BL 11/1/03; HBG 4/04; SLJ 1/04*) [919.8]

18371 Byles, Monica. *Life in the Polar Lands* (2–5). Illus. by Francis Mosley. 2000, Two-Can LB $9.95 (978-1-58728-557-8); paper $4.95 (978-1-58728-572-1). 31pp. This is a basic introduction to how plants, animals, and humans manage to survive in the Arctic and Antarctic. (Rev: SLJ 4/01) [508.311]

18372 Cerullo, Mary. *Life Under Ice* (3–5). Illus. by Bill Curtsinger. 2004, Tilbury House $16.95 (978-0-88448-246-8). 40pp. Plant and animal life above and below the waters of Antarctica are shown in eye-catching color photographs. (Rev: BL 9/15/03; HBG 4/04; SLJ 10/03) [578.777]

18373 Conlan, Kathy. *Under the Ice* (4–6). Illus. 2002, Kids Can $16.95 (978-1-55337-001-7). 56pp. This photoessay relates the author's exciting experiences doing underwater marine biology research in Antarctica. (Rev: BL 11/1/02; HBG 3/03; SLJ 12/02) [578.77]

18374 Cordoba, Yasmine A. *Igloo* (3–5). Illus. by Kimberly L. Dawson Kurnizki. Series: Native American Homes. 2001, Rourke LB $28.50 (978-1-55916-277-7). 32pp. Using well-chosen photos and a good text, this book explains the construction of the igloo, its uses, and its place in the culture of the Inuit. (Rev: SLJ 3/01) [979.8]

18375 Curlee, Lynn. *Into the Ice: The Story of Arctic Exploration* (4–6). Illus. by author. 1998, Houghton $16.00 (978-0-395-83013-0). 40pp. Attractive acrylic paintings are used to illustrate this history of Arctic exploration, emphasizing the motivation behind the fearless explorers who venture into this cold, hostile environment. (Rev: BCCB 6/98; BL 4/1/98; HB 5/98; HBG 10/98; SLJ 5/98) [998]

18376 Esbensen, Barbara J. *The Night Rainbow* (1–4). Illus. by Helen K. Davie. 2000, Orchard LB $17.99 (978-0-531-33244-3). 32pp. A poetic picture book that discusses the Northern Lights and the many images from different folk traditions that are associated with this phenomenon. (Rev: BL 3/1/00; HBG 10/00; SLJ 4/00) [538.768]

18377 Fine, Jil. *The Shackleton Expedition* (5–8). Series: Survivor. 2002, Children's LB $24.50 (978-0-516-23904-0); paper $6.95 (978-0-516-23489-2). 48pp. For reluctant readers, this is an accessible and exciting account of how Shackleton's men survived the perils of shipwreck in the ice. (Rev: SLJ 9/02) [919.8904]

18378 Foran, Jill. *Search for the Northwest Passage* (5–8). Series: Great Journeys. 2004, Weigl LB $26.00 (978-1-59036-205-1). Colorful illustrations and an attractive format will appeal to browsers seeking information about the search for a sea route to the West; a useful timeline and links to Web sites are included. (Rev: BL 11/1/04) [910]

18379 Goodman, Susan E. *Life on the Ice* (3–5). Photos by Michael J. Doolittle. 2006, Millbrook LB $22.60 (978-0-7613-2775-2). 32pp. This brief introduction to the world's polar regions explores their geographical remoteness, weather extremes, and the scientific research projects conducted there. (Rev: BL 3/15/06; SLJ 8/06) [910]

18380 Gray, Susan H. *Tundra* (2–5). Series: First Reports. 2000, Compass Point LB $22.60 (978-0-7565-0024-5). 48pp. An informative introduction to the ecosystem, with material on plants and animals, the conditions there, the importance of the biome to the global environment, and features such as the discovery of a woolly mammoth in the permafrost in Russia. (Rev: SLJ 5/01) [577.5]

18381 Green, Jen. *On the Tundra* (2–5). Illus. Series: Small World. 2002, Crabtree LB $25.27 (978-0-7787-0139-2); paper $8.95 (978-0-7787-0153-8). 32pp. This book for younger readers takes a close look at the creatures that are found in the tundra, and how plant and animal life coexist there. (Rev: BL 10/15/02; SLJ 8/02) [577.5]

18382 Hoyt-Goldsmith, Diane. *Arctic Hunter* (3–6). 1992, Holiday House LB $16.95 (978-0-8234-0972-3). 32pp. Ten-year-old Reggie and his family travel to their camp north of the Arctic Circle to add to their food supply. (Rev: BL 12/15/92; HB 1/93; SLJ 11/92*) [979.8]

18383 Johnson, Rebecca. *A Walk in the Tundra* (2–4). Illus. Series: Biomes of North America. 2000, Carolrhoda LB $23.93 (978-1-57505-157-4). 48pp. A lively account that uses maps, pictures, and text to describe the climate, flora and fauna, and the people of the tundra regions of North America. (Rev: BL 10/15/00; HBG 3/01; SLJ 12/00) [577.5]

18384 Kaplan, Elizabeth. *Tundra* (4–6). Illus. Series: Biomes of the World. 1995, Marshall Cavendish LB

$25.64 (978-0-7614-0080-6). 64pp. Material is given on the location of this frigid biome and the life it supports. (Rev: BL 12/15/95; SLJ 3/96) [551.4]

18385 Kimmel, Elizabeth C. *Ice Story: Shackleton's Lost Expedition* (4–7). Illus. 1999, Clarion $19.00 (978-0-395-91524-0). 120pp. A fine, accurate, and engrossing description of Shackleton's Imperial Transatlantic Expedition to the Antarctic — one of the great survival stories of all time. (Rev: BL 4/1/99; HBG 10/99; SLJ 4/99) [910.9]

18386 Levinson, Nancy S. *North Pole South Pole* (1–2). Illus. by Diane D. Hearn. 2002, Holiday House $14.95 (978-0-8234-1737-7). 40pp. Basic facts about the two poles for beginning readers. (Rev: HB 1/03; HBG 3/03; SLJ 12/02) [574]

18387 Levy, Janey. *Discovering the Arctic Tundra* (3–5). Series: World Habitats. 2007, Rosen LB $23.95 (978-1-4042-3787-2). 32pp. With photographs and fast facts, this volume covers location, climate, plants and animals, people, threats and conservation efforts, and so forth. (Rev: LMC 3/08; SLJ 1/08) [577.5]

18388 Love, Ann, and Jane Drake. *The Kids Book of the Far North* (2–4). Illus. 2000, Kids Can $15.95 (978-1-55074-563-4). 48pp. Topics covered in this introduction to the Arctic include climate and landscape, natural resources, exploration and settlement, and the life, past and present, of the native people. (Rev: BL 9/15/00; SLJ 1/01) [909]

18389 Lynch, Wayne. *The Arctic* (5–9). Series: Our Wild World Ecosystems. 2007, NorthWord $16.95 (978-1-55971-960-5); paper $8.95 (978-1-55971-961-2). 64pp. Lynch introduces the flora and fauna of the Arctic with interesting anecdotes about his own experiences, color photographs, sidebar features, and eco-fact boxes. (Rev: SLJ 5/07) [577.0911]

18390 Lynch, Wayne. *Arctic Alphabet: Exploring the North from A to Z* (3–5). Illus. 1999, Firefly $19.95 (978-1-55209-336-8); paper $6.95 (978-1-55209-334-4). 32pp. Using an alphabetical arrangement, the author/photographer introduces Arctic wildlife as well as the aurora borealis, glaciers, hibernation, and the Inuit. (Rev: BL 2/1/00; HBG 3/00; SLJ 2/00) [577]

18391 McMillan, Bruce. *Summer Ice: Life Along the Antarctic Peninsula* (4–6). Illus. 1995, Houghton $16.00 (978-0-395-66561-9). 48pp. A photoessay that describes the geography and the plants and animals that live on the Antarctic Peninsula. (Rev: BL 11/1/95; SLJ 9/95) [508]

18392 Markle, Sandra. *Super Cool Science: South Pole Stations Past, Present, and Future* (3–5). Illus. 1998, Walker LB $17.85 (978-0-8027-8471-1). 32pp. After describing the first research station at the South Pole built in 1956, the author describes the present facilities and their uses, with coverage on plans for a newer, larger station in the future. (Rev: BL 3/15/98; HBG 10/98; SLJ 4/98) [507]

18393 Martin, Jacqueline B. *The Lamp, the Ice, and the Boat Called Fish* (2–4). Illus. 2000, Houghton $15.00 (978-0-618-00341-9). 48pp. The story of the personnel aboard a research boat named Fish and

how they survived with the help of some natives after they were trapped in the ice during an Arctic expedition. (Rev: BCCB 2/01; BL 3/1/01; HB 3/01; HBG 10/01) [919.804]

18394 Matsen, Brad. *An Extreme Dive Under the Antarctic Ice* (4–6). Series: Incredible Deep-Sea Adventures. 2003, Enslow LB $23.93 (978-0-7660-2190-7). 48pp. Readers follow environmental scientists under the cold ice of the Antarctic and discover pollution and other threats. (Rev: HBG 4/04; SLJ 1/04) [551.46]

18395 Penner, Lucille R. *Ice Wreck* (2–4). Illus. Series: Road to Reading. 2001, Golden $11.99 (978-0-307-46408-8); paper $3.99 (978-0-307-26408-4). 48pp. An absorbing narrative about Shackleton's disastrous expedition and exciting rescue. (Rev: BL 7/01; HBG 3/02) [919.8]

18396 Penny, Malcolm. *The Polar Seas* (4–6). Illus. Series: Seas and Oceans. 1997, Raintree LB $27.12 (978-0-8172-4513-9). 48pp. An overview of the history and importance of the polar seas, as well as the dangers that tourism and the search for natural resources now pose. (Rev: BL 7/97) [551.46]

18397 Pipe, Jim. *Polar Region Survival* (4–6). Illus. Series: Extreme Habitats. 2007, Gareth Stevens LB $25.27 (978-0-8368-8248-3). 32pp. This well-designed title combines high visual appeal and accessible facts to make an attractive and informative overview of polar regions, the plants and animals that live there, how people use these regions, and the threats to the environment. (Rev: LMC 1/08; SLJ 12/07) [613.6]

18398 Pipes, Rose. *Tundra and Cold Deserts* (2–4). Series: World Habitats. 1998, Raintree LB $24.28 (978-0-8172-5010-2). 32pp. The world's tundra areas are introduced along with their physical characteristics, wildlife, climate, and uses. (Rev: BL 3/15/99; HBG 3/99) [574.5]

18399 Rootes, David. *The Arctic* (3–6). Illus. Series: Endangered People and Places. 1996, Lerner LB $22.60 (978-0-8225-2776-3). 48pp. A glimpse of the Arctic region and the people who live in this hostile environment. (Rev: BL 11/15/96; SLJ 1/97) [333.73]

18400 Sandler, Martin. *Trapped in Ice! An Amazing True Whaling Adventure* (5–8). Illus. 2006, Scholastic $16.99 (978-0-439-74363-1). 176pp. A gripping account of 1,219 people forced to abandon ship after their whaling vessels became imprisoned in Arctic ice during the early winter of 1871; includes maps, photographs, and journal accounts. (Rev: BL 4/15/06; SLJ 6/06) [639.2]

18401 Sayre, April P. *Antarctica* (5–8). Series: Seven Continents. 1998, Twenty-First Century LB $25.90 (978-0-7613-3227-5). A well-written and well-illustrated introduction to the Antarctic environment, including its geology, plants, animals, and research facilities. (Rev: BL 2/1/99; HBG 9/99; SLJ 4/99) [919.89]

18402 Scott, Elaine. *Poles Apart: Why Penguins and Polar Bears Will Never Be Neighbors* (4–8). Illus. 2004, Viking $17.99 (978-0-670-05925-6). 64pp. This fascinating overview of the two polar regions examines their physical characteristics, seasons, wildlife, magnetism, exploration, and the effects of global warming. (Rev: BL 12/1/04; SLJ 12/04) [909]

18403 Sommers, Michael A. *Antarctic Melting: The Disappearing Antarctic Ice Cap* (4–8). Series: Extreme Environmental Threats. 2006, Rosen LB $27.95 (978-1-4042-0741-7). 64pp. An examination of the impact that global warming has had on Antarctica since 1995, with discussion of the research that takes place on the continent and the work of glaciologists. (Rev: LMC 8/07; SLJ 8/07) [363.738]

18404 Steele, Philip. *Tundra* (3–5). Illus. Series: Geography Detectives. 1997, Carolrhoda LB $19.93 (978-1-57505-040-9). 32pp. The treeless plains of the Arctic and parts of Antarctica are introduced, with material on the people who live there and how these areas have changed through the centuries. (Rev: BL 8/97; SLJ 1/98) [574.5]

18405 Steger, Will, and Jon Bowermaster. *Over the Top of the World: Explorer Will Steger's Trek Across the Arctic* (4–7). Illus. 1997, Scholastic paper $17.95 (978-0-590-84860-2). 64pp. Describes the grueling, dangerous adventures involved in a journey across the Arctic Ocean. (Rev: BCCB 2/97; BL 4/15/97; SLJ 4/97*) [919.804]

18406 Stone, Lynn M. *Tundra* (1–3). Illus. Series: Biomes of North America. 2003, Rourke $20.64 (978-1-58952-687-7). 24pp. For young researchers, this is an excellent introduction to this biome, with clear, simple text, photographs, and maps. (Rev: BL 10/15/03) [577.5]

18407 Theodorou, Rod. *From the Arctic to Antarctica* (2–4). Series: Amazing Journeys. 2000, Heinemann LB $22.79 (978-1-57572-485-0). 32pp. Both the Arctic and Antarctic regions are described in this brief overview that also introduces plant and animal life. (Rev: HBG 3/01; SLJ 7/00) [998]

18408 Wadsworth, Ginger. *Tundra Discoveries* (PS–3). Illus. by John Carrozza. 1999, Charlesbridge LB $15.95 (978-0-88106-875-7); paper $6.95 (978-0-88106-876-4). 32pp. Each double-page spread chronicles a different month in the Arctic tundra and describes the changes in both animals and plants. (Rev: BL 9/1/99; HBG 3/00; SLJ 8/99) [591.75]

18409 Winner, Cherie. *Life in the Tundra* (5–8). Series: Ecosystems in Action. 2003, Lerner LB $26.60 (978-0-8225-4686-3). 72pp. In text and pictures, the Arctic tundra is presented with material on the organisms that live there and how human life has changed this ecosystem. (Rev: BL 9/15/03; HBG 10/03) [551.4]

18410 Yolen, Jane. *Welcome to the Ice House* (PS–3). Illus. by Laura Regan. 1998, Penguin $16.99 (978-0-399-23011-0). 32pp. Using illustrations that portray the bleak Arctic landscapes, the poet introduces various animals that live in this inhospitable climate. (Rev: BL 2/15/98; HBG 10/98; SLJ 3/98*) [591.7586]

18411 Yue, Charlotte, and David Yue. *The Igloo* (3–6). Illus. 1988, Houghton $16.00 (978-0-395-

44613-3). 128pp. Describes the construction and function of igloos. (Rev: BCCB 1/89; BL 9/1/88; SLJ 12/88)

United States

General

18412 Ayer, Eleanor. *Our National Monuments* (4–6). Illus. Series: I Know America. 1992, Millbrook LB $20.90 (978-1-56294-078-2). 48pp. The most important of our national monuments are highlighted and their history explained in this well-illustrated account. (Rev: BL 9/1/92; SLJ 10/92) [973]

18413 Brent, Lynnette R. *At Home: Long Ago and Today* (2–4). Series: Times Change. 2003, Heinemann LB $24.22 (978-1-4034-4531-5). 32pp. A look at how things were "at home" a century or more ago compared with today. (Rev: SLJ 5/04) [690]

18414 Brent, Lynnette R. *At School: Long Ago and Today* (2–4). Series: Times Change. 2003, Heinemann LB $24.22 (978-1-4034-4533-9). 32pp. This book, illustrated with period and contemporary photographs, contrasts a day in school today and a century or so ago. (Rev: SLJ 5/04) [372.973]

18415 Brent, Lynnette R. *Going Shopping: Long Ago and Today* (2–4). Series: Times Change. 2003, Heinemann LB $24.22 (978-1-4034-4535-3). 32pp. A comparison of what it was like to go shopping more than 100 years ago with what it's like today, illustrated with contemporary and period photographs. (Rev: SLJ 5/04) [380.1]

18416 Haskins, James, and Kathleen Benson. *Africa: A Look Back* (5–8). Series: Drama of African-American History. 2006, Benchmark LB $23.95 (978-0-7614-2148-1). 68pp. Slave narratives form a substantial portion of this survey of African American culture, tracing its roots back to the western part of Africa. (Rev: SLJ 5/07) [967]

18417 Haskins, Lori. *Spooky America: Four Real Ghost Stories* (2–3). Series: Step into Reading. 2003, Golden paper $3.99 (978-0-375-82500-2). 48pp. Truth and legend are intertwined in these illustrated stories set in Massachusetts, Virginia, Colorado, and California. (Rev: BL 10/1/03; HBG 4/04) [133.1]

18418 Hess, Debra. *The American Flag* (3–5). Series: Symbols of America. 2003, Benchmark LB $25.64 (978-0-7614-1709-5). 39pp. A look back at the many variations of the Stars and Stripes before and since the first one was made (according to legend) by Betsy Ross during the Revolutionary War. (Rev: HBG 4/04; SLJ 3/04)

18419 Hess, Debra. *The Liberty Bell* (3–5). Series: Symbols of America. 2003, Benchmark LB $25.64 (978-0-7614-1713-2). 40pp. A look at the Liberty Bell, its role in the Revolution, and why it is cracked. Also use *Statue of Liberty* (2003). (Rev: HBG 4/04; SLJ 3/04)

18420 Hopkinson, Deborah. *Up Before Daybreak: Cotton and People in America* (5–8). Illus. 2006,

Scholastic $18.99 (978-0-439-63901-9). 128pp. A concise, readable history of the American cotton industry with a focus on laborers, especially children; contains archival photographs, reading list, and bibliography. (Rev: BL 4/15/06*; HB 5/06; LMC 11/06; SLJ 6/06*) [331.7]

18421 Johnson, Linda C. *Our National Symbols* (4–6). Illus. Series: I Know America. 1992, Millbrook LB $24.90 (978-1-56294-108-6). 48pp. American symbols — historical and current, such as yellow ribbons during the Persian Gulf War — are discussed. (Rev: BL 5/15/92; SLJ 7/93) [929.9]

18422 Keenan, Sheila. *O, Say Can You See? America's Symbols, Landmarks, and Important Words* (2–5). Illus. by Ann Boyajian. 2004, Scholastic $16.95 (978-0-439-42450-9). 64pp. The bald eagle, the Pledge of Allegiance, and Veteran's Day are among the holidays, landmarks, symbols, and sayings included in this attractive guide. (Rev: BL 10/15/04) [973]

18423 Locker, Thomas. *Home: A Journey Through America* (4–6). Illus. 1998, Harcourt $16.00 (978-0-15-201473-5). 32pp. Using excerpts from poems, letters, and novels, plus outstanding full-page oil paintings, this book celebrates the beauty of various American landscapes. (Rev: BL 11/1/98; HBG 3/99; SLJ 10/98) [810.8]

18424 Magaziner, Henry Jonas. *Our Liberty Bell* (2–4). Illus. by John O'Brien. 2007, Holiday $15.95 (978-0-8234-1892-3). 32pp. The Liberty Bell's significance throughout American history is examined in this well-designed volume. (Rev: BL 6/1–15/07; LMC 11/07; SLJ 7/07) [974.8]

18425 Martin, Bill, Jr., and Michael Sampson. *I Pledge Allegiance* (K–4). Illus. by Chris Raschka. 2002, Candlewick $15.99 (978-0-7636-1648-9). 40pp. The Pledge of Allegiance, which was adopted in 1892, is explained to young readers in simple language. (Rev: BCCB 10/02; BL 9/1/02; HBG 3/03; SLJ 12/02) [323.6]

18426 Saller, Carol. *Working Children* (3–6). Illus. Series: Picture the American Past. 1998, Carolrhoda LB $22.60 (978-1-57505-276-2). 48pp. This work supplies a history of child labor, particularly in this country, and efforts to stop it. (Rev: BL 3/1/99; HBG 3/99; SLJ 1/99) [331.3]

18427 Sís, Peter. *The Train of States* (K–3). 2004, Greenwillow LB $18.89 (978-0-06-057839-8). 64pp. Eye-catching circus wagons representing each of the 50 states (the District of Columbia gets the caboose) are arranged in chronological order and accompanied by pertinent facts. (Rev: BL 10/15/04; SLJ 11/04*) [973]

18428 Sonneborn, Liz. *The Pledge of Allegiance: The Story Behind Our Patriotic Promise* (3–5). Illus. Series: America in Words and Song. 2004, Chelsea House LB $23.00 (978-0-7910-7336-0). 32pp. This slim volume provides the history of the pledge and the changes it has undergone over the years. (Rev: BL 4/1/04; SLJ 5/04) [323.0]

18429 West, Delno C., and Jean M. West. *Uncle Sam and Old Glory: Symbols of America* (2–5). Illus. 2000, Simon & Schuster $17.00 (978-0-689-82043-

4). 40pp. From the bald eagle and the Liberty Bell to Smokey the Bear, this is a history of 15 symbols, their origins, and meanings. (Rev: BCCB 1/00; BL 12/15/99; HBG 10/00; SLJ 1/00) [929.9]

18430 Yaccarino, Dan. *Go, Go America* (3–5). Illus. by author. 2008, Scholastic $17.99 (978-0-439-70338-3). 80pp. The Farley family takes readers on an entertaining and informative tour of the 50 states, with a combination of key facts and interesting trivia. (Rev: BL 3/1/08; LMC 1/08; SLJ 3/08) [973]

General History and Geography

18431 Ajmera, Maya, and Yvonne Wakim Dennis. *Children of the U.S.A* (3–6). Illus. 2008, Charlesbridge $23.95 (978-1-57091-615-1). 128pp. This photo-essay compares and contrasts children enjoying themselves in 51 American communities. (Rev: BL 3/1/08; SLJ 2/08) [305.230973]

18432 Andryszewski, Tricia. *Step by Step Along the Appalachian Trail* (4–8). 1998, Twenty-First Century LB $24.90 (978-0-7613-0273-5). A state-by-state tour of the Appalachian Trail, with material on the terrain, elevations, landmarks, and sites along the way. (Rev: BL 3/1/99; HBG 9/99; SLJ 4/99) [973]

18433 Armstrong, Jennifer. *The American Story: 100 True Tales from American History* (4–7). Illus. by Roger Roth. 2006, Knopf $34.95 (978-0-375-81256-9). 368pp. The 100 stories in this large-format collection bring American history to life and include such diverse events as Paul Revere's midnight ride, the first flight of the Wright brothers, the eruption of Mount St. Helens, and the Supreme Court decision resolving the disputed 2000 presidential election. (Rev: BCCB 10/06; BL 8/06; HBG 4/07; SLJ 8/06*) [973]

18434 Backer, Miles. *Travels with Charlie: Way Out West* (1–3). Illus. by Chuck Nitzberg. 2006, Blue Apple $15.95 (978-1-59354-134-7). Charlie the dog visits interesting and quirky sites in the western United States; maps of the states he visits, as well as a U.S. map, will help readers as they follow Charlie on his travels. (Rev: SLJ 6/06) [978]

18435 Baines, John. *The United States* (4–8). Illus. Series: Country Fact Files. 1994, Raintree LB $27.12 (978-0-8114-1857-7). 45pp. In a series of double-page spreads, basic information about the United States is given, including geography, economy, population, industry, education, government, and environment. (Rev: SLJ 7/94) [973]

18436 Beckett, Harry. *Lake Erie* (3–5). Series: Great Lakes of North America. 1999, Rourke LB $26.60 (978-0-86593-527-3). 32pp. This book introduces the history of Lake Erie as well as its geography and industries. (Rev: SLJ 2/00) [973]

18437 Beckett, Harry. *Lake Superior* (3–5). Series: Great Lakes of North America. 1999, Rourke LB $26.60 (978-0-86593-528-0). 32pp. Maps, graphs, and photographs illustrate this introduction to Lake Superior, its history, geography, and commercial value. (Rev: SLJ 2/00) [973]

18438 Beckett, Harry. *Waterways to the Great Lakes* (3–5). Series: Great Lakes of North America. 1999,

Rourke LB $26.60 (978-0-86593-529-7). 32pp. This book discusses how the Great Lakes were formed, the fur trade, the lock system, and current environmental problems. (Rev: SLJ 2/00) [973]

18439 Bockenhauer, Mark H., and Stephen F. Cunha. *Our Fifty States* (4–10). Illus. 2004, National Geographic LB $45.90 (978-0-7922-6992-2). 239pp. Maps of the states are accompanied by basic facts, photographs, and archival reproductions of key historical events; also includes the U.S. territories. (Rev: SLJ 1/05) [973]

18440 Bowden, Rob. *Settlements of the Mississippi River* (3–5). Illus. Series: Rivers Through Time. 2005, Heinemann LB $29.93 (978-1-4034-5719-6). 48pp. Traces the history and contemporary life of major settlements along the Mississippi, discussing the development of industry and the importance of environmental factors.

18441 Brownell, Barbara. *Spin's Really Wild U.S.A. Tour* (K–4). Illus. 1996, National Geographic paper $7.95 (978-0-7922-3422-7). An introduction to the geography of the United States that highlights the flora, fauna, and land formations, conducted by Spin from the National Geographic TV series. (Rev: SLJ 6/96) [910]

18442 Buckley, Susan, and Elspeth Leacock. *Journeys for Freedom: A New Look at America's Story* (4–7). Illus. by Rodica Prato. 2006, Houghton $17.00 (978-0-618-22323-7). 48pp. Twenty stories of personal struggles for freedom — ranging from the early 17th century to the late 20th century — feature quotations from primary sources. (Rev: BL 11/15/06; SLJ 1/07) [973]

18443 Buckley, Susan, and Elspeth Leacock. *Kids Make History: A New Look at America's Story* (4–8). Illus. by Randy Jones. 2006, Houghton $17.00 (978-0-618-22329-9). 48pp. Twenty stories of young people who experienced milestone events in American history — from Pocahontas in 1607 to a high school senior on 9/11 — are told in text, quotations, fictionalized dialogue, and illustrations. (Rev: SLJ 1/07) [973.09]

18444 Burleigh, Robert. *American Moments: Scenes from American History* (3–6). Trans. and illus. by Bruce Strachan. 2004, Holt $18.95 (978-0-8050-7082-8). 48pp. Eighteen chapters present scenes from American history that may lack detail but will arouse interest. (Rev: BL 7/04; SLJ 6/04) [973]

18445 Butler, Daphne. *U.S.A.* (2–4). Illus. 1992, Raintree LB $22.83 (978-0-8114-3676-2). 32pp. Color photos aid in a broad overview of the United States, described in terms of topography and lifestyle. (Rev: BL 3/15/93) [973]

18446 Cheney, Lynne. *Our 50 States: A Family Adventure Across America* (4–6). Illus. by Robin P. Glasser. 2006, Simon & Schuster $17.95 (978-0-689-86717-0). 74pp. Follow a family as they travel all over the United States, visiting interesting destinations and learning historical, geographical, and cultural facts. (Rev: BL 11/15/06; SLJ 1/07) [973]

18447 Collier, Christopher, and James Lincoln Collier. *A Century of Immigration, 1820–1924* (5–8). Series: Drama of American History. 1999, Marshall Cavendish LB $31.36 (978-0-7614-0821-5). 91pp. A compelling account that focuses on 100 years of migration to this country, with material on where the immigrants came from, why they emigrated, where they settled, and the problems of assimilation. (Rev: BL 2/15/00; HBG 10/00; SLJ 3/00) [973]

18448 Collier, Christopher, and James Lincoln Collier. *The Rise of the Cities: 1820–1920* (5–8). Illus. Series: The Drama of American History. 2001, Marshall Cavendish LB $31.36 (978-0-7614-1051-5). 96pp. In this highly illustrated volume, the Colliers paint a broad picture of the process of urbanization in the United States, tracing the problems involved and the growing prominence of cities in American life. (Rev: BL 3/15/01; HBG 10/01; SLJ 7/01) [973]

18449 Colman, Penny. *Girls: A History of Growing Up Female in America* (5–8). Illus. 2000, Scholastic paper $18.95 (978-0-590-37129-2). 192pp. Using diaries, memoirs, letters, magazine articles, and other sources, the author presents a history of girls in America from the first females to cross the Bering Strait to the present day. (Rev: BCCB 2/00; BL 2/1/00; HBG 10/00; SLJ 3/00) [305.23]

18450 Cooper, Jason. *Árboles / Trees* (4–8). Trans. by Blanca Rey. Illus. Series: La Guía de Rourke Para los Símbolos de los Estados/Rourke's Guide to State Symbols. 2002, Rourke LB $20.95 (978-1-58952-399-9). 63pp. The 50 state trees are introduced in bilingual text and illustrations. Also use *Aves / Birds*, *Banderas / Flags*, and *Flores / Flowers*. (Rev: SLJ 3/03) [582]

18451 Costain, Meredith, and Paul Collins. *Welcome to the United States of America* (3–5). Illus. Series: Countries of the World. 2001, Chelsea LB $28.00 (978-0-7910-6542-6). 32pp. This basic introduction to the land, people, and culture of the United States will be useful in work with new immigrants and ESL students. (Rev: HBG 3/02; SLJ 2/02)

18452 Dolan, Edward F. *The American Indian Wars* (5–8). Illus. 2003, Millbrook LB $29.90 (978-0-7613-1968-9). 112pp. Four hundred years of conflict are covered in this volume that looks at the causes, details the key battles and events, and provides portraits of the key participants. (Rev: BL 12/1/03) [973.04]

18453 Emsden, Katharine, ed. *Coming to America: A New Life in a New Land* (4–8). Series: Perspectives on History. 1993, Discovery paper $6.95 (978-1-878668-23-3). 64pp. Diaries, journals, and letters of immigrants from many countries are used to provide insights into their lives. (Rev: BL 11/15/93) [325.73]

18454 Firestone, Mary. *The Liberty Bell* (K–4). Illus. by Matthew Skeens. Series: American Symbols. 2006, Picture Window LB $23.93 (978-1-4048-3101-8). 24pp. Contemporary-looking illustrations accompany simple text for an introduction to one of America's best-loved symbols. (Rev: SLJ 5/07)

18455 Fischer, Maureen M. *Nineteenth Century Lumber Camp Cooking* (4–7). Series: Exploring History Through Simple Recipes. 2000, Capstone LB $23.93 (978-0-7368-0604-6). 32pp. After describing life in a lumber camp more than a hundred years ago, this book supplies some authentic recipes. (Rev: BL 3/1/01; HBG 10/01; SLJ 4/01) [973.8]

18456 Floca, Brian. *Lightship* (PS–2). Illus. 2007, Simon & Schuster $16.99 (978-1-4169-2436-4). 48pp. This is a detailed and attractive account of the role of lightships — which were used where lighthouses were not suitable; the last one in the United States was retired in 1983. (Rev: BL 2/1/07) [387.2]

18457 Garland, Michael. *Americana Adventure: A Look Again Book* (1–3). Illus. by author. 2008, Dutton $15.99 (978-0-525-47945-1). 32pp. On the 4th of July Tommy gets the first in a set of clues from his Aunt Jeanne and finds himself on a tour of the country. (Rev: BL 5/15/08; SLJ 6/08) [973]

18458 Gritzner, Charles F. *The United States of America* (4–6). Illus. Series: Modern World Nations. 2007, Chelsea House LB $30.00 (978-0-7910-9511-9). 142pp. This is a very positive overview of the United States' history, geography, government, economy, and culture. (Rev: BLO 5/5/08) [973]

18459 Haban, Rita D. *How Proudly They Wave: Flags of the Fifty States* (4–9). Illus. 1989, Lerner LB $23.93 (978-0-8225-1799-3). Pictures of the state flags are accompanied by background information. (Rev: BL 12/15/89; SLJ 3/90) [929.9]

18460 Hatt, Christine. *Slavery: From Africa to the Americas* (5–8). 1998, Bedrick $19.95 (978-0-87226-552-3). 63pp. A broad overview of slavery in America that covers slave ships, plantation life, abolitionism, the Civil War, and Reconstruction, with maps, illustrations, and reproductions of documents. (Rev: HBG 10/98; SLJ 5/98) [973]

18461 Hauser, Pierre. *Illegal Aliens* (5–8). Series: Immigrant Experience. 1996, Chelsea LB $14.95 (978-0-7910-3363-0). A history of attitudes toward immigration is followed by a discussion of illegal immigrants, where they come from, why they came, and the government's policy toward them. (Rev: SLJ 2/97) [932]

18462 Heinz, Brian J. *Nathan of Yesteryear and Michael of Today* (4–6). Illus. by Joanne Friar. 2006, Lerner LB $22.60 (978-0-7613-2893-3). 32pp. This thought-provoking picture book for older students contrasts the daily life of a 12-year-old boy living today and that of his great-great-grandfather, who lived in the 1880s. (Rev: BL 10/15/06) [303.4]

18463 Hicks, Terry Allan. *The Bald Eagle* (3–5). Series: Symbols of America. 2006, Benchmark LB $28.50 (978-0-7614-2133-7). 40pp. Information on the bald eagle and its selection as the national bird of the United States are accompanied by archival and contemporary images. Also use *Uncle Sam* (2006). (Rev: SLJ 12/06) [929.9]

18464 Isaacs, Sally Senzell. *America in the Time of Susan B. Anthony: The Story of Our Nation from Coast to Coast, from 1845 to 1928* (4–8). 1999, Heinemann LB $30.35 (978-1-57572-763-9). 48pp. Using the life of Susan B. Anthony as a framework, this work covers topics including woman's suffrage, poverty, and World War I. (Rev: SLJ 5/00) [973.9]

18465 Johnston, Robert D. *The Making of America* (5–8). Illus. 2002, National Geographic $29.95

(978-0-7922-6944-1). 224pp. An informative and balanced overview of American history, this appealing volume divides American history into eight periods; in addition to the narrative, each period includes profiles of two major figures and examines important issues of the time. (Rev: BL 1/1–15/03; HBG 3/03; SLJ 12/02*) [973]

18466 Jordan, Anne Devereaux, and Virginia Schomp. *Slavery and Resistance* (5–8). Illus. 2006, Marshall Cavendish LB $34.21 (978-0-7614-2178-8). 70pp. A well-illustrated, well-organized history of slavery in America from the first colony in Jamestown up until the Civil War. (Rev: BL 2/1/07; SLJ 5/07) [306.3]

18467 Kalman, Bobbie, and Greg Nickles. *Spanish Missions* (4–7). Illus. Series: Historic Communities. 1996, Crabtree LB $25.27 (978-0-86505-436-3); paper $7.95 (978-0-86505-466-0). 32pp. In double-page spreads, this book covers the building of the mission in the southern United States and of its functions: teaching Christianity, educating children, and supplying housing and food. (Rev: SLJ 4/97) [973]

18468 Keenan, Sheila. *Greetings from the 50 States: How They Got Their Names* (4–6). Illus. by Selina Alko. 2008, Scholastic $18.99 (978-0-439-83439-1). 112pp. In addition to the states' names and how they got them, this breezy volume looks at mottos, physical features, natural resources, history, and key people; includes the District of Columbia. (Rev: BL 12/15/08; LMC 3/09) [900]

18469 Leacock, Elspeth, and Susan Buckley. *Journeys in Time: A New Atlas of American History* (4–6). Illus. 2001, Houghton $15.00 (978-0-395-97956-3). 48pp. Twenty dramatic stories of "journeys" drawn from true accounts serve to introduce the history of America in an unusual and effective way. (Rev: BL 6/1–15/01; HB 7/01; HBG 10/01; SLJ 6/01) [973]

18470 Leacock, Elspeth, and Susan Buckley. *Places in Time: A New Atlas of American History* (4–6). Illus. 2001, Houghton $15.00 (978-0-395-97958-7). 48pp. In this companion to *Journeys in Time*, 20 significant sites — towns, battlefields, Ellis Island, even a tract house — are used to convey essential elements of American history. (Rev: BL 6/1–15/01; HB 7/01; HBG 10/01; SLJ 6/01) [911]

18471 Leedy, Loreen. *Celebrate the 50 States!* (1–3). Illus. 1999, Holiday House $17.95 (978-0-8234-1431-4). 32pp. Each page in this simple geography book introduces two states and gives basic information such as capitals, state symbols, and bits of state lore. (Rev: BL 9/1/99; HBG 3/00; SLJ 9/99) [973]

18472 Lester, Julius. *From Slave Ship to Freedom Road* (5–10). Illus. 1998, Dial $17.99 (978-0-8037-1893-7). This book combines art, history, and commentary to produce a graphically gripping history of slavery. (Rev: BL 2/15/98; HBG 9/98; SLJ 2/98*) [759.13]

18473 Lourie, Peter. *Mississippi River* (3–5). Illus. 2000, Boyds Mills $17.95 (978-1-56397-756-5). 48pp. While describing his trip on the Mississippi from Minnesota to Louisiana, the author gives facts about the waterway and the life that surrounds it. (Rev: BCCB 10/00; BL 10/1/00; HBG 3/01; SLJ 10/00) [976.81]

18474 Lourie, Peter. *On the Trail of Lewis and Clark: A Journey Up the Missouri River* (3–5). Illus. 2002, Boyds Mills $19.95 (978-1-56397-936-1). 48pp. Lourie connects his own trip up the Missouri River to the more famous journey that Lewis and Clark took years before. (Rev: BL 4/1/02; HBG 10/02; SLJ 6/02) [917.804]

18475 Lourie, Peter. *Rio Grande: From the Rocky Mountains to the Gulf of Mexico* (4–6). Illus. 1999, Boyds Mills $17.95 (978-1-56397-706-0). 46pp. In dramatic prose and stunning photos, the course of the Rio Grande and its place in American history are covered. (Rev: BCCB 4/99; BL 2/15/99; HBG 10/99; SLJ 6/99) [917.3]

18476 McCormick, Anita Louise. *The Industrial Revolution in American History* (5–8). Illus. Series: In American History. 1998, Enslow LB $26.60 (978-0-89490-985-6). A description of the causes of the Industrial Revolution and the changes that it brought to the United States up to 1946. (Rev: BL 9/1/98) [338.0973]

18477 Masoff, Joy. *We Are All Americans: Understanding Diversity* (4–7). 2006, Five Ponds $26.50 (978-0-9727156-2-1). 63pp. This celebration of immigration to America — full of photographs, maps, and diagrams — looks at the reasons for migration, the problems involved, and the contributions made by immigrants in all aspects of American life, including music, sports, games, celebrations, literature, food, and art. (Rev: SLJ 1/07) [304.8]

18478 Miller, Marilyn. *Words That Built a Nation: A Young Person's Collection of Historic American Documents* (4–8). Illus. 1999, Scholastic paper $18.95 (978-0-590-29881-0). 176pp. A collection of 37 documents important in American history — from the Mayflower Compact and the Declaration of Independence to Hillary Rodham Clinton's address to the United Nations Conference on Women and Malcolm X's "The Ballot or the Bullet" speech. (Rev: BL 10/15/99; HBG 3/00; SLJ 2/00) [973]

18479 Miller, Page Putnam. *Landmarks of American Women's History* (5–8). 2004, Oxford Univ. LB $32.95 (978-0-19-514501-4). 143pp. Landmarks — all on the National Register of Historic Places — highlighted for their importance in women's history include Taos Pueblo, New Mexico, chosen for the strong Native American women who lived there; the Wesleyan Chapel at Seneca Falls, where the first women's rights conference was held; and the Boardinghouse at Boott Cotton Mill in Lowell, Massachusetts, home to many young women who worked in the textile industry. (Rev: SLJ 9/04) [973]

18480 Nelson, Robin. *School* (3–6). Series: First Step Nonfiction. 2003, Lerner LB $18.60 (978-0-8225-4640-5). 24pp. Ideal for new readers, this book looks at how early schools differed from those we know today. Also in this series, use *Toys and*

Games (2003). (Rev: BL 11/15/03; HBG 4/04; SLJ 12/03)

18481 Neubecker, Robert. *Wow! America!* (PS–K). Illus. 2006, Hyperion $16.99 (978-0-7868-3816-5). 48pp. In this rollicking sequel to *Wow! City!* (2004), Izzy and Jo visit some of America's most famous sights. (Rev: BL 4/15/06; SLJ 6/06) [973]

18482 Newman, Shirlee P. *Slavery in the United States* (4–7). Series: Watts Library: History of Slavery. 2000, Watts LB $25.50 (978-0-531-11695-1). 64pp. This account covers the shameful American record concerning slavery with coverage from the African slave trade through plantation life, the Underground Railroad, and abolitionists to the Civil War and emancipation. (Rev: BL 3/1/01) [973]

18483 Pearl, Norman. *The Bald Eagle* (K–4). Illus. by Matthew Skeens. Series: American Symbols. 2006, Picture Window LB $23.93 (978-1-4048-2642-7). 24pp. Children will enjoy learning about how the bald eagle was selected to serve as a symbol of the United States. Contemporary-looking illustrations accompany simple text in this introduction to one of America's best-loved symbols. (Rev: SLJ 5/07)

18484 Pollard, Michael. *The Mississippi* (5–8). Illus. Series: Great Rivers. 1997, Benchmark LB $22.79 (978-0-7614-0502-3). 45pp. A history of this great river and its influence on American history, with photographs, maps, and diagrams. (Rev: HBG 3/98; SLJ 3/98) [917.7]

18485 Prevost, John. *Mississippi River* (3–4). Series: Rivers and Lakes. 2002, ABDO LB $21.35 (978-1-57765-102-4). 24pp. A solid introduction to the Mississippi, its tributaries, flora and fauna, and the ways in which it has influenced human development in the area throughout history. (Rev: HBG 10/02; SLJ 7/02) [976.81]

18486 Rawlins, Carol B. *The Colorado River* (4–8). Series: Watts Library. 1999, Watts LB $25.50 (978-0-531-11738-5). 64pp. With full-color photographs and maps that complement the text, this book traces the famous Rocky Mountain waterway from north-central Colorado through the Southwest into the Gulf of California and covers its history and uses. (Rev: BL 1/1–15/00; SLJ 2/00) [973]

18487 Reimers, David M. *A Land of Immigrants* (5–8). Series: Immigrant Experience. 1995, Chelsea LB $21.95 (978-0-7910-3361-6). An overview of immigration to the United States and Canada and how the influx influenced the culture. (Rev: BL 10/15/95; SLJ 12/95) [304.8]

18488 Roop, Peter, and Connie Roop. *A Farm Album* (2–3). Series: Long Ago and Today. 1998, Heinemann LB $19.92 (978-1-57572-601-4). 24pp. Pairing old illustrations with modern photographs, this work compares life on a farm today with that of 100 years ago. (Rev: BL 12/15/98) [973]

18489 Roop, Peter, and Connie Roop. *A Home Album* (2–3). Series: Long Ago and Today. 1998, Heinemann LB $19.92 (978-1-57572-602-1). 24pp. American home life today and 100 years ago are compared through a simple text and contrasting photographs. (Rev: BL 12/15/98) [973]

18490 Rubel, David. *Scholastic Atlas of the United States* (3–5). 2000, Scholastic $19.95 (978-0-590-72562-0). 144pp. Arranged by region and then by state, this atlas also contains a text that gives good background on each state plus maps that indicate principal towns, highways, natural resources, national parks, etc. (Rev: HBG 3/01; SLJ 2/01) [917.3]

18491 Sabuda, Robert. *America the Beautiful* (2–4). Illus. by author. 2004, Simon & Schuster $26.95 (978-0-689-84744-8). 16pp. Elaborate pop-up spreads salute natural and man-made landmarks, including Mount Rushmore, New York City, Mesa Verde, and the Golden Gate Bridge, and the verses of the well-known song. (Rev: BL 11/15/04; SLJ 11/04) [811]

18492 Sandak, Cass R. *The United States* (4–8). Illus. Series: Modern Industrial World. 1996, Raintree LB $24.26 (978-0-8172-4556-6). An examination of the economic and industrial situation in the United States, with additional information on education, living standards, and related subjects. (Rev: BL 2/15/97; SLJ 8/97) [973]

18493 Siebert, Diane. *Mississippi* (3–5). Illus. 2001, HarperCollins LB $17.89 (978-0-688-16446-1). 40pp. This volume uses free-verse to describe the history associated with the Mississippi River as well as its course from its beginnings in the north to its mouth on the Gulf of Mexico. (Rev: BL 3/15/01; HBG 10/01) [976.2]

18494 Sills, Leslie. *From Rags to Riches: A History of Girls' Clothing in America* (4–7). Illus. 2005, Holiday $16.95 (978-0-8234-1708-7). 48pp. Changes in clothing over the centuries are linked to the social mores of the time in this appealing volume. (Rev: BL 5/1/05; SLJ 8/05) [391]

18495 Stanley, George E. *The New Republic (1763–1815)* (5–8). Illus. Series: A Primary Source History of the United States. 2005, World Almanac LB $31.00 (978-0-8368-5825-9). 48pp. A simple narrative links well-chosen primary sources documenting the key events of the revolutionary period. (Rev: BL 4/1/05; SLJ 7/05)

18496 Stienecker, David L. *States* (2–5). Illus. Series: Discovering Geography. 1997, Marshall Cavendish LB $22.79 (978-0-7614-0541-2). 32pp. Using a question-and-answer approach, this book teaches youngsters how to read maps that show topics such as terrain, weather, landmarks, population, capitals and products. (Rev: BL 2/1/98; HBG 3/98) [917.3]

18497 Talbott, Hudson. *United Tweets of America* (3–5). Illus. by author. 2008, Putnam $17.99 (978-0-399-24520-6). 64pp. An impish look at the 50 states, introduced through a competition between the state birds. (Rev: BL 4/1/08; SLJ 5/08) [973]

18498 Telford, Carole, and Rod Theodorou. *Down a River* (2–6). Illus. by Stephen Lings and Jane Pickering. Series: Amazing Journeys. 1997, Heinemann LB $13.95 (978-1-57572-153-8). 32pp. This journey of the entire length of the Mississippi and Missouri rivers supplies maps, illustrations and a description of the plants and animals that live in this ecosystem. (Rev: SLJ 5/98) [917.3]

18499 Thro, Ellen, and Andrew K. Frank. *Growing and Dividing* (5–8). Series: The Making of America. 2001, Raintree LB $28.54 (978-0-8172-5704-0). 96pp. The story of the development of the eastern United States from the early days of the Republic through the clashes that led to the Civil War. (Rev: BL 4/15/01; HBG 10/01) [973.5]

18500 Travis, George. *State Facts* (3–5). Series: The Rourke Guide to State Symbols. 1999, Rourke LB $29.93 (978-1-57103-297-3). 48pp. Basic information about each state is given including nicknames, size, number of counties, and bordering states, plus colorful topographical maps. (Rev: SLJ 2/00) [973]

18501 *United States in Pictures* (5–8). Illus. Series: Visual Geography. 1995, Lerner LB $25.55 (978-0-8225-1896-9). 64pp. An attractive basic introduction to the geography, history, and people of the United States. (Rev: BL 8/95) [973]

18502 Van Zandt, Eleanor. *A History of the United States Through Art* (5–8). Illus. Series: History Through Art. 1996, Thomson Learning LB $5.00 (978-1-56847-443-4). 48pp. American history is covered in 21 double-page spreads that feature text and famous artworks. (Rev: BL 3/1/96; SLJ 2/96) [973]

18503 Wacker, Grant. *Religion in Nineteenth Century America* (5–8). Series: Religion in American Life. 2000, Oxford $32.95 (978-0-19-511021-0). 183pp. This is the story of how religion in America affected such 19th-century events as the westward movement, the Civil War, and immigration, with additional coverage of the careers of such people as Sojourner Truth and Mary Baker Eddy. (Rev: BL 6/1–15/00; HBG 10/00; SLJ 8/00) [973]

18504 Wilbur, Keith C. *Revolutionary Medicine, 1700–1800* (4–8). Illus. Series: Illustrated Living History. 1996, Chelsea $21.95 (978-0-7910-4532-9). In a large-book format, this account gives a great deal of information — some gruesome, some funny — about medicine in 18th-century America. (Rev: BL 6/1–15/97; SLJ 7/97) [973.3]

18505 Woods, Michael, and Mary B. Woods. *Seven Natural Wonders of North America* (5–8). Illus. 2009, Twenty-First Century LB $33.26 (978-0-8225-9069-9). 80pp. Dinosaur Provincial Park, Pacific Rim National Park, the redwood forests, Niagara Falls, the Grand Canyon, Yellowstone National Park, and the Paricutín Volcano are the seven wonders featured in this attractive volume. (Rev: BL 4/1/09; SLJ 5/09) [917]

18506 Yeh, Phil. *Dinosaurs Across America* (2–4). Illus. by author. 2007, NBM $12.95 (978-1-56163-509-2). 32pp. Patrick Rabbit gets a lesson on the 50 states from some humorous dinosaurs using an appealing graphic format. (Rev: BL 10/15/07; LMC 1/08; SLJ 3/08) [741.5]

18507 Yorinks, Adrienne. *Quilt of States: Piecing Together America* (5–8). Illus. 2005, National Geographic LB $29.90 (978-0-7922-7286-1). 128pp. With contributions from librarians from all 50 states, this beautifully illustrated volume offers a brief story of each state's accession to the Union, along with other pertinent facts and figures. (Rev: BL 10/1/05; SLJ 12/05) [973]

Historical Periods

NATIVE AMERICANS

18508 Abbink, Emily. *Colors of the Navajo* (2–4). Illus. by Janice L. Porter. Series: Colors of the World. 1998, Carolrhoda LB $19.93 (978-1-57505-207-6); paper $5.95 (978-1-57505-269-4). 24pp. Ten different colors are used to tie together this book about Navajo life, culture, arts, and traditions. (Rev: SLJ 12/98) [973]

18509 Adams, McCrea. *Tipi* (3–5). Illus. by Kimberly L. Dawson Kurnizki. Series: Native American Homes. 2001, Rourke LB $28.50 (978-1-55916-275-3). 32pp. This volume discusses Native American tipis and how, why, where, and by whom they were built. (Rev: SLJ 3/01) [973]

18510 Adare, Sierra. *Mohawk* (4–8). Illus. 2003, Gareth Stevens LB $26.00 (978-0-8368-3665-3). 32pp. An introduction to the history, culture, and current status of the Mohawk people, with photographs, maps, and interesting sidebar features that will be useful for reports. Also use *Apache* and *Nez Perce* (both 2003). (Rev: HBG 10/03; SLJ 9/03) [974.7004]

18511 Aloian, Molly, and Bobbie Kalman. *Nations of the Southeast* (3–5). Illus. Series: Native Nations of North America. 2006, Crabtree LB $26.60 (978-0-7787-0385-3); paper $8.95 (978-0-7787-0477-5). 32pp. An interesting overview of the Native American tribes of the American Southeast, examining their culture, language, customs, and contemporary status. (Rev: SLJ 11/06) [975.004]

18512 Alter, Judy. *Native Americans* (3–5). Series: Spirit of America: Our Cultural Heritage. 2002, Child's World LB $27.07 (978-1-56766-152-1). 32pp. This account gives an overview of the history of Native Americans, their problems, and the impact of their cultures on present-day American society. (Rev: BL 10/15/02) [973]

18513 Anderson, Dale. *The Anasazi Culture at Mesa Verde* (5–8). Series: Landmark Events in American History. 2003, World Almanac LB $31.00 (978-0-8368-5371-1). 48pp. The story of the native people from the region around the Four Corners and of their many cultural accomplishment including basketry, pottery, and urban architecture. (Rev: BL 10/15/03) [973]

18514 Andryszewski, Tricia. *The Seminoles: People of the Southeast* (3–6). Illus. Series: Native Americans. 1995, Millbrook LB $21.90 (978-1-56294-530-5). 64pp. As well as giving a history of the Seminoles, this account tells about their culture and traditions and includes a recipe, a legend, and instructions for the Seminole pole-ball game. (Rev: SLJ 1/96) [973]

18515 Baylor, Byrd. *The Desert Is Theirs* (2–4). Illus. by Peter Parnall. 1987, Macmillan $16.00 (978-0-684-14266-1); paper $5.95 (978-0-689-71105-3). 32pp. Through colorful, strong pictures and a lyric text, the life of the Papago Indians and their reverence for the desert are revealed.

18516 Bealer, Alex W. *Only the Names Remain: The Cherokees and the Trail of Tears* (4–6). Illus. by William Sauts Bock. 1996, Little, Brown paper $5.95 (978-0-316-08519-9). A history of the Cherokees, with emphasis on their tragic exile west of the Mississippi River in 1839.

18517 Beres, Cynthia Breslin. *Longhouse* (3–5). Illus. by Kimberly L. Dawson Kurnizki. 2001, Rourke LB $28.50 (978-1-55916-247-0). 32pp. This book describes the building and uses of the Native American longhouses and the part they played in the culture. (Rev: SLJ 3/01) [973]

18518 Bial, Raymond. *The Apache* (5–8). Series: Lifeways. 2000, Benchmark LB $34.21 (978-0-7614-0939-7). 128pp. Presents the dramatic, often tragic history of the Apache Indians, with biographies of leaders such as Geronimo and a description of the social and cultural life of these nomadic people. (Rev: BL 11/15/00; HBG 3/01; SLJ 3/01) [973]

18519 Bial, Raymond. *The Cheyenne* (5–8). Series: Lifeways. 2000, Benchmark LB $34.21 (978-0-7614-0938-0). 128pp. Part of the Great Plains Indian group, the Cheyenne's daily life, religious beliefs, social system, and history are introduced in this book. (Rev: BL 11/15/00; HBG 3/01; SLJ 3/01) [973]

18520 Bial, Raymond. *The Comanche* (4–8). Series: Lifeways. 1999, Benchmark LB $34.21 (978-0-7614-0864-2). 127pp. This impressive volume gives an accurate picture of the social and political life of the Comanche from their early history to the present day. (Rev: BL 3/15/00; HBG 10/00; SLJ 3/00) [973]

18521 Bial, Raymond. *The Delaware* (5–9). Series: Lifeways. 2005, Benchmark LB $23.95 (978-0-7614-1904-4). 127pp. The history, culture, traditions, and present-day life of the Native American tribe, with photographs and other visuals. (Rev: SLJ 6/06) [974.004]

18522 Bial, Raymond. *The Haida* (5–8). Series: Lifeways. 2000, Benchmark LB $34.21 (978-0-7614-0937-3). 128pp. This book describes these Native Americans of the Northwest and introduces their artistic and carving skills, their social system, beliefs, history, and daily life. (Rev: BL 11/15/00; HBG 3/01; SLJ 3/01) [973]

18523 Bial, Raymond. *The Huron* (5–8). Series: Lifeways. 2000, Benchmark LB $34.21 (978-0-7614-0940-3). 128pp. Color pictures and clear text describe this Indian group's past and present and give details of their daily life, religion, and rituals. (Rev: BL 11/15/00; HBG 3/01; SLJ 3/01) [973]

18524 Bial, Raymond. *Longhouses* (2–5). Series: American Community. 2004, Children's Pr. LB $29.00 (978-0-516-23707-7). 48pp. A look at life in the longhouses of the Iroquois living in the Great Lakes region. (Rev: SLJ 1/05) [973]

18525 Bial, Raymond. *The Mandan* (5–9). Series: Lifeways. 2002, Benchmark LB $34.21 (978-0-7614-1415-5). 126pp. Two traditional stories, a recipe, and a language guide accompany information on the history, culture, beliefs, and key figures of the Mandan people. (Rev: HBG 3/03; LMC 8/03; SLJ 6/03) [978.004]

18526 Bial, Raymond. *The Menominee* (5–9). Series: Lifeways. 2005, Benchmark LB $23.95 (978-0-7614-1903-7). 127pp. The history, culture, traditions and present-day life of the Native American tribe, with photographs and other visuals. (Rev: SLJ 6/06) [977.4004]

18527 Bial, Raymond. *The Nez Perce* (5–8). Series: Lifeways. 2001, Marshall Cavendish LB $34.21 (978-0-7614-1210-6). This attractively illustrated account gives basic material on the historical and social aspects of this Native American tribe, including their food, clothing, and culture. (Rev: BL 1/1–15/02; HBG 3/02; SLJ 4/02) [973]

18528 Bial, Raymond. *The Ojibwe* (5–8). Illus. Series: Lifeways. 1999, Marshall Cavendish LB $34.21 (978-0-7614-0863-5). 127pp. Topics covered in this introduction to the Ojibwe nation include history, traditions, beliefs, and the nation today. (Rev: BL 3/1/00; HBG 10/00; SLJ 3/00) [977]

18529 Bial, Raymond. *The Powhatan* (5–8). Series: Lifeways. 2001, Marshall Cavendish LB $34.21 (978-0-7614-1209-0). The story of the Powhatan tribe of Virginia, whose members included Pocahontas, with material on their history and various aspects of their culture. (Rev: BL 1/1–15/02; HBG 3/02) [973]

18530 Bial, Raymond. *The Pueblo* (5–8). Illus. Series: Lifeways. 1999, Marshall Cavendish LB $34.21 (978-0-7614-0861-1). 127pp. Good photographs and a lucid text combine to produce a fine introduction to the Pueblo Indians, their history, culture, traditions, present status, and notable members of the nation. (Rev: BL 3/1/00; HBG 10/00; SLJ 3/00) [978.9]

18531 Bial, Raymond. *The Seminole* (4–8). Series: Lifeways. 1999, Benchmark LB $34.21 (978-0-7614-0862-8). 127pp. Topics covered in this account of the Seminole Indians include history, daily life, religious beliefs, sacred rituals, and attitudes toward themselves. (Rev: BL 3/15/00; HBG 10/00; SLJ 3/00) [973]

18532 Bial, Raymond. *The Shoshone* (5–8). Series: Lifeways. 2001, Marshall Cavendish LB $34.21 (978-0-7614-1211-3). The story of the Native American tribe of buffalo hunters who lived in the Northwest, with material on their history, culture, language, food, and clothing. (Rev: BL 1/1–15/02; HBG 3/02) [973]

18533 Birchfield, D. L. *The Trail of Tears* (4–7). Series: Landmark Events in American History. 2003, World Almanac LB $31.00 (978-0-8368-5381-0). 48pp. A brief account of the tragic forced removal of Native American people from their lands by the U.S. government in the mid-19th century. (Rev: SLJ 6/04) [973.04]

18534 Braine, Susan. *Drumbeat . . . Heartbeat: A Celebration of the Powwow* (4–6). Photos by author. Series: We Are Still Here: Native Americans Today. 1995, Lerner LB $21.27 (978-0-8225-2656-8); paper $6.95 (978-0-8225-9711-7). 48pp. An

introduction to powwows that explains their history, where they are held, and what they mean to Native Americans today. (Rev: SLJ 9/95) [973]

18535 Brody, J. J. *A Day with a Mimbres* (4–6). Illus. by Giorgio Bacchin. Series: A Day With. 1999, Runestone LB $22.60 (978-0-8225-1917-1). 48pp. This book explores the history and daily life of this ancient Native American group who lived in the Southwest. (Rev: HBG 10/99; SLJ 10/99) [973]

18536 Broida, Marian. *Projects About American Indians of the Southwest* (3–5). Illus. Series: Hands-on History. 2003, Marshall Cavendish LB $27.07 (978-0-7614-1602-9). 48pp. The 10 simple projects outlined in this book introduce information about the Navajo, Hopi, Zuni, and Pueblo Indians. (Rev: BL 4/1/04; HBG 4/04; SLJ 4/04) [979.004]

18537 Bruchac, Joseph. *Navajo Long Walk: The Tragic Story of a Proud People's Forced March from Their Homeland* (4–8). Illus. by Shonto Begay. 2002, National Geographic $18.95 (978-0-7922-7058-4). 34pp. Using revealing words and pictures, this large picture book for older readers re-creates the shameful story of the deadly marches of the Navajo in the 1860s. (Rev: BL 5/1/02; HBG 10/02; SLJ 7/02) [979.1]

18538 Bruchac, Joseph. *The Trail of Tears* (2–4). Illus. by Diana Magnuson. Series: Step into Reading. 1999, Random LB $11.99 (978-0-679-99052-9); paper $3.99 (978-0-679-89052-2). 48pp. An easy reader that movingly tells the story of the Cherokees and the bitter 1,200-mile forced journey from Georgia to Oklahoma between 1838 and 1839. (Rev: BL 12/1/99) [973]

18539 Burgan, Michael. *The Trail of Tears* (3–5). Series: We the People. 2001, Compass Point LB $26.60 (978-0-7565-0101-3). 48pp. A well-illustrated, concise introduction to the Cherokee people and the events leading up to their removal from their lands in 1838. (Rev: SLJ 6/01) [975]

18540 Carew-Miller, Anna. *Native American Cooking* (4–7). Illus. Series: Native American Life. 2002, Mason Crest LB $19.95 (978-1-59084-131-0). 64pp. The role of the environment in Native American food choices is emphasized in this overview that is organized by region. Also use *Native American Tools and Weapons* and *What the Native Americans Wore* (both 2002). (Rev: SLJ 2/03) [641.5979]

18541 Claro, Nicole. *The Cherokee Indians* (3–5). Illus. Series: Indians of North America. 1991, Chelsea LB $25.00 (978-0-7910-1652-7). 80pp. The concentration is on the history of the Cherokee since their contact with Europeans. (Rev: BL 10/15/91) [973]

18542 Collins, David R., and Kris Bergren. *Ishi: The Last of His People* (5–8). Illus. 2000, Morgan Reynolds LB $23.95 (978-1-883846-54-1). 96pp. This is the story of Ishi, the ill-clad and half-starved man who emerged from the wilderness in California in 1911 and who was believed to be a survivor of the lost Yahi tribe. (Rev: BL 12/1/00; HBG 10/00) [979.4004]

18543 Cooper, Michael L. *Indian School: Teaching the White Man's Way* (5–10). Illus. 1999, Clarion

$18.00 (978-0-395-92084-8). 103pp. A moving photoessay about Native American children and how they were removed from their homes and uprooted from their culture to attend Indian boarding schools in an effort to "civilize" them. (Rev: BL 12/1/99; HBG 3/00; SLJ 2/00; VOYA 4/00) [370]

18544 Cory, Steven. *Pueblo Indian* (5–8). Illus. Series: American Pastfinder. 1996, Lerner LB $21.27 (978-0-8225-2976-7). Color illustrations and maps accompany this account of the Pueblo Indians and the incredible cities they built. (Rev: BL 7/96) [973]

18545 Crewe, Sabrina, and Dale Anderson. *The Anasazi Culture at Mesa Verde* (3–5). Series: Events That Shaped America. 2003, Gareth Stevens LB $26.00 (978-0-8368-3390-4). 32pp. Explores what we know about the ancient Anasazi culture of the American Southwest and why they chose to settle in Mesa Verde. (Rev: HBG 10/03; SLJ 10/03) [978.8]

18546 DeAngelis, Therese. *The Cherokee: Native Basket Weavers* (3–5). Illus. Series: America's First Peoples. 2003, Capstone LB $23.93 (978-0-7368-1535-2). 32pp. This fascinating overview of the Cherokee provides a basic introduction to the history and culture of the Native American tribe with particular focus on basket weaving skills. (Rev: SLJ 10/03)

18547 DeAngelis, Therese. *The Ojibwa: Wild Rice Gatherers* (3–5). Illus. Series: America's First Peoples. 2003, Capstone LB $23.93 (978-0-7368-1537-6). 32pp. This title from America's First Families series introduces readers to the history and culture of the Ojibwa, an Algonquian-speaking tribe that traditionally lived in the north central United States and nearby Canada. (Rev: HBG 10/03; SLJ 10/03)

18548 Delgado, James P. *Native American Shipwrecks* (5–7). Illus. Series: Watts Library: Shipwrecks. 2000, Watts LB $25.50 (978-0-531-20379-8). 64pp. This book covers the boats that Native Americans made, their uses and voyages, the culture of these peoples, and how underwater archaeologists have explored their wrecks. (Rev: BL 10/15/00) [623.8]

18549 Dennis, Yvonne Wakim, and Arlene Hirschfelder. *Children of Native America Today* (3–6). Illus. 2003, Charlesbridge $19.95 (978-1-57091-499-7). 64pp. Photos show contemporary Native American young people wearing traditional as well as modern clothes, with maps, reservation locations, and a resource list. (Rev: BL 3/1/03; HBG 10/03; SLJ 10/03) [306]

18550 Denny, Sidney G., and Ernest L. Schusky. *The Ancient Splendor of Prehistoric Cahokia* (4–8). 1997, Ozark paper $3.95 (978-1-56763-272-9). Using the findings at the Cahokia Mounds in southern Illinois as a beginning, the author re-creates the life and culture of these prehistoric American Indians. (Rev: BL 5/1/97) [977.3]

18551 Englar, Mary. *The Cherokee and Their History* (3–5). Series: We the People. 2005, Compass Point LB $26.60 (978-0-7565-1273-6). 48pp. Suitable for report writers, this history starts with an account of the Trail of Tears and then covers traditions, achievements, life today, and so forth. Also use *The Sioux and Their History* (2006). (Rev: SLJ 9/06) [973]

18552 Englar, Mary. *The Great Plains Indians: Daily Life in the 1700s* (2–4). Series: Native American Life. 2005, Capstone LB $22.60 (978-0-7368-4315-7). 24pp. A brief, attractive introduction to the tribes of the Great Plains, covering their social structure, homes, food, clothing, and traditions. (Rev: SLJ 12/05) [978.004]

18553 Englar, Mary. *The Pueblo: Southwestern Potters* (3–5). Illus. Series: America's First Peoples. 2003, Capstone LB $23.93 (978-0-7368-1538-3). 32pp. This appealing introduction to the Pueblo people of America's Southwest focuses on their traditional pottery. (Rev: HBG 10/03; SLJ 10/03)

18554 Feinstein, Stephen. *California Native Peoples* (4–6). Illus. Series: Heinemann State Studies. 2003, Heinemann LB $27.07 (978-1-4034-0341-4). 48pp. From prehistory to today, this attractively illustrated volume looks at the lives and culture of California's native peoples, with particular focus on "outside influences" that brought upheavals. (Rev: HBG 4/04; SLJ 11/03) [979.4]

18555 Ferrell, Nancy W. *The Battle of the Little Bighorn* (5–9). Series: In American History. 1996, Enslow LB $26.60 (978-0-89490-768-5). A detailed account of the Battle of Little Bighorn from various points of view on both sides, along with a review of the conflicts between the U.S. government and Native Americans, the different cultures of various tribes, key figures such as Crazy Horse and Sitting Bull, and the aftermath of the battle. (Rev: SLJ 12/96) [973.8]

18556 Fischer, Laura. *Life on the Trail of Tears* (2–4). Illus. Series: Picture the Past. 2003, Heinemann LB $22.79 (978-1-4034-3800-3). 32pp. The plight of Cherokee children is highlighted in this attractive introduction to the sad story of forced relocation. (Rev: SLJ 6/04) [973.04]

18557 Fowler, Verna. *The Menominee* (4–7). Series: Indian Nations. 2000, Raintree LB $25.69 (978-0-8172-5458-2). 48pp. Opening with a folk tale, this book describes the Menominee Indians, their life and culture, and how they were overrun in the 19th century and pushed onto a reservation in northern Wisconsin. (Rev: BL 3/15/01; HBG 10/01) [973]

18558 Freedman, Russell. *Buffalo Hunt* (4–6). Illus. 1988, Holiday House LB $21.95 (978-0-8234-0702-6). 52pp. How the Plains Indians worshiped and depended on the buffalo. (Rev: BCCB 10/88; BL 10/1/88; SLJ 10/88)

18559 Fulkerston, Chuck. *The Shawnee* (4–6). Illus. by Katherine Ace. Series: Native American People. 1992, Rourke LB $31.36 (978-0-86625-392-5). 32pp. This account emphasizes the history of the Shawnee and presents material on their everyday life and religion. (Rev: BL 12/15/92) [973]

18560 Gallimard Jeunesse, et al. *Native Americans* (PS–2). Series: First Discovery. 1998, Scholastic $12.95 (978-0-590-38153-6). 24pp. Using sturdy plastic pages, overlays, and colorful illustrations, this introduction to Native Americans emphasizes the part they have played in U.S. history. (Rev: BL 9/15/98; HBG 10/98) [973]

18561 Gibson, Karen Bush. *The Great Basin Indians: Daily Life in the 1700s* (2–4). Series: Native American Life. 2005, Capstone LB $22.60 (978-0-7368-4318-8). 24pp. A brief, attractive introduction to the tribes of the Great Basin region, covering their social structure, homes, food, clothing, and traditions. (Rev: SLJ 12/05) [979.004]

18562 Gold, Susan Dudley. *Indian Treaties* (5–8). Illus. Series: Pacts and Treaties. 1997, Twenty-First Century LB $24.90 (978-0-8050-4813-1). A history of the successive treaties under which the Native Americans gradually lost their homes and livelihood. (Rev: BL 5/15/97; SLJ 6/97) [323.1]

18563 Gorsline, Marie, and Douglas Gorsline. *North American Indians* (5–8). Illus. by Douglas Gorsline. 1978, Random paper $3.25 (978-0-394-83702-4). Major tribes are identified and briefly described. [973]

18564 Gray-Kanatiiosh, Barbara A. *Hopi* (2–4). Illus. by Charles Chimerica. Series: Native Americans. 2002, ABDO LB $22.78 (978-1-57765-598-5). 32pp. An attractive and accessible introduction to the Hopi people that covers homeland, culture, family life, mythology, crafts, war, early contact with the Europeans, and contemporary lifestyle. Also use *Inuit* (2002). (Rev: HBG 10/02; SLJ 8/02) [973]

18565 Griffin, Lana T. *The Navajo* (4–7). Illus. Series: Indian Nations. 1999, Raintree LB $25.69 (978-0-8172-5463-6). 48pp. This book describes the history of the Navajo, their everyday life, customs, and tribal government, and includes two Navajo creation stories. (Rev: BL 2/15/00; HBG 10/00; SLJ 4/00) [979.1]

18566 Gunderson, Mary. *American Indian Cooking Before 1500* (4–7). Series: Exploring History Through Simple Recipes. 2000, Capstone LB $23.93 (978-0-7368-0605-3). 32pp. This book describes the everyday life of Native Americans before Europeans arrived and gives a few simple recipes. (Rev: BL 3/1/01; HBG 10/01; SLJ 7/01) [973]

18567 Haderer, Kurt. *Journey to Native Americans* (2–5). Illus. 1999, Prestel $14.95 (3-7913-2083-1). 30pp. This is a report on Native Americans as studied by German prince Maximilian of Wied and Swiss painter Karl Bodmer in the 1830s. (Rev: BL 11/1/99; SLJ 1/00) [978]

18568 Hahn, Elizabeth. *The Creek* (4–6). Illus. by Katherine Ace. Series: Native American People. 1992, Rourke LB $27.93 (978-0-86625-393-2). 32pp. History is emphasized in this book that features the point of view of the Native Americans. (Rev: BL 12/15/92) [976]

18569 Hahn, Elizabeth. *The Pawnee* (4–6). Illus. by Katherine Ace. Series: Native American People. 1992, Rourke LB $27.93 (978-0-86625-391-8). 32pp. Everyday life of the Pawnee, their religion, history, and present-day status are covered in this illustrated account. (Rev: BL 12/15/92) [973]

18570 Haluska, Vicki. *The Arapaho Indians* (3–5). Illus. Series: Junior Library of American Indians. 1993, Chelsea LB $20.75 (978-0-7910-1657-2). 80pp. Coverage is given on both the past and the present of this Indian group, with special material on their arts and crafts. (Rev: BL 5/15/93) [973]

18571 Hicks, Terry Allan. *The Chumash* (1–4). Series: First Americans. 2007, Marshall Cavendish LB $20.95 (978-0-7614-2678-3). 48pp. An introduction to these Native Americans from the California region, covering their history, culture, beliefs, current status, and future; with an activity and a recipe. (Rev: SLJ 4/08) [979.4004]

18572 Holm, Tom. *Code Talkers and Warriors: Native Americans and World War II* (5–9). Illus. Series: Landmark Events in Native American History. 2007, Chelsea House LB $35.00 (978-0-7910-9340-5). 168pp. How Native Americans have aided their country in wars (many more than WWII are discussed), with an emphasis on Navajo and Comanche code talk. (Rev: BL 12/15/07) [940.54]

18573 Hoyt-Goldsmith, Diane. *Apache Rodeo* (3–5). Photos by Lawrence Migdale. 1995, Holiday House LB $15.95 (978-0-8234-1164-1). 32pp. The current lifestyles and traditions of the Apache people are revealed through the eyes of young Felicita. (Rev: BCCB 2/95; BL 2/1/95; SLJ 6/95) [973]

18574 Hoyt-Goldsmith, Diane. *Buffalo Days* (3–7). Illus. by Lawrence Migdale. 1997, Holiday House LB $17.95 (978-0-8234-1327-0). 32pp. By focusing on 10-year-old Clarence Three Irons, Jr., the reader is introduced to the Crow Indians of the present and their heritage, which includes celebrating Buffalo Days. (Rev: BL 11/1/97*; HBG 3/98; SLJ 12/97*) [973]

18575 Hoyt-Goldsmith, Diane. *Potlatch: A Tsimshian Celebration* (4–8). 1997, Holiday $16.95 (978-0-8234-1290-7). A 13-year-old boy explains the meaning of potlatch for the Tsimshian tribe in Alaska and describes the many rituals and activities it involves. (Rev: BL 5/1/97; SLJ 6/97) [394.2]

18576 Hoyt-Goldsmith, Diane. *Pueblo Storyteller* (3–5). Illus. by Lawrence Migdale. 1991, Holiday House LB $17.95 (978-0-8234-0864-1). 32pp. A present-day account of how a Pueblo family in New Mexico lives. (Rev: BCCB 4/91; BL 3/5/91; SLJ 5/91) [978.9]

18577 Hunter, Sally M. *Four Seasons of Corn: A Winnebago Tradition* (3–6). Illus. 1997, Lerner LB $21.27 (978-0-8225-2658-2); paper $6.95 (978-0-8225-9741-4). 40pp. The daily life of a boy who assimilates his Anglo-American heritage, along with the traditional activities of his Winnebago people. (Rev: BL 2/1/97; SLJ 3/97) [394.1]

18578 Isaacs, Sally Senzell. *Life in a Hopi Village* (1–3). Series: Picture the Past. 2000, Heinemann $21.36 (978-1-57572-314-3). A well-organized, visually attractive account that describes daily life in a Hopi village and covers such topics as food, clothing, shelter, and care of children. (Rev: HBG 3/01; SLJ 11/00) [973]

18579 Jemison, Mary. *The Diary of Mary Jemison: Captured by the Indians* (3–6). Ed. by Connie Roop and Peter Roop. Illus. Series: My Own Words. 2000, Marshall Cavendish LB $27.07 (978-0-7614-1010-2). 64pp. Based on the account published in 1824, this short, nicely illustrated book tells, in a first-person narrative, how Mary Jemison was captured by Indians at age 12 and describes her life with these Native Americans. (Rev: BL 2/15/01; HBG 3/01; SLJ 3/01) [974.7]

18580 Kalman, Bobbie. *Celebrating the Powwow* (2–4). Illus. Series: Crabapples. 1997, Crabtree paper $5.95 (978-0-86505-740-1). 32pp. Using a number of quality photos, this account describes powwows and their various components. (Rev: SLJ 1/98) [973]

18581 Kavasch, E. Barrie. *The Seminoles* (4–7). Illus. Series: Indian Nations. 1999, Raintree LB $25.69 (978-0-8172-5464-3). 48pp. This account gives a history of the Seminole Indians, with material on their society, customs, festivals, government, present-day conditions, and one of their creation myths. (Rev: BL 2/15/00; HBG 10/00; SLJ 4/00) [975.9]

18582 Keegan, Marcia. *Pueblo Girls: Growing Up in Two Worlds* (3–6). Photos by author. 1999, Clear Light $14.95 (978-1-57416-020-8). A brief look at how two girls of the San Ildefonso Pueblo in New Mexico are growing up and learning about two cultures, religions, and languages, first their Native American one and secondly that of modern America. (Rev: HBG 3/00; SLJ 10/99) [973]

18583 King, Sandra. *Shannon: An Ojibway Dancer* (4–7). Illus. by Catherine Whipple. 1993, Lerner $19.95 (978-0-8225-2752-7); paper $21.27 (978-0-8225-9643-1). 48pp. Thirteen-year-old Shannon Anderson, an Ojibway girl, prepares for the summer powwow and her part in the shawl dance. (Rev: BCCB 1/94; BL 1/15/94; SLJ 2/94) [394]

18584 Kirk, Connie Ann. *The Mohawks of North America* (4–7). Series: First Peoples. 2001, Lerner LB $23.93 (978-0-8225-4853-9). 32pp. This book focuses on the history and cultural practices of the Mohawk people and their present status in America. (Rev: BL 10/15/01; HBG 3/02) [973]

18585 Krehbiel, Randy. *Little Bighorn* (4–8). Series: Battlefields Across America. 1997, Twenty-First Century LB $26.90 (978-0-8050-5236-7). A review of the historical background and events leading up to the Battle of Little Bighorn, followed by a description of the battle itself and the site as it is today. (Rev: SLJ 1/98) [973.8]

18586 Krull, Kathleen. *One Nation, Many Tribes: How Kids Live in Milwaukee's Indian Community* (3–7). Illus. Series: A World of My Own. 1995, Dutton $15.99 (978-0-526-67440-4). 48pp. The story of the daily life and activities of Native American children who are growing up in a community in Milwaukee, Wisconsin. (Rev: BCCB 2/95; BL 2/15/95; SLJ 3/95) [977.5]

18587 La Pierre, Yvette. *Native American Rock Art: Messages from the Past* (4–8). Illus. 1994, Thomasson-Grant $16.95 (978-1-56566-064-9). 48pp. Different types and techniques of Native American rock art are discussed, with additional information

on the cultures that produced this phenomenon. (Rev: BL 12/1/94; SLJ 11/94) [709]

18588 Larson, Timothy. *Anasazi* (4–6). Series: Ancient Civilizations. 2001, Raintree LB $22.83 (978-0-7398-3575-3). 48pp. The history, culture, and daily life of the Anasazi Indians are introduced, with maps and photographs and discussion of archaeological studies and the architecture. (Rev: HBG 3/02; SLJ 6/01) [979]

18589 Lassieur, Allison. *The Apsaalooke (Crow) Nation* (2–5). Series: Native Peoples. 2002, Bridgestone LB $21.26 (978-0-7368-1103-3). 24pp. This account describes the history and lifestyle of this Native American people who lived on the plains around the Yellowstone River. (Rev: BL 6/1–15/02; HBG 3/03) [973]

18590 Lassieur, Allison. *The Arapaho Tribe* (2–5). Series: Native Peoples. 2001, Bridgestone LB $21.26 (978-0-7368-0945-0). 24pp. Covers the history, culture, and lifestyle of this Native American tribe from the Colorado-Wyoming region. (Rev: BL 3/15/02; HBG 3/02) [973]

18591 Lassieur, Allison. *The Blackfeet Nation* (2–5). Series: Native Peoples. 2001, Bridgestone LB $21.26 (978-0-7368-0946-7). 24pp. A brief, colorful introduction to the past and the present of this midwestern Native American nation whose members dyed their moccasins black. (Rev: BL 3/15/02; HBG 3/02) [973]

18592 Lassieur, Allison. *The Choctaw Nation* (2–5). Illus. Series: Native Peoples. 2001, Capstone $21.26 (978-0-7368-0832-3). 24pp. History and contemporary lifestyle are among the topics covered in this introduction to the Choctaw Indians, the first tribe forced to leave its homeland. Also use *The Shoshone People* (2001). (Rev: BL 5/15/01; HBG 10/01; SLJ 8/01) [973]

18593 Lassieur, Allison. *The Creek Nation* (2–5). Series: Native Peoples. 2001, Bridgestone LB $21.26 (978-0-7368-0947-4). 24pp. This short history of the Creek people covers present status and conditions as well as offering informative text and full-color historical photographs and illustrations. (Rev: BL 3/15/02; HBG 3/02) [973]

18594 Lassieur, Allison. *The Hopi* (2–5). Series: Native Peoples. 2002, Bridgestone LB $21.26 (978-0-7368-1102-6). 24pp. A brief account with many photographs that describes the past and present of this tribe of Pueblo Indians and gives details on the richness of the culture they developed. (Rev: BL 6/1–15/02) [973]

18595 Lassieur, Allison. *The Navajo: A Proud People* (3–5). Series: American Indians. 2005, Enslow LB $23.93 (978-0-7660-2453-3). 48pp. The history of the Navajo (properly called Diné, the book notes), with information about their accomplishments and their lives today. (Rev: SLJ 5/06) [979.1004]

18596 Lassieur, Allison. *The Pequot Tribe* (2–5). Series: Native Peoples. 2001, Bridgestone LB $21.26 (978-0-7368-0948-1). 24pp. The story of this Eastern Woodlands group of Native Americans is covered briefly in a simple text with many color illustrations. (Rev: BL 3/15/02; HBG 3/02) [973]

18597 Lavender, David. *Mother Earth, Father Sky: Pueblo Indians of the American Southwest* (5–8). Illus. 1998, Holiday $16.95 (978-0-8234-1365-2). 117pp. After introducing the geographical area of the Southwest known as Four Corners — where Arizona, New Mexico, Colorado, and Utah meet — this book traces the history and culture of the Pueblo Indians who live there. (Rev: BL 9/1/98; HBG 10/99; SLJ 11/98) [978]

18598 Lee, Georgia. *A Day with a Chumash* (4–6). Illus. by Giorgio Bacchin. Series: A Day With. 1999, Runestone LB $22.60 (978-0-8225-1918-8). 48pp. Based on archaeological and anthropological findings, this account traces the history and lifestyles of this ancient people of California. (Rev: HBG 10/99; SLJ 10/99) [973]

18599 Limberland, Dennis, and Mary Em Parrilli. *The Cheyenne* (4–7). Series: Indian Nations. 2000, Raintree LB $25.69 (978-0-8172-5469-8). 48pp. This history of the Cheyenne Indians begins with a folk tale and goes on to describe their lifestyles before and after being sent to reservations in Oklahoma and Montana. (Rev: BL 3/15/01; HBG 10/01) [973]

18600 Littlefield, Holly. *Children of the Indian Boarding Schools* (3–6). Illus. Series: Picture the American Past. 2001, Carolrhoda LB $22.60 (978-1-57505-467-4). 48pp. A brief, informative text is accompanied by moving photographs that dramatically tell the sad story of Native American children taken from their homes and sent to boarding schools to learn European customs. (Rev: BL 5/15/01; HBG 10/01; SLJ 7/01) [371.829]

18601 McCarthy, Cathy. *The Ojibwa* (4–7). Series: Indian Nations. 2000, Raintree LB $25.69 (978-0-8172-5460-5). 48pp. A history of the Ojibwa Indians that includes material on the daily life and traditions of this group that now lives in Minnesota, Wisconsin, and central Canada. (Rev: BL 3/15/01; HBG 10/01) [973]

18602 McDaniel, Melissa. *The Sac and Fox Indians* (3–5). Illus. Series: Junior Library of American Indians. 1995, Chelsea LB $25.00 (978-0-7910-1670-1); paper $25.00 (978-0-7910-2034-0). 80pp. This account tells of these Wisconsin-based Indians, their near annihilation by the French, and their part in the Black Hawk War. (Rev: BL 1/1–15/96) [977]

18603 McLester, L. Gordon, and Elisabeth Towers. *The Oneida* (4–7). Series: Indian Nations. 2000, Raintree LB $25.69 (978-0-8172-5457-5). 48pp. The Oneida left their New York lands for Wisconsin and Canada. Beginning with a folk tale, this account describes their past and present with some indication of what the future holds. (Rev: BL 3/15/01; HBG 10/01) [973]

18604 Margolin, Malcolm, and Yolanda Montijo, eds. *Native Ways: California Indian Stories and Memories* (5–8). Illus. 1996, Heyday paper $8.95 (978-0-930588-73-1). Reminiscences and stories reflect California Indian culture, both past and present. (Rev: BL 7/96) [979.4]

18605 May, Robin. *Plains Indians of North America* (4–6). Illus. 1987, Rourke LB $16.67 (978-0-86625-258-4). 48pp. Lifestyle and customs of the Plains Indians are described in this well-illustrated introduction to these indigenous people, part of the Original Peoples series. (Rev: BL 1/15/88)

18606 Mayfield, Thomas Jefferson. *Adopted by Indians: A True Story* (5–8). Ed. by Malcolm Margolin. Illus. 1997, Heyday paper $10.95 (978-0-930588-93-9). This is an adaption of the memoirs of a white man who lived with the Choinumne Indians in California for 10 years, beginning in 1850 when he was 8 years old. (Rev: BL 3/1/98) [979.4]

18607 Meli, Franco. *A Day with a Cheyenne* (4–6). Illus. by Giorgio Bacchin. Series: A Day With. 1999, Runestone LB $16.95 (978-0-8225-1920-1). 48pp. An account of the Cheyenne Indians that gives background historical information and then describes the daily life of a hunter and his son in the late 1800s. (Rev: HBG 3/00; SLJ 6/00) [973]

18608 Mercredi, Morningstar. *Fort Chipewyan Homecoming: A Journey to Native Canada* (3–6). Photos by Darren McNally. 1997, Lerner LB $21.27 (978-0-8225-2659-9); paper $6.95 (978-0-8225-9731-5). 48pp. Twelve-year-old Matthew visits relatives at Fort Chipewyan in Alberta, Canada, and learns a great deal about his Native American heritage. (Rev: SLJ 9/97) [973]

18609 Meyers, Madeleine, ed. *Cherokee Nation: Life Before the Tears* (4–8). Series: Perspectives on History. 1994, Discovery paper $6.95 (978-1-878668-26-4). 60pp. A history of the Cherokees that emphasizes the leadership of Sequoyah and the life of the tribe before their forced displacement. (Rev: BL 8/94) [970.3]

18610 Miller, Jay. *American Indian Families* (3–5). Illus. Series: True Books. 1996, Children's Book Pr. LB $25.00 (978-0-516-20133-7). 47pp. Discusses family structure and importance in various Native American tribes. (Rev: SLJ 8/97) [973]

18611 Miller, Jay. *American Indian Festivals* (2–3). Illus. Series: True Books. 1996, Children's Book Pr. LB $25.00 (978-0-516-20134-4). 47pp. Presents various festivals of Native Americans, like rain dances and thanksgiving celebrations. (Rev: BL 3/1/97; SLJ 8/97) [394.2]

18612 Miller, Jay. *American Indian Games* (2–3). Illus. Series: True Books. 1996, Children's Book Pr. LB $25.00 (978-0-516-20136-8). 47pp. With a color photograph on each page and brief text, this title presents the games Native Americans played in the past, like canoe racing and lacrosse, and how they compare with today's interests. (Rev: BL 3/15/97) [394]

18613 Monroe, Judy. *The Northwest Indians: Daily Life in the 1700s* (2–4). Series: Native American Life. 2005, Capstone LB $22.60 (978-0-7368-4316-4). 24pp. A brief, attractive introduction to the tribes of the Pacific Northwest, covering their social structure, homes, food, clothing, and traditions. (Rev: SLJ 12/05) [977.004]

18614 Mooney, Martin. *The Comanche Indians* (4–7). Illus. Series: Junior Library of American Indians. 1993, Chelsea LB $25.00 (978-0-7910-1653-4). 71pp. A historical account of the Comanches from about 1700 to the present. (Rev: SLJ 4/93) [970]

18615 Morris, Ann. *Grandma Maxine Remembers: A Native-American Family Story* (1–3). Series: What Was It Like, Grandma? 2002, Millbrook LB $22.90 (978-0-7613-2317-4). 32pp. Native American culture is explored through the memories of a grandmother who tells about her experiences as young girl. An appropriate activity, recipe, and game are appended. (Rev: BL 9/15/02; HBG 10/02; SLJ 10/02) [973]

18616 Naranjo, Tito E. *A Day with a Pueblo* (4–6). Illus. by Giorgio Bacchin. Series: A Day With. 1999, Runestone LB $16.95 (978-0-8225-1919-5). 48pp. Historical information is given about the Pueblo Indians followed by an account of an elder today and his daily activities at Taos Pueblo. (Rev: HBG 3/00; SLJ 6/00) [973]

18617 Nelson, Sharlene, and Ted Nelson. *The Makah* (4–6). Series: Watts Library. 2003, Watts LB $25.50 (978-0-531-12168-9). 63pp. An accessible introduction to the Makah people of the Northwest Pacific Coast, with material on their history and culture. (Rev: SLJ 5/04) [979.7]

18618 Nobleman, Marc Tyler. *The Battle of the Little Bighorn* (4–6). Series: We the People. 2001, Compass Point LB $26.60 (978-0-7565-0150-1). 48pp. A basic overview of Custer's last stand and the motivations of both sides in the battle. (Rev: SLJ 1/02) [973.8]

18619 Pasqua, Sandra M. *The Navajo Nation* (2–4). Illus. 2000, Bridgestone LB $21.26 (978-0-7368-0499-8). 24pp. This introduction to the largest group of Native Americans in the U.S. briefly covers their history, culture, government, and daily life. (Rev: BL 10/1/00; HBG 10/00; SLJ 12/00) [979.1]

18620 Patent, Dorothy Hinshaw. *The Buffalo and the Indians: A Shared Destiny* (4–8). Illus. by William Muñoz. 2006, Clarion $18.00 (978-0-618-48570-3). 85pp. This beautifully illustrated title explores the unique bonds — both spiritual and economic — between Native Americans and the American bison. (Rev: BL 6/1/06*; HBG 4/07; LMC 1/07; SLJ 8/06*) [978.004]

18621 Pennington, Daniel. *Itse Selu: Cherokee Harvest Festival* (K–3). Illus. by Don Stewart. 1994, Charlesbridge paper $6.95 (978-0-88106-850-4). 32pp. Little Wolf and his Cherokee family celebrate the Green Corn Festival with rituals and feasting to acknowledge the ripening of the corn. (Rev: BL 5/1/94; SLJ 7/94) [394.2]

18622 Peters, Russell. *Clambake: A Wampanoag Tradition* (3–5). Illus. by John Madama. Series: We Are Still Here: Native Americans Today. 1992, Lerner LB $21.27 (978-0-8225-2651-3); paper $6.95 (978-0-8225-9621-9). 48pp. Origins and present-day observations of the traditional ceremony that we know as a clambake. (Rev: BCCB 11/92; SLJ 12/92) [973]

18623 Philip, Neil, ed. *A Braid of Lives: Native American Childhood* (4–8). Illus. 2000, Clarion $20.00 (978-0-395-64528-4). 80pp. Twenty vignettes of one or two pages in length give a many-faceted

picture of growing up Native American in different parts of the county. (Rev: BL 10/1/00; HBG 10/01; SLJ 6/01; VOYA 4/01) [973]

18624 Philip, Neil, ed. *In a Sacred Manner I Live: Native American Wisdom* (4–8). Illus. 1997, Clarion $20.00 (978-0-395-84981-1). 93pp. More than 30 Native American leaders — including Geronimo and Cochise — are quoted on topics relating to the conduct of life and their beliefs. (Rev: BL 7/97; HBG 3/98; SLJ 12/97) [973]

18625 Press, Petra. *The Pueblo* (3–6). Series: First Reports. 2001, Compass Point LB $22.60 (978-0-7565-0082-5). 48pp. An absorbing, well-illustrated account of the Pueblo people that covers religion, society, history, culture, and lifestyle today. (Rev: SLJ 7/01) [978.9]

18626 Quigley, Mary. *Mesa Verde* (4–6). Illus. Series: Excavating the Past. 2005, Heinemann LB $31.43 (978-1-4034-5997-8). 48pp. The work of archaeologists is clearly shown in this well-illustrated exploration of the Mesa Verde site and the people who created it. (Rev: SLJ 2/06) [978.8]

18627 Rasmussen, R. Kent. *Pueblo* (3–5). Illus. by Kimberly L. Dawson Kurnizki. 2001, Rourke LB $28.50 (978-1-55916-249-4). 32pp. The amazing clay-based homes and villages of the Pueblo Indians are highlighted in this account that explains how they were built, their parts, and their many uses. (Rev: SLJ 3/01) [973]

18628 Ray, Kurt. *Native Americans and the New American Government: Treaties and Promises* (4–6). Illus. Series: Life in the New American Nation. 2004, Rosen LB $22.50 (978-0-8239-4035-6). 32pp. The often fractious relations between Native Americans and the federal government are explored. (Rev: BL 6/1–15/04) [323.1]

18629 Riehecky, Janet. *The Cree Tribe* (2–5). Series: Native Peoples. 2002, Capstone LB $21.26 (978-0-7368-1366-2). 24pp. A brief introduction to these Plains Indians with details on their past and present and an emphasis on their place in today's world. (Rev: BL 3/15/03; HBG 3/03) [973]

18630 Riehecky, Janet. *The Osage* (2–5). Series: Native Peoples. 2002, Capstone LB $21.26 (978-0-7368-1367-9). 24pp. This introduction to these Plains Indians tells about their history, culture, and how they live today. (Rev: BL 3/15/03; HBG 3/03) [973]

18631 Roessel, Monty. *Kinaalda: A Navajo Girl Grows Up* (4–7). Illus. 1993, Lerner LB $25.55 (978-0-8225-2655-1); paper $11.15 (978-0-8225-9641-7). 48pp. Celinda McKelvey, a Navajo girl, returns to the reservation to participate in her Kinaalda, the coming-of-age ceremony. (Rev: BCCB 1/94; BL 1/15/94; SLJ 2/94) [392.1]

18632 Roessel, Monty. *Songs from the Loom: A Navajo Girl Learns to Weave* (3–6). Illus. 1995, Lerner LB $21.27 (978-0-8225-2657-5); paper $6.95 (978-0-8225-9712-4). 48pp. A photoessay about weaving the Navajo way that reveals information about the culture and way of life of these people. (Rev: BL 9/15/95; SLJ 11/95) [746.1]

18633 Rose, LaVera. *Grandchildren of the Lakota* (4–6). Illus. Series: World's Children. 1998, Carolrhoda $23.93 (978-1-57505-279-3). 48pp. An introduction to the Lakota Indians, their history, how they live, and their current struggles with the U.S. government. (Rev: BL 4/1/99; HBG 3/99; SLJ 12/98) [305.23]

18634 Rosinsky, Natalie M. *The Wampanoag and Their History* (3–6). Illus. Series: We the People. 2005, Compass Point LB $26.60 (978-0-7565-0847-0). 48pp. A concise introduction to the Wampanoag people, their way of life, and the impact of the arrival of the colonists. [974]

18635 Ryan, Marla Felkins, and Linda Schmittroth, eds. *Abenaki* (3–6). Series: Tribes of Native America. 2004, Gale LB $23.70 (978-1-56711-574-1). 32pp. A richly illustrated look at the Abenaki people of northern New England and southeastern Canada, their history, and their traditional and contemporary customs. Also use *Chickasaw* and *Chinook* (both 2004). (Rev: SLJ 5/04) [974.004]

18636 Salas, Laura Purdie. *The Trail of Tears, 1838* (4–6). Illus. Series: Let Freedom Ring. 2003, Capstone LB $23.93 (978-0-7368-1559-8). 48pp. Examines the government's removal of the Cherokee from their homelands, their forced march to reservations in Indian Territory, the challenges they faced their, and their status today. (Rev: HBG 10/03; LMC 11/03; SLJ 12/03) [973.04]

18637 Santella, Andrew. *The Cherokee* (2–3). Series: True Books: American Indians. 2001, Children's Book Pr. paper $6.95 (978-0-516-27315-0). 48pp. This simple, colorful introduction to the Cherokee Indians covers topics such as their homelands, traditions and customs, history, and present status. (Rev: BL 8/1/01) [973]

18638 Schonberg, Marcia. *Ohio Native Peoples* (4–6). Illus. Series: Heinemann State Studies. 2003, Heinemann LB $27.07 (978-1-4034-0667-5). 48pp. This historical survey of the native peoples who have called Ohio home covers roughly 13,000 years of history. (Rev: HBG 4/04; SLJ 10/03) [977.1]

18639 Schwabacher, Martin. *The Huron Indians* (3–5). Illus. Series: The Junior Library of American Indians. 1995, Chelsea $25.00 (978-0-7910-2489-8); paper $8.95 (978-0-7910-2033-3). 80pp. An introduction to the history and culture of the Huron peoples, with material on how they preserve their traditions today. (Rev: BL 7/95) [392.2]

18640 Seymour, Tryntje Van Ness. *The Gift of Changing Woman* (5–8). 1993, Holt $16.95 (978-0-8050-2577-4). A description of the Apache initiation rite for young women in picture-book format, illustrated by Apache artists. (Rev: BL 11/15/93; SLJ 3/94) [299]

18641 Shemie, Bonnie. *Houses of Adobe: Native Dwellings: The Southwest* (3–5). Illus. Series: Native Dwellings. 1995, Tundra $13.95 (978-0-88776-330-4). 24pp. Various dwellings built by Indians of the Southwest — like pit houses and cliff homes — are described in double-page spreads with detailed drawings. (Rev: BL 9/1/95) [392]

18642 Shemie, Bonnie. *Mounds of Earth and Shell* (3–6). Illus. Series: Native Dwellings. 1993, Tundra $13.95 (978-0-88776-318-2). 24pp. Explores the mound-building Indians of North America, where the mounds are located, and why they were built. (Rev: BL 1/1/94) [393.1]

18643 Sherrow, Victoria. *The Iroquois Indians* (3–5). Series: Junior Library of American Indians. 1993, Chelsea LB $25.00 (978-0-7910-1655-8). 82pp. History and culture of Iroquis arts and crafts. Includes an eight-page photoessay. (Rev: BL 11/1/92) [973]

18644 Shuter, Jane, ed. *Francis Parkman and the Plains Indians* (5–8). Illus. Series: History Eyewitness. 1995, Raintree LB $24.26 (978-0-8114-8280-6). 48pp. An edited and abridged version of Parkman's autobiographical writing about the social customs, family life, and hunting practices of the Plains Indians. (Rev: BL 4/15/95) [978]

18645 Shuter, Jane. *Mesa Verde* (4–6). Series: Visiting the Past. 1999, Heinemann LB $24.22 (978-1-57572-858-2). 32pp. This work introduces the homes and lifestyle of the ancient Pueblo Indians (A.D. 500 to 1292), with coverage of their clothing, beliefs, trade, farming, and tools. (Rev: SLJ 3/00) [973.1]

18646 Siegel, Beatrice. *Indians of the Northeast Woodlands* (4–8). Illus. by William Sauts Bock. 1991, Walker LB $14.85 (978-0-8027-8157-4). 96pp. In question-and-answer format — following the original 1972 edition — this volume contains much information on Native Americans in New England. (Rev: BL 11/15/92) [973]

18647 Smith, Karla. *Virginia Native Peoples* (4–6). 2003, Heinemann LB $27.07 (978-1-4034-0363-6). 48pp. Introduces readers to the native peoples who resided in the state before and after the arrival of European settlers. (Rev: HBG 4/04; SLJ 12/03) [975.5004]

18648 Smithyman, Kathryn, and Bobbie Kalman. *Native North American Foods and Recipes* (3–5). Illus. Series: Native Nations of North America. 2006, Crabtree LB $26.60 (978-0-7787-0383-9); paper $8.95 (978-0-7787-0475-1). 32pp. Maple sugar, wild rice, squash, and corn are just a few of the foods mentioned in this survey of the Native American diet and methods of food preparation and conservation. (Rev: SLJ 11/06) [641.59]

18649 Sneve, Virginia Driving Hawk. *The Apaches* (3–6). Illus. by Ronald Himler. Series: First Americans. 1997, Holiday House LB $17.95 (978-0-8234-1287-7). 32pp. An overview of the six tribes that make up the Apache nation, accompanied by handsome illustrations. (Rev: BL 4/1/97; SLJ 7/97) [973]

18650 Sneve, Virginia Driving Hawk. *The Cherokees* (3–6). Illus. by Ronald Himler. Series: First Americans. 1996, Holiday House $17.95 (978-0-8234-1214-3). 32pp. The story of this large, important Indian group, its culture, and its present status. (Rev: BCCB 5/96; BL 2/15/96; HB 5/96; SLJ 4/96) [973]

18651 Sneve, Virginia Driving Hawk. *The Cheyennes* (K–4). Illus. Series: First Americans. 1996, Holiday

House LB $17.95 (978-0-8234-1250-1). 32pp. The story of the Cheyenne, their history, customs, and how the white man affected their lives. (Rev: BL 9/15/96; SLJ 2/97) [970]

18652 Sneve, Virginia Driving Hawk, ed. *Enduring Wisdom: Sayings from Native Americans* (3–6). Illus. by Synthia Saint James. 2003, Holiday House $16.95 (978-0-8234-1455-0). 32pp. A picture-book collection of sayings from 1647 to the present day that are backed up by helpful endnotes. (Rev: BL 3/15/03; HBG 10/03; SLJ 5/03) [970]

18653 Sneve, Virginia Driving Hawk. *The Hopis* (3–5). Illus. by Ronald Himler. Series: First Americans. 1995, Holiday House LB $16.95 (978-0-8234-1194-8). 32pp. Details are given of the religion, social structure, history, and lifestyle of the Hopi, along with a creation myth. (Rev: SLJ 10/95) [973]

18654 Sneve, Virginia Driving Hawk. *The Iroquois* (K–4). Illus. by Ronald Himler. Series: A First American Book. 1995, Holiday House LB $17.95 (978-0-8234-1163-4). 32pp. Provides a history of the Iroquois, as well as their beliefs, way of life, religion, and current situation. (Rev: BL 6/1–15/95; SLJ 7/95) [973]

18655 Sneve, Virginia Driving Hawk. *The Navajos* (K–3). Illus. by Ronald Himler. Series: First Americans. 1993, Holiday House LB $17.95 (978-0-8234-1039-2). 32pp. After a creation story, the Navajos are introduced with details given on their daily life, society, relations with other Indian groups, and their fortune after the white man came. (Rev: BCCB 10/93; BL 12/15/93; SLJ 10/93) [973]

18656 Sneve, Virginia Driving Hawk. *The Nez Perce* (K–3). Illus. by Ronald Himler. Series: First Americans. 1994, Holiday House LB $16.95 (978-0-8234-1090-3). 32pp. Beginning with a creation myth, this account continues with an exploration of the daily life and history of the Nez Perce. (Rev: BL 10/1/94) [973]

18657 Sneve, Virginia Driving Hawk. *The Seminoles: A First Americans Book* (3–5). Illus. by Ronald Himler. 1994, Holiday House LB $17.95 (978-0-8234-1112-2). 32pp. Discusses many aspects of the Seminole history and culture, including the career of Osceola, the Seminole Wars, and their living conditions today. (Rev: BCCB 7–8/94; SLJ 4/94) [973]

18658 Sneve, Virginia Driving Hawk. *The Sioux* (K–3). Illus. by Ronald Himler. Series: First Americans. 1993, Holiday House LB $16.95 (978-0-8234-1017-0). 32pp. The history of the Sioux Indians is given, with information on their social structure, daily life, ceremonies, and contemporary condition. (Rev: BCCB 10/93; BL 12/15/93; SLJ 10/93) [973]

18659 Sonneborn, Liz. *The Apache* (3–5). Illus. 2005, Watts LB $25.50 (978-0-531-12295-2). 64pp. Explores the history and culture of the Apache people, with period and contemporary illustrations and a timeline. (Rev: BL 7/05) [979.004]

18660 Sonneborn, Liz. *The New York Public Library Amazing Native American History: A Book of Answers for Kids* (5–8). 1999, Wiley paper $16.95 (978-0-471-33204-6). 169pp. Organized by regions and using a question-and-answer approach, this is a

fine overview of the history of Native Americans, ending with a chapter on contemporary conditions. (Rev: BL 5/1/00; SLJ 7/00) [970.004]

18661 Steele, Philip. *Little Bighorn* (5–8). Illus. by Richard Hook. Series: Great Battles and Sieges. 1992, Macmillan $21.00 (978-0-02-786885-2). 32pp. How General George Custer was defeated by Cheyenne and Sioux Indians in 1876. (Rev: BL 10/1/92; SLJ 2/93) [973.8]

18662 Stone, Amy M. *Creek* (4–8). Series: Native American Peoples. 2004, Gareth Stevens LB $26.00 (978-0-8368-4217-3). 32pp. History, tradition, and contemporary life are described with photographs, timeline, fact boxes, and activities. (Rev: SLJ 1/05) [973]

18663 Stout, Mary. *Blackfoot* (4–8). Series: Native American Peoples. 2004, Gareth Stevens LB $26.00 (978-0-8368-4216-6). 32pp. History, tradition, and contemporary life are described with photographs, timeline, fact boxes, and activities. (Rev: SLJ 1/05) [973]

18664 Sundling, Charles W. *Native Americans of the Frontier* (4–6). Illus. Series: Frontier Land. 2000, ABDO $24.21 (978-1-57765-042-3). 32pp. A simple text and many illustrations are used in this accessible account of the daily life of the American Plains Indians during the 19th century. (Rev: BL 10/15/00; HBG 10/00; SLJ 6/00) [978]

18665 Swentzell, Rina. *Children of Clay: A Family of Pueblo Potters* (3–5). Illus. by Bill Steen. 1992, Lerner LB $21.27 (978-0-8225-2654-4). 40pp. The family of Gia Rose of Santa Clara Pueblo takes the reader through the ancient process of pottery making. (Rev: BCCB 3/93; BL 1/15/93; SLJ 2/92) [978.9]

18666 Thompson, Linda. *The California People* (4–7). Illus. Series: Native People, Native Lands. 2003, Rourke LB $29.93 (978-1-58952-753-9). 48pp. One of a well-illustrated series on individual groups of native Americans, with attention to the negative impact of the arrival of European settlers. Other titles in the series include *People of the Northwest and Subarctic*, *People of the Great Basin*, *People of the Northeast Woodlands*, and *People of the Plains and Prairies* (all 2003). (Rev: SLJ 4/04) [979.4]

18667 Walker, Niki, and Bobbie Kalman. *Native North American Wisdom and Gifts* (3–5). Illus. Series: Native Nations of North America. 2006, Crabtree LB $26.60 (978-0-7787-0384-6); paper $8.95 (978-0-7787-0476-8). 32pp. Culture, hunting traditions, medicine and health, language, sports and games, are all covered in this survey of Native American beliefs and respect for the environment. (Rev: SLJ 11/06) [970.004]

18668 Williams, Suzanne Morgan. *Tlingit Indians* (2–4). Illus. Series: Native Americans. 2003, Heinemann LB $22.79 (978-1-4034-0868-6). 32pp. A look at the Tlingit native people of the northwest Pacific coast and their lives before and after the arrival of white settlers. (Rev: SLJ 5/04) [979.8]

18669 Wittstock, Laura W. *Ininatig's Gift of Sugar: Traditional Native Sugarmaking* (3–5). Illus. by

Dale Kakkak. Series: We Are Still Here: Native Americans Today. 1993, Lerner LB $21.27 (978-0-8225-2653-7); paper $21.27 (978-0-8225-9642-4). 48pp. Describes the traditional way of making maple sugar and syrup by Minnesota Indians. (Rev: BL 9/1/93; HB 11/93) [338.1]

18670 Wolfson, Evelyn. *Growing Up Indian* (5–7). Illus. 1986, Walker LB $11.85 (978-0-8027-6644-1). 96pp. What it was like to grow up Indian in traditional American culture before the influence of the white race. (Rev: BL 1/15/87; SLJ 3/87) [306.08997073]

18671 Wood, Leigh. *The Crow Indians* (3–5). Illus. Series: Junior Library of American Indians. 1993, Chelsea LB $25.00 (978-0-7910-1661-9). 80pp. This account tells about the past, present, and culture of the Crow Indians who now live in southeastern Montana. (Rev: BL 5/15/93) [973]

18672 Wood, Marion, and Brian Williams. *Ancient America*. Rev. ed. (5–8). Illus. Series: Cultural Atlas for Young People. 2003, Facts on File $35.00 (978-0-8160-5145-8). 96pp. Colorful topical spreads introduce readers to Native American history from the end of the Ice Age to the arrival of European explorers and conquerers. (Rev: SLJ 1/04) [970.01]

18673 Wood, Ted. *A Boy Becomes a Man at Wounded Knee* (4–6). Illus. 1992, Walker LB $16.85 (978-0-8027-8175-8). 42pp. An eight-year-old Lakota boy wants to participate in his ancestor's journey to Wounded Knee. (Rev: BCCB 12/92; BL 9/1/92; SLJ 11/92) [973.8]

18674 Woods, Geraldine. *The Navajo* (5–7). Illus. Series: Watts Library: Indians of the Americas. 2002, Watts paper $8.95 (978-0-531-16227-9). 64pp. This account includes information on history and contemporary issues and covers the Navajo code talkers, land disputes, traditions, housing, and clothing. (Rev: BL 7/02) [979.1]

18675 Young, Robert. *A Personal Tour of Mesa Verde* (4–7). Illus. Series: How It Was. 1999, Lerner LB $30.35 (978-0-8225-3577-5). 64pp. This book gives a special glimpse into the lives of the Native Americans known as the Puebloans, how they lived, and the culture they developed. (Rev: BL 6/1–15/99; HBG 10/99; SLJ 7/99) [978.8]

18676 Yue, Charlotte, and David Yue. *The Wigwam and the Longhouse* (4–9). Illus. by authors. 2000, Houghton $15.00 (978-0-395-84169-3). 118pp. A well-balanced account that describes the life and history of several tribes of Native Americans from the eastern woodlands. (Rev: HB 7/00; HBG 10/00; SLJ 10/00; VOYA 12/00) [973]

DISCOVERY AND EXPLORATION

18677 Arenstam, Peter, et al. *Mayflower 1620: A New Look at a Pilgrim Voyage* (5–9). 2003, National Geographic $17.95 (978-0-7922-6142-1). 48pp. A large-format photoessay of a voyage of the *Mayflower II* — re-creating the original journey — is the backdrop for detail about the 1620 passengers, supplies, navigation techniques, and the new country they arrived in. (Rev: BL 11/1/03; HBG 4/04; SLJ 11/03) [974.4]

18678 Armentrout, David, and Patricia Armentrout. *The Mayflower Compact* (4–7). 2004, Rourke $20.95 (978-1-59515-229-9). 48pp. The reasons for the creation of this document — a political statement signed by a group of *Mayflower* passengers — are thoroughly explored in concise text, accompanied by an array of maps and illustrations. (Rev: BL 10/15/04) [974.4]

18679 Aykroyd, Clarissa. *Exploration of the California Coast* (4–7). Series: Exploration and Discovery. 2002, Mason Crest LB $19.95 (978-1-59084-043-6). 64pp. Explorers such as Cortes and Drake are covered in this look at 16th-century California. (Rev: SLJ 12/02) [917.94041]

18680 Bowen, Andy Russell. *The Back of Beyond: A Story About Lewis and Clark* (3–5). Illus. 1997, Carolrhoda LB $21.27 (978-1-57505-010-2). 64pp. A gripping account of the journey that took Lewis and Clark to the mouth of the Columbia River in 1805. (Rev: BL 9/1/97; HB 11/97; SLJ 3/98) [917.804]

18681 Cook, Peter. *You Wouldn't Want to Sail on the Mayflower! A Trip That Took Entirely Too Long* (3–6). Illus. by Kevin Whelan. Series: You Wouldn't Want to . . . 2005, Watts LB $29.00 (978-0-531-12411-6); paper $9.95 (978-0-531-12391-1). 32pp. An engaging account of the grim realities and hardships of the Pilgrims' voyage, with cartoon art, a diagram of the ship's layout, and maps. (Rev: SLJ 3/06) [973.2]

18682 Dell, Pamela. *The Plymouth Colony* (4–6). Series: Let Freedom Ring. 2004, Capstone LB $23.93 (978-0-7368-2463-7). 48pp. With large type and bright design, this volume explores the hardships and triumphs of the Pilgrims. (Rev: SLJ 8/04) [974.4]

18683 Dyson, John. *Westward with Columbus* (4–6). Illus. by Peter Christopher. 1991, Scholastic paper $6.95 (978-0-590-43847-6). 64pp. Fact and fiction are interwoven in this account of the 1492 voyage, theorizing that Columbus used a secret map. (Rev: BL 11/15/91; SLJ 11/91) [910.4]

18684 Eisenberg, Jana. *Lewis and Clark: Path to the Pacific* (4–6). Series: Trailblazers of the West. 2005, Children's Pr. LB $24.50 (978-0-516-25126-4); paper $6.95 (978-0-516-25096-0). 48pp. The hardships on this epic expedition, and the relations with Native Americans, are portrayed in short chapters suitable for reluctant readers. (Rev: SLJ 4/06) [917.804]

18685 Faber, Harold. *Lewis and Clark: From Ocean to Ocean* (5–8). Illus. Series: Great Explorations. 2001, Benchmark LB $29.93 (978-0-7614-1241-0). 80pp. This concise, artfully illustrated volume about the journey of Lewis and Clark includes journal entries, a timeline, and Web site information. (Rev: BL 1/1–15/02; HBG 3/02; SLJ 3/02) [917.804]

18686 Gioia, Robyn. *America's Real First Thanksgiving: St. Augustine, Florida, September 8, 1565* (3–6). Illus. 2007, Pineapple LB $14.95 (978-1-56164-389-9). 48pp. The first Thanksgiving might have taken place in Florida, claims this author, when the Spanish explorer Pedro Menéndez de

Avilés feasted with the Timucua in 1565. (Rev: SLJ 6/07)

18687 Gunderson, Jessica. *The Lewis and Clark Expedition* (4–6). Illus. by Steven Erwin and Keith Williams,. Series: Graphic Library: Graphic History. 2006, Capstone LB $25.26 (978-0-7368-6493-0). 32pp. The difficulty and significance of the expedition are made clear in this graphic presentation. (Rev: SLJ 5/07)

18688 Gunderson, Mary. *Cooking on the Lewis and Clark Expedition* (3–6). 2000, Capstone LB $23.93 (978-0-7368-0354-0). 32pp. As well as historical material on the Lewis and Clark expedition, this book contains a number of modern recipes for food that might have been eaten on this memorable journey. (Rev: HBG 10/00; SLJ 12/00) [978]

18689 Hart, Avery, and Paul Mantell. *Who Really Discovered America? Unraveling the Mystery and Solving the Puzzle* (5–7). Illus. by Michael Kline. Series: A Kaleidoscope Kids Book. 2001, Williamson paper $12.95 (978-1-885593-46-7). 96pp. Several theories are presented about the discovery of America, and students are urged to examine them with open minds, using activities that help them to question and explore. (Rev: SLJ 10/01) [970.01]

18690 Johmann, Carol A. *The Lewis and Clark Expedition: Join the Corps of Discovery to Explore Uncharted Territory* (4–6). Illus. by Michael Kline. Series: Kaleidoscope Kids. 2002, Williamson paper $14.25 (978-1-885593-73-3). 112pp. This is a wide-ranging and lively history of the expedition, providing profiles of the explorers, excerpts from journals, lists of resources, and activities. (Rev: BL 1/1–15/03; SLJ 3/03) [917.804]

18691 King, David C. *Projects About the Spanish West* (3–5). Illus. Series: Hands-on History. 2005, Benchmark LB $18.95 (978-0-7614-1982-2). 47pp. The projects outlined in this book — including a yarn picture, a luminaria, an ojo de Dios (eye of God), and a piñata — are designed to help students understand the early Spanish exploration and colonization of the American West. (Rev: SLJ 4/06) [979.0046]

18692 Krensky, Stephen. *Christopher Columbus* (1–2). Illus. by Norman Green. 1991, Random paper $3.99 (978-0-679-80369-0). 32pp. This is an easy-reading book that tells about Columbus's first voyage to America. (Rev: BL 12/1/91; SLJ 12/91) [970.01]

18693 Krensky, Stephen. *Who Really Discovered America?* (4–6). Illus. 1991, Scholastic paper $2.50 (978-0-590-40854-7). 64pp. A parade of discoverers who came to North or South America are uncovered in the attempt to answer this intriguing question. (Rev: BL 1/15/88; SLJ 4/88) [970.01]

18694 Lasky, Kathryn. *The Journal of Augustus Pelletier: The Lewis and Clark Expedition* (4–6). Series: My Name Is America. 2000, Scholastic $10.95 (978-0-590-68489-7). 172pp. Fourteen-year-old Augustus Pelletier, half French and half Omaha Indian, relates his adventures into unknown territory. (Rev: HBG 10/01) [978.02]

18695 Lourie, Peter. *On the Trail of Sacagawea* (4–6). Illus. 2001, Boyds Mills $18.95 (978-1-56397-840-1). 48pp. In this handsome pictorial account of a family trip retracing the steps of Lewis and Clark, the author interweaves their contemporary experiences and historical notes. (Rev: BL 5/1/01; HBG 3/02; SLJ 4/01) [978.004]

18696 Owens, L. L. *Pilgrims in America* (4–6). 2007, Rourke LB $29.93 (978-1-60044-122-6). 48pp. A well-illustrated overview of the Pilgrims who settled in Plymouth, explaining who they were and covering their trip to the New World, the first Thanksgiving, and relations with the native peoples. (Rev: SLJ 4/07) [974.4]

18697 Patent, Dorothy Hinshaw. *Animals on the Trail with Lewis and Clark* (4–8). Illus. by William Muñoz. 2002, Clarion $18.00 (978-0-395-91415-1). 118pp. A handsome account of the Lewis and Clark expedition with emphasis on the animals that were discovered during the journey. (Rev: BCCB 5/02; BL 4/15/02*; HB 5/02; HBG 10/02; SLJ 4/02) [917.804]

18698 Pringle, Laurence. *The Dog of Discovery: A Newfoundland's Adventures with Lewis and Clark* (4–6). Illus. by Meryl Henderson. 2002, Boyds Mills $16.95 (978-1-56397-028-3). 152pp. A Newfoundland dog named Seaman was a valued member of the Lewis and Clark expedition, and his story is told here, based on entries in the explorers' journals and illustrated with drawings and photographs. (Rev: BL 12/1/02; SLJ 3/03) [917.804]

18699 Quiri, Patricia R. *The Lewis and Clark Expedition* (3–6). Series: We the People. 2000, Compass Point LB $26.60 (978-0-7565-0044-3). 48pp. A profusely illustrated, readable account of the Lewis and Clark expedition that makes for a good introductory overview. (Rev: SLJ 2/01) [917.8]

18700 Roberts, Russell. *Pedro Menendez de Aviles* (5–7). Illus. Series: Latinos in American History. 2002, Mitchell Lane LB $29.95 (978-1-58415-150-0). 48pp. This account of explorer Pedro Menendez de Aviles's efforts to procure Florida for Spain uses some fictionalized narrative to illustrate the times. (Rev: BL 10/15/02; HBG 3/03; SLJ 10/02) [975.9]

18701 Roop, Peter, and Connie Roop. *River Roads West* (5–8). Illus. 2007, Boyds Mills $19.95 (978-1-59078-430-3). 60pp. The Hudson, Ohio, and Mississippi rivers and the Erie Canal are among the American waterways introduced in this large-format book that discusses the Native American peoples who lived along them and the impact of European exploration and settlement. (Rev: BL 9/15/07; SLJ 9/07) [917]

18702 Schanzer, Rosalyn. *How We Crossed the West: The Adventures of Lewis and Clark* (3–5). Illus. 1997, National Geographic $18.00 (978-0-7922-3738-9). 48pp. A richly illustrated volume that deals with the expedition of Lewis and Clark as taken from their journals. (Rev: BL 9/15/97; HBG 3/98; SLJ 10/97*) [917.8]

18703 Stefoff, Rebecca. *Exploration and Settlement* (5–9). Series: Colonial Life. 2007, Sharpe Focus $37.95 (978-0-7656-8108-9). 96pp. With color illustrations and interesting sidebars, this volume looks at the progress of exploration in the 15th and 16th centuries and includes profiles of key explorers. (Rev: SLJ 1/08)

18704 Stefoff, Rebecca. *Exploring the New World* (4–7). Illus. Series: North American Historical Atlases. 2000, Benchmark LB $27.07 (978-0-7614-1056-0). Using historical maps and reproductions, the important explorers and their accomplishments are covered in this slim, attractive volume. (Rev: HBG 3/01; SLJ 1/01) [970.01]

18705 Stefoff, Rebecca. *Lewis and Clark* (4–7). Illus. 1992, Chelsea LB $28.00 (978-0-7910-1750-0). 80pp. A simple text and pictures of the Lewis and Clark expedition, which helped open up the West. (Rev: BL 7/92) [978.02]

18706 Steins, Richard. *Exploration and Settlement* (5–8). Illus. Series: Making of America. 2000, Raintree LB $28.54 (978-0-8172-5700-2). 96pp. This account begins with prehistoric migrations to North America and continues with European explorers, including the Spanish, English, French, and Dutch. (Rev: BL 5/1/00; HBG 10/00; SLJ 9/00) [970.01]

18707 Whiting, Jim. *Francisco Vasquez de Coronado* (5–7). Illus. Series: Latinos in American History. 2002, Mitchell Lane LB $29.95 (978-1-58415-146-3). 56pp. This account of Francisco Vasquez de Coronado's search for the lost cities of gold, and his subsequent trial for cruelty to Native Americans, uses some fictionalized narrative. (Rev: BL 10/15/02; HBG 3/03; SLJ 10/02; VOYA 6/03) [979]

18708 Wittmann, Kelly. *The European Rediscovery of America* (4–7). Series: Exploration and Discovery. 2002, Mason Crest LB $19.95 (978-1-59084-052-8). 64pp. Wittmann looks at the explorers of the 15th and 16th centuries, including Columbus and Cabot. (Rev: SLJ 12/02) [970]

COLONIAL PERIOD

18709 Allman, Melinda, ed. *Primary Sources* (5–8). Series: Thirteen Colonies. 2002, Gale LB $27.45 (978-1-59018-011-2). 112pp. A fascinating collection of primary source material for the young researcher. (Rev: BL 9/15/02; SLJ 10/02) [873.2]

18710 Altman, Linda J. *Trade and Commerce* (5–9). Series: Colonial Life. 2007, Sharpe Focus $37.95 (978-0-7656-8111-9). 96pp. With color illustrations and interesting sidebars, this volume looks at trade and commerce in the colonies. (Rev: SLJ 1/08)

18711 Appelbaum, Diana. *Giants in the Land* (2–4). Illus. by Michael McCurdy. 1993, Houghton $17.00 (978-0-395-64720-2). 32pp. An ecological story concerning the forests of giant white pines in New England that were destroyed to build ships for the British in the 18th century. (Rev: BCCB 9/93; BL 10/1/93*; SLJ 11/93*) [634.9]

18712 Barrett, Tracy. *Growing Up in Colonial America* (4–6). Illus. 1995, Millbrook LB $23.40 (978-1-56294-578-7). 96pp. Colonial settlements in the North and South are contrasted in their theories and practices of child rearing. (Rev: BL 12/15/95; SLJ 12/95) [973]

18713 Bauer, Brandy. *The Virginia Colony* (2–4). Series: Fact Finders: The American Colonies. 2005, Capstone LB $23.93 (978-0-7368-2684-6). 32pp. A very basic overview of the geography, history, religion, and everyday life of the Virginia colony, with large type and short paragraphs. (Rev: SLJ 12/05) [975.5]

18714 Boraas, Tracey. *The Salem Witch Trials* (4–6). Series: Let Freedom Ring. 2004, Capstone LB $23.93 (978-0-7368-2464-4). 48pp. A clear explanation of the trials, with background information that aids understanding plus lots of illustrations and a large-size text that will appeal to reluctant readers. (Rev: SLJ 8/04) [974.4]

18715 Britton, Tamara. *The Georgia Colony* (3–4). Series: The Colonies. 2001, ABDO LB $22.78 (978-1-57765-583-1). 32pp. The history of the colony is presented here, with information on both the settlers and the Native Americans of the area and on housing, clothing, and the economy. Also use *Roanoke: The Lost Colony* (2001). (Rev: HBG 3/02; SLJ 4/02) [975]

18716 Broida, Marian. *Projects About Colonial Life* (3–5). Illus. Series: Hands-on History. 2003, Marshall Cavendish LB $27.07 (978-0-7614-1603-6). 48pp. The easy-to-follow projects in this slim volume offer students new insights into life in colonial America. (Rev: BL 4/1/04; HBG 4/04; SLJ 3/04) [973.2]

18717 Brown, Gene. *Discovery and Settlement: Europe Meets the New World (1490–1700)* (5–7). Series: First Person America. 1993, Twenty-First Century LB $20.90 (978-0-8050-2574-3). 64pp. Using excerpts from original documents, this book covers the exploration of the United States, the Puritans, and the role of Native Americans, African Americans, and women in early colonial days. (Rev: SLJ 3/94) [973.2]

18718 Burgan, Michael. *The Boston Massacre* (3–6). Illus. Series: We the People. 2005, Compass Point LB $26.60 (978-0-7565-0832-6). 48pp. Describes the 1770 protest against the British that ended in violence. [973]

18719 Burgan, Michael. *The Salem Witch Trials* (4–6). Series: We the People. 2005, Compass Point LB $26.60 (978-0-7565-0845-6). 48pp. Details the 1692 trials and places them in historical context. (Rev: SLJ 6/05) [973.2]

18720 Burgan, Michael. *The Stamp Act of 1765* (3–6). Illus. Series: We the People. 2005, Compass Point LB $26.60 (978-0-7565-0846-3). 48pp. A concise account of the American colonists' rebellion against a new British tax. [973]

18721 Butler, Jon. *Religion in Colonial America* (5–8). Series: Religion in American Life. 2000, Oxford $32.95 (978-0-19-511998-5). 154pp. This book describes the mix of Catholics, Jews, Africans, Native Americans, Puritans, and various Protestant faiths that coexisted during colonial times. (Rev: BL 6/1–15/00; HBG 10/00) [973.2]

18722 Carlson, Laurie. *Colonial Kids: An Activity Guide to Life in the New World* (4–6). Illus. 1997, Chicago Review paper $12.95 (978-1-55652-322-

9). 160pp. Along with facts about colonial America, this book gives directions for many related projects and activities, like tying sailors' knots, steaming clams, dyeing a shirt, and stitching a sampler. (Rev: BL 2/15/98; SLJ 3/98) [973.2]

18723 Carter, E. J. *The Mayflower Compact* (4–6). Series: Historical Documents. 2003, Heinemann LB $27.07 (978-1-4034-0803-7). 48pp. A study of the Mayflower Compact, the agreement signed by Pilgrims aboard the *Mayflower* that would effectively form their government in the New World, with suitable illustrations and maps. (Rev: SLJ 5/04) [974.4]

18724 Cobb, Mary. *A Sampler View of Colonial Life: With Projects Kids Can Make* (3–5). Illus. 1999, Millbrook LB $24.90 (978-0-7613-0372-5). 64pp. This book discusses many of the home crafts of colonial times, with an emphasis on samplers and crafts projects that the reader can make. (Rev: BL 10/15/99; HBG 3/00; SLJ 1/00) [746.44]

18725 Collier, Christopher, and James Lincoln Collier. *Clash of Cultures: Prehistory–1638* (5–8). Illus. Series: Drama of American History. 1998, Marshall Cavendish LB $31.36 (978-0-7614-0436-1). This well-illustrated examination of the cultures on both sides of the Atlantic — Native American and European — in the years before and during the formation of the colonies. (Rev: BL 4/15/98*; HBG 10/98) [970.00497]

18726 Collier, Christopher, and James Lincoln Collier. *The French and Indian War* (5–8). Illus. Series: Drama of American History. 1998, Marshall Cavendish LB $31.36 (978-0-7614-0439-2). 96pp. A nicely illustrated book providing a broad perspective on the French and Indian War, and noting the conflict's importance on both sides of the Atlantic. (Rev: BL 4/15/98*; HBG 10/98) [973.2]

18727 Collier, Christopher, and James Lincoln Collier. *The Paradox of Jamestown: 1585–1700* (5–8). Illus. Series: Drama of American History. 1998, Marshall Cavendish LB $31.36 (978-0-7614-0437-8). The paradox of Jamestown's history is that it gave democratic freedom through its elected legislature while introducing the first African slaves into the colonies. (Rev: BL 4/15/98*; HBG 10/98) [975.5]

18728 Collier, Christopher, and James Lincoln Collier. *Pilgrims and Puritans: 1620–1676* (5–8). Illus. Series: Drama of American History. 1997, Marshall Cavendish LB $31.36 (978-0-7614-0438-5). 96pp. This volume describes the routes the Pilgrims and Puritans took to America, their beliefs and practices, and how present-day American life continues to be influenced by them. (Rev: BL 4/15/98*; HBG 10/98) [974.4]

18729 Daugherty, James. *The Landing of the Pilgrims* (5–7). Illus. by author. 1981, Random paper $5.99 (978-0-394-84697-2). 160pp. Based on his own writings, this is the story of the Pilgrims from the standpoint of William Bradford. [974.4]

18730 Day, Nancy. *Your Travel Guide to Colonial America* (4–8). Series: Passport to History. 2000, Lerner LB $26.50 (978-0-8225-3079-4). 96pp. Using a modern-day guidebook format, this account takes the reader back to colonial times with glimpses of the *Mayflower* and visits to such colonies as Jamestown, Virginia, and Plymouth, Massachusetts. (Rev: BL 3/1/01; HBG 10/01; SLJ 4/01) [973.2]

18731 Deady, Kathleen W. *The Massachusetts Bay Colony* (2–4). Illus. Series: Fact Finders: American Colonies. 2005, Capstone LB $23.93 (978-0-7368-2676-1). 32pp. Researchers will find solid information on the colony, covering education, religion, work, trade, and community life. (Rev: BL 10/15/05) [974.4]

18732 Deady, Kathleen W. *The New Hampshire Colony* (2–4). Series: Fact Finders: The American Colonies. 2005, Capstone LB $23.93 (978-0-7368-2677-8). 32pp. A very basic overview of the geography, history, religion, and everyday life of the New Hampshire colony, with large type and short paragraphs. (Rev: SLJ 12/05) [974.2]

18733 De Capua, Sarah E. *The Virginia Colony* (3–6). Series: Our Thirteen Colonies. 2003, Child's World LB $28.50 (978-1-56766-711-0). 40pp. A profile of colonial-era Virginia, with a concentration on its role in early steps toward U.S. nationhood. (Rev: SLJ 6/04) [975.5]

18734 Doeden, Matt. *The Boston Tea Party* (4–6). Illus. Series: Graphic History. 2005, Capstone LB $26.60 (978-0-7368-3846-7). 32pp. An eye-catching and dramatically worded graphic presentation of the tax revolt.

18735 Doherty, Craig A., and Katherine M. Doherty. *North Carolina* (5–9). Illus. Series: The Thirteen Colonies. 2005, Facts on File LB $35.00 (978-0-8160-5412-1). 116pp. Traces the history of North Carolina from the early settlers through 1787, with discussion of the Native American culture and with excerpts from primary documents, maps, and profiles of key individuals. (Rev: SLJ 8/05) [973]

18736 Doherty, Craig A., and Katherine M. Doherty. *Pennsylvania* (5–9). Illus. Series: The Thirteen Colonies. 2005, Facts on File LB $35.00 (978-0-8160-5413-8). 142pp. Traces the history of Pennsylvania from the early settlers through 1787, with discussion of the Native American culture, the Quakers, and with excerpts from primary documents, maps, and profiles of key individuals. (Rev: SLJ 8/05) [973]

18737 Doherty, Craig A., and Katherine M. Doherty. *Rhode Island* (5–9). Illus. Series: The Thirteen Colonies. 2005, Facts on File LB $35.00 (978-0-8160-5415-2). 126pp. Traces the history of Rhode Island from the early settlers through 1787, with discussion of the Native American culture and with excerpts from primary documents, maps, and profiles of key individuals. (Rev: SLJ 8/05) [973]

18738 Doherty, Kieran. *Puritans, Pilgrims, and Merchants: Founders of the Northeastern Colonies* (4–8). Illus. 1999, Oliver LB $22.95 (978-1-881508-50-2). 176pp. A history of each of the northeastern colonies is supplemented with brief biographies of such people as William Bradford, John Winthrop, Peter Stuyvesant, Anne Hutchinson, and William Penn. (Rev: BL 8/99; HBG 3/00; SLJ 1/00) [974]

18739 Doherty, Kieran. *Soldiers, Cavaliers, and Planters: Settlers of the Southeastern Colonies* (4–8). 1999, Oliver LB $22.95 (978-1-881508-51-9). This book focuses on the early southern colonies and their founders and leaders, among them Captain John Smith, Sir Walter Raleigh, and Pedro Menendez de Aviles. (Rev: BL 8/99; HBG 3/00; SLJ 10/99) [975]

18740 Dosier, Susan. *Colonial Cooking* (4–7). Illus. Series: Exploring History Through Simple Recipes. 2000, Capstone LB $23.93 (978-0-7368-0352-6). 32pp. This work covers the home life of the colonialists in the North, with material on kitchens, celebrations, food, and some recipes. (Rev: BL 8/00; HBG 10/00) [394.1]

18741 Dubois, Muriel L. *The Delaware Colony* (2–4). Series: Fact Finders: The American Colonies. 2005, Capstone LB $23.93 (978-0-7368-2673-0). 32pp. A very basic overview of the geography, history, religion, and everyday life of the Delaware colony, with large type and short paragraphs. (Rev: SLJ 12/05) [975.1]

18742 Dubois, Muriel L. *The New Jersey Colony* (2–4). Series: Fact Finders: The American Colonies. 2005, Capstone LB $23.93 (978-0-7368-2678-5). 32pp. A very basic overview of the geography, history, religion, and everyday life of the New Jersey colony, with large type and short paragraphs. (Rev: SLJ 12/05) [974.9]

18743 Egger-Bovet, Howard, and Marlene Smith-Baranzini. *US Kids History: Book of the American Colonies* (5–7). Illus. Series: Brown Paper School. 1996, Little, Brown paper $14.99 (978-0-316-22201-3). 96pp. In an informal writing style with plenty of drawings and activities, the American colonial period is introduced. (Rev: BL 8/96; SLJ 8/96) [973.2]

18744 Englar, Mary. *Dutch Colonies in America* (4–6). Series: We the People. 2008, Compass Point LB $26.60 (978-0-7565-3837-8). 48pp. An introduction to how the Dutch colonies were claimed and explored; also use *French Colonies in America* (2008). (Rev: SLJ 6/09) [974.7]

18745 Erickson, Paul. *Daily Life in the Pilgrim Colony 1636* (3–5). Illus. Series: Daily Life. 2001, Clarion $20.00 (978-0-618-05846-4). 48pp. Text, drawings, photographs, and maps describe how the Pilgrims lived at the Plymouth colony in 1636. (Rev: BL 10/1/01; HBG 3/02; SLJ 10/01) [974.4]

18746 Fischer, Laura. *Life in New Amsterdam* (2–4). Illus. Series: Picture the Past. 2003, Heinemann LB $24.22 (978-1-4034-3798-3). 32pp. A simple, illustrated account of what daily life was like in what is now New York City. (Rev: SLJ 4/04) [974.7]

18747 Fisher, Leonard Everett. *The Hatters* (4–6). Illus. Series: Colonial Craftsmen. 2000, Marshall Cavendish LB $21.36 (978-0-7614-1146-8). 48pp. This book supplies a glimpse into the hat trade of the 17th and 18th centuries with material on how different hats were made, worn, and marketed. Also use *The Potters* (2000). (Rev: BL 3/15/01; HBG 10/01) [646.5]

18748 Fisher, Leonard Everett. *The Papermakers* (4–6). Series: Colonial Craftsmen. 2000, Marshall Cavendish LB $21.36 (978-0-7614-1147-5). 48pp. A reissue of this beautifully illustrated work that describes the process of manufacturing, selling, and using paper during colonial times. Also use from the same series *The Tanners* (2000). (Rev: BL 3/15/01; HBG 10/01) [973.2]

18749 Fishkin, Rebecca. *English Colonies in America* (4–6). Series: We the People. 2008, Compass Point LB $26.60 (978-0-7565-3838-5). 48pp. An introduction to how England's culture shaped the new colonies. (Rev: SLJ 6/09) [973.2]

18750 Fradin, Dennis Brindell. *Jamestown, Virginia* (3–5). Illus. Series: Turning Points in U.S. History. 2006, Marshall Cavendish LB $29.93 (978-0-7614-2122-1). 47pp. This volume discusses Jamestown's founding, the dire conditions of its early settlers, and the critical aid provided by Native Americans as well as new arrivals to the settlement. (Rev: BL 1/1–15/07) [975.5]

18751 Fritz, Jean. *The Lost Colony of Roanoke* (3–5). Illus. by Hudson Talbott. 2004, Penguin $17.99 (978-0-399-24027-0). 64pp. Fritz interweaves facts and speculation in this captivating and well-illustrated account of the lost colony. (Rev: BL 4/1/04; HB 5/04; SLJ 5/04) [975.6]

18752 Gillis, Jennifer Blizin. *Life in Colonial Boston* (2–4). Illus. Series: Picture the Past. 2003, Heinemann LB $24.22 (978-1-4034-3795-2). 32pp. An introductory look at Boston in the late pre-Revolutionary War era (1760–1773), with information on what life was like for its residents at home, at school, and at work. (Rev: SLJ 4/04) [973]

18753 Gillis, Jennifer Blizin. *Life in New France* (2–4). Illus. Series: Picture the Past. 2003, Heinemann LB $24.22 (978-1-4034-3799-0). 32pp. A sampling of everyday colonial life in "New France" — the French colonies in eastern Canada and Louisiana — with illustrations, timelines, and maps. (Rev: SLJ 4/04) [971.01]

18754 Girod, Christina M. *South Carolina* (5–8). Series: Thirteen Colonies. 2002, Gale LB $27.45 (978-1-56006-994-2). 96pp. A history of the colony of South Carolina and its people from the early settlements to admission into the United States, told in concise prose with numerous black-and-white illustrations. (Rev: BL 9/15/02) [973.2]

18755 Gourley, Catherine. *Welcome to Felicity's World, 1774* (3–6). Illus. 1999, Pleasant $14.95 (978-1-56247-768-4). 58pp. Using double-page spreads, this book covers everyday life in Colonial Williamsburg in the 1770s, with material on such topics as the plantation village, slave laws, women, and epidemics. (Rev: BCCB 9/99; BL 9/1/99; HBG 3/00; SLJ 10/99) [973.2]

18756 Green, Carl R. *The French and Indian War* (4–6). Illus. Series: U.S. Wars. 2002, Enslow LB $25.26 (978-0-7660-5090-7). 48pp. Supported by verified and updated Web links, this is a useful overview of the French and Indian Wars. (Rev: BL 10/15/02; HBG 3/03) [973.2]

18757 Haberle, Susan E. *The South Carolina Colony* (2–4). Series: Fact Finders: The American Colonies. 2005, Capstone LB $23.93 (978-0-7368-2683-9). 32pp. A very basic overview of the geography, history, religion, and everyday life of the South Carolina colony, with large type and short paragraphs. (Rev: SLJ 12/05) [975.7]

18758 Hale, Anna W. *The Mayflower People: Triumphs and Tragedies* (5–8). Illus. 1995, Harbinger $15.95 (978-1-57140-002-4); paper $9.95 (978-1-57140-003-1). A human account of the Pilgrims that begins with their departure from Southampton, England, in 1620 and ends two years later in the New World with the death of Squanto. (Rev: BL 1/1–15/96) [974.4]

18759 Harkins, Susan, and William H. Harkins. *Jamestown: The First English Colony* (4–6). Series: Building America. 2006, Mitchell Lane LB $29.95 (978-1-58415-458-7). 48pp. A mixture of fact and educated conjecture, this well-organized overview of Jamestown underscores the difficulties faced by the settlers who established the first permanent English colony in America. (Rev: BL 10/15/06; SLJ 11/06) [975.5]

18760 Harkins, Susan Sales, and William H. Harkins. *Georgia: The Debtors Colony* (4–7). Series: Building America. 2006, Mitchell Lane LB $29.95 (978-1-58415-465-5). 48pp. A look at Georgia's early history — including climate, early industry, and population — with information on James Oglethorpe, a key figure who aimed to provide a haven in America for debtors imprisoned in England. (Rev: SLJ 2/07) [975.8]

18761 Harness, Cheryl. *Our Colonial Year* (1–3). Illus. 2005, Simon & Schuster $16.95 (978-0-689-83479-0). 40pp. Double-page spreads with short, free-verse text follow everyday life in the 13 colonies through the 12 months of the year, plus a spread for New Year's Day. (Rev: BL 12/1/05; SLJ 12/05) [973.2]

18762 Hinds, Kathryn. *Daily Living* (5–9). Series: Colonial Life. 2007, Sharpe Focus $37.95 (978-0-7656-8110-2). 96pp. With color illustrations and interesting sidebars, this volume looks at social life in the colonies, exploring food, family life, and so forth. (Rev: SLJ 1/08)

18763 Hinman, Bonnie. *Pennsylvania: William Penn and the City of Brotherly Love* (4–7). Series: Building America. 2006, Mitchell Lane LB $29.95 (978-1-58415-463-1). 48pp. This history of colonial Pennsylvania explores the reasons why William Penn established the colony in the late 17th century. (Rev: SLJ 2/07) [974.8]

18764 Hossell, Karen. *Delaware 1638–1776* (5–8). Series: Voices from Colonial America. 2006, National Geographic $21.95 (978-0-7922-6408-8). 109pp. This well-illustrated title traces the history of Delaware from the 17th-century massacre of Dutch settlers by Native Americans to the eve of the American Revolution; maps and a timeline make this useful for research. (Rev: SLJ 1/07) [975.1]

18765 Howarth, Sarah. *Colonial Places* (4–8). Illus. Series: People and Places. 1994, Millbrook LB $22.90 (978-1-56294-513-8). 48pp. Highlights various places of importance in everyday colonial life, such as the meetinghouse and the church. (Rev: BL 5/15/95; SLJ 3/95) [973]

18766 Hubbard-Brown, Janet. *The Secret of Roanoke Island* (4–7). Illus. 1991, Avon paper $3.50 (978-0-380-76223-1). 96pp. An intriguing look at this bit of history in colonial times. (Rev: BL 12/15/91) [975.63]

18767 Ichord, Loretta Frances. *Hasty Pudding, Johnnycakes, and Other Good Stuff: Cooking in Colonial America* (3–6). Illus. 1998, Millbrook LB $22.40 (978-0-7613-0369-5). 64pp. Topics related to colonial life and early Thanksgivings are covered, with background information on colonial cooking and step-by-step recipes (the original and updated versions). (Rev: BL 1/1–15/99; HBG 3/99; SLJ 2/99) [641.5973]

18768 Isaacs, Sally Senzell. *Life in a Colonial Town* (1–3). Series: Picture the Past. 2000, Heinemann LB $21.36 (978-1-57572-312-9). This well-organized account covers such topics as communication, houses, occupations, education, clothing, and food. Similar coverage for colonial cities is given in *Life in America's First Cities* (2000). (Rev: HBG 3/01; SLJ 11/00) [973.2]

18769 Italia, Bob. *The New York Colony* (3–5). Illus. Series: The Colonies. 2001, ABDO $22.78 (978-1-57765-589-3). 32pp. An overview for younger readers of the New York colony, including information on early history, settlements, everyday life, and other topics. Also use *Roanoke* (2001). (Rev: BL 1/1–15/02; HBG 3/02; SLJ 2/02) [974.7]

18770 Jackson, Shirley. *The Witchcraft of Salem Village* (4–7). Illus. 1963, Random paper $5.99 (978-0-394-89176-7). An account of the witch-hunting hysteria that hit Salem Village. [133.43097445]

18771 January, Brendan. *The Jamestown Colony* (3–6). Series: We the People. 2000, Compass Point LB $26.60 (978-0-7565-0043-6). 48pp. A heavily illustrated account of the Jamestown colony that is simple in appearance and format. (Rev: SLJ 2/01) [973.2]

18772 Kalman, Bobbie. *The Blacksmith* (3–5). Illus. by Barbara Bedell. Series: Colonial People. 2002, Crabtree LB $25.27 (978-0-7787-0747-9); paper $8.95 (978-0-7787-0793-6). 32pp. Photographs of reenactments at Williamsburg and Old Salem, North Carolina, add appeal to this description of the work of a colonial blacksmith and the equipment he used. Also use *The Milliner* and *The Woodworker* (2002). (Rev: SLJ 10/02)

18773 Kalman, Bobbie. *Colonial Crafts* (3–6). Illus. by Antoinette DeBiasi. Series: Historic Communities. 1992, Crabtree LB $25.27 (978-0-86505-490-5); paper $7.95 (978-0-86505-510-0). 32pp. This book introduces crafts from colonial America through those found in the many reconstructed craft shops in Williamsburg, Virginia. Two others in this series dealing with colonial life are: *A Colonial Town: Williamsburg* and *Tools and Gadgets* (both 1992). (Rev: SLJ 7/92) [973.2]

18774 Kalman, Bobbie. *Colonial Life* (3–6). Illus. Series: Historic Communities. 1992, Crabtree LB $25.27 (978-0-86505-491-2); paper $7.95 (978-0-86505-511-7). 32pp. Using many illustrations and simple text, this book describes how people lived during the colonial period in U.S. history. (Rev: BL 11/1/92) [973.2]

18775 Kalman, Bobbie, and Amanda Bishop. *A Slave Family* (3–5). Illus. Series: Colonial People. 2003, Crabtree LB $25.27 (978-0-7787-0746-2); paper $8.95 (978-0-7787-0792-9). 32pp. Describes the lives of slave families during America's colonial period from the early 17th century until the Revolutionary War. (Rev: SLJ 1/04)

18776 Kelly, Martin, and Melissa Kelly. *Government* (5–9). Series: Colonial Life. 2007, Sharpe Focus $37.95 (978-0-7656-8112-6). 96pp. With color illustrations and interesting sidebars, this volume looks at government in the colonies, exploring the Native American tribal organization as well as the colonial structure. (Rev: SLJ 1/08)

18777 Kent, Deborah. *In Colonial New England* (4–8). Series: How We Lived. 1999, Benchmark LB $28.50 (978-0-7614-0905-2). 72pp. Topics such as home life, childhood, religion, problems, and amusements are covered for the colonial period in New England. Companion volumes are *In the Middle Colonies* and *In the Southern Colonies* (1999). (Rev: HBG 10/00; SLJ 2/00) [973.2]

18778 King, David C. *Colonial Days: Discover the Past with Fun Projects, Games, Activities, and Recipes* (3–6). Illus. 1998, Wiley paper $12.95 (978-0-471-16168-4). 128pp. Focusing on a year in the lives of a fictional colonial family, this book outlines 40 projects, including making a sundial, dyeing yarn, and dipping candles. (Rev: BL 2/1/98; SLJ 6/98) [973]

18779 Lange, Karen. *1607: A New Look at Jamestown* (4–6). Illus. by Ira Block. 2007, National Geographic $17.95 (978-1-4263-0012-7). 48pp. In the light of new information discovered about Jamestown in the late 20th century, this book describes what we now understand about life in the colony. (Rev: BL 12/1/06; SLJ 1/07*) [973.21]

18780 Lilly, Alexandra. *Spanish Colonies in America* (4–6). Series: We the People. 2008, Compass Point LB $26.60 (978-0-7565-3840-8). 48pp. An introduction to how Spain's culture shaped the new colonies. (Rev: SLJ 6/09) [970.01]

18781 McGovern, Ann. *If You Lived in Colonial Times* (2–4). Illus. 1992, Scholastic paper $5.99 (978-0-590-45160-4). A re-creation of incidents and situations that could have occurred in the colonial period.

18782 McGovern, Ann. *If You Sailed on the Mayflower* (3–4). Illus. by Anna Devito. 1991, Scholastic paper $5.99 (978-0-590-45161-1). 80pp. In a question-and-answer format, information is given on the historic voyage and the settlement in New England.

18783 McKissack, Patricia C., and Fredrick McKissack. *Hard Labor: The First African Americans, 1619* (5–8). Illus. by Joseph Fiedler. Series: Milestone Books. 2004, Simon & Schuster paper $3.99 (978-0-689-86149-9). 64pp. Drawing on the meager evidence available, the authors reconstruct the story of the first Africans brought to America. (Rev: BL 2/15/04; SLJ 3/04) [306.3]

18784 McNeese, Tim. *Jamestown* (5–8). Illus. Series: Colonial Settlements in America. 2007, Chelsea House $30.00 (978-0-7910-9335-1). 112pp. This overview of the settlement of the colony will be helpful to report writers and includes maps and other graphics. (Rev: BL 7/07; LMC 11/07; SLJ 7/07) [973]

18785 Martin, Michael. *The Salem Witch Trials* (3–6). Illus. by Brian Bascle. Series: Graphic Library/Graphic History. 2004, Capstone LB $26.60 (978-0-7368-3847-4). 32pp. This broad overview in graphic-novel format — factual but embellished — of this chapter of American history will appeal to reluctant readers. (Rev: SLJ 7/05) [973.2]

18786 Marx, Mandy R. *The Maryland Colony* (2–4). Series: Fact Finders: The American Colonies. 2005, Capstone LB $23.93 (978-0-7368-2675-4). 32pp. A very basic overview of the geography, history, religion, and everyday life of the Maryland colony, with large type and short paragraphs. (Rev: SLJ 12/05) [975.2]

18787 Miller, Brandon M. *Good Women of a Well-Blessed Land: Women's Lives in Colonial America* (5–8). Series: People's History. 2003, Lerner LB $29.27 (978-0-8225-0032-2). 96pp. The lives and roles of women from all layers of early American society are presented in this well-written account that includes many quotations, maps, and period reproductions. (Rev: BL 5/15/03; HBG 10/03; SLJ 7/03) [305.4]

18788 Miller, Brandon M. *Growing Up in a New World* (5–8). Series: Our America. 2002, Lerner LB $26.60 (978-0-8225-0658-4). 64pp. The thrill of landing in the New World for the first time is re-created through true-life adventures of young people. (Rev: BL 2/15/03; HBG 3/03; SLJ 7/03) [973.2]

18789 Miller, Lee. *Roanoke: The Mystery of the Lost Colony* (4–7). Illus. 2007, Scholastic $18.99 (978-0-439-71266-8). 112pp. Author Miller presents her theory that the colony at Roanoke was sabotaged. (Rev: BL 6/1–15/07; LMC 10/07) [975.6]

18790 Niz, Xavier. *The Mystery of the Roanoke Colony* (4–6). Illus. by Shannon Eric Denton. Series: Graphic Library: Graphic History. 2006, Capstone LB $25.26 (978-0-7368-6494-7). 32pp. The mystery of this American colony is presented in a graphic format; information following adds depth. (Rev: SLJ 5/07)

18791 Pipe, Jim. *You Wouldn't Want to Be a Salem Witch: Bizarre Accusations You'd Rather Not Face* (3–5). Illus. by David Antram. Series: You Wouldn't Want To. 2009, Scholastic LB $29.00 (978-0-531-20821-2); paper $9.95 (978-0-531-21047-5). 32pp. Cartoon illustrations and gruesome details make it clear why you wouldn't want to be involved in the Salem witch trials. (Rev: BLO 3/17/09) [900]

18792 Roop, Connie, and Peter Roop, eds. *Pilgrim Voices: Our First Year in the New World* (4–7). Illus. 1995, Walker LB $17.85 (978-0-8027-8315-

8). 48pp. Using first-person sources, the experiences of the Pilgrims from their sea journey to the first Thanksgiving are re-created. (Rev: BL 2/1/96; SLJ 1/96) [974.4]

18793 Schumacher, Tyler. *The Georgia Colony* (2–4). Series: Fact Finders: The American Colonies. 2005, Capstone LB $23.93 (978-0-7368-2674-7). 32pp. A very basic overview of the geography, history, religion, and everyday life of the Georgia colony, with large type and short paragraphs. (Rev: SLJ 12/05) [975.8]

18794 Sewall, Marcia. *James Towne: Struggle for Survival* (3–5). Illus. 2001, Simon & Schuster $16.00 (978-0-689-81814-1). 40pp. An 18-year-old carpenter relates his experiences in the colony of Jamestown, sparing little detail of the hardships the settlers faced. (Rev: BL 6/1–15/01; HB 7/01; HBG 10/01; SLJ 6/01) [975.5]

18795 Sherrow, Victoria. *Huskings, Quiltings, and Barn Raisings: Work-Play Parties in Early America* (4–7). Illus. by Laura LoTurco. 1992, Walker LB $14.85 (978-0-8027-8188-8). 78pp. How people in early America helped each other with difficult tasks, such as clearing land and raising barns. (Rev: BL 1/15/93) [973.2]

18796 Smith, Carter, ed. *The Arts and Sciences: A Sourcebook on Colonial America* (5–8). Illus. Series: American Albums. 1991, Millbrook $25.90 (978-1-56294-037-9). 96pp. Through many well-captioned illustrations and brief text, this sourcebook traces cultural and scientific life during the U.S. colonial period. (Rev: BL 1/1/92) [973.2]

18797 Stefoff, Rebecca. *Cities and Towns* (5–9). Series: Colonial Life. 2007, Sharpe Focus $37.95 (978-0-7656-8109-6). 96pp. With color illustrations and interesting sidebars, this volume looks at the development of cities and towns from the earlier forts and fishing camps. (Rev: SLJ 1/08)

18798 Stefoff, Rebecca. *The Colonies* (4–7). Series: North American Historical Atlases. 2000, Benchmark LB $27.07 (978-0-7614-1057-7). 48pp. A slim, clearly written account that gives a history of the American colonies, important places, and outstanding people. (Rev: HBG 3/01; SLJ 1/01) [973.2]

18799 Steins, Richard. *Colonial America* (5–8). Series: Making of America. 2000, Raintree LB $28.54 (978-0-8172-5701-9). 96pp. A brief history of the colonies from 1607 to 1763 with details of their founding, composition, and history. (Rev: HBG 10/00; SLJ 8/00) [973.2]

18800 Walker, Niki. *Colonial Women* (3–5). Illus. by Barbara Bedell. Series: Colonial People. 2003, Crabtree LB $25.27 (978-0-7787-0749-3); paper $8.95 (978-0-7787-0795-0). 32pp. Examines what life was like for women during America's colonial era. (Rev: SLJ 1/04)

18801 Waters, Kate. *Tapenum's Day: A Wampanoag Indian Boy in Pilgrim Times* (3–5). Illus. by Russ Kendall. 1996, Scholastic $16.95 (978-0-590-20237-4). 40pp. Re-enactment photos of the Plimoth Plantation site in Massachusetts enhance this account of a Wampanoag Indian boy in the 1620s.

(Rev: BCCB 3/96; BL 5/1/96; HB 5/96; SLJ 5/96) [974.4]

18802 Whitehurst, Susan. *Plymouth: Surviving the First Winter* (2–4). Series: The Library of the Pilgrims. 2001, Rosen LB $21.25 (978-0-8239-5809-2). 24pp. An accessible account of the pilgrims' hard first winter, with details of housing, food, and illness. Also use *William Bradford and Plymouth: A Colony Grows* (2001). (Rev: SLJ 3/02) [974.4]

18803 Wiener, Roberta, and James R. Arnold. *Connecticut: The History of Connecticut Colony, 1633–1776* (5–8). Series: 13 Colonies. 2004, Raintree LB $31.36 (978-0-7398-6877-5). 64pp. A fact-filled and balanced discussion of the settlement of this area and the problems — political, social, and religious — that confronted the early European inhabitants. Also use *Delaware* and *Maryland* (both 2004). (Rev: SLJ 4/05) [974.6]

18804 Williams, Jean Kinney. *The Maryland Colony* (3–6). Series: Our Thirteen Colonies. 2003, Child's World LB $28.50 (978-1-56766-615-1). 40pp. Maps, prints, and other illustrations add to this presentation of Maryland's early history — from its founding in 1634 to early statehood, with coverage of colonial life, relations with Native Americans, and the roles of women and slaves. (Rev: SLJ 6/04) [975.2]

18805 Wilmore, Kathy. *A Day in the Life of a Colonial Innkeeper* (3–5). Illus. Series: Library of Living and Working in Colonial Times. 2000, Rosen $18.75 (978-0-8239-5430-8). 24pp. In this picture of life at an inn in colonial times, innkeepers Mr. and Mrs. Watkins go about their daily chores — cooking, minding the horses in the stable, cleaning the rooms, and so forth. (Rev: BL 10/15/00) [973.3]

18806 Wilmore, Kathy. *A Day in the Life of a Colonial Wigmaker* (3–5). Illus. Series: Library of Living and Working in Colonial Times. 2000, Rosen $19.95 (978-0-8239-5426-1). 24pp. Set in a colonial American wig shop, this account shows how Mr. Hawkins and his staff of wig makers accomplish such tasks as making scull caps, sewing hair onto them, and powdering the finished wigs. (Rev: BL 10/15/00) [973.3]

18807 Worth, Richard. *Colonial America: Building Toward Independence* (5–8). Series: The American Saga. 2006, Enslow LB $31.93 (978-0-7660-2569-1). 128pp. Tracing the history of the original 13 colonies from the earliest English settlements through the ratification of the Constitution, this volume will be useful for report writers seeking information on politics, government, economy, and culture. (Rev: SLJ 12/06) [973.2]

18808 Wroble, Lisa A. *Kids in Colonial Times* (1–3). Series: Kids Throughout History. 1997, Rosen LB $19.95 (978-0-8239-5118-5). 24pp. An introduction to daily life and customs in the New England colonies. (Rev: SLJ 4/98) [973.2]

18809 Yero, Judith Lloyd. *The Mayflower Compact* (4–7). Series: American Documents. 2006, National Geographic $15.95 (978-0-7922-5891-9). 40pp. Yero distinguishes fact from myth in this examination of the *Mayflower*'s voyage, the colony the Separatists create, and the document they drafted as their governing compact. (Rev: BL 9/15/06; SLJ 10/06) [974.4]

18810 Yolen, Jane, and Heidi Elizabet Yolen-Stemple. *Roanoke the Lost Colony: An Unsolved Mystery from History* (2–5). Illus. by Roger Roth. Series: Unsolved Mystery from History. 2003, Simon & Schuster $16.95 (978-0-689-82321-3). 32pp. Fact and fiction are cleverly woven together in this picture book for older children about the disappearance of the colonists of Roanoke, narrated by a young girl who aspires to be a detective. (Rev: BL 7/03; HBG 4/04; SLJ 10/03) [975]

REVOLUTIONARY PERIOD

18811 Ammon, Richard. *Valley Forge* (3–6). Illus. by Bill Farnsworth. 2004, Holiday House $16.95 (978-0-8234-1746-9). 32pp. Details of the hardships suffered by American forces during the winter of 1777–1778 are placed in historical context in this large-format book. (Rev: BL 9/15/04; SLJ 10/04) [973.3]

18812 Amstel, Marsha. *Sybil Ludington's Midnight Ride* (2–4). Illus. by Ellen Beier. 2000, Carolrhoda LB $23.93 (978-1-57505-211-3); paper $5.95 (978-1-57505-456-8). 48pp. A readable account of 16-year-old Sybil Ludington's exciting midnight ride to spread the word that the British were attacking Danbury, Connecticut. (Rev: HBG 10/00; SLJ 6/00) [973.3]

18813 Anderson, Dale. *The American Colonies Declare Independence* (5–8). Series: World Almanac Library of the American Revolution. 2005, World Almanac LB $31.00 (978-0-8368-5926-3). 48pp. Excerpts from primary sources bolster the informative, clearly written text, which is sprinkled with biographical sidebars. Also use *The Causes of the American Revolution, The Patriots Win the American Revolution*, and *Forming a New American Government* (all 2005). (Rev: SLJ 1/06) [973.3]

18814 Beller, Susan P. *The Revolutionary War* (5–8). Series: Letters from the Homefront. 2001, Benchmark LB $29.93 (978-0-7614-1094-2). 96pp. An attractive volume that brings events and living conditions during the Revolution alive through a collection of letters and other personal documents. (Rev: BL 10/15/01; HBG 3/02) [973.3]

18815 Beller, Susan P. *Yankee Doodle and the Redcoats: Soldiering in the Revolutionary War* (5–8). Illus. by Larry Day. 2003, Millbrook LB $26.90 (978-0-7613-2612-0). 96pp. This attractive book covers the plight of the Revolutionary War soldier, with artwork as well as soldiers' letters and other documents adding to the presentation. (Rev: BL 5/15/03; HBG 10/03; SLJ 9/01) [973.3]

18816 Bobrick, Benson. *Fight for Freedom: The American Revolutionary War* (5–8). 2004, Simon & Schuster $22.95 (978-0-689-86422-3). 96pp. Full-page illustrations face text and "Quick Facts" about topics ranging from the origins and progress of the war to the Continental Congresses, with profiles of key figures and maps. (Rev: BL 11/15/04; SLJ 11/04) [973.3]

18817 Bohannon, Lisa Frederiksen. *The American Revolution* (5–8). Series: Chronicle of America's Wars. 2003, Lerner LB $27.93 (978-0-8225-4717-4). 88pp. Illustrations and maps enliven this overview of the American colonies' struggle for independence, covering the two decades from the French and Indian War to the Treaty of Paris. (Rev: SLJ 3/04) [973.3]

18818 Brenner, Barbara. *If You Were There in 1776* (4–8). Illus. 1994, Bradbury $17.95 (978-0-02-712322-7). 112pp. The year 1776 is explored, with particular emphasis on the everyday life of young people in the colonies. (Rev: BCCB 6/94; BL 5/15/94; SLJ 6/94) [973.3]

18819 Brown, Don. *Let It Begin Here! April 19, 1775: The Day the American Revolution Began* (2–4). Illus. by author. 2008, Roaring Brook $17.95 (978-1-59643-221-5). 32pp. After introducing the causes of the rebellion, this picture book gives a more detailed account of the first day of fighting and the key characters involved. (Rev: BL 10/1/08; HB 1/09; SLJ 10/08) [973.3]

18820 Cheney, Lynne. *When Washington Crossed the Delaware: A Wintertime Story for Young Patriots* (2–4). Illus. by Peter M. Fiore. 2004, Simon & Schuster $16.95 (978-0-689-87043-9). 40pp. The battles of Trenton and Princeton are described in vivid prose with brief eyewitness quotations. (Rev: BL 10/1/04; SLJ 11/04) [973]

18821 Collier, Christopher, and James Lincoln Collier. *The American Revolution: 1763–1783* (5–8). Series: Drama of American History. 1998, Marshall Cavendish LB $31.36 (978-0-7614-0440-8). Using period illustrations, this is a basic history of the Revolution, with material on how the colonialists felt, major battles, and major figures. (Rev: BL 4/15/98*; HBG 10/98) [973.3]

18822 Cook, Peter. *You Wouldn't Want to Be at the Boston Tea Party! Wharf Water Tea You'd Rather Not Drink* (3–6). Illus. by David Antram. Series: You Wouldn't Want To. 2006, Watts paper $9.95 (978-0-531-12447-5). 32pp. A lively look at life in colonial Boston, with some unvarnished realities balanced by the lighthearted cartoon illustrations. (Rev: SLJ 9/06) [973.3]

18823 Crewe, Sabrina, and Dale Anderson. *Lexington and Concord* (4–6). Series: Events That Shaped America. 2004, Gareth Stevens LB $26.00 (978-0-8368-3398-0). 32pp. The story of the 1775 battle serves as the opening for a well-illustrated and well-organized discussion of the Revolutionary War. (Rev: SLJ 8/04) [973.3]

18824 Deem, James M. *Primary Source Accounts of the Revolutionary War* (5–8). Illus. Series: America's Wars Through Primary Sources. 2006, Enslow LB $33.27 (978-1-59845-004-0). 128pp. Soldiers' journal entries, letters from home, personal recollections, songs and poetry, and newspaper articles are among the primary sources included in this general history of the war. (Rev: SLJ 4/07) [973.3]

18825 Draper, Allison Stark. *George Washington Elected: How America's First President Was Chosen* (2–4). Illus. Series: Headlines from History.

2001, Rosen LB $19.95 (978-0-8239-5675-3). 24pp. Newspaper headlines and large type make for easy-reading accounts of significant events leading up to and during Washington's tenure. Also use *The Boston Tea Party: Angry Colonists Dump British Tea* (2001). (Rev: SLJ 8/01) [973.4]

18826 Edwards, Pamela Duncan. *Boston Tea Party* (1–3). Illus. by Henry Cole. 2001, Penguin $16.99 (978-0-399-23357-9). 32pp. Rhythmic text presents the key events in the lead-up to the Tea Party, enlivened by additional commentary from a crew of mice. (Rev: BCCB 6/01; BL 6/1–15/01; HBG 3/02; SLJ 7/01) [973.3]

18827 Ferrie, Richard. *The World Turned Upside Down: George Washington and the Battle of Yorktown* (5–9). Illus. 1999, Holiday $18.95 (978-0-8234-1402-4). A lavishly illustrated account of the battle that was the turning point in the Revolution, with details on strategies, personalities, and period warfare. (Rev: BL 9/1/99; HBG 3/00; SLJ 10/99) [973.3]

18828 Fleming, Thomas. *Everybody's Revolution* (4–7). Illus. 2006, Scholastic $19.99 (978-0-439-63404-5). 96pp. A fascinating introduction to the diverse heroes and heroines of many nationalities who contributed to the success of the American Revolution. (Rev: BL 10/15/06; SLJ 11/06) [973.3]

18829 Foster, Genevieve, and Joanna Foster. *George Washington's World*. Rev. ed. (5–8). Illus. 1997, Beautiful Feet paper $15.95 (978-0-9643803-4-9). 357pp. A new edition of this 50-year-old book that re-creates what was happening in the world during Washington's life, now with expanded coverage on minorities. (Rev: SLJ 3/98) [909]

18830 Fradin, Dennis Brindell. *The Declaration of Independence* (3–6). Series: Turning Points in U.S. History. 2006, Benchmark LB $29.93 (978-0-7614-2129-0). 45pp. Describes the events leading up to writing of the Declaration of Independence, its composition, and its impact on history. (Rev: SLJ 3/07) [973.3]

18831 Fradin, Dennis Brindell. *Let It Begin Here! Lexington and Concord: First Battles of the American Revolution* (2–4). Illus. by Larry Day. 2005, Walker LB $17.85 (978-0-8027-8946-4). 32pp. The story of the battles that began it all, told in an engaging style to appeal to students; with illustrations and information on key figures of the war. (Rev: BL 4/15/05) [973.3]

18832 Fradin, Dennis Brindell. *The Signers: The 56 Stories Behind the Declaration of Independence* (4–6). Illus. by Michael McCurdy. 2002, Walker $22.95 (978-0-8027-8849-8). 160pp. Report writers will find plenty of information on the 13 colonies and the important individuals of the time in this lively presentation. (Rev: HB 1/03; HBG 3/03; SLJ 11/02)

18833 Freedman, Russell. *Give Me Liberty! The Story of the Declaration of Independence* (4–7). Illus. 2000, Holiday $24.95 (978-0-8234-1448-2). 90pp. Beginning with the Boston Tea Party, this stirring account introduces characters including Patrick Henry and Paul Revere, events such as the battles at

Lexington and Concord, and ends with the Continental Congress and the drawing up of the Declaration of Independence. (Rev: BCCB 10/00; BL 10/1/00*; HB 1/01; HBG 3/01; SLJ 10/00) [973.3]

18834 Furgang, Kathy. *The Declaration of Independence and John Adams of Massachusetts* (3–4). Illus. Series: Framers of the Declaration of Independence. 2001, Rosen LB $21.25 (978-0-8239-5590-9). 24pp. Large print and visual interest make this introductory account suitable for reluctant readers. Also use *The Declaration of Independence and Richard Henry Lee of Virginia* and *The Declaration of Independence and Roger Sherman of Connecticut* (both 2002). (Rev: SLJ 5/02)

18835 Furstinger, Nancy. *The Boston Tea Party* (4–6). Illus. Series: Let Freedom Ring. 2002, Capstone LB $23.93 (978-0-7368-1093-7). 48pp. Furstinger gives a concise account of the event and places it in a simple historical context that will be useful for report writers. Also use *The Boston Massacre* (2002). (Rev: HBG 3/03; SLJ 6/02)

18836 Graves, Kerry A. *The Declaration of Independence: The Story Behind America's Founding Document* (3–5). Series: America in Words and Song. 2003, Chelsea Clubhouse LB $23.00 (978-0-7910-7334-6). 32pp. Details events leading up to America's political break from Britain and the difficulties in framing the document declaring that independence. (Rev: SLJ 5/04) [973.3]

18837 Green, Carl R. *The Revolutionary War* (4–6). Illus. Series: U.S. Wars. 2002, Enslow LB $25.26 (978-0-7660-5089-1). 48pp. Supported by verified and updated Web links, this is a useful account of the Revolutionary War. (Rev: BL 10/15/02; HBG 3/03) [973.3]

18838 Herbert, Janis. *The American Revolution for Kids* (5–8). Illus. 2002, Chicago Review paper $14.95 (978-1-55652-456-1). 160pp. A comprehensive look at the American Revolution from its causes through the early 18th century, with biographical information and interesting features. (Rev: BL 10/1/02; SLJ 11/02) [973.3]

18839 Hossell, Karen. *The Articles of Confederation* (4–6). Series: Historical Documents. 2003, Heinemann LB $27.07 (978-1-4034-0800-6). 48pp. The story of the Articles of Confederation, which served as the first Constitution of the newly independent United States, with a look at what a primary document is and how original documents are preserved. (Rev: SLJ 5/04) [342.73]

18840 Ingram, Scott. *The Battle of Valcour Bay* (4–6). Series: Triangle Histories of the American Revolution. 2003, Gale LB $22.45 (978-1-56711-778-3). 32pp. A detailed and well-illustrated account of the Revolutionary War battle of Valcour Bay on Lake Champlain. (Rev: SLJ 3/04)

18841 Jules, Jacqueline. *Unite or Die: How Thirteen States Became a Nation* (2–4). Illus. by Jef Czekaj. 2009, Charlesbridge $16.95 (978-1-58089-189-9); paper $7.95 (978-1-58089-190-5). 48pp. This picture book uses a school play with children dressed as the thirteen states as a framework for introducing the path to nationhood. (Rev: BL 1/1–15/09; SLJ 4/09) [973.3]

18842 King, David C. *Saratoga* (5–8). Illus. Series: Battlefields Across America. 1998, Twenty-First Century LB $26.90 (978-0-7613-3011-0). The significance of the battle at Saratoga in 1777, in which General Burgoyne's British army was defeated, and where and how the history of this battle is preserved today. (Rev: HBG 9/98; SLJ 8/98) [973.3]

18843 Kirby, Philippa. *Glorious Days, Dreadful Days: The Battle of Bunker Hill* (4–6). Illus. by John Edens. Series: Stories of America. 1993, Raintree LB $28.55 (978-0-8114-7226-5). 88pp. Describes the Battle of Bunker Hill and its significance to the Revolution. (Rev: HB 11/97; SLJ 9/93) [973.3]

18844 Kroll, Steven. *The Boston Tea Party* (3–6). Illus. by Peter M. Fiore. 1998, Holiday House $16.95 (978-0-8234-1316-4). 32pp. A mature picture book in which the events leading up to and during the Boston Tea Party are described, with an afterword on its consequences. (Rev: BL 9/15/98; HBG 10/98; SLJ 12/98) [973.3]

18845 Lilly, Melinda. *The Boston Tea Party* (K–2). Illus. by Patrick O'Brien. Series: Reading American History. 2002, Rourke LB $14.95 (978-1-58952-357-9). 24pp. A simple account for beginning readers that introduces the key characters behind the rebellion. (Rev: SLJ 3/03) [973.3]

18846 Maestro, Betsy. *Liberty or Death: The American Revolution: 1763–1783* (3–5). Illus. by Giulio Maestro. Series: American Story. 2005, HarperCollins $16.99 (978-0-688-08802-6). 64pp. This attractive volume provides an easy-to-understand overview of the American Revolution and the events that led up to it. (Rev: BL 11/1/05; SLJ 9/05) [973.3]

18847 Martin, Joseph Plumb. *A Revolutionary War Soldier* (3–6). Series: In My Own Words. 2000, Marshall Cavendish LB $27.07 (978-0-7614-1014-0). 64pp. Sly humor is present in diary excerpts that bring to life stirring moments in America's war for independence. (Rev: BL 3/1/01; HBG 3/01; SLJ 3/01) [973.3]

18848 Miller, Brandon M. *Declaring Independence: Life During the American Revolution* (5–8). Series: People's History. 2005, Lerner LB $29.27 (978-0-8225-1275-2). 112pp. A thorough look at what life was like during the American Revolution, using primary sources. (Rev: SLJ 9/05; VOYA 6/05) [973.3]

18849 Miller, Brandon M. *Growing Up in the Revolution and the New Nation* (4–7). Illus. Series: Our America. 2002, Lerner LB $26.60 (978-0-8225-0078-0). 64pp. An in-depth examination of the lives of children during and immediately after the American Revolution, including biographical information about real youngsters. (Rev: BL 10/15/02; HBG 3/03; SLJ 12/02) [973.3]

18850 Minor, Wendell. *Yankee Doodle America: The Spirit of 1776 from A to Z* (2–5). Illus. 2006, Putnam $16.99 (978-0-399-24003-4). 48pp. An attractive and informative alphabetical tour of colonial America. (Rev: BL 4/15/06; SLJ 4/06) [973.3]

18851 Murphy, Jim. *A Young Patriot: The American Revolution as Experienced by One Boy* (5–8). Illus. 1996, Clarion $16.00 (978-0-395-60523-3). The American Revolution as seen through the eyes of a 15-year-old volunteer. (Rev: BCCB 6/96; BL 6/1–15/96*; HB 9/96; SLJ 6/96*) [973.3]

18852 Nash, Gary B. *Landmarks of the American Revolution* (5–8). Series: American Landmarks. 2003, Oxford LB $32.95 (978-0-19-512849-9). 158pp. Landmark sites such as Independence Hall, Valley Forge National Historic Park, Faneuil Hall, and Yorktown Battlefield are introduced with excerpts from primary documents such as letters and broadsides. (Rev: SLJ 8/03) [973.3]

18853 O'Neill, Laurie A. *The Boston Tea Party* (4–8). Series: Spotlight on American History. 1996, Millbrook LB $24.90 (978-0-7613-0006-9). The causes and effects of the Boston Tea Party are discussed, along with material on the Battles of Lexington and Concord. (Rev: BL 1/1–15/97; SLJ 3/97) [973.3]

18854 Raatma, Lucia. *The Minutemen* (4–6). Series: We the People. 2005, Compass Point LB $26.60 (978-0-7565-0842-5). 48pp. Describes the role of the Minutemen and their bravery at the battles of Lexington and Concord. (Rev: SLJ 6/05)

18855 St. George, Judith. *The One and Only Declaration of Independence* (1–3). Illus. by Will Hillenbrand. 2005, Penguin $16.99 (978-0-399-23738-6). 48pp. The story of the document's search for a permanent home, presented using questions and answers with cartoon-style illustrations. (Rev: BL 3/1/05; SLJ 6/05) [973.3]

18856 Schanzer, Rosalyn. *George vs. George: The Revolutionary War as Seen by Both Sides* (5–7). Illus. 2004, National Geographic $16.95 (978-0-7922-7349-3). 64pp. The two sides' differences — and commonalities — are portrayed in an appealing combination of well-written text, colorful art, and speech balloons; sensationalist aspects detract from the overall value. (Rev: BL 11/15/04; SLJ 10/04*) [973.3]

18857 Schleifer, Jay. *Our Declaration of Independence* (4–6). Illus. Series: I Know America. 1992, Millbrook LB $20.90 (978-1-56294-205-2). 48pp. A well-illustrated history of the writing of the Declaration of Independence and its significance. (Rev: BL 9/1/92; SLJ 10/92) [973.3]

18858 Silox-Jarrett, Diane. *Heroines of the American Revolution: America's Founding Mothers* (4–6). Illus. 1998, Green Angel $19.95 (978-0-9658065-2-7). 94pp. Profiles of 25 important women who championed the colonists' cause during the American Revolution. (Rev: BL 2/15/98) [973.3]

18859 Smith, Carter, ed. *The Revolutionary War: A Sourcebook on Colonial America* (5–8). Series: American Albums. 1991, Millbrook $25.90 (978-1-56294-039-3). This volume illustrates the major events leading up to the Revolution and the battles and personalities involved. (Rev: BL 1/1/92) [973.38]

18860 Sobel, Syl. *The Declaration of Independence: How 13 Colonies Became the United States* (3–5).

Illus. by Denise Gilgannon. 2008, Barron's paper $6.99 (978-0-7641-3950-5). 48pp. A succinct introduction to the creation of the Declaration of Independence, with background information on the history and beliefs of the time and a description of the government it created. (Rev: LMC 11/08; SLJ 9/08) [973.3]

18861 Stefoff, Rebecca. *Revolutionary War* (4–7). Illus. Series: North American Historical Atlases. 2000, Benchmark LB $27.07 (978-0-7614-1058-4). Using historical maps and reproductions plus a clear text, this is a basic account of the American Revolution. (Rev: HBG 3/01; SLJ 1/01) [973.3]

18862 Weber, Michael. *The American Revolution* (5–8). Series: Making of America. 2000, Raintree LB $28.54 (978-0-8172-5702-6). 96pp. A fine overview of the American Revolution from the French and Indian War to the creation of the United States. (Rev: BL 7/00; HBG 10/00; SLJ 8/00) [973.3]

18863 Weber, Michael. *Yorktown* (4–7). Illus. Series: Battlefields Across America. 1997, Twenty-First Century LB $26.90 (978-0-8050-5226-8). 63pp. Background material on the Revolutionary War is given, along with details of the battle and the present-day condition of its site. (Rev: SLJ 1/98) [973.3]

18864 Weber, Michael. *The Young Republic* (5–8). Illus. Series: Making of America. 2000, Raintree LB $28.54 (978-0-8172-5703-3). 94pp. This well-illustrated account begins in the 1780s with the creation of the federal system, the ratification of the Constitution, and the inauguration of Washington as president in 1789. (Rev: BL 5/1/00; HBG 10/00; SLJ 9/00) [973]

18865 Whitelaw, Nancy. *The Shot Heard Round the World: The Battles of Lexington and Concord* (5–8). Illus. 2001, Morgan Reynolds LB $23.95 (978-1-883846-75-6). 112pp. Whitelaw details events from the Boston Massacre in 1770 to the first battles of the Revolution in 1775, with profiles of some of the key players. (Rev: BL 5/15/01; HBG 10/01; SLJ 7/01; VOYA 6/01) [973.3]

18866 Wilbur, Keith C. *The Revolutionary Soldier, 1775–1783* (4–8). Series: Illustrated Living History. 1996, Chelsea LB $14.95 (978-0-7910-4533-6). Topics covered in this book about the Continental Army include clothing, weapons, camp life, food, hospitals, and leisure activities. (Rev: BL 6/1–15/97; SLJ 7/97) [973.3]

18867 Winters, Kay. *Colonial Voices: Hear Them Speak* (4–7). Illus. by Larry Day. 2008, Dutton $17.99 (978-0-525-47872-0). 40pp. Fictional residents of colonial Boston offer their opinions on independence and revolution in this illustrated book by the author of *Voices of Egypt*. (Rev: BL 5/15/08; LMC 11/08; SLJ 6/08*) [973.3]

18868 Wister, Sally. *A Colonial Quaker Girl: The Diary of Sally Wister, 1777–1778* (4–6). Series: Diaries, Letters, and Memoirs. 2000, Capstone LB $23.93 (978-0-7368-0349-6). 32pp. This diary of a young girl, kept during the Revolution, reflects everyday family life during this period. (Rev: BL 10/15/00; SLJ 9/00) [973.3]

18869 Yero, Judith Lloyd. *The Declaration of Independence* (3–5). Series: American Documents. 2006, National Geographic $15.95 (978-0-7922-5397-6). 40pp. Discusses the events that led to this document and the important figures who signed it, with interesting sidebars. (Rev: SLJ 5/06) [973.3]

18870 Zeinert, Karen. *Those Remarkable Women of the American Revolution* (5–8). Illus. 1996, Millbrook LB $29.90 (978-1-56294-657-9). A fascinating account of the conditions and status of women in colonial America and their important contributions to the Revolution, from fighting and spying to fund raising. (Rev: BL 12/1/96; SLJ 3/97; VOYA 4/97) [973.3]

THE YOUNG NATION, 1789–1861

18871 Baldwin, Robert F. *New England Whaler* (5–8). Illus. Series: American Pastfinder. 1996, Lerner LB $25.55 (978-0-8225-2978-1). Life on a 19th-century whaling ship is detailed, with many maps and color photographs. (Rev: BL 7/96; SLJ 6/96) [638.2]

18872 Bial, Raymond. *The Strength of These Arms: Life in the Slave Quarters* (5–8). 1997, Houghton $16.00 (978-0-395-77394-9). This photoessay recreates daily life in the slave quarters on large plantations, contrasts it with the luxurious lifestyles of the slave holders, and documents how slaves tried to preserve their heritage, dignity, and hope. (Rev: BL 9/15/97; HBG 3/98; SLJ 11/97) [975]

18873 Bozonelis, Helen Koutras. *Primary Source Accounts of the War of 1812* (5–8). Illus. Series: America's Wars Through Primary Sources. 2006, Enslow LB $33.27 (978-1-59845-006-4). 128pp. Soldiers' journal entries, letters from the homefront, personal recollections, songs and poetry, and newspaper articles are among the primary sources included in this general history of the war. (Rev: SLJ 4/07) [973.5]

18874 Bredeson, Carmen. *The Battle of the Alamo: The Fight for Texas Territory* (5–8). Series: Spotlight on American History. 1996, Millbrook LB $24.90 (978-0-7613-0019-9). A well-organized account of the causes, events, and campaigns of the war in which much of California, Texas, and the Southwest became part of the United States. (Rev: SLJ 4/97) [973.6]

18875 Britton, Tamara. *The Alamo* (3–5). Series: Symbols, Landmarks, and Monuments. 2004, ABDO LB $22.78 (978-1-59197-518-2). 32pp. Historical and contemporary photographs add interest to this presentation of the Alamo's history and significance. (Rev: SLJ 11/04) [976.4]

18876 Burgan, Michael. *The Alamo* (3–6). Series: We the People. 2001, Compass Point LB $26.60 (978-0-7565-0097-9). 48pp. The major figures are profiled in this overview of the battle, along with maps, photographs, and paintings that bring the story to life. (Rev: SLJ 8/01) [976.4]

18877 Burgan, Michael. *The Louisiana Purchase* (5–8). Series: We the People. 2002, Compass Point LB $26.60 (978-0-7565-0210-2). 48pp. An accessible, well-illustrated account of the purchase that doubled the size of the United States. (Rev: SLJ 7/02) [973.46]

18878 Cantor, Carrie Nicholas. *The Mexican War: How the United States Gained Its Western Lands* (4–6). Illus. Series: A Proud Heritage: The Hispanic Library. 2003, Child's World LB $28.50 (978-1-56766-176-7). 40pp. A balanced account of the reasons why the United States went to war and of the progress of the war itself, with material on the prominent individuals, a timeline, and a glossary. (Rev: BL 10/15/03) [973.6]

18879 Chase, John Churchill. *Louisiana Purchase: An American Story*. Rev. ed. (5–8). Illus. 2002, Pelican paper $12.95 (978-1-58980-084-7). 96pp. The story of the Louisiana Purchase, engagingly told in comic-strip format. (Rev: BL 2/1/03) [973.4]

18880 Coleman, Wim, and Pat Perrin. *The Amazing Erie Canal and How a Big Ditch Opened Up the West* (4–7). Illus. Series: Wild History of the American West. 2006, Enslow LB $33.27 (978-1-59845-017-0). 128pp. Why was the Erie Canal built? What was its impact on American commerce and history? This richly illustrated profile answers those questions and offers a general overview of canals; 30 Internet links are provided for further research. (Rev: BL 10/15/06) [386]

18881 Collier, Christopher, and James Lincoln Collier. *Andrew Jackson's America, 1824–1850* (5–8). Illus. Series: Drama of American History. 1998, Marshall Cavendish LB $29.93 (978-0-7614-0779-9). The Colliers trace American history over an eventful 26 years that encompass great change, from the Industrial Revolution to the Trail of Tears. (Rev: BL 2/15/99; HBG 10/99) [973.56]

18882 Collier, Christopher, and James Lincoln Collier. *Building a New Nation, 1789–1801* (5–8). Illus. Series: Drama of American History. 1998, Marshall Cavendish LB $31.36 (978-0-7614-0777-5). 89pp. An account of how the Federalists began to use the Constitution as a blueprint for guiding the young nation. (Rev: BL 2/15/99) [973.4]

18883 Collier, Christopher, and James Lincoln Collier. *Hispanic America, Texas and the Mexican War, 1835–1850* (5–8). Illus. Series: Drama of American History. 1998, Marshall Cavendish LB $31.36 (978-0-7614-0780-5). 89pp. This account covers the history of Europeans in the Southwest, the Hispanic culture in the region, the doctrine of Manifest Destiny, the Mexican War, and the settling of California. (Rev: BL 2/15/99; HBG 10/99; SLJ 4/99) [979]

18884 Collier, Christopher, and James Lincoln Collier. *The Jeffersonian Republicans, 1800–1823* (5–8). Illus. Series: Drama of American History. 1998, Marshall Cavendish LB $29.93 (978-0-7614-0778-2). This lively account describes 23 eventful years in our history that include the Louisiana Purchase, the Lewis and Clark Expedition, and the War of 1812. (Rev: BL 2/15/99; HBG 10/99; SLJ 4/99) [973.46]

18885 Collier, Christopher, and James Lincoln Collier. *Slavery and the Coming of the Civil War, 1831–1861* (5–8). Illus. 1999, Marshall Cavendish LB $29.93 (978-0-7614-0817-8). 87pp. A reliable,

interesting account the traces the history of slavery in the United States, with an emphasis on the events leading up to the Civil War. (Rev: BL 2/15/00; HBG 10/00; SLJ 3/00) [973.7]

18886 Cosson, M. J. *Yankee Whalers* (4–6). Series: Events in American History. 2007, Rourke LB $29.93 (978-1-60044-140-0). 48pp. Life aboard whaling ships in the 1800s is a major focus of this volume. (Rev: BL 4/1/07; SLJ 4/07) [639.2]

18887 Coulter, Laurie. *Cowboys and Coffin Makers: One Hundred 19th-Century Jobs You Might Have Feared or Fancied* (3–6). Illus. by Martha Newbigging. 2007, Annick $25.95 (978-1-55451-068-9); paper $16.95 (978-1-55451-067-2). 96pp. Miller, stagecoach driver, farmer, butcher, laundress, and dentist are just a few of the occupations described here. Readers will learn what life was like for all sorts of people during this time in the United States. (Rev: SLJ 6/07)

18888 Currie, Stephen. *Escapes from Slavery* (5–9). Series: Great Escapes. 2003, Gale LB $29.95 (978-1-59018-276-5). 112pp. The stories of six of the approximately 60,000 slaves who escaped from captivity in pre-Civil War America. (Rev: SLJ 4/04) [973.7]

18889 Doeden, Matt. *The Battle of the Alamo* (4–6). Illus. Series: Graphic History. 2005, Capstone LB $26.60 (978-0-7368-3832-0). 32pp. An eye-catching and dramatically worded graphic presentation of the battle. [976]

18890 Doherty, Craig A., and Katherine M. Doherty. *The Erie Canal* (4–7). Illus. Series: Building America. 1996, Blackbirch LB $24.95 (978-1-56711-112-5). 48pp. Photographs and maps are used effectively in this introduction to the Erie Canal, an engineering marvel. (Rev: BL 2/15/97; SLJ 2/97) [386]

18891 Draper, Charla L. *Cooking on Nineteenth-Century Whaling Ships* (4–7). Series: Exploring History Through Simple Recipes. 2000, Capstone LB $23.93 (978-0-7368-0602-2). 32pp. As well as learning about life on a whaling ship, this book provides a series of simple recipes. (Rev: BL 3/1/01; HBG 10/01; SLJ 4/01) [974.8]

18892 Fischer, Laura. *Life in a Mississippi River Town* (2–4). Illus. Series: Picture the Past. 2003, Heinemann LB $24.22 (978-1-4034-3797-6). 32pp. A well-illustrated look at life along the Mississippi in the mid-19th century and the busy river's impact on society. (Rev: SLJ 6/04) [977]

18893 Fleischner, Jennifer. *The Dred Scott Case: Testing the Right to Live Free* (5–8). Series: Spotlight on American History. 1997, Millbrook $24.90 (978-0-7613-0005-2). An account of the life of the slave Dred Scott and the historic court case of 1857 against his owner, John Sanford. (Rev: BL 5/1/97; SLJ 4/97) [342.73]

18894 Fradin, Dennis Brindell. *The Alamo* (3–6). Series: Turning Points in U.S. History. 2006, Benchmark LB $29.93 (978-0-7614-2127-6). 45pp. A look at the famous battle, the events that led up to the fight for Texas's independence, the famous people involved, and its aftermath. (Rev: SLJ 3/07) [976.4]

18895 Fradin, Dennis Brindell. *Duel! Burr and Hamilton's Deadly War of Words* (3–6). Illus. by Larry Day. 2008, Walker $16.95 (978-0-8027-9583-0). 32pp. A fast-paced, dramatic account of the feud between Burr and Hamilton, with lots of information on the men's early lives and on their roles in the American Revolution. (Rev: BL 6/1–15/08; SLJ 7/08) [973.4]

18896 Freedman, Florence B. *Two Tickets to Freedom: The True Story of Ellen and William Craft, Fugitive Slaves* (4–8). Illus. by Ezra Jack Keats. 1971, Bedrick $12.95 (978-0-87226-330-7); paper $5.95 (978-0-87226-221-8). 96pp. An exciting story of slavery, escape, and pursuit that is based on fact. A reissue. [973.5]

18897 Gaines, Ann. *The Alamo: The Fight Over Texas* (4–6). Illus. Series: A Proud Heritage: The Hispanic Library. 2003, Child's World LB $28.50 (978-1-56766-173-6). 40pp. An even-handed description of the history of the mission, its use as a fort, and the famous battle fought there. [976.4]

18898 Gay, Kathlyn, and Martin Gay. *War of 1812* (5–8). Series: Voices of the Past. 1995, Twenty-First Century LB $25.90 (978-0-8050-2846-1). Excerpts from letters, memoirs, and official reports highlight this well-illustrated history of the War of 1812 and its consequences. (Rev: BL 12/15/95; SLJ 3/96) [973.5]

18899 Green, Carl R. *The War of 1812* (4–6). Series: U.S. Wars. 2002, Enslow LB $25.26 (978-0-7660-5092-1). 48pp. In addition to a concise discussion of the causes, progress, and resolution of the War of 1812, this book contains a lengthy listing of Web sites where students can find additional material on the subject. (Rev: BL 10/15/02; HBG 3/03) [973.5]

18900 Greene, Meg. *Slave Young, Slave Long: The American Slave Experience* (5–8). Illus. Series: People's History. 1999, Lerner LB $30.35 (978-0-8225-1739-9). Using quotations from both victims and perpetrators, and illustrated by historical prints and photographs, this book presents the story of slavery in the United States. (Rev: BL 4/1/99; HBG 10/99; SLJ 10/99) [973.0496]

18901 Gunderson, Mary. *Southern Plantation Cooking* (4–7). Illus. 2000, Capstone LB $23.93 (978-0-7368-0357-1). 32pp. This book explores life on Southern plantations during the days of slavery with emphasis on the importance of food and food preparation. A few representative recipes are provided. (Rev: BL 8/00; HBG 10/00) [394.1]

18902 Hansen, Joyce, and Gary McGowan. *Freedom Roads: Searching for the Underground Railroad* (5–8). Illus. by James Ransome. 2003, Cricket $18.95 (978-0-8126-2673-5). 176pp. This look at the history of the Underground Railroad emphasizes how much of our knowledge consists of speculation and anecdotal material rather than hard evidence. (Rev: BL 5/1/03; HB 7/03; HBG 10/03; SLJ 9/03*) [973.7]

18903 Heinrichs, Ann. *The Underground Railroad* (3–5). Series: We the People. 2001, Compass Point LB $26.60 (978-0-7565-0102-0). 48pp. Heinrichs gives a clear explanation of the causes for the devel-

opment of this route to freedom, details how it worked, and profiles key figures. (Rev: SLJ 7/01) [973.7]

18904 Isaacs, Sally Senzell. *Life on a Southern Plantation* (1–3). Series: Picture the Past. 2000, Heinemann $21.36 (978-1-57572-316-7). A well-organized account that uses double-page spreads to describe life on a southern plantation before the Civil War with coverage of the lives of both the planters and the slaves. (Rev: HBG 3/01; SLJ 11/00) [973.6]

18905 Jacobs, William J. *War with Mexico* (4–6). Illus. Series: Spotlight on American History. 1993, Millbrook LB $21.90 (978-1-56294-366-0). 64pp. The events of the 1846–1848 war with Mexico are reported, with an objective account of its causes and results. (Rev: BL 12/15/93; SLJ 1/94) [973.6]

18906 Kalman, Bobbie. *The General Store* (3–5). Illus. Series: Historic Communities. 1997, Crabtree LB $25.27 (978-0-86505-432-5); paper $7.95 (978-0-86505-462-2). 32pp. Using photos of reconstructions in such places as Old Sturbridge Village, this account describes the importance, contents, and workings of the general store in 18th- and 19th-century America. (Rev: SLJ 7/97) [381]

18907 Kalman, Bobbie. *Life on a Plantation* (3–6). Illus. Series: Historic Communities. 1997, Crabtree LB $25.27 (978-0-86505-435-6); paper $7.95 (978-0-86505-465-3). 32pp. Daily life on the plantation for both the owners and their slaves is covered, with details about working in the fields and the roles and duties of various workers. (Rev: BL 7/97) [975]

18908 Kendall, Martha E. *The Erie Canal* (4–6). Illus. 2008, National Geographic $18.95 (978-1-4263-0022-6). 128pp. With period prints and photographs and a smooth narrative, Kendall tells the story of the building of the canal and how it helped shape westward expansion. (Rev: BL 1/1–15/08; SLJ 2/08) [386]

18909 King, David C. *New Orleans* (5–8). Illus. Series: Battlefields Across America. 1998, Twenty-First Century LB $26.90 (978-0-7613-3010-3). The story of the famous 1815 battle in New Orleans in which the British were decisively defeated, including the background of the War of 1812, the role of Andrew Jackson, and the significance of this defeat to the British. (Rev: HBG 9/98; SLJ 8/98) [973.6]

18910 Leebrick, Kristal. *The United States Constitution* (3–8). Series: Let Freedom Ring. 2002, Capstone LB $23.93 (978-0-7368-1094-4). 48pp. James Madison's role in creating the constitution, the Constitutional Convention, and the ratification process are all covered here. Also use *The Declaration of Independence* (2002). (Rev: HBG 3/03; SLJ 7/02) [973.3]

18911 Levy, Janey. *The Alamo: A Primary Source History of the Legendary Texas Mission* (5–8). Illus. Series: Primary Sources in American History. 2003, Rosen LB $29.25 (978-0-8239-3681-6). 64pp. Primary sources — including maps and paintings — tell the story of the Battle of the Alamo. (Rev: BL 5/15/03; SLJ 5/03) [976.4]

18912 Levy, Janey. *The Erie Canal: A Primary Source History of the Canal That Changed America*

(5–8). 2003, Rosen LB $29.25 (978-0-8239-3680-9). 64pp. The story of the construction of the Erie Canal and its impact on commerce is revealed through primary documents and many period illustrations. (Rev: SLJ 5/03) [974.7]

18913 Lourie, Peter. *Erie Canal: Canoeing America's Great Waterway* (5–8). Illus. 1997, Boyds Mills $17.95 (978-1-56397-669-8). This colorful book about a journey along the Erie Canal also supplies historical facts about its construction and uses. (Rev: BL 7/97; HBG 3/98; SLJ 9/97) [974.7]

18914 McGowen, Tom. *The Alamo* (3–6). Series: Cornerstones of Freedom, Second Series. 2003, Children's Pr. LB $26.00 (978-0-516-24208-8). 48pp. Background information provides context for the famous events at the Alamo; details of uniforms and weapons add to the picture. (Rev: SLJ 6/03) [976.4]

18915 McKissack, Patricia C., and Fredrick McKissack. *Rebels Against Slavery: American Slave Revolts* (5–8). Illus. 1996, Scholastic paper $15.95 (978-0-590-45735-4). A fascinating account of the men and women who led revolts against slavery, including Toussaint L'Ouverture, Cinque, Harriet Tubman, and Nat Turner. (Rev: BCCB 6/96; BL 2/15/96; SLJ 3/96; VOYA 4/96) [970]

18916 Marcovitz, Hal. *The Alamo* (4–8). Illus. Series: American Symbols and Their Meanings. 2002, Mason Crest LB $18.95 (978-1-59084-037-5). 48pp. A basic and readable introduction to the history of the Alamo and its importance to Americans, with illuminating illustrations and inset features. (Rev: SLJ 9/02) [976]

18917 Marquette, Scott. *War of 1812* (4–7). Illus. Series: America at War. 2002, Rourke LB $20.95 (978-1-58952-389-0). 48pp. This book for middle-graders studies the war itself and the events that led up to it. (Rev: BL 10/15/02) [973.5]

18918 Martin, Michael. *Harriet Tubman and the Underground Railroad* (3–6). Illus. by Dave Hoover and Bill Anderson. Series: Graphic Library/Graphic History. 2004, Capstone LB $26.60 (978-0-7368-3829-0). 32pp. A graphic "novel" — factual, but embellished — about Tubman's role in the Underground Railroad; will appeal to reluctant readers. (Rev: SLJ 7/05) [973.7]

18919 Moore, Cathy. *The Daring Escape of Ellen Craft* (1–3). Illus. by Mary O. Young. Series: On My Own History. 2002, Carolrhoda LB $23.93 (978-0-87614-462-6); paper $5.95 (978-0-87614-787-0). 48pp. This is the story, based on truth, of two slaves' 1848 journey from Georgia to safety in Philadelphia, the woman disguised as a white slave master. (Rev: HBG 10/02; SLJ 4/02)

18920 Morrison, Taylor. *Coast Mappers* (4–8). Illus. 2004, Houghton $16.00 (978-0-618-25408-8). 48pp. Science and biography are interwoven in this examination of the mid-19th-century mapping of the U.S. Pacific coastline. (Rev: BL 3/15/04; SLJ 5/04) [623.89]

18921 Nofi, Albert A. *The Underground Railroad and the Civil War* (4–8). Series: Untold History of the Civil War. 2000, Chelsea $25.00 (978-0-7910-

5434-5). 64pp. A history of the dangers, devotion, excitement, and daring involved in this collaborative system that was developed to help fugitive Southern slaves reach freedom in the North or in Canada. (Rev: BL 5/15/00; HBG 10/00; SLJ 6/00) [973.7]

18922 Olson, Kay Melchisedech. *Africans in America: 1619–1865* (4–6). Series: Coming to America. 2002, Capstone LB $23.93 (978-0-7368-1204-7). 32pp. The story of the forced migrations of Africans to America, their life of slavery, their culture and contributions, and information on famous African Americans. (Rev: BL 1/1–15/03; HBG 3/03) [973]

18923 Paulson, Timothy J. *Days of Sorrow, Years of Glory, 1831–1850: From the Nat Turner Revolt to the Fugitive Slave Law* (5–9). Series: Milestones in Black American History. 1994, Chelsea paper $14.93 (978-0-7910-2552-9). An examination of the Underground Railroad, slave resistance, the Seminole Wars, and the abolition movement. (Rev: BL 11/1/94; SLJ 4/95; VOYA 12/94) [973]

18924 Pelta, Kathy. *Eastern Trails: From Footpaths to Turnpikes* (4–6). Series: American Trails. 1997, Raintree LB $28.54 (978-0-8172-4071-4). 96pp. Focusing on trails, footpaths, and emerging roads, this account traces the opening up of the American East to settlers and explorers. Also use *Trails to the West: Beyond the Mississippi* (1997). (Rev: BL 10/15/97; HBG 3/98) [973.6]

18925 Ray, Kurt. *New Roads, Canals, and Railroads in Early-19th-Century America: The Transportation Revolution* (3–5). Illus. Series: Life in the New American Nation. 2004, Rosen LB $22.50 (978-0-8239-4036-3). 32pp. A look at the growth in transport-related construction in the early 19th century.

18926 Richards, Caroline Cowles. *A 19th Century Schoolgirl: The Diary of Caroline Cowles Richards, 1852–1855* (4–8). Ed. by Kerry Graves. Illus. Series: Diaries, Letters, and Memoirs. 2000, Capstone LB $23.93 (978-0-7368-0342-7). 32pp. This diary of a young girl living in western New York State in the early 1850s describes her daily life, schooling, and her reaction to the women's rights movement. (Rev: BL 10/15/00; HBG 10/00; SLJ 9/00) [974.7]

18927 Santella, Andrew. *The Erie Canal* (4–6). Series: We the People. 2004, Compass Point LB $26.60 (978-0-7565-0679-7). 48pp. Discusses the construction of this canal in the 19th century and its importance in transporting goods. (Rev: SLJ 2/05) [386]

18928 Stefoff, Rebecca. *The War of 1812* (4–7). Illus. Series: North American Historical Atlases. 2000, Benchmark LB $27.07 (978-0-7614-1060-7). A clearly written text plus historical maps and reproductions are used to give an easy-to-read account of the War of 1812. (Rev: HBG 3/01; SLJ 1/01) [973.8]

18929 Stewart, Mark. *The Alamo, February 23–March 6, 1836* (5–7). Illus. Series: American Battlefields. 2004, Enchanted Lion $14.95 (978-1-59270-026-4). 32pp. This overview of the Battle of the Alamo offers a clear account of the conflict and an examination of the developments leading up to it; sidebars, illustrations, a timeline, and other features add to the narrative. (Rev: BL 11/1/04) [976.4]

18930 Toynton, Evelyn. *Growing Up in America: 1830 to 1860* (4–6). Illus. 1995, Millbrook LB $24.90 (978-1-56294-453-7). 96pp. Describes the life of pre-Civil War children from five social groups, including Native Americans, slaves, and farmers. (Rev: BL 4/15/95; SLJ 4/95) [973.5]

18931 Turner, Glennette Tilley. *The Underground Railroad in Illinois* (5–8). Illus. 2001, Newman Educational Publg. paper $16.95 (978-0-938990-05-5). 320pp. Using a question-and-answer format, this book focuses on the Underground Railroad in Illinois, the historical period, the problems, people who worked on the effort, and the many heroic deeds. (Rev: BL 2/15/01) [973.7]

18932 Walker, Paul R. *Remember the Alamo: Texians, Tejanos, and Mexicans Tell Their Stories* (5–8). Illus. 2007, National Geographic $17.95 (978-1-4263-0010-3). 64pp. A detailed account of the siege of the Alamo, with explanation of the events leading up to the crisis and with many firsthand descriptions. (Rev: BL 5/15/07; SLJ 8/07) [976.4]

18933 Wells, Rosemary. *Streets of Gold* (2–5). Illus. by Dan Andreasen. 1999, Dial $16.99 (978-0-8037-2149-4). 40pp. This picture book for older readers is the biography of a Russian Jewish girl who leaves the old country for a new life in America. (Rev: BCCB 7–8/99; BL 5/1/99; HBG 3/00; SLJ 6/99) [973]

18934 Whitcraft, Melissa. *Seward's Folly* (3–6). Series: Cornerstones of Freedom, Second Series. 2002, Children's Book Pr. LB $26.00 (978-0-516-22525-8). 48pp. An attractive account of the purchase of the Alaskan territory. (Rev: SLJ 12/02)

18935 Williams, Carla. *The Underground Railroad* (4–6). Series: Journey to Freedom. 2009, The Child's World LB $28.50 (978-1-60253-139-0). 32pp. A solid overview of the Underground Railroad told through personal stories, photographs, news accounts, and brief biographies. (Rev: SLJ 7/09) [973.7]

PIONEER LIFE AND WESTWARD EXPANSION

18936 Altman, Linda J. *The California Gold Rush in American History* (4–8). Illus. Series: In American History. 1997, Enslow LB $26.60 (978-0-89490-878-1). 128pp. After a brief history of the California Gold Rush, this book covers topics including frontier injustice, racial discrimination, and the place of women. (Rev: HBG 3/98; SLJ 3/98) [979.4]

18937 Ammon, Richard. *Conestoga Wagons* (2–5). Illus. 2000, Holiday House $17.95 (978-0-8234-1475-8). 32pp. This illustrated account gives the history of the vehicles used for long-distance hauling between 1750 and 1850 and discusses their construction, parts, uses, and the people who drove them. (Rev: BCCB 9/00; BL 10/1/00; HBG 3/01; SLJ 9/00) [388.3]

18938 Anderson, Dale. *Westward Expansion* (5–8). Series: The Making of America. 2001, Raintree LB $28.54 (978-0-8172-5705-7). 96pp. An attractive, balanced history of the expansion of the United States to the Pacific with many biographies of pioneers given in sidebars. (Rev: BL 4/15/01; HBG 10/01) [978]

18939 Anderson, Joan. *Spanish Pioneers of the Southwest* (3–6). Illus. 1989, Dutton paper $16.99 (978-0-525-67546-4). 64pp. A photoessay of life in mid-18th-century New Mexico. (Rev: BCCB 4/89; BL 4/15/89; SLJ 5/89)

18940 Bial, Raymond. *Cow Towns* (2–5). Series: American Community. 2004, Children's Pr. LB $29.00 (978-0-516-23706-0). 48pp. The daily lives of the people — cattlemen and prospectors, for example — who populated the towns of the early West are described plus detailed back matter and many illustrations. Also use *Frontier Settlements* and *Missions and Presidios* (both 2004). (Rev: SLJ 1/05) [978]

18941 Bial, Raymond. *Ghost Towns of the American West* (3–5). Illus. 2001, Houghton $16.00 (978-0-618-06557-8). Several western ghost towns are presented, with pictures of how they looked then and look today and details of why they were abandoned. (Rev: BCCB 2/01; BL 1/1–15/01; HB 3/01; HBG 10/01; SLJ 2/01) [978]

18942 Blackwood, Gary L. *Life on the Oregon Trail* (5–8). Series: The Way People Live. 1999, Lucent LB $28.70 (978-1-56006-540-1). 111pp. Using many excerpts from diaries, this is a thorough, appealing account of life on the Oregon Trail, which took pioneers from Missouri to the Pacific Ocean. (Rev: HBG 3/00; SLJ 8/99) [978]

18943 Blashfield, Jean F. *The California Gold Rush* (3–6). Series: We the People. 2000, Compass Point LB $26.60 (978-0-7565-0041-2). 48pp. A straightforward account of why and how people traveled to California during the Gold Rush and of the lasting effects this migration had on western history. (Rev: SLJ 3/01) [979.4]

18944 Blashfield, Jean F. *The Oregon Trail* (3–6). 2000, Compass Point LB $26.60 (978-0-7565-0045-0). 48pp. This book explains the building of the Oregon Trail, its uses, and travel conditions along it. Also use: *The Santa Fe Trail* (2000). (Rev: SLJ 3/01) [978]

18945 Brill, Marlene T. *Bronco Charlie and the Pony Express* (2–4). Illus. by Craig Orback. Series: On My Own History. 2004, Carolrhoda LB $27.93 (978-1-57505-587-9); paper $5.95 (978-1-57505-618-0). 46pp. Bronco Charlie, 11, became the youngest rider for the Pony Express in 1861 and rode bravely through various dangers. (Rev: SLJ 8/04) [383]

18946 Burnett, Linda. *Pioneers: Adventure in a New Land* (4–6). Series: Trailblazers of the West. 2005, Children's Pr. LB $24.50 (978-0-516-25127-1); paper $6.95 (978-0-516-25097-7). 48pp. The hard life of pioneers on the western frontier is portrayed in short chapters suitable for reluctant readers. (Rev: SLJ 4/06) [978.02]

18947 Calabro, Marian. *The Perilous Journey of the Donner Party* (5–8). Illus. 1999, Houghton $20.00

(978-0-395-86610-8). The story of the ill-fated Donner Party, as seen through the eyes of 12-year-old Virginia Reed. (Rev: BL 4/1/99*; HB 5/99; SLJ 5/99; VOYA 2/00) [979.4]

18948 Carlson, Laurie. *Westward Ho! An Activity Guide to the Wild West* (4–6). 1996, Chicago Review paper $12.95 (978-1-55652-271-0). 160pp. Clear directions accompany this introduction to 50 activities — like hooking rugs or keeping a trapper's journal — associated with the westward movement. (Rev: BL 10/1/96; SLJ 12/96) [978]

18949 Cobb, Mary. *The Quilt-Block History of Pioneer Days: With Projects Kids Can Make* (3–6). Illus. 1995, Millbrook LB $23.90 (978-1-56294-485-8). 64pp. A history of America's Western pioneers as seen through the patterns in their quilts plus a number of related craft projects, such as making bookmarks. (Rev: BL 4/15/95; SLJ 6/95) [746.9]

18950 Coleman, Wim, and Pat Perrin. *What Made the Wild West Wild* (4–8). Illus. Series: The Wild History of the American West. 2006, Enslow LB $33.27 (978-1-59845-016-3). 128pp. The myths and legends of the Wild West are debunked in this expansive overview of media portrayals and reality. (Rev: SLJ 1/07) [978]

18951 Collier, Christopher, and James Lincoln Collier. *Indians, Cowboys, and Farmers: And the Battle for the Great Plains* (5–8). Series: The Drama of American History. 2001, Marshall Cavendish LB $31.36 (978-0-7614-1052-2). This excellently written and illustrated account covers the history of the Great Plains from the end of the Civil War to 1910, by which time the Native Americans had been scattered and the ranchers and farmers had reached a truce. (Rev: BL 3/15/01; HBG 10/01; SLJ 7/01) [973.8]

18952 Comport, Sally Wern. *The Great Expedition of Lewis and Clark: By Private Reubin Field, Member of the Corps of Discovery* (3–4). Illus. by author. 2003, Farrar $17.00 (978-0-374-38039-7). 40pp. Writing from the point of view of Reubin Field, Edwards gives a lively account of the famous expedition, its principal characters, and its dangers and delights. (Rev: BL 8/03; HBG 4/04; SLJ 11/03) [917.8]

18953 Crewe, Sabrina, and Dale Anderson. *The California Gold Rush* (3–5). Series: Events That Shaped America. 2003, Gareth Stevens LB $26.00 (978-0-8368-3393-5). 32pp. This brief history of the mid-19th-century California Gold Rush covers the discovery of gold at Sutter's Mill and that event's impact on the state and the nation as a whole. (Rev: HBG 10/03; SLJ 10/03) [979.4]

18954 Davis, Kenneth C. *Don't Know Much About the Pioneers* (3–5). Illus. by Renée Andriani. Series: Don't Know Much About. 2003, HarperCollins LB $16.89 (978-0-06-028618-7). 48pp. Quizzes, quotations, feature sidebars, and bright illustrations make this a volume for browsing. (Rev: HBG 10/03; SLJ 6/03) [978]

18955 Dean, Arlan. *The Mormon Pioneer Trail: From Nauvoo, Illinois, to the Great Salt Lake, Utah* (2–4). Illus. Series: Famous American Trails. 2003,

Rosen LB $19.95 (978-0-8239-6476-5). 24pp. For early readers and researchers, this title explores the 1,200-mile trail, providing lots of illustrations and maps. (Rev: SLJ 6/03) [978]

18956 Dean, Arlan. *The Old Spanish Trail: From Santa Fe, New Mexico, to Los Angeles, California* (2–4). Series: Famous American Trails. 2003, Rosen LB $19.95 (978-0-8239-6480-2). 24pp. This attractive and informative survey for young readers includes maps, photographs, and illustrations. (Rev: SLJ 12/03) [979]

18957 Dean, Arlan. *The Santa Fe Trail: From Independence, Missouri, to Santa Fe, New Mexico* (2–4). Illus. Series: Famous American Trails. 2003, Rosen LB $19.95 (978-0-8239-6481-9). 24pp. For early readers and researchers, this title explores the historic wagon trail, providing lots of illustrations and maps. (Rev: SLJ 6/03) [978]

18958 DeAngelis, Gina. *The Black Cowboys* (4–8). Illus. Series: Legends of the West. 1997, Chelsea LB $30.00 (978-0-7910-2589-5); paper $9.95 (978-0-7910-2590-1). A look at the contributions of African Americans such as Jim Beckwourth and Edward Rose to the exploration and settlement of the American West. (Rev: BL 2/15/98; HBG 3/98) [978]

18959 DeAngelis, Gina. *The Wild West* (5–8). Series: Costume, Tradition, and Culture: Reflecting on the Past. 1998, Chelsea $19.75 (978-0-7910-5169-6). 64pp. Illustrated with historical collectors' cards, this account relates the legends and stories of the Wild West — its explorers, lawmen, outlaws, and Native Americans. (Rev: BL 3/15/99; HBG 10/99) [978]

18960 Delgado, James P. *Shipwrecks from the Westward Movement* (5–7). Series: Shipwrecks. 2000, Watts LB $25.50 (978-0-531-20380-4). 64pp. A discussion and exploration of the shipwrecks — from small canoes to steam-powered riverboats — that occurred as European settlers moved across America. (Rev: BL 10/15/00) [978]

18961 Duncan, Dayton. *People of the West* (5–10). Illus. 1996, Little, Brown $19.95 (978-0-316-19627-7). Individual people — both famous and less well known — describe in their own words the opening up of the West. Based on the PBS series. (Rev: BL 8/96; SLJ 10/96) [978]

18962 Fine, Jil. *The Transcontinental Railroad: Tracks Across America* (4–6). Series: Trailblazers of the West. 2005, Children's Pr. LB $24.50 (978-0-516-25128-8); paper $6.95 (978-0-516-25098-4). 48pp. This attractive title chronicles the building of the transcontinental railroad, an important step in opening up the American West, and the hardships suffered by those involved; short, well-illustrated chapters are suitable for reluctant readers. (Rev: SLJ 4/06) [385]

18963 Fisher, Leonard Everett. *The Oregon Trail* (4–6). Illus. 1990, Holiday House LB $18.95 (978-0-8234-0833-7). 64pp. A clear, readable account of the westward expansion in the 1800s. (Rev: BCCB 1/91; BL 12/15/90; HB 3/91; SLJ 1/91) [979.5]

18964 Freedman, Russell. *Children of the Wild West* (5–9). Illus. 1983, Clarion $18.00 (978-0-89919-143-0). A look at the life of the children of pioneers. (Rev: BL 1/1/90) [978]

18965 Freedman, Russell. *Cowboys of the Wild West* (5–8). Illus. 1990, Houghton paper $9.95 (978-0-395-54800-4). 128pp. Text and excellent historical photographs describe these romantic figures. (Rev: BCCB 12/85; HB 3/86) [978.02]

18966 Galford, Ellen. *The Trail West: Exploring History Through Art* (5–8). Illus. Series: Picture That! 2004, Two-Can $19.95 (978-1-58728-442-7). 64pp. Paintings serve as the vehicle to draw students into the story of westward expansion. (Rev: BL 11/1/04; SLJ 2/05) [978]

18967 Goldsmith, Connie. *Lost in Death Valley: The True Story of Four Families in California's Gold Rush* (5–8). Illus. 2001, Twenty-First Century LB $24.90 (978-0-7613-1915-3). 144pp. Using original sources, the author has re-created the story of an ill-fated pioneer trek and the shortcut that led them into Death Valley. (Rev: BL 4/1/01; HBG 10/01; SLJ 4/01; VOYA 10/01) [979.4]

18968 Graves, Kerry A. *Going to School in Pioneer Times* (4–6). Illus. Series: Going to School in History. 2001, Capstone LB $23.93 (978-0-7368-0804-0). 32pp. Today's students will enjoy this look at the one-room schoolhouse of pioneer days, introduced by historical context and illustrated with period photographs. (Rev: BL 10/15/01; HBG 3/02; SLJ 1/02) [370.977]

18969 Green, Carl R., and William R. Sanford. *The Dalton Gang* (4–8). Illus. Series: Outlaws and Lawmen of the Wild West. 1995, Enslow LB $21.26 (978-0-89490-588-9). 48pp. The story of the gang of outlaws who roamed the West during pioneer days. (Rev: BL 11/15/95) [978]

18970 Hailstone, Ruth. *The White Ox: The Journey of Emily Swain Squires* (2–5). Illus. by Dan Burr. 2009, Boyds Mills $18.95 (978-1-59078-555-3). 40pp. Dramatic art extends this story of 10-year-old Emily, a Mormon, and her grueling journey to Salt Lake City; set in 1863, this is based on the experiences of an ancestor of the author. (Rev: BL 4/15/09) [289.3092]

18971 Hatt, Christine. *The American West: Native Americans, Pioneers and Settlers* (4–7). Series: History in Writing. 1999, Bedrick $19.95 (978-0-87226-290-4). 62pp. A broad overview of frontier life in America with material on such topics as the Louisiana Purchase, Indian relocations, the Gold Rush, and a settler's daily life. (Rev: HBG 3/00; SLJ 5/99) [978]

18972 Hester, Sallie. *A Covered Wagon Girl: The Diary of Sallie Hester, 1849–1850* (4–6). Series: Diaries, Letters, and Memoirs. 2000, Capstone LB $23.93 (978-0-7368-0344-1). 32pp. Diary entries by a young pioneer girl reveal everyday life on the American frontier. (Rev: BL 10/15/00; HBG 10/00; SLJ 9/00) [978]

18973 Isaacs, Sally Senzell. *The Gold Rush* (4–6). Illus. Series: The American Adventure. 2003, Heinemann LB $25.65 (978-1-4034-2501-0). 32pp.

An accessible account of the "Fortyniners" who thronged to California in the mid-18th century. (Rev: HBG 4/04; SLJ 6/04) [979.4]

18974 Isaacs, Sally Senzell. *The Great Land Rush* (4–6). Illus. Series: The American Adventure. 2003, Heinemann LB $25.64 (978-1-4034-2505-8). 32pp. The story of the rush to settle land on the American frontier in the late 19th century, including its impact on the native people who already lived there. (Rev: HBG 4/04; SLJ 6/04) [976.6]

18975 Isaacs, Sally Senzell. *The Lewis and Clark Expedition* (4–6). Illus. Series: The American Adventure. 2003, Heinemann LB $25.64 (978-1-4034-2503-4). 32pp. The impact on the native peoples of the West and Pacific Northwest is one focus of this well-illustrated account. (Rev: HBG 4/04; SLJ 6/04) [917.8]

18976 Isaacs, Sally Senzell. *Life on a Pioneer Homestead* (1–3). Series: Picture the Past. 2000, Heinemann LB $21.36 (978-1-57572-313-6). Using double-page spreads, this well-organized account covers such basic topics as pioneer food, clothing, and rearing of children. Also use from this series *Life on the Oregon Trail* (2000). (Rev: HBG 3/01; SLJ 11/00) [978]

18977 January, Brendan. *Little Bighorn: June 25, 1876* (5–7). Series: American Battlefields. 2004, Enchanted Lion $14.95 (978-1-59270-028-8). 32pp. This overview of the Battle of Little Bighorn offers a clear-cut account of the bloody conflict and an examination of the developments leading up to it; sidebars, illustrations, a timeline, and other features add to the narrative. (Rev: BL 11/1/04) [973]

18978 Johmann, Carol A., and Elizabeth J. Rieth. *Going West! Journey on a Wagon Train to Settle a Frontier Town* (3–6). Illus. by Michael Kline. Series: Kaleidoscope Kids. 2000, Williamson paper $14.25 (978-1-885593-38-2). 96pp. As well as information on wagon trains, this book gives good background history involving the opening up of the West and outlines projects that use the crafts and skills of the pioneers. (Rev: SLJ 1/01) [978]

18979 Josephson, Judith P. *Growing up in Pioneer America: 1800 to 1890* (4–6). Series: Our America. 2002, Lerner LB $26.60 (978-0-8225-0659-1). 64pp. The lives of children in this period are described with many quotations and excerpts from diaries, letter, and memoirs. (Rev: HBG 3/03; SLJ 2/03)

18980 Kalman, Bobbie. *Bandannas, Chaps, and Ten-Gallon Hats* (3–6). Series: Life in the Old West. 1999, Crabtree LB $25.27 (978-0-7787-0073-9). 32pp. An interesting but somewhat disorganized account on the part played by cowboys in the opening up of the West. (Rev: SLJ 9/99) [978]

18981 Kalman, Bobbie. *The Gristmill* (3–6). Illus. Series: Historic Communities. 1991, Crabtree LB $25.27 (978-0-86505-486-8); paper $7.95 (978-0-86505-506-3). 32pp. Text and pictures show the construction and operation of the mill as well as the skills of the millers. (Rev: BL 7/91) [664]

18982 Kalman, Bobbie. *Home Crafts* (3–6). Illus. Series: Historic Communities. 1991, Crabtree LB

$25.27 (978-0-86505-485-1); paper $7.95 (978-0-86505-505-6). 32pp. How early settlers produced wool and other cloth and made quilts, soap, leather goods, and other necessities. (Rev: BL 7/91) [745.5]

18983 Kalman, Bobbie. *In the Barn* (3–6). Illus. Series: Historic Communities. 1997, Crabtree LB $25.27 (978-0-86505-433-2); paper $7.95 (978-0-86505-463-9). 32pp. Shows how the barn was the center of activity on a settler's farm and supplies details on its design, barn raising, and all the seasonal activities it housed. (Rev: BL 7/97) [631.2]

18984 Kalman, Bobbie. *The Kitchen* (3–6). Illus. Series: Historic Communities. 1991, Crabtree LB $25.27 (978-0-86505-484-4); paper $7.95 (978-0-86505-504-9). 32pp. The kitchen and its utensils as they existed in pioneer times are pictured and described. (Rev: BL 7/91) [643.3]

18985 Kalman, Bobbie. *A One-Room School* (3–5). Illus. Series: Historic Communities. 1994, Crabtree LB $25.27 (978-0-86505-497-4); paper $7.95 (978-0-86505-517-9). 32pp. Through pictures and text, the physical plan of a one-room school is presented, with material on supplies, routines, expected conduct, and school rules. (Rev: SLJ 9/94) [371.7]

18986 Kalman, Bobbie. *Settler Sayings* (3–5). Illus. Series: Historic Communities. 1994, Crabtree LB $25.27 (978-0-86505-498-1); paper $7.95 (978-0-86505-518-6). 32pp. In a conversational text, sayings popular with settlers are described under such headings as the kitchen and the farm. (Rev: SLJ 7/94) [973.8]

18987 Kalman, Bobbie. *Visiting a Village* (3–6). Illus. Series: Historic Communities. 1991, Crabtree $25.27 (978-0-86505-487-5); paper $7.95 (978-0-86505-507-0). 32pp. Life in a frontier village is described in this well-illustrated account. (Rev: BL 7/91) [971]

18988 Kalman, Bobbie. *Who Settled the West?* (3–6). Series: Life in the Old West. 1999, Crabtree LB $25.27 (978-0-7787-0075-3); paper $7.95 (978-0-7787-0107-1). 32pp. An eclectic collection of material about the various groups of pioneers who settled in the West. Also use *Boomtowns of the West*. (Rev: SLJ 9/99) [978]

18989 Kalman, Bobbie, and Kate Calder. *The Life of a Miner* (3–6). Series: Life in the Old West. 1999, Crabtree LB $25.27 (978-0-7787-0077-7); paper $7.95 (978-0-7787-0109-5). 32pp. This well-researched title traces the development of the mining industry in the mid-1800s and takes the reader underground to show how miners worked. (Rev: SLJ 5/00) [973.6]

18990 Kalman, Bobbie, and Kate Calder. *Women of the West* (3–6). 1999, Crabtree LB $25.27 (978-0-7787-0080-7); paper $7.95 (978-0-7787-0112-5). 32pp. Traces the roles of both white and Native American women in the history of the old West with material on daily life and hardships. (Rev: SLJ 5/00) [973.6]

18991 Kalman, Bobbie, and Tammy Everts. *A Child's Day* (3–5). Illus. by Antoinette DeBiasi. Series: Historic Communities. 1994, Crabtree LB $25.27 (978-0-86505-494-3); paper $7.95 (978-0-86505-514-8).

32pp. A day in the life of settlers' children is shown through such activities as doing chores, playing games, going to school, and visiting a fair. (Rev: SLJ 9/94) [978]

18992 Kalman, Bobbie, and Tammy Everts. *Customs and Traditions* (3–5). Illus. Series: Historic Communities. 1994, Crabtree LB $25.27 (978-0-86505-495-0); paper $7.95 (978-0-86505-515-5). 32pp. Various customs and traditions from the days of the settlers are described and their origins traced in this heavily illustrated volume. (Rev: SLJ 7/94) [973.8]

18993 Kalman, Bobbie, and David Schimpky. *Fort Life* (3–5). Illus. Series: Historic Communities. 1994, Crabtree LB $25.27 (978-0-86505-496-7); paper $7.95 (978-0-86505-516-2). 32pp. This book describes life in a fort, with details on early American defenses and the daily life of soldiers. (Rev: SLJ 9/94) [978]

18994 King, David C. *Pioneer Days: Discover the Past with Fun Projects, Games, Activities, and Recipes* (3–6). Illus. by Bobbie Moore. Series: American Kids in History. 1997, Wiley paper $12.95 (978-0-471-16169-1). 118pp. In chapters arranged by season, the daily life of pioneers is recreated through an assortment of history, culture, crafts, and stories. (Rev: SLJ 2/98) [973.5]

18995 Klausmeier, Robert. *Cowboy* (4–7). Illus. Series: American Pastfinder. 1996, Lerner LB $21.27 (978-0-8225-2975-0). 48pp. This account focuses on the huge cattle drives and the men who led them in the years following the Civil War. (Rev: BL 3/1/96; SLJ 3/96) [636.2]

18996 Klobuchar, Lisa. *The History and Activities of the Wagon Trail* (3–5). Series: Hands-on American History. 2006, Heinemann LB $27.07 (978-1-4034-6055-4). 32pp. An accessible and informative account of life on the westbound wagon trains is bolstered by illustrations and activities — a recipe, a toy, and a prairie schooner replica. (Rev: BL 9/1/06) [978]

18997 Landau, Elaine. *The Pony Express* (2–4). Illus. Series: Westward Expansion (True Book). 2006, Children's Pr. LB $25.00 (978-0-516-25873-7). 48pp. The colorful — but brief — history of the Pony Express, launched to move mail from St. Joseph, Missouri, to San Francisco in a scant ten days, is chronicled in readable text, drawings, and maps. (Rev: BL 4/1/06) [383]

18998 Landau, Elaine. *The Transcontinental Railroad* (5–8). Illus. Series: Watts Library: American West. 2005, Watts LB $25.50 (978-0-531-12326-3). 64pp. The story behind the building of the Transcontinental Railroad, with illustrations, maps, a timeline, and sidebar features. (Rev: SLJ 12/05)

18999 La Pierre, Yvette. *Welcome to Josefina's World, 1824* (3–6). Series: American Girl. 1999, Pleasant $16.95 (978-1-56247-769-1). 58pp. With excellent illustrations and good historical information, this book uses a series of double-page spreads to introduce life on the American Southwest frontier in 1824 as experienced by a young girl. (Rev: BL 1/1–15/00; HBG 3/00) [973.4]

19000 Lassieur, Allison. *The Wild West: An Interactive History Adventure* (3–5). Illus. Series: You Choose. 2008, Capstone LB $20.99 (978-1-4296-2342-1). 112pp. Put yourself right in the middle of the Wild West action as you choose between various actions; will you be a lawman or a gambler, for example? (Rev: BL 4/1/09) [978]

19001 Leeper, David R. *The Diary of David R. Leeper: Rush for Gold* (3–6). Ed. by Connie Roop and Peter Roop. Illus. Series: My Own Words. 2000, Marshall Cavendish LB $27.07 (978-0-7614-1011-9). 64pp. This book, taken from Leeper's memoirs published in 1894, tells how he crossed the country by wagon train and his life as a prospector for gold in California. (Rev: BL 2/15/01; HBG 3/01; SLJ 3/01) [979.4]

19002 Loeper, John J. *Meet the Drakes on the Kentucky Frontier* (3–5). Series: Early American Family. 1998, Marshall Cavendish LB $25.64 (978-0-7614-0845-1). 64pp. Based on fact, this account depicts the life of the Drake family, who moved to the unsettled Kentucky frontier in 1781. (Rev: HBG 10/99; SLJ 4/99) [973.3]

19003 Loeper, John J. *Meet the Wards on the Oregon Trail* (3–5). Series: Early American Family. 1998, Marshall Cavendish LB $25.64 (978-0-7614-0844-4). 64pp. Using many authentic details, this is an exciting re-creation of a family's everyday experiences as they travel on the Oregon Trail in the 1850s. (Rev: HBG 10/99; SLJ 4/99) [973.6]

19004 Markel, Rita J. *Your Travel Guide to America's Old West* (4–7). Illus. Series: Passport to History. 2003, Lerner LB $26.60 (978-0-8225-3074-9). 96pp. Information about the Old West — everything from historical anecdotes to profiles of key individuals to details of dress and behavior — is conveyed in the style of a travel guide complete with photographs and prints. (Rev: BL 2/15/04; HBG 4/04; SLJ 4/04) [917.604]

19005 Miller, Brandon M. *Buffalo Gals: Women of the Old West* (4–7). Illus. 1995, Lerner LB $30.35 (978-0-8225-1730-6). 88pp. A realistic portrait of the hardships faced by women pioneers during the 19th century on the western frontier. (Rev: BCCB 7–8/95; BL 5/1/95; SLJ 6/95*) [978]

19006 O'Donnell, Kerri. *The Gold Rush: A Primary Source History of the Search for Gold in California* (4–8). Series: Primary Sources in American History. 2003, Rosen LB $29.25 (978-0-8239-3682-3). 64pp. Timelines and reproductions of period photographs and relevant items add to the narrative in this introduction to the Gold Rush, the life of the miners, and the lawless character of the West. (Rev: SLJ 5/03) [979.4]

19007 Patent, Dorothy Hinshaw. *Homesteading: Settling America's Heartland* (2–5). Photos by William Munoz. 1998, Walker $16.95 (978-0-8027-8664-7). 32pp. Building a sod house, farming, housekeeping, schooling, and amusements are some of the subjects in this account of homesteading on the American frontier. (Rev: BL 11/1/98; HBG 10/99; SLJ 10/98) [978]

19008 Patent, Dorothy Hinshaw. *West by Covered Wagon: Retracing the Pioneer Trails* (3–6). Illus. by William Muñoz. 1995, Walker LB $16.85 (978-0-8027-8378-3). 32pp. A modern covered-wagon trip is compared to the original journeys accomplished by pioneers as they opened up the West. (Rev: BCCB 11/95; BL 11/1/95; SLJ 10/95*) [978]

19009 Pelta, Kathy. *Cattle Trails: "Get Along Little Dogies"* (5–8). Series: American Trails. 1997, Raintree LB $19.98 (978-0-8172-4073-8). A discussion of the cattle drives that were part of the history of the American West from 1850 to 1890. (Rev: SLJ 12/97) [978]

19010 Pelta, Kathy. *The Royal Roads: Spanish Trails in North America* (5–8). Series: American Trails. 1997, Raintree LB $19.98 (978-0-8172-4074-5). The story of the Spanish trails in Florida, California, New Mexico, and Texas, and the people who traveled them looking for spiritual or material gain. (Rev: SLJ 12/97) [970.01]

19011 Raabe, Emily. *Pioneers: Life as a Homesteader* (2–4). Series: Westward Ho! 2003, Rosen LB $19.95 (978-0-8239-6498-7). 24pp. An overview of what life was like for the men and women who opened up the American West. (Rev: SLJ 12/03) [978]

19012 Randolph, Ryan P. *Frontier Schools and Schoolteachers* (3–5). Illus. Series: The Library of the Westward Expansion. 2003, Rosen LB $21.25 (978-0-8239-6295-2). 24pp. Historical artwork and "Did You Know" boxes enliven this overview of schools on the American frontier. (Rev: SLJ 10/03) [371.009]

19013 Randolph, Ryan P. *Wild West Lawmen and Outlaws* (3–5). Illus. Series: The Library of the Westward Expansion. 2003, Rosen LB $21.25 (978-0-8239-6293-8). 24pp. Profiles the men who helped to put the "wild" in Wild West and the law enforcement officers who did their best to keep the peace. (Rev: SLJ 10/03) [978]

19014 Redmond, Shirley Raye. *Lewis and Clark: A Prairie Dog for the President* (1–3). Illus. by John Manders. Series: Step into Reading. 2003, Random LB $11.99 (978-0-375-81120-3); paper $3.99 (978-0-375-91120-0). 48pp. This entertaining history for beginning readers uses cartoon-style art to portray Lewis and Clark's efforts to find suitable presents to send back to President Jefferson. (Rev: BL 8/03; HBG 4/04) [917.804]

19015 Ritchie, David. *Frontier Life* (5–7). Illus. Series: Life in America 100 Years Ago. 1995, Chelsea $21.95 (978-0-7910-2842-1). 104pp. A concise overview of life on the American frontier that does not gloss over the harsh and often violent aspects. (Rev: SLJ 1/96) [973.5]

19016 Ross, Stewart. *Cowboys* (5–7). Illus. Series: Fact or Fiction? 1995, Millbrook LB $26.90 (978-1-56294-618-0). 48pp. The life of cowboys during the late 1800s is covered, with information that tries to separate fact from fable. (Rev: BL 7/95; SLJ 5/95) [978.02]

19017 Rounds, Glen. *Sod Houses on the Great Plains* (K–3). Illus. 1995, Holiday House LB $16.95 (978-

0-8234-1162-7). 32pp. An illustrated account of the construction and utilization of a sod house, home of many prairie pioneers. (Rev: BCCB 3/95; BL 3/1/95*; HB 5/95; SLJ 3/95*) [693]

19018 Saffer, Barbara. *The California Gold Rush* (5–7). Series: The American West. 2002, Mason Crest LB $19.95 (978-1-59084-060-3). 64pp. Reluctant readers will be drawn to this attractive account of the hardships of traveling to California and the life in the mining camps. (Rev: SLJ 4/02) [979.4]

19019 Salas, Laura Purdie. *The Wilderness Road, 1775* (4–6). Illus. Series: Let Freedom Ring. 2003, Capstone LB $23.93 (978-0-7368-1561-1). 48pp. Tells the story of the building of the Wilderness Road, which opened the way into Kentucky for early American settlers; includes a chapter on Daniel Boone. (Rev: HBG 10/03; SLJ 12/03) [973.2]

19020 Sanford, William R. *The Chisholm Trail in American History* (4–6). Series: In American History. 2000, Enslow LB $26.60 (978-0-7660-1345-2). 112pp. This book traces the history of the Chisholm Trail, the daily life of the cowboys who used it, and its eventual demise. (Rev: BL 7/00; HBG 3/01; SLJ 12/00) [978]

19021 Savage, Jeff. *Cowboys and Cow Towns of the Wild West* (4–7). Illus. Series: Trailblazers of the Wild West. 1995, Enslow LB $21.26 (978-0-89490-603-9). 48pp. Through the experiences of a single cowboy, the reader learns about his equipment, dangers, leisure time, cattle drives, and roundups. (Rev: SLJ 2/96) [978]

19022 Savage, Jeff. *Gunfighters of the Wild West* (3–5). Illus. Series: Trailblazers of the Wild West. 1995, Enslow LB $21.26 (978-0-89490-600-8). 48pp. This book briefly covers the lives and exploits of such gunslingers as Doc Holliday, the Earps, John Fisher King, Billy the Kid, the Jameses, the Daltons, and the Wild Bunch. (Rev: SLJ 1/96) [973.5]

19023 Savage, Jeff. *Pioneering Women of the Wild West* (3–5). Illus. Series: Trailblazers of the Wild West. 1995, Enslow LB $16.95 (978-0-89490-604-6). 48pp. The struggles and hardships of women in the Wild West are covered, with particular mention of such famous characters as Calamity Jane and Carrie Nation. (Rev: SLJ 1/96) [973.5]

19024 Schaffer, David. *The Louisiana Purchase: The Deal of the Century That Doubled the Nation* (5–8). Illus. Series: The Wild History of the American West. 2006, Enslow LB $33.27 (978-1-59845-018-7). 128pp. Tells the story behind America's negotiations to buy the vast Louisiana Territory for $15 million, or less than 3 cents an acre; includes a list of carefully selected Web sites that offer additional information. (Rev: SLJ 12/06) [973.4]

19025 Schanzer, Rosalyn. *Gold Fever! Tales from the California Gold Rush* (3–5). Illus. 1999, National Geographic $17.95 (978-0-7922-7303-5). 48pp. Beginning with the discovery of gold nuggets at Sutter's Mill in 1847, this story of the California Gold Rush is told through diaries and original writ-

ings. (Rev: BCCB 6/99; BL 4/15/99; HBG 10/99; SLJ 4/99) [979.4]

19026 Schlaepfer, Gloria G. *The Louisiana Purchase* (5–8). Illus. Series: Watts Library: American West. 2005, Watts LB $25.50 (978-0-531-12300-3). 64pp. The story behind the Louisiana Purchase and its role in America's westward expansion, with illustrations, maps, a timeline, and sidebar features. (Rev: SLJ 12/05)

19027 Schroeder, Lisa Golden. *California Gold Rush Cooking* (4–7). Series: Exploring History Through Simple Recipes. 2000, Capstone LB $23.93 (978-0-7368-0603-9). 32pp. This book discusses the California Gold Rush and everyday life of the period with details of the kinds of food eaten and some simple recipes. (Rev: BL 3/1/01; HBG 10/01; SLJ 4/01) [979.4]

19028 Shuter, Jane, ed. *Sarah Royce and the American West* (5–8). Illus. Series: History Eyewitness. 1996, Raintree LB $24.26 (978-0-8114-8286-8). The ordeals and achievements of American pioneers are chronicled in this first-person account, accompanied by many splendid illustrations. (Rev: BL 5/15/96; SLJ 6/96) [978]

19029 Sinnott, Susan. *Welcome to Kirsten's World, 1854: Growing Up in Pioneer America* (3–6). Illus. Series: American Girls Collection. 1999, Pleasant $16.95 (978-1-56247-770-7). 58pp. As seen through the eyes of a family of Swedish immigrants, this account describes frontier life in the Minnesota Territory in the 1840s. (Rev: BL 1/1–15/00; HBG 3/00) [978]

19030 Sonneborn, Liz. *The Mormon Trail* (5–8). Illus. Series: Watts Library: American West. 2005, Watts LB $25.50 (978-0-531-12317-1). 64pp. The story behind the westward trek of thousands of Mormons during the middle of the 19th century, with illustrations, maps, a timeline, and sidebar features. (Rev: SLJ 12/05)

19031 Sonneborn, Liz. *Women of the American West* (4–7). Illus. Series: Watts Library: American West. 2005, Watts LB $25.50 (978-0-531-12318-8). 64pp. Excerpts from first-person accounts offer a glimpse into what life was like for the women who helped to open the American West. (Rev: BL 10/15/05) [978]

19032 Spradlin, Michael P. *Texas Rangers: Legendary Lawmen* (2–4). Illus. by Roxie Munro. 2008, Walker $16.95 (978-0-8027-8096-6). 32pp. A picture-book history of the Texas Rangers (formed in 1823) and their exploits, this is more suitable for browsing than research. (Rev: BL 1/1–15/08; SLJ 4/08) [976.4]

19033 Steedman, Scott. *A Frontier Fort on the Oregon Trail* (4–6). Illus. Series: Inside Story. 1994, Bedrick $18.95 (978-0-87226-371-0); paper $10.95 (978-0-87226-264-5). 48pp. An examination of both the exterior and interior of a frontier fort, with details on its construction and everyday life in it. (Rev: BL 10/15/94; SLJ 9/94) [978]

19034 Stefoff, Rebecca. *First Frontier* (4–7). Series: North American Historical Atlases. 2000, Benchmark LB $24.21 (978-0-7614-1059-1). 48pp. This book presents an illustrated view of the western expansion and its effects on Native Americans, frontiersmen, speculators, and soldiers. (Rev: HBG 3/01; SLJ 1/01) [978]

19035 Stefoff, Rebecca. *The Opening of the West* (5–8). 2002, Benchmark LB $34.21 (978-0-7614-1201-4). 105pp. A collection of primary sources that includes excerpts from letters, newspaper articles, and journal entries commenting on different aspects of frontier life, exploration, and the plight of Native Americans. (Rev: HBG 10/03; SLJ 4/03) [978]

19036 Stein, R. Conrad. *In the Spanish West* (4–8). Series: How We Lived. 1999, Benchmark LB $27.07 (978-0-7614-0906-9). 72pp. This well-balanced account describes the American West under Spanish control and influence with material on history, social life, agriculture, and home life. (Rev: HBG 10/00; SLJ 3/00) [978]

19037 Stein, R. Conrad. *On the Old Western Frontier* (4–8). Series: How We Lived. 1999, Benchmark LB $28.50 (978-0-7614-0909-0). 72pp. An interesting book that gives an overview of the history and living conditions on the American frontier with material on everyday life, farming and ranching, social life, religion, Native Americans, and slaves. (Rev: HBG 10/00; SLJ 3/00) [978]

19038 Stein, R. Conrad. *Spanish Missionaries: Bringing Spanish Culture to the Americas* (3–6). Series: A Proud Heritage. 2005, Child's World LB $28.50 (978-1-59296-387-4). 40pp. A look at the missions found in various parts of the country and at key missionary leaders. (Rev: SLJ 6/05)

19039 Sundling, Charles W. *Cowboys of the Frontier* (4–6). Illus. Series: Frontier Land. 2000, ABDO $24.21 (978-1-57765-045-4). 32pp. An accessible text that describes the daily life of hardworking cattle drivers, with emphasis on the second half of the 19th century. (Rev: BL 10/15/00; HBG 10/00; SLJ 7/00) [978]

19040 Sundling, Charles W. *Explorers of the Frontier* (4–6). Series: Frontier Land. 2000, ABDO LB $24.21 (978-1-57765-044-7). 32pp. Using many easy-to-read maps and a fact-filled text, this book traces the exploits of the explorers who opened up the West. A companion volume is *Mountain Men of the Frontier* (2000). (Rev: BL 10/15/00; HBG 10/00) [978]

19041 Sundling, Charles W. *Pioneers of the Frontier* (4–6). Series: Frontier Land. 2000, ABDO LB $24.21 (978-1-57765-047-8). 32pp. The day-to-day struggles of the early pioneers of the West are recreated in text and pictures. Also use *Women of the Frontier* (2000). (Rev: BL 10/15/00; HBG 10/00) [978]

19042 Swanson, Wayne. *Why the West Was Wild* (5–8). 2004, Annick $12.95 (978-1-55037-837-5); paper $12.95 (978-1-55037-836-8). 48pp. The excitement of the Old West is captured in this lavishly illustrated survey of the region's history during the second half of the 19th century. (Rev: BL 8/04; SLJ 6/04) [978]

19043 Thompson, Linda. *The Transcontinental Railroad* (4–6). Illus. Series: Expansion of America. 2005, Rourke LB $20.95 (978-1-59515-227-5). 48pp. The who, what, where, when, and how of the railroad, with background information linking the project to America's expansion. Among the other titles in this series by this author are *The Erie Canal, The Mississippi and West,* and *The Oregon Trail* (all 2005). (Rev: BL 4/1/05) [385]

19044 Toht, David W. *Sodbuster* (3–6). Illus. by Richard Erickson. Series: American Pastfinder. 1996, Lerner LB $21.27 (978-0-8225-2977-4). 48pp. In double-page chapters, the life of early pioneers is described, with many quotes from original sources. (Rev: SLJ 3/96) [973.6]

19045 Wadsworth, Ginger. *Words West: Voices of Young Pioneers* (5–8). 2003, Clarion $18.00 (978-0-618-23475-2). 208pp. Excerpts from journals and other documents give a clear picture of the experiences of young people traveling west between 1840 and 1870. (Rev: HBG 4/04; SLJ 12/03) [917.804]

19046 Waldman, Stuart. *The Last River: John Wesley Powell and the Colorado River Exploring Expedition* (4–7). Illus. by Gregory Manchess. 2005, Mikaya $19.95 (978-1-931414-09-8). 48pp. This is the exciting story of the three-month exploration of the Colorado River led by the one-armed John Wesley Powell in 1869; excerpts from journals and letters reveal details of the dangers faced. (Rev: BL 12/15/05; SLJ 2/06) [550.92]

19047 Warren, Andrea. *Pioneer Girl: Growing Up on the Prairie* (3–6). 1998, Morrow $15.95 (978-0-688-15438-7). 96pp. Based on the memoirs of Grace McCance Snyder, this is the true story of a homesteading family in Nebraska during the late 1800s. (Rev: BCCB 12/98; BL 10/1/98; HB 11/98; HBG 3/99; SLJ 11/98) [978.2]

19048 Werther, Scott P. *The Donner Party* (5–7). Illus. 2002, Children's LB $24.50 (978-0-516-23901-9). 48pp. The fate of the Donner Party is described against the backdrop of life in America in the 1840s and the dangers of travel to the West and the Pacific. (Rev: SLJ 10/02) [979.4]

19049 Woog, Adam. *A Cowboy in the Wild West* (3–5). Illus. Series: Daily Life. 2002, Gale LB $23.70 (978-0-7377-0990-2). 48pp. An information-packed review of a cowboy's daily routine, including material on clothing, trail drives and roundups, and the overall history of cowboys. (Rev: BL 12/1/02; SLJ 8/02) [978]

19050 Worcester, Don. *Cowboy with a Camera, Erwin E. Smith: Cowboy Photographer* (3–5). 1999, Amon Carter Museum $18.95 (978-0-88360-091-7). 48pp. With photos from the turn of the last century, this book chronicles the life and work of cowboys, including roping, wrangling, and bronco busting. (Rev: BCCB 2/99; BL 1/1–15/99; HBG 10/99) [636.2]

THE CIVIL WAR

19051 Abnett, Dan. *The Battle of Gettysburg: Spilled Blood on Sacred Ground* (4–6). Illus. by Dheeraj Verma. Series: Graphic Battles of the Civil War. 2007, Rosen LB $29.25 (978-1-4042-0777-6). 48pp. This graphic-novel treatment of the crucial battle has a dramatic style that seems to bring the reader close to the action. (Rev: SLJ 5/07)

19052 Allen, Thomas B. *Harriet Tubman, Secret Agent: How Daring Slaves and Free Blacks Spied for the Union During the Civil War* (5–8). Illus. by Carla Bauer. 2006, National Geographic $16.95 (978-0-7922-7889-4). 191pp. The efforts of Tubman and other slaves to gather important information and pass it to the Union forces is the focus of this volume that includes examples of a code sometimes used. (Rev: BCCB 1/07; BL 12/1/06; HBG 4/07; LMC 5/07; SLJ 2/07*) [973.7]

19053 Anderson, Dale. *The Causes of the Civil War* (4–6). 2004, World Almanac LB $31.00 (978-0-8368-5581-4); paper $11.95 (978-0-8368-5590-6). 48pp. A concise and readable overview of the underlying causes of the Civil War, with material on key individuals, interesting sidebar features, maps, and many appropriate illustrations. Also use *A Soldier's Life in the Civil War*, *The Aftermath of the Civil War*, and *The Union Victory: (July 1863–1865)*. (Rev: SLJ 3/05) [973.7]

19054 Anderson, Dale. *The Civil War at Sea* (4–6). Series: World Almanac Library of the Civil War. 2004, World Almanac LB $31.00 (978-0-8368-5585-2). 48pp. A look at major battles at sea, with period photographs, maps, and sidebars about individuals. Also use in this series: *The Civil War in the East (1861–July 1863)*, *The Civil War in the West (1861–July 1863)*, and *The Home Fronts in the Civil War* (all 2004). (Rev: SLJ 7/04) [973.7]

19055 Armentrout, David, and Patricia Armentrout. *The Emancipation Proclamation* (4–7). Series: Documents That Shaped the Nation. 2004, Rourke $20.95 (978-1-59515-233-6). 48pp. The reasons for the creation of this document and the results of its proclamation are thoroughly explored in concise text, accompanied by an array of maps and illustrations. (Rev: BL 10/15/04) [973.7]

19056 Armstrong, Jennifer. *A Three-Minute Speech: Lincoln's Remarks at Gettysburg* (2–5). Series: Milestone Books. 2003, Aladdin paper $3.99 (978-0-689-85622-8). 96pp. This appealing introduction to the Gettysburg Address provides extensive background information. (Rev: BL 9/1/03; HBG 4/04; SLJ 9/03) [973]

19057 Arnold, James R., and Roberta Wiener. *Divided in Two: The Road to Civil War* (4–7). Series: The Civil War. 2002, Lerner LB $25.26 (978-0-8225-2312-3). 72pp. A well-designed oversize book that describes the events of 1861 that led to the outbreak of the Civil War. (Rev: BL 10/15/02; HBG 10/02; SLJ 7/02) [973.7]

19058 Arnold, James R., and Roberta Wiener. *Life Goes On: The Civil War at Home* (4–7). Series: The Civil War. 2002, Lerner LB $25.26 (978-0-8225-2315-4). 72pp. Many easy-to-follow maps and illustrations are used with a simple text to describe life on the home front in both South and North during the Civil War. (Rev: BL 10/15/02; HBG 10/02; SLJ 7/02) [973.7]

19059 Arnold, James R., and Roberta Wiener. *Lost Cause: The End of the Civil War* (4–7). Series: The

Civil War. 2002, Lerner LB $25.26 (978-0-8225-2317-8). 72pp. Beginning with the campaign of 1864, this well-illustrated account traces the Civil War to Appomattox and beyond. (Rev: BL 10/15/02; HBG 10/02; SLJ 6/02) [973.7]

19060 Arnold, James R., and Roberta Wiener. *On to Richmond: The Civil War in the East, 1861–1862* (4–7). Illus. Series: Civil War. 2002, Lerner LB $25.26 (978-0-8225-2313-0). 72pp. Early battles in the Civil War are the subject of this volume for older readers that includes timelines, notes, and lists of Web sites and battlefields to visit. (Rev: BL 10/15/02; HBG 10/02; SLJ 6/02; VOYA 6/03) [973.7]

19061 Arnold, James R., and Roberta Wiener. *River to Victory: The Civil War in the West* (4–7). Series: The Civil War. 2002, Lerner LB $25.26 (978-0-8225-2314-7). 72pp. The Civil War in the West from 1861 through 1863 is re-created in text and illustrations with many maps and sidebars on personalities and events. (Rev: BL 10/15/02; HBG 10/02; SLJ 6/02; VOYA 6/03) [973.7]

19062 Arnold, James R., and Roberta Wiener. *This Unhappy Country: The Turn of the Civil War* (4–7). Illus. Series: Civil War. 2002, Lerner LB $25.26 (978-0-8225-2316-1). 72pp. Maps and other period illustrations flesh out the events of 1863, a pivotal year in the Civil War, in this volume for older readers. (Rev: BL 10/15/02; HBG 10/02; SLJ 7/02) [973.7]

19063 Ashby, Ruth. *Gettysburg* (5–8). Series: Civil War Chronicles. 2002, Smart Apple LB $28.50 (978-1-58340-186-6). 48pp. The three days of battle are covered in some detail, and the text and photographs convey the horrible conditions. (Rev: HBG 3/03; SLJ 2/03; VOYA 4/03) [973]

19064 Beller, Susan P. *Billy Yank and Johnny Reb: Soldiering in the Civil War* (5–8). Illus. 2000, Twenty-First Century LB $26.90 (978-0-7613-1869-9). 96pp. Solid, interesting information is provided in this illustrated account that describes the everyday life of soldiers on both sides of the Civil War. (Rev: BL 10/15/00; HBG 3/01; SLJ 12/00; VOYA 2/01) [973.7]

19065 Beller, Susan P. *The Civil War* (5–8). Series: American Voices From. 2002, Benchmark LB $34.21 (978-0-7614-1204-5). 103pp. A collection of primary sources that includes speeches by Lincoln and Lee and represents people from all walks of life commenting on different aspects of the Civil War. (Rev: HBG 10/03; SLJ 4/03) [973.7]

19066 Beller, Susan P. *The Confederate Ladies of Richmond* (5–8). Illus. 1999, Twenty-First Century LB $26.90 (978-0-7613-1470-7). 96pp. The Civil War seen through the eyes and activities of the upper-class women of Richmond, the capital of the Confederacy. (Rev: BCCB 1/00; BL 12/15/99; HBG 3/00; SLJ 1/00) [973.7]

19067 Berry, Carrie. *A Confederate Girl: The Diary of Carrie Berry, 1864* (4–6). Ed. by Christy Steel and Anne Todd. Series: Diaries, Letters, and Memoirs. 2000, Capstone LB $23.93 (978-0-7368-0343-4). 32pp. These excerpts from the diary of a

10-year-old Confederate girl describe everyday life and problems behind the front lines and are supplemented by informative sidebars that give good background information. (Rev: BL 10/15/00; HBG 10/00; SLJ 9/00) [973.7]

19068 Bolotin, Norman. *Civil War A to Z: A Young Reader's Guide to Over 100 People, Places, and Points of Importance* (4–8). Illus. 2002, Dutton $19.99 (978-0-525-46268-2). 160pp. An encyclopedia-style text on the Civil War, with brief entries on important battles; politicians, generals, and other key figures; and crucial issues of the time, with photographs, a glossary, a timeline, and information on further resources. (Rev: BL 7/02; SLJ 7/02) [973.7]

19069 Brooks, Victor. *African Americans in the Civil War* (4–8). Illus. Series: Untold History of the Civil War. 2000, Chelsea $25.00 (978-0-7910-5435-2). 64pp. This book describes African American soldiers' roles in the Civil War, on both the Confederate and Union sides. (Rev: BL 5/15/00; HBG 10/00; SLJ 6/00) [355.7]

19070 Brooks, Victor. *Civil War Forts* (4–8). Illus. Series: Untold History of the Civil War. 2000, Chelsea $25.00 (978-0-7910-5438-3). 64pp. Describes the important roles played by such forts as Fort Sumter and Fort Wagner in South Carolina, Fort Fischer in North Carolina, Fort Henry and Fort Donelson in Tennessee, and the city of Vicksburg, Mississippi. (Rev: BL 5/15/00; HBG 10/00; SLJ 7/00) [973.7]

19071 Brooks, Victor. *Secret Weapons in the Civil War* (4–8). Series: Untold History of the Civil War. 2000, Chelsea $29.50 (978-0-7910-5433-8). 64pp. Covers such secret weapons and maneuvers as underwater transportation, advanced artillery, communications devices, and explosive materials. (Rev: BL 5/15/00; HBG 10/00; SLJ 7/00) [973.7]

19072 Butzer, C. M. *Gettysburg: The Graphic Novel* (4–8). Illus. by author. 2009, HarperCollins $16.99 (978-0-06-156176-4); paper $9.99 (978-0-06-156175-7). 80pp. After a brief section on the Battle of Gettysburg, Butzer moves on to present Lincoln's famous address; the graphic novel format works well and he integrates words from primary sources including letters and diaries. (Rev: BL 12/1/08; LMC 10/09; SLJ 11/08) [973.7]

19073 Clinton, Catherine. *Scholastic Encyclopedia of the Civil War* (4–7). Illus. 1999, Scholastic paper $18.95 (978-0-590-37227-5). 112pp. Using many black-and-white illustrations, this narrative gives a good chronological introduction to the Civil War, with interesting supplementary information. (Rev: BL 1/1–15/00; HBG 3/00; SLJ 5/00) [973.7]

19074 Collier, Christopher, and James Lincoln Collier. *The Civil War, 1860–1865* (5–8). Series: Drama of American History. 1999, Marshall Cavendish LB $31.36 (978-0-7614-0818-5). 95pp. A dramatic, accurate account that covers causes, leaders, battles, effects, and the immediate aftermath of the Civil War. (Rev: BL 2/15/00; HBG 10/00; SLJ 3/00) [973.7]

19075 Damon, Duane. *Growing Up In the Civil War: 1861 to 1865* (5–8). Series: Our America. 2002,

Lerner LB $26.60 (978-0-8225-0656-0). 64pp. The lives of children in this period are described with many quotations and excerpts from diaries, letters, and memoirs. (Rev: BL 2/15/03; HBG 3/03; SLJ 2/03) [973.7]

19076 Damon, Duane. *When This Cruel War Is Over* (5–8). Illus. 1996, Lerner LB $30.35 (978-0-8225-1731-3). The human side of the Civil War is stressed as the reader goes behind the scenes at the battlefields and learns about conditions on the home front. (Rev: BL 8/96; SLJ 8/96*) [973.7]

19077 Day, Nancy. *Your Travel Guide to Civil War America* (4–8). Series: Passport to History. 2000, Lerner LB $26.50 (978-0-8225-3078-7). 96pp. Using the format of a guide book, this account takes the reader back to the Civil War with coverage of topics including food, civil and military clothing, Lincoln's office, Gettysburg, and various battlefields. (Rev: BL 3/1/01; HBG 10/01; SLJ 4/01; VOYA 8/01) [073.7]

19078 Dolan, Edward F. *The American Civil War: A House Divided* (5–8). Illus. 1997, Millbrook LB $29.90 (978-0-7613-0255-1). A chronologically arranged, well-organized account of the Civil War, beginning with the shots fired at Fort Sumter. (Rev: BL 3/1/98; HBG 3/98; SLJ 3/98) [973.7]

19079 Dosier, Susan. *Civil War Cooking: The Confederacy* (4–7). Series: Exploring History Through Simple Recipes. 2000, Capstone LB $23.93 (978-0-7368-0350-2). 32pp. As well as simple, authentic recipes of Civil War times, this book tells of customs, family roles, and everyday life during this period. Also use *Civil War Cooking: The Union* (2000). (Rev: BL 8/00; HBG 10/00; SLJ 9/00) [973.7]

19080 Egger-Bovet, Howard, and Marlene Smith-Baranzini. *Book of the American Civil War* (5–7). Illus. by D. J. Simison. Series: Brown Paper School. 1998, Little, Brown paper $12.95 (978-0-316-22243-3). 95pp. Facts, photographs, illustrations, stories and appealing activities are combined in this overview of the Civil War. (Rev: SLJ 12/98) [973.7]

19081 Feinberg, Barbara S. *Abraham Lincoln's Gettysburg Address: Four Score and More . . .* (4–8). Illus. 2000, Twenty-First Century LB $24.90 (978-0-7613-1610-7). 80pp. Illustrated with period photographs, this well-researched volume reveals surprising facts about the Gettysburg Address and its delivery. (Rev: BL 11/15/00) [973.7]

19082 Ford, Carin T. *The American Civil War: An Overview* (5–8). Series: The Civil War Library. 2004, Enslow LB $23.93 (978-0-7660-2255-3). 48pp. This informative general overview of the war features maps, illustrations, and interesting sidebar features. Also use *Lincoln, Slavery, and the Emancipation Proclamation* (2004). (Rev: SLJ 3/05) [973.7]

19083 Ford, Carin T. *The Battle of Gettysburg and Lincoln's Gettysburg Address* (4–6). Series: The Civil War Library. 2004, Enslow LB $23.93 (978-0-7660-2253-9). 48pp. Background information adds to the coverage of the battle itself and to an understanding of the importance of Lincoln's speech. (Rev: SLJ 1/05) [973]

19084 Ford, Carin T. *Daring Women of the Civil War* (3–5). Series: The Civil War Library. 2004, Enslow LB $23.93 (978-0-7660-2250-8). 48pp. Primary-source quotations and reproductions add to the discussion of the role of women — from both the Union and the Confederacy — in America's Civil War. (Rev: BL 7/04; SLJ 8/04) [973.7]

19085 Ford, Carin T. *Slavery and the Underground Railroad: Bound for Freedom* (3–5). Series: The Civil War Library. 2004, Enslow LB $23.93 (978-0-7660-2251-5). 48pp. Primary-source quotations and reproductions add to the discussion of the role of the Underground Railroad and the people involved in its success. (Rev: BL 7/04; SLJ 8/04) [973]

19086 Friend, Sandra. *Florida in the Civil War: A State in Turmoil* (5–8). Illus. 2001, Millbrook LB $25.90 (978-0-7613-1973-3). 80pp. An account of Florida's involvement in the Civil War, with maps and photographs. (Rev: BL 10/15/01; HBG 3/02; SLJ 2/02; VOYA 12/01) [973.7]

19087 Fritz, Jean. *Just a Few Words, Mr. Lincoln: The Story of the Gettysburg Address* (1–3). Illus. by Charles Robinson. 1993, Penguin paper $3.99 (978-0-448-40170-6). 48pp. An easy-to-read book that tells the background of the Gettysburg Address and explains its importance. (Rev: BL 10/1/93; SLJ 10/93) [973.7]

19088 *Gettysburg: Bold Battle in the North* (4–6). Series: The Civil War. 2005, Cobblestone $17.95 (978-0-8126-7903-8). 47pp. A richly illustrated overview of this important battle. (Rev: SLJ 3/06) [973.7]

19089 Graves, Kerry A. *Going to School During the Civil War: The Confederacy* (4–6). Series: Going to School in History. 2001, Capstone LB $23.93 (978-0-7368-0802-6). 32pp. A look at schools in the South during the Civil War with information on subjects studied, the length of the school year, classroom materials, and typical activities and games. (Rev: BL 10/15/01; HBG 3/02) [973.7]

19090 Graves, Kerry A. *Going to School During the Civil War: The Union* (4–6). Series: Going to School in History. 2001, Capstone LB $23.93 (978-0-7368-0801-9). 32pp. Details of school life in the northern states include curriculum, teaching methods, and subjects taught plus sidebars on crafts and games. (Rev: BL 10/15/01; HBG 3/03) [973.7]

19091 Hama, Larry. *The Battle of Antietam: "The Bloodiest Day of Battle"* (4–6). Illus. by Scott Moore. Series: Graphic Battles of the Civil War. 2007, Rosen LB $29.25 (978-1-4042-0775-2). 48pp. Historically accurate and not overly gory, this graphic account of a key Civil War battle will hold the interest of researchers and browsers. (Rev: SLJ 5/07)

19092 Haskins, James. *The Day Fort Sumter Was Fired On: A Photo History of the Civil War* (5–8). Illus. 1995, Scholastic paper $6.95 (978-0-590-46397-3). 96pp. A short, well-illustrated history of the Civil War, with coverage of the roles of women and African Americans. (Rev: BL 7/95) [973.7]

19093 Heinrichs, Ann. *The Emancipation Proclamation* (5–8). Series: We the People. 2002, Compass Point LB $26.60 (978-0-7565-0209-6). 48pp. An accessible examination of the proclamation's creation that reveals Lincoln's careful attention to detail. (Rev: SLJ 7/02) [973.7]

19094 Herbert, Janis. *The Civil War for Kids: A History with 21 Activities* (4–8). Illus. 1999, Chicago Review paper $14.95 (978-1-55652-355-7). 166pp. As well as supplying information about leaders, battles, daily life, and the contributions of women and African Americans, this book on the Civil War includes activities such as reenactments of battles, most of which are geared toward groups. (Rev: SLJ 12/99) [973.7]

19095 High, Linda Oatman. *The Cemetery Keepers of Gettysburg* (3–5). Illus. by Laura Francesca Filippucci. 2007, Walker $16.95 (978-0-8027-8094-2). 32pp. The battle of Gettysburg is presented from the perspective of the oldest boy of a family of cemetery keepers trying to survive the Civil War while the father is off fighting. (Rev: BL 3/15/07) [973.7]

19096 Holford, David M. *Lincoln and the Emancipation Proclamation in American History* (5–8). Series: In American History. 2002, Enslow LB $26.60 (978-0-7660-1456-5). 128pp. A well-researched account that gives background material and traces the significance of this document. (Rev: BL 1/1–15/03; HBG 3/03) [973.7]

19097 Hughes, Christopher. *Antietam* (5–8). Series: Battlefields Across America. 1998, Millbrook LB $26.90 (978-0-7613-3009-7). This book describes the battle at Antietam in detail, discusses its impact on the outcome of the war and on the future of the United States, profiles the major people involved, and provides information on where the history of this battle is preserved. (Rev: HBG 9/98; SLJ 8/98) [973.7]

19098 January, Brendan. *Gettysburg, July 1–3, 1863* (5–7). Illus. Series: American Battlefields. 2004, Enchanted Lion $14.95 (978-1-59270-025-7). 32pp. This overview of the Battle of Gettysburg offers a clear account of the bloody conflict and an examination of the developments leading up to it; sidebars, illustrations, a timeline, and other features add to the narrative. (Rev: BL 11/1/04) [973]

19099 King, Wilma. *Children of the Emancipation* (2–5). Illus. Series: Picture the American Past. 2000, Carolrhoda $22.60 (978-1-57505-396-7). 48pp. This book covers the years 1860 through 1890 and examines the lives of children born as slaves, and how they fared before the Emancipation Proclamation, during the Civil War, and also during Reconstruction. (Rev: BL 6/1–15/00; HBG 10/00; SLJ 7/00) [973.7]

19100 Lincoln, Abraham. *The Gettysburg Address* (4–6). Illus. by Michael McCurdy. 1995, Houghton $14.95 (978-0-395-69824-2). 32pp. An illustrated edition of the address, with pictures that show the audience and the thoughts they might have had. (Rev: BL 10/15/95; HB 11/95; SLJ 9/95*) [973.7]

19101 McComb, Marianne. *The Emancipation Proclamation* (4–7). Illus. Series: American Documents.

2006, National Geographic LB $23.90 (978-0-7922-7936-5). 40pp. The background, nature, and impact of this important document are explained clearly, with photos and illustrations plus full texts of the Emancipation Proclamation, the Fugitive Slave Law of 1850, and Constitutional Amendments XIII through XV. (Rev: BL 2/1/06; SLJ 2/06; VOYA 8/06) [973.7]

19102 Nofi, Albert A. *Spies in the Civil War* (5–8). Series: Untold History of the Civil War. 2000, Chelsea $25.00 (978-0-7910-5427-7). 64pp. In this account readers meet famous spies (including Allan Pinkerton and Belle Boyd) and lesser-known spies of the Civil War. (Rev: HBG 10/00; SLJ 7/00) [973.7]

19103 O'Brien, Patrick. *Duel of the Ironclads: The Monitor vs. the Virginia* (2–6). Illus. 2003, Walker LB $18.85 (978-0-8027-8843-6). 40pp. A beautifully illustrated account of the battle between two state-of-the-art Civil War ships. (Rev: BL 3/15/03*; HBG 10/03; SLJ 5/03) [973.7]

19104 Ransom, Candice F. *Children of the Civil War* (3–6). Series: Picture the American Past. 1998, Carolrhoda LB $19.93 (978-0-575-05241-3). 48pp. This book, divided into three parts — before, during, and after the Civil War — uses photos to show children in such roles as soldiers, slaves, servants, prisoners, and orphans. (Rev: SLJ 1/99) [973.7]

19105 Rappaport, Doreen. *United No More! Stories of the Civil War* (4–6). Illus. by Rick Reeves. 2006, HarperCollins $16.99 (978-0-06-050599-8). 144pp. Seven stories of Civil War personalities and events give readers a feeling for the conflict. (Rev: BL 2/15/06; SLJ 2/06) [973.7]

19106 Savage, Douglas J. *Ironclads and Blockades in the Civil War* (4–8). Series: Untold History of the Civil War. 2000, Chelsea $25.00 (978-0-7910-5429-1). 64pp. A clear text and period illustrations introduce the huge ships used in the Union and Confederate navies and their efforts to block different ports during the Civil War. (Rev: BL 7/00; HBG 10/00; SLJ 9/00) [973.7]

19107 Savage, Douglas J. *Prison Camps in the Civil War* (4–8). Series: Untold History of the Civil War. 2000, Chelsea $25.00 (978-0-7910-5428-4). 64pp. This account describes the prisoner-of-war camps on both sides during the Civil War, the appalling conditions in them, and the acts of heroism that sometimes occurred. (Rev: BL 7/00; HBG 10/00; SLJ 9/00) [973.7]

19108 Savage, Douglas J. *Women in the Civil War* (4–8). Series: Untold History of the Civil War. 2000, Chelsea $25.00 (978-0-7910-5436-9). 64pp. This book describes the roles played by women in the Civil War as nurses, suppliers of support services, and crusaders for issues including suffrage and abolition. (Rev: BL 7/00; HBG 10/00; SLJ 9/00) [973.7]

19109 Schomp, Virginia. *The Civil War* (5–8). Illus. Series: Letters from the Homefront. 2001, Marshall Cavendish LB $29.93 (978-0-7614-1095-9). 95pp. After placing the conflict in historical context, Schomp uses excerpts from letters and other

accounts that bring the period to life. (Rev: BL 10/15/01; HBG 3/02; SLJ 3/02) [973.7]

19110 Sheinkin, Steve. *Two Miserable Presidents: Everything Your Schoolbooks Didn't Tell You About the Civil War* (4–8). Illus. by Tim Robinson. 2008, Roaring Brook $19.95 (978-1-59643-320-5). 224pp. This unusual take on the war and its leaders will attract reluctant history students. It focuses on the personalities but does not leave out the larger issues that led to the war and affected its outcome. (Rev: BL 4/15/08) [973.7]

19111 Sinnott, Susan. *Charley Waters Goes to Gettysburg* (3–5). Illus. 2000, Millbrook LB $22.90 (978-0-7613-1567-4). 48pp. Told from the point of view of an 8-year-old boy who is visiting the Gettysburg battlefield with his parents, this book gives information on the battle and its reenactments. (Rev: BL 3/15/00; HBG 10/00; SLJ 6/00) [973.7]

19112 Sinnott, Susan. *Welcome to Addy's World, 1864* (3–6). Series: American Girl. 1999, Pleasant $14.95 (978-1-56237-771-7). 58pp. Addy was born a slave and lived on a Southern plantation until age nine. Through her eyes, life during the last year of the Civil War is re-created in a series of double-page spreads that explore slavery and other social and political topics of the time. (Rev: BL 1/1–15/00) [973.7]

19113 Smith, Carter, ed. *One Nation Again: A Sourcebook on the Civil War* (5–8). Series: American Albums. 1993, Millbrook LB $25.90 (978-1-56294-266-3). This heavily illustrated sourcebook chronicles the peace at Appomattox and the period immediately following. (Rev: BL 3/1/93) [973.8]

19114 Smith, Carter, ed. *The Road to Appomattox: A Sourcebook on the Civil War* (5–8). Series: American Albums. 1993, Millbrook $25.90 (978-1-56294-264-9). The last battles of the Civil War are covered in this album that uses period illustrations and excerpts from first-person accounts. (Rev: BL 3/1/93) [973.7]

19115 Somerlott, Robert. *The Lincoln Assassination* (5–8). Series: In American History. 1998, Enslow LB $26.60 (978-0-89490-886-6). 128pp. Using primary sources, the author has created a gripping story of the causes of the assassination, the shooting itself, and its aftermath. (Rev: BL 7/98; SLJ 6/98) [973.7]

19116 Stanchak, John. *Civil War* (5–8). Illus. Series: Eyewitness Books. 2000, DK paper $15.99 (978-0-7894-6302-9). 64pp. This highly visual treatment presents topics related to the Civil War such as causes, battles, slavery, states' rights, weapons, and uniforms in a series of double-page spreads. (Rev: BL 1/1–15/01; HBG 3/01; SLJ 12/00) [973.7]

19117 Stanley, George E. *The Crisis of the Union (1815–1865)* (5–8). Illus. Series: A Primary Source History of the United States. 2005, World Almanac LB $31.00 (978-0-8368-5826-6). 48pp. A simple narrative links well-chosen primary sources documenting the key events of the Civil War. (Rev: BL 4/1/05)

19118 Stark, Ken. *Marching to Appomattox: The Footrace that Ended the Civil War* (4–6). Illus. by author. 2009, Putnam $17.99 (978-0-399-24212-0). 48pp. This volume offers a dramatic and highly readable account of six days in April 1865 as Southern troops worked doggedly to break out of the North's tightening noose. (Rev: BL 1/1–15/09; LMC 5/09; SLJ 1/09) [973.7]

19119 Sullivan, George. *The Civil War at Sea* (5–8). Illus. 2001, Twenty-First Century LB $27.90 (978-0-7613-1553-7). 64pp. This book tells of the struggle between the Union and Confederate forces in American bays, harbors, and rivers with material on famous ships and their commanders, important battles, and the daily life of the sailors. (Rev: BL 2/1/01; HBG 10/01; SLJ 3/01) [973.7]

19120 Walker, Sally M. *Shipwreck Search: Discovery of the H. L. Hunley* (2–4). Illus. by Elaine Verstraete. Series: On My Own Science. 2006, Lerner $25.26 (978-1-57505-878-8). 48pp. Chronicles the successful search for the wreckage of the *H. L. Hunley*, a Confederate submarine that was sunk in Charleston Harbor during the Civil War. (Rev: BL 6/1–15/06; SLJ 6/06) [973.7]

19121 Warren, Andrea. *Under Siege: Three Children at the Civil War Battle for Vicksburg* (5–8). Illus. 2009, Farrar $17.95 (978-0-374-31255-8). 176pp. Using the reminiscences of three children between the ages of 10 and 12 (including General Grant's son), this is an interesting account of the battle and of the plight of the city's residents who retreated to caves. (Rev: BL 4/15/09; HB 5/09; SLJ 5/09) [973.7]

19122 Waryncia, Lou, and Sarah Elder Hale, eds. *Antietam: Day of Courage and Sacrifice* (4–6). Series: The Civil War. 2005, Cobblestone $17.95 (978-0-8126-7904-5). 48pp. Based on articles appearing in Cobblestone publications, this book consists of short chapters covering topics including the battle, the equipment used, the mascot dogs, and the role of Clara Barton. (Rev: BL 1/1–15/06) [973.7]

19123 Weber, Michael. *Civil War and Reconstruction* (5–8). Series: The Making of America. 2001, Raintree LB $19.98 (978-0-8172-5707-1). 96pp. Using many illustrations, interesting sidebars, and an accessible text, this is a concise history of the Civil War and its immediate aftermath. (Rev: BL 4/15/01) [973.7]

19124 *Young Heroes of the North and South* (4–6). Series: The Civil War. 2005, Cobblestone $17.95 (978-0-8126-7901-4). 47pp. A compelling look at the roles played by children on the home front and the battlefield, on both sides of the Civil War. (Rev: SLJ 3/06) [973.7]

19125 Zeinert, Karen. *Those Courageous Women of the Civil War* (5–8). Illus. 1998, Millbrook LB $29.90 (978-0-7613-0212-4). 96pp. This account relates the contributions of women during the Civil War, with details on how they served as nurses, spies, writers, and workers on the home front. (Rev: BL 6/1–15/98; HBG 3/99) [973.7]

RECONSTRUCTION TO THE KOREAN WAR, 1865–1950

19126 Arnold, Caroline. *Children of the Settlement Houses* (4–7). Illus. Series: Picture the American Past. 1998, Carolrhoda LB $27.15 (978-1-57505-242-7). 48pp. Using historical photographs and a simple text, this book introduces the turn-of-the-20th-century settlement house, where the poor and new immigrants found shelter and a place to learn, explore the arts, and develop a sense of belonging. (Rev: BL 9/15/98; HBG 3/99; SLJ 1/99) [362.5]

19127 Axelrod-Contrada, Joan. *The Lizzie Borden "Axe Murder" Trial: A Headline Court Case* (5–9). Series: Headline Court Cases. 2000, Enslow LB $26.60 (978-0-7660-1422-0). 128pp. A well-documented account of the famous 1892 trial, the events that led up to it, and its aftermath. (Rev: HBG 3/01; SLJ 1/01) [973.8]

19128 Bartoletti, Susan C. *Growing Up in Coal Country* (5–8). Illus. 1996, Houghton $17.00 (978-0-395-77847-0). The life of child laborers in the coal mines of Pennsylvania 100 years ago is covered in this brilliant photoessay. (Rev: BCCB 2/97; BL 12/1/96*; SLJ 2/97*) [331.3]

19129 Bartoletti, Susan C. *Kids on Strike!* (5–8). Illus. 1999, Houghton $20.00 (978-0-395-88892-6). 208pp. This book chronicles the history of child labor in America during the 19th and early 20th centuries and features such personalities as William Randolph Hearst, Pauline Newman, and Mother Jones. (Rev: BCCB 12/99; BL 12/1/99; HBG 3/00; SLJ 12/99*; VOYA 2/00) [973.8]

19130 Brexel, Bernadette. *The Knights of Labor and the Haymarket Riot: The Fight for an Eight-Hour Workday* (5–8). Illus. Series: America's Industrial Society in the 19th Century. 2004, Rosen LB $22.50 (978-0-8239-4028-8). 32pp. For reluctant readers, this overview of the struggle to improve working conditions features large print and short chapters. Also use *The Populist Party: A Voice for the Farmers in an Industrial Society* (2004). (Rev: BL 4/1/04)

19131 Brezina, Corona. *America's Political Scandals in the late 1800s: Boss Tweed and Tammany Hall* (5–8). Illus. Series: America's Industrial Society in the 19th Century. 2004, Rosen LB $22.50 (978-0-8239-4021-9). 32pp. For reluctant readers, this overview of the political scandals of the late 19th century features large print and short chapters. (Rev: BL 4/1/04)

19132 Brown, Gene. *Conflict in Europe and the Great Depression: World War I (1914–1940)* (5–8). Series: First Person America. 1994, Twenty-First Century LB $20.90 (978-0-8050-2585-9). The period from 1914 to 1940 is re-created through excerpts from original source material and texts describing events and social conditions. (Rev: BL 5/15/94; SLJ 11/94) [973.9]

19133 Brown, Harriet. *Welcome to Kit's World — 1934: Growing Up During America's Great Depression* (3–6). Illus. Series: American Girl. 2002, Pleasant $16.95 (978-1-58485-359-6). 60pp. Double-page spreads are used in this heavily illustrated volume to describe growing up in 1934 during the Great Depression. (Rev: BL 4/15/02; HBG 10/02; SLJ 7/02) [973.9]

19134 Burgan, Michael. *The Great Depression* (4–6). Series: We the People. 2001, Compass Point LB $26.60 (978-0-7565-0152-5). 48pp. A basic overview of the causes of the Depression and the programs that were intended to alleviate its impact. (Rev: SLJ 1/02)

19135 Burgan, Michael. *The Haymarket Square Tragedy* (4–6). Series: We the People. 2005, Compass Point LB $26.60 (978-0-7565-1265-1). 48pp. The story of the 1886 Haymarket Square riot in Chicago is placed in historical and social context, with period reproductions and photographs. (Rev: SLJ 2/06) [977.311]

19136 Carter, Ron. *The Youngest Drover* (5–9). 1995, Harbour $19.95 (978-0-9643672-1-0); paper $14.95 (978-0-9643672-0-3). In 1923, when he was 15, the author's father participated in an exciting cattle drive from Alberta to Montana. (Rev: BL 1/1–15/96) [978]

19137 Cohen, Daniel. *The Alaska Purchase* (4–8). Series: Spotlight on American History. 1996, Millbrook $24.90 (978-1-56294-528-2). The story of the purchase of Alaska from Russia in 1867 and how it changed the course of American history. (Rev: BL 3/15/96; SLJ 5/96) [979.8]

19138 Collier, Christopher, and James Lincoln Collier. *Progressivism, the Great Depression, and the New Deal* (5–8). Illus. Series: The Drama of American History. 2001, Marshall Cavendish LB $31.36 (978-0-7614-1054-6). 96pp. A highly readable account that covers such topics as the stock market crash, the reformation of business practices, the Great Depression, and the social policies of the New Deal. (Rev: BL 3/15/01; HBG 10/01) [973.91]

19139 Collier, Christopher, and James Lincoln Collier. *Reconstruction and the Rise of Jim Crow, 1864–1896* (5–8). Series: Drama of American History. 1999, Marshall Cavendish LB $31.36 (978-0-7614-0819-2). 89pp. A clear, objective account of the problems facing the country after the Civil War and how they were resolved. (Rev: BL 2/15/00; HBG 10/00; SLJ 3/00) [973.8]

19140 Collier, Christopher, and James Lincoln Collier. *The Rise of Industry, 1860–1900* (5–8). Illus. Series: Drama of American History. 1999, Marshall Cavendish LB $31.36 (978-0-7614-0820-8). 89pp. A readable account of 40 years of industrialism and its effect on the United States. (Rev: BL 2/15/00; HBG 10/00; SLJ 3/00) [338.0973]

19141 Collier, Christopher, and James Lincoln Collier. *The United States Enters the World Stage: From the Alaska Purchase Through World War I* (5–8). Series: The Drama of American History. 2001, Marshall Cavendish LB $31.36 (978-0-7614-1053-9). Covering the years 1867 through 1918, this well-illustrated account traces America's emergence as a world power. (Rev: BL 3/15/01; HBG 10/01) [973.9]

19142 Coombs, Karen Mueller. *Children of the Dust Days* (3–6). Illus. Series: Picture the American Past.

2000, Carolrhoda LB $22.60 (978-1-57505-360-8). 48pp. A mainly illustrated account of the hardships associated with the Dust Bowl and the journeys of many displaced farmers to California. (Rev: BL 4/1/00; HBG 10/00; SLJ 6/00) [978]

19143 Cooper, Michael L. *Dust to Eat: Drought and Depression in the 1930s* (5–8). Illus. 2004, Clarion $17.00 (978-0-618-15449-4). 96pp. First-person accounts and period photographs convey the hopelessness of those who were caught in the grip of the Depression and the drought in the Midwest. (Rev: BL 7/04; SLJ 9/04) [973.917]

19144 Cooper, Michael L. *Remembering Manzanar: Life in a Japanese Relocation Camp* (4–8). Illus. 2002, Clarion $15.00 (978-0-618-06778-7). 68pp. This evocative account of life in a Japanese American World War II internment center tells its tale through personal accounts of survivors, quotations from the camp newspaper, and revealing photographs. (Rev: BL 1/1–15/03; HBG 10/03; SLJ 2/03) [940.54]

19145 Costantino, Maria. *Fashions of a Decade: The 1930s* (5–10). 2007, Chelsea House LB $35.00 (978-0-8160-6719-0). 64pp. With illustrations, photographs, and a helpful chronology of trends and events, this book captures the fashions of the 1930s and relates them to the conditions of the times. (Rev: SLJ 7/07)

19146 Cryan-Hicks, Kathryn, ed. *Pride and Promise: The Harlem Renaisssance* (4–8). Illus. Series: Perspectives on History. 1994, Discovery Enterprises paper $6.95 (978-1-878668-30-1). The story of the great artistic awakening in New York's Harlem and of its many leaders, including Langston Hughes. (Rev: BL 8/94) [305.896]

19147 Davis, Barbara J. *The Teapot Dome Scandal: Corruption Rocks 1920s America* (5–8). Series: Snapshots in History. 2007, Compass Point LB $31.93 (978-0-7565-3336-6). 96pp. Davis traces the corruption in the Harding administration and the scandal that erupted over oil leasing without competitive bidding. (Rev: SLJ 1/08)

19148 Degezelle, Terri. *Franklin D. Roosevelt and the Great Depression* (2–4). Illus. Series: Heinemann First Library. 2007, Heinemann LB $17.75 (978-1-4034-9670-6); paper $7.99 (978-1-4034-9678-2). 32pp. A brief biography of Roosevelt precedes simple accounts of events including the 1929 stock market crash, the Depression itself, the New Deal, World War II and discussion of family life at that time. (Rev: BL 10/15/07; LMC 1/08; SLJ 1/08) [973.917]

19149 Doak, Robin. *Struggling to Become American: 1899–1940* (5–10). Series: Latino-American History. 2007, Chelsea House LB $35.00 (978-0-8160-6443-4). 106pp. Doak looks at Latino immigration — especially from Puerto Rico, Cuba, and Mexico — and at the conditions of Hispanic laborers in the United States during World War I and the Great Depression; includes photographs, sidebars, political cartoons, maps, and so forth. (Rev: SLJ 7/07)

19150 Dolan, Edward F. *The Spanish-American War* (5–8). Illus. 2001, Millbrook LB $28.90 (978-0-

7613-1453-0). 112pp. This chronological account of the Spanish-American War includes profiles of military personnel, maps, and historical photographs. (Rev: BL 11/1/01; HBG 3/02; SLJ 11/01) [973.8]

19151 Duble, Kathleen Benner. *The Story of the Samson* (2–5). Illus. by Alexander Farquharson. 2008, Charlesbridge $16.95 (978-1-58089-183-7); paper $7.95 (978-1-58089-184-4). 32pp. The importance of the *Samson*, a schooner built in 1885 that played a part in many major events in maritime history, is revealed through conversations between a young boy, Sam, and his grandfather, who sailed aboard the ship. (Rev: BL 9/1/08) [910.4]

19152 Feinberg, Barbara S. *Black Tuesday: The Stock Market Crash of 1929* (4–7). Illus. Series: Spotlight on American History. 1995, Millbrook LB $24.90 (978-1-56294-574-9). 64pp. The causes and consequences of the great stock market crash of 1929 are interestingly retold with many photographs and illustrations. (Rev: BL 10/15/95) [338.5]

19153 Feinstein, Stephen. *The 1910s: From World War I to Ragtime Music* (5–8). Series: Decades of the 20th Century. 2001, Enslow LB $22.60 (978-0-7660-1611-8). 64pp. The events of the 1910s are covered in chapters on lifestyle and fashion, arts and entertainment, sports, politics, and science, technology, and medicine. Also use *The 1920s: From Prohibition to Charles Lindbergh* (2001). (Rev: HBG 10/02; SLJ 2/02) [973.9]

19154 Feinstein, Stephen. *The 1940s: From World War II to Jackie Robinson* (5–8). Illus. Series: Decades of the 20th Century. 2000, Enslow LB $22.60 (978-0-7660-1428-2). 64pp. A lively look at events of the 1940s, covering everything from fashion and fads to politics, science, technology, medicine, and sports. Also use *The 1930s: From the Great Depression to the Wizard of Oz* (2001) and *The 1950s: From the Korean War to Elvis* (2000). (Rev: HBG 3/01; SLJ 5/01) [973.9]

19155 Ferrell, Claudine L. *Reconstruction* (5–10). Series: Greenwood Guides to Historic Events, 1500–1900. 2003, Greenwood $51.95 (978-0-313-32062-0). 220pp. Covers key individuals involved in Reconstruction and the speeches, proclamations, and other primary documents that cast light on the events of the time. (Rev: SLJ 6/04) [973.8]

19156 Flanagan, Alice K. *The Buffalo Soldiers* (3–6). Illus. Series: We the People. 2005, Compass Point LB $26.60 (978-0-7565-0833-3). 48pp. An introduction to the first all-black regiments formed after the Civil War and nicknamed "Buffalo soldiers" by the Kiowa Indians. [973.7]

19157 Freedman, Russell. *Children of the Great Depression* (5–8). Illus. 2005, Clarion $20.00 (978-0-618-44630-8). 128pp. The works of such notable photographers as Dorothea Lange and Walker Evans, moving quotations, and the accessible text of Freedman make this a memorable photoessay. (Rev: BCCB 12/05; BL 12/15/05*; IIBG 4/05; LMC 3/06; SLJ 12/05*; VOYA 6/06) [305.23]

19158 Freedman, Russell. *Immigrant Kids* (3–7). Illus. 1995, Puffin paper $8.99 (978-0-14-037594-

7). 64pp. An account of the immigration to the United States from 1880 to 1920.

19159 Gourley, Catherine. *Welcome to Samantha's World, 1904* (3–6). Series: American Girl. 1999, Pleasant $14.95 (978-1-56247-772-1). 58pp. Using double-page spreads, this book introduces social and cultural life in America at the beginning of the 20th century. (Rev: BL 1/1–15/00; HBG 3/00) [973.9]

19160 Graves, Kerry A. *Going to School During the Great Depression* (4–6). Series: Going to School in History. 2001, Capstone LB $16.95 (978-0-7368-0800-2). 32pp. School life during the 1930s and early '40s is covered with material on subjects studied, school supplies, and typical activities and games of the time. (Rev: BL 10/15/01) [973.9]

19161 Green, Carl R. *The Spanish-American War* (4–6). Series: U.S. Wars. 2002, Enslow LB $25.26 (978-0-7660-5091-4). 48pp. Preceding a brief history of the Spanish-American War, there is a lengthy section listing Internet sites that offer students additional material on the subject. (Rev: BL 10/15/02; HBG 3/03) [973.8]

19162 Greene, Meg. *Into the Land of Freedom: African Americans in Reconstruction* (5–8). Illus. Series: People's History. 2004, Lerner LB $29.27 (978-0-8225-4690-0). 112pp. Sepia-toned photographs and historical documents and interviews add to this portrait of the situation of African Americans during Reconstruction. (Rev: BL 2/15/04*; SLJ 5/04) [973]

19163 Heinrichs, Ann. *The Dust Bowl* (3–6). Illus. Series: We the People. 2005, Compass Point LB $26.60 (978-0-7565-0837-1). 48pp. Describes the plight of people living in the Midwest during the long drought of the 1930s. [978]

19164 Herald, Jacqueline. *Fashions of a Decade: The 1920s* (5–10). 2007, Chelsea House LB $35.00 (978-0-8160-6718-3). 64pp. Photographs, illustrations, and timelines accompany text that relates the fashion of the 1920s to events and the culture of the times. (Rev: SLJ 7/07)

19165 Hoffman, Nancy. *Eleanor Roosevelt and the Arthurdale Experiment* (5–8). Illus. 2001, Linnet LB $22.50 (978-0-208-02504-3). 108pp. Hoffman includes quotations and black-and-white photographs in her account of the story of Arthurdale, a government-planned community of the 1930s. (Rev: BL 10/15/01; HBG 3/02; SLJ 12/01) [975.4]

19166 Holiday, Billie, and Arthur Herzog. *God Bless the Child* (2–5). Illus. by Jerry Pinkney. 2004, HarperCollins $16.99 (978-0-06-028797-9). 32pp. The lyrics of Billie Holiday's signature song provide the framework for this moving portrait of a black family joining the great migration from the cotton fields of the Deep South to the streets of Chicago; a CD is included. (Rev: BL 2/15/04*; SLJ 2/04) [782.42164]

19167 Houle, Michelle M. *Triangle Shirtwaist Factory Fire: Flames of Labor Reform* (4–6). Illus. Series: American Disasters. 2002, Enslow LB $23.93 (978-0-7660-1785-6). 48pp. A frank portrayal of the tragic 1911 fire and the impact it had on the labor movement. (Rev: HBG 3/03; SLJ 12/02)

19168 Isaacs, Sally Senzell. *America in the Time of Franklin Delano Roosevelt: The Story of Our Nation from Coast to Coast, from 1929 to 1948* (4–8). Series: America in the Time Of. 1999, Heinemann LB $30.35 (978-1-57572-761-5). 48pp. Using the life of Roosevelt as a framework, this account describes life in America during the Great Depression and World War II. (Rev: SLJ 5/00) [973.9]

19169 Isaacs, Sally Senzell. *Life in the Dust Bowl* (2–4). Illus. Series: Picture the Past. 2001, Heinemann LB $21.36 (978-1-58810-248-5). 32pp. A gripping introduction to the hardships of life on the plains in the 1930s, with information on society at the time. (Rev: SLJ 3/02)

19170 Jackson, Robert. *Meet Me in St. Louis: A Trip to the 1904 World's Fair* (4–7). Illus. 2004, HarperCollins $17.99 (978-0-06-009267-2). 144pp. Jackson beautifully evokes the excitement surrounding the 1904 St. Louis World's Fair, which attracted nearly 20 million people, many of them key figures of the day. (Rev: BL 2/15/04; SLJ 4/04) [907]

19171 Jernegan, Laura. *A Whaling Captain's Daughter: The Diary of Laura Jernegan, 1868–1871* (4–6). Series: Diaries, Letters, and Memoirs. 2000, Capstone LB $22.60 (978-0-7368-0319-9). Excerpts from a young girl's diary introduce the reader to life ashore and aboard a whaling ship immediately after the Civil War. (Rev: BL 10/15/00; SLJ 9/00) [973.8]

19172 Josephson, Judith P. *Growing Up in a New Century* (5–8). Illus. Series: Our America. 2002, Lerner LB $26.60 (978-0-8225-0657-7). 64pp. A look at the lives of American children of different backgrounds and situations at the dawn of the 20th century. (Rev: BL 2/1/03; HBG 3/03; SLJ 7/03) [973.91]

19173 Josephson, Judith P. *Growing Up in World War II* (5–8). Illus. Series: Our America. 2002, Lerner LB $26.60 (978-0-8225-0660-7). 64pp. A look at the lives of American children of different backgrounds and situations during World War II. (Rev: BL 2/1/03; HBG 3/03) [940.533]

19174 Kalman, Bobbie. *19th Century Girls and Women* (3–5). Illus. 1997, Crabtree LB $25.27 (978-0-86505-434-9); paper $7.95 (978-0-86505-464-6). 32pp. A realistic portrait of the life women led in both the working and wealthy classes, with details on home life, chores, health hazards, and stifling clothing. (Rev: BL 7/97; SLJ 8/97) [305.4]

19175 King, David C. *Victorian Days: Discover the Past with Fun Projects, Games, Activities, and Recipes* (4–6). Illus. by Cheryl K. Noll. Series: American Kids in History. 2000, Wiley paper $14.95 (978-0-471-33122-3). 96pp. Through an interesting text and more than 30 activities like making paper flowers and shadow puppets and following some delicious recipes, young readers can re-create life in New York in the year 1893. (Rev: SLJ 4/00) [973.8]

19176 King, David C. *World Wars and the Modern Age* (5–8). Illus. Series: American Heritage, Ameri-

can Voices. 2004, Wiley paper $12.95 (978-0-471-44392-6). 144pp. A concise overview of the profound changes seen in the United States during the decades from 1870 to 1950, with excerpts from primary sources. (Rev: BL 2/1/05; SLJ 5/05) [973]

19177 Koehler-Pentacoff, Elizabeth. *Jackson and Bud's Bumpy Ride: America's First Cross-Country Automobile Trip* (1–3). Illus. by Wes Hargis. 2009, Millbrook LB $16.95 (978-0-8225-7885-7). 32pp. This is a compelling account of a 1903 cross-country adventure in a "horseless buggy" accompanied by a dog called Bud; cartoon illustrations extend the narrative. (Rev: BL 4/15/09; LMC 10/09; SLJ 4/09) [917.3]

19178 Komatsu, Kimberly, and Kaleigh Komatsu. *In America's Shadow* (5–8). Illus. 2003, Thomas George $35.00 (978-0-9709829-0-2). 96pp. This account of the internment of Japanese Americans during World War II draws on the memories and archives of the authors' family. (Rev: BL 4/1/03) [940.531]

19179 Lassieur, Allison. *The Dust Bowl: An Interactive History Adventure* (3–5). Illus. Series: You Choose. 2008, Capstone LB $20.99 (978-1-4296-2343-8). 112pp. The reader must choose among various alternatives — to stay and Kansas and try to farm despite the dust, to leave for California, to become a government photographer, and so forth. (Rev: BL 4/1/09) [978]

19180 Littlefield, Holly. *Children of the Orphan Trains* (3–6). Illus. Series: Picture the American Past. 2001, Carolrhoda LB $22.60 (978-1-57505-466-7). 48pp. A brief, informative text is accompanied by moving photographs that dramatically tell the sad story of orphan children transported West to find work and homes. (Rev: BL 5/15/01; HBG 10/01) [362.73]

19181 McHugh, Janet. *The Great Chicago Fire* (3–6). Series: Code Red. 2007, Bearport LB $23.96 (978-1-59716-360-6). 32pp. In chapters including "Where Is the Fire Department" "Looting in the Streets," No More Water!," and "Picking Up the Pieces," McHugh describes the 1871 catastrophe. (Rev: LMC 10/07; SLJ 10/07) [977.3]

19182 Meltzer, Milton. *Driven from the Land: The Story of the Dust Bowl* (4–8). Series: Great Journeys. 1999, Benchmark LB $32.79 (978-0-7614-0968-7). 111pp. Traces the development of the Dust Bowl, its effects on the land and the people, and how many were forced to leave their farms and seek a new life elsewhere. (Rev: BL 1/1–15/00; HBG 3/00; SLJ 2/00) [973.9]

19183 Miller, Marilyn. *The Transcontinental Railroad* (5–8). Illus. 1987, Silver Burdett paper $12.36 (978-0-382-09912-0). 64pp. The great event that linked East and West by rail is portrayed with numerous illustrations. (Rev: BL 7/87; SLJ 9/87) [385.0979]

19184 Nicholson, Dorinda M. *Pearl Harbor Child: A Child's View of Pearl Harbor — from Attack to Peace* (5–8). 1998, Woodson House paper $9.95 (978-1-892858-00-9). This photoessay describes a child's experience during the bombing of Pearl Harbor, the temporary evacuation, and everyday life growing up in Hawaii during World War II. (Rev: BL 1/1–15/99) [996.9]

19185 Nobleman, Marc Tyler. *The Hindenburg* (4–6). Series: We the People. 2005, Compass Point LB $26.60 (978-0-7565-1266-8). 48pp. The story of the *Hindenburg*, the German dirigible that burst into flames as it was landing at Lakehurst, New Jersey, in 1937, is placed in historical context. (Rev: SLJ 2/06) [363.12]

19186 Porterfield, Jason. *Problems and Progress in American Politics: The Growth of the Democratic Party in the Late 1800s* (5–8). Illus. Series: America's Industrial Society in the 19th Century. 2004, Rosen LB $22.50 (978-0-8239-4026-4). 32pp. For reluctant readers, this overview of the growth of the Democratic Party features large print and short chapters. (Rev: BL 4/1/04)

19187 Ransom, Candice F. *The Day of the Black Blizzard* (1–3). Illus. by Laurie Harden. Series: On My Own History. 2009, Millbrook $25.26 (978-0-8225-7895-6). 48pp. A fictionalized account of Black Sunday (April 14, 1935) featuring 10-year-old Orry and his younger stepsister as they find themselves far from home during the worst dust storm in the country's history. (Rev: BLO 1/14/09; SLJ 3/09) [978]

19188 Rau, Dana Meachen. *The Harlem Renaissance* (4–6). Series: We the People. 2005, Compass Point LB $26.60 (978-0-7565-1264-4). 48pp. A look at the key characters and the artistic creations of the Harlem Renaissance, an African American cultural movement during the 1920s and early 1930s. (Rev: SLJ 2/06) [700]

19189 Ruth, Amy. *Growing Up in the Great Depression* (5–8). Series: Our America. 2002, Lerner LB $26.60 (978-0-8225-0655-3). 64pp. With many sidebars and quotations from original sources, this narrative re-creates the despair and courage of children growing up during the Great Depression. (Rev: BL 2/15/03; HBG 3/03) [973.9]

19190 Sandler, Martin W. *Island of Hope: The Story of Ellis Island and the Journey to America* (5–7). Illus. 2004, Scholastic $19.99 (978-0-439-53082-8). 144pp. Drawing heavily on firsthand accounts, Sandler traces immigrants' progress through the processing at Ellis Island and on into the cities and farms of their new country. (Rev: BL 4/15/04; SLJ 6/04) [304.8]

19191 Santella, Andrew. *Roosevelt's Rough Riders* (4–6). Series: We the People. 2005, Compass Point LB $26.60 (978-0-7565-1268-2). 48pp. Profiles the men from diverse walks of life who volunteered to fight as part of Roosevelt's Rough Riders during the Spanish-American War. (Rev: SLJ 2/06) [973.8]

19192 Schaefer, Adam R. *The Triangle Shirtwaist Factory Fire* (4–7). Series: Landmark Events in American History. 2003, World Almanac LB $31.00 (978-0-8368-5383-4). 48pp. An accessible account of the tragic 1911 fire in New York City, with material on the horrible working conditions and the resulting reforms in labor law. (Rev: SLJ 6/04) [974.7]

19193 Scher, Linda. *The Texas City Disaster* (3–6). Series: Code Red. 2007, Bearport LB $23.96 (978-1-59716-363-7). 32pp. Readers will learn of an explosion that killed 550 people in Texas City in 1947 and led to changes in industrial safety regulations. (Rev: LMC 10/07; SLJ 7/07)

19194 Schomp, Virginia. *World War II* (5–8). Illus. Series: Letters from the Homefront. 2001, Marshall Cavendish LB $29.93 (978-0-7614-1098-0). 96pp. Schomp uses letters written during World War II, accompanied by relevant illustrations, to give readers a real understanding of the difficulties of life on the homefront. (Rev: BL 10/15/01; HBG 3/02) [940.54]

19195 Schwartz, Eric. *Crossing the Seas: Americans Form an Empire 1890–1899* (5–8). Series: How America Became America. 2005, Mason Crest LB $22.95 (978-1-59084-910-1). 91pp. Schwartz explores America's turn to imperialism in the final decade of the 19th century. Also use *Super Power: Americans Today* (2005). (Rev: SLJ 11/05) [973]

19196 Sherrow, Victoria. *The Triangle Factory Fire* (5–8). Series: Spotlight on American History. 1995, Millbrook LB $24.90 (978-1-56294-572-5). The story of the deadly factory fire that exposed the shameful labor exploitation in this country and led to needed reforms. (Rev: SLJ 3/96) [363.37]

19197 Stanley, George E. *An Emerging World Power (1900–1929)* (5–8). Illus. Series: A Primary Source History of the United States. 2005, World Almanac LB $31.00 (978-0-8368-5828-0). 48pp. A simple narrative links well-chosen primary sources documenting the key events of the early 20th century. Also use *The Era of Reconstruction and Expansion (1865–1900)* and *The Great Depression and World War II (1929–1949)* (both 2005). (Rev: BL 4/1/05; SLJ 7/05)

19198 Stewart, Dave. *You Wouldn't Want to Sail on the Titanic! One Voyage You'd Rather Not Make* (4–6). Illus. by David Antram. Series: You Wouldn't Want To. 2001, Watts LB $29.00 (978-0-531-14604-0); paper $9.95 (978-0-531-16210-1). 32pp. The uncomfortable opportunity to imagine yourself aboard the *Titanic*. (Rev: SLJ 3/02) [910.91]

19199 Stites, Bill. *The Republican Party in the Late 1800s: A Changing Role for American Government* (5–8). Illus. Series: America's Industrial Society in the 19th Century. 2004, Rosen LB $22.50 (978-0-8239-4030-1). 32pp. For reluctant readers, this overview of the growth of the Republican Party features large print and short chapters. (Rev: BL 4/1/04)

19200 Stone, Tanya L. *The Great Depression and World War II* (5–8). Series: Making of America. 2001, Raintree LB $28.54 (978-0-8172-5710-1). 96pp. Concise text and attractive illustrations re-create the history of America from 1929 through World War II. (Rev: BL 9/15/01; HBG 10/01) [973.9]

19201 Stone, Tanya L. *The Progressive Era and World War I* (5–8). Series: Making of America. 2001, Raintree LB $28.54 (978-0-8172-5709-5). 96pp. Roughly the first 20 years of the 20th century in American history are retold in this history that also looks at home life, culture, and entertainment. (Rev: BL 9/15/01; HBG 10/01; SLJ 6/01) [973.9]

19202 Stroud, Bettye, and Virginia Schomp. *The Reconstruction Era* (5–8). Series: Drama of African-American History. 2006, Benchmark LB $23.95 (978-0-7614-2181-8). 70pp. This volume traces the history of Reconstruction and the tensions remaining between the many factions after the Civil War. (Rev: SLJ 5/07) [973.8]

19203 Uschan, Michael V. *The 1940s* (5–10). Series: Cultural History of the United States. 1998, Lucent LB $28.70 (978-1-56510-554-6). Life at home and abroad during World War II dominate this book, which also discusses the Great Depression, the New Deal, events leading up to U.S. participation in the war, the beginnings of the Cold War, the growth of suburban living, and the rise of television, with sidebars on such topics as the Holocaust, the influences of radio, movies, and comics, 1940s slang, and the first computers. (Rev: SLJ 1/99) [973.9]

19204 Warren, Andrea. *We Rode the Orphan Trains* (4–8). Illus. 2001, Houghton $18.00 (978-0-618-11712-3). 144pp. Eight moving biographical accounts of men and women, now in their 80s and 90s, who traveled to the Midwest to find new homes and families. (Rev: BCCB 11/01; BL 11/1/01; HBG 3/02; SLJ 11/01; VOYA 12/01) [362.73]

19205 Weber, Valerie, and Valerie Baker. *Traveling in Grandma's Day* (3–4). 2000, Carolrhoda LB $21.27 (978-1-57505-326-4). 32pp. A nostalgic look at traveling in the 1930s and 1940s told through first-person narratives and plenty of photographs. Also use *School in Grandma's Day, Shopping in Grandma's Day,* and *Food in Grandma's Day* (all 2000). (Rev: HBG 10/00; SLJ 6/00) [973.9]

19206 Wells, Donna. *America Comes of Age* (5–8). Series: The Making of America. 2001, Raintree LB $28.54 (978-0-8172-5708-8). 96pp. A handsomely illustrated account that traces U.S. history from Reconstruction to the beginning of the 20th century. (Rev: BL 4/15/01; HBG 10/01) [973.8]

19207 Wetterer, Margaret K., and Charles M. Wetterer. *The Snow Walker* (2–4). Illus. 1996, Carolrhoda LB $23.93 (978-0-87614-891-4); paper $5.95 (978-0-87614-959-1). 48pp. During the terrible blizzard of 1888, Milton Daub unselfishly helped his neighbors in the Bronx by delivering needed supplies. (Rev: BCCB 12/96; BL 2/15/96; SLJ 3/96) [973.9]

19208 Whitman, Sylvia. *Immigrant Children: Late 1800s to Early 1900s* (3–5). Series: Picture the American Past. 2000, Carolrhoda LB $22.60 (978-1-57505-395-0). 48pp. This book describes the lives of immigrant children who arrived in this country, many to work in mines, factories, or farms but all trying to get ahead. (Rev: HBG 10/00; SLJ 7/00) [973.9]

19209 Whitman, Sylvia. *V Is for Victory: The American Home Front During World War II* (4–7). Illus. 1993, Lerner LB $30.35 (978-0-8225-1727-6). 80pp. Rosie the Riveter, ration stamps, and the relocation of Japanese Americans are among the topics covered in this look at the United States in another time. (Rev: BL 2/15/93) [973.9]

19210 Worth, Richard. *The Harlem Renaissance: An Explosion of African-American Culture* (5–8). Illus. 2008, Enslow LB $23.95 (978-0-7660-2907-1). 128pp. This attractive overview of the Harlem Renaissance traces the origins and spirit of the movement and profiles many of its writers, artists, musicians, and thinkers. (Rev: BL 2/1/09; LMC 11/08) [700.89]

19211 Wroble, Lisa A. *Kids During the Great Depression* (3–5). Series: Kids Throughout History. 1999, Rosen LB $19.95 (978-0-8239-5255-7). 24pp. This book tells of the events preceding the Depression, its effects on people and particularly children, and the gradual recovery before World War II. (Rev: SLJ 11/99) [973.9]

19212 Wroble, Lisa A. *The New Deal and the Great Depression in American History* (5–8). Series: In American History. 2002, Enslow LB $26.60 (978-0-7660-1421-3). 128pp. A timeline, maps, chapter notes, and research topics are found in this well-researched account that concentrates on Roosevelt's economic policies during the 1930s. (Rev: BL 1/1–15/03; HBG 3/03) [973.9]

THE 1950S TO THE PRESENT

19213 Anderson, Dale. *America into a New Millennium* (5–8). Series: Making of America. 2001, Raintree LB $28.54 (978-0-8172-5712-5). 96pp. This last part of a 12-volume series presents American history from the end of the Cold War to the beginning of the 21st century. (Rev: BL 9/15/01; HBG 10/01; SLJ 6/01) [973.9]

19214 Anderson, Dale. *The Cold War Years* (5–8). Series: Making of America. 2001, Raintree LB $28.54 (978-0-8172-5711-8). 96pp. A concise, easy-to-understand text tells America's story from the end of World War II to the 1990s. (Rev: BL 9/15/01; HBG 10/01; SLJ 6/01) [973.9]

19215 Britton, Tamara. *The World Trade Center* (3–5). Series: Symbols, Landmarks, and Monuments. 2003, ABDO LB $22.78 (978-1-57765-850-4). 40pp. The design and construction of New York City's World Trade Center are described along with its destruction on September 11, 2001. (Rev: HBG 10/03; SLJ 10/03) [720]

19216 Brown, Gene. *The Nation in Turmoil: Civil Rights and the Vietnam War (1960–1973)* (5–8). Series: First Person America. 1994, Twenty-First Century LB $20.90 (978-0-8050-2588-0). An overview of the civil rights movement and the Vietnam War, highlighting excerpts from letters, diaries, and speeches. (Rev: BL 5/15/94) [973.92]

19217 Burgan, Michael. *Spying and the Cold War* (4–6). Series: On the Front Line. 2005, Raintree LB $29.93 (978-1-4109-1465-1). 48pp. This is an accessible overview of the Cold War, covering its roots and progress and looking in particular at the role of espionage; personal accounts add interest. (Rev: SLJ 12/05) [327.1209]

19218 Canwell, Diane, and Jon Sutherland. *African Americans in the Vietnam War* (5–8). Illus. Series: American Experience in Vietnam. 2005, World Almanac LB $31.00 (978-0-8368-5772-6). 48pp.

Personal stories and full-color photographs add to the information on black Americans' contributions to the conflict and the military's efforts toward integration. Also use *American Women in the Vietnam War* (2005). (Rev: BL 2/1/05) [959.705]

19219 Carter, E. J. *The Cuban Missile Crisis* (4–8). Series: 20th Century Perspectives. 2003, Heinemann LB $27.07 (978-1-4034-3806-5). 48pp. A review of the 1962 crisis in which Cuba secretly installed missiles capable of carrying nuclear warheads. (Rev: SLJ 5/04) [972.9]

19220 Feinstein, Stephen. *The 1960s: From the Vietnam War to Flower Power* (4–7). Illus. Series: Decades of the 20th Century. 2000, Enslow LB $22.60 (978-0-7660-1426-8). 64pp. An account of America's turbulent 1960s that includes lifestyles, politics, fashion, fads, and entertainment. (Rev: BL 10/15/00; HBG 3/01; SLJ 12/00) [973.92]

19221 Feinstein, Stephen. *The 1970s: From Watergate to Disco* (4–7). Series: Decades of the 20th Century. 2000, Enslow LB $22.60 (978-0-7660-1425-1). 64pp. This book covers the people and events of the 1970s along with developments in such areas as politics, science, and sports. (Rev: BL 10/15/00; HBG 3/01; SLJ 12/00) [973.9]

19222 Feinstein, Stephen. *The 1980s: From Ronald Reagan to MTV* (4–7). Series: Decades of the 20th Century. 2000, Enslow LB $22.60 (978-0-7660-1424-4). 64pp. Presents the decade's major events, important people, and developments in such areas as politics, science, the arts, and sports. (Rev: BL 10/15/00; HBG 10/00; SLJ 12/00) [973.9]

19223 Feinstein, Stephen. *The 1990s: Fom the Persian Gulf War to Y2K* (5–8). Series: Decades of the 20th Century. 2001, Enslow LB $22.60 (978-0-7660-1613-2). 64pp. The events of the 1990s are covered in chapters on lifestyle and fashion; arts and entertainment; sports; politics; and science, technology, and medicine. (Rev: HBG 10/02; SLJ 2/02) [973.9]

19224 Gard, Carolyn. *The Attack on the Pentagon on September 11, 2001* (4–8). Series: Terrorist Attacks. 2003, Rosen LB $27.95 (978-0-8239-3858-2). 64pp. In addition to describing the attack itself, Gard looks at the organization of Al-Qaeda. (Rev: SLJ 2/04) [975.5]

19225 Green, Carl R. *The Vietnam War* (4–6). Illus. Scrics: U.S. Wars. 2003, Enslow LB $25.26 (978-0-7660-5147-8). 48pp. Supported by verified and updated Web links, this is a useful introduction to the Vietnam War. (Rev: HBG 4/04)

19226 Hampton, Wilborn. *Kennedy Assassinated! The World Mourns* (5–8). Illus. 1997, Candlewick $17.99 (978-1-56402-811-2). A gripping first-person account of John Kennedy's assassination by a veteran newspaper reporter who was in Dallas that day. (Rev: BL 9/15/97; HBG 3/98; SLJ 10/97) [364.1]

19227 Isaacs, Sally Senzell. *America in the Time of Martin Luther King Jr.: The Story of Our Nation from Coast to Coast, from 1948 to 1976* (4–8). Series: America in the Time Of. 1999, Heinemann LB $30.35 (978-1-57572-780-6). 48pp. As well as describing the accomplishment of Martin Luther King, Jr., this account traces important developments during his time including the 1960s peace movement, the Vietnam War, space travel, and the Watergate scandal. (Rev: SLJ 5/00) [973.9]

19228 Koestler, Rachel. *Going to School During the Civil Rights Movement* (4–6). Illus. Series: Going to School in History. 2001, Capstone LB $23.93 (978-0-7368-0799-9). 32pp. Koestler explores the difficulties of attending school during segregation. (Rev: BL 10/15/01; HBG 3/02) [379.2]

19229 Koestler-Grack, Rachel A. *The Kent State Tragedy* (4–7). Illus. Series: American Moments. 2005, ABDO LB $25.65 (978-1-59197-934-0). 48pp. A concise overview of the deadly 1970 clash between National Guard troops and war protesters on the campus of Ohio's Kent State University. (Rev: BL 9/1/05; SLJ 11/05) [378.771]

19230 Mason, Andrew. *The Vietnam War: A Primary Source History* (5–8). Illus. Series: In Their Own Words. 2005, Gareth Stevens LB $27.00 (978-0-8368-5981-2). 48pp. Primary sources — including letters, articles, speeches, and songs — deliver the views of combatants in Vietnam and people on the home front in this well-illustrated volume. (Rev: BL 10/15/05) [959.704]

19231 Petersen, Christine. *The Iran-Contra Scandal* (4–6). Series: Cornerstones of Freedom. 2004, Children's Pr. LB $26.00 (978-0-516-24228-6). 48pp. Petersen offers a fascinating overview of the investigations into Reagan administration activities involving illegal arms sales to Iran. (Rev: SLJ 7/04) [973.927]

19232 Poffenberger, Nancy. *September 11th, 2001: A Simple Account for Children* (PS–2). Illus. 2002, Fun paper $8.95 (978-0-938293-12-5). 16pp. Drawings by schoolchildren illustrate a straightforward presentation of the events of September 11. (Rev: BL 7/02) [973.931]

19233 Santella, Andrew. *September 11, 2001* (4–6). Series: Cornerstones of Freedom, Second Series. 2002, Children's Book Pr. LB $26.00 (978-0-516-22692-7). 48pp. This presentation gives the basic facts on the attacks and the U.S. response. (Rev: SLJ 11/02)

19234 Schomp, Virginia. *The Vietnam War* (5–8). Series: Letters from the Homefront. 2001, Benchmark LB $29.93 (978-0-7614-1099-7). 96pp. Conditions on the home front during the Vietnam War are re-created through primary documents such as letters and period photographs. (Rev: BL 10/15/01; HBG 3/02; SLJ 3/02) [973.9]

19235 Stein, R. Conrad. *The Cold War* (4–6). Series: U.S. Wars. 2002, Enslow LB $25.26 (978-0-7660-5095-2). 48pp. In addition to a concise history of the causes and progress of the Cold War, this volume includes a listing of pertinent Web sites where additional material such as maps, documents, and biographies can be found. (Rev: BL 10/15/02; HBG 3/03) [973.9]

19236 Steins, Richard. *The Postwar Years: The Cold War and the Atomic Age (1950–1959)* (5–8). Series: First Person America. 1994, Twenty-First Century

LB $20.90 (978-0-8050-2587-3). Coverage of the 1950s includes first-person material on the Cold War and the Korean conflict. (Rev: BL 5/15/94; SLJ 12/94) [973.92]

19237 Walsh, Frank. *The Montgomery Bus Boycott* (5–8). Series: Landmark Events in American History. 2003, World Almanac LB $31.00 (978-0-8368-5375-9). 48pp. The story of what happened when Rosa Parks refused to give up her seat on a Montgomery, Alabama, bus in 1955. (Rev: BL 10/15/03; SLJ 9/03) [305.8]

19238 Wheeler, Jill C. *September 11, 2001: The Day That Changed America* (3–5). Illus. Series: War on Terrorism. 2002, ABDO $25.65 (978-1-57765-656-2). 64pp. This introductory volume covers the attacks, the rescue efforts, and the initial American response, with lots of photographs. Also use *Ground Zero* and *Heroes of the Day*. (Rev: BL 5/1/02; HBG 10/02; SLJ 6/02) [973.931]

19239 Young, Jeff C. *The Korean War* (4–6). Illus. Series: U.S. Wars. 2003, Enslow LB $25.26 (978-0-7660-5148-5). 48pp. Supported by verified and updated Web links, this is a useful account of the Korean War. (Rev: HBG 4/04)

19240 Young, Jeff C. *Operation Iraqi Freedom* (4–6). Illus. Series: U.S. Wars. 2003, Enslow LB $25.26 (978-0-7660-5088-4). 48pp. Supported by verified and updated Web links, this is a useful introduction to Operation Iraqi Freedom. (Rev: HBG 4/04)

19241 Zeinert, Karen. *The Valiant Women of the Vietnam War* (5–8). Illus. 2000, Millbrook LB $29.90 (978-0-7613-1268-0). 96pp. Provides a good overview of the Vietnam War and highlights the contributions of women at home and abroad during this conflict. (Rev: BL 4/1/00; HBG 10/00; SLJ 5/00) [959.704]

Regions

MIDWEST

19242 Anderson, Kathy P. *Illinois* (3–6). Illus. Series: Hello USA. 1993, Lerner LB $19.93 (978-0-8225-2723-7). 72pp. Presents the history and geography of this state, and includes biographies of famous native sons and daughters. (Rev: BL 1/15/93) [977.3]

19243 Anderson, Reuben. *Uniquely Oklahoma* (4–7). Illus. Series: Heinemann State Studies. 2004, Heinemann LB $27.07 (978-1-4034-4658-9). 48pp. In addition to providing the facts necessary for report writers, this volume emphasizes the features that distinguish Oklahoma from its neighbors. (Rev: BL 10/15/03)

19244 Anderson, Reuben. *Uniquely South Dakota* (4–7). Illus. Series: Heinemann State Studies. 2004, Heinemann LB $31.36 (978-1-4034-4662-6). 48pp. In addition to providing the facts necessary for report writers, this volume emphasizes the features that distinguish South Dakota from its neighbors. (Rev: BL 10/15/03)

19245 Ash, Stephanie. *Uniquely Minnesota* (4–7). Series: Heinemann State Studies. 2004, Heinemann LB $27.07 (978-1-4034-4494-3). 48pp. In addition to providing the facts necessary for report writers, this volume emphasizes the features that distinguish Minnesota from its neighbors. (Rev: BL 4/1/04)

19246 Aylesworth, Thomas G., and Virginia L. Aylesworth. *Eastern Great Lakes: Indiana, Michigan, Ohio* (4–7). Illus. Series: State Reports. 1995, Chelsea $19.95 (978-0-7910-3409-5). 64pp. Information is given for each of the three states covered, including major cities, history, geography, and climate. (Rev: BL 3/15/92) [977]

19247 Balcavage, Dynise. *Iowa* (5–8). Illus. Series: From Sea to Shining Sea, Second Series. 2002, Children's LB $30.50 (978-0-516-22481-7). 80pp. An attractive overview of Iowa's land, history, culture, economy, and people. (Rev: SLJ 3/03) [977.7]

19248 Baldwin, Guy. *Oklahoma* (4–8). Series: Celebrate the States. 2000, Marshall Cavendish LB $148.29 (978-0-7614-1061-4). 144pp. The beauties and hidden treasures of Oklahoma are covered in this colorful introduction to the state, its past, its present, and its people. (Rev: BL 12/15/00) [976.6]

19249 Bennett, Michelle. *Missouri* (4–8). Series: Celebrate the States. 2001, Benchmark LB $37.07 (978-0-7614-1063-8). 144pp. A logically organized, thorough introduction to Missouri with material on such topics as history, people, landmarks, and famous natives. (Rev: BL 9/15/01; HBG 10/01) [977.8]

19250 Bial, Raymond. *Nauvoo: Mormon City on the Mississippi River* (4–7). Illus. 2006, Houghton $17.00 (978-0-618-39685-6). 48pp. This richly illustrated title profiles the Illinois city of Nauvoo and the important role it played in the history of the Church of Jesus Christ of Latter-day Saints. (Rev: BL 11/1/06; SLJ 12/06) [289.3]

19251 Bjorklund, Ruth. *Kansas* (4–8). Series: Celebrate the States. 2000, Marshall Cavendish LB $37.07 (978-0-7614-0646-4). 143pp. A broad introduction to Kansas — its geography and history, its government and people, its songs and folktales, and a few of its recipes. (Rev: BL 6/1–15/00; HBG 10/00) [978.1]

19252 Bodden, Valerie. *Mount Rushmore* (3–6). Series: Modern Wonders of the World. 2006, Creative Education LB $27.10 (978-1-58341-440-8). 32pp. This is an interesting history of the memorial at Mount Rushmore, with good photographs and discussion of its contemporary importance. (Rev: SLJ 12/06) [978.3]

19253 Brandenburg, Jim. *An American Safari: Adventures on the North American Prairie* (4–6). Illus. 1995, Walker LB $17.85 (978-0-8027-8320-2). 48pp. This American photographer describes in words and pictures the western prairies and the animals that live there. (Rev: BCCB 6/95; BL 4/15/95; SLJ 8/95) [508.73]

19254 Bratvold, Gretchen. *Wisconsin* (3–6). Illus. Series: Hello USA. 1991, Lerner LB $19.93 (978-0-8225-2700-8). 72pp. An introduction to the dairy state, with full-color photos. (Rev: BL 4/15/91; SLJ 7/91) [977.5]

19255 Brill, Marlene T. *Illinois* (4–7). Illus. Series: Celebrate the States. 2005, Benchmark LB $37.07 (978-0-7614-1735-4). 144pp. A revised edition of this introduction to the state — including its history, culture, famous sites, and important individuals — with updated illustrations. (Rev: SLJ 5/06) [913.73]

19256 Brill, Marlene T. *Indiana* (4–8). Illus. Series: Celebrate the States. 1997, Marshall Cavendish LB $37.07 (978-0-7614-0147-6). An introduction to this Midwest state's agriculture, industries, famous natives, history, and geography. (Rev: BL 7/97; SLJ 8/97) [977.2]

19257 Brown, Dottie. *Ohio* (3–6). Illus. Series: Hello USA. 1992, Lerner LB $19.93 (978-0-8225-2725-1). 72pp. Ohio, the nation's seventh-largest state, is described from the days of the Indians and settlers until today. (Rev: BL 11/15/92) [977.1]

19258 Burgan, Michael. *Illinois* (5–8). Illus. Series: America the Beautiful: Third Series. 2007, Children's Pr. LB $38.00 (978-0-531-18559-9). 144pp. This new edition of the classic series entry about the state features a new design and layout, definitions of difficult words in the margins, more history and mini biographies, and project ideas in writing, art, and science. (Rev: BL 2/1/08) [8. 977.3]

19259 Butler, Dori. *M Is for Minnesota* (3–5). Illus. by Janice L. Porter. 1998, Univ. of Minnesota $16.95 (978-0-8166-3041-7). 32pp. Using an *A* through *Z* approach, this picture book covers basic facts about Minnesota. (Rev: BL 1/1–15/99; HBG 3/99; SLJ 3/99) [977.6]

19260 Carlson, Jeffrey D. *A Historical Album of Minnesota* (5–8). Illus. Series: Historical Albums. 1993, Millbrook LB $24.40 (978-1-56294-006-5). 64pp. A heavily illustrated volume that traces the history of Minnesota from Native American communities through exploration and settlement to present-day concerns. (Rev: SLJ 10/93) [977.6]

19261 Deinard, Jenny. *How to Draw Illinois' Sights and Symbols* (3–6). Illus. Series: Kid's Guide to Drawing America. 2002, Rosen LB $25.25 (978-0-8239-6069-9). 32pp. An eclectic mix of drawing exercises and basic facts about Illinois history, geography, demographics, and important features. Also use *How to Draw Missouri's Sights and Symbols* (2001). (Rev: BL 2/15/02; SLJ 7/02) [743]

19262 Derzipilski, Kathleen. *Indiana* (3–6). Illus. Series: It's My State! 2007, Marshall Cavendish LB $20.95 (978-0-7614-1927-3). 80pp. Interesting facts and a pleasing design combine to make this an engaging introduction to the Hoosier state. (Rev: SLJ 8/07)

19263 Doherty, Craig A., and Katherine M. Doherty. *The Gateway Arch* (3–6). Illus. Series: Building America. 1995, Blackbirch LB $23.70 (978-1-56711-105-7). 48pp. A description of the construction and parts of this St. Louis landmark. (Rev: BL 9/15/95; SLJ 7/95) [725]

19264 Doherty, Craig A., and Katherine M. Doherty. *Mount Rushmore* (3–6). Illus. Series: Build America. 1995, Blackbirch LB $23.70 (978-1-56711-108-8). 48pp. The story of the planning through the execution of the four gigantic heads on Mount Rushmore and the controversy concerning taking the land from the Sioux. (Rev: BL 9/15/95; SLJ 7/95) [730]

19265 Dornfeld, Margaret. *Wisconsin* (4–7). Series: It's My State! 2003, Marshall Cavendish LB $27.07 (978-0-7614-1524-4). 80pp. Using many quotations from various sources, this account supplies a basic introduction to Wisconsin, its people, and its past and present. (Rev: BL 9/15/03; HBG 4/04; SLJ 11/03) [977.5]

19266 Dykstra, Mary. *Iowa* (2–4). Series: Portraits of the States. 2006, Gareth Stevens LB $24.00 (978-0-8368-4664-5). 32pp. Young report writers will find lots of useful information in this introduction to the state, with accessible text and graphic features that add interest. (Rev: SLJ 5/06) [977.7]

19267 Edge, Laura B. *A Personal Tour of Hull-House* (4–7). Series: How It Was. 2001, Lerner LB $25.26 (978-0-8225-3583-6). 64pp. A firsthand account of the settlement house founded in Chicago by Jane Addams. (Rev: BL 8/1/01) [977.3]

19268 Fredeen, Charles. *Kansas* (3–6). Illus. Series: Hello USA. 1992, Lerner LB $19.93 (978-0-8225-2716-9). 72pp. With excellent color illustrations, this account covers the state of Kansas and includes information on history, geography, and social and economic conditions. (Rev: BL 6/1/92) [978.1]

19269 Gedatus, Gus. *Minnesota* (2–4). Series: Portraits of the States. 2006, Gareth Stevens LB $24.00 (978-0-8368-4669-0). 32pp. Young report writers will find lots of useful information in this introduction to the state, with accessible text and graphic features that add interest. (Rev: SLJ 5/06) [977.6]

19270 Hahn, Laura. *Mount Rushmore* (4–8). Illus. Series: American Symbols and Their Meanings. 2002, Mason Crest LB $18.95 (978-1-59084-027-6). 48pp. Hahn describes Gutzon Borglum's struggle to build his monument, with a helpful timeline and many illustrations. (Rev: SLJ 9/02) [730]

19271 Heinrichs, Ann. *Illinois* (3–6). Series: This Land Is Your Land. 2002, Compass Point LB $25.26 (978-0-7565-0313-0). 48pp. An overview of the geography, history, government, economy, people, and attractions of Illinois. (Rev: SLJ 2/03)

19272 Heinrichs, Ann. *Michigan* (2–5). Illus. Series: This Land Is Your Land. 2003, Compass Point LB $25.26 (978-0-7565-0323-9). 48pp. For early researchers, this introduction to basic facts about the state and its history, geography, people, government, economy, and attractions includes plenty of photographs and maps. Also use *Ohio* (2003). (Rev: SLJ 7/03) [977.4]

19273 Heinrichs, Ann. *Minnesota* (2–5). Illus. Series: This Land Is Your Land. 2003, Compass Point LB $25.26 (978-0-7565-0315-4). 48pp. This brightly illustrated profile explores Minnesota's history, people, geography, government, economy, and attractions. Also use *Ohio* and *Wisconsin* (both 2003). (Rev: SLJ 7/03) [977.6]

19274 Heinrichs, Ann. *Ohio* (3–5). Illus. by Matt Kania. Series: Welcome to the U.S.A. 2005, The Child's World LB $27.07 (978-1-59296-449-9). 40pp. Using an attractive scrapbook format featuring a family on vacation, this volume introduces the state's geography, history, people, major attractions, and state symbols. (Rev: SLJ 2/06) [977.1]

19275 Heinrichs, Ann. *South Dakota* (3–5). Illus. by Matt Kania. Series: Welcome to the U.S.A. 2005, The Child's World LB $27.07 (978-1-59296-483-3). 40pp. A basic introduction with maps, pertinent facts, discussion of the state's geography and history, plus popular destinations and cultural information. (Rev: SLJ 1/06) [979.2]

19276 Jameson, W. C. *Buried Treasures of the Great Plains* (5–8). Series: Buried Treasure. 1997, August House $11.95 (978-0-87483-486-4). Stories of buried treasure are organized by the individual states of the Great Plains region. (Rev: SLJ 7/97) [977]

19277 King, David C. *Iowa* (3–6). Illus. Series: It's My State! 2007, Marshall Cavendish LB $20.95 (978-0-7614-1928-0). 80pp. A pleasant design and interesting information make this a useful resource for students writing reports on Iowa. (Rev: SLJ 8/07)

19278 LaDoux, Rita C. *Iowa* (3–6). Illus. Series: Hello USA. 1992, Lerner LB $19.93 (978-0-8225-2724-4). 72pp. This introduction to Iowa gives capsule biographies, a timeline, fact sheets, and chapters on topics like history and geography. (Rev: BL 9/1/92) [977.7]

19279 LaDoux, Rita C. *Missouri* (3–6). Illus. Series: Hello USA. 1991, Lerner LB $19.93 (978-0-8225-2710-7). 72pp. With timelines, capsule biographies, many fact sheets, and the usual information, the state of Missouri is introduced. (Rev: BL 12/1/91) [977.8]

19280 LaDoux, Rita C. *Oklahoma* (3–6). Illus. Series: Hello USA. 1992, Lerner LB $19.93 (978-0-8225-2717-6). 72pp. Oklahoma is introduced with topics that include famous inhabitants, timelines, and fact sheets. (Rev: BL 6/1/92) [976.6]

19281 Ling, Bettina. *Wisconsin* (4–6). Series: From Sea to Shining Sea. 2002, Children's Book Pr. LB $30.50 (978-0-516-22380-3). The state of Wisconsin is introduced through a lively text, many color photographs, maps, a glossary, a timeline, and other attractive features. (Rev: BL 4/15/02) [977.5]

19282 Mader, Jan. *Michigan* (K–2). Series: Rookie Read-About Geography. 2003, Children's Pr. LB $20.50 (978-0-516-22736-8); paper $5.95 (978-0-516-27781-3). 31pp. A small-format, basic introduction to the state of Michigan suitable for beginning readers. (Rev: SLJ 10/03) [917.74]

19283 Martin, Michael A. *Ohio: The Buckeye State* (4–7). Series: World Almanac Library of the States. 2002, World Almanac LB $31.00 (978-0-8368-5124-3). 48pp. Facts, statistics, a pleasing layout, and color photographs make this a useful choice for report writers. Also use *Iowa: The Hawkeye State* (2002). (Rev: SLJ 9/02) [977.1]

19284 Murphy, Jim. *The Great Fire* (5–9). 1995, Scholastic paper $18.95 (978-0-590-47267-8). A dramatic re-creation of the great Chicago fire that combines documents, personal accounts, illustrations, photographs, and street maps to give an in-

depth view of the disaster. (Rev: BCCB 5/95; BL 6/1–15/95; HB 5/95, 9/95; SLJ 7/95) [977.3]

19285 Nobleman, Marc Tyler. *Chicago* (3–6). Series: Great Cities of the World. 2004, World Almanac LB $31.00 (978-0-8368-5036-9). 48pp. Chicago's history, geography, and economy are described, as are shopping and leisure attractions and the life of the city. (Rev: SLJ 4/05)

19286 Olien, Rebecca. *Kansas* (3–5). Illus. Series: Land of Liberty. 2003, Capstone LB $25.26 (978-0-7368-1584-0). 64pp. Bright illustrations — photographs, reproductions, charts, and maps — add to this overview of the state's geography, climate, history, people, lifestyle, economy, government, and flora and fauna. (Rev: SLJ 10/03) [978.1]

19287 Opat, Jamie Stockman. *Uniquely Nebraska* (4–7). Illus. Series: Heinemann State Studies. 2004, Heinemann LB $27.07 (978-1-4034-4649-7). 48pp. In addition to providing the facts necessary for report writers, this volume emphasizes the features that distinguish Nebraska from its neighbors. (Rev: BL 10/15/03)

19288 Pfeffer, Wendy. *The Big Flood* (K–3). Illus. by Vanessa Lubach. 2001, Millbrook LB $23.90 (978-0-7613-1653-4). 32pp. Young Patti describes the Mississippi flood of 1993 and the way the neighbors worked together to try to avert disaster. (Rev: BL 6/1–15/01; HBG 10/01; SLJ 10/01) [363.34]

19289 Porter, A. P. *Minnesota* (3–6). Illus. Series: Hello USA. 1992, Lerner LB $19.93 (978-0-8225-2718-3). 72pp. Fact sheets, timelines, and biographies of famous native sons and daughters are included in this introduction to Minnesota. (Rev: BL 6/1/92) [977.6]

19290 Porter, A. P. *Nebraska* (3–6). Illus. Series: Hello USA. 1991, Lerner LB $19.93 (978-0-8225-2708-4). 72pp. With information on the environment as well as on topics like population, industries, symbols, history, and geography, Nebraska is given good coverage. (Rev: BL 12/1/91) [978.2]

19291 Price-Groff, Claire. *Illinois* (3–6). Illus. Series: It's My State! 2002, Benchmark LB $27.07 (978-0-7614-1422-3). 80pp. The usual state information — geography, history, government, people, and economy — is presented in an appealing layout and with an activity. (Rev: BL 3/1/03; HBG 10/03; SLJ 2/03)

19292 Redmond, Jim, and D. J. Ross. *Uniquely North Dakota* (4–7). Series: Heinemann State Studies. 2004, Heinemann LB $27.07 (978-1-4034-4657-2). 48pp. In addition to providing the facts necessary for report writers, this volume emphasizes the features that distinguish North Dakota from its neighbors. (Rev: BL 4/1/04)

19293 Riggs, Kate. *Mount Rushmore* (2–4). Illus. Series: Now That's Big! 2009, Creative Education LB $24.25 (978-1-58341-705-8). 24pp. A slim introduction to the mountain and its famous sculptures. (Rev: BLO 3/11/09) [978.3]

19294 Ross, Jim, and Paul Myers, eds. *Dear Oklahoma City, Get Well Soon* (3–6). Illus. 1996, Walker LB $17.85 (978-0-8027-8437-7). 48pp. A sampling of the letters and drawings sent by children to victims of the 1995 bombing of the Oklahoma City

Federal Building. (Rev: BCCB 6/96; BL 5/15/96; SLJ 5/96) [976.6]

19295 St. Antoine, Sara, ed. *Stories from Where We Live: The Great North American Prairie* (4–8). 2001, Milkweed $19.95 (978-1-57131-630-1). 264pp. A collection of historical and contemporary stories, poems, essays, and journal entries about life on the prairie, with informative appendixes. (Rev: BL 5/15/01) [978]

19296 Schonberg, Lisa. *People of Ohio* (4–7). Illus. Series: Heinemann State Studies. 2003, Heinemann LB $27.07 (978-1-4034-0668-2). 48pp. Schonberg looks at groups of Ohioans from the original native peoples to later arrivals and at individuals who have contributed to all fields of endeavor, with many color photographs. (Rev: BL 10/15/03; HBG 4/04; SLJ 10/03) [305.8]

19297 Schonberg, Marcia. *Uniquely Ohio* (4–6). Illus. Series: Heinemann State Studies. 2003, Heinemann LB $27.07 (978-1-4034-0670-5). 48pp. Full of facts and figures about the people, places, and things that make Ohio "a one-of-a-kind place." (Rev: HBG 4/04; SLJ 10/03) [977.1]

19298 Schwabacher, Martin. *Minnesota* (4–7). Series: Celebrate the States. 1999, Benchmark LB $37.07 (978-0-7614-0658-7). 144pp. Minnesota is introduced in six chapters that cover history, geography, government and economy, people, achievements, and landmarks. (Rev: HBG 10/99; SLJ 10/99) [977.6]

19299 Sirvaitis, Karen. *Michigan* (3–5). Illus. Series: Hello USA. 1994, Lerner LB $19.93 (978-0-8225-2722-0). 72pp. With photos on every page, this account supplies a brief trip around Michigan plus historical information and material on resources, cities, and people. (Rev: BL 4/15/94) [977.4]

19300 Somervill, Barbara. *Illinois* (4–6). Illus. Series: From Sea to Shining Sea. 2001, Children's Book Pr. LB $30.50 (978-0-516-22320-9). 80pp. A good resource for report writing, this book features historical facts, maps, and information about the governmental structure and the people of Illinois. (Rev: BL 3/15/02) [977.3]

19301 Steele, Christy Lee. *Uniquely Wisconsin* (4–7). Series: Heinemann State Studies. 2004, Heinemann LB $27.07 (978-1-4034-4499-8). 48pp. In addition to providing the facts necessary for report writers, this volume emphasizes the features that distinguish Wisconsin from its neighbors. (Rev: BL 4/1/04)

19302 Sturm, Ellen. *Ohio* (3–5). Illus. Series: Land of Liberty. 2003, Capstone LB $25.26 (978-0-7368-1593-2). 64pp. Bright illustrations — photographs, reproductions, charts, and maps — add to this overview of the state's geography, climate, history, people, lifestyle, economy, government, and flora and fauna. (Rev: SLJ 10/03) [977.1]

19303 Temple, Teri, and Bob Temple. *Welcome to Badlands National Park* (3–5). Series: Visitor Guides. 2006, The Child's World LB $27.07 (978-1-59296-693-6). 32pp. An attractively presented tour of the South Dakota park, with information on its geography, history, flora, fauna, and weather. (Rev: SLJ 2/07) [917.83]

19304 Thomas, William David. *Kansas* (2–4). Series: Portraits of the States. 2006, Gareth Stevens LB $24.00 (978-0-8368-4665-2). 32pp. History, geography, economy, and other research needs — including some interesting trivia — are covered in this concise volume. (Rev: BL 7/06) [978.1]

19305 Verba, Joan M. *North Dakota* (2–6). Illus. Series: Hello USA. 1992, Lerner LB $19.93 (978-0-8225-2746-6). 72pp. This guide to the Flickertail State includes coverage of history, geography, and famous North Dakotans. (Rev: BL 12/15/92) [978.4]

19306 Wills, Charles A. *A Historical Album of Illinois* (4–8). Illus. Series: Historical Albums. 1994, Millbrook LB $24.40 (978-1-56294-482-7). 64pp. A brief history of Illinois that touches on the most important events from before the white man to the 1990s. (Rev: SLJ 3/95) [977.3]

19307 Wills, Charles A. *A Historical Album of Michigan* (4–7). Illus. Series: Historical Albums. 1996, Millbrook LB $24.40 (978-0-7613-0036-6). 64pp. Using many archival prints, drawings, photographs, and ample text, the history of Michigan is told. (Rev: BL 10/15/96) [977]

MOUNTAIN STATES

19308 Ayer, Eleanor. *Colorado* (4–8). Illus. Series: Celebrate the States. 1997, Marshall Cavendish LB $37.07 (978-0-7614-0148-3). An introduction to the Centennial State, with information on its history, geography, and people. (Rev: BL 7/97; SLJ 8/97) [978.8]

19309 Bauer, Marion Dane. *Yellowstone* (PS–2). Illus. by John Wallace. Series: Ready-to-Read Wonders of America. 2008, Aladdin LB $13.89 (978-1-4169-5405-7); paper $3.99 (978-1-4169-5404-0). 32pp. For beginning readers, this is an introduction to the geological and animals wonders of the first national park. (Rev: BL 5/15/08) [978.7]

19310 Bledsoe, Sara. *Colorado* (3–6). Illus. Series: Hello USA. 1993, Lerner LB $19.93 (978-0-8225-2750-3). 72pp. A small volume that covers Colorado's history, geography, people, industries, and landmarks. (Rev: BL 12/1/93) [978.8]

19311 Bograd, Larry. *Uniquely Wyoming* (4–7). Illus. Series: Heinemann State Studies. 2004, Heinemann LB $31.36 (978-1-4034-4666-4). 48pp. In addition to providing the facts necessary for report writers, this volume emphasizes the features that distinguish Wyoming from its neighbors. (Rev: BL 10/15/03)

19312 Doherty, Craig A., and Katherine M. Doherty. *Hoover Dam* (3–6). Illus. Series: Building America. 1995, Blackbirch LB $23.70 (978-1-56711-107-1). 48pp. Traces the construction of the Hoover Dam on the Colorado River, from its conception through its completion in 1936 to its present importance. (Rev: BL 9/15/95; SLJ 7/95) [627]

19313 Dumas, Bianca, and D. J. Ross. *Uniquely Utah* (4–7). Series: Heinemann State Studies. 2004, Heinemann LB $27.07 (978-1-4034-4663-3). 48pp. In addition to providing the facts necessary for report writers, this volume emphasizes the features that distinguish Utah from its neighbors. (Rev: BL 4/1/04)

19314 Frisch, Carlienne. *Wyoming* (3–6). Illus. Series: Hello USA. 1994, Lerner LB $19.93 (978-0-8225-2736-7). 72pp. The famous sights and attractions of Wyoming are covered, along with its history, development, and people. (Rev: BL 4/15/94; SLJ 7/94) [978.7]

19315 Graf, Mike. *Montana* (3–5). Illus. Series: Land of Liberty. 2003, Capstone LB $25.26 (978-0-7368-2184-1). 64pp. An accessible profile of Montana, covering its people, history, topography, climate, economy, and more, together with suggestions for further reading. (Rev: SLJ 3/04) [978.6]

19316 Hall, M. C. *Glacier National Park* (K–4). Series: Symbols of Freedom: National Parks. 2005, Heinemann LB $25.36 (978-1-4034-6698-3). 32pp. Large color photographs and clear text introduce the history, geography, flora, and fauna of this park; useful for basic research and reports. (Rev: SLJ 12/05) [978.6]

19317 Hall, M. C. *Grand Canyon National Park* (K–4). Series: Symbols of Freedom: National Parks. 2005, Heinemann LB $25.36 (978-1-4034-6699-0). 32pp. Large color photographs and clear text introduce the history, geography, flora, and fauna of this park; useful for basic research and reports. (Rev: SLJ 12/05) [979.1]

19318 Hall, M. C. *Rocky Mountain National Park* (K–4). Series: Symbols of Freedom: National Parks. 2005, Heinemann LB $25.36 (978-1-4034-6701-0). 32pp. Large color photographs and clear text introduce the history, geography, flora, and fauna of this park; useful for basic research and reports. (Rev: SLJ 12/05) [978.8]

19319 Hall, M. C. *Yellowstone National Park* (K–4). 2005, Heinemann LB $25.36 (978-1-4034-6702-7). 32pp. Large color photographs and clear text introduce the history, geography, flora, and fauna of this park; useful for basic research and reports. (Rev: SLJ 12/05) [978.7]

19320 Hamilton, John. *Rocky Mountain National Park* (4–6). Series: National Parks. 2008, ABDO LB $17.95 (978-1-60453-094-0). 32pp. Very informative short chapters and dazzling photographs (some full-page) make up this book about the geology, landscape, and uses of this national park. Also use *Zion National Park* (2008). (Rev: SLJ 2/09) [978.8]

19321 Heinrichs, Ann. *Colorado* (3–5). Illus. by Matt Kania. Series: Welcome to the U.S.A. 2005, The Child's World LB $24.21 (978-1-59296-572-4). 40pp. A basic introduction with maps, pertinent facts, discussion of the state's geography and history, plus popular destinations and cultural information. (Rev: SLJ 1/06) [978.8]

19322 Heinrichs, Ann. *Utah* (3–5). Illus. by Matt Kania. Series: Welcome to the U.S.A. 2005, The Child's World LB $27.07 (978-1-59296-486-4). 40pp. A basic introduction with maps, pertinent facts, discussion of the state's geography and history, plus popular destinations and cultural information. (Rev: SLJ 1/06) [978.8]

19323 Herda, D. J. *Environmental America: The Northwestern States* (4–7). Illus. Series: American Scene. 1991, Millbrook LB $22.40 (978-1-878841-10-0). 64pp. This account presents information on such topics as pollution, waste, logging, and the general condition of the environment in Idaho, Montana, Oregon, Washington, and Wyoming. (Rev: BL 8/91; SLJ 7/91) [639.9]

19324 Higgins, Nadia. *Welcome to Glacier National Park* (3–5). Series: Visitor Guides. 2006, The Child's World LB $27.07 (978-1-59296-696-7). 32pp. An attractively presented tour of the Montana park, focusing on its geography, history, flora, fauna, and weather. (Rev: SLJ 2/07) [917.86]

19325 LaDoux, Rita C. *Montana* (3–6). Illus. Series: Hello USA. 1992, Lerner LB $19.93 (978-0-8225-2714-5). 72pp. In addition to standard introductory material, coverage includes timelines about Montana and biographies of famous residents. (Rev: BL 5/15/92; SLJ 7/92) [978.6]

19326 Lauber, Patricia. *Summer of Fire: Yellowstone 1988* (3–5). Illus. 1991, Orchard $19.95 (978-0-531-05943-2). 64pp. Striking photos dramatize the fires of 1988 and their aftermath in Yellowstone National Park. (Rev: BCCB 10/91; BL 9/1/91; HB 9/91*; SLJ 9/91) [581.5]

19327 Lorbiecki, Marybeth. *Welcome to Grand Teton National Park* (3–5). Illus. Series: Visitor Guides. 2006, Child's World LB $27.07 (978-1-59296-698-1). 32pp. Despite confusing maps, this guide to the Wyoming park offers solid information for reports. (Rev: BL 10/15/06; SLJ 2/07) [917.87]

19328 Lynch, Wayne, and Aubrey Lang. *Rocky Mountains* (4–7). Illus. by Wayne Lynch. Series: Our Wild World. 2006, NorthWord $16.95 (978-1-55971-948-3); paper $8.95 (978-1-55971-949-0). 64pp. An appealing introduction to the geography, animals, and plants of the region, with full-color photographs and first-person anecdotes. (Rev: BL 10/15/06; SLJ 1/07*) [577.5]

19329 Mann, Elizabeth. *Hoover Dam* (3–6). Illus. by Alan Witschonke. Series: Wonders of the World. 2001, Mikaya $19.95 (978-1-931414-02-9). 48pp. The exciting story of Hoover Dam is presented in a well-designed package with personal anecdotes and an emphasis on the loss of life. (Rev: BL 12/1/01; HB 3/02; HBG 10/02; SLJ 12/01) [627]

19330 Maynard, Charles W. *The Rocky Mountains* (2–5). Series: Great Mountain Ranges of the World. 2004, Rosen LB $21.25 (978-0-8239-6926-5). 24pp. Full-page, full-color photographs grace each spread of this slim volume that introduces the geology, climate, plants, animals, economy, peoples, and exploration of the Rockies, with discussion of environmental issues. (Rev: SLJ 8/04) [917.8]

19331 Meister, Cari. *Yellowstone National Park* (2–4). Illus. Series: Going Places. 2000, ABDO $21.35 (978-1-57765-026-3). This tour of Yellowstone National Park includes material on history, its things to see and do, and the plants and animals. (Rev: HBG 10/00; SLJ 1/01) [917.8]

19332 O'Connor, Rebecca K., and Dennis Myers. *Uniquely Nevada* (4–7). Illus. Series: Heinemann

State Studies. 2004, Heinemann LB $27.07 (978-1-4034-4650-3). 48pp. In addition to providing the facts necessary for report writers, this volume emphasizes the features that distinguish Nevada from its neighbors. (Rev: BL 10/15/03)

19333 Patent, Dorothy Hinshaw. *When the Wolves Returned: Restoring Nature's Balance in Yellowstone* (3–5). Illus. by Cassie Hartman. 2008, Walker $17.95 (978-0-8027-9686-8). 40pp. Patent looks at the ecological harm caused by the disappearance of the wolf from Yellowstone, and the recovery that took place when they returned. (Rev: BL 2/15/08; HB 5/08; LMC 10/08; SLJ 6/08) [599.773]

19334 Petersen, David. *Bryce Canyon National Park* (2–3). Illus. Series: True Books. 1996, Children's Book Pr. LB $25.00 (978-0-516-20048-4). 48pp. A well-illustrated introduction to this national park and its amazing rock formations. Also use *Death Valley National Park* (1996). (Rev: SLJ 5/97) [917.91]

19335 Sanders, Doug. *Idaho* (4–6). Illus. Series: It's My State! 2004, Benchmark LB $27.07 (978-0-7614-1824-5). 80pp. Idaho's geography, wildlife, history, people, government, and natural resources are all covered here, with material on key individuals and famous events. (Rev: SLJ 5/05)

19336 Sirvaitis, Karen. *Utah* (3–6). Illus. Series: Hello USA. 1991, Lerner LB $19.93 (978-0-8225-2707-7). 72pp. This introduction to Utah features color illustrations on each page, facts-at-a-glance sections, and a historical timeline. (Rev: BL 8/91; SLJ 2/92) [979.2]

19337 Staub, Frank. *Yellowstone's Cycle of Fire* (3–6). Illus. Series: Earth Watch. 1994, Carolrhoda LB $21.27 (978-0-87614-778-8). 48pp. The cycle of forest fires and later renewal in Yellowstone Park is described, with major coverage of the huge fire of 1988. (Rev: BL 2/1/94; SLJ 6/94) [574.5]

19338 Stefoff, Rebecca. *Idaho* (4–8). Series: Celebrate the States. 2000, Benchmark LB $37.07 (978-0-7614-0663-1). Interesting charts, graphs, and maps are used to illustrate such topics as the people, land, history, and culture of Idaho. (Rev: BL 1/1–15/00; HBG 10/00) [978.8]

19339 Stefoff, Rebecca. *Nevada* (4–8). Series: Celebrate the States. 2001, Benchmark LB $37.07 (978-0-7614-1073-7). 144pp. This well-organized introduction to Nevada gives general information followed by a timeline and special material on tourist attractions, famous natives of Nevada, and local festivals. (Rev: BL 9/15/01; HBG 10/01) [979.3]

19340 Stefoff, Rebecca. *Utah* (4–8). Series: Celebrate the States. 2000, Marshall Cavendish LB $37.07 (978-0-7614-1064-5). 144pp. Utah's unique characteristics and places are highlighted in this account that also covers the state's history, geography, and government. (Rev: BL 12/15/00; HBG 3/01; SLJ 2/01) [979.2]

19341 Trumbauer, Lisa. *Grand Canyon* (K–2). Series: Rookie Read-About Geography. 2005, Children's Pr. LB $20.50 (978-0-516-22747-4). 31pp. This

simple easy-reader covers the basic facts about the geographic wonder. (Rev: SLJ 7/05) [979.1]

19342 Wills, Charles A. *A Historical Album of Colorado* (4–7). Illus. Series: Historical Albums. 1996, Millbrook $24.40 (978-1-56294-592-3); paper $6.95 (978-1-56294-858-0). 64pp. Using many old engravings and photographs, the history of Colorado is traced, beginning with its Native American population. (Rev: BL 7/96; SLJ 7/96) [978.8]

NORTHEAST

19343 Ashabranner, Brent. *Badge of Valor: The National Law Enforcement Officers Memorial* (5–8). Illus. 2000, Twenty-First Century LB $25.90 (978-0-7613-1522-3). 64pp. This history of the memorial, from the original proposal in the 1970s to its opening in 1991, also discusses what it stands for and reveals the heroic deeds of some important law enforcement officers. (Rev: BL 10/1/00; HBG 3/01; SLJ 1/01) [363.2]

19344 Ashabranner, Brent. *No Better Hope: What the Lincoln Memorial Means to America* (4–8). Illus. Series: Great American Memorials. 2001, Twenty-First Century LB $25.90 (978-0-7613-1523-0). 64pp. As well as telling about Lincoln and his importance to the country, this volume describes the building of the memorial and the important events that have occurred on the site. (Rev: BL 3/1/01; HBG 10/01; SLJ 7/01; VOYA 10/01) [975.3]

19345 Ashabranner, Brent. *On the Mall in Washington, D.C.: A Visit to America's Front Yard* (5–7). Illus. by Jennifer Ashabranner. 2002, Twenty-First Century LB $23.90 (978-0-7613-2351-8). 64pp. An entertaining and informative tour of the National Mall in Washington, D.C. (Rev: BL 3/15/02; HBG 10/02; SLJ 4/02) [917.5304]

19346 Ashabranner, Brent. *Remembering Korea: The Korean War Veterans Memorial* (4–8). Illus. by Jennifer Ashabranner. Series: Great American Memorials. 2001, Twenty-First Century LB $25.90 (978-0-7613-2156-9). 64pp. Ashabranner explains who the memorial honors, how much it cost, and what it represents. (Rev: BL 9/15/01; HBG 3/02; SLJ 12/01) [951.904]

19347 Ashabranner, Brent. *The Washington Monument: A Beacon for America* (4–8). Illus. by Jennifer Ashabranner. Series: Great American Memorials. 2002, Millbrook LB $25.90 (978-0-7613-1524-7). 64pp. Ashabranner presents the story behind the monument, including its planning, design, and construction, with full-color photographs and black-and-white period reproductions. (Rev: BL 9/1/02; HBG 3/03; SLJ 11/02) [975.3]

19348 Avakian, Monique. *A Historical Album of Massachusetts* (4–8). Illus. Series: Historical Albums. 1994, Millbrook LB $24.40 (978-1-56294-481-0). 64pp. A history of Massachusetts that begins with the Native American culture and ends with the 1900s, including basic material on major events and personalities. (Rev: SLJ 2/95) [974.4]

19349 Avakian, Monique, and Carter Smith, III. *A Historical Album of New York* (5–8). Illus. Series: Historical Albums. 1993, Millbrook $24.40 (978-1-

56294-005-8). 64pp. An overview of New York State history from Native American settlements to the present day, using extensive archival illustrations. (Rev: SLJ 10/93) [974.7]

19350 Aylesworth, Thomas G., and Virginia L. Aylesworth. *Upper Atlantic: New Jersey, New York* (3–8). Illus. 1995, Chelsea LB $19.95 (978-0-7910-3399-9); paper $9.95 (978-0-7910-3417-0). 64pp. Encyclopedia-like coverage of New York and New Jersey. (Rev: BL 9/1/87; SLJ 11/87)

19351 Backer, Miles. *Travels with Charlie: Travelin' the Northeast* (1–4). Illus. by Chuck Nitzberg. Series: A Search and Find Geography Book. 2006, Blue Apple $15.95 (978-1-59354-162-0). Charlie, a travel-loving mutt, takes readers on a light-hearted, seek-and-find hunt of the northeastern United States. (Rev: SLJ 2/07) [974]

19352 Barenblat, Rachel. *Massachusetts: The Bay State* (4–7). Series: World Almanac Library of the States. 2002, World Almanac LB $31.00 (978-0-8368-5123-6). 48pp. History, politics, government, culture, and state symbols are all covered, with charts, maps, photographs, biographical sketches, and a list of important events and attractions. (Rev: SLJ 6/02) [974.4]

19353 Bauer, Marion Dane. *Niagara Falls* (K–2). Illus. by John Wallace. Series: Ready-to-Read Wonders of America. 2006, Simon & Schuster LB $11.89 (978-0-689-86945-7); paper $3.99 (978-0-689-86944-0). 32pp. Basic information about the waterfall — geology and history, including daredevil feats — is presented in an attractive format suitable for beginning readers. (Rev: SLJ 6/06) [971.3]

19354 Belanger, Jeff. *Who's Haunting the White House?* (4–7). Illus. by Rick Powell. 2008, Sterling $14.95 (978-1-4027-3822-7). 64pp. A history of the White House and paranormal incidents there, with period illustrations, paintings, drawings, and prints. (Rev: BL 12/15/08; SLJ 12/08) [133.1]

19355 Benson, Laura Lee. *Washington, D.C.: A Scrapbook* (2–6). Illus. by Iris Van Rynbach. 1999, Charlesbridge LB $15.95 (978-0-88106-064-5); paper $6.95 (978-0-88106-063-8). A young African American student records a class trip to Washington, D.C., where he uses the subway line and visits such landmarks as the White House and the National Zoo. (Rev: HBG 3/00; SLJ 11/99) [975.3]

19356 Bial, Raymond. *Ellis Island: Coming to the Land of Liberty* (4–6). 2009, Houghton $18.00 (978-0-618-99943-9). 58pp. With both period and contemporary photographs, plus primary-source quotations, Bial looks at the history of the immigration center. (Rev: BCCB 9/09; BL 8/09; SLJ 6/09) [900]

19357 Bial, Raymond. *Tenement: Immigrant Life on the Lower East Side* (5–8). Illus. 2002, Houghton $16.00 (978-0-618-13849-4). 48pp. Historic photographs complement the simple, descriptive text about life in New York City tenement housing in the late 1800s and early 1900s. (Rev: BL 10/15/02; HB 11/02; HBG 3/03; SLJ 9/02) [307.76]

19358 Braithwaite, Jill. *The Statue of Liberty* (K–2). Series: Pull Ahead Books. 2003, Lerner LB $22.60 (978-0-8225-3802-8); paper $5.95 (978-0-8225-

3756-4). 32pp. For beginning report writers, this is a simple, well-illustrated look at the statue and its symbolism. (Rev: SLJ 1/04) [974.7]

19359 Britton, Tamara. *The Pentagon* (3–5). Series: Symbols, Landmarks, and Monuments. 2003, ABDO LB $22.78 (978-1-57765-849-8). 32pp. A brief history of the vast headquarters of the U.S. Department of Defense, covering the terrorist attack of September 11, 2001. (Rev: HBG 10/03; SLJ 10/03) [355.6]

19360 Britton, Tamara. *The Smithsonian Institution* (3–5). Series: Symbols, Landmarks, and Monuments. 2004, ABDO LB $22.78 (978-1-59197-521-2). 32pp. An introduction to the history and contemporary importance of the museums that make up this venerable establishment. (Rev: SLJ 11/04) [069]

19361 Britton, Tamara. *The Vietnam Veterans Memorial* (3–5). Series: Symbols, Landmarks, and Monuments. 2004, ABDO LB $22.78 (978-1-59197-523-6). 32pp. Explains the importance of this memorial and the story of its design. (Rev: SLJ 11/04) [975.3]

19362 Brown, Dottie. *Delaware* (3–6). Illus. Series: Hello USA. 1994, Lerner LB $19.93 (978-0-8225-2733-6). 72pp. A compact book that introduces Delaware's history, geography, resources, and famous people. (Rev: BL 4/15/94) [975.1]

19363 Brown, Dottie. *New Hampshire* (3–6). Illus. Series: Hello USA. 1993, Lerner LB $19.93 (978-0-8225-2730-5). 72pp. A brief, colorful introduction to New Hampshire that takes the reader on a tour of the state, covers its history, tells how the people live, and gives biographies of famous residents. (Rev: BL 12/1/93) [974.2]

19364 Burg, Ann K. *Times Square: A New York State Number Book* (2–5). Illus. by Maureen K. Brookfield. 2005, Sleeping Bear $16.95 (978-1-58536-195-3). Readers count to 100 while absorbing numerous facts — some little-known — about New York State. (Rev: SLJ 1/06) [974.7]

19365 Burgan, Michael. *Connecticut* (4–7). Series: It's My State! 2003, Marshall Cavendish LB $27.07 (978-0-7614-1523-7). 80pp. This New England state is introduced with material on its people, geography, history, cities, products, and resources. (Rev: BL 9/15/03; HBG 4/04) [974.6]

19366 Clark, Diane C. *A Kid's Guide to Washington, D.C.* Rev. ed. (4–6). Ed. by Miriam Chernick. Illus. by Richard E. Brown. 2008, Harcourt paper $14.00 (978-0-15-206125-8). 160pp. This attractive, large-format book, an update of a 1989 edition, provides lots of age-appropriate information on the sites of the capital. (Rev: BL 6/1–15/08) [917.5304]

19367 Climo, Shirley. *City! Washington, D.C.* (4–6). 1991, Macmillan LB $16.95 (978-0-02-719036-6). 64pp. An upbeat look at the nation's capital. (Rev: BL 8/91; SLJ 9/91) [917.5304]

19368 Cotter, Kristin. *New York* (3–5). Illus. Series: From Sea to Shining Sea, Second Series. 2002, Children's Book Pr. LB $30.50 (978-0-516-22485-5). 80pp. This revision of an earlier title adds information and features that will enhance its appeal to report writers. Also use *Connecticut* and *Delaware* (both 2002). (Rev: SLJ 1/03)

19369 Cowan, Mary Morton. *Timberrr: A History of Logging in New England* (5–8). Illus. 2003, Millbrook LB $25.90 (978-0-7613-1866-8). 96pp. Cowan highlights timber's historical importance in many walks of life — trade, politics, and construction, for example — and looks at changes brought by new technologies and the impact on ecology and the environment. (Rev: BL 11/15/03; HBG 4/04) [634.9]

19370 Curlee, Lynn. *Brooklyn Bridge* (3–6). Illus. 2001, Simon & Schuster $18.00 (978-0-689-83183-6). 40pp. The story of the construction of the Brooklyn Bridge with particular emphasis on the role played by the Roebling family. (Rev: BCCB 6/01; BL 4/15/01; HB 7/01; HBG 10/01; SLJ 5/01) [624]

19371 Curlee, Lynn. *Capital* (2–5). Illus. 2003, Simon & Schuster $17.95 (978-0-689-84947-3). 48pp. Stories of five important Washington, D.C., buildings portray much of American history. (Rev: BCCB 2/03; BL 1/1–15/03; HBG 10/03; SLJ 1/03) [975.3]

19372 Cytron, Barry. *Fire! The Library Is Burning* (4–7). Illus. 1988, Lerner LB $15.93 (978-0-8225-0525-9). 56pp. How workers and volunteers helped to restore the Jewish Theological Seminary in New York City when it was nearly destroyed by fire. (Rev: BL 7/88; SLJ 9/88) [027.63]

19373 Degezelle, Terri. *Ellis Island* (K–2). Series: American Symbols. 2003, Capstone LB $21.26 (978-0-7368-2292-3). 24pp. A visit to Ellis Island in New York Harbor, the place of entry to the United States for millions of immigrants, with modern and archival photos. (Rev: SLJ 4/04) [304.8]

19374 Deinard, Jenny. *How to Draw Massachusetts's Sights and Symbols* (3–6). Series: Kid's Guide to Drawing America. 2001, Rosen LB $25.25 (978-0-8239-6077-4). As well as basic facts on key sights and symbols of Massachusetts, clear instructions are given on how to draw the state seal, flag, bird, and so forth. (Rev: BL 4/15/02; SLJ 7/02) [974.4]

19375 Doak, Robin. *New Jersey* (5–8). Illus. Series: Voices from Colonial America. 2005, National Geographic LB $32.90 (978-0-7922-6680-8). 112pp. A compelling account of life in early New Jersey, from its initial settlement by the Dutch through the adoption of the Constitution. (Rev: BL 6/1–15/05; SLJ 1/06) [974.9]

19376 Doherty, Craig A., and Katherine M. Doherty. *The Statue of Liberty* (3–6). Illus. Series: Building America. 1996, Blackbirch LB $24.95 (978-1-56711-111-8). 48pp. The Statue of Liberty, from the original idea to the finished sculpture. (Rev: BL 11/15/96; SLJ 1/97) [974.7]

19377 Dornfeld, Margaret. *Maine* (4–8). Series: Celebrate the States. 2001, Benchmark LB $37.07 (978-0-7614-1071-3). 144pp. An attractive, fact-filled introduction to the state of Maine with material on history, famous places and people, and current concerns. (Rev: BL 9/15/01; HBG 10/01) [974.1]

19378 Elish, Dan. *New York* (4–7). Illus. Series: My State. 2003, Marshall Cavendish $27.07 (978-0-7614-1419-3). 80pp. Color photographs accompany information on the state's topography, wildlife, climate, population, government, industries, and resources. (Rev: BL 3/1/03; HBG 10/03) [974.7]

19379 Elish, Dan. *Washington, D.C.* (5–8). Series: Celebrate the States. 1998, Benchmark LB $37.07 (978-0-7614-0423-1). 144pp. An attractive introduction to the people and government of the U.S. capital with material on parks, landmarks, history, economics, and racial problems. (Rev: HBG 10/98; SLJ 1/99) [975.3]

19380 Engfer, LeeAnne. *Maine* (3–6). Illus. Series: Hello USA. 1991, Lerner LB $19.93 (978-0-8225-2701-5). 72pp. With many illustrations, this is a solid introduction to the New England state Maine. (Rev: BL 4/15/91; SLJ 6/91) [974.1]

19381 Foster, Mark. *Whale Port: A History of Tuckanucket* (4–7). Illus. by Gerald Foster. 2007, Houghton $18.00 (978-0-618-54722-7). 64pp. The life and times of a fictitious New England town from 1683 to today reveal how changes in population, technology, commerce, and society all affect a town's growth; detailed illustrations. (Rev: BL 12/1/07; SLJ 11/07) [338.3]

19382 Fredeen, Charles. *New Jersey* (3–6). Illus. Series: Hello USA. 1993, Lerner LB $19.93 (978-0-8225-2732-9). 72pp. The Garden State is introduced with color illustrations and informative text. (Rev: BL 7/93; SLJ 8/93) [974.9]

19383 Gibbons, Gail. *From Path to Highway: The Story of the Boston Post Road* (2–4). Illus. 1986, HarperCollins LB $14.89 (978-0-690-04514-7). 32pp. A picture-book history of the road used by early travelers and today's citizens when traveling between Boston and New York. (Rev: BCCB 6/86; BL 6/15/86; SLJ 9/86)

19384 Gleman, Amy. *Connecticut* (3–6). Illus. 1991, Lerner LB $19.93 (978-0-8225-2709-1). 72pp. In text and pictures, this book covers history, economics, and interesting features and includes a timeline, maps, and charts. (Rev: BL 10/15/91) [974.6]

19385 Goldstein, Ernest. *The Statue of Abraham Lincoln: A Masterpiece by Daniel Chester French* (5–8). Series: Art Beyond Borders. 1998, Lerner LB $28.80 (978-0-8225-2067-2). 64pp. This book provides a detailed description of the Lincoln Memorial and an introduction to the life and accomplishments of its sculptor, Daniel Chester French. (Rev: SLJ 5/98) [975.3]

19386 Graham, Amy. *Maine* (4–7). Illus. Series: States. 2002, Enslow LB $25.26 (978-0-7660-5017-4). 48pp. This well-illustrated volume offers report writers basic information on the state's land, climate, economy, government, and history, plus recommendations of Web sites that will extend their knowledge. Also use *New York* (2002). (Rev: SLJ 9/02) [974.1]

19387 Gray, Susan H. *The White House* (2–4). Series: Our Nation. 2001, Compass Point LB $19.93 (978-0-7565-0145-7). 24pp. An introduction to the interior of the executive mansion. (Rev: SLJ 1/02) [975.3]

19388 Greene, Jacqueline D. *The Triangle Shirtwaist Factory Fire* (3–5). Illus. Series: Code Red. 2007, Bearport LB $25.27 (978-1-59716-359-0). 32pp.

This study of the tragic 1911 fire that killed 146 at a New York City clothing factory examines the disaster itself, the reasons for the heavy loss of life, and the lessons that were learned by city authorities. (Rev: BL 4/1/07) [974.7]

19389 Haas, Jessie. *Fire! My Parents' Story* (4–6). Illus. 1998, Greenwillow $15.00 (978-0-688-15203-1). 72pp. Told from the standpoint of an eight-year-old girl, this is the true story of how a fire destroyed a Vermont farm and how the family eventually rebuilt and returned to their property. (Rev: BCCB 3/98; BL 5/1/98; HBG 10/98; SLJ 5/98) [974.3]

19390 Heinrichs, Ann. *Delaware* (3–5). Illus. by Matt Kania. Series: Welcome to the U.S.A. 2005, The Child's World LB $27.07 (978-1-59296-470-3). 40pp. Using an attractive scrapbook format featuring a family on vacation, this volume introduces the state's geography, history, people, major attractions, and state symbols. Also use *Maryland* (2005). (Rev: SLJ 2/06) [975.1]

19391 Heinrichs, Ann. *Pennsylvania* (2–5). Illus. Series: This Land Is Your Land. 2003, Compass Point LB $25.26 (978-0-7565-0320-8). 48pp. A brightly illustrated introduction to Pennsylvania's history, people, geography, government, economy, and attractions. (Rev: SLJ 8/03) [974.8]

19392 Hempstead, Anne. *The Statue of Liberty* (4–7). Series: Land of the Free. 2006, Heinemann LB $28.21 (978-1-4034-7004-1). 32pp. With many illustrations and interesting sidebars, this history of the Statue of Liberty details key events and examines its significance as an American symbol. (Rev: SLJ 10/06) [974.7]

19393 Hempstead, Anne. *The Supreme Court* (4–7). Series: Land of the Free. 2006, Heinemann LB $28.21 (978-1-4034-7001-0). 32pp. With many illustrations and interesting sidebars, this history of the U.S. Supreme Court details key events and examines its significance as an American symbol. Also use *The U.S. Capitol* and *The White House* (both 2006). (Rev: SLJ 10/06) [347]

19394 Herda, D. J. *Environmental America: The Northeastern States* (4–7). Illus. Series: American Scene. 1991, Millbrook LB $22.40 (978-1-878841-06-3). 64pp. This volume discusses the condition of the environment and presents information on such topics as water and land pollution in the northeastern states. (Rev: BL 8/91; SLJ 7/91) [639.9]

19395 Herda, D. J. *Ethnic America: The Northeastern States* (5–7). Illus. Series: American Scene. 1991, Millbrook LB $22.40 (978-1-56294-014-0). 64pp. In this heavily illustrated account, the ethnic groups of the area, including Native Americans, are described and their accomplishments detailed. (Rev: BL 2/1/92; SLJ 2/92) [572.973]

19396 Hess, Debra. *The White House* (3–5). Series: Symbols of America. 2003, Benchmark LB $25.64 (978-0-7614-1712-5). 40pp. The history of the White House, residence of every U.S. president since 1792, and how it has changed over the years. (Rev: HBG 4/04; SLJ 3/04)

19397 Hicks, Terry Allan. *The Capitol* (3–5). Series: Symbols of America. 2006, Benchmark LB $28.50

(978-0-7614-2132-0). 40pp. A look at the U.S. Capitol, its history, and the important role it plays as the home of America's legislative branch of government. (Rev: SLJ 12/06) [975.3]

19398 Hicks, Terry Allan. *Ellis Island* (3–5). Series: Symbols of America. 2006, Benchmark LB $28.50 (978-0-7614-2134-4). 40pp. An overview of the history of Ellis Island and its importance as a symbol of the United States. (Rev: SLJ 12/06) [4.6.8.4.3]

19399 Hicks, Terry Allan. *Washington, D.C.* (3–6). Illus. Series: It's My State! 2007, Marshall Cavendish LB $20.95 (978-0-7614-1929-9). 80pp. Interesting facts and a pleasing design combine to make this an engaging introduction to the United States capital. (Rev: SLJ 8/07)

19400 High, Linda O. *Under New York* (PS–3). Illus. by Robert Rayevsky. 2001, Holiday House $16.95 (978-0-8234-1551-9). 32pp. A richly illustrated picture book that takes the reader underground in New York City to a world of pipes, power lines, trains, and tunnels. (Rev: BL 3/1/01; HB 7/01; HBG 10/01) [974.7]

19401 Hochain, Serge. *Building Liberty: A Statue Is Born* (3–6). Trans. from French by Camilla Bozzoli. Illus. by author. 2004, National Geographic LB $25.90 (978-0-7922-6969-4). 46pp. The Statue of Liberty's story is told in four parts — design and construction, transportation across the Atlantic, fund-raising for the pedestal, and eventual erection — each involving a boy who plays a role. (Rev: SLJ 8/04) [974.7]

19402 Ingram, Scott. *Pennsylvania: The Keystone State* (4–7). Series: World Almanac Library of the States. 2002, World Almanac LB $31.00 (978-0-8368-5120-5). 48pp. Facts, statistics, a pleasing layout, and color photographs make this a useful choice for report writers. (Rev: SLJ 9/02) [974.8]

19403 Jacobs, William J. *Ellis Island* (4–6). Illus. 1990, Macmillan $17.00 (978-0-684-19171-3). 40pp. A well-written introduction to Ellis Island in the you-are-there style. (Rev: BCCB 5/90; BL 4/15/90; SLJ 6/90) [304.8]

19404 Jameson, W. C. *Buried Treasures of New England: Legends of Hidden Riches, Forgotten War Loots, and Lost Ship Treasures* (4–8). Series: Buried Treasure. 1997, August House $11.95 (978-0-87483-485-7). This account describes how these treasures were amassed and lost, and furnishes maps to indicate their general location. (Rev: SLJ 10/97) [910.4]

19405 Johnston, Joyce. *Washington, D.C.* (3–6). Illus. Series: Hello USA. 1994, Lerner LB $19.93 (978-0-8225-2751-0). 72pp. This brief introduction to Washington, D.C., tells about its history, local government, landmarks, and daily life. (Rev: BL 2/1/94) [975.3]

19406 Kennedy, Marge. *The Story of the White House* (K–2). Series: Scholastic News Nonfiction Readers. 2009, Children's Pr. LB $20.00 (978-0-531-21094-9); paper $6.95 (978-0-531-22431-1). 24pp. The White House's history and some interesting facts about the building are presented in an easy-to-read format. Also use *Having Fun at the*

White House and *Time to Eat at the White House* (2009). (Rev: SLJ 5/09) [975.3]

19407 Knox, Barbara. *New Hampshire* (3–5). Illus. Series: Land of Liberty. 2003, Capstone LB $25.26 (978-0-7368-2187-2). 64pp. A trip to Mount Monadnock opens this survey of New Hampshire, which provides all the material needed for a state report. (Rev: SLJ 2/04) [974.2]

19408 Krementz, Jill. *A Visit to Washington, D.C.* (K–3). Illus. by author. 1987, Scholastic paper $5.95 (978-0-590-40583-6). 48pp. A six-year-old tells of his home town, the nation's capital city. (Rev: BL 5/15/87; HB 7/87; SLJ 5/87)

19409 Krensky, Stephen. *What's the Big Idea?* (4–6). Illus. 2008, Charlesbridge $18.95 (978-1-58089-310-7); paper $9.95 (978-1-58089-311-4). 64pp. A brief history of Boston with mini-biographies of some of the city's major figures. (Rev: BL 3/1/08; LMC 11/08; SLJ 6/08) [330.9774]

19410 Kroll, Steven. *Ellis Island: Doorway to Freedom* (3–5). Illus. by Karen Ritz. 1995, Holiday House LB $17.95 (978-0-8234-1192-4). 32pp. This history, beginning with colonial times, concentrates on the period when Ellis Island's immigration center processed millions of immigrants. (Rev: BL 11/15/95; SLJ 1/96) [325.73]

19411 Leotta, Joan. *Massachusetts* (4–6). Series: From Sea to Shining Sea. 2001, Children's Book Pr. LB $30.50 (978-0-516-22486-2). As well as basic coverage on Massachusetts, this book includes interesting sidebars. (Rev: BL 4/15/02) [974.4]

19412 Levert, Suzanne. *Massachusetts* (4–8). Series: Celebrate the States. 2000, Benchmark LB $37.07 (978-0-7614-0666-2). A fine introduction to the people and places of the Bay State that also includes recipes, folktales, and songs. (Rev: BL 1/1–15/00; HBG 10/00; SLJ 5/00) [974.4]

19413 Louis, Nancy. *Ground Zero* (4–7). Series: War on Terrorism. 2002, ABDO LB $16.95 (978-1-57765-675-3). 48pp. This heavily illustrated, factually accurate account describes the search, recovery, and cleanup that took place after September 11, 2001, in New York City. (Rev: BL 5/15/02) [974.7]

19414 Low, William. *Old Penn Station* (2–4). Illus. 2007, Holt $16.95 (978-0-8050-7925-8). 32pp. This photoessay celebrates the grandeur of the New York City landmark that was demolished in the 1960s. (Rev: BL 3/15/07) [385.3]

19415 McAuliffe, Emily. *Connecticut Facts and Symbols*. Rev. ed. (3–5). Illus. Series: The States and Their Symbols. 2003, Capstone LB $21.26 (978-0-7368-2237-4). 24pp. A brief, illustrated overview of facts about Connecticut such as the state's nickname, motto, flag, and other symbols. (Rev: SLJ 1/04) [974.6]

19416 Marcovitz, Hal. *The Liberty Bell* (4–8). Illus. Series: American Symbols and Their Meanings. 2002, Mason Crest LB $18.95 (978-1-59084-025-2). 48pp. The history and condition of the bell are presented through text, illustrations, and a useful timeline. Also use *The White House* (2002). (Rev: SLJ 9/02) [974.8]

19417 Melman, Peter. *Uniquely New Hampshire* (4–7). Series: Heinemann State Studies. 2004, Heinemann LB $27.07 (978-1-4034-4651-0). 48pp. In addition to providing the facts necessary for report writers, this volume emphasizes the features that distinguish New Hampshire from its neighbors. (Rev: BL 4/1/04)

19418 Moose, Katherine B. *Uniquely Delaware* (4–7). Series: Heinemann State Studies. 2004, Heinemann LB $27.07 (978-1-4034-4644-2). 48pp. In addition to providing the facts necessary for report writers, this volume emphasizes the features that distinguish Delaware from its neighbors. (Rev: BL 4/1/04)

19419 Moose, Katherine B. *Uniquely Rhode Island* (4–7). Illus. Series: Heinemann State Studies. 2004, Heinemann LB $27.07 (978-1-4034-4660-2). 48pp. In addition to providing the facts necessary for report writers, this volume emphasizes the features that distinguish Rhode Island from its neighbors. (Rev: BL 10/15/03)

19420 Morgane, Wendy. *New Jersey* (4–8). Series: Celebrate the States. 2000, Benchmark LB $37.07 (978-0-7614-0673-0). This excellent introduction to New Jersey covers its history, land, government, economy, unique characteristics, and famous residents. (Rev: BL 1/1–15/00; HBG 10/00) [974.9]

19421 Mortensen, Lori. *Ellis Island* (K–2). Illus. by Matthew Skeens. Series: American Symbols. 2008, Picture Window $25.26 (978-1-4048-4705-7). 24pp. Simple text, engaging facts, and big illustrations make this a good entry-level read about Ellis Island. (Rev: BLO 10/7/08; SLJ 1/09) [304.8]

19422 Nelson, Kristin L. *The Washington Monument* (K–2). Series: Pull Ahead Books. 2003, Lerner LB $22.60 (978-0-8225-0250-0); paper $5.95 (978-0-8225-3759-5). 32pp. For beginning report writers, this is a simple, well-illustrated look at the monument and its symbolism. (Rev: SLJ 1/04) [975.3]

19423 *New York*. Rev. ed. (3–5). Series: One Nation. 2002, Capstone LB $22.60 (978-0-7368-1256-6). 48pp. A chapter on New York City's subways introduces an overview of the state's geography, history, people, lifestyle, economy, and tourist attractions. (Rev: HBG 3/03; SLJ 4/03) [974.7]

19424 *Our White House: Looking In, Looking Out* (5–8). Illus. 2008, Candlewick $29.99 (978-0-7636-2067-7). 242pp. Essays, historical fiction, and poetry from contemporary children's writers are combined with firsthand accounts from former presidents, their family members, and White House visitors to create this attractive, large-format look at the White House and its place in America's history. (Rev: BL 8/08; SLJ 9/08) [975.3]

19425 Pascoe, Elaine. *The Brooklyn Bridge* (4–6). Illus. Series: Building America. 1999, Blackbirch LB $24.95 (978-1-56711-173-6). 48pp. The story of the Brooklyn Bridge from the first proposals in 1811 to 1983 when it celebrated its 100th birthday. (Rev: BL 12/1/99; HBG 3/00; SLJ 2/00) [624]

19426 Pascoe, Elaine. *History Around You: A Unique Look at the Past, People, and Places of New York* (4–7). Illus. 2004, Gale LB $27.45 (978-1-4103-

0490-2). 80pp. Using a news-style format with maps, charts, and illustrations, Pascoe details the history of New York State and profiles famous individuals. (Rev: SLJ 3/05) [974.7]

19427 Peduzzi, Kelli. *Shaping a President: Sculpting for the Roosevelt Memorial* (3–6). Illus. 1997, Millbrook LB $23.40 (978-0-7613-0207-0); paper $9.95 (978-0-7613-0325-1). 48pp. This photoessay tells of the work of the sculptor Neil Estrin, who sculpted figures of Franklin, Eleanor, and their dog Fala, for the Roosevelt Memorial in Washington, D.C. (Rev: BL 12/1/97; HBG 3/98; SLJ 3/98) [730]

19428 Peters, Stephen. *Pennsylvania* (4–7). Series: Celebrate the States. 2000, Marshall Cavendish LB $37.07 (978-0-7614-0644-0). 144pp. An overview of the history, geography, and culture of Pennsylvania with additional material on state symbols, industry, the people, and the economy. (Rev: BL 6/1–15/00; SLJ 9/00) [974.8]

19429 Raabe, Emily. *Uniquely Vermont* (4–7). Illus. Series: Heinemann State Studies. 2005, Heinemann LB $31.36 (978-1-4034-4664-0). 48pp. In addition to providing the facts necessary for report writers, this volume emphasizes the features that distinguish Vermont from its neighbors. (Rev: BL 10/15/03)

19430 Rappaport, Doreen. *Lady Liberty: A Biography* (2–5). Illus. by Matt Tavares. 2008, Candlewick $17.99 (978-0-7636-2530-6). 60pp. Free-verse accounts by individuals involved — including sculptor Auguste Bartholdi and poet Emma Lazarus — tell the story of the creation of the Statue of Liberty. (Rev: BL 4/15/08; HB 7/08; LMC 11/08; SLJ 5/08) [974.7]

19431 Rau, Dana Meachen. *The Statue of Liberty* (2–4). Series: Our Nation. 2001, Compass Point LB $19.93 (978-0-7565-0143-3). 24pp. An introduction to the statue with information on its history, symbolism, and location. (Rev: SLJ 1/02) [974.7]

19432 Rebman, Renee C. *Life on Ellis Island* (5–8). Series: The Way People Live. 1999, Lucent LB $29.95 (978-1-56006-533-3). 95pp. With extensive use of firsthand accounts, this book relates the purpose of Ellis Island, the processing of immigrants, and the joys and hardships involved. (Rev: BL 10/15/99; HBG 10/00; SLJ 1/00) [325.1]

19433 Ross, D. J. *Uniquely Maine* (4–7). Series: Heinemann State Studies. 2004, Heinemann LB $27.07 (978-1-4034-4655-8). 48pp. In addition to providing the facts necessary for report writers, this volume emphasizes the features that distinguish Maine from its neighbors. (Rev: BL 4/1/04)

19434 Rubbino, Salvatore. *A Walk in New York* (2–5). Illus. by author. 2009, Candlewick $16.99 (978-0-7636-3855-9). 38pp. A boy and his father see the sights of New York City in this appealing volume with interesting bits of information and fold-out pages with city scenes. (Rev: HB 7/09; SLJ 5/09) [917.47]

19435 Sanders, Mark. *The White House* (3–6). Series: American Government Today. 2000, Raintree LB $22.83 (978-0-7398-1791-9). 48pp. An account that gives a history of the White House, its construction and renovations, plus details on its rooms and offices. (Rev: HBG 10/00; SLJ 8/00) [975]

19436 Schaefer, Ted, and Lola M. Schaefer. *Independence Hall* (1–3). Series: Symbols of Freedom. 2005, Heinemann LB $25.36 (978-1-4034-6664-8). 32pp. Large color photographs and clear text introduce Philadelphia's Independence Hall and the important role it played in America's history; useful for basic research and reports. (Rev: SLJ 12/05) [974.811]

19437 Schaefer, Ted, and Lola M. Schaefer. *The Vietnam Veterans Memorial* (1–3). Series: Symbols of Freedom. 2005, Heinemann LB $25.36 (978-1-4034-6659-4). 32pp. Large color photographs and clear text introduce the Washington, D.C., memorial; useful for basic research and reports. (Rev: SLJ 12/05) [959.7043]

19438 Schnurnberger, Lynn. *Kids Love New York! The A-to-Z Resource Book* (4–8). Illus. 1990, Congdon & Weed paper $133.65 (978-0-312-92415-7). 224pp. A group of suggestions for various activities in New York City.

19439 Schomp, Virginia. *New York* (4–7). Illus. Series: Celebrate the States. 2005, Benchmark LB $37.07 (978-0-7614-1738-5). 144pp. A revised edition of this introduction to the Empire State — including its history, culture, famous sites, and distinguished New Yorkers — with updated illustrations. (Rev: SLJ 5/06) [917.47]

19440 Schuman, Michael. *Delaware* (4–8). Series: Celebrate the States. 2000, Marshall Cavendish LB $37.07 (978-0-7614-0645-7). 139pp. Beginning with quotations about Delaware and its people, this account covers the basic topics plus information on folklore, food, and festivals. (Rev: BL 6/1–15/00; HBG 10/00) [975.1]

19441 Shea, Pegi Deitz. *Liberty Rising: The Story of the Statue of Liberty* (2–4). Illus. by Wade Zahares. 2005, Holt $17.95 (978-0-8050-7220-4). 44pp. Bold illustrations highlight the story of the creation of the statue; also includes a timeline and pronunciation guide. (Rev: BL 8/05; SLJ 10/05) [974.7]

19442 Smith, Marie, and Roland Smith. *N Is for Our Nation's Capital: A Washington, DC Alphabet* (K–4). Illus. by Barbara Leonard Gibson. 2005, Sleeping Bear $17.95 (978-1-58556-148-3). An inventive alphabet book that introduces historical information about the capital and the people who have worked there. (Rev: SLJ 8/05) [957.3]

19443 Somervill, Barbara. *Pennsylvania* (3–6). Illus. Series: From Sea to Shining Sea. 2003, Children's Pr. LB $30.50 (978-0-516-22388-9). 80pp. A photofilled profile covering the state's geography, people, government, lifestyle, and attractions. (Rev: SLJ 8/03) [974.8]

19444 Stevenson, Harvey. *Looking at Liberty* (3–5). Illus. by author. 2003, HarperCollins LB $17.89 (978-0-06-000101-8). 40pp. This artful blend of poetry, eye-catching artwork, and concise facts recounts the story behind the construction of the Statue of Liberty — a gift from the people of France to the people of the United States. (Rev: BL 10/1/03; HBG 10/03; SLJ 6/03)

19445 Sullivan, George. *How the White House Really Works* (5–8). Illus. 1990, Scholastic paper $3.95 (978-0-590-43403-4). Home, office, museum, and tourist attraction — how the White House operates. (Rev: BCCB 5/89; BL 5/15/89; HB 7/89) [975.3]

19446 Swain, Gwenyth. *Pennsylvania* (3–5). Illus. Series: Hello USA. 1994, Lerner LB $19.93 (978-0-8225-2727-5). 72pp. After an introductory trip around Pennsylvania, this concise book covers its history, attractions, environment, and famous people. (Rev: BL 4/15/94; SLJ 8/94) [974.8]

19447 Tagliaferro, Linda. *Destination New York* (4–8). Series: Port Cities of North America. 1998, Lerner LB $23.93 (978-0-8225-2793-0). Written with a focus on New York's economic life and its handling of goods moving in and out of the port, this book also gives information on the city's history, geography, and daily life. (Rev: HBG 3/99; SLJ 1/99) [974.7]

19448 Talbott, Hudson. *River of Dreams: The Story of the Hudson River* (4–7). Illus. by author. 2009, Putnam $17.99 (978-0-399-24521-3). 40pp. An engaging history of the river, covering its role in early settlements, shipping and the Erie Canal, the pollution that afflicted the ecosystem and efforts to clean it up, and the river's influence on art. (Rev: BL 12/15/08; HB 3/09; SLJ 3/09) [974.7]

19449 Thomas, Pamela. *Brooklyn Pops Up* (3–10). Illus. 2000, Simon & Schuster $19.95 (978-0-689-84019-7). This pop-up book takes you on a tour of this borough of New York City, including visits to Coney Island and the Brooklyn Museum. (Rev: BL 12/1/00; HBG 3/01) [917.47]

19450 Topper, Frank, and Charles A. Wills. *A Historical Album of New Jersey* (3–5). Illus. Series: Historical Album. 1995, Millbrook LB $23.40 (978-1-56294-505-3). 64pp. Beginning with the Native American culture and ending with the present day, the most important events and people in New Jersey history are touched on in a rapid overview. (Rev: SLJ 7/95) [974.9]

19451 Walsh, Frank. *New York City* (3–6). Series: Great Cities of the World. 2003, World Almanac LB $31.00 (978-0-8368-5025-3). 48pp. An overview of one of the world's most famous cities, with detail on its history, its economy, and what it's like to live there. (Rev: SLJ 3/04) [974.7]

19452 Warner, J. F. *Rhode Island* (3–6). Illus. Series: Hello USA. 1993, Lerner LB $19.93 (978-0-8225-2731-2). 72pp. In excellent color illustrations and informative text, Rhode Island and its history, geography, cities, and social and economic life are covered. (Rev: BL 1/15/93) [974]

19453 Warrick, Karen Clemens. *Independence National Historical Park* (5–8). Illus. Series: Virtual Field Trips. 2005, Enslow LB $25.26 (978-0-7660-5224-6). 48pp. A visit to Independence Park, using both print and related Web sites, that covers its historical importance, including Independence Hall and the Liberty Bell. (Rev: SLJ 5/05)

19454 Welsbacher, Anne. *New York* (3–4). Series: Checkerboard Geography. 1999, ABDO LB $22.78 (978-1-56239-891-0). 32pp. By focusing on the people, history, and geography of New York State, this simple book introduces the different regions and supplies such unusual facts as how Uncle Sam originated. (Rev: HBG 10/99; SLJ 8/99) [974.7]

19455 Whitcraft, Melissa. *The Hudson River* (4–7). Illus. Series: World of Water. 1999, Watts LB $25.50 (978-0-531-11739-2). 64pp. A handsome volume that traces the history of New York State's most important river and how it currently affects people's lives. (Rev: BL 1/1–15/00) [974.7]

19456 Wills, Charles A. *A Historical Album of Pennsylvania* (4–8). Series: Historical Albums. 1996, Millbrook LB $24.40 (978-1-56294-595-4). Beginning with its Native American origins and settlement by Europeans and the Quakers, this book traces the history of Pennsylvania from the First Continental Congress and the ratification of the United States Constitution, through the Battle of Gettysburg and President Lincoln's famous Gettysburg Address, and up to today. (Rev: BL 7/96; SLJ 7/96) [974.8]

19457 Yolen, Jane. *House, House* (3–6). Illus. 1998, Marshall Cavendish $15.95 (978-0-7614-5013-9). 32pp. Life in Hatfield, Massachusetts, in 1900 and 2000 is contrasted in a series of then-and-now photographs and explanatory text. (Rev: BL 5/15/98; HBG 10/98; SLJ 6/98) [974.4]

19458 Zschock, Martha, and Heather Zschock. *Journey Around New York from A to Z* (1–3). Illus. 2002, Commonwealth $17.95 (978-1-889833-32-3). 32pp. An alphabetical journey around New York that combines information on tourist attractions, history, neighborhoods, and public celebrations. (Rev: BL 6/1–15/02; SLJ 7/02) [917.47]

PACIFIC STATES

19459 Abbink, Emily. *Missions of the Monterey Bay Area* (4–7). Series: California Missions. 1996, Lerner LB $23.93 (978-0-8225-1928-7). 80pp. Covers the history of the missions at San Carlos Borromeo de Carmelo, San Juan Bautista, and Santa Cruz. (Rev: BL 2/15/97) [979.4]

19460 Aillaud, Cindy Lou. *Recess at 20 Below* (K–3). Illus. 2005, Alaska Northwest $15.95 (978-0-88240-604-6); paper $8.95 (978-0-88240-609-1). 32pp. Though the temperature outside can be nearly 20 degrees below zero (Fahrenheit), Alaskan schoolchildren still find a way to play outdoors. (Rev: BL 12/15/05; HB 1/06; HBG 4/06; SLJ 3/06) [371.2]

19461 Altman, Linda J. *California* (5–8). Series: Celebrate the States. 2005, Benchmark LB $37.07 (978-0-7614-1737-8). 143pp. This revised edition updates facts and adds information on the government and economy plus new, full-color photographs. (Rev: SLJ 3/06) [979.4]

19462 Ansary, Mir T. *People of California* (4–7). Illus. Series: Heinemann State Studies. 2003, Heinemann LB $27.07 (978-1-4034-0342-1). 48pp. Ansary looks at groups of people who have settled in California and offers brief biographies of individuals who have contributed to all fields of endeavor, with many color photographs. (Rev: BL 10/15/03; HBG 4/04; SLJ 11/03) [305.8]

19463 Aylesworth, Thomas G., and Virginia L. Aylesworth. *The Pacific: California, Hawaii* (3–8). Illus. 1995, Chelsea LB $19.95 (978-0-7910-3407-1); paper $8.95 (978-0-7910-3425-5). 64pp. People and places are included in this study of the West. (Rev: BL 11/1/87; SLJ 11/95)

19464 Behrens, June. *Missions of the Central Coast* (4–7). Series: California Missions. 1996, Lerner LB $23.93 (978-0-8225-1930-0). 80pp. The missions at Santa Barbara, Santa Ines, and La Purisima Concepción are discussed, with material on their history and importance. (Rev: BL 2/15/97) [979.4]

19465 Boekhoff, P. M., and Stuart A. Kallen. *California* (4–7). Illus. Series: Seeds of a Nation. 2002, Gale LB $23.70 (978-0-7377-0946-9). 48pp. The history of California before statehood is presented with material on Native Americans, missionaries, settlers, and prospectors. (Rev: BL 4/1/02) [979.4]

19466 Bratvold, Gretchen. *Oregon* (3–6). Illus. Series: Hello USA. 1991, Lerner LB $19.93 (978-0-8225-2704-6). 72pp. Topics include geography; history; and social, economic, and environmental concerns, with full-color photos. (Rev: BL 4/15/91; SLJ 6/91) [979.5]

19467 Bredeson, Carmen. *Fire in Oakland, California: Billion-Dollar Blaze* (4–8). Series: American Disasters. 1999, Enslow LB $23.93 (978-0-7660-1220-2). 48pp. A high-interest book that tells of the terrible fire in Oakland and the massive destruction it caused. (Rev: BL 10/15/99; HBG 3/00) [976.8]

19468 Britton, Tamara. *Pearl Harbor* (3–5). Series: Symbols, Landmarks, and Monuments. 2003, ABDO LB $22.78 (978-1-57765-851-1). 40pp. From the attack in 1941 to the USS Arizona Memorial, this volume provides information that will be useful to report writers. (Rev: HBG 10/03; SLJ 10/03) [940.54]

19469 Brower, Pauline. *Missions of the Inland Valleys* (4–7). Series: California Missions. 1996, Lerner LB $23.93 (978-0-8225-1929-4). 80pp. Examines four missions, including San Luis Obispo and San Miguel Arcangel, with material on their early history and their impact on the existing cultures. (Rev: BL 2/15/97) [979.4]

19470 Corral, Kimberly. *A Child's Glacier Bay* (4–8). Illus. 1998, Graphic Arts Center $15.95 (978-0-88240-503-2). A photoessay chronicling a three-week kayak trip in Alaska's Glacier Bay, told from the perspective of a 13-year-old girl. (Rev: BL 7/98; HBG 10/98; SLJ 8/98) [978.652]

19471 Cosson, M. J. *Welcome to Redwood National and State Parks* (3–5). Series: Visitor Guides. 2006, The Child's World LB $27.07 (978-1-59296-701-8). 32pp. An attractively presented tour of three California parks, focusing on their geography, history, flora, fauna, and weather. (Rev: SLJ 2/07) [917.94]

19472 Covert, Kim. *Washington* (3–5). Illus. Series: Land of Liberty. 2003, Capstone LB $25.26 (978-0-7368-2203-9). 64pp. A profile of the state of Washington, covering everything from climate and topography to people and economy, with fast facts, a recipe, and other useful material at the end. (Rev: SLJ 3/04) [979.7]

19473 Crewe, Sabrina. *Los Angeles* (4–6). Series: Great Cities of the World. 2004, World Almanac LB $31.00 (978-0-8368-5029-1). 48pp. Report writers will find useful information on Los Angeles's history, culture, lifestyle, and current problems such as traffic congestion, smog, and water shortages. (Rev: SLJ 7/04) [979.4]

19474 Dell, Pamela. *Welcome to Mount Rainier National Park* (3–5). Series: Visitor Guides. 2006, The Child's World LB $27.07 (978-1-59296-700-1). 32pp. An attractively presented tour of the Washington state park, focusing on its geography, history, flora, fauna, and weather. (Rev: SLJ 2/07) [979.7]

19475 Doak, Robin. *California 1542–1850* (5–8). Series: Voices from Colonial America. 2006, National Geographic $21.95 (978-0-7922-6391-3). 109pp. This well-illustrated title traces the history of California from its 1542 "discovery" by Juan Rodriguez Cabrillo to the frenzied Gold Rush years of the mid-19th century; maps and a timeline make this useful for research. (Rev: SLJ 1/07) [979.4]

19476 Doherty, Craig A., and Katherine M. Doherty. *The Golden Gate Bridge* (3–6). Illus. Series: Building America. 1995, Blackbirch LB $23.70 (978-1-56711-106-4). 48pp. From concept to completion, this is a thorough, engrossing description of the Golden Gate Bridge in San Francisco. (Rev: BL 9/15/95; SLJ 7/95) [624]

19477 Fandel, Jennifer. *Golden Gate Bridge* (3–6). Series: Modern Wonders of the World. 2006, Creative Education LB $27.10 (978-1-58341-437-8). 32pp. This is an attractive overview of the history of the famous bridge, the engineering challenges involved in its construction, and its importance today as a span and a symbol. (Rev: SLJ 12/06) [624.2]

19478 Feeney, Stephanie. *Hawaii Is a Rainbow* (2–6). Illus. 1985, Univ. of Hawaii $13.95 (978-0-8248-1007-8). 64pp. Color photos present the people and land of Hawaii as they present the colors of the rainbow. (Rev: BL 2/1/85; SLJ 1/86)

19479 Feeney, Stephanie. *Sun and Rain: Exploring Seasons in Hawai'i* (K–3). Illus. 2007, Univ. of Hawaii $13.95 (978-0-8248-3088-5). 48pp. Hawaii's dry and wet seasons are explored with information about the weather, plants, and animals. (Rev: BL 12/15/07) [551.5]

19480 Gaines, Ann Graham. *Hawaii* (3–6). Illus. Series: It's My State! 2007, Marshall Cavendish LB $20.95 (978-0-7614-1926-6). 32pp. Neatly designed and filled with color photographs, this overview of Hawaii provides information about the state's history, plants, animals, geography, economy, and so forth. (Rev: BL 5/15/07; SLJ 8/07) [996.9]

19481 Gill, Shelley. *Hawai'i* (5–8). Illus. by Scott Goto. 2006, Charlesbridge paper $6.95 (978-0-88106-297-7). 32pp. A boy and his father tour the state of Hawaii by kayak; as they pass each island the father tells his son a little about its history, geography, people, culture, and economy. (Rev: SLJ 8/06) [996.9]

19482 Goh, Geok Yian. *Uniquely Hawaii* (4–7). Illus. Series: Heinemann State Studies. 2004, Heinemann LB $27.07 (978-1-4034-4645-9). 48pp. In addition to providing the facts necessary for report writers, this volume emphasizes the features that make Hawaii unique. (Rev: BL 10/15/03)

19483 Goldberg, Jake. *Hawaii* (5–8). Series: Celebrate the States. 1998, Benchmark LB $37.07 (978-0-7614-0203-9). 144pp. Using fine illustrations, fact boxes, graphs, and maps, this attractive book gives an excellent introduction to Hawaii, with the added bonus of a recipe and two songs. (Rev: HBG 10/98; SLJ 1/99) [996.9]

19484 Grabowski, John, and Patricia Grabowski. *The Northwest: Alaska, Idaho, Oregon, Washington* (3–6). Series: State Reports. 1995, Chelsea LB $19.95 (978-0-7910-3406-4); paper $8.95 (978-0-7910-3424-8). 64pp. History, geography, state symbols, capitals, principal cities, and places to visit are some of the topics covered in this introduction to these four states. (Rev: SLJ 9/92) [978]

19485 Hall, M. C. *Hawaii Volcanoes National Park* (K–4). Series: Symbols of Freedom: National Parks. 2005, Heinemann LB $25.36 (978-1-4034-6700-3). 32pp. Large color photographs and clear text introduce the history, geography, flora, and fauna of this park; useful for basic research and reports. (Rev: SLJ 12/05) [919.69]

19486 Hall, M. C. *Welcome to Denali National Park* (3–5). Series: Visitor Guides. 2006, The Child's World LB $27.07 (978-1-59296-695-0). 32pp. An attractively presented tour of the Alaskan park, focusing on its geography, history, flora, fauna, and weather. (Rev: SLJ 2/07) [979.8]

19487 Harder, Dan, and Lawrence Migdale. *A Child's California* (2–4). Illus. 2000, Graphic Arts $15.95 (978-1-55868-520-8). 48pp. This introduction to California covers topics of particular interest to children and emphasizes the state's diversity and contrasts. (Rev: BL 2/1/01; SLJ 1/01) [917.94]

19488 Heinrichs, Ann. *California* (2–4). Illus. Series: This Land Is Your Land. 2002, Compass Point LB $25.26 (978-0-7565-0308-6). 48pp. Simple text with age-appropriate language and good illustrations introduce the history, geography, culture, famous people, and attractions of California. (Rev: SLJ 1/03)

19489 Heinrichs, Ann. *The California Missions* (5–8). Series: We the People. 2002, Compass Point LB $26.60 (978-0-7565-0208-9). 48pp. An accessible, well-illustrated account of the creation of Spanish missions in California and the impact on the native peoples of the region. (Rev: SLJ 7/02) [979.402]

19490 Heinrichs, Ann. *Oregon* (3–5). Illus. by Matt Kania. Series: Welcome to the U.S.A. 2005, The Child's World LB $27.07 (978-1-59296-479-6). 40pp. Using an attractive scrapbook format featuring a family on vacation, this volume introduces the state's geography, history, people, major attractions, and state symbols. (Rev: SLJ 2/06) [979.5]

19491 Henry, Judy. *Uniquely Alaska* (4–7). Illus. Series: Heinemann State Studies. 2005, Heinemann LB $31.36 (978-1-4034-4642-8). 48pp. In addition to providing the facts necessary for report writers, this volume emphasizes the features that make Alaska unique. (Rev: BL 10/15/03)

19492 Isaacs, Sally Senzell. *Life in San Francisco's Chinatown* (2–4). Illus. Series: Picture the Past. 2002, Heinemann LB $22.79 (978-1-58810-692-6). 32pp. A look at life in San Francisco for Chinese immigrants in the years from the Gold Rush through the early 20th century. (Rev: HBG 3/03; SLJ 3/03) [979.4]

19493 Johnston, Joyce. *Alaska* (3–6). Illus. Series: Hello USA. 1994, Lerner LB $19.93 (978-0-8225-2735-0). 72pp. This introduction to Alaska features a trip around the state, historical information, and material on the life-styles of its people. (Rev: BL 4/15/94; SLJ 8/94) [979.8]

19494 Kennedy, Teresa. *California* (4–6). Series: From Sea to Shining Sea. 2001, Children's Book Pr. LB $30.50 (978-0-516-22309-4). This attractive, oversize volume includes material on the land, history, people, and lifestyle of California. (Rev: BL 4/15/02) [979.4]

19495 Kimmel, Elizabeth C. *Balto and the Great Race* (3–5). Illus. 1999, Random paper $3.99 (978-0-679-89198-7). 112pp. The true story set of a dog team, led by a Siberian husky, that delivered medicine to sick children in Alaska in 1925. (Rev: BL 10/15/99; HBG 10/00; SLJ 3/00) [636.73]

19496 Knapp, Ron. *Oregon* (4–7). Illus. Series: MyReportLinks.com. 2002, Enslow LB $25.26 (978-0-7660-5021-1). 48pp. An introduction to the government, geography, and history of the state, with helpful Web sites. (Rev: BL 2/1/03; HBG 3/03; VOYA 4/03) [979.5]

19497 Labella, Susan. *Washington* (K–2). Series: Rookie Read-About Geography. 2006, Scholastic LB $20.50 (978-0-516-24993-3); paper $5.95 (978-0-516-26455-4). 32pp. A slim, square volume on Washington state that will be a good start for young researchers. (Rev: BL 7/06) [917.97]

19498 Lemke, Nancy. *Missions of the Southern Coast* (4–7). Illus. Series: California Missions. 1996, Lerner LB $23.93 (978-0-8225-1925-6). 80pp. The three missions described here are San Diego de Alcala, San Luis Rey de Francia, and San Juan Capistrano. (Rev: BL 9/15/96; SLJ 8/96) [979.4]

19499 Levi, Steven C. *Cowboys of the Sky: The Story of Alaska's Bush Pilots* (5–9). Illus. 1996, Walker LB $18.85 (978-0-8027-8332-5). The exciting life of the people who deliver medical supplies, mail, and passengers to remote areas in Alaska is vividly re-created. (Rev: BL 6/1–15/96; SLJ 7/96; VOYA 8/96) [629.13]

19500 Levinson, Nancy S. *Death Valley: A Day in the Desert* (2–3). Illus. by Diane D. Hearn. 2001, Holiday House $14.95 (978-0-8234-1566-3). 32pp. In this easily read book, Death Valley and its plants and animals are introduced with excellent drawings. (Rev: BL 4/15/01; HBG 10/01; SLJ 4/01) [508.794]

19501 McMillan, Bruce. *Salmon Summer* (K–3). Illus. 1998, Houghton $17.00 (978-0-395-84544-8). 32pp. An outstanding photoessay about 9-year-old

Alex, an Aleut boy, and his summer at his family's salmon fishing camp. (Rev: BCCB 5/98; BL 4/1/98; HB 5/98; HBG 10/98; SLJ 5/98) [639.2]

19502 MacMillan, Dianne. *Destination Los Angeles* (4–6). Illus. Series: Port Cities of North America. 1998, Lerner LB $23.93 (978-0-8225-2786-2). 80pp. Describes Los Angeles and its history but concentrates on the harbor, trade, and the cargo shipped in and out. (Rev: HBG 10/98; SLJ 3/98) [917.94]

19503 MacMillan, Dianne. *Missions of the Los Angeles Area* (4–7). Illus. Series: California Missions. 1996, Lerner LB $23.93 (978-0-8225-1927-0). 80pp. This volume gives a description and history of three missions: San Gabriel Arcangel, San Fernando Rey de España, and San Buenaventura. (Rev: BL 9/15/96; SLJ 8/96) [979.4]

19504 Mannis, Celeste Davidson. *Snapshots: The Wonders of Monterey Bay* (K–4). Photos by author. 2006, Viking $16.99 (978-0-670-06062-7). All about the varied plants and animals of California's spectacular Monterey Bay, with plenty of eye-catching photographs and clearly presented information. (Rev: SLJ 6/06*)

19505 Markle, Sandra. *After the Spill: The Exxon Valdez Disaster Then and Now* (3–5). Illus. 1999, Walker $16.95 (978-0-8027-8610-4). 32pp. A photoessay that describes the oil spill and events through mid-1999 involving the cleanup. (Rev: BL 8/99; HBG 10/99; SLJ 9/99) [363.738]

19506 Miller, Debbie S. *Big Alaska: Journey Across America's Most Amazing State* (2–4). Illus. by Jon Van Zyle. 2006, Walker $17.95 (978-0-8027-8069-0). 40pp. Sixteen of Alaska's most breathtaking natural wonders are shown in this large-format, photo-filled book that uses a bald eagle's flight as a unifying element; facts, state symbols, and Internet sites are appended. (Rev: BL 3/1/06; SLJ 5/06) [917.98]

19507 Miller, Debbie S. *Disappearing Lake: Nature's Magic in Denali National Park* (K–3). Illus. by Jon Van Zyle. 1997, Walker $15.95 (978-0-8027-8474-2). 32pp. The story of an area in Alaska's Denali National Park, which is transformed annually into a lake and then, as the waters recede, into a flowering meadow. (Rev: BCCB 2/97; BL 3/15/97; SLJ 4/97*) [508.798]

19508 Miller, Debbie S. *River of Life* (K–3). Illus. by Jon Van Zyle. 2000, Clarion $16.00 (978-0-395-96790-4). 32pp. Realistic oil paintings are used to illustrate this book that describes a year in the life of an Alaskan river and the wildlife surrounding it. (Rev: BL 3/15/00; HBG 10/00; SLJ 7/00) [577.6]

19509 Murphy, Claire R. *Children of Alcatraz: Growing Up on the Rock* (4–7). Illus. 2006, Walker $17.95 (978-0-8027-9577-9). 64pp. This is the story of the children who have grown up on Alcatraz Island over time — early Native American children, children of lighthouse keepers, children of prison authorities, and so forth — with archival photographs and a timeline. (Rev: BL 12/15/06; SLJ 11/06) [979.4]

19510 Neri, P. J. *Hawaii* (3–6). Illus. Series: From Sea to Shining Sea, Second Series. 2003, Children's Pr. LB $30.50 (978-0-516-22383-4). 80pp. A revised, photo-filled introduction to the Aloha State's geography, history, people, culture, and economy. (Rev: SLJ 12/03) [919.6]

19511 Oliver, Marilyn Tower. *Alcatraz Prison* (4–8). Series: In American History. 1998, Enslow LB $26.60 (978-0-89490-990-0). After years as first a settlement and then a fort and a lighthouse, the "Rock" became a military and federal prison. This is its history, including famous prisoners, escape attempts, and its evolution into a top tourist attraction. (Rev: HBG 3/99; SLJ 1/99) [979.4]

19512 Orr, Tamra. *California* (5–8). Illus. Series: America the Beautiful: Third Series. 2007, Children's Pr. LB $38.00 (978-0-531-18557-5). 144pp. This new edition of the classic series entry about the state features a new design and layout, definitions of difficult words in the margins, more history and mini biographies, and project ideas in writing, art, and science. (Rev: BL 2/1/08) [979.4]

19513 Otfinoski, Steve. *Washington* (4–7). Series: It's My State! 2003, Marshall Cavendish LB $27.07 (978-0-7614-1522-0). 80pp. The state of Washington, its geography, history, people, and economic development are some of the topics covered in this introduction to this Pacific state. (Rev: BL 9/15/03; HBG 4/04) [979.9]

19514 Pelta, Kathy. *California* (3–5). Illus. Series: Hello USA. 1994, Lerner LB $19.93 (978-0-8225-2738-1). 72pp. This small book is crammed with basic information about California, including its history, famous attractions, and important residents. (Rev: BL 4/15/94) [979.4]

19515 Quasha, Jennifer. *How to Draw California's Sights and Symbols* (3–6). Illus. Series: Kid's Guide to Drawing America. 2002, Rosen LB $25.25 (978-0-8239-6059-0). 32pp. An eclectic mix of California history, geography, demographics, and state sights and symbols. (Rev: BL 2/15/02; SLJ 7/02) [743]

19516 Rice, Oliver D. *Lone Woman of Ghalas-Hat* (5–7). Illus. by Charles Zafuto. 1993, California Weekly LB $13.00 (978-0-936778-52-5); paper $6.00 (978-0-936778-51-8). 32pp. The true story of the Indian woman who lived alone on a California island for 18 years. This was the basis of *Island of the Blue Dolphins*. A reissue. [979.7]

19517 Ryan, Pam Muñoz. *Our California* (PS–2). Illus. by Rafael Lopez. 2008, Charlesbridge $17.95 (978-1-58089-116-5); paper $7.95 (978-1-58089-117-2). 48pp. A rhyming text presents information about various locations in California, including Capistrano, San Francisco, Los Angeles, and Palm Springs. (Rev: BL 12/15/07; SLJ 6/08) [979.4]

19518 Seibold, J. Otto, and Vivian Walsh. *Going to the Getty: A Book About the Getty Center in Los Angeles* (4–7). Illus. 1997, Getty Museum $17.50 (978-0-89236-493-0). 32pp. This introduction to the Getty Museum in Los Angeles is a patchwork of impressions, photographs, drawings, and reproductions of artworks. (Rev: BL 2/15/98; HBG 10/98) [708]

19519 Sherrow, Victoria. *The Exxon Valdez: Tragic Oil Spill* (4–8). Series: American Disasters. 1998, Enslow LB $23.93 (978-0-7660-1058-1). 48pp. The dramatic story of the *Exxon Valdez* oil spill and the damage it caused to the Alaskan coast and its wildlife. (Rev: BL 1/1–15/99; HBG 3/99; SLJ 3/99; VOYA 4/99) [979.8]

19520 Sherrow, Victoria. *San Francisco Earthquake, 1989: Death and Destruction* (4–8). Illus. Series: American Disasters. 1998, Enslow LB $23.93 (978-0-7660-1060-4). 48pp. This account of the San Francisco earthquake incorporates many eyewitness reports. (Rev: BL 1/1–15/99; HBG 3/99; SLJ 6/99) [363.34]

19521 Staub, Frank. *Children of Hawaii* (4–6). Series: The World's Children. 1999, Carolrhoda $23.93 (978-1-57505-253-3). 48pp. Through enticing photographs of Hawaiian children, the reader learns about the history, geography, and culture of the 50th U.S. state. (Rev: BL 7/99; HBG 10/99) [996.9]

19522 Staub, Frank. *Children of the Tlingit* (3–6). Illus. Series: The World's Children. 1999, Carolrhoda LB $21.27 (978-1-57505-333-2). 48pp. A look at the daily life of several children who belong to the Tlingit people of southeastern Alaska. (Rev: BL 6/1–15/99; HBG 10/99; SLJ 10/99) [979.8]

19523 Stefoff, Rebecca. *Alaska* (4–6). Illus. Series: Celebrate the States. 2006, Benchmark LB $39.93 (978-0-7614-2153-5). 144pp. An updated edition that includes attractive photographs, maps, and graphs and covers Alaska's history, geography, government, economy, and natural and man-made landmarks; fun facts, famous people, and places to visit, plus a list of Web sites round out this useful volume. (Rev: SLJ 12/06) [979.8]

19524 Stefoff, Rebecca. *Oregon* (4–8). Illus. Series: Celebrate the States. 1997, Marshall Cavendish LB $37.07 (978-0-7614-0145-2). 140pp. A look at life in this Pacific state, along with its history, famous sights, cities, and industries. (Rev: BL 7/97; SLJ 7/97) [917.95]

19525 Stepanchuk, Carol. *Exploring Chinatown* (4–8). Illus. by Leland Wong. 2002, Pacific View LB $22.95 (978-1-881896-25-8). 64pp. This "walk" through San Francisco's Chinatown explores the Chinese culture and customs, and offers historical facts as well as a few hands-on projects. (Rev: BL 8/02; SLJ 9/02) [305.8951073]

19526 Temple, Teri, and Bob Temple. *Welcome to Hawai'i Volcanoes National Park* (3–5). Series: Visitor Guides. 2006, The Child's World LB $27.07 (978-1-59296-699-8). 32pp. An attractively presented tour of the Hawaiian state park, with information on its geography, history, flora, fauna, and weather plus discussion of the legend of Pele, the goddess of fire. (Rev: SLJ 2/07) [996.9]

19527 Uschan, Michael V. *The California Gold Rush* (5 8). Series: Landmark Events in American History. 2003, World Almanac LB $31.00 (978-0-8368-5374-2). 48pp. An attractive account of the California gold rush, famous people involved, and its consequences. (Rev: BL 10/15/03) [979.4]

19528 Webster, Christine. *Washington* (3–6). Illus. Series: From Sea to Shining Sea. 2003, Children's Pr. LB $30.50 (978-0-516-22386-5). 80pp. This photo-filled overview provides all the information on the Pacific Northwest state that report writers need. (Rev: SLJ 9/03) [979.7]

19529 White, Tekla N. *Missions of the San Francisco Bay Area* (4–7). Illus. Series: California Missions. 1996, Lerner LB $23.93 (978-0-8225-1926-3). 80pp. The history of five Spanish missions in the San Francisco Bay Area, including Santa Clara de Asis and San Rafael Arcangel. (Rev: BL 9/15/96; SLJ 8/96) [979.4]

19530 Wills, Charles A. *A Historical Album of California* (4–8). Illus. Series: Historical Albums. 1994, Millbrook LB $24.40 (978-1-56294-479-7). 64pp. A slim volume that covers the basic history of California, with material on major events and important personalities. (Rev: SLJ 3/95) [979.4]

19531 Wills, Charles A. *A Historical Album of Oregon* (4–8). Series: Historical Albums. 1995, Millbrook $24.40 (978-1-56294-594-7). A good, broad overview of Oregon's history and current political and economic situation, places to see, and other information, with many illustrations. (Rev: BL 12/15/95; SLJ 1/96) [979.5]

19532 Young, Robert. *A Personal Tour of La Purisima* (4–7). Series: How It Was. 1999, Lerner LB $30.35 (978-0-8225-3576-8). 64pp. A you-are-there visit to La Purisima — one of the 21 missions built by the Spanish in California — in which the reader experiences life in the mission as it was in 1820. (Rev: BL 6/1–15/99; HBG 10/99) [979.4]

SOUTH

19533 Alex, Nan. *North Carolina* (4–6). Series: From Sea to Shining Sea. 2001, Children's Book Pr. LB $30.50 (978-0-516-22487-9). An attractive, well-organized volume that introduces the land and people of North Carolina. Also use *Florida*, *Georgia*, *Kentucky*, and *Tennessee* (all 2001). (Rev: BL 4/15/02) [975.6]

19534 Altman, Linda J. *Arkansas* (4–8). Series: Celebrate the States. 2000, Benchmark LB $37.07 (978-0-7614-0672-3). An broad introduction to the culture, land, government, history, and unique characteristics of Arkansas, with emphasis on its inhabitants. (Rev: BL 1/1–15/00; HBG 10/00) [976.7]

19535 Ashabranner, Brent. *A Date with Destiny: The Women in Military Service for America Memorial* (5–8). Illus. 2000, Twenty-First Century LB $25.90 (978-0-7613-1472-1). 64pp. This book tells the story of the memorial outside Arlington National Cemetery that honors American women in the military and retells some of the stories of these servicewomen. (Rev: BL 2/1/00; HBG 10/00; SLJ 4/00) [355.1]

19536 Aylesworth, Thomas G., and Virginia L. Aylesworth. *The Southeast: Georgia, Kentucky, Tennessee* (3–8). Illus. 1995, Chelsea LB $21.95 (978-0-7910-3411-8); paper $9.95 (978-0-7910-3429-3). 64pp. An inviting look at this region, with color photos and map. (Rev: BL 11/1/87; SLJ 11/87)

19537 Backer, Miles. *Travels with Charlie: Down South* (1–3). Illus. by Chuck Nitzberg. Series: Travels with Charlie. 2007, Blue Apple $15.95 (978-1-59354-594-9). Readers will learn about the southern United States as they search for a dog named Charlie. Trivia, fun facts, and maps packed with sites of interest make this a fun way to learn about geography. (Rev: SLJ 8/07)

19538 Barrett, Tracy. *Kentucky* (4–7). Series: Celebrate the States. 1999, Benchmark LB $37.07 (978-0-7614-0657-0). 144pp. An attractive, concise introduction to Kentucky that covers geography, history, government and economy, people, achievements, and landmarks. (Rev: HBG 10/99; SLJ 10/99) [976.9]

19539 Barrett, Tracy. *Virginia* (4–7). Illus. Series: Celebrate the States. 2005, Benchmark LB $37.07 (978-0-7614-1734-7). 142pp. A revised edition of this introduction to the state — including its history, culture, famous sites, and important Virginians — with updated illustrations. (Rev: SLJ 5/06) [975.5]

19540 Bjorklund, Ruth. *Louisiana* (3–5). Illus. Series: It's My State. 2006, Benchmark LB $27.07 (978-0-7614-1863-4). 80pp. Report writers will find all the facts they need on the history, geography, government, and economy of Louisiana — including information on the effects of Hurricane Katrina — plus a state-themed craft. (Rev: SLJ 6/06) [976.3]

19541 Bredeson, Carmen, and Mary Dodson Wade. *Texas* (5–8). Series: Celebrate the States. 2005, Benchmark LB $37.07 (978-0-7614-1736-1). 144pp. This revised edition updates facts and adds information on the government and economy plus new, full-color photographs. (Rev: SLJ 3/06) [976.4]

19542 Brown, Dottie. *Kentucky* (3–6). Illus. Series: Hello USA. 1992, Lerner LB $19.93 (978-0-8225-2715-2). 72pp. The visual beauty of the Bluegrass State is captured in text and pictures in this introductory volume. (Rev: BL 5/15/92; SLJ 7/92) [976.9]

19543 Chang, Perry. *Florida* (5–8). Series: Celebrate the States. 1998, Benchmark LB $37.07 (978-0-7614-0420-0). A fine introduction to the history, geography, people, landmarks, and government of Florida, with material on the cultural diversity of its people. (Rev: HBG 9/98; SLJ 1/99) [975.9]

19544 Cocke, William. *A Historical Album of Virginia* (4–8). Series: Historical Albums. 1995, Millbrook paper $6.95 (978-1-56294-856-6). A broad overview of Virginia's history, using many period prints and paintings, with equal space given to past and current events, and including general information on the state. (Rev: SLJ 1/96) [975.5]

19545 Coleman, Wim, and Pat Perrin. *Colonial Williamsburg* (5–8). Illus. Series: Virtual Field Trips. 2005, Enslow LB $25.26 (978-0-7660-5220-8). 48pp. A visit to Williamsburg, using both print and related Web sites, that covers its historical importance and its portrayal of colonial life. (Rev: SLJ 5/05)

19546 Cribben, Patrick. *Uniquely West Virginia* (4–7). Illus. Series: Heinemann State Studies. 2005, Heinemann LB $31.36 (978-1-4034-4665-7). 48pp. In addition to providing the facts necessary for report writers, this volume emphasizes the features that distinguish West Virginia from its neighbors. (Rev: BL 10/15/03)

19547 Fisher, Leonard Everett. *Monticello* (4–7). Illus. by author. 1988, Holiday $18.95 (978-0-8234-0688-3). 64pp. Touring the famous home of the third president. (Rev: BCCB 6/88; BL 6/1/88; SLJ 6–7/88) [973.46]

19548 Fradin, Dennis Brindell. *Georgia* (3–5). Illus. Series: From Sea to Shining Sea. 1991, Children's Book Pr. LB $27.00 (978-0-516-03810-0). 64pp. A simple, attractive look at geography, early history, and current status of this southern state. (Rev: BL 2/1/92) [975.8]

19549 Gaines, Ann Graham. *Kentucky* (4–7). Series: It's My State! 2003, Marshall Cavendish LB $27.07 (978-0-7614-1525-1). 80pp. Full-color photographs, trivia, and recipes and crafts are included along with the standard information required for reports. (Rev: BL 9/15/03; HBG 4/04; SLJ 9/03) [976.9]

19550 George, Jean Craighead. *Everglades* (2–4). Illus. by Wendell Minor. 1995, HarperCollins LB $16.89 (978-0-06-021229-2). 32pp. A storyteller explains to five children the origins and characteristics of the Everglades and the destruction that humans have caused to this ecosystem. (Rev: BCCB 7–8/95; BL 6/1–15/95; SLJ 6/95*) [975.9]

19551 Hamilton, John. *Everglades National Park* (4–6). Series: National Parks. 2005, ABDO LB $24.21 (978-1-59197-424-6). 32pp. Full-color photographs illustrate the information on the Everglades's history, ecosystem, geology, and wildlife, plus discussion of development of this area. Also use *Glacier National Park*, *Grand Canyon National Park*, and *Great Smoky Mountains National Park* (2005). (Rev: SLJ 6/05) [975.9]

19552 Haywood, Karen Diane. *Georgia* (3–5). Illus. Series: It's My State! 2006, Benchmark LB $27.07 (978-0-7614-1862-7). 79pp. Report writers will find all the facts they need in this book that comes complete with a state-themed craft. (Rev: SLJ 6/06) [975.8]

19553 Heinrichs, Ann. *Kentucky* (2–5). Illus. Series: This Land Is Your Land. 2003, Compass Point LB $25.26 (978-0-7565-0322-2). 48pp. Introduces readers to the geography, history, government, economy, and famous citizens of the Bluegrass State. (Rev: SLJ 8/03)

19554 Heinrichs, Ann. *Maryland* (2–5). Illus. Series: This Land Is Your Land. 2003, Compass Point LB $25.26 (978-0-7565-0348-2). 48pp. An attractive introduction to Maryland with plenty of photographs and accessible information for report writers. (Rev: SLJ 8/03) [975]

19555 Heinrichs, Ann. *Tennessee* (2–5). Illus. Series: This Land Is Your Land. 2003, Compass Point LB $25.26 (978-0-7565-0319-2). 48pp. This brightly illustrated profile explores Tennessee's history, people, geography, government, economy, and attractions. (Rev: SLJ 7/03) [976.8]

19556 Heinrichs, Ann. *Virginia* (2–4). Illus. Series: This Land Is Your Land. 2002, Compass Point LB $25.26 (978-0-7565-0310-9). 48pp. Simple text and good illustrations introduce the history, geography, culture, famous people, and attractions of Virginia. (Rev: SLJ 1/03)

19557 Heinrichs, Ann. *West Virginia* (3–5). Illus. by Matt Kania. 2005, The Child's World LB $27.07 (978-1-59296-490-1). 40pp. Using an attractive scrapbook format featuring a family on vacation, this volume introduces the state's geography, history, people, major attractions, and state symbols. (Rev: SLJ 2/06) [975.4]

19558 Herda, D. J. *Environmental America: The South Central States* (4–7). Illus. Series: American Scene. 1991, Millbrook LB $22.40 (978-1-878841-09-4). 64pp. This account discusses the general state of the environment and presents information on animal species, pollution, waste, and urban sprawl for 10 states, including Georgia, Kansas, Missouri, and Texas. (Rev: BL 8/91; SLJ 7/91) [639.9]

19559 Hess, Debra. *Florida* (4–7). Series: It's My State! 2003, Marshall Cavendish LB $27.07 (978-0-7614-1527-5). 80pp. Products, resources, plants and animals, and important background material are some of the topics covered in this general introduction to Florida. (Rev: BL 9/15/03; HBG 4/04; SLJ 9/03) [975.9]

19560 Higgins, Nadia. *Welcome to Everglades National Park* (3–5). 2006, The Child's World LB $27.07 (978-1-59296-702-5). 32pp. An attractively presented tour of the South Florida park, focusing on its geography, history, flora, fauna, and weather. (Rev: SLJ 2/07) [917.59]

19561 Hoffman, Nancy. *South Carolina* (4–8). Series: Celebrate the States. 2000, Marshall Cavendish LB $37.07 (978-0-7614-1065-2). 144pp. An interesting introduction to South Carolina, with material on its land and waterways, history, government, economy, landmarks, and success stories. (Rev: BL 12/15/00; HBG 3/01) [975.7]

19562 Johnston, Joyce. *Maryland* (3–6). Illus. Series: Hello USA. 1992, Lerner LB $19.93 (978-0-8225-2713-8). 72pp. In this overview on Maryland, there are chapters on history and geography, as well as social and economic conditions. (Rev: BL 5/15/92; SLJ 10/92) [975]

19563 LaDoux, Rita C. *Georgia* (3–6). Illus. Series: Hello USA. 1991, Lerner LB $19.93 (978-0-8225-2703-9). 72pp. Geography, economics, history, and the environment are some of the topics covered in this look at a southern state. (Rev: BL 4/15/91; SLJ 6/91) [975.8]

19564 La Doux, Rita C. *Louisiana*. Rev. ed. (3–5). Illus. Series: Hello U.S.A. 2001, Lerner LB $25.26 (978-0-8225-4065-6); paper $6.95 (978-0-8225-4145-5). 84pp. This revision of the 1993 edition features a more spacious layout and some expanded content. (Rev: SLJ 2/02) [976]

19565 Leese, Jennifer. *Uniquely Maryland* (4–7). Series: State Studies. 2004, Heinemann LB $27.07

(978-1-4034-4493-6). 48pp. History, industry, tourism, and culture are among the highlights of this survey of Maryland and its characteristics. (Rev: BL 4/1/04) [975.2]

19566 Levert, Suzanne. *Louisiana* (4–8). Illus. Series: Celebrate the States. 1997, Marshall Cavendish LB $37.07 (978-0-7614-0112-4). An interesting introduction that covers the standard material needed for reports. (Rev: BL 7/97; SLJ 7/97) [976.3]

19567 Lynch, Wayne. *The Everglades* (4–7). Illus. Series: Our Wild World. 2007, NorthWord $16.95 (978-1-55971-970-4); paper $8.95 (978-1-55971-971-1). 64pp. With eye-catching color photographs and conversational narrative, Lynch introduces the flora and fauna of the Everglades and highlights the threats to this ecosystem. (Rev: BL 9/1/07; SLJ 11/07) [508.759]

19568 MacAulay, Ellen. *Arkansas* (3–5). Illus. 2002, Children's Book Pr. LB $30.50 (978-0-516-22296-7). 80pp. This revision of an earlier title adds information and features that will enhance its appeal to report writers. (Rev: SLJ 1/03)

19569 McAuliffe, Emily. *Florida Facts and Symbols*. Rev. ed. (3–5). Illus. Series: The States and Their Symbols. 2003, Capstone LB $21.26 (978-0-7368-2239-8). 24pp. A brief, illustrated overview of facts about Florida such as the state's nickname, motto, flag, and other symbols. (Rev: SLJ 1/04) [975.9]

19570 McAuliffe, Emily. *Georgia Facts and Symbols*. Rev. ed. (3–5). Illus. Series: The States and Their Symbols. 2003, Capstone LB $21.26 (978-0-7368-2240-4). 24pp. A brief overview that will serve as a source of limited facts about the state. (Rev: SLJ 1/04) [975.8]

19571 McClellan, Adam, and Martin Wilson. *Uniquely North Carolina* (4–7). Series: Heinemann State Studies. 2004, Heinemann LB $27.07 (978-1-4034-4653-4). 48pp. In addition to providing the facts necessary for report writers, this volume emphasizes the features that distinguish North Carolina from its neighbors. (Rev: BL 4/1/04)

19572 Martin, Michael A. *Alabama: The Heart of Dixie* (4–7). Series: World Almanac Library of the States. 2002, World Almanac LB $31.00 (978-0-8368-5127-4). 48pp. Full-color photographs and graphic elements this informative introduction to the state. Also use *Virginia* (2002). (Rev: SLJ 2/03) [976.1]

19573 Odinoski, Steve. *Georgia* (4–8). Series: Celebrate the States. 2000, Marshall Cavendish LB $37.07 (978-0-7614-1062-1). 144pp. An informative, attractive introduction to Georgia with material on its land, history, people, social issues, and hidden treasures. (Rev: BL 12/15/00; HBG 3/01; SLJ 2/01) [975.8]

19574 Otfinoski, Steve. *Maryland* (3–6). Illus. Series: It's My State! 2002, Benchmark LB $27.07 (978-0-7614-1421-6). 80pp. The usual state information — geography, history, government, people, and economy — is presented in an appealing layout. (Rev: HBG 10/03; SLJ 2/03)

19575 Owens, Lisa. *Uniquely Missouri* (4–7). Series: Heinemann State Studies. 2004, Heinemann LB

$27.07 (978-1-4034-4495-0). 48pp. In addition to providing the facts necessary for report writers, this volume emphasizes the features that distinguish Missouri from its neighbors. (Rev: BL 4/1/04)

19576 Pobst, Sandy. *Virginia, 1607–1776* (5–8). Illus. Series: Voices from Colonial America. 2005, National Geographic LB $32.90 (978-0-7922-6771-3). 112pp. A thorough political and social history of early Virginia, with excellent illustrations. (Rev: BL 10/15/05; SLJ 11/05) [975.5]

19577 Rauth, Leslie. *Maryland* (5–9). Series: Celebrate the States. 1999, Benchmark LB $37.07 (978-0-7614-0671-6). 144pp. This book explores Maryland with material on topics including land and waterways, government, economy, festivals, and people. (Rev: BL 1/1–15/00; HBG 10/00; SLJ 5/00) [975.2]

19578 Raven, Margot Theis. *Let Them Play* (2–5). Illus. by Chris Ellison. 2005, Sleeping Bear $16.95 (978-1-58536-260-8). In this fact-based tale from the mid-1950s, an African American Little League team from Charleston, South Carolina, is snubbed by the state's white teams and by officials of the Little League World Series. (Rev: SLJ 11/05)

19579 Ready, Anna. *Mississippi* (3–6). Illus. Series: Hello USA. 1993, Lerner LB $19.93 (978-0-8225-2743-5). 72pp. Such topics as geography, culture, history, and economics are covered in this introduction. (Rev: BL 7/93) [976.2]

19580 Santella, Andrew. *Mount Vernon* (4–6). Series: We the People. 2004, Compass Point LB $26.60 (978-0-7565-0682-7). 48pp. A look at George Washington's home, with discussion of its role as a plantation and of the slaves who worked there. (Rev: SLJ 2/05) [973]

19581 Schaefer, Ted, and Lola M. Schaefer. *Arlington National Cemetery* (1–3). Series: Symbols of Freedom. 2005, Heinemann LB $25.36 (978-1-4034-6665-5). 32pp. The burial site for many Americans who served their country is introduced in simple text and archival and contemporary photographs; includes a "Fact File" and a timeline. (Rev: SLJ 12/05) [975.5]

19582 Schaefer, Ted, and Lola M. Schaefer. *The Pentagon* (1–3). Series: Symbols of Freedom. 2005, Heinemann LB $25.36 (978-1-4034-6663-1). 32pp. Large color photographs and clear text introduce the Pentagon's role as the headquarters of the U.S. Defense Department, also covering the terrorist attack of 2001; useful for basic research and reports. (Rev: SLJ 12/05) [355.6]

19583 Schulz, Andrea. *North Carolina* (3–6). Illus. Series: Hello USA. 1994, Lerner LB $19.93 (978-0-8225-2744-2). 72pp. A colorful introduction to North Carolina's history, geography, landmarks, and life-styles. (Rev: BL 2/1/94) [975.6]

19584 Sherrow, Victoria. *Uniquely South Carolina* (4–7). Illus. Series: Heinemann State Studies. 2005, Heinemann LB $31.36 (978-1-4034-4661-9). 48pp. In addition to providing the facts necessary for report writers, this volume emphasizes the features that distinguish South Carolina from its neighbors. (Rev: BL 10/15/03)

19585 Shirley, David. *Alabama* (4–8). Series: Celebrate the States. 2000, Marshall Cavendish LB $37.07 (978-0-7614-0648-8). 141pp. An introduction to Alabama that covers its land and waterways; its history, government, and economy; and its culture and success stories. (Rev: BL 6/1–15/00; HBG 10/00) [976.1]

19586 Shirley, David. *North Carolina* (4–8). Series: Celebrate the States. 2001, Benchmark LB $37.07 (978-0-7614-1072-0). 144pp. A fine introduction to the land, history, economy, and people of North Carolina. (Rev: BL 9/15/01; HBG 10/01) [975.6]

19587 Sirvaitis, Karen. *Florida* (3–5). Illus. Series: Hello USA. 1994, Lerner LB $19.93 (978-0-8225-2728-2). 72pp. With photos on every page, this compact book contains basic background information about Florida, including its history, famous sights, and important residents. (Rev: BL 4/15/94) [973]

19588 Sirvaitis, Karen. *Tennessee* (3–6). Illus. Series: Hello USA. 1991, Lerner LB $19.93 (978-0-8225-2711-4). 72pp. This book covers the geography, history, and socioeconomic conditions, along with timelines and biographies of famous residents. (Rev: BL 12/1/91) [976.8]

19589 Sirvaitis, Karen. *Virginia* (3–6). Illus. Series: Hello USA. 1991, Lerner LB $19.93 (978-0-8225-2702-2). 72pp. With full-color photos, this is a good, fact-filled introduction to Virginia. (Rev: BL 4/15/91; SLJ 6/91) [975.5]

19590 Smith, Karla. *Virginia* (4–6). Series: Heinemann State Studies. 2003, Heinemann LB $27.07 (978-1-4034-0361-2). 48pp. A useful overview of Virginia's geography, history, people, culture, and attractions. (Rev: HBG 4/04; SLJ 12/03) [975.5]

19591 Smith, Karla. *Virginia History* (4–6). 2003, Heinemann LB $27.07 (978-1-4034-0362-9). 48pp. A useful overview of the history of Virginia. (Rev: HBG 4/04; SLJ 12/03) [975.5]

19592 Stout, Mary. *Atlanta* (4–7). Illus. Series: Great Cities of the World. 2005, World Almanac LB $31.00 (978-0-8368-5042-0). 48pp. Report writers will find useful information on Atlanta's history, culture, lifestyle, and current problems. (Rev: BL 4/15/04)

19593 Valzania, Kimberly. *Tennessee* (K–2). Series: Rookie Read-About Geography. 2003, Children's Pr. LB $20.50 (978-0-516-22699-6); paper $5.95 (978-0-516-27843-8). 31pp. For beginning readers, this is a useful introduction to Tennessee, covering the Volunteer State's geography, people, industry, agriculture, and recreation. (Rev: SLJ 10/03) [917.68]

19594 Weatherford, Carole Boston. *Sink or Swim: African-American Lifesavers of the Outer Banks* (4–8). Illus. 1999, Coastal Carolina $15.95 (978-1-928556-01-5); paper $12.95 (978-1-928556-03-9). 80pp. A history of the African Americans who participated in lifesaving efforts on the Outer Banks of North Carolina, known as "the graveyard of the Atlantic." (Rev: BL 12/15/99) [363.28]

19595 Wills, Charles A. *A Historical Album of Alabama* (4–8). Series: Historical Albums. 1995, Millbrook LB $23.40 (978-1-56294-591-6); paper $6.95 (978-1-56294-854-2). Using many period prints and engravings, the author traces the history of Alabama from prehistoric days to today, including the impact of the shift away from cotton as a main crop, the civil rights movement, and the importance of football in the state. (Rev: BL 12/15/95; SLJ 1/96) [976.1]

19596 Wills, Charles A. *A Historical Album of Florida* (4–8). Illus. Series: Historical Albums. 1994, Millbrook LB $24.40 (978-1-56294-480-3). 64pp. This compressed history of Florida deals with major events from prehistory through the 1990s. (Rev: SLJ 2/95) [975.9]

19597 Wills, Charles A. *A Historical Album of Georgia* (4–7). Illus. Series: Historical Albums. 1996, Millbrook LB $24.40 (978-0-7613-0035-9). 64pp. With many period illustrations, some in color, and a simple text, the history and geography of Georgia are presented. (Rev: BL 12/15/96) [975.8]

19598 Wilson, Martin. *Uniquely Alabama* (4–7). Series: Heinemann State Studies. 2004, Heinemann LB $27.07 (978-1-4034-4485-1). 48pp. In addition to providing the facts necessary for report writers, this volume emphasizes the features that distinguish Alabama from its neighbors. (Rev: BL 4/1/04)

19599 Wilson, Martin. *Uniquely Mississippi* (4–7). Illus. Series: Heinemann State Studies. 2004, Heinemann LB $27.07 (978-1-4034-4656-5). 48pp. In addition to providing the facts necessary for report writers, this volume emphasizes the features that distinguish Mississippi from its neighbors. (Rev: BL 10/15/03)

19600 Yolen, Jane. *Welcome to the River of Grass* (PS–3). Illus. by Laura Regan. 2001, Penguin $16.99 (978-0-399-23221-3). 32pp. Yolen examines the animal and plant life of the Everglades — and the perils the area faces — in rhythmic text accompanied by excellent illustrations. (Rev: BCCB 2/02; BL 10/1/01; HBG 3/02; SLJ 11/01) [577.68]

19601 Young, Robert. *A Personal Tour of Monticello* (4–7). Illus. Series: How It Was. 1999, Lerner LB $30.35 (978-0-8225-3575-1). 64pp. Through the eyes of Jefferson, his daughter, and one of his slaves, the reader is introduced to the home of the third president of the United States. (Rev: BL 6/1–15/99; HBG 10/99; SLJ 7/99) [975.5]

SOUTHWEST

19602 Alter, Judy. *New Mexico* (4–7). Illus. Series: MyReportLinks.com. 2002, Enslow LB $25.26 (978-0-7660-5098-3). 48pp. An introduction to the government, geography, and history of the state, with helpful Web sites. (Rev: BL 2/1/03; SLJ 4/03; VOYA 4/03) [978.9]

19603 Aylesworth, Thomas G., and Virginia L. Aylesworth. *The Southwest: Colorado, New Mexico, Texas* (3–6). Illus. 1995, Chelsea LB $19.95 (978-0-7910-3412-5); paper $9.95 (978-0-7910-3430-9). 64pp. An easy-to-use study of three southwestern states. (Rev: BL 8/88; SLJ 11/88)

19604 Bauer, Marion Dane. *The Grand Canyon* (K–2). Illus. by John Wallace. Series: Ready-to-

Read Wonders of America. 2006, Simon & Schuster LB $11.89 (978-0-689-86947-1); paper $3.99 (978-0-689-86946-4). 32pp. How the Grand Canyon was formed, and what it's like to visit it, in a format for beginning readers with cartoon-like illustrations. (Rev: SLJ 7/06) [917.91]

19605 Bjorklund, Ruth. *New Mexico* (4–7). Series: It's My State! 2003, Marshall Cavendish LB $27.07 (978-0-7614-1526-8). 80pp. Actual quotations from both famous and unknown residents of New Mexico are used to introduce this state, its people, history, wildlife, and resources. (Rev: BL 9/15/03; HBG 4/04) [978.9]

19606 Bredeson, Carmen. *The Spindletop Gusher: The Story of the Texas Oil Boom* (4–7). Illus. Series: Spotlight on American History. 1996, Millbrook LB $24.90 (978-1-56294-916-7). 64pp. A discussion of the Texas oil boom, its effects on the state and its economy, and the present status of the oil industry. (Rev: BL 3/15/96) [338.4]

19607 Corrick, James. *Uniquely Arizona* (4–7). Series: Heinemann State Studies. 2004, Heinemann LB $27.07 (978-1-4034-4486-8); paper $8.50 (978-1-4304-4501-2). 48pp. In addition to providing the facts necessary for report writers, this volume emphasizes the features that distinguish Arizona from its neighbors. (Rev: BL 4/1/04)

19608 Early, Theresa S. *New Mexico* (3–6). Illus. Series: Hello USA. 1993, Lerner LB $19.93 (978-0-8225-2748-0). 72pp. An introduction to New Mexico that includes geography, history, and social and economic conditions. (Rev: BL 7/93; SLJ 8/93) [978.9]

19609 Foster, Lynne. *Exploring the Grand Canyon: Adventures of Yesterday and Today* (3–6). Illus. by Margaret Sanfilippo. 1990, Grand Canyon Natural History Assn. paper $15.95 (978-0-938216-33-9). 150pp. This work gives a history of the Grand Canyon, the kinds of people who have been involved with it, and tips for the first-time visitor. (Rev: BL 9/1/90) [917]

19610 Garza, Carmen Lomas, and Harriet Rohmer. *Magic Windows: Ventanas Magicas* (3–7). Illus. 1999, Children's Book Pr. $15.95 (978-0-89239-157-8). 32pp. This bilingual book introduces Mexican American culture and lifestyle through an examination of *papel picado* (cut-paper art). Also see *Making Magic Windows*. (Rev: BL 5/1/99; HBG 10/99; SLJ 7/99) [745.54]

19611 Gibson, Karen Bush. *Oklahoma Facts and Symbols*. Rev. ed. (3–5). Illus. Series: The States and Their Symbols. 2003, Capstone LB $21.26 (978-0-7368-2266-4). 24pp. A brief overview that will serve as a source of limited facts about the state. (Rev: SLJ 1/04) [976.6]

19612 Hanson-Harding, Alexandra. *Texas* (4–6). Illus. Series: From Sea to Shining Sea. 2001, Children's Book Pr. LB $30.50 (978-0-516-22322-3). 80pp. A good resource for report writing, this book features historical facts, maps, and information about the governmental structure and the people of Texas. (Rev: BL 3/15/02) [976.4]

19613 Heinrichs, Ann. *Oklahoma* (2–5). Illus. Series: This Land Is Your Land. 2003, Compass Point LB $25.26 (978-0-7565-0330-7). 48pp. This brightly illustrated profile explores Oklahoma's history, people, geography, government, economy, and attractions. (Rev: SLJ 7/03) [976.6]

19614 Heinrichs, Ann. *Texas* (2–4). Illus. Series: This Land Is Your Land. 2002, Compass Point LB $25.26 (978-0-7565-0312-3). 48pp. Simple text with age-appropriate language and good illustrations introduce the history, geography, culture, famous people, and attractions of Texas. (Rev: SLJ 1/03)

19615 Herda, D. J. *Environmental America: The Southwestern States* (4–7). Illus. Series: American Scene. 1991, Millbrook LB $22.40 (978-1-878841-11-7). 64pp. This account, which discusses the state of the environment and how it can be changed for the better, covers Arizona, California, Colorado, Nevada, New Mexico, and Utah. (Rev: BL 8/91; SLJ 7/91) [639.9]

19616 Hicks, Terry Allan. *Nevada* (3–5). Illus. Series: It's My State! 2006, Benchmark LB $27.07 (978-0-7614-1860-3). 80pp. Report writers will find all the facts they need in this book that comes complete with a state-themed craft. (Rev: SLJ 6/06) [979.3]

19617 Lourie, Peter. *The Lost World of the Anasazi: Exploring the Mysteries of Chaco Canyon* (5–8). Illus. 2003, Boyds Mills $19.95 (978-1-56397-972-9). 48pp. With many full-color photographs, the author describes his trip to the ruins of Chaco Canyon and discusses the mysterious disappearance of its Anasazi residents. (Rev: BL 9/1/03; HBG 4/04; SLJ 1/04) [978.9]

19618 McDaniel, Melissa. *Arizona* (4–8). Series: Celebrate the States. 2000, Marshall Cavendish LB $37.07 (978-0-7614-0647-1). 139pp. This introduction to Arizona discusses its land, history, economy, festivals, cultural diversity, and landmarks. (Rev: BL 6/1–15/00; HBG 10/00; SLJ 9/00) [979.1]

19619 Meister, Cari. *Grand Canyon* (2–4). Series: Going Places. 2000, ABDO LB $21.35 (978-1-57765-024-9). 24pp. This well-organized introduction to the Grand Canyon describes the geological formations and supplies material on the plants, animals, and interesting sights in the area. (Rev: HBG 10/00; SLJ 1/01) [917.91]

19620 Melmed, Laura K. *Heart of Texas: A Lone Star ABC* (2–4). Illus. by Frane Lessac. 2009, Harper-Collins $17.99 (978-0-06-114283-3). 48pp. An alphabetical tour of the history, landmarks, and people of Texas. (Rev: BL 5/1/09; SLJ 4/09) [976.4]

19621 Minor, Wendell. *Grand Canyon: Exploring a Natural Wonder* (4–8). Illus. 1998, Scholastic paper $16.95 (978-0-590-47968-4). In watercolors and lyrical text, the author presents a grand portrait of the Grand Canyon. (Rev: BL 9/15/98; HBG 3/99; SLJ 8/98) [978.8]

19622 Munro, Roxie. *The Inside-Outside Book of Texas* (K–3). Illus. Series: Inside-Outside. 2001, North-South LB $16.88 (978-1-58717-051-5). 48pp. Some of the most famous places and landmarks in Texas are pictured in this attractive book with a minimum of text. (Rev: BL 4/1/01; HB 5/01; HBG 10/01; SLJ 6/01) [976.4]

19623 Pelta, Kathy. *Texas*. Rev. ed. (3–5). Illus. Series: Hello U.S.A. 2001, Lerner LB $25.26 (978-0-8225-4064-9); paper $6.95 (978-0-8225-4142-4). 84pp. This revision of a 1993 edition features a more spacious layout and some expanded content. (Rev: HBG 3/02; SLJ 2/02) [976.4]

19624 Powell, John Wesley. *Conquering the Grand Canyon* (3–6). Series: In My Own Words. 2000, Marshall Cavendish LB $24.21 (978-0-7614-1013-3). 64pp. These excerpts from the writings of John Wesley Powell describe how he felt as the first white man to view the natural wonders of the Grand Canyon. (Rev: BL 3/1/01; HBG 3/01) [978]

19625 Tweit, Susan J. *Meet the Wild Southwest: Land of Hoodoos and Gila Monsters* (4–8). Illus. 1996, Alaska Northwest paper $14.95 (978-0-88240-468-4). 124pp. An impressive collection of facts and curiosities about the natural history of the Southwest, with many appendixes that supply more-traditional information. (Rev: BL 3/1/96) [508.79]

19626 Weintraub, Aileen. *The Grand Canyon: The Widest Canyon* (3–5). Illus. Series: Great Record Breakers in Nature. 2001, Rosen $21.25 (978-0-8239-5641-8). 24pp. Jam-packed with facts, this book takes readers on a word and photo tour of the formation, history, and appeal of one of the world's natural wonders. (Rev: BL 12/15/01; SLJ 7/01) [979.1]

19627 Wills, Charles A. *A Historical Album of Texas* (4–7). Illus. Series: Historical Albums. 1995, Millbrook LB $24.40 (978-1-56294-504-6). 64pp. This account of the history of Texas from earliest times to today is also particularly noteworthy for its many illustrations. (Rev: SLJ 6/95) [976.4]

Social Institutions and Issues

Business and Economics

General

19628 Aaseng, Nathan. *Business Builders in Sweets and Treats* (5–8). Illus. Series: Business Builders. 2005, Oliver LB $24.95 (978-1-881508-84-7). 160pp. This attractive title examines food companies that succeed through satisfying America's sweet tooth. (Rev: BL 12/1/05; HBG 4/06) [338.7]

19629 Adams, Barbara J. *The Go-Around Dollar* (2–4). Illus. by Joyce A. Zarins. 1992, Macmillan LB $16.00 (978-0-02-700031-3). 32pp. The dollar is introduced within the framework of a story and the look of a picture book. (Rev: BCCB 2/92; BL 2/15/92; SLJ 5/92) [332.4]

19630 Adler, David A. *Money Madness* (PS–3). Illus. by Edward Miller. 2009, Holiday $16.95 (978-0-8234-1474-1). 32pp. A picture-book introduction to money with a look at bartering and early forms of money such as rocks and feathers as well as today's coins, bills, and checks; features bright artwork and an interesting page showing foreign money. (Rev: BCCB 3/09; BL 1/1–15/09; HB 5/09; SLJ 5/09) [332.4]

19631 Allman, Barbara. *Banking* (4–6). Illus. Series: How Economics Works. 2005, Lerner LB $25.26 (978-0-8225-2148-8). 48pp. An excellent overview of the banking system with cartoons and bright illustrations and sidebars; checking and savings accounts are among the topics covered and a glossary defines common banking terms. (Rev: BL 10/15/05) [332.1]

19632 Berger, Melvin, and Gilda Berger. *Round and Round the Money Goes: What Money Is and How We Use It* (1–3). Illus. by Jane McCreary. Series: Discovery Readers. 1993, Ideals paper $4.50 (978-0-8249-8598-1). 48pp. Many topics about money are briefly introduced in this beginner's account, including the forms money takes, why it is necessary, world monetary units, and how banks work. (Rev: SLJ 12/93) [332]

19633 Burns, Peggy. *Money* (3–5). Illus. Series: Stepping Through History. 1995, Thomson Learning LB $5.00 (978-1-56847-248-5). 32pp. As well as a history of coins and paper money, this account tells of the development of banks, credit cards, and foreign exchange. (Rev: BL 4/15/95; SLJ 6/95) [332.4]

19634 Caes, Charles J. *The Young Zillionaire's Guide to the Stock Market* (5–8). Series: Be a Zillionaire. 2000, Rosen LB $26.50 (978-0-8239-3265-8). 48pp. Basic information on the inner workings of the stock market is presented with many examples from the corporate world. (Rev: HBG 10/01; SLJ 3/01) [332.6]

19635 Condon, Daniel. *Playing the Market: Stocks and Bonds* (3–5). Series: Everyday Economics. 2004, Heinemann LB $27.07 (978-1-58810-495-3). 48pp. Condon discusses savings and investment, stocks and bonds, interest rates, and the role of the government and the Federal Reserve. (Rev: SLJ 6/04) [332.63]

19636 Cooper, Jason. *Around the World with Money* (2–4). Series: Money Power. 2002, Rourke LB $14.95 (978-1-58952-212-1). 24pp. This brief, small-format overview introduces the currencies of Canada, Mexico, the United States, and Europe. Also use *Money Through the Ages* (2002), which looks at the history of money. (Rev: SLJ 4/03) [332.4]

19637 Craats, Rennay. *Economy* (4–6). Illus. Series: USA Past, Present, Future. 2008, Weigl $29.05 (978-1-59036-980-7); paper $10.95 (978-1-59036-981-4). 48pp. Although published before the current downturn, this volume — which examines the U.S. economy by decades from 1900 to the early 2000s provides good background material, profiles of key figures, and a running timeline. (Rev: BL 5/15/09; LMC 5/09) [330.973]

19638 Craats, Rennay. *Fashion* (4–6). Illus. Series: USA Past, Present, Future. 2008, Weigl $29.05 (978-1-59036-972-2); paper $10.95 (978-1-59036-973-9). 48pp. A decade-by-decade look at a century of women's fashions, demonstrating the cyclical nature of the industry; includes profiles of key figures, and a running timeline. Also use *Trends* (2008). (Rev: BL 5/15/09; LMC 5/09) [391.00973]

19639 Downing, David. *Capitalism* (5–8). Series: Political and Economic Systems. 2002, Heinemann LB $28.50 (978-1-4034-0315-5). 64pp. In an attractive format, this book explains the capitalistic economic system, its history, key thinkers, and present status. (Rev: BL 1/1–15/03; HBG 3/03; SLJ 2/03) [330.12]

19640 Downing, David. *Communism* (5–8). Series: Political and Economic Systems. 2002, Heinemann LB $28.50 (978-1-4034-0316-2). 64pp. The theoretical basis of communism is explained with material on its application, history, important thinkers and leaders, and different movements. (Rev: BL 1/1–15/03; HBG 3/03; SLJ 2/03) [335.43]

19641 Drobot, Eve. *Money, Money, Money: Where It Comes From, How to Save It, Spend It, and Make It* (4–6). Illus. by Claudia Dávila. 2004, Maple Tree $19.95 (978-1-897066-10-2); paper $12.95 (978-1-897066-11-9). 96pp. Useful both for browsing and research, this accessible volume covers such fundamentals as the history of currency, banks and savings, credit cards, the stock market, and identity theft. (Rev: BL 1/1–15/05; SLJ 1/05) [332.4]

19642 Firestone, Mary. *Earning Money* (K–3). Illus. Series: Learning About Money. 2004, Capstone LB $21.26 (978-0-7368-2639-6). 24pp. A simple introduction to the reasons why people want to earn money and how prices of goods are established. Also use *Saving Money* and *Spending Money* (both 2004). (Rev: BL 10/15/04) [650.1]

19643 Firestone, Mary. *What Is Money?* (K–3). Series: Learning About Money. 2004, Capstone LB $21.26 (978-0-7368-2642-6). 24pp. Informative and attractive, this volume explains the basics of currency in clear text and covers such topics as bartering and the minting of new money. Also use *Earning Money* (2004), which explores ways of acquiring money and its relative worth. (Rev: BL 10/15/04) [332.4]

19644 Giesecke, Ernestine. *Your Money at Work: Taxes* (3–5). Series: Everyday Economics. 2004, Heinemann LB $27.07 (978-1-58810-494-6). 48pp. Introduces the principle of taxation, why it's necessary, different forms of taxation, and how the money collected is spent. (Rev: SLJ 6/04) [336.73]

19645 Graydon, Shari. *Made You Look: How Advertising Works and Why You Should Know* (5–9). Illus. by Warren Clark. 2003, Annick $24.95 (978-1-55037-815-3); paper $14.95 (978-1-55037-814-6). 120pp. The 8- to 14-year-old age group is an advertising target, and this title teaches readers to recognize the various techniques used and to assess products' value. (Rev: BL 12/1/03*; SLJ 12/03) [659.1]

19646 Green, Meg. *The Young Zillionaire's Guide to Investments and Savings* (5–8). Series: Be a Zillionaire. 2000, Rosen LB $23.95 (978-0-8239-3261-0). 48pp. A guide to the investment markets and methods of saving with good use of examples and case studies. (Rev: HBG 10/01; SLJ 3/01) [338.5]

19647 Hall, Margaret. *Credit Cards and Checks*. 2nd ed. (1–3). Series: Earning, Saving, Spending. 2007, Heinemann LB $28.21 (978-1-4034-9816-8). 32pp. An updated introduction to how we use checks, debit cards, and credit cards, with advice on using credit wisely. Also use *Banks* and *Money* (both 2007). (Rev: LMC 5/08; SLJ 12/07) [332.76]

19648 Hall, Margaret. *Money* (3–5). Illus. Series: Earning, Saving, Spending. 2000, Heinemann $14.95 (978-1-57572-233-7). 32pp. This history of coins and paper money also discusses their value and uses and how people earn and spend money. (Rev: BL 10/15/00) [332.4]

19649 Harman, Hollis Page. *Money $ense for Kids!* 2nd ed. (4–7). Illus. 2004, Barron's paper $14.99 (978-0-7641-2894-3). 180pp. Explains the basics of money and currency and of earning, saving, and investing, with exercises at the end of each chapter and a "Money Games" section. (Rev: SLJ 11/04) [332.024]

19650 Kummer, Patricia K. *Currency* (4–8). Series: Inventions That Shaped the World. 2004, Watts LB $30.50 (978-0-531-12341-6). 80pp. After looking at the nature of currency, this title discusses modern forms and the role of currency in our lives. (Rev: SLJ 2/05) [332.4]

19651 Loewen, Nancy. *Cash, Credit Cards, or Checks: A Book About Payment Methods* (3–5). Illus. by Brad Fitzpatrick. Series: Money Matters. 2005, Picture Window LB $25.26 (978-1-4048-0951-2). 24pp. Shopping for school necessities forms the backdrop for information on money and banking. Also use *Save, Spend, or Donate?* (2005). (Rev: SLJ 9/05) [332.4]

19652 McGowan, Eileen Nixon, and Nancy Lagow Dumas. *Stock Market Smart* (5–8). Illus. 2002, Millbrook LB $23.90 (978-0-7613-2113-2). 64pp. An accessible question-and-answer presentation on the stock market and different types of investors, with illustrations, tips on saving, activities, a glossary, and list of resources. (Rev: BL 9/1/02; HBG 3/03; SLJ 10/02) [332.63]

19653 McKissack, Patricia C., and Fredrick McKissack. *A Long Hard Journey* (5–9). Illus. 1989, Walker LB $18.85 (978-0-8027-6885-8). A 150-year saga of the organization of porters into the first black American union, the Brotherhood of Sleeping Car Porters. (Rev: BL 9/15/89; SLJ 1/90; VOYA 12/89) [331]

19654 Maestro, Betsy. *The Story of Money* (2–4). Illus. by Giulio Maestro. 1993, Houghton $17.00 (978-0-395-56242-0). 48pp. The story of the ancient Sumerians who invented the idea of making money. (Rev: BCCB 3/93; BL 3/1/93; SLJ 4/93) [332.4]

19655 Rau, Dana Meachen. *What Is a Bank?* (2–4). Illus. Series: Money and Banks. 2005, Weekly Reader LB $21.00 (978-0-8368-4873-1). 24pp. An inside (small-format) look at how a bank operates, covering checking and savings accounts, safe-deposit boxes, ATMs, and money lending. (Rev: BL 10/15/05) [332.1]

19656 Seidman, David. *The Young Zillionaire's Guide to Supply and Demand* (5–7). Series: Be a

Zillionaire. 2000, Rosen LB $26.50 (978-0-8239-3264-1). 48pp. The basic principles of supply and demand are explained, with information on how they are influenced by producers and consumers and how they help create economic conditions. (Rev: SLJ 2/01) [330]

19657 *Sold! The Origins of Money and Trade* (5–8). Series: Buried Worlds. 1994, Runestone LB $28.75 (978-0-8225-3206-4). Explains the world origins of commerce and money, with coverage of how the earliest coins were made in the West and how other cultures developed unique forms of currency. (Rev: BL 9/15/94; SLJ 9/94) [737.4]

19658 Thomas, Keltie. *The Kids Guide to Money Cent$* (4–7). Illus. by Stephen MacEachern. 2004, Kids Can $14.95 (978-1-55337-389-6); paper $7.95 (978-1-55337-390-2). 56pp. Readers follow three children — the Money Cent$ Gang — who join together to investigate the ins and outs of banking, credit, investment, and money making; quizzes and examples make the content clear and comic-strip scenes add appeal. (Rev: SLJ 7/04) [332.02]

19659 Wilson, Antoine. *The Young Zillionaire's Guide to Distributing Goods and Services* (5–7). Series: Be a Zillionaire. 2000, Rosen LB $26.50 (978-0-8239-3259-7). 48pp. This book explains how goods and services are distributed, the importance of retailing and wholesaling, how transportation affects prices and availability, and how the Internet might change these conditions. (Rev: SLJ 2/01) [330]

19660 Young, Robert. *Money* (3–6). Illus. Series: Household History. 1998, Carolrhoda LB $16.95 (978-1-57505-070-6). 48pp. A breezy account of the history of money in its various forms, including counterfeiting, credit, and even some magic tricks with coins and bills. (Rev: BL 9/1/98; HBG 9/98; SLJ 7/98) [332.4]

Consumerism

19661 Burns, Peggy. *Stores and Markets* (3–5). Illus. Series: Stepping Through History. 1995, Thomson Learning LB $5.00 (978-1-56847-344-4). 32pp. A history of the distribution of goods from ancient markets and bazaars to today's shopping malls. (Rev: BL 7/95) [381]

19662 Lewin, Ted. *How Much? Visiting Markets Around the World* (K–2). Illus. 2006, HarperCollins $16.99 (978-0-688-17552-8). 40pp. A large-format photographic tour of marketplaces on four continents, with text that enhances the images and offers the phrase "How much" in various languages. (Rev: BL 2/1/06; SLJ 1/06) [381]

19663 Mayer, Cassie. *Markets* (PS–2). Illus. Series: Our Global Community. 2007, Heinemann LB $14.50 (978-1-4034-9404-7). 24pp. Simple, short text and photographs on each page make this a useful easy-reader introduction to markets around the world. (Rev: BL 7/07) [381]

19664 Miller, Marilyn. *Behind the Scenes at the Shopping Mall* (PS–3). Illus. Series: Behind the Scenes. 1996, Raintree LB $21.40 (978-0-8172-4088-2). 32pp. Using many leading questions and cartoon–style illustrations, this book provides an inside look at the activities that make a shopping mall work. (Rev: BL 4/15/96; SLJ 12/96) [381]

19665 Yardley, Thompson. *Buy Now, Pay Later: Smart Shopping Counts* (2–3). Illus. by author. Series: Lighter Look. 1992, Millbrook LB $20.90 (978-1-56294-149-9). 39pp. In an entertaining format, facts about smart shopping and recycling are given. (Rev: SLJ 6/92) [640.73]

Money-Making Ideas and Budgeting

19666 Barkin, Carol, and Elizabeth James. *The New Complete Babysitter's Handbook* (5–7). Illus. 1995, Clarion paper $7.95 (978-0-395-66558-9). 164pp. A fine manual that covers such topics as first aid, ways to amuse children, and how to get jobs baby sitting. (Rev: BL 5/1/95; SLJ 6/95) [649.1]

19667 Bernstein, Daryl. *Better Than a Lemonade Stand! Small Business Ideas for Kids* (5–8). Illus. 1992, Beyond Words paper $9.95 (978-0-941831-75-8). The author, a 15-year-old entrepreneur, provides ideas for starting 51 different small businesses and offers advice on start-up costs, billing, and customer relations. (Rev: BL 10/1/92; SLJ 1/93) [650.1]

19668 Buckley, Annie. *Be a Better Babysitter* (5–6). Series: Girls Rock! 2006, The Child's World LB $25.64 (978-1-59296-740-7). 32pp. This introductory guide to baby-sitting explains the nature of the job, looks at its pros and cons and safety issues, and offers advice on doing a good job. (Rev: SLJ 2/07) [649]

19669 Byers, Patricia, and Julia Preston. *The Kids' Money Book* (2–6). Illus. 1983, Liberty paper $4.95 (978-0-89709-041-4). A number of ways kids can make money.

19670 Drew, Bonnie, and Noel Drew. *Fast Cash for Kids* (4–7). Illus. 1995, Career Pr. paper $13.99 (978-1-56414-154-5). 168pp. The authors present a variety of possible ways to make money. (Rev: BL 6/15/87) [658.041]

19671 Hall, Margaret. *Your Allowance* (3–5). Illus. Series: Earning, Saving, Spending. 2000, Heinemann $21.36 (978-1-57572-234-4). 32pp. This book looks seriously at budgeting one's allowance, at good consumer practices, savings accounts, and gifts to charity. (Rev: BL 10/15/00) [332.024]

19672 Halperin, Wendy A. *Once upon a Company: A True Story* (1–5). Illus. 1998, Orchard LB $17.99 (978-0-531-33089-0). 40pp. A winningly illustrated picture book about the three Halperin children who raised money for their college fund by creating and selling Christmas wreaths and, in the summer, opening a food stand. (Rev: BCCB 9/98; BL 9/1/98*; HBG 3/99; SLJ 9/98) [658]

19673 Holyoke, Nancy. *A Smart Girl's Guide to Money: How to Make It, Save It, and Spend It* (4–7). Illus. by Ali Douglass. Series: A Smart Girl's Guide. 2006, Pleasant paper $9.95 (978-1-59369-103-5). 94pp. Shopping and investing are only two of the topics covered in this user-friendly guide. (Rev: BL 5/15/06; SLJ 5/06) [332.024]

19674 Loewen, Nancy. *Lemons and Lemonade: A Book About Supply and Demand* (3–5). Illus. by Brian Jensen. Series: Money Matters. 2005, Picture Window LB $25.26 (978-1-4048-0956-7). 24pp. Karly learns about managing a small business — and about the principle of supply and demand — in this humorous entry in the series. (Rev: SLJ 9/05) [338.5]

19675 Nathan, Amy. *The Kids' Allowance Book* (4–7). Illus. 1998, Walker $15.95 (978-0-8027-8651-7). 96pp. Children ages 9 to 14 present the pros and cons of allowances and money management. (Rev: BCCB 6/98; BL 7/98; HBG 10/98; SLJ 10/98) [332.02]

19676 Otfinoski, Steven. *The Kid's Guide to Money: Earning It, Saving It, Spending It, Growing It, Sharing It* (4–8). Illus. 1996, Scholastic paper $4.95 (978-0-590-53853-4). This practical guide for kids on how to earn money and manage it responsibly includes budgeting, standard consumer advice, basic information about the stock market, credit cards, and sharing. (Rev: BL 4/1/96; SLJ 6/96; VOYA 6/96) [332.4]

19677 Weintraub, Aileen. *Everything You Need to Know About Being a Baby-Sitter: A Teen's Guide to Responsible Child Care* (5–8). 2000, Rosen LB $25.25 (978-0-8239-3085-2). 64pp. This book covers all facets of baby-sitting from preparation, responsibilities, and safety precautions to employment opportunities. (Rev: SLJ 7/00) [649]

19678 Willson, Sarah. *Pet Peeves* (1–3). Illus. by John Nez. Series: Social Studies Connects. 2005, Kane paper $4.99 (978-1-57565-149-1). 32pp. Children work together to become entrepreneurs in this story designed to support social studies. (Rev: SLJ 9/05)

19679 Zakarin, Debra M. *The Ultimate Baby-Sitter's Handbook: So You Wanna Make Tons of Money?* (4–8). Illus. 1997, Price Stern Sloan paper $4.99 (978-0-8431-7936-1). A practical, easily read guide to baby-sitting and setting up a business. (Rev: BL 9/15/97; SLJ 12/97) [649]

Retail Stores and Other Workplaces

19680 Krull, Kathleen. *Supermarket* (K–3). Illus. by Melanie Hope Greenberg. 2001, Holiday House $16.95 (978-0-8234-1546-5). 32pp. This is a fascinating and stimulating overview of what you'll find in the supermarket and how it gets there, including material on the history of shopping from barter onward and lots of interesting tidbits. (Rev: BL 9/15/01; HBG 3/02; SLJ 10/01) [381]

Ecology and Environment

General

19681 Ansary, Mir T. *Earth Day* (2–3). Illus. Series: Holiday Histories. 2002, Heinemann LB $21.36 (978-1-58810-220-1). 32pp. The author traces the history of the Earth and its natural resources, man's misappropriation of them, and the founding of Earth Day. (Rev: BL 2/1/02) [333.7]

19682 Ballard, Carol. *The Search for Better Conservation* (4–7). Illus. Series: Science Quest. 2005, Gareth Stevens LB $26.00 (978-0-8368-4553-2). 32pp. A look at how lack of conservation affects us, and what scientists are doing to tackle this problem. (Rev: BL 4/1/05)

19683 Barraclough, Sue. *Respecting Our World* (1–3). Series: Making a Difference. 2008, Sea-to-Sea LB $27.10 (978-1-59771-111-1). 32pp. Clearly written information about saving water and energy and the importance of respecting nature is accompanied by facts, hints, suggestions, and photographs. (Rev: SLJ 9/08) [333.72]

19684 Boothroyd, Jennifer. *People and the Environment* (K–2). Illus. 2008, Lerner LB $18.60 (978-0-8225-8601-2). 24pp. A brief, simple look at how people, animals, and plants interact with each other — for good and for bad. (Rev: BL 2/15/08; LMC 3/08; SLJ 3/08) [304.2]

19685 Bowden, Rob. *Water Supply: Our Impact on the Planet* (5–8). Illus. Series: 21st Century Debates. 2003, Raintree LB $28.56 (978-0-7398-5506-5). 64pp. A thought-provoking examination of the status of the world's water supply, predictions of a looming water crisis, and measures that could be taken to avert this. (Rev: BL 8/03; HBG 10/03) [363.6]

19686 Burnie, David. *Endangered Planet* (4–8). Illus. Series: Kingfisher Knowledge. 2004, Kingfisher $11.95 (978-0-7534-5776-4). 63pp. This volume looks at how human requirements threaten the flora, fauna, and resources of our planet. (Rev: BL 9/1/04; SLJ 1/05) [333.95]

19687 Chandler, Gary, and Kevin Graham. *Environmental Causes* (5–10). Series: Celebrity Activists. 1997, Twenty-First Century LB $25.90 (978-0-8050-5232-9). This book discusses how entertainers including Robert Redford, Sting, and Chevy Chase and other celebrities such as Al Gore, Ted Turner, and Jerry Greenfield support environmental causes. (Rev: SLJ 1/98) [363.7]

19688 Cherry, Lynne. *How We Know What We Know About Our Changing Climate: Scientists and Kids Explore Global Warming* (4–7). Illus. by Gary Braasch. 2008, Dawn $17.95 (978-1-58469-103-7). 66pp. Children are called to be "citizen scientists" as they learn about the scientific evidence for global warming and are armed with specific strategies to help turn things around. (Rev: BL 2/15/08; SLJ 6/08) [551.6]

19689 Coley, Mary McIntyre. *Environmentalism: How You Can Make a Difference* (4–7). Series: Take Action. 2009, Capstone LB $25.32 (978-1-4296-2797-9). 32pp. This title provides directions for correctly researching an environmental problem, making a plan, and dealing with the rejection that sometimes accompanies speaking out. (Rev: SLJ 5/09) [333.72]

19690 Dalgleish, Sharon. *Protecting Wildlife* (4–6). Illus. Series: Our World: Our Future. 2002, Chelsea LB $28.00 (978-0-7910-7021-5). 32pp. The role of humans is emphasized in this look at the impact on wildlife of vanishing habitats and changes in the weather, and simple actions that children can take are suggested. Also use *Saving Our Water* (2002). (Rev: HBG 3/03; SLJ 1/03)

19691 David, Laurie, and Cambria Gordon. *The Down-to-Earth Guide to Global Warming* (4–7). Illus. 2007, Scholastic paper $15.99 (978-0-439-02494-5). 128pp. The authors balance alarming information on climate change and its impact with practical ways in which readers can reduce their carbon footprint and details of new technologies that may help. (Rev: BL 9/15/07; SLJ 11/07) [363.738]

19692 Delano, Marfé Ferguson. *Earth in the Hot Seat: Bulletins from a Warming World* (4–6). Illus. 2009, National Geographic $16.95 (978-1-4263-0434-7). 64pp. A clear look at the subject of global warming, with information on the signs we are already seeing and the future consequences of inaction. (Rev: HB 7/09; SLJ 7/09) [363.738]

19693 Ditchfield, Christin. *Oil* (2–5). Illus. Series: True Books — Natural Resources. 2002, Children's Book Pr. LB $25.00 (978-0-516-22343-8); paper $6.95 (978-0-516-29367-7). 48pp. This book discusses oil, its procurement and processing, and the environmental impact of using oil as fuel, with simple text and excellent photographs. (Rev: BL 10/15/02) [553.2]

19694 Ditchfield, Christin. *Water* (2–5). Illus. Series: True Books — Natural Resources. 2002, Children's Book Pr. LB $25.00 (978-0-516-22345-2). 48pp. Ditchfield discusses water as a natural resource, covering in simple text and excellent photographs the forms of water, the water cycle, and the ways in which we use water. (Rev: BL 10/15/02) [553.7]

19695 Gorman, Jacqueline Laks. *Fossil Fuels* (5–8). Series: What If We Do Nothing? 2009, Gareth Stevens LB $31.00 (978-1-4339-0087-7). 48pp. A look at fossil fuels, how we use them, how they affect the climate, and the future of these fuels. (Rev: SLJ 6/09; VOYA 10/09) [333.8]

19696 Herzog, Brad. *S Is for Save the Planet: A How-to-Be-Green Alphabet* (2–4). Illus. by Linda Holt Ayriss. 2009, Sleeping Bear $17.95 (978-1-58536-428-2). 40pp. Simple eight-line poems deal with environmental topics from A to Z ("zero carbon footprint"), with informative sidebars. (Rev: BL 4/15/09; SLJ 5/09) [333.72]

19697 Hill, Lee S. *Parks Are to Share* (1–3). Series: Building Blocks Books. 1997, Carolrhoda $21.27 (978-1-57505-068-3). 32pp. This book explores all kinds of parks and their care and uses, from Yosemite National Park to Central Park in New York City. (Rev: BL 3/15/98; HBG 3/98) [363.6]

19698 Holmes, Anita. *I Can Save the Earth: A Kid's Handbook for Keeping Earth Healthy and Green* (4–6). Illus. by David Neuhaus. 1993, Simon & Schuster LB $12.95 (978-0-671-74544-8); paper $7.95 (978-0-671-74545-5). 96pp. A practical guide that offers many suggestions on ways for young people to actively help in conservation. (Rev: SLJ 7/93) [320.5]

19699 Javna, John. *50 Simple Things Kids Can Do to Save the Earth* (3–6). Illus. by Michele Montez. 1990, Andrews McMeel paper $6.95 (978-0-8362-2301-9). 156pp. This book shows how small changes can help to save the environment. (Rev: BL 6/15/90; SLJ 9/90) [333.7]

19700 Johnson, Rebecca. *Investigating the Ozone Hole* (5–8). 1994, Lerner LB $28.75 (978-0-8225-1574-6). Using interviews, documents, and firsthand research, the author charts the development and possible consequences of an ozone hole above the Antarctic. (Rev: BL 3/1/94) [551.5]

19701 Juettner, Bonnie. *Energy* (5–8). Illus. Series: Our Environment. 2004, Gale LB $26.20 (978-0-7377-1821-8). 48pp. Answers such questions as "How is energy managed?" and "Are we running out of energy?" in four chapters that feature many illustrations and large type. (Rev: SLJ 4/05) [333.79]

19702 Kerley, Barbara. *A Cool Drink of Water* (PS–3). Illus. 2002, National Geographic $16.95 (978-0-7922-6723-2). 32pp. A series of beautiful photographs with minimal text show how water is collected and carried by people throughout the world. (Rev: BL 3/15/02; HBG 10/02; SLJ 4/02*) [363.6]

19703 Léger, Diane Carmel. *Who's in Maxine's Tree?* (1–4). Illus. by Darlene Gait. 2006, Orca $17.95 (978-1-55143-346-2). Maxine is thrilled to learn that her favorite tree will be protected from loggers because it is home to an endangered species of bird. (Rev: SLJ 6/06)

19704 Levine, Shar, and Allison Grafton. *Projects for a Healthy Planet: Simple Environmental Experiments for Kids* (3–7). Illus. by Terry Chui. 1992, Wiley paper $12.95 (978-0-471-55484-4). 64pp. A worthy addition to the many ecology books on the market. (Rev: BL 8/92; SLJ 8/92) [628]

19705 Lishak, Antony. *Global Warming* (4–7). Illus. Series: What's That Got to Do with Me? 2007, Smart Apple LB $18.95 (978-1-59920-037-8). 32pp. People from around the world who have been affected by climate change — and those who fear they may be — are interviewed to demonstrate various aspects of global warming. (Rev: BL 10/15/07; LMC 1/08) [363.738]

19706 Lorbiecki, Marybeth. *Planet Patrol* (3–5). Illus. by Nancy Meyers. 2005, Two-Can $15.95 (978-1-58728-514-1); paper $8.95 (978-1-58728-518-9). 48pp. This brightly illustrated title alerts readers to a wide range of environmental threats — pollution, overpopulation, climate change, deforestation, and species extinction — and what young people can do to help save the globe and reverse some of the damage. (Rev: BL 12/1/05; SLJ 12/05) [577]

19707 Lowery, Linda, and Marybeth Lorbiecki. *Earthwise at Home* (3–5). Illus. by David Mataya. 1993, Carolrhoda LB $19.93 (978-0-87614-730-6). 48pp. This book gives tips on how to recycle, reuse, and preserve materials at home. Others in this series are *Earthwise at Play* and *Earthwise at School* (both 1993). (Rev: SLJ 5/93) [320]

19708 Mattson, Mark. *Scholastic Environmental Atlas of the United States* (3–6). Illus. 1993, Scholastic $14.95 (978-0-590-49354-3). 80pp. In this atlas, natural resources and ecological threats like water pollution and toxic dumps are pictured globally. (Rev: BL 10/15/93; SLJ 4/94) [333.7]

19709 Nakaya, Andrea C., ed. *The Environment* (5–9). Series: Introducing Issues with Opposing Viewpoints. 2006, Gale LB $33.70 (978-0-7377-3459-1). 128pp. This thought-provoking study examines the delicate balance between the preservation of our natural environment and the need for energy to fuel economic growth. (Rev: SLJ 8/06)

19710 Olien, Rebecca. *Kids Care! 75 Ways to Make a Difference for People, Animals and the Environment* (3–6). Illus. by Michael Kline. Series: Williamson Kids Can! 2007, Williamson $16.99 (978-0-8249-6793-2); paper $12.99 (978-0-8249-6792-5). 128pp. In sections on people, pets, wildlife, the environment, and kids joining together, this volume presents practical ways in which children can improve life. (Rev: SLJ 10/07) [177]

19711 Ostopowich, Melanie. *Greenpeace* (4–8). Series: International Organizations. 2002, Weigl LB $16.95 (978-1-59036-020-0). 32pp. An introduction to the goals, structure, members, and volunteers who work with this international organization. Also use *Peace Corps* (2003). (Rev: HBG 3/03; SLJ 4/03) [333.72]

19712 Oxlade, Chris. *Global Warming* (5–7). Illus. Series: Our Planet in Peril. 2002, Capstone LB $22.60 (978-0-7368-1361-7). 32pp. Attractive double-page spreads explore the concern about global warning, its causes, and options for the future. Also use *Nuclear Waste* (2003). (Rev: HBG 3/03; SLJ 4/03) [363.738]

19713 Parker, Janice, ed. *The Disappearing Forests* (5–8). Illus. Series: Understanding Global Issues. 2002, Smart Apple LB $19.95 (978-1-58340-168-2). 56pp. A great deal of information about forest use, abuse, and conservation is packed into double-paged spreads with color illustrations. (Rev: BL 10/15/02; HBG 3/03; SLJ 12/02) [634.9]

19714 Parks, Peggy. *Global Warming* (5–8). Illus. Series: Lucent Library of Science and Technology. 2004, Gale LB $29.95 (978-1-59018-319-9). 112pp. Explores the controversies surrounding the theory of global warming and the potential consequences of the Earth's rising temperature. (Rev: BL 1/05)

19715 Parks, Peggy J. *Ecotourism* (5–8). Series: Our Environment. 2005, Gale LB $26.20 (978-0-7377-3048-7). 48pp. All about how ecologically sensitive areas can be protected while being explored, with explanations of the advantages and disadvantages of this type of travel. (Rev: SLJ 5/06) [338.4]

19716 Parks, Peggy J. *Global Warming* (5–8). Illus. Series: Our Environment. 2004, Gale LB $26.20 (978-0-7377-1822-5). 48pp. Answers such questions as "Caused by humans or caused by nature?" and "What can be done?" in four chapters that feature many illustrations and large type. (Rev: SLJ 4/05) [363.738]

19717 Parry, Ann. *Greenpeace* (5–8). Illus. Series: Humanitarian Organizations. 2005, Chelsea House LB $25.00 (978-0-7910-8815-9). 32pp. Maps, timelines, factboxes, and color photographs add to this account of Greenpeace's history and mission. (Rev: SLJ 12/05)

19718 Penny, Malcolm. *Our Environment* (2–3). Series: Talking About. 1999, Raintree LB $25.69 (978-0-8172-5889-4). 32pp. A simple format and many illustrations enhance this beginner's book on conservation and environmental protection, using such everyday examples as littering. (Rev: BL 2/15/00; HBG 9/00) [333.75]

19719 Peters, Celeste, ed. *The Energy Dilemma* (5–8). Illus. Series: Understanding Global Issues. 2002, Smart Apple LB $19.95 (978-1-58340-169-9). 56pp. The information about energy sources, use, and conservation packed into these double-paged spreads with color illustrations will spark debate. (Rev: BL 10/15/02) [333.79]

19720 Pringle, Laurence. *The Environmental Movement: From Its Roots to the Challenges of a New Century* (5–8). Illus. 2000, HarperCollins $16.95 (978-0-688-15626-8). 144pp. This is a fine history of environmentalism in America, beginning with the conflicts between Native Americans and early settlers concerning natural resources and ending with current issues. (Rev: BL 4/1/00; HBG 10/00; SLJ 6/00) [363.7]

19721 Pringle, Laurence. *Global Warming: The Threat of Earth's Changing Climate* (4–8). Illus. 2001, North-South $16.95 (978-1-58717-009-6). 48pp. A straightforward account that covers topics including the causes of global warming, the signs that it is occurring, and possible solutions. (Rev: BL 4/1/01; HBG 10/01; SLJ 6/01) [363.738]

19722 Reilly, Kathleen M. *Planet Earth: 25 Environmental Projects You Can Build Yourself* (4–7). Illus. Series: Projects You Can Build Yourself. 2008, Nomad $21.95 (978-1-934670-05-7); paper $14.95 (978-1-934670-04-0). 128pp. A worm composting castle and a wind-powered bubble machine are just two of the projects in this book that teaches about the environment and important environmental issues. (Rev: BL 5/1/08) [507.8]

19723 Rockwell, Anne. *Why Are the Ice Caps Melting? The Dangers of Global Warming* (2–4). Illus. by Paul Meisel. Series: Let's-Read-and-Find-Out Science. 2006, HarperCollins $15.99 (978-0-06-054669-4); paper $5.99 (978-0-06-054671-7). 33pp. The hot-button issue of global warming is discussed in easy-to-understand language, as are the greenhouse effect and the role of carbon dioxide emissions. (Rev: BL 12/15/06; SLJ 11/06) [363.738]

19724 Rooney, Anne. *Is Our Climate Changing?* (4–8). Illus. Series: Global Questions. 2008, Arcturus LB $22.95 (978-1-84837-011-1). 48pp. What is climate change? Has the climate changed in the past? This brief title answers these and other questions in clear text and color photographs, with a final chapter that looks at the future. (Rev: BL 12/1/08; LMC 5/09) [551.6]

19725 Royston, Angela. *Global Warming* (2–3). Illus. Series: Protect Our Planet. 2008, Heinemann LB $17.75 (978-1-4329-0924-6). 32pp. A basic introduction to global warming with discussion of climate change, the loss of ice at the poles, and measures we can take to protect the planet. (Rev: BL 9/1/08) [363.738]

19726 Sayre, April P. *Trout Are Made of Trees* (K–2). Illus. by Kate Endle. 2008, Charlesbridge $15.95 (978-1-58089-137-0); paper $6.95 (978-1-58089-138-7). 32pp. Using very simple text, this book illustrates how the whole world is interconnected and that, in fact, trout are made from trees. (Rev: BL 2/15/08; HB 7/08; SLJ 4/08) [577]

19727 Seibert, Patricia. *Toad Overload: A True Tale of Nature Knocked Off Balance in Australia* (K–3). Illus. by Jan Davey Ellis. 1996, Millbrook LB $21.90 (978-1-56294-613-5). 32pp. The balance of nature in Australia is upset when large toads are imported to eat marauding beetles. (Rev: BCCB 2/96; BL 2/15/96; SLJ 4/96) [597.8]

19728 Sheehan, Sean. *Greenpeace* (5–8). Series: World Watch. 2004, Raintree LB $18.99 (978-0-7398-6612-2). 47pp. A thorough review of the sometimes controversial conservationist organization since its founding in 1970, with some graphic photographs. (Rev: BL 4/1/04; SLJ 3/04) [333.7]

19729 Sirett, Dawn. *Love Your World* (PS). Illus. 2009, DK $8.99 (978-0-7566-4590-8). 36pp. Advice for young environmentalists ranges from turning down the heat and brushing teeth without the water running to recycling and planting seeds. (Rev: BLO 4/14/09; SLJ 5/09) [333.72]

19730 Solway, Andrew. *Biofuels* (5–8). Illus. Series: Energy for the Future and Global Warming. 2007, Gareth Stevens LB $26.60 (978-0-8368-8398-5); paper $9.95 (978-0-8368-8407-4). 32pp. A brief introduction to the use of alternatives to fossil fuels — ethanol, biogas, and so forth — with an explanation of how these could benefit the environment. (Rev: BL 10/15/07) [662]

19731 Spilsbury, Louise, and Richard Spilsbury. *Water* (5–8). Series: Planet Under Pressure. 2006, Heinemann LB $31.43 (978-1-4034-8214-3). 48pp. Discusses the demand for water, its sources, and what's being done to conserve it. (Rev: SLJ 3/07)

19732 Stille, Darlene R. *Nature Interrupted: The Science of Environmental Chain Reactions* (5–7). Series: Headline Science. 2008, Compass Point LB $27.93 (978-0-7565-3949-8). 48pp. Through understandable text and helpful charts, this title clearly explains the fragile and important links between all things in the environment and how breaks in the chain can have detrimental, widespread results. (Rev: SLJ 2/09) [577.27]

19733 Strauss, Rochelle. *One Well: The Story of Water on Earth* (3–5). Illus. by Rosemary Woods. 2007, Kids Can $17.95 (978-1-55337-954-6). 32pp. The importance of water to life on earth and the connections between all uses of water are emphasized in this oversize picture book that also discusses water distribution and recycling and gives tips on conservation. (Rev: BL 2/15/07*) [553.7]

19734 Suzuki, David, and Kathy Vanderlinden. *Eco-Fun* (5–8). Illus. 2001, Douglas & McIntyre paper $10.95 (978-1-55054-823-5). 128pp. The activities in this collection reinforce some basic scientific concepts about air, water, earth, and fire, and encourage young readers to think about environmental issues and avoid pollution. (Rev: BL 6/1–15/01; SLJ 8/01) [577]

19735 Taylor, Barbara. *How to Save the Planet* (3–6). Illus. by Scoular Anderson. Series: How To. 2001, Watts LB $16.00 (978-0-531-14640-8). 96pp. Experiments back up the concepts introduced in this discussion of global warming, pollution, future

energy needs, and other important topics. (Rev: SLJ 4/02) [363.7]

19736 Tesar, Jenny. *Food and Water: Threats, Shortages and Solutions* (5–9). Series: Our Fragile Planet. 1992, Facts on File LB $21.95 (978-0-8160-2495-7). A discussion of the world's water and food supplies, threats to them, and possible solutions. (Rev: BL 6/1/92) [333.91]

19737 Toft, Kim Michelle. *The World That We Want* (PS–3). Illus. by author. 2005, Charlesbridge paper $6.95 (978-1-58089-115-8). The interconnectedness of animals, plants, and their habitats is emphasized in this book with beautiful illustrations and an environmental message. (Rev: SLJ 9/05) [577]

19738 VanCleave, Janice. *Janice VanCleave's Ecology for Every Kid* (4–7). Illus. 1996, Wiley paper $12.95 (978-0-471-10086-7). 240pp. Clear instructions and many diagrams introduce a series of experiments that highlight environmental issues. (Rev: BL 3/1/96; SLJ 4/96) [574.5]

19739 Walker, Jane. *Atmosphere in Danger* (4–6). 2005, Stargazer LB $27.10 (978-1-932799-12-5). Easy-to-understand language with helpful graphs, charts, and illustrations make this a useful introduction to the problems threatening the Earth's fragile atmosphere and the potential solutions. (Rev: SLJ 4/06) [363.739]

19740 Walsh, Melanie. *10 Things I Can Do to Help My World: Fun and Easy Eco-Tips* (PS–2). Illus. by author. 2008, Candlewick $15.99 (978-0-7636-4144-3). 40pp. Simple actions — turning off the tap when you brush your teeth — are presented in this engaging can-do book. (Rev: BLO 9/24/08; HB 1/09) [640]

19741 Wells, Robert E. *Polar Bear, Why Is Your World Melting?* (1–4). Illus. by author. 2008, Albert Whitman $16.99 (978-0-8075-6598-8); paper $6.99 (978-0-8075-6599-5). For young readers, this is an introduction to the dangers of global warming, with information on what can be done to ameliorate the situation. (Rev: BCCB 12/08; SLJ 11/08) [363.738]

19742 Whitman, Sylvia. *This Land Is Your Land: The American Conservation Movement* (5–7). Illus. 1994, Lerner LB $30.35 (978-0-8225-1729-0). 88pp. A history of the conservation movement from its beginnings in 1870 when there were efforts to save Yellowstone and ending with today's major problems such as oil spills and trash disposal. (Rev: BL 12/15/94; HB 3/94; SLJ 12/94) [363.7]

19743 Woods, Michael, and Mary B. Woods. *Environmental Disasters* (4–7). Illus. Series: Disasters Up Close. 2008, Lerner LB $27.93 (978-0-8225-6774-5). 64pp. Love Canal, Bhopal, the *Exxon Valdez* — these are only three of the disasters covered in this well-illustrated account of disasters that could have been avoided. (Rev: BL 2/15/08; SLJ 8/08) [363.7]

Cities

19744 Matsen, Bradford. *Go Wild in New York City* (4–6). Illus. 2005, National Geographic $16.95 (978-0-7922-7982-2). 80pp. Skippy the squirrel guides readers through the nature to be found in the urban landscape of New York City, with chapters on its flora and fauna, water, rocks, and air. (Rev: BL 3/15/05; SLJ 5/05) [508.747]

19745 Pancella, Peggy. *City* (K–2). Series: Neighborhood Walk. 2005, Heinemann LB $25.36 (978-1-4034-6215-2). 32pp. After a discussion of a neighborhood as part of a larger community, this book looks at various aspects of life in the city, including work, recreation, transportation, and shopping. Also use *Farm Community, Military Base, Small Town,* and *Suburb* (all 2005). (Rev: SLJ 2/06) [307.76]

19746 Parker, Philip. *Global Cities* (4–6). Illus. Series: Project Eco-City. 1995, Thomson Learning LB $7.95 (978-1-56847-286-7). 48pp. This account concentrates on the ecology and balance of nature found in large cities. (Rev: BL 6/1–15/95) [307.76]

19747 Sammis, Fran. *Cities and Towns* (2–5). Illus. Series: Discovering Geography. 1997, Marshall Cavendish LB $22.79 (978-0-7614-0540-5). 32pp. Using a question-and-answer approach, this account introduces cities and towns and outlines projects in map making, including finding houses along a newspaper route or stores in a mall. (Rev: BL 2/1/98; HBG 3/98; SLJ 4/98) [307.76]

Garbage and Waste Recycling

19748 Barraclough, Sue. *Recycling Materials* (1–3). Series: Making a Difference. 2008, Sea-to-Sea LB $27.10 (978-1-59771-108-1). 32pp. Clearly written information about recycling paper, glass, metal, and plastic is accompanied by facts, hints, suggestions, and photographs. Also use *Reducing Garbage* (2008). (Rev: SLJ 9/08) [363.72]

19749 Barraclough, Sue. *Reusing Things* (1–3). Series: Making a Difference. 2008, Sea-to-Sea LB $27.10 (978-1-59771-109-8). 32pp. Clearly written information about reusing paper, junk, clothing and other materials is accompanied by facts, hints, suggestions, and photographs. (Rev: SLJ 9/08) [363.72]

19750 Coombs, Karen Mueller. *Flush! Treating Wastewater* (3–6). Illus. 1995, Carolrhoda LB $22.60 (978-0-87614-879-2). 56pp. A history of sanitation through the centuries is given, plus a description of present-day water purification systems. (Rev: BCCB 1/96; BL 12/1/95; SLJ 12/95) [628.3]

19751 Hall, Eleanor J. *Recycling* (5–8). Illus. Series: Our Environment. 2004, Gale LB $26.20 (978-0-7377-1517-0). 48pp. Answers such questions as "What is recycling?" and "What does the future hold?" in four chapters that feature many illustrations and large type. (Rev: SLJ 4/05) [363.72]

19752 Heilman, Joan R. *Tons of Trash: Why You Should Recycle and What Happens When You Do* (3–5). 1992, Avon paper $3.50 (978-0-380-76379-5). 80pp. This lively tour of processing plants shows how garbage is recycled. (Rev: BL 4/15/92) [363.72]

19753 Love, Ann, and Jane Drake. *Trash Action: A Fresh Look at Garbage* (3–6). Illus. by Mark Thurman. 2006, Tundra paper $14.95 (978-0-88776-721-0). 76pp. Examples of trash on Mount Everest and in space draw readers into this information-packed book that looks at the growing problems of garbage and waste disposal and outlines steps that can be taken to address the situation. (Rev: SLJ 8/06) [363.72]

19754 Ring, Elizabeth. *What Rot! Nature's Mighty Recycler* (3–5). Illus. 1996, Millbrook LB $23.40 (978-1-56294-671-5). 32pp. Numerous photos and a lively text describe how nature provides organisms and processes to decompose materials naturally. (Rev: BL 2/15/96; SLJ 4/96) [574.2]

19755 Snodgrass, Mary Ellen. *Solid Waste* (4–6). Illus. Series: Environmental Awareness. 1991, Bancroft-Sage LB $19.93 (978-0-944280-28-7). 48pp. The techniques and problems of waste removal and recycling, with many color illustrations. Also use: *Water Pollution* (1991). (Rev: BL 2/15/92) [363.73]

19756 Wilcox, Charlotte. *Trash!* (3–5). Illus. 1988, Carolrhoda LB $16.95 (978-0-87614-311-7); Lerner paper $5.95 (978-0-87614-511-1). 40pp. What happens to garbage after it's collected. (Rev: BL 12/1/88; HB 1/89; SLJ 1/89)

Pollution

19757 Bellamy, Rufus. *Clean Air* (4–6). 2005, Smart Apple LB $27.10 (978-1-58340-594-9). This book takes a somewhat optimistic tack on the problem of global air pollution, citing numerous examples of programs that either have been put in place or are being considered. (Rev: SLJ 4/06) [363.739]

19758 Berger, Melvin. *Oil Spill!* (K–3). Illus. by Paul Mirocha. 1994, HarperCollins paper $5.99 (978-0-06-445121-5). 32pp. After a description of the *Exxon Valdez* catastrophe, general material on oil spills is presented, including their causes, effects, and how they can be prevented. (Rev: BL 6/1–15/94) [363.73]

19759 Brown, Paul. *Global Pollution* (5–8). Illus. Series: Face the Facts. 2003, Raintree LB $28.56 (978-0-7398-6433-3). 56pp. The effects of pollution on the environment are described in understandable terms, and practical responses from young people are suggested. (Rev: BL 11/15/03; HBG 10/03; SLJ 9/03) [303.73]

19760 Chapman, Matthew, and Rob Bowden. *Air Pollution* (5–8). Series: 21st Century Debates. 2002, Raintree LB $19.99 (978-0-7398-4874-6). 64pp. The causes of air pollution, the present situation, and possible future solutions are presented in this well-illustrated book that presents various points of view and offers topics for debate. (Rev: BL 6/1–15/02; SLJ 4/06) [363.73]

19761 Cherry, Lynne. *A River Ran Wild* (1–3). Illus. 1992, Harcourt $16.00 (978-0-15-200542-9). 40pp. Tracing the environmental history and present status of the Nashua River, which runs through New Hampshire and Massachusetts. (Rev: BL 3/15/92; HB 5/92; SLJ 5/92) [974.4]

19762 Cole, Joanna. *The Magic School Bus: At the Water Works* (2–5). Illus. by Bruce Degen. 1995, Scholastic $14.95 (978-0-614-03341-0); paper $5.99 (978-0-590-40360-3). 40pp. Scientific fun with Ms. Frizzle, the world's strangest teacher and an unflappable naturalist. (Rev: BL 11/15/86; SLJ 1/87)

19763 Gifford, Clive. *Pollution* (4–7). Illus. Series: Planet Under Pressure. 2006, Heinemann LB $31.43 (978-1-4034-7742-2). 48pp. An overview of the various types of pollution, their sources and impact, and possible future remedies. (Rev: SLJ 6/06)

19764 Green, Jen. *Reducing Air Pollution* (4–6). 2005, Gareth Stevens LB $26.00 (978-0-8368-4428-3). This easy-to-understand overview of air pollution looks at what's causing the problem, including such factors as acid rain, ozone depletion, and global warming, and examines ways in which the world can reduce its dependence on fossil fuels. (Rev: SLJ 4/06) [363.739]

19765 Ingram, Scott. *The Chernobyl Nuclear Disaster* (5–8). Series: Environmental Disasters. 2005, Facts on File $35.00 (978-0-8160-5755-9). 100pp. Ingram assesses the continuing environmental fallout from the 1986 Chernobyl nuclear disaster. (Rev: SLJ 11/05) [333.79]

19766 Leacock, Elspeth. *The Exxon Valdez Oil Spill* (5–8). Series: Environmental Disasters. 2005, Facts on File $35.00 (978-0-8160-5754-2). 100pp. A look at the environmental impact of the 1989 *Exxon Valdez* oil spill in Alaska's Prince William Sound. (Rev: SLJ 11/05) [363.7]

19767 Ostopowich, Melanie. *Water Pollution* (4–6). 2005, Weigl LB $24.45 (978-1-59036-307-2). This overview of water pollution explores the water cycle and various causes of pollution and includes a few experiments to help readers better understand the concepts involved. (Rev: SLJ 4/06) [363.739]

19768 Snodgrass, Mary Ellen. *Acid Rain* (4–6). Illus. Series: Environmental Awareness. 1991, Bancroft-Sage LB $19.93 (978-0-944280-30-0). 48pp. Basic, up-to-date information on acid rain. Also use: *Toxic Waste* (1991). (Rev: BL 2/15/92) [363.73]

19769 Snodgrass, Mary Ellen. *Air Pollution* (4–6). Illus. Series: Environmental Awareness. 1991, Bancroft-Sage LB $19.93 (978-0-944280-31-7). 48pp. Using color photos, diagrams, and straightforward information, the problems of air pollution are introduced, along with possible solutions. Also use: *Land Pollution* (1991). (Rev: BL 2/15/92) [363.73]

Population

19770 Ayer, Eleanor. *Homeless Children* (5–8). Illus. Series: Overview. 1997, Lucent LB $29.95 (978-1-56006-177-9). The causes and consequences of homelessness are explored, with a focus on children and the ways the problem is being handled. (Rev: BL 3/15/97) [362.7]

19771 Bowden, Rob. *Food Supply* (5–8). Series: 21st Century Debates. 2002, Raintree LB $27.12 (978-0-7398-4871-5). 64pp. Trends and issues regarding the food supply, and possible solutions for shortages, are presented in this look at pros and cons. (Rev: BL 6/1–15/02) [338.19]

19772 Bowden, Rob. *An Overcrowded World?* (5–8). Series: 21st Century Debates. 2002, Raintree LB $27.12 (978-0-7398-4872-2). 64pp. Using a well-organized text, plus sidebars for additional facts and statements of opinion, this colorfully illustrated volume explores the current problems of overpopulation and the dire strain it causes on the earth's supplies. (Rev: BL 6/1–15/02) [304.6]

19773 Green, Robert. *Poverty* (4–8). Series: Global Perspectives. 2008, Cherry Lake LB $27.07 (978-1-60279-126-8). 32pp. An accessible look at poverty, how we measure it, its effects, and what can be done to curb this problem. (Rev: LMC 10/08; SLJ 11/08) [362.5]

19774 McLeish, Ewan. *Overcrowded World* (5–8). Illus. Series: What If We Do Nothing? 2009, Gareth Stevens LB $31.00 (978-1-4339-0088-4). 48pp. Overpopulation and the associated problems of famine, water shortages, poverty, and homelessness are addressed in this volume that looks at the past, the current status, and the future outlook. (Rev: BL 4/15/09; SLJ 6/09; VOYA 10/09) [363.9]

19775 Mason, Paul. *Population* (4–7). Series: Planet Under Pressure. 2006, Heinemann LB $31.43 (978-1-4034-7741-5). 48pp. The problems created by overpopulation are the focus of this book that also explores the underlying reasons and possible solutions. (Rev: SLJ 6/06)

19776 Mason, Paul. *Poverty* (4–7). Illus. Series: Planet Under Pressure. 2006, Heinemann LB $31.43 (978-1-4034-7743-9). 48pp. A clear presentation of how poverty affects people around the world, with charts, photographs, and profiles. (Rev: BL 4/1/06; SLJ 6/06) [362.5]

19777 Nichelason, Margery G. *Homeless or Hopeless?* (5–8). Illus. Series: Pro/Con Issues. 1994, Lerner LB $30.35 (978-0-8225-2606-3). 112pp. After an explanation of the roots and causes of homelessness, clearly written statements debate who is responsible for homelessness and how it should be handled. (Rev: BL 6/1–15/94; SLJ 7/94) [362.5]

19778 Seymour-Jones, Carole. *Homelessness* (5–9). Series: Past and Present. 1993, Macmillan $20.00 (978-0-02-786882-1). A discussion of the causes of homelessness, the extent of the problem and who is affected, and ways to end it. (Rev: BL 8/93) [362.5]

19779 Smith, David J. *If the World Were a Village* (3–5). Illus. by Shelagh Armstrong. 2002, Kids Can $15.95 (978-1-55074-779-9). 32pp. By condensing the world's population to a "village" of 100 people, this book makes data and statistics more comprehensible — and more fascinating — for younger readers. (Rev: BL 3/1/02; HB 5/02; HBG 10/02; SLJ 5/02) [304.6]

19780 Stearman, Kaye. *Homelessness* (5–10). Illus. Series: Talking Points. 1999, Raintree LB $27.12 (978-0-8172-5312-7). 64pp. A worldwide view of homelessness, its causes — including eviction, natu-ral disasters, and war — and international efforts to combat it. (Rev: BL 9/1/99; SLJ 8/99) [363.5]

19781 Stearman, Kaye. *Why Do People Live on the Streets?* (5–7). Series: Exploring Tough Issues. 2001, Raintree LB $25.69 (978-0-7398-3232-5). 48pp. Among reasons given for homelessness are poverty and discrimination. (Rev: HBG 10/01; SLJ 7/01) [305.569]

19782 Worth, Richard. *Poverty* (5–8). Illus. Series: Overview. 1997, Lucent LB $29.95 (978-1-56006-192-2). A carefully researched title that gives a history of poverty in America, changing attitudes toward it, and current policies and practices. (Rev: BL 8/97; SLJ 9/97) [362.5]

Government and Politics

Courts and the Law

19783 Anderson, Wayne. *Brown v. Board of Education: The Case Against School Segregation* (5–8). Series: Supreme Court Cases Through Primary Sources. 2004, Rosen LB $29.25 (978-0-8239-4009-7). 64pp. Primary sources — photographs, police records, newspaper clippings, and court documents — provide details of the case and the narrative discusses the historical and social context. Also use *Plessy v. Ferguson: Legalizing Segregation* (2004). (Rev: SLJ 6/04) [345.73]

19784 Beaudry, Jo, and Lynne Ketchum. *Carla Goes to Court* (3–6). Illus. 1983, Human Sciences $16.95 (978-0-89885-088-8); paper $10.95 (978-0-89885-354-4). 32pp. The court process is explored through Carla's experience after she witnesses a burglary.

19785 Burnett, Betty. *The Trial of Julius and Ethel Rosenberg: A Primary Source Account* (5–8). Illus. Series: Great Trials of the Twentieth Century. 2004, Rosen LB $29.25 (978-0-8239-3976-3). 64pp. Primary sources — photographs, original transcripts, quotations, and so forth — give depth to this compelling account of the complex trial. (Rev: BL 4/1/04; SLJ 10/04)

19786 Crewe, Sabrina, and Michael V. Uschan. *The Scottsboro Case* (4–7). Illus. Series: Events That Shaped America. 2005, Gareth Stevens LB $26.00 (978-0-8368-3407-9). 32pp. A thorough and thought-provoking look at the infamous Scottsboro case in which nine young African Americans were accused of raping two white women. (Rev: BL 1/1–15/05; SLJ 3/05) [345.73]

19787 De Capua, Sarah E. *Serving on a Jury* (2–5). Series: True Books — Civics. 2002, Children's Book Pr. LB $25.00 (978-0-516-22329-2); paper $6.95 (978-0-516-27364-8). 48pp. Chapters in this simple book on the jury system include material on what is a jury, who can serve, how members are selected, and what they do. (Rev: BL 6/1–15/02; SLJ 10/02) [347.73]

19788 Donnelly, Karen. *Cruzan v. Missouri: The Right to Die* (5–7). Illus. Series: Supreme Court Cases Through Primary Sources. 2004, Rosen LB $29.25 (978-0-8239-4014-1). 64pp. The lengthy legal battle for a patient's right to die is chronicled in this account of the Supreme Court's decision in Cruzan v. Missouri. (Rev: BL 6/1–15/04; SLJ 6/04) [344.73]

19789 Donovan, Sandy. *Making Laws: A Look at How a Bill Becomes a Law* (4–6). Illus. Series: How Government Works. 2003, Lerner LB $25.26 (978-0-8225-1346-9). 56pp. An easily understood explanation of how an idea (the example is banning school on Fridays) can become a bill and then a law. (Rev: SLJ 3/04) [328.7]

19790 Dudley, Mark E. *Engel v. Vitale (1962): Religion and the Schools* (5–9). Series: Supreme Court Decisions. 1995, Twenty-First Century LB $25.90 (978-0-8050-3916-0). The story of the Supreme Court case on school prayer that originated with two Jewish youngsters who objected to being forced to pray every morning in a New York City school. (Rev: BL 11/15/95; SLJ 1/96; VOYA 4/96) [347]

19791 Gold, Susan Dudley. *In Re Gault (1967): Juvenile Justice* (5–9). Series: Supreme Court Decisions. 1995, Twenty-First Century LB $25.90 (978-0-8050-3917-7). Inequalities in juvenile sentencing were the subject of this Supreme Court case, an appeal of a six-year reform school sentence given to a juvenile for making an obscene phone call. (Rev: BL 11/15/95; SLJ 1/96; VOYA 4/96) [347]

19792 Goldish, Meish. *Our Supreme Court* (4–6). Illus. Series: I Know America. 1994, Millbrook LB $24.90 (978-1-56294-445-2). 48pp. An introduction to the Supreme Court that gives its history, composition, and a few historic decisions. (Rev: BL 11/15/94; SLJ 1/95) [347.73]

19793 Gorman, Jacqueline Laks. *Judge* (2–4). Series: Know Your Government. 2009, Gareth Stevens LB $21.00 (978-1-4339-0092-1); paper $5.95 (978-1-4339-0120-1). 24pp. With color photographs and clear text, Gorman introduces the various levels of judges, focusing mainly on the Supreme Court. (Rev: SLJ 6/09) [345.73]

19794 Grabowski, John. *The Death Penalty* (5–8). Series: Overview. 1999, Lucent LB $29.95 (978-1-56006-371-1). 96pp. A fair, unbiased review of the history, pro and con arguments, and present status of the death penalty in America. (Rev: BL 8/99) [364.6]

19795 Himton, Kerry. *The Trial of Sacco and Vanzetti: A Primary Source Account* (5–8). Illus. Series: Great Trials of the Twentieth Century. 2004, Rosen LB $29.25 (978-0-8239-3973-2). 64pp. Primary sources — photographs, original transcripts, quotations, and so forth — give depth to this compelling account of the complex trial. (Rev: BL 4/1/04; SLJ 6/04)

19796 Horn, Geoffrey M. *The Supreme Court* (5–8). Series: World Almanac Library of American Government. 2003, World Almanac LB $31.00 (978-0-8368-5459-6). 48pp. An excellent introduction to the U.S. Supreme Court and the important role it plays in interpreting the laws of the land. (Rev: SLJ 1/04)

19797 Linz, Kathi. *Chickens May Not Cross the Road and Other Crazy (But True) Laws* (2–4). Illus. by Tony Griego. 2002, Houghton $16.00 (978-0-618-11257-9). 32pp. A compilation of silly laws ("no tying crocodiles to fire hydrants," "no donkeys in bathtubs") from cities across the United States, each with a cartoon illustration. (Rev: BL 9/1/02; HBG 3/03; SLJ 11/02) [348.73]

19798 Naden, Corinne J., and Rose Blue. *Dred Scott: Person or Property?* (5–8). Illus. Series: Supreme Court Milestones. 2005, Benchmark LB $37.07 (978-0-7614-1841-2). 144pp. The Supreme Court's 1857 Dred Scott decision, arguably the high court's most misguided ruling ever, is examined in detail. (Rev: BL 2/1/05) [342.7]

19799 Olson, Steven P. *The Trial of John T. Scopes: A Primary Source Account* (5–8). Series: Great Trials of the Twentieth Century. 2004, Rosen LB $29.25 (978-0-8239-3974-9). 64pp. Primary sources — photographs, original transcripts, quotations, and so forth — give depth to this compelling account of the complex trial. (Rev: BL 4/1/04; SLJ 8/04) [344.73]

19800 Payment, Simone. *Roe v. Wade: The Right to Choose* (5–7). Illus. Series: Supreme Court Cases Through Primary Sources. 2004, Rosen LB $29.25 (978-0-8239-4012-7). 64pp. Illustrations are used to good effect in this overview of the issues raised in the Supreme Court's landmark decision. (Rev: BL 6/1–15/04; SLJ 6/04) [342.73]

19801 Payment, Simone. *The Trial of Leopold and Loeb: A Primary Source Account* (5–8). Illus. Series: Great Trials of the Twentieth Century. 2004, Rosen LB $29.25 (978-0-8239-3970-1). 64pp. Primary sources — photographs, original transcripts, quotations, and so forth — give depth to this compelling account of the complex trial. (Rev: BL 4/1/04; SLJ 6/04; VOYA 4/04)

19802 Roensch, Greg. *The Lindbergh Baby Kidnapping Trial: A Primary Source Account* (5–8). Series:

Great Trials of the Twentieth Century. 2004, Rosen LB $29.25 (978-0-8239-3971-8). 64pp. Primary sources — photographs, original transcripts, handwriting samples, and so forth — give depth to this account of this controversial trial. (Rev: BL 4/1/04; SLJ 8/04) [345.73]

19803 Scheppler, Bill. *The Mississippi Burning Trial: A Primary Source Account* (5–8). Illus. Series: Great Trials of the Twentieth Century. 2004, Rosen LB $29.25 (978-0-8239-3972-5). 64pp. Primary sources — photographs, original transcripts, quotations, and so forth — give depth to this compelling account of the complex trial. (Rev: BL 4/1/04; SLJ 10/04)

19804 Sonneborn, Liz. *Miranda v. Arizona: The Rights of the Accused* (5–8). Series: Supreme Court Cases Through Primary Sources. 2004, Rosen LB $29.25 (978-0-8239-4010-3). 64pp. Primary sources — photographs, police records, newspaper clippings, and court documents — provide details of the case and the narrative discusses the historical and social context. (Rev: BL 6/1–15/04; SLJ 6/04) [345.73]

United Nations and International Affairs

19805 Bradman, Tony, ed. *Give Me Shelter: Stories About Children Who Seek Asylum* (5–8). 2007, Frances Lincoln $16.95 (978-1-84507-522-4). 220pp. These gripping stories of real children seeking refuge from countries torn apart by war or strife will capture readers' hearts. (Rev: SLJ 3/08)

19806 Burger, Leslie, and Debra L. Rahm. *Red Cross / Red Crescent: When Help Can't Wait* (5–7). Illus. 1996, Lerner $22.60 (978-0-8225-2698-8). 80pp. The story of the Red Cross and the role it plays in helping people today. (Rev: BL 1/1–15/97; SLJ 1/97; VOYA 4/97) [361.7]

19807 Downing, David. *Democracy* (5–8). Illus. Series: Political and Economic Systems. 2002, Heinemann LB $28.50 (978-1-4034-0317-9). 64pp. Downing explains the history of democracy and looks at its weaknesses and benefits. Also use *Dictatorship* (2002). (Rev: BL 1/1–15/03; HBG 3/03) [321.8]

19808 *Every Human Has Rights: A Photographic Declaration for Kids* (4–8). Illus. 2009, National Geographic $17.95 (978-1-4263-0510-8). 48pp. Compelling photographs, accompanied by poems, illustrate the 30 rights covered in the Universal Declaration of Human Rights. (Rev: BL 12/15/08; SLJ 3/09) [300]

19809 Giesecke, Ernestine. *Governments Around the World* (3–5). Series: Kids' Guide. 2000, Heinemann $22.79 (978-1-57572-511-6). 32pp. This book explains different kinds of governments — democracies, communist and socialist states, monarchies, and other systems. (Rev: HBG 3/01; SLJ 10/00) [320]

19810 Grant, R. G. *Genocide* (5–10). Illus. Series: Talking Points. 1999, Raintree LB $27.12 (978-0-8172-5314-1). This book covers the Holocaust in World War II as well as more recent massacres in Cambodia, Rwanda, and Bosnia, and probes such controversies as who is guilty of genocide — the person who pulls the trigger or those who plan and organize it, and what about the bystander? (Rev: BL 9/1/99) [304.6]

19811 Grodin, Elissa. *D Is for Democracy: A Citizen's Alphabet* (5–8). Illus. by Victor Juhasz. 2004, Sleeping Bear $16.95 (978-1-58536-234-9). 40pp. From "Amendment" to "Zeitgeist," this is an exploration of key concepts, people, places, and things, with an emphasis on the United States. (Rev: BL 1/1–15/05; SLJ 10/04) [320.973]

19812 Kerley, Barbara. *A Little Peace* (1–6). 2007, National Geographic $16.95 (978-1-4263-0086-8). Photographs of children performing simple acts of peace and kindness will inspire readers. (Rev: SLJ 5/07)

19813 Kramer, Ann. *Human Rights: Who Decides?* (5–8). Series: Behind the News. 2006, Heinemann LB $32.86 (978-1-4034-8832-9). 56pp. With photographs and examples of news stories, this volume offers various viewpoints on the information we receive on human rights and asks readers how they will make up their minds. (Rev: SLJ 4/07) [323]

19814 Maddocks, Steven. *UNICEF* (5–8). Series: World Watch. 2004, Raintree LB $271.40 (978-0-7398-6617-7). 48pp. Introduces UNICEF's history, organization, and work on behalf of the world's children; sidebars provide key facts and relevant quotations. (Rev: BL 4/1/04; SLJ 6/04) [362.7]

19815 *Making It Home: Real Life Stories from Children Forced to Flee* (5–8). Illus. 2006, Dial $17.99 (978-0-8037-3083-0); paper $6.99 (978-0-14-240455-3). 144pp. The horrific impact of war on children is documented in these first-person accounts, with many photographs, from children who were displaced from their homes in Afghanistan, Bosnia, Burundi, Congo, Iraq, Kosovo, Liberia, and Sudan. (Rev: BL 12/1/05; SLJ 2/06) [305.23]

19816 Parry, Ann. *Red Cross* (4–6). Illus. Series: Humanitarian Organizations. 2005, Chelsea House LB $25.00 (978-0-7910-8814-2). 32pp. With many photographs, sidebars, and other features, this volume explores the history, mission, and core values of the Red Cross. (Rev: BL 10/15/05; SLJ 12/05) [361.77]

19817 Radunsky, Vladimir. *What Does Peace Feel Like?* (PS–3). Illus. by author. 2004, Simon & Schuster $14.95 (978-0-689-86676-0). 24pp. Students at an international school in Rome imagine what peace looks, sounds, tastes, feels, and smells like. (Rev: BL 11/1/04; SLJ 1/05) [303.6]

19818 Ross, Stewart. *United Nations* (5–8). Illus. Series: World Watch. 2004, Raintree LB $18.99 (978-0-7398-6616-0). 48pp. Ross explains the role of the United Nations as an international watchdog and provides a brief review of its history and organization. (Rev: BL 4/1/04) [341.23]

19819 Spies, Karen B. *Isolation vs. Intervention: Is America the World's Police Force?* (4–6). Illus. Series: Issues of Our Time. 1995, Twenty-First Century LB $18.90 (978-0-8050-3880-4). 64pp. Objectively presents arguments, pro and con, concerning involvement in the political and economic problems of other countries. (Rev: SLJ 2/96) [327.73]

19820 Suen, Anastasia. *Doctors Without Borders* (1–2). Series: Helping Organizations. 2002, Rosen LB $19.95 (978-0-8239-6002-6). 24pp. As well as giving a history of this humanitarian organization, this simple account describes how it works and the good work it accomplishes. (Rev: BL 6/1–15/02; SLJ 4/02) [361.7]

19821 Suen, Anastasia. *The Red Cross* (1–2). Illus. Series: Helping Organizations. 2002, Rosen LB $19.95 (978-0-8239-6003-3). 24pp. This basic introduction to the Red Cross explains how it was formed and the work it does around the world. (Rev: BL 6/1–15/02) [361.7]

19822 Suen, Anastasia. *UNICEF* (1–2). Illus. 2002, Rosen LB $19.95 (978-0-8239-6005-7). 24pp. This introduction to UNICEF and its mission also tells how volunteers can help and how youngsters can raise money to aid its programs. (Rev: BL 6/1–15/02; SLJ 3/02) [362.7]

19823 Tames, Richard. *Monarchy* (5–8). Series: Political and Economic Systems. 2002, Heinemann LB $28.50 (978-1-4034-0320-9). 64pp. A description of the concept of monarchy, followed by a history of its application, its current status, and its various forms. (Rev: BL 1/1–15/03; HBG 3/03) [321.8]

19824 *We Are All Born Free: The Universal Declaration of Human Rights in Pictures* (K–3). Illus. by John Burningham. 2008, Frances Lincoln $19.95 (978-1-84507-650-4). 64pp. Effectively illustrated by a diverse group of well-known artists, this book presents the 30 articles of the Universal Declaration of Human Rights. (Rev: BL 12/1/08; SLJ 11/08) [341.48]

United States

Civil Rights

19825 Adams, Colleen. *Women's Suffrage: A Primary Source History of the Women's Rights Movement in America* (5–8). Illus. Series: Primary Sources in American History. 2003, Rosen LB $29.25 (978-0-8239-3685-4). 64pp. Primary sources — including pamphlets and newspaper articles — tell the story of the women's rights movement in America. (Rev: BL 5/15/03) [305.42]

19826 Bradley, David, and Shelley Fisher Fishkin, eds. *The Encyclopedia of Civil Rights in America* (5–10). 1997, Sharpe Reference $299.00 (978-0-7656-8000-6). This three-volume set contains 683 alphabetically arranged articles that explore the history, meaning, and application of civil rights issues in the United States. (Rev: BL 2/15/98; SLJ 5/98) [323]

19827 Bridges, Ruby. *Through My Eyes* (3–9). Illus. 1999, Scholastic $16.95 (978-0-590-18923-1). 64pp. Ruby Bridges tells what it was like to be the first African American child at an integrated school in 1960; photographs add to the attractive presentation. (Rev: BCCB 1/00*; BL 11/15/99*; HBG 4/00; SLJ 12/99*) [379.2]

19828 Brill, Marlene T. *Let Women Vote!* (4–6). Illus. Series: Spotlight on American History. 1995, Millbrook LB $15.90 (978-0-562-94589-6). 64pp. The history of the struggle to gain the vote for U.S. women and of the key personalities involved. (Rev: BL 12/15/95; SLJ 1/96) [324.6]

19829 Crewe, Sabrina, and Dale Anderson. *The Seneca Falls Women's Rights Convention* (3–5). Series: Events That Shaped America. 2005, Gareth Stevens LB $26.00 (978-0-8368-3408-6). 32pp. A simple, straightforward account of the 1848 convention featuring direct quotations, editorial cartoons, photographs, reproductions, and newspaper clippings. (Rev: SLJ 3/05) [305.42]

19830 Davidson, Tish. *Prejudice* (4–8). Series: Life Balance. 2003, Watts LB $20.50 (978-0-531-12252-5); paper $6.95 (978-0-531-15572-1). 80pp. This book explore the causes, types, and effects of prejudice, how it can change a person's mental health, and how it has influenced human history. (Rev: BL 10/15/03) [305.8]

19831 Edwards, Pamela Duncan. *The Bus Ride That Changed History: The Story of Rosa Parks* (K–2). Illus. by Danny Shanahan. 2005, Houghton $16.00 (978-0-618-44911-8). 32pp. The story of Rosa Parks's bus ride is told in cumulative "This Is the House That Jack Built" fashion with cartoon illustrations featuring children's questions in dialogue balloons. (Rev: BL 9/1/05; SLJ 10/05) [323]

19832 Fitzgerald, Stephanie. *Struggling for Civil Rights* (4–6). Series: On the Front Line. 2005, Raintree LB $29.93 (978-1-4109-1467-5). 48pp. This is an accessible overview of the civil rights movement of the 1950s and 1960s, covering its roots and key events; personal profiles add interest. (Rev: SLJ 12/05) [323.1196]

19833 Freedman, Jeri. *America Debates Civil Liberties and Terrorism* (5–8). Series: America Debates. 2007, Rosen LB $29.25 (978-1-4042-1927-4). 64pp. Presents facts and opinions on both sides of issues including governmental surveillance and homeland security. (Rev: LMC 1/08; SLJ 11/07) [323.4]

19834 Freedman, Jeri. *America Debates Privacy Versus Security* (5–8). Series: America Debates. 2007, Rosen LB $29.25 (978-1-4042-1929-8). 64pp. Presents facts and opinions on both sides of issues including profiling and the right to privacy. (Rev: LMC 1/08; SLJ 11/07) [323.44]

19835 Freedman, Russell. *Freedom Walkers: The Story of the Montgomery Bus Boycott* (4–7). 2006, Holiday $18.95 (978-0-8234-2031-5). 114pp. First-person accounts enliven this history of the 381-day Montgomery Bus Boycott of the mid-1950s, which ended segregation on the buses. (Rev: BCCB 12/06;

BL 9/15/06; HBG 4/07; LMC 3/07; SLJ 11/06*; VOYA 10/06) [323.1196]

19836 Good, Diane L. *Brown v. Board of Education* (4–6). Series: Cornerstones of Freedom. 2004, Children's Pr. LB $26.00 (978-0-516-24225-5). 48pp. A nicely presented examination of the Supreme Court's 1954 ruling against school segregation. (Rev: SLJ 7/04) [344.73]

19837 Greenberg, Keith E. *Adolescent Rights: Are Young People Equal Under the Law?* (5–8). Illus. Series: Issues of Our Time. 1995, Twenty-First Century LB $22.90 (978-0-8050-3877-4). 64pp. This unbiased account of the controversial subject encourages readers to form their own conclusions. (Rev: SLJ 9/95) [323]

19838 Heinrichs, Ann. *The Ku Klux Klan: A Hooded Brotherhood* (4–7). Series: Journey to Freedom. 2002, Child's World LB $28.50 (978-1-56766-646-5). 40pp. This brief introduction to the Klan covers the group's origins and history, and touches on the Internet's role in spreading hate messages. (Rev: SLJ 12/02) [322.420973]

19839 Hu, Evaleen. *A Level Playing Field: Sports and Race* (5–8). Illus. Series: Sports Issues. 1995, Lerner LB $28.75 (978-0-8225-3302-3). A frank, thorough examination of the problems involving race in sports and how different athletes have dealt with them. (Rev: BL 1/1–15/96; SLJ 9/95) [796]

19840 Isler, Claudia. *The Right to Free Speech* (4–6). Series: Individual Rights and Civic Responsibility. 2001, Rosen LB $26.50 (978-0-8239-3234-4). 128pp. The history of the first amendment is followed by information on sedition, protest, obscenity, symbolic speech, and hate speech. (Rev: SLJ 2/02) [342.0853]

19841 Johnston, Norma. *Remember the Ladies: The First Women's Rights Convention* (4–6). Illus. 1995, Scholastic paper $3.50 (978-0-590-47086-5). 169pp. The story of the 1848 Women's Rights Convention in Seneca Falls, New York, includes biographies of its leaders, like Elizabeth Cady Stanton and Lucretia Mott. (Rev: BL 5/1/95) [323.34]

19842 Kelso, Richard. *Walking for Freedom: The Montgomery Bus Boycott* (3–5). Illus. by Michael Newton. 1993, Raintree LB $27.12 (978-0-8114-7218-0). 52pp. The events and personalities associated with the Montgomery bus boycott are noted. (Rev: SLJ 8/93) [323.4]

19843 Kendall, Martha E. *Failure Is Impossible: The History of American Women's Rights* (5–8). Illus. Series: People's History. 2001, Lerner LB $30.35 (978-0-8225-1744-3). 96pp. The status of women in the United States is discussed from the time of the Puritans to the present, including information on life for slaves, Native American women, and mill girls, and on equal pay and equal opportunity. (Rev: BL 5/1/01; HBG 10/01; SLJ 6/01; VOYA 8/01) [305.42]

19844 King, Casey. *Oh, Freedom! Kids Talk About the Civil Rights Movement with the People Who Made It Happen* (5–9). 1997, Random paper $12.95 (978-0-679-89005-8). In 31 interviews, children ask family members, neighbors, and friends about the part they played in the civil rights movement. (Rev: BL 4/1/97; SLJ 6/97*) [973]

19845 King, David C. *Freedom of Assembly* (4–8). Series: Land of the Free. 1997, Millbrook LB $22.90 (978-0-7613-0064-9). This book covers this basic civil right with examples throughout U.S. history and landmark court cases that helped define its limits. (Rev: BL 5/15/97; SLJ 10/97) [342.73]

19846 King, David C. *The Right to Speak Out* (4–8). Series: Land of the Free. 1997, Millbrook LB $22.90 (978-0-7613-0063-2). Background material on the freedom of speech is given, its use and abuse, and landmark courts cases that have defined it. (Rev: BL 5/15/97; SLJ 10/97) [351.81]

19847 King, Martin Luther, Jr. *I Have a Dream* (4–8). Illus. 1997, Scholastic paper $16.95 (978-0-590-20516-0). The full text of Dr. King's speech is reprinted, with illustrations by 15 award-winning African American artists. (Rev: BL 2/15/98; HBG 3/98; SLJ 11/97) [305.896]

19848 Kops, Deborah. *Women's Suffrage* (5–8). Illus. Series: People at the Center. 2004, Gale LB $24.95 (978-1-56711-772-1). 48pp. This brief but fact-filled volume introduces key leaders in the women's suffrage movement in America. (Rev: BL 5/15/04; SLJ 9/04) [324.6]

19849 Kuhn, Betsy. *Prying Eyes: Privacy in the Twenty-first Century* (5–8). Illus. 2008, Lerner LB $38.60 (978-0-8225-7179-7). 160pp. From video cameras that can track our every move to personal data stored on computers, this book looks at security/privacy issues and court cases related to them to provide an overview of the important issues in this arena. (Rev: BL 1/1–15/08; LMC 10/08; SLJ 5/08) [323.44]

19850 Landau, Elaine. *The Civil Rights Movement in America* (3–5). Series: Cornerstones of Freedom. 2003, Children's Pr. LB $26.00 (978-0-516-24219-4). 48pp. A brief, well-illustrated history of the troubled race relations in the United States and the concerted drive for equality beginning with the U.S. Supreme Court finding that school segregation was unconstitutional. (Rev: SLJ 2/04) [323]

19851 Lucas, Eileen. *Cracking the Wall: The Struggles of the Little Rock Nine* (3–5). Illus. 1998, Carolrhoda $23.93 (978-0-87614-990-4). 48pp. A simple narrative that tells of the desegregation of Central High School in Little Rock, Arkansas, and gives background information on the 1953 Supreme Court decision. (Rev: BCCB 3/98; BL 2/15/98; HBG 9/98; SLJ 6/98) [379.2]

19852 Luthringer, Chelsea. *So What Is Citizenship Anyway?* (5–8). Series: A Student's Guide to American Civics. 1999, Rosen LB $23.95 (978-0-8239-3097-5). 48pp. Describes and defines the roles and responsibilities of citizens in a democracy and encourages young people to become active in political and social affairs and issues. (Rev: HBG 10/00; SLJ 3/00; VOYA 4/00) [323.6]

19853 McKissack, Patricia C., and Fredrick McKissack. *Days of Jubilee: The End of Slavery in the United States* (5–8). 2003, Scholastic $19.99 (978-0-590-10764-8). 134pp. A combination of clear, interesting narrative, relevant quotations from primary sources, thorough historical approach, and well-chosen illustrations make this a worthwhile volume on the gradual end of slavery. (Rev: BCCB 4/03; BL 5/15/03; HBG 10/03; LMC 8/03; SLJ 5/03; VOYA 4/03) [973.7]

19854 Meyers, Madeleine, ed. *Forward into Light: The Struggle for Woman's Suffrage* (4–8). Illus. Series: Perspectives on History. 1994, Discovery paper $6.95 (978-1-878668-25-7). 64pp. The story of the long struggle for women's right to vote, including the contributions of Elizabeth Cady Stanton, Susan B. Anthony, Sojourner Truth, and other leaders. (Rev: BL 8/94) [324.6]

19855 Michelson, Richard. *As Good as Anybody: Martin Luther King Jr. and Abraham Joshua Heschel's Amazing March Toward Freedom* (2–4). Illus. by Raúl Colón. 2008, Knopf $16.99 (978-0-375-83335-9). 40pp. A clear, well-written story about the collaboration between two civil rights leaders — one an African American Baptist and the other a Polish-born rabbi. (Rev: BL 2/1/08; LMC 3/08; SLJ 5/08) [323]

19856 Miller, Jake. *The Montgomery Bus Boycott: Integrating Public Buses* (2–4). Series: The Library of the Civil Rights Movement. 2004, Rosen LB $21.25 (978-0-8239-6251-8). 24pp. Full of photographs, this is an accessible account of the major events of the bus boycott. Also use *Sit-Ins and Freedom Rides: The Power of Nonviolent Resistance* and *The March from Selma to Montgomery: African Americans Demand the Vote* (bolth 2004). (Rev: SLJ 6/04) [323.1]

19857 Morrison, Toni. *Remember: The Journey to School Integration* (5–12). Illus. 2004, Houghton $18.00 (978-0-618-39740-2). 80pp. With striking archival photographs and a fictionalized narrative based on historical fact, this fascinating book explores the impact of the American struggle for civil rights on the children who were often at its center. (Rev: BL 4/15/04; SLJ 6/04) [379.2]

19858 Pacoe, Elaine. *The Right to Vote* (4–6). Illus. Series: Land of the Free. 1997, Millbrook LB $19.90 (978-0-7613-0066-3). 48pp. Explores the principles behind the right to vote and how it was gradually awarded to all citizens. (Rev: BL 5/15/97; SLJ 5/97) [324.6]

19859 Parks, Rosa, and Gregory J. Reed. *Dear Mrs. Parks: A Dialogue with Today's Youth* (5–8). 1996, Lee & Low $16.95 (978-1-880000-45-8). This book contains a sampling of the thousands of letters sent to civil rights leader Rosa Parks and her replies. (Rev: BL 12/1/96; SLJ 12/96) [323]

19860 Price, Sean. *When Will I Get In?* (4–6). Series: American History Through Primary Sources. 2006, Raintree LB $28.21 (978-1-4109-2414-8); paper $7.99 (978-1-4109-2425-4). 32pp. An introduction for reluctant readers to the history of segregation and the important moments and people that were part of the fight for equal rights. (Rev: BL 2/1/07) [305.896]

19861 Rappaport, Doreen. *Nobody Gonna Turn Me 'Round* (4–7). Illus. by Shane W. Evans. 2006, Candlewick $19.99 (978-0-7636-1927-5). 64pp. This concluding volume of a trilogy documenting the black experience in America focuses on the stormy decade between the Montgomery bus boycott and the signing of the Voting Rights Act in August 1965, providing profiles of key figures. (Rev: BL 8/06; SLJ 10/06) [323.1196]

19862 Rappaport, Doreen. *The School Is Not White!* (2–4). Illus. by Curtis James. 2005, Hyperion $16.99 (978-0-7868-1838-9). 32pp. This inspiring true story chronicles the courageous 1960s campaign by Mae Bertha and Matthew Carter, African American sharecroppers, to ensure that their children receive a quality education. (Rev: BL 2/1/05) [323.1]

19863 Rossi, Ann. *Created Equal: Women Campaign for the Right to Vote, 1* (4–6). Series: Crossroads America. 2005, National Geographic LB $21.90 (978-0-7922-8285-3). 40pp. The campaign for women's right to vote is placed in historical context through period photographs, cartoons, and primary source material; biographical information is provided for key individuals. (Rev: SLJ 4/05) [324.6]

19864 Rossi, Ann. *Freedom Struggle: The Anti-Slavery Movement in America, 1830–1865* (4–6). Series: Crossroads America. 2005, National Geographic LB $21.90 (978-0-7922-8061-3). 40pp. Efforts to abolish slavery in the mid-19th century are placed in historical context through period photographs, cartoons, and primary source material; biographical information is provided for key individuals. (Rev: BL 4/1/04; SLJ 4/05) [323]

19865 Seidman, David. *Civil Rights* (4–6). Series: Individual Rights and Civic Responsibility. 2001, Rosen LB $26.50 (978-0-8239-3231-3). 128pp. Covers civil rights issues involving African Americans, women, Native Americans, immigrants, prisoners, and gays and lesbians. (Rev: BL 3/15/02; SLJ 2/02) [323]

19866 Sherrow, Victoria. *Freedom of Worship* (4–6). Illus. Series: Land of the Free. 1997, Millbrook LB $19.90 (978-0-7613-0065-6). 48pp. As well as discussing the right to worship as one pleases, this account covers the religious right, religious intolerance, school prayer, and cults. (Rev: BL 5/15/97; SLJ 5/97) [323.44]

19867 Shore, Diane Z., and Jessica Alexander. *This Is the Dream* (2–4). Illus. by James Ransome. 2006, HarperCollins $16.99 (978-0-06-055519-1). 40pp. Mixing archival photographs, newspaper clippings, original paintings, and rhythmic verse, the creators of this book tell the story of the civil rights movement in an unusual and effective way. (Rev: BL 2/1/06*; SLJ 1/06) [811]

19868 Stokes, John A., and Lois Wolfe. *Students on Strike: Jim Crow, Civil Rights, Brown, and Me* (5–8). Illus. 2008, National Geographic $15.95 (978-1-4263-0153-7). 48pp. The author recounts his days on strike to protest the conditions at a black high school in Virginia in 1951 and explains how this strike helped lead to school desegregation in the 1960s. (Rev: BL 3/15/08; SLJ 4/08) [371.829]

19869 Sullivan, George. *The Day the Women Got the Vote: A Photo History of the Women's Rights Movement* (5–8). Illus. 1994, Scholastic paper $6.95 (978-0-590-47560-0). 96pp. The history of the struggle for women's rights is covered in a series of 24 short photoessays. (Rev: BL 6/1–15/94; SLJ 7/94) [323.34]

19870 Turck, Mary C. *The Civil Rights Movement for Kids: A History with 21 Activities* (4–8). 2000, Chicago Review paper $14.95 (978-1-55652-370-0). 189pp. The story of the civil rights movement with coverage of key events and personalities plus a number of related activities. (Rev: SLJ 10/00) [973.9]

19871 Venable, Rose. *The Civil Rights Movement* (4–6). Series: Journey to Freedom: The African American Library. 2001, Child's World LB $28.50 (978-1-56766-917-6). 40pp. An oversize, attractive volume that supplies details on the 20th-century civil rights movement in the United States, its leaders, and their accomplishments. (Rev: BL 12/15/01; HBG 3/02; SLJ 1/02) [323]

19872 Walker, Paul R. *Remember Little Rock: The Time, the People, the Stories* (4–7). Illus. 2008, National Geographic $17.95 (978-1-4263-0402-6). 64pp. This title offers a dramatic and solidly researched account of the attempt to integrate an all-white school in Little Rock, Arkansas, in September 1957, with eyewitness accounts and news photography. (Rev: BL 2/1/09; SLJ 3/09) [379.2]

19873 Welch, Catherine A. *Children of the Civil Rights Era* (3–6). Series: Picture the American Past. 2001, Carolrhoda LB $22.60 (978-1-57505-481-0). 48pp. Large historical photographs and a simple text are used to describe how young people participated in America's civil rights movement. (Rev: BL 6/1–15/01; HBG 10/01) [323]

19874 Wilson, Reginald. *Think About Our Rights: Civil Liberties and the United States* (5–8). Illus. 1991, Walker LB $15.85 (978-0-8027-8127-7); paper $9.95 (978-0-8027-7371-5). 128pp. The focus is on such civil rights questions as integration, affirmative action, and women's rights. (Rev: SLJ 1/92) [323.4]

Constitution

19875 Allen, Kathy. *The U.S. Constitution* (PS–2). Illus. 2006, Capstone $21.26 (978-0-7368-9594-1). 32pp. This large-format picture book offers a child-friendly, very basic introduction to the U.S. Constitution. (Rev: BL 10/1/06) [342]

19876 Burgan, Michael. *The Bill of Rights* (4–6). Series: We the People. 2001, Compass Point LB $26.60 (978-0-7565-0151-8). 48pp. Burgan discusses the reasons behind the creation of the Bill of Rights, with paintings, maps, and documents. (Rev: SLJ 1/02) [342.73]

19877 Catrow, David. *We the Kids* (PS–3). Illus. 2002, Dial $16.99 (978-0-8037-2553-9). 32pp. A visually engaging, straightforward interpretation of the constitution for young readers. (Rev: BL 3/15/02; HBG 10/02; SLJ 5/02) [342.73]

19878 Collier, Christopher, and James Lincoln Collier. *Creating the Constitution, 1787* (5–8). Illus. Series: Drama of American History. 1998, Marshall Cavendish LB $31.36 (978-0-7614-0776-8). 89pp. This history of the U.S. Constitution describes the background and importance of the document and the compromises made to win ratification. (Rev: BL 2/15/99) [342.73029]

19879 Eck, Kristin. *Drafting the Constitution: Weighing the Evidence to Draw Sound Conclusions* (5–8). Illus. Series: Critical Thinking in American History. 2005, Rosen LB $26.50 (978-1-4042-0412-6). 48pp. This slim volume offers a review of the issues debated at the Constitutional Convention, plus study questions, a reading list, and a Web site with links to related online resources. (Rev: BL 10/15/05) [342.7302]

19880 Feinberg, Barbara S. *Constitutional Amendments* (5–8). Series: Inside Government. 1996, Twenty-First Century LB $22.40 (978-0-8050-4619-9). After presenting a brief history of the Constitution, this work examines the Bill of Rights and then covers the remaining amendments in chapters arranged by topic. (Rev: SLJ 12/96) [342.73]

19881 Finkelman, Paul. *The Constitution* (4–8). Series: American Documents. 2006, National Geographic LB $23.90 (978-0-7922-7975-4). 48pp. An unusually attractive introduction to the Constitution, with reproductions, photographs, and profiles of key individuals. (Rev: SLJ 2/06; VOYA 8/06) [342.73]

19882 Freedman, Russell. *In Defense of Liberty: The Story of America's Bill of Rights* (5–10). 2003, Holiday $24.95 (978-0-8234-1585-4). 196pp. A succinct explanation of the history of the Bill of Rights, discussing each amendment in turn and its particular relevance to today's controversies, with many references to cases involving young people. (Rev: BCCB 10/03*; BL 10/1/03*; HB 9/03*; HBG 4/04; SLJ 10/03*; VOYA 4/04) [342.73]

19883 Gonzales, Doreen. *A Look at the Second Amendment: To Keep and Bear Arms* (4–7). Illus. Series: MyReportLinks.com. 2007, Enslow LB $24.95 (978-1-59845-061-3). 128pp. Links to relevant Web sites enhance the text introducing students to the content and intent of the Second Amendment to the United States Constitution. (Rev: BL 10/15/07; LMC 11/07; SLJ 1/08) [344.7305]

19884 Graham, Amy. *A Look at the 18th and 21st Amendments: The Prohibition and Sale of Intoxicating Liquors* (5–8). Illus. Series: The Constitution of the United States. 2007, Enslow LB $33.27 (978-1-59845-063-7). 128pp. A clear overview of these two amendments with links to Web sites that offer additional information. (Rev: SLJ 1/08)

19885 Horn, Geoffrey M. *The Bill of Rights and Other Amendments* (5–8). Series: World Almanac Library of American Government. 2004, World Almanac LB $31.00 (978-0-8368-5475-6). 48pp. A thorough and detailed examination of the process of changing the Constitution and the issues underlying the various amendments. (Rev: SLJ 9/04) [342.73]

19886 Hubbard-Brown, Janet. *How the Constitution Was Created* (5–8). Series: The U.S. Government:

How It Works. 2007, Chelsea House LB $30.00 (978-0-7910-9420-4). 104pp. This is a thorough introduction to the Constitution, with interesting text and accompanying historical and biographical sidebars. (Rev: SLJ 1/08)

19887 Hudson, David L. *The Bill of Rights* (5–8). Illus. Series: The Constitution. 2002, Enslow LB $26.60 (978-0-7660-1903-4). 128pp. A look at the first 10 amendments to the Constitution and how they have affected the citizens of the United States. (Rev: BL 2/15/03; HBG 3/03) [342.73]

19888 Hudson, David L. *The Fourteenth Amendment: Equal Protection Under the Law* (5–8). Illus. Series: The Constitution. 2002, Enslow LB $26.60 (978-0-7660-1904-1). 128pp. What the 14th amendment to the Constitution entails and how it has affected the citizens of the United States. (Rev: BL 2/15/03; HBG 10/03) [342.73]

19889 Johnson, Linda C. *Our Constitution* (4–6). Illus. Series: I Know America. 1992, Millbrook LB $20.90 (978-1-56294-090-4). 48pp. This history of our Constitution includes an explanation of its important parts. (Rev: BL 9/1/92; SLJ 10/92) [342.73]

19890 Krull, Kathleen. *A Kids' Guide to America's Bill of Rights: Curfews, Censorship, and the 100-Pound Giant* (5–8). Illus. 1999, Avon $16.99 (978-0-380-97497-9). 224pp. After a description of the first 10 amendments, this book details famous court cases and what each amendment means to young people. (Rev: BL 12/1/99; HBG 3/00; VOYA 4/00) [342.73]

19891 Levert, Suzanne. *The Constitution* (2–5). Series: Kaleidoscope. 2002, Benchmark LB $25.64 (978-0-7614-1452-0). 48pp. An accessible overview of Constitution, its history, and its impact on the government of the united States. (Rev: HBG 3/03; SLJ 4/03) [342.73]

19892 Levy, Elizabeth. *If You Were There When They Signed the Constitution* (2–4). Illus. 1992, Scholastic paper $5.99 (978-0-590-45159-8). 80pp. All about the delegates and the U.S. Constitution. (Rev: BL 9/15/87; SLJ 11/87)

19893 Maestro, Betsy, and Giulio Maestro. *A More Perfect Union: The Story of Our Constitution* (2–4). Illus. 1987, Morrow paper $7.99 (978-0-688-10192-3). 48pp. The U.S. Constitution is explained for young readers. (Rev: BCCB 10/87; BL 9/1/87; SLJ 9/87)

19894 Sobel, Syl. *The U.S. Constitution and You* (3–5). Illus. by Denise Gilgannon. 2001, Barron's paper $6.95 (978-0-7641-1707-7). 48pp. Clear text and pen-and-ink sketches provide a concise look at the importance of the Constitution, with chapters on checks and balances and the rights of the people and of the states. (Rev: SLJ 8/01) [342.73]

19895 Taylor-Butler, Christine. *The Bill of Rights* (3–5). Illus. Series: True Book: American History. 2007, Scholastic LB $26.00 (978-0-531-12627-1); paper $6.95 (978-0-531-14777-1). 48pp. A visually engaging introduction to the basics of the Bill of Rights with fast facts, resource list, and glossary. (Rev: BL 1/1–15/08) [342.7308]

19896 Weidner, Daniel. *The Constitution: The Preamble and the Articles* (5–8). Series: The Constitution. 2002, Enslow LB $26.60 (978-0-7660-1906-5). 112pp. The history of the U.S. Constitution and its meanings are explored through personal stories and examples. (Rev: BL 2/15/03; HBG 3/03; SLJ 1/03) [342.73]

19897 Weidner, Daniel. *Creating the Constitution: The People and Events That Formed the Nation* (5–8). Series: The Constitution. 2002, Enslow LB $26.60 (978-0-7660-1905-8). 112pp. This informative volume describes how the U.S. Constitution was written and the debates that preceded its adoption. (Rev: BL 2/15/03; HBG 3/03; SLJ 1/03) [342.73]

Crime and Criminals

19898 Aaseng, Nathan. *Treacherous Traitors* (5–9). Series: Profiles. 1997, Oliver LB $19.95 (978-1-881508-38-0). This book profiles 12 Americans who were tried for treason, including Benedict Arnold, John Brown, Alger Hiss, Julius and Ethel Rosenberg, and Aldrich Ames. (Rev: SLJ 2/98) [355.3]

19899 Anderson, Wayne. *The Chicago Black Sox Trial: A Primary Source Account* (5–8). Illus. Series: Great Trials of the Twentieth Century. 2003, Rosen LB $29.25 (978-0-8239-3969-5). 64pp. This is a detailed, readable account of the 1919 Chicago Black Sox scandal and the plot to fix the World Series. (Rev: BL 4/1/04; SLJ 6/04; VOYA 4/04) [796.357]

19900 Beres, D. B. *Dusted and Busted! The Science of Fingerprinting* (4–8). Illus. Series: 24/7: Science Behind the Scenes: Forensic Files. 2007, Watts LB $25.00 (978-0-531-11822-1); paper $7.95 (978-0-531-15457-1). 64pp. Introduces the scientific process of fingerprinting through easy-to-read text, illustrations, and real-life examples. (Rev: SLJ 7/07) [363.2]

19901 Beres, D. B. *Killer at Large* (3–6). Series: 24/7: Science Behind the Scenes. 2007, Watts LB $25.00 (978-0-531-12065-1); paper $7.95 (978-0-531-17526-2). 64pp. The profiling techniques used to track down murderers is explained in three real-life case studies. Readers meet people working in this field and learn how they got there. (Rev: SLJ 6/07)

19902 Blackwood, Gary L. *Gangsters* (4–7). Series: Bad Guys. 2001, Benchmark LB $28.50 (978-0-7614-1016-4). 72pp. Al Capone is just one of the evildoers profiled in this volume that gives historical context for each "bad guy." Also use *Outlaws* and *Highwaymen* (both 2001). (Rev: HBG 3/02; SLJ 1/02) [364.106]

19903 Butterfield, Moira. *Pirates and Smugglers* (5–7). Series: Kingfisher Knowledge. 2005, Kingfisher paper $12.95 (978-0-7534-5864-8). 64pp. A broad historical survey of outlaws on the high seas, from early smugglers to today's dealers in drugs and exotic animals. (Rev: SLJ 12/05)

19904 Dahl, Michael. *Computer Evidence* (4–8). Illus. Series: Forensic Crime Solvers. 2004, Capstone LB $23.93 (978-0-7368-2698-3). 32pp. After a story that draws the readers in, Dahl looks at the use of computer evidence in tracking down and convicting criminals. Also use *Poison Evidence* (2004). (Rev: BL 5/1/04)

19905 Denega, Danielle. *Gut-Eating Bugs: Maggots Reveal the Time of Death!* (3–6). Series: 24/7: Science Behind the Scenes. 2007, Watts LB $25.00 (978-0-531-11824-5); paper $7.95 (978-0-531-17525-5). 64pp. An obscure branch of forensics, forensic entomology, is explained here in a format that will interest many readers. (Rev: SLJ 6/07)

19906 Denega, Danielle. *Have You Seen This Face? The Work of Forensic Artists* (4–8). Illus. Series: 24/7: Science Behind the Scenes: Forensic Files. 2007, Watts LB $25.00 (978-0-531-11823-8); paper $7.95 (978-0-531-15458-8). 64pp. Introduces the work of forensic artists through easy-to-read text, illustrations, and real-life examples. (Rev: SLJ 7/07) [363.2]

19907 Dickson, Louise. *Lu and Clancy's Crime Science* (2–4). Illus. by Pat Cupples. Series: Lu and Clancy. 1999, Kids Can paper $5.95 (978-1-55074-552-8). 40pp. While solving a mystery about missing pups, a Scotch terrier and a basset hound teach readers about observational skills, how to take finger and lip prints, how to analyze footprints and teeth prints, and how to perform other procedures in criminal science. (Rev: SLJ 11/99) [364]

19908 Farman, John. *The Short and Bloody History of Spies* (5–8). Illus. 2002, Lerner LB $19.93 (978-0-8225-0845-8); paper $5.95 (978-0-8225-0846-5). 96pp. A witty and fascinating account of the intriguing lives of spies, with descriptions of spying techniques and gadgets. (Rev: BL 1/1–15/03; HBG 3/03) [327.12]

19909 Fridell, Ron. *Forensic Science* (4–7). Series: Cool Science. 2006, Lerner LB $26.60 (978-0-8225-5935-1). 48pp. The history of forensic science from 1910 to today is accompanied by information on the professionals involved (medical examiners, forensic entomologists) and the equipment used; effective photographs add to the appeal. (Rev: SLJ 4/07) [363.25]

19910 Fridell, Ron. *Spy Technology* (4–7). Series: Cool Science. 2006, Lerner LB $26.60 (978-0-8225-5934-4). 48pp. A review of the kinds of technology available in the past and today — including gadgets used by the CIA and KGB and spy satellites — is followed by accounts of dangerous missions and discussion of future technologies. (Rev: SLJ 4/07) [623]

19911 Friedlander, Mark P., Jr., and Terry M. Phillips. *When Objects Talk: Solving a Crime with Science* (5–8). Illus. Series: Discovery! 2001, Lerner LB $27.93 (978-0-8225-0649-2). 120pp. A fictional mystery serves to introduce criminal investigation techniques such as fingerprints and DNA. (Rev: HBG 3/02; SLJ 2/02; VOYA 2/02) [363.25]

19912 Gifford, Clive. *Spies* (5–9). Illus. Series: Kingfisher Knowledge. 2004, Kingfisher LB $11.95

(978-0-7534-5777-1). 64pp. Stories of notable espionage achievements are included along with brisk facts, plenty of high-interest illustrations, a history of spying, and discussion of the future of this field. (Rev: BL 9/1/04; SLJ 5/05)

19913 Goldentyer, Debra. *Street Violence* (4–8). Series: Preteen Pressures. 1998, Raintree LB $25.69 (978-0-8172-5028-7). This book discusses types of street violence and how young people can protect themselves, as well as gang issues and alternatives to participation. (Rev: BL 5/15/98; HBG 10/98; SLJ 6/98) [364]

19914 Gordon, Olivia. *Cold Case File: Murder in the Mountains* (5–8). Series: Crime Solvers. 2007, Bearport LB $25.27 (978-1-59716-547-1). 32pp. After a description of the crime, the victim (a photographer who disappeared in the Rockies in the 1970s), and the accused, Gordon recounts the steps taken in the nearly 20-year effort to find the body and solve the crime. "Crime Solving Up Close" looks at forensic terminology. (Rev: LMC 1/08; SLJ 11/07) [364.152]

19915 Graham, Ian. *Crime-Fighting* (5–8). Illus. Series: Science Spotlight. 1995, Raintree LB $24.26 (978-0-8114-3840-7). 46pp. A discussion of scientific methods used in analyzing evidence at crime scenes, such as DNA testing. (Rev: SLJ 7/95) [364]

19916 Graham, Ian. *Fakes and Forgeries* (5–8). Illus. Series: Science Spotlight. 1995, Raintree LB $24.26 (978-0-8114-3843-8). 46pp. Examines famous scandals in history involving such fakes as the Loch Ness monster, counterfeit money, and the forged Hitler diaries. (Rev: SLJ 7/95) [364]

19917 Greenberg, Keith E. *Out of the Gang* (5–8). Illus. 1992, Lerner LB $19.93 (978-0-8225-2553-0). 40pp. A realistic portrait of gang life, revealed by a man who escaped it and a boy who managed to stay out of it. (Rev: BCCB 6/92; BL 6/15/92; SLJ 9/92) [364.1]

19918 Hjelmeland, Andy. *Prisons: Inside the Big House* (4–8). Illus. Series: Pro/Con Issues. 1996, Lerner LB $30.35 (978-0-8225-2607-0). Opposing viewpoints are presented on the purposes of prisons, prison conditions, and alternate forms of rehabilitation. (Rev: BL 8/96; SLJ 9/96) [365]

19919 Howard, Amanda. *Kidnapping File: The Graeme Thorne Case* (3–6). Series: Crime Solvers. 2007, Bearport LB $25.27 (978-1-59716-548-8). 32pp. An attention-grabbing account of the kidnapping of an 8-year-old boy, with details of the steps investigators took to solve the crime. Also use *Robbery File: The Museum Heist* (2007). (Rev: LMC 1/08; SLJ 11/07) [364.14]

19920 Jackson, Donna. *The Bone Detectives: How Forensic Anthropologists Solve Crimes and Uncover Mysteries of the Dead* (5–9). 1996, Little, Brown $17.95 (978-0-316-82935-9). A look at the role of forensic anthropologists in solving crimes including murder. (Rev: BCCB 4/96; BL 4/1/96; HB 5/96; SLJ 5/96*; VOYA 8/96) [363.2]

19921 Johnson, Julie. *Why Do People Join Gangs?* (5–8). Series: Exploring Tough Issues. 2001, Raintree LB $25.69 (978-0-7398-3236-3). 48pp. Johnson looks at gangs — who joins them and why, and how to get out of one — in the United States and abroad, and includes a chapter on dealing with bullies. Also use *Why Do People Fight Wars?* and *Why Are People Prejudiced?* (both 2002). (Rev: SLJ 11/01) [364.1]

19922 Joyce, Jaime. *Bullet Proof! The Evidence That Guns Leave Behind* (5–10). Series: 24/7: Science Behind the Scenes. 2007, Watts LB $25.00 (978-0-531-11820-7); paper $7.95 (978-0-531-15455-7). 64pp. Joyce uses three real cases to illustrate how ballistics experts can help to solve crimes; reluctant readers will enjoy this. (Rev: SLJ 8/07) [363.25]

19923 Lane, Brian. *Investigation of Murder* (4–6). Illus. Series: Crimebusters. 1996, Millbrook LB $20.90 (978-0-7613-0527-9). 32pp. A fictitious murder is used as the framework for this discussion of the work of police and forensic experts. (Rev: BL 1/1–15/97; SLJ 1/97) [363.2]

19924 McDonald, Fiona. *You Wouldn't Want to Meet a Body Snatcher: Criminals and Murderers You'd Rather Avoid* (3–6). Illus. by David Antram. 2009, Scholastic LB $29.00 (978-0-531-20822-9); paper $9.95 (978-0-531-21046-8). 32pp. A lighthearted review of evildoers through the ages. (Rev: BLO 3/17/09) [900]

19925 Oliver, Marilyn Tower. *Gangs: Trouble in the Streets* (5–8). 1995, Enslow LB $20.95 (978-0-89490-492-9). Discusses the roots of gangs in the 19th century, aspects of modern gang life, and how members manage to quit gangs. (Rev: BL 8/95) [364.1]

19926 Oxlade, Chris. *Crime Detection* (3–5). Illus. Series: Science Encounters. 1997, Rigby $22.79 (978-1-57572-090-6). 32pp. An introduction to detective work that covers forensic science, security, fingerprints, and how evidence is chemically treated. (Rev: SLJ 11/97) [364]

19927 Pentland, Peter, and Pennie Stoyles. *Forensic Science* (4–6). Illus. Series: Science and Scientists. 2002, Chelsea House LB $28.00 (978-0-7910-7010-9). 32pp. An overview of how blood types, fingerprints, and DNA profiling figure in forensic science, and of the career itself, with illustrations and interesting sidebars. (Rev: HBG 3/03; SLJ 4/03) [363.25]

19928 Platt, Richard. *Forensics* (5–10). Illus. Series: Kingfisher Knowledge. 2005, Kingfisher paper $12.95 (978-0-7534-5862-4). 64pp. This introduction to the use of the forensic sciences in crime investigation is presented in short blocks of text that will make it appealing to reluctant readers. (Rev: SLJ 11/05) [363.2]

19929 Powell, Jillian. *Drug Trafficking* (4–6). Illus. Series: Crimebusters. 1997, Millbrook LB $20.90 (978-0-7613-0555-2). 32pp. Using a fabricated crime as a focus, this book describes the many avenues of drug trafficking in the United States and how various agencies are combating it. (Rev: BL 6/1–15/97) [364.1]

19930 Prokos, Anna. *Guilty by a Hair! Real-Life DNA Matches!* (4–8). Illus. Series: 24/7: Science Behind the Scenes: Forensic Files. 2007, Watts LB $25.00 (978-0-531-11821-4); paper $7.95 (978-0-

531-18733-3). 64pp. In clear, engaging prose with illustrations and real-life examples, this volume discusses the science behind DNA analysis used in crime investigations. (Rev: SLJ 7/07) [363.2]

19931 Prokos, Anna. *Killer Wallpaper: True Cases of Deadly Poisonings* (5–10). Series: 24/7: Science Behind the Scenes. 2007, Watts LB $25.00 (978-0-531-12061-3); paper $7.95 (978-0-531-15459-5). 64pp. Prokos uses three real cases to illustrate the work of forensic toxicologists; reluctant readers will enjoy this. (Rev: SLJ 8/07) [363.2]

19932 Rainis, Kenneth G. *Crime-Solving Science Projects: Forensic Science Experiments* (5–9). 2000, Enslow LB $26.60 (978-0-7660-1289-9). 128pp. After defining forensic science, this book contains experiments and projects involving such areas as fingerprints, inks, writing samples, fibers, forgeries, and blood evidence. (Rev: HBG 10/01; SLJ 2/01) [363.2]

19933 Rainis, Kenneth G. *Forgery: Crime-Solving Science Experiments* (4–8). Series: Forensic Science Projects. 2006, Enslow LB $31.93 (978-0-7660-1961-4). 128pp. Rainis explores how forensic scientists identify forgeries, with 10 interesting case studies. (Rev: SLJ 5/07) [363.25]

19934 Rollins, Barbara B., and Michael Dahl. *Ballistics* (4–7). Series: Edge Books, Forensic Crime Solvers. 2004, Capstone LB $23.93 (978-0-7368-2421-7). 32pp. Report writers and reluctant readers will be attracted to this brief, concise discussion of the science of ballistics. (Rev: BL 5/1/04; SLJ 8/04) [363.25]

19935 Rollins, Barbara B., and Michael Dahl. *Blood Evidence* (4–8). Illus. Series: Forensic Crime Solvers. 2004, Capstone LB $23.93 (978-0-7368-2418-7). 32pp. Reluctant readers will be attracted to the gruesome nature of the subject matter and the often lurid presentation of facts. (Rev: BL 5/1/04; SLJ 8/04) [363.25]

19936 Rollins, Barbara B., and Michael Dahl. *Cause of Death* (4–8). Illus. Series: Forensic Crime Solvers. 2004, Capstone LB $23.93 (978-0-7368-2420-0). 32pp. This look at how crime scene technicians and medical examiners determine cause of death will draw in reluctant readers. (Rev: BL 5/1/04; SLJ 8/04) [614]

19937 Rollins, Barbara B., and Michael Dahl. *Fingerprint Evidence* (4–7). Series: Edge Books, Forensic Crime Solvers. 2004, Capstone LB $23.93 (978-0-7368-2419-4). 32pp. After a story that draws the readers in, the authors describe the features of fingerprints and discusses their use in solving crimes. (Rev: BL 5/1/04; SLJ 8/04) [363.25]

19938 Ross, Stewart. *Spies and Traitors* (5–8). Series: Fact or Fiction? 1995, Millbrook LB $26.90 (978-1-56294-648-7). A history of the people who have placed themselves above their country in the dangerous game of espionage and betrayal. (Rev: BL 11/15/95; SLJ 3/96) [355.3]

19939 Schroeder, Andreas. *Scams!* (5–8). Series: True Stories from the Edge. 2004, Annick $18.95 (978-1-55037-853-5); paper $7.95 (978-1-55037-852-8). 154pp. Ten stories reveal daring trickery,

con jobs, and scams, including the 1938 radio broadcast of *War of the Worlds* that terrified millions of Americans and the baseless claim that a tribe of cavemen had been found living in a remote corner of the Philippines. (Rev: SLJ 8/04) [364.16]

19940 Schroeder, Andreas. *Thieves!* (5–10). Series: True Stories from the Edge. 2005, Annick $18.95 (978-1-55037-933-4); paper $8.95 (978-1-55037-932-7). 164pp. Ten world-class crimes are described in compelling detail. (Rev: SLJ 3/06) [364]

19941 Sorensen, Lita. *The Scottsboro Boys Trial: A Primary Source Account* (5–8). Illus. 2003, Rosen LB $29.25 (978-0-8239-3975-6). 64pp. Sorensen dissects the sensational Scottsboro Boys rape case in Alabama that attracted media attention from around the globe. (Rev: BL 4/1/04) [345.761]

19942 Steele, Philip. *Smuggling* (5–9). Series: Past and Present. 1993, Macmillan LB $20.00 (978-0-02-786884-5). A colorful history of smuggling through the ages. (Rev: BL 8/93) [364.1]

19943 Townsend, John. *Bone Detectives* (4–6). Series: Crabtree Contact. 2008, Crabtree LB $26.60 (978-0-7787-3806-0); paper $8.95 (978-0-7787-3828-2). 32pp. A body is discovered and forensic scientists swing into action, examining the skeleton and seeking clues to the victim in fingerprints, teeth, and so forth. Also use *Forensic Evidence: Prints* (2008). (Rev: SLJ 3/09) [614]

19944 Townsend, John. *Breakouts and Blunders* (5–8). Series: True Crime. 2005, Raintree LB $31.43 (978-1-4109-1427-9). 48pp. Attempted and successful escapes through history are the subject of this book in the True Crime series, which features a scrapbook format with engaging photographs and graphics. Also use *Fakes and Forgeries* and *Kidnappers and Assassins* (both 2005). (Rev: SLJ 6/06) [365.641]

19945 Trapani, Margi. *Working Together Against Gang Violence* (4–8). Series: The Library of Social Activism. 1996, Rosen LB $16.95 (978-0-8239-2260-4). After a general discussion on gang behavior, the author gives pointers to help young people cope with the threat of gangs and suggestions for working with others against gang violence. (Rev: SLJ 2/97) [302.3]

19946 Webber, Diane. *Do You Read Me? Famous Cases Solved by Handwriting Analysis!* (5–10). Series: 24/7: Science Behind the Scenes. 2007, Watts LB $25.00 (978-0-531-12066-8); paper $7.95 (978-0-531-15456-4). 64pp. Webber uses three real cases to illustrate ways in which the study of handwriting can help to solve crimes; reluctant readers will enjoy this. (Rev: SLJ 8/07) [363.2]

19947 West, David. *Detective Work with Ballistics* (4–7). Illus. by Emanuele Boccanfuso. Series: Graphic Forensic Science. 2008, Rosen LB $21.95 (978-1-4042-1434-7). 48pp. Graphic-novel-like depictions of actual cases in which ballistic evidence pointed to the culprit make this an interesting introduction to this forensic specialty. (Rev: BL 3/15/08) [363.25]

19948 Wiese, Jim. *Detective Science: 40 Crime-Solving, Case-Breaking, Crook-Catching Activities for*

Kids (4–7). 1996, Wiley paper $12.95 (978-0-471-11980-7). 128pp. Presents 40 experiments and activities that illustrate techniques in forensic science related to observing, collecting, and analyzing evidence. (Rev: BL 4/15/96; SLJ 6/96) [363.2]

19949 Williams, Stanley, and Barbara C. Becnel. *Gangs and Drugs* (3–5). Illus. Series: Tookie Speaks Out. 1996, Rosen LB $18.75 (978-0-8239-2348-9). 24pp. A former gang leader and current prison inmate, Tookie Williams tells about the part drugs play in the gang scene. (Rev: BL 2/15/97) [364.1]

19950 Williams, Stanley, and Barbara C. Becnel. *Gangs and the Abuse of Power* (4–8). Series: Tookie Speaks Out Against Gang Violence. 1996, Rosen LB $18.75 (978-0-8239-2346-5). A former active gang member in Los Angeles tells what his life was like as a member and how to avoid his mistakes. Also use in this series *Gangs and Wanting to Belong* (1996). (Rev: SLJ 1/97) [302.3]

19951 Williams, Stanley, and Barbara C. Becnel. *Gangs and Weapons* (4–8). Series: Tookie Speaks Out Against Gang Violence. 1996, Rosen LB $18.75 (978-0-8239-2342-7). The use of weapons in gangs to gain and maintain power and how they are obtained are two of the topics covered in this cautionary account written by a former gang member who was seriously wounded in a shootout. Also use *Gangs and Your Friends* (1996). (Rev: SLJ 1/97) [302.3]

19952 Williams, Stanley, and Barbara C. Becnel. *Gangs and Your Neighborhood* (4–8). Series: Tookie Speaks Out Against Gang Violence. 1996, Rosen LB $18.75 (978-0-8239-2347-2). How gangs grow in neighborhoods and how they change them are two of the topics covered in this book about the dangers of gangs and how to avoid joining one. (Rev: SLJ 1/97) [302.3]

19953 Winchester, Elizabeth Siris. *The Right Bite: Dentists as Detectives* (4–8). Illus. Series: 24/7 Science Behind the Scenes: Forensic Files. 2007, Scholastic LB $26.00 (978-0-531-12062-0); paper $7.95 (978-0-531-18734-0). 64pp. Conversational text focuses on the work of forensic dentists and offers multiple (sometimes gruesome) examples of cases in which their findings identified victims and perpetrators; factual inserts add interest and a final section discusses the equipment used. (Rev: BL 4/1/07; SLJ 6/07) [614]

19954 Winkleman, Katherine K. *Police Patrol* (PS–3). Illus. by John S. Winkleman. 1996, Walker LB $16.85 (978-0-8027-8454-4). 32pp. Activities in a police station and the duties of police are described in words and photos. (Rev: BCCB 1/97; BL 1/1–15/97; SLJ 12/96) [363.2]

19955 Woodford, Chris. *Criminal Investigation* (4–8). Illus. Series: Science Fact Files. 2001, Raintree LB $27.12 (978-0-7398-1016-3). 45pp. A concise introduction to the forensic science with information on the newest equipment and techniques. (Rev: HBG 10/01; SLJ 1/02) [363.2]

19956 Yaffe, Rebecca M., and Lonnie F. Hoade. *When a Parent Goes to Jail: A Comprehensive*

Guide for Counseling Children of Incarcerated Parents (3–5). Illus. by Barbara S. Moody. 2000, Rayve $49.95 (978-1-877810-08-4). 45pp. This book about adults in trouble with the law goes through the incarceration process from arrest to sentencing. (Rev: SLJ 12/00) [363.2]

Elections and Political Parties

19957 Anderson, Dale. *The Democratic Party: America's Oldest Party* (5–8). Series: Snapshots in History. 2007, Compass Point LB $31.93 (978-0-7565-2450-0). 96pp. This well-designed book provides a thorough, unbiased history of the Democratic Party and includes sidebars, charts, photographs, maps, and Web sites. (Rev: SLJ 7/07) [324.2736]

19958 Anderson, Dale. *The Republican Party: The Story of the Grand Old Party* (5–8). Series: Snapshots in History. 2007, Compass Point LB $31.93 (978-0-7565-2449-4). 96pp. This history of the Republican Party presents a balanced view of the how the party formed, its values, and its highs and lows since its formation. (Rev: SLJ 7/07) [324.273]

19959 Andryszewski, Tricia. *The Reform Party* (5–8). Series: Headliners. 2000, Millbrook LB $25.90 (978-0-7613-1906-1). 64pp. This book describes the formation of the Reform Party and highlights the work of Ross Perot, Pat Buchanan, and Jesse Ventura. (Rev: BL 8/00; HBG 10/01; SLJ 1/01) [324.273]

19960 Ansary, Mir T. *Election Day* (2–3). Illus. Series: Holiday Histories. 2002, Heinemann LB $21.36 (978-1-58810-221-8). 32pp. A brief history and overview of the U.S. presidential election system. (Rev: BL 2/1/02) [324.973]

19961 Christelow, Eileen. *Vote!* (2–5). 2003, Houghton LB $16.00 (978-0-618-24754-7). 48pp. A mayoral campaign — with comic-book style art and commentary by politically minded dogs — serves to illustrate the voting process and teach helpful lessons about such related issues as voting rights, registration, fund raising, and ballot recounts. (Rev: BL 11/1/03; HBG 4/04; SLJ 12/03)

19962 De Capua, Sarah E. *Running for Public Office* (2–5). Series: True Books — Civics. 2002, Children's Book Pr. LB $25.00 (978-0-516-22333-9); paper $6.95 (978-0-516-27368-6). 48pp. A simple, large-type text and many photographs are used to introduce the positions open in public office and the steps in running for these positions, including campaigning and elections. (Rev: BL 6/1–15/02; SLJ 10/02) [324.7]

19963 De Capua, Sarah E. *Voting* (2–5). Series: True Books — Civics. 2002, Children's Book Pr. paper $6.95 (978-0-516-27365-5). 48pp. The election system is introduced in simple, large-type text with plenty of attractive color photographs. (Rev: BL 6/1–15/02) [324]

19964 Donovan, Sandy. *Running for Office: A Look at Political Campaigns* (4–6). Illus. Series: How Government Works. 2004, Lerner LB $25.26 (978-0-8225-4700-6). 56pp. The fictional tale of Samantha Brown's campaign for election as a state senator serves as a framework for details about all aspects of electioneering. (Rev: BL 5/1/04; HBG 4/04) [324.7]

19965 Giddens-White, Bryon. *National Elections and the Political Process* (4–6). Series: Our Government. 2005, Heinemann LB $28.21 (978-1-4034-6604-4). 32pp. This explanation of how elections in the United States work will be useful for report writers. (Rev: SLJ 5/06) [324.6097]

19966 Gottfried, Ted. *The 2000 Election* (5–8). Illus. 2002, Millbrook LB $25.90 (978-0-7613-2406-5). 64pp. A well-designed and detailed look at the controversial presidential election of 2000, with background information, sidebars on important people, and an electoral map and other graphics. (Rev: BL 7/02; HBG 10/02; SLJ 4/02) [324.973]

19967 Granfield, Linda. *America Votes: How Our President Is Elected* (4–6). 2003, Kids Can $16.95 (978-1-55337-086-4); paper $9.95 (978-1-55337-087-1). 64pp. This is an appealing and clear explanation of the American presidential election process, from qualifications for voting through such issues as election fraud and the role of television. (Rev: BL 9/15/03; HBG 4/04; SLJ 12/03) [324.6]

19968 Hamilton, John. *Running for Office* (3–5). Series: Government in Action! 2005, ABDO LB $22.78 (978-1-59197-822-0). 32pp. All about how one goes about being elected to public office, with discussion of the differences between the two major U.S. parties. (Rev: SLJ 7/05) [324.7]

19969 Hewson, Martha S. *The Electoral College* (5–9). 2002, Chelsea $25.00 (978-0-7910-6790-1). 64pp. Covers the history of the electoral college and details of elections of particular interest, including the 2000 Bush–Gore decision. (Rev: HBG 3/03; SLJ 2/03) [324.6]

19970 Horn, Geoffrey M. *Political Parties, Interest Groups, and the Media* (5–8). Series: World Almanac Library of American Government. 2004, World Almanac LB $31.00 (978-0-8368-5478-7). 48pp. An engaging introduction to the world of politics, the importance of money and lobbying, and the role of the press. (Rev: SLJ 9/04) [324]

19971 Landau, Elaine. *Friendly Foes: A Look at Political Parties* (4–6). Illus. Series: How Government Works. 2003, Lerner LB $25.26 (978-0-8225-1349-0). 56pp. Discusses the two major political parties in the United States, with an eye to their differences in such areas as the role of government in society; minority parties are mentioned in a final chapter. (Rev: HBG 4/04; SLJ 3/04) [324.273]

19972 Landau, Elaine. *The 2000 Presidential Election* (2–5). Series: Cornerstones of Freedom, Second Series. 2002, Children's Book Pr. LB $26.00 (978-0-516-22527-2). 48pp. A timeline and informative text help to unravel the events between the 2000 election and Gore's concession speech. (Rev: SLJ 3/03)

19973 Lindop, Edmund. *Political Parties* (5–8). Series: Inside Government. 1996, Twenty-First Century LB $24.90 (978-0-8050-4618-2). This work traces the origins of political parties and the role they play in presidential elections. (Rev: BL 9/15/96; SLJ 12/96) [324.273]

19974 Lutz, Norma Jean. *The History of Third Parties* (4–6). Series: Your Government: How It Works. 2000, Chelsea LB $25.00 (978-0-7910-5541-0). 64pp. The Abolitionists, Liberty Party, Southern Democrats, Nativists, Prohibitionists, Socialists, and Reform Party are a few of the American third parties discussed here. (Rev: HBG 9/00; SLJ 8/00) [324.273]

19975 Morris-Lipsman, Arlene. *Presidential Races: The Battle for Power in the United States* (5–8). Illus. Series: People's History. 2007, Lerner LB $30.60 (978-0-8225-6783-7). 112pp. Political cartoons, photographs, and other memorabilia add to the text of this guide to the growth in importance of presidential election campaigns; the author gives pertinent background information on each election and provides a useful chart of election results. (Rev: BL 9/15/07; SLJ 10/07) [324.973]

19976 Murphy, Patricia. *Election Day* (PS–2). Series: Rookie Read-about Holidays. 2003, Children's Book Pr. paper $5.95 (978-0-516-27488-1). 32pp. In very simple words and pictures, this book describes the activities that occur on the first Tuesday after the first Monday in November. (Rev: BL 3/15/03) [324]

19977 Murphy, Patricia J. *Voting and Elections* (K–2). Series: Let's See. 2001, Compass Point LB $19.93 (978-0-7565-0144-0). 24pp. A simple introduction to the voting process and how you register to vote. (Rev: SLJ 1/02) [324.7]

19978 Nobleman, Marc Tyler. *Election Day* (1–3). Series: Let's See. 2004, Compass Point LB $19.93 (978-0-7565-0644-5). 24pp. Using a question-and-answer format, large print, and many illustrations, this small book introduces the American election process. (Rev: BL 10/15/04) [324.6]

19979 Payan, Gregory. *The Federalists and Anti-Federalists: How and Why Political Parties Were Formed in Young America* (4–6). Illus. Series: Life in the New American Nation. 2004, Rosen LB $22.50 (978-0-8239-4038-7). 32pp. The evolution of political parties in America is chronicled from the close of the Constitutional Convention to the present. (Rev: BL 6/1–15/04) [324.2732]

19980 Santella, Andrew. *U.S. Presidential Inaugurations* (3–6). Series: Cornerstones of Freedom, Second Series. 2002, Children's Book Pr. LB $26.00 (978-0-516-22533-3). 48pp. Inaugural addresses, inaugural balls, and inaugural weather are the focus of this narrative, which also explains the role of the Electoral College and its part in the Gore-Bush presidential election. (Rev: SLJ 12/02)

19981 Staton, Hilarie. *The Progressive Party: The Success of a Failed Party* (5–8). Series: Snapshots in History. 2007, Compass Point LB $31.93 (978-0-7565-2451-7). 96pp. This history of the Progressives is well-organized and shows how the party's agenda moved forward even though the party itself didn't survive. (Rev: SLJ 7/07) [324.2732]

19982 Steins, Richard. *Our Elections* (4–6). Illus. 1994, Millbrook LB $24.90 (978-1-56294-446-9). 48pp. The process of being elected to office (primarily at the national level) is outlined in text, pictures, and diagrams. (Rev: BL 11/15/94; SLJ 12/94) [324.6]

19983 Stier, Catherine. *If I Ran for President* (3–5). Illus. by Lynne Avril. 2007, Albert Whitman $15.95 (978-0-8075-3543-1). 32pp. Through narration by six children, Stier explains the U.S. presidential election process in all its stages — from deciding to run through inauguration — with humor and cartoon illustrations. (Rev: BL 11/1/07; LMC 1/08; SLJ 9/07) [324.70973]

19984 Thomas, William David. *How Do We Elect Our Leaders?* (3–5). Illus. Series: My American Government. 2008, Gareth Stevens LB $23.93 (978-0-8368-8860-7); paper $8.95 (978-0-8368-8865-2). 32pp. A story about Ronald Reagan's candidacy introduces this informative volume that covers political parties, primaries and caucuses, conventions, and the election process. (Rev: BL 4/1/08; SLJ 6/08) [324.60]

19985 Wagner, Heather Lehr. *How the President Is Elected* (5–8). Series: The U.S. Government: How It Works. 2007, Chelsea House LB $30.00 (978-0-7910-9418-1). 95pp. This is a thorough introduction to the presidential election process (using the drama of the 2000 election to draw readers in), with interesting text and accompanying historical and biographical sidebars. (Rev: SLJ 1/08)

Federal Government and Agencies

19986 Attebury, Nancy Garhan. *Out and About at the United States Mint* (1–3). Illus. by Zachary Trover. Series: Field Trips. 2005, Picture Window LB $26.60 (978-1-4048-1151-5). 24pp. Tour the U.S. Mint along with a group of children and learn about its operations and the money produced there. (Rev: SLJ 2/06) [737.4973]

19987 Bay, Ann Phillips. *The Kid's Guide to the Smithsonian* (4–6). Illus. by Steven Rotblatt. 1996, Smithsonian Institution $26.95 (978-1-56098-734-5); paper $15.95 (978-1-56098-693-5). 160pp. A handy guide to historical information on many of the treasures of the Smithsonian. (Rev: BL 9/1/96) [069]

19988 Berger, Melvin, and Gilda Berger. *Where Does the Mail Go? A Book About the Postal System* (K–3). Illus. by Geoffrey Brittingham. Series: Discovery Readers. 1994, Ideals paper $4.50 (978-1-57102-006-2). 48pp. Explores the U.S. Postal Service by tracing a letter from posting to delivery. (Rev: SLJ 9/94) [353]

19989 Burns, Peggy. *The Mail* (3–5). Illus. Series: Stepping Through History. 1995, Thomson Learning LB $5.00 (978-1-56847-249-2). 32pp. A broad history of mail service, beginning with the ancient Persians and including material on today's computerized mail sorting and the hobby of stamp collecting. (Rev: BL 4/15/95; SLJ 6/95) [383]

19990 De Capua, Sarah E. *Becoming a Citizen* (2–5). Illus. Series: True Books — Civics. 2002, Children's Book Pr. LB $25.00 (978-0-516-22331-5); paper $6.95 (978-0-516-27366-2). 48pp. This work describes the requirements for becoming a U.S. citi-

zen and the steps one must take to become naturalized. (Rev: BL 6/1–15/02; SLJ check) [342.73]

19991 Donovan, Sandy. *Protecting America: A Look at the People Who Keep Our Country Safe* (4–6). Illus. Series: How Government Works. 2003, Lerner LB $25.26 (978-0-8225-1345-2). 56pp. A look at the U.S. armed forces and at security agencies including the FBI and CIA, all from a post-September 11 vantage point. (Rev: HBG 4/04; SLJ 3/04)

19992 Feinberg, Barbara S. *The Cabinet* (4–6). Illus. Series: Inside Government. 1995, Twenty-First Century LB $18.90 (978-0-8050-3421-9). 64pp. The history and changing composition of the cabinet are traced, with an explanation of each member's duties. (Rev: BL 9/1/95; SLJ 10/95) [353.04]

19993 Feinberg, Barbara S. *Term Limits for Congress?* (4–6). Illus. Series: Inside Government. 1996, Twenty-First Century LB $18.90 (978-0-8050-4099-9). 64pp. A clear and concise overview of the arguments for and against congressional term limits. (Rev: BL 5/15/96; SLJ 8/96) [328.73]

19994 Feldman, Ruth Tenzer. *How Congress Works: A Look at the Legislative Branch* (4–6). Illus. Series: How Government Works. 2004, Lerner LB $25.26 (978-0-8225-1347-6). 56pp. An easily understood explanation of the roles of the two houses of the legislative branch.

19995 Gibbons, Gail. *The Post Office Book: Mail and How It Moves* (K–3). Illus. by author. 1982, HarperCollins LB $15.89 (978-0-690-04199-6); paper $6.99 (978-0-06-446029-3). 32pp. A simple description of how the post office works.

19996 Giddens-White, Bryon. *The President and the Executive Branch* (4–6). Series: Our Government. 2005, Heinemann LB $28.21 (978-1-4034-6601-3). 32pp. This clear explanation of the executive power of the president of the United States will be useful for report writers. Also use *The Supreme Court and the Judicial Branch* (2005). (Rev: SLJ 5/06) [352.2309]

19997 Giesecke, Ernestine. *National Government* (3–5). Series: Kids' Guide. 2000, Heinemann $22.79 (978-1-57572-510-9). 32pp. A simple explanation of the three branches of government in the U.S. and the duties and responsibilities of each. (Rev: HBG 3/01; SLJ 10/00) [320]

19998 Gorman, Jacqueline Laks. *Member of Congress* (2–4). Series: Know Your Government. 2009, Gareth Stevens LB $21.00 (978-1-4339-0094-5); paper $5.95 (978-1-4339-0122-5). 24pp. With color photographs and clear text, Gorman compares and contrasts members of the Senate and the House of Representatives. (Rev: SLJ 6/09) [328.73]

19999 Gorman, Jacqueline Laks. *Vice President* (2–4). Series: Know Your Government. 2009, Gareth Stevens LB $21.00 (978-1-4339-0096-9); paper $5.95 (978-1-4339-0124-9). 24pp. With color photographs and clear text, Gorman introduces the job of vice president. (Rev: SLJ 6/09)

20000 Hamilton, John. *Becoming a Citizen* (3–5). Series: Government in Action! 2005, ABDO LB $22.78 (978-1-59197-642-4). 32pp. The steps to citizenship are well explained and accompanied by photographs of documents, sample questions, and the "Oath of Allegiance." (Rev: SLJ 7/05) [323.6]

20001 Hamilton, John. *The FBI* (3–5). Series: Defending the Nation. 2007, ABDO LB $22.78 (978-1-59679-757-4). 32pp. Students interested in the Federal Bureau of Investigation will find introductory information here, accompanied by photographs and sidebars. (Rev: SLJ 7/07)

20002 Hamilton, John. *How a Bill Becomes a Law* (3–5). Series: Government in Action! 2005, ABDO LB $22.78 (978-1-59197-646-2). 32pp. This look at the U.S. legislative system includes clear illustrations of the steps involved in a bill's passage. (Rev: SLJ 7/05) [328.73]

20003 Hamilton, John. *The Navy* (3–5). 2007, ABDO LB $22.78 (978-1-59679-760-4). 32pp. Students interested in the United States Navy will find introductory information here, accompanied by photographs and sidebars. (Rev: SLJ 7/07)

20004 Hamilton, John. *Special Forces* (3–5). Series: Defending the Nation. 2007, ABDO LB $22.78 (978-1-59679-759-8). 32pp. Students interested in the Army Rangers, Green Berets, Delta Force, Navy SEALs, Marine Corps Force Reconnaissance, and Air Force Special Operations will find introductory information here, accompanied by photographs and sidebars. (Rev: SLJ 7/07)

20005 Horn, Geoffrey M. *The Presidency* (5–8). Series: World Almanac Library of American Government. 2003, World Almanac LB $31.00 (978-0-8368-5458-9). 48pp. Information on the first lady, the White House, and key presidents add to the coverage here, which includes primary sources as well as many photographs and statistics. (Rev: SLJ 1/04) [973]

20006 Kassinger, Ruth G. *U.S. Census: A Mirror of America* (5–8). Illus. 1999, Raintree $28.54 (978-0-7398-1217-4). 80pp. Written before the 2000 census began, this book describes the history of the census and the methods used to count Americans. (Rev: BL 12/15/99; HBG 3/00) [304]

20007 Kennedy, Edward M. *My Senator and Me: A Dog's Eye View of Washington D.C* (2–4). Illus. by David Small. 2006, Scholastic $16.99 (978-0-439-65077-9). 56pp. Senator Kennedy's dog Splash narrates the events of a busy day on Capitol Hill. (Rev: BL 8/06; SLJ 8/06*) [328.73092]

20008 Kowalski, Kathiann M. *A Balancing Act: A Look at Checks and Balances* (4–6). Illus. Series: How Government Works. 2004, Lerner LB $25.26 (978-0-8225-1350-6). 56pp. An easily understood explanation of the principle intended to ensure that the three branches of government share power. (Rev: HBG 4/04)

20009 Kule, Elaine A. *The U.S. Mail* (2–4). Series: Transportation and Communication. 2002, Enslow LB $23.93 (978-0-7660-1892-1). 48pp. A history of the U.S. Postal Service from colonial days to the present, with material on how it works, its possible future uses, and people important in its development. (Rev: BL 9/15/02; HBG 3/03) [353]

20010 Landau, Elaine. *The President's Work: A Look at the Executive Branch* (4–6). Illus. Series: How Government Works. 2004, Lerner LB $25.26 (978-0-8225-0811-3). 56pp. A look at the president's responsibilities, enhanced by interesting sidebars and photographs. (Rev: BL 5/1/04; HBG 4/04; SLJ 3/04) [352.23]

20011 Levert, Suzanne. *The Congress* (2–5). Series: Kaleidoscope. 2002, Benchmark LB $25.64 (978-0-7614-1451-3). 48pp. An inside look at the inner workings of the House and Senate, with a description of the life of a piece of legislation, from introduction to passage. (Rev: HBG 3/03; SLJ 4/03) [328.73]

20012 McCave, Marta E. *Counting Heads, and More: The Work of the U.S. Census Bureau* (3–5). Illus. 1998, Twenty-First Century LB $24.90 (978-0-7613-3017-2). 64pp. An introduction to the U.S. Census Bureau, with information on its history, organization, functions, and the day-to-day work of its employees. (Rev: BL 12/15/98) [352.7]

20013 Ricciuti, Edward R. *Wildlife Special Agent: Protecting Endangered Species* (3–5). Illus. Series: Risky Business. 1996, Blackbirch LB $24.94 (978-1-56711-160-6). 32pp. A look at the exciting work of the people involved in the Law Enforcement Division of the U.S. Fish and Wildlife Service and how it helps protect endangered species. (Rev: SLJ 2/97) [363.11]

20014 Robb, Don. *Hail to the Chief: The American Presidency* (3–5). Illus. by Alan Witschonke. 2000, Charlesbridge LB $16.95 (978-0-88106-392-9); paper $7.95 (978-0-88106-939-6). 31pp. In 14 double-page spreads, the office of the presidency is introduced with material on duties, responsibilities and powers plus coverage of some men who have held the office and changed its character. (Rev: HBG 3/01; SLJ 3/01) [353.03]

20015 Rubel, David. *Scholastic Encyclopedia of the Presidents and Their Times*. Rev. ed. (4–8). Illus. 1997, Scholastic paper $18.95 (978-0-590-49366-6). 232pp. This fine reference book introduces each of the presidents and his administration and supplies material on related historical events, movements, and personalities. (Rev: HBG 10/01; SLJ 5/97) [920]

20016 St. George, Judith. *So You Want to Be President?* (3–5). Illus. by David Small. 2000, Penguin $17.99 (978-0-399-23407-1). 56pp. A delightful, lively compendium of facts about the presidency and the presidents covering such topics as favorite sports, appearance, pets, musical abilities, ages, and personalities. Caldecott Medal, 2001. (Rev: BCCB 7–8/00; BL 7/00*; HB 7/00; HBG 3/01; SLJ 8/00) [324.6]

20017 Sandak, Cass R. *Congressional Committees* (4–6). Illus. Series: Inside Government. 1995, Twenty-First Century LB $18.90 (978-0-8050-3425-7). 64pp. The purposes, structure, and functions of congressional committees are covered in this illustrated account. (Rev: BL 12/15/95) [328.73]

20018 Sandak, Cass R. *Lobbying* (4–6). Illus. Series: Inside Government. 1995, Twenty-First Century LB $18.90 (978-0-8050-3424-0). 64pp. An objective account that discusses the history, purposes, and results of lobbying in the U.S. Congress. (Rev: BL 12/15/95; SLJ 1/96) [324]

20019 Sandak, Cass R. *The National Debt* (5–8). Series: Inside Government. 1996, Twenty-First Century LB $22.40 (978-0-8050-3423-3). The origins and causes of the national debt are covered, with options for the future. (Rev: BL 5/15/96; SLJ 8/96) [336.3]

20020 Shea, Pegi Deitz. *The Impeachment Process* (4–6). Series: Your Government: How It Works. 2000, Chelsea LB $25.00 (978-0-7910-5538-0). 64pp. Beginning with the Watergate and Clinton scandals, this account traces the impeachment process and why the Constitution was written as it was. (Rev: HBG 9/00; SLJ 8/00) [320]

20021 Smith, Carter, ed. *Presidents in a Time of Change: A Sourcebook on the U.S. Presidency* (5–8). Illus. Series: American Albums. 1993, Millbrook $25.90 (978-1-56294-362-2). 96pp. A heavily illustrated, attractive review of the presidency from Truman to Clinton. (Rev: BL 12/1/93; SLJ 4/94; VOYA 4/94) [973.92]

20022 Smith, Carter, ed. *Presidents of a Divided Nation: A Sourcebook on the U.S. Presidency* (5–8). Series: American Albums. 1993, Millbrook $25.90 (978-1-56294-360-8). A visual sourcebook about the presidents during the Civil War and immediately after, from the Library of Congress collection on U.S. presidents. Also use *Presidents of a Growing Country*. (Rev: BL 12/1/93) [973.8]

20023 Smith, Carter, ed. *Presidents of a Growing Country: A Sourcebook on the U.S. Presidency* (5–8). Illus. Series: American Albums. 1993, Millbrook $25.90 (978-1-56294-358-5). 96pp. Through extensive use of pictorials, a thorough timeline, and concise text, this attractive book traces the presidency from Hayes through McKinley. (Rev: BL 12/1/93; SLJ 4/94) [973.8]

20024 Smith, Carter, ed. *Presidents of a Young Republic: A Sourcebook on the U.S. Presidency* (5–8). Illus. Series: American Albums. 1993, Millbrook $25.90 (978-1-56294-359-2). 96pp. A well-illustrated account that traces U.S. history from the presidency of John Quincy Adams through James Buchanan. (Rev: BL 12/1/93; SLJ 4/94) [973.5]

20025 Stein, R. Conrad. *The National Archives* (4–6). Series: Watts Library: U.S. Government and Military. 2002, Watts LB $24.00 (978-0-531-13032-2); paper $8.95 (978-0-531-16602-4). 64pp. This account presents in text and pictures a visit to the National Archives, a treasure trove that holds millions of American documents including the original Declaration of Independence. (Rev: BL 10/15/02) [069]

20026 Suen, Anastasia. *The Peace Corps* (1–2). Series: Helping Organizations. 2002, Rosen LB $19.95 (978-0-8239-6001-9). 24pp. As well as a brief description of the history and activities of the Peace Corps, this beginning reader tells how youngsters can become involved. (Rev: BL 6/1–15/02) [361.6]

20027 Sullivan, George. *Presidents at Play* (4–6). Illus. 1995, Walker LB $16.85 (978-0-8027-8334-9). 176pp. An unusual side of U.S. presidents is explored: the sports and other recreational activities they engaged in. (Rev: BL 1/1/95; SLJ 2/95) [973]

20028 Teichmann, Iris. *Immigration and the Law* (5–8). Series: Understanding Immigration. 2006, Smart Apple LB $31.35 (978-1-58340-970-1). 44pp. Covers all aspects of immigration including the laws granting admission, visas, and how to gain citizenship. (Rev: SLJ 3/07)

20029 Ventura, Jesse, and Heron Marquez. *Jesse Ventura Tells It Like It Is: America's Most Outspoken Governor Speaks Out About Government* (5–8). Illus. 2002, Lerner LB $15.95 (978-0-8225-0385-9). 64pp. A look at the U.S. government and politicians from the viewpoint of wrestler-turned-Minnesota-governor Jesse Ventura. (Rev: BL 8/02; HBG 3/03; SLJ 9/02) [977.6]

20030 Wagner, Heather Lehr. *The Central Intelligence Agency* (5–8). Illus. Series: The U.S. Government: How It Works. 2007, Chelsea House LB $30.00 (978-0-7910-9282-8). 104pp. Provides information on the Central Intelligence Agency; its history, how it influences government policies, and the kinds of jobs available there. (Rev: BL 8/07) [327]

State Government and Agencies

20031 Armentrout, David, and Patricia Armentrout. *State Seals* (3–5). Illus. Series: The Rourke Guide to State Symbols. 2001, Rourke LB $29.93 (978-1-58952-087-5). 48pp. Brief, large-print text explains the history and design of each state's seal. (Rev: SLJ 5/02) [973]

20032 Giesecke, Ernestine. *State Government* (3–5). Series: Kids' Guide. 2000, Heinemann $22.79 (978-1-57572-513-0). 32pp. An appealing, simple account that discusses the structure of state governments in the U.S. and the responsibilities involved. (Rev: HBG 3/01; SLJ 10/00) [320]

20033 Gorman, Jacqueline Laks. *Governor* (2–4). Illus. Series: Know Your Government. 2009, Gareth Stevens LB $21.00 (978-1-4339-0091-4); paper $5.95 (978-1-4339-0119-5). 24pp. An introductory look at the roles played by state governors, how governors are selected, and governors of note. (Rev: BL 3/1/09) [352.23]

Municipal Government and Agencies

20034 Flanagan, Alice K. *Mayors* (1–3). Series: Community Workers. 2001, Compass Point LB $21.26 (978-0-7565-0064-1). 32pp. This is an easily read introduction to the work of mayors, the skills and training required, and their contributions to the community. Also use *Teachers* (2001). (Rev: SLJ 5/01) [352.23]

20035 Giesecke, Ernestine. *Local Government* (3–5). Series: Kids' Guide. 2000, Heinemann $22.79 (978-1-57572-512-3). 32pp. The functions of city, country, and school district governments are explained with material on duties and responsibilities. (Rev: HBG 3/01; SLJ 10/00) [320.8]

20036 Gorman, Jacqueline Laks. *Mayor* (2–4). Series: Know Your Government. 2009, Gareth Stevens LB $21.00 (978-1-4339-0093-8); paper $5.95 (978-1-4339-0121-8). 24pp. With color photographs and clear text, Gorman introduces the job of mayor in both small towns and large cities. (Rev: SLJ 6/09) [352.23]

Social Problems and Solutions

20037 Ajmera, Maya, and John D. Ivanko. *Be My Neighbor* (PS–2). Illus. 2004, Charlesbridge $15.95 (978-1-57091-504-8). 32pp. Observations from the late Fred Rogers open this appealing introduction to the concepts of community and neighborhood, presented on horizontal spreads with photographs depicting many environments. (Rev: BL 1/1–15/05; SLJ 1/05) [307.3]

20038 Ancona, George. *Harvest* (4–7). Illus. 2001, Marshall Cavendish $15.95 (978-0-7614-5086-3). 48pp. This volume examines the difficult lives and work of Mexican migrant workers and the crops they harvest, ending with a look at the contributions of labor leader Cesar Chavez. (Rev: BL 1/1–15/02; HBG 3/02; SLJ 4/02) [331.5]

20039 Brimner, Larry Dane. *A Migrant Family* (4–8). Illus. 1992, Lerner LB $23.95 (978-0-8225-2554-7). 40pp. The daily life of 12-year-old Juan and his Mexican American family is captured in this photoessay. (Rev: BCCB 10/92; BL 9/15/92) [305.5]

20040 De Angelis, Therese. *Blackout! Cities in Darkness* (4–8). Series: American Disasters. 2003, Enslow LB $23.93 (978-0-7660-2110-5). 48pp. This book chronicles the events and people involved in some of the important blackouts that have crippled America's cities. (Rev: BL 11/15/03) [307.7]

20041 de Ruiz, Dana C., and Richard Larios. *La Causa: The Migrant Farmworkers' Story* (4–7). Illus. by Rudy Gutierrez. 1992, Raintree LB $30.40 (978-0-8114-7231-9). 92pp. The story of the founding of the United Farm Workers highlights the work of Cesar Chavez and Dolores Huerta. (Rev: BL 6/1–15/93) [331]

20042 Ditchfield, Christin. *Serving Your Community* (3–5). Series: True Book. 2004, Children's Pr. LB $25.00 (978-0-516-22802-0). 47pp. The concept of volunteerism is introduced, with discussion of what young people can do to improve the quality of life in their communities. (Rev: SLJ 8/04) [361.3]

20043 Gourley, Catherine. *Media Wizards: A Behind-the-Scenes Look at Media Manipulations* (5–9). 1999, Twenty-First Century LB $26.90 (978-0-7613-0967-3). 128pp. An informative account of how the media can manipulate the truth. (Rev: HBG 3/00; SLJ 2/00; VOYA 4/00) [380.3]

20044 Green, Jen. *Dealing with Racism* (2–4). Photos by Roger Vlitos. Illus. by Chris O'Neill. Series: How Do I Feel About. 1998, Millbrook LB $19.90 (978-0-7613-0810-2). 24pp. Using the words of children, this book defines racism, gives examples, and makes suggestions on how to stop it. (Rev: HBG 9/98; SLJ 7/98) [305.8]

20045 Green, Jen. *Racism* (2–3). Series: Talking About. 1999, Raintree LB $25.69 (978-0-7398-1375-1). 32pp. In this simple, attractive book, several examples of racism are given, with ways of dealing with them and tips on how to get along in a multicultural society. (Rev: BL 2/15/00; HBG 9/00; SLJ 7/00) [305.42]

20046 Hoyt-Goldsmith, Diane. *Migrant Worker: A Boy from the Rio Grande Valley* (4–7). Illus. 1996, Holiday $15.95 (978-0-8234-1225-9). 32pp. A photoessay about the grim living conditions endured by an 11-year-old Mexican American migrant worker. (Rev: BCCB 3/96; BL 3/1/96; SLJ 5/96) [331.5]

20047 Hull, Mary. *Ethnic Violence* (5–8). Illus. Series: Overview. 1997, Lucent LB $29.95 (978-1-56006-184-7). 112pp. Gives a history of racial prejudice that has led to violence and discusses decisions and policies that currently guide our behavior and attitudes toward this problem. (Rev: BL 8/97; SLJ 9/97) [305.8]

20048 Hurwitz, Eugene, and Sue Hurwitz. *Working Together Against Homelessness* (4–6). Illus. Series: Library of Social Activism. 1995, Rosen LB $27.95 (978-0-8239-1772-3). 64pp. A history of homelessness both nationally and globally, its present frequency, and possible solutions. (Rev: BL 2/15/95; SLJ 12/94) [362.5]

20049 James, Barbara. *Animal Rights* (5–10). Series: Talking Points. 1999, Raintree LB $27.12 (978-0-8172-5317-2). 64pp. Various aspects of the animal rights controversy are explored in an objective, straightforward manner. (Rev: BL 8/99) [179.3]

20050 Katella-Cofrancesco, Kathy. *Children's Causes* (4–6). Illus. Series: Celebrity Activist. 1998, Twenty-First Century LB $25.90 (978-0-7613-3013-4). 64pp. Each chapter in this book examines the contributions made by a celebrity to a cause involving children. (Rev: BL 8/98; HBG 9/98) [361.7]

20051 Katella-Cofrancesco, Kathy. *Economic Causes* (4–6). Illus. Series: Celebrity Activist. 1998, Twenty-First Century LB $25.90 (978-0-7613-3014-1). 64pp. Focuses on how celebrities, including Sharon Stone (Planet Hope) and former President Carter (Habitat for Humanity), support causes involving poverty and related problems. (Rev: BL 8/98; HBG 9/98) [361.7]

20052 Marsico, Katie. *Racism* (4–8). Series: Global Perspectives. 2008, Cherry Lake LB $27.07 (978-1-60279-134-3). 32pp. An accessible look at racism and its causes, history, and ways to alleviate this problem. (Rev: SLJ 11/08) [305.8]

20053 Newman, Shirlee P. *Child Slavery in Modern Times* (4–7). Illus. Series: Watts Library: History of Slavery. 2000, Watts LB $25.50 (978-0-531-11696-8). 64pp. From Europe to Asia and Africa, this book explores the deplorable lives of servitude forced on child laborers and slaves, and how some have escaped. (Rev: BL 2/15/01; SLJ 3/01) [306.3]

20054 Rondeau, Amanda. *Do Something in Your Community* (K–2). Illus. Series: Do Something About It! 2004, ABDO LB $19.93 (978-1-59197-572-4). 24pp. Photographs of people who contribute to the community — doctors and firefighters, for example — are accompanied by short descriptions of their roles. Also use *Do Something in Your Family* (2004). (Rev: BL 11/1/04) [361]

20055 Rondeau, Amanda. *Volunteering* (1–3). 2003, ABDO LB $19.93 (978-1-57765-882-5). 24pp. Numerous examples of volunteer activities are shown in full-color photographs and simple text. (Rev: HBG 10/03; SLJ 6/03) [361.3]

20056 Siegel, Danny. *Mitzvah Magic: What Kids Can Do to Change the World* (3–8). Illus. by Naomi Eisenberger. 2002, Kar-Ben paper $8.95 (978-1-58013-034-9). 64pp. Siegel has amassed a large number of suggestions for children who want to help others. (Rev: BL 10/1/02) [302]

20057 Siegel, Danny. *Tell Me a Mitzvah: Little and Big Ways to Repair the World* (3–6). Illus. by Judith Friedman. 1993, Kar-Ben paper $7.95 (978-0-929371-78-8). 64pp. Profiles of 12 people who have made the world a better place by performing mitzvahs, or good deeds. (Rev: SLJ 3/94) [307.1]

20058 Steins, Richard. *Censorship: How Does It Conflict with Freedom?* (5–9). Series: Issues of Our Time. 1995, Twenty-First Century LB $22.90 (978-0-8050-3879-8). A clearly written introduction to censorship, its history, and the various positions possible toward it. (Rev: BL 7/95; SLJ 9/95) [363.3]

20059 Suen, Anastasia. *Habitat for Humanity* (1–2). Series: Helping Organizations. 2002, Rosen LB $19.95 (978-0-8239-6006-4). 24pp. A beginning reader that describes how this organization provides housing for the poor and tells how such people as President Carter participate in its work. (Rev: BL 6/1–15/02; SLJ 3/02) [361.7]

20060 Tipp, Stacey L. *Child Abuse: Detecting Bias* (5–7). Series: Opposing Viewpoints Juniors. 1991, Greenhaven LB $22.45 (978-0-89908-611-8). 32pp. Four different issues involving child abuse (e.g., whether abusers should be sent to prison) are presented from various points of view. (Rev: BL 5/15/92; SLJ 3/92) [362.7]

20061 Wolf, Bernard. *Homeless* (2–4). Illus. 1995, Orchard LB $17.99 (978-0-531-08736-7). 46pp. The plight of a homeless family caught up in the New York City welfare system is the subject of this affecting picture book. (Rev: BCCB 3/95; BL 2/15/95; HB 5/95; SLJ 4/95) [362.5]

Religion and Holidays

General and Miscellaneous

20062 Abrams, Judith Z. *The Secret World of Kabbalah* (5–9). Illus. 2006, Lerner paper $9.95 (978-1-58013-224-4). 80pp. This interesting introduction to Kabbalah defines this form of Jewish mysticism as "the journey to come as closely in touch with God as you can." (Rev: SLJ 12/06) [296.16]

20063 Ajmera, Maya, and Cynthia Pon. *Faith* (1–3). Illus. 2009, Charlesbridge $16.95 (978-1-58089-177-6); paper $7.95 (978-1-58089-178-3). 48pp. An exploration of the many ways in which people practice their faiths around the world, with large photographs and brief captions. (Rev: BL 3/1/09; SLJ 3/09) [200]

20064 Alexander, Cecil Frances. *All Things Bright and Beautiful* (PS–3). Illus. by Anna Vojtech. 2004, North-South LB $16.50 (978-0-7358-1893-4). A beautifully — and inventively — illustrated version of this 19th-century song. (Rev: SLJ 11/04) [264]

20065 Baring-Gould, Sabine. *Now the Day Is Over* (PS–2). Illus. by Preston McDaniels. 2001, Morehouse $17.95 (978-0-8192-1868-1). 32pp. Graceful illustrations of a little boy, animals, and angels accompany the four verses of the song. (Rev: BL 6/1–15/01) [242]

20066 Barnes, Trevor. *Islam* (5–8). Illus. Series: World Faiths. 2005, Kingfisher paper $6.95 (978-0-7534-5882-2). 40pp. Originally published in 1999 as part of *The Kingfisher Book of Religions: Festivals, Ceremonies, and Beliefs from Around the World*, this 40-page expanded volume provides a wide-ranging overview of Islam and its followers. (Rev: BL 10/1/05; SLJ 10/05; VOYA 6/06) [297]

20067 Bedard, Michael. *The Wolf of Gubbio* (2–4). Illus. 2001, Stoddart $15.95 (978-0-7737-3250-6). 24pp. The story of Saint Francis of Assisi and how his ability to talk to animals saved the city of Gubbio from a hungry wolf is retold through the voice of a young child. (Rev: BCCB 6/01; BL 4/15/01) [398.22]

20068 Birdseye, Debbie H., and Tom Birdseye. *What I Believe: Kids Talk About Faith* (4–7). 1996, Holiday $15.95 (978-0-8234-1268-6). 32pp. Children from six faiths explain what their religion means to them. (Rev: BL 12/15/96; SLJ 2/97) [200]

20069 Bolick, Nancy O., and Sallie Randolph. *Shaker Inventions* (4–6). Illus. by Melissa Francisco. 1990, Walker LB $13.85 (978-0-8027-6934-3). 96pp. A rundown on many inventions by the Shakers, and a general introduction to their way of life. (Rev: SLJ 9/90) [289]

20070 Borchard, Therese. *Taste and See: The Goodness of the Lord* (PS–K). Illus. by Phyllis V. Saroff. 2000, Paulist Press $9.95 (978-0-8091-6665-7). 32pp. With images that use the five senses, children are made to feel that God is everywhere and in all living things. (Rev: BL 10/1/00; HBG 3/01) [231]

20071 Brown, Alan, and Andrew Langley. *What I Believe: A Young Person's Guide to the Religions of the World* (4–7). Illus. 1999, Millbrook LB $24.90 (978-0-7613-1501-8). 64pp. Young people of eight major faiths explain their religion's principal tenets, rituals, holy days, and celebrations. (Rev: BL 10/1/99; HBG 3/00; SLJ 2/00) [291]

20072 Brown, Tricia. *Salaam: A Muslim American Boy's Story* (K–3). Photos by Ken Cardwell. 2006, Holt $17.95 (978-0-8050-6538-1). A young Muslim American boy explains the basic tenets of his faith and the customs and rituals associated with it; full of photographs, this also includes a glossary. (Rev: SLJ 12/06) [073]

20073 Capek, Michael. *A Personal Tour of a Shaker Village* (4–7). Series: How It Was. 2001, Lerner LB $30.35 (978-0-8225-3584-3). 64pp. An account of life in a Shaker village, seen through the eyes of people who lived there. (Rev: BL 8/1/01; HBG 10/01; SLJ 8/01) [289.8]

20074 Carew-Miller, Anna. *Buddha: Father of Buddhism* (2–5). Illus. by Paolo d'Altan. Series: Great Names. 2002, Mason Crest LB $19.95 (978-1-59084-137-2). This account of Buddha's life blends fact and fiction and conveys information on the religion as well as the man. (Rev: SLJ 8/03) [294.3]

20075 Carlstrom, Nancy White. *Does God Know How to Tie Shoes?* (PS–K). Illus. by Lori McElrath-Eslick. 1993, Eerdmans $15.00 (978-0-8028-5074-4). 32pp. A child questions her parents about the nature of God, and the answers are correlated with passages from the Bible. (Rev: BL 12/1/93; SLJ 3/94)

20076 Chaikin, Miriam. *Angels Sweep the Desert Floor: Bible Legends About Moses in the Wilderness* (4–7). Illus. by Alexander Koshkin. 2002, Clarion $19.00 (978-0-395-97825-2). 102pp. This collection of stories mixes religious history and rabbinic literature to tell the story of the Israelites' 40 years in the wilderness. (Rev: BL 10/1/02; HB 11/02; HBG 3/03; SLJ 9/02) [296.1]

20077 Chalfonte, Jessica. *I Am Muslim* (1–4). Illus. Series: Religions of the World. 1996, Rosen LB $18.75 (978-0-8239-2375-5). 24pp. An introduction to the Muslim religion and the world of Islam as seen through the eyes of Ahmet, a boy living in Detroit. (Rev: SLJ 2/97) [297]

20078 Conover, Sarah, and Freda Crane. *Beautiful Signs/Ayat Jamilah: A Treasury of Islamic Wisdom for Children and Parents* (5–7). Illus. by Valerie Wahl. Series: Little Light of Mine. 2004, Eastern Washington Univ. paper $19.95 (978-0-910055-94-9). 200pp. Muslim folktales, fables, stories from the Koran, and historic tales originate from countries around the world. (Rev: BL 10/15/04; SLJ 8/04) [297.1]

20079 Das, Rasamandala. *Hinduism* (4–6). Series: Religions of the World. 2005, World Almanac LB $31.00 (978-0-8368-5867-9). 48pp. A photo-filled introduction to Hinduism and its history, beliefs, rites, and holidays. (Rev: SLJ 1/06) [294.5]

20080 Demi. *Buddha* (4–6). Illus. 1996, Holt $18.95 (978-0-8050-4203-0). 32pp. In this picture book for older children, the story of Buddha's life and teachings is effectively retold. (Rev: BCCB 6/96; BL 4/1/96; HB 9/96; SLJ 6/96) [294.3]

20081 Demi. *Buddha Stories* (3–6). Illus. 1997, Holt $16.95 (978-0-8050-4886-5). 32pp. Ten of the author's favorite Buddha stories, or jakatas, are elegantly retold with excellent illustrations. (Rev: BCCB 4/97; BL 2/15/97; SLJ 6/97) [294.3]

20082 Demi. *The Legend of St. Nicholas* (2–5). Illus. by author. 2003, Simon & Schuster $19.95 (978-0-689-84681-6). 40pp. Young readers will be fascinated by this beautifully illustrated biography of the real St. Nicholas, who devoted his life to relieving the suffering of others. (Rev: BL 10/1/03; HBG 4/04; SLJ 10/03)

20083 Dillon, Leo, and Diane Dillon. *To Every Thing There Is a Season: Verses from Ecclesiastes* (4–7). Illus. 1998, Scholastic paper $16.95 (978-0-590-47887-8). 40pp. Using verses from Ecclesiastes such as "A time to be born and a time to die," the artists have created a stunning picture book on the cycle of life. (Rev: BCCB 11/98; BL 10/1/98*; HB 9/98; HBG 3/99; SLJ 9/98) [223]

20084 Dineen, Jacqueline. *Births* (3–6). Series: Ceremonies and Celebrations. 2001, Raintree LB $25.69 (978-0-7398-3267-7). 32pp. Traditions surrounding births are explored in six major religions, covering topics from circumcision, baptism, and naming ceremonies to gifts, clothing, food, and horoscopes. Also use *Weddings* (2001). (Rev: SLJ 9/01) [392.12]

20085 Douglass, Susan L. *Ramadan* (1–3). Series: On My Own Holidays. 2003, Carolrhoda LB $25.26 (978-0-87614-932-4); paper $5.95 (978-1-57505-584-8). 48pp. An excellent introduction to the holy month of fasting observed by Muslims each year, with helpful information about the basic beliefs and practices of Islam. (Rev: BL 10/15/03; HBG 4/04; SLJ 8/03)

20086 Faber, Doris. *The Amish* (3–5). Illus. by Michael Erkel. 1990, Doubleday $17.95 (978-0-385-44518-4). An enlightening look at the people, who live plainly, in harmony with nature. (Rev: BL 1/15/91) [973.08]

20087 *A Faith Like Mine* (3–5). Illus. 2005, DK $19.99 (978-0-7566-1177-4). 80pp. Children of different religious backgrounds describe the basics of their faith and what they like about their religion; includes background information on major and minor world religions. (Rev: BL 10/1/05; SLJ 11/05) [291]

20088 Ganeri, Anita. *Buddhism* (4–6). Series: Religions of the World. 2005, World Almanac LB $31.00 (978-0-8368-5865-5). 48pp. A photo-filled introduction to Buddhism and its history, beliefs, rites, and holidays. (Rev: SLJ 1/06) [294.3]

20089 Ganeri, Anita. *Buddhist Stories* (1–6). Illus. by Tracey Fennell. Series: Traditional Religious Tales. 2006, Picture Window LB $26.60 (978-1-4048-1311-3). 32pp. The stories in this appealing collection chronicle the life of the Buddha, focusing in particular on his lifelong search for enlightenment. (Rev: SLJ 4/06) [294.3]

20090 Ganeri, Anita. *Hindu Stories* (1–6). Illus. by Carole Gray. Series: Traditional Religious Tales. 2006, Picture Window LB $26.60 (978-1-4048-1309-0). 32pp. The seven stories in this collection are prime examples of classical Hindu mythology and include colorful tales about such deities and demons as Krishna the cowherd, Ganesh the elephant god, and Holika the demon princess. (Rev: SLJ 4/06) [294.5]

20091 Ganeri, Anita. *Journey's End: Death and Mourning* (4–6). Illus. 1999, Bedrick LB $15.95 (978-0-87226-289-8). 32pp. This book looks at death rituals in six major religions: Hinduism, Buddhism, Sikhism, Islam, Judaism, and Christianity. (Rev: BL 5/15/99; HBG 9/99; SLJ 3/99) [291.3]

20092 Ganeri, Anita. *Sikh Stories* (1–6). Illus. by Rachael Phillips. Series: Traditional Religious Tales. 2006, Picture Window LB $26.60 (978-1-4048-1314-4). 32pp. This collection of stories documents incidents from the lives of Sikh spiritual leaders, emphasizing the moral lessons exemplified. (Rev: SLJ 4/06) [294.6]

20093 Ganeri, Anita. *Wedding Days: Celebrations of Marriage* (4–6). Illus. 1999, Bedrick LB $15.95

(978-0-87226-288-1). 32pp. Covers marriage and marriage customs in six religions: Hinduism, Buddhism, Sikhism, Islam, Judaism, and Christianity. (Rev: BL 5/15/99; SLJ 3/99) [291.3]

20094 Gellman, Marc. *And God Cried, Too: A Kid's Book of Healing and Hope* (2–5). Illus. by Harry Bliss. 2002, HarperCollins LB $17.89 (978-0-06-009887-2); paper $5.99 (978-0-06-009886-5). 128pp. A fictional story about a young angel-in-training opens this thought-provoking book that deals with questions that challenge faith. (Rev: BL 10/1/02; SLJ 12/02) [291.2]

20095 Gellman, Marc, and Thomas Hartman. *How Do You Spell God? Answers to the Big Questions from Around the World* (5–8). Illus. by Joseph A. Smith. 1995, Morrow $17.99 (978-0-688-13041-1). 224pp. A priest and a rabbi have written this introduction to the world's most important religions: Judaism, Christianity, Islam, Buddhism, and Hinduism. (Rev: BCCB 7–8/95; BL 6/1–15/95; SLJ 5/95) [200]

20096 Glossop, Jennifer. *The Kids Book of World Religions* (3–6). Illus. by John Mantha. 2003, Kids Can $15.95 (978-1-55074-959-5). 64pp. Students writing reports will find this a useful source of information on the basic tenets of the world's major religions. (Rev: BL 4/15/03; HBG 10/03; SLJ 4/03) [291]

20097 Gold, Susan Dudley. *Religions of the Western Hemisphere* (5–8). Illus. Series: Comparing Continents. 1997, Twenty-First Century $23.40 (978-0-8050-5603-7). This work explores the history and influence of religions, beliefs, and customs on life in the United States, Canada, and Latin America, with discussion of the roles of religious leaders in government, economy, and everyday life. (Rev: BL 2/1/98; SLJ 3/98) [200]

20098 Goodnough, David. *Cult Awareness: A Hot Issue* (5–8). Series: Hot Issues. 2000, Enslow LB $27.93 (978-0-7660-1196-0). 64pp. This book explains the nature of cults and how they differ as well as giving information on many groups including Jehovah's Witnesses, Unification Church, Hare Krishna, Shakers, Mormons, and Church of Scientology. (Rev: BL 6/1–15/00; HBG 10/00; SLJ 6/00) [291.9]

20099 Gunderson, Cory. *Religions of the Middle East* (3–5). Series: World in Conflict: The Middle East. 2004, ABDO LB $25.65 (978-1-59197-412-3). 48pp. A comparative description of the major religion of the Middle East — Islam, Judaism, Christianity, Druze, and Hinduism. (Rev: SLJ 5/04) [200]

20100 Hodges, Margaret. *The Legend of Saint Christopher* (3–6). Illus. by Richard J. Watson. 2002, Eerdmans $18.00 (978-0-8028-5077-5). 32pp. Hodges retells the story of how Saint Christopher got the name that means "Christ bearer." (Rev: BCCB 12/02; BL 10/1/02; HBG 3/03; SLJ 11/02) [242]

20101 Hoffman, Lawrence A., and Wolfson Ron. *What You Will See Inside a Synagogue* (3–5). Illus. 2004, SkyLight Paths $17.99 (978-1-59473-012-2). 32pp. Introduces readers to the rituals and places of worship of three branches of American Judaism —

Conservative, Reconstruction, and Reform. (Rev: BL 1/1–15/05; SLJ 2/05) [296.4]

20102 *I Believe: The Nicene Creed* (1–3). Illus. by Pauline Baynes. 2004, Eerdmans $16.00 (978-0-8028-5258-8). 32pp. The Nicene Creed, a basic outline of Christian doctrine used by Eastern Orthodox, Roman Catholic, and most Protestant denominations, is examined line by line in this beautifully illustrated book. (Rev: BL 7/03; HBG 4/04; SLJ 11/03) [238]

20103 Israel, Fred L. *The Amish* (5–8). Illus. Series: Immigrant Experience. 1996, Chelsea LB $14.95 (978-0-7910-3368-5). The story of this conservative division of the Mennonites, why they settled in the United States, and their contributions to the nation. (Rev: BL 7/96; SLJ 10/96) [305.6]

20104 Jaffe, Nina. *The Mysterious Visitor: Stories of the Prophet Elijah* (4–6). Illus. 1997, Scholastic $19.95 (978-0-590-48422-0). 112pp. Eight Jewish stories that involve the prophet Elijah are retold. (Rev: BCCB 6/97; BL 5/1/97; HBG 3/98; SLJ 6/97*) [222]

20105 Jani, Mahendra, and Vandana Jani. *What You Will See Inside a Hindu Temple* (4–6). Illus. by Neirah Bhargava. Series: What You Will See Inside. 2005, SkyLight Paths $17.99 (978-1-59473-116-7). 32pp. Attractive double-page spreads look inside a typical Hindu temple and introduce the fundamental beliefs, rituals, and ceremonies of Hinduism. (Rev: BL 1/1–15/06; SLJ 2/06) [294.5]

20106 *Jesus Loves Me!* (K–2). Illus. by Tim Warnes. 2006, Simon & Schuster $12.95 (978-1-4169-0065-8). A happy family of bears living in a forest celebrate the classic Christian children's song; the music is appended. (Rev: SLJ 3/06) [242]

20107 Johari, Harish, and Vatsala Sperling. *How Ganesh Got His Elephant Head* (1–4). Illus. by Pieter Weltevrede. 2003, Bear & Company $15.95 (978-1-59143-021-6). 32pp. Traditional illustrations highlight the Hindu story of how Ganesh got his elephant head, which is amplified with a tale of Ganesh's rivalry with his brother. (Rev: BL 12/1/03; SLJ 1/04)

20108 John Paul II. *Every Child a Light: The Pope's Message to Young People* (4–7). Ed. by Jerome M. Vereb. Illus. 2002, Boyds Mills $16.95 (978-1-56397-090-0). 48pp. Using photographs and snippets from Pope John Paul II's writings for children and teens, this is an inspirational book of comments and advice for youngsters. (Rev: BL 6/1–15/02; HBG 10/02; SLJ 5/02) [248.8]

20109 Keane, Michael. *What You Will See Inside a Catholic Church* (3–6). Illus. 2002, SkyLight Paths $17.95 (978-1-893361-54-6). 32pp. Readers are introduced to the layout, ceremonies, and rituals of a Roman Catholic church. (Rev: BL 3/15/03; SLJ 9/03) [264]

20110 Keene, Michael. *Judaism* (5–8). Series: Religions of the World. 2005, World Almanac LB $31.00 (978-0-8368-5869-3). 48pp. A basic introduction to the beliefs and practices of Judaism around the world, with a chronology of important events. (Rev: SLJ 2/06) [296]

20111 Khan, Rukhsana. *Muslim Child: Understanding Islam Through Stories and Poems* (4–6). Illus. by Patty Gallinger. 2002, Whitman $16.99 (978-0-8075-5307-7). 104pp. A series of vignettes told by children about living as a Muslim in various countries around the world. (Rev: BL 2/15/02; HBG 10/02; SLJ 2/02) [297]

20112 Kimmel, Eric A. *Brother Wolf, Sister Sparrow: Stories About Saints and Animals* (3–6). Illus. by John Winch. 2003, Holiday House $18.95 (978-0-8234-1724-7). 64pp. This collection of well-illustrated stories explores several saints' relationships with animals and includes the tale of a bargain Francis of Assisi struck with a wolf and an account of how angels helped Saint Brigid to replace the butter and milk she'd given to the needy. (Rev: BL 4/1/03; HBG 10/03; SLJ 5/03) [398.22]

20113 Kroll, Virginia. *I Wanted to Know All About God* (PS–1). Illus. by Debra R. Jenkins. 1994, Eerdmans $15.00 (978-0-8028-5078-2). 32pp. A book about the nature of God that emphasizes human relationships and the wonders of nature. (Rev: BL 2/15/94; SLJ 8/94) [231.2]

20114 Krull, Kathleen, ed. *Songs of Praise* (PS–1). Illus. by Kathryn Hewitt. 1989, Harcourt paper $5.95 (978-0-15-277109-6). 32pp. A collection of 15 hymns. (Rev: BCCB 9/88; BL 11/15/88)

20115 Kushner, Lawrence, and Karen Kushner. *Because Nothing Looks Like God* (PS–2). Illus. by Dawn Majewski. 2001, Jewish Lights $17.99 (978-1-58023-092-6). 32pp. The concept of God is explored in this picture book filled with paintings of nature scenes. (Rev: BL 1/1–15/01; SLJ 2/01) [291.2]

20116 Lehman-Wilzig, Tami. *Keeping the Promise: A Torah's Journey* (1–5). Illus. by Craig Orback. 2004, Lerner LB $16.95 (978-1-58013-117-9); paper $6.95 (978-1-58013-118-6). The story of a tiny Torah scroll that is passed from a Dutch rabbi to a young boy in Bergen-Belsen who years later gives it to Ilan Ramon, the Israeli astronaut, who took it with him on the tragic *Columbia* mission. (Rev: BCCB 4/04; SLJ 8/04) [296.4]

20117 Le Joly, Edward, and Jaya Chaliha, eds. *Stories Told by Mother Teresa* (2–4). Illus. by Allan Drummond. 2000, Element Books $15.95 (978-1-902618-65-4). 32pp. These 11 moving stories derived from the personal experiences of Mother Teresa describe acts of sacrifice, faith, and devotion by ordinary people. (Rev: BL 3/15/00; HBG 9/00) [271.97]

20118 Lester, Julius. *When the Beginning Began: Stories About God, the Creatures, and Us* (4–8). Illus. 1999, Harcourt $17.00 (978-0-15-201138-3). Using parts of Genesis and creation stories from Jewish legends, this wondrous retelling adds thought-provoking human interest to the stories that end with Adam and Eve. (Rev: BL 4/15/99*; SLJ 5/99) [296.1]

20119 Lincoln, Frances. *A Family Treasury of Prayers* (4–8). 1996, Simon & Schuster $16.00 (978-0-689-80956-9). Classic art works illustrate this lovely collection of prayers from famous sources. (Rev: BL 10/1/96; SLJ 10/96; VOYA 6/97) [242]

20120 Lindbergh, Reeve. *The Circle of Days* (PS–3). Illus. by Cathie Felstead. 1998, Candlewick $15.99 (978-0-7637-0357-8). 32pp. This adaptation of the writings of St. Francis of Assisi translates the cycle of creation, life, and death in nature into simple, flowing prose and detailed illustrations. (Rev: BL 4/1/98*) [242]

20121 Llewellyn, Claire. *Saints and Angels* (3–6). 2003, Houghton $14.95 (978-0-7534-5588-3). 64pp. This lushly illustrated book focuses primarily on the Christian saints — organized into such logical groups as martyrs, thinkers, and disciples — but also devotes a section to angels. (Rev: BL 10/1/03; HBG 4/04)

20122 Lutz, Norma Jean. *The History of the Black Church* (5–8). Illus. Series: African American Achievers. 2001, Chelsea $30.00 (978-0-7910-5822-0). 112pp. Historical and contemporary photographs illustrate this history of African American religious life and institutions. (Rev: BL 10/1/01; HBG 3/02; SLJ 12/01) [277.3]

20123 MacMillan, Dianne. *Diwali: Hindu Festival of Lights* (4–8). Series: Best Holiday Books. 1997, Enslow LB $23.93 (978-0-89490-817-0). This book on the Hindu Diwali festival discusses its significance and relationship to the history, culture, and people of India, and includes material on the food, crafts, instruments, and costumes of the festival. (Rev: SLJ 8/97) [294.5]

20124 Mulvihill, Margaret. *The Treasury of Saints and Martyrs* (5–7). Illus. 1999, Viking $19.99 (978-0-670-88789-7). 80pp. A handsome, oversize book about the lives of 40 saints from the beginning of Christianity to the present day. (Rev: BL 10/1/99; HBG 10/00; SLJ 3/00) [270.029]

20125 Nomura, Noriko S. *I Am Shinto* (K–3). Illus. Series: Religions of the World. 1996, Rosen LB $18.75 (978-0-8239-2380-9). 24pp. In double-page spreads, various aspects of the Shinto religion are introduced, including Dami spirits, shrines, and purification rituals. (Rev: SLJ 11/96) [299]

20126 Novesky, Amy. *Elephant Prince: The Story of Ganesh* (PS–2). Illus. by Belgin K. Wedman. 2004, Mandala $16.95 (978-1-886069-16-9). 32pp. A beautifully illustrated story of how the Hindu god Ganesh acquired his elephant head. (Rev: BL 1/1–15/05; SLJ 2/05) [294.5]

20127 Paul, John. *For the Children: Words of Love and Inspiration from His Holiness John Paul II* (4–7). Illus. 2000, Scholastic paper $16.95 (978-0-439-14902-0). 32pp. Letters and speeches by Pope John Paul II and photographs of children from around the world are used to illustrate inspirational messages about such subjects as hope, faith, and school. (Rev: BL 3/1/00; HBG 10/00; SLJ 3/00) [248.8]

20128 Raimondo, Lois. *The Little Lama of Tibet* (K–4). Illus. 1994, Scholastic $15.95 (978-0-590-46167-2). 40pp. This photoessay deals with the everyday life of Ling Rinpoche, a six-year-old high lama in the Tibetan Buddhist religion. (Rev: BCCB 1/94; BL 1/1/94; HB 9/94; SLJ 3/94) [294.3]

20129 Rotner, Shelley, and Sheila M. Kelly. *Many Ways: How Families Practice Their Beliefs and Religions* (K–2). Illus. by Shelley Rotner. 2005, Millbrook $16.95 (978-0-7613-2873-5). 32pp. A simple child-friendly introduction to the customs followed by believers of six religions: Buddhism, Christianity, Hinduism, Islam, Judaism, and Sikhism. (Rev: BL 10/1/05) [200]

20130 Rushton, Lucy. *Birth Customs* (4–6). Illus. Series: Religions. 1993, Thomson Learning LB $22.83 (978-1-56847-030-6). 32pp. This book examines the rituals and customs associated with birth as found in many of the world's religions. A companion volume is: *Death Customs* (1993). (Rev: BL 6/1–15/93; SLJ 7/93) [291.2]

20131 Sasso, Sandy Eisenberg. *God in Between* (PS–3). Illus. by Sally Sweetland. 1998, Jewish Lights $16.95 (978-1-879045-86-6). 32pp. Two townspeople are disappointed when their journey to find God ends unsuccessfully — until they realize that God is found while reaching out to others in need. (Rev: BL 10/15/98; HBG 9/98; SLJ 9/98) [211]

20132 Schwartz, Howard. *Invisible Kingdoms: Jewish Tales of Angels, Spirits, and Demons* (3–5). Illus. by Stephen Fieser. 2002, HarperCollins LB $18.89 (978-0-06-027856-4). 80pp. Schwartz retells nine varied tales peopled with angels, ghosts, and demons. (Rev: BL 10/1/02; HB 11/02; HBG 3/03; SLJ 10/02) [398.2]

20133 Self, David. *Christianity* (5–8). Series: Religions of the World. 2005, World Almanac LB $31.00 (978-0-8368-5866-2). 48pp. A basic introduction to the beliefs and practices of Christianity, with a chronology of important events. (Rev: SLJ 2/06)

20134 Sevastiades, Philemon D. *I Am Eastern Orthodox* (1–4). Illus. Series: Religions of the World. 1996, Rosen LB $19.95 (978-0-8239-2377-9). 24pp. The unique qualities of this church are covered through the story of Anastasia and her brother, who is the priest of her church in Chicago. (Rev: SLJ 2/97) [291]

20135 Sevastiades, Philemon D. *I Am Protestant* (1–4). Illus. Series: Religions of the World. 1996, Rosen LB $18.75 (978-0-8239-2378-6). 24pp. Focusing on Yvonne, a Southern African American girl who is an Evangelical Protestant, this and other branches of Protestantism and their beliefs are covered. (Rev: SLJ 2/97) [280]

20136 Sevastiades, Philemon D. *I Am Roman Catholic* (K–3). Illus. Series: Religions of the World. 1996, Rosen LB $19.95 (978-0-8239-2376-2). 24pp. Such Roman Catholic institutions, beliefs, and rituals as the Trinity, the Pope, baptism, Mass, confession, communion, and confirmation are discussed. (Rev: SLJ 11/96) [282]

20137 Sita, Lisa. *Worlds of Belief: Religion and Spirituality* (5–8). Series: Our Human Family. 1995, Blackbirch LB $27.45 (978-1-56711-125-5). Using many illustrations, this book gives a tour of the

world's religions, with an emphasis on the similarities rather than the differences. (Rev: SLJ 1/96) [200]

20138 Stanton, Sue. *Child's Guide to the Mass* (PS–3). Illus. by H. M. Alan. 2001, Paulist Press $9.95 (978-0-8091-6682-4). 32pp. Using a light-hearted approach, this book explains the parts of the Roman Catholic Mass and what each means. (Rev: BL 3/15/01; HBG 10/01) [264]

20139 Sugarman, Joan G., and Grace R. Freeman. *Inside the Synagogue* (K–3). Illus. 1984, UAHC paper $7.00 (978-0-8074-0268-9). In text and photos, the Jewish house of worship is introduced. (Rev: SLJ 3/85)

20140 Teece, Geoff. *Christianity* (3–7). Illus. Series: Religion in Focus. 2004, Smart Apple LB $18.95 (978-1-58340-465-2). This slim, photo-filled volume introduces the history, beliefs, and practices of Christianity, covering festivals, sacred places, and a list of denominations. Also use *Buddhism* (2004). (Rev: BL 10/1/04) [202]

20141 Thompson, Jan. *Islam* (5–8). Series: World Religions. 2005, Walrus paper $12.95 (978-1-55285-654-3). 58pp. Using a question-and-answer format, this attractive introduction explores the history and beliefs of Islam; a first-person account by a 15-year-old Muslim boy in London starts the book. (Rev: BL 10/15/05) [297]

20142 Tompert, Ann. *Saint Nicholas* (2–4). Illus. 2000, Boyds Mills $15.95 (978-1-56397-844-9). 32pp. A retelling of the legends surrounding St. Nicholas and the attributes that made him one of the most beloved of all saints. (Rev: BCCB 10/00; BL 10/1/00; HBG 3/01) [398.2]

20143 Visconte, Guido. *Clare and Francis* (4–7). Illus. by Bimba Landmann. 2004, Eerdmans $20.00 (978-0-8028-5269-4). 40pp. Eye-catching artwork highlights the inspiring stories of saints Clare and Francis in this picture book for older readers. (Rev: BL 2/1/04*; SLJ 6/04) [270]

20144 Waldman, Neil. *The Promised Land: The Birth of the Jewish People* (4–7). Illus. 2002, Boyds Mills $21.95 (978-1-56397-332-1). 40pp. Waldman interweaves information on religious tradition and the experiences of the Jewish people over time in this handsome volume. (Rev: BL 10/1/02; HBG 3/03; SLJ 9/02) [909]

20145 Wallace, Holly. *Islam: Budi's Story* (3–5). Illus. Series: This Is My Faith. 2007, Barron's paper $4.99 (978-0-7641-3475-3). 32pp. Budi, a young Indonesian Muslim, introduces his family and neighbors and describes the ways in which his religion affects his life. (Rev: BL 4/1/07) [297]

20146 Weiss, Bernard P. *I Am Jewish* (1–4). Illus. Series: Religions of the World. 1996, Rosen LB $15.93 (978-0-8239-2349-6). 24pp. This explanation of Judaism shows the links between the religion, Jewish history, and the country of Israel. (Rev: SLJ 2/97) [296]

20147 *What You Will See Inside a Mosque* (3–6). Series: What You Will See Inside. 2003, SkyLight Paths $16.95 (978-1-893361-60-7). 32pp. Two small New York mosques are featured in this introduction to the fundamentals of Islam and how and where Muslims worship. (Rev: BL 10/1/03; SLJ 2/04) [297.3]

20148 Wilkinson, Philip. *Buddhism* (5–8). Illus. 2003, DK $15.99 (978-0-7894-9833-5). 64pp. An attractive, well-illustrated overview of the teachings and symbols of Buddhism, with information on history, different forms, important sites, and art and artifacts. (Rev: BL 1/1–15/04) [294.3]

20149 Wilson, Karma. *I Will Rejoice: Celebrating Psalm 118* (PS–2). Illus. by Amy June Bates. 2007, Zondervan $14.99 (978-0-310-71117-9). 32pp. Based on the psalm that reads "This is the day that the Lord has made, and I will rejoice and be glad in it," this book urges children to find happiness and joy in the world around them. (Rev: BL 10/1/06)

20150 Zarin, Cynthia. *Saints Among the Animals* (5–8). Illus. by Leonid Gore. 2006, Atheneum $17.95 (978-0-689-85031-8). 96pp. An attractive collection of ten stories about saints interacting with animals; brief biographies of the saints are appended. (Rev: BL 12/1/06; SLJ 1/07) [270]

Bible Stories

20151 Aaseng, Rolf E. *Augsburg Story Bible* (4–8). Illus. by Annegert Fuchshuber. 1992, Augsburg LB $19.99 (978-0-8066-2607-9). 270pp. This copiously illustrated version of the Bible is only slightly abridged. (Rev: SLJ 7/92) [222]

20152 Alexander, Pat. *My First Bible* (PS–1). Illus. by Leon Baxter. 2002, Good Bks. $14.99 (978-1-56148-360-0). 480pp. A collection of more than 60 stories from the Old and New Testaments, with amusing, cartoon-style illustrations. (Rev: SLJ 12/02)

20153 *And It Was Good* (PS–2). Illus. by Harold H. Nofziger. 1993, Herald $12.99 (978-0-8361-3634-0). The Creation story is reproduced with brightly colored collages and a text from the New Revised Standard Version of the Bible. (Rev: SLJ 12/93) [222]

20154 Beneduce, Ann Keay. *Moses: The Long Road to Freedom* (2–4). Illus. by Gennady Spirin. 2004, Scholastic $16.95 (978-0-439-35225-3). 32pp. The striking artwork of Gennady Spirin enhances this retelling of the story of Moses and how he led his people out of Egypt to freedom. (Rev: BL 4/1/04; SLJ 3/04) [222]

20155 Bogot, Howard I., and Mary K. Bogot, retels. *Seven Animal Stories for Children* (K–3). Illus. by Harry Araten. 1997, Pitspopany $16.95 (978-0-943706-40-5); paper $9.95 (978-0-943706-41-2). 45pp. A collection of Bible stories and Jewish folktales that tell about such people as Noah, Solomon, David, and Jonah. (Rev: HBG 3/98; SLJ 12/97) [226]

20156 Boroson, Martin. *Becoming Me* (K–3). Illus. by Christopher Gilvan-Cartwright. 2000, SkyLight Paths $16.95 (978-1-893361-11-9). 32pp. The Bible

creation story as told from the standpoint of God. (Rev: BL 7/00; SLJ 10/00) [291.2]

20157 Boss, Sarah Jane. *Mary's Story* (3–5). Illus. by Helen Cann. 1999, Barefoot Bks. $16.95 (978-1-901223-44-6). 48pp. Using biblical sources as well as folk traditions, this book re-creates the life of Mary, the mother of Jesus. (Rev: BL 10/1/99; SLJ 10/99) [224]

20158 Brett, Jan. *On Noah's Ark* (PS–1). Illus. by author. 2003, Penguin $16.99 (978-0-399-24028-7). Noah's granddaughter is the focus of this beautifully illustrated retelling with detailed watercolors of the ark's occupants. (Rev: BL 10/1/03; HBG 4/04; SLJ 9/03)

20159 Brunelli, Roberto. *A Family Treasury of Bible Stories: One for Each Week of the Year* (4–8). Illus. 1997, Abrams $24.95 (978-0-8109-1248-9). A collection of 52 short stories from the Old and New Testaments. (Rev: BL 10/1/97; SLJ 2/98) [220.9]

20160 Chaikin, Miriam, adapt. *Exodus* (3–5). Illus. by Charles Mikolaycak. 1987, Holiday House LB $15.95 (978-0-8234-0607-4). 32pp. The story of the Israelites' flight out of Egypt. (Rev: BCCB 5/87; BL 5/15/87; HB 5/87)

20161 Chancellor, Deborah, retel. *DK Children's Everyday Bible: A Bible Story for Every Day of the Year* (K–4). Illus. by Anna C. Leplar. 2002, DK $19.99 (978-0-7894-8858-9). 383pp. Retellings of Old and New Testament stories for each day of the year. (Rev: HBG 10/03; SLJ 12/02)

20162 Clements, Andrew. *Noah and the Ark and the Animals* (PS–2). Illus. 1992, Scholastic paper $4.95 (978-0-590-44457-6). 28pp. Subdued watercolors enhance this retelling. (Rev: SLJ 8/04) [226.7]

20163 Connolly, Sean. *New Testament Miracles* (5–10). Series: Art Revelations. 2004, Enchanted Lion $18.95 (978-1-59270-012-7). 32pp. Presents brief retellings of 12 miracles performed by Jesus Christ, each illustrated by a well-known painting by an eminent artist, such as Rembrandt, El Greco, and Tintoretto. (Rev: SLJ 8/04) [226.7]

20164 Crossley-Holland, Kevin. *How Many Miles to Bethlehem?* (1–3). Illus. by Peter Malone. 2004, Scholastic LB $16.95 (978-0-439-67642-7). 32pp. Illustrations with a Renaissance flavor form a backdrop for the characters who introduce themselves and their role in the story of the Nativity. (Rev: BL 10/1/04; SLJ 10/04) [232.92]

20165 Demi. *Mary* (4–7). 2006, Simon & Schuster $19.95 (978-0-689-87692-9). 48pp. Traces the story of the mother of Jesus from the days preceding her birth through her ascension into heaven. (Rev: BL 10/1/06; SLJ 11/06) [232.91]

20166 dePaola, Tomie. *Mary: The Mother of Jesus* (K–3). Illus. 1995, Holiday House LB $16.95 (978-0-8234-1018-7). 32pp. This account combines stories from the Bible with popular legends to create a life of Mary. (Rev: BCCB 11/95; BL 9/1/95; SLJ 12/95) [232.91]

20167 dePaola, Tomie. *The Miracles of Jesus* (3–6). Illus. by author. 1987, Holiday House LB $17.95 (978-0-8234-0635-7). 32pp. These one-page adaptations from the New Testament include the 12 miracles of Jesus. (Rev: BL 11/1/87; SLJ 10/87)

20168 dePaola, Tomie. *The Parables of Jesus* (3–6). Illus. by author. 1987, Holiday House LB $17.95 (978-0-8234-0636-4). 32pp. Seven retellings of the parables of Jesus, such as "The Good Samaritan" and "The Mustard Seed." (Rev: BL 11/1/87; SLJ 10/87)

20169 dePaola, Tomie. *Tomie dePaola's Book of Bible Stories* (K–3). Illus. 1990, Penguin $25.99 (978-0-399-21690-9). 128pp. A collection of stories from the Old and New Testaments. (Rev: BCCB 11/90; BL 10/15/90; SLJ 12/90*) [220]

20170 De Regniers, Beatrice S. *David and Goliath* (1–3). Illus. by Scott Cameron. 1996, Orchard LB $16.99 (978-0-531-08796-1). 32pp. The story of the shepherd boy David and his deadly confrontation with Goliath. (Rev: BL 3/15/96; SLJ 3/96) [222]

20171 Devon, Paddie. *The Grumpy Shepherd* (PS–2). Illus. 1995, Abingdon paper $7.00 (978-0-687-00129-3). 32pp. A grumpy shepherd named Joram changes his attitude when he meets Jesus. (Rev: BL 12/1/95)

20172 Downey, Lynn. *This Is the Earth That God Made* (PS–1). Illus. by Benrei Huang. 2000, Augsburg $8.99 (978-0-8066-3960-4). In this good-natured look at the Creation, images such as mountains, fountains, seas, winds, animals, and bees gradually appear, ending with a human family giving thanks. (Rev: SLJ 9/00) [224]

20173 Fischer, Chuck, and Curtis Flowers. *In the Beginning: The Art of Genesis* (5–8). Illus. by Bruce Foster. 2008, Little, Brown $35.00 (978-0-316-11842-2). 12pp. This artful pop-up book highlights stories from the Book of Genesis, including the Garden of Eden, Noah's Ark, the Tower of Babel, and Jacob's Ladder. (Rev: BL 2/1/09*)

20174 Fisher, Leonard Everett. *David and Goliath* (K–3). Illus. 1993, Holiday House LB $15.95 (978-0-8234-0997-6). 32pp. An expertly illustrated retelling of the Bible story of the brave lad who saved the land of the Israelites. (Rev: BL 5/1/93*; SLJ 6/93) [222]

20175 Fisher, Leonard Everett. *Moses* (PS–4). Illus. 1995, Holiday House LB $15.95 (978-0-8234-1149-8). 32pp. The life of Moses and the salvation of the Jewish people are portrayed in double-page spreads. (Rev: BCCB 5/95; BL 5/15/95; SLJ 5/95) [222]

20176 Gellman, Marc. *Does God Have a Big Toe? Stories About Stories in the Bible* (4–6). Illus. by Oscar de Mejo. 1989, HarperCollins $16.95 (978-0-06-022432-5); paper $7.99 (978-0-06-440453-2). 96pp. A look at familiar tales in the Bible through new eyes. (Rev: BL 10/15/89; HB 3/90; SLJ 12/89) [221]

20177 Gellman, Marc. *God's Mailbox: More Stories About Stories in the Bible* (4–7). Illus. by Debbie Tilley. 1996, Morrow $15.00 (978-0-688-13169-2). 92pp. Some stories retold from the Bible, including the Creation, Garden of Eden, Jacob's ladder, the Exodus, and Moses receiving the Ten Commandments. (Rev: BCCB 5/96; SLJ 3/96) [222]

20178 Goble, Paul. *Song of Creation* (K–3). Illus. by author. 2004, Eerdmans $16.00 (978-0-8028-5271-

7). 32pp. This richly illustrated celebration of God and the wonders of nature draws on *The Book of Common Prayer*. (Rev: BL 10/1/04; SLJ 10/04) [242]

20179 Graham, Lorenz. *How God Fix Jonah* (3–5). Illus. 2000, Boyds Mills $17.95 (978-1-56397-698-8). 156pp. This collection of biblical-story poems contains tales from both the Testaments told from a West African native's viewpoint. (Rev: BL 10/1/00; HBG 10/01; SLJ 12/00) [220.9]

20180 Greenberg, Blu, and Linda Tarry. *King Solomon and the Queen of Sheba* (2–5). Illus. by Avi Katz. 1997, Pitspopany $16.95 (978-0-943706-90-0). 48pp. The biblically based story of the Ethiopian queen, her love for the wise, Jewish king, Solomon, and their child. (Rev: SLJ 5/98)

20181 Greenfield, Karen R. *Sister Yessa's Story* (2–5). Illus. by Claire Ewart. 1992, HarperCollins $15.00 (978-0-06-020278-1). As she walks through the woods, Yessa gathers animals for her brother's ark. (Rev: SLJ 8/92)

20182 Grimes, Nikki. *At Break of Day* (PS–3). Illus. by Paul Morin. 1999, Eerdmans $17.00 (978-0-8028-5104-8). 32pp. In this version of the creation story, God and his Son work together to produce the universe and its wonders. (Rev: BL 10/1/99; HBG 4/00; SLJ 1/00) [231.7]

20183 Grindley, Sally, and Jan Barger. *Bible Stories for the Young* (PS–2). Illus. 1998, Little Tiger $16.95 (978-1-888444-42-1). 96pp. Twenty well-known stories from the Old and New Testaments are presented in language and pictures suitable for a young audience. (Rev: BCCB 2/99; BL 10/1/98; HBG 9/99; SLJ 10/98) [220.9]

20184 Gunney, Lynn Tuttle. *Meet Jesus: The Life and Lessons of a Beloved Teacher* (K–3). Illus. by Jane Conteh-Morgan. 2007, Skinner $12.00 (978-1-55896-524-9). 36pp. A simple, clearly written introduction to the life of Jesus and his teachings and parables. (Rev: BL 10/1/07) [232.9]

20185 Harrison, James. *My Very First Bible* (PS–2). Illus. by Diana Mayo. 2005, DK $12.99 (978-0-7566-0983-2). 80pp. Twenty-five key stories from both Testaments are told in clear prose and appealing illustrations. (Rev: BL 3/1/04; SLJ 5/05) [220.9]

20186 Hodges, Margaret. *Moses* (3–5). Illus. by Barry Moser. 2006, Harcourt $16.00 (978-0-15-200946-5). 32pp. From his birth and placement in the bulrushes to his retrieval of the Ten Commandments, this handsome volume highlights Moses' achievements and the obstacles he faced. (Rev: BL 10/1/06; SLJ 12/06) [222.1]

20187 Hoffman, Mary, retel. *A First Bible Story Book* (K–2). Illus. by Julie Downing. 1998, DK $12.99 (978-0-7894-1555-4). 80pp. A basic Bible storybook that contains easy-to-read narratives from both the Old and New Testaments. (Rev: HBG 9/99; SLJ 2/99) [221.9]

20188 Hoffman, Mary. *Kings and Queens of the Bible* (K–3). Illus. by Christina Balit. 2008, Holt $16.95 (978-0-8050-8837-3). 40pp. Retells the stories of Old Testament kings and queens (Moses, David, Soloman, Esther, Balkis, Jezebel, and Belshazzar); includes occasional violent scenes plus an appendix of the books of the Bible in which the figures appear. (Rev: BL 10/1/08; SLJ 11/08) [220.9]

20189 Johnson, James W. *The Creation* (K–4). Illus. by James Ransome. 1994, Holiday House LB $18.95 (978-0-8234-1069-9). 32pp. The story of the first seven days of the world is told in the paintings and a poem by a famous African American writer. (Rev: BL 4/15/94; HB 9/94; SLJ 5/94*) [811]

20190 Joslin, Mary. *The Paraclete Treasury of Angel Stories* (K–3). Illus. by Elena Temporin. 2008, Paraclete $18.95 (978-1-55725-572-3). 32pp. An accessible collection of Bible stories, verses, and prayers about angels. (Rev: BL 5/1/08) [220.9]

20191 Jules, Jacqueline. *Abraham's Search for God* (K–3). Illus. by Natascia Ugliano. 2007, Kar-Ben $17.95 (978-1-58013-243-5). 32pp. Abraham came early to the belief that there was one God, according to this retelling of a legend based on the Bible. (Rev: BL 10/1/07; SLJ 9/07) [222]

20192 Jules, Jacqueline. *Benjamin and the Silver Goblet* (K–3). Illus. by Natascia Ugliano. 2009, Lerner LB $17.95 (978-0-8225-8757-6); paper $8.95 (978-0-8225-8758-3). Joseph, sold into slavery in Egypt but risen to become a powerful man, tests his brothers the honesty of his brothers in this Bible story. (Rev: SLJ 4/09) [222]

20193 Jules, Jacqueline. *Sarah Laughs* (PS–3). Illus. by Natascia Ugliano. 2008, Lerner $17.95 (978-0-8225-7216-9). 32pp. Sarah, the wife of Abraham and elderly mother of young Isaac, is the focus of this picture book that draws on legend as well as the Bible story. (Rev: BL 10/1/08; SLJ 6/08) [222]

20194 Kimmel, Eric A. *Why the Snake Crawls on Its Belly* (K–3). Illus. by Allen Davis. 2001, Pitspopany $14.95 (978-1-930143-20-3). 32pp. This very readable pourquoi story relates how God punishes the snake for tempting Adam and Eve in the garden of Eden. (Rev: BL 10/1/01; HBG 3/02; SLJ 12/01)

20195 Koralek, Jenny. *The Coat of Many Colors* (PS–2). Illus. by Pauline Baynes. 2004, Eerdmans $16.00 (978-0-8028-5277-9). 32pp. The Old Testament story of Joseph is retold in a lively way and enhanced with art that evokes the time and the setting. (Rev: BL 10/15/04; SLJ 11/04) [224]

20196 Koralek, Jenny. *The Moses Basket* (3–5). Illus. by Pauline Baynes. 2003, Eerdmans $16.00 (978-0-8028-5251-9). This beautifully realized retelling relates how Moses's mother gave up her infant son rather than see him killed. (Rev: HBG 4/04; SLJ 10/03) [221.9]

20197 Lane, Leena. *Angels Among Us* (1–3). Illus. by Elena Baboni. 2007, Eerdmans $17.00 (978-0-8028-5321-9). 29pp. This oversize picture book contains 12 biblical stories in which angels appear to humans. (Rev: BL 10/1/07; SLJ 11/07) [220.9]

20198 Lee, Young Shin. *Traitors, Kings, and the Big Break* (3–5). Illus. by Jung Sun Hwang. Series: Manga Bible. 2008, Zondervan paper $6.99 (978-0-310-71290-9). 208pp. King David and Solomon feature in this upbeat manga version of the first and second book of Kings from the Old Testament. (Rev: BLO 7/29/08) [222]

20199 *The Lord Is My Shepherd* (PS–2). Illus. by Anne Wilson. 2003, Eerdmans $16.00 (978-0-8028-5250-2). 32pp. The 23rd psalm is accompanied by expressive art. (Rev: BL 2/1/03; HBG 10/03; SLJ 7/03) [223]

20200 Lottridge, Celia B. *Stories from Adam and Eve to Ezekiel: Retold from the Bible* (4–7). Illus. by Gary Clement. 2004, Groundwood $24.95 (978-0-88899-490-5). 192pp. Some of the best-loved stories from the Hebrew Bible are engagingly adapted in this attractively illustrated volume. (Rev: BL 10/1/04; SLJ 4/05) [220]

20201 Lottridge, Celia B. *Stories from the Life of Jesus* (5–7). Illus. by Linda Wolfsgruber. 2004, Douglas & McIntyre $24.95 (978-0-88899-497-4). 128pp. Lottridge draws on the first four books of the New Testament for this illustrated collection of stories. (Rev: BL 5/1/04; HB 7/04; SLJ 11/04) [232.9]

20202 McCarthy, Michael, retel. *The Story of Daniel in the Lions' Den* (PS–3). Illus. by Giuliano Ferri. 2003, Barefoot Bks. $16.99 (978-1-84148-209-5). The Old Testament story is retold in rhyme in this beautifully illustrated picture book. (Rev: BL 6/1–15/03; HBG 10/03; SLJ 5/03) [224.5]

20203 McCarthy, Michael. *The Story of Noah and the Ark* (PS–K). Illus. by Giuliano Ferri. 2001, Barefoot Bks. $16.99 (978-1-84148-361-0). 32pp. Wonderful illustrations show the animals arrayed around the decks, the roiling seas, and the arrival of the dove. (Rev: BL 10/1/01; HBG 3/02; SLJ 11/01) [222]

20204 McGee, Marni. *The Colt and the King* (PS–3). Illus. by John Winch. 2002, Holiday House $16.95 (978-0-8234-1695-0). 32pp. Told from the standpoint of the donkey that carried Jesus into Jerusalem on Palm Sunday, this is a beautifully illustrated retelling of a Bible story. (Rev: BCCB 4/02; BL 4/1/02; HB 3/02; HBG 10/02; SLJ 4/02)

20205 Matthews, Caitlin. *The Blessing Seed: A Creation Myth for the New Millennium* (1–5). Illus. by Alison Dexter. 1998, Barefoot Bks. $14.95 (978-1-901223-28-6). 32pp. An enthralling new version of the world's beginnings, using the Judeo-Christian creation story as a basis, supplemented with mystical interpretations. (Rev: BL 10/15/98; SLJ 9/98) [291.2]

20206 Mayer, Marianna. *Young Jesus of Nazareth* (2–4). Illus. 1999, Morrow LB $15.89 (978-0-688-16728-8). 32pp. From the Nativity to the Sermon on the Mount, this is a retelling of stories about the youthful Jesus. (Rev: BCCB 11/99; BL 10/1/99; HBG 4/00; SLJ 12/99) [232.92]

20207 Oberman, Sheldon. *The Wisdom Bird: A Tale of Solomon and Sheba* (K–4). Illus. by Neil Waldman. 2000, Boyds Mills $15.95 (978-1-56397-816-6). 32pp. Drawing on many sources, including the Bible, African folklore, and Jewish tales, this is the story of Sheba's request that Solomon build her a palace out of bird's beaks. (Rev: BCCB 10/00; BL 10/1/00; HBG 3/01; SLJ 10/00)

20208 *Paradise* (2–5). Illus. by Fiona French. 2004, Frances Lincoln $15.95 (978-1-84507-007-6). An eye-catching version of the Creation story, based on the King James translation of the Bible. (Rev: SLJ 6/04) [222.1]

20209 Paterson, Katherine. *The Angel and the Donkey* (1–4). Illus. by Alexander Koshkin. 1996, Clarion $15.95 (978-0-395-68969-1). 34pp. Based on passages in the Hebrew Bible, this is the story of Pethor, a soothsayer, and his encounter with Moses. (Rev: BCCB 4/96; BL 3/1/96; SLJ 3/96) [222]

20210 Paterson, Katherine. *The Light of the World: The Life of Jesus for Children* (K–3). Illus. by François Roca. 2008, Scholastic $17.99 (978-0-545-01172-3). 48pp. Rich paintings accompany this telling of the life of Jesus, highlighting his disciples and some of the parables. (Rev: BCCB 2/08; BL 1/1–15/08; HB 5/08; SLJ 1/08) [232.9]

20211 Pilling, Ann. *A Kingfisher Treasury of Bible Stories, Poems, and Prayers for Bedtime* (3–6). Illus. 2000, Kingfisher $18.95 (978-0-7534-5329-2). 96pp. Poetry, songs, and Bible stories from the Old and New Testaments are included in this anthology aimed at Christian children. (Rev: BL 10/1/00; HBG 10/01) [242]

20212 Pinkney, Jerry. *Noah's Ark* (2–5). Illus. by author. 2002, North-South LB $16.50 (978-1-58717-202-1). 40pp. Pinkney offers a fresh take on the popular story while keeping his narrative fairly close to the standard version. Caldecott Honor Book, 2004. (Rev: BCCB 1/03; BL 10/1/02; HB 1/03; HBG 3/03; SLJ 11/02*) [222]

20213 *Psalm Twenty-Three* (PS–3). Illus. by Tim Ladwig. 1997, Eerdmans $17.00 (978-0-8028-5160-4); paper $8.00 (978-0-8028-5163-5). 32pp. This version of the famous psalm pictures two African American children growing up in a bleak, urban neighborhood. (Rev: BL 10/1/97; HBG 3/98) [123.2]

20214 Ray, Jane. *Adam and Eve and the Garden of Eden* (K–3). Illus. 2005, Eerdmans $17.00 (978-0-8028-5278-6). 32pp. A beautiful picture-book presentation of the story of the creation and fall of the first humans. (Rev: BL 4/1/05; SLJ 5/05) [222]

20215 Rock, Lois, ed. *Words of Gold: A Treasury of Bible Poetry and Wisdom* (4–6). Illus. 2000, Eerdmans $18.00 (978-0-8028-5199-4). 48pp. Using 22 double-page spreads, this book contains passages from the Old and New Testaments covering the story of the Jewish people from Abraham to Revelations. (Rev: BL 4/1/00; HBG 9/00; SLJ 9/00) [220.9]

20216 Ross, Lillian H. *Daughters of Eve: Strong Women of the Bible* (5–7). Illus. 2000, Barefoot Bks. $19.99 (978-1-902283-82-1). 96pp. Fictionalized accounts that expand on the material given in the Bible and Apocrypha about 12 strong women and their deeds. (Rev: BL 10/1/00; HBG 10/01; SLJ 11/00) [220.9]

20217 Sasso, Sandy Eisenberg. *Adam and Eve's First Sunset: God's New Day* (K–4). Illus. by Joani Keller Rothenberg. 2003, Jewish Lights $17.95 (978-1-58023-177-0). 32pp. Based on a Talmudic lesson, this is the story of how God helped Adam and Eve build a fire on their first night in the Garden of Eden. (Rev: BL 1/1–15/04; SLJ 3/04) [222]

20218 Sasso, Sandy Eisenberg. *But God Remembered: Stories of Women from Creation to the Promised Land* (3–6). Illus. by Bethanne Andersen. 1995, Jewish Lights $16.95 (978-1-879045-43-9). 32pp. In this picture book, the stories of several almost-forgotten women in the Old Testament are retold. (Rev: BL 9/1/95*; SLJ 12/95) [221.9]

20219 Sasso, Sandy Eisenberg. *Cain and Abel: Finding the Fruits of Peace* (K–3). Illus. by Joani Keller Rothenberg. 2001, Jewish Lights $16.95 (978-1-58023-123-7). 32pp. This retelling of a biblical parable encourages children to think about the harmful consequences of jealousy and anger. (Rev: BL 11/15/01; HBG 10/02; SLJ 2/02) [222.1]

20220 Sasso, Sandy Eisenberg. *Naamah, Noah's Wife* (PS–K). Illus. by Bethanne Andersen. 2002, Jewish Lights $7.95 (978-1-893361-56-0). 24pp. This board-book version of *Noah's Wife: The Story of Naamah* (2002) shows Naamah gathering seeds and planting them aboard the ark, and then restocking the earth's plant life after the flood. (Rev: BL 1/1–15/03) [222]

20221 Schmidt, Gary D., retel. *The Blessing of the Lord: Stories from the Old and New Testaments* (5–8). Illus. 1997, Eerdmans $20.00 (978-0-8028-3789-9). Using 25 Old and New Testament stories as a focus, these insightful accounts describe how biblical personalities react to such events as Daniel's struggle with the lions and Jesus causing nets to be filled with fish. (Rev: BL 11/1/97; HBG 3/98; SLJ 10/97) [222]

20222 Shaw, Luci. *The Genesis of It All* (K–3). Illus. by Sr. Huai-Kuang Miao. 2006, Paraclete $17.95 (978-1-55725-480-1). 32pp. This child-friendly retelling of the creation story imagines what God was thinking as He gave form to the world and breathed life into man and beast; the beautiful art progresses from black and white to color, and the author emphasizes that the story is speculation not fact. (Rev: BL 10/1/06) [222]

20223 Spier, Peter, retel. *Noah's Ark* (PS–K). Illus. by Peter Spier. 1977, Dell paper $7.99 (978-0-440-40693-8). 44pp. Vital, humorous, detailed pictures present a panorama of the animals and their voyage in the ark. Caldecott Medal winner, 1978.

20224 Spirin, Gennady. *Gennady Spirin's Creation* (K–3). Illus. by author. Series: Master Illustrators. 2008, Zonderkidz $14.99 (978-0-310-71084-4). 32pp. Handsome watercolors illustrate the creation story as told at the beginning of Genesis. (Rev: BL 6/1–15/08; SLJ 3/08) [223]

20225 *Stories from the Bible* (5–7). Illus. by Lisbeth Zwerger. 2002, North-South $19.95 (978-0-7358-1413-4). 160pp. Sophisticated paintings illustrate verbatim excerpts from the King James version of both the Old and New Testaments. (Rev: BCCB 9/02; BL 4/1/02; HB 7/02; HBG 10/02; SLJ 5/02) [220.5]

20226 *The Story of Noah and the Ark: According to the Book of Genesis: From the King James Bible* (3–5). Illus. by Gennady Spirin. 2004, Holt $18.95 (978-0-8050-6181-9). 32pp. This retelling of the bible story of Noah's Ark is set apart by Spirin's strikingly beautiful oil illustrations. (Rev: BL 4/15/04; HB 7/04; SLJ 4/04) [222]

20227 Topek, Susan Remick. *Ten Good Rules* (PS–K). Illus. by Rosalyn Schanzer. 1992, Kar-Ben paper $5.95 (978-0-929371-28-3). 32pp. In modern language, the Ten Commandments and their meanings are presented in an attractive concept book. (Rev: SLJ 7/92) [222]

20228 Ward, Elaine. *Old Testament Women* (5–10). Series: Art Revelations. 2004, Enchanted Lion $18.95 (978-1-59270-011-0). 32pp. Paintings by masters accompany stories about 18 women including Rachel, Ruth, and Bathsheba. (Rev: SLJ 8/04) [224]

20229 Watts, Murray. *The Bible for Children* (K–4). Illus. by Helen Cann. 2002, Good Bks. $23.99 (978-1-56148-362-4). 352pp. Watts vividly retells more than 200 stories from both Old and New Testaments in this handsome volume that includes a map, a glossary, and indexes of people and places. (Rev: BL 10/1/02; HBG 3/03; SLJ 1/03) [220.9]

20230 Wildsmith, Brian. *Exodus* (3–5). Illus. 1999, Eerdmans $20.00 (978-0-8028-5175-8). 36pp. A lushly illustrated and detailed life of Moses, from his beginnings in Egypt to his arrival in the promised land. (Rev: BL 2/15/99; HBG 9/99; SLJ 1/99) [222]

20231 Wildsmith, Brian. *Jesus* (PS–3). Illus. 2000, Eerdmans $20.00 (978-0-8028-5212-0). 32pp. Using quotes from the four gospels, the illustrator covers the important incidents in the life of Jesus beginning with the Nativity story and ending with Jesus' death and resurrection. (Rev: BCCB 1/01; BL 2/1/01; HBG 10/01) [224]

20232 Wildsmith, Brian. *Joseph* (K–4). Illus. 1997, Eerdmans $20.00 (978-0-8028-5161-1). 40pp. A handsome, well-told version of the biblical story of Joseph. (Rev: BL 2/1/98; HBG 3/98) [222]

20233 Williams, Marcia. *God and His Creations: Tales from the Old Testament* (K–2). Illus. 2004, Candlewick $15.99 (978-0-7636-2211-4). 40pp. Comic-strip interpretations make accessible several well-known Old Testament stories. (Rev: BL 3/15/04; SLJ 5/04) [221.9]

20234 Winch, John. *Two by Two* (PS). 2004, Holiday House $16.95 (978-0-8234-1840-4). 32pp. This retelling of the story of Noah's Ark, recounted in a lush blend of poetic narrative and detailed artwork, focuses on the flood itself and not the spiritual aspects of the Bible story. (Rev: BL 10/1/04; SLJ 10/04)

20235 Winthrop, Elizabeth, adapt. *He Is Risen: The Easter Story* (4–7). Illus. by Charles Mikolaycak. 1985, Holiday $17.95 (978-0-8234-0547-3). 32pp. The Easter story taken from parts of the King James version of the Bible and dramatically illustrated. (Rev: BCCB 4/85; HB 7/85; SLJ 4/85)

Holidays and Holy Days

General and Miscellaneous

20236 Addasi, Maha. *The White Nights of Ramadan* (K–3). Illus. by Ned Gannon. 2008, Boyds Mills $16.95 (978-1-59078-523-2). 32pp. This is the story of how Noor, a young Kuwaiti girl, performs the rituals of Girgian, three days in the middle of the holy month of Ramadan. (Rev: BL 7/08; LMC 11/08; SLJ 9/08) [297.3]

20237 Ansary, Mir T. *Columbus Day* (K–2). Series: Holiday Histories. 1998, Heinemann LB $21.36 (978-1-57572-702-8). 32pp. Though somewhat oversimplified, this is a history of Columbus Day and the celebration of the discovery of America. (Rev: SLJ 2/99) [394]

20238 Ansary, Mir T. *Labor Day* (2–3). Illus. Series: Holiday Histories. 1998, Heinemann LB $21.36 (978-1-57572-703-5). 32pp. This holiday book explains how workers banded together to fight poor working conditions and how, in time, this national holiday was born. (Rev: BL 1/1–15/99; SLJ 2/99) [394.264]

20239 Ansary, Mir T. *Martin Luther King Jr. Day* (2–3). Series: Holiday Histories. 1998, Heinemann LB $21.36 (978-1-57572-873-5). 32pp. This easy reader examines the history of Martin Luther King Day, tells how it is celebrated, and why it is important. (Rev: BL 12/15/98) [394.2]

20240 Ansary, Mir T. *Memorial Day* (2–3). Series: Holiday Histories. 1998, Heinemann LB $21.36 (978-1-57572-874-2). 32pp. Gives the history of Memorial Day, explaining how and why we celebrate it. (Rev: BL 12/15/98) [394.2]

20241 Ansary, Mir T. *Veterans Day* (2–3). Illus. Series: Holiday Histories. 1998, Heinemann LB $13.95 (978-1-57572-876-6). 32pp. A discussion of Veterans Day — its origins, history, and its growing importance after World Wars I and II. (Rev: BL 1/1–15/99) [394.264]

20242 Barner, Bob. *Parade Day: Marching Through the Calendar Year* (PS–1). Illus. 2003, Holiday House $16.95 (978-0-8234-1690-5). 32pp. A parade for each month — some for holidays, others (such as a pet parade) just for fun. (Rev: BL 2/15/03; HBG 10/03; SLJ 4/03)

20243 Barrett, Anna Pearl. *Juneteenth: Celebrating Freedom in Texas* (3–6). Illus. by Gary Laronde. 1999, Eakin $12.95 (978-1-57168-180-5). 80pp. This book tells how the author and her family celebrated in 1945 the 80th Juneteenth, the holiday that celebrates the emancipation of African Americans from slavery. (Rev: SLJ 8/99)

20244 Batmanglij, Najmieh. *Happy Nowruz: Cooking with Children to Celebrate the Persian New Year* (4–8). Illus. 2008, Mage $40.00 (978-1-933823-16-4). 120pp. This attractive spiral-bound book combines the history and customs of the Persian New Year with recipes. (Rev: BL 6/1–15/08) [641.59]

20245 Bennett, Kelly. *Flag Day* (PS–2). Series: Rookie Read-about Holidays. 2003, Children's

Book Pr. LB $20.50 (978-0-516-22862-4); paper $5.95 (978-0-516-27755-4). 32pp. An easy-to-read book that introduces the holiday celebrated on June 14, with details on its origin and observances. (Rev: BL 3/15/03) [394]

20246 Brady, April A. *Kwanzaa Karamu: Cooking and Crafts for a Kwanzaa Feast* (4–6). Illus. 1995, Carolrhoda LB $21.27 (978-0-87614-842-6); paper $6.95 (978-0-87614-633-0). 64pp. Following a general introduction to Kwanzaa, this book introduces crafts and gives 18 recipes for appropriate food. (Rev: BL 4/15/95) [641.59]

20247 Brill, Marlene T. *Veterans Day* (1–3). Illus. Series: On My Own Holidays. 2005, Carolrhoda LB $25.26 (978-1-57505-699-9); paper $5.95 (978-1-57505-766-8). 48pp. The origins and traditions of Veterans Day are introduced with many illustrations and a short glossary.

20248 Campbell, Louisa. *A World of Holidays! Family Festivities All Over the World!* (3–5). Illus. by Michael Bryant. Series: Family Ties. 1993, Silver Moon LB $14.95 (978-1-881889-08-3). 60pp. Using a ficticious framework, five holidays from such places as Pakistan, Japan, and Namibia are introduced. (Rev: SLJ 2/94) [394.2]

20249 Chambers, Catherine. *Carnival* (4–6). Illus. Series: World of Holidays. 1998, Raintree LB $25.69 (978-0-8172-4613-6). 32pp. Reveals the African influences that have shaped the pre-Lenten celebration of Carnival and provides suitable activities such as recipes and mask-making. (Rev: BL 5/1/98; HBG 9/98) [394.25]

20250 Chambers, Catherine. *Chinese New Year* (3–5). Illus. Series: World of Holidays. 1997, Raintree LB $25.70 (978-0-8172-4605-1). 31pp. With many color photos and several craft ideas, this book supplies background information on this spring celebration of good fortune and success and the rituals that surround it. (Rev: BL 6/1–15/97) [394.261]

20251 Chandler, Clare. *Harvest Celebrations* (2–4). Illus. Series: Festivals. 1998, Millbrook LB $20.90 (978-0-7613-0964-2). 32pp. This book outlines the best-known and most popular harvest celebrations around the world. (Rev: BL 3/1/99; HBG 3/99; SLJ 4/99) [394.264]

20252 Chocolate, Deborah N. *My First Kwanzaa Book* (PS–2). Illus. by Cal Massey. 1992, Scholastic $10.95 (978-0-590-45762-0). 32pp. A celebration of African American cultural heritage for the very young. (Rev: BCCB 2/93; BL 9/1/92) [394.2]

20253 Cooper, Jason. *Arbor Day* (1–3). Illus. Series: Holiday Celebrations. 2003, Rourke LB $20.64 (978-1-58952-217-6). 24pp. An attractive and informative overview of Arbor Day, the holiday's origins, and the contributions trees make to a healthy environment. (Rev: BL 4/1/03) [394.26]

20254 Dean, Sheri. *Flag Day / Día de la bandera* (K–2). Trans. by Tatiana Acosta and Guillermo Gutiérrez. Series: Our Country's Holidays / Las fiestas de nuestra nación. 2006, Weekly Reader LB $21.00 (978-0-8368-6518-9). 24pp. In English and Spanish, this is an introduction to the history behind Flag Day, with a look at the customs associated with

the celebration. Also use *The Fourth of July / Cuatro de Julio, Martin Luther King Jr. Day / Día de Martin Luther King Jr.,*, and *Presidents' Day / Día de los presidentes* (all 2006). (Rev: SLJ 10/06) [394.263]

20255 Ditchfield, Christin. *Memorial Day* (2–4). Series: A True Book. 2003, Children's Pr. LB $25.00 (978-0-516-22783-2). 48pp. A concise look at Memorial Day (formerly known as Decoration Day) and the various ways in which it is observed. (Rev: SLJ 1/04) [394.262]

20256 Doering, Amanda. *Cinco de Mayo: Day of Mexican Pride* (1–3). Series: First Facts: Holidays and Culture. 2005, Capstone LB $21.26 (978-0-7368-5387-3). 24pp. A craft, a story, and photographs accompany a brief introduction to the holiday and an explanation of why it is important; suitable for beginning readers. Also use *Day of the Dead* (2005). (Rev: SLJ 5/06) [394.2]

20257 Erlbach, Arlene. *Happy Birthday, Everywhere!* (3–5). Illus. 1997, Millbrook LB $24.90 (978-0-7613-0007-6). 48pp. With accompanying food and craft projects, this book describes birthday celebrations around the world. (Rev: BL 12/1/97; HBG 3/98; SLJ 2/98) [394.2]

20258 Erlbach, Arlene. *Happy New Year, Everywhere!* (K–3). Illus. by Sharon L. Holm. 2000, Millbrook LB $23.90 (978-0-7613-1707-4). 48pp. Lavish double-page spreads introduce New Year celebrations in 20 countries, including Belgium, Haiti, Iran, and Israel. (Rev: BL 11/1/00; HBG 3/01; SLJ 12/00) [394.261]

20259 Fisher, Leonard E. *To Bigotry No Sanction: The Story of the Oldest Synagogue in America* (5–8). Illus. 1998, Holiday $16.95 (978-0-8234-1401-7). Beginning with the expulsion of the Jews from Spain in 1492, the author traces the history of Jews in America, including the 1763 building — with George Washington's blessing — of the Touro Synagogue. (Rev: BCCB 4/99; BL 2/1/99; HBG 10/99; SLJ 3/99) [296.097457]

20260 Fradin, Dennis Brindell. *Columbus Day* (2–4). Illus. Series: Best Holiday Books. 1990, Enslow LB $23.93 (978-0-89490-233-8). 48pp. Highlights of the explorer's life and his four voyages. (Rev: BL 5/1/90) [970.01]

20261 Freeman, Dorothy R. *St. Patrick's Day*. Rev. ed. (3–5). Illus. Series: Best Holiday Books. 2008, Enslow LB $23.93 (978-0-89490-383-0). 48pp. This easily read account describes the origins of St. Patrick's Day and how it is celebrated. (Rev: BL 10/1/92) [394.2]

20262 Freeman, Dorothy R., and Dianne MacMillan. *Kwanzaa*. Rev. ed. (3–5). Illus. Series: Best Holiday Books. 2008, Enslow LB $23.93 (978-0-89490-381-6). 48pp. A full treatment of this African American holiday. (Rev: BL 10/1/92) [394.2]

20263 Ganeri, Anita. *Hindu Festivals Throughout the Year* (3–6). Illus. Series: A Year of Festivals. 2003, Smart Apple LB $24.25 (978-1-58340-372-3). 30pp. After a short introduction to the religion, chronological chapters explain the origins and customs of the major festivals of Hinduism. Also use

Muslim Festivals Throughout the Year (2003). (Rev: SLJ 12/03) [294.5]

20264 Gibbons, Gail. *Groundhog Day* (PS–2). Illus. 2007, Holiday $16.95 (978-0-8234-2003-2). 32pp. This examination of the February holiday is accompanied by Gibbons's usual clear illustrations and augmented with information about groundhogs. (Rev: BL 1/1–15/07) [394.261]

20265 Gibbons, Gail. *St. Patrick's Day* (2–4). Illus. 1994, Holiday House LB $17.95 (978-0-8234-1119-1). 32pp. As well as telling the story of St. Patrick's life, this simple account describes how we celebrate his day and the symbols connected with it. (Rev: BCCB 2/94; BL 2/1/94; SLJ 4/94) [394.2]

20266 Gilley, Jeremy. *Peace One Day: How September 21 Became World Peace Day* (4–6). Illus. by Karen Blessen. 2005, Putnam $16.99 (978-0-399-24330-1). 48pp. British filmmaker Gilley tells the story behind World Peace Day, an annual observance he worked diligently to establish. (Rev: BL 10/1/05; SLJ 9/05) [303.6]

20267 Gnojewski, Carol. *Cinco de Mayo: Celebrating Hispanic Pride* (3–5). Illus. Series: Finding Out About Holidays. 2002, Enslow LB $23.93 (978-0-7660-1575-3). 48pp. Simple text and colorful photographs cover many aspects of Cinco de Mayo, from its history to the way it is celebrated today. (Rev: BL 12/15/02; HBG 3/03; SLJ 11/02) [394.26972]

20268 Gnojewski, Carol. *Day of the Dead: A Latino Celebration of Family and Life* (3–5). Illus. Series: Finding Out About Holidays. 2005, Enslow LB $23.93 (978-0-7660-1780-1). 48pp. A history of this Mexican holiday, with discussion of how it is celebrated today and its emphasis on family. (Rev: BL 6/1–15/05) [394.264]

20269 Gnojewski, Carol. *Martin Luther King, Jr., Day: Honoring a Man of Peace* (2–4). Series: Finding Out About Holidays. 2002, Enslow LB $23.93 (978-0-7660-1574-6). 48pp. Information on the holiday and how it is celebrated follows a brief introduction to King's life. (Rev: HBG 3/03; SLJ 12/02)

20270 Gogerly, Liz. *Autumn* (2–4). Series: Holidays Around the World. 2004, Rourke $19.95 (978-1-59515-198-8). The holidays of September to November — and how they're celebrated in different parts of the globe — are profiled with many photographs. Also use *Spring* (2004). (Rev: BL 11/15/04) [394.264]

20271 Harris, Zoe, and Suzanne Williams. *Pinatas and Smiling Skeletons* (4–8). Illus. 1998, Pacific View LB $19.95 (978-1-881896-19-7). This book introduces six festivals celebrated in Mexico: the Feast of the Virgin of Guadalupe, Christmas, Carnaval, Corpus Christi, Independence Day, and the Day of the Dead. (Rev: BL 3/15/99; HBG 3/99; SLJ 3/99) [394.26972]

20272 Heiligman, Deborah. *Celebrate Diwali* (1–3). Series: Holidays Around the World. 2006, National Geographic $15.95 (978-0-7922-5922-0). 32pp. A look at the customs associated with the celebration of the Hindu holiday, in India and in four other countries. (Rev: SLJ 1/07) [294.5]

20273 Heiligman, Deborah. *Celebrate Independence Day* (K–3). Series: Holidays Around the World. 2007, National Geographic $15.95 (978-1-4263-0074-5). 32pp. The author discusses how and why people around the United States celebrate the Fourth of July. A locator map shows where every photograph in the book was taken. (Rev: SLJ 8/07)

20274 Heiligman, Deborah. *Celebrate Ramadan and Eid al-Fitr* (1–3). Series: Holidays Around the World. 2006, National Geographic $15.95 (978-0-7922-5926-8). 32pp. A look at these Islamic observances and their religious significance as well as the associated customs and rituals. (Rev: SLJ 1/07) [297.3]

20275 Heinrichs, Ann. *Chinese New Year* (K–3). Illus. by Benrei Huang. Series: Holidays, Festivals, and Celebrations. 2006, The Child's World LB $24.21 (978-1-59296-572-4). 32pp. Examines the history, customs, and symbols of this holiday and includes a recipe and a craft. Also use *Saint Patrick's Day* (2006). (Rev: SLJ 9/06) [394.261]

20276 Heinrichs, Ann. *Cinco de Mayo* (2–3). Illus. by Kathleen Petelinsek. Series: Holidays, Festivals, and Celebrations. 2006, The Child's World LB $24.21 (978-1-59296-573-1). 32pp. Information about the holiday and how it is celebrated, plus photographs of the festivities, Spanish words, and a craft to try; also use *Día de los Muertos* (2006). (Rev: SLJ 5/06) [394.2]

20277 Hoyt-Goldsmith, Diane. *Celebrating a Quinceañera: A Latina's 15th Birthday Celebration* (3–6). Photos by Lawrence Migdale. 2002, Holiday House $16.95 (978-0-8234-1693-6). 30pp. A detailed description of a young woman's preparations for and celebration of her quinceanera, the ritual coming of age at 15. (Rev: HBG 3/03; SLJ 9/02) [395.24]

20278 Hoyt-Goldsmith, Diane. *Celebrating Chinese New Year* (3–5). Illus. 1998, Holiday House $17.95 (978-0-8234-1393-5). 32pp. A richly illustrated book that traces the activities of a Chinese American family in San Francisco as they prepare for and participate in Chinese New Year. (Rev: BL 12/1/98; HBG 3/99; SLJ 2/99) [394.261]

20279 Hoyt-Goldsmith, Diane. *Celebrating Kwanzaa* (4–6). Illus. by Lawrence Migdale. 1993, Holiday House LB $17.95 (978-0-8234-1048-4). 32pp. A photoessay about a Chicago family's celebration of Kwanzaa that explains the origins and meanings of the Seven Principles. (Rev: BCCB 11/93; BL 10/1/93*) [394.2]

20280 Hoyt-Goldsmith, Diane. *Celebrating Ramadan* (2–5). Illus. by Lawrence Migdale. 2001, Holiday House $17.95 (978-0-8234-1581-6). 32pp. This informative picture-book introduction to Islam and the month of Ramadan features a fourth-grade New Jersey boy named Ibraheem. (Rev: BCCB 12/01; BL 10/1/01; HB 1/02; HBG 3/02; SLJ 8/01) [297]

20281 Hoyt-Goldsmith, Diane. *Cinco de Mayo: Celebrating the Traditions of Mexico* (3–5). Illus. 2008, Holiday $16.95 (978-0-8234-2107-7). 32pp. Rosie and her Mexican American family enjoy the Cinco de Mayo celebration in their California community. (Rev: BL 3/15/08; SLJ 4/08) [394.262]

20282 Hoyt-Goldsmith, Diane. *Mardi Gras: A Cajun Country Celebration* (4–6). Illus. 1995, Holiday House LB $17.95 (978-0-8234-1184-9). 32pp. A story of the rituals of Mardi Gras plus a history of the Cajun people and even a recipe for gumbo. (Rev: BL 10/1/95; SLJ 11/95) [394.2]

20283 Hoyt-Goldsmith, Diane. *Three Kings Day: A Celebration at Christmastime* (2–5). Illus. by Lawrence Migdale. 2004, Holiday House $16.95 (978-0-8234-1839-8). 32pp. Dia de los Tres Reyes is seen from the point of view of a 10-year-old girl living in New York's Puerto Rican community. (Rev: BL 9/15/04; SLJ 10/04) [263]

20284 Jackson, Ellen. *The Autumn Equinox: Celebrating the Harvest* (2–5). Illus. by Jan Davey Ellis. 2000, Millbrook LB $22.90 (978-0-7613-1354-0). Harvest festivals, past and present, from around the world are described with attractive craft projects, games, and recipes. (Rev: HBG 3/01; SLJ 11/00) [394.3]

20285 Jackson, Ellen. *The Spring Equinox: Celebrating the Greening of the Earth* (3–5). Illus. by Jan Davey Ellis. 2002, Millbrook LB $24.90 (978-0-7613-1955-9). 32pp. Many of the holidays associated with spring — including Passover, Easter, Earth Day, and Holi — are highlighted in a series of illustrated double-page spreads. (Rev: BL 4/15/02; HBG 10/02; SLJ 6/02) [394.262]

20286 Jango-Cohen, Judith. *Chinese New Year* (1–3). Illus. by Jason Chin. Series: On My Own Holidays. 2005, Carolrhoda LB $25.26 (978-1-57505-653-1); paper $5.95 (978-1-57505-763-7). 48pp. The origins and traditions of the Chinese New Year are introduced with many illustrations and a short glossary. (Rev: BL 1/1–15/05) [394.261]

20287 Jeffrey, Laura S. *Celebrate Ramadan* (5–8). Illus. Series: Celebrate Holidays. 2007, Enslow LB $23.95 (978-0-7660-2774-9). 112pp. Report writers and others wanting to know about this Muslim holiday will find the facts they need here, as well as more general information about Islam in America. (Rev: BL 10/1/07; SLJ 11/07) [297.3]

20288 Jones, Lynda. *Kids Around the World Celebrate! The Best Feasts and Festivals from Many Lands* (3–6). Illus. by Michelle Nidenoff. Series: Kids Around the World. 1999, Wiley paper $12.95 (978-0-471-34527-5). 124pp. Each chapter covers the customs of different cultures organized by themes, like giving thanks and celebrating New Year; for each there are a number of hands-on activities. (Rev: SLJ 2/00) [394.3]

20289 Jordan, Denise M. *Juneteenth* (1–3). Series: Holiday Histories. 2003, Heinemann LB $22.79 (978-1-4034-3505-7). 32pp. The story of the unofficial holiday (June 19th) that celebrates the end of slavery. (Rev: SLJ 5/04) [394.263]

20290 Kadodwala, Dilip. *Divali* (4–6). Illus. Series: World of Holidays. 1998, Raintree LB $25.70 (978-0-8172-4616-7). 32pp. Discusses the origins, methods of celebrating, and the many gods and goddesses

involved in the Hindu holiday of Diwali. (Rev: BL 5/1/98; HBG 9/98) [294.5]

20291 Kadodwala, Dilip. *Holi* (3–5). Illus. Series: World of Holidays. 1997, Raintree LB $25.70 (978-0-8172-4610-5). 31pp. A description of this joyous Hindu spring festival and how it is observed. (Rev: BL 6/1–15/97) [294.5]

20292 Kaplan, Leslie C. *Chinese New Year* (2–4). Series: Library of Holidays. 2004, Rosen LB $19.95 (978-0-8239-6658-5). 24pp. Brief, illustrated chapters introduce the history and traditions of this month-long holiday. (Rev: SLJ 8/04) [394.261]

20293 Kaplan, Leslie C. *Cinco de Mayo* (2–4). Series: Library of Holidays. 2004, Rosen LB $19.95 (978-0-8239-6662-2). 24pp. A brief introduction to Cinco de Mayo, with information on history and tradition paired with full-page photographs. (Rev: SLJ 8/04) [394.26972]

20294 Kaplan, Leslie C. *Flag Day* (2–4). Series: Library of Holidays. 2004, Rosen LB $19.95 (978-0-8239-6659-2). 24pp. A brief introduction to the patriotic holiday, with information on history and tradition paired with full-page photographs. (Rev: SLJ 8/04) [394.263]

20295 Katz, Karen. *My First Chinese New Year* (PS–K). Illus. 2004, Holt $14.95 (978-0-8050-7076-7). 32pp. A young girl and her family prepare for the annual celebration in this simple introduction. (Rev: BL 2/1/05) [394.2]

20296 Kerven, Rosalind. *Id-ul-Fitr* (3–5). Illus. Series: World of Holidays. 1997, Raintree LB $25.69 (978-0-8172-4609-9). 31pp. After giving a brief introduction to Islam, describes the celebration that marks the end of the sacred month of Ramadan. (Rev: BL 6/1–15/97) [297]

20297 Kindersley, Barnabas, and Anabel Kindersley. *Celebrations!* (2–6). Illus. Series: Children Just Like Me. 1997, DK $17.99 (978-0-7894-2027-5). 63pp. Using double-page spreads, a number of holidays from around the world are featured, such as Christmas in Germany and Diwali in India. (Rev: HBG 3/98; SLJ 1/98) [394.2]

20298 Krasno, Rena. *Floating Lanterns and Golden Shrines: Celebrating Japanese Festivals* (3–5). Illus. by Toru Sugita. 2000, Pacific View $19.95 (978-1-881896-21-0). 49pp. Important celebrations for both Japanese and Japanese Americans are covered in this attractive book. (Rev: HBG 9/00; SLJ 6/00) [394.2]

20299 Krishnaswami, Uma. *Holi* (K–2). Illus. Series: Rookie Read-about Holidays. 2003, Children's Pr. LB $20.50 (978-0-516-22863-1). 32pp. For beginning readers, this is a well-illustrated basic description of the Hindu festival of Holi. (Rev: BL 5/1/03; SLJ 6/03) [294.5]

20300 Landau, Elaine. *Columbus Day — Celebrating a Famous Explorer* (3–6). Series: Finding Out About Holidays. 2001, Enslow LB $23.93 (978-0-7660-1573-9). 48pp. After introducing Christopher Columbus, this account describes the history of the holiday that honors him and tells how it is celebrated. (Rev: BL 9/15/01; HBG 3/02; SLJ 9/01) [394.2]

20301 Landau, Elaine. *Earth Day: Keeping Our Planet Clean* (3–6). Series: Finding Out About Holidays. 2002, Enslow LB $23.93 (978-0-7660-1778-8). 48pp. A look at the founding of Earth Day in 1970 by Senator Gaylord Nelson and how Earth Day is observed today. (Rev: BL 7/02; HBG 10/02; SLJ 7/02) [333.7]

20302 Landau, Elaine. *Independence Day: Birthday of the United States* (3–6). Series: Finding Out About Holidays. 2001, Enslow LB $23.93 (978-0-7660-1571-5). 48pp. Short chapters and plenty of color photographs introduce the history of the July 4th holiday and how it is celebrated today. (Rev: BL 9/15/01; HBG 3/02; SLJ 9/01) [394]

20303 Landau, Elaine. *Mardi Gras: Parades, Costumes, and Parties* (3–6). Series: Finding Out About Holidays. 2002, Enslow LB $23.93 (978-0-7660-1776-4). 48pp. The origins of Mardi Gras are explained, with material on how the holiday is observed in locations including New Orleans. (Rev: BL 7/02; HBG 10/02; SLJ 8/02) [394.2]

20304 Landau, Elaine. *St. Patrick's Day: Parades, Shamrocks, and Leprechauns* (3–6). Series: Finding Out About Holidays. 2002, Enslow LB $23.93 (978-0-7660-1777-1). 48pp. SaintPatrick is introduced along with material on the symbols connected with this holiday and ways it is observed. (Rev: BL 7/02; HBG 3/03; SLJ 10/02) [394.2]

20305 Landau, Elaine. *Veteran's Day: Remembering Our War Heroes* (3–6). Series: Finding Out About Holidays. 2002, Enslow LB $23.93 (978-0-7660-1775-7). 48pp. Landau traces the origins of this holiday and details how it is observed across the United States. (Rev: BL 7/02; HBG 10/02) [394.264]

20306 Liestman, Vicki. *Columbus Day* (2–3). Illus. by Rick Hanson. Series: On My Own. 1991, Carolrhoda LB $23.93 (978-0-87614-444-2). 56pp. The history of this holiday, plus the life of the explorer, illustrated with colorful paintings. (Rev: BCCB 10/91; BL 9/1/91; SLJ 9/91) [970.01]

20307 Livingston, Myra Cohn. *Festivals* (K–3). Illus. by Leonard Everett Fisher. 1996, Holiday House $17.95 (978-0-8234-1217-4). 32pp. Fourteen of the world's festivals, both common and obscure, are introduced in poetry and paintings. (Rev: BCCB 5/96; BL 5/1/96; SLJ 7/96) [811]

20308 Lowery, Linda. *Day of the Dead* (K–3). Illus. by Barbara Knutson. Series: On My Own Holidays. 2003, Carolrhoda LB $25.26 (978-0-87614-914-0); paper $5.95 (978-1-57505-581-7). 48pp. A lively, easy-reader introduction to the Mexican holiday. (Rev: HBG 4/04; SLJ 11/03) [394.266]

20309 Luenn, Nancy. *Celebrations of Light: A Year of Holidays Around the World* (3–5). Illus. 1998, Simon & Schuster $16.00 (978-0-689-31986-0). 32pp. Describes 12 festivals of light, including Christmas, Hanukkah, Buddha's Birthday, and the Swedish Luciadagen. (Rev: BL 9/15/98; HBG 3/99; SLJ 12/98) [394.2]

20310 MacMillan, Dianne. *Mardi Gras* (3–5). Series: Best Holiday. 1997, Enslow LB $23.93 (978-0-89490-819-4). 48pp. Gives a description and history of this holiday with religious roots, with details on

how it is celebrated around the world, particularly in New Orleans. (Rev: BL 12/15/97; HBG 3/98; SLJ 8/97) [394.2]

20311 MacMillan, Dianne. *Martin Luther King, Jr. Day*. Rev. ed. (3–5). Illus. Series: Best Holiday Books. 2008, Enslow LB $23.93 (978-0-89490-382-3). 48pp. This easy-to-read book describes how Martin Luther King, Jr. Day originated and how it is celebrated in schools and towns. (Rev: BL 10/1/92; SLJ 1/93) [323]

20312 MacMillan, Dianne. *Presidents Day* (3–5). Illus. Series: Best Holiday. 1997, Enslow LB $23.93 (978-0-89490-820-0). 48pp. An introduction to the day on which Americans pay tribute to their presidents and a discussion of the ways in which it is celebrated. (Rev: BL 7/97) [973.4]

20313 Marchant, Kerena. *Id-ul-Fitr* (3–5). Series: Festivals. 1998, Millbrook LB $22.90 (978-0-7613-0963-5). 32pp. An explanation of this Muslim festival is followed by colorful descriptions of how it is celebrated around the world. (Rev: HBG 3/99; SLJ 4/99) [297]

20314 Martinet, Jeanne, comp. *The Year You Were Born, 1986* (2–6). Illus. by Judy Lanfredi. Series: Day-By-Day Record Of. 1993, Tambourine paper $7.95 (978-0-688-11968-3). This book, like the others in the series, gives facts and assorted trivia for each day of the featured year. (Rev: SLJ 2/94) [793.21]

20315 Marx, David F. *Chinese New Year* (PS–1). Series: Rookie Read-about Holidays. 2002, Children's Book Pr. paper $5.95 (978-0-516-27375-4). 32pp. An introduction for very young readers to the rituals of the Chinese New Year. Also use *Ramadan*. (Rev: SLJ 9/02) [394.2]

20316 Mercer, Abbie. *Happy St. Patrick's Day* (2–4). Series: Holiday Fun. 2007, Rosen LB $21.25 (978-1-4042-3811-4). 24pp. Along with historical information and discussion of the symbols and activities associated with this holiday, this volume includes a recipe and a craft. (Rev: SLJ 2/08) [394.262]

20317 Mobin-Uddin, Asma. *The Best Eid Ever* (K–3). Illus. by Laura Jacobsen. 2007, Boyds Mills $16.95 (978-1-59078-431-0). 32pp. Aneesa and her grandmother celebrate Eid al-Adha, an Islamic holiday, and plan to help two girls who have escaped from a war-torn country; a glossary and pronunciation guide are helpful. (Rev: BL 1/1–15/08; LMC 3/08; SLJ 12/07) [297.3]

20318 Murray, Julie. *Kwanzaa* (1–3). Illus. Series: Holidays. 2003, ABDO LB $21.35 (978-1-57765-955-6). 24pp. Examines Kwanzaa's adaptation from an African harvest festival and looks at some of the activities associated with the holiday. (Rev: HBG 10/03; SLJ 10/03) [394.261]

20319 Nelson, Robin. *Constitution Day* (K–2). Illus. Series: First Step Nonfiction: American Holidays. 2009, Lerner LB $19.93 (978-0-7613-4930-3). 24pp. A simple look at the holiday that was enacted in 2005 and the reasons why we recognize this day. (Rev: BL 6/1–15/09) [394.263]

20320 Nelson, Robin. *Juneteenth* (K–2). Illus. Series: First Step Nonfiction - American Holidays. 2009,

Lerner LB $19.93 (978-0-7613-4934-1). 24pp. Texas slaves heard about the Emancipation Proclamation two years late — on Juneteenth. (Rev: BL 6/1–15/09) [394.263]

20321 Nelson, Vaunda Micheaux, and Drew Nelson. *Juneteenth* (2–4). Illus. by Mark Schroder. Series: On My Own Holidays. 2006, Lerner $25.26 (978-1-57505-876-4); paper $5.95 (978-0-8225-5974-0). 48pp. The story behind the Juneteenth holiday is told for beginning readers. (Rev: BL 2/1/06; SLJ 3/06) [394.263]

20322 Nobleman, Marc Tyler. *Martin Luther King Jr. Day* (1–3). Series: Let's See. 2004, Compass Point LB $19.93 (978-0-7565-0646-9). 24pp. For young researchers, this is an introduction to this holiday, using questions as chapter headings. (Rev: SLJ 1/05) [394.261]

20323 Otto, Carolyn. *Celebrate Chinese New Year: With Fireworks, Dragons, and Lanterns* (1–4). Illus. 2008, National Geographic $15.95 (978-1-4263-0381-4). 32pp. Well-written narrative and color photographs show how Chinese New Year is celebrated in a variety of countries. (Rev: BL 12/15/08; SLJ 1/09) [394.261]

20324 Otto, Carolyn. *Celebrate Cinco de Mayo with Fiestas, Music, and Dance* (1–4). Illus. Series: Holidays Around the World. 2008, National Geographic $15.95 (978-1-4263-0215-2). 32pp. An attractive account of the origins of and traditions associated with Cinco de Mayo both in the United States and south of the border, with lots of photographs, a bibliography, a glossary, and recipes. (Rev: BL 4/15/08; SLJ 4/08) [394.262]

20325 Penner, Lucille R. *Celebration: The Story of American Holidays* (3–5). Illus. by Ib Ohlsson. 1993, Macmillan LB $15.95 (978-0-02-770903-2). 79pp. A discussion of the origins of and celebrations associated with 13 important American holidays, e.g., Columbus Day, Veterans Day, Martin Luther King Day, Halloween, and New Year's Day. (Rev: SLJ 11/93) [394.2]

20326 Petelinsek, Kathleen, and E. Russell Primm. *Holidays and Celebrations / Días de fiesta y celebraciones* (K–2). Illus. by Nichole Day Diggins. Series: Talking Hands. 2006, The Child's World LB $21.36 (978-1-59296-453-6). 24pp. Students demonstrate simple holiday-related words using American Sign Language; the text is in both English and Spanish. (Rev: SLJ 6/06) [419]

20327 Porter, A. P. *Kwanzaa* (2–4). Illus. by Janice L. Porter. 1991, Carolrhoda LB $21.27 (978-0-87614-668-2). 56pp. African Americans celebrate their rich history and culture by observing Kwanzaa. (Rev: BCCB 12/91; BL 12/1/91) [394.2]

20328 Reynolds, Betty. *Japanese Celebrations: Cherry Blossoms, Lanterns and Stars!* (3–5). Illus. 2006, Turtle $16.95 (978-0-8048-3658-6). 48pp. A chronological survey of Japanese holidays throughout the year, covering food, dress, decoration, symbols, and so forth. (Rev: BL 12/1/06; SLJ 12/06) [394.2]

20329 Roberts, Russell. *Holidays and Celebrations in Colonial America* (4–6). Illus. Series: Building America. 2006, Mitchell Lane LB $29.95 (978-1-58415-467-9). 48pp. This attractive title, which features a timeline, glossary, and calendar, briefly profiles the holidays celebrated during America's colonial period and examines how those that are still observed today have changed over the years. (Rev: BL 11/1/06) [394.26973]

20330 Robinson, Fay. *Chinese New Year: A Time for Parades, Family, and Friends* (3–6). Illus. Series: Finding Out About Holidays. 2001, Enslow LB $23.93 (978-0-7660-1631-6). 48pp. This detailed account gives the history behind this traditional holiday and explains how Chinese Americans celebrate it. (Rev: BL 9/15/01; HBG 3/02; SLJ 1/02) [394.261]

20331 Roop, Connie, and Peter Roop. *Let's Celebrate Earth Day* (1–3). Illus. by Gwen Connelly. 2001, Millbrook LB $22.90 (978-0-7613-1812-5). 32pp. Information on the history and purpose of Earth Day is presented in a question-and-answer format. (Rev: BL 5/1/01; HBG 10/01) [363.7]

20332 Rosinsky, Natalie M. *Juneteenth* (1–3). Series: Let's See. 2004, Compass Point LB $19.93 (978-0-7565-0770-1). 24pp. For young researchers, this is an introduction to this holiday, using questions as chapter headings. (Rev: SLJ 1/05) [394.2]

20333 Rosinsky, Natalie M. *Presidents' Day* (1–3). Illus. Series: Let's See. 2004, Compass Point LB $19.93 (978-0-7565-0773-2). 24pp. Using a question-and-answer format, large print, and many illustrations, this small book discusses the history of Presidents' Day and how it honors Washington and Lincoln. (Rev: BL 10/15/04) [394.201]

20334 Ross, Kathy. *The Best Birthday Parties Ever! A Kid's Do-It-Yourself Guide* (2–5). Illus. by Sharon L. Holm. 1999, Millbrook LB $24.90 (978-0-7613-1410-3). 78pp. This do-it-yourself guide to great birthday parties includes instructions on invitations, hats, decorations, cakes, favors, and games. (Rev: HBG 4/00; SLJ 11/99) [394.2]

20335 San Vicente, Luis. *The Festival of Bones / El Festival de las Calaveras: The Little-Bitty Book for the Day of the Dead* (PS–3). Illus. by author. 2002, Cinco Puntos $14.95 (978-0-938317-67-8). 32pp. Dancing skeletons accompany the text describing the Mexican festival known as the Day of the Dead, or el Día de los Muertos. (Rev: HBG 3/03; SLJ 3/03) [394.266]

20336 Schaefer, Lola M. *Chinese New Year* (PS–2). Series: Holidays and Celebrations. 2000, Capstone LB $17.26 (978-0-7368-0660-2). 24pp. A simple beginning reader that introduces the traditions and meaning behind the Chinese New Year. (Rev: HBG 3/01; SLJ 12/00) [394.2]

20337 Schaefer, Lola M. *Cinco de Mayo* (PS–2). Series: Holidays and Celebrations. 2000, Capstone LB $17.26 (978-0-7368-0661-9). 24pp. The traditions and customs surrounding the Mexican Independence Day are outlined in this simple book for beginning readers. (Rev: HBG 3/01; SLJ 12/00) [394.2]

20338 Schuh, Mari C. *Flag Day* (PS–2). Series: National Holidays. 2003, Capstone LB $17.26 (978-0-7368-1652-6). 24pp. For beginning readers, this is an introduction to Flag Day and its history. (Rev: HBG 10/03; SLJ 9/03) [394.203]

20339 Schuh, Mari C. *Labor Day* (PS–2). Series: National Holidays. 2003, Capstone LB $17.26 (978-0-7368-1653-3). 24pp. For beginning readers, this is an introduction to Labor Day and its history. (Rev: HBG 10/03) [394.204]

20340 Schuh, Mari C. *New Year's Day* (K–2). Series: Holidays and Celebrations. 2002, Capstone LB $17.26 (978-0-7368-1446-1). 24pp. Double-page spreads with bright full-page photographs on the left and a brief text on the right introduce the history, traditions, and celebrations that surround New Year's Day. (Rev: BL 1/1–15/03; HBG 3/03) [394.2]

20341 Schuh, Mari C. *St. Patrick's Day* (K–2). Illus. Series: Holidays and Celebrations. 2002, Capstone $17.26 (978-0-7368-1447-8). 24pp. This small, square book about Saint Patrick's Day includes discussion of the holiday's symbols and traditions and includes reference sources and a glossary. (Rev: BL 1/1–15/03; HBG 3/03) [296.4]

20342 Scott, Geoffrey. *Labor Day* (1–4). Illus. by Cherie R. Wyman. 1982, Carolrhoda LB $18.60 (978-0-87614-178-6). 48pp. A simple book about the first Labor Day.

20343 Senker, Cath. *Winter* (2–4). Illus. Series: Holidays Around the World. 2004, Rourke $19.95 (978-1-59515-199-5). Holidays that take place from December to February are included here, with Christmas in Zimbabwe and Id ul-Fitr in Canada among those featured; a chart lists dates through 2006. Also use *Summer* (2004). (Rev: BL 11/15/04) [394.261]

20344 Shahan, Sherry. *Fiesta! A Celebration of Latino Festivals* (1–3). Illus. by Paula Barragán. 2009, August House $16.95 (978-0-87483-861-9). 32pp. A month-by-month look at various holidays celebrated in Latin American countries, including Mexico's Fiesta de San Antonio Abad and Brazil's Águas de Oxalá. (Rev: BL 4/1/09; LMC 8/09; SLJ 4/09) [394.2698]

20345 Sievert, Terri. *Ramadan: Islamic Holy Month* (K–2). Illus. Series: First Facts: Holidays and Culture. 2006, Capstone LB $21.26 (978-0-7368-5392-7). 24pp. This photo-filled title introduces young readers to the Islamic holiday, exploring its religious significance and traditions. (Rev: BL 4/1/06) [297.3]

20346 Simonds, Nina, et al. *Moonbeams, Dumplings and Dragon Boats: A Treasury of Chinese Holiday Tales, Activities and Recipes* (4–6). Illus. by Meilo So. 2002, Harcourt $20.00 (978-0-15-201983-9). 80pp. This vibrantly illustrated book for older readers examines five Chinese holidays and includes stories, recipes, and crafts related to each. (Rev: BL 10/15/02; HBG 3/03; SLJ 11/02*) [394.26]

20347 Sita, Lisa. *Coming of Age* (2–5). Series: World Celebrations and Ceremonies. 1998, Blackbirch LB $21.20 (978-1-56711-276-4). 24pp. Presenting facts and maps about each country highlighted, this account describes the ceremonies associated with the rites of passage that lead to adulthood in ten

countries on six continents. (Rev: HBG 3/99; SLJ 4/99) [612]

20348 Tabor, Nancy María Grande. *Celebrations / Celebraciones* (PS–3). Illus. 2004, Charlesbridge $16.95 (978-1-57091-575-8). 32pp. Shared holidays and individual Mexican and U.S. holidays are introduced in both Spanish and English. (Rev: BL 3/1/04; SLJ 4/04) [394.26972]

20349 Taylor, Charles A. *Juneteenth: A Celebration of Freedom* (5–8). Illus. by author. 2002, Open Hand $19.95 (978-0-940880-68-9). 32pp. A well-organized account of this holiday, which celebrates emancipation, with a discussion of the history of slavery. (Rev: SLJ 11/02) [394.2]

20350 Thompson, Jan. *Christian Festivals* (3–6). Illus. Series: Celebrate! 1997, Heinemann $22.79 (978-0-431-06961-6). 48pp. Familiar Christian holidays such as Christmas, Lent, Ascension Day, and Easter are explained through the experiences of three children. (Rev: BL 8/97; SLJ 12/97) [263]

20351 Trueit, Trudi. *Kwanzaa* (1–3). Series: Rookie Read-about Holidays. 2006, Children's Pr. LB $20.50 (978-0-531-12458-1); paper $5.95 (978-0-531-11839-9). 32pp. This colorful introduction to the holiday examines its history and customs and provides a holiday-related recipe and craft. (Rev: SLJ 10/06) [394.2]

20352 Verma, Jatinder. *The Story of Divaali* (1–3). Illus. by Nilesh Mistry. 2002, Barefoot Bks. $16.99 (978-1-84148-936-0). 40pp. Verma effectively retells the complex story, based on the Sanskrit *Ramayana*, of the lighting of lamps that started the celebration of the Hindu festival of Diwali. (Rev: BL 1/1–15/03; HBG 3/03; SLJ 11/02) [294.5]

20353 Viesti, Joe, and Diane Hall. *Celebrate! In Southeast Asia* (2–5). Illus. 1996, Lothrop LB $15.93 (978-0-688-13489-1). 32pp. Such countries as Vietnam, Thailand, Malaysia, and the Philippines are represented in this explanation of nine celebrations. (Rev: BCCB 10/96; BL 9/1/96; SLJ 9/96) [394.2]

20354 Walsh, Kieran. *Chinese New Year* (2–3). Series: Holiday Celebrations. 2003, Rourke LB $20.64 (978-1-58952-215-2). 24pp. Provides basic information about how the holiday began and how it is celebrated. Also use *Cinco de Mayo* (2003). (Rev: BL 9/15/03; SLJ 1/03) [394.261]

20355 Walsh, Kieran. *Cinco de Mayo* (1–3). Illus. Series: Holiday Celebrations. 2003, Rourke LB $20.64 (978-1-58952-221-3). 24pp. The Mexican holiday comes to life with discussions of the festivities that take place as well as the origin of the celebration. (Rev: BL 4/1/03) [394.26972]

20356 Walter, Mildred P. *Kwanzaa: A Family Affair* (PS–2). Illus. by Cheryl Carrington. 1995, Lothrop $15.00 (978-0-688-11553-1). 80pp. Background material, ways of celebrating the holiday, and crafts and gifts are all covered in this introduction to Kwanzaa. (Rev: BL 9/15/95) [394.2]

20357 Waters, Kate, and Madeline Slovenz-Low. *Lion Dancer: Ernie Wan's Chinese New Year* (PS–3). 1990, Scholastic paper $5.99 (978-0-590-43047-0). 32pp. This account describes how a Chinese-American family celebrates the lunar New Year. (Rev: HB 7/90; SLJ 2/90) [391.2]

20358 Whitman, Sylvia. *Under the Ramadan Moon* (PS–2). Illus. by Sue Williams. 2008, Albert Whitman $15.99 (978-0-8075-8304-3). 32pp. This rhythmic picture-book introduction to the Muslim month of Ramadan follows a family at home and at the mosque. (Rev: BL 10/1/08; SLJ 9/08) [297.3]

20359 Wilkinson, Philip. *A Celebration of Customs and Rituals of the World* (5–8). Illus. 1996, Facts on File $44.00 (978-0-8160-3479-6). A discussion of customs and rituals connected with birth, death, marriage, and coming-of-age. (Rev: BL 4/1/96; VOYA 6/96) [394.2]

20360 Wilson, Sule Greg C. *Kwanzaa! Africa Lives in a New World Festival* (4–7). Series: The Library of African American Arts and Culture. 1999, Rosen LB $27.95 (978-0-8239-1857-7). 64pp. This book begins with a history of slavery and the civil rights movement, then explains the origins and meaning of Kwanzaa. (Rev: SLJ 10/99) [641.59]

Christmas

20361 Box, Su. *Behind the Scenes Christmas* (3–5). Illus. by Jo Blake. 2006, Abingdon $14.00 (978-0-687-49121-6). 29pp. Arranged in question-and-answer format and featuring excerpted Bible stories, this colorful book pieces together the events surrounding the birth of Jesus Christ. (Rev: SLJ 10/06)

20362 Chambers, Catherine. *Christmas* (3–5). Illus. Series: World of Holidays. 1997, Raintree LB $25.70 (978-0-8172-4608-2). 31pp. This book explains the origins of Christmas and how it is observed around the world, along with decorating ideas and some craft projects. (Rev: BL 6/1–15/97) [394.2]

20363 *Christmas in Colonial and Early America* (4–7). Illus. 1996, World Book $19.00 (978-0-7166-0875-2). 80pp. The evolution of Christmas celebrations is traced through more than 100 years of American history to the end of the 19th century. (Rev: BL 11/1/96) [394.26]

20364 *Christmas in Greece* (5–10). Illus. Series: Christmas Around the World. 2000, World Book $19.00 (978-0-7166-0859-2). 80pp. This account focuses on the religious practices of the Greek Orthodox Church at Christmastime, which begins with a long fasting period. (Rev: BL 9/1/00) [398.2]

20365 *Christmas in Switzerland* (4–6). Illus. 1995, World Book $19.00 (978-0-7166-0895-0). 80pp. This book introduces Swiss customs and traditional activities surrounding Christmas. (Rev: BL 9/15/95) [394.26]

20366 Davis, Katherine, et al. *The Little Drummer Boy* (K–3). Illus. by Kristina Rodanas. 2001, Clarion $15.00 (978-0-395-97015-7). 32pp. An attractive rendering of the traditional Christmas song about the little boy and the value of gifts. (Rev: BL 9/1/01; HBG 3/02; SLJ 10/01) [782.42]

20367 Erlbach, Arlene. *Christmas — Celebrating Life, Giving, and Kindness* (3–6). Series: Finding Out About Holidays. 2001, Enslow LB $23.93 (978-0-7660-1576-0). 48pp. In a series of short chapters that include many attractive color photographs, this book explores the history of Christmas and tells how it is observed in the United States. (Rev: BL 9/15/01; HBG 3/02; SLJ 10/01) [394.2]

20368 Erlbach, Arlene, and Herb Erlbach. *Merry Christmas, Everywhere!* (K–2). Illus. by Sharon L. Holm. 2002, Millbrook $23.90 (978-0-7613-1956-6); paper $8.95 (978-0-7613-1699-2). 48pp. Fine illustrations and maps introduce Christmas traditions in countries around the world, accompanied by illustrations, recipes, and crafts. (Rev: BL 9/15/02; HBG 3/03; SLJ 10/02) [394.2663]

20369 *The First Christmas* (3–7). Illus. 1992, Simon & Schuster paper $17.00 (978-0-671-79364-7). 30pp. This Christmas story, in the words of Isaiah, St. Matthew, and St. Luke, is illustrated with the work of such artists as Botticelli and Fra Filippo Lippi. (Rev: BL 11/1/92) [226]

20370 Flanagan, Alice K. *Christmas* (2–3). Series: Holidays and Festivals. 2001, Compass Point LB $23.93 (978-0-7565-0085-6). 32pp. An easy-to-read picture book that describes the origins of Christmas and the many ways in which it is celebrated. (Rev: BL 10/15/01; SLJ 10/01) [394]

20371 Foreman, Michael. *Michael Foreman's Christmas Treasury* (3–6). 2000, Pavilion $22.95 (978-1-86205-197-3). 124pp. A delightful collection of songs, stories, poems, and carols. (Rev: BL 12/1/00) [394.26]

20372 French, Fiona. *Bethlehem* (PS–3). Illus. 2001, HarperCollins $15.95 (978-0-06-029623-0). 32pp. Stained-glass style illustrations illuminate the story of the first Christmas as told in the King James version of the gospels of St. Luke and St. Matthew. (Rev: BL 10/15/01; HBG 3/02; SLJ 10/01) [226]

20373 Graham-Barber, Lynda. *Ho Ho Ho! The Complete Book of Christmas Words* (4–6). Illus. by Betsy Lewin. 1993, Bradbury $16.00 (978-0-02-736933-5). 128pp. A collection of words associated with Christmas, with their definitions and derivations. (Rev: BL 10/1/93) [394.2]

20374 Hickman, Martha W. *A Baby Born in Bethlehem* (K–5). Illus. by Giuliano Ferri. 1999, Whitman $15.95 (978-0-8075-5522-4). 32pp. Simplified biblical verses tell the story of Jesus' birth and the visits by the shepherds and the magi. (Rev: BCCB 11/99; BL 9/1/99; HBG 4/00; SLJ 10/99) [232]

20375 Hoyt-Goldsmith, Diane. *Las Posadas: An Hispanic Christmas Celebration* (3–6). Illus. 1999, Holiday House $17.95 (978-0-8234-1449-9). 32pp. Using a Hispanic American family as a focus, this book explains the nine-night celebration known as Las Posadas, which tells the story of Mary and Joseph's journey to Bethlehem and the birth of Jesus. (Rev: BL 10/1/99; HBG 4/00; SLJ 10/99) [394.266]

20376 Jeffers, H. Paul. *Legends of Santa Claus* (4–7). Series: A&E Biography. 2000, Lucent LB $27.93 (978-0-8225-4983-3). 112pp. This book recounts the tales, legends, and myths about Santa Claus and sorts the truth from the fiction. (Rev: BL 12/15/00; HBG 3/01) [394.2]

20377 Kelley, Emily. *Christmas Around the World.* Rev. ed. (2–3). Illus. by Joni Oeltjenbruns. Series: On My Own Holidays. 2003, Carolrhoda LB $25.26 (978-0-87614-915-7); paper $5.95 (978-1-57505-580-0). 48pp. This revised edition introduces young readers to Christmas traditions in Australia, China, Ethiopia, Germany, Lebanon, Mexico, Russia, and Sweden. (Rev: HBG 4/04; SLJ 10/03)

20378 Kurelek, William. *A Northern Nativity: Christmas Dreams of a Prairie Boy* (1–3). Illus. by author. 1976, Tundra paper $9.95 (978-0-88776-099-0). Twenty paintings of the Holy Family transferred to various locales, accompanied by a lyrical text.

20379 Lankford, Mary D. *Christmas Around the World* (2–5). Illus. 1995, Morrow $16.89 (978-0-688-12167-9). 48pp. An examination of Christmas traditions in 12 countries. (Rev: BL 9/15/95) [394.2]

20380 Lankford, Mary D. *Christmas USA* (3–5). Illus. by Karen Dugan. 2006, HarperCollins $16.99 (978-0-688-15012-9). 48pp. A regional look at the various Christmas customs in the United States, including instructions for various crafts, recipes, and a timeline of popular Christmas toys over the years. (Rev: BL 11/15/06; SLJ 10/06) [394.2663]

20381 Murray, Julie. *Christmas* (1–3). Series: Holidays. 2003, ABDO LB $21.35 (978-1-57765-951-8). 24pp. Explores the origins of the holiday, as well as many of the activities, foods, and customs associated with it. (Rev: HBG 10/03; SLJ 10/03) [394.2663]

20382 *The Nativity* (PS–3). Illus. by Julie Vivas. 1988, Harcourt $13.95 (978-0-15-200535-1). 34pp. A retelling using Bible verses and earthy, sometimes humorous illustrations. A reissue. (Rev: HB 11/88)

20383 Nazoa, Aquiles. *A Small Nativity* (1–3). Trans. by Hugh Hazelton. Illus. by Ana Palmero Caceres. 2007, Groundwood $9.95 (978-0-88899-839-2). 44pp. Featuring contemporary characters but more traditional, rich artwork, this is an appealing retelling of the Nativity story. (Rev: BL 10/15/07; HB 11/07) [863]

20384 Onyefulu, Ifeoma. *An African Christmas* (K–2). Illus. 2005, Frances Lincoln $15.95 (978-1-84507-387-9). 32pp. A young Nigerian boy Afam hopes to create his own mask and to dance in the traditional Mmo masquerade. (Rev: BL 11/1/05) [394.2]

20385 Ouwendijk, George. *Santas of the World* (3–6). Series: Looking Into the Past: People, Places, and Customs. 1998, Chelsea LB $28.00 (978-0-7910-4678-4). 64pp. A overview of the Santa Claus legend is followed by an examination of Christmas gift-giving customs in 24 countries and regions. (Rev: HBG 9/98; SLJ 10/98) [394.26]

20386 Pingry, Patricia A. *Joseph's Story* (1–3). Illus. by George Hinke. 1998, Ideals $16.95 (978-0-8249-4092-8). The traditional stories surrounding the birth of Jesus are retold from the standpoint of Joseph, Mary's husband. (Rev: SLJ 10/98) [394.2]

20387 Roop, Peter, and Connie Roop. *Let's Celebrate Christmas* (3–5). Illus. 1997, Millbrook LB $22.90 (978-0-7613-0115-8). 32pp. As well as a history of the customs surrounding Christmas, this book contains crafts, puzzles, and riddles. (Rev: BL 9/1/97; HBG 3/98; SLJ 10/97) [394]

20388 Ross, Michael Elsohn. *A Mexican Christmas* (K–3). Photos by Felix Rigau. 2002, Carolrhoda LB $23.93 (978-0-87614-601-9). 40pp. Christmas customs in Oaxaca are described in text and photographs. (Rev: HBG 3/03; SLJ 10/02) [394.2663]

20389 Schuh, Mari C. *Christmas* (PS–2). Series: Holidays and Celebrations. 2002, Capstone LB $17.26 (978-0-7368-0979-5). 24pp. An overview of holiday traditions in the United States for beginning readers. (Rev: HBG 3/02; SLJ 10/02)

20390 Steiner, Joan. *Look-Alikes Christmas* (K–4). Photos by Ogden Gigli. 2003, Little, Brown $14.95 (978-0-316-81187-3). Challenges young readers to name the everyday objects that have been used to construct nine three-dimensional holiday scenes, including Santa's workshop, a cathedral, and a scene from the *Nutcracker* ballet. (Rev: HB 11/03; HBG 4/04; SLJ 10/03) [793.73]

Easter

20391 Chambers, Catherine. *Easter* (4–6). Series: A World of Holidays. 1998, Raintree LB $25.70 (978-0-8172-4615-0). 32pp. Tells the story of Easter and Christ's resurrection, and covers the secular aspects of this spring celebration, such as Easter eggs, bunnies, and baskets. (Rev: BL 6/1–15/98; HBG 9/98) [394.2]

20392 Joslin, Mary. *On That Easter Morning* (K–3). Illus. by Helen Cann. 2006, Good Bks. $16.00 (978-1-56148-517-8). The biblical account of Jesus's last days on Earth, leading to his crucifixion and resurrection, is retold and accompanied by beautiful artwork. (Rev: SLJ 5/06) [232.9]

20393 Kennedy, Pamela. *An Easter Celebration: Traditions and Customs from Around the World* (4–6). Illus. 1991, Ideals $10.95 (978-0-8249-8506-6). 32pp. Color photos and historical drawings add to this handy volume on Easter celebrations. (Rev: BL 3/15/91) [394.2]

20394 Knudsen, Shannon. *Easter Around the World* (1–3). Illus. Series: On My Own Holidays. 2005, Carolrhoda LB $25.26 (978-1-57505-655-5). 48pp. The origins and traditions of Easter are introduced with many illustrations and a short glossary.

20395 Landau, Elaine. *Easter: Parades, Chocolates, and Celebration* (2–5). Illus. Series: Finding Out About Holidays. 2004, Enslow LB $23.93 (978-0-7660-2172-3). 48pp. Informative text and colorful photographs present the history and religious significance of Easter, plus traditional symbols and contemporary ways of celebrating this holiday. (Rev: SLJ 4/05)

20396 Schuh, Mari C. *Easter* (K–2). Series: Holidays and Celebrations. 2002, Capstone LB $17.26 (978-0-7368-1445-4). 24pp. This small, square book uses full-page photographs and a brief text to present the meaning of Easter, its symbols, celebrations, and importance. (Rev: BCCB 2/02; BL 1/1–15/03; HBG 3/03) [394.2]

20397 Stalcup, Ann. *Ukrainian Egg Decoration: A Holiday Tradition* (3–5). Series: Crafts of the World. 1999, Rosen $21.25 (978-0-8239-5335-6). 24pp. This photoessay covers the history and lore of the Ukrainian tradition of creating beautifully patterned eggs at Easter. Also features one craft project. (Rev: SLJ 4/99) [394.2]

Halloween

20398 Chambers, Catherine. *All Saints, All Souls, and Halloween* (3–5). Illus. Series: World of Holidays. 1997, Raintree LB $25.70 (978-0-8172-4606-8). 31pp. An explanation of the origins of this holiday as an observance for the spirits of the dead, customs associated with it, and a number of craft activities. (Rev: BL 6/1–15/97) [394.2]

20399 Flanagan, Alice K. *Halloween* (2–3). Series: Holidays and Festivals. 2001, Compass Point LB $23.93 (978-0-7565-0086-3). 32pp. An attractive picture book that describes the origins of Halloween and how it is celebrated by youngsters today. (Rev: BCCB 10/02; BL 10/15/01; SLJ 1/02) [745.5]

20400 Gibbons, Gail. *Halloween* (PS–1). Illus. by author. 1984, Holiday House LB $16.95 (978-0-8234-0524-4); paper $6.95 (978-0-8234-0577-0). 32pp. Halloween history and traditions are explained in this simple picture book.

20401 Gibbons, Gail. *Halloween Is . . .* (PS–2). Illus. 2002, Holiday House $17.95 (978-0-8234-1758-2). 32pp. A larger, revised version with new, enhanced illustrations of the 1984 *Halloween*, describing the holiday's history and traditions. (Rev: BL 9/15/02; HBG 3/03) [394.2646]

20402 Greene, Carol. *The Story of Halloween* (3–5). Illus. by Linda Bronson. 2004, HarperCollins LB $16.89 (978-0-06-029560-8). 40pp. The history of Halloween is covered from its origins in the Celtic festival of Samhain to present-day problems with trick-or-treating. (Rev: BL 9/1/04; SLJ 8/04) [394]

20403 Limburg, Peter R. *Weird! The Complete Book of Halloween Words* (4–7). Illus. by Betsy Lewin. 1989, Macmillan LB $13.95 (978-0-02-759050-0). 128pp. This book defines 41 words and expressions, such as trick or treat, associated with Halloween. (Rev: BL 9/1/89; SLJ 9/89) [394]

20404 Mercer, Abbie. *Happy Halloween* (2–4). Series: Holiday Fun. 2007, Rosen LB $21.25 (978-1-4042-3806-0). 24pp. Along with discussion of the traditions and activities associated with this holiday, this volume includes a recipe and a craft. (Rev: SLJ 2/08) [394.2646]

20405 Robinson, Fay. *Halloween — Costumes and Treats on All Hallows' Eve* (3–6). Series: Finding Out About Holidays. 2001, Enslow LB $23.93 (978-0-7660-1632-3). 48pp. The origins of Halloween are described, with material on how this holiday has evolved and how it is currently celebrated in the United States. (Rev: BL 9/15/01; HBG 3/02; SLJ 9/01) [745.5]

20406 Roop, Peter, and Connie Roop. *Let's Celebrate Halloween* (3–5). Illus. 1997, Millbrook LB $22.90 (978-0-7613-0113-4); paper $6.95 (978-0-7613-

0284-1). 32pp. Includes a number of crafts, like making a haunted house and different masks, as well as a history of Halloween and its significance. (Rev: BL 9/1/97; HBG 3/98; SLJ 8/97) [745.5]

20407 Trumbauer, Lisa. *Computer Fun Halloween* (2–5). Illus. by Sydney Wright. Series: Click It! 1999, Millbrook LB $21.90 (978-0-7613-1560-5). 32pp. These projects involving a computer and a paint program give directions on how to make decorations, masks and costumes, party invitations, place cards, and more. (Rev: HBG 4/00; SLJ 2/00) [745.5]

20408 Wolff, Ferida, and Dolores Kozielski. *Halloween Fun for Everyone* (1–6). Illus. by Judy Lanfredi. 1997, Morrow paper $7.95 (978-0-688-15257-4). 79pp. After a history of Halloween, this book gives directions on how to make costumes, games, decorations, and holiday food. (Rev: SLJ 1/98) [745.5]

20409 Zocchi, Judy. *On Halloween Night / La noche de Halloween* (2–4). Illus. by Rebecca Wallis. 2005, Dingles LB $15.50 (978-1-891997-76-1). A cartoon-filled bilingual introduction to the history and rituals of Halloween. (Rev: SLJ 2/06) [745.5]

Jewish Holy Days and Celebrations

20410 Adler, David A. *The Kids' Catalog of Jewish Holidays* (4–7). Illus. 1996, Jewish Publication Soc. paper $15.95 (978-0-8276-0581-7). 244pp. Thirteen major and several minor Jewish holidays are introduced, along with activities, songs, and recipes. (Rev: BL 12/15/96; SLJ 3/97) [296.4]

20411 Baum, Maxie. *I Have a Little Dreidel* (PS–K). Illus. by Julie Paschkis. 2006, Scholastic $9.99 (978-0-439-64997-1). 32pp. Illustrations full of interesting details enhance this retelling of the traditional Hanukkah song. (Rev: BL 9/15/06; HB 11/06; HBG 4/07; SLJ 10/06) [782.42]

20412 Ben-Zvi, Rebecca Tova. *Four Sides, Eight Nights: A New Spin on Hanukkah* (2–4). Illus. by Susanna Natti. 2005, Roaring Brook $16.95 (978-1-59643-059-4). 48pp. Dreidels — their composition and rules and technique of the game — are the focus of this Hanukkah book that also touches on holiday food and the stories of Judith and Hannah. (Rev: BL 11/1/05; SLJ 10/05) [296.4]

20413 Brinn, Ruth Esrig. *Jewish Holiday Crafts for Little Hands* (PS–4). Illus. by Katherine J. Kahn. 1993, Kar-Ben paper $10.95 (9-929371-47-X). 127pp. Using 11 different Jewish holidays as a focus, this unique craft book gives an average of a dozen simple projects for each. (Rev: SLJ 10/93) [296.4]

20414 Burstein, Chaya M. *The Jewish Kids Catalog* (3–7). Illus. by author. 1983, Jewish Publication Soc. paper $15.95 (978-0-8276-0215-1). 224pp. An introduction to Jewish holidays, traditions, and crafts.

20415 Chaikin, Miriam. *Menorahs, Mezuzas, and Other Jewish Symbols* (5–9). 1990, Clarion $17.00 (978-0-89919-856-9). A Jewish historian explains some of the symbols of the faith. (Rev: BL 1/15/91; HB 5/91; SLJ 1/91) [296.4]

20416 Clark, Anne, et al. *Hanukkah* (4–6). Series: A World of Holidays. 1998, Raintree LB $25.70 (978-0-8172-4614-3). 32pp. Tells the story of Hanukkah, its traditions, symbols, and heroes, such as Judah Maccabee and others who faced incredible odds. (Rev: BL 6/1–15/98; HBG 9/98) [296.4]

20417 Cone, Molly. *The Story of Shabbat* (2–5). Illus. 2000, HarperCollins LB $14.89 (978-0-06-027945-5). 40pp. A discussion of the weekly Jewish holiday — its history, customs, and such practices as abstaining from work and studying the Torah. (Rev: BL 4/1/00; HBG 9/00; SLJ 8/00) [296.4]

20418 Cooper, Ilene. *Jewish Holidays All Year Round: A Family Treasury* (3–5). Illus. by Elivia Savadier. 2002, Abrams $18.95 (978-0-8109-0550-4). 80pp. Details of the rituals that take place at home and in the synagogue are given in this overview of the holidays of the Jewish year, with an activity and recipe for each celebration. (Rev: HBG 3/03; SLJ 3/03) [296.4]

20419 David, Jo, and Daniel B. Syme. *The Book of the Jewish Life* (5–8). Illus. 1997, UAHC paper $13.95 (978-0-8074-0628-1). This book explores common Jewish traditions in such areas as birth and naming, religious schools, bar/bat mitzvahs, confirmation, marriage, and mourning. (Rev: SLJ 9/98) [296]

20420 Feinstein, Edward. *Tough Questions Jews Ask: A Young Adult's Guide to Building a Jewish Life* (5–7). 2003, Jewish Lights $14.99 (978-1-58023-139-8). 128pp. Rabbi Feinstein effectively answers hypothetical questions posed by an imagined class of thoughtful young students. (Rev: BL 4/1/03) [296.7]

20421 Ferro, Jennifer. *Jewish Foods and Culture* (3–5). Series: Festive Foods and Celebrations. 1999, Rourke LB $27.93 (978-1-57103-303-1). 48pp. Bar and bat mitzvahs, Passover, and Purim are three facets of Jewish life that are featured, along with recipes, in this book that also discusses Jewish history and culture. (Rev: SLJ 2/00) [296.4]

20422 Fishman, Cathy Goldberg. *Hanukkah* (2–3). Illus. by Mary O'Keefe Young. Series: On My Own Holidays. 2003, Carolrhoda LB $25.26 (978-1-57505-195-6); paper $5.95 (978-1-57505-583-1). 48pp. A simple history of the Jewish holiday, with a look at how it is celebrated today and instructions on how to play dreidel. (Rev: HBG 4/04; SLJ 10/03) [296.4]

20423 Fishman, Cathy Goldberg. *On Sukkot and Simchat Torah* (K–3). Illus. by Melanie Hall. 2006, Lerner $17.95 (978-1-58013-165-0). 32pp. Follows a Jewish family preparing a sukkah for the Sukkot harvest festival, and enjoying the celebration that accompanies the completion of the Torah reading on Simchat Torah. (Rev: BL 10/1/06; SLJ 9/06) [296.4]

20424 Goldin, Barbara D. *Ten Holiday Jewish Children's Stories* (K–3). Illus. by Jeffrey Allon. 2000, Pitspopany $16.95 (978-0-943706-47-4); paper $9.95 (978-0-943706-48-1). 48pp. A lively collec-

tion of ten stories, each of which stems from a tradition or practice associated with a Jewish holiday. (Rev: BL 10/1/00)

20425 Groner, Judye, and Madeline Wikler. *All About Passover* (2–4). Illus. by Kinny Kreiswirth. 2000, Kar-Ben paper $5.95 (978-1-58013-060-8). 32pp. A concise guide to this holiday, with a summary of the Passover story, details on suitable preparations, including cooking the seder meal, and a description of the seder itself. (Rev: BL 10/1/00) [296.4]

20426 Groner, Judye, and Madeline Wikler. *All About Sukkot* (1–5). Illus. by Kinny Kreiswirth. 1998, Kar-Ben paper $5.95 (978-1-58013-018-9). 32pp. This book gives information on the origins and history of this Jewish festival, on how it is celebrated and the connection between Sukkot and Thanksgiving, and provides suitable prayers, a story, and some poems. (Rev: SLJ 3/99) [296.4]

20427 Heiligman, Deborah. *Celebrate Hanukkah with Light, Latkes, and Dreidels* (1–3). Illus. Series: Holidays Around the World. 2006, National Geographic $15.95 (978-0-7922-5924-4). 32pp. A colorful introduction to the history and traditions of Hanukkah, with photographs from countries around the world; appended materials include prayers, a recipe for latkes, a bibliography, and a glossary. (Rev: BL 10/15/06) [296.35]

20428 Heiligman, Deborah. *Celebrate Passover* (3–5). Illus. Series: Holidays Around the World. 2007, National Geographic LB $23.90 (978-1-4263-0019-6); paper $15.95 (978-1-4263-0018-9). 32pp. Introduces to the Jewish holiday and its religious significance, customs, and rituals in communities around the world. (Rev: BL 3/15/07) [296.4]

20429 Heiligman, Deborah. *Celebrate Rosh Hashanah and Yom Kippur* (K–3). Series: Holidays Around the World. 2007, National Geographic $15.95 (978-1-4263-0076-9). 32pp. The author discusses how and why Jewish people around the world observe these High Holy Days. Includes a note for teachers and parents by Rabbi Shira Stern. (Rev: SLJ 8/07)

20430 Hildebrandt, Ziporah. *This Is Our Seder* (PS–2). Illus. by Robin Roraback. 1999, Holiday House $15.95 (978-0-8234-1436-9). 32pp. Wonderful illustrations and a simple text introduce each of the items associated with a Passover seder. (Rev: BL 3/1/99; HBG 9/99; SLJ 4/99) [296.4]

20431 Hoyt-Goldsmith, Diane. *Celebrating Hanukkah* (3–6). Illus. by Lawrence Migdale. 1996, Holiday House $17.95 (978-0-8234-1252-5). 32pp. A photoessay about Hanukkah and how it is celebrated in the United States. (Rev: BCCB 11/96; BL 9/1/96) [296.4]

20432 Hoyt-Goldsmith, Diane. *Celebrating Passover* (2–5). Illus. 2000, Holiday House $16.95 (978-0-8234-1420-8). 32pp. A 9-year-old boy explains the origins of Passover and how he and his extended family celebrate it. (Rev: BL 5/1/00; HBG 9/00; SLJ 6/00) [296.4]

20433 Kimmel, Eric A. *Wonders and Miracles: A Passover Companion* (4–8). Illus. 2004, Scholastic $18.95 (978-0-439-07175-8). 144pp. In addition to a description of the holiday and its rituals, Kimmel provides stories, songs, prayers, poems, and recipes. (Rev: BL 2/15/04*; SLJ 2/04) [296.4]

20434 Kolatch, Alfred J. *The Jewish Child's First Book of Why* (PS–4). Illus. by Harry Araten. 1992, Jonathan David $14.95 (978-0-8246-0354-0). 32pp. Fifteen questions and answers dealing mainly with Jewish holidays. (Rev: BL 4/15/92) [296.4]

20435 Kropf, Latifa Berry. *It's Challah Time!* (PS–1). Illus. by Tod Cohen. 2002, Kar-Ben LB $12.95 (978-1-58013-036-3). 24pp. Color photographs show happy young children making challah for the Sabbath, singing blessings, and tasting the final product. (Rev: BL 10/1/02; HBG 3/03; SLJ 12/02) [641.5]

20436 Kropf, Latifa Berry. *It's Purim Time!* (PS). Photos by Tod Cohen. 2005, Lerner LB $12.95 (978-1-58013-153-7). Preschool children enjoy a fun-filled Purim, selecting costumes, making noise-makers, and having traditional snacks. (Rev: SLJ 8/05) [296.4]

20437 Kropf, Latifa Berry. *It's Shofar Time!* (1–3). Illus. by Tod Cohen. 2006, Kar-Ben $12.95 (978-1-58013-158-2). 24pp. Color photographs show children enjoying the traditions associated with the Jewish holiday of Rosh Hashanah. (Rev: BL 10/1/06) [296.4]

20438 Metter, Bert. *Bar Mitzvah, Bat Mitzvah: The Ceremony, the Party, and How the Day Came to Be* (4–7). Illus. by Joan Reilly. 2007, Clarion $15.00 (978-0-618-76772-4); paper $5.95 (978-0-618-76773-1). 80pp. This book about the coming-of-age ceremony for Jewish children (and now adults) covers its history but does not leave out the fun part — the party — and even includes details about the parties of some celebrities. (Rev: BL 7/07; SLJ 11/07) [296.4]

20439 Murray, Julie. *Hanukkah* (1–3). Series: Holidays. 2003, ABDO LB $21.35 (978-1-57765-953-2). 24pp. Provides a brief history of the holiday as well as a look at some of the associated traditions. (Rev: HBG 10/03; SLJ 10/03) [296.4]

20440 Musleah, Rahel, and Michael Klayman. *Sharing Blessings: Children's Stories for Exploring the Spirit of the Jewish Holidays* (3–5). Illus. 1997, Jewish Lights $18.95 (978-1-879045-71-2). 64pp. Through the observances of a single family, all the major Jewish holidays are introduced and explained. (Rev: BL 10/1/97; HBG 3/98; SLJ 9/97) [296.4]

20441 Podwal, Mark. *A Sweet Year: A Taste of the Jewish Holidays* (K–6). Illus. by author. 2003, Doubleday LB $14.99 (978-0-385-90869-6). Lyrical prose and striking artwork offer an excellent introduction to the traditions and foods of the Jewish holidays. (Rev: HBG 4/04; SLJ 8/03) [296.4]

20442 Rose, David, and Gill Rose. *Passover* (3–5). Illus. Series: World of Holidays. 1997, Raintree LB $25.70 (978-0-8172-4607-5). 31pp. This book explains the origins of Passover and the Seder that accompanies it, along with many activities and craft projects. (Rev: BL 6/1–15/97) [296.4]

20443 Ross, Kathy. *Crafts for Hanukkah* (2–4). Illus. 1996, Millbrook LB $24.90 (978-1-56294-919-8);

paper $6.95 (978-0-7613-0078-6). 48pp. Outlines crafts associated with Hanukkah, like making dreidels and menorahs. (Rev: BL 9/1/96) [745.594]

20444 Scharfstein, Sol. *Understanding Jewish Holidays and Customs: Historical and Contemporary* (4–7). Illus. 1999, KTAV $27.50 (978-0-88125-634-5); paper $18.95 (978-0-88125-626-0). 186pp. From ancient Jewish traditions to the present day, this highly visual volume describes the history, customs, and teaching of Judaism. (Rev: BL 10/1/99; HBG 3/00; SLJ 2/00) [296.4]

20445 Schecter, Ellen. *The Family Haggadah* (3–6). Illus. 1999, Viking $13.99 (978-0-670-88341-7). 80pp. For use by both parents and children, this guide to a Passover seder has instructions for table settings, a version of the service, and some traditional prayers and music. (Rev: BCCB 3/99; BL 5/15/99; SLJ 6/99) [296.4]

20446 Schuh, Mari C. *Passover* (K–2). Illus. Series: Holidays and Celebrations. 2002, Capstone $17.26 (978-0-7368-1448-5). 24pp. Colorful photographs and simple text explain the meaning, history, and traditions of the Passover celebration in this small, square book. (Rev: BL 1/1–15/03; HBG 3/03) [394.262]

20447 Siegel, Bruce H. *The Magic of Kol Nidre: A Yom Kippur Story* (1–4). Illus. by Shelly O. Haas. 1998, Kar-Ben $16.95 (978-1-58013-003-5); paper $6.95 (978-1-58013-002-8). The meanings behind Kol Nidre, the opening prayer of the Yom Kippur eve service, are explored in this book illustrated with realistic watercolors. (Rev: HBG 3/99; SLJ 3/99) [296.4]

20448 Techner, David, and Judith Hirt-Manheimer. *A Candle for Grandpa* (K–3). Illus. by Joel Iskowitz. 1993, UAHC $13.95 (978-0-8074-0507-9). Using the first anniversary of the death of a boy's grandfather as a focus, this book presents Jewish funeral practices. (Rev: SLJ 10/93) [296.4]

20449 Wood, Angela. *Jewish Festivals* (4–6). Illus. Series: Celebrate! 1997, Heinemann $22.79 (978-0-431-06962-3). 48pp. A boy in Jerusalem and a girl in Chicago explain how their families celebrate a number of Jewish holidays and holy days. (Rev: SLJ 12/97) [221.6]

20450 Wood, Angela. *Judaism* (5–8). Illus. Series: World Religions. 1995, Thomson Learning LB $24.26 (978-1-56847-376-5). 48pp. An informative, clearly written text on Judaism, with a glossary, bibliography, and map of regions in which the religion flourishes. (Rev: BL 9/1/95; SLJ 11/95) [296]

Thanksgiving

20451 Anderson, Laurie Halse. *Thank You, Sarah: The Woman Who Saved Thanksgiving* (K–3). Illus. by Matt Faulkner. 2002, Simon & Schuster $16.95 (978-0-689-84787-5). 40pp. Humorous illustrations accompany this true tale of a woman who campaigned for almost four decades to make Thanksgiving a national holiday. (Rev: BL 12/15/02; HBG 3/03; SLJ 12/02) [394.2649]

20452 Bruchac, Joseph. *Squanto's Journey: The Story of the First Thanksgiving* (4–8). Illus. by Greg Shed. 2000, Harcourt $17.00 (978-0-15-201817-7). 32pp. A picture book for older readers about the Pilgrims, the first Thanksgiving, and the important role played by the Paluxet Indian Squanto in helping the colony survive. (Rev: BL 9/1/00; HBG 3/01; SLJ 11/00) [394.2]

20453 Fink, Deborah F. *It's a Family Thanksgiving! A Celebration of an American Tradition for Children and Their Families* (K–4). Illus. by Kinny Kreiswirth. 2000, Harmony Hearth paper $9.95 (978-0-9678871-0-4). 32pp. History, foods, and traditions are covered in this book about Thanksgiving that also contains recipes and craft projects. (Rev: BL 9/15/00) [394.2]

20454 Gibbons, Gail. *Thanksgiving Day* (PS–2). Illus. by author. 1983, Holiday House LB $16.95 (978-0-8234-0489-6); paper $6.95 (978-0-8234-0576-3). 32pp. A very simple introduction to Thanksgiving Day.

20455 Grace, Catherine O'Neill, and Margaret M. Bruchac. *1621: A New Look at Thanksgiving* (K–4). Illus. by Sisse Brimberg and Cotton Coulson. 2001, National Geographic $17.95 (978-0-7922-7027-0). 48pp. This appealing and informative photoessay presents the historically correct story of the first Thanksgiving, as reenacted at the Plimoth Plantation. (Rev: BL 9/1/01; HBG 10/02; SLJ 9/01*) [394.2649]

20456 Graham-Barber, Lynda. *Gobble! The Complete Book of Thanksgiving Words* (4–6). Illus. by Betsy Lewin. 1993, Avon paper $3.99 (978-0-380-71963-1). 128pp. In readable fashion, all the words associated with this holiday are featured. (Rev: BL 1/1/91; SLJ 11/91) [394.2]

20457 Greenwood, Barbara. *A Pioneer Thanksgiving: A Story of Harvest Celebrations in 1841* (3–6). Illus. by Heather Collins. 1999, Kids Can $14.95 (978-1-55074-744-7); paper $6.95 (978-1-55074-574-0). 48pp. This book about a family's Thanksgiving celebration in 1841 includes recipes, craft projects, and games. (Rev: BCCB 11/99; BL 9/1/99; HBG 4/00; SLJ 9/99) [394]

20458 Hayward, Linda. *The First Thanksgiving* (1–3). Illus. by James Watling. Series: Step into Reading. 1990, Random LB $11.99 (978-0-679-90218-8); paper $3.99 (978-0-679-80218-1). 48pp. This easy-to-read book tells about the journey of the Pilgrims and of their first colony. (Rev: BCCB 11/90; BL 12/1/90) [394.2]

20459 Heinrichs, Ann. *Thanksgiving* (K–3). Illus. by Charles Jordan. Series: Holidays, Festivals, and Celebrations. 2006, The Child's World LB $24.21 (978-1-59296-582-3). 32pp. Examines the history, customs, and symbols of this holiday and includes a recipe and a craft. (Rev: SLJ 9/06) [394.2649]

20460 Landau, Elaine. *Thanksgiving Day: A Time to Be Thankful* (3–6). Illus. Series: Finding Out About Holidays. 2001, Enslow LB $23.93 (978-0-7660-1572-2). 48pp. A general introduction to this traditional American holiday, its history, and how it is

celebrated. (Rev: BL 9/15/01; HBG 3/02; SLJ 1/02) [394.2649]

20461 MacMillan, Dianne. *Thanksgiving Day* (4–8). Series: Best Holiday Books. 1997, Enslow LB $23.93 (978-0-89490-822-4). In spite of a dull format, this book gives solid information about Thanksgiving, its history, common traditions, and modern observances. (Rev: SLJ 8/97) [394.2]

20462 Mercer, Abbie. *Happy Thanksgiving* (2–4). Series: Holiday Fun. 2007, Rosen LB $21.25 (978-1-4042-3807-7). 24pp. Along with descriptions of typical Thanksgiving activities, traditions, and foods, this volume includes historical information, a recipe, and a craft. (Rev: SLJ 2/08) [394.2649]

20463 Miller, Marilyn. *Thanksgiving* (4–6). Series: A World of Holidays. 1998, Raintree LB $25.69 (978-0-8172-4612-9). 32pp. This book discusses America's Thanksgiving Day and compares it with similar harvest festivals in such countries as the Czech Republic and Sierra Leone. (Rev: BL 6/1–15/98; HBG 9/98) [394.2]

20464 Schuh, Mari C. *Thanksgiving Day* (PS–1). Series: National Holidays. 2003, Capstone LB $17.26 (978-0-7368-1654-0). 24pp. This slim title examines the history of Thanksgiving Day, which was declared a national holiday in the 1860s. (Rev: HBG 10/03; SLJ 9/03) [394.2]

Valentine's Day

20465 Bulla, Clyde Robert. *The Story of Valentine's Day* (3–5). Illus. by Susan Estelle Kwas. 1999, HarperCollins LB $14.89 (978-0-06-027884-7). 40pp. This well-illustrated volume discusses the origins of Valentine's Day, shows how it is celebrated, and presents a few related projects. (Rev: BL 2/1/99; HBG 9/99; SLJ 6/99) [394.2618]

20466 Flanagan, Alice K. *Valentine's Day* (2–4). Illus. by Shelley Dieterichs. Series: Holidays and Festivals. 2001, Compass Point LB $23.93 (978-0-7565-0088-7). 32pp. Flanagan tells readers about the origins of Valentine's Day (as a Roman festival) and details how we celebrate the holiday today. (Rev: BL 10/15/01; SLJ 1/02) [394.2618]

20467 Fradin, Dennis Brindell. *Valentine's Day* (3–5). Illus. 1990, Enslow LB $23.93 (978-0-89490-237-6). 48pp. A look at how this holiday has been celebrated over the years. (Rev: BL 8/90; SLJ 2/91) [394.2]

20468 Gibbons, Gail. *Valentine's Day* (PS–1). Illus. by author. 1986, Holiday House LB $16.95 (978-0-8234-0572-5); paper $6.95 (978-0-8234-0764-4). 32pp. History, meaning, and customs of Valentine's Day with simple drawings in bright colors. (Rev: BCCB 2/86; BL 12/15/85)

20469 Gibbons, Gail. *Valentine's Day Is . . .* (PS–1). Illus. 2006, Holiday $17.95 (978-0-8234-1852-7). 32pp. In spreads introduced by the title phrase, Gibbons explores the origins and customs of Valentine's Day. (Rev: BL 2/1/06; SLJ 3/06) [394.2681]

20470 Graham-Barber, Lynda. *Mushy! The Complete Book of Valentine Words* (4–8). Illus. by Betsy Lewin. 1993, Avon paper $3.50 (978-0-380-71650-

0). 122pp. An explanation of the words, symbols, and customs concerning Valentine's Day. (Rev: BCCB 3/91; BL 2/15/91; SLJ 5/91) [394.2]

20471 Kessel, Joyce K. *Valentine's Day* (2–4). Illus. by Karen Ritz. 1981, Carolrhoda LB $13.13 (978-0-87614-166-3); Lerner paper $5.95 (978-0-87614-502-9). 48pp. An easily read account of the origins of this holiday and the traditions surrounding it.

20472 Landau, Elaine. *Valentine's Day: Candy, Love, and Hearts* (3–6). Series: Finding Out About Holidays. 2002, Enslow LB $23.93 (978-0-7660-1779-5). 48pp. Material on Saint Valentine is included with information on the symbols connected with the holiday and the ways in which it is celebrated. (Rev: BL 7/02; HBG 10/02; SLJ 10/02) [394.2]

20473 Sabuda, Robert. *Saint Valentine* (K–4). Illus. 1992, Macmillan $16.95 (978-0-689-31762-0). 32pp. Mosaiclike illustrations accompany the story of the gentle Christian physician and priest who lived in Rome during the Christian persecutions. (Rev: BL 11/15/92; SLJ 11/92) [270.1]

20474 Trueit, Trudi. *Valentine's Day* (K–2). Illus. Series: Rookie Read-about Holidays. 2006, Scholastic LB $20.50 (978-0-531-12461-1). 32pp. Brief information and stock photographs introduce beginning readers to Valentine's Day. (Rev: BL 1/1–15/07) [394.2618]

Prayers

20475 Attenborough, Liz, ed. *The Children's Book of Poems, Prayers and Meditations* (4–6). Illus. 1998, Element Books $19.95 (978-1-901881-85-1). 128pp. From St. Francis of Assisi to Bob Dylan and Maya Angelou, this is a fine collection of meditative poems dealing with such topics as the nature of time and brotherly love. (Rev: BL 12/15/98; HBG 3/99; SLJ 1/99) [808.81]

20476 Brooks, Jeremy. *My First Prayers* (K–2). Illus. by Laurie Fournier. 2009, Frances Lincoln $16.95 (978-1-84507-535-4). A collection of prayers from many nations. (Rev: SLJ 6/09)

20477 Brooks, Jeremy. *A World of Prayers* (PS–1). Illus. by Elena Gomez. 2006, Eerdmans $16.00 (978-0-8028-5285-4). 32pp. A collection of more than 25 prayers from around the world, organized by category rather than religion. (Rev: BL 12/15/05; SLJ 2/06) [204]

20478 Carlstrom, Nancy White. *Glory* (PS–2). Illus. by Debra R. Jenkins. 2001, Eerdmans $17.00 (978-0-8028-5143-7). 32pp. Animals — and one little girl — joyfully reflect the glory of God in this prayer with bright, bold illustrations. (Rev: BL 10/1/01; HBG 3/02; SLJ 12/01) [811]

20479 *A Children's Treasury of Prayers* (PS–1). Illus. by Linda Bleck. 2006, Sterling $12.95 (978-1-4027-2982-9). 32pp. This child-friendly collection of prayers offers examples from a number of religions, including Christianity, Hinduism, Islam, and Judaism. (Rev: BL 10/1/06) [204]

20480 Dearborn, Sabrina, ed. *A Child's Book of Blessings* (3–6). Illus. 1999, Barefoot Bks. $16.95 (978-1-84148-010-7). 40pp. A collection of simple blessings from various world cultures and religions. (Rev: BL 10/1/99; SLJ 2/00) [291.43]

20481 Field, Rachel. *Prayer for a Child* (1–3). Illus. by Elizabeth Orton Jones. 1968, Macmillan LB $14.00 (978-0-02-735190-3); paper $5.99 (978-0-02-043070-4). 32pp. A prayer bespeaking the faith, hope, and love of little children. Caldecott Medal winner, 1945.

20482 *Give Us This Day: The Lord's Prayer* (PS–4). Illus. by Tasha Tudor. 1989, Penguin $12.99 (978-0-399-21442-4). 32pp. Children in New England a century ago highlight the lovely paintings that illustrate the words of this Christian prayer. (Rev: BL 2/1/88)

20483 Groner, Judye, and Madeline Wikler. *Thank You, God! A Jewish Child's Book of Prayers* (PS–2). Illus. by Shelly O. Haas. 1994, Kar-Ben $16.95 (978-0-929371-65-8). 32pp. A series of blessings and prayers involving Jewish traditions, written in Hebrew letters with an English translation. (Rev: BL 3/15/94; SLJ 4/94) [296.7]

20484 Jelenek, Frank. X. *Journey to the Heart: Centering Prayer for Children* (1–4). Illus. by Ann Boyajian. 2007, Paraclete $14.95 (978-1-55725-482-5). 32pp. Jelenek introduces the concept of contemplative prayer to young children. (Rev: BL 10/1/07) [248.3]

20485 Kangas, Juli. *A Child's Book of Prayers* (PS–K). Illus. by author. 2008, Dial $32.00 (978-0-8037-3054-0). 32pp. Families seeking blessings and meditations will appreciate this collection of 26 short prayers accompanied by colorful, child-centered illustrations. (Rev: BL 12/1/07; SLJ 7/08) [204]

20486 Knowlton, Laurie L. *God Be in My Heart: Poems and Prayers for Children* (K–3). Illus. 1999, Boyds Mills $11.95 (978-1-56397-646-9). 32pp. A charming collection of 11 Christian prayers — some from history and others written by the author. (Rev: BL 4/1/99; HBG 9/99; SLJ 4/99) [291.4]

20487 Ladwig, Tim. *The Lord's Prayer* (PS–4). 2000, Eerdmans $17.00 (978-0-8028-5180-2). 32pp. Full-page paintings are used with the text of the Lord's Prayer to tell the story of an African American father and daughter who help an elderly neighbor. (Rev: BCCB 12/00; BL 10/1/00; SLJ 1/01) [226.9]

20488 *The Lord Is My Shepherd* (PS–2). Illus. by Regolo Ricci. 2007, Tundra $18.95 (978-0-88776-776-0). 24pp. Illustrations of nature and the changing seasons accompany the words of the 23rd Psalm. (Rev: BL 10/1/07; SLJ 11/07) [223]

20489 *The Lord Is My Shepherd: The Twenty-Third Psalm* (2–4). Illus. by Gennady Spirin. 2008, Philomel $17.99 (978-0-399-24527-5). 32pp. A handsomely illustrated version of the Old Testament psalm, with ornate scenes in lush colors. (Rev: BL 1/1–15/08; SLJ 5/08) [223]

20490 Moser, Barry. *Psalm 23* (K–2). Illus. by author. 2008, Zondervan $14.99 (978-0-310-71085-1). 32pp. The comfort and peace of this prayer is retained with fresh Caribbean island illustrations. (Rev: BL 1/1–15/08; SLJ 3/08) [223]

20491 O'Keefe, Susan Heyboer. *Angel Prayers: Prayers for All Children* (PS–1). Illus. by Sophia Suzan. 1999, Boyds Mills $15.95 (978-1-56397-683-4). A warm, gentle collection of prayers addressed to God and angels, plus several blessings. (Rev: HBG 4/00; SLJ 12/99) [242]

20492 Rock, Lois. *A Child's Book of Graces* (PS–2). Illus. by Allison Jay. 2006, Good Bks. $5.95 (978-1-56148-514-7). 28pp. Prayers for before (and after) meals from many sources, Christian and non-Christian. (Rev: BL 7/06) [242]

20493 Rock, Lois, comp. *My Very First Prayers* (PS–2). Illus. by Alex Ayliffe. 2003, Good Bks. $14.99 (978-1-56148-371-6). 159pp. This collection of prayers covers family, friends, pets, holidays, love, nature, and the seasons. (Rev: SLJ 1/04) [242]

20494 Rylant, Cynthia. *Give Me Grace: A Child's Daybook of Prayers* (PS–K). Illus. 1999, Simon & Schuster $12.00 (978-0-689-82293-3). 32pp. A simple book of seven prayers, one for each day of the week. (Rev: BL 10/1/99; HBG 4/00; SLJ 12/99) [291.4]

20495 Simmons, Justine. *God, Can You Hear Me?* (PS–4). Illus. by Robert Papp. 2007, HarperCollins $16.99 (978-0-06-115397-6). Children ask God their tough questions in this book that reassures readers that God cares about the problems in their lives. The author appears on the MTV program "Run's House." (Rev: SLJ 8/07)

20496 Tickle, Phyllis. *This Is What I Pray Today: The Divine Hours Prayers for Children* (PS–1). Illus. by Elsa Warnick. 2007, Dutton $15.99 (978-0-525-47828-7). 32pp. This illustrated book offers three short simple prayers for different parts of each day of the week. (Rev: BL 10/1/07) [811]

20497 Winter, Rebecca. *Prayers for Children* (2–4). Illus. by Helen Cann. 2005, Good Bks. $14.99 (978-1-56148-470-6). 160pp. More than 200 prayers, traditional and new, come from different countries and cover a wide variety of subjects. (Rev: BL 6/1–15/05) [242]

Social Groups

Ethnic Groups

20498 Aliotta, Jerome J. *The Puerto Ricans* (5–8). Series: Land of Immigrants. 1995, Chelsea LB $21.95 (978-0-7910-3360-9). This account provides an extensive history of Puerto Ricans living in the United States, their struggles, traditions, and way of life. (Rev: BL 10/15/95) [305.868]

20499 Archibald, Erika F. *A Sudanese Family* (4–7). Illus. Series: Journey Between Two Worlds. 1997, Lerner paper $8.95 (978-0-8225-9753-7). 56pp. Introduces Dei Jock Dei and his family, who left Sudan to escape religious persecution and, through the help of a church, settled in Atlanta, Georgia. (Rev: BL 6/1–15/97; SLJ 7/97) [975.8]

20500 Ashabranner, Brent. *The New African Americans* (5–9). Illus. 1999, Linnet LB $22.50 (978-0-208-02420-6). 105pp. After a brief history of early African immigration and slavery, this account focuses on present-day immigrants — where they come from and their reception in the United States. (Rev: BCCB 12/99; BL 10/15/99; HB 11/99; HBG 3/00; VOYA 12/00) [304.87]

20501 Bandon, Alexandra. *Dominican Americans* (5–8). Illus. Series: Footsteps to America. 1995, New Discovery $22.00 (978-0-02-768152-9). 111pp. A readable account of why many residents of the Dominican Republic left their country to come to the United States and the conditions they found. (Rev: SLJ 8/95) [973]

20502 Banks, William H., Jr. *The Black Muslims* (5–10). Series: African-American Achievers. 1996, Chelsea LB $21.95 (978-0-7910-2593-2); paper $30.00 (978-0-7910-2594-9). The story of the founding of the Nation of Islam, its leaders, the Million Man March, and the reign of Louis Farrakhan. (Rev: SLJ 5/97) [323]

20503 Behnke, Alison. *Mexicans in America* (4–8). Series: In America. 2004, Lerner LB $27.93 (978-0-8225-3955-1). 80pp. The reasons for Mexican migration to the United States and the life the new-comers find when they arrive are discussed in engaging narrative, with personal stories, notes on key figures, illustrations, and a timeline. (Rev: SLJ 3/05) [304.8]

20504 Berg, Lois Anne. *An Eritrean Family* (4–7). Illus. Series: Journey Between Two Worlds. 1997, Lerner LB $22.60 (978-0-8225-3405-1); paper $8.95 (978-0-8225-9755-1). 64pp. The story of the Kiklu family, which fled Eritrea in eastern Africa in 1978, spent 10 years in a refugee camp, and resettled in Minnesota. (Rev: BL 6/1–15/97; SLJ 8/97) [304.895]

20505 Berger, Melvin, and Gilda Berger. *Where Did Your Family Come From? A Book About Immigrants* (2–3). Illus. by Robert Quackenbush. Series: Discovery Readers. 1993, Ideals paper $4.50 (978-0-8249-8610-0). 48pp. A simple text about the waves of immigration to the United States. (Rev: BCCB 4/93; BL 7/93; SLJ 6/93) [325.73]

20506 Binns, Tristan Boyer. *Chinese Americans* (3–5). Series: We Are America. 2003, Heinemann LB $24.22 (978-1-4034-0162-5). 32pp. Binns explores the challenges and hardships faced by Chinese immigrants to America and the many contributions they have made to society as a whole. Also use *Mexican Americans* (2003). (Rev: HBG 10/03; SLJ 8/03) [973]

20507 Birdseye, Debbie H., and Tom Birdseye. *Under Our Skin: Kids Talk About Race* (4–8). 1997, Holiday $15.95 (978-0-8234-1325-6). In separate chapters, six 8th-grade students in Oregon from different racial and ethnic backgrounds talk about race and what racism means to them. (Rev: HBG 3/98; SLJ 4/98) [572.973]

20508 Bolden, Tonya. *Tell All the Children Our Story: Memories and Mementos of Being Young and Black in America* (4–8). Illus. 2002, Abrams $24.95 (978-0-8109-4496-1). 128pp. From the first recorded birth of a black child in the United States to the Million Man March, this book describes the African American experience through both personal and historical accounts, using a scrapbook format. (Rev:

BL 2/15/02; HB 3/02; HBG 10/02; SLJ 3/02*; VOYA 4/02) [973]

20509 Bryan, Nichol. *Haitian Americans* (3–5). Series: One Nation. 2004, ABDO LB $22.78 (978-1-57765-982-2). 32pp. A look at immigration from Haiti (both legal and illegal), the reasons behind it, what happens to the immigrants once they are in the United States, and the contributions they make to the culture in their new country. Also use *Mexican Americans* (2004). (Rev: HBG 4/04; SLJ 3/04) [973]

20510 Burgan, Michael. *African Americans* (3–5). Illus. Series: Our Cultural Heritage. 2004, Child's World LB $27.07 (978-1-59296-012-5). 32pp. Covers migration from America to the United States, emphasizing that in the early years few came by choice, with material on native culture, ethnic background, and contributions to present-day American society. [973]

20511 Burgan, Michael. *Italian Immigrants* (5–8). Series: Immigration to the United States. 2004, Facts on File $35.00 (978-0-8160-5681-1). 96pp. After an overview of the reasons underlying immigration in general, this illustrated volume looks at the circumstances of migrants from Italy, the group's history in the United States, and the contemporary situation, with sidebar features, a timeline, and a glossary. (Rev: SLJ 4/05)

20512 Cannarella, Deborah. *Cuban Americans* (3–5). Illus. Series: Our Cultural Heritage. 2004, Child's World LB $27.07 (978-1-59296-013-2). 32pp. Covers Cuban migration to the United States, with material on native culture, ethnic background, and the impact on present-day American society.

20513 Catalano, Julie. *The Mexican Americans* (5–8). Illus. Series: Immigrant Experience. 1995, Chelsea LB $14.95 (978-0-7910-3359-3); paper $9.95 (978-0-7910-3381-4). 100pp. This book traces the reasons for leaving Mexico, the immigrants' reception in the United States, and their contributions and achievements. (Rev: BL 11/15/95; SLJ 1/96) [973]

20514 Cavan, Seamus. *The Irish-American Experience* (5–7). Illus. Series: Coming to America. 1993, Millbrook LB $23.40 (978-1-56294-218-2). 64pp. Beginning with the potato famine that forced millions of Irish to come to America, this is the story of the rise of Irish Americans to positions of prominence. (Rev: BCCB 4/93; BL 6/1–15/93) [973]

20515 Clinton, Catherine. *The Black Soldier: 1492 to the Present* (5–8). Illus. 2000, Houghton $17.00 (978-0-395-67722-3). 128pp. This history of African Americans in the army begins with colonial slaves who were given muskets to fight the Indians and continues through each of America's wars to the present with emphasis on the slow progress toward equality in the ranks. (Rev: BCCB 10/00; BL 9/15/00; HBG 3/01; SLJ 10/00; VOYA 2/01) [355]

20516 Cole, Harriette, and John Pinderhuges. *Coming Together: Celebrations for African American Families* (4–12). Illus. 2003, Hyperion $22.99 (978-0-7868-0753-6). 128pp. Traditions surrounding celebrations including Christmas, Kwanzaa, and naming ceremonies are covered here, with accompanying crafts, menu suggestions, and activities. (Rev: BL 12/15/03; HBG 4/04; VOYA 2/04) [306.8]

20517 Cole, Melanie, et al. *Famous People of Hispanic Heritage* (4–7). Series: Contemporary American Success Stories. 1997, Mitchell Lane LB $21.95 (978-1-883845-44-5); paper $12.95 (978-1-883845-43-8). 96pp. This useful series, now in nine volumes, profiles famous Hispanics, past and present, from around the world. (Rev: BL 3/15/98; HBG 3/98) [920]

20518 Cole, Michael D. *The Los Angeles Riots: Rage in the City of Angels* (5–9). Series: American Disasters. 1999, Enslow LB $23.93 (978-0-7660-1219-6). An account of the police beating of Rodney King in Los Angeles and the subsequent riots, the worst in U.S. history. (Rev: BL 2/1/99; HBG 10/99; SLJ 6/99) [979.494053]

20519 Coleman, Lori. *Vietnamese in America* (4–8). Series: In America. 2004, Lerner LB $27.93 (978-0-8225-3951-3). 72pp. The reasons for Vietnamese migration to the United States and the life the newcomers find when they arrive are discussed in engaging narrative, with personal stories, notes on key figures, illustrations, and a timeline. Also use *Koreans in America* (2004). (Rev: BL 11/15/04; SLJ 3/05) [973]

20520 Cunningham, Kevin. *Canadian Americans* (3–5). Illus. Series: Our Cultural Heritage. 2004, Child's World LB $27.07 (978-1-59296-178-8). 32pp. Covers Canadian migration to the United States, with material on native culture, ethnic background, and contributions to present-day American society.

20521 Daley, William. *The Chinese Americans* (5–8). Illus. 1995, Chelsea LB $21.95 (978-0-7910-3357-9); paper $9.95 (978-0-7910-3379-1). 112pp. The background and culture of this group are explained, as well as its adjustment to life in America. (Rev: BL 1/1/88) [973.04951]

20522 De Capua, Sarah E. *Irish Americans* (3–5). Series: Spirit of America: Our Cultural Heritage. 2002, Child's World LB $27.07 (978-1-56766-155-2). 32pp. De Capua discusses the reasons for Irish migration to the United States and the lasting contributions this group has made. (Rev: BL 10/15/02) [973]

20523 Di Franco, J. Philip. *The Italian Americans* (5–8). Illus. 1995, Chelsea LB $14.95 (978-0-7910-3353-1); paper $9.95 (978-0-7910-3375-3). 112pp. A heavily illustrated discussion of the culture that Italian immigrants left behind and their contributions to American life. (Rev: BL 1/1/88) [973.0451]

20524 Feelings, Tom. *Tommy Traveler in the World of Black History* (5–8). 1991, Black Butterfly $13.95 (978-0-86316-202-2). A history of African Americans seen through the eyes of a boy who imagines himself participating in the important events. (Rev: BL 9/15/91; SLJ 2/92) [973]

20525 Fitterer, C. Ann. *German Americans* (3–5). Series: Spirit of America: Our Cultural Heritage. 2002, Child's World LB $27.07 (978-1-56766-151-

4). 32pp. Fitterer discusses German migration to the United States and the contributions of this community. (Rev: BL 10/15/02; SLJ 2/03) [973]

20526 Fitterer, C. Ann. *Russian Americans* (3–5). Series: Spirit of America: Our Cultural Heritage. 2002, Child's World LB $27.07 (978-1-56766-158-3). 32pp. Russian migration to the United States is discussed in this richly illustrated account that includes material on famous immigrants. (Rev: BL 10/15/02; SLJ 12/02) [973]

20527 Franchino, Vicky. *Italian Americans* (3–5). Series: Spirit of America: Our Cultural Heritage. 2002, Child's World LB $27.07 (978-1-56766-153-8). 32pp. How Italian immigrants changed American life is one of the topics discussed in this simple account of why and how they came to this country, their reception, and a rundown of famous Italian Americans. Also use *British Americans* and *Spanish Americans* (both 2002). (Rev: BL 10/15/02) [973]

20528 Freeman, Dena. *How People Live* (3–6). 2003, DK $29.99 (978-0-7894-9867-0). 304pp. Organized by continent, this ambitious volume full of photographs explores many different cultures and is suitable for browsing. (Rev: HBG 4/04; SLJ 2/04) [306]

20529 Frost, Helen. *Russian Immigrants: 1860–1915* (4–6). Series: Coming to America. 2002, Capstone LB $23.93 (978-0-7368-1209-2). 32pp. After a look at why Russians left their country to migrate to the United States, this account covers their destinations, culture, and contributions. (Rev: BL 1/1–15/03; HBG 3/03; SLJ 3/03) [973]

20530 Gabor, A. *Polish Americans* (4–6). Illus. Series: Cultures of America. 1995, Marshall Cavendish $19.95 (978-1-76140-154-1). 80pp. After a description of life in Poland, this account describes the history of Polish Americans and various aspects of their culture. (Rev: BL 7/95) [305.89]

20531 Galicich, Anne. *The German Americans* (5–8). Illus. Series: Immigrant Experience. 1995, Chelsea LB $19.95 (978-0-7910-3362-3); paper $13.25 (978-0-7910-3384-5). 120pp. This account traces the history of German Americans, from their reasons for leaving Germany and their initial reception in the United States to their present status. (Rev: BL 4/1/89) [973]

20532 Gernand, Renee. *The Cuban Americans* (5–8). Illus. 1995, Chelsea LB $21.95 (978-0-7910-3354-8); paper $9.95 (978-0-7910-3376-0). 112pp. The contributions of Cuban Americans and reasons why they came to America. (Rev: BL 2/1/89) [973.0468729]

20533 Goldish, Meish. *Immigration: How Should It Be Controlled?* (4–6). Illus. Series: Issues of Our Time. 1994, Twenty-First Century LB $18.90 (978-0-8050-3182-9). 64pp. Contains historical information about immigration plus material on citizenship laws, illegal aliens, and the pros and cons of allowing more immigrants into the United States. (Rev: SLJ 7/94) [304.8]

20534 Goldstein, Margaret J. *Irish in America* (5–8). Series: In America. 2004, Lerner LB $27.93 (978-0-8225-3950-6). 80pp. This overview of Irish migration to the United States looks at the underlying reasons for the exodus and explores the lives of the

new arrivals and the traditions they maintained. (Rev: BL 11/15/04) [973]

20535 Goldstein, Margaret J. *Japanese in America* (4–7). Series: In America. 2006, Lerner LB $27.93 (978-0-8225-3952-0). 80pp. The author discusses the history of U.S.-Japan relations and the course of Japanese immigration to America from the 1800s to today, including the internments during World War II; profiles of famous Japanese Americans are appended. (Rev: SLJ 5/06) [973.0495]

20536 Greenfield, Eloise, and Lessie Jones Little. *Childtimes: A Three-Generation Memoir* (5–8). Illus. by Jerry Pinkney. 1979, HarperCollins LB $16.89 (978-0-690-03875-0); paper $9.99 (978-0-06-446134-4). 160pp. The childhoods of three generations of African American women.

20537 Haberle, Susan E. *Jewish Immigrants: 1880–1924* (4–6). Series: Coming to America. 2002, Capstone LB $23.93 (978-0-7368-1207-8). 32pp. A brief overview of why Jews left Europe, plus an account of where they settled in America, their cultural contributions, and a list of famous Jewish Americans. (Rev: BL 1/1–15/03; HBG 3/03) [973]

20538 Hamanaka, Sheila. *The Journey: Japanese Americans, Racism and Renewal* (5–9). Illus. by author. 1990, Orchard LB $20.99 (978-0-531-08449-6). 39pp. With brief text, this book is a series of paintings from a large mural that describes the injustices suffered by Japanese Americans at the beginning of World War II. (Rev: BL 3/15/90; HB 5/90; SLJ 5/90; VOYA 6/90) [940.54]

20539 Harkrader, Lisa. *South Korea* (5–8). Illus. Series: Top Ten Countries of Recent Immigrants. 2004, Enslow LB $25.26 (978-0-7660-5181-2). 48pp. Information on South Korea — culture, history, climate, and people — accompanies an explanation of the reasons for migration to the United States and discussion of the contributions of this community; supported by Web links. (Rev: SLJ 3/05) [304]

20540 Heinrichs, Ann. *French Americans* (3–5). Illus. Series: Our Cultural Heritage. 2004, Child's World LB $27.07 (978-1-59296-180-1). 32pp. Covers French migration to the United States, with material on the group's native culture, ethnic background, and the impact they have had on present-day American society.

20541 Heinrichs, Ann. *Norwegian Americans* (3–5). Illus. Series: Our Cultural Heritage. 2004, Child's World LB $27.07 (978-1-59296-182-5). 32pp. Covers Norwegian migration to the United States, with material on the group's native culture, ethnic background, and the impact they have had on present-day American society.

20542 Herron, Carolivia. *Always an Olivia* (1–3). Illus. by Jeremy Tugeau. 2007, Lerner $17.95 (978-0-8225-7049-3). 32pp. Using a fictionalized framework in which Great-grandma Olivia tells Carol Olivia about their family's experiences beginning during the Spanish Inquisition, Herron traces her African American-Jewish roots. (Rev: BL 11/1/07; LMC 11/07; SLJ 10/07) [813.54]

20543 Hopkinson, Deborah. *Shutting Out the Sky* (5–12). Illus. 2003, Scholastic $17.95 (978-0-439-

37590-0). 144pp. Five personal stories of young immigrants, striking photographs, and excerpts from primary documents form the backbone of this history of immigration to New York City in the late 19th century. (Rev: BL 11/1/03*; HBG 4/04; SLJ 12/03*; VOYA 6/04) [307.76]

20544 Horton, Casey. *The Jews* (4–8). Series: We Came to North America. 2000, Crabtree LB $25.27 (978-0-7787-0187-3); paper $8.95 (978-0-7787-0201-6). 32pp. As well as discussing the reasons why Jews left Europe, this account describes the trip across the Atlantic, reception in America, and the many contributions to the United States. (Rev: SLJ 10/00) [973]

20545 Hossell, Karen. *Pakistani Americans* (3–5). Series: We Are America. 2004, Heinemann LB $24.22 (978-1-4034-5023-4). 32pp. A story about a young Pakistani's arrival in America introduces this overview of immigration from Pakistan that looks at history, cultural life, and contributions to the United States, with a map, a chart, and a timeline. (Rev: SLJ 11/04) [973]

20546 Hoyt-Goldsmith, Diane. *Hoang Anh: A Vietnamese-American Boy* (3–5). Illus. by Lawrence Migdale. Series: Cornerstones of Freedom. 1992, Holiday House LB $16.95 (978-0-8234-0948-8). 32pp. Color photos and a first-person narrative describe the life of a Vietnamese boy living in California. (Rev: BCCB 4/92; BL 4/15/92; HB 5/92; SLJ 4/92) [378.1]

20547 Hunter, David. *Teen Life Among the Amish and Other Alternative Communities: Choosing a Lifestyle* (5–8). Series: Youth in Rural North America. 2007, Mason Crest LB $22.95 (978-1-4222-0017-9). 96pp. Hunter introduces readers to the traditions and beliefs of Amish and other alternative communities found around the United States and Canada (including monasteries and kibbutzim), emphasizing how teens in these groupings cope with their different lifestyles; includes many photographs. (Rev: LMC 3/08; SLJ 2/08)

20548 Ingram, Scott. *Greek Immigrants* (5–8). Series: Immigration to the United States. 2004, Facts on File $35.00 (978-0-8160-5689-7). 96pp. After an overview of the reasons underlying immigration in general, this illustrated volume looks at the circumstances of migrants from Greece, the group's history in the United States, and the contemporary situation, with sidebar features, a timeline, and a glossary. Also use *Japanese Immigrants* and *Polish Immigrants* (both 2004). (Rev: BL 4/1/04; HB 3/04; SLJ 4/05)

20549 Kitano, Harry. *The Japanese Americans*. 2nd ed. (5–8). Photos by Richard Hewett. Series: Land of Immigrants. 1995, Chelsea LB $19.95 (978-0-7910-3358-6); paper $9.95 (978-0-7910-3380-7). 92pp. The story of Japanese Americans and their traditions and contributions to American life and culture. (Rev: BL 10/15/95; VOYA 2/96) [305]

20550 Knight, Margy B. *Who Belongs Here? An American Story* (4–7). Illus. by Anne S. O'Brien. 1993, Tilbury House $16.95 (978-0-88448-110-2). 40pp. The story of 10-year-old Nari, who survived

the killing fields of Cambodia and found a new life in the United States. (Rev: BL 3/1/94; SLJ 10/93) [305.895]

20551 Koenig, Angela T. *Pakistani Americans* (3–5). Series: Spirit of America: Our Cultural Heritage. 2003, Child's World LB $27.07 (978-1-59296-017-0). 32pp. Explores the history behind immigration to the United States from Pakistan, the influences this ethnic group has had on American culture, and life today. (Rev: SLJ 2/04) [973]

20552 Kroll, Virginia. *With Love, to Earth's Endangered Peoples* (3–6). Illus. by Roberta Collier-Morales. 1998, Dawn $17.95 (978-1-883220-83-9); paper $8.95 (978-1-883220-82-2). This book deals with such endangered peoples as the Australian aborigine, the Inuit, the Toda of India, and the Ainu of Japan. (Rev: HBG 3/99; SLJ 12/98) [910]

20553 Kuropas, Myron B. *Ukrainians in America* (5–7). Illus. Series: In America. 1996, Lerner LB $19.93 (978-0-8225-1043-7). 80pp. The story of Ukrainian immigrants to the United States, their cultural traditions, and their contributions to American life. (Rev: BL 3/15/96; SLJ 3/96) [973]

20554 Kyuchukov, Hristo, and Ian Hancock. *A History of the Romani People* (3–5). Illus. 2005, Boyds Mills $19.95 (978-1-56397-962-0). 48pp. An introductory overview of the history, culture, and language of the Roma or Gypsy people. (Rev: BL 12/1/05; SLJ 11/05) [909]

20555 Leder, Jane. *A Russian Jewish Family* (5–8). Series: Journey Between Two Worlds. 1996, Lerner LB $22.60 (978-0-8225-3401-3); paper $8.95 (978-0-8225-9744-5). This account compares the living conditions of a Jewish family in Russia and in their new American home. (Rev: BL 11/1/96; SLJ 11/96) [977.3]

20556 Levete, Sarah. *Being an Immigrant* (3–5). Series: Let's Talk About. 2007, Stargazer LB $27.10 (978-1-59604-084-7). 32pp. Readers will learn why immigrants come to the United States and what it's like to be part of an immigrant family. (Rev: SLJ 6/07)

20557 Lingen, Marissa. *The Jewish Americans* (4–7). Illus. Series: We Came to America. 2002, Mason Crest LB $19.95 (978-1-59084-109-9). 64pp. Lingen traces the history of Jewish migration to the United States and provides a list of Jewish Americans of note. (Rev: SLJ 9/02) [973.049]

20558 Lingen, Marissa. *The Jewish Americans* (5–8). Illus. Series: Major American Immigration. 2008, Mason Crest $22.95 (978-1-4222-0611-9). 64pp. Lingen provides a thorough overview of Jewish migration to the United States going back to the colonial and revolutionary eras, with information on German Jews, Jews from Eastern Europe, and the impact of the Holocaust, plus profiles of key figures. (Rev: BL 5/15/09) [973]

20559 Lock, Donna. *The Polish Americans* (5–8). Illus. Series: We Came to America. 2002, Mason Crest LB $19.95 (978-1-59084-112-9). 64pp. A look at the customs and contributions of this ethnic group, including information on famous Polish Americans, with a bibliography, glossary, timeline, and resources for tracing ancestors. (Rev: BL 7/02) [305.891]

20560 Lomas Garza, Carmen. *Family Pictures / Cuadros de Familia* (3–7). Illus. 1990, Children's Book Pr. paper $7.95 (978-0-89239-108-0). 32pp. A Mexican American artist shares memories of her childhood in Texas. (Rev: BCCB 10/90; BL 6/1/90; SLJ 11/90*) [306]

20561 McDaniel, Melissa. *Japanese Americans* (3–5). Series: Spirit of America: Our Cultural Heritage. 2002, Child's World LB $27.07 (978-1-56766-154-5). 32pp. The history of Japanese migration to the United States is discussed, with material on the the discrimination the new citizens faced and the many ways in which they have changed American culture. (Rev: BL 10/15/02; SLJ 12/02) [973]

20562 McGill, Allyson. *The Swedish Americans* (5–8). Series: Immigrant Experience. 1997, Chelsea $19.95 (978-0-7910-4551-0); paper $9.95 (978-0-7910-4552-7). 107pp. Explains why Swedes have emigrated from their homeland, their reception in the United States, and their contributions to the nation. (Rev: BL 10/15/97) [322.4]

20563 McQuinn, Anna. *My Friend Jamal* (PS–1). Illus. by author. Series: My Friend. 2008, Annick $17.95 (978-1-55451-123-5); paper $8.95 (978-1-55451-122-8). 32pp. Two immigrant boys — Jamal from Somalia and Joseph from Poland — enjoy a close friendship despite their different lives. (Rev: BL 6/1–15/08; SLJ 6/08) [823]

20564 Maestro, Betsy. *Coming to America: The Story of Immigration* (K–3). Illus. by Susannah Ryan. 1996, Scholastic $16.95 (978-0-590-44151-3). 40pp. A picture-book introduction to what the many waves of immigrants have meant to the United States. (Rev: BCCB 2/96; BL 2/1/96; SLJ 5/96) [304]

20565 Magocsi, Paul R. *The Russian Americans* (5–8). Illus. Series: Immigrant Experience. 1995, Chelsea LB $21.95 (978-0-7910-3367-8). 110pp. Coverage includes reasons for leaving Russia, customs and traditions, contributions to their new nation, and famous Russian Americans. (Rev: BL 11/15/95; SLJ 1/96) [973]

20566 Mendez, Adriana. *Cubans in America* (5–7). Illus. Series: In America. 1994, Lerner LB $19.93 (978-0-8225-1953-9). 80pp. An account that describes why Cubans left their homeland, where they live in the United States, their lifestyles, and their contributions to society. (Rev: BL 8/94; SLJ 8/94) [973]

20567 Morris, Ann. *Grandma Esther Remembers: A Jewish-American Family Story* (1–3). Series: What Was It Like, Grandma? 2002, Millbrook LB $22.90 (978-0-7613-2318-1). 32pp. In double-page spreads (with a picture opposite a page of simple text), a Jewish American grandmother describes her life in the old country and her early experiences in the United States. (Rev: BL 9/15/02; HBG 10/02; SLJ 6/02) [973]

20568 Morris, Ann. *Grandma Francisca Remembers: A Mexican-American Family Story* (1–3). Illus. by Peter Linenthal. Series: What Was It Like, Grandma? 2002, Millbrook LB $22.90 (978-0-7613-2315-0). 32pp. Some Spanish vocabulary, a recipe for stew, and instructions for making a sock doll accompany this account of the activities of a young Mexican American girl and her grandmother. (Rev: BL 2/15/02; HBG 10/02; SLJ 4/02) [973]

20569 Morris, Ann. *Grandma Lai Goon Remembers: A Chinese-American Family Story* (1–3). Series: What Was It Like, Grandma? 2002, Millbrook LB $22.90 (978-0-7613-2314-3). 32pp. Activities such as making a Chinese doll, making Chinese buns, and playing a Chinese game complement the story of a Chinese American grandmother's life. (Rev: BL 9/15/02; HBG 10/02; SLJ 6/02) [973]

20570 Morris, Ann. *Grandma Lois Remembers: An African-American Family Story* (1–3). Series: What Was It Like, Grandma? 2002, Millbrook LB $22.90 (978-0-7613-2316-7). 32pp. An African American grandmother tells the family history to her grandson, with appended activities and games. (Rev: BL 9/15/02; HBG 10/02; SLJ 3/02) [976.1]

20571 Morris, Ann. *Grandma Susan Remembers: A British-American Family Story* (1–3). Series: What Was It Like, Grandma? 2002, Millbrook LB $22.90 (978-0-7613-2319-8). 32pp. A grandmother who was born in Britain recalls her childhood and the culture of the land she left. Activities are appended. (Rev: BL 9/15/02; HBG 10/02; SLJ 6/02) [973]

20572 Muggamin, Howard. *The Jewish Americans* (5–8). Series: Immigrant Experience. 1995, Chelsea LB $19.95 (978-0-7910-3365-4); paper $9.95 (978-0-7910-3387-6). An examination of Jewish Americans, their history of immigration and their reception in this country, and their achievements and contributions. (Rev: BL 11/15/95) [973]

20573 Murphy, Nora. *A Hmong Family* (4–7). Illus. Series: Journey Between Two Worlds. 1997, Lerner LB $27.15 (978-0-8225-3406-8); paper $8.95 (978-0-8225-9756-8). 64pp. After fleeing Laos in 1975 to escape the Communists, this family spent time in a refugee camp in Thailand before settling in Minneapolis, Minnesota. (Rev: BL 6/1–15/97; SLJ 8/97) [305.895]

20574 Nichols, Catherine. *African American Culture* (4–6). Series: Discovering the Arts. 2006, Advantage World LB $125.70 (978-1-59515-516-0). 48pp. A concise history of African American arts, introducing key figures and placing them in historical context. (Rev: BL 2/1/06) [704.03]

20575 Ochoa, George. *The New York Public Library Amazing Hispanic American History: A Book of Answers for Kids* (4–9). 1998, Wiley paper $12.95 (978-0-471-19204-6). Using a question-and-answer format, this work explores such topics as Hispanic American identity and history, cultural groups, accomplishments, and immigrant experiences. (Rev: BL 12/1/98; SLJ 11/98) [973]

20576 O'Connor, Karen. *Dan Thuy's New Life in America* (4–8). Illus. 1992, Lerner LB $19.93 (978-0-8225-2555-4). 40pp. A photoessay of a 13-year-old Vietnamese girl and her family, newly arrived in San Diego. (Rev: BL 9/15/92; SLJ 9/92) [325]

20577 O'Connor, Karen. *A Kurdish Family* (5–8). Series: Journey Between Two Worlds. 1996, Lerner LB $22.60 (978-0-8225-3402-0); paper $8.95 (978-0-8225-9743-8). This work describes the living conditions endured by a Kurdish family in their homeland and their new life in the United States. (Rev: BCCB 12/96; BL 11/1/96; SLJ 11/96) [305.891]

20578 O'Hara, Megan. *Irish Immigrants: 1840–1920* (4–6). Series: Coming to America. 2001, Capstone LB $23.93 (978-0-7368-0795-1). 32pp. This account, complete with many reader activities, takes a quick look at Irish history, explains why the migrants left their country, and describes their reception in the United States and their contributions to American life. (Rev: BL 10/15/01; HBG 3/02; SLJ 1/02) [973]

20579 Olson, Kay Melchisedech. *Chinese Immigrants: 1850–1900* (4–6). Series: Coming to America. 2001, Capstone LB $23.93 (978-0-7368-0793-7). 32pp. Using many sidebars, recipes, and suggested activities, this book tells how and why the Chinese originally came to the United States and the contributions they have made to American culture. (Rev: BL 10/15/01; HBG 3/02) [973]

20580 Olson, Kay Melchisedech. *French Immigrants: 1840–1940* (4–6). Series: Coming to America. 2002, Capstone LB $23.93 (978-0-7368-1205-4). 32pp. Covers the reasons why French citizens left their country for America and gives details of their struggle to retain their traditions, of their contributions, and the lives of famous immigrants and their descendants. (Rev: BL 1/1–15/03; HBG 3/03) [973]

20581 Omoto, Susan. *Hmong Milestones in America: Citizens in a New World* (5–8). Illus. 2003, John Gordon Burke $27.00 (978-0-934272-57-5); paper $15.00 (978-0-934272-56-8). 64pp. The author introduces the Hmong people's history and traditions and traces the steps of Hmong refugees who migrated to the United States, profiling five individuals who have found success in their new country. (Rev: BL 4/15/03) [973]

20582 Orr, Tamra. *The Korean Americans* (5–8). Illus. Series: Major American Immigration. 2009, Mason Crest LB $22.95 (978-1-4222-0612-6). 64pp. Orr provides a thorough overview of migration from Korea to the United States, with information on the history of Korea, the reasons for leaving the country, and the "picture brides" who arrived here in the early 20th century, plus profiles of key figures. (Rev: BL 5/15/09) [973]

20583 Parker, Lewis K. *Why Japanese Immigrants Came to America* (2–5). Series: Coming to America. 2003, Rosen LB $19.95 (978-0-8239-6463-5). 24pp. A brief overview of the experience of Japanese immigrants to America, the first major wave of whom arrived in Hawaii in 1885. (Rev: SLJ 10/03) [973]

20584 Parker, Lewis K. *Why Mexican Immigrants Came to America* (2–5). Series: Coming to America. 2003, Rosen LB $19.95 (978-0-8239-6459-8). 24pp. Examines the reasons underlying Mexican immigration to the United States and the contributions this group has made to American society. (Rev: SLJ 10/03) [304.8]

20585 Parker, Lewis K. *Why Vietnamese Immigrants Came to America* (2–5). Series: Coming to America. 2003, Rosen LB $19.95 (978-0-8239-6461-1). 24pp. Focuses on the influx of Vietnamese immigrants that began in the 1960s, emphasizing the contributions this group has made to American society. (Rev: SLJ 10/03) [304.8]

20586 Patrick, Diane. *The New York Public Library Amazing African American History: A Book of Answers for Kids* (5–9). Illus. 1998, Wiley paper $12.95 (978-0-471-19217-6). Using a question-and-answer format, this book traces the history of African Americans from slavery to the present day. (Rev: BL 2/15/98; SLJ 4/98) [973]

20587 Paulson, Timothy J. *Irish Immigrants* (5–8). Series: Immigration to the United States. 2004, Facts on File $35.00 (978-0-8160-5682-8). 96pp. After an overview of the reasons underlying immigration in general, this illustrated volume looks at the circumstances of migrants from Ireland, the group's history in the United States, and the contemporary situation, with sidebar features, a timeline, and a glossary. (Rev: SLJ 4/05)

20588 Perl, Lila. *North Across the Border: The Story of the Mexican Americans* (5–9). Series: Great Journeys. 2001, Benchmark LB $32.79 (978-0-7614-1226-7). 112pp. The economic and social reasons for Mexican migration to the north through history are presented in text, quotations from primary sources, and many illustrations and maps. (Rev: BL 1/1–15/02; HBG 10/02; SLJ 3/02) [973.0468]

20589 Peterson, Tiffany. *Greek Americans* (3–5). Series: We Are America. 2004, Heinemann LB $24.22 (978-1-4034-5021-0). 32pp. A personal story introduces this overview of immigration from Greece that looks at history, cultural life, and contributions to the United States, with a map, a chart, and a timeline. Also use *Japanese Americans* (2004), which includes material on internment. (Rev: SLJ 11/04) [973]

20590 Petrillo, Valerie. *A Kid's Guide to Asian American History: More than 90 Activities* (3–6). 2007, Chicago Review paper $14.95 (978-1-55652-634-3). 256pp. Crafts, games, and other activities introduce various aspects of Asian American cultures. (Rev: BL 4/15/07; SLJ 5/07) [973.3]

20591 Petrillo, Valerie. *A Kid's Guide to Latino History: More than 50 Activities* (4–8). Illus. 2009, Chicago Review paper $14.95 (978-1-55652-771-5). 208pp. This is a sweeping introduction to the history of Hispanic Americans in the United States, covering the countries they came from, the reasons they left, and their reception and contributions here, with profiles of key figures and discussion of such issues as bilingual education; activities include crafts, dancing, writing stories, and so forth. (Rev: BL 6/1–15/09) [973]

20592 Press, Petra. *Puerto Ricans* (4–6). Illus. Series: Cultures of America. 1996, Marshall Cavendish LB $19.95 (978-0-7614-0160-5). 80pp. A nicely illustrated description of the island of Puerto Rico details the customs, traditions, and contributions of its people. (Rev: BL 5/15/96) [973]

20593 Raatma, Lucia. *Chinese Americans* (3–5). Illus. Series: Spirit of America: Our Cultural Heritage. 2002, Child's World LB $27.07 (978-1-56766-149-1). 32pp. An overview of the Chinese American experience that includes maps, timelines, and other visuals. (Rev: BL 10/15/02) [973]

20594 Raatma, Lucia. *Polish Americans* (3–5). Series: Spirit of America: Our Cultural Heritage. 2002, Child's World LB $27.07 (978-1-56766-157-6). 32pp. Provides a history of Polish migration to this country, with emphasis on the many contributions this group has made to American life and culture. (Rev: BL 10/15/02) [973]

20595 Raatma, Lucia. *Swedish Americans* (3–5). Series: Spirit of America: Our Cultural Heritage. 2002, Child's World LB $27.07 (978-1-56766-159-0). 32pp. Swedish migration to the United States is the topic of this work, with material on the group's native culture, ethnic background, and the impact they have had on present-day American society. (Rev: BL 10/15/02) [973]

20596 Rappaport, Doreen. *Free at Last! Stories and Songs of Emancipation* (4–8). Illus. by Shane W. Evans. 2004, Candlewick $19.99 (978-0-7636-1440-9). 64pp. First-hand accounts form the basis of this portrait of the black experience from emancipation to the 1954 Supreme Court decision declaring school segregation illegal. (Rev: BL 2/15/04*; HB 5/04; SLJ 2/04) [973]

20597 Rappaport, Doreen. *No More! Stories and Songs of Slave Resistance* (4–7). Illus. by Shane W. Evans. 2002, Candlewick $17.99 (978-0-7636-0984-9). 64pp. A collection of narratives, prose, poetry, and songs that describe the African slave experience and the various forms of rebellion that took place. (Rev: BCCB 4/02; BL 2/15/02; HB 3/02; HBG 10/02; SLJ 2/02*) [306.3]

20598 Rohmer, Harriet, ed. *Honoring Our Ancestors: Stories and Pictures by Fourteen Artists* (3–6). Illus. 1999, Children's Book Pr. $15.95 (978-0-89239-158-5). 32pp. A diverse group of artists from various ethnic groups honor family members and describe how they succeeded in America. (Rev: BCCB 3/99; BL 2/1/99; HBG 9/99; SLJ 6/99) [759.13]

20599 Rosenberg, Pam. *Jewish Americans* (3–5). Illus. Series: Our Cultural Heritage. 2004, Child's World LB $27.07 (978-1-59296-181-8). 32pp. Covers Jewish migration to the United States, with material on the group's native culture, ethnic background, and the impact they have had on present-day American society.

20600 Sanders, Nancy I. *D Is for Drinking Gourd: An African American Alphabet* (2–4). Illus. by E. B. Lewis. 2007, Sleeping Bear $17.95 (978-1-58536-293-6). 32pp. Four-line poems paired with watercolor paintings and historical information introduce African American topics from abolitionists through Harlem Renaissance, Malcolm X, and roots. (Rev: BL 9/1/07; LMC 1/08; SLJ 1/08) [973]

20601 Sawyers, June S. *Famous Firsts of Scottish-Americans* (4–8). Illus. 1996, Pelican $13.95 (978-1-56554-122-1). Brief biographies of 30 Americans of Scottish descent, including Neil Armstrong, Alexander Calder, Herman Melville, and Patrick Henry. (Rev: BL 6/1–15/97) [920]

20602 Schouweiler, Thomas. *Germans in America* (5–7). Illus. Series: In America. 1994, Lerner LB $19.93 (978-0-8225-0245-6). 72pp. The causes and results of German immigration to the United States are outlined, with good coverage of their contributions and important figures. (Rev: BL 1/15/95; SLJ 12/94) [973]

20603 Secakuku, Susan. *Meet Mindy: A Native Girl from the Southwest* (5–8). Photos by John Harrington. Series: My World: Young Native Americans Today. 2003, Beyond Words paper $15.95 (978-1-58270-091-5). 48pp. A Hopi teen named Mindy talks about her life and heritage in this full-color photoessay. (Rev: BL 4/1/03; SLJ 3/03) [979.1004]

20604 Silverman, Robin L. *A Bosnian Family* (4–7). Illus. Series: Journey Between Two Worlds. 1997, Lerner LB $27.15 (978-0-8225-3404-4); paper $8.95 (978-0-8225-9754-4). 64pp. The story of Velma Dusper, her homeland of Bosnia, and her journey with her family to freedom and a new home in North Dakota. (Rev: BL 6/1–15/97; SLJ 7/97) [304.8]

20605 Smith, Charles R., Jr. *I Am America* (1–3). Photos by author. 2003, Scholastic $14.95 (978-0-439-43179-8). Striking color photographs and simple text show children of multiple races and ethnicities. (Rev: HBG 4/04; SLJ 11/03) [305.23]

20606 Stanek, Muriel. *We Came from Vietnam* (4–6). Illus. 1985, Whitman LB $12.99 (978-0-8075-8699-0). 48pp. Photos and text focus on the Nguyen family from Vietnam, now settled in Chicago. (Rev: BCCB 11/85; BL 11/1/85)

20607 Straub, Deborah G., ed. *African American Voices* (5–8). Illus. 1996, Gale $126.00 (978-0-8103-9497-1). 320pp. This is a collection of excerpts from important speeches delivered by a vast array of African Americans, past and present. (Rev: SLJ 2/97) [973]

20608 Taus-Bolstad, Stacy. *Puerto Ricans in America* (5–8). Series: In America. 2004, Lerner LB $27.93 (978-0-8225-3953-7). 80pp. This overview of Puerto Rican migration to the United States looks at the motivations for moving and explores the lives of the new arrivals and the traditions they maintained. (Rev: BL 11/15/04) [304.8]

20609 Teitelbaum, Michael. *Chinese Immigrants* (5–8). Series: Immigration to the United States. 2004, Facts on File $35.00 (978-0-8160-5687-3). 96pp. After an overview of the reasons underlying immigration in general, this illustrated volume looks at the circumstances of migrants from China, the group's history in the United States, and the contemporary situation, with sidebar features, a timeline, and a glossary. (Rev: SLJ 4/05)

20610 Temple, Bob. *The Arab Americans* (5–8). Illus. Series: We Came to America. 2002, Mason Crest LB $19.95 (978-1-59084-102-0). 64pp. Temple reviews the history of Arab immigration to North America, the group's customs and contributions, and famous Arab Americans, with the aid of photographs, a timeline, and glossary. (Rev: BL 7/02; SLJ 9/02) [305.892]

20611 Todd, Anne M. *Italian Immigrants: 1880–1920* (4–6). Series: Coming to America. 2001, Capstone LB $23.93 (978-0-7368-0796-8). 32pp. The rich heritage and cultural contributions of Italian Americans are covered in this book that also explores why and how they came to the United States. (Rev: BL 10/15/01; HBG 3/02) [973]

20612 Trumbauer, Lisa. *German Immigrants* (5–8). Series: Immigration to the United States. 2004, Facts on File $35.00 (978-0-8160-5683-5). 96pp. After an overview of the reasons underlying immigration in general, this illustrated volume looks at the circumstances of migrants from Germany, the group's history in the United States, and the contemporary situation, with sidebar features, a timeline, and a glossary. Also use *Russian Immigrants* (2004). (Rev: SLJ 4/05)

20613 Wallner, Rosemary. *Greek Immigrants: 1890–1920* (4–6). Series: Coming to America. 2002, Capstone LB $23.93 (978-0-7368-1206-1). 32pp. Using many primary sources, this book traces the causes of Greek immigration and provides information on the Greek immigrants' journeys, culture, integration, and contributions. (Rev: BL 1/1–15/03; HBG 3/03; SLJ 3/03) [973]

20614 Wallner, Rosemary. *Japanese Immigrants: 1850–1950* (4–6). Series: Coming to America. 2001, Capstone LB $16.95 (978-0-7368-0797-5). 32pp. A century of Japanese migration to the United States is detailed with material on their contributions, cultural heritage, and treatment on arrival. (Rev: BL 10/15/01) [973]

20615 Wallner, Rosemary. *Polish Immigrants: 1890–1920* (4–6). Series: Coming to America. 2002, Capstone LB $23.93 (978-0-7368-1208-5). 32pp. The exodus from Poland to America is traced through text, timelines, maps, and personal memoirs, with material on such topics as Polish culture, contributions to American life, and famous Polish Americans. (Rev: BL 1/1–15/03; HBG 3/03) [973]

20616 Watts, J. F. *The Irish Americans* (5–8). Series: Immigrant Experience. 1995, Chelsea paper $9.95 (978-0-7910-3388-3). A lively, informative account of why the Irish came to America, the conditions they found here, and how they have fared. (Rev: BL 10/15/95) [973]

20617 Weber, Valerie J. *I Come from Afghanistan* (2–4). Illus. Series: This Is My Story. 2006, Gareth Stevens LB $21.00 (978-0-8368-7233-0). 24pp. Afghan American Bahishta, age 9, introduces readers to her family, Muslim faith, and cultural heritage in this series entry. (Rev: BL 1/1–15/07) [973]

20618 Weitzman, Elizabeth. *I Am Jewish American* (K–3). Series: Our American Family. 1998, Rosen LB $19.95 (978-0-8239-5006-5). 24pp. A young girl living in Chicago describes her feelings about her family and the Jewish American community of which she is a part. (Rev: SLJ 9/98) [973]

20619 Williams, Jean Kinney. *Asian Indian Americans* (3–5). Series: Spirit of America: Our Cultural Heritage. 2003, Child's World LB $27.07 (978-1-

59296-015-6). 32pp. A brief look at the history of Indian immigration to the United States and an assessment of the community's contributions to American culture and society. (Rev: SLJ 2/04) [973]

20620 Wolf, Bernard. *Coming to America: A Muslim Family's Story* (3–5). Illus. 2003, Lee & Low $17.95 (978-1-58430-086-1); paper $7.95 (978-1-58430-177-6). 48pp. This bright photoessay offers useful insights into Islam and its adherents as it tells the story of a Muslim family's migration from Egypt to the United States. (Rev: BL 4/1/03; HB 5/03; HBG 10/03; SLJ 5/03) [305.892]

20621 Worth, Richard. *Mexican Immigrants* (5–8). Series: Immigration to the United States. 2004, Facts on File $35.00 (978-0-8160-5690-3). 96pp. After an overview of the reasons underlying immigration in general, this illustrated volume looks at the circumstances of migrants from Mexico, the group's history in the United States, and the contemporary situation, with sidebar features, a timeline, and a glossary. Also use *Jewish Immigrants* and *Africans in America* (both 2004). (Rev: SLJ 4/05) [304.8]

20622 Wu, Dana Ying-Hul, and Jeffrey Dao-Sheng Tung. *The Chinese-American Experience* (5–7). Illus. Series: Coming to America. 1993, Millbrook LB $22.40 (978-1-56294-271-7). 64pp. The story of Chinese immigration to the United States, from exploitation, prejudice, and discrimination to gradual acceptance. (Rev: BL 6/1–15/93) [973]

20623 Yoder, Carolyn P. *Asian Indian Americans* (3–5). Series: We Are America. 2003, Heinemann LB $24.22 (978-1-4034-0167-0). 32pp. Yoder explores the challenges and hardships faced by Indian immigrants to America and the many contributions they have made to society as a whole. Also use *Italian Americans* (2003). (Rev: HBG 10/03; SLJ 8/03) [973]

Terrorism

20624 Bingley, Richard. *Terrorism* (5–9). Series: Face the Facts. 2003, Raintree LB $28.56 (978-0-7398-6852-2). 56pp. An examination of terrorism, its causes, and the efforts being made to combat it. (Rev: SLJ 4/04) [303.6]

20625 Deedy, Carmen A., and Wilson Kimeli Naiyomah. *14 Cows for America* (2–4). Illus. by Thomas Gonzalez. 2009, Peachtree $17.95 (978-1-56145-490-7). 36pp. A beautifully illustrated true story of an act of kindness and generosity from Africa to the United States after the tragedy of 9/11. (Rev: BL 7/09; LMC 11/09; SLJ 8/09*) [327.676073]

20626 Greene, Jacqueline D. *The 2001 World Trade Center Attack* (3–4). Series: Code Red. 2007, Bearport LB $23.96 (978-1-59716-365-1). 32pp. This look at the terrorist attacks of September 11, 2001, describes what happened that day and how emergency workers responded. (Rev: SLJ 8/07)

20627 Hamilton, John. *Behind the Terror* (4–7). Series: War on Terrorism. 2002, ABDO LB $16.95

(978-1-57765-679-1). 48pp. Using an accessible text and color photographs, this book reports on various international terrorist organizations, their leaders, and their tactics. (Rev: BL 5/15/02) [909.9]

20628 Hamilton, John. *Operation Enduring Freedom* (4–7). Series: War on Terrorism. 2002, ABDO LB $25.65 (978-1-57765-665-4). 48pp. Using many color photographs and a matter-of-fact text, this book covers various aspects of the U.S. war against terrorism. (Rev: BL 5/15/02; HBG 10/02) [973.9]

20629 Hamilton, John. *Operation Noble Eagle* (4–7). Series: War on Terrorism. 2002, ABDO LB $25.65 (978-1-57765-664-7). 48pp. A look at U.S. efforts to police and defend its borders as part of the war on terroism. (Rev: BL 5/15/02; HBG 10/02) [973.9]

20630 Lalley, Patrick. *9.11.01: Terrorists Attack the U.S* (4–7). Illus. 2002, Raintree LB $31.40 (978-0-7398-6021-2). 48pp. A compact look at the terrorist attacks of September 11, 2001, their causes, the world of Islam, the history of the World Trade Center, and personal stories related to the attacks. (Rev: BL 4/1/02; HBG 10/02; SLJ 5/02; VOYA 8/02) [303.6250]

20631 Louis, Nancy. *Heroes of the Day* (4–7). Series: War on Terrorism. 2002, ABDO LB $25.65 (978-1-57765-658-6). 48pp. This account of September 11, 2001, describes through pictures and case studies the gallant feats of firefighters, police, and those who fought back on Flight 93. (Rev: BL 5/15/02; HBG 10/02; SLJ 6/02) [973.9]

20632 Louis, Nancy. *United We Stand* (4–7). Series: War on Terrorism. 2002, ABDO LB $25.65 (978-1-57765-660-9). 48pp. In text and pictures, this account describes the support offered to the victims of the terrorist attacks of September 11, 2001, and their families. (Rev: BL 5/15/02; HBG 10/02) [909.9]

20633 Margulies, Phillip. *Al-Qaeda: Osama Bin Laden's Army of Terrorists* (5–7). Illus. Series: Inside the World's Most Infamous Terrorist Organizations. 2003, Rosen LB $27.95 (978-0-8239-3817-9). 64pp. Al-Qaeda's history, missions, methods, and structure are described, with a detailed profile of Osama Bin Laden. (Rev: BL 10/15/03) [973.93]

20634 Marquette, Scott. *America Under Attack* (4–7). Illus. Series: America at War. 2002, Rourke LB $20.95 (978-1-58952-386-9). 48pp. This book for middle graders explains in simple terms the September 11, 2001 attacks and other acts of terrorism against the United States, as well as discussing resulting legislation and changing opinions in America. (Rev: BL 10/15/02) [973.931]

20635 Roden, Katie. *Terrorism* (4–6). Illus. Series: Crimebusters. 1997, Millbrook LB $20.90 (978-0-7613-0556-9). 32pp. Using many text boxes, photos, diagrams, file folder formats, and a fabricated crime to set the stage, this book studies the causes and effects of terrorism. (Rev: BL 6/1–15/97; SLJ 9/97) [363.2]

20636 Rosaler, Maxine. *Hamas: Palestinian Terrorists* (5–7). Illus. Series: Inside the World's Most Infamous Terrorist Organizations. 2003, Rosen LB $27.95 (978-0-8239-3820-9). 64pp. Hamas's history, missions, methods, and structure are described, with profiles of key figures. (Rev: BL 10/15/03) [950.940]

20637 Sherrow, Victoria. *The Oklahoma City Bombing: Terror in the Heartland* (4–8). Illus. Series: American Disasters. 1998, Enslow LB $23.93 (978-0-7660-1061-1). 48pp. Using many first-person descriptions, this account of the Oklahoma City bombing ends with the sentencing of Timothy McVeigh and Terry Nichols. (Rev: BL 1/1–15/99; HBG 3/99; SLJ 3/99) [364.16]

20638 Sherrow, Victoria. *The World Trade Center Bombing: Terror in the Towers* (4–8). Illus. Series: American Disasters. 1998, Enslow LB $23.93 (978-0-7660-1056-7). An illustrated discussion of the events and individuals leading up to the 1993 World Trade Center bombing. (Rev: BL 1/1–15/99; HBG 3/99; SLJ 3/99; VOYA 4/99) [363.2]

20639 Stewart, Gail B. *Terrorism* (4–6). Illus. Series: Understanding Issues. 2002, Gale LB $26.20 (978-0-7377-1287-2). 48pp. Taking September 11, 2001, as a starting point, this account explores the causes and effects of terrorism and the measures taken to combat it. (Rev: BL 6/1–15/02; SLJ 9/02) [303.6]

20640 Uschan, Michael V. *The Beslan School Siege and Separatist Terrorism* (5–8). Illus. Series: Terrorism in Today's World. 2005, World Almanac LB $186.00 (978-0-8368-6555-4). 48pp. The deadly 2004 attack on a Russian school by Chechen Muslim terrorists is only the first of several attacks described in this volume on independence movements that use violence. (Rev: BL 4/1/06) [947.5]

20641 Wachtel, Alan. *September 11: A Primary Source History* (5–8). Illus. Series: In Their Own Words. 2009, Gareth Stevens LB $27.00 (978-1-4339-0048-8). 48pp. With narrative text and numerous photographs, plus excerpts from primary sources — including transcripts of phone conversations aboard the planes and firsthand accounts from responders and eyewitnesses — this volume covers the attack itself and the aftermath. (Rev: BL 4/1/09) [973.931]

Personal Development

Behavior

General

20642 Andrews, Linda Wasmer. *Meditation* (3–6). Illus. Series: Life Balance. 2004, Watts LB $20.50 (978-0-531-12219-8). 79pp. Explores different forms of meditation, including yoga, zen, and transcendental meditation, and discusses how they can be used to reduce stress and improve mental well-being. (Rev: SLJ 7/04) [158.1]

20643 Barber, Nicola. *First Day of School* (K–1). Series: The Big Day! 2009, Rosen LB $21.25 (978-1-4358-2839-1). 24pp. This simple book looks at typical concerns about school — getting ready, saying goodbye, making friends, and so forth. (Rev: SLJ 7/09) [372.12]

20644 Barber, Nicola. *Moving to a New House* (K–1). Series: The Big Day! 2009, Rosen LB $21.25 (978-1-4358-2841-4). 24pp. Typical problems involved in moving — adjusting to a new neighborhood and finding new friends — are the focus of this volume. (Rev: SLJ 7/09) [648]

20645 Barron, T. A. *The Hero's Trail: A Guide for Heroic Life* (4–7). Illus. 2002, Putnam $15.99 (978-0-399-23860-4). 160pp. This collection of anecdotes about both real and fictional characters aims to define heroism, and explores how one can lead a heroic life. (Rev: BL 10/15/02; HBG 3/03; SLJ 12/02; VOYA 12/02) [170]

20646 Becker, Helaine. *Like a Pro: 101 Simple Ways to Do Really Important Stuff* (4–6). Illus. by Claudia Dávila. Series: Planet Earth News. 2006, Maple Tree $21.95 (978-1-897066-53-9); paper $9.95 (978-1-897066-54-6). 160pp. From changing a bike tire to telling jokes to making friends, this friendly, practical guide offers instructions and advice. (Rev: SLJ 6/06) [646.7]

20647 Berger, Terry. *I Have Feelings* (1–5). Illus. 1971, Human Sciences $18.95 (978-0-87705-021-6); paper $10.95 (978-0-89885-342-1). 32pp. Text and photos show children that their feelings and emotions — good and bad — are natural.

20648 Borden, Sara, et al. *Middle School: How to Deal* (4–6). Illus. by Yuki Hatori. 2005, Chronicle LB $15.50 (978-0-8118-4845-9); paper $9.95 (978-0-8118-4497-0). 96pp. Advice from five 7th-grade girls on everything academic and social, with a dictionary of online chat conventions. (Rev: BL 6/1 15/05) [373.236]

20649 Buckley, Annie. *Hero Girls* (2–5). Series: Girls Rock! 2006, The Child's World LB $25.64 (978-1-59296-744-5). 32pp. Profiles American girls whose courage or other attributes can be classed as heroic; suitable for browsing by beginning readers. (Rev: SLJ 4/07) [305.2]

20650 Canfield, Jack, et al. *Chicken Soup for the Girl's Soul: Real Stories by Real Girls About Real Stuff* (4–6). 2005, Health Communications paper $14.95 (978-0-7573-0313-5). 345pp. Real-life stories tackle a wide variety of topics, including dealing with peer pressure, parental divorce, surviving middle school, first loves, and friendship. (Rev: SLJ 2/06) [158.1]

20651 Damm, Antje. *Ask Me* (PS–3). Trans. from German by Doris Orgel. Illus. by author. 2003, Millbrook $14.95 (978-0-7613-1845-3). 220pp. This is a compilation of questions, ranging from the fairly basic to the thought-provoking and accompanied by imaginative illustrations, that can be used to prompt discussion. (Rev: BCCB 3/03; BL 4/1/03; HBG 10/03; SLJ 3/03) [306.874]

20652 Doak, Robin. *Caring* (3–6). Series: Character Education. 2003, Raintree LB $24.26 (978-0-7398-5778-6). 32pp. Photographs and text illustrate the importance of compassion and caring. (Rev: HBG 3/03; SLJ 4/03)

20653 Doudna, Kelly. *Honestly!* (K–3). Illus. Series: Character Concepts. 2007, ABDO LB $13.95 (978-1-59928-735-5). 24pp. Examples of children behaving honestly — and a brief story about a boy who makes the decision to be honest — will help children grasp the concept and practice it in their lives. (Rev: SLJ 6/07)

20654 Doudna, Kelly. *Keep Your Cool!* (K–3). Illus. Series: Character Concepts. 2007, ABDO LB $13.95 (978-1-59928-736-2). 24pp. Stories of children nipping temper tantrums in the bud provide examples of good behavior. (Rev: SLJ 6/07)

20655 Dylan, Matthew. *Respect* (3–6). Series: Character Education. 2003, Raintree LB $24.26 (978-0-7398-5780-9). 32pp. This slim book examines respect from a number of points of view, including respect for authority, self, others, women, property rights, and the environment. (Rev: HBG 3/03; SLJ 4/03) [179]

20656 Edelman, Marian Wright. *I Can Make a Difference* (2–4). Illus. by Barry Moser. 2005, HarperCollins $20.89 (978-0-06-028052-9). 112pp. This oversize collection of poems, stories, songs, quotations, art, and folk tales, organized in 12 sections dealing with such topics as honesty, courage, and compassion, includes selections from a wide variety of sources that emphasize children's capacity to make a difference. (Rev: BL 11/1/05) [808.8]

20657 Erlbach, Arlene. *Worth the Risk: True Stories About Risk Takers, Plus How You Can Be One, Too* (5–9). Illus. 1999, Free Spirit paper $12.95 (978-1-57542-051-6). 127pp. These are 20 case studies of teenagers who took risks, from defying the dominant cliques in school to entering a burning house to save siblings. (Rev: BL 5/1/99; SLJ 8/99) [158]

20658 Finn, Carrie. *Kids Talk About Bravery* (K–2). Illus. by Amy Bailey Muehlenhardt. Series: Kids Talk Jr. 2006, Picture Window LB $25.26 (978-1-4048-2314-3). 32pp. A question-and-answer format and simple language are used to discuss children's fears and ways of tackling them. (Rev: SLJ 1/07) [179]

20659 Fitzhugh, Karla. *Body Image* (5–9). Series: Health Issues. 2004, Steck-Vaughn LB $32.79 (978-0-7398-6891-1). Body image and such related issues as cosmetic surgery, piercing, tattooing, eating disorders, and physical culture are examined in appealing text with informative charts and sidebars. (Rev: SLJ 11/05) [155.2]

20660 Fleischman, Paul, ed. *Cannibal in the Mirror* (5–10). Photos by John Whalen. 2000, Twenty-First Century LB $24.90 (978-0-7613-0968-0). 64pp. This thought-provoking book takes 27 quotations that describe barbarous behavior of primitive societies and pairs each with a telling photograph of similar behavior in modern American society. (Rev: BL 4/15/00; HBG 10/00; SLJ 4/00) [150]

20661 Fleming, Robert. *Rescuing a Neighborhood: The Bedford-Stuyvesant Volunteer Ambulance Corps* (4–8). Illus. 1995, Walker LB $16.85 (978-0-8027-8330-1). 48pp. The story of how two determined, dedicated men organized emergency response services in their inner-city neighborhood. (Rev: BL 5/1/95; SLJ 9/95) [362]

20662 Frost, Helen. *Feeling Angry* (PS–1). Series: Emotions. 2000, Capstone LB $17.26 (978-0-7368-0668-8). 24pp. Nine full-color photos and nine short sentences are used to illustrate anger. Others in the series are *Feeling Happy* and *Feeling Scared* (both 2000). (Rev: HBG 3/01; SLJ 1/01) [152.4]

20663 Gardner, Richard A. *The Girls and Boys Book About Good and Bad Behavior* (3–6). Illus. by Al Lowenheim. 1990, Creative Therapeutics paper $21.95 (978-0-933812-21-5). 221pp. This book talks about ethics and values. (Rev: SLJ 12/90) [155.5]

20664 Hartman, Holly, ed. *Girlwonder: Every Girl's Guide to the Fantastic Feats, Cool Qualities, and Remarkable Abilities of Women and Girls* (4–8). Illus. 2003, Houghton paper $9.95 (978-0-618-31939-8). 234pp. A browsable look at famous women and their accomplishments, interspersed with information and advice on topics ranging from romance to fashion. (Rev: SLJ 5/04) [305.235]

20665 Holyoke, Nancy. *A Smart Girl's Guide to Boys: Surviving Crushes, Staying True to Yourself, and Other Love Stuff* (4–6). Illus. 2001, Pleasant $9.95 (978-1-58485-368-8). 112pp. Age-appropriate advice on dealing with boys, first kisses, and balancing friends and boyfriends is interwoven with magazine-style quizzes and letters from girls. (Rev: BL 8/01; SLJ 9/01) [305.23]

20666 Hovanec, Erin M. *Get Involved! A Girl's Guide to Volunteering* (5–8). Series: Girls' Guides. 1999, Rosen LB $27.95 (978-0-8239-2985-6). 48pp. Two case studies of successful volunteers are given in this account that explains where to volunteer, how to approach organizations, and how to determine one's interests. (Rev: HBG 10/00; SLJ 1/00; VOYA 2/00) [361]

20667 Hughes, Monica. *First Day at School* (PS–2). Series: My First. 2004, Raintree LB $18.56 (978-1-4109-0643-4); paper $5.50 (978-1-4109-0669-4). 24pp. Simple language introduces young readers to what happens on the first day of school — coatrooms, classrooms, playtime, and so forth. Also use *First Vacation* (2004). [371]

20668 Inwald, Robin. *Cap It Off with a Smile: A Guide for Making Friends* (K–3). Illus. by author. 1994, Hilson Pr. $16.95 (978-1-885738-00-4). This book offers practical tips to young people on how they can make friends. (Rev: SLJ 12/94) [158]

20669 Jackson, Ellen. *Sometimes Bad Things Happen* (PS–2). Photos by Shelley Rotner. 2002, Millbrook LB $22.90 (978-0-7613-2810-0); paper $7.95 (978-0-7613-1734-0). Children are reassured that while bad things do happen, there are ways to cope and people who will want to help. (Rev: BL 11/15/02; HBG 3/03; SLJ 2/03)

20670 Johnston, Marianne. *Dealing with Anger* (2–4). Illus. Series: Conflict Resolution Library. 1996, Rosen LB $19.95 (978-0-8239-2325-0). 24pp. This simple introduction to anger defines it, explains its different forms, and tells how to handle it. (Rev: SLJ 9/96) [152.4]

20671 Karnes, Frances A., and Suzanne M. Bean. *Girls and Young Women Leading the Way: 20 True Stories About Leadership* (5–8). Illus. 1993, Free Spirit paper $12.95 (978-0-915793-52-5). 160pp. Contains case histories of 20 girls who changed their communities by starting projects such as collecting food for the homeless or starting a recycling program. (Rev: SLJ 12/93) [307.1]

20672 Kevi. *Don't Talk to Strangers* (K–3). Illus. Series: Hip Kid Hop. 2003, Scholastic $13.95 (978-0-439-31385-8). This attractive title, packaged with an audio CD, uses a rap rhyme to teach young readers how to recognize and behave around strangers. (Rev: HBG 10/03; SLJ 9/03)

20673 Kincher, Jonni. *Psychology for Kids II: 40 Fun Experiments That Help You Learn About Others* (4–6). Illus. 1995, Free Spirit paper $17.95 (978-0-915793-83-9). 157pp. This second volume supplies more activities and projects to help explore the world of human behavior. (Rev: BL 7/95) [155.2]

20674 King, Bart. *The Big Book of Girl Stuff* (4–8). Illus. by Jennifer Kalis. 2006, Gibbs Smith paper $19.99 (978-1-58685-819-3). 320pp. A lighthearted, well-organized guide to a great many topics of interest to growing girls, including why boys smell bad, etiquette, dieting, how to shop, and how to get a boy's attention. (Rev: SLJ 1/07) [646.7]

20675 Klingel, Cynthia A. *Friendliness* (K–3). 2007, The Child's World LB $21.36 (978-1-59296-669-1). 24pp. Using a question-and-answer format, Klingel discusses friendliness and its benefits, with many pertinent examples. Also use *Generosity* (2007). (Rev: SLJ 11/07) [177]

20676 Lester, Julius. *Let's Talk About Race* (K–3). Illus. by Karen Barbour. 2005, HarperCollins LB $17.89 (978-0-06-028598-2). 32pp. Lester emphasizes that racial identity is only one of the many elements in an individual's makeup. (Rev: BL 2/1/05; SLJ 1/05) [305.8]

20677 Lewis, Barbara A. *The Kid's Guide to Service Projects: Over 500 Service Ideas for Young People Who Want to Make a Difference* (4–7). 1995, Free Spirit paper $12.95 (978-0-915793-82-2). 175pp. After an introduction on how to organize and conduct service projects, this book gives details on 500 ideas from running errands for seniors to working for voter registration. (Rev: SLJ 7/95) [307]

20678 Lewis, Barbara A. *The Kid's Guide to Social Action: How to Solve the Social Problems You Choose — and Turn Creative Thinking into Positive Action*. Rev. ed. (4–8). 1998, Free Spirit paper $18.95 (978-1-57542-038-7). An inspirational guide that shows how young people can make a difference by becoming involved in social action, such as instigating a cleanup of toxic waste, lobbying, or youth rights campaigns. (Rev: SLJ 1/99) [361.6]

20679 Lewis, Barbara S. *Being Your Best: Character Building for Kids 7–10* (4–6). Illus. 1999, Free Spirit paper $14.95 (978-1-57542-063-9). 148pp. A child-centered book that presents ten positive character traits and suggests practical ways and activities to develop and strengthen them. (Rev: BL 5/15/00) [155.2]

20680 MacGregor, Cynthia. *Think for Yourself: A Kid's Guide to Solving Life's Dilemmas and Other Sticky Problems* (3–6). Illus. by Susan Norberg Farias. 2003, Lobster paper $7.95 (978-1-894222-73-0). 96pp. Readers learn to identify problems and to work out solutions for themselves. (Rev: SLJ 2/04) [170]

20681 Madison, Lynda. *The Feelings Book: The Care and Keeping of Your Emotions* (4–6). Illus. by Norm Bendell. 2002, Pleasant paper $8.95 (978-1-58485-528-6). 104pp. Madison tackles the topic of the emotional upheavals that many youngsters experience as they near their teens and offers tips on identifying and coping with strong feelings. (Rev: BL 12/1/02; SLJ 10/02) [155.43]

20682 Mattern, Joanne. *Do You Share?* (PS–1). Illus. Series: Are You a Good Friend? 2007, Gareth Stevens LB $19.93 (978-0-8368-9275-8); paper $5.95 (978-0-8368-8280-3). 24pp. Photographs and a brief text illustrate many ways in which children enjoy sharing. (Rev: BL 10/15/07) [177]

20683 Mayer, Cassie. *Being Honest* (K–1). Series: Citizenship. 2007, Heinemann LB $20.71 (978-1-4034-9484-9). 24pp. What is being honest? How can you be honest? This title answers such questions with simple vocabulary and helpful examples. (Rev: BL 9/1/07; SLJ 11/07) [179]

20684 Meiners, Cheri J. *Be Polite and Kind* (PS–1). Illus. by Meredith Johnson. 2004, Free Spirit paper $10.95 (978-1-57542-151-3). 40pp. This attractive picture book is designed to teach the simple virtues of courtesy and kindness. (Rev: BL 5/1/04; SLJ 8/04) [177]

20685 Meiners, Cheri J. *Join In and Play* (PS–1). Illus. by Meredith Johnson. 2004, Free Spirit paper $10.95 (978-1-57542-152-0). 40pp. The basic skills children need to interact happily with others are clearly communicated in this attractive picture book. (Rev: BL 5/1/04; SLJ 8/04) [790]

20686 *The Milestones Project: Celebrating Childhood Around the World* (PS–2). Photos by Richard Steckel and Michele Steckel. Illus. 2004, Tricycle $17.95 (978-1-58246-132-8). 64pp. Children around the world are shown in "milestone moments" — birthdays, losing a tooth, haircuts, playing with toys, and so forth. (Rev: BL 1/1–15/05; SLJ 11/04) [305.23]

20687 Montanari, Donata. *Children Around the World* (PS–K). Illus. by author. 2001, Kids Can $14.95 (978-1-55337-064-2). 32pp. Readers are introduced to children in countries around the world who describe their lives in simple sentences that highlight their similarities and differences. (Rev: HBG 3/02; SLJ 12/01) [390.083]

20688 Moore-Mallinos, Jennifer. *Do You Have a Secret?* (PS–3). Illus. by Marta Fàbrega. Series: Let's Talk About It! 2005, Barron's paper $6.95 (978-0-7641-3170-7). 31pp. Moore-Mallinos explains the difference between good secrets and bad ones, and gives advice on getting help from adults. (Rev: SLJ 10/05)

20689 Navarra, Tova. *The Kids' Guidebook: Great Advice to Help Kids Cope*. Rev. ed. (4–6). Illus. by Tom Kerr. 2002, Barron's paper $12.99 (978-0-7641-2066-4). 128pp. Advice on coping with difficult situations, from power outages and dealing with strangers to the death of a loved one. (Rev: SLJ 3/03)

20690 Nelson, Robin. *Being a Leader* (K–1). Illus. Series: First Step Nonfiction: Citizenship. 2003,

Lerner LB $18.60 (978-0-8225-1287-5). 23pp. A basic look at what it takes to be a leader and how to become a good leader at home, school, and in the community. (Rev: HBG 4/04; SLJ 11/03) [303.3]

20691 Nikola-Lisa, W. *How We Are Smart* (4–7). Illus. by Scan Quails. 2006, Lee & Low $16.95 (978-1-58430-254-4). 32pp. A picture book for older readers that looks at different kinds of intelligence, using double-page spreads about 12 famous people to illustrate these concepts. (Rev: BL 4/1/06; SLJ 6/06) [811]

20692 Pendleton, Scott. *The Ultimate Guide to Student Contests, Grades K–6* (4–6). 1998, Walker paper $14.95 (978-0-8027-7513-9). 208pp. A directory of organizations that sponsor student competitions or reward outstanding student work, arranged by subject. (Rev: BL 3/15/98; SLJ 9/98) [370]

20693 Raatma, Lucia. *Determination* (2–4). Series: Character Education. 2002, Capstone LB $22.60 (978-0-7368-1387-7). 24pp. The characteristic is described, with examples of how to show determination and a famous person who exhibits it. Also use *Loyalty* and *Leadership* (both 2002). (Rev: HBG 3/03; SLJ 2/03)

20694 Raatma, Lucia. *Loyalty* (K–4). Illus. Series: 21st Century Junior Library Character Education. 2009, Cherry Lake LB $22.80 (978-1-60279-326-2). 24pp. An overview of what loyalty means, with specific examples illustrating how loyalty applies in the home, school, and community. (Rev: BL 4/1/09) [179]

20695 Roberts, Cynthia. *Tolerance* (K–2). Illus. Series: Learn About Values. 2007, Child's World LB $14.95 (978-1-59296-678-3). 24pp. Roberts shows the benefits of tolerant behavior in a variety of settings — at school, at home, with younger children. (Rev: BL 10/15/07) [179]

20696 Robinson, Sharon. *Jackie's Nine: Jackie Robinson's Values to Live By* (5–8). Illus. 2001, Scholastic paper $15.95 (978-0-439-23764-2). 183pp. A collection of inspirational writings, selected by baseball legend Jackie Robinson's daughter and organized under headings including "Courage" and "Determination," that include material by and about such well-known individuals as Christopher Reeve and Oprah Winfrey. (Rev: BL 7/01; HBG 10/01; SLJ 6/01; VOYA 8/01) [158]

20697 Romain, Trevor. *How to Do Homework Without Throwing Up* (3–6). Illus. by author. 1997, Free Spirit paper $8.95 (978-1-57542-011-0). 67pp. Using humorous text and drawings, this work supplies a positive approach to homework with many tips on how to do it efficiently. (Rev: SLJ 5/97) [371.3]

20698 Rosenthal, Amy Krouse. *Cookies: Bite Size Life Lessons* (PS–1). Illus. by Jane Dyer. 2006, HarperCollins $12.99 (978-0-06-058081-0). 40pp. Baking cookies serves as the framework for defining words and concepts in this attractive and child-friendly book. (Rev: BCCB 9/06; BL 4/1/06*; HBG 10/06; SLJ 5/06) [179]

20699 Rotner, Shelley, and Sheila Kelly. *What Can You Do? A Book About Discovering What You Do Well* (PS–1). Photos by Shelley Rotner. Illus. 2001, Millbrook LB $22.90 (978-0-7613-2119-4). 24pp. With illustrations and text that show a variety of activities and talents, the authors ask readers to determine what they can do best. (Rev: BL 4/15/01; HBG 10/01; SLJ 9/01) [153.9]

20700 Salzmann, Mary Elizabeth. *I Am a Good Citizen* (K–2). Series: Building Character. 2003, ABDO LB $19.93 (978-1-57765-825-2). 23pp. A simple explanation of the character traits and behavior that make a good citizen. Also use *I Am Fair* (2003). (Rev: HBG 10/03; SLJ 9/03) [323.6]

20701 Sanders, Pete, and Steve Myers. *Feeling Violent* (3–6). Illus. by Mike Lacey. Series: What Do You Know About. 1997, Millbrook LB $20.90 (978-0-7613-0700-6). 32pp. This book explores violence, its different forms, its causes, and how to handle it. (Rev: HBG 9/98; SLJ 4/98) [616.8]

20702 Scheunemann, Pam. *Patriotism* (1–3). Series: United We Stand. 2003, ABDO LB $19.93 (978-1-57765-880-1). 24pp. A look at pride in one's country, with simple text and relevant, multicultural photographs. (Rev: HBG 10/03; SLJ 6/03) [323.6]

20703 Schuette, Sarah L. *I Am Cooperative* (PS–2). Series: Character Values. 2002, Capstone LB $17.26 (978-0-7368-1439-3). 24pp. Photographs and simple text are used to explain how to be cooperative. Also use *I Am Honest*, *I Am Respectful*, and *I Am Responsible*. (Rev: HBG 3/03; SLJ 3/03)

20704 Schuette, Sarah L. *Soy bondadosa / I Am Caring* (PS–2). Trans. by Martin Luis Guzman Ferrer. Series: Pebble Bilingual Books. 2003, Capstone LB $17.26 (978-0-7368-2301-2). 24pp. Good, caring behavior is illustrated and described in English and Spanish. Also use *Soy respetuoso/I Am Respectful*, *Soy cooperativa/I Am Cooperative*, and *Soy responsable/I Am Responsible* (all 2003). (Rev: SLJ 4/04) [395]

20705 Sheindlin, Judy. *Judge Judy Sheindlin's You Can't Judge a Book by Its Cover: Cool Rules for School* (2–5). Illus. by Bob Tore. 2001, HarperCollins LB $14.89 (978-0-06-029484-7). Judge Judy looks at common choices young students have to make, presenting a range of possible decisions, some sensible and some clearly not. (Rev: HBG 10/01; SLJ 7/01) [170]

20706 Sherman, Joanne. *Because It's My Body!* (PS–2). Illus. by John S. Gurney. Series: Keep `em Safe. 2002, S.A.F.E. for Children paper $14.95 (978-0-9711735-0-7). 30pp. This text presents clear strategies for dealing with unwelcome attention, even from friends and family. (Rev: SLJ 12/02)

20707 Silverman, Robin L. *Reaching Your Goals* (4–8). Illus. Series: Life Balance. 2004, Watts LB $20.50 (978-0-531-12342-3); paper $6.95 (978-0-531-16691-8). 80pp. Practical advice on building self-confidence, making smart decisions, and focusing on achievable goals. (Rev: BL 10/15/03)

20708 Small, Mary. *Being a Good Citizen: A Book About Citizenship* (K–2). Illus. by Stacey Previn. Series: Way to Be! 2005, Picture Window LB $25.26 (978-1-4048-1050-1). 24pp. A slim overview of simple ways in which children can be good citizens and help improve their communities, such as picking up trash and planting flowers. (Rev: SLJ 12/05) [323.6]

20709 Small, Mary. *Being Fair: A Book About Fairness* (K–2). Illus. by Stacey Previn. Series: Way to Be! 2005, Picture Window LB $25.26 (978-1-4048-1051-8). 24pp. A slim overview of simple ways in which children can be fair in their dealings with others. Also use *Being Responsible, Being Respectful,* and *Being Trustworthy* (2005). (Rev: SLJ 12/05) [179]

20710 Swain, Gwenyth. *Smiling* (PS–1). Illus. Series: Small Worlds. 1999, Carolrhoda $19.93 (978-1-57505-256-4). 24pp. Children from around the world, including China, Australia, Sudan, and Mexico, display a variety of smiles in this happy book about childhood. (Rev: BL 6/1–15/99; HBG 9/99; SLJ 6/99) [153.6]

20711 Thomas, Pat. *I'm Telling the Truth: A First Look at Honesty* (K–3). Illus. by Lesley Harker. Series: A First Look At. 2006, Barron's paper $6.99 (978-0-7641-3214-8). 29pp. Introduces the concept of honesty, explains its importance in dealing with others, and offers suggestions about how to incorporate this character trait into everyday life. (Rev: SLJ 9/06) [179.9]

20712 Thong, Roseanne. *Wish: Wishing Traditions Around the World* (K–3). Illus. by Elisa Kleven. 2008, Chronicle $16.99 (978-0-8118-5716-1). 44pp. Wishing traditions around the world — blowing dandelion fluff, tossing coins into fountains, and so forth — are the focus of this well-illustrated volume. (Rev: BL 12/1/08; SLJ 4/09) [398]

20713 Waber, Bernard. *Courage* (K–3). Illus. 2002, Houghton $12.00 (978-0-618-23855-2). 40pp. Waber introduces the concept of courage with amusing illustrations and examples that younger readers can understand. (Rev: BCCB 2/03; BL 12/15/02; HBG 3/03; SLJ 12/02) [179]

20714 Waters, Jennifer. *Be a Good Friend!* (K–1). Series: Spyglass Books. 2002, Compass Point LB $19.93 (978-0-7565-0376-5). 24pp. For beginning readers, this book lists the qualities that make a good friend. Also use *Be a Good Sport!* (2002). (Rev: SLJ 1/03)

20715 Williams, Venus, and Serena Williams. *Venus and Serena: Serving from the Hip* (5–8). Illus. 2005, Houghton paper $14.00 (978-0-618-57653-1). 144pp. The successful Williams sisters offer practical advice on self-respect, friendship, financial security, and other pertinent topics. (Rev: BL 5/15/05; SLJ 4/05) [796.342]

20716 Zimmerman, Bill. *100 Things Guys Need to Know* (5–9). 2005, Free Spirit paper $13.95 (978-1-57542-167-4). Effective graphic design will draw teenage boys into this self-help guide that touches on a wide variety of topics, including body image, dating, school, friendship, and family. (Rev: SLJ 11/05) [305.235]

Etiquette

20717 Best, Alyse. *Miss Best's Etiquette for Young People: Manners for Real People in Today's World* (3–7). Illus. 1991, PEP paper $9.95 (978-0-945033-02-8). 137pp. Advice is given to young people on proper behavior for both formal and informal social events. (Rev: BL 9/15/91) [395]

20718 Cabot, Meg. *Princess Lessons* (5–7). Illus. by Chesley McLaren. Series: Princess Diaries. 2003, HarperCollins $12.99 (978-0-06-052677-1). 144pp. Princess Mia gives lighthearted — and often quite practical — tips on behaving like a real princess. (Rev: BL 5/15/03; HBG 10/03; VOYA 10/03) [646.7]

20719 Doudna, Kelly. *Excuse Me* (PS–1). Series: Good Manners. 2001, ABDO LB $19.93 (978-1-57765-574-9). 24pp. Simple text suitable for beginning readers introduces the basic concept of apologizing, accompanied by illustrations of children in appropriate situations. Also in this series are *Please* and *Thank You.* (Rev: HBG 3/02; SLJ 4/02) [395.1]

20720 Doudna, Kelly. *Right on Time!* (K–3). Illus. Series: Character Concepts. 2007, ABDO LB $13.95 (978-1-59928-740-9). 24pp. This book shows the importance of punctuality through examples of children being on time. (Rev: SLJ 6/07)

20721 Dougherty, Karla. *The Rules to Be Cool: Etiquette and Netiquette* (5–9). Series: Teen Issues. 2001, Enslow LB $22.60 (978-0-7660-1607-1). 64pp. Respect and consideration for others are the key elements of Dougherty's rules of behavior, with an emphasis on politeness, kindness, and courtesy, on the Internet as well as at home and at school. (Rev: HBG 3/02; SLJ 10/01) [395]

20722 Finn, Carrie. *Manners in Public* (PS–2). Illus. by Chris Lensch. Series: Way to Be! 2007, Picture Window LB $23.93 (978-1-4048-3153-7). 24pp. This book gives examples of children behaving as they should, with photographs that emphasize that being polite makes everyone happy. Also use *Manners on the Playground* (2007). (Rev: SLJ 6/07)

20723 Gibbs, Lynne. *Don't Slurp Your Soup! A First Guide to Letter Writing, E-Mail Etiquette, and Other Everyday Manners* (K–2). Illus. by John Eastwood. 2003, McGraw-Hill $14.95 (978-1-57768-556-2). 32pp. A lighthearted introduction to the basic rules of behavior, this guide covers table manners, party invitations, and phone etiquette. (Rev: BL 4/1/03; HBG 4/04; SLJ 8/03) [390]

20724 Goldberg, Whoopi. *Whoopi's Big Book of Manners* (K–3). Illus. by Olo. 2006, Hyperion $15.99 (978-0-7868-5295-6). A funny, chatty guide to proper etiquette. (Rev: SLJ 11/06) [395]

20725 Hample, Stoo. *Book of Bad Manners* (3–5). Illus. by author. 2006, Candlewick $15.99 (978-0-7636-2933-5). Examples of bad behavior are paired with lively drawings of the evil deeds, bound to amuse young readers. (Rev: SLJ 9/06) [395.12]

20726 Holyoke, Nancy. *A Smart Girl's Guide to Manners* (4–7). Illus. by Cathi Mingus. 2005, Pleasant paper $9.95 (978-1-58485-983-3). 120pp. A nice mix of good manners that ranges from introductions to cell phone etiquette to how and when to write real thank-you notes. (Rev: BL 11/1/05; SLJ 1/06; VOYA 12/05) [395]

20727 James, Elizabeth, and Carol Barkin. *Social Smarts: Manners for Today's Kids* (4–7). Illus. 1996, Clarion paper $7.95 (978-0-395-81312-6). 103pp. Table manners and responsible, appropriate public behavior are two topics covered. (Rev: BL 9/1/96; SLJ 9/96) [395]

20728 Lauber, Patricia. *What You Never Knew About Fingers, Forks, and Chopsticks* (2–5). Illus. by John Manders. 1999, Simon & Schuster $16.00 (978-0-689-80479-3). 40pp. An amusing, fascinating look at manners and eating utensils, from the Stone Age to the present. (Rev: BCCB 12/99; BL 9/1/99*; HBG 4/00; SLJ 9/99) [394.1]

20729 Post, Peggy, and Cindy Post Senning. *Emily's Everyday Manners* (PS–2). Illus. by Steve Björkman. 2006, HarperCollins $16.99 (978-0-06-076174-5). 32pp. Emily and Ethan outline the basics of good behavior. (Rev: BL 10/15/06) [395.1]

20730 Raatma, Lucia. *Politeness* (K–2). Series: Character Education. 2002, Capstone LB $22.60 (978-0-7368-1134-7). 24pp. A how-to guide for the very young that provides a definition of politeness, shows how to display it, and offers some practice ideas. Also use *Self-Respect* and *Sportsmanship* (2002). (Rev: SLJ 6/02) [395.1]

20731 Senning, Cindy Post, and Peggy Post. *Emily Post's Table Manners for Kids* (4–8). Illus. by Steve Björkman. 2009, HarperCollins $15.99 (978-0-06-111709-1). 96pp. When can you eat with your fingers? Which fork do I use? Everything today's child needs to know about proper meal etiquette and just why these things matter. (Rev: BL 4/1/09) [395.5]

20732 Smith, Mavis. *Mind Your Manners, Ben Bunny: A Lift-the-Flap Book About Table Manners* (PS–K). Illus. by author. 1998, Scholastic $8.95 (978-0-590-06844-4). This book uses flaps and advice from a crow to teach Ben Bunny and two friends proper table manners. (Rev: HBG 3/99; SLJ 7/98) [395]

20733 Stewart, Marjabelle Young, and Ann Buchwald. *What to Do When and Why* (4–7). 1988, Luce $14.95 (978-0-88331-105-9). An easily read introduction to the basics of good manners and behavior.

20734 Thomas, Pat. *My Manners Matter: A First Look at Being Polite* (K–3). Illus. by Lesley Harker. 2006, Barron's paper $6.99 (978-0-7641-3212-4). 29pp. Introduces the concept of politeness, examines its importance in dealing with others, and offers suggestions about how to behave politely. (Rev: SLJ 9/06) [179.9]

20735 Willems, Mo. *Time to Say "Please"!* (PS–3). Illus. by author. 2005, Hyperion $15.99 (978-0-7868-5293-2). Mice give children playful tips on correct behavior. (Rev: SLJ 8/05) [395.1]

20736 Zemke, Deborah. *Don't Feed the Babysitter to Your Boa Constrictor: 43 Ridiculous Rules Every Kid Should Know* (2–3). Series: I'm Going to Read! 2006, Sterling paper $3.95 (978-1-4027-3429-8). 24pp. A funny, easy-reader collection of nonsensical rules for children — including "Never eat anything that's still moving" and "Don't eat spaghetti through your nose." (Rev: BL 11/1/06; SLJ 12/06) [818]

Family Relationships

20737 Adamson, Heather. *Families in Many Cultures* (PS–2). Illus. Series: Life Around the World. 2007, Capstone LB $14.95 (978-1-4296-0019-4). 24pp. Families in eight countries around the world are shown enjoying time together in this simple volume suitable for beginning readers. (Rev: BL 10/15/07; LMC 5/08; SLJ 1/08) [306.85]

20738 Aldape, Virginia Totorica. *David, Donny, and Darren: A Book About Identical Triplets* (2–4). Illus. Series: Meeting the Challenge. 1997, Lerner LB $21.27 (978-0-8225-2584-4). 40pp. Using a first-person narrative, this is the story of an identical triplet and how his life is different from those of average kids. (Rev: BL 3/15/98; HBG 3/98) [306.875]

20739 Ancona, George. *Mis abuelos / My Grandparents* (K–2). Photos by author. Illus. Series: Somos Latinos. 2005, Children's Pr. LB $21.00 (978-0-516-25294-0). 32pp. In this photo-filled bilingual picture book, Latino American children talk about their relationships with their grandparents. Also in this series: *Mis juegos / My Games, Mi música / My Music, Mis comidas / My Foods, Mis fiestas / My Celebrations,* and *Mis quehaceres / My Chores.* (Rev: SLJ 2/06) [977.5]

20740 Barber, Nicola. *A New Baby Arrives* (K–1). Series: The Big Day! 2009, Rosen LB $21.25 (978-1-4358-2842-1). 24pp. This simple book looks at typical concerns — sharing with a new baby, helping, bath time, and so forth. (Rev: SLJ 7/09) [306.875]

20741 Bingham, Jane. *Why Do Families Break Up?* (4–8). Series: Exploring Tough Issues. 2004, Raintree LB $29.93 (978-0-7398-6683-2). 48pp. Every member of the family is considered in this comprehensive examination of divorce and how individuals of different ages cope. (Rev: SLJ 2/05) [306.8]

20742 Brown, Laurie Krasny, and Marc Brown. *Dinosaurs Divorce: A Guide for Changing Families* (PS–3). Illus. by Marc Brown. 1988, Little, Brown $15.95 (978-0-316-11248-2); paper $7.95 (978-0-316-10996-3). 32pp. These green, somewhat crocodilian dinosaurs demonstrate all the feelings and problems children encounter with divorce in the family. (Rev: SLJ 10/86)

20743 Charlish, Anne. *Divorce* (5–10). Series: Talking Points. 1999, Raintree LB $27.12 (978-0-8172-5310-3). 64pp. An overview of the causes of divorce, the legal aspects, and the difficult adjustments that must be made. (Rev: BL 8/99) [306.89]

20744 Cole, Joanna. *The New Baby at Your House.* Rev. ed. (PS–1). Illus. by Margaret Miller. 1998,

Morrow $15.89 (978-0-688-13898-1). 48pp. A revision of the standard account on adjustments that are made in a family when a new baby arrives. (Rev: BL 3/1/98; HBG 9/98; SLJ 4/98) [306.875]

20745 Cooper, Kay. *Where Did You Get Those Eyes? A Guide to Discovering Your Family History* (5–7). Illus. by Anthony Accardo. 1988, Walker LB $14.85 (978-0-8027-6803-2). A helpful guide for researching the family tree. (Rev: BCCB 11/88; BL 1/15/89; SLJ 2/89)

20746 Currie, Stephen. *Adoption* (5–8). Illus. Series: Overview. 1997, Lucent LB $29.95 (978-1-56006-183-0). 96pp. A well-illustrated account of the history of adoption and present-day practices, procedures, and problems. (Rev: BL 5/15/97; SLJ 4/97) [362.7]

20747 Drescher, Joan. *Your Family, My Family* (K–3). Illus. by author. 1980, Walker LB $13.85 (978-0-8027-6383-9). 32pp. All kinds of family arrangements, such as single parents and working mothers, are described.

20748 Gardner, Richard A. *Boys and Girls Book About Divorce* (5–8). Illus. 1992, Bantam paper $6.99 (978-0-553-27619-0). 160pp. A self-help book written for adolescents trying to cope with parental marriage problems. [306.8]

20749 Gelber, Carol. *Love and Marriage Around the World* (5–7). 1998, Millbrook LB $23.90 (978-0-7613-0102-8). 72pp. From courtship to the wedding, this book introduces marriage customs from around the world and among different ethnic groups. (Rev: BCCB 7–8/98; HBG 10/98; SLJ 6/98) [392]

20750 Goldentyer, Debra. *Divorce* (4–8). Series: Preteen Pressures. 1998, Raintree LB $25.69 (978-0-8172-5030-0). 48pp. This work discusses the reasons for divorce, the legal aspects, the effect on children, remarriage, and relationships with new family members. (Rev: BL 5/15/98; HBG 10/98; SLJ 6/98) [306.8]

20751 Greenberg, Keith E. *Family Abuse: Why Do People Hurt Each Other?* (3–6). Illus. 1997, Twenty-First Century LB $21.99 (978-0-8050-3183-6). 64pp. An easily read book that explores physical, emotional, and sexual abuse of children as well as neglect and abuse of spouses, the elderly, and the disabled. (Rev: SLJ 9/94) [362.7]

20752 Greenberg, Keith E. *Zack's Story: Growing Up with Same-Sex Parents* (5–7). Illus. Series: Meeting the Challenge. 1996, Lerner LB $21.27 (978-0-8225-2581-3). 32pp. A true account of 11-year-old Zack, who is growing up with his lesbian mother and her lover, whom he has grown to regard as a second mother. (Rev: BL 10/15/96; SLJ 3/97) [306]

20753 Hughes, Monica. *First Brother or Sister* (PS–2). Series: My First. 2004, Raintree LB $18.56 (978-1-4109-0644-1). 24pp. Color photographs and simple narrative are tailor-made for only children whose families are awaiting the arrival of a new baby. (Rev: BL 4/1/04) [306.875]

20754 Isler, Claudia. *Caught in the Middle: A Teen Guide to Custody* (5–8). Series: The Divorce Resource. 2000, Rosen LB $27.95 (978-0-8239-

3109-5). 64pp. This book about divorce uses many actual case histories to explore such questions as what happens to the children when parents divorce and whether grandparents get visitation rights. (Rev: SLJ 6/00) [306.8]

20755 Jackson, Ellen. *Here Come the Brides* (3–5). Illus. by Carol Heyer. 1998, Walker LB $16.85 (978-0-8027-8469-8). 32pp. Brides, wedding customs, symbols, and attire are a few of the topics covered in this overview of wedding practices in different cultures. (Rev: BL 5/1/98; HBG 9/98; SLJ 4/98) [392.5]

20756 Johnson, Julie. *My Stepfamily* (2–4). Series: How Do I Feel About. 1998, Millbrook LB $19.90 (978-0-7613-0868-3). 24pp. Four children explain their feelings about being part of a stepfamily and how they have dealt with various situations. (Rev: HBG 9/99; SLJ 4/99) [646.7]

20757 Kandel, Bethany. *Trevor's Story: Growing Up Biracial* (2–4). Illus. Series: Meeting the Challenge. 1997, Lerner LB $21.27 (978-0-8225-2583-7). 40pp. A first-person narrative in which a boy talks about the racism he has had to face growing up with a white mother and an African American father. (Rev: BL 3/15/98; HBG 3/98) [362.1]

20758 Kinkade, Sheila. *My Family* (PS–2). Illus. by Elaine Little. 2006, Charlesbridge $16.95 (978-1-57091-662-5); paper $6.95 (978-1-57091-691-5). 32pp. In double-page spreads, this full-color photoessay shows the diversity and similarities of families around the world. (Rev: BL 1/1–15/06; SLJ 2/06) [306.85]

20759 Koh, Frances M. *Adopted from Asia: How It Feels to Grow Up in America* (5–8). 1993, East-West $16.95 (978-0-9606090-6-2). 95pp. The author has gathered stories, impressions, and opinions from 11 young people who were born in Korea and adopted by Caucasian Americans. (Rev: BL 2/15/94) [306.874]

20760 Krementz, Jill. *How It Feels to Be Adopted* (5–8). Illus. 1988, Knopf paper $15.00 (978-0-394-75853-4). Interviews with 19 young people, ages 8 to 16, on how it feels to be adopted. [362.7]

20761 Krementz, Jill. *How It Feels When Parents Divorce* (4–8). Illus. 1988, Knopf paper $15.00 (978-0-394-75855-8). Boys and girls, ages 8 to 16, share their experiences dealing with divorced parents. [306.8]

20762 Krohn, Katherine. *You and Your Parents' Divorce* (5–8). Series: Family Matters. 2001, Rosen LB $26.50 (978-0-8239-3354-9). 48pp. Krohn writes about the practicalities and emotional problems of divorce in a style suitable for reluctant readers. (Rev: SLJ 8/01) [155.44]

20763 Kuklin, Susan. *Families* (3–5). Illus. 2006, Hyperion $15.99 (978-0-7868-0822-9). 40pp. Kuklin explores the diversity of families in America through interviews of children who have single, mixed-race, divorced, immigrant, gay, and lesbian parents; photographs are included on the double-page spreads. (Rev: BL 12/15/05; SLJ 1/06*) [306.85]

20764 Landau, Elaine. *Sibling Rivalry: Brothers and Sisters at Odds* (3–6). Illus. 1994, Millbrook LB $19.90 (978-1-56294-328-8). 64pp. Factors that influence sibling rivalry, such as family size, gender, and divorce, are discussed, with tips on how to understand and lessen the problem. (Rev: BL 5/1/94; SLJ 4/94) [306]

20765 Leibowitz, Julie. *Finding Your Place: A Teen Guide to Life in a Blended Family* (5–8). 2000, Rosen LB $27.95 (978-0-8239-3114-9). 64pp. This book explores possible problems and solutions for members of blended families. (Rev: SLJ 6/00) [645.7]

20766 Lindsay, Jeanne W. *Do I Have a Daddy? A Story About a Single-Parent Child* (PS–2). Illus. by Jami Moffett. 2000, Morning Glory $14.95 (978-1-885356-62-8); paper $7.95 (978-1-885356-63-5). 48pp. A single mother reassures her son that, although he does not have a father, his uncle and grandfather will be there to help him. (Rev: BL 5/15/00; HBG 9/00; SLJ 7/00) [306.85]

20767 MacGregor, Cynthia. *The Divorce Helpbook for Kids* (4–7). 2001, Impact paper $13.95 (978-1-886230-39-2). 112pp. In this candid, honest book, a divorced mother gives advice to children about how to survive their parent's divorce. (Rev: BL 2/1/02; SLJ 3/02) [306.89]

20768 MacGregor, Cynthia. *Jigsaw Puzzle Family: The Stepkids' Guide to Fitting It Together* (5–8). Series: Rebuilding Books. 2005, Impact paper $12.95 (978-1-886230-63-7). 128pp. Offers reassuring, practical advice — with an emphasis on talking through problems and seeking solutions — for stepchildren who are having difficulty adjusting to life in a blended family. (Rev: BL 9/1/05; SLJ 10/05) [306.874]

20769 McMahon, Patricia, and Conor Clarke McCarthy. *Just Add One Chinese Sister* (PS–2). Illus. by Karen A. Jerome. 2005, Boyds Mills $16.95 (978-1-56397-989-7). A compelling story of the adoption of a Chinese girl, conveyed through a scrapbook created by Claire and her American mother with contributions by her new big brother Conor. (Rev: BL 8/05; SLJ 2/05) [362.734]

20770 Moore-Mallinos, Jennifer. *When My Parents Forgot How to Be Friends* (PS–3). Illus. by Marta Fàbrega. Series: Let's Talk About It! 2005, Barron's paper $6.95 (978-0-7641-3172-1). 31pp. A girl talks about her unhappiness and uncertainty when her parents were preparing to separate; the situation improves when her dad moves out. (Rev: SLJ 10/05) [306.89]

20771 Morris, Ann. *Families* (PS–1). Illus. 2000, HarperCollins LB $17.89 (978-0-688-17199-5). 32pp. Different kinds of families around the world are introduced in this photo-essay that uses very little text. (Rev: BL 5/15/00; HBG 9/00; SLJ 5/00) [306.85]

20772 Morris, Ann. *Loving* (PS–2). Illus. by Ken Heyman. 1990, Lothrop LB $15.93 (978-0-688-06341-2). 32pp. Clear photos focus on children, their families, and their pets. Also use *On the Go* (1990). (Rev: BL 1/1/91; SLJ 1/91) [306.7]

20773 Murphy, Patricia J. *Divorce and Separation* (2–4). Illus. Series: Tough Topics. 2007, Heinemann LB $17.75 (978-1-4034-9775-8). 32pp. This title takes a frank but encouraging look at the lifestyle changes and emotional challenges associated with divorce and separation. (Rev: BL 1/1–15/08; LMC 3/08; SLJ 6/08) [306.89]

20774 Powell, Jillian. *Adoption* (2–3). Series: Talking About. 1999, Raintree LB $25.69 (978-0-8172-5890-0). 32pp. Stories with happy endings enhance this simple account of adoptions — their meaning, reasons, and effects on children's feelings. (Rev: BL 2/15/00; HBG 9/00) [362.7]

20775 Powell, Jillian. *Family Breakup* (1–3). Photos by Martyn F. Chillmaid. Series: Talking About. 1999, Raintree LB $25.69 (978-0-8172-5542-8). 32pp. Covers children's concerns when a family is breaking up — why this happens, what becomes of the children, who one can talk to, and what a stepfamily is. (Rev: HBG 9/99; SLJ 7/99) [306.8]

20776 Raum, Elizabeth. *New Brothers and Sisters* (1–3). Series: Tough Topics. 2008, Heinemann LB $25.36 (978-1-4329-0820-1); paper $7.99 (978-1-4329-0825-6). 32pp. Raum provides guidance for siblings expecting a new baby in chapters with titles such as "Why Do I Have to Wait So Long?" and "What If I Feel Left Out?" (Rev: SLJ 11/08) [306.875]

20777 Rosenberg, Maxine B. *Living with a Single Parent* (4–7). 1992, Macmillan $14.95 (978-0-02-777915-8). 160pp. In interview format, this topic is presented through the opinions of youngsters from eight to 13. (Rev: BCCB 2/93; BL 11/15/92; SLJ 12/92) [306.85]

20778 Rotner, Shelley, and Sheila Kelly. *Lots of Grandparents* (PS–1). Illus. 2001, Millbrook $23.90 (978-0-7613-2313-6). 24pp. A collection of color photographs showing grandparents of various ethnicities engaged in many activities. (Rev: BL 9/1/01; HBG 3/02; SLJ 9/01) [306.874]

20779 Rubel, Nicole. *Twice As Nice: What It's Like to Be a Twin* (3–5). 2004, Farrar $16.50 (978-0-374-31836-9). 32pp. An entertaining exploration of the biology, psychology, and advantages and disadvantages of being — and parenting — a twin. (Rev: BL 11/15/04; SLJ 11/04) [306.875]

20780 Sanders, Pete, and Steve Myers. *Divorce and Separation* (4–8). Illus. Series: What Do You Know About. 1997, Millbrook LB $23.90 (978-0-7613-0574-3). An introduction to separation and divorce, with an emphasis on tips to help youngsters adjust and cope. (Rev: SLJ 10/97) [306.8]

20781 Sheldon, Annette. *Big Sister Now: A Story About Me and Our New Baby* (PS). Illus. by Karen Maizel. 2006, Magination $14.95 (978-1-59147-243-8); paper $9.95 (978-1-59147-244-5). 32pp. A little girl has some difficulty adjusting to the presence of her new baby brother; a note at the end gives parents advice on easing the transition. (Rev: BL 8/06; SLJ 2/07) [306.875]

20782 Simon, Norma. *All Kinds of Families* (4–6). Illus. by Joe Lasker. 1976, Whitman LB $16.99

(978-0-8075-0282-2). 40pp. Explores various kinds of families and their problems.

20783 Snow, Judith E. *How It Feels to Have a Gay or Lesbian Parent: A Book by Kids for Kids of All Ages* (5–8). 2004, Haworth $19.95 (978-1-56023-419-7); paper $12.95 (978-1-56023-420-3). 110pp. Diverse reflections on what it means to have a gay or lesbian parent come from children, young adults, and adults (up to age 31). (Rev: BL 1/1–15/05; SLJ 10/04) [306.874]

20784 Stein, Sara Bonnett. *On Divorce* (2–4). Illus. 1979, Walker $10.95 (978-0-8027-6344-0); paper $4.95 (978-0-8027-7226-8). Photographs and text cover this subject in an elementary fashion.

20785 Taylor, Maureen. *Through the Eyes of Your Ancestors: A Step-by-Step Guide to Uncovering Your Family's History* (5–9). Illus. 1999, Houghton paper $8.95 (978-0-395-86982-6). Budding researchers learn how to investigate family history, from conducting interviews to visiting genealogical libraries. (Rev: BCCB 5/99; BL 3/1/99; HB 5/99; HBG 10/99; SLJ 5/99) [929.1]

20786 Thomas, Pat. *My Family's Changing* (PS–2). Illus. by Lesley Harker. 1999, Barron's paper $6.95 (978-0-7641-0995-9). 32pp. A beginning book about divorce and how it affects different members of the family. (Rev: BL 5/15/99; SLJ 6/99) [306.89]

20787 Tym, Kate, and Penny Worms. *Coping with Families: A Guide to Taking Control of Your Life* (5–8). Series: Get Real. 2004, Raintree LB $28.56 (978-1-4109-0574-1). 48pp. Expert advice and case studies are presented in an appealing format, plus a list of hotline numbers. Also use *Coping with Friends* (2004). (Rev: SLJ 5/05)

20788 Weitzman, Elizabeth. *Let's Talk About Foster Homes* (K–2). Illus. Series: Let's Talk. 1996, Rosen LB $18.75 (978-0-8239-2310-6). 24pp. After defining what a foster home is, this title explains why some children are placed in one and the adjustments that they must make. Other family problems are explored in *Let's Talk About Staying in a Shelter, Let's Talk About When a Parent Dies,* and *Let's Talk About Your Parents' Divorce* (all 1996). (Rev: SLJ 12/96) [362.7]

20789 Wolfman, Ira. *Climbing Your Family Tree: Online and Off-Line Genealogy for Kids.* Rev. ed. (5–9). Illus. by Tim Robinson. 2002, Workman paper $13.95 (978-0-7611-2539-6). 228pp. A wide-ranging look at genealogy and the ways of tracing family names through document research, interviews, and the World Wide Web. (Rev: SLJ 2/03; VOYA 10/03) [929]

Personal Problems and Relationships

20790 Adams, Lisa K. *Dealing with Teasing* (K–4). Series: Conflict Resolution Library. 1997, Rosen LB $19.95 (978-0-8239-5070-6). 24pp. This book explains the different kinds of teasing — from the innocent to the harmful — and how to cope when teasing gets out of hand. (Rev: SLJ 4/98) [152.4]

20791 Allman, Toney. *Mean Behind the Screen: What You Need to Know About Cyberbullying* (5–8). Illus. Series: What's the Issue? 2008, Compass Point LB $20.99 (978-0-7565-4145-3). 48pp. A solid introduction to cyberbullying and its consequences. (Rev: BL 4/1/09) [302.3]

20792 Cohen-Posey, Kate. *How to Handle Bullies, Teasers and Other Meanies: A Book That Takes the Nuisance out of Name Calling and Other Nonsense* (4–7). 1995, Rainbow paper $8.95 (978-1-56825-029-8). 91pp. A practical book that offers useful suggestions on how to handle bullies. (Rev: BCCB 12/95; BL 11/15/95) [646.7]

20793 Cordes, Helen. *Girl Power in the Mirror: A Book About Girls, Their Bodies, and Themselves* (5–8). Illus. 2000, Lerner LB $30.35 (978-0-8225-2691-9). 112pp. This book for girls explains proper attitudes about appearance and gives coping strategies concerning pressures about one's looks. Also use *Girl Power in the Classroom: A Book About Girls, Their Fears, and Their Future* (2000). (Rev: BL 5/15/00; HBG 10/00; SLJ 5/00) [306.4]

20794 Crist, James J. *What to Do When You're Scared and Worried: A Guide for Kids* (5–8). Illus. by Michael Chesworth. 2004, Free Spirit paper $9.99 (978-1-57542-153-7). 123pp. Reassuring words and sound advice for young people troubled by such diverse issues as school exams, bullies, terrorism, nightmares, monsters, and the dark. (Rev: SLJ 7/04) [152.4]

20795 Dee, Catherine, ed. *The Girls' Book of Wisdom: Empowering, Inspirational Quotes from Over 400 Fabulous Females* (5–8). Illus. by Lou M. Pollack. 1999, Little, Brown paper $8.95 (978-0-316-17956-0). 192pp. A collection of quotations from more than 400 famous women grouped under such headings as "Friends," "Happiness," and "Leadership." (Rev: SLJ 12/99; VOYA 4/00) [305.23]

20796 Erlbach, Arlene. *The Middle School Survival Guide* (5–7). Illus. by Helen Flook. 2003, Walker $16.95 (978-0-8027-8852-8); paper $8.95 (978-0-8027-7657-0). 160pp. The author offers tips on a wide variety of topics of interest to this age group (homework, drugs, sex, and so forth), interspersed with advice from students themselves. (Rev: BL 9/15/03; SLJ 9/03) [373.18]

20797 Finn, Carrie. *Kids Talk About Bullying* (K–2). Illus. by Amy Bailey Muehlenhardt. Series: Kids Talk Jr. 2006, Picture Window LB $25.26 (978-1-4048-2315-0). 32pp. A question-and-answer format and simple language are used to discuss bullying and ways of coping with it. (Rev: SLJ 1/07) [303.6]

20798 Foltz, Linda Lee. *Kids Helping Kids: Break the Silence of Sexual Abuse* (4–9). 2003, Lighthouse Point $21.95 (978-0-9637966-8-4); paper $14.95 (978-0-9637966-9-1). 141pp. Personal stories from young people and adults who suffered abuse as children illustrate the guilt and shame typically experienced and show how to get help. (Rev: SLJ 9/03) [362.7]

20799 Gellman, Marc. *"Always Wear Clean Underwear!" and Other Ways Parents Say "I Love You"* (4–7). 1997, Morrow $14.95 (978-0-688-14492-0).

128pp. Some kids think that the expressions featured in this book are parental nagging, but the message really is that parents care. (Rev: BL 10/1/97; HBG 3/98; SLJ 11/97) [306.874]

20800 Goldentyer, Debra. *Child Abuse* (4–8). Series: Preteen Pressures. 1998, Raintree LB $25.69 (978-0-8172-5032-4). 48pp. This work describes the types, causes, and effects of child abuse and supplies material on how to change an abusive situation. (Rev: BL 5/15/98; HBG 10/98) [362.7]

20801 Greenberg, Judith E. *A Girl's Guide to Growing Up: Making the Right Choices* (5–8). Illus. 2000, Watts LB $24.00 (978-0-531-11592-3). 144pp. Lots of personal stories are quoted in this guidance book for preteen and teenage girls dealing with such subjects as school, risky behaviors, dating, sex, self-esteem, eating disorders, and cliques. (Rev: BL 2/15/01; SLJ 4/01; VOYA 6/01) [305.23]

20802 Halperin, Wendy A. *Love Is . . .* (PS–3). Illus. 2001, Simon & Schuster $16.00 (978-0-689-82980-2). 32pp. Different kinds of love are explored in this unusually beautiful picture book. (Rev: BL 1/1–15/01*; HBG 10/01; SLJ 2/01) [242]

20803 Heegaard, Mary E. *Coping with Death and Grief* (4–6). 1990, Lerner LB $19.93 (978-0-8225-0043-8). 64pp. This account helps children understand how the grieving process promotes emotional growth. (Rev: BL 11/1/90; SLJ 11/90) [155.6]

20804 Johnson, Julie. *Bullies and Gangs* (2–4). Photos by Roger Vlitos. Illus. by Chris O'Neill. Series: How Do I Feel About. 1998, Millbrook LB $19.90 (978-0-7613-0807-2). 24pp. This work describes how and why bullies behave the way they do and how to cope with them. (Rev: HBG 9/98; SLJ 7/98) [646.7]

20805 Johnston, Marianne. *Dealing with Bullying* (K–3). Illus. Series: Conflict Resolution Library. 1996, Rosen LB $19.95 (978-0-8239-2374-8). 24pp. A helpful book that helps young people understand bullies and offers techniques for self-protection. (Rev: SLJ 1/97) [155.5]

20806 Johnston, Marianne. *Let's Talk About Being Shy* (4–8). Illus. Series: Let's Talk. 1996, Rosen LB $19.95 (978-0-8239-2304-5). 24pp. The causes and possible cures of shyness are covered in this straightforward discussion. Also use *Let's Talk About Being Afraid* (1996). (Rev: BL 3/15/97) [155.4]

20807 Kent, Susan. *Let's Talk About Needing Extra Help at School* (3–5). Series: Let's Talk. 2000, Rosen LB $19.95 (978-0-8239-5422-3). 24pp. Using actual cases and realistic photos, this book explores the many reasons why kids might need extra help at school and what they can do about it. (Rev: SLJ 2/01) [371.2]

20808 Krohn, Katherine. *Everything You Need to Know About Birth Order* (5–9). Series: Need to Know Library. 2000, Rosen LB $27.95 (978-0-8239-3228-3). 64pp. An interesting book that looks at a number of theories about how birth order affects people. (Rev: SLJ 12/00) [306.85]

20809 Levete, Sarah. *Being Jealous* (1–3). Illus. by Chris O'Neill. Series: How Do I Feel About. 1999,

Millbrook LB $19.90 (978-0-7613-0911-6). 24pp. The experiences of five youngsters in the same class are used to explore the concept of jealousy. (Rev: BL 9/15/99; HBG 9/99; SLJ 12/99) [152.4]

20810 Lound, Karen. *Girl Power in the Family: A Book About Girls, Their Rights, and Their Voice* (5–10). Series: Girl Power. 2000, Lerner LB $30.35 (978-0-8225-2692-6). 80pp. A book that explores the problems of growing up female today with material on gender roles, biases, and relationships. (Rev: HBG 10/00; SLJ 6/00) [303.6]

20811 McIntyre, Tom. *The Behavior Survival Guide for Kids: How to Make Good Choices and Stay out of Trouble* (4–7). Illus. by Chris Sharp. 2003, Free Spirit paper $14.95 (978-1-57542-132-2). 167pp. This accessible guide offers concrete suggestions for dealing with behavior disorders and improving relations with teachers, family members, and friends. (Rev: SLJ 1/04) [649]

20812 Medina, Sarah. *Sad* (PS–K). Illus. Series: Feelings. 2007, Heinemann LB $21.36 (978-1-4034-9293-7). 24pp. In the form of questions and answers, this small volume tackles the topic of sadness and offers reassuring advice. (Rev: BL 4/15/07) [152.4]

20813 Middleton, Don. *Dealing with Competitiveness* (2–4). Series: Conflict Resolution Library. 1999, Rosen $19.95 (978-0-8239-5267-0). 24pp. An attractive introduction to this difficult subject that uses fictional anecdotes to explain the nature of competitiveness and its problems and solutions. Also use (from the same series and author) *Dealing with Secrets* (1998). (Rev: SLJ 4/99) [155]

20814 Moehn, Heather. *Everything You Need to Know About Cliques* (5–8). Series: Need to Know Library. 2001, Rosen LB $27.95 (978-0-8239-3326-6). 64pp. Moehn uses first-person narratives to introduce such topics as making friends, peer pressure, bullies, insecurity, and popularity, with a look at how cliques continue after high school. (Rev: SLJ 12/01) [158.25]

20815 Moroney, Trace. *When I'm Feeling Angry* (PS). Illus. 2006, School Specialty $9.95 (978-0-7696-4424-0). 18pp. A bunny describes what makes him mad and what it's like to feel angry; readers learn when it's OK to feel angry and when they need to control their behavior. Also use *When I'm Feeling Scared* (2006). (Rev: BL 3/1/06) [152.4]

20816 Nelson, Robin. *Working with Others* (K–3). Series: Pull Ahead Books. 2006, Lerner LB $22.60 (978-0-8225-3488-4). 32pp. Easy-to-understand advice about how to work well with others, covering such topics as conflict resolution, respect for others' opinions, patience, and discussing all sides of an issue. (Rev: SLJ 8/06) [303.69]

20817 Polland, Barbara K. *We Can Work it Out: Conflict Resolution for Children* (K–3). Illus. by Craig DeRoy. 2000, Tricycle $13.95 (978-1-58246-031-4). 64pp. This book poses questions about various kinds of behavioral problems (e.g., teasing, poor sportsmanship) and enables children to solve these problems through self-direction. (Rev: BL 1/1–15/01; HBG 10/01) [303.6]

20818 Powell, Jillian. *Talking About Bullying* (2–3). Illus. Series: Talking About. 1999, Raintree LB $25.70 (978-0-8172-5535-0). 32pp. This book explains to young children why kids become bullies and how to cope with them. (Rev: BL 7/99; HBG 9/99; SLJ 7/99) [371.58]

20819 Radabaugh, Melinda. *Sleeping Over* (PS–1). Series: First Time. 2003, Heinemann LB $18.50 (978-1-4034-0231-8). 24pp. Reassuring text and photographs introduce various kinds of sleepovers. (Rev: HBG 10/03; SLJ 9/03) [793.2]

20820 Rashkin, Rachel. *Feeling Better: A Kid's Book About Therapy* (4–8). Illus. by Bonnie Adamson. 2005, Magination paper $9.95 (978-1-59147-238-4). 48pp. Presented in journal format, this volume uses 12-year-old Maya's experiences with a therapist to offer useful insights into the process and its value. (Rev: SLJ 11/05) [618.92]

20821 Raum, Elizabeth. *Bullying* (1–3). Series: Tough Topics. 2008, Heinemann LB $25.36 (978-1-4329-0818-8); paper $7.99 (978-1-4329-0823-2). 32pp. After defining bullying, Raum discusses what to do to avoid bullying and what to do if you see bullying taking place. Also use *Fighting* and *Peer Pressure* (both 2008). (Rev: SLJ 11/08) [302.3]

20822 Rimm, Sylvia. *See Jane Win for Girls: A Smart Girl's Guide to Success* (5–9). Illus. 2003, Free Spirit paper $13.95 (978-1-57542-122-3). 131pp. Rimm offers practical advice on social and academic achievement and general life skills, with quizzes, activities, and success stories. (Rev: LMC 10/03; SLJ 6/03) [305.235]

20823 Romain, Trevor. *Bullies Are a Pain in the Brain* (3–7). Illus. by author. 1997, Free Spirit paper $8.95 (978-1-57542-023-3). 105pp. Explains why bullies act the way they do, types of bullying, and ways to cope with it. (Rev: SLJ 2/98) [371.5]

20824 Romain, Trevor. *Cliques, Phonies, and Other Baloney* (3–8). Illus. by author. 1998, Free Spirit paper $8.95 (978-1-57542-045-5). 136pp. This book deals with social groups centered around friendships (many false and destructive) and suggests ways to form and hold solid friendships. (Rev: SLJ 4/99) [177]

20825 Ross, Dave. *A Book of Friends* (PS–3). Illus. by Laura Rader. 1999, HarperCollins LB $12.89 (978-0-06-028362-9). This simple picture book shows in words and pictures how to be a good friend. (Rev: HBG 9/99; SLJ 7/99) [177]

20826 Spelman, Cornelia Maude. *Your Body Belongs to You* (K–3). Illus. by Teri Weidner. 1997, Whitman LB $13.95 (978-0-8075-9474-2). 24pp. An introduction to child sexual abuse, with a special section of advice for parents. (Rev: BL 9/1/97; HBG 3/98; SLJ 9/97) [613.6]

20827 *Yikes! A Smart Girl's Guide to Surviving Tricky, Sticky, Icky Situations* (4–8). Illus. by Bonnie Timmons. Series: American Girl Library. 2002, Pleasant paper $8.95 (978-1-58485-530-9). 87pp. Advice on everything from dealing with teachers and friends to coping with embarrassing situations and dangerous incidents. (Rev: SLJ 12/02) [305.23]

Careers

General and Miscellaneous

20828 Alagna, Magdalena. *War Correspondents: Life Under Fire* (5–10). Series: Extreme Careers. 2003, Rosen LB $26.50 (978-0-8239-3798-1). 64pp. The dangers of wartime assignments are emphasized in this volume that also stresses job requirements that include a good education and broad knowledge of world events. (Rev: BL 9/15/03; SLJ 11/03) [808]

20829 Bauld, Jane Scoggins. *We Need Librarians* (PS–1). Series: Helpers in Our Schools. 2000, Capstone LB $13.25 (978-0-7368-0531-5). 24pp. The many roles of school librarians are discussed in this beginning reader. (Rev: HBG 9/00; SLJ 10/00) [027]

20830 Bauld, Jane Scoggins. *We Need Principals* (PS–1). Series: Helpers in Our Schools. 2000, Capstone LB $17.26 (978-0-7368-0532-2). 24pp. For beginning readers, this is a book about school principals and what they do. (Rev: HBG 9/00; SLJ 10/00) [371]

20831 Bourgeois, Paulette. *Garbage Collectors* (PS–2). Illus. by Kim LaFave. Series: In My Neighborhood. 1998, Kids Can $12.95 (978-1-55074-440-8). 32pp. Using realistic paintings as illustrations, this book describes the duties of garbage collectors and how waste is recycled. (Rev: BL 4/15/98; HBG 10/98; SLJ 6/98) [363.72]

20832 Bourgeois, Paulette. *Postal Workers* (PS–2). Illus. by Kim LaFave. 1999, Kids Can $12.95 (978-1-55074-504-7). 32pp. This work introduces the many types of postal workers — from those who work in the post office to mail carriers. (Rev: BL 7/99; HBG 9/99; SLJ 7/99) [383.4973]

20833 Buckley, Annie & James Buckley, Jr. *Inside Photography* (3–5). Series: Reading Rocks! 2007, The Child's World LB $24.21 (978-1-59296-867-1). 32pp. This volume introduces three photographers — specializing in fashion, news, and animals — and looks at their techniques. (Rev: SLJ 1/08) [770]

20834 Cefrey, Holly. *Archaeologists: Life Digging Up Artifacts* (5–10). Series: Extreme Careers. 2004, Rosen LB $26.50 (978-0-8239-3963-3). 64pp. This is an introduction to the field of archeology, its problems, its opportunities, and its rewards. (Rev: BL 5/15/04) [930]

20835 *Food* (5–9). Series: Discovering Careers for Your Future. 2005, Ferguson $21.95 (978-0-8160-5848-8). 92pp. Education and training, salaries, and outlook for the field are all covered here along with a description of the kinds of daily activities found in various positions. (Rev: SLJ 1/06)

20836 Franks, Katie. *I Want to Be a Baseball Player* (2–4). Series: Dream Jobs. 2007, Rosen LB $21.25 (978-1-4042-3622-6). 24pp. Who wouldn't want to be a professional baseball player? Plenty of photographs and information about the career path to the pros will appeal to beginning and reluctant readers. (Rev: SLJ 7/07)

20837 Gibson, Karen Bush. *Child Care Workers* (K–3). Series: Community Helpers. 2000, Bridgestone LB $22.60 (978-0-7368-0622-0). 24pp. A solid introduction to various people who are involved in child care. (Rev: HBG 3/01; SLJ 2/01) [649]

20838 Gorman, Jacqueline Laks. *Librarian / El Bibliotecario* (PS–2). Photos by Gregg Andersen. Series: People in My Community/La Gente de Mi Comunidad. 2002, Gareth Stevens LB $21.00 (978-0-8368-3310-2). 24pp. Full-color photographs and single-sentence descriptions, in English and in Spanish, introduce various aspects of a librarian's job. (Rev: SLJ 3/03)

20839 Greenberg, Keith E. *Window Washer: At Work Above the Clouds* (2–5). Illus. Series: Risky Business. 1995, Blackbirch LB $16.95 (978-1-56711-154-5). 32pp. The dangers involved and the safety measures required are stressed in this career book about two men who wash windows at the World Trade Center in New York City. (Rev: SLJ 8/95) [646.2]

20840 Greene, Meg. *Careers in the National Guards' Search and Rescue Unit* (5–9). Series: Careers in Search and Rescue Operations. 2003, Rosen LB $26.50 (978-0-8239-3836-0). 64pp. This account describes the vital role that citizen-soldiers play in the line of defense and tells of their search-and-rescue activities during the terrorist attacks of September 11, 2001. (Rev: BL 10/15/03; SLJ 4/04) [335]

20841 Hayhurst, Chris. *Astronauts: Life Exploring Outer Space* (4–7). Series: Extreme Careers. 2001, Rosen LB $26.50 (978-0-8239-3364-8). 64pp. A high-interest look at the extensive skills required to become an astronaut, with brief coverage of space exploration and profiles of astronauts. (Rev: SLJ 1/02) [629]

20842 *History* (4–8). Illus. Series: Discovering Careers for Your Future. 2001, Ferguson LB $21.95 (978-0-89434-391-9). 92pp. A useful introduction to the career opportunities in this field, with information on the skills required, potential earnings, and job outlook. (Rev: SLJ 11/01) [331.702]

20843 Hurwitz, Jane. *Choosing a Career in Animal Care* (4–8). Illus. Series: World of Work. 1996, Rosen LB $17.95 (978-0-8239-2268-0). 64pp. Various careers in working with animals are described, along with the education required, desirable character traits, and ways to break into the field. (Rev: SLJ 8/97) [371.7]

20844 Hyland, Tony. *Miners and Drillers* (4–6). Series: Extreme Jobs. 2007, Smart Apple LB $27.10 (978-1-58340-741-7). 32pp. Readers interested in exciting, sometimes risky jobs will enjoy exploring what a miner or driller does and how to go about becoming one. Also use *Divers* (2007). (Rev: SLJ 8/07)

20845 Jacobs, Shannon K. *Healers of the Wild: People Who Care for Injured and Orphaned Wildlife* (4–7). Illus. 1998, Coyote Moon paper $19.95 (978-0-9661070-0-5). 212pp. The process of helping orphaned, injured, or displaced wildlife is covered thoroughly under three operational headings: rescue, rehabilitation, and release. (Rev: BL 10/1/98) [339.946]

20846 Jaspersohn, William. *A Week in the Life of an Airline Pilot* (4–8). Illus. 1991, Little, Brown $14.95 (978-0-316-45822-1). 96pp. A close-up look at the duties and lives of members of an airline crew. (Rev: BL 3/15/91; HB 5/91; SLJ 5/91) [629.132]

20847 Kiland, Taylor Baldwin. *The U.S. Navy and Military Careers* (5–8). Series: U.S. Armed Forces and Military Careers. 2006, Enslow LB $31.93 (978-0-7660-2523-3). 128pp. Straightforward and informative, this title provides a history of the Navy, looks at its role in the nation's defense, and details various jobs within this branch of the armed forces. (Rev: SLJ 6/07)

20848 Klein, Hilary Dole. *A Day with a Chef* (1–3). Illus. Series: Reading Rocks! 2007, Child's World LB $24.21 (978-1-59296-857-2). 32pp. Readers learn about the varied work involved in being a chef — planning menus, ordering supplies, managing the staff — as well as the training needed and the

vocabulary of this trade. (Rev: BL 1/1–15/08; SLJ 1/08) [641.5092]

20849 Leboutillier, Nate. *A Day in the Life of a Zookeeper* (K–3). Series: First Facts: Community Helpers at Work. 2004, Capstone LB $21.26 (978-0-7368-2632-7). 24pp. Using a question-and-answer format and full-color photographs, this volume looks at the tasks a zookeeper performs. (Rev: SLJ 1/05) [636]

20850 Lee, Barbara. *Working with Animals* (4–8). Illus. Series: Exploring Careers. 1996, Lerner LB $23.93 (978-0-8225-1759-7). 112pp. Profiles of 12 careers involving animals, such as veterinarian, animal shelter worker, or pet sitter. (Rev: BL 2/15/97) [591]

20851 Liebman, Dan. *I Want to Be a Teacher* (K–2). Series: I Want to Be. 2001, Firefly LB $14.95 (978-1-55209-572-0). 24pp. A teacher's typical working day is described with a color photograph and two or three lines of text on each page in this easily read book. (Rev: BL 12/15/01; HBG 10/01) [371.1]

20852 Lowenstein, Felicia. *What Does a Teacher Do?* (K–2). Illus. Series: What Does a Community Helper Do? 2006, Enslow LB $21.26 (978-0-7660-2321-5). 24pp. Outlines in easy-to-understand language the job requirements and everyday responsibilities of a teacher. (Rev: SLJ 4/06) [371.1]

20853 Loy, Jessica. *When I Grow Up: A Young Person's Guide to Interesting and Unusual Occupations* (4–6). 2008, Holt $16.95 (978-0-8050-7717-9). Young people looking to the future will find interesting options here, among them master cheese maker, chocolatier, lobsterman, kite designer, and pet photographer. (Rev: LMC 1/09; SLJ 3/09) [331.702]

20854 Manley, Claudia B. *Secret Agents: Life as a Professional Spy* (4–7). Series: Extreme Careers. 2001, Rosen LB $26.50 (978-0-8239-3369-3). 64pp. A high-interest look at the extensive skills required to become an intelligence agent and the kinds of intelligence that are gathered (strategic, tactical, counterintelligence), with material on the history of espionage and on real-life and fictional spies. (Rev: SLJ 1/02) [327.12]

20855 Maze, Stephanie. *I Want to Be a Fashion Designer* (3–6). Illus. Series: I Want to Be. 2000, Harcourt $18.00 (978-0-15-201862-7); paper $9.00 (978-0-15-201938-9). 48pp. This large-format book uses double-page spreads to explore the world of fashion design and covers such topics as trade shows, education, and how a designer works. (Rev: BL 3/1/00; SLJ 4/00) [746.9]

20856 Minden, Cecelia. *Coaches* (1–2). Series: Neighborhood Helpers. 2006, The Child's World LB $24.21 (978-1-59296-561-8). 32pp. This attractive overview introduces young children to the role and responsibilities of a coach, plus the equipment and training needed. (Rev: SLJ 8/06) [796]

20857 Monroe, Judy. *A Day in the Life of a Librarian* (K–3). Series: First Facts: Community Helpers at Work. 2004, Capstone LB $21.26 (978-0-7368-2630-3). 24pp. Using a question-and-answer format and full-color photos, this volume looks at the tasks a librarian performs. (Rev: SLJ 1/05)

20858 Morris, Ann. *That's Our Librarian!* (K–3). Photos and illus. by Peter Linenthal. Series: That's Our School. 2003, Millbrook LB $22.90 (978-0-7613-2400-3). Readers are introduced to elementary school librarian Maria Rodriguez and all the responsibilities of her job. Also use *That's Our Teacher!* (2003). (Rev: HBG 4/04; SLJ 11/03) [027.8]

20859 Murdico, Suzanne J. *Bomb Squad Experts: Life Defusing Explosive Devices* (5–10). Series: Extreme Careers. 2004, Rosen LB $26.50 (978-0-8239-3968-8). 64pp. A look at the career opportunities in bomb squads, with material on training, salaries, and working conditions. (Rev: BL 5/15/04) [363]

20860 Pasternak, Ceel. *Cool Careers for Girls with Animals* (5–8). Series: Cool Careers for Girls. 1998, Impact $19.95 (978-1-57023-108-7); paper $12.95 (978-1-57023-105-6). Veterinarian, pet sitter, bird handler, animal trainer, and horse-farm owner are among the careers covered, supplemented by interviews with women who work in each field. (Rev: SLJ 4/99; VOYA 8/99) [371.7]

20861 Pasternak, Ceel, and Linda Thornburg. *Cool Careers for Girls in Food* (5–10). Series: Cool Careers for Girls. 2000, Impact $19.95 (978-1-57023-127-8); paper $12.95 (978-1-57023-120-9). 128pp. The 11 women featured in this book are involved in various aspects of the food industry such as cheese making, baking, wine making, selling health food, and cooking for the military. (Rev: SLJ 2/00) [641]

20862 Payment, Simone. *Frontline Marines: Fighting in the Marine Combat Arms Units* (5–8). Illus. Series: Extreme Careers. 2007, Rosen LB $26.50 (978-1-4042-0946-6). 64pp. Students looking for exciting careers may want to look into the combat arms units of the U.S. Marines, suggests this book, which tells readers what these units do and explains the training involved. (Rev: BL 7/07) [359.9]

20863 *Publishing* (5–9). Series: Discovering Careers for Your Future. 2005, Ferguson LB $21.95 (978-0-8160-5845-7). 92pp. Education and training, salaries, and outlook for the field are all covered here along with a description of the kinds of daily activities found in various positions. (Rev: SLJ 1/06)

20864 Rau, Dana Meachen. *Baker* (PS–K). Series: Benchmark Rebus. 2007, Marshall Cavendish LB $15.95 (978-0-7614-2623-3). 24pp. For young children, this overview of the job of a baker contains an appealing mix of rebus, text, and image. (Rev: SLJ 12/07) [641.8]

20865 Reeves, Diane L. *Career Ideas for Kids Who Like Art* (5–9). Illus. Series: Career Ideas for Kids Who Like. 1998, Facts on File $23.00 (978-0-8160-3681-3). An upbeat book that explores a variety of art-related careers, including many peripheral ones such as chef, animator, and photojournalist, with suggestions on how to test one's suitability for each area and reports from people working in the field. (Rev: SLJ 10/98; VOYA 8/98) [791]

20866 Reeves, Diane L. *Career Ideas for Kids Who Like Math* (4–8). Illus. by Nancy Bond. 2000, Facts on File $23.00 (978-0-8160-4095-7). 186pp. Presents an amazing array of careers available for the mathematically inclined, arranged alphabetically with good solid information on each. (Rev: HBG 10/00; SLJ 9/00) [510]

20867 Reeves, Diane L. *Career Ideas for Kids Who Like Talking* (5–9). Illus. by Nancy Bond. Series: Career Ideas for Kids. 1998, Facts on File $23.00 (978-0-8160-3683-7); paper $12.95 (978-0-8160-3689-9). 154pp. This is a guide to careers in communications, from hotel manager to publicist to broadcaster, with reports from people in the field, tests to check one's aptitude, and lists of resources. (Rev: SLJ 10/98) [331.7]

20868 Reeves, Diane L. *Career Ideas for Kids Who Like Writing* (5–9). Illus. Series: Career Ideas for Kids Who Like. 1998, Facts on File $23.00 (978-0-8160-3685-1); paper $12.95 (978-0-8160-3691-2). A look at 15 careers related to writing, among them advertising copywriter, author, bookseller, editor, grant writer, journalist, librarian, literary agent, and publicist, with a self-test for each one and a profile of a person working in the field. (Rev: SLJ 3/99) [808]

20869 Ring, Susan. *Animal Watch* (2–4). Series: On the Job. 2003, Chelsea Clubhouse LB $23.00 (978-0-7910-7409-1). 24pp. Explores three jobs that involve the study of animals: zoologist, entomologist, and ornithologist. (Rev: HBG 10/03; SLJ 10/03) [590]

20870 Rosenberg, Aaron. *Cryptologists: Life Making and Breaking Codes* (5–10). Series: Extreme Careers. 2004, Rosen LB $26.50 (978-0-8239-3965-7). 64pp. After some background material on the history of codes, this volume discusses career opportunities as a cryptologist. (Rev: BL 5/15/04; SLJ 5/90) [410]

20871 Rotner, Shelley, and Ken Kreisler. *Everybody Works* (PS–1). Photos by Shelley Rotner. 2003, Millbrook LB $23.93 (978-0-7613-1751-7). In addition to jobs that interest youngsters — police, firefighters, and so forth — this book looks at lower-profile occupations and at volunteerism, hobbies, and even working animals. (Rev: HBG 10/03; SLJ 7/03) [331.7]

20872 Roza, Greg. *Careers in the Coast Guard's Search and Rescue Unit* (5–9). Series: Careers in Search and Rescue Operations. 2003, Rosen LB $26.50 (978-0-8239-3835-3). 64pp. This book covers the search and rescue operations involving the Coast Guard with particular emphasis on their vital role during the September 11, 2001, attacks. (Rev: BL 10/15/03; SLJ 4/04) [355]

20873 Schomp, Virginia. *If You Were a Farmer* (3–4). Series: If You Were A. 2000, Benchmark LB $22.79 (978-0-7614-1001-0). 32pp. The daily routines of a farmer and the equipment used are included in this simple career book. (Rev: BL 11/15/00; HBG 3/01; SLJ 3/01) [631]

20874 Schomp, Virginia. *If You Were a Teacher* (1–3). Series: If You Were A. 1999, Benchmark LB

$22.79 (978-0-7614-0916-8). 32pp. After a brief history of teaching, there is coverage of various kinds of teachers in this attractive book. (Rev: HBG 9/00; SLJ 3/00) [371.7]

20875 Schomp, Virginia. *If You Were an Astronaut* (3–4). Series: If You Were A. 1997, Marshall Cavendish LB $22.79 (978-0-7614-0618-1). 32pp. Covers the education, training, and duties of astronauts. (Rev: BL 2/15/98; HBG 3/98; SLJ 2/98) [629]

20876 Simon, Charnan. *Lewis the Librarian* (K–2). Illus. by Rebecca Thornburgh. Series: Magic Door to Learning. 2006, The Child's World LB $21.36 (978-1-59296-624-0). 24pp. An inviting basic introduction to the role of a librarian. (Rev: SLJ 2/07) [020.92]

20877 Stein, R. Conrad. *The U.S. Marine Corps and Military Careers* (5–8). Series: U.S. Armed Forces and Military Careers. 2006, Enslow LB $31.93 (978-0-7660-2521-9). 128pp. This overview of careers in the U.S. Marine Corps discusses expectations, duties, and pay scales as well as the Marines' role in national defense. (Rev: SLJ 6/07)

20878 Stockdale, Linda. *ABC Career Book for Girls / El Libro de Carreras para Niñas* (K–3). Illus. by John Schafer. 1996, Columbia Univ. Pr. paper $9.95 (978-1-884830-00-6). 31pp. Using the letters of the alphabet, this book describes a wide range of occupations in English and Spanish. (Rev: SLJ 2/97) [331.7]

20879 Sweeney, Alyse. *Welcome to the Library* (K–2). Series: Scholastic News Nonfiction Readers. 2006, Children's Pr. LB $20.00 (978-0-531-16841-7). 24pp. Basic information for beginning readers about libraries and the work of librarians, with seven highlighted words that are featured in bold in the text. (Rev: SLJ 1/07) [027]

20880 Sweeney, Alyse. *Who Works at the Zoo?* (K–2). Series: Scholastic News Nonfiction Readers. 2006, Children's Pr. LB $20.00 (978-0-531-16842-4). 24pp. For beginning readers interested in working at a zoo, this book provides basic information. (Rev: SLJ 1/07) [590.73]

20881 Talbert, Marc. *Holding the Reins: A Ride Through Cowgirl Life* (5–7). Photos by Barbara Van Cleve. 2003, HarperCollins $16.99 (978-0-06-029255-3). 105pp. The demanding but exhilarating lives of modern-day cowgirls are shown here as the author follows four teens through the seasons. (Rev: BCCB 4/03; BL 1/1–15/03; HBG 10/03; SLJ 4/03) [978]

20882 Thompson, Lisa. *Creating Cuisine: Have You Got What It Takes to Be a Chef?* (5–8). Illus. Series: On the Job. 2008, Compass Point LB $19.95 (978-0-7565-3625-1). 48pp. An inside look at professional kitchens and the training to become a restaurant cook. (Rev: BL 4/1/08) [641.5092]

20883 Turner, Chérie. *Adventure Tour Guides: Life on Extreme Outdoor Adventures* (5–10). Series: Extreme Careers. 2003, Rosen LB $26.50 (978-0-8239-3793-6). 64pp. A look at the profession of guiding excursions such as white-water rafting and

mountain climbing, with material on qualifications and future possibilities. (Rev: BL 9/15/03) [908]

20884 Willett, Edward. *Careers in Outer Space: New Business Opportunities* (4–9). Series: The Career Resource Library. 2002, Rosen LB $31.95 (978-0-8239-3358-7). 92pp. An interesting look at opportunities in the fields of science, math, engineering, technology, communication, and, of course, aeronautics, with information on required skills and training and on the pros and cons of working in the public and private sectors. (Rev: SLJ 6/02) [629.4]

Arts and Entertainment

20885 Aaseng, Nathan. *Wildshots: The World of the Wildlife Photographer* (5–8). Illus. 2001, Millbrook LB $29.90 (978-0-7613-1551-3). 80pp. This account describes the work of a wildlife photographer and tells exciting stories about unusual encounters. (Rev: BL 3/1/01*; HBG 10/01; SLJ 3/01; VOYA 10/01) [778.9]

20886 Amara, Philip. *So, You Wanna Be a Comic Book Artist?* (5–8). Illus. by Pop Mhan. 2001, Beyond Words paper $9.95 (978-1-58270-058-8). 160pp. A comprehensive, engaging look at the world of comic-book illustration, with tips on everything from buying supplies to submitting work to publishers. (Rev: BL 1/1–15/02; SLJ 4/02) [808]

20887 *Art* (4–8). Illus. Series: Discovering Careers for Your Future. 2001, Ferguson LB $21.95 (978-0-89434-388-9). 92pp. A useful introduction to career opportunities in art, with information on the skills required, potential earnings, and job outlook. (Rev: SLJ 11/01) [702.373]

20888 Burton, Marilee. *Artists at Work* (2–4). Series: On the Job. 2003, Chelsea Clubhouse LB $23.00 (978-0-7910-7410-7). 24pp. Introduces young readers to theatrical producer/costume designer Julie Taymor, architect/sculptor Maya Lin, and jazz trumpeter Wynton Marsalis. (Rev: HBG 10/03; SLJ 10/03) [700]

20889 Christelow, Eileen. *What Do Illustrators Do?* (2–4). Illus. 1999, Clarion $16.00 (978-0-395-90230-1). 40pp. Showing two illustrators — both working on a version of *Jack and the Beanstalk* — this book explores the illustration process and its finished product. (Rev: BCCB 5/99; BL 3/1/99; HB 5/99; HBG 9/99; SLJ 11/99) [741.6]

20890 Dubois, Muriel L. *I Like Music* (1–3). 2000, Bridgestone LB $22.60 (978-0-7368-0632-9). 24pp. Opposite each full-page photo, there is a description of a music-related occupation such as composer, conductor, sound engineer, or disc jockey. (Rev: HBG 3/01; SLJ 2/01) [780]

20891 Hyland, Tony. *Stunt Performers* (4–6). Series: Extreme Jobs. 2007, Smart Apple LB $27.10 (978-1-58340-739-4). 32pp. Readers interested in exciting, sometimes risky jobs will enjoy exploring what a stunt performer does and how to go about becoming one. (Rev: SLJ 8/07)

20892 Johnson, Marlys H. *Careers in the Movies* (5–9). Series: Career Resource Library. 2001, Rosen LB $31.95 (978-0-8239-3186-6). 122pp. Job descriptions and qualifications are clearly laid out in this guide for aspiring filmmakers that also discusses the history of the industry and the basic steps in film production. (Rev: SLJ 8/01) [791.43]

20893 Lee, Barbara. *Working in Sports and Recreation* (5–9). Illus. Series: Exploring Careers. 1996, Lerner LB $23.93 (978-0-8225-1762-7). Twelve people involved in careers related to sports and recreation talk candidly about their professions. (Rev: BL 2/15/97) [796]

20894 Lehn, Barbara. *What Is an Artist?* (PS–2). Illus. by Carol Krauss. 2002, Millbrook LB $21.90 (978-0-7613-2259-7). 32pp. An introduction of the concept of "artist," presented in a friendly format for younger readers. (Rev: BL 12/15/02; HBG 3/03) [709]

20895 Libal, Joyce, and Rae Simons. *Professional Athlete and Sports Official* (5–9). Series: Careers with Character. 2003, Mason Crest LB $22.95 (978-1-59084-321-5). 90pp. The importance of character traits such as integrity, respect, fairness, and self-discipline when seeking careers in sports is emphasized here. (Rev: HBG 10/03; SLJ 4/03) [796]

20896 Lyon, George E. *A Sign* (K–4). Illus. by Chris K. Soentpiet. 1998, Orchard $15.95 (978-0-531-30073-2). 32pp. As a child, the author wanted to pursue many different careers, but finally she decided that the best one would be writing. (Rev: BL 2/15/98; HBG 9/98; SLJ 3/98) [813]

20897 McLaglen, Mary, et al. *You Can Be a Woman Movie Maker* (4–8). Series: You Can Be a Woman. 2003, Cascade Pass $19.95 (978-1-880599-64-8); paper $14.95 (978-1-880599-63-1). 71pp. Three women — a producer, an independent filmmaker, and an executive producer — talk about their jobs, how they got into the movie industry, and what a day on the job is like. Interviews and film clips are on an accompanying DVD. (Rev: SLJ 4/04) [791.43]

20898 Nathan, Amy. *Meet the Musicians: From Prodigy (or Not) to Pro* (5–8). Illus. 2006, Holt $17.95 (978-0-8050-7743-8). 156pp. Profiles of members of the New York Philharmonic give readers a good understanding of the different roles of various instruments and the careers of professional musicians. (Rev: BL 3/15/06; SLJ 5/06; VOYA 6/06) [750.92]

20899 Nathan, Amy. *The Young Musician's Survival Guide: Tips from Teens and Pros* (5–8). 2000, Oxford $21.99 (978-0-19-512611-2). 126pp. A thorough study of how to break into the music world, with information on working with music teachers, conductors, and peers, and tips on practicing, choosing an instrument, and handling fears and frustrations. (Rev: BL 4/1/00; HBG 10/00; SLJ 6/00) [780]

20900 Parks, Peggy J. *Musician* (4–7). Illus. Series: Exploring Careers. 2004, Gale LB $26.20 (978-0-7377-2067-9). 48pp. In addition to a description of the work that musicians (including DJs) do, there is a frank assessment of the opportunities available. (Rev: BL 3/15/04) [780]

20901 Parks, Peggy J. *Writer* (4–7). Illus. Series: Exploring Careers. 2004, Gale LB $26.20 (978-0-7377-2069-3). 48pp. The ups and downs of a career in writing are frankly discussed in this slim guide. (Rev: BL 3/15/04) [808]

20902 Pasternak, Ceel, and Linda Thornburg. *Cool Careers for Girls in Sports* (5–10). Series: Cool Careers for Girls. 1999, Impact $19.95 (978-1-57023-107-0); paper $12.95 (978-1-57023-104-9). 120pp. A golf pro, basketball player, ski instructor, sports broadcaster, trainer, sports psychologist, and athletic director are among the 10 women profiled in this overview of careers for women in sports. (Rev: SLJ 7/99; VOYA 8/99) [796]

20903 *Radio and Television* (5–9). Series: Discovering Careers for Your Future. 2005, Ferguson LB $21.95 (978-0-8160-5846-4). 92pp. Education and training, salaries, and outlook for the field are all covered here along with a description of the kinds of daily activities found in various positions. (Rev: SLJ 1/06)

20904 Reeves, Diane L., and Peter Kent. *Career Ideas for Kids Who Like Sports* (5–9). Illus. Series: Career Ideas for Kids Who Like. 1998, Facts on File $23.00 (978-0-8160-3684-4); paper $12.95 (978-0-8160-3690-5). The 15 sports-related careers highlighted in this volume include coach, athlete, agent, sportscaster, and sports equipment manufacturer, with accompanying material on necessary skills, opportunities, duties, and a report from someone in the field. (Rev: SLJ 6/99) [796]

20905 Schomp, Virginia. *If You Were a Ballet Dancer* (3–4). Illus. Series: If You Were A. 1997, Marshall Cavendish LB $22.79 (978-0-7614-0616-7). 32pp. This introduction to a career in ballet tells about practicing, performing, styles of dance, costumes, and terminology. (Rev: BL 2/15/98; HBG 3/98; SLJ 2/98) [792.8]

20906 Schomp, Virginia. *If You Were a Musician* (3–4). Series: If You Were A. 2000, Benchmark LB $22.79 (978-0-7614-1002-7). 32pp. Using color photos and a simple text, this career book covers a typical day in the life of a musician. (Rev: BL 11/15/00; HBG 3/01; SLJ 3/01) [780]

20907 Sommers, Michael A. *Wildlife Photographers: Life Through a Lens* (5–10). Series: Extreme Careers. 2003, Rosen LB $26.50 (978-0-8239-3638-0). 64pp. A concise explanation of the work of wildlife photographers, the attributes needed, and the training and tenacity required to enter this field. (Rev: BL 9/15/03; SLJ 5/03) [771]

Business

20908 *Advertising and Marketing* (5–9). Series: Discovering Careers for Your Future. 2005, Ferguson $21.95 (978-0-8160-5847-1). 92pp. Education and training, salaries, and outlook for the field are all covered here along with a description of the kinds of daily activities found in various positions. (Rev: SLJ 1/06)

Engineering, Technology, and Trades

20909 Boekhoff, P. M. *What Does a Construction Worker Do?* (K–2). Illus. Series: What Does a Community Helper Do? 2006, Enslow LB $21.26 (978-0-7660-2326-0). 24pp. Outlines in easy-to-understand language the job requirements and everyday responsibilities of a construction worker. (Rev: SLJ 4/06) [690]

20910 Brown, Marty. *Webmaster* (4–8). Series: Coolcareers.com. 2000, Rosen LB $23.95 (978-0-8239-3111-8). 44pp. This volume describes a Web page, types of networks, servers, browsers, and protocols and introduces some careers in Web-related areas. (Rev: SLJ 6/00) [004]

20911 *Computers* (4–8). Illus. Series: Discovering Careers for Your Future. 2001, Ferguson LB $21.95 (978-0-89434-389-6). 92pp. A useful introduction to the career opportunities in this field, with information on the skills required, potential earnings, and job outlook. (Rev: SLJ 11/01) [004.02373]

20912 Frew, Katherine. *Plumber* (5–8). Series: Great Jobs. 2004, Children's Pr. LB $24.50 (978-0-516-24088-6). 48pp. This appealing, photo-filled title focuses on the plumbing trade, looking at job requirements, training, and tools, as well as providing a history of the plumbing business and a look at a typical day at work. (Rev: SLJ 7/04) [696]

20913 Hovanec, Erin M. *Careers as a Content Provider for the Web* (5–8). Series: The Library of E-Commerce and Internet Careers. 2001, Rosen LB $26.50 (978-0-8239-3418-8). 64pp. A basic guide to career opportunities in the high-tech sector, with personal stories, information on skills needed and how to get started, and lists of recommended resources, many of which are on the Web. Also use *E-Tailing: Careers Selling Over the Web* (2001). (Rev: SLJ 4/02) [004]

20914 Hyland, Tony. *Astronauts* (4–6). Series: Extreme Jobs. 2007, Smart Apple LB $27.10 (978-1-58340-743-1). 32pp. An interesting overview of what it takes to become an astronaut. (Rev: SLJ 8/07)

20915 Hyland, Tony. *High-rise Workers* (4–6). Series: Extreme Jobs. 2007, Smart Apple LB $27.10 (978-1-58340-742-4). 32pp. Readers interested in exciting, sometimes risky jobs will enjoy exploring what high-rise workers do and how to go about becoming one. (Rev: SLJ 8/07)

20916 McGinty, Alice B. *Software Designer* (4–8). Series: Coolcareers.com. 2000, Rosen LB $23.95 (978-0-8239-3149-1). 48pp. This book explains what a software engineer does, the skills required, education needed, and future prospects. (Rev: SLJ 6/00) [004]

20917 Mazor, Barry. *Multimedia and New Media Developer* (4–8). Series: Coolcareers.com. 2000, Rosen LB $26.50 (978-0-8239-3102-6). 45pp. This work explains the nature of multimedia careers, the training and skills necessary, and the job opportunities. (Rev: SLJ 6/00) [004]

20918 O'Donnell, Annie. *Computer Animator* (4–8). Series: Coolcareers.com. 2000, Rosen LB $23.95 (978-0-8239-3101-9). 44pp. This book gives a brief history of animation and explains how it is used today, the specialized roles of animators, educational requirements, and the future of the industry. (Rev: SLJ 6/00) [004]

20919 Oleksy, Walter. *Video Game Designer* (4–8). Series: Coolcareers.com. 2000, Rosen LB $23.95 (978-0-8239-3117-0). 47pp. This account explains how video games work and how they are designed, with material on the careers involved and the qualifications necessary. (Rev: SLJ 6/00) [794.8]

20920 Oleksy, Walter. *Web Page Designer* (4–8). Series: Coolcareers.com. 2000, Rosen LB $26.50 (978-0-8239-3112-5). 47pp. This well-illustrated account, which features case studies of several teenagers, gives information on Web page construction, what a designer does, the training required, and the job outlook. (Rev: SLJ 6/00) [004]

20921 Overcamp, David. *Electrician* (5–8). Series: Great Jobs. 2004, Children's Pr. LB $24.50 (978-0-516-24086-2); paper $6.95 (978-0-516-25924-6). 48pp. This appealing, photo-filled title focuses on the work of an electrician, looking at job requirements, training, and tools, as well as providing a history of the field and a look at a typical day at work. (Rev: SLJ 7/04) [621.3]

20922 Reeves, Diane L., and Peter Kent. *Career Ideas for Kids Who Like Computers* (5–9). Illus. by Nancy Bond. Series: Career Ideas for Kids. 1998, Facts on File $23.00 (978-0-8160-3682-0). 167pp. An upbeat, breezy introduction to careers related to computers, providing aptitude tests and information on educational requirements, working conditions, activities, etc. (Rev: SLJ 6/99) [004]

20923 Schomp, Virginia. *If You Were a Construction Worker* (3–4). Illus. Series: If You Were A. 1997, Marshall Cavendish LB $22.79 (978-0-7614-0617-4). 32pp. This title describes the different jobs involved in a construction project, the various kinds of buildings these people work on, and some of the world's great structures, such as the Empire State Building and the pyramids. (Rev: BL 2/15/98; HBG 3/98) [624]

20924 Spilsbury, Richard. *Design and Technical Art* (3–6). Illus. Series: Art off the Wall. 2006, Heinemann LB $32.86 (978-1-4034-8289-1). 56pp. Professional designers and engineers and their techniques using computer-aided design (CAD) are featured. Readers who would like to design cars will be especially interested in this book. (Rev: SLJ 5/07)

20925 Weintraub, Aileen. *Auto Mechanic* (5–8). Series: Great Jobs. 2004, Children's Pr. LB $24.50 (978-0-516-24090-9). 48pp. This appealing, photo-filled title focuses on the work of an auto mechanic, looking at job requirements, training, and tools, as well as providing a history of the trade and a look at a typical day at work. (Rev: SLJ 7/04) [629.28]

20926 White, Katherine. *Oil Rig Workers: Life Drilling for Oil* (5–10). Series: Extreme Careers. 2003, Rosen LB $26.50 (978-0-8239-3797-4). 64pp.

A look at the lives of oil rig workers and day-to-day activities on a rig. (Rev: BL 9/15/03) [665.5]

Health and Medicine

20927 Asher, Dana. *Epidemiologists: Life Tracking Deadly Diseases* (5–10). Series: Extreme Careers. 2003, Rosen LB $26.50 (978-0-8239-3633-5). 64pp. A concise explanation of the work of epidemiologists, the history of this discipline, and the training required to enter this field, with a case study. (Rev: BL 5/15/03; SLJ 5/03) [614.4]

20928 Aylmore, Angela. *We Work at the Hospital* (PS–K). Series: Where We Work. 2006, Raintree LB $21.36 (978-1-4109-2246-5). 24pp. A basic introduction to what doctors, nurses, and other healthcare workers do, with color photographs and simple text. (Rev: SLJ 7/06) [362.1]

20929 Brill, Marlene T. *Doctors* (K–2). Series: Pull Ahead Books. 2004, Lerner LB $22.60 (978-0-8225-1689-7). The important role that doctors play in maintaining a healthy community is shown in brief text and and full-color photographs in this small-format book. (Rev: BL 10/15/04) [610]

20930 Fluet, Connie. *A Day in the Life of a Nurse* (K–3). Series: First Facts: Community Helpers at Work. 2004, Capstone LB $21.26 (978-0-7368-2631-0). 24pp. Using a question-and-answer format and full-color photos, Fluet looks at the tasks a nurse performs. (Rev: SLJ 1/05) [610]

20931 Gorman, Jacqueline Laks. *Dentist / El Dentista* (PS–2). Photos by Gregg Andersen. Series: People in My Community/La Gente de Mi Comunidad. 2002, Gareth Stevens LB $21.00 (978-0-8368-3307-2). 24pp. Full-color photographs and single-sentence descriptions, in English and in Spanish, introduce various aspects of a dentist's work. Also use *Doctor / El Medico* (2002). (Rev: HBG 3/03; SLJ 3/03)

20932 Kalman, Bobbie. *Hospital Workers in the Emergency Room* (1–4). Illus. Series: My Community and Its Helpers. 2004, Crabtree LB $25.27 (978-0-7787-2095-9); paper $8.95 (978-0-7787-2123-9). 32pp. A simple review of the tasks assigned to emergency room workers and the education necessary for a career in this field. (Rev: BL 5/1/04; SLJ 6/05)

20933 Lee, Barbara. *Working in Health Care and Wellness* (4–8). Illus. Series: Exploring Careers. 1996, Lerner LB $23.93 (978-0-8225-1760-3). This book profiles 12 people who are in health care professions and includes the pros and cons of each career. (Rev: BL 2/15/97) [610.69]

20934 Liebman, Dan. *I Want to Be a Doctor* (PS–1). Illus. Series: I Want to Be. 2000, Firefly LB $14.95 (978-1-55209-463-1); paper $3.99 (978-1-55209-461-7). 24pp. Using a simple text and many full-color photos, this book introduces the medical profession. (Rev: BL 9/15/00; HBG 9/00; SLJ 9/00) [610]

20935 Liebman, Dan. *I Want to Be a Nurse* (K–2). Series: I Want to Be. 2001, Firefly LB $14.95 (978-1-55209-568-3). 24pp. With color photographs and two or three lines of simple text on each page, the working day of a nurse is described. (Rev: BL 12/15/01; HBG 10/01) [610]

20936 Lowenstein, Felicia. *What Does a Doctor Do?* (1–3). Series: What Does a Community Helper Do? 2005, Enslow LB $21.26 (978-0-7660-2542-4). 24pp. This easy-reader chapter book looks at the important tasks that doctors perform to preserve the health of the communities in which they live and also examines career opportunities in the field of medicine. (Rev: SLJ 11/05)

20937 Miller, Heather. *What Does a Dentist Do?* (K–2). Illus. Series: What Does a Community Helper Do? 2006, Enslow LB $21.26 (978-0-7660-2323-9). 24pp. Outlines in easy-to-understand language the job requirements and everyday responsibilities of a dentist. (Rev: SLJ 4/06) [617.6]

20938 Minden, Cecelia. *Nurses* (1–2). Series: Neighborhood Helpers. 2006, The Child's World LB $24.21 (978-1-59296-566-3). 32pp. This attractive overview introduces young children to the role and responsibilities of a nurse, plus the equipment and training needed and the nature of the workplace. (Rev: SLJ 8/06) [610]

20939 Pasternak, Ceel, and Linda Thornburg. *Cool Careers for Girls in Health* (5–9). Series: Cool Careers for Girls. 1999, Impact $19.95 (978-1-57023-125-4); paper $12.95 (978-1-57023-118-6). 160pp. This book describes health-related careers for girls — as doctors, nurses, dentists, personal trainers, medical technologists, physical therapists, and dietitians. (Rev: SLJ 10/99) [610]

20940 Schomp, Virginia. *If You Were a Doctor* (3–4). Series: If You Were A. 2000, Benchmark LB $22.79 (978-0-7614-1000-3). 32pp. Full-color photographs and an easy text are used to describe the daily routines of a doctor. (Rev: BL 11/15/00; HBG 3/01) [610]

20941 Simon, Charnan. *My Mother Is a Doctor* (K–2). Illus. by Patrick Girouard. Series: Magic Door to Learning. 2006, The Child's World LB $21.36 (978-1-59296-620-2). 24pp. An inviting basic introduction to doctors and their work, taking young readers through a typical day in a doctor's office. (Rev: SLJ 2/07) [610.69]

Police and Fire Fighters

20942 Aylmore, Angela. *We Work at the Fire Station* (PS–K). Series: Where We Work. 2006, Raintree LB $21.36 (978-1-4109-2243-4). 24pp. A basic introduction to what fire fighters do, with color photographs and simple text. (Rev: SLJ 7/06) [628.9]

20943 Binney, Greg A. *Careers in the Federal Emergency Management Agency's Search and Rescue Unit* (5–9). Illus. Series: Careers in Search and Rescue Operations. 2003, Rosen LB $26.50 (978-0-8239-3832-2). 64pp. Starting with September 11,

2001, this volume explores the work of the teams that specialize in search and rescue after disasters such as tornadoes, hazardous materials spills, and building collapses, with material on the training required. (Rev: BL 10/15/03) [363.3]

20944 Bourgeois, Paulette. *Fire Fighters* (PS–2). Illus. by Kim LaFave. Series: In My Neighborhood. 1998, Kids Can $12.95 (978-1-55074-438-5). 32pp. This book about fire fighters and their duties highlights fires in various settings and the ways fire fighters approach them. (Rev: BL 4/15/98; HBG 10/98; SLJ 6/98) [363.37]

20945 Bourgeois, Paulette. *Police Officers* (1–3). Series: Kids Can Read. 2004, Kids Can $14.95 (978-1-55337-742-9); paper $3.95 (978-1-55337-743-6). 32pp. After describing a fictional police investigation, Bourgeois moves on to discuss police duties and children's safety. (Rev: BL 11/15/04) [363.2]

20946 Bourgeois, Paulette. *Police Officers* (PS–2). Illus. by Kim LaFave. Series: My Neighborhood. 1999, Kids Can $12.95 (978-1-55074-502-3). 32pp. This picture book explains the basic duties of police officers. (Rev: BL 7/99; HBG 9/99; SLJ 7/99) [363.2]

20947 Croce, Nicholas. *Detectives: Life Investigating Crimes* (5–10). Series: Extreme Careers. 2003, Rosen LB $26.50 (978-0-8239-3796-7). 64pp. As well as exploring the exciting side of detective work, this account explains the qualifications and training needed and the techniques that help do this job well. (Rev: BL 9/15/03) [340]

20948 Fall, Mitchell. *Careers in Fire Departments' Search and Rescue Unit* (5–9). Series: Careers in Search and Rescue Operations. 2003, Rosen LB $26.50 (978-0-8239-3833-9). 64pp. This account pays tribute to the heroism of fire departments' search and rescue operations particularly during the September 11, 2001 attacks and also gives a career guide to this occupation. (Rev: BL 10/15/03) [363]

20949 Fine, Jil. *Bomb Squad Specialist* (4–8). Series: Danger Is My Business. 2003, Children's Pr. LB $24.50 (978-0-516-24340-5). 48pp. An illustrated glimpse of the perilous life of a bomb squad member in an age of terrorism, including information on how bombs work and how they are detected and disarmed. (Rev: SLJ 3/04) [363.2]

20950 Fortney, Mary T. *Fire Station Number 4: The Daily Life of Firefighters* (2–4). Illus. 1998, Carolrhoda LB $22.60 (978-1-57505-089-8). 48pp. Using the fire station at Livermore, a suburb of San Francisco, as home base, this photo-essay clearly details the day-to-day activities in a fire station and the duties and responsibilities of typical fire fighters. (Rev: BL 10/1/98; HBG 3/99; SLJ 1/99) [363.37]

20951 Freedman, Jeri. *Careers in Emergency Medical Response Team's Search and Rescue Unit* (5–9). Illus. Series: Careers in Search and Rescue Operations. 2003, Rosen LB $26.50 (978-0-8239-3831-5). 64pp. Starting with September 11, 2001, this volume explores the various roles played by emergency response teams, the use of equipment

including helicopters and ambulances, and the training required. (Rev: BL 10/15/03) [616.0]

20952 Ghione, Yvette. *This Is Daniel Cook at the Fire Station* (K–3). 2006, Kids Can $12.95 (978-1-55453-075-5); paper $4.95 (978-1-55453-076-2). In this companion to the popular Canadian-produced TV show, the young host invites readers to join him on a tour of a fire station. (Rev: SLJ 11/06) [628.9]

20953 Giacobello, John. *Bodyguards: Life Protecting Others* (5–10). Series: Extreme Careers. 2003, Rosen LB $26.50 (978-0-8239-3795-0). 64pp. This book explores the duties and responsibilities of a bodyguard and includes information how to stay safe on the job and get ahead in this profession. (Rev: BL 9/15/03; SLJ 11/03) [340]

20954 Gorman, Jacqueline Laks. *Firefighter / El Bombero* (PS–2). Photos by Gregg Andersen. Series: People in My Community/La Gente de Mi Comunidad. 2002, Gareth Stevens LB $21.00 (978-0-8368-3309-6). 24pp. Full-color photographs and single-sentence descriptions, in English and in Spanish, introduce various aspects of a fire fighter's job. Also use *Police Officer / El Policía* (2002). (Rev: SLJ 3/03)

20955 Gorrell, Gena K. *Catching Fire: The Story of Firefighting* (4–6). Illus. 1999, Tundra $16.95 (978-0-88776-430-1). 144pp. After giving a history of fire fighting, this account describes different kinds of fires and the methods used to combat them. (Rev: BCCB 5/99; BL 6/1–15/99) [363.37]

20956 Greenberg, Keith E. *Bomb Squad Officer: Expert with Explosives* (2–4). Illus. Series: Risky Business. 1995, Blackbirch LB $22.45 (978-1-56711-155-2). 32pp. A career book, set in New Jersey, that explains the work of the men who remove and dismantle or detonate suspicious objects. (Rev: SLJ 2/96) [363]

20957 Hayward, Linda. *A Day in the Life of a Firefighter* (PS–K). Series: Dorling Kindersley Readers: Jobs People Do. 2001, DK $14.99 (978-0-7894-7366-0); paper $3.99 (978-0-7894-7365-3). 32pp. In this beginning reader that uses a limited vocabulary and simple sentences, the daily life of a fire fighter is portrayed. (Rev: BL 8/1/01; HBG 10/01) [363]

20958 Hubbell, Patricia. *Police: Hurry! Helping! Saving!* (PS–1). Illus. by Viviana Garofoli. 2008, Marshall Cavendish $14.99 (978-0-7614-5421-2). A lively, simple introduction to law enforcement jobs and roles. (Rev: SLJ 9/08) [363.2]

20959 Kalman, Bobbie. *Firefighters to the Rescue!* (1–4). Illus. Series: My Community and Its Helpers. 2004, Crabtree LB $25.27 (978-0-7787-2096-6); paper $8.95 (978-0-7787-2124-6). 32pp. A simple review of the work of fire fighters and the education necessary for a career in this field. (Rev: BL 5/1/04; SLJ 6/05) [363.37]

20960 Knudsen, Shannon. *Police Officers* (K–2). 2004, Lerner LB $22.60 (978-0-8225-1693-4). 32pp. The important role that police officers play in the community is shown in brief text and and full-color photographs in this small-format book. (Rev: BL 10/15/04) [363.2]

20961 Landau, Elaine. *Smokejumpers* (3–6). Illus. 2002, Millbrook LB $23.90 (978-0-7613-2324-2). 48pp. An excellent tribute to the life and work of the gallant men and women who jump from planes to fight forest fires. (Rev: BCCB 3/02; BL 6/1–15/02; HBG 10/02; SLJ 7/02) [634.9]

20962 Liebman, Dan. *I Want to Be a Police Officer* (PS–1). Illus. Series: I Want to Be. 2000, Firefly LB $14.95 (978-1-55209-467-9); paper $3.99 (978-1-55209-465-5). 24pp. Full-color photographs and a brief text introduce police officers and what they do. (Rev: BL 6/1–15/00; SLJ 9/00) [363.2]

20963 Plum, Jennifer. *Careers in Police Departments' Search and Rescue Unit* (5–9). Series: Careers in Search and Rescue Operations. 2003, Rosen LB $26.50 (978-0-8239-3834-6). 64pp. This account highlights the role of police officers in search and rescue operations, particularly their acts of heroism during the attacks of September 11, 2001. (Rev: BL 10/15/03) [363]

20964 Pohl, Kathleen. *What Happens at a Firehouse?* (PS–2). Series: Where People Work. 2006, Gareth Stevens LB $21.00 (978-0-8368-6887-6). 24pp. This small-format book combines cartoons and clear photographs with facts about day-to-day activities inside a firehouse. (Rev: BL 1/1–15/07) [628.9]

20965 Rau, Dana Meachen. *Firefighter* (PS–1). Illus. Series: Benchmark Rebus. 2007, Marshall Cavendish LB $15.95 (978-0-7614-2617-2). 24pp. Double-page spreads with large color photographs and simple large-type text introduce the work of a fire fighter; a small-format book suitable for young children. (Rev: BL 10/15/07; SLJ 12/07) [628.9]

20966 Rau, Dana Meachen. *Police Officer* (PS–K). Series: Benchmark Rebus. 2007, Marshall Cavendish LB $15.95 (978-0-7614-2618-9). 24pp. For young children, this overview of the job of a police officer contains an appealing mix of rebus, text, and image. (Rev: SLJ 12/07) [363.2]

20967 Royston, Angela. *Fire Fighters* (1–3). Illus. Series: Eyewitness Reader. 1998, DK paper $3.99 (978-0-7894-2960-5). 32pp. Using photographs and a simple text, this easy reader describes a house fire and the role of fire fighters in controlling it. (Rev: BL 7/98) [628.9]

20968 Schomp, Virginia. *If You Were a Firefighter* (3–4). Series: If You Were A. 1997, Marshall Cavendish LB $22.79 (978-0-7614-0615-0). 32pp. In this simple career book, the training and responsibilities of fire fighters are introduced. (Rev: BL 2/15/98; HBG 3/98) [363]

20969 Schomp, Virginia. *If You Were a Police Officer* (3–4). Series: If You Were A. 1997, Marshall Cavendish LB $22.79 (978-0-7614-0614-3). 32pp. The everyday activities of a police officer are described in this simple career book. (Rev: BL 2/15/98; HBG 3/98) [363]

20970 Simon, Charnan. *Firefighter Tom to the Rescue!* (K–2). Illus. by Joel Snyder. Series: Magic Door to Learning. 2006, The Child's World LB $21.36 (978-1-59296-621-9). 24pp. An inviting basic introduction to firefighters' role in the community and a typical day on the job. (Rev: SLJ 2/07) [628.9]

20971 Sweeney, Alyse. *A Very Busy Firehouse* (K–2). Series: Scholastic News Nonfiction Readers. 2006, Children's Pr. LB $20.00 (978-0-531-16840-0). 24pp. Basic information for beginning readers, with seven highlighted words that are featured in bold in the text. (Rev: SLJ 1/07) [628.9]

20972 Winkleman, Katherine K. *Firehouse* (2–4). Illus. by John S. Winkleman. 1994, Walker $15.85 (978-0-8027-8317-2). 32pp. Facts about firehouses, past and present, and how they operate are presented in this fascinating behind-the-scenes look. (Rev: BCCB 10/94; BL 10/1/94; SLJ 1/95) [363.37]

Science

20973 Collard, Sneed B., III. *A Firefly Biologist at Work* (4–6). Illus. Series: Wildlife Conservation Society. 2001, Watts LB $24.50 (978-0-531-11798-9). 48pp. Readers learn about the career of a firefly researcher, with information both about fireflies themselves and about the life and interests of a biologist. (Rev: BL 12/1/01; SLJ check) [595.7]

20974 Ghez, Andrea Mia, and Judith Cohen. *You Can Be a Woman Astronomer* (3–5). Illus. by David Katz. 1995, Cascade Pass paper $6.00 (978-1-880599-17-4). 38pp. A career book in which the author tells how she became a scientist and of the excitement and wonder of using telescopes and other tools of the astronomer. (Rev: SLJ 1/96) [520]

20975 Hammonds, Heather. *Geologists* (4–6). 2004, Smart Apple LB $27.10 (978-1-58340-543-7). 32pp. Following an overview of the science and its history, this volume discusses geology today, the duties of geologists and equipment used, the future of the profession, and how to become a geologist. (Rev: BL 10/15/04; SLJ 2/05) [551]

20976 Haydon, Julie. *Astronomers* (4–6). Illus. Series: Scientists at Work. 2004, Smart Apple LB $27.10 (978-1-58340-541-3). 32pp. Following an overview of the science and its history, this volume discusses astronomy today, the duties of astronomers and equipment used, the future of the profession, and how to become an astronomer. (Rev: BL 10/15/04; SLJ 2/05) [520]

20977 Hayhurst, Chris. *Arctic Scientists: Life Studying the Arctic* (5–10). Series: Extreme Careers. 2003, Rosen LB $26.50 (978-0-8239-3794-3). 64pp. This guide to the life and work of Arctic scientists indicates exciting areas of research such as the plant and animal life and the effects of global warming. (Rev: BL 9/15/03; SLJ 11/03) [500]

20978 Hayhurst, Chris. *Volcanologists: Life Exploring Volcanoes* (5–10). Series: Extreme Careers. 2003, Rosen LB $26.50 (978-0-8239-3637-3). 64pp. This career guide explains what is necessary to become a serious student of volcanoes and what to expect when one becomes a volcanologist. (Rev: BL 9/15/03) [551.2]

20979 Higginson, Mel. *Scientists Who Study Ancient Temples and Tombs* (1–2). Illus. Series: Scientists. 1994, Rourke LB $18.60 (978-0-86593-376-7). 24pp. A simple introduction to archaeologists, what they do, the education necessary, and some of their important discoveries. (Rev: SLJ 2/95) [930]

20980 Higginson, Mel. *Scientists Who Study Fossils* (1–2). Illus. Series: Scientists. 1994, Rourke LB $18.60 (978-0-86593-375-0). 24pp. This basic book describes what paleontologists do, what sort of education and training they require, and some of their important accomplishments. (Rev: SLJ 2/95) [560]

20981 Higginson, Mel. *Scientists Who Study Ocean Life* (1–2). Illus. Series: Scientists. 1994, Rourke LB $18.60 (978-0-86593-371-2). 24pp. Describes the science of oceanography, as well as the training required and discoveries of these scientists who study the oceans. (Rev: SLJ 2/95) [551.46]

20982 Higginson, Mel. *Scientists Who Study the Earth* (1–2). Illus. Series: Scientists. 1994, Rourke LB $18.60 (978-0-86593-372-9). 24pp. A basic introduction to the work that geologists do and how they prepare for it. (Rev: SLJ 2/95) [557]

20983 Higginson, Mel. *Scientists Who Study Wild Animals* (1–2). Illus. Series: Scientists. 1994, Rourke LB $18.60 (978-0-86593-374-3). 24pp. Careers in animal biology are introduced briefly, with a description of the education and training necessary. (Rev: SLJ 2/95) [591]

20984 Jackson, Donna. *Extreme Scientists: Exploring Nature's Mysteries from Perilous Places* (4–8). Illus. Series: Scientists in the Field. 2009, Houghton $18.00 (978-0-618-77706-8). 80pp. Jackson shows the work of scientists who face danger in the field — a meteorologist who flies into hurricanes, a biologist who goes deep into caves, an ecologist who climbs high into tall redwoods — and discusses their motivations. (Rev: BCCB 6/09; BL 5/15/09; HB 7/09; SLJ 7/09) [509.2]

20985 Lehn, Barbara. *What Is a Scientist?* (K–2). 1998, Millbrook $21.90 (978-0-7613-1272-7). 32pp. Outlines the various steps in the scientific method — designing experiments, making observations, and so forth — and introduces the work of different kinds of scientists. (Rev: HBG 3/99; SLJ 4/99) [500]

20986 McElroy, Lisa. *Meet My Grandmother: She's a Deep Sea Explorer* (2–4). Series: Grandmothers at Work. 2000, Millbrook LB $22.90 (978-0-7613-1720-3). 32pp. A young boy introduces his grandmother, Sylvia Earle, who regularly swims with sharks as she explores the ocean's depths. (Rev: BL 9/15/00; HBG 3/01; SLJ 1/01) [551.46]

20987 McGlone, Catherine. *Visiting Volcanoes with a Scientist* (1–3). Illus. Series: I Like Science! 2004, Enslow LB $21.26 (978-0-7660-2269-0). 24pp. Readers follow a volcanologist through work in the field and learn how to make a model volcano using everyday materials. (Rev: BL 4/1/04; SLJ 2/05) [551.21]

20988 Murdico, Suzanne J. *Forensic Scientists: Life Investigating Sudden Death* (5–12). Series: Extreme Careers. 2004, Rosen LB $26.50 (978-0-8239-3966-

4). 64pp. A look at this rapidly growing science and the career opportunities offered. (Rev: BL 5/15/04) [363.2]

20989 Pasternak, Ceel, and Linda Thornburg. *Cool Careers for Girls in Engineering* (5–8). Series: Cool Careers for Girls. 1999, Impact $19.95 (978-1-57023-126-1); paper $12.95 (978-1-57023-119-3). 132pp. Examines engineering specializations — such as computer, biomedical, civil, and agricultural — and the opportunities for women in these fields. (Rev: SLJ 1/00) [620]

20990 Reeves, Diane L. *Career Ideas for Kids Who Like Science* (5–9). Illus. by Nancy Bond. Series: Career Ideas for Kids. 1998, Facts on File $23.00 (978-0-8160-3680-6); paper $12.95 (978-0-8060-3686-1). 165pp. An upbeat, breezy introduction to 15 careers, providing aptitude tests and information on educational requirements, working conditions, activities, etc. (Rev: SLJ 9/98) [500]

20991 Swinburne, Stephen. *The Woods Scientist* (4–8). Photos by Susan C. Morse. Illus. Series: Scientists in the Field. 2003, Houghton $16.00 (978-0-618-04602-7). 48pp. Swinburne describes his fascinating expeditions in the company of a conservationist and ecologist in the woods of Vermont, and provides lots of information on risks to wildlife. (Rev: BCCB 3/03; BL 3/15/03; HBG 10/03; SLJ 4/03) [591.73]

20992 Williams, Judith. *Discovering Dinosaurs with a Fossil Hunter* (1–3). Illus. by Michael W. Skrepnick. Series: I Like Science! 2004, Enslow LB $21.26 (978-0-7660-2267-6). 24pp. Readers follow a paleontologist through work in the field and learn how to re-create a plant fossil. (Rev: BL 4/1/04; SLJ 2/05) [567.9]

Transportation

20993 Gorman, Jacqueline Laks. *Bus Driver / El Conductor del Autobús* (PS–2). Photos by Gregg Andersen. Series: People in My Community/La Gente de Mi Comunidad. 2002, Gareth Stevens LB $21.00 (978-0-8368-3306-5). 24pp. Full-color photographs and single-sentence descriptions, in English and in Spanish, introduce various aspects of a bus driver's job. (Rev: HBG 3/03; SLJ 3/03)

20994 Liebman, Dan. *I Want to Be a Truck Driver* (K–2). Series: I Want to Be. 2001, Firefly LB $14.95 (978-1-55209-576-8). 24pp. The daily life of a truck driver is described using a brief text and color photographs on each page. (Rev: BL 12/15/01; HBG 10/01) [629.24]

20995 Royston, Angela. *Truck Trouble* (1–3). Illus. Series: Eyewitness Reader. 1998, DK paper $3.99 (978-0-7894-2958-2). 32pp. This easy reader describes the problems — a flat tire and a rainstorm — encountered by a truck driver who is making a special delivery to a children's hospital. (Rev: BL 7/98) [629.2]

20996 Schomp, Virginia. *If You Were a Pilot* (1–3). Series: If You Were A. 1999, Benchmark LB

$22.79 (978-0-7614-0919-9). 32pp. A brief, attractive introduction to what a pilot does, plus a discussion of different kinds of planes. (Rev: HBG 9/00; SLJ 3/00) [629.132]

20997 Schomp, Virginia. *If You Were a Truck Driver* (3–4). Series: If You Were A. 2000, Benchmark LB $22.79 (978-0-7614-1003-4). 32pp. Covers the daily life of a truck driver, with information on the care and handling of trucks. (Rev: BL 11/15/00; HBG 3/01) [629.24]

20998 Trumbauer, Lisa. *What Does a Truck Driver Do?* (K–2). Illus. Series: What Does a Community Helper Do? 2006, Enslow LB $21.26 (978-0-7660-2324-6). 24pp. Outlines in easy-to-understand language the job requirements and everyday responsibilities of a truck driver. (Rev: SLJ 4/06) [388.324]

Veterinarians

20999 Aylmore, Angela. *We Work at the Vet's* (PS–K). Series: Where We Work. 2006, Raintree LB $21.36 (978-1-4109-2245-8). 24pp. A basic introduction to what veterinarians and their assistants do, with color photographs and simple text. (Rev: SLJ 7/06) [636.089]

21000 Ermitage, Kathleen. *Veterinarian* (2–4). Series: Workers You Know. 2000, Raintree LB $25.70 (978-0-8172-5592-3). 32pp. Describes a day in the life of a vet, including routine diagnoses, emergency procedures, and follow-up activities. (Rev: HBG 9/00; SLJ 11/00) [636.089]

21001 Jackson, Donna. *ER Vets: Life in an Animal Emergency Room* (5–8). Illus. 2005, Houghton $17.00 (978-0-618-43663-7). 96pp. A behind-the-scenes look at life in a veterinary emergency clinic and the frustrations and joys to be found working there. (Rev: BL 11/1/05; SLJ 1/06*) [636.089]

21002 Kalman, Bobbie. *Veterinarians Help Keep Animals Healthy* (1–4). Illus. Series: My Community and Its Helpers. 2004, Crabtree LB $25.27 (978-0-7787-2097-3); paper $8.95 (978-0-7787-2125-3). 32pp. A simple review of the work of veterinarians

and the education necessary for a career in this field. (Rev: SLJ 6/05) [636]

21003 Leake, Diyan. *Vets* (PS–1). Illus. Series: People in Our Community. 2008, Heinemann LB $17.75 (978-1-4329-1192-8). 24pp. A basic introduction to the work of vets, with bright photographs. (Rev: BLO 7/31/08) [636.089]

21004 Liebman, Dan. *I Want to Be a Vet* (PS–1). Illus. Series: I Want to Be. 2000, Firefly LB $14.95 (978-1-55209-471-6); paper $3.99 (978-1-55209-469-3). 24pp. A very simple introduction to what veterinarians do and how they are prepared for their jobs. (Rev: BL 9/15/00; HBG 9/00; SLJ 2/01) [636]

21005 Minden, Cecelia. *Veterinarians* (1–2). Series: Neighborhood Helpers. 2006, The Child's World LB $24.21 (978-1-59296-571-7). 32pp. This attractive overview introduces young children to the role and responsibilities of a vet, plus the equipment and training needed. (Rev: SLJ 8/06) [636]

21006 Owen, Ann. *Caring for Your Pets: A Book About Veterinarians* (PS–3). Illus. by Eric Thomas. Series: Community Workers. 2004, Picture Window LB $25.26 (978-1-4048-0087-8). 24pp. A simple first look at the many tasks of veterinarians as they work with pets, livestock, and wild animals. (Rev: SLJ 4/04) [636]

21007 Patrick, Jean L. S. *Cows, Cats, and Kids: A Veterinarian's Family at Work* (3–6). Illus. by Alvis Upitis. 2003, Boyds Mills $17.95 (978-1-56397-111-2). 48pp. A rural vet's wife describes the family's love of animals and the ways in which her children are able to help their father. (Rev: BL 3/1/03; HBG 10/03; SLJ 4/03) [636.089]

21008 Schomp, Virginia. *If You Were a Veterinarian* (3–4). Series: If You Were A. 1997, Marshall Cavendish LB $22.79 (978-0-7614-0613-6). 32pp. In this simple career book, the everyday activities of a veterinarian are described, with some information on the educational background necessary. (Rev: BL 2/15/98; HBG 3/98; SLJ 2/98) [636]

21009 Simon, Charnan. *The Best Vet in the World* (K–2). Illus. by Carol Schwartz. Series: Magic Door to Learning. 2006, The Child's World LB $21.36 (978-1-59296-628-8). 24pp. An inviting basic introduction to the veterinary profession. (Rev: SLJ 2/07) [636]

Health and the Human Body

Aging and Death

21010 Dennison, Amy, and Allie Dennison. *Our Dad Died: The True Story of Three Kids Whose Lives Changed* (3–7). Illus. by authors. 2003, Free Spirit paper $9.95 (978-1-57542-135-3). 107pp. Three young siblings recount their initial reaction to the sudden and unexpected death of their father and how, with support from their mother, they learned to live with this loss. (Rev: SLJ 1/04) [155.9]

21011 Helmer, Diana Star. *Let's Talk About When Someone You Know Is in a Nursing Home* (PS–2). Photos by Seth Dinnerman. Series: Let's Talk. 1999, Rosen LB $19.95 (978-0-8239-5190-1). 24pp. A simply written account that answers questions that children might have about nursing homes, including how to be comfortable when visiting. (Rev: SLJ 12/99) [362]

21012 Hyde, Margaret O., and Lawrence E. Hyde. *Meeting Death* (5–8). 1989, Walker LB $15.85 (978-0-8027-6874-2). After a history of how various cultures regard death, the authors discuss this phenomenon, the concept of grieving, and how to face death. (Rev: BL 1/1/90; SLJ 11/89) [306.9]

21013 Jackson, Aariane R. *Can You Hear Me Smiling? A Child Grieves a Sister* (2–4). Series: New Child and Family Press Titles. 2004, Child Welfare League of America $9.95 (978-0-87868-835-7). 40pp. Nine-year-old Aariane discusses the conflicting emotions she experienced after the sudden death of her older sister. (Rev: BL 7/04) [155.9]

21014 Johnston, Marianne. *Let's Talk About Going to a Funeral* (1–4). Series: Let's Talk. 1998, Rosen LB $19.95 (978-0-8239-5038-6). 24pp. This book describes what happens before, during, and after a funeral and discusses grieving, the cemetery, the grave, and cremation. (Rev: SLJ 7/98) [393]

21015 Krementz, Jill. *How It Feels When a Parent Dies* (4–7). Illus. 1988, Knopf paper $15.00 (978-0-394-75854-1). 128pp. Eighteen experiences of parental death are recounted.

21016 LeShan, Eda. *Learning to Say Good-bye: When a Parent Dies* (5–7). Illus. by Paul Giovanopoulos. 1976, Avon paper $8.00 (978-0-380-40105-5). 96pp. A sympathetic explanation of the many reactions children have to death.

21017 Murphy, Patricia J. *Death* (PS–3). Series: Tough Topics. 2007, Heinemann LB $25.36 (978-1-4034-9778-9). 32pp. A sensitive discussion of the nature of death, why people die, funerals, and the ways people feel after a death. (Rev: SLJ 12/07) [155.9]

21018 Peacock, Carol Antoinette. *Death and Dying* (4–8). Illus. Series: Life Balance. 2004, Watts LB $20.50 (978-0-531-12370-6); paper $6.95 (978-0-531-16728-1). 80pp. A practical guide to dealing with death and dying, with advice on seeking help when necessary. (Rev: BL 10/15/03)

21019 Rebman, Renee C. *Euthanasia and the "Right to Die": A Pro/Con Issue* (5–8). Illus. Series: Pro/Con Issues. 2002, Enslow LB $27.93 (978-0-7660-1816-7). 64pp. An objective examination of both sides of the issue of euthanasia. (Rev: BL 9/1/02; HBG 3/03) [179.7]

21020 Sanders, Pete, and Steve Myers. *When People Die* (3–6). Illus. by Mike Lacey. Series: Choices and Decisions. 2005, Stargazer LB $27.10 (1-59604-076-9). 32pp. This reassuring title covers with sensitivity the topics of death, grieving, and funerals, and also discusses euthanasia. (Rev: SLJ 4/06) [155.9]

21021 Stalfelt, Pernilla. *The Death Book* (2–4). Illus. 2002, Groundwood $15.95 (978-0-88899-482-0). 32pp. A straightforward yet lighthearted look at death, including the customs surrounding it, what might happen when we die, and an "interview" with a ghost. (Rev: BL 2/1/03; HBG 3/03; SLJ 8/03) [306.9]

21022 Wilson, Antoine. *You and a Death in Your Family* (5–8). Series: Family Matters. 2001, Rosen LB $26.50 (978-0-8239-3355-6). 48pp. Wilson provides concise, readable advice on coping with the death of a relative or pet and stresses that youngsters should seek help when necessary. (Rev: SLJ 8/01) [155.9]

Alcohol, Drugs, and Smoking

21023 Boyd, George A. *Drugs and Sex* (5–10). Illus. Series: Drug Abuse Prevention Library. 1994, Rosen LB $17.95 (978-0-8239-1538-5). A careful examination of the hazards of combining drugs and sex, including unsafe sex, pregnancy, AIDS, and other sexually transmitted diseases. (Rev: BL 6/1–15/94; SLJ 5/94) [613.9]

21024 Bryant-Mole, Karen. *Drugs* (2–3). Series: Talking About. 1999, Raintree LB $25.69 (978-0-8172-5887-0). 32pp. Large pages, large type, big color photos, and short sentences introduce, from a child's point of view, drugs and their use and misuse. (Rev: BL 2/15/00; HBG 9/00; SLJ 5/00) [362.29]

21025 Clayton, Lawrence. *Alcohol Drug Dangers* (4–7). Illus. Series: Drug Dangers. 1999, Enslow LB $27.93 (978-0-7660-1159-5). 64pp. Using real-life case histories, this book describes the effects of alcohol on the body and mind. (Rev: BL 8/99; HBG 10/99) [362.292]

21026 Clayton, Lawrence. *Diet Pill Drug Dangers* (5–9). Series: Drug Dangers. 1999, Enslow LB $19.95 (978-0-7660-1158-8). With liberal use of case histories, this book explores the dangers of diet pill use, their effects on the human body, and prevention techniques. (Rev: HBG 10/99; SLJ 9/99) [362.29]

21027 Galas, Judith C. *Drugs and Sports* (5–8). Illus. Series: Overview. 1997, Lucent LB $29.95 (978-1-56006-185-4). A look at the kinds of illegal drugs taken by athletes, the reasons for their use, and the ways in which their use can be detected. (Rev: BL 3/15/97) [362.29]

21028 Green, Carl R. *Nicotine and Tobacco* (4–8). Illus. Series: Drugs. 2005, Enslow LB $25.26 (978-0-7660-5283-3). 48pp. Fictional scenarios are combined with information on the addictive qualities of nicotine and the dangers of smoking and other forms of tobacco use; Web links extend the text. (Rev: SLJ 11/05) [362.2]

21029 Green, Jen. *Alcohol* (2–3). Series: Talking About. 1999, Raintree LB $25.69 (978-0-8172-5888-7). 32pp. A simple but colorfully illustrated introduction to alcohol — what it is and how it affects the human body. (Rev: BL 2/15/00; HBG 9/00) [613.8]

21030 Grosshandler-Smith, Janet. *Working Together Against Drinking and Driving* (4–8). Series: The Library of Social Activism. 1996, Rosen LB $16.95 (978-0-8239-2259-8). With an emphasis on prevention, the author presents a general discussion on drinking and driving and its consequences, followed by pointers on how to avoid embarrassing situations and how to handle peer pressure about drinking. (Rev: SLJ 2/97) [613.8]

21031 Hanan, Jessica. *When Someone You Love Is Addicted* (5–9). Series: Drug Abuse Prevention Library. 1999, Rosen LB $27.95 (978-0-8239-2831-6). A short book that begins with teenage case histories and then discusses treatments and resources for young people with drug problems. (Rev: SLJ 7/99) [362.29]

21032 Hyde, Margaret O. *Know About Drugs*. 4th ed. (5–8). 1995, Walker LB $15.85 (978-0-8027-8395-0). 93pp. An introduction to drugs including marijuana, alcohol, PCP, inhalants, crack/cocaine, heroin, and nicotine. (Rev: BL 7/90; SLJ 3/96) [362.2]

21033 Hyde, Margaret O. *Know About Smoking*. Rev. ed. (5–8). Illus. 1995, Walker LB $14.85 (978-0-8027-8400-1). 100pp. After a history of tobacco and nicotine, this book describes their effects on the body, addiction prevention, and the role of advertising in smoking. (Rev: BL 7/90; SLJ 9/95) [362.2]

21034 Hyde, Margaret O., and John F. Setaro. *Alcohol 101: An Overview for Teens* (5–10). 1999, Twenty-First Century LB $24.90 (978-0-7613-1274-1). 128pp. Kinds of alcohol and their effects are described, with material on alcoholism and binge drinking. (Rev: HBG 3/00; SLJ 3/00; VOYA 12/00) [613.8]

21035 Kreiner, Anna. *Let's Talk About Drug Abuse* (1–4). Illus. Series: Let's Talk. 1996, Rosen LB $19.95 (978-0-8239-2302-1). 24pp. Various kinds of drugs and their effects on the human body are introduced. (Rev: BL 3/1/97; SLJ 12/96) [362.29]

21036 Landau, Elaine. *Hooked: Talking About Addiction* (5–10). Illus. 1995, Millbrook LB $22.90 (978-1-56294-469-8). 64pp. This account defines addiction broadly — from use of alcohol and drugs to various forms of compulsive behavior — and gives suggestions for recovery. (Rev: BL 1/1–15/96; SLJ 1/96) [362.29]

21037 Lawler, Jennifer. *Drug Testing in Schools: A Pro/Con Issue* (5–8). Series: Hot Issues. 2000, Enslow LB $27.93 (978-0-7660-1367-4). 64pp. The pros and cons of drug testing in schools are presented in an unbiased manner with sections on methods of drug testing, policies of various organizations, and the opinions of students, teachers, and parents. (Rev: HBG 3/01; SLJ 12/00) [362.29]

21038 Lee, Mary Price, and Richard S. Lee. *Drugs and the Media* (5–10). Illus. Series: Drug Abuse Prevention Library. 1994, Rosen LB $17.95 (978-0-8239-1537-8). This book shows that the media often unintentionally glamorize drug use and describes how teens can evaluate the media's mixed messages. (Rev: BL 6/1–15/94; SLJ 5/94) [070.4]

21039 Levete, Sarah. *Drugs* (3–5). Series: Let's Talk About. 2007, Stargazer LB $27.10 (978-1-59604-090-8). 32pp. Questions and answers about drugs address their dangers in a straightforward way. Also use *Alcohol* (2007). (Rev: SLJ 8/07)

21040 Littell, Mary Ann. *Heroin Drug Dangers* (5–8). Series: Drug Dangers. 1999, Enslow LB $27.93 (978-0-7660-1156-4). A short, well-illustrated book that describes the physiological effects of heroin, the dangers of its use, and how to resist its temptations. (Rev: BL 9/15/99; HBG 3/00) [362.29]

21041 McGuire, Paula. *Alcohol* (4–8). Illus. Series: Preteen Pressures. 1998, Raintree LB $25.69 (978-0-8172-5026-3). 48pp. Topics discussed in this practical account include peer pressure to drink, the physical effects of alcohol, underage drinking, alcoholic parents, and ways to seek help. (Rev: BL 4/15/98; HBG 10/98) [362.29]

21042 Monroe, Judy. *Inhalant Drug Dangers* (5–9). 1999, Enslow LB $27.93 (978-0-7660-1153-3). Using case histories — such as the story of Ian, who is addicted to inhaling fabric protector — this slim volume tells of the effects and dangers of inhalants. (Rev: BL 8/99; HBG 10/99; SLJ 9/99) [362.29]

21043 Monroe, Judy. *Steroid Drug Dangers* (5–8). Illus. Series: Drug Dangers. 1999, Enslow LB $27.93 (978-0-7660-1154-0). Case histories, facts, and statistics introduce the reader to steroid drugs and their legal and illegal uses, their effects and dangers, and the organizations that promote safe usage. (Rev: BL 9/15/99; HBG 3/00) [362.29]

21044 Murdico, Suzanne J. *Drug Abuse* (4–8). Series: Preteen Pressures. 1998, Raintree LB $25.69 (978-0-8172-5027-0). 48pp. This work discusses drug abuse, with emphasis on healthy alternatives and solutions to typical drug-related problems faced by many young people. (Rev: BL 5/15/98; HBG 10/98) [362.2]

21045 Murphy, Patricia J. *Avoiding Drugs* (1–3). Series: Pull Ahead. 2005, Lerner LB $22.60 (978-0-8225-2867-8); paper $5.95 (978-0-8225-2779-4). 32pp. Alcohol, tobacco, and "non-medicinal" drugs are defined and discussed in clear text and photographs; a question-and-answer section offers practice in rejecting drug offers. (Rev: SLJ 3/06) [362.29]

21046 Nolan, Meghan, ed. *Let's Clear the Air: 10 Reasons Not to Start Smoking* (5–8). Illus. by Deanna Staffo. 2007, Lobster paper $14.95 (978-1-897073-66-7). 192pp. In personal essays, young people reveal the reasons why they don't smoke — reasons ranging from the deaths of loved ones to the smell and the cost. (Rev: BL 1/1–15/08; LMC 1/08; SLJ 3/08) [613.85]

21047 Robbins, Paul R. *Crack and Cocaine Drug Dangers* (5–9). Series: Drug Dangers. 1999, Enslow LB $27.93 (978-0-7660-1155-7). Charts, photographs, fact boxes, and a succinct text are used to discuss crack cocaine, its effects, and how to avoid its use. (Rev: BL 9/15/99; HBG 3/00) [362.29]

21048 Sanders, Pete. *Smoking* (4–7). Illus. Series: What Do You Know About. 1996, Millbrook LB $23.90 (978-0-7613-0536-1). 32pp. Covers the effects of smoking and ways in which youngsters can avoid getting hooked. (Rev: SLJ 3/97) [362.2]

21049 Sanders, Pete, and Steve Myers. *Drinking Alcohol* (4–8). Illus. Series: What Do You Know About. 1997, Millbrook LB $23.90 (978-0-7613-0573-6). An introduction to alcohol use and abuse, with material on how alcohol affects the body and behavior. (Rev: SLJ 10/97) [613.8]

21050 Schleifer, Jay. *Methamphetamine: Speed Kills* (5–9). Series: Drug Abuse Prevention Library. 1999, Rosen LB $25.25 (978-0-8239-2512-4). An introduction to this drug, its effects, the crime and violence associated with it, and agencies and organizations where help is available. (Rev: SLJ 7/99; VOYA 4/00) [362.29]

21051 Sherry, Clifford J. *Drugs and Eating Disorders* (5–10). Illus. Series: Drug Abuse Prevention Library. 1994, Rosen LB $17.95 (978-0-8239-1540-8). Shows how diet pills and other weight-loss products can lead to drug abuse and, in some cases, addiction. (Rev: BL 6/1–15/94; SLJ 6/94) [616.85]

21052 Sherry, Clifford J. *Inhalants* (5–10). 1994, Rosen LB $17.95 (978-0-8239-1704-4). A look at inhalants, where they are found, and how they affect the body. (Rev: BL 2/15/95; SLJ 3/95) [362.29]

21053 Simpson, Carolyn. *Methadone* (5–9). Series: Drug Abuse Prevention Library. 1997, Rosen LB $25.25 (978-0-8239-2286-4). The dangers of heroin are discussed, followed by an objective discussion of the pros and cons of methadone, the legal drug used to combat heroin addiction. (Rev: SLJ 11/97) [362.29]

21054 Somdahl, Gary L. *Marijuana Drug Dangers* (5–8). Series: Drug Dangers. 1999, Enslow LB $27.93 (978-0-7660-1214-1). 64pp. After introducing marijuana and its effects, this account covers its misuse and abuse and ways to resist it. (Rev: BL 11/15/99; HBG 3/00) [362.29]

21055 Taylor, Clark. *The House That Crack Built* (3–8). Illus. by Jan T. Dicks. 1992, Chronicle paper $6.95 (978-0-8118-0123-2). 36pp. An old children's rhyme is turned into a dark verse, with a relentless rap beat, about drugs. (Rev: BL 4/15/92; SLJ 6/92) [362.29]

21056 Wax, Wendy. *Say No and Know Why: Kids Learn About Drugs* (4–7). Illus. by Toby McAfee. 1992, Walker LB $13.85 (978-0-8027-8141-3). 80pp. A serious look at drug problems as a 6th-grade class in the Bronx, New York, gets a visit from a local nurse and an assistant district attorney. (Rev: BL 1/15/93; SLJ 10/92) [362.29]

21057 Weitzman, Elizabeth. *Let's Talk About Smoking* (4–8). Illus. Series: Let's Talk. 1996, Rosen LB $19.95 (978-0-8239-2307-6). 24pp. This book explains why people smoke, its effects, and ways to avoid starting, with tips on how to give up. (Rev: BL 3/15/97; SLJ 1/97) [362.29]

21058 Westcott, Patsy. *Why Do People Take Drugs?* (5–7). Series: Exploring Tough Issues. 2001, Raintree LB $25.69 (978-0-7398-3231-8). 48pp. Drugs from caffeine to cocaine are explored, with discussion of society's attitudes toward drugs, legal issues, and the reasons some people are more tempted to abuse substances. (Rev: HBG 10/01; SLJ 7/01) [362.29]

Bionics and Transplants

21059 Beecroft, Simon. *Super Humans: A Beginner's Guide to Bionics* (5–7). Illus. by Ian Thompson and Stephen Sweet. Series: Future Files. 1998, Millbrook LB $23.40 (978-0-7613-0621-4). 32pp. This work explores such futuristic topics as cloning humans, gene manipulation, electronic body parts, and life extension. (Rev: HBG 10/98; SLJ 10/98) [617.9]

21060 Fullick, Ann. *Rebuilding the Body* (5–8). Illus. Series: Science at the Edge. 2002, Heinemann LB $27.86 (978-1-58810-700-8). 64pp. An insightful volume about transplant procedures, including a section on how the organs of the body function and a discussion about ethics. (Rev: BL 10/15/02; HBG 3/03; SLJ 4/03) [617.9]

21061 Jango-Cohen, Judith. *Bionics* (4–6). 2006, Lerner LB $26.60 (978-0-8225-5937-5). 48pp. Covers the topic of bionics and how mechanical parts can replace human parts and can help the senses. (Rev: SLJ 3/07) [617]

21062 Rosaler, Maxine. *Bionics* (5–9). Series: Science on the Edge. 2003, Gale LB $24.95 (978-1-56711-784-4). 48pp. This account explores the science of fusing artificial parts with human parts to aid body functions and comments on the controversy surround this new science. (Rev: BL 10/15/03; SLJ 3/04) [174]

Disabilities, Physical and Mental

21063 Abeel, Samantha. *What Once Was White* (5–8). Illus. by Charles R. Murphy. 1993, Village $19.95 (978-0-941653-13-8). The author is a 13-year-old learning-disabled student who can't tell time but writes sensitive interpretations of a group of watercolor paintings. (Rev: SLJ 9/93*) [618.62]

21064 Aseltine, Lorraine, et al. *I'm Deaf and It's Okay* (3–5). Illus. by Helen Cogancherry. 1986, Whitman LB $15.99 (978-0-8075-3472-4). 40pp. A boy copes with the frustrations of deafness. (Rev: BL 5/15/86; SLJ 8/86)

21065 Baldwin, Carol. *Autism* (4–6). Illus. Series: Health Matters. 2002, Heinemann LB $24.22 (978-1-4034-0250-9). 32pp. Examines the causes and symptoms of autism and offers an inspiring profile of Scottish artist Richard Wawro, who has become world-famous despite his autism. (Rev: HBG 10/03; SLJ 5/03) [616.8]

21066 Bardhan-Quallen, Sudipta. *Autism* (3–6). Series: Understanding Diseases and Disorders. 2005, Gale LB $26.20 (978-0-7377-2167-6). 48pp. A well-presented look at the symptoms, diagnosis, treatment, and research relating to autism. (Rev: SLJ 8/05) [616.8]

21067 Dendy, Chris A. Zeigler, and Alex Zeigler. *A Bird's-Eye View of Life with ADD and ADHD: Advice from Young Survivors* (5–9). 2003, Cherish

the Children paper $19.95 (978-0-9679911-3-9). 180pp. A guide to ADD and ADHD, written by a dozen teenagers with these disorders with the aim of helping others cope, with advice on succeeding in school, medication, driving, and so forth. (Rev: SLJ 4/04) [618.9]

21068 Dinner, Sherry H. *Nothing to Be Ashamed Of: Growing Up with Mental Illness in Your Family* (5–10). 1989, Lothrop LB $12.93 (978-0-688-08482-0). A psychologist gives good advice to those who live with a mentally ill person. (Rev: BL 6/1/89; SLJ 4/89; VOYA 8/89) [616.89]

21069 Dwight, Laura. *Brothers and Sisters* (K–3). Photos by author. 2005, Star Bright $15.95 (978-1-887734-80-6). Stories of children's lives with disabilities are told by siblings of the impaired and in some cases by the impaired children themselves. (Rev: SLJ 11/05)

21070 Dwight, Laura. *We Can Do It!* (PS–3). Illus. 1992, Checkerboard $7.95 (978-1-56288-301-0). 36pp. Children with various disabilities are shown at home, at play, and at school. (Rev: BL 1/15/93) [305]

21071 Dwyer, Kathleen M. *What Do You Mean I Have a Learning Disability?* (3–6). 1991, Walker LB $15.85 (978-0-8027-8103-1). 48pp. Feelings of inferiority are related in this story of a ten-year-old boy who fails in school. (Rev: BCCB 9/91; BL 9/1/91; SLJ 11/91) [371.9]

21072 Dwyer, Kathleen M. *What Do You Mean I Have Attention Deficit Disorder?* (4–6). Illus. 1996, Walker LB $15.85 (978-0-8027-8393-6). 128pp. Patrick doesn't know why he can't pay attention in school until he is diagnosed as having ADD. (Rev: BCCB 9/96; BL 8/96; SLJ 8/96) [618.92]

21073 Gordon, Melanie Apel. *Let's Talk About Dyslexia* (2–4). Series: Let's Talk. 1999, Rosen LB $19.95 (978-0-8239-5199-4). 24pp. This book describes problems with reading and gives several examples of reading difficulties. (Rev: SLJ 3/99) [371.92]

21074 Gray, Shirley W. *Good Mental Health* (2–4). Illus. Series: Living Well. 2003, Child's World LB $27.07 (978-1-59296-082-8). 32pp. Worry, stress, depression, and other mental problems are discussed. (Rev: SLJ 2/04) [616.89]

21075 Hall, David E. *Living with Learning Disabilities: A Guide for Students* (5–8). 1993, Lerner LB $19.93 (978-0-8225-0036-0). This book explains what learning disabilities are, what causes them, how they can be detected, and today's techniques for treatment. (Rev: BL 1/1/94; SLJ 4/94) [371.9]

21076 Heelan, Jamee Riggio. *Can You Hear a Rainbow? The Story of a Deaf Boy Named Chris* (K–3). Illus. by Nicola Simmonds. 2002, Peachtree $14.95 (978-1-56145-268-2). Chris tells the reader how sign language and other aids help him to cope with his deafness. (Rev: HBG 10/02; SLJ 9/02) [362.42]

21077 Heelan, Jamee Riggio. *The Making of My Special Hand: Madison's Story* (PS–3). Photos by author. Illus. by Nicola Simmonds. 2000, Peachtree $14.95 (978-1-56145-186-9). Described the process of making a prosthesis for a girl who was born with one hand, from taking a plaster cast to connecting the electrode and battery and giving occupational therapy. (Rev: BL 4/1/00; HBG 3/01; SLJ 9/00) [617.5]

21078 Heelan, Jamee Riggio. *Rolling Along: The Story of Taylor and His Wheelchair* (PS–4). Illus. by Nicola Simmonds. 2000, Peachtree $14.95 (978-1-56145-219-4). 32pp. The true story of Taylor, who was born with cerebral palsy and uses a wheelchair. (Rev: BL 9/1/00; HBG 3/01; SLJ 12/00) [616.6]

21079 Kent, Susan. *Let's Talk About Stuttering* (3–5). Series: Let's Talk. 2000, Rosen LB $19.95 (978-0-8239-5423-0). 24pp. As well as explaining what causes stuttering and who is most likely to stutter, this book tells how to deal with teasing and how to get help. (Rev: SLJ 2/01) [616.85]

21080 Landau, Elaine. *Blindness* (4–7). Illus. Series: Understanding Illness. 1994, Twenty-First Century LB $24.90 (978-0-8050-2992-5). 64pp. Both the emotional and scientific aspects of blindness are covered, with an excellent chapter on prevention. (Rev: BL 12/15/94; SLJ 2/95) [617.7]

21081 Landau, Elaine. *Deafness* (4–7). Illus. Series: Understanding Illness. 1994, Twenty-First Century LB $24.90 (978-0-8050-2993-2). 64pp. Beginning with the story of a deaf child, this book explores the causes of deafness, the scientific and emotional factors involved, treatments, and problems in adjusting. (Rev: BL 12/15/94; SLJ 2/95) [617.8]

21082 Landau, Elaine. *Dyslexia* (3–6). Series: Life Balanc. 2004, Watts LB $20.50 (978-0-531-12217-4). 79pp. An informative and practical guide that describes dyslexia and talks about ways to cope with the problem, mentioning famous people who have dealt with this "learning difference." (Rev: SLJ 7/04) [616.85]

21083 Landau, Elaine. *Schizophrenia* (4–8). Illus. Series: Life Balance. 2004, Watts LB $20.50 (978-0-531-12215-0); paper $6.95 (978-0-531-16614-7). 80pp. An overview of the causes, symptoms, and treatment of this mental condition, with true stories of sufferers. (Rev: BL 10/15/03)

21084 Lauren, Jill. *Succeeding with LD: 20 True Stories About Real People with LD* (5–8). Illus. 1997, Free Spirit paper $14.95 (978-1-57542-012-7). 160pp. Case studies of 20 people ages 10 to 61 who have overcome various learning difficulties. (Rev: BL 6/1–15/97; SLJ 7/97; VOYA 8/97) [371.92]

21085 Lee, Mary Price, and Richard S. Lee. *Everything You Need to Know About Natural Disasters and Post-Traumatic Stress Disorder* (5–9). Series: Need to Know Library. 1996, Rosen LB $17.95 (978-0-8239-2053-2). This book explains how such disasters as hurricanes, floods, and earthquakes can cause post-traumatic stress disorder and how to get help and counseling. (Rev: SLJ 6/96; VOYA 8/96) [155.5]

21086 Leigh, Vanora. *Mental Illness* (5–10). Series: Talking Points. 1999, Raintree LB $27.12 (978-0-8172-5311-0). 64pp. This book defines mental illness, gives examples, and discusses causes, treat-

ments, and how to stay mentally healthy. (Rev: BL 8/99; SLJ 8/99) [362.2]

21087 Lennard-Brown, Sarah. *Autism* (5–8). Illus. Series: Health Issues. 2003, Raintree LB $28.56 (978-0-7398-6422-7). 64pp. An in-depth introduction to autism, with attention to the difficulties people with autism face and what is being done to help them. (Rev: SLJ 5/04) [616.89]

21088 Levete, Sarah. *Learning Difficulties* (3–5). Series: Let's Talk About. 2007, Stargazer LB $27.10 (978-1-59604-089-2). 32pp. Dyslexia, autism, and ADHD are explained for elementary students who may know others with these conditions or have them themselves. Basic information and an airy design combine for a good introduction. (Rev: SLJ 6/07)

21089 McCarthy-Tucker, Sherri. *Coping with Special-Needs Classmates* (5–8). 1993, Rosen LB $25.25 (978-0-8239-1598-9). 115pp. First-person accounts describe physical, mental, and emotional problems faced by some young people. (Rev: SLJ 8/93) [616]

21090 McCully, Emily Arnold. *My Heart Glow: Alice Cogswell, Thomas Gallaudet and the Birth of American Sign Language* (1–3). Illus. by author. 2008, Hyperion $15.99 (978-1-4231-0028-7). 40pp. Alice Cogswell, who became deaf after suffering spotted fever, inspired neighbor Thomas Gallaudet to investigate methods of educating the deaf; imagined dialogue is intermingled with quotations and historical material. (Rev: BCCB 9/08; BL 6/1–15/08; HB 7/08; LMC 5/08; SLJ 7/08) [370]

21091 MacKinnon, Christy. *Silent Observer* (K–4). Illus. 1993, Gallaudet Univ. $15.95 (978-1-56368-022-9). 48pp. The journal of a young deaf girl growing up in Nova Scotia at the end of the 19th century and her experiences at a boarding school. (Rev: BL 1/15/94; SLJ 3/94) [362.4]

21092 McMahon, Patricia. *Dancing Wheels* (3–7). Illus. 2000, Houghton $16.00 (978-0-395-88889-6). 48pp. Founded by a woman born with spina bifida, the Dancing Wheels project teaches people to "dance" from their wheelchairs. (Rev: BL 10/1/00; HBG 3/01; SLJ 11/00) [792.8]

21093 McNey, Martha. *Leslie's Story: A Book About a Girl with Mental Retardation* (3–5). Illus. 1996, Lerner LB $21.27 (978-0-8225-2576-9). 32pp. The lifestyle and limitations of a mentally retarded girl are explained. (Rev: BL 7/96; SLJ 9/96) [362.3]

21094 Meyer, Donald, ed. *Views from Our Shoes: Growing Up with a Brother or Sister with Special Needs* (4–6). Illus. 1997, Woodbine paper $15.95 (978-0-933149-98-4). 106pp. Using the words of 45 youngsters ages four to 18 as a focus, this book tells what it is like living with a sibling who has a physical or mental disability. (Rev: BL 1/1–15/98; SLJ 4/98) [362.1]

21095 Moore-Mallinos, Jennifer. *It's OK to Be Me!* (K–3). Illus. by Marta Fàbrega. Series: Live and Learn. 2007, Barron's paper $6.99 (978-0-7641-3584-2). 32pp. A wheelchair-bound boy who feels isolated at school eventually makes the basketball team. (Rev: BL 5/15/07) [306.8]

21096 Nemiroff, Marc A., and Jane Annunziata. *Help Is on the Way: A Child's Book About ADD* (K–3). Illus. by Margaret Scott. 1998, Magination $14.95 (978-1-55798-505-7). 60pp. A picture book for children who suffer from attention deficit disorder, with material on its symptoms, the emotions it causes, and treatments that are available. (Rev: SLJ 9/98) [371.9]

21097 Pigache, Philippa. *ADHD* (4–8). Series: Just the Facts. 2004, Heinemann LB $27.07 (978-1-4034-5142-2). 56pp. The symptoms, causes, and treatment of attention deficit hyperactivity disorder are described, with discussion of continuing research. (Rev: SLJ 5/05)

21098 Powell, Jillian. *Talking About Disability* (2–3). Illus. Series: Talking About. 1999, Raintree LB $25.70 (978-0-8172-5537-4). 32pp. Large pages, big type, and color photographs introduce children to physical and mental disabilities. (Rev: BL 7/99; HBG 9/99) [362.4]

21099 Quinn, Patricia O. *Attention, Girls! A Guide to Learn All About Your AD/HD* (3–8). Illus. by Carl Pearce. 2009, Magination $16.95 (978-1-4338-0447-2); paper $12.95 (978-1-4338-0448-9). 128pp. A readable, girl-centered look at AD/HD with advice and tips from the author who is a physician living with AD/HD. (Rev: BL 7/09) [618.92]

21100 Resh, Kimberly, ed. *Our Friend Mikayla* (K–3). Illus. 2007, Bubel/Aiken Foundation $14.95 (978-1-4243-0734-0). 48pp. School children describe the experience of slowly welcoming Mikayla into their classroom and helping her to enjoy school despite her many disabilities. (Rev: SLJ 6/07)

21101 Riggs, Stephanie. *Never Sell Yourself Short* (3–6). Illus. 2001, Whitman $16.99 (978-0-8075-5563-7). 32pp. Through text and photographs, readers learn how Josh, a 14-year-old dwarf, enjoys his life despite obstacles. (Rev: BCCB 1/02; BL 9/1/01; HBG 3/02; SLJ 11/01) [618.92]

21102 Rissman, Rebecca. *We All Move* (PS–K). Illus. Series: Disabilities and Differences. 2009, Heinemann LB $14.50 (978-1-4329-2150-7). 24pp. Introduces physical and mental differences and looks at the ways in which people cope with various disabilities. (Rev: BL 4/1/09) [612]

21103 Rotner, Shelley, and Sheila Kelly. *The A.D.D. Book for Kids* (K–3). Illus. 2000, Millbrook LB $22.90 (978-0-7613-1722-7). 32pp. This photoessay describes attention deficit disorder and its various symptoms and coping mechanisms. (Rev: BL 4/15/00; HBG 9/00; SLJ 7/00) [618.9]

21104 Shapiro, Ouisie. *Autism and Me: Sibling Stories* (3–6). Illus. by Steven Vote. 2009, Albert Whitman $16.99 (978-0-8075-0487-1). 32pp. Young siblings with brothers and sisters who have autism express the frustrations and rewards they feel. (Rev: BL 3/15/09; SLJ 5/09) [618.92]

21105 Silverstein, Alvin, et al. *Scoliosis* (3–5). Series: My Health. 2002, Watts LB $25.50 (978-0-531-12046-0); paper $6.95 (978-0-531-16639-0). 48pp. The causes of this abnormal curvature of the spine are covered with material on how it affects young

people and how it can be treated. (Rev: BL 12/15/02) [616]

21106 Stein, Sara Bonnett. *About Handicaps* (2–3). Illus. 1974, Walker $14.95 (978-0-8027-6174-3); paper $8.95 (978-0-8027-7225-1). 48pp. A book about learning to accept people who have physical handicaps.

21107 Taylor, John F. *The Survival Guide for Kids with ADD or ADHD* (3–5). Illus. by Tad Herr. 2006, Free Spirit paper $13.95 (978-1-57542-195-7). 119pp. This child-friendly guide to coping with ADD/ADHD offers information and advice on such topics as making friends, success at school, medications, eating sensibly, and so forth. (Rev: SLJ 12/06) [618.92]

21108 Thornton, Denise. *Physical Disabilities: The Ultimate Teen Guide* (5–10). Series: It Happened to Me. 2007, Scarecrow $42.00 (978-0-8108-5300-3). 162pp. In interviews, teens with disabilities describe how they cope at school, with technology and tools, getting around, sports, and so forth. (Rev: SLJ 10/07) [362.40835]

21109 Trueit, Trudi. *ADHD* (3–6). Illus. Series: Life Balance. 2004, Watts LB $20.50 (978-0-531-12261-7). 79pp. Trueit looks at the learning and behavioral problems faced by children — and adults — who suffer from the disorder and discusses some of the more popular methods of treatment. (Rev: SLJ 7/04) [618.92]

21110 Westcott, Patsy. *Living with Blindness* (3–5). 1999, Raintree LB $25.69 (978-0-8172-5741-5). 32pp. This book shows how blind people go about their daily lives and informs the reader about how the eye functions, kinds of visual impairment, and the causes of cataracts, glaucoma, and other conditions. (Rev: HBG 9/00; SLJ 4/00) [617.7]

Disease and Illness

21111 Abrams, Liesa. *Chronic Fatigue Syndrome* (5–7). Illus. Series: Diseases and Disorders. 2003, Gale LB $32.45 (978-1-59018-039-6). 96pp. The symptoms of and treatments for this mysterious condition and related medical problems are covered here, along with the research being undertaken. (Rev: SLJ 7/03) [616]

21112 Aldape, Virginia Totorica. *Nicole's Story: A Book About a Girl with Juvenile Rheumatoid Arthritis* (3–5). Illus. 1996, Lerner LB $21.27 (978-0-8225-2578-3). 40pp. The case history of a young girl who has rheumatoid arthritis. (Rev: BL 7/96; SLJ 9/96) [362.1]

21113 Ali, Rasheda. *I'll Hold Your Hand So You Won't Fall: A Child's Guide to Parkinson's Disease* (2–4). Illus. 2005, Merit $19.95 (978-1-873413-13-5). 40pp. Rasheda Ali, daughter of Muhammad Ali, describes the disease that afflicts her father and its debilitating symptoms. (Rev: SLJ 10/05) [616.8]

21114 Arnold, Lynda. *My Mommy Has AIDS* (PS–3). Illus. by Rosemont School of the Holy Child Students. 1998, Dream $18.95 (978-1-892073-01-3).

32pp. This story about a boy and his sick mother is a first-person narrative describing AIDS, how to avoid infection, and current treatments. (Rev: SLJ 5/99) [616.97]

21115 Baldwin, Carol. *Asthma* (4–6). Illus. Series: Health Matters. 2002, Heinemann LB $24.22 (978-1-4034-0248-6). 32pp. Examines the causes and symptoms of asthma and offers an inspiring profile of Olympic gold medalist Jackie Joyner-Kersee. (Rev: HBG 10/03; SLJ 5/03) [616.2]

21116 Baldwin, Carol. *Sickle Cell Disease* (4–6). Illus. Series: Health Matters. 2002, Heinemann LB $22.79 (978-1-4034-0252-3). 32pp. Examines the causes and symptoms of this disease and describes the condition of Rev. Jesse Jackson, who carries the genetic trait for this disease. (Rev: HBG 10/03; SLJ 5/03) [616.1]

21117 Ballard, Carol. *AIDS and Other Epidemics* (5–8). Illus. Series: What If We Do Nothing? 2009, Gareth Stevens LB $31.00 (978-1-4339-0085-3). 48pp. HIV/AIDS, SARS, and malaria are among the diseases addressed in this volume that looks at the past, the current status, and the future outlook. (Rev: BL 4/15/09; SLJ 6/09) [614.5]

21118 Bardhan-Quallen, Sudipta. *AIDS* (4–6). Illus. Series: Understanding Diseases and Disorders. 2005, Gale LB $26.20 (978-0-7377-2638-1). 48pp. This overview of HIV/AIDS examines the virus and its symptoms, diagnosis, and treatment; also covered are research and availability of medication in the Third World; full-color photographs and quotations from young patients add to the succinct text. (Rev: BL 7/05; SLJ 8/05) [616.97]

21119 Barnard, Bryn. *Outbreak! Plagues That Changed History* (5–8). Illus. by author. 2005, Crown LB $19.99 (978-0-375-92986-1). 48pp. Information on microbes and the study of microorganisms precedes details of specific epidemics. (Rev: SLJ 2/06) [614.4]

21120 Bee, Peta. *Living with Asthma* (3–5). Illus. Series: Living With. 1999, Raintree $27.12 (978-0-8172-5568-8). 32pp. This work discusses the causes and nature of asthma, various medications and treatments, and gives advice on how friends and family can help. (Rev: BL 8/99; HBG 9/99) [618.92]

21121 Berger, Melvin. *Germs Make Me Sick!* Rev. ed. (K–3). Illus. by Marylin Hafner. Series: Let's-Read-and-Find-Out. 1995, HarperCollins paper $5.99 (978-0-06-445154-3). 32pp. In this easily read book, germs and viruses and their effects on the human body are introduced. (Rev: BL 10/1/95; SLJ 3/96) [616.9]

21122 Bjorklund, Ruth. *Asthma* (4–7). Illus. Series: Health Alert. 2004, Benchmark LB $28.50 (978-0-7614-1803-0). 64pp. In addition to describing the causes and treatment of asthma, this attractive title opens with a case history and also includes lists of famous people who suffer from the condition. (Rev: SLJ 5/05)

21123 Bjorklund, Ruth. *Food-Borne Illnesses* (4–7). Illus. Series: Health Alert. 2005, Marshall Cavendish LB $19.95 (978-0-7614-1917-4). 64pp. This is a wide-ranging exploration of illnesses that can be caused by contaminated food — including those resulting from bacteria, poor hygiene, poor handling, and terrorism — and the treatments and preventions available. (Rev: SLJ 6/06) [615.9]

21124 Blake, Claire, et al. *The Paper Chain* (PS–2). Illus. by Kathy Parkinson. 1998, Health paper $8.95 (978-0-929173-28-3). 30pp. As seen through the eyes of Marcus and Ben, this book deals with breast cancer and what happens when their mother undergoes surgery, chemotherapy, and radiation. (Rev: SLJ 6/98) [616.99]

21125 Bowman-Kruhm, Mary. *Everything You Need to Know About Down Syndrome* (4–7). Series: Need to Know Library. 2000, Rosen LB $25.25 (978-0-8239-2949-8). 63pp. Describes the causes, symptoms, and treatment of Down syndrome, and looks at the education and family life of individuals with this condition. (Rev: HBG 10/00; SLJ 3/00) [362.1]

21126 Bridge, Chris. *Andrew's Story: A Book About a Boy Who Beat Cancer* (2–4). Illus. 2001, Lerner LB $21.27 (978-0-8225-2587-5). 32pp. A straightforward account of a boy's battle with cancer written in a 9-year-old's voice. (Rev: BL 1/1–15/02; HBG 3/02; SLJ 12/01) [362.1]

21127 Brill, Marlene T. *Alzheimer's Disease* (4–7). Illus. Series: Health Alert. 2004, Benchmark LB $28.50 (978-0-7614-1799-6). 64pp. In addition to describing the diagnosis and treatment of Alzheimer's disease, this attractive title opens with a case history and also includes lists of famous people who suffer from the condition. (Rev: SLJ 5/05) [362.19]

21128 Bryan, Jenny. *Asthma* (5–10). Illus. Series: Just the Facts. 2004, Heinemann LB $27.07 (978-1-4034-4599-5). 56pp. A well-organized explanation of asthma, illustrated with numerous color photographs and providing material on how air pollution and smoking are factors in causing or aggravating the disease. (Rev: SLJ 6/04) [616.2]

21129 Bryan, Jenny. *Diabetes* (5–10). Illus. Series: Just the Facts. 2004, Heinemann LB $27.07 (978-1-4034-4600-8). 56pp. An illustrated overview of the disease, including causes and treatments and the effects of diet and cultural factors. (Rev: SLJ 6/04) [616.4]

21130 Bryan, Jenny. *What's Wrong with Me? What Happens When You're Sick, and Ways to Stay Healthy* (2–4). Illus. 1995, Thomson Learning LB $5.00 (978-1-56847-199-0). 32pp. In this book about illnesses, double-page spreads reveal possible causes and treatments for various symptoms. (Rev: BL 3/15/95) [616]

21131 Bueche, Shelley. *The Ebola Virus* (4–7). Illus. Series: Parasites. 2003, Gale LB $24.95 (978-0-7377-1780-8). 32pp. Although it's part of the Parasites series, this book focuses on the Ebola virus, which causes an infectious illness and is found widely in Central Africa. (Rev: BL 3/1/04; SLJ 6/04) [616.9]

21132 Burnfield, Alexander. *Multiple Sclerosis* (5–8). Series: Just the Facts. 2004, Heinemann LB $27.07 (978-1-4034-4602-2). 56pp. An accessible explanation of multiple sclerosis, its symptoms, treatment, and the efforts being made to find new treatments and a cure. (Rev: SLJ 6/04) [616.8]

21133 Butler, Dori. *My Grandpa Had a Stroke* (K–2). Illus. by Nicole Wong. 2007, Magination $14.95 (978-1-59147-806-5); paper $8.95 (978-1-59147-807-2). 32pp. Ryan's safe world is shaken when his grandfather has a stroke and moves to Ryan's house, but the young boy finds a way for the two to continue their fishing expeditions; this informative story conveys lots of information about strokes and depicts the young boy's fears. (Rev: BL 7/07; SLJ 7/07) [616.8]

21134 Carter, Alden R. *I'm Tougher than Diabetes!* (2–4). Illus. 2001, Whitman $16.99 (978-0-8075-1572-3). 32pp. A first-person account from the perspective of a pre-teen girl about the management of Type 1 diabetes, with color photographs and frequently asked questions. (Rev: BL 1/1–15/02; HBG 3/02; SLJ 5/02) [616.4]

21135 Casil, Amy Sterling. *Hantavirus* (4–6). Series: Epidemics. 2005, Rosen LB $27.95 (978-1-4042-0254-2). 64pp. Casil offers basic information, suitable for report writers, about the discovery of this virus; its carriers, symptoms, and prevention; outbreaks; and any dangers of its use in bioterrorism. (Rev: SLJ 10/05) [616.9]

21136 Cefrey, Holly. *Syphilis and Other Sexually Transmitted Diseases* (5–8). Illus. Series: Epidemics. 2001, Rosen LB $27.95 (978-0-8239-3488-1). 64pp. Cefrey describes historic outbreaks and treatments, as well as the symptoms and cure, of syphilis and other sexually transmitted diseases. (Rev: BL 3/15/02) [616.95]

21137 Cefrey, Holly. *Yellow Fever* (5–8). Series: Epidemics. 2002, Rosen LB $27.95 (978-0-8239-3489-8). 64pp. Yellow fever, spread by mosquitoes, was the cause of several epidemics in American cities during the 19th century before a cure was found by dedicated doctors who risked their lives. (Rev: BL 8/02) [616]

21138 Connelly, John P., and Leonard Berlow. *You're Too Sweet: A Guide for the Young Diabetic* (4–6). Illus. 1968, Astor-Honor $14.95 (978-0-8392-1173-0). The cause and treatment of diabetes from the standpoint of a 9-year-old boy.

21139 Davies, Nicola. *What's Eating You? Parasites — The Inside Story* (4–6). Illus. by Neal Layton. 2007, Candlewick $12.99 (978-0-7636-3460-5). 62pp. Fleas, lice, tapeworms, and other parasites are described in this book, which provides details about their life cycle and "host"/habitat. (Rev: BCCB 1/08; BL 12/1/07; HB 1/08; LMC 5/08; SLJ 3/08) [591.6]

21140 DerKazarian, Susan. *You Have Head Lice!* (PS–2). Illus. Series: Rookie Read-About Health. 2005, Children's Pr. LB $20.50 (978-0-516-25879-9); paper $5.95 (978-0-516-27920-6). 32pp. A small-format, matter-of-fact look at head lice and their transmission and treatment. (Rev: BL 6/1–15/05) [616.5]

21141 DiConsiglio, John. *When Birds Get Flu and Cows Go Mad!* (5–7). Illus. Series: 24/7 Science Behind the Scenes: Medical Files. 2007, Scholastic LB $26.00 (978-0-531-12069-9); paper $7.95 (978-0-531-17528-6). 64pp. A lively discussion of bird flu, mad cow disease, E. coli bacteria, and other food-borne and headline-grabbing illnesses. (Rev: BL 12/1/07; LMC 3/08) [616.9]

21142 Donnellan, William L. *The Miracle of Immunity* (5–8). Illus. Series: The Story of Science. 2002, Benchmark LB $29.93 (978-0-7614-1425-4). 79pp. A history of mankind's discoveries about diseases and about the body's vulnerabilities and abilities to fend off infections, from the earliest times through AIDS. (Rev: HBG 3/03; LMC 5/03; SLJ 5/03) [616.07]

21143 Donnelly, Karen. *Everything You Need to Know About Lyme Disease* (5–8). Illus. Series: Need to Know Library. 2000, Rosen LB $27.95 (978-0-8239-3216-0). 64pp. This book explains how Lyme disease was discovered, how it is transmitted, its symptoms, and its treatments. (Rev: BL 12/1/00) [616.9]

21144 Donnelly, Karen. *Leprosy (Hansen's Disease)* (5–8). Series: Epidemics. 2002, Rosen LB $27.95 (978-0-8239-3498-0). 64pp. This is the story of leprosy, the disease that created social outcasts of its victims, and of a man named Hansen who discovered an effective treatment. (Rev: BL 8/02) [616.9]

21145 Draper, Allison Stark. *Ebola* (5–8). Illus. Series: Epidemics. 2002, Rosen LB $27.95 (978-0-8239-3496-6). 64pp. Discusses the Ebola virus in both scientific and human terms. Also use *Mad Cow Disease* (2002). (Rev: BL 8/02; SLJ 6/02) [616.9]

21146 Fassler, David, and Kelly McQueen. *What's a Virus, Anyway? The Kids' Book About AIDS* (K–4). 1993, Waterfront $10.95 (978-0-914525-14-1). 67pp. This book describes what AIDS is through an explanation of what a virus is and how some viruses attack our immune system. A reissue. (Rev: BL 6/1/90) [616]

21147 Favor, Lesli J. *Bacteria* (5–8). Illus. Series: Germs: The Library of Disease-Causing Organisms. 2004, Rosen LB $26.50 (978-0-8239-4491-0). 48pp. An informative, illustrated discussion of bacteria, covering their discovery, how they survive, and the dangers they pose to humans. (Rev: SLJ 1/05) [616]

21148 Foley, Ronan. *World Health: The Impact on Our Lives* (5–8). Illus. Series: 21st Century Debates. 2003, Raintree LB $28.56 (978-0-7398-5507-2). 64pp. A thorough and thought-provoking exploration of the health status of countries around the world and the reasons for the wide disparity between wealthy and poor nations. (Rev: BL 8/03; HBG 10/03; SLJ 7/03) [362.1]

21149 Forbes, Anna. *Kids with AIDS* (2–5). Illus. Series: AIDS Awareness Library. 1996, Rosen LB $19.95 (978-0-8239-2372-4). 24pp. Essential facts about AIDS are presented simply, with a focus on living with the disease and that being with AIDS- or HIV-infected individuals need not involve a health risk. (Rev: SLJ 1/97) [616.97]

21150 Forbes, Anna. *When Someone You Know Has AIDS* (3–5). Illus. Series: The AIDS Awareness Library. 1996, Rosen LB $19.95 (978-0-8239-2369-4). 24pp. A simple introduction to AIDS that covers its causes, effects, and treatments. Also use *Where Did AIDS Come From?* (1996). (Rev: SLJ 12/96) [616.97]

21151 Getz, David. *Purple Death: The Mysterious Flu of 1918* (3–5). Illus. 2000, Holt $16.00 (978-0-8050-5751-5). 86pp. This account describes the deadliest six months in human history — the 1918 flu epidemic that infected 2 billion people. (Rev: BCCB 12/00; BL 12/1/00; HBG 3/01; SLJ 2/01) [614.5]

21152 Gillie, Oliver. *Cancer* (5–8). Series: Just the Facts. 2004, Heinemann LB $27.07 (978-1-4034-5144-6). 56pp. Provides accessible explanations of cancer itself, plus the symptoms, diagnosis, and surgery, chemotherapy, and radiation involved in its treatment. (Rev: SLJ 2/05) [616.99]

21153 Gillie, Oliver. *Sickle Cell Disease* (5–8). Series: Just the Facts. 2004, Heinemann LB $27.07 (978-1-4034-4603-9). 56pp. An examination of sickle cell anemia presented in an accessible style, with coverage of symptoms, treatment, and research. (Rev: SLJ 6/04) [616.1]

21154 Gilman, Laura Anne. *Coping with Cerebral Palsy* (5–9). Series: Coping. 2001, Rosen LB $31.95 (978-0-8239-3150-7). 92pp. This is a self-help book that looks at ways to deal with school, work, and travel as well as coping with other people and their attitudes. (Rev: SLJ 2/02) [616.836]

21155 Glaser, Jason. *Chicken Pox* (1–3). Series: First Facts: Health Matters. 2005, Capstone LB $21.26 (978-0-7368-4288-4). 24pp. Basic information on the causes, symptoms, and treatment of chickenpox is presented in simple text. Also use *Flu* and *Pinkeye* (both 2005). (Rev: SLJ 12/05) [618.92]

21156 Gold, Susan Dudley. *Sickle Cell Disease* (4–7). Illus. Series: Health Watch. 2001, Enslow LB $23.93 (978-0-7660-1662-0). 48pp. Readers are introduced to the symptoms and treatment of this disease through the true story of a young African American boy called Keone who received a successful stem-cell transplant. (Rev: HBG 3/02; SLJ 12/01) [616.1]

21157 Goldstein, Margaret J. *Everything You Need to Know About Multiple Sclerosis* (5–8). Series: Need to Know Library. 2001, Rosen LB $27.95 (978-0-8239-3292-4). 64pp. An introduction to multiple sclerosis, its symptoms and treatment, and how it affects the nervous system, along with information on the importance of treating the emotional impact of this disease. (Rev: SLJ 5/01) [616]

21158 Goodnough, David. *Eating Disorders: A Hot Issue* (5–8). Series: Hot Issues. 1999, Enslow LB $27.93 (978-0-7660-1336-0). 64pp. This is a clear introduction to anorexia nervosa, bulimia, and binge eating with material and case studies on symptoms, causes, and consequences but little coverage of prevention and treatment. (Rev: HBG 3/00; SLJ 1/00) [618.92]

21159 Gordon, Melanie Apel. *Let's Talk About Head Lice* (2–4). Series: Let's Talk. 1999, Rosen LB $13.95 (978-1-56838-276-0). 24pp. The habits of head lice are covered plus material on how they are transmitted and how to get rid of them. (Rev: SLJ 3/99) [595.7]

21160 Gordon, Sherri Mabry. *Peanut Butter, Milk, and Other Deadly Threats: What You Should Know About Food Allergies* (5–9). Series: Issues in Focus Today. 2006, Enslow LB $31.93 (978-0-7660-2529-5). 112pp. This information-packed survey of food allergies identifies common culprit foods, explains the mechanics of allergic reactions, and also reports on medical research to find better treatments. (Rev: SLJ 11/06) [616.97]

21161 Gray, Susan H. *Living with Cystic Fibrosis* (3–5). Series: Living Well. 2002, Child's World LB $27.07 (978-1-56766-105-7). 32pp. The nature of cystic fibrosis is discussed with details on how it affects the body, its causes, and how to live with it, plus anecdotes from people who suffer from the illness. Also use *Living with Cerebral Palsy* (2002). (Rev: BL 10/15/02) [616]

21162 Gray, Susan H. *Living with Juvenile Rheumatoid Arthritis* (3–5). Illus. Series: Living Well. 2002, Child's World LB $27.07 (978-1-56766-104-0). 32pp. First-hand accounts from children with juvenile rheumatoid arthritis enhance the information on the disease, from diagnosis to treatment. (Rev: BL 10/15/02; SLJ 3/03) [618.92]

21163 Gutman, Bill. *Harmful to Your Health* (5–8). Illus. Series: Focus on Safety. 1996, Twenty-First Century LB $24.90 (978-0-8050-4144-6). This volume outlines the problems inherent in drugs, alcohol, AIDS, steroids, and sexual abuse, with material on how to be alert to their dangers. (Rev: BL 2/1/97; SLJ 2/97) [616.86]

21164 Haney, Johannah. *Juvenile Diabetes* (4–7). Illus. Series: Health Alert. 2004, Benchmark LB $28.50 (978-0-7614-1798-9). 63pp. In addition to describing the treatment and possible complications of juvenile diabetes, this attractive title opens with a case history and also includes lists of famous people who suffer from the condition. (Rev: SLJ 5/05)

21165 Hawkins, Trisha. *Everything You Need to Know About Measles and Rubella* (4–8). Series: Need to Know Library. 2001, Rosen LB $27.95 (978-0-8239-3322-8). 64pp. Simple text and photographs describe the diseases and methods of prevention and treatment, and discuss public-health issues. Also use *Everything You Need to Know About Chicken Pox and Shingles* (2001). (Rev: SLJ 8/01) [616.9]

21166 Hayhurst, Chris. *Cholera* (5–9). Series: Epidemics. 2001, Rosen LB $27.95 (978-0-8239-3345-7). 64pp. In a readable style, Hayhurst discusses the history of cholera, formerly a deadly disease, and explains how its treatment was developed. Also use *Polio* and *Smallpox* (both 2001). (Rev: SLJ 7/01) [616.9]

21167 Hayhurst, Chris. *E. Coli* (4–7). Series: Epidemics. 2004, Rosen LB $27.95 (978-0-8239-4201-5). 64pp. A look at the transmission, treatment, and prevention of this bacterium, with an emphasis on the importance of washing hands and food before eating. (Rev: SLJ 8/04) [616.9]

21168 Hicks, Terry Allan. *Allergies* (4–8). Illus. Series: Health Alert. 2005, Benchmark LB $19.95 (978-0-7614-1918-1). 64pp. All about what allergies are, what brings them on, and how they are treated, with colorful sidebars and features that add to the text. (Rev: SLJ 5/06) [616.97]

21169 Hirschmann, Kris. *Salmonella* (4–7). Illus. Series: Parasites. 2003, Gale LB $24.95 (978-0-7377-1785-3). 32pp. This fascinating examination of Salmonella bacteria, responsible for a wide variety of illnesses in the United States and elsewhere, is supplemented with numerous photos and microscopic views of the title bacteria. (Rev: BL 3/1/04) [615.4]

21170 Hoffmann, Gretchen. *Mononucleosis* (4–8). Illus. Series: Health Alert. 2005, Benchmark LB $19.95 (978-0-7614-1915-0). 64pp. All about what "mono" is, its symptoms, and its treatment, with graphic features that add to the text. (Rev: SLJ 5/06) [616.9]

21171 Hyde, Margaret O., and Elizabeth Forsyth. *Diabetes* (4–7). Illus. 2003, Watts LB $26.00 (978-0-531-12209-9). 96pp. Case studies of young people add to the easy-to-understand coverage of the disease, its different types, causes, symptoms, and popular methods of treatment. (Rev: SLJ 2/04) [616.4]

21172 Hyde, Margaret O., and Elizabeth Forsyth. *The Disease Book: A Kid's Guide* (5–8). Illus. 1997, Walker LB $17.85 (978-0-8027-8498-8). A simple, straightforward overview of the causes, symptoms, and treatments of more than 100 physical and mental diseases. (Rev: BL 9/15/97; HBG 3/98; SLJ 11/97) [616]

21173 Hyde, Margaret O., and Elizabeth Forsyth. *Living with Asthma* (4–6). Illus. 1995, Walker LB $15.85 (978-0-8027-8287-8). 96pp. The physical and emotional aspects of asthma are introduced, with several case histories of people who cope with this condition. (Rev: BL 6/1–15/95; SLJ 7/95) [362]

21174 Isle, Mick. *Everything You Need to Know About Food Poisoning* (4–8). Illus. Series: Need to Know Library. 2001, Rosen LB $27.95 (978-0-8239-3396-9). 64pp. Safe ways to prepare food are the main focus of this book, which also describes the symptoms and treatment of food poisoning. (Rev: SLJ 10/01) [615.954]

21175 Jukes, Mavis, and Lilian Cheung. *Be Healthy! It's a Girl Thing: Food, Fitness, and Feeling Great* (5–8). Illus. by Debra Ziss. 2003, Crown LB $18.99 (978-0-679-99029-1); paper $12.95 (978-0-679-89029-4). 160pp. The authors take a matter-of-fact, motivational approach to changes that arrive with puberty and the steps girls can take to be healthy and avoid weight gain and eating disorders. (Rev: BL 1/1–15/04; SLJ 12/03) [613]

21176 Katz, Bobbi. *Germs! Germs! Germs!* (1–2). Illus. by Steve Björkman. Series: Beginning Reader: Science. 1996, Scholastic $3.99 (978-0-590-67295-5). 40pp. The contributions and havoc caused by germs are revealed from their point of view. (Rev: BL 2/1/97) [616]

21177 Katz, Bobbi. *Lots of Lice* (1–3). Illus. by Steve Björkman. Series: Hello Reader! 1998, Scholastic paper $3.99 (978-0-590-10834-8). 40pp. A funny and informative book for beginning readers that tells about lice, how one gets them, and what to do about them — as told from the standpoint of one of the lice. (Rev: BL 11/1/98; SLJ 2/99) [613]

21178 Lamb, Kirsten. *Cancer* (5–8). Series: Health Issues. 2002, Raintree LB $28.54 (978-0-7398-5219-4). 64pp. An informative account that covers various kinds of cancer, giving real-life stories, and also deals with issues and choices facing teens today. (Rev: BL 12/15/02; HBG 3/03; SLJ 3/03) [616.99]

21179 Landau, Elaine. *Allergies* (4–7). Illus. Series: Understanding Illness. 1994, Twenty-First Century LB $24.90 (978-0-8050-2989-5). 64pp. After a case history that explores allergies in personal terms, an objective presentation is given of their causes, effects, and treatment. (Rev: BL 12/15/94; SLJ 2/95) [616.97]

21180 Landau, Elaine. *Cancer* (4–7). Illus. Series: Understanding Illness. 1994, Twenty-First Century LB $24.90 (978-0-8050-2990-1). 64pp. This book explains the many types of cancer, their causes, present-day treatments, and possible developments in the future. (Rev: BL 12/15/95; SLJ 2/95) [616.99]

21181 Landau, Elaine. *Epilepsy* (4–7). Illus. Series: Understanding Illness. 1994, Twenty-First Century LB $24.90 (978-0-8050-2991-8). 64pp. Following the story of a youngster who has epilepsy, this account describes the disorder, its emotional and medical aspects, and treatments. (Rev: BL 12/15/94; SLJ 2/95) [616.8]

21182 Lassieur, Allison. *Head Lice* (3–5). Illus. Series: My Health. 2000, Watts LB $25.50 (978-0-531-11624-1). 48pp. Using amazing photos taken with microscopes, this account introduces head lice, their physical characteristics, how they are transmitted, and how to get rid of them. (Rev: BL 6/1–15/00) [616.5]

21183 Lennard-Brown, Sarah. *Asthma* (5–8). Illus. Series: Health Issues. 2002, Raintree LB $28.54 (978-0-7398-5218-7). 64pp. Color photographs and straightforward text explain the symptoms, diagnosis, and treatment of asthma. (Rev: BL 12/15/02; HBG 3/03) [616.2]

21184 Lynette, Rachel. *Leprosy* (5–8). Illus. Series: Understanding Diseases and Disorders. 2005, Gale LB $26.20 (978-0-7377-3172-9). 48pp. Straightforward text discusses the plight of leprosy patients around the world and through history; causes, treatments, and transmission are also discussed. (Rev: SLJ 6/06) [616.9]

21185 McGuire, Paula. *AIDS* (4–8). Series: Preteen Pressures. 1998, Raintree LB $25.69 (978-0-8172-5025-6). 48pp. Straight facts and statistics are given on AIDS, including methods of prevention and stories of people with HIV/AIDS, such as Magic Johnson and the late Ryan White. (Rev: BL 5/15/98; HBG 10/98) [616,97]

21186 Margulies, Phillip. *Creutzfeldt-Jakob Disease* (4–7). Series: Epidemics. 2004, Rosen LB $27.95 (978-0-8239-4199-5). 64pp. Examines the history and current state of knowledge about this rare disorder that affects the brain and is related to Mad Cow Disease. Also use *West Nile Virus* (2004). (Rev: SLJ 8/04) [616.8]

21187 Margulies, Phillip. *Diphtheria* (4–6). Series: Epidemics. 2005, Rosen LB $27.95 (978-1-4042-0253-5). 64pp. Suitable for report writers, this book covers the nature of diphtheria, important outbreaks of the disease, treatment, and efforts to prevent future epidemics. (Rev: SLJ 10/05) [616.9]

21188 Margulies, Phillip. *Everything You Need to Know About Rheumatic Fever* (5–8). Series: The Need to Know Library. 2004, Rosen LB $27.95 (978-0-8239-4509-2). 64pp. After a brief history of the disease and the discovery of its cause, this volume discusses symptoms, treatment, and the concern that the disease may become more prevalent as bacteria develop resistance to antibiotics. (Rev: SLJ 4/05)

21189 Marrin, Albert. *Dr. Jenner and the Speckled Monster: The Search for the Smallpox Vaccine* (4–8). Illus. 2002, Dutton $19.99 (978-0-525-46922-3). 96pp. This highly readable and detailed account describes the impact of smallpox from the time of the Aztecs, major outbreaks over the years, the way the virus works, the work of Jenner in developing a vaccine, and the virus's potential as a weapon of mass destruction. (Rev: BL 11/15/02; HB 11/02; HBG 3/03; SLJ 1/03; VOYA 12/02) [614.5]

21190 Marx, Trish, and Dorita Beh-Eger. *I Heal: The Children of Chernobyl in Cuba* (3–6). Illus. 1996, Lerner LB $21.27 (978-0-8225-4897-3). 48pp. This book contains the story of two young victims of the Chernobyl nuclear disaster and of their medical treatment in Cuba. (Rev: BCCB 12/96; BL 12/1/96; SLJ 10/96) [618.92]

21191 Massari, Francesca. *Everything You Need to Know About Cancer* (5–9). Series: Need to Know Library. 2000, Rosen LB $27.95 (978-0-8239-3164-4). 64pp. This book defines what cancer is and looks at its causes, prevention, symptoms, diagnosis, and treatment. (Rev: HBG 10/00; SLJ 8/00) [616.99]

21192 Moehn, Heather. *Everything You Need to Know When Someone You Know Has Leukemia* (5–10). Series: Need to Know Library. 2000, Rosen LB $27.95 (978-0-8239-3121-7). 64pp. The basic facts about leukemia are covered with material on its various types and treatments, possible causes, and the emotional aspects of the illness. (Rev: SLJ 9/00) [616.99]

21193 Monroe, Judy. *Cystic Fibrosis* (5–9). Illus. Series: Perspectives on Disease and Illness. 2001, Capstone LB $25.26 (978-0-7368-1026-5). 64pp. A straightforward account of the symptoms, diagnosis, and treatment of this disease, with discussion of the impact on the life of the patient and other family members. Also use *Breast Cancer* (2001). (Rev: HBG 3/02; SLJ 3/02) [616.3]

21194 Moore-Mallinos, Jennifer. *I Have Asthma* (PS–2). Illus. by Rosa M. Curto. 2007, Barron's paper $6.99 (978-0-7641-3785-3). 32pp. At soccer practice a boy experiences his first asthma attack, is taken to the hospital where he learns how to deal with it, and returns to the playing field in this simple and informative picture book. (Rev: BL 11/1/07; SLJ 3/08) [616.238]

21195 Moragne, Wendy. *Allergies* (5–8). Series: Twenty-First Century Medical Library. 1999, Twenty-First Century LB $26.90 (978-0-7613-1359-5). 128pp. After general material on allergies, their causes and treatment, this account describes specific allergies involving food, skin, rhinitis, drugs, and insects. (Rev: HBG 3/00; SLJ 3/00) [616.97]

21196 Morgan, Sally. *Germ Killers: Fighting Disease* (5–8). Series: Science at the Edge. 2002, Heinemann LB $27.86 (978-1-58810-699-5). 64pp. Current advances in fighting disease are outlined with their current applications and future possibilities. (Rev: BL 10/15/02; HBG 3/03) [616]

21197 Murphy, Patricia J. *Illness* (PS–3). Series: Tough Topics. 2007, Heinemann LB $25.36 (978-1-4034-9777-2). 32pp. A sensitive discussion of the nature of illness, different kinds of illnesses, diagnosis, treatment, and how to cope when others are ill. (Rev: SLJ 12/07) [155.9]

21198 Niner, Holly L. *I Can't Stop! A Story About Tourette Syndrome* (1–3). Illus. by Meryl Treatner. 2005, Albert Whitman $16.99 (978-0-8075-3620-9). 32pp. Nathan learns to deal with his Tourette syndrome in this realistic story that is bolstered by factual information contributed by a doctor. (Rev: BL 11/15/05)

21199 Nye, Bill, and Kathleen W. Zoehfeld. *Bill Nye the Science Guy's Great Big Book of Tiny Germs* (4–7). Illus. by Bryn Barnard. 2005, Hyperion $16.99 (978-0-7868-0543-3). 48pp. Solid information on bacteria and viruses is presented in an appealing and lively format. (Rev: BL 6/1–15/05; SLJ 7/05) [579]

21200 Peacock, Carol Antoinette. *Sugar Was My Best Food: Diabetes and Me* (3–6). Illus. 1998, Whitman $13.99 (978-0-8075-7646-5). 55pp. An 11-year-old boy describes his daily experiences in coping with diabetes, which he has had since age nine. (Rev: BL 8/98; HBG 9/98; SLJ 6/98) [362.1]

21201 Pincus, Dion. *Everything You Need to Know About Cerebral Palsy* (4–7). Series: Need to Know Library. 2000, Rosen LB $27.95 (978-0-8239-2960-3). 64pp. The causes and characteristics of cerebral palsy are discussed with material on the treatments and the daily life of those affected. (Rev: HBG 10/00; SLJ 3/00) [618.92]

21202 Powell, Jillian. *Asthma* (K–2). Illus. Series: Feeling Sick? 2008, Black Rabbit LB $18.95 (978-1-84234-472-9). 32pp. Powell looks at the causes, symptoms, and treatment of this common problem, and includes anecdotes about typical asthma experiences. (Rev: BL 4/1/08) [616.2]

21203 Ramen, Fred. *SARS (Severe Acute Respiratory Syndrome)* (4–6). Series: Epidemics. 2005, Rosen LB $27.95 (978-1-4042-0258-0). 64pp. Offers basic information, suitable for report writers, about the various outbreaks of Severe Acute Respiratory Syndrome and the symptoms, treatment, and research efforts. (Rev: SLJ 10/05) [614.5]

21204 Ramen, Fred. *Sleeping Sickness and Other Parasitic Tropical Diseases* (5–8). Series: Epidemics. 2002, Rosen LB $27.95 (978-0-8239-3499-7). 64pp. After a history of parasitic diseases around the globe and the role played by bloodsucking killers like the tsetse fly, this account describes the treatments now available. (Rev: BL 8/02; SLJ 7/02) [616]

21205 Ray, Kurt. *Typhoid Fever* (5–8). Illus. Series: Epidemics. 2002, Rosen LB $27.95 (978-0-8239-3572-7). 64pp. An introduction to the history and treatment of typhoid fever, including coverage of Typhoid Mary. (Rev: BL 3/15/02) [614.5]

21206 Romano, Amy. *Germ Warfare* (5–8). Illus. Series: Germs: The Library of Disease-Causing Organisms. 2004, Rosen LB $26.50 (978-0-8239-4493-4). 48pp. An informative, illustrated overview of the history and current status of germ warfare, with discussion of what we can do to protect ourselves. (Rev: SLJ 1/05) [358]

21207 Rosaler, Maxine. *Botulism* (4–7). Series: Epidemics. 2004, Rosen LB $27.95 (978-0-8239-4197-1). 64pp. A look at outbreaks of botulism and their causes and prevention. (Rev: SLJ 8/04) [614.5]

21208 Routh, Kristina. *Down Syndrome* (5–8). Series: Just the Facts. 2004, Heinemann LB $27.07 (978-1-4034-5145-3). 56pp. An informative overview of this disease and its diagnosis and treatment, stressing the individuality of children with the syndrome. (Rev: SLJ 2/05) [362.1]

21209 Routh, Kristina. *Meningitis* (5–8). Illus. Series: Just the Facts. 2004, Heinemann LB $27.07 (978-1-4034-5146-0). 56pp. The symptoms of meningitis are provided along with a thorough explanation of the disease and its diagnosis and treatment. (Rev: SLJ 2/05)

21210 Roy, Jennifer. *Depression* (4–7). Illus. Series: Health Alert. 2004, Benchmark LB $28.50 (978-0-7614-1800-9). 64pp. In addition to describing the causes and treatment of depression, this attractive title opens with a case history and also includes lists of famous people who suffer from the condition. (Rev: SLJ 5/05)

21211 Royston, Angela. *Why Do My Eyes Itch? And Other Questions About Allergies* (3–5). Illus. Series: Body Matters. 2002, Heinemann LB $24.22 (978-1-4034-0207-3). 32pp. All kinds of allergies are introduced in concise, simple text with many illustrations. (Rev: SLJ 4/03) [616.97]

21212 Sanders, Pete, and Steve Myers. *Anorexia and Bulimia* (4–8). Illus. by Mike Lacy and Liz Sawyer. Series: What Do You Know About. 1999, Millbrook LB $23.90 (978-0-7613-0914-7). 32pp. Using an actual case study as a beginning, this book explores the causes, effects, and treatment of these eating disorders and covers the behavioral patterns of those afflicted. (Rev: HBG 10/99; SLJ 10/99) [618.92]

21213 Schwartz, Robert H., and Peter M. G. Deane. *Coping with Allergies* (4–7). Series: Coping. 1999, Rosen LB $31.95 (978-0-8239-2511-7). 160pp.

After a rundown of the types and causes of allergies, this account describes their physical and emotional impact and current treatments. (Rev: BL 2/15/00) [616.97]

21214 Senker, Cath. *World Health Organization* (5–8). Series: World Watch. 2004, Raintree LB $18.99 (978-0-7398-6614-6). 48pp. The world's health problems and what is being done to combat them are the focus of this somber title, which looks at both the developing world and the wealthiest of nations. (Rev: BL 4/1/04; SLJ 3/04) [362.1]

21215 Sheen, Barbara. *Diabetes* (5–7). Illus. Series: Diseases and Disorders. 2003, Gale LB $32.45 (978-1-59018-244-4). 112pp. The symptoms of and treatments for diabetes are covered here, with discussion of alternative treatments, how diabetics manage their disease, and the research being undertaken. (Rev: SLJ 7/03) [616.4]

21216 Shein, Lori. *AIDS* (5–8). Series: Overview. 1998, Lucent LB $29.95 (978-1-56006-193-9). A concise overview of the AIDS epidemic in the late 20th century, the attempts to treat and restrict the spread of the disease, and the controversies surrounding it. (Rev: BL 8/98) [616.99]

21217 Sherrow, Victoria. *Polio Epidemic: Crippling Virus Outbreak* (4–7). Series: American Disasters. 2001, Enslow LB $23.93 (978-0-7660-1555-5). 48pp. In this readable account, Sherrow looks at the history of polio, its treatment, the epidemic in the United States that started in 1952, and the creation of the polio vaccine. (Rev: HBG 3/02; SLJ 3/02) [362.1]

21218 Silverstein, Alvin. *The Asthma Update* (5–8). 2006, Enslow LB $31.93 (978-0-7660-2482-3). 128pp. A thorough look at asthma, its symptoms, history, treatments, and the research being done in hopes of finding a cure. (Rev: BL 12/1/06) [616.2]

21219 Silverstein, Alvin. *The Food Poisoning Update* (5–8). Illus. Series: Disease Update. 2007, Enslow LB $23.95 (978-0-7660-2748-0). 128pp. A clear introduction to what causes food poisoning, how it affects the body, and how it can be avoided. (Rev: BL 12/1/07; SLJ 2/08) [615.9]

21220 Silverstein, Alvin, et al. *Allergies* (3–5). Series: My Health. 1999, Watts LB $25.50 (978-0-531-11581-7). 48pp. This simple work with entertaining drawings and photos explains, from a child's point of view, what allergies are, the different kinds, and how they can be treated. (Rev: BL 10/15/99; HBG 4/00; SLJ 12/99) [616]

21221 Silverstein, Alvin, et al. *The Flu and Pneumonia Update* (5–8). Illus. Series: Disease Update. 2006, Enslow LB $31.93 (978-0-7660-2480-9). 104pp. Symptoms, treatment, history, and new research are all included in this discussion of flu and pneumonia. (Rev: BL 4/1/06; SLJ 9/06) [616.2]

21222 Silverstein, Alvin, et al. *Lyme Disease* (4–7). Illus. 2000, Watts LB $25.50 (978-0-531-11751-4). 64pp. This book introduces Lyme disease, its symptoms, history, the tick that carries it, prevention, and treatments. (Rev: BL 10/15/00) [616.9]

21223 Silverstein, Alvin, and Virginia Silverstein. *The Breast Cancer Update* (5–9). Illus. Series: Disease Update. 2007, Enslow LB $31.93 (978-0-7660-2747-3). 128pp. Symptoms, treatment, history, and new research are all included in this concise discussion of breast cancer. (Rev: SLJ 2/08)

21224 Silverstein, Alvin, and Virginia Silverstein. *Parkinson's Disease* (4–6). Illus. Series: Diseases and People. 2002, Enslow LB $26.60 (978-0-7660-1593-7). 128pp. Actor Michael J. Fox's diagnosis of Parkinson's serves as an introduction to the history, causes, symptoms, and treatment of this disease. (Rev: HBG 3/03; SLJ 12/02)

21225 Silverstein, Alvin, and Virginia Silverstein. *Vaccinations* (3–5). Series: My Health. 2002, Watts paper $6.95 (978-0-531-15564-6). 48pp. Using many visuals and a clear, simple text, this book describes how vaccinations were developed, how they work, and the various types. (Rev: BL 6/1–15/02; SLJ 8/02) [614.4]

21226 Simpson, Carolyn. *Everything You Need to Know About Asthma* (5–10). Illus. Series: Need to Know Library. 1998, Rosen LB $27.95 (978-0-8239-2567-4). Vital background information is given about the causes and effects, symptoms, and treatments of asthma. (Rev: SLJ 10/98) [616.2]

21227 Smart, Paul. *Everything You Need to Know About Mononucleosis* (5–9). Series: Need to Know Library. 1998, Rosen LB $27.95 (978-0-8239-2550-6). 64pp. A straightforward presentation about the "kissing disease," which is often undiagnosed or mistaken for the flu and which requires long periods of rest for recovery. (Rev: SLJ 10/98) [616]

21228 Spray, Michelle. *Growing Up with Scoliosis: A Young Girl's Story* (5–9). Illus. by author. 2002, Book Shelf paper $12.95 (978-0-9714160-3-1). 119pp. An autobiographical account of the treatment of scoliosis and the emotional impact on the patient, with clear illustrations. (Rev: SLJ 12/02) [362.19673]

21229 Stewart, Gail B. *Sleep Disorders* (5–8). Illus. Series: Diseases and Disorders. 2002, Gale LB $32.45 (978-1-56006-909-6). 112pp. Insomnia, narcolepsy, apnea, and night terrors are among the problems discussed here, with material on treatments, new research, and attitudes toward people who are always tired. (Rev: SLJ 3/03) [616.8498]

21230 Stone, Tanya L. *Medical Causes* (5–10). Series: Celebrity Activists. 1997, Twenty-First Century LB $25.90 (978-0-8050-5233-6). The contributions of such celebrity activists as Elizabeth Taylor, Elton John, Paul Newman, Jerry Lewis, and Linda Ellerbee to various medical causes are highlighted, with material on each of their causes. (Rev: SLJ 1/98) [616]

21231 Susman, Edward. *Multiple Sclerosis* (4–7). Series: Diseases and People. 1999, Enslow LB $26.60 (978-0-7660-1185-4). 128pp. A description of this debilitating disease that attacks the nervous system. (Rev: HBG 3/00; SLJ 2/00) [616]

21232 Taylor-Butler, Christine. *Food Allergies* (3–5). Illus. Series: True Book: Health and the Human Body. 2008, Children's Pr. LB $26.00 (978-0-531-16858-5); paper $6.95 (978-0-531-20732-1). 48pp. Peanuts, milk, and wheat are among the substances

covered in this accessible and attractive overview that includes a useful "Hidden Dangers" spread. (Rev: BL 6/1–15/08; LMC 8/08) [618.92]

21233 Thomas, Pat. *Why Is It So Hard to Breathe?* (PS–2). Illus. by Lesley Harker. Series: A First Look At. 2008, Barron's paper $6.99 (978-0-7641-3898-0). 32pp. This title explains what asthma is and how it can be managed and features discussion questions for parents and children and colorful illustrations showing how a little boy learns to use his inhaler. (Rev: BLO 9/17/08) [616.2]

21234 Tsubakiyama, Margaret. *Lice Are Lousy! All About Headlice* (3–5). Illus. 1999, Millbrook $23.90 (978-0-7613-1316-8). 32pp. A breezy but fact-filled introduction to head lice, their habits, how you get them, and how to get rid of them. (Rev: BL 8/99; HBG 9/99; SLJ 9/99) [616.5]

21235 Viegas, Jennifer. *Parasites* (5–8). Illus. Series: Germs: The Library of Disease-Causing Organisms. 2004, Rosen LB $26.50 (978-0-8239-4494-1). 48pp. An informative, illustrated discussion of parasites, covering how they survive and the dangers they pose to humans. (Rev: SLJ 1/05) [574.5]

21236 Wainwright, Tabitha. *You and an Illness in Your Family* (5–8). Series: Family Matters. 2001, Rosen LB $26.50 (978-0-8239-3352-5). 48pp. Concise, readable advice is accompanied by full-page photographs of young teens and the recommendation to seek help when necessary. (Rev: SLJ 8/01) [610]

21237 Ward, Brian. *Epidemic* (4–7). Illus. Series: Eyewitness Books. 2000, DK $15.99 (978-0-7894-6296-1). 64pp. This book covers the nature of epidemics, their causes, how they are spread and contained, and gives examples from history. (Rev: BL 12/1/00; HBG 10/01) [614.4]

21238 Watters, Debbie. *Where's Mom's Hair? A Family's Journey Through Cancer* (2–5). 2005, Second Story paper $10.95 (978-1-896764-94-8). 32pp. This photo-essay documents how family members lovingly supported a cancer-stricken mother as she underwent the rigors of chemotherapy. (Rev: BL 10/1/05; SLJ 7/05) [362.196]

21239 Weiss, Jonathan H. *Breathe Easy: Young People's Guide to Asthma* (4–7). Illus. 1994, Magination paper $9.95 (978-0-945354-62-8). 64pp. An account that describes the causes of asthma, what happens during an attack, and how to manage this condition. (Rev: BL 2/15/95) [618.92]

21240 Weitzman, Elizabeth. *Let's Talk About When Someone You Love Has Alzheimer's Disease* (1–4). Illus. Series: Let's Talk. 1996, Rosen LB $18.75 (978-0-8239-2306-9). 24pp. A discussion of the nature of Alzheimer's disease, the changes it causes, and how to adjust to it. (Rev: BL 3/1/97; SLJ 8/96) [618.97]

21241 Westcott, Patsy. *Living with Epilepsy* (3–5). Series: Living With. 1999, Raintree LB $27.12 (978-0-8172-5570-1). 32pp. This book introduces epilepsy and explains the causes, different kinds of seizures, and treatment options. (Rev: BL 8/99; HBG 9/99) [616.8]

21242 Whelan, Jo. *Diabetes* (5–8). Series: Health Issues. 2002, Raintree LB $28.54 (978-0-7398-5220-0). 64pp. Case histories of youngsters with diabetes are used to explain the nature of this disease, the problems it produces, and the treatments available. (Rev: BL 12/15/02; HBG 3/03) [616.4]

21243 Woolf, Alex. *Death and Disease* (5–8). Series: Medieval Realms. 2004, Gale LB $29.95 (978-1-59018-533-9). 48pp. Black Death, leprosy, and other diseases are discussed, with their impact on society, and the practice of medicine in general is described. (Rev: BL 4/1/04; SLJ 3/05) [610]

21244 Yount, Lisa. *Cancer* (5–8). Series: Overview. 1999, Lucent LB $29.95 (978-1-56006-363-6). 111pp. This objective overview explains how cancer cells develop, types of cancer, causes, and past and present treatments, both traditional and alternative. (Rev: BL 9/15/99; HBG 3/00; SLJ 7/99) [616.994]

21245 Zonta, Pat. *Jessica's X-Ray* (2–5). Illus. by Clive Dobson. 2002, Firefly $19.95 (978-1—6); paper $8.95 (978-1-55297-577-0). 28pp. When Jessica breaks her arm, the doctor orders X-rays and the reader is introduced to the whys and hows of this diagnostic tool. (Rev: BL 5/1/02; HBG 10/02; SLJ check) [616.0750]

Doctors and Medicine

21246 Casterline, Linda. *Natural-born Killers: A Chapter Book* (3–7). Series: True Tales. 2004, Children's Pr. LB $22.50 (978-0-516-23725-1). 48pp. Discusses various poisonous plants and animals that have been used in modern medicine to save lives. (Rev: BL 12/1/04; SLJ 2/05) [578.6]

21247 Dowswell, Paul. *Medicine* (5–8). Illus. Series: Great Inventions. 2001, Heinemann LB $25.64 (978-1-58810-213-3). 48pp. A chronological look at new medical instruments and procedures over the ages, with diagrams and information on the inventors. (Rev: HBG 3/02; SLJ 2/02) [610]

21248 Freedman, Jeri. *Stem Cell Research* (5–8). Illus. Series: America Debates. 2007, Rosen LB $21.95 (978-1-4042-1928-1). 64pp. A technical and detailed examination of the issues surrounding stem cell research and the ethical questions that it provokes. (Rev: BL 12/1/07; LMC 1/08; SLJ 2/08) [616]

21249 Green, Jen. *Medicine* (4–7). Illus. Series: Routes of Science. 2004, Gale LB $23.70 (978-1-4103-0168-0). 40pp. A look at the history of medicine and the scientific process, with profiles of key individuals and their discoveries, a chronology, and discussion of future advances. (Rev: SLJ 5/05)

21250 Hughes, Monica. *First Visit to the Dentist* (PS–2). Series: My First. 2004, Raintree LB $18.56 (978-1-4109-0645-8); paper $5.50 (978-1-4109-0671-7). 24pp. Simple language introduces young readers to what happens at the dentist — waiting rooms, examination, cleaning and polishing, and so forth.

21251 Ichord, Loretta Frances. *Toothworms and Spider Juice: An Illustrated History of Dentistry* (5–8). Illus. 2000, Millbrook LB $24.90 (978-0-7613-1465-3). 96pp. A history of dentistry that reveals many of the barbaric treatments of the past and how superstition and ignorance gradually gave way to modern practices. (Rev: BCCB 2/00; BL 2/15/00; HBG 10/00; SLJ 2/00) [617.6]

21252 Jefferis, David. *Bio Tech: Frontiers of Medicine* (4–8). Illus. Series: Megatech. 2001, Crabtree paper $8.95 (978-0-7787-0061-6). 32pp. An eye-catching look at future medical possibilities such as artificial body parts, enhanced use of robots, special foods, and so forth. (Rev: SLJ 6/02) [660.6]

21253 Lindsay, Judy. *The Story of Medicine: From Acupuncture to X Rays* (4–6). Illus. 2003, Oxford LB $26.50 (978-0-19-521984-5). 40pp. The history of medicine, from ancient times to the modern day, is presented in this lively and accessible book full of reproductions. (Rev: HBG 4/04; SLJ 4/04) [610]

21254 Manson, Ainslie. *House Calls: The True Story of a Pioneer Doctor* (3–6). Illus. by Mary Jane Gerber. 2001, Groundwood $15.95 (978-0-88899-446-2). 56pp. Though the narrator of this book is a fictional girl, the story details the real life of an early 19th-century rural Canadian doctor with information on tools and treatment. (Rev: BL 2/1/02; HBG 3/02; SLJ 12/01) [610.92]

21255 Miller, Brandon M. *Just What the Doctor Ordered: The History of American Medicine* (5–8). Series: People's History. 1997, Lerner LB $30.35 (978-0-8225-1737-5). A history of American medicine from early Indian ceremonies and remedies to today's use of laser surgery, placing medical developments in a historical context, such as the role disease played in the Revolutionary and Civil Wars. (Rev: SLJ 5/97*) [610.9]

21256 Snedden, Robert. *Medical Ethics: Changing Attitudes 1900–2000* (4–7). 1999, Raintree LB $28.54 (978-0-8172-5893-1). 64pp. Beginning with Hippocrates, this book gives a history of bioethics and follows with coverage of topics including reproductive rights, euthanasia, organ donation, psychiatry, eugenics, and cloning. (Rev: HBG 10/00; SLJ 5/00) [616]

21257 Townsend, John. *Scalpels, Stitches and Scars: A History of Surgery* (4–7). Illus. Series: A Painful History of Medicine. 2005, Raintree LB $32.86 (978-1-4109-1332-6). 56pp. Gory it may be but this title conveys accurate facts and the eye-catching illustrations will entice browsers. (Rev: BL 5/15/05; SLJ 7/05) [617]

21258 Van Steenwyk, Elizabeth. *Frontier Fever: The Silly, Superstitious — and Sometimes Sensible — Medicine of the Pioneers* (5–8). Illus. 1995, Walker LB $16.85 (978-0-8027-8403-2). 160pp. A history of medicine in the United States from colonial times through the 19th century, including information on the training of caregivers. (Rev: BL 7/95; SLJ 12/95; VOYA 12/95) [610]

21259 Winkler, Kathy. *Radiology* (4–8). Series: Inventors and Inventions. 1996, Benchmark LB $25.64 (978-0-7614-0075-2). This work outlines the history of radiology, provides short profiles of leaders in the field, and describes the effects of too many x-rays on tissue, how x-rays are made, their use in diagnosis and treatment, and other medical imaging such as ultrasound and MRIs. (Rev: BL 7/96; SLJ 9/96) [616.07]

21260 Woods, Michael, and Mary B. Woods. *The History of Medicine* (5–8). Series: Major Inventions Through History. 2005, Twenty-First Century LB $26.60 (978-0-8225-2336-9). 56pp. An attractive look at medical developments through time and their impact on our lives. (Rev: SLJ 1/06) [610]

21261 Woods, Samuel. *The Pediatrician* (3–5). Illus. Series: Doctors in Action. 1998, Blackbirch LB $21.20 (978-1-56711-237-5). 24pp. Introduces the branch of medicine that deals with children and their health problems, and provides many examples of good patient-doctor relationships. (Rev: BL 12/15/98; HBG 3/99) [618.92]

Genetics

21262 Allan, Tony. *Understanding DNA: A Breakthrough in Medicine* (5–8). Illus. Series: Point of Impact. 2002, Heinemann LB $25.64 (978-1-58810-557-8). 32pp. A history of genetics with profiles of the important scientists and discussion of future uses of this knowledge in cloning, medicine, and production of food. (Rev: SLJ 9/02) [572.8609]

21263 Beatty, Richard. *Genetics* (4–8). Illus. Series: Science Fact Files. 2001, Raintree LB $27.12 (978-0-7398-1015-6). 42pp. Cells, chromosomes, genes, and genetic engineering are covered here, with profiles of key scientists. (Rev: HBG 10/01; SLJ 1/02) [660]

21264 Bornstein, Sandy. *What Makes You What You Are: A First Look at Genetics* (5–8). Illus. by Frank Cecala. 1989, Silver Burdett paper $6.95 (978-0-671-68650-5). 115pp. This book affords a fine introduction to cell structure, dominant and recessive traits, and heredity. (Rev: SLJ 1/90) [573.2]

21265 Boskey, Elizabeth. *America Debates Genetic DNA Testing* (5–8). Series: America Debates. 2007, Rosen LB $29.25 (978-1-4042-1926-7). 64pp. Presents facts and opinions on both sides of issues including prenatal and adult genetic testing. (Rev: LMC 1/08; SLJ 11/07) [362.196]

21266 Butterfield, Moira. *Genetics* (5–8). Illus. Series: 21st Century Science. 2003, Smart Apple LB $27.10 (978-1-58340-350-1). 44pp. An accessible, large-format volume on genetics, cloning, and the use of genes in medicine and food engineering, with attractive full-color photographs. (Rev: BL 12/1/03) [576.5.]

21267 Gallant, Roy A. *The Treasure of Inheritance* (5–8). Illus. Series: The Story of Science. 2002, Benchmark LB $29.93 (978-0-7614-1426-1). 78pp. A history of mankind's discoveries about genetics and heredity, starting with the earliest efforts to improve crops and animals, with material on today's and future genetic engineering and the mapping of

the human genome. (Rev: HBG 3/03; LMC 5/03; SLJ 5/03) [576.5]

21268 George, Linda. *Gene Therapy* (5–9). Series: Science on the Edge. 2003, Gale LB $24.95 (978-1-56711-786-8). 48pp. This book explain how genetic engineering can not only have applications in health and industry but also can arouse a great deal of controversy. (Rev: BL 10/15/03) [660]

21269 Jefferis, David. *Cloning: Frontiers of Genetic Engineering* (5–7). Series: Megatech. 1999, Crabtree LB $25.27 (978-0-7787-0048-7). 32pp. This account discusses the history of genetic discoveries and theories, cell reproduction, and the present and possible future of genetic engineering with plants, animals, and humans. (Rev: SLJ 9/99) [174.957]

21270 Morgan, Sally. *Body Doubles: Cloning Plants and Animals* (5–8). Illus. Series: Science at the Edge. 2002, Heinemann LB $27.86 (978-1-58810-698-8). 64pp. A discussion of the scientific and ethical issues of cloning, with excellent diagrams. (Rev: BL 10/15/02; HBG 3/03) [660.6]

21271 Nardo, Don. *Cloning* (5–9). Illus. Series: Science on the Edge. 2003, Gale $24.95 (978-1-56711-782-0). 48pp. A concise overview of the techniques involved in cloning and the ways this science can be applied, with a balanced presentation of the pro and con arguments. (Rev: BL 10/15/03; SLJ 2/04) [660.6]

21272 Nicolson, Cynthia Pratt. *Baa! The Most Interesting Book You'll Ever Read About Genes and Cloning* (4–6). Illus. by Rose Cowles. Series: Mysterious You. 2001, Kids Can $14.95 (978-1-55074-856-7); paper $6.95 (978-1-55074-886-4). 40pp. Nicolson provides succinct definitions and descriptions of genetics and cloning-related issues in an easy-to-read volume. (Rev: BL 1/1–15/02; HBG 3/02) [572.8]

21273 Phelan, Glen. *Double Helix: The Quest to Uncover the Structure of DNA* (5–8). Series: Science Quest. 2006, National Geographic $17.95 (978-0-7922-5541-3). 59pp. From Mendel's early experiments with pea plants through Crick and Watson's race to solve the mystery of DNA, this is an accessible and informative history that also looks at the wide range of social and scientific areas influenced by the discovery. (Rev: SLJ 4/07) [572.8]

21274 Silverstein, Alvin, et al. *DNA* (4–8). Series: Science Concepts. 2002, Millbrook LB $26.90 (978-0-7613-2257-3). 64pp. This book examines the structure of DNA and clearly explains its components and functions and includes current topics such as the genome project, genetic engineering, gene therapy, and cloning. (Rev: BL 9/15/02; HBG 3/03; SLJ 11/02) [574.87]

21275 Simpson, Kathleen. *Genetics: From DNA to Designer Dogs* (4–6). Illus. Series: National Geographic Investigates. 2008, National Geographic $17.95 (978-1-4263-0361-6). 64pp. An absorbing introduction to genetics covering everything from Mendel's early work to what we know today about plant, animal, and human genetics and how this knowledge can help us in various ways. (Rev: BL 1/1–15/09) [576.5]

21276 Wells, Donna. *Biotechnology* (3–6). Illus. Series: Inventors and Inventions. 1996, Marshall Cavendish LB $25.64 (978-0-7614-0046-2). 63pp. Cell structure, DNA, and ways of altering genetic makeup are discussed, with short profiles of past and current leaders in the field. (Rev: BL 7/96; SLJ 9/96) [660]

Hospitals

21277 Attebury, Nancy Garhan. *Out and About at the Hospital* (1–3). Illus. by Zachary Trover. Series: Field Trips. 2005, Picture Window LB $26.60 (978-1-4048-1148-5). 24pp. Takes readers on a tour of a typical hospital, explaining its purpose and the roles of people who work there. (Rev: SLJ 2/06) [362.11]

21278 Barber, Nicola. *Going to the Hospital* (K–1). Series: The Big Day! 2009, Rosen LB $21.25 (978-1-4358-2840-7). 24pp. This simple book looks at typical concerns — feeling sick, staying overnight, having an operation, visitors, and so forth. (Rev: SLJ 7/09) [362.11]

21279 Brink, Benjamin. *David's Story: A Book About Surgery* (3–5). Illus. 1996, Lerner LB $21.27 (978-0-8225-2577-6). 32pp. A step-by-step account of a boy undergoing surgery. (Rev: BL 12/1/96; SLJ 10/96) [617.5]

21280 Dooley, Virginia. *Tubes in My Ears: My Trip to the Hospital* (PS–1). Illus. by Miriam Katin. 1996, Mondo paper $4.95 (978-1-57255-118-3). 32pp. The experiences of a young boy when he goes to a hospital for the first time to treat an ear infection. (Rev: BL 5/1/96; SLJ 6/96) [362.1]

21281 Johnston, Marianne. *Let's Talk About Going to the Hospital* (1–4). Series: Let's Talk. 1998, Rosen LB $19.95 (978-0-8239-5036-2). 24pp. Two-page sections cover such hospital-related topics as admission, meals, IV tubes, blood tests, anesthesia, and surgery. (Rev: SLJ 4/98) [362.1]

21282 Miller, Marilyn. *Behind the Scenes at the Hospital* (PS–3). Illus. 1996, Raintree LB $22.83 (978-0-8172-4087-5). 32pp. The workers and activities that make hospitals function are introduced in a simple question-and-answer format. (Rev: BL 4/15/96; SLJ 12/96) [362.1]

21283 Murphy, Patricia J. *Everything You Need to Know About Staying in the Hospital* (5–8). Series: Need to Know Library. 2001, Rosen LB $27.95 (978-0-8239-3325-9). 64pp. This volume explains the basic hospital process from admission to discharge and follows a patient through a typical day. (Rev: SLJ 5/01) [362.1]

21284 Pascoe, Elaine, ed. *Crash: The Body in Crisis* (5–8). Illus. Series: Body Story. 2003, Gale LB $24.95 (978-1-4103-0062-1). 48pp. Two people are badly hurt in a car crash — he is unconscious, she has a ruptured spleen — and readers accompany them to the emergency room and the operating room as they fight for their lives. (Rev: SLJ 4/04) [617.1]

21285 Rosenberg, Maxine B. *Mommy's in the Hospital Having a Baby* (PS–1). Illus. by Robert Maass.

1997, Clarion $15.00 (978-0-395-71813-1). 29pp. Questions are answered about what happens in a hospital when mommy is having a baby, including "How do I behave on visits?" (Rev: BL 4/1/97; SLJ 5/97) [618.4]

21286 Stein, Sara Bonnett. *A Hospital Story* (1–3). Illus. 1984, Walker paper $8.95 (978-0-8027-7222-0). A fine introduction to hospitals and what a hospital stay involves.

The Human Body

General

21287 Aliki. *My Feet* (PS–1). Illus. Series: Let's-Read-and-Find-Out. 1990, HarperCollins LB $15.89 (978-0-690-04815-5). 32pp. Children are asked to consider the uniqueness of their feet. (Rev: BL 10/1/90; HB 11/90; SLJ 11/90) [612]

21288 Aliki. *My Hands* (1–3). Illus. by author. 1990, HarperCollins LB $15.89 (978-0-690-04880-3); paper $5.99 (978-0-06-445096-6). 32pp. The structure and uses of our hands are presented.

21289 Allison, Linda. *Blood and Guts: A Working Guide to Your Own Little Insides* (5–8). 1976, Little, Brown paper $14.99 (978-0-316-03443-2). An off-putting title but a fine explanation of the functions of the human body.

21290 Balkwill, Fran. *Cells Are Us* (4–5). Illus. by Mic Rolph. 1993, Carolrhoda LB $19.93 (978-0-87614-762-7). 32pp. This book introduces the many types of cells found in the human body. Other related books by the same author are: *Cell Wars* and *DNA Is Here to Stay* (both 1993). (Rev: SLJ 4/93) [611]

21291 Batten, Mary. *Who Has a Belly Button?* (K–4). Illus. by Higgins Bond. 2004, Peachtree $15.95 (978-1-56145-235-4). All about belly buttons — what they are, where they come from, what animals' belly buttons are like, and so forth. (Rev: SLJ 5/04) [612.6]

21292 Berger, Melvin, and Gilda Berger. *Why Don't Haircuts Hurt? Questions and Answers About the Human Body* (3–5). Series: Question and Answer. 1999, Scholastic $12.95 (978-0-590-13079-0); paper $5.95 (978-0-590-08569-4). 48pp. Using questions that children might ask about the human body, this account supplies concise, well-organized answers, which are illustrated with many original paintings. (Rev: BL 11/15/99; SLJ 12/99) [612]

21293 Berger, Melvin, and Gilda Berger. *You're Tall in the Morning but Shorter at Night and Other Amazing Facts About the Human Body* (2–5). Illus. Series: Speedy Facts. 2004, Scholastic paper $7.99 (978-0-439-62536-4). 48pp. An entertaining and lively presentation of amazing and informative facts about the human body. [611]

21294 Borenstein, Gerri. *Therapy* (4–8). Illus. Series: Life Balance. 2003, Watts paper $6.95 (978-0-531-15585-1). 80pp. This friendly, reassuring introduction explains what therapy consists of, the different kinds of professionals involved, and the ways in which privacy is maintained. (Rev: BL 10/15/03; SLJ 12/03) [616.89]

21295 Calabresi, Linda. *Human Body* (4–7). Illus. Series: Insiders. 2008, Simon & Schuster $16.99 (978-1-4169-3861-3). 64pp. Cross-sections, computer-aided graphics, and other visual wonders offer amazing views of the body in this large-format book that provides text information in snippets and sidebars. (Rev: BL 3/1/08; SLJ 5/08) [612]

21296 Cobb, Vicki. *Your Body Battles a Skinned Knee* (K–3). Illus. by Andrew N. Harris. 2009, Millbrook LB $25.26 (978-0-8225-6814-8). 32pp. A simple, accessible explanation — with cartoon illustrations and characters including Skin Cell and Platelet — of how the body heals after an injury. Also use *Your Body Battles a Stomachache* and *Your Body Battles a Cold* (2009). (Rev: BL 1/1–15/09; SLJ 4/09) [617.5]

21297 Cole, Joanna. *The Magic School Bus: Inside the Human Body* (2–5). Illus. by Bruce Degen. 1989, Scholastic $15.95 (978-0-590-41426-5); paper $5.99 (978-0-590-41427-2). Ms. Frizzle's class goes on a guided tour of the human body. (Rev: BCCB 4/89; BL 4/15/89; HB 5/89)

21298 Darling, Kathy. *There's a Zoo on You!* (3–5). Illus. 2000, Millbrook LB $24.90 (978-0-7613-1357-1). 48pp. The supermagnified photographs in this book are of the bacteria, fungi, and other organisms that live in or on the human body. (Rev: BL 11/1/00; HBG 9/00; SLJ 7/00) [579]

21299 Ewald, Wendy. *The Best Part of Me: Children Talk About Their Bodies in Pictures and Words* (1–3). Illus. 2001, Little, Brown $16.95 (978-0-316-70306-2). 32pp. In their own words, youngsters describe what they like best about their bodies. (Rev: BL 9/1/01; HBG 3/02; SLJ 10/01) [810.8]

21300 Fisher, Gary L., and Rhoda Woods Cummings. *The Survival Guide for Kids with LD (Learning Differences)* (5–8). Illus. 1990, Free Spirit paper $9.95 (978-0-915793-18-1). A book that explains various kinds of learning disabilities and how to cope with them. (Rev: BL 7/90; SLJ 6/90) [371.9]

21301 Ganeri, Anita. *Alive: The Living, Breathing Human Body Book* (5–7). Illus. 2007, DK $24.99 (978-0-7566-3211-3). Visual and audio effects accompany amazing graphics and text in this comprehensive and attention-grabbing pop-up anatomy book. (Rev: SLJ 3/08)

21302 Giacobello, John. *Everything You Need to Know About Anxiety and Panic Attacks* (5–9). Series: Need to Know Library. 2000, Rosen LB $27.95 (978-0-8239-3219-1). 64pp. This book explains anxiety attacks' causes, symptoms, and treatments in a reassuring tone. (Rev: SLJ 1/01) [616]

21303 Gold, Susan Dudley. *Attention Deficit Disorder* (4–8). Series: Health Watch. 2000, Enslow LB $23.93 (978-0-7660-1657-6). 48pp. This account focuses on one boy from childhood to college and how he coped with attention deficit disorder. Several young people are profiled in the companion volume *Bipolar Disorder and Depression* (2000). (Rev: HBG 10/01; SLJ 2/01) [618.92]

21304 Hawcock, David. *The Amazing Pop-Up Pull-Out Body in a Book* (2–4). Illus. 1997, DK $19.99 (978-0-7894-2052-7). 9pp. Unfolding pages in this book brings out a full-length 3-D skeleton, accompanied by facts about the human body. (Rev: BL 12/15/97) [612]

21305 Jefferis, David. *Human Body* (3–6). Illus. Series: Record Breakers. 2003, Raintree LB $25.69 (978-0-7398-6322-0). 32pp. An attractively illustrated collection of fascinating trivia about the human body. (Rev: HBG 10/03; SLJ 7/03)

21306 Kahn, Ada P., and Ronald M. Doctor. *Phobias* (4–8). Series: Life Balance. 2003, Watts LB $20.50 (978-0-531-12256-3); paper $6.95 (978-0-531-15575-2). 80pp. This book discusses the causes of phobias, the different types, how they affect people, and their treatment. (Rev: BL 10/15/03) [616.85]

21307 Kim, Melissa L. *The Endocrine and Reproductive Systems* (5–10). Illus. Series: Human Body Library. 2003, Enslow LB $23.93 (978-0-7660-2020-7). 48pp. Kim uses a conversational style to introduce detailed facts about these two body systems, with useful graphics and some practical advice. (Rev: BL 4/15/03; HBG 10/03) [612.4]

21308 Klingel, Cynthia, and Robert B. Noyed. *Feet* (PS–1). Photos by Gregg Andersen. Series: Let's Read About Our Bodies. 2002, Gareth Stevens LB $21.00 (978-0-8368-3064-4). 24pp. Full-page, full-color close-ups and minimal text present toes, feet, and shoes. Also use *Nose* and *Skin* (2002). (Rev: HBG 10/02; SLJ 5/02) [612.98]

21309 Kroll, Virginia. *Hands!* (PS–1). Illus. by Cathryn Falwell. 1997, Boyds Mills $9.95 (978-1-56397-051-1). 32pp. In this unusual picture book, hands are seen fulfilling a variety of tasks. (Rev: BL 9/15/97; HBG 3/98; SLJ 12/97) [612]

21310 Levine, Shar, and Leslie Johnstone. *First Science Experiments: The Amazing Human Body* (PS–2). Illus. by Steve Harpster. 2006, Sterling LB $14.95 (978-1-4027-2437-4). 48pp. Simple activities using handy materials help students answer a wide range of questions, from "Do people with big ears hear better than people with small ears?" to "How can I tell how fast my heart is beating?" and "Why does my tummy growl or grumble when I am hungry?" (Rev: SLJ 11/06) [612.0078]

21311 Manning, Mick, and Brita Granström. *Under Your Skin: Your Amazing Body* (1–3). Illus. by Mick Manning. 2007, Albert Whitman $16.95 (978-0-8075-8313-5). 32pp. This friendly introduction to the human body offers simple explanations written in a lively tone with an appealing lift-the-flap format. (Rev: BL 9/15/07; SLJ 6/08) [612]

21312 Murray, Julie. *The Body* (2–4). Illus. Series: That's Gross! A Look at Science. 2009, ABDO LB $17.95 (978-1-60453-554-9). 32pp. Snot, flatulence, farts, earwax — this exploration of all things icky about the body will attract an audience. (Rev: BL 5/15/09) [612]

21313 Myers, Jack. *On Top of Mount Everest: And Other Explorations of Science in Action* (4–6). Illus. by John Rice. 2005, Boyds Mills $17.95 (978-1-59078-252-1). 64pp. A collection of science-related articles that have appeared in the magazine *Highlights for Children*, most relating to interesting abilities of the human body. (Rev: SLJ 8/05)

21314 Parker, Steve. *Allergies* (5–8). Series: Just the Facts. 2004, Heinemann LB $27.07 (978-1-4034-4598-8). 56pp. A comprehensive and accessible overview of allergies, their causes, symptoms, and treatment. (Rev: SLJ 6/04) [616.97]

21315 Parker, Steve. *Human Body: An Interactive Guide to the Inner Workings of the Body* (4–7). Illus. Series: Discoverology. 2008, Barron's $18.99 (978-0-7641-6083-7). 32pp. Pop-ups, pullouts, gatefolds, cutaways, X-ray images, spinning wheels, and other visual elements make this guide to anatomy effective and interesting. (Rev: BL 6/1–15/08; SLJ 8/08) [612]

21316 Pascoe, Elaine, ed. *Out of Control: Brain Function and Immune Reactions* (5–8). Illus. Series: Body Story. 2003, Gale LB $24.95 (978-1-4103-0063-8). 48pp. This fact-packed book looks first at a baby's brain function, before and after birth, and how its capabilities grow as he learns, then traces the reaction of a young woman's immune system as it copes with a severe allergic reaction to a wasp sting. (Rev: SLJ 4/04) [612.8]

21317 Perols, Sylvaine. *The Human Body* (PS–1). Trans. from French by Jennifer Riggs. Illus. by author. Series: First Discovery. 1996, Scholastic $12.95 (978-0-590-73876-7). With the uses of transparencies, the skeleton and different systems and organs of the human body are introduced. (Rev: BL 10/15/96; SLJ 2/97) [612]

21318 Powell, Jillian. *Moving* (1–3). Series: The Body in Action. 2004, Smart Apple LB $18.95 (978-1-58340-437-9). 32pp. Powell explores human movement and explains the parts of the body involved in various activities and how injuries can occur. (Rev: BL 11/1/04) [612.7]

21319 Pringle, Laurence. *Everybody Has a Bellybutton* (PS–3). Illus. by Clare Wood. 1997, Boyds Mills $14.95 (978-1-56397-009-2). 32pp. A simple account of the growth of a fetus from a single cell to the birth of a baby. (Rev: BL 9/15/97; HBG 3/98; SLJ 10/97) [612]

21320 Reilly, Kathleen M. *The Human Body: 25 Fantastic Projects* (5–9). Illus. by Shawn Braley. 2008, Nomad paper $15.95 (978-1-9346702-4-8). 120pp. Experiments (many of which need adult supervision) show how various processes of the human body work and are accompanied by excellent descriptions. (Rev: SLJ 2/09)

21321 Rosenberg, Marsha Sarah. *Everything You Need to Know When a Brother or Sister Is Autistic* (5–9). Series: Need to Know Library. 2000, Rosen LB $27.95 (978-0-8239-3123-1). 64pp. Autism is defined and described, with material on its diagnosis and treatment plus coverage of how this condition can affect other members of the family. (Rev: SLJ 8/00) [616.8]

21322 Ross, Michael Elsohn. *Body Cycles* (PS–1). Illus. by Gustav Moore. Series: Cycles. 2002, Millbrook LB $22.40 (978-0-7613-1816-3). Young readers are introduced to the ways in which the body uses oxygen, blood, and nutrients. (Rev: HBG 10/02; SLJ 8/02) [612]

21323 Saltz, Gail. *Amazing You! Getting Smart About Your Private Parts* (PS–2). Illus. by Lynne Cravath. 2005, Button $15.99 (978-0-525-47389-3). 32pp. Cheerful cartoons and straightforward text offer age-appropriate information about reproduction, birth, development, and the difference between boys' and girls' bodies. (Rev: BL 6/1–15/05; SLJ 5/05) [612.6]

21324 Sanders, Pete, and Steve Myers. *Dyslexia* (4–8). Illus. by Mike Lacy and Liz Sawyer. Series: What Do You Know About. 1999, Millbrook LB $23.90 (978-0-7613-0915-4). 32pp. Using a case study, this book explores one boy's problems with dyslexia, its causes, symptoms, and treatment. (Rev: HBG 10/99; SLJ 10/99) [617.7]

21325 Seuling, Barbara. *From Head to Toe: The Amazing Human Body and How It Works* (3–4). Illus. by Edward Miller. 2002, Holiday House $16.95 (978-0-8234-1699-8). 32pp. An accessible overview of the various body systems, omitting reproduction, with clear illustrations and several experiments. (Rev: SLJ 11/02) [612]

21326 Sprung, Barbara. *Stress* (4–8). Illus. Series: Preteen Pressures. 1998, Raintree LB $25.69 (978-0-8172-5033-1). 48pp. A concise, practical account of the types and causes of stress in young people and how to manage it. (Rev: BL 4/15/98; HBG 10/98; SLJ 6/98) [155.4]

21327 Stewart, David. *How Your Body Works: A Good Look Inside Your Insides* (1–3). Illus. by Carolyn Franklin. Series: Amaze. 2008, Children's Pr. LB $26.00 (978-0-531-20444-3); paper $8.95 (978-0-531-20455-9). 32pp. A bright and appealing introduction to the body, looking at the senses as well as internal organs and systems. (Rev: BL 4/1/08) [612]

21328 Swanson, Diane. *You Are Weird: Your Body's Peculiar Parts and Funny Functions* (2–4). Illus. by Kathy Boake. 2009, Kids Can $16.95 (978-1-55453-282-7); paper $7.95 (978-1-55453-283-4). 40pp. Full of surprising, humorously delivered facts, this is an accessible introduction to the human body. (Rev: BL 3/15/09) [612]

21329 Szpirglas, Jeff. *Gross Universe: Your Guide to All Disgusting Things Under the Sun* (3–6). Illus. by Michael Cho. 2004, Maple Tree $21.95 (978-1-894379-64-9); paper $12.95 (978-1-894379-65-6). 64pp. Cartoon characters add details to the entertaining narrative about various bodily unpleasantnesses. (Rev: BCCB 5/04; SLJ 11/04) [612]

21330 Taylor-Butler, Christine. *Tiny Life on Your Body* (2–3). Series: Rookie Read-About Science. 2005, Children's Pr. LB $20.50 (978-0-516-25299-5); paper $4.95 (978-0-516-25480-7). 32pp. For beginning readers, this is an introduction to the kinds of bacteria — good and bad — that can be found on the human body. (Rev: SLJ 4/06) [612]

21331 VanCleave, Janice. *The Human Body for Every Kid: Easy Activities That Make Learning Science Fun* (5–7). Illus. Series: Science for Every Kid. 1995, Wiley paper $12.95 (978-0-471-02408-8). 240pp. The various systems in the human body are introduced and decribed, with many projects and experiments. (Rev: BL 4/15/95; SLJ 5/95) [612]

21332 Walker, Richard. *Body* (4–7). Illus. 2005, DK $19.99 (978-0-7566-1371-6). 96pp. With a spiral binding, acetate overlays, and computer-generated 3-D images, this volume gives an in-depth view of the human body; there is an accompanying CD. (Rev: BL 12/1/05; SLJ 3/06) [611]

21333 Walker, Richard. *How the Incredible Human Body Works . . . by the Brainwaves* (2–4). Illus. by Lisa Swerling. 2007, DK $19.99 (978-0-7566-3145-1). 64pp. Humorous illustrations add to this overview of the systems, organs, and operation of the human body. (Rev: BL 12/1/07; LMC 1/08; SLJ 11/07) [612]

21334 Walker, Richard. *Human Body* (5–9). Illus. Series: DK/Google e.guides. 2005, DK $17.99 (978-0-7566-1009-8). 96pp. This highly illustrated guide introduces readers to the human body and provides a link to a Web site that serves as a gateway to additional resources. (Rev: SLJ 8/05) [612]

21335 Walker, Richard. *The Kingfisher First Human Body Encyclopedia* (3–5). 1999, Kingfisher $16.95 (978-0-7534-5177-9). 112pp. Using a topical arrangement, this book offers an outstanding look at the inside and outside of the human body. (Rev: BL 12/1/99; HBG 4/00; SLJ 11/99) [612]

21336 Walker, Richard. *Ouch! How Your Body Makes It Through a Very Bad Day* (5–8). Illus. 2007, DK $16.99 (978-0-7566-2536-8). 72pp. Wonderfully gross, this day starts with some sneezes and progresses through a variety of events including urinating, sweating, vomiting, and being stung by a bee; the accompanying CD-ROM adds an inside view to these processes. (Rev: LMC 10/07; SLJ 7/07)

21337 Waters, Jennifer. *All Kinds of People: What Makes Us Different* (K–2). Illus. Series: Spyglass Books. 2002, Compass Point LB $19.93 (978-0-7565-0377-2). 24pp. Eight spreads look at how people differ in physical appearance, personality, and ways of moving and communicating. (Rev: SLJ 4/03)

21338 Wiese, Jim. *Head to Toe Science: Over 40 Eye-Popping, Spine-Tingling, Heart-Pounding Activities That Teach Kids* (4–8). Illus. 2000, Wiley paper $12.95 (978-0-471-33203-9). 120pp. A collection of experiments and projects that is arranged by body systems (e.g., nervous, digestive), accompanied by good instructions and scientific explanations. (Rev: BL 7/00; SLJ 7/00) [612]

21339 Wiltshire, Paula. *Dyslexia* (5–8). Illus. Series: Health Issues. 2002, Raintree LB $28.54 (978-0-7398-5221-7). 64pp. Color photographs and straightforward text introduce dyslexia's symptoms and treatment and explain how it affects learning, with tips on how to cope with the disability. (Rev: BL 12/15/02; HBG 3/03; SLJ 3/03) [616.85]

21340 Winston, Robert M. L. *What Makes Me Me?* (4–6). 2004, DK $15.99 (978-0-7566-0325-0). 96pp. In this creative approach to human biology, full of questions and activities, Winston takes readers on a fascinating journey through the body and

then concentrates on the mind. (Rev: BL 12/1/04) [612]

21341 Zucker, Faye. *Depression* (4–8). Series: Life Balance. 2003, Watts LB $20.50 (978-0-531-12259-4); paper $6.95 (978-0-531-15578-3). 80pp. This friendly, reassuring introduction explains the causes, diagnosis, and treatment of depression. (Rev: BL 10/15/03; SLJ 12/03) [616.85]

Circulatory System

21342 Ballard, Carol. *The Heart and Circulatory System* (5–8). Illus. Series: The Human Body. 1997, Raintree LB $18.98 (978-0-8172-4800-0). Topics discussed in this nicely illustrated volume include how blood is made, how it is pumped through the body, and how the heart and circulation system work together. (Rev: BL 6/1–15/97; SLJ 8/97) [612.1]

21343 Frost, Helen. *The Circulatory System* (K–2). Illus. Series: Human Body Systems. 2000, Capstone LB $17.26 (978-0-7368-0648-0). 24pp. A small-format, basic introduction for beginning readers. (Rev: HBG 10/01; SLJ 4/01) [612.1]

21344 Gray, Susan H. *The Circulatory System* (3–6). Illus. Series: The Human Body. 2003, Child's World LB $27.07 (978-1-59296-036-1). 32pp. A clear and detailed description of the functions of the circulatory system, using a child-friendly approach. (Rev: BL 2/1/04) [612.1]

21345 Parker, Steve. *Heart, Lungs, and Blood* (5–9). Illus. Series: Our Bodies. 2004, Raintree LB $28.56 (978-0-7398-6621-4). 48pp. Details of the human body's circulatory system are accompanied by information on keeping them healthy. (Rev: BL 8/04) [612.1]

21346 Parramon, Merce. *How Our Blood Circulates* (5–7). Illus. by Marcel Socias. Series: Invisible World. 1994, Chelsea LB $17.55 (978-0-7910-2127-9). 31pp. Double-page spreads introduce the circulatory system and discuss such topics as blood cells, clotting, the heart and its functions, and the lymphatic system. (Rev: SLJ 8/94) [612]

21347 Rau, Dana Meachen. *My Heart and Blood* (PS–3). Illus. Series: Bookworms: What's Inside Me? 2004, Benchmark LB $21.36 (978-0-7614-1779-8). 31pp. A simple overview of the circulatory system, with photographs, diagrams, and X-rays. (Rev: SLJ 2/05) [612]

21348 Romanek, Trudee. *Squirt! The Most Interesting Book You'll Ever Read About Blood* (4–7). Illus. by Rose Cowles. Series: Mysterious You. 2006, Kids Can $14.95 (978-1-55337-776-4); paper $7.95 (978-1-55337-777-1). 160pp. This fascinating book with an engaging format discusses the human circulatory system, with information about other animals and their blood, too. (Rev: BL 5/15/06; HBG 10/06) [612.1]

21349 Sandeman, Anna. *Blood* (1–3). Illus. Series: Body Books. 1996, Millbrook LB $18.90 (978-0-7613-0477-7). 32pp. An introduction to the composition and function of blood and the circulatory system, with clearly labeled artwork. (Rev: BL 4/15/96; SLJ 4/96) [612.1]

21350 Showers, Paul. *A Drop of Blood* (K–2). Illus. by Edward Miller. Series: Let's Read-and-Find-Out. 2004, HarperCollins LB $5.99 (978-0-06-009110-1); paper $16.89 (978-0-06-009109-5). 128pp. This updated edition features a new, vampire slant and retains the earlier clear overview of blood and the human circulatory system. (Rev: BL 8/04; SLJ 7/04) [612]

21351 Showers, Paul. *Hear Your Heart* (2–5). Illus. by Holly Keller. Series: Let's-Read-and-Find-Out. 2001, HarperCollins LB $15.89 (978-0-06-025411-7); paper $5.99 (978-0-06-445139-0). 32pp. An amusing introduction to the human heart accompanied by activities such as making a stethoscope, taking a pulse, and listening to heartbeats. (Rev: BL 1/1–15/01; HBG 10/01) [612.1]

21352 Viegas, Jennifer. *The Heart: Learning How Our Blood Circulates* (5–9). Illus. Series: 3-D Library of the Human Body. 2002, Rosen LB $27.95 (978-0-8239-3532-1). 48pp. An introduction to the anatomy and function of the human heart and the circulatory system that includes illustrations, diagrams, a glossary, and other aids. (Rev: BL 7/02) [612.1]

Digestive and Excretory Systems

21353 Ballard, Carol. *The Stomach and Digestive System* (5–8). Illus. Series: The Human Body. 1997, Raintree LB $25.68 (978-0-8172-4801-7). Topics discussed in this nicely illustrated volume include the digestive organs, how they work together, how food is tasted, and where nutrients are stored. (Rev: BL 6/1–15/97; SLJ 8/97) [612.3]

21354 Bryan, Jenny. *Digestion: The Digestive System* (4–6). Illus. Series: Body Talk. 1993, Dillon LB $13.95 (978-0-87518-564-4). 48pp. A clear, informative text and large captioned illustrations tell about the digestive system and related topics. (Rev: SLJ 10/93) [612]

21355 Brynie, Faith Hickman. *101 Questions About Food and Digestion That Have Been Eating at You . . . Until Now* (5–8). Illus. 2002, Millbrook LB $27.90 (978-0-7613-2309-9). 176pp. A question-and-answer format succeeds in conveying lots of food for thought, with details on digestive functions, digestive disorders, food safety, fat cells, Mad Cow disease, vitamins, and so forth. (Rev: BL 1/1–15/03; HBG 3/03; SLJ 3/03) [612.3]

21356 Cho, Shinta. *The Gas We Pass: The Story of Farts* (PS–2). Trans. by Amanda Mayer Stinchecum. Illus. 1994, Kane $12.95 (978-0-916291-52-5). 28pp. This book tells about the causes, production, and effects of farts in a variety of animals, mainly humans. (Rev: BL 10/1/94; SLJ 11/94) [612.3]

21357 Frost, Helen. *The Digestive System* (K–2). Illus. Series: Human Body Systems. 2000, Capstone LB $17.26 (978-0-7368-0649-7). 24pp. This is a simple introduction to the digestive system that

includes clearly labeled diagrams and full-color photographs. (Rev: HBG 10/01; SLJ 4/01) [612.3]

21358 Goodman, Susan E. *Gee Whiz! It's All About Pee* (4–6). Illus. by Elwood H. Smith. 2006, Viking $15.99 (978-0-670-06064-1). 40pp. This companion to *The Truth About Poop* (2004) provides facts and trivia — often unexpected and humorous — about pee, with cartoon illustrations. (Rev: BL 11/1/06; SLJ 11/06) [612.4]

21359 Goodman, Susan E. *The Truth About Poop* (4–6). Illus. by Elwood H. Smith. 2004, Viking $15.99 (978-0-670-03674-5). 40pp. Cartoon artwork accompanies matter-of-fact information about human and animal waste and the history of toilets and sewage. (Rev: BL 5/15/04; SLJ 7/04) [612.3]

21360 Jakab, Cheryl. *Digestive System* (3–5). Illus. Series: Our Body. 2007, Smart Apple LB $27.10 (978-1-58340-737-0). 32pp. The anatomy and functions of this system of the body are covered, as well as diseases and conditions that can affect it and how to keep it healthy. (Rev: SLJ 7/07)

21361 Lambourne, Mike. *Down the Hatch: Find Out About Your Food* (2–3). Illus. by Thompson Yardley. Series: Lighter Look. 1992, Millbrook LB $20.90 (978-1-56294-150-5). 39pp. In simple text and cartoonlike illustrations, the story of food and nutrition is presented. (Rev: SLJ 6/92) [641]

21362 Llewellyn, Claire. *Eating* (1–3). Series: Body in Action. 2004, Smart Apple LB $27.10 (978-1-58340-436-2). The digestive system, senses of smell and taste, the body's use of nutrients, and various types of food are all covered here, along with information on healthy eating and food allergies. (Rev: BL 11/1/04) [612.3]

21363 Parker, Steve. *Digestion* (5–9). Illus. Series: Our Bodies. 2004, Raintree LB $28.56 (978-0-7398-6620-7). 48pp. Details of the human body's digestive system are accompanied by information on keeping them healthy. (Rev: BL 8/04) [612]

21364 Petrie, Kristin. *The Digestive System* (3–5). Illus. Series: The Human Body. 2006, ABDO LB $22.78 (978-1-59679-710-9). 32pp. Why and how we eat and how our bodies use food are all covered here, with diagrams, photographs, and interesting facts to keep readers engaged. (Rev: SLJ 5/07)

21365 Rau, Dana Meachen. *My Stomach* (PS–3). Illus. Series: Bookworms: What's Inside Me? 2004, Benchmark LB $21.36 (978-0-7614-1782-8). 31pp. A simple overview of the stomach's role in digestion, with photographs, diagrams, and X-rays. (Rev: SLJ 2/05) [612.3]

21366 Royston, Angela. *Why Do I Vomit? And Other Questions About Digestion* (3–5). Illus. Series: Body Matters. 2002, Heinemann LB $24.22 (978-1-4034-0206-6). 32pp. In easy-to-understand language and many illustrations, Royston gives an inside look at the gastrointestinal system and some of its most obvious manifestations. (Rev: HBG 10/03; SLJ 4/03) [612.3]

21367 Showers, Paul. *What Happens to a Hamburger?* (K–3). Illus. by Edward Miller. Series: Let's-Read-and-Find-Out Science. 2001, HarperCollins LB $15.89 (978-0-06-027948-6); paper $5.99 (978-

0-06-445183-3). 32pp. A new edition of this interesting easy reader that explains the mysteries of digestion. (Rev: BL 4/15/01; HBG 10/01) [612.3]

21368 Silverstein, Alvin, et al. *The Excretory System* (5–8). Illus. Series: Human Body Systems. 1994, Twenty-First Century LB $29.90 (978-0-8050-2834-8). A discussion on the human system of waste elimination. (Rev: BL 3/15/95; SLJ 3/95) [612.4]

21369 Simon, Seymour. *Guts: Our Digestive System* (5–8). Illus. 2005, HarperCollins LB $17.89 (978-0-06-054652-6). 32pp. Photographs and straightforward yet fascinating text present the digestive system. (Rev: BL 3/1/05; SLJ 4/05) [612.3]

21370 Toriello, James. *The Stomach: Learning How We Digest* (5–9). Series: 3-D Library of the Human Body. 2002, Rosen LB $27.95 (978-0-8239-3536-9). 48pp. Using outstanding diagrams and clear explanations, the digestive system is highlighted with material on each of its parts and their functions. (Rev: BL 7/02; SLJ 7/02) [612.3]

Nervous System

21371 Andrews, Linda Wasmer. *Intelligence* (4–8). Series: Life Balance. 2003, Watts paper $6.95 (978-0-531-16608-6). 80pp. This book explores the concept of intelligence, how it is measured, and how it affects daily life. (Rev: BL 10/15/03) [612]

21372 Ballard, Carol. *How Do We Think?* (3–5). Series: How Your Body Works. 1998, Raintree LB $25.70 (978-0-8172-4740-9). 32pp. This book includes material on learning, memory, information processing, and message transmittal and provides activities on mental reactions and memory testing. (Rev: BL 5/15/98; HBG 9/98; SLJ 7/98) [612.8]

21373 Degezelle, Terri. *Your Brain* (K–2). Illus. Series: The Bridgestone Science Library. 2002, Capstone LB $22.60 (978-0-7368-1147-7). 24pp. An attractive, basic overview of the brain with "Fun Facts" and an easy activity. (Rev: SLJ 7/02) [612.8]

21374 Funston, Sylvia, and Jay Ingram. *It's All in Your Head: A Guide to Your Brilliant Brain*. 2nd ed. (3–6). Illus. by Gary Clement. 2005, Maple Tree $16.95 (978-1-897066-43-0); paper $9.95 (978-1-897066-44-7). 64pp. Answering questions in conversational text, this book explores the makeup and workings of the human brain, touches on brain research, and includes experiments and puzzles. (Rev: SLJ 1/06) [612.8]

21375 Garfield, Patricia. *The Dream Book: A Young Person's Guide to Understanding Dreams* (5–8). 2002, Tundra paper $9.95 (978-0-88776-594-0). 124pp. The author, a psychologist, explains the meanings of common (and uncommon) dreams and suggests how to use dreams to good effect. (Rev: BL 9/15/02; SLJ 9/02; VOYA 8/02) [154.6]

21376 Hayhurst, Chris. *The Brain and Spinal Cord: Learning How We Think, Feel, and Move* (5–9). Series: 3-D Library of the Human Body. 2002, Rosen LB $27.95 (978-0-8239-3528-4). 48pp. Exceptional illustrations and a clear text are used to explain the composition of the brain with explana-

tions of how it works and how emotions influence our thoughts. (Rev: BL 7/02; SLJ 7/02) [612.8]

21377 Innes, Brian. *Powers of the Mind* (4–7). Series: Unsolved Mysteries. 1999, Raintree LB $25.69 (978-0-8172-5488-9). 48pp. A balanced account that explores the powers of the brain in such controversial areas as moving objects, planting thoughts, and predicting events. (Rev: BL 5/15/99; HBG 10/99) [612.8]

21378 Jakab, Cheryl. *Nervous System* (3–5). Illus. Series: Our Body. 2007, Smart Apple LB $27.10 (978-1-58340-735-6). 32pp. The anatomy and functions of this system of the body are covered, as well as diseases and conditions that can affect it and how to keep it healthy. (Rev: SLJ 7/07)

21379 Nettleton, Pamela Hill. *Think, Think, Think: Learning About Your Brain* (K–3). Illus. by Becky Shipe. Series: The Amazing Body. 2004, Picture Window LB $25.26 (978-1-4048-0252-0). 24pp. A simple explanation of how the brain works, with an activity and discussion of protective gear and brain scans. (Rev: SLJ 11/04) [612.8]

21380 Newquist, H. P. *The Great Brain Book: An Inside Look at the Inside of Your Head* (5–8). Illus. by Keith Kasnot. 2005, Scholastic $18.95 (978-0-439-45895-5). 160pp. The structure of the brain, its inner workings, and the history of our knowledge of this organ are all discussed in detail; interesting anecdotes add to the presentation. (Rev: BL 6/1–15/05; SLJ 9/05) [612.8]

21381 Parker, Steve. *Brain and Nerves* (4–6). Illus. by Ian Thompson. Series: Look at Your Body. 1998, Millbrook LB $20.90 (978-0-7613-0812-6). 31pp. This explanation of the nervous system covers the brain, spinal cord, and nerves, with additional material on such topics as memory, headaches, and meningitis. (Rev: HBG 9/98; SLJ 10/98) [612]

21382 Parker, Steve. *The Brain and Nervous System* (5–9). Illus. Series: Our Bodies. 2004, Raintree LB $28.56 (978-0-7398-6619-1). 48pp. Details of the human body's brain and nervous system are accompanied by information on keeping them healthy. (Rev: BL 8/04)

21383 Routh, Kristina. *Epilepsy* (5–10). Illus. Series: Just the Facts. 2004, Heinemann LB $27.07 (978-1-4034-4601-5). 56pp. An overview of epilepsy, with attention to its effect on individuals when it comes to driving, sports, education, and employment. (Rev: SLJ 6/04) [616.8]

21384 Sandeman, Anna. *Brain* (1–2). Illus. Series: Body Books. 1996, Millbrook LB $18.90 (978-0-7613-0490-6). 32pp. With a simple text and full-color photos and diagrams, the brain is explored and explanations are given on how it works. (Rev: BL 10/15/96; SLJ 1/97) [612]

21385 Showers, Paul. *Sleep Is for Everyone* (PS–1). Illus. by Wendy Watson. Series: Let's-Read-and-Find-Out. 1997, HarperCollins LB $15.89 (978-0-06-025393-6). 32pp. This simple science book explains what sleep is, why it is necessary, and what happens if we do without it. (Rev: BL 8/97; SLJ 8/97) [612.8]

21386 Silverstein, Alvin, et al. *The Nervous System* (5–8). Illus. Series: Human Body Systems. 1994, Twenty-First Century LB $28.90 (978-0-8050-2835-5). 96pp. The human nervous system and how it functions and can malfunction are described, with information on the systems of other animals. (Rev: BL 3/15/95; SLJ 5/95) [612.8]

Respiratory System

21387 Frost, Helen. *The Respiratory System* (K–2). Illus. Series: Human Body Systems. 2000, Capstone LB $17.26 (978-0-7368-0652-7). 24pp. Simple, brief text introduces the respiratory system, with clearly labeled diagrams and full-color photographs. (Rev: HBG 10/01; SLJ 4/01) [612]

21388 Furgang, Kathy. *My Lungs* (K–3). Illus. Series: My Body. 2001, Rosen LB $21.25 (978-0-8239-5575-6). 24pp. A basic overview of the lungs, their anatomy, how they function, and diseases of the lung, with helpful illustrations. (Rev: SLJ 9/01) [612.2]

21389 Hayhurst, Chris. *The Lungs: Learning How We Breathe* (5–9). Series: 3-D Library of the Human Body. 2002, Rosen LB $27.95 (978-0-8239-3534-5). 48pp. Amazing computer graphics are used to explain the composition of the lungs, how they work, and what keeps them healthy. (Rev: BL 7/02) [612.6]

21390 Jakab, Cheryl. *Respiratory System* (3–5). Illus. Series: Our Body. 2007, Smart Apple LB $27.10 (978-1-58340-736-3). 32pp. The anatomy and functions of this system of the body are covered, as well as diseases and conditions that can affect it and how to keep it healthy. (Rev: SLJ 7/07)

21391 Nettleton, Pamela Hill. *Breathe in, Breathe Out: Learning About Your Lungs* (K–3). Illus. by Becky Shipe. Series: The Amazing Body. 2004, Picture Window LB $25.26 (978-1-4048-0254-4). 24pp. A simple explanation of how the lungs work, with breathing activities and discussion of asthma and inhalers. (Rev: SLJ 11/04) [612.2]

21392 Parker, Steve. *Lungs* (4–6). Illus. Series: Look at Your Body. 1996, Millbrook LB $20.90 (978-0-7613-0530-9). 32pp. A well-organized, clearly illustrated description of lungs and their functions. (Rev: BL 11/1/96) [612.2]

21393 Parker, Steve. *The Lungs and Respiratory System* (5–8). Illus. Series: The Human Body. 1997, Raintree LB $18.98 (978-0-8172-4803-1). This nicely illustrated volume examines the organs used in breathing, tells how the respiratory system works, and explains what happens when it fails. (Rev: BL 6/1–15/97; SLJ 8/97) [612.2]

21394 Silverstein, Alvin, et al. *The Respiratory System* (5–8). Illus. Series: Human Body Systems. 1994, Twenty-First Century LB $29.90 (978-0-8050-2831-7). The purpose and process of breathing are discussed, with the text and illustrations focusing on the human respiratory system. (Rev: BL 3/15/95; SLJ 4/95) [612.2]

21395 Simon, Seymour. *Lungs: Your Respiratory System* (3–6). Illus. 2007, Collins $16.99 (978-0-06-

054654-0). 32pp. From simple breathing to coughing, hiccups, and other respiratory problems, this is a clear overview of the lungs and their importance to human life. (Rev: BL 12/1/06; SLJ 4/07) [612.2]

Senses

21396 Aliki. *My Five Senses* (PS–1). Illus. by author. 1989, HarperCollins paper $5.99 (978-0-06-445083-6). 32pp. A young boy finds that he is learning about the world through the marvels of his five senses. (Rev: SLJ 1/90) [152.1]

21397 Ballard, Carol. *How Do Our Ears Hear?* (3–5). Illus. Series: How Your Body Works. 1998, Raintree LB $25.70 (978-0-8172-4737-9). 32pp. Using attractive double-page spreads, this book explains the anatomy of the ear, its role in hearing and balance, and methods for coping with a hearing loss. (Rev: BL 4/15/98; HBG 9/98) [612.8]

21398 Ballard, Carol. *How Do Our Eyes See?* (3–5). Illus. Series: How Your Body Works. 1998, Raintree LB $25.70 (978-0-8172-4736-2). 32pp. Double-page spreads and clearly labeled diagrams introduce the structure and functions of the eyes along with material on optical illusions, optometry, and vision problems. (Rev: BL 4/15/98; HBG 9/98) [612.8]

21399 Ballard, Carol. *How Do We Feel and Touch?* (3–5). Series: How Your Body Works. 1998, Raintree LB $25.70 (978-0-8172-4739-3). 32pp. Informative photos and drawings help explain the sense of touch, with added activities such as creating a "feely" box and using a test to determine different degrees of sensitivity. (Rev: BL 5/15/98; HBG 9/98) [612.8]

21400 Ballard, Carol. *How Do We Taste and Smell?* (3–5). Series: How Your Body Works. 1998, Raintree LB $25.70 (978-0-8172-4738-6). 32pp. Good explanations, fine diagrams and photos, and a few related activities are used to explain how we are able to smell and taste. (Rev: BL 5/15/98; HBG 9/98; SLJ 7/98) [612.8]

21401 Beck, Esther. *Cool Odor Decoders: Fun Science Projects About Smells* (4–6). 2008, ABDO LB $16.95 (978-1-59928-909-0). 32pp. Five high-interest experiments with detailed, illustrated instructions follow discussion about the scientific method, keeping a journal, and safety. (Rev: SLJ 2/08) [612.8]

21402 Byles, Monica. *Experiment with Senses* (2–5). Illus. Series: Science Experiments. 1994, Lerner LB $19.93 (978-0-8225-2455-7). 32pp. Fifteen experiments explain the senses, how they operate, and how they send messages to the brain. (Rev: BL 3/1/94; SLJ 4/94) [612.8]

21403 Cobb, Vicki. *Follow Your Nose: Discover Your Sense of Smell* (3–5). Illus. Series: Five Senses. 2000, Millbrook LB $22.90 (978-0-7613-1521-6). 32pp. This book blends facts and humor in an exploration of the sense of smell and also offers suggestions for easy experiments. (Rev: BL 11/15/00; HBG 3/01) [612.8]

21404 Cobb, Vicki. *Open Your Eyes: Discover Your Sense of Sight* (2–5). Illus. by Cynthia C. Lewis.

Series: The Five Senses. 2002, Millbrook LB $22.90 (978-0-7613-1705-0). An appealing look at the eye, the parts of the eye, and how the eye works, with easy experiments and optical illusions. (Rev: HBG 10/02; SLJ 5/02) [612.84]

21405 Cobb, Vicki. *Perk up Your Ears: Discover Your Sense of Hearing* (3–6). Illus. by Cynthia C. Lewis. Series: The Five Senses. 2001, Millbrook LB $22.90 (978-0-7613-1704-3). An entertaining overview of hearing that encourages children to do lots of experimenting. (Rev: HBG 3/02; SLJ 4/02) [612.8]

21406 Cobb, Vicki. *Your Tongue Can Tell: Discover Your Sense of Taste* (3–5). Illus. Series: Five Senses. 2000, Millbrook LB $21.90 (978-0-7613-1473-8). 32pp. As well as giving an entertaining introduction to the sense of taste, this book supplies many ideas for activities and simple projects. (Rev: BL 11/15/00; HBG 3/01) [612.8]

21407 Cole, Joanna. *The Magic School Bus Explores the Senses* (2–4). Illus. by Bruce Degen. 1999, Scholastic $15.95 (978-0-590-44697-6). 48pp. The Magic School Bus travels with its passengers through an eye, an ear, a nose, and a mouth as it explores the human senses. (Rev: BL 2/15/99; HB 7/99; HBG 9/99; SLJ 2/99) [612.8]

21408 Cole, Joanna. *You Can't Smell a Flower with Your Ear! All About Your Five Senses* (1–3). Illus. by Mavis Smith. 1994, Penguin paper $3.99 (978-0-448-40469-1). 48pp. Using everyday experiences as examples, the five senses are introduced in this easy-to-read book. (Rev: BL 1/1/95) [612.8]

21409 Furgang, Kathy. *My Ears* (K–3). Illus. Series: My Body. 2001, Rosen LB $21.25 (978-0-8239-5572-5). 24pp. A basic overview of the ears, their anatomy, how they function, and diseases of the ear, with helpful illustrations. (Rev: SLJ 9/01) [612.8]

21410 Gordon, Sharon. *Seeing* (1–2). Illus. Series: Rookie Read-About Health. 2001, Children's Book Pr. paper $5.95 (978-0-516-25990-1). 32pp. Very young readers are encouraged to think about their eyes and their ability to see. Also use *Smelling* (2001). (Rev: BL 12/1/01) [612.8]

21411 Litchfield, Ada B. *A Button in Her Ear* (1–3). Illus. by Eleanor Mill. 1976, Whitman LB $16.99 (978-0-8075-0987-6). 32pp. A simple introduction to hearing problems and correctional devices such as the hearing aid.

21412 Martin, Paul D. *Messengers to the Brain: Our Fantastic Five Senses* (4–6). Illus. 1984, National Geographic LB $12.50 (978-0-87044-504-0). 104pp. A well-illustrated explanation of how the organs of the human body send messages to the brain, which acts as a message center.

21413 Murphy, Patricia J. *Hearing* (2–4). Illus. Series: A True Book. 2003, Children's Pr. paper $6.95 (978-0-516-26970-2). 47pp. A simple, large-print look at the ear and our sense of hearing. Also use *Taste* and *Touch* (both 2003). (Rev: SLJ 7/03) [612.8]

21414 O'Brien-Palmer, Michelle. *Sense-Abilities: Fun Ways to Explore the Senses: Activities for Children 4 to 8* (PS–2). Illus. by Fran Lee. 1998, Chica-

go Review paper $12.95 (978-1-55652-327-4). 166pp. With a single chapter devoted to each of the senses, this activity book contains facts and experiments that explore various sensory experiences. (Rev: SLJ 1/99) [612.8]

21415 Olien, Rebecca. *Hearing* (PS–1). Series: First Facts, The Senses. 2005, Capstone LB $21.26 (978-0-7368-4301-0). 24pp. This slim introduction to hearing includes an experiment to help young readers understand how this sense works. Also use *Tasting* and *Touching* (both 2005). (Rev: SLJ 1/06) [612.8]

21416 Parker, Steve. *Senses* (4–6). Series: Look at Your Body. 1997, Millbrook LB $20.90 (978-0-7613-0602-3). 32pp. In this visually appealing, clearly written book, the five senses are introduced and explored, with interesting accompanying activities. (Rev: BL 1/1–15/98; HBG 3/98) [612]

21417 Parker, Steve. *The Senses* (5–9). Illus. Series: Our Bodies. 2004, Raintree LB $28.56 (978-0-7398-6624-5). 48pp. Details of the human senses are accompanied by information on keeping them healthy. (Rev: BL 8/04) [612]

21418 Parramon, J. M., and J. J. Puig. *Hearing* (PS–1). Illus. by Maria Rius. 1985, Barron's paper $7.99 (978-0-8120-3563-6). 32pp. An easy introduction to the sense of hearing. (Rev: BL 9/1/85)

21419 Parramon, J. M., and J. J. Puig. *Sight* (PS–1). Illus. by Maria Rius. 1985, Barron's paper $6.95 (978-0-8120-3564-3). 32pp. The sense of sight is explained to young readers. (Rev: BL 9/1/85; SLJ 11/85)

21420 Parramon, J. M., and J. J. Puig. *Smell* (PS–1). Illus. by Maria Rius. 1985, Barron's paper $7.99 (978-0-8120-3565-0). 32pp. An easy explanation of the sense of smell. (Rev: BL 9/1/85)

21421 Parramon, J. M., and J. J. Puig. *Taste* (PS–1). Illus. by Maria Rius. 1985, Barron's paper $7.99 (978-0-8120-3566-7). 32pp. Easy reading about the sense of taste. (Rev: BL 9/1/85)

21422 Parramon, J. M., and J. J. Puig. *Touch* (PS–1). Illus. by Maria Rius. 1985, Barron's paper $6.95 (978-0-8120-3567-4). 32pp. An easy-to-read explanation of the sense of touch. (Rev: BL 9/1/85)

21423 Pringle, Laurence. *Hearing* (3–6). Illus. Series: Explore Your Senses. 1999, Marshall Cavendish LB $25.64 (978-0-7614-0735-5). 32pp. Using a large format and clear diagrams, this book discusses the structure of the ear, how it operates, possible malfunctions, and how to preserve hearing. (Rev: BL 2/1/00; HBG 9/00; SLJ 3/00) [612.8]

21424 Pringle, Laurence. *Smell* (3–6). Series: Explore Your Senses. 1999, Marshall Cavendish LB $25.64 (978-0-7614-0737-9). 32pp. A clear text, diagrams, and photographs are used to explain how the sense of smell works, problems that can occur, and the differences between animals and humans. (Rev: BL 2/15/00; HBG 9/00; SLJ 3/00) [612]

21425 Pringle, Laurence. *Taste* (3–6). Illus. Series: Explore Your Senses. 1999, Marshall Cavendish LB $25.64 (978-0-7614-0736-2). 32pp. The structure of the tongue, taste buds, taste cells, and the relationship between smell and taste are some of the subjects covered in this large-format book. (Rev: BL 2/1/00; HBG 9/00; SLJ 3/00) [612.8]

21426 Pringle, Laurence. *Touch* (3–6). Series: Explore Your Senses. 1999, Marshall Cavendish LB $25.64 (978-0-7614-0738-6). 32pp. A fresh look at the sense of touch that uses many color diagrams, photos, and an accessible text. (Rev: BL 2/15/00; HBG 9/00) [612]

21427 Sandeman, Anna. *Senses* (1–2). Illus. Series: Body Books. 1995, Millbrook LB $18.90 (978-1-56294-944-0). 32pp. Body organs that are involved with the senses, like eyes, are discussed in this simple introduction that also mentions such topics as color blindness and the ears' role in balance. (Rev: BL 12/15/95; SLJ 2/96) [612.8]

21428 Schuette, Sarah L. *Taking Care of My Ears* (PS–1). Illus. Series: Keeping Healthy. 2005, Capstone LB $21.26 (978-0-7368-4259-4). 24pp. An easy-to-understand explanation of the sense of hearing plus basic information about ear care. (Rev: BL 10/15/05) [613]

21429 Schuh, Mari. *The Sense of Touch* (K–3). Series: Blastoff! Readers. The Senses. 2007, Children's Pr. LB $20.00 (978-0-531-14747-4). 24pp. With diagrams, clear text, and fun facts, Schuh introduces the sense of touch in both humans and animals. *The Sense of Hearing, The Sense of Sight, The Sense of Smell,* and *The Sense of Taste* (all 2007). (Rev: SLJ 2/08) [612.8]

21430 Sherman, Josepha. *The Ear: Learning How We Hear* (5–9). Series: 3-D Library of the Human Body. 2002, Rosen LB $26.50 (978-0-8239-3529-1). 48pp. Using amazing illustrations and clear explanations, Sherman introduces the ear, its anatomy, uses, operation, and problems that can develop. (Rev: BL 7/02) [612.8]

21431 Showers, Paul. *Look at Your Eyes* (PS–2). Illus. by True Kelley. Series: Let's-Read-and-Find-Out. 1992, HarperCollins LB $15.89 (978-0-06-020189-0). 32pp. A little boy looks in the bathroom mirror and begins to think about his eyes. (Rev: BL 1/1/93) [612.8]

21432 Sideri, Simona. *Let's Look at Eyes* (PS–K). Illus. by Sheilagh Noble. Series: Let's Look At. 2004, Smart Apple LB $22.80 (978-1-58340-495-9). 30pp. Young children compare their eyes and sight with those of animals, including owls, eagles, camels, lobsters, and wasps. Also use *Let's Look at Feet* (2004). (Rev: BL 1/1–15/05) [573.8]

21433 Silverstein, Alvin, and Virginia Silverstein. *Earaches* (3–5). Series: My Health. 2002, Watts paper $6.95 (978-0-531-15562-2). 48pp. This book describes, in a simple text and many pictures, how the ear functions, what can cause earaches, and how to treat them. (Rev: BL 6/1–15/02) [612.8]

21434 Silverstein, Alvin, and Virginia Silverstein. *Smelling and Tasting* (4–6). Illus. by Anne Canevari Green. Series: Senses and Sensors. 2002, Twenty-First Century LB $25.90 (978-0-7613-1667-1). 64pp. Human and animal senses of smell and taste are covered in this well-organized and readable volume. Also use *Touching and Feeling* (2002). (Rev: BL 3/15/02; HBG 10/02; SLJ 8/02)

21435 Suhr, Mandy. *Taste* (PS–1). Illus. by Mike Gordon. Series: I'm Alive. 1994, Carolrhoda LB $14.95 (978-0-87614-836-5). 32pp. Why and how we taste is covered in a nontechnical way, with simple activities and projects to amplify the text. From the same series, also use *Touch* (1994). (Rev: SLJ 12/94) [152.1]

21436 Viegas, Jennifer. *The Eye: Learning How We See* (5–9). Illus. Series: 3-D Library of the Human Body. 2002, Rosen LB $27.95 (978-0-8239-3530-7). 48pp. This volume on the anatomy and function of the human eye includes illustrations, diagrams, a glossary, and other aids. (Rev: BL 7/02) [612.8]

21437 Viegas, Jennifer. *The Mouth and Nose: Learning How We Taste and Smell* (5–9). Series: 3-D Library of the Human Body. 2002, Rosen LB $26.50 (978-0-8239-3535-2). 48pp. The mouth and nose are featured in this heavily illustrated account that covers their composition, functions, and how they work together. (Rev: BL 7/02) [612]

21438 Woodward, Kay. *Hearing* (1–4). Series: Our Senses. 2005, Gareth Stevens LB $23.00 (978-0-8368-4406-1). 24pp. A book on how the sense of hearing works in humans and animals, with simple text, eye-catching illustrations, and related activities. Also use *Touch, Taste, Smell,* and *Sight* (all 2005). (Rev: SLJ 7/05) [612.8]

Skeletal-Muscular System

21439 Arnold, Caroline. *The Skeletal System* (3–4). Illus. 2004, Lerner LB $25.26 (978-0-8225-5140-9). 48pp. The skeleton and bones are introduced in simple, concise text. (Rev: SLJ 2/05) [612.7]

21440 Balestrino, Philip. *The Skeleton Inside You* (2–4). Illus. by True Kelley. 1989, HarperCollins paper $5.99 (978-0-06-445087-4). 32pp. Color illustrations help to explain the body's structure. (Rev: BL 6/15/89)

21441 Ballard, Carol. *How Do We Move?* (3–5). Series: How Your Body Works. 1998, Raintree LB $25.70 (978-0-8172-4741-6). 32pp. This book explains how the skeletal and muscular systems work and includes activities such as creating a model of a muscle. (Rev: BL 5/15/98; HBG 9/98) [612]

21442 Ballard, Carol. *The Skeleton and Muscular System* (5–8). Illus. Series: Human Body. 1997, Raintree $18.98 (978-0-8172-4805-5). 48pp. This well-organized book introduces in text and pictures such topics as muscles and how they work, joint diseases, bones, and skeletal diseases. (Rev: SLJ 2/98) [612]

21443 Barner, Bob. *Dem Bones* (K–3). Illus. 1996, Chronicle $14.95 (978-0-8118-0827-9). 32pp. The human skeleton is introduced by using the words of the old song "Dem Dry Bones." (Rev: BL 12/1/96; SLJ 11/96) [611]

21444 Cobb, Vicki. *Your Body Battles a Broken Bone* (3–6). Illus. by Andrew N. Harris. Series: Body Battles. 2009, Millbrook LB $25.26 (978-0-8225-7468-2). 32pp. This title explains and cleverly illustrates how the body's cells act like a troop to fix a broken bone, and additionally clarifies the concept through photomicrographs. (Rev: SLJ 5/09) [617.4]

21445 Degezelle, Terri. *Your Bones* (K–2). Illus. Series: The Bridgestone Science Library. 2002, Capstone LB $22.60 (978-0-7368-1146-0). 24pp. An attractive, basic overview of bones with "Fun Facts" and an easy activity. (Rev: SLJ 7/02) [612.7]

21446 Frost, Helen. *The Muscular System* (K–2). Illus. Series: Human Body Systems. 2000, Capstone LB $17.26 (978-0-7368-0650-3). 24pp. Short, simple text introduces the muscular system, accompanied by full-color illustrations. (Rev: HBG 10/01; SLJ 4/01) [612]

21447 Gold, Susan Dudley. *The Musculoskeletal System and the Skin* (5–10). Illus. Series: Human Body Library. 2003, Enslow LB $23.93 (978-0-7660-2023-8). 48pp. Gold uses a conversational style to introduce detailed facts about the skeletal system, with useful graphics and some practical advice. (Rev: BL 4/15/03; HBG 10/03; SLJ 10/03) [612.7]

21448 Johnson, Rebecca. *The Muscular System* (2–4). Series: Early Bird Body Systems. 2004, Lerner LB $25.26 (978-0-8225-1248-6). Photographs and diagrams add to the easy-to-understand text; a word list starts the book and print and Web resources are appended. (Rev: BL 10/15/04; SLJ 2/05) [612.7]

21449 Macnair, Patricia Ann. *Movers and Shapers* (3–5). Series: Bodyscope. 2004, Houghton $9.95 (978-0-7534-5791-7). 40pp. The importance of physical fitness is emphasized in this attractive overview of the musculoskeletal system. (Rev: BL 10/15/04) [612.7]

21450 Oleksy, Walter. *The Head and Neck: Learning How We Use Our Muscles* (5–9). Series: 3-D Library of the Human Body. 2002, Rosen LB $26.50 (978-0-8239-3531-4). 48pp. The muscles of the head and neck and their roles in controlling the sense organs, chewing and swallowing, facial expressions, and conveying emotions are explained in this well-illustrated account. (Rev: BL 7/02) [612.7]

21451 Parker, Steve. *Skeleton* (4–6). Illus. Series: Look at Your Body. 1996, Millbrook LB $20.90 (978-0-7613-0529-3). 32pp. The human skeleton, its composition, and its uses are covered, with extensive, unusual illustrations like X-rays and CAT scans. (Rev: BL 11/1/96) [611]

21452 Parker, Steve. *The Skeleton and Muscles* (5–9). Illus. Series: Our Bodies. 2004, Raintree LB $28.56 (978-0-7398-6622-1). 48pp. Details of the human body's skeletal and muscular systems are accompanied by information on keeping them healthy. (Rev: BL 8/04) [612.7]

21453 Rau, Dana Meachen. *My Bones and Muscles* (PS–3). Illus. Series: Bookworms: What's Inside Me? 2004, Benchmark LB $21.36 (978-0-7614-1777-4). 31pp. A simple overview of bones, skeleton, and muscles, with photographs, diagrams, and X-rays. (Rev: SLJ 2/05) [612.7]

21454 Sherman, Josepha. *The Upper Limbs: Learning How We Use Our Arms, Elbows, Forearms, and Hands* (5–9). Series: 3-D Library of the Human Body. 2002, Rosen LB $27.95 (978-0-8239-3537-

6). 48pp. The parts of the arm and hand are examined with illustrated material on how the muscles in these areas function and receive support from the skeletal structure. (Rev: BL 7/02) [612.7]

21455 Silverstein, Alvin, et al. *Broken Bones* (3–5). Series: My Health. 2001, Watts LB $25.50 (978-0-531-11781-1). This book describes what happens when bones get broken, the causes, treatments available, and how mending takes place. (Rev: BL 1/1–15/02; SLJ 8/01) [612.7]

21456 Silverstein, Alvin, et al. *The Muscular System* (5–8). Illus. Series: Human Body Systems. 1994, Twenty-First Century $29.90 (978-0-8050-2836-2). Full-color diagrams, drawings, and photographs highlight this survey of the human muscular system. (Rev: BL 3/15/95; SLJ 5/95) [612.7]

21457 Viegas, Jennifer. *The Lower Limbs: Learning How We Use Our Thighs, Knees, Legs, and Feet* (5–9). Series: 3-D Library of the Human Body. 2002, Rosen LB $26.50 (978-0-8239-3533-8). 48pp. The bones and muscles of the legs and feet and their functions are described in a clear text and exceptional illustrations. (Rev: BL 7/02; SLJ 7/02) [612.7]

Skin and Hair

21458 Baines, Becky. *Your Skin Holds You In: A Book About Your Skin* (1–2). Series: Zig Zag. 2008, National Geographic $14.95 (978-1-4263-0311-1). 32pp. Thirteen short sentences and large illustrations featuring children of diverse backgrounds convey key facts about skin. (Rev: HB 9/08; LMC 11/08; SLJ 11/08) [612.7]

21459 Degezelle, Terri. *Taking Care of My Hair* (PS–2). Series: Keeping Healthy. 2005, Capstone LB $21.26 (978-0-7368-4261-7). 24pp. Easy-to-understand advice about hair care, in an oversize format with large color photographs. Also use *Taking Care of My Skin* (2005). (Rev: SLJ 12/05) [646.7]

21460 Glaser, Jason. *Head Lice* (1–3). Series: First Facts: Health Matters. 2005, Capstone LB $21.26 (978-0-7368-4291-4). 24pp. In simple text, this basic title looks at the causes, symptoms, and treatment of head lice. (Rev: SLJ 12/05) [616.5]

21461 Kinch, Michael P. *Warts* (3–5). Illus. Series: My Health. 2000, Watts LB $25.50 (978-0-531-11625-8). 48pp. Different kinds of warts are discussed, with material and activities related to how they are transmitted, how they grow, and how they can be eliminated. (Rev: BL 6/1–15/00) [616.5]

21462 Radabaugh, Melinda. *Getting a Haircut* (PS–1). Series: First Time. 2003, Heinemann LB $18.50 (978-1-4034-0225-7). 24pp. Reasons for getting a haircut and the experiences involved are emploerd in simple, reassuring text plus pictures and a quiz. (Rev: HBG 10/03; SLJ 9/03) [646.7]

21463 Sandeman, Anna. *Skin, Teeth, and Hair* (1–2). Illus. Series: Body Books. 1996, Millbrook LB $18.90 (978-0-7613-0489-0). 32pp. For beginning readers, this colorful account explains the composition and use in the human body of skin, teeth, and hair. (Rev: BL 10/15/96; SLJ 1/97) [612]

21464 Showers, Paul. *Your Skin and Mine* (PS–3). Illus. by Kathleen Kuchera. Series: Let's-Read-and-Find-Out. 1991, HarperCollins paper $5.99 (978-0-06-445102-4). 32pp. A look at skin, with simple experiments to show skin reactions. (Rev: BL 10/15/91; SLJ 8/91) [612.7]

21465 Silverstein, Alvin, et al. *Is That a Rash?* (3–5). Illus. Series: My Health. 2000, Watts LB $25.50 (978-0-531-11637-1). 48pp. With many suggested activities and excellent color photos, this account introduces skin problems — their causes and treatments. (Rev: BL 6/1–15/00) [616.5]

21466 Tyler, Michael. *The Skin You Live In* (PS–2). Illus. by David Lee Csicsko. 2005, Chicago Children's Museum $14.95 (978-0-9759580-0-1). Skin's physical properties and different shades are among the features explored in rhyming verse. (Rev: SLJ 5/05)

21467 Yagyu, Genichiro. *All About Scabs* (K–3). Trans. by Amanda Mayer Stinchecum. Illus. 1998, Kane $12.95 (978-0-916291-82-2). 28pp. This attention-getting book tells what a scab is, how it is formed, its uses, and what eventually happens to it. (Rev: BL 1/1–15/99; HBG 3/99; SLJ 2/99) [617.1]

Teeth

21468 Cobb, Vicki. *Your Body Battles a Cavity* (3–6). Illus. by Andrew N. Harris. Series: Body Battles. 2009, Millbrook LB $25.26 (978-0-8225-7469-9). 32pp. This title explains and cleverly illustrates how the body's cells act like a troop to get rid of plaque and additionally clarifies the concept through photomicrographs. (Rev: SLJ 5/09) [617.6]

21469 Copeland, Cynthia L. *The Tooth Fairy Tells All* (K–3). Illus. by author. Series: Silly Millies. 2002, Millbrook LB $17.90 (978-0-7613-2805-6); paper $4.99 (978-0-7613-1785-2). 31pp. This gentle exchange between the Tooth Fairy and the Wisdom Tooth provides useful information about teeth — including the different types — and how best to care for them. (Rev: HBG 3/03; SLJ 8/03)

21470 Degezelle, Terri. *Taking Care of My Teeth* (PS–2). Series: Keeping Healthy. 2005, Capstone LB $21.26 (978-0-7368-4264-8). 24pp. Easy-to-understand advice about dental care, in an oversize format with large color photographs. Also use *Taking Care of My Skin* (2005). (Rev: SLJ 12/05) [617.6]

21471 Keller, Laurie. *Open Wide: Tooth School Inside* (2–4). Illus. 2000, Holt $16.95 (978-0-8050-6192-5). 32pp. A fun book that explores the different kinds of teeth, dental care, and the causes of tooth decay. (Rev: BCCB 9/00; BL 5/1/00; HB 5/00; HBG 9/00; SLJ 5/00) [617.6]

21472 Lee, Jordan. *Coping with Braces and Other Orthodontic Work* (4–9). Series: Coping. 1998, Rosen LB $31.95 (978-0-8239-2721-0). 95pp. A book about braces, their purposes, and the problems they can cause. (Rev: SLJ 11/98) [612.3]

21473 McGinty, Alice B. *Staying Healthy: Dental Care* (K–3). Series: The Library of Healthy Living. 1998, Rosen LB $18.75 (978-0-8239-5139-0). 24pp. A fine introduction to teeth that covers such topics as different types of teeth, parts of a tooth, dental hygiene, and problems such as decay and cavities. (Rev: SLJ 9/98) [612.3]

21474 Miller, Edward. *The Tooth Book: A Guide to Healthy Teeth and Gums* (K–3). Illus. by author. 2008, Holiday $16.95 (978-0-8234-2092-6). 32pp. Facts and advice are dispensed with a dollop of humor and history, plus engaging images. (Rev: BL 2/15/08; SLJ 2/08) [617.6]

21475 Murkoff, Heidi. *What to Expect When You Go to the Dentist* (1–3). Illus. by Laura Rader. Series: What To Expect Kids. 2002, HarperCollins $10.99 (978-0-694-01328-9). 32pp. Angus the dog gives good advice and some projects to prepare youngsters for their first visit to a dentist. (Rev: BL 6/1–15/02; HBG 10/02) [617.601]

21476 Showers, Paul. *How Many Teeth?* (PS–2). Illus. by True Kelley. Series: Let's-Read-and-Find-Out. 1991, HarperCollins paper $5.99 (978-0-06-445098-0). 32pp. A full-color, funny, informative book showing a multiracial classroom. (Rev: BL 6/15/91; SLJ 10/91) [612.3]

Hygiene, Physical Fitness, and Nutrition

21477 Baptiste, Baron. *My Daddy Is a Pretzel* (PS–3). Illus. by Sophie Fatus. 2004, Barefoot Bks. $16.99 (978-1-84148-151-7). 48pp. An attractive introduction to basic yoga poses. (Rev: BL 10/15/04; SLJ 1/05) [613]

21478 Brown, Laurie Krasny, and Marc Brown. *Dinosaurs Alive and Well! A Guide to Good Health* (PS–3). Illus. 1990, Little, Brown paper $6.95 (978-0-316-11009-9). 32pp. Using dinosaurs, the basic principles of nutrition and hygiene are covered. Also use *Dinosaurs Travel* (1990). (Rev: BCCB 5/90; BL 5/15/90; HB 5/90; SLJ 4/90*) [613]

21479 Chryssicas, Mary Kaye. *I Love Yoga* (3–5). Photos by Angela Coppola. 2005, DK $12.99 (978-0-7566-1400-3). 48pp. Follows six children as they learn the basic techniques and positions of hatha yoga. (Rev: BL 11/15/05; SLJ 5/06) [613.7]

21480 Cole, Babette. *The Sprog Owner's Manual (or How Kids Work)* (K–3). 2006, Trafalgar paper $9.99 (978-0-09-944765-8). 32pp. Tips on health and grooming issues for kids ("sprogs" is a British term), presented with lots of humor. (Rev: BL 5/1/06) [823.914]

21481 Crump, Marguerite. *Don't Sweat It! Every Body's Answers to Questions You Don't Want to Ask: A Guide for Young People* (5–9). Illus. by Chris Sharp. 2002, Free Spirit paper $12.95 (978-1-57542-114-8). 118pp. Crump tackles potentially embarrassing questions about personal hygiene. (Rev: SLJ 1/03; VOYA 2/03) [613.0433]

21482 D'Aluisio, Faith. *What the World Eats* (4–8). 2008, Tricycle $22.99 (978-1-5824-6246-2). 160pp. What do people eat around the world? This is a fascinating survey of expenses, ingredients, and meals shared with 25 families in 21 countries; with statistics on obesity, access to water, and other key factors. (Rev: BL 7/08*; SLJ 7/08) [641.300]

21483 Dalgleish, Sharon. *Exercise and Rest* (3–5). Illus. Series: Healthy Choices. 2007, Black Rabbit LB $18.95 (978-1-58340-755-4). 32pp. Square, colorful pages looks at the importance of both exercise and rest, recommending 30 minutes of exercise three or four times a week. (Rev: BL 4/1/07) [613.7]

21484 Dawson, Mildred L. *Beauty Lab: How Science Is Changing the Way We Look* (5–10). 1997, Silver Moon $14.95 (978-1-881889-84-7). This work on health and hygiene contains chapters on skin, eyes, teeth, fitness, and hair. (Rev: SLJ 3/97) [613.7]

21485 De Brunhoff, Laurent. *Babar's Yoga for Elephants* (2–4). Illus. 2002, Abrams $16.95 (978-0-8109-1021-8). 48pp. The sage elephant Babar re-creates yoga poses, which kids may be tempted to do as well, in this nonfiction book best read with an adult nearby. (Rev: BL 10/15/02; HBG 3/03; SLJ 4/03) [613.7]

21486 Ehrlich, Fred. *Does an Elephant Take a Bath?* (PS–K). Illus. by Emily Bolam. Series: Early Experiences. 2005, Blue Apple LB $13.50 (978-1-59354-111-8); paper $5.95 (978-1-59354-123-1). 32pp. Illustrations of animals in bathtubs are followed by views of the animals using their natural methods of hygiene in this book that also shows how humans keep clean; a small, square book. (Rev: BL 10/15/05) [617.6]

21487 Feeney, Kathy. *Get Moving: Tips on Exercise* (K–3). Series: Your Health. 2001, Capstone LB $22.60 (978-0-7368-0973-3). 24pp. The importance of exercise is stressed through simple text and an activity pyramid. (Rev: HBG 3/02; SLJ 4/02) [613.7]

21488 Frost, Helen. *Drinking Water* (K–2). 2000, Capstone LB $17.26 (978-0-7368-0534-6). 24pp. This book explains simply why drinking water is a necessary part of one's diet. (Rev: HBG 9/00; SLJ 10/00) [613.2]

21489 Frost, Helen. *Eating Right* (K–2). Series: Food Guide Pyramid. 2000, Capstone LB $17.26 (978-0-7368-0535-3). 24pp. A very simple introduction to nutrition and the food pyramid. (Rev: HBG 9/00; SLJ 10/00) [613.2]

21490 Gordon, Sharon. *Exercise* (3–5). Series: Rookie Read-About Health. 2002, Children's Book Pr. paper $5.95 (978-0-516-26950-4). 32pp. This easy-reader explains how exercise builds strong muscles and shows how children can have fun while doing favorite activities. (Rev: BL 12/15/02) [613.7]

21491 Gordon, Sharon. *Keeping Clean* (3–5). Series: Rookie Read-About Health. 2002, Children's Book Pr. LB $20.50 (978-0-516-22572-2); paper $5.95 (978-0-516-26951-1). 32pp. From bathing after exercise to washing one's hands before eating, this is a simple guide to personal hygiene and on how to keep germs from spreading. (Rev: BL 12/15/02) [613]

21492 Gordon, Sharon. *You Are What You Eat* (3–5). Series: Rookie Read-About Health. 2002, Children's Book Pr. LB $20.50 (978-0-516-22573-9); paper $5.95 (978-0-516-26952-8). 32pp. This book uses simple language to explain such nutritional facts as why breakfast is the most important meal of the day and why an apple is a better snack than potato chips. (Rev: BL 12/15/02) [613]

21493 Gray, Shirley W. *Exercising for Good Health* (2–4). Illus. Series: Living Well. 2003, Child's World LB $27.07 (978-1-59296-081-1). 32pp. Outlines the many benefits of regular exercise and describes the effects of specific activities on overall health. (Rev: SLJ 2/04) [613.7]

21494 Green, Emily K. *Fruits* (K–3). Illus. Series: New Food Guide Pyramid. 2006, Children's Pr. LB $18.50 (978-1-60014-005-1). 24pp. Explains the importance of fruit in the diet, referring to the new food guide pyramid. Also use *Grains; Meat and Beans; Oils; Milk, Yogurt, and Cheese; Vegetables,* and *Oils* (all 2006). (Rev: SLJ 5/07)

21495 King, Hazel. *Carbohydrates for a Healthy Body* (4–6). Illus. Series: Body Needs. 2003, Heinemann LB $27.07 (978-1-4034-0756-6). 48pp. A clearly written and well illustrated introduction to the role and value of carbohydrates in nutrition. (Rev: HBG 10/03; SLJ 4/04) [612.3]

21496 Koellhoffer, Tara, ed. *Food and Nutrition* (4–6). Series: Science News for Kids. 2006, Chelsea House $30.00 (978-0-7910-9121-0). 110pp. A wide-ranging collection of articles on food and nutrition that originally appeared on the Science News for Kids Web site. (Rev: BL 6/1–15/06) [613.2]

21497 Landau, Elaine. *A Healthy Diet* (4–7). Series: Watts Library. 2003, Watts LB $25.50 (978-0-531-12027-9). 63pp. Landau explains the basics of good nutrition; the benefits of vitamins, minerals, and exercise; and the dangers of fad diets. (Rev: SLJ 9/03) [613.2]

21498 Leedy, Loreen. *The Edible Pyramid: Good Eating Every Day.* Rev. ed. (PS–2). 2007, Holiday $17.95 (978-0-8234-2074-2); paper $6.95 (978-0-8234-2075-9). 32pp. This updated version of the 1994 guide retains the same charming animal characters and illustrations. (Rev: BL 5/1/07; SLJ 5/07) [613.2]

21499 Luby, Thia. *Children's Book of Yoga: Games and Exercises Mimic Plants and Animals and Objects* (PS–7). 1998, Clear Light $14.95 (978-1-57416-003-1). 112pp. Brief, clear instructions are used to introduce yoga exercises — from the very easy to the more complex. (Rev: SLJ 10/98) [181.45]

21500 Mainland, Pauline. *A Yoga Parade of Animals: A First Fun Picture Book of Yoga* (2–6). Photos by Katie Vandyck. Illus. by Chris Perry. 1998, Element Books $15.95 (978-1-901881-65-3). This book shows children how they can assume the shapes and positions of various animals and supplies information about yoga and its history. (Rev: HBG 3/99; SLJ 11/98) [613.7]

21501 Miller, Edward. *The Monster Health Book: A Guide to Eating Healthy, Being Active and Feeling Great for Monsters and Kids!* (2–4). Illus. by author. 2006, Holiday $16.95 (978-0-8234-1956-2). 40pp. Basic health and nutrition facts and advice are presented in an enticing but brief format that may require amplification by adults. (Rev: BL 5/15/06; SLJ 6/06) [613.7]

21502 Mitchell, Melanie. *Eating Well* (K–3). Illus. Series: Pull Ahead Books. 2006, Lerner LB $22.60 (978-0-8225-2449-6). 32pp. An informative guide to the food pyramid and the fundamentals of healthy eating. (Rev: SLJ 8/06) [613.2]

21503 Murray, Julie. *Home* (2–4). Series: That's Gross! A Look at Science. 2009, ABDO LB $17.95 (978-1-60453-555-6). 32pp. A look at all the icky stuff in our homes — from bacteria and bugs to the spray of a flushing toilet. Also use *Icky, Sticky, Gross Stuff in Your School* (2009). (Rev: BL 5/15/09) [577.5]

21504 Nelson, Robin. *Staying Clean* (PS–1). Illus. Series: Pull-Ahead Books: Health. 2005, Lerner LB $22.60 (978-0-8225-2368-0); paper $5.95 (978-0-8225-2773-2). 32pp. Hand washing, brushing teeth, and avoiding head lice are among the topics addressed in simple text with full-color photographs. (Rev: BL 1/1–15/06) [613]

21505 Parker, Steve. *Professor Protein's Fitness, Health, Hygiene and Relaxation Tonic* (4–6). Illus. by Rob Shone. 1996, Millbrook LB $23.90 (978-0-7613-0494-4). 48pp. A witty presentation of material about fitness, health, and hygiene, with accompanying humorous cartoons. (Rev: SLJ 1/97) [613]

21506 Pascoe, Elaine, ed. *Spreading Menace: Salmonella Attack and the Hunger Craving* (5–8). Illus. Series: Body Story. 2003, Gale LB $24.95 (978-1-4103-0064-5). 48pp. Two stories show how the body can react to food — Mike is infected with salmonella, and George's hunger is giving him a weight problem. (Rev: SLJ 4/04) [615.9]

21507 Petrie, Kristin. *The Food Pyramid* (2–4). Illus. Series: Nutrition. 2004, ABDO LB $22.78 (978-1-59197-403-1). 32pp. A look at food groups, nutrition, serving sizes, and healthy eating in general, illustrated with photographs and other graphics. (Rev: HBG 4/04; SLJ 4/04) [613.2]

21508 Petrie, Kristin. *Nutrition Anyone?* (2–4). Illus. Series: Nutrition. 2004, ABDO LB $22.78 (978-1-59197-404-8). 32pp. Clear text and graphics introduce good nutrition and why it is necessary. (Rev: HBG 4/04; SLJ 4/04) [613.2]

21509 Petrie, Kristin. *Vitamins Are Vital* (2–4). Illus. Series: Nutrition. 2004, ABDO LB $22.78 (978-1-59197-406-2). 32pp. An exploration of the role of vitamins and minerals in nutrition, aimed at helping children have a healthful and balanced diet. (Rev: HBG 4/04; SLJ 4/04) [613.2]

21510 Powell, Jillian. *Exercise and Your Health* (2–5). Illus. Series: Health Matters. 1997, Raintree LB $25.69 (978-0-8172-4927-4). 32pp. Explains how exercise affects good health and gives tips on types of exercises, warming-up and cooling activi-

ties, proper dress, and ways to design a personalized program. (Rev: HBG 3/98; SLJ 2/98) [613.7]

21511 Powell, Jillian. *Food and Your Health* (2–5). Illus. Series: Health Matters. 1997, Raintree LB $25.69 (978-0-8172-4925-0). 32pp. Explains how food is digested, what constitutes good nutrition, problem foods, and data on proper body weight. (Rev: HBG 3/98; SLJ 2/98) [613.2]

21512 Rockwell, Lizzy. *The Busy Body Book: A Kid's Guide to Fitness* (PS–1). Illus. by author. 2004, Crown LB $17.99 (978-0-375-92203-9). Children of diverse backgrounds are shown in activities from yoga to rollerblading, and there is information on how the body works and the important role of exercise. (Rev: SLJ 1/04) [612]

21513 Rockwell, Lizzy. *Good Enough to Eat: A Kid's Guide to Food and Nutrition* (K–4). Illus. 1999, HarperCollins $17.99 (978-0-06-027434-4). 40pp. A nutritional guide for preschoolers that tells them about food groups, good eating habits, and how proper nutrition can keep them healthy and growing. (Rev: BL 1/1–15/99; HBG 9/99; SLJ 1/99) [613.2]

21514 Royston, Angela. *Eat Well* (K–2). Series: Safe and Sound. 1999, Heinemann LB $13.95 (978-1-57572-982-4). 32pp. This basic book on nutrition explains the food pyramid and the nutrients that are essential for good health. Exercise is given a similar treatment in the author's *A Healthy Body* (1999). (Rev: SLJ 1/00) [613]

21515 Royston, Angela. *Get Some Exercise!* (1–3). Series: Look After Yourself. 2003, Heinemann LB $22.79 (978-1-4034-4440-0). 32pp. The mechanics and benefits of exercise are clearly explained in easy-to-understand text. Also use *Get Some Rest!* (2003). (Rev: SLJ 2/04) [613.7]

21516 Royston, Angela. *Proteins for a Healthy Body* (4–6). Illus. Series: Body Needs. 2003, Heinemann LB $27.07 (978-1-4034-0759-7). 48pp. A description of the various types of proteins — hormones, antibodies, and enzymes — and how they are important in nutrition, with a look at how vegetarians can get enough of them on a restricted diet. (Rev: HBG 10/03; SLJ 4/04) [612.3]

21517 Royston, Angela. *Vitamins and Minerals for a Healthy Body* (4–6). Illus. Series: Body Needs. 2003, Heinemann LB $27.07 (978-1-4034-0758-0). 48pp. A look at the importance of vitamins and minerals in maintaining a healthy body, and at their role in preventing disease. (Rev: HBG 10/03; SLJ 4/04) [612.3]

21518 Savage, Jeff. *Fundamental Strength Training* (5–9). Photos by Jimmy Clarke. Series: Fundamental Sports. 1998, Lerner LB $26.40 (978-0-8225-3461-7). 64pp. This beginner's manual discusses weight machines, training without weights, and various exercises for developing specific parts of the body. (Rev: HBG 10/99; SLJ 2/99) [613.7]

21519 Schuh, Mari C. *Being Active* (PS–2). Series: Healthy Eating with MyPyramid. 2006, Capstone LB $21.26 (978-0-7368-5368-2). 24pp. This simple, bright volume focuses on activities that promote physical fitness, including bicycling, swimming, baseball, volleyball, taking care of pets, and playing with friends. Also use *Drinking Water* (2006). (Rev: SLJ 8/06) [613.7]

21520 Schuh, Mari C. *Healthy Snacks* (PS–2). Illus. by author. Series: Healthy Eating with MyPyramid. 2006, Scholastic LB $21.26 (978-0-7368-5369-9). 24pp. A companion to the new USDA food pyramid, explaining which snacks are best to eat in simple language and photographs. (Rev: BL 5/15/06; SLJ 8/06) [641.5]

21521 Schwartz, Ellen. *I'm a Vegetarian: Amazing Facts and Ideas for Healthy Vegetarians* (5–8). Illus. by Farida Zaman. 2002, Tundra paper $9.95 (978-0-88776-588-9). 112pp. The social aspects of being a vegetarian are handled here with humor and sensitivity. (Rev: BL 7/02; SLJ 9/02) [613.2]

21522 Serafin, Kim. *Everything You Need to Know About Being a Vegetarian* (5–8). Series: Need to Know Library. 1999, Rosen LB $27.95 (978-0-8239-2951-1). 64pp. This book explains vegetarianism and its various varieties, the reasons why people become vegetarians, the nature of their diets, social problems involved, and names celebrities who are vegetarians. (Rev: SLJ 1/00; VOYA 4/00) [613.2]

21523 Silverstein, Alvin, et al. *Eat Your Vegetables! Drink Your Milk!* (3–5). Series: My Health. 2000, Watts paper $6.95 (978-0-531-16507-2). 48pp. This is a beginner's guide to nutrition and the part played by foods in maintaining a healthy body. (Rev: BL 9/15/00) [613]

21524 Silverstein, Alvin, and Virginia Silverstein. *Physical Fitness* (3–5). Series: My Health. 2002, Watts paper $6.95 (978-0-531-15563-9). 48pp. Using photographs, cartoons, and other visuals plus a simple text, this book describes the importance of physical fitness and how to maintain it. (Rev: BL 6/1–15/02) [613.7]

21525 VanCleave, Janice. *Janice VanCleave's Food and Nutrition for Every Kid: Easy Activities That Make Learning Science Fun* (4–8). Illus. Series: Science for Every Kid. 1999, Wiley paper $12.95 (978-0-471-17665-7). Each of the 25 chapters in this book contains information about food, including food groups, the relationship between energy and food, how to read nutrition labels, and vitamins and minerals, plus dozens of easily performed projects that demonstrate these facts and concepts. (Rev: SLJ 8/99) [641.3]

21526 Weiss, Stefanie Iris. *Everything You Need to Know About Being a Vegan* (5–8). Series: Need to Know Library. 1999, Rosen LB $27.95 (978-0-8239-2958-0). 64pp. This book discusses vegans, people who do not eat or use animal products (usually for religious reasons), their lifestyles, diets, and possible social problems. (Rev: SLJ 1/00; VOYA 4/00) [613.2]

21527 Whitford, Rebecca. *Little Yoga: A Toddler's First Book of Yoga* (PS). Illus. by Martina Selway. 2005, Holt $9.95 (978-0-8050-7879-4). 28pp. Nine simple yoga exercises for children are shown in eye-catching spreads. (Rev: BL 10/1/05; SLJ 11/05) [613.7]

21528 Williams, Kara. *Frequently Asked Questions About MyPyramid: Eating Right* (5–8). Illus. 2007, Rosen LB $20.95 (978-1-4042-1974-8). 63pp. Introduces the 2005 version of the food pyramid as well as information on diet, nutrition, the human body, and exercise. (Rev: BL 6/1–15/07; LMC 10/07) [613.2]

21529 Zahensky, Barbara A. *Diet Fads* (4–8). Series: Danger Zone. Dieting and Eating Disorders. 2007, Rosen LB $27.95 (978-1-4042-1999-1). 64pp. Fad and crash diets and the dangers of overeating and excessive weight loss are the focus of this practical guide. (Rev: LMC 10/07; SLJ 9/07) [613.2]

Safety and Accidents

21530 Boelts, Maribeth. *A Kid's Guide to Staying Safe Around Water* (K–3). Series: The Kids' Library of Personal Safety. 1997, Rosen LB $18.75 (978-0-8239-5078-2). 24pp. This simple book on water safety presents basic rules for situations in a pool, lake, or ocean, plus coverage on swimming lessons, sunscreen, and what to do if someone is in trouble. (Rev: SLJ 4/98) [613.7]

21531 Boelts, Maribeth, and Darwin Boelts. *Kids to the Rescue! First Aid Techniques for Kids* (3–6). Illus. by Marina Megale. 1992, Parenting LB $17.95 (978-0-943990-83-5). 72pp. This book helps children react properly to 14 different medical emergencies and includes directions for appropriate actions in each case. (Rev: SLJ 9/92) [616.04]

21532 Chaiet, Donna, and Francine Russell. *The Safe Zone: A Kid's Guide to Personal Safety* (4–7). Illus. 1998, Morrow paper $6.95 (978-0-688-16091-3). 160pp. This book alerts youngsters to danger signs, gives advice on body language and self-esteem, and offers tips on how to avoid threatening situations. (Rev: BL 4/1/98; HBG 10/98) [613.6]

21533 Gale, Karen Buhler. *The Kids' Guide to First Aid: All About Bruises, Burns, Stings, Sprains and Other Ouches* (4–6). Illus. by Michael Kline. 2002, Williamson paper $14.25 (978-1-885593-58-0). 128pp. Readers learn to distinguish between situations they can handle and when they need to call for help, and gain useful information on stopping bleeding, applying bandages, and dealing with choking. (Rev: SLJ 4/02) [616.04]

21534 Gordon, Sharon. *Bruises* (1–2). Series: Rookie Read-About Health. 2002, Children's Book Pr. paper $5.95 (978-0-516-26872-9). 31pp. Readers learn why bruises change color and how to treat them, with reminders of the protection that proper clothing can offer. Also use *Cuts and Scrapes* (2001). (Rev: SLJ 8/02) [616.04]

21535 Gutman, Bill. *Be Aware of Danger* (5–8). Illus. Series: Focus on Safety. 1996, Twenty-First Century LB $24.90 (978-0-8050-4142-2). Situations that could be dangerous to young people are highlighted and preventive measures outlined. (Rev: BL 2/1/97; SLJ 2/97) [613.6]

21536 Gutman, Bill. *Hazards at Home* (4–8). Series: Focus on Safety. 1996, Twenty-First Century LB $24.90 (978-0-8050-4141-5). A look at sources of potential accidents in the home with information on prevention and first-aid procedures. (Rev: SLJ 9/96) [363.1]

21537 Gutman, Bill. *Recreation Can Be Risky* (4–8). Series: Focus on Safety. 1996, Holt LB $24.90 (978-0-8050-4143-9). The author gives practical suggestions for enjoying such activities as baseball, biking, or hiking while also keeping safe through warm-up exercises, proper equipment, correct clothing, etc. (Rev: BL 7/96; SLJ 9/96; VOYA 10/96) [790]

21538 Llewellyn, Claire. *Around Town* (PS–2). Illus. by Mike Gordon. Series: Watch Out! 2006, Barron's paper $5.99 (978-0-7641-3326-8). 32pp. Readers learn about some of the dangers they might face in an urban setting, such as dogs, getting lost, and construction sites. Also use *At Home, Near Water,* and *On the Road* (2006). (Rev: SLJ 10/06)

21539 MacGregor, Cynthia. *Ten Steps to Staying Safe* (2–4). Illus. Series: Abduction Prevention Library. 1998, Rosen LB $19.95 (978-0-8239-5248-9). 24pp. This book focuses on the inherent dangers of being with strangers and how to protect oneself in these situations. (Rev: BL 2/1/99) [613.6]

21540 MacGregor, Cynthia. *What to Do If You Get Lost* (2–4). Illus. Series: Abduction Prevention Library. 1998, Rosen LB $19.95 (978-0-8239-5250-2). 24pp. This is a practical guide for children who get separated from familiar places and people, telling how they can get help. (Rev: BL 2/1/99) [613.6]

21541 Mattern, Joanne. *Safety at School* (K–3). Series: Safety First. 1999, ABDO LB $21.35 (978-1-57765-070-6). 24pp. This book tells youngsters how to stay safe at school. Also use *Safety in Public Places* (1999). (Rev: HBG 4/00; SLJ 1/00) [613.6]

21542 Mattern, Joanne. *Safety on the Go* (K–3). Series: Safety First. 1999, ABDO LB $21.35 (978-1-57765-075-1). 24pp. This account tells children how to remain safe while using public transportation. Also use *Safety in the Water* and *Safety on Your Bicycle* (both 1999). (Rev: HBG 4/00; SLJ 1/00) [613.6]

21543 O'Shei, Tim. *How to Survive on a Deserted Island* (4–6). Illus. 2008, Capstone LB $17.99 (978-1-4296-2282-0). 32pp. Building a shelter, finding water, building a fire, and finding food are just a few of the tasks you will learn to achieve in this handy guide. (Rev: BL 4/1/09) [613.6]

21544 Pendziwol, Jean E. *Once Upon a Dragon: Stranger Safety Tips for Kids (and Dragons)* (PS–2). Illus. by Martine Gourbault. 2006, Kids Can $14.95 (978-1-55337-722-1); paper $6.95 (978-1-55337-969-0). 32pp. This companion to *No Drag-*

ons for Tea: Fire Safety for Kids (and Dragons) uses fairy-tale characters as stand-ins for strangers, easing the scariness of this difficult topic. (Rev: BL 5/15/06; SLJ 6/06)

21545 Raatma, Lucia. *Bicycle Safety* (2–4). Illus. Series: Living Well. 2003, Child's World LB $27.07 (978-1-59296-085-9). 32pp. A simple story about a child riding a bicycle is followed by easy-to-understand safety rules. Also use *School Safety* and *Internet Safety* (both 2003). (Rev: SLJ 3/04) [796.6]

21546 Roberts, Robin. *Sports Injuries: How to Stay Safe and Keep on Playing* (5–8). Series: Get in the Game! With Robin Roberts. 2001, Millbrook LB $23.90 (978-0-7613-2116-3). 48pp. This general sports book that targets girls as a primary audience discusses safety in a variety of sports and how to cope with injuries. (Rev: BL 9/15/01; HBG 3/02; SLJ 1/02) [790]

Sleep and Dreams

21547 Feeney, Kathy. *Sleep Well: Why You Need to Rest* (K–3). Series: Your Health. 2001, Capstone LB $22.60 (978-0-7368-0970-2). 24pp. Simple text and illustrations stress the importance of sleep and discuss sleepwalking and nightmares. (Rev: HBG 3/02; SLJ 4/02) [612.82]

21548 Gordon, Sharon. *A Good Night's Sleep* (3–5). Series: Rookie Read-About Health. 2002, Children's Book Pr. LB $20.50 (978-0-516-22570-8). 32pp. After explaining the reasons why sleep is important, this easy-reader gives a few hints on how to fall asleep fast. (Rev: BL 12/15/02) [616.5]

21549 Romanek, Trudee. *Zzz . . .: The Most Interesting Book You'll Ever Read About Sleep* (3–6). Illus. by Rose Cowles. 2002, Kids Can $14.95 (978-1-55074-944-1); paper $7.95 (978-1-55074-946-5). 40pp. With lively, amusing illustrations and an interesting text, this book covers such topics related to sleep as REM sleep, dreams, sleep cycles, snoring, and yawning. (Rev: BL 6/1–15/02; HBG 10/02; SLJ 6/02) [612.8]

21550 Swain, Ruth Freeman. *Bedtime!* (PS–3). Illus. by Cat B. Smith. 1999, Holiday House $15.95 (978-0-8234-1444-4). 32pp. This history of beds highlights simple mats, dorm bunks, hammocks, Pullman sleepers, Murphy beds, and so on. (Rev: BL 9/15/99; HBG 3/00; SLJ 11/99) [392.3]

21551 Trueit, Trudi. *Dreams and Sleep* (4–8). Illus. Series: Life Balance. 2004, Watts LB $20.50 (978-0-531-12260-0). 80pp. Discusses why we dream and what dreams mean and gives advice on getting a good night's sleep. (Rev: BL 10/15/03) [616.5]

Sex Education and Reproduction

Babies

21552 Anderson, Rachel. *Hello Peanut* (PS). Illus. by Debbie Harter. Series: Hodder Toddler. 2004, Hodder paper $8.95 (978-0-340-85248-4). A toddler follows the progress of her mother's pregnancy with great interest. (Rev: SLJ 2/04)

21553 Bernhard, Emery. *A Ride on Mother's Back: A Day of Baby Carrying Around the World* (K–2). Illus. by Durga Bernhard. 1996, Harcourt $16.00 (978-0-15-200870-3). 40pp. Various ways of carrying babies reflect cultural differences around the world. (Rev: BL 10/15/96; SLJ 10/96) [392]

21554 Cole, Joanna. *When You Were Inside Mommy* (PS). Illus. by Maxie Chambliss. 2001, Harper-Collins $7.99 (978-0-688-17043-1). 32pp. Basic facts about a child's development are presented in this small-format picture book. (Rev: BL 8/01; HBG 3/02; SLJ 12/01) [612.6]

21555 Davis, Jennifer. *Before You Were Born* (PS–2). Illus. by Laura Cornell. 1998, Workman $10.95 (978-0-7611-1200-6). 24pp. The nine months of prenatal development are chronicled in a simple text with thumbnail drawings and told from a pregnant woman's point of view. (Rev: HBG 3/99; SLJ 9/98) [612]

21556 Dilley, Becki, and Keith Dilley. *Sixty Fingers, Sixty Toes: See How the Dilley Sextuplets Grow* (PS). Photos by E. Anthony Valainis. 1998, Walker $15.95 (978-0-8027-8613-5). 32pp. In a series of photographs, the life and activities of the Dilley sextuplets are covered from infancy through age four. (Rev: HBG 9/98; SLJ 7/98) [305]

21557 Douglas, Ann. *Baby Science: How Babies Really Work!* (PS–2). Illus. by Helene Desputeaux. 1998, Firefly $17.95 (978-1-895688-83-2). 32pp. The behavioral habits of babies during the first year of life are explored in this colorful picture book. (Rev: BL 1/1–15/99; SLJ 12/98) [305.232]

21558 Heiligman, Deborah. *Babies: All You Need to Know* (K–2). Illus. by Laura Freeman. Series: Jump into Science. 2002, National Geographic $16.95 (978-0-7922-8205-1). 32pp. Young readers learn how babies grow, what they eat, how they learn, and so forth. (Rev: BCCB 10/02; BL 10/1/02; HBG 3/03; SLJ 10/02) [612.6]

21559 Murkoff, Heidi. *What to Expect When the New Baby Comes Home* (PS–K). Illus. by Laura Rader. 2001, HarperCollins $8.99 (978-0-694-01327-2). 32pp. Angus the Answer Dog guides readers through answers to such questions as "What do new babies eat?" and "Can I play with the new baby?" (Rev: BL 7/01; HBG 10/01; SLJ 6/01) [305.232]

21560 Nanao, Jun. *Contemplating Your Bellybutton* (PS–K). Trans. by Amanda Mayer Stinchecum. Illus. by Tomoko Hasegawa. 1995, Kane $11.95 (978-0-916291-60-0). 32pp. Young Tettchan is told how he got his belly button and the purpose it serves. (Rev: BL 1/1–15/96; SLJ 12/95) [611.95]

21561 Sears, William, et al. *Baby on the Way* (K–3). Illus. by Renée Andriani. 2001, Little, Brown $12.95 (978-0-316-78767-3). 32pp. A reassuring, colorfully illustrated book that tells young children about the effects of pregnancy on the mother. (Rev: BL 9/15/01; HBG 3/02; SLJ 10/01) [618.2]

21562 Sears, William, et al. *What Baby Needs* (K–3). Illus. by Renée Andriani. 2001, Little, Brown $12.95 (978-0-316-78828-1). 32pp. A readable look at the changes boys and girls can expect when they become big brothers or sisters. (Rev: BL 9/15/01; HBG 3/02; SLJ 10/01) [649]

21563 Stein, Sara Bonnett. *Oh, Baby!* (PS–1). Illus. by Holly Anne Shelowitz. 1993, Walker LB $15.85 (978-0-8027-8262-5). 32pp. Using a series of baby pictures, physical and mental developments during the first year of a child's life are outlined. (Rev: BL 3/1/94*; SLJ 12/93*) [305]

21564 Thomas, Shelley M. *A Baby's Coming to Your House!* (PS–1). Illus. by Eric Futran. 2001, Whitman $15.95 (978-0-8075-0502-1). 32pp. Using funny family pictures as illustrations, this book explains to youngsters the changes that take place when a new baby enters the house — like the appearance of high chairs and messy diapers. (Rev: BL 3/15/01; HBG 10/01) [305.2]

Reproduction

21565 Butler, Dori. *My Mom's Having a Baby!* (2–4). Illus. by Carol Thompson. 2005, Whitman $16.95 (978-0-8075-5344-2). 32pp. For children who are ready for a detailed treatment of intercourse, conception, gestation, and birth, this book discusses it all and is enhanced with cartoon-style illustrations. (Rev: BL 4/1/05; SLJ 5/05) [618.2]

21566 Cole, Joanna. *How You Were Born* (PS–3). Illus. by Margaret Miller. 1993, Morrow paper $7.99 (978-0-688-12061-0). 48pp. Fetal development is tracked in text and color pictures, plus tips are given on how to use this book with children. (Rev: BL 6/1–15/93; SLJ 4/93*) [612]

21567 Fullick, Ann. *Test Tube Babies: In Vitro Fertilization* (5–8). Series: Science at the Edge. 2002, Heinemann LB $27.86 (978-1-58810-703-9). 64pp. This attractive book balances hard science with thought-provoking discussion on this controversial topic. (Rev: BL 10/15/02; HBG 3/03; SLJ 4/03) [613.9]

21568 Girard, Linda Walvoord. *You Were Born on Your Very First Birthday* (PS). Illus. by Christa Kieffer. 1983, Whitman paper $5.95 (978-0-8075-9456-8). 32pp. A simple introduction to pregnancy and birth.

21569 Orr, Tamra. *Test Tube Babies* (5–9). Series: Science on the Edge. 2003, Gale LB $24.95 (978-1-56711-788-2). 48pp. This book discusses in vitro fertilization, and how it has helped many but also caused a great deal of controversy. (Rev: BL 10/15/03; SLJ 3/04) [612]

21570 Overend, Jenni. *Welcome with Love* (1–3). Illus. by Julie Vivas. 2000, Kane $15.95 (978-0-916291-96-9). 32pp. A direct, graphic treatment of childbirth showing the members of a close family participating in a home delivery. (Rev: BCCB 6/00; BL 3/15/00; HBG 9/00; SLJ 4/00) [618.4]

21571 Parker, Steve. *Reproduction* (5–9). Illus. Series: Our Bodies. 2004, Raintree LB $28.56 (978-0-7398-6623-8). 48pp. Details of the human body's reproductive organs and how they function are accompanied by information on keeping them healthy. (Rev: BL 8/04) [612.6]

21572 Parker, Steve. *The Reproductive System* (5–8). Illus. Series: Human Body. 1997, Raintree LB $18.98 (978-0-8172-4806-2). 48pp. A well-organized, straightforward account that covers male and female anatomy, genes, fertility problems, contraception, STDs, and human development from conception to adolescence. (Rev: SLJ 2/98) [613.9]

21573 Rozakis, Laurie. *Teen Pregnancy: Why Are Kids Having Babies?* (5–8). Illus. Series: Issues of Our Time. 1993, Twenty-First Century LB $22.90 (978-0-8050-2569-9). 64pp. A slim, easily read account that explains birth control and deplores the

fact that teens do not have access to information about it. (Rev: SLJ 2/94) [612.6]

21574 Sandeman, Anna. *Babies* (2–4). Illus. Series: Body Books. 1996, Millbrook LB $18.90 (978-0-7613-0478-4). 31pp. Clear information is given on conception, pregnancy, childbirth, and the growth of babies. (Rev: SLJ 6/96) [613.9]

21575 Silverstein, Alvin, et al. *The Reproductive System* (5–8). Illus. Series: Human Body Systems. 1994, Twenty-First Century LB $16.95 (978-0-8050-2838-6). Reproduction in the plant and animal worlds is introduced, focusing on the human system and body parts. (Rev: BL 3/15/95) [612.6]

Sex Education and Puberty

21576 Arredia, Joni. *Sex, Boys, and You: Be Your Own Best Girlfriend* (5–9). Illus. 1998, Perc Publg. paper $15.95 (978-0-9653203-2-0). A self-help book for younger teen girls with advice on how to accept oneself, when to say "no" to sex, how to assess one's strengths and weaknesses, and how to develop healthy relationships with boys. (Rev: SLJ 10/98) [305.23]

21577 Bailey, Jacqui. *Sex, Puberty and All That Stuff: A Guide to Growing Up* (5–10). Illus. by Jan McCafferty. 2004, Barron's paper $12.99 (978-0-7641-2992-6). 112pp. In this comprehensive volume full of lighthearted illustrations, Bailey covers the wide range of changes that affect young people, emphasizing the individual's right to choose and the need to resist peer pressure. (Rev: SLJ 1/05) [613.9]

21578 Brewer, Janet Neff. *In God's Image* (PS–K). Illus. 1998, Bridge Resources $14.99 (978-1-57895-055-3). 32pp. Using a Christian framework that stresses God's love, this book on sex education explains to the very young how babies grow inside mothers, the differences between a boy's and a girl's body, what "bad" touching is about, and how to cope with various emotions. (Rev: BL 10/1/98) [241]

21579 Dunham, Kelli. *The Boy's Body Book: Everything You Need to Know for Growing Up YOU* (4–7). Illus. by Steve Björkman. 2007, Sterling paper $9.95 (978-1-933662-74-9). 112pp. This is a straightforward review of the changes to expect during puberty; it also discusses stress, friendship, peer pressure, and family problems such as divorce. (Rev: LMC 1/08; SLJ 10/07) [612.6]

21580 Dunham, Kelli. *The Girl's Body Book: Everything You Need to Know for Growing up You* (4–7). Illus. by Laura Tallardy. 2008, Applesauce paper $9.95 (978-1-60433-004-5). 128pp. This friendly introduction to puberty covers physical and emotional changes and offers practical guidance. (Rev: LMC 1/09; SLJ 11/08) [612]

21581 Feinmann, Jane. *Everything a Girl Needs to Know About Her Periods* (5–9). Illus. 2003, Ronnie Sellers paper $14.95 (978-1-56906-555-6). 144pp. This useful and reassuring guide to the female body changes of puberty focuses largely on the menstrual cycle. (Rev: BL 2/1/04) [618.083]

21582 Girard, Linda Walvoord. *My Body Is Private* (PS–3). Illus. by Rodney Pate. 1984, Whitman LB $14.95 (978-0-8075-5320-6); paper $6.95 (978-0-8075-5319-0). 32pp. A girl of seven or eight talks about unwarranted touching of one's body by another in this lesson on prevention of sexual abuse.

21583 Gordon, Sol, and Judith Gordon. *A Better Safe Than Sorry Book: A Family Guide for Sexual Assault Prevention* (PS–1). Illus. 1992, Prometheus paper $13.98 (978-0-87975-768-7). A book that approaches the subjects of sexual abuse and threats from strangers in a nonscary manner. (Rev: BL 11/15/85)

21584 Gravelle, Karen, and Nick Castro. *What's Going on Down There? Answers to Questions Boys Find Hard to Ask* (5–10). Illus. by Robert Leighton. 1998, Walker paper $8.95 (978-0-8027-7540-5). 128pp. Straightforward information for boys covers such topics as physical changes, sexual intercourse, peer pressure, and pregnancy and birth. (Rev: BL 11/1/98; HB 1/99; HBG 3/99; SLJ 12/98) [613]

21585 Harris, Robie H. *It's Not the Stork! A Book About Girls, Boys, Babies, Bodies, Families, and Friends* (K–3). Illus. by Michael Emberley. 2006, Candlewick $16.99 (978-0-7636-0047-1). 64pp. A frank, sensitive, and inevitably controversial discussion of gender differences, human anatomy, sexuality, and reproduction. (Rev: BCCB 10/06; BL 6/1–15/06; HBG 4/07; LMC 1/07; SLJ 9/06*) [613.9]

21586 Harris, Robie H. *It's So Amazing: A Book About Eggs, Sperm, Birth, Babies, and Families* (2–5). Illus. by Michael Emberley. 1999, Candlewick $21.99 (978-0-7636-0051-8). 80pp. An outstanding book that explains human reproduction and birth in straightforward prose and bold, colorful illustrations. (Rev: BCCB 2/00; BL 1/1–15/00*; HBG 4/00; SLJ 2/00) [612.6]

21587 Johnson, Eric W. *People, Love, Sex, and Families: Answers to Questions That Preteens Ask* (5–8). Illus. 1985, Walker LB $14.85 (978-0-8027-6605-2). 144pp. Based on the results of a survey of 1,000 preteens, this book covers a broad range of topics, from sexual abuse to venereal disease to divorce and incest. (Rev: BL 3/15/86) [306.707]

21588 Jukes, Mavis. *Growing Up: It's a Girl Thing: Straight Talk About First Bras, First Periods and Your Changing Body* (4–8). Illus. 1998, Knopf paper $10.00 (978-0-679-89027-0). Essential information about the changes girls experience during puberty, with half the book devoted to what to expect and how to plan for their first period, presented in an easy, big-sister style. (Rev: BL 11/1/98; SLJ 11/98) [612]

21589 Jukes, Mavis. *It's a Girl Thing: How to Stay Healthy, Safe, and in Charge* (5–9). Illus. 1996, Knopf paper $12.00 (978-0-679-87392-1). This guide to puberty for girls discusses such topics as menstruation, drinking and drugs, body changes, contraceptives, sexually transmitted diseases, and

sexual abuse and harassment. (Rev: SLJ 6/96*) [612.6]

21590 Kemp, Kristen. *Healthy Sexuality* (5–10). Illus. Series: Life Balance. 2004, Watts LB $20.50 (978-0-531-12336-2); paper $6.95 (978-0-531-16689-5). 80pp. Covering both boys and girls, this easy-to-understand volume looks at physical and emotional changes and provides practical tips on handling difficult decisions and confusing feelings. (Rev: BL 10/15/03; SLJ 4/05)

21591 Kleven, Sandy. *The Right Touch: A Read-Aloud Story to Help Prevent Child Sexual Abuse* (PS–3). Illus. by Jody Bergsma. 1998, Illumination Arts $15.95 (978-0-935699-10-4). 32pp. This book instructs children on how to deal with unwanted and inappropriate touching. (Rev: SLJ 7/98) [306]

21592 Loulan, JoAnn, and Bonnie Worthen. *Period: A Girl's Guide to Menstruation with a Parent's Guide*. Rev. ed. (5–7). Illus. 2001, Book Peddlers paper $9.99 (978-0-916773-96-0). 96pp. This practical guide to menstruation is arranged by such questions as "What do I do when I get my first period?" and "What kind of exercise can I do?" (Rev: BL 2/1/01; HBG 10/01) [612.6]

21593 Madaras, Lynda. *On Your Mark, Get Set, Grow! A "What's Happening to My Body?" Book for Younger Boys* (4–6). Illus. by Paul Gilligan. 2008, Newmarket $22.00 (978-1-55704-780-0); paper $12.00 (978-1-55704-781-6). 119pp. For boys, this companion book to the *Ready, Set, Grow* also takes a humorous and accessible look at puberty and contains many questions and quotations from boys themselves. (Rev: BL 5/15/08; SLJ 5/08) [613]

21594 Madaras, Lynda. *Ready, Set, Grow! A "What's Happening to My Body?" Book for Younger Girls* (2–5). Illus. by Linda Davick. 2003, Newmarket $22.00 (978-1-55704-587-4); paper $12.00 (978-1-55704-565-2). 125pp. This spin-off guide to puberty is aimed at the girls who are now going through this experience at a younger age and includes medical tips and upbeat discussion. (Rev: HBG 4/04; SLJ 11/03) [612.6]

21595 Marsh, Carole. *AIDS to Zits: A "Sextionary" for Kids* (3–7). 1987, Gallopade $29.95 (978-1-55609-263-3); paper $19.95 (978-1-55609-210-7). 28pp. This dictionary contains definitions of about 100 words related to sexuality. (Rev: BL 12/1/89) [613.951]

21596 Mosatche, Harriet S., and Karen Unger. *Too Old for This, Too Young for That! Your Survival Guide for the Middle-School Years* (5–8). Illus. 2000, Free Spirit paper $14.99 (978-1-57542-067-7). 200pp. This guide to the early years of puberty contains material on self-esteem, family relationships, friendships, and activities; also included is a lengthy section on bodily changes and such events as the onset of menstruation, erections, and ejaculation. (Rev: BL 7/00; SLJ 9/00) [646.7]

21597 Movsessian, Shushann. *Puberty Girl* (4–7). Illus. 2005, Allen & Unwin paper $15.95 (978-1-74114-104-7). 128pp. A frank and friendly guide covering such topics as body changes, conflict resolution, and personal boundaries, as well as the changes that puberty brings in the opposite sex. (Rev: BL 10/15/05; SLJ 10/05; VOYA 10/05) [612.6]

21598 Pascoe, Elaine, ed. *Teen Dreams: The Journey Through Puberty* (5–8). Illus. Series: Body Story. 2003, Gale LB $24.95 (978-1-4103-0061-4). 48pp. Puberty and the many changes it brings are the topic of this arresting and informative book, seen from the points of view of a teenage boy and girl. (Rev: SLJ 4/04) [612.6]

21599 Pfeifer, Kate Gruenwald. *Boy's Guide to Becoming a Teen* (4–7). Ed. by Amy B. Middleman. 2006, Jossey-Bass paper $12.95 (978-0-7879-8343-7). 128pp. A guide to handling the physical, emo-

tional, and social changes that accompany puberty in boys. (Rev: BL 5/15/06; SLJ 5/07) [613]

21600 Pfeifer, Kate Gruenwald. *Girl's Guide to Becoming a Teen* (4–7). Ed. by Amy B. Middleman. 2006, Jossey-Bass paper $12.95 (978-0-7879-8344-4). 128pp. A guide to handling the physical, emotional, and social changes that accompany puberty in girls. (Rev: BL 5/15/06; SLJ 5/07) [613]

21601 Price, Geoff. *Puberty Boy* (5–8). 2006, Allen & Unwin paper $15.95 (978-1-74114-563-2). 128pp. A frank and friendly guide with an Australian accent that covers the important physical and emotional changes that accompany puberty. (Rev: BL 7/06; SLJ 9/06; VOYA 8/06) [612]

Physical and Applied Sciences

General Science

Miscellaneous

21602 Aaseng, Nathan. *Yearbooks in Science: 1930–1939* (5–8). Illus. Series: Yearbooks in Science. 1995, Twenty-First Century LB $22.90 (978-0-8050-3433-2). 80pp. An overview of the accomplishments in science in the 1930s arranged by such divisions as physics and chemistry. (Rev: BL 12/1/95; SLJ 1/96) [609]

21603 Aaseng, Nathan. *Yearbooks in Science: 1940–1949* (5–8). Illus. Series: Yearbooks in Science. 1995, Twenty-First Century LB $22.90 (978-0-8050-3434-9). An important decade in scientific discovery is chronicled, with emphasis on the impact of these advances on society. (Rev: BL 1/1–15/96; SLJ 5/96) [609]

21604 Arnold, Nick. *The Stunning Science of Everything: Science with the Squishy Bits Left In!* (4–8). Illus. by Tony De Saulles. 2006, Scholastic $10.99 (978-0-439-87777-0). 96pp. This lighthearted look at science, brightly illustrated with cartoons, examines such diverse topics as the Big Bang theory, atoms, insects, humans, dinosaurs, and the universe. (Rev: HBG 4/07; LMC 3/07; SLJ 2/07; VOYA 2/07) [500]

21605 Beres, Samantha. *101 Things Every Kid Should Know About Science* (4–7). Illus. 1998, Lowell House paper $9.95 (978-1-56565-916-2). 96pp. This information-packed book supplies basic scientific facts organized under headings such as chemistry, physics, biology, and geography. (Rev: BL 10/15/98; SLJ 12/98) [500]

21606 Boring, Mel, and Leslie Dendy. *Guinea Pig Scientists: Bold Self-Experimenters in Science and Medicine* (5–9). Illus. by C. B. Mordan. 2005, Holt $19.95 (978-0-8050-7316-4). 224pp. Scientists who served as their own guinea pigs — demonstrating their passion for science and often their foolhardiness — are the topic of this appealing volume. (Rev: BL 7/05*; SLJ 7/05*; VOYA 6/05) [616]

21607 Day, Trevor. *Genetics* (4–7). Illus. Series: Routes of Science. 2004, Gale LB $24.95 (978-1-4103-0301-1). 40pp. A detailed examination of the development of genetics as a science, with profiles of key individuals and their discoveries, a chronology, and discussion of future advances. (Rev: SLJ 5/05)

21608 Dolan, Graham. *The Greenwich Guide to Time and the Millennium* (4–7). Illus. by Jeff Edwards. 1999, Heinemann $16.95 (978-1-57572-802-5). 48pp. Covers such subjects as time zones, calendars, centuries, and longitude. (Rev: SLJ 9/99) [529]

21609 Dotlich, Rebecca Kai. *What Is Science?* (PS–2). Illus. by Sachiko Yoshikawa. 2006, Holt $16.95 (978-0-8050-7394-2). 32pp. A trio of children and their dog get a simple, poetic tour of the world of science. (Rev: BL 9/15/06; SLJ 11/06) [500]

21610 Ehrlich, Robert. *What If? Mind-Boggling Science Questions for Kids* (4–6). Illus. 1998, Wiley paper $13.95 (978-0-471-17608-4). 192pp. Chapters on such subjects as time, the earth, and the planets provide explanations for intriguing science puzzlers. (Rev: BL 6/1–15/98; SLJ 10/98) [500]

21611 Fridell, Ron. *Genetic Engineering* (4–6). Illus. Series: Cool Science. 2005, Lerner LB $26.60 (978-0-8225-2633-9). 48pp. With many interesting examples and an attractive layout, this introduction explores how this cutting-edge branch of science is paving the way for new species of plant and animal life and also helping to deal with human health problems. (Rev: SLJ 12/05) [660.6]

21612 Gutfreund, Geraldine M. *Yearbooks in Science: 1970–1979* (5–8). Illus. Series: Yearbooks in Science. 1995, Twenty-First Century LB $22.90 (978-0-8050-3437-0). A decade of new scientific concepts and inventions is discussed, with profiles of the scientists behind them. (Rev: BL 1/1–15/96; SLJ 5/96) [609]

21613 Hickman, Pamela. *The Night Book: Exploring Nature After Dark with Activities, Experiments and Information* (3–6). Illus. 1999, Kids Can $12.95

(978-1-55074-318-0); paper $6.95 (978-1-55074-306-7). 48pp. This is a collection of activities exploring the night world, including starlight, stargazing, night vision, and such nocturnal creatures as owls and fireflies. (Rev: BL 2/15/99; SLJ 8/99) [591.5]

21614 Hoyt, Beth Caldwell, and Erica Ritter. *The Ultimate Girls' Guide to Science: From Backyard Experiments to Winning the Nobel Prize!* (4–8). Illus. 2004, Beyond Words paper $9.95 (978-1-58270-092-2). 128pp. Designed to pique girls' interest in the study of science, this attractive title offers brief profiles of famous female scientists as well as the major branches of science and also provides instructions for a number of scientific experiments. (Rev: SLJ 8/04) [500]

21615 Kramer, Stephen. *Hidden Worlds: Looking Through a Scientist's Microscope* (4–7). Illus. Series: Scientists in the Field. 2001, Houghton $16.00 (978-0-618-05546-3). 61pp. Striking photographs, mostly taken with electron microscopes by scientist Dennis Kunkel, serve to illustrate this explanation of how scientists use microscopes in their work. (Rev: BL 8/01; HB 1/02; HBG 3/02; SLJ 9/01*) [570]

21616 Kramer, Stephen. *How to Think Like a Scientist: Answering Questions by the Scientific Method* (3–5). Illus. 1987, HarperCollins LB $16.89 (978-0-690-04565-9). 48pp. An intriguing account of the ways in which questions are asked, and how scientists try to make sure they are answered correctly. (Rev: BCCB 1/87; BL 5/15/87; SLJ 5/87)

21617 McGowen, Tom. *The Beginnings of Science* (5–8). Illus. 1998, Twenty-First Century LB $26.90 (978-0-7613-3016-5). 80pp. Beginning with primitive people and their use of magic, fire, counting, writing, and astronomy, this book traces the history of science up to the 16th century. (Rev: BL 12/1/98; HBG 3/99) [509]

21618 McGowen, Tom. *Yearbooks in Science: 1900–1919* (5–8). Illus. Series: Yearbooks in Science. 1995, Twenty-First Century LB $22.90 (978-0-8050-3431-8). 80pp. An overview of human achievements in science and technology during the first 20 years of the 20th century, how they helped humanity, and the men and women involved. (Rev: BL 12/1/95; SLJ 1/96) [609]

21619 McGowen, Tom. *Yearbooks in Science: 1960–1969* (5–8). Illus. Series: Yearbooks in Science. 1996, Twenty-First Century LB $22.90 (978-0-8050-3436-3). Developments in the history of science and technology during the 1960s are covered in an exciting step-by-step approach. (Rev: BL 1/1–15/96; SLJ 5/96) [609]

21620 Martin, Paul D. *Science: It's Changing Your World* (5–8). Illus. 1985, National Geographic LB $12.50 (978-0-87044-521-7). 104pp. An overview of the science field today, crediting computers and lasers with the vast growth of scientific information. (Rev: BL 9/15/85; SLJ 10/85) [500]

21621 Masoff, Joy. *Oh, Yuck! The Encyclopedia of Everything Nasty* (4–8). Illus. by Terry Sirrell. 2001, Workman paper $14.95 (978-0-7611-0771-2).

212pp. This unsavory, fact-filled look at smells, noises, creepy-crawlies, toilets, and other fascinating topics even includes some suitably gross experiments. (Rev: SLJ 5/01) [031.02]

21622 Murphy, Glenn. *Why Is Snot Green?* (3–6). Illus. by Mike Phillips. 2009, Roaring Brook paper $9.95 (978-1-59643-500-1). 240pp. Facts and fun are combined in this conversational, question-and-answer look at scientific topics ranging from outer space ("What is space made of?") to animals ("Do rabbits fart?"), the human body, and the future. (Rev: BCCB 6/09; BL 3/1/09; SLJ 6/09) [500]

21623 Myers, Jack. *On the Trail of the Komodo Dragon: And Other Explorations of Science in Action* (3–6). Illus. 1999, Boyds Mills $17.95 (978-1-56397-761-9). 63pp. A collection of 11 "Science Reporting" columns from *Highlights for Children* that explore unusual topics, such as how horses sleep and why cats can often fall safely. (Rev: BL 2/15/99; HBG 9/99; SLJ 4/99) [591]

21624 Newton, David E. *Yearbooks in Science: 1920–1929* (5–8). Illus. Series: Yearbooks in Science. 1995, Twenty-First Century LB $22.90 (978-0-8050-3432-5). 80pp. The history of scientific advances in the 1920s, with chapters on various fields that explain the breakthroughs, how they helped humanity, and the scientists involved. (Rev: BL 12/1/95; SLJ 1/96) [609]

21625 O'Meara, Stephen James. *Are You Afraid Yet? The Science Behind Scary Stuff* (5–8). Illus. by Jeremy Kaposy. 2009, Kids Can $17.95 (978-1-55453-294-0); paper $9.95 (978-1-55453-295-7). 80pp. O'Meara uses classic horror themes to look at scientific facts; he links vampirism to the blood disease porphyria, for example. (Rev: BL 3/15/09) [001.944]

21626 Pentland, Peter, and Pennie Stoyles. *Kitchen Science* (4–6). Illus. Series: Science and Scientists. 2002, Chelsea House LB $27.00 (978-0-7910-7014-7). 32pp. A clear overview of the scientific phenomena involved in basic foodstuffs as well as the various ways in which they are prepared and preserved, with illustrations, interesting sidebars, and information on careers in kitchen science. Also use *Party Science* and *Toy and Game Science* (both 2002). (Rev: HBG 3/03; SLJ 4/03) [641.5]

21627 Raab, Brigitte. *Where Does Pepper Come From? And Other Fun Facts* (K–3). Trans. from German by J. Alison James. Illus. by Manuela Olten. 2006, North-South $15.95 (978-0-7358-2070-8). A humorous and lively question-and-answer format provides answers to a wide variety of science questions. (Rev: SLJ 10/06)

21628 Rice, David L. *Lifetimes* (3–6). Illus. 1997, Dawn $16.95 (978-1-883220-58-7); paper $7.95 (978-1-883220-59-4). 32pp. Various activities are interspersed with facts about a number of animals, plants, and astronomical bodies. (Rev: BL 6/1–15/97; SLJ 2/98) [574.3]

21629 Rosinsky, Natalie M. *How Scientists Work* (3–5). Series: Simply Science. 2004, Compass Point LB $21.26 (978-0-7565-0596-7). 32pp. Introduces readers to the scientific method of research. (Rev: SLJ 8/04) [507]

21630 Ross, Michael Elsohn. *Re-Cycles* (K–2). Illus. by Gustav Moore. 2002, Millbrook LB $22.90 (978-0-7613-1818-7). 32pp. Readers learn how water and soil are constantly being recycled for reuse, and how humans can contribute to nature's efforts. (Rev: BL 11/1/02; HBG 3/03; SLJ 1/03) [551.3]

21631 Schwartz, David M. *Q Is for Quark: A Science Alphabet Book* (4–9). Illus. by Kim Doner. 2001, Tricycle $15.95 (978-1-58246-021-5). 64pp. An entertaining and informative alphabet book from atom to Zzzzzzzz that doesn't hesitate to tackle difficult topics. (Rev: HBG 3/02; SLJ 11/01) [500]

21632 *Science Detectives: How Scientists Solved Six Real-Life Mysteries* (3–5). Illus. by Rose Cowles. 2006, Kids Can $15.95 (978-1-55337-994-2); paper $8.95 (978-1-55337-995-9). 48pp. An interesting selection of mysteries that were eventually solved through scientific means — including a typhoid outbreak in New York and a plunge in the number of vultures in central Asia. (Rev: BL 10/15/06) [501]

21633 Shields, Carol Diggory. *BrainJuice: Science, Fresh Squeezed!* (4–7). Illus. by Richard Thompson. 2003, Handprint $14.95 (978-1-59354-005-0). 64pp. A humorous, rhyming look at grade-school science with appealing illustrations and useful mnemonic devices. (Rev: SLJ 3/04) [500]

21634 Stein, Sara Bonnett. *The Science Book* (4–8). Illus. by author. 1980, Workman paper $9.95 (978-0-89480-120-4). 288pp. A whole-earth approach to strange and fascinating science facts.

21635 Sullivan, Navin. *Time* (4–7). Series: Measure Up! 2006, Marshall Cavendish LB $20.95 (978-0-7614-2321-8). 48pp. This entertaining volume provides a history of the way humans have measured time, up to the present day and including the new rule for Daylight Saving Time. (Rev: LMC 8/07; SLJ 6/07) [529]

21636 Sullivan, Navin. *Weight* (4–7). Illus. Series: Measure Up! 2006, Marshall Cavendish LB $20.95 (978-0-7614-2324-9). 48pp. Topics such as gravity and buoyancy are covered in this well-designed book about weight. (Rev: LMC 8/07; SLJ 6/07)

21637 Swanson, Diane. *Nibbling on Einstein's Brain* (5–8). Illus. by Warren Clark. 2001, Firefly paper $14.95 (978-1-55037-686-9). 112pp. Swanson looks at "bad" science and examines the difference between sound scientific theory and hype, teaching kids how to ask the right questions when analyzing advertisers' claims. (Rev: BL 2/15/02; HBG 3/02; SLJ 11/01) [507.2]

21638 Swanson, Diane. *Turn It Loose: The Scientist in Absolutely Everybody* (4–6). Illus. by Warren Clark. 2004, Annick $29.95 (978-1-55037-851-1); paper $14.95 (978-1-55037-850-4). 120pp. Swanson offers activities to help young people polish their scientific skills and profiles a number of scientists and others who have demonstrated scientific thinking. (Rev: BL 6/1–15/04; SLJ 6/04) [500]

21639 Tocci, Salvatore. *Experiments with Magic* (2–4). Illus. Series: A True Book. 2003, Children's Pr. LB $25.00 (978-0-516-22788-7). 48pp. Basic scientific principles are demonstrated through

"magic" tricks in this attractive book that is suitable for beginning readers. (Rev: SLJ 4/04) [507.8]

21640 Wilkes, Angela. *Your World: A First Encyclopedia* (K–2). 1999, Kingfisher $24.95 (978-0-7534-5217-2). 320pp. Questions and answers are given on such topics as the universe, the environment, prehistoric life, plants, animals, the human body, people, and places. (Rev: BL 12/1/99; HBG 4/00; SLJ 2/00) [030]

21641 Wollard, Kathy. *How Come?* (5–9). 1993, Workman paper $12.95 (978-1-56305-324-5). Provides answers to some common and not-so-common questions about ordinary things. (Rev: BL 5/1/94) [500]

21642 Wollard, Kathy. *How Come Planet Earth?* (4–7). Illus. by Debra Solomon. 1999, Workman paper $12.95 (978-0-7611-1239-6). 332pp. This book contains 125 science questions asked by children involving subjects such as warts, dust, cholesterol, and volcanoes. (Rev: SLJ 5/00) [500]

Experiments and Projects

21643 Bardhan-Quallen, Sudipta. *Championship Science Fair Projects: 100 Sure-to-Win Experiments* (5–9). Illus. 2005, Sterling $19.95 (978-1-4027-1138-1). 208pp. Clearly defined science projects (more than 100 at varying levels of difficulty) are accompanied by lists of materials, illustrations, and extension activities. (Rev: BL 8/05; SLJ 9/05; VOYA 8/05) [507]

21644 Bardhan-Quallen, Sudipta. *Last-Minute Science Fair Projects* (4–7). Illus. 2007, Sterling $19.95 (978-1-4027-1690-4). 112pp. A guide to science experiments that can be done in a short amount of time using common household materials. (Rev: BL 5/15/07) [507.8]

21645 *The Big Book of Nature Projects* (4–6). Illus. 1997, Thames & Hudson paper $16.95 (978-0-500-01773-9). 128pp. An attractive large-format paperback that introduces a wide variety of nature projects for both indoors and outdoors with easy instructions. (Rev: BL 7/97; SLJ 1/98) [507.8]

21646 Buttitta, Hope. *It's Not Magic, It's Science! 50 Science Tricks that Mystify, Dazzle and Astound!* (4–6). Illus. by Tom LaBaff and Orrin Lundgren. 2005, Sterling $14.95 (978-1-57990-622-1). 80pp. Each "magic track" in this book demonstrates a scientific principle, making it a fun exploration of basic concepts. (Rev: SLJ 9/05) [793.8]

21647 Calhoun, Yael. *Plant and Animal Science Fair Projects Using Beetles, Weeds, Seeds, and More* (5–8). Illus. Series: Biology! Best Science Projects. 2005, Enslow LB $26.60 (978-0-7660-2368-0). 128pp. Great ideas for biology-based science fair projects, with plenty of information for performing and presenting each activity correctly plus helpful charts and graphs. (Rev: SLJ 7/06) [570]

21648 Carrow, Robert. *Put a Fan in Your Hat! Inventions, Contraptions, and Gadgets Kids Can Build* (5–8). Illus. by Rick Brown. 1997, McGraw-Hill paper $14.95 (978-0-07-011658-0). 139pp. Interesting projects include making a natural battery, building a motor, and creating a hat with a cooling fan. (Rev: BL 4/15/97; SLJ 5/97) [507]

21649 Chapman, Gillian, and Pam Robson. *Exploring Time* (3–5). Illus. 1995, Millbrook LB $19.90 (978-1-56294-559-6). 32pp. Fourteen projects of varying difficulty related to time, such as creating a timeline and a sundial. (Rev: BL 11/1/95; SLJ 3/96) [529]

21650 Cobb, Vicki. *See for Yourself: More Than 100 Experiments for Science Fairs and Projects* (3–8). Illus. by Dave Klug. 2001, Scholastic $16.95 (978-0-439-09010-0); paper $7.95 (978-0-439-09011-7). 192pp. A collection of experiments and activities arranged by topic, with a notation of the level of difficulty. (Rev: HBG 10/02; SLJ 3/02) [507.8]

21651 Cobb, Vicki, and Kathy Darling. *Wanna Bet? Science Challenges to Fool You* (3–6). Illus. by Meredith Johnson. 1993, Lothrop $15.00 (978-0-688-11213-4). 128pp. This book of experiments and projects for young people covers such areas as physics, chemistry, mathematics, physiology, and electricity. (Rev: BL 5/1/93; SLJ 8/93) [793]

21652 Cobb, Vicki, and Kathy Darling. *We Dare You! Hundreds of Science Bets, Challenges, and Experiments You Can Do at Home* (3–7). Illus. by True Kelley and Meredith Johnson. 2008, Skyhorse $19.95 (978-1-60239-225-0). 321pp. More than 200 well-explained experiments are presented in chapters with headings such as "Energy Entrapments" and "Mathematical Duplicity." (Rev: SLJ 9/08) [507.8]

21653 Cole, Joanna. *The Magic School Bus and the Science Fair Expedition* (2–4). Illus. by Bruce Degen. Series: Magic School Bus. 2006, Scholastic $15.99 (978-0-590-10824-9). 32pp. Ms. Frizzle and her students travel on the bus to a nearby museum in search of inspiration for the upcoming science fair. (Rev: BL 9/15/06) [507.8]

21654 Coulter, George, and Shirley Coulter. *Science in Art* (3–4). Illus. Series: Science Projects. 1995, Rourke LB $13.95 (978-0-86625-519-6). 32pp. Six science activities are included in this volume, each of which explores some aspect of art, color, or artists' materials. Companion volumes are *Science in Food* and *Science in History* (both 1995). (Rev: SLJ 1/96) [507]

21655 Duensing, Edward. *Talking to Fireflies, Shrinking the Moon: Nature Activities for All Ages* (5–9). Illus. 1997, Fulcrum paper $15.95 (978-1-55591-310-6). More than 40 nature activities are included in this volume, including how to hypnotize a frog, weave a daisy chain, and whistle for woodchucks. (Rev: VOYA 10/97) [507]

21656 Falk, John H., et al. *Bubble Monster: And Other Science Fun* (PS–3). Illus. by Charles C. Somerville. 1996, Chicago Review paper $17.95 (978-1-55652-301-4). 168pp. Five scientific areas — patterns, matter, communication, the human body, and technology — are covered in a series of activities that require some adult help. (Rev: SLJ 4/97) [507]

21657 Fox, Tom. *Snowball Launchers, Giant-Pumpkin Growers, and Other Cool Contraptions* (5–8). Illus. by Joel Holland. 2006, Sterling paper $9.95 (978-0-8069-5515-5). 127pp. A collection of 20 creative projects with clear instructions and explanations of scientific principles. (Rev: BL 1/1–15/07; SLJ 3/07)

21658 Gardner, Robert. *Kitchen Chemistry: Science Experiments to Do at Home* (4–8). Illus. 1989, Silver Burdett paper $4.95 (978-0-671-67576-9). 136pp. These entertaining and instructive experiments can be performed in the kitchen with everyday equipment and supplies. [542]

21659 Gardner, Robert. *Science Around the House* (4–6). Illus. 1989, Silver Burdett paper $4.95 (978-0-671-68139-5). 136pp. Simple experiments using everyday objects are detailed in this reissued project book.

21660 Gibson, Gary. *Making Shapes* (3–5). Photos by Roger Vlitos. Illus. by Tony Kenyon. Series: Science for Fun. 1995, Millbrook LB $22.90 (978-1-56294-631-9). 32pp. In double-page spreads, experiments in shape making and shifting are described, as well as how they illustrate various principles of science. (Rev: SLJ 3/96) [507]

21661 Gibson, Gary. *Making Things Change* (3–5). Illus. Series: Science for Fun. 1995, Millbrook LB $20.90 (978-1-56294-645-6). 32pp. Double-page spreads are used to introduce a series of experiments and projects that illustrate how objects and materials can change their forms and structures. (Rev: BL 12/15/95) [507.8]

21662 Graham, John, et al. *Hands-On Science* (4–6). Illus. by David Le Jars. Series: Hands-On. 2002, Kingfisher paper $10.95 (978-0-7534-5440-4). 160pp. More than 100 easy-to-follow, nicely presented experiments teach students about basic science concepts. (Rev: SLJ 8/02)

21663 Haduch, Bill. *Science Fair Success Secrets: How to Win Prizes, Have Fun, and Think Like a Scientist* (5–8). Illus. by Philip Scheuer. 2002, Dutton paper $10.99 (978-0-525-46534-8). 128pp. A handy and appealing introduction to how to conduct a science experiment, with examples of award-winning projects, a list of ideas, and metric conversion tables. (Rev: BL 12/1/02; SLJ 3/03) [507]

21664 Harris, Elizabeth Snoke. *First Place Science Fair Projects for Inquisitive Kids* (4–7). Illus. 2005, Sterling LB $19.95 (978-1-57990-493-7). 127pp. Project ideas in biology, chemistry, and physics mostly involve everyday materials and are presented in accessible text with an eight-week schedule and clear photographs. (Rev: SLJ 3/06) [507]

21665 Harris, Elizabeth Snoke. *Yikes! Wow! Yuck! Fun Experiments for Your First Science Fair* (4–7). Illus. by Nora Thompson. 2008, Sterling $12.95 (978-1-57990-930-7). 112pp. The breezy, light-hearted tone of this book will appeal to young scientists looking for simple but interesting projects. (Rev: BL 4/15/08; SLJ 6/08) [507.8]

21666 Hartzog, John Daniel. *Everyday Science Experiments in the Kitchen* (PS–3). Series: Science Suprises. 2000, Rosen $21.25 (978-0-8239-5456-8).

24pp. Eight simple experiments are outlined from using lemon juice to shine a penny to creating a celery straw. (Rev: SLJ 9/00) [509]

21667 Hauser, Jill F. *Gizmos and Gadgets: Creating Science Contraptions That Work (and Knowing Why)* (4–7). Illus. by Michael Kline. Series: Kids Can! 1999, Williamson paper $14.25 (978-1-885593-26-9). 144pp. Outlines the construction of all sorts of gadgets from objects found in kitchen and garage closets and relates each to such scientific topics as motion, energy, balancing, and gravity. (Rev: SLJ 1/00) [745]

21668 Hauser, Jill F. *Science Play! Beginning Discoveries for 2- to 6-Year-Olds* (PS–K). Illus. by Michael Kline. Series: Little Hands. 1998, Williamson paper $12.95 (978-1-885593-20-7). 135pp. Basic science concepts are taught in this book for preschoolers that contains 65 simple activities. (Rev: SLJ 1/99) [507.8]

21669 Hirschfeld, Robert, and Nancy White. *The Kids' Science Book: Creative Experiences for Hands-on Fun* (2–5). Illus. by Loretta Braren. Series: Kids Can! 1995, Williamson paper $14.25 (978-0-913589-88-5). 157pp. An interesting collection of games, experiments, and activities that illustrate various principles of science and are fun to perform. (Rev: SLJ 12/95) [507]

21670 Hurd, Will. *Changing States: Solids, Liquids, and Gases* (3–6). Illus. 2009, Heinemann LB $22.00 (978-1-4329-2312-9). 48pp. Experiments with easy-to-obtain materials and parental warnings. (Rev: BL 6/1–15/09) [530.4]

21671 Lempke, Donald B., and Thomas K. Adamson. *Lessons in Science Safety with Max Axiom, Super Scientist* (5–8). Illus. by Tod Smith. Series: Graphic Science. 2006, Capstone LB $26.60 (978-0-7368-6834-1). 32pp. This graphic-novel approach to teaching safe science procedures features an appealing adult. (Rev: BL 3/15/07) [507.8]

21672 Levine, Shar. *Sports Science* (3–5). Illus. by Leslie Johnstone. 2006, Sterling $19.95 (978-1-4027-1520-4). 80pp. A collection of 26 science experiments, each with a sports connection, that illustrate such scientific principles as gravity, aerodynamics, and buoyancy. (Rev: BL 12/1/06; SLJ 12/06) [507.8]

21673 Levine, Shar, and Leslie Johnstone. *Everyday Science: Fun and Easy Projects for Making Practical Things* (4–6). Illus. by Ed Shems. 1995, Wiley paper $9.95 (978-0-471-11014-9). 97pp. The science behind everyday objects is explored in this book of 25 simple projects under such headings as Light and Optics, Heat, Earth Science, Electricity, and Chemistry. (Rev: SLJ 8/95) [507]

21674 Levine, Shar, and Leslie Johnstone. *Science Around the World: Travel Through Time and Space with Fun Experiments and Projects* (3–6). Illus. by Laurel Aiello. 1996, Wiley paper $12.95 (978-0-471-11916-6). 84pp. This project book presents activities from ten countries around the world, including making paper and creating a sand timer. (Rev: SLJ 7/96) [507]

21675 Markle, Sandra. *Exploring Autumn: A Season of Science Activities, Puzzlers, and Games* (4–7). Illus. Series: Exploring Seasons. 1991, Avon paper $3.50 (978-0-380-71910-5). 160pp. Science, history, myth, quizzes, and more are combined in this book on seasonal activities in the classroom and home. (Rev: BL 1/1/91; SLJ 1/92) [574.5]

21676 Markle, Sandra. *Super Science Secrets: Exploring Nature Through Games, Puzzles and Activities* (1–3). Illus. 1997, Longstreet $14.95 (978-1-56352-396-0). 36pp. Scientific topics like evaporation, static electricity, and animal defenses are examined, with follow-up questions and simple experiments. (Rev: SLJ 9/97) [507]

21677 Mason, Adrienne. *Living Things* (K–4). Series: Starting with Science. 1998, Kids Can LB $14.95 (978-1-55074-343-2). 32pp. Basic science concepts about life are examined, using 13 simple experiments such as "worm farming," "hairy egg heads," and "baking beasts." (Rev: BL 5/15/98; HBG 9/98; SLJ 5/98) [507.8]

21678 Mercer, Bobby. *The Leaping, Sliding, Sprinting, Riding Science Book: 50 Super Sports Science Activities* (4–7). Illus. by Tom LaBaff. 2007, Sterling $14.95 (978-1-57990-785-3). 80pp. Sports moves are used to illustrate scientific principles in this activity book with step-by-step instructions, discussions of the science, and lots of lively illustrations. (Rev: BL 5/1/07; SLJ 5/07) [796]

21679 Muller, Eric. *While You're Waiting for the Food to Come* (4–6). Illus. 1999, Orchard $15.95 (978-0-531-30199-9); paper $8.95 (978-0-531-07144-1). 96pp. An appealing experiment book that contains simple projects, arranged like a menu, designed to be performed where food is served. (Rev: BCCB 9/99; BL 1/1–15/00; HBG 4/00; SLJ 10/99) [507]

21680 Murphy, Pat. *Exploratopia* (4–7). Illus. 2006, Little, Brown $29.99 (978-0-316-61281-4). 384pp. From San Francisco's Exploratorium, this is an interesting selection of facts, activities, and hands-on experiments that encourage students to learn about and explore the world around them. (Rev: BL 12/1/06; SLJ 1/07) [507.8]

21681 Murphy, Pat, et al. *The Science Explorer Out and About: Fantastic Science Experiments Your Family Can Do Anywhere!* (3–8). Illus. by Jason Gorski. Series: Exploratorium Science-at-Home-Book. 1997, Holt paper $12.95 (978-0-8050-4537-6). 127pp. A wide variety of science experiments are outlined, many that can be performed alone and others that require adult help. (Rev: SLJ 2/98) [507]

21682 Newcomb, Rain, and Bobby Mercer. *Crash It! Smash It! Launch It!* (5–8). Illus. by Rain Newcomb. 2006, Sterling $14.95 (978-1-57990-795-2). 80pp. More than 40 experiments provide great entertainment as well as scientific knowledge. (Rev: BL 11/1/06; SLJ 12/06) [507.8]

21683 Nye, Bill. *Bill Nye the Science Guy's Big Blast of Science* (5–8). Illus. 1993, Addison-Wesley paper $16.00 (978-0-201-60864-9). 172pp. Matter, heat, light, electricity, magnetism, weather, and space are among the topics introduced in this quick and entertaining tour of the world of science. (Rev: BL 2/15/94) [507.8]

21684 Potter, Jean. *Science in Seconds with Toys: Over 100 Experiments You Can Do in Ten Minutes or Less* (2–5). 1998, Wiley paper $12.95 (978-0-471-17900-9). 131pp. Each page contains a separate easy-to-perform activity that answers a question involving a simple scientific principle. (Rev: SLJ 4/98) [507.8]

21685 Richards, Roy. *101 Science Surprises: Exciting Experiments with Everyday Materials* (3–5). Illus. 1993, Sterling $17.95 (978-0-8069-8822-1). 104pp. The activities and experiments presented in this book represent various branches of science and vary in difficulty. (Rev: BL 9/1/93; SLJ 6/93) [507.8]

21686 Richards, Roy. *101 Science Tricks: Fun Experiments with Everyday Materials* (4–8). Illus. by Alex Pang. 1992, Sterling $16.95 (978-0-8069-8388-2). 104pp. Interesting, easy-to-do science and math activities emphasize the underlying principles. (Rev: BL 2/1/92; SLJ 1/92) [507.8]

21687 Ross, Michael E. *Sandbox Scientist: Real Science Activities for Little Kids* (PS–2). Illus. by Mary Anne Lloyd. 1995, Chicago Review paper $12.95 (978-1-55652-248-2). 206pp. Simple experiments and activities introduce young children to the principles involving such components as light and water. (Rev: BL 2/1/96) [372.3]

21688 Ross, Michael Elsohn. *Toy Lab* (4–6). Illus. by Tim Seeley. Series: You Are the Scientist. 2002, Carolrhoda LB $23.93 (978-0-87614-456-5). 48pp. Toys such as slinkies, silly putty, frisbees, and blocks are all put to good use as readers learn about gravity, flight, motion, and other basic concepts. (Rev: HBG 3/03; SLJ 2/03)

21689 Rybolt, Thomas R., and Leah M. Rybolt. *Science Fair Success with Scents, Aromas, and Smells* (5–8). Series: Science Fair Success. 2002, Enslow LB $26.60 (978-0-7660-1625-5). 112pp. Several science fair projects using the sense of smell are presented with clear instructions and easy-to-find materials. (Rev: BL 5/15/02; HBG 10/02; SLJ 11/02) [507]

21690 *Science Fairs: Ideas and Activities* (4–8). 1998, World Book $15.00 (978-0-7166-4498-9). Using many diagrams and logical step-by-step explanations, this work offers science projects in such areas as space, earth science, geology, botany, and machines. (Rev: SLJ 1/99) [507]

21691 Smith, Norman F. *How to Do Successful Science Projects*. Rev. ed. (5–8). Illus. 1990, Messner paper $5.95 (978-0-671-70686-9). This guide gives many fine tips and concentrates on the applications of the scientific method. (Rev: BL 7/90) [507.8]

21692 Sobey, Ed. *Wrapper Rockets and Trombone Straws: Science at Every Meal* (4–7). Illus. 1996, McGraw-Hill paper $14.95 (978-0-07-021745-4). 137pp. Using simple items found in restaurants such as glasses, straws, and napkins, a number of simple tricks and experiments are introduced. (Rev: BL 3/1/97; SLJ 6/97) [500]

21693 Tocci, Salvatore. *Experiments with Sports* (2–4). Illus. Series: True Books. 2003, Children's Pr. paper $6.95 (978-0-516-27807-0). 48pp. A book of experiments that demonstrate how basic scientific principles apply to sports. (Rev: SLJ 4/04) [507.8]

21694 Tocci, Salvatore. *Science Fair Success in the Hardware Store* (5–8). Series: Science Fair Success. 2000, Enslow LB $26.60 (978-0-7660-1287-5). 128pp. A group of science fair projects that use materials and objects found in a hardware store, with clear explanations of the scientific principles behind each project. (Rev: BL 4/15/00; HBG 10/00) [507]

21695 Tocci, Salvatore. *Science Fair Success Using Supermarket Products* (5–8). Series: Science Fair Success. 2000, Enslow LB $26.60 (978-0-7660-1288-2). 128pp. Using common items found in a supermarket, this work outlines a number of excellent science projects that demonstrate important scientific principles. (Rev: BL 4/15/00; HBG 10/00; SLJ 4/00) [507]

21696 Tocci, Salvatore. *Using Household Products* (5–8). Series: Science Fair Success. 2002, Enslow LB $26.60 (978-0-7660-1626-2). This useful volume outlines a number of science fair projects that can be done using materials found around the house. (Rev: BL 4/15/02; HBG 10/02) [509]

21697 UNESCO. *700 Science Experiments for Everyone* (5–8). Illus. 1964, Doubleday $19.95 (978-0-385-05275-7). 252pp. An excellent collection of experiments, noted for its number of entries and breadth of coverage.

21698 VanCleave, Janice. *Janice VanCleave's Animals* (4–6). Illus. Series: Spectacular Science Projects. 1992, Wiley paper $10.95 (978-0-471-55052-5). 84pp. This book contains many easy-to-follow projects involving animals. (Rev: BL 1/1/93; SLJ 2/93) [591]

21699 VanCleave, Janice. *Janice VanCleave's Biology for Every Kid: 101 Easy Experiments That Really Work* (4–7). Illus. 1989, Wiley paper $12.95 (978-0-471-50381-1). 224pp. This book outlines simple experiments that use readily available equipment and supplies. (Rev: BL 2/15/90) [574]

21700 VanCleave, Janice. *Janice VanCleave's Guide to More of the Best Science Fair Projects* (4–8). 2000, Wiley paper $14.95 (978-0-471-32627-4). 156pp. After general information about the scientific method, research, and presentation, this book outlines about 50 projects in the areas of astronomy, biology, earth science, engineering, physical science, and mathematics. (Rev: SLJ 5/00) [509]

21701 VanCleave, Janice. *Janice VanCleave's Guide to the Best Science Fair Projects* (3–6). Illus. 1997, Wiley paper $14.95 (978-0-471-14802-9). 144pp. An excellent experiment book that covers 50 science projects in the life and physical sciences, astronomy, mathematics, and engineering. (Rev: BL 3/15/97; SLJ 4/97) [507.8]

21702 VanCleave, Janice. *Janice VanCleave's 203 Icy, Freezing, Frosty, Cool and Wild Experiments* (4–7). 1999, Wiley paper $12.95 (978-0-471-25223-8). 122pp. An excellent book filled with easily performed experiments in such areas as biology, chemistry, earth science, and physics. (Rev: SLJ 4/00) [507.8]

21703 VanCleave, Janice. *Janice VanCleave's 202 Oozing, Bubbling, Dripping and Bouncing Experiments* (4–6). Illus. 1996, Wiley paper $12.95 (978-0-471-14025-2). 120pp. Fun and learning are combined in these experiments that investigate astronomy, biology, chemistry, earth science, and physics. (Rev: SLJ 2/97) [507]

21704 Vecchione, Glen. *100 First Prize Make It Yourself Science Fair Projects* (4–8). Illus. 1998, Sterling $19.95 (978-0-8069-0703-1). The projects outlined in this good resource for project ideas range from the simple to complex and cover a wide range of branches of science. (Rev: SLJ 4/99) [507]

21705 Voth, Danna. *Kidsource: Science Fair Handbook* (5–8). Illus. 1998, Lowell House paper $9.95 (978-1-56565-514-0). This source provides excellent advice on selecting, preparing, and presenting science projects, with material on choosing workable topics, equipment needed, safety, measuring devices, and record keeping. (Rev: BL 2/15/99; SLJ 5/99) [507]

21706 Wiese, Jim. *Magic Science: 50 Jaw-Dropping, Mind-Boggling, Head-Scratching Activities for Kids* (4–6). Illus. 1998, Wiley paper $12.95 (978-0-471-18239-9). 128pp. The author explains the science behind 50 magic tricks, which are divided into six categories: matter, reactions, water, air, force and energy, and electricity and magnetism. (Rev: BL 5/15/98) [507.8]

21707 Wiese, Jim. *Rocket Science: 50 Flying, Floating, Flipping, Spinning Gadgets Kids Create Themselves* (3–6). Illus. 1995, Wiley paper $12.95 (978-0-471-11357-7). 128pp. Principles related to physics, electricity, optics, acoustics, and other branches of science are explored in a number of interesting projects and experiments. (Rev: BL 12/1/95; SLJ 3/96) [507.8]

21708 Wyatt, Valerie. *The Science Book for Girls and Other Intelligent Beings* (3–5). Illus. by Pat Cupples. 1997, Kids Can paper $12.95 (978-1-55074-113-1). 80pp. Introduces various science experiments from different branches of science, as well as several female scientists, like Mary Leakey and Sally Ride. (Rev: SLJ 10/97) [509]

21709 Wyler, Rose. *Science Fun with Peanuts and Popcorn* (2–4). Illus. 1986, Simon & Schuster paper $4.95 (978-0-671-62452-1). 48pp. Simple experiments that explain scientific principles. Also use: *Science Fun with Mud and Dirt* (1986). (Rev: BL 7/86; SLJ 11/86)

Astronomy

General

21710 Asimov, Isaac. *The Birth of Our Universe* (5–8). Illus. Series: Isaac Asimov's 21st Century Library of the Universe. 2005, Gareth Stevens LB $26.00 (978-0-8368-3964-7). 32pp. This is an update of a 1995 edition on the origins of the universe, with illustrations and photographs. (Rev: BL 3/1/05) [523.1]

21711 Asimov, Isaac. *How Did We Find Out About Comets?* (5–7). Illus. 1975, Walker LB $10.85 (978-0-8027-6204-7). 64pp. An introduction to comets and our knowledge and attitudes about them since ancient times. [523.6]

21712 Berger, Melvin, and Gilda Berger. *Do Stars Have Points? Questions and Answers About Stars and Planets* (3–5). Illus. Series: Question and Answer. 1999, Scholastic $12.95 (978-0-590-13080-6); paper $5.95 (978-0-590-08570-0). 48pp. Using a question-and-answer format, this book covers important facts in astronomy involving the solar system and the universe. (Rev: BL 11/1/99; SLJ 2/00) [523]

21713 Bonnet, Bob, and Dan Keen. *Science Fair Projects: Flight, Space and Astronomy* (4–6). Illus. by Frances Zweifel. 1997, Sterling $16.95 (978-0-8069-9450-5). 95pp. A collection of 53 clever astronomy-related experiments that vary considerably in difficulty and in the nature of the equipment involved. (Rev: SLJ 2/98) [520]

21714 Bortz, Fred. *Collision Course! Cosmic Impacts and Life on Earth* (4–7). Illus. 2001, Millbrook LB $25.90 (978-0-7613-1403-5). 72pp. A straightforward discussion of an intriguing subject that includes material on past collisions and on detecting and perhaps deflecting future "near Earth objects." (Rev: BL 5/1/01; HBG 10/01; SLJ 5/01) [523.44]

21715 Bredeson, Carmen. *What Do Astronauts Do?* (1–3). Illus. Series: I Like Space! 2008, Enslow LB $22.60 (978-0-7660-2942-2). 32pp. "What do astronauts eat and how do they go to the bathroom?"

Simple design and text with a question-and-answer format and color photographs present fascinating space-related facts. (Rev: SLJ 9/08) [629.45]

21716 Campbell, Ann-Jeanette. *The New York Public Library: Amazing Space: A Book of Answers for Kids* (5–8). Illus. 1997, Wiley paper $12.95 (978-0-471-14498-4). This question-and-answer book introduces space exploration, the solar system, individual planets, galaxies, and related phenomena. (Rev: SLJ 7/97) [523]

21717 Davis, Kenneth C. *Don't Know Much About Space* (3–7). Illus. by Sergio Ruzzier. Series: Don't Know Much About. 2001, HarperCollins LB $19.89 (978-0-06-028602-6); paper $6.99 (978-0-06-440835-6). 144pp. An entertaining, informal, question-and-answer introduction to astronomy. (Rev: BL 9/15/01; HBG 3/02; SLJ 8/01) [520]

21718 Delafosse, Claude, et al. *Hidden World: Space* (PS–2). Series: First Discovery. 2000, Scholastic $12.95 (978-0-439-14826-9). 24pp. For the very young, this is a colorful, well-illustrated introduction to space and what it means. (Rev: BL 8/00) [523]

21719 Dyer, Alan. *Space* (5–8). Illus. Series: Insiders. 2007, Simon & Schuster $16.99 (978-1-4169-3860-6). 64pp. An introduction to the big bang, the solar system, stars and nebulas, galaxies, and so forth, with eye-catching illustrations. (Rev: LMC 10/07; SLJ 12/07) [520]

21720 Fleisher, Paul. *The Big Bang* (5–8). Illus. Series: Great Ideas in Science. 2005, Twenty-First Century LB $27.93 (978-0-8225-2133-4). 80pp. Students with a real interest in science will benefit most from this overview of theories about the creation of the universe, from creation myths onward. (Rev: BL 12/1/05; SLJ 12/05) [523.1]

21721 Gardner, Robert. *Far-Out Science Projects About Earth's Sun and Moon* (3–6). Illus. by Tom LaBaff. Series: Rockin' Earth Science Experiments. 2007, Enslow LB $23.93 (978-0-7660-2736-7). 48pp. A book of basic projects that show how the sun and moon affect our planet. (Rev: SLJ 8/07) [523.7078]

21722 Gifford, Clive. *The Kingfisher Facts and Records Book of Space: The Ultimate Information Database* (4–6). Illus. 2001, Kingfisher $14.95 (978-0-7534-5363-6). 64pp. Among the topics covered in this fact-packed volume are the solar system, the Milky Way and other galaxies, astronomical equipment, and man's journeys into space. (Rev: HBG 10/02; SLJ 12/01) [520]

21723 Grady, Monica. *Stardust from Space* (K–3). Illus. by Lucia deLeiris. 2007, Frances Lincoln $16.95 (978-1-84507-570-5). 32pp. The formation of planets and other objects in the solar system is explored and accompanied by large, appealing illustrations. (Rev: BL 12/1/07; SLJ 4/08) [523.1125]

21724 Graham, Ian. *Voyage Through Space* (4–6). Illus. by Sebastian Quigley and Gary Slater. Series: Discoverology. 2007, Barron's $18.99 (978-0-7641-6062-2). 30pp. With wheels, pull-tabs, flaps, and pop-ups, this effective volume gives a nice introduction to the solar system, stars, and galaxies, as well as details of human exploration; more suitable for display than circulation. (Rev: SLJ 1/08) [520]

21725 Graun, Ken, and Suzanne Maly. *Our Galaxy and the Universe* (4–6). Illus. Series: 21st Century Astronomy. 2002, Ken Pr. $15.95 (978-1-928771-08-1). 36pp. Excellent illustrations add to the appeal of this look at the stars. (Rev: SLJ 12/02)

21726 Halpern, Paul. *Faraway Worlds: Planets Beyond Our Solar System* (3–6). Illus. by Lynette R. Cook. 2004, Charlesbridge $16.95 (978-1-57091-616-8); paper $6.95 (978-1-57091-617-5). 32pp. This strikingly illustrated slim volume looks at planets exising beyond our solar system and discusses how they are studied by scientists. (Rev: BL 8/04; SLJ 3/05) [523.2]

21727 Hirst, Robin, and Sally Hirst. *My Place in Space* (3–4). Illus. by Roland Harvey. 1992, Orchard paper $6.95 (978-0-531-07030-7). 40pp. A sky show from earth to solar system to the outer reaches of the universe. (Rev: BCCB 3/90; BL 4/1/90; HB 5/91; SLJ 4/90) [520]

21728 Jackson, Ellen. *The Mysterious Universe: Supernovae, Dark Energy, and Black Holes* (5–8). Illus. Series: Scientists in the Field. 2008, Houghton $18.00 (978-0-618-56325-8). 64pp. Astronomer Alex Filippenko and his work at key observatories is the focus of this book that also describes such phenomena as supernovae and black holes in accessible text with informative diagrams and spectacular photographs. (Rev: BL 6/1–15/08; SLJ 6/08) [523.8]

21729 Jefferis, David. *Black Holes and Other Bizarre Space Objects* (5–8). Illus. Series: Science Frontiers. 2006, Crabtree LB $26.60 (978-0-7787-2856-6); paper $8.95 (978-0-7787-2870-2). 32pp. Double-page spreads with color photographs and informative sidebars explore the life of stars, black holes, gamma-ray bursts, space telescopes, and so forth. (Rev: BL 4/1/06) [523.8]

21730 Jefferis, David. *Star Spotters: Telescopes and Observatories* (4–6). Illus. Series: Our Solar System. 2009, Crabtree LB $26.60 (978-0-7787-3725-4); paper $8.95 (978-0-7787-3742-1). 32pp. A brief, attractive, and easy-to-understand overview of telescopes and observatories — both on Earth and orbiting far above — and of the important information they provide; with a "Young Astronomer" section. Also use *Space Probes: Exploring Beyond Earth* and *Galaxies: Immense Star Islands* (both 2009). (Rev: LMC 10/09; SLJ 5/09) [522]

21731 Love, Ann, and Jane Drake. *The Kids' Book of the Night Sky* (4–6). Illus. by Heather Collins. 2004, Kids Can $19.95 (978-1-55337-357-5). 144pp. The authors offer a potpourri of basic astronomy facts, sky folklore, charts, and suggestions for art and science projects, leavened with light humor and helpful illustrations. (Rev: BL 4/15/04; SLJ 7/04) [520]

21732 Macy, Sue. *Are We Alone? Scientists Search for Life in Space* (4–8). Illus. 2004, National Geographic $18.95 (978-0-7922-6567-2). 96pp. Modern scientific efforts to find extraterrestrial life are discussed along with the popularity of flying saucers, crop circles, and other theories. (Rev: BL 10/1/04; SLJ 12/04*) [001.9]

21733 Maynard, Christopher. *The Young Scientist Book of Stars and Planets* (4–7). Illus. 1978, EDC LB $14.95 (978-0-88110-313-7); paper $6.95 (978-0-86020-094-9). 32pp. Attractive illustrations and plentiful experiments and projects add to this book's appeal.

21734 Mechler, Gary. *National Audubon Society First Field Guide: Night Sky* (4–6). Series: First Field Guide. 1999, Scholastic $17.95 (978-0-590-64085-5); paper $8.95 (978-0-590-64086-2). 160pp. This atlas to the night sky identifies and gives information on the most common stars and constellations. (Rev: BL 10/15/99) [523]

21735 Miles, Lisa, and Alastair Smith. *The Usborne Complete Book of Astronomy and Space* (3–4). Illus. by Gary Bines and Peter Bull. 1998, EDC paper $14.95 (978-0-7460-3104-9). 96pp. A clear introduction to astronomy and famous astronomers, plus tips for stargazers and sky photographers. (Rev: SLJ 1/99) [523]

21736 Miotto, Enrico. *The Universe: Origins and Evolution* (5–8). Series: Beginnings. 1995, Raintree LB $24.26 (978-0-8114-3334-1). This basic outline of the history of the universe begins with the Big Bang theory and finishes with the "Big Crunch" that may end time. (Rev: BL 4/15/95) [523.1]

21737 Moeschl, Richard. *Exploring the Sky: 100 Projects for Beginning Astronomers* (5–8). Illus. 1992, Chicago Review paper $16.95 (978-1-55652-160-7). 320pp. Many ideas for experiments and observations in an information-packed book. (Rev: BL 5/1/89)

21738 Oleksy, Walter. *Mapping the Skies* (5–7). Series: Watts Library: Geography. 2002, Watts LB $25.50 (978-0-531-12031 6); paper $8.95 (978-0-531-16635-2). 64pp. From the ancient Greeks and Romans through Galileo to astronomers today, this is a history of how the stars, planets, and space have been mapped. (Rev: BL 10/15/02) [520]

21739 Orr, Tamra. *The Telescope* (4–8). Series: Inventions That Shaped the World. 2004, Watts LB $30.50 (978-0-531-12344-7). 80pp. Describes the invention of the telescope, the impact of the knowledge imparted, and future possibilities. (Rev: BL 4/1/04; SLJ 2/05) [522]

21740 Oxlade, Chris. *The Mystery of Black Holes* (4–6). Series: Can Science Solve? 1999, Heinemann LB $22.79 (978-1-57572-808-7). 32pp. Using a dynamic format, this book supplies a brief overview of theories concerning the existence of black holes. (Rev: SLJ 1/00) [523]

21741 Petty, Kate. *The Sun Is a Star: And Other Amazing Facts About the Universe* (1–3). Illus. by Francis Phillips and Ian Thompson. Series: I Didn't Know That. 1997, Millbrook LB $19.90 (978-0-7613-0567-5). 32pp. As well as introducing the sun, this book describes other parts of the solar system, black holes, the Milky Way, and other parts of the universe. (Rev: SLJ 9/97) [523]

21742 Rabe, Tish. *There's No Place Like Space: All About Our Solar System* (K–3). Illus. by Aristides Ruiz. Series: The Cat in the Hat's Learning Library. 1999, Random LB $11.99 (978-0-679-99115-1). 44pp. Using rhyming couplets and cartoon-like illustrations, this is a basic introduction to space and the solar system. (Rev: HBG 9/00; SLJ 3/00) [523]

21743 Rau, Dana Meachen. *Black Holes* (3–5). Illus. Series: Our Solar System. 2005, Compass Point $23.93 (978-0-7565-0849-4). 32pp. Good coverage of a tricky topic, describing black holes' nature and formation, with photographs and illustrations adding to the appeal. (Rev: SLJ 8/05) [523.8]

21744 Redfern, Martin. *The Kingfisher Young People's Book of Space* (4–6). 1998, Kingfisher $19.95 (978-0-7534-5136-6). 95pp. This work contains a short history of astronomy, a tour of the universe with material on galaxies and the solar system, a rundown on space exploration, and a list of questions about space still to be answered. (Rev: HBG 3/99; SLJ 2/99) [523]

21745 Roza, Greg. *The Incredible Story of Telescopes* (3–6). Illus. Series: A Kid's Guide to Incredible Technology. 2004, Rosen LB $19.95 (978-0-8239-6715-5). 24pp. The history and technology of telescopes are discussed in concise terms, with material on Hubble and on future developments. (Rev: SLJ 2/05) [681]

21746 Ruiz, Andres L. *The Origin of the Universe* (4–9). Series: Sequences of Earth and Space. 1997, Sterling $12.95 (978-0-8069-9744-5). In simple, concise language, this work discusses various theories concerning the origin of the universe, including the Big Bang theory. (Rev: BL 12/15/97) [523]

21747 Schorer, Lonnie Jones. *Kids to Space: A Space Traveler's Guide* (5–9). Illus. 2006, Apogee paper $29.95 (978-1-894959-42-1). 304pp. Organized in almost 100 categories, this volume includes thousands of questions about space posed by children and answered by experts including NASA engineers, former astronauts, and astronomy professors. (Rev: SLJ 12/06) [500.5]

21748 Simon, Seymour. *The Universe* (3–6). 1998, Morrow LB $17.89 (978-0-688-15302-1). In a series of double-page spreads, this book introduces topics related to the universe, including nebulas, galaxies, the Big Bang, quasars, stars, and planets. (Rev: HBG 3/99; SLJ 5/98) [523]

21749 Sparrow, Giles. *Cosmic! The Ultimate 3-D Guide to the Universe* (3–6). Illus. by Richard Ferguson. 2008, DK $24.99 (978-0-7566-4021-7). 16pp. Pop-up illustrations, gatefold pages, lift-flaps, illustrations, and text present information on the universe. (Rev: BLO 12/16/08) [523.1]

21750 Stott, Carole. *Astronomy* (4–6). Illus. 2003, Kingfisher $16.95 (978-0-7534-5582-1). 64pp. This engaging introduction to astronomy explores the history of the science, how the universe was viewed by earlier civilizations, and the tools of the astronomer. (Rev: HBG 4/04; SLJ 11/03) [520]

21751 Verdet, Jean-Pierre. *The Universe* (PS–2). Illus. Series: First Discovery. 1997, Scholastic $11.95 (978-0-590-96212-4). 24pp. From the endless cosmos to exploding stars and a view of our blazing sun, this brilliantly illustrated book introduces the universe. (Rev: BL 2/1/98) [520]

21752 Vogt, Gregory L. *Deep Space Astronomy* (5–8). Illus. 1999, Twenty-First Century LB $25.90 (978-0-7613-1369-4). 80pp. This look beyond our own star system covers such topics as the development of space-based detectors, information-gathering techniques, and recent discoveries. (Rev: BL 1/1–15/00; HBG 3/00; SLJ 2/00) [520]

21753 Whitfield, David. *Northern Lights* (2–4). Illus. Series: Science Matters. 2006, Weigl $24.45 (978-1-59036-413-0). 24pp. Readers will be fascinated to learn about the phenomenon of the northern lights and the science behind it. Photographs and other graphics, as well as related information and activities, add to this book's appeal. (Rev: SLJ 5/07)

21754 Wiese, Jim. *Cosmic Science: Over 40 Gravity-Defying, Earth-Orbiting, Space-Cruising Activities for Kids* (4–6). Illus. 1997, Wiley paper $12.95 (978-0-471-15852-3). 128pp. Principles of astronomy and space technology are explored through a series of engaging projects with common materials that involve topics like gravity, orbits, planets, and space travel. (Rev: BL 7/97; SLJ 7/97) [929.4]

21755 Wills, Susan, and Steven Wills. *Astronomy: Looking at the Stars* (5–8). Illus. Series: Innovators. 2001, Oliver $21.95 (978-1-881508-76-2). 144pp. A good starting point for research into astronomy, with profiles of individuals including Ptolemy, Copernicus, Galileo, and Newton. (Rev: HBG 10/02; SLJ 2/02) [520.922]

Earth

21756 Alessandrello, Anna. *The Earth: Origins and Evolution* (4–8). Illus. Series: Beginnings — Origins and Evolution. 1995, Raintree LB $24.26 (978-0-8114-3331-0). 48pp. An oversize book with lavish illustrations that discusses the theories concerning the formation of the earth, its structure and composition, and ways in which it is changing. (Rev: BL 4/15/95; SLJ 6/95) [550]

21757 Bailey, Jacqui. *Sun Up, Sun Down: The Story of Day and Night* (2–4). Illus. by Matthew Lilly. Series: Science Works. 2004, Picture Window LB $26.60 (978-1-4048-0567-5). 31pp. A clear and attractive look at the Earth's rotation and the changes in light, explaining how light rays travel, how shadows are formed, and so forth. (Rev: SLJ 8/04) [525.35]

21758 Branley, Franklyn M. *What Makes Day and Night?* (1–3). Illus. by Arthur Dorros. 1986, Harper-Collins paper $5.99 (978-0-06-445050-8). 32pp. A clear, simple explanation of the rotation of the earth. (Rev: BL 3/15/86; SLJ 9/86)

21759 Davis, Kenneth C. *Don't Know Much About Planet Earth* (3–6). Illus. by Tom Bloom. Series: Don't Know Much About. 2001, HarperCollins LB $19.89 (978-0-06-028600-2); paper $7.99 (978-0-06-440834-9). 144pp. A question-and-answer format with cartoonlike drawings makes an attractive backdrop for this overview of the earth's physical and environmental features, as well as today's political divisions and a timeline of historical highlights. (Rev: BL 12/15/01; HBG 3/02; SLJ 8/01) [910]

21760 Gallant, Roy A. *Earth's Place in Space* (5–8). Series: The Story of Science. 1999, Benchmark LB $28.50 (978-0-7614-0963-2). 80pp. Using a chronological approach, this account traces our knowledge of the earth and its place in the solar system and space. (Rev: BL 2/15/00; HBG 3/00; SLJ 2/00) [525]

21761 Karas, G. Brian. *On Earth* (K–3). Illus. 2005, Penguin $16.99 (978-0-399-24025-6). 32pp. Large double-page spreads featuring attractive illustrations discuss the passage of time, the seasons, and the Earth's obit, rotation, and tilt. (Rev: BL 5/1/05; SLJ 5/05) [525]

21762 Kerrod, Robin. *Planet Earth* (4–6). Series: Planet Library. 2000, Lerner LB $21.27 (978-0-8225-3902-5). 32pp. This book discusses the earth's formation, its journey through space, its drifting continents, its waters and weather, and its many forms of life. (Rev: BL 10/15/00; HBG 3/01) [525]

21763 Miller, Ron. *Earth and the Moon* (5–7). Illus. Series: Worlds Beyond. 2003, Twenty-First Century LB $25.90 (978-0-7613-2358-7). 96pp. NASA photographs and computer-generated images are used throughout this account of the origin, composition, and evolution the Earth and its moon. (Rev: HBG 10/03; SLJ 8/03) [525]

21764 Nadeau, Isaac. *Learning About Earth's Cycles with Graphic Organizers* (3–6). 2005, Rosen LB $21.25 (978-1-4042-2807-8). This title uses a wide variety of graphic organizers, including concept webs, compare/contrast charts, Venn diagrams, graphs, timelines, and KWL charts, to introduce readers to Earth's natural cycles, including tidal ebb and flow; seasonal changes; and day and night. (Rev: SLJ 11/05)

21765 Nicolson, Cynthia P. *The Earth* (2–5). Illus. Series: Starting with Space. 1997, Kids Can $14.95 (978-1-55074-314-2). 40pp. Appropriate folktales and projects are included, along with information about the earth and night and day. (Rev: BL 9/1/97; SLJ 9/97) [525]

21766 Patent, Dorothy Hinshaw. *Shaping the Earth* (4–7). Illus. 2000, Clarion $18.00 (978-0-395-85691-8). 88pp. The evolution of the earth is traced in this compelling book that describes how the surface has changed and continues to change, with coverage of plate tectonics, ice ages, natural disasters, and descriptions of its natural wonders. (Rev: BL 3/15/00; HBG 10/00; SLJ 4/00) [550]

21767 Pettigrew, Mark. *Planet Earth* (3–6). Series: Science World. 2004, Stargazer LB $27.10 (978-1-932799-28-6). 32pp. Basic facts about the Earth — its structure, movement, atmosphere, and so forth — are introduced in concise text with good diagrams, photographs, and a project, all presented in picture-book format. (Rev: BL 12/1/04) [551]

21768 Riley, Peter D. *Earth* (4–5). Series: Cycles in Science. 1998, Heinemann LB $22.79 (978-1-57572-620-5). 32pp. This colorfully illustrated book looks at the earth's major cycles, including orbits, rotations, seasons, time zones, and the sun's life. (Rev: SLJ 7/98) [525]

21769 Ross, Michael E. *Earth Cycles* (1–3). Illus. by Gustav Moore. 2001, Millbrook $22.40 (978-0-7613-1815-6). 32pp. The earth's rotation pattern is described with material on the reasons for night and day and the causes of seasons, plus why the moon appears to change shape during a lunar month. (Rev: BL 1/1–15/01; HBG 10/01) [525]

21770 Vogt, Gregory L. *Earth* (2–4). Illus. Series: Gateway Solar System. 1996, Millbrook LB $22.90 (978-1-56294-602-9). 32pp. A beginning introduction to the planet, its composition, and its place in the solar system. (Rev: BL 4/15/96; SLJ 5/96) [550]

21771 Whitehouse, Patricia. *The Earth* (2–4). Illus. Series: Space Explorer. 2004, Heinemann LB $24.21 (978-1-4034-5150-7). 32pp. A slim overview of the Earth, discussing its composition, axis, and rotation, with fascinating photographs from space and final Earth facts. [550]

Moon

21772 Bourgeois, Paulette. *The Moon* (3–4). Illus. by Bill Slavin. Series: Starting with Space. 1997, Kids Can $14.95 (978-1-55074-157-5). 40pp. This introduction to the moon includes material on its features, phases, and tides, important lunar landings, and legends about the moon from around the world. (Rev: SLJ 9/97) [523.3]

21773 Branley, Franklyn M. *What the Moon Is Like* (1–3). Illus. by True Kelley. Series: Let's-Read-and-Find-Out. 2000, HarperCollins LB $15.89 (978-0-06-027993-6). 40pp. An updated version of this standard title that includes important new material about the moon and its composition. (Rev: BL 6/1–15/00; HBG 9/00; SLJ 7/00) [559.9]

21774 Crelin, Bob. *Faces of the Moon* (2–4). Illus. by Leslie Evans. 2009, Charlesbridge $16.95 (978-1-57091-785-1). 36pp. The moon's phases are explained through poetry, prose, and illustrations. (Rev: BL 7/09; SLJ 7/09) [523.3]

21775 Gardner, Robert. *Science Project Ideas About the Moon* (4–7). Illus. Series: Science Project Ideas. 1997, Enslow LB $25.26 (978-0-89490-844-6). 96pp. After giving basic information about the moon, this book outlines projects involving ways of observing the moon and how to make models to show its movements. (Rev: BL 12/1/97; HBG 3/98) [523.3]

21776 Gibbons, Gail. *The Moon Book* (2–4). Illus. 1997, Holiday House LB $16.95 (978-0-8234-1297-6). 32pp. An introductory description of the moon, its orbit and phases, its place in eclipses, and its effects of the earth's oceans. (Rev: BCCB 7–8/97; BL 5/1/97; SLJ 4/97) [523.3]

21777 Graham, Ian. *The Best Book of the Moon* (2–5). Series: The Best Book Of. 1999, Kingfisher $10.95 (978-0-7534-5174-8). 31pp. A fine introduction to the moon with material on its composition, exploration including the *Apollo* and *Prospector* missions, and lunar and solar eclipses. (Rev: HBG 9/99; SLJ 5/99) [523.3]

21778 Kerrod, Robin. *The Moon* (4–6). Series: Planet Library. 2000, Lerner LB $21.27 (978-0-8225-3900-1). 32pp. The moon's formation, history, orbit, and makeup are covered, plus material on the moon landing. (Rev: BL 10/15/00; HBG 3/01; SLJ 11/00) [523.3]

21779 Krupp, E. C. *The Moon and You* (3–6). Illus. by Robin R. Krupp. 1993, Macmillan LB $15.00 (978-0-02-751142-0). 48pp. In picture-book format, this account covers all the basic facts about the moon, including its formation, phases, and exploration. (Rev: BL 11/1/93; SLJ 2/94) [523.3]

21780 *Our Satellite: The Moon* (3–6). Illus. Series: Window on the Universe. 1994, Barron's $12.95 (978-0-8120-6369-1). 32pp. In double-page spreads, features of the moon are explained, such as lunar eclipses and the appearance of the moon's far side. (Rev: BL 4/15/94; SLJ 5/94) [523.3]

21781 Rosen, Sidney. *Where Does the Moon Go?* (2–4). Illus. 1992, Carolrhoda LB $19.93 (978-0-87614-685-9). 40pp. In excellent photos, clever illustrations, and simple text, the moon and its phases are introduced. (Rev: SLJ 11/92) [523.3]

21782 Simon, Seymour. *The Moon* (2–4). 2003, Simon & Schuster $17.95 (978-0-689-83563-6). 32pp. This revised edition adds new photographs and color reproductions. (Rev: BL 10/15/03; SLJ 1/04) [559.9]

21783 Siy, Alexandra. *Footprints on the Moon* (3–5). Illus. 2001, Charlesbridge $16.95 (978-1-57091-408-9). 32pp. This heavily illustrated book covers human fascination with the moon throughout history and then focuses on Project Apollo and the moon landings. (Rev: BL 2/1/01; HBG 10/01; SLJ 2/01) [629.45]

21784 Tomecek, Steve. *Moon* (K–3). Illus. by Lisa Chauncy Guida. Series: Jump into Science. 2005, National Geographic LB $25.90 (978-0-7922-8304-1). 32pp. An entertaining introduction to the moon for young children. (Rev: BL 3/1/05) [523.3]

21785 Whitehouse, Patricia. *The Moon* (2–4). Illus. Series: Space Explorer. 2004, Heinemann LB $24.21 (978-1-4034-5152-1). 32pp. A slim overview of the moon, covering topics including its size, composition, climate, and different phases. (Rev: BL 7/02; HBG 10/02) [523.3]

Planets

21786 Aguilar, David A. *11 Planets: A New View of the Solar System* (5–8). Illus. 2008, National Geographic $16.95 (978-1-4263-0236-7). 48pp. The author includes the eight planets and three dwarf planets in his calculation of the main celestial bodies in the solar system; attractive color paintings and photographs accompany the text. (Rev: BL 5/1/08; SLJ 9/08) [523]

21787 Berger, Melvin. *Discovering Jupiter: The Amazing Collision in Space* (3–6). Illus. by Tom Leonard. 1995, Scholastic paper $4.95 (978-0-590-48824-2). 55pp. After covering the general facts we know about Jupiter, this account tells of the Comet Shoemaker-Levy 9 and its crash into the planet. (Rev: SLJ 3/96) [523.4]

21788 Bortolotti, Dan. *Exploring Saturn* (4–8). Illus. 2003, Firefly $19.95 (978-1-55297-766-8); paper $9.95 (978-1-55297-765-1). 64pp. This highly visual volume with readable text presents facts about Saturn, explains how and when we acquired this knowledge, and looks at the Cassini-Huygens mission. (Rev: BL 12/1/03; SLJ 5/04) [523.46]

21789 Branley, Franklyn M. *The Planets in Our Solar System* (K–2). Illus. by Kevin O'Malley. Series: Let's-Read-and-Find-Out. 1998, HarperCollins LB $15.89 (978-0-06-027770-3); paper $5.99 (978-0-06-445178-9). 31pp. The planets of our solar system are described — their similarities, differences, and distinctive characteristics. (Rev: SLJ 6/98) [523.4]

21790 Cole, Michael D. *Living on Mars: Mission to the Red Planet* (4–6). Illus. Series: Countdown to Space. 1999, Enslow LB $23.93 (978-0-7660-1121-2). 48pp. This book covers our findings through the late 1990s from the exploration of Mars and discusses the possibility of visiting and colonizing this planet in the future. (Rev: BL 12/1/98; HBG 9/99; SLJ 4/99) [919.9]

21791 Feinstein, Stephen. *Saturn* (4–7). Illus. Series: Solar System. 2005, Enslow LB $25.26 (978-0-7660-5304-5). 48pp. Useful for reports, this clearly written title includes links to Web sites for further research. (Rev: SLJ 12/05) [523.46]

21792 Gallant, Roy A. *Planets* (2–4). Illus. Series: Kaleidoscope. 2000, Marshall Cavendish LB $25.64 (978-0-7614-1033-1). 48pp. With colorful illustrations, each of the planets of our solar system is introduced with a brief descriptive text. (Rev: BL 1/1–15/01; HBG 10/01) [523.4]

21793 Gibbons, Gail. *The Planets*. Rev. ed. (K–2). Illus. by author. 2005, Holiday House $16.95 (978-0-8234-1957-9). There are few changes in this revised edition of the popular introductory guide to the planets that was first published in 1993. (Rev: SLJ 11/05) [523.4]

21794 Gifford, Clive. *How to Live on Mars* (3–6). Illus. by Scoular Anderson. Series: How To. 2001, Watts LB $16.00 (978-0-531-14647-7). 96pp. Experiments back up the concepts introduced in this discussion of the possibilities of traveling to and living on Mars. (Rev: SLJ 4/02) [523.4]

21795 Goldstein, Margaret J. *Uranus* (2–3). Illus. Series: Our Universe. 2003, Lerner LB $22.60 (978-0-8225-4654-2). 32pp. This solid introduction to Uranus examines the huge planet's physical characteristics, distance from the sun, rotation axis, and 15 moons. Also use *Saturn* and *Venus* (both 2003). (Rev: SLJ 1/04) [523.47]

21796 Gustafson, John. *Planets, Moons and Meteors: The Young Stargazer's Guide to the Galaxy* (4–8). Illus. 1992, Simon & Schuster LB $12.95 (978-0-671-72534-1); paper $6.95 (978-0-671-72535-8). 64pp. This guidebook tells how and when to observe the solar system and provides basic information about the planets. (Rev: BL 11/1/92) [523]

21797 Kerrod, Robin. *Jupiter* (4–6). Illus. Series: Planet Library. 2000, Lerner $21.27 (978-0-8225-3907-0). 32pp. Jupiter, the largest of the planets, is presented in text and pictures with material on its formation, makeup, atmosphere, and the space probes that have gathered information about it. Two others in this series are *Mars* and *Mercury and Venus*. (Rev: BL 10/15/00; HBG 3/01) [523.45]

21798 Kerrod, Robin. *Saturn* (4–6). Series: Planet Library. 2000, Lerner LB $21.27 (978-0-8225-3909-4). 32pp. Breathtaking photographs and a clear text introduce Saturn, the planet of swirling clouds, bright rings, and 18 moons. (Rev: BL 10/15/00; HBG 3/01; SLJ 1/01) [523.4]

21799 Kerrod, Robin. *Uranus, Neptune, and Pluto* (4–6). Series: Planet Library. 2000, Lerner LB $21.27 (978-0-8225-3908-7). 32pp. An exploration of the planets on the edge of our solar system, beginning with the ringed gas giants, Uranus and Neptune, and ending with mysterious Pluto. (Rev: BL 10/15/00; HBG 3/01; SLJ 1/01) [513.4]

21800 Landau, Elaine. *Pluto: From Planet to Dwarf* (2–4). Illus. Series: True Books: Space. 2008, Scholastic LB $26.00 (978-0-531-12566-3). 48pp. Pluto's changed status to dwarf planet is clearly explained along with information about a space probe scheduled to reach Pluto in 2015. (Rev: BL 12/1/07) [523.48]

21801 Leedy, Loreen, and Andrew Schuerger. *Messages from Mars* (2–4). 2006, Holiday $16.95 (978-0-8234-1954-8). 40pp. In 2106, six children take a trip to Mars, tour the planet, visit the sites of century-old landings, and send messages home reporting on their travels and discoveries. (Rev: BL 9/15/06; SLJ 10/06) [523.43]

21802 Miller, Ron. *Jupiter* (5–8). Series: Worlds Beyond. 2002, Millbrook LB $25.90 (978-0-7613-

2356-3). 64pp. An excellent oversize volume that explores the largest of the planets with amazing full-page color illustrations and a detailed text. Also use *Venus* (2002). (Rev: BL 8/02; HBG 3/03; SLJ 8/02) [523.4]

21803 Miller, Ron. *Mercury and Pluto* (5–8). Series: Worlds Beyond. 2003, Millbrook LB $25.90 (978-0-7613-2361-7). 80pp. Information on these planets and their discoveries is presented clearly, with helpful illustrations. Also use *Saturn* (2003). (Rev: BL 11/15/03; SLJ 12/03) [523.4]

21804 Miller, Ron. *Saturn* (5–8). Series: Worlds Beyond. 2003, Millbrook LB $25.90 (978-0-7613-2360-0). 80pp. A colorful volume that describes the discovery of the solar system and supplies details about the planet Saturn and its many rings. (Rev: BL 11/15/03; SLJ 12/03) [523.4]

21805 Miller, Ron. *Uranus and Neptune* (5–7). Illus. Series: Worlds Beyond. 2003, Twenty-First Century LB $25.90 (978-0-7613-2357-0). 80pp. NASA photographs and computer-generated images are used throughout this account of the discovery and exploration of these two planets and what we know about their origin, composition, and evolution. (Rev: HBG 10/03; SLJ 8/03) [523.47]

21806 Moore, Patrick. *The Planets* (K–3). Illus. Series: Starry Sky. 1995, Millbrook LB $23.90 (978-1-56294-624-1). 24pp. The size and makeup of the planets are discussed in this beginning astronomy book that also looks at the possibility of interplanetary travel. (Rev: SLJ 7/95) [523.4]

21807 Nicolson, Cynthia P. *The Planets* (2–5). Series: Starting with Space. 1998, Kids Can $12.95 (978-1-55074-512-2). Using a question-and-answer format and NASA mission photos, this concise book introduces the planets to a young audience. (Rev: BL 8/98; HBG 3/99; SLJ 10/98) [523.4]

21808 O'Connell, Kim A. *Mercury* (4–7). Illus. Series: Solar System. 2005, Enslow LB $25.26 (978-0-7660-5209-3). 48pp. A blend of easy-to-understand narrative, vivid color photographs, and links to related online resources introduce Mercury. Also use *Pluto* (2005). (Rev: SLJ 12/05) [523.4]

21809 Rau, Dana Meachen. *Jupiter* (3–5). Illus. Series: Our Solar System. 2002, Compass Point LB $23.93 (978-0-7565-0198-3). 32pp. An appealing introduction to the planet, with large photographs. Also use *Mars*, *Mercury*, and *Venus* (all 2002). (Rev: BL 5/15/02; SLJ 7/02) [523.45]

21810 Scherer, Glenn, and Marty Fletcher. *Neptune* (4–6). Illus. Series: The Solar System. 2005, Enslow LB $25.26 (978-0-7660-5211-6). 48pp. A useful overview of our knowledge about Neptune (including its planetoid, Sedna), with 30 recommended Internet links. (Rev: SLJ 11/05)

21811 Scherer, Glenn, and Marty Fletcher. *Uranus* (4–6). Illus. Series: The Solar System. 2005, Enslow LB $25.26 (978-0-7660-5307-6). 48pp. A useful overview of our knowledge about Uranus, with 30 recommended Internet links. (Rev: SLJ 11/05) [523.4]

21812 Scott, Elaine. *Mars and the Search for Life* (5–8). Illus. 2008, Clarion $17.00 (978-0-618-

76695-6). 60pp. Is there water on the Red Planet? Scott addresses this and other questions while discussing what we know about the planet, the various explorations that have already taken place, and possible future missions. (Rev: BCCB 12/08; BL 12/1/08; HB 1/09; SLJ 1/09) [576.8]

21813 Scott, Elaine. *When is a Planet Not a Planet?* (3–6). Illus. 2007, Clarion $17.00 (978-0-618-89832-9). 40pp. Pluto's reclassification serves as the introduction for a discussion of astronomy and the discovery of planets and other celestial bodies. (Rev: BL 9/1/07; HB 11/07; LMC 1/08; SLJ 10/07) [523.48]

21814 Simon, Seymour. *Destination: Jupiter.* Rev. ed. (3–5). Illus. 1998, Morrow $15.95 (978-0-688-15620-6). 32pp. This update of the 1985 edition includes information on the findings of the Hubble space telescope, material on the *Galileo* space probe, and basic information about the planet. (Rev: BL 4/15/98; HBG 9/98; SLJ 5/98) [523.45]

21815 Simon, Seymour. *Jupiter* (2–4). Illus. 1988, Morrow paper $6.95 (978-0-688-08403-5). 32pp. A detailed look at Jupiter, enhanced by photographs taken mostly from unmanned spacecraft. (Rev: BCCB 12/85; BL 9/15/85; SLJ 10/85)

21816 Simon, Seymour. *Mars* (2–5). Illus. 1987, Morrow paper $6.99 (978-0-688-09928-2). 32pp. Lucid text and spectacular photos highlight this detailed study of the Red Planet. (Rev: BL 10/15/87; HB 11/87; SLJ 12/87)

21817 Simon, Seymour. *Neptune* (4–8). Illus. 1991, Morrow $17.89 (978-0-688-09632-8). 32pp. The voyage of *Voyager II* as it swept past Neptune provided scientists with more information on this planet than they had ever had. (Rev: BCCB 4/91; BL 2/15/91; HB 5/91; SLJ 4/91) [523.4]

21818 Simon, Seymour. *Planets Around the Sun* (1–3). Series: See More Readers. 2002, North-South $13.95 (978-1-58717-145-1); paper $3.95 (978-1-58717-146-8). 32pp. The plants and the solar system are introduced in this beginning reader. (Rev: BL 7/02; HBG 10/02; SLJ 6/02) [523.2]

21819 Simon, Seymour. *Saturn* (2–4). Illus. 1985, Morrow paper $6.99 (978-0-688-08404-2). 32pp. Lots of information about Saturn and its rings, enhanced with color photographs. (Rev: BL 9/15/85; HB 1/86; SLJ 10/85)

21820 Simon, Seymour. *Uranus* (2–5). Illus. 1987, Morrow paper $7.99 (978-0-688-09929-9). 32pp. Descriptions and photos of its five moons highlight this look at Uranus, which was not recognized as a planet until 1781. (Rev: BL 10/15/87; HB 11/87; SLJ 12/87)

21821 Skurzynski, Gloria. *Discover Mars* (4–6). 1998, National Geographic $17.95 (978-0-7922-7099-7). 44pp. An overview of what we know about Mars, a rundown on space probes in the area, and plenty of illustrations — some in 3–D that require special glasses, which are provided. (Rev: SLJ 11/98) [523.4]

21822 Stefoff, Rebecca. *Pluto* (3–5). Illus. Series: Blastoff. 2003, Marshall Cavendish LB $28.50 (978-0-7614-1404-9). 64pp. A fascinating, well-

illustrated account of the discovery of the planet Pluto and the continuing scientific debate about whether it is a true planet or not. (Rev: BL 4/1/03; HBG 3/03) [523.48]

21823 Stone, Tanya L. *Mercury* (3–5). Illus. Series: Blastoff. 2003, Marshall Cavendish LB $28.50 (978-0-7614-1403-2). 64pp. Stone explains the history of our knowledge of Mercury and what we may learn from new expeditions to the planet; a glossary, bibliography, and list of Web sites follow the text. (Rev: BL 4/1/03; HBG 3/03) [523.41]

21824 Vogt, Gregory L. *Jupiter* (3–4). Series: Galaxy. 2000, Capstone LB $22.60 (978-0-7368-0512-4). 24pp. This book and the others listed cover basic facts and material on atmospheres, rings, physical features, and moons. Others are *Neptune, Pluto,* and *Uranus* (all 2000). (Rev: HBG 9/00; SLJ 9/00) [523.4]

21825 Vogt, Gregory L. *Mars* (3–6). Illus. Series: Gateway Solar System. 1994, Millbrook LB $22.90 (978-1-56294-392-9). 31pp. Color and black-and-white photos and drawings highlight this introduction to Mars and its geography. Also use *Pluto* (1994). (Rev: BL 7/94; SLJ 5/94) [523.4]

21826 Vogt, Gregory L. *Mercury* (3–6). Illus. Series: Gateway Solar System. 1994, Millbrook LB $22.90 (978-1-56294-390-5). 32pp. A useful introduction to the planet Mercury that includes material on Project Mariner and its findings. (Rev: BL 7/94; SLJ 5/94) [523.4]

21827 Vogt, Gregory L. *Pluto* (2–4). Illus. Series: Gateway Solar System. 1994, Millbrook LB $22.90 (978-1-56294-393-6). 32pp. This introduction to Pluto describes its origins plus a history of what we know about it and things we should find out in the future. Also use *Venus* (1994). (Rev: BL 7/94; SLJ 5/94) [523.1]

21828 Vogt, Gregory L. *Saturn* (3–5). Illus. Series: Gateway Solar System. 1993, Millbrook LB $19.90 (978-1-56294-332-5). 32pp. This introduction to Saturn includes material on its cloud layers, magnetic field, and thousands of rings. (Rev: SLJ 11/93) [523.2]

21829 Vogt, Gregory L. *Uranus* (3–5). Illus. Series: Gateway Solar System. 1993, Millbrook LB $22.90 (978-1-56294-330-1). 32pp. Sharp, full-color illustrations and a brief text introduce the salient features of Uranus, including its moons, rings, and atmosphere. (Rev: SLJ 11/93) [523.2]

Solar System

21830 Branley, Franklyn M. *The Sun and the Solar System* (4–6). Illus. Series: Secrets of Space. 1996, Twenty-First Century LB $25.90 (978-0-8050-4475-1). 80pp. Traces the origin of the solar system and the place of the earth and its moon within it. (Rev: BL 12/15/96; SLJ 1/97) [523.2]

21831 Bredeson, Carmen. *What Is the Solar System?* (1–3). Illus. Series: I Like Space! 2008, Enslow LB $22.60 (978-0-7660-2944-6). 32pp. "Is Pluto a planet?" Simple design and text with a question-and-answer format and color photographs present fascinating space-related facts. (Rev: SLJ 9/08) [523.2]

21832 Croswell, Ken. *Ten Worlds: Everything That Orbits the Sun* (4–6). 2006, Boyds Mills $19.95 (978-1-59078-423-5). 56pp. A large-format exploration of the solar system with striking images of the planets. (Rev: BL 8/06; SLJ 7/06) [523.4]

21833 Gallan, Roy. *Comets, Asteroids, and Meteorites* (2–4). Series: Kaleidoscope. 2000, Marshall Cavendish LB $25.64 (978-0-7614-1034-8). 48pp. An up-to-date account that combines good visuals with an exciting text in this examination of these visitors from space. (Rev: BL 1/1–15/01; HBG 10/01) [523]

21834 Goldsmith, Mike. *Solar System* (K–3). Series: Kingfisher Young Knowledge. 2004, Kingfisher $8.95 (978-0-7534-5773-3). 47pp. Using two-page chapters with large text and eye-catching photographs, planets, asteroids, comets, and meteoroids are introduced. (Rev: SLJ 4/05) [523.4]

21835 Graun, Ken. *Our Earth and the Solar System* (4–6). Illus. 2001, Ken Pr. $15.95 (978-1-928771-02-9). 36pp. A large-format, interesting guide to the solar system that also looks at the equipment we use to look at these bodies. (Rev: BL 5/1/01; SLJ 6/01) [523.2]

21836 Hansen, Rosanna, and Robert A. Bell. *My First Book About Space* (3–6). Illus. 1985, Simon & Schuster $13.00 (978-0-671-60262-8). The solar system is explained, including each planet, discussed in terms of appearance, atmosphere, orbit, and revolutions. (Rev: BCCB 7–8/86; BL 12/1/85; SLJ 2/86)

21837 Jenkins, Alvin. *Next Stop Neptune: Experiencing the Solar System* (2–5). Illus. by Steve Jenkins. 2004, Houghton $16.00 (978-0-618-41603-5). 40pp. Colorful collage illustrations subsitute for photographs in this well-written introduction to the solar system. (Rev: BL 10/15/04; SLJ 10/04) [523.2]

21838 Kerrod, Robin. *Asteroids, Comets, and Meteors* (4–6). Series: Planet Library. 2000, Lerner LB $21.27 (978-0-8225-3905-6). 32pp. This book explores the smallest members of the solar system and tells how they were formed, how they shaped the surface of the planets and moons, and how they sometimes light up our sky. (Rev: BL 10/15/00; HBG 3/01) [523.4]

21839 Kerrod, Robin. *The Solar System* (4–6). Illus. Series: Planet Library. 2000, Lerner $21.27 (978-0-8225-3903-2). 32pp. A discussion on the formation of the sun, the planets, their moons, and the asteroid belt is followed by additional coverage of topics such as orbiting stars, space exploration, and the search for extraterrestrial life. (Rev: BL 10/15/00; HBG 3/01; SLJ 11/00) [523.2]

21840 Kudlinski, Kathleen V. *Boy, Were We Wrong About the Solar System!* (1–3). Illus. by John Rocco. 2008, Dutton $15.99 (978-0-525-46979-7). 32pp. Kudlinski provides a lighthearted overview of some of the scientific concepts of the universe that have proved quite wrong. (Rev: BCCB 11/08; BL 12/1/08; LMC 1/09; SLJ 11/08) [523.2]

21841 Leedy, Loreen. *Postcards from Pluto: A Tour of the Solar System* (1–3). Illus. 1993, Holiday House LB $17.95 (978-0-8234-1000-2). 32pp. A group of children are introduced to the solar system via a spaceship tour conducted by a robot, Dr. Quasar. (Rev: BL 10/15/93; SLJ 10/93) [523.2]

21842 Marsh, Carole. *Asteroids, Comets, and Meteors* (4–6). Illus. Series: Secrets of Space. 1996, Twenty-First Century LB $25.90 (978-0-8050-4473-7). 64pp. The history of our knowledge of these bodies from outer space is traced, with descriptions of the nature of each. (Rev: BL 12/15/96; SLJ 1/97) [523.4]

21843 Miller, Ron. *The Sun* (5–8). Illus. Series: Worlds Beyond. 2002, Millbrook LB $25.90 (978-0-7613-2355-6). 64pp. Miller explores the nature and structure of the sun and the importance of solar energy. (Rev: BL 4/1/02; HBG 10/02; SLJ 5/02) [523.7]

21844 Mitton, Jacqueline. *The Planet Gods: Myths and Facts About the Solar System* (2–4). Illus. by Christina Balit. 2008, National Geographic LB $25.90 (978-1-4263-0449-1); paper $7.95 (978-1-4263-0448-4). 32pp. Gorgeous artwork is just one of the highlights of this title about space that includes lush language, poetic references, solid facts, and information on mythology. (Rev: BLO 1/13/09) [523.2]

21845 Moore, Patrick. *The Sun and Moon* (K–3). Illus. Series: Starry Sky. 1995, Millbrook LB $23.90 (978-1-56294-622-7). 24pp. A description of the sun and moon is given, with an explanation of their movements and eclipses. (Rev: SLJ 7/95) [523]

21846 Peddicord, Jane Ann. *Night Wonders* (2–4). Illus. 2005, Charlesbridge paper $6.95 (978-1-57091-878-0). 32pp. Eye-catching full-color images of the moon, sun, stars, and planets are paired with appealing verse and brief descriptive narrative. (Rev: SLJ 4/05) [523]

21847 Poynter, Margaret. *Killer Asteroids* (3–6). Illus. Series: Weird and Wacky Science. 1996, Enslow LB $23.93 (978-0-89490-616-9). 48pp. Violent clashes involving asteroids and the earth are described, along with coverage of a comet's encounter with Jupiter. (Rev: SLJ 5/96) [551.3]

21848 Rau, Dana Meachen. *The Solar System* (2–3). 2000, Compass Point LB $21.26 (978-0-7565-0036-8). 32pp. After discussing the sun, the author conducts a quick tour of the solar system including meteors, comets, and moons. (Rev: SLJ 2/01) [523.4]

21849 Rosen, Sidney. *Can You Hitch a Ride on a Comet?* (1–3). Illus. by Dean Lindberg. Series: A Question of Science. 1993, Carolrhoda LB $19.93 (978-0-87614-773-3). 40pp. Using a question-and-answer format, all sorts of information is given about comets, including their formation, discovery, and tracking. (Rev: BL 10/15/93) [525.6]

21850 Simon, Seymour. *Comets, Meteors, and Asteroids* (3–5). Illus. 1994, Morrow LB $14.93 (978-0-688-12710-7). 32pp. These three space bodies are described, with material on their composition and differences. (Rev: BL 9/15/94; SLJ 8/94) [523.6]

21851 Simon, Seymour. *Our Solar System* (2–6). Illus. 1992, Morrow $20.89 (978-0-688-09993-0). 72pp. A quick tour of the solar system, with many of NASA's striking photos. (Rev: BL 10/15/92; HB 11/92; SLJ 10/92) [523.2]

21852 Theodorou, Rod. *Across the Solar System* (2–4). Series: Amazing Journeys. 2000, Heinemann LB $22.79 (978-1-57572-486-7). 32pp. In this journey into outer space there are double-page spreads with information on each planet including distance from the sun, size, and length of a day and year. (Rev: HBG 3/01; SLJ 7/00) [523.4]

21853 VanCleave, Janice. *Janice VanCleave's Solar System: Mind-Boggling Experiments You Can Turn into Science Fair Projects* (4–6). Illus. by Laurel Aiello. Series: Spectacular Science Projects. 2000, Wiley paper $10.95 (978-0-471-32204-7). 90pp. Twenty interesting experiments involving the solar system are outlined with material on how to turn them into science projects. (Rev: SLJ 6/00) [523.4]

21854 Vogt, Gregory L. *Asteroids, Comets, and Meteors* (2–4). Illus. by Mark Alan Stamaty. Series: Gateway Solar System. 1996, Millbrook LB $22.90 (978-1-56294-601-2). 32pp. A beginning introduction to these celestial bodies and their characteristics. (Rev: BL 4/15/96; SLJ 5/96) [523.6]

21855 Whitehouse, Patricia. *The Planets* (2–4). Illus. Series: Space Explorer. 2004, Heinemann LB $24.21 (978-1-4034-5153-8). 32pp. A slim survey of the solar system and the individual planets, defining what makes a planet and ending with a listing of quick facts.

Stars

21856 Asimov, Isaac. *The Life and Death of Stars* (5–8). Illus. Series: Isaac Asimov's 21st Century Library of the Universe. 2005, Gareth Stevens LB $26.00 (978-0-8368-3967-8). 32pp. A revised, well-illustrated edition of a previously published book, this discusses the birth of stars, profiles different types of stars, and looks at the future of our Sun. Also in this series: *Black Holes, Pulsars, and Quasars*, *The Milky Way and Other Galaxies*, *Our Planetary System*, and *Comets and Meteors* (all 2005). (Rev: BL 3/1/05; SLJ 8/05)

21857 Bendick, Jeanne. *The Stars: Lights in the Night Sky* (2–4). Illus. by Chris Forsey. Series: Early Bird Astronomy. 1991, Millbrook LB $19.90 (978-1-878841-00-1). 32pp. Ideas and theories about stars and their formation are presented in a clear and simple text and with many diagrams. (Rev: BL 9/1/91; SLJ 8/91) [523.8]

21858 Berger, Melvin, and Gilda Berger. *Where Are the Stars During the Day? A Book About Stars* (3–5). Illus. by Blanche Sims. Series: Discovery Readers. 1993, Ideals paper $4.50 (978-0-8249-8607-0). 48pp. An easy-to-read book that introduces

the stars, sun, and constellations. (Rev: BCCB 4/93; SLJ 5/93) [523]

21859 Branley, Franklyn M. *The Big Dipper* (K–2). Illus. by Ed Emberley. 1991, HarperCollins paper $5.99 (978-0-06-445100-0). 32pp. An introduction to the composition, mythology, and location of the Big and Little Dippers.

21860 Branley, Franklyn M. *The Sky Is Full of Stars* (2–4). Illus. by Felicia Bond. 1981, HarperCollins paper $5.99 (978-0-06-445002-7). 40pp. A simple introduction to constellations and star watching.

21861 Branley, Franklyn M. *Star Guide* (4–6). Illus. by Ellen Eagle. 1997, Macmillan paper $9.10 (978-0-02-862019-0). 64pp. An exploration of what stars are made of, how they change, and how they are formed. (Rev: BL 8/87; SLJ 9/87)

21862 Croswell, Ken. *See the Stars* (4–8). Illus. 2000, Boyds Mills $16.95 (978-1-56397-757-2). 32pp. Twelve constellations are introduced in double-page spreads, with material on where and when to look for them. (Rev: BL 11/1/00; HBG 3/01; SLJ 10/00) [523]

21863 Gallan, Roy. *Stars* (2–4). Series: Kaleidoscope. 2000, Marshall Cavendish LB $25.64 (978-0-7614-1036-2). 48pp. This book introduces stars, how they are born and die, and their constellations. (Rev: BL 1/1–15/01; HBG 10/01) [523]

21864 Gibbons, Gail. *Galaxies, Galaxies!* (2–3). Illus. by author. 2006, Holiday House $16.95 (978-0-8234-2002-5). 32pp. In addition to describing five forms of galaxies, Gibbons discusses telescopes and the study of astronomy. (Rev: SLJ 12/06) [523.1]

21865 Gibbons, Gail. *Stargazers* (1–3). Illus. 1992, Holiday House LB $16.95 (978-0-8234-0983-9). 32pp. With full-color artwork, the author explains what stars are and how we look at them. (Rev: BCCB 1/93; BL 10/15/92; SLJ 10/92) [520]

21866 Gustafson, John. *Stars, Clusters and Galaxies* (5–8). Illus. Series: Young Stargazer's Guide to the Galaxy. 1993, Simon & Schuster LB $18.95 (978-0-671-72536-5); paper $6.95 (978-0-671-72537-2). 64pp. Introduces stars, binary stars, star clusters, nebulae, and galaxies, and provides tips for viewing the night sky through binoculars and telescopes. (Rev: BL 7/93; SLJ 6/93; VOYA 10/93) [523.8]

21867 MacKall, Dandi Daley. *Seeing Stars* (PS–K). Illus. by Claudine Gevry. 2006, Simon & Schuster $9.99 (978-1-4169-0361-1). 16pp. An introduction to the constellations for very young children, with sparkling gold outlining stars that shine above people of many backgrounds. (Rev: BL 5/1/06) [520]

21868 Mitton, Jacqueline. *Once upon a Starry Night: A Book of Constellations* (K–4). Illus. by Christina Balit. 2004, National Geographic $16.95 (978-0-7922-6332-6). 26pp. Ten brief, richly illustrated tales about the constellations are drawn from the mythology of ancient Greece and Rome. (Rev: BL 1/1–15/04; SLJ 1/04) [523.8]

21869 Mitton, Jacqueline. *Zodiac* (2–4). Illus. by Christina Balit. 2005, Frances Lincoln $16.95 (978-1-84507-074-8). 44pp. This is an attractive introduction to the 12 constellations that make up the zodiac, also providing information on the fundamentals of astronomy and on the mythology surrounding these stars. (Rev: BL 11/15/05; SLJ 1/06) [133.5]

21870 Mitton, Jacqueline. *Zoo in the Sky: A Book of Animal Constellations* (K–3). Illus. by Christina Balit. 1998, National Geographic $17.95 (978-0-7922-7069-0). 32pp. This attractive introduction to the animal constellations uses sparkling silver stars to outline each of them in the night sky. (Rev: BL 11/1/98; HBG 3/99; SLJ 12/98) [523.8]

21871 Moore, Patrick. *The Stars* (K–3). Illus. Series: Starry Sky. 1995, Millbrook LB $23.90 (978-1-56294-623-4). 24pp. A beginning astronomy book that describes the birth and death of stars and the composition of the Milky Way and other galaxies. (Rev: SLJ 7/95) [523.8]

21872 Nicolson, Cynthia P. *The Stars* (4–6). 1998, Kids Can $14.95 (978-1-55074-524-5). The stars are introduced in a question-and-answer format with good photographs and a glossary of terms. (Rev: BL 8/98; HBG 3/99; SLJ 10/98) [523.8]

21873 Nicolson, Cynthia Pratt. *Discover the Stars* (1–3). Illus. by Bill Slavin. Series: Kids Can Read. 2006, Kids Can $14.95 (978-1-55337-898-3); paper $3.95 (978-1-55337-899-0). 32pp. Using a question-and-answer format, this easy reader introduces basic information about the stars, including constellations, galaxies, the typical life cycle of a star, and how we observe them. (Rev: BL 3/15/06; SLJ 8/06) [523.8]

21874 Pearce, Q. L. *The Stargazer's Guide to the Galaxy* (4–8). Illus. by Mary Ann Fraser. 1991, Tor paper $6.99 (978-0-8125-9423-2). 60pp. In this introduction to star gazing in the Northern Hemisphere, material covered includes a look at the night sky in each of the four seasons. (Rev: SLJ 12/91) [523]

21875 Purslow, Frances. *Constellations* (2–4). Illus. Series: Science Matters. 2006, Weigl $24.45 (978-1-59036-410-9). 24pp. An introduction to the constellations for the young reader or researcher with photographs and other graphics as well as an astronomy-related craft. (Rev: SLJ 5/07)

21876 Rau, Dana Meachen. *The Milky Way and Other Galaxies* (3–5). Illus. Series: Our Solar System. 2005, Compass Point $23.93 (978-0-7565-0853-1). 32pp. After a discussion of our own galaxy, Rau describes others including quasars, clusters, and superclusters; photographs and illustrations add to the appeal. (Rev: SLJ 8/05) [523.1]

21877 Rey, H. A. *Find the Constellations*. 2nd ed. (4–6). Illus. by author. 2008, Houghton $20.00 (978-0-547-13140-5); paper $9.99 (978-0-547-13178-8). 72pp. This updated version includes an explanation of why Pluto is no longer a planet, new data for all the planets, charts, and a list of current books for further reading. (Rev: SLJ 2/09) [523.8]

21878 Rosen, Sidney. *Where's the Big Dipper?* (2–4). Illus. by Dean Lindberg. Series: A Question of Science. 1996, Carolrhoda $14.95 (978-0-87614-883-9). 40pp. In a question-and-answer format, this book supplies a simple introduction to deep space, with a focus on the Big Dipper. (Rev: SLJ 4/96) [523]

21879 Sasaki, Chris. *Constellations: A Glow-in-the-Dark Guide to the Night Sky* (1–4). Illus. by Alan Flinn. 2006, Sterling $12.95 (978-1-4027-0385-0). 48pp. Introduces some of the best-known constellations, with the mythology behind them, and glow-in-the-dark outlines that will show when the lights are turned off. (Rev: SLJ 8/06) [523.8]

21880 Simon, Seymour. *Galaxies* (2–5). Illus. 1988, Morrow paper $7.99 (978-0-688-10992-9). 32pp. Engrossing photographs highlight this look at galaxies. (Rev: BCCB 4/88; BL 3/1/88; SLJ 5/88)

21881 Simon, Seymour. *The Stars* (3–5). Illus. 1986, Morrow $16.89 (978-0-688-05856-2); paper $6.99 (978-0-688-09237-5). 32pp. Large photos and diagrams highlight the story of the life cycles of stars, giving a sense of their great numbers and relationship to earth. (Rev: BCCB 10/86; BL 9/1/86; SLJ 12/86)

21882 Tomecek, Steve. *Stars* (K–3). Illus. by Sachiko Yoshikawa. 2003, National Geographic $16.95 (978-0-7922-6955-7). 32pp. A boy introduces young readers to the stars in this book that includes a star activity. (Rev: BL 2/1/03; HBG 10/03; SLJ 5/03) [523.8]

21883 Whitehouse, Patricia. *The Stars* (2–4). Illus. Series: Space Explorer. 2004, Heinemann LB $24.21 (978-1-4034-5156-9). 32pp. A slim overview of stars, looking at the Milky Way and other galaxies, the ways in which stars are born and grow, and the changing night sky. [523.8]

Sun and the Seasons

21884 Anderson, Maxine. *Explore Spring! 25 Great Ways to Learn About Spring* (1–4). Illus. by Alexis Frederick-Frost. 2007, Nomad paper $12.95 (978-0-9785037-4-1). 92pp. This activity book with good solid science, engaging experiments, and humorous illustrations looks at such topics as the seasons, spring's role in the growth of plants and trees, and spring weather. (Rev: LMC 11/07; SLJ 10/07)

21885 Bourgeois, Paulette. *The Sun* (2–5). Illus. Series: Starting with Space. 1997, Kids Can $14.95 (978-1-55074-158-2). 40pp. As well as providing information about the sun, stars, and the seasons, this work contains folktales and projects. (Rev: BL 9/1/97; SLJ 9/97) [523.7]

21886 Branley, Franklyn M. *The Sun: Our Nearest Star* (1–3). Illus. by Don Madden. 1988, HarperCollins LB $14.89 (978-0-690-04678-6). 32pp. An easily read book about the sun and its importance in our lives. Update of 1962 edition.

21887 Branley, Franklyn M. *Sunshine Makes the Seasons* (3–4). Illus. by Giulio Maestro. 1988, HarperCollins paper $4.99 (978-0-06-445019-5). 32pp. A very simple account that explains the seasons by exploring the relationship of the sun to the earth and its orbit. Update of 1974 edition.

21888 Dolan, Graham. *The Greenwich Guide to the Seasons* (3–6). Illus. Series: Greenwich Guide To. 2001, Heinemann LB $22.79 (978-1-58810-044-3).

32pp. Color photographs and clear text introduce the seasons, with a glossary and other aids. (Rev: BL 10/15/01) [525]

21889 Fowler, Allan. *The Sun Is Always Shining Somewhere* (1–2). Illus. Series: Rookie Readers. 1991, Children's Book Pr. LB $20.50 (978-0-516-04906-9). 32pp. This simple introduction to astronomy tells about the sun and the earth's rotation around it. (Rev: BL 8/91) [523.7]

21890 Glaser, Linda. *It's Fall!* (2–4). Illus. by Susan Swan. 2001, Millbrook $21.90 (978-0-7613-1758-6). 32pp. A young boy observes the changes that occur in nature in the fall, with suggested nature activities for the season. (Rev: BL 9/15/01; HBG 3/02; SLJ 10/01)

21891 Jackson, Ellen. *The Summer Solstice* (2–4). Illus. 2001, Millbrook LB $21.90 (978-0-7613-1623-7). 32pp. An attractive resource that explains the summer solstice, why it is the longest day of the year, and its cultural significance. (Rev: BL 4/1/01; HBG 10/01; SLJ 5/01) [394.263]

21892 Jackson, Ellen. *The Winter Solstice* (2–4). Illus. 1994, Millbrook LB $23.40 (978-1-56294-400-1). 32pp. The customs and beliefs surrounding the winter solstice are explored in many cultures, e.g., the ancient Britons, Romans, and Peruvians. (Rev: BL 2/15/94; SLJ 4/94) [394.2]

21893 Kerrod, Robin. *The Sun* (4–6). Series: Planet Library. 2000, Lerner LB $21.27 (978-0-8225-3901-8). 32pp. This work explains how the sun was formed, its role in the solar system, in the galaxy, and beyond, and what the future holds. (Rev: BL 10/15/00; HBG 3/01; SLJ 1/01) [523.7]

21894 Latta, Sara. *What Happens in Spring?* (PS–2). Illus. Series: I Like the Seasons! 2006, Enslow LB $21.26 (978-0-7660-2419-9). 24pp. Answers a parade of questions about spring ("What are the first signs . . ."), and provides an experiment and a glossary of seasonally related terms. Also use *What Happens in Winter?* (2006). (Rev: SLJ 12/06) [508.2]

21895 Lin, Grace, and Ranida T. McKneally. *Our Seasons* (1–3). Illus. by Grace Lin. 2006, Charlesbridge $15.95 (978-1-57091-360-0). 32pp. Questions and answers about the seasons, with paintings and haiku to accompany the factual information. (Rev: BL 7/06; SLJ 8/06) [508.2]

21896 Markle, Sandra. *Exploring Winter* (3–6). Illus. by author. 1984, Avon paper $2.99 (978-0-380-71321-9). 160pp. Science and recreation are mixed in this book about winter and activities that are associated with it.

21897 Martin, Bill, Jr., and Michael Sampson. *I Love Our Earth* (PS–2). Illus. by Dan Lipow. 2006, Charlesbridge $14.95 (978-1-58089-106-6). 32pp. Impressive color photographs and minimal text celebrate the wonders of nature and the changing seasons. (Rev: BL 2/1/06; SLJ 2/06) [525]

21898 Meyer, Mary L. *Spring* (2–3). Series: Seasons. 2002, Smart Apple LB $21.35 (978-1-58340-143-9). 24pp. The weather, animals, plants, and activities of spring are presented in concise text with attractive full-color photographs. Also use *Fall* (2002). (Rev: HBG 10/03; SLJ 2/03)

21899 Pfeffer, Wendy. *A New Beginning: Celebrating the Spring Equinox* (1–3). Illus. by Linda Bleck. 2008, Dutton $17.99 (978-0-525-47874-4). 40pp. Learn about the arrival of spring and how it is celebrated in different cultures. (Rev: BL 12/1/07; SLJ 3/08) [394.26]

21900 Pfeffer, Wendy. *The Shortest Day: Celebrating the Winter Solstice* (K–4). Illus. by Jesse Reisch. 2003, Dutton $16.99 (978-0-525-46968-1). History and astronomy are combined in this easy-to-understand overview of the winter landmark. (Rev: HBG 4/04; SLJ 9/03) [394.261]

21901 Pfeffer, Wendy. *We Gather Together: Celebrating the Harvest Season* (1–3). Illus. by Linda Bleck. 2006, Dutton $17.99 (978-0-525-47669-6). 40pp. This companion to *The Shortest Day: Celebrating the Winter Solstice* provides information on the autumnal equinox, ways in which humans and animals prepare for the winter during this season; facts on the harvest and its many celebrations around the world, plus experiments and activities. (Rev: BL 12/1/06; SLJ 11/06) [508.2]

21902 Pipe, Jim. *The Sun* (3–5). Illus. Series: Earthwise. 2004, Stargazer LB $27.10 (978-1-932799-46-0). 32pp. An excellent introduction to the sun and its energy, this attractively illustrated volume supplements its facts and figures with suggested activities. (Rev: BL 10/15/04) [523.7]

21903 Rockwell, Anne. *Four Seasons Make a Year* (K–2). Illus. by Megan Halsey. 2004, Walker $15.95 (978-0-8027-8883-2). 32pp. A young girl on a farm guides readers through the seasons, following the progress of a sunflower she planted in spring. (Rev: BL 2/15/04; SLJ 4/04) [508]

21904 Schuette, Sarah L. *Let's Look at Spring* (K–2). Series: Investigate the Seasons. 2006, Capstone LB $19.93 (978-0-7368-6707-8). 24pp. The attractive and simple design will draw young readers into this introduction. Also use *Let's Look at Fall, Let's Look at Summer,* and *Let's Look at Winter* (all 2006). (Rev: SLJ 5/07)

21905 Simon, Seymour. *Spring Across America* (3–5). Illus. 1996, Hyperion LB $16.49 (978-0-7868-2056-6). 32pp. A book about spring as it develops in various sections of our country. A sequel to *Autumn Across America* (1993) and *Winter Across America* (1994). (Rev: BL 3/1/96; SLJ 4/96) [508.73]

21906 Simon, Seymour. *The Sun* (3–5). Illus. 1986, Morrow paper $6.99 (978-0-688-09236-8). 32pp. A look at the structure and atmosphere of this "middle-size" star. (Rev: BCCB 10/86; BL 9/1/86; SLJ 12/86)

21907 Vogt, Gregory L. *The Sun* (2–4). Illus. Series: Gateway Solar System. 1996, Millbrook LB $22.90 (978-1-56294-600-5). 32pp. An introduction to the star of our solar system and its life-sustaining force. (Rev: BL 4/15/96; SLJ 7/96) [523.7]

21908 Whitehouse, Patricia. *The Sun* (2–4). Illus. Series: Space Explorer. 2004, Heinemann LB $24.21 (978-1-4034-5157-6). 32pp. A slim overview of the sun and its composition, size, and temperature, with material on solar flares, eclipses, and solar wind. [523.7]

Biological Sciences

General

21909 Arnold, Katya. *Let's Find It! My First Nature Guide* (PS–1). Illus. 2002, Holiday House $16.95 (978-0-8234-1539-7). 32pp. Young readers search for plants and animals in painted scenes of habitats in this colorful introduction to nature. (Rev: BL 8/02; HBG 3/03; SLJ 10/02) [570]

21910 Batten, Mary. *Aliens from Earth: When Animals and Plants Invade Other Ecosystems* (3–5). Illus. by Beverly J. Doyle. 2003, Peachtree $15.95 (978-1-56145-236-1). 32pp. A narrative overview of the results of animal and plant migrations to new home ecosystems, with full-page illustrations. (Rev: BL 3/1/03; HBG 10/03; SLJ 5/03) [577]

21911 Biesiot, Elizabeth. *Natural Treasures Field Guide for Kids* (3–6). Illus. 1996, Roberts Rinehart paper $12.95 (978-1-57098-082-4). 64pp. A paperback that explains the lives of wild animals by examining such evidence as paw prints, nests, and night sounds. (Rev: BL 9/1/96; SLJ 7/96) [591]

21912 Bottone, Frank G., Jr. *The Science of Life: Projects and Principles for Beginning Biologists* (5–8). Illus. 2001, Chicago Review paper $14.95 (978-1-55652-382-3). 126pp. Twenty-five projects introduce readers to the basics of biology and the rigors of scientific research. (Rev: SLJ 11/01) [570.78]

21913 Cheshire, Gerard. *Living World* (1–4). Illus. by Janet Baker, et al. Series: World of Wonder. 2008, Children's Pr. LB $29.00 (978-0-531-24026-7); paper $9.95 (978-0-531-23822-6). 32pp. Answering such questions as "What's the Deadliest Creature on Earth," this book looks at various forms of life on our planet and includes acetate overlays. (Rev: SLJ 3/09)

21914 *DK Nature Encyclopedia* (5–8). 1998, DK paper $29.99 (978-0-7894-3411-1). A browsable reference book that covers topics including classification of living things, ecology, the origins and evolution of life, specific animal and plant groups, and the inner workings of plants and animals, all in a series of beautifully illustrated double-page spreads. (Rev: BL 12/1/98; SLJ 2/99) [574]

21915 Doris, Ellen. *Woods, Ponds, and Fields* (4–7). Illus. Series: Real Kids Real Science. 1994, Thames & Hudson $16.95 (978-0-500-19006-7). 64pp. A book that gives background essays as well as step-by-step directions for nature study projects in all seasons. (Rev: BL 9/1/94) [508]

21916 Drake, Jane, and Ann Love. *Alien Invaders: Species That Threaten Our World* (4–6). Illus. by Mark Thurman. 2008, Tundra $19.95 (978-0-88776-798-2). 56pp. This title presents a variety of natural disasters that occur when invaders in the form of plants, animals, bacteria, and viruses are introduced into a new habitat. (Rev: BL 3/15/08; SLJ 6/08) [578.6]

21917 Early, Bobbi. *Tiny Life in a Puddle* (2–3). Series: Rookie Read-About Science. 2005, Children's Pr. LB $20.50 (978-0-516-25272-8); paper $4.95 (978-0-516-25475-3). 32pp. For beginning readers, this is an introduction to the kinds of bacteria — good and bad — that can be found in a small puddle of water. (Rev: SLJ 4/06) [579.176]

21918 Emory, Jerry. *Dirty, Rotten, Dead? A Worm's-eye View of Death, Decomposition . . . and Life* (5–8). Illus. 1996, Harcourt paper $15.00 (978-0-15-200695-2). Along with a number of experiments and ecological projects, this book discusses death and recycling in nature, including such topics as the parts of the human body that become waste (e.g. hair, nails, skin), digestion and human excretion, processing of sewage, water pollution, diseases of the immune system, and contemporary mortuary practices. (Rev: SLJ 8/96) [628.4]

21919 Gallant, Roy A. *The Wonders of Biodiversity* (5–8). Illus. Series: The Story of Science. 2002, Benchmark $29.93 (978-0-7614-1427-8). 80pp. Gallant discusses the importance of biodiversity, the plight of species that are affected by loss of habitat and other environmental factors, and species interdependence. (Rev: HBG 3/03; SLJ 2/03) [578]

21920 Goodman, Susan E. *Nature Did It First!* (PS–2). Illus. 2003, Millbrook LB $21.90 (978-0-7613-2413-3). 24pp. This attractive picture book teaches younger children about everyday products and processes that have their roots in nature. (Rev: BL 5/1/03; HBG 10/03) [508]

21921 Green, Jen. *In a Backyard* (2–5). Illus. Series: Small World. 2002, Crabtree LB $25.27 (978-0-7787-0141-5); paper $8.95 (978-0-7787-0155-2). 32pp. This book for younger readers takes a close look at the creatures that might be found in a backyard, and how plant and animal life coexist there. (Rev: BL 10/15/02) [591.75]

21922 Johnson, Rebecca. *Mighty Animal Cells* (5–7). Illus. by Jack Desrocher. Series: Microquests. 2007, Lerner LB $29.27 (978-0-8225-7137-7). 48pp. Animal cell structure and cell division, followed by human cells, are discussed in chapters such as "Meet the Organelles," "What Cells Do," and "Cells with Special Talents" in this reader-friendly but information-packed book with cartoon illustrations to spice up the text. (Rev: BL 10/15/07; HB 1/08*; SLJ 11/07) [571.6]

21923 Jones, Jennifer B. *Who Lives in the Snow?* (PS–3). Illus. by Consie Powell. 2001, Court Wayne $15.95 (978-1-57098-287-3). 32pp. Cutaway illustrations give young readers a glimpse below the surface of a snowy meadow to see what happens to plants, insects, and animals during winter. (Rev: BL 11/15/01) [591.4]

21924 Kalman, Bobbie. *Forest Food Chains* (2–4). Illus. Series: Food Chains. 2004, Crabtree LB $25.27 (978-0-7787-1943-4); paper $6.95 (978-0-7787-1989-2). 32pp. All about the dynamics of food chains and food webs in the forest. (Rev: BL 3/15/05) [577.3]

21925 Kalman, Bobbie, and Jacqueline Langille. *What Are Food Chains and Webs?* (3–5). Series: Science of Living Things. 1998, Crabtree LB $25.27 (978-0-86505-876-7); paper $6.95 (978-0-86505-888-0). 32pp. This book uses clear photographs, illustrations, charts, and short chapters to describe food chains and explain their various levels and types. A game is included to enhance the learning process. (Rev: SLJ 11/98) [574.5]

21926 Kalman, Bobbie, and Jacqueline Langille. *What Is a Life Cycle?* (3–5). Series: Science of Living Things. 1998, Crabtree LB $25.27 (978-0-86505-874-3); paper $6.95 (978-0-86505-886-6). 32pp. Using many visuals and a concise text, this book traces life cycles from birth to adulthood of a number of plants and animals, including humans. (Rev: SLJ 11/98) [508]

21927 Kelsey, Elin. *Strange New Species: Astonishing Discoveries of Life on Earth* (5–8). Illus. 2005, Maple Tree $24.95 (978-1-897066-31-7). 96pp. A large-format, well-illustrated introduction to plant and animal classification and to newly discovered species. (Rev: BL 10/15/05; SLJ 2/06) [578]

21928 Knight, Tim. *Dramatic Displays* (3–5). Series: Amazing Nature. 2003, Heinemann LB $24.22 (978-1-4034-0721-4). 32pp. An attractive look at nature's use of camouflage, mimicry, and brilliant color displays, more suitable for browsers than for report writers. Also use *Ferocious Fighters* and *Fantastic Feeders* (2003). (Rev: HBG 10/03; SLJ 7/03) [591.4]

21929 Knight, Tim. *Super Survivors* (3–5). Series: Amazing Nature. 2003, Heinemann LB $24.22 (978-1-4034-0723-8). 32pp. How plants and animals adapt to their surroundings in order to survive and thrive is the subject of this photo-illustrated volume. Also in this series is *Incredible Life Cycles* (2003), which looks at the more unusual features of the life cycles of plants and animals. (Rev: HBG 4/04; SLJ 3/04) [578.4]

21930 Lindstrom, Karin. *Tiny Life on Plants* (2–3). Series: Rookie Read-About Science. 2005, Children's Pr. LB $20.50 (978-0-516-25297-1); paper $4.95 (978-0-516-25478-4). 32pp. For beginning readers, this is an introduction to the kinds of bacteria — good and bad — that thrive on the surface of plants. (Rev: SLJ 4/06) [577.852]

21931 MacAulay, Kelley, and Bobbie Kalman. *Backyard Habitats* (K–2). Illus. Series: Introducing Habitats. 2006, Crabtree LB $25.27 (978-0-7787-2957-0); paper $6.95 (978-0-7787-2985-3). 32pp. For beginning readers, this inviting volume introduces the diversity of animal and plant life that can be found in many backyards. (Rev: BL 10/15/06) [577.5]

21932 McNamara, Ken. *It's True: We Came from Slime* (4–6). Illus. by Andrew Plant. Series: It's True. 2006, Annick $19.95 (978-1-55037-953-2); paper $5.95 (978-1-55037-952-5). 96pp. Eye-catching artwork highlights this fascinating look at the origins of life on Earth — from primordial ooze through evolution across more than 3.5 billion years of history. (Rev: BL 4/1/06) [576.8]

21933 Manning, Mick, and Brita Granström. *Snap!* (PS–2). Illus. by authors. 2006, Frances Lincoln $14.95 (978-1-84507-408-1). A lighthearted look at the food chain in which one creature after another is gobbled up by a larger animal. (Rev: SLJ 11/06) [577.16]

21934 Mattern, Joanne. *What Grassland Animals Eat* (1–2). Illus. Series: Nature's Food Chains. 2007, Weekly Reader LB $19.93 (978-0-8368-6872-2); paper $5.95 (978-0-8368-6879-1). 24pp. Beginning readers learning about food chains will find this book on the food chain on a grassland helpful. Also use *What River Animals Eat, What Sea Animals Eat,* and *What Polar Animals Eat* (all 2007). (Rev: SLJ 8/07)

21935 Morrison, Gordon. *Nature in the Neighborhood* (2–5). Illus. 2004, Houghton $16.00 (978-0-618-35215-9). 32pp. This attractively illustrated title introduces readers to the abundance of plant and animal life that can be found in areas ranging from their own backyards to train tracks and vacant lots. (Rev: BL 12/1/04; SLJ 10/04) [508]

21936 Murray, Julie. *Backyard* (2–5). Illus. Series: That's Gross! A Look at Science. 2009, ABDO $17.95 (978-1-60453-553-2). 32pp. A look at all the icky stuff in the backyard — centipedes, worms, poop of all kinds, and so forth. (Rev: BL 5/15/09) [591.75]

21937 Parker, Steve. *Survival and Change* (4–7). Series: Life Processes. 2001, Heinemann LB $21.36 (978-1-57572-340-2). 32pp. Parker considers how organisms evolve and looks at how species behave under threat and the origin of new species in this concise book with diagrams, charts, and color photographs. (Rev: HBG 10/01; SLJ 7/01) [578.4]

21938 Peters, Lisa Westberg. *Our Family Tree: An Evolution Story* (K–3). Illus. by Lauren Stringer. 2003, Harcourt $17.00 (978-0-15-201772-9). This oversize picture book, with conversational text and many bright illustrations, is fairly successful in its ambitious mission; adults may want to explain the timeline and final notes. (Rev: BL 3/15/03; HBG 10/03; SLJ 5/03) [576.8]

21939 Quinlan, Susan E. *The Case of the Monkeys That Fell from the Trees: And Other Mysteries in Tropical Nature* (5–8). Illus. 2003, Boyds Mills $15.95 (978-1-56397-902-6). 171pp. Quinlan introduces plant and animal mysteries in South and Central American tropical forests and shows how scientists approached solving them. (Rev: BL 3/1/03; HBG 10/03; SLJ 3/03; VOYA 10/03) [508.313]

21940 Rockwell, Anne. *Growing Like Me* (PS–K). Illus. by Holly Keller. 2001, Harcourt $15.00 (978-0-15-202202-0). 24pp. This simple book about change and development in the plant and animal world shows an organism on one page and what it becomes on the next (e.g., a caterpillar and then a butterfly). (Rev: BL 3/1/01; HB 9/01; HBG 3/02) [571.8]

21941 Ross, Michael Elsohn. *Life Cycles* (2–4). Illus. by Gustav Moore. 2001, Millbrook LB $22.40 (978-0-7613-1817-0). 32pp. Young readers are introduced to the concept of life cycles through the stories of a sunflower, a mushroom, and a grasshopper. (Rev: BL 8/01; HBG 3/02; SLJ 1/02) [571.8]

21942 Salas, Laura Purdie. *Are You Living? A Song About Living and Nonliving Things* (PS–2). Illus. by Viviana Garofoli. Series: Science Songs. 2008, Picture Window LB $18.99 (978-1-4048-5302-7). 24pp. This variation on the "Are You Sleeping?" song explores the characteristics of living and nonliving things, looking at characteristics such as locomotion and nutrition. (Rev: BL 4/1/09; SLJ 5/09) [570]

21943 Silverstein, Alvin, et al. *Symbiosis* (5–9). Series: Science Concepts. 1998, Twenty-First Century LB $26.90 (978-0-7613-3001-1). 64pp. The concept of cooperation in nature for mutual benefit is explored, with explanations of various forms of symbiotic partnerships including the relationships humans have with animals, plants, fungi, and microorganisms. (Rev: HBG 3/99; SLJ 2/99) [574.5]

21944 Singer, Marilyn. *What Stinks?* (4–6). 2006, Darby Creek $17.95 (978-1-58196-035-8). 64pp. The use of scent in the animal and plant kingdoms — to mark territory, to attract mates, and so forth —

is presented in an entertaining format full of wordplay and illustrations. (Rev: BL 5/1/06) [591.5]

21945 Strauss, Rochelle. *Tree of Life: The Incredible Biodiversity of Life on Earth* (3–6). Illus. by Margot Thompson. 2004, Kids Can $16.95 (978-1-55337-669-9). 40pp. This large-format book presents a visual representation — using the branches of a tree — of the diversity of species, from bacteria on up. (Rev: BL 12/1/04; SLJ 10/04) [578]

21946 Thomas, Keltie. *Nature Shockers* (4–6). Illus. by Greg Hall. Series: Planet Earth News. 2005, Maple Tree $16.95 (978-1-897066-29-4); paper $9.95 (978-1-897066-30-0). 64pp. Oddities of nature — including everything from a tree that's wrapped itself around a bicycle to the discovery of a strange-looking salamander — are reported in tabloid style. (Rev: BL 10/15/05; SLJ 1/06) [508]

21947 Thornhill, Jan. *Before and After: A Book of Nature Timescapes* (PS–3). Illus. 1997, National Geographic $16.00 (978-0-7922-7093-5). 32pp. Using different habitats, this book pictures a variety of animals and plants using a single dramatic incident, like the charge of a lioness, to show before-and-after situations. (Rev: BL 10/1/97; HBG 3/98; SLJ 9/97) [577]

21948 Triefeldt, Laurie. *Plants and Animals* (4–8). Illus. Series: World of Wonder. 2007, Quill Driver $19.95 (978-1-884956-72-0). 100pp. By the author of a nationally syndicated newspaper column called World of Wonder, this book, a companion to *People and Places*, covers a huge amount of material and will be helpful to report writers. (Rev: BL 4/1/08) [570]

21949 Trumbauer, Lisa. *Tiny Life in Your Home* (2–3). 2005, Children's Pr. LB $20.50 (978-0-516-25274-2); paper $4.95 (978-0-516-25477-7). 32pp. This fascinating title gives a close-up look at the diversity of microscopic life forms — mostly bacteria — that can be found in the average home. (Rev: SLJ 4/06) [579.1755]

21950 Turner, Pamela. *Life on Earth — and Beyond* (5–8). Illus. 2008, Charlesbridge $19.95 (978-1-58089-133-2); paper $11.95 (978-1-58089-134-9). 112pp. Readers follow NASA astrobiologist Chris McKay as he searches for microbes in extreme environments on Earth — in hopes of determining if life can survive in extreme environments in space. (Rev: BL 2/1/08; SLJ 3/08) [571.0919]

21951 Wallace, Holly. *Classification* (4–7). Series: Life Processes. 2006, Heinemann LB $20.50 (978-1-4034-8845-9). 32pp. A clear and colorful introduction to the classification of plants and animals. (Rev: BL 10/15/06) [570.1]

Animal Life

General

21952 Aaseng, Nathan. *Nature's Poisonous Creatures* (5–9). Series: Scientific American Sourcebooks. 1997, Twenty-First Century LB $28.90 (978-0-8050-4690-8). After a general introduction to animal poisons, why they are produced, and their composition, this book devotes separate chapters to such venom-bearing vertebrates and invertebrates as sea wasps, blue-ringed octopi, African killer bees, and marine toads. (Rev: BL 2/1/98; SLJ 8/98) [591.6]

21953 Ablow, Gail. *A Horse in the House and Other Strange but True Animal Stories* (2–4). Illus. by Kathy Osborn. 2007, Candlewick $17.99 (978-0-7636-2838-3). 40pp. Truth really *is* stranger than fiction as each of these 16 tales proves; source notes document authenticity. (Rev: BL 9/15/07; LMC 1/08) [590]

21954 Armentrout, David, and Patricia Armentrout. *Animals* (PS–2). Series: 50 Words About. 2002, Rourke LB $19.95 (978-1-58952-341-8). 32pp. Simple definitions are given for 50 words about animals (camouflage, extinct, and so forth), along with a sentence that includes the word. (Rev: SLJ 3/03) [590]

21955 Arnold, Caroline. *Australian Animals* (1–3). 2000, HarperCollins LB $15.89 (978-0-688-16767-7). 48pp. Seventeen Australian animals are introduced in four sections that represent individual biomes. (Rev: HBG 3/01; SLJ 10/00) [591]

21956 Aston, Dianna. *An Egg Is Quiet* (PS–2). Illus. by Sylvia Long. 2006, Chronicle $16.95 (978-0-8118-4428-4). 32pp. This exploration of eggs — from fish eggs to bird eggs — offers a blend of factual and poetic text plus detailed illustrations. (Rev: BL 4/15/06; SLJ 6/06) [591.4]

21957 Aston, Dianna. *Mama's Wild Child / Papa's Wild Child* (PS–2). Illus. by Nora Hilb. 2006, Charlesbridge $14.95 (978-1-57091-590-1). In this appealing "flip-me-over" book, a mother and father separately tell their child how various parents in the animal kingdom take care of their offspring. (Rev: SLJ 3/06) [591.56]

21958 *Atlas of Animals* (PS–2). Illus. Series: First Discovery. 1996, Scholastic $12.95 (978-0-590-58280-3). 24pp. Using a highly visual approach, this short book discusses the animals found in the various regions of the world. (Rev: BL 10/15/96) [591]

21959 Barrow, Lloyd H. *Science Fair Projects Investigating Earthworms* (5–8). Series: Science Fair Success. 2000, Enslow LB $26.60 (978-0-7660-1291-2). 104pp. This book contains a fascinating number of experiments involving earthworms, with very explicit directions and explanations of the scientific principles behind each project. (Rev: BL 4/15/00; HBG 10/00) [595.1]

21960 Berger, Melvin, and Gilda Berger. *Do Tarantulas Have Teeth? Questions and Answers About Poisonous Creatures* (3–5). Illus. by Jim Effler. Series: Scholastic Question and Answer. 2000, Scholastic $14.95 (978-0-439-09578-5); paper $5.95 (978-0-439-14877-1). 48pp. Using a question-and-answer format and bright, realistic illustrations, this title presents information on the methods poisonous animals use to inject their venom, how they hunt and feed, and their physical characteristics. (Rev: HBG 3/01; SLJ 5/01) [591]

21961 Bial, Raymond. *A Handful of Dirt* (3–5). Photos by author. 2000, Walker $16.95 (978-0-8027-8698-2). 32pp. This set of photographs with accompanying text examines life found underground from invertebrates to the mammals and reptiles that burrow into the earth. (Rev: BCCB 5/00; HBG 9/00; SLJ 4/00) [591]

21962 Bishop, Nic. *Backyard Detective: Critters Up Close* (1–3). Illus. 2002, Scholastic $16.95 (978-0-439-17478-7). 48pp. Photographic collages show "life-sized" animals and insects found in backyards across the United States, along with two pages of informational text about each and a section of nature projects. (Rev: BL 10/15/02; HBG 3/03; SLJ 10/02) [591.75]

21963 Bloom, Steve. *Untamed: Animals Around the World* (4–7). Illus. by Emmanuelle Zicot. 2005, Abrams $18.95 (978-0-8109-5956-9). 75pp. Enthralling photographs of wild animals are accompanied by brief facts and an environmentalist message. (Rev: BL 12/1/05) [636]

21964 Browning, Bel. *Animal Welfare* (5–8). Illus. Series: Face the Facts. 2003, Raintree LB $28.56 (978-0-7398-6430-2). 56pp. Hot issues in animal protection such as whaling, intensive farming, and zoos are discussed, and practical responses from young people are suggested. (Rev: BL 11/15/03; HBG 10/03) [364.1]

21965 Cassie, Brian. *Say It Again* (1–3). Illus. by David Mooney. 2000, Charlesbridge LB $16.95 (978-0-88106-341-7); paper $6.95 (978-0-88106-342-4). This unusual animal book features, in picture and text, 12 creatures whose names involve a repetitive sound, such as a killy-killy and a caracara. (Rev: HBG 9/00; SLJ 3/00) [591]

21966 Cobb, Allan B. *Super Science Projects About Animals and Their Habitats* (4–8). Series: Psyched for Science. 2000, Rosen LB $26.50 (978-0-8239-3175-0). 48pp. Six hand-on activities are introduced to help children observe animals and to study their adjustments to climate, habitat, and food. (Rev: SLJ 9/00) [591]

21967 Collard, Sneed B. *Science Warriors: The Battle Against Invasive Species* (5–8). Series: Scientists in the Field. 2008, Houghton $17.00 (978-0-618-75636-0). 48pp. Collard presents some of the 6,200 invasive plant and animal species that are currently "accidental guests" of the United States and explains how scientists try to combat the damage they cause; photographs illustrate the scale of the problem. (Rev: BCCB 12/08; BL 12/1/08; HB 1/09; SLJ 1/09) [578.6]

21968 Crenson, Victoria. *Horseshoe Crabs and Shorebirds: The Story of a Food Web* (2–4). Illus. by Annie Cannon. 2003, Marshall Cavendish $16.95 (978-0-7614-5115-0). 32pp. Wildlife on the Delaware Bay is the focus of this informative picture-book exploration full of attractive and atmospheric paintings. (Rev: BL 11/1/03; HBG 4/04; SLJ 12/03)

21969 *Do Bears Give Bear Hugs? First Questions and Answers About Animals* (PS–1). Series: Library of First Questions and Answers. 1994, Time-Life

$14.95 (978-0-7835-0870-2). 47pp. A fun book that explores some common questions about animals. (Rev: SLJ 8/94) [591]

21970 Donald, Rhonda Lucas. *Animal Rights: How You Can Make a Difference* (4–7). Series: Take Action. 2009, Capstone LB $25.32 (978-1-4296-2796-2). 32pp. This title provides directions for dealing with animal rights issues, making a plan (how to rescue dogs, raising money for a shelter), and dealing with the rejection that sometimes accompanies speaking out. (Rev: SLJ 5/09) [179]

21971 Donovan, Sandra. *Animals of Rivers, Lakes, and Ponds* (2–4). Series: Animals of the Biomes. 2003, Raintree LB $25.70 (978-0-7398-5690-1). 48pp. The great blue heron, giant water bugs, raccoons, and snapping turtles are featured in this introduction. Also use *Desert Animals*, which looks at roadrunners, scorpions, camels, and Gila monsters. (Rev: HBG 3/03; SLJ 2/03)

21972 Doris, Ellen. *Meet the Arthropods* (4–7). 1996, Thames & Hudson $16.95 (978-0-500-19010-4). 64pp. Such arthropods as the horseshoe crab, potato beetle, and praying mantis are introduced with photographs and activities. (Rev: BL 10/15/96) [595.2]

21973 Ehrlich, Fred. *Does a Seal Smile?* (PS–2). Illus. by Emily Bolam. Series: Early Experiences. 2006, Blue Apple $13.50 (978-1-59354-168-2); paper $5.95 (978-1-59354-169-9). 32pp. An entertaining look at the different ways in which humans and animals communicate. (Rev: BL 8/06) [153.6]

21974 Elliott, Leslee. *Mind-Blowing Mammals* (3–6). Illus. Series: Amazing Animals. 1995, Sterling $14.95 (978-0-8069-1270-7); paper $9.95 (978-0-8069-1271-4). 64pp. Introduces some amazing mammals with full-color photos on each page. (Rev: SLJ 4/95) [591]

21975 Fowler, Allan. *Animals Under the Ground* (1–3). Series: Rookie Readers. 1997, Children's Book Pr. $20.50 (978-0-516-20427-7). 32pp. An easy-to-read science book that introduces basic material about such animals as moles. (Rev: BL 12/15/97; HBG 3/98) [591]

21976 Fredericks, Anthony D. *Fearsome Fangs* (4–6). Illus. Series: Watts Library. 2002, Watts LB $25.50 (978-0-531-11966-2). 63pp. Animals with alarming teeth — including some prehistoric beasts — are profiled here, with information on physical features, behavior, distribution, habitat, prey, and relationship with humans. (Rev: SLJ 1/03) [591.47]

21977 Ganeri, Anita. *Animal Life Cycles* (K–3). Illus. Series: Nature's Patterns. 2005, Heinemann LB $16.95 (978-1-4034-5894-0). 32pp. In simple language, this volume introduces the life cycles of reptiles, insects, mammals, and amphibians. (Rev: SLJ 6/05)

21978 Ganeri, Anita. *Animals* (4–7). Series: Inside and Outside Guide. 2006, Heinemann LB $29.29 (978-1-4034-9084-1). 32pp. This attractive guide provides in-depth introductions to 12 animals, with double-page spreads focusing on each animal's identifying characteristics and behaviors. (Rev: BL 10/15/06) [571.3]

21979 Ganeri, Anita. *The Hunt for Food* (1–5). Illus. Series: Life Cycle. 1997, Millbrook LB $22.90 (978-0-7613-0304-6). 32pp. This book deals with animals in a meadow and their feeding habits throughout the four seasons. (Rev: BL 12/1/97; HBG 3/98; SLJ 1/98) [577.4]

21980 George, Jean Craighead. *Morning, Noon, and Night* (PS–3). Illus. by Wendell Minor. 1999, HarperCollins LB $17.89 (978-0-06-023629-8). 32pp. An easy-reader about a full day from Maine to California and the activities of such animals as antelopes, lizards, and cardinals. (Rev: HBG 9/99; SLJ 4/99) [591]

21981 Glassman, Jackie. *Amazing Arctic Animals* (K–3). Illus. by Lisa Bonforte. Series: All Aboard Science Reader. 2002, Grosset paper $3.99 (978-0-448-42844-4). 48pp. Animals including the polar bear, arctic tern, caribou, snowy owl, and arctic fox are introduced with colored illustrations. (Rev: SLJ 6/03) [591.7]

21982 Gordon, Sharon. *Guess Who Grabs* (K–2). Series: Bookworms: Guess Who. 2003, Benchmark LB $21.36 (978-0-7614-1557-2). 31pp. Young readers are challenged to identify an animal that "grabs" (an octopus), with clues about characteristics, habitat, and so forth. Also use *Guess Who Changes* and *Guess Who Hides* (both 2003). (Rev: HBG 4/04; SLJ 4/04)

21983 Guiberson, Brenda Z. *Exotic Species: Invaders in Paradise* (4–6). Illus. 1999, Twenty-First Century LB $24.90 (978-0-7613-1319-9). 80pp. Using examples including starlings, kudzu, and zebra mussels, this account reveals the disastrous results that occur when a foreign species is introduced into a different ecosystem. (Rev: BL 7/99; HBG 4/00; SLJ 9/99) [577]

21984 Halfmann, Janet. *Life in a Garden* (5–7). Photos by David Liebman. 2000, Creative LB $22.60 (978-1-58341-072-1). This book explores such life forms found in a garden as fungi, beetles, slugs, snails, and aphids. (Rev: SLJ 8/00) [635]

21985 Hanly, Sheila. *The Big Book of Animals* (PS–2). Illus. 1997, DK $14.99 (978-0-7894-1485-4). 48pp. In a book arranged by habitat, more than 300 familiar or little-known animals are introduced and pictured. (Rev: BL 7/97; HBG 3/98) [590]

21986 Hanna, Jack, and Rick A. Prebeg. *Jungle Jack Hanna's Safari Adventure* (3–5). Illus. 1996, Scholastic $12.95 (978-0-590-67322-8). 44pp. The animals of Kenya and Uganda are introduced in this handsomely illustrated account. (Rev: BL 10/15/96; SLJ 11/96) [591.96]

21987 Hansen, Rosanna. *Caring Animals* (2–4). Illus. Series: True Tales. 2003, Children's Pr. LB $22.50 (978-0-516-22912-6); paper $4.95 (978-0-516-24603-1). 48pp. Introduces animals that help people, from dolphins to a seeing-eye horse. (Rev: BL 1/1–15/04) [362.404]

21988 Heller, Ruth. *"Galápagos" Means "Tortoises"* (3–5). Illus. by author. 2000, Sierra Club $14.95 (978-0-87156-917-2). 41pp. The animals and birds of the Galapagos Islands are described in this book of rhymes and accompanying realistic paintings. (Rev: SLJ 3/01) [985]

21989 Hiller, Ilo. *Introducing Mammals to Young Naturalists* (5–9). Illus. 1990, Texas A & M Univ. $9.00 (978-0-89096-427-9). An introduction to a number of mammals, from the common squirrel to the exotic armadillo. (Rev: BL 7/90) [599]

21990 Hodge, Deborah. *Polar Animals* (PS–1). Illus. by Pat Stephens. Series: Who Lives Here? 2008, Kids Can LB $14.95 (978-1-55453-043-4); paper $5.95 (978-1-55453-044-1). 24pp. A simple introduction to polar animals including penguins, foxes, and whales, with eye-catching photographs. (Rev: BL 4/1/08; LMC 10/08) [591.75]

21991 Hodgkins, Fran. *Animals Among Us: Living with Suburban Wildlife* (5–8). Illus. 2000, Linnet LB $19.50 (978-0-208-02478-7). 116pp. This book discusses the behavior and lifestyles of animals such as deer, coyotes, bears, skunks, and bats that live in suburbs, close to their original haunts. (Rev: BL 6/1–15/00; HB 7/00; HBG 10/00; SLJ 9/00; VOYA 12/00) [591.7]

21992 Jackson, Donna. *The Wildlife Detectives: How Forensic Scientists Fight Crimes Against Nature* (3–7). Illus. 2000, Houghton $17.00 (978-0-395-86976-5). 48pp. This book introduces the forensic scientists who track down criminals who harm wild animals. (Rev: BL 4/1/00; HBG 9/00; SLJ 7/00) [363.28]

21993 Jefferis, David. *Animal Kingdom* (3–6). Illus. Series: Record Breakers. 2003, Raintree LB $25.69 (978-0-7398-6321-3). 32pp. Good for browsing, this attractive volume identifies such animal record-holders as the smallest bird, largest sea creature, longest migrator, best camouflage, and so forth. (Rev: HBG 10/03; SLJ 7/03) [591]

21994 Jenkins, Steve. *Actual Size* (1–3). Illus. 2004, Houghton $16.00 (978-0-618-37594-3). 32pp. Striking cut-paper collages portray animals — and parts of animals — in real size, so that an earthworm appears in full size while only the eyes of a giant squid can be accommodated. (Rev: BL 5/15/04; HB 5/04; SLJ 6/04) [591.4]

21995 Jenkins, Steve. *Biggest, Strongest, Fastest* (PS–3). Illus. 1995, Ticknor $16.00 (978-0-395-69701-6). 32pp. Double-page collages illustrate some of the animal kingdom's record holders. (Rev: BCCB 6/95; BL 2/1/95*; HB 7/95; SLJ 5/95*) [591]

21996 Jenkins, Steve, and Robin Page. *What Do You Do with a Tail Like This?* (PS–2). Illus. 2003, Houghton $15.00 (978-0-618-25628-0). 32pp. The tails, mouths, and other parts of different animals are rendered in cut paper, illustrating interesting animal facts. Caldecott Honor Book, 2004. (Rev: BCCB 3/03; BL 2/15/03*; HBG 10/03; SLJ 3/03) [573.8]

21997 Johnson, Sylvia A. *Silkworms* (4–7). Illus. 1982, Lerner paper $5.95 (978-0-8225-9557-1). 48pp. The life cycle of the silkworm, told in text and striking color pictures. [595.78]

21998 Kalman, Bobbie. *Food Chains and You* (2–4). Illus. Series: Food Chains. 2004, Crabtree LB

$25.27 (978-0-7787-1942-7); paper $6.95 (978-0-7787-1988-5). 32pp. A simple look at the relationship between producers and consumers of energy (both herbivores and carnivores), with discussion of humans' food choices.

21999 Kaner, Etta. *Animals at Work: How Animals Build, Dig, Fish and Trap* (2–4). Illus. by Pat Stephens. 2001, Kids Can $10.95 (978-1-55074-673-0); paper $5.95 (978-1-55074-675-4). 40pp. Activities, a game, and a quiz are provided in this basic look at the work various animals have to do to find food, shelter, and mates. (Rev: HBG 3/02; SLJ 10/01) [591.5]

22000 Knapp, Ron. *Bloodsuckers* (3–6). Illus. Series: Weird and Wacky Science. 1996, Enslow LB $23.93 (978-0-89490-614-5). 48pp. An interesting look at such creatures as vampire bats, leeches, fleas, lice, mosquitoes, and lampreys. (Rev: SLJ 6/96) [591]

22001 Kneidel, Sally. *Slugs, Bugs, and Salamanders: Discovering Animals in Your Garden* (5–7). Illus. by Anna-Maria L. Crum. 1997, Fulcrum paper $16.95 (978-1-55591-313-7). 120pp. As well as introducing backyard insects and other small creatures, this account gives a number of tips on growing healthy flowers and vegetables. (Rev: SLJ 10/97) [595.7]

22002 Kratter, Paul. *The Living Rain Forest: An Animal Alphabet* (PS–2). Illus. 2004, Charlesbridge $17.95 (978-1-57091-603-8). 64pp. Striking acrylic-and-watercolor illustrations introduces 26 animals of the rain forest. (Rev: BL 2/1/04; SLJ 4/04) [591.734]

22003 Lauber, Patricia. *Fur, Feathers, and Flippers: How Animals Live Where They Do* (4–8). Illus. 1994, Scholastic paper $4.95 (978-0-590-45072-0). 48pp. Using various habitats such as the grasslands of East Africa as examples, this photo-essay describes how animals have adapted to their different environments. (Rev: BL 12/1/94*; SLJ 12/94) [591.5]

22004 Martin, James W. R. *In a House* (2–5). Series: Small World. 2002, Crabtree LB $25.27 (978-0-7787-0140-8); paper $8.95 (978-0-7787-0154-5). 32pp. From bugs and rodents to insects and worms, this is a rundown of the animal life that can be found inside a house. (Rev: BL 10/15/02) [591]

22005 Maynard, Christopher. *Micromonsters: Life Under the Microscope* (3–5). Illus. Series: Eyewitness Reader. 1999, DK LB $12.99 (978-0-7894-4757-9); paper $3.99 (978-0-7894-4756-2). 48pp. Tapeworms, fleas, and lice are among the monsters introduced in this book illustrated with magnifications of microscope photographs. (Rev: BL 12/15/99; HBG 4/00) [595]

22006 Maze, Stephanie, ed. *Beautiful Moments in the Wild: Animals and Their Colors* (PS–K). Series: Moments in the Wild. 2002, Moonstone $15.00 (978-0-9707768-7-7). 32pp. An attractive picture book showing the diversity of animal colors in full-color shots. (Rev: SLJ 3/03)

22007 Miles, Victoria. *Wild Science: Amazing Encounters Between Animals and the People Who Study*

Them (5–8). Series: Scientists in the Field. 2004, Raincoast paper $18.95 (978-1-55192-618-6). 168pp. This photo-filled volume introduces readers to scientists who study animals and describes memorable moments with animals in the wilderness. (Rev: BL 12/1/04; SLJ 12/04) [591.68]

22008 Murawski, Darlyne A. *Animal Faces* (PS–2). Photos by author. 2005, Sterling LB $12.95 (978-1-4027-2295-0). A nature photographer offers close-up views of the faces of a wide variety of animals, introduced by brief poems. (Rev: SLJ 3/06) [590]

22009 Myers, Jack, ed. *The Puzzle of the Platypus and Other Explorations of Science in Action* (3–5). Illus. by John Rice. 2008, Boyds Mills $17.95 (978-1-59078-556-0). 64pp. Each story in this collection of eleven short essays reprinted from *Highlights* magazine tells how a scientist was able to unravel a mystery about some kind of animal; resource list. (Rev: BL 3/1/08; LMC 3/08; SLJ 6/08) [590]

22010 Palazzo, Tony. *The Biggest and the Littlest Animals* (4–7). Illus. by author. 1973, Lion LB $13.95 (978-0-87460-225-8). 40pp. Many ways of comparing animals, including size and mobility, are explored.

22011 Pascoe, Elaine, ed. *Into Wild California* (3–6). Series: The Jeff Corwin Experience. 2004, Gale LB $24.95 (978-1-56711-858-2). 48pp. In a spin-off of his Animal Planet TV series, Corwin introduces such creatures as bears, snakes, sea otters, and bobcats that make California their home. (Rev: SLJ 4/04) [591.9]

22012 Pascoe, Elaine, ed. *Into Wild Madagascar* (3–6). Series: The Jeff Corwin Experience. 2004, Gale LB $24.95 (978-1-56711-855-1). 48pp. Jeff Corwin of television's Animal Planet is the "host" for this survey of the threatened wildlife of Madagascar, from chameleons to lemurs. (Rev: SLJ 4/04) [591.9]

22013 Pascoe, Elaine. *Snails and Slugs* (4–7). Series: Nature Close-Up. 1998, Blackbirch LB $23.70 (978-1-56711-181-1). 48pp. Outstanding photographs, an interesting text, and several easy-to-do projects highlight this introduction to snails and slugs. (Rev: BL 9/15/98; HBG 3/99) [594.3]

22014 Patkau, Karen. *Creatures: Yesterday and Today* (2–4). Illus. by author. 2008, Tundra $18.95 (978-0-88776-833-0). 32pp. Using double-page spreads with bold computer-generated graphics and simple text Patkau looks at prehistoric animals and their modern-day descendants. (Rev: BL 4/1/08; SLJ 6/08) [591.38]

22015 Paul, Tessa. *In Fields and Meadows* (2–5). Illus. Series: Animal Trackers. 1997, Crabtree LB $22.60 (978-0-86505-585-8); paper $7.95 (978-0-86505-593-3). 32pp. Using evidence like footprints, teeth marks, holes, nests, and hair or fur, about a dozen creatures that live in fields and meadows are described. (Rev: HBG 3/98; SLJ 10/97) [591]

22016 Pearce, Q. L. *Piranhas and Other Wonders of the Jungle* (3–6). Illus. by Mary Ann Fraser. Series: Amazing Science. 1990, Simon & Schuster paper $5.95 (978-0-671-70690-6). 64pp. Sketches of ani-

mals found in the jungle, such as driver ants and vampire bats. (Rev: SLJ 2/91) [591]

22017 Pfeffer, Wendy. *Icy Antarctic Waters* (3–5). Series: Living on the Edge. 2002, Benchmark LB $25.64 (978-0-7614-1438-4). 40pp. The Weddell seal, emperor penguin, and minke whale are highlighted in this colorful, easy-to-read overview of Antarctic animals. (Rev: HBG 10/03; SLJ 6/03) [591.77]

22018 Pope, Joyce. *Living Fossils: Animals Unchanged by Time* (3–6). Illus. by Stella Stilwell and Helen Ward. Series: Curious Creatures. 1992, Raintree LB $5.00 (978-0-8114-3151-4). 46pp. Many examples of animals that exist in prehistoric form, from dragonflies to horseshoe crabs, are explored in this volume. A companion volume is *Two Lives: Metamorphosis in the Natural World* (1992). (Rev: SLJ 5/92) [591]

22019 Powell, Jillian. *Animal Rights* (2–3). Series: Talking About. 1999, Raintree LB $25.69 (978-0-7398-1374-4). 32pp. This simple account shows how society's use of animals can conflict with the animals' needs and how this dilemma can be tackled. (Rev: BL 2/15/00; HBG 9/00) [346]

22020 Presnall, Judith Janda. *Animal Actors* (4–6). Series: Animals with Jobs. 2002, Gale LB $23.70 (978-0-7377-0934-6). 48pp. Animals that work in television and movies are profiled here with information on their training and care. Also use *Navy Dolphins* (2002). (Rev: SLJ 3/02) [791.43]

22021 Pringle, Laurence. *Animal Monsters: The Truth About Scary Creatures* (4–6). Illus. 1997, Marshall Cavendish $15.95 (978-0-7614-5003-0). 64pp. The truth about such feared animals as alligators, killer bees, and tarantulas — and why they are not as dangerous as many believe. (Rev: BL 9/1/97; HBG 3/98; SLJ 10/97) [591]

22022 Pye, Claire. *The Wild World of the Future* (4–8). Illus. 2003, Firefly $24.95 (978-1-55297-727-9); paper $14.95 (978-1-55297-725-5). 96pp. This lively, attractive volume speculates on the animals of the future, basing the projections on previous evolutionary development. (Rev: BL 7/03; SLJ 6/03) [576.8]

22023 Ross, Michael E. *Rolypolyology* (4–6). Illus. Series: Backyard Creatures. 1996, Carolrhoda LB $19.95 (978-0-87614-862-4). 48pp. Several common backyard creatures and their habits are described with interesting accompanying activities. (Rev: BL 3/15/96; SLJ 7/96) [595.3]

22024 Ruiz, Andres L. *Metamorphosis* (3–5). Illus. by Francisco Arredondo. Series: Cycles of Life. 1997, Sterling $12.95 (978-0-8069-9325-6). 32pp. In double-page spreads, Ruiz explains how some creatures transform themselves into another life form, such as tadpoles becoming frogs. (Rev: SLJ 6/97) [591]

22025 Ruurs, Margriet. *Wild Babies* (PS–2). Illus. by Andrew Kiss. 2003, Tundra $14.95 (978-0-88776-627-5). 32pp. Young animals and birds found in a North American forest are shown in lush, detailed paintings that provide intriguing hints of the next animal. (Rev: HBG 10/03; SLJ 2/03)

22026 Schubert, Ingrid, and Dieter Schubert. *Amazing Animals* (1–3). Trans. from Dutch by Leigh Sauerwein. 1995, Front St. $16.95 (978-1-886910-05-8). Using catchy rhymes and pleasant illustrations, this book shows how common animals live, reproduce, and deal with danger. (Rev: SLJ 1/96) [591]

22027 Shedd, Warner. *The Kids' Wildlife Book: Exploring Animal Worlds Through Indoor/Outdoor Experiences* (2–6). Illus. by Loretta Braren. Series: Kids Can! 1994, Williamson paper $12.95 (978-0-913589-77-9). 156pp. This book of projects and experiments features common mammals, amphibians, and birds of Canada and the United States. (Rev: SLJ 8/94) [591]

22028 Silverstein, Alvin, et al. *Vertebrates* (3–6). Illus. Series: Kingdoms of Life. 1996, Twenty-First Century LB $21.40 (978-0-8050-3517-9). 64pp. Vertebrates — animals with enclosed spinal cords — are introduced, with many color photos. (Rev: BL 6/1–15/96) [596]

22029 Siwanowicz, Igor. *Animals Up Close* (4–8). Illus. by author. 2009, DK $16.99 (978-0-7566-4513-7). 96pp. Dramatic close-up photographs display the features of small creatures of all kinds; fascinating for browsing, this book also offers enough information for reports. (Rev: BLO 5/27/09; SLJ 8/09) [500]

22030 Spada, Ada. *Fangs, Claws and Talons: Animal Predators* (3–6). Trans. by Amy Gulick. Illus. by Filippo Cappellini. 2007, Sterling $9.95 (978-1-60059-150-1). 48pp. This large-format book describes a variety of predators including snakes, raptors, big cats, and even tyrannosaurs. (Rev: BL 12/1/07; LMC 1/08) [591.5]

22031 Squire, Ann O. *African Animals* (2–3). Series: True Books — Animals. 2001, Children's Book Pr. LB $23.00 (978-0-516-22186-1). 48pp. A compact guide to the most common animals of Africa is presented in a simple text with color photographs on each page. (Rev: BL 12/15/01) [599]

22032 Stetson, Emily. *Kids' Easy-to-Create Wildlife Habitats* (2–5). Illus. by J. Susan Stone. Series: Quick Starts for Kids! 2004, Williamson paper $12.95 (978-0-8249-8665-0). 128pp. Offering solid information, illustrations, and activities, this wide-format book introduces the wildlife found in many communities and the foods that may bring them into the open. (Rev: BL 12/1/04; SLJ 3/05) [639.9]

22033 Stewart, Melissa. *Why Are Animals Orange?* (K–3). Illus. Series: Rainbow of Animals. 2009, Enslow LB $16.95 (978-0-7660-3250-7). 32pp. Butterflies can be orange, as can tigers, fish, and other animals. This photo-essay looks at the reasons why this coloring can be beneficial. (Rev: BL 4/1/09) [591.47]

22034 Suen, Anastasia. *ASPCA* (1–2). Series: Helping Organizations. 2002, Rosen LB $19.95 (978-0-8239-6004-0). 24pp. As well as a history of this organization, this easily read account describes how it works and how young people can get involved. (Rev: BL 6/1–15/02; SLJ 4/02) [179.3]

22035 Thornhill, Jan. *I Found a Dead Bird: The Kids' Guide to the Cycle of Life and Death* (3–6). Illus. 2006, Maple Tree $21.95 (978-1-897066-70-6); paper $9.95 (978-1-897066-71-3). 64pp. An attractive, thought-provoking approach to such sensitive topics as death and decomposition that covers scientific and social aspects. (Rev: SLJ 10/06)

22036 Tildes, Phyllis L. *Eye Guess: A Foldout Guessing Game* (PS–2). Illus. 2005, Charlesbridge $9.95 (978-1-57091-650-2). 36pp. Each of eight foldouts shows close-ups of an animal's eye and part of the face; there are a few facts about each animal and a tantalizing glimpse of the next animal. (Rev: BL 9/1/05) [590]

22037 Votaw, Carol. *Waking Up Down Under* (PS–1). Illus. by Susan Banta. 2007, NorthWord $15.95 (978-1-55971-976-6). Rhyming verses describe 12 Australian animals and how they greet the day (or night). (Rev: SLJ 12/07) [591.994]

22038 Wadsworth, Ginger. *River Discoveries* (2–4). Illus. by Paul Kratter. 2002, Charlesbridge $16.95 (978-1-57091-418-8); paper $6.95 (978-1-57091-419-5). 32pp. An introduction to the varied wildlife that surrounds and depends on a river, describing the activities of 13 types of animals over a 24-hour period. (Rev: BL 9/15/02; HBG 3/03; SLJ 8/02) [591.76]

22039 Ward, Jennifer. *Forest Bright, Forest Night* (K–3). Illus. by Jamichael Henterly. Series: Sharing Nature with Children. 2005, Dawn $16.95 (978-1-58469-066-5); paper $8.95 (978-1-58469-067-2). Diurnal animals go about daytime errands in the first part of this attractive book; readers flip it over to find these animals asleep and the nocturnal residents of the forest moving about. (Rev: SLJ 10/05) [591.5]

22040 Whyman, Kate. *The Animal Kingdom* (5–8). Illus. 1999, Raintree LB $27.12 (978-0-8172-5885-6). 48pp. A valuable account that introduces animal classification basics through text, sidebars, diagrams, and many eye-catching color photographs. (Rev: BL 2/1/00) [596]

22041 Woods, Geraldine. *Animal Experimentation and Testing: A Pro/Con Issue* (5–8). Series: Hot Issues. 1999, Enslow LB $27.93 (978-0-7660-1191-5). 64pp. The controversial subject of using animals in experiments is discussed with a history of the problem, arguments for and against, and a summary of important actions taken by government and individual groups. (Rev: HBG 3/00; SLJ 3/00) [179.3]

Amphibians and Reptiles

GENERAL AND MISCELLANEOUS

22042 Allen, Nancy Kelly. *Whose Food Is This: A Look at What Animals Eat — Seeds, Bugs, and Nuts* (PS–2). Illus. by Derrick Alderman and Denise Shea. Series: Whose Is It? 2004, Picture Window LB $25.26 (978-1-4048-0607-8). 24pp. Rhythmic question-and-answer format and colorful collages introduce the wide variety of foods that animals eat. Also use *Whose Sound Is This? A Look at Animal*

Noises — Chirps, Clicks, and Hoots (2004). (Rev: BL 11/1/04) [591.5]

22043 Arnosky, Jim. *Slither and Crawl: Eye to Eye with Reptiles* (2–4). Illus. by Jim Aronsky. 2009, Sterling $14.95 (978-1-4027-3986-6). 32pp. A large-format look at reptiles—mostly North American—with eye-catching life-size paintings and details of physical features, diet, hibernation, and so forth. (Rev: BL 4/1/09; LMC 8/09; SLJ 6/09) [597.9]

22044 Behler, John. *National Audubon Society First Field Guide: Reptiles* (4–8). 1999, Scholastic $17.95 (978-0-590-05467-6); paper $11.95 (978-0-590-05487-4). This richly illustrated manual discusses common characteristics of North American reptiles, then presents individual species under four groups: crocodiles, turtles, lizards, and snakes. (Rev: BL 3/15/99; SLJ 7/99) [597.9]

22045 Bredeson, Carmen. *Fun Facts About Salamanders!* (1–3). Series: I Like Reptiles and Amphibians! 2007, Enslow LB $21.26 (978-0-7660-2790-9). 24pp. The crisp narrative uses a question-and-answer format to provide basic information about salamanders; illustrated with color photographs. (Rev: SLJ 10/07) [597.6]

22046 Brenner, Barbara, and Bernice Chardiet. *Where's That Reptile?* (2–4). Illus. Series: Hide and Seek. 1993, Scholastic $10.95 (978-0-590-45212-0). 32pp. An interactive book that introduces a variety of reptiles to primary-age children. (Rev: BL 10/15/93; SLJ 1/94) [597.9]

22047 Burns, Diane L. *Frogs, Toads and Turtles* (3–6). Illus. 1997, NorthWord paper $6.95 (978-1-55971-593-5). 48pp. A paperback field guide that introduces the world of 30 amphibians, with coverage of their habitats, food, and appearance. (Rev: BL 8/97) [597.8]

22048 Cassie, Brian. *National Audubon Society First Field Guide: Amphibians* (4–6). Series: First Field Guide. 1999, Scholastic $17.95 (978-0-590-63982-8); paper $8.95 (978-0-590-64008-4). 160pp. This field guide, with more than 450 full-color illustrations, introduces 50 easily found amphibians, with material on their characteristics and habitats. (Rev: BL 10/15/99) [597.5]

22049 Chermayeff, Ivan. *Scaly Facts* (PS–1). Illus. 1995, Harcourt $11.00 (978-0-15-200109-4). 32pp. Reptiles are introduced through brief, simple text and dynamic illustrations. (Rev: BL 4/1/95; SLJ 7/95) [597.9]

22050 Dennard, Deborah. *Reptiles* (5–7). Illus. by Jennifer O. Dewey. Series: Our Wild World. 2004, NorthWord $16.95 (978-1-55971-880-6). 191pp. A compilation of four shorter books published by NorthWord in 2003, this volume examines the physical characteristics, natural habitat, diet, and behavior of alligators, crocodiles, lizards, snakes, and turtles. (Rev: SLJ 8/04) [597.9]

22051 Holub, Joan. *Why Do Snakes Hiss? And Other Questions About Snakes, Lizards, and Turtles* (1–2). Illus. by Anna DiVito. Series: Easy-to-Read. 2004, Penguin $14.99 (978-0-8037-3000-7). 48pp. Using an attractive question-and-answer format, this vol-

ume explores the characteristics and behavior of the reptile family. (Rev: BL 11/1/04; SLJ 11/04) [597.9]

22052 Jango-Cohen, Judith. *Desert Iguanas* (PS–2). Series: Pull Ahead Books. 2001, Lerner LB $22.60 (978-0-8225-3635-2). 32pp. A color photograph and two lines of simple text are found on each page of this attractive basic introduction to these desert reptiles. (Rev: BL 6/1–15/01; HBG 10/01) [597.9]

22053 Kalman, Bobbie, and Jacqueline Langille. *What Is an Amphibian?* (2–5). Series: Science of Living Things. 1999, Crabtree LB $25.27 (978-0-86505-934-4); paper $6.95 (978-0-86505-952-8). 32pp. Amphibians and their general characteristics, habits, and habitats are covered plus material on some specific members of the group in this lavishly illustrated book. (Rev: SLJ 3/00) [597.8]

22054 Llewellyn, Claire. *Question Time: Reptiles* (3–5). Illus. Series: Question Time. 2002, Kingfisher $11.95 (978-0-7534-5451-0); paper $6.95 (978-0-7534-5463-3). 32pp. Topics covered in a question-and-answer format include the different types of reptiles, and their characteristics, habitat, and defense mechanisms. (Rev: HBG 3/03; SLJ 2/03)

22055 Miller, Ruth. *Reptiles* (4–6). Series: Animal Kingdom. 2004, Raintree LB $32.79 (978-1-4109-1052-3). 64pp. The common characteristics of reptiles are explained, followed by descriptions of various orders of reptiles and selected specific species plus discussion of endangered status and evolution. Also use *Amphibians* (2004). (Rev: BL 5/1/04; SLJ 6/05)

22056 Miller, Sara S. *Salamanders: Secret Silent Lives* (3–5). Series: Animals in Order. 1999, Watts LB $26.50 (978-0-531-11568-8). 48pp. This book discusses the amphibian class known as salamanders and gives a pictorial glimpse into their types, lives, structure, habits, and homes. (Rev: BL 12/15/99; HBG 4/00) [597.6]

22057 Murray, Peter. *Amphibians* (3–6). Series: Science Around Us. 2004, Child's World LB $27.07 (978-1-59296-271-6). 32pp. Eye-catching photographs and interesting "Did You Know?" features draw the reader into this overview of amphibians. Also use *Reptiles* (2004). (Rev: SLJ 3/05) [597.8]

22058 Pascoe, Elaine, ed. *Into Wild Louisiana* (3–6). Series: The Jeff Corwin Experience. 2004, Gale LB $24.95 (978-1-4103-0060-7). 48pp. Readers visit the swamp creatures of backwoods Louisiana, from alligators to frogs, guided by Jeff Corwin of TV's *Animal Planet*. (Rev: SLJ 4/04)

22059 Savage, Stephen. *Amphibians* (2–4). Series: What's the Difference? 2000, Raintree LB $25.69 (978-0-7398-1359-1). 32pp. This book introduces a number of amphibians that live on water, land, or both. (Rev: BL 10/15/00; HBG 3/01) [597.6]

22060 Savage, Stephen. *Reptiles* (2–4). Series: What's the Difference? 2000, Raintree LB $25.69 (978-0-7398-1358-4). 32pp. This book explores the similarities and differences in the class known as reptiles and introduces such creatures as crocodiles, rattlesnakes, and tortoises. (Rev: BL 10/15/00; HBG 3/01; SLJ 1/01) [597.96]

22061 Sill, Cathryn. *About Amphibians: A Guide for Children* (PS–2). Illus. by John Sill. 2001, Peachtree $15.95 (978-1-56145-234-7). 40pp. An introduction for young children that has colorful, realistic paintings facing brief text. (Rev: BL 5/15/01; HBG 10/01; SLJ 6/01) [597.8]

22062 Sill, Cathryn. *About Reptiles: A Guide for Children* (PS–2). Illus. by John Sill. 1999, Peachtree $15.95 (978-1-56145-183-8). 40pp. This introduction to reptiles in general and snakes in particular is aimed at young children and has a colorful, realistic painting on one page followed by brief text on the facing page. (Rev: BL 6/1–15/99; HBG 9/99; SLJ 7/99) [597.9]

22063 Spilsbury, Richard, and Louise Spilsbury. *Classifying Reptiles* (4–6). Series: Classifying Living Things. 2003, Heinemann LB $24.22 (978-1-4034-0848-8). 32pp. This title examines the scientific classification of reptiles, including identification of the phyllum, class, and order of different types of reptiles. (Rev: HBG 10/03; SLJ 11/03) [597.9]

22064 Spilsbury, Richard, and Louise Spilsbury. *The Life Cycle of Amphibians* (3–5). Illus. Series: From Egg to Adult. 2003, Heinemann LB $24.22 (978-1-4034-0785-6). 32pp. A brief overview of amphibians, examining the creatures' physical characteristics, habitat, diet, and life cycle. (Rev: HBG 4/04; SLJ 10/03) [597.8]

22065 Squire, Ann O. *Chinese Giant Salamander: The World's Biggest Amphibian* (K–2). Illus. Series: SuperSized! 2007, Bearport LB $21.28 (978-1-59716-386-6). 24pp. Report writers will get lots of mileage from this introduction to the Chinese giant salamander, filled with facts about and photographs of the big amphibian. (Rev: SLJ 8/07)

22066 Stewart, Melissa. *Amphibians* (2–3). Series: True Books — Animals. 2001, Children's Book Pr. LB $25.00 (978-0-516-22037-6). 48pp. In this colorful, simple volume, a variety of amphibians are introduced with material on their appearance, habits, and distinctive characteristics. (Rev: BL 12/15/01) [597.6]

22067 Theodorou, Rod. *Amphibians* (2–4). Series: Animal Babies. 1999, Heinemann LB $21.36 (978-1-57572-950-3). 32pp. The babies of about half a dozen species of amphibians are presented, with material on their anatomy, life cycles, and habits. (Rev: SLJ 4/00) [597.6]

22068 Wilkes, Sarah. *Amphibians* (5–9). Series: World Almanac Library of the Animal Kingdom. 2006, World Almanac LB $31.00 (978-0-8368-6208-9). 48pp. This colorful guide identifies common species of amphibians and examines their physical characteristics, habitats, diets, behaviors, and life cycles. (Rev: SLJ 12/06) [597.5]

22069 Wilson, Hannah. *Life-Size Reptiles* (3–6). Illus. 2007, Sterling $9.95 (978-1-4027-4542-3). 28pp. From lizards to turtles, geckos to Komodo dragons, this is a large-format introduction to things reptile with fold-out illustrations. (Rev: BL 6/1–15/07; SLJ 8/07) [597.9]

22070 Winner, Cherie. *Everything Reptile: What Kids Really Want to Know About Reptiles* (3–5). 2004, NorthWord $10.95 (978-1-55971-146-3); paper $7.95 (978-1-55971-164-7). 63pp. A basic introduction, using a question-and-answer format with plenty of photographs. (Rev: SLJ 11/04) [597.9]

22071 Winner, Cherie. *Salamanders* (3–6). Illus. Series: Nature Watch. 1993, Carolrhoda LB $23.93 (978-0-87614-757-3). 48pp. Various kinds of salamanders are introduced, with material given on life cycle, habits, and endangered status. (Rev: BL 8/93) [597.6]

22072 Zabludoff, Marc. *The Reptile Class* (5–9). Illus. Series: Family Trees. 2005, Benchmark LB $32.79 (978-0-7614-1820-7). 95pp. Habits, habitats, and other aspects of this varied class of animals; an engaging book with plenty of facts for report writers. (Rev: SLJ 6/06) [597.9]

ALLIGATORS AND CROCODILES

22073 Arnosky, Jim. *Crocodile Safari* (2–5). Illus. by author. 2009, Scholastic $21.99 (978-0-439-90356-1). 40pp. Arnosky sprinkles informative text about crocodiles with anecdotes about his own experiences in the mangrove swamps of Florida. (Rev: BL 12/1/08; LMC 5/09; SLJ 2/09) [597.98]

22074 Bare, Colleen S. *Never Kiss an Alligator!* (2–4). Illus. 1994, Puffin paper $6.99 (978-0-14-055257-7). 32pp. Sharp color photos highlight this close-up look at the alligator. (Rev: BCCB 9/89; BL 9/1/89; SLJ 8/89) [597.98]

22075 Clarke, Ginjer L. *Baby Alligator* (1–3). Illus. by Neecy Twinem. 2000, Penguin paper $3.99 (978-0-448-42095-0). 48pp. For beginning readers, this is a simple introduction to alligators that traces the life cycle from hatching from an egg in the spring to waiting out the winter in a dark tunnel. (Rev: BL 7/00; HBG 9/00) [597.98]

22076 Feigenbaum, Aaron. *American Alligators: Freshwater Survivors* (3–5). Series: America's Animal Comebacks. 2008, Bearport LB $25.27 (978-1-59716-503-7). 32pp. With eye-catching photographs and an appealing format, this volume looks at the reasons for the decline in the alligator population (hunting, pollution, loss of habitat) and the measures that succeeded in bring them back from the brink of extinction. (Rev: SLJ 2/08) [597.98]

22077 Fitzgerald, Patrick J. *Croc and Gator Attacks* (4–7). Series: Animal Attack! 2000, Children's paper $6.95 (978-0-516-23514-1). 48pp. Aimed at the reluctant reader, this book tells true stories of attacks by crocodiles and alligators and gives information about these species and their differences. (Rev: SLJ 2/01) [597.98]

22078 Jango-Cohen, Judith. *Crocodiles* (4–6). Series: Animals Animals. 2002, Benchmark LB $25.64 (978-0-7614-1446-9). 48pp. This is an oversize book filled with excellent photographs and text covering the anatomy, habits, food, and habitats of crocodiles. (Rev: BL 12/15/02; HBG 3/03; SLJ 2/03) [597.98]

22079 Jango-Cohen, Judith. *Crocodiles* (5–8). Series: AnimalWays. 2000, Marshall Cavendish LB $31.36 (978-0-7614-1136-9). 112pp. This book examines the habitat, range, classification, evolution, anatomy, behavior, and endangered status of the crocodile. (Rev: BL 1/1–15/01; HBG 3/01) [597.98]

22080 Kallen, Stuart A., and P. M. Boekhoff. *Alligators* (4–6). Series: Nature's Predators. 2002, Gale LB $23.70 (978-0-7377-0642-0). Color photographs are used with a simple text to describe characteristics of alligators and their habitats, with coverage on how they kill their prey and how they also are hunted. (Rev: BL 1/1–15/02; SLJ 6/02) [597.98]

22081 Llewellyn, Claire. *Crocodile* (PS–3). Illus. by Simon Mendez. Series: Starting Life. 2004, NorthWord $16.95 (978-1-55971-900-1). 23pp. On pages that grow progressively wider, the stages of a crocodile's development are traced, with information on such topics as habitat, diet, and predatory behavior plus realistic illustrations. (Rev: SLJ 11/04) [597.98]

22082 Markle, Sandra. *Crocodiles* (2–5). Illus. Series: Animal Predators. 2004, Carolrhoda LB $25.26 (978-1-57505-726-2). 40pp. Concise text and clear, full-page photographs introduce the life cycle of the crocodile and its physical characteristics, habitat, diet, and predatory behavior. (Rev: BL 9/15/04; SLJ 10/04) [597.98]

22083 Muñoz, William. *Waiting Alligators* (PS–2). Series: Pull Ahead Books. 1999, Lerner LB $22.60 (978-0-8225-3615-4). 32pp. Using interactive material, this simple science book introduces alligators and includes many photos, a map, a body diagram, glossary, and index. (Rev: BL 8/99; HBG 9/99) [597.98]

22084 Noonan, Diana. *The Crocodile* (2–4). Illus. Series: Life Cycles. 2002, Chelsea LB $23.00 (978-0-7910-6964-6). 32pp. Handsome photographs and simple text describe the life cycle, habitat, appearance, and predators of the crocodile, in a small, square, photo-essay format. (Rev: BL 1/1–15/03; HBG 3/03) [597.98]

22085 Robinson, Claire. *Crocodiles* (2–3). Illus. Series: In the Wild. 1997, Heinemann $18.50 (978-1-57572-133-0). 24pp. A simple introduction to crocodiles that tells how they live, communicate, find food, and raise their young. (Rev: BL 2/1/98; SLJ 4/98) [597.98]

22086 Rockwell, Anne. *Who Lives in an Alligator Hole?* (K–3). Illus. by Lizzy Rockwell. Series: Let's-Read-and-Find-Out Science. 2006, HarperCollins $15.99 (978-0-06-028530-2); paper $4.99 (978-0-06-445200-7). 40pp. This informational picture book gives facts on the history and habitat of alligators; it also discusses threats to their existence, how their surroundings have changed, conservation efforts, and their key role in helping other species to survive. (Rev: BL 12/1/06; SLJ 11/06) [597.98]

22087 Scherer, Glenn, and Marty Fletcher. *The American Crocodile: Help Save This Endangered Species!* (5–7). Illus. Series: Saving Endangered Species. 2007, Enslow $33.27 (978-1-59845-041-5). 128pp. Report writers will welcome the information included in this volume and at the recommended Web links. (Rev: SLJ 11/07) [597.98]

22088 Simon, Seymour. *Crocodiles and Alligators* (3–6). Illus. 1999, HarperCollins LB $16.89 (978-0-

06-027474-0). 32pp. Basic information about alligators and crocodiles is given, including their history, differences, habitats, food, reproduction, and endangered status. (Rev: BL 4/1/99; HBG 9/99; SLJ 6/99) [597.98]

22089 Snyder, Trish. *Alligator and Crocodile Rescue: Changing the Future for Endangered Wildlife* (4–8). Series: Firefly Animal Rescue. 2006, Firefly LB $19.95 (978-1-55297-920-4); paper $9.95 (978-1-55297-919-8). 64pp. Examines the work being done to protect alligators and crocodiles in their natural habitats and also looks at the physical characteristics, diets, behaviors, and life cycles of these reptiles. (Rev: SLJ 12/06) [597.98]

22090 Souza, D. M. *Roaring Reptiles: A Book About Crocodilians* (3–5). Illus. Series: Creatures All Around Us. 1992, Carolrhoda LB $14.95 (978-0-87614-710-8). 40pp. Close-up photographs and lively text introduce the types of crocodilians found in North America. (Rev: BL 10/1/92; SLJ 12/92) [597.98]

22091 Spilsbury, Richard. *Alligator* (4–6). Illus. Series: Animals Under Threat. 2004, Heinemann LB $18.95 (978-1-4034-4857-6). 48pp. The life cycle of the alligator and threats to its survival are explored in this blend of narrative and eye-catching color photography.

22092 Staub, Frank. *Alligators* (2–4). Photos by author. Illus. Series: Early Bird Nature Books. 1995, Lerner LB $25.26 (978-0-8225-3007-7). 48pp. Discusses the appearance and habits of alligators, as well as the role they play in their environment. (Rev: SLJ 8/95) [597.6]

22093 Tourville, Amanda Doering. *A Crocodile Grows Up* (1–3). Illus. by Michael Denman and William J. Huiett. Series: Wild Animals. 2006, Picture Window LB $25.26 (978-1-4048-3157-5). 24pp. A crocodile's development from birth to full independence is described in brief text and realistic illustrations. (Rev: SLJ 4/07) [597.98]

22094 Walker, Sally M. *Crocodiles* (4–6). Illus. Series: Nature Watch. 2003, Lerner LB $25.26 (978-1-57505-345-5). 48pp. An attractive introduction to crocodiles, how and where they live, and their life cycle. (Rev: HBG 4/04)

FROGS AND TOADS

22095 Aloian, Molly, and Bobbie Kalman. *Endangered Frogs* (3–5). Illus. Series: Earth's Endangered Animals. 2006, Crabtree LB $25.27 (978-0-7787-1872-7). 32pp. Large text and clear color photographs focus on threatened frog species, presenting basic information about physical characteristics, diet, habitat, and behavior, and discussing the specific threats they face. (Rev: SLJ 1/07) [597.8]

22096 Arnosky, Jim. *All About Frogs* (2–4). Illus. Series: All About. 2002, Scholastic $16.95 (978-0-590-48164-9). 32pp. Excellent illustrations accompany the in-depth information about the anatomy and habitats of various species of frogs in this book for younger readers. (Rev: BL 2/1/02; HB 3/02; HBG 10/02; SLJ 3/02) [597.8]

22097 Berman, Ruth. *Climbing Tree Frogs* (PS–2). Series: Pull Ahead Books. 1998, Lerner LB $22.60 (978-0-8225-3605-5). 32pp. This unusual branch of the frog family is introduced with a series of thoughtful questions, color photos, maps, and simple text. (Rev: BL 2/15/99; HBG 3/99; SLJ 6/99) [597.8]

22098 Bishop, Nic. *Nic Bishop Frogs* (2–4). Illus. 2008, Scholastic $17.99 (978-0-439-87755-8). 48pp. Compelling photographs and clear text — covering anatomy, diet, reproduction, and so forth — make this a very appealing volume. (Rev: BL 1/1–15/08; HB 3/08; LMC 3/08; SLJ 2/08*) [597.8]

22099 Bredeson, Carmen. *Fun Facts About Frogs!* (PS–2). Series: I Like Reptiles and Amphibians! 2007, Enslow LB $21.26 (978-0-7660-2788-6). 24pp. Eye-catching photographs and clear text make this a useful introduction for beginning readers. (Rev: SLJ 1/08) [597.8]

22100 Bredeson, Carmen. *Poison Dart Frogs Up Close* (1–3). Series: Zoom in on Animals! 2008, Enslow LB $21.26 (978-0-7660-3077-0). 24pp. Simple text and close-up color photographs introduce body parts, babies, and other important characteristics. (Rev: SLJ 11/08) [597.87]

22101 Chrustowski, Rick. *Hop Frog* (PS–3). Illus. by author. 2003, Holt $15.95 (978-0-8050-6688-3). The life cycle of a leopard frog is told in an entertaining narrative. (Rev: HBG 10/03; SLJ 5/03) [597.8]

22102 Cowley, Joy. *Red-Eyed Tree Frog* (PS–K). Illus. by Nic Bishop. 1999, Scholastic $16.95 (978-0-590-87175-4). 32pp. In this stunning work, the feeding habits of several animals in a rain forest in Central America are described from a tree frog's point of view. (Rev: BCCB 3/99; BL 5/15/99*; HB 3/99; HBG 9/99; SLJ 3/99) [597.8]

22103 Delafosse, Claude. *Frogs* (PS–2). Illus. Series: First Discovery. 1997, Scholastic $12.95 (978-0-590-93782-5). 24pp. With a highly visual approach, this book introduces frogs using excellent drawings and a brief text. (Rev: BL 2/15/97) [597.8]

22104 Dell'Oro, Suzanne Paul. *Hiding Toads* (PS–2). Series: Pull Ahead Books. 1999, Lerner $22.60 (978-0-8225-3626-0); paper $5.95 (978-0-8225-3630-7). 32pp. Using questions and plenty of close-up photographs, this is a simple overview of the behavior and physical characteristics of toads. (Rev: BL 12/15/99; HBG 4/00) [597.8]

22105 Dewey, Jennifer O. *Poison Dart Frogs* (K–3). Illus. 1998, Boyds Mills $15.95 (978-1-56397-655-1). This introduction to the many kinds of poison dart frogs of Latin American rain forests explains how they release a poison through their skin that is used by hunters on blowpipe darts. (Rev: BCCB 4/98; BL 3/1/98; HB 3/98; HBG 9/98; SLJ 4/98) [597.8]

22106 Ganeri, Anita. *From Tadpole to Frog* (1–3). Illus. Series: How Living Things Grow. 2006, Heinemann LB $25.36 (978-1-4034-7859-7). 32pp. How a tadpole grows to be a frog, presented in an easy-to-read format. (Rev: SLJ 6/06) [597.8]

22107 Gibbons, Gail. *Frogs* (K–3). Illus. 1993, Holiday House LB $16.95 (978-0-8234-1052-1). 32pp. Colorful water scenes and a simple text depict frogs in all stages of development from spawn to maturity. (Rev: BL 10/15/93; SLJ 12/93) [597.8]

22108 Glaser, Linda. *Fabulous Frogs* (PS–1). Illus. by Loretta Krupinski. 1999, Millbrook LB $22.90 (978-0-7613-0424-1). An enjoyable picture book that presents the life of a frog from mating to birth and growth, plus material on such varieties as the leopard frog, spring peeper, and bullfrog. (Rev: HBG 9/99; SLJ 5/99) [597.8]

22109 Godwin, Sam. *The Trouble with Tadpoles: A First Look at the Life Cycle of a Frog* (K–1). Illus. Series: First Look: Science. 2004, Picture Window LB $25.26 (978-1-4048-0654-2). 32pp. In simple language with cartoon-style illustrations, this volume describes the life cycle of frogs.

22110 Greenberg, Dan. *Frogs* (5–8). Series: Animal-Ways. 2000, Marshall Cavendish LB $31.36 (978-0-7614-1138-3). 112pp. As well as chapters devoted to the amazing variety of frogs, this book discusses their anatomy, habits, and survival skills. (Rev: BL 1/1–15/01; HBG 3/01) [597.8]

22111 Hawes, Judy. *Why Frogs Are Wet* (K–3). Illus. by Mary Ann Fraser. Series: Let's-Read-and-Find-Out. 2000, HarperCollins LB $15.89 (978-0-06-028162-5); paper $5.99 (978-0-06-445195-6). 40pp. The physical characteristics, life cycle, evolution, and behavior of frogs are introduced in this revision of the 1968 title. (Rev: BL 9/15/00; HBG 3/01) [597.8]

22112 Hickman, Pamela. *A New Frog: My First Look at the Life Cycle of an Amphibian* (PS–2). Illus. by Heather Collins. Series: My First Look At. 1999, Kids Can $6.95 (978-1-55074-615-0). 20pp. A beginning science book that explains the life cycle of a frog, using rhymes, factual text, and watercolor paintings. (Rev: BL 6/1–15/99; HBG 9/99; SLJ 8/99) [571.8]

22113 Johnson, Sylvia A. *Tree Frogs* (4–6). Illus. 1986, Lerner LB $22.60 (978-0-8225-1467-1). 48pp. A look at the characteristics, environment, breeding, and life cycles of the tree frog. (Rev: BL 10/1/86; SLJ 11/86)

22114 Llewellyn, Claire. *Frog* (K–4). Illus. by Simon Mendez. Series: Starting Life. 2003, NorthWord $16.95 (978-1-55971-869-1). 23pp. A look at the life cycle of a frog, from egg to tadpole to adult, and the environment in which frogs live. (Rev: SLJ 4/04) [597.8]

22115 Magloff, Lisa. *Watch Me Grow: Frog* (PS–2). Series: Watch Me Grow. 2003, DK $7.99 (978-0-7894-9629-4). 24pp. This attractive title provides a close-up look — from the perspective of the animal — at the early life cycle of a frog from the tadpole stage. (Rev: BL 10/15/03) [597.8]

22116 Mara, William P. *The Fragile Frog* (3–6). Illus. 1996, Whitman LB $16.99 (978-0-8075-2580-7). 48pp. A description is given of the life cycle of this tiny frog, whose existence is now threatened. (Rev: BL 11/1/96; SLJ 11/96) [597.8]

22117 Markle, Sandra. *Slippery, Slimy Baby Frogs* (3–5). 2006, Walker $16.95 (978-0-8027-8062-1). 32pp. This compelling photo-essay pairs interesting facts about frogs and their development with beautiful photographs, including some great close-ups. (Rev: BL 5/1/06; SLJ 5/06) [597.8]

22118 Miller, Sara S. *Frogs and Toads: The Leggy Leapers* (3–5). Series: Animals in Order. 2000, Watts LB $26.50 (978-0-531-11632-6). 48pp. A brief introduction to animal classification is followed by a description of frogs and toads, their similarities, differences, and life cycles. (Rev: BL 10/15/00) [597.8]

22119 Netherton, John. *Red-Eyed Tree Frogs* (2–3). Series: Early Bird Nature Books. 2000, Lerner LB $25.26 (978-0-8225-3037-4). 48pp. An introduction to these colorful rain forest amphibians — with their orange feet, lime green skin, blue stripes, and big red eyes. (Rev: BL 7/00; HBG 3/01) [597.8]

22120 Noonan, Diana. *The Frog* (2–4). Series: Life Cycles. 2002, Chelsea LB $23.00 (978-0-7910-6966-0). 32pp. This account follows the life cycle of this amphibian from egg to tadpole and finally the growth of lungs and legs needed to live on land. (Rev: BL 12/15/02; HBG 3/03) [597.8]

22121 Pfeffer, Wendy. *From Tadpole to Frog* (PS–1). Illus. by Holly Keller. Series: Let's-Read-and-Find-Out. 1994, HarperCollins paper $5.99 (978-0-06-445123-9). 32pp. This simple science book shows one year in the life cycle of a frog, beginning with the end of its hibernation in the spring. (Rev: BL 8/94; HB 7/94; SLJ 11/94) [597.8]

22122 Rau, Dana Meachen. *The Frog in the Pond* (PS–1). Series: Benchmark Rebus. 2006, Benchmark LB $22.79 (978-0-7614-2310-2). 24pp. With its child-friendly blend of rebuses and easy-to-understand text, this easy reader describes the physical characteristics, life cycle, and daily activities of frogs. (Rev: SLJ 12/06) [597.8]

22123 Rau, Dana Meachen. *Guess Who Jumps* (PS–K). Series: Bookworms. Guess Who. 2009, Marshall Cavendish $15.95 (978-0-7614-2908-1). 32pp. Fun for browsing, this book asks readers to identify a frog using the clues in the text and images. (Rev: SLJ 6/09) [597.8]

22124 Robinson, Fay. *Fantastic Frogs* (1–2). Illus. by Jean Cassels. Series: Hello Reader! 2000, Scholastic paper $3.99 (978-0-590-52269-4). 32pp. Different varieties of frogs like brown, green, and jungle frogs are introduced in this beginning reader with material on their looks and behavior. (Rev: BL 2/15/01) [597.8]

22125 Royston, Angela. *Life Cycle of a Frog* (2–3). Illus. Series: Life Cycle. 1998, Heinemann $21.36 (978-1-57572-613-7). 32pp. Using a color photograph and a continuing timeline on each page, the development of a frog is traced from egg to full-grown adult, who, in turn, produces eggs. (Rev: BL 4/15/98; SLJ 7/98) [597.8]

22126 Somervill, Barbara. *Cane Toad* (3–6). Series: Animal Invaders. 2008, Cherry Lake LB $26.26 (978-1-60279-115-2). 32pp. A solid introduction to the invasive cane toad and the threat it presents in Australia, with color photographs and maps. (Rev: SLJ 9/08) [597.8]

22127 Souza, D. M. *Frogs, Frogs Everywhere* (3–5). Illus. Series: Creatures All Around Us. 1995, Carolrhoda LB $19.93 (978-0-87614-825-9). 40pp. Physical and behavioral characteristics of frogs are attractively presented, along with various species and habitats. (Rev: BL 4/15/95; SLJ 9/95) [597.8]

22128 Spilsbury, Louise. *Frog* (K–2). Series: Life Cycles. 2005, Heinemann LB $20.64 (978-1-4034-6772-0). 24pp. Brief text consisting of questions and answers suitable for beginning readers and bold photographs focus on the life cycle of the frog. (Rev: SLJ 7/05) [597.8]

22129 Starosta, Paul. *The Frog: Natural Acrobat* (3–6). Photos by author. Series: Animal Close-Ups. 1996, Charlesbridge paper $6.95 (978-0-88106-437-7). 27pp. A simple account with plenty of photos that tells about the various species, habitats, life cycles, and behavior of frogs. (Rev: SLJ 1/97) [597.8]

22130 Stone, Tanya L. *Toads* (3–5). Series: Wild America. 2002, Gale LB $24.94 (978-1-56711-646-5). 24pp. A close-up look at these amphibians that gives material on where they live and their physical features, life cycle, and habits. (Rev: BL 10/15/02) [597.8]

22131 Tagholm, Sally. *The Frog* (2–3). Illus. by Bert Kitchen. Series: Animal Lives. 2000, Kingfisher $9.95 (978-0-7534-5215-8). 32pp. After a series of pictures depicting the daily activities of a frog and its mating procedures, this account focuses on the development of an egg to adulthood. (Rev: BL 5/15/00; HBG 3/01; SLJ 8/00) [597.8]

22132 Wallace, Karen. *Tale of a Tadpole* (PS–2). Series: Eyewitness Reader. 1998, DK $3.99 (978-0-7894-3437-1); paper $14.99 (978-0-7894-3761-7). 32pp. The growth cycle of a frog from egg to mature adult is traced in a spare text with well-chosen photographs. (Rev: HBG 3/99; SLJ 4/99) [597.8]

22133 Wechsler, Doug. *Bullfrogs* (3–6). Series: The Really Wild Life of Frogs. 2002, Rosen LB $21.25 (978-0-8239-5855-9). 24pp. The bullfrog's physical characteristics, habitat, diet, predators, and so forth are presented with close-up photographs and boxed features. Also use *Leopard Frogs*, *Treefrogs*, and *Wood Frogs* (all 2002). (Rev: SLJ 5/02) [597.89]

22134 White, William. *All About the Frog* (4–8). Illus. Series: Sterling Color Nature. 1992, Sterling $14.95 (978-0-8069-8274-8). 72pp. A brief history of the frog and a discussion of its anatomy, reproduction, food, adaptations, and likely future. (Rev: BL 7/92; SLJ 9/92) [597.8]

22135 Whiting, Jim. *Frogs in Danger* (3–5). Series: A Robbie Reader. On the Verge of Extinction: Crisis in the Environment. 2007, Mitchell Lane LB $25.70 (978-1-58415-585-0). 32pp. After explaining what is happening to frogs, Whiting discusses the impact of global warming and other threats and looks ahead to the future; a "What You Can Do" section will help emerging activists. (Rev: LMC 1/08; SLJ 11/07)

22136 Winer, Yvonne. *Frogs Sing Songs* (PS–3). Illus. by Tony Oliver. 2003, Charlesbridge $16.95 (978-1-57091-548-2); paper $6.95 (978-1-57091-549-9). 32pp. Frogs and their sounds are presented in a lyrical text combined with realistic watercolor illustrations and a strong environmental message. (Rev: BL 4/1/03; HBG 10/03; SLJ 7/03) [597.8]

22137 Zollman, Pam. *A Tadpole Grows Up* (K–1). Series: Scholastic News Nonfiction Readers. 2005, Children's Pr. LB $20.00 (978-0-516-24947-6). 24pp. This photo-filled book introduces the life cycle of frogs and toads, focusing in particular on survival strategies of tadpoles. (Rev: SLJ 4/06) [597.8]

LIZARDS

22138 Cowley, Joy. *Chameleon, Chameleon* (K–2). Illus. 2005, Scholastic $16.95 (978-0-439-66653-4). 32pp. The panther chameleon of Madagascar is the focus of this compelling photo-essay. (Rev: BL 2/15/05; SLJ 4/05) [597.95]

22139 Darling, Kathy. *Komodo Dragon: On Location* (4–6). Illus. by Tara Darling. Series: On Location. 1997, Lothrop LB $16.89 (978-0-688-13777-9). 40pp. Color photographs enliven the description of this reptile, its habits, and its habitat on Komodo Island. (Rev: BCCB 5/97; BL 2/15/97; SLJ 4/97) [597.95]

22140 Greenaway, Theresa. *Snakes* (4–7). Series: The Secret World of . . . 2001, Raintree LB $18.98 (978-0-7368-3510-7). 48pp. A look at the world of snakes with material on their structure, habitats, behavior, food, mating habits, and enemies. (Rev: BL 10/15/01) [597.96]

22141 Kalman, Bobbie. *Endangered Komodo Dragons* (3–5). Illus. Series: Earth's Endangered Animals. 2004, Crabtree LB $25.27 (978-0-7787-1857-4); paper $6.95 (978-0-7787-1903-8). 32pp. In addition to discussion of their endangered status, this volume covers these animals' habitat, behavior, life cycle, and so forth. (Rev: SLJ 6/05)

22142 Lunis, Natalie. *Komodo Dragon: The World's Biggest Lizard* (K–2). Illus. Series: SuperSized! 2007, Bearport LB $21.28 (978-1-59716-392-7). 24pp. A fact-filled introduction to the big lizard, with eye-catching photographs. (Rev: SLJ 8/07)

22143 MacKen, JoAnn Early. *Gila Monsters / Monstruos de Gila* (2–4). Trans. by Tatiana Acosta and Guillermo Gutiérrez. Series: Animals That Live in the Desert / Animales del desierto. 2005, Weekly Reader LB $21.00 (978-0-8368-4841-0). 24pp. A beginning book with facts about gila monsters in both English and Spanish. (Rev: SLJ 6/06) [597.95]

22144 Marsico, Katie. *A Komodo Dragon Hatchling Grows Up* (1–2). 2007, Children's Pr. LB $19.00 (978-0-531-17477-7). 24pp. The development of a Komodo dragon is the topic of this vocabulary-building book with interesting photographs. (Rev: SLJ 7/07)

22145 Mattern, Joanne. *Lizards* (3–6). Series: Animals, Animals. 2001, Benchmark LB $25.64 (978-0-7614-1259-5). 48pp. In addition to describing physical characteristics, behavior, habitat, and so forth of more than two dozen species, Mattern looks at related folklore and at the animals' relationship with humans. (Rev: HBG 10/02; SLJ 6/02) [597.95]

22146 Maynard, Thane. *Komodo Dragons* (3–4). Series: New Naturebooks. 2006, The Child's World LB $27.07 (978-1-59296-642-4). 32pp. An introductory overview of this large lizard, with vivid color photographs. (Rev: SLJ 2/07) [597.95]

22147 Montgomery, Sy. *The Snake Scientist* (5–8). Series: Scientists in the Field. 1999, Houghton $16.00 (978-0-395-87169-0). This account captures the excitement of scientific discovery by focusing on a zoologist and young students who are studying the red-sided garter snake in Canada. (Rev: BCCB 4/99; BL 2/15/99; HB 7/99; HBG 9/99; SLJ 5/99) [597.96]

22148 Pipe, Jim. *The Giant Book of Snakes and Slithery Creatures* (4–8). Illus. 1998, Millbrook LB $27.90 (978-0-7613-0804-1). This richly illustrated, oversize volume contains details about snakes, lizards, and amphibians. (Rev: BL 8/98; HBG 9/98; SLJ 12/98) [597.9]

22149 Schnieper, Claudia. *Chameleons* (3–6). Illus. by Max Meier. Series: Nature Watch. 1989, Carolrhoda LB $19.93 (978-0-87614-341-4). 48pp. Introduces the life cycle, physical characteristics, and habits of chameleons. (Rev: BL 9/15/89; HB 11/89; SLJ 10/89) [597.95]

22150 Schnieper, Claudia. *Lizards* (3–6). Illus. by Max Meier. Series: Nature Watch. 1990, Carolrhoda LB $19.95 (978-0-87614-405-3). 48pp. Characteristics and reproductive patterns are covered, with color photos. (Rev: BCCB 10/90; BL 6/15/90; SLJ 9/90) [597.95]

22151 Stefoff, Rebecca. *Chameleon* (2–4). Illus. Series: From the Living Things. 1996, Marshall Cavendish LB $22.79 (978-0-7614-0118-6). 32pp. The African chameleon, its life history, and its habits are presented in brief text and colorful photos. (Rev: BL 2/1/97; SLJ 3/97) [597.95]

22152 Welsbacher, Anne. *Komodo Dragons* (3–5). Series: Predators in the Wild. 2002, Capstone LB $23.93 (978-0-7368-1066-1). 32pp. Basic information about the komodo dragon's life, habitat, diet, and endangered status is presented in a format that will suit both browsers and report writers. (Rev: SLJ 8/02) [597.95]

SNAKES

22153 Behler, Deborah, and John Behler. *Snakes* (5–8). Series: AnimalWays. 2001, Marshall Cavendish LB $31.36 (978-0-7614-1265-6). 112pp. Brilliant photographs highlight this fine introduction to snakes, their habitats, behavior, species, evolution, and anatomy. (Rev: BL 3/15/02; HBG 10/02) [597.96]

22154 Berman, Ruth. *Buzzing Rattlesnakes* (PS–2). Series: Pull Ahead Books. 1998, Lerner LB $22.60 (978-0-8225-3603-1). 32pp. An innovative book that uses questions to introduce the topic of rattlesnakes, their homes, food, and habits. (Rev: BL 2/15/99; HBG 3/99; SLJ 1/99) [597.96]

22155 Bredeson, Carmen. *Fun Facts About Snakes!* (PS–2). Series: I Like Reptiles and Amphibians! 2007, Enslow LB $21.26 (978 0 7660-2787-9). 24pp. Eye-catching photographs and clear text make this a useful introduction for beginning readers. (Rev: SLJ 1/08) [597.96]

22156 Demuth, Patricia. *Snakes* (1–3). Illus. by Judith Moffatt. 1993, Penguin paper $3.99 (978-0-448-40513-1). 48pp. An introduction to snakes, their habits, size, and food. (Rev: BL 7/93; SLJ 7/93) [597.66]

22157 Editors of Time for Kids. *Snakes!* (1–3). Illus. Series: Time For Kids Science Scoops. 2005, HarperCollins $14.99 (978-0-06-057637-0); paper $3.99 (978-0-06-057636-3). 32pp. Simple text suitable for beginning readers and bright illustrations present basic information on snakes, plus a profile of a scientist who works with them.

22158 Feldman, Heather. *Cottonmouths* (3–5). Series: The Really Wild Life of Snakes. 2004, Rosen LB $21.25 (978-0-8239-6722-3). 24pp. The behavior, physical characteristics, and habitat of the cottonmouth are featured in this colorfully illustrated account. Also use *Diamondbacks* and *Milk Snakes* (both 2004). (Rev: SLJ 2/05) [597.96]

22159 Fiedler, Julie. *Vipers* (2–4). Series: Scary Snakes. 2007, Rosen LB $21.25 (978-1-4042-3833-6). 24pp. A basic introduction to vipers' characteristics, habitat, diet, and so forth, suitable for beginning report writers. Also use *Rattlesnakes* and *Boas* (2007). (Rev: SLJ 4/08) [597.96]

22160 Gibbons, Gail. *Snakes* (1–3). Illus. by author. 2008, Holiday $16.95 (978-0-8234-2122-0). 32pp. Snake basics are delivered in straightforward style and illustrated with dozens of different species. (Rev: BL 2/15/08; SLJ 4/08) [597.96]

22161 Llewellyn, Claire. *Some Snakes Spit Poison and Other Amazing Facts About Snakes* (2–4). Illus. Series: I Didn't Know That. 1997, Millbrook LB $19.90 (978-0-7613-0561-3). 32pp. Strange facts about unusual snakes and their behavior are given along with basic facts about the life span, food, and reproduction of snakes. (Rev: HBG 3/98; SLJ 10/97) [597.96]

22162 MacKen, JoAnn Early. *Rattlesnakes / Serpientes de cascabel* (2–4). Trans. by Tatiana Acosta and Guillermo Gutiérrez. Series: Animals That Live in the Desert / Animales del desierto. 2005, Weekly Reader LB $21.00 (978-0-8368-4843-4). 24pp. A beginning book with facts about rattlesnakes in both English and Spanish. (Rev: SLJ 6/06) [597.96]

22163 Mason, Adrienne. *Snakes* (2–4). Illus. by Nancy Gray Ogle. Series: Wildlife. 2005, Kids Can $10.95 (978-1-55337-627-9); paper $6.95 (978-1-55337-628-6). 32pp. In addition to introducing the physical characteristics and behavior of snakes, this overview discusses their usefulness to humans and the reasons why people are afraid of snakes. (Rev: BL 5/1/05; SLJ 6/05) [597.96]

22164 Pascoe, Elaine, ed. *Into Wild Arizona* (3–6). Series: The Jeff Corwin Experience. 2004, Gale LB $24.95 (978-1-4103-0058-4). 48pp. Jeff Corwin of TV's *Animal Planet* guides a tour of the wildlife of Arizona, concentrating on its snakes. (Rev: SLJ 4/04)

22165 Patent, Dorothy Hinshaw. *Slinky Scaly Slithery Snakes* (K–3). Illus. by Kendahl Jan Jubb. 2000, Walker LB $17.85 (978-0-8027-8744-6). 32pp. This colorful introduction to snakes explains how they move, their body parts, where they live, and how they can eat animals larger than themselves. (Rev: BL 12/1/00; HBG 3/01; SLJ 3/01) [597.96]

22166 Penner, Lucille R. *S-S-Snakes!* (1–2). Illus. by Peter Barrett. Series: Step into Reading. 1994, Random paper $3.99 (978-0-679-84777-9). 32pp. An easy-to-read book about snakes, their structure, and their habits. (Rev: BL 1/1/95; SLJ 2/95) [597.96]

22167 Pringle, Laurence. *Snakes! Strange and Wonderful* (2–5). Illus. by Meryl Henderson. Series: Strange and Wonderful. 2004, Boyds Mills $15.95 (978-1-59078-003-9). 32pp. Realistic illustrations and lively, concise text present an interesting and fact-filled introduction to snakes and their diverse behaviors. (Rev: BL 12/1/04*; SLJ 9/04) [597.96]

22168 Robinson, Fay. *Great Snakes!* (2–3). Illus. by Jean Day Zallinger. 1996, Scholastic paper $3.99 (978-0-590-26243-9). 32pp. In an easily read format, this counting book introduces various snakes. (Rev: BL 11/15/96) [597.96]

22169 Ruth, Maria Mudd. *Snakes* (3–6). Series: Animals, Animals. 2001, Benchmark LB $25.64 (978-0-7614-1262-5). 48pp. In addition to describing physical characteristics, behavior, habitat, locomotion, and so forth of more than a dozen species, Mattern looks at related folklore and at the animals' relationship with humans. (Rev: HBG 10/02; SLJ 6/02) [597.96]

22170 Schnieper, Claudia. *Snakes: Silent Hunters* (3–5). Illus. Series: Nature Watch. 1995, Carolrhoda LB $25.26 (978-0-87614-881-5); paper $7.95 (978-0-87614-952-2). 48pp. An introduction to snakes organized under such headings as physical characteristics, reproduction, hunting, and self-defense. (Rev: BL 10/1/95; SLJ 12/95) [597.96]

22171 Smith, Molly. *Green Anaconda: The World's Heaviest Snake* (K–2). Illus. Series: SuperSized! 2007, Bearport LB $21.28 (978-1-59716-391-0). 24pp. Report writers will get lots of mileage from this introduction to the anaconda, filled with facts about and photographs of the scary snake. (Rev: SLJ 7/07)

22172 Thomson, Sarah L. *Amazing Snakes!* (K–2). Illus. Series: I Can Read Book. 2006, HarperCollins $15.99 (978-0-06-054462-1). 32pp. This photo-filled beginning reader introduces young students to snakes, offering easy-to-understand basic information about the reptiles' physical characteristics and behavior. (Rev: BL 12/15/05; SLJ 7/06) [597.96]

22173 Welsbacher, Anne. *Anacondas* (3–6). Series: Predators in the Wild. 2001, Capstone LB $23.93 (978-0-7368-0785-2). 32pp. Myths about the anaconda are presented along with facts in this general introduction to the snake's characteristics and habitat. (Rev: HBG 10/01; SLJ 1/02) [597.96]

TURTLES AND TORTOISES

22174 Bredeson, Carmen. *Fun Facts About Turtles!* (1–3). Series: I Like Reptiles and Amphibians! 2007, Enslow LB $21.26 (978-0-7660-2785-5). 24pp. The crisp narrative uses a question-and-answer format to provide basic information about turtles; illustrated with color photographs. (Rev: LMC 11/07; SLJ 10/07) [597.92]

22175 Cerullo, Mary. *Sea Turtles: Ocean Nomads* (3–6). Photos by Jeffrey L. Rotman. Illus. 2003, Dutton $17.99 (978-0-525-46649-9). 32pp. A handsome photo-essay on these endangered animals and their fascinating lives. (Rev: BL 5/15/03; HBG 10/03; SLJ 7/03) [597.92]

22176 Chrustowski, Rick. *Turtle Crossing* (1–3). Illus. 2006, Holt $16.95 (978-0-8050-7498-7). 32pp. A painted turtle's life is portrayed in large-scale art and a simple narrative that offers a satisfying circular structure. (Rev: BL 3/1/06; SLJ 6/06) [597.92]

22177 Cooper, Jason. *Loggerhead Turtle* (1–3). Series: Life Cycles. 2002, Rourke LB $17.95 (978-1-58952-354-8). 24pp. Handsome photographs and simple text describe the life cycle, habitat, appearance, and behavior of these animals. (Rev: SLJ 12/02) [597.92]

22178 Davies, Nicola. *One Tiny Turtle* (PS–4). Illus. by Janet Chapman. 2001, Candlewick $15.99 (978-0-7636-1549-9). 32pp. An appealing overview of the loggerhead sea turtle, introduced by the story of one turtle's life from hatching to laying her own eggs on the beach of her birth. (Rev: BCCB 11/01; BL 12/1/01; HBG 3/02; SLJ 12/01) [597.92]

22179 Fletcher, Marty, and Glenn Scherer. *The Green Sea Turtle: Help Save This Endangered Species!* (5–7). Illus. Series: Saving Endangered Species. 2006, Enslow LB $33.27 (978-1-59845-033-0). 128pp. A well-illustrated look at the plight of the endangered green sea turtle, with an overview of its physical characteristics, diet, habitat, and behavior. (Rev: SLJ 9/06) [597.92]

22180 Gibbons, Gail. *Sea Turtles* (2–4). Illus. 1995, Holiday House LB $16.95 (978-0-8234-1191-7). 32pp. This account covers the anatomy, life cycle, diet, and habitat of the sea turtle and how it differs from other members of its reptile family. (Rev: BL 10/1/95; SLJ 10/95) [597.92]

22181 Guiberson, Brenda Z. *Into the Sea* (2–4). Illus. by Alix Berenzy. 1996, Holt $16.95 (978-0-8050-2263-6). 28pp. The life of a sea turtle from being hatched to becoming an egg-laying adult. (Rev: BCCB 9/96; BL 9/15/96; HB 11/96; SLJ 9/96*) [597.92]

22182 Hall, Kirsten. *Leatherback Turtle: The World's Heaviest Reptile* (K–2). Illus. Series: SuperSized! 2007, Bearport LB $21.28 (978-1-59716-393-4). 24pp. Report writers will get lots of mileage from this introduction to the leatherback turtle, filled with facts about and photographs of this big reptile. (Rev: SLJ 7/07)

22183 Hickman, Pamela. *Turtle Rescue: Changing the Future for Endangered Wildlife* (4–8). Series: Firefly Animal Rescue. 2006, Firefly $19.95 (978-1-55297-916-7); paper $9.95 (978-1-55297-915-0). 64pp. Hickman provides a detailed but accessible overview of the dangers facing turtles around the world and what is being done to protect them. (Rev: SLJ 6/06) [597.92]

22184 Holling, Holling C. *Minn of the Mississippi* (4–6). Illus. by author. 1951, Houghton $21.00 (978-0-395-17578-1); paper $11.95 (978-0-395-27399-9). A snapping turtle's trip down the Mississippi.

22185 Jacobs, Lee. *Turtles* (3–5). Series: Wild America. 2003, Gale LB $24.94 (978-1-56711-571-0). 24pp. A brief and basic introduction to turtles and their habitat, diet, physical appearance, and behavior. (Rev: SLJ 11/03) [597.92]

22186 Kalman, Bobbie. *The Life Cycle of a Sea Turtle* (2–4). Illus. Series: The Life Cycle. 2001, Crabtree LB $25.27 (978-0-7787-0652-6); paper $6.95 (978-0-7787-0682-3). 32pp. After a general description of the sea turtle, the author clearly explains its life cycle and discusses what can be done to curb human encroachment. (Rev: SLJ 6/02) [597.92]

22187 Korman, Susan. *Box Turtle at Silver Pond Lake* (K–3). Illus. by Stephen Marchesi. Series: Smithsonian Backyard. 2001, Smithsonian Institution $15.95 (978-1-56899-860-2). 32pp. A female box turtle's daily life is presented in simple text with realistic illustrations. (Rev: BL 9/15/01; HBG 10/01; SLJ 8/01)

22188 Lang, Aubrey. *Baby Sea Turtle* (PS–1). Illus. Series: Nature Babies. 2007, Fitzhenry & Whiteside $13.95 (978-1-55041-728-9); paper $7.95 (978-1-55041-746-3). 32pp. This volume full of eye-catching photographs provides fascinating information about the leatherback sea turtle's life cycle. (Rev: BL 5/15/07; SLJ 7/07) [597.92]

22189 Laskey, Elizabeth. *Sea Turtles* (4–6). Illus. Series: Sea Creatures. 2003, Heinemann LB $22.79 (978-1-4034-0962-1). 32pp. A clear overview of sea turtles and their lives, using a question-and-answer format. (Rev: HBG 10/03; SLJ 11/03) [597.9]

22190 Lepthien, Emilie U. *Sea Turtles* (3–4). Illus. Series: True Books. 1996, Children's Book Pr. LB $25.00 (978-0-516-20161-0). 48pp. An introduction to sea turtles that covers their environment, physiology, feeding, mating, nesting, and current endangered status. (Rev: SLJ 6/97) [597.92]

22191 Lockwood, Sophie. *Sea Turtles* (4–7). Illus. Series: World of Reptiles. 2006, Child's World LB $29.93 (978-1-59296-550-2). 40pp. In addition to the kind of information needed for reports, Lockwood discusses conservation, how scientists track turtles, and the turtle's appearances in folklore and art. (Rev: BL 4/1/06) [597.92]

22192 Martin-James, Kathleen. *Sturdy Turtles* (PS–2). Series: Pull Ahead Books. 1999, Lerner $22.60 (978-0-8225-3627-7); paper $5.95 (978-0-8225-3631-4). 32pp. This book uses provocative questions, outstanding photos, and simple text to describe turtles, their habits, and habitats. (Rev: BL 12/15/99; HBG 4/00) [597.92]

22193 Mason, Janeen. *Ocean Commotion: Sea Turtles* (3–5). Illus. 2006, Pelican $15.95 (978-1-58980-434-0). 32pp. Follow the journey of a female loggerhead sea turtle from the time she hatches on a Florida beach to the day she returns to mate and lay eggs of her own. (Rev: BL 12/1/06; SLJ 12/06) [597.92]

22194 Monroe, Mary Alice. *Turtle Summer: A Journal for My Daughter* (2–3). Photos by Barbara J. Bergwerf. Illus. by Lisa Downey. 2007, Sylvan Dell $15.95 (978-0-9777423-5-6); paper $8.95 (978-0-9777423-7-0). In a scrapbook format, a mother organizes photos and information about the sea turtles that she and her daughter observe on the beach. Readers are encouraged to compile their own scrapbooks about what they observe in nature. (Rev: SLJ 6/07)

22195 Noonan, Diana. *The Green Turtle* (2–4). Series: Life Cycles. 2002, Chelsea LB $23.00 (978-0-7910-6967-7). 32pp. The story of this endangered reptile that lives and mates in the sea is told with material on how the female goes ashore to lay her eggs and what happens when the young hatch. (Rev: BL 12/15/02; HBG 3/03) [597.92]

22196 Rathmell, Donna. *Carolina's Story: Sea Turtles Get Sick Too!* (2–4). Illus. 2005, Sylvan Dell $15.95 (978-0-9764943-0-0). 32pp. A sick loggerhead turtle's rehabilitation in South Carolina is documented in sensitive text and photographs. (Rev: BL 8/05; SLJ 11/05)

22197 Rebman, Renee C. *Turtles and Tortoises* (3–5). Series: Animals, Animals. 2006, Benchmark LB $19.95 (978-0-7614-2239-6). 48pp. An introduction to the anatomy, behavior, and habitat of turtles and tortoises, in addition to other aspects of these animals and their lives. Color photographs give readers a close-up look. (Rev: SLJ 5/07)

22198 Sayre, April P. *Turtle, Turtle, Watch Out!* (PS–2). Illus. by Lee Christiansen. 2000, Orchard LB $17.99 (978-0-531-33285-6). 32pp. A lovely nature book with some fictional touches that covers the life cycle of a sea turtle and how a boy protected one turtle's eggs so they could hatch. (Rev: BL 8/00; HBG 3/01; SLJ 10/00) [597.92]

22199 Schafer, Susan. *Turtles* (2–5). Series: Perfect Pets. 1998, Benchmark LB $25.64 (978-0-7614-0796-6). 31pp. This book deals with turtles as pets and gives material on physical characteristics, behavior patterns, and tips on caring and raising them. (Rev: HBG 9/99; SLJ 5/99) [597.92]

22200 Souza, D. M. *What's Under That Shell? A Book About Turtles* (3–5). Illus. Series: Creatures All Around Us. 1992, Carolrhoda LB $14.95 (978-0-87614-712-2). 40pp. Various varieties of turtles and tortoises are introduced in color photographs and a lively text. (Rev: BL 10/1/92; SLJ 12/92) [597.92]

22201 Stefoff, Rebecca. *Turtles* (4–8). Illus. Series: AnimalWays. 2007, Marshall Cavendish LB $23.95 (978-0-7614-2539-7). 110pp. Report writers will find plenty of valuable information about turtles' anatomy, habitat, evolution, and appearances in literature and legend as well as discussion of conservation efforts and many attractive photographs. (Rev: BL 2/8/08) [597.92]

22202 Theodorou, Rod. *Leatherback Sea Turtle* (2–4). Illus. Series: Animals in Danger. 2001, Heinemann LB $21.36 (978-1-57572-272-6). 32pp. Basic information about the sea turtle and its endangered status. (Rev: BL 7/01; HBG 10/01) [597.2]

Animal Behavior and Anatomy

GENERAL

22203 Arnold, Caroline. *Did You Hear That? Animals with Super Hearing* (3–5). Illus. by Cathy Trachok. 2001, Charlesbridge $16.95 (978-1-57091-404-1). 32pp. This book full of color pictures introduces bats' and dolphins' echolocation skills, rhinos' ability to communicate over long distances, and other facts to do with animal hearing. (Rev: BL 12/1/01; HBG 3/02; SLJ 8/01) [591.59]

22204 Arnold, Caroline. *Mealtime for Zoo Animals* (PS–3). Illus. by Richard Hewett. Series: Zoo Animals. 1999, Carolrhoda LB $21.27 (978-1-57505-286-1). 32pp. Unusual color photographs and a simple text show a variety of zoo animals and how and what they eat. (Rev: BL 6/1–15/99; HBG 9/99) [636.088]

22205 Arnold, Caroline. *Noisytime for Zoo Animals* (PS–3). Illus. by Richard Hewett. Series: Zoo Animals. 1999, Carolrhoda LB $21.27 (978-1-57505-289-2). 32pp. All sorts of noises made by zoo animals are portrayed in lively photographs and a simple text. (Rev: BL 6/1–15/99; HBG 9/99) [636.088]

22206 Arnold, Caroline. *Playtime for Zoo Animals* (PS–3). Series: Zoo Animals. 1999, Carolrhoda LB $21.27 (978-1-57505-287-8); paper $9.95 (978-1-57505-391-2). 32pp. A very simple text identifies 15 zoo animals shown at play in full-page illustrations, and stresses similarities between human and animal behavior. (Rev: BL 6/1–15/99; HBG 9/99) [591.51]

22207 Arnold, Caroline. *Sleepytime for Zoo Animals* (PS–3). Series: Zoo Animals. 1999, Carolrhoda LB $21.27 (978-1-57505-290-8); paper $9.95 (978-1-57505-393-6). 32pp. The sleeping habits of zoo animals are shown in full-page color photos and a brief text. (Rev: BL 6/1–15/99; HBG 9/99; SLJ 8/99) [591]

22208 Arnold, Caroline. *Splashtime for Zoo Animals* (PS–3). Series: Zoo Animals. 1999, Carolrhoda LB $21.27 (978-1-57505-288-5); paper $9.95 (978-1-57505-394-3). 32pp. A simple, engaging text and full-page color photos of zoo animals show that animals bathe in ways often similar to their human counterparts. (Rev: BL 6/1–15/99; HBG 9/99; SLJ 8/99) [591]

22209 Arnosky, Jim. *Wild Tracks! A Guide to Nature's Footprints* (1–3). Illus. by author. 2008, Sterling $14.95 (978-1-4027-3985-9). 32pp. With full-color paintings, pencil sketches, fold-out pages, and accessible text, Arnosky provides information about the tracks of a variety of North American animals. (Rev: BL 4/1/08; SLJ 6/08) [591.47]

22210 Aruego, Jose, and Ariane Dewey. *Weird Friends: Unlikely Allies in the Animal Kingdom*

(1–3). Illus. 2002, Harcourt $16.00 (978-0-15-202128-3). 40pp. Fourteen symbiotic relationships among animals are explained and brightly illustrated. (Rev: BL 5/15/02; HBG 10/02; SLJ 4/02) [577.8]

22211 Bancroft, Henrietta, and Richard G. Van Gelder. *Animals in Winter* (PS–1). Illus. by Helen K. Davie. Series: Let's-Read-and-Find-Out. 1997, HarperCollins LB $15.89 (978-0-06-027158-9). 32pp. An easily read title that describes how some animals prepare for winter and how others don't. (Rev: BL 12/1/96; SLJ 3/97) [591.54]

22212 Batten, Mary. *Please Don't Wake the Animals: A Book About Sleep* (PS–3). Illus. by Higgins Bond. 2008, Peachtree $16.95 (978-1-56145-393-1). 32pp. A look at how a variety of animals sleep (by day, by night; in danger, in safety), with information on hibernation too. (Rev: BL 7/08; LMC 5/08; SLJ 8/08) [591.5]

22213 Black, Sonia. *Animal Mysteries: A Chapter Book* (3–5). Series: True Tales. 2005, Children's Pr. LB $22.50 (978-0-516-25187-5). 48pp. This interesting book looks at examples of amazing animal behavior, such as the loggerhead turtle's ability to navigate by using the ocean's magnetic fields. (Rev: SLJ 1/06) [590]

22214 Bonnett-Rampersaud, Louise. *How Do You Sleep?* (PS). Illus. by Kristin Kest. 2005, Marshall Cavendish $14.95 (978-0-7614-5231-7). 32pp. A look at the sleeping habits of seven creatures, including human siblings, bears, and birds. (Rev: BL 10/1/05; SLJ 11/05) [573.8]

22215 Bonsignore, Joan. *Stick Out Your Tongue! Fantastic Facts, Features, and Functions of Animal and Human Tongues* (2–3). Illus. by John T. Ward. 2001, Peachtree $15.95 (978-1-56145-230-9). 32pp. A look at how animals of all kinds use their tongues with comparisons to similar human behavior. (Rev: BL 8/01; HBG 3/02; SLJ 11/01) [612.8]

22216 Butler, John. *Can You Cuddle Like a Koala?* (PS). Illus. by author. 2003, Peachtree $15.95 (978-1-56145-298-9). In this charming blend of rhyming text and colorful artwork, young readers will learn how various animals move. (Rev: HBG 4/04; SLJ 1/04)

22217 Carlson-Voiles, Polly. *Someone Walks By: The Wonders of Winter Wildlife* (K–3). Illus. by author. 2008, Raven $18.95 (978-0-9801045-5-4); paper $12.95 (978-0-9801045-6-1). 32pp. This attractive picture book follows a variety of animals as they adapt to winter living in the northern woods. (Rev: BL 12/1/08; SLJ 6/09) [591.723]

22218 Challoner, Jack. *Wet and Dry* (K–4). Illus. Series: Start-Up Science. 1996, Raintree LB $24.26 (978-0-8172-4322-7). 32pp. Using both text and experiments, this book discusses the different habitats of water and land and the creatures that exist in/on them. (Rev: SLJ 2/97) [530]

22219 Collard, Sneed B. *Animals Asleep* (PS–3). Illus. by Anik McGrory. 2004, Houghton $15.00 (978-0-618-27697-4). 32pp. Readers can choose between brief, large-print information and more detailed smaller text in this chatty overview of ani-

mals' sleeping habits. (Rev: BL 3/1/04; SLJ 5/04) [591.56]

22220 Collard, Sneed B. *Teeth* (1–3). Illus. by Phyllis V. Saroff. 2008, Charlesbridge $16.95 (978-1-58089-120-2); paper $7.95 (978-1-58089-121-9). 32pp. Animal teeth are the focus of this informative and colorful large-format picture book. (Rev: BL 3/1/08; SLJ 2/08) [591.4]

22221 Collard, Sneed B., III. *Leaving Home* (PS–3). Illus. by Joan Dunning. 2002, Houghton $15.00 (978-0-618-11454-2). 32pp. This unique book for younger readers explores the various ways in which animals leave their homes upon maturation. (Rev: BL 3/1/02; HBG 10/02; SLJ 4/02) [591.5]

22222 Cooper, Jason. *Antlers and Horns* (K–2). Series: Let's Look at Animals. 2007, Rourke LB $21.35 (978-1-60044-168-4). 24pp. Photos of animals that have antlers and horns are accompanied by brief text explaining what they are used for. (Rev: SLJ 6/07)

22223 Cooper, Jason. *Hooves and Claws* (K–2). Series: Let's Look at Animals. 2007, Rourke LB $21.35 (978-1-60044-173-8). 24pp. Photos of animals' hooves and claws are accompanied by brief text explaining what they are used for. (Rev: SLJ 6/07)

22224 Crump, Donald J., ed. *How Animals Behave: A New Look at Wildlife* (5–8). Illus. 1984, National Geographic LB $12.50 (978-0-87044-505-7). 104pp. A general, colorful introduction to why and how animals perform such functions as courting, living together, and caring for their young. [591.5]

22225 Crump, Donald J., ed. *Secrets of Animal Survival* (4–8). Illus. 1983, National Geographic LB $12.50 (978-0-87044-431-9). 104pp. The survival tactics of animals in five geographical environments are discussed.

22226 Davies, Nicola. *Extreme Animals: The Toughest Creatures on Earth* (3–5). Illus. by Neal Layton. 2006, Candlewick $12.99 (978-0-7636-3067-6). 58pp. Reveals some of the world's most resilient creatures and how they've adapted to habitats that humans couldn't last minutes in. (Rev: BL 12/1/06; SLJ 12/06*) [590]

22227 Ehrlich, Fred. *You Can't Use Your Brain If You're a Jellyfish* (K–3). Illus. by Amanda Haley. 2005, Blue Apple $15.95 (978-1-59354-090-6). 44pp. A lighthearted but fact-packed look at the brains of a diverse range of creatures — from invertebrates to humans. (Rev: BL 12/1/05; SLJ 11/05) [612.8]

22228 Facklam, Margery. *Bugs for Lunch* (PS–3). Illus. by Sylvia Long. 1999, Charlesbridge LB $15.95 (978-0-88106-271-7); paper $6.95 (978-0-88106-272-4). 32pp. This work highlights the creatures that eat insects, including bats, bears, aardvarks, rainbow trout, praying mantises, and Venus flytraps. (Rev: BL 2/1/99; HBG 9/99; SLJ 3/99) [591.5]

22229 Flegg, Jim. *Animal Movement* (4–7). Illus. by David Hosking. Series: Wild World. 1991, Millbrook LB $17.90 (978-1-878137-21-0). 32pp. Various ways animals move and at what speeds are discussed in this well-illustrated book. (Rev: BL 1/1/91; SLJ 2/92) [591.18]

22230 Fraser, Mary Ann. *Where Are the Night Animals?* (PS–1). Illus. Series: Let's-Read-and-Find-Out. 1999, HarperCollins LB $15.89 (978-0-06-027718-5). 32pp. Several nocturnal animals are introduced, including the coyote, skunk, harvest mouse, barn owl, opossum, raccoon, bat, and tree frog. (Rev: BL 2/15/99; HBG 9/99; SLJ 1/99) [591.5]

22231 Fredericks, Anthony D. *Animal Sharpshooters* (5–7). Illus. Series: Watts Library: Animals. 1999, Watts LB $25.50 (978-0-531-11700-2). 64pp. This book focuses on the strange adaptations some animals have made to protect themselves and to find food. (Rev: BL 12/1/99; SLJ 12/99) [591.47]

22232 Funston, Sylvia. *Animal Feelings* (3–5). Illus. by Pat Stephens. Series: The Secret Life of Animals. 1998, Owl paper $9.95 (978-1-895688-81-8). 48pp. An investigation of emotions in both wild and domestic animals is included in this book that also emphasizes that animals should be treated with compassion and respect. (Rev: SLJ 3/99) [591]

22233 Funston, Sylvia. *Animal Smarts* (4–6). Illus. 1997, Firefly $19.95 (978-1-895688-66-5). 48pp. Explores the levels of intelligence in various mammals, birds, and insects, with material on how they think, solve problems, and understand human language. (Rev: BL 2/1/98; SLJ 4/98) [591.5]

22234 Gardner, Robert, and David Webster. *Science Project Ideas About Animal Behavior* (4–8). Illus. Series: Science Project Ideas. 1997, Enslow LB $25.26 (978-0-89490-842-2). A workmanlike compilation of projects involving animal behavior, such as the language of honeybees, with full background information and clear instructions. (Rev: BL 12/15/97; HBG 3/98; SLJ 2/98) [591]

22235 Gilpin, Daniel. *Life-Size Killer Creatures* (3–6). Illus. 2006, Sterling $9.95 (978-1-4027-2701-6). 28pp. This oversized book with numerous eye-catching foldouts shows life-size illustrations of several predatory animals and offers basic facts on each. (Rev: BL 12/1/06; SLJ 12/1/06) [590]

22236 Goodman, Susan E. *Claws, Coats, and Camouflage: The Ways Animals Fit into Their World* (2–5). Illus. by Michael Doolittle. 2001, Millbrook $22.90 (978-0-7613-1865-1). 48pp. The ways in which animals (and finally, humans) adapt to their worlds are presented in broad categories with brief text and photographs. (Rev: BL 12/1/01; HBG 3/02; SLJ 1/02) [591.4]

22237 Greenaway, Theresa. *Paws and Claws* (3–5). Illus. by Ann Savage, et al. Series: Head to Tail. 1995, Raintree LB $5.00 (978-0-8114-8266-0). 39pp. An appealing introduction to various kinds of animal feet and their uses for movement, digging, climbing, etc. (Rev: SLJ 5/95) [591]

22238 Hall, Kirsten. *Tracking Animals: A Chapter Book* (3–5). Series: True Tales. 2005, Children's Pr. LB $22.50 (978-0-516-25186-8). 48pp. An interesting exploration of scientists' ability to track animals and study their behavior using technology. (Rev: SLJ 1/06) [591.5]

22239 Hartley, Karen, and Chris Macro. *Hearing in Living Things* (K–2). Series: Sense. 2000, Heinemann LB $21.36 (978-1-57572-246-7). 32pp. An overview that explains hearing in animals and uses as examples such animals as bats, frogs, insects, owls, elephants, and humans. Also use *Tasting in Living Things* (2000). (Rev: HBG 3/01; SLJ 8/00) [591]

22240 Hickman, Pamela. *Animal Senses: How Animals See, Hear, Taste, Smell and Feel* (3–5). Illus. 1998, Kids Can $10.95 (978-1-55074-423-1). 40pp. In double-page spreads with text and accompanying activities, this book explores the senses of such animals as frogs, bats, butterflies, and deer. (Rev: BL 5/15/98; HBG 9/98; SLJ 5/98) [573.8]

22241 Hickman, Pamela. *Animals Eating* (3–5). Illus. 2001, Kids Can $10.95 (978-1-55074-577-1); paper $5.95 (978-1-55074-579-5). 40pp. After a general discussion of animal mouths, tongues, and teeth, this book explains how various animals eat and drink. It also gives a number of interesting simple activities. (Rev: BL 3/15/01; HBG 10/01) [591.5]

22242 Hickman, Pamela. *Animals in Motion: How Animals Swim, Jump, Slither and Glide* (3–5). Illus. 2000, Kids Can $10.95 (978-1-55074-573-3); paper $5.95 (978-1-55074-575-7). 40pp. This book on animal locomotion classifies animals by how they move — running, hopping, slipping, swimming, and climbing, for example. (Rev: BL 5/1/00; HBG 9/00; SLJ 9/00) [573.7]

22243 Hirschi, Ron. *When Morning Comes* (1–4). Photos by Thomas D. Mangelsen. 2000, Boyds Mills $16.95 (978-1-56397-767-1). Using striking photographs, this book on nature study shows various forms of wildlife in the morning. A companion volume is *When Night Comes* (2000). (Rev: BL 10/15/00; HBG 3/01; SLJ 12/00) [508]

22244 Hirschi, Ron. *When Night Comes* (1–3). Illus. by Thomas D. Mangelsen. 2000, Boyds Mills $16.95 (978-1-56397-766-4). 32pp. The activities of such animals as otters, raccoons, and coyotes at night are described in excellent photos and a simple text. (Rev: BL 10/15/00; HBG 3/01; SLJ 12/00) [591.5]

22245 James, Ray. *Teeth and Fangs* (K–2). Series: Let's Look at Animals. 2007, Rourke LB $21.35 (978-1-60044-174-5). 24pp. Photos of animals' teeth — and, in some cases, fangs — are accompanied by brief text explaining what they are used for. (Rev: SLJ 6/07)

22246 Jenkins, Steve, and Robin Page. *Animals in Flight* (PS–3). Illus. by Steve Jenkins. 2001, Houghton $16.00 (978-0-618-12351-3). 32pp. The wonder of flight is explained in simple prose and sensational cut-paper collages. (Rev: BCCB 12/01; BL 12/15/01; HBG 3/02; SLJ 11/01) [573.7]

22247 Jenkins, Steve, and Robin Page. *Move!* (PS–2). Illus. 2006, Houghton $16.00 (978-0-618-64637-1). 32pp. This engaging picture book shows diverse members of the animal kingdom in motion. (Rev: BL 3/15/06; SLJ 6/06*) [573.7]

22248 Jocelyn, Marthe. *Eats* (K–1). Illus. by Tom Slaughter. 2007, Tundra $15.95 (978-0-88776-820-

0). A simple look at who eats what — worms eat apples, birds eat worms — with appealing illustrations. (Rev: SLJ 12/07)

22249 Kajikawa, Kimiko. *Sweet Dreams: How Animals Sleep* (PS–1). Illus. 1999, Holt $15.95 (978-0-8050-5890-1). Animals including a chipmunk, flamingo, bear, and bat are pictured and described while asleep. (Rev: BL 4/1/99; HBG 9/99; SLJ 4/99) [591.5]

22250 Kalman, Bobbie. *How Do Animals Adapt?* (1–3). Series: Science of Living Things. 2000, Crabtree LB $25.27 (978-0-86505-980-1); paper $6.95 (978-0-86505-957-3). 32pp. This beginning science book on animal adaptations includes camouflage, hibernation, and migration. (Rev: SLJ 11/00) [591]

22251 Kalman, Bobbie. *How Do Animals Find Food?* (2–4). Illus. Series: The Science of Living Things. 2001, Crabtree LB $25.27 (978-0-86505-986-3); paper $6.95 (978-0-86505-963-4). 32pp. Colorful illustrations present details of animals of various kinds and their ways of killing and devouring their prey. (Rev: SLJ 12/01) [591.5]

22252 Kaner, Etta. *Animal Groups: How Animals Live Together* (K–3). Illus. by Pat Stephens. 2004, Kids Can $10.95 (978-1-55337-337-7); paper $5.95 (978-1-55337-338-4). 40pp. For browsers, this is an interesting introduction to how animals behave, from hunting to grooming to raising young. (Rev: SLJ 5/04) [591.56]

22253 Karwoski, Gail L. *River Beds: Sleeping in the World's Rivers* (1–3). Illus. by Connie McLennan. 2008, Sylvan Dell $16.95 (978-0-9777423-4-9); paper $8.95 (978-1-934359-31-0). 32pp. It's evening and a boy goes around the world in a rowboat visiting animals who make their homes in or near the water. (Rev: BL 8/08; LMC 10/08) [591.76]

22254 Karwoski, Gail L. *Water Beds: Sleeping in the Ocean* (PS–1). Illus. by Connie McLennan. 2005, Sylvan Dell $15.95 (978-0-9764943-1-7). 32pp. An educational and attractive bedtime book that conveys facts about the sleeping habits of water mammals. (Rev: SLJ 6/06) [599.5]

22255 Kenah, Katherine. *Predator Attack!* (K–2). Illus. Series: Extreme Readers. 2004, McGraw-Hill paper $3.95 (978-0-7696-3176-9). 32pp. This photo-filled book introduces, with drama, such predators as the shark, tiger, alligator, cheetah, and polar bear. (Rev: BL 4/15/04) [591.5]

22256 Kudlinski, Kathleen V. *The Sunset Switch* (PS–2). Illus. by Lindy Burnett. 2005, NorthWord $15.95 (978-1-55971-916-2). Some animals settle in for the night while their nocturnal friends set off to hunt in this book that can double as a bedtime story and inspiration to learn more about animals. (Rev: SLJ 7/05) [591.5]

22257 MacDonald, Suse. *Peck Slither and Slide* (PS–1). Illus. 1997, Harcourt $15.00 (978-0-15-200079-0). 48pp. The ways that animals move and travel are illustrated, and the words that describe their motions — for example, *wade* and *slither* — are explained. (Rev: BL 4/1/97; SLJ 4/97) [591]

22258 McGrath, Susan. *The Amazing Things Animals Do* (4–7). Illus. 1989, National Geographic $8.95

(978-0-87044-709-9). 96pp. Unusual animal behavior is shown in such areas as communication, motion, raising young, and survival. (Rev: SLJ 2/90) [591.5]

22259 Matero, Robert. *Animals Asleep* (3–6). Illus. 2000, Millbrook LB $25.90 (978-0-7613-1652-7). 80pp. Covers the sleep and rest habits of humans and animals, including bears, woodchucks, bats, hummingbirds, lobsters, and frogs. (Rev: BL 11/1/00; HBG 3/01; SLJ 2/01) [579.5]

22260 Mayo, Margaret. *Roar!* (K–2). Illus. by Alex Ayliffe. 2007, Carolrhoda $15.95 (978-0-7613-9473-0). 32pp. A rhyming celebration of wild animals and their behaviors — climbing, prowling, stretching, fishing, jumping . . . . (Rev: BL 1/1–15/08; SLJ 10/07) [590]

22261 Moses, Brian. *Winking, Blinking, Wiggling, and Waggling* (2–3). Illus. Series: Eyewitness Reader. 2000, DK paper $3.99 (978-0-7894-5413-3). 32pp. This book for beginning readers describes fascinating facts about animals that have unusual eyes and ears. (Rev: BL 4/15/00; HBG 9/00; SLJ 8/00) [573.8]

22262 Mostue, Trude. *Wild About Animals: A Book of Beastly Behaviour* (4–6). 2000, Madcap $24.95 (978-0-233-99684-4). 112pp. A total of 26 mammals — some familiar, like the elephant, and others not so, like the hyrax — are introduced with four-page descriptions of each animal, its habits, and habitats. (Rev: SLJ 1/01) [591]

22263 Myers, Jack. *How Dogs Came from Wolves: And Other Explorations of Science in Action* (3–6). Illus. by John Rice. 2001, Boyds Mills $17.95 (978-1-56397-411-3). 64pp. A professor of zoology presents 12 fascinating animal abilities and adaptations, such as elephant "speech" and dog domestication. (Rev: BL 9/15/01; HBG 3/02; SLJ 10/01) [590]

22264 Myers, Jack. *What Happened to the Mammoths? And Other Explorations of Science in Action* (4–6). Illus. 2000, Boyds Mills $17.95 (978-1-56397-801-2). 64pp. A collection of articles from *Highlights for Children* magazine that explores such aspects of animal behavior as the seal's ability to dive and the cat's purr. (Rev: BL 3/1/00; HBG 9/00; SLJ 6/00) [591]

22265 Nail, Jim. *Whose Tracks Are These? A Clue Book of Familiar Forest Animals* (PS–3). Illus. by Hyla Skudder. 1994, Roberts Rinehart $13.95 (978-1-879373-89-1). Presents six guessing games in which readers are challenged to identify various common forest creatures through their tracks and a description of their habits. (Rev: SLJ 9/94) [591]

22266 Nichols, Catherine. *Animal Masterminds: A Chapter Book* (2–5). Series: True Tales. 2003, Children's Pr. LB $22.50 (978-0-516-22913-3). 48pp. Four animals with amazing abilities are the focus of this appealing volume that introduces new terms with care. (Rev: SLJ 1/04) [591.5]

22267 Nunn, Daniel. *Ears* (PS–2). Series: Spot the Difference. 2006, Heinemann LB $20.71 (978-1-4034-8473-4). 24pp. Compares the ears of a cricket, chimpanzee, and bat, with color photographs illustrating the differences. (Rev: SLJ 2/07) [591.44]

22268 Nunn, Daniel. *Eyes* (PS–2). Series: Spot the Difference. 2006, Heinemann LB $20.71 (978-1-4034-8474-1). 24pp. Color photographs allow readers to compare the eyes of such animals ranging from moles to gorillas. (Rev: SLJ 2/07)

22269 Page, Robin, and Steve Jenkins. *Sisters and Brothers: Sibling Relationships in the Animal World* (2–4). Illus. by Steve Jenkins. 2008, Houghton $16.00 (978-0-618-37596-7). 32pp. From termites and spiders to bears and elephants, this book offers an attractive peek into the many varied relationships among animal siblings. (Rev: BL 4/1/08; HB 5/08; LMC 11/08; SLJ 7/08) [591]

22270 Patkau, Karen. *Creatures Great and Small* (K–3). Illus. by author. 2006, Tundra LB $17.95 (978-0-88776-754-8). Large and small animals are juxtaposed on spreads that show relative sizes and give a good impression of the environments they inhabit. (Rev: SLJ 11/06) [591.4]

22271 Pearce, Q. L. *Great Predators of the Land* (3–5). Illus. by Ed Yakovetic. 1999, Tor paper $12.95 (978-0-312-85981-7). 57pp. A mostly pictorial presentation that deals with various methods used to capture prey and highlights animals including tigers and eagles. Also use *Great Predators of the Sea* (1999). (Rev: SLJ 3/00) [591]

22272 Pipe, Jim. *The Giant Book of Creatures of the Night* (3–5). Illus. 1998, Millbrook LB $25.90 (978-0-7613-0858-4). 32pp. An entertaining, oversize book with copious illustrations and lots of information about night creatures, including various insects as well as birds and animals. (Rev: BL 12/15/98; HBG 3/99) [591.5]

22273 Riha, Susanne. *Animal Journeys: Life Cycles and Migrations* (4–6). Illus. by author. Series: Animals in the Wild. 1999, Blackbirch LB $22.45 (978-1-56711-426-3). 30pp. This colorful book describes the life cycle and migration patterns of both land and water animals. (Rev: HBG 4/00; SLJ 4/00) [591.52]

22274 Ross, Michael Elsohn. *Mama's Milk* (PS–1). Illus. by Ashley Wolff. 2007, Tricycle $12.95 (978-1-58246-181-6). Human and animal mothers are shown nursing their babies in this book that is perfect for little ones who are curious about breast-feeding. (Rev: SLJ 5/07)

22275 Rylant, Cynthia. *The Journey: Stories of Migration* (2–4). Illus. by Lambert Davis. 2006, Scholastic $16.99 (978-0-590-30717-8). 48pp. Migrations of the desert locust, the blue whale, the American silver eel, the monarch butterfly, the caribou, and the Arctic tern are described in separate chapters in this large-format, well-illustrated book. (Rev: BL 12/1/05; SLJ 3/06) [591.56]

22276 Savage, Stephen. *Skin* (2–4). Illus. Series: Adaptation for Survival. 1995, Thomson Learning LB $5.00 (978-1-56847-353-6). 32pp. Describes the skin covering on a variety of animals, including humans and other mammals, reptiles, birds, fish, and shellfish. (Rev: SLJ 3/96) [591]

22277 Sayre, April P. *Splish! Splash! Animal Baths* (PS–1). Illus. 2000, Millbrook LB $21.90 (978-0-7613-1821-7). 32pp. Lots of photos and a spare text

are used to introduce unusual grooming techniques in the animal kingdom, such as chimpanzees picking fleas off each other. (Rev: BL 4/1/00; HBG 9/00; SLJ 5/00) [591.56]

22278 Settel, Joanne. *Exploding Ants: Amazing Facts About How Animals Adapt* (4–8). Illus. 1999, Simon & Schuster $16.00 (978-0-689-81739-7). 40pp. Lurid details of animal life, such as predatory fireflies, regurgitating birds, and bloodsuckers, are presented in this attention-getting collection of biological facts. (Rev: BCCB 3/99; BL 4/15/99; HBG 10/99; SLJ 4/99) [591.5]

22279 Shalev, Zahavit. *Water Hole* (3–5). Illus. Series: 24 Hours. 2005, DK $12.99 (978-0-7566-1126-2). 48pp. A colorful and information-packed look at the animals — elephants, giraffes, wildebeest, hawks, and so forth — that use a water hole over a 24-hour period. (Rev: BL 5/15/05) [591.74]

22280 Singer, Marilyn. *Eggs* (1–4). Illus. by Emma Stevenson. 2008, Holiday House $16.95 (978-0-8234-1727-8). 32pp. Realistic paintings and smooth text introduce eggs of many shapes and sizes and explain their functions. (Rev: BL 4/1/08; HB 5/08; LMC 10/08; SLJ 4/08) [591.4]

22281 Singer, Marilyn. *A Pair of Wings* (2–3). Illus. by Anne Wertheim. 2001, Holiday House $16.95 (978-0-8234-1547-2). 32pp. A fascinating introduction to all the ways in which animals' wings are used in addition to simple flying. (Rev: BL 5/15/01; HBG 10/01; SLJ 6/01) [591.47]

22282 Singer, Marilyn. *Venom* (5–8). Illus. 2007, Darby Creek $19.95 (978-1-58196-043-3). 96pp. Poisonous animals and insects of the land, sea, and air are featured in this book, with plenty of strange facts and weird photographs. (Rev: BL 10/1/07; SLJ 11/07) [592.16]

22283 Souza, D. M. *Look What Feet Can Do* (2–4). Illus. Series: Look What Animals Can Do. 2006, Lerner LB $22.60 (978-0-7613-9460-0). 48pp. An interesting look at all the ways in which animals — from slugs to ostriches — can use their feet. (Rev: BL 10/15/06) [573.9]

22284 Souza, D. M. *Look What Mouths Can Do* (2–4). Series: Look What Animals Can Do. 2006, Lerner LB $22.60 (978-0-7613-9462-4). 48pp. This photo-filled, chatty volume with large type shows the varied ways in which animals use their mouths. Also use *Look What Tails Can Do* and *Look What Whiskers Can Do* (both 2006). (Rev: SLJ 12/06) [573.9]

22285 Stewart, Melissa. *When Rain Falls* (PS–2). Illus. by Constance R. Bergum. 2008, Peachtree $16.95 (978-1-56145-438-9). What do animals do when the rain falls? Stewart looks at the various fascinating actions they take. (Rev: LMC 10/08; SLJ 4/08) [591.72]

22286 Stockland, Patricia M. *Red Eyes or Blue Feathers: A Book About Animal Colors* (K–2). Illus. Series: Animal Wise. 2005, Picture Window LB $25.26 (978-1-4048-0931-4). 24pp. With color photographs, this volume introduces the varied colors found in animals and the ways in which they enable survival. Also use *Pointy, Long or Round: A Book*

About Animal Shapes, Strange Dances and Long Flights: A Book About Animal Behaviors, and *Stripes, Spots, or Diamonds: A Book About Animal Patterns* (all 2005).

22287 Swanson, Diane. *Animals Can Be So Playful* (K–1). Illus. by Rose Cowles. Series: Animals Can Be So. 2002, Douglas & McIntyre $10.95 (978-1-55054-900-3). 24pp. Various animals are seen at play in a series of excellent color photographs and an accompanying simple text. (Rev: BL 4/1/02) [591.5]

22288 Swanson, Diane. *Headgear That Hides and Plays* (2–4). Series: Up Close. 2001, Greystone $9.95 (978-1-55054-819-8). 32pp. Beginning with the human skull, this book describes the head structure of a number of animals from birds to the musk ox and tells how their heads help them to compete, court, and defend themselves. (Rev: BL 8/1/01; SLJ 1/02) [591]

22289 Swanson, Diane. *Noses That Plow and Poke* (2–4). Series: Up Close. 2000, Greystone $9.95 (978-1-55054-715-3). 30pp. A colorful, well-organized book that examines — up-close — noses on a number of animals and their uses beyond breathing. Also use *Tails That Talk and Fly, Feet That Suck and Feed,* and *Teeth That Stab and Grind.* (Rev: HB 7/03; HBG 10/03; SLJ 4/00) [591]

22290 Swanson, Diane. *Skin That Slimes and Scares* (2–4). Series: Up Close. 2001, Greystone $9.95 (978-1-55054-817-4). 32pp. This interesting science book starts with the human skin and then describes the outer coverings of different animals, from the armored skin of an African rhino to the poison-packed needles on the back of a red lionfish. (Rev: BL 8/1/01; SLJ 1/02) [591]

22291 Took, Atif. *Animal Encounters: A Chapter Book* (3–5). Series: True Tales. 2005, Children's Pr. LB $22.50 (978-0-516-25190-5). 48pp. This title examines encounters — friendly and dangerous — between humans and animals. (Rev: SLJ 1/06) [590]

22292 Walker, Niki, and Bobbie Kalman. *How Do Animals Move?* (1–3). Series: Science of Living Things. 2000, Crabtree LB $25.27 (978-0-86505-981-8); paper $6.95 (978-0-86505-958-0). 32pp. Using pictures and a very simple text, this book introduces such forms of animal locomotion as swimming, running, flying, and jumping. (Rev: SLJ 11/00) [591]

22293 Wells, Robert E. *What's Faster Than a Speeding Cheetah?* (K–4). Illus. 1997, Whitman LB $16.99 (978-0-8075-2280-6); paper $6.95 (978-0-8075-2281-3). 32pp. The author explores the concept of speed in the animal kingdom by focusing on the cheetah, the fastest animal. (Rev: BL 10/1/97; HBG 3/98; SLJ 1/98) [531]

22294 Woelfle, Gretchen. *Animal Families, Animal Friends* (1–3). Illus. by Robert Hynes. 2005, North-Word $15.95 (978-1-55971-901-8). Animal relationships are explored in three areas: parent-child, family group or pack, and larger communities. (Rev: LMC 10/05; SLJ 5/05)

BABIES

22295 Arnold, Caroline. *Mother and Baby Zoo Animals* (PS–3). Series: Zoo Animals. 1999, Carolrhoda LB $21.27 (978-1-57505-285-4); paper $9.95 (978-1-57505-390-5). 32pp. Similarities between human and animal behavior are stressed in this delightful book that introduces several zoo animals and how they care for their young. (Rev: BL 6/1–15/99; HBG 9/99) [591.3]

22296 Ashman, Linda. *Babies on the Go* (PS–2). Illus. by Jane Dyer. 2003, Harcourt $16.00 (978-0-15-201894-8). 32pp. This beautiful picture book looks at the diverse ways in which animal mothers — including humans — transport their young from one place to another. (Rev: BL 5/1/03; HBG 10/03; SLJ 5/03) [591.56]

22297 Batten, Mary. *Hey, Daddy! Animal Fathers and Their Babies* (K–3). Illus. by Higgins Bond. 2002, Peachtree $15.95 (978-1-56145-272-9). 32pp. Detailed illustrations are paired with descriptive text to introduce animal fathers that share in parenting. (Rev: BL 10/1/02; HBG 3/03; SLJ 12/02) [591.56]

22298 Bentley, Dawn. *Busy Little Beaver* (PS–2). Illus. by Beth Stover. Series: Read-and-Discover Atlantic Wilderness Adventures. 2003, Soundprints paper $3.95 (978-1-59249-011-0). 48pp. This appealing book follows a male beaver as he prepares a suitable home for his mate and the new babies that are soon to arrive. (Rev: SLJ 1/04)

22299 Bredeson, Carmen. *Baby Animals of the Grasslands* (K–2). Series: Nature's Baby Animals. 2008, Enslow LB $15.95 (978-0-7660-3006-0). 24pp. Engaging photographs show baby animals at home in the grasslands. (Rev: BLO 2/9/09; LMC 1/09) [591.74]

22300 Bull, Schuyler. *Crocodile Crossing* (K–4). Illus. by Alan Male. Series: Amazing Animal Adventures. 2003, Soundprints $15.95 (978-1-59249-051-6); paper $6.95 (978-1-59249-052-3). 27pp. A Nile crocodile waits for her hatchlings to emerge from the egg and then tries to protect them from the multiple threats around the waterhole. (Rev: HBG 4/04; SLJ 2/04) [597.98]

22301 Collard, Sneed B. *Animal Dads* (PS–2). Illus. by Steve Jenkins. 1997, Houghton $16.00 (978-0-395-83621-7). 32pp. The role of fathers in the animal kingdom is presented in large type and beautiful collages. (Rev: BCCB 5/97; BL 5/15/97; SLJ 6/97*) [591.56]

22302 Darling, Kathy. *Arctic Babies* (K–3). Illus. by Tara Darling. 1996, Walker LB $16.85 (978-0-8027-8414-8). 32pp. Using full-color photos of each animal, the author introduces a variety of babies from a lynx kitten to a baby beluga whale. (Rev: BL 4/15/96; SLJ 4/96) [591.9]

22303 Darling, Kathy. *Desert Babies* (3–5). Illus. by Tara Darling. 1997, Walker LB $16.85 (978-0-8027-8480-3). 32pp. An introduction to deserts, with a focus on the young animals found there, their size, food, enemies, and world location. (Rev: BCCB 3/97; BL 4/1/97; SLJ 3/97) [591.909]

22304 Dewey, Jennifer O. *Family Ties: Raising Wild Babies* (4–6). Illus. 1998, Marshall Cavendish

$15.95 (978-0-7614-5037-5). 80pp. Using case histories involving five different animals, these accounts demonstrate the strong — often fierce — drive to protect the family. (Rev: BL 10/1/98; HBG 3/99; SLJ 10/98) [591.5]

22305 Fraser, Mary Ann. *How Animal Babies Stay Safe* (PS–1). Illus. Series: Let's-Read-and-Find-Out Science. 2002, HarperCollins $15.95 (978-0-06-028803-7). 40pp. An introduction to the many ways in which nature protects baby animals, from camouflage to parental supervision. (Rev: BL 2/1/02; HBG 10/02; SLJ 2/02) [591.56]

22306 Greve, Meg. *Tap, Tap, Tap: What's Hatching?* (PS). Illus. Series: Rourke Board Books. 2009, Rourke $5.99 (978-1-60472-430-1). 16pp. Attractive color photographs and rhymed sentences provide a few easily absorbed facts about animals that hatch from eggs. (Rev: BL 5/15/09) [591.4]

22307 Hickman, Pamela. *Animals and Their Young: How Animals Produce and Care for Their Babies* (3–5). Illus. by Pat Stephens. 2003, Kids Can $10.95 (978-1-55337-061-1); paper $5.95 (978-1-55337-062-8). 40pp. This picture-book-format account shows animals' reproductive habits and care of the young. (Rev: BL 3/1/03; HBG 10/03; SLJ 6/03) [591.56]

22308 Kajikawa, Kimiko. *Close to You: How Animals Bond* (PS–1). Illus. 2008, Holt $16.95 (978-0-8050-8123-7). 32pp. Photographs of baby animals bonding with adult animals are paired with brief descriptions ("Porcupines brush with a prickly nose"). (Rev: BL 5/1/08; SLJ 5/08) [591.3]

22309 Maze, Stephanie, ed. *Tender Moments in the Wild: Animals and Their Babies* (PS–2). 2001, Moonstone $15.00 (978-0-9707768-0-8). Adult animals caring for their young are shown in attractive spreads with minimal text. (Rev: SLJ 12/01)

22310 Schofield, Jennifer. *Animal Babies in Ponds and Rivers* (PS–K). Illus. Series: Animal Babies. 2004, Kingfisher $7.95 (978-0-7534-5790-0). 32pp. Using a simple question-and-answer format that involves young readers, this volume introduces seven baby animals found in ponds and rivers. Also use *Animal Babies in Grasslands*. (Rev: BL 4/1/04; SLJ 10/04) [591.76]

22311 Simon, Seymour. *Baby Animals* (1–3). Series: See More Readers. 2002, North-South paper $3.95 (978-1-58717-171-0). 32pp. Double-page spreads containing a brief text opposite a color photograph introduce a number of different baby animals with material on how they are raised. (Rev: BL 7/02; HBG 3/03; SLJ 10/02) [591.3]

22312 Squire, Ann O. *Animal Babies* (2–3). Series: True Books — Animals. 2001, Children's Book Pr. LB $25.00 (978-0-516-22188-5). 48pp. The young of many species are presented in colorful pictures and simple text. (Rev: BL 12/15/01) [591.3]

22313 Stockdale, Susan. *Carry Me! Animal Babies on the Move* (PS–2). Illus. 2005, Peachtree $15.95 (978-1-56145-328-3). 32pp. Bright illustrations show how 14 varied animals — including a baboon and an alligator — carry their young. (Rev: BL 5/1/05; SLJ 4/05) [591.56]

22314 Wallace, Karen. *Wild Baby Animals* (K–3). Illus. Series: Eyewitness Reader. 2000, DK $12.99 (978-0-7894-5420-1); paper $3.99 (978-0-7894-5419-5). 32pp. Beginning readers will enjoy this book on various animal babies, their body parts, behavior, protection, and diet. (Rev: BL 7/00; HBG 9/00) [591.3]

CAMOUFLAGE

22315 Fowler, Allan. *Hard-to-See Animals* (1–2). Series: Rookie Readers. 1997, Children's Book Pr. LB $20.50 (978-0-516-20548-9). 32pp. This book introduces animal camouflage, with striking photos and minimal text, suitable for beginning readers. (Rev: BL 11/15/97; HBG 3/98; SLJ 10/97) [591]

22316 Helman, Andrea. *Hide and Seek: Nature's Best Vanishing Acts* (2–4). Illus. 2008, Walker $16.95 (978-0-8027-9690-5). 40pp. With a wide format and high-quality photographs, this is an arresting collection of examples of animal camouflages. (Rev: BL 3/1/08; HB 3/08; LMC 3/08*; SLJ 7/08) [591.47]

22317 Holmes, Anita. *Can You Find Us?* (1–2). Illus. 2000, Benchmark $21.36 (978-0-7614-1108-6). 32pp. A beginner reader that explores animal camouflage and challenges children to find small animals hidden in their surroundings. (Rev: BL 12/1/00; HBG 3/01; SLJ 2/01) [591.47]

22318 Kalman, Bobbie. *What Are Camouflage and Mimicry?* (2–4). Illus. Series: The Science of Living Things. 2001, Crabtree LB $25.27 (978-0-86505-985-6); paper $6.95 (978-0-86505-962-7). 32pp. Dramatic close-up photographs with informative captions accompany details of animals' efforts to become invisible. (Rev: SLJ 12/01) [591]

22319 Patent, Dorothy Hinshaw. *Bold and Bright: Black-and-White Animals* (K–3). Illus. by Kendahl Jan Jubb. 1998, Walker LB $16.85 (978-0-8027-8673-9). 32pp. This work presents a number of black-and-white animals, such as the skunk and the penguin, and shows how this coloration has helped them survive. (Rev: BL 9/1/98; HBG 3/99; SLJ 10/98) [591.42]

22320 Schwartz, David M., and Yael Schy. *Where in the Wild?* (1–3). Illus. by Dwight Kuhn. 2007, Tricycle $15.95 (978-1-58246-207-3). 32pp. Combining poetry, photography, and gatefolds with facts, this clever book challenges readers to find animals against their camouflage. (Rev: BL 11/1/07; LMC 1/08; SLJ 8/07) [590]

22321 Swanson, Diane. *Animals Can Be So Hard to See* (K–1). Illus. by Rose Cowles. Series: Animals Can Be So. 2002, Douglas & McIntyre $10.95 (978-1-55054-901-0). 24pp. Using double-page spreads with a color photograph on one side and simple text on the other, the camouflaging abilities of a variety of animals are explored. (Rev: BL 4/1/02; SLJ 8/02) [591.47]

22322 Weber, Belinda. *Animal Disguises* (K–3). Illus. Series: Kingfisher Young Knowledge. 2004, Kingfisher $8.95 (978-0-7534-5772-6). 47pp. Using two-page chapters with large text and eye-catching photographs, Weber introduces camouflage and the various animals that use this disguise. (Rev: BL 4/15/04*; SLJ 4/05) [591]

COMMUNICATION

22323 Jenkins, Steve. *Slap, Squeak, and Scatter: How Animals Communicate* (K–3). Illus. 2001, Houghton $16.00 (978-0-618-03376-8). 48pp. An introduction to the many wonderful ways in which animals communicate with each other. (Rev: BL 5/15/01; HBG 10/01; SLJ 5/01) [591.59]

22324 Kaner, Etta. *Animal Talk: How Animals Communicate Through Sight, Sound and Smell* (2–4). Illus. by Greg Douglas. 2002, Kids Can $10.95 (978-1-55074-982-3); paper $5.95 (978-1-55074-984-7). 40pp. Double-page spreads with photographs and original artwork explain how a variety of animals communicate through smell, sound, and body language. (Rev: BL 4/15/02; HBG 10/02; SLJ 7/02) [581.59]

22325 Sayre, April P. *Secrets of Sound: Studying the Calls and Songs of Whales, Elephants, and Birds* (4–7). Illus. 2002, Houghton $17.00 (978-0-618-01514-6). 64pp. Fascinating profiles of scientists who study animal sounds serve to introduce readers to a number of scientific concepts. (Rev: BL 12/1/02; HB 9/02; HBG 3/03; SLJ 10/02) [559.159]

22326 Schlein, Miriam. *Hello, Hello!* (K–2). Illus. by Daniel Kirk. 2002, Simon & Schuster $16.95 (978-0-689-83435-6). 32pp. This simple picture book shows how different animals greet each other. (Rev: BL 6/1–15/02; HB 7/02; HBG 10/02; SLJ 7/02) [591.59]

DEFENSES

22327 Bennett, Paul. *Escaping from Enemies* (1–4). Illus. Series: Nature's Secrets. 1995, Thomson Learning LB $21.40 (978-1-56847-358-1). 32pp. Describes how animals defend themselves by fighting, running, or resorting to trickery. (Rev: SLJ 8/95) [591]

22328 Jenkins, Steve. *What Do You Do When Something Wants to Eat You?* (PS–3). Illus. 1997, Houghton $16.00 (978-0-395-82514-3). 32pp. In this thrilling science book illustrated with paper collages, 14 different animals employ unusual tricks of nature to escape their predators. (Rev: BL 12/1/97; HBG 3/98; SLJ 11/97) [591.47]

22329 Kaner, Etta. *Animal Defenses: How Animals Protect Themselves* (2–5). Illus. by Pat Stephens. 1999, Kids Can $10.95 (978-1-55074-419-4). 40pp. Each section of this book is devoted to a particular type of defense, with several animals used as examples. (Rev: BL 4/15/99; HBG 9/99; SLJ 6/99) [591.47]

22330 Page, Robin, and Steve Jenkins. *How Many Ways Can You Catch a Fly?* (PS–3). Illus. by Steve Jenkins. 2008, Houghton $16.00 (978-0-618-96634-9). 32pp. A close and engaging look at how a variety of animals escape danger, avoid predators, and survive and thrive. (Rev: BL 9/1/08) [591.5]

22331 Souza, D. M. *Packed with Poison! Deadly Animal Defenses* (1–3). Illus. by Jack Harris. Series: On My Own Science. 2006, Millbrook LB $25.26 (978-1-57505-877-1). 48pp. For new readers, an introduction to several animals — spiders, scorpions, jellyfish, and so forth — that use poison as a defense. (Rev: SLJ 6/06) [591.65]

HIBERNATION

22332 Berger, Melvin, and Gilda Berger. *What Do Animals Do in Winter? How Animals Survive the Cold* (2–4). Illus. Series: Discovery Readers. 1995, Ideals paper $4.50 (978-1-57102-041-3). 48pp. Such winter survival tactics as hibernation and migration are presented with many examples. (Rev: BL 12/1/95; SLJ 2/96) [591.54]

22333 Ganeri, Anita. *Hibernation* (K–3). Series: Nature's Patterns. 2005, Heinemann LB $16.95 (978-1-4034-5895-7). 32pp. In simple langue, this volume introduces the stages of animal hibernation. (Rev: SLJ 6/05)

22334 Hickman, Pamela. *Animals Hibernating: How Animals Survive Extreme Conditions* (3–5). Illus. by Pat Stephens. Series: Animal Behavior. 2005, Kids Can $12.95 (978-1-55337-662-0); paper $5.95 (978-1-55337-663-7). 40pp. Hickman explains the reasons for hibernation and distinguishes between animals that go into true hibernation and those that merely retreat into deep sleep. (Rev: BL 11/1/05; SLJ 10/05) [591.56]

22335 Seuling, Barbara. *Winter Lullaby* (PS–1). Illus. by Greg Newbold. 1998, Harcourt $16.00 (978-0-15-201403-2). 32pp. Poetic language and colorful acrylic paintings are used to tell where such animals as bees, ducks, and mice spend the winter. (Rev: BL 9/1/98; HBG 3/99; SLJ 9/98) [591.54]

HOMES

22336 Crump, Donald J., ed. *Animal Architects* (3–8). Illus. 1987, National Geographic LB $12.50 (978-0-87044-617-7). 104pp. Chapters on animal builders are divided according to techniques — mound builders, weavers, excavators, and so on. (Rev: BL 12/15/87)

22337 Gregoire, Elizabeth. *Whose House Is This? A Look at Animal Homes — Webs, Nests, and Shells* (PS–2). Illus. by Derrick Alderman and Denise Shea. Series: Whose Is It? 2004, Picture Window LB $25.26 (978-1-4048-0608-5). 24pp. Rhythmic question-and-answer format and colorful collages introduce a wide variety of animal habitats. (Rev: BL 11/1/04) [591.56]

22338 Hickman, Pamela. *It's Moving Day!* (PS–2). Illus. by Geraldo Valério. 2008, Kids Can $16.95 (978-1-55453-074-8). 32pp. A single burrow is home to a revolving variety of creatures and often their young — first a woodchuck, then a rabbit, followed by a salamander, and so forth. (Rev: BL 5/1/08; LMC 5/08; SLJ 6/08) [591.56]

22339 Jenkins, Steve, and Robin Page. *I See a Kookaburra! Discovering Animal Habitats Around the World* (K–3). Illus. by Steve Jenkins. 2005, Houghton $16.00 (978-0-618-50764-1). A bright I Spy game that introduces six habitats — the American

Southwest, an English coastal tide pool, the Amazon rain forest, African grasslands, an Australian forest, and a Midwest pond — and the wildlife found there. (Rev: BCCB 5/05; BL 8/05; HB 5/05; SLJ 5/05) [591]

22340 Robinson, W. Wright. *How Mammals Build Their Amazing Homes* (5–8). Illus. by Carlyn Iverson. Series: Animal Architects. 1999, Blackbirch LB $27.44 (978-1-56711-381-5). 64pp. After defining what a mammal is, this account shows the homes of animals including beavers, chimpanzees, squirrels, prairie dogs, and moles, and describes how they are constructed. (Rev: HBG 3/00; SLJ 5/00) [591.56]

22341 Ryan, Pam Muñoz. *Armadillos Sleep in Dugouts: And Other Places Animals Live* (K–2). Illus. by Diane deGroat. 1997, Hyperion LB $14.89 (978-0-7868-2222-5). About 30 animal homes, from a beaver lodge to a woody thicket for deer, are described in text and pictures in this simple science book. (Rev: HBG 3/98; SLJ 12/97) [591]

22342 Shields, Carol Diggory. *Homes* (PS–3). Illus. by Svjetlan Junakovic. Series: Animagicals. 2001, Handprint $9.95 (978-1-929766-27-7). 32pp. Rhyming riddles give clues about animal homes hidden under the flaps in this tall-format picture book. (Rev: BL 2/1/02; HBG 3/02; SLJ 2/02) [811]

22343 Squire, Ann O. *Animal Homes* (2–3). Series: True Books — Animals. 2001, Children's Book Pr. LB $25.00 (978-0-516-22189-2). 48pp. Various kinds of animal homes are presented with well-captioned color pictures on each page plus a few lines of accompanying text. (Rev: BL 12/15/01) [591.56]

22344 Stockland, Patricia M. *Sand, Leaf, or Coral Reef: A Book About Animal Habitats* (K–2). Illus. Series: Animal Wise. 2005, Picture Window LB $25.26 (978-1-4048-0932-1). 24pp. With color photographs, this volume introduces the varied places where animals make their homes.

22345 Zoehfeld, Kathleen W. *What Lives in a Shell?* (PS–1). Illus. by Helen K. Davie. Series: Let's-Read-and-Find-Out. 1994, HarperCollins paper $5.99 (978-0-06-445124-6). 32pp. A simple science book that introduces such creatures as snails, turtles, crabs, and oysters that use their shells as homes. (Rev: BL 8/94; HB 11/94; SLJ 9/94) [591.4]

REPRODUCTION

22346 Gill, Shelley. *The Egg* (K–3). Illus. by Jo-Ellen Bosson. 2001, Charlesbridge $16.95 (978-1-57091-377-8). 32pp. A fact-filled book about eggs and egg-bearers with attractive illustrations and humorous text. (Rev: BCCB 2/01; BL 11/1/01; HBG 3/02; SLJ 7/01) [591.4]

22347 Hickman, Pamela. *Animals and Their Mates: How Animals Attract, Fight for and Protect Each Other* (2–5). Illus. by Pat Stephens. 2004, Kids Can $5.95 (978-1-55337-546-3). 40pp. A broad range of mating rituals — many involving unexpected behaviors — are presented. (Rev: BL 10/15/04) [591.56]

22348 Posada, Mia. *Guess What Is Growing Inside This Egg* (K–3). Illus. 2007, Millbrook $15.95 (978-

0-8225-6192-7). 32pp. On the first spread of each pair, a close-up of an egg is accompanied by a rhyming clue; on the second spread, the answer is given as well as basic information about the animal in question. (Rev: BL 4/1/07) [591.4]

Animal Species

GENERAL AND MISCELLANEOUS

22349 Anderson, Jill. *Zebras* (PS–2). Series: Wild Ones. 2005, NorthWord $12.95 (978-1-55971-926-1); paper $6.95 (978-1-55971-927-8). With lots of photographs, many of them close-ups, this simple text introduces basic facts about zebras. (Rev: HBG 4/06; SLJ 1/06) [599.72]

22350 Arnold, Caroline. *A Zebra's World* (PS–2). Illus. by author. Series: Caroline Arnold's Animals. 2006, Picture Window LB $26.60 (978-1-4048-1324-3). 24pp. A baby zebra grows up and learns to fend for himself in this appealing fact-packed title. (Rev: LMC 11/06; SLJ 6/06) [599.72]

22351 Arnosky, Jim. *Raccoons and Ripe Corn* (PS–1). Illus. by author. 1991, Morrow paper $6.99 (978-0-688-10489-4). 32pp. An autumn night with mother and baby raccoon eating corn in the field. (Rev: BL 9/1/87; SLJ 9/87)

22352 Barbé-Julien, Colette. *Little Hippopotamuses* (1–3). Series: Born to Be Wild. 2005, Gareth Stevens LB $23.00 (978-0-8368-4736-9). 24pp. A close-up look at what life is like for baby hippopotamuses, including their relationships with their parents; suitable for browsers. (Rev: SLJ 2/06) [599.63]

22353 Barnes, Julia. *Camels and Llamas at Work* (3–5). Series: Animals at Work. 2006, Gareth Stevens LB $24.00 (978-0-8368-6222-5). 32pp. Camels and llamas are not only used as pack animals; full-color photographs show them in various roles and the text discusses the animals' physical characteristics and relationship with humans. (Rev: SLJ 1/07) [636.2]

22354 Berman, Ruth. *American Bison* (3–6). Illus. by Cheryl Walsh Bellville. Series: Nature Watch. 1992, Carolrhoda LB $25.26 (978-0-87614-697-2). 48pp. The lifestyle, habitat, and current status of the American buffalo is covered in text and pictures. (Rev: BL 8/92; SLJ 10/82) [599.73]

22355 Brimner, Larry Dane. *Polar Mammals* (3–4). Illus. Series: A True Book. 1996, Children's Book Pr. LB $25.00 (978-0-516-20042-2). 48pp. An introduction to the Arctic biome, followed by general information on the many different mammals that live there. (Rev: SLJ 4/97) [590]

22356 Butler, John. *Whose Baby Am I?* (PS). Illus. 2001, Viking $10.99 (978-0-670-89683-7). 24pp. Nine animal babies ask "Whose baby am I?" and the answer is found by turning the page. (Rev: BL 6/1–15/01; HBG 10/01; SLJ 7/01) [591.39]

22357 Butterfield, Moira. *Fast, Strong, and Striped: What Am I?* (PS–3). Illus. by Wayne Ford. Series: What Am I? 1997, Raintree LB $15.98 (978-0-8172-4583-2); paper $7.95 (978-0-8172-7229-6). 32pp. Using double-page spreads, clues are given about an animal by introducing its physical characteristics, habitat, and diet and then identifying it. Also use *Brown, Fierce, and Furry: What Am I?* (1997). (Rev: SLJ 7/97) [591]

22358 Caper, William. *American Bison: A Scary Prediction* (3–4). Series: America's Animal Comebacks. 2007, Bearport LB $25.27 (978-1-59716-504-4). 32pp. With eye-catching photographs and an appealing design, Caper looks at how the iconic American bison almost disappeared and at efforts being made to help them on the comeback trail. (Rev: LMC 1/08; SLJ 12/07) [599.64]

22359 Carson, Mary Kay. *Emi and the Rhino Scientist* (5–8). Illus. Series: Scientists in the Field. 2007, Houghton $18.00 (978-0-618-64639-5). 64pp. Emi, a rhinoceros at the Cincinnati Zoo, gives birth in captivity (which is unusual for a rhino) thanks to the help of scientist Terri Roth in this exciting and informative account. (Rev: BL 12/1/07; HB 11/07; SLJ 11/07) [599.66]

22360 Clarke, Ginjer L. *Platypus!* (PS–1). Illus. by Paul Mirocha. Series: Step into Reading. 2004, Random paper $3.99 (978-0-375-82417-3). 32pp. This friendly introduction to the platypus provides simple, engaging text and close-up illustrations. (Rev: BL 7/04) [599.2]

22361 Collard, Sneed B., III. *In the Rain Forest Canopy* (3–6). Series: Science Adventures. 2005, Benchmark LB $25.64 (978-0-7614-1954-9). 43pp. Readers meet a scientist who studies creatures that live high in the canopy of the rain forest. (Rev: SLJ 5/06) [578.734]

22362 Collard, Sneed B., III. *A Platypus, Probably* (K–3). Illus. by Andrew Plant. 2005, Charlesbridge $16.95 (978-1-57091-583-3); paper $6.95 (978-1-57091-584-0). 32pp. An accessible and attractive introduction to the platypus. (Rev: BL 9/15/05; SLJ 9/05) [599.2]

22363 Delafosse, Claude. *Under the Ground: Hidden World* (PS–2). Series: First Discovery. 1999, Scholastic $12.95 (978-0-590-43813-1). 24pp. For young children, this colorful, well-illustrated account introduces underground animals such as moles and worms. (Rev: BL 6/1–15/99; SLJ 7/99) [591]

22364 Dossenbach, Hans D. *Beware! We Are Poisonous: How Animals Defend Themselves* (4–6). Illus. 1998, Blackbirch LB $23.70 (978-1-56711-215-3). 40pp. Many poisonous animals are discussed including some that are relatively harmless, such as the tarantula, and others that mimic poisonous ones to avoid predators. (Rev: BL 12/1/98; HBG 3/99) [591.6]

22365 Fowler, Allan. *It Could Still Be a Mammal* (1–2). Illus. Series: Rookie Readers. 1990, Children's Book Pr. LB $20.50 (978-0-516-04903-8). 32pp. The nature of mammals and some examples are covered in this easily read science book. (Rev: BL 2/1/91) [599]

22366 Fredericks, Anthony D. *Zebras* (2–3). Series: Early Bird Nature Books. 2000, Lerner LB $25.26 (978-0-8225-3043-5). 48pp. A fact-filled text and amazing color photos explore how zebras live and grow in their native Africa or in zoos around the world. (Rev: BL 7/00; HBG 3/01) [599.72]

22367 Gibbons, Gail. *Pigs* (PS–2). Illus. 1999, Holiday House $16.95 (978-0-8234-1441-3). This book introduces various breeds of pigs, their physical characteristics, their history and habits, and common myths about them. (Rev: BL 3/15/99; HBG 9/99; SLJ 5/99) [636.4]

22368 Glaser, Linda. *Hello Squirrels! Scampering Through the Seasons* (K–2). Illus. by Gay Holland. 2006, Millbrook LB $22.60 (978-0-7613-2887-2). 32pp. An appealing look at the first year of a squirrel's life, narrated from the perspective of a young child and including realistic drawings. (Rev: BL 4/15/06) [599.36]

22369 Grassy, John, and Chuck Keene. *National Audubon Society First Field Guide: Mammals* (4–8). Series: Audubon Society First Field Guide. 1998, Scholastic paper $17.95 (978-0-590-05471-3). 160pp. An attractive guide to mammals, with maps showing habitats, a picture of each animal, and basic descriptive text. (Rev: SLJ 4/99) [599]

22370 Green, Jen, and David Burnie. *Mammal* (5–9). Illus. Series: DK/Google e.guides. 2005, DK $17.99 (978-0-7566-1139-2). 96pp. This highly illustrated guide introduces readers to the evolution and diversity of mammals and provides a link to a Web site that serves as a gateway to additional resources. (Rev: SLJ 8/05) [599]

22371 Guidoux, Valérie. *Little Zebras* (1–3). Series: Born to Be Wild. 2005, Gareth Stevens LB $23.00 (978-0-8368-4741-3). 24pp. This attractive title introduces the physical and behavioral characteristics of zebras and examines the role of zebra parents in feeding their young and protecting them from predators. (Rev: SLJ 2/06) [599.72]

22372 Haas, Robert B. *African Critters* (3–5). Illus. 2008, National Geographic $17.95 (978-1-4263-0317-3). 96pp. Wildlife photographer Haas shows real life for animals from antelope to zebra in clear text and arresting photographs. (Rev: BL 7/08; SLJ 9/08)

22373 Hare, Tony. *Animal Fact-File: Head-to-Tail Profiles of More Than 90 Mammals* (4–8). 1999, Facts on File paper $18.95 (978-0-8160-4016-2). From aardvarks to wombats, this is an alphabetical guide to more than 90 mammals with details including classification, size, coloration, and habits. (Rev: SLJ 9/99; VOYA 6/00) [599]

22374 Harman, Amanda. *Rhinoceroses* (3–5). Illus. Series: Endangered! 1996, Benchmark LB $22.79 (978-0-7614-0290-9). 32pp. The ferocious rhinoceros is described, with material on its habits, habitats, and why it is on the endangered list. (Rev: SLJ 2/97) [599.72]

22375 Hatkoff, Isabella, and Craig Hatkoff. *Owen and Mzee: The Language of Friendship* (K–4). Photos by Peter Greste. 2007, Scholastic $16.99 (978-0-439-89959-8). This appealing sequel to *Owen and Mzee: The True Story of a Remarkable Friendship* continues the story of the bond between the baby hippo orphaned by the Indian Ocean tsunami and an ancient tortoise, focusing on how the two creatures communicate with one another. (Rev: BL 12/15/06*; SLJ 2/07*) [599.63]

22376 Hatkoff, Isabella, and Craig Hatkoff. *Owen and Mzee: The True Story of a Remarkable Friendship* (1–3). Illus. by Peter Greste. 2006, Scholastic $16.99 (978-0-439-82973-1). 32pp. A baby hippo and a giant tortoise form an unlikely bond following the hippo's rescue from the 2004 tsunami; photographs bring the unusual situation to life. (Rev: BL 5/15/06; SLJ 5/06*) [599.63]

22377 Hoban, Tana. *A Children's Zoo* (PS). Illus. 1985, Greenwillow $16.89 (978-0-688-05204-1). 24pp. Appealing portraits of 11 common zoo animals. (Rev: BCCB 10/85; BL 9/1/85; SLJ 10/85)

22378 Hooper, Meredith. *Antarctic Journal: The Hidden Worlds of Antarctica's Animals* (5–7). Illus. by Lucia deLeiris. 2001, National Geographic $16.95 (978-0-7922-7188-8). An exciting account of a summer the author spent at Palmer Station in the Antarctic and the wildlife there. (Rev: BL 6/1–15/01; HBG 10/01; SLJ 3/01) [988]

22379 Jango-Cohen, Judith. *Camels* (3–6). Illus. Series: Animals, Animals. 2004, Benchmark $25.64 (978-0-7614-1750-7). 47pp. A well-written overview of these animals, providing all the information needed for report writing plus additional material of interest. (Rev: BL 3/15/04; SLJ 2/05) [599.63]

22380 Jango-Cohen, Judith. *Hippopotamuses* (3–5). Illus. Series: Animals, Animals. 2006, Marshall Cavendish LB $28.50 (978-0-7614-2238-9). 47pp. This series entry combines full-color photographs and facts about hippos, including a chapter about interaction with humans. (Rev: BL 1/1–15/07) [599.63]

22381 Jango-Cohen, Judith. *Rhinoceroses* (3–6). Illus. Series: Animals, Animals. 2004, Benchmark $25.64 (978-0-7614-1753-8). 47pp. A well-written overview of these animals, providing all the information needed for report writing plus additional material of interest. (Rev: BL 4/15/04; HB 3/04; SLJ 2/05) [599.72]

22382 Jarrow, Gail, and Paul Sherman. *Naked Mole-Rats* (4–7). Illus. Series: Nature Watch. 1996, Carolrhoda LB $28.75 (978-0-87614-995-9). 48pp. An informative introduction to the naked mole-rat, a most unusual animal that seems to copy habits from a variety of other species. (Rev: SLJ 10/96) [599.32]

22383 Johnson, Sylvia A. *Ferrets* (3–6). Illus. 1997, Carolrhoda LB $25.26 (978-1-57505-014-0). 48pp. Several types of wild and domestic ferrets and their cousins, including otters and skunks, are introduced, with a concentration on efforts to save the black-footed ferret. (Rev: BL 7/97; HBG 3/98; SLJ 8/97) [636]

22384 Kalman, Bobbie. *The Life Cycle of a Beaver* (2–4). Illus. Series: Life Cycle. 2006, Crabtree LB $25.20 (978-0-7787-0628-1); paper $6.95 (978-0-7787-0702-8). 32pp. Report writers will find this a useful and interesting resource. Diet, habitat, behavior, and other aspects of beavers are covered. Photographs and illustrations accompany the text, and vocabulary words appear in bold font. (Rev: SLJ 5/07)

22385 Komiya, Teruyuki. *Life-Size Zoo* (PS–2). Illus. by Toyofumi Fukuda. 2009, Seven Footer $17.95 (978-1-934734-20-9). 48pp. This oversize book presents excellent, proportionally sized photographs of animals or parts of animals — a whole meerkat but a tiger's head — and encourages readers to notice salient features; facts are appended. (Rev: BL 4/15/09; LMC 10/09; SLJ 6/09) [500]

22386 Lambilly-Bresson, Élisabeth de. *Animals in the Desert* (PS–2). Series: Animal Show and Tell. 2007, Gareth Stevens LB $17.27 (978-0-8368-8204-9). 16pp. In simple first-person narratives, desert animals describe their key characteristics and behaviors; with eye-catching full-page photographs. Also use *Animals in the Jungle, Animals of the Mountains,* and *Animals of the Ocean* (all 2007). (Rev: SLJ 3/08)

22387 Landau, Elaine. *Raccoons: Scavengers of the Night* (2–3). Series: Animals after Dark. 2007, Enslow LB $22.60 (978-0-7660-2767-1). 32pp. Photographs of raccoons accompany information about their nocturnal behavior and their scavenging habits. (Rev: SLJ 8/07)

22388 Lang, Aubrey. *Baby Ground Squirrel* (2–4). Photos by Wayne Lynch. Series: Nature Babies. 2004, Fitzhenry & Whiteside $13.95 (978-1-55041-797-5); paper $5.95 (978-1-55041-799-9). 36pp. Full-color photographs follow the development of a litter of baby ground squirrels on the Western Canadian prairie. (Rev: BCCB 7–8/04; SLJ 2/05)

22389 Lang, Aubrey. *Baby Porcupine* (1–4). Photos by Wayne Lynch. Series: Nature Babies. 2006, Fitzhenry & Whiteside $13.95 (978-1-55041-560-5); paper $6.95 (978-1-55041-562-9). 36pp. Filled with photographs of a baby porcupine's growth until it's able to survive without its mother's protection and guidance. (Rev: SLJ 6/06) [599.35]

22390 Lang, Aubrey. *Baby Sloth* (1–4). Photos by Wayne Lynch. Series: Nature Babies. 2005, Fitzhenry & Whiteside $13.95 (978-1-55041-825-5); paper $5.95 (978-1-55041-827-9). 36pp. After a fascinating account of their trip to Panama's rain forests, the authors supply basic information on baby sloths — habitat, diet, relationship with their mothers, and so forth. (Rev: SLJ 4/05)

22391 Latta, Jan. *Rudy the Rhinoceros* (K–4). Series: Wild Animal Families. 2006, Gareth Stevens LB $23.93 (978-0-8368-7771-7). 24pp. In a first-"person" account, Rudy describes what it's like to be a rhinoceros, giving readers facts about his species in an enjoyable and engaging format. (Rev: SLJ 5/07)

22392 MacKen, JoAnn Early. *Jackrabbits / Liebres americanas* (2–4). Trans. by Tatiana Acosta and Guillermo Gutiérrez. Series: Animals That Live in the Desert / Animales del desierto. 2005, Weekly Reader LB $21.00 (978-0-8368-4842-7). 24pp. A beginning book with facts about jackrabbits in both English and Spanish. (Rev: SLJ 6/06) [599.32]

22393 Markle, Sandra. *Animals Robert Scott Saw: An Adventure in Antarctica* (4–7). Illus. by Phil. Series: Explorers. 2008, Chronicle LB $16.99 (978-0-8118-4918-0). 48pp. As the title indicates, this book focuses on the animals that explorer Scott took with him to the South Pole in 1912 and those he observed on the way. (Rev: BL 4/1/08) [919.8]

22394 Markle, Sandra. *Musk Oxen* (K–4). Series: Animal Prey. 2007, Lerner LB $25.26 (978-0-8225-6064-7). 40pp. Eye-catching photographs and clear, readable text discuss musk oxen, their social structure, and how they deal with predators, mainly wolves that target the young or weak. (Rev: SLJ 4/07) [599.64]

22395 Marrin, Albert. *Saving the Buffalo* (5–7). 2006, Scholastic $18.99 (978-0-439-71854-7). 128pp. This well-written, well-illustrated history traces the fortunes of the American bison from the days when huge herds covered the plains to near extinction at the end of the 19th century and then to an amazing recovery over the past century or so. (Rev: SLJ 12/06*) [599.64]

22396 Mason, Adrienne. *Skunks* (2–4). Illus. by Nancy Gray Ogle. 2006, Kids Can LB $10.95 (978-1-55337-733-7); paper $6.95 (978-1-55337-734-4). 32pp. This picture-book introduction to skunks covers the often-maligned creature's physical characteristics, diet, habitat, behavior, and interaction with humans. (Rev: SLJ 9/06) [599.74]

22397 Merrick, Patrick. *Raccoons* (3–4). Series: New Naturebooks. 2006, The Child's World LB $27.07 (978-1-59296-647-9). 32pp. An introductory overview of this nocturnal mammal, with vivid color photographs. (Rev: SLJ 2/07) [599.76]

22398 Midge, Tiffany. *Buffalo* (PS–3). Illus. by Diana Magnuson. Series: Animal Lore and Legend. 1995, Scholastic $4.95 (978-0-590-22489-5). 32pp. The food, habitats, and behavior of buffalo are described, along with three Indian folktales about them. (Rev: SLJ 3/96) [591.52]

22399 Miller, Sara S. *Horses and Rhinos: What They Have in Common* (3–5). Series: Animals in Order. 1999, Watts LB $26.50 (978-0-531-11586-2). 48pp. After a general introduction to animal classification, this beautifully illustrated book discusses horses and rhinos — how they are considered alike and how they differ. (Rev: BL 12/15/99; HBG 4/00) [591]

22400 Montgomery, Sy. *Quest for the Tree Kangaroo: An Expedition to the Cloud Forest of New Guinea* (5–8). Illus. by Nic Bishop. 2006, Houghton $18.00 (978-0-618-49641-9). 80pp. Join researchers on a challenging expedition to the cloud forests of Papua New Guinea to learn more about the rare Matschie's tree kangaroo. Sibert Honor Book, 2007. (Rev: BL 12/1/06; SLJ 12/06*) [599.2]

22401 Moore, Heidi. *A Mob of Meerkats* (3–5). Series: Animal Groups. 2004, Heinemann LB $24.22 (978-1-4034-4694-7). 32pp. A basic introduction to the animal and its characteristics, using a question-and-answer format and including color close-ups. (Rev: SLJ 9/04)

22402 Morgan, Ben. *DK Guide to Mammals: A Wild Journey with These Extraordinary Beasts* (4–6). Illus. 2003, DK $15.99 (978-0-7894-9581-5). 64pp. For browsers, an excellent overview of mammals, covering topics from the purely physical to the social — "Urban Living," for example. (Rev: HBG 4/04; SLJ 1/04) [599]

22403 Murray, Peter. *Rhinos* (4–7). Series: The World of Mammals. 2005, Child's World LB $29.93 (978-1-59296-502-1). 40pp. Arresting photographs and engaging text introduce the anatomy, behavior, habitat, and life cycle of the rhinoceros as well as the threats to the animal's survival in the wild. (Rev: SLJ 3/06) [599.72]

22404 Nelson, Kristin L. *Clever Raccoons* (PS–2). Series: Pull Ahead Books. 2000, Lerner LB $22.60 (978-0-8225-3763-2); paper $5.95 (978-0-8225-3644-4). 32pp. This simple science book covers raccoons — their homes, when they are active, and how they use their paws. (Rev: BL 9/15/00; HBG 3/01) [599.32]

22405 Nelson, Kristin L. *Spraying Skunks* (2–3). Series: Pull Ahead Books. 2003, Lerner LB $22.60 (978-0-8225-4670-2); paper $5.95 (978-0-8225-3598-0). 32pp. An introduction to skunks and their habits that contains many color photographs and a map activity. (Rev: BL 3/15/03; HBG 10/03) [599.74]

22406 Nicholson, Darrel. *Wild Boars* (2–4). Illus. 1987, Carolrhoda LB $23.93 (978-0-87614-308-7). 48pp. Full-color photos highlight the habits and characteristics of the boar, introduced in the United States 100 years ago. (Rev: BCCB 9/87; BL 7/87; SLJ 9/87)

22407 Older, Jules. *Pig* (K–3). Illus. by Lyn Severance. 2004, Charlesbridge paper $6.95 (978-0-88106-110-9). 32pp. Children will enjoy browsing through the pages of this colorfully illustrated introduction to pigs and their place in the world. (Rev: BL 8/04; SLJ 9/04) [636.4]

22408 Otfinoski, Steven. *Skunks* (4–6). Series: Animals Animals. 2008, Marshall Cavendish LB $20.95 (978-0-7614-2929-6). 48pp. *Skunks* is packed with information regarding habitat, adaptations, and humanity's impact and includes excellent photographs. (Rev: SLJ 2/09) [599.76]

22409 Penny, Malcolm. *Black Rhino* (3–6). Illus. Series: Natural World. 2001, Raintree LB $27.12 (978-0-7398-4438-0). 48pp. A fine guide to the black rhinoceros with accessible text, memorable photographs, a glossary, and list of Web sites. (Rev: BL 12/15/01; HBG 10/02) [599.66]

22410 Perry, Phyllis J. *Buffalo* (3–5). Illus. Series: Animals, Animals. 2005, Benchmark LB $17.95 (978-0-7614-1866-5). 48pp. Report writers will find plenty of clear photographs and maps plus well-organized information about the bison and its physical characteristics, diet, habitat, and behavior. (Rev: SLJ 2/06) [599.64]

22411 *Polar Animals* (PS–2). Illus. by Paul Hess. 1996, De Agostini $6.95 (978-1-899883-36-3). Humorous rhymes accompany paintings that describe eight animals from the polar regions. (Rev: SLJ 12/96) [591]

22412 Pringle, Laurence. *Strange Animals, New to Science* (4–7). Illus. 2002, Marshall Cavendish $16.95 (978-0-7614-5083-2). 112pp. The results of scientists' efforts to discover new animal species are presented here, with color photographs and coverage of the reasons behind disappearing habitats.

(Rev: BCCB 9/02; BL 7/02; HBG 10/02; SLJ 8/02) [591.68]

22413 Pyers, Greg. *Why Am I a Mammal?* (3–5). Illus. Series: Classifying Animals. 2005, Raintree LB $27.50 (978-1-4109-2016-4); paper $7.85 (978-1-4109-2023-2). 32pp. Introduces readers to the process of scientific classification and then examines the unique characteristics of mammals. (Rev: SLJ 4/06) [599]

22414 Rake, Jody Sullivan. *Meerkats* (PS–2). Illus. Series: Pebble Plus: African Animals. 2008, Capstone LB $14.95 (978-1-4296-1249-4). 32pp. Rake uses close-up photographs and limited-vocabulary text to introduce the meerkat and its behavior, anatomy, habitat, and diet. (Rev: BL 4/1/08) [599.74]

22415 Rau, Dana Meachen. *Guess Who Grunts* (PS–K). Series: Bookworms. Guess Who. 2009, Marshall Cavendish $15.95 (978-0-7614-2906-7). 32pp. Fun for browsing, this book asks readers to identify a pig using the clues in the text and images. (Rev: SLJ 6/09) [636.4]

22416 Rau, Dana Meachen. *The Rabbit in the Garden* (PS–1). Series: Benchmark Rebus. 2006, Benchmark LB $22.79 (978-0-7614-2308-9). 24pp. This colorful easy reader, which features a blend of rebuses and easy-to-understand text, follows a typical day in the life of a rabbit and describes physical characteristics, habitat, diet, and behavior. (Rev: SLJ 12/06) [599.32]

22417 Rebman, Renee C. *Anteaters* (3–5). Series: Animals, Animals. 2006, Benchmark LB $19.95 (978-0-7614-2234-1). 48pp. An introduction to the anatomy, behavior, diet, and habitat of anteaters. Color photographs give readers a close-up look. (Rev: SLJ 5/07)

22418 Ring, Susan. *Project Hippopotamus* (3–6). Illus. Series: Zoo Life. 2002, Weigl LB $15.15 (978-1-59036-013-2). 32pp. This volume looks at both the good and bad aspects of raising hippopotamuses in zoos, and discusses their natural habitat, physiology, and so forth, using color photographs and featured sidebars. (Rev: BL 12/15/02; HBG 3/03) [599.63]

22419 Robbins, Ken. *Thunder on the Plains: The Story of the American Buffalo* (3–5). Illus. 2001, Simon & Schuster $16.00 (978-0-689-83025-9). 32pp. An introduction to the American buffalo, its place in American history, and why its population went from 50 million to near extinction. (Rev: BL 12/1/00; HBG 10/01; SLJ 3/01) [599.64]

22420 Rodriguez, Ana María. *Secret of the Singing Mice . . . and More!* (4–6). Series: Animal Secrets Revealed! 2008, Enslow LB $23.93 (978-0-7660-2956-9). 48pp. Full-color pictures and interesting information about how scientists discovered and proved their theories about mice, bats, and other small animals. (Rev: SLJ 2/09) [599]

22421 Royer, Anne. *Little Marmots* (3–5). Illus. Series: Born to Be Wild. 2005, Gareth Stevens LB $23.00 (978-0-8368-4439-9). 24pp. A simply worded look at young marmots and their lives, with large photographs.

22422 Savage, Stephen. *Mammals* (2–4). Illus. Series: What's the Difference? 2000, Raintree $25.69 (978-0-7398-1354-6). 32pp. This book reveals common characteristics and differences among mammals and discusses habitats, babies, food, and locomotion. (Rev: BL 10/15/00; HBG 3/01) [599]

22423 *Savanna Animals: Fun Facts and Stuff to Do* (PS–K). Illus. Series: Padded Animal Board Books. 2006, ME Media $7.95 (978-1-58925-798-6). 24pp. This richly illustrated board book introduces young readers to the animals of the African savanna, including elephants and chimpanzees. (Rev: BL 10/15/06) [591.74]

22424 Short, Joan, et al. *Platypus* (3–4). Illus. by Andrew Wichlinski. 1997, Mondo paper $4.95 (978-1-57255-195-4). 22pp. There is coverage on the anatomy, habits, and habitat of this unusual animal, with a cross-section drawing of its underground burrow. (Rev: SLJ 8/97) [599]

22425 Sill, Cathryn. *About Mammals: A Guide for Children* (1–2). Illus. by John Sill. 1997, Peachtree $14.95 (978-1-56145-141-8). 32pp. In this very simple volume with full-color paintings, several mammals and their habits are introduced to young children. (Rev: BL 6/1–15/97; SLJ 6/97) [500]

22426 Silverstein, Alvin, et al. *The Mustang* (4–8). Series: Endangered in America. 1997, Millbrook $24.90 (978-0-7613-0048-9). Examines the life cycle and behavior of the mustang, the reasons it has become endangered, and the measures being taken to ensure its survival. (Rev: BL 3/15/97; SLJ 6/97) [636.1]

22427 Souza, D. M. *Skunks Do More Than Stink!* (3–5). Illus. 2002, Millbrook LB $21.90 (978-0-7613-2503-1). 32pp. This volume is filled with photographs and easily understandable text about the lives of skunks. (Rev: BL 3/1/02; HBG 10/02; SLJ 3/02) [599.76]

22428 Spilsbury, Richard. *Black Rhino* (4–6). Illus. Series: Animals Under Threat. 2004, Heinemann LB $27.07 (978-1-4034-4859-0); paper $8.50 (978-1-4034-5433-1). 48pp. The rhinoceros and its characteristics are described before discussion of poaching, relocation, tourism, and other environmental concerns. (Rev: SLJ 1/05) [599.66]

22429 Spilsbury, Richard, and Louise Spilsbury. *A Mob of Kangaroos* (3–5). Series: Animal Groups. 2004, Heinemann LB $24.22 (978-1-4034-4690-9). 32pp. A basic introduction to the animal and its characteristics, using a question-and-answer format and including color close-ups. (Rev: SLJ 9/04)

22430 Squire, Ann O. *Anteaters, Sloths, and Armadillos* (3–5). Series: Animals in Order. 1999, Watts LB $22.00 (978-0-531-11515-2). 48pp. After a general introduction to animal classification, this book discusses three oddities of the animal world. (Rev: BL 8/99; HBG 9/99) [591]

22431 Staub, Frank. *Mountain Goats* (2–5). Photos by author. Series: Early Bird Nature Books. 1994, Lerner LB $25.26 (978-0-8225-3000-8). 48pp. A simple text and excellent photos are used to introduce mountain goats of the American Northwest. (Rev: SLJ 8/94) [599]

22432 Stewart, Melissa. *Hippopotamuses* (2–3). Series: Animals. 2002, Children's Book Pr. LB $25.00 (978-0-516-22200-4). 48pp. The anatomy, life cycle, and habits of the hippopotamus are covered in a simple, large-type text and many color photographs. Also use *Rhinoceroses* and *Zebras* (both 2002). (Rev: BL 8/02) [599.63]

22433 Stone, Tanya L. *Skunk* (3–5). Series: Wild America. 2002, Gale LB $21.20 (978-1-56711-641-0). 24pp. A photo-essay on this much-shunned animal with material on its appearance, unusual abilities, food, and life cycle. (Rev: BL 10/15/02; SLJ 2/03) [599.74]

22434 Stuart, Dee. *The Astonishing Armadillo* (3–6). Illus. Series: Nature Watch. 1993, Carolrhoda LB $25.26 (978-0-87614-769-6). 48pp. The amazing armadillo is featured in text and sharp color photos. (Rev: BL 8/93) [599.3]

22435 Swan, Erin Pembrey. *Camels and Pigs: What They Have in Common* (3–5). Series: Animals in Order. 1999, Watts LB $26.50 (978-0-531-11585-5). 47pp. This title deals with 14 specific animals from the Artiodactyla, or "even-toed," order, which includes camels, llamas, deer, and pigs. (Rev: SLJ 11/99) [599]

22436 Swanson, Diane. *Skunks* (2–4). Series: Welcome to the World of Animals. 2002, Gareth Stevens LB $24.00 (978-0-8368-3317-1). 32pp. A slim volume that provides information on the animal's home, diet, communication, and lifestyle. (Rev: HBG 3/03; SLJ 3/03) [599.74]

22437 Swinburne, Stephen. *Armadillo Trail* (K–3). Illus. by Bruce Hiscock. 2009, Boyds Mills $16.95 (978-1-59078-463-1). 32pp. This engaging picture book follows a mother armadillo as she gives birth to four pups and raises them to start families of their own. (Rev: BL 2/1/09; SLJ 3/09) [599.3]

22438 Theodorou, Rod. *Black Rhino* (K–2). Illus. Series: Animals in Danger. 2000, Heinemann LB $21.36 (978-1-57572-262-7). 32pp. The endangered black rhino is introduced, with information on diet, habitat, life cycle, and so on, as well as the reasons why the animal is imperiled. (Rev: HBG 10/03; SLJ 4/01) [599]

22439 Toda, Kyoko. *Animal Faces* (PS). Trans. from Japanese by Amanda Mayer Stinchecum. Photos by Akira Satoh. 1996, Kane $16.95 (978-0-916291-62-4). 53pp. This book shows how animal faces differ, even within a particular species. (Rev: SLJ 11/96) [591]

22440 Walker, Sally M. *Hippos* (4–6). Illus. Series: Nature Watch. 1998, Carolrhoda LB $25.26 (978-1-57505-078-2). 48pp. Two types of hippos are introduced, with material on physical characteristics, life cycles, habits, communication, and habitats. (Rev: BL 5/1/98; HBG 9/98; SLJ 4/98) [599.63]

22441 Walker, Sally M. *Rhinos* (4–6). Illus. 1996, Carolrhoda LB $25.26 (978-1-57505-008-9). 48pp. An introduction to rhinos that stresses their endangered status and conservation efforts. (Rev: BL 12/1/96; SLJ 12/96*) [599.72]

22442 Webber, Desiree Morrison. *The Buffalo Train Ride* (4–7). Illus. by Sandy Shropshire. 1999, Eakin $14.95 (978-1-57168-275-8). 91pp. This is a history of the American buffalo, how it was hunted to near extinction, and the modern efforts to make sure it survives, with special attention to the work of William Hornaday. (Rev: HBG 3/00; SLJ 3/00) [591.52]

22443 Winter, Jeanette. *Mama: A True Story in Which a Baby Hippo Loses His Mama During a Tsunami, but Finds a New Home and a New Mama* (K–2). Illus. 2006, Harcourt $16.00 (978-0-15-205495-3). 32pp. In this affecting, well-illustrated picture book, a baby hippo is separated from his mother during a tsunami and later, at a wildlife preserve, adopts a giant tortoise as a surrogate parent. (Rev: BL 4/1/06; SLJ 5/06) [599.63]

APE FAMILY

22444 Bredeson, Carmen. *Orangutans Up Close* (1–3). Series: Zoom in on Animals! 2008, Enslow LB $21.26 (978-0-7660-3078-7). 24pp. Simple text and close-up color photographs introduce body parts, babies, and other important characteristics. (Rev: SLJ 11/08) [599.88]

22445 Climo, Shirley. *Monkey Business: Stories from Around the World* (3–5). Illus. by Erik Brooks. 2005, Holt $18.95 (978-0-8050-6392-9). 128pp. Climo has gathered monkey-related folktales, proverbs, historical facts, and scientific information in one entertaining volume. (Rev: BL 5/15/05; SLJ 6/05) [599.8]

22446 Darling, Kathy. *Lemurs on Location* (3–5). Illus. Series: On Location. 1998, Lothrop $16.95 (978-0-688-12539-4). 32pp. Three species of Madagascar lemurs are introduced in text and color illustrations, with material on their physical characteristics, habits, diet, and social organization. (Rev: BL 4/15/98; HBG 3/99; SLJ 5/98) [599.8]

22447 Darling, Tara, and Kathy Darling. *How to Babysit an Orangutan* (2–4). Illus. 1996, Walker LB $16.85 (978-0-8027-8467-4). 32pp. The description of the activities and functions of Camp Leakey on Borneo, where orphaned orangutans are cared for. (Rev: BL 12/15/96; HB 11/96; SLJ 10/96) [599.88]

22448 Eason, Sarah. *Save the Orangutan* (1–3). Illus. by Andrew Geeson and Marijke Veldhoven. Series: Save the . . . 2009, Rosen LB $23.95 (978-1-4358-2811-7). 32pp. Colorful spreads present answers to common questions in this solid introduction to the endangered orangutan. (Rev: SLJ 6/09) [599.883]

22449 Fleisher, Paul. *Gorillas* (5–8). Illus. Series: AnimalWays. 2000, Marshall Cavendish LB $28.50 (978-0-7614-1140-6). 104pp. Color photographs and clear text introduce gorillas, their scientific classification, physical and behavioral characteristics, and relationship to humans. (Rev: BL 1/1–15/01; HBG 3/01) [599.884]

22450 Gallimard Jeunesse. *Monkeys and Apes* (PS–2). Series: First Discovery. 1999, Scholastic $12.95 (978-0-590-87610-0). 24pp. Using many color photos and a brief text, this colorful book introduces different members of the ape family and explains their differences. (Rev: BL 6/1–15/99; HBG 9/99; SLJ 8/99) [599.88]

22451 Goodall, Jane. *The Chimpanzee Family Book* (4–6). Illus. 1997, North-South paper $8.95 (978-1-55858-803-5). 72pp. Illustrated with photographs, this is an affectionate portrayal of a family of chimps. (Rev: BL 7/89; HB 7/89; SLJ 6/89) [599.88]

22452 Goodall, Jane. *The Chimpanzees I Love: Saving Their World and Ours* (5–8). Illus. 2001, Scholastic paper $18.95 (978-0-439-21310-3). 80pp. Jane Goodall combines details of her own life researching chimpanzees with fact-filled descriptions of the animals' behavior and a cry for chimpanzee protection. (Rev: BL 12/1/01; HB 1/02; HBG 3/02; SLJ 9/01*) [599]

22453 Green, Carl R. *The Gorilla* (3–7). Series: Endangered and Threatened Animals. 2004, Enslow LB $25.26 (978-0-7660-5060-0). 48pp. Supplemented by a lengthy list of links to online resources, this overview of the gorilla explores its behavior and physical characteristics, as well as the threats it faces. (Rev: BL 6/1–15/04)

22454 Harman, Amanda. *South American Monkeys* (4–6). Illus. Series: Endangered! 1996, Benchmark LB $22.79 (978-0-7614-0218-3). 32pp. The monkeys of South America are introduced, with material on how they differ from their African counterparts and why they are endangered. (Rev: SLJ 8/96) [599.88]

22455 Hatkoff, Craig, and Juliana Hatkoff. *Looking for Miza: The True Story of the Mountain Gorilla Family Who Rescued One of Their Own* (2–5). Illus. by Peter Greste. 2008, Scholastic $16.99 (978-0-545-08540-3). 40pp. This moving photo-essay tells the story of a father gorilla going to rescue his young daughter when the mother disappears in the Democratic Republic of Congo's Virunga National Park. (Rev: BCCB 12/08; BL 12/15/08; LMC 5/09; SLJ 2/09) [599.884]

22456 Horton, Casey. *Apes* (3–6). Illus. Series: Endangered! 1996, Benchmark LB $25.64 (978-0-7614-0212-1). 32pp. Several species of great and lesser apes are introduced, with material on habitats, physical traits, behavior, and endangered status. (Rev: SLJ 3/96) [599.88]

22457 Jango-Cohen, Judith. *Gorillas* (4–6). Series: Animals Animals. 2002, Benchmark LB $25.64 (978-0-7614-1444-5). 48pp. The world of the giant gorilla is explored in this volume that covers topics including physical characteristics, habitat, care of the young, food, and social life. (Rev: BL 12/15/02; HBG 3/03) [599.884]

22458 Jenkins, Martin. *Ape* (K–3). Illus. by Vicky White. 2007, Candlewick $16.99 (978-0-7636-3471-1). 45pp. Compelling illustrations combine with interesting text to introduce the orangutan, chimpanzee, bonobo, and gorilla, showing their daily lives and family relationships and including a final section about threats to their survival and comparisons with human beings. (Rev: HB 1/08; LMC 5/08*; SLJ 3/08) [599.88]

22459 Kalman, Bobbie. *Endangered Mountain Gorillas* (3–5). Illus. Series: Earth's Endangered Ani-

mals. 2004, Crabtree LB $25.27 (978-0-7787-1855-0); paper $6.95 (978-0-7787-1901-4). 32pp. In addition to discussion of their endangered status, this volume covers these animals' habitat, behavior, life cycle, and so forth. (Rev: SLJ 6/05) [599.884]

22460 Kalman, Bobbie, and Hadley Dyer. *Endangered Chimpanzees* (3–5). Illus. Series: Earth's Endangered Animals. 2005, Crabtree LB $25.27 (978-0-7787-1859-8); paper $6.95 (978-0-7787-1905-2). 32pp. After giving a clear overview of the chimpanzee's physical characteristics, life cycle, and behavior, the authors discuss the reasons the animal is endangered and measures being taken to reduce the threat. (Rev: SLJ 12/05) [599.885]

22461 Kalman, Bobbie, and Heather Levigne. *What Is a Primate?* (3–5). Illus. by Barbara Bedell. Series: Science of Living Things. 1999, Crabtree LB $25.27 (978-0-86505-922-1); paper $6.95 (978-0-86505-950-4). 32pp. Double-page spreads are used to introduce primates of different species like gorillas, gibbons, orangutans, chimpanzees, and bonobos. (Rev: SLJ 12/99) [599.8]

22462 Kane, Karen. *Mountain Gorillas* (2–3). Series: Early Bird Nature Books. 2001, Lerner LB $22.60 (978-0-8225-3040-1). 48pp. An easy-to-read text and numerous color photographs highlight this introduction to mountain gorillas that covers their life cycle, habits, anatomy, and habitats. (Rev: BL 8/1/01) [599.884]

22463 Kendell, Patricia. *Gorillas* (K–2). Series: In the Wild. 2003, Raintree LB $25.70 (978-0-7398-5497-6). 32pp. Designed for beginning readers, this colorfully illustrated book provides a basic overview of gorillas, including their habitat, diet, behavior, and the reasons the species is endangered. (Rev: HBG 10/03; SLJ 10/03) [599.8]

22464 Laman, Tim. *Face to Face with Orangutans* (3–5). Illus. by Cheryl Knott. Series: Face to Face with Animals. 2009, National Geographic $16.95 (978-1-4263-0464-4). 32pp. Striking photo spreads are combined with crisp text and fast facts, with information on the threats this animal faces. (Rev: BL 4/1/09) [599.88]

22465 Lewin, Ted, and Betsy Lewin. *Gorilla Walk* (4–8). 1999, Lothrop LB $17.89 (978-0-688-16510-9). A beautifully illustrated book about the Lewins' trip to Uganda to study mountain gorillas. (Rev: BL 8/99; HBG 4/00; SLJ 9/99) [599.8]

22466 Lockwood, Sophie. *Baboons* (4–7). Series: The World of Mammals. 2005, Child's World LB $29.93 (978-1-59296-497-0). 40pp. Arresting photographs and engaging text introduce the anatomy, behavior, habitat, and life cycle of the baboon as well as the threats to the animal's survival in the wild. (Rev: SLJ 3/06) [599.8]

22467 Martin, Patricia A. *Chimpanzees* (3–5). Series: True Books. 2000, Children's Book Pr. LB $21.50 (978-0-516-24013-8). 48pp. Large text and color photos introduce chimpanzees, their habits, food, and homes. (Rev: BL 5/15/00) [599.88]

22468 Milton, Joyce. *Gorillas: Gentle Giants of the Forest* (1–3). Illus. by Bryn Barnard. Series: Step into Reading. 1997, Random paper $3.99 (978-0-

679-87284-9). 48pp. This easy-to-read account introduces gorillas, where they live, what they eat, and how they move. (Rev: BL 5/1/97; SLJ 8/97) [598.98]

22469 Orme, David. *Orangutan* (4–6). Illus. Series: Animals Under Threat. 2005, Heinemann LB $29.93 (978-1-4034-5586-4). 48pp. The life cycle of the orangutan and threats to its survival are explored in this blend of narrative and eye-catching color photography.

22470 Pimm, Nancy Roe. *The Heart of the Beast: Eight Great Gorilla Stories* (4–7). Illus. 2007, Darby Creek $18.95 (978-1-58196-054-9). 111pp. True stories about famous gorillas provide information on their mental and physical development, behavior, and diet. (Rev: BL 6/1–15/07; SLJ 12/07) [599.884]

22471 Powzyk, Joyce. *In Search of Lemurs: My Days and Nights in a Madagascar Rain Forest* (4–7). Illus. 1998, National Geographic $17.95 (978-0-7922-7072-0). 48pp. The author describes and illustrates her journey into the wilds of Madagascar and the many animals, plants, and birds she encountered, culminating in the elusive lemur. (Rev: BL 9/15/98; HBG 3/99; SLJ 10/98) [599.8]

22472 Robinson, Claire. *Chimpanzees* (2–3). Illus. Series: In the Wild. 1997, Heinemann $21.36 (978-1-57572-136-1). 24pp. A simple introduction to chimpanzees with close-up views of family life, information on how apes use tools, and material about their endangered status. (Rev: BL 2/1/98) [599.885]

22473 Spilsbury, Richard, and Louise Spilsbury. *A Troop of Chimpanzees* (3–5). Series: Animal Groups. 2003, Heinemann LB $24.22 (978-1-4034-0746-7). 32pp. This photo-filled overview of chimpanzees looks at behavior, diet, habitat, physical appearance, and social structure. (Rev: HBG 10/03; SLJ 9/03) [599.885]

22474 Stefoff, Rebecca. *Chimpanzees* (4–7). Illus. Series: AnimalWays. 2003, Benchmark LB $31.36 (978-0-7614-1579-4). 112pp. A richly illustrated look at chimpanzees, from their physiology to their interaction with humans. (Rev: SLJ 3/04)

22475 Stefoff, Rebecca. *The Primate Order* (5–9). Illus. Series: Family Trees. 2005, Benchmark LB $32.79 (978-0-7614-1816-0). 92pp. Habits, habitats, and human-like aspects of this order of animals; an engaging book with plenty of facts for report writers. (Rev: SLJ 6/06) [599.8]

22476 Stone, Lynn M. *Baboons* (1–3). Illus. Series: Monkey Discovery Library. 1991, Rourke LB $18.60 (978-0-86593-067-4). 24pp. A brief introduction to baboons: physical traits, behavior, and habitats. Also use: *Chimpanzees; Gorillas;* and *Snow Monkeys* (all 1990). (Rev: SLJ 6/91) [599.8]

22477 Taylor, Marianne. *Mountain Gorilla* (4–6). Illus. Series: Animals Under Threat. 2004, Heinemann LB $27.07 (978-1-4034-4861-3); paper $8.50 (978-1-4034-5435-5). 48pp. The mountain gorilla and its characteristics are described before discussion of problems with habitat, tourism, and conservation. (Rev: SLJ 1/05) [599.884]

22478 Thomson, Sarah L. *Amazing Gorillas!* (K–2). Illus. Series: I Can Read. 2005, HarperCollins LB $16.89 (978-0-06-054460-7). 32pp. Close-up color photographs add to the simple text in this informative introduction that looks at gorillas and their diet, habitat, physical characteristics, and endangered status. (Rev: BL 5/1/05) [599.884]

22479 Turner, Pamela S. *Gorilla Doctors: Saving Endangered Great Apes* (3–5). Illus. Series: Scientists in the Field. 2005, Houghton $17.00 (978-0-618-44555-4). 48pp. Exciting accounts of real events add drama to this exploration of the work of veterinarians in east central Africa. (Rev: BL 6/1–15/05) [333.95]

22480 Zabludoff, Marc. *Monkeys* (3–6). Series: AnimalWays. 2007, Marshall Cavendish LB $23.95 (978-0-7614-2535-9). 108pp. After an overview of monkey history, this volume looks at monkey anatomy, behavior, relationship with humans, and so forth. (Rev: SLJ 5/08) [599.8]

BATS

22481 Bair, Diane, and Pamela Wright. *Bat Watching* (2–5). Series: Wildlife Watching. 1999, Capstone $19.93 (978-0-7638-0318-6). 48pp. An introduction to bats, their habits, habitats, and practical advice on how, when, and where to observe them. (Rev: BL 2/15/00) [599.4]

22482 Berman, Ruth. *Squeaking Bats* (PS–2). Series: Pull Ahead Books. 1998, Lerner LB $22.60 (978-0-8225-3602-4). 32pp. An interactive text, color photos, and a body diagram are used to explore the fascinating world of bats. (Rev: BL 2/15/99; HBG 3/99; SLJ 1/99) [599.4]

22483 Earle, Ann. *Zipping, Zapping, Zooming Bats* (2–3). Illus. by Henry Cole. 1995, HarperCollins LB $15.89 (978-0-06-023480-5). 32pp. Coverage is given on various types of bats and their body structure, senses, eating habits, and homes. (Rev: BCCB 2/96; BL 8/95; SLJ 8/95) [599.4]

22484 Gibbons, Gail. *Bats* (K–3). Illus. 1999, Holiday House $16.95 (978-0-8234-1457-4). 32pp. An introduction to bats that discusses their physical characteristics, habits, food, and lifestyle. (Rev: BL 9/1/99; HBG 4/00; SLJ 1/00) [599.4]

22485 Glaser, Linda. *Beautiful Bats* (PS–K). Illus. by Sharon L. Holm. 1997, Millbrook LB $22.90 (978-0-7613-0254-4). 32pp. Basic information about bats is given in the body of this simple science book, with six pages of additional details at the back of the book. (Rev: HBG 3/98; SLJ 12/97) [599.4]

22486 Greenaway, Theresa. *The Secret Life of Bats* (4–7). Series: The Secret World of . . . 2002, Raintree LB $27.12 (978-0-7398-4982-8). 48pp. An accessible, attractive volume that begins with little-known facts about bats and continues with information on their structure, habits, food, and habitats. (Rev: BL 8/02) [599.4]

22487 Landau, Elaine. *Bats: Hunters of the Night* (2–3). Series: Animals after Dark. 2007, Enslow LB $22.60 (978-0-7660-2772-5). 32pp. Photographs of bats accompany information about their nocturnal behavior and their peculiar habits and abilities. (Rev: LMC 10/07; SLJ 8/07)

22488 Milton, Joyce. *Bats: Creatures of the Night* (1–3). Illus. by Judith Moffatt. 1993, Penguin paper $3.99 (978-0-448-40193-5). 48pp. Simple vocabulary and short sentences are used to convey basic information about bats and their habits. (Rev: BL 12/1/93; SLJ 2/94) [599.4]

22489 Penny, Malcolm. *How Bats "See" in the Dark* (3–5). Illus. Series: Nature's Mysteries. 1996, Benchmark LB $22.79 (978-0-7614-0455-2). 32pp. The facts about bats are interestingly presented with details on how we uncovered their secrets and what questions remain unanswered. (Rev: SLJ 2/97) [599.4]

22490 Pringle, Laurence. *Bats! Strange and Wonderful* (3–5). 2000, Boyds Mills $15.95 (978-1-56397-327-7). 32pp. This book gives basic information about various types of bats and their habitats and lifestyles, and exposes popular myths about these misunderstood mammals. (Rev: BCCB 4/00; BL 3/15/00; HBG 9/00; SLJ 6/00) [599.4]

22491 Ruff, Sue, and Don E. Wilson. *Bats* (5–8). Series: AnimalWays. 2000, Marshall Cavendish LB $31.36 (978-0-7614-1137-6). 112pp. Some of the topics that are covered include anatomy, habits, range, classification, habitats, evolution, and survival skills. (Rev: BL 1/1–15/01; HBG 3/01) [599.4]

22492 Simon, Seymour. *Amazing Bats* (1–3). Series: SeeMore Readers. 2005, Chronicle Bks. LB $14.50 (978-1-58717-261-8); paper $3.95 (978-1-58717-262-5). This photo-filled title provides beginning readers with an attractive overview of bats' physical characteristics, habitat, diet, and behavior. (Rev: SLJ 11/05)

22493 Stuart, Dee. *Bats: Mysterious Flyers of the Night* (3–6). Illus. Series: Nature Watch. 1994, Carolrhoda LB $25.26 (978-0-87614-814-3). 48pp. With outstanding photographs, this is a fine introduction to bats and their habits, food, and habitats. (Rev: BL 9/15/94; SLJ 10/94) [599.4]

22494 Vogel, Julia. *Bats* (2–4). Illus. Series: Our Wild World. 2007, NorthWord $10.95 (978-1-55971-968-1); paper $7.95 (978-1-55971-969-8). 48pp. This easy-to-understand and eye-catching guide to bats introduces a variety of different species, as well as general information about the flying mammals' physical characteristics, habitat, diet, predators, prey, and behavior. (Rev: BL 3/15/07) [599.4]

22495 Welsbacher, Anne. *Vampire Bats* (3–6). Series: Predators in the Wild. 2001, Capstone LB $23.93 (978-0-7368-0787-6). 32pp. Myths about the vampire bat are presented along with facts in this general introduction to the animal's characteristics and habitat. (Rev: HBG 10/01; SLJ 1/02) [599.4]

22496 Wheeler, Jill C. *Bumblebee Bats* (3–5). Illus. Series: Bats, Set II. 2005, ABDO LB $21.35 (978-1-59679-320-0). 24pp. Introduces the bumblebee bat, which is found in Thailand and is the world's smallest bat species. (Rev: SLJ 2/06) [599.4]

BEARS

22497 Berman, Ruth. *Fishing Bears* (PS–2). Series: Pull Ahead Books. 1998, Lerner LB $22.60 (978-0-8225-3601-7). 32pp. For beginning readers, this introduction to bears, their habits, and habitats uses color photographs, questions and answers, and an easy-to-read text. (Rev: BL 2/15/99; HBG 3/99; SLJ 1/99) [599.74]

22498 Calabro, Marian. *Operation Grizzly Bear* (5–8). Illus. 1989, Macmillan $13.95 (978-0-02-716241-7). An account by two naturalists on a 12-year study of silvertip bears in Yellowstone Park. (Rev: BL 3/15/90; VOYA 4/90) [599.74]

22499 Davies, Nicola. *Ice Bear: In the Steps of the Polar Bear* (K–2). Illus. by Gary Blythe. 2005, Candlewick $16.99 (978-0-7636-2759-1). 32pp. Basic information about polar bears — and admiration for their survival — is delivered in a friendly narrative that also touches on what the Inuit have learned from these animals. (Rev: BL 12/1/05; SLJ 2/06) [599.796]

22500 Deady, Kathleen W. *Grizzly Bears* (3–5). Series: Predators in the Wild. 2002, Capstone LB $23.93 (978-0-7368-1063-0). 32pp. Basic information about grizzly bears' lives, habitat, diet, and endangered status is presented in a format that will suit both browsers and report writers. (Rev: SLJ 8/02) [599.74]

22501 DuTemple, Lesley A. *Polar Bears* (2–3). Series: Early Bird Nature Books. 1998, Lerner LB $25.26 (978-0-8225-3025-1). 48pp. An easily read, extremely attractive introduction to polar bears that covers their life cycle and habitats. (Rev: BL 3/15/98; HBG 9/98; SLJ 7/98) [599.74]

22502 Eason, Sarah. *Save the Polar Bear* (1–3). Illus. by Andrew Geeson and Marijke Veldhoven. Series: Save the . . . 2009, Rosen LB $23.95 (978-1-4358-2810-0). 32pp. Colorful spreads present answers to common questions in this solid introduction to the endangered polar bear. (Rev: SLJ 6/09) [599.786]

22503 Fraggalosch, Audrey. *Great Grizzly Wilderness: A Story of the Pacific Rain Forest* (K–3). Illus. by Donald G. Eberhart. Series: Habitats. 2000, Soundprints $15.95 (978-1-56899-838-1). This highly pictorial account traces one year in the lives of a British Columbia grizzly bear and her cubs. (Rev: HBG 3/01; SLJ 1/01) [599.7]

22504 Gaines, Richard Marshall. *When Bears Attack!* (4–6). Series: When Wild Animals Attack! 2006, Enslow LB $23.93 (978-0-7660-2669-8). 48pp. Readers will come away from this book with a healthy respect for bears and their wild ways. The author also discusses conservation of bear habitats. (Rev: SLJ 7/07)

22505 Gibbons, Gail. *Grizzly Bears* (K–4). Illus. by author. 2003, Holiday House $16.95 (978-0-8234-1793-3). All about grizzly bears — where they live, what they eat, and what's being done to protect them. (Rev: HBG 4/04; SLJ 3/04) [599.7]

22506 Gibbons, Gail. *Polar Bears* (2–4). Illus. 2001, Holiday House $16.95 (978-0-8234-1593-9). 32pp. An accessible, nicely illustrated introduction to the habitat, behavior, diet, and anatomy of the polar bear. (Rev: BL 9/15/01; HBG 3/02; SLJ 9/01) [599.786]

22507 Greene, Jacqueline D. *Grizzly Bears: Saving the Silvertip* (3–4). Series: America's Animal Comebacks. 2007, Bearport LB $25.27 (978-1-59716-533-4). 32pp. With eye-catching photographs and an appealing design, Greene looks at threats to the grizzly and at efforts to bring them back from the brink of extinction. (Rev: SLJ 12/07) [599.7]

22508 Guidoux, Valérie. *Little Polar Bears* (1–3). Series: Born to Be Wild. 2005, Gareth Stevens LB $23.00 (978-0-8368-4739-0). 24pp. This colorful overview of polar bear cubs focuses on the role that their parents play in finding food for their offspring and protecting them from predators. (Rev: SLJ 2/06) [599.786]

22509 Hatkoff, Juliana, and Isabella Hatkoff. *Knut: How One Little Polar Bear Captivated the World* (2–4). Illus. 2007, Scholastic $16.99 (978-0-545-04716-6). 40pp. Enchanting photographs of Knut, a polar bear born in a German zoo and abandoned by his mother, accompany a text describing the role of the zookeeper who raised him. (Rev: BCCB 12/07; BL 12/15/07; SLJ 1/08) [599.786]

22510 Hirschi, Ron. *Our Three Bears* (3–5). Illus. 2008, Boyds Mills $16.95 (978-1-59078-015-2). 32pp. An attractive introduction to the bears — black, grizzly, and polar — that live in North America. (Rev: BL 11/15/08; LMC 1/09; SLJ 10/08) [599.78]

22511 Hirschi, Ron. *Searching for Grizzlies* (3–5). Illus. 2005, Boyds Mills $15.95 (978-1-59078-014-5). 32pp. Beautiful photographs, factual text, and excerpts from notebooks make this a fascinating introduction to the grizzly bear, with enough information for report writers. (Rev: BL 9/1/05; SLJ 9/05) [599.784]

22512 Hodge, Deborah. *Bears: Polar Bears, Black Bears and Grizzly Bears* (K–3). Illus. by Pat Stephens. Series: Wildlife. 1997, Kids Can $10.95 (978-1-55074-269-5). 32pp. Discusses bears' food, habitats, hibernation, and life cycle. (Rev: BL 9/15/97; SLJ 9/97) [599.78]

22513 Horton, Casey. *Bears* (3–5). Illus. Series: Endangered! 1996, Benchmark LB $25.64 (978-0-7614-0211-4). 32pp. Different species of bears are introduced, with their habitats, physical traits, behavior, and endangered status. (Rev: SLJ 3/96) [599.74]

22514 Hunt, Joni Phelps. *A Band of Bears: The Rambling Life of a Lovable Loner* (5–8). Series: Jean-Michel Cousteau Presents. 2007, London Town paper $8.95 (978-0-9766134-5-9). 48pp. With eye-catching photographs and stories of close encounters with these animals, this book looks at bears' characteristics, behavior, intelligence, and the threats to their survival. (Rev: SLJ 11/07) [599.78]

22515 Lang, Aubrey. *The Adventures of Baby Bear* (K–2). Illus. by Wayne Lynch. Series: Nature Babies. 2001, Fitzhenry & Whiteside $13.95 (978-1-55041-670-1). 28pp. Readers accompany two young bear cubs from birth to adolescence, in a pho-

tographic presentation with simple text and a page of facts. (Rev: BL 12/15/01; SLJ 2/02) [599.78]

22516 Lang, Aubrey. *Baby Grizzly* (2–4). Photos by Wayne Lynch. Series: Nature Babies. 2006, Fitzhenry & Whiteside $13.95 (978-1-55041-577-3); paper $6.95 (978-1-55041-579-7). 36pp. This photo-filled title follows the development of three grizzly cubs as they stay by their mother's side in the wilds of Alaska. (Rev: SLJ 11/06) [599.784]

22517 Lang, Aubrey. *Baby Polar Bear* (2–3). Illus. by Wayne Lynch. Series: Nature Babies. 2008, Fitzhenry & Whiteside $15.95 (978-1-55455-101-9); paper $7.95 (978-1-55455-102-6). 36pp. A handsome portrayal of a female polar bear looking after her two cubs. (Rev: BL 9/15/08) [599.786]

22518 Leathers, Dan. *Polar Bears on the Hudson Bay* (3–6). Illus. Series: A Robbie Reader: On the Verge of Extinction: Crisis in the Environment. 2007, Mitchell Lane LB $17.95 (978-1-58415-586-7). 32pp. Global warming and growth in tourism are two of the threats described in this overview of the animals and their habitat; there are close-up photographs and "What You Can Do" sections. (Rev: BL 10/15/07; LMC 1/08; SLJ 11/07) [599.786]

22519 Lockwood, Sophie. *Polar Bears* (5–8). Illus. Series: World of Mammals. 2005, Child's World LB $29.93 (978-1-59296-501-4). 40pp. This slim but richly illustrated title looks at polar bears' physical characteristics, behavior, diet, relationship with the Inuit people, and the growing threats to their survival. (Rev: BL 10/15/05) [599.786]

22520 Markle, Sandra. *Polar Bears* (3–7). Series: Animal Predators. 2004, Carolrhoda LB $25.26 (978-1-57505-730-9). 40pp. Describes the life of a female polar bear in the Arctic — behavior, diet, communication, life cycle, and so forth. (Rev: SLJ 1/05) [599.786]

22521 Montgomery, Sy. *Search for the Golden Moon Bear: Science and Adventure in the Asian Tropics* (5–9). 2004, Houghton $17.00 (978-0-618-35650-8). 80pp. Nature writer Montgomery describes her search across war-torn Southeast Asia for the elusive golden moon bear. (Rev: BL 12/1/04; SLJ 12/04) [599.78]

22522 Murray, Julie. *Black Bears* (2–3). Illus. Series: Animal Kingdom. 2005, ABDO LB $21.35 (978-1-59197-302-7). 24pp. For beginning readers, this is an introduction to the black bear and its physical characteristics, habitat, and diet. (Rev: SLJ 5/05) [599]

22523 Murray, Julie. *Grizzly Bears* (1–3). Illus. Series: Animal Kingdom. 2002, ABDO LB $21.35 (978-1-57765-715-6). 24pp. For beginning readers, this photo-filled book offers a basic introduction to the life of the grizzly bear. (Rev: SLJ 4/03) [599.784]

22524 Patent, Dorothy Hinshaw. *Looking at Bears* (2–5). Photos by William Munoz. 1994, Holiday House LB $15.95 (978-0-8234-1139-9). 40pp. An attractive book on bears that covers such subjects as classification, behavior, food, reproduction, hibernation, and evolution. (Rev: BL 12/1/94; SLJ 1/95) [599.74]

22525 Patent, Dorothy Hinshaw. *A Polar Bear Biologist at Work* (4–6). Series: Wildlife Conservation Society. 2001, Watts LB $24.50 (978-0-531-11850-4). 48pp. Basic information on polar bears is enlivened by the portrayal of biologist Chuck Jonkel at work and by his comments on bears and the environment. (Rev: SLJ 11/01) [599.786]

22526 Patent, Dorothy Hinshaw. *Polar Bears* (3–6). Series: Nature Watch. 2000, Carolrhoda $25.26 (978-1-57505-020-1). 48pp. The biggest and strongest animal of the arctic, the polar bear is the subject of this simple science book that contains outstanding color photographs. (Rev: BL 3/15/00; HBG 9/00; SLJ 7/00) [599.78]

22527 Penny, Malcolm. *Polar Bear* (2–4). Series: Natural World. 2000, Raintree LB $27.12 (978-0-7398-1060-6). 48pp. This fine introduction to the polar bear, with clear photos and a good layout, covers topics including appearance, life cycle, mating, food, and habits. (Rev: HBG 9/00; SLJ 7/00) [599.7]

22528 Preston-Mafham, Rod. *The Secret Life of Bears* (4–7). Series: The Secret World of . . . 2002, Raintree LB $27.12 (978-0-7398-4983-5). 48pp. In this attractive volume readers learn why bears behave as they do, how they feed, communicate, and reproduce, and what dangers face their future. (Rev: BL 8/02) [599.74]

22529 Robinson, Claire. *Bears* (2–3). Series: In the Wild. 1997, Heinemann $21.36 (978-1-57572-134-7). 24pp. In this simple introduction to bears, such topics as food, care of cubs, and communication are covered. (Rev: BL 2/15/98) [599.74]

22530 Ryder, Joanne. *A Pair of Polar Bears: Twin Cubs Find a Home at the San Diego Zoo* (K–2). Illus. 2006, Simon & Schuster $16.95 (978-0-689-85871-0). 32pp. This engaging photo-essay chronicles the story of two orphaned polar bear cubs who find a home at the San Diego Zoo. (Rev: BL 2/1/06; SLJ 3/06) [599.786]

22531 Sartore, Joel. *Face to Face with Grizzlies* (2–5). Illus. Series: Face to Face with Animals. 2007, National Geographic $16.95 (978-1-4263-0050-9). 32pp. This close-up look at the grizzly bear describes the author/photographer's encounters with these huge animals and introduces readers to their physical characteristics, habitat, diet, behavior, and the threats to their survival. (Rev: BL 4/1/07) [599.784]

22532 Shea, Therese. *Bears* (PS–2). 2006, Rosen LB $19.95 (978-1-4042-3524-8). 24pp. An up-close look at various bears, with facts on their physical characteristics, the food they eat, their habitat, caring for their young, and their enemies. (Rev: SLJ 3/07) [599.78]

22533 Silverstein, Alvin, et al. *The Grizzly Bear* (3–6). Illus. Series: Endangered in America. 1998, Millbrook LB $22.40 (978-0-7613-0265-0). 64pp. This book describes the life cycle, physical characteristics, and habits of the grizzly and why it is now considered an endangered animal. (Rev: BL 9/1/98; HBG 9/98) [639.97]

22534 Stefoff, Rebecca. *Bears* (5–8). Series: AnimalWays. 2001, Marshall Cavendish LB $31.36 (978-0-7614-1268-7). 112pp. Various species of bears are introduced in text and color photographs with additional material on their location, anatomy, habits, and behavior. (Rev: BL 3/15/02; HBG 10/02) [599.74]

22535 Stone, Jason, and Jody Stone. *Grizzly Bear* (2–4). Illus. 2000, Blackbirch $21.20 (978-1-56711-342-6). 24pp. Striking photos and a straightforward text are used to introduce grizzly bears, their physical characteristics, habits, hibernation, food, and habitats. (Rev: BL 12/15/00; HBG 3/01) [599.784]

22536 Stone, Jason, and Jody Stone. *Polar Bear* (2–4). Series: Wild Bears! 2000, Blackbirch LB $24.94 (978-1-56711-344-0). 24pp. This stunningly illustrated book describes the physical characteristics and homes of the polar bear, its food, mating, care of young, and interaction with humans. (Rev: BL 12/15/00; HBG 3/01) [599.7]

22537 Stone, Lynn M. *Grizzlies* (3–6). Illus. Series: Nature Watch. 1993, Carolrhoda LB $25.26 (978-0-87614-800-6). 48pp. Outstanding color photos and clear text are used to introduce grizzlies, their habitats, food, and family life. (Rev: BL 1/15/94; SLJ 2/94) [599.74]

22538 Swinburne, Stephen. *Black Bear: North America's Bear* (3–4). 2003, Boyds Mills $15.95 (978-1-59078-023-7). 32pp. This comprehensive, photo-filled overview covers the black bear's habitat, diet, and behavior, looks at the bear's history in Yellowstone, and clears up some common misconceptions. (Rev: BL 1/1–15/04; HBG 4/04; SLJ 11/03) [599.78]

22539 Thomas, Keltie. *Bear Rescue: Changing the Future for Endangered Wildlife* (4–8). Series: Firefly Animal Rescue. 2006, Firefly LB $19.95 (978-1-55297-922-8); paper $9.95 (978-1-55297-921-1). 64pp. Focuses on work that's being done on behalf of threatened bear species, including Indian sloth bears, Chinese black bears, and polar bears. (Rev: SLJ 12/06) [599.78]

22540 Tracqui, Valerie. *The Brown Bear: Giant of the Mountains* (3–5). Illus. Series: Animal Close-Ups. 1998, Charlesbridge paper $6.95 (978-0-88106-439-1). 32pp. Introduces brown bears and discusses their habitats, characteristics, habits, and life cycles. (Rev: BL 5/15/98) [599.74]

BIG CATS

22541 Arnold, Caroline. *Bobcats* (2–3). Series: Early Bird Nature Books. 1998, Lerner LB $25.26 (978-0-8225-3021-3). 48pp. A very attractive introduction to the world of the bobcat and its life cycle. (Rev: BL 3/15/98; HBG 9/98; SLJ 3/98) [599.74]

22542 Ball, Jacqueline, and Kit Carlson. *The Leopard Son: A True Story* (3–5). Illus. 1996, McGraw-Hill $14.95 (978-0-07-016061-3). 32pp. The animals and vegetation of the Serengeti are seen through the eyes of a young leopard. (Rev: BL 11/1/96; SLJ 1/97) [599.74]

22543 Barfuss, Matto H. *My Cheetah Family* (4–6). Trans. by Amy Gelman. Illus. by author. 1999, Carolrhoda LB $17.95 (978-1-57505-377-6). 48pp.

This photo-essay chronicles the life of a female cheetah and her cubs on the Serengeti Plain. (Rev: HBG 4/00; SLJ 12/99) [599.74]

22544 Barrett, Jalma. *Bobcat* (3–5). Series: Wildcats of North America. 1998, Blackbirch LB $24.94 (978-1-56711-257-3). 24pp. Excellent photographs and an appealing, simple text are used to introduce the North American bobcat, its habits, and habitats. (Rev: BL 12/15/98; HBG 3/99; SLJ 11/98) [599.74]

22545 Barrett, Jalma. *Cougar* (3–5). Illus. Series: Wildcats of North America. 1998, Blackbirch LB $21.20 (978-1-56711-258-0). 24pp. A discussion of the cougar — also known as the panther, puma, or mountain lion — that includes material on its life cycle and physical features. (Rev: BL 12/1/98; HBG 3/99) [599.73]

22546 Barrett, Jalma. *Feral Cat* (3–5). Series: Wildcats of North America. 1998, Blackbirch LB $22.45 (978-1-56711-260-3). 24pp. The world of the feral cat is explored in photographs and an appealing text. (Rev: BL 12/15/98; HBG 3/99; SLJ 11/98) [599.74]

22547 Barrett, Jalma. *Lynx* (3–5). Illus. Series: Wildcats of North America. 1998, Blackbirch LB $22.45 (978-1-56711-259-7). 24pp. Introduces the lynx, with material on its habits, habitats, and physical features. (Rev: BL 12/1/98; HBG 3/99; SLJ 11/98) [599.75]

22548 Becker, John E. *Wild Cats: Past and Present* (5–8). Illus. by Mark Hallett. 2008, Darby Creek $18.95 (978-1-58196-052-5). 80pp. Lions, tigers, jaguars, and cheetahs are among the wild cats covered in this well-illustrated, large-format book that covers history, environmental threats, and conservation and will attract both researchers and browsers. (Rev: BL 3/15/08; SLJ 6/08) [599.75]

22549 Bortolotti, Dan. *Tiger Rescue: Changing the Future for Endangered Wildlife* (3–8). Series: Firefly Animal Rescue. 2003, Firefly LB $19.95 (978-1-55297-599-2); paper $9.95 (978-1-55297-558-9). 64pp. A look at how and why tigers are an endangered species and what can be done to help them, with profiles of some of the people involved in the effort. (Rev: BL 1/1–15/04; SLJ 4/04) [333.9]

22550 Chancellor, Deborah. *Tiger Tales: And Big Cat Stories* (2–4). Illus. by Peter Dennis. Series: Eyewitness Reader. 2000, DK $14.99 (978-0-7894-5424-9); paper $3.99 (978-0-7894-5423-2). 48pp. A beginning reader that features lions, tigers, and other big cats and incidents in which they clash with humans. (Rev: HBG 9/00; SLJ 7/00) [599.74]

22551 Chottin, Ariane. *Little Leopards* (3–5). Illus. Series: Born to Be Wild. 2005, Gareth Stevens LB $23.00 (978-0-8368-4438-2). 24pp. A simply worded look at young leopards and their lives, with large photographs.

22552 Costello, Emily. *Realm of the Panther: A Story of South Florida's Forests* (K–3). Illus. by Wes Siegrist. Series: Habitats. 2000, Soundprints $15.95 (978-1-56899-847-3). A richly illustrated account that focuses on a pair of yearling panthers in the Big Cypress National Preserve in Florida. (Rev: HBG 3/01; SLJ 1/01) [599.74]

22553 Darling, Kathy. *Lions* (3–6). Series: Nature Watch. 2000, Carolrhoda $25.26 (978-1-57505-404-9). 48pp. The unique life of the lion is described in this simple book that contains a wealth of attention-getting color photographs. (Rev: BL 3/15/00; HBG 9/00) [599.74]

22554 DuTemple, Lesley A. *Tigers* (2–4). Photos by Lynn M. Stone. Series: Early Bird Nature Books. 1996, Lerner LB $25.26 (978-0-8225-3010-7). 48pp. Beginning readers will find this an interesting introduction to tigers, their characteristics, and their endangered status. (Rev: SLJ 9/96) [599.74]

22555 Eason, Sarah. *Save the Tiger* (1–3). Illus. by Andrew Geeson and Marijke Veldhoven. Series: Save the . . . 2009, Rosen LB $23.95 (978-1-4358-2813-1). 32pp. Colorful spreads present answers to common questions in this solid introduction to the endangered tiger. (Rev: SLJ 6/09) [599.74]

22556 Estigarribia, Diana. *Cheetahs* (3–6). Illus. Series: Animals, Animals. 2004, Benchmark $25.64 (978-0-7614-1749-1). 46pp. A well-written overview of these animals, providing all the information needed for report writing plus additional material of interest. (Rev: SLJ 2/05) [599.74]

22557 Feinstein, Stephen. *The Jaguar: Help Save This Endangered Species!* (4–7). Illus. Series: Saving Endangered Species. 2008, Enslow LB $24.95 (978-1-59845-065-1). 128pp. Part of the MyReportLinks.com series, this introduction to jaguars and the threats they face features Web sites that report writers can access for more information. (Rev: BL 2/15/08) [599.75]

22558 Gaines, Richard Marshall. *When Tigers Attack!* (4–6). Series: When Wild Animals Attack! 2006, Enslow LB $23.93 (978-0-7660-2665-0). 48pp. Readers will come away from this book with a healthy respect for tigers and their wild ways. The author also discusses conservation of tiger habitats. (Rev: LMC 3/07; SLJ 7/07)

22559 Gallimard Jeunesse, et al. *Lions* (PS–2). Series: First Discovery. 2000, Scholastic $12.95 (978-0-439-14824-5). 24pp. A beginner's look at lions in a heavily illustrated book that presents their physical characteristics, homes, and family life. (Rev: BL 8/00; HBG 3/01) [599.74]

22560 Greenberg, Dan. *Leopards* (4–6). Series: Animals Animals. 2002, Benchmark LB $25.64 (978-0-7614-1448-3). 48pp. This simple introduction to leopards examines, in text and photographs, their anatomy, habitats, behavior, and eating habits. (Rev: BL 12/15/02; HBG 3/03) [599.6]

22561 Hansen, Rosanna. *Caring for Cheetahs: My African Adventure* (3–6). Illus. 2007, Boyds Mills $16.95 (978-1-59078-387-0). 32pp. Cheetahs saved by the Cheetah Conservation Fund in Namibia are featured in beautiful color photos, along with plenty of information about the big cats in general and one rescued cheetah in particular. (Rev: BCCB 4/07; BL 2/15/07; SLJ 3/07) [599.75]

22562 Harman, Amanda. *Leopards* (3–5). Illus. Series: Endangered! 1996, Benchmark LB $25.64 (978-0-7614-0223-7). 32pp. Introduces the three species of leopards and their characteristics and describes the circumstances that have caused them to be placed on the endangered list. (Rev: SLJ 8/96) [599.74]

22563 Harman, Amanda. *Tigers* (4–6). Illus. Series: Endangered! 1996, Benchmark LB $22.79 (978-0-7614-0215-2). 32pp. The world of the tiger is introduced, with material on its hunting skills, habitats, parenting habits, and endangered status. (Rev: SLJ 4/96) [599.74]

22564 Hewitt, Joan. *A Tiger Cub Grows Up* (1–3). Series: Baby Animals. 2001, Carolrhoda LB $21.27 (978-1-57505-163-5); paper $6.95 (978-0-8225-0089-6). 32pp. For beginning readers, this colorful account describes the youth of a tiger cub in a brief, simple text. (Rev: BL 10/15/01; HBG 3/02; SLJ 10/01) [599.74]

22565 Hodge, Deborah. *Wild Cats: Cougars, Bobcats and Lynx* (K–3). Illus. by Nancy Gray Ogle. Series: Wildlife. 1997, Kids Can $10.95 (978-1-55074-267-1). 32pp. Double-page spreads cover such topics about these big cats as their homes, food, habits, and relations with humans. (Rev: BL 9/15/97; SLJ 9/97) [599.75]

22566 Hughes, Monica. *Tiger Cub* (K–2). Illus. Series: I Love Reading. 2006, Bearport LB $19.96 (978-1-59716-155-8). 24pp. Facts about tigers — their physical appearance, habitat, endangered status, and behavior — are given in concise answers to questions posed on colorful double-page spreads; a small-format book suitable for beginning readers. (Rev: BL 4/1/06) [599.756]

22567 Jordan, Billy. *Lion* (3–5). Illus. Series: Natural World. 1999, Raintree $27.12 (978-0-7398-1057-6). 48pp. This book, illustrated with many stunning photographs, introduces the lion and how it lives. (Rev: BL 10/15/99; HBG 4/00) [599.757]

22568 Kendell, Patricia. *Leopards* (K–2). Series: In the Wild. 2003, Raintree LB $25.70 (978-0-7398-5496-9). 32pp. Designed for beginning readers, this photo-filled overview of leopards provides basic information about the big cat's habitat, diet, behavior, and how it raises its young. (Rev: HBG 10/03; SLJ 10/03) [599.7]

22569 Landau, Elaine. *Big Cats: Hunters of the Night* (2–3). 2007, Enslow LB $22.60 (978-0-7660-2770-1). 32pp. Photographs of big cats accompany information about their nocturnal behavior and their hunting abilities. (Rev: SLJ 8/07*)

22570 Landau, Elaine. *Fierce Cats* (3–5). Illus. Series: Fearsome, Scary, and Creepy Animals. 2003, Enslow LB $23.93 (978-0-7660-2062-7). 48pp. Landau offers a dramatic overview of the fierce behavior of leopards, cheetahs, and other big cats and documents some real-life attacks on humans. (Rev: BL 10/15/03; HBG 4/04) [599.7]

22571 Latta, Jan. *Timba the Tiger* (K–4). Series: Wild Animal Families. 2006, Gareth Stevens LB $23.93 (978-0-8368-7772-4). 24pp. In a first-"person" account, Timba describes what it's like to be a tiger, giving readers facts about these big cats in an enjoyable and engaging format. Also use *Lisa the Lion* (2006). (Rev: SLJ 5/07)

22572 Lumpkin, Susan. *Small Cats* (5–8). Series: Great Creatures of the World. 1993, Facts on File $17.95 (978-0-8160-2848-1). A handsome oversized volume about the smaller wild cats, with many photographs and charts. (Rev: BL 2/15/93) [599.74]

22573 MacKen, JoAnn Early. *Cougars / Puma* (2–4). Trans. by Tatiana Acosta and Guillermo Gutiérrez. Series: Animals That Live in the Mountains / Animales de las montañas. 2006, Weekly Reader LB $21.00 (978-0-8368-6448-9). 24pp. A beginning book with facts about cougars in both English and Spanish. (Rev: SLJ 6/06) [599.75]

22574 MacKen, JoAnn Early. *Tigers* (K–2). Series: Animals I See at the Zoo. 2002, Gareth Stevens LB $21.00 (978-0-8368-3276-1). 24pp. Large type and clear pictures make this introduction appealing to beginning readers. (Rev: HBG 3/03; SLJ 2/03)

22575 MacMillan, Dianne. *Cheetahs* (3–5). Illus. Series: Nature Watch. 1998, Carolrhoda $25.26 (978-1-57505-044-7). 48pp. An attractive title that introduces the cheetah and tells about its anatomy, habitats, behavior, and its endangered status. (Rev: BL 2/15/98; HBG 9/98) [599.74]

22576 Markle, Sandra. *Lions* (2–5). Illus. Series: Animal Predators. 2004, Carolrhoda LB $25.26 (978-1-57505-727-9). Concise text and clear, full-page photographs introduce the life cycle of the lion and its physical characteristics, habitat, diet, and predatory behavior. (Rev: BL 9/15/04; SLJ 10/04) [599.757]

22577 Markle, Sandra. *Outside and Inside Big Cats* (2–4). Series: Outside Inside. 2003, Simon & Schuster $16.95 (978-0-689-82299-5). 40pp. This overview of the big cats, including cougars, leopards, lions, and tigers, looks in particular at their predatory characteristics. (Rev: BL 10/1/03; HB 7/03; HBG 4/04; SLJ 8/03) [599.75]

22578 Middleton, Don. *Jaguars* (2–4). Illus. Series: Big Cats. 1998, Rosen $21.25 (978-0-8239-5210-6). 24pp. A simple, easy-to-read introduction to jaguars that describes their characteristics, habits, and danger of extinction. (Rev: BL 2/1/99) [599.75]

22579 Middleton, Don. *Tigers* (2–4). Illus. Series: Big Cats. 1998, Rosen $21.25 (978-0-8239-5213-7). 24pp. The appearance, behavior, and mating habits of tigers are introduced along with a discussion of their endangered status. (Rev: BL 2/1/99) [599.756]

22580 Milton, Joyce. *Big Cats* (1–3). Illus. by Silvia Duran. Series: All Aboard Reading. 1994, Penguin paper $3.99 (978-0-448-40564-3). 48pp. An easy-to-read book that introduces such big cats as leopards, tigers, lions, jaguars, cougars, and cheetahs. (Rev: BCCB 4/95; BL 1/1/95; HB 3/94; SLJ 2/95) [599.74]

22581 O'Brien, Patrick. *Sabertooth* (2–4). Illus. by author. 2008, Holt $16.95 (978-0-8050-7105-4). 32pp. This large-format volume looks at the prehistoric cats with long, sharp teeth; illustrations compare sizes with modern tigers. (Rev: BL 8/08; LMC 8/08; SLJ 7/08) [569.74]

22582 Patent, Dorothy Hinshaw. *Big Cats,* (2–4). Illus. by Kendahl Jan Jubb. 2005, Walker $16.95 (978-0-8027-8968-6). 32pp. An excellent overview

— covering physical characteristics, diet, habitat, and behavior — of the world's big cat species, including the cheetah, cougar, jaguar, leopard, lion, and tiger. (Rev: BL 11/15/05; SLJ 12/05) [599.75]

22583 Robinson, Claire. *Lions* (2–3). Series: In the Wild. 1997, Heinemann $21.36 (978-1-57572-132-3). 24pp. A heavily illustrated introduction to lions that uses double-page spreads to cover such topics as behavior, food, habitats, and care of young. (Rev: BL 2/15/98) [599.74]

22584 Schafer, Susan. *Tigers* (3–5). Illus. Series: Animals, Animals. 2000, Benchmark LB $25.64 (978-0-7614-1170-3). 48pp. Color photographs and brief, readable text introduce these big cats and their anatomy, behavior, diet, reproduction, and so on. Also use *Lions* (2000). (Rev: HBG 3/01; SLJ 7/01) [599.756]

22585 Schlaepfer, Gloria G. *Cheetahs* (5–8). Series: AnimalWays. 2001, Marshall Cavendish LB $31.36 (978-0-7614-1266-3). 112pp. Cheetahs are introduced with material on anatomy, species identification, habitats, behavior, and endangered status. (Rev: BL 3/15/02; HBG 10/02) [599.7]

22586 Schneider, Jost. *Lynx* (4–7). Illus. 1994, Carolrhoda LB $28.75 (978-0-87614-844-0). 48pp. The life cycle, habits, and behavior of the lynx are described. (Rev: BL 1/15/95; SLJ 3/95) [599.74]

22587 Silverstein, Alvin, et al. *The Florida Panther* (4–7). Illus. Series: Endangered in America. 1997, Millbrook $24.90 (978-0-7613-0049-6). 64pp. Explains why the Florida panther has become endangered, with material on its life cycle and behavior and the efforts being made to save it. (Rev: BL 3/15/97; SLJ 6/97) [599.74]

22588 Simon, Seymour. *Big Cats* (K–3). 1991, HarperCollins LB $17.89 (978-0-06-021647-4). 40pp. The life and characteristics of big cats all over the world, with large color photos. (Rev: BCCB 6/91; BL 5/1/91; SLJ 5/91) [599.74]

22589 Spilsbury, Louise, and Richard Spilsbury. *Save the Bengal Tiger* (2–4). Series: Save Our Animals! 2006, Heinemann LB $25.36 (978-1-4034-7803-0). 32pp. Information about the threats to these tigers and the decline in their population is accompanied by information on their diet, habitat, and so forth, and on the ways in which readers can help. Also use *Save the Black Rhino, Save the Giant Panda, Save the Blue Whale,* and *Save the Florida Manatee* (all 2006). (Rev: SLJ 9/06) [599.75]

22590 Spilsbury, Louise, and Richard Spilsbury. *Watching Lions in Africa* (1–3). Series: Wild World. 2006, Heinemann LB $25.36 (978-1-4034-7222-9). 32pp. Provides details about lions' characteristics, diet, reproduction, predators, and so forth, with photographs, a world map, and a "Tracker's Guide." (Rev: SLJ 7/06) [599.757]

22591 Spilsbury, Richard. *Bengal Tiger* (4–6). Illus. Series: Animals Under Threat. 2004, Heinemann LB $27.07 (978-1-4034-4858-3). 48pp. The life cycle of the threatened Bengal tiger is explored in this blend of narrative and eye-catching color photography. (Rev: BL 8/04; SLJ 1/05) [599.756]

22592 Squire, Ann O. *Cheetahs* (2–4). Illus. Series: True Book. 2005, Children's Pr. LB $25.00 (978-0-516-22792-4); paper $6.95 (978-0-516-27932-9). 48pp. An appealing look at the cheetah and its characteristics, with discussion of its endangered status and plenty of arresting color photographs. (Rev: BL 6/1–15/05) [599.759]

22593 Stone, Lynn M. *Cougars* (2–3). Series: Early Bird Nature Books. 1997, Lerner LB $25.26 (978-0-8225-3013-8). 48pp. These large cats, noted for their speed and ferocity, are introduced with stunning photos and a simple text. (Rev: BL 9/15/97; SLJ 10/97) [599.74]

22594 Stone, Lynn M. *Cougars* (3–6). Illus. Series: Nature Watch. 1999, Carolrhoda LB $25.26 (978-1-57505-050-8). 48pp. Topics discussed in this colorful volume include the cougar's anatomy, habitats, reproduction, hunting, and relations with humans. (Rev: BL 9/1/99; HBG 9/99) [599.75]

22595 Suen, Anastasia. *A Tiger Grows Up* (K–2). Illus. by Michael L. Denman and William J. Huiett. Series: Wild Animals. 2005, Picture Window LB $25.26 (978-1-4048-0987-1). 24pp. Minimal text paired with vivid paintings, in an oversize format, follow a Bengal tiger and her three cubs as they learn to fend for themselves. (Rev: BL 10/15/05) [599.756]

22596 Sullivan, Jody. *Cheetahs: Spotted Speedsters* (1–3). Illus. Series: Wild World of Animals. 2002, Capstone LB $22.60 (978-0-7368-1393-8). 24pp. Facts about the fleet-footed cheetah include habitat, reproduction, behavior, and physical characteristics. (Rev: BL 1/1–15/03; HBG 3/03) [599]

22597 Swinburne, Stephen. *Bobcat: North America's Cat* (3–6). Illus. 2001, Boyds Mills $15.95 (978-1-56397-843-2). 32pp. Using a first-person narrative, the author describes his encounters with the bobcat and gives many background facts about this animal. (Rev: BL 4/1/01; HBG 10/01; SLJ 8/01) [599.75]

22598 Taylor, Bonnie Highsmith. *Ezra: A Mountain Lion* (3–5). Illus. Series: Cover-to-Cover Books. 2000, Perfection Learning $16.95 (978-0-7807-9313-2); paper $8.95 (978-0-7891-5166-7). 56pp. The reader learns through text and color photos about the life cycle of a mountain lion named Ezra. (Rev: BL 2/1/01) [599.75]

22599 Thapar, Valmik. *Tiger* (3–5). Illus. Series: Natural World. 1999, Raintree $27.12 (978-0-7398-1055-2). 48pp. This book introduces the tiger, labels the parts of its body, and explains how it lives. (Rev: BL 10/15/99; HBG 4/00) [599.766]

22600 Theodorou, Rod. *Bengal Tiger* (K–2). Illus. Series: Animals in Danger. 2000, Heinemann LB $21.36 (978-1-57572-267-2). 32pp. A look at the Bengal tiger and its life cycle, habitat, habits, and diet, with a section on its endangered status and efforts to save the species. (Rev: HBG 3/01; SLJ 4/01) [599.756]

22601 Thompson, Sharon E. *Built for Speed: The Extraordinary, Enigmatic Cheetah* (5–8). Illus. 1998, Lerner LB $27.93 (978-0-8225-2854-8). 88pp. The habits and lifestyle of this endangered animal are introduced with full-color illustrations. (Rev: BL 6/1–15/98; HBG 10/98) [599.75]

22602 Tourville, Amanda Doering. *A Jaguar Grows Up* (1–3). Illus. by Michael Denman and William J. Huiett. Series: Wild Animals. 2006, Picture Window LB $25.26 (978-1-4048-3159-9). 24pp. A jaguar's development from birth to full independence is described in brief text and realistic illustrations. (Rev: SLJ 4/07) [599.75]

22603 Von Zumbusch, Amelie. *Cheetahs* (PS–2). Series: Safari Animals. 2007, Rosen LB $21.25 (978-1-4042-3614-1). 24pp. The photographs are the focus of this simple introduction to these big cats. (Rev: SLJ 5/07)

22604 Von Zumbusch, Amelie. *Lions* (PS–2). Series: Safari Animals. 2007, Rosen LB $21.25 (978-1-4042-3612-7). 24pp. The photographs are the focus of this simple introduction to these big cats. (Rev: SLJ 5/07)

22605 Walker, Sarah, ed. *Big Cats* (3–5). Series: Eye Wonder. 2002, DK paper $9.99 (978-0-7894-8548-9). 48pp. A brilliantly illustrated look at tigers, lions, and other big cats and how and where they live. (Rev: BL 6/1–15/02; HBG 10/02) [599.74]

COYOTES, FOXES, AND WOLVES

22606 Bailey, Jill. *Gray Wolf* (4–6). Illus. Series: Animals Under Threat. 2005, Heinemann LB $29.93 (978-1-4034-5583-3). 48pp. The life cycle of the gray wolf and threats to its survival are explored in this blend of narrative and eye-catching color photography.

22607 Berman, Ruth. *Watchful Wolves* (PS–2). Illus. by William Muñoz. Series: Pull Again Books. 1998, Lerner LB $22.60 (978-0-8225-3600-0). 32pp. Questions with answers and colorful photos are used to explore the world of wolves with material on their habits, habitats, and social behavior. (Rev: BL 2/1/99; HBG 3/99; SLJ 1/99) [599.773]

22608 Brandenburg, Jim. *To the Top of the World: Adventures with Arctic Wolves* (5–7). Illus. 1993, Walker LB $17.85 (978-0-8027-8220-5). 44pp. Amazing color photographs highlight this account of a photographer's experiences living near a pack of Arctic wolves. (Rev: BCCB 11/93; BL 1/1/94*; SLJ 12/93*) [599.74]

22609 Chottin, Ariane. *Little Foxes* (3–5). Illus. Series: Born to Be Wild. 2005, Gareth Stevens LB $23.00 (978-0-8368-4435-1). 24pp. A simply worded look at young foxes and their lives, with large photographs.

22610 George, Jean Craighead. *The Wolves Are Back* (3–5). Illus. by Wendell Minor. 2008, Dutton $16.99 (978-0-525-47947-5). 32pp. Lovely paintings and clear text describe how the wolf was reintroduced into Yellowstone Park in the mid-1990s and the effect this has had on the whole ecosystem. (Rev: BL 4/1/08; IIB 5/08; LMC 5/08; SLJ 3/08) [599.773]

22611 Gibbons, Gail. *Wolves* (2–4). Illus. 1994, Holiday House LB $16.95 (978-0-8234-1127-6). 32pp. The habitat, life cycle, and habits of the gray (tim-

ber) wolf are explored in large color drawings and a detailed text. (Rev: BL 9/15/94; SLJ 9/94) [599.74]

22612 Goldish, Meish. *Gray Wolves: Return to Yellowstone* (3–4). Series: America's Animal Comebacks. 2007, Bearport LB $25.27 (978-1-59716-502-0). 32pp. With eye-catching photographs and an appealing design, Goldish looks at how the gray wolf almost disappeared and at efforts to bring them back to Yellowstone. (Rev: SLJ 12/07) [599.773]

22613 Goldish, Meish. *Red Wolves: And Then There Were (Almost) None* (3–6). Series: America's Animal Comebacks. 2009, Bearport LB $25.27 (978-1-59716-742-0). 32pp. Goldish traces the red wolf's struggle to survive and scientists' efforts to bring this animal back into its natural habitat. (Rev: SLJ 5/09) [599.74]

22614 Greenaway, Theresa. *Wolves, Wild Dogs, and Foxes* (4–7). Illus. Series: Secret World Of. 2001, Raintree LB $27.12 (978-0-7398-3507-4). 48pp. Report writers will find information here about wolves, wild dogs, and foxes, including their diet, habitat, and behavior, with photographs and interesting facts. (Rev: BL 10/15/01; HBG 3/02; SLJ 1/02) [599.77]

22615 Greenberg, Dan. *Wolves* (4–6). Series: Animals Animals. 2002, Benchmark LB $25.64 (978-0-7614-1447-6). 48pp. A colorful introduction to wolves, their physical characteristics, social behavior, and hunting strategies. (Rev: BL 12/15/02; HBG 3/03) [599.773]

22616 Gunzi, Christiane. *The Best Book of Wolves and Wild Dogs* (3–5). Illus. by Mike Rowe. 2003, Kingfisher $12.95 (978-0-7534-5574-6). 31pp. Young dog lovers will delight in this richly illustrated overview of wild canines, including African wild dogs, gray wolves of North America, Australian dingoes, and the jackals of southern Europe. (Rev: HBG 10/03; SLJ 11/03) [599.773]

22617 Harrington, Fred H. *The Ethiopian Wolf* (2–4). Series: The Library of Wolves and Wild Dogs. 2002, Rosen LB $21.25 (978-0-8239-5767-5). 24pp. Basic information about this wolf is accompanied by full-page photographs. Also use *The Dingo* and *The African Wild Dog* (2002). (Rev: SLJ 6/02)

22618 Havard, Christian. *The Fox: Playful Prowler* (PS–3). Illus. Series: Animal Close-Ups. 1995, Charlesbridge paper $6.95 (978-0-88106-434-6). 28pp. Using clear, colorful photos and a simple text, this is an attractive introduction to foxes and their lifestyle. (Rev: BL 4/15/95) [599.74]

22619 Heinz, Brian J. *The Wolves* (K–3). Illus. by Bernie Fuchs. 1996, Dial LB $15.89 (978-0-8037-1636-0). 32pp. The life of wolves and the activities of the pack are chronicled in this entertaining picture book. (Rev: BL 9/15/96*; SLJ 10/96) [599.74]

22620 Hodge, Deborah. *Wild Dogs: Wolves, Coyotes and Foxes* (K–3). Series: Wildlife. 1997, Kids Can $10.95 (978-1-55074-360-9). 32pp. Effective illustrations highlight these double-page spreads introducing these "wild dogs" and their lives, food, habits, and sleep. (Rev: BL 9/15/97; SLJ 11/97) [599.74]

22621 Horton, Casey. *Wolves* (3–5). Illus. Series: Endangered! 1996, Benchmark LB $25.64 (978-0-7614-0213-8). 32pp. Different species of wolves are discussed, with material on habitats, physical traits, behavior, and endangered status. (Rev: SLJ 3/96) [599.74]

22622 Johnson, Sylvia A., and Alice Aamodt. *Wolf Pack: Tracking Wolves in the Wild* (5–8). Illus. 1985, Lerner paper $27.93 (978-0-8225-9526-7). 96pp. Fascinating details of the lives of these animals that travel in packs and share hunting, raising the young, and protection. (Rev: BCCB 12/85; BL 2/1/86; SLJ 1/86) [599.74442]

22623 Kalman, Bobbie. *Endangered Wolves* (3–5). Illus. Series: Earth's Endangered Animals. 2004, Crabtree LB $25.27 (978-0-7787-1854-3); paper $6.95 (978-0-7787-1900-7). 32pp. In addition to discussion of their endangered status, this volume covers these animals' habitat, behavior, life cycle, and so forth. (Rev: SLJ 6/05) [599.74]

22624 Kalman, Bobbie, and Amanda Bishop. *The Life Cycle of a Wolf* (2–5). Illus. by Margaret Amy Reiach. Series: The Life Cycle. 2002, Crabtree LB $25.27 (978-0-7787-0657-1); paper $6.95 (978-0-7787-0687-8). 32pp. Report writers and browsers will find value in this easily read account of the life and habits of wolves that includes plenty of illustrations. (Rev: SLJ 10/02)

22625 Lang, Aubrey. *Baby Fox* (1–3). Photos by Wayne Lynch. Series: Nature Babies. 2002, Fitzhenry & Whiteside $13.95 (978-1-55041-688-6). 36pp. Browsers will enjoy following the story of a female fox finding a mate, giving birth to pups, and rearing them. (Rev: SLJ 12/02)

22626 Mara, Wil. *Coyotes* (4–6). Series: Animals Animals. 2008, Marshall Cavendish LB $20.95 (978-0-7614-2928-9). 48pp. *Coyotes* is packed with information regarding habitat, adaptations, and humanity's impact and includes excellent photographs. (Rev: SLJ 2/09) [599.77]

22627 Markle, Sandra. *Jackals* (2–5). Series: Animal Scavengers. 2005, Lerner LB $25.26 (978-0-8225-3197-5). 40pp. A well-written overview of jackals and their physical characteristics, diet, habitat, and behavior, with a focus on foraging for food. (Rev: SLJ 2/06) [599.77]

22628 Markle, Sandra. *Wolverines* (2–5). Series: Animal Scavengers. 2005, Lerner LB $25.26 (978-0-8225-3198-2). 40pp. A well-written overview of wolverines and their physical characteristics, diet, habitat, and behavior, with a focus on foraging for food. (Rev: SLJ 2/06) [599.76]

22629 Markle, Sandra. *Wolves* (3–6). Illus. Series: Animal Predators. 2004, Carolrhoda LB $25.26 (978-1-57505-732-3). 40pp. Concise text and clear, full-page photographs introduce the life cycle of the wolf and its physical characteristics, habitat, diet, and predatory behavior. (Rev: SLJ 10/04) [599.74]

22630 Martin, Patricia A. Fink. *Gray Wolves* (2–3). Series: Animals. 2002, Children's Book Pr. paper $6.95 (978-0-516-27472-0). 48pp. An attractive, well-designed beginning chapter book that intro-

duces gray wolves, their social life, habits, homes, and food. (Rev: BL 8/02) [599.773]

22631 Mason, Cherie. *Wild Fox* (3–5). Illus. by JoEllen M. Stammen. 1993, Down East $15.95 (978-0-89272-319-5). 32pp. This picture book tells about the author's encounter with a lame red fox. (Rev: BL 6/1–15/93; SLJ 8/93*) [599.7]

22632 Montardre, Helene. *Little Wolves* (3–5). Illus. Series: Born to Be Wild. 2005, Gareth Stevens LB $23.00 (978-0-8368-4440-5). 24pp. A simply worded look at young wolves and their lives, with large photographs.

22633 Murdico, Suzanne J. *Coyote Attacks* (4–7). 2000, Children's paper $6.95 (978-0-516-23513-4). 48pp. As well as covering the causes of coyote attacks on animals and humans, this account gives basic information on coyotes, their habitat, survival techniques, behavior, and preferred food. (Rev: SLJ 3/01) [599.74]

22634 Parker, Barbara Keevil. *North American Wolves* (4–6). Illus. Series: Nature Watch. 1998, Carolrhoda LB $25.26 (978-1-57505-095-9). 48pp. A superior account that describes the North American wolf's physical characteristics, habitat, social behavior, hunting habits, family care, and means of communication. (Rev: BL 12/1/98; HBG 3/99; SLJ 11/98) [599.773]

22635 Perry, Phyllis J. *Crafty Canines* (3–5). Illus. 1999, Watts LB $25.50 (978-0-531-11680-7). 64pp. An introduction to the physical characteristics, behavior, and habitats of North American coyotes, foxes, and wolves. (Rev: BL 11/1/99; HBG 4/00) [599.77]

22636 Silverstein, Alvin, et al. *The Red Wolf* (4–8). Illus. Series: Endangered Species. 1994, Millbrook LB $24.90 (978-1-56294-416-2). 48pp. The story of the red wolf, once thought to have become extinct in the United States, and the efforts to reintroduce it in North Carolina. (Rev: BL 4/15/95) [333.95]

22637 Swanson, Diane. *Coyotes* (2–4). Series: Welcome to the World of Animals. 2002, Gareth Stevens LB $24.00 (978-0-8368-3313-3). 32pp. A slim volume that provides information on the animal's home, diet, communication, and lifestyle. (Rev: SLJ 3/03)

22638 Swinburne, Stephen. *Coyote: North America's Dog* (4–6). Illus. 1999, Boyds Mills $15.95 (978-1-56397-765-7). 32pp. The author, a veteran park ranger who knows these animals well, describes the coyote and supplies details on the animals' life and habits. (Rev: BL 10/15/99; HBG 4/00; SLJ 11/99) [599.77]

22639 van Frankenhuyzen, Robbyn Smith. *Saving Samantha: A True Story* (K–2). Illus. by Gijsbert van Frankenhuyzen. 2004, Sleeping Bear $17.95 (978-1-58536-220-2). 48pp. A fox pup named Samantha is the focus of this frank story about rehabilitating animals and returning them to the wild. (Rev: BL 7/04; SLJ 9/04) [599.775]

22640 Weide, Bruce, and Patricia Tucker. *There's a Wolf in the Classroom!* (3–5). Illus. 1995, Carolrhoda LB $22.60 (978-0-87614-939-3). 56pp. After a general introduction to gray wolves, this book gives details on raising Koani, from cub to an adult wolf that can be taken into classrooms. (Rev: BCCB 12/95; BL 9/1/95; SLJ 10/95) [599.74]

22641 Winner, Cherie. *Coyotes* (3–6). Illus. Series: Nature Watch. 1995, Carolrhoda LB $25.26 (978-0-87614-938-6). 48pp. With color photos on each page and an interesting text, the world of the coyote is introduced, with material on its habitats, family life, and place in America's folklore. (Rev: BL 10/15/95) [599.74]

DEER FAMILY

22642 Arnold, Caroline. *Tule Elk* (3–6). Illus. by Richard Hewett. Series: Nature Watch. 1989, Carolrhoda LB $14.95 (978-0-87614-343-8). 48pp. This account is highlighted with data on structure, habits, and preservation techniques on this nearly extinct species of elk. (Rev: BL 9/15/89; HB 11/89; SLJ 9/89) [599.73]

22643 DuTemple, Lesley A. *North American Moose* (3–6). Series: Nature Watch. 2000, Carolrhoda LB $25.26 (978-1-57505-426-1). 48pp. An introduction to these gentle giants of the north, how and where they live, and their life cycle. (Rev: BL 5/15/00; HBG 10/01) [599.73]

22644 Estigarribia, Diana. *Moose* (3–5). Illus. Series: Animals, Animals. 2005, Benchmark LB $17.95 (978-0-7614-1870-2). 48pp. Report writers will find plenty of clear photographs and maps plus well-organized information about the moose and its physical characteristics, diet, habitat, and behavior. (Rev: SLJ 2/06) [599.65]

22645 Heuer, Karsten. *Being Caribou: Five Months on Foot with a Caribou Herd* (3–6). Illus. 2007, Walker $17.95 (978-0-8027-9565-6). 48pp. Heuer tells the fascinating story of a five-month trip with a caribou herd whose Arctic birthing grounds are threatened by oil drilling. (Rev: BCCB 2/07; BL 4/15/07; HBG 10/07) [599.65]

22646 Hinshaw Patent, Dorothy. *White-Tailed Deer* (2–4). Series: Early Bird Nature Books. 2004, Lerner LB $25.26 (978-0-8225-3052-7). This engaging overview ntroduces early readers to the white-tailed deer's physical characteristics, habitat, diet, behavior, and life cycle. (Rev: BL 12/15/04)

22647 Hiscock, Bruce. *The Big Caribou Herd: Life in the Arctic National Wildlife Refuge* (2–5). Illus. 2003, Boyds Mills $16.95 (978-1-59078-010-7). 32pp. Beautiful watercolor paintings illustrate this account of a caribou herd's migration through Alaska's Arctic National Wildlife Refuge. (Rev: BL 2/1/03; HBG 10/03; SLJ 3/03) [599.73]

22648 Hodge, Deborah. *Deer, Moose, Elk and Caribou* (3–5). Illus. Series: Wildlife. 1998, Kids Can $10.95 (978-1-55074-435-4). 32pp. Using colorful pictures, diagrams, and sidebars, this work introduces the moose, its habitats, life cycle, survival techniques, and reproductive process. (Rev: BL 1/1–15/99; HBG 3/99; SLJ 2/99) [599.65]

22649 Love, Pamela. *A Moose's Morning* (K–3). Illus. by Lesia Sochor. 2007, Down East $15.95 (978-0-89272-733-9). In a gentle style, this book takes the reader along as a young moose and his mother spend their day in the wild. (Rev: SLJ 6/07)

22650 Mara, Wil. *Deer* (4–6). Series: Animals Animals. 2008, Marshall Cavendish LB $20.95 (978-0-7614-2926-5). 48pp. *Deer* is packed with information regarding habitat, adaptations, and humanity's impact and includes excellent photographs. (Rev: SLJ 2/09) [599.65]

22651 Stefoff, Rebecca. *Deer* (3–6). Series: Animal-Ways. 2007, Marshall Cavendish LB $23.95 (978-0-7614-2534-2). 108pp. After looking at the physical characteristics of deer (sharp senses, unique antlers), this volume discusses their history, classification, diet, family life, and so forth as well as looking at particular kinds of deer and their conservation status. (Rev: SLJ 5/08) [599.65]

22652 Stewart, Melissa. *Antelope* (2–3). Series: Animals. 2002, Children's Book Pr. LB $25.00 (978-0-516-22198-4). 48pp. An attractively designed beginning chapter book that introduces the antelope, its life cycle, and how and where it lives. (Rev: BL 8/02) [599.73]

22653 Sullivan, Jody. *Deer: Graceful Grazers* (1–3). Series: Wild World of Animals. 2002, Capstone LB $22.60 (978-0-7368-1394-5). 24pp. Using a simple text, colorful images, and large type, this is a beginner's introduction to the world of the deer. (Rev: BL 1/1–15/03; HBG 3/03) [599.73]

ELEPHANTS

22654 Arnold, Katya. *Elephants Can Paint Too!* (1–3). Illus. 2005, Simon & Schuster $16.95 (978-0-689-86985-3). 40pp. Asian elephants' ability to paint is compared with the author's young human students in this affecting and informative picture book; the unemployed elephants' plight is explained, and additional facts are provided. (Rev: BCCB 11/05; BL 8/05; HBG 4/06; LMC 1/06; SLJ 9/05) [599.67]

22655 Barnes, Julia. *Elephants at Work* (3–5). Series: Animals at Work. 2006, Gareth Stevens LB $24.00 (978-0-8368-6224-9). 32pp. Full-color photographs show elephants being used in various roles and the text discusses the animal's physical characteristics, ability to learn commands, and relationship with humans. (Rev: SLJ 1/07) [636.9]

22656 Buckley, Carol. *Just for Elephants* (3–6). 2006, Tilbury House $16.95 (978-0-88448-283-3). This is the moving story of an aging circus elephant finding refuge after years of performing and then neglect in a zoo; the author's elephant sanctuary in Tennessee is the real star of this true story. (Rev: BL 12/15/06; SLJ 1/07) [639.97]

22657 Buckley, Carol. *Travels with Tarra* (3–5). Illus. 2002, Tilbury House $16.95 (978-0-88448-241-3). 40pp. Buckley tells the story of Tarra, the elephant she trained to do circus acts before creating an elephant sanctuary for Tarra's retirement. (Rev: BL 10/1/02; HBG 3/03) [599.67]

22658 Darling, Kathy. *The Elephant Hospital* (3–5). Illus. by Tara Darling. 2002, Millbrook LB $23.90 (978-0-7613-1723-4). 40pp. This is the story of a hospital for sick elephants that was founded in Thailand in 1994. (Rev: BCCB 7–8/02; BL 4/15/02; HBG 10/02; SLJ 4/02) [636.9]

22659 Douglas-Hamilton, Oria. *The Elephant Family Book* (3–5). Illus. 1996, North-South paper $8.95 (978-1-55858-549-2). 60pp. A beautifully illustrated book about this endangered species. (Rev: BL 1/1/91; HB 9/90; SLJ 4/91) [599.6]

22660 Hall, Kirsten. *African Elephant: The World's Biggest Land Mammal* (K–2). Illus. Series: Super-Sized! 2007, Bearport LB $21.28 (978-1-59716-387-3). 24pp. Report writers will get lots of mileage from this introduction to the African elephant, filled with facts about and photographs of the largest land mammal. (Rev: LMC 10/07; SLJ 8/07)

22661 Harman, Amanda. *Elephants* (3–5). Illus. Series: Endangered! 1996, Benchmark LB $22.79 (978-0-7614-0221-3). 32pp. After an introduction to the two species of elephants and their characteristics, this book describes why they are considered endangered. (Rev: SLJ 8/96) [599.6]

22662 Helfer, Ralph. *The World's Greatest Elephant* (1–3). Illus. by Ted Lewin. 2006, Philomel $16.99 (978-0-399-24190-1). 48pp. The amazing true story of the lifelong relationship between a boy and an elephant, who performed in circuses in Germany and the United States and had many adventures. (Rev: BCCB 4/06; BL 2/1/06*; HBG 10/06; SLJ 2/06) [791.3]

22663 Jonas, Ann. *Little Elephants* (3–5). Illus. Series: Born to Be Wild. 2005, Gareth Stevens LB $23.00 (978-0-8368-4434-4). 24pp. A simply worded look at young elephants and their lives, with large color photographs.

22664 Kalman, Bobbie. *Endangered Elephants* (3–5). Illus. Series: Earth's Endangered Animals. 2005, Crabtree LB $25.27 (978-0-7787-1860-4); paper $6.95 (978-0-7787-1906-9). 32pp. The dangers elephants face are highlighted in this photo-essay that also covers physical characteristics, diet, behavior, habitat, and life cycle. (Rev: BL 9/15/05; SLJ 12/05) [599.67]

22665 Latta, Jan. *Ella the Elephant* (K–4). Series: Wild Animal Families. 2006, Gareth Stevens LB $23.93 (978-0-8368-7768-7). 24pp. In a first-"person" account, Ella describes what it's like to be an elephant, giving readers facts about her species in an enjoyable and engaging format. (Rev: SLJ 5/07)

22666 Lewin, Ted, and Betsy Lewin. *Elephant Quest* (4–9). Illus. by authors. 2000, HarperCollins $15.95 (978-0-688-14111-0). 47pp. This account of the flora and fauna of Botswana's Moremi Reserve also describes the authors' search for elephants. (Rev: HB 1/01; HBG 3/01; SLJ 9/00) [599.67]

22667 MacMillan, Dianne. *Elephants: Our Last Land Giants* (3–6). Illus. Series: Nature Watch. 1993, Lerner LB $19.93 (978-0-87614-770-2). 48pp. A well-organized look at the animal's physical, social, and behavioral characteristics, with excellent full-color photos. (Rev: BL 1/15/94; SLJ 2/94) [599.6]

22668 Magloff, Lisa. *Elephant* (1–2). Illus. Series: Watch Me Grow. 2005, DK $7.99 (978-0-7566-1155-2). 24pp. An appealing look at how elephants develop, with eye-catching illustrations.

22669 Morgan, Jody. *Elephant Rescue: Changing the Future for Endangered Wildlife* (4–7). Illus. Series: Firefly Animal Rescue. 2005, Firefly $19.95 (978-1-55297-595-4); paper $9.95 (978-1-55297-594-7). 64pp. This photo-filled book documents the many threats facing the world's remaining herds of African and Asian elephants, and discusses elephant physiology, behavior, and habitat. (Rev: BL 2/15/05; SLJ 5/05) [599.67]

22670 Murray, Julie. *Elephants* (2–3). Illus. Series: Animal Kingdom. 2005, ABDO LB $21.35 (978-1-59197-314-0). 24pp. For beginning readers, this is an introduction to the elephant and its physical characteristics, habitat, and diet. (Rev: SLJ 5/05) [599.6]

22671 Overbeck, Cynthia. *Elephants* (4–7). Illus. 1981, Lerner LB $22.60 (978-0-8225-1452-7). 48pp. Elephants and their life cycle and habitats are discussed in this well-illustrated volume. [599]

22672 Ring, Susan. *Project Elephant* (3–6). Illus. Series: Zoo Life. 2002, Weigl LB $15.15 (978-1-59036-016-3). 32pp. Ring looks at elephants born in captivity and at the good and bad aspects of being raised in a zoo, with information on the animals' natural habitat and physiology. (Rev: BL 12/15/02; HBG 3/03) [599.67]

22673 Robinson, Claire. *Elephants* (2–3). Series: In the Wild. 1997, Heinemann $21.36 (978-1-57572-135-4). 24pp. A heavily illustrated introduction to elephants that covers topics like how they move, find food, and raise their young. (Rev: BL 2/15/98) [599.6]

22674 Schlaepfer, Gloria G. *Elephants* (5–9). Illus. Series: AnimalWays. 2003, Marshall Cavendish $31.36 (978-0-7614-1390-5). 112pp. In addition to material on physical characteristics, behavior, habitats, and threats, Schlaepfer touches on the animal's roles in history, mythology, religion, and literature. (Rev: BL 3/15/03; HBG 3/03) [599.67]

22675 Schmidt, Jeremy. *In the Village of the Elephants* (3–6). Illus. by Ted Wood. 1994, Walker LB $16.85 (978-0-8027-8227-4). 32pp. This book focuses on an elephant keeper who works with other mahouts and their elephants in a wildlife sanctuary in India. (Rev: BCCB 3/94; BL 4/15/94; SLJ 5/94) [636]

22676 Schwabacher, Martin. *Elephants* (4–6). Illus. 2000, Marshall Cavendish LB $25.64 (978-0-7614-1168-0). 32pp. A useful volume that describes the physical structure of the elephant and gives coverage on its habitats, behavior, mating habits, life cycle, and food. (Rev: BL 3/15/01; HBG 3/01) [599.67]

22677 Smith, Roland. *African Elephants* (2–4). Photos by Gerry Ellis. Illus. Series: Early Bird Nature Books. 1995, Lerner LB $25.26 (978-0-8225-3006-0). 48pp. Beginning with a map of Africa, this account describes the African elephant, its habits and habitats, and why it is scarce and valuable. (Rev: SLJ 8/95) [599.6]

22678 Sobol, Richard. *An Elephant in the Backyard* (PS–2). Illus. 2004, Penguin $17.99 (978-0-525-47288-9). 32pp. A 4-year-old elephant is the focus of this photo-essay about elephants' roles in the everyday life of a Thai village. (Rev: BL 6/1–15/04; SLJ 7/04) [636.9]

22679 Stewart, Melissa. *Elephants* (2–3). Series: Animals. 2002, Children's Book Pr. LB $25.00 (978-0-516-22199-1); paper $6.95 (978-0-516-26990-0). 48pp. This beginning chapter book uses attractive color photographs and a simple text to introduce the elephant and explain where and how it lives and raises its family. (Rev: BL 8/02) [599.6]

22680 Travers, Will. *Elephant* (3–5). Series: Natural World. 1999, Raintree $27.12 (978-0-7398-1056-9). 48pp. Through amazing photos and brief text, this book traces the life cycle of the elephant from its first steps in the African savanna through learning essential skills to finally taking its place as an adult in the herd. (Rev: BL 10/15/99; HBG 4/00) [599.6]

22681 Turner, Matt. *Asian Elephant* (4–6). Illus. Series: Animals Under Threat. 2005, Heinemann LB $29.93 (978-1-4034-5581-9). 48pp. The life cycle of the Asian elephant and threats to its survival are explored in this blend of narrative and eye-catching color photography.

GIRAFFES

22682 Anderson, Jill. *Giraffes* (PS–K). Illus. Series: Wild Ones. 2005, North Word $12.95 (978-1-55971-928-5); paper $6.95 (978-1-55971-929-2). 24pp. This photo-filled title chronicles a day in the life of a giraffe and provides basic information about the animal's physical appearance, habitat, diet, and behavior. (Rev: BL 10/15/05; HBG 4/06; SLJ 1/06) [599.665]

22683 Jango-Cohen, Judith. *Giraffes* (3–5). Illus. Series: Animals, Animals. 2001, Benchmark LB $25.64 (978-0-7614-1258-8). 48pp. In addition to the usual information on the species, this book discusses the giraffe's discovery and naming, and its relationship with humans. (Rev: HBG 10/02; SLJ 2/02) [599.638]

22684 Leach, Michael. *Giraffe* (3–6). Illus. Series: Natural World. 2001, Raintree LB $27.12 (978-0-7398-4435-9). 48pp. Fascinating facts about giraffes are expressed in breezy, clear terms, with memorable close-up photographs, a glossary, and a list of Web sites. (Rev: BL 12/15/01; HBG 10/02) [599.638]

22685 Marie, Christian. *Little Giraffes* (3–5). Illus. Series: Born to Be Wild. 2005, Gareth Stevens LB $23.00 (978-0-8368-4436-8). 24pp. A simply worded look at young giraffes and their lives, with large color photographs.

22686 Parker, Barbara Keevil. *Giraffes* (4–6). Illus. Series: Nature Watch. 2003, Lerner LB $25.26 (978-1-57505-346-2). 48pp. An attractive introduction to these long-necked animals, how and where they live, and their life cycle. (Rev: HBG 4/04)

22687 St. George, Judith. *Zarafa: The Giraffe Who Walked to the King* (1–3). Illus. by Britt Spencer. 2009, Philomel $16.99 (978-0-399-25049-1). 40pp. In 1824 an elegant and good-natured giraffe called Zarafa — a gift from one ruler to another — started a long journey from Egypt to Paris, making friends and impressing crowds along the way. (Rev: BL 5/1/09; LMC 10/09; SLJ 6/09) [599.638092]

22688 Tourville, Amanda Doering. *A Giraffe Grows Up* (1–3). Illus. by Michael Denman and William J. Huiett. Series: Wild Animals. 2006, Picture Window LB $25.26 (978-1-4048-3158-2). 24pp. A giraffe's development from birth to full independence is described in brief text and realistic illustrations. (Rev: SLJ 4/07) [599.638]

22689 Underwood, Deborah. *Watching Giraffes in Africa* (1–3). Series: Wild World. 2006, Heinemann LB $25.36 (978-1-4034-7230-4). 32pp. Provides details about giraffes' characteristics, diet, reproduction, predators, and so forth, with photographs, a world map, and a "Tracker's Guide." (Rev: SLJ 7/06) [599.638]

MARSUPIALS

22690 Anderson, Jill. *Kangaroos* (PS–2). Series: Wild Ones. 2006, NorthWord $12.95 (978-1-55971-935-3); paper $6.95 (978-1-55971-936-0). This photo-filled title offers an excellent visual introduction to kangaroos and is appropriate for preschoolers and early elementary students. (Rev: HBG 10/06; SLJ 8/06)

22691 Arnold, Caroline. *A Wombat's World* (K–3). Illus. by author. Series: Caroline Arnold's Animals. 2008, Picture Window LB $19.95 (978-1-4048-3986-1). 24pp. This title follows the events in a wombat's life over the course of a year as she gives birth and raises her young to maturity. (Rev: BL 3/15/08; SLJ 8/08) [599.24]

22692 Bredeson, Carmen. *Kangaroos Up Close* (1–3). Series: Zoom in on Animals! 2008, Enslow LB $21.26 (978-0-7660-3079-4). 24pp. Simple text and close-up color photographs introduce body parts, babies, and other important characteristics. (Rev: SLJ 11/08) [599.2]

22693 Burt, Denise. *Kangaroos* (3–6). Series: Nature Watch. 2000, Carolrhoda $25.26 (978-1-57505-388-2). 48pp. This attractive volume uses a number of color photos to introduce the kangaroo, its physical characteristics, habits, and homes. (Rev: BL 3/15/00; HBG 9/00) [599.2]

22694 Burt, Denise. *Koalas* (3–6). Illus. Series: Nature Watch. 1999, Carolrhoda $25.26 (978-1-57505-380-6). 48pp. Colorful photographs and clear text introduce koalas, their food, physical characteristics, lifestyles, habitats, and mating habits. (Rev: BL 12/15/99; HBG 4/00) [599.2]

22695 Collard, Sneed B. *Pocket Babies and Other Amazing Marsupials* (4–7). Illus. 2007, Darby Creek $18.95 (978-1-58196-046-4). 72pp. A large-format introduction to marsupials around the world — including the opossum, kangaroo, koala, and wombat — and to the efforts being made to save the many endangered marsupials. (Rev: BL 9/15/07; SLJ 10/07) [599.2]

22696 Dennard, Deborah. *Koala Country: The Story of an Australian Eucalyptus Forest* (2–4). Illus. Series: Wild Habitat. 2001, Soundprints $15.95 (978-1-56899-887-9). 32pp. An appealing look at a day in the life of a koala, covering the animal's diet, habitat, and nocturnal and reproductive activities.

(Rev: BL 6/1–15/01; HBG 10/01; SLJ 11/01) [599.1]

22697 French, Jackie. *How to Scratch a Wombat: Where to Find It . . . What to Feed It . . . Why It Sleeps All Day* (3–5). Illus. by Bruce Whatley. 2009, Clarion $15.00 (978-0-618-86864-3). 86pp. All about wombats and their physical characteristics and behavior, with engaging anecdotes and advice on dealing with these Australian marsupials. (Rev: BL 2/1/09; SLJ 3/09) [599.2]

22698 Hewett, Joan. *A Kangaroo Joey Grows Up* (1–3). Illus. by Richard Hewett. Series: Baby Animals. 2001, Lerner LB $21.27 (978-1-57505-165-9); paper $6.95 (978-0-8225-0091-9). 32pp. Beginning readers will enjoy this basic book about a young kangaroo joey. (Rev: BL 10/15/01; HBG 3/02; SLJ 10/01) [599.2]

22699 Inskipp, Carol. *Koala* (4–6). Illus. Series: Animals Under Threat. 2005, Heinemann LB $29.93 (978-1-4034-5585-7). 48pp. The life cycle of the koala and threats to its survival are explored in this blend of narrative and eye-catching color photography. [599.1]

22700 Kalman, Bobbie. *The Life Cycle of a Koala* (2–4). Illus. Series: The Life Cycle. 2001, Crabtree LB $25.27 (978-0-7787-0655-7); paper $6.95 (978-0-7787-0685-4). 32pp. After a general description of the koala, the author clearly explains its life cycle and discusses what can be done to curb human encroachment. (Rev: SLJ 6/02) [599.1]

22701 Kalman, Bobbie, and Heather Levigne. *What Is a Marsupial?* (1–3). Series: Science of Living Things. 2000, Crabtree LB $25.27 (978-0-86505-978-8); paper $6.95 (978-0-86505-955-9). 32pp. This beginning science book introduces in text and pictures such marsupials as the kangaroo, koala, and opossum. (Rev: SLJ 11/00) [599.1]

22702 Lang, Aubrey. *Baby Koala* (K–3). Illus. Series: Nature Babies. 2005, Fitzhenry & Whiteside $13.95 (978-1-55041-874-3); paper $5.95 (978-1-55041-876-7). 36pp. This appealing photo-essay follows a koala mother and baby as they browse on eucalyptus in an Australian forest. (Rev: BL 2/1/05; SLJ 4/05) [599.25]

22703 Levine, Michelle. *Jumping Kangaroos* (K–2). Illus. Series: Pull Ahead Books. 2005, Lerner LB $22.60 (978-0-8225-2421-2); paper $5.95 (978-0-8225-2440-3). 32pp. All about kangaroos, their behavior and habitat, designed for the beginning reader. (Rev: BL 3/15/05) [599.2]

22704 Markle, Sandra. *Finding Home* (K–3). Illus. by Alan Marks. 2008, Charlesbridge $15.95 (978-1-58089-122-6). 32pp. The story of a mother koala who manages to survive raging bushfires and protect her young joey in the face of multiple challenges. (Rev: BL 2/15/08; HB 3/08; LMC 10/08; SLJ 2/08) [599.2]

22705 Markle, Sandra. *Tasmanian Devils* (2–5). Series: Animal Scavengers. 2005, Lerner LB $25.26 (978-0-8225-3199-9). 40pp. A well-written overview of the ill-tempered Tasmanian devil and its physical characteristics, diet, habitat, and behavior, with a focus on foraging for food. (Rev: SLJ 2/06) [599.2]

22706 Marsico, Katie. *A Kangaroo Joey Grows Up* (1–2). 2007, Children's Pr. LB $19.00 (978-0-531-17476-0). 24pp. The development of a baby kangaroo is the topic of this vocabulary-building book with interesting photographs. (Rev: SLJ 8/07)

22707 Murray, Peter. *Kangaroos* (4–7). Series: The World of Mammals. 2005, Child's World LB $29.93 (978-1-59296-499-4). 40pp. Arresting photographs and engaging text introduce the anatomy, behavior, habitat, and life cycle of the kangaroo as well as the threats to the animal's survival in the wild. (Rev: SLJ 3/06) [599.2]

22708 Noonan, Diana. *The Kangaroo* (2–4). Illus. Series: Life Cycles. 2002, Chelsea LB $23.00 (978-0-7910-6968-4). 32pp. Handsome images and simple text describe the life cycle, habitat, appearance, and predators of the kangaroo, in a small, square, photo-essay format. (Rev: BL 1/1–15/03; HBG 3/03) [599.2]

22709 Otfinoski, Steven. *Koalas* (2–5). Illus. Series: Animals Animals. 2007, Marshall Cavendish LB $23.95 (978-0-7614-2526-7). 48pp. Reference aids including a glossary and additional resources make this overview on koalas useful for research. (Rev: BL 12/1/07) [599.2]

22710 Penny, Malcolm. *The Secret Life of Kangaroos* (4–7). Series: The Secret World of . . . 2002, Raintree LB $27.12 (978-0-7398-4986-6). 48pp. A visually interesting look at the world of the kangaroo with material on behavior, anatomy, reproduction, and how pollution and habitat destruction have affected these animals. (Rev: BL 8/02) [599.2]

22711 Royston, Angela. *Life Cycle of a Kangaroo* (PS–3). Series: Life Cycle. 1998, Heinemann LB $21.36 (978-1-57572-615-1). 32pp. Using a color photo and four lines of text per page, this book introduces the kangaroo and its life cycle. (Rev: BL 5/15/98; SLJ 6/98) [599]

22712 Sill, Cathryn. *About Marsupials: A Guide for Children* (K–2). Illus. by John Sill. 2006, Peachtree $15.95 (978-1-56145-358-0). 48pp. Kangaroos, wombats, and wallabies are only three of the marsupials covered in this useful, well-illustrated guide. (Rev: BL 2/15/06; SLJ 5/06) [599.2]

22713 Sotzek, Hannelore, and Bobbie Kalman. *A Koala Is Not a Bear!* (1–3). Illus. by Barbara Bedell. Series: Crabapples. 1997, Crabtree paper $5.95 (978-0-86505-739-5). 32pp. After distinguishing between this marsupial and bears, this book introduces their subspecies and traits and habits. (Rev: SLJ 9/97) [599.1]

22714 Spilsbury, Louise, and Richard Spilsbury. *Watching Kangaroos in Australia* (1–3). Series: Wild World. 2006, Heinemann LB $25.36 (978-1-4034-7225-0). 32pp. Provides details about kangaroos' characteristics, diet, reproduction, predators, and so forth, with photographs, a world map, and a "Tracker's Guide." (Rev: SLJ 7/06) [599.2]

22715 Swan, Erin Pembrey. *Meat-Eating Marsupials* (3–5). Series: Animals in Order. 2002, Watts LB $26.50 (978-0-531-11628-9). 48pp. After a general introduction to these pouched animals, individual species are featured in descriptive text and striking color photographs. (Rev: BL 3/15/02) [599.1]

22716 Tesar, Jenny. *What on Earth Is a Quokka?* (3–4). Illus. Series: What on Earth? 1996, Blackbirch LB $24.94 (978-1-56711-104-0). 32pp. Describes the characteristics and habitat of this cat-sized marsupial that lives in Australia. (Rev: SLJ 3/97) [599.1]

22717 Theodorou, Rod. *Koala* (2–4). Illus. Series: Animals in Danger. 2001, Heinemann LB $21.36 (978-1-57572-271-9). 32pp. Basic information about the koala and its endangered status. (Rev: BL 7/01; HBG 10/01) [599.2]

22718 Twinem, Neecy. *High in the Trees* (PS–3). Illus. by author. Series: Animal Clues Board Books. 1996, Charlesbridge $4.95 (978-0-88106-940-2). Close-up pictures of parts of an animal are revealed to be those of a koala in this picture puzzle book. (Rev: SLJ 12/96) [599.74]

PANDAS

22719 Arnold, Caroline. *A Panda's World* (PS–2). Illus. by author. Series: Caroline Arnold's Animals. 2006, Picture Window LB $26.60 (978-1-4048-1322-9). 24pp. A baby panda grows up and learns to fend for himself in this appealing fact-packed title. (Rev: LMC 11/06; SLJ 6/06) [[599.789]

22720 Bortolotti, Dan. *Panda Rescue: Changing the Future for Endangered Wildlife* (3–8). Series: Firefly Animal Rescue. 2003, Firefly LB $19.95 (978-1-55297-598-5); paper $9.95 (978-1-55297-557-2). 64pp. Threats to the panda's survival and efforts to protect them from extinction are examined in detail, with profiles of some of the key individuals involved. (Rev: BL 1/1–15/04; SLJ 4/04) [599.789]

22721 Bredeson, Carmen. *Giant Pandas Up Close* (PS–3). Series: Zoom in on Animals. 2006, Enslow LB $21.26 (978-0-7660-2496-0). 24pp. Eye-catching full-color close-ups show key physical characteristics of the panda, and the text gives basic details on diet, habitat, life cycle, and so forth. (Rev: SLJ 11/06) [599.789]

22722 Claybourne, Anna. *Giant Panda* (4–6). Illus. Series: Animals Under Threat. 2005, Heinemann LB $29.93 (978-1-4034-5582-6). 48pp. The life cycle of the giant panda and threats to its survival are explored in this blend of narrative and eye-catching color photography. [599.74]

22723 Crossingham, John, and Bobbie Kalman. *Endangered Pandas* (3–5). Illus. Series: Earth's Endangered Animals. 2005, Crabtree LB $25.27 (978-0-7787-1858-1); paper $6.95 (978-0-7787-1904-5). 32pp. After giving a clear overview of the giant panda's physical characteristics, life cycle, and behavior, the authors discuss the reasons the animal is endangered and measures being taken to reduce the threat. (Rev: SLJ 12/05) [599.789]

22724 Dudley, Karen. *Giant Pandas* (3–6). Illus. Series: Untamed World. 1997, Raintree LB $28.54 (978-0-8172-4566-5). 64pp. This presentation includes material on the panda's classification, life span, behavior, and endangered status, plus the

myths and legends that surround this animal. (Rev: SLJ 8/97) [599.74]

22725 Eason, Sarah. *Save the Panda* (1–3). Illus. by Andrew Geeson and Marijke Veldhoven. Series: Save the . . . 2009, Rosen LB $23.95 (978-1-4358-2812-4). 32pp. Colorful spreads present answers to common questions in this solid introduction to the endangered panda. (Rev: SLJ 6/09) [599.789]

22726 Gibbons, Gail. *Giant Pandas* (K–3). Illus. 2002, Holiday House $16.95 (978-0-8234-1761-2). 32pp. Simple text and watercolors introduce facts about pandas in the wild and in zoos. (Rev: BL 1/1–15/03; HBG 10/03; SLJ 12/02) [599.789]

22727 Green, Carl R. *The Giant Panda* (3–7). Series: Endangered and Threatened Animals. 2004, Enslow LB $25.26 (978-0-7660-5061-7). 48pp. Supplemented by a lengthy list of links to online resources, this overview of the giant panda explores its behavior and physical characteristics, as well as the threats it faces. (Rev: BL 6/1–15/04) [599.789]

22728 Jiguang, Xin, and Markus Kappeler. *The Giant Panda* (5–7). Trans. by Noel Simon. Illus. 1984, China Books paper $9.95 (978-0-8351-1388-5). 118pp. China's giant panda is introduced in its natural habitat. (Rev: BL 12/15/86; HB 1/87; SLJ 12/86) [599]

22729 Leeson, Tom, and Pat Leeson. *Panda* (2–4). Illus. Series: Wild Bears! 2000, Blackbirch $24.94 (978-1-56711-341-9). 24pp. Using a direct text and quality photos, this book covers topics related to pandas, such as the world population, physical characteristics, behavior, diet, and endangered status. (Rev: BL 12/15/00; HBG 3/01) [599.789]

22730 Nagda, Ann Whitehead. *Panda Math: Learning About Subtraction from Hua Mei and Mei Sheng* (3–5). Illus. 2005, Holt $16.95 (978-0-8050-7644-8). 32pp. Using two giant panda siblings at the San Diego Zoo as the framework, this book teaches the fundamentals of subtraction as it considers topics including bamboo consumption, sleep habits, weight, and life expectancy. (Rev: BL 9/15/05; SLJ 9/05) [513.2]

22731 Penny, Malcolm. *Giant Panda* (2–4). Series: Natural World. 2000, Raintree LB $27.12 (978-0-7398-1063-7). 48pp. Clear photos and a good layout distinguish this book about the giant panda, its habitat, mating, diet, and endangered status. (Rev: HBG 9/00; SLJ 7/00) [599.74]

22732 Ryder, Joanne. *Little Panda* (K–3). Illus. 2001, Simon & Schuster $16.95 (978-0-689-84310-5). 32pp. This photo-essay chronicles the birth and early life of Hua Mei, a panda born at the San Diego Zoo. (Rev: BL 4/15/01; HB 5/01; HBG 10/01; SLJ 7/01*) [599.789]

22733 Ryder, Joanne. *Panda Kindergarten* (PS–3). Illus. by Katherine Feng. 2009, HarperCollins $17.99 (978-0-06-057850-3). 32pp. A photo-essay about panda cubs at a Chinese zoo. (Rev: BCCB 9/09; BL 6/1–15/09; HB 9/09) [599.789]

RODENTS

22734 Bastian, Lois Brunner. *Chipmunk Family* (3–5). Illus. Series: Wildlife Conservation Society

Books. 2000, Watts LB $24.50 (978-0-531-11683-8). 48pp. Photographed in the author's backyard in New Jersey, this is a stunning book that focuses on a mother chipmunk and how she raises her brood. (Rev: BL 2/15/01) [599.36]

22735 Conniff, Richard. *Rats! The Good, the Bad, and the Ugly* (3–5). Illus. 2002, Crown $15.95 (978-0-375-81207-1). 37pp. A volume packed with information, anecdotes, and color photographs covering the biology, mythology, and history of rats. (Rev: BCCB 12/02; BL 12/15/02; HBG 3/03; SLJ 1/03) [599.35]

22736 Gallagher, Kristin Ellersbusch. *Cottontail Rabbits* (PS–2). Series: Pull Ahead Books. 2000, Lerner LB $22.60 (978-0-8225-3617-8); paper $5.95 (978-0-8225-3623-9). 32pp. Using many questions built into the text, this attractive easy reader introduces the cottontail rabbit, its physical characteristics, habits, food, and habitats. (Rev: BL 8/00; HBG 3/01) [599.32]

22737 Hipp, Andrew. *The Life Cycle of a Mouse* (PS–2). Illus. by Dwight Kuhn. Series: Life Cycle Of. 2002, Rosen LB $19.95 (978-0-8239-5866-5). 24pp. This book for beginning readers follows the life of a mouse from conception to adulthood. (Rev: BL 12/15/02) [599.35]

22738 Hodge, Deborah. *Beavers* (3–5). Illus. Series: Wildlife. 1998, Kids Can $10.95 (978-1-55074-429-3). 32pp. As well as the habitats, appearance, survival techniques, and life cycle of the beaver, this work discusses the animal's incredible building skills. (Rev: BL 1/1–15/99; HBG 3/99; SLJ 2/99) [599.37]

22739 Holub, Joan. *Why Do Rabbits Hop?* (K–2). Illus. 2003, Dial paper $3.99 (978-0-14-230120-3). 48pp. An interesting introduction to rabbits in a question-and-answer format for beginning readers. (Rev: BL 11/15/02; HBG 10/03; SLJ 2/03) [636.9]

22740 Jacobs, Lee. *Beaver* (3–5). Series: Wild America. 2003, Gale LB $24.94 (978-1-56711-566-6). 24pp. This colorful volume introduces young readers to the beaver, examining the toothy creature's physical characteristics, habitat, and behavior. (Rev: SLJ 11/03) [599.37]

22741 Jango-Cohen, Judith. *Porcupines* (3–5). Illus. Series: Animals, Animals. 2005, Benchmark LB $17.95 (978-0-7614-1868-9). 48pp. Report writers will find plenty of clear photographs and maps plus well-organized information about the porcupine and its physical characteristics, diet, habitat, and behavior. (Rev: SLJ 2/06) [599.35]

22742 Kalman, Bobbie, and Jacqueline Langille. *What Is a Rodent?* (2–5). Series: Science of Living Things. 1999, Crabtree LB $25.27 (978-0-86505-923-8); paper $6.95 (978-0-86505-951-1). 32pp. Excellent photos and an informative text introduce rodents, their characteristics, and habitat, as well as giving information on specific members of the group. (Rev: SLJ 3/00) [599.32]

22743 Lorbiecki, Marybeth. *Prairie Dogs* (2–4). Illus. Series: Our Wild World. 2004, NorthWord $10.95 (978-1-55971-883-7). 48pp. This photo-filled book dramatizes the plight of prairie dogs,

facing increasing pressure from the rapid spread of human development into their habitat. (Rev: BL 3/15/04; SLJ 10/04) [599.36]

22744 Markle, Sandra. *Porcupines* (K–4). Series: Animal Prey. 2007, Lerner LB $25.26 (978-0-8225-6439-3). 40pp. Eye-catching photographs and clear, readable text discuss how porcupines, nocturnal rodents, repel predators with their sharp quills. (Rev: SLJ 4/07) [599.35]

22745 Marrin, Albert. *Oh, Rats! The Story of Rats and People* (3–5). Illus. by C. B. Mordan. 2006, Dutton $16.99 (978-0-525-47762-4). 48pp. All about rats and everything they do to both assist and annoy people, with red-accented illustrations. (Rev: BL 7/06; SLJ 8/06*) [599.35]

22746 Martin-James, Kathleen. *Building Beavers* (PS–2). Series: Pull Ahead Books. 1999, Lerner $22.60 (978-0-8225-3628-4); paper $5.95 (978-0-8225-3632-1). 32pp. This introduction to the physical characteristics and habits of the beaver includes a map activity, a body diagram, and many close-up color photos. (Rev: BL 12/15/99; HBG 4/00; SLJ 3/00) [599.32]

22747 Miller, Sara S. *Rodents: From Mice to Muskrats* (3–5). Illus. Series: Animals in Order. 1998, Watts LB $26.50 (978-0-531-11488-9). 48pp. Using a scientific classification, this book describes, in photos and text, 14 species of rodents, their various habitats, and ways to observe these creatures. (Rev: BL 9/15/98; HBG 3/99) [599.35]

22748 Miller, Sara Swan. *Rabbits, Pikas, and Hares* (3–5). Series: Animals in Order. 2002, Watts LB $26.50 (978-0-531-11634-0). 48pp. Following a general explanation of animal classification, this attractive volume describes in text and color photographs several species of rabbits and related animals. (Rev: BL 3/15/02) [599.32]

22749 Old, Wendie. *The Groundhog Day Book of Facts and Fun* (K–3). Illus. by Paige Billin-Frye. 2004, Whitman LB $16.99 (978-0-8075-3066-5). 40pp. Punxsutawney Phil, groundhogs in general, and information on other animal forecasters around the world are all included in this volume. (Rev: BL 12/15/04; SLJ 1/05)

22750 Pascoe, Elaine. *Mice* (3–6). Illus. by Dwight Kuhn. Series: Nature Close-Up. 2005, Gale LB $24.95 (978-1-4103-0537-4). 48pp. The life cycle of mice, as well as their physical characteristics, different breeds, diet, and behavior, are examined in this book full of eye-catching photographs that also addresses the care of pet mice. (Rev: BL 2/1/06) [599.35]

22751 Powell, Sandy. *Rats* (2–4). Illus. 1994, Lerner LB $25.26 (978-0-8225-3003-9). 48pp. The characteristics, habits, and life cycle of various species of rats are described. (Rev: BL 1/1/95) [599.32]

22752 Ricciuti, Edward R. *What on Earth Is a Capybara?* (3–5). Illus. Series: What on Earth? 1995, Blackbirch LB $17.95 (978-1-56711-097-5). 32pp. The habitat, characteristics, and behavior of this unusual rodent are described in pictures and text. (Rev: SLJ 11/95) [636.3]

22753 Richardson, Adele D. *Groundhogs: Woodchuck, Marmots, and Whistle Pigs* (1–3). Illus. Series: Wild World of Animals. 2002, Capstone LB $22.60 (978-0-7368-1397-6). 24pp. A simple introduction to the groundhog's appearance, behavior, and other basic facts is followed by a glossary and list of resources. Also use *Beavers* (2002). (Rev: BL 1/1–15/03; HBG 3/03; SLJ 4/03) [599]

22754 Rounds, Glen. *Beaver* (PS–2). Illus. by author. 1999, Holiday House $16.95 (978-0-8234-1440-6). With text and drawings, this book shows many beaver activities including tree cutting, bark eating, and dam building. (Rev: BCCB 6/99; HB 5/99; HBG 9/99; SLJ 7/99*) [599.32]

22755 Savage, Stephen. *Mouse* (3–6). Illus. Series: Animal Neighbors. 2008, Rosen LB $23.95 (978-1-4358-4990-7). 32pp. This title includes details about a mouse's life and habitat and has clear, easy text and large photographs which help explain a mouse's anatomy. Also use *Rat* (2008). (Rev: SLJ 5/09) [599.35]

22756 Sill, Cathryn. *About Rodents: A Guide for Children* (K–3). Illus. by John Sill. 2008, Peachtree $15.95 (978-1-56145-454-9). 32pp. Each rodent in this attractive picture book — which introduces everything from mice and squirrels to chinchillas and capybaras — gets a full spread with a watercolor painting and a sentence or two of text, with additional information at the back of the book. (Rev: BL 9/15/08) [599.35]

22757 Souza, D. M. *What's a Lemming?* (4–5). Series: Creatures All Around Us. 1998, Carolrhoda $22.60 (978-1-57505-088-1). 40pp. This book on the tiny rodents found in subarctic regions tells of their appearance, mating, life cycle, habits, and food. (Rev: HBG 3/99; SLJ 1/99) [599.32]

22758 Staub, Frank. *Prairie Dogs* (2–3). Series: Early Bird Nature Books. 1998, Lerner $25.26 (978-0-8225-3038-1). 48pp. This work introduces the prairie dog, its habitat, and its unique burrows. (Rev: BL 10/15/98; HBG 3/99; SLJ 1/99) [599.32]

22759 Stone, Tanya L. *Rabbits* (3–5). Series: Wild America. 2002, Gale LB $24.94 (978-1-56711-645-8). 24pp. Rabbits in the wild are featured in this picture-filled account that describes appearance, life cycle, food, and survival skills. Also use *Squirrels* (2002). (Rev: BL 10/15/02) [599.32]

22760 Tagholm, Sally. *The Rabbit* (2–3). Illus. by Bert Kitchen. Series: Animal Lives. 2000, Kingfisher $9.95 (978-0-7534-5214-1). 32pp. After a description of the daily routines of a rabbit and its mating habits, this account details the building of a nest by the female, the birth of little rabbits, and their care until adulthood. (Rev: BL 5/15/00; HBG 3/01; SLJ 8/00) [599.32]

22761 Zuchora-Walske, Christine. *Peeking Prairie Dogs* (PS–2). Series: Pull Ahead Books. 1999, Lerner $22.60 (978-0-8225-3616-1); paper $5.95 (978-0-8225-3622-2). 32pp. The prairie dog's physical characteristics, habitats, and habits are introduced in a simple text with a color picture on each page. (Rev: BL 12/15/99; HBG 4/00; SLJ 3/00) [599.32]

SHEEP AND GOATS

22762 Green, Emily. *Goats* (PS–2). Illus. Series: Blastoff! Readers. 2007, Scholastic LB $18.50 (978-0-531-17552-1). 24pp. Short descriptions of goats and their characteristics make this book useful for beginning readers. (Rev: BL 5/15/07; SLJ 6/07) [636.3]

22763 Lang, Aubrey. *Baby Mountain Sheep* (K–3). Illus. 2008, Fitzhenry & Whiteside $15.95 (978-1-55455-042-5); paper $6.95 (978-1-55455-043-2). 36pp. With many color photographs, this attractive volume traces the first year in the life of a young Dall's sheep, born in the Alaskan mountains. (Rev: BL 2/15/08; SLJ 3/08) [599.649]

22764 MacKen, JoAnn Early. *Bighorn Sheep / Carnero de Canadá* (2–4). Trans. by Tatiana Acosta and Guillermo Gutiérrez. Series: Animals That Live in the Mountains / Animales de las montañas. 2006, Weekly Reader LB $21.00 (978-0-8368-6446-5). 24pp. A beginning book with facts about bighorn sheep in both English and Spanish; also use *Mountain Goats / Cabra montés* (2006). (Rev: SLJ 6/06) [599.649]

22765 Urbigkit, Cat. *The Shepherd's Trail* (2–4). Illus. 2008, Boyds Mills $16.95 (978-1-59078-509-6). 32pp. Urbigkit follows the migration of sheep herds in the U.S. West, explaining why they change habitats, how they move, and when breeding and shearing take place. (Rev: BL 1/1–15/08; SLJ 3/08) [636.300978]

Birds

GENERAL AND MISCELLANEOUS

22766 Arnold, Caroline. *Birds: Nature's Magnificent Flying Machines* (3–4). Illus. by Patricia J. Wynne. 2003, Charlesbridge $16.95 (978-1-57091-516-1); paper $6.95 (978-1-57091-572-7). 32pp. Arnold take a close look at the physical mechanics behind birds' flight, examining such topics as taking off, hovering, gliding, altering direction, soaring, and landing. (Rev: BL 6/1–15/03; HBG 4/04; SLJ 12/03) [598]

22767 Arnold, Caroline. *House Sparrows Everywhere* (3–6). Illus. Series: Nature Watch. 1992, Carolrhoda LB $25.26 (978-0-87614-696-5). 48pp. Gives details on the house sparrow's life cycle, how it was introduced into the United States, and how its population has grown. (Rev: BL 7/92) [598.8]

22768 Arnold, Caroline. *Ostriches and Other Flightless Birds* (3–6). Illus. by Richard Hewett. Series: Nature Watch. 1990, Carolrhoda LB $25.26 (978-0-87614-377-3). 48pp. Smooth text and sharp photos tell of the amazing ostrich and other flightless birds. (Rev: BL 3/1/90; SLJ 7/90) [598.5]

22769 Arnosky, Jim. *All About Turkeys* (1–4). Illus. Series: All About. 1998, Scholastic $15.95 (978-0-590-48147-2). 32pp. Using double-page spreads, this book introduces wild turkeys, their bodies, habitats, behavior, and food. (Rev: BL 10/15/98; HBG 3/99; SLJ 11/98) [598.6]

22770 Arnosky, Jim. *Watching Water Birds* (1–4). Illus. 1997, National Geographic $16.00 (978-0-7922-7073-7). 32pp. An informal introduction to such diving birds as loons, grebes, mallards, wood ducks, Canada geese, gulls, and herons. (Rev: BL 10/1/97; SLJ 10/97*) [598.179]

22771 Aziz, Laurel. *Hummingbirds: A Beginner's Guide* (5–8). Illus. 2002, Firefly LB $19.95 (978-1-55209-487-7); paper $9.95 (978-1-55209-374-0). 64pp. This heavily illustrated book offers a great deal of information about hummingbirds, including their bills, metabolism, flight, nesting, and migration. (Rev: BL 6/1–15/02; HBG 10/02) [598.7]

22772 Bateman, Robert. *Bateman's Backyard Birds* (4–7). Illus. 2005, Barron's $14.99 (978-0-7641-5882-7). 48pp. Wildlife artist Bateman introduces readers to numerous North American species of birds and the joys of birding in this beautifully illustrated guide. (Rev: BL 10/15/05) [598]

22773 Berman, Ruth. *Peacocks* (2–5). Photos by Richard Hewett. Series: Early Bird Nature Books. 1996, Lerner LB $25.26 (978-0-8225-3009-1). 47pp. A clear, succinct text and full-color photographs are used to introduce the members of the peafowl family. (Rev: SLJ 5/96) [598]

22774 Carney, Margaret. *Where Does a Tiger-Heron Spend the Night?* (PS–1). Illus. by Melanie Watt. 2002, Kids Can $15.95 (978-1-55337-022-2). 32pp. Rhyming text, rich acrylic artwork, and a lift-the-flap format combine to present facts about birds for younger readers. (Rev: BCCB 9/02; BL 3/15/02; HBG 10/02; SLJ 5/02) [598]

22775 Chermayeff, Ivan. *Feathery Facts* (PS–1). Illus. 1995, Harcourt $11.00 (978-0-15-200110-0). 32pp. Short, simple text and attractive illustrations are used to introduce the world of birds. (Rev: BL 4/1/95; SLJ 7/95) [598]

22776 Chrustowski, Rick. *Blue Sky Bluebird* (1–3). 2004, Holt $16.95 (978-0-8050-7104-7). 32pp. This overview of the bluebird's physical characteristics, diet, mating habits, and migratory patterns includes vivid and detailed illustrations. (Rev: BL 8/04; SLJ 4/04) [598.8]

22777 Collard, Sneed B., III. *Beaks!* (K–3). Illus. by Robin Brickman. 2002, Charlesbridge $16.95 (978-1-57091-387-7); paper $6.95 (978-1-57091-388-4). 32pp. Striking artwork and engrossing text about birds and their beaks will fascinate younger readers. (Rev: BL 8/02; HBG 3/03; SLJ 8/02) [573.3]

22778 Collard, Sneed B., III. *Wings* (3–5). Illus. by Robin Brickman. 2008, Charlesbridge $16.95 (978-1-57091-611-3); paper $7.95 (978-1-57091-612-0). 32pp. This is a fascinating look at the many animals that have wings, wing design, and the freedom of movement that these wings provide. (Rev: LMC 10/08; SLJ 2/08) [591.47]

22779 Copeland, Cynthia L., and Alexandra P. Lewis. *Funny Faces, Wacky Wings, and Other Silly Big Bird Things* (K–3). Series: Silly Millies. 2002, Millbrook LB $17.90 (978-0-7613-2863-6); paper $4.99 (978-0-7613-1788-3). 28pp. This overview of the world of big birds looks at the physical characteristics and behavior of such creatures as the ostrich, penguin, and bustard in an appealing blend of colorful illustrations and easy-to-read narrative. (Rev: HBG 3/03; SLJ 8/03)

22780 Demuth, Patricia. *Cradles in the Trees: The Story of Bird Nests* (1–3). Illus. by Suzanne Barnes. 1994, Macmillan LB $14.95 (978-0-02-728466-9). 32pp. Describes and pictures a number of different bird nests and the way in which each meets the special needs of a species. (Rev: BL 9/15/94; SLJ 11/94) [598.2]

22781 Dewey, Jennifer O. *Paisano, the Roadrunner* (4–6). Illus. by Wyman Meinzer. 2002, Millbrook LB $23.90 (978-0-7613-1250-5). 48pp. The author relates — in photographs, diary entries, and narrative — her experiences with a roadrunner she named "Paisano." (Rev: BCCB 9/02; BL 5/15/02; HB 7/02; HBG 10/02; SLJ 8/02) [598.7]

22782 Doris, Ellen. *Ornithology* (4–7). Illus. Series: Real Kids Real Science. 1994, Thames & Hudson $16.95 (978-0-500-19008-1). 64pp. An excellent manual on how to study birds in their natural habitats, with accompanying activities for all seasons. (Rev: BL 9/1/94) [598]

22783 DuTemple, Lesley A. *North American Cranes* (3–6). Illus. Series: Nature Watch. 1999, Carolrhoda $25.26 (978-1-57505-302-8). 48pp. Includes material on the physical characteristics and life cycles of the sandhill crane and the whooping crane. (Rev: BL 5/1/99; HBG 9/99; SLJ 4/99) [598.3]

22784 Gans, Roma. *How Do Birds Find Their Way?* (PS–3). Illus. by Paul Mirocha. Series: Let's-Read-and-Find-Out. 1996, HarperCollins LB $15.89 (978-0-06-020225-5); paper $5.99 (978-0-06-445150-5). 32pp. Various kinds of birds that migrate are introduced and the mysteries connected with their semiannual flights are explored. (Rev: BL 2/1/96; SLJ 4/96) [598.2]

22785 Garelick, May. *What Makes a Bird a Bird?* (K–3). Illus. 1995, Mondo paper $4.95 (978-1-57255-008-7). 32pp. In a series of questions and answers, the distinctive characteristics of birds are enumerated. (Rev: BL 8/95) [598.2]

22786 Goodman, Susan E. *Saving the Whooping Crane* (2–5). Illus. by Phyllis V. Saroff. Series: On My Own Science. 2007, Millbrook LB $25.26 (978-0-8225-6748-6). 48pp. How a group of scientists went to extreme measures to rear baby whooping cranes. (Rev: SLJ 10/07) [598.3]

22787 Guiberson, Brenda Z. *Mud City: A Flamingo Story* (K–3). Illus. 2005, Holt $16.95 (978-0-8050-7177-1). 32pp. From egg through mating and having a chick, this volume follows the life cycle of a flamingo. (Rev: BL 5/15/05; SLJ 5/05) [598.3]

22788 Guibert, Francoise de. *Sing, Nightingale, Sing!* (3–5). Illus. by Chiaki Miyamoto. 2006, Kane $13.95 (978-1-929132-98-0). 48pp. This brightly illustrated guide translated from French introduces 51 bird species, each with an illustration and a paragraph of text, and is accompanied by an audio CD of the birds' songs. (Rev: BL 4/1/06) [598]

22789 Hall, Kirsten. *Great Bustard: The World's Heaviest Flying Bird* (K–2). Illus. Series: Super-Sized! 2007, Bearport LB $21.28 (978-1-59716-

390-3). 24pp. Report writers will get lots of mileage from this introduction to the bustard, filled with facts about and photographs of the big bird. (Rev: SLJ 7/07)

22790 Harrison, George H. *Backyard Bird Watching for Kids* (2–5). Illus. 1997, Willow Creek $14.95 (978-1-57223-089-7). 64pp. Describes the joys of bird watching and introduces 20 popular backyard birds, with material on their calls, food, and habitats. (Rev: BL 12/1/97) [598]

22791 Haus, Robyn. *Make Your Own Birdhouses and Feeders* (3–6). Illus. Series: Quick Starts for Kids! 2001, Williamson paper $8.95 (978-1-885593-55-9). 64pp. A detailed guide for younger readers to feeding and providing shelter for wild birds. (Rev: BL 2/15/02; SLJ 12/01) [690]

22792 Herkert, Barbara. *Birds in Your Backyard* (K–3). Illus. by author. Series: A Sharing Nature with Children Book. 2001, Dawn $17.95 (978-1-58469-026-9); paper $8.95 (978-1-58469-025-2). 35pp. Tips on attracting birds to your backyard, instructions for building a birdhouse, and advice on binoculars accompany descriptions of a variety of birds and maps showing birds commonly found in North America. (Rev: HBG 3/02; SLJ 5/02) [598]

22793 Hewitt, Joan. *A Flamingo Chick Grows Up* (1–3). Series: Baby Animals. 2001, Carolrhoda LB $21.27 (978-1-57505-164-2); paper $6.95 (978-0-8225-0090-2). 32pp. Using excellent photographs, short sentences, large print, and simple vocabulary, this attractive book describes a flamingo chick's growth to adulthood. (Rev: BL 10/15/01; HBG 3/02; SLJ 10/01) [598]

22794 Hickman, Pamela. *Starting with Nature Bird Book* (2–4). Illus. by Heather Collins. Series: Starting with Nature. 2000, Kids Can $12.95 (978-1-55074-471-2); paper $5.95 (978-1-55074-810-9). 32pp. An introduction to birds that gives basic material on species, homes, migration, songs, and banding as well as advice to bird watchers and a series of activities including making a birdhouse. (Rev: HBG 9/00; SLJ 7/00) [598]

22795 Hoose, Phillip. *The Race to Save the Lord God Bird* (5–8). 2004, Farrar $20.00 (978-0-374-36173-0). 208pp. The sad tale of the ivory-billed woodpecker's decline is interwoven with discussion of the scientific and sociological implications. (Rev: BL 6/1–15/04; SLJ 9/04) [598.7]

22796 Horton, Casey. *Parrots* (3–6). Illus. Series: Endangered! 1996, Benchmark LB $22.79 (978-0-7614-0222-0). 32pp. This account focuses on eight species of parrots from around the world and why they are endangered. (Rev: SLJ 9/96) [598.71]

22797 Jango-Cohen, Judith. *Hovering Hummingbirds* (2–3). Series: Pull Ahead Books. 2003, Lerner LB $22.60 (978-0-8225-4666-5). 32pp. In this book, ideal for beginning readers, author Judith Jango-Cohen examines the life cycle, physical characteristics, behavior, and habitat of hummingbirds. (Rev: BL 11/15/03; HBG 10/03)

22798 Jenkins, Priscilla B. *A Nest Full of Eggs* (1–3). Illus. by Lizzy Rockwell. 1995, HarperCollins LB $15.89 (978-0-06-023442-3). 32pp. By observing a pair of robins build a nest and raise a family, two youngsters learn about birds and their habits. (Rev: BCCB 7–8/95; BL 6/1–15/95; SLJ 8/95) [598.8]

22799 Johnson, Sylvia A. *Albatrosses of Midway Island* (3–6). Illus. by Frans Lanting. 1990, Carolrhoda LB $19.93 (978-0-87614-391-9). 48pp. Amazing facts and statistics about the wondrous albatross. (Rev: BL 3/1/90; SLJ 7/90) [598.4]

22800 Johnson, Sylvia A. *Crows* (4–6). Illus. Series: Nature Watch. 2004, Carolrhoda LB $25.26 (978-1-57505-628-9). Along with information on the crow's habitat, diet, behavior, migratory patterns, and life cycle, this photo-filled overview discusses West Nile virus and crows' increasing taste for city dwelling. (Rev: BL 12/1/04; SLJ 4/05) [598.8]

22801 Kelly, Irene. *It's a Hummingbird's Life* (1–3). Illus. 2003, Holiday House $16.95 (978-0-8234-1658-5). 32pp. An appealing look at a year in the life of the ruby-throated hummingbird, including its annual migration south in search of warmer weather. (Rev: BL 4/1/03; HBG 10/03; SLJ 6/03) [598.7]

22802 Kenyon, Linda. *Rainforest Bird Rescue: Changing the Future for Endangered Wildlife* (4–8). Series: Firefly Animal Rescue. 2006, Firefly LB $19.95 (978-1-55407-153-1); paper $9.95 (978-1-55407-152-4). 64pp. This book discusses the threats to the tropical bird species that live in the world's rain forests, habitat that is rapidly disappearing, and profiles the men and women who are crusading to save them. (Rev: SLJ 12/06) [598.1734]

22803 Kirby, Pamela F. *What Bluebirds Do* (K–3). Illus. 2009, Boyds Mills $18.95 (978-1-59078-614-7). 32pp. Excellent images document the lives of a family of Eastern Bluebirds. (Rev: BL 4/15/09; SLJ 5/09) [598.8]

22804 Klein, Tom. *Loon Magic for Kids* (2–4). Illus. 1990, NorthWord paper $6.95 (978-1-55971-121-0). 48pp. This colorful account includes information on the behavior and life cycle of the loon. (Rev: BL 6/1/90; SLJ 3/91) [598.4]

22805 Latimer, Jonathan P., and Karen Stray Nolting. *Bizarre Birds* (3–6). Series: Peterson Field Guides for Young Naturalists. 1999, Houghton paper $5.95 (978-0-395-92279-8). 48pp. Using double-page spreads, this field guide describes and pictures a number of birds that are unusual for their appearance, habits, mating rituals, habitats, or other considerations. (Rev: BL 6/1–15/99; SLJ 8/99) [598]

22806 Latimer, Jonathan P., and Karen Stray Nolting. *Shorebirds* (3–6). Illus. Series: Peterson Field Guides for Young Naturalists. 1999, Houghton $15.00 (978-0-395-95212-2); paper $5.95 (978-0-395-92278-1). 48pp. A wide variety of shore birds that live near fresh water as well as oceans and the Gulf of Mexico are described in a series of colorful double-page spreads. (Rev: BL 6/1–15/99; SLJ 8/99) [598.3]

22807 Llamas, Andreu. *Birds Conquer the Sky* (4–8). Illus. by Miriam Ferrón and Miguel Ferrón. Series: Development of the Earth. 1996, Chelsea LB $17.55 (978-0-7910-3455-2). 32pp. A science book that explains the evolution of birds from prehistoric land birds onward and defines their characteristics. (Rev: SLJ 7/96) [598]

22808 London, Jonathan. *Flamingo Sunset* (K–3). Illus. by Kristina Rodanas. 2008, Marshall Cavendish $16.99 (978-0-7614-5384-0). 32pp. Readers follow a flamingo family through a year during which a chick grows up; with attractive illustrations and discussion of conservation efforts. (Rev: BL 4/15/08; LMC 8/08; SLJ 7/08) [598.3]

22809 London, Jonathan. *Gone Again Ptarmigan* (K–3). Illus. by Jon Van Zyle. 2001, National Geographic $16.95 (978-0-7922-7561-9). 32pp. The life cycle of the Arctic ptarmigan is covered in this picture book that shows how its feathers change color to offer camouflage in both winter and summer. (Rev: BL 1/1–15/01; HBG 10/01) [598.6]

22810 Lynne, Cherry. *Flute's Journey: The Life of a Wood Thrush* (K–3). Illus. 1997, Harcourt $15.00 (978-0-15-292853-7). 40pp. The story of a single wood thrush's journey from Maryland to a Central American rain forest and back. (Rev: BCCB 5/97; BL 4/1/97; SLJ 7/97) [599.8]

22811 MacKen, JoAnn Early. *Roadrunners / Correcaminos* (2–4). Trans. by Tatiana Acosta and Guillermo Gutiérrez. Series: Animals That Live in the Desert / Animales del desierto. 2005, Weekly Reader LB $21.00 (978-0-8368-4844-1). 24pp. A beginning book with facts about roadrunners in both English and Spanish. (Rev: SLJ 6/06) [598.7]

22812 McMillan, Bruce. *Wild Flamingos* (3–5). Illus. 1997, Houghton $17.00 (978-0-395-84545-5). 32pp. Introduces the flamingos of Bonaire in the Caribbean using clear text and spectacular photos. (Rev: BL 7/97; HB 9/97; SLJ 8/97*) [598.3]

22813 McNulty, Faith. *Peeping in the Shell: A Whooping Crane Is Hatched* (2–4). Illus. by Irene Brady. 1986, HarperCollins $11.95 (978-0-06-024134-6). 64pp. The process of hatching a whooping crane egg, with a personal narrative. (Rev: BCCB 10/86; BL 1/1/87; SLJ 12/86)

22814 Mania, Cathy, and Robert Mania. *Woodpecker in the Backyard* (3–5). Series: Wildlife Conservation Society Books. 2000, Watts LB $24.50 (978-0-531-11799-6). 48pp. A heavily illustrated book that describes the physical characteristics of the woodpecker and gives material on its habits, lifestyle, food, and homes. (Rev: BL 3/15/01) [598]

22815 Markle, Sandra. *Vultures* (3–5). Illus. Series: Animal Scavenger. 2005, Lerner LB $25.26 (978-0-8225-3195-1). 40pp. Vultures' role as scavengers is the focus of this volume full of dramatic photographs that looks in particular at the vultures of the African savannah, the Gulf Coast of Florida, and the Peruvian jungle. (Rev: BL 12/1/05) [598.9]

22816 Marsico, Katie. *A Peachick Grows Up* (1–2). 2007, Children's Pr. LB $19.00 (978-0-531-17480-7). 24pp. The development of a baby peacock is the topic of this vocabulary-building book with interesting photographs. (Rev: SLJ 8/07)

22817 Martin, Gilles. *Birds* (5–8). Illus. 2005, Abrams $18.95 (978-0-8109-5878-4). 80pp. An oversize book full of color photographs of birds, plus watercolor sketches and brief, quite advanced

text that comments on various aspects of the birds. (Rev: BL 5/1/05; SLJ 5/05) [598.22]

22818 Martin, Patricia A. Fink. *California Condors* (2–3). Series: Animals. 2002, Children's Book Pr. LB $25.00 (978-0-516-22161-8). 48pp. With a color photograph on almost every page and large type throughout, this is a simple but informative introduction to the California condor. (Rev: BL 8/02) [598.9]

22819 Maynard, Thane. *Ostriches* (3–4). Series: New Naturebooks. 2006, The Child's World LB $27.07 (978-1-59296-645-5). 32pp. An introductory overview of this huge bird, with vivid color photographs. (Rev: SLJ 2/07) [598.5]

22820 Miller, Sara Swan. *Wading Birds: From Herons to Hammerheads* (3–5). Series: Animals in Order. 2001, Watts LB $26.50 (978-0-531-11630-2). 32pp. The traits and behavior of wading birds are discussed with full-color photographs of various species and a simple text. (Rev: BL 6/1–15/01) [598.3]

22821 Miller, Sara Swan. *Woodpeckers, Toucans, and Their Kin* (4–6). Series: Animals in Order. 2003, Watts LB $26.50 (978-0-531-12243-3). 47pp. Introduces readers to birds that are members of the piciforme order, with information on representative species and their habitats. (Rev: SLJ 7/03) [598]

22822 Parker, Edward. *Birds* (5–8). Photos by author. Series: Rain Forest. 2003, Raintree LB $27.12 (978-0-7398-5239-2). 48pp. Birds that are found in rain forests are the topic of this overview that describes the dangers posed by humans through hunting, pollution, and agriculture. (Rev: HBG 3/03; SLJ 1/03) [598]

22823 Patent, Dorothy Hinshaw. *Pigeons* (3–6). Illus. 1997, Clarion $16.00 (978-0-395-69848-8). 78pp. An introduction to pigeons that covers their history, homes, uses, and intelligence. (Rev: BL 9/1/97; SLJ 10/97) [598.6]

22824 Patent, Dorothy Hinshaw. *Wild Turkeys* (2–3). Series: Early Bird Nature Books. 1999, Lerner LB $25.26 (978-0-8225-3026-8). 48pp. A well-written, handsomely illustrated guide to the life cycle, habits, and physical characteristics of wild turkeys. (Rev: BL 8/99; HBG 9/99; SLJ 5/99) [598]

22825 Pericoli, Matteo. *The True Story of Stellina* (K–3). Illus. 2006, Knopf $15.95 (978-0-375-83273-4). 40pp. In lyrical text and appealing art, Pericoli describes his wife's care for a baby finch she rescued from a busy New York City intersection. (Rev: BCCB 4/06; BL 2/1/06*; HBG 10/06; LMC 5/06; SLJ 4/06) [636.6]

22826 Posada, Mia. *Robins: Songbirds of Spring* (K–3). Illus. by author. 2004, Carolrhoda LB $15.95 (978-1-57505-615-9). After a description in rhyming text of the life cycle of the American robin and its migratory and other behaviors, a detailed section gives additional facts and tips. (Rev: SLJ 5/04) [598.8]

22827 Post, Hans, and Kees Heij. *Sparrows* (PS–2). Illus. by Irene Goede. 2008, Boyds Mills $16.95 (978-1-59078-570-6). 32pp. An appealing and informative large-format look at the life cycle of the house sparrow. (Rev: BL 8/08; LMC 10/08) [598.8]

22828 Powell, Jillian. *Eggs* (3–5). Illus. Series: Everyone Eats. 1997, Raintree LB $17.98 (978-0-8172-4759-1). 32pp. This book introduces eggs — their sizes, from caviar to ostrich; the construction, production, and nutritional value of chickens' eggs; rituals connected with eggs; and two recipes. (Rev: SLJ 8/97) [598.6]

22829 Pringle, Laurence. *Crows! Strange and Wonderful* (2–4). Illus. by Bob Marstall. 2002, Boyds Mills $15.95 (978-1-56397-899-9). 32pp. This is an absorbing, well-illustrated account of the life and behavior of the crow, showing the bird's intelligence, adaptability, and amazing ability to communicate. (Rev: BCCB 12/02; BL 11/1/02; HBG 3/03; SLJ 9/02) [598.964]

22830 Pyers, Greg. *Why Am I a Bird?* (3–5). Illus. Series: Classifying Animals. 2005, Raintree LB $27.50 (978-1-4109-2014-0); paper $7.85 (978-1-4109-2021-8). 32pp. Introduces readers to the process of scientific classification and then examines the unique physical characteristics — such as feathers, wings, and hollow bones — of birds as a class. (Rev: SLJ 4/06) [598]

22831 Rau, Dana Meachen. *The Robin in the Tree* (PS–1). 2006, Benchmark LB $22.79 (978-0-7614-2304-1). 24pp. With its child-friendly blend of rebuses and easy-to-understand text, this easy reader follows a typical day in a robin's life, providing basic information about the bird's physical characteristics, habitat, diet, behavior, and life cycle. (Rev: SLJ 12/06) [598.8]

22832 Rauzon, Mark J. *Parrots Around the World* (3–5). Series: Animals in Order. 2001, Watts LB $26.50 (978-0-531-11688-3). 32pp. Following a discussion of the parrot family, various species are introduced through color photographs and a brief text that describes anatomy, habits, and habitats. Also use *Pelicans, Cormorants, and Their Kin* (2002). (Rev: BL 6/1–15/01) [598.71]

22833 Reynolds, Cynthia Furlong. *The Far-Flung Adventures of Homer the Hummer* (1–3). Illus. by Catherine McClung. 2005, Mitten $17.95 (978-1-58726-269-2). 32pp. In the spring a ruby-throated hummingbird called Homer leaves the jungles of Costa Rica on a long and dangerous journey north to the United States, where he meets a female called Ruby in an artist's garden. (Rev: BL 9/1/05; SLJ 12/05)

22834 Ricciuti, Edward R. *Birds* (4–6). Illus. Series: Our Living World. 1993, Blackbirch LB $19.95 (978-1-56711-038-8). 64pp. This introduction covers general topics related to birds. (Rev: SLJ 8/93) [598]

22835 Robinson, Fay. *Singing Robins* (PS–2). Series: Pull Ahead Books. 2000, Lerner $22.60 (978-0-8225-3641-3). 32pp. With four lines of simple text and a color photo on each page, this book tells of the bird with the beautiful orange breast feathers and the pretty blue eggs. (Rev: BL 5/15/00; HBG 9/00) [598.8]

22836 Roop, Peter, and Connie Roop. *Seasons of the Crane* (2–6). Illus. 1989, Walker LB $15.85 (978-0-8027-6860-5). 48pp. With outstanding photos and lucid text, the migratory habits of this endangered bird are described. (Rev: BL 8/89; SLJ 9/89) [598.31]

22837 Savage, Stephen. *Birds* (2–4). Illus. Series: What's the Difference? 2000, Raintree $25.69 (978-0-7398-1356-0). 32pp. A most attractive volume that presents a number of different birds and explains their common characteristics, along with material on their nests, food, and how they care for their young. (Rev: BL 10/15/00; HBG 3/01) [598]

22838 Sayre, April P. *The Hungry Hummingbird* (K–3). Illus. by Gay Holland. 2001, Millbrook LB $22.90 (978-0-7613-1951-1). 32pp. A hungry little hummingbird searches for food in this beautifully illustrated book. (Rev: BL 11/15/01; HBG 3/02; SLJ 11/01) [598.7]

22839 Sexton, Colleen. *Puffins* (K–3). Series: Blastoff! Readers: Oceans Alive. 2009, Children's Pr. LB $20.00 (978-0-531-21714-6). 24pp. With color photographs and clearly defined scientific terms, this simple book introduces beginning readers to the puffin. (Rev: SLJ 6/09) [598.3]

22840 Sill, Cathryn. *About Birds: A Guide for Children* (3–6). Illus. by John Sill. 1991, Peachtree $14.95 (978-1-56145-028-2). 40pp. This very simple introduction to birds describes common species and their characteristics. (Rev: BL 12/15/91; SLJ 2/92*) [598]

22841 Smith, Roland. *Vultures* (2–3). Series: Early Bird Nature Books. 1998, Lerner LB $25.26 (978-0-8225-3011-4). 48pp. A sympathetic, easily read introduction to the world of the vulture, including the ways they find and eat their food, their life cycle, and habitats. (Rev: BL 3/15/98; HBG 9/98; SLJ 3/98) [598]

22842 Spaulding, Dean T. *Feeding Our Feathered Friends* (4–6). Series: Birder's Bookshelf. 1997, Lerner LB $19.93 (978-0-8225-3175-3). 56pp. This book covers many aspects of backyard bird feeding, like how to build bird feeders, where and when to hang them, their contents, and how to keep squirrels away. (Rev: BL 3/15/98; HBG 3/98; SLJ 4/98) [598]

22843 Spaulding, Dean T. *Housing Our Feathered Friends* (4–6). Illus. Series: Birder's Bookshelf. 1997, Lerner LB $19.93 (978-0-8225-3176-0). 56pp. As well as supplying information on nests and other conveniences birds use as homes, this book gives directions on how to make a number of birdhouses. Also use: *Protecting Our Feathered Friends* (1997). (Rev: BL 10/15/97; HBG 3/98; SLJ 9/97) [690]

22844 Spaulding, Dean T. *Watching Our Feathered Friends* (4–6). Series: Birder's Bookshelf. 1997, Lerner LB $19.93 (978-0-8225-3177-7). 56pp. This book introduces the hobby of bird watching, with material on its history, how to use a field guide, the best times and places for birding, and the necessary equipment. (Rev: BL 3/15/98; HBG 3/98) [598]

22845 Spilsbury, Richard, and Louise Spilsbury. *A Murder of Crows* (3–5). Series: Animal Groups. 2003, Heinemann LB $24.22 (978-1-4034-0742-9). 32pp. In this attractively illustrated book readers learn about the crow's habitat, diet, hierarchical social structure, and behavior in groups. (Rev: HBG 10/03; SLJ 9/03) [598.8]

22846 Staub, Frank. *Herons* (2–5). Illus. Series: Early Bird. 1997, Lerner LB $25.26 (978-0-8225-3017-6). 48pp. Text and wonderful photos introduce a variety of heron species and their behavior and habitats. (Rev: BL 7/97; SLJ 8/97) [598.3]

22847 Stewart, Melissa. *A Place for Birds* (K–3). Illus. by Higgins Bond. 2009, Peachtree $16.95 (978-1-56145-474-7). 28pp. This attractive title highlights the ways in which humans threaten the lives of birds, recommends environmentally conscious behavior, and includes species maps of North America. (Rev: BL 3/15/09; SLJ 5/09) [598]

22848 Stone, Lynn M. *Sandhill Cranes* (2–3). Series: Early Bird Nature Books. 1998, Lerner LB $25.26 (978-0-8225-3027-5). 48pp. This easily read, beautifully illustrated account introduces the sand hill crane and its life cycle, with material on its habitat, food, and enemies. (Rev: BL 3/15/98; HBG 9/98; SLJ 7/98) [597]

22849 Swinburne, Stephen. *Unbeatable Beaks* (PS–3). Illus. by Joan Paley. 1999, Holt $15.95 (978-0-8050-4802-5). Using colorful collages and a singsong verse, this book introduces 39 birds each with a distinctive beak and also includes a quiz to match the birds with their beaks. (Rev: BCCB 11/99; HBG 4/00; SLJ 11/99) [598]

22850 Taylor, Kenny. *Puffins* (5–9). Series: WorldLife Library. 1999, Voyageur paper $16.95 (978-0-89658-419-8). 72pp. Outstanding photographs and conservation awareness are highlights of this introduction to puffins, their characteristics, habitats, and habits. (Rev: BL 8/99) [598.3]

22851 Tesar, Jenny. *What on Earth Is a Bustard?* (3–5). Illus. Series: What on Earth? 1996, Blackbirch LB $24.94 (978-1-56711-102-6). 32pp. Examines the world of the bustard, a ground-dwelling bird found in grasslands on several continents. (Rev: SLJ 2/97) [598]

22852 Townsend, Emily Rose. *Woodpeckers* (PS–2). 2004, Capstone LB $17.26 (978-0-7368-2070-7). 24pp. Presents basic information on woodpeckers in a small format with brief text facing full-color close-up photographs. (Rev: SLJ 8/04) [598]

22853 Underwood, Deborah. *Colorful Peacocks* (2–3). Series: Pull Ahead Books. 2006, Lerner LB $22.60 (978-0-8225-5930-6). 32pp. This colorful introduction to peacocks examines the birds' physical characteristics, diet, behavior, and habitat, and looks at how peacock parents care for their young. (Rev: SLJ 9/06) [598.6]

22854 Wechsler, Doug. *Bizarre Birds* (3–5). Illus. 1999, Boyds Mills $17.95 (978-1-56397-760-2). 48pp. This description of birds with unique habits — such as strange food preferences — offers scientific explanations for their behavior. (Rev: BL 1/1–15/00; HBG 4/00; SLJ 11/99) [598]

22855 Weidensaul, Scott, and National Audubon Society, eds. *National Audubon Society First Field Guide: Birds* (4–8). Illus. 1998, Scholastic paper $17.95 (978-0-590-05446-1). After a general introduction to ornithology, this guide describes and pictures several species of birds, including markings, eating, mating and nesting habits, migration, and endangered status. (Rev: BL 8/98; SLJ 10/98) [598]

22856 Welsbacher, Anne. *Wading Birds* (K–2). Photos by John Netherton. Series: Pull Ahead Books. 1999, Lerner LB $22.60 (978-0-8225-3614-7). 32pp. This book focuses on herons as wading birds and describes their physical characteristics, food, where they live, and how they bring up their young. (Rev: HBG 9/99; SLJ 5/99) [598]

22857 Wilkes, Angela. *Question Time: Birds* (3–5). Illus. Series: Question Time. 2002, Kingfisher $11.95 (978-0-7534-5450-3); paper $6.95 (978-0-7534-5462-6). 32pp. Topics covered in a question-and-answer format include the different types of birds, and their characteristics, habitat, and defense mechanisms. (Rev: HBG 3/03; SLJ 2/03)

22858 Williams, Nick. *How Birds Fly* (3–5). Illus. Series: Nature's Mysteries. 1996, Benchmark LB $22.79 (978-0-7614-0454-5). 32pp. The flight of birds is explained through an investigation of the internal and external design of their bodies in this book that gives many different examples and descriptions to amplify the text. (Rev: SLJ 2/97) [598]

22859 Willis, Nancy C. *The Robins in Your Backyard* (K–3). Illus. 1996, Cucumber Island Storytellers $15.95 (978-1-887813-21-1). 32pp. The life of robins is covered, with material on mating habits and nest building. (Rev: BCCB 6/97; BL 1/1–15/97; SLJ 7/97) [598.8]

22860 Willis, Nancy Carol. *Red Knot: A Shorebird's Incredible Journey* (2–4). 2006, Birdsong $15.95 (978-0-9662761-4-5); paper $6.95 (978-0-9662761-5-2). 32pp. Using the form of journal entries, this picture book follows the red knot shorebird on its incredible 20,000-mile annual migration. (Rev: BL 6/1–15/06; SLJ 7/06) [598.3]

22861 Winner, Cherie. *Everything Bird: What Kids Really Want to Know About Birds* (3–4). 2007, NorthWord LB $10.95 (978-1-55971-962-9); paper $7.95 (978-1-55971-963-6). 64pp. Questions and answers about birds provide plenty of interesting information about these feathered friends. With photographs. (Rev: SLJ 8/07)

22862 Winner, Cherie. *Woodpeckers* (3–6). Series: Nature Watch. 2000, Carolrhoda LB $25.26 (978-1-57505-445-2). 48pp. This colorful introduction to the varieties of woodpeckers explains why they tap holes in wood. (Rev: BL 7/00; HBG 10/01) [598]

22863 Zim, Herbert S., and Ira N. Gabrielson. *Birds* (5–8). Illus. 1991, Western paper $21.27 (978-0-307-64053-6). A guide to the most commonly seen birds, with accompanying illustrations and basic materials. [598]

BEHAVIOR

22864 Bash, Barbara. *Urban Roosts: Where Birds Nest in the City* (3–5). Illus. 1992, Little, Brown paper $6.95 (978-0-316-08312-6). 32pp. This unusual nature study shows that wildlife can thrive in an urban setting. (Rev: BCCB 3/91; BL 1/1/91*; HB 1/91; SLJ 11/90*) [598]

22865 Johnson, Sylvia A. *Inside an Egg* (5–8). Illus. 1982, Lerner LB $31.95 (978-0-8225-1472-5); paper $5.95 (978-0-8225-9522-9). 48pp. An excellently illustrated account tracing the growth of a chicken in an egg until it is hatched. [598]

22866 Johnson, Sylvia A. *Songbirds: The Language of Song* (3–6). Series: Nature Watch. 2000, Carolrhoda LB $25.26 (978-1-57505-483-4). 48pp. This book introduces a number of songbirds and describes their songs. (Rev: BL 3/1/01; HBG 10/01) [598]

22867 Kelly, Irene. *Even an Ostrich Needs a Nest: Where Birds Begin* (1–3). Illus. by author. 2009, Holiday $16.95 (978-0-8234-2102-2). 32pp. An appealing and informative look at bird nests, the materials used, and how they are constructed. (Rev: BL 3/1/09; SLJ 6/09) [598.156]

22868 Stevens, Ann Shepard. *Strange Nests* (2–5). Illus. by Jennifer O. Dewey. 1998, Millbrook LB $21.90 (978-0-7613-0413-5). 31pp. Covers the nests and building habits of 11 common North American birds, including robins, swallows, eagles, wrens, house sparrows, Baltimore orioles, and crows. (Rev: HBG 9/99; SLJ 7/99) [598]

22869 Winer, Yvonne. *Birds Build Nests* (PS–3). Illus. by Tony Oliver. 2002, Charlesbridge $16.95 (978-1-57091-500-0); paper $6.95 (978-1-57091-501-7). 32pp. A lovely book of poetic text and beautiful, realistic illustrations that introduces the nesting habits of various species of birds to younger readers. (Rev: BL 3/1/02; HBG 10/02; SLJ 3/02) [598.156]

DUCKS, GEESE, AND SWANS

22870 Cooper, Jason. *Canada Goose* (1–3). Series: Life Cycles. 2002, Rourke LB $17.95 (978-1-58952-351-7). 24pp. Handsome photographs and simple text describe the life cycle, habitat, appearance, and behavior of these animals. (Rev: SLJ 12/02)

22871 Goldin, Augusta. *Ducks Don't Get Wet* (PS–2). Illus. Series: Let's-Read-and-Find-Out. 1999, HarperCollins LB $15.89 (978-0-06-027882-3); paper $5.99 (978-0-06-445187-1). 32pp. Explains why ducks don't get wet in water and introduces several types of wild ducks, their habits, diet, migration, and habitats. (Rev: BL 8/99*; HBG 9/99; SLJ 6/99) [598.4]

22872 Helget, Nicole. *Swans* (4–7). Series: Living Wild. 2008, Smart Apple LB $32.80 (978-1-58341-659-4). 48pp. With excellent color photographs and extensive explanatory text this book looks at the seven species of swans, including humanity's influence on and involvement with the birds. (Rev: SLJ 2/09) [598.4]

22873 Hickman, Pamela. *A New Duck: My First Look at the Life Cycle of a Bird* (PS–K). Illus. by Heather Collins. Series: My First Look At. 1999, Kids Can $6.95 (978-1-55074-613-6). 20pp. The nesting habits of a pair of mallards and the hatching and growth of their ducklings are covered in attractive pictures and simple text. (Rev: HBG 9/99; SLJ 8/99) [598.4]

22874 Hipp, Andrew. *The Life Cycle of a Duck* (PS–2). Illus. by Dwight Kuhn. Series: Life Cycle Of. 2002, Rosen LB $19.95 (978-0-8239-5868-9). 24pp. This book for beginning readers follows the life of a duck from conception to adulthood. (Rev: BL 12/15/02) [598.4]

22875 Horton, Tom. *Swanfall: Journey of the Tundra Swans* (4–6). Illus. by David Harp. 1991, Walker LB $16.85 (978-0-8027-8107-9). 48pp. All about migration and the life of a swan family for one year. (Rev: BCCB 2/92; BL 12/15/91) [598.4]

22876 Llewellyn, Claire. *Duck* (K–3). Illus. by Simon Mendez. Series: Starting Life. 2004, NorthWord $16.95 (978-1-55971-878-3). 32pp. An innovative picture-book layout enhances the journey of the mallard duck from egg to adult. (Rev: BL 4/15/04; SLJ 11/04) [598.4]

22877 Loomis, Jennifer A. *A Duck in a Tree* (K–3). Illus. 1996, Stemmer $18.95 (978-0-88045-136-9). 40pp. A year in the lives of two wood ducks includes raising a family and migrating to Florida. (Rev: BL 2/1/97) [598.4]

22878 Mara, Wil. *Ducks* (4–6). Series: Animals Animals. 2008, Marshall Cavendish LB $20.95 (978-0-7614-2927-2). 48pp. *Ducks* clearly defines various types of ducks, their habits and habitats, and how humans affect them. (Rev: SLJ 2/09) [598.4]

22879 Miller, Sara S. *Waterfowl: From Swans to Screamers* (3–5). Series: Animals in Order. 1999, Watts LB $26.50 (978-0-531-11584-8). 48pp. After a discussion of animal classification, water birds are introduced and several are pictured and described. (Rev: BL 12/15/99; HBG 4/00) [598.4]

22880 Osborn, Elinor. *Project UltraSwan* (3–6). Illus. 2002, Houghton $16.00 (978-0-618-14528-7). 64pp. This is a fascinating and readable account of how scientists using ultralight aircraft are working to help trumpeter swans to rediscover their migratory routes. (Rev: BCCB 12/02; BL 12/15/02; HB 1/03; HBG 3/03; SLJ 6/03) [598.4]

22881 Savage, Stephen. *Duck* (K–2). Illus. by Stephen Lings. Series: Observing Nature. 1995, Thomson Learning LB $21.20 (978-1-56847-328-4). 32pp. Using double-page spreads, very basic information is given on the life cycle of the mallard duck. (Rev: SLJ 10/95) [598.4]

22882 Savage, Stephen. *Duck* (3–6). Illus. Series: Animal Neighbors. 2008, Rosen LB $23.95 (978-1-4358-4988-4). 32pp. This title includes details about a duck's life and habitat and has clear easy text and large photographs which help explain a duck's anatomy. (Rev: SLJ 5/09) [598.4]

22883 Sayre, April P. *Honk, Honk, Goose! Canada Geese Start a Family* (K–3). Illus. by Huy Voun Lee. 2009, Holt $16.95 (978-0-8050-7103-0). 32pp.

A pair of geese mate mate, build a nest, protect the eggs, and nurture the young; detailed information appears at the back of the book. (Rev: BL 3/1/09; HB 5/09; SLJ 4/09)

22884 Spilsbury, Louise. *Duck* (K–2). Series: Life Cycles. 2005, Heinemann LB $20.64 (978-1-4034-6771-3). 24pp. Simple easy-reader questions and answers about ducks and how they grow are accompanied by color photographs. (Rev: SLJ 7/05) [598.4]

22885 Stockland, Patricia M. *On the Duck Pond* (K–2). Illus. by Todd Ouren. Series: Barnyard Buddies. 2008, ABDO LB $17.95 (978-1-60270-027-7). 24pp. Simple facts about ducks are presented in two formats — information about a fictional family of ducks in larger type, with specific features highlighted in smaller type alongside; clear illustrations and a labeled diagram are also included. (Rev: BL 10/15/07; SLJ 2/08) [636.5]

22886 Stone, Lynn M. *Swans* (2–3). Series: Early Bird Nature Books. 1997, Lerner LB $23.93 (978-0-8225-3019-0). 48pp. A well-written introduction for beginners to these handsome birds, with a simple text and many color photos. (Rev: BL 9/15/97; SLJ 10/97) [598.4]

22887 Wallace, Karen. *Duckling Days* (1). Illus. Series: Eyewitness Reader. 1999, DK paper $3.99 (978-0-7894-3994-9). 32pp. Six ducks hatch from mother duck's eggs, one of them a loner in this easily read book. (Rev: BL 5/15/99; HBG 9/99) [598.4]

22888 Watts, Barrie. *Duck* (K–3). Illus. 2002, Smart Apple LB $24.25 (978-1-58340-197-2). 32pp. This easy-to-read book about ducks includes loads of facts and excellent photography. (Rev: BL 10/15/02; HBG 3/03) [598.4]

EAGLES, HAWKS, AND OTHER BIRDS OF PREY

22889 Arnold, Caroline. *Saving the Peregrine Falcon* (4–6). Illus. 1985, Lerner paper $25.26 (978-0-87614-523-4). 48pp. Once threatened because its eggs were weakened by the pesticide DDT, the peregrine falcon can now be seen in American cities. The story of their comeback. (Rev: BCCB 3/85; BL 4/1/85; SLJ 3/85)

22890 Bailey, Jill. *Birds of Prey* (5–8). Illus. 1988, Facts on File $17.55 (978-0-8160-1655-6). In brief, lavishly illustrated chapters, various characteristics of birds of prey are explored and the most important types are described. (Rev: SLJ 1/89) [598]

22891 Bailey, Jill. *The Secret Life of Falcons* (4–7). Series: The Secret World of . . . 2002, Raintree LB $27.12 (978-0-7398-4985-9). 48pp. This book describes the anatomy and habits of the falcon with material on how they feed, communicate, and reproduce. (Rev: BL 8/02) [598.9]

22892 Bardhan-Quallen, Sudipta. *Flying Eagle* (K–3). Illus. by Deborah Kogan Ray. 2009, Charlesbridge $15.95 (978-1-57091-671-7). 32pp. A tawny eagle soars over the Serengeti in search of food for his young, giving readers a view of the wildlife below and the dangers of life there; effective watercolors are accompanied by simple rhymes. (Rev: BL 4/1/09; SLJ 3/09) [598.9]

22893 Bernhard, Emery. *Eagles: Lions of the Sky* (PS–3). Illus. by Durga Bernhard. 1994, Holiday House LB $15.95 (978-0-8234-1105-4). 32pp. Many aspects of the life of eagles, including mating, eating, flying, hunting, and parenting, are discussed in this richly illustrated book. (Rev: BL 2/1/94; HB 5/94; SLJ 5/94) [598.9]

22894 Collard, Sneed B. *Birds of Prey: A Look at Daytime Raptors* (4–7). Illus. 1999, Watts LB $25.50 (978-0-531-20363-7). 64pp. Eagles, hawks, ospreys, falcons, and vultures of North America are introduced with material on the appearance and habits of each. (Rev: BL 10/15/99; HBG 3/00) [598.9]

22895 Colman, C. H. *The Bald Eagle's View of American History* (1–4). Illus. by Joanne Friar. 2006, Charlesbridge paper $5.95 (978-1-58089-301-5). 48pp. Postage-stamp depictions of the bald eagle illustrate this history of the bird, threats to its existence, and its importance as a symbol. (Rev: SLJ 1/07) [929.9]

22896 Evert, Laura, and Wayne Lynch. *Birds of Prey* (3–6). Illus. by Sherry Neidigh and John F. McGee. Series: Our Wild World. 2005, NorthWord $16.95 (978-1-55971-925-4). 191pp. An attractive, well-organized and easily accessible introduction to the four major subdivisions of raptors: eagles, falcons, owls, and vultures. (Rev: SLJ 11/05)

22897 Gibbons, Gail. *Soaring with the Wind: The Bald Eagle* (3–5). Illus. 1998, Morrow $16.99 (978-0-688-13730-4). 32pp. Excellent full-color illustrations dominate this account of the bald eagle, its characteristics, behavior, life cycle, struggle for survival, and its emergence as a national symbol. (Rev: BL 4/15/98; HBG 3/99; SLJ 4/98) [598.9]

22898 Goldish, Meish. *Bald Eagles: A Chemical Nightmare* (3–5). Series: America's Animal Comebacks. 2008, Bearport LB $25.27 (978-1-59716-505-1). 32pp. With eye-catching photographs and an appealing format, this volume looks at the reasons for the decline in the eagle population (mainly hunting and pesticides) and the measures that succeeded in bring them back from the brink of extinction. (Rev: LMC 1/08; SLJ 2/08) [598.9]

22899 Goldish, Meish. *California Condors: Saved by Captive Breeding* (3–6). Series: America's Animal Comebacks. 2009, Bearport LB $25.27 (978-1-59716-741-3). 32pp. Goldish traces the condor's struggle to survive and scientists' efforts to bring this animal back into its natural habitat. (Rev: SLJ 5/09)

22900 Hodge, Deborah. *Eagles* (2–5). Illus. Series: Kids Can! 2000, Kids Can $10.95 (978-1-55074-715-7); paper $5.95 (978-1-55074-717-1). 32pp. After a general look at eagles around the world, this account focuses on two American breeds and gives information on their habitats, food, physical characteristics, flight, behavior, and young. (Rev: BL 11/1/00; HBG 3/01) [598.9]

22901 Horton, Casey. *Eagles* (4–6). Illus. Series: Endangered! 1996, Benchmark LB $25.64 (978-0-

7614-0214-5). 32pp. The endangered eagle is presented, with individual chapters on eight species. (Rev: SLJ 4/96) [598.9]

22902 Latimer, Jonathan P., and Karen Stray Nolting. *Birds of Prey* (3–6). Illus. Series: Peterson Field Guides for Young Naturalists. 1999, Houghton paper $5.95 (978-0-395-92277-4). 48pp. A general introduction to birds of prey is followed by 20 double-page spreads that introduce the appearance and habits of such birds as eagles, hawks, falcons, and owls. (Rev: BL 6/1–15/99; SLJ 8/99) [598.9]

22903 Laubach, Christyna, et al. *Raptor! A Kid's Guide to Birds of Prey* (4–7). Illus. 2002, Storey paper $14.95 (978-1-58017-445-9). 128pp. A large-format treasure trove of facts about raptors, with information on individual species, identification, habits, habitat, range maps, and so forth. (Rev: BL 12/1/02; HBG 3/03; SLJ 10/02) [598.9]

22904 Lynch, Wayne. *Falcons* (3–5). Photos by author. Illus. by Sherry Neidigh. Series: Our Wild World. 2005, NorthWord $10.95 (978-1-55971-911-7); paper $7.95 (978-1-55971-912-4). 47pp. With eye-catching photographs and readable text, this book discusses the physical characteristics, life cycle, diet, habitat, and family life of the falcons of North America. Also use *Vultures* (2005). (Rev: SLJ 8/05) [598.9]

22905 McCarthy, Meghan. *City Hawk: The Story of Pale Male* (PS–3). Illus. by author. 2007, Simon & Schuster $15.99 (978-1-4169-3359-5). Bird watchers follow a red-tailed hawk as he and his mate make a nest and raise their young on a Central Park building in 1991. (Rev: BCCB 10/07; LMC 1/08; SLJ 10/07) [598.9]

22906 MacKen, JoAnn Early. *Golden Eagles / Águila real* (2–4). Trans. by Tatiana Acosta and Guillermo Gutiérrez. Series: Animals That Live in the Mountains / Animales de las montañas. 2006, Weekly Reader LB $21.00 (978-0-8368-6450-2). 24pp. A beginning book with facts about golden eagles in both English and Spanish. (Rev: SLJ 6/06) [598.9]

22907 Martin-James, Kathleen. *Soaring Bald Eagles* (PS–2). Series: Pull Ahead Books. 2001, Lerner LB $22.60 (978-0-8225-3636-9). 32pp. A few lines of simple text plus a color photograph on each page present the world of bald eagles to beginning readers. (Rev: BL 6/1–15/01; HBG 10/01) [598.9]

22908 Morrison, Gordon. *Bald Eagle* (PS–4). Illus. 1998, Houghton $16.00 (978-0-395-87328-1). 32pp. Using watercolor paintings that trace the life cycle of two bald eagles, from hatching to producing an egg of their own, this is a fine introduction to these majestic birds of prey. (Rev: BL 6/1–15/98; HBG 3/99; SLJ 5/98) [598.9]

22909 Patent, Dorothy Hinshaw. *The Bald Eagle Returns* (4–8). Illus. 2000, Clarion $16.00 (978-0-395-91416-8). 68pp. This book not only discusses the successful efforts to save the bald eagle but also gives material on its anatomy, habitats, mating, and behavior. (Rev: BCCB 1/01; BL 10/15/00; HBG 10/01; SLJ 11/00) [598.9]

22910 Patent, Dorothy Hinshaw. *Eagles of America* (4–6). Photos by William Munoz. 1995, Holiday

House $15.95 (978-0-8234-1198-6). 40pp. Bald and golden eagles are described, with information on their habits and endangered status. (Rev: BL 3/1/96; SLJ 2/96) [598.9]

22911 Povey, Karen D. *Falcons* (4–6). Illus. Series: Nature's Predators. 2005, Gale LB $26.20 (978-0-7377-2347-2). 48pp. In four brief chapters, the lives of falcons are explored with material on the food they eat and how they catch it.

22912 Priebe, Mac. *The Peregrine Falcon* (2–5). Illus. by Jennifer Priebe. 1999, Mindfull $15.95 (978-0-9669551-9-4). 32pp. This environmental success story tells how the peregrine falcon was saved from extinction by the banning of the pesticide DDT. (Rev: SLJ 4/00) [598.9]

22913 Rauzon, Mark. *Golden Eagles of Devil Mountain* (3–5). Series: Wildlife Conservation Society Books. 2000, Watts LB $24.50 (978-0-531-11787-3). 48pp. The golden eagle is introduced, with material on its anatomy, behavioral patterns, life cycle, and habitat. (Rev: BL 3/15/01) [598.9]

22914 Sayre, April P. *Vulture View* (K–2). Illus. by Steven Jenkins. 2007, Holt $16.95 (978-0-8050-7557-1). 32pp. Brief, rhyming text and brilliant-colored collage backgrounds show the lives of vultures, ending with a more-detailed informational spread about "nature's cleanup crew." (Rev: BCCB 11/07; BL 11/1/07; HB 11/07; SLJ 12/07) [598.9]

22915 Schulman, Janet. *Pale Male: Citizen Hawk of New York City* (1–3). Illus. by Meilo So. 2008, Knopf $16.99 (978-0-375-84558-1). 40pp. The story of a red-tailed hawk who nested on a ledge of an exclusive New York City building and the resulting clash between residents and environmentalists. (Rev: BL 2/15/08; HB 3/08; LMC 3/08; SLJ 1/08) [598.9]

22916 Silverstein, Alvin, et al. *The California Condor* (3–6). Illus. Series: Endangered in America. 1998, Millbrook LB $22.40 (978-0-7613-0264-3). 64pp. In addition to a description of the characteristics and habits of the California condor, this book explains why the species has declined in number and outlines efforts to save it. (Rev: BL 9/1/98; HBG 9/98) [639.97]

22917 Stone, Lynn M. *Vultures* (3–6). Illus. Series: Nature Watch. 1993, Carolrhoda LB $14.95 (978-0-87614-768-9). 48pp. The life cycle of the vulture is covered, and material is given on its habitat and food. (Rev: BL 8/93; SLJ 8/93*) [598.9]

22918 Swinburne, Stephen. *In Good Hands: Behind the Scenes at a Center for Orphaned and Injured Birds* (3–6). Illus. 1998, Sierra Club $16.95 (978-0-87156-397-2). 32pp. A behind-the-scenes visit to the Vermont Raptor Center where orphaned or injured birds of prey, such as owls and eagles, are cared for. (Rev: BL 7/98; HBG 3/99; SLJ 8/98) [639.9]

22919 Unwin, Mike. *Peregrine Falcon* (4–6). Illus. Series: Animals Under Threat. 2004, Heinemann LB $18.95 (978-1-4034-4862-0). 48pp. The life cycle of the peregrine falcon and threats to its survival are explored in this blend of narrative and eye-catching color photography.

GULLS AND OTHER SEA BIRDS

22920 Bentley, Dawn. *Welcome Back, Puffin!* (PS–2). Illus. by Beth Stover. Series: Read-and-Discover Atlantic Wilderness Adventures. 2003, Soundprints paper $3.95 (978-1-59249-009-7). 48pp. This appealing title follows a female puffin and her mate as they make their annual visit to an island; soon after they arrive, the female lays a single egg, and she and her mate keep it warm until it hatches, after which they're kept busy gathering food for the hatchling that eats ten times a day. (Rev: SLJ 1/04)

22921 Gibbons, Gail. *Gulls . . . Gulls . . . Gulls* (3–5). Illus. 1997, Holiday House LB $16.95 (978-0-8234-1323-2). 32pp. Brief text and watercolor pictures are used to explore the world of the gull, its structure, diet, habits, mating behavior, and migration. (Rev: BL 9/1/97; HBG 3/98; SLJ 9/97) [598.3]

22922 Holling, Holling C. *Seabird* (4–6). 1978, Houghton $20.00 (978-0-395-18230-7); paper $11.95 (978-0-395-26681-6). A gull accompanies a whaling expedition.

22923 Kress, Stephen W., and Pete Salmansohn. *Project Puffin: How We Brought Puffins Back to Egg Rock* (3–6). Illus. 1997, Tilbury House $16.95 (978-0-88448-170-6). 40pp. A first-person narrative about the project starting in 1973 that had as a goal bringing puffins back to Eastern Egg Rock off the Maine coast. (Rev: BCCB 7–8/97; BL 8/97) [636.9]

22924 McMillan, Bruce. *Nights of the Pufflings* (2–4). Illus. 1995, Houghton $16.00 (978-0-395-70810-1). 32pp. On an island off the coast of Iceland, children help young puffins succeed in their first flight. (Rev: BCCB 3/95; BL 3/15/95; SLJ 3/95*) [598.3]

22925 Miller, Sara S. *Shorebirds: From Stilts to Sanderlings* (3–5). Illus. Series: Animals in Order. 2000, Watts LB $26.50 (978-0-531-11596-1). 48pp. Introductory material on animal classification is followed by an overview of shorebirds, their varieties, habits, structure, and care of young. (Rev: BL 9/15/00) [598.29]

22926 Quinlan, Susan E. *Puffins* (3–5). Illus. 1999, Lerner LB $25.26 (978-1-57505-090-4). 48pp. Three species of puffins are introduced, with material on their life cycles, habits, and habitats. (Rev: BL 1/1–15/99; HBG 9/99; SLJ 2/99) [598.3]

22927 Webb, Sophie. *Looking for Seabirds: Journal from an Alaskan Voyage* (4–6). Illus. 2004, Houghton $16.00 (978-0-618-21235-4). 48pp. The author conveys the excitement of research in this fact-filled account of a shipboard bird-counting expedition. (Rev: BL 4/15/04; HB 5/04; SLJ 5/04) [598.177]

22928 Welsbacher, Anne. *Flying Brown Pelicans* (K–2). Photos by John Netherton. Series: Pull Ahead Books. 1999, Lerner LB $22.60 (978-0-8225-3613-0). 32pp. A colorful introduction to pelicans that includes material on appearance, habits, habitats, a map, and a physiological diagram. (Rev: HBG 9/99; SLJ 5/99) [598]

22929 Zecca, Katherine. *A Puffin's Year* (PS–3). Illus. 2007, Down East $15.95 (978-0-89272-742-1). 32pp. Clearly written and well designed, this appealing book about puffins' life cycle includes a conservation message from the National Audubon Society. (Rev: BL 5/1/07; SLJ 8/07) [598.3]

OWLS

22930 Browne, Vee. *Owl* (PS–3). Illus. by Diana Magnuson. Series: Animal Lore and Legend. 1995, Scholastic paper $4.95 (978-0-590-22488-8). 32pp. Factual information is given about owls on their characteristics, habitats, species, and food, as well as three folktales. (Rev: SLJ 3/96) [598.9]

22931 Epple, Wolfgang. *Barn Owls* (3–6). Illus. by Manfred Rogl. Series: Nature Watch. 1992, Carolrhoda LB $25.26 (978-0-87614-742-9). 48pp. This informative book looks at the life cycle, habitat, and feeding habits of the barn owl. (Rev: BCCB 1/93*; BL 10/1/92; SLJ 1/93) [598.97]

22932 Esbensen, Barbara J. *Tiger with Wings: The Great Horned Owl* (3–5). Illus. by Mary B. Brown. 1991, Orchard $16.95 (978-0-531-05940-1). 32pp. This deadly hunter, with stripes and a catlike face, is known as a tiger with wings. (Rev: BL 9/1/91; HB 9/91; SLJ 8/91*) [598.97]

22933 Gibbons, Gail. *Owls* (K–3). Illus. 2005, Holiday House $16.95 (978-0-8234-1880-0). 32pp. All about the owls that are native to North America, with watercolor illustrations and a section about an owl family. (Rev: BL 3/15/05; SLJ 4/05) [598.9]

22934 Hiscock, Bruce. *Ookpik: The Travels of a Snowy Owl* (K–3). Illus. by author. 2008, Boyds Mills $16.95 (978-1-59078-461-7). 32pp. A snowy owl hatches in the arctic tundra and migrates to a farm in the Adirondacks, facing many challenges along the way; with a final page of facts. (Rev: BL 1/1–15/08; LMC 3/08; SLJ 6/08) [598.9]

22935 Jarvis, Kila, and Denver W. Holt. *Owls: Whoo Are They?* (3–5). Illus. 1996, Mountain paper $12.00 (978-0-87842-336-1). 64pp. This introduction to owls includes descriptions of the 19 species found in North America. (Rev: BL 8/96; SLJ 12/96) [598.9]

22936 Landau, Elaine. *Owls: Hunters of the Night* (2–4). Illus. Series: Animals after Dark. 2007, Enslow LB $16.95 (978-0-7660-2768-8). 32pp. Large color photographs accompany basic facts about owls' physical characteristics and behavior. (Rev: BL 5/15/07; LMC 10/07; SLJ 8/07) [598.9]

22937 Lang, Aubrey. *Baby Owl* (1–3). Photos by Wayne Lynch. Series: Nature Babies. 2004, Fitzhenry & Whiteside $11.95 (978-1-55041-796-8); paper $5.95 (978-1-55041-798-2). 36pp. Full-color photographs follow the development of three baby great horned owls from hatching to independence. (Rev: SLJ 2/05) [598.9]

22938 Lynch, Wayne. *Owls* (3–5). Photos by author. Illus. by Sherry Neidigh. Series: Our Wild World. 2005, NorthWord $10.95 (978-1-55971-914-8); paper $7.95 (978-1-55971-915-5). 47pp. With eye-catching photographs and readable text, this book discusses the physical characteristics, life cycle, diet, habitat, and family life of the owls of North America. (Rev: SLJ 8/05) [598.9]

22939 Markle, Sandra. *Owls* (3–6). Illus. Series: Animal Predators. 2004, Carolrhoda LB $25.26 (978-1-

57505-729-3). 40pp. Concise text and clear, full-page photographs introduce the life cycle of the owl and its physical characteristics, habitat, diet, and predatory behavior. (Rev: SLJ 12/04)

22940 Richardson, Adele D. *Owls: Flat-Faced Flyers* (1–3). Series: Wild World of Animals. 2002, Capstone LB $22.60 (978-0-7368-1396-9). 24pp. For beginning readers, this is an attractive introduction to owls, their appearance, habits, care of young, and habitats. (Rev: BL 1/1–15/03; HBG 3/03) [598.9]

22941 Silverstein, Alvin, et al. *The Spotted Owl* (4–8). Illus. Series: Endangered Species. 1994, Millbrook LB $24.90 (978-1-56294-415-5). 48pp. The story of the spotted owl, its endangered status, efforts to protect it, and the conflicts with the timber industry. (Rev: BL 4/15/95) [333.95]

22942 Stefoff, Rebecca. *Owl* (K–3). Series: Living Things. 1997, Marshall Cavendish LB $22.79 (978-0-7614-0443-9). 32pp. This simple introduction to the owl contains short bits of basic information and many colorful photos. (Rev: BL 2/15/98; HBG 3/98) [598.9]

22943 Townsend, Emily Rose. *Owls* (PS–2). Series: Woodland Animals. 2004, Capstone LB $17.26 (978-0-7368-2068-4). 24pp. Presents basic information on owls in a small format with brief text facing full-color close-up photographs. (Rev: SLJ 8/04) [598]

22944 Warhol, Tom. *Owls* (3–6). Series: AnimalWays. 2007, Marshall Cavendish LB $23.95 (978-0-7614-2537-3). 112pp. Information on owl lore and legend precedes details of owl evolution; types of owls; owl anatomy, characteristics, behavior, and reproduction; and threats to their survival. (Rev: SLJ 5/08) [598.9]

PENGUINS

22945 Arnold, Caroline. *A Penguin's World* (PS–2). Illus. Series: Caroline Arnold's Animals. 2006, Picture Window LB $26.60 (978-1-4048-1323-6). 24pp. With an accessible blend of paper collage artwork and easy-to-understand text, this picture book introduces basic facts about Adelie penguins and their family life. (Rev: BL 4/1/06; LMC 11/06; SLJ 6/06) [598.47]

22946 Barner, Bob. *Penguins, Penguins, Everywhere!* (PS–2). Illus. 2007, Chronicle $14.95 (978-0-8118-5664-5). 32pp. Basic information about penguins is couched in appealing rhyming text accompanied by bold illustrations. (Rev: BL 4/1/07) [598.47]

22947 Bonners, Susan. *A Penguin Year* (K–4). Illus. by author. 1981, Delacorte $9.43 (978-0-440-00170-6). 48pp. An introduction to the lifestyle of penguins of the South Pole.

22948 Bredeson, Carmen. *Emperor Penguins Up Close* (PS–3). Series: Zoom in on Animals! 2006, Enslow LB $21.26 (978-0-7660-2497-7). 24pp. Eye-catching full-color close-ups show key physical characteristics of the penguins, and the text gives basic details on diet, habitat, life cycle, and so forth. (Rev: SLJ 11/06) [598.47]

22949 Daigle, Evelyne. *The World of Penguins* (4–6). Trans. from French by Geneviève Wright. Illus. by

Daniel Grenier. 2007, Tundra $18.95 (978-0-88776-799-9). 48pp. Penguins' habitat, diet, anatomy, behavior, and distribution are all covered here, along with information about the author's 2003 trip to Antarctica to view the penguins. With photographs and illustrations. (Rev: SLJ 5/07)

22950 Fontanel, Beatrice. *The Penguin: A Funny Bird* (2–4). Illus. by Andre Fatras. 1992, Charlesbridge paper $6.95 (978-0-88106-426-1). 28pp. The growth, development, and behavior of this "funny bird" are presented in color photos and large format. (Rev: BL 2/1/93) [598]

22951 Gibbons, Gail. *Penguins!* (2–4). Illus. 1998, Holiday House $16.95 (978-0-8234-1388-1). With pen-and-ink and watercolor paintings, the author introduces different species of penguins and describes their characteristics, food, habits, and enemies. (Rev: BL 11/1/98; HBG 3/99; SLJ 11/98) [598.47]

22952 Guiberson, Brenda Z. *The Emperor Lays an Egg* (K–3). Illus. by Joan Paley. 2001, Holt $16.95 (978-0-8050-6204-5). 32pp. Colorful text and lovely collages depict a year in the life of a family of emperor penguins, showing the father's incredible care for the egg, the necessary swimming skills, and the struggle to stay warm in the frigid air. (Rev: BL 12/1/01; HB 1/02; HBG 3/02; SLJ 12/01*) [598.47]

22953 Hanel, Rachael. *Penguins* (4–7). Series: Living Wild. 2008, Smart Apple LB $32.80 (978-1-58341-658-7). 48pp. With excellent color photographs and extensive explanatory text this book looks at the 17 species of penguins, including humanity's influence on and involvement with the birds. (Rev: SLJ 2/09) [598.47]

22954 Jacquet, Luc. *March of the Penguins* (3–5). Illus. by Jerome Maison. 2005, National Geographic $30.00 (978-0-7922-6190-2). 160pp. A companion to the movie, this book also tells the story of emperor penguins' life cycle, and features many striking images; back matter includes a behind-the-scenes look at the making of the movie and additional information about the emperor penguins that were its stars. (Rev: BL 11/15/05) [598.47]

22955 Jango-Cohen, Judith. *Penguins* (3–5). Illus. Series: Animals, Animals. 2001, Benchmark LB $25.64 (978-0-7614-1260-1). 48pp. In addition to the usual information on the species, this book discusses the penguin's discovery and naming, and its relationship with humans. (Rev: HBG 10/02; SLJ 2/02) [598.47]

22956 Johnson, Sylvia A. *Penguins* (4–7). Illus. 1981, Lerner LB $22.60 (978-0-8225-1453-4). 48pp. Handsome photographs enliven the text of this introduction to penguins and their habitats. [598]

22957 Jonas, Ann. *Little Penguins* (1–3). Series: Born to Be Wild. 2005, Gareth Stevens LB $23.00 (978-0-8368-4738-3). 24pp. This colorful title introduces the physical and behavioral characteristics of penguins and examines how adult birds feed their offspring and protect them from predators. (Rev: SLJ 2/06) [598.4]

22958 Kalman, Bobbie. *The Life Cycle of an Emperor Penguin* (2–4). Illus. Series: Life Cycle. 2006, Crabtree LB $25.20 (978-0-7787-0630-4); paper $6.95 (978-0-7787-0704-2). 32pp. Report writers will find this a useful and interesting resource. Diet, habitat, behavior, and other aspects of emperor penguins are covered. Photographs and illustrations accompany the text, and vocabulary words appear in bold font. (Rev: SLJ 5/07)

22959 Kalman, Bobbie. *Penguins* (2–4). Illus. Series: Crabapples. 1995, Crabtree paper $5.95 (978-0-86505-724-1). 32pp. Color photos and text are used to give basic facts about the habits, anatomy, food, and enemies of penguins. (Rev: SLJ 5/96) [598.4]

22960 Lang, Aubrey. *Baby Penguin* (K–2). Illus. by Wayne Lynch. Series: Nature Babies. 2001, Fitzhenry & Whiteside $13.95 (978-1-55041-675-6). 28pp. Excellent photographs and a brief text present young penguins from birth to adolescence. (Rev: BL 12/15/01; SLJ 2/02) [598.47]

22961 Lynch, Wayne. *Penguins!* (4–7). Illus. 1999, Firefly LB $19.95 (978-1-55209-421-1); paper $9.95 (978-1-55209-424-2). 64pp. An appealing book that introduces penguins and their various species with coverage of their evolution, food, life cycle, habits, and habitats. (Rev: BCCB 12/99; BL 9/15/99; HBG 3/00) [598.47]

22962 McMillan, Bruce. *Penguins at Home: Gentoos of Antarctica* (3–6). Illus. 1993, Houghton $17.00 (978-0-395-66560-2). 32pp. A photo-essay on the Gentoo penguins of Antarctica that describes their anatomy, behavior, and mating cycle. (Rev: BCCB 9/93; BL 11/15/93; SLJ 12/93) [598]

22963 Markert, Jenny. *Penguins* (1–3). Illus. Series: New Naturebooks. 2007, Child's World LB $18.95 (978-1-59296-850-3). 32pp. Easily read text and large bright photographs introduce facts about penguins. (Rev: BL 10/1/07; SLJ 2/08) [598.47]

22964 Markle, Sandra. *A Mother's Journey* (K–3). Illus. by Alan Marks. 2005, Charlesbridge $16.95 (978-1-57091-621-2). 32pp. This handsome picture book chronicles the arduous journey of a female Emperor penguin from laying an egg through hunting for food for the newborn chick. (Rev: BL 9/1/05; SLJ 9/05) [598.47]

22965 Noonan, Diana. *The Emperor Penguin* (2–4). Series: Life Cycles. 2002, Chelsea LB $23.00 (978-0-7910-6965-3). 32pp. This account covers the life cycle of the Antarctic emperor penguin and how these animals grow, mate, incubate their eggs, and feed their chicks. (Rev: BL 12/15/02; HBG 3/03) [598.42]

22966 Patent, Dorothy Hinshaw. *Looking at Penguins* (3–5). Illus. by Graham Robertson. 1993, Holiday House LB $16.95 (978-0-8234-1037-8). 40pp. Various kinds of penguins are introduced, with material on their world habitats and on the endangered emperor penguin. (Rev: BL 1/1/94; SLJ 1/94*) [598]

22967 *Penguins* (PS–2). Illus. Series: First Discovery. 1996, Scholastic $12.95 (978-0-590-73877-4). 24pp. Using interactive techniques and interesting visuals, this book answers basic questions about penguins. (Rev: BL 10/15/96) [598.441]

22968 Pringle, Laurence. *Penguins!* (3–7). Series: Strange and Wonderful. 2007, Boyds Mills $16.95 (978-1-59078-090-9). 32pp. Report writers will find plenty of material in this book that covers the 17 species of penguins and their behavior, with realistic double-page watercolor illustrations. (Rev: BL 2/15/07; SLJ 4/07) [516]

22969 Raatma, Lucia. *Penguins* (2–4). Series: First Reports. 2001, Compass Point LB $22.60 (978-0-7565-0058-0). 48pp. Young report writers will quickly find basic information on penguins here. (Rev: HBG 4/04; SLJ 7/01) [598]

22970 Rau, Dana Meachen. *Guess Who Swims* (PS–K). Series: Bookworms. Guess Who. 2009, Marshall Cavendish $15.95 (978-0-7614-2974-6). 32pp. Fun for browsing, this book asks readers to identify a penguin using the clues in the text and images. (Rev: SLJ 6/09) [598.47]

22971 Robinson, Claire. *Penguins* (2–3). Series: In the Wild. 1997, Heinemann $21.36 (978-1-57572-137-8). 24pp. A heavily illustrated introduction to penguins that uses double-page spreads to cover such topics as behavior, food, habitats, and care of young. (Rev: BL 2/15/98; SLJ 4/98) [598.4]

22972 Rodriguez, Ana María. *Secret of the Puking Penguins . . . and More!* (5–7). Illus. Series: Animal Secrets Revealed! 2008, Enslow LB $17.95 (978-0-7660-2955-2). 48pp. Unusual habits of a variety of animals are revealed along with the ways in which scientists establish these facts. (Rev: BL 12/1/08; SLJ 3/09) [597.9]

22973 Schlein, Miriam. *What's a Penguin Doing in a Place Like This?* (3–5). Illus. 1997, Millbrook LB $23.90 (978-0-7613-0003-8). 48pp. A guide to 17 species of penguins, arranged by habitat. (Rev: BL 6/1–15/97; SLJ 7/97) [598.4]

22974 Simon, Seymour. *Penguins* (2–4). Illus. 2007, HarperCollins $16.99 (978-0-06-028395-7). 32pp. Eye-catching, full-page photographs accompany clear text about penguins and their lives. (Rev: BL 9/15/07; SLJ 10/07) [598.47]

22975 Spilsbury, Louise, and Richard Spilsbury. *Watching Penguins in Antarctica* (1–3). Series: Wild World. 2006, Heinemann LB $25.36 (978-1-4034-7223-6). 32pp. Provides details about penguins' characteristics, diet, reproduction, predators, and so forth, with photographs, a world map, and a "Tracker's Guide." (Rev: SLJ 7/06) [598.47]

22976 Spilsbury, Richard, and Louise Spilsbury. *A Rookery of Penguins* (3–5). Illus. Series: Animal Groups. 2004, Heinemann LB $24.22 (978-1-4034-4691-6). 32pp. Easy-to-understand narrative and plenty of color photographs provide a good overview of penguins and their behaviors and habitats. (Rev: BL 4/15/04; SLJ 9/04) [598.47]

22977 Stefoff, Rebecca. *Penguin* (K–3). Series: Living Things. 1997, Marshall Cavendish LB $22.79 (978-0-7614-0446-0). 32pp. Using double-page spreads and many color photos, the habits, homes, and behavior of penguins are introduced very simply. (Rev: BL 2/15/98; HBG 3/98) [598.4]

22978 Stefoff, Rebecca. *Penguins* (4–8). Illus. Series: AnimalWays. 2005, Benchmark LB $21.95 (978-0-7614-1743-9). 112pp. Beautiful photographs enrich this well-organized volume that provides basic information on the penguin's characteristics, habits, and habitat. (Rev: SLJ 5/06) [598.4]

22979 Stone, Lynn M. *Penguins* (2–4). Series: Bird Discovery Library. 1989, Rourke LB $18.60 (978-0-86592-325-6). 24pp. Introduces penguins, with brief text, color photos, and a glossary on the effects of pollution on penguins. Also use: *Vultures* (1989). (Rev: SLJ 11/89) [598.4]

22980 Stone, Lynn M. *Penguins* (2–4). Illus. Series: Early Bird Nature Books. 1998, Lerner LB $25.26 (978-0-8225-3022-0). 48pp. Questions are used throughout this book to explain important facts about penguins, their habits, family life, and homes. (Rev: BL 12/1/98; HBG 3/99) [598.47]

22981 Tatham, Betty. *Penguin Chick* (2–3). Illus. by Helen K. Davie. Series: Let's-Read-and-Find-Out Science. 2002, HarperCollins $16.99 (978-0-06-028594-4); paper $5.99 (978-0-06-445206-9). 40pp. An account for younger readers of an emperor penguin chick's survival in an often ruthless habitat. (Rev: BL 3/1/02; HB 5/02; HBG 10/02; SLJ 3/02) [598.47]

22982 Teitelbaum, Michael. *Baby Penguin Slips and Slides* (PS–1). Illus. Series: Photo Adventure Book. 2009, Treasure Bay $9.95 (978-1-60115-285-5); paper $4.99 (978-1-60115-286-2). 24pp. Color photographs show penguins as they make their way through the day. (Rev: BL 6/1–15/09)

22983 Webb, Sophie. *My Season with Penguins: An Antarctic Journal* (4–8). Illus. by author. 2000, Houghton $15.00 (978-0-395-92291-0). 48pp. Journal entries plus effective drawings show the joys and tribulations of a two-month stay in the Antarctic studying penguins and their behavior. (Rev: HB 11/00; HBG 3/01; SLJ 12/00) [598]

Conservation of Endangered Species

22984 Astorga, Amalia, and Gary Paul Nabhan. *Efrain of the Sonoran Desert: A Lizard's Life Among the Seri People* (2–6). Illus. by Janet K. Miller. 2001, Cinco Puntos $15.95 (978-0-938317-55-5). 32pp. The fascinating story of how an endangered lizard can flourish within a special community. (Rev: BL 12/15/01; HBG 3/02; SLJ 12/01) [305.8975]

22985 Barnes, Simon. *Planet Zoo* (4–7). Illus. 2001, Orion $29.95 (978-1-85881-488-9). 264pp. An overview of 100 endangered species that conveys information in a conversational manner. (Rev: BL 8/01; SLJ 8/01) [578.68]

22986 Casterline, Linda. *Rare Animals: A Chapter Book* (2–5). Series: True Tales. 2003, Children's Pr. LB $22.50 (978-0-516-22914-0). 48pp. Written in simple language, this volume introduces four endangered animals — the whopping crane, elephant, monk seal, and polar bear — and discusses what is being done to protect them. (Rev: SLJ 2/04) [591.68]

22987 Chandler, Gary, and Kevin Graham. *Guardians of Wildlife* (4–8). Illus. Series: Making a Better World. 1996, Twenty-First Century LB $25.90 (978-0-8050-4626-7). 64pp. Solutions to overhunting, poaching, and overfishing are explored, as well as new wildlife management techniques. (Rev: BL 12/15/96; SLJ 4/97) [639.9]

22988 Collard, Sneed B., III. *In the Wild* (3–6). Series: Science Adventures. 2005, Benchmark LB $28.50 (978-0-7614-1955-6). 43pp. Readers meet scientists at Zoo Atlanta who work with endangered primates. (Rev: SLJ 5/06) [599.8]

22989 Dobson, David. *Can We Save Them? Endangered Species of North America* (4–5). Illus. by James M. Needham. 1997, Charlesbridge $16.95 (978-0-88106-823-8); paper $6.95 (978-0-88106-822-1). 32pp. Features 12 North American species of endangered wildlife, including Florida panthers, tree snails, gray bats, peregrine falcons, and wildflowers. (Rev: BL 4/1/97; SLJ 7/97) [591.52]

22990 Fowler, Allan. *It Could Still Be Endangered* (K–2). Illus. Series: Rookie Readers. 2000, Children's Book Pr. $20.50 (978-0-516-21208-1). 32pp. Full-page colors photos introduce the concept of endangerment and introduce several animals large and small that are on the endangered list. (Rev: BL 1/1–15/01) [333.95]

22991 Hirschi, Ron. *Lions, Tigers, and Bears: Why Are Big Predators So Rare?* (3–6). Illus. by Thomas D. Mangelsen. 2007, Boyds Mills $16.95 (978-1-59078-435-8). 32pp. Hirschi explains the many and varied threats facing cougars, polar bears, lions, cheetahs, tigers, grizzly bears, and killer whales; the wide format and eye-catching photographs make this a compelling book. (Rev: BL 10/15/07; LMC 1/08; SLJ 9/07) [591.3]

22992 Jenkins, Steve. *Almost Gone: The World's Rarest Animals* (1–3). Illus. Series: Let's-Read-and-Find-Out Science. 2006, HarperCollins $16.99 (978-0-06-053598-8); paper $5.99 (978-0-06-053600-8). 40pp. Striking cut-paper collages and brief text introduce 21 animal species that are endangered. (Rev: BL 12/1/05; SLJ 2/06*) [574.529]

22993 Kendell, Patricia. *WWF* (5–8). Series: World Watch. 2004, Raintree LB $27.14 (978-0-7398-6615-3). 48pp. Introduces the World Wildlife Fund's history, organization, and work on behalf of the endangered animals; sidebars provide key facts and relevant quotations. (Rev: BL 4/1/04; SLJ 6/04) [333.95]

22994 Lessem, Don. *Dinosaurs to Dodos: An Encyclopedia of Extinct Animals* (4–7). Illus. 1999, Scholastic paper $16.95 (978-0-590-31684-2). 112pp. Moving through 12 time periods, this book describes each period and how geological changes caused the extinction of certain species and the creation of new ones. (Rev: BL 11/1/99; HBG 3/00; SLJ 11/99) [560]

22995 Lovett, Sarah. *Extremely Weird Endangered Species* (3–6). Illus. by Mary Sundstrom and Sally Blakemore. Series: Extremely Weird. 1997, Davidson LB $21.27 (978-1-884756-26-9); John Muir paper $5.95 (978-0-562-61280-4). 48pp. This colorful book introduces such unusual endangered species as manatees, bats, guans, rhinos, and condors. (Rev: SLJ 7/92) [574]

22996 McClung, Robert M. *Lost Wild America: The Story of Our Extinct and Vanishing Wildlife.* Rev. ed. (5–8). Illus. 1993, Shoe String LB $30.00 (978-0-208-02359-9). A history of American wildlife management from pioneer days to the present, with information on extinct and endangered species. (Rev: BL 1/1/94; SLJ 2/94*; VOYA 2/94) [591.5]

22997 McDaniel, Melissa. *Mysterious Nature: A Chapter Book* (3–6). Series: True Tales. 2005, Children's Pr. LB $22.50 (978-0-516-25183-7); paper $4.95 (978-0-516-25453-1). 48pp. Scientists discuss the causes of mysterious animal extinctions around the world; clear illustrations add to the easy-reading text. (Rev: SLJ 5/06) [591.68]

22998 McLimans, David. *Gone Fishing: Ocean Life by the Numbers* (2–4). Illus. by author. 2008, Walker $16.99 (978-0-8027-9770-4). 40pp. Endangered marine creatures and their habitats are introduced along with "Ocean Facts by the Numbers"; illustrations are numbers made up of creatures' bodies. (Rev: BL 12/1/08; LMC 11/08; SLJ 10/08) [591.77]

22999 Nirgiotis, Nicholas, and Theodore Nigiortis. *No More Dodos: How Zoos Help Endangered Wildlife* (5–8). Illus. 1996, Lerner LB $23.93 (978-0-8225-2856-2). An introduction to the many organizations that are trying to protect and preserve endangered wildlife worldwide. (Rev: BCCB 2/97; BL 2/15/97; SLJ 2/97) [639.9]

23000 Penny, Malcolm. *Endangered Species* (5–8). Series: 21st Century Debates. 2002, Raintree LB $27.12 (978-0-7398-4873-9). 64pp. Topics covered in this well-illustrated book include a history of conservation, how species become endangered, methods for protection such as captive breeding, and saving habitats. (Rev: BL 6/1–15/02) [591]

23001 Radley, Gail. *Forests and Jungles* (2–5). Illus. by Jean Sherlock. Series: Vanishing From. 2001, Carolrhoda LB $22.60 (978-1-57505-405-6); paper $6.95 (978-1-57505-567-1). 32pp. The plight of endangered species as humans threaten their habitats serves as an introduction to double-page spreads about specific animals. Also use *Grasslands and Deserts* and *The Skies* (both 2001). (Rev: HBG 3/02; SLJ 10/01) [591]

23002 Salmansohn, Pete, and Stephen W. Kress. *Saving Birds: Heroes Around the World* (4–7). Illus. 2003, Tilbury House $16.95 (978-0-88448-237-6). 40pp. Efforts to save endangered bird species are detailed in informative text and arresting, full-color photographs. (Rev: BL 3/15/03; HBG 10/03; SLJ 5/03) [333.95]

23003 Sheehan, Sean. *Endangered Species* (5–8). Illus. Series: What If We Do Nothing? 2009, Gareth Stevens LB $31.00 (978-1-4339-0086-0). 48pp. The threats to both plants and animals, along with factors such as ecotourism and the exotic pet market, are addressed in this volume that looks at the past, the current status, and the future outlook. (Rev: BL 4/15/09; SLJ 6/09) [333.95]

23004 Stuart, Gene S. *Wildlife Alert: The Struggle to Survive* (3–6). Illus. 1980, National Geographic LB $12.50 (978-0-87044-323-7). 104pp. This book outlines the steps being taken to help endangered animals around the world.

23005 Thomas, Peggy. *Big Cat Conservation* (5–8). Illus. Series: Science of Saving Animals. 2000, Twenty-First Century LB $25.90 (978-0-7613-3231-2). 64pp. This book focuses on seven species, including panthers, cheetahs, and tigers, and discusses wildlife conservation programs, challenges, and successes. (Rev: BL 6/1–15/00; HBG 10/00; SLJ 7/00) [333.95]

23006 Thomas, Peggy. *Bird Alert* (5–8). Series: The Science of Saving Animals. 2000, Twenty-First Century LB $25.90 (978-0-7613-1457-8). 64pp. This book discusses conservation programs designed to save endangered bird species and tells how youngsters can get involved in saving birds. (Rev: BL 10/15/00; HBG 10/01; SLJ 12/00) [591.52]

23007 Thomas, Peggy. *Marine Mammal Preservation* (5–8). Series: The Science of Saving Animals. 2000, Twenty-First Century LB $25.90 (978-0-7613-1458-5). 64pp. Focuses on endangered marine mammals and describes a wide range of conservation programs. (Rev: BL 10/15/00; HBG 10/01; SLJ 1/01) [574.92]

23008 Thomas, Peggy. *Reptile Rescue* (5–8). Illus. Series: Science of Saving Animals. 2000, Twenty-First Century LB $25.90 (978-0-7613-3232-9). 64pp. A description of various conservation programs and how they operate in relation to several reptile species, including tortoises, crocodiles, and snakes. (Rev: BL 6/1–15/00; HBG 10/00; SLJ 7/00) [333.95]

23009 Turbak, Gary. *Mountain Animals in Danger* (1–4). Illus. by Lawrence Ormsby. 1994, Northland LB $14.95 (978-0-87358-573-6). 32pp. Introduces ten endangered species, like the gray wolf, bald eagle, and spotted owl. (Rev: BL 2/1/95; SLJ 2/95) [599]

Insects and Arachnids

GENERAL AND MISCELLANEOUS

23010 Anderson, Margaret J. *Bizarre Insects* (3–6). Illus. Series: Weird and Wacky Science. 1996, Enslow LB $23.93 (978-0-89490-613-8). 48pp. Fascinating facts and lots of pictures highlight this account of unusual insects and their habits. (Rev: SLJ 6/96) [595.7]

23011 Ashley, Susan. *Fireflies* (1–4). Series: Let's Read About Insects. 2004, Weekly Reader LB $21.00 (978-0-8368-4053-7); paper $5.95 (978-0-8368-4060-5). 24pp. The life cycle of fireflies is described in small-format, easy-to-read text with close-up photographs. (Rev: SLJ 2/05)

23012 Bailey, Jill. *Mosquito* (1–3). Illus. by Alan Male. Series: Bug Books. 1998, Heinemann LB $21.36 (978-1-57572-663-2). 32pp. Large photos of mosquitoes accompanied by short paragraphs of text introduce such subjects as mating, physical structure, life cycle, and diet. (Rev: HBG 9/99; SLJ 1/99) [595.77]

23013 Barner, Bob. *Bug Safari* (1–3). Illus. 2004, Holiday House $16.95 (978-0-8234-1707-0). 32pp. In this colorful journey into the world of insects, a young boy follows a trail of ants and discovers an alternative perspective on a picnic lunch. (Rev: BL 4/15/04; SLJ 3/04) [595.7]

23014 Barner, Bob. *Bugs! Bugs! Bugs!* (PS–1). Illus. 1999, Chronicle $12.95 (978-0-8118-2238-1). 32pp. A rhyming text and bold color illustrations effectively introduce the world of bugs. (Rev: BL 7/99; SLJ 8/99) [595.7]

23015 Becker, Helaine. *The Insecto-Files* (3–6). Illus. by Claudia Dávila. 2009, Maple Tree $22.95 (978-1-897349-46-5); paper $10.95 (978-1-897349-47-2). 64pp. This is a bright, lively introduction to insects and their important characteristics, including facts, interesting sidebars, quizzes, experiments, and activities. (Rev: LMC 10/09; SLJ 7/09) [595.7]

23016 Berger, Melvin. *Buzz! A Book About Insects* (1–2). Illus. 2000, Scholastic $3.99 (978-0-439-08748-3). 40pp. This easy-to-read science book uses color photographs to introduce various insects, explain their physical characteristics, and show the changes from caterpillar to butterfly. (Rev: BL 10/1/00) [595.7]

23017 Berger, Melvin. *Killer Bugs* (4–8). Illus. 1990, Avon paper $3.50 (978-0-380-76036-7). 88pp. This account explores the world of killer bees, fire ants, and other such bugs. (Rev: BL 12/15/90) [595.7]

23018 Berger, Melvin, and Gilda Berger. *How Do Flies Walk Upside Down? Questions and Answers About Insects* (3–5). Illus. Series: Question and Answer. 1999, Scholastic $12.95 (978-0-590-13082-0); paper $5.95 (978-0-590-08572-4). 48pp. An attractive book that describes the characteristics of insects in a question-and-answer format. (Rev: BL 11/1/99; SLJ 12/99) [595.7]

23019 Blobaum, Cindy. *Insectigations! 40 Hands-on Activities to Explore the Insect World* (3–6). Illus. by Gail Rattray. 2005, Chicago Review paper $12.95 (978-1-55652-568-1). 133pp. From collecting and drawing insects to raising mealworms, keeping a scientific journal, and gardening for butterflies, this useful volume offers both activities and facts. (Rev: SLJ 1/06) [595.7]

23020 Brenner, Barbara, and Bernice Chardiet. *Where's That Insect?* (2–4). Illus. by Carol Schwartz. 1995, Scholastic paper $4.99 (978-0-590-45211-3). 32pp. Simple facts are presented about 14 kinds of insects. (Rev: BL 8/93; SLJ 3/93) [595.7]

23021 Bulion, Leslie. *Hey There, Stink Bug!* (4–6). 2006, Charlesbridge $12.95 (978-1-58089-304-6). 48pp. Poems about bugs full of dramatic and often gross details are designed to fascinate the older elementary student. (Rev: BL 7/06; SLJ 7/06) [595.7]

23022 Burnie, David. *Bug Hunter* (4–6). Illus. Series: Nature Activities. 2005, DK paper $9.99 (978-0-7566-1030-2). 72pp. Bright, attractive double-page spreads explore the study of bugs (insects, spiders, and some worms) and provide activities. (Rev: BL 7/05) [595.7]

23023 Burnie, David. *Insect* (5–9). Illus. Series: DK/Google e.guides. 2005, DK $17.99 (978-0-7566-1010-4). 96pp. This highly illustrated guide introduces readers to the life cycle, behavior, diet, and habitat of insects and provides a link to a Web site that serves as a gateway to additional resources. (Rev: SLJ 8/05)

23024 Crowley, Ned. *Ugh! A Bug!* (K–2). Series: Silly Millies. 2005, Millbrook LB $18.60 (978-0-7613-3450-7); paper $4.99 (978-0-7613-2475-1). 32pp. This photo-filled title with rhyming text introduces young readers to 25 kinds of insects, provides some fascinating facts, and includes a "pictionary" index. (Rev: SLJ 11/05)

23025 Dewey, Jennifer O. *Bedbugs in Our House: True Tales of Insect, Bug, and Spider Discovery* (4–6). Illus. 1997, Marshall Cavendish $14.95 (978-0-7614-5006-1). 64pp. Using personal encounters with insects as a focus, the author presents details about all sorts of creatures, including fireflies, locusts, and spiders. (Rev: BL 1/1–15/98; HBG 9/98) [595.7]

23026 Dixon, Norma. *Focus on Flies* (3–6). Illus. 2008, Fitzhenry & Whiteside $18.95 (978-1-55005-128-5). 32pp. Dixon provides an engaging, conversational introduction to insects including houseflies, fruit flies, and mosquitoes, covering their history, physical characteristics, metamorphosis, role in pollination, and so forth, plus their ability to spread disease. (Rev: BL 12/15/08; SLJ 4/09) [595.77]

23027 Doris, Ellen. *Entomology* (4–6). Illus. by Len Rubenstein. 1993, Thames & Hudson $16.95 (978-0-500-19004-3). 64pp. In this project book, the classification of insects is covered, along with their habitats and metamorphosis and ideas for field trips and collecting specimens. (Rev: BL 10/1/93; SLJ 9/93) [595.7]

23028 Dussling, Jennifer. *Bugs! Bugs! Bugs!* (2–4). Series: Eyewitness Reader. 1998, DK paper $3.99 (978-0-7894-3438-8). 32pp. Using lavish illustrations, a chatty text, information boxes, and fact pages, this book introduces a variety of insects, their physical characteristics, habits, food, and life cycles. (Rev: HBG 3/99; SLJ 1/99) [595.7]

23029 Fischer-Nagel, Heiderose, and Andreas Fischer-Nagel. *The Housefly* (3–6). Illus. Series: Nature Watch. 1990, Carolrhoda LB $19.95 (978-0-87614-374-2). 48pp. A well-organized text with many details about the housefly. (Rev: BL 6/15/90; SLJ 9/90) [595.7]

23030 Frost, Helen. *Praying Mantises* (PS–3). Series: Insects. 2001, Capstone LB $17.26 (978-0-7368-0853-8). 24pp. Spare text and full-page color photographs — often close-up shots — offer basic information on praying mantises. Also use *Walkingsticks* (2001). (Rev: HBG 3/02; SLJ 9/01) [959.7]

23031 Gilpin, Daniel. *Centipedes, Millipedes, Scorpions and Spiders* (4–6). Illus. Series: Animal Kingdom Classification. 2005, Compass Point LB $29.26 (978-0-7565-1254-5). 48pp. Spiders and other members of the arachnid family, including mites, scorpions, and ticks, are introduced in informative spreads with eye-catching illustrations. (Rev: BL 11/1/05) [595.6]

23032 Glaser, Linda. *Dazzling Dragonflies: A Life Cycle Story* (K–3). Illus. by Mia Posada. 2008, Lerner LB $22.60 (978-0-8225-6753-0). 32pp. The life cycle of the dragonfly is clearly presented for younger readers. (Rev: BL 12/1/07; LMC 10/08; SLJ 8/08) [595.7]

23033 Gray, Susan H. *Emerald Ash Borer* (3–6). Series: Animal Invaders. 2008, Cherry Lake LB $26.26 (978-1-60279-112-1). 32pp. A solid introduction to the invasive borer and the threat it presents to ash trees, with color photographs and maps. (Rev: SLJ 9/08) [595.76]

23034 Hartley, Karen, et al. *Cockroach* (K–3). Series: Heinemann First Library. 1999, Heinemann LB $21.36 (978-1-57572-797-4). 32pp. Through amazing color photos and a simple text, the cockroach is introduced, with material on types, food, habitats, and life cycle. (Rev: BL 6/1–15/99; HBG 9/99) [595.7]

23035 Hartley, Karen, et al. *Fly* (1–4). Illus. Series: Bug Books. 2000, Heinemann LB $21.36 (978-1-57572-548-2). 32pp. Traces the life cycle of the fly, with illustrations and text that also cover its habitats and food. (Rev: BL 7/00) [595.77]

23036 Hartley, Karen, et al. *Grasshopper* (K–3). Illus. Series: Heinemann First Library. 1999, Heinemann LB $21.36 (978-1-57572-798-1). 32pp. A large labeled drawing of a grasshopper's body is accompanied by descriptions in pictures and text of its life cycle, habits, habitats, and unique characteristics. (Rev: BL 6/1–15/99; HBG 9/99) [595]

23037 Hartley, Karen, et al. *Head Louse* (1–4). Illus. Series: Bug Books. 2000, Heinemann LB $21.36 (978-1-57572-549-9). 32pp. Close-up photos are used to introduce the life cycle of the head louse, its food, and habits. (Rev: BL 7/00) [616.5]

23038 Hartley, Karen, et al. *Termite* (K–3). Series: Heinemann First Library. 1999, Heinemann LB $21.36 (978-1-57572-800-1). 32pp. The termite is introduced in stunning photographs and a simple text that gives basic information about varieties, habits, habitats, and their destructive behavior. (Rev: BL 6/1–15/99; HBG 9/99) [595.7]

23039 Hawes, Judy. *Fireflies in the Night* (PS–3). Illus. by Ellen Alexander. Series: Let's-Read-and-Find-Out. 1991, HarperCollins $13.95 (978-0-06-022484-4); paper $5.99 (978-0-06-445101-7). 32pp. Full-color illustrations help to explain the world of fireflies. A remake of the original 1963 edition. (Rev: BL 11/15/91; SLJ 3/92) [595.76]

23040 Heinrichs, Ann. *Grasshoppers* (2–4). Series: Nature's Friends. 2002, Compass Point LB $22.60 (978-0-7565-0166-2). 32pp. Grasshoppers, their anatomy and life cycle, and their relationship to humans are covered in simple text and clear close-up photographs. (Rev: SLJ 7/02) [595.7]

23041 Hickman, Pamela. *Bug Book* (3–5). Illus. Series: Starting with Nature. 1999, Kids Can $12.95 (978-1-55074-475-0). 32pp. Using double-page spreads and fact boxes, this is an attractive introduc-

tion to insects including beetles, moths, termites, and butterflies. (Rev: BL 2/1/99; HBG 9/99) [595.7]

23042 Hipp, Andrew. *Orchid Mantises* (3–5). Series: The Really Wild Life of Insects. 2003, Rosen LB $21.25 (978-0-8239-6239-6). 24pp. Mantises that can mimic the flower of an orchid are the focus of this interesting, well-illustrated volume. (Rev: SLJ 1/04) [595.7]

23043 Hipp, Andrew. *Peanut-Head Bugs* (3–5). Series: The Really Wild Life of Insects. 2003, Rosen LB $21.25 (978-0-8239-6242-6). 24pp. An excellent overview of members of the Fulgoridae family, found throughout much of Latin America and commonly called peanut-head bugs. (Rev: SLJ 1/04) [595.7]

23044 Hirschmann, Kris. *Lice* (4–6). Illus. Series: Parasites. 2003, Gale LB $24.95 (978-0-7377-1784-6). 32pp. The physical and behavioral characteristics of lice are introduced, with information on how they spread disease to humans. (Rev: SLJ 6/04) [614.4]

23045 Holland, Gay. *Look Closer: An Introduction to Bug-Watching* (1–4). Illus. 2003, Millbrook LB $22.90 (978-0-7613-2664-9). 32pp. Aphids, spittlebugs, and dragonflies are among the bugs introduced in this guide that combines realistic illustrations with easy-to-read text. (Rev: BL 6/1–15/03; HBG 10/03; SLJ 9/03) [595.7]

23046 Holmes, Anita. *Insect Detector* (1–2). Illus. Series: We Can Read About — Nature! 2000, Benchmark $21.36 (978-0-7614-1110-9). 32pp. A beginning reader that defines the characteristics of an insect and asks if particular creatures such as a scorpion or a spider would meet these criteria. (Rev: BL 12/1/00; HBG 3/01; SLJ 2/01) [595.7]

23047 Hughes, Monica. *Pill Bugs* (PS–2). Illus. Series: Creepy Creatures. 2003, Raintree LB $18.56 (978-1-4109-0624-3). 24pp. A close-up look at the diet, anatomy, habitat, and life cycle of pill bugs, for beginning readers. (Rev: BL 2/15/04) [595.3]

23048 Jackson, Donna. *The Bug Scientists* (4–7). Illus. Series: Scientists in the Field. 2002, Houghton $16.00 (978-0-618-10868-8). 48pp. In addition to describing a variety of professional jobs related to insects, this colorful volume presents excellent information about insects and how they live. (Rev: BCCB 6/02; BL 4/1/02; HB 5/02; HBG 10/02; SLJ 4/02) [595.7]

23049 Jarrow, Gail. *Chiggers* (4–6). Series: Parasites. 2003, Gale LB $24.95 (978-0-7377-1778-5). 32pp. A close-up look at these tiny bloodsucking mites, with color photographs and first-person accounts of chigger encounters. (Rev: SLJ 6/04) [616.9]

23050 Johnson, Jinny. *Children's Guide to Insects and Spiders* (3–5). Illus. 1997, Simon & Schuster $19.95 (978-0-689-81163-0). 64pp. Using a large format, the author identifies and describes families of insects and spiders and furnishes drawings and photos of body parts and stages of life cycles. (Rev: BL 5/1/97; SLJ 11/97) [595.7]

23051 Johnson, Sylvia A. *Fireflies* (4–6). 1986, Lerner LB $22.60 (978-0-8225-1485-5). 48pp. Life cycle, breeding, environment, and characteristics of the firefly. (Rev: BL 10/1/86; SLJ 11/86)

23052 Johnson, Sylvia A. *Ladybugs* (5–8). Illus. by Yuko Sato. 1983, Lerner LB $22.60 (978-0-8225-1481-7). 48pp. A description of the ladybug, its habits, behavior, and uses. [595.7]

23053 Johnson, Sylvia A. *Water Insects* (3–6). Illus. by Modoki Masuda. 1989, Lerner LB $22.60 (978-0-8225-1489-3). 48pp. Various kinds of aquatic insects are pictured and described. (Rev: BL 2/15/90; SLJ 4/90) [595]

23054 Karapetkova, Holly. *Katydid? Katy Didn't!* (PS). Illus. Series: Rourke Board Books. 2009, Rourke $5.99 (978-1-60472-427-1). 16pp. Attractive color photographs and chanting wordplay provide a few easily absorbed facts about katydids. (Rev: BL 5/15/09) [595.7]

23055 Kite, L. Patricia. *Cockroaches* (2–3). Series: Early Bird Nature Books. 2001, Lerner LB $25.26 (978-0-8225-3046-6). 48pp. Using a simple text and color photographs on each page, this book effectively introduces the life cycle of the cockroach with material on its habits, anatomy, and homes. Also use *Fireflies* (2001). (Rev: BL 8/1/01; HBG 10/01) [595.7]

23056 Kite, L. Patricia. *Insect: Facts and Folklore* (3–6). Illus. 2001, Millbrook LB $29.90 (978-0-7613-1822-4). 80pp. Fascinating information (mixing facts, folklore, and interesting anecdotes) about insects, all colorfully presented. (Rev: BL 9/1/01; HBG 3/02; SLJ 10/01) [595.7]

23057 Kneidel, Sally. *Pet Bugs: A Kid's Guide to Catching and Keeping Touchable Insects* (4–6). Illus. 1994, Wiley paper $12.95 (978-0-471-31188-1). 117pp. Describes 25 insects; how they live, eat, and reproduce; and how they can be kept as specimens. (Rev: BL 7/94; SLJ 9/94) [638]

23058 Llewellyn, Claire. *The Best Book of Bugs* (3–5). 1998, Kingfisher $10.95 (978-0-7534-5118-2). 33pp. A lavishly illustrated book that introduces insects and spiders and describes more than 20 different species, including information on the life cycles of honeybees, dragonflies, and butterflies. (Rev: HBG 9/98; SLJ 7/98) [595.7]

23059 Llewellyn, Claire. *Some Bugs Glow in the Dark: And Other Amazing Facts About Insects* (1–3). Illus. by Mike Taylor, et al. Series: I Didn't Know That. 1997, Millbrook LB $19.90 (978-0-7613-0562-0). 32pp. As well as explaining what insects are, this book covers amazing facts about their speed, size, weight, metamorphosis, and unusual behavior. (Rev: SLJ 9/97) [595.7]

23060 Lockwood, Sophie. *Dragonflies* (4–6). Series: The World of Insects. 2007, The Child's World LB $29.93 (978-1-59296-821-3). 40pp. Crisp writing and sharp photographs offer substantive insight into various aspects of dragonfly life. Also use *Flies* (2007). (Rev: SLJ 3/08) [595.7]

23061 McLaughlin, Molly. *Dragonflies* (2–6). Illus. 1988, Walker LB $15.85 (978-0-8027-6847-6). 48pp. The life cycle of dragonflies plus information on different varieties are provided with outstanding

photographs. (Rev: BCCB 10/89; BL 8/89*; SLJ 9/89) [595.7]

23062 Markle, Sandra. *Creepy, Crawly Baby Bugs* (3–5). Illus. 1996, Walker LB $16.85 (978-0-8027-8444-5). 32pp. The growth cycle of insects is explored, with emphasis on each infant stage. (Rev: BL 11/15/96; SLJ 4/97*) [595.7]

23063 Markle, Sandra. *Insects* (1–3). Illus. Series: Biggest! Littlest! 2009, Boyds Mills $16.95 (978-1-59078-512-6). 24pp. Looking at insects both tiny and large, Markle identifies the characteristics that make them successful. (Rev: BCCB 4/09; BL 3/15/09; LMC 8/09; SLJ 3/09) [595.7]

23064 Markle, Sandra. *Praying Mantises: Hungry Insect Heroes* (2–4). Illus. 2008, Lerner LB $27.93 (978-0-8225-7300-5). 48pp. With clear, eye-catching photographs, an animated text, and numerous sidebars, this is a thorough and interesting overview of the praying mantis. (Rev: BL 4/1/08; SLJ 2/08) [595.7]

23065 Markle, Sandra. *Termites: Hardworking Insect Families* (2–5). Series: Insect World. 2008, Lerner LB $27.93 (978-0-8225-7301-2). 48pp. Eye-catching illustrations and simple diagrams are combined with interestingly presented facts about these insects and two activities. (Rev: LMC 10/08; SLJ 2/08) [595.7]

23066 Meister, Cari. *Mosquitoes* (2–4). Illus. Series: Checkerboard Science and Nature Library: Insects. 2001, ABDO LB $21.35 (978-1-57765-464-3). 24pp. An introduction to mosquitoes and their structure, diet, habitat, and habits. (Rev: BL 10/15/01; HBG 10/01) [595.77]

23067 Miller, Sara S. *True Bugs: When Is a Bug Really a Bug?* (3–5). Illus. Series: Animals in Order. 1998, Watts LB $26.50 (978-0-531-11479-7). 48pp. The classification of animals is explained, followed by a profile of 14 common insects with material on their physical characteristics, behavior, and life cycles. (Rev: BL 1/1–15/99; HBG 3/99) [595.7]

23068 Miller, Sara Swan. *Grasshoppers and Crickets of North America* (3–5). Series: Animals in Order. 2002, Watts $26.50 (978-0-531-12170-2). 48pp. This colorful volume explores insect jumpers of the orthopteran order, which includes grasshoppers, crickets, and katydids. (Rev: BL 9/15/02) [595]

23069 Murawski, Darlyne A. *Bug Faces* (K–4). Illus. 2000, National Geographic $16.95 (978-0-7922-7557-2). 32pp. Huge, sometimes scary photographs in gorgeous color show close-up views of such creatures as a spider, cockroach, bumblebee, deer fly, and weevil. (Rev: BL 11/15/00; HBG 3/01; SLJ 11/00) [595.7]

23070 Nathan, Emma. *What Do You Call a Group of Butterflies? And Other Insect Groups* (3–5). Illus. 2000, Blackbirch LB $21.20 (978-1-56711-359-4). 24pp. This simple science book uses questions and answers to give basic facts about insects and to reveal each one's group name, such as a colony of ants. (Rev: BL 12/1/00; HBG 3/01) [595.7]

23071 Needham, Karen, and Launi Lucas. *Strange Beginnings* (K–2). Illus. by Launi Lucas. 2002,

Tradewind paper $6.95 (978-1-896580-11-1). An attractive introduction to the various insects that emerge from water to spend their often brief adult lives in the air. (Rev: SLJ 9/02) [595.7176]

23072 Oppenheim, Joanne. *Have You Seen Bugs?* (K–3). Illus. by Ron Broda. 1998, Scholastic $15.95 (978-0-590-05963-3). 32pp. A series of charming verses and paper sculptures introduce moths, bees, spiders, and several insects, and describe their life cycles and characteristics. (Rev: BL 4/1/98; HBG 9/98; SLJ 9/98) [595.7]

23073 Parker, Janice. *Cockroaches, Cocoons, and Honeycombs: The Science of Insects* (3–5). Series: Science@Work. 1999, Raintree LB $27.12 (978-0-7398-0135-2). 48pp. This book about insects presents interesting facts, diagrams, and lots of appended information, along with material on careers related to the study of insects. (Rev: SLJ 3/00) [595.7]

23074 Parker, Nancy W., and Joan Richards Wright. *Bugs* (K–3). Illus. by Nancy W. Parker. 1987, Morrow paper $6.99 (978-0-688-08296-3). A picture-book format provides solid facts on bugs — including 16 common insects. (Rev: BL 11/1/87; SLJ 10/87)

23075 Pascoe, Elaine. *Ant Lions and Lacewings* (4–8). Photos by Dwight Kuhn. Series: Nature Close-Up. 2005, Gale LB $24.95 (978-1-4103-0310-3). 48pp. Eye-catching close-ups illustrate information on these insects' life cycles and eating habits. Also use *Mantids and Their Relatives* (2005). (Rev: SLJ 6/05)

23076 Pascoe, Elaine. *Crickets and Grasshoppers* (4–7). Series: Nature Close-Up. 1998, Blackbirch LB $23.70 (978-1-56711-176-7). 48pp. Easy projects introduce youngsters to these insects in this book illustrated with color photographs. (Rev: BL 9/15/98; HBG 3/99) [595.7]

23077 Pascoe, Elaine. *Flies* (4–7). Series: Nature Close-Up. 2000, Blackbirch LB $27.44 (978-1-56711-149-1). 48pp. This introduction to flies uses stunning photographs and text to describe their body parts, life cycle, and how to observe them; a few focused experiments are also included. (Rev: BL 4/15/00; HBG 3/01; SLJ 9/00) [595.7]

23078 Pascoe, Elaine. *Spittlebugs: And Other Sap Tappers* (3–5). Photos by Dwight Kuhn. Series: Nature Close-Up. 2003, Gale LB $24.95 (978-1-56711-430-0). 48pp. A close-up study, with eye-catching photographs, of the insect order Homoptera, covering life cycle, behavior, characteristics, and how they may be harmful or beneficial. (Rev: SLJ 3/04) [595.7]

23079 Pipe, Jim. *The Giant Book of Bugs and Creepy Crawlies* (4–8). Illus. 1998, Millbrook LB $27.90 (978-0-7613-0716-7). Exotic and common insects and spiders are presented in this oversize book with eye-catching pictures and fascinating text. (Rev: BL 8/98) [595.7]

23080 Pringle, Laurence. *A Dragon in the Sky: The Story of a Green Darner Dragonfly* (3–5). Illus. 2001, Scholastic $18.95 (978-0-531-30315-3). 64pp. The reader follows a green darner from egg to mating in this attractive, large-format book. (Rev: BL 6/1–15/01; HB 7/01; HBG 10/01; SLJ 8/01) [595.7]

23081 Pyers, Greg. *Grasshoppers up Close* (2–4). Illus. Series: Minibeasts Up Close. 2005, Raintree LB $27.50 (978-1-4109-1529-0). 32pp. A simple introduction to grasshoppers and their physical characteristics, habitat, senses, locomotion, and reproduction, with large-scale color photographs.

23082 Pyers, Greg. *Why Am I an Insect?* (3–5). Illus. Series: Classifying Animals. 2005, Raintree LB $27.50 (978-1-4109-2019-5); paper $7.85 (978-1-4109-2026-3). 32pp. Introduces readers to the process of scientific classification and then examines the unique characteristics of insects. (Rev: SLJ 4/06) [595.7]

23083 Rabe, Tish. *On Beyond Bugs! All About Insects* (K–3). Series: The Cat in the Hat's Learning Library. 1999, Random LB $11.99 (978-0-679-97303-4). 45pp. A beginning reader that contains basic facts about insects in rhyming couplets. (Rev: HBG 9/00; SLJ 3/00) [595.7]

23084 Robinson, W. Wright. *How Insects Build Their Amazing Homes* (5–8). Illus. by Carlyn Iverson. Series: Animal Architects. 1999, Blackbirch LB $24.95 (978-1-56711-375-4). 64pp. After defining what an insect is, this book shows how termites, wasps, ants, and bees construct their houses and nests. (Rev: HBG 3/00; SLJ 5/00) [595.7]

23085 Rockwell, Anne. *Bugs Are Insects* (K–3). Illus. by Steve Jenkins. Series: Let's-Read-and-Find-Out Science. 2001, HarperCollins $15.95 (978-0-06-028568-5); paper $17.89 (978-0-06-028569-2). 32pp. Rockwell makes clear the distinctions between insects and spiders and the characteristics of bugs and beetles. (Rev: BCCB 7–8/01; BL 5/1/01; HB 9/01; HBG 3/02; SLJ 10/01) [595.7]

23086 Ross, Michael E. *Cricketology* (4–6). Illus. Series: Backyard Buddies. 1996, Carolrhoda LB $19.93 (978-0-87614-985-0). 48pp. The classification, life cycle, and habits of crickets are discussed in this science activity book. (Rev: BL 7/96; SLJ 8/96) [595.7]

23087 Savage, Stephen. *Insects* (2–4). Series: What's the Difference? 2000, Raintree LB $25.69 (978-0-7398-1355-3). 32pp. This book points out similar characteristics among insects — such as the three parts of their bodies — but also shows how they can differ in size, color, and shape. (Rev: BL 10/15/00; HBG 3/01; SLJ 1/01) [595.7]

23088 Sayre, April P. *Ant, Ant, Ant: An Insect Chant* (K–3). Illus. by Trip Park. 2005, NorthWord $15.95 (978-1-55971-922-3). With a rhyming chant as its narrative line, this colorful and humorous picture book introduces 60 American insects and highlights their unusual features; a companion to *Trout, Trout, Trout! A Fish Chant* (2004). (Rev: SLJ 12/05) [595.7]

23089 Schaffer, Donna. *Pillbugs* (2–4). Illus. Series: Life Cycle. 1999, Capstone LB $22.60 (978-0-7368-0212-3). 24pp. This book introduces pillbugs (also known as rolypolies or wood lice) and explains their structure, habits, habitats, and reproductive cycle. (Rev: BL 7/99) [595.3]

23090 Schaffer, Donna. *Silkworms* (2–4). Illus. Series: Life Cycle. 1999, Capstone LB $22.60 (978-0-7368-0213-0). 24pp. Covers the life story of the silkworm, with material on how the cocoons are used to produce silk thread. (Rev: BL 7/99) [595.78]

23091 Selsam, Millicent E., and Ron Goor. *Backyard Insects* (K–3). Illus. 1988, Scholastic paper $4.99 (978-0-590-42256-7). 40pp. How backyard insects camouflage themselves for protection.

23092 Sexton, Colleen. *Cicadas* (1–3). Series: Blast Off! Readers: World of Insects. 2007, Children's Pr. LB $18.50 (978-0-531-17567-5). 24pp. Facts about cicadas are accompanied by close-up photographs, making this a useful book for beginning report writers. (Rev: SLJ 8/07)

23093 Sexton, Colleen. *Praying Mantises* (1–3). Series: Blast Off! Readers: World of Insects. 2007, Children's Pr. LB $18.50 (978-0-531-17569-9). 24pp. Facts about praying mantises are accompanied by close-up photographs, making this a useful book for beginning report writers. (Rev: SLJ 8/07)

23094 Sill, Cathryn. *About Arachnids: A Guide for Children* (PS–2). Illus. by John Sill. 2003, Peachtree $15.95 (978-1-56145-038-1). 40pp. Clear simple sentences and naturalistic paintings present basic information about arachnids. (Rev: BL 3/1/03) [595.4]

23095 Sill, Cathryn. *About Insects: A Guide for Children* (PS–2). Illus. by John Sill. Series: About Books. 2000, Peachtree $15.95 (978-1-56145-207-1). 48pp. Naturalistic paintings present several insects and their characteristics. (Rev: BL 2/1/00; HBG 9/00; SLJ 7/00) [595.7]

23096 Siy, Alexandra. *Mosquito Bite* (2–4). Illus. by Dennis Kunkel. 2005, Charlesbridge $15.95 (978-1-57091-591-8). 32pp. Information on the mosquito is presented within the framework of a story about children playing outside on a summer night; arresting magnified photographs show the insect and its parts. (Rev: BL 6/1–15/05) [595.77]

23097 Smithyman, Kathryn, and Bobbie Kalman. *Insects in Danger* (3–5). Illus. Series: The World of Insects. 2006, Crabtree LB $25.27 (978-0-7787-2344-8). 32pp. This brightly illustrated volume considers the dangers facing certain insect species, including the pressure put on some insects by the migratory patterns of other animals. (Rev: SLJ 1/07) [595.7168]

23098 Solway, Andrew. *Classifying Insects* (4–6). Series: Classifying Living Things. 2003, Heinemann LB $24.22 (978-1-4034-0849-5). 32pp. This introduction to the scientific classification of animals provides an overview of the ways in which insects differ from other animals and also how different insect species differ from each other; among the insects examined are ants, butterflies, bees, dragonflies, cockroaches, and grasshoppers. (Rev: HBG 10/03; SLJ 11/03) [595.7]

23099 Souza, D. M. *Insects Around the House* (3–5). Illus. Series: Creatures All Around Us. 1991, Carolrhoda LB $22.60 (978-0-87614-438-1). 40pp. Describes household insects, from termites under the front steps to caterpillars in the carpet. Also use:

Insects in the Garden (1991). (Rev: BL 4/15/91; SLJ 7/91) [595.7]

23100 Souza, D. M. *What Bit Me?* (3–5). Illus. Series: Creatures All Around Us. 1991, Carolrhoda LB $22.60 (978-0-87614-440-4). 40pp. In pictures and text, this book introduces creatures that can bite and sting, such as water bugs, ticks, and mosquitoes. (Rev: BL 4/15/91; SLJ 7/91) [595.7]

23101 Spilsbury, Richard, and Louise Spilsbury. *The Life Cycle of Insects* (3–5). Illus. Series: From Egg to Adult. 2003, Heinemann LB $24.22 (978-1-4034-0786-3). 32pp. This overview of insect life looks at where they live, what they eat, and how they differ from other types of animals. (Rev: HBG 4/04; SLJ 10/03) [595.7]

23102 Stewart, Melissa. *Maggots, Grubs, and More: The Secret Lives of Young Insects* (4–6). 2003, Millbrook LB $24.90 (978-0-7613-2658-8). 63pp. This photo-filled look at the world of insects details the life cycles of more than 20 insect species, including ants, mosquitoes, and yellow jackets. (Rev: HBG 4/04; SLJ 1/04) [595.7]

23103 Swanson, Diane. *Bugs Up Close* (3–5). Photos by Paul Davidson. 2007, Kids Can $16.95 (978-1-55453-138-7); paper $8.95 (978-1-55453-139-4). 40pp. Full of useful information, this large-format volume also provides huge close-ups of insects and their parts, and discusses each part in turn — legs, wings, eyes, antennae, and so forth. (Rev: LMC 11/07*; SLJ 11/07) [595.7]

23104 Telford, Carole, and Rod Theodorou. *Through a Termite City* (3–5). Series: Amazing Journeys. 1997, Heinemann LB $22.79 (978-1-57572-155-2). 32pp. Organized like a journey, this trek through a termite mound in Africa reveals details on termite life, food, and society. (Rev: SLJ 4/98) [595.7]

23105 Theodorou, Rod. *Insects* (2–4). Series: Animal Babies. 1999, Heinemann LB $21.36 (978-1-57572-880-3). 32pp. Several insect species are introduced with material on their characteristics, habits, habitats, and life cycles. (Rev: SLJ 4/00) [595.7]

23106 Tokuda, Yukihisa. *I'm a Pill Bug* (PS–2). Illus. by Kiyoshi Takahashi. Series: Nature: A Child's Eye View. 2006, Kane paper $7.95 (978-1-929132-95-9). 28pp. This attractive picture book provides a wealth of information about pill bugs, including what they eat, how they defend themselves, their reproductive habits, why they live near people, and why they shed their shells. (Rev: BL 4/1/06*) [595.372]

23107 VanCleave, Janice. *Bugs C* (PS–2). Series: Play and Find Out. 1999, Wiley $29.95 (978-0-471-17664-0). 121pp. A series of entertaining experiments and projects that explores such topics as life cycles, movement, communication, feeding, and camouflage. (Rev: HBG 9/99; SLJ 4/99) [595.7]

23108 VanCleave, Janice. *Janice VanCleave's Insects and Spiders: Mind-Boggling Experiments You Can Turn into Science Fair Projects* (3–5). Illus. by Doris Ettlinger. Series: Spectacular Science Projects. 1998, Wiley paper $10.95 (978-0-471-16396-1). 92pp. Divided into 20 chapters arranged by specific questions about insects and spiders, each supplying a step-by-step activity to answer the question, with variations on that project and ways of turning it into a science fair entry. (Rev: SLJ 6/98) [595]

23109 Wangberg, James K. *Do Bees Sneeze? And Other Questions Kids Ask About Insects* (4–6). Illus. 1997, Fulcrum paper $17.95 (978-1-55591-963-4). 194pp. A noted entomologist answers 200 questions about insects that were actually asked him by children, like "Do bugs have emotions?" (Rev: BL 1/1–15/98; SLJ 4/98) [595.7]

23110 Wilkes, Sarah. *Insects* (5–9). Series: World Almanac Library of the Animal Kingdom. 2006, World Almanac LB $31.00 (978-0-8368-6211-9). 48pp. A helpful introduction to members of the insect kingdom, this guide looks at physical characteristics that help to define this group as a whole, as well as specific species, habitats, diets, behaviors, and life cycles. (Rev: SLJ 12/06) [595.7]

23111 Wilsdon, Christina, and National Audubon Society, eds. *National Audubon Society First Field Guide: Insects* (4–8). Illus. 1998, Scholastic paper $17.95 (978-0-590-05447-8). Following a general introduction to entomology, specific insects are pictured and information is given on such topics as their eating, mating and social habits, physical structure, habitats, and identification markings. (Rev: BL 8/98; SLJ 10/98) [595]

23112 Winner, Cherie. *Everything Bug: What Kids Really Want to Know About Insects and Spiders* (3–6). Series: Kids' FAQs. 2004, North Word $10.95 (978-1-55971-890-5). 64pp. In a question-and-answer format, this compendium of facts is suitable for browsing. (Rev: BL 2/15/04; SLJ 7/04) [595]

23113 *The World in Your Backyard: And Other Stories of Insects and Spiders* (3–5). Illus. 1990, Zaner-Bloser $10.95 (978-0-88309-132-6). 63pp. Eighteen articles and stories from *Highlights for Children* magazine. (Rev: SLJ 6/90) [595.7]

23114 York, Penelope, ed. *Bugs* (3–5). 2002, DK LB $17.99 (978-0-7894-8553-3). 48pp. A colorful introduction to insects, their characteristics, life cycles, habitats, and varieties. (Rev: BL 6/1–15/02; HBG 10/02) [595.7]

23115 Zabludoff, Marc. *The Insect Class* (5–9). Illus. Series: Family Trees. 2005, Benchmark LB $29.93 (978-0-7614-1819-1). 95pp. Habits, habitats, and other aspects of this varied class of animals; an engaging book with plenty of facts for report writers. (Rev: SLJ 6/06) [595.7]

23116 Zakowski, Connie. *The Insect Book: A Basic Guide to the Collection and Care of Common Insects for Young Children* (3–5). Illus. 1996, Rainbow paper $8.95 (978-1-56825-037-3). 64pp. A practical beginner's guide to collecting, caring for, and studying insects. (Rev: BL 12/1/96; SLJ 5/97) [595.7]

23117 Zuchora-Walske, Christine. *Leaping Grasshoppers* (PS–2). Series: Pull Ahead Books. 2000, Lerner $22.60 (978-0-8225-3634-5). 32pp. This simple, colorful introduction to grasshoppers explains the reasons why they hop: to find food, to avoid predators, and to find mates. (Rev: BL 5/15/00; HBG 9/00) [595.7]

ANTS

23118 Allen, Judy. *Are You an Ant?* (PS–1). Series: Backyard Books. 2002, Kingfisher $9.95 (978-0-7534-5365-0). 32pp. A young ant faces many challenges on the road to adulthood in this beginning science book. (Rev: BL 6/1–15/02; SLJ 7/02) [595.79]

23119 Berman, Ruth. *Ants* (2–3). Illus. Series: Early Bird Nature Books. 1996, Lerner LB $25.26 (978-0-8225-3012-1). 48pp. The formica ant and its community are described in this introduction to the ant world. (Rev: BL 8/96; SLJ 7/96) [595.78]

23120 Brenner, Barbara. *Thinking About Ants* (2–3). Illus. by Carol Schwartz. 1997, Mondo $14.95 (978-1-57255-210-4). 32pp. In a readable style, 11 types of ants are introduced, with material on their bodies, colors, diet, colonies, and enemies. (Rev: BL 6/1–15/97; SLJ 10/97) [595.79]

23121 Dorros, Arthur. *Ant Cities* (K–2). Illus. by author. 1987, HarperCollins paper $5.99 (978-0-06-445079-9). 32pp. A simplified explanation of the ant world: jobs of worker ants, operation of the ant hill, social divisions of the ant colony. (Rev: BCCB 3/87; BL 2/15/87; SLJ 8/87)

23122 Fleisher, Paul. *Ants* (5–8). Series: Animal-Ways. 2001, Marshall Cavendish LB $31.36 (978-0-7614-1269-4). 112pp. This introduction to ants and their habits and habitats also includes fine color images and material on species identification, anatomy, and classification. (Rev: BL 3/15/02; HBG 10/02) [595.79]

23123 Gomel, Luc. *The Ant: Energetic Worker* (3–6). Illus. by Remy Amann and Dominique Stoffell. Series: Face-to-Face. 2001, Charlesbridge $9.95 (978-1-57091-451-5). 32pp. This is a detailed look at ants and the ant world, with arresting photographs. (Rev: BL 10/15/01; HBG 3/02) [595.79]

23124 Greenaway, Theresa. *Ants* (4–7). Series: The Secret World of . . . 2001, Raintree LB $18.98 (978-0-7368-3511-4). 48pp. After presenting interesting and unusual facts about ants, this book examines their structure, homes, behavior, and enemies. (Rev: BL 10/15/01) [595.79]

23125 Greve, Meg. *Can an Ant Carry Me?* (PS). Illus. 2009, Rourke $5.99 (978-1-60472-425-7). 16pp. Attractive color photographs and rhymed sentences provide a few easily absorbed facts about ants. (Rev: BL 5/15/09) [595.79]

23126 Hodge, Deborah. *Ants* (1–3). Illus. Series: Denver Museum of Nature and Science. 2004, Kids Can $14.95 (978-1-55337-066-6). 32pp. Simple narrative and detailed photographs combine to offer young readers an introduction to the world of ants; instructions for three related projects are included. (Rev: BL 4/1/04; SLJ 6/04) [595.79]

23127 Lockwood, Sophie. *Ants* (4–6). Series: The World of Insects. 2007, The Child's World LB $29.93 (978-1-59296-817-6). 40pp. Crisp writing and sharp photographs offer substantive insight into various aspects of ant life. (Rev: SLJ 3/08) [595.79]

23128 Micucci, Charles. *The Life and Times of the Ant* (1–4). Illus. 2003, Houghton $16.00 (978-0-618-00559-8). 32pp. Micucci provides an impressive amount of information about the life and physique of the ant in a brightly illustrated picture-book format. (Rev: BL 4/15/03; HB 5/03; HBG 10/03; SLJ 5/03) [595.79]

23129 Morris, Ting. *Ant* (2–4). Illus. by Desiderio Sanzi. Series: Creepy Crawly World. 2004, Smart Apple LB $27.10 (978-1-58340-376-1). 32pp. Introduces ants' characteristics, habitat, diet, defense mechanisms, and life cycle, using realistic paintings and diagrams. (Rev: HB 11/96; SLJ 6/05)

23130 Pascoe, Elaine. *Ants* (4–7). Series: Nature Close-Up. 1998, Blackbirch LB $23.70 (978-1-56711-183-5). 48pp. Using outstanding photographs, this book introduces ants and a series of projects designed to teach more about these creatures. (Rev: BL 9/15/98; HBG 3/99; SLJ 3/99) [595.78]

23131 Sayre, April P. *Army Ant Parade* (PS–2). Illus. by Rick Chrustowski. 2002, Holt $16.95 (978-0-8050-6353-0). 32pp. This beautifully illustrated book for younger readers gives a detailed description of an army ant swarm in a Central American jungle. (Rev: BCCB 3/02; BL 3/1/02; HB 9/02; HBG 3/03; SLJ 5/02) [595.79]

23132 Stefoff, Rebecca. *Ant* (K–3). Series: Living Things. 1997, Marshall Cavendish LB $22.79 (978-0-7614-0447-7). 32pp. A colorful introduction to the world of ants that describes colonies, homes and food. (Rev: BL 2/15/98; HBG 3/98; SLJ 3/98) [595.79]

BEES AND WASPS

23133 Ashley, Susan. *Bees* (1–3). Series: Let's Read About Insects. 2004, Weekly Reader LB $21.00 (978-0-8368-4051-3); paper $5.95 (978-0-8368-4058-2). 24pp. The life cycle of bees is described in small-format, easy-to-read text with close-up photographs. (Rev: SLJ 2/05) [595.79]

23134 Chinery, Michael. *How Bees Make Honey* (3–5). Illus. Series: Nature's Mysteries. 1996, Benchmark LB $22.79 (978-0-7614-0453-8). 32pp. In this introduction to bees, such topics as a bee's anatomy, life cycle, enemies, nectar gathering, and honey production are covered. (Rev: SLJ 2/97) [595.79]

23135 Cole, Joanna. *The Magic School Bus Inside a Beehive* (3–5). Illus. by Bruce Degen. 1996, Scholastic $15.95 (978-0-590-44684-6). 48pp. Mrs. Frizzle's school bus becomes a beehive in this exploration of the anatomy, activities, and social structure of bees. (Rev: BCCB 10/96; BL 9/1/96; HB 11/96; SLJ 10/96) [585.79]

23136 Fischer-Nagel, Heiderose, and Andreas Fischer-Nagel. *Life of the Honeybee* (2–5). Illus. 1986, Carolrhoda paper $6.95 (978-0-87614-470-1). 48pp. A simply written science book showing the work of three kinds of bees. (Rev: BCCB 4/86; BL 4/15/86; SLJ 2/86)

23137 Gibbons, Gail. *The Honey Makers* (1–4). Illus. 1997, Morrow $16.89 (978-0-688-11387-2). 32pp. An informative picture book that introduces honeybees and their society. (Rev: BCCB 4/97; BL 3/15/97; SLJ 5/97) [595.79]

23138 Glaser, Linda. *Brilliant Bees* (K–3). Illus. by Gay Holland. 2003, Millbrook LB $22.90 (978-0-7613-2670-0); paper $8.95 (978-0-7613-1943-6). A young girl looks at bees' behavior and habits in simple text and large colored pictures; four pages at the back of the book add factual information. (Rev: HBG 4/04; SLJ 1/04) [595.79]

23139 Guidoux, Valérie. *Little Bees* (3–5). Illus. Series: Born to Be Wild. 2005, Gareth Stevens LB $16.50 (978-0-7368-4433-8). 32pp. A simply worded look at young bees and their lives, with large color photographs.

23140 Hodge, Deborah. *Bees* (1–3). Illus. Series: Denver Museum of Nature and Science. 2004, Kids Can $14.95 (978-1-55337-065-9). 32pp. Suggestions for simple projects supplement this attractive examination of the life cycle of bees. (Rev: BL 4/1/04; SLJ 6/04) [595.79]

23141 Jango-Cohen, Judith. *Bees* (3–5). Series: Animals, Animals. 2006, Benchmark LB $19.95 (978-0-7614-2235-8). 48pp. An introduction to the anatomy, behavior, and habitat of bees, in addition to other aspects of these insects and their lives. Color photographs give readers a close-up look. (Rev: SLJ 5/07)

23142 Johnson, Sylvia A. *Wasps* (4–6). Illus. 1984, Lerner LB $22.60 (978-0-8225-1460-2). 48pp. A year in the life of a wasp is presented in a clear text and fascinating illustrations.

23143 Landau, Elaine. *Killer Bees* (4–6). Series: Fearsome, Scary, and Creepy Animals. 2003, Enslow LB $23.93 (978-0-7660-2061-0). 48pp. Landau offers a dramatic overview of killer bees and documents some real-life attacks on humans. (Rev: BL 10/15/03; HBG 10/03; SLJ 2/04) [595.79]

23144 Markle, Sandra. *Hornets: Incredible Insect Architects* (2–5). Series: Insect World. 2008, Lerner LB $27.93 (978-0-8225-7297-8). 48pp. Eye-catching illustrations and simple diagrams are combined with interestingly presented facts about these insects and two activities. (Rev: LMC 10/08; SLJ 2/08) [595.79]

23145 Rau, Dana Meachen. *Guess Who Stings* (PS–K). Series: Bookworms. Guess Who. 2009, Marshall Cavendish $15.95 (978-0-7614-2973-9). 32pp. Fun for browsing, this book asks readers to identify a honeybee using the clues in the text and images. (Rev: SLJ 6/09) [595.79]

23146 Riley, Joelle. *Buzzing Bumblebees* (2–3). Series: Pull Ahead Books. 2003, Lerner LB $22.60 (978-0-8225-4668-9). 32pp. An excellent introduction to the physical characteristics, behavior, and life cycle of the bumblebee, this book is suitable for beginning readers. (Rev: BL 11/15/03; HBG 10/03)

23147 Sayre, April P. *The Bumblebee Queen* (1–3). Illus. by Patricia J. Wynne. 2005, Charlesbridge $14.95 (978-1-57091-362-4). 32pp. The life of a bumblebee queen, accompanied by additional bee information and detailed watercolor illustrations. (Rev: BL 3/1/05; SLJ 4/05) [595.79]

23148 Starosta, Paul. *The Bee* (2–4). Illus. Series: Animal Close-Ups. 2005, Charlesbridge paper $6.95 (978-1-57091-629-8). 28pp. Plenty of close-up photographs accompany information about the life cycle of honeybees and the important role they play in nature. (Rev: BL 9/15/05) [575.79]

BEETLES

23149 Allen, Judy. *Are You a Ladybug?* (PS–1). Illus. by Tudor Humphries. Series: Backyard Books. 2000, Kingfisher $9.95 (978-0-7534-5241-7). 32pp. A beginner's book that explains in text and pictures what a ladybug is, what it eats, and how it grows from egg to first flight. (Rev: BL 5/15/00; HBG 3/01; SLJ 9/00) [595.76]

23150 Ashley, Susan. *Ladybugs* (1–4). Series: Let's Read About Insects. 2004, Weekly Reader LB $21.00 (978-0-8368-4055-1); paper $5.95 (978-0-8368-4062-9). 24pp. The life cycle of ladybugs is described in small-format, easy-to-read text with close-up photographs. (Rev: SLJ 2/05) [595.76]

23151 Chrustowski, Rick. *Bright Beetle* (PS–2). Illus. 2000, Holt $15.95 (978-0-8050-6058-4). 32pp. The life cycle of the ladybug, its habits, and physical characteristics are covered in this good introduction for beginning scientists. (Rev: BL 6/1–15/00; HBG 9/00; SLJ 5/00) [595.76]

23152 Fischer-Nagel, Heiderose, and Andreas Fischer-Nagel. *Life of the Ladybug* (2–5). Illus. 1986, Carolrhoda LB $19.95 (978-0-87614-240-0). 48pp. The life cycle of the ladybug with full-color, informative photographs. (Rev: BCCB 3/86; BL 5/15/86; SLJ 4/86)

23153 Hartley, Karen, and Chris Macro. *Ladybug* (1–3). Illus. by Alan Male. Series: Bug Books. 1998, Heinemann LB $21.36 (978-1-57572-662-5). 32pp. Double-page spreads, each with a large photo of a ladybug, introduce such topics as structure, behavior, enemies, food, and life cycle. (Rev: HBG 9/99; SLJ 1/99) [595.7]

23154 Jango-Cohen, Judith. *Hungry Ladybugs* (2–3). Series: Pull Ahead Books. 2003, Lerner LB $22.60 (978-0-8225-4667-2). 32pp. The life cycle and physical characteristics of the ladybird beetle, one of nature's most efficient pest-killers and commonly known as the ladybug, is explored in this short book suitable for beginning readers. (Rev: BL 11/15/03; HBG 10/03)

23155 Johnson, Sylvia A. *Beetles* (4–7). Illus. 1982, Lerner LB $22.60 (978-0-8225-1476-3). 48pp. Color photography highlights this account that concentrates on the scarab beetle.

23156 Llewellyn, Claire. *Ladybug* (PS–3). Illus. by Simon Mendez. Series: Starting Life. 2004, North-Word $16.95 (978-1-55971-892-9). 23pp. On pages that grow progressively wider, the stages of a ladybug's development are traced, with information on such topics as habitat and diet plus realistic illustrations. (Rev: SLJ 11/04) [595.76]

23157 Lockwood, Sophie. *Beetles* (4–6). Illus. Series: World of Insects. 2007, Child's World LB $20.95 (978-1-59296-819-0). 40pp. All about beetles — their life cycle, anatomy, diversity, and ubiquity —

with a look at their relationship with humans. (Rev: BL 10/15/07) [595.76]

23158 McEvey, Shane F. *Beetles* (3–5). Series: Insects and Spiders. 2001, Chelsea LB $28.00 (978-0-7910-6600-3). 32pp. Beetle facts of all kinds are amplified by information on how scientists collect and study them and by tips on keeping beetles as pets. Also use *Bugs* (2001). (Rev: HBG 3/02; SLJ 2/02) [595.76]

23159 Mason, Adrienne. *Mealworms: Raise Them, Watch Them, See Them Change* (3–5). Illus. 1998, Kids Can $12.95 (978-1-55074-448-4). 24pp. Gives the life story of mealworms (the larval stage of the darkling beetle) and tips on how to raise and observe them. (Rev: BL 6/1–15/98; HBG 9/98; SLJ 9/98) [638.5]

23160 Murray, Peter. *Beetles* (1–4). Series: Naturebooks. 2003, Child's World LB $25.64 (978-1-56766-976-3). 32pp. Large-print text and close-up photographs explore beetles' many varieties, physical characteristics, habitat, diet, and behavior. (Rev: SLJ 12/03) [595.76]

23161 Pallotta, Jerry. *The Beetle Alphabet Book* (PS–2). Illus. by David Biedrzycki. 2004, Charlesbridge $16.95 (978-1-57091-551-2). 32pp. An arresting alphabet of bugs, providing brightly illustrated information with a dollop of humor. (Rev: BL 2/1/04; SLJ 5/04) [595.76]

23162 Posada, Mia. *Ladybugs: Red, Fiery, and Bright* (PS–2). Illus. by author. 2002, Carolrhoda LB $15.95 (978-0-87614-334-6). A rhythmic look at ladybugs and their life cycle and behavior. (Rev: HBG 10/02; SLJ 5/02) [595.7]

23163 Pyers, Greg. *Ladybugs up Close* (2–4). Illus. Series: Minibeasts Up Close. 2005, Raintree LB $27.50 (978-1-4109-1530-6). 32pp. A simple introduction to ladybugs and their physical characteristics, habitat, senses, and reproduction, with large-scale color photographs.

23164 Ross, Michael E. *Ladybugology* (3–5). Photos by Brian Grogan. Illus. by Darren Erickson. Series: Backyard Buddies. 1998, Carolrhoda $19.93 (978-1-57505-051-5). 48pp. This introduction to ladybugs describes their structure and habits and outlines a number of activities that involve capturing and observing them. (Rev: BL 7/98; SLJ 3/98) [595.7]

23165 Sexton, Colleen. *Beetles* (1–3). Series: Blast Off! Readers: World of Insects. 2007, Children's Pr. LB $18.50 (978-0-531-17566-8). 24pp. Facts about beetles are accompanied by close-up photographs, making this a useful book for beginning report writers. (Rev: SLJ 8/07)

23166 Tracqui, Valerie. *Face-to-Face with the Ladybug* (3–6). Series: Face-to-Face. 2002, Charlesbridge $9.95 (978-1-57091-453-9). 32pp. The physical characteristics, habits, life cycle, and habitats of the industrious, colorful ladybug are featured in this attractive volume. (Rev: BCCB 10/02; BL 9/15/02; HBG 3/03) [595.76]

CATERPILLARS, BUTTERFLIES, AND MOTHS

23167 Allen, Judy. *Are You a Butterfly?* (PS–1). Illus. by Tudor Humphries. Series: Backyard Books. 2000, Kingfisher $9.95 (978-0-7534-5240-0). 32pp. By allowing the child to imagine that he or she is the insect discussed, this simple book goes through the stages of growth from egg and caterpillar to chrysalis and butterfly. (Rev: BL 10/15/00; HBG 10/01) [544.2]

23168 Bishop, Nic. *Nic Bishop Butterflies and Moths* (2–4). Illus. by author. 2009, Scholastic $17.99 (978-0-439-87757-2). 48pp. Fine color photos and well-written text make this title a fly away winner. (Rev: BCCB 5/09; BL 6/1–15/09; HB 7/09; SLJ 6/09) [595.78]

23169 Cassie, Brian, and Jerry Pallotta. *The Butterfly Alphabet Book* (PS–2). Illus. by Mark Astrella. 1995, Charlesbridge paper $6.95 (978-0-88106-894-8). From an Apollo butterfly to a Zephyr Metalmark, this alphabet book features amazing butterflies with descriptions of their characteristics. (Rev: SLJ 12/95) [595.78]

23170 Ehlert, Lois. *Waiting for Wings* (PS–1). Illus. 2001, Harcourt $17.00 (978-0-15-202608-0). 38pp. Using a short rhyming text and glowing illustrations, this book covers the life cycle of the butterfly, with information on physical characteristics, diet, and behavior. (Rev: BL 3/1/01*; HB 5/01; HBG 10/01) [595.78]

23171 Fischer-Nagel, Heiderose, and Andreas Fischer-Nagel. *Life of the Butterfly* (4–6). Illus. 1987, Lerner paper $7.95 (978-0-87614-484-8). 48pp. Clear, readable text and color photos detail the life of a peacock butterfly. (Rev: BL 4/1/87; SLJ 5/87)

23172 Frost, Helen. *Monarch and Milkweed* (PS–2). Illus. by Leonid Gore. 2008, Atheneum $17.99 (978-1-4169-0085-6). 40pp. The interdependent life cycles of the monarch butterfly and the milkweed plant are presented with maps and illustrations. (Rev: BL 1/1–15/08; SLJ 1/08) [595.78]

23173 Frost, Helen. *Moths* (PS–3). Series: Insects. 2001, Capstone LB $17.26 (978-0-7368-0852-1). 24pp. Spare text and full-page color photographs — often close-up shots — offer basic information on moths. (Rev: HBG 3/02; SLJ 9/01) [595.78]

23174 Gibbons, Gail. *Monarch Butterfly* (1–3). Illus. 1989, Holiday House LB $16.95 (978-0-8234-0773-6). 32pp. The basic life cycle of the monarch butterfly from egg to adult. (Rev: BCCB 12/89; BL 11/1/89; HB 11/89; SLJ 12/89) [595.78]

23175 Glaser, Linda. *Magnificent Monarchs* (K–3). Illus. by Gay Holland. 2000, Millbrook LB $21.40 (978-0-7613-1700-5). This is a very attractive work on monarch butterflies and their amazing lives and migrations. (Rev: HBG 10/01; SLJ 1/01) [595.78]

23176 Hamilton, Kersten. *The Butterfly Book: A Kid's Guide to Attracting, Raising, and Keeping Butterflies* (3–6). Illus. 1997, John Muir paper $8.95 (978-1-56261-309-9). 40pp. Introduces 20 species of butterflies and how to attract and keep them, as well as describing their life cycle, anatomy, and habits. (Rev: BL 7/97) [595.78]

23177 Hartley, Karen, et al. *Caterpillar* (K–3). Series: Heinemann First Library. 1999, Heinemann LB $21.36 (978-1-57572-795-0). 32pp. Different kinds of caterpillars are introduced, with material on lifestyles and habitats, richly illustrated with full-page color photographs that accompany a simple text. (Rev: BL 6/1–15/99; HBG 9/99) [595.78]

23178 Heiligman, Deborah. *From Caterpillar to Butterfly* (PS–1). Illus. by Bari Weissman. Series: Let's-Read-and-Find-Out. 1996, HarperCollins paper $5.99 (978-0-06-445129-1). 31pp. Using a classroom setting, this book shows children watching the miracle of the metamorphosis from caterpillar to butterfly. (Rev: SLJ 8/96) [595.78]

23179 Kalman, Bobbie. *The Life Cycle of a Butterfly* (2–4). Illus. Series: The Life Cycle. 2001, Crabtree LB $25.27 (978-0-7787-0650-2); paper $6.95 (978-0-7787-0680-9). 32pp. After a general description of the butterfly, the author clearly explains the stages of its life cycle and discusses what can be done to curb human encroachment. (Rev: SLJ 6/02) [595.789]

23180 Kalman, Bobbie, and Robin Johnson. *Endangered Butterflies* (3–5). Illus. Series: Earth's Endangered Animals. 2006, Crabtree LB $25.27 (978-0-7787-1870-3). 32pp. Large text and clear color photographs focus on endangered butterfly species, presenting basic information about physical characteristics, diet, habitat, behavior, and discussing the specific threats they face. (Rev: SLJ 1/07) [595.78]

23181 Lasky, Kathryn. *Monarchs* (4–6). Illus. by Christopher G. Knight. 1993, Harcourt paper $11.00 (978-0-15-255297-8). 64pp. The life cycle of the monarch butterfly is presented with details of its mammoth migration. Also tells how communities have helped preserve this species. (Rev: BCCB 11/93; BL 11/15/93; HB 11/93; SLJ 9/93*) [595.78]

23182 List, Ilka Katherine. *Moths and Butterflies of North America* (3–5). Series: Animals in Order. 2002, Watts LB $26.50 (978-0-531-11597-8). 48pp. After a general discussion of animal classification, this book describes in words and pictures 15 species of moths and butterflies that live in North America. (Rev: BL 3/15/02) [595.78]

23183 Llewellyn, Claire. *Butterfly* (K–4). Illus. by Simon Mendez. Series: Starting Life. 2003, NorthWord $16.95 (978-1-55971-868-4). 23pp. The life cycle of a butterfly is detailed in words and paintings, together with a combined glossary and index; the unusual graduated page sizes add appeal. (Rev: SLJ 4/04) [595.78]

23184 Loewen, Nancy. *Flying Colors: Butterflies in Your Backyard* (PS–2). Illus. by Rick Peterson. Series: Backyard Bugs. 2005, Picture Window LB $25.26 (978-1-4048-1143-0). 24pp. Butterflies' importance as plant pollinators is emphasized in this large, horizontal volume that includes an activity and a craft project. (Rev: BL 12/1/05) [595.78]

23185 Markle, Sandra. *Luna Moths: Masters of Change* (2–5). Series: Insect World. 2008, Lerner LB $27.93 (978-0-8225-7302-9). 48pp. Eye-catching illustrations and simple diagrams are combined with interestingly presented facts about these insects and two activities. (Rev: LMC 10/08; SLJ 2/08) [595.78]

23186 Meister, Cari. *Butterflies* (2–4). Illus. Series: Checkerboard Science and Nature Library: Insects. 2001, ABDO LB $21.35 (978-1-57765-459-9). 24pp. This is an attractive, basic introduction to butterflies. (Rev: BL 10/15/01; HBG 10/01) [595.78]

23187 Morris, Ting. *Butterfly* (2–4). Illus. by Desiderio Sanzi. Series: Creepy Crawly World. 2004, Smart Apple LB $27.10 (978-1-58340-379-2). 32pp. Introduces butterflies' characteristics, habitat, diet, defense mechanisms, and life cycle, using realistic paintings and diagrams. (Rev: SLJ 6/05)

23188 Murawski, Darlyne A. *Face to Face with Caterpillars* (3–6). Photos by author. Series: Face to Face. 2007, National Geographic $16.95 (978-1-4263-0052-3). 32pp. Close-up photographs by the author provide a new perspective on caterpillars, with facts suitable for report writers. (Rev: SLJ 6/07)

23189 Noonan, Diana. *The Butterfly* (2–4). Series: Life Cycles. 2002, Chelsea LB $23.00 (978-0-7910-6963-9). 32pp. Full-color illustrations show the various stages in the life cycle of the butterfly from egg to caterpillar and pupa to the mature butterfly. (Rev: BL 12/15/02; HBG 3/03) [595.78]

23190 Patent, Dorothy Hinshaw. *Fabulous Fluttering Tropical Butterflies* (1–3). Illus. by Kendahl Jan Jubb. 2003, Walker LB $17.85 (978-0-8027-8839-9). 32pp. With bright illustrations, this book describes tropical butterflies' life cycles and looks at individual species and at butterflies' lives in the rainforest and in zoos. (Rev: BL 5/1/03; HBG 10/03; SLJ 5/03) [595.78]

23191 Preston-Mafham, Rod. *The Secret Life of Butterflies and Moths* (4–7). Series: The Secret World of . . . 2002, Raintree LB $27.12 (978-0-7398-4984-2). 48pp. Beginning with little-known facts about butterflies and moths, this book explores their life cycles, behavior, mating habits, enemies, food, and habitats. (Rev: BL 8/02) [595.78]

23192 Pringle, Laurence. *An Extraordinary Life: The Story of a Monarch Butterfly* (3–6). Illus. by Bob Marstall. 1997, Orchard LB $19.99 (978-0-531-33002-9). 32pp. The life cycle of a single monarch butterfly and its migration from Massachusetts to Mexico. (Rev: BCCB 5/97; BL 3/15/97*; HB 5/97; SLJ 5/97) [595.78]

23193 Pyers, Greg. *Butterflies up Close* (2–4). Illus. Series: Minibeasts Up Close. 2005, Raintree LB $27.50 (978-1-4109-1528-3). 32pp. A simple introduction to butterflies and their physical characteristics, habitat, senses, and reproduction, with large-scale color photographs.

23194 Rabe, Tish. *My, Oh My — a Butterfly! All About Butterflies* (1–2). Illus. by Aristides Ruiz and Joe Mathieu. Series: The Cat in the Hat's Learning Library. 2007, Random $11.99 (978-0-375-82882-9). 45pp. Rhyming, Dr. Seuss-style text introduces facts about different types of butterflies in an engaging way. (Rev: SLJ 8/07)

23195 Rea, Ba. *Monarch! Come Play with Me* (K–2). Illus. by author. 2006, Bas Relief paper $10.95

(978-0-9657472-5-7). 32pp. A young girl's conversation with a monarch caterpillar that is concentrating on metamorphosis offers insights into the process. (Rev: SLJ 8/06) [595]

23196 Ring, Elizabeth. *Night Flier* (1–3). Photos by Dwight Kuhn. 1994, Millbrook LB $21.90 (978-1-56294-467-4). 32pp. The life cycle of the cecropia moth is chronicled from its hatching. (Rev: BL 10/1/94; SLJ 12/94) [595.78]

23197 Rockwell, Anne. *Becoming Butterflies* (PS–2). Illus. by Megan Halsey. 2002, Walker LB $16.85 (978-0-8027-8798-9). 32pp. The story of the metamorphosis of monarch butterflies is told in a clear, concise manner for young readers. (Rev: BCCB 5/02; BL 3/15/02; HBG 10/02; SLJ 3/02) [595.78]

23198 Rosenblatt, Lynn. *Monarch Magic! Butterfly Activities and Nature Discoveries* (3–6). Illus. Series: Good Times! 1998, Williamson paper $14.25 (978-1-885593-23-8). 96pp. This work covers many topics involving the monarch butterfly, including physical characteristics, feeding habits, habitats, and migratory patterns plus material on how to raise them and protect them from extinction. (Rev: BL 12/1/98; SLJ 4/99) [595.78]

23199 Ross, Michael E. *Caterpillarology* (3–5). Photos by Brian Grogan. Illus. by Darren Erickson. Series: Backyard Buddies. 1998, Carolrhoda LB $19.93 (978-1-57505-055-3). 48pp. A great deal of scientific information is presented about caterpillars in an entertaining way, with experiments and instructions on how to capture and release them. (Rev: BL 7/98; SLJ 3/98) [595.78]

23200 Schlaepfer, Gloria G. *Butterflies* (4–8). Illus. Series: AnimalWays. 2005, Benchmark LB $21.95 (978-0-7614-1745-3). 112pp. Beautiful photographs of butterfly specimens enrich this well-organized volume that provides basic information on the butterfly's characteristics, habits, and habitat. (Rev: SLJ 5/06) [595.78]

23201 Spilsbury, Louise. *Butterfly* (K–2). Series: Life Cycles. 2005, Heinemann LB $20.64 (978-1-4034-6770-6). 24pp. Brief text and bold photographs suitable for beginning readers focus on the life cycle of the butterfly. (Rev: SLJ 7/05) [595.78]

23202 Stewart, Melissa. *Butterflies* (4–7). Illus. by Andrew Recher. Series: Our Wild World. 2007, NorthWord LB $10.95 (978-1-55971-966-7); paper $7.95 (978-1-55971-967-4). 48pp. The behavior, physical characteristics and life cycles of butterflies are presented in great detail with many photographs. (Rev: SLJ 7/07) [595.78]

23203 Stewart, Melissa. *A Place for Butterflies* (K–3). Illus. by Higgins Bond. 2006, Peachtree $16.95 (978-1-56145-357-3). 32pp. This richly illustrated book takes readers on a tour of butterfly habitats where human intervention has helped the insects to survive. (Rev: BL 3/15/06; SLJ 6/06) [595.7]

23204 Swinburne, Stephen. *A Butterfly Grows* (PS–1). Illus. Series: Green Light Readers. 2009, Houghton $12.99 (978-0-15-206422-8). 24pp. For beginning readers, this simple and colorful book follows the development of a butterfly. (Rev: BL 5/1/09; SLJ 10/09) [595.78]

23205 Swinburne, Stephen. *Wings of Light: The Migration of the Yellow Butterfly* (K–3). Illus. by Bruce Hiscock. 2006, Boyds Mills $15.95 (978-1-59078-082-4). 32pp. Traces the migration of the cloudless sulphur butterfly from its winter home in Mexico's Yucatan to its summer range in the northeastern United States. (Rev: BL 4/1/06; SLJ 5/06) [595.78]

23206 Wallace, Nancy Elizabeth. *Fly, Monarch! Fly!* (K–2). Illus. by author. 2008, Marshall Cavendish $16.99 (978-0-7614-5425-0). 40pp. A rabbit family — mother, father, Minna, and Pip — visit Butterfly Place and learn all about monarch butterflies' life cycle through a series of exhibits; a craft, tips for a butterfly garden, and additional facts close this attractive book. (Rev: BL 6/1–15/08; LMC 10/08; SLJ 8/08) [595.78]

23207 Waxman, Laura Hamilton. *Monarch Butterflies* (2–3). Series: Pull Ahead Books. 2003, Lerner LB $22.60 (978-0-8225-4669-6). 32pp. Suitable for beginning readers, this book follows the beautiful monarch butterfly through each stage of its life cycle. (Rev: BL 11/15/03; HBG 10/03)

23208 Wilner, Yvonne. *Butterflies Fly* (2–5). Illus. by Karen Lloyd-Jones. 2001, Charlesbridge LB $16.95 (978-1-57091-446-1). 32pp. A poetic text with large illustrations shows butterflies of the world in their natural habitats. (Rev: BL 2/15/01; HBG 10/01; SLJ 2/01) [595.78]

23209 Zemlicka, Shannon. *From Egg to Butterfly* (K–2). Series: Start to Finish. 2003, Lerner LB $18.60 (978-0-8225-0713-0). 24pp. Full of photographs, this basic introduction suitable for beginning readers follows the life cycle of a butterfly. (Rev: SLJ 9/03) [595.78]

SPIDERS AND SCORPIONS

23210 Allen, Judy. *Are You a Spider?* (PS–1). Illus. by Tudor Humphries. Series: Backyard Books. 2000, Kingfisher $9.95 (978-0-7534-5243-1). 32pp. The reader becomes a newly hatched spider and learns how to spin threads, make webs, and watch out for dangers such as birds. (Rev: BL 10/15/00; HBG 10/01) [595.4]

23211 Allman, Toney. *From Spider Webs to Man-Made Silk* (4–7). Illus. Series: Imitating Nature. 2005, Gale LB $24.95 (978-0-7377-3124-8). 48pp. An introduction to scientists' attempts to replicate spider silk in the laboratory. (Rev: BL 10/15/05; LMC 3/06) [595.4]

23212 Bailey, Jill. *How Spiders Make Their Webs* (3–5). Illus. Series: Nature's Mysteries. 1996, Benchmark LB $22.79 (978-0-7614-0456-9). 32pp. Using a large number of illustrations, this account describes a variety of spider constructions and how they are made. (Rev: SLJ 2/97) [595.4]

23213 Berger, Melvin. *Spinning Spiders* (K–4). Illus. by S. D. Schindler. Series: Let's-Read-and-Find-Out Science. 2003, HarperCollins LB $16.89 (978-0-06-028697-2); paper $5.99 (978-0-06-445207-6). 33pp. The differences between arachnids and insects are

clearly explained, and five types of spiders are profiled with full-color illustrations. (Rev: HBG 10/03; SLJ 9/03) [595.4]

23214 Berger, Melvin, and Gilda Berger. *Do All Spiders Spin Webs? Questions and Answers About Spiders* (3–5). Illus. by Roberto Osti. Series: Scholastic Question and Answer. 2000, Scholastic $14.95 (978-0-439-09586-0); paper $6.99 (978-0-439-14881-8). 48pp. The authors give informative answers to such questions as "What happens when an enemy bites off a spider's leg?" Also use *Tarantulas* (2001). (Rev: HBG 3/01; SLJ 5/01) [595.4]

23215 Berman, Ruth. *Spinning Spiders* (PS–2). Illus. by David T. Roberts. Series: Pull Ahead Books. 1998, Lerner LB $22.60 (978-0-8225-3604-8). 32pp. Using questions within the text, this book introduces spiders and their habits along with information on the differences between spiders and insects, spider webs, egg sacs, and spiderlings. (Rev: BL 2/1/99; HBG 3/99; SLJ 6/99) [595.4]

23216 Bishop, Nic. *Nic Bishop Spiders* (3–5). Photos by author. 2007, Scholastic $16.99 (978-0-439-87756-5). 48pp. Striking close-up photographs and conversational text introduce more than 15 arachnids and their behavior. (Rev: BCCB 10/07; HB 3/08; SLJ 11/07)

23217 Bredeson, Carmen. *Tarantulas Up Close* (1–3). Series: Zoom in on Animals! 2008, Enslow LB $21.26 (978-0-7660-3076-3). 24pp. A simple introduction to tarantulas with sharp, close-up color photographs and clear text. (Rev: SLJ 9/08) [595.4]

23218 Dallinger, Jane. *Spiders* (4–7). Illus. 1981, Lerner LB $22.60 (978-0-8225-1456-5). 48pp. Excellent color photographs complement the text.

23219 Dinaberg, Leslie. *Spider Life* (2–5). Series: Boys Rock! 2006, The Child's World LB $25.64 (978-1-59296-737-7). 32pp. A good choice for beginning and reluctant readers (girls as well as boys), this colorful volume looks at spiders' physical and behavioral characteristics, habitat, diet, predators, and life cycle. (Rev: SLJ 2/07) [595.4]

23220 Ganeri, Anita. *From Egg to Spider* (1–3). Illus. Series: How Living Things Grow. 2006, Heinemann LB $25.36 (978-1-4034-7860-3). 32pp. The life cycle of the garden spider, presented in an easy-to-read format. (Rev: SLJ 6/06) [595.4]

23221 Gibbons, Gail. *Spiders* (1–2). Illus. 1993, Holiday House LB $16.95 (978-0-8234-1006-4). 32pp. An introductory account with stunning drawings of spiders, plus their structure, behavior, and important species. (Rev: BL 4/15/93; SLJ 7/93) [595.4]

23222 Glaser, Linda. *Spectacular Spiders* (K–2). Illus. by Gay Holland. 1998, Millbrook LB $22.90 (978-0-7613-0353-4). 32pp. A young girl explains the habits and behavior of garden spiders, including their diet and how they spin webs. (Rev: BL 1/1–15/99; HBG 3/99; SLJ 3/99) [595.4]

23223 Greenaway, Theresa. *Spiders* (4–7). Series: The Secret World of . . . 2001, Raintree LB $18.98 (978-0-7368-3509-1). 48pp. An information-crammed text and attractive illustrations introduce spiders, how and where they live, and their behavior. (Rev: BL 10/15/01) [595.4]

23224 Hartley, Karen, et al. *Spider* (K–3). Series: Heinemann First Library. 1999, Heinemann LB $21.36 (978-1-57572-799-8). 32pp. Different kinds of spiders are pictured in full-color photos with textual material on habits, physical characteristics, and life cycles. (Rev: BL 6/1–15/99; HBG 9/99) [595.4]

23225 Hughes, Monica. *Spiders* (PS–2). Illus. 2003, Raintree LB $18.56 (978-1-4109-0622-9). 24pp. A close-up look at the diet, anatomy, habitat, and life cycle of spiders, for beginning readers. (Rev: BL 2/15/04) [595.4]

23226 Kallen, Stuart A. *Spiders* (4–6). Illus. Series: Nature's Predators. 2001, Gale LB $23.70 (978-0-7377-0630-7). 48pp. Spiders' methods of hunting, catching, and eating their prey are presented, with illustrations. (Rev: BL 10/15/01) [595.4]

23227 Kalman, Bobbie. *Web Weavers and Other Spiders* (2–5). Illus. Series: Crabapples. 1997, Crabtree paper $5.95 (978-0-86505-732-6). 32pp. A description of how spiders live is given, with material on physical characteristics, web building, defenses, and mating behavior. (Rev: BL 7/97; SLJ 7/97) [595.4]

23228 McGinty, Alice B. *The Jumping Spider* (3–6). 2001, Rosen LB $18.75 (978-0-8239-5568-8). 24pp. Two-page chapters with arresting photographs discuss topics such as the spider's anatomy, behavior, habitat, and relationship to humans. Other titles in this series include *The Black Widow* and *The Tarantula* (both 2001). (Rev: SLJ 3/02) [595.4]

23229 Markle, Sandra. *Sneaky, Spinning Baby Spiders* (2–5). Illus. 2008, Walker $16.99 (978-0-8027-9697-4). 32pp. Featuring clear photographs, this volume focuses on baby spiders and how their mothers care (or fail to care) for them. (Rev: BCCB 11/08; BL 12/1/08; HB 1/09; LMC 1/09; SLJ 10/08) [595.4]

23230 Montgomery, Sy. *The Tarantula Scientist* (4–7). Photos by Nic Bishop. Series: Scientists in the Field. 2004, Houghton $18.00 (978-0-618-14799-1). 80pp. This informative, photo-filled book chronicles the day-to-day field work of arachnologist Sam Marshall as he searches for tarantulas in the French Guianan rain forest. (Rev: BL 3/15/04; HB 7/04; SLJ 5/04) [595.4]

23231 Morley, Christine. *Freaky Facts About Spiders* (2–4). Illus. Series: Freaky Facts About. 2007, Two-Can $13.95 (978-1-58728-596-7); paper $8.95 (978-1-58728-597-4). 32pp. A colorful introduction to spiders and their weirder characteristics, full of graphic elements that will appeal to reluctant readers. (Rev: BL 3/15/07) [595.4]

23232 Murawski, Darlyne. *Spiders and Their Webs* (2–5). 2004, National Geographic $16.95 (978-0-7922-6979-3). 32pp. Dramatic telephoto shots of spiders are paired with basic facts and information on unusual behaviors. (Rev: BL 12/1/04; SLJ 3/05) [595.4]

23233 Murray, Peter. *Spiders and Scorpions* (3–6). Series: Science Around Us. 2004, Child's World LB $27.07 (978-1-59296-273-0). 32pp. Eye-catching photographs and interesting "Did You Know?" features draw the reader into this overview of spiders and scorpions. (Rev: SLJ 3/05) [595.4]

23234 Ross, Michael E. *Spiderology* (3–6). Illus. 2000, Carolrhoda LB $19.93 (978-1-57505-387-5); paper $6.95 (978-1-57505-438-4). 48pp. After describing how to collect and observe spiders humanely, this book suggests a number of activities to learn more about them. (Rev: BL 5/15/00; HBG 9/00; SLJ 7/00) [595.4]

23235 Schnieper, Claudia. *Amazing Spiders* (3–6). Illus. by Max Meier. 1989, Carolrhoda LB $23.93 (978-0-87614-342-1). 48pp. In often startling photos and a clear text, spiders are introduced. (Rev: BL 9/15/89; HB 11/89; SLJ 8/89) [595.4]

23236 Simon, Seymour. *Spiders*. Rev. ed. (3–6). 2007, Collins $16.99 (978-0-06-089104-6); paper $6.99 (978-0-06-089103-9). 32pp. A new edition of the guide to spiders that provides stunning photographs and smooth, informative text, making it a browsing pleasure as well as a resource for reports. (Rev: HB 11/03; SLJ 3/08) [595.4]

23237 Souza, D. M. *Eight Legs* (3–5). Illus. Series: Creatures All Around Us. 1991, Carolrhoda LB $22.60 (978-0-87614-441-1). 40pp. Close-up photographs and clear explanations introduce spiders, scorpions, and other crawling creatures with eight legs. (Rev: BL 4/15/91; SLJ 7/91) [595.4]

23238 Squire, Ann O. *Spiders of North America* (3–5). Series: Animals in Order. 2000, Watts LB $26.50 (978-0-531-11516-9). 48pp. This book explains the animal classification system and then goes on to describe arachnids and introduce different varieties of spiders and their behavior. (Rev: BL 4/15/00) [595.4]

23239 Storad, Conrad J. *Tarantulas* (2–3). Series: Early Bird Nature Books. 1998, Lerner LB $25.26 (978-0-8225-3024-4). 48pp. This easily read, beautifully illustrated account introduces the tarantula, its life cycle, and its feeding habits. (Rev: BL 3/15/98; HBG 9/98; SLJ 7/98) [595.4]

23240 Time For Kids Eds., and Nicole Iorio. *Spiders!* (2–3). Illus. Series: Time For Kids Science Scoops. 2005, HarperCollins $14.99 (978-0-06-057635-6); paper $3.99 (978-0-06-057634-9). 48pp. Simple text suitable for beginning readers and bright illustrations present basic information on spiders, plus a profile of a scientist who works with them. (Rev: SLJ 3/05) [595.4]

23241 Winer, Yvonne. *Spiders Spin Webs* (PS–3). Illus. by Karen Lloyd-Jones. 1998, Charlesbridge $15.95 (978-0-88106-983-9); paper $6.95 (978-0-88106-984-6). 32pp. This visually exciting field guide introduces 15 types of spiders and their characteristics. (Rev: BL 7/98; HBG 3/99; SLJ 11/98) [595.4]

23242 Zabludoff, Marc. *Spiders* (4–8). Illus. Series: AnimalWays. 2005, Benchmark LB $21.95 (978-0-7614-1747-7). 112pp. Beautiful photographs enrich this well-organized volume that provides basic information on the insect's characteristics, habits, and habitat. (Rev: SLJ 5/06) [595.4]

23243 Zollman, Pam. *A Spiderling Grows Up* (K–1). Series: Scholastic News Nonfiction Readers. 2005, Children's Pr. LB $20.00 (978-0-516-24946-9). 24pp. Covers the life cycle of a spider, with a focus on spider eggs and young spiderlings and their survival tactics. (Rev: SLJ 4/06) [595.4]

Land Invertebrates

23244 Allen, Judy. *Are You a Snail?* (PS–1). Illus. by Tudor Humphries. Series: Backyard Books. 2000, Kingfisher $9.95 (978-0-7534-5242-4). 32pp. An introduction to snails that discusses their appearance, food, and how they grow from egg to adult. (Rev: BL 5/15/00; HBG 3/01; SLJ 9/00) [594]

23245 Blaxland, Beth. *Annelids: Earthworms, Leeches, and Sea Worms* (3–5). Illus. Series: Invertebrates. 2002, Chelsea LB $28.00 (978-0-7910-6993-6). 32pp. Close-up photographs, straightforward text, and an enticing layout introduce the annelid invertebrates. Also use *Cephalopods: Octopuses, Squids, and Their Relatives* and *Myriapods: Centipedes, Millipedes, and Their Relatives* (2002). (Rev: BL 12/1/02; HBG 3/03) [592]

23246 Buholzer, Theres. *Life of the Snail* (2–5). Illus. 1987, Carolrhoda LB $23.93 (978-0-87614-246-2). 48pp. Close-up photos highlight the story of this small, fascinating animal. (Rev: BL 3/15/87; SLJ 6–7/87)

23247 Campbell, Sarah C. *Wolfsnail: A Backyard Predator* (PS–2). Illus. by author. 2008, Boyds Mills $16.95 (978-1-59078-554-6). 32pp. Simple text and close-up photographs introduce the tiny wolfsnail, which eats smaller snails and slugs. (Rev: BL 4/1/08; HB 7/08; LMC 10/08; SLJ 5/08) [594]

23248 Dell'Oro, Suzanne Paul. *Tunneling Earthworms* (PS–2). Series: Pull Ahead Books. 2000, Lerner LB $22.60 (978-0-8225-3762-5). 32pp. A lavishly illustrated book that introduces the earthworm, its anatomy, food, and how it is able to move through earth. (Rev: BL 3/1/01; HBG 10/01) [595]

23249 Dixon, Norma. *Lowdown on Earthworms* (2–4). Illus. 2005, Fitzhenry & Whiteside $16.95 (978-1-55041-114-0). 32pp. This attractive title digs into the anatomy, behavior, and habitat of earthworms and describes worm-related projects. (Rev: BL 9/1/05) [592.64]

23250 Fredericks, Anthony D. *Slugs* (2–3). Series: Early Bird Nature Books. 2000, Lerner LB $25.26 (978-0-8225-3041-1). 48pp. A beginning science book that describes, in pictures and text, what a slug looks like, where it lives, how it reproduces, and how it survives in spite of predators. (Rev: BL 5/15/00; HBG 9/00) [595]

23251 Glaser, Linda. *Wonderful Worms* (PS–2). Illus. by Loretta Krupinski. 1992, Millbrook LB $21.90 (978-1-56294-062-1). 32pp. A close peek at the wriggly world of earthworms. (Rev: BL 1/15/93; SLJ 3/93) [595]

23252 Hartley, Karen, et al. *Centipede* (1–3). Illus. 2006, Heinemann LB $17.75 (978-1-4034-8295-2). 31pp. A simple question-and-answer format and eye-catching photographs introduce the life cycle of the centipede, as well as the invertebrate's physical characteristics, diet, habitat, and predators. (Rev: BL 9/15/06) [595.6]

23253 Hartley, Karen, and Chris Macro. *Snail* (1–3). Illus. by Alan Male. Series: Bug Books. 1998, Heinemann LB $21.36 (978-1-57572-664-9). 32pp. Large color photos of snails and short paragraphs of text are used to explain the physical structure, behavior, food, and life cycle of the snail. (Rev: HBG 9/99; SLJ 1/99) [594.3]

23254 Heinrichs, Ann. *Worms* (1–3). Illus. Series: Nature's Friends. 2004, Compass Point LB $22.60 (978-0-7565-0589-9). 32pp. Worms' anatomy and life cycle are covered in simple text and clear close-up photographs.

23255 Johnson, Sylvia A. *Snails* (4–6). Illus. 1982, Lerner LB $22.60 (978-0-8225-1475-6). 48pp. The structure, habits, and life cycle of a snail.

23256 Knudsen, Michelle. *A Slimy Story* (K–2). Illus. by Paige Billin-Frye. Series: Science Solves It! 2004, Kane paper $4.99 (978-1-57565-144-6). 32pp. Dan can't think what he can give his mother for her birthday until he realizes that earthworms are the perfect present for a gardener; scientific facts are interwoven into the text. (Rev: SLJ 1/05) [595]

23257 McLaughlin, Molly. *Earthworms, Dirt, and Rotten Leaves: An Exploration in Ecology* (4–6). Illus. 1986, Avon paper $3.50 (978-0-380-71074-4). 96pp. Activities that lead to an understanding of the behavior and appearance of earthworms. (Rev: BCCB 2/87; BL 2/1/87; SLJ 3/87)

23258 Miller, Ruth. *Arthropods* (4–6). Series: Animal Kingdom. 2004, Raintree LB $25.70 (978-1-4109-1049-3). 64pp. The common characteristics of arthropods are explained, followed by descriptions of various orders of arthropods and selected specific species plus discussion of endangered status and evolution. (Rev: SLJ 6/05)

23259 Parker, Steve. *Nematodes, Leeches and Other Worms* (4–6). Illus. Series: Animals Kingdom Classification. 2006, Compass Point LB $29.26 (978-0-7565-1615-4). 48pp. Concise, well-written text, color photographs, diagrams, and charts cover the physical characteristics, habitat, diet, and behavior of worms. (Rev: SLJ 11/06) [592]

23260 Pfeffer, Wendy. *Wiggling Worms at Work* (K–3). Illus. by Steve Jenkins. Series: Let's-Read-and-Find-Out Science. 2004, HarperCollins $15.99 (978-0-06-028448-0). 40pp. Solid information on the earthworm and its characteristics are followed by advice on observing worms in their native habitat. (Rev: BL 2/15/04; SLJ 3/04) [592]

23261 Ross, Michael E. *Millipedeology* (3–6). Illus. Series: Backyard Buddies. 2000, Carolrhoda LB $19.93 (978-1-57505-398-1); paper $6.95 (978-1-57505-436-0). 48pp. This book shows how to collect and humanely study millipedes, with experiments that can be performed to learn more about them. (Rev: BL 5/15/00; HBG 9/00; SLJ 7/00) [595.6]

23262 Ross, Michael E. *Snailology* (4–6). Illus. Series: Backyard Buddies. 1996, Carolrhoda LB $19.95 (978-0-87614-894-5). 48pp. Various types of snails are introduced, with material on their classification, physical structure, and habits. (Rev: BL 7/96; SLJ 8/96) [594]

23263 Ross, Michael E. *Wormology* (4–6). Illus. 1996, Carolrhoda LB $14.95 (978-0-87614-937-9). 48pp. Worms and their classification, structure, and habits are introduced, with several activities and experiments. (Rev: BL 3/15/96; SLJ 7/96) [595.1]

Marine and Freshwater Life

GENERAL AND MISCELLANEOUS

23264 Allen, Judy. *Whales and Dolphins* (1–3). Illus. by Mike Bostock. Series: I Wonder Why: Flip the Flaps. 2008, Kingfisher $7.95 (978-0-7534-6225-6). 32pp. This attractive introduction to whales and dolphins features half-page flaps. (Rev: BL 4/1/08) [599.5]

23265 Armstrong, Pam. *Young Explorer's Guide to Undersea Life* (3–5). Illus. 1996, Monterey Bay $12.95 (978-1-878244-10-9). 64pp. Some plants and about 20 animals that live in or around the sea are described. (Rev: BL 9/15/96; SLJ 9/96) [574.92]

23266 Batten, Mary. *The Winking, Blinking Sea: All About Bioluminescence* (3–5). 2000, Millbrook LB $20.90 (978-0-7613-1550-6). Large photos of 11 bioluminescent sea creatures are presented opposite a paragraph or two of descriptive text. (Rev: BCCB 6/00; HBG 9/00; SLJ 7/00) [591.92]

23267 Berger, Melvin. *Dive! A Book of Deep-Sea Creatures* (1–2). Illus. Series: Hello Reader! 2000, Scholastic $3.99 (978-0-439-08747-6). 40pp. This easy reader introduces the marine life found on the ocean floor, with color photographs mostly at a close range. (Rev: BL 10/1/00) [591.77]

23268 Berger, Melvin, and Gilda Berger. *Do Whales Have Belly Buttons? Questions and Answers About Whales and Dolphins* (3–5). Series: Question and Answer. 1999, Scholastic $12.95 (978-0-590-13081-3); paper $5.95 (978-0-590-08571-7). 48pp. Simple questions related to whales and dolphins are asked and answered in a clear and precise way in this book illustrated with dramatic, often beautiful, paintings. (Rev: BL 11/15/99; SLJ 12/99) [599.5]

23269 Butterworth, Chris. *Sea Horse: The Shyest Horse in the Sea* (K–2). Illus. by John Lawrence. 2006, Candlewick $16.99 (978-0-7636-2989-2). 32pp. Lovely, detailed illustrations and appealing narrative combined with facts trace the life cycle of an endangered sea horse. (Rev: BCCB 10/06; BL 4/15/06*; HB 7/06; HBG 10/06; SLJ 6/06*) [597]

23270 Cerullo, Mary. *Sea Soup: Phytoplankton* (4–7). Illus. 1999, Tilbury House $16.95 (978-0-88448-208-6). 40pp. An introduction to the microscopic world of tiny plants known as phytoplankton and their contributions to life on this planet. (Rev: BL 3/15/00; SLJ 5/00) [578.77]

23271 Cerullo, Mary. *Sea Soup: Zooplankton* (4–7). Illus. by Bill Curtsinger. 2001, Tilbury House $16.95 (978-0-88448-219-2). 48pp. An inviting introduction to the world of tiny drifting animals known as zooplankton, with intriguing photographs. (Rev: BL 7/01; HBG 10/01; SLJ 8/01) [592.1776.]

23272 Cerullo, Mary. *The Truth About Dangerous Sea Creatures* (3–5). Photos by Jeffrey L. Rotman. Illus. by Michael Wertz. 2003, Chronicle $15.95 (978-0-8118-4050-7). 46pp. The dangers posed by jellyfish, giant squid, sharks, octopi, and other marine animals are examined in text and illustrations. (Rev: SLJ 12/03) [591.77]

23273 Collard, Sneed B., III. *In the Deep Sea* (3–6). Illus. Series: Science Adventures. 2005, Benchmark LB $25.64 (978-0-7614-1952-5). 43pp. Readers meet a scientist who studies creatures of the deep sea that use bioluminescence. (Rev: SLJ 5/06) [572]

23274 Delafosse, Claude. *Under the Sea: Hidden World* (PS–2). Series: First Discovery. 1999, Scholastic $12.95 (978-0-590-10992-5). 24pp. This beginning science book explores life in the ocean depths through many color pictures and a simple text. (Rev: BL 6/1–15/99; SLJ 7/99) [591]

23275 Demuth, Patricia. *Way Down Deep: Strange Ocean Creatures* (1–3). Illus. by Jim Deal. Series: All Aboard Reading. 1995, Penguin paper $3.99 (978-0-448-40851-4). 48pp. This easy-to-read science book introduces youngsters to the amazing creatures found at the bottom of the ocean. (Rev: BL 1/1–15/96; SLJ 6/96) [551.46]

23276 Earle, Sylvia A. *Dive! My Adventures in the Deep Frontier* (3–7). Illus. 1999, National Geographic $18.95 (978-0-7922-7144-4). 64pp. This photo-essay contains a spectacular view of underwater life as experienced by the author, an eminent marine biologist. (Rev: BCCB 6/99; BL 2/15/99*; HBG 9/99; SLJ 3/99) [627]

23277 Earle, Sylvia A. *Sea Critters* (1–4). Illus. by Wolcott Henry. 2000, National Geographic $16.95 (978-0-7922-7181-9). 32pp. Color photos and a lyrical text are used to introduce such unusual sea creatures as Christmas-tree worms, sea squirts, sponges, and moray eels. (Rev: BL 11/1/00; HBG 3/01; SLJ 9/00) [591.7]

23278 Feeney, Stephanie, and Ann Fielding. *Sand to Sea: Marine Life of Hawaii* (2–4). Illus. by Ed Robinson. 1989, Univ. of Hawaii $13.95 (978-0-8248-1180-8). 64pp. A look at the fascinating sea life in Hawaii. (Rev: BL 11/1/89) [574]

23279 Grupper, Jonathan. *Destination: Deep Sea* (1–4). 2000, National Geographic $16.95 (978-0-7922-7693-7). 31pp. A beautiful collection of photographs and informative text present many sea creatures, from the inhabitants of coral reefs to dolphins, whales, and sea otters. (Rev: BL 10/15/00; HBG 3/01; SLJ 9/00) [591.92]

23280 Halfmann, Janet. *Life in the Sea* (5–7). Series: LifeViews. 2000, Creative LB $22.60 (978-1-58341-074-5). 25pp. All life in the sea is discussed with a focus on the tiniest — plankton, algae, sea spiders, coral, and worms. (Rev: SLJ 8/00) [591.92]

23281 Hirschmann, Kris. *Moray Eels* (4–6). Illus. Series: Creatures of the Sea. 2003, Gale LB $23.70 (978-0-7377-0985-8). 48pp. Introduces the moray eel, with color photographs and readable text. (Rev: SLJ 3/03) [597]

23282 Jenkins, Steve. *Down, Down, Down: A Journey to the Bottom of the Sea* (2–4). Illus. by author. 2009, Houghton $17.00 (978-0-618-96636-3). 40pp. Starting with the surface and the birds and the sea animals that emerge into the air, Jenkins explores deeper and deeper into the ocean, identifying the animals that live at each layer. (Rev: BCCB 7–8/09; BL 4/1/09; HB 5/09; SLJ 4/09) [591.779]

23283 Johnson, Jinny. *Simon and Schuster Children's Guide to Sea Creatures* (4–7). 1998, Simon & Schuster $19.95 (978-0-689-81534-8). 80pp. This book contains broad coverage of the invertebrates, birds, mammals, and fish found in various parts of the oceans and their shores. (Rev: HBG 10/98; SLJ 5/98) [591]

23284 Kalman, Bobbie. *AB Sea* (K–3). Illus. Series: Crabapples. 1995, Crabtree paper $5.95 (978-0-86505-725-8). 32pp. An alphabet book that uses full-color pictures of marine life to illustrate the ABCs. (Rev: SLJ 4/96) [574.92]

23285 Kalman, Bobbie, and Heather Levigne. *What Is a Whale?* (2–4). Series: Science of Living Things. 1999, Crabtree LB $25.27 (978-0-86505-935-1); paper $6.95 (978-0-86505-953-5). 32pp. This introduction to whales, dolphins, and other cetaceans is well illustrated and informative. (Rev: SLJ 4/00) [599]

23286 Kramer, Jennifer Evans. *Ocean Hide and Seek* (K–3). Illus. by Gary R. Phillips. 2009, Sylvan Dell $16.95 (978-1-934359-91-4); paper $8.95 (978-1-60718-036-4). 32pp. Large illustrations and four-line verses show how marine animals use various forms of camouflage for protection. (Rev: BL 3/15/09; SLJ 6/09) [591.77]

23287 Leardi, Jeanette. *Southern Sea Otters: Fur-tastrophe Avoided* (3–4). Series: America's Animal Comebacks. 2007, Bearport LB $25.27 (978-1-59716-534-1). 32pp. With eye-catching photographs and an appealing design, Leardi looks at threats to the sea otters that lived off the coast of California and at efforts to bring them back from the brink. (Rev: SLJ 12/07) [599.769]

23288 Lindeen, Carol K. *Sea Horses* (K–3). Series: Under the Sea. 2004, Capstone LB $21.26 (978-0-7368-3662-3). 24pp. A simple, easy-to-read description of the sea horse, with bright photographs. (Rev: SLJ 7/05) [597]

23289 O'Neill, Michael Patrick. *Ocean Magic* (1–4). Photos by author. 2008, Batfish $19.95 (978-0-9728653-5-7). 45pp. Mainly for browsers, this book features eye-catching photographs of underwater life in diverse environments and discusses the need for conservation. (Rev: LMC 5/08; SLJ 3/08)

23290 Pallotta, Jerry. *The Freshwater Alphabet Book* (1–4). Illus. by David Biedrzycki. 1996, Charlesbridge $15.95 (978-0-88106-901-3). Freshwater fish and crustaceans are used, along with a mythical monster or two, in this nicely illustrated alphabet book. (Rev: SLJ 4/96) [597]

23291 Parker, Steve. *Sponges, Jellyfish and Other Simple Animals* (4–6). Illus. Series: Animal Kingdom Classification. 2006, Compass Point LB $29.26 (978-0-7565-1614-7). 48pp. Concise, well-written text, color photographs, diagrams, and charts cover the physical characteristics, habitat, diet, and behavior of animals such as sea anemones, corals, sponges, and jellyfish. (Rev: SLJ 11/06) [592]

23292 Redmond, Shirley Raye. *Tentacles! Tales of the Giant Squid* (1–3). Illus. by Bryn Barnard. Series: Step into Reading. 2003, Random LB $11.99 (978-0-375-91307-5); paper $3.99 (978-0-375-81307-8). 48pp. For beginning readers, facts and myths about the giant squid are presented with photographs and paintings. (Rev: BL 7/03; HBG 4/04) [594]

23293 Rhodes, Mary Jo, and David Hall. *Partners in the Sea* (2–4). Photos by David Hall. Series: Undersea Encounters. 2005, Children's Pr. LB $27.00 (978-0-516-24397-9). 48pp. This photo-filled title explores the symbiotic relationship between different forms of marine life. (Rev: BL 10/15/05) [591.77]

23294 Rinard, Judith E. *Amazing Animals of the Sea* (5–8). Illus. 1981, National Geographic LB $12.50 (978-0-87044-387-9). 104pp. Whales, dolphins, sea otters, sea lions, seals, manatees, and other marine mammals are described.

23295 Rustad, Martha E. H. *Stingrays* (PS–1). Series: Blastoff! Readers: Oceans Alive. 2007, Children's Pr. LB $18.50 (978-0-531-17570-5). 24pp. Basic information about stingrays is accompanied by photographs in this introduction for young students. (Rev: SLJ 6/07)

23296 Savage, Stephen. *Animals of the Oceans* (2–6). Illus. Series: Animals by Habitat. 1997, Raintree LB $22.83 (978-0-8172-4753-9). 32pp. Readers are taken on a tour of vast underwater habitats and encounter such animals as the moray eel, green turtle, and sea anemone. (Rev: BL 5/15/97; SLJ 8/97) [591.9]

23297 Sheather, Allan. *Neptune's Nursery* (2–3). Illus. by Kim Michelle Toft. 2000, Charlesbridge LB $16.95 (978-1-57091-391-4); paper $6.95 (978-1-57091-392-1). 32pp. A rhyming text and stunning paintings introduce a number of marine animals and their young. (Rev: BL 12/15/00; HBG 3/01; SLJ 10/00) [591.77]

23298 Souza, D. M. *Sea Snakes* (2–3). Illus. Series: Creatures All Around Us. 1998, Carolrhoda LB $19.93 (978-1-57505-263-2). 40pp. An illustrated study of the habits, life cycles, and reproductive behavior of sea snakes and sea kraits, including a fact summary and glossary. (Rev: BL 12/1/98; HBG 3/99; SLJ 3/99) [597.96]

23299 Stone, Lynn M. *The Food Chain* (2–4). Illus. Series: Under the Sea Discovery Library. 2001, Rourke LB $20.64 (978-1-58952-113-1). 24pp. A look at how food is used to provide energy and at the structure of the food chain found in the underwater world. (Rev: BL 12/15/01; SLJ 3/02) [577.7]

23300 Stone, Lynn M. *Getting Around* (2–3). Series: Under the Sea. 2001, Rourke LB $20.64 (978-1-58952-110-0). 24pp. Text and full-page color photographs provide a simple introduction to the locomotion of various sea animals. (Rev: BL 3/15/02; SLJ 3/02) [591.7]

23301 Stone, Lynn M. *Life of the Kelp Forest* (2–3). Series: Under the Sea. 2001, Rourke LB $20.64 (978-1-58952-112-4). 24pp. The vegetation and marine life found in an ocean kelp forest are introduced with simple text and full-page photographs. (Rev: BL 3/15/02; SLJ 2/02) [589.4]

23302 Stone, Lynn M. *Partners* (2–4). Illus. Series: Under the Sea Discovery Library. 2001, Rourke LB $20.64 (978-1-58952-114-8). 24pp. Underwater partnerships such as parasites and symbiotic relationships are the focus of this slim volume with full-color double-page spreads. (Rev: BL 12/15/01; SLJ 2/02) [591.77]

23303 Taylor-Butler, Christine. *A Home in the Coral Reef* (1–3). 2006, Children's Pr. LB $20.00 (978-0-516-25344-2). 24pp. This easy-to-understand introduction to the coral reef looks at the nature of the coral, its climate, flora, and the animals that call it home. (Rev: SLJ 2/07) [574.9]

23304 Treat, Rose. *The Seaweed Book: How to Find and Have Fun with Seaweed* (4–7). Illus. 1995, Star Bright paper $5.95 (978-1-887724-00-5). 32pp. The identification, collection, and preservation of various kinds of seaweed. (Rev: BL 2/1/96) [589.45]

23305 Vogel, Carole G. *Ocean Wildlife* (5–9). Series: The Restless Sea. 2003, Watts LB $30.50 (978-0-531-12324-9); paper $12.95 (978-0-531-16681-9). 95pp. A thorough examination of marine life, from algae to whales, with an emphasis on those species facing extinction through pollution, overfishing, and other manmade threats. (Rev: SLJ 3/04) [591.77]

23306 Zabludoff, Marc. *The Protoctist Kingdom* (5–9). Series: Family Trees. 2005, Benchmark LB $32.79 (978-0-7614-1818-4). 95pp. Habits, habitats, and other aspects of this newly classified kingdom of animals that includes algae; an engaging book with plenty of facts for report writers. (Rev: SLJ 6/06) [579]

CORALS AND JELLYFISH

23307 Collard, Sneed B. *Lizard Island: Science and Scientists on Australia's Great Barrier Reef* (5–7). Illus. 2000, Watts LB $26.00 (978-0-531-11719-4). 144pp. A lively and absorbing description of the work of scientists studying the forms of life on the Great Barrier Reef. (Rev: BL 2/1/01; SLJ 5/01; VOYA 12/01) [577.7]

23308 Collard, Sneed B. *One Night in the Coral Sea* (3–5). Illus. by Robin Brickman. 2005, Charlesbridge $15.95 (978-1-57091-389-1). 32pp. Collard describes a unique spawning of millions of eggs by the coral of the Great Barrier Reef. (Rev: BL 5/15/05) [593.6]

23309 Collard, Sneed B., III. *On the Coral Reefs* (4–7). Illus. Series: Science Adventures. 2005, Marshall Cavendish LB $25.64 (978-0-7614-1953-2). 48pp. In addition to a profile of a marine biologist who studies fish that eat parasites living on other fish, Collard presents information on scientific research methods and on global warming and other environmental threats. (Rev: BL 2/1/06; SLJ 5/06) [577.7]

23310 Earle, Sylvia A. *Coral Reefs* (K–2). Illus. by Bonnie Matthews. Series: Jump into Science. 2003, National Geographic $16.95 (978-0-7922-6953-3). 32pp. A young swimmer describes the passing world of a coral reef, explaining its ecology, plants,

and sea life, illustrated by vivid paintings and accompanied by a map and an activity. (Rev: BL 1/1–15/03; HBG 10/03; SLJ 5/03) [577.7]

23311 Earle, Sylvia A. *Hello, Fish! Visiting the Coral Reef* (PS–4). Photos by Wolcott Henry. 1999, National Geographic $15.95 (978-0-7922-7103-1). Stunning photography is featured in a series of double-page spreads that introduce 12 fish that live in the waters around coral reefs. (Rev: BCCB 6/99; HBG 9/99; SLJ 3/99) [574]

23312 Fleisher, Paul. *Coral Reef* (3–5). Series: Webs of Life. 1997, Marshall Cavendish LB $22.79 (978-0-7614-0432-3). 40pp. This look at life in a coral reef explains how they are formed and the kinds of life found within them. (Rev: BL 2/15/98; HBG 3/98; SLJ 4/98) [574.9]

23313 Furgang, Kathy. *Let's Take a Field Trip to a Coral Reef* (3–5). Illus. Series: Neighborhoods in Nature. 2000, Rosen LB $21.25 (978-0-8239-5445-2). 24pp. This book looks at the formation of coral reefs, the types of plants and animals found there, and the impact of human activities. (Rev: SLJ 4/01) [574.9]

23314 George, Twig C. *Jellies: The Life of Jellyfish* (K–3). Illus. 2000, Millbrook LB $21.90 (978-0-7613-1659-6). 32pp. Handsome photographs introduce jellyfish, their many varieties, special features, and beauty. (Rev: BL 5/1/00; HBG 9/00; SLJ 8/00) [593.5]

23315 Gibbons, Gail. *Coral Reefs* (K–3). Illus. by author. 2007, Holiday $16.95 (978-0-8234-2080-3). 32pp. With her signature style — watercolor pictures, text boxes, labels, definitions, maps, and more — Gibbons takes the reader on an exploration of the ecology of coral reefs. (Rev: BL 12/1/07; SLJ 1/08) [577.7]

23316 Green, Jen. *A Coral Reef* (2–5). Series: Small World. 2002, Crabtree LB $25.27 (978-0-7787-0138-5); paper $8.95 (978-0-7787-0152-1). 32pp. The variety of life found in a coral reef is described in a simple text with stunning pictures. (Rev: BL 10/15/02; SLJ 8/02) [574.5]

23317 Herriges, Ann. *Jellyfish* (K–3). Series: Blastoff! Readers: Oceans Alive! 2006, Children's Pr. LB $16.95 (978-1-60014-018-1). 24pp. Habitat, anatomy, and characteristics of the jellyfish are covered in large text accompanied by eye-catching photographs. (Rev: SLJ 2/07) [593.5]

23318 Johansson, Philip. *The Coral Reef: A Colorful Web of Life* (3–5). Illus. Series: Wonderful Water Biomes. 2007, Enslow LB $17.95 (978-0-7660-2813-5). 48pp. A colorful look at coral reefs and the varied plants and animals found within them. (Rev: BL 10/1/07; LMC 11/07) [577.7]

23319 Johnson, Rebecca. *The Great Barrier Reef: A Living Laboratory* (5–8). 1992, Lerner LB $28.75 (978-0-8225-1596-8). A look at the world's largest coral reef, off the coast of Australia. (Rev: BL 5/15/92; SLJ 7/92) [574.9943]

23320 Kalman, Bobbie. *Life in the Coral Reef* (2–5). Illus. Series: Crabapples. 1997, Crabtree LB $22.60 (978-0-86505-629-9); paper $5.95 (978-0-86505-729-6). 32pp. A description of how coral reefs are formed, their interdependence with other animals and plants, and methods used to save them. (Rev: BL 7/97) [574.5]

23321 Lunis, Natalie. *Gooey Jellyfish* (1–3). Series: No Backbone! The World of Invertebrates. 2007, Bearport LB $21.28 (978-1-59716-510-5). 24pp. An engaging overview of these animals' physical characteristics, habitat, diet, and behavior, with excellent photographs, appealing layout, useful glossary, and accompanying, informative Web site. (Rev: LMC 3/08; SLJ 12/07) [593.5]

23322 Martin-James, Kathleen. *Floating Jellyfish* (PS–2). Series: Pull Ahead Books. 2001, Lerner LB $22.60 (978-0-8225-3766-3). 32pp. Each page contains two lines of simple text and a color photograph in this introduction to jellyfish for beginning readers. (Rev: BL 6/1–15/01; HBG 10/01) [593.5]

23323 Pyers, Greg. *Coral Reef Explorer* (2–4). Illus. Series: Perspectives: Habitat Explorer. 2004, Raintree LB $25.70 (978-1-4109-0515-4). 32pp. This photo-filled exploration of Australia's Great Barrier Reef and other reefs offers readers important information about coral reefs, the abundant life found there, and their fragility. (Rev: BL 4/1/04) [577.7]

23324 Rhodes, Mary Jo, and David Hall. *Life on a Coral Reef* (4–6). Photos by David Hall. Series: Undersea Encounters. 2006, Children's Pr. LB $27.00 (978-0-516-24395-5). 48pp. A look at life on a coral reef, with facts on life cycles, reproduction, and threats from pollution. (Rev: SLJ 3/07) [574]

23325 Telford, Carole, and Rod Theodorou. *Inside a Coral Reef* (2–6). Illus. by Stephen Lings and Jane Pickering. Series: Amazing Journeys. 1997, Heinemann LB $22.79 (978-1-57572-154-5). 32pp. Using a journey format with maps and other illustrations, this account introduces readers to the Great Barrier Reef and its flora and fauna. (Rev: SLJ 5/98) [574.9]

CRUSTACEANS

23326 Blaxland, Beth. *Crustaceans: Crabs, Crayfishes, and Their Relatives* (4–6). Series: Invertebrates. 2002, Chelsea LB $28.00 (978-0-7910-6994-3). 32pp. Blaxland defines crustaceans and describes their physical characteristics, life cycles, habitats, senses, food, and means of self-defense. (Rev: HBG 3/03; SLJ 1/03)

23327 Greenaway, Theresa. *Crabs* (4–6). Illus. Series: The Secret World Of. 2001, Raintree LB $27.12 (978-0-7398-3506-7). 48pp. An attractive, well-organized account of the life cycle, anatomy, and habits of the crab, with information on the animal's place in the ecosystem and interesting material on peculiar features or unusual subspecies. (Rev: BL 10/15/01; HBG 3/02; SLJ 1/02) [595.3]

23328 Grimm, Phyllis W. *Crayfish* (2–3). Series: Early Bird Nature Books. 2000, Lerner LB $25.26 (978-0-8225-3030-5). 48pp. A look at this unusual sea creature that has eight legs, two large claws, four antennae, and many mouth parts. (Rev: BL 10/15/00; HBG 3/01; SLJ 2/01) [595.3]

23329 Holling, Holling C. *Pagoo* (4–6). Illus. 1957, Houghton $20.00 (978-0-395-06826-7); paper

$11.95 (978-0-395-53964-4). 96pp. Life cycle of the hermit crab.

23330 Johnson, Sylvia A. *Crabs* (4–6). Illus. 1982, Lerner LB $22.60 (978-0-8225-1471-8). 48pp. A look at the structure and life cycle of various crabs.

23331 Kite, L. Patricia. *Down in the Sea: The Crab* (2–4). Illus. 1994, Whitman LB $14.95 (978-0-8075-1709-3). 32pp. Photographs and simple text introduce the crab, with interesting material on how they communicate. (Rev: BL 6/1–15/94; SLJ 5/94) [595.3]

23332 Lunis, Natalie. *Crawling Crabs* (1–3). Series: No Backbone! The World of Invertebrates. 2007, Bearport LB $21.28 (978-1-59716-509-9). 24pp. An engaging overview of crabs' physical characteristics, habitat, diet, and behavior, with excellent photographs, appealing layout, useful glossary, and accompanying, informative Web site. (Rev: LMC 3/08; SLJ 12/07) [595.3]

23333 Marsico, Katie. *A Baby Lobster Grows Up* (1–2). 2007, Children's Pr. LB $19.00 (978-0-531-17475-3). 24pp. The development of a lobster is the topic of this vocabulary-building book with interesting photographs. (Rev: SLJ 7/07)

23334 Sexton, Colleen. *Shrimp* (K–3). 2009, Children's Pr. LB $20.00 (978-0-531-21716-0). 24pp. With color photographs and clearly defined scientific terms, this simple book introduces beginning readers to the characteristics and behavior of shrimp. (Rev: SLJ 6/09) [595.3]

23335 Sill, Cathryn. *About Crustaceans: A Guide for Children* (PS–2). Illus. by John Sill. Series: About . . . 2004, Peachtree $15.95 (978-1-56145-301-6). 40pp. Brief, large-print text and precise watercolor paintings introduce the world of crustaceans, including barnacles, crabs, and lobsters. (Rev: BL 5/1/04; SLJ 6/04) [595.3]

DOLPHINS AND PORPOISES

23336 Barnes, Julia. *The Secret Lives of Dolphins* (3–5). Illus. Series: The Secret Lives of Animals. 2007, Gareth Stevens LB $17.95 (978-0-8368-7656-7). 32pp. Characteristics common to most dolphins are the focus of this clearly written volume. (Rev: BL 5/15/07; LMC 11/07) [599.53]

23337 Crisp, Marty. *Everything Dolphin: What Kids Really Want to Know About Dolphins* (3–5). 2004, NorthWord $10.95 (978-1-55971-042-8); paper $7.95 (978-1-55971-049-7). 63pp. A basic introduction, using a question-and-answer format with plenty of photographs. (Rev: SLJ 11/04) [599.5]

23338 Fowler, Allan. *Friendly Dolphins* (1–2). Series: Rookie Readers. 1997, Children's Book Pr. LB $20.50 (978-0-516-20428-4). 32pp. Introduces dolphins, with striking photos and minimal text suitable for beginning readers. (Rev: BL 11/15/97; HBG 3/98; SLJ 10/97) [599.5]

23339 Greenaway, Theresa. *Whales* (4–7). Illus. Series: Secret World Of. 2001, Raintree LB $27.12 (978-0-7398-3508-1). 48pp. A look at whales' diet, habitat, and behavior, with photographs and interesting facts. (Rev: BL 10/15/01; HBG 3/02) [599.5]

23340 Greenberg, Dan. *Whales* (5–9). Illus. Series: AnimalWays. 2003, Marshall Cavendish $31.36 (978-0-7614-1389-9). 110pp. In addition to material on physical characteristics, behavior, habitats, and threats, Greenberg touches on the animal's roles in history, mythology, religion, and literature. (Rev: BL 3/15/03; HBG 3/03) [599.5]

23341 Hall, Howard. *A Charm of Dolphins: The Threatened Life of a Flippered Friend* (5–8). Series: Jean-Michel Cousteau Presents. 2007, London Town paper $8.95 (978-0-9766134-8-0). 48pp. With eye-catching photographs and stories of close encounters with these animals, this book looks at dolphins' characteristics, behavior, intelligence, and the threats to their survival. (Rev: SLJ 11/07) [599.53]

23342 Hirschi, Ron. *Dolphins* (4–6). Series: Animals Animals. 2002, Benchmark LB $25.64 (978-0-7614-1443-8). 48pp. An oversize book filled with excellent photographs and a simple text that introduces dolphins and their structure, habits, and homes. (Rev: BL 12/15/02; HBG 3/03) [599.5]

23343 Horton, Casey. *Dolphins* (3–5). Illus. Series: Endangered! 1996, Benchmark LB $22.79 (978-0-7614-0216-9). 32pp. A basic introduction to dolphins, their characteristics, habitats, and structure is given through text and full-color photos. (Rev: SLJ 3/96) [599.5]

23344 Morris, Robert A. *Dolphin* (K–3). Illus. by Mamoru Funai. 1975, HarperCollins $6.93 (978-0-06-024337-1). 64pp. A simple account of the first five months of this lovable sea mammal.

23345 Pascoe, Elaine, adapt. *Animal Intelligence: Why Is This Dolphin Smiling?* (5–8). 1997, Blackbirch $17.95 (978-1-56711-226-9). This book reports on the scientific research on communication between dolphins and humans, with reports on such projects as one by John Lilly to create, via computer, dolphin equivalents of human words. (Rev: HBG 3/98; SLJ 12/97) [599.5]

23346 Pfeffer, Wendy. *Dolphin Talk: Whistles, Clicks, and Clapping Jaws* (1–2). Illus. by Helen K. Davie. Series: Let's-Read-and-Find-Out Science. 2003, HarperCollins LB $16.89 (978-0-06-028802-0); paper $5.99 (978-0-06-445210-6). 33pp. Dolphins' many ways of communicating are conveyed in understandable text. (Rev: HBG 4/04; SLJ 1/04) [599.53]

23347 Read, Andrew. *Porpoises* (5–8). Illus. Series: WorldLife Library. 1999, Voyageur paper $16.95 (978-0-89658-420-4). 72pp. With many color illustrations and large print, this book introduces porpoises, their characteristics, behavior, habitats, and how humans study them. (Rev: BL 8/99; VOYA 2/00) [599.53]

23348 Simon, Seymour. *Dolphins* (1–4). Illus. 2009, HarperCollins $17.99 (978-0-06-028393-3). 32pp. With full-page color photographs, Simon looks at dolphins, their relationship to porpoises and whales, their anatomy and characteristics, and their experiences with humans. (Rev: BL 4/1/09; HB 7/09; SLJ 5/09) [599.53]

23349 Spilsbury, Richard, and Louise Spilsbury. *A School of Dolphins* (3–5). Illus. Series: Animal Groups. 2004, Heinemann LB $24.22 (978-1-4034-4692-3). 32pp. Easy-to-understand narrative and plenty of color photographs provide a good overview of dolphins and their behaviors and habitats. (Rev: BL 4/15/04) [599.53]

23350 Sweeney, Diane, and Michelle Reddy. *Dolphin Babies: Making a Splash* (4–6). Photos by Jeff Smith. Illus. by Jim Corey. 1998, Roberts Rinehart paper $14.95 (978-1-57098-194-4). 64pp. Using remarkable photos and a brief text, this book chronicles the pregnancy of four dolphins and the subsequent births at the Dolphin Learning Center in Hawaii. (Rev: SLJ 9/98) [599.5]

23351 Thomson, Sarah L. *Amazing Dolphins!* (K–3). Series: I Can Read. 2006, HarperCollins $16.99 (978-0-06-054453-9). 32pp. For beginning readers, this introduces the world of dolphins, discussing their physical characteristics, communications, habitat, behavior, and how they care for their young. (Rev: BL 6/1–15/06; SLJ 7/06) [599.53]

23352 Walker, Sally M. *Dolphins* (3–6). Illus. Series: Nature Watch. 1999, Carolrhoda LB $25.26 (978-1-57505-221-2). 48pp. This attractive introduction to dolphins includes material on their physical characteristics, communication, behavior, life cycle, and relations with people. (Rev: BL 9/1/99; HBG 9/99) [599.53]

FISH

23353 Arnold, Caroline. *Shockers of the Sea and Other Electrical Animals* (1–3). Illus. by Crista Forest. 1999, Charlesbridge $15.95 (978-0-88106-873-3); paper $6.95 (978-0-88106-874-0). 32pp. Covers electric fish and how they use this attribute for purposes such as getting food, defense, and communication. (Rev: BL 10/15/99; HBG 4/00; SLJ 1/00) [597]

23354 Arnosky, Jim. *Crinkleroot's 25 Fish Every Child Should Know* (PS–3). Illus. 1993, Bradbury LB $12.95 (978-0-02-705844-4). 32pp. A picture-book field guide that introduces with paintings and brief text 25 common species of fish. (Rev: BL 9/1/93; SLJ 9/93) [597]

23355 Bailey, Jill. *How Fish Swim* (3–5). Illus. by Colin Newman. Series: Nature's Mysteries. 1996, Benchmark LB $22.79 (978-0-7614-0451-4). 32pp. This work covers how fish and other aquatic animals move and the different anatomical specializations that make locomotion possible. (Rev: SLJ 2/97) [597]

23356 Einhorn, Kama. *My First Book About Fish* (PS–1). Illus. by Christopher Moroney. Series: Sesame Subjects. 2006, Random paper $7.99 (978-0-375-83513-1). Muppets Grover and Elmo, the latter accompanied by his pet goldfish, team up to introduce basic information about fish, including their physical characteristics, habitat, diet, and behavior. (Rev: SLJ 12/06) [597]

23357 Gallimard Jeunesse. *Fish* (PS–2). Illus. Series: First Discovery. 1998, Scholastic $12.95 (978-0-590-38155-0). 24pp. Using overlays and colorful illustrations, this book introduces several types of fish and describes how fish breathe, reproduce, eat, and protect themselves. (Rev: BL 9/15/98; HBG 9/98) [579]

23358 Herriges, Ann. *Sea Horses* (K–3). Series: Blastoff! Readers: Oceans Alive! 2006, Children's Pr. LB $16.95 (978-1-60014-020-4). 24pp. Habitat, anatomy, and characteristics of sea horses are covered in large text accompanied by eye-catching photographs. Also use *Sea Stars* (2006). (Rev: SLJ 2/07) [597]

23359 Hirschi, Ron. *Salmon* (3–6). Series: Nature Watch. 2000, Carolrhoda LB $25.26 (978-1-57505-482-7). 48pp. Amazing photos and a clear text describe how salmon change from egg to fry to grown fish that then complete the cycle by making a journey upstream to reproduce. (Rev: BL 10/15/00; HBG 10/01) [597.55]

23360 Hirschmann, Kris. *Rays* (4–7). Illus. 2003, Gale LB $23.70 (978-0-7377-0988-9). 48pp. Hirschmann presents basic information about the ray's anatomy, movement, feeding, defense, reproduction, and man's fascination with this fish. (Rev: BL 3/1/03) [597.3]

23361 Hodge, Deborah. *Salmon* (3–5). Illus. by Nancy Gray Ogle. Series: Wildlife. 2002, Kids Can $10.95 (978-1-55074-961-8); paper $5.95 (978-1-55074-963-2). 32pp. Atlantic and Pacific salmon are covered along with subspecies in a flowing text and detailed paintings. (Rev: HBG 10/02; SLJ 7/02) [597.56]

23362 Jango-Cohen, Judith. *Clinging Sea Horses* (PS–2). Series: Pull Ahead Books. 2000, Lerner LB $22.60 (978-0-8225-3764-9); paper $5.95 (978-0-8225-3767-0). 32pp. Stunning underwater photos bring to life this unique fish whose young grow in a pouch on the father's body. (Rev: BL 8/00; HBG 3/01; SLJ 1/01) [597]

23363 Kurlansky, Mark. *The Cod's Tale* (3–5). Illus. by S. D. Schindler. 2001, Penguin $17.99 (978-0-399-23476-7). 48pp. Kurlansky looks at the surprisingly fascinating relationship between cod and humans, presenting basic facts about the fish itself (including how to cook it) and exploring its importance throughout history. (Rev: BCCB 10/01; BL 12/1/01; HB 11/01; HBG 3/02; SLJ 10/01) [639.2]

23364 Landau, Elaine. *Electric Fish* (3–5). Series: A True Book. 1999, Children's Book Pr. LB $21.00 (978-0-513-20660-1). 48pp. With stunning photos and a simple text, this account introduces fish that produce electricity and explains the causes and effects of this phenomenon. (Rev: BL 8/99) [597]

23365 Laskey, Elizabeth. *Seahorses* (4–6). Series: Sea Creatures. 2003, Heinemann LB $22.79 (978-1-4034-0963-8). 32pp. Examines the tiny marine animal's physical characteristics, habitat, diet, and behavior. (Rev: HBG 10/03; SLJ 11/03) [597]

23366 Pascoe, Elaine. *Freshwater Fish* (4–8). Photos by Dwight Kuhn. Series: Nature Close-Up. 2005, Gale LB $24.95 (978-1-4103-0308-0). 48pp. Eye-catching close-ups illustrate information on the life cycles and eating habits of freshwater fish. (Rev: SLJ 6/05)

23367 Pyers, Greg. *Why Am I a Fish?* (3–5). Illus. Series: Classifying Animals. 2005, Raintree LB $27.50 (978-1-4109-2015-7); paper $7.85 (978-1-4109-2022-5). 32pp. Introduces readers to the process of scientific classification and then examines the unique physical characteristics — such as fins, gills, and a streamlined body — of fish as a class. (Rev: SLJ 4/06) [597]

23368 Rodriguez, Ana María. *Secret of the Suffocating Slime Trap . . . and More!* (4–6). 2008, Enslow LB $23.93 (978-0-7660-2954-5). 48pp. How scientists discovered fish species that use secretions for many purposes is explained though interesting text and photographs. (Rev: SLJ 2/09) [597]

23369 Royston, Angela. *Life Cycle of a Salmon* (PS–3). Series: Life Cycle. 2000, Heinemann LB $21.36 (978-1-57572-212-2). 32pp. From egg to adult, this book explains the life cycle of a salmon, using a simple text and full-color photos on each page. (Rev: BL 5/15/00; HBG 3/01) [597.55]

23370 Rustad, Martha E. H. *Parrotfish* (K–3). Series: Blastoff! Readers: Oceans Alive. 2007, Children's Pr. LB $20.00 (978-0-531-14739-9). 24pp. For beginning readers, this is an easily read, colorful introduction to these fish. Also use *Sharks* (2007). (Rev: SLJ 2/08) [597]

23371 Savage, Stephen. *Fish* (2–4). Series: What's the Difference? 2000, Raintree LB $25.69 (978-0-7398-1357-7). 32pp. Fish can be as different as a goldfish and a shark, but this book points out their common features (e.g., gills) as well as salient differences. (Rev: BL 10/15/00; HBG 3/01) [597]

23372 Schach, David. *Sea Dragons* (PS–1). Series: Blastoff! Readers: Oceans Alive! 2007, Children's Pr. LB $18.50 (978-0-531-17563-7). 24pp. This entry in the series covers this fish by briefly discussing habitat, diet, behavior, and so on, with bright photographs and resources for additional information. (Rev: SLJ 6/07)

23373 Sexton, Colleen. *Clown Fish* (PS–1). 2007, Children's Pr. LB $18.50 (978-0-531-17562-0). 24pp. Briefly discusses habitat, diet, behavior, and so on, with bright photographs and resources for additional information. (Rev: SLJ 6/07)

23374 Sexton, Colleen. *Lionfish* (K–3). Series: Blastoff! Readers: Oceans Alive. 2009, Children's Pr. LB $20.00 (978-0-531-21713-9). 24pp. With color photographs and clearly defined scientific terms, this book introduces beginning readers to the lionfish, an interesting predator. (Rev: SLJ 6/09) [597]

23375 Sill, Cathryn. *About Fish: A Guide for Children* (PS–1). Illus. by John Sill. 2002, Peachtree $15.95 (978-1-56145-256-9). 40pp. Watercolor illustrations and simple text describe for preschoolers how fish live and move. Also use *About Amphibians* (2001). (Rev: BL 3/1/02; HBG 10/02; SLJ 6/02) [597]

23376 Spilsbury, Richard, and Louise Spilsbury. *Classifying Fish* (4–6). Series: Classifying Living Things. 2003, Heinemann LB $24.22 (978-1-4034-0846-4). 32pp. The principles of scientific classification are covered along with an introduction to some of the many groupings of fish. (Rev: HBG 10/03; SLJ 11/03) [597]

23377 Spilsbury, Richard, and Louise Spilsbury. *The Life Cycle of Fish* (3–5). Illus. Series: From Egg to Adult. 2003, Heinemann LB $24.22 (978-1-4034-0783-2). 32pp. A photo-filled overview of the life cycle of fish, with material on habitat, diet, and life expectancy. (Rev: HBG 4/04; SLJ 10/03) [597]

23378 Stefoff, Rebecca. *Sea Horse* (2–4). Illus. Series: From the Living Things. 1996, Marshall Cavendish LB $22.79 (978-0-7614-0116-2). 32pp. Various kinds of sea horses are described, along with their habits and life cycles. (Rev: BL 2/1/97; SLJ 3/97) [597]

23379 Stewart, Melissa. *Fishes* (2–3). Series: True Books. 2001, Children's Book Pr. LB $25.00 (978-0-516-22038-3). 48pp. This book looks at a number of kinds of fish and points out similarities as well as differences. (Rev: BL 3/15/01) [597]

23380 Stewart, Melissa. *How Do Fish Breathe Underwater?* (2–4). Series: Tell Me Why, Tell Me How. 2006, Marshall Cavendish LB $28.50 (978-0-7614-2109-2). 32pp. In brief chapters with easy-to-understand text and eye-catching full-color photos, the author discusses how fish breathe. (Rev: BL 10/15/06; SLJ 12/06) [573.2]

23381 Stockdale, Susan. *Fabulous Fishes* (PS–3). Illus. by author. 2008, Peachtree $15.95 (978-1-56145-429-7). 32pp. Fishes of all kinds are introduced in simple rhymes and clear illustrations. (Rev: BL 4/1/08; LMC 3/08; SLJ 4/08) [597]

23382 Stone, Lynn M. *Ocean Hunters* (2–3). Series: Under the Sea. 2001, Rourke LB $20.64 (978-1-58952-111-7). 24pp. A basic introduction to various sea animals and how they find, kill, and eat their food. (Rev: BL 3/15/02) [597]

23383 Walker, Sally M. *Fossil Fish Found Alive: Discovering the Coelacanth* (5–8). Illus. 2002, Carolrhoda LB $17.95 (978-1-57505-536-7). 64pp. An engaging look at the search for and study of coelacanths, a fish believed to be extinct until 1938. (Rev: BL 3/15/02; HB 1/03; HBG 3/03; SLJ 5/02*) [597.3]

23384 Walker, Sally M. *Sea Horses* (2–4). Series: Early Bird Nature Books. 2003, Lerner LB $25.26 (978-0-8225-3051-0). 48pp. Newly independent readers will enjoy this basic introduction to the life cycle of the sea horse, covering habitat, diet, and reproduction. (Rev: HBG 4/04; SLJ 11/03) [597]

23385 Walker, Sally M. *Sea Horses* (3–6). Illus. Series: Nature Watch. 1999, Lerner $25.26 (978-1-57505-317-2). 48pp. The sea horse is introduced with many color photographs and material on its physical characteristics, bonding rituals, classification, and the mythology surrounding these small animals. (Rev: BL 5/1/99; HBG 9/99; SLJ 11/99) [597]

23386 Walker, Sally M. *Seahorse Reef: A Story of the South Pacific* (1–3). Illus. by Steven J. Petruccio. Series: Smithsonian Oceanic. 2001, Smithsonian Institution $15.95 (978-1-56899-869-5). 32pp. Information about the sea horse — behavior, habitat, and reproduction — is presented through the story of one sea horse and his mate. (Rev: BL 9/15/01; HBG 10/01; SLJ 8/01) [597]

23387 Weber, Valerie J. *Anglerfish* (3–5). Series: Weird Wonders of the Deep. 2005, Gareth Stevens LB $23.00 (978-0-8368-4560-0). 24pp. A look at the unusual anglerfish and its ability to swallow prey much larger than itself. (Rev: SLJ 8/05) [597]

23388 Weber, Valerie J. *Coelacanth: The Living Fossil* (3–5). Series: Weird Wonders of the Deep. 2005, Gareth Stevens LB $23.00 (978-0-8368-4561-7). 24pp. An introduction to a interesting fish that lived 400 million years ago and had no backbone — and still exists today. (Rev: SLJ 8/05) [597.3]

23389 Wilkes, Sarah. *Fish* (5–9). Series: World Almanac Library of the Animal Kingdom. 2006, World Almanac LB $31.00 (978-0-8368-6210-2). 48pp. This brightly illustrated guide to fish introduces specific species, physical characteristics, habitats, diets, behaviors, and life cycles. (Rev: SLJ 12/06) [597]

23390 Winkelman, Barbara Gaines. *Puffer's Surprise* (2–3). 2005, Soundprints $15.95 (978-1-59249-032-5); paper $6.95 (978-1-59249-034-9). 32pp. A fascinating day in the life of a tiny puffer fish is chronicled in beautiful illustratations and simple but detailed text. (Rev: BL 12/1/03; HBG 4/04)

23391 Zim, Herbert S., and Hurst H. Shoemaker. *Fishes* (5–8). Illus. by James G. Irving. 1991, Western paper $21.27 (978-0-307-64059-8). 160pp. This is a basic guide to both fresh and saltwater species.

MOLLUSKS, SPONGES, AND STARFISH

23392 Blaxland, Beth. *Echinoderms: Sea Stars, Sea Urchins, and Their Relatives* (4–6). Series: Invertebrates. 2002, Chelsea LB $28.00 (978-0-7910-6996-7). 32pp. Blaxland defines echinoderms and describes their physical characteristics, life cycles, habitats, senses, food, and means of self-defense. (Rev: HBG 3/03; SLJ 1/03)

23393 Esbensen, Barbara J. *Sponges Are Skeletons* (1–4). Illus. by Holly Keller. Series: Let's-Read-and-Find-Out. 1993, HarperCollins LB $15.89 (978-0-06-021037-3). 32pp. This account tells about the original bath sponges and how they originated on the ocean floor. (Rev: BL 12/1/93; SLJ 2/94) [593.4]

23394 Gilpin, Daniel. *Snails, Shellfish and Other Mollusks* (4–6). Illus. Series: Animal Kingdom Classification. 2006, Compass Point LB $29.26 (978-0-7565-1613-0). 48pp. Concise, well-written text, color photographs, diagrams, and charts cover the physical characteristics, habitat, diet, and behavior of mollusks. (Rev: SLJ 11/06)

23395 Lunis, Natalie. *Prickly Sea Stars* (1–3). Series: No Backbone! The World of Invertebrates. 2007, Bearport LB $21.28 (978-1-59716-508-2). 24pp. An engaging overview of these animals' physical characteristics, habitat, diet, and behavior, with excellent photographs, appealing layout, useful glossary, and accompanying, informative Web site. (Rev: LMC 3/08; SLJ 12/07) [593.9]

23396 Morgan, Sally. *Sponges and Other Minor Phyla* (4–6). Series: Animal Kingdom. 2004, Raintree LB $32.79 (978-1-4109-1053-0). 64pp. The common characteristics of sponges and other minor phyla are explained, followed by descriptions of various orders within this classification and selected specific species, plus discussion of endangered status and evolution. (Rev: SLJ 6/05)

23397 Rustad, Martha E. H. *Sea Urchins* (K–3). Series: Blastoff! Readers: Oceans Alive. 2007, Children's Pr. LB $20.00 (978-0-531-14741-2). 24pp. For beginning readers, this is an easily read, colorful introduction to these marine animals. (Rev: SLJ 2/08) [593.9]

23398 Sill, Cathryn. *About Mollusks: A Guide for Children* (K–2). Illus. by John Sill. 2005, Peachtree $15.95 (978-1-56145-331-3). A simple introduction to mollusks, with large, realistic watercolors. (Rev: BL 2/1/04; HB 5/04; SLJ 4/05)

23399 Zuchora-Walske, Christine. *Spiny Sea Stars* (PS–2). Series: Pull Ahead Books. 2001, Lerner LB $22.60 (978-0-8225-3765-6). 32pp. A variety of starfish and their habits and habitats are presented with a simple, basic text and attractive color photographs. (Rev: BL 6/1–15/01; HBG 10/01) [593.9]

OCTOPUS

23400 Herriges, Ann. *Octopuses* (K–3). Series: Blastoff! Readers: Oceans Alive! 2006, Children's Pr. LB $16.95 (978-1-60014-019-8). 24pp. Habitat, anatomy, and characteristics of the octopus are covered in large text accompanied by eye-catching photographs. (Rev: SLJ 2/07) [594]

23401 Hirschi, Ron. *Octopuses* (3–6). Series: Nature Watch. 2000, Carolrhoda $25.26 (978-1-57505-386-8). 48pp. An informative text about the octopus, its daily life, and how it uses its eight arms for swimming, eating, catching prey, and even tasting food. (Rev: BL 3/15/00; HBG 9/00; SLJ 7/00) [594]

23402 Lindeen, Carol K. *Octopuses* (K–3). Series: Under the Sea. 2004, Capstone LB $21.26 (978-0-7368-3661-6). 24pp. A simple, easy-to-read description of the octopus, with bright photographs. (Rev: SLJ 7/05) [594]

23403 Markle, Sandra. *Octopuses* (3–5). Illus. Series: Animal Prey. 2007, Lerner $25.26 (978-0-8225-6063-0). 40pp. Stunning color photography highlights this well-written introduction to the octopus that covers its physical characteristics, habitat, diet, behavior, and life cycle. (Rev: BL 4/1/07) [594]

23404 Matsen, Brad. *The Incredible Hunt for the Giant Squid* (4–6). Illus. Series: Incredible Deep-Sea Adventures. 2003, Enslow LB $23.93 (978-0-7660-2192-1). 48pp. An engaging overview of what is known about the mysterious creature, focusing primarily on efforts to track down the elusive squid in its deep habitat. (Rev: HBG 4/04; SLJ 1/04) [594]

23405 Souza, D. M. *Sea Creatures with Many Arms* (2–3). Illus. Series: Creatures All Around Us. 1998, Carolrhoda LB $19.93 (978-1-57505-262-5). 40pp. The life cycle, habits, and reproduction of squid, octopuses, cuttlefish, and chambered nautiluses are introduced through color photos and clear captions. (Rev: BL 12/1/98; HBG 3/99; SLJ 3/99) [594]

23406 Spirn, Michele. *Octopuses* (3–6). Series: Smart Animals. 2006, Bearport LB $25.27 (978-1-59716-250-0). 32pp. The octopus's intelligence and ability to solve problems are discussed here; a facts page gives details about physical characteristics and so forth and a diagram labels body parts. (Rev: SLJ 1/07) [594]

23407 Stefoff, Rebecca. *Octopus* (K–3). Illus. Series: Living Things. 1996, Marshall Cavendish LB $22.79 (978-0-7614-0119-3). 32pp. This colorful introduction to the octopus uses short bits of information and many illustrations on double-page spreads. Also use in this series *Starfish, Giant Turtle,* and *Praying Mantis.* (Rev: BL 3/15/97; SLJ 3/97) [597.92]

23408 Zuchora-Walske, Christine. *Giant Octopuses* (PS–2). Series: Pull Ahead Books. 1999, Lerner $22.60 (978-0-8225-3633-8); paper $5.95 (978-0-8225-3637-6). 32pp. The physical characteristics and habits of the octopus are covered with a brief text and a color photo on each page plus a body diagram, map, glossary, and simple index. (Rev: BL 12/15/99; HBG 4/00) [594.56]

SEA MAMMALS

23409 Arnold, Caroline. *Super Swimmers* (2–4). Illus. by Patricia J. Wynne. 2007, Charlesbridge $16.95 (978-1-57091-588-8); paper $6.95 (978-1-57091-589-5). 32pp. A wide variety of marine mammals are introduced in this clear text with well-chosen illustrations. (Rev: BL 2/1/07) [599.5]

23410 Arnosky, Jim. *All About Manatees* (K–3). Illus. by author. 2008, Scholastic paper $5.99 (978-0-439-90361-5). 32pp. For young readers, this is a clear introduction to manatees — their physical characteristics, habitat, and endangered status — with eye-catching illustrations. (Rev: BL 6/1–15/08; LMC 10/08; SLJ 8/08) [599.55]

23411 Boyle, Doe. *Otter on His Own: The Story of a Sea Otter.* 2nd ed. (K–2). Illus. by Robert Lawson. 2002, Soundprints $15.95 (978-1-56899-129-0); paper $6.95 (978-1-931465-53-3). 31pp. A revision of the exciting story of an otter pup's childhood, with plenty of facts about sea otters. (Rev: HBG 3/03; SLJ 11/02) [599.74]

23412 Cossi, Olga. *Harp Seals* (3–6). Illus. 1991, Carolrhoda LB $23.93 (978-0-87614-437-4). 48pp. The life cycle, migratory patterns, and behavior of the Arctic harp seal are described. (Rev: BCCB 4/91; BL 5/5/91; SLJ 6/91) [599.74]

23413 Darling, Kathy. *Walrus: On Location* (1–4). Illus. by Tara Darling. Series: On Location. 1991, Lothrop $14.95 (978-0-688-09032-6). 40pp. Watching the walrus who come to shore every year on Round Island off the coast of Alaska. (Rev: BL 8/91; SLJ 12/91) [599.74]

23414 Fetty, Margaret. *Sea Lions* (3–6). Series: Smart Animals. 2006, Bearport LB $25.27 (978-1-59716-274-6). 32pp. Sea lions' intelligence is clearly shown in stories of their ability to communicate and their work for the U.S. Navy; a facts page gives details about physical characteristics and so forth. (Rev: SLJ 1/07) [599.79]

23415 Goldish, Meish. *Florida Manatees: Warm Water Miracles* (2–4). Illus. Series: America's Animal Comebacks. 2007, Bearport LB $18.95 (978-1-59716-507-5). 32pp. Goldish recounts the manatee's recovery from near-extinction and looks at the many challenges the animal still faces and at today's conservation efforts. (Rev: BL 10/15/07) [599.5509]

23416 Grace, Eric S. *Seals* (4–6). Illus. by Fred Bruemmer. Series: Sierra Club Wildlife Library. 1994, Little, Brown paper $7.95 (978-0-316-32291-1). 62pp. This slim, oversized volume supplies an attractive, well-organized introduction to seals and their cousins, sea lions and walruses. (Rev: BL 1/15/92; SLJ 2/92*) [599.74]

23417 Harman, Amanda. *Manatees and Dugongs* (3–5). Illus. Series: Endangered! 1996, Benchmark LB $22.79 (978-0-7614-0294-7). 32pp. These endangered sea creatures are described in text and pictures, with material on their habitats, lifestyles, and how they can be helped. (Rev: SLJ 2/97) [599.5]

23418 Hewett, Joan. *A Harbor Seal Grows Up* (1–3). Illus. by Richard Hewett. Series: Baby Animals. 2001, Lerner LB $21.27 (978-1-57505-166-6); paper $6.95 (978-0-8225-0092-6). 32pp. A book for beginning readers about a baby harbor seal being raised in captivity. (Rev: BL 10/15/01; HBG 3/02; SLJ 10/01) [599.79]

23419 Hirschi, Ron. *Seals* (4–6). Series: Animals Animals. 2002, Benchmark LB $25.64 (978-0-7614-1445-2). 48pp. Pictures and text present these animals' anatomy, diet, habits, and social interactions. (Rev: BL 12/15/02; HBG 3/03; SLJ 2/03) [599.74]

23420 Hodgkins, Fran. *Andre: The Famous Harbor Seal* (K–3). Illus. by Yetti Frenkel. 2003, Down East $16.95 (978-0-89272-594-6). 32pp. The real-life story of Andre the harbor seal traces the animal's life from its 1961 adoption as a pup by a Maine harbormaster to its death in 1986. (Rev: SLJ 1/04) [599.79]

23421 Hurd, Edith Thacher. *The Song of the Sea Otter* (4–6). Illus. by Jennifer O. Dewey. 1989, Sierra Club paper $5.95 (978-0-316-38323-3). 40pp. In a harbor on the Pacific coast, a baby sea otter explores his world. A reissue.

23422 Johnson, Sylvia A. *Elephant Seals* (3–6). Illus. 1989, Lerner LB $22.60 (978-0-8225-1487-9). 48pp. The story of these animals, hunted almost to extinction, along the California and Mexico coasts. (Rev: BL 3/1/89)

23423 Leon, Vicki. *A Raft of Sea Otters: The Playful Life of a Furry Survivor*. 2nd ed. (4–7). Illus. 2005, London Town paper $7.95 (978-0-9666490-4-8). 48pp. This accessible introduction to the sea otter and its physical characteristics, behavior, diet, habitat, life cycle, and conservation threats is a picture-book-size revision of an earlier edition and contains excellent photographs. (Rev: BL 7/05) [599.7695]

23424 Lindeen, Carol K. *Seals* (K–3). Series: Under the Sea. 2004, Capstone LB $21.26 (978-0-7368-3663-0). 24pp. A simple, easy-to-read description of the seal, with bright photographs. (Rev: SLJ 7/05) [599.79]

23425 Marsico, Katie. *A Manatee Calf Grows Up* (PS–2). Illus. Series: Scholastic News Nonfiction Readers: Life Cycles. 2007, Children's Pr. LB $20.00 (978-0-531-17479-1). 24pp. This photo-filled title traces the life cycle of a female manatee, introducing young readers to the marine mammal's physical and behavioral characteristics, habitat, and diet. (Rev: BL 3/15/07) [599.55]

23426 Martin, Patricia A. Fink. *Manatees* (2–3). Series: Animals. 2002, Children's Book Pr. paper $6.95 (978-0-516-27473-7). 48pp. Color photographs on almost every page and large-type text are used to introduce these endangered sea mammals and explain their life cycle, habits, and habitats. (Rev: BL 8/02) [599.5]

23427 Meeker, Clare Hodgson. *Lootas, Little Wave Eater: An Orphaned Sea Otter's Story* (3–5). Photos by C. J. Casson. 1999, Sasquatch paper $12.95 (978-1-57061-164-3). 43pp. Describes the early life of a young sea otter and how she was rescued after a boating accident and raised in the Seattle Aquarium. (Rev: SLJ 1/00) [599.74]

23428 Richardson, Adele D. *Manatees: Peaceful Plant-Eaters* (1–3). Series: Wild World of Animals. 2002, Capstone LB $22.60 (978-0-7368-1395-2). 24pp. This endangered aquatic mammal is introduced with many color photographs, large type, and simple language. (Rev: BL 1/1–15/03; HBG 3/03) [599.55]

23429 Sexton, Colleen. *Seals* (PS–1). Series: Blastoff! Readers: Oceans Alive. 2007, Children's Pr. LB $18.50 (978-0-531-17564-2). 24pp. This entry covers seals by briefly discussing habitat, diet, behavior, and so on, with bright photos and resources for additional information. (Rev: SLJ 6/07)

23430 Sexton, Colleen. *Walruses* (K–3). Series: Blastoff! Readers: Oceans Alive. 2007, Children's Pr. LB $20.00 (978-0-531-14742-9). 24pp. For beginning readers, this is an easily read, colorful introduction to these sea mammals. (Rev: SLJ 2/08) [599.79]

23431 Silverstein, Alvin, et al. *The Manatee* (4–7). Illus. Series: Endangered in America. 1995, Millbrook LB $24.90 (978-1-56294-551-0). 64pp. A profile of this sea creature, its lifestyle and habits, and how it became an endangered species. (Rev: BL 10/15/95; SLJ 1/96) [599.5]

23432 Staub, Frank. *Manatees* (2–3). Series: Early Bird Nature Books. 1998, Lerner $25.26 (978-0-8225-3023-7). 48pp. Good illustrations and simple text are used to introduce this endangered sea mammal. (Rev: BL 10/15/98; HBG 3/99; SLJ 1/99) [599.5]

23433 Staub, Frank. *Sea Lions* (2–3). Series: Early Bird Nature Books. 2000, Lerner LB $25.26 (978-0-8225-3018-3). 48pp. This simple introduction to the California sea lion covers its habitat, appearance, behavior, and the dangers it faces. (Rev: BL 5/15/00; HBG 9/00) [599]

23434 Stille, Darlene R. *I Am a Seal: The Life of an Elephant Seal* (K–3). Illus. by Todd Ouren. Series: I

Live in the Ocean. 2004, Picture Window LB $25.26 (978-1-4048-0598-9). 24pp. An elephant seal describes its life — diet, activities, and so forth. (Rev: SLJ 1/05) [599.74]

23435 Swinburne, Stephen. *Saving Manatees* (4–6). 2006, Boyds Mills $16.95 (978-1-59078-319-1). 40pp. This tour of Florida's manatee country includes discussions with biologists and park rangers and a class of fourth-graders swimming with manatees, as well as information on the mammal's physical appearance, diet, behavior, and habitat, plus the threats it faces. (Rev: BL 9/1/06; SLJ 11/06) [599.5]

23436 Tatham, Betty. *Baby Sea Otter* (PS–2). Illus. by Joan Paley. 2005, Holt $16.95 (978-0-8050-7504-5). 32pp. With some tender and some exciting moments, this book follows the life of a sea otter from birth through mating and caring for its own pups. (Rev: BL 11/1/05; SLJ 9/05) [599.769]

23437 Theodorou, Rod. *Florida Manatee* (K–2). Illus. Series: Animals in Danger. 2000, Heinemann LB $21.36 (978-1-57572-265-8). 32pp. This is an introductory overview of the manatee, with basic information on the animal, its diet and habitat, and the reasons it is endangered. (Rev: HBG 3/01; SLJ 4/01) [599.5]

23438 Walker, Sally M. *Manatees* (3–6). Illus. Series: Nature Watch. 1999, Carolrhoda $25.26 (978-1-57505-299-1). 48pp. Amazing photographs are used to illustrate this introduction to the manatee, its physical characteristics, lifestyle, habits, and habitats. (Rev: BL 12/15/99; HBG 4/00) [599.55]

23439 Weber, Valerie. *Squids* (2–4). Illus. Series: Weird Wonders of the Deep. 2005, Gareth Stevens LB $23.00 (978-0-8368-4564-8). 24pp. A small-format but informative introduction to the many types of squid and their characteristics. (Rev: BL 5/1/05) [594]

SHARKS

23440 Arnosky, Jim. *All About Sharks* (1–4). Illus. by author. Series: All About. 2003, Scholastic $15.95 (978-0-590-48166-3). Easy-to-understand text and attractive illustrations present facts about sharks in an accessible manner. (Rev: BL 7/03; HBG 4/04; SLJ 6/03) [597.3]

23441 Berger, Melvin. *Chomp! A Book About Sharks* (1–3). Series: Hello Reader! 1999, Scholastic paper $3.99 (978-0-590-52298-4). Lots of introductory information about sharks is given in this book for beginning readers. (Rev: SLJ 7/99) [597.31]

23442 Burnham, Brad. *The Hammerhead Shark* (1–4). Illus. Series: Underwater World of Sharks. 2001, Rosen LB $18.75 (978-0-8239-5584-8). 24pp. A fact-filled, easy-to-read book about the odd-looking hammerhead shark, with full-color photographs and a list of Web sites. (Rev: BL 12/15/01) [597.3]

23443 Cerullo, Mary. *The Truth About Great White Sharks* (4–7). Illus. 2000, Chronicle $14.95 (978-0-8118-2467-5). 48pp. A fascinating account with excellent underwater photographs that explores such topics about sharks as physical characteristics,

behavior, feeding habits, and the difficulty of studying them. (Rev: BL 4/1/00; SLJ 7/00) [597.3]

23444 Cole, Joanna. *Hungry, Hungry Sharks* (1–3). Illus. by Patricia J. Wynne. 1986, Random paper $3.99 (978-0-394-87471-5). 48pp. Different kinds of sharks are explained in simple terms. (Rev: BL 8/86)

23445 Del Prado, Dana. *Terror Below! True Shark Stories* (2–3). Illus. by Stephen Marchesi. Series: All Aboard Reading. 1997, Grosset paper $3.99 (978-0-448-41124-8). 47pp. Three true stories about encounters with sharks in which the victims lived to tell their stories. (Rev: SLJ 10/97) [597.31]

23446 Ellwood, Nancy, and Margaret Parrish. *Sharkpedia* (4–6). Illus. 2008, DK $12.99 (978-0-7566-3761-3). 124pp. Conversational yet thorough, this attractive volume offers lots of information on sharks present and past, their physical characteristics and behavior, shark mythology and appearances in literature, and so forth. (Rev: BLO 8/28/08) [500]

23447 Fowler, Allan. *The Best Way to See a Shark* (1–2). Illus. Series: Rookie Readers. 1995, Children's Book Pr. LB $20.50 (978-0-516-06032-3). 32pp. In a small format, this colorful book introduces sharks and their bodies, types, and habits. (Rev: BL 7/95) [596.31]

23448 Gibbons, Gail. *Sharks* (2–4). Illus. 1992, Holiday House LB $16.95 (978-0-8234-0960-0). For the primary level, this account presents basic general facts as well as specific data on 12 common sharks. (Rev: BL 5/1/92; SLJ 7/92) [597.31]

23449 Harman, Amanda. *Sharks* (4–6). Illus. Series: Endangered! 1996, Benchmark LB $17.95 (978-0-7614-0220-6). 32pp. This account concentrates on three kinds of sharks — the great white, the whale, and the basking — and tells about the differences in their anatomies and why they are endangered. (Rev: SLJ 8/96) [597]

23450 Johnston, Marianne. *Sharks Past and Present* (3–5). Illus. 2000, Rosen LB $21.25 (978-0-8239-5206-9). 24pp. The shark's anatomy is discussed, as well as its 400-million-year history and why it has changed so little during that time. (Rev: BL 12/1/00) [567.3]

23451 Llewellyn, Claire. *The Best Book of Sharks* (3–5). Illus. by Ray Grinaway and Roger Stewart. Series: The Best Book Of. 1999, Kingfisher $12.95 (978-0-7534-5173-1). 31pp. A book about sharks that contains information on body structure, teeth, species, life cycle, and shark attacks. (Rev: HBG 4/00; SLJ 2/00) [597]

23452 McMillan, Beverly, and John A. Musick. *Sharks* (3–7). Illus. Series: Insiders. 2008, Simon & Schuster $16.99 (978-1-4169-3867-5). 64pp. Open wide for close-up views in this introduction to everything shark delivered in an easy conversational tone with double-page spreads, detailed diagrams, photographs, and a glossary. (Rev: BL 9/15/08; SLJ 9/08) [597.3]

23453 Maestro, Betsy. *A Sea Full of Sharks* (3–6). Illus. by Giulio Maestro. 1997, Scholastic paper $5.99 (978-0-590-43101-9). 32pp. An informative look at this feared but fascinating creature. (Rev: BL 1/1/91; SLJ 10/90) [597.31]

23454 Mallory, Kenneth. *Swimming with Hammerhead Sharks* (3–7). Illus. Series: Scientists in the Field. 2001, Houghton $16.00 (978-0-618-05543-2). 48pp. Vivid photographs and first-person narrative depict the excitement of swimming with sharks and describe this creature of the deep. (Rev: BL 4/1/01; HB 7/01; HBG 10/01; SLJ 7/01*) [597.3]

23455 Markle, Sandra. *Great White Sharks* (3–6). Illus. Series: Animal Predators. 2004, Carolrhoda LB $25.26 (978-1-57505-731-6). 40pp. Concise text and clear, full-page photographs introduce the life cycle of the great white shark and its physical characteristics, habitat, diet, and predatory behavior. (Rev: SLJ 12/04) [597]

23456 Markle, Sandra. *Tough, Toothy, Baby Sharks* (4–6). Illus. 2007, Walker $16.95 (978-0-8027-9593-9). 32pp. Eye-catching photographs and easy-to-understand text make this an unusually appealing book about baby sharks and how they mature. (Rev: BL 9/1/07; LMC 1/08; SLJ 12/07) [597.3]

23457 Nelson, Kristin L. *Hunting Sharks* (2–3). Series: Pull Ahead Books. 2003, Lerner LB $22.60 (978-0-8225-4671-9). 32pp. This fascinating book explores the physical characteristics, behavior, and life cycle of the shark and is suitable for beginning readers. (Rev: BL 11/15/03; HBG 10/03)

23458 O'Neill, Michael Patrick. *Shark Encounters* (2–4). Illus. 2008, Batfish $19.95 (978-0-9728653-4-0). 45pp. Eye-catching photographs make this an appealing introduction to sharks, more suitable for browsing than for research although it does discuss sharks' importance to the ecosystem and the threats they face. (Rev: BLO 6/17/08; LMC 3/08; SLJ 3/08) [597.3]

23459 Parker, Steve. *Sharks* (3–5). Illus. Series: What If. 1996, Millbrook LB $19.90 (978-0-7613-0456-2); paper $6.95 (978-0-7613-0471-5). 32pp. Using questions and answers, various characteristics of sharks are highlighted. (Rev: SLJ 6/96) [597.13]

23460 Pringle, Laurence. *Sharks! Strange and Wonderful* (3–5). Illus. 2001, Boyds Mills $15.95 (978-1-56397-863-0). 32pp. A picture book for older children that explains the shark's anatomy and habits, and introduces several different species. (Rev: BL 4/15/01; HBG 10/01; SLJ 8/01) [597.3]

23461 Rockwell, Anne. *Little Shark* (K–2). Illus. by Megan Halsey. 2005, Walker $15.95 (978-0-8027-8955-6). Readers follow the growth and maturing of a baby blue shark in this simple text with pertinent facts presented in bubbles. (Rev: BL 2/1/04*; SLJ 4/05) [597]

23462 Shea, Therese. *Sharks* (PS–2). Series: Big Bad Biters. 2006, Rosen LB $19.95 (978-1-4042-3519-1). 24pp. A look at the world of sharks and learn about their physical characteristics, habitat, what they eat, how they raise their young, and their enemies in the sea. (Rev: SLJ 3/07) [597.3]

23463 Sieswerda, Paul L. *Sharks* (5–8). Series: AnimalWays. 2001, Marshall Cavendish LB $31.36 (978-0-7614-1267-0). 112pp. Photographs, maps, and text introduce many species of sharks, their behavior, anatomy, and habitats. (Rev: BL 3/15/02; HBG 10/02) [597.31]

23464 Simon, Seymour. *Sharks* (2–4). Illus. 1995, HarperCollins LB $15.89 (978-0-06-023032-6). 32pp. Basic information about sharks, including life cycles, anatomy, and habits, is given with full-color illustrations. (Rev: BL 10/15/95; HB 11/95; SLJ 9/95) [597]

23465 Smith, Miranda. *Sharks* (4–6). Illus. Series: Kingfisher Knowledge. 2008, Kingfisher $12.95 (978-0-7534-6194-5). 64pp. An attractive introduction to the various types of sharks, their anatomy, life cycle, diet, migrations, and relationship with humans, with information on the need for conservation. (Rev: SLJ 9/08) [597.3]

23466 Spilsbury, Richard. *Great White Shark* (4–6). Illus. Series: Animals Under Threat. 2004, Heinemann LB $31.43 (978-1-4034-4860-6). 48pp. Striking color photographs enhance this overview of the great white shark and the environmental threats it faces. (Rev: BL 8/04) [597.3]

23467 Stille, Darlene R. *I Am a Shark: The Life of a Hammerhead Shark* (K–3). Illus. by Todd Ouren. Series: I Live in the Ocean. 2004, Picture Window LB $25.26 (978-1-4048-0599-6). 24pp. A hammerhead shark describes its life — diet, activities, and so forth. (Rev: SLJ 1/05) [597]

23468 Strong, Mike. *Shark! The Truth Behind the Terror* (4–6). Series: High Five Reading. 2002, Capstone LB $23.93 (978-0-7368-9547-7). 48pp. The combination of simple text describing sharks and shark attacks plus eye-catching photographs will attract reluctant readers. (Rev: HBG 10/03; SLJ 5/03) [597.3]

23469 Thomson, Sarah L. *Amazing Sharks!* (K–2). Illus. Series: I Can Read. 2005, HarperCollins $15.99 (978-0-06-054458-4). 32pp. Short sentences and bright photographs make this overview of sharks and shark behavior suitable for beginning readers. (Rev: BL 10/1/05; SLJ 1/06) [597.3]

23470 Troll, Ray. *Sharkabet: A Sea of Sharks from A to Z* (2–4). Illus. 2002, Graphic Arts paper $8.95 (978-1-55868-519-2). 40pp. From angel sharks to zebra sharks (and including some non-shark species), Troll includes many interesting shark facts in this unusual and beautifully illustrated alphabet book. (Rev: BL 9/1/02; HBG 10/02; SLJ 5/02) [597.3]

23471 Vadon, Catherine. *Meet the Shark* (K–4). Illus. by Vincent Boyer and Charles Dutertre. 2007, Two-Can $15.95 (978-1-58728-598-1). 45pp. Using cartoon characters and clear, interesting text, Vadon covers sharks' anatomy, behavior, and reproduction, and emphasizes the grave threats to their survival, dispelling myths about their violent character. (Rev: LMC 1/08; SLJ 12/07) [597.3]

23472 Ward, Nathalie. *Do Sharks Ever . . .?* (3–4). Illus. by Tessa Morgan. 1999, Down East paper $9.95 (978-0-89272-438-3). Using a question-and-answer format, this book covers topics related to sharks including physical characteristics, species, life cycle, food, and mating. (Rev: SLJ 2/00) [597.31]

23473 Woods, Bob. *Shark Attack!* (2–5). Series: Boys Rock! 2006, The Child's World LB $25.64 (978-1-59296-734-6). 32pp. A non-alarmist overview of the danger posed by sharks, suitable for beginning and reluctant readers (girls as well as boys). (Rev: SLJ 2/07) [597.3]

23474 Zoehfeld, Kathleen W. *Great White Shark: Ruler of the Sea* (PS–3). Illus. by Steven J. Petruccio. Series: Smithsonian Oceanic. 1995, Soundprints $15.95 (978-1-56899-122-1). 31pp. The life cycle of a great white shark, the Ruler of the Sea, which grows to 20 feet in length in adulthood. (Rev: SLJ 6/95) [597]

23475 Zollman, Pam. *A Shark Pup Grows Up* (K–1). Series: Scholastic News Nonfiction Readers. 2005, Children's Pr. LB $20.00 (978-0-516-24945-2). 24pp. Covers the life cycle of a shark, with a focus on newborn pups and their survival tactics. (Rev: SLJ 4/06) [597.3]

SHELLS

23476 Berkes, Marianne. *Seashells by the Seashore* (PS–2). Illus. by Robert Noreika. 2002, Dawn $16.95 (978-1-58469-035-1); paper $8.95 (978-1-58469-034-4). 32pp. Using rhyme and lovely illustrations, this picture book combines a lesson in counting with a lesson in seashell identification. (Rev: BL 3/1/02; HBG 10/02; SLJ check) [594.147]

23477 Cassie, Brian. *Shells* (4–6). Series: National Audubon Society First Field Guides. 2000, Scholastic $17.95 (978-0-590-64233-0); paper $8.95 (978-0-590-64258-3). 160pp. With more than 450 color photographs, this attractive volume focuses on about 50 of the most easily found shells and their characteristics. (Rev: BL 8/00; SLJ 1/01) [591]

23478 Lember, Barbara Hirsch. *The Shell Book* (K–3). Photos by author. 1997, Houghton $17.00 (978-0-395-72030-1). 32pp. Two-page layouts are used to introduce and describe several seashells that are found along the North American coastline. (Rev: SLJ 4/97) [594]

WHALES

23479 Arnold, Caroline. *A Killer Whale's World* (PS–2). Illus. by author. Series: Caroline Arnold's Animals. 2006, Picture Window LB $26.60 (978-1-4048-1321-2). 24pp. A baby killer whale grows up and learns to fend for himself in this appealing fact-packed title. (Rev: LMC 11/06; SLJ 6/06) [599.53]

23480 Carrick, Carol. *Whaling Days* (3–6). Illus. by David Frampton. 1993, Houghton $15.95 (978-0-395-50948-7). 40pp. With an emphasis on conservation, this is a history of whaling, from ancient times to the present. (Rev: BCCB 7–8/93; BL 5/1/93*; HB 5/93; SLJ 5/93*) [639.2]

23481 Carwardine, Mark. *Killer Whale* (3–5). Series: Natural World. 1999, Raintree $27.12 (978-0-7398-1058-3). 48pp. Illustrated with brilliant color photos, this book describes the life cycle of the killer whale from being a 400-pound baby, to learning to hunt with other members of the pod, and finally

reaching maturity. (Rev: BL 10/15/99; HBG 4/00) [599.5]

23482 Chrisp, Peter. *The Whalers* (4–6). Illus. 1995, Thomson Learning LB $18.98 (978-1-56847-421-2). 48pp. A history of whaling from ancient to modern times, with information on present-day efforts to protect whales. (Rev: BL 2/15/96; SLJ 3/96) [639.2]

23483 Collard, Sneed B. *A Whale Biologist at Work* (3–5). Illus. Series: Wildlife Conservation Society Books. 2000, Watts LB $24.50 (978-0-531-11786-6). 48pp. This book focuses on a marine biologist's observations of humpback and blue whales off the Pacific coast of North America. (Rev: BL 2/15/01; SLJ 3/01) [578.77]

23484 Delafosse, Claude, and Ute Fuhr. *Whales* (PS–3). Illus. Series: First Discovery. 1993, Scholastic $12.95 (978-0-590-47130-5). 24pp. This interactive, highly visual beginner's book introduces whales, how and where they live, and what they eat. (Rev: BL 11/15/93; HB 3/93; SLJ 4/94) [599.5]

23485 DuTemple, Lesley A. *Whales* (2–3). Illus. Series: Early Bird Nature Books. 1996, Lerner LB $25.26 (978-0-8225-3008-4). 48pp. Several kinds of whales are introduced, with descriptions of their appearance and behavior. (Rev: BL 8/96; SLJ 7/96) [599.5]

23486 Esbensen, Barbara J. *Baby Whales Drink Milk* (PS–1). Illus. by Lambert Davis. Series: Let's-Read-and-Find-Out. 1994, HarperCollins paper $5.99 (978-0-06-445119-2). 32pp. This book explains why whales are not fish and in so doing covers the characteristics of mammals. (Rev: BL 2/15/94; SLJ 3/94) [599.5]

23487 Gibbons, Gail. *Whales* (PS–1). Illus. 1991, Holiday House LB $16.95 (978-0-8234-0900-6). 32pp. The world of the fascinating whale, with good photos. (Rev: BL 10/15/91; HB 11/91; SLJ 12/91) [599.5]

23488 Greenberg, Dan. *Whales* (4–6). Illus. Series: Animals Animals. 2000, Marshall Cavendish LB $25.64 (978-0-7614-1167-3). 32pp. A useful book that introduces several types of whales and supplies information on their habitats, mating habits, structure, and behavior. (Rev: BL 3/15/01; HBG 3/01) [599.5]

23489 Harman, Amanda. *Whales* (4–6). Illus. Series: Endangered! 1996, Benchmark LB $25.64 (978-0-7614-0219-0). 32pp. Different species of whales are introduced, with coverage on why they have been hunted to near extinction and the efforts being made to save them. (Rev: SLJ 8/96) [599.5]

23490 Hodge, Deborah. *Whales: Killer Whales, Blue Whales and More* (K–3). Series: Wildlife. 1997, Kids Can $10.95 (978-1-55074-356-2). 32pp. In a series of double-page spreads, various whales are introduced, with material on food, habitats, and mobility. (Rev: BL 9/15/97; SLJ 11/97) [599.5]

23491 Hodgkins, Fran. *The Whale Scientists: Solving the Mystery of Whale Strandings* (5–8). Illus. Series: Scientists in the Field. 2007, Houghton $18.00 (978-0-618-55673-1). 32pp. A look at scientists' efforts to understand why whales sometimes strand themselves on beaches, seemingly waiting for death;

with accounts of efforts to rescue these huge mammals. (Rev: BL 12/1/07; HB 1/08; SLJ 12/07) [599.5]

23492 Hopkins, Ellen. *Orcas: High Seas Supermen* (3–7). Illus. 2000, Perfection Learning $17.95 (978-0-7807-9670-6); paper $8.96 (978-0-7891-5258-9). 56pp. For reluctant readers, this attractive book introduces different species of whales, their habitats, food, and methods of communication. (Rev: BL 11/1/00) [599.5]

23493 Hoyt, Erich. *Whale Rescue: Changing the Future for Endangered Wildlife* (4–6). Illus. Series: Animal Rescue. 2005, Firefly $19.95 (978-1-55297-601-2); paper $9.95 (978-1-55297-600-5). 64pp. An interesting discussion of international efforts to conserve the world's whales, with coverage of the various species and their characteristics plus information on whale researchers. (Rev: BL 8/05; SLJ 12/05) [599.5]

23494 Inskipp, Carol. *Killer Whale* (4–6). Illus. Series: Animals Under Threat. 2005, Heinemann LB $29.93 (978-1-4034-5584-0). 48pp. The life cycle of the killer whale and threats to its survival are explored in this blend of narrative and eye-catching color photography.

23495 Kant, Tanya. *The Migration of a Whale* (K–3). Illus. by Mark Bergin. Series: Amaze. 2008, Children's Pr. LB $26.00 (978-0-531-24049-6); paper $8.95 (978-0-531-23803-5). 32pp. "What Do Whales Eat? Why Do Whales Migrate? What Happens After Mating?" This simple introduction to whale migration, with colorful illustrations and well-organized chapters, includes a "Words to Remember" section. (Rev: SLJ 3/09)

23496 Kelsey, Elin. *Finding Out About Whales* (4–8). Illus. Series: Science Explorers. 1998, Owl $19.95 (978-1-895688-79-5); paper $9.95 (978-1-895688-80-1). This book discusses how information is gathered about whales and introduces five different species: blue, humpback, beluga, gray, and killer. (Rev: BL 3/1/99; SLJ 3/99) [595.5]

23497 Kurth, Linda Moore. *Keiko's Story: A Killer Whale Goes Home* (4–6). 2000, Millbrook $24.90 (978-0-7613-1500-1). 72pp. An informative, enjoyable read about Keiko, the killer whale who played in the movie *Free Willy* and the efforts to return him to the wild. (Rev: HBG 4/04; SLJ 9/00) [595.5]

23498 Leon, Vicki. *A Pod of Killer Whales: The Mysterious Life of the Intelligent Orca* (5–8). Series: Jean-Michel Cousteau Presents. 2007, London Town paper $8.95 (978-0-9766134-7-3). 48pp. With eye-catching photographs and stories of close encounters with these animals, this book looks at killer whales' characteristics, behavior, intelligence, and the threats to their survival. (Rev: SLJ 11/07) [599.53]

23499 Lockwood, Sophie. *Whales* (4–7). Illus. Series: World of Mammals. 2008, Child's World LB $20.95 (978-1-59296-930-2). 40pp. Well-suited to report writers, this surprisingly comprehensive title discusses whale behavior and physiology and includes information on conservation. (Rev: BLO 6/17/08; SLJ 6/08) [599.5]

23500 McMillan, Bruce. *Going on a Whale Watch* (PS–3). Illus. 1993, Scholastic $19.95 (978-0-590-72826-3). 40pp. Readers go on a whale watch and watch two children watching the whales. (Rev: BL 10/15/92; SLJ 4/93) [599.5]

23501 Markle, Sandra. *Killer Whales* (3–6). Series: Animal Predators. 2004, Carolrhoda LB $25.26 (978-1-57505-728-6). The killer whale's skill as a hunter is emphasized in this attractive overview. (Rev: BL 12/1/04; SLJ 1/05) [599.53]

23502 Pringle, Laurence. *Whales! Strange and Wonderful* (3–5). Illus. by Meryl Henderson. 2003, Boyds Mills $15.95 (978-1-56397-439-7). 32pp. Whales and their physical and behavioral characteristics are introduced, with brief information on whaling history and current conservation efforts. (Rev: BL 3/15/03; HBG 10/03; SLJ 4/03) [599.53]

23503 Rau, Dana Meachen. *Guess Who Hunts* (PS–K). Series: Bookworms. Guess Who. 2009, Marshall Cavendish $15.95 (978-0-7614-2907-4). 32pp. Fun for browsing, this book asks readers to identify a whale using the clues in the text and images. (Rev: SLJ 6/09) [599.5]

23504 Reiter, Chris. *The Blue Whale* (4–7). Series: Endangered and Threatened Animals. 2003, Enslow LB $25.26 (978-0-7660-5055-6). 48pp. Standard information on the blue whale and its endangered status is accompanied by links to Web sites for further research. (Rev: HBG 10/03; SLJ 6/03) [599.5]

23505 Short, Joan, and Bettina Bird. *Whales* (3–5). Illus. by Deborah Savin. 1997, Mondo paper $4.95 (978-1-57255-190-9). 31pp. Colorful illustrations are used to cover such particulars about whales as anatomy, swimming, breathing, feeding, and communication. (Rev: SLJ 9/97) [599.5]

23506 Simon, Seymour. *Killer Whales* (1–3). Series: See More Readers. 2002, North-South paper $3.95 (978-1-58717-142-0). 32pp. Stunning photographs placed opposite a few lines of text give basic information about killer whales in this beginning reader. (Rev: BL 7/02; HBG 10/02; SLJ 4/02) [599.5]

23507 Skerry, Brian. *A Whale on Her Own: The True Story of Wilma the Beluga Whale* (3–4). Photos by author. 2000, Blackbirch LB $26.19 (978-1-56711-431-7). 32pp. This true story tells of the friendly relationship that developed between a diver and a beluga whale in Chedabucto Bay, Nova Scotia. (Rev: HBG 9/00; SLJ 10/00) [595.5]

23508 Smyth, Karen C. *Crystal: The Story of a Real Baby Whale* (3–6). Illus. 1986, Down East paper $10.95 (978-0-89272-327-0). 96pp. The first year in the life of a humpback whale. (Rev: BL 8/86; SLJ 4/87)

23509 Sobol, Richard. *Adelina's Whales* (2–5). Illus. 2003, Penguin $17.99 (978-0-525-47110-3). 32pp. Readers meet 10-year-old Adelina, who lives in a simple home in Baja California and each winter awaits the arrival of gray whales in the lagoon — and of the tourists who watch them; facts about the gray whale and a foreword about protectionist efforts accompany this photo-essay. (Rev: BL 7/03; HBG 10/03; SLJ 9/03) [639]

23510 Stille, Darlene R. *I Am a Whale: The Life of a Humpback Whale* (K–3). Illus. by Todd Ouren. Series: I Live in the Ocean. 2004, Picture Window LB $25.26 (978-1-4048-0600-9). 24pp. A humpback whale describes its life — diet, activities, and so forth. (Rev: SLJ 1/05) [599.5]

23511 Stonehouse, Bernard. *Whales: A Visual Introduction to Whales, Dolphins, and Porpoises* (4–6). Illus. Series: Animal Watch. 1998, Facts on File LB $16.95 (978-0-8160-3922-7). 48pp. Maps, photos, paintings, and double-page spreads are used to introduce readers to the world of cetaceans. (Rev: BL 12/1/98) [599.5]

23512 Stoops, Erik D., et al. *Whales* (3–6). Illus. 1995, Sterling $16.95 (978-0-8069-0566-2). 80pp. Using a question-and-answer format, this book provides basic facts about whales, including why they don't drown. (Rev: BL 12/1/95; SLJ 1/96) [599.5]

23513 Thomson, Sarah L. *Amazing Whales!* (1–3). Illus. Series: I Can Read! 2005, HarperCollins LB $17.89 (978-0-06-054466-9). 32pp. Simple, easy-reader text introduces blue whales, killer whales, sperm whales, dolphins, and porpoises and their characteristics, communication, and endangered status. (Rev: BL 5/15/05; SLJ 1/05) [599.5]

Microscopes and Microbiology

23514 Latta, Sara. *The Good, the Bad, the Slimy: The Secret Life of Microbes* (5–8). Photos by Dennis Kunkel. 2006, Enslow LB $31.93 (978-0-7660-1294-3). 128pp. Bright photography and clear explanations will engage browsers and please report writers. (Rev: LMC 5/07; SLJ 8/07)

23515 Lee, Kimberly Fekany. *Cells* (4–6). Illus. Series: Mission: Science. 2008, Compass Point LB $26.60 (978-0-7565-3954-2). 40pp. An appealing exploration of the structure of plant and animal cells, cell movement, and cell reproduction; also includes many photographs and illustrations plus an activity. (Rev: LMC 3/09; SLJ 6/09) [571.6]

23516 Levine, Shar, and Leslie Johnstone. *The Ultimate Guide to Your Microscope* (5–9). 2008, Sterling paper $9.95 (978-1-4027-4329-0). 144pp. After covering the basics of using a microscope, this volume presents 41 hands-on activities. (Rev: LMC 10/08; SLJ 11/08) [570.28]

23517 Selsam, Millicent E. *Greg's Microscope* (K–3). Illus. by Arnold Lobel. 1963, HarperCollins paper $3.99 (978-0-06-444144-5). 64pp. Greg and his parents observe small household items through a microscope.

23518 Silverstein, Alvin, et al. *Cells* (4–8). Series: Science Concepts. 2002, Millbrook LB $26.90 (978-0-7613-2254-2). 64pp. The functions and components of plant and animal cells are discussed along with such topics as cloning, cell fusion, and stem cell research. (Rev: BL 9/15/02; HBG 3/03) [574.87]

23519 Thomas, Peggy. *Bacteria and Viruses* (5–8). Illus. Series: Lucent Library of Science and Technology. 2005, Gale LB $29.95 (978-1-59018-438-7). 112pp. Introduces the scientists who discovered bacteria and viruses and how we fight ones that harm us and attempt to use others to our benefit. (Rev: BL 1/05)

23520 Walker, Richard. *Microscopic Life* (4–8). Illus. Series: Kingfisher Knowledge. 2004, Kingfisher $11.95 (978-0-7534-5778-8). 63pp. A well-illustrated look at the tiniest living things — bacteria, viruses, mites, fungi, and molds, for example — and how we study them and attempt to use them to our benefit. (Rev: BL 9/1/04; SLJ 1/05) [579]

Oceanography

GENERAL

23521 Berger, Melvin, and Gilda Berger. *What Makes an Ocean Wave? Questions and Answers About Oceans and Ocean Life* (3–6). Illus. 2001, Scholastic $14.95 (978-0-439-09588-4). 48pp. In question-and-answer format, this title tackles topics of interest both to browsers and report writers. (Rev: BL 7/01; HBG 10/01) [551.46]

23522 Castaldo, Nancy F. *Oceans: An Activity Guide for Ages 6–9* (3–5). Illus. 2002, Chicago Review paper $14.95 (978-1-55652-443-1). 134pp. All about the world's oceans, including their plant and animal life, folklore, and currents and tides, with related crafts and experiments. (Rev: BL 5/15/02; SLJ 3/02) [372.3]

23523 Chambers, Catherine. *Oceans and Seas* (3–5). Series: Mapping Earthforms. 2000, Heinemann LB $21.36 (978-1-57572-526-0). 32pp. A basic overview that describes the characteristics of oceans and seas, life within them, and how environmental factors like global warming affect them. (Rev: HBG 3/01; SLJ 8/00) [551.46]

23524 Cobb, Allan B. *Super Science Projects About Oceans* (4–7). Series: Psyched for Science. 2000, Rosen LB $26.50 (978-0-8239-3174-3). 48pp. Although the format is unattractive, this book contains six fine experiments that explore concepts involving the ocean. (Rev: SLJ 7/00) [551.46]

23525 Davies, Nicola. *Oceans and Seas* (K–3). Series: Kingfisher Young Knowledge. 2004, Houghton $8.95 (978-0-7534-5758-0). 48pp. Attractive double-page spreads with many illustrations and diagrams present basic information on salt water, tides, and marine plants and animals and the dangers they face. (Rev: BL 9/1/04) [551.46]

23526 Gray, Samantha. *Ocean* (3–5). Illus. Series: Eye Wonder. 2001, DK LB $17.99 (978-0-7894-8180-1); paper $9.99 (978-0-7894-7852-8). 48pp. The ocean, marine animals, and marine research are among the topics tackled in this fact-filled book. (Rev: BL 12/1/01; HBG 3/02) [591.77]

23527 Harrison, David L. *Oceans: The Vast, Mysterious Deep* (2–3). Illus. by Cheryl Nathan. Series: Earthworks. 2003, Boyds Mills $15.95 (978-1-59078-018-3). 32pp. The oceans, their movement, and the life they support are shown in bright illustrations and brief, informative text. (Rev: BL 1/1–15/04; HBG 4/04; SLJ 1/04) [577.7]

23528 Hirschi, Ron. *Ocean Seasons* (1–3). Illus. by Kirsten Carlson. 2007, Sylvan Dell $15.95 (978-0-

9777423-2-5); paper $8.95 (978-1-9343591-6-7). An engaging exploration of the ways in which the seasons affect the oceans and ocean wildlife, looking in particular at marine and land ecology in the Pacific Northwest; with attractive illustrations and well-written text. (Rev: LMC 11/07; SLJ 10/07) [577.7]

23529 Hodge, Susie. *Ocean Survival* (4–6). Illus. Series: Extreme Habitats. 2007, Gareth Stevens LB $25.27 (978-0-8368-8247-6). 32pp. This well-designed title combines high visual appeal and accessible facts to make an attractive and informative overview of the oceans, the plants and animals that live there, how people use the oceans, and the threats the oceans face. (Rev: LMC 1/08; SLJ 12/07) [551.46]

23530 Kalman, Bobbie. *The ABCs of Oceans* (2–4). Illus. Series: ABCs of the Natural World. 2007, Crabtree LB $26.60 (978-0-7787-3412-3); paper $7.95 (978-0-7787-3432-1). 32pp. Butterfly fish, camouflage, dolphins, and eels are among the topics covered in this alphabetical look at the oceans that also includes krait, nudibranchs, and zones of the ocean. (Rev: BL 10/15/07; LMC 5/08) [591.77]

23531 Kraske, Robert. *The Voyager's Stone* (4–6). Illus. 1995, Orchard LB $16.99 (978-0-531-08740-4). 96pp. The framework of a message in a bottle cast into the sea is used to introduce oceanography, currents, and sea life. (Rev: BCCB 3/95; BL 3/1/95; SLJ 3/95) [551.46]

23532 Lambert, David. *The Mediterranean Sea* (4–6). Illus. Series: Seas and Oceans. 1997, Raintree LB $27.12 (978-0-8172-4512-2). 48pp. Describes the role of the Mediterranean throughout history, its features and formations, and the plant and animal life it supports. (Rev: BL 7/97) [551.46]

23533 Lambert, David. *The Pacific Ocean* (4–6). Illus. Series: Seas and Oceans. 1996, Raintree LB $18.98 (978-0-8172-4507-8). 48pp. Ocean life, currents, the formation of islands, and pollution are a few of the topics discussed in this introduction to the Pacific Ocean. (Rev: BL 1/1–15/97) [551.46]

23534 Littlefield, Cindy A. *Awesome Ocean Science!* (3–5). Illus. by Sarah Rakitin. Series: Kids Can. 2003, Williamson paper $12.95 (978-1-885593-71-9). 120pp. This informative book looks at the water cycle, the oceans and their animal life, and at conservation, and provides simple projects that illustrate or reinforce some of the basic concepts. (Rev: BL 1/1–15/03; SLJ 5/03) [551.46]

23535 McMillan, Beverly, and John A. Musick. *Oceans* (5–8). Illus. Series: Insiders. 2007, Simon & Schuster $16.99 (978-1-4169-3859-0). 64pp. An introduction to Earth's oceans, marine life, ocean migrations, sea vents, coastal and polar seas, and so forth, with eye-catching illustrations. (Rev: LMC 10/07; SLJ 12/07) [551.46]

23536 Markle, Sandra. *Down, Down, Down in the Ocean* (3–5). Illus. by Bob Marstall. 1999, Walker LB $17.85 (978-0-8027-8655-5). 32pp. This is a dramatic journey through the different levels of life in the ocean told in double-page spreads. (Rev: HBG 4/00; SLJ 11/99) [551.46]

23537 Morgan, Nina. *The Caribbean and the Gulf of Mexico* (4–6). Illus. Series: Seas and Oceans. 1996, Raintree LB $18.98 (978-0-8172-4508-5). 48pp. For these two bodies of water, material is presented on such topics as ocean life, shipping, tourism, currents, and people. (Rev: BL 1/1–15/97) [917.29]

23538 Morgan, Nina. *The North Sea and the Baltic Sea* (4–6). Illus. Series: Seas and Oceans. 1996, Raintree LB $27.12 (978-0-8172-4510-8). 48pp. These two European bodies of water are introduced, with coverage on their importance, history, shipping routes, and plant and animal life. (Rev: BL 1/1–15/97) [551.46]

23539 Penny, Malcolm. *The Indian Ocean* (4–6). Illus. Series: Seas and Oceans. 1997, Raintree LB $27.12 (978-0-8172-4514-6). 48pp. The history of the world's third-largest ocean, the migration and exploration paths that people took from Europe to Asia, and the marine life it supports. (Rev: BL 7/97) [551.46]

23540 Pyers, Greg. *Ocean Explorer* (2–4). Illus. Series: Habitat Explorer. 2004, Raintree LB $25.70 (978-1-4109-0510-9). 32pp. This photo-filled exploration of oceans looks at the plants and animals found there, plus environmental threats posed by pollution and development.

23541 Ricciuti, Edward R. *Ocean* (4–6). Illus. Series: Biomes of the World. 1995, Marshall Cavendish LB $25.64 (978-0-7614-0079-0). 64pp. With clear explanations and full-color photos, the world's ocean environment and its animal and plant life are introduced. (Rev: BL 12/15/95) [551.46]

23542 Sauvain, Philip. *Oceans* (3–5). Illus. Series: Geography Detectives. 1997, Carolrhoda LB $19.93 (978-1-57505-043-0). 32pp. This account identifies and describes the world's oceans, explains the saltwater ecosystem, and explores coastlines, the ocean floor, tides, and marine plant and animal life. (Rev: BL 8/97; SLJ 1/98) [551.46]

23543 Sayre, April P. *Ocean* (4–7). Illus. Series: Exploring Earth's Biomes. 1996, Twenty-First Century LB $25.90 (978-0-8050-4084-5). 80pp. An introduction to the nature and composition of oceans and the animal and plant life that they support. (Rev: BL 10/15/96; SLJ 1/97) [551.46]

23544 Stone, Lynn M. *Oceans* (1–3). Illus. Series: Biomes of North America. 2003, Rourke $20.64 (978-1-58952-686-0). 24pp. For young researchers, this is an excellent introduction to this biome, with clear, simple text, photographs, and maps. (Rev: BL 10/15/03) [577.7]

23545 VanCleave, Janice. *Janice VanCleave's Oceans for Every Kid: Easy Activities That Make Learning Science Fun* (5–7). Illus. Series: Science for Every Kid. 1996, Wiley paper $12.95 (978-0-471-12453-5). 256pp. This book gives good background information about oceans plus a number of entertaining and instructive projects and activities. (Rev: BL 4/15/96; SLJ 5/96) [551.46]

23546 Vogel, Carole G. *Dangerous Crossings* (5–8). Illus. Series: The Restless Sea. 2003, Watts LB $30.50 (978-0-531-12325-6); paper $12.95 (978-0-531-16679-6). 79pp. Ranging widely from tales of endurance at sea to pirates and problems created by global warming, this is an arresting account. (Rev: BL 1/1/04; SLJ 1/04) [910.4]

23547 Vogel, Carole G. *Human Impact* (5–9). Series: The Restless Sea. 2003, Watts LB $30.50 (978-0-531-12323-2). 95pp. An examination of how mankind is endangering the sea and its creatures through activities including coastal development, global warming, and oil spills. (Rev: SLJ 3/04) [333.91]

23548 Waterlow, Julia. *The Atlantic Ocean* (4–6). Illus. Series: Seas and Oceans. 1996, Raintree LB $18.98 (978-0-8172-4509-2). 48pp. Such topics as geography, currents, history, and economic and recreational importance are covered in relation to the Atlantic Ocean. (Rev: BL 1/1–15/97) [551.46]

23549 Waterlow, Julia. *The Red Sea and the Arabian Gulf* (4–6). Illus. Series: Seas and Oceans. 1997, Raintree LB $27.12 (978-0-8172-4515-3). 48pp. An overview of the history and importance of these bodies of water, with information on the coral reefs and animals of the Red Sea and oil reserves of the Arabian Gulf. (Rev: BL 7/97) [551.46]

23550 Woodward, John. *Oceans Atlas: An Amazing Aquatic Adventure* (4–6). Illus. 2007, DK $19.99 (978-0-7566-2557-3). 96pp. Readers will enjoy the photographs and maps of the world's oceans and their features. Facts about ocean exploration, oceanographers, conservation efforts, and the 2004 tsunami add interest. With transparent overlays and an interactive CD-ROM. (Rev: SLJ 5/07)

23551 Young, Karen Romano. *Across the Wide Ocean: The Why, How, and Where of Navigation for Humans and Animals at Sea* (5–7). Illus. by author. 2007, HarperCollins $18.99 (978-0-06-009086-9). 80pp. Before satellite global positioning technology, humans had to use many different methods to navigate at sea, and this book creatively explores many of these methods as well as those of sea creatures including turtles and whales. (Rev: SLJ 7/07) [623.89]

COMMERCIAL FISHING

23552 Love, Ann, and Jane Drake. *Fishing* (2–4). Illus. by Pat Cupples. Series: America at Work. 1999, Kids Can $12.95 (978-1-55074-457-6). 31pp. This book introduces the fishing industry on both coasts by visiting a fish farm, taking a voyage on a trawler, and studying the life cycles and habitats of various fish. (Rev: HBG 4/00; SLJ 11/99) [639]

CURRENTS, TIDES, AND WAVES

23553 Adamson, Thomas K. *Tsunamis* (2–4). Illus. 2005, Capstone LB $22.60 (978-0-7368-5248-7). 24pp. This volume, which explores the causes and destructive capacities of tsunamis, includes information on the December 26, 2004, tragedy. (Rev: BL 6/1–15/05) [551.40]

23554 Allen, Judy, et al. *Higher Ground* (5–8). Illus. 2006, Chrysalis paper $8.99 (978-1-84458-581-6). 156pp. First-person accounts of survivors and rescue workers mixed with fictional treatments based

on fact portray the impact on children of the deadly Indian Ocean tsunami of December 2004. (Rev: BCCB 5/06; BL 2/1/06; SLJ 3/06) [363.349]

23555 Fine, Jil. *Tsunamis* (3–5). Illus. Series: Natural Disaster. 2006, Children's Pr. LB $24.50 (978-0-531-12444-4). 48pp. A photo-filled exploration of tsunamis and the geological events that can cause these massive tidal waves, focusing in particular on the deadly Indian Ocean tsunami of December 2004. (Rev: BL 11/1/06) [551.46]

23556 Hamilton, John. *Tsunamis* (3–4). Series: Nature's Fury. 2005, ABDO LB $24.21 (978-1-59679-333-0). 32pp. Well-chosen color photographs and clear text explore tsunamis, their causes and impact, and specific tidal waves of the past. (Rev: SLJ 3/06) [551.55]

23557 Karwoski, Gail L. *Tsunami: The True Story of an April Fools' Day Disaster* (4–7). Illus. by John MacDonald. 2006, Darby Creek $17.95 (978-1-58196-044-0). 64pp. Karwoski tells the story of a devastating 1946 tsunami, and expands the coverage to other destructive waves and their causes, effects, and the measures being taken to alert residents to their arrival. (Rev: SLJ 1/07) [363.34]

23558 Lampton, Christopher. *Tidal Wave* (4–6). Illus. Series: Disaster! 1992, Houghton paper $5.70 (978-0-395-62464-7). 40pp. This explanation of the causes and effects of tidal waves includes many color photos and detailed descriptions of important tidal-wave disasters of the past. (Rev: BL 3/15/92) [363.3]

23559 Morris, Ann, and Heidi Larson. *Tsunami: Helping Each Other* (2–4). 2005, Millbrook $15.95 (978-0-7613-9501-0). 48pp. Focusing on the experiences of two Thai brothers, 8-year-old Chaiya and 12-year-old Chaipreak, who lose their father to the tsunami, this is a more personal treatment than many of the books about tsunamis and includes many photographs of the disaster and the progress toward recovery. (Rev: BL 12/1/05; SLJ 7/06) [959.304]

23560 Morrison, Taylor. *Tsunami Warning* (4–6). Illus. 2007, Houghton $17.00 (978-0-618-73463-4). 32pp. Morrison discusses the tsunamis of 1946 and 1957 in this overview of warning systems and how they work. (Rev: BL 2/1/07) [551.47]

23561 Steele, Christy. *Tsunamis* (3–5). Illus. 2001, Raintree LB $22.83 (978-0-7398-4706-0). 32pp. The authors look at our knowledge of tidal waves and their causes, and discuss the ways in which we can protect ourselves from danger. (Rev: HBG 3/02; SLJ 2/02) [551.55]

23562 Stewart, Gail B. *Catastrophe in Southern Asia: The Tsunami of 2004* (5–8). Series: Overview. 2005, Gale LB $29.95 (978-1-59018-831-6). 112pp. An information-packed review of the tsunami itself, the human costs of the disaster, and the reconstruction efforts. (Rev: SLJ 12/05)

23563 Torres, John A. *Disaster in the Indian Ocean: Tsunami 2004* (5–8). Illus. Series: Monumental Milestones: Great Events of Modern Times. 2005, Mitchell Lane LB $29.95 (978-1-58415-344-3). 48pp. This slim volume, uneven in its coverage, nonetheless offers a chilling overview of the devastating Indian Ocean tsunami of December 2004 and includes a number of eyewitness accounts. (Rev: BL 10/15/05; SLJ 12/05) [909]

23564 Vogel, Carole G. *Savage Waters* (5–8). Illus. Series: The Restless Sea. 2003, Watts LB $30.50 (978-0-531-12321-8); paper $12.95 (978-0-531-16682-6). 79pp. An entertaining and attractive discussion of the origins of the world's oceans and seas and the forces that influence waves, tides, and tsunamis. Also use *Shifting Shores* (2003). (Rev: BL 1/1/04; SLJ 1/04) [551.46]

23565 Wade, Mary Dodson. *Tsunami: Monster Waves* (4–8). Series: American Disasters. 2002, Enslow LB $23.93 (978-0-7660-1786-3). 48pp. This book explains in photographs and text how these giant sea swells are created, how they are tracked, and their effects. (Rev: BL 6/1–15/02; HBG 10/02; SLJ 10/02) [551.55]

SEASHORES AND TIDAL POOLS

23566 Arnosky, Jim. *Beach Combing: Exploring the Seashore* (PS–2). 2004, Penguin $15.99 (978-0-525-47104-2). 32pp. Arnosky explores the wonders of a tropical beach and its wildlife. (Rev: BL 7/04; SLJ 7/04) [578.769]

23567 Arnosky, Jim. *Following the Coast* (3–5). Illus. 2004, HarperCollins $15.99 (978-0-688-17117-9). 32pp. The life and landmarks of the salt marshes of the Atlantic Coast, from Florida northward to Delaware, are the focus of this attractive blend of narrative and artwork. (Rev: BL 2/15/04; SLJ 5/04) [591.769]

23568 Brenner, Barbara. *One Small Place by the Sea* (2–4). Illus. by Tom Leonard. 2004, HarperCollins $16.99 (978-0-688-17182-7). 32pp. The abundant life in a tidal pool is explored in accessible text and realistic illustrations. (Rev: BL 3/1/04; SLJ 4/04) [577.69]

23569 Cohat, Elisabeth. *The Seashore* (PS–2). Illus. by Pierre de Hugo. Series: First Discovery. 1995, Scholastic $12.95 (978-0-590-20303-6). A spiral-bound book with transparencies that show the many organisms found in tidal pools. (Rev: SLJ 9/95) [591]

23570 Cooper, Ann. *Along the Seashore* (3–5). Illus. Series: Wild Wonders. 1997, Roberts Rinehart paper $9.95 (978-1-57098-121-0). 46pp. A little book that introduces animals associated with seas and seashores: the seal, cormorant, hermit crab, raccoon, osprey, sea star, dolphin, gull, and sea trout. (Rev: BL 7/97; SLJ 8/97) [577.7]

23571 Darling, Kathy. *Seashore Babies* (3–5). Illus. by Tara Darling. 1997, Walker LB $16.85 (978-0-8027-8477-3). 32pp. Seashores are introduced, with details of the young of the creatures found there and their lives and enemies. (Rev: BL 4/1/97; SLJ 3/97) [591.3]

23572 Davidson, Avelyn. *Beach Biology* (3–5). Illus. 2007, Children's Pr. LB $25.00 (978-0-531-17764-8); paper $6.95 (978-0-531-15495-3). 36pp. A well-designed introduction to topics including tides, waves and currents, rocky and sandy shores, coral reefs, and so forth. (Rev: LMC 1/08; SLJ 11/07) [577.5]

23573 Fleisher, Paul. *Tide Pool* (3–5). Illus. Series: Webs of Life. 1997, Marshall Cavendish LB $22.79 (978-0-7614-0431-6). 40pp. This wet-and-dry environment is introduced, along with the animals and plants that thrive under conditions where flooding occurs twice a day. (Rev: BL 2/15/98; HBG 3/98; SLJ 4/98) [574.5]

23574 Giesecke, Ernestine. *Seashore Plants* (K–3). Illus. Series: Heinemann First Library. 1999, Heinemann $21.36 (978-1-57572-828-5). 32pp. Ten plants, six from sandy shores such as sea oats and eelgrass and four from rocky shores including kelp and rock weed, are introduced in full-page photos and a brief text. (Rev: BL 6/1–15/99; SLJ 8/99) [581.769]

23575 Hunter, Anne. *What's in the Tide Pool?* (K–2). Illus. 2000, Houghton $5.95 (978-0-618-01510-8). 32pp. Ten animals that live in tidal pools, such as the sea anemone, herring gull, hermit crab, and barnacle, are introduced in this little book. (Rev: BL 9/15/00; HBG 3/01) [578.769]

23576 Johansson, Philip. *The Seashore: A Saltwater Web of Life* (4–6). Illus. Series: Wonderful Water Biomes. 2007, Enslow LB $23.93 (978-0-7660-2811-1). 48pp. After an account of a midnight search for a leatherback turtle on a tropical beach, this title looks at the plants and animals that live on seashores. (Rev: SLJ 1/08) [577.69]

23577 Kudlinski, Kathleen V. *The Seaside Switch* (K–2). Illus. by Lindy Burnett. 2007, NorthWord $16.95 (978-1-55971-964-3). 32pp. An appealing look at the changing of the tides and the seashore and the effects on the varied life there. (Rev: BL 3/15/07) [577.69]

23578 Malnig, Anita. *Where the Waves Break: Life at the Edge of the Sea* (3–5). Illus. 1985, Carolrhoda LB $14.95 (978-0-87614-226-4); Lerner paper $7.95 (978-0-87614-477-0). 48pp. An introduction to life at the sea's edge, including descriptions of starfish, brittle stars, snails, and seaweed. (Rev: BL 6/1/85; HB 9/85; SLJ 5/85)

23579 Paul, Tessa. *By the Seashore* (2–5). Illus. Series: Animal Trackers. 1997, Crabtree LB $22.60 (978-0-86505-587-2); paper $7.95 (978-0-86505-595-7). 32pp. Ten creatures found at the seashore are introduced and identified by the evidence they leave behind, like prints, holes, nests, and hair or fur. (Rev: HBG 3/98; SLJ 10/97) [591]

23580 Pipes, Rose. *Coasts and Shores* (2–4). Series: World Habitats. 1998, Raintree LB $24.26 (978-0-8172-5008-9). 32pp. This book describes the physical features of coastal regions with material on climates, wildlife, human interaction, and the need for protection. (Rev: BL 3/15/99; HBG 3/99) [591]

23581 Pringle, Laurence. *Come to the Ocean's Edge* (K–3). Illus. by Michael Chesworth. 2003, Boyds Mills $15.95 (978-1-56397-779-4). 32pp. Watercolor paintings depict the shoreline and the wildlife found there in daytime and at night. (Rev: BL 2/1/04; HBG 4/04; SLJ 10/03) [577.7]

23582 Sayre, April P. *Seashore* (4–7). Illus. Series: Exploring Earth's Biomes. 1996, Twenty-First Century LB $25.90 (978-0-8050-4085-2). 80pp. The composition of seashores and the life that they support are covered in this nicely illustrated account. (Rev: BL 10/15/96; SLJ 1/97) [574.5]

23583 Serafini, Frank. *Looking Closely Along the Shore* (PS–3). Illus. 2008, Kids Can $15.95 (978-1-55453-141-7). 40pp. Close-up photographs and an interactive format make this an appealing introduction to seashore plants and animals. (Rev: BLO 6/17/08; LMC 10/08; SLJ 4/08) [578.769]

23584 Silverstein, Alvin, and Virginia Silverstein. *Life in a Tidal Pool* (4–6). Illus. by Pamela Carroll and Walter Carroll. 1990, Little, Brown $14.95 (978-0-316-79120-5). 60pp. The tidal pool habitat is explored. (Rev: SLJ 10/90) [574]

23585 Theodorou, Rod. *Along the Seashore* (2–4). Series: Amazing Journeys. 2000, Heinemann LB $22.79 (978-1-57572-483-6). 32pp. This brief overview of seashores focuses on several specific plants and animals found there. (Rev: HBG 3/01; SLJ 7/00) [591]

23586 Waldron, Melanie. *Coasts* (3–5). Series: Mapping Earthforms. 2007, Heinemann LB $28.21 (978-1-4034-9605-8). 32pp. With maps, diagrams, tables, and color photographs, this title looks at how coasts were formed, the action of tides and waves, erosion, plants and animals, and important examples (one chapter is titled "A Way of Life — Iceland"). (Rev: SLJ 10/07) [508.314]

23587 Wechsler, Doug. *Marvels in the Muck: Life in the Salt Marshes* (3–6). Illus. by author. 2008, Boyds Mills $17.95 (978-1-59078-588-1). 48pp. This year in the life of a salt marsh follows the seasons in text and photographs. (Rev: BL 12/1/08; LMC 3/09; SLJ 12/08) [578.769]

23588 Zim, Herbert S., and Lester Ingle. *Seashores* (5–8). Illus. 1991, Western $21.27 (978-0-307-64496-1). 160pp. This is a guide to animals and plants found along the beaches.

UNDERWATER EXPLORATION

23589 Collard, Sneed B., III. *The Deep-Sea Floor* (2–4). Illus. by Gregory Wenzel. 2003, Charlesbridge $16.95 (978-1-57091-402-7); paper $6.95 (978-1-57091-403-4). 32pp. A look at the amazing discoveries gleaned from the exploration of the deep-sea floor, including plant and animal life and geologic finds, with watercolor illustrations. (Rev: BL 2/1/03; HBG 10/03; SLJ 7/03) [591.779]

23590 Gibbons, Gail. *Sunken Treasure* (2–5). Illus. 1988, HarperCollins LB $15.89 (978-0-690-04736-3); paper $6.99 (978-0-06-446097-2). 32pp. Searching for the cargo of the Atocha, a Spanish galleon sunk off Florida in 1622. (Rev: BCCB 10/88; BL 10/15/88; HB 9/88)

23591 Lindop, Laurie. *Venturing the Deep Sea* (4–8). Series: Science on the Edge. 2005, Twenty-First Century LB $27.93 (978-0-7613-2701-1). 80pp. A behind-the-scenes look at the technology employed by modern-day undersea explorers, with a clear explanation of the types of knowledge these researchers are seeking. (Rev: SLJ 8/06; VOYA 4/06) [551.46]

23592 Mallory, Kenneth. *Diving to a Deep-Sea Volcano* (4–7). Illus. 2006, Houghton $17.00 (978-0-618-33205-2). 64pp. Take a dive with marine biologists as they explore deep-sea volcanoes and the creatures that live and thrive around them; scientific method, adventure, biography, and insight into a career are intertwined in this portrait of a marine biologist's work in an underwater habitat. (Rev: BL 12/1/06; SLJ 2/07) [551.2]

23593 Matsen, Brad. *The Incredible Record-Setting Deep-Sea Dive of the Bathysphere* (4–6). Series: Incredible Deep-Sea Adventures. 2003, Enslow LB $23.93 (978-0-7660-2188-4). 48pp. An attractive look at early bathyspheres and undersea discoveries. Also use *The Incredible Submersible Alvin Discovers a Strange Deep-Sea World* (2003), about more-recent explorations. (Rev: HBG 4/04; SLJ 1/04) [551.46]

23594 Pitkin, Linda. *Journey Under the Sea* (3–6). Illus. 2003, Oxford $19.95 (978-0-19-521972-2). 48pp. In words and pictures, marine photographer Pitkin paints a vivid portrait of her visit to coral reefs off the coast of Indonesia. (Rev: BL 2/15/04; HBG 4/04) [578]

23595 Platt, Richard. *Shipwreck* (4–9). Series: Eyewitness Books. 1997, Knopf LB $20.99 (978-0-679-98569-3). An overview of the causes and consequences of the world's most famous maritime disasters. (Rev: BL 12/15/97) [387.2]

23596 Sandler, Michael. *Oceans: Surviving in the Deep Sea* (3–5). Illus. Series: X-treme Places. 2005, Bearport LB $25.27 (978-1-59716-087-2). 32pp. This overview of the deep ocean environment is given added punch by the first-person account of marine biologist Dr. Sylvia Earle, who has explored the ocean depths in submersibles and pressurized suits. (Rev: SLJ 1/06) [551.46]

23597 Sloan, Frank. *Titanic*. Rev. ed. (5–8). 1998, Raintree $19.98 (978-0-8172-4091-2). This thorough account of the *Titanic* and its sinking covers the structure of the ship, why it sank, the inquiries that followed, the many attempts to find and explore the wreckage, and movies and plays inspired by it. (Rev: BL 9/1/98; HBG 9/99; SLJ 2/99) [910]

23598 Sullivan, George. *To the Bottom of the Sea: The Exploration of Exotic Life, the Titanic, and Other Secrets of the Oceans* (4–6). Illus. 1999, Twenty-First Century LB $24.90 (978-0-7613-0352-7). 80pp. A history of underwater exploration with fascinating information on contemporary accomplishments and discoveries such as locating the *Titanic*. (Rev: BL 10/1/99; HBG 4/00; SLJ 10/99) [551.46]

23599 *Sunk! Exploring Underwater Archaeology* (5–8). Series: Buried Worlds. 1994, Lerner LB $28.75 (978-0-8225-3205-7). Provides a general overview of how archaeologists interpret underwater discoveries to learn about aspects of ancient trade, commerce, and history. (Rev: BL 10/15/94; SLJ 9/94) [930.1]

Pets

GENERAL AND MISCELLANEOUS

23600 Altman, Linda J. *Parrots* (4–6). Illus. Series: Perfect Pets. 2000, Marshall Cavendish LB $25.64 (978-0-7614-1102-4). 32pp. Full-color photographs and accessible text introduce parrots, their physical characteristics, and how to care for them. (Rev: BL 3/15/01; HBG 3/01) [636.6]

23601 Barnes, Julia. *Pet Guinea Pigs* (2–5). 2006, Gareth Stevens LB $24.00 (978-0-8368-6779-4). 32pp. This handy guide full of advice on caring for a guinea pig also examines the qualities that make them desirable pets, looks at how they communicate, and explores the guinea pig's roots in the wild. Also use *Pet Rabbits* (2006). (Rev: SLJ 2/07) [636.9]

23602 Barnes, Julia. *Pet Parakeets* (2–5). 2006, Gareth Stevens LB $24.00 (978-0-8368-6780-0). 32pp. This handy guide full of advice on caring for a parakeet also examines the qualities that make them such popular pets, looks at how they communicate, and explores their roots in the wild. (Rev: SLJ 12/06) [636.6]

23603 Bjorklund, Ruth. *Rabbits* (2–4). Series: Great Pets. 2007, Marshall Cavendish LB $19.95 (978-0-7614-2708-7). 48pp. A solid introduction to the pleasures and responsibilities of caring for rabbits. (Rev: LMC 8/08; SLJ 4/08) [636.932]

23604 Bozzo, Linda. *My First Bird* (1–3). Series: My First Pet Library from the American Humane Association. 2007, Enslow LB $22.60 (978-0-7660-2749-7). 32pp. New pet owners will learn all the facts about caring for birds and will enjoy looking at the pictures of birds and their owners. (Rev: SLJ 6/07)

23605 Buckmaster, Marjorie L. *Freshwater Fishes* (2–4). Series: Great Pets. 2007, Marshall Cavendish LB $19.95 (978-0-7614-2712-4). 48pp. A solid introduction to the pleasures and responsibilities of caring for fish. (Rev: LMC 8/08; SLJ 4/08) [639.34]

23606 Curran, Wanda L. *Your Guinea Pig: A Kid's Guide to Raising and Showing* (4–6). Illus. 1995, Storey paper $14.95 (978-0-88266-889-5). 160pp. Topics in this book on how to keep guinea pigs as pets include selecting, feeding, mating, and showing. (Rev: BL 9/1/95) [636]

23607 Davis, Kathryn Gibbs. *Wacky White House Pets* (2–4). Illus. by David Johnson. 2004, Scholastic LB $16.95 (978-0-439-44373-9). 48pp. Presidential pets have included John Quincy Adam's alligator, Reagan's First Fish, and Coolidge's raccoon; all White House occupants are mentioned in the appendix to this entertaining book. (Rev: BL 10/1/04; SLJ 11/04) [636.088]

23608 Doudna, Kelly. *Frisky Ferrets* (K–2). Illus. by C. A. Nobens. Series: Perfect Pets. 2007, ABDO LB $19.93 (978-1-59928-748-5). 24pp. Caring for ferrets looks like fun in this book that combines photographs and drawings of ferrets and their happy owners. (Rev: SLJ 7/07)

23609 Engfer, LeeAnne. *My Pet Lizards* (3–6). Photos by Andy King. Series: All About Pets. 1999, Lerner LB $22.60 (978-0-8225-2263-8). 64pp. An unusual book that deals with lizards as pets with material on how to acquire them, care for them, feed them, handle them, and detect health problems. (Rev: HBG 9/99; SLJ 8/99) [597.95]

23610 Fritzsche, Peter. *Hamsters* (2–5). Illus. Series: Complete Pet Owner's Manual. 2008, Barron's paper $7.99 (978-0-7641-3927-7). 64pp. A comprehensive introduction to the care of hamsters, with information on their physical characteristics and behavior. (Rev: BLO 7/31/08) [636.935]

23611 Ganeri, Anita. *Guinea Pigs* (1–3). Series: A Pet's Life. 2003, Heinemann LB $22.79 (978-1-4034-3996-3). 32pp. All about pet guinea pigs and how to care for them, with detailed information on their physiology and life cycle. (Rev: SLJ 6/04) [636.9]

23612 Ganeri, Anita. *Hamsters* (1–3). Series: A Pet's Life. 2003, Heinemann LB $22.79 (978-1-4034-3997-0). 32pp. Presents clear information on hamsters and their physiology, habits, and care and feeding; suitable for beginning readers. (Rev: SLJ 6/04) [636.9]

23613 Ganeri, Anita. *Rabbits* (1–3). Series: A Pet's Life. 2003, Heinemann LB $22.79 (978-1-4034-3995-6). 32pp. A book on keeping rabbits as pets, with help on their care and feeding, habits, and physiology. (Rev: SLJ 6/04) [636.9]

23614 Gelman, Amy. *My Pet Ferrets* (2–5). Photos by Andy King. Series: All About Pets. 2000, Lerner LB $22.60 (978-0-8225-2264-5). 64pp. The care and feeding of ferrets are covered in this book that also gives details on grooming, bathing, and even litter-box training. (Rev: BL 1/1–15/01; HBG 3/01; SLJ 11/00) [636]

23615 Gibbons, Gail. *Rabbits, Rabbits and More Rabbits!* (K–3). Illus. 2000, Holiday House $16.95 (978-0-8234-1486-4). 32pp. Simple text and colored drawings introduce different types of rabbits, their physical characteristics, habits, behavior, and how to care for them. (Rev: BCCB 3/00; BL 1/1–15/00; HBG 9/00; SLJ 3/00) [636.9]

23616 Gutman, Bill. *Adopting Pets: How to Choose Your New Best Friend* (3–6). Illus. by Anne Canevari Green. Series: Pet Friends. 2001, Millbrook LB $22.90 (978-0-7613-1863-7). 64pp. This book gives special tips on choosing a pet with attention to topics such as the kind of home and food it will need and the attention required. (Rev: BCCB 3/01; BL 3/1/01; HBG 10/01) [636]

23617 Gutman, Bill. *Becoming Best Friends with Your Hamster, Guinea Pig, or Rabbit* (3–6). Illus. 1997, Millbrook LB $21.90 (978-0-7613-0201-8). 64pp. Practical advice on the care of these pets, with tips on how to make their lives comfortable. (Rev: BCCB 6/97; BL 8/97; SLJ 7/97) [636]

23618 Gutman, Bill. *Becoming Best Friends with Your Iguana, Snake, or Turtle* (3–6). Illus. by Anne Canevari Green. Series: Pet Friends. 2001, Millbrook LB $24.90 (978-0-7613-1862-0). 64pp.

Explains the special needs of reptiles that are kept as pets. (Rev: BL 3/1/01; HBG 10/01) [636]

23619 Hamilton, Lynn. *Caring for Your Bird* (3–5). Illus. 2002, Weigl LB $16.95 (978-1-59036-037-8). 32pp. A guide to choosing and looking after a feathered pet with information on different avian breeds. (Rev: BL 12/1/02; HBG 3/03) [636.6]

23620 Haney, Johannah. *Turtles* (2–4). Series: Great Pets. 2007, Marshall Cavendish LB $19.95 (978-0-7614-2709-4). 48pp. A solid introduction to the pleasures and responsibilities of caring for turtles. (Rev: LMC 8/08; SLJ 4/08) [639.3]

23621 Hansen, Elvig. *Guinea Pig* (3–6). Illus. 1992, Carolrhoda LB $23.93 (978-0-87614-681-1). 48pp. Charming, informative photos explore the life and care of guinea pigs. (Rev: BL 6/15/92; SLJ 8/92) [636]

23622 Hansen, Rosanna. *Animal Rescuers: A Chapter Book* (2–5). Series: True Tales. 2003, Children's Pr. LB $22.50 (978-0-516-22915-7). 48pp. Heroic animals featured in these four tales include the guide dog named Salty that led his owner from the World Trade Center on 9/11. (Rev: SLJ 1/04) [636.088]

23623 Hernandez-Divers, Sonia. *Geckos* (4–8). Illus. Series: Keeping Unusual Pets. 2003, Heinemann LB $25.64 (978-1-4034-0282-0). 48pp. An appealing and informative introduction to geckos that provides much practical guidance on actually keeping one as a pet. Also use *Chinchillas*, *Ferrets*, *Snakes* (all 2002), and *Rats* (2003). (Rev: BL 3/15/03; HBG 10/03; SLJ 4/03) [639.3]

23624 Hinds, Kathryn. *Hamsters and Gerbils* (4–6). Illus. Series: Perfect Pets. 2000, Marshall Cavendish LB $25.64 (978-0-7614-1104-8). 32pp. Gives tips on housing, feeding, training, and keeping these pets safe. (Rev: BL 3/15/01; HBG 3/01) [636]

23625 Hinds, Kathryn. *Rabbits* (2–5). Series: Perfect Pets. 1998, Benchmark LB $25.64 (978-0-7614-0793-5). 32pp. The physical characteristics of rabbits, how they live, and tips on caring for them are given in this simple book with color photos. (Rev: HBG 9/99; SLJ 5/99) [636.932]

23626 Jenkins, Steve. *Dogs and Cats* (1–3). Illus. 2007, Houghton $16.00 (978-0-618-50767-2). 40pp. Start at one end and you read about dogs and their characteristics; from the other end you have cats; and in the middle of this appealing and informative package, a portrait of a dog and cat happily coexisting. (Rev: BCCB 6/07; BL 5/1/07; HB 5/07; SLJ 5/07) [636.7]

23627 Keenan, Sheila. *Animals in the House: A History of Pets and People* (4–6). Illus. by author. 2007, Scholastic $17.99 (978-0-439-69286-1). 112pp. This eye-catching volume provides a history of how humans began to keep pets, chapters on specific animals, and finally a chapter about how humans have dealt with the death of pets throughout the ages. (Rev: BL 7/07; SLJ 7/07) [636.088]

23628 Kennedy, Marge. *Pets at the White House* (PS–1). Illus. Series: Scholastic News Nonfiction Readers. 2009, Scholastic LB $20.00 (978-0-531-21096-3); paper $6.95 (978-0-531-22433-5). 24pp. A cheerful collective overview of presidential pets,

which include seven goats and a herd of sheep, with highlighted vocabulary and opportunities to practice counting. (Rev: BL 4/1/09; SLJ 5/09) [975.3]

23629 Kent, Deborah. *Animal Helpers for the Disabled* (5–7). Illus. Series: Watts Library: Disability. 2003, Watts LB $25.50 (978-0-531-12017-0). 64pp. Stories of animal accomplishments draw readers into this account, which covers the history of service animals, the kinds of animals used, and the training they undergo. (Rev: BL 10/15/03; LMC 11/03; SLJ 9/03) [636.08]

23630 Leavitt, Amie Jane. *Care for a Pet Chimpanzee* (2–4). 2007, Mitchell Lane LB $25.70 (978-1-58415-607-9). 32pp. Is a chimpanzee the right pet for your family? Probably not, but this straightforward book will help readers understand the pros and cons of chimp ownership. Also use *Care for a Pet Tarantula* and *Care for a Pet Mouse* (both 2007). (Rev: LMC 1/08; SLJ 10/07) [636.9885]

23631 McKay, Sindy. *About Pets* (K–2). Series: We Both Read. 2003, Treasure Bay $7.99 (978-1-891327-41-4). 40pp. Designed to be read together by a child and an adult, this book looks at what's involved in caring for a pet. (Rev: HBG 10/03; SLJ 7/03) [636.088]

23632 McNicholas, June. *Ferrets* (3–6). Series: Keeping Unusual Pets. 2002, Heinemann LB $25.64 (978-1-4034-0281-3). 48pp. A pratical, no-nonsense guide to the choice and responsibilities of caring for such a pet. (Rev: HBG 10/03; SLJ 4/03) [636.9]

23633 Miller, Michaela. *Guinea Pigs* (K–2). Series: Pets. 1997, Heinemann LB $21.36 (978-1-57572-575-8). 24pp. A simple introduction to guinea pigs, their care and feeding, and how to treat them as pets. (Rev: SLJ 4/98) [636]

23634 Nelson, Robin. *Pet Frog* (PS). Series: Classroom Pets. 2002, Lerner LB $18.60 (978-0-8225-1271-4). 24pp. With only a few sentences of text and full-page color illustrations, this book introduces the frog as a pet and describes its care and feeding. Also use *Pet Guinea Pig*, *Pet Hamster*, and *Pet Hermit Crab* (all 2002). (Rev: BL 10/15/02; HBG 3/03; SLJ 10/02) [597.8]

23635 Nelson, Robin. *Pet Hamster* (PS–K). Illus. Series: Classroom Pets. 2002, Lerner LB $18.60 (978-0-8225-1269-1). 24pp. A preschooler's introduction to the care and feeding of classroom hamsters, with relevant facts, a glossary, and an index. Also use *Pet Guinea Pig* (2002). (Rev: BL 10/15/02; HBG 3/03) [636.9]

23636 Nelson, Robin. *Pet Hermit Crab* (PS–K). Illus. Series: Classroom Pets. 2002, Lerner LB $18.60 (978-0-8225-1270-7). 24pp. A preschooler's introduction to the care and feeding of classroom hermit crabs, with relevant facts, a glossary, and an index. (Rev: HBG 3/03)

23637 Rayner, Matthew. *Hamster* (2–4). Photos by Frank Greenaway. Series: I Am Your Pet. 2004, Gareth Stevens LB $24.00 (978-0-8368-4104-6). 32pp. Practical information on selecting and caring for a hamster is presented in clear text with dialogue bubbles giving the hamster's point of view plus colorful fact boxes. (Rev: SLJ 8/04) [636]

23638 Richardson, Adele. *Caring for Your Hamster* (K–3). Illus. Series: First Facts, Positively Pets. 2006, Capstone LB $21.26 (978-0-7368-6387-2). 24pp. Hamster selection, care and feeding, health, safety, relations in the wild, and behavior are all covered in this attractive, concise title that includes commentary by a cartoon hamster. (Rev: SLJ 12/06) [636]

23639 Richardson, Adele. *Caring for Your Hermit Crab* (K–3). Illus. Series: First Facts, Positively Pets. 2006, Capstone LB $21.26 (978-0-7368-6388-9). 24pp. Hermit crab selection, care and feeding, health, safety, and roots in the wild are all covered in this attractive, concise title that includes commentary by a cartoon crab. (Rev: SLJ 12/06) [639]

23640 Rockwell, Anne. *My Pet Hamster* (K–2). Illus. by Bernice Lum. Series: Let's-Read-and-Find-Out Science. 2002, HarperCollins LB $17.89 (978-0-06-028565-4). 33pp. Facts about hamsters blend easily with the text about a young girl selecting, looking after, and playing with her pet. (Rev: HBG 3/03; SLJ 12/02) [636]

23641 Ross, Veronica. *My First Hamster* (K–2). Illus. Series: My First Pet. 2002, Thameside LB $24.25 (978-1-930643-75-8). 32pp. A basic guide to caring for a hamster, with information on diet and hygiene. (Rev: BL 3/1/03) [636.935]

23642 Royston, Angela. *Life Cycle of a Guinea Pig* (PS–3). Series: Life Cycle. 1998, Heinemann LB $21.36 (978-1-57572-614-4). 32pp. With a color photo and four or five lines of text per page, this book explains the life cycle of the guinea pig and gives a timeline to help identify stages of development. (Rev: BL 5/15/98; SLJ 6/98) [636]

23643 Salzmann, Mary Elizabeth. *Brilliant Birds* (K–2). Illus. by C. A. Nobens. Series: Perfect Pets. 2007, ABDO LB $19.93 (978-1-59928-744-7). 24pp. Caring for birds looks like fun in this book that combines photographs and drawings of birds and their happy owners. (Rev: SLJ 7/07)

23644 Salzmann, Mary Elizabeth. *Goofy Guinea Pigs* (K–2). Illus. by C. A. Nobens. 2007, ABDO LB $19.93 (978-1-59928-749-2). 24pp. Information on guinea pigs is paired with photographs and drawings of these furry animals and their happy owners. (Rev: SLJ 7/07)

23645 Schafer, Susan. *Lizards* (4–6). Series: Perfect Pets. 2000, Marshall Cavendish LB $25.64 (978-0-7614-1103-1). 32pp. History, folklore, and practical tips are included in this introduction to the care, feeding, and raising of pet lizards. (Rev: BL 3/15/01; HBG 3/01) [595.95]

23646 Silverstein, Alvin, et al. *Snakes and Such* (3–6). Illus. Series: What a Pet! 1999, Twenty-First Century LB $23.90 (978-0-7613-3229-9). 48pp. In pictures and text, this book explores the idea that such reptiles and amphibians as chameleons, geckos, iguanas, as well as frogs and toads, can be kept as pets. (Rev: BL 8/99; HBG 4/00; SLJ 10/99) [639.3]

23647 Simon, Seymour. *Pets in a Jar: Collecting and Caring for Small Wild Animals* (4–6). Illus. by Betty Fraser. 1979, Puffin paper $6.99 (978-0-14-049186-

9). How to catch and care for such small wild creatures as snails, toads, and ants.

23648 Starosta, Paul. *Face-to-Face with the Hamster* (3–4). Photos by author. Series: Face-to-Face. 2004, Charlesbridge $9.95 (978-1-57091-456-0). 25pp. Colorful photographs accompany bright text on the characteristics and care of hamsters. (Rev: SLJ 2/05) [636]

23649 Stevens, Kathryn. *Parakeets* (PS–2). Illus. Series: Pet Care for Kids. 2009, Child's World LB $21.36 (978-1-60253-186-4). 24pp. With large color photographs and simple text, this is an introduction to the care of parakeets. (Rev: BL 4/1/09) [636.6]

23650 Verdick, Elizabeth. *Tails Are Not for Pulling* (PS). Illus. by Marieka Heinlen. 2005, Free Spirit $7.95 (978-1-57542-180-3). Preschoolers will learn the right and wrong way to play with a pet from this simple board book. (Rev: SLJ 6/06) [636.088]

23651 Wexler, Jerome. *Pet Hamsters* (3–6). Illus. 1992, Whitman LB $15.95 (978-0-8075-6525-4). 48pp. Personal advice from a hamster raiser on the care and handling of these pets. (Rev: BCCB 2/93; BL 2/15/93; SLJ 2/93) [636]

CATS

23652 Arnold, Caroline. *Cats: In from the Wild* (4–7). Photos by Richard Hewett. 1993, Carolrhoda LB $19.93 (978-0-87614-692-7). 48pp. Domestic and wild cats are highlighted with comparisons and contrasts. (Rev: BL 8/93) [636.8]

23653 Barnes, Julia. *Pet Cats* (3–5). Illus. Series: Pet Pals. 2006, Gareth Stevens $24.00 (978-0-8368-6776-3). 32pp. This guide to cats provides tips about care and feeding as well as exploring cat behavior, human-feline interaction, and the diversity of cat breeds. (Rev: BL 10/15/06; SLJ 2/07) [636.8]

23654 Bidner, Jenni. *Is My Cat a Tiger? How Your Pet Compares to Its Wild Cousins* (3–5). Illus. 2007, Sterling $9.95 (978-1-57990-815-7). 64pp. Clearly written and illustrated with crisp photos, this book examines cats' behavior in relationship to the larger cat family, presenting information about the body language and curious antics of these pets. (Rev: BL 1/1–15/07) [636.8]

23655 Bozzo, Linda. *My First Cat* (K–2). Illus. Series: My First Pet Library. 2007, Enslow LB $16.95 (978-0-7660-2750-3). 32pp. Provides very basic information about choosing and caring for a cat. (Rev: BL 9/1/07; SLJ 8/07) [636.8]

23656 Fowler, Allan. *It Could Still Be a Cat* (1–2). Illus. Series: Rookie Readers. 1993, Children's Book Pr. LB $20.50 (978-0-516-06015-6). 32pp. The cat family is introduced in this easy-to-read book for beginners. (Rev: BL 3/1/94) [636.8]

23657 George, Jean Craighead. *How to Talk to Your Cat* (2–4). Illus. by Paul Meisel. 2000, HarperCollins LB $13.89 (978-0-06-027969-1). 40pp. After a history of the domestication of cats, this account tells how and what they communicate with humans. (Rev: BCCB 4/00; BL 12/15/99; HB 3/00; HBG 9/00; SLJ 2/00) [636.8]

23658 Gibbons, Gail. *Cats* (PS–2). Illus. by author. 1996, Holiday House LB $16.95 (978-0-8234-1253-

2). Watercolor illustrations are used to introduce a number of breeds of cats, their characteristics, and behavior. (Rev: SLJ 12/96) [636.8]

23659 Gutman, Bill. *Becoming Your Cat's Best Friend* (3–6). Illus. Series: Pet Friends. 1997, Millbrook LB $21.90 (978-0-7613-0200-1). 64pp. This book expresses the cat's point of view and gives advice on how to make the pet and its owner happy with the relationship. (Rev: BCCB 6/97; BL 8/97; SLJ 7/97) [636.8]

23660 Hart, Joyce. *Cats* (2–4). Series: Great Pets. 2007, Marshall Cavendish LB $19.95 (978-0-7614-2710-0). 48pp. A solid introduction to the pleasures and responsibilities of caring for cats. (Rev: LMC 8/08; SLJ 4/08) [636.8]

23661 Hinds, Kathryn. *Cats* (2–5). Series: Perfect Pets. 1998, Benchmark LB $25.64 (978-0-7614-0794-2). 31pp. As well as a history of cats and their role in mythology, this simple book describes their physical characteristics and how to take care of them. (Rev: HBG 9/99; SLJ 5/99) [636.8]

23662 Holub, Joan. *Why Do Cats Meow?* (1–2). Illus. Series: Easy-to-Read. 2001, Dial paper $3.99 (978-0-14-056788-5). 48pp. This informative, easy-to-read book, with many photos and cartoons, discusses behavioral traits of cats and provides material on breeds and their characteristics. (Rev: BCCB 2/01; BL 2/15/01) [636.8]

23663 Jeffrey, Laura S. *Cats: How to Choose and Care for a Cat* (3–5). Illus. Series: American Humane Pet Care Library. 2004, Enslow LB $23.93 (978-0-7660-2516-5). 48pp. Offers a wide array of information on cats and their care, including tips on selecting the right cat, steps to prevent the loss of a pet, cat allergies, and how to cope with feline misbehavior. (Rev: BL 10/15/04; SLJ 2/05) [636.8]

23664 Mattern, Joanne. *The American Shorthair Cat* (4–7). Illus. Series: Learning About Cats. 2002, Capstone LB $23.93 (978-0-7368-1300-6). 48pp. Beautiful photographs of frisky felines are accompanied by data about the physical characteristics and personality, with a glossary, bibliography, and lists of addresses and Web sites. Also use *The Manx Cat* (2002). (Rev: BL 12/1/02; HBG 3/03) [636.8]

23665 Overbeck, Cynthia. *Cats* (4–6). Illus. by Shin Yoshino. 1983, Lerner LB $22.60 (978-0-8225-1480-0). 48pp. This work concentrates on domestic cats and their habits and appearance.

23666 Quasha, Jennifer. *The Manx: The Cat with No Tail* (2–4). Illus. Series: Kids Can! 2000, Rosen LB $21.25 (978-0-8239-5512-1). 24pp. Many color close-ups are used to present the Manx cat, its characteristics, habits, and the myth about how it lost its tail. (Rev: BL 10/15/00) [636.8]

23667 Quasha, Jennifer. *Shorthaired Cats in America* (2–4). Illus. 2000, Rosen LB $18.75 (978-0-8239-5513-8). 24pp. This is a general book about cats that covers American attitudes toward them, their history from the Mayflower to today, their part in the Salem witch trials, and similar material. (Rev: BL 10/15/00) [636.8]

23668 Rau, Dana Meachen. *Guess Who Purrs* (PS–K). Series: Bookworms. Guess Who. 2009, Marshall

Cavendish $15.95 (978-0-7614-2972-2). 32pp. Fun for browsing, this book asks readers to identify a cat using the clues in the text and images. (Rev: SLJ 6/09) [636.8]

23669 Rayner, Matthew. *Cat* (2–4). Photos by Jane Burton. Series: I Am Your Pet. 2004, Gareth Stevens LB $24.00 (978-0-8368-4102-2). 32pp. Practical information on selecting and caring for a cat is presented in clear text with dialogue bubbles giving the cat's point of view plus colorful fact boxes. (Rev: SLJ 8/04) [636.8]

23670 Ring, Susan. *Caring for Your Cat* (3–5). Illus. 2002, Weigl LB $16.95 (978-1-59036-032-3). 32pp. A detailed introduction to the various breeds of cat and how to care for one — in more than the strict physical sense — with photographs and a list of relevant Web sites. (Rev: BL 12/1/02; HBG 3/03) [636.8]

23671 Roca, Núria. *Let's Take Care of Our New Cat* (K–3). Illus. by Rosa M. Curto. Series: Let's Take Care of. 2006, Barron's paper $6.99 (978-0-7641-3452-4). 35pp. An appealing introduction to the care and feeding of a cat, with watercolor illustrations. (Rev: SLJ 2/07) [636.8]

23672 Rosen, Michael J., ed. *Purr . . . Children's Book Illustrators Brag About Their Cats* (2–5). Illus. 1996, Harcourt $18.00 (978-0-15-200837-6). 48pp. Paintings and text illustrate the moods and activities of a variety of cats. (Rev: BL 4/1/96; SLJ 5/96) [636.8]

23673 Ross, Veronica. *My First Cat* (K–2). Illus. Series: My First Pet. 2002, Thameside LB $24.25 (978-1-930643-72-7). 32pp. A basic guide to choosing and caring for a cat. (Rev: BL 3/1/03; HBG 3/03) [636.8]

23674 Simon, Seymour. *Cats* (2–3). Illus. 2004, HarperCollins $16.99 (978-0-06-028940-9). 40pp. Full-color photographs and clear text explore basic facts about cats — breeds, intelligence, diet, and so forth. (Rev: BL 3/15/04; SLJ 6/04) [599.75]

23675 Singer, Marilyn. *Cats to the Rescue* (4–7). Illus. by Jean Cassels. 2006, Holt $16.95 (978-0-8050-7433-8). 160pp. This collection of true cat stories focuses on feats ranging from catching tens of thousands of mice to detecting a gas leak. (Rev: BL 9/15/06; SLJ 11/06) [636.8]

23676 Stefoff, Rebecca. *Cats* (4–7). Series: AnimalWays. 2003, Benchmark LB $31.36 (978-0-7614-1577-0). 112pp. A well-illustrated study of cats, their evolution, behavior, and human attitudes toward them. (Rev: SLJ 3/04) [636.8]

23677 Tildes, Phyllis L. *Calico's Cousins: Cats from Around the World* (K–3). Illus. 1999, Charlesbridge LB $15.95 (978-0-88106-648-7); paper $6.95 (978-0-88106-649-4). 32pp. General information about different breeds of cats is given in this book that features beautiful watercolor art. (Rev: BL 2/1/99; HBG 9/99; SLJ 3/99) [636.8]

DOGS

23678 Ajmera, Maya, and Alex Fisher. *A Kid's Best Friend* (1–3). Illus. 2002, Charlesbridge $15.95 (978-1-57091-513-0); paper $6.95 (978-1-57091-

514-7). 32pp. Photographs of children and their dogs show that dogs are friends and helpers everywhere in the world. (Rev: BL 9/1/02; HBG 3/03; SLJ 8/02) [636.7]

23679 Altman, Linda J. *Big Dogs* (4–6). Series: Perfect Pets. 2000, Marshall Cavendish LB $25.64 (978-0-7614-1101-7). 32pp. Filled with historical and factual material, this book introduces several breeds of large dogs and gives tips for raising and caring for them. (Rev: BL 3/15/01; HBG 3/01) [636.7]

23680 Altman, Linda J. *Small Dogs* (2–5). Series: Perfect Pets. 1998, Benchmark LB $25.64 (978-0-7614-0795-9). 32pp. Young dog lovers will enjoy this simple introduction to dogs that gives some history plus behavioral traits and tips on caring for them. (Rev: HBG 9/99; SLJ 5/99) [636.7]

23681 Anderson, Bendix. *Security Dogs* (2–4). Illus. Series: Dog Heroes. 2005, Bearport LB $25.27 (978-1-59716-015-5). 32pp. Features dogs who work to keep people safe, with photographs and factoids emphasizing their helpfulness to humans. (Rev: SLJ 8/05) [363.2]

23682 Arnold, Caroline. *A Guide Dog Puppy Grows Up* (3–5). Photos by Richard Hewett. 1991, Harcourt $16.95 (978-0-15-232657-9); paper $7.00 (978-0-15-201557-2). 48pp. The life and training of a golden retriever named Honey. (Rev: BCCB 3/91; BL 4/15/91; HB 5/91; SLJ 5/91) [362.4]

23683 Barnes, Julia. *Pet Dogs* (2–5). 2006, Gareth Stevens LB $24.00 (978-0-8368-6777-0). 32pp. This handy guide full of advice on caring for a dog also examines the qualities that make cats such popular pets, looks at how they communicate, and explores the dog's roots in the wild. (Rev: SLJ 2/07) [636.7]

23684 Benjamin, Carol Lea. *Dog Training for Kids*. Rev. ed. (5–8). Illus. 1988, Howell Book House $18.95 (978-0-87605-541-0). A simple guide to dog training that emphasizes the goal of having fun with a dog you are proud of. (Rev: SLJ 4/89) [636.7]

23685 Bidner, Jenni. *Is My Dog a Wolf? How Your Dog Compares to Its Wild Cousin* (4–6). 2006, Sterling $9.95 (978-1-57990-732-7). 64pp. Using many vivid photographs, this is a fascinating look at the similarities — and differences — between domestic dogs and wild wolves. (Rev: BL 9/1/06; SLJ 10/06) [636.7]

23686 Bozzo, Linda. *My First Dog* (1–3). Series: My First Pet Library from the American Humane Association. 2007, Enslow LB $22.60 (978-0-7660-2754-1). 32pp. New pet owners will learn all the facts about caring for dogs and will enjoy looking at the pictures of dogs and their owners. (Rev: SLJ 6/07)

23687 Calmenson, Stephanie. *May I Pet Your Dog? The How-to Guide for Kids Meeting Dogs (and Dogs Meeting Kids)* (PS–2). Illus. by Jan Ormerod. 2007, Clarion $9.95 (978-0-618-51034-4). 32pp. A dachshund named Harry patiently explains how to approach an unfamiliar dog. (Rev: SLJ 4/07)

23688 Calmenson, Stephanie. *Rosie: A Visiting Dog's Story* (PS–3). Illus. by Justin Sutcliffe. 1994, Houghton $16.00 (978-0-395-65477-4). 48pp. The true story of the dog Rosie, who is being trained to be a visiting dog to help those who are sad or lonely. (Rev: BL 4/15/94; HB 7/94; SLJ 4/94) [636.7]

23689 Calmenson, Stephanie. *Shaggy, Waggy Dogs (and Others)* (K–3). Illus. by Justin Sutcliffe. 1998, Clarion $15.00 (978-0-395-77605-6). 48pp. Twenty canine breeds are introduced in a series of four-line poems and clear color photographs. (Rev: BL 5/1/98; HBG 9/98; SLJ 7/98) [636.7]

23690 Collard, Sneed B., III. *Shep: Our Most Loyal Dog* (2–4). Illus. by Joanna Yardley. 2006, Sleeping Bear $16.95 (978-1-58536-259-2). This is the moving story of Shep, a sheepdog that watched its master's coffin being loaded onto a train in Montana and met every passenger train arriving at that station from that day until his death more than five years later. (Rev: SLJ 8/06) [636.737]

23691 Coren, Stanley. *Why Do Dogs Have Wet Noses?* (2–4). Illus. 2006, Kids Can $12.95 (978-1-55337-657-6). 64pp. The famous dog expert offers a wealth of doggy facts in an appealing format suited more to browsing than report writing. (Rev: BL 4/15/06; SLJ 5/06) [636.7]

23692 Crisp, Marty. *Everything Dog: What Kids Really Want to Know About Dogs* (2–5). 2003, NorthWord $9.95 (978-1-55971-839-4); paper $6.95 (978-1-55971-854-7). 64pp. Friendly and attractive, this is nonetheless a fact-filled volume suitable for browsing. (Rev: BL 5/15/03; SLJ 6/03) [636.7]

23693 Crosby, Jeff, and Shelley Jackson. *Little Lions, Bull Baiters and Hunting Hounds* (2–4). Illus. by Jeff Crosby. 2008, Tundra $19.95 (978-0-88776-815-6). 72pp. Best for browsers, this is an attractive introduction to a variety of breeds of dogs, with painted portraits that occasionally show confrontations with other animals. (Rev: BL 6/1–15/08; SLJ 5/08) [636.7]

23694 Feldman, Heather. *The Story of the Golden Retriever* (2–4). Illus. Series: Dogs Throughout History. 2000, Rosen $21.25 (978-0-8239-5514-5). 24pp. This history of the golden retriever also describes its physical characteristics and its roles in rescue missions and as a guide dog. (Rev: BL 10/15/00) [636.752]

23695 Flowers, Pam, and Ann Dixon. *Big-Enough Anna: The Little Sled Dog Who Braved the Arctic* (PS–3). Illus. by Bill Farnsworth. 2003, Alaska Northwest $15.95 (978-0-88240-577-3); paper $8.95 (978-0-88240-580-3). In this inspiring real-life story, Anna, a sled dog that was the runt of her litter, takes over as lead dog on an arduous journey across the North American Arctic. (Rev: HBG 4/04; SLJ 1/04) [636.73]

23696 Gallimard Jeunesse. *Dogs* (PS–2). Series: First Discovery. 1999, Scholastic $12.95 (978-0-590-87608-7). 24pp. A heavily illustrated, simple introduction to dogs, their characteristics, and some of the important breeds. (Rev: BL 6/1–15/99; HBG 9/99) [636.7]

23697 Gibbons, Gail. *Dogs* (K–2). Illus. by author. 1996, Holiday House LB $16.95 (978-0-8234-1226-

6). An easy-to-read overview of dogs and their history, breeds, and anatomy. (Rev: BCCB 5/96; HB 5/96; SLJ 9/96) [636.7]

23698 Gorrell, Gena K. *Working Like a Dog: The Story of Working Dogs Through History* (4–8). Illus. 2003, Tundra $16.95 (978-0-88776-589-6). 160pp. A comprehensive and very appealing look at dogs' services to man throughout history — as hunters and trackers, bomb sniffers, guide dogs, and companions, to name but a few. (Rev: BL 11/1/03; SLJ 12/03) [636.73]

23699 Grogan, John. *Marley: A Dog like No Other* (4–7). Illus. 2007, HarperCollins $16.99 (978-0-06-124033-1). 208pp. An adaptation of Grogan's book for adults, *Marley & Me*, this story of a hopelessly out-of-control but lovable dog who dies too soon will touch young readers. (Rev: BL 7/07; SLJ 7/07) [636.752]

23700 Guy, Foglesong Ginger. *Perros! Perros! / Dogs! Dogs! A Story in English and Spanish* (PS–K). Illus. by Sharon Glick. 2006, Greenwillow $16.99 (978-0-06-083574-3). 32pp. Dogs of all sizes and shapes are the focus of this simple bilingual book. (Rev: BL 9/1/06; SLJ 10/06) [468.1]

23701 Halls, Kelly Milner. *Wild Dogs: Past and Present* (4–7). Illus. 2005, Darby Creek $18.95 (978-1-58196-027-3). 64pp. A wide-ranging introduction to dogs and their history, with attractive design, many photographs, and lots of factboxes about dogs both wild and domestic. (Rev: BL 12/1/05; SLJ 11/05) [599.77]

23702 Hart, Joyce. *Big Dogs* (2–4). Series: Great Pets. 2007, Marshall Cavendish LB $19.95 (978-0-7614-2707-0). 48pp. A solid introduction to the pleasures and responsibilities of caring for large dogs. (Rev: LMC 8/08; SLJ 4/08) [636.7]

23703 Hengel, Katherine. *Brainy Brittanys* (2–3). Illus. Series: Dog Daze. 2009, ABDO LB $16.95 (978-1-60453-616-4). 24pp. For beginning readers, this volume offers a blend of facts, stories, photographs, and art relating to Brittany spaniels. (Rev: BL 4/1/09) [636.752]

23704 Jackson, Emma. *A Home for Dixie: The True Story of a Rescued Puppy* (2–4). Illus. by Bob Carey. 2008, HarperCollins $16.99 (978-0-06-144962-8). 40pp. A young girl finds the pet she has been longing for in this affecting photo-essay. (Rev: BL 6/1–15/08; SLJ 5/08) [636.7]

23705 Jeffrey, Laura S. *Dogs: How to Choose and Care for a Dog* (2–5). Illus. Series: American Humane Pet Care Library. 2004, Enslow LB $23.93 (978-0-7660-2520-2). 48pp. Appealing full-color photographs accompany advice on choosing and caring for a dog. (Rev: SLJ 2/05) [636.7]

23706 Kehret, Peg. *Shelter Dogs: Amazing Stories of Adopted Strays* (3–5). Illus. 1999, Whitman $15.99 (978-0-8075-7334-1). 134pp. A collection of eight true stories about shelter dogs that went on to great things — starring on TV, for example. (Rev: BCCB 4/99; BL 5/1/99; HBG 9/99; SLJ 10/99) [636.7]

23707 Kirk, Daniel. *Dogs Rule!* (3–5). Illus. by author. 2003, Disney $18.99 (978-0-7868-1949-2). 48pp. In this large-format collection of dog-related

poetry and accompanying CD, Kirk manages to celebrate just about every aspect of canine behavior. (Rev: BL 10/15/03; HBG 4/04; SLJ 12/03)

23708 Lauber, Patricia. *The True-or-False Book of Dogs* (1–3). Illus. by Rosalyn Schanzer. 2003, HarperCollins $15.99 (978-0-06-029767-1). 32pp. This brightly illustrated book uses a true-or-false format to convey a wide range of facts and figures about dogs and their history. (Rev: BL 11/1/03; HBG 4/04; SLJ 12/03)

23709 Lawrenson, Diana. *Guide Dogs: From Puppies to Partners* (4–6). 2002, Allen & Unwin paper $7.95 (978-1-86508-246-2). 32pp. The breeding, care, and training of guide dogs are covered in this title from Australia, with profiles of several dogs and their partners and an interesting chart of commands. (Rev: SLJ 10/02)

23710 McDaniel, Melissa. *Disaster Search Dogs* (2–4). Illus. Series: Dog Heroes. 2005, Bearport LB $25.27 (978-1-59716-012-4). 32pp. Dogs that work to find people in trouble are the focus of this photo-filled volume. Also use *Guide Dogs* (2005). (Rev: SLJ 8/05) [363.2]

23711 Mehus-Roe, Kristin. *Dogs for Kids! Everything You Need to Know About Dogs* (4–7). Illus. 2007, Bowtie paper $14.95 (978-1-931993-83-8). 384pp. From a history of dogs to information on breeds, anatomy, and behavior to advice on care and training — as the title says, this book is all you need. (Rev: BL 2/15/08; SLJ 6/07) [636.7]

23712 Meister, Cari. *Basset Hounds* (3–5). Series: Dogs. 2001, ABDO $21.35 (978-1-57765-478-0). 24pp. A simple colorful introduction to this breed of dog that describes its physical and behavioral characteristics and gives tips on proper care. Other titles in this series include *Boxers, Greyhounds*, and *Saint Bernards* (all 2001). (Rev: BL 12/15/01; HBG 3/02) [636.7]

23713 Meister, Cari. *Bulldogs* (3–5). Series: Dogs. 2001, ABDO $21.35 (978-1-57765-476-6). 24pp. Attractive color photographs show bulldogs playing, eating, and sleeping, and a simple text describes the breed, its many varieties, and its characteristics. (Rev: BL 12/15/01; HBG 3/02) [636.7]

23714 Moore, Eva. *Buddy: The First Seeing Eye Dog* (2–3). Illus. by Don Bolognese. 1996, Scholastic paper $3.99 (978-0-590-26585 0). 48pp. In simple prose, this book traces the beginning of the Seeing Eye movement in the 1930s. (Rev: BL 11/15/96) [392.4]

23715 Mulvany, Martha. *The Story of the Boxer* (2–4). Illus. Series: Dogs Throughout History. 2000, Rosen $21.25 (978-0-8239-5519-0). 24pp. This history of the boxer also describes its physical characteristics and its reputation for loyalty and courage. (Rev: BL 10/15/00) [636.73]

23716 O'Neill, Amanda. *Dogs* (3–5). 1999, Kingfisher $15.95 (978-0-7534-5175-5). 63pp. This oversize introduction to dogs covers such topics as physical features, evolution, history, breeds, behavior, and care. (Rev: HBG 9/99; SLJ 7/99) [636.7]

23717 O'Sullivan, Robyn. *More than Man's Best Friend: The Story of Working Dogs* (2–4). Illus.

Series: National Geographic Science Chapters. 2006, National Geographic $17.90 (978-0-7922-5940-4). 40pp. Six chapters look at the different kinds of jobs performed by working dogs; photos and easy vocabulary make this suitable for young readers. (Rev: BL 10/15/06) [636.7]

23718 Otto, Carolyn. *Our Puppies Are Growing* (1). Illus. by Mary Morgan. Series: Let's-Read-and-Find-Out. 1998, HarperCollins paper $4.95 (978-0-06-445169-7). 32pp. In this book for beginning readers, the experiences of a preschooler whose dog has five puppies help readers learn about the dog's pregnancy, the birth process, and the care of the newborn puppies. (Rev: BL 11/1/98; HBG 3/99; SLJ 7/99) [636.7]

23719 Patent, Dorothy Hinshaw. *Dogs: The Wolf Within* (3–6). Illus. by William Muñoz. 1993, Carolrhoda LB $19.93 (978-0-87614-691-0); paper $7.95 (978-0-87614-604-0). 48pp. This book describes the relationship between the habits of the domesticated dog and its distant ancestor, the wolf. (Rev: BCCB 7–8/93; BL 6/1–15/93) [599]

23720 Patent, Dorothy Hinshaw. *Right Dog for the Job: Ira's Path from Service Dog to Guide Dog* (3–5). 2004, Walker $16.95 (978-0-8027-8915-0). 32pp. A puppy's training to be a guide dog is followed in loving detail in this appealing and informative photo-essay. (Rev: BL 6/1–15/04; SLJ 6/04)

23721 Paulsen, Gary. *My Life in Dog Years* (5–10). Illus. 1998, Delacorte $15.95 (978-0-385-32570-7). The famous novelist tells about eight wonderful dogs that he has known and loved over the years. (Rev: BCCB 3/98; BL 1/1–15/98; SLJ 3/98; VOYA 4/98) [636.7]

23722 Presnall, Judith Janda. *Police Dogs* (4–7). Illus. Series: Animals with Jobs. 2002, Gale LB $23.70 (978-0-7377-0631-4). 48pp. This well-illustrated account describes the various ways in which dogs are used to fight crime. (Rev: BL 4/1/02) [363.2]

23723 Presnall, Judith Janda. *Rescue Dogs* (4–6). Series: Animals with Jobs. 2002, Gale LB $23.70 (978-0-7377-1361-9). 48pp. Individual rescue dogs are profiled in this well-written overview of these animals and their training. (Rev: SLJ 9/03) [636.7]

23724 Rappaport, Jill. *Jack and Jill: The Miracle Dog with a Happy Tail to Tell* (2–4). Photos by Linda Solomon. 2009, HarperCollins $17.99 (978-0-06-173136-5). A German Shepherd loses a leg and survives cancer in this moving story that will help children facing a similar situation. (Rev: SLJ 6/09) [636.737]

23725 Rayner, Matthew. *Dog* (2–4). Photos by Jane Burton. Series: I Am Your Pet. 2004, Gareth Stevens LB $24.00 (978-0-8368-4103-9). 32pp. Practical information on selecting and caring for a dog is presented in clear text with dialogue bubbles giving the dog's point of view plus colorful fact boxes. (Rev: SLJ 8/04) [636.7]

23726 Roca, Núria. *Let's Take Care of Our New Dog* (K–3). Illus. by Rosa M. Curto. Series: Let's Take Care of . . . 2006, Barron's paper $6.99 (978-0-7641-3455-5). 35pp. An appealing introduction to the care and feeding of a dog, with watercolor illustrations. (Rev: SLJ 2/07) [636.7]

23727 Rock, Maxine. *Totally Fun Things to Do with Your Dog* (3–6). Illus. 1998, Wiley paper $12.95 (978-0-471-19754-6). 128pp. An informative manual for young dog owners on training, suitable activities, and building bonds of trust and friendship between owner and dog. (Rev: BL 6/1–15/98) [636]

23728 Rosenthal, Lisa. *A Dog's Best Friend: An Activity Book for Kids and Their Dogs* (4–7). Illus. by Bonnie Matthews. 1999, Chicago Review paper $12.95 (978-1-55652-362-5). 181pp. This book that gives hints on how to choose a dog and care for a puppy offers 60 projects related to these subjects including crafts, recipes, and games. (Rev: SLJ 1/00) [636.7]

23729 Ross, Veronica. *My First Dog* (PS–2). Series: My First. 2002, Raintree LB $24.95 (978-1-930643-71-0). 32pp. Simple language introduces young readers to dogs and their care. (Rev: HBG 3/03)

23730 Royston, Angela. *Life Cycle of a Dog* (PS–3). Series: Life Cycle. 2000, Heinemann LB $21.36 (978-1-57572-209-2). 32pp. This book describes a dog's life cycle with a simple text and color photos on each page. (Rev: BL 5/15/00; HBG 3/01) [636.7]

23731 Seibert, Patricia. *Mush! Across Alaska in the World's Longest Sled-Dog Race* (2–4). Illus. 1992, Houghton paper $5.70 (978-0-395-64537-6). 32pp. Focusing on the work dogs of the 1,000-plus-mile Iditarod race from Anchorage to Nome. (Rev: BL 9/15/92; SLJ 11/92) [798.8]

23732 Selsam, Millicent E. *How Puppies Grow* (1–2). Illus. 1990, Scholastic paper $2.99 (978-0-590-42736-4). 32pp. The stages in a puppy's life — from birth through walking, seeing, eating, and playing — described in excellent photographs and simple text.

23733 Selsam, Millicent E., and Joyce Hunt. *A First Look at Dogs* (1–3). Illus. by Harriett Springer. 1981, Walker LB $9.85 (978-0-8027-6421-8). 32pp. A history of dogs and an introduction to present breeds.

23734 Silverstein, Alvin, et al. *Different Dogs* (4–7). Series: What a Pet! 2000, Twenty-First Century LB $23.90 (978-0-7613-1371-7). 48pp. Several different breeds of dogs are introduced in pictures and text plus information on cost, food, housing, and training. (Rev: HBG 10/00; SLJ 5/00) [636.7]

23735 Simon, Seymour. *Dogs* (2–3). Illus. 2004, HarperCollins $16.99 (978-0-06-028942-3). 40pp. Full-color photographs and clear text explore basic facts about dogs — breeds, intelligence, diet, and so forth. (Rev: BL 3/15/04; SLJ 6/04) [636.7]

23736 Singer, Marilyn. *A Dog's Gotta Do What a Dog's Gotta Do* (3–6). Illus. 2000, Holt $16.00 (978-0-8050-6074-4). 86pp. This book on working dogs includes material on their roles as defenders, herders, detectives, rescuers, and entertainers. (Rev: BCCB 11/00; BL 11/15/00; HBG 3/01; SLJ 2/01) [636.7]

23737 Stone, Lynn M. *Beagles* (K–2). Series: Eye to Eye with Dogs. 2002, Rourke LB $17.95 (978-1-58952-325-8). 24pp. From puppyhood to adult status, this is an introduction to beagles and their behavior, characteristics, and care. Other titles in this series include *German Shepherds*, *Golden Retrievers*, *Labrador Retrievers*, and *Poodles* (all 2002). (Rev: BL 10/15/02) [636.7]

23738 Stone, Lynn M. *Dachshunds* (K–2). Series: Eye to Eye with Dogs. 2002, Rourke LB $17.95 (978-1-58952-326-5). 24pp. The five short sections in this simple book give information on dachshunds' characteristics, history, appearance, and care, and discuss how dachshunds help people. (Rev: BL 10/15/02) [636.7]

23739 Storer, Pat. *Your Puppy, Your Dog: A Kid's Guide to Raising a Happy, Healthy Dog* (4–6). Illus. 1997, Storey paper $14.95 (978-0-88266-959-5). 172pp. Chapters in this complete dog care manual cover such subjects as feeding, walking, playing, grooming, and toilet needs. (Rev: BL 12/15/97) [636.7]

23740 Tagliaferro, Linda. *Therapy Dogs* (2–4). Illus. Series: Dog Heroes. 2005, Bearport LB $25.27 (978-1-59716-018-6). 32pp. Features dogs that work to help people with special needs, with photographs and factoids emphasizing their helpfulness to humans. (Rev: SLJ 8/05) [363.2]

23741 Temple, Bob. *Chihuahuas* (3–5). Series: Dogs. 2000, ABDO LB $21.35 (978-1-57765-419-3). 24pp. This heavily illustrated book covers the history of this breed, its structure, habits, and required care and feeding. Also use from the same series: *Pugs*, *Scottish Terriers*, and *Shih Tzus* (all 2000). (Rev: BL 3/15/01; HBG 3/01) [636.7]

23742 Temple, Bob. *Jack Russell Terriers* (3–5). Illus. Series: Dogs. 2000, ABDO $21.35 (978-1-57765-424-7). 24pp. This book introduces terriers, their physical characteristics, habits, how to care for them, and their special needs. Similar material is found in *Siberian Huskies* (2000). (Rev: BL 3/15/01; HBG 3/01) [636.755]

23743 Tracqui, Valerie. *The Dog: Loyal Companion* (2–4). Trans. from French by Lisa Laird. Photos by Marie-Luce Hubert and Jean-Louis Klein. Series: Face-to-Face. 2002, Charlesbridge $9.95 (978-1-57091-452-2). 32pp. A celebration of dogs' relationship with humans, their ability to follow commands, and their contributions to the lost and handicapped. (Rev: SLJ 8/02) [636.7]

23744 Turner, Pamela S. *Hachiko: The True Story of a Loyal Dog* (1–3). Illus. by Yan Nascimbene. 2004, Houghton $16.00 (978-0-618-14094-7). 32pp. This small-format picture book tells the moving story of Hachiko, the devoted dog who spent nearly 10 years at a Tokyo train station, waiting in vain for the return of his dead master. (Rev: BL 4/15/04*; HB 7/04; SLJ 5/04) [636.7]

23745 Urbigkit, Cat. *Brave Dogs, Gentle Dogs: How They Guard Sheep* (K–2). Illus. 2005, Boyds Mills $15.95 (978-1-59078-317-7). 32pp. Photographs of Wyoming ranch dogs accompany the text on guardian dogs, trained to tend and protect flocks of sheep. (Rev: BL 3/1/05; SLJ 3/05) [636.737]

23746 Wahman, Wendy. *Don't Lick the Dog: Making Friends with Dogs* (PS–2). Illus. by author. 2009,

Holt $16.95 (978-0-8050-8733-8). 32pp. A humorous, rhyming guide to meeting and interacting with dogs. (Rev: BL 3/15/09; SLJ 5/09) [636.7]

23747 White, Nancy. *Why Do Dogs Do That?* (2–4). Illus. by Gioia Fiammenghi. 1995, Scholastic paper $4.99 (978-0-590-26597-3). 32pp. Through answers to 24 simple questions, such common canine behavior as tail wagging is explained. (Rev: BL 2/15/96) [599]

23748 Williams, Chris. *One Incredible Dog! Kizzy* (1–5). Illus. by Judith Friedman. 2006, Keene LB $15.95 (978-0-9766805-5-0). This photo-essay documents a day in the life of Kizzy, a therapy dog that offers a kind and interested ear to children and adults practicing reading and speaking. (Rev: SLJ 2/07) [636.7]

23749 Wood, Selina. *Dog* (4–6). Illus. Series: Owning a Pet. 2008, Black Rabbit LB $18.95 (978-1-59771-056-5). 32pp. Wood offers sensible advice on the selection, care, and training of dogs. (Rev: BL 4/1/08) [636.7]

FISH

23750 Barnes, Julia. *Pet Goldfish* (2–5). Series: Pet Pals. 2006, Gareth Stevens LB $24.00 (978-0-8368-6778-7). 32pp. This handy guide full of advice on caring for goldfish also examines their history. (Rev: SLJ 12/06) [639.3]

23751 Coleman, Lori. *My Pet Fish* (3–6). Illus. Series: All About Pets. 1998, Lerner LB $22.60 (978-0-8225-2262-1). 64pp. This book supplies basic information on aquariums, the equipment involved, and the problems of maintenance. (Rev: BL 9/1/98; HBG 9/98) [639.34]

23752 Nelson, Robin. *Pet Fish* (PS–K). Illus. Series: Classroom Pets. 2002, Lerner LB $18.60 (978-0-8225-1267-7). 24pp. A preschooler's introduction to the care and feeding of classroom fish, with fish facts, a glossary, and an index. (Rev: BL 10/15/02; HBG 3/03) [639.34]

23753 Richardson, Adele. *Caring for Your Fish* (K–3). Illus. Series: First Facts, Positively Pets. 2006, Capstone LB $21.26 (978-0-7368-6386-5). 24pp. Fish selection, care and feeding, health, and safety are all covered in this attractive, concise title that includes commentary by a cartoon fish. (Rev: SLJ 12/06) [639.34]

23754 Salzmann, Mary Elizabeth. *Flashy Fish* (K–2). Illus. by C. A. Nobens. 2007, ABDO LB $19.93 (978-1-59928-747-8). 24pp. Caring for fish looks like fun in this book that combines photographs and drawings of fish and their happy owners. (Rev: SLJ 7/07)

HORSES AND PONIES

23755 Ancona, George. *Man and Mustang* (3–6). Illus. 1992, Macmillan LB $15.95 (978-0-02-700802-9). 48pp. Black-and-white photos help to tell the story of how the Bureau of Land Management manages the growing population of wild mustangs. (Rev: BCCB 4/92; BL 3/15/92; HB 7/92; SLJ 4/92) [636.1]

23756 Arnosky, Jim. *Wild Ponies* (PS–3). Illus. by author. Series: One Whole Day. 2002, National Geographic $16.95 (978-0-7922-7121-5). 32pp. Bright illustrations and simple rhyming text introduce the small ponies of Assateague Island and the other animals that live there. (Rev: HBG 3/03; SLJ 10/02)

23757 Barnes, Julia. *Horses at Work* (3–5). Series: Animals at Work. 2006, Gareth Stevens LB $24.00 (978-0-8368-6225-6). 32pp. Full-color photographs show horses working in many roles and the text discusses the animal's physical characteristics, ability to learn commands, and relationship with humans. (Rev: SLJ 1/07) [636.1]

23758 Budd, Jackie. *Horses* (3–8). Illus. 1995, Kingfisher $15.95 (978-1-85697-566-7). 64pp. Drawings and text cover such subjects related to horses as anatomy, breeds, care, and grooming. (Rev: BL 10/1/95; SLJ 12/95) [636.1]

23759 Budd, Jackie. *Seasons of the Horse: A Practical Guide to Year-Round Equine Care* (5–12). 2007, T.F.H. $29.95 (978-0-7938-0611-9). 272pp. Well-organized and visually pleasing, this book provides a complete guide to caring for a horse, including nutrition and exercise. (Rev: SLJ 3/08)

23760 Budiansky, Stephen. *The World According to Horses: How They Run, See, and Think* (4–8). Illus. 2000, Holt $17.95 (978-0-8050-6054-6). 101pp. This book explores horses' behavior — such as their sight and thinking powers — and goes on to explain how this knowledge was gained through observation and experiments. (Rev: BCCB 5/00; BL 3/1/00; HB 5/00; HBG 10/00; SLJ 7/00; VOYA 6/00) [636.1]

23761 Crisp, Marty. *Everything Horse: What Kids Really Want to Know About Horses* (3–5). Series: Kids' FAQs. 2005, NorthWord $10.95 (978-1-55971-920-9); paper $7.95 (978-1-55971-921-6). 63pp. Answers to frequently asked questions about horses, with photographs and a diagram of a horse's body. (Rev: SLJ 9/05)

23762 Dell, Pamela. *Thoroughbreds* (2–4). Illus. Series: Majestic Horses. 2007, Child's World LB $17.95 (978-1-59296-786-5). 24pp. This introduction to Thoroughbred horses covers their history, their physical characteristics, and their achievements. (Rev: BL 5/1/07) [636.1]

23763 Draper, Judith. *My First Horse and Pony Book* (2–4). Illus. 2005, Kingfisher $9.95 (978-0-7534-5878-5). 48pp. All about looking after and riding horses and ponies, with details of the animals' physical characteristics and discussion of Western and English riding, proper clothing, jumping, and so forth. (Rev: BL 7/05; SLJ 8/05) [636.1]

23764 Draper, Judith. *My First Horse and Pony Care Book* (2–4). Photos by Matthew Roberts. 2006, Kingfisher $9.95 (978-0-7534-5989-8). 48pp. Feeding, grooming, tack cleaning, and safety tips are all covered in this British import that focuses on English-style equipment. (Rev: SLJ 1/07) [636.1]

23765 Dubowski, Cathy E., and Mark Dubowski. *A Horse Named Seabiscuit* (2–4). Illus. by Mark Rowe. Series: All Aboard Reading. 2003, Grosset paper $3.99 (978-0-448-43342-4). 47pp. The story

of the famous Depression-era race horse is told in lively, well-illustrated narrative. (Rev: BL 1/1–15/04; HBG 4/04; SLJ 4/04) [636.1]

23766 Farley, Walter. *Man O' War* (4–6). Illus. 1983, Random paper $4.99 (978-0-394-86015-2). 352pp. The story of the famous racehorse.

23767 Funny Cide Team. *A Horse Named Funny Cide* (2–4). Illus. by Barry Moser. 2006, Putnam $16.99 (978-0-399-24462-9). 32pp. This is a beautifully illustrated tribute to the little race horse that overcame a number of obstacles to win both the Kentucky Derby and Preakness in 2003. (Rev: BL 4/15/06; SLJ 5/06) [798.4]

23768 Gibbons, Gail. *Horses!* (K–3). Illus. by author. 2003, Holiday House $16.95 (978-0-8234-1703-2). Browsers and report writers will enjoy Gibbons's exploration of horses' history, physical characteristics and breeds, life cycle, and care and grooming. (Rev: HBG 4/04; SLJ 12/03) [636.1]

23769 Hansen, Rosanna. *Panda: A Guide Horse for Ann* (3–5). Illus. by Neil Soderstrom. 2005, Boyds Mills $19.95 (978-1-59078-184-5). 48pp. This photo-essay presents the heartwarming story of Panda, a miniature horse trained to be a guide for a blind woman. (Rev: BL 1/1–15/06; SLJ 10/05) [362.40483]

23770 Hayden, Kate. *Horse Show* (1–3). Series: Dorling Kindersley Readers. 2001, DK $12.99 (978-0-7894-7372-1); paper $3.99 (978-0-7894-7371-4). 32pp. An introduction to gymkhanas and the preparations that horses and riders undergo, for beginning readers. (Rev: HBG 10/01; SLJ 6/01) [798.24]

23771 Henry, Marguerite. *Album of Horses* (5–8). Illus. by Wesley Dennis. 1951, Macmillan paper $11.99 (978-0-689-71709-3). 112pp. A beautifully illustrated guide to 20 breeds of horses.

23772 Hill, Cherry. *Horse Care for Kids* (4–8). Illus. 2002, Storey $23.95 (978-1-58017-476-3); paper $16.95 (978-1-58017-407-7). 128pp. A very practical guide for young horse lovers and their parents using clear prose and topnotch illustrations to cover everything from selecting a horse and instructor to proper care and equine psychology. (Rev: BL 12/1/02; HBG 3/03; SLJ 1/03) [636.1]

23773 Holub, Joan. *Why Do Horses Neigh?* (K–2). Illus. Series: Dial Easy-to-Read. 2003, Dial paper $3.99 (978-0-14-230119-7). 48pp. Beginning readers will enjoy this introduction to horses that presents interesting material in a question-and-answer format. (Rev: BL 11/15/02; HBG 10/03; SLJ 2/03) [636.1]

23774 Isenbart, Hans-Heinrich. *Birth of a Foal* (2–5). Illus. 1986, Carolrhoda LB $22.60 (978-0-87614-239-4). 48pp. Complemented by color photos, the phases of fetal development and the birth process are detailed. (Rev: BL 4/1/86; HB 5/86; SLJ 3/86)

23775 Jauck, Andrea. *Assateague: Island of the Wild Ponies* (2–4). Illus. 1997, Sierra Club paper $7.95 (978-0-939365-59-3). 32pp. A color photo-essay to interest horse fans. (Rev: BCCB 5/93; BL 3/15/93; SLJ 6/93) [599.72]

23776 Jeffrey, Laura S. *Horses: How to Choose and Care for a Horse* (3–5). Illus. Series: American

Humane Pet Care Library. 2004, Enslow LB $23.93 (978-0-7660-2519-6). 48pp. This helpful guide to horses and their care offers tips on selecting the right breed for your needs and on grooming, housing, and diet. (Rev: BL 10/15/04; SLJ 2/05) [636.1]

23777 Jurmain, Suzanne. *Once upon a Horse: A History of Horses and How They Shaped Our History* (5–9). Illus. 1989, Lothrop $15.95 (978-0-688-05550-9). A history of the horse and how it has been domesticated and used by humans. (Rev: BL 12/15/89; SLJ 1/90; VOYA 4/90) [636.1]

23778 Kelley, Brent. *Horse Breeds of the World* (4–8). Series: Horse Library. 2001, Chelsea $25.00 (978-0-7910-6652-2). 64pp. In addition to basic facts about nearly 40 types of horses around the world, this account looks briefly at the horse's evolutionary history and related species. (Rev: HBG 3/02; SLJ 3/02) [636.1]

23779 Libby, Barbara M. *I Rode the Red Horse: Secretariat's Belmont Race* (1–3). Illus. by author. 2003, Blood-Horse $16.95 (978-1-58150-096-7). 32pp. Triple Crown-winner Secretariat's victory at the Belmont Stakes in 1973 is told in the words of jockey Ron Turcotte. (Rev: BL 7/03; HBG 10/03) [798.4]

23780 McKerley, Jennifer. *Man O' War: Best Racehorse Ever* (1–3). Illus. by Terry Widener. Series: Step into Reading. 2005, Random LB $11.99 (978-0-375-93164-2); paper $3.99 (978-0-375-83164-5). 48pp. The exciting story of the famous, independent-minded racehorse who was the grandfather of Seabiscuit. (Rev: BL 11/1/05; SLJ 1/06) [798.4]

23781 Meltzer, Milton. *Hold Your Horses! A Feedbag Full of Fact and Fable* (4–8). Illus. 1995, HarperCollins LB $16.89 (978-0-06-024478-1). 160pp. The place of horses in history is explored in this account that looks at horses' role in art, war, sports, and work. (Rev: BCCB 12/95; BL 11/15/95; SLJ 12/95*) [636.1]

23782 Momatiuk, Yva, and John Eastcott. *Face to Face with Wild Horses* (5–8). Illus. Series: Face to Face with Animals. 2009, National Geographic $16.95 (978-1-4263-0466-8). 32pp. Riveting close-up photographs show wild horses in their own environment; back matter includes sections on How You Can Help, It's Your Turn, and Facts at a Glance. (Rev: BL 4/1/09) [599.665]

23783 Parker, Jane. *The Fantastic Book of Horses* (4–6). Illus. Series: Fantastic Book Of. 1997, Millbrook LB $22.40 (978-0-7613-0566-8). 40pp. The care, uses, and breeds of horses are introduced in this copiously illustrated book with foldout sections. (Rev: SLJ 8/97) [636.1]

23784 Patent, Dorothy Hinshaw. *Horses* (3–5). Illus. by William Muñoz. Series: Understanding Animals. 1994, Carolrhoda LB $19.95 (978-0-87614-766-5). 48pp. This excellent introduction to the world of horses includes material on their history, types, behavior, and current uses. (Rev: BCCB 3/94; BL 4/1/94; SLJ 3/94) [636.1]

23785 Patent, Dorothy Hinshaw. *Horses* (2–3). Series: Early Bird Nature Books. 2001, Lerner LB $25.26 (978-0-8225-3045-9). 48pp. With color photographs on each page and a simple text, this book introduces the life cycle of the horse with material on its anatomy, habits, and relationship to humans. (Rev: BL 8/1/01; HBG 10/01) [636.1]

23786 Penny, Malcolm. *The Secret Life of Wild Horses* (4–7). Series: The Secret World of . . . 2002, Raintree LB $27.12 (978-0-7398-4987-3). 48pp. A page of little-known facts about wild horses introduces this book that explores the horse's life, habits, mating, behavior, and threats to its future. (Rev: BL 8/02) [636.1]

23787 Peterson, Chris. *Wild Horses* (3–8). Illus. 2003, Boyds Mills $16.95 (978-1-56397-745-9). 32pp. Peterson presents photographs of and information about the horses living in the Wild Horse Sanctuary in the Black Hills of South Dakota. (Rev: BL 2/15/03; HBG 10/03; SLJ 3/03) [599.665]

23788 Peterson, Cris. *Horsepower: The Wonder of Draft Horses* (K–4). Photos by Alvis Upitis. 1997, Boyds Mills $16.95 (978-1-56397-626-1). A photo-essay that introduces the history, physical characteristics, and functions of the draft horse, with special coverage on Belgians, Percherons, and Clydesdales. (Rev: BCCB 4/97; SLJ 4/97) [636.1]

23789 Presnall, Judith Janda. *Horse Therapists* (4–7). Illus. Series: Animals with Jobs. 2002, Gale LB $23.70 (978-0-7377-0615-4). 48pp. Numerous photographs show how horses are used in various therapeutic situations including exercise for people with physical and mental disabilities. (Rev: BL 4/1/02; SLJ 3/02) [636.1]

23790 Price, Steven D. *The Kids' Book of the American Quarter Horse* (3–5). Illus. 2000, Lyons paper $19.95 (978-1-55821-975-5). 159pp. As well as telling how to choose, care for, and ride quarter horses, this account tells their history and explains the functions of the American Quarter Horse Association. (Rev: BL 2/1/00) [636.1]

23791 Pritchard, Louise. *I Love Ponies: A First Pony Guide* (2–4). Illus. 2007, Barron's paper $11.99 (978-0-7641-3790-7). 64pp. Cartoon and color photos illustrate this introduction to ponies. (Rev: SLJ 4/08)

23792 Ransford, Sandy. *Horse and Pony Breeds* (3–5). Photos by Bob Langrish. Series: Kingfisher Riding Club. 2003, Kingfisher $14.95 (978-0-7534-5575-3). 64pp. An attractive guide to horse and pony breeds from around the world. (Rev: HBG 10/03; SLJ 7/03) [636.1]

23793 Ransford, Sandy. *The Kingfisher Illustrated Horse and Pony Encyclopedia* (4–8). Photos by Bob Langrish. Illus. 2004, Kingfisher $24.95 (978-0-7534-5781-8). 224pp. After describing the history and various breeds of horses, this comprehensive and highly illustrated volume explains how to care for horses and how to ride them well and safely. (Rev: BL 3/1/05; SLJ 1/05) [636.1]

23794 Richter, Judy. *Riding for Kids* (4–8). 2003, Storey Kids $23.95 (978-1-58017-511-1); paper $16.95 (978-1-58017-510-4). 128pp. An introduction to horsemanship, from caring for horses and riding equipment to advice on safety, showing, and jumping. (Rev: BL 1/1–15/04; SLJ 3/04) [798.2]

23795 Simon, Seymour. *Horses* (2–4). Illus. 2006, HarperCollins $16.99 (978-0-06-028944-7). 40pp. Basic facts about horses — their history, physical characteristics, breeds, and so forth — are accompanied by eye-catching photographs. (Rev: BL 12/1/05; SLJ 2/06) [636.1]

23796 Stefoff, Rebecca. *Horses* (5–8). Illus. Series: AnimalWays. 2000, Marshall Cavendish LB $31.36 (978-0-7614-1139-0). 112pp. A well-illustrated account that describes the physical and behavioral characteristics of horses, their place in the classification system, and their relationships with humans. (Rev: BL 1/1–15/01) [599.884]

23797 Tracqui, Valerie. *The Horse: Faster Than the Wind* (3–6). Illus. by Gilles Delaborde. Series: Face-to-Face. 2001, Charlesbridge $9.95 (978-1-57091-450-8). 32pp. Clear text and photographs introduce the horse, with information on habitat, behavior, and reproduction. (Rev: BL 10/15/01; HBG 3/02) [599.665]

23798 van der Linde, Laurel. *From Mustangs to Movie Stars: Five True Horse Legends of Our Time* (4–7). Illus. 1995, Millbrook LB $24.40 (978-1-56294-456-8). 71pp. Biographies of five famous horses are recounted, from the racer Native Dancer to Cass Olé, who was the star of the film *The Black Stallion*. (Rev: BCCB 12/95; SLJ 12/95) [636.1]

23799 Vogel, Julia. *Wild Horses* (2–4). Illus. 2004, NorthWord $10.95 (978-1-55971-881-3). 48pp. Vogel examines the threats facing the last remaining herds of wild mustangs roaming the western United States. (Rev: BL 3/15/04; SLJ 10/04) [599.665]

23800 Yerxa, Leo. *Ancient Thunder* (K–3). Illus. by author. 2006, Groundwood $18.95 (978-0-88899-746-3). This handsome book with a spare text and illustrations that appear to be painted shirts celebrates the wild horses that roamed the Great Plains and their contributions to the Native Americans living there. (Rev: SLJ 11/06) [599.665]

Zoos and Marine Aquariums

23801 Aliki. *My Visit to the Zoo* (PS–2). Illus. 1997, HarperCollins LB $15.89 (978-0-06-024943-4). 40pp. A young girl acts as guide in a zoo and introduces the purposes of zoos as well as many of the animals that are kept there. (Rev: BL 7/97; HB 9/97; HBG 3/98; SLJ 10/97) [590]

23802 Altman, Joyce. *Dear Bronx Zoo* (3–6). Illus. by Sue Goldberg. 1992, Avon paper $3.50 (978-0-380-71649-4). 102pp. The answers to questions most frequently asked by Bronx Zoo visitors. (Rev: BL 1/1/91; SLJ 3/91) [590.74]

23803 Hanna, Jack. *Jungle Jack Hanna's What Zookeepers Do* (2–3). Illus. by Rick A. Prebeg. Series: Hello Reader! 1998, Scholastic paper $3.99 (978-0-590-67324-2). 48pp. A fascinating subject and dramatic photos make this easy-to-read book a popular one on zookeepers and their duties, such as feeding the tigers and caring for newly hatched eagle chicks. (Rev: BL 11/1/98) [636.088]

23804 Laidlaw, Rob. *Wild Animals in Captivity* (4–7). Illus. 2008, Fitzhenry & Whiteside $19.95 (978-1-55455-025-8). 48pp. Animal rights emerge front and center in this passionate, well-researched and convincing case for replacing zoos with wildlife sanctuaries and conservation centers. (Rev: BLO 2/5/09; SLJ 7/08) [636.088]

23805 Morecroft, Richard, and Alison Mackay. *Zoo Album* (3–5). Illus. by Karen Lloyd-Diviny. 2004, Enchanted Lion $17.95 (978-1-59270-032-5). 48pp. Vivid artwork and an easy-to-follow narrative introduce animals in Australian zoos, with interesting anecdotes by caretakers. (Rev: BL 12/1/04; SLJ 2/05) [590.73]

23806 Nagda, Ann Whitehead, and Cindy Bickel. *Tiger Math* (3–6). Illus. 2000, Holt $16.00 (978-0-8050-6248-9). 30pp. This account traces the growth and maturation of a Siberian tiger cub who was cared for at the Denver Zoo after his mother died when he was only ten weeks old. (Rev: BCCB 9/00; BL 10/1/00; HBG 3/01; SLJ 10/00) [511]

23807 Patent, Dorothy Hinshaw. *Back to the Wild* (4–6). Photos by William Munoz. 1997, Harcourt $18.00 (978-0-15-200280-0). 69pp. This account shows how present-day zoos are helping save endangered animals and gives four case studies where tamarins, red wolves, lemurs, and the black-footed ferret have been rescued. (Rev: SLJ 4/97) [590]

23808 Pfeffer, Wendy. *Popcorn Park Zoo: A Haven with a Heart* (3–6). Illus. by J. Gerard Smith. 1992, Simon & Schuster paper $16.95 (978-0-671-74589-9). 64pp. A unique zoo in New Jersey that cares for animals that are sick, old, hurt, abused, or unwanted. (Rev: BL 6/1/92; SLJ 7/92) [590]

23809 Rinard, Judith E. *Zoos Without Cages* (5–8). Illus. 1981, National Geographic LB $12.50 (978-0-87044-340-4). 104pp. A description of the new zoos that strive to reproduce the natural habitat of the enclosed animals. [590.74]

Botany

General and Miscellaneous

23810 Bang, Molly, and Penny Chrisholm. *Living Sunlight: How Plants Bring the Earth to Life* (PS–3). Illus. by Molly Bang. 2009, Scholastic $16.99 (978-0-545-04422-6). 40pp. Bang offers a clear explanation of photosynthesis and its importance. (Rev: BCCB 4/09; BL 12/1/08; HB 5/09; LMC 5/09; SLJ 2/09) [572]

23811 Ganeri, Anita. *Plant Life Cycles* (K–3). Series: Nature's Patterns. 2005, Heinemann LB $16.95 (978-1-4034-5896-4). 32pp. In simple languge, this volume introduces the life cycles of plants. (Rev: SLJ 6/05)

23812 Garassino, Alessandro. *Plants: Origins and Evolution* (4–8). Illus. Series: Beginnings — Origins and Evolution. 1995, Raintree LB $24.26 (978-0-8114-3332-7). 48pp. This treatment of plant evolution includes good factual data and discussion of several important concepts. (Rev: BL 4/15/95) [581.3]

23813 Greenaway, Theresa. *The Plant Kingdom* (5–8). Illus. 1999, Raintree LB $27.12 (978-0-8172-5886-3). 48pp. Using diagrams, sidebars, and color photographs, this account introduces the basics of plant classification while also covering such topics as photosynthesis and plant reproduction. (Rev: BL 2/1/00) [580]

23814 Kudlinski, Kathleen V. *What Do Roots Do?* (K–3). Illus. by David Schuppert. 2005, NorthWord $15.95 (978-1-55971-896-7). This colorfully illustrated picture book explores in rhyming verse the role of roots in the lives of plants, flowers, and trees. (Rev: SLJ 12/05) [581.4]

23815 Lerner, Carol. *Cactus* (4–7). Illus. 1992, Morrow LB $14.89 (978-0-688-09637-3). 32pp. After explaining the parts of the cactus and how it can exist in near-waterless environments, this account describes different species. (Rev: BCCB 10/92; HB 1/93; SLJ 12/92) [635.7]

23816 Murphy, Patricia J. *Peeking at Plants with a Scientist* (1–3). Series: I Like Science! 2004, Enslow LB $21.26 (978-0-7660-2266-9). 24pp. The work of a botanist is portrayed in question-and-answer format and many photographs. (Rev: SLJ 8/04) [580]

23817 Overbeck, Cynthia. *Carnivorous Plants* (4–8). Illus. by Kiyashi Shimizu. 1982, Lerner LB $31.95 (978-0-8225-1470-1). 48pp. A survey of these plants and how they evolved. [581.5]

23818 Pascoe, Elaine. *Slime, Molds, and Fungus* (4–7). Series: Nature Close-Up. 1998, Blackbirch LB $23.70 (978-1-56711-182-8). 48pp. Stunning photographs, good background information, and a number of interesting projects help introduce the world of fungi. (Rev: BL 9/15/98; HBG 3/99; SLJ 3/99) [589.2]

23819 Patent, Dorothy Hinshaw. *Plants on the Trail with Lewis and Clark.* (5–8). Photos by William Muñoz. 2003, Clarion $18.00 (978-0-618-06776-3). 102pp. This introduction to the trees and plants seen by Lewis and Clark also discusses Lewis's training as a botanist and his contributions to the field. (Rev: BL 3/1/03; HBG 10/03; SLJ 5/03) [581.978]

23820 Schaefer, Lola M. *Pick, Pull, Snap! Where Once a Flower Bloomed* (PS–1). Illus. by Lindsay Barrett George. 2003, Greenwillow $16.99 (978-0-688-17834-5). 32pp. Attractively illustrated flaps and fold-outs add to the appeal of this introduction to the basics of plant growth. (Rev: BL 5/1/03; HBG 10/03; SLJ 7/03) [571.8]

23821 Silverstein, Alvin, et al. *Photosynthesis* (5–9). Series: Science Concepts. 1998, Twenty-First Century LB $26.90 (978-0-7613-3000-4). 63pp. Photosynthesis is explained, with a history of the discoveries about the process and material on related issues including acid rain and the greenhouse effect. (Rev: HBG 3/99; SLJ 2/99) [581.1]

Flowers

23822 Farndon, John. *Flowers* (2–5). Illus. Series: World of Plants. 2006, Gale LB $23.70 (978-1-4103-0423-0). 24pp. Diagrams and photographs supplement the clear text describing flowers and the role they play in the overall life of the plant. (Rev: SLJ 2/07)

23823 Holmes, Anita. *Flowers and Friends* (K–2). Series: We Can Read About — Science! 2000, Benchmark LB $21.36 (978-0-7614-1113-0). 32pp. An easy-to-read book that describes the process of pollination through the perception of various creatures. (Rev: HBG 3/01; SLJ 2/01) [582]

23824 Hood, Susan, and National Audubon Society, eds. *Wildflowers* (5–8). Illus. 1998, Scholastic paper $17.95 (978-0-590-05464-5). Fifty common wildflowers are pictured and described, along with information on what equipment to use and what to look for to observe and study wildflowers (leaves, blooms, habitat, height, range). (Rev: BL 8/98; SLJ 8/98) [583]

23825 Johnson, Sylvia A. *Morning Glories* (4–7). Illus. 1985, Lerner LB $22.60 (978-0-8225-1462-6). 48pp. Color photographs display the stages of this plant's development. (Rev: BCCB 3/86; BL 4/15/86; SLJ 4/86)

23826 Pascoe, Elaine. *Flowers* (3–5). Photos by Dwight Kuhn. Series: Nature Close-Up. 2003, Gale LB $24.95 (978-1-56711-432-4). 48pp. Beautiful photographs of flowering plants are accompanied by introductory information on their importance to ecology and their usefulness to mankind. (Rev: SLJ 3/04) [575.6]

23827 Ryden, Hope. *Wildflowers Around the Year* (4–6). Illus. 2001, Clarion $17.00 (978-0-395-85814-1). 48pp. A handsome book on wildflowers that gives details on characteristics, uses in food or medicine, and fertilization. (Rev: BL 3/1/01; HB 3/01; HBG 10/01) [582.13]

23828 Souza, D. M. *Freaky Flowers* (4–7). Series: Watts Library. 2002, Watts LB $25.50 (978-0-531-11981-5). 64pp. Flowering plants are the main focus in this discussion of basic botany, the ways in which flowers attract pollinators, and the environmental dangers plants are facing. (Rev: SLJ 7/02) [582]

23829 Wade, Mary Dodson. *Flowers Bloom!* (K–2). Series: I Like Plants! 2009, Enslow LB $21.26 (978-0-7660-3157-9). 24pp. Using a question-and-answer format, this book provides a simple explanation of how flowers grow and bloom, with color photographs and an activity. (Rev: SLJ 4/09) [582.13]

23830 Weiss, Ellen. *From Bulb to Daffodil* (1–2). Series: Scholastic News Nonfiction Reader. 2007, Children's Pr. LB $20.00 (978-0-531-18534-6); paper $6.95 (978-0-531-18787-6). 24pp. For beginning readers, this is an easy-to-follow explanation of how bulbs grow into flowers. (Rev: SLJ 12/07) [635.9]

23831 Winner, Cherie. *The Sunflower Family* (4–7). Illus. 1996, Carolrhoda LB $23.93 (978-1-57505-007-2); paper $7.95 (978-1-57505-029-4). 48pp. Growth patterns, structures, and reproduction are topics covered in this account of the sunflower family, including thistles, daisies, and asters. (Rev: BL 10/1/96; SLJ 10/96) [583]

Foods and Farming

GENERAL

23832 Artley, Bob. *Once Upon a Farm* (4–9). Illus. by author. 2000, Pelican $21.95 (978-1-56554-753-7). 127pp. Fine watercolors accompany a readable look at the seasons as experienced by the author while growing up on a farm in Iowa. (Rev: SLJ 12/00) [630]

23833 Bial, Raymond. *The Farms* (4–7). Photos by author. Illus. Series: Building America. 2001, Benchmark LB $27.07 (978-0-7614-1332-5). 56pp. An interesting, beautifully illustrated look at the ways in which farms developed in America, with information on their structure and significance to the country as a whole. Also use *The Mills* (2001). (Rev: HBG 3/02; SLJ 2/02*) [630]

23834 Bowden, Rob. *Food and Farming* (5–8). Illus. Series: Sustainable World. 2004, Gale LB $26.20 (978-0-7377-1899-7). 48pp. Bowden looks at conventional methods of farming and at the new focus on sustainable agriculture, providing lots of facts and statistics and highlighting choices we all can make that may improve the future. (Rev: BL 4/15/04; SLJ 10/04) [338]

23835 Damerow, Gail. *Your Chickens: A Kid's Guide to Raising and Showing* (4–7). Illus. 1993, Storey paper $14.95 (978-0-88266-823-9). 160pp. A straightforward, practical guide on raising prize-winning chickens that is both thorough and filled with information. (Rev: BL 5/15/94; SLJ 1/94) [636.5]

23836 Damerow, Gail. *Your Goats: A Kid's Guide to Raising and Showing* (4–7). Illus. 1993, Storey paper $14.95 (978-0-88266-825-3). 176pp. This is a complete guide to raising, breeding, and showing goats, with many useful tips and helpful illustrations. (Rev: BL 5/15/94; SLJ 1/94) [636.3]

23837 Hughes, Meredith S. *Glorious Grasses: The Grains* (5–8). Series: Plants We Eat. 1999, Lerner LB $26.60 (978-0-8225-2831-9). A description of the history, cultivation, processing, and dietary importance of wheat, rice, corn, millet, barley, oats, and rye, plus recipes and activities. (Rev: BL 7/99; HBG 10/99; SLJ 8/99) [633.1]

23838 Hughes, Meredith S. *Tall and Tasty: Fruit Trees* (5–8). Series: Plants We Eat. 2000, Lerner LB $31.95 (978-0-8225-2837-1). 80pp. This book explores the world of apples, peaches, mangoes, and other fruits that grow on trees and explains each one's life cycle, and how the fruit has migrated during its history. (Rev: BL 4/15/00; HBG 10/00) [641.3]

23839 Lasky, Kathryn. *Sugaring Time* (4–7). Illus. 1998, Center for Applied Research paper $4.95 (978-0-87628-350-9). 64pp. Through photographs and text, the process of maple sugar production in New England is described.

23840 Olney, Ross R. *The Farm Combine* (4–8). Illus. 1984, Walker LB $10.85 (978-0-8027-6568-0). 64pp. The development of the reaper and thrash-er is discussed, with information on today's combine harvester.

FARMS, RANCHES, AND FARM ANIMALS

23841 Bell, Rachael. *Cows* (K–3). Series: Farm Animals. 2000, Heinemann LB $21.36 (978-1-57572-529-1). 32pp. Using double-page spreads, this book introduces cows and their uses as a source of meat and milk. Also use *Pigs* (2000). (Rev: HBG 3/01; SLJ 7/00) [630]

23842 Drake, Jane, and Ann Love. *Farming* (3–4). Illus. by Pat Cupples. Series: America at Work. 1998, Kids Can $12.95 (978-1-55074-451-4). 31pp. Factual information about a vegetable farm and a cattle ranch, including chores, processes, and equipment, is introduced by fictional children who live on these farms and ranches. (Rev: HBG 3/99; SLJ 12/98) [630]

23843 Feldman, Thea. *Who You Callin' Chicken?* (3–5). Photos by Stephen Green-Armytage. 2003, Abrams $14.95 (978-0-8109-4593-7). Chickens of all kinds feature in this lively photographic survey. (Rev: HBG 4/04; SLJ 12/03) [636.5]

23844 Ghione, Yvette. *This Is Daniel Cook at the Farm* (K–3). 2006, Kids Can $12.95 (978-1-55453-077-9); paper $4.95 (978-1-55453-078-6). In this companion to the popular Canadian-produced TV show, the young host invites readers to join him on a journey of discovery around a busy farmyard. (Rev: SLJ 11/06) [636]

23845 Gibbons, Gail. *Chicks and Chickens* (1–3). Illus. by author. 2003, Holiday House $16.95 (978-0-8234-1700-1). Using cartoon illustrations and simple narrative, Gibbons examines the life cycle of chickens. (Rev: HBG 10/03; SLJ 7/03) [636.5]

23846 Gibbons, Gail. *Farming* (PS–2). Illus. by author. 1988, Holiday House LB $16.95 (978-0-8234-0682-1); paper $6.95 (978-0-8234-0797-2). 32pp. Farm landscapes through the seasons. (Rev: BL 6/1/88; SLJ 8/88)

23847 Graff, Nancy P. *The Strength of the Hills: A Portrait of a Family Farm* (4–6). Illus. by Richard Howard. 1989, Little, Brown $14.95 (978-0-316-32277-5). 80pp. This account highlights life on a family dairy farm in Vermont. (Rev: BL 11/15/89; SLJ 4/90*) [338.1]

23848 Hill, Lee S. *Farms Feed the World* (1–3). Series: Building Blocks Books. 1997, Carolrhoda LB $14.60 (978-1-57505-075-1). 32pp. This book takes the reader on a visit to many kinds of farms around the world, from a wheat field in Montana to a rice paddy in Indonesia. (Rev: BL 3/15/98; HBG 3/98) [630]

23849 Kalman, Bobbie. *Hooray for Sheep Farming!* (K–3). Series: Hooray for Farming! 1997, Crabtree LB $25.27 (978-0-86505-655-8); paper $7.95 (978-0-86505-669-5). 32pp. This book describes the habits and physical structure of sheep, different kinds of wool, and the everyday routines on a sheep farm. (Rev: HBG 3/98; SLJ 4/98) [630]

23850 Kant, Tanya. *How an Egg Grows into a Chicken* (K–3). Illus. by Carolyn Franklin. Series: Amaze. 2008, Children's Pr. LB $26.00 (978-0-531-24047-

2); paper $8.95 (978-0-531-23801-1). 32pp. "Why do chickens lay eggs? Why do they sit on them?" This simple introduction to a chicken's life cycle, with colorful illustrations and well-organized chapters, includes two experiments. (Rev: SLJ 3/09) [636.5]

23851 Miller, Sara S. *Chickens* (2–3). Series: True Books. 2000, Children's Book Pr. LB $25.00 (978-0-516-21576-1). 32pp. A simple introduction to chickens that describes their anatomy, uses, homes, and habits. (Rev: BL 1/1–15/01) [636.5]

23852 Miller, Sara S. *Cows* (2–3). Illus. Series: True Books. 2000, Children's Book Pr. LB $25.00 (978-0-516-21577-8). 48pp. Covers dairy cows and their domestication as well as giving information on dairy products and life on a dairy farm. (Rev: BL 1/1–15/01) [636.3]

23853 Miller, Sara S. *Pigs* (2–3). Series: True Books. 2000, Children's Book Pr. LB $25.00 (978-0-516-21579-2). 32pp. Using colorful pictures and a minimum of text, this farm animal is introduced with material on its anatomy, habits, and uses. (Rev: BL 1/1–15/01) [636.3]

23854 Miller, Sara S. *Sheep* (2–3). Illus. Series: True Books. 2000, Children's Book Pr. LB $25.00 (978-0-516-21580-8). 48pp. This book introduces sheep and sheep farming with material on the animal's use both for food and wool. (Rev: BL 1/1–15/01) [636.3]

23855 Morck, Irene. *Old Bird* (2–4). Illus. by Muriel Wood. 2003, Fitzhenry & Whiteside $15.95 (978-1-55041-695-4). 32pp. An aging horse named Bird is determined to prove she can pull her weight around the farm in this novel based on a true story. (Rev: SLJ 10/03) [813]

23856 Munro, Roxie. *Ranch* (2–4). 2004, Bright Sky $16.95 (978-1-931721-37-0). 36pp. Readers are introduced to all aspects of a cattle ranch and the people who work there. (Rev: BL 7/04; SLJ 9/04) [636.2]

23857 Peterson, Chris. *Amazing Grazing* (3–5). Illus. by Alvis Upitis. 2002, Boyds Mills $16.95 (978-1-56397-942-2). 32pp. Color photographs and a lucid text show how three Montana cattle ranchers are using environment-friendly practices. (Rev: BL 4/1/02; HBG 10/02; SLJ 4/02) [636.0845]

23858 Peterson, Chris. *Clarabelle: Making Milk and So Much More* (1–3). Illus. 2007, Boyds Mills $16.95 (978-1-59078-310-8). 32pp. A look at the dairy industry, featuring a day in the life of Clarabelle the cow; color photographs add to the informative text. (Rev: BL 9/1/07; SLJ 10/07) [636.2]

23859 Peterson, Cris. *Century Farm: One Hundred Years on a Family Farm* (2–4). Illus. 1999, Boyds Mills $17.95 (978-1-56397-710-7). 32pp. Traces the changes in farm life over a century and includes material on the machinery used, the tasks performed, and the different farm animals. (Rev: BCCB 3/99; BL 3/1/99; HBG 9/99; SLJ 4/99) [636.2]

23860 Pipe, Jim. *Farm Animals* (PS–1). Illus. Series: Read and Play. 2007, Stargazer LB $22.80 (978-1-59604-112-7). 32pp. Very basic facts about farm

animals are presented with eye-catching photographs and a "Let's Play" section with easy games. (Rev: BL 4/15/07) [636]

23861 Powell, Jillian. *From Calf to Cow* (PS–3). Series: How Do They Grow? 2001, Raintree LB $25.69 (978-0-7398-4426-7). 32pp. Brief text and large, full-color photographs follow calves through birth and growth. Also use *From Chick to Chicken* and from *From Piglet to Pig* (both 2001). (Rev: HBG 3/02; SLJ 1/02) [636.2]

23862 Rendon, Marcie, and Cheryl Walsh Bellville. *Farmer's Market: Families Working Together* (4–6). Illus. 2001, Carolrhoda $23.93 (978-1-57505-462-9). 48pp. A look at truck farming and the sale of the produce at farmers' markets, with profiles of two Midwest families. (Rev: BL 5/1/01; HBG 10/01) [635]

23863 Rosen, Michael J. *Our Farm: Four Seasons with Five Kids on One Family's Farm* (3–7). Photos by author. 2008, Darby Creek $18.95 (978-1-58196-067-9). 144pp. An interesting photo-essay covering a year on an Ohio family farm. (Rev: SLJ 9/08) [630]

23864 Schuh, Mari C. *Chickens on the Farm* (PS–2). Series: On the Farm. 2001, Capstone LB $17.26 (978-0-7368-0991-7). 24pp. Spare text and full-color photographs convey simple facts about chickens. Also use *Pigs on the Farm* and *Sheep on the Farm* (both 2001). (Rev: HBG 3/02; SLJ 1/02) [636.5]

23865 Sklansky, Amy E. *Where Do Chicks Come From?* (K–2). Illus. by Pam Paparone. Series: Let's-Read-and-Find-Out. 2005, HarperCollins LB $16.89 (978-0-06-028893-8); paper $5.99 (978-0-06-445212-0). 40pp. Follows the development of a chick from the moment of fertilization until it hatches from the egg roughly three weeks later. (Rev: BL 2/1/05; SLJ 2/05) [636.5]

23866 Sweeney, Alyse. *Let's Visit a Dairy Farm* (K–2). Series: Scholastic News Nonfiction Readers. 2006, Children's Pr. LB $20.00 (978-0-531-16843-1). 24pp. Basic information for beginning readers, with seven highlighted words that are featured in bold in the text. (Rev: SLJ 1/07) [069]

23867 Urbigkit, Cat. *A Young Shepherd* (1–3). Illus. 2006, Boyds Mills $15.95 (978-1-59078-364-1). 32pp. This photo-essay documents a year in the life of a 12-year-old boy who tends his own sheep on a Wyoming ranch. (Rev: BL 2/15/06; SLJ 5/06) [636]

23868 Webber, Desiree Morrison. *Bone Head: Story of the Longhorn* (4–7). Illus. by Sandy Shropshire. 2003, Eakin $16.95 (978-1-57168-763-0). 74pp. The longhorn's characteristics and the reasons for its early success but decline with the arrival of the railroad are explored in appealing text and archival photographs. (Rev: SLJ 2/04) [636.2]

23869 Wolfman, Judy. *Life on a Cattle Farm* (4–6). Illus. by David Lorenz Winston. Series: Life on a Farm. 2001, Carolrhoda LB $23.93 (978-1-57505-516-9). 48pp. A photo-illustrated look at activities on a Pennsylvania cattle farm, told from a teenager's point of view. Also use *Life on a Crop Farm*, *Life on a Goat Farm*, and *Life on a Horse Farm* (all

2001). (Rev: BL 11/15/01; HBG 3/02; SLJ 11/01) [636.2]

23870 Wolfman, Judy. *Life on a Pig Farm* (3–5). Illus. 1998, Carolrhoda $23.93 (978-1-57505-237-3). 48pp. This photo-essay describes life on a pig farm, as experienced by three sisters. (Rev: BL 10/15/98; HBG 3/99; SLJ 3/99) [636.4]

FOODS

23871 Allen, Nancy Kelly. *Whose Work Is This? A Look at Things Animals Make-Pearls, Milk, and Honey* (PS–2). Illus. Series: Whose Is It? Science. 2004, Picture Window LB $25.26 (978-1-4048-0612-2). 24pp. A rhythmic question-and-answer format and colorful collages introduce the wide variety of foods that animals produce.

23872 Bial, Raymond. *The Super Soybean* (4–6). Illus. 2007, Albert Whitman $16.95 (978-0-8075-7549-9). 32pp. This well-organized title with many photographs introduces the history and characteristics of the soybean and looks at the surprising number and variety of soy products. (Rev: BL 9/1/07; LMC 1/08; SLJ 10/07) [633.3]

23873 Bryant-Mole, Karen. *Food* (PS–3). Illus. Series: Picture This! 1997, Rigby $18.50 (978-1-57572-150-7). 24pp. Various kinds of food are introduced, cooking methods are discussed, and the principles of good nutrition are mentioned. (Rev: BL 10/15/97; SLJ 12/97) [641.3]

23874 Burleigh, Robert. *Chocolate: Riches from the Rainforest* (3–6). Illus. 2002, Abrams $16.95 (978-0-8109-5734-3). 40pp. Traces the rich history of chocolate, from the Aztecs to Hershey's. (Rev: BL 3/1/02; HBG 10/02; SLJ 4/02) [641.3]

23875 Burns, Diane L. *Cranberries: Fruit of the Bogs* (3–5). Illus. by Cheryl Walsh Bellville. 1994, Carolrhoda LB $22.60 (978-0-87614-822-8). 48pp. A book about cranberry growing and activities during and after harvesting. (Rev: BL 12/1/94; SLJ 3/95) [633.76]

23876 Burns, Diane L. *Sugaring Season: Making Maple Syrup* (1–5). Illus. 1990, Carolrhoda $22.60 (978-0-87614-420-6); paper $5.95 (978-0-87614-554-8). 32pp. Crisp photos and good diagrams help to explain the maple syrup process. (Rev: BL 11/1/90; SLJ 12/90) [664]

23877 Calì, Davide. *I Love Chocolate* (K–3). Illus. by Evelyn Daviddi. 2009, Tundra $12.95 (978-0-88776-912-2). A delicious exploration of all the good things about chocolate. (Rev: SLJ 4/09) [641.3]

23878 Chandler, Gary, and Kevin Graham. *Natural Foods and Products* (4–8). Illus. Series: Making a Better World. 1996, Twenty-First Century LB $25.90 (978-0-8050-4623-6). This work discusses genetically engineered foods, safe eco-friendly methods of growing crops, and companies that engage in safe practices. (Rev: BL 12/15/96; SLJ 1/97) [333.76]

23879 Charlip, Remy. *Peanut Butter Party: Including the History, Uses, and Future of Peanut Butter* (K–4). Illus. by author. 1999, Tricycle $14.95 (978-1-883672-69-0). Peanut butter is celebrated in a book that covers its history and outlines such activities as recipes for foods with peanut butter, edible arts and crafts, riddles, games, a one-act play on the subject, and a series of clever illustrations. (Rev: BCCB 7–8/99; HBG 9/99; SLJ 6/99) [641.3]

23880 Cobb, Vicki. *Junk Food* (3–5). Illus. by Michael Gold. Series: Where's the Science Here? 2005, Millbrook LB $23.93 (978-0-7613-2773-8). 48pp. Candy, corn chips, and soda are among the popular products explored here; clear text and easy projects will grab attention. (Rev: BL 10/15/05; HBG 4/06; SLJ 2/06) [664]

23881 Cooper, Jason. *Beef* (1–3). Series: Farm to Market. 1997, Rourke LB $19.27 (978-0-86625-617-9). 24pp. This book describes how North American beef cattle are raised, slaughtered, processed, and marketed. (Rev: SLJ 6/98) [641]

23882 Cooper, Jason. *Dairy Products* (1–3). Series: Farm to Market. 1997, Rourke LB $19.27 (978-0-86625-619-3). 24pp. After a description of how dairy cattle are raised, this book covers their products, how they are processed, and how they are marketed. (Rev: SLJ 6/98) [637]

23883 Cooper, Jason. *Poultry* (1–3). Series: Farm to Market. 1997, Rourke LB $19.27 (978-0-86625-618-6). 24pp. This book shows how different types of poultry are raised, processed, and marketed. (Rev: SLJ 6/98) [598]

23884 D'Amico, Joan, and Karen Eich Drummond. *The Science Chef: 100 Fun Food Experiments and Recipes for Kids* (4–6). Illus. 1994, Wiley paper $12.95 (978-0-471-31045-7). 192pp. Simple experiments introduce various properties of foods and give youngsters a chance to be cooks. (Rev: BL 11/1/94; SLJ 12/94) [641.3]

23885 dePaola, Tomie. *The Popcorn Book* (1–3). Illus. 1978, Holiday House LB $16.95 (978-0-8234-0314-1); paper $6.95 (978-0-8234-0533-6). 32pp. While Tony makes a plate of popcorn, Tiny relates interesting facts about this delicious food.

23886 Eagen, Rachel. *The Biography of Bananas* (4–7). Illus. Series: How Did That Get Here? 2005, Crabtree LB $26.60 (978-0-7787-2483-4). 32pp. This richly illustrated title offers a wealth of information about the science and business of producing bananas. (Rev: BL 3/1/06) [634]

23887 Erlbach, Arlene. *Soda Pop* (3–6). Illus. 1994, Lerner LB $19.95 (978-0-8225-2386-4). 48pp. Tells about the origins, history, and manufacture of soda pop, with recipes for making various kinds at home. Also use *Peanut Butter* (1994). (Rev: BL 5/1/94) [663]

23888 Fleisher, Paul. *Ice Cream Treats: The Inside Scoop* (4–6). Photos by David O. Saunders. 2001, Carolrhoda LB $23.93 (978-1-57505-268-7). 48pp. This is an appealing overview of the history of ice cream, with a tour of a factory and a few simple recipes. (Rev: HBG 10/01; SLJ 7/01) [641.8]

23889 Frost, Helen. *The Grain Group* (K–2). Series: Food Guide Pyramid. 2000, Capstone LB $17.26 (978-0-7368-0538-4). 24pp. This text for beginning readers introduces different grains and explains their importance in the food pyramid. (Rev: HBG 9/00; SLJ 10/00) [633.1]

23890 Gibbons, Gail. *Ice Cream: The Full Scoop* (K–2). 2006, Holiday $16.95 (978-0-8234-2000-1). 32pp. A delicious history of ice cream from the days of Marco Polo to the present, with a tour of a contemporary factory. (Rev: BL 6/1–15/06; SLJ 8/06) [641.8]

23891 Greenstein, Elaine. *Ice-Cream Cones for Sale!* (K–2). Illus. 2003, Scholastic $15.95 (978-0-439-32728-2). 32pp. Greenstein tells the "real" story behind the ice-cream cone, taking care to delineate the boundaries between known fact and speculative fiction. (Rev: BL 5/1/03; HB 9/03; HBG 4/04; SLJ 9/03) [637.4]

23892 Harbison, Elizabeth M. *Loaves of Fun: A History of Bread with Activities and Recipes from Around the World* (3–6). Illus. 1997, Chicago Review paper $12.95 (978-1-55652-311-3). 91pp. A history of bread from ancient times to the present day, with several activities and 24 recipes. (Rev: BL 5/1/97; SLJ 9/97) [641.8]

23893 Hartzog, John Daniel. *Everyday Science Experiments with Food* (PS–3). 2000, Rosen $21.25 (978-0-8239-5460-5). 24pp. The eight projects outlined in this simple science book include recipes for making butter and homemade soda. (Rev: SLJ 9/00) [641.3]

23894 Hughes, Meredith S. *Flavor Foods: Spices and Herbs* (5–8). Series: Plants We Eat. 2000, Lerner LB $26.60 (978-0-8225-2835-7). 88pp. This book explains how roots, leaves, flowers, seeds, fruit, and bark of some plants are transformed in the seasonings that flavor so many dishes. (Rev: BL 7/00; HBG 10/00) [633.8]

23895 Jango-Cohen, Judith. *The History of Food* (5–8). Series: Major Inventions Through History. 2005, Twenty-First Century LB $26.60 (978-0-8225-2484-7). 56pp. Addresses inventions in the food industry such as canning, pasteurization, and genetically modified crops. (Rev: SLJ 2/06)

23896 Johnson, Sylvia A. *Wheat* (4–6). Illus. by Masaharu Susuki. 1990, Lerner LB $22.60 (978-0-8225-1490-9). 48pp. The life cycle of the wheat plant is described, with material on harvesting and processing. (Rev: BL 4/15/90; SLJ 8/90) [633.1]

23897 Jones, Carol. *Cheese* (4–7). Illus. Series: From Farm to You. 2002, Chelsea $28.00 (978-0-7910-7005-5). 32pp. This is an absorbing account of the techniques used in manufacturing cheese and the history of cheese, with an overview of the many varieties and a map of cheese eating around the world. Also use *Pasta and Noodles* (2002). (Rev: BL 11/1/02; HBG 3/03) [641.3]

23898 Keller, Kristin Thoennes. *From Maple Trees to Maple Syrup* (1–3). Series: First Facts: From Farm to Table. 2004, Capstone LB $21.26 (978-0-7368-2634-1). 24pp. This easy reader traces the various steps involved in the production of maple syrup and includes a simple recipe. Also use *From Oranges to Orange Juice* and *From Peanuts to Peanut Butter* (both 2004). (Rev: SLJ 2/05) [641.3]

23899 Keller, Stella. *Ice Cream* (PS). Illus. by John Holm. Series: Real Readers. 1989, Raintree LB $21.40 (978-0-8172-3523-9). 32pp. This easily read account describes the history of ice cream. (Rev: BL 2/1/90) [637.4]

23900 King, Hazel. *Milk and Yogurt* (3–5). Series: Food in Focus. 1998, Heinemann LB $14.95 (978-1-57572-657-1). 32pp. This work gives a history of milk and yogurt, plus material on their processing, nutritional value, nutrients, and related experiments and recipes. (Rev: SLJ 2/99) [636.2]

23901 Landau, Elaine. *Popcorn!* (2–4). Illus. by Brian Lies. 2003, Charlesbridge $16.95 (978-1-57091-442-3); paper $6.95 (978-1-57091-443-0). 32pp. An entertaining look at the history of the popular snack, with humorous illustrations. (Rev: BL 2/1/03; HBG 10/03; SLJ 4/03) [646.6]

23902 Landau, Elaine. *Wheat* (2–4). Series: True Books. 1999, Children's Book Pr. LB $25.00 (978-0-516-21029-2). 48pp. Where wheat is grown, its appearance, uses, and nutritional value are topics covered in this colorful introduction. (Rev: BL 10/15/99) [633.1]

23903 Levenson, George. *Bread Comes to Life: A Garden of Wheat and a Loaf to Eat* (PS–1). 2004, Tricycle $15.95 (978-1-58246-114-4). 32pp. All kinds of bread feature in this rhythmic and appetizing volume. (Rev: BL 10/1/04) [641.8]

23904 Mandell, Muriel. *Simple Kitchen Experiments: Learning Science with Everyday Foods* (4–6). Illus. 1994, Sterling paper $4.95 (978-0-8069-8415-5). 128pp. The kitchen becomes a chemistry lab in this book of simple experiments and projects, such as degassing beans. (Rev: BL 5/1/94; SLJ 8/93) [641.3]

23905 Martino, Teresa. *Pizza!* (PS). Illus. by Brigid Faranda. Series: Real Readers. 1989, Raintree LB $21.40 (978-0-8172-3533-8). 32pp. This easy-to-read account describes the development of pizza from its beginnings 1,000 years ago. (Rev: BL 2/1/90) [641.8]

23906 Meltzer, Milton. *Food* (4–8). Illus. 1998, Millbrook LB $24.90 (978-0-7613-0354-1). 96pp. A fascinating history of food and how it affects our lives. (Rev: BL 1/1–15/99; HBG 3/99; SLJ 1/99) [641.3]

23907 Morgan, Sally. *Superfoods: Genetic Modification of Foods* (5–8). Series: Science at the Edge. 2002, Heinemann LB $27.86 (978-1-58810-702-2). 64pp. A look at the history and genetic alteration of foods, with discussion of the controversy this has created. (Rev: BL 10/15/02; HBG 3/03; SLJ 4/03) [174.957]

23908 Morris, Neil. *Do You Know Where Your Food Comes From?* (4–7). Illus. 2006, Heinemann LB $32.86 (978-1-4034-8575-5). 56pp. In this informative book students learn all about the global food market, where and how their food is produced, and how to make good food choices. (Rev: BL 12/1/06; SLJ 4/07) [363.8]

23909 Nelson, Robin. *From Flower to Honey* (K–2). Series: Start to Finish. 2003, Lerner LB $18.60 (978-0-8225-0717-8). 24pp. Full of photographs, this basic introduction suitable for beginning readers follows the cycle of honey creation. (Rev: HBG 3/03; SLJ 9/03) [638]

23910 Nottridge, Rhoda. *Sugars* (3–6). Illus. Series: Food Facts. 1993, Carolrhoda LB $19.93 (978-0-87614-796-2). 32pp. Covers such topics as the various forms of sugars, the ways they are made, and their uses, with some simple recipes and activities. (Rev: SLJ 10/93) [613.2]

23911 Older, Jules. *Ice Cream* (3–6). Illus. by Lyn Severance. 2002, Charlesbridge $16.95 (978-0-88106-111-6); paper $6.95 (978-0-88106-112-3). 32pp. A fact-packed, colorful, and lighthearted book about the history of ice cream and important ice cream inventions, such as the cone and the banana split. (Rev: BL 2/15/02; HBG 10/02; SLJ 5/02) [641.8]

23912 Paulsen, Gary. *The Tortilla Factory* (1–4). Illus. by Ruth W. Paulsen. 1995, Harcourt $16.00 (978-0-15-292876-6). 32pp. Simple text and paintings show how kernels of corn become flour and eventually tortillas. (Rev: BL 6/1–15/95; HB 7/95; SLJ 7/95) [641.8]

23913 Peters, Celeste. *Peppers, Popcorn, and Pizza: The Science of Food* (3–5). Series: Science@Work. 1999, Raintree LB $27.12 (978-0-7398-0136-9). 48pp. This account illustrates how food is related to everyday life through technology, careers, society, and the environment. (Rev: SLJ 3/00) [641]

23914 Peterson, Cris. *Harvest Year* (1–3). Illus. by Alvis Upitis. 1996, Boyds Mills $19.95 (978-1-56397-571-4). 28pp. Using a month-by-month arrangement, various crops grown in the United States are highlighted. (Rev: BL 9/15/96; SLJ 11/96) [641]

23915 Polin, C. J. *The Story of Chocolate* (2–4). Illus. Series: DK Readers. 2004, DK $14.99 (978-0-7566-0991-7); paper $3.99 (978-0-7566-0992-4). 48pp. From harvesting of beans to production of candy bars, this is a simple introduction to chocolate and its history. (Rev: BL 2/1/05) [641.3]

23916 Powell, Jillian. *Milk* (3–5). Illus. Series: Everyone Eats. 1997, Raintree LB $17.98 (978-0-8172-4766-9). 32pp. This book introduces milk from different animals, but it focuses on the production, uses, and nutritional value of cow's milk. (Rev: SLJ 8/97) [636.2]

23917 Powell, Jillian. *Pasta* (1–4). Illus. Series: Everyone Eats. 1997, Raintree LB $17.98 (978-0-8172-4760-7). 32pp. A tour of a pasta-producing facility and a guide to the various shapes of pasta highlight this account, which includes a few tasty recipes. (Rev: SLJ 7/97) [664]

23918 Reynolds, Jan. *Cycle of Rice, Cycle of Life: A Story of Sustainable Farming* (4–7). Illus. 2009, Lee & Low $19.95 (978-1-60060-254-2). 48pp. This photo essay describes Balinese rice farming and its importance to the community. (Rev: BL 6/1–15/09; SLJ 6/09) [633.1]

23919 Ridgewell, Jenny. *Fruit and Vegetables* (3–5). Series: Food in Focus. 1998, Heinemann LB $14.95 (978-1-57572-656-4). 32pp. A history of fruits and vegetables is given with material on their cultiva-

tion, food value, and processing as well as recipes and a few experiments. (Rev: SLJ 2/99) [634]

23920 Ridley, Sarah. *A Chocolate Bar* (3–5). Illus. Series: How It's Made. 2006, Gareth Stevens LB $24.00 (978-0-8368-6293-5). 32pp. This attractive volume traces the history of a chocolate bar from a cacao farm in Ghana to the factory in which the final product is made; suitable both for reports and browsing. (Rev: BL 4/1/06) [664]

23921 Robbins, Ken. *Food for Thought: The Stories Behind the Things We Eat* (2–4). Illus. by author. 2009, Roaring Brook $17.95 (978-1-59643-343-4). 48pp. A luscious compilation of facts and legends about the fruit and vegetables that we eat. (Rev: BCCB 5/09; BL 3/15/09; HB 5/09; LMC 8/09; SLJ 5/09) [641.3]

23922 Rotner, Shelley, and Gary Goss. *Where Does Food Come From?* (PS–2). Illus. 2006, Millbrook LB $22.60 (978-0-7613-2935-0). 32pp. The origins of the foods we eat — and the many varieties available — are presented in simple, informative text and color photographs. (Rev: BL 3/1/06; SLJ 5/06) [664]

23923 Royston, Angela. *How Is Chocolate Made?* (2–4). Illus. Series: How Are Things Made? 2005, Heinemann LB $24.21 (978-1-4034-6641-9). 32pp. Follows the chocolate manufacturing process from the harvesting of cacao beans to the delivery of the finished product to a retailer's shelves. (Rev: BL 9/15/05) [641.3]

23924 Swain, Ruth Freeman. *How Sweet It Is (and Was): The History of Candy* (1–3). Illus. by John O'Brien. 2003, Holiday House $16.95 (978-0-8234-1712-4). 32pp. This entertaining, illustrated history of sugary delights includes anecdoes, facts, a timeline, recipes, and a bibliography. (Rev: BL 10/15/03; HBG 4/04; SLJ 11/03)

23925 Thomas, Ann. *Dairy Products* (K–4). Series: Food. 2002, Chelsea Clubhouse LB $23.00 (978-0-7910-6980-6). 32pp. A simple introduction to milk (including goat and soy milks), cheese, yogurt, and other dairy products. Also use *Meat and Protein* and *Vegetables* (both 2002). (Rev: HBG 3/03; SLJ 2/03)

23926 Thomson, Ruth. *Rice* (3–5). Illus. by Prodeepta Das. Series: Threads. 1990, Garrett LB $15.93 (978-0-944483-71-8). 26pp. The story of rice, from its growth in paddies to its uses in many cultures. (Rev: BL 2/1/91; SLJ 5/91) [633.1]

23927 Wardlaw, Lee. *Bubblemania* (4–8). 1997, Simon & Schuster paper $4.99 (978-0-689-81719-9). A thorough history of chewing gum, including descriptions of how gum is made, marketed, and distributed. (Rev: BL 10/1/97; SLJ 1/98) [641.3]

23928 Wardlaw, Lee. *We All Scream for Ice Cream: The Scoop on America's Favorite Dessert* (4–7). Illus. by Sandra Forrest. 2000, HarperTrophy paper $4.95 (978-0-380-80250-0). 216pp. A history of this frozen dessert from ancient times to the present with a concentration on modern times and such variations as Eskimo pies and the Good Humor business. (Rev: SLJ 11/00) [637]

23929 *What Makes Popcorn Pop? First Questions and Answers About Food* (K–2). Series: Library of

First Questions and Answers. 1994, Time-Life $14.95 (978-0-7835-0862-7). 47pp. Cartoonlike illustrations help answer such questions about food as how potato chips are made and why Swiss cheese has holes. (Rev: SLJ 8/94) [641]

23930 Woods, Samuel G. *Chocolate: From Start to Finish* (3–5). Photos by Gale Zucker. Series: Made in the USA. 1999, Blackbirch LB $23.70 (978-1-56711-391-4). 32pp. An attractive book that takes the reader to a chocolate factory in Pennsylvania where they see the manufacturing process from raw material to finished product. (Rev: HBG 4/00; SLJ 2/00) [633.7]

FRUITS

23931 Anderson, Sara. *Fruit* (PS–1). Illus. by author. 2007, Handprint $8.95 (978-1-59354-188-0). A bright board-book introduction to various types of fruit. (Rev: SLJ 2/08)

23932 Cook, Deanna F. *Kids' Pumpkin Projects* (3–6). Illus. 1998, Williamson paper $8.95 (978-1-885593-21-4). 104pp. Discusses the planting and cultivating of pumpkins and contains craft and cooking ideas arranged by the seasons. (Rev: BL 10/15/98; SLJ 9/98) [745.5]

23933 Farmer, Jacqueline. *Apples* (3–5). Illus. by Phyllis L. Tildes. 2007, Charlesbridge $16.95 (978-1-57091-694-6); paper $6.95 (978-1-57091-695-3). 32pp. From pollination and grafting to apple juice and cider, this is an information-filled overview of apples. (Rev: BL 6/1–15/07; SLJ 9/07) [634]

23934 Farmer, Jacqueline. *Pumpkins!* (1–3). Illus. by Phyllis L. Tildes. 2004, Charlesbridge paper $6.95 (978-1-57091-558-1). 32pp. Facts about pumpkins are followed by instructions for cooking and carving them and interesting tidbits such as world pumpkin records. (Rev: BL 8/04; SLJ 7/04) [635]

23935 Frost, Helen. *The Fruit Group* (K–2). Series: Food Guide Pyramid. 2000, Capstone LB $17.26 (978-0-7368-0537-7). 24pp. This easy-to-read guide to good health through eating properly introduces the fruit group and gives examples. (Rev: HBG 9/00; SLJ 10/00) [634]

23936 Ganeri, Anita. *From Seed to Apple* (1–3). Illus. Series: How Living Things Grow. 2006, Heinemann LB $25.36 (978-1-4034-7862-7). 32pp. How a Red Delicious apple grows from a seed, presented in an easy-to-read format. (Rev: SLJ 6/06) [583]

23937 Gibbons, Gail. *Apples* (2–3). Illus. 2000, Holiday House $16.95 (978-0-8234-1497-0). 32pp. This introduction to apples includes information on their history, varieties, parts, and development from blossom to fruit. (Rev: BL 8/00; HBG 3/01; SLJ 9/00) [634]

23938 Gibbons, Gail. *The Berry Book* (PS–2). Illus. 2002, Holiday House $16.95 (978-0-8234-1697-4). 32pp. A well-illustrated introduction to North American berries, including a few simple recipes. (Rev: BL 3/1/02; HBG 10/02; SLJ 3/02) [634]

23939 Gibbons, Gail. *The Pumpkin Book* (K–3). Illus. 1999, Holiday House $17.95 (978-0-8234-1465-9). 32pp. After a discussion of how pumpkins grow and reproduce, the author explains their roles in Hal-

loween and Thanksgiving celebrations and gives some craft projects. (Rev: BL 9/1/99; HBG 4/00; SLJ 9/99) [635]

23940 Goldsen, Louise. *Fruit* (PS–2). Illus. by P. M. Valet. Series: First Discovery. 1991, Scholastic paper $12.95 (978-0-590-45233-5). Through the use of overlays, several kinds of fruit are depicted in various stages, such as the ripening of an apple. (Rev: SLJ 6/92) [641]

23941 Harris, Calvin. *Apple Harvest* (PS–2). Series: All About Fall. 2007, Capstone LB $19.93 (978-1-4296-0023-1). 24pp. With attractive illustrations, this book for beginning readers looks at growing, picking, and eating apples. (Rev: SLJ 4/08) [634]

23942 Hubbell, Will. *Apples Here!* (PS–1). Illus. 2002, Whitman $16.99 (978-0-8075-0397-3). 32pp. The life of apples, from buds to blossoms to fruit, is the subject of this informative book. (Rev: BL 10/15/02; HBG 3/03; SLJ 9/02) [634.11]

23943 Hughes, Meredith S. *Yes, We Have Bananas: Fruits from Shrubs and Vines* (5–8). Series: Plants We Eat. 1999, Lerner LB $26.60 (978-0-8225-2836-4). 80pp. A fascinating introduction to bananas, pineapples, grapes, berries, and melons with material on how and where they grow, their cultivation and marketing, plus fun recipes and activities. (Rev: BL 11/15/99; HBG 3/00; SLJ 3/00) [641]

23944 Johnson, Sylvia A. *Apple Trees* (5–8). Illus. by Hiro Koike. 1983, Lerner LB $31.95 (978-0-8225-1479-4). 48pp. The story of the apple tree and seed and fruit formation.

23945 Landau, Elaine. *Apples* (2–4). Illus. Series: True Books. 1999, Children's Book Pr. LB $25.00 (978-0-516-21024-7). 48pp. This book gives a history of apples, shows how they grow, introduces different species, and supplies a few simple recipes. (Rev: BL 10/15/99) [634]

23946 Levenson, George. *Pumpkin Circle: The Story of a Garden* (PS–3). Illus. 1999, Tricycle $15.95 (978-1-58246-004-8). 40pp. This book, illustrated with excellent photographs, traces the life cycle of a pumpkin from seed to a mature plant that produces more seeds. (Rev: BL 10/15/99; HB 11/99; HBG 4/00; SLJ 10/99) [635]

23947 Maestro, Betsy. *How Do Apples Grow?* (5–8). Illus. by Giulio Maestro. Series: Let's-Read-and-Find-Out. 1992, HarperCollins LB $16.89 (978-0-06-020056-5). 32pp. The development of the apple from bud to fruit. (Rev: BL 12/15/91; HB 1/92; SLJ 2/92) [582]

23948 Pfeffer, Wendy. *From Seed to Pumpkin* (PS–2). Illus. by James G. Hale. Series: Let's-Read-and-Find-Out Science. 2004, HarperCollins LB $5.99 (978-0-06-445190-1); paper $17.89 (978-0-06-028039-0). 40pp. Children watch a pumpkin grow from seed to maturity; two activities round out this volume for beginning readers. (Rev: BL 10/1/04; SLJ 10/04) [583]

23949 Powell, Jillian. *Fruit* (1–4). Illus. Series: Everyone Eats. 1997, Raintree LB $17.98 (978-0-8172-4765-2). 32pp. Describes how fruit are grown, and some of the varieties, legends, and traditional customs surrounding them, with a few tasty recipes. (Rev: SLJ 7/97) [634]

23950 Robbins, Ken. *Pumpkins* (PS–2). 2006, Roaring Brook $14.95 (978-1-59643-184-3). 32pp. Full of dramatic color photographs, this celebration of the pumpkin traces its growing cycle and offers step-by-step instructions for carving a jack-o'-lantern. (Rev: BL 9/1/06; SLJ 8/06) [635]

23951 Robinson, Fay. *We Love Fruit!* (1–2). Illus. Series: Rookie Readers. 1992, Children's Book Pr. LB $20.50 (978-0-516-06006-4). 32pp. Various kinds of fruit are pictured in color photos and identified in a simple text. An oversized edition of this title is available. (Rev: BL 12/15/92; SLJ 2/93) [641.3]

23952 Smucker, Anna Egan. *Golden Delicious: A Cinderella Apple Story* (1–3). Illus. by Kathleen Kemly. 2008, Albert Whitman $16.99 (978-0-8075-2987-4). 32pp. A hundred years ago, the Stark brothers dreamed of cultivating the perfect apple and this is the delicious true story of how they did it. (Rev: BL 8/08) [634.11]

23953 Watts, Barrie. *Pumpkin* (K–3). Illus. 2002, Smart Apple LB $24.25 (978-1-58340-199-6). 32pp. This easy-to-read book about pumpkins includes lots of facts and excellent photography. Also use *Bean* (2002). (Rev: BL 10/15/02; HBG 3/03; SLJ 2/03) [635]

23954 Weiss, Ellen. *From Pit to Peach Tree* (1–2). Series: Scholastic News Nonfiction Reader. 2007, Children's Pr. LB $20.00 (978-0-531-18538-4); paper $6.95 (978-0-531-18791-3). 24pp. For beginning readers, this is an easy-to-follow explanation of how peaches grow. (Rev: SLJ 12/07) [634]

NUTRITION

23955 Inglis, Jane. *Fiber* (4–6). Illus. Series: Food Facts. 1993, Carolrhoda LB $19.93 (978-0-87614-793-1). 32pp. This nutrition book focuses on the natural fiber the body needs and how to obtain it. (Rev: BL 11/15/93; SLJ 10/93) [613.2]

23956 Nottridge, Rhoda. *Additives* (4–6). Illus. Series: Food Facts. 1993, Carolrhoda LB $19.93 (978-0-87614-794-8). 32pp. The value of such food additives as preservatives and flavorings is discussed, with an analysis of their possible harmful effects. (Rev: BL 11/15/93; SLJ 10/93) [664]

23957 Nottridge, Rhoda. *Fats* (4–6). Illus. Series: Food Facts. 1993, Lerner LB $19.93 (978-0-87614-779-5). 32pp. Introduces saturated and unsaturated fats and tells how much should be consumed in the daily diet. (Rev: BL 11/15/93; SLJ 10/93) [613.2]

23958 Nottridge, Rhoda. *Vitamins* (3–6). Illus. Series: Food Facts. 1993, Carolrhoda LB $14.95 (978-0-87614-795-5). 32pp. This book introduces the classification of vitamins, where they are found, their properties and uses, and some experiments and recipes connected with vitamins. (Rev: SLJ 10/93) [613.2]

23959 Roth, Ruby. *That's Why We Don't Eat Animals: A Book About Vegans, Vegetarians, and All Living Things* (3–6). Illus. by author. 2009, North Atlantic $16.95 (978-1-55643-785-4). 48pp. Roth describes animals' lives in factory farms, and compares this with their lives in the wild in this affecting introduction vegetarianism and veganism. (Rev: BL 4/15/09) [641.5]

VEGETABLES

23960 Aliki. *Corn Is Maize: The Gift of the Indians* (2–4). Illus. by author. 1976, HarperCollins LB $15.89 (978-0-690-00975-0); paper $5.99 (978-0-06-445026-3). 40pp. A simply written, comprehensive treatment of corn, its origins, how it is husbanded and harvested, and its many uses.

23961 Anderson, Sara. *Vegetables* (PS–1). Illus. by author. 2007, Handprint $8.95 (978-1-59354-189-7). A bright board-book introduction to various types of vegetables. (Rev: SLJ 2/08)

23962 De Bourgoing, Pascale. *Vegetables in the Garden* (PS–3). Illus. by Gilbert Houbre. Series: First Discovery. 1994, Scholastic $11.95 (978-0-590-48326-1). 24pp. In this well-illustrated interactive book, small children learn about gardens and different kinds of vegetables and how they grow. (Rev: BL 11/15/94) [635]

23963 Fowler, Allan. *Taking Root* (1–2). Series: Rookie Readers. 2000, Children's Book Pr. LB $20.50 (978-0-516-21591-4). 32pp. This simple science book introduces taproots that we eat including carrots, beets, and radishes. (Rev: BL 4/15/00) [641.6]

23964 Gibbons, Gail. *Corn* (K–3). Illus. by author. 2008, Holiday $16.95 (978-0-8234-2169-5). 32pp. From the ancient Mayans and the Pilgrims to today's multiple uses of corn, this is a clearly written overview. (Rev: BL 11/15/08; SLJ 10/08) [633.1]

23965 Hughes, Meredith S. *Cool as a Cucumber, Hot as a Pepper* (5–8). Series: Foods We Eat. 1999, Lerner LB $26.60 (978-0-8225-2832-6). This lively book on vegetables gives botanical information, details on growing and harvesting, the history of many of these plants, and a number of mouth-watering recipes. (Rev: BL 7/99; HBG 10/99; SLJ 8/99) [635]

23966 Hughes, Meredith S. *Spill the Beans and Pass the Peanuts: Legumes* (5–8). Series: Plants We Eat. 1999, Lerner LB $31.95 (978-0-8225-2834-0). 80pp. Peas and beans are two of the legumes introduced in this book that explains, in an entertaining way, their origins, how they grow, their appearance, and nutritional value, plus giving the occasional recipe or activity. (Rev: BL 10/15/99; HBG 3/00; SLJ 12/99) [641.6]

23967 Hughes, Meredith S. *Stinky and Stringy* (5–8). Series: Plants We Eat. 1999, Lerner LB $31.95 (978-0-8225-2833-3). 88pp. Stem and bulb vegetables onions and garlic are introduced with interesting historical information, details about their cultivation, harvesting and marketing, and a few tempting recipes. (Rev: BL 7/99; HBG 10/99; SLJ 8/99) [635]

23968 Hughes, Meredith S., and E. Thomas Hughes. *Buried Treasure: Roots and Tubers* (4–7). Series: Plants We Eat. 1998, Lerner LB $26.60 (978-0-

8225-2830-2). 96pp. Covering such vegetables as potatoes, sweet potatoes, carrots, turnips, beets, and radishes, this account describes the origin, history, cultivation, and importance of each. (Rev: HBG 3/99; SLJ 4/99) [635]

23969 Kudlinski, Kathleen V. *Popcorn Plants* (2–3). Series: Early Bird Nature Books. 1998, Lerner $25.26 (978-0-8225-3014-5). 48pp. The life cycle of the popcorn plant is traced in excellent photos and simple text. (Rev: BL 10/15/98; HBG 3/99; SLJ 1/99) [633.1]

23970 Landau, Elaine. *Corn* (2–4). Illus. 1999, Children's Book Pr. LB $25.00 (978-0-516-21026-1). 48pp. A history of corn is accompanied by descriptions of different species and how they grow plus a few simple tasty recipes. (Rev: BL 10/15/99) [633.1]

23971 Nelson, Robin. *From Kernel to Corn* (PS–2). Illus. Series: Start to Finish. 2003, Lerner $18.60 (978-0-8225-4659-7). 24pp. This small, colorful picture book uses simple language to describe corn's progress from initial planting to delivery to market. (Rev: BL 4/15/03; HBG 10/03; SLJ 7/03) [633.1]

23972 Robinson, Fay. *Vegetables, Vegetables!* (1–2). Illus. Series: Rookie Readers. 1994, Children's Book Pr. LB $20.50 (978-0-516-06030-9). 32pp. An easily read book that introduces various vegetables and shows ways in which they are prepared as food. (Rev: BL 4/15/95) [635]

23973 Weiss, Ellen. *From Eye to Potato* (1–2). Series: Scholastic News Nonfiction Reader. 2007, Children's Pr. LB $20.00 (978-0-531-18535-3); paper $6.95 (978-0-531-18788-3). 24pp. For beginning readers, this is an easy-to-follow explanation of how potatoes grow. (Rev: SLJ 12/07) [635]

Fungi

23974 Royston, Angela. *Life Cycle of a Mushroom* (PS–3). Series: Life Cycle. 2000, Heinemann LB $21.36 (978-1-57572-210-8). 32pp. Using a color photo and four or five lines of text on each page, this book describes different mushrooms and gives their basic life cycle. (Rev: BL 5/15/00; HBG 3/01) [589.2]

23975 Tesar, Jenny. *Fungi* (5–7). Illus. Series: Our Living World. 1994, Blackbirch LB $24.95 (978-1-56711-044-9). 64pp. A volume that explains what a fungus is, how the various types reproduce and grow, their unique characteristics, and how they fit into food webs and chains. (Rev: BL 12/1/94) [589.2]

Leaves and Trees

23976 Brenner, Barbara. *One Small Place in a Tree* (2–4). Illus. by Tom Leonard. 2004, HarperCollins $16.99 (978-0-688-17180-3). 32pp. The abundant life found in a single tree is captured in easy-to-understand narrative and realistic artwork. (Rev: BL 3/1/04; SLJ 4/04) [577.3]

23977 Bulla, Clyde Robert. *A Tree Is a Plant* (PS–1). Illus. by Stacey Schuett. Series: Let's-Read-and-Find-Out Science. 2001, HarperCollins LB $5.99 (978-0-06-445196-3); paper $15.89 (978-0-06-028172-4). 34pp. Vivid paintings grace this new version of the book first published in 1960 that portrays the life cycle of an apple tree and discusses how the different parts of a tree work. (Rev: BL 12/15/01; HBG 10/02; SLJ 11/01) [583]

23978 Cassie, Brian. *National Audubon Society First Field Guide: Trees* (4–8). 1999, Scholastic $17.95 (978-0-590-05472-0); paper $8.95 (978-0-590-05490-4). After a general, illustrated introduction to the characteristics and types of North American trees, this field guide then categorizes the trees according to the shape of their leaves. (Rev: BL 3/15/99; SLJ 7/99) [582.16]

23979 Dorros, Arthur. *A Tree Is Growing* (2–4). Illus. by S. D. Schindler. 1997, Scholastic $15.95 (978-0-590-45300-4). 32pp. In double-page spreads, various types of trees and leaves are introduced, with material on how trees grow. (Rev: BCCB 6/97; BL 2/1/97; SLJ 3/97) [582.16]

23980 Farndon, John. *Leaves* (2–5). Illus. 2006, Gale LB $23.70 (978-1-4103-0422-3). 24pp. Diagrams and photographs supplement the clear text describing leaves and the role they play in the overall life of the plant. (Rev: SLJ 2/07)

23981 Fischer-Nagel, Heiderose, and Andreas Fischer-Nagel. *Fir Trees* (3–6). Illus. Series: Nature Watch. 1989, Carolrhoda LB $19.93 (978-0-87614-340-7). 48pp. The development and growth of the conifers. (Rev: BL 10/15/89; SLJ 1/90) [585.2]

23982 Fleisher, Paul. *Oak Tree* (3–5). Illus. Series: Webs of Life. 1997, Marshall Cavendish LB $22.79 (978-0-7614-0434-7). 40pp. Describes an Eastern deciduous forest and the plant and animal life that surrounds an oak tree. (Rev: BL 2/15/98; HBG 3/98) [583]

23983 Fowler, Allan. *Maple Trees* (1–2). Series: Rookie Read-About Science. 2001, Children's Book Pr. LB $20.50 (978-0-516-21684-3). 32pp. For beginning readers, a simple text with color illustrations introduces trees, their varieties, parts, and growth cycles. (Rev: BL 1/1–15/02) [582.16]

23984 Gardner, Robert, and David Webster. *Science Project Ideas About Trees* (5–8). Illus. Series: Science Project Ideas. 1997, Enslow LB $25.26 (978-0-89490-846-0). The parts of trees and their functions are described, with activities involving leaves, seeds, flowers, roots, and twigs. (Rev: BL 12/1/97; HBG 3/98; SLJ 2/98) [582.16]

23985 Gerber, Carole. *Leaf Jumpers* (PS–1). Illus. by Leslie Evans. 2004, Charlesbridge $15.95 (978-1-57091-497-3). 32pp. The leaves of eight common trees — including the red maple, birch, and ginkgo — are introduced in simple, lyrical text and striking autumnal colors. (Rev: BL 9/1/04; SLJ 8/04) [575.5]

23986 Gerber, Carole. *Winter Trees* (PS–2). Illus. by Leslie Evans. 2008, Charlesbridge $15.95 (978-1-58089-168-4). 32pp. A little boy and his dog appreciate the beauty of bare trees in the snow in this beautifully illustrated book that melds fact and poetry. (Rev: BL 7/08) [582.16]

23987 Gibbons, Gail. *Tell Me, Tree: All About Trees for Kids* (PS–3). Illus. 2002, Little, Brown $15.95 (978-0-316-30903-5). 32pp. An oversize basic guide that introduces different kinds of trees, and explains their parts and how each operates. (Rev: BL 4/1/02; HB 7/02; HBG 10/02; SLJ 3/02) [582.16]

23988 Godwin, Sam. *From Little Acorns: A First Look at the Life Cycle of a Tree* (K–1). Illus. by Simone Abel. Series: First Look : Science. 2004, Picture Window LB $25.26 (978-1-4048-0658-0). 32pp. In simple language with cartoon-style illustrations, a mother squirrel and her babies discuss how an oak tree grows. (Rev: BL 10/15/04; SLJ 3/05) [571.8]

23989 Guillain, Charlotte. *Leaves* (PS–K). Illus. Series: Spot the Difference. 2008, Heinemann LB $14.50 (978-1-4329-0944-4). 24pp. Basic facts about leaves are presented attractively in this small, horizontal book. (Rev: BL 4/1/08; LMC 10/08) [581.4]

23990 Hickman, Pamela. *Tree Book* (3–5). Illus. 1999, Kids Can $12.95 (978-1-55074-485-9). 32pp. An introduction to trees, how they grow and reproduce, and their parts, plus a few related activities and projects. (Rev: BL 2/1/99; HBG 9/99) [582.16]

23991 Holmes, Bonnie. *Quaking Aspen* (2–4). Series: Nature Watch. 1999, Carolrhoda $25.26 (978-1-57505-351-6). 48pp. This illustrated book about the aspen tree includes material on its location, characteristics, ecology, and possible future endangerments. (Rev: BL 10/1/99; HBG 4/00) [583]

23992 Johnson, Sylvia A. *How Leaves Change* (3–5). Illus. 1986, Lerner LB $22.60 (978-0-8225-1483-1); paper $5.95 (978-0-8225-9513-7). 48pp. Explains how and why leaves change color in the fall. (Rev: BCCB 4/87; BL 1/15/87; SLJ 3/87)

23993 Jorgensen, Lisa. *Grand Trees of America: Our State and Champion Trees* (4–7). Illus. 1992, Roberts paper $8.95 (978-1-879373-15-0). 120pp. This book describes the official tree of each state and introduces the National Register of Big Trees. (Rev: BL 2/15/93) [582.16]

23994 Lauber, Patricia. *Be a Friend to Trees* (2–4). Illus. by Holly Keller. Series: Let's-Read-and-Find-Out. 1994, HarperCollins LB $15.89 (978-0-06-021529-3). 32pp. The many uses of trees — such as providing homes for birds and supplying wood for construction — are outlined, with material on trees' structure, parts, and how their leaves make food. (Rev: BCCB 1/94; BL 6/1–15/94; SLJ 3/94) [582.16]

23995 Llewellyn, Claire. *Tree* (K–3). Illus. by Simon Mendez. 2004, NorthWord $16.95 (978-1-55971-879-0). 32pp. An innovative picture-book layout chronicles the life cycle of an apple tree, tracing its progress from seedling to a mature, fruit-bearing adult. (Rev: BL 4/15/04; SLJ 11/04) [634]

23996 Maestro, Betsy. *Why Do Leaves Change Color?* (K–4). Illus. by Loretta Krupinski. Series: Let's-Read-and-Find-Out. 1994, HarperCollins LB $15.89 (978-0-06-022874-3). 32pp. This book explains the process that causes leaf color change in

the autumn and why leaves fall from the trees. (Rev: BCCB 11/94; BL 11/15/94; SLJ 7/95) [582.16]

23997 Miller, Debbie S. *Are Trees Alive?* (K–3). Illus. by Stacey Schuett. 2002, Walker LB $17.85 (978-0-8027-8802-3). 32pp. This colorful picture book explains how trees live and survive in different environments. (Rev: BL 6/1–15/02; HBG 10/02; SLJ 5/02) [582.16]

23998 Morrison, Gordon. *Oak Tree* (4–6). Illus. 2000, Houghton $16.00 (978-0-395-95644-1). 32pp. A year in the life of an oak tree is described in this appealing account that uses a picture-book format. (Rev: BL 3/1/00; HBG 9/00; SLJ 6/00) [583]

23999 Pascoe, Elaine. *The Ecosystem of a Fallen Tree* (3–5). Photos by Dwight Kuhn. Series: The Library of Small Ecosystems. 2003, Rosen LB $22.50 (978-0-8239-6308-9). 32pp. In this photo-filled overview of the plant and animal life that can be sustained in the remains of a downed tree, students will learn that ecosystems come in all sizes. (Rev: SLJ 11/03) [577]

24000 Pascoe, Elaine. *The Ecosystem of an Apple Tree* (3–5). Photos by Dwight Kuhn. Series: The Library of Small Ecosystems. 2003, Rosen LB $22.50 (978-0-8239-6304-1). 32pp. An overview of the animal and plant life associated with the apple tree. (Rev: SLJ 11/03) [577]

24001 Pascoe, Elaine. *Leaves and Trees* (4–7). Series: Nature Close-Up. 2001, Blackbirch LB $23.70 (978-1-56711-474-4). 32pp. Easy projects and a simple text are used to introduce the nature of trees and leaves and the living processes involved. (Rev: BL 9/15/01; HBG 3/02) [582.16]

24002 Patent, Dorothy Hinshaw. *Apple Trees* (2–3). Series: Early Bird Nature Books. 1998, Lerner LB $23.93 (978-0-8225-3020-6). 48pp. An easily read introduction to the apple tree and its life cycle, told in a simple text with attractive color photographs. (Rev: BL 3/15/98; HBG 9/98; SLJ 4/98) [582.16]

24003 Pfeffer, Wendy. *A Log's Life* (K–3). Illus. by Robin Brickman. 1997, Simon & Schuster paper $16.00 (978-0-689-80636-0). 32pp. The life cycle of an oak tree and its many roles in the forest ecology. (Rev: BL 9/15/97; HBG 3/98; SLJ 9/97) [574.5]

24004 Reed-Jones, Carol. *The Tree in the Ancient Forest* (K–3). Illus. by Christopher Canyon. 1995, Dawn $16.95 (978-1-883220-32-7); paper $7.95 (978-1-883220-31-0). 32pp. The food cycle of interdependence that involves both plants and animals and a 300-year-old fir tree is the subject of this stunning picture book. (Rev: BL 7/95; SLJ 9/95) [574]

24005 Royston, Angela. *Life Cycle of an Oak Tree* (PS–3). Series: Life Cycle. 2000, Heinemann LB $21.36 (978-1-57572-211-5). 32pp. From acorn to giant oak, this book describes the life cycle of an oak tree using a few lines of text and a color photo on each page. (Rev: BL 5/15/00; HBG 3/01) [583]

24006 Souza, D. M. *Wacky Trees* (3–6). Series: Watts Library. 2003, Watts LB $25.50 (978-0-531-12210-5). 63pp. The oddities of the tree world, including such giants as the sequoia and the baobab, are examined in this illustrated work. (Rev: SLJ 4/04) [582.16]

24007 Spicer, Maggee, and Richard Thompson. *We'll All Go Exploring* (PS–1). Illus. by Kim LaFave. 2003, Fitzhenry & Whiteside $16.95 (978-1-55041-732-6). 36pp. Three young explorers find out about different kinds of trees and the wildlife found near them in this lively rhyming-text picture book. (Rev: BL 5/1/03; SLJ 5/03) [811]

24008 Vieira, Linda. *The Ever-Living Tree: The Life and Times of a Coast Redwood* (2–5). Illus. by Christopher Canyon. 1994, Walker LB $15.85 (978-0-8027-8278-6). 32pp. The life of a 2,000-year-old redwood, with details of some important events that occurred during its life. (Rev: BL 3/1/94; SLJ 5/94) [584]

24009 Wadsworth, Ginger. *Giant Sequoia Trees* (2–4). Photos by Frank Staub. Series: Early Bird Nature Books. 1995, Lerner LB $25.26 (978-0-8225-3001-5). 48pp. A photo-essay about the world's largest tree, the sequoia, with details on its parts, environment, and life cycle. (Rev: SLJ 10/95) [582]

24010 Zim, Herbert S., and Alexander C. Martin. *Trees* (5–8). Illus. 1991, Western paper $21.27 (978-0-307-64056-7). 160pp. A small, handy volume packed with information and color illustrations that help identify our most important trees. [582.16]

Plants

24011 Aaseng, Nathan. *Meat-Eating Plants* (3–6). Illus. Series: Weird and Wacky Science. 1996, Enslow LB $23.93 (978-0-89490-617-6). 48pp. Such plants as bladderworts, sundews, pitcher plants, and Venus's-flytraps are described, along with their methods of obtaining food. (Rev: SLJ 5/96) [581.5]

24012 *Atlas of Plants* (1–3). Illus. by Sylvaine Perols. Series: First Discovery Atlases. 1996, Scholastic $12.95 (978-0-590-58113-4). Using extensive captions and maps, this atlas tells where plants come from. (Rev: SLJ 9/96) [581.5]

24013 Bash, Barbara. *Desert Giant: The World of the Saguaro Cactus* (3–6). Illus. 1989, Little, Brown paper $5.95 (978-0-685-33583-3). 32pp. The Tohono O'odham Indians — the Desert People — gather the fruit of the saguaro in a centuries-old harvest ritual. (Rev: BL 3/15/89; HB 3/89)

24014 Farndon, John. *Roots* (2–5). Illus. 2006, Gale LB $23.70 (978-1-4103-0421-6). 24pp. Diagrams and photographs supplement the clear text describing roots and the role they play in the overall life of the plant. Also use *Stems* (2006). (Rev: SLJ 2/07)

24015 Godwin, Sam. *A Seed in Need: A First Look at the Plant Cycle* (K–1). Illus. Series: First Look: Science. 2004, Picture Window LB $25.26 (978-1-4048-0920-8). 32pp. In simple language with cartoon-style illustrations, this volume describes the life cycle of plants.

24016 Goodman, Emily. *Plant Secrets* (PS–2). Illus. by Phyllis L. Tildes. 2009, Charlesbridge $16.95 (978-1-58089-204-9). 40pp. Goodman explores the life cycles of four plants — the rose, the oak, the pea, and the tomato — identifying "secrets" at key stages of development (seed, plant, flower, and fruit). (Rev: BCCB 4/09; BL 3/15/09; SLJ 3/09) [580]

24017 Goodman, Susan E. *Seeds, Stems, and Stamens: The Ways Plants Fit into Their World* (2–4). Illus. by Michael Doolittle. 2001, Millbrook LB $22.90 (978-0-7613-1874-3). 48pp. A clear look at how plants adapt to their environments, with stunning photographs and questions to stimulate investigation. (Rev: BL 9/15/01; HBG 3/02; SLJ 11/01) [581.4]

24018 Guiberson, Brenda Z. *Cactus Hotel* (PS–3). Illus. by Megan Lloyd. 1991, Holt $16.95 (978-0-8050-1333-7). 32pp. The life cycle of the giant saguaro cactus. (Rev: BL 6/15/91; SLJ 7/91) [574.5]

24019 Halfmann, Janet. *Plant Tricksters* (3–6). Series: Watts Library. 2003, Watts LB $25.50 (978-0-531-12278-5); paper $8.95 (978-0-531-16371-9). 63pp. With plenty of close-up photographs, this is a study of the unusual mechanisms by which some plants survive — from being unusually smelly to trying to fool the eye. (Rev: SLJ 4/04) [581.4]

24020 Hickman, Pamela. *Starting with Nature Plant Book* (2–4). Illus. by Heather Collins. Series: Starting with Nature. 2000, Kids Can $12.95 (978-1-55074-483-5); paper $5.95 (978-1-55074-812-3). 32pp. This introductory account describes groups of plants and plant parts and gives material on state flowers, endangered plants, and outlines of several related activities. (Rev: HBG 9/00; SLJ 7/00) [581]

24021 Kalman, Bobbie. *How a Plant Grows* (3–5). Illus. by Barbara Bedell. Series: Crabapples. 1996, Crabtree paper $5.95 (978-0-86505-728-9). 32pp. An introduction to plants that covers topics like structure, photosynthesis, pollination, carnivorous plants, and the importance of plants in the food chain. (Rev: SLJ 7/97) [581.5]

24022 Kite, L. Patricia. *Dandelion Adventures* (PS–2). Illus. by Anca Hariton. 1998, Millbrook $21.90 (978-0-7613-0037-3); paper $6.95 (978-0-7613-0377-0). 32pp. This appealing picture book describing the life cycle of a dandelion begins with the landing of seed parachutes and ending with new plants producing their own flowers and seeds. (Rev: BL 3/15/98; HBG 3/99; SLJ 7/98) [583]

24023 Kudlinski, Kathleen V. *Dandelions* (2–3). Series: Early Bird Nature Books. 1999, Lerner LB $25.26 (978-0-8225-3016-9). 48pp. This attractive account, suitable for beginning readers, describes the characteristics of a dandelion and outlines its life cycle. (Rev: BL 10/15/99; HBG 4/00; SLJ 1/00) [583]

24024 Kudlinski, Kathleen V. *Venus Flytraps* (2–5). Illus. Series: Early Bird Nature Books. 1998, Lerner LB $25.26 (978-0-8225-3015-2). 48pp. This photo-essay uses amazing color photos and a simple text to describe the habitats of the Venus's-flytrap and how and why it kills insects. (Rev: BL 12/1/98; HBG 3/99; SLJ 3/99) [583]

24025 Llamas, Andreu. *Plants Under the Sea* (4–6). Illus. by Luis Rizo. Series: Incredible World of Plants. 1996, Chelsea LB $17.55 (978-0-7910-3468-2). 32pp. Familiar and less common ocean plants are described and pictured, along with their relation to aquatic animal life. Also use *The Vegetation of Rivers, Lakes, and Swamps* (1996). (Rev: SLJ 7/96) [581]

24026 Lucht, Irmgard. *The Red Poppy* (K–3). Trans. by Frank Jacoby-Nelson. Illus. 1995, Hyperion LB $14.49 (978-0-7868-2043-6). 32pp. A year in the life of a poppy plant is explored in this large-format picture book. (Rev: BCCB 6/95; BL 4/1/95; SLJ 6/95*) [583]

24027 Overbeck, Cynthia. *Cactus* (3–6). Illus. by Shabo Hans. 1982, Lerner paper $5.95 (978-0-8225-9556-4). 48pp. A description of the cactus and how it lives.

24028 Pascoe, Elaine. *The Ecosystem of a Milkweed Patch* (3–5). Photos by Dwight Kuhn. Series: The Library of Small Ecosystems. 2003, Rosen LB $22.50 (978-0-8239-6309-6). 32pp. Introduces the animals and plants that live within a milkweed patch and also to the ways in which they interact. (Rev: SLJ 11/03) [577.4]

24029 Penny, Malcolm. *How Plants Grow* (3–5). Illus. by Stuart Lafford. Series: Nature's Mysteries. 1996, Benchmark LB $22.79 (978-0-7614-0452-1). 32pp. Topics like flowering, pollination, seed production, and growth are covered in this elementary book about plants. (Rev: SLJ 2/97) [581.5]

24030 *Plants* (K–4). Series: Starting with Science. 1998, Kids Can LB $10.95 (978-1-55074-193-3). 32pp. Thirteen safe and simple experiments with plants, such as creating "super soil," are presented in this beginning science activity book. (Rev: BL 5/15/98; HBG 9/98; SLJ 5/98) [581]

24031 Posada, Mia. *Dandelions: Stars in the Grass* (PS–2). Illus. by author. 2000, Carolrhoda LB $15.95 (978-1-57505-383-7). The life cycle of a dandelion is covered in bright acrylic illustrations and a text that includes unusual facts and a recipe for dandelion salad. (Rev: HBG 9/00; SLJ 5/00) [581]

24032 Royston, Angela. *Flowers, Fruits, and Seeds* (K–3). Series: Heinemann First Library. 1999, Heinemann LB $21.36 (978-1-57572-822-3). 32pp. Through color photos and a brief text, this book introduces the life cycle of various fruits from pollination of flowers through development of the fruit and production of seeds. Also use the companion book by the same author, *How Plants Grow*. (Rev: BL 6/1–15/99; SLJ 1/00) [634]

24033 Royston, Angela. *Life Cycle of a Bean* (2–3). Illus. Series: Life Cycle. 1998, Heinemann $21.36 (978-1-57572-612-0). 32pp. Using a colorful photograph and a timeline on each page, this book describes the stages in the maturation of a bean plant and its eventual production of a new seed. (Rev: BL 4/15/98; SLJ 7/98) [583]

24034 Royston, Angela. *Plants and Us* (K–3). Series: Heinemann First Library. 1999, Heinemann LB $21.36 (978-1-57572-825-4). 32pp. Attractive illustrations and a short text are used to explain the relationship between plants and humankind, with material on plants' various uses in everyday life.

Also use *Strange Plants* by the same author. (Rev: BL 6/1–15/99) [581]

24035 Silverstein, Alvin, et al. *Plants* (3–6). Illus. Series: Kingdoms of Life. 1996, Twenty-First Century LB $21.40 (978-0-8050-3519-3). 64pp. Scientific classification of life on earth is explained, focusing on the world of plants and its diversity. (Rev: BL 6/1–15/96; SLJ 7/96) [581]

24036 Souza, D. M. *Plant Invaders* (3–6). Series: Watts Library. 2003, Watts LB $25.50 (978-0-531-12211-2). 63pp. An illustrated look at invasive plants, such as kudzu, that spread widely and pose a significant threat to the ecosystem. (Rev: SLJ 4/04) [581.6]

24037 VanCleave, Janice. *Janice VanCleave's Plants: Mind-Boggling Experiments You Can Turn into Science Fair Projects* (3–7). Illus. 1997, Wiley paper $10.95 (978-0-471-14687-2). 96pp. Twenty projects and experiments involving plants, their parts, and their growth cycles are presented with clear, easy-to-follow instructions. (Rev: BL 2/15/97; SLJ 3/97) [581]

24038 Wade, Mary Dodson. *Plants Live Everywhere!* (K–2). 2009, Enslow LB $21.26 (978-0-7660-3155-5). 24pp. Using a question-and-answer format, this book provides a simple explanation of plant habitats of all kinds, with color photographs and an activity. Also use *People Need Plants* and *Plants Grow!* (both 2009). (Rev: SLJ 4/09)

24039 Wexler, Jerome. *Queen Anne's Lace* (3–6). Illus. 1994, Whitman LB $16.99 (978-0-8075-6710-4). 32pp. An examination of this common weed, exploring its structure, roots, seeds, and flowers. (Rev: BCCB 6/94; BL 4/15/94; SLJ 6/94) [583]

Seeds

24040 Aston, Dianna. *A Seed Is Sleepy* (PS–2). Illus. by Sylvia Long. 2007, Chronicle $16.95 (978-0-8118-5520-4). 32pp. Using poetic text and lush watercolors, this picture book explores the mysteries of seeds and how they are transformed into colorful plants and flowers of very varying sizes. (Rev: BL 3/15/07) [581.4]

24041 Burns, Diane L. *Berries, Nuts and Seeds* (4–7). Illus. by John F. McGee. 1996, NorthWord paper $7.95 (978-1-55971-573-7). 42pp. Each page in this guide is devoted to a description of a single berry, nut, or seed. (Rev: BL 2/15/97) [582.13]

24042 Farndon, John. *Seeds* (2–5). Illus. 2006, Gale LB $23.70 (978-1-4103-0419-3). 24pp. Diagrams and photographs supplement the clear text describing seeds and the role they play in the overall life of the plant. (Rev: SLJ 2/07)

24043 Gibbons, Gail. *From Seed to Plant* (PS–3). Illus. 1991, Holiday House LB $16.95 (978-0-8234-0872-6). 32pp. How seeds grow into plants and how flowering plants produce seeds. (Rev: BL 3/1/91; HB 7/91; SLJ 7/91) [581.3]

24044 Jordan, Helene J. *How a Seed Grows* (3–6). Illus. by Loretta Krupinski. Series: Let's-Read-and-Find-Out. 1992, HarperCollins LB $15.89 (978-0-06-020185-2); paper $5.99 (978-0-06-445107-9).

32pp. A boy and a girl plant seeds and watch them grow. (Rev: BL 8/92; SLJ 7/92) [582]

24045 MacKen, JoAnn Early. *Flip, Float, Fly: Seeds on the Move* (K–3). Illus. by Pam Paparone. 2008, Holiday $16.95 (978-0-8234-2043-8). 32pp. Seeds of all kinds are shown benefiting from their abilities to float, roll, stick to clothing, drift on water, and so forth. (Rev: BL 4/15/08; LMC 11/08; SLJ 5/08) [581.4]

24046 Pascoe, Elaine. *Plants with Seeds* (2–5). Photos by Dwight Kuhn. Series: A Kid's Guide to the Classification of Living Things. 2003, Rosen LB $22.50 (978-0-8239-6314-0). 32pp. A richly illustrated, slim guide to plants that use seeds to repro-duce, with color photographs and a useful glossary. Also use *Plants Without Seeds* (2003). (Rev: SLJ 7/03) [580]

24047 Richards, Jean. *A Fruit Is a Suitcase for Seeds* (PS–2). Illus. by Anca Hariton. 2002, Millbrook LB $21.90 (978-0-7613-1622-0). 32pp. An accessible and very visual introduction to seeds and how they are dispersed. (Rev: HBG 10/02; SLJ 5/02) [581.467]

24048 Wade, Mary Dodson. *Seeds Sprout!* (K–2). 2009, Enslow LB $21.26 (978-0-7660-3154-8). 24pp. Using a question-and-answer format, this book provides a simple explanation of seeds and how they create plants, with color photographs and an activity. (Rev: SLJ 4/09) [581.4]

24049 Angliss, Sarah. *Gold* (4–8). Series: The Elements. 1999, Marshall Cavendish LB $25.64 (978-0-7614-0887-1). 32pp. Easy-to-follow diagrams, fact boxes, and color illustrations accompany an informative text that introduces gold, where it is mined and processed, its properties, value, and uses. (Rev: BL 2/15/00; HBG 10/00) [546]

24050 Baxter, Roberta. *Chemical Reaction* (4–8). Illus. Series: The Kidhaven Science Library. 2004, Gale LB $26.20 (978-0-7377-2072-3). 48pp. Clear, concise text, supported by full-color photographs and diagrams, describes many types of reactions — oxidation and photosynthesis, for example — and discusses their uses. (Rev: SLJ 6/05)

24051 Beatty, Richard. *Copper* (4–8). Series: The Elements. 2000, Marshall Cavendish LB $25.64 (978-0-7614-0945-8). 32pp. This book identifies the element copper, defines its properties and describes its uses in everyday life, especially in electrical cables. (Rev: BL 1/1–15/01; HBG 10/01; SLJ 2/01) [546]

24052 Beatty, Richard. *The Lanthanides* (4–8). Series: The Elements. 2007, Marshall Cavendish LB $19.95 (978-0-7614-2687-5). 32pp. This detailed and thorough overview of the 15 metal elements in the Lanthanides provides fact boxes and clear explanations in a graphically pleasing format. (Rev: SLJ 3/08)

24053 Beatty, Richard. *Manganese* (5–8). Illus. Series: The Elements. 2004, Marshall Cavendish LB $25.64 (978-0-7614-1813-9). 32pp. Easy-to-follow diagrams, fact boxes, and color illustrations accompany an informative text that introduces manganese and its properties, value, and uses. (Rev: BL 12/1/04)

24054 Beatty, Richard. *Phosphorus* (4–8). Series: The Elements. 2000, Marshall Cavendish LB $25.64 (978-0-7614-0946-5). 32pp. This book describes this nonmetallic element, lists its properties, tells how it behaves, and discusses such uses as matches and fertilizers. (Rev: BL 1/1–15/01; HBG 10/01; SLJ 2/01) [546]

24055 Beatty, Richard. *Sulfur* (4–8). Series: The Elements. 2000, Marshall Cavendish LB $25.64 (978-0-7614-0948-9). 32pp. Introduces this nonmetallic element, its characteristics, various compounds, and uses in everyday life, with color photographs, easy-to-follow diagrams, fact boxes, and a clear text. (Rev: BL 1/1–15/01; HBG 10/01; SLJ 2/01) [546]

24056 Brandolini, Anita. *Fizz, Bubble and Flash! Element Explorations and Atom Adventures for Hands-On Science Fun!* (4–7). Illus. by Michael Kline. Series: Kids Can! 2003, Williamson paper $14.25 (978-1-885593-83-2). 127pp. A friendly narrative and cartoon-style drawing present activities that illustrate basic scientific concepts. (Rev: BL 1/1–15/04; SLJ 11/03) [546]

24057 Cobb, Allan. *Cadmium* (4–8). Series: The Elements. 2007, Marshall Cavendish LB $19.95 (978-0-7614-2686-8). 32pp. This well-designed overview of cadmium is thorough and also includes a section on how the element relates to the health of human beings. (Rev: SLJ 3/08)

24058 Cooper, Chris. *Arsenic* (4–8). Illus. Series: The Elements. 2006, Benchmark LB $19.95 (978-0-7614-2203-7). 32pp. A basic guide to arsenic's properties and uses (including as a poison and in industrial applications). (Rev: SLJ 5/07) [546]

24059 Farndon, John. *Aluminum* (4–8). Series: The Elements. 2000, Marshall Cavendish LB $25.64 (978-0-7614-0947-2). 32pp. This silvery, metallic element is introduced, with material on its individual characteristics, how it behaves, and its many uses in everyday life. (Rev: BL 1/1–15/01; HBG 10/01) [546]

24060 Farndon, John. *Calcium* (5–8). 1999, Benchmark LB $25.64 (978-0-7614-0888-8). 32pp. An attractive, readable book that explains calcium's atomic structure, where and how it occurs in nature, its reactions, compounds, and uses. (Rev: BL 2/15/00; HBG 10/00; SLJ 6/00) [540]

24061 Farndon, John. *Chemicals* (3–6). Series: Science Experiments. 2002, Marshall Cavendish LB $25.64 (978-0-7614-1466-7). 32pp. Simple experiments with easy-to-follow instructions explore the nature and properties of chemicals. (Rev: BL 12/15/02; HBG 3/03; SLJ 4/03) [540]

24062 Farndon, John. *Hydrogen* (5–8). Illus. Series: Elements. 1999, Marshall Cavendish LB $25.64 (978-0-7614-0886-4). 32pp. As well as explaining hydrogen's place on the periodic table, this account traces the history of its discovery, its properties, reactive combinations, and uses. (Rev: BL 2/15/00; HBG 10/00; SLJ 6/00) [546]

24063 Farndon, John. *Nitrogen* (5–8). Series: The Elements. 1998, Benchmark LB $25.64 (978-0-7614-0877-2). An informative science book that introduces nitrogen's properties, reactions, place in the periodic table, and importance in the human body and the environment, and environmental issues relating to nitrogen such as pollution from noxious gases and acid rain. (Rev: HBG 10/99; SLJ 2/99) [540]

24064 Farndon, John. *Oxygen* (5–8). Series: The Elements. 1998, Benchmark LB $25.64 (978-0-7614-0879-6). 32pp. Oxygen, its properties, uses, and various chemical combinations are covered in this informative text that also discusses the ozone layer. (Rev: HBG 10/99; SLJ 2/99) [540]

24065 Gray, Leon. *Iodine* (5–8). Series: Elements (Group 7). 2004, Marshall Cavendish $25.64 (978-0-7614-1812-2). This introduction to iodine examines the importance of this substance to body chemistry, as well as how it was discovered, where it is found, and its physical characteristics. (Rev: BL 12/1/04) [546]

24066 Jackson, Tom. *Lithium* (4–8). Illus. Series: The Elements. 2006, Benchmark LB $19.95 (978-0-7614-2199-3). 32pp. A basic guide to lithium's properties and uses in batteries and pharmaceuticals. (Rev: SLJ 5/07) [546]

24067 Lepora, Nathan. *Molybdenum* (4–8). Illus. Series: The Elements. 2006, Benchmark LB $19.95 (978-0-7614-2201-3). 32pp. A basic guide to molybdenum's properties and uses (including its medical applications). (Rev: SLJ 5/07) [546]

24068 Madgwick, Wendy. *Super Materials* (K–3). Series: Science Starters. 1999, Raintree LB $22.83 (978-0-8172-5555-8). 32pp. The properties of various materials are explored in a dozen simple projects using everyday materials: for example, how crystals are formed, why sugar disappears in water, and where metals come from. (Rev: BL 6/1–15/99; HBG 9/99) [540]

24069 Mebane, Robert C., and Thomas R. Rybolt. *Salts and Solids* (4–6). Illus. Series: Everyday Material Science Experiments. 1995, Twenty-First Century LB $18.90 (978-0-8050-2841-6). 64pp. Each of the experiments that explore the properties of salts and solids is accompanied by an explanation of what should happen and why. (Rev: BL 9/15/95; SLJ 8/95) [530]

24070 O'Daly, Anne. *Sodium* (4–8). Series: The Elements. 2001, Marshall Cavendish LB $25.64 (978-0-7614-1271-7). 32pp. Diagrams and full-color illustrations are used to introduce sodium and its characteristics and importance in everyday life. (Rev: BL 3/15/02; HBG 3/02) [546]

24071 Richards, Jon. *Chemicals and Reactions* (3–6). Illus. 2000, Millbrook LB $21.90 (978-0-7613-1160-7). 32pp. Using common household items, experiments involving chemical reactions are accompanied with sidebars that explain how each works. (Rev: BL 8/00; HBG 3/01) [540]

24072 Roza, Greg. *Calcium* (5–8). Illus. Series: Understanding the Elements of the Periodic Table. 2007, Rosen LB $26.50 (978-1-4042-1963-2). 48pp. This reader-friendly volume contains a full overview of calcium, including basic information and interesting sidebar features such as the amount of calcium found in different foods. (Rev: SLJ 3/08)

24073 Saucerman, Linda. *Chlorine* (5–8). Illus. Series: Understanding the Elements of the Periodic Table. 2007, Rosen LB $26.50 (978-1-4042-1962-5). 48pp. Little-known facts interspersed among basic details make this book about chlorine an interesting read. (Rev: SLJ 3/08)

24074 Sommers, Michael A. *Phosphorus* (5–8). Illus. 2007, Rosen LB $26.50 (978-1-4042-1960-1). 48pp. An easy to understand overview of phosphorus, including attractive graphics and interesting, little known facts (includes charts, diagrams, illustrations, photos, reproductions, bibliography, further reading, glossary, index and Web sites). (Rev: SLJ 3/08)

24075 Sparrow, Giles. *Nickel* (5–8). Illus. Series: The Elements. 2004, Marshall Cavendish LB $25.64 (978-0-7614-1811-5). 32pp. Easy-to-follow diagrams, fact boxes, and color illustrations accompany an informative text that introduces nickel and its properties, value, and uses. (Rev: BL 12/1/04)

24076 Stimola, Aubrey. *Sulfur* (5–8). Illus. 2007, Rosen LB $26.50 (978-1-4042-1961-8). 48pp. This basic overview of sulfur is well-organized and easy to understand, and contains interesting facts such as the use of sulfur in medicine (includes charts, diagrams, illustrations, photos, reproductions, bibliography, further reading, glossary, index and Web sites). (Rev: SLJ 3/08)

24077 Thomas, Jens. *Silicon* (4–8). Series: The Elements. 2001, Marshall Cavendish LB $25.64 (978-0-7614-1274-8). 32pp. Thomas introduces this important element and its origins, discovery, and many uses. (Rev: BL 3/15/02; HBG 3/02) [546]

24078 Tocci, Salvatore. *Carbon* (2–3). Illus. Series: True Book - Elements. 2004, Children's Pr. LB $25.00 (978-0-516-22828-0); paper $6.95 (978-0-516-27848-3). 48pp. An exploration of the characteristics of carbon and what makes it special. Also use *Calcium* and *Nitrogen* (both 2004).

24079 Tocci, Salvatore. *The Periodic Table* (2–3). Illus. Series: True Book - Elements. 2004, Children's Pr. LB $25.00 (978-0-516-22833-4). 48pp. Introduces the periodic table, how it was developed, and how it is organized, with some fun facts at the end. [546.8]

24080 Uttley, Colin. *Magnesium* (4–8). Series: The Elements. 1999, Marshall Cavendish LB $25.64 (978-0-7614-0889-5). 32pp. This book explores magnesium, a silvery metallic element important in living organisms, and explains its place in the periodic table, as well as its forms, uses, and properties. (Rev: BL 2/15/00; HBG 10/00) [546]

24081 VanCleave, Janice. *Janice VanCleave's Molecules* (4–6). Illus. 1992, Wiley paper $10.95 (978-0-471-55054-9). 86pp. The principles of cohesion, adhesion, density, diffusion, and emulsion are explored, with clear line drawings. (Rev: BL 1/15/93; SLJ 2/93) [540]

24082 Van Gorp, Lynn. *Elements* (4–6). Illus. Series: Mission: Science. 2008, Compass Point LB $26.60 (978-0-7565-3951-1). 40pp. An appealing exploration of matter and the elements, the periodic table, reactions, and so forth; also includes many photographs and illustrations plus an activity. (Rev: LMC 3/09; SLJ 6/09) [540]

24083 Watt, Susan. *Chlorine* (4–8). Series: The Elements. 2001, Marshall Cavendish LB $25.64 (978-0-7614-1272-4). 32pp. Using diagrams, photographs, and a concise text, this book introduces this active, nonmetallic element with material on its composition, characteristics, and many uses — including as a disinfectant and in water purification. (Rev: BL 3/15/02; HBG 3/02) [546]

24084 Watt, Susan. *Cobalt* (4–8). Illus. Series: The Elements. 2006, Benchmark LB $19.95 (978-0-7614-2200-6). 32pp. A basic guide to cobalt's properties and uses. (Rev: SLJ 5/07) [546]

24085 Watt, Susan. *Lead* (4–8). Series: The Elements. 2001, Marshall Cavendish LB $25.64 (978-0-7614-1273-1). 32pp. Explores the history, origins, discovery, characteristics, and uses of this heavy metallic element in everyday life. (Rev: BL 3/15/02; HBG 3/02) [546]

24086 Watt, Susan. *Mercury* (5–8). Illus. Series: The Elements. 2004, Marshall Cavendish LB $25.64 (978-0-7614-1814-6). 32pp. Easy-to-follow diagrams, fact boxes, and color illustrations accompany an informative text that introduces mercury and its properties, value, and uses. (Rev: BL 12/1/04)

24087 Watt, Susan. *Silver* (4–8). Illus. Series: The Elements. 2002, Benchmark LB $25.64 (978-0-7614-1464-3). 32pp. A concise introduction to this element, its history, where it is found and how it is mined, and its many uses. Also in this series is *Potassium* (2002). (Rev: HBG 3/03; LMC 5/03; SLJ 4/03) [546]

24088 Watt, Susan. *Zirconium* (4–8). Series: The Elements. 2007, Marshall Cavendish LB $19.95 (978-0-7614-2688-2). 32pp. This volume covers all aspects of zirconium including its use in dating some rocks and minerals. (Rev: SLJ 3/08)

24089 West, Krista. *Bromine* (4–8). Series: The Elements. 2007, Marshall Cavendish LB $19.95 (978-0-7614-2685-1). 32pp. The element bromine is covered in detail in this attractively designed volume. (Rev: SLJ 3/08)

Geology and Geography

Earth and Geology

24090 Bailey, Jacqui. *The Birth of the Earth* (3–5). Illus. by Matthew Lilly. Series: Cartoon History of the Earth. 2001, Kids Can $16.95 (978-1-55337-071-0); paper $7.95 (978-1-55337-080-2). 32pp. A comic-book-style presentation of the origin of the planet. (Rev: BL 10/15/01; HBG 3/02; SLJ 1/02) [523.1]

24091 Bannan, Jan G. *Letting Off Steam* (3–7). Illus. 1989, Carolrhoda LB $21.27 (978-0-87614-300-1). 48pp. This book explains and illustrates how underground heat can cause hot springs, geysers, and other phenomena. (Rev: BCCB 12/89; BL 9/15/89; HB 9/89; SLJ 9/89) [551.3]

24092 Blobaum, Cindy. *Geology Rocks! 50 Hands-On Activities to Explore the Earth* (4–6). Illus. by Michael Kline. Series: A Kaleidoscope Kids Book. 2000, Williamson paper $14.25 (978-1-885593-29-0). 96pp. Each chapter introduces a different concept in geology with accompanying projects and plenty of sidebars to furnish interesting information on geologists, land formations, the scientific method, etc. (Rev: SLJ 3/00) [551]

24093 Burton, Virginia Lee. *Life Story* (3–5). Illus. by author. 1989, Houghton $22.00 (978-0-395-16030-5); paper $10.95 (978-0-395-52017-8). A work about the changes that have taken place on the earth and in its flora and fauna, from the beginning of time until the present.

24094 Calhoun, Yael. *Earth Science Fair Projects Using Rocks, Minerals, Magnets, Mud, and More* (5–8). Illus. Series: Earth Science! Best Science Projects. 2005, Enslow LB $26.60 (978-0-7660-2363-5). 128pp. More than 20 geology-related projects are introduced with clear instructions and interesting background information. (Rev: BL 11/1/05) [550]

24095 Campbell, Ann-Jeanette, and Ronald Rood. *The New York Public Library Incredible Earth: A Book of Answers for Kids* (4–7). Illus. 1996, Wiley paper $14.95 (978-0-471-14497-7). 192pp. Questions and answers involving science, collected from the reference department of the New York Public Library. (Rev: BL 9/15/96; SLJ 1/97) [550]

24096 Christian, Spencer, and Antonia Felix. *What Makes the Grand Canyon Grand? The World's Most Awe-Inspiring Natural Wonders* (4–6). Series: Spencer Christian's World of Wonders. 1998, Wiley paper $12.95 (978-0-471-19617-4). 116pp. Chapters on canyons, wild waters, caves, mountains, forests, glaciers, and icebergs are accompanied by many experiments and projects in this book on the world's geographical wonders. (Rev: SLJ 4/98) [550]

24097 Coady, Christopher, and Meredith Hooper. *The Island That Moved* (3–5). 2004, Penguin $16.99 (978-0-670-05882-2). An imaginary island off the coast of Antarctica serves as the focus for an exploration of geologic and climate change, continental drift, and plate tectonics. (Rev: BL 8/04; SLJ 12/04) [551.1]

24098 Cole, Joanna. *The Magic School Bus: Inside the Earth* (2–5). Illus. by Bruce Degen. 1987, Scholastic paper $5.99 (978-0-590-40760-1). 48pp. In picture-book format, geology is introduced as a school bus journeys to the center of the earth. (Rev: BL 1/1/88)

24099 Dewey, Jennifer O. *Mud Matters* (4–6). 1998, Marshall Cavendish $14.95 (978-0-7416-5014-6). 65pp. The author, a native of the Southwest, describes all kinds of mud, its characteristics, uses, and the part it played in her childhood, when she became acquainted with flash floods, sinkholes, and other manifestations of mud. (Rev: BL 8/98*) [553.6]

24100 Downs, Sandra. *Shaping the Earth: Erosion* (5–8). Series: Exploring Planet Earth. 2000, Twenty First Century LB $24.90 (978 0 7613 1414 1). 64pp. This book explores the force of erosion and how such phenomena as wind, waves, floods, rain, acid rain, freezing, and thawing can change the face of the land. (Rev: HBG 10/00; SLJ 7/00) [551]

24101 Friend, Sandra. *Sinkholes* (4–7). Illus. 2002, Pineapple $18.95 (978-1-56164-258-8). 96pp. This volume uncovers the geological and ecological causes of sinkholes, holes in the earth's surface that occur naturally, sometimes with devastating consequences. (Rev: BL 8/02; HBG 10/02) [551.44]

24102 Gallant, Roy A. *Dance of the Continents* (5–8). Series: The Story of Science. 1999, Benchmark LB $29.93 (978-0-7614-0962-5). 80pp. This book covers geological theory from the ancient Greeks to modern plate tectonics with material on earthquakes, volcanoes, geysers, and other phenomena. (Rev: BL 2/15/00; HBG 3/00; SLJ 3/00) [551]

24103 Gardner, Robert. *Super Science Projects About Earth's Soil and Water* (3–5). Illus. Series: Rockin' Earth Science Experiments. 2007, Enslow LB $23.93 (978-0-7660-2735-0). 48pp. The experiments and projects outlined here teach important lessons about soil and water, touching on such topics as the makeup of soil, evaporation, and pollution of aquifers; scientific principles are reinforced, and symbols flag projects especially suited to science fairs. (Rev: BL 4/1/07) [631.4078]

24104 George, Linda. *Plate Tectonics* (4–9). Illus. 2003, Gale LB $23.70 (978-0-7377-1405-0). 48pp. Concise information on the movement of continents, the formation of mountains, and volcanic and earthquake activity is presented with full-color photographs and diagrams. (Rev: SLJ 10/03) [551.1]

24105 Goodman, Billy. *Natural Wonders and Disasters* (4–7). Illus. Series: Planet Earth. 1991, Little, Brown $17.95 (978-0-316-32016-0). 96pp. Full-color photographs help to explain the earth's natural wonders as well as such disasters as floods and typhoons. (Rev: BL 12/1/91; SLJ 1/92) [550]

24106 Hooper, Meredith. *The Pebble in My Pocket: A History of Our Earth* (3–5). Illus. by Chris Coady. 1996, Viking $18.99 (978-0-670-86259-7). 40pp. From molten rock to the formation of mountains, this is a concise history of the earth. (Rev: BL 7/96; SLJ 4/96) [552]

24107 Llewellyn, Claire. *Our Planet Earth* (K–3). Illus. Series: Scholastic First Encyclopedia. 1997, Scholastic paper $14.95 (978-0-590-87929-3). 77pp. An introductory book on the Earth's origins, physical geography, and the life forms that inhabit our planet. (Rev: SLJ 2/98) [910]

24108 McNulty, Faith. *How to Dig a Hole to the Other Side of the World* (2–4). Illus. by Marc Simont. 1979, HarperCollins paper $6.99 (978-0-06-443218-4). 32pp. A journey to the center of the earth.

24109 O'Neill, Catherine. *Natural Wonders of North America* (4–6). Illus. 1984, National Geographic LB $12.50 (978-0-87044-519-4). 104pp. Many of the wonders of North America, such as a Mexican volcano and life far north in Alaska, are shown in color photographs.

24110 Pellant, Chris. *Rocks and Fossils* (K–3). Series: Kingfisher Young Knowledge. 2003, Kingfisher $8.95 (978-0-7534-5619-4). 47pp. Bright, clear photographs and easy-to-read text convey information on rocks and fossils, crystals, and ero-

sion, plus suggested activities. (Rev: HBG 4/04; SLJ 4/04) [552]

24111 Redfern, Martin. *The Kingfisher Young People's Book of Planet Earth* (4–8). 1999, Kingfisher $21.95 (978-0-7534-5180-9). 96pp. A useful, enjoyable look at the earth's geology, atmosphere, and weather. (Rev: HBG 10/00; SLJ 2/00) [525]

24112 Redmond, Jim, and Ronda Redmond. *Landslides and Avalanches* (3–5). Illus. Series: Nature on the Rampage. 2001, Raintree LB $22.83 (978-0-7398-4704-6). 32pp. The authors look at our knowledge of landslides and avalanches and their causes, and discuss the ways in which we can protect ourselves from danger. (Rev: HBG 3/02; SLJ 2/02) [551.3]

24113 Robson, Pam. *Mountains and Our Moving Earth* (2–4). Illus. by Tony Kenyon. Series: Geography for Fun. 2001, Millbrook LB $22.90 (978-0-7613-2166-8). 32pp. Step-by-step instructions for projects that reinforce the information given here on geology, weather and erosion, and earthquakes and volcanoes. (Rev: HBG 10/01; SLJ 9/01) [551.43]

24114 Savan, Beth. *Earthwatch: Earthcycles and Ecosystems* (3–7). Illus. by Pat Cupples. 1992, Addison-Wesley paper $9.95 (978-0-201-58148-5). 96pp. Earth cycles — such as those of water, earth, and air — are explained; contemporary ecology problems are introduced; and simple activities are outlined. (Rev: SLJ 7/92) [550]

24115 Silverstein, Alvin, et al. *Plate Tectonics* (5–8). Illus. Series: Science Concepts. 1998, Twenty-First Century LB $26.90 (978-0-7613-3225-1). 64pp. An account that includes an introduction to the earth's crust and mantle, an explanation of plate tectonics theory, and information on the prediction of volcanic eruptions and earthquakes. (Rev: BL 2/1/99; HBG 10/99; SLJ 5/99) [555.1]

24116 Storad, Conrad J. *Earth's Crust* (2–4). Series: Early Bird Earth Science. 2006, Lerner $25.26 (978-0-8225-5944-3). 48pp. This attractive, readable overview of the earth's geological makeup examines the structure of the planet, changes in its crust, plate tectonics, and such features as mountains, volcanoes, and faults. (Rev: BL 9/1/06; SLJ 1/07) [851.1]

24117 VanCleave, Janice. *Janice VanCleave's A+ Projects in Earth Science: Winning Experiments for Science Fairs and Extra Credit* (5–10). Illus. 1999, Wiley paper $12.95 (978-0-471-17770-8). 240pp. Thirty projects varying in complexity are included in this exploration of topography, minerals, atmospheric composition, the ocean floor, and erosion. (Rev: BL 12/1/98; SLJ 6/99) [550]

24118 VanCleave, Janice. *Janice VanCleave's Gravity* (4–6). Illus. 1992, Wiley paper $10.95 (978-0-471-55050-1). 86pp. Problems that explain how gravity affects the environment, with clear line drawings. (Rev: BL 1/15/93; SLJ 2/93) [531]

24119 Verdet, Jean-Pierre. *Atlas of the Earth* (PS–2). Illus. Series: First Discovery. 1997, Scholastic $12.95 (978-0-590-96211-7). 24pp. This atlas introduces the different surfaces and regions of the earth, from the ocean floor to the dry stretches of the Sahara desert. (Rev: BL 2/1/98; HBG 3/98) [550]

24120 Williams, Brian. *Earth Time* (4–6). Series: About Time. 2002, Smart Apple LB $24.25 (978-1-58340-210-8). 32pp. An exploration of geologic and evolutionary time that looks at the forms of life appearing in each era. (Rev: HBG 3/03; SLJ 12/02)

24121 Zike, Dinah. *The Earth Science Book: Activities for Kids* (3–6). Illus. by Jessie J. Flores. 1993, Wiley paper $12.95 (978-0-471-57166-7). 119pp. Earth science concepts and environmental issues are presented. (Rev: SLJ 7/93) [551]

Earthquakes and Volcanoes

24122 Asimov, Isaac. *How Did We Find Out About Volcanoes?* (5–7). Illus. by David Wool. 1981, Avon paper $1.95 (978-0-380-59626-3). 64pp. An overview of volcanoes, from Pompeii to Mount St. Helens. [550]

24123 Bauer, Marion Dane. *Natural Disasters: Earthquake!* (PS–2). Illus. by John Wallace. Series: Ready-to-Read Natural Disasters. 2009, Aladdin paper $3.99 (978-1-4169-2551-4). 32pp. Bauer looks at what causes earthquakes and explores traditional beliefs, what scientists know now, and what remains a mystery; for beginning readers. (Rev: BLO 6/19/09) [551.22]

24124 Berger, Melvin, and Gilda Berger. *Why Do Volcanoes Blow Their Tops?* (3–5). Series: Scholastic Question and Answer. 2000, Scholastic LB $14.95 (978-0-439-09580-8). 48pp. Answers basic questions about volcanoes and earthquakes with plenty of eye-catching illustrations. (Rev: BL 12/15/00; HBG 3/01; SLJ 2/01) [551.2]

24125 Branley, Franklyn M. *Earthquakes* (K–3). Illus. by Megan Lloyd. Series: Let's-Read-and-Find-Out Science. 2005, HarperCollins LB $16.89 (978-0-06-028009-3); paper $5.99 (978-0-06-445188-8). 40pp. An update of the 1990 edition, with photographs and diagrams of what happens when earthquakes strike. (Rev: BL 3/1/05; SLJ 4/05) [551.22]

24126 Branley, Franklyn M. *Volcanoes* (1–3). Illus. by Marc Simont. 1986, HarperCollins paper $5.99 (978-0-06-445059-1). 32pp. A simple look at the whys and hows of volcanoes. (Rev: BL 6/15/89; HB 5/85; SLJ 9/85)

24127 Branley, Franklyn M. *Volcanoes* (PS–2). Illus. by Megan Lloyd. Series: Let's-Read-and-Find-Out. 2008, HarperCollins $16.99 (978-0-06-028011-6); paper $5.99 (978-0-06-445189-5). 32pp. This new edition of a 1985 title features new artwork, a page of facts, and directions for making a baking soda and vinegar eruption. (Rev: BLO 3/3/08; SLJ 8/08) [551.21]

24128 Bunce, Vincent. *Volcanoes* (4–6). Series: Restless Planet. 2000, Raintree LB $27.12 (978-0-7398-1327-0). 48pp. Different volcanic landforms are illustrated and explained, along with various kinds

of eruptions, their effects, and disaster relief efforts. (Rev: HBG 9/00; SLJ 12/00) [551.2]

24129 Burleigh, Robert, adapt. *Volcanoes: Journey to the Crater's Edge* (5–9). Photos by Philippe Bourseiller. Illus. by David Giraudon. 2003, Abrams $14.95 (978-0-8109-4590-6). 75pp. Volcanoes, lava lakes, ash plumes, and other related phenomena are beautifully illustrated in this oversized photo-essay. (Rev: BL 1/1–15/04; SLJ 12/03) [550]

24130 Challen, Paul. *Volcano Alert!* (4–6). Illus. Series: Disaster Alert! 2004, Crabtree LB $26.60 (978-0-7787-1570-2); paper $8.95 (978-0-7787-1602-0). 32pp. In addition to describing volcanoes, there is colorfully presented material on early beliefs and myths associated with them, discussion of advances in predicting eruptions, tips on staying safe, and an experiment. (Rev: SLJ 3/05) [551.2]

24131 Claybourne, Anna. *Volcanoes* (3–6). Illus. 2007, Kingfisher $16.95 (978-0-7534-6137-2). 64pp. This well-designed, oversized volume arranges information about volcanoes in chapters titled "World of Volcanoes," "Exploding Earth," "Famous Eruptions," "Changing Landscapes," "Volcanoes and People," "Studying Volcanoes," and "Volcano Data." (Rev: SLJ 10/07) [551.2]

24132 Drohan, Michele Ingber. *Earthquakes* (2–4). Illus. Series: Natural Disasters. 1999, Rosen $21.25 (978-0-8239-5285-4). 24pp. Full-page photographs and large type are used in this book that explains the causes and effects of earthquakes. (Rev: BL 9/15/99) [551.22]

24133 Fradin, Judy, and Dennis Fradin. *Volcanoes* (4–6). Illus. Series: Witness to Disaster. 2007, National Geographic $16.95 (978-0-7922-5376-1). 48pp. This volume is filled with compelling facts, photographs, and accounts of famous volcanoes and eruptions. (Rev: BL 6/1–15/07; SLJ 10/07) [551.21]

24134 Harper, Kristine C. *The Mount St. Helens Volcanic Eruptions* (5–8). Series: Environmental Disasters. 2005, Facts on File $35.00 (978-0-8160-5757-3). 100pp. The environment impact of Mount St. Helens' eruptions is examined in this title from the Environmental Disasters series. (Rev: SLJ 11/05)

24135 Harrison, David L. *Earthquakes: Earth's Mightiest Moments* (K–3). Illus. by Cheryl Nathan. Series: Earthworks. 2004, Boyds Mills $15.95 (978-1-59078-243-9). After a dramatic account of an 1811 earthquake in Missouri, Harrison presents clear, reader-friendly explanations of plate tectonics and the study of earthquakes. (Rev: SLJ 11/04) [551.2]

24136 Harrison, David L. *Volcanoes: Nature's Incredible Fireworks* (1–3). Illus. by Cheryl Nathan. Series: Earthworks. 2002, Boyds Mills $15.95 (978-1-56397-996-5). 32pp. The forces underlying volcanic eruptions are discussed here, with rich and informative illustrations. (Rev: BL 7/02; HBG 3/03; SLJ 9/02) [551.21]

24137 Lindop, Laurie. *Probing Volcanoes* (5–8). Illus. Series: Science on the Edge. 2003, Millbrook LB $26.90 (978-0-7613-2700-4). 80pp. A lively introduction to the history of volcanoes and eruptions, the scientists who dare to study volcanoes, and techniques for collecting data and forecasting volcanic activity. (Rev: BL 12/1/03; SLJ 1/04) [551.21]

24138 Maslin, Mark. *Earthquakes* (4–6). Series: Restless Planet. 2000, Raintree LB $27.12 (978-0-7398-1328-7). 48pp. This book explains the causes, measurement, hazards, and effects of both earthquakes and tsunamis. (Rev: HBG 9/00; SLJ 12/00) [551.2]

24139 Mehta-Jones, Shilpa. *Earthquake Alert!* (4–6). Illus. Series: Disaster Alert! 2004, Crabtree LB $26.60 (978-0-7787-1572-6); paper $8.95 (978-0-7787-1604-4). 32pp. In addition to describing earthquakes, there is colorfully presented material on early beliefs and myths associated with them, discussion of advances in predicting events, tips on staying safe, and an experiment. (Rev: SLJ 3/05) [551.2]

24140 Meister, Cari. *Earthquakes* (4–6). Illus. Series: Nature's Fury. 1999, ABDO LB $24.21 (978-1-57765-083-6). 32pp. This account presents a history of earthquakes, how they are predicted, and how to stay safe. Also use *Volcanoes* (1999). (Rev: HBG 4/00; SLJ 12/99) [551.2]

24141 Nicholson, Cynthia Pratt. *Volcano!* (2–5). Illus. Series: Disaster. 2001, Kids Can $14.95 (978-1-55074-908-3); paper $6.95 (978-1-55074-966-3). 32pp. A tabloid-style format with sensational headlines draws attention to this survey of volcanoes, famous volcanic eruptions, and the work of volcanologists. (Rev: BL 12/1/01; HBG 3/02) [551.21]

24142 Nicolson, Cynthia Pratt. *Earthquake!* (3–6). Illus. 2002, Kids Can $14.95 (978-1-55074-949-6); paper $6.95 (978-1-55074-968-7). 32pp. Using double-page spreads that contain concise text and dramatic photographs, various aspects of earthquakes and their causes and effects are covered. (Rev: BL 5/1/02; HBG 10/02; SLJ 5/02) [551.22]

24143 Prager, Ellen. *Earthquakes* (K–3). Illus. by Susan Greenstein. Series: Jump into Science. 2002, National Geographic $16.95 (978-0-7922-8202-0). 32pp. This is a colorful book that explains simply what earthquakes are, where and why they occur, and their effects. (Rev: BL 6/1–15/02; HBG 10/02) [551.22]

24144 Reed, Jennifer B. *Earthquakes: Disaster and Survival, 2005* (4–7). Illus. Series: Disaster and Survival. 2005, Enslow LB $23.93 (978-0-7660-2381-9). 48pp. Major earthquakes and their effects are detailed in text and personal accounts, with a chapter devoted to the December 2004 Asian tsunami. (Rev: BL 5/1/05; SLJ 10/05) [363.34]

24145 Rogers, Daniel. *Earthquakes* (3–4). Series: Geography Starts Here. 1999, Raintree LB $25.69 (978-0-8172-5546-6). 32pp. Covers many topics including faults, plate movement, shock waves, methods of measurement, and kinds of destruction. (Rev: HBG 9/99; SLJ 7/99) [551.2]

24146 Rogers, Daniel. *Volcanoes* (3–4). Series: Geography Starts Here. 1999, Raintree LB $25.69 (978-0-8172-5547-3). 32pp. The causes of volcanic eruptions are covered along with how they occur, their effects, and the ecological consequences. (Rev: HBG 9/99; SLJ 7/99) [551.2]

24147 Rubin, Ken. *Volcanoes and Earthquakes* (4–7). Illus. Series: Insiders. 2007, Simon & Schuster $16.99 (978-1-4169-3862-0). 64pp. Vivid illustrations accompany informative text, charts, and graphs introducing earthquakes and volcanoes and some of the important disasters that have taken place. (Rev: SLJ 10/07) [551.21]

24148 Rusch, Elizabeth. *Will It Blow? Become a Volcano Detective at Mount St. Helens* (4–6). Illus. by K. E. Lewis. 2007, Sasquatch $18.95 (978-1-57061-510-8); paper $13.95 (978-1-57061-509-2). 46pp. Readers will learn how scientists predict whether a volcano will erupt as they read about the "clues" that lead to this conclusion. Cartoon drawings, experiments, and case studies add interest. (Rev: SLJ 7/07)

24149 Simon, Seymour. *Danger! Earthquakes* (1–3). Illus. Series: SeeMore Readers. 2002, North-South paper $3.95 (978-1-58717-140-6). 32pp. Double-page spreads that use color photographs and diagrams explain the causes and impact of earthquakes. (Rev: BL 4/15/02; HBG 10/02; SLJ 3/02) [551.22]

24150 Simon, Seymour. *Danger! Volcanoes* (1–3). Series: See More Readers. 2002, North-South $13.95 (978-1-58717-181-9). 32pp. Outstanding pictures and a brief, simple text are the highlights in this first reader that explores the world of volcanoes. (Rev: BL 7/02; HBG 3/03; SLJ 8/02) [551.2]

24151 Simon, Seymour. *Volcanoes* (1–3). Illus. 1988, Morrow LB $15.89 (978-0-688-07412-8). 32pp. How volcanoes are formed and erupt, with well-known examples. (Rev: BCCB 10/88; HB 9/88; SLJ 12/88)

24152 VanCleave, Janice. *Earthquakes: Mind-Boggling Experiments You Can Turn into Science Fair Projects* (4–6). Illus. Series: Spectacular Science Projects. 1993, Wiley paper $10.95 (978-0-471-57107-0). 88pp. This is a collection of projects involving the movements of the earth, along with good scientific explanations and simple directions. (Rev: BL 5/1/93; SLJ 7/93) [551.2]

24153 VanCleave, Janice. *Janice VanCleave's Volcanoes: Mind-Boggling Experiments You Can Turn into Science Fair Projects* (4–7). Illus. 1994, Wiley paper $10.95 (978-0-471-30811-9). 89pp. Twenty experiments that explore the properties of erupting volcanoes using simple materials that can often be found around the house. (Rev: BL 7/94; SLJ 8/94) [551.2]

24154 Waldron, Melanie. *Volcanoes* (3–5). Series: Mapping Earthforms. 2007, Heinemann LB $28.21 (978-1-4034-9606-5). 32pp. With maps, diagrams, tables, and color photographs, this title looks at how volcanoes were formed, what happens during an eruption, the impact on population and wildlife, and important examples (one chapter is titled "A Way of Life — Montserrat"). (Rev: SLJ 10/07) [551.21]

24155 Walker, Sally M. *Earthquakes* (3–6). Illus. Series: Earth Watch. 1996, Carolrhoda LB $21.27 (978-0-87614-888-4). 48pp. A clearly written text and powerful color photos highlight this award-winning book. (Rev: BL 4/15/96; SLJ 6/96) [551.2]

24156 Walker, Sally M. *Volcanoes: Earth's Inner Fire* (3–6). Illus. Series: Earth Watch. 1994, Carolrhoda LB $21.27 (978-0-87614-812-9). 56pp. Many color photographs and clear text are used to explain the causes, locations, and effects of volcanoes. (Rev: BL 1/15/95) [551.2]

24157 Watson, Nancy. *Our Violent Earth* (4–8). Illus. 1982, National Geographic LB $12.50 (978-0-87044-388-6). 104pp. A discussion of such phenomena as earthquakes, volcanoes, and floods. [363.3]

24158 Winchester, Simon. *The Day the World Exploded: The Earthshaking Catastrophe at Krakatoa* (5–8). Adapted by Dwight Jon Zimmerman. Illus. by Jason Chin. 2008, HarperCollins $22.99 (978-0-06-123982-3). 96pp. After looking at volcanoes and the reasons for eruptions plus the culture and economy of the region at the time, Winchester describes the 1883 disaster and its aftermath; an adaptation of a book for adults titled *Krakatoa* (2003). (Rev: SLJ 11/08; VOYA 8/08) [363.3495]

24159 Woods, Michael, and Mary B. Woods. *Volcanoes* (4–6). Series: Disasters Up Close. 2006, Lerner LB $27.93 (978-0-8225-4715-0). 64pp. With charts, photographs, and quotes from survivors, this book clearly demonstrates the devastating power of volcanic eruptions, and provides information on the formation of volcanoes and the ways we measure their activity. (Rev: SLJ 1/07) [551.21]

24160 Worth, Richard. *The San Francisco Earthquake* (5–8). Illus. Series: Environmental Disasters. 2005, Facts on File $35.00 (978-0-8160-5756-6). 100pp. Worth examines how the San Francisco earthquake of 1906 affected the region's environment. (Rev: SLJ 11/05) [363.34]

Icebergs and Glaciers

24161 Bundey, Nikki. *Ice and the Earth* (3–5). Series: The Science of Weather. 2000, Carolrhoda LB $21.27 (978-1-57505-472-8). 32pp. Along with some interesting experiments, this book describes how ice affects the earth, how it is created, and what would happen if there was no ice on the earth. Also use a companion work *Ice and People* (2000). (Rev: BL 12/15/00; HBG 3/01) [551.3]

24162 George, Michael. *Glaciers* (3–8). Illus. 1991, Creative Ed. LB $25.30 (978-0-88682-401-3). 40pp. Formations and types of glaciers, as well as their future effects, are explained. (Rev: BL 12/15/91; SLJ 3/92) [551.3]

24163 Harrison, David L. *Glaciers: Nature's Icy Caps* (1–3). Illus. by Cheryl Nathan. Series: Earthworks. 2006, Boyds Mills $15.95 (978-1-59078-372-6). 32pp. A solid introduction to glaciers, with digital illustrations and large maps. (Rev: BL 4/1/06; SLJ 8/06) [551.31]

Physical Geography

General and Miscellaneous

24164 Baldwin, Carol. *Living in the Tundra* (3–6). Series: Living Habitats. 2003, Heinemann LB $24.22 (978-1-4034-2991-9). 32pp. The plants and animals of the tundra are presented in question-and-answer format, with brief discussion of human interference. (Rev: HBG 4/04; SLJ 2/04) [577.5]

24165 Blaustein, Daniel. *The Everglades and the Gulf Coast* (4–7). 1999, Benchmark LB $28.50 (978-0-7614-0896-3). 64pp. In addition to a tour of the wetlands of the southeastern United States, this book describes how the plants and animals there interact and how this changes human life. (Rev: HBG 10/00; SLJ 4/00) [574.5]

24166 Burnie, David. *Shrublands* (5–8). Series: Biomes Atlases. 2003, Raintree LB $31.42 (978-0-7398-5514-0). 64pp. This comprehensive overview of shrublands describes the climate, flora and fauna, people, and future of these areas, and includes good maps. (Rev: SLJ 9/03) [577.3]

24167 Collard, Sneed B. *Our Natural Homes* (3–6). Illus. by James M. Needham. Series: Our Perfect Planet. 1996, Charlesbridge paper $6.95 (978-0-88106-928-0). An introduction to the plant and animal life found in such North and South American biomes as tundra, boreal forest, mountains, grasslands, deserts, rain forests, and chaparral. (Rev: SLJ 10/96) [910]

24168 Cone, Patrick. *Wildfire* (3–7). Illus. 1996, Carolrhoda $14.95 (978-0-87614-936-2); paper $7.95 (978-1-57505-027-0). 48pp. After a general description of wildfires, discusses their causes, effects, and possible preventive measures that can be taken. (Rev: BL 2/15/97; SLJ 1/97) [574.5]

24169 Gibbons, Gail. *Marshes and Swamps* (2–3). Illus. 1998, Holiday House LB $16.95 (978-0-8234-1347-8). 32pp. Fresh and saltwater wetlands are introduced, as well as the amazing variety of animals and plants that are found in them. (Rev: BCCB 4/98; BL 3/15/98; HBG 9/98; SLJ 5/98) [551.41]

24170 Godkin, Celia. *Sea Otter Inlet* (1–3). Illus. by author. 1998, Fitzhenry & Whiteside $15.95 (978-1-55041-080-8). Ecosystems and the balance of nature are explored in this account of what happens to a kelp bed when the otters are killed or driven off by hunters. (Rev: SLJ 1/99) [574]

24171 Guiberson, Brenda Z. *Spoonbill Swamp* (1–3). Illus. by Megan Lloyd. 1995, Holt paper $6.95 (978-0-8050-3385-4). 32pp. This story depicts a day in the lives of a mother spoonbill and a mother alligator in a southern swamp. (Rev: BL 3/15/92; SLJ 3/92) [591.5]

24172 Harrison, David L. *Caves: Mysteries Beneath Our Feet* (1–3). Illus. by Cheryl Nathan. 2001, Boyds Mills $15.95 (978-1-56397-915-6). 32pp. A general discussion of caves follows the story of the discovery of New York's Howe Caverns in 1842. (Rev: BL 9/15/01; HBG 3/02; SLJ 10/01) [551.447]

24173 Jenkins, Steve. *Hottest, Coldest, Highest, Deepest* (PS–3). Illus. 1998, Houghton $16.00 (978-0-395-89999-1). 32pp. A geographical picture book describing superlative locations — the deepest lake, highest mountain, and places that are the hottest, coldest, windiest, etc. (Rev: BCCB 1/99; BL 8/98; HBG 3/99; SLJ 8/98) [910]

24174 Jennings, Terry. *Coasts and Islands* (3–6). Illus. Series: Restless Earth. 2003, Thameside LB $24.25 (978-1-931983-18-1). 32pp. Diagrams, photographs, and paintings combine with the text to illustrate how islands, coral reefs, and atolls are created and how water and earth interact. (Rev: BL 12/1/02; HBG 3/03) [551.457]

24175 Johansson, Philip. *The Frozen Tundra: A Web of Life* (3–5). Illus. Series: World of Biomes. 2004, Enslow LB $23.93 (978-0-7660-2176-1). 48pp. Plants and animals of the tundra are introduced here, along with information on the climate and seasons and the cycle of life. (Rev: BL 4/1/04) [577.5]

24176 Johansson, Philip. *Marshes and Swamps: A Wetland Web of Life* (4–6). Illus. Series: Wonderful Water Biomes. 2007, Enslow LB $23.93 (978-0-7660-2814-2). 48pp. After an account of a herpetologist's expedition into the New Jersey salt marshes, this title looks at the plants and animals that live in such habitats. (Rev: SLJ 1/08) [577.68]

24177 Johnson, Rebecca. *A Journey into a Wetland* (3–6). Illus. by Phyllis V. Saroff. Series: Biomes of North America. 2004, Lerner LB $23.93 (978-1-57505-593-0). 48pp. This appealing blend of easy-to-understand narrative and colorful illustrations explores the plants and animals found in and around a wetlands habitat. (Rev: BL 5/1/04) [577.68]

24178 Kalman, Bobbie, and Jacqueline Langille. *What Is a Biome?* (3–5). Series: Science of Living Things. 1998, Crabtree LB $25.27 (978-0-86505-875-0); paper $6.95 (978-0-86505-887-3). 32pp. Different types of ecological communities such as grasslands and deserts are described, with maps, photographs, charts, and short, interesting chapters. (Rev: SLJ 11/98) [591]

24179 Kramer, Stephen. *Caves* (3–6). Photos by Kenrick L. Day. Series: Caves. 1995, Carolrhoda LB $19.93 (978-0-87614-447-3); paper $7.95 (978-0-87614-896-9). 48pp. Using color photos, diagrams, and maps plus an interesting text, this book supplies a fascinating introduction to caves and their exploration. (Rev: BCCB 7–8/95; BL 4/15/95; SLJ 7/95) [557.4]

24180 Marsico, Katie. *A Home on the Tundra* (1–3). 2006, Children's Pr. LB $20.00 (978-0-516-25345-9). 24pp. This easy-to-understand introduction to the tundra as a natural habitat looks at the nature of the land itself, its climate, flora, and the animals that call it home. (Rev: SLJ 2/07) [577.5]

24181 Marx, Irish. *Everglades Forever: Restoring America's Great Wetland* (3–5). Illus. 2004, Lee & Low $17.95 (978-1-58430-164-6). 40pp. A Florida fifth-grade class's exploration of the Everglades serves as an appealing framework for information on this ecosystem and the perils it faces. (Rev: BL 2/1/05; SLJ 1/05) [508.759]

24182 Perenyi, Constance. *Wild Wild West: Wildlife Habitats of Western North America* (K–3). Illus. 1993, Sasquatch paper $8.95 (978-0-912365-90-9). 32pp. Ten geographical areas, including the Arctic tundra, Rocky Mountains, Sonoran Desert, and a coral reef, are described and pictured in colorful collages. (Rev: BL 12/15/93; SLJ 12/93) [508.78]

24183 Pipes, Rose. *Islands* (2–4). Series: World Habitats. 1998, Raintree LB $24.26 (978-0-8172-5009-6). 32pp. The physical characteristics of islands are presented with material on shore life, general geography, and various kinds of wildlife. (Rev: BL 3/15/99; HBG 3/99) [551.4]

24184 Pipes, Rose. *Wetlands* (2–4). Series: World Habitats. 1998, Raintree LB $24.28 (978-0-8172-5001-0). 32pp. A nicely illustrated and well-laid out book on the ecology of wetlands, their climate, physical features, and plant and animal life. (Rev: BL 5/15/98; HBG 9/98) [574.5]

24185 Quigley, Mary. *Wetlands Explorer* (2–4). Illus. Series: Habitat Explorer. 2004, Raintree LB $25.70 (978-1-4109-0514-7). 32pp. This photo-filled exploration of wetlands looks at the plants and animals found there, plus environmental threats posed by pollution and development.

24186 Regan, Colm. *People of the Islands* (4–6). Series: Wide World. 1998, Raintree LB $18.98 (978-0-8172-5064-5). 48pp. Island environments are introduced with material on their geography and ecology and how humans live in these environments. (Rev: HBG 3/99; SLJ 2/99) [551.4]

24187 Ricciuti, Edward R. *Chaparral* (5–7). Illus. Series: Biomes of the World. 1996, Benchmark LB $25.64 (978-0-7614-0137-7). 64pp. An examination of the climate, vegetation, and life cycles of the chaparral, the biome situated between desert and grassland or forest and grassland, as in western North America from Oregon to Baja California. (Rev: SLJ 7/96) [574.5]

24188 Sauvain, Philip. *Rivers and Valleys* (4–7). Illus. Series: Geography Detectives. 1996, Carolrhoda LB $23.95 (978-0-87614-996-6). 32pp. In two-page spreads, rivers and valleys are introduced, with material on geology, flood control, wildlife, and tourism. (Rev: SLJ 3/97) [551.48]

24189 Sayres, Meghan Nuttall. *The Shape of Betts Meadow: A Wetlands Story* (K–3). Illus. by Joanne Friar. 2002, Millbrook LB $22.90 (978-0-7613-2115-6). 32pp. A stunning picture book set in Washington State that shows how a local doctor purchased a dry meadow and restored it to its original condition as a wetland. (Rev: BL 6/1–15/02; HBG 10/02; SLJ 4/02) [333.91]

24190 Staub, Frank. *America's Wetlands* (4–6). Illus. 1995, Carolrhoda LB $21.27 (978-0-87614-827-3). 48pp. The ecology of wetlands is described, with emphasis on their importance for the survival of wildlife. (Rev: BL 4/1/95; SLJ 5/95) [574.5]

24191 Steele, Philip. *Islands* (3–5). Illus. Series: Geography Detectives. 1996, Carolrhoda LB $19.93 (978-0-87614-997-3). 32pp. Double-page spreads introduce islands, their composition, and how they have been changed by humankind. (Rev: BL 9/1/96; SLJ 9/96) [551.4]

24192 Stille, Darlene R. *Wetlands* (2–4). Illus. Series: True Books. 1999, Children's Book Pr. LB $25.00 (978-0-516-21512-9). 48pp. A simple text and many photographs are used to introduce wetlands, their climate and geography, and the plants and animals that exist there. (Rev: BL 10/15/99) [578.768]

24193 Stone, Lynn M. *Wetlands* (1–3). Illus. Series: Biomes of North America. 2003, Rourke LB $20.64 (978-1-58952-688-4). 24pp. For young researchers, this is an excellent introduction to this biome, with clear, simple text, photographs, and maps. [574.5]

24194 Warhol, Tom. *Chaparral and Scrub* (5–8). Series: Earth's Biomes. 2006, Marshall Cavendish LB $32.79 (978-0-7614-2195-5). 80pp. Report writers will appreciate this attractive introduction to the characteristics of this biome and its plants and animals; also use *Tundra* (2006). (Rev: LMC 8/07; SLJ 8/07) [577.3]

24195 Wojahn, Rebecca Hogue, and Donald Wojahn. *A Tundra Food Chain: A Who-Eats-What Adventure in the Arctic* (3–6). Illus. Series: Follow That Food Chain. 2009, Lerner LB $30.60 (978-0-8225-7500-9). 64pp. Polar animals are introduced in this attractive "choose your own adventure" introduction to plant and animal life on the tundra. (Rev: SLJ 6/09) [577.5]

24196 Zollman, Pam. *Gulf of Mexico* (1–2). Series: Rookie Read-About Geography. 2006, Children's Pr. LB $20.50 (978-0-516-25035-9). 32pp. Geographical and geological facts about this body of water are presented in an airy format that will appeal to beginning readers. (Rev: SLJ 6/06) [911.6364]

Deserts

24197 Arnold, Caroline. *Watching Desert Wildlife* (3–6). Photos by Arthur Arnold. 1994, Carolrhoda LB $25.26 (978-0-87614-841-9). 48pp. The desert environment is first explained, and then its wildlife is introduced in text and excellent photographs. (Rev: BL 12/1/94; SLJ 1/95) [574.5]

24198 Benduhn, Tea. *Living in Deserts* (3–4). Series: Life on the Edge. 2007, Gareth Stevens LB $19.93 (978-0-8368-8341-1). 24pp. After an introduction to deserts and the desert climate, Benduhn looks at the people of desert areas, the life they lead, and the problems they face. (Rev: LMC 1/08; SLJ 12/07) [910.915]

24199 Brown, John. *Journey into the Desert* (3–6). 2003, Oxford LB $19.95 (978-0-19-515777-2). 48pp. A camping trip forms the backdrop for a photo-filled introduction to the landscape, plants, and wildlife of the Sonoran Desert. (Rev: HBG 10/03; SLJ 8/03) [508.3154]

24200 Chambers, Catherine. *Deserts* (3–5). Series: Mapping Earthforms. 2000, Heinemann LB $21.36 (978-1-57572-522-2). 32pp. Deserts and desert life plus environmental factors that affect deserts are introduced in a large, bold text and numerous illustrations. (Rev: HBG 3/01; SLJ 8/00) [574.5]

24201 Fleisher, Paul. *Saguaro Cactus* (3–5). Series: Webs of Life. 1997, Marshall Cavendish LB $22.79 (978-0-7614-0433-0). 40pp. An introduction to this gigantic cactus found in the Southwest, with material on how it survives in a hostile environment. (Rev: BL 2/15/98; HBG 3/98) [635.9]

24202 Fredericks, Anthony D. *Around One Cactus: Owls, Bats and Leaping Rats* (K–4). Illus. by Jennifer DiRubbio. Series: Sharing Nature with Children. 2003, Dawn $16.95 (978-1-58469-051-1); paper $7.95 (978-1-58469-052-8). A cumulative tale, told in verse, about the natural life surrounding a Saguaro cactus, colorfully illustrated with detailed drawings. (Rev: HBG 4/04; SLJ 4/04) [591.754]

24203 Giesecke, Ernestine. *Desert Plants* (K–3). Series: Heinemann First Library. 1999, Heinemann LB $21.36 (978-1-57572-821-6). 32pp. A colorful beginning book that introduces desert plants and explains a little about their ecosystem and how they have adapted. (Rev: BL 6/1–15/99; SLJ 8/99) [574.4]

24204 Green, Jen. *A Saguaro Cactus* (2–4). Series: Small Worlds. 1999, Crabtree LB $25.27 (978-0-7787-0134-7); paper $8.95 (978-0-7787-0148-4). 32pp. The desert ecosystem of the Sonoran Desert is introduced with material on the plants and animals found there. (Rev: SLJ 2/00) [574.5]

24205 Hyde, Natalie. *Desert Extremes* (2–5). Illus. Series: Extreme Nature. 2008, Crabtree LB $26.60 (978-0-7787-4500-6); paper $8.95 (978-0-7787-4517-4). 32pp. Clear photographs accompany informative text describing the plants, animals, and people of deserts around the world. (Rev: BLO 3/11/09) [578.754]

24206 Jenkins, Martin. *Deserts* (3–6). Illus. Series: Endangered People and Places. 1996, Lerner LB $22.60 (978-0-8225-2775-6). 48pp. In this account that combines geography and sociology, deserts and the survival of their inhabitants are described. (Rev: BL 11/15/96; SLJ 11/96) [333.73]

24207 Jernigan, Gisela. *Sonoran Seasons: A Year in the Desert* (3–6). Illus. by E. Wesley Jernigan. 1994, Harbinger paper $10.95 (978-0-943173-91-7). For every month of the year, a different plant from the Sonoran Desert is introduced, most of them edible. (Rev: SLJ 6/94) [581.5]

24208 Johnson, Rebecca. *A Walk in the Desert* (2–5). Illus. by Phyllis V. Saroff. Series: Biomes of North America. 2001, Carolrhoda LB $23.93 (978-1-57505-152-9). 48pp. As well as the climate of the desert, this account covers its flora and fauna and their interactions. (Rev: HBG 10/01; SLJ 3/01) [574.5]

24209 Lambert, David. *People of the Deserts* (4–6). Series: Wide World. 1998, Raintree LB $18.98 (978-0-8172-5063-8). 48pp. The physical geography and ecology of desert regions are discussed with material on the human cultures in these areas. (Rev: HBG 3/99; SLJ 2/99) [551.4]

24210 Lazaroff, David. *Correctamundo! Prickly Pete's Guide to Desert Facts and Cactifracts* (K–3). Illus. by Preston Neel. 2001, Arizona-Sonora Desert Museum paper $14.95 (978-1-886679-17-7). A bright, lively question-and-answer introduction to desert plants and animals, conducted by a packrat named Prickly Pete. (Rev: SLJ 8/01) [574.5]

24211 Le Rochais, Marie-Ange. *Desert Trek: An Eye-Opening Journey Through the World's Driest Places* (3–5). Trans. by George L. Newman. Illus. 2001, Walker LB $18.85 (978-0-8027-8766-8). 40pp. Dramatic spreads and brief text show the diversity of desert landscapes around the world, with features ranging from plants, animals, and oases to people hunting and working. (Rev: BL 6/1–15/01; HBG 10/01; SLJ 9/01) [577.54]

24212 Low, Robert. *Peoples of the Desert* (2–5). Illus. Series: People and Their Environments. 1996, Rosen LB $19.95 (978-0-8239-2296-3). 24pp. Two nomadic tribes, one from the Sahara and the other from the Kalahari, are featured in this discussion of human life in a desert environment. (Rev: BL 10/15/96; SLJ 1/97) [966]

24213 Moss, Miriam. *This Is the Oasis* (K–2). Illus. by Adrienne Kennaway. 2005, Kane $14.95 (978-1-929132-76-8). Lush illustrations enhance this large-format introduction to the people, plants, and animals of a Saharan oasis. (Rev: SLJ 3/06) [574.5]

24214 Patent, Dorothy Hinshaw. *Life in a Desert* (5–8). Series: Ecosystems in Action. 2003, Lerner LB $26.60 (978-0-8225-2140-2). 72pp. This account explores the plant and animal life in deserts and how human intervention has changed this ecosystem. (Rev: BL 9/15/03; HBG 10/03) [574.5]

24215 Pfeffer, Wendy. *Hot Deserts* (3–5). Series: Living on the Edge. 2002, Benchmark LB $25.64 (978-0-7614-1440-7). 40pp. This easy-to-read overview of the animals and plants that flourish in desert climates opens with a map. (Rev: HBG 10/03; SLJ 6/03) [577.54]

24216 Pipe, Jim. *Desert Survival* (4–6). Illus. Series: Extreme Habitats. 2007, Gareth Stevens LB $25.27 (978-0-8368-8245-2). 32pp. This well-designed title combines high visual appeal and accessible facts to make an attractive and informative overview of deserts, the plants and animals that live there, how people use deserts, and the threats the deserts face. (Rev: LMC 1/08; SLJ 12/07) [577.54]

24217 Pipes, Rose. *Hot Deserts* (2–4). Illus. Series: World Habitats. 1998, Raintree LB $24.28 (978-0-8172-5004-1). 32pp. Color photos and a large, clear text introduce deserts, their climate, vegetation, and the people and animals populating them. (Rev: BL 4/15/98; HBG 9/98) [577.54]

24218 Pratt-Serafini, Kristin Joy. *Saguaro Moon: A Desert Journal* (3–6). Illus. 2002, Dawn $16.95 (978-1-58469-037-5); paper $7.95 (978-1-58469-036-8). 32pp. Factual information about desert plant and animal life is presented in the form of a nature journal written by a girl named Megan, who has recently moved to Arizona. (Rev: BL 10/15/02; HBG 3/03; SLJ 9/02) [508.3154]

24219 Pyers, Greg. *Desert Explorer* (2–4). Illus. Series: Habitat Explorer. 2004, Raintree LB $25.70 (978-1-4109-0507-9). 32pp. This photo-filled exploration of deserts looks at the plants and animals

found there, plus environmental threats to this habitat.

24220 Ricciuti, Edward R. *Desert* (4–6). Illus. Series: Biomes of the World. 1996, Benchmark LB $25.64 (978-0-7614-0134-6). 64pp. Deserts of the world are identified and described, with coverage on their plant and animal life. (Rev: SLJ 7/96) [574.9]

24221 Ruth, Maria Mudd. *The Deserts of the Southwest* (5–8). Series: Ecosystems of North America. 1998, Benchmark LB $28.50 (978-0-7614-0899-4). After an overview of the deserts of the Southwest and how they were formed, this book introduces desert plants and wildlife, how they interact, adaptations they have made to the desert environment, and the impact of human development. (Rev: HBG 10/99; SLJ 2/99) [591]

24222 Salzmann, Mary Elizabeth. *In the Desert* (K–1). Illus. Series: What Do You See? 2001, ABDO LB $19.93 (978-1-57765-564-0). 24pp. Colorful double-page spreads introduce the desert in simple language for beginning readers. (Rev: HBG 3/02; SLJ 3/02) [577.54]

24223 Sandler, Michael. *Deserts: Surviving in the Sahara* (3–5). Illus. Series: X-treme Places. 2005, Bearport LB $25.27 (978-1-59716-085-8). 32pp. A compelling overview of deserts and the challenges to their human and animal inhabitants is given added punch by the inclusion of the story of René Caillié, who crossed the Sahara in 1828. (Rev: SLJ 1/06) [916.6]

24224 Savage, Stephen. *Animals of the Desert* (3–6). Illus. Series: Animals by Habitat. 1997, Raintree LB $22.83 (978-0-8172-4750-8). 32pp. After a discussion of the world's deserts and how they differ, this book introduces five basic animals groups found in deserts, like mammals, birds, and reptiles. (Rev: BL 5/15/97; SLJ 8/97) [591.5]

24225 Sayre, April P. *Desert* (4–7). Illus. Series: Exploring Earth's Biomes. 1994, Twenty-First Century LB $25.90 (978-0-8050-2825-6). 64pp. After a general introduction to deserts, a specific one is explored in brief chapters with excellent illustrations. (Rev: BL 1/1/95*; SLJ 1/95) [574.5]

24226 Sill, Cathryn. *Deserts* (1–4). Illus. by John Sill. Series: About Habitats. 2007, Peachtree $16.95 (978-1-56145-390-0). 48pp. The landscape, flora, and fauna of the desert are introduced in appealing illustrations and accessible text. (Rev: BL 4/1/07) [577.54]

24227 Steele, Philip. *Deserts* (4–6). Illus. Series: Geography Detectives. 1996, Carolrhoda LB $19.93 (978-0-87614-998-0). 32pp. This introduction to deserts and the life found in them discusses such topics as the differences between hot and cold deserts, their landscape features, and how they are still being created. (Rev: SLJ 9/96) [574.5]

24228 Stone, Lynn M. *Deserts* (1–3). Illus. Series: Biomes of North America. 2003, Rourke LB $20.64 (978-1-58952-683-9). 24pp. For young researchers, this is an excellent introduction to this biome, with clear, simple text, photographs, and maps. [574.5]

24229 Storad, Conrad J. *Saguaro Cactus* (3–5). Photos by Paula Jansen. Series: Early Bird Nature

Books. 1994, Lerner LB $25.26 (978-0-8225-3002-2). 48pp. After a general introduction to cacti, this account focuses on the physical appearance and life cycle of the saguaro. (Rev: SLJ 8/94) [583]

24230 Wallace, Marianne D. *America's Deserts: Guide to Plants and Animals* (3–5). Illus. 1996, Fulcrum paper $15.95 (978-1-55591-268-0). 48pp. After a general discussion of the flora and fauna of deserts, this account focuses on specific deserts, like Mojave and Death Valley. (Rev: BL 4/1/96; SLJ 7/96) [574.973]

24231 Warhol, Tom. *Desert* (5–8). Series: Earth's Biomes. 2006, Marshall Cavendish LB $32.79 (978-0-7614-2194-8). 80pp. Report writers will appreciate this attractive introduction to the characteristics of this biome and its plants and animals. (Rev: SLJ 8/07) [577.54]

Forests and Rain Forests

24232 Art, Henry W., and Michael W. Robbins. *Woods Walk* (4–6). Illus. 2003, Storey $21.95 (978-1-58017-477-0); paper $14.95 (978-1-58017-452-7). 128pp. A broad overview of the plants and animals found in the woodlands of the eastern and western United States. (Rev: HBG 4/04; SLJ 6/03) [508.352]

24233 Baldwin, Carol. *Living in a Rain Forest* (3–6). Series: Living Habitats. 2003, Heinemann LB $24.22 (978-1-4034-2992-6). 32pp. The plants and animals of the rain forest are presented in question-and-answer format, with brief discussion of human interference. (Rev: HBG 4/04; SLJ 2/04) [577.34]

24234 Baldwin, Carol. *Living in the Taiga* (3–6). Series: Living Habitats. 2003, Heinemann LB $24.22 (978-1-4034-2994-0). 32pp. The plants and animals of the taiga are presented in question-and-answer format, with brief discussion of human interference. (Rev: HBG 4/04; SLJ 2/04) [577.3]

24235 Benduhn, Tea. *Living in Tropical Rain Forests* (3–4). Series: Life on the Edge. 2007, Gareth Stevens LB $19.93 (978-0-8368-8344-2). 24pp. After an introduction to rain forests and the climate of these areas, Benduhn looks at the people who live there, the life they lead, and the problems they face. (Rev: LMC 1/08; SLJ 12/07) [910.915]

24236 Bishop, Nic. *Forest Explorer: A Life-Size Field Guide* (K–4). Photos by author. 2004, Scholastic $17.95 (978-0-439-17480-0). 48pp. An attractive introductory guide to the trees and animal life found in deciduous forests. (Rev: BL 1/1–15/04; SLJ 3/04) [591.734]

24237 Butterfield, Moira. *Animals in Trees* (K–3). Series: Looking At. 1999, Raintree LB $24.26 (978-0-7398-0110-9). 32pp. For beginning readers, this book introduces in a simple text and pictures such animals as the squirrel, marmoset, macaw, and ocelot. (Rev: HBG 9/00; SLJ 3/00) [591]

24238 Castaldo, Nancy F. *Rainforests: An Activity Guide for Ages 6–9* (2–6). Illus. 2003, Chicago Review paper $14.95 (978-1-55652-476-9). 133pp. This engaging collection of resources and activities is designed to help young readers gain a better understanding of the different types of rainforests and the animals and plants that are common to each. (Rev: SLJ 11/03) [577.34]

24239 Chinery, Michael. *Poisoners and Pretenders* (5–8). Series: Secrets of the Rainforests. 2000, Crabtree LB $25.27 (978-0-7787-0219-1); paper $7.95 (978-0-7787-0229-0). 32pp. After a brief description of a rain forest, this book looks at animals found there and their mimicry, camouflage, venom, natural selection, and adaptation to the environment. Also use *Predators and Prey* (2000). (Rev: SLJ 2/01) [574.5]

24240 Cole, Melissa. *Forests* (3–6). Photos by Tom Leeson and Pat Leeson. Series: Wild America Habitats. 2003, Gale LB $21.20 (978-1-56711-802-5). 24pp. Describes the unique characteristics of the forest habitat and the plants and animals that thrive within it. Also use *Rain Forests* (2003). (Rev: SLJ 2/04) [577.3]

24241 Collard, Sneed B. *The Forest in the Clouds* (2–4). Illus. by Michael Rothman. 2000, Charlesbridge $16.95 (978-0-88106-985-3); paper $6.95 (978-0-88106-986-0). 32pp. In double-page spreads, the Monteverde Cloud Forest in Costa Rica is introduced with material on its climate, animals, and plants. (Rev: BL 6/1–15/00; HBG 3/01; SLJ 8/00) [577.34]

24242 Dorros, Arthur. *Rain Forest Secrets* (3–5). Illus. 1990, Scholastic $15.95 (978-0-590-43369-3). 32pp. A picture-book introduction to rain forests. (Rev: BCCB 9/90; BL 9/1/90; SLJ 2/91) [574.5]

24243 Drake, Jane, and Ann Love. *Forestry* (3–4). Illus. by Pat Cupples. Series: America at Work. 1998, Kids Can $12.95 (978-1-55074-462-0). 31pp. A young boy is taken into a forest where he learns about forestry, the lumbering industry, and associated environmental concerns. (Rev: HBG 3/99; SLJ 12/98) [574.5]

24244 Fleisher, Paul. *Forest Food Webs* (2–5). Illus. Series: Early Bird Food Webs. 2007, Lerner LB $26.60 (978-0-8225-6729-5). 48pp. This book describes the interrelationship between plants and animals in the forest. (Rev: BL 12/1/07) [577.3]

24245 George, Jean Craighead. *One Day in the Tropical Rain Forest* (3–6). Illus. by Gary Allen. 1990, HarperCollins $15.99 (978-0-690-04767-7). 64pp. The tropical rain forest is introduced in a narrative that proceeds through the course of a day. (Rev: BCCB 3/90; BL 4/15/90; HB 5/90; SLJ 8/90) [508]

24246 Gibbons, Gail. *Nature's Green Umbrella: Tropical Rain Forests* (3–5). Illus. 1994, Morrow $15.89 (978-0-688-12354-3). 32pp. The ecosystem of the rain forest is explained, with material on how these resources should be protected and preserved. (Rev: BL 6/1–15/94; SLJ 7/94) [574.5]

24247 Giesecke, Ernestine. *Forest Plants* (K–3). Series: Heinemann First Library. 1999, Heinemann LB $21.36 (978-1-57572-823-0). 32pp. Different plants that grow in forests are presented with a full-color photo followed by a few lines of explanatory text. (Rev: BL 6/1–15/99) [574]

24248 Godkin, Celia. *Fire!* (1–3). 2006, Fitzhenry & Whiteside $17.95 (978-1-55041-889-7). 40pp. Double-page spreads show the role fire plays in forest ecology, with a frightening blaze followed by returning animals and plants. (Rev: BL 8/06; SLJ 11/06) [577.24]

24249 Goodman, Susan E. *Bats, Bugs, and Biodiversity: Adventures in the Amazonian Rain Forest* (4–8). Illus. 1995, Simon & Schuster $16.00 (978-0-689-31942-6). Some junior high students learn first-hand about the Amazon rain forest and its endangered ecology. (Rev: BL 12/1/97) [508]

24250 Green, Jen. *A Dead Log* (2–4). Series: Small Worlds. 1999, Crabtree LB $25.27 (978-0-7787-0136-1). 32pp. This book presents the animals and plants that might be associated with a fallen log in a North American deciduous forest. (Rev: SLJ 2/00) [574.5]

24251 Grupper, Jonathan. *Destination: Rain Forest* (4–6). Illus. 1997, National Geographic $16.00 (978-0-7922-7018-8). 32pp. Using brilliant photos, this book introduces the rain forest as a habitat, as well as the animals found there. (Rev: BL 11/1/97; HBG 3/98; SLJ 10/97) [578.734]

24252 Guiberson, Brenda Z. *Life in the Boreal Forest* (2–5). Illus. by Gennady Spirin. 2009, Holt $16.99 (978-0-8050-7718-6). 40pp. Beautiful illustrations and compelling text describe the taigas of the northern hemisphere, the plants and animals that live there, the threats they face, and their importance to the environment. (Rev: BL 7/09; LMC 10/09; SLJ 9/09) [578.73]

24253 Guiberson, Brenda Z. *Rain, Rain, Rainforest* (K–3). Illus. by Steve Jenkins. 2004, Holt $16.95 (978-0-8050-6582-4). 32pp. Basic information on day-to-day life and survival in the rain forest is conveyed in an attractive blend of picturesque narrative and colorful paper-cut collages. (Rev: BL 5/1/04; HB 7/04; SLJ 6/04) [577.34]

24254 Hickman, Pamela. *In the Woods* (3–5). Series: See, Make and Do. 1998, Formac paper $9.95 (978-0-88780-412-0). 64pp. A book about woodland exploration and the animals and plants one might encounter, with several suggestions for craft projects. (Rev: BL 12/1/98) [557.3]

24255 Jackson, Kay. *Rain Forests* (4–7). Illus. Series: Our Environment. 2007, Gale LB $23.70 (978-0-7377-3624-3). 48pp. This well-illustrated volume explores why rain forests are important; what people, plants, and animals live there; why these areas are endangered; and what their future may hold. (Rev: BL 12/1/07) [577.34]

24256 Jackson, Tom. *Tropical Forests* (5–8). Series: Biomes Atlases. 2003, Raintree LB $31.42 (978-0-7398-5250-7). 64pp. This comprehensive overview of tropical forests describes the climate, flora and fauna, people, and future of these areas, and includes good maps. (Rev: SLJ 9/03) [577.34]

24257 Johanasen, Heather, and Sindy McKay. *About the Rain Forest* (1–2). Illus. Series: We Both Read. 2000, Treasure Bay $7.99 (978-1-891327-23-0); paper $3.99 (978-1-891327-24-7). 44pp. Using side-by-side texts, one for adults and the other for children, this book introduces the rain forest, its

climate, ecosystem, and animals. (Rev: BL 7/00) [574.5]

24258 Johansson, Philip. *The Dry Desert: A Web of Life* (3–5). Illus. Series: A World of Biomes. 2004, Enslow LB $23.93 (978-0-7660-2200-3). 48pp. An engaging introduction to the flora and fauna of the desert and to the work of the scientists who study the biome.

24259 Johansson, Philip. *The Forested Taiga: A Web of Life* (3–6). Illus. Series: A World of Biomes. 2004, Enslow LB $23.93 (978-0-7660-2197-6). 48pp. Introduces readers to the physical characteristics, climate, flora, and fauna of the forested taiga, a vast subpolar region dominated by conifers. (Rev: SLJ 8/04) [577.3]

24260 Johansson, Philip. *The Temperate Forest: A Web of Life* (3–5). Illus. Series: World of Biomes. 2004, Enslow LB $23.93 (978-0-7660-2198-3). 48pp. A biologist's interest in a black bear in North Carolina serves as an introduction to this study of plant and animal interaction in temperate forests. (Rev: BL 4/1/04; SLJ 8/04) [577.3]

24261 Johansson, Philip. *The Tropical Rain Forest: A Web of Life* (3–6). Illus. Series: World of Biomes. 2004, Enslow LB $23.93 (978-0-7660-2199-0). 48pp. An engaging introduction to the flora and fauna of the rain forest and to the work of the scientists who study the biome. (Rev: SLJ 8/04) [577.34]

24262 Johnson, Linda Carlson. *Rain Forests: A Pro/Con Issue* (4–8). Series: Hot Issues. 1999, Enslow LB $21.95 (978-0-7660-1202-8). 64pp. This book describes the rain forests of the world, how political and economic interests are destroying them, efforts to save them, and the pros and cons of conserving them. (Rev: HBG 10/00; SLJ 4/00) [574.5]

24263 Johnson, Rebecca. *A Walk in the Boreal Forest* (2–4). Illus. by Phyllis V. Saroff. Series: Biomes of North America. 2000, Carolrhoda LB $23.93 (978-1-57505-156-7). 48pp. This book takes the reader to a forest of tall conifers and tells about its plants and animals and their interdependence. (Rev: BL 10/15/00; HBG 3/01; SLJ 3/01) [574.5]

24264 Johnson, Rebecca. *A Walk in the Rain Forest* (2–5). Illus. by Phyllis V. Saroff. Series: Biomes of North America. 2001, Carolrhoda LB $23.93 (978-1-57505-154-3). 48pp. Examines the climate of the rain forest and its flora and fauna. (Rev: HBG 10/01; SLJ 3/01) [574.5]

24265 Kaplan, Elizabeth. *Taiga* (5–7). Illus. Series: Biomes of the World. 1996, Benchmark LB $25.64 (978-0-7614-0135-3). 64pp. This account discusses the climate, animal and plant life, soil, and seasonal changes in the taiga, the extensive forest in the Northern Hemisphere. (Rev: SLJ 7/96) [574.5]

24266 Kaplan, Elizabeth. *Temperate Forest* (4–6). Illus. Series: Biomes of the World. 1995, Marshall Cavendish LB $25.64 (978-0-7614-0082-0). 64pp. Four types of temperate forests are introduced, with material on locations, animals, plants, and possible future problems. (Rev: BL 12/15/95; SLJ 3/96) [574.5]

24267 Knight, Tim. *Journey into the Rainforest* (3–5). Illus. by Juan Pablo Moreiras and Tim Knight. 2001, Oxford $19.95 (978-0-19-521751-3). 48pp. Readers take a colorful tour through a rain forest, observing the vegetation and wildlife as they go and learning about the ecosystem's intricacies and endangered status. (Rev: BL 9/15/01; HBG 3/02; SLJ 10/01) [577.34]

24268 Lasky, Kathryn. *The Most Beautiful Roof in the World: Exploring the Rainforest Canopy* (5–8). 1997, Harcourt paper $9.00 (978-0-15-200897-0). The canopy of plants and animals found in the rain forest of Belize is explored by the author, a biologist, who also explains the methods scientists use to conduct research in this often challenging environment. (Rev: BL 4/1/97; SLJ 4/97) [574.5]

24269 Levinson, Nancy S. *Rain Forests* (K–2). Illus. by Diane D. Hearn. 2008, Holiday $15.95 (978-0-8234-1899-2). 40pp. A useful introduction to rain forests around the world and the animals and plants found in them. (Rev: BL 5/1/08; SLJ 5/08) [577.34]

24270 Levy, Janey. *Discovering Rain Forests* (3–5). Series: World Habitats. 2007, Rosen LB $23.95 (978-1-4042-3782-7). 32pp. With photographs and fast facts, this volume covers location, climate, plants and animals, people, threats and conservation efforts, and so forth. (Rev: LMC 3/08; SLJ 1/08) [577.34]

24271 Lewington, Anna. *Antonio's Rain Forest* (3–5). Illus. by Edward Parker. 1993, Carolrhoda LB $22.60 (978-0-87614-749-8). 48pp. A first-person narrative by an 8-year-old boy of the rain forest. (Rev: BL 3/1/93; SLJ 3/93) [338]

24272 Lewington, Anna, and Edward Parker. *People of the Rain Forests* (4–7). Series: Wide World. 1998, Raintree $18.98 (978-0-8172-5061-4). 48pp. As well as introducing rain forests, this book describes the people who live there, their tribal customs, their homes — including cities — and their everyday lives. (Rev: HBG 3/99; SLJ 1/99) [574.5]

24273 MacMillan, Dianne. *Life in a Deciduous Forest* (5–8). Series: Ecosystems in Action. 2003, Lerner LB $26.60 (978-0-8225-4684-9). 72pp. This book explores the ecosystem, its flora and fauna, where trees shed their leaves in autumn. (Rev: BL 9/15/03; HBG 10/03) [574.5]

24274 Montgomery, Sy. *Encantado: Pink Dolphin of the Amazon* (5–8). Illus. by Diane Taylor-Snow. 2002, Houghton $18.00 (978-0-618-13103-7). 80pp. The author describes the flora and fauna of the South American rain forest seen in her unsuccessful journey to locate the encantado, the elusive pink dolphin. (Rev: BL 4/1/02; HB 7/02; HBG 10/02; SLJ 5/02*) [599.53]

24275 Morrison, Marion. *The Amazon Rain Forest and Its People* (5–8). Series: People and Places. 1993, Thomson Learning LB $24.26 (978-1-56847-087-0). After a general history and a description of the region's plants, animals, and people, the author discusses the dangers developers pose to this rain forest. (Rev: BL 11/1/93) [333.75]

24276 Morrison, Taylor. *Wildfire* (4–6). Illus. 2006, Houghton $17.00 (978-0-618-50900-3). 48pp. Explores the contradiction between the destruction caused by wildfires and their beneficial impact on forests; with descriptions of the roles of firefighters, scientists, and foresters. (Rev: BL 4/1/06; SLJ 5/06) [634.9]

24277 Moss, Miriam. *Jungle Song* (PS–2). Illus. by Adrienne Kennaway. 2004, Lincoln $15.95 (978-1-84507-039-7). 32pp. A young tapir is lured away from his mother by a spider and explores the lush and busy South American rain forest. (Rev: BL 10/1/04; SLJ 10/04)

24278 O'Hare, Ted. *Vanishing Rain Forest* (1–3). Photos by Lynn M. Stone. Series: Rain Forests Today. 2005, Rourke LB $14.95 (978-1-59515-156-8). 24pp. An attractive introduction to the threats to world's rain forests from pollution and wholesale deforestation. Other titles in this series include *Animals of the Rain Forest*, *Plants of the Rain Forest*, and *People of the Rain Forest* (all 2005). (Rev: BL 1/1–15/05) [333.75]

24279 Oldfield, Sara. *Rain Forests* (3–6). Illus. Series: Endangered People and Places. 1996, Lerner LB $22.60 (978-0-8225-2778-7). 48pp. The location, geography, and natural life of rain forests are described, plus material on the threats to these regions and how conservation efforts are proceeding. (Rev: BL 11/15/96; SLJ 1/97) [333.75]

24280 Parker, Edward. *People* (5–8). Photos by author. Series: Rain Forest. 2003, Raintree LB $27.12 (978-0-7398-5242-2). 48pp. An introduction to the various peoples of the rain forest. (Rev: HBG 3/03; SLJ 1/03) [304.2]

24281 Parker, Edward. *Rain Forest Mammals* (5–9). Illus. Series: Rain Forest. 2002, Raintree LB $27.12 (978-0-7398-5241-5). 48pp. Mammals of the rain forest and the importance of preserving their habitat are introduced in close-up color photographs and a catchy layout, with a glossary, bibliography, and list of related organizations. Also use *Rain Forest Reptiles and Amphibians* (2002). (Rev: BL 12/1/02; HBG 3/03) [599]

24282 Pipes, Rose. *Forests and Woodlands* (2–4). Series: World Habitats. 1998, Raintree LB $24.28 (978-0-8172-5007-2). 32pp. A general description of the physical features of forests is followed by material on climate, wildlife, uses, and protection efforts. (Rev: BL 3/15/99; HBG 3/99) [574.5]

24283 Pipes, Rose. *Rain Forests* (2–4). Illus. Series: World Habitats. 1998, Raintree LB $24.28 (978-0-8172-5003-4). 32pp. Rain forests are introduced in color photographs and clear text, with material on animal and plant life, climate, and conservation. (Rev: BL 4/15/98; HBG 9/98) [577.4]

24284 Pirotta, Saviour. *People in the Rain Forest* (2–4). Illus. Series: Deep in the Rain Forest. 1998, Raintree LB $25.69 (978-0-8172-5137-6). 32pp. Rain forests in Peru, Indonesia, and New Guinea are highlighted in this account of the various peoples of the rain forest, their different habitats, how they live, and how their environments are being threatened. (Rev: BL 1/1–15/99; HBG 3/99) [304.2]

24285 Pyers, Greg. *Forest Explorer* (2–4). Illus. Series: Habitat Explorer. 2004, Raintree LB $25.70

(978-1-4109-0508-6). 32pp. This photo-filled exploration of forests looks at the plants and animals found there, plus environmental threats posed by pollution and development. Also use *Rain Forest Explorer* (2004).

24286 Rapp, Valerie. *Life in an Old Growth Forest* (5–8). Series: Ecosystems in Action. 2002, Lerner LB $26.60 (978-0-8225-2135-8). 72pp. In pictures and text, this book introduces life in an established forest with material on the interdependence of organisms there, and how human intervention has changed this ecosystem. (Rev: BL 12/15/02; HBG 3/03; SLJ 2/03) [574.5]

24287 Ricciuti, Edward R. *Rainforest* (4–6). Illus. Series: Biomes of the World. 1995, Marshall Cavendish LB $25.64 (978-0-7614-0081-3). 64pp. The world's rain forest biome is described, with material on this ecological system, its animals, plants, and current threats of destruction. (Rev: BL 12/15/95) [574.5]

24288 Ross, Suzanne. *What's in the Rainforest?* (3–5). Illus. by author. 1991, Enchanted Rainforest paper $5.95 (978-0-9629895-0-6). 48pp. Using an alphabetical approach, this is a well-organized introduction to the plants and animals found in a rain forest. (Rev: SLJ 3/92) [574.5]

24289 Sandler, Michael. *Rain Forests: Surviving in the Amazon* (3–5). Illus. Series: X-treme Places. 2005, Bearport LB $25.27 (978-1-59716-089-6). 32pp. This colorful overview of the world's rain forests includes the harrowing survival story of Yossi Ghinsberg, who became lost in the wilds of the Amazon basin. (Rev: SLJ 1/06) [578.734]

24290 Sauvain, Philip. *Rain Forests* (3–5). Illus. Series: Geography Detectives. 1997, Carolrhoda LB $19.93 (978-1-57505-041-6). 32pp. Identifies and describes the world's rain forests and the lush plants and diverse peoples and animals that live in them, with information on the many industrial threats to rain forests' survival. (Rev: BL 8/97) [574.5]

24291 Savage, Stephen. *Animals of the Rain Forest* (3–6). Illus. Series: Animals by Habitat. 1997, Raintree LB $22.83 (978-0-8172-4751-5). 32pp. The rain forest habitat is introduced, with focus on the five categories of animal life found there, such as mammals, birds, and amphibians. (Rev: BL 5/15/97) [591.9]

24292 Sayre, April P. *Taiga* (4–7). Illus. Series: Exploring Earth's Biomes. 1994, Twenty-First Century LB $25.90 (978-0-8050-2830-0). 64pp. This book clearly describes the swampy, carnivorous forest and the wildlife found, for example, in northern Canada, where the tundra ends. (Rev: BL 1/15/95; SLJ 2/95) [574.5]

24293 Sayre, April P. *Temperate Deciduous Forest* (4–7). Illus. Series: Exploring Earth's Biomes. 1994, Twenty-First Century LB $25.90 (978-0-8050-2828-7). 64pp. Deciduous forests are introduced with material on their composition, uses, and the animal and other plant life found within their community. (Rev: BL 1/1/95*; SLJ 1/95) [574.5]

24294 Sayre, April P. *Tropical Rain Forest* (4–7). Illus. Series: Exploring Earth's Biomes. 1994,

Twenty-First Century LB $25.90 (978-0-8050-2826-3). 64pp. The structure and contents of rain forests are explored with information on the plants, animals, and people that exist in this habitat. (Rev: BL 1/1/95; SLJ 1/95) [574.5]

24295 Serafini, Frank. *Looking Closely Through the Forest* (K–3). Photos by author. 2008, Kids Can $15.95 (978-1-55453-212-4). Guessing game questions draw readers through the forest with answers and facts revealed at the turn of each page. (Rev: LMC 10/08; SLJ 4/08) [578.73]

24296 Silver, Donald M. *Why Save the Rain Forest?* (3–5). Illus. by Patricia J. Wynne. 1993, Messner LB $23.00 (978-0-671-86609-9); paper $6.95 (978-0-671-86610-5). 48pp. A handsome volume that shows the amazing diversity of life in a rain forest and the consequences of destroying this environment. (Rev: SLJ 3/94) [574.5]

24297 Staub, Frank. *America's Forests* (3–6). Illus. 1999, Carolrhoda $15.95 (978-1-57505-265-6). 48pp. Different types of forests that exist in North America are introduced with material on kinds of trees and a basic woodland ecosystem. (Rev: BL 5/1/99; HBG 9/99; SLJ 7/99) [577.3]

24298 Stille, Darlene R. *Tropical Rain Forests* (2–4). Illus. 1999, Children's Book Pr. LB $25.00 (978-0-516-21511-2). 48pp. The climate and geography of tropical rain forests are discussed with coverage on their plants and animals. (Rev: BL 10/15/99) [578.734]

24299 Stone, Lynn M. *Forests* (1–3). Illus. Series: Biomes of North America. 2003, Rourke LB $20.64 (978-1-58952-684-6). 24pp. For young researchers, this is an excellent introduction to this biome, with clear, simple text, photographs, and maps. [574.5]

24300 Telford, Carole, and Rod Theodorou. *Up a Rainforest Tree* (3–5). Series: Amazing Journeys. 1997, Heinemann LB $22.79 (978-1-57572-156-9). 32pp. This trek through the layers of the Amazon rain forest is well organized, but the illustrations are often too small for clarity. (Rev: SLJ 4/98) [574.5]

24301 Welsbacher, Anne. *Life in a Rainforest* (5–8). Series: Ecosystems in Action. 2003, Lerner LB $26.60 (978-0-8225-4685-6). 72pp. This illustrated account covers the plant and animal life in rain forests and explains how human intervention has changed, and often endangered, this ecosystem. (Rev: BL 9/15/03; HBG 10/03) [574.5]

24302 Woods, Mae. *Insects of the Rain Forest* (2–4). Series: Rain Forest. 1999, ABDO LB $21.35 (978-1-57765-023-2). 24pp. This book presents the insects found in the rain forest with outstanding photos and an interesting text. Also use *People of the Rain Forest* and *Protecting the Rain Forest* (both 1999). (Rev: HBG 4/00; SLJ 1/00) [574.5]

Mountains

24303 Benduhn, Tea. *Living in Mountains* (3–4). Series: Life on the Edge. 2007, Gareth Stevens LB $19.93 (978-0-8368-8342-8). 24pp. After an introduction to mountains and the climate of these areas, Benduhn looks at the people of mountain areas, the life they lead, and the problems they face. (Rev: LMC 1/08; SLJ 12/07) [910.914]

24304 Chambers, Catherine. *Mountains* (3–5). Series: Mapping Earthforms. 2000, Heinemann LB $21.36 (978-1-57572-525-3). 32pp. A basic overview of mountains presented in double-page spreads illustrated with photographs, maps, and charts. (Rev: HBG 3/01; SLJ 8/00) [551.4]

24305 Cobb, Vicki. *This Place Is High* (3–5). Illus. by Barbara Lavallee. Series: Imagine Living Here. 1989, Walker LB $13.85 (978-0-8027-6883-4). Set in the high Andes, this is a book on an unusual climate zone in South America. A companion volume is *This Place Is Wet* (1989), about the rain forest of the Amazon River. (Rev: SLJ 10/89) [551.4]

24306 Cumming, David. *Mountains* (5–8). Illus. Series: Habitats. 1995, Thomson Learning LB $24.26 (978-1-56847-388-8). 48pp. Material covered includes the geology of mountains, their formation, and the life they support, and the effects of industry, tourism, and transportation. (Rev: BL 2/1/96) [551.4]

24307 Gill, Shelley. *Up on Denali* (2–4). Illus. by Shannon Cartwright. 2006, Sasquatch $16.95 (978-1-57061-366-1); paper $10.95 (978-1-57061-365-4). 32pp. Explores the geology and plants and animals of Denali, North America's tallest mountain, in an appealing and humorous blend of fact and fiction. (Rev: BL 6/1–15/06) [551.43]

24308 Green, Jen. *People of the Mountains* (4–6). Series: Wide World. 1998, Raintree LB $18.98 (978-0-8172-5062-1). 48pp. The geography and ecology of mountain environments are discussed plus material on the human cultures in these areas. (Rev: HBG 3/99; SLJ 2/99) [551.4]

24309 Grupper, Jonathan. *Rocky Mountains* (4–6). Series: Destination. 2001, National Geographic LB $16.95 (978-0-7922-7722-4). 32pp. This book introduces the Rockies, how they were formed, their composition, and their animals and plants. (Rev: BL 3/1/01; HBG 10/01) [978]

24310 Harrison, David L. *Mountains: The Tops of the World* (1–3). Illus. by Cheryl Nathan. 2005, Boyds Mills $16.95 (978-1-59078-326-9). 32pp. Explores the ways in which mountains were created and provides explanations for such puzzling phenomena as the discovery of a fish fossil on a mountaintop. (Rev: BL 11/1/05; SLJ 10/05) [551.43]

24311 Jennings, Terry. *Mountains* (3–6). Illus. 2003, Thameside LB $24.25 (978-1-931983-19-8). 32pp. Vivid photographs help to explain how mountains are formed and eroded, their importance in our climate, and the kind of life there. (Rev: BL 12/1/02; HBG 3/03) [551.432]

24312 Levy, Janey. *Discovering Mountains* (3–5). Series: World Habitats. 2007, Rosen LB $23.95 (978-1-4042-3785-8). 32pp. With photographs and fast facts, this volume covers location, climate, plants and animals, people, threats and conservation efforts, and so forth. (Rev: LMC 3/08; SLJ 1/08) [551.4]

24313 Locker, Thomas. *Mountain Dance* (K–4). Illus. by author. 2001, Harcourt $17.00 (978-0-15-

202622-6). Verse and oil paintings describe various kinds of mountains and how they were formed, in an informative combination that appends additional details. (Rev: BCCB 2/02; HBG 3/02; SLJ 10/01) [551.4]

24314 Low, Robert. *Peoples of the Mountains* (2–4). Illus. Series: Peoples and Their Environments. 1996, Rosen LB $18.75 (978-0-8239-2298-7). 24pp. After a definition of a mountain environment, this book tells about people who live in the Himalayas, Andes, and the mountains of China. (Rev: SLJ 1/97) [551.4]

24315 Maynard, Charles W. *The Appalachians* (2–5). Series: Great Mountain Ranges of the World. 2004, Rosen LB $21.25 (978-0-8239-6695-0). 24pp. Geology, history, climate, flora and fauna, and economy are all discussed in this easy-to-read, large-format volume. (Rev: SLJ 8/04) [917.4]

24316 Maynard, Charles W. *The Himalayas* (2–5). Series: Great Mountain Ranges of the World. 2004, Rosen LB $21.25 (978-0-8239-6694-3). 24pp. Geology, history, climate, flora and fauna, and economy are all discussed in this easy-to-read, large-format volume. (Rev: SLJ 8/04) [915.496]

24317 Pipes, Rose. *Mountains and Volcanoes* (2–4). Series: World Habitats. 1998, Raintree LB $24.28 (978-0-8172-5006-5). 32pp. This work discusses mountains — their geographic features, evolution, weather, wildlife, and human life — and volcanoes. (Rev: BL 5/15/98; HBG 9/98) [551.4]

24318 Pyers, Greg. *Mountain Explorer* (2–4). Illus. Series: Habitat Explorer. 2004, Raintree LB $25.70 (978-1-4109-0509-3). 32pp. This photo-filled exploration of mountains looks at the plants and animals found there, plus environmental threats posed by pollution and development.

24319 Rotter, Charles. *Mountains* (5–8). Illus. Series: Images. 1994, Creative Editions LB $23.95 (978-0-88682-596-6). 40pp. How mountains are formed is discussed, with material on how they change and the life they support. (Rev: SLJ 12/94) [551.4]

24320 Rotter, Charles. *Mountains: The Towering Sentinels* (4–6). Series: LifeViews. 2002, Creative Editions LB $24.25 (978-1-58341-123-0). 32pp. The various types of mountains are detailed, with information on climate, ecosystems, and environmental concerns. (Rev: HBG 3/03; SLJ 1/03)

24321 Sandler, Michael. *Mountains: Surviving on Mt. Everest* (3–5). Series: X-treme Places. 2005, Bearport LB $25.27 (978-1-59716-086-5). 32pp. The first-person account of Temba Tsheri Sherpa, a Nepalese climber who lost fingers to frostbite during a successful assault on Mount Everest, gives added punch to this overview of mountain climbing. (Rev: SLJ 1/06) [796.52]

24322 Sill, Cathryn. *Mountains* (K–4). Illus. by John Sill. Series: About Habitats. 2009, Peachtree $16.95 (978-1-56145-469-3). Simple, descriptive text and detailed illustrations of the plants and animals that inhabit various mountain locations combine to create an appealing volume. (Rev: SLJ 5/09) [577.5]

24323 Stronach, Neil. *Mountains* (4–8). Series: Endangered People and Places. 1996, Lerner LB

$22.60 (978-0-8225-2777-0). Geological aspects of mountains are covered, as well as the adjustments people make to live in mountainous regions. (Rev: SLJ 11/96) [333.73]

24324 Tocci, Salvatore. *Alpine Tundra: Life on the Tallest Mountain* (4–7). Series: Biomes and Habitats. 2005, Watts LB $25.50 (978-0-531-12365-2). 63pp. Introduces the climate, flora, and fauna found high above sea level on the world's highest mountains. Also use *Arctic Tundra: Life at the North Pole* (2005). (Rev: SLJ 7/05) [577.5]

Ponds, Rivers, and Lakes

24325 Amos, William Hopkins. *Life in Ponds and Streams* (PS–3). Illus. 1981, National Geographic LB $16.95 (978-0-87044-404-3). 32pp. Simple descriptions of pond life, plus outstanding photographs.

24326 Arnosky, Jim. *The Brook Book: Exploring the Smallest Streams* (K–3). Illus. by author. 2008, Dutton $15.99 (978-0-525-47716-7). 32pp. Beautiful watercolor artwork enhances this exploration of the ecology of brooks and streams. (Rev: BL 12/1/07; HB 3/08; LMC 10/08; SLJ 1/08) [574.5]

24327 Baron, Robert. *Hudson: The Story of a River* (2–5). Illus. by Thomas Locker. 2004, Fulcrum $17.95 (978-1-55591-512-4). 32pp. Breathtaking landscape paintings bring this natural history of the Hudson River Valley to life. (Rev: BL 5/15/04; SLJ 6/04) [974.7]

24328 Bauer, Marion Dane. *The Mighty Mississippi* (1–2). Illus. by John Wallace. Series: Wonders of America. 2007, Simon & Schuster LB $11.89 (978-0-689-86951-8); paper $3.99 (978-0-689-86950-1). 32pp. An introduction to the Mississippi River, with pleasing color illustrations and simple phrases for the beginning reader. (Rev: SLJ 5/07)

24329 Bryan, Dale-Marie. *The Colorado River* (1–2). Series: Rookie Read-About Geography. 2006, Children's Pr. LB $20.50 (978-0-516-25033-5). 32pp. Beginning readers and report writers will get all the facts about this grand river in this well-designed book. (Rev: SLJ 6/06) [917.91]

24330 Castaldo, Nancy F. *River Wild: An Activity Guide to North American Rivers* (4–7). Illus. 2006, Chicago Review $14.95 (978-1-55652-585-8). 150pp. From a general introduction to the water cycle and watersheds, this volume narrows in on specific rivers in North America and the flora and fauna found there, even offering profiles of riverkeepers. (Rev: BL 3/1/06; SLJ 6/06) [372.8991]

24331 Chambers, Catherine, and Nicholas Lapthorn. *Rivers*. Rev. ed. (3–5). Series: Mapping Earthforms. 2007, Heinemann LB $28.21 (978-1-4034-9604-1). 32pp. With maps, diagrams, tables, and color photographs, this title looks at how rivers are formed; river landscapes, plants, and animals; the future of rivers; and important examples (one chapter is titled "A Way of Life — Bangladesh"). (Rev: SLJ 10/07) [508.316]

24332 Cooper, Ann. *Around the Pond* (3–5). Illus. Series: Wild Wonders. 1998, Roberts Rinehart paper $9.95 (978-1-57098-223-1). 48pp. Using a series of four-page sections, this book describes such pond life as the bullfrog, blackbird, skunk, heron, dragonfly, grebe, turtle, diving beetle, and muskrat. (Rev: BL 12/1/98; SLJ 6/99) [591.763]

24333 Cumming, David. *Rivers and Lakes* (5–8). Series: Habitats. 1995, Thomson Learning LB $24.26 (978-1-56847-389-5). The plant and animal life that is supported by lakes and rivers is introduced, with accompanying information on geology and pollution. (Rev: BL 2/1/96) [551.48]

24334 Giesecke, Ernestine. *Pond Plants* (K–3). Series: Heinemann First Library. 1999, Heinemann LB $21.36 (978-1-57572-826-1). 32pp. Each of the ten pond plants that are introduced are illustrated with a full-color photo plus a few lines of large-print text. (Rev: BL 6/1–15/99) [574]

24335 Giesecke, Ernestine. *River Plants* (K–3). Series: Heinemann First Library. 1999, Heinemann LB $21.36 (978-1-57572-827-8). 32pp. Color photos and a few lines of simple text are used to introduce about ten plants that are found in rivers. (Rev: BL 6/1–15/99) [574]

24336 Giesecke, Ernestine. *Wetland Plants* (K–3). Series: Heinemann First Library. 1999, Heinemann LB $21.36 (978-1-57572-830-8). 32pp. About ten common plants found in wetlands are identified and, for each, there is a color photograph and a few lines of explanatory text. (Rev: BL 6/1–15/99; SLJ 8/99) [574]

24337 Gilpin, Daniel. *The Snake River* (4–8). Illus. Series: Rivers of North America. 2003, Gareth Stevens LB $26.00 (978-0-8368-3761-2). 32pp. Following the course of the Snake RIver in the Northwestern United States, with attention to the plant and animal life along it and its role in history. (Rev: SLJ 3/04)

24338 Gray, Leon. *The Missouri River* (4–8). Illus. Series: Rivers of North America. 2003, Gareth Stevens LB $26.00 (978-0-8368-3758-2). 32pp. A trip along the Missouri, the longest river in the United States, from its source to its confluence with the Mississippi, with a look at the history that has been made on its banks. (Rev: SLJ 3/04)

24339 Harris, Tim. *The Mackenzie River* (4–8). Illus. Series: Rivers of North America. 2003, Gareth Stevens LB $26.00 (978-0-8368-3756-8). 32pp. A visit to the Mackenzie River in Canada's Northwest Territories and the people, plants, and animals who have lived along it. (Rev: SLJ 3/04)

24340 Harrison, David L. *Rivers: Nature's Wondrous Waterways* (K–3). Illus. by Cheryl Nathan. 2002, Boyds Mills $15.95 (978-1-56397-968-2). 32pp. Using verse and color illustrations, this basic science book explains how rivers are formed, how they support life, and their importance in conservation and pollution. (Rev: BL 4/1/02; HBG 10/02; SLJ 5/02) [551.48]

24341 Hawkes, Steve. *The Tennessee River* (4–8). Illus. Series: Rivers of North America. 2003, Gareth Stevens LB $26.00 (978-0-8368-3763-6). 32pp. A trip along the length of the Tennessee River, with information on its history, natural attributes, and its effect on the people who live along its path. (Rev: SLJ 3/04)

24342 Heinz, Brian J. *Butternut Hollow Pond* (2–4). Illus. by Bob Marstall. 2000, Millbrook LB $22.90 (978-0-7613-0268-1). 32pp. This beautiful study of a day and night on a pond introduces many forms of animal life and demonstrates the food chain and the interdependence of creatures. (Rev: BL 1/1–15/01*; HBG 3/01; SLJ 3/01) [591.763]

24343 Himmelman, John. *Frog in a Bog* (PS–2). Illus. 2004, Charlesbridge $15.95 (978-1-57091-517-8). 32pp. A detailed and colorful look at life in a bog, for frogs and for all the other plants and animals found there. (Rev: BL 2/15/04; SLJ 3/04) [591.76]

24344 Hunter, Anne. *What's in the Pond?* (PS–2). Illus. by author. 1999, Houghton $5.95 (978-0-395-91224-9). Attractive color drawings are used to introduce pond life including several insects, a bluegill, a red-winged blackbird, a painted turtle, a frog, a tadpole, and a muskrat. Also use *What's Under the Log?* (1999). (Rev: HBG 4/00; SLJ 11/99) [574]

24345 Jackson, Tom. *The Arkansas River* (4–8). Illus. Series: Rivers of North America. 2003, Gareth Stevens LB $26.00 (978-0-8368-3752-0). 32pp. Tracing the Arkansas River its entire length of nearly 1,500 miles, with coverage of the people who have lived along it over the centuries and its importance to them. (Rev: SLJ 3/04)

24346 Jackson, Tom. *The Ohio River* (4–8). Illus. Series: Rivers of North America. 2003, Gareth Stevens LB $26.00 (978-0-8368-3759-9). 32pp. Following the Ohio River from Pittsburgh to its confluence with the Mississippi at Cairo, Illinois, with material on the people and places found along its banks. (Rev: SLJ 3/04)

24347 Johnson, Rebecca. *A Journey into a Lake* (3–6). Illus. by Phyllis V. Saroff. Series: Biomes of North America. 2004, Lerner LB $23.93 (978-1-57505-594-7). 48pp. The flora and fauna found in and around lakes are clearly described in striking text and illustrations that will please report writers and browsers. (Rev: BL 5/1/04) [577.63]

24348 Kalman, Bobbie, and Hadley Dyer. *Wetland Food Chains* (3–5). Illus. Series: Food Chains. 2006, Crabtree LB $25.20 (978-0-7787-1952-6); paper $6.95 (978-0-7787-1999-1). 32pp. An introduction to this biome, the plants and animals that live there, and how their interconnection functions. (Rev: SLJ 6/07)

24349 Kirkpatrick, Rena K. *Look at Pond Life* (K–2). Illus. 1978, Raintree paper $4.95 (978-0-8114-6901-2). 32pp. An introduction to the subject through brief text and many illustrations.

24350 Morrison, Gordon. *Pond* (3–6). Illus. 2002, Houghton $16.00 (978-0-618-10271-6). 32pp. Wonderful watercolors, descriptive text, and detailed insets show life in and around a pond through the seasons of the year. (Rev: BL 1/1–15/03; HBG 3/03; SLJ 10/02) [577.63]

24351 Pipes, Rose. *Rivers and Lakes* (2–4). Series: World Habitats. 1998, Raintree LB $24.28 (978-0-

8172-5002-7). 32pp. The geographical features of rivers and lakes are introduced with material on plant and animal life found in and around them, and how to protect them in the future. (Rev: BL 5/15/98; HBG 9/98) [574.5]

24352 Pyers, Greg. *River Explorer* (2–4). Illus. Series: Habitat Explorer. 2004, Raintree LB $25.70 (978-1-4109-0512-3). 32pp. This photo-filled exploration of rivers looks at the plants and animals found in and around them, plus environmental threats posed by pollution and development.

24353 Rapp, Valerie. *Life in a River* (5–8). Illus. Series: Ecosystems in Action. 2002, Lerner LB $26.60 (978-0-8225-2136-5). 72pp. The first title in a new series about ecosystems, this volume uses the example of the Columbia River to explain the concept and the interrelationship of rivers, animals, and humans. (Rev: BL 10/15/02; HBG 3/03; SLJ 1/03; VOYA 2/03) [577.6]

24354 Sayre, April P. *Lake and Pond* (4–7). Illus. Series: Exploring Earth's Biomes. 1996, Twenty-First Century LB $25.90 (978-0-8050-4089-0). 80pp. A colorful introduction to lake and pond habitats and the life forms found within them. (Rev: BL 6/1–15/96; SLJ 6/96) [574.05]

24355 Sayre, April P. *River and Stream* (4–7). Illus. Series: Exploring Earth's Biomes. 1996, Twenty-First Century LB $25.90 (978-0-8050-4088-3). 80pp. In a clearly written, informative style, this book presents material on rivers and streams, their ecology, and the various creatures and plants living in and around them. (Rev: BL 6/1–15/96; SLJ 6/96) [574.5]

24356 Schulte, Mary. *Great Salt Lake* (1–2). Series: Rookie Read-About Geography. 2006, Children's Pr. LB $20.50 (978-0-516-25034-2). 32pp. Beginning readers and report writers will get all the facts about this unusual lake in this well-designed book. (Rev: SLJ 6/06) [979.2]

24357 Sill, Cathryn. *Wetlands* (K–3). Illus. by John Sill. 2008, Peachtree $16.95 (978-1-56145-432-7). 32pp. From swamp to marsh to meadow to bog, this title covers the variety, features and environmental significance of wetlands. (Rev: BLO 3/3/08; SLJ 5/08) [578.768]

24358 Stewart, Melissa. *Life in a Lake* (5–8). Series: Ecosystems in Action. 2002, Lerner LB $26.60 (978-0-8225-2138-9). 72pp. The diversity and interdependence of life in a typical lake are introduced with material on how this ecosystem works and how man's interference has changed the balance of nature. (Rev: BL 12/15/02; HBG 3/03) [551.48]

24359 Viera, Linda. *The Mighty Mississippi: The Life and Times of America's Greatest River* (3–5). Illus. by Higgins Bond. 2005, Walker LB $17.85 (978-0-8027-8944-0). 32pp. Viera explores the geology and history of America's mighty Mississippi River. (Rev: BL 10/1/05; SLJ 11/05) [917.7]

24360 Walker, Sally M. *Life in an Estuary* (5–8). Series: Ecosystems in Action. 2002, Lerner LB $26.60 (978-0-8225-2137-2). 72pp. A look at life at the tidal mouths of rivers and the diversity of life in these areas, its interdependence, the balance of nature, and how human interaction has changed this ecosystem. (Rev: BL 12/15/02; HBG 3/03; SLJ 2/03) [574]

24361 Wechsler, Doug. *Frog Heaven: Ecology of a Vernal Pool* (3–6). 2006, Boyds Mills $17.95 (978-1-59078-253-8). 48pp. This is a vivid, richly illustrated, and thorough exploration of life in a vernal pool in Delaware over the period of a year. (Rev: BL 11/1/06*; HBG 4/07; LMC 3/08; SLJ 11/06) [577.63]

24362 Zollman, Pam. *Lake Tahoe* (1–2). Series: Rookie Read-About Geography. 2006, Children's Pr. LB $20.50 (978-0-516-25036-6). 32pp. Geographical and geological facts about this body of water are presented in an airy format that will appeal to beginning readers. (Rev: SLJ 6/06) [917.9438]

Prairies and Grasslands

24363 Bannatyne-Cugnet, Jo. *A Prairie Year* (3–5). Illus. by Yvette Moore. 1994, Tundra $16.95 (978-0-88776-334-2). 32pp. A month-by-month account of the experiences and activities involved in prairie life. (Rev: BL 1/15/95; SLJ 2/95) [630]

24364 Butterfield, Moira. *Animals on Plains and Prairies* (K–3). Series: Looking At. 1999, Raintree LB $24.26 (978-0-7398-0109-3). 32pp. Such grassland animals as the giraffe, termite, vulture, and agama lizard are introduced in this beginning reader. (Rev: HBG 9/00; SLJ 3/00) [574.5]

24365 Cole, Melissa. *Prairies* (3–6). Photos by Tom Leeson and Pat Leeson. Series: Wild America Habitats. 2003, Gale LB $22.45 (978-1-56711-807-0). 24pp. Examines the overall ecology and climate of the prairie, as well as the specific plant and animal species that flourish there. (Rev: SLJ 2/04) [577.4]

24366 Collard, Sneed B. *The Prairie Builders: Reconstructing America's Lost Grasslands* (5–8). Illus. 2005, Houghton $17.00 (978-0-618-39687-0). 72pp. This wide-format look at a project to regenerate tallgrass prairie and populate it with native plants and animals includes excellent photographs. (Rev: BL 6/1–15/05; SLJ 8/05*) [635.9]

24367 Green, Jen. *Under a Stone* (2–4). Series: Small Worlds. 1999, Crabtree LB $25.27 (978-0-7787-0137-8); paper $8.95 (978-0-7787-0151-4). 32pp. Highlights the animals and plants found on a North American prairie. (Rev: SLJ 2/00) [574.5]

24368 Himmelman, John. *Mouse in a Meadow* (PS–2). Illus. 2005, Charlesbridge $15.95 (978-1-57091-250-4); paper $6.95 (978-1-57091-521-5). 32pp. A close-up view of wildlife in a typical North American meadow. (Rev: BL 3/1/05; SLJ 5/05) [578.74]

24369 Hoare, Ben. *Temperate Grasslands* (5–8). Series: Biomes Atlases. 2003, Raintree LB $31.42 (978-0-7398-5249-1). 64pp. This comprehensive overview of grasslands describes the climate, flora and fauna, people, and future of these areas, and includes good maps. (Rev: SLJ 9/03) [577.4]

24370 Hunter, Anne. *What's in the Meadow?* (K–2). Illus. 2000, Houghton $5.95 (978-0-618-01512-2). 32pp. Ten animals that live in meadows — includ-

ing the woolly bear caterpillar, spittlebug, firefly, and meadowlark — are introduced with material on this habitat. (Rev: BL 9/15/00; HBG 3/01) [591.74]

24371 Johansson, Philip. *The Wide Open Grasslands: A Web of Life* (3–5). Illus. Series: A World of Biomes. 2004, Enslow LB $23.93 (978-0-7660-2201-0). 48pp. An engaging introduction to the flora and fauna of the grasslands and to the work of the scientists who study the biome. [577.4]

24372 Kalman, Bobbie, and Hadley Dyer. *Australian Outback Food Chains* (3–5). Illus. Series: Food Chains. 2006, Crabtree LB $25.20 (978-0-7787-1950-2); paper $6.95 (978-0-7787-1996-0). 32pp. An introduction to this habitat, the plants and animals that live there, and how their interconnection functions. (Rev: SLJ 6/07)

24373 Kalman, Bobbie, and Hadley Dyer. *Savanna Food Chains* (3–5). Illus. Series: Food Chains. 2006, Crabtree LB $25.20 (978-0-7787-1952-6); paper $6.95 (978-0-7787-1998-4). 32pp. An introduction to this biome, the plants and animals that live there, and how their interconnection functions. (Rev: SLJ 6/07)

24374 Knapp, Brian. *What Do We Know About Grasslands?* (4–6). Illus. 1992, Bedrick LB $15.95 (978-0-87226-359-8). 40pp. Among the topics covered are the importance of grasslands and their locations, ecology, and outlook. (Rev: BL 2/15/93; SLJ 1/93) [574]

24375 Levy, Janey. *Discovering the Tropical Savanna* (3–5). Series: World Habitats. 2007, Rosen LB $23.95 (978-1-4042-3783-4). 32pp. With photographs and fast facts, this volume covers location, climate, plants and animals, people, threats and conservation efforts, and so forth. (Rev: LMC 3/08; SLJ 1/08) [304.2]

24376 Lion, David C. *A Home on the Prairie* (1–3). Series: Scholastic News Nonfiction Readers. 2006, Children's Pr. LB $20.00 (978-0-516-25346-6). 24pp. This easy-to-understand introduction to the prairie as a natural habitat looks at the nature of the land itself, its climate, flora, and the animals that call it home. (Rev: SLJ 2/07) [574.5]

24377 Low, Robert. *Peoples of the Savanna* (2–5). Illus. Series: People and Their Environments. 1996, Rosen LB $18.75 (978-0-8239-2299-4). 24pp. Describes life in a grassland habitat and how this environment has shaped the lifestyles of the people who live there. (Rev: BL 11/15/96; SLJ 1/97) [304.2]

24378 Ormsby, Alison. *The Prairie* (5–8). Series: Ecosystems of North America. 1998, Benchmark LB $28.50 (978-0-7614-0897-0). A description of the prairie ecosystem and an examination of how the plants and animals in prairies affect one another and their environments. (Rev: HBG 10/99; SLJ 2/99) [551.4]

24379 Patent, Dorothy Hinshaw. *Life in a Grassland* (5–8). Series: Ecosystems in Action. 2002, Lerner LB $26.60 (978-0-8225-2139-6). 72pp. Using excellent pictures and a clear text, this volume explores the flora and fauna of different kinds of grasslands, with material on conservation. (Rev: BL 12/15/02; HBG 3/03) [574.5]

24380 Patent, Dorothy Hinshaw. *Prairies* (3–6). Illus. by William Muñoz. 1996, Holiday House LB $15.95 (978-0-8234-1277-8). 40pp. The ecology of prairie environments is covered, with striking photos and clear text. (Rev: BCCB 2/97; BL 11/1/96; SLJ 2/97) [574.5]

24381 Pipes, Rose. *Grasslands* (2–4). Series: World Habitats. 1998, Raintree LB $24.28 (978-0-8172-5005-8). 32pp. A well-organized account that explains the grassland ecology and gives examples of it around the world using text and pictures. (Rev: BL 5/15/98; HBG 9/98) [574.5]

24382 Quigley, Mary. *Prairie Explorer* (2–4). Illus. Series: Habitat Explorer. 2004, Raintree LB $25.70 (978-1-4109-0513-0). 32pp. This photo-filled exploration of prairies looks at the plants and animals found there, plus environmental threats posed by pollution and development.

24383 Ricciuti, Edward R. *Grassland* (4–6). Illus. Series: Biomes of the World. 1996, Benchmark LB $25.64 (978-0-7614-0136-0). 64pp. The world's grasslands are identified and described, with material on their vegetation and animal life and the environmental threats they face. (Rev: SLJ 7/96) [574.5]

24384 Rotter, Charles. *The Prairie* (5–8). Illus. Series: Images. 1994, Creative Editions LB $17.95 (978-0-88682-598-0). 40pp. The nature of prairie grasslands is introduced, with material on the animals and plants found there. (Rev: SLJ 12/94) [574.5]

24385 Savage, Stephen. *Animals of the Grasslands* (2–6). Illus. Series: Animals by Habitat. 1997, Raintree LB $22.83 (978-0-8172-4752-2). 32pp. Worldwide locations and characteristics of grasslands are highlighted, with material on such animals as coyotes, zebras, prairie dogs, emus, and termites. (Rev: BL 5/15/97) [591.9]

24386 Sayre, April P. *Grassland* (4–7). Illus. Series: Exploring Earth's Biomes. 1994, Twenty-First Century LB $25.90 (978-0-8050-2827-0). 64pp. A well-organized, clearly written account that explains what grasslands are and where they exist and the interaction of the creatures who live in this biome. (Rev: BL 1/15/95; SLJ 2/95) [574.5]

24387 Staub, Frank. *America's Prairies* (3–6). Illus. Series: Earth Watch. 1994, Carolrhoda LB $21.27 (978-0-87614-781-8). 48pp. The three kinds of prairies found in the United States are introduced, with coverage of the animals and plants found in each and the environmental hazards. (Rev: BL 2/1/94) [574.5]

24388 Steele, Philip. *Grasslands* (3–5). Illus. Series: Geography Detectives. 1997, Carolrhoda LB $19.93 (978-1-57505-042-3). 32pp. Discusses the grassland ecosystem in both temperate and tropical areas, with coverage on how they have been changed by agriculture and urbanization. (Rev: BL 8/97) [574.5]

24389 Stille, Darlene R. *Grasslands* (2–4). Series: True Books. 1999, Children's Book Pr. LB $25.00 (978-0-516-21509-9). 48pp. Grasslands and prairies are introduced in a book that contains a color pic-

ture and six lines of text on each page. (Rev: BL 10/15/99) [574.5]

24390 Stone, Lynn M. *Grasslands* (1–3). Illus. Series: Biomes of North America. 2003, Rourke LB $20.64 (978-1-58952-685-3). 24pp. For young researchers, this is an excellent introduction to this biome, with clear, simple text, photographs, and maps. [574.5]

24391 Toupin, Laurie Peach. *Life in the Temperate Grasslands* (4–7). Series: Biomes and Habitats. 2005, Watts LB $25.50 (978-0-531-12385-0). 63pp. Introduces the climatic conditions, plants, and wildlife of the world's temperate grasslands. Also use *Savannas: Life in the Tropical Grasslands* (2005). (Rev: SLJ 7/05) [577.4]

Rocks, Minerals, and Soil

24392 Bourgeois, Paulette. *The Amazing Dirt Book* (3–5). Illus. by Craig Terlson. Series: Children's Activities. 1990, Addison-Wesley paper $8.95 (978-0-201-55096-2). 80pp. Facts on such appealing matters as dust mites and worms. (Rev: BL 12/1/90; SLJ 3/91) [631.4]

24393 Bourgeois, Paulette. *The Dirt on Dirt* (3–6). Illus. by Martha Newbigging. 2008, Kids Can $15.95 (978-1-55453-101-1); paper $7.95 (978-1-55453-102-8). 32pp. An appealing introduction to dirt in all its forms, with experiments and activities. (Rev: BL 3/1/08; LMC 3/08; SLJ 5/08) [631.4]

24394 Ditchfield, Christin. *Soil* (2–5). Series: True Books — Natural Resources. 2002, Children's Book Pr. LB $25.00 (978-0-516-22344-5); paper $6.95 (978-0-516-29368-4). 48pp. This book covers such topics as how soil is formed, what it is made of, what it's used for, and how we can protect this important resource. (Rev: BL 10/15/02) [631.5]

24395 Eid, Alain. *1000 Photos of Minerals and Fossils* (5–9). Photos by Michel Viard. 2000, Barron's paper $24.95 (978-0-7641-5218-4). 127pp. An oversized, nicely illustrated volume that introduces minerals in their natural and refined states with material on sites, fossils, and jewelry. (Rev: SLJ 10/00) [548]

24396 Estigarribia, Diana. *Learning About Rocks, Weathering, and Erosion with Graphic Organizers* (3–6). Series: Graphic Organizers in Science. 2005, Rosen LB $21.25 (978-1-4042-2806-1). 24pp. This title uses a wide variety of graphic organizers, including concept webs, compare/contrast charts, Venn diagrams, graphs, timelines, and KWL charts, to illustrate geological concepts. (Rev: SLJ 11/05)

24397 Farndon, John. *Rock and Mineral* (5–9). Illus. Series: DK/Google e.guides. 2005, DK $17.99 (978-0-7566-1140-8). 96pp. This highly illustrated guide introduces readers to the basics of geology and provides a link to a Web site that serves as a gateway to additional resources. (Rev: SLJ 8/05) [552]

24398 Farndon, John. *Rocks and Minerals* (3–6). Series: Science Experiments. 2002, Marshall Cavendish LB $25.64 (978-0-7614-1468-1). 32pp.

Clear illustrations and good step-by-step instructions are used to present a series of experiments that reveal the nature and properties of rocks and minerals. (Rev: BL 12/15/02; HBG 3/03; SLJ 4/03) [552]

24399 Faulkner, Rebecca. *Igneous Rock* (4–6). Series: Geology Rocks! 2007, Raintree LB $31.43 (978-1-4109-2747-7). 48pp. Categories of rocks, minerals, identification, and formation are among the topics covered in this appealing and well-organized, high-interest introduction to igneous rock, with color photographs. (Rev: LMC 10/08; SLJ 3/08) [552]

24400 Faulkner, Rebecca. *Sedimentary Rock* (4–6). Series: Geology Rocks! 2007, Raintree LB $31.43 (978-1-4109-2748-4); paper $8.99 (978-1-4109-2756-9). 48pp. Rock formation and fossils are among the topics covered in this appealing and well-organized, high-interest introduction to sedimentary rock, with color photographs. (Rev: LMC 10/08; SLJ 3/08) [552]

24401 Flanagan, Alice K. *Rocks* (2–3). Series: Simply Science. 2000, Compass Point LB $21.26 (978-0-7565-0033-7). 32pp. This book explains how the three types of rocks are formed with examples of each as well as information on erosion and how to be a rock hound. (Rev: SLJ 2/01) [552]

24402 Gallant, Roy A. *Minerals* (3–5). Illus. Series: Kaleidoscope. 2000, Marshall Cavendish $25.64 (978-0-7614-1039-3). 48pp. An interesting look at minerals and rocks that begins with simple material and moves on to more complex topics such as mineral replacement. (Rev: BL 2/1/01; HBG 3/01) [549]

24403 Gallant, Roy A. *Rocks* (5–8). Series: Earth Sciences. 2000, Marshall Cavendish LB $25.64 (978-0-7614-1042-3). 48pp. Illustrations and full-spread diagrams introduce rocks and minerals and their properties, forms, and uses. (Rev: BL 3/1/01; HBG 3/01; SLJ 3/01) [552.2]

24404 Gans, Roma. *Let's Go Rock Collecting* (2–4). Illus. by Holly Keller. 1997, HarperCollins paper $5.99 (978-0-06-445170-3). 32pp. An introduction to rocks, how they were formed, their composition, their uses, and how to collect them. (Rev: BL 5/15/97; SLJ 8/97) [552]

24405 Kallen, Stuart A. *Gems* (4–7). Illus. Series: Wonders of the World. 2003, Gale LB $23.70 (978-0-7377-1028-1). 48pp. The formation of precious stones, their mining, and individual stones of note are all covered here. (Rev: BL 5/1/03) [553.8]

24406 Klein, James. *Gold Rush! The Young Prospector's Guide to Striking It Rich* (3–6). Illus. 1998, Tricycle paper $9.95 (978-1-883672-64-5). 96pp. This book provides a history of gold and gold prospecting and gives tips on good prospecting locations, tools, and what to do if you hit pay dirt. (Rev: BL 4/15/98) [622]

24407 Marzollo, Jean. *I Am a Rock* (1). Illus. by Judith Moffatt. Series: Hello Reader! 1998, Scholastic paper $3.99 (978-0-590-37222-0). 32pp. In this easy reader, a child named Marble visits the Rock Hall of Fame where one can identify 12 different rocks. (Rev: BL 7/98) [552]

24408 Milne, Jean. *The Story of Diamonds* (5–8). 2000, Linnet LB $21.50 (978-0-208-02476-3). 113pp. A book that explains where diamonds are found and how they are mined, evaluated, cut, polished, and used as jewels or in industry. (Rev: BL 2/1/00; HBG 10/00; SLJ 6/00; VOYA 4/01) [553.8]

24409 Oxlade, Chris. *Rock* (2–3). Series: Materials, Materials, Materials. 2002, Heinemann LB $22.79 (978-1-58810-585-1). 32pp. Using a few lines of text and a color picture on each page, this is a simple introduction to rocks, their composition, structure, and uses. (Rev: BL 6/1–15/02) [552]

24410 Oxlade, Chris. *Soil* (2–3). Series: Materials, Materials, Materials. 2002, Heinemann LB $22.79 (978-1-58810-587-5). 32pp. The composition of soil and its properties, uses, and formation are topics covered in this easily-read beginning science book. (Rev: BL 6/1–15/02) [631.5]

24411 Ricciuti, Edward R., and National Audubon Society, eds. *National Audubon Society First Field Guide: Rocks and Minerals* (5–8). Illus. 1998, Scholastic paper $17.95 (978-0-590-05463-8). A guide to equipment and techniques for observation and general information on geology, followed by an examination of 50 common rocks, their composition, texture, color, and environment. (Rev: BL 8/98; SLJ 8/98) [552]

24412 Richardson, Adele D. *Rocks* (2–4). Illus. Series: The Bridgestone Science Library. 2001, Capstone LB $22.60 (978-0-7368-0953-5). 24pp. Rock types, rock formation, and the Mohs scale of hardness are covered in this slim volume. (Rev: HBG 3/02; SLJ 2/02) [552]

24413 Spickert, Diane Nelson. *Earthsteps: A Rock's Journey Through Time* (3–6). Illus. 2000, Fulcrum $17.95 (978-1-55591-986-3). 32pp. The story of a rock and its transformation over 250 million years to a grain of sand. (Rev: BL 1/1–15/01; SLJ 1/01) [551.3]

24414 Staedter, Tracy. *Rocks and Minerals* (4–8). Series: Reader's Digest Pathfinders. 1999, Reader's Digest $16.99 (978-1-57584-290-5). 64pp. An outstanding introduction to geology is organized in three sections — "Rocks," "Minerals," and "Collecting Rocks and Minerals" — with "discovery paths" featuring personal accounts, hands-on activities, vocabulary, and facts. (Rev: SLJ 11/99) [552]

24415 Stewart, Melissa. *Extreme Rocks and Minerals! Q & A* (3–6). 2007, Collins $16.99 (978-0-06-089982-0); paper $6.99 (978-0-06-089981-3). 48pp. Well-designed and on-target, this title offers a clearly organized and well-illustrated overview of rocks and minerals. (Rev: SLJ 4/08) [552]

24416 Thorson, Kristine, and Robert Thorson. *Stone Wall Secrets* (3–5). Illus. by Gustav Moore. 1998, Tilbury House $16.95 (978-0-88448-195-9). A history and geology lesson on rocks and their uses, from the shale formed eons ago in prehistoric seas to the construction of a stone fence surrounding a New England farm. (Rev: SLJ 11/98) [552]

24417 Tomecek, Steve. *Dirt* (1–3). Illus. by Nancy Woodman. Series: Jump into Science. 2002, National Geographic $16.95 (978-0-7922-8204-4). 31pp.

This discussion of soil's composition, inhabitants, and uses combines scientific fact with appealing humor. (Rev: BCCB 11/02; HBG 3/03; SLJ 10/02) [631.5]

24418 Trueit, Trudi. *Rocks, Gems, and Minerals* (4–7). Series: Watts Library. 2003, Watts LB $25.50 (978-0-531-12195-5); paper $8.95 (978-0-531-16241-5). 63pp. This attractive volume introduces readers to rocks, gems, and minerals and examines the natural forces that created them. (Rev: SLJ 1/04) [552]

24419 VanCleave, Janice. *Rocks and Minerals* (4–6). Illus. Series: Spectacular Science Projects. 1996, Wiley paper $10.95 (978-0-471-10269-4). 96pp. In easy-to-follow steps, a series of experiments and other activities illustrate the properties and uses of rocks and minerals. (Rev: BL 3/15/96; SLJ 3/96) [552]

24420 Walker, Sally M. *Rocks* (2–4). Series: Early Bird Earth Science. 2006, Lerner LB $25.26 (978-0-8225-5947-4). 48pp. This attractive, readable overview of rocks and crystals examines the three families into which rocks are divided and also how they're formed. (Rev: BL 9/1/06; SLJ 1/07) [352]

24421 Wallace, Nancy Elizabeth. *Rocks! Rocks! Rocks!* (PS–2). Illus. by author. 2009, Marshall Cavendish $17.99 (978-0-7614-5528-8). 48pp. Mama and Buddy Bear study rocks at the Nature Center and learn about bedrock, erosion, and so forth. (Rev: BL 4/1/09; SLJ 6/09) [552]

Mathematics

General

24422 Aber, Linda Williams. *Who's Got Spots?* (2–3). Illus. by Gioia Fiammenghi. Series: Math Matters. 2000, Kane paper $4.95 (978-1-57565-099-9). 32pp. In this early math book, there is an outbreak of chicken pox and kids use this opportunity to create charts and graphs to record who has been sick and predict who will stay well. (Rev: SLJ 2/01) [001.4]

24423 Aboff, Marcie. *Mike's Mystery* (1–3). Illus. by Amy Bailey Muehlenhardt. Series: Read It! Readers: Math. 2007, Picture Window LB $19.93 (978-1-4048-3667-9). 32pp. Mike and his friends count down as they gather books toward their final donation goal. How many are left to go? Will they win a pizza party? (Rev: SLJ 2/08) [513.2]

24424 Adler, David A. *Fraction Fun* (2–4). Illus. by Nancy Tobin. 1996, Holiday House LB $16.95 (978-0-8234-1259-4). A clear, concise introduction to fractions using plenty of real-life situations as examples and for fun. (Rev: BCCB 12/96; SLJ 11/96) [513.2]

24425 Adler, David A. *Working with Fractions* (1–3). Illus. by Edward Miller. 2007, Holiday $32.00 (978-0-8234-2010-0). 32pp. With a birthday party as the setting, Adler uses such items as pizza, cake, children, and balloons to illustrate properties of fractions. (Rev: BL 11/15/07; LMC 1/08; SLJ 10/07) [513.2]

24426 Axelrod, Amy. *Pigs at Odds: Fun with Math and Games* (2–4). Illus. by Sharon McGinley-Nally. 2000, Simon & Schuster $14.00 (978-0-689-81566-9). In this entertaining concept book starring the Pig family at a carnival, the concept of probability is explored. (Rev: HBG 3/01; SLJ 1/01)

24427 Bodach, Vijaya Khisty. *Bar Graphs* (PS–2). 2007, Capstone LB $23.93 (978-1-4296-0040-8). 32pp. Using simple text and child-friendly examples, this book leads readers through the process of sorting items and representing quantity on a graph.

Also use *Pictographs* and *Tally Charts* (both 2007). (Rev: LMC 1/08; SLJ 2/08) [510]

24428 Bodach, Vijaya Khisty. *Pie Graphs* (K–2). Illus. 2007, Capstone LB $17.95 (978-1-4296-0042-2). 32pp. Eight child-friendly examples illustrate the usefulness of pie charts and show how to create them. (Rev: BL 10/15/07; LMC 1/08; SLJ 2/08) [510]

24429 Bruce, Sheila. *Everybody Wins!* (2–3). Illus. by Paige Billin-Frye. Series: Math Matters. 2001, Kane paper $4.95 (978-1-57565-101-9). 32pp. Readers learn the usefulness of math skills as they see friends agreeing to share. Also use *Keep Your Distance*. (Rev: SLJ 12/01) [513]

24430 Caron, Lucille, and Philip M. St. Jacques. *Fractions and Decimals* (4–8). Illus. Series: Math Success. 2000, Enslow LB $22.60 (978-0-7660-1430-5). 64pp. Many examples accompany explanations of how to add, subtract, multiply, and divide fractions and decimals. Also use *Addition and Subtraction* (2001). (Rev: HBG 3/01; SLJ 7/01) [513.2]

24431 Cleary, Brian P. *The Action of Subtraction* (K–4). Illus. by Brian Gable. Series: Math Is CATegorical. 2006, Millbrook LB $15.95 (978-1-76139-461-4). 32pp. Cartoon-style illustrations and a rap-style rhyming text introduce subtraction with child-friendly examples. (Rev: SLJ 11/06) [513.2]

24432 Clemson, Wendy, and David Clemson. *Digging for Dinosaurs* (2–3). Illus. Series: Math Adventures. 2007, Gareth Stevens LB $25.27 (978-0-8368-7838-7); paper $8.95 (978-0-8368-8137-0). 32pp. Readers will learn that math does come in handy in the real world as they explore how paleontologists manipulate data in their study of dinosaurs. (Rev: SLJ 5/07)

24433 Clemson, Wendy, and David Clemson. *Firefighters to the Rescue* (2–3). Illus. Series: Math Adventures. 2007, Gareth Stevens LB $25.27 (978-0-8368-7839-4); paper $8.95 (978-0-8368-8138-7). 32pp. Would-be firefighters will be fascinated to learn how math is used in this job. Photographs of real-world heroes using math will inspire reluctant students. (Rev: SLJ 5/07)

24434 Clemson, Wendy, and David Clemson. *Ocean Giants* (2–3). Illus. Series: Math Adventures. 2007, Gareth Stevens LB $25.27 (978-0-8368-7840-0); paper $8.95 (978-0-8368-8139-4). 32pp. Readers will be fascinated to learn that even scuba divers use math. The photographs of deep-sea divers will inspire even reluctant students of mathematics. (Rev: SLJ 5/07)

24435 Clemson, Wendy, and David Clemson. *Rocket to the Moon* (2–3). Illus. Series: Math Adventures. 2007, Gareth Stevens LB $25.27 (978-0-8368-7841-7); paper $8.95 (978-0-8368-8140-0). 32pp. Math is essential to space exploration, as readers will discover in this book. Photographs of astronauts and explanations of how data are used by them will spur a new interest in math. (Rev: SLJ 5/07)

24436 Day, Eileen M. *I'm Good at Math* (PS–1). Series: I'm Good At. 2003, Heinemann LB $18.50 (978-1-4034-0901-0). 24pp. Basic mathematical skills, from counting to measuring, are introduced with large photographs. (Rev: HBG 4/04; SLJ 4/04) [510]

24437 Dobson, Christina. *The Pizza Counting Book* (1–3). Illus. by Matthew Holmes. 2004, Charlesbridge $16.95 (978-0-88106-338-7); paper $6.95 (978-0-88106-339-4). 32pp. Pizzas and their toppings are used to teach young readers such basic mathematical concepts as fractions, large numbers, addition, and subtraction. (Rev: BL 8/03; HBG 4/04; SLJ 11/03) [513.2]

24438 Dodds, Dayle Ann. *Full House: An Invitation to Fractions* (K–3). Illus. by Ann Carter. 2007, Candlewick $16.99 (978-0-7636-2468-2). 32pp. A rhyming text and humorous illustrations frame this story about fractions set at Miss Bloom's guest house, Strawberry Inn. (Rev: BL 12/1/07; SLJ 12/07) [513.6]

24439 Gifford, Scott. *Piece = Part = Portion: Fractions = Decimals = Percents* (3–5). 2004, Tricycle $14.95 (978-1-58246-102-1). 32pp. A strong visual approach enhances clear explanations of the relationships between various mathematical concepts. (Rev: BL 12/15/03; HBG 4/04; SLJ 11/03)

24440 Goldstone, Bruce. *Great Estimations* (2–4). 2006, Holt $16.95 (978-0-8050-7446-8). 32pp. Through eye-catching photographs of well-arranged items, readers learn progressively to recognize larger and larger quantities, from groupings of 10 to 100 to 1000, and then to estimate amounts. (Rev: BL 9/1/06; SLJ 11/06) [519.5]

24441 Goldstone, Bruce. *Greater Estimations* (2–4). Illus. 2008, Holt $16.95 (978-0-8050-8315-6). 32pp. Readers who have mastered *Great Estimations* (2006) can now tackle groupings up to 10,000 and learn strategies for estimating length, weight, volume, and so forth. (Rev: BLO 7/29/08; LMC 3/09; SLJ 9/08) [519.5]

24442 Harris, Trudy. *Splitting the Herd: A Corral of Odds and Evens* (K–2). Illus. by Russell Julian. 2008, Lerner $16.95 (978-0-8225-7466-8). 32pp. Miss Emma's cattle keep straying onto Cowboy

Kirby's land, causing problems. Whose cows are whose? And how to sort them out? Their first effort at division in not a success in this entertaining introduction to a mathematical concept. (Rev: BLO 10/7/08; LMC 1/09; SLJ 10/08) [513]

24443 Haven, Kendall. *Marvels of Math: Fascinating Reads and Awesome Activities* (5–8). Illus. 1998, Teacher Ideas paper $23.50 (978-1-56308-585-7). This book chronicles 16 turning points in the history of mathematics, including the discovery of zero and the story of the first female to become a professor of mathematics. (Rev: VOYA 4/99) [510]

24444 Holub, Joan. *Riddle-Iculous Math* (2–5). Illus. by Regan Dunnick. 2003, Whitman $16.99 (978-0-8075-4996-4). 32pp. Puns, rhymes, jokes, and cartoons add appeal to learning basic mathematical tasks. (Rev: BL 10/15/03; HBG 4/04; SLJ 3/04)

24445 King, Andrew. *Exploring Shapes* (2–5). Illus. Series: Math for Fun. 1998, Millbrook LB $20.90 (978-0-7613-0851-5). 32pp. Various shapes are introduced in this mathematics book with projects for each shape. (Rev: BL 1/1–15/99; HBG 3/99; SLJ 2/99) [516]

24446 Lee, Cora, and Gillian O'Reilly. *The Great Number Rumble: A Story of Math in Surprising Places* (4–6). Illus. by Virginia Gray. 2007, Annick $24.95 (978-1-55451-032-0); paper $14.95 (978-1-55451-031-3). 104pp. Who wouldn't want to get rid of math? Sam, upset when his school district wants to cut math from the curriculum, expounds on the value and applications of mathematics. (Rev: SLJ 6/07)

24447 Leech, Bonnie Coulter. *Mesopotamia: Creating and Solving Word Problems* (4–8). Series: Math for the Real World. 2007, Rosen LB $23.95 (978-1-4042-3357-7). 32pp. Ancient number systems are among the mathematical concepts highlighted in this overview of the civilization of Mesopotamia that covers its people, buildings, writings, and calendars. (Rev: SLJ 2/07) [510]

24448 Leedy, Loreen. *It's Probably Penny* (1–3). Illus. 2007, Holt $16.95 (978-0-8050-7389-8). 32pp. Lisa uses her dog Penny to anchor her probability calculations — for example, Will Penny want to go for a walk? (Rev: BL 4/1/07) [519.2]

24449 Leedy, Loreen. *Measuring Penny* (2–4). Illus. 1998, Holt $16.95 (978-0-8050-5360-9). 32pp. An attractively illustrated introduction to the world of measurement. (Rev: BL 4/1/98*; HB 7/98; HBG 9/98; SLJ 4/98) [530.8]

24450 Leedy, Loreen. *Mission Addition* (PS–3). Illus. 1997, Holiday House LB $17.95 (978-0-8234-1307-2). 32pp. Through many practical applications, the animal creatures of Miss Prime's class explore the mysteries of addition. (Rev: BL 10/15/97; HBG 3/98; SLJ 8/97) [513.2]

24451 Littlefield, Cindy A. *Real-World Math for Hands-On Fun!* (3–5). Illus. by Michael Kline. Series: A Williamson Kids Can! Book. 2001, Williamson paper $12.95 (978-1-885593-51-1). 128pp. Numbers, shapes, measurements, time, probability, and money are all discussed here, with puzzles, activities, and experiments that include a water clock, a pyramid of clay, and a pendulum made from a plastic bottle. (Rev: SLJ 3/02) [510]

24452 Lobosco, Michael L. *Mental Math Workout* (3–7). 1998, Sterling $16.95 (978-1-895569-27-8). 80pp. There are 34 projects in this book, each of which interestingly explores a different idea or concept in mathematics. (Rev: SLJ 10/98) [510]

24453 Long, Lynette. *Dazzling Division: Games and Activities That Make Math Easy and Fun* (2–5). Illus. 2000, Wiley $12.95 (978-0-471-36983-7). 122pp. A large-format book that explains division and outlines many activities that explore this concept. (Rev: BL 12/15/00; SLJ 1/01) [513]

24454 Long, Lynette. *Fabulous Fractions: Games and Activities that Make Math Easy and Fun* (2–6). Illus. 2001, Wiley $12.95 (978-0-471-36981-3). 128pp. Games and projects are used to teach youngsters the nature of fractions and how they can be manipulated. (Rev: BL 4/1/01; SLJ 7/01) [513.2]

24455 Long, Lynette. *Marvelous Multiplication: Games and Activities That Make Math Easy and Fun* (2–5). Illus. 2000, Wiley $12.95 (978-0-471-36982-0). 122pp. Multiplication is explained in this large-format paperback with cheerful drawings and a number of related activities. (Rev: BL 12/15/00) [513.2]

24456 Murphy, Stuart J. *Divide and Ride* (PS–3). Illus. by George Ulrich. Series: MathStart. 1997, HarperCollins LB $15.89 (978-0-06-026777-3). 40pp. Principles of division are demonstrated as 11 friends visit various carnival attractions. Also in this series, use *Too Many Kangaroo Things to Do!* (1996), which covers multiplication; *Jump, Kangaroo, Jump!* (1999), which looks at division and fractions; *Mall Mania* (1996), which deals with addition; and *Shark Swimathon* (2001), which teaches subtraction. (Rev: BL 2/1/97; SLJ 3/97) [513.2]

24457 Murphy, Stuart J. *Lemonade for Sale* (1–3). Illus. by Tricia Tusa. Series: MathStart. 1998, HarperCollins LB $15.89 (978-0-06-027441-2); paper $5.99 (978-0-06-446715-5). 31pp. Four children operate a lemonade stand and use a bar graph to chart their progress in this simple introduction to graphs. (Rev: SLJ 5/98)

24458 Murphy, Stuart J. *Probably Pistachio* (1–3). Illus. by Marsha Winborn. Series: MathStart. 2001, HarperCollins LB $15.89 (978-0-06-028029-1); paper $5.99 (978-0-06-446734-6). 40pp. Throughout his day, Stuart makes predictions based on sound reasoning in this entertaining concept book about probability. Also use *Betcha!* (1997), about estimating; *Safari Park* (2002), about finding unknowns; and *Same Old Horse* (2005), about prediction theory. (Rev: BL 2/15/01; HBG 10/01; SLJ 3/01) [519.2]

24459 Murphy, Stuart J. *The Sundae Scoop* (1–3). Illus. by Cynthia Jabar. 2003, HarperCollins paper $5.99 (978-0-06-446250-1). 40pp. A story of the various flavor combinations available at an ice-cream booth illustrates a basic math concept in a way sure to appeal. (Rev: BL 1/1–15/03; HBG 10/03) [511]

24460 Nagda, Ann Whitehead. *Cheetah Math: Learning About Division from Baby Cheetahs* (3–5). 2007, Holt $16.95 (978-0-8050-7645-5). 32pp. A clever way to introduce a math concept to animal lovers, this book combines photographs of cheetahs, math problems, and animal facts. (Rev: SLJ 8/07)

24461 Nagda, Ann Whitehead, and Cindy Bickel. *Polar Bear Math: Learning About Fractions from Klondike and Snow* (3–5). Illus. 2004, Holt $16.95 (978-0-8050-7301-0). 29pp. The care of two polar bears cubs, Klondike and Snow, is used as a way to introduce fractions — looking at such topics as milk consumption, polar bear weight, and so forth. (Rev: SLJ 9/04) [513.2]

24462 Neuschwander, Cindy. *Sir Cumference and the Great Knight of Angleland: A Math Adventure* (1–4). Illus. by Wayne Geehan. 2001, Charlesbridge LB $16.95 (978-1-57091-170-5); paper $6.95 (978-1-57091-169-9). 32pp. The pun-full exploits of Radius, son of Sir Cumference and Lady Di of Ameter, involve the mastery of angles, squares, circles, and so forth, in this story that can be read on several levels. (Rev: HBG 3/02; SLJ 2/02) [516]

24463 Neuschwander, Cindy. *Sir Cumference and the Isle of Immeter: A Math Adventure* (3–6). Illus. by Wayne Geehan. 2006, Charlesbridge paper $6.95 (978-1-57091-681-6). 32pp. Per pays a visit to her uncle and aunt — Sir Cumference and Lady Di of Ameter — and with her cousin Radius uses skills of establishing perimeter and area to solve a riddle about the Isle of Immeter. (Rev: SLJ 8/06) [516]

24464 Penner, Lucille R. *Clean-Sweep Campers* (2–3). Illus. by Paige Billin-Frye. Series: Math Matters. 2000, Kane paper $4.95 (978-1-57565-096-8). 32pp. Using a story about a messy cabin at summer camp, this book effectively introduces fractions. (Rev: SLJ 2/01) [513.2]

24465 Pistoia, Sara. *Counting* (1–3). Illus. Series: Mighty Math. 2002, Child's World LB $24.21 (978-1-56766-114-9). 24pp. Counting by fives and tens is shown with clear examples and advice from cartoon character Math Mutt. Also use *Money*, which discusses counting change. (Rev: SLJ 3/03)

24466 Reisberg, Joanne A. *Zachary Zormer: Shape Transformer* (2–4). Illus. by David Hohn. Series: Math Adventures. 2006, Charlesbridge paper $6.95 (978-1-57091-876-6). 32pp. A forgetful but resourceful student comes up with some ingenious ways to measure area, perimeter, length, and width. (Rev: SLJ 8/06) [516]

24467 Ribke, Simone T. *Grouping at the Dog Show* (1–2). Series: Rookie Read-about Math. 2006, Children's Pr. LB $20.50 (978-0-516-24959-9). 32pp. For beginning readers, an introduction to the concept of grouping, using different attributes of different breeds of dogs. (Rev: SLJ 6/06) [511.3]

24468 Ribke, Simone T. *Pet Store Subtraction* (K–2). Series: Rookie Read-about Math. 2006, Children's Pr. LB $20.50 (978-0-516-29673-9). 32pp. A pet store employee uses subtraction skills to determine how many new animals and supplies she needs to order. (Rev: SLJ 12/06) [513.2]

24469 Roy, Jennifer, and Gregory Roy. *Graphing in the Desert* (2–4). Series: Math All Around. 2006, Benchmark LB $28.50 (978-0-7614-2262-4). 32pp. Introduces different types of graphs and uses them to convey information about the Sonoran Desert and its flora and fauna. (Rev: SLJ 12/06) [518]

24470 Roy, Jennifer, and Gregory Roy. *Multiplication on the Farm* (2–4). Illus. Series: Math All Around. 2006, Benchmark LB $28.50 (978-0-7614-2268-6). 32pp. This title focuses on multiplication and gives multiple examples of how it can be used to make important calculations on the farm. (Rev: SLJ 12/06) [513.2]

24471 Roy, Jennifer, and Gregory Roy. *Subtraction at School* (K–3). Series: Math All Around. 2005, Benchmark LB $25.64 (978-0-7614-2003-3). 32pp. Everyday situations are used to illustrate the principles of subtraction. Also use *Sorting at the Ocean* and *Patterns in Nature* (both 2005). (Rev: SLJ 3/06)

24472 Sargent, Brian. *Guess the Order* (1–2). Series: Rookie Read-about Math. 2006, Children's Pr. LB $20.50 (978-0-516-24963-6). 32pp. An introduction to the mathematical concept of placing things in order using pictures from a day at a carnival; for beginning readers. (Rev: SLJ 6/06) [513.2]

24473 Sargent, Brian. *Slumber Party Problem Solving* (1–2). Series: Rookie Read-about Math. 2006, Children's Pr. LB $20.50 (978-0-516-24962-9). 32pp. For beginning readers, this book has a girl using basic math to plan a slumber party. (Rev: SLJ 6/06) [513]

24474 Schwartz, David M. *G Is For Googol: A Math Alphabet Book* (3–5). Illus. 1998, Tricycle $15.95 (978-1-883672-58-4). 56pp. An alphabet book that uses terms in mathematics, from abacus to zillion, for each letter. (Rev: BL 10/15/98; HBG 3/99) [510]

24475 Shea, Therese. *America's Electoral College: Choosing the President: Comparing and Analyzing Charts, Graphs, and Tables* (4–8). Series: Math for the Real World. 2007, Rosen LB $23.95 (978-1-4042-3358-4). 32pp. Results of various elections, including the controversial 2000 polls, are used to demonstrate fundamental mathematical principles. (Rev: SLJ 2/07) [324.6097]

24476 Shea, Therese. *The Great Barrier Reef: Using Graphs and Charts to Solve Word Problems* (4–8). Series: Math for the Real World. 2007, Rosen LB $23.95 (978-1-4042-3359-1). 32pp. Charts and graphs are used to show the number of species found on the reef, the percentages of coral, the number of visitors, and so forth. (Rev: SLJ 2/07) [510]

24477 Shea, Therese. *The Transcontinental Railroad: Using Proportions to Solve Problems* (4–8). Series: Math for the Real World. 2007, Rosen LB $23.95 (978-1-4042-3361-4). 32pp. The cost of laying the track, number of rails laid in a period, and other interesting aspects of construction of the railroad are considered using ratios, proportions, and other mathematical techniques. (Rev: SLJ 2/07) [513.24]

24478 Skinner, Daphne. *Tightwad Tod* (1–3). Illus. by John Nez. Series: Math Matters. 2001, Kane paper $4.95 (978-1-57565-109-5). 32pp. Tod has $20 to spend, and the story follows his purchases and deducts the amounts spent, in this book that includes three math problems. (Rev: SLJ 1/02) [512.9]

24479 Stewart, Melissa. *Giraffe Graphs* (K–2). Series: Rookie Read-about Math. 2006, Children's Pr. LB $20.50 (978-0-516-23798-5). 32pp. Students on a class trip to the zoo use graphs and charts to keep track of the animals they've seen. (Rev: SLJ 12/06) [511]

24480 Stienecker, David L. *Addition* (3–5). Illus. by Richard Maccabe. Series: Discovering Math. 1995, Benchmark LB $22.79 (978-0-7614-0593-1). 32pp. An introductory math book that explains the principles of addition and gives puzzles and exercises on applying these concepts. Also use *Division, Fractions*, and *Multiplication* (all 1995). (Rev: SLJ 4/96) [510]

24481 Sullivan, Navin. *Area, Distance, and Volume* (4–7). Illus. Series: Measure Up. 2006, Marshall Cavendish LB $29.93 (978-0-7614-2323-2). 44pp. Includes information on the history of measuring area, distance, and volume along with how to measure each and the devices used. (Rev: BL 2/15/07; SLJ 6/07) [598.47]

24482 Tang, Greg. *The Best of Times: Math Strategies That Multiply* (2–3). Illus. by Harry Briggs. 2002, Scholastic $16.95 (978-0-439-21044-7). 32pp. A rhyming approach to remembering the multiplication tables from one to ten. (Rev: BL 11/1/02; HBG 3/03; SLJ 9/02) [513.2]

24483 Tang, Greg. *Math-Terpieces* (2–4). 2003, Scholastic $16.95 (978-0-439-44388-3). 32pp. The paintings of 12 great artists are used in exercises that develop mathematics problem-solving skills. (Rev: BL 7/03; HBG 4/04; SLJ 8/03) [510]

24484 Townsend, Donna. *Apple Fractions* (1–2). Series: Rookie Read-about Math. 2004, Scholastic LB $5.95 (978-0-516-24670-3). 32pp. Using apples and apple muffins as examples, author Donna Townsend introduces beginning readers to the concept of fractions. (Rev: BL 10/15/04)

24485 Wingard-Nelson, Rebecca. *Division Made Easy* (1–4). Illus. by Tom LaBaff. Series: Making Math Easy. 2005, Enslow LB $23.93 (978-0-7660-2511-0). 48pp. An easy-to-understand introduction to the fundamentals of division. Also use *Multiplication Made Easy* and *Word Problems Made Easy* (2005). (Rev: SLJ 1/06) [513.2]

24486 Woods, Mary B., and Michael Woods. *Ancient Computing: From Counting to Calendars* (5–8). Series: Ancient Technologies. 2000, Runestone LB $25.26 (978-0-8225-2997-2). 88pp. From the invention of the abacus and sundials to the creation of calculators and computers, this is a history of counting with material on the development of the calendar. (Rev: BL 9/15/00; HBG 3/01; SLJ 1/01) [510]

24487 Wyatt, Valerie. *The Math Book for Girls and Other Beings Who Count* (3–6). Illus. 2000, Kids Can $14.95 (978-1-55074-830-7); paper $9.95 (978-1-55074-584-9). 64pp. A well-organized, cheerful book that introduces such math concepts as proportion in an entertaining way. (Rev: BCCB 11/00; BL 2/15/01; HBG 10/01; SLJ 11/00) [510.8]

24488 Zaslavsky, Claudia. *Number Sense and Nonsense: Building Math Creativity and Confidence Through Number Play* (3–6). Illus. 2001, Chicago Review paper $14.95 (978-1-55652-378-6). 120pp. Readers are encouraged to develop "number sense" rather than learning by rote, in chapters that introduce mathematical concepts, look at money and measurement, and provide puzzles, games, and some history. (Rev: SLJ 7/01) [510]

24489 Ziefert, Harriet. *Rabbit and Hare Divide an Apple* (1–2). Illus. by Emily Bolam. Series: Viking Math Easy-to-Read. 1998, Viking paper $3.99 (978-0-14-038820-6). 32pp. In this easy reader, the math concept of fractions is taught through a story about Rabbit, Hare, and wily Mr. Raccoon. (Rev: BL 2/1/98; HBG 9/98; SLJ 2/98)

Geometry

24490 King, Andrew. *Plotting Points and Position* (2–5). Illus. Series: Math for Fun. 1998, Millbrook LB $20.90 (978-0-7613-0852-2). 32pp. An activity book that explores plotting coordinates, measuring angles, and different kinds of symmetry. (Rev: BL 1/1–15/99; HBG 3/99; SLJ 2/99) [516.16]

24491 Riggs, Sandy. *Circles* (2–4). Illus. by Richard Maccabe. Series: Discovering Shapes. 1996, Benchmark LB $22.79 (978-0-7614-0458-3). 32pp. Circles are introduced through a series of games, puzzles, and crafts. Also use *Triangles* (1996). (Rev: SLJ 2/97) [516]

24492 Roy, Jennifer, and Gregory Roy. *Shapes in Transportation* (2–4). Illus. Series: Math All Around. 2006, Benchmark LB $28.50 (978-0-7614-2265-5). 32pp. Using traffic signs, bridges, buildings, and other transport-related items, this volume introduces shapes of all kinds and discusses such topics as angles and dimensions. (Rev: SLJ 12/06) [516]

24493 Sargent, Brian. *Grandfather's Shape Story* (K–2). Series: Rookie Read-about Math. 2006, Children's Pr. LB $20.50 (978-0-516-29919-8). 32pp. A grandfather entertains his granddaughter with tangrams while telling her a story. (Rev: SLJ 12/06) [793.74]

24494 Stienecker, David L. *Rectangles* (2–4). Series: Discovering Shapes. 1996, Benchmark LB $22.79 (978-0-7614-0460-6). 32pp. A slim volume in which rectangles are explored through games, art ideas, and problems to solve. Also use *Patterns, Polygons,* and *Three-Dimensional Shapes* (all 1996). (Rev: SLJ 2/97) [516]

24495 VanCleave, Janice. *Geometry for Every Kid: Easy Activities That Make Learning Geometry Fun* (4–6). Illus. Series: Science for Every Kid. 1994, Wiley paper $12.95 (978-0-471-31141-6). 221pp. Through interesting activities, this book explains geometry from simple shapes and angles to coordinate graphing. (Rev: BL 10/15/94; SLJ 12/94) [516]

Mathematical Puzzles

24496 Adler, David A. *Calculator Riddles* (3–5). Illus. by Cynthia Fisher. 1995, Holiday House $14.95 (978-0-8234-1186-3). 42pp. A series of clever riddles and problems in arithmetic that can be answered using a calculator. (Rev: BL 11/1/95; SLJ 11/95) [513.2]

24497 Adler, David A. *Easy Math Puzzles* (2–5). Illus. by Cynthia Fisher. 1997, Holiday House LB $15.95 (978-0-8234-1283-9). 32pp. A book of challenging, often very tricky math puzzles that sometimes involve the quirks of language and logic. (Rev: BCCB 5/97; BL 3/1/97; SLJ 6/97) [818]

24498 Adler, David A. *You Can, Toucan, Math: Word Problem-Solving Fun* (1–3). Illus. by Edward Miller. 2006, Holiday $16.95 (978-0-8234-1919-7). 32pp. This collection of 20 bird-themed word problems — rhyming riddles posing math questions — covers the basics of addition, subtraction, multiplication, and division. (Rev: BL 8/06; HBG 4/07; SLJ 10/06) [511.3]

24499 Ball, Johnny. *Go Figure! A Totally Cool Book About Numbers* (4–7). Illus. 2005, DK $15.99 (978-0-7566-1374-7). 96pp. A fascinating volume for math-minded youngsters and adults, introducing number-related games and puzzles as well as more sophisticated mathematical disciplines, such as chaos theory, fractals, and topology. (Rev: BL 10/15/05; SLJ 1/06) [510]

24500 Barber, Patti. *First Number Book* (PS–1). Illus. by Mandy Stanley. 2001, Kingfisher $12.95 (978-0-7534-5338-4). 48pp. More than a counting book, this brightly illustrated guide also looks at shapes and sizes and addition and subtraction and includes beginning mathematical puzzles and exercises. (Rev: BL 10/1/01; SLJ 7/01) [513.2]

24501 Blum, Raymond. *Math Tricks, Puzzles and Games* (4–7). Illus. 1994, Sterling $14.95 (978-0-8069-0582-2). 96pp. Kids who like math will particularly enjoy these tricks, mathematical games and puzzles, and calculator riddles. (Rev: BL 11/1/94) [793.7]

24502 Burns, Marilyn. *The I Hate Mathematics! Book* (5–8). Illus. by Martha Hairston. 1975, Little, Brown paper $14.99 (978-0-316-11741-8). 128pp. A lively collection of puzzles and other mind stretchers that illustrate mathematical concepts.

24503 Cushman, Jean. *Do You Wanna Bet? Your Chance to Find Out About Probability* (3–6). Illus. by Martha Weston. 1991, Houghton $16.00 (978-0-395-56516-2). 102pp. A slight plot line aids in the explanation of probability and moves on to guessing games, coin tossing, and breaking codes. (Rev: BCCB 2/92; BL 1/1/92; SLJ 12/91) [519.2]

24504 Ferris, Julie. *Galaxy Getaway: A Math Puzzle Adventure* (2–4). Series: Math for Martians. 2000, Larousse paper $5.95 (978-0-7534-5276-9). 32pp. Zeno, a young Martian, must solve a number of math problems and decipher codes in order to rescue a pet. Also use: *Planet Omicron: A Math Puzzle Adventure* (2000). (Rev: SLJ 9/00) [793.7]

24505 Fisher, Valorie. *How High Can a Dinosaur Count? And Other Math Mysteries* (1–3). Illus. 2006, Random $16.95 (978-0-375-83608-4). 40pp. Fifteen entertaining math mysteries are presented with interesting text and eye-catching illustrations. (Rev: BL 1/1–15/06; SLJ 2/06*) [513]

24506 Gardner, Martin. *Perplexing Puzzles and Tantalizing Teasers* (4–7). Illus. by Laszlo Kubinyi. 1988, Dover paper $7.95 (978-0-486-25637-5). 256pp. An assortment of math problems, visual teasers, and tricky questions to challenge young, alert minds; perky drawings. [793.73]

24507 Lewis, J. Patrick. *Arithme-Tickle: An Even Number of Odd Riddle-Rhymes* (2–4). Illus. by Frank Remkiewicz. 2002, Harcourt $16.00 (978-0-15-216418-8). 32pp. A book of puzzles and problems that entertain while testing elementary mathematics skills, with illustrations. (Rev: BL 5/15/02; HBG 10/02; SLJ 4/02) [513]

24508 Salvadori, Mario, and Joseph P. Wright. *Math Games for Middle School: Challenges and Skill-Builders for Students at Every Level* (5–8). Illus. 1998, Chicago Review paper $14.95 (978-1-55652-288-8). 176pp. After explaining the concepts involved in such mathematical areas as geometry, arithmetic, graphing, and linear equations, this work presents a series of puzzles for readers to solve. (Rev: BL 11/1/98) [510]

24509 Sharp, Richard M., and Seymour Metzner. *The Sneaky Square and 113 Other Math Activities for Kids* (4–8). Illus. 1990, TAB $15.95 (978-0-8306-8474-8); paper $8.95 (978-0-8306-3474-3). 134pp. Readers are challenged to solve classic as well as new math and logic problems. (Rev: BL 1/1/91) [793.7]

24510 Tang, Greg. *The Grapes of Math: Mind-Stretching Math Riddles* (3–5). Illus. by Harry Briggs. 2001, Scholastic $16.99 (978-0-439-21033-1). Each riddle and the rhyming clues that accompany it, can be answer by applying simple math skills like adding, subtracting, and multiplying. (Rev: BCCB 3/01; HBG 10/01; SLJ 3/01) [793.7]

24511 Tang, Greg. *Math Appeal: Mind-Stretching Math Riddles* (2–4). Illus. by Harry Briggs. 2003, Scholastic $16.95 (978-0-439-21046-1). 40pp. Counting and adding puzzles encourage children to find answers in creative ways. (Rev: BL 2/15/03; HBG 10/03; SLJ 2/03) [510]

24512 Tang, Greg. *Math for All Seasons: Mind-Stretching Math Riddles* (1–3). Illus. by Harry Briggs. 2002, Scholastic $16.95 (978-0-439-21042-3). 40pp. Each spread of this book for younger readers features a different math riddle, as well as clues to counting in different ways. (Rev: BL 2/1/02; HBG 10/02; SLJ 3/02) [513]

24513 Tang, Greg. *Math Potatoes: Mind-Stretching Brain Food* (3–5). Illus. by Harry Briggs. 2005, Scholastic $16.99 (978-0-439-44390-6). 40pp. Games involving humorous rhymes and appealing illustrations teach readers how to approach grouping

numbers efficiently. (Rev: BL 7/05; SLJ 8/05) [793.74]

24514 Wells, Alison. *Subtraction* (3–5). Illus. by Richard Maccabe. Series: Discovering Math. 1995, Benchmark LB $22.79 (978-0-7614-0594-8). 32pp. Principles of subtraction are introduced, with many puzzles and games that apply these concepts in problem-solving situations. (Rev: SLJ 4/96) [510]

24515 Zaslavsky, Claudia. *More Math Games and Activities from Around the World* (3–7). Illus. 2003, Chicago Review paper $14.95 (978-1-55652-501-8). 160pp. More than 70 inventive math games and activities are accompanied by historical background. (Rev: SLJ 1/04) [793.7]

Metric System

24516 Murphy, Stuart J. *Polly's Pen Pal* (PS–3). Illus. by Rémy Simard. Series: MathStart. 2005, HarperCollins $15.99 (978-0-06-053168-3); paper $5.99 (978-0-06-053170-6). 33pp. Polly's (e-mail) pen pal lives in Canada, and through her Polly learns about the metric system. (Rev: SLJ 7/05)

Numbers and Number Systems

24517 Adler, David A. *Fun with Roman Numerals* (2–4). Illus. by Edward Miller. 2008, Holiday $16.95 (978-0-8234-2060-5). 32pp. A bright and accessible introduction to roman numerals, with attractive illustrations. (Rev: BLO 10/7/08; SLJ 11/08) [513.5]

24518 Anno, Mitsumasa. *Anno's Mysterious Multiplying Jar* (4–6). Illus. by author. 1983, Penguin $20.99 (978-0-399-20951-2). 48pp. Everyday objects are used to explain factorials.

24519 Geisert, Arthur. *Roman Numerals I to MM: Numberabillia Romana Uno ad Duo Mila* (2–4). Illus. 1996, Houghton $16.00 (978-0-395-74519-9). 32pp. Using groups of pigs as examples, Roman numerals are introduced, and later other objects test the reader's knowledge. (Rev: BCCB 3/96; BL 5/1/96; HB 9/96; SLJ 9/96) [513.5]

24520 Massin. *Fun with Numbers* (2–4). Illus. by Les Chats Pelés. 1995, Harcourt $22.65 (978-0-15-200962-5). A boy and his dog travel through time from ancient Egypt, Mesopotamia, and Rome, to India and Europe to trace the origins and development of numbers and our counting system. (Rev: SLJ 2/96) [512]

24521 Murphy, Stuart J. *Coyotes All Around* (1–3). Illus. by Steve Björkman. Series: MathStart. 2003, HarperCollins paper $5.99 (978-0-06-051531-7). 31pp. The concept of rounding is introduced in a western setting. (Rev: HBG 4/04; SLJ 2/04) [519.5]

24522 Murphy, Stuart J. *Earth Day — Hooray!* (1–3). Illus. by Renée Andriani. Series: MathStart. 2004, HarperCollins $16.99 (978-0-06-000127-8); paper

$5.99 (978-0-06-000129-2). 40pp. Readers learn about place value as well as the benefits of recycling in this accessible and humorous book. Also use *More or Less (2005)*, about comparing numbers. (Rev: BL 1/1–15/04) [513]

24523 Schmandt-Besserat, Denise. *The History of Counting* (3–5). Illus. by Michael Hays. 1999, Morrow $18.99 (978-0-688-14118-9). 48pp. This oversize book traces the history of numbers and counting from primitive people through the Sumerians, Greeks, and Romans to the Arabs who brought Hindu numbers to Europe where this Arabic system was adopted. (Rev: BCCB 11/99; BL 8/99*; HBG 4/00; SLJ 8/99) [513.5]

24524 Schwartz, David M. *How Much Is a Million?* (K–3). Illus. by Steven Kellogg. 1985, Lothrop LB $18.89 (978-0-688-04050-5); Morrow paper $6.99 (978-0-688-09933-6). 40pp. Using images that children can enjoy — such as "one million kids standing on each other's shoulders would be taller than . . ." — the concepts of million, billion, and trillion are explained. (Rev: BCCB 7–8/85; BL 6/15/85; HB 7/85)

24525 Stienecker, David L. *Numbers* (3–5). Illus. by Richard Maccabe. Series: Discovering Math. 1995, Benchmark LB $22.79 (978-0-7614-0597-9). 32pp. This introductory math book introduces the world of numbers and supplies many problems, with answers at the back of the book. (Rev: SLJ 4/96) [512]

Statistics

24526 Leedy, Loreen. *The Great Graph Contest* (2–4). Illus. 2005, Holiday $16.95 (978-0-8234-1710-0). 32pp. Gonk the toad and Beezy the lizard compete in a graph contest in a lively tale displaying all kinds of graphs and methods of gathering data. (Rev: BL 8/05; SLJ 9/05*)

24527 Long, Lynette. *Great Graphs and Sensational Statistics: Games and Activities That Make Math Easy and Fun* (4–7). Illus. 2004, Wiley paper $12.95 (978-0-471-21060-3). 118pp. The games and activities in this large-format paperback will give new insights into the value of statistics and graphs and how the latter can be used to visually represent the former. (Rev: BL 5/1/04; SLJ 11/04) [372.7]

24528 Nechaev, Michelle Wagner. *Making Graphs* (PS–1). Illus. Series: I Can Do Math. 2004, Gareth Stevens LB $22.00 (978-0-8368-4111-4). 24pp. A question-and-answer format and abundant photographs introduce the use of graphs to visually represent different characteristics. (Rev: BL 4/1/04) [001.4]

Time, Clocks, and Calendars

24529 Cobb, Annie. *The Long Wait* (1–3). Illus. by Liza Woodruff. Series: Math Matters. 2000, Kane paper $4.59 (978-1-57565-094-4). 32pp. Introduces

the concept of estimating time, using a simple easy-to-read story about two boys waiting in line for a thrill ride. (Rev: SLJ 6/00)

24530 Dolan, Graham. *The Greenwich Guide to Day and Night* (3–6). Illus. Series: Greenwich Guide To. 2001, Heinemann LB $22.79 (978-1-58810-042-9). 32pp. Dolan explains how day becomes night, with photographs, a glossary, and other aids. Also use *The Greenwich Guide to Measuring Time* (2001). (Rev: BL 10/15/01) [525]

24531 Farndon, John. *Time* (3–6). Series: Science Experiments. 2002, Marshall Cavendish LB $25.64 (978-0-7614-1470-4). 32pp. Through simple experiments using common household objects, the nature and properties of time are explored. (Rev: BL 12/15/02; HBG 3/03) [529]

24532 Jenkins, Martin. *The Time Book: A Brief History from Lunar Calendars to Atomic Clocks* (3–5). Illus. by Richard Holland. 2009, Candlewick $18.99 (978-0-7636-4112-2). 64pp. A comprehensive look at the notion of time and the various systems of measuring it. (Rev: BL 5/1/09; LMC 10/09) [529]

24533 Koscielniak, Bruce. *About Time: A First Look at Time and Clocks* (2–5). Illus. 2004, Houghton $16.00 (978-0-618-39668-9). 32pp. After a general discussion of the basic concepts of time, Koscielniak traces the development of clocks from sundials onward. (Rev: BL 12/1/04; SLJ 11/04) [529.7]

24534 Kummer, Patricia K. *The Calendar* (5–8). Illus. Series: Inventions That Shaped the World. 2005, Watts LB $30.50 (978-0-531-12340-9). 80pp. Traces the development of calendars from prehistoric times, with period and contemporary illustrations, lists of recommended resources, and a calendar. (Rev: BL 5/15/05) [529]

24535 Murphy, Stuart J. *Get Up and Go!* (1–3). Illus. by Diane Greenseid. Series: MathStart. 1996, HarperCollins LB $15.89 (978-0-06-025882-5). 40pp. The concept of time as measured by minutes and displayed on timelines is explored in this imaginative picture book. Also use *Rodeo Time* (2006), about time and schedules. (Rev: BL 10/15/96; SLJ 12/96) [513.2]

24536 Nagda, Ann Whitehead, and Cindy Bickel. *Chimp Math: Learning About Time from a Baby Chimpanzee* (2–5). Illus. 2002, Holt $16.95 (978-0-8050-6674-6). 32pp. This is a delightful and effective combination, presenting both the story of young chimp Jiggs being raised by humans and the various methods of timekeeping — clocks, calendars, timelines, charts — that recorded his growth and development. (Rev: BL 11/1/02; HB 9/02; HBG 3/03; SLJ 9/02) [529]

24537 Older, Jules. *Telling Time* (PS–2). Illus. by Megan Halsey. 2000, Charlesbridge $16.95 (978-0-88106-396-7); paper $6.95 (978-0-88106-397-4). 32pp. As well as exploring the concept of time, this picture book explains ways in which it is measured and covers topics including how to tell time, calendars, and different kinds of numbers. (Rev: BL 3/1/00; HBG 9/00; SLJ 3/00) [529]

24538 Richards, Kitty. *It's About Time, Max!* (1–3). Illus. by Gioia Fiammenghi. Series: Math Matters.

2000, Kane paper $4.95 (978-1-57565-088-3). 32pp. After losing his digital watch, a young boy must learn how to tell time using analog timepieces in this easy-to-read concept book. (Rev: SLJ 6/00)

24539 Skurzynski, Gloria. *On Time: From Seasons to Split Seconds* (2–5). Illus. 2000, National Geographic $17.95 (978-0-7922-7503-9). 48pp. This heavily illustrated book discusses time and seasons, years, months, and days, with additional coverage on the development of clocks and calendars. (Rev: BL 3/1/00; HBG 9/00; SLJ 7/00) [529]

24540 Somervill, Barbara. *The History of the Calendar* (3–6). Series: Our Changing World: The Timeline Library. 2006, The Child's World LB $27.07 (978-1-59296-436-9). 32pp. Two students and their teacher explore how different cultures have measured days, months, and years through the ages. (Rev: SLJ 7/06) [529]

24541 Verdet, Andre. *All About Time* (PS–2). Illus. by Celine Bour-Chollet, et al. Series: First Discovery. 1995, Scholastic $12.95 (978-0-590-42795-1). This book about time includes material on clocks and watches, time zones, seasons, phases of the moon, months of the year, and how a person can budget time. (Rev: SLJ 3/96) [529]

24542 Wells, Robert E. *How Do You Know What Time It Is?* (2–5). Illus. 2002, Whitman $16.99 (978-0-8075-7939-8); paper $6.95 (978-0-8075-7940-4). 32pp. In picture-book format, the author traces the history of timekeeping — from sundials to quartz crystals, from lunar and solar calendars to the one we know today. (Rev: BL 12/1/02; HBG 3/03; SLJ 1/03) [529]

24543 Williams, Brian. *Calendars* (4–6). Series: About Time. 2002, Smart Apple LB $24.25 (978-1-58340-207-8). 32pp. The need for keeping time and the various methods used over the centuries are explained in text and illustrations. (Rev: HBG 3/03; SLJ 12/02) [909.83]

Weights and Measures

24544 Cato, Sheila. *Measuring* (1–4). Illus. by Sami Sweeten. Series: A Question of Math Book. 1999, Carolrhoda LB $25.26 (978-1-57505-323-3). 32pp. The concept of measurement, what it involves, and several types are covered briefly in a series of double-page spreads each containing a problem. (Rev: HBG 4/00; SLJ 11/99) [530.8]

24545 Chrismer, Melanie. *Math Tools* (1–2). Series: Rookie Read-about Math. 2006, Children's Pr. LB $20.50 (978-0-516-24961-2). 32pp. For beginning readers, an introduction to the tools used to measure distance, time, volume, and other quantities. (Rev: SLJ 6/06) [681]

24546 Cleary, Brian P. *On the Scale, a Weighty Tale* (K–4). Illus. by Brian Gable. Series: Math Is CATegorical. 2008, Lerner $15.95 (978-0-8225-7851-2). 32pp. A lighthearted introduction to systems of measuring weight. (Rev: BLO 9/17/08) [530.8]

24547 Gresko, Marcia S. *Measuring* (PS–1). Illus. Series: I Can Do Math. 2004, Gareth Stevens LB $22.00 (978-0-8368-4112-1). 24pp. A question-and-answer format and abundant photographs introduce the concept of measurement and the various standards that are used to measure height, weight, length, temperature, and time. (Rev: BL 4/1/04) [530.8]

24548 King, Andrew. *Measuring Weight and Time* (2–5). Series: Math for Fun. 1998, Millbrook LB $20.90 (978-0-7613-0854-6); paper $5.95 (978-0-7613-0748-8). 32pp. Using interactive games, projects, and colorful artwork, this book explains how we measure weight and time. (Rev: BL 2/15/99; HBG 9/99) [530.8]

24549 Long, Lynette. *Measurement Mania: Games and Activities that Make Math Easy and Fun* (2–6). Illus. 2001, Wiley $12.95 (978-0-471-36980-6). 128pp. Forty activities are outlined, such as measuring the length of a smile, in this entertaining book that teaches the rudiments of measurement. (Rev: BL 4/1/01; SLJ 7/01) [513.2]

24550 Loughran, Donna. *How Long Is It?* (1–2). Series: Rookie Read-about Math. 2004, Scholastic LB $5.95 (978-0-516-24671-0). 32pp. Photographs and brief text introduce linear measures and the use of rulers. (Rev: BL 10/15/04)

24551 Murphy, Stuart J. *Bigger, Better, Best!* (K–3). Illus. by Marsha Winborn. Series: MathStart. 2002, HarperCollins paper $5.99 (978-0-06-446247-1). 33pp. A story of siblings choosing rooms in a new house is a backdrop for teaching about measurements and area. Also use *Room for Ripley* (1999), which introduces liquid measurements. (Rev: HBG 3/03; SLJ 1/03) [516]

24552 Murphy, Stuart J. *Super Sand Castle Saturday* (1–3). Illus. by Julia Gorton. Series: MathStart. 1999, HarperCollins LB $15.89 (978-0-06-027613-3). The concept of measurement is introduced by three friends trying to determine who built the tallest sand castle with the longest moat and the longest wall. (Rev: HBG 10/99; SLJ 7/99)

24553 Roy, Jennifer, and Gregory Roy. *Measuring at Home* (2–4). Series: Math All Around. 2006, Benchmark LB $28.50 (978-0-7614-2263-1). 32pp. Everyday items such as a ruler, thermometer, and measuring cup are used to introduce the concepts of measuring area, weight, volume, and time. (Rev: SLJ 12/06) [516]

24554 Schwartz, David M. *Millions to Measure* (1–4). Illus. by Steven Kellogg. 2003, HarperCollins LB $18.89 (978-0-06-623784-8). 40pp. Marvelosissimo the Mathematical Magician explains the history of measures and measurement (with an appendix on the metric system) in this informative and entertaining book. (Rev: BL 2/1/03*; HB 3/03; HBG 10/03; SLJ 3/03) [530.8]

24555 Scott, Janine. *Why We Measure* (K–2). Illus. 2003, Compass Point LB $19.93 (978-0-7565-0449-6). 24pp. Introduces the concept of measurement and the various tools that can be used to gauge length, weight, speed, and quantity. (Rev: SLJ 12/03) [530.8]

Meteorology

General

24556 Gardner, Robert. *Stellar Science Projects About Earth's Sky* (3–6). Illus. by Tom LaBaff. Series: Rockin' Earth Science Experiments. 2007, Enslow LB $23.93 (978-0-7660-2732-9). 48pp. A book of basic projects involving the earth's atmosphere for beginning researchers. (Rev: SLJ 8/07) [551.5078]

24557 Locker, Thomas. *Cloud Dance* (3–5). Illus. 2000, Harcourt $17.00 (978-0-15-202231-0). 32pp. This picture book for older readers is a mixture of fiction, science, and art as it describes the beauty of the sky during the different seasons. (Rev: BL 10/1/00; HBG 3/01; SLJ 11/00) [551.5]

24558 Malone, Peter. *Close to the Wind: The Beaufort Scale* (4–8). Illus. by author. 2007, Putnam $16.99 (978-0-399-24399-8). 40pp. An informative picture book that explains the history and use of the Beaufort scale that measures wind force at sea. (Rev: BL 6/1–15/07; LMC 11/07; SLJ 5/07) [551.51]

24559 Smith, Trevor. *Earth's Changing Climate* (5–8). Series: Understanding Global Issues. 2003, Smart Apple $19.95 (978-1-58340-358-7). 56pp. Topics including global warming are discussed in this well-organized look at the world's climate, how it is gradually changing, and what can be done about it. (Rev: BL 11/15/03; SLJ 12/03) [551.6]

24560 Sullivan, Navin. *Temperature* (4–7). Series: Measure Up! 2006, Marshall Cavendish LB $20.95 (978-0-7614-2322-5). 48pp. This well-designed book about temperature includes at-home experiments and easy-to-follow charts. (Rev: LMC 8/07; SLJ 6/07)

24561 Vogel, Carole G. *Nature's Fury: Eyewitness Reports of Natural Disasters* (3–6). Illus. 2000, Scholastic $16.95 (978-0-590-11502-5). 128pp. Taken from historical archives and newspapers, this book features 13 eyewitness accounts of 13 disasters including flash floods, earthquakes, blizzards, and tornadoes. (Rev: BL 12/15/00; HBG 3/01) [551]

Air

24562 Bauer, Marion Dane. *Wind* (K–2). Illus. by John Wallace. Series: Ready-to-Read. 2003, Simon & Schuster paper $3.99 (978-0-689-85443-9). 32pp. For beginning readers, this is an attractively illustrated simple introduction to wind and its properties. (Rev: HBG 4/04; SLJ 1/04) [551.51]

24563 Branley, Franklyn M. *Air Is All Around You* (PS–2). Illus. by Holly Keller. 1986, HarperCollins paper $4.99 (978-0-06-445048-5). 32pp. Cheery children and an orange cat demonstrate the properties of air. (Rev: BL 4/15/86; SLJ 12/86)

24564 Bundey, Nikki. *Wind and People* (3–5). Series: The Science of Weather. 2000, Carolrhoda LB $21.27 (978-1-57505-495-7). 32pp. This book, which contains some simple experiments, shows how wind affects our lives — from causing snowdrifts and sandstorms to powering sailboats and creating energy. (Rev: BL 12/15/00; HBG 3/01) [551.5]

24565 Cobb, Vicki. *I Face the Wind* (PS–2). Illus. by Julia Gorton. Series: Vicki Cobb Science Play. 2003, HarperCollins LB $17.89 (978-0-688-17841-3). For beginning readers, Cobb explains the properties of wind and suggests appropriate demonstrations. (Rev: HB 7/03; HBG 10/03; SLJ 8/03) [551.51]

24566 Friend, Sandra. *Earth's Wild Winds* (5–8). Illus. Series: Exploring Planet Earth. 2002, Twenty-First Century LB $24.90 (978-0-7613-2673-1). 63pp. Report writers will find good material in this attractively presented coverage of all kinds of winds that also looks at the ways in which humans have attempted to harness wind power. (Rev: HBG 3/03; SLJ 10/02) [551.518]

24567 Gallant, Roy A. *Atmosphere: Sea of Air* (4–8). Illus. Series: Earthworks. 2003, Marshall Cavendish $29.93 (978-0-7614-1366-0). 80pp. An intriguing and well-presented look at how changes in the atmosphere affect us — from storms to beautiful rainbows and sunsets — and how we affect the atmosphere. (Rev: BL 3/15/03; HBG 3/03; SLJ 4/06) [551.51]

24568 Gardner, Robert. *Science Project Ideas About Air* (4–7). Series: Science Project Ideas. 1997, Enslow LB $25.26 (978-0-89490-838-5). 96pp. The properties of air are explored in a series of experiments and projects with easy-to-follow directions. (Rev: BL 12/15/97; HBG 3/98; SLJ 4/98) [678.5]

24569 Gardner, Robert, and David Webster. *Experiments with Balloons* (4–7). Illus. Series: Getting Started in Science. 1995, Enslow LB $20.95 (978-0-89490-669-5). 104pp. More than a dozen experiments explore balloons and the properties of air. (Rev: BL 12/1/95; SLJ 3/96) [507.8]

24570 Kaner, Etta. *Who Likes the Wind?* (PS–2). Illus. by Marie Lafrance. Series: Exploring the Elements. 2006, Kids Can $14.95 (978-1-55337-839-6). 32pp. Children's questions about the wind are answered in attractive illustrations using foldout pages. Also use *Who Likes the Rain?* (2007). (Rev: BL 4/1/06) [551.51]

24571 Madgwick, Wendy. *Up in the Air* (K–3). Illus. Series: Science Starters. 1999, Raintree $25.70 (978-0-8172-5325-7). 32pp. Concepts and activities related to air are presented in large double-page spreads that deal with topics including air pressure, wind, and how to make a paper airplane. (Rev: BL 6/1–15/99; HBG 9/99) [553]

24572 Murphy, Bryan. *Experiment with Air* (2–4). Illus. Series: Science Experiments. 1992, Lerner LB $19.93 (978-0-8225-2452-6). 32pp. Introduces, in simple terms, concepts involving air pressure, how things fly, and how sound waves travel. (Rev: BL 6/15/92; SLJ 10/92) [533.6]

24573 Vogt, Gregory L. *The Atmosphere: Planetary Heat Engine* (5–8). Illus. Series: Earth's Spheres. 2007, Lerner $29.27 (978-0-7613-2841-4). 80pp. Examines a wide array of topics, including the composition of our air, weather and climate, and the use of satellites and other tools to study the atmosphere. (Rev: BL 4/1/07; SLJ 5/07) [551.5]

Storms

24574 Berger, Melvin, and Gilda Berger. *Hurricanes Have Eyes but Can't See and Other Amazing Facts About Wild Weather* (2–5). Illus. Series: Speedy Facts. 2004, Scholastic paper $7.99 (978-0-439-62534-0). 48pp. An entertaining and lively presentation of amazing and informative facts about storms.

24575 Boskey, Madeline. *Natural Disasters: A Chapter Book* (2–5). Series: True Tales. 2003, Children's Pr. LB $22.50 (978-0-516-22918-8). 48pp. This imaginative overview of natural disasters transports reluctant readers into the eye of the storm on a hurricane hunter plane, to the edge of a volcano that may erupt at any moment, and into a truck chasing tornadoes. (Rev: SLJ 2/04) [904]

24576 Branley, Franklyn M. *Flash, Crash, Rumble, and Roll* (K–3). Illus. by True Kelley. Series: Let's-Read-and-Find-Out. 1999, HarperCollins LB $15.89 (978-0-06-027859-5); paper $5.99 (978-0-06-445179-6). 32pp. A new edition of the classic science book that explains the causes and effects of storms to youngsters and contains accompanying activities. Also use: *Rain and Hail* (1983). (Rev: BL 7/99; HBG 9/99; SLJ 6/99) [551.55]

24577 Branley, Franklyn M. *Tornado Alert* (K–4). Illus. by Giulio Maestro. 1988, HarperCollins LB $16.89 (978-0-690-04688-5); paper $5.99 (978-0-06-445094-2). 32pp. An explanation of these powerful storms that hold great fear and fascination for children. (Rev: BCCB 9/88; BL 9/1/88; SLJ 11/88)

24578 Bredeson, Carmen. *The Mighty Midwest Flood: Raging Rivers* (4–8). Series: American Disasters. 1999, Enslow LB $23.93 (978-0-7660-1221-9). 48pp. This account describes the terrible midwestern flood of 1993 and gives background information on the Mississippi River complex and on the causes of floods. (Rev: BL 10/15/99; HBG 3/00) [363.4]

24579 Burby, Liza N. *Tornadoes* (2–3). Illus. Series: Extreme Weather. 1999, Rosen $21.25 (978-0-8239-5289-2). 24pp. Using amazing photographs, this book introduces tornadoes with material on their causes, their impact, the possibility of prediction, and where they are commonly found. (Rev: BL 9/15/99) [551.55]

24580 Ceban, Bonnie J. *Tornadoes: Disaster and Survival* (4–7). Series: Deadly Disasters. 2005, Enslow LB $23.93 (978-0-7660-2383-3). 48pp. Explores the science behind tornadoes and offers advice about how to prepare for and survive such natural disasters. (Rev: SLJ 10/05) [551.5]

24581 Challen, Paul. *Hurricane and Typhoon Alert!* (4–6). Illus. Series: Disaster Alert! 2004, Crabtree LB $26.60 (978-0-7787-1575-7); paper $8.95 (978-0-7787-1607-5). 32pp. In addition to describing hurricanes and typhoons, there is colorfully presented material on early beliefs and myths associated with them, discussion of advances in predicting storms, tips on staying safe, and an experiment. (Rev: SLJ 3/05) [551.5]

24582 Demarest, Chris. *Hurricane Hunters! Riders on the Storm* (2–4). Illus. 2006, Simon & Schuster $17.95 (978-0-689-86168-0). 40pp. Pastel paintings introduce the work of the pilots and planes that fly into hurricanes on weather reconnaissance missions. (Rev: BL 2/1/06; SLJ 6/06) [551.55]

24583 Doeden, Matt. *Hurricanes* (K–3). Illus. Series: Pull Ahead Books: Forces of Nature. 2008, Lerner LB $22.60 (978-0-8225-7906-9). 32pp. An overview of hurricanes, cyclones, and typhoons, looking at how they form, when and where they strike, and how we can prepare for them. (Rev: BL 4/1/08; LMC 5/08) [551.55]

24584 Drohan, Michele Ingber. *Floods* (2–4). Illus. Series: Natural Disasters. 1999, Rosen $21.25 (978-0-8239-5288-5). 24pp. The causes of floods are explained and their effect on people and places covered in this simple introduction that uses many color photographs. (Rev: BL 9/15/99) [551.48]

24585 Gibbons, Gail. *Tornadoes* (1–3). Illus. by author. 2009, Holiday $16.95 (978-0-8234-2216-6).

32pp. A dramatic, fact-filled introduction to tornadoes and the destruction they cause, highlighting two spectacular events, and providing tips on keeping safe. (Rev: BL 6/1–15/09; SLJ 6/09) [551.55]

24586 Gibson, Karen Bush. *The Fury of Hurricane Andrew, 1992* (3–5). Illus. Series: Robbie Reader: Natural Disasters. 2006, Mitchell Lane LB $25.70 (978-1-58415-416-7). 32pp. Explores the economic and social impact of the devastating 1992 hurricane, with photographs, personal stories, and resources for further research. (Rev: BL 4/1/06; SLJ 5/06) [363.34]

24587 Godkin, Celia. *Hurricane!* (3–4). Illus. by author. 2008, Fitzhenry & Whiteside $19.95 (978-1-55455-080-7). Godkin looks at how people and animals in a fictional Florida town prepare for a storm, the storm itself, and the aftermath as residents assess the damage. (Rev: LMC 5/09; SLJ 11/08) [551.55]

24588 Goin, Miriam Busch. *Storms!* (PS–2). Illus. 2009, National Geographic LB $11.90 (978-1-4263-0395-1); paper $3.99 (978-1-4263-0394-4). 32pp. Color photos add drama to this absolutely furious weather narrative. (Rev: BL 6/1–15/09) [551.55]

24589 Gow, Mary. *Johnstown Flood: The Day the Dam Burst* (4–8). Series: American Disasters. 2003, Enslow LB $23.93 (978-0-7660-2109-9). 48pp. The story of the terrible Pennsylvania flood of 1889 that resulted in more than 2,000 deaths. (Rev: BL 11/15/03; HBG 10/03) [973.8]

24590 Greenberg, Keith E. *Storm Chaser: Into the Eye of a Hurricane* (4–7). Series: Risky Business. 1997, Blackbirch LB $24.94 (978-1-56711-161-3). 48pp. Tells about the people who track the paths of hurricanes and the dangers they often face. (Rev: BL 10/15/97; HBG 3/98; SLJ 12/97) [551.55]

24591 Harper, Kristine C. *Hurricane Andrew* (5–8). Series: Environmental Disasters. 2005, Facts on File $35.00 (978-0-8160-5759-7). 100pp. The impact of 1992's Hurricane Andrew on Florida's wetlands is seen as a warning about the need to be more prepared. (Rev: SLJ 11/05) [551.5]

24592 Hayden, Kate. *Twisters!* (2–3). Illus. Series: DK Readers. 2000, DK $12.99 (978-0-7894-5708-0); paper $3.99 (978-0-7894-5709-7). 32pp. An easy reader that uses a story about Rob, a farmer in Texas, to explain the causes, characteristics, and effects of tornadoes. (Rev: BL 10/1/00; HBG 3/01; SLJ 1/01) [551.55]

24593 Hopping, Lorraine Jean. *Wild Weather: Blizzards!* (2–3). Illus. by Jody Wheeler. Series: Hello Reader! 1999, Scholastic paper $3.99 (978-0-590-39730-8). 48pp. After describing several terrible blizzards, there is a discussion of what causes blizzards in this easy reader. (Rev: BCCB 1/99; BL 5/15/99; SLJ 5/99) [551.55]

24594 Hopping, Lorraine Jean. *Wild Weather: Lightning!* (1–4). Illus. by Jody Wheeler. Series: Hello Reader! 1999, Scholastic paper $3.99 (978-0-590-52285-4). 47pp. The story of lightning from classical mythology to its study using modern computer technology, with tales from survivors of lightning strikes. (Rev: SLJ 8/99) [551.5]

24595 Kahl, Jonathan D. *Storm Warning: Tornadoes and Hurricanes* (3–6). Illus. Series: How's the Weather? 1993, Lerner LB $21.27 (978-0-8225-2527-1). 64pp. An introduction to tornadoes and hurricanes with information on their causes, characteristics, and effects. (Rev: BL 5/15/93) [551]

24596 Kramer, Stephen. *Lightning* (3–6). Illus. by Warren Faidley. Series: Nature in Action. 1992, Carolrhoda LB $19.95 (978-0-87614-659-0). 48pp. A clear text and many full-color photos explain the hows and whys of lightning. (Rev: BCCB 9/92; BL 6/15/92; SLJ 7/92*) [551.5]

24597 Kramer, Stephen. *Tornado* (3–6). Illus. Series: Nature in Action. 1992, Carolrhoda LB $19.93 (978-0-87614-660-6). 48pp. This book shows how and where tornadoes usually form and the damage they can cause. (Rev: BL 11/1/92; SLJ 11/92) [551.53]

24598 Langley, Andrew. *Hurricanes, Tsunamis, and Other Natural Disasters* (4–6). Series: Kingfisher Knowledge. 2006, Kingfisher $12.95 (978-0-7534-5975-1). 64pp. This well-illustrated volume examines a wide range of natural disasters and looks at the ways in which humans respond and what they are doing to better predict or prevent these disasters in the future. (Rev: BL 9/1/06; SLJ 10/06) [363.34]

24599 Larson, Kirby, and Mary Nethery. *Two Bobbies: A True Story of Hurricane Katrina, Friendship, and Survival* (K–3). Illus. by Jean Cassels. 2008, Walker $16.99 (978-0-8027-9754-4). 32pp. The inspiring story of a cat and a dog who survived Hurricane Katrina through mutual devotion and the help of a volunteer shelter. (Rev: BL 9/1/08; SLJ 9/08) [636.08]

24600 Lindop, Laurie. *Chasing Tornadoes* (5–8). Illus. Series: Science on the Edge. 2003, Millbrook LB $26.90 (978-0-7613-2703-5). 80pp. A lively introduction to tornadoes, the scientists who dare to study them, and techniques for collecting data and forecasting tornado activity. (Rev: BL 12/1/03; SLJ 1/04) [551.55]

24601 McGrath, Barbara Barbieri, comp. *The Storm: Students of Biloxi, Mississippi, Remember Hurricane Katrina* (3–8). Illus. 2006, Charlesbridge $18.95 (978-1-58089-172-1). 64pp. Artwork and writings show the impact of the storm on K–12 students in Biloxi; the book is divided into four sections: "Evacuation," "Storm," "Aftermath," and "Hope." (Rev: SLJ 12/06) [976.2]

24602 Meister, Cari. *Hurricanes* (4–6). Illus. Series: Nature's Fury. 1999, ABDO LB $24.21 (978-1-57765-080-5). 32pp. A history of hurricanes is included along with material on their causes, effects, and how to stay safe during one. (Rev: HBG 4/00; SLJ 12/99) [551.5]

24603 Miller, Mara. *Hurricane Katrina Strikes the Gulf Coast* (5–8). Series: Deadly Disasters. 2006, Enslow LB $23.93 (978-0-7660-2803-6). 48pp. The story of Hurricane Katrina and its disastrous impact on the Gulf Coast in 2005 is accompanied by personal stories plus information on other deadly storms. (Rev: BL 7/06; SLJ 9/06) [363.34]

24604 Nicolson, Cynthia Pratt. *Hurricane!* (4–8). Illus. Series: Disaster. 2002, Kids Can $14.95 (978-1-55074-906-9); paper $6.95 (978-1-55074-970-0). 32pp. An accessible text and many photographs provide information on hurricane formation and intensity, on the preparations for major hurricanes, and on famous storms of the past. (Rev: HBG 3/03; SLJ 12/02) [551.552]

24605 Nicolson, Cynthia Pratt. *Tornado!* (3–6). Illus. 2003, Kids Can $14.95 (978-1-55337-951-5); paper $6.95 (978-1-55337-972-0). 32pp. The nature and power of tornadoes are described in this oversize volume that includes easy experiments and accounts of notable tornadoes. (Rev: BL 4/1/03) [551.55]

24606 Otfinoski, Steven. *Blizzards* (4–6). Illus. Series: When Disaster Strikes! 1994, Twenty-First Century LB $18.90 (978-0-8050-3093-8). 64pp. This book explains why blizzards occur, provides safety tips, and tells about famous storms of the past. (Rev: BL 10/15/94; SLJ 9/94) [363.3]

24607 Prokos, Anna. *Tornadoes* (4–6). Series: The Ultimate 10 Natural Disasters. 2008, Gareth Stevens LB $31.00 (978-0-8368-9153-9). 48pp. Prokos looks at 10 significant tornadoes and the destruction they caused, with color photographs, eyewitness accounts, maps and charts, and statistics; a final section covers ways to prepare for such events. (Rev: LMC 3/09; SLJ 3/09) [551.55]

24608 Rotter, Charles. *Hurricanes: Storms of the Sea* (4–6). Series: LifeViews. 2002, Creative Editions LB $24.25 (978-1-58341-020-2). 32pp. A revised edition with updated text and new photographs that describes hurricanes and their causes and includes two projects. (Rev: HBG 3/03; SLJ 1/03) [551.5]

24609 Royston, Angela. *Floods* (2–4). Illus. Series: Wild Weather. 2009, Black Rabbit LB $18.95 (978-1-59566-584-3). 32pp. What causes floods, the kinds of floods and mudslides that occur, their destructive power, and what can be done to prevent and prepare for these disasters are all covered here. (Rev: BL 4/1/09) [500]

24610 Ryback, Carol, and Jayne Keedle. *Hurricanes* (4–6). Series: The Ultimate 10 Natural Disasters. 2008, Gareth Stevens LB $31.00 (978-0-8368-9152-2). 48pp. This volume looks at 10 significant hurricanes and the destruction they caused, with color photographs, eyewitness accounts, maps and charts, and statistics; a final section covers ways to prepare for such events. (Rev: LMC 3/09; SLJ 3/09) [551.55]

24611 Scavuzzo, Wendy. *Tornado Alert!* (4–6). Illus. Series: Disaster Alert! 2004, Crabtree LB $26.60 (978-0-7787-1571-9); paper $8.95 (978-0-7787-1603-7). 32pp. In addition to describing tornadoes, there is colorfully presented material on early beliefs and myths associated with them, discussion of advances in predicting storms, tips on staying safe, and an experiment. (Rev: SLJ 3/05) [551.55]

24612 Sherrow, Victoria. *Hurricane Andrew: Nature's Rage* (4–8). Series: American Disasters. 1998, Enslow LB $23.93 (978-0-7660-1057-4). The story of the storm that caused millions of dollars of damage on the Atlantic Coast, told in dramatic text and pictures. (Rev: BL 1/1–15/99; HBG 3/99; VOYA 4/99) [551.5]

24613 Sherrow, Victoria. *Plains Outbreak Tornadoes: Killer Twisters* (4–8). Series: American Disasters. 1998, Enslow LB $23.93 (978-0-7660-1059-8). The causes and effects of the giant tornadoes that occur in the Midwest, with details of some of the most horrendous. (Rev: BL 1/1–15/99; HBG 3/99) [551.55]

24614 Simon, Seymour. *Hurricanes*. Rev. ed. (3–5). 2007, Collins $16.99 (978-0-06-117072-0); paper $6.99 (978-0-06-117071-3). 32pp. An updated edition of the 2003 volume, with colorful photographs, thorough explanations of how hurricanes are formed and behave, and details of important storms. (Rev: LMC 3/04; SLJ 5/08) [551.55]

24615 Simon, Seymour. *Lightning* (3–6). Illus. 1997, Morrow $17.89 (978-0-688-14639-9). 32pp. A dramatic, fact-packed description of the causes of lightning, different types, and its effects. (Rev: BL 3/15/97*; SLJ 5/97) [551.319]

24616 Simon, Seymour. *Storms* (3–5). Illus. 1989, Morrow LB $15.89 (978-0-688-07414-2); paper $6.99 (978-0-688-11708-5). 32pp. Explaining how storms occur. (Rev: BCCB 3/89; BL 3/1/89; SLJ 4/89)

24617 Simon, Seymour. *Super Storms* (1–3). Series: Sec More Readers. 2002, North-South $13.95 (978-1-58717-137-6); paper $3.95 (978-1-58717-138-3). 32pp. Violent storms and their causes are covered in this beginning reader that uses double-page spreads consisting each of a large color picture opposite a few lines of text. (Rev: BL 7/02; HBG 10/02) [551.5]

24618 Simon, Seymour. *Tornadoes* (4–8). 1999, Morrow LB $16.89 (978-0-688-14647-4). Well-organized text discusses the weather conditions that give rise to tornadoes, how they form, where they are most likely to occur, and how scientists predict and track them, supplemented by large, riveting photographs showing meteorologists at work, a variety of tornadoes, and the devastation caused by major tornadoes. (Rev: BCCB 4/99; BL 5/99; HBG 9/99; SLJ 6/99) [551.55]

24619 Souza, D. M. *Hurricanes* (3–6). Illus. Series: Nature in Action. 1996, Carolrhoda LB $19.95 (978-0-87614-861-7); paper $19.93 (978-0-87614-955-3). 48pp. The causes and effects of hurricanes are covered, as well as forecasting devices. (Rev: BL 8/96; SLJ 11/96) [551.55]

24620 Souza, D. M. *Powerful Waves* (3–6). Illus. 1992, Carolrhoda LB $19.95 (978-0-87614-661-3). 48pp. Deals with tsunamis — misnamed tidal waves — how they develop, and the disasters they cause. (Rev: BL 11/1/92; SLJ 11/92) [551]

24621 Stewart, Mark. *Blizzards and Winter Storms* (4–6). Series: The Ultimate 10 Natural Disasters. 2008, Gareth Stevens LB $31.00 (978-0-8368-9150-8). 48pp. Stewart looks at 10 significant blizzards and the destruction they caused, with color photographs, eyewitness accounts, maps and charts, and statistics; a final section covers ways to prepare for such events. (Rev: LMC 3/09; SLJ 3/09) [551.55]

24622 Torres, John A. *Hurricane Katrina and the Devastation of New Orleans* (4–7). Series: Monumental Milestones. 2006, Mitchell Lane $29.95 (978-1-58415-473-0). 48pp. An interview with a newlywed couple who lost everything in the storm draws readers into this account of the devastation. (Rev: BL 9/1/06) [363.34]

24623 Webster, Christine. *Storms* (2–4). Illus. 2006, Weigl $24.45 (978-1-59036-418-5). 24pp. An engaging and detailed introduction to storms, their meteorological origins, extreme phenomena such as hail and tornadoes, and the technologies that allow us to predict and track them. (Rev: BL 12/1/06) [551.55]

24624 Woods, Michael, and Mary B. Woods. *Hurricanes* (4–6). Series: Disasters Up Close. 2006, Lerner LB $27.93 (978-0-8225-4710-5). 64pp. With charts, photographs, and quotes from survivors, this book clearly demonstrates the power of hurricanes, and provides quick facts plus tips on preparing for a storm. (Rev: SLJ 1/07) [551.5]

24625 Woods, Michael, and Mary B. Woods. *Tornadoes* (5–8). Illus. Series: Disasters Up Close. 2006, Lerner $27.93 (978-0-8225-4714-3). 64pp. Eyewitness accounts add to this well-illustrated overview of tornadoes and the destruction they can cause. (Rev: BL 10/15/06) [551.55]

Water

24626 Bauer, Marion Dane. *Snow* (K–2). Illus. by John Wallace. Series: Ready to Read. 2003, Simon & Schuster paper $3.99 (978-0-689-85437-8). 31pp. Facts about snow become part of this gentle story about a child and dog enjoying a wintry day. (Rev: HBG 4/04; SLJ 1/04) [551.57]

24627 Berger, Melvin, and Gilda Berger. *Water, Water Everywhere: A Book About the Water Cycle* (2–4). Illus. Series: Discovery Readers. 1995, Ideals paper $4.50 (978-1-57102-042-0). 48pp. In addition to the water cycle, this book discusses a city's water system, sewage, and how to conserve water. (Rev: BL 12/1/95; SLJ 2/96) [551.48]

24628 Bundey, Nikki. *Rain and People* (3–5). Illus. Series: Science of Weather. 2000, Carolrhoda $21.27 (978-1-57505-494-0). 32pp. This volume describes how fresh water and rain are involved in health, agriculture, construction, and power. A companion volume *Rain and the Earth* (2000), discusses the water cycle, clouds, water pollution, and ecosystems. (Rev: BL 10/15/00; HBG 3/01) [551.57]

24629 Bundey, Nikki. *Snow and the Earth* (3–5). Series: The Science of Weather. 2000, Carolrhoda LB $21.27 (978-1-57505-471-1). 32pp. This account, with a few experiments, shows how important snow is to the well-being of the earth and its people, animals, and plants. (Rev: BL 12/15/00; HBG 3/01) [551.57]

24630 Cobb, Vicki. *Squirts and Spurts: Science Fun with Water* (3–6). Illus. 2000, Millbrook LB $24.90 (978-0-7613-1572-8). 48pp. The mechanics behind hydraulics, vacuum pressure, and other forms of moving water are explored in this entertaining activity book that uses a cartoon format. (Rev: BCCB 11/00; BL 10/15/00; HBG 3/01; SLJ 3/01) [507.8]

24631 Farndon, John. *Water* (3–6). Series: Science Experiments. 2000, Marshall Cavendish LB $25.64 (978-0-7614-1087-4). 32pp. Covers the properties of water, its three states, and the ways it can be manipulated, along with related experiments and projects. (Rev: BL 3/15/01; HBG 3/01) [553.7]

24632 Fiarotta, Noel, and Phyllis Fiarotta. *Great Experiments with H²O* (4–6). Illus. 1997, Sterling paper $9.95 (978-0-8069-4259-9). 80pp. These simple hands-on experiments demonstrate why water freezes, rises as steam, condenses, and evaporates. (Rev: BL 12/1/97) [553.7]

24633 Fowler, Allan. *It Could Still Be Water* (1–2). Illus. Series: Rookie Readers. 1992, Children's Book Pr. LB $20.50 (978-0-516-06003-3). 32pp. This is a simple introduction to water and its many uses. It is also available in an oversized "Big Book" edition. (Rev: BL 12/15/92) [553.7]

24634 Gallant, Roy A. *Water* (5–8). Series: Earth Sciences. 2000, Marshall Cavendish LB $25.64 (978-0-7614-1040-9). 48pp. This work introduces the importance of water on the earth, its three states, and the water cycle. (Rev: BL 3/1/01; HBG 3/01; SLJ 5/01) [551.57]

24635 Gallant, Roy A. *Water: Our Precious Resource* (4–8). Illus. Series: Earthworks. 2003, Marshall Cavendish $29.93 (978-0-7614-1365-3). 80pp. A thought-provoking and well-presented overview of the sources of water; the ways in which we use, misuse, and recycle water; and efforts to preserve this vital natural resource. (Rev: BL 3/15/03; HBG 3/03; SLJ 2/03) [553.7]

24636 Godwin, Sam. *The Drop Goes Plop: A First Look at the Water Cycle* (K–1). Illus. by Simone Abel. Series: First Look : Science. 2004, Picture Window LB $25.26 (978-1-4048-0657-3). 32pp. In simple language with cartoon-style illustrations, a mother bird explains to her baby how a single drop of water fits into the water cycle. (Rev: BL 10/15/04) [551.48]

24637 Hamilton, Kersten. *This Is the Ocean* (PS–2). Illus. by Lorianne Siomades. 2001, Boyds Mills $14.95 (978-1-56397-890-6). 32pp. Using rhyming couplets and lovely three-dimensional collages, this book presents the water cycle to a young audience. (Rev: BL 4/15/01; HBG 10/01; SLJ 6/01) [551.46]

24638 Locker, Thomas. *Water Dance* (3–5). Illus. 1997, Harcourt $16.00 (978-0-15-201284-7). 32pp. Using a fictionalized format, this account poetically traces the phases of the water cycle. (Rev: BCCB 5/97; BL 3/1/97; SLJ 4/97) [551]

24639 Madgwick, Wendy. *Water Play* (K–3). Illus. Series: Science Starters. 1999, Raintree $25.69 (978-0-8172-5326-4). 32pp. The composition, states, and uses of water are explored in large double-page spreads with activities such as constructing a rain measure, observing surface tension, and making a bubble wand. (Rev: BL 6/1–15/99; HBG 9/99) [532]

24640 Marzollo, Jean. *I Am Water* (1–2). Illus. by Judith Moffatt. 1996, Scholastic paper $3.99 (978-0-590-26587-4). 32pp. In a beginning reader, the various forms of water are introduced. (Rev: BL 9/15/96*) [553.7]

24641 Morgan, Sally, and Adrian Morgan. *Water* (4–7). Illus. Series: Designs in Science. 1994, Facts on File $23.00 (978-0-8160-2982-2). 48pp. The importance and uses of water are described, with information on water storage, filtering, and conservation, plus activities and experiments. (Rev: BL 7/94) [533.7]

24642 Morrison, Gordon. *A Drop of Water* (K–3). 2006, Houghton $16.00 (978-0-618-58557-1). 32pp. A gentle account of the water cycle, following the path of a drop of rainwater as it makes its way downhill past different settings, plants, and animals. (Rev: BL 8/06; SLJ 10/06) [508]

24643 Nadeau, Isaac. *Learning About the Water Cycle with Graphic Organizers* (3–6). Series: Graphic Organizers in Science. 2005, Rosen LB $21.25 (978-1-4042-2808-5). 24pp. This title uses a wide variety of graphic organizers, including concept webs, compare/contrast charts, Venn diagrams, graphs, timelines, and KWL charts, to introduce readers to the water cycle. (Rev: SLJ 11/05)

24644 Nelson, Robin. *We Use Water* (PS–K). Illus. Series: First Step Nonfiction: Water. 2003, Lerner LB $18.60 (978-0-8225-4594-1). 24pp. This introduction for beginning readers to the properties and uses of water looks at familiar scenarios such as hand washing, fire fighting, and ice cubes. Also use *Where Is Water?* (2003). (Rev: BL 10/15/03; HBG 4/04) [553.7]

24645 Oxlade, Chris. *Water* (2–3). Series: Materials, Materials, Materials. 2002, Heinemann LB $22.79 (978-1-58810-588-2). 32pp. Color photographs and an easy text are used to introduce water, its properties, and its uses. (Rev: BL 6/1–15/02) [533.7]

24646 Robinson, Fay. *Where Do Puddles Go?* (1–2). Illus. Series: Rookie Readers. 1995, Children's Book Pr. LB $20.50 (978-0-516-06036-1). 32pp. In very simple language and many color photographs, the water cycle is introduced to young children. (Rev: BL 7/95) [551.57]

24647 Royston, Angela. *Water: Let's Look at a Puddle* (K–3). Illus. Series: Read and Learn: Material Detectives. 2005, Heinemann LB $14.95 (978-1-4034-7676-0). 24pp. Examples from daily life — What happens to a frozen puddle? What makes a puddle dry up? — make basic science concepts clear. (Rev: BL 12/1/05) [553.7]

24648 Schaefer, Lola M. *This Is the Rain* (PS–1). Illus. by Jane Wattenberg. 2001, Greenwillow LB $16.89 (978-0-688-17040-0). 32pp. Simple, rhythmic text echoes the movement of water through its cycle from sea to sky to streams in this book with inventive illustrations. (Rev: BCCB 10/01; BL 12/15/01; HBG 3/02; SLJ 9/01) [551]

24649 Seuling, Barbara. *Drip! Drop! How Water Gets to Your Tap* (K–2). Illus. by Nancy Tobin. 2000, Holiday House $15.95 (978-0-8234-1459-8). After describing the water cycle, this concise account tells how reservoir water is collected, filtered, and sent through a water-treatment plant before reaching houses and apartments. (Rev: BCCB 1/01; HBG 10/01; SLJ 2/01) [546]

24650 Stewart, Melissa. *The Wonders of Water* (2–4). Illus. Series: Investigate Science. 2004, Compass Point LB $21.26 (978-0-7565-0637-7). 32pp. Text, illustrations, and activities introduce the characteristics and importance of water. (Rev: SLJ 3/05) [553.7]

24651 Swanson, Diane. *The Wonder in Water* (3–5). 2006, Annick $19.95 (978-1-55037-937-2); paper $8.95 (978-1-55037-936-5). 44pp. The many faces of water — from beads of human perspiration to raindrops to the world's largest oceans — are explored in conversational text with lots of interesting sidebars, photographs, and diagrams. (Rev: BL 1/1–15/06) [553.7]

24652 Waldman, Neil. *The Snowflake: A Water Cycle Story* (1–5). Illus. by author. 2003, Millbrook LB $23.90 (978-0-7613-1762-3). This beautiful overview follows a single drop of water from snowflake through the entire water cycle and back to snowflake. (Rev: BL 11/1/03; HBG 4/04; SLJ 12/03) [551.48]

24653 Walker, Sally M. *Water Up, Water Down: The Hydrologic Cycle* (3–6). Illus. Series: Earth Watch. 1992, Carolrhoda LB $21.27 (978-0-87614-695-8). 48pp. This includes a description of the water cycle and material on erosion, flooding, caves, and other interesting aspects. (Rev: BL 1/15/93; SLJ 12/92) [551]

24654 Wells, Robert E. *Did a Dinosaur Drink This Water?* (1–3). Illus. by author. 2006, Albert Whitman $16.99 (978-0-8075-8839-0); paper $6.95 (978-0-8075-8840-6). This cartoon-style introduction to the water cycle takes readers on a world tour to explore a wide variety of issues, including water's importance in sustaining the life of plants and animals; its three states; water use policies; conservation efforts; and water pollution. (Rev: BL 12/1/06; SLJ 2/07) [551.48]

24655 Wick, Walter. *A Drop of Water* (3–6). Illus. 1997, Scholastic $16.95 (978-0-590-22197-9). 40pp. The properties of water are explored in amazing photographs and activities. (Rev: BCCB 2/97; BL 2/1/97*; HB 3/97; SLJ 3/97) [546]

Weather

24656 Armentrout, David, and Patricia Armentrout. *Weather* (PS–2). Illus. 2002, Rourke LB $19.95 (978-1-58952-346-3). 32pp. Simple definitions are given for 50 words about weather (arid, breeze, and so forth), along with a sentence that includes the word. (Rev: HBG 3/03; SLJ 3/03)

24657 Arnold, Caroline. *El Niño: Stormy Weather for People and Wildlife* (4–8). Illus. 1998, Clarion $16.00 (978-0-395-77602-5). A brief overview of El Niño, its causes and history, and how tracking and forecasting are used to make predictions. (Rev: BL 10/1/98; HBG 10/99; SLJ 12/98) [551.6]

24658 Banqueri, Eduardo. *Weather* (4–8). Illus. by Estudio Marcel Socías and Gabi Marfil. Series: Field Guides. 2006, Enchanted Lion $16.95 (978-1-59270-059-2). 33pp. This information-packed guide explores a broad array of weather-related topics, including seasonal change, climatic zones, the science of meteorology, clouds, winds, storms, and the atmosphere. (Rev: SLJ 1/07) [551.5]

24659 Berger, Melvin, and Gilda Berger. *Can It Rain Cats and Dogs? Questions and Answers About Weather* (3–5). Series: Question and Answer. 1999, Scholastic $12.95 (978-0-590-13083-7); paper $5.95 (978-0-590-08573-1). 148pp. Basic facts about weather are introduced using a question-and-answer format and entertaining illustrations. (Rev: BL 11/15/99; SLJ 2/00) [551.5]

24660 Berger, Melvin, and Gilda Berger. *How's the Weather? A Look at Weather and How It Changes* (K–2). Illus. by John E. Cymerman. Series: Discovery Readers. 1993, Ideals paper $4.50 (978-0-8249-8599-8). 48pp. A basic introduction to weather that touches on such topics as air pressure, water vapor, weather maps, lightning, hurricanes, and tornadoes. (Rev: SLJ 3/94) [551.5]

24661 Bredeson, Carmen. *El Niño and La Niña: Deadly Weather* (4–8). Series: American Disasters. 2002, Enslow LB $23.93 (978-0-7660-1551-7). 48pp. A well-researched account of these two weather phenomena, their effects, and how they can be traced. (Rev: BL 6/1–15/02; HBG 10/02; SLJ 6/02) [551.6]

24662 Breen, Mark, and Kathleen Friestad. *The Kids' Book of Weather Forecasting* (3–5). Illus. Series: Kids Can! 2000, Williamson paper $14.25 (978-1-885593-39-9). 140pp. This book explains the complex subject of weather forecasting and includes such activities as making a barometer, a rain gauge, and a tornado. (Rev: BL 2/1/01; SLJ 1/01) [551.63]

24663 Brotak, Edward. *Wild About Weather: 50 Wet, Windy and Wonderful Activities* (3–6). 2004, Lark Books $19.95 (978-1-57990-468-5). 128pp. In addition to 50 activities with clear instructions, Brotak provides lots of entertainingly presented facts, diagrams, and photographs. (Rev: BL 12/1/04) [551.6]

24664 Burby, Liza N. *Heat Waves and Droughts* (2–3). Illus. Series: Extreme Weather. 1999, Rosen $21.25 (978-0-8239-5292-2). 24pp. Dramatic photographs illustrate this beginning book on heat waves and droughts and their causes and effects. (Rev: BL 9/15/99) [551.5]

24665 Carson, Mary Kay. *Weather Projects for Young Scientists* (4–7). 2007, Chicago Review paper $14.95 (978-1-55652-629-9). 160pp. A detailed look at weather basics is intertwined with more than 40 projects, many appropriate for science fairs, and a few career profiles. (Rev: BL 12/1/06; SLJ 3/08) [551.5078]

24666 Christian, Spencer, and Antonia Felix. *Can It Really Rain Frogs? The World's Strangest Weather Events* (3–7). Series: Spencer Christian's World of Wonders. 1997, Wiley paper $13.95 (978-0-471-15290-3). 115pp. Strange facts about the weather

are combined with many related activities, experiments, and projects. (Rev: SLJ 4/98) [551.5]

24667 Cobb, Allan B. *Weather Observation Satellites* (5–9). Series: The Library of Satellites. 2003, Rosen LB $26.50 (978-0-8239-3856-8). 64pp. This book shows how the development of satellites from the 1960s on has provided us with clear weather observations and accurate forecasts. (Rev: BL 11/15/03) [551.6]

24668 DeWitt, Lynda. *What Will the Weather Be?* (K–3). Illus. by Carolyn Croll. Series: Let's-Read-and-Find-Out. 1993, HarperCollins paper $5.99 (978-0-06-445113-0). 32pp. An illustrated introduction to weather forecasting. (Rev: BCCB 6/91; BL 5/1/91; SLJ 7/91) [551.6]

24669 Drake, Jane, and Ann Love. *Snow Amazing: Cool Facts and Warm Tales* (3–5). Illus. by Mark Thurman. 2004, Tundra $19.95 (978-0-88776-670-1). 80pp. Snow lore and facts are at the center of this compendium of diverse facts, figures, and folktales, including details of the animals that inhabit arctic regions. (Rev: BL 2/1/05; SLJ 12/04) [551.57]

24670 Estigarribia, Diana. *Learning About Weather with Graphic Organizers* (3–6). Series: Graphic Organizers in Science. 2005, Rosen LB $21.25 (978-1-4042-2803-0). 24pp. This title uses a wide variety of graphic organizers, including concept webs, compare/contrast charts, Venn diagrams, graphs, timelines, and KWL charts, to introduce topics such as global warming, the greenhouse effect, seasonal change, and weather forecasting. (Rev: SLJ 11/05)

24671 Farndon, John. *Weather* (3–6). Illus. Series: Science Experiments. 2000, Marshall Cavendish LB $25.64 (978-0-7614-1089-8). 32pp. In addition to material on topics including sunlight, winds, clouds, and storms, this book outlines such projects as making a rain gauge and a weather vane. (Rev: BL 3/15/01; HBG 3/01) [551.6]

24672 Gardner, Robert. *Science Project Ideas About Rain* (4–7). Series: Science Project Ideas. 1997, Enslow LB $25.26 (978-0-89490-843-9). 96pp. Clear explanations and functional drawings and diagrams for a number of activities that study rain, its causes, and its effects. (Rev: BL 12/15/97; HBG 3/98; SLJ 1/98) [551.55]

24673 Gardner, Robert. *Wild Science Projects About Earth's Weather* (4–6). Illus. by Tom LaBaff. Series: Rockin' Earth Science Experiments. 2007, Enslow LB $23.93 (978-0-7660-2734-3). 48pp. These projects concerning weather are appropriate for science fairs and are accompanied by safety precautions and detailed directions. (Rev: SLJ 6/07)

24674 Gibbons, Gail. *Weather Words and What They Mean* (1–3). Illus. by author. 1990, Holiday House LB $16.95 (978-0-8234-0805-4). Various broad terms — such as temperature, air pressure, moisture, and wind — are defined, with breakdowns into more-specific terms. (Rev: BCCB 4/90; SLJ 5/90) [551.6]

24675 Gold, Susan Dudley. *Blame It on El Niño* (5–9). 1999, Raintree LB $28.54 (978-0-7398-1376-8). 96pp. Covers El Niño, La Niña, how scientists predict and track them, and the effects of each globally. (Rev: HBG 3/00; SLJ 4/00) [551.6]

24676 Kahl, Jonathan D. *Hazy Skies: Weather and the Environment* (4–6). Illus. 1998, Lerner LB $21.27 (978-0-8225-2530-1). 64pp. After providing a history of air pollution, this book links it to such weather-related topics as the ozone layer and global warming. (Rev: BL 3/15/98; HBG 9/98) [363.73]

24677 Kahl, Jonathan D. *Weather Watch: Forecasting the Weather* (5–8). Series: How's the Weather? 1996, Lerner LB $21.27 (978-0-8225-2529-5). This work provides basic information on weather systems, maps, and forecasting tools, the history of weather forecasting and keeping weather records, and directions for making a weather station. (Rev: BL 6/1–15/96; SLJ 6/96) [551.6]

24678 Kahl, Jonathan D. *Weatherwise: Learning About the Weather* (4–6). Illus. 1992, Lerner LB $21.27 (978-0-8225-2525-7). 64pp. Topics covered include atmosphere, winds, storms, and forecasting. (Rev: SLJ 8/92) [551.6]

24679 Kaner, Etta. *Who Likes the Snow?* (PS–2). Illus. by Marie Lafrance. Series: Exploring the Elements. 2006, Kids Can $14.95 (978-1-55337-842-6). This slim book uses questions and flaps to offer interesting information about snow. (Rev: SLJ 12/06) [551.51]

24680 Kramer, Stephen. *Avalanche* (3–6). Illus. by Patrick Cone. Series: Nature in Action. 1992, Carolrhoda LB $19.93 (978-0-87614-422-0). 48pp. Examining different types of snowslides, and how and when they occur. (Rev: BCCB 9/92; BL 6/15/92; SLJ 9/92) [551.57]

24681 Markle, Sandra. *A Rainy Day* (K–3). Illus. by Cathy Johnson. 1993, Orchard LB $16.99 (978-0-531-08576-9). 32pp. A simple explanation of how clouds form and why rain falls. (Rev: BCCB 3/93; BL 3/1/93; SLJ 7/93) [551]

24682 Marsico, Katie. *Snowy Weather Days* (K–2). Series: Scholastic News Nonfiction Readers. 2006, Children's Pr. LB $20.00 (978-0-531-16773-1). 24pp. Basic information for beginning readers, with seven highlighted words that are featured in bold in the text. Also use *Wild Weather Days* (2006). (Rev: SLJ 1/07) [551.57]

24683 Michaels, Pat. *W Is for Wind: A Weather Alphabet* (1–4). Illus. by Melanie Rose. 2005, Sleeping Bear $16.95 (978-1-58536-237-0). A rhyming alphabet book about the weather with useful information for young elementary students. (Rev: SLJ 7/05) [428.1]

24684 Nelson, Robin. *A Rainy Day* (PS–1). Illus. Series: Weather. 2001, Lerner LB $17.27 (978-0-8225-0173-2); paper $4.25 (978-0-8225-1962-1). 23pp. In a small format for beginning readers, some simple facts about rainy days are accompanied by bold illustrations. Also use *A Snowy Day* and *A Sunny Day* (both 2001). (Rev: HBG 3/02; SLJ 4/02) [551.57]

24685 Pipe, Jim. *Weather* (3–5). Illus. Series: Earthwise. 2004, Stargazer LB $27.10 (978-1-932799-47-7). 32pp. An excellent introduction to the forces that create our weather, this attractively illustrated vol-

ume supplements its facts and figures with suggested activities. (Rev: BL 10/15/04) [551.5]

24686 Rockwell, Anne. *Clouds* (PS–1). Illus. by Frane Lessac. Series: Let's-Read-and-Find-Out Science Stage 1. 2008, Collins $16.99 (978-0-06-445220-5); paper $5.99 (978-0-06-029101-3). 40pp. For beginning readers, this is a simple picture-book introduction to clouds and the kinds of weather they accompany. (Rev: BL 12/15/08; SLJ 12/08) [551.57]

24687 Rodgers, Alan, and Angella Streluk. *Cloud Cover* (3–6). Illus. Series: Measuring the Weather. 2002, Heinemann LB $22.79 (978-1-58810-686-5). 32pp. Fog, ultraviolet radiation, types of cloud, and cloud cover in itself are all discussed — with their benefits and potential dangers — in this attractive titles. (Rev: HBG 3/03; SLJ 4/03) [551.5]

24688 Rodgers, Alan, and Angella Streluk. *Forecasting the Weather* (3–6). Illus. Series: Measuring the Weather. 2002, Heinemann LB $22.79 (978-1-58810-687-2). 32pp. Many of the tools used by meteorologists are examined here. Also use *Wind and Air Pressure* (2002). (Rev: HBG 3/03; SLJ 4/03) [551.6]

24689 Rosenberg, Pam. *Sunny Weather Days* (K–2). Series: Scholastic News Nonfiction Readers. 2006, Children's Pr. LB $20.00 (978-0-531-16770-0). 24pp. This colorful picture book introduces young readers to the properties of the sun and introduces seven weather-related vocabulary words. (Rev: SLJ 1/07) [551.5]

24690 Rupp, Rebecca. *Weather! Watch How Weather Works* (4–8). Illus. 2003, Storey Kids paper $14.95 (978-1-58017-420-6). 136pp. A well-illustrated and appealing introduction to the science of weather, with numerous experiments and projects. (Rev: SLJ 5/04) [551.6]

24691 Rustad, Martha E. H. *Today Is Hot* (PS–3). 2005, Capstone LB $21.26 (978-0-7368-5343-9). 24pp. A very basic introduction to climate and weather, emphasizing aspects that affect a child's life. Also in this series: *Today Is Cold, Today Is Rainy,* and *Today Is Snowy* (all 2005). (Rev: SLJ 7/06) [551.5]

24692 Saunders-Smith, Gail. *La lluvia / Rain* (K–2). Trans. by Mart'n Luis Guzm n Ferrer. Series: Pebble Bilingual Books. 2003, Capstone LB $17.26 (978-0-7368-2309-8). 24pp. An introduction to rain and rainstorms in English and Spanish, illustrated with photographs. (Rev: SLJ 4/04) [551.5]

24693 Sayre, April P. *El Niño and La Niña: Weather in the Headlines* (4–8). Illus. 2000, Twenty-First Century LB $25.90 (978-0-7613-1405-9). 80pp. An exploration of this complex Pacific Ocean phenomenon that produces unusual weather conditions that affect the entire world. (Rev: BL 9/15/00; HBG 3/01) [551.6]

24694 Silverstein, Alvin, et al. *Weather and Climate* (4–7). Illus. Series: Science Concepts. 1998, Twenty-First Century LB $26.90 (978-0-7613-3223-7). 64pp. This book introduces weather by explaining earth's atmosphere, rotation, and different climates with material on air and water movements, cloud formation, and climate changes. (Rev: BL 5/1/99; HBG 10/99) [551.5]

24695 Solway, Andrew. *A Pirate Adventure: Weather* (3–6). Illus. Series: Raintree Fusion. 2005, Raintree LB $28.21 (978-1-4109-1926-7). 32pp. An exciting voyage on an 18th-century ship serves as the backdrop for information about wind, weather, and weather forecasting. (Rev: SLJ 5/06) [551.6]

24696 Souza, D. M. *Northern Lights* (5–7). Illus. 1994, Carolrhoda LB $23.95 (978-0-87614-799-3); paper $7.95 (978-0-87614-629-3). 48pp. A description of the northern lights and an explanation of what causes them. (Rev: BL 1/15/94) [538]

24697 Stein, Paul. *Forecasting the Climate of the Future* (5–7). Series: The Library of Future Weather and Climate. 2001, Rosen LB $29.25 (978-0-8239-3413-3). 64pp. A fascinating, well-organized account that looks at long-range weather predictions and at the use and accuracy of computer models in forecasting future weather patterns, especially with regard to global warming. Also use *Storms of the Future* (2001), which looks at whether global warming might cause stronger storms. (Rev: SLJ 4/02) [551.5]

24698 Stein, Paul. *Ice Ages of the Future* (5–7). Series: The Library of Future Weather and Climate. 2001, Rosen LB $29.25 (978-0-8239-3415-7). 64pp. A look at the possibility that the greenhouse effect and other factors could in fact cause a wave of colder rather than warmer air. (Rev: SLJ 11/01) [551.6]

24699 Stonehouse, Bernard. *Snow, Ice and Cold* (5–7). 1993, Macmillan LB $21.00 (978-0-02-788530-9). 45pp. This work tells about how cultures and individuals have adjusted to severe cold climates. (Rev: SLJ 7/93) [551.6]

24700 VanCleave, Janice. *Janice VanCleave's Weather: Mind-Boggling Experiments You Can Turn into Science Fair Projects* (3–6). Illus. Series: Janice VanCleave's Spectacular Science Projects. 1995, Wiley paper $10.95 (978-0-471-03231-1). 89pp. Intriguing questions about the weather are answered in 20 easily performed experiments and projects. (Rev: SLJ 8/95) [551.6]

24701 Vogel, Carole G. *Weather Legends: Native American Lore and the Science of Weather* (4–8). Illus. 2001, Millbrook LB $29.90 (978-0-7613-

1900-9). 80pp. Native American weather myths are paired with scientific information about actual weather phenomena. (Rev: BL 9/1/01; HBG 3/02; SLJ 10/01) [398.2]

24702 Williams, Judith. *How Does the Sun Make Weather?* (1–3). Illus. Series: I Like Weather! 2005, Enslow LB $21.26 (978-0-7660-2317-8). 24pp. Preceded by a glossary and using questions as most chapter headers, this volume introduces the sun's influence on our weather. Also use: *Why Is It Raining?* and *Why Is It Windy?* (2005). (Rev: BL 4/1/05) [551.6]

24703 Williams, Terry Tempest, and Ted Major. *The Secret Language of Snow* (4–8). Illus. by Jennifer O. Dewey. 1984, Pantheon $10.95 (978-0-394-96574-1). 144pp. Different words for snow in the Eskimo language are used to explore this phenomenon.

24704 Williams, Zella, ed. *Experiments on the Weather* (3–5). Series: Do-It-Yourself Science. 2007, Rosen LB $23.95 (978-1-4042-3663-9). 24pp. Young scientists will find these weather-related projects informative. Instructions are included for an anemometer, a barometer, and a thermometer, as well as other activities. (Rev: SLJ 5/07)

24705 Wills, Susan, and Steven Wills. *Meteorology: Predicting the Weather* (5–7). Series: Innovators. 2004, Oliver LB $21.95 (978-1-881508-61-8). 144pp. Introduces seven scientists who have made substantial contributions to the science of meteorology. (Rev: SLJ 7/04) [920]

24706 *Wind and Weather* (4–6). Illus. Series: Voyages of Discovery. 1995, Scholastic $19.95 (978-0-590-47646-1). 45pp. Using die-cut pages, transparencies, foldouts, and stickers, this attractively illustrated book explains the atmosphere, weather, storms, climates, and precipitation. (Rev: SLJ 5/96) [551.5]

24707 Wyatt, Valerie. *FAQ Weather* (4–6). Illus. by Brian Share. 2000, Kids Can $12.95 (978-1-55074-582-5); paper $6.95 (978-1-55074-815-4). 40pp. Using a question-and-answer format, this book covers many aspects of weather including winds, clouds, precipitation, and global warming. (Rev: SLJ 8/00) [551.6]

Physics

General

24708 Bonnet, Bob, and Dan Keen. *Science Fair Projects: Physics* (4–7). Illus. 2000, Sterling $17.95 (978-0-8069-0707-9). 96pp. This large-format book presents 47 projects demonstrating concepts in physics and using common materials as equipment. (Rev: BL 2/1/00; SLJ 4/00) [530]

24709 Boothroyd, Jennifer. *What Is a Liquid?* (K–2). Illus. Series: States of Matter. 2007, Lerner LB $17.27 (978-0-8225-6838-4). 24pp. A very basic introduction to the liquid state of matter, with brief text and large photographs. (Rev: SLJ 5/07)

24710 Boothroyd, Jennifer. *What Is a Solid?* (K–2). Illus. Series: States of Matter. 2007, Lerner LB $17.27 (978-0-8225-6836-0). 24pp. A very basic introduction to the solid state of matter, with brief text and large photographs. (Rev: SLJ 5/07)

24711 Challoner, Jack. *Big and Small* (K–4). Illus. Series: Start-Up Science. 1996, Raintree LB $24.26 (978-0-8172-4319-7). 32pp. Information and experiments are combined in this attractive beginner's science book about size. (Rev: SLJ 2/97) [153.7]

24712 Challoner, Jack. *Floating and Sinking* (K–4). Illus. Series: Start-Up Science. 1996, Raintree LB $16.98 (978-0-8172-4317-3). 32pp. The concepts of floating and sinking are explored in a simple, conversational text with many attractive pictures. (Rev: SLJ 2/97) [530]

24713 Claybourne, Anna. *The Nature of Matter* (4–6). Illus. Series: Gareth Stevens Vital Science: Physical Science. 2007, Gareth Stevens LB $26.60 (978-0-8368-8088-5); paper $11.95 (978-0-8368-8097-7). 48pp. A straightforward look at various forms of matter and their properties. (Rev: SLJ 1/08) [530]

24714 Cregan, Elizabeth R. *The Atom* (4–6). Illus. Series: Mission: Science. 2008, Compass Point LB $26.60 (978-0-7565-3953-5). 40pp. An appealing exploration of the structure of the atom, cathode rays and electrons, radioactivity, the future, and key scientists involved in research; also includes many photographs and illustrations plus an activity. (Rev: LMC 3/09; SLJ 6/09) [539.7]

24715 Durant, Penny R. *Bubblemania! Learn the Secrets to Creating Millions of Spectacular Bubbles!* (4–8). 1994, Avon paper $3.99 (978-0-380-77373-2). 86pp. Through a series of easy experiments, surface tension, bubble formation, and the uses of bubbles are explained. (Rev: SLJ 7/94) [530]

24716 Evans, Neville. *The Science of Gravity* (5–8). Illus. Series: Science World. 2000, Raintree LB $25.69 (978-0-7398-1323-2). 32pp. Explores the force of gravity and how it affects our lives, with additional material on air resistance, mass, and invisible forces. (Rev: BL 9/15/00; HBG 10/00) [531]

24717 Farndon, John. *Buoyancy* (3–6). Series: Science Experiments. 2002, Marshall Cavendish LB $25.64 (978-0-7614-1467-4). 32pp. The nature of buoyancy is explained through a simple text, color photographs, and an explanatory experiment in each chapter. (Rev: BL 12/15/02; HBG 3/03) [530]

24718 Gallant, Roy A. *The Ever-Changing Atom* (5–8). Series: The Story of Science. 1999, Benchmark LB $29.93 (978-0-7614-0961 8). 80pp. Using a chronological approach, this book traces how and what we have found out about the atom and its structure. (Rev: BL 2/15/00; HBG 3/00; SLJ 2/00) [539]

24719 Gardner, Robert. *Experiments with Bubbles* (4–7). Illus. Series: Getting Started in Science. 1995, Enslow LB $26.60 (978-0-89490-666-4). 104pp. The properties of bubbles are explored in a series of experiments, each a little more complex than the last. (Rev: BL 12/1/95; SLJ 3/96) [530.4]

24720 Gardner, Robert. *Melting, Freezing, and Boiling Science Projects with Matter* (3–5). Series: Fantastic Physical Science Experiments. 2006, Enslow LB $23.93 (978-0-7660-2589-9). 48pp. Nine science projects that explore the properties of matter are introduced in double-page spreads, with discussion of the principles demonstrated. Also use *Sizzling Science Projects with Heat and Energy* (2006). (Rev: BL 9/15/06) [507]

24721 Goodstein, Madeline. *Fish Tank Physics Projects* (5–8). Series: Science Fair Success. 2002, Enslow LB $26.60 (978-0-7660-1624-8). 112pp. Using a common fish tank and its contents, various aspects of laws of physics are presented in the form of science fair projects. (Rev: BL 5/15/02; HBG 10/02; SLJ 11/02) [621.9]

24722 Goodstein, Madeline. *Sports Science Projects: The Physics of Balls in Motion* (5–8). Illus. Series: Science Fair Success. 1999, Enslow LB $26.60 (978-0-7660-1174-8). 128pp. This book contains 40 projects that use the properties of different sports balls to demonstrate principles of physics. (Rev: BL 2/15/00; HBG 10/00; SLJ 3/00) [530]

24723 Hammond, Richard. *Can You Feel the Force?* (5–8). Illus. 2006, DK $15.99 (978-0-7566-2033-2). 96pp. Light, matter, friction, gravity, velocity — these and other basic physics principles are explained in a reader-friendly format that includes experiments, captions, sidebars, and other eye-catching elements. (Rev: SLJ 10/06) [530]

24724 Hodge, Deborah, and Adrienne Mason. *Solids, Liquids, and Gases* (K–4). Illus. Series: Starting with Science. 1998, Kids Can $14.95 (978-1-55074-195-7). 32pp. Uses simple science activities to demonstrate the three states of matter and such phenomena as air pressure and condensation. (Rev: BL 4/15/98; HBG 9/98; SLJ 6/98) [530.4]

24725 Hopwood, James. *Cool Gravity Activities: Fun Science Projects About Balance* (4–6). Series: Cool Science. 2008, ABDO LB $16.95 (978-1-59928-908-3). 32pp. Five high-interest experiments with detailed, illustrated instructions follow discussion about the scientific method, keeping a journal, and safety. Also use *Cool Dry Ice Devices: Fun Science Projects with Dry Ice* and *Cool Distance Assistants: Fun Science Projects to Propel Things* (both 2008). (Rev: LMC 5/08; SLJ 2/08) [531]

24726 Jerome, Kate Boehm. *Atomic Universe: The Quest to Discover Radioactivity* (5–8). Series: Science Quest. 2006, National Geographic $17.95 (978-0-7922-5543-7). 59pp. An attractive and informative history of radioactivity, profiling key figures and placing the discovery and subsequent developments in scientific and social context. (Rev: SLJ 4/07) [539.7]

24727 Juettner, Bonnie. *Molecules* (4–8). Illus. 2004, Gale LB $26.20 (978-0-7377-2076-1). 48pp. Clear, concise text, supported by full-color photographs and diagrams, describes the characteristics of atoms and molecules. (Rev: SLJ 6/05)

24728 McGrath, Susan. *Fun with Physics* (5–9). Illus. 1986, National Geographic LB $12.50 (978-0-87044-581-1). An introduction to physics that uses everyday situations as examples and supplies a smattering of experiments. (Rev: SLJ 6/87) [530]

24729 Mason, Adrienne. *Touch It! Materials, Matter and You* (K–2). Illus. by Claudia Dávila. Series: Primary Physical Science. 2005, Kids Can $12.95 (978-1-55337-760-3); paper $5.95 (978-1-55337-

761-0). 32pp. This easy-to-understand approach to science introduces the various properties of matter and suggests simple activities and projects. (Rev: BL 10/15/05) [530]

24730 Morgan, Sally, and Adrian Morgan. *Materials* (4–7). Illus. Series: Designs in Science. 1994, Facts on File $23.00 (978-0-8160-2985-3). 48pp. Basic properties of matter and materials are explored in a series of experiments using everyday materials. (Rev: BL 7/94) [620.1]

24731 Parker, Barry. *The Mystery of Gravity* (5–8). Illus. Series: The Story of Science. 2002, Benchmark $29.93 (978-0-7614-1428-5). 78pp. Parker traces our understanding of gravity from the early Greek philosophers through Einstein and Hubble, with discussion of the Big Bang theory and black holes. (Rev: HBG 3/03; SLJ 2/03) [531]

24732 Rosinsky, Natalie M. *Sinking and Floating* (3–5). Series: Simply Science. 2004, Compass Point LB $21.26 (978-0-7565-0598-1). 32pp. Rosinsky examines why some objects float while others sink, looking in detail at such scientific principles as water displacement and density. (Rev: SLJ 8/04) [532]

24733 Silverstein, Alvin, and Virginia Silverstein. *Forces and Motion* (4–8). Illus. Series: Science Concepts, Second Series. 2008, Twenty-First Century LB $31.93 (978-0-8225-7514-6). 112pp. With photographs, diagrams, and examples that attract young readers, this volume provides clear explanations of forces, motion, gravity, and simple machines. Also use *Matter* (2008). (Rev: SLJ 12/08) [531]

24734 Snedden, Robert. *Forces and Motion* (4–6). Illus. Series: Gareth Stevens Vital Science: Physical Science. 2007, Gareth Stevens LB $26.60 (978-0-8368-8087-8); paper $11.95 (978-0-8368-8096-0). 48pp. Speed, acceleration, gravity, and friction are among the topics covered in this straightforward overview that includes features on Galileo, Newton, and Pascal. (Rev: SLJ 1/08) [531]

24735 Spilsbury, Richard. *What Are Solids, Liquids, and Gases? Exploring Science with Hands-on Activities* (3–4). Illus. Series: In Touch with Basic Science. 2008, Enslow LB $22.60 (978-0-7660-3094-7). 32pp. Introduces solids, liquids, and gases, with activities that demonstrate scientific principles. (Rev: SLJ 3/09) [530.4078]

24736 Stille, Darlene R. *Physical Change: Reshaping Matter* (5–8). Illus. Series: Exploring Science. 2005, Compass Point LB $27.93 (978-0-7565-1257-6). 48pp. An attractive format with plenty of graphics adds to the appeal of this brief discussion of the states of matter. (Rev: SLJ 7/06) [530]

24737 Stille, Darlene R. *Solids, Liquids, and Gases* (2–4). Illus. Series: Science Around Us. 2004, Child's World LB $27.07 (978-1-59296-225-9). 32pp. In simple, easy-to-understand language supplemented by bright photographs, Stille introduces readers to the differences between the three basic states of matter. (Rev: BL 11/1/04) [530.4]

24738 Stringer, John. *The Science of a Spring* (5–8). Illus. Series: Science World. 2000, Raintree LB $25.69 (978-0-7398-1322-5). 32pp. Leaf and coil springs are introduced as well as the balance of forces in physics, the limits of springs, and their uses in such common objects as staplers. (Rev: BL 9/1/00; HBG 10/00; SLJ 8/00) [531]

24739 Tiner, John Hudson. *Gravity* (4–7). Series: Understanding Science. 2002, Smart Apple $24.25 (978-1-58340-157-6). 32pp. Through a number of simple projects, colorful illustrations, and a clear text, the fundamentals of gravity are explored. (Rev: BL 3/15/03; HBG 3/03) [531]

24740 Twist, Clint. *Light and Sound* (K–1). Illus. Series: Check It Out! 2005, Bearport LB $19.96 (978-1-59716-060-5). 24pp. Presents the basics of the science behind light and sound. (Rev: BL 10/15/05) [535]

24741 Williams, Zella, ed. *Experiments with Physical Science* (3–5). Series: Do-It-Yourself Science. 2007, Rosen LB $23.95 (978-1-4042-3659-2). 24pp. Young scientists will find these physics-related projects informative. Instructions are included to investigate sound waves, vibrations, friction, and gravity, as well as other phenomena. (Rev: SLJ 5/07)

Energy and Motion

General

24742 Asimov, Isaac. *How Did We Find Out About Solar Power?* (5–8). Illus. by David Wool. 1981, Walker LB $12.85 (978-0-8027-6423-2). 64pp. An explanation of how man has benefited from solar power from the earliest time until today. [621.47]

24743 Bonnet, Bob, and Dan Keen. *Science Fair Projects: Energy* (4–6). Illus. 1998, Sterling $16.95 (978-0-8069-9793-3). 96pp. Such sources of energy as sunlight, batteries, microwave ovens, and light-bulbs are used in this collection of 55 simple activities about energy and the various forms it takes. (Rev: BL 3/1/98; SLJ 6/98) [531]

24744 Bradley, Kimberly Brubaker. *Energy Makes Things Happen* (1–3). Illus. by Paul Meisel. Series: Let's-Read-and-Find-Out Science. 2003, Harper-Collins LB $16.89 (978-0-06-028909-6); paper $5.99 (978-0-06-445213-7). 40pp. An entertaining introduction to energy and its sources and uses, for young readers. (Rev: BL 2/1/03; HBG 10/03; SLJ 1/03) [531]

24745 Bradley, Kimberly Brubaker. *Forces Make Things Move* (1–3). Illus. by Paul Meisel. Series: Let's-Read-and-Find-Out Science. 2005, Harper-Collins $15.99 (978-0-06-028906-5); paper $5.99 (978-0-06-445214-4). 40pp. Using a toy car as an example, this is a basic exploration of the physics of motion and such related concepts as inertia, friction, and gravity. (Rev: BL 9/15/05) [531]

24746 Cobb, Vicki. *I Fall Down* (PS–1). Illus. by Julia Gorton. Series: Science Play. 2004, Harper-Collins LB $17.89 (978-0-688-17843-7). 40pp. Exercises introduce the concept of gravity. (Rev: BL 2/1/05) [531]

24747 Cobb, Vicki. *Whirlers and Twirlers: Science Fun with Spinning* (3–5). Illus. by Steve Haefele. 2001, Millbrook LB $24.90 (978-0-7613-1573-5). 64pp. A lighthearted introduction to the physics involved in the motion of spinning, with experiments with tops, pinwheels, and other objects. (Rev: BL 10/15/01; HBG 3/02; SLJ 1/02) [531]

24748 Cruden, Gabriel. *Energy Alternatives* (5–8). Illus. Series: Lucent Library of Science and Technology. 2005, Gale LB $29.95 (978-1-59018-530-8). 112pp. A look at the importance of finding alternatives to existing energy sources, covering such technologies as solar, wind, and geothermal power. (Rev: BL 1/05)

24749 de Pinna, Simon. *Forces and Motion* (3–5). Series: Science Projects. 1998, Raintree $25.69 (978-0-8172-4962-5). 48pp. A brief explanation of force and motion is followed by a series of activities, with each double-page spread dealing with a different aspect of the subject. (Rev: BL 3/15/98; HBG 9/98) [531.6]

24750 de Pinna, Simon. *Transfer of Energy* (4–6). Illus. Series: Gareth Stevens Vital Science: Physical Science. 2007, Gareth Stevens LB $26.60 (978-0-8368-8091-5); paper $11.95 (978-0-8368-8100-4). 48pp. A straightforward overview of the nature of energy, its forms, and its sources. (Rev: SLJ 1/08) [531]

24751 Doherty, Paul, and Don Rathjen. *The Spinning Blackboard and Other Dynamic Experiments on Force and Motion* (4–8). Illus. Series: Exploratorium Science Snackbook. 1996, Wiley paper $13.95 (978-0-471-11514-4). The many activities in this well-organized, attractive book reveal important characteristics of force and motion. (Rev: BL 4/15/96; SLJ 6/96) [531]

24752 Driscoll, Laura. *Slow Down, Sara!* (1–3). Illus. by Page Eastburn O'Rourke. Series: Science Solves It! 2003, Kane paper $4.99 (978-1-57565-125-5). 32pp. This appealing title from the Science Solves It! series focuses on the principle of friction and its impact on speed; young Sara has a need for speed, but she discovers that sometimes it makes sense to slow down. (Rev: SLJ 10/03)

24753 Egendorf, Laura K., ed. *Energy Alternatives* (5–9). Series: Introducing Issues with Opposing Viewpoints. 2006, Gale LB $33.70 (978-0-7377-3458-4). 120pp. Presents basic information about alternatives to fossil fuel-driven energy, along with diverse views on the feasibility and practicality of these alternative energy sources. (Rev: SLJ 8/06) [333.79]

24754 Farndon, John. *Energy* (3–6). Series: Science Experiments. 2002, Marshall Cavendish LB $25.64 (978-0-7614-1469-8). 32pp. The nature and forms of energy are introduced through a series of easy-to-follow experiments and a simple explanatory text with many color photographs and diagrams. (Rev: BL 12/15/02; HBG 3/03) [531.6]

24755 Farndon, John. *Motion* (3–6). Series: Science Experiments. 2002, Marshall Cavendish LB $25.64 (978-0-7614-1471-1). 32pp. The properties of motion are revealed to the young scientist through several easy-to-follow activities using common household materials. (Rev: BL 12/15/02; HBG 3/03) [531]

24756 Gardner, Robert. *Experiments with Motion* (5–8). Series: Getting Started in Science. 1995, Enslow LB $20.95 (978-0-89490-667-1). Projects using simple equipment illustrate the laws of motion and the ways in which motion differs in various situations. (Rev: BL 2/1/96; SLJ 2/96; VOYA 6/96) [531]

24757 Gardner, Robert. *Science Project Ideas About the Sun* (4–7). Series: Science Project Ideas. 1997, Enslow LB $25.26 (978-0-89490-845-3). 96pp. The sun and solar energy are the subjects of this book that illustrates important concepts through a number of interesting projects and experiments. (Rev: BL 12/15/97; HBG 3/98; SLJ 1/98) [697.78]

24758 Gutnik, Martin J., and Natalie B. Gutnik. *Projects That Explore Energy* (5–8). Illus. Series: Investigate! 1994, Millbrook LB $21.40 (978-1-56294-334-9). 72pp. A lucid, well-organized series of projects and experiments that explore power, force, and energy sources and resources. (Rev: BL 8/94; SLJ 6/94) [333.79]

24759 Landau, Elaine. *The History of Energy* (5–8). Series: Major Inventions Through History. 2005, Twenty-First Century LB $26.60 (978-0-8225-3806-6). 56pp. An attractive look at developments through time in the use of various forms of energy (fire, wind, water, coal, steam, oil and gasoline, electricity, and so forth) and their application in transportation and other sectors. (Rev: SLJ 1/06)

24760 Lew, Kristi. *Goodbye, Gasoline: The Science of Fuel Cells* (5–7). Series: Headline Science. 2008, Compass Point LB $27.93 (978-0-7565-3521-6). 48pp. Understandable text and helpful charts educate readers as they delve into the science of fuel cells as alternative, clean energy and learn about the negative impact that gasoline has on our environment. (Rev: LMC 5/09*; SLJ 2/09) [621.31]

24761 Madgwick, Wendy. *On the Move* (K–3). Series: Science Starters. 1999, Raintree LB $25.70 (978-0-8172-5333-2). 32pp. Energy and motion are explored in this book through a dozen simple activities that use items found in the home to answer questions like why running shoes increase speed, how you keep your balance, and why ice is slippery. (Rev: BL 6/1–15/99; HBG 9/99) [531]

24762 Petersen, Christine. *Wind Power* (3–5). Illus. Series: True Book (Environment and Conservation). 2004, Children's Pr. LB $25.00 (978-0-516-22809-9). 48pp. This thought-provoking look at at the potential of wind power discusses current and future uses of the technology. (Rev: BL 6/1–15/04) [621.31]

24763 Riley, Peter D. *Energy* (4–5). Series: Cycles in Science. 1998, Heinemann LB $21.36 (978-1-57572-617-5). 32pp. An overview of the world of energy that touches on topics such as kinds of energy, how potential energy becomes kinetic, nuclear energy, electricity, magnetism, and ecological issues. (Rev: SLJ 7/98) [531.6]

24764 Silverstein, Alvin, et al. *Energy* (4–7). Illus. Series: Science Concepts. 1998, Twenty-First Century LB $26.90 (978-0-7613-3222-0). 64pp. Photographs, diagrams, and illustrations help to introduce six types of energy: electrical, magnetic, light, heat, sound, and nuclear. (Rev: BL 5/1/99; HBG 10/99) [621.042]

24765 Spilsbury, Richard, and Louise Spilsbury. *What Are Forces and Motion? Exploring Science with Hands-on Activities* (3–4). Illus. Series: In Touch with Basic Science. 2008, Enslow LB $22.60 (978-0-7660-3095-4). 32pp. Introduces Newton's laws of motion and some simple machines, with activities that demonstrate scientific principles. (Rev: LMC 1/09; SLJ 3/09)

24766 Stille, Darlene R. *Waves: Energy on the Move* (5–8). Illus. Series: Exploring Science. 2005, Compass Point LB $27.93 (978-0-7565-1259-0). 48pp. An attractive format with plenty of graphics adds to the appeal of this brief discussion of waves in water, light, air, and other media. (Rev: SLJ 7/06) [531]

24767 Sullivan, Navin. *Speed* (4–7). Illus. Series: Measure Up! 2006, Marshall Cavendish LB $20.95 (978-0-7614-2325-6). 48pp. In addition to providing an overview of the science of speed, this volume includes high-quality graphics, information about historical versus modern methods, and at-home experiments. (Rev: LMC 8/07; SLJ 6/07)

24768 Walker, Niki. *Generating Wind Power* (5–8). Illus. Series: Energy Revolution. 2007, Crabtree LB $25.20 (978-0-7787-2913-6); paper $8.95 (978-0-7787-2927-3). 32pp. Wind is explored as an alternative energy source in this well-designed volume. Also use *Harnessing Power from the Sun* and *Biomass: Fueling Change* (both 2007). (Rev: SLJ 7/07)

24769 Woelfle, Gretchen. *The Wind at Work: An Activity Guide to Windmills* (4–8). 1997, Chicago Review paper $14.95 (978-1-55652-308-3). The history, types, and uses of windmills are covered, with many activities and a discussion of the future of wind power. (Rev: BL 9/1/97; SLJ 10/97*) [621.4]

24770 Woodford, Chris. *Energy* (4–7). Illus. Series: See for Yourself. 2007, DK $14.99 (978-0-7566-2561-0). 64pp. This introductory guide to energy provides an easy-to-understand definition, offers examples of both kinetic and potential energy, identifies major energy sources, explains the processes through which energy is released, and discusses the problems inherent in energy usage. (Rev: BL 4/1/07) [333.79]

24771 Woodruff, John. *Energy* (3–5). Series: Science Projects. 1998, Raintree $25.69 (978-0-8172-4961-8). 48pp. The properties, uses, and kinds of energy are covered in a series of double-page spreads that give brief explanations followed by simple activities. (Rev: BL 3/15/98; HBG 9/98) [333]

Coal, Gas, and Oil

24772 Ditchfield, Christin. *Coal* (2–5). Series: True Books — Natural Resources. 2002, Children's Book Pr. LB $25.00 (978-0-516-22342-1). 48pp. This simple introduction to coal explains how it is formed, where it is found, how it is used, and how it affects our environment. (Rev: BL 10/15/02) [622]

Nuclear Energy

24773 Cole, Michael D. *Three Mile Island: Nuclear Disaster* (4–8). Series: American Disasters. 2002, Enslow LB $23.93 (978-0-7660-1556-2). 48pp. An informative, well-researched account of the disaster that affected the development of nuclear power plants in this country. (Rev: BL 6/1–15/02; HBG 10/02; SLJ 6/02) [621.48]

24774 Holland, Gini. *Nuclear Energy* (3–6). Illus. Series: Inventors and Inventions. 1996, Marshall Cavendish LB $25.64 (978-0-7614-0047-9). 63pp. The story of the discoverers of nuclear energy, its uses, and current problems and possibilities are covered, with many color photos. (Rev: BL 7/96; SLJ 9/96) [333.692]

24775 Wilcox, Charlotte. *Powerhouse: Inside a Nuclear Power Plant* (4–8). Illus. 1996, Carolrhoda LB $27.15 (978-0-87614-945-4); paper $7.95 (978-0-87614-979-9). 48pp. A history of nuclear energy is followed by a description of how a power plant operates and the dangers that are present. (Rev: BL 10/1/96; SLJ 9/96) [621.48]

Solar Energy

24776 Petersen, Christine. *Solar Power* (3–5). Illus. Series: True Book (Environment and Conservation). 2004, Children's Pr. LB $25.00 (978-0-516-22807-5). 48pp. The energy of the sun and its potential as a source of power are explored in this photo-filled, small-format book. (Rev: BL 6/1–15/04) [612.47]

Light and Color

24777 Asimov, Isaac. *How Did We Find Out About Lasers?* (5–7). Illus. by Erika Kors. 1990, Walker LB $13.85 (978-0-8027-6936-7). 64pp. A readable introduction to laser science by the veteran writer. (Rev: BL 8/90; SLJ 11/90) [621.36]

24778 Bang, Molly. *My Light* (1–3). Illus. 2004, Scholastic $16.95 (978-0-439-48961-4). 48pp. Highly visual and accessible, this picture book introduces four ways of making electricity and explores the energy provided by the sun. (Rev: BL 2/1/04*; HB 5/04; SLJ 4/04) [621]

24779 Boekhoff, P. M., and Stuart A. Kallen. *Lasers* (4–5). Illus. Series: Kidhaven Science Library. 2002, Gale LB $23.70 (978-0-7377-0944-5). 48pp. A discussion of the discovery of lasers and of their uses today in such fields as industry, medicine, recreation, and the armed forces. (Rev: BL 5/1/02; SLJ 9/02) [621.36]

24780 Branley, Franklyn M. *Day Light, Night Light: Where Light Comes From* (K–3). Illus. by Stacey Schuett. Series: Let's-Read-and-Find-Out. 1998,

HarperCollins LB $16.89 (978-0-06-027295-1). 32pp. In this book about light, topics like darkness, heat, light sources, reflection, vision, and the speed of light are discussed. (Rev: BL 12/1/97; HBG 9/98; SLJ 2/98) [535]

24781 Day, Trevor. *Light* (3–5). Illus. Series: Science Projects. 1998, Raintree $25.69 (978-0-8172-4943-4). 48pp. With explanatory text and simple activities, this account covers such topics as the nature of light, vision, shadows, photography, reflections, refraction, and color. (Rev: BL 3/15/98; HBG 9/98) [538]

24782 Farndon, John. *Color* (3–6). Illus. Series: Science Experiments. 2000, Marshall Cavendish LB $25.64 (978-0-7614-1092-8). 32pp. Topics covered include the spectrum, primary colors, pigment, mixing colors, and color blindness, with many interesting activities such as making a color wheel and creating a spectrum. (Rev: BL 3/15/01; HBG 3/01) [535.6]

24783 Farndon, John. *Lights and Optics* (3–6). Series: Science Experiments. 2000, Marshall Cavendish LB $25.64 (978-0-7614-1090-4). 32pp. Explores properties of light and optics and outlines projects that apply the principles established. (Rev: BL 3/15/01; HBG 3/01) [535]

24784 Fox, Mary V. *Lasers* (3–6). Illus. Series: Inventors and Inventions. 1996, Benchmark LB $25.64 (978-0-7614-0067-7). 63pp. The history of laser technology, with profiles of several scientists involved in this branch of science and its effects in such areas as medicine. (Rev: BL 3/15/96; SLJ 6/96) [621.36]

24785 Gardner, Robert. *Dazzling Science Projects with Light and Color* (4–6). Illus. by Tom LaBaff. Series: Fantastic Physical Science Experiments. 2006, Enslow LB $23.93 (978-0-7660-2587-5). 48pp. Experiments involving readily available materials demonstrate the properties of light and color and how the two interact; advice on developing these into science fair projects follows. (Rev: SLJ 8/06) [535]

24786 Gardner, Robert. *Experiments with Light and Mirrors* (4–7). Illus. 1995, Enslow LB $20.95 (978-0-89490-668-8). 112pp. Properties of light are explained and demonstrated using equipment such as mirrors and cardboard. (Rev: BL 2/1/96; SLJ 3/96) [535.2]

24787 Madgwick, Wendy. *Light and Dark* (K–3). Series: Science Starters. 1999, Raintree LB $22.83 (978-0-8172-5556-5). 32pp. Double-page spreads introduce about a dozen projects that explore the topic of light including demonstrations on how rainbows are formed, why shadows change, and how lenses work. (Rev: BL 6/1–15/99; HBG 9/99) [535.2]

24788 Sitarski, Anita. *Cold Light: Creatures, Discoveries, and Inventions that Glow* (4–7). Illus. 2007, Boyds Mills $16.95 (978-1-59078-468-6). 48pp. An interesting introduction to the phenomenon of luminescence — found in animals that glow but also in light-emitting diodes — this will appeal to report writers and browsers. (Rev: BL 12/1/07; LMC 1/08; SLJ 10/07) [535.35]

24789 Stille, Darlene R. *Manipulating Light: Reflection, Refraction, and Absorption* (5–8). Illus. Series: Exploring Science. 2005, Compass Point LB $27.93 (978-0-7565-1258-3). 48pp. An attractive format with plenty of graphics adds to the appeal of this brief discussion of the nature of light. (Rev: SLJ 7/06) [535]

24790 Tocci, Salvatore. *Experiments with Colors* (2–4). Illus. Series: A True Book. 2003, Children's Pr. LB $25.00 (978-0-516-22785-6). 48pp. A simple and attractive explanation of what creates color, how we perceive it, and how optical illusions work. (Rev: SLJ 4/04) [535.6]

24791 Trumbauer, Lisa. *All About Light* (PS–1). Series: Rookie Read-About Science. 2004, Scholastic LB $4.95 (978-0-516-25842-3). 31pp. Simple text and color photographs introduce beginning readers to the concept of light, including its sources and basic characteristics. (Rev: BL 9/1/04) [535]

24792 Whitfield, David. *Rainbows* (2–4). Illus. Series: Science Matters. 2006, Weigl $24.45 (978-1-59036-414-7). 24pp. Readers will be fascinated to learn about the science behind rainbows. Photographs and other graphics, as well as related information and activities, add to this book's appeal. (Rev: SLJ 5/07)

Magnetism and Electricity

24793 Bartholomew, Alan. *Electric Mischief* (4–7). Series: Kids Can Do It. 2002, Kids Can $12.95 (978-1-55074-923-6); paper $5.95 (978-1-55074-925-0). 48pp. An activity book that outlines simple, safe experiments with electricity. (Rev: BL 3/15/03; HBG 3/03; SLJ 12/02) [537]

24794 Berger, Melvin. *Switch On, Switch Off* (K–3). Illus. by Carolyn Croll. 1989, HarperCollins LB $15.89 (978-0-690-04786-8); paper $5.99 (978-0-06-445097-3). 32pp. Explaining the mysteries of electricity. (Rev: BL 4/15/89; HB 5/89)

24795 Cole, Joanna. *The Magic School Bus and the Electric Field Trip* (2–4). Illus. by Bruce Degen. Series: Magic School Bus. 1997, Scholastic $15.95 (978-0-590-44682-2). 56pp. Mrs. Frizzle's class visits a power plant to find out how electricity is made in this entertaining science book filled with facts, jokes, and puns. (Rev: BL 10/15/97; HBG 3/98; SLJ 11/97) [621.3]

24796 Cosner, Sharon. *The Light Bulb* (4–6). Illus. 1984, Walker LB $10.85 (978-0-8027-6527-7). 64pp. A history of various forms of lighting, the light bulb, and the electrical industry.

24797 de Pinna, Simon. *Electricity* (3–5). Series: Science Projects. 1998, Raintree $25.70 (978-0-8172-4945-8). 48pp. The properties of electricity are covered in a series of double-page spreads, each of which covers a different aspect of the subject and outlines three or four simple acitivities. (Rev: BL 3/15/98; HBG 9/98) [621.3]

24798 Dreier, David. *Electrical Circuits: Harnessing Electricity* (5–7). Illus. Series: Exploring Science: Physical Science. 2007, Compass Point LB $19.95 (978-0-7565-3267-3). 48pp. A user-friendly introduction to electricity and how we use it, with good graphics and interesting sidebar features. (Rev: BL 12/1/07; LMC 1/08) [537]

24799 Evans, Neville. *The Science of a Light Bulb* (5–8). Illus. Series: Science World. 2000, Raintree LB $25.69 (978-0-7398-1325-6). 32pp. This work explains how Edison invented the light bulb, describes its parts, and tells how light is produced and how we see it. (Rev: BL 9/15/00; HBG 10/00) [535]

24800 Farndon, John. *Electricity* (3–6). Series: Science Experiments. 2000, Marshall Cavendish LB $25.64 (978-0-7614-1086-7). 32pp. Each chapter contains information on different aspects and applications of electricity plus experiments that illustrate key principles. (Rev: BL 3/15/01; HBG 3/01) [537]

24801 Good, Keith. *Zap It! Exciting Electricity Activities* (3–7). Series: Design It! 2000, Lerner LB $21.27 (978-0-8225-3565-2). 30pp. An activity book that explores concepts in electricity and contains projects involving electric circuits, pressure pads, and different kinds of switches. (Rev: HBG 9/00; SLJ 6/00) [537]

24802 Levine, Shar, and Leslie Johnstone. *Magnet Power!* (2–4). Illus. by Steve Harpster. Series: First Science Experiments. 2006, Sterling $14.95 (978-1-4027-2438-1). 48pp. Clearly explained experiments and activities demonstrate the properties of magnets. (Rev: BL 11/1/06) [538]

24803 Madgwick, Wendy. *Magnets and Sparks* (K–3). Series: Science Starters. 1999, Raintree LB $25.70 (978-0-8172-5328-8). 32pp. A basic introduction to electricity and magnetism that includes more than a dozen activities using items found in the home to explore topics such as how electricity travels, what magnets attract, and how flashlights work. (Rev: BL 6/1–15/99; HBG 9/99) [537]

24804 Nankivell-Aston, Sally, and Dorothy Jackson. *Science Experiments with Electricity* (3–6). Series: Science Experiments. 2000, Watts paper $6.95 (978-0-531-15443-4). 32pp. This book of simple electricity projects includes building simple switches and circuits with additional material on scientific method and safety. (Rev: SLJ 3/01) [537]

24805 Parker, Steve. *Electricity and Magnetism* (4–6). Illus. Series: Gareth Stevens Vital Science: Physical Science. 2007, Gareth Stevens LB $26.60 (978-0-8368-8085-4); paper $11.95 (978-0-8368-8094-6). 48pp. A straightforward introduction to electricity and magnetism and their importance in our lives. (Rev: SLJ 1/08) [537]

24806 Rau, Dana Meachen. *Electricity and Magnetism* (2–4). Illus. Series: Real World Science. 2009, Cherry Lake LB $27.07 (978-1-60279-459-7). 32pp. With bright illustrations and clear text, this title looks at static and current electricity and the relationship between electricity and magnets. (Rev: BL 4/1/09) [537]

24807 Seuling, Barbara. *Flick a Switch: How Electricity Gets to Your Home* (1–3). Illus. by Nancy Tobin. 2003, Holiday House $16.95 (978-0-8234-1729-2). 32pp. An easy-to-understand narrative is combined with bright cartoon illustrations to help young readers learn some basics about electricity — where it comes from and how it gets to where it's needed. (Rev: BL 9/1/03; HBG 4/04; SLJ 11/03)

24808 Spilsbury, Richard. *What Is Electricity and Magnetism? Exploring Science with Hands-on Activities* (3–4). Illus. Series: In Touch with Basic Science. 2008, Enslow LB $22.60 (978-0-7660-3096-1). 32pp. Motors, generators, and electromagnetism are among the topics discussed, with activities that demonstrate scientific principles. (Rev: SLJ 3/09) [537]

24809 Tiner, John Hudson. *Magnetism* (4–7). Series: Understanding Science. 2002, Smart Apple LB $24.25 (978-1-58340-158-3). 32pp. Using clear explanations, simple projects, and good illustrations, the concept of magnetism is introduced. (Rev: BL 3/15/03; HBG 3/03) [538.4]

24810 VanCleave, Janice. *Janice VanCleave's Electricity: Mind-Boggling Experiments You Can Turn into Science Fair Projects* (5–7). Illus. 1994, Wiley paper $10.95 (978-0-471-31010-5). 96pp. As well as providing a discussion on the nature of electricity, this book offers 20 informative experiments that move from the very simple to the more complex. (Rev: BL 12/1/94; SLJ 11/94) [537]

24811 VanCleave, Janice. *Magnets: Mind-Boggling Experiments You Can Turn into Science Fair Projects* (4–6). Illus. Series: Spectacular Science Projects. 1993, Wiley paper $10.95 (978-0-471-57106-3). 88pp. Using magnets and the principles of magnetism, this book offers clear directions in developing many interesting science projects. Also use: *Animals; Gravity;* and *Molecules* (all 1993). (Rev: BL 5/1/93; SLJ 7/93) [538]

24812 Walker, Sally M. *Electricity* (3–5). Photos by Andy King. Illus. Series: Early Bird Energy. 2005, Lerner LB $25.26 (978-0-8225-2919-4). 48pp. After a basic explanation of how electricity works, this volume looks at static electricity, currents, circuits, and so forth and suggests a number of activities that use materials including batteries, light bulbs, and aluminum foil. (Rev: BL 12/1/05) [537]

24813 Woodford, Chris, and Martin Clowes. *Electricity* (4–7). Illus. 2004, Gale LB $23.70 (978-1-4103-0165-9). 40pp. A detailed examination of the development of electricity, with profiles of key individuals and their discoveries, a chronology, and discussion of future advances. (Rev: SLJ 5/05)

Optical Illusions

24814 Illusionworks. *Amazing Optical Illusions* (3–5). Illus. 2005, Firefly LB $16.95 (978-1-55297-961-7); paper $5.95 (978-1-55237-962-2). 32pp. Twenty-nine optical illusions challenge readers. (Rev: SLJ 8/05) [152]

24815 Simon, Seymour. *Now You See It, Now You Don't: The Amazing World of Optical Illusions.* Rev. ed. (3–6). Illus. 1998, Morrow $17.99 (978-0-688-16152-1). 96pp. This interesting discussion of optical illusions uses good illustrations and clear explanations. (Rev: BL 10/15/98; HBG 3/99) [152.14]

Simple Machines

24816 Armentrout, David, and Patricia Armentrout. *An Inclined Plane* (1–3). Illus. Series: How Can I Experiment With . . . ? 2002, Rourke LB $19.95 (978-1-58952-333-3). 32pp. This volume teaches younger readers, through illustration, narrative, and experimentation, about inclined planes. Other titles in this series include *A Lever, A Screw, A Wedge,* and *A Wheel* (all 2002). (Rev: BL 10/15/02; SLJ 3/03) [621.8]

24817 Gardner, Robert. *Sensational Science Projects with Simple Machines* (4–6). Illus. by Tom LaBaff. Series: Fantastic Physical Science Experiments. 2006, Enslow LB $23.93 (978-0-7660-2585-1). 48pp. The experiments and projects in this volume are designed to help readers understand the workings of simple machines — such as inclined planes, levers, and pulleys — and to incorporate them in exciting science fair projects. (Rev: SLJ 8/06) [621.8]

24818 Good, Keith. *Gear Up! Marvelous Machine Projects* (3–7). Series: Design It! 2000, Lerner LB $21.27 (978-0-8225-3566-9). 30pp. Simple machines like pulleys, levers, crankshafts, gear wheels, and conveyor belts are explored in this book of projects that apply the principles behind these machines. (Rev: HBG 9/00; SLJ 6/00) [621.8]

24819 Hodge, Deborah, and Adrienne Mason. *Simple Machines* (K–4). Illus. Series: Starting with Science. 1998, Kids Can $14.59 (978-1-55074-311-1). 32pp. This activity book uses double-page spreads to present science activities involving pulleys, levers, and other simple machines. (Rev: BL 4/15/98; HBG 9/98; SLJ 6/98) [621.8]

24820 Oxlade, Chris. *Levers* (K–2). Illus. Series: Useful Machines. 2003, Heinemann LB $22.79 (978-1-4034-3662-7). 32pp. Information on how these simple machines work are followed by illustrations of levers in action in everyday situations. Also use *Pulleys* (2003). (Rev: BL 2/15/04) [021.8]

24821 Royston, Angela. *Screws* (2–4). Illus. Series: Machines in Action. 2000, Heinemann LB $22.79 (978-1-57572-322-8). 32pp. An easy-to-read introduction to how screws work and the different kinds of screws we find in objects all around us. Also use *Springs* (2000). (Rev: HBG 3/01; SLJ 4/01) [621.8]

24822 Solway, Andrew. *Castle Under Siege! Simple Machines* (3–5). Illus. 2005, Raintree LB $28.21 (978-1-4109-1918-2). 32pp. Covering the construction of a medieval castle and its forms of defense, this book also introduces simple machines —

wedges, inclined planes, levers, and so forth. (Rev: SLJ 4/06) [621.8]

24823 Sugiura, Kuniko. *Pulleys to the Rescue* (2–3). Illus. Series: First Facts: Simple Machines to the Rescue. 2006, Capstone LB $21.26 (978-0-7368-6748-1). 24pp. Readers will learn that pulleys are simple machines that make simple tasks easier in this introduction that includes photographs, fast facts, and an easy experiment. Also use *Screws to the Rescue* and *Wedges to the Rescue* (both 2006). (Rev: SLJ 8/07)

24824 Thales, Sharon. *Inclined Planes to the Rescue* (2–3). Series: Simple Machines to the Rescue. 2006, Capstone LB $21.26 (978-0-7368-6752-8). 24pp. A simple introduction to a simple machine using real-world examples is accompanied by an easy-to-perform experiment. Also use *Levers to the Rescue and Wheels* and *Axles to the Rescue* (both 2006). (Rev: SLJ 5/07)

24825 Tieck, Sarah. *Inclined Planes* (2–4). Series: Buddy Books: Simple Machines. 2006, ABDO $21.35 (978-1-59679-818-2). 32pp. A concise explanation of inclined planes and their importance, with illustrations that aid comprehension. (Rev: BL 10/15/06) [621.8]

24826 Walker, Sally M., and Roseann Feldmann. *Inclined Planes and Wedges* (2–4). Photos by Andy King. 2001, Lerner LB $25.26 (978-0-8225-2221-8). 47pp. A concise explanation of these simple machines, that increases in complexity as the reader progresses through the book, with simple experiments and clear illustrations. Also use *Pulleys* and *Wheels and Axles* (both 2001). (Rev: HBG 3/02; SLJ 2/02) [621.8]

24827 Welsbacher, Anne. *Wedges* (2–3). Illus. Series: Understanding Simple Machines. 2000, Capstone $22.60 (978-0-7368-0614-5). 24pp. This book introduces wedges, their parts, and how they are used in axes, knives, scissors, doorstops, and zippers. (Rev: BL 12/1/00; HBG 3/01; SLJ 12/00) [621.8]

24828 Whittle, Fran, and Sarah Lawrence. *Simple Machines* (3–5). Illus. Series: Design and Create. 1997, Raintree $17.98 (978-0-8172-4889-5). 32pp. How to make a cookie crusher and a bubble machine are among the 12 projects nicely presented in double-page spreads to outline each activity and give background information. (Rev: BL 2/1/98; HBG 3/98) [621.8]

Sound

24829 Cobb, Vicki. *Bangs and Twangs: Science Fun with Sound* (3–6). Illus. 2000, Millbrook LB $24.90 (978-0-7613-1571-1). 48pp. Using a cartoon format, this lively activity book explores different aspects of sound including pitch and the physiology of hearing. (Rev: BCCB 11/00; BL 10/15/00; HBG 3/01; SLJ 3/01) [534.078]

24830 de Pinna, Simon. *Sound* (3–5). Series: Science Projects. 1998, Raintree $25.69 (978-0-8172-4944-1). 48pp. The properties of sound are explored in a

series of double-page spreads that give simple explanations followed by three or four simple activities. (Rev: BL 3/15/98; HBG 9/98) [534]

24831 Farndon, John. *Sound and Hearing* (3–6). Series: Science Experiments. 2000, Marshall Cavendish LB $25.64 (978-0-7614-1091-1). 32pp. The properties of sound and the process of hearing are explored with a series of experiments to illustrate different concepts and applications. (Rev: BL 3/15/01; HBG 3/01) [534]

24832 Gibson, Gary. *Hearing Sounds* (3–5). Illus. Series: Science for Fun. 1995, Millbrook LB $20.90 (978-1-56294-614-2). 32pp. Basic concepts involving sound are introduced through a series of simple activities and projects, with simple instructions and clear, often amusing illustrations. (Rev: BL 7/95) [534]

24833 Kaner, Etta. *Sound Science* (3–5). Illus. by Louise Phillips. 1992, Addison-Wesley paper $11.00 (978-0-201-56758-8). 96pp. The 40-plus experiments and projects in this book, which can be done with easily obtained materials, explore various aspects of sound. (Rev: SLJ 6/92) [530]

24834 Madgwick, Wendy. *Super Sound* (K–3). Series: Science Starters. 1999, Raintree LB $25.70 (978-0-8172-5327-1). 32pp. The properties of sound are explored in this book of simple projects that include topics such as how sound travels, whether two ears are better than one, and the possibility of trapping sound. (Rev: BL 6/1–15/99; HBG 9/99) [534]

24835 Morgan, Sally, and Adrian Morgan. *Using Sound* (4–7). Illus. Series: Designs in Science. 1994, Facts on File $23.00 (978-0-8160-2981-5). 48pp. The properties of sound and their relation to everyday life are covered in the text and a number of experiments using readily available materials. (Rev: BL 7/94) [534]

24836 Parker, Steve. *The Science of Sound: Projects and Experiments with Music and Sound Waves* (4–7). Illus. Series: Tabletop Scientist. 2005, Heinemann LB $29.29 (978-1-4034-7281-6). 32pp. The 12 experiments and projects in this collection demonstrate the basic scientific principles of sound waves. (Rev: SLJ 12/05)

24837 Pfeffer, Wendy. *Sounds All Around* (PS–2). Illus. by Holly Keller. Series: Let's-Read-and-Find-Out. 1999, HarperCollins LB $15.89 (978-0-06-027712-3). 32pp. This book about sound covers such topics as decibels, vibration, communication, and radar with examples for the animal kingdom and suggested activities. (Rev: BL 3/1/99; HBG 9/99; SLJ 1/99) [534]

24838 Trumbauer, Lisa. *All About Sound* (PS–1). Series: Rookie Read-About Science. 2004, Scholastic LB $4.95 (978-0-516-25847-8). 31pp. Simple text and color photographs introduce beginning readers to the basic characteristics of sound. (Rev: BL 9/1/04) [534]

24839 Wright, Lynne. *The Science of Noise* (5–8). Illus. Series: Science World. 2000, Raintree LB $25.69 (978-0-7398-1324-9). 32pp. This account describes how sound is produced, how it travels, how we hear it, and how it can be changed. (Rev: BL 9/1/00; HBG 10/00; SLJ 8/00) [534]

Space Exploration

24840 Aldrin, Buzz. *Look to the Stars* (1–3). Illus. by Wendell Minor. 2009, Putnam $17.99 (978-0-399-24721-7). 40pp. The *Apollo 11* astronaut presents an interesting overview of aviation and space flight from early theories of Newton and Galileo through the developments by such figures as the Wright brothers and Robert Goddard to concepts for colonies on Mars. (Rev: BL 12/1/08; HB 5/09; SLJ 4/09) [629.409]

24841 *The Amazing International Space Station* (4–6). Illus. by Rose Cowles. 2003, Kids Can $15.95 (978-1-55337-380-3); paper $8.95 (978-1-55337-523-4). 48pp. An appealing, highly visual and information-packed look at life aboard the International Space Station. (Rev: HBG 4/04; SLJ 4/04) [629.44]

24842 Angliss, Sarah. *Cosmic Journeys: A Beginner's Guide to Space and Time Travel* (5–7). Illus. by Alex Pang, et al. Series: Future Files. 1998, Millbrook LB $23.90 (978-0-7613-0620-7). 32pp. This book explores such topics as traveling to other solar systems, time travel, black holes, and parallel universes. (Rev: HBG 10/98; SLJ 10/98) [629.4]

24843 Barter, James. *Space Stations* (5–8). Illus. Series: Lucent Library of Science and Technology. 2005, Gale LB $29.95 (978-1-59018-106-5). 112pp. Explores the space stations that have been used for many years as medical laboratories and platforms for space study. (Rev: BL 1/05)

24844 Berger, Melvin, and Gilda Berger. *Can You Hear a Shout in Space? Questions and Answers About Space Exploration* (3–6). Illus. 2001, Scholastic $14.95 (978-0-439-09582-2); paper $5.95 (978-0-439-14879-5). 48pp. In question-and-answer format, this title tackles topics of interest both to browsers and report writers. (Rev: BL 7/01; HBG 10/01) [629.4]

24845 Berliner, Don. *Living in Space* (4–6). Illus. 1993, Lerner LB $22.60 (978-0-8225-1599-9). 72pp. The living conditions of travelers in space are covered. (Rev: BL 7/93) [629.47]

24846 Beyer, Mark. *Crisis in Space: Apollo 13* (3–4). Illus. Series: Survivor. 2002, Children's Book Pr. LB $24.50 (978-0-516-23903-3). 48pp. A suspenseful account of the problems encountered on the *Apollo 13* mission and the dangers the astronauts faced. (Rev: SLJ 6/02) [629.45]

24847 Blackwood, Gary L. *Alien Astronauts* (4–6). Series: Secrets of the Unexplained. 1998, Benchmark LB $29.93 (978-0-7614-0469-9). 80pp. As well as a historical look at UFO sightings, this book covers the types of sightings and the most common varieties. (Rev: HBG 9/99; SLJ 3/99) [001.9]

24848 Branley, Franklyn M. *Floating in Space* (K–3). Illus. by True Kelley. Series: Let's-Read-and-Find-Out. 1998, HarperCollins LB $15.89 (978-0-06-025433-9). 32pp. Life in space is covered in this book describing weightlessness, space suits, the food astronauts eat, and the activities aboard a space shuttle. (Rev: BCCB 4/98; BL 12/1/97; HBG 9/98; SLJ 2/98) [629.47]

24849 Branley, Franklyn M. *Is There Life in Outer Space?* (PS–3). Illus. by Edward Miller. Series: Let's-Read-and-Find-Out. 1999, HarperCollins paper $5.99 (978-0-06-445192-5). 31pp. A beginning science book that explores what we know about life on the planets and in outer space. (Rev: HBG 4/00; SLJ 10/99) [523]

24850 Bredeson, Carmen. *The Challenger Disaster: Tragic Space Flight* (4–8). Series: American Disasters. 1999, Enslow LB $23.93 (978-0-7660-1222-6). 48pp. An account of the 1986 tragedy. (Rev: BL 10/15/99; HBG 3/00) [629.5]

24851 Bredeson, Carmen. *John Glenn Returns to Orbit: Life on the Space Shuttle* (4–7). Series: Countdown to Space. 2000, Enslow LB $23.93 (978-0-7660-1304-9). 48pp. This is the story of John Glenn, now a famous politician, his return to space, and the different conditions he encountered. (Rev: BL 8/00; HBG 10/00) [629.4]

24852 Bredeson, Carmen. *NASA Planetary Spacecraft: Galileo, Magellan, Pathfinder, and Voyager* (4–7). Series: Countdown to Space. 2000, Enslow

LB $23.93 (978-0-7660-1303-2). 48pp. This gives a good rundown on the NASA spacecraft used to explore planets, their individual missions, and their findings. (Rev: BL 9/15/00; HBG 10/01) [629.4]

24853 Bredeson, Carmen. *Our Space Program* (3–5). Series: I Know America. 1999, Millbrook LB $24.90 (978-0-7613-0952-9). 48pp. This history of the first 50 years of the space program contains material on the space race with the Soviet Union, prominent astronauts, and major successes, failures, and disasters. (Rev: HBG 9/99; SLJ 5/99) [629.45]

24854 Brenner, Barbara. *Planetarium: The Museum That Explores the Many Wonders of Our Solar System* (1–4). Illus. by Ron Miller. Series: Bank Street Museum Book. 1993, Bantam LB $9.50 (978-0-533-35428-3). 48pp. On a trip to a planetarium, the reader visits outer space and learns about the solar system. (Rev: BL 9/1/93; SLJ 8/93) [520]

24855 Briggs, Carole S. *Women in Space* (4–7). Series: A&E Biography. 1999, Lerner LB $27.93 (978-0-8225-4937-6). 112pp. Includes profiles of astronauts including Sally Ride, Mae Jemison, Shannon Lucid, Eileen Collins, and two of their Russian counterparts. (Rev: SLJ 5/99) [629.45]

24856 Britton, Tamara. *NASA* (3–5). Series: Symbols, Landmarks, and Monuments. 2005, ABDO LB $22.78 (978-1-59197-836-7). 32pp. American space exploration and the key role of the National Aeronautics and Space Administration are the focus of this informative book that includes photographs and graphics. (Rev: SLJ 9/05) [354.79]

24857 Burleigh, Robert. *One Giant Leap* (1–3). Illus. by Mike Wimmer. 2009, Philomel $16.99 (978-0-399-23883-3). 40pp. Using rich language and eye-catching illustrations, Burleigh describes the moon landing on July 20, 1969; an author's note adds historical context. (Rev: BCCB 7–8/09; BL 12/1/08; SLJ 4/09) [629.45]

24858 Caper, William. *The Challenger Space Shuttle Explosion* (3–4). 2007, Bearport LB $23.96 (978-1-59716-367-5). 32pp. Part of the Code Red series, this book looks at the terrible shuttle accident of 1986, how it happened, and the effects that it had on the space program. (Rev: SLJ 8/07)

24859 Chaikin, Andrew, and Victoria Kohl. *Mission Control, This is Apollo: The Story of the First Voyages to the Moon* (5–8). Illus. by Alan Bean. 2009, Viking $23.99 (978-0-670-01156-8). 128pp. A compelling wide-format account of the Apollo program, with interesting anecdotes, informative sidebars, excellent photographs, and paintings by former astronaut Bean. (Rev: BL 5/1/09; HB 7/09*; SLJ 5/09; VOYA 6/09) [900]

24860 Clay, Rebecca. *Space Travel and Exploration* (4–8). Illus. Series: Secrets of Space. 1995, Twenty-First Century LB $23.90 (978-0-8050-4474-4). A history of modern space exploration, covering manned flights, space stations, space probes, and telescopes. (Rev: BL 7/97; SLJ 1/98) [629.5]

24861 Cole, Michael D. *Challenger: America's Space Tragedy* (4–6). Illus. Series: Countdown to Space. 1995, Enslow LB $23.93 (978-0-89490-544-5). 48pp. This tragic event is movingly described.

Two other titles in this series are *Friendship 7: First American in Orbit* and *Vostok 1: First Human in Space* (both 1995). (Rev: SLJ 2/96) [523]

24862 Cole, Michael D. *Galileo Spacecraft: Mission to Jupiter* (4–7). Series: Countdown to Space. 1999, Enslow LB $23.93 (978-0-7660-1119-9). 48pp. *Galileo*'s journey to Jupiter is described with details of the preparations for the flight and its findings. Photographs, a glossary, and Web sites round out the coverage. (Rev: BL 2/15/99; HBG 10/99; SLJ 5/99) [629.45]

24863 Cole, Michael D. *Moon Base: First Colony on Space* (4–7). Series: Countdown to Space. 1999, Enslow LB $23.93 (978-0-7660-1118-2). 48pp. A futuristic look at what a space colony on the moon might look like and the problems involved in creating it. (Rev: BL 2/15/99; HBG 10/99; SLJ 5/99) [629.45]

24864 Cole, Michael D. *NASA Space Vehicles: Capsules, Shuttles, and Space Stations* (4–7). Series: Countdown to Space. 2000, Enslow LB $23.93 (978-0-7660-1308-7). 48pp. Gives a rundown on these specialized vehicles plus a description of space stations and how they operate, with full-color photographs and clear, readable text. (Rev: BL 5/15/00; HBG 10/00; SLJ 12/00) [629.4]

24865 Cole, Michael D. *Space Emergency: Astronauts in Danger* (4–8). Illus. Series: Countdown to Space. 2000, Enslow LB $23.93 (978-0-7660-1307-0). 48pp. An explosion on the command module of *Apollo 13* and a faulty landing bag on *Friendship 7* are two of the emergencies described in this book on crises in space exploration. (Rev: BL 2/1/00; HBG 10/00; SLJ 12/00) [629.45]

24866 Cole, Michael D. *Space Launch Disaster: When Liftoff Goes Wrong* (4–7). Series: Countdown to Space. 2000, Enslow LB $23.93 (978-0-7660-1309-4). 48pp. This is a rundown of problems that can occur during the liftoff of space vehicles, with examples of actual disasters, many caught on camera. (Rev: BL 3/15/00; HBG 10/00; SLJ 8/00) [629]

24867 Davis, Amanda. *Extraterrestrials: Is There Life in Outer Space?* (2–4). Series: Exploring Space. 1997, Rosen LB $21.25 (978-0-8239-5058-4). 24pp. Colorful illustrations enliven this explanation of the conditions that led to life on earth and to our current quest for proof of life on other planets. (Rev: SLJ 4/98) [001.9]

24868 Dyer, Alan. *Mission to the Moon* (5–7). 2009, Simon & Schuster $19.99 (978-1-4169-7935-7). 80pp. This well-organized package of clear narrative, color photographs, quotations, and DVD of video clips presents a good overview of the space race and the U.S. Apollo missions. (Rev: LMC 10/09; SLJ 4/09)

24869 Dyson, Marianne J. *Home on the Moon: Living on a Space Frontier* (5–8). Illus. 2003, National Geographic $18.95 (978-0-7922-7193-2). 64pp. Dyson, a former NASA mission controller, discusses the resources available on the moon, explores the possibilities of building facilities there, and suggests activities. (Rev: BL 7/03; HBG 10/03; SLJ 9/03) [919.91]

24870 Dyson, Marianne J. *Space Station Science: Life in Free Fall* (4–7). Illus. 1999, Scholastic paper $16.95 (978-0-590-05889-6). 128pp. Written by a former member of a NASA control team, this work explores living and working in space including details on a space station bathroom. (Rev: BL 11/15/99; HBG 10/00; SLJ 12/99) [629.45]

24871 English, June A., and Thomas D. Jones. *Mission: Earth: Voyage to the Home Planet* (4–7). Illus. 1996, Scholastic paper $16.95 (978-0-590-48571-5). 48pp. The space program is introduced, with special coverage of the flights of the shuttle *Endeavor* in 1994 and its environmental studies. (Rev: BL 10/15/96; SLJ 10/96) [550]

24872 Fallen, Anne-Catherine. *USA from Space* (4–7). Illus. 1997, Firefly LB $19.95 (978-1-55209-159-3); paper $7.95 (978-1-55209-157-9). 48pp. Excellent satellite pictures of parts of the earth are contained in this book, which also explains the value of satellite imagery in tracking pollution, population, and natural disasters. (Rev: BL 3/1/98; SLJ 12/97) [917.3]

24873 Farbman, Melinda, and Frye Gaillard. *Spacechimp: NASA's Ape in Space* (4–7). Series: Countdown to Space. 2000, Enslow LB $23.93 (978-0-7660-1478-7). 48pp. The story of how animals in general have helped the space program and how one chimp's voyage into space contributed to progress. (Rev: BL 8/00; HBG 10/00) [629.4]

24874 Feldman, Heather. *Dennis Tito: The First Space Tourist* (2–3). Series: Space Firsts. 2003, Rosen LB $21.25 (978-0-8239-6249-5). 24pp. The true story of a 60-year-old man who paid a reported $20 million to spend a week aboard the International Space Station. (Rev: SLJ 3/04) [910]

24875 Feldman, Heather. *Skylab: The First American Space Station* (2–3). Series: Space Firsts. 2003, Rosen LB $21.25 (978-0-8239-6248-8). 24pp. An interesting look at Skylab and its significance in space exploration. (Rev: SLJ 3/04) [629.44]

24876 Feldman, Heather. *Sputnik: The First Satellite* (2–3). Series: Space Firsts. 2003, Rosen LB $21.25 (978-0-8239-6244-0). 24pp. An ideal choice for young readers with no memory of the race for space between the Soviet Union and the United States, this book profiles the Soviets' Sputnik 1, the first satellite to be launched into space by humans. (Rev: SLJ 11/03) [629.46]

24877 Fox, Mary V. *Rockets* (3–6). Illus. Series: Inventors and Inventions. 1996, Benchmark LB $25.64 (978-0-7614-0063-9). 63pp. Rocket pioneers are profiled, along with their discoveries and the changes these have caused in the modern world. (Rev: BL 3/15/96; SLJ 3/96) [621.43]

24878 Fox, Mary V. *Satellites* (3–6). Illus. Series: Inventors and Inventions. 1996, Marshall Cavendish LB $25.64 (978-0-7614-0049-3). 63pp. Details in an informal text and many interesting photos the story of satellites, their uses, and their creators. (Rev: BL 7/96; SLJ 8/96) [629.43]

24879 Gaffney, Timothy R. *Secret Spy Satellites: America's Eyes in Space* (4–7). Series: Countdown to Space. 2000, Enslow LB $23.93 (978-0-7660-1402-2). 48pp. With sharp illustrations and a strong narrative, this book describes U.S. spy satellites, their purposes, and findings. (Rev: BL 9/15/00; HBG 10/01) [629.4]

24880 Gallant, Roy A. *Space Stations* (2–4). Illus. Series: Kaleidoscope. 2000, Marshall Cavendish LB $25.64 (978-0-7614-1035-5). 48pp. This account briefly covers, in text and color pictures, space stations *Salyut, Skylab,* and *Mir* with a little information on the International Space Station. (Rev: BL 1/1–15/01; HBG 10/01) [629.44]

24881 Goldsmith, Mike. *Space* (4–7). Illus. Series: Kingfisher Voyages. 2005, Kingfisher $14.95 (978-0-7534-5910-2). 60pp. An appealing overview of space exploration, with concise text, good photographs, and a foreword and comments by astronaut Sally Ride. (Rev: BL 10/15/05) [629.45]

24882 Goodman, Susan E. *Ultimate Field Trip 5: Blasting Off to Space Academy* (3–5). Illus. Series: Ultimate Field Trip. 2001, Simon & Schuster $17.00 (978-0-689-83044-0). 48pp. This book follows 16 young people through a week-long training session at the U.S. Space Academy and includes the children's own comments and some space facts. (Rev: BL 5/1/01; HBG 10/01; SLJ 6/01) [629.45]

24883 Graham, Ian. *The Best Book of Spaceships* (1–4). Illus. 1998, Kingfisher $10.95 (978-0-7534-5133-5). 33pp. This introduction to space exploration pictures various space vehicles, the Hubble telescope, parts of a space suit, and everyday life in space, while also giving simple explanations of gravity and the solar system. (Rev: BL 12/15/98; HBG 3/99; SLJ 3/99) [629.47]

24884 Green, Carl R. *Apollo 11 Rockets to First Moon Landing: A MyReportLinks. com Book* (4–6). Illus. Series: Space Flight Adventures and Disasters. 2004, Enslow LB $25.26 (978-0-7660-5164-5). 48pp. Thorough chapter notes support this well-researched account of the dramatic story; Web links extend the book. Also use *The Gemini 4 Spacewalk Mission* (2004). (Rev: BL 10/1/04; SLJ 1/05) [029.45]

24885 Harris, Alan, and Paul Weissman. *The Great Voyager Adventure: A Guided Tour Through the Solar System* (4–8). Illus. 1990, Simon & Schuster paper $16.95 (978-0-671-72538-9). 80pp. Two scientists introduce the missions, paths, and discoveries of the Voyager spacecraft. (Rev: BL 2/1/91; SLJ 2/91) [523.4]

24886 Hilliard, Richard. *Ham the Astrochimp* (3–5). Illus. by author. 2007, Boyds Mills $16.95 (978-1-59078-459-4). Young readers will fascinated to learn that a chimpanzee was sent into space in 1961 as part of the Mercury space program. Illustrated by the author, who also wrote *Godspeed, John Glen, Neil, Buzz and Mike Go to the Moon,* and *Lucky 13: Survival in Space.* (Rev: LMC 11/07; SLJ 8/07)

24887 Holden, Henry M. *Living and Working Aboard the International Space Station: A MyReportLinks. com Book* (4–6). Series: Space Flight Adventures and Disasters. 2004, Enslow LB $25.26 (978-0-7660-5168-3). 48pp. This inside look at space station is supported by thorough chapter notes and extended by Web links. (Rev: BL 10/1/04; SLJ 2/05) [029.44]

24888 Holden, Henry M. *The Tragedy of the Space Shuttle Challenger* (4–8). Illus. Series: Space Flight Adventures and Disasters. 2004, Enslow LB $25.26 (978-0-7660-5165-2). 48pp. An account of the ill-fated *Challenger* mission, backed up by a list of Web sites that provide additional information. (Rev: BL 10/1/04; SLJ 2/05) [629.5]

24889 Jefferis, David. *Alien Lifesearch: Quest for Extraterrestrial Organisms* (4–6). Illus. Series: Megatech. 1999, Crabtree LB $25.27 (978-0-7787-0049-4). 32pp. This work explores the possibility of planets supporting life, alien searches, and UFO mysteries. (Rev: BL 8/99) [516.8]

24890 Johnson, Rebecca. *Satellites* (4–6). Illus. Series: Cool Science. 2005, Lerner LB $26.60 (978-0-8225-2908-8). 48pp. With many interesting examples and an attractive layout, this introduction explores the history and science of the artificial satellites that orbit the earth and gather all sorts of data. (Rev: SLJ 12/05) [629.46]

24891 Kennedy, Gregory. *The First Men in Space* (5–7). Illus. Series: World Explorers. 1991, Chelsea LB $21.95 (978-0-7910-1324-3). 111pp. This book covers the early years and accomplishments of both Soviet and American space programs. (Rev: SLJ 8/91) [629.44]

24892 Kerrod, Robin. *Dawn of the Space Age* (5–7). Illus. Series: The History of Space Exploration. 2005, World Almanac LB $31.00 (978-0-8368-5705-4). 48pp. A well-illustrated history of space exploration, from the ideas of Cyrano de Bergerac to the modern Mars probes. Also recommended in this series are *Space Probes*, *Space Shuttles*, and *Space Stations* (all 2004). (Rev: SLJ 3/05) [629.4]

24893 Kupperberg, Paul. *Spy Satellites* (4–8). Illus. Series: Library of Satellites. 2003, Rosen LB $26.50 (978-0-8239-3854-4). 64pp. The author discusses the history of U.S. spy satellites and how the country has used the information they have gleaned. (Rev: BL 5/15/03; SLJ 1/04) [327.1273]

24894 McCarthy, Meghan. *Astronaut Handbook* (K–3). Illus. by author. 2008, Knopf $16.99 (978-0-375-84459-1). 40pp. Aspiring astronauts will enjoy this lighthearted introduction to the training required before taking off for space. (Rev: BCCB 7–8/08; BL 6/1–15/08; HB 7/08; LMC 8/08; SLJ 7/08) [629.45]

24895 Markle, Sandra. *Pioneering Space* (5–8). 1992, Atheneum LB $14.95 (978-0-689-31748-4). A look at space travel and how people may succeed in living in space. (Rev: BL 9/1/92; SLJ 2/93) [629.4]

24896 Marsh, Carole. *Unidentified Flying Objects and Extraterrestrial Life* (5–8). Series: Secrets of Space. 1996, Twenty-First Century LB $25.90 (978-0-8050-4472-0). This book touches on a wide range of topics associated with UFOs, including a history of famous sightings, but the emphasis is on major SETI (Search for Extra Terrestrial Intelligence) projects undertaken to detect alien radio signals. The author concludes that there is no definitive proof of the existence of intelligent life outside Earth. (Rev: BL 12/1/96; SLJ 12/96) [001.9]

24897 Mason, Paul. *Space Race* (3–5). Series: Space Busters. 2002, Raintree LB $25.69 (978-0-7398-4851-7). 32pp. The Apollo Program is the major focus of this look at efforts to win the space competition. (Rev: HBG 10/02; SLJ 4/02) [629.45]

24898 Murphy, Patricia J. *Exploring Space with an Astronaut* (1–3). Series: I Like Science! 2004, Enslow LB $21.26 (978-0-7660-2268-3). 24pp. In addition to a discussion of life in space, this title introduces readers to an astronaut and offers a night sky activity. (Rev: SLJ 2/05) [629.5]

24899 Nicolson, Cynthia P. *Exploring Space* (3–5). Illus. Series: Starting with Space. 2000, Kids Can $12.95 (978-1-55074-711-9). 40pp. A basic book that covers the huge topic of space exploration in a clear, well-organized way. (Rev: BL 12/1/00; HBG 10/01) [629.4]

24900 O'Brien, Patrick. *You Are the First Kid on Mars* (K–3). Illus. by author. 2009, Putnam $16.99 (978-0-399-24634-0). 32pp. This compelling, well-illustrated imagining of a trip to Mars conveys lots of information about science and space travel. (Rev: BL 5/1/09; SLJ 7/09) [919.9]

24901 Platt, Richard. *Moon Landing: A Pop-Up Celebration of Apollo 11* (3–5). Illus. by David Hawcock. 2008, Candlewick $29.99 (978-0-7636-4046-0). 10pp. Pop-ups of a rocket, a lunar module, a spaceship, and the moon are bolstered by many fold-out flaps and pullout minibooks that present lots of information about the Apollo program. (Rev: BLO 12/16/08; SLJ 1/09) [629.45]

24902 Ride, Sally, and Susan Okie. *To Space and Back* (3–7). Illus. 1986, Lothrop $21.99 (978-0-688-06159-3); Morrow paper $14.99 (978-0-688-09112-5). 96pp. The first American woman in space describes her experiences aboard the shuttle. (Rev: BCCB 10/86; BL 11/1/86; SLJ 11/86)

24903 Schyffert, Bea Uusma. *Man Who Went to the Far Side of the Moon* (3–6). 2003, Chronicle $14.95 (978-0-8118-4007-1). 80pp. With scrapbook-style illustrations and fascinating details, this story of astronaut Michael Collins, who circled the moon while fellow astronauts Neil Armstrong and Buzz Aldrin walked on its surface, is full of tension and suspense. (Rev: BL 11/1/03; HBG 4/04; SLJ 10/03)

24904 Sherman, Josepha. *Deep Space Observation Satellites* (4–8). Illus. Series: Library of Satellites. 2003, Rosen LB $26.50 (978-0-8239-3852-0). 64pp. The author discusses the history of U.S. observation satellites and how the country has benefited from their discoveries. (Rev: BL 5/15/03) [522]

24905 Siy, Alexandra. *Cars on Mars: Roving the Red Planet* (5–8). Illus. by author. 2009, Charlesbridge $18.95 (978-1-57091-462-1). 58pp. The fascinating story of the Mars rovers built to last for three months but still exploring the Martian terrain more than five years later. (Rev: BL 8/09*; LMC 11/09; SLJ 7/09) [919.9]

24906 Stone, Jerry. *One Small Step: Celebrating the First Men on the Moon* (4–8). 2009, Roaring Brook $24.95 (978-1-59643-491-2). This "scrapbook" offers a wealth of perspectives on the first moon landing. (Rev: SLJ 6/09)

24907 Sullivan, George. *The Day We Walked on the Moon: A Photo History of Space Exploration* (5–8). Illus. 1990, Scholastic paper $4.95 (978-0-685-58532-0). 80pp. The history of U.S. space exploration, showing the accomplishments of both the United States and the Soviet Union. (Rev: BL 9/1/90; SLJ 2/91) [629.4]

24908 Thimmesh, Catherine. *Team Moon: How 400,000 People Landed Apollo 11 on the Moon* (5–10). 2006, Houghton $19.95 (978-0-618-50757-3). 80pp. A breathless account of all the behind-the-scenes work that went into the Apollo space program, with plenty of photographs. Sibert Medal, 2007. (Rev: SLJ 6/06) [629.45]

24909 Vogt, Gregory L. *Apollo Moonwalks: The Amazing Lunar Missions* (4–7). Series: Countdown to Space. 2000, Enslow LB $23.93 (978-0-7660-1306-3). 48pp. This account focuses on the moonwalks during the *Apollo 11* expedition and details what was found. (Rev: BL 8/00; HBG 10/00) [629.4]

24910 Vogt, Gregory L. *Disasters in Space Exploration*. Rev. ed. (5–8). 2003, Millbrook LB $25.90 (978-0-7613-2895-7). 79pp. An illustrated survey of serious accidents that have befallen the U.S. and Russian space programs, what caused them, and what was learned from them. This revised edition includes the *Columbia* space shuttle disaster of February 2003. (Rev: SLJ 3/04) [363.12]

24911 Vogt, Gregory L. *Spacewalks: The Ultimate Adventures in Orbit* (4–7). Series: Countdown to Space. 2000, Enslow LB $23.93 (978-0-7660-1305-6). 48pp. This gives a history of spacewalks, tells who were the pioneers, and explains their purpose. (Rev: BL 8/00; HBG 10/00) [629.4]

24912 Whitehouse, Patricia. *Space Travel* (2–4). Illus. Series: Space Explorer. 2004, Heinemann LB $24.21 (978-1-4034-5155-2). 32pp. A brief introduction to space travel, with lots of photographs, short paragraphs, and large type. (Rev: BL 1/1–15/05; SLJ 2/05) [910]

24913 Whitehouse, Patricia. *Working in Space* (1–3). Illus. Series: Space Explorer. 2004, Heinemann LB $24.21 (978-1-4034-5158-3); paper $6.95 (978-1-4034-5662-5). 32pp. For young readers, this is a colorful introduction to the kind of work carried out in space. Companion books are *Space Equipment* and *Living in Space* (both 2004). (Rev: SLJ 2/05) [629]

24914 Woodford, Chris. *Space Dramas* (3–5). Illus. Series: Space Busters. 2002, Raintree LB $25.69 (978-0-7398-4850-0). 32pp. Natural space events such as comet collisions are described along with disasters that have hit manned and unmanned missions outside our atmosphere. (Rev: HBG 10/02; SLJ 4/02) [629.45]

24915 Wunsch, Susi Trautmann. *The Adventures of Sojourner: The Mission to Mars that Thrilled the World* (5–9). 1998, Mikaya LB $22.95 (978-0-9650493-5-1); paper $9.95 (978-0-9650493-6-8). 60pp. This book describes the construction of the *Sojourner* rover and its performance on Mars after landing on July 4, 1997. (Rev: SLJ 2/99*) [629.5]

Technology, Engineering, and Industry

General and Miscellaneous Industries and Inventions

24916 Allman, Toney. *From Fish Gills to Underwater Breathing* (4–6). Series: Imitating Nature. 2006, Gale LB $22.45 (978-0-7377-3608-3). 32pp. All about an inventor's attempts to design a diving vest that would mimic fish gills. Part of an interesting series that helps readers to see the practical applications of scientific principles that also includes *From Octopus Eyes to Powerful Lenses* (2006). (Rev: SLJ 5/07)

24917 Alphin, Elaine M. *Irons* (3–6). Series: Household History. 1998, Carolrhoda LB $16.95 (978-1-57505-238-0). 48pp. This book traces the history of this important household appliance and its many uses. (Rev: HBG 9/98; SLJ 7/98) [643]

24918 Alphin, Elaine M. *Toasters* (3–6). Series: Household History. 1998, Carolrhoda LB $16.95 (978-1-57505-243-4). 48pp. A history of toasters, how they operate, and how they are used. (Rev: HBG 9/98; SLJ 7/98) [643]

24919 Alphin, Elaine M. *Vacuum Cleaners* (3–5). Illus. Series: Household History. 1997, Carolrhoda $22.60 (978-1-57505-018-8). 48pp. A fascinating history of the vacuum cleaner with an explanation of how it works. (Rev: BL 1/1–15/98; HBG 3/98) [683]

24920 Baker, Christopher W. *A New World of Simulators: Training with Technology* (5–8). Illus. 2001, Millbrook LB $23.90 (978-0-7613-1352-6). 48pp. An introduction to the uses of simulators and their importance in training workers who operate complex technologies such as those found in airplanes, ships, and nuclear power plants. (Rev: BL 8/01; HBG 3/02; SLJ 8/01) [003]

24921 Bryant-Mole, Karen. *Toys* (PS–3). Series: Picture This! 1997, Rigby $18.50 (978-1-57572-057-9). 24pp. Many toys are shown in this heavily

illustrated, interactive book. Also use *Games* (1997). (Rev: BL 10/15/97; SLJ 12/97) [745.592]

24922 *CDs, Super Glue, and Salsa Series 2: How Everyday Products Are Made* (5–10). 1996, Gale LB $126.00 (978-0-7876-0870-5). This two-volume set tells how 30 everyday products are made, including air bags, bungee cords, contact lenses, ketchup, pencils, soda bottles, and umbrellas. (Rev: SLJ 8/97) [658.5]

24923 Cobb, Vicki. *Fireworks* (4–8). Photos by Michael Gold. Series: Where's the Science Here? 2005, Lerner LB $23.93 (978-0-7613-2771-4). 48pp. A well-illustrated, engaging text covers the history and science of pyrotechnics; experiments require adult supervision. Also recommended in this series are *Junk Food* and *Sneakers* (both 2005). (Rev: SLJ 2/06)

24924 Collicutt, Paul. *This Rocket* (PS–2). Illus. 2005, Farrar $16.00 (978-0-374-37484-6). 32pp. A colorful overview of rockets and spacecraft ranging from Fourth of July fireworks to the space shuttle. (Rev: BL 12/1/05; SLJ 9/05) [621.43]

24925 Colman, Penny. *Toilets, Bathtubs, Sinks, and Sewers: A History of the Bathroom* (5–8). 1994, Atheneum $16.00 (978-0-689-31894-8). A fascinating look at sanitation systems and inventions related to personal hygiene from ancient times to the present. (Rev: BCCB 2/95; BL 1/1/95; SLJ 3/95) [643]

24926 Cooper, Elisha. *Ice Cream* (1–3). Illus. 2002, HarperCollins LB $15.89 (978-0-06-001424-7). 40pp. An entertaining look at the production of ice cream, tracing its way from cow to consumer. (Rev: BL 5/15/02; HB 5/02; HBG 10/02; SLJ 5/02) [637.4]

24927 Crump, Donald J., ed. *How Things Work* (5–7). Illus. 1984, National Geographic LB $12.50 (978-0-87044-430-2). 104pp. A handsome volume that explains the mechanics of a variety of objects from toasters to space shuttles. [600]

24928 Ditchfield, Christin. *Wood* (2–5). Series: True Books — Natural Resources. 2002, Children's Book Pr. LB $25.00 (978-0-516-22346-9). 48pp. This simple account shows the importance of wood in such industries as building and paper-making, and tells how we can protect this resouce from forest fires and pollution. (Rev: BL 10/15/02) [674]

24929 Drake, Jane, and Ann Love. *Mining* (2–4). Illus. by Pat Cupples. Series: America at Work. 1999, Kids Can $12.95 (978-1-55074-508-5). 31pp. Trish and Jamie learn how the steel blades on their ice skates were made by visiting a mine and then a steel mill and observing the processes in each. (Rev: HBG 4/00; SLJ 11/99) [672]

24930 Englart, Mindi Rose. *Pens* (3–5). Series: Made in the USA. 2002, Gale LB $23.70 (978-1-56711-487-4). 32pp. The evolution of writing pens is described along with a detailed view of how they are made today. (Rev: BL 9/15/02) [681]

24931 Erlbach, Arlene. *The Kids' Invention Book* (4–6). Illus. 1997, Lerner LB $22.60 (978-0-8225-2414-4). 64pp. Beginning with 15-year-old Chester Greenwood, who invented earmuffs in 1873, this book introduces over a dozen young people and their inventions. (Rev: BL 2/1/98; HBG 3/98) [608]

24932 Erlbach, Arlene. *Teddy Bears* (3–5). Illus. 1997, Carolrhoda $22.60 (978-1-57505-019-5); paper $7.95 (978-1-57505-222-9). 48pp. Provides the history of the teddy bear, discusses the problem of identifying the first maker, and describes the industry today. (Rev: BL 1/1–15/98; HBG 3/98) [745.594]

24933 *Fantastic Feats and Failures* (4–8). Illus. by Jane Kurisu. 2004, Kids Can paper $9.95 (978-1-55337-634-7). 52pp. Highs and lows of engineering (the Brooklyn Bridge in the first category, for example, and the Tacoma Narrows in the latter) are reviewed in this fascinating large-format book. (Rev: BL 9/15/04) [624.1]

24934 Feigenbaum, Aaron. *Emergency at Three Mile Island* (3–6). Series: Code Red. 2007, Bearport LB $23.96 (978-1-59716-364-4). 32pp. Part of a series on the causes and costs of disasters, this book discusses the accident at this nuclear power plant and how it could have been much more serious. (Rev: SLJ 7/07)

24935 Goldberg, Jan. *Earth Imaging Satellites* (5–9). Series: The Library of Satellites. 2003, Rosen LB $26.50 (978-0-8239-3853-7). 64pp. A survey of the various satellites and how their images of the earth's surface measure pollution, locate forest fires, find earthquake faults, and measure the size of polar caps. (Rev: BL 11/15/03) [629.46]

24936 Graham, Ian. *Machines and Inventions* (1–4). Illus. by David Antram, et al. Series: World of Wonder. 2008, Children's Pr. LB $29.00 (978-0-531-24027-4); paper $9.95 (978-0-531-23823-3). 32pp. Answering such questions as "How Do People Keep Clean," this book looks at devices that make our lives easier and includes acetate overlays with cutaway details. (Rev: SLJ 3/09)

24937 Harper, Charise Mericle. *Imaginative Inventions* (2–4). Illus. 2001, Little, Brown $14.95 (978-0-316-34725-9). 32pp. An imaginative look at the origins of products ranging from chewing gum and doughnuts to roller skates and high-heeled shoes. (Rev: BL 12/15/01; HBG 3/02; SLJ 10/01) [609]

24938 Jones, Charlotte F. *Mistakes That Worked* (4–6). Illus. by John O'Brien. 1994, Doubleday paper $11.95 (978-0-385-32043-6). 82pp. An entertaining look at successful mistakes, such as the ice cream vendor who ran out of dishes and invented the cone. (Rev: BCCB 10/91; BL 10/15/91*; SLJ 10/91) [609]

24939 Jones, George. *My First Book of How Things Are Made: Crayons, Jeans, Peanut Butter, Guitars and More* (3–5). Illus. 1995, Scholastic $12.95 (978-0-590-48004-8). 64pp. The manufacturing process of eight objects common in children's lives — including grape jelly, footballs, orange juice, blue jeans, and books — are enumerated. (Rev: SLJ 2/96) [658.5]

24940 Kassinger, Ruth G. *Iron and Steel: From Thor's Hammer to the Space Shuttle* (5–7). Illus. Series: Material World. 2003, Millbrook LB $25.90 (978-0-7613-2111-8). 80pp. The different ways in which humans have used and processed iron and steel through the ages is the focus of this book. (Rev: BL 5/15/03; HBG 10/03; SLJ 1/04) [669]

24941 Kerrod, Robin. *New Materials: Present Knowledge, Future Trends* (5–9). Illus. Series: 21st Century Science. 2003, Smart Apple LB $27.10 (978-1-58340-353-2). 44pp. Numerous diagrams, photographs, and drawings help to explain the processing of raw materials and the need to conserve our limited resources. (Rev: SLJ 1/04) [620.11]

24942 Koscielniak, Bruce. *Looking at Glass Through the Ages* (3–6). Illus. by author. 2006, Houghton $16.00 (978-0-618-50750-4). From the earliest faience of ancient Egypt to today's optical fiber, this is a fascinating review of glassmaking, covering everything from magnifying lenses to stained glass, lead crystal, and neon tubes. (Rev: SLJ 8/06) [666]

24943 Kuklin, Susan. *From Head to Toe: How a Doll Is Made* (1–3). Illus. 1994, Hyperion $15.95 (978-1-56282-666-6). 32pp. The step-by-step creation of a doll is shown using imaginative photos and a text that introduces each worker. (Rev: BCCB 5/94; BL 5/1/94*; HB 5/94; SLJ 5/94) [688.7]

24944 Landau, Elaine. *The History of Everyday Life* (5–8). Series: Major Inventions Through History. 2005, Twenty-First Century LB $26.60 (978-0-8225-3808-0). 56pp. Fireplaces, washing machines, and microwave ovens are among the inventions discussed here that have improved our everyday lives. (Rev: SLJ 2/06)

24945 Llewellyn, Claire. *Paper* (2–4). Series: Material World. 2002, Watts LB $24.00 (978-0-531-14629-3). 30pp. A well-illustrated look at paper and the ways it is used; with "Fast Facts," related activities, and a glossary. (Rev: SLJ 5/03) [620.1]

24946 Lockie, Mark. *Biometric Technology* (5–8). Series: Science at the Edge. 2002, Heinemann LB $27.86 (978-1-58810-701-5). 64pp. Lockie explores the study of biometry and its applications in such areas as voice-speaker identification and facial recognition. (Rev: BL 10/15/02; HBG 3/03) [609]

24947 *Machines and Inventions* (5–9). Series: Understanding Science and Nature. 1993, Time-Life $17.95 (978-0-8094-9704-1). Using a question-and-answer format, double-page spreads look at a variety of inventions including the box camera, printing press, and dynamite. (Rev: BL 1/15/94; SLJ 6/94) [621.8]

24948 Markle, Sandra. *Science Surprises* (4–5). Illus. by June Otani. 1996, Scholastic paper $3.99 (978-0-590-48401-5). 63pp. Six science surprises — like the invention of photography and the discoveries of penicillin and Velcro/TM — are described, along with 11 fascinating experiments to expand on scientific principles. (Rev: SLJ 7/97) [507]

24949 Nelson, Robin. *From Wax to Crayon* (1–3). Series: Start to Finish. 2003, Lerner LB $18.60 (978-0-8225-4660-3). 24pp. Traces the creation of a crayon, full-page color photographs. (Rev: HBG 10/03; SLJ 8/03) [741.2]

24950 Nobleman, Marc Tyler. *The Telephone* (2–4). Series: Fact Finders: Great Inventions. 2003, Capstone LB $23.93 (978-0-7368-2218-3). 32pp. A simple and attractive introduction to the invention of the telephone, how it works, and the effect it has had on society, ending with instructions for making a phone with cups and string. (Rev: SLJ 6/04) [621.385]

24951 Oxlade, Chris. *Glass* (2–3). Series: Materials, Materials, Materials. 2001, Heinemann LB $21.36 (978-1-58810-154-9). 32pp. Though in a compact format, this book contains lots of information about how glass is manufactured, its history, forms, and uses. (Rev: BL 10/15/01) [666]

24952 Oxlade, Chris. *Paper* (2–3). Series: Materials, Materials, Materials. 2001, Heinemann LB $21.36 (978-1-58810-156-3). 32pp. An attractive, introductory look at paper, how it is produced, its uses, and its recycling and conservation. (Rev: BL 10/15/01) [676]

24953 Oxlade, Chris. *Plastic* (2–3). Series: Materials, Materials, Materials. 2001, Heinemann LB $21.36 (978-1-58810-157-0). 32pp. Using a compact format with a color illustration and text on each page, this introductory work explains what plastics are, how they are made, their uses, and their role in conservation. (Rev: BL 10/15/01) [547.7]

24954 Oxlade, Chris. *Rubber* (2–3). Series: Materials, Materials, Materials. 2002, Heinemann LB $22.79 (978-1-58810-586-8). 32pp. This book provides a simple, clear introduction to rubber, its properties, where it comes from, and its uses in everyday life. (Rev: BL 6/1–15/02) [633.8]

24955 Oxlade, Chris. *Wood* (2–3). Illus. Series: Materials, Materials, Materials. 2001, Heinemann LB $21.36 (978-1-58810-158-7). 32pp. A discussion of where wood comes from and how it is made into products we use, with photographs. (Rev: BL 10/15/01) [674]

24956 Packard, Mary. *High-Tech Inventions: A Chapter Book* (3–7). Series: True Tales. 2004, Children's Pr. LB $22.50 (978-0-516-23728-2). 48pp. A clear and attractive look at the history of computers and at new and future developments, such as a cock-roach that might be used for search-and-rescue operations. (Rev: SLJ 2/05) [004]

24957 Raum, Elizabeth. *The Story Behind Toilets* (2–4). Illus. Series: True Stories. 2009, Raintree LB $19.75 (978-1-4329-2350-1). 32pp. A fascinating look at the history of toilets — with a great timeline — and contemporary debates about pay toilets, waste treatment, and sanitation in general. (Rev: BL 4/1/09; SLJ 10/09) [696]

24958 Rocker, Megan. *How It Happens at the Fireworks Factory* (K–3). Illus. Series: How It Happens. 2005, Oliver $19.95 (978-1-881508-97-7). 32pp. An inside look at the operation of a factory. Also use *How It Happens at the Cereal Company* (2005).

24959 Romanek, Trudee. *Switched On, Flushed Down, Tossed Out: Investigating the Hidden Workings of Your Home* (3–5). Illus. by Stephen MacEachern. 2005, Annick paper $12.95 (978-1-55037-902-0). 48pp. Casey, who has a vivid imagination, is curious about the workings of all kinds of household features — plumbing, electricity, thermostats, phones — and his funny theories are balanced by clear explanations of the real thing. (Rev: BL 7/05; SLJ 12/05) [643]

24960 Romanek, Trudee, and Pat Cupples. *The Technology Book for Girls: And Other Advanced Beings* (3–6). 2001, Kids Can $14.95 (978-1-55074-936-6); paper $8.95 (978-1-55074-619-8). 56pp. The workings of a variety of everyday items — remote controls, smoke detectors, lasers, and so forth — are detailed in this lighthearted book that also profiles women with science-based careers. (Rev: HBG 10/01; SLJ 6/01) [604.83]

24961 St. George, Judith. *So You Want to Be an Inventor?* (3–5). Illus. by David Small. 2002, Penguin $16.99 (978-0-399-23593-1). 56pp. A spirited and informative look at inventors and their inventions with eye-catching and amusing illustrations. (Rev: BCCB 10/02; BL 8/02; HB 9/02; HBG 3/03; SLJ 9/02) [608]

24962 Sandler, Martin W. *Inventors* (5–8). Series: Library of Congress Books. 1996, HarperCollins $24.95 (978-0-06-024923-6). Concentrating on the late 19th and 20th centuries, the book is divided into sections on inventors, transportation, communication, and entertainment. (Rev: SLJ 2/96) [608]

24963 Slavin, Bill. *Transformed: How Everyday Things Are Made* (4–7). Illus. 2005, Kids Can $24.95 (978-1-55337-179-3). 160pp. A behind-the-scenes look at the manufacturing process for a wide array of everyday products. (Rev: BL 10/15/05; SLJ 1/06) [670]

24964 Smith, Ryan A. *Trading Cards: From Start to Finish* (3–5). Illus. Series: Made in the U.S.A. 2005, Gale LB $23.70 (978-1-4103-0374-5). 48pp. A behind-the-scenes glimpse at how trading cards are manufactured and distributed. (Rev: BL 9/15/05) [976]

24965 Soucie, Gary. *What's the Difference Between . . . Lenses and Prisms and Other Scientific Things?* (3–6). Illus. by Jeff Domm. 1995, Wiley paper $9.95 (978-0-471-08626-0). 85pp. This book describes the differences in technology between two similar commodities, e.g., soap and detergent; iron and steel. (Rev: SLJ 2/96) [609]

24966 Taylor, Barbara. *Be an Inventor* (5–9). Illus. 1987, Harcourt $11.95 (978-0-15 205950-7); paper $7.95 (978-0-15-205951-4). A discussion of the process of invention and some examples plus coverage of entries in a *Weekly Reader* invention contest. (Rev: BL 12/15/87; SLJ 3/88) [608]

24967 Thimmesh, Catherine. *Girls Think of Everything* (4–7). Illus. 2000, Houghton $16.00 (978-0-395-93744-0). 64pp. A fresh, breezy account about women whose inventions include the windshield wiper, chocolate chip cookies, and Glo-paper. (Rev: BCCB 5/00; BL 3/15/00; HB 5/00; HBG 10/00; SLJ 4/00) [609.2]

24968 Tomecek, Stephen M. *What a Great Idea! Inventions That Changed the World* (3–6). Illus. by Dan Stuckenschneider. 2003, Scholastic $18.95 (978-0-590-68144-5). 128pp. This attractively illustrated chronology — divided into five time periods — identifies the major inventions of human civilization from the hand axe and wheel to the airplane and computer. (Rev: BL 4/1/03; HBG 10/03; SLJ 4/03) [609]

24969 Whiting, Jim. *James Watt and the Steam Engine* (5–8). Series: Uncharted, Unexplored, and Unexplained: Scientific Advancements of the 19th Century. 2006, Mitchell Lane LB $29.95 (978-1-58415-371-9). 48pp. Brief biographical information about Watt is accompanied by a more detailed discussion of his invention and its importance. (Rev: SLJ 5/06) [621]

24970 Wilkinson, Philip, and Jacqueline Dineen. *Art and Technology Through the Ages* (5–8). Illus. Series: Ideas That Changed the World. 1995, Chelsea LB $14.95 (978-0-7910-2769-1). A survey of the evolution of art and communications, from cave paintings through advanced digital recording and computer graphics. (Rev: SLJ 11/95; VOYA 2/96) [501.4]

24971 Williams, Marcia. *Hooray for Inventors!* (3–5). Illus. 2005, Candlewick $16.99 (978-0-7636-2760-7). 40pp. This attractive large-format book tells the stories behind some of the world's most notable inventions and their creators, pairing a lighthearted text full of asides and snippets of dialogue. (Rev: BL 12/1/05; SLJ 12/05) [609.2]

24972 Woodford, Chris, and Jon Woodcock. *Cool Stuff 2.0 and How It Works* (4–8). Illus. by Darren Awuah, et al. 2007, DK $24.99 (978-0-7566-3207-6). 256pp. More than 100 new "cool" items are featured in this updated edition full of things that appeal to kids, such as robot cars and "silent flight" aircraft. (Rev: SLJ 3/08)

24973 Woods, Michael, and Mary B. Woods. *The History of Communication* (5–8). Series: Major Inventions Through History. 2005, Twenty-First Century LB $26.60 (978-0-8225-3807-3). 56pp. An attractive look at developments through time in methods of communication — the printing press, telephone, radio, television, and the Internet — and the impact on our lives. (Rev: SLJ 1/06) [302.2]

24974 Woods, Samuel. *Recycled Paper* (3–5). Series: Made in the USA. 2000, Blackbirch LB $24.94 (978-1-56711-395-2). 32pp. The process of recycling paper is covered from the collection of old paper to the production of new paper. (Rev: BL 12/15/00; HBG 3/01; SLJ 12/00) [686.2]

24975 Wyatt, Valerie. *Inventions* (3–5). Illus. by Matthew Fernandes. Series: Frequently Asked Questions. 2003, Kids Can $12.95 (978-1-55337-403-9); paper $6.95 (978-1-55337-404-6). 40pp. A bright question-and-answer format is used to present information about a variety of inventions. (Rev: HBG 10/03; SLJ 7/03) [608]

24976 Zuckerman, Amy, and James Daly. *2030: A Day in the Life of Tomorrow's Kids* (K–3). Illus. by John Manders. 2009, Dutton $16.99 (978-0-525-47860-7). 32pp. This light look at the future follows a boy through a typical day featuring a talking dog, a smart wristwatch, magnetically hovering skateboards, and other wonders. (Rev: BCCB 4/09; BL 1/1–15/09; LMC 5/09; SLJ 3/09) [601]

Aeronautics and Airplanes

24977 Barton, Byron. *Airplanes* (PS). Illus. by author. 1986, HarperCollins LB $17.89 (978-0-690-04532-1). 32pp. Simple words and brightly colored artwork portray the roles of airplanes. (Rev: BL 8/86; SLJ 9/86)

24978 Berliner, Don. *Aviation: Reaching for the Sky* (5–8). Illus. Series: Innovators. 1997, Oliver LB $21.95 (978-1-881508-33-5). 144pp. A thorough history of aviation, beginning with early hot-air balloons and dirigibles and continuing through the Wright Brothers and Sikorsky's helicopter to supersonic jets. (Rev: BL 5/1/97; SLJ 7/97) [629.133]

24979 Bingham, Caroline. *Big Book of Airplanes* (2–5). Illus. 2001, DK $14.99 (978-0-7894-6521-4). 32pp. A stunning fact-filled picture book about all kinds of planes, from jumbo jets to the tiny "Gee Bee" and the space plane X-33. (Rev: BL 3/1/01; HBG 10/01) [629.133]

24980 Britton, Tamara. *Air Force One* (3–5). Series: Symbols, Landmarks, and Monuments. 2004, ABDO LB $22.78 (978-1-59197-520-5). 32pp. A look at the aircraft that have been used to transport the president, especially Air Force One, which has become a symbol of the office itself. (Rev: SLJ 11/04) [387.7]

24981 Carson, Mary Kay. *The Wright Brothers for Kids: How They Invented the Airplane: 21 Activities Exploring the Science and History of Flight* (4–8). Illus. by Laura D'Argo. 2003, Chicago Review paper $14.95 (978-1-55652-477-6). 146pp. After an account of the achievements of the Wrights and other early airplane enthusiasts, 21 activities allow readers to investigate some of the basic principles and to learn about equipment and means of communication. (Rev: SLJ 6/03) [629.13]

24982 Cole, Michael D. *TWA Flight 800: Explosion in Midair* (4–8). Series: American Disasters. 1999,

Enslow LB $23.93 (978-0-7660-1217-2). A dramatic account of the air tragedy. (Rev: BL 1/1–15/99; HBG 10/99) [629.136]

24983 Davis, Meredith. *Up and Away! Taking a Flight* (2–4). Illus. by Ken Dubrowski. 1997, Mondo paper $4.95 (978-1-57255-214-2). 23pp. An international flight is covered from entering the airport to reaching the final destination. (Rev: SLJ 1/98) [629.133]

24984 Feigenbaum, Aaron. *The Hindenburg Disaster* (3–6). Series: Code Red. 2007, Bearport LB $23.96 (978-1-59716-361-3). 32pp. In chapters including "Why Airships Can Fly," "A Floating Hotel," "The Crash," and "What Happened?," Feigenbaum describes the 1937 catastrophe. (Rev: LMC 10/07; SLJ 10/07) [363.12]

24985 Gaffney, Timothy R. *Hurricane Hunters* (4–7). Series: Aircraft. 2001, Enslow LB $23.93 (978-0-7660-1569-2). 48pp. Information on the planes that investigate hurricanes is accompanied by quotations from the pilots and scientists who fly in them. (Rev: HBG 3/02; SLJ 2/02) [551.55]

24986 Ghione, Yvette. *This Is Daniel Cook on a Plane* (K–3). 2006, Kids Can $12.95 (978-1-55453-081-6); paper $4.95 (978-1-55453-082-3). In this companion to the popular Canadian-produced TV show, the young host takes readers on a flight in a small airplane, introducing them to the parts of the airplane, flying techniques, and safety procedures. (Rev: SLJ 11/06) [629.13]

24987 Graham, Ian. *Aircraft* (3–5). Illus. Series: How Machines Work. 2008, Smart Apple LB $18.95 (978-1-59920-292-1). 32pp. Fast facts, drawings, diagrams, and photographs accompany text explaining how the engines, wings, controls, and so forth work. (Rev: BL 12/1/08) [629.133]

24988 Graham, Ian. *You Wouldn't Want to Be on the Hindenburg! A Transatlantic Trip You'd Rather Skip* (3–5). Illus. by David Antram. 2009, Scholastic LB $29.00 (978-0-531-20823-6); paper $9.95 (978-0-531-21049-9). 32pp. This detailed cartoon account of the design, construction, and dangers of airships also described the disaster. (Rev: BLO 3/17/09) [900]

24989 Hansen, Ole Steen. *Amazing Flights: The Golden Age* (4–7). Illus. Series: The Story of Flight. 2003, Crabtree LB $25.27 (978-0-7787-1202-2); paper $8.95 (978-0-7787-1218-3). 32pp. Double-page spreads present text, feature sidebars, color photographs, and paintings on the people and events of flying after World War I — air races, barnstormers, Lindbergh, and more. (Rev: BL 10/15/03) [629.13]

24990 Hansen, Ole Steen. *Commercial Aviation* (4–7). Series: The Story of Flight. 2003, Crabtree $25.27 (978-0-7787-1205-3). 32pp. The history and development of airlines and other forms of commercial aviation are discussed with coverage of present-day problems. (Rev: BL 10/15/03) [629.13]

24991 Hansen, Ole Steen. *Modern Military Aircraft* (4–7). Illus. Series: The Story of Flight. 2003, Crabtree LB $25.27 (978-0-7787-1204-6); paper $8.95 (978-0-7787-1220-6). 32pp. A highly visual overview of military aircraft since World War II, with a spotter's guide. (Rev: BL 10/15/03) [623.]

24992 Hill, Lee S. *The Flyer Flew! The Invention of the Airplane* (2–4). Illus. by Craig Orback. Series: On My Own Science. 2006, Millbrook LB $25.26 (978-1-57505-758-3). 48pp. This easy-reader chapter book tells the story of the Wright brothers' invention, discusses their scientific approach, and explains terms such as pitch and air pressure. (Rev: SLJ 8/06) [629.13]

24993 Hodgkins, Fran. *How People Learned to Fly* (1–3). Illus. by True Kelley. Series: Let's-Read-and-Find-Out Science. 2007, Collins $15.99 (978-0-06-029558-5); paper $5.99 (978-0-06-445221-2). 33pp. An introduction to the history of aircraft and the scientific principles that keep them aloft. (Rev: SLJ 10/07) [629.133]

24994 Homan, Lynn M., and Thomas Reilly. *Women Who Fly* (5–8). Illus. by Rosalie M. Shepherd. 2004, Pelican $14.95 (978-1-58980-160-8). 104pp. Women's efforts to establish a foothold in the male-dominated field of aviation are recounted in this book that is suitable for browsers. (Rev: BL 7/04; SLJ 9/04) [629.13]

24995 Hunter, Ryan Ann. *Into the Air: A Timeline of Flight* (2–4). 2003, National Geographic $16.95 (978-0-7922-5120-0). 48pp. Hunter reaches way back in history to begin her beautifully illustrated history of flight, starting with prehistory's flying reptiles and continuing through the ages to the developments of human flight. (Rev: BL 12/15/03; HBG 4/04)

24996 Hunter, Ryan Ann. *Take Off!* (PS–1). Illus. by Edward Miller. 2000, Holiday House $15.95 (978-0-8234-1466-6). 32pp. All kinds of airplanes — from the Wright brothers' craft to the 1,000-seat plane of the future — are introduced in this brightly illustrated volume that ends with directions on making a paper airplane. (Rev: BCCB 7–8/00; BL 2/15/00; HBG 9/00; SLJ 9/00) [629.13]

24997 Malam, John. *Airport: Behind the Scenes, Check-in to Take-off* (3–5). Illus. Series: Building Works. 2000, Bedrick $16.95 (978-0-87226-586-8). 32pp. This book supplies an illustrated guided tour of an airport and its facilities plus a history of airports and a glossary of terms. (Rev: BL 7/00; HBG 9/00) [387.7]

24998 Masters, Nancy Robinson. *The Airplane* (4–8). Series: Inventions That Shaped the World. 2004, Watts LB $30.50 (978-0-531-12360-7). 80pp. An interesting overview of the discovery and development of flight, with discussion of its impact on our lives today and in the future. (Rev: SLJ 2/05) [629.13]

24999 Maynard, Chris. *Aircraft* (5–8). Illus. Series: Need for Speed. 1999, Lerner LB $23.93 (978-0-8225-2485-4); paper $7.95 (978-0-8225-9855-8). 32pp. Using double-page spreads, this work introduces high-speed aircraft. (Rev: BL 1/1–15/00; HBG 3/00; SLJ 2/00) [629.133]

25000 Miller, Marilyn. *Behind the Scenes at the Airport* (PS–3). Illus. 1996, Raintree LB $21.40 (978-0-8172-4086-8). 32pp. Using a question-and-answer approach, the activities that make an airport work are pictured. (Rev: BL 4/15/96; SLJ 12/96) [387.7]

25001 Millspaugh, Ben. *Aviation and Space Science Projects* (5–8). Illus. 1992, TAB paper $9.95 (978-0-8306-2156-9). 133pp. The principles of flight are explored in 19 projects that vary in difficulty and complexity. (Rev: BL 1/15/92; SLJ 6/92) [629.1]

25002 Molzahn, Arlene Bourgeois. *Airplanes* (2–4). Illus. Series: Transportation and Communication. 2003, Enslow LB $23.93 (978-0-7660-2026-9). 48pp. An easy-to-read history of airplanes and their use in enabling various forms of communication. Also use *Ships and Boats* (2003). (Rev: HBG 10/03)

25003 O'Brien, Patrick. *Fantastic Flights: One Hundred Years of Flying on the Edge* (3–6). 2003, Walker $17.95 (978-0-8027-8880-1); paper $18.85 (978-0-8027-8881-8). 40pp. Seventeen significant flights — from Otto Lilienthal's glider experiments to the landing of the spacecraft Pathfinder on Mars — are introduced in colorful spreads. (Rev: BL 9/1/03; HBG 4/04; SLJ 11/03) [629.13]

25004 Old, Wendie. *To Fly: The Story of the Wright Brothers* (3–5). Illus. by Robert Andrew Parker. 2002, Clarion $16.00 (978-0-618-13347-5). 48pp. An attractive, large-format introduction to the brothers and their accomplishments with good coverage of the basic principles of flight. (Rev: BL 10/1/02; HB 11/02; HBG 3/03; SLJ 10/02) [629.13]

25005 Otfinoski, Steven. *Taking Off: Planes Then and Now* (2–4). Illus. Series: Here We Go! 1996, Benchmark LB $22.79 (978-0-7614-0407-1). 32pp. A history of airplanes that is notable for its informative large-print text and spectacular photos. (Rev: SLJ 2/97) [629.133]

25006 Oxlade, Chris. *Airplanes: Uncovering Technology* (4–8). Illus. Series: Uncovering. 2006, Firefly $16.95 (978-1-55407-134-0). 52pp. A well-illustrated survey of developments in air travel, with four overlay pages and a look at future possibilities. (Rev: SLJ 2/07) [629.133]

25007 Oxlade, Chris. *Plane* (4–6). Series: Take It Apart. 2002, Thameside $24.25 (978-1-930643-95-6). 32pp. Readers get an inside look at the various parts of a plane with cutaway illustrations, in-depth diagrams, and fact boxes. (Rev: BL 1/1–15/03; HBG 3/03) [629.133]

25008 Pallotta, Jerry, and Fred Pallotta. *The Airplane Alphabet Book* (2–4). Illus. by Rob Bolster. 1997, Charlesbridge $16.95 (978-0-88106-907-5). 32pp. Presents 26 airplanes plus information about the history of flight. (Rev: BL 2/1/97; SLJ 7/97) [629]

25009 Parker, Steve. *What's Inside Airplanes?* (4–8). Illus. Series: What's Inside? 1995, Bedrick LB $17.95 (978-0-87226-394-9). 45pp. Elaborate illustrations show various types of airplanes and describe their parts, including pistons, propellers, fuel tanks, and landing gear. (Rev: SLJ 12/95) [629.133]

25010 Priceman, Marjorie. *Hot Air: The (Mostly) True Story of the First Hot-Air Balloon Ride* (K–3). Illus. 2005, Simon & Schuster $16.95 (978-0-689-82642-9). 40pp. The Montgolfier brothers' first successful hot-air balloon flight is detailed with humor,

great illustrations, and a little embellishment. Caldecott Honor Book, 2006. (Rev: BL 7/05; SLJ 7/05) [629.133]

25011 Provensen, Alice, and Martin Provensen. *The Glorious Flight Across the Channel with Louis Bleriot* (1–5). Illus. by authors. 1983, Puffin paper $4.95 (978-0-317-63651-2). 40pp. The story of a historic flight by a French aviation pioneer. Caldecott Medal winner, 1984.

25012 Riehle, Mary Ann McCabe. *A Is for Airplane: An Aviation Alphabet* (2–4). Illus. by David Craig. 2009, Sleeping Bear $16.95 (978-1-58536-358-2). 32pp. This attractive alphabet book provides lots of history, science, and biographical information. (Rev: BLO 3/5/09) [629.1]

25013 Rinard, Judith E. *The Story of Flight* (3–6). Illus. 2002, Firefly $16.95 (978-1-55297-642-5); paper $8.95 (978-1-55297-694-4). 64pp. From balloon travel to possible manned space flights to Mars, this well-illustrated overview of the history of flight was published in cooperation with the National Air and Space Museum. (Rev: BL 12/15/02; HBG 3/03; SLJ 12/02) [629.1]

25014 Roberts, Cynthia. *Rescue Helicopters* (2–4). Series: Machines at Work. 2007, The Child's World LB $21.36 (978-1-59296-835-0). 24pp. Beginning and reluctant readers will enjoy this introduction to these helicopters and how they are used to rescue people in distress. Features many photographs. (Rev: SLJ 8/07)

25015 Santella, Andrew. *Air Force One* (4–7). Illus. 2003, Millbrook LB $24.90 (978-0-7613-2617-5). 48pp. An overview of the aircraft that have transported United States presidents, with an inside look at today's Air Force One. (Rev: BL 2/15/03; HBG 10/03; SLJ 8/03) [387.7]

25016 Sherrow, Victoria. *The Hindenburg Disaster: Doomed Airship* (4–8). Series: American Disasters. 2002, Enslow LB $23.93 (978-0-7660-1554-8). 48pp. Excellent illustrations and a clear text are used to tell the story of the destruction of the mighty German dirigible. (Rev: BL 6/1–15/02; HBG 10/02; SLJ 6/02) [629.133]

25017 *The Story of Flight* (4–6). Illus. Series: Voyages of Discovery. 1995, Scholastic $19.95 (978-0-590-47643-0). 45pp. Using die-cut pages, transparencies, foldouts, and stickers, this attractive book traces the history of flight and airplanes from ancient times to the present. (Rev: SLJ 5/96) [629]

Building and Construction

General

25018 *Architecture and Construction* (4–6). Illus. Series: Voyages of Discovery. 1995, Scholastic $19.95 (978-0-590-47644-7). 45pp. An introduction to architecture that spans the subject from simple shelters to such constructions as a Japanese paper house, skyscrapers, castles, and Frank Lloyd Wright's Fallingwater, with brief text and many illustrations, transparencies, foldouts, stickers, and a spiral binding. (Rev: SLJ 5/96) [720]

25019 Ardagh, Philip. *A Hole in the Road* (PS–K). Illus. by Tig Sutton. Series: British Mighty Machines. 2003, Thameside LB $24.25 (978-1-931983-02-0). 32pp. A burst water pipe causes a hole in the road and a great deal of digging, earth moving, and paving involving a variety of large machines. (Rev: BL 12/1/02; HBG 3/03) [621.8]

25020 Boring, Mel. *Incredible Constructions: And the People Who Built Them* (4–7). Illus. 1985, Walker LB $13.85 (978-0-8027-6560-4). Hoover Dam, the Statue of Liberty, and other structures are featured in this history of engineering marvels. (Rev: BL 6/1/85; SLJ 8/86) [620]

25021 Britton, Tamara. *The Empire State Building* (3–5). Series: Symbols, Landmarks, and Monuments. 2005, ABDO LB $22.78 (978-1-59197-834-3). 32pp. All about the famous New York landmark, with information on its history, construction, and importance. (Rev: SLJ 9/05)

25022 Britton, Tamara. *The Golden Gate Bridge* (3–5). Series: Symbols, Landmarks, and Monuments. 2005, ABDO LB $22.78 (978-1-59197-835-0). 32pp. All about the famous California landmark, with information on its history, its construction, and its importance. (Rev: SLJ 9/05) [624]

25023 Caney, Steven. *Steven Caney's Ultimate Building Book* (4–8). Illus. by Lauren House. 2006, Running Pr. $29.95 (978-0-7624-0409-4). 596pp. Starting with a history of construction and the basic techniques involved, Caney looks at the ways design and technology intersect and suggests a wide range of kid-tested building projects. (Rev: SLJ 1/07*) [624]

25024 Cash, Terry. *Bricks* (3–5). Illus. by Ed Barber. Series: Threads. 1990, Garrett LB $15.93 (978-0-944483-68-8). 26pp. The history of bricks, how they are made, and their many uses are explored. (Rev: BL 2/1/91; SLJ 5/91) [666]

25025 Delafosse, Claude. *Construction* (PS–2). Illus. Series: First Discovery. 1997, Scholastic paper $12.95 (978-0-590-93783-2). 24pp. Various forms of building and their processes are introduced simply with interesting visuals that encourage interaction. (Rev: BL 2/15/97) [338.476]

25026 *Do Buildings Have Bones? First Questions and Answers About Buildings* (PS–3). Illus. Series: Time-Life Library of First Questions and Answers. 1995, Time-Life $14.95 (978-0-7835-0900-6). 48pp. A series of questions and answers supplies basic information about buildings and construction. (Rev: BL 8/95) [720]

25027 Donovan, Sandy. *The Channel Tunnel* (4–7). Series: Great Building Feats. 2003, Lerner LB $27.93 (978-0-8225-4692-4). 96pp. Using many black-and-white illustrations, diagrams, and maps, this is the exciting story of the underwater engineering marvel that links England and France. (Rev: BL 11/15/03; HBG 10/03; SLJ 11/03) [624.1]

25028 Dreyer, Francis. *Lighthouses* (4–7). Photos by Philip Plisson. 2005, Abrams $18.95 (978-0-8109-5958-3). 78pp. A fascinating and strikingly beauti-

ful overview of lighthouses — of the past and present — and of the courage and loneliness of the men and women who tend them. (Rev: BL 1/1–15/06) [387.1]

25029 DuTemple, Lesley A. *The Hoover Dam* (4–7). Series: Great Building Feats. 2003, Lerner LB $27.93 (978-0-8225-4691-7). 96pp. This story traces the dam's construction from the planning stages through its technically difficult and dangerous construction and places this impressive structure in historical context. (Rev: BL 11/15/03; HBG 10/03; SLJ 11/03) [627]

25030 Farbman, Melinda. *Bridges* (2–4). Series: Transportation and Communication. 2001, Enslow LB $23.93 (978-0-7660-1647-7). 48pp. Basic facts are given on the history of bridges and their present-day construction in this heavily illustrated volume. (Rev: BL 3/15/02; HBG 3/02) [624]

25031 Gonzales, Doreen. *Seven Wonders of the Modern World* (4–7). Illus. Series: Seven Wonders of the World. 2005, Enslow LB $25.26 (978-0-7660-5292-5). 48pp. Profiles seven marvels of modern construction, including the Panama Canal, Toronto's CN Tower, and the Empire State Building in New York City; the text is extended by constantly updated links to Web sites. (Rev: SLJ 11/05)

25032 Good, Keith. *Build It! Activities for Setting Up Super Structures* (3–7). Series: Design It! 2000, Lerner LB $21.27 (978-0-8225-3567-6). 30pp. This book of projects explores ideas for bridges, domes, structures that collapse, and pop-ups in a clear format with good directions. (Rev: HBG 9/00; SLJ 6/00) [624]

25033 Goodman, Susan E. *Skyscraper* (2–5). 2004, Knopf $18.99 (978-0-375-91309-9). 40pp. The myriad details involved in designing and building a skyscraper are accompanied by personal stories that draw the reader into the process. (Rev: BL 12/1/04*; SLJ 2/05) [720]

25034 Greene, Meg. *The Eiffel Tower* (5–8). Series: Building World Landmarks. 2004, Gale LB $24.95 (978-1-56711-315-0). 48pp. The story of the construction of the Eiffel Tower, which when completed in 1899 was the tallest human-made structure in the world. (Rev: SLJ 7/04) [725]

25035 Gresko, Marcia S. *The Grand Coulee Dam* (4–6). Illus. Series: Building America. 1999, Blackbirch LB $23.70 (978-1-56711-174-3). 48pp. The story of the construction of the Grand Coulee Dam, the largest single producer of hydroelectric power in the U.S. since World War II. (Rev: BL 12/1/99; HBG 4/00; SLJ 2/00) [627]

25036 Hill, Lee S. *Bridges Connect* (1–3). Illus. Series: Building Blocks Books. 1997, Carolrhoda $14.60 (978-1-57505-021-8). 32pp. Using color photos and a simple text, the structure of bridges is introduced. Also use *Canals Are Water Roads* and *Dams Give Us Power* (both 1997). (Rev: BL 9/15/97; SLJ 7/97) [624]

25037 Hill, Lee S. *Monuments Help Us Remember* (1–3). Illus. Series: Building Blocks Books. 2000, Carolrhoda $21.27 (978-1-57505-475-9). 32pp. This simple book takes the reader on a tour of the world's most famous monuments, including the Statue of Liberty. (Rev: BL 9/15/00; HBG 3/01) [720]

25038 Hill, Lee S. *Roads Take Us Home* (1–3). Illus. Series: Building Blocks Books. 1997, Carolrhoda LB $21.27 (978-1-57505-022-5). 32pp. Types of roads and their construction are introduced in color photos and a simple text. Also use *Towers Reach High* (1997). (Rev: BL 9/15/97; SLJ 7/97) [388.1]

25039 Hill, Lee S. *Tunnels Go Underground* (1–3). Illus. Series: Building Blocks Books. 2000, Carolrhoda $14.60 (978-1-57505-429-2). 32pp. Many different kinds of tunnels are covered, from mining tunnels in Pennsylvania to the tunnel that runs under the English Channel. (Rev: BL 9/15/00; HBG 3/01) [725]

25040 Hudson, Cheryl W. *Construction Zone* (K–3). Illus. by Richard Sobol. 2006, Candlewick $15.99 (978-0-7636-2684-6). 32pp. A fascinating behind-the-scenes glimpse of the construction of a building designed by noted architect Frank Gehry, featuring eye-catching photographs and definitions of specialized vocabulary. (Rev: BL 9/1/06; SLJ 6/06) [690]

25041 Hunter, Ryan Ann. *Cross a Bridge* (PS–2). Illus. by Edward Miller. 1998, Holiday House LB $15.95 (978-0-8234-1340-9). A simple picture book that describes various kinds of bridges. (Rev: BL 4/1/98; HBG 9/98; SLJ 3/98) [625]

25042 Hunter, Ryan Ann. *Dig a Tunnel* (PS–2). Illus. by Edward Miller. 1999, Holiday House $15.95 (978-0-8234-1391-1). 24pp. Beginning with the tunnels dug by animals like moles, this book continues with explanations of how humans have dug tunnels throughout history and the tools they used. (Rev: BCCB 5/99; BL 3/15/99; HBG 9/99; SLJ 4/99) [624.1]

25043 Hunter, Ryan Ann. *Into the Sky* (PS–2). Illus. by Edward Miller. 1998, Holiday House $15.95 (978-0-8234-1372-0). 32pp. This is a heavily illustrated history of the skyscraper (ending with Japan's planned 196-floor Sky City 1000), with details on how they are built and problems encountered during construction. (Rev: BL 9/15/98; HBG 3/99; SLJ 9/98) [720]

25044 Jefferis, David. *Megastructures* (3–6). Series: Record Breakers. 2003, Raintree LB $25.69 (978-0-7398-6324-4). 32pp. In this overview of large-scale structures, part of the Record Breakers series, author David Jefferis looks at massive tunnels, bridges, castles, and domes. (Rev: HBG 10/03; SLJ 7/03)

25045 Johmann, Carol A., and Elizabeth J. Rieth. *Bridges! Amazing Structures to Design, Build and Test* (4–6). Illus. Series: Kaleidoscope Kids. 1999, Williamson paper $14.25 (978-1-885593-30-6). 96pp. Bridge construction, design, mechanics, and maintenance are covered in this paperback that also contains several interesting projects. (Rev: BL 1/1–15/00; SLJ 3/00) [624]

25046 Kirkwood, Jon. *The Fantastic Cutaway Book of Giant Buildings* (4–7). Illus. 1997, Millbrook paper $9.95 (978-0-7613-0629-0). 40pp. Using double-page spreads, outstanding graphics, and many fact boxes, this book features a wide variety of

structures including the Statue of Liberty, the pyramids, the Colosseum, churches, operas houses, Grand Central Station, Munich's Olympic stadium, and skyscrapers. (Rev: BL 4/1/98; HBG 10/98) [720]

25047 Leboutillier, Nate. *Eiffel Tower* (3–6). Series: Modern Wonders of the World. 2006, Creative Education LB $27.10 (978-1-58341-438-5). 32pp. Leboutillier tells the story of the construction of the tower — in the face of much protest and technical challenges — and documents its history, including many unusual feats, and its contemporary importance as a symbol. (Rev: SLJ 12/06) [725]

25048 Levy, Debbie. *The World Trade Center* (4–6). Illus. Series: Great Structures in History. 2005, Gale LB $26.20 (978-0-7377-2071-6). 48pp. Chronicles the six-year construction project — including design and excavation, their symbolism, and the eventual destruction of the towers. (Rev: BL 12/1/05) [720]

25049 Macaulay, David. *Unbuilding* (5–8). Illus. by author. 1980, Houghton $19.00 (978-0-395-29457-4); paper $6.95 (978-0-395-45360-5). 128pp. A book that explores the concept of tearing down the Empire State Building.

25050 Macaulay, David. *Underground* (5–10). Illus. by author. 1983, Houghton $19.00 (978-0-395-24739-6); paper $9.95 (978-0-395-34065-3). An exploration in text and detailed drawings of the intricate network of systems under city streets. [624]

25051 MacKen, JoAnn Early. *Digging Tunnels* (PS–1). Illus. Series: Building World Landmarks. 2008, Capstone LB $14.95 (978-1-4296-1234-0). 32pp. Macken uses full-page color photographs and large, simple text to show types of tunnels and how they are built. (Rev: BL 8/08; SLJ 8/08) [624.1]

25052 Mann, Elizabeth. *The Brooklyn Bridge* (4–7). Illus. Series: Wonders of the World. 1996, Mikaya $19.95 (978-0-9650493-0-6). 48pp. The story of the building of the Brooklyn Bridge is told through the eyes of a family. (Rev: BL 2/1/97; SLJ 6/97*) [624]

25053 Mann, Elizabeth. *Empire State Building* (3–8). Illus. by Alan Witschonke. Series: Wonders of the World Books. 2003, Mikaya $19.95 (978-1-931414-06-7). 48pp. With a four-page foldout, period photographs, and full-color illustrations, this story of the skyscraper's construction will please both browsers and report writers. (Rev: BL 2/1/04; SLJ 4/04) [974.7]

25054 Mattern, Joanne. *The Chunnel* (5–8). Series: Building World Landmarks. 2004, Gale LB $24.95 (978-1-56711-301-3). 48pp. The story of the long delays and eventual construction of the tunnel under the English Channel, linking England and France, with a focus on the new technology involved. (Rev: SLJ 7/04) [624.1]

25055 Mellentin, Kath. *Let's Build an Airport* (K–3). Illus. 1998, Zero to Ten LB $14.95 (978-1-84089-026-6). 32pp. From the decision to build an airport to the opening day celebrations this is a step-by-step account of how an airport is built. (Rev: BL 3/1/99; HBG 3/99) [629.136]

25056 Murray, Julie. *Golden Gate Bridge* (2–3). Illus. Series: All Aboard America. 2003, ABDO LB

$21.35 (978-1-57765-672-2). 24pp. A brief history of the huge San Francisco suspension bridge. (Rev: HBG 10/03; SLJ 11/03) [624]

25057 Neumann, Dietrich. *Joe and the Skyscraper: The Empire State Building in New York City* (2–4). Illus. Series: Where We Live. 2000, Prestel $14.95 (3-7913-2103-X). 32pp. Seen through the eyes of a 16-year-old waterboy, this is the story of the construction of the Empire State Building. (Rev: BL 4/15/00*; SLJ 4/00) [720.483]

25058 Owens, Thomas S. *Football Stadiums* (5–8). Illus. Series: Sports Palaces. 2001, Millbrook LB $25.90 (978-0-7613-1764-7). 64pp. Rather than highlighting individual stadiums, this book covers general topics such as their design, replacement, funding, amenities, and history. (Rev: BL 4/1/01; HBG 10/01; SLJ 4/01) [796.332]

25059 Oxlade, Chris. *Skyscrapers* (3–5). Series: Building Amazing Structures. 2000, Heinemann LB $22.79 (978-1-57572-278-8). 32pp. This colorful book introduces skyscrapers and describes their construction, materials, and functions with many examples of historical and contemporary buildings. Also use *Stadiums* and *Tunnels* (both 2000). (Rev: HBG 10/01; SLJ 3/01) [720.4]

25060 Oxlade, Chris. *Skyscrapers: Uncovering Technology* (4–6). Series: Uncovering. 2006, Firefly $16.95 (978-1-55407-136-4). 52pp. This overview of the world's skyscrapers — past, present, and future — looks briefly at some of the most notable structures, as well as the design and technological challenges involved in building them, and offers several mylar overlays. (Rev: BL 10/15/06; SLJ 2/07) [720]

25061 Richards, Jon. *Diggers and Other Construction Machines* (1–3). Illus. 1999, Millbrook LB $23.90 (978-0-7613-0905-5). 40pp. An informative book that highlights all kinds of diggers and allied machinery, along with details of tunnel construction. (Rev: BL 8/99; HBG 9/99) [624.1]

25062 Roza, Greg. *The Incredible Story of Skyscrapers* (3–6). Illus. Series: A Kid's Guide to Incredible Technology. 2004, Rosen LB $21.25 (978-0-8239-6716-2). 24pp. Discusses the challenges and techniques of building skyscrapers, with a look at some famous buildings and at the potential size of future ones. (Rev: SLJ 2/05) [720]

25063 Severance, John B. *Skyscrapers: How America Grew Up* (5–9). Illus. 2000, Holiday $18.95 (978-0-8234-1492-5). 96pp. Beginning with an explanation of the architectural breakthroughs that made the building of skyscrapers possible, this account traces the construction of these buildings from 1851 to the end of the 20th century. (Rev: BL 6/1–15/00; HB 9/00; HBG 10/00; SLJ 7/00; VOYA 4/01) [720]

25064 Stone, Lynn M. *Bridges* (3–5). Illus. Series: How Are They Built? 2001, Rourke LB $29.93 (978-1-58952-135-3). 48pp. How, why, and where bridges are built, with photographs, a glossary, and other features. Also use *Dams* (2001). (Rev: BL 10/15/01) [624]

25065 Stone, Lynn M. *Roads and Highways* (3–5). Series: How Are They Built? 2001, Rourke LB $29.93 (978-1-58952-138-4). 48pp. Following information on the history of roads, this book gives details on highway construction today, the materials used, and the techniques employed. (Rev: BL 10/15/01) [625.7]

25066 Stone, Lynn M. *Skyscrapers* (3–5). Series: How Are They Built? 2001, Rourke LB $29.93 (978-1-58952-139-1). 48pp. Background material on skyscrapers is followed by coverage of how they are built, their design, materials used, and present-day practices and concerns. (Rev: BL 10/15/01) [720]

25067 Sturges, Philemon. *Bridges Are to Cross* (3–6). Illus. by Giles Laroche. 1998, Penguin $15.99 (978-0-399-23174-2). 32pp. A series of double-page spreads show the beauty and usefulness of bridges — from the Brooklyn Bridge to Chenonceau, where a bridge is part of the castle. (Rev: BL 12/15/98) [624.2]

25068 Sullivan, George. *Built to Last: Building America's Amazing Bridges, Dams, Tunnels, and Skyscrapers* (5–8). Illus. 2005, Scholastic $18.99 (978-0-439-51737-9). 128pp. Seventeen marvels of American engineering — including the Erie Canal, Hoover Dam, Brooklyn Bridge, and Boston's "Big Dig" — are presented in chronological chapters with good illustrations and fact boxes that add historical and technological context. (Rev: BL 12/1/05; SLJ 3/06*; VOYA 8/06) [624]

25069 Woods, Mary B., and Michael Woods. *Ancient Construction: From Tents to Towers* (5–8). Illus. Series: Ancient Technologies. 2000, Runestone LB $25.26 (978-0-8225-2998-9). 88pp. From Stonehenge and the Colosseum to the Eiffel Tower and the Golden Gate Bridge, this is a history of building and construction. (Rev: BL 9/15/00; HBG 3/01; SLJ 1/01) [720]

25070 Yuan, Margaret Speaker. *The Royal Gorge Bridge* (5–8). Series: Building World Landmarks. 2004, Gale LB $24.95 (978-1-56711-352-5). 48pp. Examines the engineering and construction challenges involved in the 1929 construction of Colorado's Royal Gorge Bridge. (Rev: SLJ 7/04) [624.2]

25071 Zaunders, Bo. *The Great Bridge-Building Contest* (3–5). Illus. by Roxie Munro. 2004, Abrams $16.95 (978-0-8109-4929-4). 32pp. With fine illustrations, this is the story of 19th-century cabinetmaker Lemuel Chenoweth's successful bid to design a bridge. (Rev: BL 12/1/04; SLJ 3/05) [624.2]

Houses

25072 Andersen, Jenna. *How It Happens at the Building Site* (K–3). Illus. Series: How It Happens. 2004, Oliver $19.95 (978-1-881508-95-3). 32pp. An inside look at the work that goes into the construction of a home. (Rev: BL 1/1–15/05) [690]

25073 Bial, Raymond. *The Houses* (4–8). Illus. Series: Building America. 2001, Marshall Cavendish LB $27.07 (978-0-7614-1335-6). 56pp. A history of different types of housing in the United States that includes excellent photographs and drawings. (Rev: BL 3/1/02; HBG 3/02) [392.3]

25074 Gallimard Jeunesse, and Claude Delafosse. *Houses* (PS–2). Series: First Discovery. 1998, Scholastic $12.95 (978-0-590-38152-9). 24pp. Sturdy plastic pages and overlays are used to describe the construction of a house and its parts. (Rev: BL 9/15/98; HBG 9/98) [690]

25075 Gustafson, Angela. *Imagine a House: A Journey to Fascinating Houses Around the World* (2–5). Illus. 2003, Out of the Box $16.95 (978-0-9726849-0-3). 32pp. A dozen houses around the world serve as examples of the diversity of architecture and creativity. (Rev: SLJ 2/04) [392.3]

25076 Hill, Lee S. *Homes Keep Us Warm* (1–3). Illus. Series: Building Blocks Books. 2000, Carolrhoda $21.27 (978-1-57505-430-8). 32pp. This book explores all kinds of homes, from huts made with animal skins to city apartments, farmhouses, and bungalows. (Rev: BL 9/15/00; HBG 3/01) [690]

25077 Komatsu, Yoshio. *Wonderful Houses Around the World* (3–5). Trans. from Japanese by Katy Bridges and Naoko Amemiya. Photos by author. Illus. by Akira Nishiyama. 2004, Shelter $14.95 (978-0-936070-35-3); paper $8.95 (978-0-936070-34-6). 43pp. A Mongolian yurt, a Chinese circular tulou, and a Tunisian underground home are among the 10 houses included, with cutaway diagrams and information on decor and inhabitants. (Rev: SLJ 4/05)

25078 Newhouse, Maxwell. *The House That Max Built* (PS–2). Illus. by author. 2008, Tundra $18.95 (978-0-88776-774-6). 24pp. A detailed look at how houses are constructed, covering all phases from design through foundation, framing, siding, plumbing, and so forth, ending with landscaping and a glossary of the tradesmen involved. (Rev: BL 4/15/08; SLJ 5/08) [690]

25079 Stone, Lynn M. *Houses* (3–5). Series: How Are They Built? 2001, Rourke LB $19.95 (978-1-58952-137-7). 48pp. After some historical material, this book describes how houses are built today and the materials used. (Rev: BL 10/15/01) [690]

Clothing, Textiles, and Jewelry

25080 Bryant-Mole, Karen. *Clothes* (K–3). Illus. Series: Picture This! 1997, Rigby $18.50 (978-1-57572-149-1). 24pp. This book shows what clothes are made of and which should be worn on different occasions. (Rev: BL 10/15/97) [646]

25081 Carlson, Laurie. *Queen of Inventions: How the Sewing Machine Changed the World* (3–5). Illus. 2003, Millbrook LB $22.90 (978-0-7613-2706-6). 32pp. The history of the sewing machine and its impact on home and commercial garment-making, with illustrations and photographs. (Rev: BL 2/15/03; HBG 10/03; SLJ 4/03) [681]

25082 Dixon, Annabelle. *Wool* (3–5). Illus. by Ed Barber. Series: Threads. 1990, Garrett LB $15.93 (978-0-944483-73-2). 26pp. The nature of wool, its

origins, and its uses are explored in text and pictures. (Rev: BL 2/1/91) [677.31]

25083 Elgin, Kathy. *France* (3–5). Series: Costume Around the World. 2008, Chelsea Clubhouse LB $28.00 (978-0-7910-9766-3). 32pp. Elgin introduces the traditional costumes of France and discusses the influences of climate, culture, religion, and so forth. (Rev: LMC 11/08; SLJ 9/08)

25084 Greenberg, Keith E. *Bill Bowerman and Phil Knight: Building the Nike Empire* (3–4). Illus. by Dick Smolinski. Series: Partners. 1994, Blackbirch LB $20.56 (978-1-56711-085-2). 47pp. The story of the pair who created the Nike empire and the production of the first "waffle sole" using a waffle iron. (Rev: SLJ 1/95) [391]

25085 Hoobler, Dorothy, and Thomas Hoobler. *Vanity Rules: A History of American Fashion and Beauty* (5–8). Illus. 2000, Twenty-First Century LB $28.90 (978-0-7613-1258-1). 160pp. From the painted bodies of early Native Americans to today's body piercing, this is a history of the quest for personal beauty in America. (Rev: BL 4/1/00; HBG 10/00; SLJ 5/00) [391]

25086 Kalman, Bobbie. *18th Century Clothing* (3–6). Illus. Series: Historic Communities. 1993, Crabtree LB $25.27 (978-0-86505-492-9); paper $7.95 (978-0-86505-512-4). 32pp. Many illustrations and simple text show how people of all levels of society dressed in the 18th century. A companion volume is: *19th Century Clothing* (1993). (Rev: BL 8/93; SLJ 9/93) [391]

25087 Lawlor, Laurie. *Where Will This Shoe Take You? A Walk Through the History of Footwear* (5–8). Illus. 1996, Walker LB $18.85 (978-0-8027-8435-3). 144pp. This is a history of footwear, from sandals worn by the ancients to the sneakers popular today. (Rev: BCCB 1/97; BL 11/15/96; SLJ 5/97; VOYA 6/97) [391]

25088 Llewellyn, Claire. *Silk* (2–4). Illus. Series: Material World. 2002, Watts LB $24.00 (978-0-531-14630-9). 30pp. A well-illustrated look at silk, how it is manufactured, and the various types; with "Fast Facts," related activities, and a glossary. (Rev: SLJ 5/03) [677]

25089 Miller, Brandon M. *Dressed for the Occasion: What Americans Wore, 1620–1970* (5–8). 1999, Lerner LB $30.35 (978-0-8225-1738-2). A fascinating look at men's and women's fashions throughout history and how they reflect society's culture and values. (Rev: BCCB 5/99; BL 4/1/99; SLJ 9/99) [391]

25090 Morris, Ann. *Shoes, Shoes, Shoes* (PS–2). Illus. 1995, Lothrop LB $14.93 (978-0-688-13667-3). 32pp. Thirty-one shoes from a variety of cultures are identified and pictured. (Rev: BCCB 10/95; BL 10/1/95; SLJ 1/96) [391]

25091 Nelson, Robin. *From Cotton to T-Shirt* (PS–2). Illus. Series: Start to Finish. 2003, Lerner $18.60 (978-0-8225-4661-0). 24pp. This colorful picture book traces the production of a T-shirt from the picking of the cotton that will be its main ingredient through each step of the manufacturing process. (Rev: BL 4/15/03; HBG 10/03; SLJ 7/03) [633.5]

25092 Nelson, Robin. *From Sheep to Sweater* (1–3). Series: Start to Finish. 2003, Lerner LB $18.60 (978-0-8225-0716-1). 24pp. This accessible overview follows the process of a wool sweater's creation from shearing of the sheep to finished product. (Rev: HBG 10/03; SLJ 8/03) [746.43]

25093 Nichelason, Margery G. *Shoes* (3–5). Illus. 1997, Carolrhoda $22.60 (978-1-57505-047-8). 48pp. From the first shoes worn by the Egyptians to today's latest trends, this is the surprising history of footwear through the years. (Rev: BL 1/1–15/98; HB 5/97; HBG 3/98) [391.4]

25094 Oxlade, Chris. *Cotton* (2–3). Series: Materials, Materials, Materials. 2002, Heinemann LB $22.79 (978-1-58810-584-4). 32pp. With a color picture and brief text on each page, this is a basic introduction to cotton and how it is grown, processed, and made into other things. (Rev: BL 6/1–15/02) [633.5]

25095 Oxlade, Chris. *Wool* (2–3). Illus. Series: Materials, Materials, Materials. 2001, Heinemann LB $21.36 (978-1-58810-159-4). 32pp. Photographs accompany detailed information about where wool comes from and how it is made into products we use. (Rev: BL 10/15/01) [677]

25096 Reynolds, Helen. *Jewelry and Accessories* (3–8). Illus. Series: A Fashionable History of Costume. 2003, Raintree LB $25.70 (978-1-4109-0029-6). 32pp. Traces the evolution of accessories and jewelry from the beginning of recorded history to the present. (Rev: HBG 10/03; SLJ 9/03) [391.4]

25097 Reynolds, Helen. *The Shoe* (3–8). Illus. Series: A Fashionable History of Costume. 2003, Raintree LB $25.70 (978-1-4109-0027-2). 32pp. Traces the evolution of footwear from the beginning of recorded history to the present. (Rev: HBG 10/03; SLJ 9/03) [391.4]

25098 Shaskan, Kathy. *How Underwear Got Under There: A Brief History* (5–8). Illus. by Regan Dunnick. 2007, Dutton $16.99 (978-0-525-47178-3). 48pp. Shaskan takes a lighthearted look at the history of nether garments, looking at their various roles (protection, warmth, modesty, support, and so forth) and at changes in fashion and social attitudes; a lack of sources makes this most suitable for browsing. (Rev: BCCB 9/07; LMC 11/07; SLJ 8/07) [391.4]

25099 Straus, Lucy. *The Story of Shoes* (PS). Illus. by Mas Miyamoto. Series: Real Readers. 1989, Raintree LB $21.40 (978-0-8172-3534-5). 32pp. This easily read account describes how shoes evolved from ancient times. (Rev: BL 2/1/90) [391]

25100 Tythacott, Louise. *Jewelry* (4–8). Illus. Series: Traditions Around the World. 1995, Thomson Learning LB $24.26 (978-1-56847-229-4). 48pp. A history of jewelry, why it is worn, and the variety of materials and designs used. (Rev: SLJ 7/95) [739.27]

25101 Weaver, Janice. *From Head to Toe: Bound Feet, Bathing Suits, and Other Bizarre and Beautiful Things* (5–8). Illus. by Francis Blake. 2003, Tundra paper $16.95 (978-0-88776-654-1). 80pp. History and culture are interwoven in this account of fashion fads over the years, mostly in the West. (Rev: SLJ 2/04) [391]

25102 Whitty, Helen. *Protective Clothing* (3–8). Illus. Series: Clothing. 2001, Chelsea LB $22.95 (978-0-7910-6574-7). 32pp. An interesting look at apparel that includes aprons, armor, firefighting suits, and space suits. Also use *You Are What You Wear* and *Underwear* (both 2001). (Rev: HBG 3/02; SLJ 12/01) [745]

25103 Woods, Samuel G. *Kids' Clothes from Start to Finish* (3–5). Series: Made in the USA. 2001, Blackbirch LB $23.70 (978-1-56711-483-6). 32pp. The steps in the manufacture of children's clothing from design to finished product are discussed in this colorful, easily read account. (Rev: BL 3/15/02; HBG 3/02) [687]

25104 Woods, Samuel G. *Sneakers: From Start to Finish* (3–5). Illus. Series: Made in the USA. 1999, Blackbirch LB $23.70 (978-1-56711-393-8). 32pp. The manufacture of sneakers is covered in this book that gives a tour of the New Balance Athletic Shoe factory in Lawrence, Massachusetts. (Rev: BL 12/1/99; HBG 4/00; SLJ 3/00) [685]

Computers and Automation

25105 Bailey, Diane. *Cyber Ethics* (4–6). Illus. Series: Cyber Citizenship and Cyber Safety. 2008, Rosen LB $19.95 (978-1-4042-1349-4). 48pp. Privacy, plagiarism, and bullying are among the topics discussed in this accessible volume. (Rev: BL 4/1/08; LMC 10/08; SLJ 7/08) [175]

25106 Baker, Christopher W. *Let There Be Life! Animating with the Computer* (4–6). Illus. 1997, Walker LB $17.85 (978-0-8027-8473-5). 48pp. An overview of the basics of computer animation, illustrated with stills from feature films, shorts, and commercials. (Rev: BL 1/1–15/98; HBG 3/98) [778.2]

25107 Baker, Christopher W. *Robots Among Us: The Challenges and Promises of Robotics* (5–8). Illus. Series: New Century Technology. 2002, Millbrook LB $23.90 (978-0-7613-1969-6). 48pp. A lavishly illustrated account that describes the science of robotics, current developments, and what might be expected in the future. (Rev: BL 6/1–15/02; HBG 10/02; SLJ 9/02) [629.8]

25108 Baker, Christopher W. *Scientific Visualization: The New Eyes of Science* (5–8). Illus. Series: New Century Technology. 2000, Millbrook LB $23.90 (978-0-7613-1351-9). 48pp. This book explores the ways in which computers enable scientists to study the universe and simulate events such as the creation of a black hole. (Rev: BL 4/1/00; HBG 3/01; SLJ 6/00) [507.2]

25109 Bingham, Jane. *Internet Freedom: Where Is the Limit?* (5–8). Series: Behind the News. 2006, Heinemann LB $32.86 (978-1-4034-8833-6). 56pp. Short news stories highlight the problems involved in the freedom we find on the Internet and chapters discuss how to evaluate the stories behind the news and the pros and cons of Internet regulation. (Rev: SLJ 4/07)

25110 Chorlton, Windsor. *The Invention of the Silicon Chip: A Revolution in Daily Life* (5–8). Series: Point of Impact. 2002, Heinemann LB $25.64 (978-1-58810-554-7). 32pp. Chorlton explores computers before and after the invention of the chip, introduces key players in the field, and discusses the impact of this new technology on society. (Rev: SLJ 9/02) [621.3815]

25111 Cook, Peter, and Scott Manning. *Why Doesn't My Floppy Disk Flop? And Other Kids' Computer Questions Answered by the CompuDudes* (3–5). Illus. 1999, Wiley paper $12.95 (978-0-471-18429-4). 90pp. Using a question-and-answer approach, this book covers hardware, software, the Internet, good computer practices, and the future of computers. (Rev: BL 9/1/99) [004]

25112 Domaine, Helena. *Robotics* (4–6). Illus. Series: Cool Science! 2005, Lerner LB $26.60 (978-0-8225-2112-9). 48pp. An attractive, colorful exploration of the history of robotics and the ways in which this technology is likely to affect life in the future. (Rev: BL 9/1/05; SLJ 12/05) [629.8]

25113 Douglas, Julie. *The Internet* (2–4). Series: Transportation and Communication. 2002, Enslow LB $23.93 (978-0-7660-1889-1). 48pp. A basic introduction to the Internet that supplies material on what it is, its history, people behind it, safety while online, and possible future developments. (Rev: BL 9/15/02; HBG 3/03) [004]

25114 Drake, Jim. *Computers All Around Us* (2–4). Illus. Series: Log On to Computers. 1999, Heinemann LB $21.36 (978-1-57572-784-4). 32pp. An easily read oversize book that explains the many uses of computers in such places as grocery stores, factories, and offices. (Rev: BL 7/99; SLJ 11/99) [004]

25115 Drake, Jim. *Computers and School* (2–4). Series: Log On to Computers. 1999, Heinemann LB $14.95 (978-1-57572-785-1). 32pp. Large color photographs and a concise text are used to explore the ways computers can be used to gather information to help in school assignments and other related activities. (Rev: BL 7/99; SLJ 12/99) [004]

25116 Drake, Jim. *Play with Computers* (2–4). Series: Log On to Computers. 1999, Heinemann LB $21.36 (978-1-57572-786-8). 32pp. Double-page spreads featuring large print and bright photographs explore various ways children can use the computer for recreation. (Rev: BL 7/99; SLJ 11/99) [004]

25117 Drake, Jim. *What Is a Computer?* (2–4). Illus. Series: Log On to Computers. 1999, Heinemann LB $21.36 (978-1-57572-787-5). 32pp. A large-size book that gives a history of computers, explains software and hardware, and relates computers to the everyday life of youngsters. (Rev: BL 7/99; SLJ 12/99) [004]

25118 Fritz, Sandy. *Robotics and Artificial Intelligence* (5–10). Illus. Series: Hot Science. 2003, Smart Apple LB $28.50 (978-1-58340-364-8). 48pp. After describing robots' contributions in space, in the workplace, in danger spots, and in medicine, Fritz speculates on the future possibilities. (Rev: BL 12/1/03; HBG 4/04; SLJ 4/04) [629.8]

25119 Gallimard Jeunesse, et al. *Internet* (PS–2). Series: First Discovery. 2000, Scholastic $12.95 (978-0-439-14825-2). 24pp. A beginning look at computers and the Internet with large illustrations and clear, simple explanations. (Rev: BL 8/00; HBG 3/01; SLJ 11/00) [004]

25120 Herumin, Wendy. *Censorship on the Internet: From Filters to Freedom of Speech* (5–12). Series: Issues in Focus. 2004, Enslow LB $26.60 (978-0-7660-1946-1). 128pp. A look at the various ways we restrict the free exchange of information over the Internet and the pros and cons of doing so. (Rev: SLJ 4/04) [303.48]

25121 Jefferis, David. *Artificial Intelligence: Robotics and Machine Evolution* (5–7). Series: Megatech. 1999, Crabtree paper $8.95 (978-0-7787-0056-2). 32pp. This is a survey of the variety of robotic devices in use at the end of the 20th century, some of the advances that are being made, and a glimpse into the future. (Rev: SLJ 9/99) [004]

25122 Jefferis, David. *Internet: Electronic Global Village* (4–8). Illus. Series: Megatech. 2001, Crabtree paper $8.95 (978-0-7787-0062-3). 32pp. An eye-catching look at the development of the Internet and the World Wide Web and their uses in communication and commerce. (Rev: SLJ 6/02) [4.678]

25123 Jones, David. *Mighty Robots: Mechanical Marvels That Fascinate and Frighten* (5–8). Illus. 2006, Annick $24.95 (978-1-55037-929-7); paper $14.95 (978-1-55037-928-0). 126pp. Artificial intelligence, mobility, and various robot roles are discussed in this look at the past, present, and future of robots. (Rev: BL 2/1/06) [629.8]

25124 Jortberg, Charles A. *The Internet* (4–6). Illus. Series: Kids and Computers. 1997, ABDO LB $24.21 (978-1-56239-727-2). 38pp. A history of the Internet, how to use it, and a listing of important sites for kids. (Rev: BL 6/1–15/97; HBG 3/98) [004.6]

25125 Knittel, John, and Michael Soto. *Everything You Need to Know About the Dangers of Computer Hacking* (5–8). Illus. 2000, Rosen LB $25.25 (978-0-8239-3034-0). 64pp. This book points out the differences between a hacker and a cracker and, through this, discusses beneficial and harmful computer actions and how to avoid the latter. (Rev: BL 4/1/00; SLJ 5/00) [364.16]

25126 Lauber, Patricia. *Get Ready for Robots!* (K–3). Illus. by True Kelley. 1987, HarperCollins $12.95 (978-0-690-04576-5). 32pp. An introduction to robots that work in space, under water, and in factories. (Rev: BCCB 3/87; BL 2/15/87; SLJ 6–7/87)

25127 Lawler, Jennifer. *Cyberdanger and Internet Safety: A Hot Issue* (5–10). Series: Hot Issues. 2000, Enslow LB $27.93 (978-0-7660-1368-1). 64pp. As well as introducing the Internet, this account explains how people abuse it with hidden identities, threatening or obscene material, loss of privacy, hacking, con tricks, pranks, and hoaxes. (Rev: HBG 3/01; SLJ 1/01; VOYA 4/01) [004.6]

25128 Lemke, Donald. *Steve Jobs, Steve Wozniak, and the Personal Computer* (4–6). Illus. by Tod Smith. Series: Graphic Library: Inventions and Discovery. 2006, Capstone LB $26.60 (978-0-7368-6488-6). 32pp. A graphic-novel presentation of the story of Apple Computer, profiling its two young creators; the art has less value than the information presented but will attract some students to this history. (Rev: BL 10/15/06) [621.39092]

25129 Lindsay, Dave. *Dave's Quick 'n' Easy Web Pages: An Introductory Guide to Creating Web Sites.* 2nd ed. (5–9). Illus. by Sean Lindsay. 2001, Erin $11.95 (978-0-9690609-8-7). 116pp. Young Dave, Webmaster of the popular Redwall site, gives good, basic information on HTML coding and Web page design. (Rev: SLJ 8/01) [005.7]

25130 Loughran, Donna. *Using the Internet Safely* (3–5). Series: Technology and You. 2003, Raintree LB $27.12 (978-0-7398-4697-1). 48pp. A guide to avioding the pitfalls of the Web, with diagrams and "Techno Tips." (Rev: HBG 10/03; SLJ 4/03) [004.67]

25131 McCormick, Anita Louise. *The Internet: Surfing the Issues* (5–10). Series: Issues in Focus. 1998, Enslow LB $26.60 (978-0-89490-956-6). 128pp. A guide to the history, mechanics, and use of the Internet that also covers such topics as surfing, child pornography, hate groups, and censorship. (Rev: BL 10/1/98; SLJ 12/98) [004]

25132 MacDonald, Joan Vos. *Cybersafety: Surfing Safely Online* (5–7). Illus. Series: Teen Issues. 2001, Enslow LB $22.60 (978-0-7660-1580-7). 64pp. Various dangers of venturing online are covered, from viruses and other problems that can infect your computer to activities such as hacking, cyberstalking, and copying software illegally. (Rev: HBG 3/02; SLJ 12/01) [004.6]

25133 Mason, Adrienne, ed. *Robots: From Everyday to Out of This World* (3–7). Illus. 2008, Kids Can $16.95 (978-1-55453-203-2). 32pp. A fascinating introduction to robots at work and at play with snappy text, easy reading sidebars, cartoon graphics, and color photographs. (Rev: BL 9/1/08) [629.8]

25134 Oxlade, Chris. *My First E-Mail Guide* (K–2). Illus. Series: My First Computer Guides. 2007, Heinemann LB $25.36 (978-1-4329-0017-5). 32pp. An easy-to-read introduction to everything email — writing messages, correct etiquette, adding attachments, junk mail, and so forth. Also use *My First Internet Guide* (2007). (Rev: SLJ 12/07) [004.692]

25135 Pascoe, Elaine, adapt. *Virtual Reality: Beyond the Looking Glass* (4–6). Series: New Explorers. 1997, Blackbirch LB $17.95 (978-1-56711-228-3). 48pp. An interesting look at virtual reality, its nature, history, uses, and future. (Rev: HBG 3/98; SLJ 6/98) [006]

25136 Perry, Robert L. *Personal Computer Communications* (4–7). Illus. Series: Watts Library: Computer Science. 2000, Watts paper $8.95 (978-0-531-16483-9). 64pp. This work covers such topics as modems, networks, satellite and wireless technology, and the future of communications. (Rev: BL 10/15/00) [004.16]

25137 Raum, Elizabeth. *The History of the Computer* (2–3). Series: Inventions That Changed the World. 2007, Heinemann LB $25.36 (978-1-4034-9649-2).

32pp. After looking at the equipment we used before the invention of the computer, Raum traces developments from the early monster machines to today's notebooks and examines how the Internet has changed our lives. (Rev: SLJ 11/07) [004]

25138 Rooney, Anne. *Computers: Faster, Smaller, and Smarter* (5–9). Illus. Series: The Cutting Edge. 2005, Heinemann LB $32.86 (978-1-4034-7426-1). 56pp. Looks at the technology behind computers of the past, present, and future; a high-tech design completes the package. (Rev: SLJ 6/06) [004]

25139 Roza, Greg. *The Incredible Story of Computers and the Internet* (3–6). Illus. Series: A Kid's Guide to Incredible Technology. 2004, Rosen LB $21.25 (978-0-8239-6717-9). 24pp. The structure of the Internet and the technology of accessing it are explained in concise terms, with discussion of safe behavior and future developments. (Rev: SLJ 2/05) [004.67]

25140 Sabbeth, Carol. *Kids' Computer Creations: Using Your Computer for Art and Craft Fun* (3–6). Illus. by Loretta Braren. Series: Kids Can! 1995, Williamson paper $12.95 (978-0-913589-92-2). 158pp. An interesting collection of computer activities grouped by subjects like "Around the House," "Fun and Games," and "Wearable Art." (Rev: SLJ 6/96) [005.1]

25141 Selfridge, Benjamin, and Peter Selfridge. *A Kid's Guide to Creating Web Pages for Home and School* (5–10). Illus. 2004, Chicago Review paper $19.95 (978-1-56976-180-9). 110pp. Simple instructions on creating Web pages using HTML are accompanied by helpful illustrations and sample finished pages. (Rev: SLJ 2/05) [005.7]

25142 Spangenburg, Ray, and Kit Moser. *Savvy Surfing on the Internet: Searching and Evaluating Web Sites* (5–8). Illus. Series: Issues in Focus. 2001, Enslow LB $26.60 (978-0-7660-1590-6). 112pp. Readers are encouraged to view much of the information on the Internet with healthy suspicion and are given advice on efficient searching for and assessment of Web sites. (Rev: HBG 3/02; SLJ 12/01) [004.6]

25143 Steinhauser, Peggy L. *Mousetracks: A Kid's Computer Idea Book* (K–5). Illus. 1997, Tricycle paper $12.95 (978-1-883672-48-5). 94pp. The 70 projects in this book are designed to help youngsters develop their computer skills. (Rev: SLJ 8/97) [004]

25144 Thomas, Peggy. *Artificial Intelligence* (5–8). Illus. Series: Lucent Library of Science and Technology. 2005, Gale LB $29.95 (978-1-59018-437-0). 112pp. An interesting overview of progress in efforts to create machines that can think like humans. (Rev: BL 1/05) [004]

25145 Trumbauer, Lisa. *Computer Fun Math* (3–5). Illus. by Sydney Wright. Series: Click It! 1999, Millbrook LB $20.90 (978-0-7613-1504-9); paper $5.95 (978-0-7613-0996-3). 32pp. This book explains how to create simple graphs, charts, and measuring tools, and how to understand math concepts using the computer. Adult help may be required to understand the directions. Also use

Computer Fun Science. (Rev: HBG 4/00; SLJ 12/99) [004]

25146 Wan, Guofang. *Virtually True: Questioning Online Media* (4–7). Illus. Series: Fact Finders. Media Literacy. 2006, Capstone LB $22.60 (978-0-7368-6767-2). 32pp. Designed to awaken skepticism about online media, this book discusses the motivations of those who produce online content and the influence this media has on society. (Rev: SLJ 6/07)

25147 Ward-Johnson, Chris. *Computers: A Magic Mouse Guide* (1–4). Illus. Series: Magic Mouse Guides. 2003, Enslow LB $22.60 (978-0-7660-2263-8). 32pp. Suitable for beginners, this basic guide is presented in the form of a story about Ben, Liza, and Hari, who are learning to use a computer. (Rev: HBG 4/04; SLJ 8/03) [004]

25148 Ward-Johnson, Chris. *E-mail: A Magic Mouse Guide* (1–4). Illus. Series: Magic Mouse Guides. 2003, Enslow LB $22.60 (978-0-7660-2261-4). 32pp. Ben and Hari learn to communicate electronically in this attractive and informative volume for beginners. Also use *Internet* (2003). (Rev: HBG 4/04; SLJ 8/03) [004.692]

25149 Williams, Brian. *Computers* (5–8). Illus. Series: Great Inventions. 2001, Heinemann LB $25.64 (978-1-58810-210-2). 48pp. A chronological look at computers and their predecessors, from the abacus onward, with diagrams and information on the inventors. (Rev: HBG 3/02; SLJ 2/02) [004]

25150 Wolinsky, Art. *Communicating on the Internet* (4–8). Series: The Internet Library. 1999, Enslow LB $22.60 (978-0-7660-1260-8). 64pp. This book on how to communicate safely and effectively on the Internet includes material on e-mail problems, computer etiquette, chat rooms, and newsgroups. (Rev: HBG 3/00; SLJ 3/00) [004]

25151 Wolinsky, Art. *The History of the Internet and the World Wide Web* (5–9). Illus. Series: Internet Library. 1999, Enslow LB $22.60 (978-0-7660-1261-5). 64pp. This volume explains how the Internet evolved during the Cold War and how it transfers and distributes information. (Rev: BL 12/15/99; HBG 3/00; SLJ 1/00; VOYA 2/00) [004.67]

25152 Wolinsky, Art. *Internet Power Research Using the Big6 Approach*. Rev. ed. (3–8). Illus. Series: The Internet Library. 2005, Enslow LB $22.60 (978-0-7660-1563-0). 64pp. Shows readers how to apply the "Big6" method to research done on the Internet; a revision of a 2002 title. (Rev: SLJ 11/05) [025.04]

25153 Wolinsky, Art. *Safe Surfing on the Internet* (4–8). Illus. 2003, Enslow LB $22.60 (978-0-7660-2030-6). 64pp. Wolinksy presents information on safe use of the Internet and topics including proper use of language, copyright, privacy, and plagiarism. (Rev: HBG 10/03; LMC 8/03; SLJ 7/03) [004.67]

25154 Woodford, Chris. *Digital Technology* (4–7). Series: Science in Focus. 2006, Chelsea House LB $27.00 (978-0-7910-8861-6). 48pp. A clear introduction to the world of digital technology, covering topics including smart cards, computer-aided design, mobile phones, and so forth in easy-to-understand language. (Rev: BL 10/15/06) [621.381]

25155 Worland, Gayle. *The Computer* (2–4). Series: Fact Finders: Great Inventions. 2003, Capstone LB $23.93 (978-0-7368-2215-2). 32pp. An introduction to computers — how they came to be, how they work, and how they have changed daily life — with a final page of facts and an activity (writing a message in binary code). (Rev: SLJ 6/04) [004]

25156 Wright, David. *Computers* (5–8). Series: Inventors and Inventions. 1995, Benchmark LB $25.64 (978-0-7614-0064-6). A look at the development of the computer, with brief profiles of important people in its history and an examination of the uses of computers in the world today. (Rev: SLJ 6/96) [004]

Electronics

25157 Hoare, Stephen. *Digital Revolution* (3–6). Series: 20th Century Inventions. 1998, Raintree LB $27.12 (978-0-8172-4897-0). 48pp. This work introduces digital technology and such applications as compact discs, television, telephones, DVDs, watches, and cameras. (Rev: HBG 3/99; SLJ 2/99) [621.38]

25158 Oxlade, Chris. *Electronics: MP3s, TVs, and DVDs* (5–9). Illus. Series: The Cutting Edge. 2005, Heinemann LB $32.86 (978-1-4034-7427-8). 56pp. Looks at the technology behind popular electronic devices and at predictions about gadgets of the future; a high-tech design completes the package. (Rev: SLJ 6/06)

Machinery

25159 Berger, Melvin, and Gilda Berger. *Telephones, Televisions and Toilets: How They Work and What Can Go Wrong* (2–3). Illus. by Don Madden. Series: Discovery Readers. 1993, Ideals paper $4.50 (978-0-8249-8608-7). 48pp. Cartoons and simple text explain the inner workings of these three machines. (Rev: BL 7/93) [632.6]

25160 Low, William. *Machines Go to Work* (PS–1). Illus. by author. 2009, Holt $14.95 (978-0-8050-8759-8). 42pp. With motion, bright images, and fold-outs that expose additional images, this is a satisfying look at powerful machines (a helicopter, a tugboat, a cement mixer, and so forth). (Rev: BL 3/15/09; HB 7/09; SLJ 5/09*) [621.8]

25161 Mitchell, Joyce Slayton. *Knuckleboom Loaders Load Logs: A Trip to the Sawmill* (K–3). Illus. 2003, Overlook $14.95 (978-1-58567-368-1). 40pp. This feast of powerful machines used in the harvesting, hauling, and processing of forest products will appeal to the big-truck crowd. (Rev: BL 2/1/04; HBG 4/04; SLJ 3/04) [634]

25162 Peterson, Cris. *Fantastic Farm Machines* (1–3). Illus. by David R. Lundquist. 2006, Boyds Mills $17.95 (978-1-59078-271-2). 32pp. Peterson gives readers a personal tour of the high-tech equipment used on today's farms. (Rev: BL 2/15/06; SLJ 3/06) [631.3]

25163 Silverman, Buffy. *Simple Machines* (3–6). Illus. 2009, Heinemann LB $22.00 (978-1-4329-2310-5). 48pp. Examples and experiments in building simple machines with parental guidance advised. (Rev: BL 6/1–15/09) [621.8]

25164 VanCleave, Janice. *Machines: Mind-Boggling Experiments You Can Turn into Science Fair Projects* (4–6). Illus. Series: Spectacular Science Projects. 1993, Wiley paper $10.95 (978-0-471-57108-7). 88pp. Simple machines that can be made and operated are featured in this collection of fascinating science projects. (Rev: BL 5/1/93; SLJ 7/93) [521.8]

25165 Wallace, Karen. *Big Machines* (K–2). Series: Eyewitness Reader. 2000, DK LB $14.99 (978-0-7894-5412-6); paper $3.99 (978-0-7894-5411-9). 32pp. This book presents pictures and text on such big machines as a crane, a bulldozer, a front loader, a dump truck, and an excavator. (Rev: HBG 9/00; SLJ 7/00) [621.8]

25166 Whitehouse, Patty. *Moving Machines* (K–2). Illus. 2006, Rourke LB $14.95 (978-1-60044-192-9). 24pp. This attractive title explores the wide range of machines used to move materials, ranging from simple pulleys, shovels, and wheelbarrows to cherry pickers and scissor lifts. (Rev: BL 10/15/06) [621.8]

Metals

25167 Oxlade, Chris. *Metal* (2–3). Series: Materials, Materials, Materials. 2001, Heinemann LB $21.36 (978-1-58810-155-6). 32pp. With color photographs and brief text on each page, the story of what metals are is covered plus where they are found and extracted, and their uses in everyday life. (Rev: BL 10/15/01) [669]

25168 Ridley, Sarah. *A Metal Can* (2–4). Illus. Series: How It's Made. 2006, Gareth Stevens $24.00 (978-0-8368-6702-2). 32pp. This photo-filled title traces the life cycle of an aluminum soda can from the mining of the raw material — bauxite — to the recycling bin. (Rev: BL 10/15/06) [670]

Telegraph, Telephone, and Telecommunications

25169 Byers, Ann. *Communications Satellites* (5–9). Series: The Library of Satellites. 2003, Rosen LB $26.50 (978-0-8239-3851-3). 64pp. From the first important communications satellites launched in 1962, this account traces the growth of this technology and its possible future developments. (Rev: BL 11/15/03; SLJ 1/04) [001.51]

25170 Hegedus, Alannah, and Kaitlin Rainey. *Bleeps and Blips to Rocket Ships: Great Inventions in Communications* (5–9). Illus. by Bill Slavin. 2001, Tundra paper $17.95 (978-0-88776-452-3). 88pp. This is a fact-packed and appealing look at the field of communications, with information on history and inventors and inventions as well as suggested activities. (Rev: SLJ 8/01) [609.71]

25171 Maddison, Simon. *Telecoms: Present Knowledge, Future Trends* (5–9). Illus. Series: 21st Century Science. 2003, Smart Apple LB $27.10 (978-1-58340-352-5). 44pp. Numerous diagrams, photographs, and drawings add to this overview of the history of telecommunications and the status of current technology. (Rev: SLJ 1/04) [384]

25172 Mattern, Joanne. *From Radio to the Wireless Web* (2–4). Series: Transportation and Communication. 2002, Enslow LB $23.93 (978-0-7660-1893-8). 48pp. This book explains the development of telecommunications, present uses, possible future developments, and people involved in its history. (Rev: BL 9/15/02; HBG 10/02) [384]

25173 Mattern, Joanne. *Telephones* (2–4). Series: Transportation and Communication. 2002, Enslow LB $23.93 (978-0-7660-1888-4). 48pp. From Alexander Graham Bell to the cell phones of today, this is the history of the telephone with material on how it works and possible future developments. (Rev: BL 9/15/02; HBG 10/02) [384.6]

25174 Nelson, Robin. *Communication* (3–6). Series: First Step Nonfiction. 2003, Lerner LB $18.60 (978-0-8225-4638-2). 24pp. For beginning readers, old and new in the field of communication are paired to good effect on double-page spreads. (Rev: BL 11/15/03; HBG 4/04; SLJ 12/03)

25175 Oxlade, Chris. *Telecommunications* (3–6). Illus. Series: 20th Century Inventions. 1997, Raintree LB $27.12 (978-0-8172-4813-0). 48pp. After a brief introduction to telecommunications, this account focuses on such topics as the telephone, telegraph, radio, television, and computers. (Rev: BL 6/1–15/97) [384]

25176 Raum, Elizabeth. *The History of the Telephone* (2–3). Series: Inventions That Changed the World. 2007, Heinemann LB $25.36 (978-1-4034-9650-8). 32pp. After looking at the status quo before the invention of the telephone, Raum traces the history of this service from party lines to cell phones. (Rev: SLJ 11/07) [621.385]

25177 Streissguth, Thomas. *Communications: Sending the Message* (5–8). Series: Innovators. 1997, Oliver LB $21.95 (978-1-881508-41-0). A compact, easy-to-understand history of communication from earliest times, through Gutenberg, Edison, and Marconi, to the present "information highway." (Rev: SLJ 2/98) [001.51]

Television, Motion Pictures, Radio, and Recording

25178 Abraham, Philip. *Television and Movies* (4–7). Illus. Series: American Pop Culture. 2004, Children's Pr. LB $24.50 (978-0-516-24074-9); paper $6.95 (978-0-516-25946-8). 48pp. Traces the technological and cultural development of TV and movies in the United States. (Rev: SLJ 1/05)

25179 Anderson, Carol D., and Robert Sheely. *Techno Lab: How Science Is Changing Entertainment* (4–6). Illus. 1995, Silver Moon $14.95 (978-1-881889-63-2). 64pp. This fascinating book traces the influence of science and technology on movies, recorded music, television, video games, and virtual reality. (Rev: BL 1/1–15/96; SLJ 12/95) [791.4]

25180 Biel, Jackie. *Video* (3–6). Illus. Series: Inventors and Inventions. 1996, Marshall Cavendish LB $25.64 (978-0-7614-0048-6). 63pp. The story of this important modern invention and the people who brought it into being. (Rev: BL 7/96; SLJ 8/96) [621.388]

25181 Feeney, Kathy. *Television* (2–4). Series: Transportation and Communication. 2001, Enslow LB $23.93 (978-0-7660-1644-6). 48pp. A simple, well-illustrated volume on the history of television, its development, and its many uses. (Rev: BL 3/15/02; HBG 3/02) [384.55]

25182 Hahn, Don. *Disney's Animation Magic: A Behind-the-Scenes Look at How an Animated Film Is Made* (4–6). Illus. 1996, Disney $16.89 (978-0-7868-5041-9). 96pp. Using a team from the Disney studio as case studies, this book traces the various steps and processes involved in creating an animated film. (Rev: BL 9/1/96; SLJ 10/96) [791.43]

25183 Hamilton, Jake. *Special Effects: In Film and Television* (4–8). Illus. 1998, DK $17.95 (978-0-7849-2813-4). This is an intriguing glimpse at special effects in film and television, using double-page spreads that each focus on a different aspect of production, such as storyboards, makeup, and stunts. (Rev: BCCB 9/98; BL 8/98; VOYA 10/98) [791.43]

25184 Mattern, Joanne. *The History of Radio* (2–4). Illus. Series: Transportation and Communication. 2002, Enslow LB $23.93 (978-0-7660-2027-6). 48pp. An easy-to-read account of the invention and long popularity of radio. (Rev: HBG 10/03) [621]

25185 Oxlade, Chris. *Movies* (3–5). Illus. Series: Science Encounters. 1997, Rigby $22.79 (978-1-57572-088-3). 32pp. An introduction to movie making that gives a basic history of motion pictures, tells how the film camera works, and covers stunts, different types of film, animation, and computer enhancement. (Rev: SLJ 11/97) [791]

25186 Raum, Elizabeth. *The History of the Camera* (2–3). Series: Inventions That Changed the World. 2007, Heinemann LB $25.36 (978-1-4034-9647-8). 32pp. After looking at the images we used before the development of the camera, Raum traces the camera's history from early daguerrotypes to today's digital and cell-phone cameras. (Rev: SLJ 11/07) [771.309]

25187 Riehecky, Janet. *Television* (3–6). Illus. Series: Inventors and Inventions. 1996, Marshall Cavendish LB $25.64 (978-0-7614-0045-5). 63pp. The history of television and the people behind its development are chronicled, with many photographs and an informal text. (Rev: BL 7/96; SLJ 8/96) [384.55]

25188 Somervill, Barbara. *The History of the Motion Picture* (3–6). Series: Our Changing World: The Timeline Library. 2006, The Child's World LB $27.07 (978-1-59296-440-6). 32pp. From moving shadows to computer video clips, this book traces the evolution of moving images and looks forward into the future. (Rev: SLJ 7/06) [791.43]

25189 Spilsbury, Richard. *Cartoons and Animation* (4–7). Illus. Series: Art off the Wall. 2006, Heinemann LB $23.00 (978-1-4034-8287-7). 56pp. Surveys the history, techniques, and movie applications of cartooning and animation, and includes bold color illustrations of familiar characters and animators at work. (Rev: BL 1/1–15/07; SLJ 5/07) [741.5]

25190 Worland, Gayle. *The Radio* (2–4). Series: Fact Finders: Great Inventions. 2003, Capstone LB $23.93 (978-0-7368-2217-6). 32pp. A basic history of radio — how it works, who its pioneers were, and the impact it has had on civilization. (Rev: SLJ 6/04) [621.384]

Transportation

General

25191 Abramson, Andra Serlin. *Heavy Equipment Up Close* (2–4). Illus. Series: Up Close. 2008, Sterling $9.95 (978-1-4027-4799-3). 24pp. Full-color photographs show construction equipment (dump trucks, dozers, tractors, cranes, and so forth) up close in this large-format book that also provides the correct terminology and lots of interesting facts. (Rev: BL 4/1/08; LMC 8/08) [623.74]

25192 Anderson, Catherine. *Fire Truck Factory* (PS–2). Illus. Series: Read and Learn. 2005, Heinemann LB $18.50 (978-1-4034-6162-9). 24pp. The construction of a fire truck is shown in clear photographs and short, simple sentences. (Rev: BL 5/1/05; SLJ 5/05) [629.225]

25193 Bial, Raymond. *The Canals* (4–8). Illus. Series: Building America. 2001, Marshall Cavendish LB $27.07 (978-0-7614-1336-3). 56pp. This history of the U.S. canal system and how it works includes excellent photographs and illustrations that help to explain the technical aspects of canals. (Rev: BL 3/1/02; HBG 3/02; SLJ 2/02*) [386]

25194 Bridges, Sarah. *I Drive a Bulldozer* (PS–2). Illus. by Derrick Alderman and Denise Shea. Series: Working Wheels. 2004, Picture Window LB $25.26 (978-1-4048-0613-9). 24pp. A large-format volume that shows a bulldozer driver day at work. Also use *I Drive a Dump Truck* and *I Drive a Snowplow* (2004). (Rev: SLJ 3/05) [621.8]

25195 Brimner, Larry Dane. *Subway: A Brief History of Underground Mass Transit* (3–6). Illus. by Neil Waldman. 2004, Boyds Mills $15.95 (978-1-59078-176-0). 32pp. This attractively illustrated overview explores the history of New York City's century-old subway, the forces behind its development, and the impact it had on the city. (Rev: BL 10/15/04; SLJ 3/05) [388.4]

25196 Burns, Peggy, and Peter Chrisp. *Travel* (3–5). Illus. Series: Stepping Through History. 1995, Thomson Learning LB $5.00 (978-1-56847-343-7). 32pp. A history of travel and transportation from ancient days to the superjets of today. (Rev: BL 7/95) [629]

25197 Coppendale, Jean. *Fire Trucks and Rescue Vehicles* (PS–2). Illus. Series: QEB First Book Of. 2007, Black Rabbit LB $16.95 (978-1-59566-342-9). 24pp. This title features trucks and fireboats, urgent action, and big color pictures. (Rev: BLO 3/3/08) [629.225]

25198 David, Jack. *Motocross Racing* (3–5). Series: Torque: Action Sports. 2007, Children's Pr. LB $20.00 (978-0-531-18491-2). 24pp. With lots of clear, bright photographs and simple text, this volume looks at the equipment and experiences of this sport. Also use *Enduro Motocycles, Cruisers,* and *Choppers* in the companion Torque: Motorcycles series (all 2007). (Rev: SLJ 7/08) [796.7]

25199 DuTemple, Lesley A. *New York Subways* (4–7). Illus. Series: Great Building Feats. 2003, Lerner LB $27.93 (978-0-8225-0378-1). 80pp. DuTemple presents the history of the subway system with details of its difficult construction, continuing financial problems, and the damage caused in the destruction of the World Trade Center. (Rev: BL 1/1–15/03; HBG 10/03) [388.4]

25200 Francis, Dorothy. *Our Transportation System* (3–4). Illus. Series: I Know America. 2002, Millbrook LB $24.90 (978-0-7613-2366-2). 48pp. A historical look at transportation in the United States, from roads to rail, water, and air. (Rev: BL 2/1/02; HBG 10/02) [388]

25201 *Go! The Whole World of Transportation* (5–10). Illus. 2006, DK $26.99 (978-0-7566-2224-4). 240pp. This wide-ranging, visually fascinating journey through the world of transportation touches on everything from buses and ferries to speedboats and fighter jets. (Rev: SLJ 2/07*) [388]

25202 Goodman, Susan. *Choppers!* (K–2). Photos by Michael J. Doolittle. Series: Step into Reading. 2004, Random LB $11.99 (978-0-375-92517-7); paper $3.99 (978-0-375-82517-0). 48pp. For beginning readers, a look at the history and uses of helicopters. (Rev: SLJ 5/05)

25203 Goodman, Susan E. *Motorcycles!* (PS–2). Illus. by Michael Doolittle. Series: Step into Reading. 2007, Random LB $11.99 (978-0-375-94116-0); paper $3.99 (978-0-375-84116-3). 48pp. Beginning readers will imagine themselves riding the motorcycles and racing bikes featured in this photograph-filled book. (Rev: BL 6/1–15/07; SLJ 10/07) [629.227]

25204 Hamilton, John. *Transportation: A Pictorial History of the Past One Thousand Years* (4–7). Illus. Series: The Millennium. 2000, ABDO LB $25.65 (978-1-57765-361-5). 48pp. A history of 1,000 years of transportation that includes animals, ships, trains, bicycles, motorcycles, cars, airplanes, and spacecraft. (Rev: BL 7/00; HBG 10/00; SLJ 10/00) [388.21]

25205 Herbst, Judith. *The History of Transportation* (5–8). Series: Major Inventions Through History. 2005, Twenty-First Century LB $26.60 (978-0-8225-2496-0). 56pp. From the wheel to the airplane, technological innovations involving transport have had a profound impact on our lives as shown in this attractive, well-written volume. (Rev: SLJ 2/06) [973]

25206 *Let's Get to Work! / ¡Vamos a trabajar!* (PS–2). Illus. by Gaétan Evrard. 2005, Two-Can $6.95 (978-1-58728-512-7). This attractive bilingual board book introduces young readers to a variety of vehicles and their names in both English and Spanish; also use *Let's Go! / ¡Vamos a Viajar!* (2005). (Rev: SLJ 10/05)

25207 McKendry, Joe. *Beneath the Streets of Boston: Building America's First Subway* (3–5). Illus. 2005, Godine $19.95 (978-1-56792-284-4). 48pp. A fascinating and detailed look at America's first subway and the social and technical issues surrounding it. (Rev: BL 6/1–15/05) [625.4]

25208 Maynard, Christopher. *Extreme Machines* (3–6). Series: Eyewitness Reader. 2000, DK paper $3.99 (978-0-7894-5417-1). 48pp. A visually appealing book that looks at machines from drag cars to helicopters. (Rev: HBG 9/00; SLJ 8/00) [629.04]

25209 Mayo, Margaret. *Choo Choo Clickety-Clack!* (PS–K). Illus. by Alex Ayliffe. 2005, Carolrhoda $14.95 (978-1-57505-819-1). 32pp. Brightly colored pages with eye-catching graphics and lively words introduce various modes of transportation. (Rev: BL 2/15/05; SLJ 5/05) [629]

25210 Mayo, Margaret. *Dig Dig Digging* (PS). Illus. by Alex Ayliffe. 2002, Holt $14.95 (978-0-8050-6840-5). 32pp. A rhyming book, with illustrations, about tractors, fire engines, helicopters, and other favorite vehicles. (Rev: BL 5/15/02; HBG 10/02; SLJ 5/02) [629.225]

25211 Nelson, Robin. *Transportation* (3–6). Series: First Step Nonfiction. 2003, Lerner LB $18.60 (978-0-8225-4636-8). 24pp. Suitable for beginning readers, this book uses double-page spreads to show how transportation has changed over the years. (Rev: BL 11/15/03; HBG 4/04; SLJ 12/03)

25212 Prince, April Jones. *What Do Wheels Do All Day?* (PS–2). Illus. by Giles Laroche. 2006, Houghton $16.00 (978-0-618-56307-4). 32pp. This oversized picture book explores wheels of every size and description and the wide range of tasks they perform. (Rev: BL 4/15/06; SLJ 6/06) [621.8]

25213 Richards, Julie. *Canals and Aqueducts* (4–6). Illus. Series: Smart Structures. 2003, Smart Apple LB $24.25 (978-1-58340-347-1). 32pp. The science and history of canals, from Venice to Panama, is explored in this well-illustrated book. (Rev: SLJ 3/04) [627]

25214 Tong, Willabel L. *Cars, Boats, Trains, and Planes* (PS). Illus. by Jeff Cummins. 1998, Orchard $12.95 (978-0-531-30058-9). In this interactive book, all kinds of transportation vehicles pop-out at the reader. (Rev: BL 1/1–15/99) [629.04]

25215 Tourville, Amanda Doering. *Bulldozers* (PS–2). Illus. by Zachary Trover. Series: Mighty Machines. 2009, Magic Wagon LB $18.95 (978-1-60270-621-7). 32pp. For machinery fans, this offers bright images and details of key working parts. (Rev: BL 4/1/09) [629.225]

25216 Wilkinson, Philip, and Jacqueline Dineen. *Transportation* (5–8). Illus. 1995, Chelsea LB $21.95 (978-0-7910-2768-4). An informative, simple overview of inventions and changes that created the modern transportation systems of today. (Rev: VOYA 2/96) [629]

Automobiles and Trucks

25217 Anderson, Jenna. *How It Happens at the Truck Plant* (1–3). Photos by Bob Wolfe and Diane Wolfe. Series: How It Happens. 2002, Oliver LB $19.95 (978-1-881508-93-9). 32pp. How trucks are manufactured is described in text and photographs. (Rev: HBG 10/02; SLJ 12/02) [629]

25218 Barton, Byron. *Trucks* (PS). Illus. by author. 1986, HarperCollins LB $17.89 (978-0-690-04530-7). 32pp. Bright colors and simple text describe the role of trucks. (Rev: BL 8/86; SLJ 9/86)

25219 Boucher, Jerry. *Fire Truck Nuts and Bolts* (K–3). Illus. 1993, Carolrhoda LB $22.60 (978-0-87614-783-2); paper $5.95 (978-0-87614-619-4). 40pp. An examination of the construction of a fire truck and its many parts. (Rev: BL 11/1/93; SLJ 12/93) [629.255]

25220 Burgan, Michael. *The World's Fastest Cars* (3–8). Illus. Series: Built for Speed. 2000, Capstone LB $23.93 (978-0-7368-0570-4). 48pp. Dragsters, Indie 500 race cars, and other fast automobiles are covered in this visually appealing account that will be attractive to reluctant readers. (Rev: HBG 10/01; SLJ 6/01) [629.228]

25221 Collicutt, Paul. *This Truck* (PS–1). Illus. by author. 2004, Farrar $15.00 (978-0-374-37496-9). From the front endpapers showing vintage models to the back endpapers' contemporary examples, this is an appealing and colorful look at big rigs. (Rev: SLJ 7/04) [629.224]

25222 Cooper, Wade. *On the Road* (PS–1). Illus. Series: Scholastic Reader. 2008, Scholastic LB $3.99 (978-0-545-00720-7). 32pp. Vehicles from cement mixers to sports cars are presented in photographs and rhymes geared to brand-new readers. (Rev: BL 1/1–15/08) [629.046]

25223 Flammang, James M. *Cars* (2–4). Illus. Series: Transportation and Communication. 2001, Enslow LB $23.93 (978-0-7660-1646-0). 48pp. Car lovers will enjoy this easy-reading look at automobiles past and present with black-and-white and color photographs, a timeline, a glossary, and lists of fur-

ther resources. (Rev: BL 10/15/01; HBG 3/02) [629.222]

25224 Hubbell, Patricia. *Cars: Rushing! Honking! Zooming!* (PS–2). Illus. by Megan Halsey. 2006, Marshall Cavendish $14.99 (978-0-7614-5296-6). 32pp. Rhyming text and intricate illustrations introduce everything from family cars to limousines and hot rods. (Rev: BL 11/1/06; SLJ 11/06)

25225 Italia, Bob. *Great Auto Makers and Their Cars* (4–6). Illus. 1993, Oliver LB $19.95 (978-1-881508-08-3). 160pp. The founders of ten automobile companies — like Henry Ford, Horace Dodge, Karl Benz, Soichiro Honda, and Ferruccio Lamborghini — are profiled with details on the obstacles they overcame. (Rev: SLJ 11/93) [629.2]

25226 Jango-Cohen, Judith. *Dump Trucks* (2–3). Series: Pull Ahead Books. 2002, Lerner LB $22.60 (978-0-8225-0688-1); paper $5.95 (978-0-8225-0602-7). 32pp. This colorful account introduces dump trucks, explains their parts, tells how they work, and describes their functions. (Rev: BL 8/02; HBG 3/03) [629.224]

25227 Jango-Cohen, Judith. *Fire Trucks* (2–3). Series: Pull Ahead Books. 2002, Lerner LB $22.60 (978-0-8225-0077-3); paper $5.95 (978-0-8225-0604-1). 32pp. After describing the parts of a fire truck in text and pictures, this book explains how they work and the jobs they do. (Rev: BL 8/02; HBG 3/03) [629.255]

25228 Johnstone, Mike. *Monster Trucks* (5–8). Series: Need for Speed. 2002, Lerner LB $23.93 (978-0-8225-0388-0). 32pp. In stunning action-filled text and pictures, this book highlights huge trucks that weigh thousands of pounds and stand more than 10 feet high. (Rev: BL 8/02; HBG 10/02; SLJ 7/02) [629.225]

25229 Juettner, Bonnie. *Hybrid Cars* (4–7). Illus. Series: A Great Idea!: Going Green. 2009, Norwood House LB $18.95 (978-1-59953-193-9). 48pp. Juettner places the development of hybrid cars in historical context and discusses research into alternative fuels; the photographs will attract browsers. (Rev: BL 4/1/09) [629.22]

25230 Kilby, Don. *On the Road* (PS–K). Illus. 2003, Kids Can $14.95 (978-1-55337-379-7). 24pp. Double-page spreads show bright illustrations of a variety of trucks and tractors at work. (Rev: BL 5/1/03; HBG 10/03; SLJ 5/03) [629.224]

25231 Levinson, Nancy S. *Cars: A Holiday House Reader, Level 2* (1–3). Trans. and illus. by Jacqueline Rogers. Series: Holiday House Reader. 2004, Holiday House $14.95 (978-0-8234-1614-1). 32pp. Benz, Daimler, and Ford are among the prominent names in this overview for beginning readers of the early days of the automobile. (Rev: BL 11/15/04) [629.2]

25232 Lichtenheld, Tom. *Everything I Know About Cars: A Collection of Made-Up Facts, Educated Guesses, and Silly Pictures About Cars, Trucks, and Other Zoomy Things* (2–4). Illus. by author. 2005, Simon & Schuster $16.95 (978-0-689-84382-2). A zany, large-format introduction to cars and car parts, with some facts and some fake facts plus lots of cartoons and good advice on drawing cars. (Rev: BCCB 4/05; BL 1/1–15/05; SLJ 5/05) [388.3]

25233 Lindeen, Mary. *Trucks* (PS–3). 2007, Children's Pr. LB $18.50 (978-1-60014-063-1). 24pp. The basics about trucks for young readers, clearly presented and accompanied by engaging photographs. (Rev: SLJ 7/07)

25234 McKenna, A. T. *Corvette* (5–7). Series: Ultimate Car. 2000, ABDO LB $24.21 (978-1-57765-127-7). 32pp. This introduction to this famous sports car includes material on its design, construction, and records it has broken. Similar material appears in companion books *Ferrari, Jaguar, Lamborghini, Mustang,* and *Porsche* (all 2000). (Rev: BL 3/1/01; HBG 10/01) [629]

25235 Maurer, Tracy. *License Plates* (3–5). Series: The Rourke Guide to State Symbols. 1999, Rourke LB $29.93 (978-1-57103-298-0). 48pp. In addition to showing three or four historic and modern license plates for each state, this book includes a few interesting facts and the state motto. (Rev: SLJ 2/00) [629.2]

25236 Mitchell, Joyce Slayton. *Crashed, Smashed, and Mashed* (1–3). Illus. by Steven Borns. 2001, Tricycle $14.95 (978-1-58246-034-5). 32pp. Photos and text show an automobile junkyard and describe what happens to old cars when they are recycled. (Rev: BL 3/15/01; HBG 10/01) [629.2]

25237 Mitchell, Joyce Slayton. *Tractor-Trailer Trucker: A Powerful Truck Book* (2–5). Illus. 2000, Tricycle $14.95 (978-1-58246-010-9). 40pp. Written like a manual, this book gives detailed instructions on how to drive and care for a big rig. (Rev: BL 4/1/00; HBG 9/00; SLJ 8/00) [629.2844]

25238 Mitton, Tony. *Cool Cars* (PS–3). Illus. by Ant Parker. 2005, Kingfisher $9.95 (978-0-7534-5802-0). Introduces all kinds of cars — family cars, taxis, race cars, and so forth — with an appealing blend of rhyming text and dynamic artwork. (Rev: BL 7/05; SLJ 6/05) [629.222]

25239 Molzahn, Arlene Bourgeois. *Fire Engines* (2–4). Illus. Series: Transportation and Communication. 2001, Enslow LB $23.93 (978-0-7660-1643-9). 48pp. The ever-popular fire engine is featured here, with photographs of vehicles past and present, a timeline, a glossary, and lists of further resources. (Rev: BL 10/15/01; HBG 3/02) [628.9]

25240 Molzahn, Arlene Bourgeois. *Highways and Freeways* (2–4). Series: Transportation and Communication. 2002, Enslow LB $23.93 (978-0-7660-1891-4). 48pp. This book traces the development of road transportation, how networks developed, their importance, and possible future developments. (Rev: BL 9/15/02; HBG 3/03) [388.11]

25241 Molzahn, Arlene Bourgeois. *Police and Emergency Vehicles* (2–4). Series: Transportation and Communication. 2002, Enslow LB $23.93 (978-0-7660-1890-7). 48pp. Various kinds of emergency vehicles are presented with background history, details of people who were important in their development, and potential future improvements. (Rev: BL 9/15/02; HBG 3/03) [629.04]

25242 Nelson, Kristin L. *Farm Tractors* (2–3). Series: Pull Ahead Books. 2002, Lerner LB $22.60 (978-0-8225-0690-4); paper $5.95 (978-0-8225-0607-2). 32pp. Farm tractors are introduced with many photographs and large-type text and coverage is given on the jobs they do like towing a plow, seed drill, or a mower. (Rev: BL 8/02; HBG 3/03; SLJ 10/02) [621.8]

25243 Nelson, Kristin L. *Monster Trucks* (2–3). Series: Pull Ahead Books. 2002, Lerner LB $22.60 (978-0-8225-0691-1); paper $5.95 (978-0-8225-0605-8). 32pp. The world of monster trucks is introduced in color photographs and a simple text with material on their structure and functions such as heavy towing. (Rev: BL 8/02; HBG 3/03) [629.225]

25244 Newhouse, Maxwell. *Let's Go for a Ride* (K–4). Illus. by author. 2006, Tundra $16.95 (978-0-88776-748-7). From the earliest automobiles through the "glory days" of the 1950s, this friendly, first-person overview gives a good feeling of the joys of driving as they change over time. (Rev: SLJ 4/06) [629.222]

25245 Nielsen, L. Michelle. *Vintage Cars: 1919–1930* (4–6). Series: Automania! 2006, Crabtree LB $25.20 (978-0-7787-3011-8); paper $8.95 (978-0-7787-3033-0). 32pp. Plenty of photographs of cool cars from the 1920s will draw in readers. The text discusses which models were most popular and how cars evolved during this time. (Rev: SLJ 8/07)

25246 Otfinoski, Steven. *Around the Track: Race Cars Then and Now* (2–4). Series: Here We Go! 1997, Benchmark LB $22.79 (978-0-7614-0608-2). 32pp. A colorful introduction to race cars, including Grand Prix cars, dragsters, carts, and a few of historical importance. (Rev: HBG 3/98; SLJ 4/98) [629.2]

25247 Otfinoski, Steven. *Behind the Wheel: Cars Then and Now* (2–4). Illus. Series: Here We Go! 1996, Benchmark LB $22.79 (978-0-7614-0403-3). 32pp. A simple text and spectacular photos are used to give a brief history of cars — past, present, and future. (Rev: SLJ 2/97) [629.27]

25248 Oxlade, Chris. *Car* (4–6). Illus. Series: Take It Apart. 2002, Thameside $24.25 (978-1-930643-94-9). 32pp. The mechanically minded will particularly enjoy this look at cars that uses cutaways and detailed diagrams to show its major parts. (Rev: BL 1/1–15/03; HBG 3/03) [629.222]

25249 Raby, Philip. *Racing Cars* (5–8). Series: Need for Speed. 1999, Lerner LB $23.93 (978-0-8225-2487-8). 32pp. Using an attention-getting format with plenty of color, action photographs, and sidebars, this book covers such topics as Le Mans, dragsters, the Camel T, dune buggies, and carting. (Rev: BL 1/1–15/00; HBG 3/00; SLJ 2/00) [623.8]

25250 Raum, Elizabeth. *The History of the Car* (2–3). Series: Inventions That Changed the World. 2007, Heinemann LB $25.36 (978-1-4034-9648-5). 32pp. After looking at the transport we used before the invention of the car, Raum traces developments from the earliest automobiles to new fuel alternatives and examines how cars have changed our lives. (Rev: SLJ 11/07) [629.22209]

25251 Roberts, Cynthia. *Tow Trucks* (PS). Illus. Series: Machines at Work. 2007, Child's World LB $22.79 (978-1-59296-836-7). 24pp. With close-up photographs and dramatic photographs, this small book looks at the different tasks these vehicles can perform and the equipment they use to do the job. (Rev: BL 4/15/07) [629.225]

25252 Schaefer, Margaret A. *Let's Build a Car* (3–5). Illus. by Patrick T. McRae. 1992, Ideals paper $4.95 (978-0-8249-8536-3). 32pp. Every page shows a step in car production. (Rev: BL 12/1/90) [629.23]

25253 Simon, Seymour. *Seymour Simon's Book of Trucks* (K–4). 2000, HarperCollins LB $16.89 (978-0-06-028481-7). A highly appealing book that contains pictures and information on a large number of trucks and the various jobs they do. (Rev: HBG 9/00; SLJ 7/00) [629.28]

25254 Steggall, Susan. *The Life of a Car* (PS–2). Illus. by author. 2008, Holt $16.95 (978-0-8050-8747-5). 32pp. A very simple look at a car's life from construction through recycling, with minimal text. (Rev: BL 4/15/08; SLJ 5/08) [629.222]

25255 Sturges, Philemon. *I Love Trucks!* (PS). Illus. by Shari Halpern. 1999, HarperCollins $17.99 (978-0-06-027819-9). 32pp. A number of trucks in action are pictured in this simple introduction. (Rev: BCCB 3/99; BL 2/1/99; HBG 9/99; SLJ 3/99) [629.224]

25256 Walker, Sloan, and Andrew Vasey. *The Only Other Crazy Car Book* (3–6). Illus. 1984, Walker LB $11.85 (978-0-8027-6517-8). 48pp. There is usually one "oddball" auto to a page, including origins and special features, such as the "Roach Coach," which looks like a giant insect.

25257 Wheeler, Jill C. *Alternative Cars* (3–5). Illus. Series: Checkerboard Science Library: Eye on Energy. 2008, ABDO LB $16.95 (978-1-59928-803-1). 32pp. After a discussion of the internal combustion engine and its disadvantages, this title looks at hybrid, diesel, hydrogen fuel-cell, electric, and other alternatives. (Rev: BL 2/15/08) [629.22]

25258 Whitman, Sylvia. *Get Up and Go! The History of American Road Travel* (5–8). Illus. 1996, Lerner LB $30.35 (978-0-8225-1735-1). 88pp. From primitive pathways to modern superhighways, this is a history of American roads and the vehicles that traveled them. (Rev: BL 10/15/96; SLJ 10/96; VOYA 2/97) [388.1]

25259 Wright, David K. *The Story of Chevy Impalas* (1–3). Illus. Series: Classic Cars. 2002, Gareth Stevens LB $23.00 (978-0-8368-3190-0). 24pp. Young automobile enthusiasts will enjoy seeing how the Impala has changed over the years. (Rev: BL 10/15/02; HBG 3/03) [629.222]

25260 Wright, David K. *The Story of Ford Thunderbirds* (1–3). Series: Classic Cars. 2002, Gareth Stevens LB $23.00 (978-0-8368-3191-7). 24pp. The history of the legendary Ford Thunderbird is told with bright full-page photographs and a simple text. (Rev: BL 10/15/02; HBG 3/03) [629]

25261 Wright, David K. *The Story of Model T Fords* (1–3). Series: Classic Cars. 2002, Gareth Stevens LB $23.00 (978-0-8368-3192-4). 24pp. The Model

T Ford holds a unique position in the history of the automobile. Its story is told here in beginning text and many pictures. (Rev: BL 10/15/02; HBG 3/03) [639]

25262 Wright, David K. *The Story of Porsches* (1–3). Series: Classic Cars. 2002, Gareth Stevens LB $23.00 (978-0-8368-3193-1). 24pp. The story of this pioneering European automobile is told in full-page color pictures and a beginning-reader text. (Rev: BL 10/15/02; HBG 3/03) [629]

25263 Wright, David K. *The Story of Volkswagen Beetles* (1–3). Illus. Series: Classic Cars. 2002, Gareth Stevens LB $23.00 (978-0-8368-3194-8). 24pp. Traces the history of the Volkswagen Beetle, from its inception in the 1930s to its revival in the 1990s. (Rev: BL 10/15/02; HBG 3/03) [629.222]

25264 Zronik, John. *Street Cred* (4–6). Series: Automania! 2006, Crabtree LB $25.20 (978-0-7787-3006-4); paper $8.95 (978-0-7787-3028-6). 32pp. Slick, souped-up cars are the focus of this book that includes plenty of photographs of customized rides. (Rev: SLJ 8/07)

Railroads

25265 Barton, Byron. *Trains* (PS). Illus. by author. 1986, HarperCollins LB $17.89 (978-0-690-04534-5). 32pp. Explaining the role of trains for the youngest readers. (Rev: BL 8/86; SLJ 9/86)

25266 *Big Book of Trains: National Railway Museum, York, England* (3–5). Illus. 1998, DK $14.99 (978-0-7894-3436-4). 32pp. This book begins with the early steam locomotives in England and America and ends with today's bullet trains and monorails. In addition to highlighting in pictures 50 different trains, there is a pullout section on the Channel Tunnel. (Rev: BL 1/1–15/99; HBG 3/99) [625.1]

25267 Crews, Donald. *Freight Train* (PS–K). Illus. by author. 1978, Greenwillow $17.89 (978-0-688-84165-2); Morrow paper $6.99 (978-0-688-11701-6). 32pp. A description in text and pictures of the various cars included in a freight train, from engine to caboose.

25268 Crowther, Robert. *Trains: A Pop-Up Railroad Book* (2–4). Illus. by author. 2006, Candlewick $17.99 (978-0-7636-3082-9). Suitably linear pop-ups supply a lot of information about train history and engineering. (Rev: SLJ 10/06) [625]

25269 Curlee, Lynn. *Trains* (4–6). Illus. by author. 2009, Atheneum $19.99 (978-1-4169-4848-3). 48pp. A history of railroads from the earliest steam engines to today's new technologies. (Rev: BCCB 5/09; BL 4/1/09; SLJ 6/09) [385.09]

25270 Gallimard Jeunesse. *Trains* (PS–2). Illus. Series: First Discovery. 1998, Scholastic $12.95 (978-0-590-38156-7). 24pp. This colorful book uses a number of overlays to answer basic questions about a variety of trains. (Rev: BL 9/15/98; HBG 9/98) [625.1]

25271 Gibbons, Gail. *Trains* (PS–1). Illus. by author. 1987, Holiday House LB $16.95 (978-0-8234-0640-1); paper $6.95 (978-0-8234-0699-9). 32pp. Describing the essentials of train transportation. (Rev: BL 5/1/87; SLJ 5/87)

25272 Houghton, Gillian. *The Transcontinental Railroad: A Primary Source History of America's First Coast-to-Coast Railroad* (4–8). Series: Primary Sources in American History. 2003, Rosen LB $29.25 (978-0-8239-3684-7). 64pp. Timelines and reproductions of period photographs and relevant items add to the narrative in this introduction to the planning and construction of the railroad in the mid-19th century. (Rev: SLJ 5/03) [385]

25273 Kay, Verla. *Iron Horses* (K–4). Illus. by Michael McCurdy. 1999, Penguin $16.99 (978-0-399-23119-3). 32pp. In double-page spreads, illustrated with scratchboard drawings, this picture book portrays the labor, hardships, and excitement of constructing the transcontinental railroad. (Rev: BCCB 7–8/99; BL 6/1–15/99; HB 7/99; HBG 9/99; SLJ 7/99) [625.4]

25274 Lindeen, Mary. *Trains* (PS–3). 2007, Children's Pr. LB $18.50 (978-1-60014-062-4). 24pp. The basics about trains for young readers, clearly presented and accompanied by engaging photographs. (Rev: SLJ 7/07)

25275 Maynard, Chris. *High-Speed Trains* (5–8). Series: Need for Speed. 2002, Lerner LB $23.93 (978-0-8225-0387-3). 32pp. This action-packed book looks at fast trains from around the world, propelled by steam, oil, magnets, and electricity. (Rev: BL 8/02; HBG 10/02) [625.1]

25276 O'Brien, Patrick. *Steam, Smoke, and Steel: Back in Time with Trains* (K–2). Illus. 2000, Charlesbridge $16.95 (978-0-88106-969-3); paper $6.95 (978-0-88106-972-3). 32pp. A boy describes the different trains driven by six generations of his family in this history of railroads and trains. (Rev: BL 7/00; HBG 3/01; SLJ 8/00) [385]

25277 Perry, Phyllis. *Trains* (2–4). Series: Transportation and Communication. 2001, Enslow LB $23.93 (978-0-7660-1645-3). 32pp. In an attractive format, this book supplies information on the history, development, and use of trains in North America. (Rev: BL 10/15/01; HBG 3/02) [625.1]

25278 Petty, Kate. *Some Trains Run on Water: And Other Amazing Facts About Rail Transportation* (1–3). Illus. by Ross Walton and Jo Moore. Series: I Didn't Know That. 1997, Millbrook LB $19.90 (978-0-7613-0609-2). 32pp. Strange-but-true facts involving trains, past and present, presented with several projects that don't require adult supervision. (Rev: HBG 9/98; SLJ 3/98) [625.2]

25279 Simon, Seymour. *Seymour Simon's Book of Trains* (PS–3). Illus. 2002, HarperCollins LB $18.89 (978-0-06-028476-3). 40pp. An oversized volume with striking photographs of trains coupled with simple but fascinating information ranging from early steam locomotives to today's high-speed trains. (Rev: BCCB 3/02; BL 2/15/02; HB 5/02; HBG 10/02; SLJ 5/02) [385]

25280 Stille, Darlene R. *Freight Trains* (K–2). Illus. Series: Transportation. 2001, Compass Point LB $21.26 (978-0-7565-0148-8). 32pp. Simple descrip-

tions and an attractive layout will appeal to young train fans. (Rev: BL 12/15/01) [625.1]

25281 Uschan, Michael V. *The Transcontinental Railroad* (4–7). Series: Landmark Events in American History. 2003, World Almanac LB $31.00 (978-0-8368-5382-7). 48pp. In accessible language and with plenty of illustrations, this is the story of the railroad that spanned the nation. (Rev: SLJ 6/04) [385]

25282 Weitzman, David. *A Subway for New York* (4–7). Illus. 2005, Farrar $17.00 (978-0-374-37284-2). 40pp. The story behind the early-20th-century construction of New York City's first subway is presented in picture-book format. (Rev: BL 12/1/05; SLJ 2/06) [625.4]

25283 Yancey, Diane. *Camels for Uncle Sam* (4–7). Illus. 1995, Hendrick-Long $16.95 (978-0-937460-91-7). 92pp. The story of the experiment that involved importing camels to the Southwest in the 1850s to help in railroad construction. (Rev: BL 9/15/95) [357]

25284 Zimmermann, Karl. *All Aboard! Passenger Trains Around the World* (4–7). Illus. 2006, Boyds Mills $19.95 (978-1-59078-325-2). 48pp. Photo-filled double-page spreads show the excitement of travel by train and interweave history, geography, commerce, and technology. (Rev: BL 2/15/06; SLJ 6/06) [385]

25285 Zimmermann, Karl. *Steam Locomotives: Whistling, Chugging, Smoking Iron Horses of the Past* (4–8). Illus. 2004, Boyds Mills $19.95 (978-1-59078-165-4). 48pp. Informative and photo-filled, this is an appealing history of steam engines. (Rev: BL 2/1/04; SLJ 7/04) [625.26]

Ships, Boats, and Lighthouses

25286 Ardagh, Philip. *All at Sea* (PS–K). Illus. by Tig Sutton. Series: British Mighty Machines. 2003, Thameside LB $24.25 (978-1-931983-04-4). 32pp. Young boat lovers will enjoy the parade of yachts, submarines, aircraft carrier, hovercraft, ferry, and other vessels portrayed here in bright illustrations and simple words. (Rev: BL 12/1/02; HBG 3/03) [387.2]

25287 Barton, Byron. *Boats* (PS). Illus. by author. 1986, HarperCollins LB $16.89 (978-0-690-04536-9). 32pp. Recreational and functional roles of boats are explained in simple text and bright colors. (Rev: BL 8/86; SLJ 9/86)

25288 Beech, Linda Ward. *The Exxon Valdez's Deadly Oil Spill* (3–4). Series: Code Red. 2007, Bearport LB $23.96 (978-1-59716-366-8). 32pp. Part of the Code Red series, this book looks at how the 1989 spill happened, how it was contained and cleaned, and the effects that it had on wildlife. (Rev: LMC 10/07; SLJ 8/07)

25289 *Boats* (PS–3). Illus. Series: First Discovery. 1993, Scholastic $12.95 (978-0-590-47131-2). 24pp. A book for small children that introduces boats from around the world and explains their differences. (Rev: BL 1/1/94) [623.8]

25290 *Boats and Ships* (4–6). Illus. 1996, Scholastic $19.95 (978-0-590-47647-8). 48pp. Transparencies, flaps, and windows are used to introduce various ships and boats. (Rev: BL 12/15/96) [623]

25291 Bornhoft, Simon. *High Speed Boats* (5–8). Series: Need for Speed. 1999, Lerner LB $23.93 (978-0-8225-2488-5). 32pp. Using a jazzy, attention-getting format with action photographs, sidebars with statistics and interesting facts, and different type sizes, this book covers present and future speedboats. (Rev: BL 1/1–15/00; HBG 3/00) [629.222]

25292 Burgan, Michael. *The Titanic* (3–6). Illus. Series: We the People. 2004, Compass Point LB $26.60 (978-0-7565-0614-8). 48pp. This entry in the We the People series chronicles the tragic history of the *Titanic* from the construction of the mammoth ocean liner through its ill-fated encounter with a North Atlantic iceberg to the discovery of its remains on the ocean floor in the mid-1980s. (Rev: BL 5/1/04) [910]

25293 Caper, William. *Nightmare on the Titanic* (3–6). Series: Code Red. 2007, Bearport LB $23.96 (978-1-59716-362-0). 32pp. Could the sinking of the *Titanic* have been prevented? This book, part of the Code Red series, looks at the facts surrounding this tragedy, a popular subject with young readers. (Rev: SLJ 7/07)

25294 Collicutt, Paul. *This Boat* (PS–3). Illus. 2001, Farrar $15.00 (978-0-374-37495-2). 32pp. A number of different boats are presented in this picture book, including sailboats, paddle-powered riverboats, a submarine, and an aircraft carrier. (Rev: BL 3/15/01; HBG 10/01) [623.8]

25295 Delgado, James P. *Wrecks of American Warships* (5–7). Series: Shipwrecks. 2000, Watts LB $25.50 (978-0-531-20376-7). 64pp. This book describes how underwater archaeologists have discovered and explored such warships as the *Constitution*, *Philadelphia*, *Alabama*, and *Arizona*. (Rev: BL 10/15/00) [623.8]

25296 Doeden, Matt. *The Sinking of the Titanic* (3–5). Illus. Series: Graphic History. 2005, Capstone LB $26.60 (978-0-7368-3834-4). 32pp. An eye-catching and dramatically worded presentation of the sinking. (Rev: BL 2/1/05) [910]

25297 Frederick, Dawn. *How It Happens at the Boat Factory* (1–3). Photos by Bob Wolfe and Diane Wolfe. Series: How It Happens. 2002, Oliver LB $19.95 (978-1-881508-90-8). 32pp. How boats are manufactured is described in text and photographs. (Rev: HBG 10/02; SLJ 12/02)

25298 Houghton, Gillian. *The Wreck of the Andrea Gail: Three Days of a Perfect Storm* (4–6). 2003, Rosen LB $25.25 (978-0-8239-3677-9). 48pp. This account of the 1991 loss of the fishing boat *Andrea Gail,* featured in the film *Perfect Storm,* examines possible causes. (Rev: SLJ 9/03) [910]

25299 Hubbell, Patricia. *Boats: Speeding! Sailing! Cruising!* (PS–1). Illus. by Megan Halsey. 2009, Marshall Cavendish $17.99 (978-0-7614-5524-0). 32pp. Boats and ships of all kinds — from canoes to aircraft carriers — are shown in varied illustrations with rhyming text. (Rev: BCCB 4/09; BL 3/15/09; SLJ 3/09)

25300 Jenkins, Martin. *Titanic* (4–6). Illus. by Brian Sanders. 2007, Candlewick $29.99 (978-0-7636-3468-1). An impressive *Titanic* pop-up is accompanied by a text account of the disaster. (Rev: SLJ 10/07) [910.9163]

25301 Kalman, Maira. *Fireboat: The Heroic Adventures of the John J. Harvey* (2–6). Illus. 2002, Penguin $16.99 (978-0-399-23953-3). 48pp. A beautifully and sensitively presented account of the work of the *John J. Harvey* fireboat, from its launch in 1931 through its restoration in the 1990s and its role in fighting fires in New York City on September 11, 2001. (Rev: BL 9/1/02; HB 9/02*; HBG 3/03; SLJ 9/02*) [974.71044]

25302 Kently, Eric. *The Story of the Titanic* (4–8). Illus. by Steve Noon. 2001, DK paper $17.99 (978-0-7894-7943-3). 32pp. Details of life aboard ship, double-page spreads, cutaways and cross-sections, facts and trivia, and a well-designed layout are just a few of the features of this beautifully designed large-format book. (Rev: BL 12/15/01; HBG 3/02; SLJ 12/01) [363.1]

25303 Macaulay, David. *Ship* (5–8). 1993, Houghton $19.95 (978-0-395-52439-8). A fictional caravel is featured in this exploration of historical seagoing vessels and the work of underwater archaeologists. (Rev: BCCB 11/93; BL 10/15/93*; SLJ 11/93) [387.2]

25304 Maestro, Betsy, and Giulio Maestro. *Ferryboat* (PS–1). Illus. by Giulio Maestro. 1986, HarperCollins LB $15.89 (978-0-690-04520-8). 32pp. The story of ferryboats, centered around one river crossing. (Rev: BCCB 7–8/86; BL 6/15/86; HB 5/86)

25305 Matsen, Brad. *The Incredible Search for the Treasure Ship Atocha* (4–6). Series: Incredible Deep-Sea Adventures. 2003, Enslow LB $23.93 (978-0-7660-2193-8). 48pp. This is the detailed story of the discovery of the wreck of the Spanish treasure ship *Nuestra Señora de Atocha* that sank in a hurricane in 1622. (Rev: HBG 4/04; SLJ 3/04) [909]

25306 Mayell, Hillary. *Shipwrecks* (5–8). Illus. Series: Man-Made Disasters. 2004, Gale LB $29.95 (978-1-59018-058-7). 112pp. Period photographs enhance the impact of stories of shipwrecks of all kinds — from fishing boats to luxury liners — during the 19th and 20th centuries. (Rev: SLJ 7/04) [910.4]

25307 Otfinoski, Steven. *Into the Wind: Sailboats Then and Now* (2–4). Illus. Series: Here We Go! 1996, Benchmark LB $22.79 (978-0-7614-0405-7). 32pp. This simple, well-illustrated account gives a history of sailboats and shows many types and sizes from all over the world, with details on their important features. (Rev: HB 9/96; SLJ 2/97) [623.8]

25308 Rotner, Shelley. *Boats Afloat* (PS–K). Illus. 1998, Orchard $15.95 (978-0-531-30112-8). 32pp. Colorful photographs introduce various types of boats to very young children. (Rev: BL 11/1/98; HBG 3/99; SLJ 11/98) [623.8]

25309 *Sailing Ships: A Lift-the-Flap Discovery* (3–6). Illus. by Thomas Bayley. 1998, Orchard $16.95 (978-0-531-30065-7). This interactive book contains fold-outs of many sailing ships including the *Mayflower* and the *Santa Maria*. (Rev: BL 1/1–15/99; HBG 9/98) [623.8]

25310 Sherrow, Victoria. *Titanic* (2–4). Series: Scholastic History Readers. 2002, Scholastic paper $3.99 (978-0-439-26706-9). 48pp. First-person accounts enliven this illustrated account for beginning readers. (Rev: SLJ 4/03) [910]

25311 Sutherland, John, and Diane Canwell. *Aircraft Carriers* (4–6). Illus. Series: Amazing Ships. 2007, Gareth Stevens LB $23.93 (978-0-8368-8376-3). 32pp. An attractive, basic introduction to these large vessels, with detailed drawings, photographs, and statistics. Also use *Container Ships and Oil Tankers* and *Cruise Ships* (both 2007). (Rev: SLJ 1/08) [623.825]

25312 Van Rynbach, Iris. *Safely to Shore: America's Lighthouses* (3–5). Illus. by author. 2003, Charlesbridge $16.95 (978-1-57091-434-8); paper $6.95 (978-1-57091-435-5). 32pp. Twenty-two of the most famous American lighthouses are profiled, with information on equipment, history, and keepers. (Rev: HBG 4/04; SLJ 1/04) [387.1]

25313 Wargin, Kathy-Jo. *The Edmund Fitzgerald: The Song of the Bell* (K–3). Illus. by Gijsbert van Frankenhuyzen. 2003, Sleeping Bear $17.95 (978-1-58536-126-7). The bell that was retrieved from the *Edmund Fitzgerald* after it sank in Lake Superior in 1975 brings immediacy to this narrative and poem about the storm that took the sailors' lives. (Rev: BL 1/1/04; HBG 4/04; SLJ 2/04) [917.74]

25314 Wilkinson, Philip. *Ships* (4–7). Illus. 2000, Kingfisher $16.95 (978-0-7534-5280-6). 64pp. Straightforward text and handsome illustrations cover maritime history from the earliest sailing ships and discuss piracy, the slave trade, and superstitions about the sea. (Rev: BL 2/1/01; HBG 10/01; SLJ 1/01) [623.8]

25315 Zimmermann, Karl. *Steamboats: The Story of Lakers, Ferries, and Majestic Paddle-Wheelers* (4–7). Illus. 2007, Boyds Mills $19.95 (978-1-59078-434-1). 48pp. Carefully researched by an aficionado, this detailed examination of the history, purpose, and engineering of steamboats contains biographical information and excellent archival and modern illustrations. (Rev: BL 1/1–15/07; SLJ 4/07) [623.82]

Weapons, Submarines, and the Armed Forces

25316 Aaseng, Nathan. *The Marine Corps in Action* (4–8). Series: U.S. Military Branches and Careers. 2001, Enslow LB $26.60 (978-0-7660-1637-8). 128pp. An attractive introduction to all aspects of the Marine Corps that looks at the future of this military branch and the number of women and minorities included. (Rev: HBG 3/02; SLJ 4/02) [359.9]

25317 Benson, Michael. *The U.S. Army* (4–6). Illus. Series: U.S. Armed Forces. 2004, Lerner LB $26.60 (978-0-8225-1645-3). 64pp. An introductory overview of the Army and its history, recruitment and training, equipment, and day-to-day routines. (Rev: BL 1/1–15/05; SLJ 3/05) [355]

25318 Benson, Michael. *The U.S. Marine Corps* (4–7). Illus. Series: U.S. Armed Forces. 2004, Lerner LB $26.60 (978-0-8225-1648-4). 64pp. Introduces the history of the Marine Corps, followed by information on recruitment, training, and daily life. (Rev: BL 1/05; SLJ 3/05) [359.6]

25319 Bledsoe, Karen, and Glen Bledsoe. *Helicopters: High-Flying Heroes* (4–6). Series: Mighty Military Machines. 2006, Enslow LB $23.93 (978-0-7660-2663-6). 48pp. Describes how military helicopters are used in a variety of tasks that display their nimbleness and versatility. (Rev: SLJ 4/07) [358.4]

25320 Byers, Ann. *America's Star Wars Program* (5–7). Series: The Library of Weapons of Mass Destruction. 2005, Rosen LB $27.95 (978-1-4042-0287-0). 64pp. Photographs and text document the development of 20th-century missiles and America's controversial "Star Wars" strategy. (Rev: SLJ 11/05) [623]

25321 Demarest, Chris L. *Mayday! Mayday! A Coast Guard Rescue* (K–2). Illus. by author. 2004, Simon & Schuster $16.95 (978-0-689-85161-2). 40pp. Rhyming text and eye-catching illustrations follow a Coast Guard helicopter team as it locates a yacht in trouble and rescues everybody aboard. (Rev: BL 9/1/04; SLJ 7/04) [303.12]

25322 Donovan, Sandy. *The U.S. Air Force* (4–7). Illus. Series: U.S. Armed Forces. 2004, Lerner LB $26.60 (978-0-8225-1436-7). 64pp. Introduces the history of the Air Force, followed by information on recruitment, training, and daily life. Also use *U.S. Air Force Special Operations* (2004). (Rev: BL 1/05; SLJ 3/05) [358.4]

25323 Egan, Tracie. *Weapons of Mass Destruction and North Korea* (5–7). Series: The Library of Weapons of Mass Destruction. 2005, Rosen LB $27.95 (978-1-4042-0296-2). 64pp. Explores what the West knows about North Korea's efforts to build stockpiles of biological, chemical, and — potentially — nuclear weapons. (Rev: SLJ 11/05) [623]

25324 Gartman, Gene. *Life in Army Basic Training* (4–6). Illus. Series: On Duty. 2000, Children's Book Pr. LB $24.50 (978-0-516-23347-5). 48pp. Written by a man who served in the military, this book goes through the routines and demands of basic training with information on weapons and various fitness programs. (Rev: BL 2/1/01) [355.5]

25325 Goldberg, Jan. *Green Berets: The U.S. Army Special Forces* (5–7). Series: Inside Special Operations. 2003, Rosen LB $26.50 (978-0-8239-3808-7). 64pp. An overview of the history, mission, training, and equipment of the Special Forces. (Rev: BL 7/03) [356]

25326 Gonen, Rivka. *Charge! Weapons and Warfare in Ancient Times* (5–8). Illus. 1993, Lerner LB $23.93 (978-0-8225-3201-9). 72pp. A look at the development of weapons from sticks and stones to battering rams. (Rev: BCCB 12/93; BL 2/1/94; SLJ 2/94) [355.8]

25327 Graham, Ian. *You Wouldn't Want to Be in the First Submarine! An Undersea Expedition You'd Rather Avoid* (3–5). Illus. by David Antram. 2008, Scholastic LB $29.00 (978-0-531-20702-4); paper $9.95 (978-0-531-21912-6). 32pp. A historical look at submarines highlighting the dangerous *Hunley*, built by the Confederates during the Civil War. (Rev: BL 12/1/08) [973.7]

25328 Gurstelle, William. *The Art of the Catapult: Build Greek Ballistae, Roman Onagers, English Trebuchets, and More Ancient Artillery* (5–12). Illus. 2004, Chicago Review paper $14.95 (978-1-55652-526-1). 172pp. Information on history, physics, and military tactics, plus step-by-step instructions for the construction of 10 working catapults. (Rev: SLJ 11/04) [623.4]

25329 Hamilton, John. *Armed Forces* (4–7). Illus. Series: War on Terrorism. 2002, ABDO LB $25.65 (978-1-57765-674-6). 48pp. An introduction to the U.S. military and the roles these services play in protecting the country, with color photographs, a glossary, and list of Web sites. (Rev: BL 8/02; HBG 10/02) [355]

25330 Hamilton, John. *Weapons of War* (4–7). Illus. Series: War on Terrorism. 2002, ABDO LB $25.65 (978-1-57765-673-9). 48pp. This account describes the weapons currently available to U.S. military personnel, including fighter planes, bombers, helicopters, bombs, missiles, and ships. (Rev: BL 5/1/02; HBG 10/02) [623.4]

25331 Hamilton, John. *Weapons of War: A Pictorial History of the Past One Thousand Years* (4–7). Illus. Series: The Millennium. 2000, ABDO LB $25.65 (978-1-57765-362-2). 48pp. In a short space, this book traces 1,000 years of weapons including small weaponry, ships, firearms, military airplanes, tanks, missiles, and bombs. (Rev: BL 7/00; HBG 10/00; SLJ 10/00) [623.4]

25332 Hasan, Tahara. *Anthrax Attacks Around the World* (4–8). Series: Terrorist Attacks. 2003, Rosen LB $27.95 (978-0-8239-3859-9). 64pp. Examines the use of anthrax as a terrorist weapon and includes accounts of its use in Japan, the Soviet Union, and the United States. (Rev: SLJ 2/04) [303.6]

25333 Herbst, Judith. *The History of Weapons* (5–8). Series: Major Inventions Through History. 2005, Twenty-First Century LB $26.60 (978-0-8225-3805-9). 56pp. An attractive look at the evolution of weapons from rocks and sticks to today's weapons of mass destruction. (Rev: SLJ 1/06) [623.4]

25334 Hibbert, Adam. *Chemical and Biological Warfare* (5–9). Series: Face the Facts. 2003, Raintree LB $28.56 (978-0-7398-6847-8). 56pp. Part of a series on international issues, this volume examines the powers and dangers of chemical and biological weapons. (Rev: SLJ 4/04) [358]

25335 Kennedy, Robert C. *Life as an Army Demolition Expert* (4–6). Illus. Series: On Duty. 2000, Children's Book Pr. LB $24.50 (978-0-516-23346-8); paper $6.95 (978-0-516-23546-2). 48pp. This work gives historical background plus an explanation of work today in this specialized area of the U.S. Army. (Rev: BL 2/1/01) [358]

25336 Kennedy, Robert C. *Life with the Navy Seals* (4–7). Series: On Duty. 2000, Children's LB $24.50 (978-0-516-23351-2). 48pp. A look at this special branch of the U.S. Navy with material on its responsibilities, training, and career opportunities. (Rev: BL 3/1/01) [359]

25337 Meltzer, Milton. *Weapons and Warfare: From the Stone Age to the Space Age* (5–9). Illus. 1996, HarperCollins LB $17.89 (978-0-06-024876-5). This work describes the evolution of weapons from clubs to the H-bomb, including how these weapons have been used and misused through the ages. (Rev: BCCB 2/97; BL 12/1/96; SLJ 1/97) [355.02]

25338 Myers, Walter Dean. *USS Constellation: Pride of the American Navy* (4–8). 2004, Holiday House $16.95 (978-0-8234-1816-9). 86pp. Myers presents the colorful history of the *USS Constellation,* the last of America's all-sail fighting ships, in this volume with extensive illustrations and other materials. (Rev: BL 7/04; HB 7/04; SLJ 8/04) [359.8]

25339 Payan, Gregory, and Alexander Guelke. *Life on a Submarine* (4–6). Illus. Series: On Duty. 2000, Children's Book Pr. LB $24.50 (978-0-516-23349-9). 48pp. The glamorous and arduous aspects of life aboard a navy submarine are covered, including exercise and sleeping arrangements. (Rev: BL 2/1/01) [359.9]

25340 Richie, Jason. *Weapons: Designing the Tools of War* (5–10). Illus. 2000, Oliver LB $21.95 (978-1-881508-60-1). 144pp. Using separate chapters for different categories of weapons — for example, submarines, battleships, and tanks — this is a history of the development of weaponry from 300 B.C. to today. (Rev: BL 5/1/00; HBG 10/00; SLJ 8/00) [623]

25341 Roza, Greg. *The Incredible Story of Aircraft Carriers* (3–6). Illus. Series: A Kid's Guide to Incredible Technology. 2004, Rosen LB $21.25 (978-0-8239-6714-8). 24pp. A concise look at how and why aircraft carriers are built and at the role they play and the planes they carry, with a layout diagram and discussion of the future for these huge ships. (Rev: SLJ 2/05) [359.9]

25342 Sutherland, John, and Diane Canwell. *Submarines* (4–6). Illus. Series: Amazing Ships. 2007, Gareth Stevens LB $23.93 (978-0-8368-8379-4). 32pp. An attractive, basic introduction to these underwater vessels, with detailed drawings, photographs, and statistics. (Rev: SLJ 1/08) [623.825]

25343 Thompson, Gare. *The Monitor: The Iron Warship that Changed the World* (2–4). Series: All Aboard Reading. 2003, Penguin paper $3.99 (978-0-448-43245-8). 48pp. This fascinating book recounts not only the Civil War history of the ironclad *Monitor* but also the successful 20th-century search for its underwater wreck site. (Rev: BL 12/15/03; HBG 4/04)

25344 Wolny, Philip. *Weapons Satellites* (5–9). Series: The Library of Satellites. 2003, Rosen LB $26.50 (978-0-8239-3855-1). 64pp. This account explores the growing technology of weapon satellites that are capable of knocking out enemies' satellites, and launching attacks from outer space. (Rev: BL 11/15/03; SLJ 1/04) [629.46]

25345 Woods, Mary B., and Michael Woods. *Ancient Warfare: From Clubs to Catapults* (5–8). Series: Ancient Technologies. 2000, Runestone LB $25.26 (978-0-8225-2999-6). 96pp. The weaponry of ancient civilizations including Greece and China.

(Rev: BCCB 12/00; BL 9/15/00; HBG 3/01; SLJ 1/01) [623]

25346 Yomtov, Nel. *Navy SEALS in Action* (3–6). Illus. Series: Special Ops. 2008, Bearport LB $18.95 (978-1-59716-630-0). 32pp. An overview of the SEALS' history, training, equipment, and operations, with plenty of color photographs. (Rev: BL 4/1/08) [359.9]

25347 Zeinert, Karen, and Mary Miller. *The Brave Women of the Gulf Wars: Operation Desert Storm and Operation Iraqi Freedom* (5–8). Illus. Series: Women at War. 2005, Twenty-First Century LB $30.60 (978-0-7613-2705-9). 112pp. Highlights women's roles in the Persian Gulf military campaigns. (Rev: BL 10/1/05; SLJ 11/05) [956.7]

Recreation

Crafts

General and Miscellaneous

25348 Albregts, Lisa, and Elizabeth Cape. *Best Friends: Tons of Crazy, Cool Things to Do with Your Girlfriends* (4–8). Illus. 1998, Chicago Review paper $12.95 (978-1-55652-326-7). Arranged by seasons, this activity book contains crafts, games, dances, snacks, and skits to amuse girls when they get together. (Rev: BL 3/1/99; SLJ 1/99) [796.083]

25349 Birdseye, Tom. *A Kids' Guide to Building Forts* (5–8). Illus. by Bill Klein. 1993, Harbinger paper $11.95 (978-0-943173-69-6). 62pp. A guide to the building of 19 kinds of forts, from the very simple to the more complex, some of which can be turned into clubhouses. (Rev: SLJ 9/93) [745.5]

25350 Blanchette, Peg, and Terri Thibault. *Really Cool Felt Crafts* (3–5). Illus. Series: Quick Starts for Kids! 2002, Williamson paper $8.95 (978-1-885593-80-1). 64pp. This book of easy-to-make felt projects includes instructions accompanied by drawings, and a section of full-sized templates. (Rev: BL 12/15/02; SLJ 1/03) [746]

25351 Bledsoe, Karen. *Chinese New Year Crafts* (K–5). Illus. Series: Fun Holiday Crafts Kids Can Do! 2005, Enslow LB $22.60 (978-0-7660-2347-5). 32pp. The ten crafts presented use everyday materials and include a dragon-streamer puppet, a ribbon lantern, and Chinese zodiac pictures. (Rev: SLJ 6/05) [394.261]

25352 Boonyadhistarn, Thiranut. *Fingernail Art: Dazzling Fingers and Terrific Toes* (4–8). Illus. Series: Snap Books: Crafts. 2006, Capstone LB $25.26 (978-0-7368-6474-9). 32pp. This colorful, well-thought-out guide offers interesting tips on decorating nails. (Rev: SLJ 2/07) [646.7]

25353 Boonyadhistarn, Thiranut. *Stamping Art: Imprint Your Designs* (4–8). Illus. Series: Snap Books: Crafts. 2006, Capstone LB $25.26 (978-0-7368-6477-0). 32pp. Simple, step-by-step instructions guide readers through a variety of stamping

projects that use accessible materials. (Rev: SLJ 2/07) [761]

25354 Boston, Lisa. *Sing! Play! Create! Hands-On Learning for 3- to 7-Year-Olds* (PS–2). Illus. by Sarah Cole. Series: A Williamson Little Hands Book. 2006, Williamson $14.95 (978-0-8249-6781-9); paper $12.95 (978-0-8249-6780-2). 126pp. Crafts, poems, and songs are among the activities suggested here and centered around a pond, garden, zoo, and farm. (Rev: SLJ 8/06) [372.21]

25355 Braman, Arlette N. *Create! The Best Crafts and Activities from Many Lands* (3–6). Illus. by Jo-Ellen Bosson. Series: Kids Around the World. 1999, Wiley paper $12.95 (978-0-471-29005-6). 116pp. From Amish quilts to Zulu woven baskets this craft book includes both ancient and modern crafts from a variety of cultures, all introduced with clear directions. (Rev: SLJ 12/99) [745]

25356 Broida, Marian. *Projects About Nineteenth-Century Chinese Immigrants* (3–5). Illus. Series: Hands-on History. 2005, Benchmark LB $18.95 (978-0-7614-1978-5). 48pp. Crafts — a miner's scale, an abacus, a fan — plus recipes and other projects are accompanied by historical and cultural information. (Rev: SLJ 5/06)

25357 Broida, Marian. *Projects About Nineteenth-Century European Immigrants* (3–5). Illus. Series: Hands-on History. 2005, Benchmark LB $18.95 (978-0-7614-1980-8). 47pp. Through the varied projects in this book, students will learn the details of the sometimes-difficult lives of 19th-century immigrants from Europe; cultural and historical notes precede the activities. (Rev: SLJ 5/06) [973.5085]

25358 Brownrigg, Sheri. *Hearts and Crafts* (4–8). Illus. 1995, Tricycle paper $9.95 (978-1-883672-28-7). Clear instructions show how to complete a variety of Valentine's Day projects, including making necklaces and candles. (Rev: BL 3/1/96; SLJ 3/96) [745.5]

25359 Caney, Steven. *Steven Caney's Playbook* (3–5). Illus. 1975, Workman paper $9.95 (978-0-

911104-38-7). 240pp. All sorts of activities involving discarded or inexpensive materials, thoroughly and clearly presented.

25360 Carlson, Laurie. *EcoArt! Earth-Friendly Art and Craft Experiences for 3- to 9-Year-Olds* (K–4). Illus. by Loretta Braren. 1993, Williamson paper $14.25 (978-0-913589-68-7). 160pp. Over 100 arts and crafts activities using natural, recyclable, or reusable materials. (Rev: BL 2/15/93; SLJ 4/93) [745.5]

25361 Castaldo, Nancy F. *Rainy Day Play! Explore, Create, Discover, Pretend* (PS–1). Illus. by Loretta Braren. Series: A Little Hands Book. 1996, Williamson paper $12.95 (978-1-885593-00-9). 142pp. A collection of 64 ideas for activities, crafts, and games that are attractively presented and will afford hours of enjoyment. (Rev: SLJ 2/97) [745.5]

25362 Castaldo, Nancy F. *Winter Day Play! Activities, Crafts, and Games for Indoors and Out* (PS–3). Illus. 2001, Chicago Review paper $13.95 (978-1-55652-381-6). 161pp. The more than 70 suggested activities range from scientific projects and artistic endeavors to parties and cooking. (Rev: SLJ 12/01) [790]

25363 Chapman, Gillian, and Pam Robson. *Art from Fabric: With Projects Using Rags, Old Clothing and Remnants* (3–5). Illus. Series: Salvaged! 1995, Thomson Learning LB $21.40 (978-1-56847-381-9). 32pp. This book contains several creative projects and crafts using old fabrics or fibers, on double-page spreads. (Rev: SLJ 1/96) [745.5]

25364 Check, Laura. *Create Your Own Candles: 30 Easy-to-Make Designs* (5–8). Illus. by Norma Jean Martin-Jourdenais. 2004, Williamson paper $8.95 (978-0-8249-8663-6). 61pp. Safety is stressed in this guide to exciting (and complex) candle creations. (Rev: SLJ 11/04) [745.593]

25365 Cherkerzian, Diane, and Colleen Van Blaricom. *Merry Things to Make* (3–5). Illus. 1999, Boyds Mills paper $7.95 (978-1-56397-838-8). 64pp. A wide range of craft ideas using simple materials are presented with good step-by-step instructions. (Rev: BL 9/1/99; SLJ 10/99) [745.59]

25366 Craig, Rebecca. *Gorgeous Gifts* (3–6). Photos by Andy Crawford. Series: Ecocrafts. 2007, Kingfisher paper $7.95 (978-0-7534-5967-6). 48pp. With clear instructions and photographs, this book shows how to use recyclables to create attractive gifts. Also use *Dream Bedroom* (2007). (Rev: SLJ 2/08) [745.5]

25367 Dall, Mary Doerfler. *Little Hands Create! Art and Activities for Kids Ages 3 to 6* (PS–2). Illus. by Sarah Rakitin. 2004, Williamson paper $12.95 (978-0-8249-8664-3). 120pp. Children will need help with these activities, most of which — egg-carton boats and twisted-paper jewelry, for example, use everyday materials. (Rev: BL 1/1–15/05) [745.5]

25368 D'Cruz, Anna-Marie. *Make Your Own Musical Instruments* (3–4). Series: Do It Yourself Projects! 2009, Rosen LB $23.95 (978-1-4358-2854-4). 24pp. Castanets, bongo drums, washboard, and maracas are among the instruments featured in this guide that provides color photographs and clear directions.

Also use *Make Your Own Puppets* (2009). (Rev: SLJ 7/09) [784.192]

25369 Dickins, Rosie. *Art Treasury: Pictures, Paintings, and Projects* (4–7). 2007, Usborne LB $19.99 (978-0-7945-1452-5). 96pp. Each of the art projects in this exciting collection is inspired by an existing work of art. (Rev: BL 4/1/07) [709]

25370 Dickinson, Gill, and Cheryl Owen. *Creative Crafts for Kids: Over 100 Projects for Two to Ten Year Olds* (4–10). 2007, Sterling LB $24.95 (978-0-600-61590-3). 256pp. Paper crafts, jewelry, holiday decorations, food crafts, and even good-smelling crafts for children and their teachers or adult friends are presented in a pleasant format. Materials lists and step-by-step instructions make this user-friendly. (Rev: SLJ 5/07)

25371 Drake, Jane, and Ann Love. *The Kids Winter Handbook* (3–5). Illus. by Heather Collins. 2001, Kids Can $18.95 (978-1-55337-033-8); paper $12.95 (978-1-55074-969-4). 127pp. Crafts, recipes, games, and other activities are geared to indoor and outdoor winter entertainment. (Rev: HBG 3/02; SLJ 11/01) [790.1]

25372 Ehlert, Lois. *Snowballs* (PS–3). Illus. 1995, Harcourt $16.00 (978-0-15-200074-5). 32pp. All kinds of materials are used to create and decorate a snow family in this book of craft ideas. (Rev: BCCB 11/95; BL 12/1/95; SLJ 11/95)

25373 Erlbach, Arlene, and Herb Erlbach. *Mother's Day Crafts* (3–5). Illus. Series: Fun Holiday Crafts Kids Can Do! 2005, Enslow LB $22.60 (978-0-7660-2348-2). 32pp. Ten original gifts for Mom that students will enjoy making; photographs help them picture the finished product. (Rev: SLJ 8/05) [745.594]

25374 Freixenet, Anna. *Creating with Mosaics* (3–6). Series: Crafts for All Seasons. 2000, Blackbirch LB $23.70 (978-1-56711-440-9). 32pp. This appealing craft book shows how to create attractive mosaics using items like beads, balls of aluminum foil, beans, seeds, and buttons. (Rev: SLJ 2/01) [745]

25375 Friday, Megan. *Pet Crafts: Everything You Need to Become Your Pet's Craft Star!* (4–6). Photos by Steve Giraud. Illus. by Diana Fisher. Series: Craft Star. 2009, Walter Foster paper $8.95 (978-1-60058-600-2). 64pp. A collection of 15 easy-to-make projects for pets — toys, clothing, treats, and so forth. (Rev: SLJ 6/09) [745.5]

25376 *Fun-to-make Crafts for Easter* (3–6). 2005, Boyds Mills $15.95 (978-1-59078-340-5); paper $7.95 (978-1-59078-365-8). 64pp. Greeting cards, holiday decorations, and clothing are among the 150 crafts suggested. Also use *Fun-to-Make Crafts for Every Day* (2005). (Rev: SLJ 6/05)

25377 *Fun-to-Make Crafts for Halloween* (3–6). 2005, Boyds Mills $15.95 (978-1-59078-343-6); paper $7.95 (978-1-59078-368-9). 63pp. The crafts and projects here include edible treats, masks, decorations, gifts, and other goodies for Halloween and the entire harvest season. (Rev: SLJ 9/05)

25378 Furstinger, Nancy. *Creative Crafts for Critters* (2–4). Illus. by Philippe Beha. 2001, Stoddart paper $8.95 (978-0-7737-6135-3). 48pp. Pet lovers will find lots of craft ideas for animal toys, clothing, and nutrition. (Rev: SLJ 1/02) [745.5]

25379 Gabriel, Faith K. *Nifty Thrifty Animal Crafts* (1–3). Illus. Series: Nifty Thrifty Crafts for Kids. 2007, Enslow LB $22.60 (978-0-7660-2779-4). 32pp. These simple, animal-themed crafts use readily available materials, and each includes some facts about the featured animal. (Rev: SLJ 5/07)

25380 Garner, Lynne. *African Crafts: Fun Things to Make and Do from West Africa* (4–6). Illus. 2008, Chicago Review $12.95 (978-1-55652-748-7). 48pp. Ghana is the main focus of this crafts book that also includes information on history and culture. (Rev: BL 5/1/08; SLJ 10/08) [745.5]

25381 Gessat, Audrey. *Crafts from Salt Dough* (2–4). Trans. from French by Cheryl L. Smith. Series: Step by Step. 2002, Capstone LB $22.60 (978-0-7368-1475-1). 32pp. Tips on working with dough accompany instructions for making items including a candleholder and a clown pencil. Also use *Crafts from Felt* and *Crafts from Modeling Clay* (both 2002). (Rev: HBG 3/03; SLJ 2/03)

25382 Gnojewski, Carol. *Cinco de Mayo Crafts* (K–5). Illus. Series: Fun Holiday Crafts Kids Can Do! 2005, Enslow LB $22.60 (978-0-7660-2344-4). 32pp. The ten crafts presented use everyday materials and include a sombrero and a paper poncho. (Rev: SLJ 6/05)

25383 Gould, Roberta. *Kidtopia: 'Round the Country and Back Through Time in 60 Projects* (2–7). 2000, Tricycle paper $13.95 (978-1-58246-026-0). 152pp. Divided into sections that cover American history and geography, this book contains many related projects, crafts, party ideas, and games. (Rev: SLJ 12/00) [745]

25384 Gould, Roberta. *Making Cool Crafts and Awesome Art: A Kids' Treasure Trove of Fabulous Fun* (2–5). Photos by author. 1998, Williamson paper $12.95 (978-1-885593-11-5). 160pp. This welcome addition to craft collections includes simple instructions to make a variety of objects from easy-to-find materials. Many of the projects represent foreign cultures and, in these cases, background material is given. (Rev: SLJ 4/98) [745.5]

25385 Griffith, Saul, and Nick Dragotta. *Howtoons: The Possibilities Are Endless* (5–8). Illus. by Nick Dragotta. 2007, HarperCollins paper $15.99 (978-0-06 076158-5). 112pp. A comic book and a project book in one, this will appeal to readers who are reluctant to pick up ordinary craft books; the "crafts" go beyond origami and include a marshmallow shooter, a tree swing, a rocket, and a flute. (Rev: BL 12/15/07; SLJ 5/08) [741.5]

25386 Halls, Kelly Milner, ed. *Look What You Can Make with Craft Sticks: Over 80 Pictured Crafts and Dozens of Other Ideas* (2–4). Photos by Hank Schneider. 2002, Boyds Mills paper $5.95 (978-1-56397-997-2). 48pp. Younger children may need help with some of the projects here, which use everyday materials to make a wide variety of items. Also use *Look What You Can Make with Plastic Bottles and Tubs: Over 80 Pictured Crafts and Dozens of Other Ideas* (2002). (Rev: SLJ 4/02) [745.5]

25387 Halls, Kelly Milner, ed. *Look What You Can Make with Plastic-Foam Trays: Over 90 Pictured Crafts and Dozens of Other Ideas* (K–3). Illus. 2003, Boyds Mills paper $5.95 (978-1-59078-078-7). 48pp. Child-friendly ideas for using plastic-foam trays in a variety of inventive ways. (Rev: SLJ 2/03)

25388 Hankin, Rosie. *Crafty Kids: Fun Projects for You and Your Toddler* (K–2). Illus. by author. 2006, Barron's paper $8.99 (978-0-7641-3542-2). 64pp. Adults and young children work together on the 28 simple projects here, many of them created from paper plates with a variety of adornments. (Rev: BL 1/1–15/07; SLJ 12/06) [745.5]

25389 Hauser, Jill F. *Little Hands Celebrate America! Learning About the U.S.A. Through Crafts and Activities* (K–5). Illus. by Michael Kline. Series: A Williamson Little Hands Book. 2004, Williamson paper $14.29 (978-1-885593-93-1). 128pp. Easy projects and activities introduce American symbols, sights, traditions, and holidays. (Rev: SLJ 11/04) [973]

25390 Hebert, Holly. *60 Super Simple Crafts* (3–6). Illus. by Leo Abbett. 1996, Lowell House paper $6.95 (978-1-56565-385-6). 80pp. Simple instructions are given for 60 crafts projects, most of which involve material found in the home or at local craft shops. (Rev: SLJ 2/97) [745.5]

25391 Hendry, Linda. *Cat Crafts* (4–6). Illus. Series: Kids Can Do It! 2002, Kids Can $12.95 (978-1-55074-964-9); paper $5.95 (978-1-55074-921-2). 40pp. Using double-page spreads, this book outlines 17 cat-related projects. (Rev: BL 4/1/02; HBG 10/02; SLJ 6/02) [745.5]

25392 Hendry, Linda. *Dog Crafts* (4–6). Illus. Series: Kids Can Do It! 2002, Kids Can $12.95 (978-1-55074-960-1); paper $5.95 (978-1-55074-962-5). 40pp. Seventeen projects, such as making jewelry and toys, and all related to dogs, are presented in double-page spreads with easy-to-follow instructions. (Rev: BL 4/1/02; HBG 10/02; SLJ 6/02) [745.5]

25393 Hendry, Linda. *Making Gift Boxes* (4–8). Illus. by author. Series: Kids Can! 1999, Kids Can paper $5.95 (978-1-55074-503-0). 40pp. The 14 boxes included in this fine craft book with clear instructions include a photo box, a garden box to grow seeds, a box for storing CDs, and a treasure box with false compartments. (Rev: SLJ 12/99) [745]

25394 Henry, Sandi. *Kids' Art Works! Creating with Color, Design, Texture and More* (K–5). Illus. by Norma Jean Martin-Jourdenais. Series: A Williamson Kids Can! Book. 2000, Williamson paper $12.95 (978-1-885593-35-1). 138pp. Sixty artistic creations using household materials; for example, a pasta fish, a Swiss cheese candle, and a sandpaper relief print. (Rev: SLJ 3/00) [745]

25395 *Holiday and Everyday Projects: Festive and Fun Creations* (2–5). Illus. Series: Crafty Kids. 2003, McGraw-Hill $12.95 (978-1-57768-528-9). 48pp. Projects for Easter, Halloween, and Mother's Day are among those included in this volume with easy-to-follow instructions and illustrations. (Rev: HBG 4/04; SLJ 12/03) [745.5]

25396 Hollow, Michele C. *Nifty Thrifty Sports Crafts* (1–3). Illus. Series: Nifty Thrifty Crafts for Kids. 2007, Enslow LB $22.60 (978-0-7660-2782-4). 32pp. Crafts for children who enjoy playing and watching sports. Easy-to-find, inexpensive materials make this teacher- and parent-friendly. (Rev: SLJ 8/07)

25397 Hosking, Wayne. *Asian Kites* (3–6). Illus. Series: Asian Arts and Crafts for Creative Kids. 2005, Tuttle $12.95 (978-0-8048-3545-9). 63pp. A thorough how-to guide to making 15 kites from China, Japan, Korea, Malaysia, and Thailand, with historical and cultural background. (Rev: SLJ 9/05)

25398 Hunter, Dette. *38 Ways to Entertain Your Grandparents* (K–2). Illus. by Deirdre Betteridge. 2002, Annick LB $19.95 (978-1-55037-749-1); paper $9.95 (978-1-55037-748-4). 48pp. Hunter deftly interweaves Sarah's story of all the entertaining things she does with her grandparents with instructions for young readers to do likewise, including rules for games, recipes, and craft projects. (Rev: BL 12/1/02; HBG 3/03; SLJ 4/03) [793]

25399 Irvin, Christine M. *Egg Carton Mania* (2–4). Illus. Series: Craft Mania. 2002, Children's Book Pr. LB $23.50 (978-0-516-22277-6). 32pp. Projects using egg cartons range from finger puppets to a double-decker bus. (Rev: BL 1/1–15/03; SLJ check) [745.5]

25400 Johnson, Ginger. *Make Your Own Christmas Ornaments* (3–5). Illus. by Norma Jean Martin-Jourdenais. Series: Quick Starts for Kids! 2002, Williamson paper $8.95 (978-1-885593-79-5). 64pp. A collection of 25 ornaments with clear instructions and photographs of finished products. (Rev: BL 12/15/02; SLJ 10/02)

25401 Jovinelly, Joann, and Jason Netelkos. *The Crafts and Culture of a Medieval Monastery* (4–8). Illus. Series: Crafts of the Middle Ages. 2006, Rosen LB $29.25 (978-1-4042-0759-2). 48pp. Crafts and history are interwoven in this interesting that looks at the history of monasteries, life within them, and the work that took place in scriptoria, gardens, and hospitals; crafts include prayer beads and a plague mask. Also use *The Crafts and Culture of a Medieval Town* (2006). (Rev: SLJ 4/07) [271.0094]

25402 Kerina, Jane. *African Crafts* (5–8). Illus. by Tom Feelings and Marylyn Katzman. 1970, Lion LB $13.95 (978-0-87460-084-1). Many projects arranged geographically by the region in Africa where they originated.

25403 Kimble-Ellis, Sonya. *Traditional African American Arts and Activities* (3–7). Illus. Series: Celebrating Our Heritage. 2002, Wiley paper $12.95 (978-0-471-41046-1). 120pp. The projects featured in this title will teach students something about traditional culture, foods, holidays, crafts, and games. (Rev: SLJ 8/02)

25404 King, Penny, and Clare Roundhill. *Out of This World: Lots of Space Pictures to Make* (2–6). Illus. Series: Making Pictures. 1997, Rigby $14.95 (978-1-57572-193-4). 29pp. This craft book introduces 12 space-related activities, like making a rocket from a cardboard tube. Others in the series are *Secrets of the Sea: Lots of Underwater Pictures to Make* and *Spooky Things: Lots of Spooky Pictures to Make* (both 1997). (Rev: SLJ 12/97) [745.5]

25405 Kohl, MaryAnn F., and Jean Potter. *Global Art: Activities, Projects, and Inventions from Around the World* (3–6). Illus. by Rebecca Van Slyke. 1998, Gryphon paper $14.95 (978-0-87659-190-1). 189pp. A series of crafts that vary in difficulty, are arranged by continent, and explore the world's different cultures and habitats. (Rev: SLJ 10/98) [745]

25406 Kranz, Linda. *Let's Rock! Rock Painting for Kids* (1–6). Illus. 2003, NorthWord paper $11.95 (978-1-55971-870-7). 48pp. A comprehensive introduction to rock painting, including recommendations for the best kinds of rocks and paint to use, painting techniques, and special designs. (Rev: SLJ 10/03) [751.4]

25407 Lehne, Judith Logan. *The Never-Be-Bored Book: Quick Things to Make When There's Nothing to Do* (4–6). Illus. by Morissa Lipstein. 1993, Sterling $17.95 (978-0-8069-1254-7). 128pp. Over 40 projects are included in this useful craft book, plus recipes for many ingredients including clay, dough, and natural dyes. (Rev: BL 5/15/93) [745.5]

25408 Lewis, Amanda. *Making Memory Books* (3–6). Illus. by Esperanca Melo. Series: Kids Can! 1999, Kids Can paper $6.95 (978-1-55074-567-2). 40pp. This craft book shows how to create a book for memorabilia with instructions on creating stencils, decorations, different types of lettering, templates, stamps, etc. (Rev: SLJ 2/00) [745]

25409 Lipsey, Jennifer. *I Love to Collage* (2–4). Illus. Series: My Favorite Art Book. 2006, Sterling $9.95 (978-1-57990-770-9). 48pp. Provides lots of practical, well-described ideas for making collages from materials ranging from leaves to candy wrappers to pasta. (Rev: BL 12/15/06; SLJ 12/06) [702]

25410 Love, Ann, and Jane Drake. *Kids and Grandparents: An Activity Book* (3–6). Illus. by Heather Collins. 2000, Kids Can $17.95 (978-1-55074-784-3); paper $10.95 (978-1-55074-492-7). 160pp. A collection of over 90 games, crafts, recipes, and activities for children and their grandparents together with a "Making Memories" section on creating a memory book, a relative map, and a family tree. (Rev: HBG 10/00; SLJ 5/00) [745]

25411 Luxbacher, Irene. *The Jumbo Book of Outdoor Art* (3–6). Photos by Ray Boudreau and Doug Hall. Illus. by author. 2006, Kids Can paper $16.95 (978-1-55337-680-4). 144pp. This large-format volume provides step-by-step instructions for nearly 60 outdoor art projects and activities. (Rev: SLJ 11/06) [704.9]

25412 McGraw, Sheila. *Gifts Kids Can Make* (4–8). Photos by Sheila McGraw and Joy von Tiedemann. 1994, Firefly paper $9.95 (978-1-895565-35-5). 96pp. A craft book that gives directions for making 14 simple gifts, such as a cotton sock doll and a hobby horse, using easily obtainable materials. (Rev: SLJ 12/94) [745]

25413 MacLeod, Elizabeth. *Gifts to Make and Eat* (4–7). Illus. by June Bradford. Series: Kids Can Do It! 2001, Kids Can $12.95 (978-1-55074-956-4); paper $6.95 (978-1-55074-958-8). 40pp. Kids learn through step-by-step instructions how to make an array of edible and craft gifts. (Rev: BL 11/1/01; HBG 3/02; SLJ 2/02) [641.5]

25414 Martin, Laura C. *Nature's Art Box: From T-Shirts to Twig Baskets, 65 Cool Projects for Crafty Kids to Make with Natural Materials You Can Find Anywhere* (4–8). Illus. by David Cain. 2003, Storey paper $16.95 (978-1-58017-490-9). 215pp. These projects use natural materials such as twigs, moss, gourds, stones, shells, flowers, and leaves to make articles including wreaths, necklaces, and a chess set. (Rev: HBG 10/03; SLJ 8/03*) [745.5]

25415 Martin, Laura C. *Recycled Crafts Box* (3–7). Illus. 2004, Storey Kids $19.95 (978-1-58017-523-4). 96pp. A craft book with an environmental twist, this volume offers great project ideas plus information on recycling and the history of trash. (Rev: BL 3/15/04; SLJ 7/04) [363.72]

25416 Merrill, Yvonne Y. *Hands-On Latin America: Art Activities for All Ages* (4–8). Illus. Series: Hands-On. 1998, Kits paper $20.00 (978-0-9643177-1-0). 84pp. A collection of 30 interesting, affordable arts and crafts projects inspired by the ancient cultures of Latin America. (Rev: BL 9/1/98; SLJ 8/98) [980.07]

25417 Milord, Susan. *Hands Around the World: 365 Creative Ways to Build Cultural Awareness and Global Respect* (3–6). Illus. 1992, Williamson paper $14.29 (978-0-913589-65-6). 160pp. One craft, recipe, or project is offered for each day of the year. (Rev: BL 1/1/93; SLJ 1/93) [306]

25418 Mitchell, Mari Rutz. *Creating Clever Castles and Cars (from Boxes and Other Stuff): Kids Ages 3–8 Make Their Own Pretend Play Spaces* (PS–3). Illus. by Michael Kline. 2006, Williamson $14.95 (978-0-8249-6783-3); paper $12.95 (978-0-8249-6782-6). 128pp. Directions for making pretend-play items such as a fairy house, a barn, a fire engine, and a pyramid; the crafts are of varying levels of difficulty and all include illustrations and a list of needed supplies. (Rev: SLJ 7/06) [745.5]

25419 Monaghan, Kathleen, and Hermon Joyner. *You Can Weave! Projects for Young Weavers* (4–7). Illus. 2001, Sterling $19.95 (978-0-87192-493-3). 104pp. Step-by-step instructions and photographs guide young crafters through weaving projects of varying complexity. (Rev: BL 11/1/01) [746.41]

25420 Monaghan, Kimberly. *Organic Crafts: 75 Earth-Friendly Art Activities* (3–5). Illus. 2007, Chicago Review $14.95 (978-1-55652-640-4). 160pp. The crafts, games, and activities in this collection use natural, renewable materials such as leaves and twigs, pebbles and shells. (Rev: BL 4/1/07) [745.5]

25421 Mueller, Stephanie R., and Ann E. Wheeler. *101 Great Gifts from Kids: Fabulous Gifts Every Child Can Make* (PS–3). Illus. 2002, Gryphon House paper $14.95 (978-0-87659-279-3). 174pp. Gift ideas that vary in difficulty and may require some adult help are accompanied by line drawings of the process involved and the end product. (Rev: SLJ 9/02) [745.5]

25422 Murillo, Kathy Cano. *The Crafty Diva's Lifestyle Makeover: Awesome Ideas to Spice Up Your Life!* (5–12). Illus. by Carrie Wheeler. 2005, Watson-Guptill paper $12.95 (978-0-8230-1008-0). 144pp. The Crafty Diva is back with this collection of easy-to-follow instructions for 50 projects that cover everything from room makeovers to fashion accessories. (Rev: SLJ 9/05)

25423 National Wildlife Federation. *Wild and Crafty* (1–7). Series: Ranger Rick's NatureScope. 1999, Chelsea LB $21.95 (978-0-7910-4884-9). 94pp. Step-by-step directions are given for 31 nature crafts (mostly model or puppet making) each with an assigned grade level. (Rev: SLJ 5/99) [745.5]

25424 Niven, Felicia Lowenstein. *Nifty Thrifty Music Crafts* (1–3). Illus. Series: Nifty Thrifty Crafts for Kids. 2007, Enslow LB $22.60 (978-0-7660-2784-8). 32pp. Crafts for children who enjoy playing and listening to music. Easy-to-find, inexpensive materials make this teacher- and parent-friendly. (Rev: SLJ 8/07)

25425 Otten, Jack. *Watch Me Make a Bird Feeder* (PS–2). Series: Making Things. 2002, Children's Book Pr. paper $4.95 (978-0-516-23497-7). 24pp. The process of making a bird feeder is simply explained in language that will suit challenged early readers. Also use *Watch Me Plant a Garden* (2002). (Rev: SLJ 6/02) [690.89]

25426 Owen, Cheryl. *Gifts for Kids to Make* (2–4). 2006, Sterling $14.95 (978-0-600-61502-6). 128pp. More than 50 projects involve sewing, art, clay and dough, and other materials, some of which require adult supervision. (Rev: BL 1/1–15/07; SLJ 12/06) [745.5083]

25427 Phillips, Matt. *Make Your Own Fun Frames!* (3–6). Illus. by Stan Jaskiel. 2001, Williamson paper $8.95 (978-1-885593-64-1). 63pp. Basic instructions for making frames and matting, cropping photographs, and hanging frames are accompanied by design suggestions using a variety of everyday materials. (Rev: SLJ 6/02) [749.7]

25428 Ponte, June. *Fun and Simple Southeastern State Crafts* (2–4). Illus. Series: Fun and Simple State Crafts. 2008, Enslow LB $17.95 (978-0-7660-2935-4). 48pp. Crafts associated with West Virginia, Virginia, North Carolina, South Carolina, Georgia, and Florida are accompanied by pages of facts. (Rev: BL 12/15/08) [745.50975]

25429 Powell, Michelle. *Beadwork* (3–5). Illus. Series: Step-by-Step. 2002, Heinemann LB $25.64 (978-1-4034-0696-5). 32pp. Color photographs show each step in creating beadwork projects. (Rev: BL 12/15/02; HBG 3/03) [745.58]

25430 Powell, Michelle. *Mosaics* (4–7). Series: Step-by-Step. 2001, Heinemann LB $24.22 (978-1-57572-332-7). 32pp. A number of fascinating projects creating mosaics are described with step-by-step instructions and many colorful illustrations. (Rev: BL 8/1/01; HBG 10/01; SLJ 10/01) [745]

25431 Powell, Michelle, and Judy Balchin. *Crafty Activities: Over 50 Fun and Easy Things to Make* (4–7). Illus. 2007, Search paper $19.95 (978-1-84448-250-4). 160pp. Fifty crafts involving mosaics, printing, lettering, papier-mâché, card-making, and origami, attractively and clearly presented for the young crafter. (Rev: BL 12/15/07; SLJ 1/08) [745]

25432 Press, Judy. *All Around Town: Exploring Your Community Through Craft Fun* (PS–3). Illus. Series: Little Hands. 2002, Williamson paper $12.95 (978-1-885593-68-9). 128pp. Projects using everyday materials that will introduce youngsters to community institutions such as schools, libraries, and gas stations are shown with instructions and illustrations. (Rev: BL 1/1–15/03; SLJ 4/03) [307]

25433 Press, Judy. *Around-the-World Art and Activities: Visiting the 7 Continents Through Craft Fun* (PS–2). Illus. by Betsy Day. Series: Little Hands. 2001, Williamson paper $14.29 (978-1-885593-45-0). 128pp. Activities, which are coded by level of difficulty, include making travel-related items such as a passport and suitcase, and cultural items such as totem poles, leis, nesting Russian dolls, gaucho belts, and Korean drums. (Rev: SLJ 5/01) [745]

25434 Press, Judy. *ArtStarts for Little Hands! Fun and Discoveries for 3- to 7-Year-Olds* (PS–2). Illus. by Karol Kaminski. 2000, Williamson paper $12.95 (978-1-885593-37-5). 118pp. A fresh and amusing book that presents simple activities using everyday materials under such themes as animals, seasons, transportation, colors, and gardens. (Rev: SLJ 10/00) [745]

25435 Press, Judy. *At the Zoo: Explore the Animal World with Craft Fun* (PS–3). Illus. by Jenny Campbell. Series: A Little Hands Book. 2002, Williamson paper $12.95 (978-1-885593-61-0). 126pp. Crafts using widely available materials are grouped in broad categories such as "African Safari" and "Tropical Forest" that are introduced by a map and brief general information, followed by individual animal projects. (Rev: SLJ 8/02)

25436 Press, Judy. *Vroom! Vroom! Making 'Dozers, 'Copters, Trucks, and More* (2–6). Illus. by Michael Kline. Series: Little Hands. 1997, Williamson paper $12.95 (978-1-885593-04-7). 160pp. Both craft and transportation enthusiasts can use this simple guide to making several vehicles with ordinary materials and good step-by-step directions. (Rev: SLJ 8/97) [745.5]

25437 Price, Pam. *Cool Rubber Stamp Art* (4–6). Illus. Series: Cool Crafts. 2005, ABDO LB $22.78 (978-1-59197-743-8). 32pp. A terra-cotta flowerpot, wrapping paper, and a canvas beach bag are among the projects shown, with advice on safety, creativity, and seeking help from adults. Also use *Cool Scrapbooks* (2005). (Rev: SLJ 6/05)

25438 *Recyclables* (4–6). Trans. from Spanish by Colleen Coffey. Series: Let's Create! 2004, Gareth Stevens LB $24.00 (978-0-8368-4018-6). 32pp. Projects using recyclables — cardboard, paper, and plastic, in particular — include a milk-carton cow and an egg-carton tree. (Rev: SLJ 11/04) [745.5]

25439 Rhatigan, Joe. *Soapmaking: 50 Fun and Fabulous Soaps to Melt and Pour* (4–6). Series: Kids' Crafts. 2003, Lark Books $19.95 (978-1-57990-416-6). 112pp. More than 50 diverse soap projects follow basic information and are accompanied by tips for budding entrepreneurs. (Rev: BL 12/15/03; SLJ 6/04)

25440 Rhodes, Vicki. *Pumpkin Decorating* (4–8). 1997, Sterling $10.95 (978-0-8069-9574-8). Clear directions and full-color photographs demonstrate more than 80 designs for pumpkins. (Rev: SLJ 12/97) [745.5]

25441 Rice, Melanie. *The Complete Book of Children's Activities* (PS–K). Illus. by Chris Barker. 1993, Kingfisher paper $9.95 (978-1-85697-907-8). 120pp. For the very young, this is a collection of learning activities, games, and construction projects. (Rev: BL 5/1/93) [372]

25442 Robinson, Fay. *Father's Day Crafts* (3–5). Illus. 2005, Enslow LB $22.60 (978-0-7660-2343-7). 32pp. Ten original gifts for Dad that students will enjoy making. Photographs help them picture the finished product. (Rev: SLJ 8/05)

25443 Robinson, Fay. *Halloween Crafts* (3–5). Illus. Series: Fun Holiday Crafts Kids Can Do! 2004, Enslow LB $22.60 (978-0-7660-2236-2). 32pp. Ten craft ideas that involve easily found, inexpensive materials are shown with simple instructions. (Rev: SLJ 7/04) [745.594]

25444 Robinson, Fay. *Hispanic-American Crafts Kids Can Do!* (3–5). Series: Multicultural Crafts Kids Can Do! 2006, Enslow LB $22.60 (978-0-7660-2459-5). 32pp. Easy-to-follow instructions are provided for ten crafts that originated in various corners of Latin America. (Rev: BL 8/06) [745.5089]

25445 Ross, Kathy. *All-Girl Crafts* (2–4). Illus. by Elaine Garvin. Series: Girl Crafts. 2005, Lerner LB $25.26 (978-0-7613-2776-9); paper $7.95 (978-0-7613-2391-4). 48pp. Clear directions and lists of required items are a strong feature of this collection of 22 craft projects designed to appeal to elementary-school girls and including doll furniture, a change purse, fancy envelopes, and a pillow-doll pajama bag. (Rev: BL 12/15/05; SLJ 10/05) [745.5]

25446 Ross, Kathy. *All New Crafts for Kwanzaa* (K–3). Illus. by Sharon L. Holm. 2006, Lerner LB $25.26 (978-0-7613-3401-9); paper $7.95 (978-0-8225-3435-8). 48pp. This new version of a 1994 title by the same authors includes additional projects related to the holiday. (Rev: BL 1/1–15/07; SLJ 10/06) [745.594]

25447 Ross, Kathy. *All New Crafts for Thanksgiving* (3–5). Illus. by Sharon L. Holm. 2005, Millbrook LB $25.26 (978-0-7613-2922-0); paper $7.95 (978-0-7613-2398-3). 48pp. More than 20 Thanksgiving-themed craft ideas use readily available materials and vary in difficulty. (Rev: BL 10/1/05) [745.594]

25448 Ross, Kathy. *All New Crafts for Valentine's Day* (1–3). Illus. by Barbara Leonard. 2002, Millbrook LB $23.90 (978-0-7613-2553-6); paper $7.95 (978-0-7613-1576-6). 48pp. Easy crafts are accompanied by step-by-step instructions and bright watercolor paintings. (Rev: HBG 3/03; SLJ 11/02) [745.594]

25449 Ross, Kathy. *Christmas Decorations Kids Can Make* (3–5). Illus. 1999, Millbrook $23.40 (978-0-7613-1565-0). 64pp. An old-fashioned craft book that uses ordinary materials to create such seasonal gifts and ornaments as figures of the three kings. (Rev: BL 12/15/99; HBG 3/00) [594]

25450 Ross, Kathy. *Christmas Ornaments Kids Can Make* (2–5). Illus. 1998, Millbrook LB $23.40 (978-0-7613-0366-4). 64pp. Thirty projects for making Christmas ornaments are well-presented in this easy-to-follow craft book. (Rev: BL 10/15/98; HBG 3/99; SLJ 10/98) [745.594]

25451 Ross, Kathy. *Christmas Presents Kids Can Make* (4–6). Illus. by Sharon L. Holm. 2001, Millbrook LB $24.40 (978-0-7613-1754-8). 64pp. The author provides new ideas for 29 creative Christmas gifts using everyday items. (Rev: BL 9/15/01; HBG 3/02; SLJ 10/01) [745.5]

25452 Ross, Kathy. *Community Workers* (K–2). Illus. by Jan Barger. Series: Crafts for Kids Who Are Learning About. 2005, Millbrook LB $25.26 (978-0-7613-2743-1). 48pp. Twenty crafts introduce children to the activities of various community workers, including firefighters, dentists, shopkeepers, and librarians. (Rev: SLJ 1/06) [745.5]

25453 Ross, Kathy. *Crafts for All Seasons* (3–5). Illus. 2000, Millbrook $19.95 (978-0-7613-1346-5). 176pp. Drawing widely on the material in the author's four seasonal craft books, this spiral-bound volume contains 80 projects with clear instructions. (Rev: BL 10/15/00; HBG 10/01) [745.5]

25454 Ross, Kathy. *Crafts for Christian Values* (K–4). Illus. by Sharon L. Holm. 2000, Millbrook LB $24.90 (978-0-7613-1618-3). 63pp. A book of 28 craft projects, each related to a particular Christian value — such as a bookmark that honors one's parents. (Rev: HBG 10/01; SLJ 2/01) [745]

25455 Ross, Kathy. *Crafts for Kids Who Are Wild About Deserts* (3–5). Illus. Series: Kids Who Are Wild About. 1998, Millbrook LB $22.40 (978-0-7613-0954-3). 48pp. A book of ingenious craft projects related to deserts, such as an egg-carton rattlesnake and a sand art necklace. (Rev: BL 3/15/99; HBG 10/99; SLJ 4/99) [745.5]

25456 Ross, Kathy. *Crafts for Kids Who Are Wild About Dinosaurs* (3–5). Illus. Series: Crafts for Kids Who Are Wild About. 1997, Millbrook LB $22.40 (978-0-7613-0053-3); paper $8.95 (978-0-7613-0177-6). 48pp. Twenty projects involving dinosaurs and using everyday objects are described. (Rev: BL 2/1/97; SLJ 6/97) [745.5]

25457 Ross, Kathy. *Crafts for Kids Who Are Wild About Oceans* (3–5). Illus. Series: Crafts for Kids Who Are Wild About. 1998, Millbrook LB $22.40 (978-0-7613-0262-9); paper $7.95 (978-0-7613-0331-2). 48pp. Using excellent illustrations and clear instructions, this book describes a series of ocean-related craft projects such as making a clam puppet and a water-spouting whale. (Rev: BL 4/15/98; HBG 10/98; SLJ 5/98) [745.5]

25458 Ross, Kathy. *Crafts for Kids Who Are Wild About Outer Space* (3–5). Illus. Series: Crafts for Kids Who Are Wild About. 1997, Millbrook LB $22.40 (978-0-7613-0054-0); paper $7.95 (978-0-7613-0176-9). 48pp. Various aspects of outer space are presented in 20 craft projects that use commonplace items. (Rev: BL 2/1/97; SLJ 6/97) [745.5]

25459 Ross, Kathy. *Crafts for Kids Who Are Wild About Polar Life* (3–5). Illus. Series: Kids Who Are Wild About. 1998, Millbrook LB $22.40 (978-0-7613-0955-0). 48pp. A penguin pin, a walrus mask, and an arctic fox cup puppet are three of the clever craft projects related to the Arctic that are found in this volume. (Rev: BL 3/15/99; HBG 10/99; SLJ 4/99) [745.5]

25460 Ross, Kathy. *Crafts for Kids Who Are Wild About Reptiles* (3–5). Illus. Series: Crafts for Kids Who Are Wild About. 1998, Millbrook LB $22.40 (978-0-7613-0263-6); paper $7.95 (978-0-7613-0332-9). 48pp. Twenty reptile-related projects such as making a shedding snake and constructing a tiny turtle are included in this clearly written and well-illustrated craft book. (Rev: BL 4/15/98; HBG 10/98; SLJ 5/98) [745.59]

25461 Ross, Kathy. *Crafts for Valentine's Day* (2–5). Illus. by Sharon L. Holm. Series: Holiday Crafts. 1995, Millbrook LB $24.90 (978-1-56294-489-6). 47pp. Twenty simple holiday projects using readily available materials are described on double-page spreads, with color illustrations and step-by-step instructions. (Rev: SLJ 4/95) [745.5]

25462 Ross, Kathy. *Crafts from Your Favorite Bible Stories* (3–5). Illus. 2000, Millbrook LB $24.90 (978-0-7613-1619-0). 64pp. Using simple materials such as lunch bags and pipe cleaners, this book offers 27 craft projects from both the Old and New Testaments such as making Noah's ark or Joseph's coat of many colors. (Rev: BL 6/1–15/00; HBG 10/00; SLJ 8/00) [268]

25463 Ross, Kathy. *Crafts from Your Favorite Children's Songs* (PS–2). Illus. by Vicky Enright. 2001, Millbrook LB $24.40 (978-0-7613-1912-2). 47pp. Crafts designed to accompany familiar songs are presented with simple instructions. (Rev: HBG 10/01; SLJ 5/01) [745.5]

25464 Ross, Kathy. *Crafts from Your Favorite Children's Stories* (1–4). Illus. by Elaine Garvin. 2001, Millbrook LB $24.90 (978-0-7613-1772-2). 47pp. Young children may need help with some of these projects, which include a "Bear Hug Puppet," a spinning Dorothy house on its way to Oz, and a Sourdough Sam. (Rev: HBG 3/02; SLJ 9/01) [745.5]

25465 Ross, Kathy. *Crafts from Your Favorite Nursery Rhymes* (3–5). Illus. by Elaine Garvin. 2002, Millbrook LB $24.90 (978-0-7613-2523-9); paper $8.95 (978-0-7613-1589-6). 48pp. Simple directions and clear illustrations accompany projects of varying difficulty; young children will need some help with these activities related to popular rhymes. (Rev: BL 1/1–15/03; HBG 3/03; SLJ 12/02) [745.5]

25466 Ross, Kathy. *Crafts to Celebrate God's Creation* (3–5). Illus. 2001, Millbrook LB $24.90 (978-

0-7613-1621-3). 64pp. Using the creation story in Genesis as a focus, this craft book gives directions for making such items as a "sunrise puppet," flying birds, and a beaded pin in the shape of a cross. (Rev: BL 1/1–15/01; HBG 10/01) [268.432]

25467 Ross, Kathy. *Crafts to Make in the Fall* (3–5). Illus. by Vicky Enright. Series: Crafts for All Seasons. 1998, Millbrook LB $23.40 (978-0-7613-0318-3); paper $9.95 (978-0-7613-0335-0). 63pp. Twenty-nine craft projects, with a wide range of difficulty, are included in this book that involves autumn themes and holidays like Columbus Day and Thanksgiving. (Rev: HBG 3/99; SLJ 2/99) [745]

25468 Ross, Kathy. *Crafts to Make in the Spring* (K–4). Illus. by Vicky Enright. 1998, Millbrook LB $23.40 (978-0-7613-0316-9); paper $9.95 (978-0-7613-0333-6). 63pp. This book contains 29 simple crafts described in double-page spreads and inspired by spring and such holidays as Passover and Easter. (Rev: HBG 10/98; SLJ 6/98) [745]

25469 Ross, Kathy. *Crafts to Make in the Winter* (K–3). Illus. by Vicky Enright. Series: Crafts for All Seasons. 1999, Millbrook LB $23.40 (978-0-7613-0319-0). 64pp. The use of accessible materials and good step-by-step instructions make this a fine craft book about making things that are winter-related. (Rev: BL 12/15/99; HBG 3/00; SLJ 1/00) [745.5]

25470 Ross, Kathy. *Earth-Friendly Crafts: Clever Ways to Reuse Everyday Items* (3–6). Illus. by Celine Malepart. 2009, Millbrook LB $26.60 (978-0-8225-9099-6). 48pp. A collection of projects that encourage kids to reduce, reuse, and recycle. (Rev: BL 12/15/08) [745.5]

25471 Ross, Kathy. *Every Day Is Earth Day* (2–4). Illus. by Sharon L. Holm. Series: Holiday Crafts. 1995, Millbrook LB $21.90 (978-1-56294-490-2). 47pp. After a general discussion of Earth Day, presents 20 crafts that reflect an interest in conserving natural resources and recycling materials. (Rev: SLJ 5/95) [745.5]

25472 Ross, Kathy. *Girlfriends' Get-Together Craft Book* (1–5). Illus. by Nicole in den Bosch. Series: Girl Crafts. 2007, Millbrook LB $25.26 (978-0-7613-3408-8). 48pp. Filled with great ideas for girls who like wearable and decorative crafts, this book will inspire fun sleepover projects. (Rev: SLJ 6/07)

25473 Ross, Kathy. *Kathy Ross Crafts Numbers* (PS–1). Illus. by Jan Barger. Series: Learning Is Fun! 2003, Millbrook LB $23.90 (978-0-7613-2105-7); paper $7.95 (978-0-7613-1697-8). 48pp. Numbers and the ways they are used in everyday life form the central theme of this large-format collection of crafts; included among the simple projects are a birthday cake pin, a toy alarm clock, and playing-card counters. (Rev: BL 4/15/03; HBG 10/03) [745.5]

25474 Ross, Kathy. *Kathy Ross Crafts Triangles, Rectangles, Circles, and Squares* (PS–1). Illus. by Jan Barger. Series: Learning Is Fun! 2002, Millbrook LB $23.90 (978-0-7613-2104-0); paper $7.95 (978-0-7613-1696-1). 48pp. Projects that introduce basic geometric shapes include puppets, jewelry, games, and hanging objects. (Rev: HBG 3/03; SLJ 1/03)

25475 Ross, Kathy, ed. *Look What You Can Make with Dozens of Household Items!* (4–6). Photos by Hank Schneider. Series: Look What You Can Make With. 2003, Boyds Mills $24.99 (978-1-59078-058-9). 384pp. Common household items are used to create a wide range of crafts. (Rev: BL 12/15/02) [745]

25476 Ross, Kathy. *Make Yourself a Monster! A Book of Creepy Crafts* (2–5). Illus. by Sharon Hawkins Vargo. 1999, Millbrook LB $22.90 (978-0-7613-1556-8). 45pp. Twenty 20 monster-themed crafts include making a slimy monster mitt puppet and a Dracula soap dispenser. (Rev: HBG 3/00; SLJ 4/00) [745]

25477 Ross, Kathy. *Play-Doh Animal Fun* (K–4). Illus. by Sharon Hawkins Vargo. 2002, Millbrook LB $24.40 (978-0-7613-2506-2). 48pp. Twenty animals to make with play-doh range from simple clams to a rattlesnake with a rattle. Also use *Play-Doh Art Projects* (2002). (Rev: HBG 10/02; SLJ 5/02) [745.5]

25478 Ross, Kathy. *The Scrapbooker's Idea Book* (3–5). Illus. by Nicole in den Bosch. Series: Girl Crafts. 2006, Millbrook LB $25.26 (978-0-7613-2777-6). 48pp. An excellent introduction to scrapbooking, with step-by-step instructions for 22 projects. (Rev: SLJ 9/06)

25479 Ross, Kathy. *Star-Spangled Crafts* (4–6). Illus. by Sharon L. Holm. 2003, Millbrook LB $23.90 (978-0-7613-2853-7). 48pp. Twenty-two crafts with patriotic themes include an American eagle magnet and an Uncle Sam tissue box. (Rev: HBG 10/03; SLJ 7/03)

25480 Ross, Kathy. *Step-by-Step Crafts for Summer* (3–4). Illus. by Jennifer Emery. 2007, Boyds Mills $15.95 (978-1-59078-360-3). 48pp. Twenty summer-themed crafts include projects for picnics, parades, patios, playgrounds, and more. (Rev: SLJ 7/07)

25481 Ross, Kathy. *Step-by-Step Crafts for Winter* (K–3). Illus. by Jennifer Emery. 2006, Boyds Mills $15.95 (978-1-59078-449-5); paper $6.95 (978-1-59078-358-0). 48pp. Step-by-step instructions for 20 winter-themed crafts using everyday materials include projects appropriate for Christmas, Kwanzaa, Hanukkah, Lincoln's Birthday, and Valentine's Day. (Rev: SLJ 12/06) [745]

25482 Sadler, Judy Ann. *Christmas Crafts from Around the World* (4–6). 2003, Kids Can $12.95 (978-1-55337-427-5); paper $6.95 (978-1-55337-428-2). 40pp. This guide offers step-by-step instructions for making 17 Christmas crafts with origins in countries around the world. (Rev: BL 12/15/03; HBG 4/04; SLJ 10/03)

25483 Sadler, Judy Ann. *Jumbo Book of Easy Crafts* (3–5). Illus. 2001, Kids Can $14.95 (978-1-55074-811-6). 208pp. Crafts using everyday items — paper plates, popsicle sticks, aluminum foil, beans, beads, and so forth — are arranged by type of material. (Rev: BL 6/1–15/01; SLJ 7/01) [745.5]

25484 Sadler, Judy Ann. *The Kids Can Press Jumbo Book of Crafts* (2–6). Illus. by Caroline Price. 1998, Kids Can paper $14.95 (978-1-55074-375-3). 208pp. This book contains an array of easy and inexpensive craft projects, including making papier-mâché bowls, cord-covered bottles, and collage frames. (Rev: SLJ 12/98) [745]

25485 Sanders, Nancy I. *Old Testament Days: An Activity Guide* (4–6). Illus. 1999, Chicago Review paper $14.95 (978-1-55652-354-0). 144pp. This craft book contains 80 projects related to incidents in the Old Testament, such as making a sleeping mat similar to that used by Abraham. (Rev: BL 10/15/99; SLJ 12/99) [372.89]

25486 Schwarz, Renee. *Birdhouses* (4–7). Illus. Series: Kids Can Do It! 2005, Kids Can $12.95 (978-1-55337-549-4); paper $6.95 (978-1-55337-550-0). 40pp. Nine different birdhouse projects for children to tackle, with illustrated instructions and photographs of the finished products. (Rev: BL 4/1/05; SLJ 5/05) [690]

25487 Schwarz, Renee. *Funky Junk* (4–7). Series: Kids Can Do It! 2002, Kids Can $12.95 (978-1-55337-387-2); paper $5.95 (978-1-55337-388-9). 48pp. Using easily found materials, this craft book supplies details on how to make unusual conversation pieces. (Rev: BL 3/15/03; HBG 10/03; SLJ 4/03) [745.5]

25488 Simons, Robin. *Recyclopedia: Games, Science Equipment and Crafts from Recycled Materials* (5–8). Illus. by author. 1976, Houghton paper $13.95 (978-0-395-59641-8). Clear directions complemented by good illustrations characterize this book of interesting projects using waste materials.

25489 Souter, Gillian. *Holiday Handiworks* (3–6). Illus. Series: Handy Crafts. 2002, Gareth Stevens LB $26.00 (978-0-8368-3050-7). 48pp. A well-organized collection of crafts with clear instructions, aimed at holidays including Easter, Passover, Kwanzaa, and Chinese New Year. Also use *Rainy Day Fun* and *Terrific Toys* (both 2002). (Rev: HBG 10/02; SLJ 6/02) [745.5]

25490 Stetson, Emily, and Vicky Congdon. *Little Hands Fingerplays and Action Songs: Seasonal Rhymes and Creative Play for 2- to 6-Year-Olds* (PS–1). Illus. by Betsy Day. Series: Little Hands. 2001, Williamson paper $12.95 (978-1-885593-53-5). 128pp. Suggestions for songs, games, and crafts are organized by season and accompanied by brief facts and short reading lists. (Rev: SLJ 11/01) [793.4]

25491 Temko, Florence. *Traditional Crafts from Africa* (2–5). Illus. 1996, Lerner LB $23.93 (978-0-8225-2936-1). 64pp. Clear instructions and excellent illustrations are used in the presentation of several African craft projects. (Rev: BL 9/1/96; SLJ 10/96) [745]

25492 Temko, Florence. *Traditional Crafts from China* (5–7). Illus. Series: Culture Crafts. 2001, Lerner LB $23.93 (978-0-8225-2939-2). 64pp. After a few words about crafts in general, this volume carefully outlines a number of projects relating to Chinese culture, including instructions for picture scrolls and tanagrams. (Rev: BL 2/15/01; HBG 10/01; SLJ 4/01) [745]

25493 Temko, Florence. *Traditional Crafts from Japan* (3–5). Illus. by Randall Gooch. Series: Culture Crafts. 2001, Lerner LB $23.93 (978-0-8225-2938-5). 64pp. Eight traditional Japanese handicrafts are presented with instructions for making them and explanations of their significance in Japanese culture. (Rev: HBG 10/01; SLJ 4/01) [745]

25494 Temko, Florence. *Traditional Crafts from Mexico and Central America* (3–6). Photos by Robert L. Wolfe and Diane Wolfe. Illus. by Randall Gooch. Series: Culture Crafts. 1996, Lerner LB $23.93 (978-0-8225-2935-4). 64pp. After a brief introduction to the area, this book describes eight traditional crafts with clear instructions and a number of helpful illustrations. (Rev: BCCB 2/97; SLJ 12/96) [745.5]

25495 Temko, Florence. *Traditional Crafts from the Caribbean* (5–7). Illus. Series: Culture Crafts. 2001, Lerner LB $23.93 (978-0-8225-2937-8). 64pp. Step-by-step instructions with clear diagrams are given for a number of craft projects relating to Caribbean culture including yarn dolls, Puerto Rican masks, and metal cutouts. (Rev: BL 2/15/01; HBG 10/01; SLJ 4/01) [745]

25496 Thomas, John E., and Danita Pagel. *The Ultimate Book of Kid Concoctions* (PS–4). Illus. by Robb Durr and Zachariah Durr. 1998, Kid Concoctions paper $14.95 (978-0-9661088-0-4). 80pp. Features about 65 recipes and activities using common kitchen supplies to make items like sidewalk chalk, finger paints, and scratch-and-sniff stickers. (Rev: SLJ 3/98) [745.5]

25497 Torres, Laura. *Best Friends Forever! 199 Projects to Make and Share* (5–8). Illus. 2004, Workman paper $13.95 (978-0-7611-3274-5). 148pp. Craft ideas that will appeal to young teens — bracelets, key chains, picture frames, and so forth — are clearly explained and organized into chapters such as "Cool Notes" and "Home and School." (Rev: SLJ 2/05) [745.5]

25498 Trottier, Maxine. *Native Crafts: Inspired by North America's First Peoples* (3–6). Illus. 2000, Kids Can $12.95 (978-1-55074-854-3); paper $5.95 (978-1-55074-549-8). 40pp. Sixteen projects (all requiring adult help) from the traditional arts and crafts of Native Americans are presented with step-by-step instructions and pictures of the finished products. (Rev: BL 7/00; HBG 10/00; SLJ 6/00) [745.5]

25499 Van Vleet, Carmella. *Great Ancient Egypt Projects You Can Build Yourself* (4–6). Illus. 2006, Nomad paper $14.95 (978-0-9771294-5-4). 122pp. More than two dozen hands-on activities explore life in ancient Egypt — everything from hieroglyphs and papyrus to perfume and pyramids — and are supplemented by background information. (Rev: SLJ 2/07) [932]

25500 Wagner, Lisa. *Cool Melt and Pour Soap* (4–7). Photos by Kelly Doudna. Illus. Series: Cool Crafts. 2005, ABDO LB $22.78 (978-1-59197-741-4). 32pp. Coloring, fragrance, and packaging are all covered in this guide to projects using soap. (Rev: SLJ 7/05)

25501 Wagner, Lisa. *Cool Painted Stuff* (4–6). Illus. Series: Cool Crafts. 2005, ABDO LB $22.78 (978-1-59197-742-1). 32pp. A fancy flowerpot and a mini-tote are among the projects shown, with advice on safety, creativity, and seeking help from adults. (Rev: SLJ 6/05)

25502 Walsh, Danny, et al. *The Cardboard Box Book: 25 Things to Make and Do with Empty Boxes* (3–5). Photos by Martin Norris. Illus. by Josh Halloran. 2006, Watson-Guptill paper $12.95 (978-0-8230-0610-6). 112pp. The authors — a father and sons — offer a number of kid-tested ways to convert empty boxes to better use. (Rev: SLJ 2/07) [745.54]

25503 Warwick, Ellen. *Stuff for Your Space* (4–6). Series: Kids Can Do It! 2004, Kids Can $12.95 (978-1-55337-398-8). 40pp. Well-illustrated advice and instructions for boys and girls on decorating their individual living spaces. (Rev: BL 2/15/04; SLJ 4/04) [745]

25504 West, Robin. *My Very Own Birthday: A Book of Cooking and Crafts* (2–4). Photos by Robert L. Wolfe and Diane Wolfe. Illus. by Jackie Urbanovic. Series: My Very Own Holiday. 1996, Carolrhoda LB $21.27 (978-0-87614-980-5). 64pp. Five birthday parties using different themes are described, along with recipes and craft projects. (Rev: SLJ 5/96) [745.5]

25505 West, Robin. *My Very Own Christmas: A Book of Cooking and Crafts* (PS–1). Illus. by Susan S. Burke. 1993, Carolrhoda LB $21.27 (978-0-87614-722-1). 64pp. This book contains a variety of Christmas crafts and a number of recipes. (Rev: BL 8/93) [394.2]

25506 White, Linda. *Haunting on a Halloween* (5–7). Illus. by Fran Lee. 2002, Gibbs Smith paper $9.95 (978-1-58685-112-5). 64pp. Everything young party planners need to host a Halloween get-together, with instructions for crafts, food, decorations, and costumes. (Rev: BL 9/15/02) [745.594]

25507 *A World of Things to Do* (2–5). Illus. 1987, National Geographic LB $12.50 (978-0-87044-615-3). 104pp. All sorts of activities for even the most hard to please, from kitchen science experiments to holiday ideas. (Rev: BL 5/15/87)

25508 Zakarin, Debra Mostow. *Happening Hanukkah: Creative Ways to Celebrate* (4–6). Illus. by Amanda Haley. 2002, Grosset paper $5.99 (978-0-448-42869-7). 64pp. A treasure trove of Hanukkah gift ideas plus suggestions for parties, food, and games. (Rev: SLJ 10/02)

American Historical Crafts

25509 Beard, D. C. *The American Boys' Handy Book: What to Do and How to Do It* (5–7). Illus. 1983, Godine paper $12.95 (978-0-87923-449-2). 392pp. A facsimile edition of a manual first published in 1882. [790.194]

25510 Broida, Marian. *Projects About Plantation Life* (3–5). Series: Hands-on History. 2003, Benchmark LB $27.07 (978-0-7614-1605-0). 48pp. Introduced by appropriate background, illustrations, and maps, this book offers detailed instructions on re-creating things from the period — from crafts to recipes. Also use *Projects About Westward Expansion* (2003). (Rev: BL 2/15/04; HBG 4/04; SLJ 3/04)

25511 D'Amato, Janet, and Alex D'Amato. *Indian Crafts* (1–4). Illus. by authors. 1968, Lion LB $13.95 (978-0-87460-088-9). An excellent introduction to Indian crafts through projects and activities.

25512 Greenwood, Barbara. *Pioneer Crafts* (4–8). Illus. 1997, Kids Can paper $6.95 (978-1-55074-359-3). This guide gives directions for 17 projects such as candle making, soap carving, and basket weaving. (Rev: BL 9/15/97; SLJ 9/97) [745.5]

25513 Kalman, Bobbie. *Pioneer Projects* (3–6). Illus. by Marc Crabtree. Series: Historic Communities. 1997, Crabtree LB $25.27 (978-0-86505-437-0); paper $7.95 (978-0-86505-467-7). 32pp. Authentic crafts and activities engaged in by early American settlers are outlined, including step-by-step directions for building a model of a pioneer town. (Rev: BL 7/97; SLJ 8/97) [745.5]

25514 Kuntz, Lynn. *Celebrate the USA: Hands-on History Activities for Kids* (3–5). Illus. by Mark A. Hicks. 2007, Gibbs Smith paper $7.95 (978-1-58685-846-9). 80pp. Twenty-five activities accompany information about America's history, people, landscape, holidays, songs, and more, presented in an engaging format. (Rev: SLJ 7/07)

25515 Merrill, Yvonne Y. *Hands-On Rocky Mountains: Art Activities About Anasazi, American Indians, Settlers, Trappers, and Cowboys* (4–8). Illus. 1996, Kits paper $16.95 (978-0-9643177-2-7). Historical groups from the Rocky Mountain region — early people, American Indians, trappers, settlers, and cowboys — are introduced and, for each, a series of craft projects is outlined. (Rev: BL 1/1–15/97; SLJ 4/97) [745.5]

25516 Temko, Florence. *Traditional Crafts from Native North America* (2–4). Illus. Series: Culture Crafts. 1997, Lerner LB $23.93 (978-0-8225-2934-7). 64pp. Introduces the major cultural areas of North American Indians and gives directions for making such objects as baskets, cornhusk dolls, and dream catchers. (Rev: BL 10/1/97; SLJ 7/97) [745.5]

25517 Tull, Mary, et al. *North America* (4–7). Series: Artisans Around the World. 1999, Raintree LB $27.12 (978-0-7398-0117-8). 48pp. North American folk art is surveyed, from peoples including the Haida of western Canada, New Mexico's Pueblos, the Pennsylvanian German Americans, and African Americans. (Rev: BL 10/15/99; HBG 3/00) [970]

25518 Yamane, Linda. *Weaving a California Tradition: A Native American Basketmaker* (3–6). Illus. Series: We Are Still Here: Native Americans Today. 1996, Lerner $21.27 (978-0-8225-2660-5); paper $6.95 (978-0-8225-9730-8). 48pp. The story of California basket weaving, its present status, and the people who engage in it. (Rev: BL 1/1–15/97; SLJ 2/97) [746.41]

Clay and Other Modeling Crafts

25519 Arima, Elaine. *The Kids 'n' Clay Ceramics Book: HandBuilding and Wheel-Throwing Projects from the Kids 'N' Clay Pottery Studio* (3–8). Illus. 2000, Tricycle paper $16.95 (978-1-883672-89-8). 128pp. A ceramic project book for middle and junior high grades that involves creating both handmade and wheel-thrown objects including a breakfast bowl, bookends, and a porcupine. (Rev: BL 3/1/00; SLJ 8/00) [738]

25520 Carlson, Maureen. *Clay Characters for Kids* (3–8). Photos by author. 2003, North Light paper $12.99 (978-1-58180-286-3). 79pp. This photo-filled guide to modeling figures out of polymer clay outlines 30 projects that will require a degree of adut supervision. (Rev: SLJ 12/03) [731.4]

25521 *Clay* (3–6). Series: Let's Create! 2003, Gareth Stevens LB $24.00 (978-0-8368-3746-9). 32pp. This plentifully illustrated primer on working creatively with clay details a dozen projects, with suggestions for further reading and a list of Web resources. (Rev: SLJ 4/04) [738]

25522 Dixon, Annabelle. *Clay* (3–5). Illus. by Ed Barber. Series: Threads. 1990, Garrett LB $15.93 (978-0-944483-69-5). 26pp. The nature of clay, where it is found, and its uses in pottery and model crafts are discussed. (Rev: BL 2/1/91; SLJ 4/91) [553.6]

25523 Good, Keith. *Shape It! Magnificent Projects for Molding Materials* (3–7). Series: Design It! 2000, Lerner LB $21.27 (978-0-8225-3568-3). 30pp. This is a book of craft projects that involve molding materials such as salt dough, plaster, air-drying clay, and edible materials like cookie dough. (Rev: HBG 10/00; SLJ 6/00) [745.5]

25524 Reid, Barbara. *Fun with Modeling Clay* (1–4). Illus. 1998, Kids Can paper $5.95 (978-1-55074-510-8). 40pp. After such basics as modeling balls, pancakes, and snakes from clay, this craft book goes on to such projects as fruit baskets, cars and trains, and underwater scenes. (Rev: BL 9/1/98) [731.4]

25525 Ross, Kathy. *Play-Doh Fun and Games* (K–4). Illus. by Sharon Vargo. Series: Play-Doh Fun. 2003, Millbrook LB $24.90 (978-0-7613-2507-9). 48pp. Detailed instructions for 20 game and toy projects that can be made using Play-Doh and/or other readily available materials. (Rev: HBG 10/03; SLJ 6/03)

25526 Rowe, Christine. *The Children's Book of Pottery* (4–7). Illus. 1989, Trafalgar $24.95 (978-0-7134-5995-1). 64pp. A good British import about pottery making. (Rev: BL 12/1/89) [738.1]

25527 Scheunemann, Pam. *Cool Clay Projects* (4–7). Photos by Anders Hanson. Illus. Series: Cool Crafts. 2005, ABDO LB $22.78 (978-1-59197-740-7). 32pp. Clear, step-by-step instructions for a number of clay projects are accompanied by full-color photos and tips about safety. (Rev: SLJ 7/05) [731.4]

25528 Speechley, Greta. *Clay Modeling* (3–6). Series: Step-by-Step. 2000, Heinemann LB $24.22 (978-1-57572-326-6). 32pp. This book shows how to create figures including a cat, a tiger, a flowerpot, and a bowl using air-drying clay. (Rev: BL 10/15/00; HBG 10/01; SLJ 12/00) [745.5]

Costume and Jewelry Making

25529 Baker, Diane. *Jazzy Jewelry: Power Beads, Crystals, Chokers, and Illusion and Tattoo Styles* (5–9). Illus. by Alexandra Michaels. 2001, Williamson paper $12.95 (978-1-885593-47-4). 144pp. Jewelry projects for bead lovers include chokers, headbands, and bobby pins, all presented with black-and-white line drawings and guidance on color choice, clasps and knots, and proper storage. (Rev: SLJ 7/01) [745.594]

25530 Baker, Diane. *Make Your Own Hairwear: Beaded Barrettes, Clips, Dangles and Headbands* (4–8). Illus. by Alexandra Michaels. 2001, Williamson paper $8.95 (978-1-885593-63-4). 63pp. Easy instructions guide readers through the steps of making hair accessories using beads, shells, rhinestones, and other materials. (Rev: SLJ 4/02) [745.58]

25531 Boonyadhistarn, Thiranut. *Beading: Bracelets, Barrettes, and Beyond* (4–8). Illus. Series: Snap Books: Crafts. 2006, Capstone LB $25.26 (978-0-7368-6472-5). 32pp. Simple, step-by-step instructions guide readers through a variety of fashion accessories that use accessible materials. (Rev: SLJ 2/07) [745.58]

25532 Casey, Moe. *The Most Excellent Book of Dress Up* (3–5). Illus. Series: Most Excellent Book Of. 1997, Millbrook LB $19.90 (978-0-7613-0550-7); paper $6.95 (978-0-7613-0575-0). 32pp. Using many photos and drawings, this colorful book gives easy, step-by-step instructions for making various costumes. (Rev: BL 6/1–15/97; SLJ 8/97) [646.4]

25533 Cummings, Richard. *101 Costumes for All Ages, All Occasions* (5–9). Illus. 1987, Plays paper $12.95 (978-0-8238-0286-9). A variety of easily made costumes are described from Frankenstein and Captain Hook to Cleopatra and even a tube of toothpaste. (Rev: BL 1/1/88) [792.026]

25534 Di Salle, Rachel, and Ellen Warwick. *Junk Drawer Jewelry* (4–7). Photos by Ray Boudreau. Illus. by Jane Kurisu. Series: Kids Can Do It. 2006, Kids Can $12.95 (978-1-55337-965-2); paper $6.95 (978-1-55337-966-9). 40pp. This innovative craft book offers step-by-step instructions for making jewelry using odds and ends found in the junk drawer at home. (Rev: SLJ 11/06) [745.5]

25535 Gayle, Katie. *Snappy Jazzy Jewelry* (4–7). Illus. 1996, Sterling $14.95 (978-0-8069-3854-7). 48pp. Making necklaces and earrings are two of the craft projects described, with many helpful photographs. (Rev: BL 5/15/96; SLJ 6/96) [745.594]

25536 Gryski, Camilla. *Friendship Bracelets* (3–6). Illus. 1993, Morrow paper $6.95 (978-0-688-12437-3). 48pp. Instructions are given on how to make friendship bracelets from different materials, plus material on creating other forms of jewelry. (Rev: BL 10/1/93; SLJ 9/93) [746]

25537 Newcomb, Rain. *Girls' World Book of Jewelry: 50 Cool Designs to Make* (5–8). Series: Kids Crafts. 2004, Lark Books paper $14.95 (978-1-57990-473-9). 128pp. Up-to-date designs are accompanied by well-thought-out instructions and advice in this large-format volume. (Rev: BL 12/15/04; SLJ 4/05)

25538 Sadler, Judy Ann. *Beading: Bracelets, Earrings, Necklaces and More* (4–8). Illus. Series: Kids Can! 1998, Kids Can paper $6.95 (978-1-55074-338-8). 40pp. Using photographs and simple instructions, directions are given for making a simple beading loom and creating necklaces and bracelets. (Rev: BL 5/15/98) [745.594]

25539 Sadler, Judy Ann. *Easy Braids, Barrettes and Bows* (3–7). Illus. 1997, Kids Can paper $6.95 (978-1-55074-325-8). 40pp. Discusses various hairstyles, like cornrows and ponytails, and gives instructions on making pieces of hair jewelry. (Rev: BL 10/15/97; SLJ 11/97) [646.7]

25540 Sadler, Judy Ann. *Hemp Jewelry* (4–7). Illus. Series: Kids Can Do It! 2005, Kids Can $12.95 (978-1-55337-774-0); paper $6.95 (978-1-55337-775-7). 40pp. Sixteen projects for boys and girls using hemp, with drawings and photographs to illustrate the steps and the results. (Rev: BL 3/15/05; SLJ 5/05) [746.4]

25541 Scheunemann, Pam. *Cool Beaded Jewelry* (4–7). Photos by Anders Hanson. Illus. Series: Cool Crafts. 2005, ABDO LB $22.78 (978-1-59197-739-1). 32pp. Step-by-step instructions and full-color photographs guide the user through beaded jewelry projects. (Rev: SLJ 7/05) [745]

25542 Sensier, Danielle. *Costumes* (5–7). Illus. Series: Traditions Around the World. 1994, Thomson Learning LB $24.26 (978-1-56847-227-0). 48pp. The rituals and uses involved in costumes are introduced, as well as a general discussion of clothing in various regions and cultures. (Rev: BL 2/1/95; SLJ 3/95) [391]

Drawing and Painting

25543 Ames, Lee J. *Draw Fifty Airplanes, Aircraft and Spacecraft* (3–7). Illus. by author. 1987, Doubleday paper $8.95 (978-0-385-23629-4). 64pp. Simple directions for drawing various airborne articles, from the Wright brothers' plane to the Saturn V rocket. Also use: *Draw Fifty Boats, Ships, Trucks and Trains* (1976); *Draw Fifty Vehicles* (1997); *Draw Fifty Buildings and Other Structures* (1980).

25544 Ames, Lee J. *Draw Fifty Baby Animals: The Step-by-Step Way to Draw Kittens, Lambs, Chicks, and Other Adorable Offspring* (3–5). Illus. by author. 2003, Broadway paper $8.95 (978-0-7679-1284-6). In this step-by-step guide, author Lee J. Ames shows young readers how to draw pictures of baby animals — both wild and domesticated. (Rev: SLJ 11/03) [743.6]

25545 Ames, Lee J. *Draw Fifty Cats* (4–7). Illus. 1986, Doubleday paper $8.95 (978-0-385-24640-8). 64pp. Step-by-step ways of drawing different breeds and poses of cats. Also use *Draw Fifty Holiday Decorations* (1987). (Rev: BL 11/15/86) [743.69752]

25546 Ames, Lee J. *Draw Fifty Dogs* (4–6). Illus. by author. 1981, Doubleday paper $8.95 (978-0-385-23431-3). 64pp. Six steps are used to draw several species. Also use: *Draw Fifty Animals* (1985); *Draw Fifty Dinosaurs and Other Prehistoric Animals* (1977); *Draw Fifty Horses* (1984).

25547 Ames, Lee J. *Draw Fifty Famous Cartoons* (4–6). Illus. by author. 1985, Doubleday paper $8.95 (978-0-385-19521-8). 64pp. How to draw such characters as Dick Tracy and the Flintstones.

25548 Ames, Lee J. *Draw Fifty Monsters, Creeps, Superheroes, Demons, Dragons, Nerds, Dirts, Ghouls, Giants, Vampires, Zombies and Other Curiosa* (4–6). Illus. by author. 1986, Doubleday paper $8.95 (978-0-385-17639-2). 64pp. How to draw a variety of curiosities.

25549 Ames, Lee J., and Ric Estrada. *Draw Fifty Aliens, UFOs, Galaxy Ghouls, Milky Way Marauders, and Other Extraterrestrial Creatures* (3–5). Illus. Series: Draw 50. 1998, Doubleday paper $8.95 (978-0-385-49145-7). A step-by-step guide to drawing 50 creatures and objects from outer space. (Rev: BL 1/1–15/99; SLJ 6/99) [743]

25550 Artell, Mike. *Funny Cartooning for Kids* (3–6). Illus. by author. 2007, Sterling LB $17.95 (978-1-4027-2260-8). 128pp. This guide emphasizes the importance of humor in cartooning and explains the basics — exaggeration, simplification, anthropomorphism, and so forth. (Rev: SLJ 4/07) [741.5]

25551 Balchin, Judy. *Creative Lettering* (4–7). Series: Step-by-Step. 2001, Heinemann LB $24.22 (978-1-57572-331-0). 32pp. Using easy-to-find materials, this craft book gives clear directions for several fascinating lettering projects. (Rev: BL 8/1/01; HBG 10/01) [745.6]

25552 Balchin, Judy. *Decorative Painting* (4–7). Series: Step-by-Step. 2001, Heinemann LB $24.22 (978-1-57572-330-3). 32pp. With easy-to-follow directions and illustrations that describe each step, this colorful book contains a number of simple projects that decorate with paints. (Rev: BL 8/1/01; HBG 10/01; SLJ 10/01) [745]

25553 Baron, Nancy. *Getting Started in Calligraphy* (5–8). 1979, Sterling paper $13.95 (978-0-8069-8840-5). This well-organized text shows how to draw letters with beauty and grace. [745.6]

25554 Barr, Steve. *1-2-3 Draw Cartoon Aliens and Space Stuff: A Step-by-Step Guide* (3–6). Illus. by author. 2003, Peel paper $8.99 (978-0-939217-71-7). 62pp. Easy-to-follow instructions show progressively difficult drawings first in black-and-white and finally in color. Also use *1-2-3 Draw Cartoon Wildlife* (2003). (Rev: SLJ 5/03) [741.5]

25555 Barr, Steve. *1-2-3 Draw Cartoon Animals* (2–5). Illus. 2002, Peel paper $8.99 (978-0-939217-

48-9). 64pp. Easy, step-by-step directions guide budding young artists to draw a variety of animals using a cartoon style. Also use *1-2-3 Draw Cartoon Faces* and *1-2-3 Draw Cartoon People* (both 2002). (Rev: BL 1/1–15/03) [741.5]

25556 Bergin, Mark. *Robots* (5–8). Illus. by author. Series: How to Draw. 2008, PowerKids LB $18.95 (978-1-4358-2521-5). 32pp. After discussion of perspective, tools, and materials, Bergin shows how to draw droids and robots, showing the progression of a drawing from its basic shape and form to the final detailing and shading. (Rev: BLO 10/7/08) [743]

25557 Butterfield, Moira. *Fun with Paint* (4–8). Illus. Series: Creative Crafts. 1994, Random paper $6.99 (978-0-679-83942-2). 47pp. This simple introduction to painting covers various media and a number of creative projects, including making your own paints. (Rev: SLJ 3/94) [745]

25558 Carreiro, Carolyn. *Hand-Print Animal Art* (3–5). Illus. by Carolyn Carreiro and A. J. Greenwood. Series: Kids Can! 1997, Williamson paper $14.95 (978-1-885593-09-2). 144pp. Instructions are given for creating 63 animal shapes by placing paint on one's hands and fingers and stamping them on paper. (Rev: BCCB 3/98; SLJ 4/98) [745.5]

25559 ComicsKey Staff. *How to Draw Kung Fu Comics* (4–8). 2004, ComicsOne paper $19.95 (978-1-58899-394-6). 160pp. Cheung's instructions on creating architecture and perspective are particularly valuable. (Rev: BL 8/04) [741.5]

25560 Court, Rob. *How to Draw Cars and Trucks* (4–6). Illus. Series: The Scribbles Institute. 2005, Child's World LB $24.21 (978-1-59296-148-1). 32pp. In addition to introducing the basics, Court focuses readers on the composition and purpose of the objects they are drawing. Also use *How to Draw Dinosaurs* (2005). (Rev: BL 4/1/05) [743]

25561 DuBosque, Doug. *Draw Desert Animals* (3–6). Illus. 1996, Peel paper $8.95 (978-0-939217-26-7). 64pp. Beginning with simple shapes like circles and squares, teaches the reader to draw a variety of desert animals. (Rev: BL 12/15/96; SLJ 3/97) [743]

25562 DuBosque, Doug. *Draw Dinosaurs*. Rev. ed. (3–6). Illus. 1997, Peel paper $8.95 (978-0-939217-22-9). 64pp. A fine art book that presents easily followed directions for drawing a wide variety of dinosaurs, with interesting facts about each. (Rev: BL 12/15/97) [743.6]

25563 DuBosque, Doug. *Draw! Grassland Animals: A Step-by-Step Guide* (4–7). Illus. by author. 1996, Peel paper $8.99 (978-0-939217-25-0). 63pp. A step-by-step description of how to draw 31 animals from grasslands around the world. (Rev: SLJ 9/96) [741]

25564 DuBosque, Doug. *Draw Insects* (4–8). 1997, Peel paper $8.99 (978-0-939217-28-1). A carefully constructed drawing book that gives simple directions for drawing more than 80 insects, including millipedes, ticks, and spiders. (Rev: SLJ 6/98) [741.2]

25565 DuBosque, Doug. *Draw 3-D: A Step-by-Step Guide to Perspective Drawing* (4–9). Illus. by author. 1999, Peel paper $8.99 (978-0-939217-14-

4). 63pp. Using easy-to-follow sketches, the author introduces the techniques of 3-D drawing, beginning with basic concepts involving depth and progressing to more difficult areas such as multiple vanishing points. (Rev: SLJ 5/99; VOYA 8/99) [741.2]

25566 DuBosque, Doug. *Learn to Draw Now!* (5–8). Illus. by author. Series: Learn to Draw. 1991, Peel paper $8.99 (978-0-939217-16-8). 64pp. A simple, easily followed manual on how to draw that contains many interesting practice exercises. (Rev: SLJ 8/91) [743]

25567 Ewing, Patrick Aloysius, and Linda L. Louis. *In the Paint* (2–5). Illus. 1999, Abbeville $15.95 (978-0-7892-0542-1). 64pp. Patrick Ewing talks about his favorite pastime — painting — and how young people can use color, shapes, and texture to create their own works. (Rev: BL 7/99; HBG 10/99; SLJ 11/99) [751]

25568 Gray, Peter. *Heroes and Villains* (5–8). Series: Kid's Guide to Drawing. 2006, Rosen LB $25.25 (978-1-4042-3330-0). 32pp. Shows clearly how to draw manga heroes and villains and offers guidance on getting facial expressions just right. (Rev: BL 9/1/06; SLJ 9/06) [741.5]

25569 Hart, Chris. *Drawing the New Adventure Cartoons: Cool Spies, Evil Guys and Action Heroes* (4–10). Illus. by author. 2008, Sixth & Spring paper $19.95 (978-1-933027-60-9). 128pp. Both entertaining and educational, this book gives detailed instructions, and amusing side notes, that show how to create adventure characters. (Rev: SLJ 2/09) [741.5]

25570 Hart, Christopher. *The Cartoonist's Big Book of Drawing Animals* (2–6). Illus. by author. 2008, Watson-Guptill paper $21.95 (978-0-8230-1421-7). 224pp. Dogs, cats, horses, bears, and penguins are among the animals featured in this step-by-step approach to drawing cartoon figures with many facial expressions. (Rev: SLJ 3/09) [741.5]

25571 Hart, Christopher. *Kids Draw Anime* (4–8). Illus. 2002, Watson-Guptill paper $10.95 (978-0-8230-2690-6). 128pp. Instructions on how to draw anime (Japanese cartoons) characters, with many colorful examples. (Rev: BL 2/1/03; SLJ 11/02) [741.5]

25572 Hart, Christopher. *Kids Draw Funny and Spooky Holiday Characters* (3–6). Illus. by author. 2001, Watson-Guptill paper $10.95 (978-0-8230-2626-5). 64pp. Cartoon drawing for Halloween and Christmas are the focus of this guide that covers the basic principles of showing movement and good positioning of characters. (Rev: SLJ 9/01) [741.5]

25573 Hart, Christopher. *Kids Draw Manga* (3–8). Illus. by author. Series: Kids Draw. 2004, Watson-Guptill paper $10.95 (978-0-8230-2623-4). 64pp. For beginners, this is a guide to the basics of manga, showing how to draw a number of characters, poses, and action moves. (Rev: SLJ 9/04) [741.5]

25574 Hart, Christopher. *Manga Mania: How to Draw Japanese Comics* (5–9). Illus. 2001, Watson-Guptill paper $19.95 (978-0-8230-3035-4). 144pp. Hart looks at the techniques for drawing typical

Japanese comic characters and animals, providing examples of published manga along with an introduction to the various genres of manga and an interview with a manga publisher. (Rev: BL 7/01; SLJ 7/01) [741.5]

25575 Hart, Christopher. *Manga Mania Chibi and Furry Characters: How to Draw the Adorable Mini-People and Cool Cat-Girls of Japanese Comics* (5–12). Illus. 2006, Watson-Guptill paper $19.95 (978-0-8230-2977-8). 144pp. Fans of these super-cute manga characters will appreciate the step-by-step directions in this informative book. (Rev: SLJ 5/06) [741.5]

25576 Hart, Christopher. *Mecha Mania: How to Draw the Battling Robots, Cool Spaceships, and Military Vehicles of Japanese Comics* (4–8). Illus. 2002, Watson-Guptill paper $19.95 (978-0-8230-3056-9). 128pp. Instructions on how to draw the high-tech, scary, fanciful machines and weapons that fill the pages of Japanese comic books. (Rev: BL 2/1/03; SLJ 4/03) [741.5]

25577 Hart, Christopher. *Xtreme Art: Draw Manga Monsters!* (1–4). Illus. by author. Series: Xtreme Art. 2005, Watson-Guptill paper $6.95 (978-0-8230-0372-3). 64pp. A simple guide to drawing in the manga style for children; also use *Draw Mini Manga!* (2005). (Rev: SLJ 9/05) [741.5]

25578 Hart, Christopher. *Kids Draw Animals* (3–6). Illus. by author. Series: Kids Draw. 2003, Watson-Guptill paper $10.95 (978-0-8230-2631-9). 64pp. Organized by topics, this is an easy-to-understand, step-by-step guide to drawing cartoons of animals. (Rev: SLJ 11/03) [743.6]

25579 Henson, Paige. *Drawing with Charcoal and Pastels* (3–5). Series: How to Paint and Draw. 1999, Rourke LB $26.60 (978-1-57103-313-0). 32pp. This book gives background information on charcoal and pastels, shows techniques for using them, suggests ideas and projects, and explains how to clean up when you're finished. Also use *Drawing with Markers* and *Painting with Face Paints* (both 1999). (Rev: SLJ 1/00) [741.2]

25580 Henson, Paige. *Drawing with Pencils* (1–3). Series: How to Paint and Draw. 1999, Rourke LB $26.60 (978-1-57103-310-9). 32pp. This book contains a little history, information about supplies, and plenty of easy art projects for budding artists. Also use *Painting with Tempera* and *Painting with Watercolors* (both 1999). (Rev: SLJ 2/00) [742]

25581 Hodge, Anthony. *Drawing* (4–8). Series: Mastering Art. 2004, Stargazer LB $.00 (978-1-932799-01-9). 32pp. Along with basic information on materials, colors, and techniques, this slim volume looks at drawing the human body. Also use *Painting* (2004). (Rev: BL 11/1/04) [741.2]

25582 Lacey, Sue. *Animals* (2–5). Series: Start with Art. 1999, Millbrook LB $21.90 (978-0-7613-3263-3). 32pp. Various step-by-step projects are introduced using actual artworks to inspire creativity, such as Picasso's model of a goat or a Stubbs painting of a horse. Also use in the same series: *People* (1999). (Rev: HBG 3/00; SLJ 1/00) [741.2]

25583 Levin, Freddie. *1-2-3 Draw: Cars, Trucks, and Other Vehicles* (3–5). Illus. 2002, Peel paper $8.99 (978-0-939217-43-4). 64pp. A large-format paperback that shows how to draw 24 vehicles including a race car, cement truck, and a school bus. (Rev: BL 4/15/02; SLJ 7/02) [743]

25584 Levin, Freddie. *1-2-3 Draw: Dinosaurs and Other Prehistoric Animals: A Step by Step Guide* (1–5). Illus. by author. 2000, Peel paper $8.95 (978-0-939217-41-0). 64pp. Using three basic shapes — circles, ovals, and eggs — the author shows how to draw 24 different prehistoric animals. The same techniques are applied in *1-2-3-Draw: Pets and Farm Animals* (2000). (Rev: SLJ 3/01) [742]

25585 Lewis, Amanda. *Lettering: Make Your Own Cards, Signs, Gifts and More* (4–8). Illus. 1997, Kids Can paper $6.95 (978-1-55074-232-9). This book describes calligraphy and gothic lettering techniques, covering such topics as typefaces, displays, types of pens to purchase, how to determine pen size, and how to use pens, as well as explaining how to make letterhead stationery and newsletters on the computer. (Rev: BL 10/15/97; SLJ 1/98) [745.6]

25586 Lipsey, Jennifer. *I Love to Finger Paint!* (1–3). Series: My Very Favorite Art Book. 2006, Sterling $9.95 (978-1-57990-771-6). 48pp. This attractive guide to finger painting lists essential supplies, explores various techniques, and describes several projects. (Rev: BL 6/1–15/06) [751.4]

25587 Lipsey, Jennifer. *I Love to Paint!* (3–5). Illus. 2006, Lark $9.95 (978-1-57990-630-6). 48pp. Finger painting, watercolors, scratch art, and sponge painting are among the painting techniques introduced in this attractive and well-organized guide. (Rev: BL 2/15/06) [751.4]

25588 Luxbacher, Irene. *The Jumbo Book of Art* (3–8). Illus. by author. 2003, Kids Can paper $14.95 (978-1-55074-762-1). 208pp. Drawing, use of color, sculpting, and mixed media are the focus of this book full of interesting art projects. (Rev: SLJ 11/03) [701]

25589 Luxbacher, Irene. *123 I Can Draw!* (1–3). Illus. by author. Series: Starting Art. 2008, Kids Can $14.95 (978-1-55453-039-7); paper $5.95 (978-1-55453-152-3). 24pp. This friendly book offers clear, easy directions for drawing such items as faces, features, expressions, and figures. (Rev: SLJ 4/08) [741.2]

25590 Luxbacher, Irene. *123 I Can Paint!* (1–3). Illus. Series: Starting Art. 2007, Kids Can LB $12.95 (978-1-55453-037-3); paper $5.95 (978-1-55453-150-9). 24pp. Mixing colors, perspective, and brush techniques are among the topics discussed in this introduction to painting. (Rev: BL 10/15/07; SLJ 10/07) [751.4]

25591 Lynn, Sara, and Diane James. *Play with Paint* (PS–3). Illus. 1993, Carolrhoda LB $12.44 (978-0-87614-755-9). 24pp. This beginning craft book contains simple projects with brief explanations using everyday materials. A companion volume is: *Play with Paper* (1993). (Rev: BL 5/1/93) [750]

25592 Masiello, Ralph. *Ralph Masiello's Ancient Egypt Drawing Book* (3–6). Illus. by author. 2008,

Charlesbridge $16.95 (978-1-57091-533-8); paper $7.95 (978-1-57091-534-5). A step-by-step guide to drawing Egyptian symbols and pictures — each with its own commentary. (Rev: SLJ 9/08)

25593 Masiello, Ralph. *Ralph Masiello's Dragon Drawing Book* (3–6). Illus. by author. 2007, Charlesbridge $16.95 (978-1-57091-531-4); paper $7.95 (978-1-57091-532-1). 32pp. Eleven cool dragons and other mythical creatures from cultures around the world are included in this well-designed, step-by-step drawing guide. (Rev: BL 7/07; SLJ 9/07) [743.6]

25594 Mayne, Don. *Draw Your Own Cartoons* (3–8). Illus. by author. 2001, Williamson paper $8.95 (978-1-885593-76-4). 64pp. A cartoon-like atmosphere prevails in this guide that teaches readers to draw characters. (Rev: SLJ 6/01) [741.5]

25595 Mayne, Don. *Drawing Horses (That Look Real)* (4–8). Illus. by author. Series: Quick Starts for Kids! 2002, Williamson paper $8.95 (978-1-885593-74-0). 64pp. Cartoonlike instructions take young artists step by step through using basic shapes to draw horses and to show movement and character. (Rev: SLJ 4/03) [743.6]

25596 Murawski, Laura. *How to Draw Cats* (2–5). Illus. by author. Series: A Kid's Guide to Drawing. 2001, Rosen LB $21.25 (978-0-8239-5549-7). 24pp. Information about each breed precedes instructions on how to draw it in stages that begin with basic shapes and proceed to add details. Also use *How to Draw Dogs* (2001). (Rev: SLJ 8/01) [741]

25597 *Paper and Paint: Hands-on Crafts for Everyday Fun* (2–5). Illus. Series: Crafty Kids. 2003, McGraw-Hill $12.95 (978-1-57768-527-2). 48pp. Paper and paint projects that may need adult help are included in this volume with easy-to-follow instructions and illustrations. (Rev: HBG 4/04; SLJ 12/03) [745.54]

25598 Peffer, Jessica. *DragonArt: How to Draw Fantastic Dragons and Fantasy Creatures* (5–12). Illus. by author. 2005, Impact paper $19.99 (978-1-58180-657-1). 127pp. Beautiful creatures from the author's imagination fill the pages of this well-written book and will inspire young artists to develop their own fantasy style. (Rev: SLJ 5/06) [743]

25599 Pellowski, Michael M. *The Art of Making Comic Books* (4–8). Illus. 1995, Lerner LB $25.55 (978-0-8225-2304-8). A history of comic books, plus drawing techniques and advice on how to become a comic book artist. (Rev: BCCB 2/96; BL 1/1–15/96; SLJ 1/96) [741.5]

25600 Peterson, Tiffany. *Watercraft* (3–6). Series: Draw It! 2003, Heinemann LB $24.22 (978-1-4034-0214-1). 32pp. Author Tiffany Peterson offers guidance for drawing and painting pictures of various watercraft, including jet skis, river boats, and sailing ships. Also in this series are *Sports Stars*, *Fashion Design*, and *Sea Creatures* (both 2003). (Rev: BL 11/15/03; HBG 10/03; SLJ 10/03)

25601 Reinagle, Damon J. *Draw! Medieval Fantasies* (4–8). Illus. 1995, Peel paper $8.99 (978-0-939217-30-4). 64pp. A how-to drawing book that gives simple instructions on creating such medieval subjects

as dragons and castles. (Rev: BL 1/1–15/96; SLJ 3/96) [743]

25602 Reinagle, Damon J. *Draw Alien Fantasies* (3–6). Illus. 1996, Peel paper $8.99 (978-0-939217-31-1). 64pp. Easy-to-follow directions are given for drawing a number of creatures from outer space. (Rev: BL 12/15/96; SLJ 3/97) [741.2]

25603 Reinagle, Damon J. *Draw Sports Figures* (4–8). Illus. 1997, Peel paper $8.99 (978-0-939217-32-8). In six chapters arranged by sport or sports category, the author gives easy-to-follow instructions on how to draw action figures. (Rev: SLJ 6/98) [742]

25604 Robins, Deri. *Painting* (2–5). Illus. Series: Learn Art. 2004, QEB LB $27.10 (978-1-59566-046-6). 32pp. Creativity is emphasized in this look at how colors interact and the various techniques for applying them. (Rev: SLJ 4/05) [750]

25605 Robins, Deri. *Special Effects* (3–5). Series: QEB Learn Art. 2004, QEB LB $27.10 (978-1-59566-047-3). 32pp. Using glitter paint and making mosaics and collages are among the projects presented here with clear step-by-step directions. (Rev: BL 11/1/04; SLJ 4/05) [741.2]

25606 Roche, Art. *Art for Kids: Comic Strips: Create Your Own Comic Strips from Start to Finish* (4–8). Illus. by author. 2007, Sterling LB $17.95 (978-1-57990-788-4). 112pp. This is a practical guide to creating a comic strip, with tips on story ideas, design, creating characters, and writing jokes. (Rev: BCCB 5/07; LMC 8/07; SLJ 5/07) [741.5]

25607 Roche, Art. *Cartooning: The Only Cartooning Book You'll Ever Need to Be the Artist You've Always Wanted to Be* (3–6). Illus. by author. Series: Art for Kids. 2005, Sterling $17.95 (978-1-57990-623-8). 111pp. An engaging guide to the basics of cartooning, encouraging young artists to seek their own style. (Rev: SLJ 7/05) [741.5]

25608 Russon, Jacqueline. *Face Painting* (1–4). Photos by Steve Shott. Illus. by Mei Lim. Series: First Craft Books. 1998, Carolrhoda LB $12.95 (978-1-57505-099-7). 22pp. There are ten simple craft projects in this book that give directions for painting faces to resemble a cat, mermaid, teddy bear, bunny, etc. (Rev: HBG 10/98; SLJ 4/98) [741.2]

25609 Russon, Jacqueline. *Face Painting* (3–7). Illus. Series: First Arts and Crafts. 1994, Thomson Learning LB $5.00 (978-1-56847-197-6). 32pp. An amazing number of ideas for creative face painting, with clear instructions and many illustrations. (Rev: BL 1/1/95; SLJ 12/94) [745.5]

25610 Sabbeth, Carol. *Crayons and Computers: Computer Art Activities for Kids Ages 4 to 8* (PS–4). 1998, Chicago Review paper $16.95 (978-1-55652-289-5). 159pp. Using a PC or Mac, any type of printer, and software such as Windows Paintbrush, ClarisWorks, or Kid Pix, this book gives instructions on over 50 craft and project ideas, including using the computer to draw a picture and, after printing it, coloring it. (Rev: SLJ 7/98) [741]

25611 Silver, Patricia. *Face Painting* (1–4). Illus. by Louise Phillips. 2000, Kids Can $12.95 (978-1-55074-845-1); paper $6.95 (978-1-55074-689-1).

40pp. A fine introduction to face painting that includes 16 of the most commonly requested faces with rules for safety and cleanup tips. (Rev: BL 9/15/00; SLJ 10/00) [745.5]

25612 Solga, Kim, et al. *Art Fun!* (1–6). Photos by Pamela Monfort. Illus. Series: Art and Activities for Kids. 1997, North Light paper $19.99 (978-0-89134-833-7). 216pp. This activity book introduces projects involving painting, drawing, printmaking, and sculpting. (Rev: SLJ 1/98) [741.2]

25613 Stephens, Jay. *Heroes!* (4–7). Illus. by author. 2007, Sterling $12.95 (978-1-57990-934-5). 64pp. How to draw superheroes, masks, action moves, and so forth, with lots of great examples. (Rev: BL 12/1/07; SLJ 8/07) [741.5]

25614 Stephens, Jay. *Monsters! Draw Your Own Mutants, Freaks and Creeps* (4–6). Illus. by author. 2007, Sterling LB $12.95 (978-1-57990-935-2). 64pp. The author guides readers in developing their own artistic style while supplying plenty of inspiration. (Rev: SLJ 8/07)

25615 Tecco, Betsy Dru. *How to Draw Egypt's Sights and Symbols* (3–6). Illus. Series: A Kid's Guide to Drawing the Countries of the World. 2004, Rosen LB $26.50 (978-0-8239-6682-0). 48pp. After background information on Egypt, step-by-step instructions guide readers through sketching scenes including a camel, a date palm, a pyramid, and the mask of King Tut. Also use *How to Draw France's Sights and Symbols* and *How to Draw Japan's Sights and Symbols* (both 2004). (Rev: SLJ 3/05) [743]

25616 Temple, Kathryn. *Drawing* (5–8). Illus. Series: Art for Kids. 2005, Sterling $17.95 (978-1-57990-587-3). 112pp. A comprehensive and clearly written guide to equipment and techniques, with useful illustrations and practical exercises at the end of each section. (Rev: BL 5/1/05; SLJ 9/05) [741.2]

25617 Wallace, Mary. *I Can Make Art* (4–8). Series: I Can Make. 1997, Firefly paper $6.95 (978-1-895688-65-8). Art and crafts are combined in these 12 projects involving such techniques as watercolor, still life, chalk drawing, print making, and collage. (Rev: SLJ 12/97) [741.2]

25618 Walsh, Patricia. *Aircraft* (3–6). Illus. Series: Draw It! 2000, Heinemann LB $22.79 (978-1-57572-347-1). 32pp. From the Wright brothers' flying machine to a modern Bell JetRanger helicopter, this chronologically arranged book describes aircraft and gives directions for sketching them. (Rev: BL 2/1/01; HBG 10/01) [743]

25619 Walsh, Patricia. *Cars* (3–6). Series: Draw It! 2000, Heinemann LB $22.79 (978-1-57572-348-8). 32pp. Using colored lines to show each step, this book shows how to draw cars in six easy steps. Also use from the same art series: *Dinosaurs*, *Space Vehicles*, and *Wild Animals* (all 2000). (Rev: BL 3/1/01; HBG 10/01) [741.2]

25620 Walsh, Patricia. *Woodland Animals* (3–6). Illus. 2000, Heinemann LB $22.79 (978-1-57572-352-5). 32pp. Introducing a single animal per double-page spread, this book describes such animals as the skunk, woodpecker, and porcupine with clear instructions on how to draw each. (Rev: BL 2/1/01; HBG 10/01; SLJ 2/01) [743]

25621 Wellford, Lin. *Painting on Rocks for Kids* (K–3). Illus. 2002, North Light paper $12.99 (978-1-58180-255-9). 64pp. Step-by-step instructions and tips on technique accompany ideas for making cars, flowers, dinosaurs, fish, food, and other items from painted stones and rocks. (Rev: SLJ 1/03) [745.7]

25622 Wheeler, Annie. *Painting on a Canvas: Art Adventures for Kids* (5–8). Illus. by Debra Spina Dixon. 2006, Gibbs Smith $9.95 (978-1-58685-839-1). 63pp. These projects are designed to get children's creative juices flowing and to introduce them to some of the techniques used by such world-famous artists as Matisse, Michelangelo, and Picasso. (Rev: SLJ 11/06) [701]

25623 Zemke, Deborah. *Doodle a Zoodle* (3–5). 2006, Blue Apple $12.95 (978-1-59354-140-8). Gives step-by-step instructions for drawing 39 "zoodles" — animals, such as squirrels and jackrabbits, that have double letters in their names; brief information is provided on each animal. (Rev: SLJ 12/06) [743]

25624 Zemke, Deborah. *2 Is for Toucan: Oodles of Doodles from 0 to 42* (3–5). Illus. by author. 2005, Handprint $12.95 (978-1-59354-075-3). Step-by-step instructions show how to do creative doodles integrating art and numbers; a spiral binding allows the book to open flat. (Rev: SLJ 9/05) [741]

Masks and Mask Making

25625 D'Cruz, Anna-Marie. *Make Your Own Masks* (3–4). Series: Do It Yourself Projects! 2009, Rosen LB $23.95 (978-1-4358-2853-7). 24pp. Step-by-step directions show how to make a selection of masks from diverse cultures. (Rev: SLJ 7/09) [646.4]

25626 Earl, Amanda, and Danielle Sensier. *Masks* (5–7). Illus. Series: Traditions Around the World. 1994, Thomson Learning LB $24.26 (978-1-56847-226-3). 48pp. This multicultural introduction to masks discusses their origins and uses in religion, festivals, and the theater. (Rev: BL 2/1/95; SLJ 3/95) [391.43]

25627 Schwarz, Renee. *Making Masks* (4–6). Series: Kids Can Do It! 2002, Kids Can $12.95 (978-1-55074-929-8); paper $5.95 (978-1-55074-931-1). 40pp. A basic volume on making masks from a various of easily obtained materials. (Rev: BL 9/15/02; HBG 3/03; SLJ 12/02) [731.785]

Paper Crafts

25628 Alexander, Chris. *Sort-of-Difficult Origami* (2–5). Illus. 2008, Capstone LB $18.95 (978-1-4296-2023-9). 32pp. Moderately difficult origami models include a tulip and stem, a penguin, a seal, and a goldfish. (Rev: BL 12/15/08) [736]

25629 Balchin, Judy. *Papier Mâché* (4–7). Illus. Series: Step-by-Step. 2000, Heinemann LB $24.22 (978-1-57572-328-0). 32pp. Combines easy-to-follow projects with information on how papier-mâché has been used over the centuries, including applications in construction and furniture. (Rev: BL 10/15/00; HBG 10/01; SLJ 12/00) [745.54]

25630 Blanchette, Peg, and Terri Thibault. *Make Your Own Cool Cards: 40 Awesome Notes and Invitations!* (2–4). Series: Quick Starts for Kids! 2004, Ideals Publications paper $8.95 (978-1-885593-96-2). 64pp. Sixteen projects that use easy-to-obtain materials are presented in detail with clear illustrations. (Rev: BL 12/15/03)

25631 Bliss, Helen. *Paper* (3–6). Series: Craft Workshop. 1998, Crabtree LB $19.96 (978-0-86505-781-4). 32pp. This book presents a history of paper as well as various paper-related activities such as making paper, masks, puppets, etc. (Rev: SLJ 9/98) [745]

25632 Borja, Robert, and Corinne Borja. *Making Chinese Papercuts* (4–7). Illus. by authors. 1980, Whitman LB $15.99 (978-0-8075-4948-3). A clear explanation of an ancient art with many examples and photographs.

25633 Burke, Judy, ed. *Look What You Can Make with Paper Bags* (3–5). Illus. 1999, Boyds Mills paper $5.95 (978-1-56397-717-6). 48pp. Paper bags and other easily found materials are used in this series of creative craft projects, some of which require adult help. (Rev: BL 7/99; SLJ 5/99) [745.54]

25634 Carter, David A., and James Diaz. *The Elements of Pop-Up: A Pop-Up Book for Aspiring Paper Engineers* (3–8). Photos by Keith Sutter. Illus. by authors. 1999, Simon & Schuster $35.00 (978-0-689-82224-7). Instructions are given for constructing more than 50 pop-ups with working models of each. (Rev: BL 12/15/99; HBG 3/00; SLJ 2/00) [745.5]

25635 Carter, Tamsin. *Handmade Cards* (3–5). Illus. Series: Step-by-Step. 2002, Heinemann LB $25.64 (978-1-4034-0698-9). 32pp. This volume provides simple instructions, explained one step at a time, for creating and decorating greeting cards. (Rev: BL 12/15/02; HBG 3/03) [745.594]

25636 Check, Laura. *The Kids' Guide to Making Scrapbooks and Photo Albums! How to Collect, Design, Assemble, Decorate* (4–6). Illus. by Betsy Day. 2002, Williamson paper $12.95 (978-1-885593-59-7). 128pp. Check discusses the best ways to use images to tell stories as well as giving practical instructions for creating scrapbooks and albums. (Rev: SLJ 7/02) [745.593]

25637 Churchill, E. Richard. *Holiday Paper Projects* (3–6). Illus. by James Michaels. 1993, Sterling $14.95 (978-0-8069-8512-1). 128pp. Various paper crafts related to holidays are outlined with simple instructions that usually only involve cutting, folding, and pasting. (Rev: SLJ 12/93) [745]

25638 Fiarotta, Phyllis, and Noel Fiarotta. *Papercrafts Around the World* (4–6). Illus. 1996, Sterling $19.95 (978-0-8069-3990-2). 96pp. Paper crafts and projects from 31 countries are included with easy-to-follow instructions. (Rev: BL 7/96; SLJ 8/96) [745.54]

25639 Garza, Carmen Lomas. *Making Magic Windows: Creating Papel Picado / Cut-Paper Art* (3–7). 1999, Children's Book Pr. paper $9.95 (978-0-89239-159-2). 61pp. This bilingual book gives directions on making festive papel picado (cut paper) banners associated with the Southwest and Mexican Americans. (Rev: BL 5/1/99) [745.54]

25640 Grummer, Arnold E. *Paper by Kids* (5–7). Illus. 1990, Macmillan $12.95 (978-0-87518-191-2). 116pp. A clear, well-organized guide to papermaking.

25641 Harbo, Christopher L. *The Kids' Guide to Paper Airplanes* (4–7). Illus. 2009, Capstone LB $23.93 (978-1-4296-2274-5). 32pp. Detailed, step-by-step directions show how to make a variety of arrows, missiles, and planes, with tips on increasing flight time. (Rev: BL 12/15/08; SLJ 5/09) [745.592]

25642 Henry, Sally. *Paper Folding* (3–6). Illus. Series: Make Your Own Art. 2008, PowerKids LB $18.95 (978-1-4358-2507-9). 32pp. This fold-your-own title offers an introduction to techniques and equipment followed by a number of inventive projects. (Rev: BL 12/15/08) [736]

25643 Henry, Sandi. *Cut-Paper Play! Dazzling Creations from Construction Paper* (K–5). Illus. by Norma Jean Jourdenais. Series: Kids Can! 1997, Williamson paper $12.95 (978-1-885593-05-4). 160pp. In this book, which indicates the relative difficulty of each activity, there are projects that include making a desktop robot, a frog, and a mosaic snowman. (Rev: SLJ 9/97) [745.5]

25644 Hufford, Deborah. *Greeting Card Making: Send Your Personal Message* (3–5). Illus. Series: Snap Books Crafts. 2005, Capstone LB $25.26 (978-0-7368-4385-0). 32pp. Clear directions will help readers create a variety of greeting cards, including pop-ups, collage cards, mosaic cards, and photo cards. (Rev: BL 12/15/05) [745.594]

25645 Irvin, Christine M. *Paper Plate Mania* (K–2). Illus. Series: Craft Mania. 2002, Children's Book Pr. LB $23.50 (978-0-516-21675-1). 32pp. Masks and sun catchers are among the many inventive uses for paper plates suggested in this book that emphasizes the importance of recycling. Also use *Paper Cup Mania* (2002). (Rev: SLJ 9/02) [745.54]

25646 Irvine, Joan. *How to Make Pop-Ups* (3–7). Illus. by Barbara Reid. 1988, Morrow paper $6.95 (978-0-688-07902-4). 96pp. Instructions on how to create three-dimensional wonders. (Rev: BL 4/15/88; SLJ 3/88)

25647 Irvine, Joan. *How to Make Super Pop-Ups* (4–7). Illus. 1992, Morrow $14.00 (978-0-688-10690-4); paper $6.95 (978-0-688-11521-0). 96pp. Lots of ideas and directions for making three-dimensional paper constructions with moving parts. (Rev: BL 1/15/93) [745]

25648 Johnson, Ginger. *Paper-Folding Fun! 50 Awesome Crafts to Weave, Twist and Curl* (3–5). Illus. Series: Kids Can. 2002, Williamson paper $12.95 (978-1-885593-67-2). 128pp. Step-by-step directions accompany each idea for making objects from paper, including jewelry, mobiles, and books. (Rev: BL 11/1/02) [745.54]

25649 Kelly, Emery J. *Paper Airplanes: Models to Build and Fly* (4–8). Illus. 1997, Lerner LB $23.93 (978-0-8225-2401-4). This is a practical manual on making and flying paper airplanes, with good coverage of the principles of aerodynamics. (Rev: BL 12/1/97; HBG 3/98; SLJ 2/98) [745.592]

25650 Lafosse, Michael G. *Making Origami Christmas Decorations Step by Step* (2–4). Illus. by author. Series: Kid's Guide to Origami. 2002, Rosen LB $21.25 (978-0-8239-5874-0). 24pp. Nine projects related to Christmas are suitable for beginning folders. (Rev: SLJ 10/02)

25651 Lafosse, Michael G. *Making Origami Masks Step by Step* (2–6). Illus. Series: A Kid's Guide to Origami. 2004, Rosen LB $21.25 (978-0-8239-6703-2). 24pp. Well-explained projects are suitable for different levels of expertise. Also use *Making Origami Puzzles Step by Step* and *Making Origami Science Experiments Step by Step* (both 2004). (Rev: SLJ 11/04) [745.592]

25652 Lafosse, Michael G. *Origami Activities* (4–6). Illus. Series: Asian Arts and Crafts for Creative Kids. 2004, Tuttle $12.95 (978-0-8048-3497-1). 64pp. Step-by-step instructions guide readers through 15 increasingly difficult projects. (Rev: SLJ 8/04) [736]

25653 Lassus, Irene, and Marie-Anne Voituriez. *Papier Mâché* (2–5). Series: I Made It Myself! 2005, Gareth Stevens LB $23.00 (978-0-8368-5966-9). 24pp. Following an introduction to the properties of papier mâché and the ways to work with it, nine projects include beads, candy, and a crocodile. (Rev: SLJ 2/06) [745.54]

25654 Lewis, Amanda. *The Jumbo Book of Paper Crafts* (3–6). Illus. by Jane Kurisu. 2002, Kids Can paper $14.95 (978-1-55074-940-3). 160pp. Easy, illustrated techniques and instructions teach older children how to create a multitude of crafts with paper and cardboard. (Rev: BL 12/15/02; SLJ 12/02) [745]

25655 Llimós, Anna. *Easy Cardboard Crafts in 5 Steps* (2–4). Series: Easy Crafts in Five Steps. 2008, Enslow LB $22.60 (978-0-7660-3083-1). 32pp. A notebook, a drum, and a hang-glider are among the 14 projects provided here. Also use *Easy Cloth Crafts in Five Steps* (2008). (Rev: SLJ 4/08) [745.54]

25656 McGee, Randel. *Paper Crafts for Christmas* (2–5). Illus. Series: Paper Craft Fun for Holidays. 2009, Enslow LB $17.95 (978-0-7660-2952-1). 48pp. A brief history of the holiday and its traditions precedes such projects as a holly wreath, snowflake ornaments, a paper plate angel, and a pop-up chimney card. (Rev: BL 4/1/09) [745.594]

25657 McGee, Randel. *Paper Crafts for Halloween* (2–5). Illus. Series: Paper Craft Fun for Holidays.

2009, Enslow LB $17.95 (978-0-7660-2947-7). 48pp. A brief history of the holiday and its traditions precedes such projects as a flying bat, a haunted house, a black cat, and a skull headdress. (Rev: BL 4/1/09; SLJ 4/09) [745.594]

25658 McGee, Randel. *Paper Crafts for Valentine's Day* (2–5). Illus. 2008, Enslow LB $17.95 (978-0-7660-2948-4). 48pp. This craft book opens with an introduction to Valentine's Day followed by eight simple projects. (Rev: BL 12/15/08; SLJ 11/08) [745.594]

25659 Newell, Keith. *Look and Make with Paper* (4–5). Photos by Steve Shott. Illus. by Michael Evans. Series: Look and Make. 2004, Sea-to-Sea LB $27.10 (978-1-932889-24-6). 32pp. Well-designed projects — such as paper sandals — use paper and glue and are presented with clear instructions and a photograph of the final product. (Rev: SLJ 4/05) [745.54]

25660 Nguyen, Duy. *Monster Origami* (5–7). Illus. 2007, Sterling paper $9.95 (978-1-4027-4014-5). 96pp. This how-to origami book provides easy-to-understand instructions on creating amazing paper monsters. (Rev: SLJ 3/08)

25661 *Paper* (3–6). Series: Let's Create! 2003, Gareth Stevens LB $24.00 (978-0-8368-3747-6). 32pp. An attractive introduction to paper crafts, including 12 projects and additional suggested resources. (Rev: SLJ 4/04) [745.54]

25662 *Papier-Mache* (3–4). Illus. Series: Let's Create! 2004, Gareth Stevens LB $24.00 (978-0-8368-4017-9). 32pp. Simple projects created by children may still require some adult help. Also use *Stones and "Stuff"* and *Metal* (both 2004). (Rev: BL 6/1–15/04; SLJ 11/04) [745.5]

25663 Powell, Michelle. *Printing* (4–7). Illus. Series: Step-by-Step. 2000, Heinemann LB $24.22 (978-1-57572-329-7). 32pp. Various easy-to-follow printing projects are presented along with material on printing methods from ancient Egypt onward. (Rev: BL 10/15/00; HBG 10/01) [761]

25664 Ross, Kathy, ed. *Look What You Can Make with Newspapers, Magazines, and Greeting Cards: Over 80 Pictured Crafts and Dozens of Other Ideas* (2–4). Photos by Hank Schneider. 2002, Boyds Mills paper $5.95 (978-1-56397-566-0). 48pp. Final products include dolls with clothes, boxes, banks, signs and cards, and mobiles; the illustrations enhance the written instructions. (Rev: SLJ 4/02) [745.54]

25665 Schwarz, Renee. *Papier-Mâché* (4–6). Illus. by author. Series: Kids Can! 2000, Kids Can $12.95 (978-1-55074-833-8); paper $6.95 (978-1-55074-727-0). 40pp. This work outlines 11 projects in papier-mâché with tips on getting the proper supplies, preparing the paste, and sanding and fixing mistakes. (Rev: HBG 10/00; SLJ 6/00) [745.5]

25666 Seix, Victoria. *Creating with Papier-Mâché* (3–6). Series: Crafts for All Seasons. 2000, Blackbirch LB $23.70 (978-1-56711-439-3). 32pp. Fifteen projects using either paper strips or paper pulp are outlined in this attractive craft book. (Rev: SLJ 2/01) [745.5]

25667 Siomades, Lorianne, ed. *Look What You Can Make With Boxes: Over 90 Pictured Crafts and Dozens of Other Ideas* (4–6). Photos by Hank Schneider. 1998, Boyds Mills paper $5.95 (978-1-56397-704-6). 48pp. Different kinds of boxes (cereal, greeting card, etc.) and simple materials, such as glue and paints, are used to create toys, games, decorations, and various useful objects in this easy-to-use craft manual. (Rev: SLJ 6/98) [745.5]

25668 Stevens, Clive. *Paperfolding* (4–7). Series: Step-by-Step. 2001, Heinemann LB $24.22 (978-1-57572-333-4). 32pp. Easy-to-find materials are used in a number of exciting paper folding projects, each of which is described in clear, detailed directions with step-by-step illustrations. (Rev: BL 8/1/01; HBG 10/01; SLJ 10/01) [745.5]

25669 Walter, F. Virginia. *Super Toys and Games from Paper* (4–6). Illus. 1993, Sterling $19.95 (978-1-895569-06-3). 104pp. Directions are given for almost 90 paper toys and games, such as newspaper golf clubs and cardboard-tube hammers. (Rev: BL 1/1/94; SLJ 12/93) [745.592]

25670 Watson, David. *Papermaking* (4–7). Series: Step-by-Step. 2000, Heinemann LB $24.22 (978-1-57572-327-3). 32pp. This book shows how you can use old paper to make new paper and create a number of wonderful art objects following simple step-by-step directions. (Rev: BL 10/15/00; HBG 10/01) [745.5]

25671 West, Robin. *Dinosaur Discoveries: How to Create Your Own Prehistoric World* (3–6). Illus. 1989, Carolrhoda $19.95 (978-0-87614-351-3). 72pp. Directions for creating models of dinosaurs using scissors, glue, and construction paper. (Rev: BL 11/15/89; SLJ 12/89) [745.54]

Printmaking

25672 Luxbacher, Irene. *1-2-3 I Can Make Prints!* (PS–3). Illus. by author. 2008, Kids Can LB $14.95 (978-1-55453-040-3); paper $5.95 (978-1-55453-153-0). 24pp. This volume offers easy kid-friendly printmaking projects with step-by-step instructions. (Rev: BLO 3/3/08; SLJ 4/08) [760.28]

Sewing and Needle Crafts

25673 Blanchette, Peg, and Terri Thibault. *12 Easy Knitting Projects* (3–6). Illus. by Norma Jean Martin-Jourdenais. Series: Quick Starts for Kids! 2006, Williamson $12.95 (978-0-8249-6784-0); paper $8.95 (978-0-8249-6785-7). 63pp. Offering features for both beginners and more advanced knitters, this book provides basic information about knitting and step-by-step instructions for 12 projects of differing complexity, including a scarf, doggy turtleneck sweater, and a poncho. (Rev: SLJ 8/06) [746.4]

25674 Bradberry, Sarah. *Kids Knit! Simple Steps to Nifty Projects* (4–8). Photos by Michael Hnatov. Illus. by Kim Coxey. 2004, Sterling $14.95 (978-0-8069-7733-1). 96pp. Simple, clear instructions and illustrations add to the value of this book full of appealing projects. (Rev: BL 12/15/04; SLJ 2/05)

25675 Clewer, Carolyn. *Kids Can Knit: Fun and Easy Projects for Small Knitters* (3–7). 2003, Barron's paper $16.95 (978-0-7641-2718-2). 128pp. The reader gradually moves from simple techniques to more sophisticated projects. (Rev: BL 12/15/03; SLJ 3/04)

25676 Gibbons, Gail. *The Quilting Bee* (K–2). Illus. by author. 2004, HarperCollins $17.99 (978-0-688-16397-6). Adults and children participate in a quilting circle, from initial planning to displaying the final product; historical information is included as is a concept for an author and illustrator quilt. (Rev: SLJ 5/04) [746.46]

25677 Guy, Lucinda. *Kids Learn to Crochet* (2–4). Illus. by Francois Hall. 2008, Trafalgar paper $15.95 (978-1-57076-395-3). 96pp. Presented with lists of materials, templates for felt pieces, and tips, the projects here include flowers, a bag, and a pen topper. (Rev: SLJ 3/09) [745.5]

25678 Guy, Lucinda. *Kids Learn to Knit* (2–4). Illus. by Francois Hall. 2007, Trafalgar $14.95 (978-1-57076-335-9). 96pp. After basic instructions for beginners, this book includes six simple projects suitable for this age group, with clear instructions and advice on troubleshooting problems such as dropped stitches. (Rev: BL 12/15/06) [746.43]

25679 Kinsler, Gwen Blakley, and Jackie Young. *Crocheting* (4–7). Series: Kids Can Do It! 2003, Kids Can $12.95 (978-1-55337-176-2); paper $6.95 (978-1-55337-177-9). 48pp. A simple introduction to crocheting with many easily followed diagrams and clear directions. (Rev: BL 3/15/03; HBG 10/03; SLJ 4/03) [745.5]

25680 Mahren, Sue. *Make Your Own Teddy Bears and Bear Clothes* (3–6). Illus. by Stan Jaskiel. Series: Quick Starts for Kids! 2001, Williamson paper $8.95 (978-1-885593-75-7). 64pp. Patterns for two teddy bears are followed by patterns for clothing that are clear and easy to follow using only scissors, needle, and thread. Also use *Kids' Easy Knitting Projects* and *Kids' Easy Quilting Projects* (both 2001). (Rev: SLJ 7/01) [745.592]

25681 Nicholas, Kristin, and John Gruen. *Kids' Embroidery: Projects for Kids of All Ages* (3–7). 2004, Stewart, Tabori & Chang $19.95 (978-1-58479-366-3). 144pp. Step-by-step instructions guide readers through 15 colorful embroidery projects. (Rev: BL 12/15/04)

25682 Okey, Shannon. *Knitgrrl: Learn to Knit with 15 Fun and Funky Projects* (5–8). Photos by Shannon Fagan. Illus. 2005, Watson-Guptill paper $9.95 (978-0-8230-2618-0). 96pp. Up-to-date designs are shown clearly and explained in detail. (Rev: BL 12/15/05*; SLJ 11/05; VOYA 12/05) [746.43]

25683 Okey, Shannon. *Knitgrrl 2: Learn to Knit with 16 All-New Patterns* (4–7). 2006, Watson-Guptill paper $9.99 (978-0-8230-2619-7). 96pp. This sequel to *Knitgrrl* (2005) offers step-by-step instructions for 16 new projects, including bracelets, a sports bottle holder, and a cardigan. (Rev: BL 6/1–15/06; SLJ 6/06) [746]

25684 O'Reilly, Susie. *Knitting and Crochet* (3–5). Illus. Series: Arts and Crafts. 1994, Thomson Learning LB $21.40 (978-1-56847-221-8). 32pp. A good handicraft book that explains the basic stitches, gives directions for many projects, and encourages young knitters to create their own patterns. (Rev: SLJ 1/95) [745.5]

25685 Ronci, Kelli. *Kids Crochet: Projects for Kids of All Ages* (4–8). Photos by John Gruen. Illus. by Lena Corwin. 2005, Stewart, Tabori & Chang $19.95 (978-1-58479-413-4). 128pp. A poncho, a quilt, and a tool pouch are among the 15 crocheting projects presented, which are introduced by detailed coverage of techniques. (Rev: BL 5/15/04; SLJ 6/05) [745.5]

25686 Sadler, Judy Ann. *Corking* (4–8). Illus. Series: Kids Can! 1998, Kids Can paper $5.95 (978-1-55074-265-7). 32pp. Provides directions for a handmade knitting device that is used to create knit tubes or corks popular in toys and headbands. (Rev: BL 5/15/98) [746.4]

25687 Sadler, Judy Ann. *Embroidery* (4–8). Illus. by June Bradford. Series: Kids Can Do It! 2004, Kids Can $12.95 (978-1-55337-616-3); paper $6.95 (978-1-55337-617-0). 40pp. In addition to a thorough introduction to embroidery and various stitches, Sadler provides nine projects that progress in difficulty. (Rev: SLJ 8/04) [746.44]

25688 Sadler, Judy Ann. *Knitting* (4–6). Series: Kids Can Do It! 2002, Kids Can $12.95 (978-1-55337-050-5); paper $6.95 (978-1-55337-051-2). 40pp. The basic stitches in knitting are described in text and color illustrations, followed by a series of easily accomplished knitting projects. (Rev: BL 9/15/02; HBG 3/03; SLJ 11/02) [746.43]

25689 Sadler, Judy Ann. *Making Fleece Crafts* (4–7). Illus. by June Bradford. 2000, Kids Can $12.95 (978-1-55074-847-5); paper $6.95 (978-1-55074-739-3). 40pp. Fifteen colorful and inviting projects using fleece including mittens, a scarf, and a jester's hat. (Rev: BL 9/15/00; SLJ 9/00) [745]

25690 Sadler, Judy Ann. *Quick Knits* (5–8). Illus. by Esperanca Melo. 2006, Kids Can $12.95 (978-1-55337-963-8); paper $6.95 (978-1-55337-964-5). 40pp. Clear instructions, appealing projects, and suggestions for personalizing these are features of this introduction to knitting. (Rev: BL 1/1–15/07; SLJ 12/06) [746.43]

25691 Sadler, Judy Ann. *Simply Sewing* (4–8). Illus. by Jane Kurisu. Series: Kids Can Do It! 2004, Kids Can $12.95 (978-1-55337-659-0); paper $6.95 (978-1-55337-660-6). 48pp. Detailed instructions for 12 projects — a makeup bag and a jeans skirt, for example — follow basic information on sewing by hand and by machine. (Rev: BL 12/15/04; SLJ 11/04)

25692 Sadler, Judy Ann, et al. *The Jumbo Book of Needlecrafts* (4–7). Illus. by Esperanca Melo, et al. 2005, Kids Can paper $16.95 (978-1-55337-793-1).

208pp. After advice on getting started, step-by-step directions guide readers through a range of needlecraft projects. (Rev: SLJ 5/05)

25693 Stoppleman, Monica, and Carol Crowe. *Fabric* (3–6). Series: Craft Workshop. 1998, Crabtree LB $19.96 (978-0-86505-779-1). 32pp. A history of fabrics and related craft projects (some of which require adult supervision) make up this brief introduction to an interesting subject. (Rev: SLJ 9/98) [745]

25694 Storms, Biz. *All-American Quilts* (4–7). Illus. by June Bradford. Series: Kids Can Do It! 2003, Kids Can paper $6.95 (978-1-55337-539-5). 40pp. Instructions are provided for making quilts with American themes — eagles, flags, and so forth. (Rev: BL 12/15/03; SLJ 1/04) [746.46]

25695 Storms, Biz. *Quilting* (4–7). Illus. by June Bradford. Series: Kids Can Do It! 2001, Kids Can $12.95 (978-1-55074-967-0); paper $5.95 (978-1-55074-805-5). 40pp. Easy-to-follow, step-by-step instructions take kids through quilting projects of varying difficulty. (Rev: BL 11/1/01; HBG 3/02; SLJ 2/02) [746.46]

25696 Warwick, Ellen. *Injeanuity* (5–8). Illus. by Bernice Lum. 2006, Kids Can $12.95 (978-1-55337-681-1). 80pp. Seventeen projects involving jeans and a sewing machine are shown with clear directions. (Rev: BL 6/1–15/06; SLJ 6/06) [746.9]

25697 Wenger, Jennifer, et al. *Teen Knitting Club: Chill Out and Knit Some Cool Stuff* (5–9). Illus. 2004, Artisan $17.95 (978-1-57965-244-9). 128pp. Children who already know how to knit will derive the most benefit from this collection of 35 appealing projects. (Rev: BL 12/15/04; SLJ 2/05)

25698 Willing, Karen Bates, and Julie Bates Dock. *Fabric Fun for Kids: Step-by-Step Projects for Children (and Their Grown-ups)* (4–9). 1997, Now & Then LB $17.95 (978-0-9641820-4-2); paper $12.95 (978-0-9641820-5-9). 55pp. From simple sewing projects to more complex quilting work, this book gives good step-by-step instructions, provides a rundown on necessary sewing tools and materials, and discusses methods for putting designs on fabrics. (Rev: SLJ 4/98) [746.46]

25699 Wilson, Sule Greg C. *African American Quilting: The Warmth of Tradition* (4–7). Illus. Series: Library of African American Arts and Culture. 1999, Rosen LB $27.95 (978-0-8239-1854-6). 64pp. This book traces African influences on textile patterns and techniques particularly as they have been applied to quilting by African Americans. (Rev: BL 2/15/00; SLJ 9/99) [746.46]

Toys and Dolls

25700 Hall, Patricia. *The Real-for-Sure Story of Raggedy Ann* (PS–3). Illus. by Joni Gruelle Wannamaker. 2001, Pelican $15.95 (978-1-56554-763-6). 32pp. A story about the origins of the doll, portraying the details of her clothes and the way the first dolls were made. (Rev: HBG 10/01; SLJ 11/01) [688.7]

25701 Kay, Helen. *The First Teddy Bear* (K–3). Illus. by Susan Detwiler. 1985, Stemmer $14.95 (978-0-88045-042-3). 40pp. A simple tale of the history of this well-loved stuffed animal. (Rev: BCCB 2/86; BL 11/15/85; SLJ 1/86)

25702 Polacco, Patricia. *Betty Doll* (3–5). Illus. 2001, Penguin $16.99 (978-0-399-23638-9). 32pp. In this picture book for older children, Polacco tells the story of her mother's precious Betty Doll, which accompanied her mother on many journeys until her death, when the doll was passed on to her daughter. (Rev: BL 8/01; HBG 10/01; SLJ 4/01) [973.4]

25703 Sadler, Judy Ann. *Beanbag Buddies and Other Stuffed Toys* (4–7). Illus. by June Bradford. Series: Kids Can! 1999, Kids Can paper $5.95 (978-1-55074-590-0). 40pp. Using clear directions and many step-by-step illustrations, this book offers many ideas on how to create a variety of stuffed toys. (Rev: SLJ 10/99) [745]

Woodworking

25704 Ellenwood, Everett. *Woodcarving* (4–7). Illus. Series: Kidcrafts. 2009, Fox Chapel paper $14.95 (978-1-56523-366-9). 122pp. A succinct look at this craft and the wood, tools, and techniques involved, with seven woodcarving projects. (Rev: SLJ 7/09) [736]

25705 Gibbons, Gail. *Tool Book* (K–3). Illus. by author. 1982, Holiday House LB $16.95 (978-0-8234-0444-5); paper $6.95 (978-0-8234-0694-4). 32pp. An introduction to various simple tools and their uses.

25706 Hendry, Linda, and Lisa Rebnord. *Making Picture Frames* (4–6). Photos by Frank Baldassarra. Illus. by Linda Hendry. Series: Kids Can! 1999, Kids Can paper $5.95 (978-1-55074-505-4). 40pp. This clearly illustrated book presents basic picture-frame construction plus variations for more appealing products. (Rev: SLJ 5/99) [684]

25707 Robertson, J. Craig, and Barbara Robertson. *The Kids' Building Workshop: 15 Woodworking Projects for Kids and Parents to Build Together* (3–7). Illus. 2004, Storey Kids paper $12.95 (978-1-58017-488-6). 136pp. After discussing tools and techniques, 15 projects — a bird house, a stool, for example — are presented in order of increasing difficulty. (Rev: SLJ 2/05) [684]

25708 Walker, Lester. *Housebuilding for Children* (4–7). Illus. 1977, Overlook paper $16.95 (978-0-87951-332-0). 176pp. The construction of six different kinds of houses, including a tree house, is clearly described in text and pictures.

Hobbies

General and Miscellaneous

25709 Adkins, Jan. *The Art and Industry of Sandcastles* (4–6). Illus. 1982, Walker paper $9.95 (978-0-8027-7205-3). This is an illustrated guide to basic construction of sandcastles plus amazing background information.

25710 Blakey, Nancy. *Go Outside! Activities for Outdoor Adventures* (3–7). Photos by Dana Dean Doering. 2002, Tricycle paper $14.95 (978-1-58246-064-2). 144pp. Double-page spreads suggest outdoor activities for each of the seasons, some for learning and some for pure fun. (Rev: BL 4/15/02; SLJ 9/02) [796]

25711 Brent, Lynnette R. *At Play: Long Ago and Today* (2–4). Series: Times Change. 2003, Heinemann LB $24.22 (978-1-4034-4532-2). 32pp. A look at how various everyday activities have changed over the past century or so, with photographs illustrating "then" and "now." (Rev: SLJ 5/04) [790.1]

25712 Burgess, Ron. *Be a Clown! Techniques from a Real Clown* (K–3). Illus. by Heather Barberie. 2001, Williamson paper $8.95 (978-1-885593-57-3). 63pp. Aspiring clowns will appreciate this guide to clown costumes and makeup, actions and gags, and magic tricks, along with some historical information about traditional clowns and clowning. (Rev: SLJ 10/01) [791.3]

25713 Burnie, David. *Bird Watcher* (3–6). Illus. Series: Smithsonian Nature Activity Guides. 2005, DK paper $9.99 (978-0-7566-1029-6). 72pp. All sorts of fun and facts for children fascinated by birds, including experiments, crafts, and photographs. (Rev: SLJ 8/05) [598]

25714 Cook, Nick. *Roller Coasters; or, I Had So Much Fun, I Almost Puked* (4–7). Illus. 1998, Carolrhoda LB $22.60 (978-1-57505-071-3). 56pp. This intriguing book describes the excitement of a roller-coaster ride and discusses the history, types, construction, and safety features of various roller coasters. (Rev: BCCB 6/98; BL 4/15/98; HBG 10/98) [791]

25715 Hunter, Dette. *38 Ways to Entertain Your Babysitter* (2–4). Illus. by Stephen MacEachern. 2003, Annick LB $19.95 (978-1-55037-795-8); paper $9.95 (978-1-55037-794-1). 48pp. A story about two siblings' efforts to keep their babysitter happy provides the framework for a collection of three dozen or so entertaining activities, each accompanied by easy-to-follow instructions. (Rev: SLJ 1/04) [793]

25716 Kiralfy, Bob. *The Most Excellent Book of How to Be a Cheerleader* (3–5). Series: Most Excellent Book Of. 1997, Millbrook LB $19.90 (978-0-7613-0617-7); paper $6.95 (978-0-7613-0631-3). 32pp. A step-by-step guide to cheerleading, with examples of moves and chants and tips on how to look the part. (Rev: BL 11/15/97; HBG 10/98; SLJ 3/98) [761.6]

25717 Mitchelson, Mitch. *The Most Excellent Book of How to Be a Juggler* (3–5). Series: Most Excellent Book Of. 1997, Millbrook LB $19.90 (978-0-7613-0618-4); paper $6.95 (978-0-7613-0632-0). 32pp. A step-by-step guide to juggling, with examples of techniques, routines, and tips for giving an effective performance. (Rev: BL 11/15/97; HBG 10/98) [790]

25718 Perkins, Catherine. *The Most Excellent Book of How to Be a Clown* (3–5). Illus. 1996, Millbrook LB $19.90 (978-0-7613-0486-9); paper $6.95 (978-0-7613-0499-9). 32pp. Hints on makeup and presentations plus suggestions for routines are given for aspiring clowns. (Rev: BL 6/1–15/96; SLJ 6/96) [791.3]

25719 Stetson, Emily. *Knots to Know: 40 Hitches, Loops, Bends and Bindings* (3–6). Illus. by Marc Nadel and Sarah Rakitin. 2002, Williamson paper $8.95 (978-1-885593-70-2). 64pp. A simple guide to the types and uses of knots, with step-by-step instructions on how to tie them. (Rev: BL 8/02; SLJ 9/02) [623.88]

25720 Swain, Ruth Freeman. *Hairdo! What We Do and Did to Our Hair* (K–2). Illus. by Cat B. Smith.

2002, Holiday House $16.95 (978-0-8234-1522-9). 32pp. Entertaining facts about hair and hairstyles through the ages. (Rev: BL 12/15/02; HBG 3/03; SLJ 10/02) [391.5]

25721 Walker, Lester. *Block Building for Children: Making Buildings of the World with the Ultimate Construction Toy* (2–6). Illus. 1995, Overlook $22.95 (978-0-87951-609-3). 167pp. The 18 block-building projects in this book include a city of the future and the Emerald City of Oz. (Rev: SLJ 1/96) [621]

Cooking

25722 Amari, Suad. *Cooking the Lebanese Way*. Rev. ed. (5–10). Series: Easy Menu Ethnic Cookbooks. 2003, Lerner LB $25.26 (978-0-8225-4116-5). 72pp. Revised to include low-fat and vegetarian foods, this introduction to Lebanese cooking contains about 40 recipes, clearly explained and well-illustrated. (Rev: BL 9/15/02; HBG 3/03) [641.5]

25723 Bacon, Josephine. *Cooking the Israeli Way*. Rev. ed. (5–10). Series: Easy Menu Ethnic Cookbooks. 2002, Lerner LB $25.26 (978-0-8225-4112-7). 72pp. After a general introduction to Israel, this book discusses cooking terms and ingredients, and then gives a series of tantalizing recipes with clear instructions. (Rev: BL 7/02; HBG 10/02) [641]

25724 Bastyra, J., and C. Bradley. *Look and Make Cooking* (4–5). Photos by Howard Allman. Illus. by Michael Evans. Series: Look and Make. 2004, Sea-to-Sea LB $27.10 (978-1-932889-22-2). 32pp. Well-designed recipes are introduced by reminders about safety and the importance of gathering ingredients and equipment in advance. (Rev: SLJ 4/05)

25725 Bastyra, Judy. *Fun Food* (1–4). Photos by Michael Michaels and Steve Shott. Illus. by Mei Lim. Series: First Craft Books. 1998, Carolrhoda LB $12.95 (978-1-57505-204-5). 22pp. This book contains ten projects, each involving three simple steps, that result in such goodies as an ice-cream clown or a shortbread house. (Rev: SLJ 4/98) [745]

25726 Bisignano, Alphonse. *Cooking the Italian Way*. Rev. ed. (5–10). Series: Easy Menu Ethnic Cookbooks. 2001, Lerner $25.26 (978-0-8225-4113-4); paper $7.95 (978-0-8225-4161-5). 72pp. A revised edition that now includes vegetarian and low-fat recipes as well as an expanded introductory section on the country, the people, and the culture. (Rev: HBG 3/02; SLJ 9/01) [641]

25727 Blain, Diane. *The Boxcar Children Cookbook* (3–5). Illus. by L. Kate Deal and Eileen M. Neill. 1991, Whitman paper $9.95 (978-0-8075-0856-5). 96pp. Each of the simple recipes in this book is related to the Boxcar Children series. (Rev: BL 1/15/92; SLJ 11/91) [641]

25728 Brennan, Georgeanne. *Green Eggs and Ham Cookbook* (3–6). Photos by Frankie Frankeny. 2006, Random $16.95 (978-0-679-88440-8). 64pp. Diverse recipes requiring different levels of skill and varied ingredients (no green coloring) are featured here. (Rev: SLJ 2/07) [641.5]

25729 Buck-Murray, Marian. *The Mash and Smash Cookbook: Fun and Yummy Recipes Every Kid Can Make!* (3–6). Illus. 1997, Wiley paper $12.95 (978-0-471-17969-6). 128pp. A collection of recipes that are named to appeal to kids, with interesting sidebars containing background information about the ingredients. (Rev: BL 1/1–15/98; SLJ 2/98) [641.5]

25730 Bugni, Alice. *Moose Racks, Bear Tracks, and Other Alaska Kidsnacks: Cooking with Kids Has Never Been So Easy!* (K–5). Illus. by Shannon Cartwright. 1999, Sasquatch paper $8.95 (978-1-57061-214-5). This clever, fanciful book contains recipes and step-by-step instructions for the preparation of 25 easy-to-make snacks with enticing names. (Rev: SLJ 12/99) [641]

25731 Chung, Okwha, and Judy Monroe. *Cooking the Korean Way*. Rev. ed. (5–10). Illus. Series: Easy Menu Ethnic Cookbooks. 2003, Lerner LB $25.26 (978-0-8225-4115-8). 48pp. Tempting recipes and a brief look at where they come from. (Rev: BL 8/88; HBG 3/03; SLJ 9/88) [641.59519]

25732 Cook, Deanna F. *The Kids' Multicultural Cookbook: Food and Fun Around the World* (3–6). Illus. 1995, Williamson paper $14.25 (978-0-913589-91-5). 160pp. This collection of activities, recipes, and games includes material on various regions of the world. (Rev: BL 3/15/96; SLJ 2/96) [641.59]

25733 Cornell, Kari. *Holiday Cooking Around the World*. Rev. ed. (5–10). Illus. Series: Easy Menu Ethnic Cookbooks. 2002, Lerner LB $25.26 (978-0-8225-4128-8); paper $7.95 (978-0-8225-4159-2). 72pp. Beginning cooks will appreciate the clear instructions and varied options in this appealing book that includes cultural and social information. (Rev: BL 1/1–15/02; HBG 10/02; SLJ 5/02) [641.5]

25734 Coronado, Rosa. *Cooking the Mexican Way*. Rev. ed. (5–10). Series: Easy Menu Ethnic Cookbooks. 2002, Lerner LB $25.26 (978-0-8225-4117-2). 72pp. Recipes organized by type of meal are preceded by a section that covers the geography, culture, and festivals and by information on equipment, ingredients, and eating customs. Other titles in this series include *Cooking the East African Way* and *Cooking the Spanish Way* (both 2001). (Rev: HBG 3/02; SLJ 2/02) [641]

25735 Dahl, Roald, and Felicity Dahl. *Roald Dahl's Even More Revolting Recipes* (4–6). Illus. by Quentin Blake. 2001, Viking $17.99 (978-0-670-03515-1). 64pp. A follow-up to *Revolting Recipes* (1994), this volume includes 31 new recipes inspired by Dahl's books. (Rev: BL 2/1/02; HBG 3/02; SLJ 11/01) [641.5]

25736 D'Amico, Joan, and Karen Eich Drummond. *The Healthy Body Cookbook: Fun Activities and Delicious Recipes for Kids* (4–6). Illus. by Tina Cash-Walsh. 1999, Wiley paper $12.95 (978-0-471-18888-9). 192pp. The 56 recipes in this book are arranged according to the part of the body they benefit, e.g., heart, muscles, teeth, hair, nerves. (Rev: SLJ 2/99) [641]

25737 D'Amico, Joan, and Karen Eich Drummond. *The Science Chef Travels Around the World: Fun Food Experiments and Recipes for Kids* (4–8). Illus. 1996, Wiley paper $12.95 (978-0-471-11779-7). An entertaining combination of simple science experiments and international cooking, with recipes from 14 countries and activities that demonstrate scientific principles of various cooking and baking processes. (Rev: BL 2/1/96; SLJ 3/96) [641.5]

25738 D'Amico, Joan, and Karen Eich Drummond. *The United States Cookbook: Fabulous Foods and Fascinating Facts from All 50 States* (4–6). Illus. by Jeff Cline and Tina Cash-Walsh. 2000, Wiley paper $12.95 (978-0-471-35839-8). 186pp. This cookbook, which is divided into seven regions and then individual states, gives basic information about each state followed by tempting recipes and food and cooking tips. (Rev: BL 5/15/00; SLJ 5/00) [641]

25739 Davis, Robin. *The Star Wars Cookbook: Wookiee Cookies and Other Galactic Recipes* (3–5). Photos by Frankie Frankeny. 1998, Chronicle $14.95 (978-0-8118-2184-1). 60pp. Standard recipes, many using prepared foods, are recycled using *Star Wars* lingo in a spiral-bound cookbook. (Rev: SLJ 1/99) [641]

25740 Dooley, Norah. *Everybody Cooks Rice* (K–3). Illus. 1991, Carolrhoda LB $15.95 (978-0-87614-412-1); paper $6.95 (978-0-87614-591-3). 32pp. A story that shows the different ways Americans cook and eat rice. (Rev: BCCB 5/91; BL 4/15/91; SLJ 6/91) [641.6]

25741 Dunnington, Rose. *The Greatest Cookies Ever: Dozens of Delicious, Chewy, Chunky, Fun and Foolproof Recipes* (4–8). Photos by Stewart O'Shields. 2005, Sterling $9.95 (978-1-57990-627-6). 96pp. More than 70 recipes are included in this spiral-bound guide to cookie making, with useful information about measuring, substitutions, types of mixers, and safety. (Rev: BL 1/1–15/06; SLJ 2/06) [641.8]

25742 Engfer, Lee, ed. *Desserts Around the World.* Rev. ed. (4–6). Series: Easy Menu Ethnic Cookbooks. 2003, Lerner LB $18.45 (978-0-8225-0926-4). 72pp. This expanded edition gives recipes and background material on simple desserts as prepared in different countries and cultures and features low-fat recipes. (Rev: BL 6/15/92) [641.8]

25743 Fauchald, Nick. *Holy Guacamole!* (1–3). Illus. by Rick Peterson. Series: Kids Dish. 2008, Picture Window LB $18.95 (978-1-4048-3995-3). 32pp. After an introductory section with tips on cooking, equipment, and healthy eating, Fauchald provides simple recipes for snacks and drinks including pita chips with hummus, quesadilla bites, fruit kabobs, milkshakes, and of course guacamole. (Rev: BL 4/1/08) [641.5]

25744 Frankeny, Frankie, and Wesley Martin. *The Star Wars Cookbook II: Darth Malt and More Galactic Recipes* (3–5). Photos by Frankie Frankeny. 2000, Chronicle $15.95 (978-0-8118-2803-1). 62pp. A delightful cookbook with 29 recipes in five categories: breakfasts, snacks, main courses, desserts, and drinks. (Rev: SLJ 11/00) [641]

25745 Gardella, Tricia, comp. *Writers in the Kitchen: Children's Book Authors Share Memories of Their Favorite Recipes* (4–6). 1998, Boyds Mills paper $14.95 (978-1-56397-713-8). 247pp. One hundred and fifty authors and illustrators of children's books, including Paula Danziger and Jerry Spinelli, talk about food and share a favorite recipe. (Rev: SLJ 12/98) [641]

25746 Gillies, Judi, and Jennifer Glossop. *The Jumbo Vegetarian Cookbook* (4–8). Illus. 2002, Kids Can paper $14.95 (978-1-55074-977-9). 256pp. An introduction to the vegetarian lifestyle, including nutrition and recipes. (Rev: BCCB 7–8/02; BL 3/1/02; SLJ 7/02) [641.5]

25747 Gillies, Judi, and Jennifer Glossop. *The Kids Can Press Jumbo Cookbook* (5–8). Illus. 2000, Kids Can paper $14.95 (978-1-55074-621-1). 256pp. After a few cooking tips, this book provides recipes that range from the simple (scrambled eggs) to the difficult (crepes and carrot cake). (Rev: BL 5/1/00; SLJ 6/00) [641.8]

25748 Gioffre, Rosalba. *The Young Chef's French Cookbook* (4–7). Series: I'm the Chef! 2001, Crabtree LB $25.27 (978-0-7787-0282-5); paper $8.95 (978-0-7787-0296-2). 32pp. This oversize book uses double-page spreads to present 15 appetizing French recipes along with good background material, clear directions, and excellent illustrations. (Rev: BL 10/15/01) [641]

25749 Gioffre, Rosalba. *The Young Chef's Italian Cookbook* (4–7). Series: I'm the Chef! 2001, Crabtree LB $25.27 (978-0-7787-0279-5). 32pp. Along with good background material, clear instructions are presented for 15 Italian dishes in this well-illustrated, oversize book. (Rev: BL 10/15/01; SLJ 11/01) [641]

25750 Gold, Rozanne. *Kids Cook 1-2-3: Recipes for Young Chefs Using Only 3 Ingredients* (3–6). Illus. by Sara Pinto. 2006, Bloomsbury $17.95 (978-1-58234-735-6). 144pp. A beginner's cookbook offering 125 recipes that use only three ingredients for each meal of the day. (Rev: BL 12/1/06; SLJ 3/07)

25751 Goldish, Meish. *Bug-a-licious* (2–5). Illus. Series: Extreme Cuisine. 2009, Bearport LB $16.96 (978-1-59716-757-4). 24pp. Goldish explores global insect delicacies — termites, grasshoppers, dragonflies, and so forth — with full-page illustrations. (Rev: BL 4/1/09; SLJ 6/09) [641.6]

25752 Goodwin, Bob, and Candi Perez. *A Taste of Spain* (4–6). Illus. Series: Food Around the World. 1995, Thomson Learning LB $22.83 (978-1-56847-188-4). 48pp. Basic information is given about the history and culture of Spain, followed by material on Spanish food and a group of representative recipes. (Rev: SLJ 3/95) [641]

25753 Hargittai, Magdolna. *Cooking the Hungarian Way.* Rev. ed. (5–10). Series: Easy Menu Ethnic Cookbooks. 2002, Lerner LB $25.26 (978-0-8225-4132-5). 72pp. After an introduction to Hungary and its cuisine, there are about 40 clearly presented recipes from appetizers through desserts. (Rev: BL 9/15/02; HBG 3/03) [641.5]

25754 Harrison, Supenn, and Judy Monroe. *Cooking the Thai Way*. Rev. ed. (5–10). Series: Easy Menu Ethnic Cookbooks. 2002, Lerner LB $25.26 (978-0-8225-4124-0); paper $7.95 (978-0-8225-0608-9). 72pp. The country of Thailand is introduced followed by general information on its foods and several easy-to-follow recipes. (Rev: BL 9/15/02) [641.5]

25755 Hill, Barbara W. *Cooking the English Way*. Rev. ed. (5–10). Series: Easy Menu Ethnic Cookbooks. 2002, Lerner LB $25.26 (978-0-8225-4105-9). 72pp. The land and people of England are briefly introduced followed by material on their favorite dishes and easy-to-follow recipes. (Rev: BL 9/15/02) [641.5]

25756 Hill, Mary. *Let's Make Pizza* (PS–1). Series: In the Kitchen. 2002, Children's Book Pr. paper $4.95 (978-0-516-24020-6). 24pp. For beginning readers, this is a simple introduction to the ingredients of a pizza and the technique for making one. Also use *Let's Make Tacos* (2002). (Rev: SLJ 2/03)

25757 Hopkinson, Deborah. *Fannie in the Kitchen: The Whole Story from Soup to Nuts of How Fannie Farmer Invented Recipes with Precise Measurements* (K–3). Illus. by Nancy Carpenter. 2001, Simon & Schuster $16.00 (978-0-689-81965-0). 40pp. Fannie Farmer teaches a young girl to cook in this fictionalized account that is interspersed with excerpts from Farmer's cookbook. (Rev: BCCB 6/01; BL 5/15/01*; HB 5/01; HBG 10/01; SLJ 5/01*) [641.5]

25758 Ichord, Loretta Frances. *Double Cheeseburgers, Quiche, and Vegetarian Burritos: American Cooking from the 1920s Through Today* (5–8). Illus. by Jan Davey Ellis. 2007, Lerner $25.26 (978-0-8225-5969-6). 64pp. This title traces American cuisine from 1920 to the present, with chapters highlighting such trends as TV dinners, fast food, and the rise of organic foods; recipes round out a volume useful for both reports and browsing. (Rev: BL 1/1–15/07; SLJ 5/07) [394.1]

25759 Ichord, Loretta Frances. *Pasta, Fried Rice, and Matzoh Balls: Immigrant Cooking in America* (3–5). Illus. by Jan Davey Ellis. 2006, Millbrook LB $25.26 (978-0-7613-2913-8). 64pp. French, Italian, Jewish, Polish, Portuguese, Spanish, and Swedish immigrant recipes are included, as well as a few foreign phrases and customs. (Rev: SLJ 5/06) [394.1]

25760 Ichord, Loretta Frances. *Skillet Bread, Sourdough, and Vinegar Pie: Cooking in Pioneer Days* (3–5). Illus. by Jan Davey Ellis. 2003, Millbrook LB $24.90 (978-0-7613-1864-4). 64pp. This fascinating overview of pioneer cuisine features a number of classic recipes as well as a look at unique food preparation challenges faced by early Americans. (Rev: HBG 10/03)

25761 Jacques, Brian. *The Redwall Cookbook* (3–7). Illus. by Christopher Denise. 2005, Philomel paper $24.99 (978-0-399-23791-1). 96pp. "Hare's Paw-spring Vegetable Soup" and "Savoury Squirrel Bakes" are among the recipes grouped by season and introduced by a tale about preparations for a feast; the recipes themselves are quite complex. (Rev: SLJ 1/06)

25762 Katzen, Mollie. *Honest Pretzels: And 64 Other Amazing Recipes for Cooks Ages 8 and Up* (4–6). Illus. 1999, Tricycle $19.95 (978-1-883672-88-1). 192pp. Here is a collection of 64 vegetarian recipes designed for older children. (Rev: BL 11/1/99; HBG 3/00; SLJ 9/99) [641.5]

25763 Katzen, Mollie. *Salad People and More Real Recipes* (PS–2). Illus. 2005, Ten Speed $17.95 (978-1-58246-141-0). 96pp. Healthy, kid-tested recipes for a range of tastes include instructions for children and for adults. (Rev: BL 11/15/05*; SLJ 11/05*) [641.5]

25764 Katzen, Mollie, and Ann Henderson. *Pretend Soup and Other Real Recipes: A Cookbook for Preschoolers and Up* (PS–3). Illus. by Mollie Katzen. 1994, Tricycle $17.95 (978-1-883672-06-5). 95pp. Using pictures as well as text, 17 simple recipes are presented that are easy enough for youngsters to prepare with little supervision. (Rev: HB 7/94; SLJ 6/94*) [641]

25765 Kaufman, Cheryl Davidson. *Cooking the Caribbean Way*. Rev. ed. (5–10). Illus. Series: Easy Menu Ethnic Cookbooks. 2002, Lerner $25.26 (978-0-8225-4103-5). 72pp. A variety of dishes featuring the spices and fresh fruits that come from these islands are provided in this expanded edition that includes low-fat and vegetarian foods. (Rev: BL 8/88; SLJ 9/88) [641.59729]

25766 *Kids' First Cookbook: Delicious-Nutritious Treats to Make Yourself!* (K–3). 1999, American Cancer Society $13.95 (978-0-944235-19-5). 88pp. A cookbook with 53 nutritionally sound recipes plus information on how to read a food label, kitchen safety, and a guide to the food pyramid. (Rev: SLJ 3/00) [641]

25767 Lagasse, Emeril. *Emeril's There's a Chef in My Family! Recipes to Get Everybody Cooking* (5–10). Photos by Quentin Bacon. Illus. by Charles Yuen. 2004, HarperCollins $22.99 (978-0-06-000439-2). 209pp. Seventy-six recipes are presented with clear instructions that focus on the enjoyment of cooking. (Rev: SLJ 7/04) [641.5]

25768 Lagasse, Emeril. *Emeril's There's a Chef in My Soup: Recipes for the Kid in Everyone* (5–8). Illus. by Charles Yuen. 2002, HarperCollins $22.99 (978-0-688-17706-5). 256pp. The famed TV chef presents a series of simple recipes for main dishes, pasta, desserts, breakfast and lunch items, and salads. (Rev: BL 5/1/02; HBG 10/02) [641.5]

25769 Lagasse, Emeril. *Emeril's There's a Chef in My World!* (5–8). Illus. 2006, HarperCollins $22.99 (978-0-06-073926-3). 224pp. The famous chef adds to his successful series with a basic introduction to sandwiches, meals, snacks, and more from around the world, with sections on basic skills, safety, and equipment for beginners; cultural facts accompany each recipe. (Rev: BL 12/1/06; SLJ 2/07) [641.59]

25770 Lee, Frances. *The Young Chef's Chinese Cookbook* (4–7). Illus. Series: I'm the Chef! 2001, Crabtree LB $25.27 (978-0-7787-0280-1); paper $8.95 (978-0-7787-0294-8). 40pp. Fifteen child-friendly recipes for Chinese dishes are presented with step-by-step directions and photographs. (Rev: BL 10/15/01; SLJ 11/01) [641.5951]

25771 Lewis, Sara. *Kids' Baking: 60 Delicious Recipes for Children to Make* (4–7). 2006, Sterling $12.95 (978-0-600-61561-3). 144pp. Well-illustrated recipes for cakes, cookies, and breads are suitable for children working with adult help. (Rev: BL 12/1/06) [641.8]

25772 Locricchio, Matthew. *The Cooking of Greece* (5–10). Photos by Jack McConnell. Illus. Series: Superchef. 2004, Benchmark LB $29.93 (978-0-7614-1729-3). 80pp. Recipes follow an informative overview of regional cuisines in Greece and the ingredients commonly used. (Rev: SLJ 4/05)

25773 Locricchio, Matthew. *The Cooking of India* (4–8). Photos by Jack McConnell. Illus. Series: Superchef. 2004, Benchmark $29.93 (978-0-7614-1730-9). 80pp. Clear instructions guide readers through the steps involved in making dishes from various areas of India; fresh ingredients are recommended and safety is emphasized. Also use *The Cooking of Thailand* (2004). (Rev: SLJ 2/05) [641.5954]

25774 McCulloch, Julie. *The Caribbean* (3–6). Illus. Series: World of Recipes. 2001, Heinemann LB $25.64 (978-1-58810-153-2). 48pp. Recipes, arranged by difficulty, follow information on the region and typical food choices. (Rev: BL 8/01; HBG 10/01) [641.59]

25775 McCulloch, Julie. *China* (3–6). Illus. Series: World of Recipes. 2001, Heinemann LB $25.64 (978-1-58810-152-5). 48pp. Recipes, arranged by difficulty, follow information on China and the kinds of foods eaten there. (Rev: BL 8/01; HBG 10/01; SLJ 10/01) [641.5951]

25776 McCulloch, Julie. *India* (4–6). Illus. Series: A World of Recipes. 2001, Heinemann LB $25.64 (978-1-58810-085-6). 48pp. A discussion of the history and traditions of Indian food is accompanied by a selection of typical recipes, most of which require adult participation. Also use *Mexico*. (Rev: HBG 10/01; SLJ 12/01) [641.5954]

25777 McCulloch, Julie. *Japan* (4–6). Illus. by Nicholas Beresford-Davies. Series: A World of Recipes. 2001, Heinemann LB $25.64 (978-1-58810-087-0). 48pp. Step-by-step instructions clearly show how to make dishes that are typical of Japanese cuisine, accompanied by advice on handling chopsticks. Also use *China* (2001). (Rev: HBG 10/01; SLJ 10/01) [641.5952]

25778 McKenley, Yvonne. *A Taste of the Caribbean* (4–6). Illus. Series: Food Around the World. 1995, Thomson Learning LB $22.83 (978-1-56847-187-7). 48pp. Describes the food of the Caribbean islands, gives several recipes, and supplies basic background information on Caribbean history and culture. (Rev: SLJ 3/95) [641]

25779 MacLeod, Elizabeth. *Bake and Make Amazing Cakes* (4–6). Illus. by June Bradford. Series: Kids Can Do It! 2001, Kids Can $12.95 (978-1-55074-849-9); paper $5.95 (978-1-55074-848-2). 40pp. A

collection of child-friendly cake recipes with easy-to-follow instructions. (Rev: SLJ 6/01) [641.8653]

25780 MacLeod, Elizabeth. *Bake and Make Amazing Cookies* (3–8). Illus. by June Bradford. Series: Kids Can Do It! 2004, Kids Can $12.95 (978-1-55337-631-6); paper $6.95 (978-1-55337-632-3). 40pp. Organized under headings such as "Holidays" and "Seasons," these are simple recipes for a wide variety of enticing cookies. (Rev: SLJ 2/05) [641.8]

25781 MacLeod, Elizabeth. *Bake It and Build It* (2–6). Illus. 1998, Kids Can paper $6.95 (978-1-55074-427-9). 40pp. This combination cooking and craft book shows how to make objects such as a cookie castle, an edible flower wreath, and cookie flowers out of various kinds of cookies, oatmeal, and different doughs. (Rev: BL 12/1/98; SLJ 1/99) [745.5]

25782 Madavan, Vijay. *Cooking the Indian Way* (5–8). Illus. 1985, Lerner LB $19.93 (978-0-8225-0911-0). 52pp. Cultural information is detailed plus both vegetarian and nonvegetarian recipes. (Rev: SLJ 9/85) [641.5954]

25783 Marchant, Kerena. *Hindu Cookbook* (3–5). Photos by Zul Mukhida. Series: Holiday Cookbooks from Around the World. 2001, Raintree LB $25.69 (978-0-7398-3264-6). 32pp. Marchant looks at three Hindu holidays (Holi, Divali, and Ganesh Chaturthi), describes how they are celebrated, and provides appropriate recipes, with appealing photographs. Also use *Chinese Cookbook* (2001). (Rev: SLJ 8/01) [641.5]

25784 Montgomery, Bertha Vining, and Constance Nabwire. *Cooking the West African Way*. Rev. ed. (5–10). Series: Easy Menu Ethnic Cookbooks. 2002, Lerner LB $25.26 (978-0-8225-4163-9). 72pp. An appealing introduction to West African cuisine, with information on the land, people, and culture, and several low-fat and vegetarian recipes. (Rev: HBG 10/02; SLJ 5/02) [641.5966]

25785 Munsen, Sylvia. *Cooking the Norwegian Way*. Rev. ed. (5–10). Series: Easy Menu Ethnic Cookbooks. 2002, Lerner LB $25.26 (978-0-8225-4118-9). 72pp. A revised edition of an earlier publication that gives information on the country and culture in addition to a selection of typical recipes. (Rev: BL 7/02; SLJ 9/02) [641.59]

25786 Nathan, Joan. *The Children's Jewish Holiday Kitchen: 70 Ways to Have Fun with Your Kids and Make Your Family's Celebrations Special* (4–6). Illus. 1995, Schocken $24.00 (978-0-8052-4130-3). 176pp. Seventy recipes arranged by holiday and by the degree of difficulty and need for supervision. (Rev: BL 10/15/95) [641.5]

25787 Nguyen, Chi, and Judy Monroe. *Cooking the Vietnamese Way* (5–10). Illus. Series: Easy Menu Ethnic Cookbooks. 2002, Lerner $25.26 (978-0-8225-4125-7). 72pp. The authors introduce the land and people of Vietnam before giving recipes for regional dishes, including low-fat and vegetarian selections. (Rev: BL 9/15/85; SLJ 9/85) [641]

25788 Osseo-Asare, Fran. *A Good Soup Attracts Chairs: A First African Cookbook for American Kids* (5–9). 1993, Pelican $18.95 (978-0-88289-

816-2). A basic cookbook for youngsters that explores African cooking past and present and gives more than 35 recipes. (Rev: BL 10/15/93; SLJ 8/93) [641.5966]

25789 Parnell, Helga. *Cooking the German Way*. Rev. ed. (5–10). Illus. Series: Easy Menu Ethnic Cookbooks. 2002, Lerner $25.26 (978-0-8225-4107-3). 72pp. This expanded edition now includes low-fat and vegetarian recipes as well as such treats as Black Forest torte and apple cake. (Rev: BL 8/88) [641.5943]

25790 Parnell, Helga. *Cooking the South American Way*. Rev. ed. (5–10). Series: Easy Menu Ethnic Cookbooks. 2002, Lerner LB $25.26 (978-0-8225-4121-9). 72pp. The continent of South America is introduced followed by about 40 clearly presented recipes from several different countries. (Rev: BL 9/15/02; HBG 3/03) [641.5]

25791 Plotkin, Gregory, and Rita Plotkin. *Cooking the Russian Way*. Rev. ed. (5–10). Illus. Series: Easy Menu Ethnic Cookbooks. 2002, Lerner LB $25.26 (978-0-8225-4120-2). 48pp. Included along with history and information are such recipes as Russian honey spice cake. (Rev: BL 10/15/86) [641.5947]

25792 Pratt, Dianne. *Hey Kids! You're Cookin' Now! A Global Awareness Cooking Adventure* (4–6). Illus. 1998, Harvest Hill $19.95 (978-1-886862-07-4). 160pp. Seventeen cooking projects, along with the necessary recipes and directions, are including in this handy volume dealing with such edibles as pizza and chocolate pudding and some non-edibles such as glue and play clay. (Rev: BL 12/15/98; SLJ 3/99) [641.5]

25793 Pulleyn, Micah, and Sarah Bracken. *Kids in the Kitchen: 100 Delicious, Fun and Healthy Recipes to Cook and Bake* (3–5). Illus. 1994, Sterling $24.95 (978-0-8069-0447-4). 112pp. Gives background information on food preparation for boys and girls plus lots of recipes, many of which require no cooking. (Rev: BL 7/94; SLJ 8/94) [641.5]

25794 Raabe, Emily. *An Easter Holiday Cookbook* (2–5). Series: Festive Foods for the Holidays. 2001, Rosen LB $19.50 (978-0-8239-5624-1). 24pp. Spring holidays and their foods are presented with large print and colorful illustrations. Also use *A Passover Holiday Cookbook* (2001). (Rev: SLJ 2/02) [641.568]

25795 Ralph, Judy, and Ray Gompf. *The Peanut Butter Cookbook for Kids* (5–7). Illus. 1995, Hyperion paper $10.95 (978-0-7868-1028-4). 96pp. An amazing collection of recipes involving peanut butter, including soups, snacks, and main dishes. (Rev: BL 10/1/95; SLJ 9/95) [641.6]

25796 Rotner, Shelley, and Julia P. Hellums. *Hold the Anchovies!* (K–2). Illus. 1996, Orchard LB $16.99 (978-0-531-08857-9). 32pp. The pizza, its ingredients, and methods of preparation are presented with a recipe for basic pizza dough. (Rev: BL 9/15/96; SLJ 10/96) [641.8]

25797 Sanger, Amy Wilson. *Yum Yum Dim Sum* (PS–K). Illus. by author. 2003, Tricycle $6.95 (978-

1-58246-108-3). This appealing blend of rhyming text and mixed-media artwork introduces children to dim sum. (Rev: SLJ 1/04)

25798 Scherie, Strom. *Stuffin' Muffin: Muffin Pan Cooking for Kids* (4–6). Illus. by Dave Ferry. 1982, Young People's Pr. paper $18.95 (978-0-9606964-9-9). 100pp. A variety of foods without sugar or salt that can be made in muffin tins.

25799 Sheen, Barbara. *Foods of Brazil* (4–6). Illus. 2007, Gale LB $32.45 (978-0-7377-3773-8). 64pp. After a history of the food eaten in Brazil, this volume explores the dishes of different regions and the specialties made for feasts. Also use *Foods of Ethiopia, Foods of Spain,* and *Foods of the Caribbean* (2007). (Rev: SLJ 5/08) [641.5981]

25800 Sheen, Barbara. *Foods of Greece* (4–6). Illus. Series: Taste of Culture. 2005, Gale LB $27.45 (978-0-7377-3033-3). 64pp. Eight recipes introduce the cuisine of Greece, with sidebars that add information plus a map, Web sites, and other features. (Rev: BL 1/1–15/06; SLJ 4/06) [394.1]

25801 Sheen, Barbara. *Foods of Italy* (4–8). Series: A Taste of Culture. 2005, Gale LB $27.45 (978-0-7377-3034-0). 64pp. Cultural and historical notes add to the simple, traditional recipes provided. Also use *Foods of Mexico* (2005). (Rev: SLJ 2/06) [641]

25802 Skrepcinski, Denice, et al. *Cody Coyote Cooks! A Southwest Cookbook for Kids* (4–6). Illus. 1996, Tricycle paper $14.95 (978-1-883672-37-9). 96pp. Recipes along with legends, history, and geographical facts highlight this book about cooking and eating in Texas, Arizona, and New Mexico. (Rev: BL 10/15/96; SLJ 10/96) [641]

25803 Townsend, Sue, and Caroline Young. *Indonesia* (5–8). Illus. Series: A World of Recipes. 2003, Heinemann LB $27.07 (978-1-4034-0976-8). 48pp. After a discussion of Indonesian food and ingredients, clear directions, with illustrations, are given for recipes that are graded by ease of preparation. Also use *Russia* and *Vietnam* (both 2003). (Rev: HBG 4/04; SLJ 9/03)

25804 Vaughan, Jenny, and Penny Beauchamp. *Christmas Foods* (3–7). Series: A World of Recipes. 2004, Heinemann LB $30.00 (978-1-4034-4697-8). 48pp. Christmas dishes from around the world have straightforward directions and color photographs. (Rev: BL 6/1–15/04) [641.5]

25805 Vaughan, Jenny, and Penny Beauchamp. *Festival Foods* (3–7). Series: World of Recipes. 2004, Heinemann LB $30.00 (978-1-4034-4699-2). 48pp. The easy-to-follow recipes here focus on dishes for festive occasions worldwide. (Rev: BL 6/1–15/04) [745.594]

25806 Villios, Lynne W. *Cooking the Greek Way*. Rev. ed. (5–10). Illus. Series: Easy Menu Ethnic Cookbooks. 2003, Lerner LB $25.26 (978-0-8225-4131-8). 52pp. The young cook is introduced to the cuisine of Greece, with a chapter covering utensils and ingredient needs and a glossary of basic cooking terms. Recipes are varied and easy to prepare. (Rev: BL 7/02; SLJ 9/02) [641]

25807 Wagner, Lisa. *Cool Cuisine for Super Sleepovers: Easy Recipes for Kids to Cook* (4–6). Series:

Cool Cooking. 2007, ABDO LB $15.95 (978-1-59928-721-8). 32pp. Easy-to-follow, tasty recipes will inspire young cooks to treat their friends to superior sleepover fare. (Rev: SLJ 7/07)

25808 Wagner, Lisa. *Cool Foods for Fun Fiestas: Easy Recipes for Kids to Cook* (4–6). Series: Cool Cooking. 2007, ABDO LB $15.95 (978-1-59928-722-5). 32pp. This collection of Mexican-inspired party foods will help young cooks prepare for a fiesta; clear photographs and instructions will allow them to work mostly independently. (Rev: SLJ 7/07)

25809 Wagner, Lisa. *Cool Lunches to Make and Take: Easy Recipes for Kids to Cook* (4–6). Series: Cool Cooking. 2007, ABDO LB $15.95 (978-1-59928-723-2). 32pp. Children will enjoy preparing and packing their own lunches if they use this easy-to-follow guide with photographs. (Rev: SLJ 7/07)

25810 Wagner, Lisa. *Cool Meals to Start Your Wheels: Easy Recipes for Kids to Cook* (3–6). Series: Cool Cooking. 2007, ABDO LB $22.78 (978-1-59928-724-9). 32pp. Interesting, tasty, and healthy breakfast recipes for children. Many require no baking or little preparation, so students may work somewhat independently. (Rev: SLJ 8/07)

25811 Wagner, Lisa. *Cool Pizza to Make and Bake: Easy Recipes for Kids to Cook* (3–6). 2007, ABDO LB $22.78 (978-1-59928-725-6). 32pp. Recipes for many variations on this favorite food are featured, along with tips on technique and safety precautions. (Rev: SLJ 8/07)

25812 Wagner, Lisa. *Cool Sweets and Treats to Eat: Easy Recipes for Kids to Cook* (3–6). Series: Cool Cooking. 2007, ABDO LB $22.78 (978-1-59928-726-3). 32pp. Snacks and treats for after school and summer days are featured here. Many require no baking or little preparation, so students may work somewhat independently. (Rev: SLJ 8/07)

25813 Waldee, Lynne Marie. *Cooking the French Way* (5–10). Illus. 2002, Lerner LB $25.26 (978-0-8225-4106-6). 48pp. A nicely illustrated introduction to French recipes including breads and sauces. (Rev: HBG 3/02; SLJ 2/02) [641.5944]

25814 Walker, Barbara M. *The Little House Cookbook* (5–7). Illus. by Garth Williams. 1979, HarperCollins paper $9.99 (978-0-06-446090-3). 256pp. Frontier food, such as green pumpkin pie from the Little House books, served up in tasty, easily used recipes.

25815 Warner, Margaret Brink, and Ruth Ann Hayward. *What's Cooking? Favorite Recipes from Around the World* (5–8). Illus. 1981, Little, Brown $16.95 (978-0-316-35252-9). A collection of recipes from more than 30 countries contibuted by American teenagers who also supply information on their ethnic origins. [641.5]

25816 Weston, Reiko. *Cooking the Japanese Way*. Rev. ed. (5–8). Illus. Series: Easy Menu Ethnic Cookbooks. 2002, Lerner LB $25.26 (978-0-8225-4114-1). 48pp. Directions for preparing traditional foods are given along with lists of terms, ingredients, and utensils. (Rev: HBG 3/02) [641.5952]

25817 White, Linda. *Cooking on a Stick: Campfire Recipes for Kids* (3–6). Illus. 1996, Gibbs Smith paper $9.95 (978-0-87905-727-5). 48pp. In addition to covering campfire cooking, this book discusses equipment and fire making. (Rev: BL 4/1/96) [641.5]

25818 Wilkes, Angela. *The Children's Quick and Easy Cookbook* (4–6). Illus. 1997, DK $16.99 (978-0-7894-2026-8). 96pp. Not nearly as "quick and easy" as the title would suggest, this book nevertheless contains some good recipes in an attractive format. (Rev: BL 12/15/97; HBG 3/98; SLJ 1/98) [641.5]

25819 Williamson, Sarah A. *Bake the Best-Ever Cookies!* (3–6). Illus. by Tom Ernst. Series: Quick Starts for Kids! 2001, Williamson paper $8.95 (978-1-885593-56-6). 64pp. Simple recipes follow basic information on equipment and ingredients and a number of frequently asked questions. (Rev: SLJ 11/01) [641.8654]

25820 Williamson, Sarah A., and Zachary Williamson. *Kids Cook! Fabulous Food for the Whole Family* (4–6). Illus. by Loretta Trezzo-Baren. 1992, Williamson paper $12.95 (978-0-913589-61-8). 157pp. Using recipes at three levels of difficulty, this book contains 153 recipes of foods that are fun to prepare. (Rev: SLJ 7/92) [641.5]

25821 Yolen, Jane, and Heidi Stemple. *Fairy Tale Feasts: A Literary Cookbook for Young Readers and Eaters* (K–3). Illus. by Philippe Beha. 2006, Interlink $24.95 (978-1-56656-643-8). 224pp. A tasty, oversized collection of 20 fairy tales accompanied by kid-friendly recipes, presented in four sections: breakfast, lunch, dinner, and desert. (Rev: BL 11/1/06; SLJ 11/06) [641.5]

25822 Yu, Ling. *Cooking the Chinese Way*. Rev. ed. (5–10). Illus. Series: Easy Menu Ethnic Cookbooks. 2001, Lerner LB $25.26 (978-0-8225-4104-2). 72pp. From appetizers to desserts, with attractive illustrations, this is a revised and expanded edition. (Rev: HBG 3/02) [641.5]

25823 Zamojska-Hutchins, Danuta. *Cooking the Polish Way*. Rev. ed. (5–10). Illus. Series: Easy Menu Ethnic Cookbooks. 2002, Lerner LB $25.26 (978-0-8225-4119-6). 52pp. Simple Polish recipes include traditional dishes such as pierogi. Glossary of terms, plus listing of utensils and ingredients used. (Rev: BL 7/02; HBG 10/02) [641.5]

25824 Zanzarella, Marianne. *The Good Housekeeping Illustrated Children's Cookbook* (5–8). Illus. 1997, Morrow $17.95 (978-0-688-13375-7). A visually appealing cookbook containing a number of excellent recipes, some of which require adult supervision. (Rev: BL 12/15/97; HBG 3/98; SLJ 1/98) [641.5]

Gardening

25825 Björk, Christina. *Linnea's Windowsill Garden* (1–5). Trans. by Joan Sandin. Illus. by Lena Anderson. 1988, Farrar $13.00 (91-29-59064-7). 60pp.

Linnea takes readers on a tour of her indoor garden. (Rev: BCCB 12/88; BL 1/15/89; SLJ 11/88) [635]

25826 Burns, Kate, and Dawn Apperley. *How Does Your Garden Grow?* (K–2). Illus. 1998, Levinson $10.95 (978-1-899607-51-8). In this interactive garden book, flowers and vegetables pop-up from seeds. (Rev: BL 1/1–15/99; SLJ 1/99) [635]

25827 Houle, Michelle E. *Lindsey Williams: Gardening for Impoverished Families* (4–7). Illus. Series: Young Heroes. 2007, Gale LB $27.45 (978-0-7377-3867-4). 48pp. Young author Williams has won many awards for her agricultural activism; here she talks about ways to have good food without spending a fortune and about the importance and rewards of volunteering. (Rev: BL 2/15/08) [363.8]

25828 Kite, L. Patricia. *Gardening Wizardry for Kids* (3–6). 1995, Barron's paper $16.95 (978-0-8120-1317-7). 220pp. A guide to windowsill and kitchen gardens, with informative explanations, projects and experiments. (Rev: BL 8/95) [635]

25829 Lerner, Carol. *My Backyard Garden* (4–6). Illus. 1998, Morrow $16.00 (978-0-688-14755-6). 48pp. Advice and inspiration are supplied in this book about planting and caring for a backyard vegetable garden. (Rev: BL 3/15/98; HBG 10/98; SLJ 4/98) [635]

25830 Lerner, Carol. *My Indoor Garden* (3–7). Illus. 1999, Morrow LB $15.89 (978-0-688-14754-9). 48pp. Pen-and-watercolor drawings are used to illustrate this guide to indoor gardening, the necessary tools, conditions, and the types of suitable plants. (Rev: BL 6/1–15/99; HB 7/99; HBG 10/99; SLJ 4/99) [635.9]

25831 Lock, Deborah, ed. *Grow It, Cook It: Simple Gardening Projects and Delicious Recipes* (3–6). Illus. 2008, DK $15.99 (978-0-7566-3367-7). 80pp. Covering everything from plant and gardening basics (growth cycles, soil, pests, and so forth) to individual fruits and vegetables to recipes and projects, this is a handy and appealing volume. (Rev: BL 5/1/08) [641.5]

25832 Lovejoy, Sharon. *Roots, Shoots, Buckets and Boots: Gardening Together with Children* (1–4). Illus. by author. 1999, Workman paper $13.95 (978-0-7611-1056-9). 159pp. A fine how-to book on gardening with lore, tips, techniques, and ideas for adults and children to share including a list of the top 20 plans for kids. (Rev: SLJ 2/00) [635]

25833 MacLeod, Elizabeth. *Grow It Again* (3–5). Illus. Series: Kids Can! 1999, Kids Can paper $5.95 (978-1-55074-558-0). 40pp. Using discarded parts of plants — carrot tops, avocado pits, and potato buds — this guide shows how to grow new vegetables and fruits and supplies a few tasty recipes and interesting projects. (Rev: BL 6/1–15/99; SLJ 6/99) [635]

25834 Maurer, Tracy Nelson. *Growing Flowers* (1–4). Series: Green Thumb Guides. 2000, Rourke LB $23.93 (978 1-55916-251-7). 24pp. A very simple gardening guide that includes material on what, where, and when to plant plus information on weeding, watering, and other gardening tips. Also use

Growing House Plants and *Growing Vegetables* (both 2000). (Rev: SLJ 1/01) [635]

25835 Morris, Karyn. *The Kids Can Press Jumbo Book of Gardening* (3–6). Illus. 2000, Kids Can $14.95 (978-1-55074-690-7). 240pp. Some of the topics covered in this information-packed volume include fruit, vegetable, and flower gardens; native plants; gardens that attract wildlife; and group projects. (Rev: BL 7/00) [635]

25836 Nichol, Barbara. *One Small Garden* (3–6). Illus. by Barry Moser. 2001, Tundra $17.95 (978-0-88776-475-2). 56pp. A Toronto garden is the focus of this lyrical narrative describing plants, animals, and even the people who have enjoyed it. (Rev: BL 12/15/01; HBG 3/02; SLJ 12/01) [635]

25837 Rhoades, Diane. *Garden Crafts for Kids: 50 Great Reasons to Get Your Hands Dirty* (3–6). Illus. 1995, Sterling $21.95 (978-0-8069-0998-1). 144pp. A complete guide for the beginning gardener, from choosing the right spot, to selecting seeds and plants, preparing the soil, and growing healthy plants. (Rev: SLJ 8/95*) [635]

25838 Van Hage, Mary An. *Little Green Thumbs* (3–6). Photos by Lucy Tizard. Illus. by Bettina Paterson. 1996, Millbrook LB $22.40 (978-1-56294-270-0). 32pp. An activity book that offers 12 indoor and outdoor projects for each of the seasons, like building a dinosaur-theme terrarium or planting an orange tree. (Rev: SLJ 7/96) [635]

Magic

25839 Baker, James W. *Illusions Illustrated: A Professional Magic Show for Young Performers* (5–8). Illus. by Jeanette Swofford. 1994, Lerner paper $6.95 (978-0-8225-9512-0). 120pp. Directions on how to put on a magic show with 10 different tricks.

25840 Broekel, Ray, and Laurence B. White. *Hocus Pocus: Magic You Can Do* (4–6). Illus. by Mary Thelen. 1984, Whitman LB $13.95 (978-0-8075-3350-5). 48pp. Twenty simple tricks for beginners.

25841 Burgess, Ron. *Kids Make Magic: The Complete Guide to Becoming an Amazing Magician* (3–6). Illus. by Marie Ferrante-Doyle and Sarah Rakitin. Series: Kids Can! 2003, Williamson paper $12.95 (978-1-885593-87-0). 127pp. Step-by-step tips for aspiring magicians, from the tricks themselves to advice on setting up a magic show. Includes a detailed resource guide. (Rev: SLJ 3/04) [793.8]

25842 Clibbon, Meg. *Imagine You're a Wizard!* (K–4). Illus. by Lucy Clibbon. Series: Imagine This! 2003, Annick $19.95 (978-1-55037-793-4); paper $7.95 (978-1-55037-792-7). All about wizards and how to become one, with ideas for projects. (Rev: SLJ 3/04) [133.4]

25843 Cobb, Vicki. *Magic . . . Naturally! Science Entertainments and Amusements* (4–6). Illus. 1993, HarperCollins LB $17.89 (978-0-06-022475-2). 150pp. A group of experiments that demonstrate the magic found in many scientific phenomena. (Rev: BL 10/15/93; SLJ 10/93) [793.8]

25844 Colbert, David. *The Magical Worlds of Harry Potter: A Treasury of Myths, Legends, and Fascinating Facts* (5–9). Illus. 2001, Lumina $14.95 (978-0-9708442-0-0). 223pp. Information on more than 50 topics in Harry's universe — such as alchemy, Grindylows, and Voldemort — arranged in alphabetical order. (Rev: SLJ 2/02) [823]

25845 Gordon, Henry. *It's Magic* (4–6). Illus. 1989, Prometheus paper $15.98 (978-0-87975-545-4). 92pp. A treasury of simple magic tricks. (Rev: BL 12/1/89) [793.8]

25846 Jones, Richard. *That's Magic! 40 Foolproof Tricks to Delight, Amaze and Entertain* (5–8). Illus. 2001, New Holland $19.95 (978-1-85974-668-4). 112pp. Simple instructions and photographs teach the beginning magician a few tricks. (Rev: BL 1/1–15/02; SLJ 1/02) [793.8]

25847 Keable, Ian. *The Big Book of Magic Fun* (5–9). Photos by Steve Tanner. Illus. 2005, Barron's paper $14.99 (978-0-7641-3222-3). 192pp. Step-by-step instructions, with photographs, are given for 40 tricks plus discussion of suitable props and a history of different kinds of magic and famous performers. (Rev: SLJ 3/06) [793.8]

25848 McMaster, Shawn. *Magic Tricks: Absolutely Everything You Need to Know About Magic!* (3–6). Illus. by Mike Moran. 2000, Lowell House paper $9.95 (978-0-7373-0231-8). 119pp. As well as a number of tricks, this book gives a history of sleight-of-hand performances and spells out the skills required to become a magician. (Rev: SLJ 8/00) [793.8]

25849 McMaster, Shawn. *60 Super Simple Magic Tricks* (3–6). Illus. by Leo Abbett. 1996, Lowell House paper $6.95 (978-1-56565-384-9). 80pp. Simple instructions are used to describe clearly 60 magic tricks, with additional information on effective presentations and examples of magician's patter. (Rev: SLJ 2/97) [783.9]

25850 Rigney, Francis. *A Beginner's Book of Magic* (4–6). Illus. 1963, Devin $9.95 (978-0-8159-5103-2). This is a do-it-yourself book of tricks, magic, and stunts.

25851 Wenzel, Angela. *Do You See What I See? The Art of Illusion* (5–8). Trans. from German by Rosie Jackson. 2001, Prestel $14.95 (978-3-7913-2488-3). 29pp. Tricks with perspective and color, coded messages, and hidden images are all presented in this attractive volume that makes for excellent browsing. (Rev: HBG 3/02; SLJ 2/02) [152]

25852 *Wizardology: The Book of the Secrets of Merlin* (5–8). Illus. 2005, Candlewick $19.99 (978-0-7636-2895-6). 32pp. This follow-up to *Dragonology* offers a variety of information for wannabe wizards. (Rev: BL 10/15/05)

25853 Zenon, Paul. *Simple Sleight-of-Hand: Card and Coin Tricks for the Beginning Magician* (4–7). Illus. 2007, Rosen LB $21.95 (978-1-4042-1070-7). 64pp. Written by a practicing magician, this book walks the reader through 13 tricks that will astound

and amaze; photographs provide additional explanation. (Rev: BL 11/15/07; SLJ 1/08) [793.8]

Model Making

25854 Bliss, Helen, and Ruth Thomson. *Models* (2–6). Series: Craft Workshop. 1998, Crabtree paper $8.95 (978-0-86505-788-3). 32pp. A well-organized craft book that offers instruction on how to make miniature objects from various countries and cultures. (Rev: SLJ 10/98) [745]

25855 Simon, Seymour. *The Paper Airplane Book* (3–6). Illus. by Byron Barton. 1971, Puffin paper $6.99 (978-0-14-030925-6). Using how-to-make paper airplanes as the takeoff point, the author explains why planes fly and how changes in their construction can cause variations in flight.

Photography and Filmmaking

25856 Evans, Art. *First Photos: How Kids Can Take Great Pictures* (4–6). Illus. 1993, Photo Data Research paper $9.95 (978-0-9626508-7-1). 64pp. Focuses on disposable cameras and gives good tips on topics like composition, light, point of view, and camera handling. (Rev: BL 12/15/92; SLJ 9/93) [770]

25857 Friedman, Debra. *Picture This: Fun Photography and Crafts* (4–7). Series: Kids Can Do It! 2003, Kids Can $12.95 (978-1-55337-046-8); paper $5.95 (978-1-55337-047-5). 48pp. An easy-to-follow project book that combines photographs and crafts. (Rev: BL 3/15/03; HBG 10/03; SLJ 4/03) [770]

25858 Hilton, Jonathan, and Barrie Watts. *Photography* (4–6). Illus. Series: First Guide. 1994, Millbrook LB $24.90 (978-1-56294-398-1). 96pp. Basic photographic equipment is introduced, with techniques and tips on taking a variety of photos, from still lifes to portraits. (Rev: BL 12/15/94) [770]

25859 Lasky, Kathryn. *Think Like an Eagle: At Work with a Wildlife Photographer* (3–7). Illus. by Christopher G. Knight and Jack Swedberg. 1992, Little, Brown $15.95 (978-0-316-51519-1). 48pp. Following a wildlife photographer through the seasons and across the country. (Rev: BCCB 3/92; BL 6/1/92; SLJ 4/92) [778.9]

25860 Morgan, Terri, and Shmuel Thaler. *Photography: Take Your Best Shot* (5–8). Illus. Series: Media Workshop. 1991, Lerner LB $21.27 (978-0-8225-2302-4). 72pp. A comprehensive and well-put-together guide to photography that covers cameras, film, developing, composition, lighting, and special effects, as well as discussing career opportunities. (Rev: BL 10/1/91; SLJ 11/91) [771]

25861 Price, Susanna, and Tim Stephens. *Click! Fun with Photography* (4–8). 1997, Sterling $14.95 (978-0-8069-9541-0). A fine introduction to photography that covers both beginning and advanced subjects, including the operation of various cameras, exposure, lighting, different types of photography, and filters. (Rev: SLJ 8/97) [771]

25862 Shulman, Mark, and Hazlitt Korg. *Attack of the Killer Video Book: Tips and Tricks for Young Directors* (5–8). Illus. by Martha Newbigging. 2004, Annick $24.95 (978-1-55037-841-2); paper $12.95 (978-1-55037-840-5). 64pp. Practical advice on all aspects of movie making will be helpful for aspiring directors. (Rev: BL 5/15/04; SLJ 6/04) [778.59]

25863 Varriale, Jim. *Take a Look Around: Photography Activities for Young People* (5–8). Illus. 1999, Millbrook LB $24.90 (978-0-7613-1265-9). 32pp. Photographs taken by children in a summer camp photography class illustrate the importance of such elements as light and camera angles, framing, creating mood, and photographing action. (Rev: BL 3/15/00; HBG 3/00; SLJ 12/99; VOYA 2/00) [770]

Stamp, Coin, and Other Types of Collecting

25864 Dyson, Cindy. *Rare and Interesting Stamps* (5–8). Series: Costume, Tradition, and Culture: Reflecting on the Past. 1998, Chelsea $19.75 (978-0-7910-5171-9). The stories behind 25 rare and unusual stamps start with Britain's first one-penny stamp, which bore a portrait of Queen Victoria. (Rev: BL 3/15/99; HBG 10/99) [769.56]

25865 Hubley, Dan, and Mary Hubley. *Kids Collect: Amazing Collections for Fun, Crafts, and Science Fair Projects* (3–6). Illus. 2002, Bluefish Bay paper $13.95 (978-0-9707267-1-1). 176pp. Provides tips on the selection of an item to collect; the development of the collection itself through buying, trading, and selling; and using the collection as part of a science fair or other school project. (Rev: SLJ 3/03)

25866 Owens, Thomas S. *Collecting Baseball Cards: 21st Century Edition*. Rev. ed. (4–8). 2001, Millbrook LB $26.90 (978-0-7613-1708-1). 80pp. An entertaining introduction to collecting baseball cards, with information on the history of the industry, on how to determine the condition of cards, and how to use the Internet to buy and sell. (Rev: HBG 10/01; SLJ 7/01) [796]

25867 Owens, Thomas S. *Collecting Baseball Memorabilia* (4–6). Illus. 1996, Millbrook LB $26.90 (978-1-56294-579-4). 96pp. Ticket stubs, team schedules, autographs, and other related items are described, with hints for collectors on how to get them and how to organize and preserve a collection. (Rev: SLJ 6/96) [796.357]

25868 Owens, Thomas S. *Collecting Comic Books: A Young Person's Guide* (5–8). 1995, Millbrook LB $26.90 (978-1-56294-580-0). A beginner's guide to comic book collecting, with sections on kinds of collections, sources, and organizations. (Rev: BL 2/1/96; SLJ 1/96) [741.5]

25869 Owens, Thomas S. *Collecting Stock Car Racing Memorabilia* (4–8). Illus. 2001, Millbrook LB $26.90 (978-0-7613-1853-8). 80pp. NASCAR fans in particular will appreciate this practical and detailed guide to collecting, which includes extensive lists of useful addresses. (Rev: BL 12/15/01; HBG 3/02; SLJ 11/01) [796.72]

25870 Pellant, Chris. *Collecting Gems and Minerals: Hold the Treasures of the Earth in the Palm of Your Hand* (5–8). Illus. 1998, Sterling $14.95 (978-0-8069-9760-5). 80pp. After explaining how gems and minerals are formed, this book discusses necessary equipment for the hunter, where to look, how to identify specimens, and how to organize one's collection. (Rev: BL 6/1–15/98; SLJ 8/98) [553.8]

Jokes, Puzzles, Riddles, Word Games

Jokes and Riddles

25871 Adler, David A. *The Dinosaur Princess and Other Prehistoric Riddles* (2–6). Illus. 1988, Holiday House LB $14.95 (978-0-8234-0686-9). 64pp. An assortment of jokes and riddles and laughs with dinosaurs as the focus. (Rev: BL 5/1/88; SLJ 9/88)

25872 Becker, Helaine. *Boredom Blasters: Brain Bogglers, Awesome Activities, Cool Comics, Tasty Treats, and More . . .* (4–6). Illus. by Claudia Dávila. 2004, Maple Tree $21.95 (978-1-897066-02-7); paper $9.95 (978-1-897066-03-4). 160pp. Cures for boredom include stories, jokes and riddles, tricks, games, and foods. (Rev: SLJ 1/05) [818]

25873 Becker, Helaine. *Funny Business: Clowning Around, Practical Jokes, Cool Comedy, Cartooning, and More* (5–8). Illus. by Claudia Dávila. 2005, Maple Tree $21.95 (978-1-897066-40-9); paper $9.95 (978-1-897066-41-6). 160pp. Tips on body language, stand-up routines, clowning, and so forth are accompanied by discussion of various types of humor, a self-quiz, and recipes for delights including "Moose Droppings." (Rev: SLJ 1/06) [808.7]

25874 Bell-Rehwoldt, Sheri. *The Kids' Guide to Pranks, Tricks, and Practical Jokes* (3–6). Illus. 2008, Capstone LB $23.99 (978-1-4296-2275-2). 32pp. This well-illustrated book gives instructions for harmless tricks and jokes such as "fake vomit" and "rattlesnake eggs." (Rev: SLJ 5/09) [793.8]

25875 Brewer, Paul. *You Must Be Joking!* (3–5). Illus. 2003, Cricket $15.95 (978-0-8126-2661-2). 128pp. More than 200 jokes are accompanied by tips for effective delivery. (Rev: BL 2/1/04; HBG 4/04; SLJ 2/04) [818]

25876 Burns, Diane L., and Andy Burns. *Home on the Range: Ranch-Style Riddles* (2–5). Illus. by Susan S. Burke. Series: You Must Be Joking! 1994, Lerner LB $14.60 (978-0-8225-2341-3). A collection of zany riddles about life on the range. (Rev: SLJ 8/94) [818]

25877 Calmenson, Stephanie. *Kindergarten Kids: Riddles, Rebuses, Wiggles, Giggles, and More!* (PS–K). Illus. by Melissa Sweet. 2005, HarperCollins LB $16.89 (978-0-06-000714-0). 32pp. This well-illustrated collection of riddles and rhymes celebrates typical kindergarten activities. (Rev: BL 8/05; SLJ 8/05) [811]

25878 Charlip, Remy. *Arm in Arm: A Collection of Connections, Endless Tales, Reiterations, and Other Echolalia* (K–3). Illus. 1997, Tricycle $16.95 (978-1-883672-50-8). 48pp. Verbal and visual plays on words are revealed through a series of riddles, jokes, and puzzles. (Rev: BL 9/1/97; HBG 3/98) [808]

25879 Chmielewski, Gary. *The Classroom Zone: Jokes, Riddles, Tongue Twisters and "Daffynitions"* (3–5). Illus. by Jim Caputo. Series: The Funny Zone. 2008, Norwood House LB $19.95 (978-1-59953-145-8). 24pp. A collection of funny school-themed jokes and riddles, many of them new, with tips on creating your own. Also use *Let's Eat in the Funny Zone, Let's Go in the Funny Zone*, and *The Science Zone* (all 2008). (Rev: LMC 10/08; SLJ 7/08) [818]

25880 Christopher, Matt. *Baseball Jokes and Riddles* (2–4). Illus. 1996, Little, Brown paper $4.50 (978-0-316-14081-2). 48pp. Trivia and lots of jokes and riddles about baseball highlight this amusing collection. (Rev: BL 4/1/96; SLJ 6/96) [796.357]

25881 Eckstein, Joan, and Joyce Gleit. *The Best Joke Book for Kids Number 4* (3–6). Illus. by Joe Kohl. 1991, Avon paper $3.50 (978-0-380-76263-7). 64pp. There are riddles, knock-knocks, jokes, and tongue twisters in this book arranged by subjects. (Rev: BL 9/15/91) [793.73]

25882 Eisenberg, Lisa. *Silly School Riddles* (1–3). Illus. by Elwood H. Smith. 2008, Dial $14.99 (978-0-8037-3165-3). 40pp. A slightly uneven collection of jokes, riddles, and puns. (Rev: BL 8/08) [398.6]

25883 Fisher, Doris. *Happy Birthday to Whooo? A Baby Animal Riddle Book* (K–3). Illus. by Lisa Downey. 2006, Sylvan Dell $15.95 (978-0-9768823-1-2). Birth announcements give relevant details about new animal arrivals, and readers must turn the page to find out the animal in question. (Rev: SLJ 10/06)

25884 Hall, Katy, and Lisa Eisenberg. *Piggy Riddles* (PS–2). Illus. by Renée Andriani. Series: Dial Easy-to-Read. 2004, Dial $14.99 (978-0-8037-2855-4). 40pp. The unifying theme throughout this brightly illustrated book of riddles is pigs. (Rev: BL 3/1/04; SLJ 7/04) [818]

25885 Hall, Katy, and Lisa Eisenberg. *Simms Taback's Great Big Book of Spacey, Snakey, Buggy Riddles* (K–3). Illus. by Simms Taback. 2008, Viking $17.99 (978-0-670-01121-6). 64pp. A very lively collection of riddles enhanced by illustrations that offer clues. (Rev: BL 9/1/08) [818]

25886 Helmer, Marilyn. *Critter Riddles* (1–3). Illus. by Eric Parker. Series: Kids Can Read. 2003, Kids Can $14.95 (978-1-55337-445-9); paper $3.95 (978-1-55337-411-4). 32pp. Animal-themed jokes and riddles teach vocabulary and wordplay. Also use the food-related *Yummy Riddles* (2003). (Rev: HBG 10/03; SLJ 5/03) [818]

25887 Helmer, Marilyn. *Yucky Riddles* (K–2). Illus. by Eric Parker. Series: Kids Can Read. 2003, Kids Can $14.95 (978-1-55337-448-0); paper $3.95 (978-1-55337-414-5). 32pp. Cartoon art accompanies jokes and riddles that feature both humor and suitable grossness. (Rev: BL 1/1–15/04; HBG 4/04) [818.54]

25888 Helmer, Marilyn, and Jane Kurisu. *Funtime Riddles* (2–3). Series: Kids Can Read. 2004, Kids Can $14.95 (978-1-55337-579-1). 32pp. This collection of pun-filled riddles and jokes focuses on athletics and other leisure activities. (Rev: BL 6/1–15/04; SLJ 5/04) [818.5]

25889 Helmer, Marilyn, and Jane Kurisu. *Recess Riddles* (2–3). Series: Kids Can Read. 2004, Kids Can $14.95 (978-1-55337-577-7). 32pp. Easy-to-read school-related riddles and jokes include many puns. (Rev: BL 6/1–15/04; SLJ 5/04) [818.5]

25890 Hills, Tad. *Knock, Knock! Who's There? My First Book of Knock-Knock Jokes* (PS–1). Illus. by author. 2000, Simon & Schuster $6.99 (978-0-689-83413-4). Using flaps to conceal answers, this is an amusing collection of old and new knock-knock jokes. (Rev: SLJ 8/00) [818]

25891 Holub, Joan. *Geogra-fleas! Riddles All over the Map* (1–3). Illus. by Regan Dunnick. 2004, Whitman LB $16.99 (978-0-8075-2818-1). Funny facts and riddles are presented by a little brown dog. (Rev: SLJ 11/04) [398.6]

25892 Jansen, John. *Class Act: Riddles for School* (3–5). Illus. by Susan S. Burke. Series: You Must Be Joking! 1995, Lerner paper $3.95 (978-0-8225-9673-8). Riddles that take schools, students, and teachers as their subjects. Also use *Playing Possum: Riddles About Kangaroos, Koalas, and Other Marsupials* (1995). (Rev: SLJ 9/95)

25893 Joyce, Susan, comp. and ed. *ABC School Riddles* (2–5). Illus. by Freddie Levin. 2001, Peel $13.95 (978-0-939217-54-0). This simple book presents one riddle for each letter of the alphabet. (Rev: HBG 10/01; SLJ 1/01)

25894 Keller, Charles. *Driving Me Crazy: Fun on Wheels Jokes* (2–6). Illus. by Lee Lorenz. 1989, Pippin $13.95 (978-0-945912-05-7). A collection of jokes and riddles that deal with driving and vehicles. (Rev: BL 7/89) [398]

25895 Keller, Charles. *It's Raining Cats and Dogs: Cat and Dog Jokes* (2–6). Illus. by Robert Quackenbush. 1988, Pippin $13.95 (978-0-945912-01-9). 40pp. Pleasing nonsense for young readers. Also use: *Colossal Fossils: Dinosaur Riddles* (1991, Simon & Schuster paper). (Rev: BCCB 11/88; BL 2/15/89; SLJ 2/89)

25896 Keller, Charles. *King Henry the Ape: Animal Jokes* (2–6). Illus. by Edward Frascino. 1990, Pippin LB $13.95 (978-0-945912-08-8). 40pp. Animal guffaws sure to delight young readers. (Rev: BL 3/15/90; SLJ 4/90) [818]

25897 Keller, Charles. *The Planet of the Grapes: Show Biz Jokes and Riddles* (2–5). Illus. by Mischa Richter. 1992, Pippin $13.95 (978-0-945912-17-0). All the performing arts are included in this collection of zany jokes. (Rev: SLJ 12/92) [808.7]

25898 Keller, Charles, ed. *Take Me to Your Liter: Science and Math Jokes* (3–6). Illus. by Gregory Filling. 1991, Pippin LB $13.95 (978-0-945912-13-2). 40pp. Jokes and silly riddles about a serious subject. (Rev: BL 5/15/91; SLJ 7/91) [398.2]

25899 Lewis, J. Patrick. *Scien-Trickery: Riddles in Science* (1–4). Illus. by Frank Remkiewicz. 2004, Harcourt $16.00 (978-0-15-216681-6). 32pp. Eighteen brain-teasing riddles feature colorful illustrations that provide hints and humor. (Rev: BL 2/15/04; SLJ 4/04) [811]

25900 Lupton, Hugh. *Riddle Me This! Riddles and Stories to Challenge Your Mind* (4–6). Illus. by Sophie Fatus. 2003, Barefoot Bks. $19.99 (978-1-84148-169-2). 64pp. Riddles and riddle-related stories and poems, often with a humorous twist, are accompanied by folk-art illustrations. (Rev: BL 12/1/03; HBG 4/04; SLJ 4/04)

25901 Maestro, Giulio. *Riddle Roundup* (3–5). Illus. 1989, Houghton paper $7.95 (978-0-89919-537-7). 64pp. Puns, homonyms, and homographs for wordplay lovers. (Rev: BL 12/15/89; SLJ 2/90) [818]

25902 Martin, Jannelle. *ABC Math Riddles* (1–4). Illus. by Freddie Levin. 2003, Peel $13.95 (978-0-939217-57-1). Colorfully illustrated riddles introduce key mathematical terms. (Rev: HBG 4/04; SLJ 2/04) [510]

25903 Marzollo, Jean. *I Spy: Gold Challenger!* (2–5). Illus. by Walter Wick. Series: I Spy. 1998, Scholastic $13.99 (978-0-590-04296-3). 40pp. Objects are hidden in each photo in this puzzle book with appropriate riddles under each picture. (Rev: BL 1/1–15/99; HBG 3/99) [793.735]

25904 Marzollo, Jean. *I Spy Spooky Night* (2–5). Illus. by Walter Wick. 1996, Scholastic $13.99 (978-0-590-48137-3). 40pp. Riddles give clues to objects hidden in accompanying pictures. (Rev: BL 9/15/96; SLJ 9/96*) [793.73]

25905 Morrison, Lillian. *Guess Again! Riddle Poems* (K–3). Illus. by Christy Hale. 2006, August House $16.95 (978-0-87483-730-8). 48pp. A collection of

23 rhyming riddles — some simple some challenging — with colorful illustrations. (Rev: BL 5/1/06; SLJ 6/06) [811]

25906 Most, Bernard. *Zoodles* (PS–2). Illus. 1992, Harcourt $13.95 (978-0-15-299969-8). 32pp. An iguana who hogs all the food is a "piguana" in this riddle book that combines animal names. (Rev: BL 10/15/92; SLJ 1/93) [818]

25907 Peterson, Scott. *Plugged In: Electric Riddles* (3–5). Illus. by Susan S. Burke. Series: You Must Be Joking! 1995, Lerner paper $1.98 (978-0-8225-9700-1). Very funny jokes and riddles that involve appliances found around the house. (Rev: SLJ 9/95)

25908 Roop, Peter, and Connie Roop. *Holiday Howlers: Jokes for Punny Parties!* (1–3). Illus. by Brian Gable. Series: Make Me Laugh! 2003, Carolrhoda LB $19.93 (978-1-57505-645-6); paper $4.95 (978-1-57505-705-7). 32pp. Very corny jokes are tied to holidays and other important calendar dates, from Thanksgiving to Election Day. (Rev: HBG 4/04) [793]

25909 Rosenberg, Pam, comp. *Baseball Jokes* (2–3). Illus. by Patrick Girouard. Series: Laughing Matters. 2007, The Child's World LB $22.79 (978-1-59296-705-6). 24pp. Simple, silly jokes for the early elementary set on a fun and familiar topic. Bright, goofy illustrations add to the humor. Also use *Bug Jokes, Gross-Out Jokes, Monster Jokes,* and *Outdoor Jokes* (all 2007) plus *Historical Jokes* and *School Jokes* (both 2005). (Rev: SLJ 5/07)

25910 Rosenbloom, Joseph. *Biggest Riddle Book in the World* (3–6). Illus. by Joyce Behr. 1979, Sterling paper $6.95 (978-0-8069-8884-9). About 2,000 old and new riddles arranged under various subjects and amusingly illustrated.

25911 Rosenbloom, Joseph. *School Jokes* (2–4). Illus. by Steve Harpster. Series: Giggle Fit. 2003, Sterling $12.95 (978-0-402-70440-9). 48pp. This entertaining title is loaded with knock-knock jokes, puns, joke dialogues, and riddles.

25912 Rosenbloom, Joseph. *The World's Best Sports Riddles and Jokes* (2–6). Illus. by Sanford Hoffman. 1988, Sterling paper $3.95 (978-0-8069-6846-9). 128pp. Young sports fans will enjoy these gaffaws. (Rev: BL 5/1/88)

25913 Rosenbloom, Joseph. *The Zaniest Riddle Book in the World* (3–6). Illus. by Sanford Hoffman. 1984, Sterling paper $4.95 (978-0-8069-6252-8). 128pp. A riddle book arranged by topics.

25914 Schultz, Sam. *Animal Antics: The Beast Jokes Ever!* (K–4). Illus. by Brian Gable. 2003, Carolrhoda LB $19.93 (978-1-57505-640-1); paper $4.95 (978-1-57505-702-6). 31pp. Animal-themed jokes and wordplay will entertain young readers. (Rev: SLJ 1/04) [972.91]

25915 Schultz, Sam. *Monster Mayhem: Jokes to Scare You Silly!* (1–3). Illus. by Brian Gable. Series: Make Me Laugh! 2003, Carolrhoda LB $19.93 (978-1-57505-642-5); paper $4.95 (978-1-57505-708-8). 32pp. Lots of silly jokes and riddles about monsters, with bright cartoon illustrations. (Rev: HBG 4/04) [793]

25916 Schwartz, Alvin. *Witcracks: Jokes and Jests from American Folklore* (3–6). Illus. by Glen Rounds. 1973, HarperCollins LB $14.89 (978-0-397-31475-1). 128pp. All sorts of humor associated with America's past, from old riddles to knock-knock jokes.

25917 Shields, Carol Diggory. *Sports* (PS–3). Illus. by Svjetlan Junakovic. Series: Animagicals. 2001, Handprint $9.95 (978-1-929766-28-4). 32pp. Rhyming riddles give clues about animals hidden under the flaps in this tall-format picture book. (Rev: BL 2/1/02; HBG 3/02; SLJ 2/02) [811]

25918 Steig, William. *C D B!* (3–6). Illus. by author. 1987, Simon & Schuster paper $3.95 (978-0-671-66689-7). 48pp. When each set of letters and/or numbers is repeated aloud and riddle buffs apply a bit of imagination, the amusing caption accompanying each cartoon becomes apparent. Also use: *C D C!* (1986, Farrar).

25919 Swanson, June. *Out to Dry: Riddles About Deserts* (2–5). Illus. by Susan S. Burke. Series: You Must Be Joking! 1994, Lerner LB $14.60 (978-0-8225-2343-7). A cornucopia of groaners dealing with deserts. More riddles can be found in *Summit Up: Riddles About Mountains* (1994). (Rev: SLJ 8/94) [818.5]

25920 Terban, Marvin. *Funny You Should Ask: How to Make Up Jokes and Riddles with Wordplay* (4–6). Illus. by John O'Brien. 1992, Houghton paper $7.95 (978-0-395-58113-1). 64pp. How word manipulation works and how kids can become schoolyard hams. (Rev: BCCB 2/93; BL 10/1/92; SLJ 12/92) [808.7]

25921 Thaler, Mike. *Frankenstein's Pantyhose* (2–4). Illus. 1990, Avon paper $2.50 (978-0-380-75613-1). 92pp. This collection of jokes and riddles contains a special section of cigar jokes. (Rev: BL 3/15/90)

Puzzles

25922 Adshead, Paul. *Puzzle Island* (2–5). Illus. 1991, Child's Play $14.99 (978-0-85953-402-4); paper $7.99 (978-0-85953-403-1). 24pp. This puzzle book contains visual clues to decode a secret message and learn the identity of an extinct species. (Rev: BL 6/1/91) [793.73]

25923 Gardner, Martin. *Classic Brainteasers* (4–6). Illus. 1995, Sterling $14.95 (978-0-8069-1260-8). 96pp. An entertaining book of classic puzzles that involve math, science, and logic. (Rev: BL 5/1/95) [793.73]

25924 Garland, Michael. *The Great Easter Egg Hunt* (PS–2). Illus. Series: Look Again. 2005, Dutton $15.99 (978-0-525-47357-2). 32pp. Rhyming clues lead Tommy and readers to more than 200 objects hidden in the elaborate collage artwork. (Rev: BL 2/15/05; SLJ 2/05) [793.73]

25925 Kidslabel. *Spot 7 School* (K–4). 2006, Chronicle $12.95 (978-0-8118-5324-8). Readers are challenged to identify objects in photographs and at the same time to solve riddles that continue throughout the book. (Rev: SLJ 10/06)

25926 Ljungkvist, Laura. *Follow the Line Through the House* (K–3). Illus. by author. 2007, Viking $16.99 (978-0-670-06225-6). Children will enjoy this combination of hide-and-seek and treasure hunt in which line drawings against patterned designs guide readers to hidden objects. (Rev: HB 7/07; SLJ 6/07)

25927 McMillan, Bruce. *Sense Suspense: A Guessing Game for the Five Senses* (PS–1). Illus. 1994, Scholastic $15.95 (978-0-590-47904-2). 32pp. A puzzle book that introduces the five senses and challenges youngsters to determine objects from close-up details. (Rev: BCCB 12/94; BL 12/1/94; SLJ 12/94*) [793.73]

25928 Marks, Jennifer L. *School Times: A Spot-It Challenge* (PS–2). 2009, Capstone LB $23.99 (978-1-4296-2218-9). 32pp. Similar to *I Spy* books, this volume provide visual challenges in a school setting. Also use *Fun and Games: A Spot-It Challenge* and *Mean Machines: A Spot-It Challenge* (both 2009). (Rev: SLJ 5/09)

25929 Marzollo, Jean. *I Spy: A Book of Picture Riddles* (K–4). Illus. 1992, Scholastic $13.99 (978-0-590-45087-4). 48pp. Readers are asked to search out certain items from collages or montages. (Rev: BCCB 2/92; BL 5/15/92; SLJ 4/92) [793.73]

25930 Marzollo, Jean. *I Spy: Extreme Challenger: A Book of Picture Riddles* (K–3). Photos by alter Wick. 2000, Scholastic $13.99 (978-0-439-19900-1). 40pp. This book contains 12 double-page picture puzzles with accompanying riddles. (Rev: BL 10/1/00; HBG 3/01; SLJ 12/00) [793.73]

25931 Marzollo, Jean. *I Spy A to Z: A Book of Pictures and Riddles* (PS–2). Illus. by Walter Wick. 2009, Scholastic $13.99 (978-0-545-10782-2). 56pp. Elements of phonics and letter recognition are introduced to this familiar series while standard observation skills are engaged. (Rev: BLO 6/16/09; SLJ 7/09)

25932 Marzollo, Jean. *I Spy Fantasy: A Book of Picture Riddles* (1–3). Illus. by Walter Wick. 1994, Scholastic $13.99 (978-0-590-46295-2). 40pp. In a series of photographic collages, children are challenged to find hidden objects. (Rev: BL 12/1/94; SLJ 10/94) [793.3]

25933 Marzollo, Jean. *I Spy Super Challenger! A Book of Picture Riddles* (PS–2). Illus. by Walter Wick. Series: I Spy. 1997, Scholastic $13.99 (978-0-590-34128-8). 32pp. This detailed picture puzzle book defies the reader to find a needle in the haystack, as well as other eye-dazzling problems. (Rev: BL 10/1/97; HBG 3/98; SLJ 9/97) [793.735]

25934 Marzollo, Jean. *I Spy Treasure Hunt: A Book of Picture Riddles* (K–3). Illus. by Walter Wick. Series: I Spy. 1999, Scholastic $13.99 (978-0-439-04244-4). 40pp. A series of picture puzzles in which children are asked to find hidden objects in the illustrations as well as solving the mystery of the pirate's hidden treasure. (Rev: BL 11/15/99; HBG 10/00; SLJ 1/00) [793.73]

25935 Marzollo, Jean. *I Spy Year-Round Challenger! A Book of Picture Riddles* (PS–2). Illus. by Walter Wick. 2001, Scholastic $13.99 (978-0-439-31634-7). 40pp. A book of double-page picture puzzles with holiday themes, one for each of the 12 months. (Rev: BL 2/1/02; HBG 10/02; SLJ 4/02) [793.73]

25936 Onishi, Satoru. *Who's Hiding?* (PS–2). Illus. by author. 2007, Kane $14.95 (978-1-933605-24-1). 32pp. A hide-and-seek book in which a different animal is partially hidden on each page, making for an entertaining but not too difficult challenge for little ones. (Rev: SLJ 5/07)

25937 Phillips, Dee. *Find It at the Beach* (K–3). Series: Can You Find It? 2005, Gareth Stevens LB $23.00 (978-0-8368-6298-0). 24pp. This hunt for animals and objects found at the beach will prompt children to study the detailed photographs. Also use *Find It in a Rain Forest*, *Find It in the Desert*, and *Find It on the Farm* (all 2005). (Rev: SLJ 6/06) [578.7699]

25938 Philpot, Lorna, and Graham Philpot. *Find Anthony Ant* (PS–1). Illus. by Lorna Philpot. 2006, Sterling $12.95 (978-1-905417-10-0). 24pp. Children will enjoy hunting for Anthony on each spread of this detailed book featuring "The Ants Go Marching." (Rev: BL 5/15/06)

25939 Riedler, Isabella. *Tricky Puzzles for Clever Kids* (2–5). Illus. 2001, Sterling paper $5.95 (978-0-8069-6753-0). 128pp. A collection of challenging visual puzzles illustrated in black and white. (Rev: BL 2/15/02) [793.73]

25940 Swinburne, Stephen. *Guess Whose Shadow?* (PS–K). Illus. 1999, Boyds Mills $15.95 (978-1-56397-724-4). 32pp. Shadows are introduced in a series of photographs and then readers are asked to identify objects by their shadows. (Rev: BCCB 4/99; BL 3/1/99; HBG 10/99; SLJ 4/99) [770]

25941 White, Graham. *Secrets of the Pyramids: A Maze Adventure* (3–6). Illus. 2002, National Geographic paper $8.95 (978-0-7922-6938-0). 32pp. Fans of mazes will enjoy helping 12-year-old Hemon look for his father in the pyramid, and will learn about ancient Egypt in the process. (Rev: SLJ 11/02) [793.7]

25942 Whybrow, Ian. *Faraway Farm* (PS–K). Illus. by Alex Ayliffe. 2006, Carolrhoda LB $14.95 (978-1-57505-938-9). Rhyming text encourages readers to locate specific animals and inanimate objects in the illustrations that chronicle a day in the life of Farmer Flat and his family. (Rev: SLJ 11/06)

25943 Wick, Walter. *Can You See What I See? Once Upon a Time* (PS–2). Illus. by author. 2006, Scholastic $13.99 (978-0-439-61777-2). 40pp. Twelve classic fairy tales are the setting for this new picture puzzle book; each spread comes with a list of items to find in each fairy tale scene. (Rev: BL 12/1/06; SLJ 2/07) [793.3]

25944 Wick, Walter. *Can You See What I See? Cool Collections: Picture Puzzles to Search and Solve* (K–2). 2004, Scholastic $13.95 (978-0-439-61772-7). 40pp. In this colorful assortment of picture puzzles, Wick focuses on some of the diverse objects that people collect, including seashells, buttons, stuffed animals, and model cars. (Rev: BL 12/1/04; SLJ 10/04) [793.73]

25945 Wick, Walter. *Can You See What I See? Dream Machine: A Picture Adventure to Search and Solve* (PS–2). Photos by author. 2003, Scholastic $13.99 (978-0-439-39950-0). 35pp. A dozen picture puzzles each offer multiple challenges, including search-and-find quests, mazes, and matching games. (Rev: HBG 4/04; SLJ 11/03) [793.73]

25946 Wick, Walter. *Can You See What I See? Picture Puzzles to Search and Solve* (K–3). Illus. 2002, Scholastic $13.95 (978-0-429-16391-3). 40pp. A collection of clever picture puzzles that test the visual perception of young readers. (Rev: BL 4/15/02; HBG 10/02; SLJ 3/02) [792.73]

25947 Wick, Walter. *Can You See What I See? Seymour Makes New Friends* (PS–K). Illus. Series: Seymour. 2006, Scholastic $8.99 (978-0-439-61780-2). 32pp. Readers must seek out specific objects on the spreads while Seymour makes a seesaw and two rabbits. (Rev: BL 2/1/06; SLJ 2/06) [793.73]

Word Games

25948 McCall, Francis, and Patricia Keeler. *A Huge Hog Is a Big Pig: A Rhyming Word Game* (K–3).

Illus. 2002, HarperCollins LB $16.89 (978-0-06-029766-4). 32pp. "A wet hound is . . . a soggy doggy!" and other wondrous rhymes are accompanied by photographs of children from a mix of races and of the appropriate animals. (Rev: BL 12/15/01; HBG 10/02; SLJ 2/02)

25949 Most, Bernard. *Hippopotamus Hunt* (1–3). Illus. 1994, Harcourt $14.95 (978-0-15-234520-4). 32pp. Explores the pastime of finding words within words and, using *hippopotamus* as an example, comes up with 53 new words. (Rev: BL 9/1/94; SLJ 11/94)

25950 Rosenbloom, Joseph. *World's Toughest Tongue Twisters* (3–5). Illus. 1987, Sterling paper $4.95 (978-0-8069-6596-3). 128pp. More than 500 tongue twisters, alphabetically from A to Z.

25951 Schnur, Steven. *Autumn: An Alphabet Acrostic* (K–3). Illus. by Leslie Evans. 1997, Clarion $16.00 (978-0-395-77043-6). 32pp. An alphabet book that uses autumn and acrostic poems as a framework. (Rev: BL 9/1/97; HBG 3/98; SLJ 9/97) [793.73]

25952 Steig, William. *CDB!* Rev. ed. (PS–4). Illus. 2000, Simon & Schuster $16.00 (978-0-689-83160-7). 48pp. The great word-game book of 30 years ago is now reissued with color drawings. (Rev: BL 4/1/00; HBG 10/00) [793.734]

Mysteries, Monsters, Curiosities, and Trivia

25953 Allman, Toney. *Werewolves* (4–7). Series: Monsters. 2004, Gale LB $26.20 (978-0-7377-2620-6). 48pp. An examination of the origins of the werewolf, with references to and illustrations from movie and TV appearances by these monsters. (Rev: SLJ 4/05) [398]

25954 Asimov, Isaac. *Is There Life in Outer Space?* (3–5). Illus. Series: Isaac Asimov's 21st Century Library of the Universe. 2004, Gareth Stevens LB $26.00 (978-0-8368-3950-0). 32pp. A revised, well-illustrated edition of a previously published book, this offers thoughtful discussion of the possibility of alien life, with material on the development of life on Earth and on exploration of Mars. (Rev: SLJ 3/05) [576.8]

25955 Aslan, Madalyn. *What's Your Sign? A Cosmic Guide for Young Astrologers* (5–9). Illus. by Jennifer Kalis. 2002, Grosset $12.99 (978-0-448-42693-8). A lively, spiral-bound guide to the 12 signs of the zodiac and the personality traits they represent, with information on the underlying mythology and lists of famous people born under each sign. (Rev: SLJ 9/02) [133.5]

25956 Bardhan-Quallen, Sudipta. *The Real Monsters* (5–8). Illus. by Josh Cochran. Series: Mysteries Unwrapped. 2008, Sterling paper $5.95 (978-1-4027-3776-3). 88pp. This volume looks into stories about ghosts, werewolves, vampires, mummies, zombies and other monsters. (Rev: SLJ 6/09) [001.944]

25957 Becker, Helaine. *Are You Psychic? The Official Guide for Kids* (4–6). Illus. by Claudia Dávila. 2005, Maple Tree $16.95 (978-1-897066-20-1); paper $9.95 (978-1-897066-21-8). 64pp. Telepathy, mind reading, and fortune telling are among the psychic abilities introduced in this breezy volume that includes activities. (Rev: SLJ 5/05) [001.9]

25958 Blackwood, Gary L. *Enigmatic Events* (5–8). Illus. Series: Unsolved History. 2005, Marshall Cavendish LB $20.95 (978-0-7614-1889-4). 80pp. Explores some of history's most enduring mysteries — the disappearance of the dinosaurs and of the

Mary Celeste, to name only two. (Rev: BL 3/1/06; SLJ 3/06) [904]

25959 Blackwood, Gary L. *Extraordinary Events and Oddball Occurrences* (4–7). Illus. Series: Secrets of the Unexplained. 1999, Marshall Cavendish LB $29.93 (978-0-7614-0748-5). 80pp. A book that covers such unusual occurrences as strange things falling from the sky, teleportation, and unexplained appearances and disappearances. (Rev: BL 3/1/00; HBG 10/00) [001.9]

25960 Blackwood, Gary L. *Fateful Forebodings* (4–6). Series: Secrets of the Unexplained. 1998, Benchmark LB $28.50 (978-0-7614-0467-5). 80pp. This book covers the origins and practices of such forms of fortune telling as astrology, tarot-card reading, tea-leaf reading, and the I Ching. (Rev: HBG 10/99; SLJ 3/99) [133.3]

25961 Blackwood, Gary L. *Long-Ago Lives* (4–7). Illus. Series: Secrets of the Unexplained. 1999, Marshall Cavendish LB $19.95 (978-0-7614-0747-8). 80pp. A look at the subject of reincarnation. (Rev: BL 3/1/00; HBG 10/00) [133.9]

25962 Blackwood, Gary L. *Paranormal Powers* (4–6). Series: Secrets of the Unexplained. 1998, Benchmark LB $28.50 (978-0-7614-0468-2). 80pp. This book explores psychic abilities such as telepathy, clairvoyance, precognition, body magnetism, pain control, and spoon bending. (Rev: HBG 10/99; SLJ 3/99) [001.9]

25963 Burns, Jan. *Crop Circles* (4–6). Series: Wonders of the World. 2005, Gale LB $26.20 (978-0-7377-3063-0). 48pp. A slim overview of the history of crop circles over the past century, with discussion of the various theories about these strange phenomena. (Rev: SLJ 12/05) [001.94]

25964 Campbell, Peter A. *Alien Encounters* (5–7). Illus. 2000, Millbrook LB $23.90 (978-0-7613-1402-8). 48pp. An overview of eight supposed encounters between humans and aliens. (Rev: BL 7/00; HBG 10/00; SLJ 4/00) [001.9]

25965 Crisp, Tony. *Super Minds: People with Amazing Mind Power* (4–7). Illus. by Mary Kuper. 1999,

Element Books paper $4.95 (978-1-901881-03-5). 128pp. A survey of near-death experiences, feral children's case histories, and instances of strange mental powers. (Rev: SLJ 5/99) [001.9]

25966 Deem, James M. *How to Find a Ghost* (5–8). Illus. 1990, Avon paper $3.25 (978-0-380-70829-1). 144pp. An attempt to explain how to have a supernatural experience. (Rev: BCCB 11/88; BL 11/1/88; SLJ 11/88) [133.1]

25967 Delrio, Martin. *The Loch Ness Monster* (3–5). Series: Unsolved Mysteries. 2002, Rosen LB $25.25 (978-0-8239-3564-2). 48pp. Here is a rundown on the many sightings and stories surrounding the Lock Ness monster, including the expeditions that tried and failed to find the truth. (Rev: BL 10/15/02) [001.9]

25968 Demolay, Jack. *Atlantis: The Mystery of the Lost City* (3–5). Illus. by author. Series: Jr. Graphic Mysteries. 2006, Rosen LB $22.50 (978-1-4042-3407-9). 24pp. Readers will be fascinated by the mystery of Atlantis, presented here with engaging artwork and background information. (Rev: SLJ 5/07)

25969 Donkin, Andrew. *Atlantis: The Lost City?* (2–4). Illus. Series: DK Readers. 2000, DK $14.99 (978-0-7894-6681-5). 48pp. The first part of this book discusses the legend of Atlantis; the second half tells of the search for this lost city at sites around the world. (Rev: BL 12/15/00; HBG 10/01) [001.94]

25970 Donkin, Andrew. *Bermuda Triangle* (2–4). Series: Eyewitness Reader. 2000, DK paper $3.99 (978-0-7894-5415-7). 48pp. An easily read study of the Bermuda Triangle that favors explanations leaning toward the supernatural — blaming UFOs or the lost continent of Atlantis. (Rev: HBG 10/00; SLJ 8/00) [001.9]

25971 Dumont-Le Cornec, Elisabeth. *Wonders of the World: Natural and Man-Made Majesties* (5–9). Illus. by Laureen Topalian. 2007, Abrams $24.95 (978-0-8109-9417-1). 150pp. Seventy-one striking sites around the world, both natural and man-made and featured on the UNESCO World Heritage list, are shown in beautiful photographs. (Rev: BL 12/15/07) [031.02]

25972 Farman, John. *The Short and Bloody History of Ghosts* (4–6). Illus. by author. Series: Short and Bloody Histories. 2002, Lerner LB $19.93 (978-0-8225-0837-3); paper $5.95 (978-0-8225-0838-0). 96pp. Ghosts and other supernatural beings are the focus of this overview of sightings around the world today and in the past, with most of the events occurring in Britain. (Rev: HBG 3/03; SLJ 2/03)

25973 Fecher, Sarah, and Clare Oliver. *Freaky Facts About Natural Disasters* (3–5). Illus. Series: Freaky Facts. 2006, Two-Can $13.95 (978-1-58728-539-4); paper $8.95 (978-1-58728-542-4). 32pp. Great for browsing, this is an overview of the impact of events ranging from extreme weather to earthquakes and volcanic eruptions. (Rev: BL 4/15/06) [363.34]

25974 French, Jackie. *The Little Book of Big Questions* (3–6). Illus. by Martha Newbigging. 2000, Annick $19.95 (978-1-55037-655-5); paper $9.95

(978-1-55037-654-8). 127pp. Fifteen subject-oriented chapters cover such areas as the universe, animal intelligence, extraterrestrials, and mortality. (Rev: HBG 3/01; SLJ 11/00) [001.9]

25975 Gilman, Laura Anne. *Yeti, the Abominable Snowman* (3–5). Illus. Series: Unsolved Mysteries. 2002, Rosen LB $26.50 (978-0-8239-3565-9). 48pp. The author presents historical accounts of the elusive yeti of the Himalayas. (Rev: BL 10/15/02) [001.944]

25976 Gorman, Jacqueline Laks. *The Bermuda Triangle* (3–5). Illus. Series: X Science: An Imagination Library. 2002, Gareth Stevens LB $23.00 (978-0-8368-3196-2). 24pp. An introduction to the mysterious Bermuda Triangle, with discussion of theories, evidence, and research. Also use *Bigfoot* and *The Loch Ness Monster* (both 2002). (Rev: HBG 3/03; SLJ 2/03) [001.9]

25977 Grace, N. B. *UFO Mysteries* (2–5). Series: Boys Rock! 2006, The Child's World LB $25.64 (978-1-59296-738-4). 32pp. A good choice for beginning and reluctant readers (girls as well as boys), this is a photo-filled exploration of the search for life outside our solar system and of the possibility that other life forms have visited earth. (Rev: SLJ 2/07) [001.942]

25978 Halls, Kelly Milner. *Tales of the Cryptids: Mysterious Creatures That May or May Not Exist* (4–7). Illus. by Rick Spears. 2006, Darby Creek $18.95 (978-1-58196-049-5). 72pp. A fun, close-up look at cryptozoology, the study of legendary animals (that may or may not be real) such as the Loch Ness Monster and Bigfoot. (Rev: BL 11/15/06; SLJ 12/06) [001.944]

25979 Herbst, Judith. *Hoaxes* (3–4). Illus. Series: The Unexplained. 2004, Lerner LB $26.60 (978-0-8225-1629-3). 48pp. Crop circles, fairy photographs, moon-men, and other famous and less-well-known hoaxes and publicity stunts are described. Also in this series is *Monsters* (2004). (Rev: SLJ 2/05) [001.9]

25980 Hillman, Ben. *How Big Is It?* (3–5). Illus. Series: What's the Big Idea? 2007, Scholastic $14.99 (978-0-439-91808-4). 48pp. Twenty-two giant items — a polar bear, a huge spider, an airship, a redwood — are juxtaposed with other objects to illustrate their size; conversational narrative provides key information. (Rev: BL 11/15/07; SLJ 2/08) [153.7]

25981 Ho, Oliver. *Mutants and Monsters* (4–6). Illus. by Josh Cochran. Series: Mysteries Unwrapped. 2008, Sterling paper $5.95 (978-1-4027-3642-1). 96pp. Bigfoot, the Jersey Devil, and Nessie are among the beings included in this survey of curiosities that is good for browsing. (Rev: BL 7/08; SLJ 7/08) [001.944]

25982 Huang, Chungliang Al. *The Chinese Book of Animal Powers* (5–7). Illus. 1999, HarperCollins LB $16.89 (978-0-06-027729-1). 40pp. The 12 animals of the Chinese zodiac are introduced in double-page spreads, and the characteristics and powers of each are outlined. (Rev: BCCB 12/99; BL 1/1–15/00; HBG 3/00) [133.5]

25983 Hubbard-Brown, Janet. *The Curse of the Hope Diamond* (4–7). Illus. 1991, Avon paper $2.99 (978-0-380-76222-4). 96pp. A mystery style is used to introduce historical information about this jewel and the bad luck it seems to carry. (Rev: BL 12/15/91) [736.23]

25984 Innes, Brian. *The Bermuda Triangle* (4–7). Illus. Series: Unsolved Mysteries. 1999, Raintree LB $30.40 (978-0-8172-5485-8). 48pp. The author explores many theories that have been proposed to explain disappearances off the southeast coast of the U.S. (Rev: BL 5/15/99; HBG 10/99) [001.94]

25985 Innes, Brian. *The Cosmic Joker* (4–7). Illus. Series: Unsolved Mysteries. 1999, Raintree LB $25.69 (978-0-8172-5487-2). 48pp. This book introduces Charles Fort, the Cosmic Joker, and the many strange facts and coincidences he has uncovered. (Rev: BL 5/15/99; HBG 10/99; SLJ 9/99) [001.94]

25986 Innes, Brian. *Giant Humanlike Beasts* (4–7). Series: Unsolved Mysteries. 1999, Raintree LB $30.40 (978-0-8172-5484-1). 48pp. This account explores stories about the Abominable Snowman, or yeti, and other sightings of primitive creatures, while questioning the possibility of living links with Neanderthals. (Rev: BL 5/15/99; HBG 10/99; SLJ 9/99) [001.9]

25987 Innes, Brian. *Millennium Prophecies* (5–8). Illus. 1999, Raintree LB $30.40 (978-0-8172-5486-5). All sorts of prophecies relating to the calendar and the millennium are explored in this attractive volume. (Rev: BL 5/15/99; HBG 10/99; SLJ 9/99; VOYA 10/99) [001.7]

25988 Innes, Brian. *Mysterious Healing* (5–8). Illus. Series: Unsolved Mysteries. 1999, Raintree LB $25.69 (978-0-8172-5489-6). Hands-on healing, acupuncture, iridology, and auras are some of the subjects discussed in this volume. (Rev: BL 5/15/99; HBG 10/99; SLJ 9/99; VOYA 10/99) [001.7]

25989 Jackson, Ellen. *The Book of Slime* (2–4). Illus. by Jan Davey Ellis. 1997, Millbrook LB $21.40 (978-0-7613-0042-7). 32pp. Describes various forms of slime in nature, including human mucus and saliva, along with their uses, slime jokes, and some recipes. (Rev: BL 3/15/97; SLJ 6/97) [001.9]

25990 Kallen, Stuart A. *Dreams* (4–8). Illus. Series: The Mystery Library. 2004, Gale LB $29.95 (978-1-59018-288-8). 112pp. In this volume in the Mystery Library, Kallen examines topics including dream science, the interpretation of dreams, and telepathic dreaming. Also use *Ghosts, Possessions and Exorcisms*, and *Shamans* (all 2004). (Rev: BL 5/15/04) [154.6]

25991 Kallen, Stuart A. *Fortune-Telling* (4–8). Illus. Series: Mystery Library. 2004, Gale LB $29.95 (978-1-59018-289-5). 112pp. This exploration of the history and mystery of fortune-telling separates fact from fiction. (Rev: BL 5/15/04) [133.3]

25992 Kallen, Stuart A. *The Loch Ness Monster* (3–6). Illus. Series: Mysteriousand Unknown. 2008, Reference Point LB $25.95 (978-1-60152-059-3). 104pp. Kallen chronicles sightings of Nessie, the various expeditions to find the monster, and looks at the many hoaxes that have been perpetrated. (Rev: BLO 3/5/09) [001.944]

25993 Kemp, Gillian. *Tea Leaves, Herbs, and Flowers: Fortune-Telling the Gypsy Way* (5–9). Illus. by Mary Kuper. Series: Elements of the Extraordinary. 1998, Element Books paper $5.95 (978-1-901881-92-9). 128pp. A look at the art of reading tea leaves and the lore and language of flowers. (Rev: SLJ 1/99) [133.3]

25994 Krensky, Stephen. *Frankenstein* (4–7). Illus. Series: Monster Chronicles. 2006, Lerner LB $26.60 (978-0-8225-5923-8). 48pp. A survey of the folklore and fiction featuring Frankenstein's monster, including excerpts from the famous Mary Shelley novel. Also use *Vampires* and *Werewolves* (both 2006). (Rev: SLJ 2/07) [823]

25995 Landau, Elaine. *ESP* (4–6). Illus. Series: Mysteries of Science. 1996, Millbrook LB $20.90 (978-0-7613-0012-0). 48pp. The amazing phenomenon known as extrasensory perception is explored in an account that separates fact from fiction. (Rev: BL 10/15/96; SLJ 11/96) [133.8]

25996 Landau, Elaine. *Fortune Telling* (4–6). Illus. Series: Mysteries of Science. 1996, Millbrook LB $22.90 (978-0-7613-0013-7). 48pp. Various methods of future telling are covered, with material that debunks the claims of supposed clairvoyants. (Rev: BL 10/15/96; SLJ 11/96) [133.3]

25997 Landau, Elaine. *Near-Death Experiences* (4–6). Illus. Series: Mysteries of Science. 1995, Millbrook LB $20.90 (978-1-56294-543-5). 48pp. An objective account that surveys the evidence concerning the possible truth behind reported near-death experiences. (Rev: BL 12/15/95; SLJ 4/96) [133.9]

25998 Landau, Elaine. *UFOs* (4–6). Illus. Series: Mysteries of Science. 1995, Millbrook LB $20.90 (978-1-56294-542-8). 48pp. The controversy concerning UFO sightings is reported in an objective way, with many intriguing photographs. (Rev: BL 12/15/95; SLJ 4/96) [001.9]

25999 Larkspur, Penelope. *The Secret Life of Fairies* (3–5). Illus. 1999, Kids Can $14.95 (978-1-55074-547-4). 32pp. This account presents an inside look at fairy life including homes, dress, and food. (Rev: BL 11/1/99; HBG 3/00) [813.48]

26000 Messenger, Norman. *Imagine* (3–5). Illus. 2005, Candlewick $17.99 (978-0-7636-2757-7). 32pp. This inventively constructed book, with folds, wheels, and flaps, offers a variety of visual stimuli and puzzles. (Rev: BL 1/1–15/06) [793.73]

26001 Miller, Karen. *Monsters and Water Beasts: Creatures of Fact or Fiction?* (4–6). Illus. by Sergio Ruzzier. 2007, Holt $17.95 (978-0-8050-7902-9). 88pp. Legends of creatures such as Bigfoot and sea serpents are thoroughly described in this book, along with scientific information that could possibly rule out the creatures' existence. (Rev: BL 5/1/07; SLJ 7/07) [398.24]

26002 Miller, Raymond H. *Vampires* (4–7). Series: Monsters. 2004, Gale LB $26.20 (978-0-7377-2619-0). 48pp. An examination of the origins of the vampire, with references to and illustrations from movie and TV appearances by these monsters. (Rev: SLJ 4/05) [398]

26003 Myers, Janet Nuzum. *Strange Stuff: True Stories of Odd Places and Things* (5–8). Illus. 1999, Linnet LB $19.50 (978-0-208-02405-3). A collection of curiosities — items about zombies, quicksand, scorpions, poisonous snakes, black holes, Bigfoot, mermaids, voodoo, the Bermuda Triangle, and feral children raised by wolves. (Rev: HBG 3/00; SLJ 7/99; VOYA 2/00) [001.9]

26004 Nardo, Don. *Atlantis* (5–8). Illus. Series: The Mystery Library. 2004, Gale LB $29.95 (978-1-59018-287-1). 112pp. The author examines whether the ancient story of the lost continent of Atlantis — as described by Plato — could be true. (Rev: BL 5/15/04; SLJ 4/04) [001.94]

26005 Nardo, Don, and Bradley Steffens. *Medusa* (4–7). Series: Monsters. 2004, Gale LB $26.20 (978-0-7377-2617-6). 48pp. Describes the mythological personage, telling the story of Perseus killing Medusa, and showing her role in paintings, sculptures, movie stills, and computer games. Also use *Cyclops* (2004). (Rev: SLJ 4/05) [398.2]

26006 Nickell, Joe. *The Magic Detectives: Join Them in Solving Strange Mysteries* (3–7). Illus. 1989, Prometheus paper $15.98 (978-0-87975-547-8). 115pp. Each of the 30 brief chapters explores a mysterious phenomenon, such as Bigfoot. (Rev: BCCB 12/89; BL 12/1/89) [133]

26007 *1001 Questions and Answers* (3–7). Illus. 1995, DK $16.95 (978-1-78940-205-6). 64pp. More than 1,000 fascinating questions and amazing answers covering science and invention, history, the natural world, and recreation are detailed, with matching photographs. (Rev: BL 1/1–15/96) [031.02]

26008 O'Neill, Catherine. *Amazing Mysteries of the World* (3–8). Illus. 1983, National Geographic LB $12.50 (978-0-87044-502-6). 104pp. Stonehenge, Easter Island, and Bigfoot are three of the many mysteries explored.

26009 Oxlade, Chris. *The Mystery of Crop Circles* (4–6). Series: Can Science Solve? 1999, Heinemann LB $22.79 (978-1-57572-804-9). 32pp. This book examines the strange phenomenon known as crop circles, unusual circular patterns that appear in crop fields, and covers the various theories about them. (Rev: SLJ 8/99) [001.9]

26010 Oxlade, Chris. *The Mystery of the Bermuda Triangle* (4–6). Series: Can Science Solve? 1999, Heinemann LB $22.79 (978-1-57572-811-7). 32pp. A variety of natural explanations are examined in this dramatic presentation of material on the Bermuda Triangle. (Rev: SLJ 1/00) [001.9]

26011 Pascoe, Elaine. *Fooled You! Fakes and Hoaxes Through the Years* (4–6). Illus. by Laurie Keller. 2005, Holt $16.95 (978-0-8050-7528-1). 96pp. Pascoe tells the stories behind some of the world's most infamous hoaxes, including the Cardiff Giant, Bigfoot, crop circles, and Piltdown Man. (Rev: BL 9/15/05; SLJ 11/05) [001.9]

26012 *Pick Me Up* (4–8). Illus. 2006, DK $29.99 (978-0-7566-2159-9). 351pp. This attractive, child-friendly compilation of facts and figures offers information on a wide variety of topics, including nature, fashion, math, politics, popular culture, geography, music, movies, and technology. (Rev: SLJ 12/06) [900]

26013 Powell, Jillian. *Body Decoration* (4–8). Illus. Series: Traditions Around the World. 1995, Thomson Learning LB $24.26 (978-1-56847-276-8). 48pp. An interesting book that explains the uses of body decoration in history and discusses tattooing, face painting, and body piercing. (Rev: SLJ 7/95) [617]

26014 Reid, Lori. *Hand Reading: Discover Your Future* (5–9). Illus. Series: Elements of the Extraordinary. 1998, Element Books paper $5.95 (978-1-901881-82-0). Palmistry is explained in detail, including the meaning of the shape of the hand and nails and of each line and curve, and how hand gestures can reveal clues to personalities. (Rev: SLJ 1/99) [133.6]

26015 Reynolds, Helen. *Makeup and Body Decoration* (3–8). Illus. Series: A Fashionable History of Costume. 2003, Raintree LB $25.70 (978-1-4109-0028-9). 32pp. Chronicles the history of body decoration and makeup from the beginning of recorded history to the present. (Rev: HBG 10/03; SLJ 9/03) [391.6]

26016 *Ripley's Believe It or Not!* (4–7). Illus. 2004, Ripley $25.95 (978-1-893951-73-0). 256pp. Packed with fascinating trivia and fun for browsing, this appealing volume focuses on weird and amazing facts. (Rev: SLJ 2/05) [031.02]

26017 Roleff, Tamara L., ed. *Black Magic and Witches* (5–8). Series: Fact or Fiction? 2003, Gale paper $18.70 (978-0-7377-1319-0). 127pp. A good starting point for debate over witchcraft, with essays for and against witches, magic, and Harry Potter, and some history of persecution of witches. (Rev: SLJ 3/03) [133.43]

26018 Rosen, Michael J. *Balls! Round 2* (4–7). Illus. by John Margeson. Series: Balls! 2008, Darby Creek $18.95 (978-1-58196-066-2). 80pp. This sequel to *Balls!* (2006) introduces even more balls — bocce, croquet, meatballs, even the Magic Eight ball — with all kinds of facts, puzzles, experiments, and fun. (Rev: BLO 6/17/08; SLJ 7/08) [796.3]

26019 Savage, Candace. *Wizards: An Amazing Journey Through the Last Great Age of Magic* (5–8). Illus. 2003, Greystone $17.95 (978-1-55054-943-0). 80pp. An appealing, oversize book full of information on witchcraft and wizardry in the late 17th century, when science and sorcery were not far apart. (Rev: BL 6/1–15/03; VOYA 8/03) [133]

26020 Scalora, Suza. *The Fairies: Photographic Evidence of the Existence of Another World* (3–5). Illus. 1999, HarperCollins $21.99 (978-0-06-028234-9). 48pp. The author spent a year investigating the phenomenon of fairies and the results, including names, sightings, location, history, and photographs, are found in this intriguing book. (Rev: BL 11/1/99; HBG 3/00; SLJ 1/00) [001.9]

26021 Simon, Seymour. *Strange Mysteries from Around the World*. Rev. ed. (4–6). Illus. 1997, Morrow $16.00 (978-0-688-14636-8). 64pp. An updating of the 1980 title that describes nine unusual events, such as strange lights that periodically appear in the sky. (Rev: BL 2/15/97; SLJ 4/97) [001.9]

26022 Slade, Arthur. *Monsterology: Fabulous Lives of the Creepy, the Revolting, and the Undead* (5–8). Illus. by Derek Mah. 2005, Tundra paper $8.95 (978-0-88776-714-2). 95pp. Dracula, Medusa, Dr. Jekyll/Mr. Hyde, and Sasquatch are among the characters profiled in this entertaining volume, each with a list of loves and hates, favorite saying, and fashion rating. (Rev: SLJ 2/06; VOYA 2/06)

26023 Spirn, Michele Sobel. *Mysterious People: A Chapter Book* (3–6). Series: True Tales. 2005, Children's Pr. LB $22.50 (978-0-516-25181-3); paper $4.95 (978-0-516-25454-8). 48pp. A compelling account of four people who met mysterious fates — Queen Nefertiti, Kaspar Hauser, Ishi, and a 5,000-year-old corpse called Otzi — and how they were discovered. (Rev: SLJ 5/06) [920]

26024 Stiekel, Bettina, ed. *The Nobel Book of Answers: The Dalai Lama, Mikhail Gorbachev, Shimon Peres, and Other Nobel Prize Winners Answer Some of Life's Most Intriguing Questions for Young People* (3–6). 2003, Simon & Schuster $14.95 (978-0-689-86310-3). 272pp. Some of life's most intriguing questions are addressed — if not answered — in this collection of writings by 22 Nobel Price winners, including Bishop Desmond Tutu, mathematician Enrico Bombieri, and geneticist Richard J. Roberts. (Rev: BL 10/15/03; HBG 4/04; SLJ 11/03)

26025 Stirling, Janet. *UFOs* (3–5). Illus. Series: Unsolved Mysteries. 2002, Rosen LB $25.25 (978-0-8239-3566-6). 48pp. An account of UFO sightings over time, from early glimpses of Army blimps to the continuing flying saucer reports. (Rev: BL 10/15/02) [001.942]

26026 Szpirglas, Jeff. *They Did What?! Your Guide to Weird and Wacky Things People Do* (3–6). Illus. by Dave Whamond. 2005, Maple Tree $16.95 (978-1-897066-22-5); paper $9.95 (978-1-897066-23-2). 64pp. A fascinating look at weird human behavior and inventions (think pet rocks, hoaxes, air-guitar competitions, and so forth). (Rev: SLJ 3/06) [031.02]

26027 Thomas, Lyn. *What? What? What? Astounding, Weird, Wonderful and Just Unbelievable Facts* (3–5). Illus. by Dianne Eastman. 2003, Maple Tree $19.95 (978-1-894379-51-9); paper (978-1-894379-52-6). 128pp. This cleverly illustrated collection of trivia is loaded with facts and figures about a little bit of everything, from animals and human anatomy to haunted houses and inventions. (Rev: BL 6/1–15/03) [031.02]

26028 Wallace, Holly. *The Mystery of Atlantis* (4–6). Series: Can Science Solve? 1999, Heinemann LB $22.79 (978-1-57572-803-2). 32pp. This account examines the efforts to prove the existence of the lost continent of Atlantis and looks at theories concerning its location and destruction. (Rev: SLJ 8/99) [001.9]

26029 Wallace, Holly. *The Mystery of the Abominable Snowman* (4–6). Series: Can Science Solve? 1999, Heinemann LB $22.79 (978-1-57572-810-0). 32pp. The possible existence of the abominable snowman is explored in this dramatic account with eye-catching illustrations. (Rev: SLJ 1/00) [001.9]

26030 Watkins, Graham. *Ghosts and Poltergeists* (3–5). Series: Unsolved Mysteries. 2002, Rosen LB $26.50 (978-0-8239-3563-5). 48pp. This book explores actual case histories of hauntings and poltergeist activity, as well as a look into the way a real ghost hunter works. (Rev: BL 10/15/02) [133.1]

26031 Watts, Claire, and Robert Nicholson. *Super Heroes* (3–6). Illus. Series: Info Adventure. 1995, Thomson Learning paper $6.00 (978-1-56847-316-1). 31pp. An introduction to many mythical and legendary heroes plus coverage on such modern marvels as Batman, James Bond, Tarzan, the Terminator, and Indiana Jones. (Rev: SLJ 12/95) [001.9]

26032 Wells, Robert E. *What's Older Than a Giant Tortoise?* (PS–3). Illus. 2004, Whitman LB $16.99 (978-0-8075-8831-4); paper $6.95 (978-0-8075-8832-1). 32pp. A giant tortoise takes young readers on a wide-ranging tour of items that are even older than he is; included are a giant sequoia tree, the pyramids of Egypt, and Mount Everest. (Rev: BL 10/15/04; SLJ 1/05) [500]

26033 Wetzel, Charles. *Haunted U.S.A* (5–8). Illus. by Josh Cochran. Series: Mysteries Unwrapped. 2008, Sterling paper $5.95 (978-1-4027-3735-0). 86pp. An eerie look at ghosts and apparitions, haunted houses, and mysteries across the United States, including on the Hollywood screen. (Rev: SLJ 6/09) [133.1]

26034 Wood, Ted. *Ghosts of the Southwest: The Phantom Gunslinger and Other Real-Life Hauntings* (4–6). Illus. 1997, Walker LB $17.85 (978-0-8027-8483-4). 48pp. A trip through Arizona, New Mexico, Texas, and Oklahoma, with stops in locales where ghosts reside. (Rev: BL 3/1/97; SLJ 4/97) [133.1]

26035 Wood, Ted. *Ghosts of the West Coast: The Lost Souls of the Queen Mary and Other Real-Life Hauntings* (3–6). Illus. 1999, Walker LB $17.85 (978-0-8027-8669-2). 48pp. A chronicle of reported sightings of ghosts in California, Oregon, and Washington with information on who saw the phantoms, and when and where. (Rev: BCCB 7–8/99; BL 4/15/99; HBG 10/99; SLJ 6/99) [133.1]

26036 Yolen, Jane, and Heidi Stemple. *Meet the Monsters* (K–2). Illus. by Patricia D. Ludlow. 1996, Walker LB $16.85 (978-0-8027-8442-1). A number of strange creatures — like zombies, vampires, mummies, and Medusa — are introduced in double-page spreads. (Rev: SLJ 11/96) [001.9]

Sports and Games

General and Miscellaneous

26037 Ajmera, Maya, and John D. Ivanko. *Come Out and Play* (PS–2). Series: It's a Kid's World. 2001, Charlesbridge LB $15.95 (978-1-57091-385-3); paper $6.95 (978-1-57091-386-0). Photographs and simple text show the differences and similarities in children's play around the world. (Rev: HBG 10/01; SLJ 8/01) [790]

26038 Ajmera, Maya, and Michael Regan. *Let the Games Begin!* (3–5). Illus. 2000, Charlesbridge LB $16.95 (978-0-88106-067-6); paper $6.95 (978-0-88106-068-3). 32pp. This book examines the philosophy of sports and sportsmanship with double-page spreads on topics such as practice, teamwork, competition, and rules. (Rev: BL 4/1/00; HBG 10/00; SLJ 5/00) [796]

26039 Alexander, Kyle. *Pro Wrestling's Most Punishing Finishing Moves* (4–7). Series: Pro Wrestling Legends. 2000, Chelsea $25.00 (978-0-7910-5833-6). 64pp. This book describes the most effective finishing moves in the sport of wrestling and fighters who use them. (Rev: BL 3/1/01; HBG 3/01) [796.8]

26040 Alexander, Kyle. *The Women of Pro Wrestling* (4–7). Illus. Series: Pro Wrestling Legends. 2000, Chelsea $25.00 (978-0-7910-5839-8); paper $25.00 (978-0-7910-5840-4). 64pp. After introducing several famous women pro wrestlers, this account describes women's roles in this sport in and out of the ring. (Rev: BL 10/15/00; HBG 3/01) [796.812]

26041 Bell-Rehwoldt, Sheri. *The Kids' Guide to Classic Games* (3–6). Series: Edge Books: Kids' Guides. 2008, Capstone LB $23.99 (978-1-4296-2273-8). 32pp. Offers clear instructions for many traditional games such as Old Maid and Red Rover. (Rev: SLJ 5/09) [790.1]

26042 Bellville, Cheryl Walsh. *Flying in a Hot Air Balloon* (3–5). Illus. 1993, Carolrhoda LB $22.60 (978-0-87614-750-4). 48pp. An introduction to hot-air ballooning past and present that uses a rally in

Minnesota as a framework. (Rev: BCCB 3/94; BL 1/1/94; SLJ 2/94) [797.5]

26043 Bellville, Cheryl Walsh. *Rodeo* (1–3). Illus. by author. 1985, Lerner paper $5.95 (978-0-87614-492-3). 32pp. A brief introduction to rodeos, highlighted with color photos. (Rev: BL 4/1/85; HB 7/85; SLJ 4/85)

26044 Birkemoe, Karen. *Strike a Pose: The Planet Girl Guide to Yoga* (5–10). Illus. by Heather Collett. Series: Planet Girl. 2007, Kids Can $12.95 (978-1-55337-004-8). 96pp. This is a practical, easy-going guide to yoga poses, breathing, meditation, and uses in sports. (Rev: SLJ 8/07) [613.7]

26045 Bizley, Kirk. *Inline Skating* (4–7). Series: Radical Sports. 1999, Heinemann LB $24.22 (978-1-57572-942-8). 32pp. As well as a history of inline skating, this book tells how to get started and gives information on equipment, techniques, terms, and safety. (Rev: SLJ 4/00) [796]

26046 Boardman, Bob. *Red Hot Peppers: The Skookum Book of Jump Rope Games, Rhymes, and Fancy Footwork* (3–6). Illus. by Diane Boardman. 1993, Sasquatch paper $8.95 (978-0-912365-74-9). 64pp. A collection of directions for jump-rope and other games, from simple to highly complex. (Rev: BL 7/93) [796.2]

26047 Bryant-Mole, Karen. *Games* (PS–3). Series: Picture This! 1997, Rigby $18.50 (978-1-57572-151-4). 24pp. Various games are introduced, with material on where they are played and the importance of healthy recreation. (Rev: BL 10/15/97) [790]

26048 Burgess, Ron. *Yo-Yo! Tips and Tricks from a Pro* (3–6). Illus. by author. 2001, Williamson paper $8.95 (978-1-885593-54-2). 64pp. Burgess shows simple and complex yo-yo techniques in easy-to-follow line drawings. (Rev: SLJ 1/02) [796.2]

26049 Caldwell, Michaela. *The Girls' Yoga Book: Stretch Your Body, Open Your Mind, and Have Fun!* (4–6). Illus. by Claudia Dávila. 2005, Maple Tree $16.95 (978-1-897066-24-9); paper $9.95 (978-1-897066-25-6). 64pp. This book emphasizes the psychological benefits of yoga in a bright and vibrant format. (Rev: SLJ 5/06) [613.7]

26050 Campbell, Guy. *The Boys' Book of Survival: How to Survive Anything, Anywhere* (4–7). Illus. by Simon Ecob. 2009, Scholastic paper $9.99 (978-0-545-08536-6). 128pp. How to deal with everything from avalanches to zombie invasions. (Rev: BLO 3/16/09) [796.54]

26051 Chalmers, Aldie. *In-Line Skating* (3–6). Illus. Series: Fantastic Book Of. 1997, Millbrook LB $22.40 (978-0-7613-0623-8). 40pp. This introduction to inline skating covers equipment, safety gear, stretching exercises, drills, techniques, and tips for beginners. (Rev: HBG 3/98; SLJ 3/98) [796.9]

26052 Chapman, Garry. *Air* (3–5). Series: Extreme Sports. 2001, Chelsea LB $28.00 (978-0-7910-6609-6). 32pp. Sky diving, bungee jumping, sky surfing, and other aerial sports are covered in this attractively illustrated volume. (Rev: BL 10/15/01; HBG 3/02) [796]

26053 Chapman, Garry. *Mountains* (3–5). Series: Extreme Sports. 2001, Chelsea LB $28.00 (978-0-7910-6610-2). 32pp. Mountain climbing, adventure racing, mountain biking, and extreme hiking are highlighted in this book that also covers weather conditions, safety precautions, and competitions. (Rev: BL 10/15/01; HBG 3/02; SLJ 12/01) [796.5]

26054 Chapman, Garry. *Rivers* (3–5). Illus. Series: Extreme Sports. 2001, Chelsea LB $28.00 (978-0-7910-6608-9). 32pp. This account looks at "extreme" water sports (such as white-water kayaking and riverboarding), with information on required gear, terminology, and stunts, accompanied by photographs. (Rev: BL 10/15/01; HBG 3/02; SLJ 12/01) [797.1]

26055 Chapman, Garry. *Snow* (3–5). Series: Extreme Sports. 2001, Chelsea LB $16.95 (978-0-7910-6606-5). 32pp. A variety of snow sports such as skiing and sledding are presented, with descriptions of unique winter environments. (Rev: BL 10/15/01) [796.95]

26056 Chapman, Garry. *Streets* (3–5). Illus. Series: Extreme Sports. 2001, Chelsea LB $28.00 (978-0-7910-6612-6). 32pp. "Extreme" sports such as BMX riding, luge racing, and inline skating that can be practiced on the street are covered here, with information on required gear, terminology, and stunts, accompanied by photographs. (Rev: BL 10/15/01; HBG 3/02) [796.2]

26057 Cole, Joanna, and Stephanie Calmenson. *The Eentsy, Weentsy Spider* (PS–1). Illus. by Alan Tiegreen. 1991, Morrow paper $8.99 (978-0-688-10805-2). 64pp. Thirty-eight rhymes that demonstrate the fun children have performing the actions. (Rev: BL 10/15/91; SLJ 10/91) [793.4]

26058 Cole, Joanna, and Stephanie Calmenson. *Fun on the Run: Travel Games and Songs* (3–6). Illus. by Alan Tiegreen. 1999, Morrow $17.00 (978-0-688-14660-3). 126pp. Good descriptions with detailed playing steps are given in this inventive book of games useful while traveling, particularly by car. (Rev: HBG 3/00; SLJ 10/99) [790]

26059 Cole, Joanna, and Stephanie Calmenson. *Pin the Tail on the Donkey and Other Party Games* (K–3). Illus. by Alan Tiegreen. 1993, Morrow LB $14.89 (978-0-688-11892-1). 48pp. A picture book with 20 simple party games. (Rev: BL 8/93) [793]

26060 Coleman, Lori. *Beginning Strength Training* (4–7). Photos by Jimmy Clarke. Series: Beginning Sports. 1998, Lerner LB $27.15 (978-0-8225-3511-9). 64pp. This abridged version of *Jeff Savage's Fundamental Strength Training* is a beginner's book on body development. (Rev: HBG 10/99; SLJ 2/99) [796]

26061 Connolly, Helen. *Field Hockey: Rules, Tips, Strategy, and Safety* (4–8). Series: Sports from Coast to Coast. 2005, Rosen LB $26.50 (978-1-4042-0182-8). 48pp. This title puts the spotlight on field hockey, including a brief history of the sport as well as a look at its rules, equipment, training, and so forth. (Rev: SLJ 10/05)

26062 Corbett, Doris, and John Cheffers, eds. *Unique Games and Sports Around the World: A Reference Guide* (4–9). Illus. 2001, Greenwood $85.00 (978-0-313-29778-6). 407pp. More than 300 games and sports are organized by continent and then by country, with details of the number of players, equipment, rules, and so forth, and indications of whether this is a suitable game for the classroom or playground. (Rev: SLJ 8/01) [790.1]

26063 Crossingham, John. *Cheerleading in Action* (4–7). Series: Sports in Action. 2003, Crabtree LB $25.27 (978-0-7787-0333-4); paper $6.95 (978-0-7787-0353-2). 32pp. This is a colorful, attractive introduction to cheerleading, the cheers, costumes, duties, and its importance in sports. (Rev: BL 11/15/03) [791]

26064 Crossingham, John. *In-Line Skating in Action* (4–7). Series: Sports in Action. 2002, Crabtree LB $25.27 (978-0-7787-0328-0); paper $6.95 (978-0-7737-0348-3). 32pp. A fine introduction to this fast-growing sport with easy-to-follow descriptions of moves and techniques. (Rev: BL 1/1–15/03; SLJ 10/03) [796.9]

26065 Crossingham, John. *Lacrosse in Action* (4–7). Series: Sports in Action. 2002, Crabtree LB $25.27 (978-0-7787-0329-7); paper $6.95 (978-0-7737-0349-0). 32pp. A clear, concise introduction to lacrosse that discusses techniques, equipment, rules, and safety precautions. (Rev: BL 1/1–15/03) [796.34]

26066 Crossingham, John. *Spike It Volleyball* (2–4). Illus. Series: Sports Starters. 2008, Crabtree LB $18.95 (978-0-7787-3143-6). 32pp. This introduction to volleyball explains scoring, tactics, basic moves, and other important factors in a well-designed easy-to-read format. (Rev: BL 9/1/08) [796.325]

26067 Crossingham, John. *Wrestling in Action* (4–7). Series: Sports in Action. 2003, Crabtree LB $25.27 (978-0-7787-0336-5); paper $6.95 (978-0-7787-0356-3). 32pp. This introduction to wrestling describes basic moves, skills, and rules. (Rev: BL 11/15/03) [796.8]

26068 Crossingham, John, and Sarah Dann. *Volleyball in Action* (4–6). Series: Sports in Action. 1999, Crabtree LB $25.27 (978-0-7787-0164-4); paper $6.95 (978-0-7787-0176-7). 32pp. This well-organized account introduces volleyball and supplies information on techniques, equipment, rules, and safety considerations. (Rev: SLJ 6/00) [796.32]

26069 Crossingham, John, and Bobbie Kalman. *Skiing in Action* (3–5). Illus. Series: Sports in Action. 2004, Crabtree LB $25.27 (978-0-7787-0337-2); paper $6.95 (978-0-7787-0357-0). 32pp. For beginning skiers, this is an attractive and useful introduction to equipment, technique, and vocabulary. (Rev: BL 4/1/04; SLJ 6/05) [796.93]

26070 Ditchfield, Christin. *Wrestling* (2–4). Illus. Series: True Books. 2000, Children's Book Pr. LB $25.00 (978-0-516-21611-9). 48pp. This simple introduction to wrestling contains material on its history and how it is played and judged. (Rev: BL 9/15/00) [796.8]

26071 Donkin, Andrew. *Danger on the Mountain: Scaling the World's Highest Peaks* (2–4). Illus. Series: Dorling Kindersley Readers. 2001, DK $14.99 (978-0-7894-7386-8); paper $3.99 (978-0-7894-7385-1). 48pp. Donkin presents details of some famous expeditions as well as discussing the hazards involved and the way climbing equipment has changed over the years. (Rev: HBG 10/01; SLJ 11/01) [796.52]

26072 Drake, Jane, and Ann Love. *The Kids Summer Games Book* (3–6). Illus. 1998, Kids Can paper $10.95 (978-1-55074-465-1). 176pp. This book includes a section on teams as well as ideas and rules for summer games, in and out of the water. (Rev: BL 5/15/98; SLJ 5/98) [796]

26073 Eckart, Edana. *I Can Bowl* (K–2). Series: Sports. 2002, Children's Book Pr. paper $4.95 (978-0-516-24028-2). 24pp. This slim volume for beginning readers shows Emma bowling with her father and discusses equipment and safety. Also use *I Can Swim*, *I Can Play Soccer*, and *I Can Ride a Bike* (all 2002). (Rev: SLJ 9/02) [794.6]

26074 Edwardes, Dan. *Parkour* (4–7). Illus. 2009, Crabtree LB $19.95 (978-0-7787-3821-3); paper $8.95 (978-0-7787-3842-8). 32pp. A fascinating look at the athletes who use urban environments as their gyms. (Rev: BL 6/1–15/09) [796.04]

26075 Egan, Tracie. *Water Polo: Rules, Tips, Strategy, and Safety* (4–8). Series: Sports from Coast to Coast. 2005, Rosen LB $26.50 (978-1-4042-0186-6). 48pp. Introduces readers to the sport of water polo, along with its rules, training, and equipment. (Rev: SLJ 10/05)

26076 Erlbach, Arlene. *Sidewalk Games Around the World* (3–5). Illus. 1997, Millbrook LB $24.90 (978-0-7613-0008-3). 64pp. Informal sidewalk games from 26 countries are introduced, with material on the country and the games and their rules. (Rev: BL 5/1/97; SLJ 5/97) [796.1]

26077 Fine, John C. *Free Spirits in the Sky* (3–5). Illus. 1994, Atheneum $14.95 (978-0-689-31705-7). 32pp. With color photos on each page, this book gives a history of ballooning, tells how balloons fly, and explains the different types. (Rev: BL 1/15/94; SLJ 3/94) [797.5]

26078 Gay, Kathlyn. *They Don't Wash Their Socks! Sports Superstitions* (3–5). Illus. by John Kerschbaum. 1990, Walker LB $14.85 (978-0-8027-6917-6). 114pp. Superstitions from many sports are highlighted. (Rev: SLJ 6/90) [796]

26079 Gedatus, Gus. *In-Line Skating for Fitness* (4–7). Series: Nutrition and Fitness. 2001, Capstone LB $25.26 (978-0-7368-0707-4). 64pp. Inline skating is introduced with an emphasis on fitness benefits and the necessity of a healthy diet. (Rev: BL 9/15/01; HBG 10/01) [796]

26080 Giddens, Sandra, and Owen Giddens. *Volleyball: Rules, Tips, Strategy, and Safety* (4–8). Series: Sports from Coast to Coast. 2005, Rosen LB $26.50 (978-1-4042-0185-9). 48pp. Introduces the sport of volleyball — including its rules, equipment, and strategies. (Rev: SLJ 10/05) [796.32]

26081 Gordon, John. *The Kids Book of Golf* (3–6). Illus. 2001, Kids Can $14.95 (978-1-55337-017-8); paper $7.95 (978-1-55074-617-4). 48pp. History, equipment, technique, rules, competitions, and humorous anecdotes are all included here, along with diagrams and full-color photographs showing children and famous golfers. (Rev: HBG 10/01; SLJ 7/01) [796.352]

26082 Griffin, Margot. *The Sleepover Book* (2–7). Illus. by Jane Kurisu. 2001, Kids Can paper $14.95 (978-1-55074-522-1). 144pp. These sleepover activities range from making a music video, cooking midnight snacks, treasure hunts, games and crafts, and, of course, telling scary stories. (Rev: SLJ 6/01) [793.21]

26083 Gryski, Camilla. *Cat's Cradle, Owl's Eyes: A Book of String Games* (4–7). Illus. by Tom Sankey. 1984, Morrow LB $15.93 (978-0-688-03940-0); paper $6.95 (978-0-688-03941-7). 80pp. Explanations of 21 string figures, plus variations. [793.9]

26084 Gryski, Camilla. *Let's Play: Traditional Games of Childhood* (K–3). Illus. by Dusan Petricic. 1998, Kids Can $14.95 (978-1-55074-497-2). 47pp. A few of the games and activities that are described in this helpful manual are jacks, marbles, hopscotch, clapping games, and jump-rope rhymes. (Rev: HBG 10/98; SLJ 5/98) [790]

26085 Gryski, Camilla. *Many Stars and More String Games* (4–8). Illus. by Tom Sankey. 1985, Morrow paper $7.95 (978-0-688-05792-3). 80pp. Figures taken from a range of cultures to be mastered by agile fingers. (Rev: BL 12/15/85; SLJ 1/86) [793.9]

26086 Gryski, Camilla. *Super String Games* (4–6). Illus. by Tom Sankey. 1988, Morrow paper $6.95 (978-0-688-07684-9). 80pp. Advanced string games with harder-to-learn patterns. (Rev: BL 3/1/88; SLJ 8/88)

26087 Hall, Godfrey. *Games* (5–7). Illus. Series: Traditions Around the World. 1995, Thomson Learning LB $24.26 (978-1-56847-345-1). 48pp. An oversize book that covers, in text and large color pictures, various games played in different regions around the world. (Rev: BL 6/1–15/95; SLJ 9/95) [790.1]

26088 Hayhurst, Chris. *Wakeboarding! Throw a Tantrum* (4–8). Series: Extreme Sports. 2000, Rosen LB $26.50 (978-0-8239-3008-1). 64pp. This new water sport is described with material on the equipment needed and the necessary safety precautions. (Rev: BL 6/1–15/00; SLJ 8/00) [797.1]

26089 Herzog, Brad. *P Is for Putt* (3–6). Illus. by Bruce Langton. 2005, Sleeping Bear $16.95 (978-1-58536-252-3). 40pp. An alphabetical format is used to introduce various facts about the game of golf. (Rev: BL 5/1/05) [796.352]

26090 Hort, Lenny. *Treasure Hunts! Treasure Hunts! Treasure and Scavenger Hunts to Play with Friends and Family* (3–6). 2000, HarperCollins $15.95 (978-0-688-17245-9); paper $7.95 (978-0-688-17177-3). 80pp. This book supplies information for all sorts of treasure-hunting games with material on number of players, and where, when, and how to play. (Rev: BL 6/1–15/00; HBG 10/00; SLJ 11/00) [796.1]

26091 Howes, Chris. *Caving* (4–8). Series: Radical Sports. 2003, Heinemann LB $25.64 (978-1-58810-626-1). 32pp. Technique, safety, gear, and other vital aspects are covered in this introduction to the sport. (Rev: BL 2/15/03; HBG 3/03) [796.52]

26092 Hoyt-Goldsmith, Diane. *Lacrosse: The National Game of the Iroquois* (3–6). Illus. 1998, Holiday House $16.95 (978-0-8234-1360-7). 32pp. After an introduction to the Iroquois Confederacy, this book traces the history of lacrosse and its past and present roles in the life of the Iroquois. (Rev: BL 6/1–15/98; HBG 10/98; SLJ 6/98) [796.3]

26093 Hu, Evaleen. *A Big Ticket: Sports and Commercialism* (4–7). Illus. 1998, Lerner LB $28.75 (978-0-8225-3305-4). 96pp. This well-organized book explains the connections between sports and the media, including broadcast rights, endorsement contracts, pop culture, and the impact of television. (Rev: BL 7/98; HBG 10/98) [338.4]

26094 Hull, Mary. *The Composite Guide to Golf* (5–7). Series: Composite Guide. 1998, Chelsea LB $18.65 (978-0-7910-4726-2). 64pp. An introduction to the game of golf and its history, along with highlights of the game's pioneers and current stars including Tiger Woods. (Rev: HBG 10/98; SLJ 9/98) [796.352]

26095 Hunter, Matt. *Pro Wrestling's Greatest Tag Teams* (4–7). Series: Pro Wrestling Legends. 2000, Chelsea $25.00 (978-0-7910-5835-0). 64pp. This title covers such tag teams as the Road Warriors, the Midnight Express, the Nasty Boys, Public Enemy, and Harlem Heat. (Rev: BL 10/15/00; HBG 3/01) [796.8]

26096 Hunter, Matt. *Ric Flair: The Story of the Wrestler They Call "The Natural Boy"* (4–7). Series: Pro Wrestling Legends. 2000, Chelsea $25.00 (978-0-7910-5825-1). 64pp. The story of the wrestler who has been at the top of his sport for most of the last three decades. (Rev: BL 10/15/00; HBG 3/01) [796.8]

26097 Jaffe, Elizabeth Dana. *Dominoes* (1–4). Illus. Series: Games Around the World. 2001, Compass Point LB $22.60 (978-0-7565-0132-7). 32pp. Varia-

tions of dominoes games are presented with instructions and diagrams, along with a section on using them to create a domino effect. (Rev: SLJ 10/01) [795.3]

26098 Jaffe, Elizabeth Dana. *Juggling* (3–5). Series: Games Around the World. 2002, Compass Point LB $22.60 (978-0-7565-0191-4). 32pp. This work contains a history of juggling and describes equipment and basic techniques, using colorful illustrations. (Rev: BL 5/15/02; SLJ 7/02) [793.8]

26099 Jenkins, Steve. *The Top of the World: Climbing Mount Everest* (2–6). Illus. by author. 1999, Houghton $16.00 (978-0-395-94218-5). After a history of climbing on Mount Everest, the author discusses necessary equipment, climbing routes, dangers, and the physical effects on climbers. (Rev: BCCB 4/99; HBG 10/99; SLJ 5/99) [796.5]

26100 Johnson, Neil. *Fire and Silk: Flying in a Hot Air Balloon* (K–3). Illus. 1991, Little, Brown $15.95 (978-0-316-46959-3). 32pp. The facts and feel of ballooning in a nonfiction book that reads like an adventure story. (Rev: BCCB 4/91; BL 5/1/91; HB 7/91; SLJ 7/91) [797.5]

26101 Jones, Jen. *Cheer Tryouts: Making the Cut* (3–7). Illus. Series: Snap Books Cheerleading. 2005, Capstone LB $25.26 (978-0-7368-4361-4). 32pp. The focus here is on preparation — from good nutrition and regular stretching to practicing drills and a good attitude; part of a series that also includes *Cheer Squad: Building Spirit and Getting Along* (2005). (Rev: SLJ 1/06) [791.6]

26102 Kalman, Bobbie. *Extreme Wakeboarding* (3–10). Illus. Series: Extreme Sports: No Limits! 2006, Crabtree LB $25.27 (978-0-7787-1680-8); paper $6.95 (978-0-7787-1726-3). 32pp. The history wakeboarding is covered here, as well as the fundamental techniques, equipment, and safety considerations. (Rev: SLJ 2/07) [797.3]

26103 Kalman, Bobbie, and John Crossingham. *Extreme Climbing* (4–8). Series: Extreme Sports No Limits! 2004, Crabtree LB $25.27 (978-0-7787-1671-6). 32pp. Explores the full spectrum of climbing sports, looking at the specific challenges of each and offering readers valuable advice about equipment, climbing techniques, locations, and difficulty ratings, as well as profiles of notable climbers. (Rev: BL 9/1/04)

26104 Kalman, Bobbie, and John Crossingham. *Extreme Skydiving* (3–10). Illus. Series: Extreme Sports: No Limits! 2006, Crabtree LB $25.27 (978-0-7787-1684-6); paper $6.95 (978-0-7787-1730-0). 32pp. This colorful introduction to skydiving chronicles the sport's long history, which can be traced back to the late 18th century, and describes its different disciplines and required equipment. (Rev: SLJ 2/07)

26105 Kalman, Bobbie, and John Crossingham. *Extreme Sports* (4–8). Series: Extreme Sports No Limits! 2004, Crabtree LB $25.27 (978-0-7787-1673-0). 32pp. All manner of extreme sports are covered in this overview. (Rev: BL 9/1/04)

26106 Kalman, Bobbie, and Sarah Dann. *Bowling in Action* (4–7). Series: Sports in Action. 2003, Crabtree LB $25.27 (978-0-7787-0335-8); paper $6.95 (978-0-7787-0355-6). 32pp. This well-illustrated introduction to bowling includes material on equipment, techniques, rules, and bowling alleys. (Rev: BL 11/15/03) [794.6]

26107 Kaminker, Laura. *In-Line Skating! Get Aggressive* (5–8). Series: Extreme Sports. 1999, Rosen LB $26.50 (978-0-8239-3012-8). 64pp. This book provides information for both beginning and advanced inline skaters and covers topics including equipment, history, techniques, and safety tips. (Rev: SLJ 4/00) [796]

26108 Kent, Deborah. *Athletes with Disabilities* (5–7). Illus. Series: Watts Library: Disabilities. 2003, Watts LB $25.50 (978-0-531-12019-4). 64pp. Achievements of disabled athletes are accompanied by the history of such events as the Special Olympics and by information on new games, equipment, and techniques that widen horizons. (Rev: BL 10/15/03; SLJ 9/03) [371.9]

26109 Klein, Adam G. *Hunting* (2–4). Illus. Series: Checkerboard Adventure Library: Outdoor Adventure! 2008, ABDO LB $16.95 (978-1-59928-960-1). 32pp. A general overview of hunting's history, the reasons why people hunt, equipment, and so forth. (Rev: BL 4/1/08) [799.2]

26110 Klingel, Cynthia, and Robert B. Noyed. *Yo-Yo Tricks* (3–5). Series: Games Around the World. 2002, Compass Point LB $22.60 (978-0-7565-0193-8). 32pp. The development of the yo-yo is covered in this volume, along with colorful illustrations and diagrams that describe techniques and moves. (Rev: BL 5/15/02; SLJ 7/02) [796]

26111 Kramer, S. A. *To the Top! Climbing the World's Highest Mountain* (2–4). Illus. by Thomas La Padula. 1993, Random paper $3.99 (978-0-679-83885-2). 47pp. An account of how Edmund Hillary and Tenzing Norgay conquered Mount Everest in 1953. (Rev: BCCB 6/93; SLJ 8/93) [796.5]

26112 Krause, Peter. *Fundamental Golf* (5–8). Photos by Andy King. Series: Fundamental Sports. 1995, Lerner LB $27.15 (978-0-8225-3454-9). 64pp. A clear introduction to golf that covers history, equipment, swings, rules, and courses. (Rev: SLJ 9/95) [796.352]

26113 Lehn, Barbara. *What Is an Athlete?* (PS–2). Illus. by Carol Krauss. 2002, Millbrook LB $21.90 (978-0-7613-2258-0). 32pp. An introduction of the concept of "athlete," presented in a friendly format for younger readers. (Rev: BL 12/15/02; HBG 3/03) [796]

26114 Lewin, Ted. *At Gleason's Gym* (4–7). Illus. by author. 2007, Roaring Brook $17.95 (978-1-59643-231-4). 40pp. The history of the famous Gleason's Gym (where Muhammad Ali and Jake La Motta trained) is told as readers follow the progress of 9-year-old Sugar Boy Younan, already showing great promise as a boxer. (Rev: BL 9/1/07*; SLJ 10/07) [796.83]

26115 Lindeen, Carol K. *Let's Downhill Ski!* (PS–1). Series: Sports and Activities. 2006, Capstone LB $21.26 (978-0-7368-6359-9). 24pp. A large-format, simply written introduction that covers basic tech-

niques, equipment, and safety and includes color photographs. (Rev: SLJ 2/07) [796.9]

26116 Lourie, Peter. *First Dive to Shark Dive* (5–8). Illus. 2006, Boyds Mills $17.95 (978-1-59078-068-8). 48pp. This attractive, interesting photoessay documents a 12-year-old girl's introduction to scuba diving among sharks. (Rev: BL 2/15/06; SLJ 6/06) [797.2]

26117 Lowe, Ayana, ed. *Come and Play: Children of Our World Having Fun* (K–3). Illus. 2008, Bloomsbury $16.95 (978-1-59990-245-6). 64pp. Full-page photographs of children playing in diverse settings around the world are accompanied by simple verses by New York City children. (Rev: BL 7/08; SLJ 8/08) [808.81]

26118 MacAulay, Kelley, and Bobbie Kalman. *Extreme Skiing* (3–9). Illus. Series: Extreme Sports: No Limits! 2006, Crabtree LB $25.27 (978-0-7787-1682-2); paper $6.95 (978-0-7787-1728-7). 32pp. This slim, well-illustrated volume looks at freestyle skiing, offering a brief history of the sport and touching on such topics as skiing styles, equipment, and competition rules. (Rev: SLJ 2/07) [797.937]

26119 Manley, Claudia B. *Competitive Volleyball for Girls* (4–7). Illus. Series: Sportsgirl. 2001, Rosen LB $26.50 (978-0-8239-3404-1). 64pp. An introduction to the rules of volleyball, the training necessary, and the special opportunities for girls, with material on nutrition and the dangers of overtraining. (Rev: SLJ 3/02) [796.325]

26120 Mason, Paul. *Skiing* (4–8). Illus. 2003, Heinemann LB $25.64 (978-1-58810-628-5). 32pp. Technique, safety, gear, and profiles of famous skiers are all covered in this introduction to the sport. (Rev: BL 2/15/03; HBG 3/03) [796.93]

26121 Mayo, Terry. *The Illustrated Rules of In-line Hockey* (3–5). Illus. by Ned Butterfield. Series: Illustrated Sports. 1996, Ideals paper $6.95 (978-1-57102-064-2). 32pp. An introduction to inline hockey, with a history of the sport, an explanation of the rules, a look at different positions and signals, and discussion of sportsmanship. (Rev: SLJ 8/96) [796.2]

26122 Miller, Thomas. *Taking Time Out: Recreation and Play* (5–8). Illus. Series: Our Human Family. 1995, Blackbirch LB $27.45 (978-1-56711-128-6). 80pp. Divided into five broad geographic areas, this account describes how people enjoy themselves at play in various cultures. (Rev: SLJ 1/96) [794]

26123 Mott, Evelyn Clarke. *Balloon Ride* (K–3). Illus. 1991, Walker LB $14.85 (978-0-8027-8126-0). Megan takes her first trip in a hot-air balloon in this nonfiction account with photos by the author. (Rev: SLJ 10/91) [797.5]

26124 Nicholson, Lois. *The Composite Guide to Lacrosse* (4–8). Series: The Composite Guide. 1998, Chelsea LB $18.65 (978-0-7910-4719-4). 64pp. A fine guide to lacrosse, giving its history, how it is played today, and portraits of the game's greatest players. (Rev: HBG 3/99; SLJ 12/98) [796.34]

26125 Orozco, Jose-Luis. *Diez Deditos and Other Play Rhymes and Action Songs from Latin America*

(PS–1). Illus. by Elisa Kleven. 1997, Dutton $19.99 (978-0-525-45736-7). 48pp. Thirty-four finger rhymes and songs in English and the original Spanish are included in this attractive collection. (Rev: BCCB 3/98; BL 1/1–15/98; HB 3/98; HBG 3/98) [782.42]

26126 Oxlade, Chris. *Rock Climbing* (4–8). Illus. Series: Extreme Sports. 2003, Lerner LB $22.60 (978-0-8225-1240-0). 32pp. An appealing introduction to the history, equipment, techniques, safety concerns, and challenges of this sport. (Rev: BL 3/1/04; SLJ 5/04) [790.52]

26127 Paros, Lawrence, and Ben Joshua Paros. *Smash Caps: The Official Milkcap Fun Book* (3–6). Illus. by Kuo W. Yang. 1995, Avon paper $7.99 (978-0-380-78459-2). 55pp. An introduction to POGS, a game originally from Hawaii, which is played with caps from different bottles. (Rev: SLJ 1/96) [796]

26128 Payan, Gregory. *Essential Snowmobiling for Teens* (5–9). Series: Outdoor Life. 2000, Children's paper $6.95 (978-0-516-23558-5). 48pp. The invention of the snowmobile is covered plus material on license requirements, trail permits, equipment, clothing, safety, driving techniques, and maintenance. (Rev: SLJ 2/01) [796.94]

26129 Peters, Craig. *Chants, Cheers, and Jumps* (5–8). Illus. Series: Let's Go Team. 2003, Mason Crest $19.95 (978-1-59084-535-6). 64pp. Readers will learn the difference between cheers and chants and how to do various jumps. Also use *Competitive Cheerleading* (2003). (Rev: BL 10/15/03; SLJ 9/03) [791.6]

26130 Peters, Craig. *Cheerleading Stars* (5–8). Series: Let's Go Team. 2003, Mason Crest LB $19.95 (978-1-59084-533-2). 64pp. This book highlights the careers and accomplishments of a select group of star cheerleaders. (Rev: BL 10/15/03; HBG 4/04) [791]

26131 Peters, Craig. *Techniques of Dance for Cheerleading* (5–8). Series: Let's Go Team. 2003, Mason Crest LB $19.95 (978-1-59084-531-8). 64pp. The importance of stretching and safety measures are emphasized in this volume that discusses choreography and the similarities and differences between cheerleading and dancing. (Rev: SLJ 9/03) [791.6]

26132 Ripoll, Oriol. *Play with Us: 100 Games from Around the World* (3–5). Illus. 2005, Chicago Review paper $16.95 (978-1-55652-594-0). 128pp. Ball games, card games, checkers, hopscotch — these are only a few of the 100 games, both indoor and outdoor, included in this international collection that is indexed by continent. (Rev: BL 11/15/05; SLJ 1/06) [793]

26133 Roberts, Jeremy. *Rock and Ice Climbing! Top the Tower* (4–8). Illus. Series: Extreme Sports. 2000, Rosen LB $26.50 (978-0-8239-3009-8). 64pp. This book on climbing covers the dangers, different climbing styles, equipment, techniques, and venues, and profiles some young climbers. (Rev: BL 3/15/00; SLJ 8/00) [796.52]

26134 Roberts, Robin. *Sports for Life: How Athletes Have More Fun* (5–8). Illus. Series: Get in the Game! 2000, Millbrook LB $23.90 (978-0-7613-1407-3). 48pp. This account, mainly for girls, explains how to enjoy sports through applying discipline, patience, cooperation, health, and the sheer fun of competition. (Rev: BL 1/1–15/01; HBG 3/01) [796]

26135 Roberts, Robin. *Which Sport Is Right for You?* (5–8). Series: Get in the Game! 2001, Millbrook LB $23.90 (978-0-7613-2117-0). 48pp. Written with girls in mind, this short book explores how to choose a sport that is right for one's capabilities and interests. (Rev: BL 9/15/01; HBG 3/02; SLJ 1/02) [796]

26136 Roper, Ingrid. *Yo-Yos: Tricks to Amaze Your Friends* (3–6). 2001, HarperCollins $15.95 (978-0-688-14663-4). 64pp. A guide to different kinds of yo-yos and yo-yo technique that starts with the basic and progresses to the more advanced. (Rev: BL 5/15/01; HBG 10/01; SLJ 8/01) [796.2]

26137 Rosen, Michael J. *Balls!* (4–7). 2006, Darby Creek $18.95 (978-1-58196-030-3). 72pp. Balls used in all sorts of sports and their history, choice of shape, and method of construction are the topic of lighthearted discussion. (Rev: BL 6/1–15/06) [796.3]

26138 Ross, Dan. *Pro Wrestling's Greatest Wars* (4–7). Illus. Series: Pro Wrestling Legends. 2000, Chelsea $25.00 (978-0-7910-5837-4); paper $25.00 (978-0-7910-5838-1). 64pp. Some of the great feuds in wrestling history, such as Harlem Heat vs. the Nasty Boys, are described in this fast read. (Rev: BL 10/15/00; HBG 3/01) [796.812]

26139 Rowe, Julian. *Recreation* (4–7). Illus. Series: Science Encounters. 1997, Rigby paper $25.55 (978-1-57572-092-0). 32pp. Shows how science is used in theme park rides, backpacking and camping equipment, computer games, television, scuba diving, and hang gliding. (Rev: SLJ 10/97) [796]

26140 Rowe, Julian. *Sports* (4–7). Illus. Series: Science Encounters. 1997, Rigby paper $25.55 (978-1-57572-089-0). 32pp. Shows how science is used in such sports-related topics as the design of equipment, protective clothing, and sports medicine. (Rev: SLJ 10/97) [796]

26141 Ryan, Pat. *Rock Climbing* (4–7). Illus. Series: World of Sports. 2000, Smart Apple LB $16.95 (978-1-887068-57-4). 32pp. In addition to covering the origins and evolution of rock climbing, this book discusses the basics of the sport, equipment, and star athletes. (Rev: BL 9/15/00) [796.52]

26142 Schindler, John E. *Hang Gliding and Parasailing* (2–5). Series: Extreme Sports: An Imagination Library Series. 2005, Gareth Stevens LB $23.00 (978-0-8368-4540-2); paper $5.95 (978-0-8368-4547-1). 24pp. An introduction to this "extreme" sport, with brief text and colorful photographs suitable for reluctant readers. (Rev: SLJ 9/05) [797.5]

26143 Schindler, John E. *Skydiving* (2–5). 2005, Gareth Stevens LB $23.00 (978-0-8368-4543-3); paper $5.95 (978-0-8368-4550-1). 24pp. A basic introduction to this "extreme" sport, with brief text and colorful photographs that will appeal to reluctant readers. (Rev: SLJ 9/05) [797.5]

26144 Schindler, John E. *Triathlons* (2–5). 2005, Gareth Stevens LB $23.00 (978-0-8368-4544-0); paper $5.95 (978-0-8368-4551-8). 24pp. A basic introduction to this "extreme" sport, with brief text and colorful photographs that will appeal to reluctant readers. (Rev: SLJ 9/05) [796.42]

26145 Schwartz, Ellen. *I Love Yoga: A Guide for Kids and Teens* (5–12). Illus. by Ben Hodson. 2003, Tundra paper $9.95 (978-0-88776-598-8). 122pp. Illustrated instructions for 18 basic poses are accompanied by breathing and relaxation exercises, discussion of the benefits of yoga, and a description of the different types of yoga practiced around the world. (Rev: SLJ 12/03; VOYA 10/03) [613.7]

26146 Seeberg, Tim. *Rock Climbing* (3–5). Illus. Series: Kids' Guides to the Outdoors. 2004, Child's World LB $25.64 (978-1-59296-033-0). 32pp. A useful guide for young people new to this sport, this book is loaded with tips about equipment and what to expect. [796.5]

26147 Shahan, Sherry. *Dashing Through the Snow: The Story of the Jr. Iditarod* (4–7). Illus. 1997, Millbrook $24.90 (978-0-7613-0208-7); paper $9.95 (978-0-7613-0143-1). 48pp. All aspects of the 150-mile Junior Iditarod are touched upon in this account, including how these young mushers communicate with their dogs. (Rev: BL 3/1/97; SLJ 4/97) [798]

26148 Sheely, Robert, and Louis Bourgeois. *Sports Lab: How Science Has Changed Sports* (4–7). Illus. Series: Science Lab. 1994, Silver Moon $14.95 (978-1-881889-49-6). 60pp. Traces the effect on sports of applying findings from such branches of science as aerodynamics, psychology, and medicine. (Rev: SLJ 9/94) [617.1]

26149 Sherman, Josepha. *Barrel Racing* (4–6). Series: Rodeo. 2000, Heinemann LB $21.36 (978-1-57572-503-1). 32pp. Barrel racing training, skills, equipment, and schedules are covered here. Three other titles on rodeo events are *Bronc Riding*, *Bull Riding* and *Steer Wrestling* (all 2000). (Rev: BL 10/15/00; HBG 3/01; SLJ 8/00) [791.8]

26150 Sherman, Josepha. *Ropers and Riders* (4–6). Series: Rodeo. 2000, Heinemann LB $21.36 (978-1-57572-506-2). 32pp. A colorful book that features these stars of the rodeo, their skills, training, and lifestyles. (Rev: BL 10/15/00; HBG 3/01; SLJ 9/00) [791.8]

26151 Sherman, Josepha. *Welcome to the Rodeo!* (4–6). Illus. Series: Rodeo. 2000, Heinemann $21.36 (978-1-57572-508-6). 32pp. An introduction to rodeos with material on the various riding and roping competitions and on famous rodeo stars. (Rev: BL 10/15/00; HBG 3/01; SLJ 9/00) [791.8]

26152 Silas, Elizabeth, and Diane Goodney. *Yoga* (4–8). Illus. Series: Life Balance. 2003, Watts LB $20.50 (978-0-531-12258-7); paper $6.95 (978-0-531-15577-6). 80pp. Information on the spiritual and philosophical aspects of yoga follows chapters on basic yoga moves. (Rev: BL 10/15/03) [613.7]

26153 Skreslet, Laurie, and Elizabeth MacLeod. *To the Top of Everest* (5–9). Illus. 2001, Kids Can $16.95 (978-1-55074-721-8). 56pp. Skreslet relates his lifelong ambition to climb Everest and his actual experiences doing so, with many facts about the mountain and the dangers involved and stunning photographs of his adventure. (Rev: BCCB 10/01; BL 9/15/01; HBG 3/02; SLJ 9/01*) [796.52]

26154 Smith, Graham. *Karting* (4–8). Series: Radical Sports. 2002, Heinemann LB $25.64 (978-1-58810-624-7). 32pp. The sport of karting is introduced with discussion of equipment selection, basic skills, fitness and training, and safety. (Rev: BL 2/15/03; HBG 3/03) [796.7]

26155 Steiner, Andy. *Girl Power on the Playing Field: A Book About Girls, Their Goals, and Their Struggles* (5–10). Series: Girl Power. 2000, Lerner LB $30.35 (978-0-8225-2690-2). 96pp. This book explains women's roles in sports with good personal guidance for young girls on participation and goals. (Rev: HBG 10/00; SLJ 6/00) [796]

26156 Steiner, Andy. *A Sporting Chance: Sports and Gender* (4–8). Series: Sports Issues. 1995, Lerner LB $28.75 (978-0-8225-3300-9). An overview of the hurdles that female athletes have had to overcome and the persistent inequality between men and women in sports at all levels, from Little League to the pros. (Rev: BL 1/1–15/96; SLJ 1/96) [796]

26157 Sullivan, George. *Any Number Can Play: The Numbers Athletes Wear* (4–8). Illus. 2000, Millbrook LB $23.90 (978-0-7613-1557-5). 80pp. A fascinating glimpse at players' devotion to their assigned numbers, along with information on retired and banned numbers and who uses the number 13. (Rev: BL 12/15/00; HBG 3/01; SLJ 2/01; VOYA 2/01) [796]

26158 Sullivan, George. *Don't Step on the Foul Line: Sports Superstitions* (4–8). Illus. 2000, Millbrook LB $23.90 (978-0-7613-1558-2). 80pp. This is an intriguing look at superstitions, customs, and traditions associated with many different sports. (Rev: BL 12/15/00; HBG 3/01; SLJ 2/01; VOYA 2/01) [796.357]

26159 Szwast, Ursula. *Cheerleading* (3–6). Series: Get Going! Hobbies. 2005, Heinemann LB $27.79 (978-1-4034-6116-2). 32pp. This guide reviews basic moves and positions and discusses both competitive cheerleading and the history of cheerleading. (Rev: SLJ 3/06) [791.6]

26160 Takeda, Pete. *Climb! Your Guide to Bouldering, Sport Climbing, Trad Climbing, Ice Climbing, Alpinism, and More* (4–9). Illus. Series: Extreme Sports. 2002, National Geographic paper $8.95 (978-0-7922-6744-7). 64pp. An attractive guide to climbing of all types — sport, wall, ice, alpine, and so forth — and to the equipment, techniques, and dangers. (Rev: SLJ 1/03) [796.5223]

26161 Tate, Nikki. *Behind the Scenes: The Racehorse* (5–8). Illus. 2008, Fitzhenry & Whiteside $22.95 (978-1-55455-018-0); paper $12.95 (978-1-55455-032-6). 72pp. Readers get an inside look at horse racing — breeding, training, jockeys and grooms, and so forth — and learn about both the glamor and the sometimes dangerous and harsh realities. (Rev: BL 2/1/08; SLJ 2/08) [798]

26162 Valliant, Doris. *Going to College* (5–8). Series: Let's Go Team. 2003, Mason Crest LB $19.95 (978-1-59084-541-7). 64pp. This well-illustrated, breezy account describes the function of cheerleading in college sports activities. (Rev: BL 10/15/03; SLJ 1/04) [791]

26163 Valliant, Doris. *The History of Cheerleading* (5–8). Series: Let's Go Team. 2003, Mason Crest LB $19.95 (978-1-59084-534-9). 64pp. Using many illustrations, this slim volume describes the history and function of cheerleading at various levels in this country. (Rev: BL 10/15/03; HBG 4/04; SLJ 1/04) [791]

26164 Wells, Don. *For the Love of Golf* (3–5). Illus. Series: For the Love of Sports. 2005, Weigl LB $24.45 (978-1-59036-296-9). 24pp. Colorful double-page spreads present the fundamentals of golf, as well as the history of the game and information on famous players. (Rev: BL 9/1/05) [796.352]

26165 Willard, Keith. *Ballooning* (4–7). Illus. Series: World of Sports. 2000, Smart Apple LB $16.95 (978-1-887068-51-2). 32pp. This brief introduction to ballooning mentions star balloonists, different kinds of ballooning, the origins of this sport, and how one becomes proficient at it. (Rev: BL 9/15/00) [797.5]

26166 Willker, Joshua D. G. *Everything You Need to Know About the Dangers of Sports Gambling* (5–10). Illus. Series: Need to Know Library. 2000, Rosen LB $27.95 (978-0-8239-3229-0). 64pp. This brief, well-written book surveys the world of gambling on sports, its legal and illegal aspects, and how it has ruined the careers of many fine athletes. (Rev: BL 1/1–15/01) [796]

26167 Wood, Ted. *Iditarod Dream: Dusty and His Sled Dogs Compete in Alaska's Jr. Iditarod* (2–5). Illus. 1996, Walker LB $17.85 (978-0-8027-8407-0). 48pp. Dusty, a 15-year-old Alaskan boy, prepares for and later enters the 158-mile Junior Iditarod. (Rev: BCCB 4/96; BL 3/15/96; SLJ 5/96) [798]

26168 Wulffson, Don L. *Toys! Amazing Stories Behind Some Great Inventions* (4–6). Illus. 2000, Holt $15.95 (978-0-8050-6196-3). 136pp. The story behind such toys as Mr. Potato Head, Slinky, Silly Putty, kites, checkers, and Parcheesi is told in 25 illustrated chapters each dealing with a different game or toy. (Rev: BCCB 6/00; BL 6/1–15/00; HBG 3/01; SLJ 9/00) [688.7]

26169 Wurdinger, Scott, and Leslie Rapparlie. *Ice Climbing* (5–9). Series: Adventure Sports. 2006, Creative Education LB $31.35 (978-1-58341-393-7). 48pp. This well-designed guide to ice climbing familiarizes readers with the sport's history, equipment, competitions, and safety measures. (Rev: SLJ 12/06) [796.52]

26170 Wurdinger, Scott, and Leslie Rapparlie. *Rock Climbing* (5–9). Series: Adventure Sports. 2006, Creative Education LB $31.35 (978-1-58341-394-4). 48pp. Using many eye-catching photographs, this slim volume introduces to rock climbing and examines the sport's history, equipment, competitions, and safety measures. (Rev: SLJ 12/06) [796.5]

Automobile Racing

26171 Benson, Michael. *Crashes and Collisions* (5–8). Series: Race Car Legends. 1997, Chelsea $25.00 (978-0-7910-4435-3). Multi-car pileups in car racing and the people who have survived them are the focus of this exciting volume. (Rev: HBG 3/98; SLJ 2/98) [629.228]

26172 Braun, Eric. *Hot Rods* (3–5). Illus. Series: Motor Mania. 2006, Lerner LB $26.60 (978-0-8225-3531-7). 48pp. A basic introduction to these customized cars and how they're raced as well as information on their history, how they're built, and what they look like. (Rev: BL 10/1/06; SLJ 3/07) [629.228]

26173 Buckley, James. *NASCAR* (5–8). Illus. Series: Eyewitness Books. 2005, DK LB $19.99 (978-0-7566-1193-4). 72pp. A visual pleasure for NASCAR fans, full of information about people, places, individual races, engineering advances, and so forth. (Rev: BL 9/1/05) [796.72]

26174 Caldwell, Dave. *Speed Show: How NASCAR Won the Heart of America* (5–8). 2006, Kingfisher $16.95 (978-0-7534-6011-5). 128pp. The history of NASCAR, the basics of stock car racing, its famous drivers, its fans, and so forth are all described in this very readable book by a *New York Times* sports writer. (Rev: BL 11/15/06; SLJ 3/07) [796.720973]

26175 Doeden, Matt. *NASCAR's Wildest Wrecks* (3–6). Series: Edge Books/NASCAR Racing. 2004, Capstone LB $23.93 (978-0-7368-3775-0). 32pp. An overview of famous NASCAR crashes, complete with color photographs, and of the safety measures prompted by these accidents. (Rev: SLJ 7/05) [796.72]

26176 Doeden, Matt. *Stock Cars* (3–5). Illus. Series: Motor Mania. 2006, Lerner LB $26.60 (978-0-8225-3530-0). 48pp. Describes stock cars and their history, racing, and famous drivers. (Rev: SLJ 3/07) [796.72]

26177 Dooling, Michael. *The Great Horse-less Carriage Race* (2–4). Illus. 2002, Holiday House $16.95 (978-0-8234-1640-0). 32pp. Car lovers will particularly appreciate this lively picture-book presentation of the country's first car race, which took place in Chicago in 1895, with competitors reaching the heady average speed of 7 mph. (Rev: BCCB 2/03; BL 11/15/02; HBG 3/03; SLJ 12/02) [796.72]

26178 Eagen, Rachel. *NASCAR* (4–7). Series: Automania. 2006, Crabtree $26.60 (978-0-7787-3007-1). 32pp. An excellent, photo-filled overview of NASCAR's history, rules, safety measures, cars, and leading drivers. (Rev: BL 9/1/06) [796.720973]

26179 Egan, Erin. *Hottest Race Cars* (4–6). Illus. Series: Wild Wheels! 2007, Enslow LB $17.95 (978-0-7660-2871-5). 48pp. All about "open-wheel" cars and drivers, race strategy, and traditions with full-color photographs. (Rev: BL 10/15/07) [796.72]

26180 Franks, Katie. *I Want to Be a Race Car Driver* (3–5). Illus. Series: Dream Jobs. 2007, Rosen LB $15.95 (978-1-4042-3623-3). 24pp. Safety, pits stops, and famous races and drivers are all covered in this brief introduction to stock-car racing. (Rev: BL 6/1–15/07; SLJ 7/07) [796.72]

26181 Herzog, Brad. *R Is for Race: A Stock Car Alphabet* (3–5). 2006, Sleeping Bear $16.95 (978-1-58536-272-1). 32pp. The variety of formats in this A to Z of auto racing will suit readers of different ages and needs. (Rev: BL 8/06) [796.72]

26182 Johnstone, Mike. *NASCAR* (5–8). Series: Need for Speed. 2002, Lerner LB $23.93 (978-0-8225-0389-7). 32pp. A look at the fast-growing sport of NASCAR auto racing, with detailed descriptions of the drivers, their cars, and the circuits. (Rev: BL 8/02; HBG 10/02; SLJ 7/02) [796.7]

26183 Kelley, K. C. *Hottest NASCAR Machines* (5–7). Series: Wild Wheels! 2007, Enslow LB $23.93 (978-0-7660-2869-2). 48pp. Colorful photographs and helpful fact boxes highlight interesting information on cars used on the NASCAR circuit. Also use *Hottest Muscle Cars* and *Hottest Sports Cars* (both 2007). (Rev: SLJ 4/08)

26184 Kirkwood, Jon. *The Fantastic Book of Car Racing* (4–6). Illus. Series: Fantastic Book Of. 1997, Millbrook LB $22.40 (978-0-7613-0565-1). 39pp. A heavily illustrated book with foldout sections on the subject of car racing, its excitement, and its allure. (Rev: SLJ 8/97) [796.7]

26185 Miller, Tim. *Vroom!* (4–6). 2006, Tundra paper $17.95 (978-0-88776-755-5). 64pp. A large-format introduction to the many different types of auto racing, featuring facts and history on each and plenty of action photographs. (Rev: BL 11/15/06) [796]

26186 Morganelli, Adrianna. *Formula One* (4–6). Series: Automania! 2006, Crabtree LB $25.20 (978-0-7787-3009-5); paper $8.95 (978-0-7787-3031-6). 32pp. The Grand Prix races in Europe and their amazing cars are the focus here. The photographs will thrill race fans. (Rev: SLJ 8/07)

26187 Parr, Danny. *Lowriders* (4–7). Illus. Series: Wild Rides! 2001, Capstone LB $23.93 (978-0-7368-0928-3). 32pp. This volume on "lowrider" cars discusses the types of vehicles that are popular, the history of this trend, and the competitions that are held. (Rev: BL 10/15/01; HBG 3/02) [628.28]

26188 Pearce, Al. *Famous Tracks* (4–8). Series: Race Car Legends: Collector's Edition. 2005, Chelsea House LB $25.00 (978-0-7910-8692-6). 77pp. Four well-known racetracks are the focus of this readable title full of photographs. (Rev: SLJ 5/06; VOYA 4/06) [796.72]

26189 Piehl, Janet. *Formula One Race Cars* (3–5). Illus. 2006, Lerner LB $26.60 (978-0-8225-5929-0). 48pp. Describes Formula One racing cars and their history and famous drivers. (Rev: SLJ 3/07)

26190 Schaefer, A. R. *The Daytona 500* (4–7). Illus. Series: NASCAR Racing. 2004, Capstone LB $23.93 (978-0-7368-2423-1). 32pp. This slim volume celebrates one of America's most famous automobile racing venues and some of the illustrious drivers who achieved fame there. (Rev: BL 4/1/04) [790.72]

26191 Schaefer, A. R. *Racing with the Pit Crew* (3–6). Series: Edge Books/NASCAR Racing. 2005, Capstone paper $7.95 (978-0-7368-5235-7). 32pp. A look at the work performed by the pit crew and the safety and other concerns they must monitor. Also use *The History of NASCAR* (2005). (Rev: SLJ 7/05) [796.72]

26192 Stewart, Mark, and Mike Kennedy. *NASCAR at the Track* (4–6). Series: The Science of NASCAR. 2008, Lerner LB $27.93 (978-0-8225-8741-5). 48pp. Stewart explores the differences between the various NASCAR tracks in this eye-catching volume that includes problems to solve. Also use *NASCAR in the Pits* (2008). (Rev: LMC 10/08; SLJ 4/08) [796.72]

26193 Stewart, Mark, and Mike Kennedy. *NASCAR in the Driver's Seat* (4–6). Illus. Series: Science of NASCAR. 2008, Lerner LB $27.93 (978-0-8225-8737-8). 48pp. NASCAR racing scenarios are used to introduce basic mathematical and physical principles in this accessible and visually pleasing book that includes problems to solve and experiments. (Rev: BL 4/1/08; SLJ 4/08) [796.72]

26194 Sullivan, George. *Burnin' Rubber: Behind the Scenes in Stock Car Racing* (4–6). 1998, Millbrook LB $22.90 (978-0-7613-1256-7). 48pp. A look at NASCAR racing, with interesting behind-the-scenes information on this uniquely American sport. (Rev: HBG 3/99; SLJ 1/99) [796.7]

Baseball

26195 Aretha, David. *Power in Pinstripes: The New York Yankees* (4–7). Illus. Series: Sensational Sports Teams. 2007, Enslow LB $24.95 (978-1-59845-044-6). 128pp. Fans of this winning team will enjoy this book that includes the ball club's history, its top players, its World Series achievements, and lots of links to Web sites. (Rev: BL 7/07) [796.357]

26196 Aylesworth, Thomas G. *The Kids' World Almanac of Baseball* (4–8). Illus. 1996, World Almanac $8.95 (978-0-88687-787-3). 288pp. An entertaining compendium of baseball facts. (Rev: BL 6/1/90) [796.357]

26197 Brown, Jonatha A. *Baseball* (1–3). Series: My Favorite Sport. 2005, Weekly Reader LB $21.00 (978-0-8368-4337-8). 24pp. For beginning readers, this is an introduction to the history and sport of baseball, defining key terms. (Rev: SLJ 5/05)

26198 Burke, Jim. *Take Me Out to the Ball Game* (2–4). Illus. 2006, Little, Brown $16.99 (978-0-316-75819-2). 32pp. Burke uses the classic song as the backdrop for the story of a famous 1908 game between the New York Giants and the Chicago Cubs. (Rev: BL 4/1/06; SLJ 4/06) [796.357]

26199 Christopher, Matt. *Great Moments in Baseball History* (3–5). 1996, Little, Brown paper $4.95 (978-0-316-14130-7). 104pp. Describes nine important baseball events, involving such luminaries as Babe Ruth and Reggie Jackson. (Rev: SLJ 5/96) [796.357]

26200 Coleman, Janet Wyman, and Elizabeth V. Warren. *Baseball for Everyone: Stories from the Great Game* (4–6). 2003, Abrams $16.95 (978-0-8109-4580-7). 48pp. Based on an exhibition at the American Folk Art Museum, this attractively illustrated volume uses many interesting anecdotes in chronicling the history of baseball. (Rev: BL 9/1/03; HBG 4/04; SLJ 10/03) [796.357]

26201 Cook, Sally, and James Charlton. *Hey Batta Batta Swing!* (3–5). Illus. by Ross MacDonald. 2007, Simon & Schuster $17.99 (978-1-4169-1207-1). 56pp. This buoyant history of baseball's early years provides fascinating facts about team names, players' numbers, equipment, and so forth; antique typography and colorful illustrations recalling early cartoons complement the lively text. (Rev: BL 1/1–15/07) [796.3]

26202 Curlee, Lynn. *Ballpark: The Story of America's Baseball Fields* (4–6). Illus. 2005, Simon & Schuster $17.95 (978-0-689-86742-2). 48pp. All about baseball stadiums, both the loved and the not-so-loved, from the mid-1800s through today. (Rev: BL 3/15/05; SLJ 3/05) [796.357]

26203 Driscoll, Laura. *Negro Leagues: All-Black Baseball* (3–5). Illus. by Tracy Mitchell. Series: Smart About History. 2002, Grosset paper $5.99 (978-0-448-42684-6). 32pp. Through Emily's report on her visit to the National Baseball Hall of Fame, readers learn about the history of the Negro Leagues and the famous African American players. (Rev: BL 9/1/02; HBG 3/03; SLJ 12/02) [796.35764]

26204 Fuerst, Jeffrey B. *The Kids' Baseball Workout: A Fun Way to Get in Shape and Improve Your Game* (5–8). Illus. by Anne Canevari Green. 2002, Millbrook LB $24.90 (978-0-7613-2307-5). 80pp. This book offers exercises, stretches, and skills that will help young baseball players improve their game. (Rev: BL 9/1/02; HBG 10/02; SLJ 7/02) [796.357]

26205 Gardner, Robert, and Dennis Shortelle. *The Forgotten Players: The Story of Black Baseball in America* (5–8). Illus. 1993, Walker LB $13.85 (978-0-8027-8249-6). 120pp. A discussion of the challenges that faced the players of the Negro Leagues. (Rev: BL 2/15/93; SLJ 4/93) [769.357]

26206 Gay, Douglas, and Kathlyn Gay. *The Not-So-Minor Leagues* (5–8). Illus. 1996, Millbrook LB $23.40 (978-1-56294-921-1). 96pp. The history, importance, and present status of the minor leagues in baseball. (Rev: BL 5/15/96; SLJ 6/96) [796.357]

26207 Gibbons, Gail. *My Baseball Book* (PS–3). Illus. 2000, HarperCollins $6.99 (978-0-688-17137-7). 24pp. An attractive introduction to baseball that describes the playing field, positions, equipment, and game plays. (Rev: BCCB 4/00; BL 5/1/00; HBG 10/00; SLJ 6/00) [796.357]

26208 Grabowski, John. *The Boston Red Sox Baseball Team* (4–6). Series: Great Sports Teams. 2001, Enslow $23.93 (978-0-7660-1488-6). 48pp. This introduction to the Boston Red Sox gives lively information on the team's past, present, and future prospects. (Rev: BL 9/15/01; HBG 10/01) [796.357]

26209 Gutelle, Andrew. *Baseball's Best: Five True Stories* (2–4). Illus. by Cliff Spohn. 1990, Random paper $3.99 (978-0-394-80983-0). 48pp. Special moments in the careers of five famous players. (Rev: BCCB 6/90; BL 6/1/90) [796.357]

26210 Healy, Dennis. *The Illustrated Rules of Baseball* (3–5). Illus. Series: Illustrated Sports. 1995, Ideals paper $6.95 (978-1-57102-017-8). 32pp. The baseball diamond, playing positions, equipment, and rules are covered in this introduction to baseball. (Rev: BL 7/95; SLJ 5/95) [798.357]

26211 Isadora, Rachel. *Nick Plays Baseball* (2–4). Illus. 2001, Penguin $15.99 (978-0-399-23231-2). 32pp. Using a fictional story about Nick and his team as a framework, this oversize picture book gives information on batting, pitching, equipment, playing positions, and the rules of the game. (Rev: BCCB 2/01; BL 2/15/01; HBG 3/02) [796.357]

26212 Jensen, Julie. *Beginning Baseball* (3–5). Photos by Andy King. Series: Beginning Sports. 1995, Lerner LB $22.60 (978-0-8225-3505-8). 80pp. The fundamentals of baseball — like throwing, hitting, fielding, and baserunning — are presented, along with a history of the game. (Rev: SLJ 2/96) [796.357]

26213 Kasoff, Jerry. *Baseball Just for Kids: Skills, Strategies and Stories to Make You a Better Ballplayer* (3–7). Illus. 1996, Grand Slam paper $12.95 (978-0-9645826-7-5). 159pp. Baseball rules, techniques, tips, jokes, and trivia are included in this book that shows that the author loves the game. (Rev: SLJ 4/97) [796.357]

26214 Kellogg, David. *True Stories of Baseball's Hall of Famers* (4–8). Illus. 2000, Bluewood $8.95 (978-0-912517-41-4). 144pp. Using a chronological approach, this book profiles 60 Hall of Famers and tells why each is there. (Rev: BL 10/15/00; VOYA 8/01) [796.357]

26215 Kennedy, Mike. *Baseball* (2–4). Series: True Books — Sports. 2002, Children's Book Pr. LB $25.00 (978-0-516-22334-6). 48pp. Using large type and many color photographs, this is a simple introduction to baseball, its history, and how it is played. (Rev: BL 9/1/02; SLJ check) [796.357]

26216 Kisseloff, Jeff. *Who Is Baseball's Greatest Pitcher?* (5–7). Illus. 2003, Cricket $15.95 (978-0-8126-2685-8). 192pp. The author presents profiles of 33 pitchers, with relevant statistics, and challenges the reader to choose the best and justify this decision. (Rev: BL 7/03; HBG 10/03; SLJ 5/03) [796.359]

26217 Krasner, Steven. *Play Ball Like the Pros: Tips for Kids from 20 Big League Stars* (5–9). Illus. 2002, Peachtree paper $12.95 (978-1-56145-261-3). 160pp. Each chapter features a professional player talking about the position he plays and giving tips to the young athlete. (Rev: BL 5/1/02; SLJ 6/02; VOYA 10/03) [796.357]

26218 Layden, Joe. *The Great American Baseball Strike* (5–8). Series: Headliners. 1995, Millbrook LB $25.90 (978-1-56294-930-3). A discussion of the issues that led to the 1995 baseball strike, with a review of the history of professional baseball and of the stormy relationship between the owners and players. (Rev: BL 11/15/95; SLJ 1/96) [796.357]

26219 Mackel, Kathy. *MadCat* (5–8). 2005, Harper-Collins LB $16.89 (978-0-06-054870-4). 192pp. Madelyn Catherine (aka MadCat), catcher on her local girls' fast-pitch softball team, is at the center of this story about sports, team play, and family involvement. (Rev: BL 2/15/05; SLJ 3/05)

26220 Mackin, Bob. *Record-Breaking Baseball Trivia* (5–8). 2000, Douglas & McIntyre $6.95 (978-1-55054-757-3). 128pp. Questions, answers, and quizzes cover topics including baseball history, team play, World Series facts, and trivia from the plate and mound. (Rev: BL 9/15/00) [796.357]

26221 Nelson, Kadir. *We Are the Ship: The Story of Negro League Baseball* (5–8). Illus. by author. 2008, Hyperion $18.99 (978-0-7868-0832-8). 96pp. Beautiful illustrations accompany a history of the league told by an anonymous but proud former player. (Rev: BL 2/1/08; SLJ 1/08) [796.357]

26222 Nevius, Carol. *Baseball Hour* (1–3). Illus. by Bill Thomson. 2008, Marshall Cavendish $16.99 (978-0-7614-5380-2). 32pp. Photorealistic art and brief rhyming text bring a baseball practice session to life. (Rev: BL 4/1/08; LMC 10/08; SLJ 6/08) [796.357]

26223 Nitz, Kristin Wolden. *Softball* (5–9). Series: Play-by-Play. 2000, Lerner paper $23.93 (978-0-8225-9875-6). 80pp. Good basic information about softball is given including history, rules, equipment, and positions. (Rev: SLJ 9/00) [796.357]

26224 Omoth, Tyler. *The Story of the Chicago Cubs* (3–6). Illus. Series: Baseball: The Great American Game. 2007, Creative Education $22.95 (978-1-58341-482-8). 48pp. Omoth offers a history of the Chicago baseball team, including details of the many defeats the team has suffered in recent years. (Rev: BL 10/15/07) [796.357]

26225 Owens, Thomas S. *The Atlanta Braves Baseball Team* (4–6). Series: Great Sports Teams. 1998, Enslow LB $18.95 (978-0-7660-1021-5). 48pp. Provides a history of the Atlanta Braves and highlights their most famous players and exciting seasons. (Rev: BL 5/15/98; HBG 10/98) [796.357]

26226 Patrick, Jean L. S. *The Girl Who Struck Out Babe Ruth* (2–3). Illus. by Jeni Reeves. 2000, Lerner $23.93 (978-1-57505-397-4); paper $5.95 (978-1-57505-455-1). 48pp. In 1931, 17-year-old Jackie Mitchell, a pitcher in the minor leagues, played in an exhibition game in which she struck out Babe Ruth and Lou Gehrig. (Rev: BCCB 6/00; BL 4/15/00; HBG 10/00; SLJ 8/00) [796.357]

26227 Pietrusza, David. *The Baltimore Orioles Baseball Team* (4–6). Series: Great Sports Teams. 2000, Enslow LB $23.93 (978-0-7660-1283-7). 48pp. Covers the history of the Baltimore Orioles, the team's best players, and its performance today and tomorrow. (Rev: BL 5/15/00; HBG 10/00) [796.357]

26228 Pietrusza, David. *The Cleveland Indians Baseball Team* (4–6). Series: Great Sports Teams. 2001, Enslow $23.93 (978-0-7660-1491-6). 48pp. Using fast-paced writing and many photographs, Pietrusza supplies a good thumbnail sketch of the team, its

famous players, and outstanding games. (Rev: BL 9/15/01; HBG 3/02) [796.357]

26229 Pietrusza, David. *The New York Yankees Baseball Team* (4–6). Illus. 1998, Enslow LB $23.93 (978-0-7660-1018-5). 48pp. A brief, well-illustrated account of the history of the Yankees, with emphasis on star players and important coaches. (Rev: BL 4/1/98; HBG 10/98) [796.357]

26230 Pietrusza, David. *The St. Louis Cardinals Baseball Team* (4–6). Series: Great Sports Teams. 2001, Enslow $23.93 (978-0-7660-1490-9). 48pp. An exciting introduction to the team with material on its history, key players, exciting seasons, and present status. (Rev: BL 9/15/01; HBG 3/02)

26231 Pietrusza, David. *The San Francisco Giants Baseball Team* (4–6). Series: Great Sports Teams. 2000, Enslow LB $23.93 (978-0-7660-1284-4). 48pp. Plenty of sports action is included in this introduction to the past, present, and future of the San Francisco Giants. (Rev: BL 5/15/00; HBG 10/00) [795.357]

26232 Preller, James. *McGwire and Sosa: A Season to Remember* (4–7). Illus. 1998, Simon & Schuster paper $5.99 (978-0-689-82871-3). 32pp. An oversize paperback that traces the baseball season that brought Sosa and McGwire to the nation's attention and made them sports heroes. (Rev: BL 1/1–15/99) [796.357]

26233 Sandler, Michael. *Baseball: The 2004 Boston Red Sox* (3–5). Illus. Series: Upsets and Comebacks. 2006, Bearport LB $25.27 (978-1-59716-165-7). 32pp. Full of photographs, this tells the story of Red Sox' triumphant 2004 season; with trivia, timeline, bibliography, glossary, and Web sites. (Rev: BL 4/1/06; SLJ 7/06) [796.357]

26234 Shaughnessy, Dan. *The Legend of the Curse of the Bambino* (2–4). Illus. by C. F. Payne. 2005, Simon & Schuster $16.95 (978-0-689-87235-8). 32pp. A father tells his daughter about Babe Ruth and the "curse" that kept the Boston Red Sox from winning the World Series until 2004. (Rev: BL 3/15/05; SLJ 5/05) [796.357]

26235 Stewart, Mark, and Mike Kennedy. *Long Ball: The Legend and Lore of the Home Run* (3–5). Illus. 2006, Millbrook LB $22.60 (978-0-7613-2779-0). 64pp. Containing photographs and reproductions of baseball cards and magazine covers, this attractive book chronicles the history of the home run and profiles some of baseball's most notable long-ball hitters. (Rev: BL 4/1/06; SLJ 6/06; VOYA 6/06) [796.357]

26236 Sublett, Anne. *The Illustrated Rules of Softball* (3–5). Illus. by Patrick Kelley. Series: Illustrated Sports. 1996, Ideals paper $6.95 (978-1-57102-063-5). 32pp. After a brief history of baseball, this account presents an explanation of rules and a look at various positions and signals, plus a glossary and discussion of sportsmanship. (Rev: SLJ 8/96) [796.357]

26237 Suen, Anastasia. *The Story of Baseball* (1–3). Illus. Series: Sports History. 2002, Rosen LB $19.95 (978-0-8239-6000-2). 24pp. A basic, easy-to-read introduction to the sport. (Rev: BL 5/15/02) [796.357]

26238 Sullivan, George. *Baseball's Boneheads, Bad Boys, and Just Plain Crazy Guys* (5–8). Illus. by Anne Canevari Green. 2003, Millbrook LB $23.90 (978-0-7613-2321-1); paper $8.95 (978-0-7613-1928-3). 64pp. An amusing collection of anecdotes that show the humor, superstitions, and general nuttiness of baseball players. (Rev: BL 7/03; HBG 10/03; SLJ 11/03) [790.357]

26239 Thomas, Keltie. *How Baseball Works* (3–6). Illus. by Greg Hall. 2004, Maple Tree $19.95 (978-1-894379-60-1). 64pp. A detailed overview of baseball and its history and techniques, plus information on famous players. (Rev: BL 5/15/04; SLJ 11/04) [796]

26240 Thomas, Ron, and Joe Herran. *Getting into Baseball* (2–4). Illus. by Nives Porcellato and Andy Craig. Series: Getting into Sports. 2005, Chelsea House LB $28.00 (978-0-7910-8808-1). After a brief history of the game, this book covers rules, equipment, clothing, and competitions and provides color photographs, useful diagrams, and interesting trivia. (Rev: SLJ 12/05) [796.357]

26241 Weatherford, Carole Boston. *A Negro League Scrapbook* (2–4). Illus. 2005, Boyds Mills $19.95 (978-1-59078-091-6). 48pp. The colorful history of baseball's Negro Leagues is documented in an interesting scrapbook format. (Rev: BL 2/1/05; SLJ 3/05) [796.357]

26242 Will, Sandra. *Baseball for Fun!* (2–4). Illus. Series: Sports for Fun. 2003, Compass Point LB $25.26 (978-0-7565-0428-1). 48pp. Covering rules, necessary skills, and key figures, this is an attractive introduction for beginning readers. (Rev: SLJ 6/03) [796.357]

26243 Wong, Stephen. *Baseball Treasures* (4–7). Illus. by Susan Einstein. 2007, HarperCollins $16.99 (978-0-06-114464-6). 64pp. An inside look at the Smithsonian Institution's collection of baseball memorabilia, revealing how much the equipment has changed since the early days of the game. (Rev: BL 12/15/07) [796.3570]

26244 Young, Robert. *A Personal Tour of Camden Yards* (4–7). Series: How It Was. 1999, Lerner LB $30.35 (978-0-8225-3578-2). 64pp. Designed to remind fans of famous old ballparks, this book visits Camden Yards, home of the Baltimore Orioles. The reader inspects the field, visits the old warehouse, and views the game from a skybox. (Rev: BL 6/1–15/99; HBG 10/99) [796.357]

Basketball

26245 Aretha, David. *The Detroit Pistons Basketball Team* (4–6). Series: Great Sports Teams. 2001, Enslow LB $23.93 (978-0-7660-1487-9). 48pp. In narrative and pictures, this volume highlights the history and achievements of the Detroit Pistons with material on their key players and important seasons,

past and present. (Rev: BL 12/15/01; HBG 3/02) [796.323]

26246 Aretha, David. *The Seattle SuperSonics Basketball Team* (4–6). Illus. Series: Great Sports Teams. 1999, Enslow LB $23.93 (978-0-7660-1102-1). 48pp. A history of the Seattle SuperSonics is given, with information on famous players past and present and descriptions of important games. (Rev: BL 3/15/99; HBG 10/99) [796.323]

26247 Bennett, Frank. *The Illustrated Rules of Basketball* (3–5). Illus. 1994, Ideals paper $6.95 (978-1-57102-021-5). 32pp. Following the history of basketball, provides a detailed discussion of each rule. (Rev: BL 9/15/94; SLJ 11/94) [796.323]

26248 Coleman, Lori. *Girls' Basketball: Making Your Mark on the Court* (3–6). Series: Girls Got Game. 2006, Capstone LB $25.26 (978-0-7368-6821-1). 32pp. Especially for girls, this overview of basketball will get readers excited about the sport. (Rev: SLJ 7/07)

26249 Dixon, Tamecka, and Judith Cohen. *You Can Be a Woman Basketball Player* (3–6). Illus. 1999, Cascade Pass $13.95 (978-1-880599-40-2); paper $7.00 (978-1-880599-38-9). 40pp. As well as the story of Tamecka Dixon, a player on the Los Angeles Sparks, this book explains the fundamentals of basketball, its positions, and the duties of each team member. (Rev: BL 8/99; SLJ 9/99) [796.323]

26250 Gibbons, Gail. *My Basketball Book* (K–2). Illus. 2000, HarperCollins $6.99 (978-0-688-17140-7). 24pp. This small-format paperback book contains the basics of basketball with coverage of equipment, positions, and rules. (Rev: BL 9/15/00; HBG 3/01; SLJ 11/00) [796.323]

26251 Glenn, Mike. *Lessons in Success from the NBA's Top Players* (5–7). Illus. 1998, Visions 3000 paper $14.95 (978-0-9649795-5-0). 126pp. This noted sportsman tells about his career in the NBA while introducing each of the NBA teams and its strengths. (Rev: BL 7/98) [796.323]

26252 Kelley, James S. *The Central Division* (3–5). Illus. Series: Above the Rim. 2008, Child's World LB $19.95 (978-1-59296-982-1). 40pp. Basketball's Central Division — its history, players, and interesting facts and figures — is the focus of this slim volume with full-color photographs. (Rev: BL 4/1/08) [796.323]

26253 Kennedy, Mike. *Basketball* (3–5). Series: True Books — Sports. 2002, Children's Book Pr. LB $25.00 (978-0-516-22335-3). 48pp. Covers the basic elements of basketball, its history, and superstars, with color photographs on each page plus large type and simple text. (Rev: BL 1/1–15/03) [796.323]

26254 Kramer, S. A. *Hoop Stars* (2–3). Illus. by Mitchell Heinze. 1995, Penguin paper $3.99 (978-0-448-40943-6). 48pp. Hakeem Olajuwon, Charles Barkley, Shaquille O'Neal, and David Robinson are the NBA stars briefly profiled in this beginning reader. (Rev: BL 1/1–15/96; SLJ 3/96) [796.323]

26255 Lace, William W. *The Los Angeles Lakers Basketball Team* (4–6). Illus. Series: Great Sports Teams. 1998, Enslow LB $18.95 (978-0-7660-

1020-8). 48pp. After a short introduction on Magic Johnson, this account focuses on the history of the team on which he played, with emphasis on their finest moments, their star players, and famous coaches. (Rev: BL 4/1/98; HBG 10/98) [796.323]

26256 Lannin, Joanne. *A History of Basketball for Girls and Women: From Bloomers to the Big Leagues* (5–9). Illus. Series: Sports Legacy. 2000, Lerner LB $26.63 (978-0-8225-3331-3); paper $9.95 (978-0-8225-9863-3). 144pp. From the creation of basketball in 1891 to today, this account describes women's roles. (Rev: BL 1/1–15/01; HBG 3/01; SLJ 2/01; VOYA 4/01) [796.323]

26257 Morris, Greggory. *Basketball Basics* (4–6). Illus. by Tim Engelland. 1979, Prentice Hall $6.95 (978-0-13-072256-0). A player and coach explain four specific skills to young players.

26258 Owens, Thomas S. *Basketball Arenas* (5–8). Illus. Series: Sports Palaces. 2002, Millbrook LB $25.90 (978-0-7613-1766-1). 64pp. Lots of basketball lore and history are included in a visit to the Boston Garden, Chicago Stadium, and the old Madison Square Garden. (Rev: BL 6/1–15/02; HBG 10/02) [796.323]

26259 Parselle, Matt. *Basketball: Learn How to Be a Star Player* (3–5). Illus. by Mel Pickering. Series: Sports Club. 2000, Two-Can $9.95 (978-1-58728-000-9). 32pp. This basic book on basketball explains different kinds of passes and the rules of the game, as well as giving some history and profiles of a few important players. (Rev: SLJ 3/01) [796.323]

26260 Roberts, Robin. *Basketball Year: What It's Like to Be a Woman Pro* (4–6). Illus. Series: Get in the Game! 2000, Millbrook $21.90 (978-0-7613-1406-6). 48pp. This account follows women of the WNBA as they train, travel, play games, and try to lead normal lives. (Rev: BL 9/1/00; HBG 10/00; SLJ 8/00) [796.323]

26261 Rutledge, Rachel. *The Best of the Best in Basketball* (4–7). Illus. Series: Women in Sports. 1998, Millbrook LB $24.90 (978-0-7613-1301-4). 64pp. After a history of basketball, this account highlights women's role and covers today's most important female players. (Rev: BL 2/15/99; HBG 10/99; SLJ 3/99) [796.323]

26262 Schulz, Randy. *The New York Knicks Basketball Team* (4–6). Series: Great Sports Teams. 2000, Enslow LB $23.93 (978-0-7660-1281-3). 48pp. The New York Nicks are profiled with material on the team's history, greatest players, and most exciting games. (Rev: BL 9/15/00; HBG 10/01) [796.323]

26263 Stewart, Mark. *The Miami Heat* (3–5). Illus. Series: Team Spirit. 2006, Norwood House LB $18.95 (978-0-599-53009-6). 48pp. An attractive profile of professional basketball's Miami Heat, examining the team's brief history, its standout players, and performance. (Rev: BL 4/1/06) [796.323]

26264 Stewart, Mark. *The NBA Finals* (5–10). Series: Watts History of Sports. 2003, Watts LB $34.50 (978-0-531-11955-6). 95pp. National Basketball Association finals over more than half a century are detailed year by year, with ample information on the teams and the players. (Rev: SLJ 3/04) [797]

26265 Stewart, Mark, and Mike Kennedy. *Swish: The Quest for Basketball's Perfect Shot* (5–8). Illus. 2009, Millbrook LB $25.26 (978-0-8225-8752-1). 64pp. This wide-ranging volume covers basketball history, famous shots, key players, remarkable plays, scoring, and so forth. (Rev: BL 1/1–15/09; SLJ 5/09) [796.3230973]

26266 Thomas, Keltie. *How Basketball Works* (5–8). Illus. 2005, Maple Tree $16.95 (978-1-897066-18-8); paper $6.95 (978-1-897066-19-5). 64pp. A lively overview of basketball's history, equipment, training, and skills, with interesting anecdotes and factoids. (Rev: BL 5/15/05) [796.323]

26267 Vancil, Mark. *NBA Basketball Offense Basics* (4–8). Illus. 1996, Sterling $16.95 (978-0-8069-4892-8). 96pp. Action photographs and lively text demonstrate such techniques as dribbling, passing, and shooting. (Rev: BL 9/1/96) [796.332]

26268 Wilker, Josh. *The Harlem Globetrotters* (5–10). Series: African-American Achievers. 1996, Chelsea LB $21.95 (978-0-7910-2585-7); paper $8.95 (978-0-7910-2586-4). This is a chronologically arranged history of the Harlem Globetrotters, the basketball team that has been entertaining crowds since 1927. (Rev: SLJ 3/97) [796.357]

Bicycles

26269 Bach, Julie. *Bicycling* (4–7). Illus. Series: World of Sports. 2000, Smart Apple LB $16.95 (978-1-887068-53-6). 32pp. A brief introduction to bicycling that gives material on the origins and evolution of the sport, equipment, and techniques, plus coverage of the sport's star athletes. (Rev: BL 9/15/00) [796.6]

26270 Bizley, Kirk. *Mountain Biking* (4–7). Series: Radical Sports. 1999, Heinemann LB $24.22 (978-1-57572-944-2). 32pp. Color photographs and a simple text introduce mountain biking, its history, equipment, skills, and safety concerns. (Rev: SLJ 5/00) [796.6]

26271 Buckley, Annie. *Be a Better Biker* (5–6). Series: Girls Rock! 2006, The Child's World LB $25.64 (978-1-59296-741-4). 32pp. As well as advice on safety and maintenance, this volume (which is suitable for boys too) covers the history of bicycles and the various types available today. (Rev: SLJ 2/07) [796.6]

26272 Cole, Steve. *Kids' Easy Bike Care: Tune-Ups, Tools and Quick Fixes* (5–9). Illus. by Sarah Rakitin. Series: Quick Starts for Kids! 2003, Williamson paper $8.95 (978-1-885593-86-3). 64pp. A detailed and accessible guide to the parts of a bicycle and their maintenance, bicycle safety, and preparing an emergency kit, with cartoon illustrations. (Rev: SLJ 12/03) [629.28]

26273 Crossingham, John. *Cycling in Action* (4–7). Illus. by Bonna Rouse. Series: Sports in Action. 2002, Crabtree LB $25.27 (978-0-7787-0118-7); paper $6.95 (978-0-7787-0124-8). 32pp. Photographs and drawings illustrate important concepts in this introduction to the sport of cycling that covers equipment and technique. (Rev: BL 9/1/02) [796.4]

26274 Deady, Kathleen W. *BMX Bikes* (4–7). Illus. Series: Wild Rides! 2001, Capstone LB $23.93 (978-0-7368-0925-2). 32pp. Bicycle motocross fans will enjoy the color photographs and concise text that explains the equipment and skills needed for BMX (bicycle motocross) racing. (Rev: BL 10/15/01; HBG 3/02) [629.22]

26275 Dick, Scott. *BMX* (4–8). Series: Radical Sports. 2002, Heinemann LB $25.64 (978-1-58810-623-0). 32pp. This introduction to bicycle motocross gives material on equipment, skills, training, and safety. (Rev: BL 2/15/03; HBG 3/03) [796.6]

26276 Erlbach, Arlene. *Bicycles* (3–5). Illus. Series: How It's Made. 1994, Lerner LB $19.93 (978-0-8225-2388-8); paper $6.95 (978-0-8225-9740-7). 48pp. The story of the bicycle is told, from its early design to the sleek machines of today. (Rev: BL 3/15/95) [629]

26277 Freeman, Gary. *Motocross* (4–8). Series: Radical Sports. 2002, Heinemann LB $25.64 (978-1-58810-627-8). 32pp. The sport of cross-country racing on motorcycles is introduced, with an emphasis on safety and skill development. (Rev: BL 2/15/03; HBG 3/03) [796.7]

26278 Gibbons, Gail. *Bicycle Book* (K–4). Illus. 1995, Holiday House LB $16.95 (978-0-8234-1199-3). 32pp. A short book that covers such topics as the history of the bicycle, its types, care tips, and safety rules. (Rev: BL 12/1/95; SLJ 1/96) [629.227]

26279 Haduch, Bill. *Go Fly a Bike! The Ultimate Book About Bicycle Fun, Freedom, and Science* (4–8). Illus. by Chris Murphy. 2004, Dutton $16.99 (978-0-525-47024-3). 112pp. Packed with facts and cartoon illustrations, this comprehensive guide covers everything from the history of bicycling to practical tips for bike care and repair. (Rev: BL 2/1/04; SLJ 3/04) [796.6]

26280 Hayhurst, Chris. *Bicycle Stunt Riding!* (4–8). Series: Extreme Sports. 2000, Rosen LB $26.50 (978-0-8239-3011-1). 64pp. In this book, readers will learn about stunts like the vert and mega spin as well as finding out about the bikes and the safety equipment needed to start this sport. (Rev: BL 6/1–15/00) [629]

26281 Hayhurst, Chris. *Mountain Biking: Get on the Trail* (4–8). Illus. Series: Extreme Sports. 2000, Rosen LB $26.50 (978-0-8239-3013-5). 64pp. Stressing safety throughout, this book covers topics including the history of mountain biking, why mountain bikes are different than others, and riding techniques. (Rev: BL 3/15/00; SLJ 8/00) [796.6]

26282 Hinman, Bonnie. *Extreme Cycling with Dale Holmes* (2–4). Illus. Series: Robbie Reader: Extreme Sports. 2006, Mitchell Lane LB $16.95 (978-1-58415-487-7). 32pp. This high-interest volume combines information on extreme cycling with a biographical profile of British-born BMX bike racer Dale Holmes. (Rev: BL 10/15/06) [796.6]

26283 Jensen, Julie. *Beginning Mountain Biking* (4–6). Photos by Andy King. Series: Beginning Sports. 1996, Lerner LB $21.27 (978-0-8225-3509-

6). 63pp. A very simple, short account that introduces mountain biking to a young audience. (Rev: SLJ 2/97) [796.6]

26284 King, Andy. *Fundamental Mountain Biking* (5–9). Series: Fundamental Sports. 1996, Lerner LB $27.15 (978-0-8225-3459-4). This introduction to mountain biking discusses its history, equipment, maneuvers, competitions, tricks, safety reminders, and repair tips. (Rev: SLJ 2/97) [796.64]

26285 Maestro, Betsy, and Giulio Maestro. *Bike Trip* (2–4). Illus. 1992, HarperCollins $16.00 (978-0-06-022731-9). 32pp. Young Joshua tells a simple story of a bike trip he takes with his family from their rural home into town. (Rev: BL 1/1/92; SLJ 3/92) [796.6]

26286 Maurer, Tracy Nelson. *BMX Freestyle* (3–6). Series: Radsports. 2001, Rourke LB $29.93 (978-1-58952-102-5). 48pp. Safety is emphasized in this account of BMX history, equipment, and techniques. (Rev: SLJ 5/02) [796.62]

26287 Otfinoski, Steven. *Pedaling Along: Bikes Then and Now* (1–3). Illus. Series: Here We Go! 1996, Benchmark LB $22.79 (978-0-7614-0402-6). 32pp. A copiously illustrated history of bicycles, from their invention to modern bikes. (Rev: SLJ 6/97) [629]

26288 Pinchuk, Amy. *The Best Book of Bikes* (4–7). Illus. 2003, Maple Tree paper $12.95 (978-1-894379-44-1). 64pp. Diagrams, color photographs, and fascinating facts add to the appeal of the maintenance advice, racing strategies, and stunts provided. (Rev: BCCB 9/03; SLJ 9/03) [629.227]

26289 Raby, Philip, and Simon Nix. *Motorbikes* (5–8). Illus. Series: Need for Speed. 1999, Lerner LB $23.93 (978-0-8225-2486-1); paper $23.93 (978-0-8225-9854-1). 32pp. A variety of motorbikes are introduced including dirt, motorcross, and land speed bikes. (Rev: BL 1/1–15/00; HBG 3/00; SLJ 2/00) [629.227]

26290 Schoenherr, Alicia, and Rusty Schoenherr. *Mountain Biking* (4–6). Series: Kids' Guides. 2005, The Child's World LB $25.64 (978-1-59296-209-9). 32pp. An introduction to mountain biking, describing its history and equipment and key athletes and competitions, with plenty of photographs and a glossary. (Rev: SLJ 7/05) [796.6]

26291 Wurdinger, Scott, and Leslie Rapparlie. *Mountain Biking* (5–9). Series: Adventure Sports. 2006, Creative Education LB $31.35 (978-1-58341-396-8). 48pp. Using many eye-catching photographs, this slim volume introduces the popular sport's history, equipment, competitions, and safety measures. (Rev: SLJ 12/06) [796.6]

Camping and Backpacking

26292 Brunelle, Lynn. *Camp Out! The Ultimate Kids' Guide* (5–12). Illus. by Brian Biggs and Elara Tanguy. 2007, Workman paper $11.95 (978-0-7611-4122-8). 384pp. This volume is packed with information about camping out, covering equipment, planning, and skills, and offering games, activities, recipes, nature tips, and so forth. (Rev: SLJ 2/08)

26293 Ching, Jacqueline. *Camping: Have Fun, Be Smart* (3–6). Series: Explore the Outdoors. 2000, Rosen LB $27.95 (978-0-8239-3173-6). 64pp. A basic introduction to camping that includes material on setting up a camp, gear and clothing, and different types of tents. (Rev: SLJ 1/01) [796.54]

26294 Drake, Jane, and Ann Love. *The Kids Campfire Book* (4–8). Illus. 1998, Kids Can paper $12.95 (978-1-55074-539-9). This manual describes how to select a location, build safe campfires, and later douse them, suggests fireside activities, including some science demonstrations, and offers safe cooking tips. (Rev: BL 3/15/98; HBG 9/98; SLJ 4/98) [796.54]

26295 Ghione, Yvette. *This Is Daniel Cook on a Hike* (K–3). 2006, Kids Can $12.95 (978-1-55453-079-3); paper $4.95 (978-1-55453-080-9). In this companion to the popular Canadian-produced TV show, the young host takes readers on a walk in the woods, introducing them to hiking equipment, safety precautions, and the animals and plants they encounter. (Rev: SLJ 11/06) [796.51]

26296 Loy, Jessica. *Follow the Trail: A Young Person's Guide to the Great Outdoors* (2–6). Illus. 2003, Holt $18.95 (978-0-8050-6195-6). 48pp. This slim volume uses the story of a camping trip to convey information about identifying wildflowers and trees, building a campfire, and avoiding such perils as poison ivy, snakes, and bears. (Rev: BL 4/1/03; HBG 10/03; SLJ 6/03) [796.54]

26297 McManus, Patrick F. *Kid Camping from Aaaaiii! to Zip* (5–7). Illus. by Roy Doty. 1979, Avon paper $3.99 (978-0-380-71311-0). 128pp. A practical camping guide presented in an amusing way.

26298 Mader, Jan. *Let's Go Camping!* (PS–1). Series: Sports and Activities. 2006, Capstone LB $21.26 (978-0-7368-6360-5). 24pp. A large-format, simply written introduction that covers basic techniques, equipment, and safety and includes color photographs. (Rev: SLJ 2/07) [796.54]

26299 Seeberg, Tim. *Camping* (3–5). Illus. Series: Kids' Guides to the Outdoors. 2004, Child's World LB $25.64 (978-1-59296-032-3). 32pp. For children with no experience of camping, the tips on safety, equipment, and advance planning provided here will be helpful. (Rev: BL 5/15/04) [796.54]

26300 Weber, Sandra. *Two in the Wilderness: Adventures of a Mother and Daughter in the Adirondack Mountains* (3–5). Photos by Carl E. Heilman. Illus. 2005, Boyds Mills $19.95 (978-1-59078-182-1). 48pp. This photoessay covers a 12-day journey the author took with her preteen daughter through New York's Adirondack Mountains, describing various physical and meteorological challenges as well as the geological and historical sights along the way; excerpts from daughter Marcy's journal add another perspective. (Rev: BL 7/05; SLJ 11/05) [508.747]

Chess

26301 Basman, Michael. *Chess for Kids* (4–8). Illus. 2001, DK paper $12.99 (978-0-7894-6540-5). 44pp. A guide to the game of chess that includes everything from the basic moves and important strategies to information on the game's origins and the roles the game has played in arenas ranging from literature to history. (Rev: BL 7/01; HBG 10/01) [794.1]

26302 Kidder, Harvey. *The Kids' Book of Chess* (4–8). Illus. by Kimberly Bulcken. 1990, Workman paper $15.95 (978-0-89480-767-1). 96pp. Using their origins in the Middle Ages as a focus, this book explains the role of each chess piece and the basics of the game. (Rev: SLJ 2/91) [794.1]

26303 Nottingham, Ted, et al. *Chess for Children* (4–6). Illus. 1994, Sterling $16.95 (978-0-8069-0452-8). 128pp. Three experts explain chess, the meaning and use of each piece, strategies, famous games, and the accomplishments of famous players. (Rev: BL 5/1/94) [794.1]

26304 Nottingham, Ted, and Bob Wade. *Winning Chess: Piece by Piece* (4–8). Illus. 1999, Sterling $17.95 (978-0-8069-9955-5). 128pp. This book is for chess players who already know the basics and are ready to improve their techniques. (Rev: BL 11/15/99) [794.1]

Fishing

26305 Arnosky, Jim. *Hook, Line, and Seeker: A Beginners Guide to Fishing, Boating, and Watching Water Wildlife* (4–6). Illus. 2005, Scholastic $12.95 (978-0-439-45584-8). 192pp. Outdoorsman (and illustrator) Arnosky draws on personal experience in this information-packed guide to boating, fishing, and wildlife watching. (Rev: BL 8/05; VOYA 4/06) [799.1]

26306 Morey, Shaun. *Incredible Fishing Stories for Kids* (3–6). Illus. 1993, Incredible Fishing Stories paper $11.95 (978-0-9633691-1-6). 96pp. These true stories tell how young anglers have made record catches. (Rev: BL 9/1/93)

26307 Schmidt, Gerald D. *Let's Go Fishing: A Book for Beginners* (4–7). Illus. by Brian W. Payne. 1990, Roberts Rinehart paper $11.95 (978-0-911797-84-8). 96pp. This practical guide to freshwater fishing includes material on tackle and kinds of fish. (Rev: BL 3/1/91; SLJ 5/91) [799.1]

26308 Seeberg, Tim. *Freshwater Fishing* (3–5). Illus. Series: Great Outdoors. 2004, Child's World LB $25.64 (978-1-59296-035-4). 32pp. A useful guide for young people planning their first fishing trip, this book is loaded with tips about equipment and what to expect. Also use *Fly-Fishing* (2004). (Rev: BL 5/15/04) [799.1]

26309 Solomon, Dane. *Fishing: Have Fun, Be Smart* (3–6). Illus. Series: Explore the Outdoors. 2000, Rosen $26.50 (978-0-8239-3168-2). This introduction to fishing includes material on fresh and salt water varieties and the equipment needed. (Rev: SLJ 1/01) [799.1]

Football

26310 Gibbons, Gail. *My Football Book* (K–2). Illus. 2000, HarperCollins $6.99 (978-0-688-17139-1). 24pp. Equipment, the playing field, positions, and basic rules are covered in this small-format paperback introduction to football. (Rev: BL 9/15/00; HBG 3/01; SLJ 11/00) [796.332]

26311 Gitlin, Marty. *Football Skills* (4–6). Illus. Series: How to Play Like a Pro. 2008, Enslow LB $17.95 (978-0-7660-3203-3). 48pp. This introduction to football basics looks at separate skills — passing, receiving, and so forth — and highlights the importance of good sportsmanship and safety. (Rev: BLO 2/9/09) [796.332]

26312 Goin, Kenn. *Football for Fun!* (2–4). Illus. Series: Sports for Fun. 2003, Compass Point LB $25.26 (978-0-7565-0430-4). 48pp. Covering rules, necessary skills, and key figures, this is an attractive introduction for beginning readers. (Rev: SLJ 6/03) [796.332]

26313 Herzog, Brad. *T Is for Touchdown: A Football Alphabet* (3–5). Illus. by Mark Braught. 2004, Sleeping Bear $16.95 (978-1-58536-233-2). Football facts abound in this informative, alphabetical picture book, written in easy rhymes, that covers history, rules, teams and players, and famous plays. (Rev: SLJ 2/05)

26314 Kennedy, Mike. *Football* (3–5). Series: True Books — Sports. 2002, Children's Book Pr. LB $25.00 (978-0-516-22336-0). 48pp. Large type and a simple text plus plenty of well-captioned color photographs are highlights of this basic introduction to football, its history, rules, and key players. (Rev: BL 1/1–15/03) [796.332]

26315 Kessler, Leonard. *Kick, Pass, and Run* (1–2). Illus. 1996, HarperCollins paper $3.99 (978-0-06-444210-7). 64pp. An easily read reissue of a book that introduces football and its rules. (Rev: BL 11/15/96) [796.332]

26316 Lace, William W. *The Pittsburgh Steelers Football Team* (4–6). Series: Great Sports Teams. 1999, Enslow LB $23.93 (978-0-7660-1099-4). 48pp. Using action photos and numerous quotes, this is a history of the Steelers and an account of their most famous moments. (Rev: BL 4/15/98; HBG 10/99) [796.332]

26317 Macnow, Glen. *The Denver Broncos Football Team* (4–6). Series: Great Sports Teams. 2001, Enslow $23.93 (978-0-7660-1489-3). 48pp. A simple account that gives information on the history of the team, its star players, and most exciting seasons. (Rev: BL 9/15/01; HBG 3/02) [796.332]

26318 Madden, John, and Bill Gutman. *John Madden's Heroes of Football: The Story of America's Game* (5–8). 2006, Dutton $18.99 (978-0-525-47698-6). 80pp. The former NFL coach and popular

football commentator chronicles the history of professional football, looking at how the game has changed over the years and profiling some of its best-known players and coaches. (Rev: BL 9/1/06; SLJ 2/07) [796.332092]

26319 Mader, Jan. *Let's Play Football!* (PS–1). Series: Sports and Activities. 2006, Capstone LB $21.26 (978-0-7368-6361-2). 24pp. A large-format, simply written introduction that covers basic techniques, equipment, and safety and includes color photographs. (Rev: SLJ 2/07) [796.332]

26320 Molzahn, Arlene Bourgeois. *The San Francisco 49ers Football Team* (4–6). Series: Great Sports Teams. 2000, Enslow LB $23.93 (978-0-7660-1280-6). 48pp. As well as giving a history of this great team, this short book describes the team's best players. (Rev: BL 9/15/00; HBG 10/01) [796.48]

26321 O'Shei, Tim. *The Chicago Bears Football Team* (4–6). Series: Great Sports Teams. 2001, Enslow LB $23.93 (978-0-7660-1285-1). 48pp. The history of the Chicago Bears is given in text and pictures with coverage of key seasons, important players, and future outlook. (Rev: BL 12/15/01; HBG 3/02) [796.48]

26322 Patey, R. L. *The Illustrated Rules of Football* (3–5). Illus. by Eleanor Hoyt. Series: Illustrated Sports. 1995, Ideals paper $6.95 (978-1-57102-049-9). 32pp. Introduces football's basic plays and techniques, equipment, and the rules. (Rev: BL 10/15/95; SLJ 1/96) [796.332]

26323 Stewart, Mark. *Football: A History of the Gridiron Game* (4–6). Illus. 1998, Watts LB $34.50 (978-0-531-11493-3). 144pp. A history of football from rugbylike competitions in England to the big-business sport it is today. (Rev: BL 4/1/99; HBG 10/99) [796.332]

26324 Stewart, Mark. *The Michigan Wolverines* (4–6). Illus. Series: Team Spirit-College Football. 2009, Norwood House LB $19.95 (978-1-59953-278-3). 48pp. For football fans, this volume traces the history of the famous team and looks at key games and players. (Rev: BL 4/1/09) [796.332]

26325 Sullivan, George. *All About Football* (3–5). Illus. 1990, Penguin paper $10.99 (978-0-399-21907-8). 128pp. Numerous photos aid in the telling of the game's development, history, complexities, and notable personalities through the years. (Rev: BCCB 12/87; BL 2/1/88)

26326 Woods, Bob. *NFC North* (4–6). Series: Inside the NFL. 2005, Child's World LB $28.50 (978-1-59296-513-7). 48pp. Introduces the four teams that make up the NFC North division of the National Football League, with discussion of their history and famous games and players. (Rev: BL 9/1/05) [796.332]

Gymnastics

26327 Bragg, Linda Wallenberg. *Fundamental Gymnastics* (3–6). Photos by Andy King. Illus. Series: Fundamental Sports. 1995, Lerner LB $22.60 (978-

0-8225-3453-2). 80pp. A brief history of gymnastics is given, including six events for boys and four for girls and basic moves and workouts. (Rev: SLJ 3/96) [796.44]

26328 Bray-Moffatt, Naia. *I Love Gymnastics* (K–3). Photos by avid Handley. Illus. 2005, DK $12.99 (978-0-7566-1011-1). 48pp. Excellent photographs show a young girl's introduction to the world of gymnastics, showing both basic and advanced moves. (Rev: BL 9/1/05; SLJ 5/06) [796.44]

26329 Ditchfield, Christin. *Gymnastics* (2–4). Illus. Series: True Books. 2000, Children's Book Pr. LB $25.00 (978-0-516-21063-6). 48pp. A simple introduction to gymnastics that describes some of the events, their history, and the equipment. (Rev: BL 9/15/00) [796.44]

26330 Kalman, Bobbie, and John Crossingham. *Gymnastics in Action* (4–7). Series: Sports in Action. 2002, Crabtree LB $25.27 (978-0-7787-0330-3); paper $6.95 (978-0-7737-0350-6). 32pp. Various branches of gymnastics are introduced in text and pictures with coverage of techniques, equipment, and basic movements. (Rev: BL 1/1–15/03) [796.44]

26331 Kuklin, Susan. *Going to My Gymnastics Class* (4–6). Illus. 1991, Macmillan LB $13.95 (978-0-02-751236-6). 40pp. The experiences of preschoolers at gymnastics class. (Rev: BCCB 10/91; BL 8/91; SLJ 12/91) [796.44]

26332 Readhead, Lloyd. *Gymnastics* (3–6). Illus. Series: Fantastic Book Of. 1997, Millbrook LB $22.40 (978-0-7613-0622-1). 32pp. Covers gymnastics techniques, training, warm-up exercises, and equipment, with an eight-page foldout section on competitions. (Rev: BL 3/15/98; HBG 3/98) [796.44]

Horsemanship

26333 Bolt, Betty. *Jumping* (4–8). Series: Horse Library. 2001, Chelsea $25.00 (978-0-7910-6657-7). 64pp. Show jumping, eventing, and steeplechase riding are all covered in detail here. Also use *Western Riding*. (Rev: HBG 3/02; SLJ 3/02) [798.4]

26334 Davis, Caroline. *The Young Equestrian* (5–8). Illus. 2000, Firefly $29.95 (978-1-55209-495-2); paper $19.95 (978-1-55209-484-6). 128pp. With a generous use of color photographs, this account devotes chapters to riding aids and techniques, choosing schools and proper equipment, buying and caring for a horse, and competitions. (Rev: BL 2/15/01; SLJ 2/01; VOYA 2/01) [798.2]

26335 Haas, Jessie. *Safe Horse, Safe Rider: A Young Rider's Guide to Responsible Horsekeeping* (4–7). Illus. 1994, Storey paper $16.95 (978-0-88266-700-3). 160pp. This guide to horsemanship stresses safety and covers such topics as understanding horse behavior. (Rev: BL 1/1/95) [636.1]

26336 Kimball, Cheryl. *Horse Showing for Kids* (4–8). Illus. 2004, Storey paper $16.95 (978-1-58017-501-2). 151pp. A comprehensive guide to showing horses, covering preparations for both horse and rider/handler, plus advice on safety,

sportsmanship, and appropriate attire (for animals and humans). (Rev: SLJ 2/05) [798.2]

26337 Kirksmith, Tommie. *Ride Western Style: A Guide for Young Riders* (4–8). Illus. 1991, Howell Book House $16.95 (978-0-87605-895-4). 212pp. Background information and step-by-step instructions for young people interested in learning to ride Western style. (Rev: BL 4/1/92; SLJ 7/92) [798.2]

26338 Mickle, Shelley Fraser. *Barbaro: America's Horse* (4–8). 2007, Simon & Schuster LB $16.89 (978-1-4169-4866-7); paper $8.99 (978-1-4169-4865-0). 147pp. The tragic story of racehorse Barbaro is told in straightforward but moving text, with lots of details about horses, racing, and genetic choices, plus many photographs. (Rev: SLJ 7/07) [636.1]

26339 Ransford, Sandy. *First Riding Lessons* (3–7). Illus. 2002, Kingfisher $14.95 (978-0-7534-5454-1). 64pp. This no-nonsense book takes young horse fans through choosing a riding instructor, learning about different types of mounts, basic lessons and exercises, and a brief view of equine competitions. (Rev: BL 1/1–15/03; HBG 3/03; SLJ 12/02) [798.2]

Ice Hockey

26340 Adelson, Bruce. *Hat Trick Trivia: Secrets, Statistics, and Little-Known Facts About Hockey* (4–7). Illus. 1998, Lerner LB $23.93 (978-0-8225-3315-3). 64pp. History, statistics, and trivia are combined in this lively discussion of hockey and its players. (Rev: BL 1/1–15/99) [796.962]

26341 Aretha, David. *The Montreal Canadiens Hockey Team* (4–6). Series: Great Sports Teams. 1998, Enslow LB $23.93 (978-0-7660-1022-2). 48pp. This book contains a history of the team and a rundown of their most valuable players and most exciting seasons. (Rev: BL 5/15/98; HBG 10/98) [796.48]

26342 Ayers, Tom. *The Illustrated Rules of Ice Hockey* (3–5). Illus. by Eleanor Hoyt. Series: Illustrated Sports. 1995, Ideals paper $6.95 (978-1-57102-048-2). 32pp. This book introduces the dimensions and parts of a hockey rink, the player's equipment, and basic rules of ice hockey. (Rev: BL 10/15/95; SLJ 1/96) [796.962]

26343 Brown, Jonatha A. *Hockey* (1–3). Series: My Favorite Sport. 2005, Weekly Reader LB $21.00 (978-0-8368-4340-8). 24pp. For beginning readers, this is an introduction to the history and sport of hockey, defining key terms. (Rev: SLJ 5/05)

26344 Carson, Paul, and Sean Rossiter. *Hockey the NHL Way: Tips from the Pros* (4–6). Illus. 2001, Sterling paper $9.95 (978-1-55054-864-8). 64pp. Excellent photographs accompany advice on skills and sportsmanship for young hockey fans from professional players and coaches. (Rev: BL 2/1/02) [796.962]

26345 Foley, Mike. *Fundamental Hockey* (4–8). Series: Fundamental Sports. 1996, Lerner LB $27.15 (978-0-8225-3456-3). The basics of ice hockey are introduced, accompanied by a brief history of the sport and an explanation of what the various players do. (Rev: SLJ 3/96) [796.962]

26346 Jensen, Julie, adapt. *Beginning Hockey* (4–8). Photos by Andy King. Series: Beginning Sports. 1996, Lerner LB $22.60 (978-0-8225-3506-5). 80pp. An introduction to hockey, its history, and the techniques and skills used by the players. (Rev: SLJ 3/96) [796.964]

26347 Kennedy, Mike. *Ice Hockey* (5–7). Series: Watts Library. 2003, Watts LB $25.50 (978-0-531-12273-0). 64pp. This overview explores the history of the sport, its rules, and styles of play, and provides information on some of the key players. (Rev: SLJ 2/04) [796.962]

26348 McFarlane, Brian. *Real Stories from the Rink* (5–8). Illus. by Steve Nease. 2002, Tundra paper $14.95 (978-0-88776-604-6). 96pp. Entertaining true stories give insight into ice hockey's history, rules, and players. (Rev: BL 2/15/03; SLJ 4/03) [796.962]

26349 McKinley, Michael, and Suzanne Levesque. *Ice Time: The Story of Hockey* (5–8). Illus. 2006, Tundra $18.95 (978-0-88776-762-3). 80pp. This history of ice hockey focuses mainly on the development and current status of the game in Canada, also covering international stars. (Rev: BL 12/1/06; SLJ 1/07) [796.962]

26350 O'Shei, Tim. *The Detroit Red Wings Hockey Team* (4–6). Series: Great Sports Teams. 2000, Enslow LB $23.93 (978-0-7660-1282-0). 48pp. Profiles the Detroit Red Wings, their history, great moments from the past, and famous players. (Rev: BL 9/15/00; HBG 10/01) [796.962]

26351 Wilson, Stacy. *The Hockey Book for Girls* (4–7). Illus. 2000, Kids Can $12.95 (978-1-55074-860-4); paper $6.95 (978-1-55074-719-5). 40pp. This book, by the former captain of Canada's women's Olympic hockey team, introduces ice hockey's rules, positions, strategies, and training and includes interviews with star players. (Rev: BL 3/1/01; HBG 3/01; SLJ 12/00) [796.962]

Ice Skating

26352 Cranston, Patty. *The Best on Ice: The World's Top Figure Skaters* (2–5). Illus. 1999, Kids Can paper $4.95 (978-1-55074-581-8). 32pp. This book on figure skating focuses on the careers of three young stars: Michelle Kwan, Todd Eldredge, and Tara Lipinski. (Rev: BL 10/15/99) [796.91]

26353 Helmer, Diana Star, and Thomas S. Owens. *The History of Figure Skating* (2–4). Series: Sports Throughout History. 2000, Rosen LB $19.95 (978-0-8239-5472-8). 24pp. This book gives a history of figure skating and information on equipment, along with biographical details on famous skaters. (Rev: SLJ 12/00) [796.91]

26354 Lindeen, Carol K. *Let's Ice-Skate!* (K–2). Series: Sports and Activities. 2005, Capstone LB $21.26 (978-0-7368-5360-6). 24pp. An attractive

introduction to the sport for beginning readers. (Rev: SLJ 6/06) [796.91]

26355 Macnow, Glen. *The Philadelphia Flyers Hockey Team* (4–6). Series: Great Sports Teams. 2000, Enslow LB $23.93 (978-0-7660-1279-0). 48pp. With a generous number of color and black-and-white photos, this slim book traces the history of the Philadelphia Flyers, their star players, and their greatest successes. (Rev: BL 3/15/00; HBG 10/00) [796.964]

26356 Schwartz, Heather E. *Girls' Figure Skating: Ruling the Rink* (3–6). Series: Girls Got Game. 2006, Capstone LB $25.26 (978-0-7368-6822-8). 32pp. An introduction to a popular sport, with tips on form, safety, terminology, and more, including profiles of famous skaters and lots of color photographs. (Rev: SLJ 7/07)

26357 Wilkes, Debbi. *The Figure Skating Book: A Young Person's Guide to Figure Skating* (4–8). Illus. 2000, Firefly LB $19.95 (978-1-55209-444-0); paper $12.95 (978-1-55209-445-7). 128pp. The author, an Olympic silver medalist, gives practical advice on figure skating from buying skates to simple and complicated skating techniques. (Rev: BL 7/00; SLJ 4/00) [796.9]

Indoor Games

26358 Bonner, Lori. *Putting on a Party: Adventure Parties for Kids* (3–6). Illus. by Fran Lee. 2004, Gibbs Smith paper $9.95 (978-1-58685-232-0). 63pp. Provides creative ideas for invitations, decorations, games and activities, and party foods with adventure themes — a polar expedition and a safari, for example. (Rev: SLJ 7/04) [793.2]

26359 Collis, Len. *Card Games for Children* (K–6). Illus. by Terry Carter and Bob George. 1989, Barron's paper $6.95 (978-0-8120-4290-0). 95pp. A collection of 41 card games with easily followed directions involving different numbers of players. (Rev: SLJ 3/90) [795.4]

26360 Erlbach, Arlene. *Video Games* (4–6). Illus. 1995, Lerner LB $19.95 (978-0-8225-2389-5). 48pp. An explanation of how video games came to be, how they are constructed, and how they work. (Rev: BL 8/95; SLJ 6/95) [794.8]

26361 Klingel, Cynthia, and Robert B. Noyed. *Card Tricks* (3–5). Series: Games Around the World. 2002, Compass Point LB $22.60 (978-0-7565-0190-7). 32pp. After background material on playing cards, this illustrated book highlights several baffling card tricks and shows how to perform them. (Rev: BL 5/15/02; SLJ 7/02) [795.4]

26362 Sheinwold, Alfred. *101 Best Family Card Games* (5–12). Illus. 1993, Sterling paper $5.95 (978-0-8069-8635-7). A book filled with games enjoyed by many age groups. (Rev: BL 2/15/93) [795.4]

Motor Bikes and Motorcycles

26363 Maurer, Tracy Nelson. *ATV Riding* (4–6). Illus. Series: Radsports. 2002, Rourke LB $20.95 (978-1-58952-276-3). 48pp. A jargon- and action-filled introduction to a "radical" sport, with photographs and Web sites. (Rev: BL 2/15/03) [796.7]

26364 Smedman, Lisa. *From Boneshakers to Choppers: The Rip-Roaring History of Motorcycles* (5–8). Illus. 2007, Annick $24.95 (978-1-55451-016-0); paper $14.95 (978-1-55451-015-3). 120pp. Covering all types of motorcycles, as well as all types of riders, this well-illustrated book will be popular with fans of transportation, extreme sports, history, and American popular culture. (Rev: BL 11/15/07) [629.227]

26365 Stuart, Dee. *Motorcycles* (2–4). Series: Transportation and Communication. 2001, Enslow LB $23.93 (978-0-7660-1648-4). 48pp. Using simple language and many illustrations, this short book describes the history and present developments related to motorcycles and their uses. (Rev: BL 3/15/02; HBG 3/02) [7796.7]

Olympic Games

26366 Fischer, David. *The Encyclopedia of the Summer Olympics* (4–8). Illus. Series: Watts Reference. 2003, Watts LB $37.00 (978-0-531-11886-3). 160pp. Events from archery to wrestling are organized in alphabetical order, with historical information from the first games to the forthcoming 2004 games, profiles of athletes, lists of gold medal winners, information on rules and equipment, and fast facts. (Rev: SLJ 12/03) [796.4]

26367 Gaff, Jackie. *Ancient Olympics* (3–6). Series: The Olympics. 2003, Heinemann LB $24.22 (978-1-4034-4676-3). 32pp. A concise look at the Ancient Olympics, with many illustrations and graphics, sidebars, and explanations of what the games involved as far back as 776 b.c. (Rev: SLJ 5/04) [796.48]

26368 Kristy, Davida. *Coubertin's Olympics: How the Games Began* (5–8). 1995, Lerner LB $26.63 (978-0-8225-3327-6). How the Olympic games began and information about Baron Pierre de Coubertin, their founder. (Rev: BL 8/95; SLJ 11/95) [338.4]

26369 Middleton, Haydn. *Ancient Olympic Games* (3–7). Series: Olympics. 1999, Heinemann LB $22.79 (978-1-57572-450-8). 32pp. This account describes the first Olympic Games, the nature of the events, and when and where they were held. (Rev: BL 4/15/00; SLJ 1/00) [796.49]

26370 Middleton, Haydn. *Crises at the Olympics* (3–7). Illus. Series: Olympics. 1999, Heinemann LB $22.79 (978-1-57572-452-2). 32pp. This account describes some of the scandals, controversies, and tragedies that have occurred at the Olympic Games

including the 1972 terrorism attack in Munich and the current drug testing of athletes. (Rev: BL 12/15/99; SLJ 1/00) [796.48]

26371 Middleton, Haydn. *Great Olympic Moments* (3–7). Series: Olympics. 1999, Heinemann LB $22.79 (978-1-57572-451-5). 32pp. Some of the great Olympic moments in modern times are retold in this exciting book. (Rev: BL 4/15/00) [796.49]

26372 Middleton, Haydn. *Modern Olympic Games* (3–7). Illus. 1999, Heinemann LB $22.79 (978-1-57572-453-9). 32pp. This account gives a history of the games from 1896 to the present with material on how new events are chosen and how the winter games came into being. (Rev: BL 12/15/99) [796.48]

26373 Middleton, Haydn. *Modern Olympics* (4–8). Series: The Olympics. 2003, Heinemann LB $16.95 (978-1-4034-4677-0). 32pp. A concise look at the modern games, with many illustrations, graphics, and sidebars, plus discussion of terrorism incidents, drug use, the choice of host cities, and the Paralympics. (Rev: SLJ 5/04) [796.48]

Running and Jogging

26374 Griffis, Molly Levite. *The Great American Bunion Derby* (5–10). 2003, Eakin $15.95 (978-1-57168-801-9); paper $9.95 (978-1-57168-810-1). 87pp. The story of a poor part-Cherokee farm boy who joined a marathon run across the United States in the late 1920s and won the $25,000 top prize. (Rev: BL 1/1–15/04; SLJ 3/04) [796.42]

26375 Hughes, Morgan. *Track and Field: The Jumps: Instructional Guide to Track and Field* (4–8). Series: Compete Like a Champion. 2001, Rourke LB $27.93 (978-1-57103-290-4). 48pp. This book includes material on the long jump, the triple jump, the high jump, and the pole vault, along with training tips. Also use in the same series *Track and Field: Middle and Long Distance Runs* and *Track and Field: The Sprints* (both 2001). (Rev: SLJ 3/01) [796.42]

26376 Manley, Claudia B. *Competitive Track and Field for Girls* (4–7). Illus. Series: Sportsgirl. 2001, Rosen LB $26.50 (978-0-8239-3408-9). 64pp. An introduction to the rules of track and field competitions, the training necessary, and the special opportunities for girls, with material on nutrition and the dangers of overtraining. (Rev: SLJ 3/02) [796.42]

Sailing and Boating

26377 Bass, Scott. *Kayaking* (4–6). Series: Kids' Guides. 2005, The Child's World LB $25.64 (978-1-59296-208-2). 32pp. An introduction to kayaking, describing its history and equipment and key athletes and competitions, with plenty of photographs and a glossary. (Rev: SLJ 7/05) [797.12]

26378 Ditchfield, Christin. *Kayaking, Canoeing, Rowing, and Yachting* (2–4). Illus. Series: True Books. 2000, Children's Book Pr. LB $25.00 (978-0-516-21610-2). 48pp. Introduces a range of water sports in a simple text with many color photos. (Rev: BL 9/15/00) [797.1]

26379 Kalman, Bobbie. *A Canoe Trip* (2–4). Illus. 1995, Crabtree paper $5.95 (978-0-86505-719-7). 32pp. Covers the parts of a canoe, safety considerations, and basic strokes. Also use *Summer Camp* (1994). (Rev: SLJ 7/95) [797.1]

26380 Revell, Phil. *Kayaking* (4–7). Series: Radical Sports. 1999, Heinemann LB $24.22 (978-1-57572-943-5). 32pp. A history of kayaks and kayaking is followed by material on basic skills, equipment, safety concerns, and competitions. (Rev: SLJ 5/00) [797.1]

26381 Wilson, Rich. *Racing a Ghost Ship: The Incredible Journey of Great American II* (3–6). Illus. 1996, Walker LB $17.85 (978-0-8027-8417-9). 48pp. Photographs, maps, and diagrams enliven this account of a voyage from San Francisco around the Cape Horn to Boston in 1993. (Rev: BL 10/1/96; SLJ 11/96) [910.4]

Martial Arts

26382 Ancona, George. *Capoeira: Game! Dance! Martial Art!* (2–4). Illus. 2007, Lee & Low $18.95 (978-1-58430-268-1). 32pp. Capoeira — a Brazilian blend of dance, martial art, and game — is shown in eye-catching photographs of students practicing in California. (Rev: BL 4/15/07) [793.3]

26383 Atwood, Jane. *Capoeira: A Martial Art and a Cultural Tradition* (5–8). Series: The Library of African American Arts and Culture. 1999, Rosen LB $27.95 (978-0-8239-1859-1). Capoeira, a unique martial art developed by African slaves in Brazil, is described, along with its history and preparations for its debut in the 2004 Olympic games. (Rev: SLJ 8/99) [796.8]

26384 Queen, J. Allen. *Learn Karate* (4–8). 1999, Sterling $17.95 (978-0-8069-8136-9). An excellent manual that covers the basics of karate — kicks, blocks, and stances — as well as stretches, meditation, safety, equipment, and sparring. (Rev: SLJ 5/99) [796.8]

26385 Rielly, Robin L. *Karate for Kids* (5–8). Illus. Series: The Martial Arts for Kids. 2004, Tuttle paper $13.95 (978-0-8048-3534-3). 48pp. After an overview of the history of karate, this appealing volume with clear illustrations looks at the moves, rules and etiquette, uniform and belts, and so forth. (Rev: BL 9/1/04; SLJ 2/05) [796.815]

26386 Scandiffio, Laura. *The Martial Arts Book* (3–5). Illus. by Nicolas Debon. 2003, Firefly paper $9.95 (978-1-55037-776-7). 64pp. The focus of this overview is the origins and evolution of various martial arts, looking at the spiritual aspects and overall benefits. (Rev: BL 4/15/03) [796.8]

Skateboarding

26387 Burke, L. M. *Skateboarding! Surf the Pavement* (5–8). Series: Extreme Sports. 1999, Rosen LB $26.50 (978-0-8239-3014-2). 64pp. This book supplies information for beginning and advanced skateboarders with coverage of history, techniques, equipment, and safety considerations. (Rev: SLJ 4/00) [796]

26388 Crossingham, John. *Skateboarding in Action* (4–7). Series: Sports in Action. 2002, Crabtree LB $25.27 (978-0-7787-0117-0); paper $6.95 (978-0-7787-0123-1). 32pp. A well-illustrated introduction to skateboarding with good material on equipment and injury prevention. (Rev: BL 9/1/02; SLJ 11/02) [795.2]

26389 Dieterich, Alice. *Tony Hawk and Andy MacDonald Ride* (2–3). Series: All Aboard Science Reader Station Stop. 2003, Penguin paper $3.99 (978-0-448-43160-4). 48pp. Skateboarding stars Tony Hawk and Andy MacDonald share some of their boarding experiences with readers. (Rev: BL 10/15/03; HBG 4/04; SLJ 1/04)

26390 Freimuth, Jeri. *Extreme Skateboarding Moves* (4–7). Illus. Series: Behind the Moves. 2001, Capstone LB $23.93 (978-0-7368-0783-8). 32pp. Skateboard slang is just one appealing part of this account of proper equipment and technique, with safety tips and some tricks. (Rev: BL 6/1–15/01; HBG 10/01; SLJ 9/01) [796.22]

26391 Hocking, Justin. *Awesome Obstacles: How to Build Your Own Skateboard Ramps and Ledges* (4–6). Illus. Series: Skateboarder's Guide to Skate Parks, Half-Pipes, Bowls, and Obstacles. 2005, Rosen LB $26.50 (978-1-4042-0337-2). 48pp. Along with advice on safety, this volume provides plans for the construction of six wooden ramps and boxes. (Rev: BL 9/1/05) [796.22]

26392 Horsley, Andy. *Skateboarding* (4–7). Illus. Series: To the Limit. 2001, Raintree LB $25.69 (978-0-7398-3163-2). 32pp. A brief history of skateboarding is included here along with material on equipment, moves, and some advice on turning pro. (Rev: BL 6/1–15/01) [796.22]

26393 Loizos, Constance. *Skateboard! Your Guide to Street, Vert, Downhill, and More* (4–9). Illus. Series: Extreme Sports. 2002, National Geographic paper $8.95 (978-0-7922-8229-7). 64pp. An attractive guide to skateboarding equipment, technique, rules, etiquette, jargon, and safety. (Rev: SLJ 1/03) [796.22]

26394 Maurer, Tracy Nelson. *Skateboarding* (3–6). Series: Radsports. 2001, Rourke LB $29.93 (978-1-58952-104-9). 48pp. Safety is emphasized in this account of skateboarding's history, equipment, and techniques that includes "Pro Spotlights." (Rev: SLJ 5/02) [796.22]

26395 Spencer, Russ. *Skateboarding* (4–6). Series: Kids' Guides. 2005, The Child's World LB $25.64 (978-1-59296-210-5). 32pp. An introduction to skateboarding, describing its history and equipment and key athletes and competitions, with plenty of photographs and a glossary. (Rev: SLJ 7/05) [796.2]

26396 Werner, Doug. *Skateboarder's Start-Up: A Beginner's Guide to Skateboarding* (4–8). 2000, Tracks paper $11.95 (978-1-884654-13-8). 144pp. Using a question-and-answer format, this introduction to skateboarding covers such subjects as equipment, history, and basic skating and technical tricks. (Rev: SLJ 12/00) [795.2]

Snowboarding

26397 Barr, Matt, and Chris Moran. *Snowboarding* (4–8). Illus. Series: Extreme Sports. 2003, Lerner LB $22.60 (978-0-8225-1242-4). 32pp. An appealing introduction to the history, equipment, techniques, safety concerns, and stars of this increasingly popular sport. (Rev: BL 3/1/04; SLJ 5/04; VOYA 6/04) [790.9]

26398 Brown, Gillian C. P. *Snowboarding* (5–8). Illus. Series: X-treme Outdoors. 2003, Children's LB $24.50 (978-0-516-24322-1); paper $6.95 (978-0-516-24383-2). 48pp. Equipment, technique, competition, and safety are covered here, as well as a history of this sport. (Rev: BL 4/15/03; SLJ 10/03) [796.9]

26399 Crossingham, John. *Snowboarding in Action* (4–7). Illus. by Bonna Rouse. Series: Sports in Action. 2002, Crabtree LB $25.27 (978-0-7787-0119-4); paper $6.95 (978-0-7787-0125-5). 32pp. Aspiring snowboarders will find much of interest here, including basic techniques. (Rev: BL 9/1/02; SLJ 11/02) [796.9]

26400 Degezelle, Terri. *Let's Snowboard!* (K–2). Series: Sports and Activities. 2005, Capstone LB $21.26 (978-0-7368-5366-8). 24pp. An attractive introduction to the sport for beginning readers, with emphasis on equipment and safety. (Rev: SLJ 6/06) [796.9]

26401 Fraser, Andy. *Snowboarding* (4–7). Series: Radical Sports. 1999, Heinemann LB $24.22 (978-1-57572-946-6). 32pp. This book covers the history of snowboarding, the equipment and clothing needed, techniques, terms, and how to get started. (Rev: SLJ 4/00) [796.9]

26402 Hayhurst, Chris. *Snowboarding! Shred the Powder* (5–8). Series: Extreme Sports. 1999, Rosen LB $26.50 (978-0-8239-3010-4). 64pp. The book supplies both beginning and advanced information on this sport, including material on history, equipment, techniques, and safety considerations. (Rev: SLJ 4/00; VOYA 6/00) [796.9]

26403 Herran, Joe, and Ron Thomas. *Snowboarding* (5–8). Illus. Series: Action Sports. 2003, Chelsea LB $28.00 (978-0-7910-7003-1). 32pp. Basic information on this sport's gear and performance is accompanied by biographical details about snowboarding champions. (Rev: BL 4/15/03; HBG 10/03) [796.9]

26404 Jensen, Julie, adapt. *Beginning Snowboarding* (4–8). Series: Beginning Sports. 1996, Lerner LB $27.15 (978-0-8225-3507-2). An introduction to snowboarding, with material on equipment, basic maneuvers, types of competition, and advanced stunts. (Rev: SLJ 3/96) [796.9]

26405 Lurie, John. *Fundamental Snowboarding* (4–8). Series: Fundamental Sports. 1996, Lerner LB $27.15 (978-0-8225-3457-0). With eye-catching photographs, the equipment and principles of snowboarding are covered, with material on basic and advanced maneuvers, skills, and stunts. (Rev: SLJ 3/96) [796.9]

26406 Woods, Bob. *Snowboarding* (4–6). Series: Kids' Guides. 2005, The Child's World LB $25.64 (978-1-59296-211-2). 32pp. An introduction to snowboarding, describing its history and equipment and key athletes and competitions, with plenty of photographs and a glossary. (Rev: SLJ 7/05) [796.9]

Soccer

26407 Bizley, Kirk. *Soccer* (K–2). Series: You Can Do It! 1999, Heinemann LB $19.92 (978-1-57572-962-6). 24pp. Colorful photos and cartoons are used to cover basic topics about soccer: warm-up exercises, moves, playing areas, rules, and safety. (Rev: SLJ 1/00) [796.334]

26408 Blackall, Bernie. *Soccer* (4–8). Illus. by Vasja Koman. Series: Top Sport. 1999, Heinemann LB $21.36 (978-1-57572-840-7). 32pp. This introduction to soccer covers history, equipment, rules, skills, and a few male and female stars. (Rev: SLJ 12/99) [796.334]

26409 Brown, Jonatha A. *Soccer* (1–3). Series: My Favorite Sport. 2005, Weekly Reader LB $21.00 (978-0-8368-4341-5). 24pp. For beginning readers, this is an introduction to the history and sport of soccer, defining key terms. (Rev: SLJ 5/05)

26410 Buckley, James, Jr. *Soccer Superstars* (2–5). Series: Boys Rock! 2006, The Child's World LB $25.64 (978-1-59296-736-0). 32pp. A good choice for beginning and reluctant readers (girls as well as boys), this colorful book looks at the status of soccer and profiles some of the game's most popular players. (Rev: SLJ 2/07) [796.3]

26411 Buckley, James, Jr. *Soccer Superwomen* (1–3). Series: Girls Rock! 2006, The Child's World LB $25.64 (978-1-59296-750-6). 32pp. Introduces readers to some of the world's best female soccer players and looks at the overall popularity of soccer. (Rev: SLJ 2/07) [796.3]

26412 Coleman, Lori. *Girls' Soccer: Going for the Goal* (3–6). Series: Girls Got Game. 2006, Capstone LB $25.26 (978-0-7368-6823-5). 32pp. Especially for girls, this overview of soccer will get readers excited about the sport. (Rev: SLJ 7/07)

26413 Coleman, Lori. *Soccer* (5–9). Series: Play-by-Play. 2000, Lerner paper $23.93 (978-0-8225-9876-3). 64pp. A fine introduction to the rules, equipment, and tactics of soccer with historical coverage through 1999. (Rev: SLJ 9/00) [796.334]

26414 Diehl, David. *Goal!* (PS–1). Illus. by author. 2008, Sterling $5.95 (978-1-60059-241-6). 28pp. A board book primer introducing the basics of soccer. (Rev: BLO 8/28/08) [796.3]

26415 Gibbons, Gail. *My Soccer Book* (PS–3). Illus. 2000, HarperCollins $6.99 (978-0-688-17138-4). 24pp. This accessible guide describes the playing field, equipment, rules, and the method of scoring. (Rev: BCCB 4/00; BL 5/1/00; HBG 10/00; SLJ 6/00) [796.334]

26416 Goin, Kenn. *Soccer for Fun!* (2–4). Illus. Series: Sports for Fun. 2003, Compass Point LB $25.26 (978-0-7565-0431-1). 48pp. Covering rules, necessary skills, and key figures, this is an attractive introduction for beginning readers. (Rev: SLJ 6/03) [796.334]

26417 Helmer, Diana Star, and Thomas S. Owens. *The History of Soccer* (2–4). Series: Sports Throughout History. 2000, Rosen LB $18.75 (978-0-8239-5467-4). 24pp. In addition to a history of soccer, this book profiles some championship players. (Rev: SLJ 12/00) [796.334]

26418 Lineker, Gary. *Soccer* (3–8). Series: Superguides. 2000, DK $9.99 (978-0-7894-5425-6). 44pp. Bright clear photographs and a straightforward text explain the fundamentals of soccer and give sound advice on improving one's game. (Rev: BL 6/1–15/00; HBG 10/00; SLJ 8/00) [796.334]

26419 Mackin, Bob. *Soccer the Winning Way: Play Like the Pros* (4–7). Illus. 2002, Douglas & McIntyre paper $10.95 (978-1-55054-825-9). 62pp. A guide to mastering crucial soccer skills, with photographs and words of wisdom from the pros. (Rev: BL 5/15/02) [796]

26420 Otten, Jack. *Soccer* (1–6). Series: Sports Training. 2002, Rosen LB $19.95 (978-0-8239-5972-3). 24pp. A brief and basic introduction to the sport that will be useful for reluctant readers and ESL students. (Rev: SLJ 3/02) [796.334]

26421 Owens, Thomas S., and Diana Star Helmer. *Soccer* (5–8). Series: Game Plan. 2000, Twenty-First Century LB $26.90 (978-0-7613-1400-4). 64pp. This introduction to soccer covers the different positions, game strategy, and memorable games and players of the past. (Rev: HBG 10/00; SLJ 7/00) [796.334]

26422 Page, Jason. *Soccer: Learn How to Be a Star Player* (3–5). Illus. by Mel Pickering. Series: Sports Club. 2000, Two-Can $9.95 (978-1-58728-001-6). 32pp. Soccer rules are explained along with some important plays and techniques, a little history, and profiles of important players. (Rev: SLJ 3/01) [796.334]

26423 Saunders, Catherine. *Play Soccer* (3–6). Photos by Russell Sadur. 2006, DK LB $12.99 (978-0-7566-2032-5). 63pp. This is a practical book that will help soccer players improve their passing and control of the ball; photographs demonstrate techniques. (Rev: SLJ 7/06) [796.334]

26424 Scott, Nina S. *The Thinking Kids Guide to Successful Soccer* (5–8). 1998, Millbrook LB $21.90 (978-0-7613-0324-4). An insider's look at strategies for kids playing soccer, including topics

not frequently addressed such as dealing with inexperienced coaches, unfair calls from referees, not getting enough playing time, and pressures of competition. The author encourages kids to have a good time and not to worry about making mistakes. (Rev: BL 5/15/99; HBG 9/99; SLJ 4/99) [796.334]

26425 Sherman, Josepha. *Competitive Soccer for Girls* (4–7). Series: Sportsgirl. 2001, Rosen LB $26.50 (978-0-8239-3405-8). 64pp. An introduction to the rules of soccer, the training necessary, and the special opportunities for girls, with material on nutrition and the dangers of overtraining. (Rev: SLJ 3/02) [796.334]

26426 Stewart, Mark. *The World Cup* (5–10). Series: The Watts History of Sports. 2003, Watts LB $34.50 (978-0-531-11957-0). 96pp. An overview of the international soccer championship that takes place every four years, this volume, which will be useful for reports, starts with the 1930 games and includes information on teams and players. (Rev: SLJ 3/04) [796.3]

26427 Suen, Anastasia. *The Story of Soccer* (1–3). Illus. Series: Sports History. 2002, Rosen LB $19.95 (978-0-8239-5998-3). 24pp. A basic, easy-to-read introduction to the sport. (Rev: BL 5/15/02; SLJ 3/02) [796.334]

26428 Thomas, Ron, and Joe Herran. *Getting into Soccer* (2–4). Illus. by Nives Porcellato and Andy Craig. Series: Getting into Sports. 2005, Chelsea House LB $28.00 (978-0-7910-8806-7). After a brief history of the game, this book covers rules, equipment, clothing, and competitions and provides color photographs, useful diagrams, and interesting trivia. (Rev: SLJ 12/05) [796.334]

26429 Venturini, Tisha Lea, and Judith Cohen. *You Can Be a Woman Soccer Player* (2–5). Illus. 2000, Cascade Pass $13.95 (978-1-880599-49-5); paper $7.00 (978-1-880599-48-8). 40pp. This is basically a biography of Venturini, a World Cup soccer player, plus tips on how to play the game and a brief history of the sport. (Rev: BL 10/1/00) [796.334]

26430 Wukovits, John. *The Composite Guide to Soccer* (4–8). 1998, Chelsea LB $28.00 (978-0-7910-4718-7). A basic guide to the history, rules, positions, and playing techniques of this sport, with material on its European popularity. (Rev: HBG 3/99; SLJ 12/98; VOYA 6/99) [796.334]

Surfing

26431 Barker, Amanda. *Windsurfing* (4–7). Series: Radical Sports. 1999, Heinemann LB $24.22 (978-1-57572-948-0). 32pp. After a history of windsurfing, this book describes equipment, safety tips, and basic skills. (Rev: SLJ 5/00) [797.2]

26432 Chapman, Garry. *Surf* (3–5). Series: Extreme Sports. 2001, Chelsea LB $28.00 (978-0-7910-6611-9). 32pp. This book covers the history of surfing, safety in the surf, and the extreme sports that began as spin-offs of traditional surfing. (Rev: BL 10/15/01; HBG 3/02; SLJ 12/01) [797.2]

26433 Maurer, Tracy Nelson. *Surfing* (4–6). Illus. Series: Radsports. 2002, Rourke LB $20.95 (978-1-58952-280-0). 48pp. A jargon- and action-filled introduction to a "radical" sport, with photographs and Web sites. (Rev: BL 2/15/03) [797.3]

Swimming and Diving

26434 Bizley, Kirk. *Swimming* (K–2). Series: You Can Do It! 1999, Heinemann LB $19.92 (978-1-57572-963-3). 24pp. A beginners guide to swimming with material on topics including water wings, basic strokes, and safety rules. (Rev: SLJ 1/00) [797.2]

26435 Crossingham, John, and Niki Walker. *Swimming in Action* (4–7). Series: Sports in Action. 2002, Crabtree LB $25.27 (978-0-7787-0331-0); paper $6.95 (978-0-7737-0351-3). 32pp. Color photographs and many diagrams are used with a clear text to describe swimming basics, with tips on various strokes and safety. (Rev: BL 1/1–15/03; SLJ 10/03) [977.2]

26436 Peterson, Sue H. *Swim with Me: A New Fun Approach to Learning to Swim* (PS–2). Illus. by Rama Von Baringer. 1999, Tricycle $12.95 (978-1-883672-94-2). 20pp. This book is intended for parents who are trying to prepare their children for swimming by showing how to teach floating, jumping in, gliding, proper breathing, and how to feel at home in the water. (Rev: SLJ 9/99) [797.2]

26437 Vander Hook, Sue. *Scuba Diving* (4–7). Illus. Series: World of Sports. 2000, Smart Apple LB $16.95 (978-1-887068-59-8). 32pp. After a section on star scuba divers, this account describes the origins and evolution of the sport, its equipment, hazards, and techniques. (Rev: BL 9/15/00) [797.2]

Tennis

26438 Blackall, Bernie. *Tennis* (4–8). Illus. by Vasja Koman. Series: Top Sport. 1999, Heinemann $21.36 (978-1-57572-842-1). 32pp. Double-page spreads present topics including the history of tennis, its equipment and rules, and important skills, plus a rundown on famous stars of the sport. (Rev: SLJ 12/99) [796.342]

26439 Crossingham, John. *Tennis in Action* (4–7). Series: Sports in Action. 2002, Crabtree LB $25.27 (978-0-7787-0116-3); paper $6.95 (978-0-7787-0122-4). 32pp. A fine introduction to tennis told through a concise text with easy-to-follow descriptions and material on equipment, rules, and techniques. (Rev: BL 9/1/02; SLJ 11/02) [796.342]

26440 Ditchfield, Christin. *Tennis* (1–3). Series: A True Book. 2003, Children's Pr. LB $25.00 (978-0-516-22589-0). 48pp. Rules, scoring, and other basics of the game are outlined in simple text and photographs, plus profiles of some of the key players. (Rev: SLJ 6/03) [796.342]

26441 Kaiman, Bobbie, and Sarah Dann. *Badminton in Action* (4–7). Series: Sports in Action. 2003, Crabtree LB $25.27 (978-0-7787-0334-1); paper $6.95 (978-0-7787-0354-9). 32pp. This basic introduction to badminton includes material on racquets, courts, rules, and strategies. (Rev: BL 11/15/03) [796.34]

26442 Muskat, Carrie. *The Composite Guide to Tennis* (5–7). Series: Composite Guide. 1998, Chelsea LB $12.95 (978-0-7910-4728-6). 64pp. Past and present tennis stars are mentioned along with a general introduction to the game. (Rev: HBG 10/98; SLJ 9/98) [796.342]

26443 Rutledge, Rachel. *The Best of the Best in Tennis* (4–7). Illus. 1998, Millbrook LB $24.90 (978-0-7613-1303-8). 64pp. Using a lively text and many color photographs, this work gives a history of women in tennis and a rundown of today's most important female players. (Rev: BL 2/15/99; HBG 10/99; SLJ 3/99) [796.342]

26444 Tym, Wanda. *The Illustrated Rules of Tennis* (3–5). Illus. Series: Illustrated Sports. 1995, Ideals paper $6.95 (978-1-57102-016-1). 32pp. Such topics as equipment, the tennis court, scoring, and the rules are covered in this introduction to tennis. (Rev: BL 7/95; SLJ 6/95) [796.342]

Track and Field

26445 Crossingham, John, and Bobbie Kalman. *Track Events in Action* (3–5). Illus. by Bonna Rouse. Series: Sports in Action. 2004, Crabtree LB $25.27 (978-0-7787-0339-6). 32pp. For beginning sprinters, steeplechasers, and other track enthusiasts, this is an attractive and useful introduction to equipment, technique, and vocabulary. (Rev: SLJ 6/05) [796.42]

26446 Kalman, Bobbie. *Field Events in Action* (3–5). Illus. Series: Sports in Action. 2004, Crabtree LB $25.27 (978-0-7787-0340-2); paper $6.95 (978-0-7787-0360-0). 32pp. For beginning enthusiasts of high and long jumps, pole vault, javelin throwing, and other field events, this is an attractive and useful introduction to equipment, technique, and vocabulary. (Rev: SLJ 6/05) [796.42]

26447 Knotts, Bob. *Track and Field* (2–4). Illus. Series: True Books. 2000, Children's Book Pr. LB $25.00 (978-0-516-21066-7). 48pp. Various track and field events are introduced in a simple text with material on their history and how they are judged. (Rev: BL 9/15/00) [796.42]

Author and Illustrator Index

Authors and illustrators are arranged alphabetically by last name, followed by book titles — which are also arranged alphabetically — and the text entry number. Book titles may refer to those that appear as a main entry or as an internal entry mentioned in the annotation. Fiction titles are indicated by (F) following the entry number.

One Ted Falls Out of Bed, 486(F)
Tickling Tigers, 2074(F)
The Wishing Club, 4284(F)
Currie, Philip J. *The Newest and Coolest Dinosaurs*, 16842
Currie, Stephen. *Adoption*, 20746
Escapes from Slavery, 18888
Miracles, Saints, and Superstition, 17302
Currie-Mcghee, Leanne K. *Emmanuel Ofosu Yeboah*, 16181
Currier, Katrina Saltonstall. *Kai's Journey to Gold Mountain*, 11018(F)
Curry, Barbara K. *Sweet Words So Brave*, 13794
Curry, Jane Louise. *The Black Canary*, 9036(F)
Brave Cloelia, 17223
Hold Up the Sky and Other Native American Tales from Texas and the Southern Plains, 12737
Curry, Tom. *The Bootmaker and the Elves*, 1418(F)
Buckamoo Girls, 2457(F)
Galileo's Universe, 15521
Curtis, Carolyn. *I Took the Moon for a Walk*, 3404(F)
Curtis, Chara M. *No One Walks on My Father's Moon*, 10386(F)
Curtis, Christopher Paul. *Bud, Not Buddy*, 10120(F)
Mr. Chickee's Funny Money, 8058(F)
The Watsons Go to Birmingham — 1963, 8536(F)
Curtis, Edward S. *Weave Little Stars into My Sleep*, 815
Curtis, Jamie Lee. *I'm Gonna Like Me*, 3405(F)
Is There Really a Human Race? 3406(F)
Today I Feel Silly, 5735(F)
Curtis, Marci. *Big Brother, Little Brother*, 4010(F)
Curtis, Neil. *Pirates Eat Porridge*, 4899(F)
Curtis, Sandra R. *Gabriel's Ark*, 10121(F)
Curtis, Stacy. *Raymond and Graham Rule the School*, 11610(F)
Curtiss, A. B. *In the Company of Bears*, 2075(F)
Curto, Rosa M. *I Have Asthma*, 21194
Let's Take Care of Our New Cat, 23671
Let's Take Care of Our New Dog, 23726
Let's Take Care of Our New Hamster, 6321(F)
Curtsinger, Bill. *Life Under Ice*, 18372
Sea Soup, 23271
Cushman, Doug. *Albert's Gift for Grandmother*, 3163(F)
The Amazing Trail of Seymour Snail, 2344(F)
Aunt Eater Loves a Mystery, 7311(F)
Aunt Eater's Mystery Halloween, 7036(F)
Aunt Eater's Mystery Vacation, 7312(F)
Dirk Bones and the Mystery of the Haunted House, 7313(F)
Dirk Bones and the Mystery of the Missing Books, 7314(F)
Fourth of July Mice! 6740(F)
Halloween Mice! 7084(F)
Inspector Hopper's Mystery Year, 7315(F)
¡Marimba! 127(F)
Mystery at the Club Sandwich, 2076(F)
The Mystery of the Monkey's Maze, 8059(F)
Thanksgiving Mice! 7197(F)
Tyrannosaurus Math, 2652(F)
Valentine Mice! 7215(F)
What a Day It Was at School! 13479
What Dads Can't Do, 3191(F)
What Grandmas Can't Do, 3192(F)
What Moms Can't Do, 3193(F)
What Teachers Can't Do, 3194(F)

Cushman, Jean. *Do You Wanna Bet?* 24503
Cushman, Karen. *The Ballad of Lucy Whipple*, 10858(F)
Matilda Bone, 10615(F)
Rodzina, 11019(F)
Cusimano, Maryann K. *You Are My I Love You*, 2077(F)
Cutbill, Andy. *The Cow That Laid an Egg*, 4700(F)
Cutchins, Judy. *Giant Predators of the Ancient Seas*, 16843
Cutler, Jane. *Common Sense and Fowls*, 3407(F)
Guttersnipe, 5347(F)
Leap, Frog, 8651(F)
Mr. Carey's Garden, 6006(F)
Rose and Riley, 2078(F)
Rose and Riley Come and Go, 7316(F)
Cuyler, Margery. *The Biggest, Best Snowman*, 7037(F)
Bullies Never Win, 6466(F)
The Bumpy Little Pumpkin, 7037(F)
From Here to There, 3408(F)
Groundhog Stays Up Late, 2079(F)
Hooray for Reading Day! 6467(F)
Monster Mess! 1143(F)
100th Day Worries, 475(F)
Please Play Safe! 3409(F)
Roadsigns, 12943
Skeleton Hiccups, 4701(F)
Stop, Drop, and Roll, 6468(F)
That's Good! That's Bad! 4702(F)
That's Good! That's Bad! In the Grand Canyon, 4703(F)
Weird Wolf, 9037(F)
We're Going on a Lion Hunt, 6469(F)
Cvijanovic, Adam. *The Ledgerbook of Thomas Blue Eagle*, 10691(F)
Cwiklik, Robert. *A. Philip Randolph and the Labor Movement*, 14664
Bill Clinton, 15029
Stokely Carmichael and Black Power, 14593
Cymerman, John E. *How's the Weather?* 24660
It's Just a Game, 3450(F)
Cyrus, Kurt. *The Clue of the Linoleum Lederhosen*, 11283(F)
Mammoths on the Move, 16950
Oddhopper Opera, 13507
Pest Fest, 2164
Sixteen Cows, 6401(F)
Tadpole Rex, 5117(F)
Word Builder, 3697(F)
Cytron, Barry. *Fire! The Library Is Burning*, 19372
Czarnota, Lorna MacDonald. *Medieval Tales That Kids Can Read and Tell*, 12125
Czech, Jan M. *An American Face*, 5736(F)
The Coffee Can Kid, 4011(F)
Czekaj, Jef. *Unite or Die*, 18841
Czernecki, Stefan. *Aziz the Storyteller*, 1305(F)
For Sure! For Sure! 11940
The Girl Who Lost Her Smile, 5271(F)
Holy Molé! 5499
Lilliput 5357, 1144(F)
Mama God, Papa God, 12893
Pancho's Pinata, 6856
The Sleeping Bread, 12864
Zorah's Magic Carpet, 1145(F)

D'Aluisio, Faith. *What the World Eats*, 21482
Da Costa, Deborah. *Hanukkah Moon*, 7109(F)
Dabaji, Mona Trad. *Lebanon 1-2-3*, 445

Dabcovich, Lydia. *The Ghost on the Hearth*, 1468(F)
Dabrowski, Kristen. *My Second Monologue Book*, 16751
Dacey, Bob. *Davy Crockett*, 13686
D'Adamo, Francesco. *Iqbal*, 10387(F)
Daddo, Andrew. *Goodnight, Me*, 707
Dadey, Debbie. *Leprechauns Don't Play Basketball*, 9038(F)
Shooting Star, 14194
This Side of Magic, 9039
Will Rogers, 14226(F)
Dahl, Felicity. *Revolting Recipes*, 25735
Dahl, Michael. *Ballistics*, 19934
Blood Evidence, 19935
Cause of Death, 19936
Computer Evidence, 19904
Double Bones, 16844
Eggs and Legs, 476(F)
England, 17920
Fingerprint Evidence, 19937
From the Garden, 477
Hands Down, 478(F)
If You Were a Noun, 16449
If You Were an Adjective, 16450
If You Were an Adverb, 16449
Last Son of Krypton, 9040
Long Arm, 16844
Lots of Ladybugs! Counting by Fives, 478(F)
Monster Fish, 16844
The Museum Monsters, 9041(F)
One Big Building, 477
Pie for Piglets, 476(F), 478(F)
Poison Evidence, 19904
The Tall, Tall Slide, 7317(F)
Dahl, Roald. *The Enormous Crocodile*, 2080(F)
Revolting Recipes, 25735
Vile Verses, 13012
The Witches, 9042(F)
Dahlberg, Maurine F. *The Story of Jonas*, 10788(F)
Daigle, Evelyne. *The World of Penguins*, 22949
Daigneault, Sylvie. *All on a Sleepy Night*, 706(F)
Daitch, Richard W. *Northwest Territories*, 18179
Dakos, Kalli. *The Bug in Teacher's Coffee*, 13433
Dal Sasso, Cristiano. *Animals*, 16845
Dalal, Anita. *Argentina*, 18317
Brazil, 18318
India, 17670
Myths of Oceania, 12911
Myths of Pre-Columbian America, 17268
Myths of Russia and the Slavs, 12912
Dalby, Danny Brooks. *Lara Ladybug*, 7357(F)
Dale, Anna. *Whispering to Witches*, 9043(F)
Dale, Penny. *The Jamie and Angus Stories*, 7355(F)
Jamie and Angus Together, 7356(F)
Dale, Shelley. *Tales from the Homeplace*, 11009(F)
Daley, Michael J. *Rat Trap*, 11701(F)
Shanghaied to the Moon, 11702(F)
Space Station Rat, 9044(F), 11701(F)
Daley, William. *The Chinese Americans*, 20521
Dalgleish, Sharon. *Exercise and Rest*, 21483
Protecting Wildlife, 19690
Dalgliesh, Alice. *The Bears on Hemlock Mountain*, 6007(F)
Courage of Sarah Noble, 10720(F)
The Thanksgiving Story, 7184(T)
Dall, Mary Doerfler. *Little Hands Create!* 25367

Lew, Kristi. *Goodbye, Gasoline*, 24760
Lewin, Betsy. *Aunt Minnie and the Twister*, 4344(F)
 Aunt Minnie McGranahan, 4345(F)
 Click, Clack, Moo, 2063(F)
 Click, Clack, Quackity-Quack, 42(F)
 Click, Clack, Splish, Splash, 473(F)
 Cowgirl Kate and Cocoa, 7691(F)
 Dooby Dooby Moo, 2064(F)
 Duck for President, 2065(F)
 Elephant Quest, 22666
 Giggle, Giggle, Quack, 2066(F)
 Gobble! 20456
 Gorilla Walk, 22465
 Heat Wave, 5613(F)
 Ho Ho Ho! 20373
 Horse Song, 17754
 A Hug Goes Around, 4260(F)
 Is It Far to Zanzibar? Poems About Tanzania, 13440
 Mushy! 20470
 My Tooth Is About to Fall Out, 7534(F)
 No Such Thing, 771(F)
 Partners, 7692(F)
 Promises, 4486(F)
 Purrfectly Purrfect, 9348(F)
 Rain or Shine, 7693(F)
 School Days, 7694(F)
 So, What's It Like to Be a Cat? 6168(F)
 Thump, Quack, Moo, 2068(F)
 Top to Bottom Down Under, 17818
 Two Eggs, Please, 3118(F)
 Weird! 20403
 Wiley Learns to Spell, 7515(F)
Lewin, Hugh. *Jafta*, 5483(F)
Lewin, Ted. *At Gleason's Gym*, 26114
 Barn Savers, 3523(F)
 The Doorman, 5764(F)
 Elephant Quest, 22666
 Gorilla Walk, 22465
 High as a Hawk, 5284(F)
 Horse Song, 17754
 How Much? Visiting Markets Around the World, 19662
 Lost City, 17276
 National Velvet, 8395(F)
 Nilo and the Tortoise, 6182(F)
 One Green Apple, 6441(F)
 Paperboy, 5460(F)
 Pennies in a Jar, 5320(F)
 Peppe the Lamplighter, 5286(F)
 The Potato Man, 3622(F)
 Sami and the Time of the Troubles, 5407(F)
 The Search for Grissi, 10272(F)
 Top to Bottom Down Under, 17818
 Touch and Go, 13918
 Winter Shoes for Shadow Horse, 4121(F)
 The World's Greatest Elephant, 22662
Lewington, Anna. *Antonio's Rain Forest*, 24271
 Mexico, 18235
 People of the Rain Forests, 24272
 What Do We Know About the Amazonian Indians? 18337
Lewis, Alan K. *I Grew Up on a Farm*, 5484(F)
Lewis, Alexandra P. *Funny Faces, Wacky Wings, and Other Silly Big Bird Things*, 22779
Lewis, Amanda. *The Jumbo Book of Paper Crafts*, 25654
 Lettering, 25585
 Making Memory Books, 25408
Lewis, Barbara A. *The Kid's Guide to Service Projects*, 20677
 The Kid's Guide to Social Action, 20678
Lewis, Barbara S. *Being Your Best*, 20679
Lewis, Beverly. *Catch a Falling Star*, 10214(F), 10215(F)

The Chicken Pox Panic, 8743(F)
The Crazy Christmas Angel Mystery, 11248(F)
The Double Dabble Surprise, 8743(F)
Frog Power, 11616(F)
Holly's First Love, 9836(F)
Night of the Fireflies, 10215(F)
Secret Summer Dreams, 9836(F)
Whispers down the Lane, 8744(F)
Lewis, Brenda Ralph. *Meat-Eating Dinosaurs*, 16900
 Plant-Eating Dinosaurs, 16901
 Prehistoric Creatures in the Sea and Sky, 16902
 Small and Deadly Dinosaurs, 16903
Lewis, C. S. *The Horse and His Boy*, 9366(F), 9367(F)
 The Magician's Nephew, 9366(F)
Lewis, Celeste. *Lost*, 6138(F)
Lewis, Claudia. *Long Ago in Oregon*, 13121(F)
Lewis, Cynthia C. *Dilly's Big Sister Diary*, 4210(F)
 Dilly's Summer Camp Diary, 11410(F)
 Open Your Eyes, 21404
 Perk up Your Ears, 21405
Lewis, E. B. *Bippity Bop Barbershop*, 3811(F)
 Circle Unbroken, 4353(F)
 Coming on Home Soon, 5682(F)
 Creativity, 4596(F)
 D Is for Drinking Gourd, 20600
 Danitra Brown, Class Clown, 4542(F)
 Dirt on Their Skirts, 5579(F)
 Down the Road, 4389(F)
 Faraway Home, 4187(F)
 Happy Feet, 5523(F)
 Homegrown House, 4489
 I Love My Hair! 3812(F)
 I Want to Be Free, 5609(F)
 Joe-Joe's First Flight, 5882(F)
 Keeping the Night Watch, 13226
 Lily Brown's Paintings, 3558(F)
 Little Cliff and the Cold Place, 5630(F)
 The Magic Tree, 12236
 My Best Friend, 4585(F)
 My Rows and Piles of Coins, 5528(F)
 The Negro Speaks of Rivers, 13298
 Night Boat to Freedom, 10821(F)
 Night Running, 5315(F)
 The Other Side, 4606(F)
 Pitching In for Eubie, 4289(F)
 Talkin' About Bessie, 13670
 This Little Light of Mine, 16571
 Virgie Goes to School with Us Boys, 5774(F)
Lewis, Elizabeth. *Mexican Art and Culture*, 18236
Lewis, Gill. *The Most Precious Thing*, 2562(F)
Lewis, H. B. *My Penguin Osbert in Love*, 1350(F)
Lewis, J. Patrick. *Arithme-Tickle*, 24507
 Big Is Big (and Little, Little), 265
 Birds on a Wire, 13130
 Blackbeard, 13122
 Castles, 13129
 Earth and Me, 5193(F)
 Earth and Us — Continuous, 13527
 Earth and You, 16771
 Freedom Like Sunlight, 13301
 Galileo's Universe, 15521
 Heroes and She-roes, 13123
 Once Upon a Tomb, 13458
 Please Bury Me in the Library, 13124
 Scien-Trickery, 25899
 The Snowflake Sisters, 6917(F)
 The Stolen Smile, 10569(F)
 Tulip at the Bat, 13459
 The Underwear Salesman, 13125

Vherses, 13126
Wing Nuts, 13386
A World of Wonders, 13127
The World's Greatest Poems, 13128
Lewis, Jan. *Small Bad Wolf*, 7721(F)
Lewis, K. E. *Will It Blow?* 24148
Lewis, Kevin. *Dinosaur Dinosaur*, 2563(F)
 My Truck Is Stuck! 2564(F)
 The Runaway Pumpkin, 7067(F)
Lewis, Kim. *Good Night, Harry*, 774(F)
 Hooray for Harry, 1404(F)
 A Puppy for Annie, 6183(F)
 Seymour and Henry, 2565(F)
 The Shepherd Boy, 3604(F)
Lewis, Maggie. *Morgy Coast to Coast*, 7881(F), 10216(F)
 Morgy's Musical Summer, 7882(F)
Lewis, Naomi. *The Snow Queen*, 12016(F)
Lewis, Naomi, retel. *Elf Hill*, 12015(F)
Lewis, Paeony. *I'll Always Love You*, 2566(F)
 No More Cookies! 3605(F)
 No More Yawning! 775(F)
Lewis, Paul Owen. *The Jupiter Stone*, 1405(F)
Lewis, Richmond. *Batman*, 9943(F)
Lewis, Rob. *Brothers and Sisters*, 2567(F)
 Grandpa at the Beach, 7516(F)
 Grandpa Comes to Stay, 4211(F)
 Too Much Trouble for Grandpa, 7517(F)
Lewis, Rose. *Every Year on Your Birthday*, 6779(F)
 I Love You Like Crazy Cakes, 5485(F)
Lewis, Sara. *Kids' Baking*, 25771
Lewis, Thomas P. *Hill of Fire*, 18237
Lewis, Wendy A. *In Abby's Hands*, 6184(F)
Lewis, Zoe. *Keisha Discovers Harlem*, 11077(F)
Lewison, Wendy C. *Shy Vi*, 2568(F)
Lewison, Wendy Cheyette. *Two Is for Twins*, 266(F)
Leznoff, Glenda. *Pigmalion*, 2569(F)
L'Homme, Erik. *Tales of a Lost Kingdom*, 12697
Li, Xiao Jun. *Nekane, the Lamina and the Bear*, 12637
 The Perfect Orange, 12223
Lia, Simone. *Billy Bean's Dream*, 1406(F)
Liano, Dante. *The Girl from Chimel*, 16120
 The Honey Jar, 12879
Liao, Jimmy. *The Sound of Colors*, 5807(F)
Libal, Joyce. *Professional Athlete and Sports Official*, 20895
Libby, Barbara M. *I Rode the Red Horse*, 23779
Liberman, Sherri. *Historical Atlas of Azerbaijan*, 18002
Libura, Krystyna. *What the Aztecs Told Me*, 17277
Licata, Renora. *Princess Diana*, 16049
Lichtenberg, Andre. *Brazil*, 18338
Lichtenheld, Tom. *Duck! Rabbit!* 297
 Everything I Know About Cars, 25232
 Everything I Know About Monsters, 9368(F)
 It's Not Fair! 5853(F)
 What Are You So Grumpy About? 5808(F)
 What's with This Room? 4212(F)
 Yes Day! 3739(F)
Lichtman, Wendy. *Do the Math*, 7883(F)
Liddell, Janice. *Imani and the Flying Africans*, 12841
Lieber, Susan F. *Parks for the People*, 14892
Liebman, Dan. *I Want to Be a Doctor*, 20934
 I Want to Be a Mechanic, 6647
 I Want to Be a Nurse, 20935
 I Want to Be a Police Officer, 20962
 I Want to Be a Teacher, 20851
 I Want to Be a Truck Driver, 20994

Title Index

This index contains both main entry titles and internal titles cited within entries. References are to entry numbers, not page numbers. Fiction titles are indicated by (F) following the entry number.

Turkey, 17853, 17854, 17865, 17869

Turkey Bowl, 7176(F)

A Turkey for Thanksgiving, 7179(F)

The Turkey Girl: A Zuni Cinderella Story, 12777

Turkey in Pictures, 17855

Turkey Surprise, 7172(F)

Turkeys Together, 7745(F)

The Turn-Around, Upside-Down Alphabet Book, 58

Turn It Loose: The Scientist in Absolutely Everybody, 21638

Turn of the Century, 17039

The Turnip, 12428

Turnip Soup, 4907(F)

Turns on a Dime, 10210(F)

Turtle and Snake's Spooky Halloween, 7704(F)

The Turtle and the Monkey: A Philippine Tale, 12392

Turtle Crossing, 22176

Turtle Dreams, 7238(F)

Turtle Girl, 4005(F)

Turtle in the Sea, 5914(F)

Turtle Rescue: Changing the Future for Endangered Wildlife, 22183

Turtle Splash! Countdown at the Pond, 497(F)

Turtle Spring, 6416(F)

Turtle Summer: A Journal for My Daughter, 22194

Turtle Tracks, 6280(F)

Turtle, Turtle, Watch Out! 22198

Turtles, 22185, 22199, 22201, 23620

Turtles and Tortoises, 22197

Turtle's Race with Beaver: A Traditional Seneca Story, 1957(F)

The Tuskegee Airmen, 17381, 17386

The Tuskegee Airmen Story, 5418(F)

Tut, Tut, 9591(F)

Tutankhamen's Gift, 16170

Tutankhamun: The Mystery of the Boy King, 16169

Tut's Mummy: Lost . . . and Found, 7335(F)

Tuttle's Red Barn: The Story of America's Oldest Family Farm, 10413

TV Rex, 1488(F)

TV Takeover: Questioning Television, 16746

TV's Forgotten Hero: The Story of Philo Farnsworth, 15497

TWA Flight 800: Explosion in Midair, 24982

'Twas the Day After Christmas, 13419

'Twas the Night Before Christmas; or, Account of a Visit from St. Nicholas, 13415

Tweedle-Dee-Dee, 16606

The Twelfth of June, 10342(F)

The Twelve Dancing Princesses, 12426

The Twelve Days of Christmas, 16629

The Twelve Days of Christmas: A Pinata for the Pinon Tree, 16628

The Twelve Days of Christmas Dogs, 16615

The Twelve Days of Kindergarten: A Counting Book, 614

The Twelve Days of Springtime: A School Counting Book, 615

The Twelve Days of Winter: A School Counting Book, 616(F)

12 Easy Knitting Projects, 25673

Twelve Hats for Lena: A Book of Months, 3574(F)

1200, 17101

Twelve Lizards Leaping: A New Twelve Days of Christmas, 16627

The Twelve Months, 12606

Twelve Plump Cookies, 7257(F)

Twelve Rounds to Glory: The Story of Muhammad Ali, 15841

Twelve-Year-Old Vows Revenge After Being Dumped by Extraterrestrial on First Date, 11478(F)

The 20th Century Children's Book Treasury: Celebrated Picture Books and Stories to Read Aloud, 1613(F)

The 20th Century Children's Poetry Treasury, 13198

Twenty and Ten, 11139(F)

Twenty Heartbeats, 5405(F)

20 Hungry Piggies: A Number Book, 522

Twenty-One Balloons, 11344(F)

Twenty-One Elephants and Still Standing, 5572(F)

26 Fairmount Avenue, 14323

26 Letters and 99 Cents, 78(F)

Twenty-six Princesses, 254(F)

2030: A Day in the Life of Tomorrow's Kids, 24976

Twice a Hero: Polish American Heroes of the American Revolution, 16001

Twice As Nice: What It's Like to Be a Twin, 20779

Twice My Size, 6246(F)

Twice Upon a Marigold: Part Comedy, Part Tragedy, Part Two, 11983(F)

Twice Yours: A Parable of God's Gift, 4089(F)

The Twiddle Twins' Haunted House, 9141(F)

Twiddle Twins' Music Box Mystery, 9141(F)

Twilight Comes Twice, 5143(F)

Twilight Hunt: A Seek-and-Find Book, 6264(F)

Twilight in Grace Falls, 8725(F)

The Twin Giants, 7480(F)

The Twin Princes, 4625(F)

Twin to Twin, 4298(F)

The Twinkie Squad, 7877(F)

Twinkle, Twinkle, Little Star, 876(F), 16591

Twinkle, Twinkle, Little Star: And Other Favorite Bedtime Rhymes, 895

Twist: Yoga Poems, 13270

A Twist in the Tail: Animal Stories from Around the World, 12149

Twister, 3229(F)

Twisters! 24592

Two at the Zoo: A Counting Book, 632

Two Bad Ants, 3054(F)

Two Bad Bears, 2794(F)

Two Bad Pilgrims, 4846(F)

Two Bear Cubs, 12784

Two Bobbies: A True Story of Hurricane Katrina, Friendship, and Survival, 24599

The Two Brothers, 11062(F)

Two by Two, 20234

Two Christmas Mice, 6858(F)

Two Eggs, Please, 3118(F)

Two False Moves, 9858(F)

Two Fools and a Horse: An Original Tale, 9053(F)

Two Hot Dogs with Everything, 11868(F)

Two Hundred Thirteen Valentines, 11559(F)

Two in the Wilderness: Adventures of a Mother and Daughter in the Adirondack Mountains, 26300

2 Is for Toucan: Oodles of Doodles from 0 to 42, 25624

Two Is for Twins, 266(F)

Two Lands, One Heart: An American Boy's Journey to His Mother's Vietnam, 17779

Two Little Trains, 6615(F)

Two Lives: Metamorphosis in the Natural World, 22018

Two Messy Friends, 7251(F)

Two-Minute Drill, 11885(F)

Two Miserable Presidents: Everything Your Schoolbooks Didn't Tell You About the Civil War, 19110

The Two Mountains: An Aztec Legend, 12873

Two Mrs. Gibsons, 4140(F)

Two of a Kind, 9818(F)

Two of Everything: A Chinese Folktale, 12314

The Two of Them, 3884(F)

The Two Princesses of Bamarre, 9363(F)

Two Shoes, Blue Shoes, New Shoes! 3453(F)

Two Shoes, New Shoes, 3538(F)

The 2000 Election, 19966

The 2001 World Trade Center Attack, 20626

The 2000 Presidential Election, 19972

Two Tickets to Freedom: The True Story of Ellen and William Craft, Fugitive Slaves, 18896

2 x 2=Boo! A Set of Spooky Multiplication Stories, 7066(F)

The Two Tyrones, 7454(F)

Two Under Par, 10039(F)

Two Ways to Count to Ten: A Liberian Folktale, 12232

Two's Company, 7675(F)

Tycho Brahe: Pioneer of Astronomy, 15397

The Tygrine Cat, 9240(F)

Typhoid Fever, 21205

Tyra Banks, 14089

Tyrannosaurus and Other Dinosaurs of North America, 16854

Tyrannosaurus Math, 2652(F)

Tyrannosaurus Time, 16930

Tyrannosaurus Was a Beast, 13360(F)

Tyrone the Horrible, 3158(F)

Ty's Triple Trouble, 10232

Tyson the Terrible, 2231(F)

USA from Space, 24872

UFO Mysteries, 25977

UFOs, 25998, 26025

Uganda, 17512, 17517

Ugh! A Bug! 23024

The Uglified Ducky: A Maynard Moose Tale, 11965(F)

The Ugly Duckling, 11948(F), 11949(F), 11950, 12053(F)

Ugly Fish, 6175(F)

The Ugly Goddess, 10454(F)

The Ugly Princess and the Wise Fool, 11990(F)

The Ugly Pumpkin, 7051(F)

The Ugly Vegetables, 4214(F)

Uh-Oh! 3548(F)

Uh-oh, Cleo, 4096(F)

Uh-oh, Cleo: Underpants on My Head, 4097(F)

Uh Oh! Gotta Go! Potty Tales from Toddlers, 3625

Uh-oh! It's Mama's Birthday! 4444(F)

Ukraine, 17984, 17989, 18001, 18013

Ukrainian Egg Decoration: A Holiday Tradition, 20397

Ukrainians in America, 20553

The Ultimate Baby-Sitter's Handbook: So You Wanna Make Tons of Money? 19679

The Ultimate Book of Kid Concoctions, 25496

Ultimate Field Trip 5: Blasting Off to Space Academy, 24882

Subject/Grade Level Index

All entries are listed by subject and then according to grade level suitability (see the key at the foot of pages for grade level designations). Subjects are arranged alphabetically and subject heads may be subdivided into nonfiction (e.g., "Trucks") and fiction (e.g., "Trucks — Fiction"). References to entries are by entry number, not page number.

A

Aardema, Verna
PI: 14263
Aaron, Hank — Fiction
PI: 5477
Aaron, Henry
PI: 15718 IJ: 15719
Abdul, Paula
IJ: 14074
Abdul-Jabbar, Kareem
IJ: 15783
Abenaki Indians — Fiction
PI: 10683 IJ: 8023, 8731
Abenaki Indians — Folklore
I: 12727
Abilities
P: 20699
Abolition — Biography
PI: 14775 I: 14510, 14774, 15231 IJ: 14612, 14683, 15244
Abolition — Fiction
I: 9960, 10887 IJ: 10815
Abolitionists
See Slavery
Abominable snowman
See also Yeti
I: 26029 IJ: 25986
Aborigines (Australia)
I: 17805, 17823 IJ: 17803, 17827
Aborigines (Australia) — Art
IJ: 16192, 16220
Aborigines (Australia) — Fiction
P: 5264 I: 10377
Aborigines (Australia) — Folklore
P: 12396
Abortion
IJ: 19800
Abraham (Bible) — Fiction
I: 11241

Acadia — Fiction
I: 10719
Acceptance — Fiction
P: 1865
Accidents
P: 21534 I: 21531, 21533 IJ: 21284, 21536
Accidents — Fiction
P: 4326, 7632 I: 10112, 10372, 11020 IJ: 7954
Acid rain
I: 19768
Acropolis (Greece)
IJ: 17208
Acting
PI: 16751 IJ: 13605, 16749, 16753
Acting — Biography
P: 15925 PI: 14094, 14108, 14124, 14139, 14146, 14148, 14152, 14172, 14179, 14187, 14211, 14215, 14217–19, 14230–31, 14239, 14241, 14251, 14255 I: 14099, 14117, 14127, 14138, 14225, 14253, 14262 IJ: 14093, 14107, 14109–10, 14112, 14118, 14120, 14136, 14163, 14166, 14178, 14183, 14190, 14203–6, 14213–14, 14220, 14227, 14232, 14929
Acting — Careers
PI: 16734
Acting — Fiction
P: 6476 PI: 5377 I: 11053, 11373, 11599 IJ: 11104
Activism
See also Social action
IJ: 19687, 21230
Activism — Biography
IJ: 16020
Activism — Fiction
P: 3457 IJ: 7913, 10299
Ada, Alma Flor
I: 14264
Adams, Abigail
P: 15203 I: 15201 IJ: 15007, 15200, 15202
Adams, Ansel
I: 13822

Adams, John
P: 15006 PI: 18834 I: 15005 IJ: 15002–4, 15007
Adams, John Quincy
P: 15010 I: 15009, 15011 IJ: 15008
Adams, John Quincy — Fiction
PI: 5456 I: 10811
Adams, Samuel
P: 14740 I: 14742, 14744 IJ: 14741, 14743
Addams, Jane
PI: 15204 IJ: 15205–7, 19267
Addictions
See also Alcohol and alcohol abuse; Drugs and drug abuse; Smoking
IJ: 21036, 21163
Addition (mathematics)
P: 455, 24456 I: 24480 IJ: 24430
Adirondack Mountains (N.Y.)
I: 26300
Adjectives
P: 16438, 16450
Adler, David A.
I: 14265
Adoption
See also Foster care; Stepfamilies
P: 20769, 20774 IJ: 20746, 20759–60
Adoption — Fiction
P: 1873, 2121, 2309, 3149, 3950, 3966, 3998, 4011–12, 4044, 4056, 4117, 4165, 4172, 4184, 4200, 4281, 4286, 4302, 4316, 4322, 4433, 4437, 4442, 4497, 4509, 5485, 5823, 5839, 5855, 6779, 7449, 7481, 12017 PI: 1933, 3961, 8535 I: 7917, 10047, 10373 IJ: 8168, 8509, 8669, 8758, 10210, 10310, 10921, 11017, 11897
Adoption — Poetry
P: 13273

Adu, Freddy
I: 15907
Adventure stories — Fiction
P: 1355, 1524–25, 1967, 1982, 2976, 3164, 3224, 3226–29, 3232, 3234–37, 3242–43, 3245, 3251, 3254–55, 3260, 3265–67, 3269, 3273, 3277–78, 3283–84, 3286, 3289, 5397, 5505, 5543, 6007, 6182, 6931, 7290, 7293, 7635, 7757, 8060, 11609 PI: 3238, 5472, 5943, 8126, 8133, 8157–58, 8191, 8967, 9232, 10776, 10796, 10817, 10997, 11002 I: 7910, 7969, 7995, 8010–11, 8013, 8036–38, 8045, 8073–75, 8080, 8084, 8104, 8116, 8125, 8128, 8140, 8143, 8183, 8190, 8209, 8216, 8257–58, 8262, 8265, 8268, 8280–81, 8286, 8292, 8296–97, 8311–15, 8331, 8346, 8348, 8354, 8357–58, 8362, 8381, 8461, 9486, 9539, 9654, 9897, 9953, 10415, 10492, 10526, 10657, 10789, 10792, 10864, 11134, 11185, 11532, 11762, 16765 IJ: 3271, 7774, 7780, 7789, 7792, 7798, 7821, 7956, 7971, 7986, 7988–89, 7999, 8012, 8015, 8022, 8039, 8052, 8055, 8065–66, 8069–70, 8072, 8085, 8088–89, 8091, 8098, 8101–2, 8105, 8114, 8117, 8123–24, 8132, 8134, 8136, 8141, 8144–45, 8148–49, 8151, 8155, 8160–62, 8170–71, 8178, 8185, 8188, 8208, 8211, 8218, 8231, 8236, 8240, 8243, 8245, 8250–51, 8254–55, 8259, 8261, 8263–64, 8266, 8270–71, 8273–74, 8283, 8295, 8303, 8309–10, 8319–20, 8325–26, 8334–37, 8347, 8349, 8351, 8353, 8356, 8365, 8367, 8370, 8376, 8384–85, 8390, 8392, 8578, 8722, 8745, 8819,

P = Primary; PI = Primary-Intermediate; I = Intermediate; IJ = Intermediate-Junior High

P = Primary; PI = Primary-Intermediate; I = Intermediate; IJ = Intermediate-Junior High

P = Primary; PI = Primary-Intermediate; I = Intermediate; IJ = Intermediate-Junior High

P = Primary; PI = Primary-Intermediate; I = Intermediate; IJ = Intermediate-Junior High

P = Primary; PI = Primary-Intermediate; I = Intermediate; IJ = Intermediate-Junior High

P = Primary; PI = Primary-Intermediate; I = Intermediate; IJ = Intermediate-Junior High

P = Primary; PI = Primary-Intermediate; I = Intermediate; IJ = Intermediate-Junior High

22886, 22905, 22914, 22942, 23604, 23643, 23649, 24171
PI: 22766, 22773, 22790, 22794, 22804, 22813, 22829, 22836–37, 22846, 22860–61
I: 22767–68, 22781, 22788, 22799–800, 22805–6, 22812, 22821, 22823, 22830, 22832, 22834, 22840, 22843, 22851, 22854, 22857–58, 22875, 22918, 22923, 22925, 22927, 23619 **IJ:** 18450, 22771–72, 22782, 22795, 22807, 22817, 22822, 22855, 22863, 22890, 22972

Birds — Beaks
P: 22777, 22849

Birds — Behavior
P: 22920

Birds — Eggs
P: 22920 **IJ:** 22865

Birds — Evolution
I: 16938

Birds — Experiments and projects
PI: 12173 **I:** 22791

Birds — Fiction
P: 2116, 2446, 2580, 2667, 2865, 2871, 5131, 5152, 5324, 5878, 5958, 5963, 5966, 5969, 6018, 6035, 6071, 6098, 6137, 6143, 6198, 6251, 6336, 6355, 6418, 6560, 7345, 7652
PI: 3216, 5933, 9562 **I:** 8465, 9146, 10482 **IJ:** 8426, 8860, 10286

Birds — Folklore
P: 12123, 12202, 12903
PI: 12173, 12824 **I:** 12178
IJ: 12160

Birds — Nests
P: 22780, 22867, 22869
PI: 22868 **I:** 22864

Birds — Pets
PI: 23602

Birds — Poetry
P: 13344, 13361, 13363
I: 13362, 13378, 13380
IJ: 13319

Birds — Songs
I: 22788, 22866

Birds — Wading
I: 22820

Birds of prey
See also individual species, e.g., Eagles
I: 22902, 22918 **IJ:** 22890, 22894, 22903

Birmingham (AL) — Poetry
I: 13258

Birth
P: 21566, 21568, 21570
I: 20084, 20130

Birth — Fiction
P: 1684, 4371

Birth order
IJ: 20808

Birthdays
PI: 16690, 20314, 20334

Birthdays — Crafts
PI: 20334, 25504 **I:** 20257

Birthdays — Fiction
P: 640, 1320, 1585, 1786, 1809, 2200, 2216, 2393, 2514, 2594, 2881, 2896, 3163, 3223, 3949, 4366, 4394, 4583, 5348,

5775, 6086, 6752, 6754, 6756, 6758–66, 6768, 6770–91, 6793–800, 6802–8, 7292, 7320, 7333, 7366, 7395, 7448, 7460, 7653, 7713, 7724, 7728
PI: 6753, 6757, 6792, 8943, 9815, 11416 **I:** 10934, 11253

Birthdays — Poetry
P: 13399 **PI:** 13398

Bismarck (ship)
IJ: 17413

Bison
P: 14999, 22398 **PI:** 22358
I: 18558, 22354, 22410, 22419 **IJ:** 18620, 22395, 22442

Bison — Fiction
P: 5370, 5912 **PI:** 6024, 11125

Biting — Fiction
P: 2755

Black, Jack
I: 14099

Black, Shirley Temple
I: 14100

Black (color) — Fiction
P: 3535

Black Death
IJ: 17303, 17328

Black Death — Fiction
IJ: 10588

Black Elk
I: 14944

Black holes
I: 21740, 21743

Blackbeard — Fiction
I: 9950

Blackberries — Fiction
P: 6276

Blackfeet Indians
PI: 18591

Blackouts (electric)
IJ: 20040

Blacks — Biography
IJ: 15890

Blacksmiths — Biography
IJ: 13996

Blacksmiths — Fiction
P: 4121

Blackwell, Elizabeth
I: 15394, 15396 **IJ:** 15395

Blades, Ruben
IJ: 14101–2

Blair, Bonnie
I: 15915

Blair, Tony
I: 16019

Blanchard, Jean-Pierre
PI: 13647

Blankets — Fiction
P: 1974, 2996, 3695, 5728

Blessings
I: 20480

Blessings — Fiction
P: 3914

Blind
P: 7229 **PI:** 15596, 16419
I: 21110, 23769 **IJ:** 21080

Blind — Biography
P: 15250, 15255, 15402
PI: 15251, 15261, 15398
I: 15227, 15253–54, 15257–60, 15401 **IJ:** 15226, 15252, 15256, 15399–400

Blind — Fiction
P: 4243, 5115, 5588, 5729
PI: 5807 **I:** 7800, 8459, 8497, 10340, 10354, 10374
IJ: 8344, 8509, 10333

Blizzard of 1888 — Fiction
I: 10873 **IJ:** 11035

Blizzards
P: 5204, 24593 **PI:** 19207
I: 24606, 24621

Blizzards — Fiction
P: 5165, 5212, 5428, 6809, 8100 **IJ:** 8231

Blood
P: 21349

Blood — Biography
I: 15461

Blood-sucking animals
I: 22000

Bloomer, Amelia — Fiction
P: 5341

Bloomer, Elizabeth
IJ: 16020

Bluebirds
P: 22803

Blues (music)
IJ: 16561

Blues (music) — Biography
PI: 14240

Blues (music) — Fiction
P: 2713, 5763

Blues (music) — Poetry
IJ: 13171

Blume, Judy
PI: 14288–89

Bly, Nellie
PI: 14763, 14766 **I:** 14528, 14765 **IJ:** 14764

BMX
IJ: 26275

Boa constrictors — Fiction
P: 3048

Board books
P: 228, 249, 264, 356, 495, 665, 1092, 2355, 3695, 25206

Board books — Fiction
P: 3084, 7130

Boarding schools — Fiction
IJ: 9908

Boars
PI: 22406

Boas
PI: 22159

Boats
See Ships and boats

Bobcats
P: 22541, 22565 **I:** 22544, 22597

Body decoration
IJ: 26013, 26015

Body image
IJ: 20659

Bodybuilding
IJ: 26060

Bodybuilding — Biography
P: 15912

Bodyguards — Careers
IJ: 20953

Bogs
P: 24343

Bogs — Fiction
P: 5192

Boitano, Brian
IJ: 15846

Bolivia
I: 18333 **IJ:** 18310, 18348

Bolivia — Fiction
IJ: 10668

Bomb squads — Careers
PI: 20956 **IJ:** 20859, 20949

Bombs — Fiction
IJ: 10632

Bonaparte, Napoleon
PI: 5319 **IJ:** 15128, 17941

Bonaparte, Napoleon — Fiction
I: 10379

Bonds
I: 19635

Bones
P: 5083, 21445 **I:** 21444, 21455

Bonetta, Sarah Forbes
IJ: 16021

Bonilla, Bobby
IJ: 15721

Book clubs — Fiction
I: 9823 **IJ:** 7814–15

Book fairs — Fiction
P: 6556

Book making
PI: 16393

Books — Fiction
P: 1113, 1317

Books and reading
P: 16264, 16390, 16395–96
PI: 16392, 16409 **IJ:** 16410, 16515

Books and reading — Biography
IJ: 15541

Books and reading — Fiction
P: 1180, 1244, 1293, 2021, 2897, 3331, 3358, 3366, 3697, 3783, 4827, 5539, 5594, 6070, 6443, 6467, 6490, 6734
PI: 4762, 5410 **I:** 7830, 10584 **IJ:** 7815, 11807

Books for beginning readers
P: 216, 483–84, 559, 5207, 6272, 6448, 6817, 7036, 7199, 7229, 7258, 7271, 7329, 7335, 7348, 7441, 7457, 7488, 7519, 7552, 7556, 7615, 7626, 7645, 7663, 7668, 7708, 7716, 12572, 12825, 13433, 13701, 13711, 13957, 14493, 14812, 14814, 14816, 14869, 14874, 14977, 15006, 15125, 15127, 15175–76, 15189, 15322, 15343, 15387, 15423, 15504, 15507, 15650, 15763, 15863, 15908, 16091, 16162, 16306, 16389–90, 16452, 16717, 16782, 16833–34, 16879, 16992, 17052, 17160, 17902, 17943, 17976, 18163, 18195, 18200, 18386, 18692, 18845, 19014, 19282, 19309, 19341, 19353, 19406, 19593, 19604, 19663, 20026, 20059, 20245, 20256, 20308, 20336–39, 20389, 20458, 20474, 20719, 20736–37, 20829–30, 20879, 21121, 21177, 21330, 21337, 21343, 21408, 21488–89, 21818, 21889, 21917, 21930–31, 21934, 21949, 21973, 21975, 21980, 21982, 22075, 22099, 22106, 22122,

P = Primary; PI = Primary-Intermediate; I = Intermediate; IJ = Intermediate-Junior High

Cajun people — Folklore
P: 12851, 12853
PI: 12477–78 I: 12813

Calcium
IJ: 24060, 24072

Calculation (mathematics)
IJ: 24486

Calculators
I: 24496

Caldecott, Randolph
IJ: 13837

Caldecott Medal
IJ: 13811

Calder, Alexander
P: 13838

Calendars
I: 24540, 24543 IJ: 24534

Calendars — Jewish
P: 311

Calendars — Poetry
P: 13528

California
See also Gold Rush
(California)
P: 19517 PI: 19487–88
I: 8230, 18554, 19471, 19494,
19514–15 IJ: 19461–63,
19512, 19516

California — Animals
I: 22011

California — Biography
IJ: 14737, 14739, 16047

California — Fiction
P: 6909, 7295 PI: 8460
I: 8216, 11129 IJ: 8028,
8255, 8548, 8787, 10858,
10866, 11203

California — History
IJ: 14736, 18467, 18679,
19459, 19464–65, 19469,
19475, 19489, 19498, 19503,
19530, 19532

California condors
I: 22916

California Gold Rush
See Gold Rush (California)

California Indians
IJ: 18604

Calligraphy
IJ: 25553, 25585

Calligraphy — Fiction
P: 5591 PI: 10486

Calusa Indians — Fiction
IJ: 8039

Cambodia
P: 17732 IJ: 17780

Cambodia — Biography
I: 16031

Cambodia — Fiction
P: 5488–89 IJ: 10477

Cambodian Americans
IJ: 20550

Camden Yards (Baltimore)
IJ: 26244

Camels
I: 22353, 22379

Camels — Fiction
P: 6070 PI: 8453 IJ: 10889

Camera
I: 25186

Cameroon
IJ: 17579

Cameroon — Folklore
P: 12276

Camouflage (biology)
P: 23286

**Camouflage (biology) —
Fiction**
P: 2041

Campanella, Roy
PI: 15722

Campbell, Ben Nighthorse
IJ: 14945

Campfires
IJ: 26294

Camps and camping
P: 26298 PI: 16682, 26296
I: 25817, 26293, 26299–300
IJ: 26292, 26294, 26297

**Camps and camping —
Fiction**
P: 2106, 2521, 2611, 2906,
3414, 3648, 3746, 4136, 4317,
4730, 5756, 5819, 7230, 7310,
7346 PI: 4224, 4388, 7866,
9830 I: 7803, 7882, 7903,
8287, 8602, 9812, 9831, 9849,
10280, 10303, 10332, 11389,
11410 IJ: 7875, 8101, 8170,
10108, 10139, 11059, 11447

Canada
P: 51, 5517, 18184, 18195,
18200 PI: 18172, 18187,
18194, 18198, 21091
I: 13911, 18169–70,
18173–75, 18179–80, 18183,
18185–86, 18188–89,
18191–92, 18202, 18210,
18212 IJ: 18167, 18171,
18181, 18199, 18204, 18209,
18214, 19295

Canada — Biography
P: 14392 PI: 16042 I: 14142
IJ: 15677, 15890, 15945,
15954

Canada — Fiction
P: 3237, 3252, 4552, 5558–59,
5941 PI: 5297, 5465, 8133,
8581, 9870, 10245, 10380,
10846 I: 7967, 8010, 8120,
8358, 10354, 10393, 10395,
10797, 11173, 11597, 11612,
11818, 11859 IJ: 8065, 8072,
8119, 8333, 8371, 8589, 8592,
8770, 8819, 10185, 10382–84,
10389, 10401–2, 10404,
10420, 10426–27, 11426

Canada — Folklore
P: 12719 PI: 12718
I: 10428, 12717

Canada — Geography
IJ: 16764

Canada — History
PI: 18753 I: 13664, 18203
IJ: 18178

Canadian Americans
I: 20520

Canals
I: 25213 IJ: 18259, 18890,
25193

Canals — Fiction
IJ: 10805

Canals — History
I: 18925

Cancer
P: 3823, 21124 PI: 21126,
21238 IJ: 15909, 21152,
21178, 21180, 21191, 21244

Cancer — Fiction
P: 4279, 4362, 4486, 5794,
5832, 5886 PI: 10363

IJ: 7849, 7854, 7925, 8716,
10100, 11904

**Cancer in animals —
Biography**
PI: 23724

Candlemaking
IJ: 25364

Candlemaking — Fiction
IJ: 9634

Candy
P: 23924 I: 17049

Candy — Fiction
P: 7030

Canoes and canoeing
PI: 26378–79

**Canoes and canoeing —
Fiction**
P: 3289 I: 10854 IJ: 8101

Canyons — Poetry
I: 13506

Cape Cod — Fiction
P: 3241

Cape Town (South Africa)
IJ: 17548

Capitalism
IJ: 19639

Capoeira (martial art)
PI: 26382 IJ: 26383

Capone, Al
IJ: 14778

Capital punishment
See Death penalty

Capybaras
I: 22752

Carbon
P: 24078

Card games
PI: 26359 IJ: 26362

Card tricks
I: 26361

Cardinals (birds) — Fiction
P: 1481

Careers
P: 20034, 20829–32,
20848–49, 20851–52,
20856–58, 20864, 20871,
20874, 20876, 20878–80,
20890, 20894, 20909,
20928–32, 20934–38,
20941–42, 20944, 20946,
20952, 20954, 20957–60,
20962, 20964–67, 20970–71,
20979–83, 20985, 20987,
20993–96, 20998–99,
21002–6, 21009, 23816,
25452 PI: 20836, 20839,
20869, 20873, 20875,
20888–89, 20896, 20905–6,
20923, 20940, 20956,
20968–69, 20972, 20986,
20997, 21000, 21008
I: 20833, 20844, 20853,
20855, 20891, 20914–15,
20924, 20955, 20961,
20973–76, 21007, 22525
IJ: 16547, 16612, 20828,
20834–35, 20840–43,
20845–47, 20850, 20854,
20859–63, 20865–68, 20870,
20872, 20877, 20881–87,
20892–93, 20895, 20897–904,
20907–8, 20910–13,
20916–22, 20925–27, 20933,
20939, 20943, 20947–49,
20951, 20953, 20963,
20977–78, 20984, 20988,
20990–91, 21001

Careers — Fiction
P: 24, 3344, 3508, 4448, 6537,
6573 I: 8798

Careers — Poetry
IJ: 13278

Caribbean Islands
I: 16570, 18284–86, 18295,
18307 IJ: 18282, 18300

**Caribbean Islands —
Cookbooks**
I: 25774, 25778, 25799
IJ: 25765

**Caribbean Islands —
Crafts**
IJ: 25495

**Caribbean Islands —
Fiction**
P: 3251 PI: 1084, 7178
IJ: 8344, 10394

**Caribbean Islands —
Folklore**
P: 12074, 12888–89, 12891,
12893, 12895–96 PI: 12886,
12894 I: 12146, 12167

**Caribbean Islands —
Holidays**
I: 18286

**Caribbean Islands —
Poetry**
PI: 13051 I: 13060

Caribbean Sea
I: 23537

Caribou
PI: 22647 I: 22645

Caribou — Fiction
P: 949, 5227, 6050

Carisbrooke Castle
I: 17946

Carle, Eric
IJ: 13839

Carlson, Chester
I: 15406

Carmichael, Stokely
I: 14593

Carnival (holiday)
I: 20249

Carnival of the Animals
P: 16567

Carnivorous plants
PI: 24024 I: 24011

**Caroline, Princess of
Monaco**
I: 16027

Carols
See Christmas — Songs and
carols

Carothers, Wallace
I: 15407

Carousels — Fiction
P: 3644

Carr, Emily
IJ: 13840–41

Carrey, Jim
IJ: 14110

Carrots — Fiction
P: 1369

Cars
P: 63

Carson, Kit
I: 13661

Carson, Kit — Fiction
I: 10867

Carson, Rachel
PI: 15409 I: 15408,
15410–13 IJ: 15414

P = Primary; PI = Primary-Intermediate; I = Intermediate; IJ = Intermediate-Junior High

P = Primary; PI = Primary-Intermediate; I = Intermediate; IJ = Intermediate-Junior High

P = Primary; PI = Primary-Intermediate; I = Intermediate; IJ = Intermediate-Junior High

P = Primary; PI = Primary-Intermediate; I = Intermediate; IJ = Intermediate-Junior High

P = Primary; PI = Primary-Intermediate; I = Intermediate; IJ = Intermediate-Junior High

Deserts — Fiction
P: 5095, 6228 I: 8398
Deserts — Plants
P: 24203, 24210
Deserts — Poetry
P: 13533 PI: 86, 13505
Design
See also Fashion; Graphic
design; Industrial design
PI: 16229 I: 16225, 16253
Design — Careers
I: 20924
DesJarlait, Patrick
IJ: 13878
de Soto, Hernando
I: 13690 IJ: 13691
Desserts
I: 25742
Desserts — Fiction
PI: 11345
Detective stories
See Mystery stories
Detectives — Biography
IJ: 14902–3
**Detroit Pistons (basketball
team)**
I: 26245
**Detroit Red Wings (hockey
team)**
I: 26350
Devers, Gail
I: 15888
Devil — Fiction
PI: 1280 I: 8891
Dewey Decimal System
I: 16385
de Zavala, Lorenzo
IJ: 14727
Dia de los Tres Reyes
PI: 20283
Diabetes
PI: 21134 I: 21138, 21200
IJ: 21129, 21164, 21171,
21215, 21242
Diabetes — Fiction
IJ: 11898
Diamonds
IJ: 24408
Diana, Princess of Wales
I: 16049 IJ: 16048, 16050–51
Diaries
See also Journals
I: 18847, 18868, 18972,
19067, 19171, 19624
IJ: 10572, 14499, 16078,
16490, 16512, 18926
Diaries — Fiction
P: 4257, 4695–97 PI: 6599,
7818–19, 7943, 8734–35,
8796, 10636, 10769, 10846,
10915 I: 4272, 7941, 7959,
8781, 9432, 10071, 10416,
10459, 10547, 10562, 10728,
10768, 11644 IJ: 7790, 7868,
8413, 8700, 9844, 10010,
10249, 10281, 10333, 10388,
10397, 10404, 10441, 10450,
10484, 10566, 10635, 10682,
10706, 10851, 10866, 10903,
11040, 11045, 11106, 11397,
11473, 11645
DiCaprio, Leonardo
IJ: 14120
Dickens, Charles
IJ: 14326–27

Dickinson, Emily — Fiction
P: 5691 I: 9792
Dictatorship
IJ: 19807
Dictionaries
See also Word books
P: 16470
Dictionaries — Fiction
P: 2269
Diet pills
IJ: 21026
Diets and dieting
See also Eating disorders
IJ: 21051
Diets and dieting — Fiction
P: 4925
Differences
P: 209
Differences — Fiction
P: 1453
Digestive system
P: 21357, 21361–62, 21365,
21367 I: 21354, 21360,
21364, 21366 IJ: 21353,
21355, 21363, 21369–70
Diggers (machinery)
P: 25061
Digital technology
I: 25157
Dilley sextuplets
P: 21556
DiMaggio, Joe
I: 15727
Dimas, Trent
I: 15917
Diners — Fiction
P: 2039
Dingoes
PI: 22617
Dinosaurs
See also Fossils; Paleontology;
Prehistoric animals
P: 6272, 7259, 16806–9,
16813, 16818–19, 16823,
16825, 16830, 16834, 16839,
16844, 16848–49, 16853,
16859, 16862, 16864, 16871,
16873, 16878–79, 16888,
16909, 16917–18, 16921,
16940, 16942, 16951, 16953,
16956, 16960, 20742 PI: 143,
15403, 16805, 16811,
16816–17, 16836–37, 16840,
16854, 16856, 16863, 16875,
16880, 16889, 16892,
16894–95, 16907, 16923,
16930–31, 16933–37, 16948,
16954–55, 16958 I: 16814–15, 16820–21,
16832, 16850–51, 16855,
16867–70, 16872, 16876,
16882–85, 16891, 16896,
16898–903, 16906, 16913–15,
16924–25, 16928–29, 16938,
16944, 16947, 16957, 16962,
25562, 25671 IJ: 15364,
16822, 16831, 16838, 16842,
16847, 16852, 16857, 16877,
16887, 16893, 16904, 16908,
16911, 16926, 16945, 16952,
17009
Dinosaurs — Crafts
I: 16910, 25456
**Dinosaurs — Drawing and
painting**
PI: 25584

Dinosaurs — Fiction
P: 977, 992, 1104, 1146,
1182–83, 1240, 1257, 1539,
1656, 1723, 1892–93, 2010,
2017, 2119, 2172, 2229, 2231,
2563, 2606, 2700, 2906, 3001,
3146, 3158, 3253, 3350, 4072,
4666–67, 4900, 5087, 5720,
5926, 5938, 6038, 6969, 7045,
7150, 7225, 7265, 7433–34,
7531, 7607, 7737 PI: 4935,
7370, 8452 I: 9278, 9969,
11315 IJ: 11707
**Dinosaurs — Jokes and
riddles**
PI: 25871
Dinosaurs — Models
I: 16886 IJ: 16841
Dinosaurs — Poetry
P: 13322, 13439 PI: 13360
I: 13167, 13248
Dinosaurs — Size
P: 16959
Diogenes — Fiction
P: 5645
Dion, Celine
I: 14121 IJ: 14122
Diphtheria
I: 21187
Dippers (stars)
See Big and Little Dippers
Dirigibles — Fiction
I: 11101
Dirt
I: 24393
Disabilities
See also Learning disabilities;
Mental handicaps; Physical
disabilities
P: 21069 IJ: 21108
Disabilities — Biography
IJ: 16181
Disabilities — Fiction
P: 10435 IJ: 10348
Disabilities — Sports
IJ: 26108
Disasters
I: 19193 IJ: 17053, 19743
**Discovery and exploration
— Fiction**
IJ: 10722
Discrimination
See Prejudice; Racism
Diseases and illness
See also Epidemics; Medicine;
and specific diseases, e.g.,
AIDS
P: 21197 PI: 21130, 21130
I: 21135, 21187 IJ: 17317,
21123, 21131, 21136,
21141–42, 21148, 21156,
21163, 21165, 21169, 21172,
21196, 21205, 21230, 21236
**Diseases and illness —
Fiction**
P: 2057, 3133, 3214, 4228,
4341, 4403, 4452, 4486, 4589,
5582, 7458 IJ: 10369
Disney, Walt
I: 13880 IJ: 13879
Diving (sport) — Biography
PI: 15930
Diving (sport) — Careers
I: 20844

Division
P: 456, 24442, 24456, 24485
PI: 24453 I: 24460, 24480
Division — Fiction
P: 2622
Divorce
P: 20742, 20770, 20775,
20786 PI: 20773, 20784
IJ: 20741, 20743, 20748,
20750, 20754, 20761–62,
20767, 20780
Divorce — Fiction
P: 2535, 3953, 3983, 4127,
5694, 5712, 5721, 5772, 5844,
5859, 5871, 5873 PI: 5868,
6603, 8652, 8735, 10023,
11337, 11342 I: 8403, 8610,
9375, 9694, 10009, 10022,
10031, 10062, 10069,
10077–78, 10191, 10258,
10300, 11341, 11914
IJ: 5770, 7781, 7790, 7862,
8413, 8604, 8614, 8618, 8728,
8818–19, 9869, 10045, 10123,
10181, 10281, 11418
Divorce — Parents
IJ: 10350
Diwali (Hindu holiday)
P: 20272, 20352 I: 20290
IJ: 20123
**Diwali (Hindu holiday) —
Fiction**
P: 6739
Dix, Dorothea
IJ: 15238
Dixon, Cromwell — Fiction
P: 5538
Dixon, Tamecka
I: 26249
DNA
IJ: 21262, 21273–74
Doctors
See also Medicine
P: 130
Doctors — Biography
PI: 15607 I: 14974–75,
15341, 15345, 15396, 15461,
15577 IJ: 15333, 15347,
15395, 15545, 15655
Doctors — Careers
P: 20929, 20931, 20934,
20936, 20941 PI: 20940
I: 21261
Doctors — Fiction
P: 2057, 3385, 3640, 7458
Doctors — History
I: 21254
Doctors — Women
I: 15345 IJ: 15347
Doctors Without Borders
P: 19820
Dodos — Fiction
P: 1493
Dog adoption
PI: 23704
Dogs
See also Guide dogs; Police
dogs; Sled dogs; Therapy
dogs; Working dogs
P: 5517, 7708, 23626, 23678,
23686–89, 23696–97, 23700,
23703, 23708, 23714, 23718,
23726, 23729–30, 23732–33,
23735, 23737–38, 23744,
23746, 24599 PI: 20007,
23680, 23683, 23690–94,
23702, 23705, 23715, 23725,

23743, 23747 **I:** 18698, 19495, 22616, 23679, 23682, 23685, 23706, 23709, 23712, 23716, 23719, 23723, 23727, 23739, 23741–42, 23749, 25546 **IJ:** 22614, 23684, 23699, 23701, 23711, 23721, 23728, 23734

Dogs — Art
IJ: 16275

Dogs — Biography
P: 15148

Dogs — Crafts
I: 25392

Dogs — Fiction
P: 96, 609, 957, 974, 976, 994, 1122, 1142, 1588, 1660, 1741, 1758, 1769, 1998, 2039, 2094, 2124, 2411, 2427, 2487, 2595, 2663, 2665, 3287, 3378, 3671, 3983, 4064, 4517, 4538, 4549, 4639, 4647, 4657, 4679–80, 4698, 4733, 4736, 4811, 4886, 4894–95, 4925, 4974, 5019, 5065, 5323, 5375, 5384, 5645, 5683, 5917, 5919, 5921–23, 5942, 5948, 5951–52, 5965, 5971, 5983, 5987, 5992–96, 5999, 6010–11, 6014, 6018–19, 6021, 6030, 6032, 6034, 6039, 6042–43, 6065–67, 6072, 6079, 6089, 6092, 6094, 6097, 6102, 6104, 6117, 6122–26, 6128, 6133, 6135, 6138, 6144–45, 6149, 6152–53, 6156, 6158, 6162–63, 6166, 6171–72, 6179–80, 6183–84, 6186, 6194, 6196, 6200–1, 6205–7, 6210, 6221, 6226, 6234–35, 6239, 6250, 6255, 6257, 6259–60, 6262, 6266, 6268, 6273, 6277, 6279, 6285, 6289–90, 6295, 6302, 6312, 6317, 6319, 6326, 6332, 6335, 6338, 6346, 6364, 6366, 6370, 6372, 6379, 6381, 6384, 6389, 6398–400, 6402, 6407, 6410, 6413, 6419, 6686, 6806, 6876, 6981, 7026, 7030, 7241, 7249, 7268, 7271–72, 7327, 7351, 7409, 7431, 7466, 7479, 7495–96, 7505, 7530, 7537, 7554, 7578, 7598, 7624, 7630, 7640–41, 7657, 7659, 7666, 7684, 8399, 8407, 8414, 8490, 11284, 11290, 12096 **PI:** 982, 1932, 2093, 2442, 2776, 3216, 5315, 5640, 5731, 5970, 6081, 6409, 7096, 7512, 7547, 7584, 8157, 8164, 8424, 8440, 8454, 8498–99, 8515–16, 8959, 9292, 10113, 10260, 11513, 11572, 11840 **I:** 6363, 7891, 7918, 8032, 8076, 8394, 8400, 8403, 8410–11, 8415, 8418, 8442, 8445, 8464, 8467, 8470, 8473–74, 8488, 8506, 8511–12, 8523, 8784, 9486, 10016, 10059, 10068, 10130, 10217, 10252, 10300, 10340, 10419, 10865, 10920, 10937, 11015, 11227, 11246, 11384, 11389, 11508, 12727 **IJ:** 7893, 7898, 7911, 8066, 8132, 8149, 8162, 8273, 8413, 8417, 8430, 8434–35, 8437, 8441, 8463, 8471, 8476, 8478–79, 8481, 8485, 8487, 8509–10, 9597, 9683, 10294,

10321, 10891, 11175, 11204, 11514, 11613

Dogs — Jokes and riddles
PI: 25895

Dogs — Poetry
P: 13316, 13321, 13330–31, 13333, 13365, 13370
PI: 13352, 13354, 13382
I: 23707

Dogs — Stories
I: 8419

Dole, Elizabeth
I: 15239

Dollhouses — Fiction
I: 11274 **IJ:** 9532

Dolls
P: 24943, 25700 **I:** 25702

Dolls — Fiction
P: 1085, 1133, 1272, 1412, 1427, 1437, 4513, 5624, 5762, 6580, 6955, 6980, 7222
I: 8896, 9408–9, 10898
IJ: 8378

Dolphins
P: 16, 23264, 23338, 23344, 23346, 23348, 23351
PI: 23285 **I:** 22020, 23268, 23336–37, 23342–43, 23349–50, 23352, 23511
IJ: 23341, 23345, 24274

Dolphins — Fiction
P: 1452, 5910, 6212
PI: 6265, 8428 **I:** 8128
IJ: 11729

Domagk, Gerhard
I: 15460

Domestic violence —
Fiction
IJ: 10335

Domingo, Plácido
IJ: 14123

Dominica
I: 18302

Dominican Americans
IJ: 18288, 20501

Dominican Republic
P: 18278 **I:** 18304 **IJ:** 20501

Dominican Republic —
Biography
IJ: 15754

Dominican Republic —
Fiction
P: 5272 **IJ:** 8600

Dominoes
P: 26097

Donkeys
IJ: 8447

Donkeys — Fiction
P: 2984, 2987, 3421, 6823, 7274

Donner Party
IJ: 18947, 19048

Donner Party — Fiction
I: 10898 **IJ:** 10927

Dorris, Michael
IJ: 14328

Douglas, Stephen
I: 14797

Douglass, Frederick
P: 14595, 14601
PI: 14597–98 **I:** 14596, 14599 **IJ:** 14600

Douty, Sheila Cornell
I: 15728

Doves — Fiction
P: 5688 **I:** 9431

Down syndrome
IJ: 21125, 21208

Down syndrome —
Biography
IJ: 14109, 16108

Down syndrome — Fiction
P: 67, 4436, 4605, 5750
PI: 4434, 10370

Doyle, Sir Arthur Conan
IJ: 14329

Dr. Seuss
P: 14340, 14344 **PI:** 14342, 14346 **I:** 14343, 14345
IJ: 14341

Dracula
I: 9527

Dragon Boat festival
I: 17618

Dragon dances — Fiction
P: 6794

Dragonflies
P: 23032 **PI:** 23061
I: 23060, 23080

Dragons
P: 1847, 2118, 2773, 6947, 7065 **PI:** 9324, 12186
I: 12927 **IJ:** 9581, 9779

Dragons — Fiction
P: 816, 1110, 1159, 1205, 1459, 1462, 1472, 1497, 1558, 1568, 1680–81, 1727, 2182, 7528, 7728, 10490 **PI:** 1047, 1251, 9000, 9150, 9461, 9602
I: 9025, 9069, 9100, 9124, 9320, 9387–88, 9410, 9561, 9649, 9675, 9712, 9748–49, 11783 **IJ:** 9026, 9051, 9062, 9065, 9068, 9155, 9176, 9373, 9457, 9646, 9780, 9788, 9918, 11967

Dragons — Folklore
P: 12140 **PI:** 12503

Dragons — Songs
P: 16611

Drake, Sir Francis
IJ: 13692–93, 17931

Drama
IJ: 16752

Drawing and painting
See also Art; Crafts
P: 16198–99, 22654, 25362, 25577, 25580, 25586, 25589–91, 25608, 25621
PI: 25555, 25567, 25570, 25582, 25584, 25596–97, 25604, 25612 **I:** 16270, 19261, 25411, 25543–44, 25546, 25548–50, 25554, 25558, 25560–62, 25572, 25578–79, 25583, 25587, 25592–93, 25600, 25602, 25615, 25618–20, 25623
IJ: 16214, 25545, 25552, 25556–57, 25559, 25563–66, 25568–69, 25571, 25573–76, 25581, 25588, 25594–95, 25598, 25601, 25603, 25606, 25613, 25616–17, 25622

Drawing and painting —
Computers
PI: 25610

Drawing and painting —
Fiction
P: 988, 1096, 1231, 1286, 1384, 2641, 3444, 3558, 3562, 3623, 4358, 6475, 6488, 6512, 6539, 7467 **PI:** 9523
I: 11927 **IJ:** 11145

Drawing and painting —
Instruction
I: 25614

Dreams and dreaming
I: 21549 **IJ:** 21375, 21551, 25990

Dreams and dreaming —
Fiction
P: 761, 783, 824, 878, 1004, 1442, 1467, 1531, 1536, 1541, 1574, 1710, 1720, 2760, 3989, 4159, 4379, 5195, 5354, 5810, 5938, 6038, 6838 **PI:** 1178, 1692, 5498 **IJ:** 9197, 9382

Dreams and dreaming —
Poetry
I: 12977

Dred Scott Case
IJ: 18893

Dress
See Clothing and dress;
Fashion

Drew, Charles
I: 15461

Drinker, Edward
IJ: 15346

Drinking and driving
IJ: 21030

Droughts
P: 24664

Droughts — Fiction
PI: 1005 **I:** 8019, 10172
IJ: 11061

Drugs and drug abuse
See also specific drugs, e.g.,
Cocaine
P: 21024, 21035, 21045
I: 19929, 19949, 21039
IJ: 21023, 21026–27, 21031–32, 21037–38, 21044, 21051, 21056, 21058

Druids — Fiction
IJ: 12476

Drums
I: 16633

Du Bois, W. E. B.
I: 14602

Ducks and geese
P: 22870–71, 22873–74, 22876–77, 22881, 22883–85, 22887–88 **I:** 22878, 22882

Ducks and geese — Fiction
P: 606, 1543, 1561, 2277, 2438, 2594, 2810, 3017, 4015, 5916, 5934, 6048, 6127, 6151, 6155, 6157, 6195, 6253, 6274, 6295, 6311, 6350, 6373, 6387, 7264 **PI:** 2811, 5953, 8191 **I:** 8401, 8416

Duff, Hilary
PI: 14124

Dugongs
I: 23417

Dump trucks
P: 25226

Duncan, Isadora
IJ: 14125

Duncan, Tim
IJ: 15796–98

Dunham, Katherine
IJ: 14126

Dust Bowl
PI: 19169 **I:** 19142, 19163, 19179 **IJ:** 19143, 19182

Dust Bowl — Fiction
I: 10393 **IJ:** 11099

P = Primary; PI = Primary-Intermediate; I = Intermediate; IJ = Intermediate-Junior High

Dust storms
P: 19187
Dwarfism
I: 21101
Dwarfism — Fiction
I: 10343
Dysgraphia
IJ: 14285
Dyslexia
PI: 21073 I: 21082, 21088
IJ: 21300, 21324, 21339
Dyslexia — Fiction
P: 5755 I: 10324–25
Dyson, Esther
IJ: 15462–63

E

E-mail
P: 25134, 25148 PI: 16497
E-mail — Fiction
I: 10274
E-mail — Fiction
IJ: 10010
E. coli bacteria
IJ: 21167
Eagles
See also Bald eagles
P: 16418, 22892–93, 22895,
22907 PI: 18483, 22900,
22906, 22908 I: 18463,
22896–98, 22901, 22910,
22913 IJ: 22909
Eagles — Fiction
P: 1703, 6245
Eagles — Folklore
P: 12786
Earaches
I: 21433
Earhart, Amelia
P: 13694, 13698, 13701
PI: 13695–97, 13704
I: 13699 IJ: 13700, 13702–3
Earle, Sylvia
PI: 20986 IJ: 15464
Early Bird Body Systems
PI: 21439
Earnhardt, Dale, Jr.
IJ: 15707
Earp, Wyatt
I: 14799 IJ: 14798
Ears
P: 21409, 21428, 22267
PI: 21413 I: 21397, 21423,
21433 IJ: 21430
Earth
See also Geology
P: 21758, 24107 PI: 21765,
21770–71, 24098, 24108
I: 21759, 21762, 21764,
21767–68, 24090, 24093,
24099 IJ: 21756, 21760,
21763, 21766, 24095, 24111
Earth — Fiction
P: 5076
Earth — Folklore
I: 12770
Earth — Poetry
P: 13527 PI: 13030
Earth — Rotation
P: 21761, 21769 PI: 21757

Earth Day
P: 19681, 20331 PI: 6744
I: 20301
Earth Day — Crafts
PI: 25471
Earth Day — Fiction
P: 7622
Earth science
I: 24097 IJ: 16838
**Earth science —
Experiments and projects**
IJ: 24117
Earth science — Songs
P: 16693
Earth sciences
I: 24121
Earthmovers
P: 6635
Earthquakes
P: 24123, 24125, 24135,
24143, 24149 PI: 24132,
24145 I: 15620, 24124,
24138–40, 24142, 24155,
24561 IJ: 19520, 24144,
24147, 24157
**Earthquakes —
Experiments and projects**
I: 24152
Earthquakes — Fiction
I: 9432 IJ: 8290
Earthworms
P: 23248, 23256, 23260
I: 23245
**Earthworms —
Experiments and projects**
PI: 23249 IJ: 21959
East Africa
I: 17490
East Africa — History
IJ: 17498
**East Africa — Kings and
queens**
IJ: 17498
Easter
P: 7006, 7013, 20392, 20394,
20396 PI: 20395 I: 20391,
20393 IJ: 20235
Easter — Cookbooks
PI: 25794
Easter — Fiction
P: 2358, 7007–8, 7010–12,
7014–15, 7017–21, 7650,
7743
Easter — Poetry
P: 7016, 13399 PI: 13418
IJ: 13391
Easter eggs
I: 20397
Easter Island
I: 17839 IJ: 17799, 17830
Easter Island — Fiction
PI: 5285
Eastern Europe
P: 12402 IJ: 17851
Eastern Europe — Fiction
P: 7120
Eastern Orthodox religion
P: 20134
Eastman, Charles
I: 15465
Eastman, George
PI: 15466
Eastwood, Alice
I: 15467

Eating disorders
See also specific disorders,
e.g., Anorexia, Bulimia
IJ: 21051, 21158, 21212
Eating utensils — History
PI: 20728
Eavesdropping — Fiction
PI: 8735
Echinoderms
P: 23397 I: 23392
Ecology and environment
See also Conservation; Global
warming; Pollution
P: 648, 16550, 19683–84,
19718, 19726–27, 19729,
19737, 19740–41, 20331,
22847, 24004, 24189, 24248
PI: 16771, 19696, 22984,
24957 I: 18397, 19690,
19698–99, 19706–8, 19733,
19735, 19746, 19767, 22126,
22135, 23078, 23572, 23857,
24114, 24167, 24216, 24242,
24246, 24387, 24651, 25420
IJ: 16221, 17472, 17617,
17665, 18389, 18403, 19323,
19394, 19558, 19615,
19686–87, 19689, 19700–1,
19709, 19715, 19717,
19720–21, 19731–32, 19734,
19743, 19751, 21919, 22795,
23547, 24134, 24166, 24262,
24369, 24591, 24748, 24753,
24770, 25229
**Ecology and environment
— Biography**
P: 15571–72 PI: 15409
I: 15408 IJ: 15618
**Ecology and environment
— Experiments and
projects**
I: 19704 IJ: 19722, 19738
**Ecology and environment
— Fiction**
P: 1197, 1424, 1694, 2418,
2719, 3316, 3428, 3632, 3782,
5085, 5091, 5108, 5147, 5161,
5244–45, 5964, 12035, 19703
PI: 1251, 5075, 5088, 9962,
11628 I: 7797, 8374, 8987
IJ: 7817, 7844, 7994, 8061,
9015, 9048
**Ecology and environment
— Folklore**
IJ: 12121
Economics and business
See also Capitalism; Supply
and demand (economics);
Money-making ideas
IJ: 19381, 19656, 19659
**Economics and business —
Biography**
PI: 15649 I: 15636
IJ: 15342, 15351, 15392,
15459, 15623, 15635
**Economics and business —
Sports**
IJ: 26093
Economy (U.S.)
I: 19637
Ecosystems
P: 19737, 24170 PI: 22038
I: 21983, 23999–4000, 24028,
24036 IJ: 24353
Ecotourism
IJ: 19715

Ecuador
I: 18312 IJ: 17279, 18327,
18342
Ecuador — Fiction
I: 10306
Ederle, Gertrude
PI: 15918
Edison, Thomas Alva
P: 15470–72, 15476
I: 15474–75 IJ: 15468–69,
15473, 15477–78
Edmonds, Emma
IJ: 15240
Edo
P: 17597
Education
See also Schools; Teachers
IJ: 16399
Education — Biography
PI: 14587–88, 14698–700
IJ: 14589, 15267, 16123
Education — Fiction
P: 5372
Education — History
IJ: 17335
Edwards, Jonathan
IJ: 14800
Eels — Fiction
P: 6288
Efron, Zac
I: 14127
Eggs
P: 21956, 22280, 22346,
22348 I: 22828 IJ: 22865
Eggs — Fiction
P: 1543, 2305, 4649, 4851,
4854 I: 11315
Egypt
P: 18082, 18084, 18089,
18096 PI: 17115, 18085,
18094, 18098 I: 18080,
18083, 18086, 18088, 18095,
25615 IJ: 17154, 17167,
17176, 18090–93, 18097,
18099–100
Egypt — Art
P: 16306 I: 17138 IJ: 16309
Egypt — Biography
P: 16088 I: 16081 IJ: 16141,
16169
Egypt — Crafts
I: 17139, 25499 IJ: 17142
Egypt — Fiction
P: 1670, 2893, 5684
PI: 10439, 10444 I: 10410,
10446, 10459, 10461
IJ: 7939, 8733, 9753, 10441,
10449, 10454
Egypt — Folklore
P: 12251 I: 12244, 12691
IJ: 12241
Egypt — Graphic novels
I: 10434
Egypt — History
P: 7335, 16306, 17128, 17132,
17160 PI: 10460, 16170,
17124, 17157, 17168
I: 13268, 16030, 16314,
17037, 17112, 17114, 17117,
17123, 17130, 17135–39,
17141, 17147, 17149, 17152,
17161–64, 17169, 17171–72,
17174, 17177, 18087, 25941
IJ: 16038, 17113, 17116,
17120, 17122, 17125–27,
17129, 17131, 17133–34,
17140, 17142–45, 17150–51,

P = Primary; PI = Primary-Intermediate; I = Intermediate; IJ = Intermediate-Junior High

P = Primary; PI = Primary-Intermediate; I = Intermediate; IJ = Intermediate-Junior High

P = Primary; PI = Primary-Intermediate; I = Intermediate; IJ = Intermediate-Junior High

P = Primary; PI = Primary-Intermediate; I = Intermediate; IJ = Intermediate-Junior High

P = Primary; PI = Primary-Intermediate; I = Intermediate; IJ = Intermediate-Junior High

Grand Coulee Dam
I: 25035
Grand Teton National Park
I: 19327
Grandfathers — Fiction
P: 848, 1014, 1106, 1222, 1686, 1797, 1980, 2145, 2364, 3278, 3280, 3418, 3522, 3524, 3541, 3584, 3622, 3876, 3882, 3892, 3899, 3937, 3968, 4018, 4030, 4040, 4040, 4066, 4085, 4093, 4114, 4141, 4157, 4196, 4201, 4204, 4209, 4239, 4243, 4256, 4283, 4315, 4334, 4379, 4415, 4430, 4468, 4477, 4490, 4505, 4577, 4803, 5256, 5309, 5381, 5513, 5549, 5582, 5623, 5667, 5700, 5870, 5878, 5880, 5949, 6378, 7073, 7200, 7277, 7504, 7586, 7658, 8605, 10168 **PI:** 3884, 4063, 4378, 5758, 8701 **I:** 8613, 8665, 8801, 8816, 8821, 8845, 9037, 10182, 10308, 10408 **IJ:** 7782, 7928, 8117, 8208, 8368, 8646, 8663, 8790, 8832, 9230, 10019, 10106, 10365, 10522, 11213, 11919
Grandfathers — Folklore
IJ: 12303
Grandmothers — Fiction
P: 1186, 3163, 3192, 3497, 3615, 3662, 3780, 3872, 3916, 3928, 3931–32, 3934, 3955–56, 3958–60, 3970, 3977, 3981, 3988, 4006, 4013, 4019, 4021, 4031, 4049, 4091, 4105–7, 4118, 4158, 4162, 4167, 4177, 4181, 4192, 4205, 4216–17, 4227, 4232, 4246, 4266, 4282, 4288, 4293, 4309, 4313, 4315, 4319, 4325, 4339, 4352, 4355, 4391, 4398, 4414, 4421, 4443, 4447, 4452, 4454, 4464, 4474, 4479, 4489, 4493, 4504, 4513, 4586, 4640, 4787, 4955, 4968, 4994, 5317, 5402, 5568, 5619, 5636, 5785, 5788, 6729, 7004, 7536, 7723, 11604 **PI:** 1064, 3888, 4180, 8619, 10233, 11243, 11502 **I:** 4125, 8601, 8626, 8636, 8664, 8721, 9042, 10009, 10020, 10178, 10231, 10992 **IJ:** 7887, 7934, 8606, 8727, 8805, 8830, 8841, 10147, 10170, 10251
Grandparents
P: 4004, 20739, 20778
Grandparents — Crafts
I: 25410
Grandparents — Fiction
P: 301, 2505, 3370, 3895, 3985, 4050–51, 4111, 4119, 4124, 4169, 4292, 4369, 4396, 4483, 5062, 5712, 6446, 7535 **I:** 10063, 11409 **IJ:** 7935, 10075, 10269
Grandparents — Games
I: 25410
Grandparents — Poetry
PI: 13152 **I:** 13074
Grant, Amy
I: 14144
Grant, Ulysses S.
IJ: 15040–41
Graphic design
I: 16226

Graphic novels — Fairy tales
P: 6693
Graphic novels — Fiction
P: 1507, 2208, 3242, 6687–92, 6694, 6697–98, 6700, 7410, 9879, 9927, 9972, 11273, 25577 **PI:** 6696, 6699, 9878, 9906, 9914, 9928–29, 9932, 9938, 9940, 9945, 9954, 9956, 9962, 9970, 9978–79, 10004 **I:** 8106, 8292, 9558, 9674, 9875, 9881–83, 9885–86, 9890, 9895–97, 9901, 9909–13, 9916, 9921, 9923, 9931, 9934, 9939, 9941, 9946, 9949, 9952–53, 9960–61, 9968–69, 9976, 9980, 9988–89, 9991, 9994–95, 9997–98, 10003, 11718, 12003, 16288 **IJ:** 6695, 8334, 8443, 9004, 9259, 9472, 9871, 9873–74, 9876–77, 9880, 9884, 9889, 9891–92, 9894, 9898–900, 9902–3, 9907–8, 9915, 9917–19, 9922, 9924, 9926, 9930, 9933, 9935, 9937, 9942–44, 9947–48, 9951, 9955, 9957–59, 9966–67, 9971, 9977, 9981–82, 9984–87, 9990, 9992–93, 9996, 10000–2, 10005–8, 10118, 10623, 11252, 12067, 12200, 12429, 12967, 17931, 25568, 25575
Graphic novels — Mythology
I: 12922 **IJ:** 12935
Graphs
P: 24422, 24427, 24457, 24479, 24528 **PI:** 24469, 24526 **IJ:** 24527
Grasshoppers
P: 23036, 23117 **PI:** 23040, 23081 **I:** 23068 **IJ:** 23076
Grasshoppers — Fiction
P: 7521
Grasslands
See also Prairies
P: 21934, 24370, 24390 **PI:** 24367, 24377, 24381, 24389 **I:** 17488, 24371, 24373–75, 24383, 24388 **IJ:** 24369, 24379, 24384, 24386, 24391
Grasslands — Animals
P: 24364 **PI:** 24385
Gratitude — Fiction
P: 3485, 3859
Gravity
P: 24746 **IJ:** 24716, 24731, 24739
Gravity — Experiments and projects
I: 24118, 24725
Great Barrier Reef
PI: 23323, 23325 **I:** 17802 **IJ:** 17801, 23307, 23319, 24476
Great Britain
See also England; Scotland; Wales; Northern Ireland
I: 17925–26, 17940 **IJ:** 17924, 17932
Great Britain — Biography
I: 16178 **IJ:** 13692–93, 16033–36, 16050, 16177, 16179

Great Britain — Fiction
IJ: 10624
Great Britain — Folklore
See also England — Folklore; Scotland — Folklore; Wales — Folklore
P: 12026, 12154, 12460, 12462–64, 12470–71, 12473, 12475, 12485, 12487–93, 12499, 12501, 12508, 12511–12, 12520–21, 12538–39, 12542, 12548, 12550, 12552 **PI:** 12479–80, 12496, 12500, 12503 **I:** 12502, 12506–7 **IJ:** 12531, 12545
Great Britain — History
IJ: 17921, 17923, 17941
Great Depression
See Depression, Great
Great Expectations — **Adaptations**
IJ: 10623
Great Lakes
See also specific lakes, e.g., Lake Superior
I: 18438
Great Plains
See Plains (U.S.)
Great Salt Lake
P: 24356
Great Smoky Mountains National Park
I: 19551
Great Wall (China)
I: 17639 **IJ:** 17623, 17632
Greece
P: 17950, 17957, 17972 **PI:** 10544, 17954, 17963 **I:** 17180 **IJ:** 17959, 17961, 17964, 17969
Greece — Ancient
See Greece — History
Greece — Art
IJ: 16310–11, 17189
Greece — Biography
PI: 16146 **IJ:** 16013, 16145
Greece — Christmas
IJ: 20364
Greece — Cookbooks
I: 25800 **IJ:** 25772, 25806
Greece — Crafts
IJ: 17183, 17191
Greece — Fiction
P: 5547, 5645 **I:** 10538 **IJ:** 10522
Greece — Folklore
P: 12555, 12558–59, 12590 **PI:** 12565, 12584 **I:** 12553–54, 12556, 12577
Greece — Graphic novels
I: 9974
Greece — History
P: 17181 **PI:** 10418, 17193, 17206, 17211–14 **I:** 17087, 17182, 17184, 17188, 17194–95, 17199–200, 17202, 17209–10, 17215, 26369 **IJ:** 16311–12, 16312, 17092, 17183, 17185–87, 17189–91, 17196–98, 17201, 17203, 17205, 17207–8
Greece — Mythology
P: 12581, 12587, 12936, 12943, 12953, 12968 **PI:** 12580, 12938, 12940,

12945–46, 12958, 12964, 17192 **I:** 12576, 12924, 12937, 12941, 12944, 12947, 12952, 12954, 12956–57, 12960, 12962, 12969 **IJ:** 9697, 12949–51, 12955, 12965, 12967, 17198, 26005
Greece — Mythology — Fiction
IJ: 9696, 9698, 11332, 11493
Greed — Fiction
P: 3784
Greed — Folklore
P: 12428 **I:** 12219
Greek (language)
I: 16363
Greek Americans
I: 20589, 20613 **IJ:** 20548
Greek Americans — Fiction
P: 5309
Green turtles
PI: 22195
Greenberg, Hank
P: 15734
Greene, Nathanael
IJ: 14834
Greenhouse effect
IJ: 19721
Greenland
P: 18027
Greenland — Fiction
IJ: 9326, 9644
Greenpeace
IJ: 19711, 19717, 19728
Gretzky, Wayne — Fiction
P: 1451
Grief
PI: 21013 **I:** 21010
Grief — Fiction
P: 2505, 3925, 4005, 4325, 4381, 4421, 5324, 5996, 7034 **PI:** 10043 **I:** 8607, 8801, 10056, 10344, 11107, 11186 **IJ:** 7841, 7911, 7922, 7936, 8646, 10128, 10220
Grief — Poetry
IJ: 13058
Griffins — Fiction
I: 9466
Grimke, Sarah and Angelina
IJ: 15244
Grimm brothers
IJ: 14350
Grissom, Gus
I: 13709
Grizzly bears
P: 22503, 22523 **PI:** 22505, 22507, 22516, 22531, 22535 **I:** 22500, 22511, 22533, 22537 **IJ:** 22498
Grizzly bears — Fiction
P: 6241 **IJ:** 8306, 8396
Grooming
IJ: 21484
Gross, Elly Berkovits
IJ: 16077
Groundhog Day
P: 20264
Groundhog Day — Fiction
P: 2368, 2671, 2838
Groundhogs
P: 20264, 22749, 22753
Groundhogs — Fiction
P: 1792, 3009

P = Primary; PI = Primary-Intermediate; I = Intermediate; IJ = Intermediate-Junior High

P = Primary; PI = Primary-Intermediate; I = Intermediate; IJ = Intermediate-Junior High

P = Primary; PI = Primary-Intermediate; I = Intermediate; IJ = Intermediate-Junior High

P = Primary; PI = Primary-Intermediate; I = Intermediate; IJ = Intermediate-Junior High

Hypnotism — Fiction
P: 5033, 7735 PI: 2701

I

Ibn Battuta
I: 17065

Ice — Poetry
IJ: 13560

Ice ages
I: 17876 IJ: 16976

Ice ages — Fiction
PI: 2543

Ice climbing
IJ: 26103, 26133, 26169

Ice cream
P: 23890–91, 23899, 24926
IJ: 23928

Ice cream — History
I: 23888, 23911

Ice hockey
PI: 133 I: 11843, 26341–42,
26344, 26350, 26355
IJ: 26340, 26345–49

Ice hockey — Biography
IJ: 15931–32, 15954

Ice hockey — Fiction
P: 1451, 1828, 3663, 5804,
6588–89 PI: 5803 I: 11915
IJ: 11816, 11829–32, 11856,
11858, 11898–99, 11919

Ice hockey — Women
IJ: 26351

Ice mummies
IJ: 16991

Ice skating
See also Figure skating; Ice
hockey
P: 26354 PI: 26353
IJ: 26357

Ice skating — Biography
PI: 26352 I: 15700, 15849,
15853, 15915 IJ: 15691,
15846–47, 15850, 15852

Ice skating — Fiction
P: 1270, 2454, 2496, 2973,
3145, 3315, 7601 I: 10528,
11893 IJ: 11878

Icebergs
See Glaciers and icebergs

Iceland
PI: 18040, 22924 IJ: 18033,
18047

Iceland — Fiction
P: 2633, 5514, 6216, 6313–14

Id-ul-Fitr (Islamic holiday)
P: 20274 I: 20296

Idaho
I: 19335 IJ: 19323, 19338

Idar, Jovita
IJ: 14733

**Identity (psychology) —
Fiction**
P: 3196, 6525 I: 11670
IJ: 8687

Iditarod (Junior)
PI: 26167 IJ: 26147

**Iditarod Sled Dog Race
(AK)**
PI: 15944, 23731, 26167
IJ: 15916

**Iditarod Sled Dog Race
(AK) — Fiction**
P: 5942 PI: 8518 IJ: 8254

Iglesias, Enrique
PI: 14159

Igloos
I: 18374, 18411

Iguanas
P: 22052

Iliad **(mythology)**
IJ: 12955

Illegal aliens
IJ: 18461

Illegal aliens — Fiction
PI: 10287 IJ: 8549

Illinois
I: 19242, 19261, 19271,
19291, 19300 IJ: 19255,
19258

Illinois — Fiction
I: 10272

Illinois — History
IJ: 18931, 19250, 19306

Illiteracy — Fiction
P: 3339 IJ: 11835

Illness
See Diseases and illness; and
specific illnesses, e.g.,
Diabetes

Illustrators
IJ: 16189

Illustrators — Biography
PI: 13953

**Imaginary animals —
Fiction**
P: 8, 10, 18, 60, 65, 148, 195,
200, 204, 276, 427, 441–42,
481, 491, 504, 514, 516, 559,
590, 606, 640, 719, 724, 739,
757, 779, 784, 789, 791, 791,
793, 814, 827, 834, 837, 851,
856–57, 866, 894, 928, 955,
958, 958–59, 962, 968–69,
973, 980–81, 999, 1022, 1148,
1195, 1246, 1269, 1301, 1350,
1360, 1377, 1401, 1404,
1410–11, 1429, 1486, 1489,
1492, 1549, 1573, 1583, 1591,
1595, 1612, 1616–17, 1656,
1672, 1714, 1749, 1767–80,
1780–90, 1793–803, 1805–25,
1825–47, 1849–56, 1856–57,
1859–64, 1864–68, 1871–76,
1878–82, 1884–98, 1898–904,
1906, 1908–31, 1934–54,
1954–64, 1964–74, 1974–78,
1980–85, 1987–92,
1994–2009, 2013–22,
2024–27, 2027–40, 2040–42,
2042–58, 2060–66, 2068–86,
2088–90, 2092, 2094–126,
2128–34, 2134–54, 2156–63,
2165–69, 2171, 2173–78,
2178–82, 2184–87, 2189–211,
2211–13, 2215–25, 2227–28,
2230, 2232–35, 2237–39,
2239–53, 2255, 2257–60,
2262–66, 2268–69, 2269–77,
2279–332, 2332–47, 2349–87,
2389–96, 2398–99, 2401–10,
2412–26, 2428–35, 2437–41,
2443–52, 2452–56, 2458–62,
2464–65, 2465–77, 2479–503,
2505–12, 2514–17, 2519,
2521–24, 2526–42, 2545–48,
2550–58, 2558–62, 2564–88,
2590–603, 2605, 2607–21,
2623–49, 2651–62, 2664,
2666–86, 2686–700, 2702–11,
2713–50, 2750–51, 2751–75,
2777–79, 2781–87, 2787–808,
2808–10, 2812–24, 2826–57,
2859–61, 2861–63, 2865–70,
2872–73, 2875–88, 2890–96,
2898–904, 2904–9, 2911–14,
2914–18, 2920–22, 2924–37,
2939–41, 2944–47, 2947–59,
2959, 2961–63, 2965–81,
2983–95, 2997–3000, 3002–5,
3007–29, 3031–44, 3046–50,
3050–57, 3059–60, 3062–64,
3064–72, 3074–102, 3102–7,
3109, 3111, 3114, 3114–19,
3119–30, 3132–45, 3148–58,
3160–69, 3171, 3173–81,
3183–99, 3201–2, 3204–15,
3217–23, 4033, 4130, 4215,
4527, 4537, 4625, 4630, 4654,
4658, 4695–97, 4700, 4721,
4783, 4786, 4794, 4797, 4806,
4809, 4834–35, 4843, 4852,
4856, 4858, 4879, 4911, 4923,
4923, 4931, 4937–38, 4941,
4944, 4947, 4960, 4963, 4987,
5006, 5011, 5011, 5016,
5027–28, 5037, 5053, 5053,
5057, 5059–60, 5060–61,
5064, 5201, 5215, 5224, 5258,
5506, 5612, 5889, 5893, 5959,
5990, 6204, 6211, 6690, 6698,
6703, 6705, 6711–12, 6762,
6773, 6775, 6777, 6784, 6784,
6790, 6790, 6796–97, 6812,
6814, 6821, 6830, 6842–44,
6847, 6849–50, 6854,
6857–58, 6871, 6876–78,
6882, 6896, 6910, 6918, 6933,
6948, 6962, 6968, 6975, 6977,
6981, 6985, 6996, 7006–7,
7009, 7014–15, 7018–20,
7032, 7063, 7088, 7095, 7100,
7171, 7173–74, 7177,
7179–80, 7183, 7185, 7189,
7206, 7208–9, 7224, 7227,
7233–34, 7237, 7240,
7247–48, 7261, 7269–70,
7273, 7275, 7278–85, 7299,
7311, 7323–24, 7331, 7343,
7346–47, 7349, 7363, 7367,
7382–83, 7385, 7397, 7414,
7426–27, 7429–30, 7447,
7447–48, 7451, 7471, 7488,
7492–93, 7501, 7516–17,
7520, 7522–24, 7526, 7530,
7557–59, 7562, 7569, 7577,
7579, 7581, 7588–90, 7618,
7620, 7624, 7626, 7663–65,
7675–76, 7680–82, 7687–88,
7698, 7701, 7719, 7721, 7725,
7738–41, 7743, 7747,
7749–51, 7755–56, 7758,
7760–61, 9357, 9739, 11965,
11965, 12135, 12190, 12461,
12509, 12513, 12723, 12887,
13003, 13473, 16679 PI: 888,
1047, 1535, 1804, 1848, 1883,
1932–33, 1979, 2011, 2059,
2059, 2091, 2093, 2188, 2267,
2348, 2388, 2397, 2442, 2457,
2478, 2518, 2543–44, 2589,
2650, 2701, 2776, 2811, 2825,
2874, 2964, 3045, 3061, 3112,
3147, 3159, 3170, 3203, 3216,
5761, 5817, 7235, 7379, 7446,
7498, 7633–34, 7660, 7736,
7805, 7869, 8005, 8009, 8454,
8879, 8879, 8997, 8999, 9019,
9184, 9186, 9194, 9232, 9264,
9330, 9365, 9416, 9471, 9530,
9565, 9673, 9746, 11304–5,
11530, 11840, 13196, 24426
I: 1907, 2278, 3182, 8032,
8131, 8281, 8292, 8883, 8886,
8906, 9012, 9089, 9115, 9185,
9187–89, 9217–18, 9311,
9313, 9403, 9531, 9558–59,
9604, 9687, 9713, 9881, 9896,
9910–13, 9976, 9994, 11315,
11365–66, 11384, 11387,
11407, 11466 IJ: 1791, 9250,
9253, 9358, 9389, 9925,
11385, 11406, 11408, 11711

**Imaginary friends —
Fiction**
P: 1542 PI: 1413, 8768
IJ: 10192

Imagination — Fiction
P: 1017, 1154, 1206, 1260,
1263, 1286, 1373, 1383, 1423,
1633, 1639–40, 1664, 1758,
1765, 2000, 2298, 3073, 3297,
3532, 3558, 3709, 3799, 4072,
4078, 4419, 4710, 4771, 6469
PI: 11528 I: 9676, 10201,
10300, 11287

Immigration — Fiction
P: 5269, 5347, 5408, 5558,
6551 PI: 8581, 8844, 9870
IJ: 8532

Immigration — Poetry
I: 13149

Immigration (Canada)
IJ: 18201

**Immigration (Canada) —
Fiction**
I: 10414, 10422–23 IJ: 9808

Immigration (U.S.)
See also Illegal aliens
P: 16022, 19373, 19421,
20505, 20563–64, 20567,
20569, 20571 PI: 7138,
18933, 19492, 20583–85
I: 11034, 19158, 19403,
19410, 20506, 20509, 20522,
20525–27, 20529, 20533,
20537, 20551, 20556, 20561,
20578–80, 20593–95, 20598,
20611, 20613–15, 20619–20,
20623, 25357, 25759
IJ: 15323, 17733, 17908,
18282, 18288, 18447, 18453,
18461, 18477, 18487, 19395,
19432, 20028, 20499–501,
20504, 20511, 20531, 20535,
20539, 20543, 20548, 20557,
20559, 20562, 20573, 20581,
20587–88, 20602, 20604,
20609, 20612, 20621

**Immigration (U.S.) —
Biography**
IJ: 14348

**Immigration (U.S.) —
Fiction**
P: 3955, 3964, 3984, 4071,
4188, 4370, 5270, 5335, 5416,
5482, 5552, 5574, 5596, 5655,
5681, 5692, 5747, 5760, 5846,
5899, 6441, 6511, 10999
PI: 5680, 5689, 6547, 6736,
7027, 7178, 11062 I: 6845,
7880, 8540, 8545, 8587, 8849,
10137, 10385, 10542
IJ: 8531, 8549, 8571, 10080,
10825, 10994, 11018, 11027,
11039, 11042, 11048, 11086,
11111

P = Primary; PI = Primary-Intermediate; I = Intermediate; IJ = Intermediate-Junior High

Interior decoration
See Room decoration
International organizations
IJ: 22993
International relations
PI: 19812
International Space Station
I: 24841
Internet
See also World Wide Web
P: 25119 PI: 25113
I: 25105, 25124, 25139
IJ: 25109, 25120, 25122,
25127, 25131–32, 25142,
25146, 25150–53
Internet — Biography
IJ: 15360, 15463, 15605
**Interpersonal relations —
Fiction**
I: 7912
**Interracial families —
Fiction**
P: 4014, 5867
Inuit
P: 18193, 19501 I: 18177,
18180, 18207–8, 18213,
18364, 18374, 18382, 18411
IJ: 18168, 18197
Inuit — Art
I: 16315 IJ: 18197
Inuit — Fiction
P: 1632, 4164, 5188, 5387,
5601, 5643, 5965, 6386
PI: 5465 I: 10694 IJ: 8254,
8345, 9326
Inuit — Folklore
P: 12720, 12722 I: 12721
IJ: 12798
Inuit — History
IJ: 16987
Inuit — Language
IJ: 24703
Inuit — Poetry
PI: 13185
Invasive species
IJ: 21967
Inventors and inventions
See also specific inventions,
e.g., Telephones
P: 24936 PI: 24937
I: 13217, 17057, 20069,
24916, 24931, 24938, 24948,
24961, 24971, 24975, 25175
IJ: 15357, 17040, 21247,
23895, 24944, 24962, 24962,
24966, 24972, 25110, 25149,
25205
**Inventors and inventions —
African American**
IJ: 15357
**Inventors and inventions —
Biography**
P: 13862, 14606, 14804,
14808, 14815, 15381, 15387,
15470–72, 15476, 15503,
15515, 15562, 15564, 15587,
15595, 15652–53, 15664,
15671 PI: 14806, 14811,
14817–18, 15330, 15379,
15382, 15457, 15494, 15517,
15543, 15561, 15658–59,
15663, 15668 I: 13863,
13865, 14807, 14820, 15372,
15383–84, 15386, 15388,
15407, 15475, 15496, 15513,
15544, 15576, 15660, 15665,
15672 IJ: 13866, 13868,

13870–72, 14822, 15332,
15348, 15378, 15380, 15385,
15468–69, 15473, 15477–78,
15497, 15505, 15516, 15548,
15642, 15654, 15661–62,
15666–67, 15670
**Inventors and inventions —
Fiction**
P: 4323, 5036, 5538 I: 9883,
11287, 11363, 11369, 11509
IJ: 15389
**Inventors and inventions —
History**
I: 24968 IJ: 17018, 24947
**Inventors and inventions —
Poetry**
P: 13089
**Inventors and inventions —
Women**
IJ: 24967
Invertebrates
I: 23245, 23259, 23291,
23326, 23392
Investing (business)
I: 19635 IJ: 19646, 19649,
19652
Iodine
IJ: 24065
Iowa
PI: 19266 I: 19277–78
IJ: 19247, 19283
Iowa — Fiction
I: 9319
iPods
IJ: 15554
Iran
See also Persia
PI: 18124, 18136 I: 18123,
19231 IJ: 18127, 18133–34,
18140, 18149, 20244
Iran — Biography
IJ: 16134
Iran — Folklore
P: 12688
Iran-Iraq War
IJ: 17464
Iraq
See also Gulf War (1991);
Operation Iraqi Freedom
P: 18156 PI: 18155
I: 18131, 18146, 18159
IJ: 18122, 18137
Iraq — Biography
IJ: 16086–87
Iraq — Fiction
P: 5591
Iraq — Folklore
P: 12690
Ireland
P: 17912 PI: 17929, 17934
I: 17915, 17944 IJ: 17913,
17933, 17936, 17939
Ireland — Fiction
P: 1024, 1173, 5681, 11986,
12528 PI: 1370 I: 10385,
10620, 10627, 11266
IJ: 7791, 7915, 8469, 9385,
10246, 10622, 10628–30,
10633, 10656, 10918, 11207,
11743, 12476
Ireland — Folklore
P: 2515, 12481–82, 12525–26,
12535, 12541 I: 12465,
12472, 12483, 12506
IJ: 12510, 12514–15

Ireland — History
P: 16135 I: 17935 IJ: 17908,
17937
Ireland — Poetry
IJ: 12514
Ireland, Northern
See Northern Ireland
Irish Americans
I: 20522, 20578 IJ: 20514,
20534, 20587, 20616
**Irish Americans —
Biography**
IJ: 14348
Irish Americans — Fiction
P: 5592 PI: 5689, 6736
I: 11071 IJ: 10825, 10836,
10967, 11032, 11070
Iron — History
IJ: 24940
**Irons (household
appliances)**
I: 24917
Iroquois Indians
PI: 18654 I: 26092
Iroquois Indians — Crafts
I: 18643
**Iroquois Indians —
Folklore**
PI: 12725
Irvin, Monte
IJ: 15735
Irving, Washington
PI: 14367 IJ: 14366
Ishi
IJ: 18542
Islam
See also Muslims; Muslim
Americans
P: 20072, 20077, 20085,
20317 PI: 6719, 12689
I: 18135, 20111, 20145,
20147, 20296, 20620
IJ: 18071, 20066, 20078,
20141, 20502
Islam — Art
IJ: 16190
Islam — Biography
IJ: 16125
Islam — Fiction
PI: 6716 IJ: 10386
Islam — Folklore
P: 12700, 12704, 12707,
12709, 12713
Islam — History
I: 18148
Islam — Holidays
See also specific holidays,
e.g., Id-ul-Fitr, Ramadan
P: 20274 I: 20263, 20313
Islamic Empire
I: 18066
Islands
P: 5634, 7645, 16766
PI: 23775, 24183 I: 24174,
24186, 24191 IJ: 19516
Islands — Fiction
P: 2869, 3136, 3805, 4239,
5239, 5417 PI: 3216 I: 8246,
8530, 8665, 9647, 10786,
11174 IJ: 8255, 8367, 10368,
10532
Israel
P: 18106, 20146 PI: 18107,
18109, 18117 I: 18101,
18112–13 IJ: 18067,
18103–5, 18114, 18116

Israel — Biography
IJ: 16015, 16102
Israel — Cookbooks
IJ: 25723
Israel — Fiction
I: 10424, 10429 IJ: 10253,
10381, 10409
Israel — History
I: 17105 IJ: 18068, 18110,
18115
Israeli-Arab relations
See Arab-Israeli relations
Issa
I: 14368
Istanbul
I: 17849 IJ: 17850
Italian Americans
I: 20527, 20611, 20623
IJ: 20511, 20523
**Italian Americans —
Fiction**
P: 3908, 4019, 5400
PI: 5286, 6547 I: 8809,
10056, 11086, 11047,
11086, 11093, 11164
**Italian Canadians —
Fiction**
I: 10414
Italy
PI: 17955, 17958, 17962,
17970 IJ: 17953, 17956,
17968, 17973
Italy — Biography
PI: 14073 IJ: 13929, 15520,
16111, 16119
Italy — Cookbooks
I: 17960 IJ: 25726, 25749,
25801
Italy — Fiction
P: 1163 PI: 10517, 10597
I: 10533 IJ: 8698, 8913,
9098, 10529, 10579, 11900
Italy — Folklore
P: 6862, 12438, 12562–64,
12566, 12569–70, 12574,
12583 I: 12568
Italy — History
See also Pompeii (Italy);
Roman Empire; Rome —
History
PI: 17247 IJ: 16320, 17249,
17341, 17343
Italy — Holidays
I: 17960
Italy — Poetry
I: 13015
Ive, Jonathan
IJ: 15554
Ives, Charles
I: 14051
Ivory Coast
IJ: 17578, 17600
Iwo Jima, Battle of
IJ: 17397
**Iwo Jima, Battle of —
Biography**
I: 14959

J

Jackals
PI: 22627

Johnson, Jimmie
I: 15711

Johnson, Judy
IJ: 15740

Johnson, Lady Bird
P: 15249

Johnson, Lyndon B.
IJ: 14560, 15067–69

Johnson, Magic
IJ: 15807

Johnson, Mamie "Peanut"
IJ: 15741

Johnston, Joseph E.
I: 14865

Johnstown Flood
IJ: 24589

Jokes and riddles
P: 40, 94, 270, 909, 6215,
6928, 7622, 7760, 25877–78,
25882, 25884–91, 25899,
25902, 25905–6, 25908–9,
25915 PI: 13019, 24444,
25871, 25876, 25880,
25893–97, 25904, 25911–12,
25914, 25919, 25921, 25925
I: 25872, 25874–75, 25879,
25881, 25892, 25898,
25900–01, 25907, 25910,
25913, 25916, 25918, 25920
IJ: 25873

**Jokes and riddles —
Folklore**
IJ: 12206

Jokes and riddles — Poetry
IJ: 13244

Jonas Brothers
IJ: 14165

Jones, John Paul
P: 14869 I: 14868
IJ: 14866–67, 14870

Jones, Marion
IJ: 15889

Jones, Quincy
IJ: 14052

Joplin, Scott
PI: 14054 I: 14055
IJ: 14053

Jordan, Barbara
I: 14613

Jordan, Michael
P: 15810 I: 15809 IJ: 15808

Jordan, Michael — Fiction
PI: 5783

Jordan (country)
IJ: 18143, 18154, 18158

Joseph, Chief
I: 14960–61

Joseph (Bible)
PI: 20232

Journalism
P: 16510 I: 13818, 16499
IJ: 16379, 16490, 16511,
16513, 16531, 16535

Journalism — Biography
PI: 14763, 14766 I: 14528,
14765 IJ: 14417, 14764,
15319, 15617

Journalism — Careers
IJ: 20828

Journalism — Fiction
IJ: 3361, 7824, 7964, 11674

Journals
See also Diaries
IJ: 13882, 14728, 16512,
16536

Journals — Fiction
P: 5219 I: 10385, 10877,
11560, 11642, 11657, 11895
IJ: 8772, 10924, 10936,
10950, 11126

**Juana Ines de la Cruz,
Sister**
P: 14370 I: 14369

Juarez, Benito
PI: 16100

Judaism
See also Jews; Jews —
History
P: 20139, 20146 I: 20101
IJ: 20062, 20110, 20144,
20415, 20419–20, 20444,
20450

Judaism — Fiction
P: 4179, 4261

Judges
PI: 19793

Judicial system
PI: 19793

Juggling
I: 25717, 26098

Juggling — Fiction
P: 6859

Julia, Raul
IJ: 14166

Julius Caesar **(play)**
IJ: 13598

July Fourth
I: 20302

July Fourth — Fiction
P: 6701, 6749–50

Juneteenth
P: 20320, 20332 PI: 20321
I: 20243 IJ: 20349

Jungles
I: 22016

Jungles — Fiction
P: 1183, 1323, 1693, 1831,
7560

Junk — Fiction
P: 3855

Junkyards — Automobiles
P: 25236

Jupiter (planet)
PI: 21815, 21824 I: 21787,
21797, 21809, 21814
IJ: 21802, 24862

Jury system
PI: 19787

Justice — Fiction
IJ: 8184

Justice — Folklore
IJ: 12151

K

Kahanamoku, Duke
IJ: 15927

Kahlo, Frida
P: 13904 PI: 13903
I: 13898, 13900, 13905
IJ: 13897, 13899, 13901–2

Kahne, Kasey
I: 15712

**Kaiulani, Princess of
Hawaii**
I: 14963 IJ: 14962

Kalahari Desert
I: 17552 IJ: 17547

Kander, Lizzie
IJ: 14871

Kangaroos
P: 22690, 22692, 22698,
22703, 22706, 22711, 22714
PI: 22708 I: 22429, 22693
IJ: 22707, 22710

Kangaroos — Fiction
P: 2467, 6199, 7299

Kansas
PI: 19304 I: 19268, 19286
IJ: 19251

Kansas — Fiction
P: 7253 PI: 10915 I: 8459,
10879, 10887 IJ: 8412,
10988

Karan, Donna
IJ: 15559

Karate
IJ: 26384–85

Karate — Fiction
P: 2841, 5818 PI: 7900
I: 9843 IJ: 11891, 11923,
11932

Karts and karting
IJ: 26154

Katydids
P: 23054 I: 23068

Katydids — Fiction
P: 6348

Kayaks and kayaking
I: 26377 IJ: 19470, 26380

**Kayaks and kayaking —
Fiction**
P: 7542

Kazakhstan
IJ: 17998

Keaton, Buster
I: 14167

Keats, Ezra Jack
I: 13906

Kehret, Peg
IJ: 14371

Keller, Helen
P: 15250, 15255 PI: 15251,
15261 I: 15253–54,
15257–60 IJ: 15252, 15256

Kellerman, Annette
I: 15928

Kelley, Florence
PI: 15262

Kelly, Emmett, Sr.
IJ: 14168

Kelp forests
P: 23301

Kennedy, John F.
P: 15074, 15078 PI: 15070
I: 15072, 15077 IJ: 14560,
15071, 15073, 15075–76,
19226

Kennedy, Robert F.
IJ: 14872

Kenny, Elizabeth
I: 15560

Kent State University
IJ: 19229

Kente cloth
P: 17575

Kentucky
PI: 19553 I: 19533, 19542
IJ: 19536, 19538, 19549

Kentucky — Fiction
P: 4007 I: 10290 IJ: 8614,
11148

Kenya
P: 17508, 17510
PI: 17504–5, 20625 I: 17488,
17507 IJ: 17485–87, 17492,
17500, 17513–14, 17522–23,
17527

Kenya — Biography
P: 15571–72 IJ: 16110

Kenya — Fiction
P: 3992, 5322, 5336, 5346,
5654 I: 10448 IJ: 10457

Kerrigan, Nancy
I: 15849

Key, Francis Scott
P: 14874, 16653 I: 14873

Kidd, Captain — Fiction
I: 11407

Kidd, Jason
PI: 15812 I: 15811

Kidnapping
I: 19919 IJ: 19944

Kidnapping — Fiction
P: 2405, 3260, 7667 I: 7996
IJ: 7960, 8014, 8136, 8179,
8187, 8264, 8277, 9018, 9359,
10101, 10127, 10163, 10466,
11094

Killer bees
I: 23143

Kindergarten
P: 6586

Kindergarten — Fiction
P: 310, 2003, 6532, 6576,
6583

Kindness — Fiction
P: 1970, 3085

King, Coretta Scott
P: 14615, 14617 IJ: 14614,
14616

King, Martin Luther, Jr.
See also Martin Luther King
Day
P: 14618–19, 14623, 14626,
14630–31, 14633, 14635
PI: 14620, 14622, 14627–29,
14634, 14637, 19855
I: 14624 IJ: 14621, 14625,
14632, 14636, 19227, 19847

**King, Martin Luther, Jr. —
Fiction**
P: 5436, 5626, 6536 PI: 9055

King, Stephen
I: 14372

King Arthur — Fiction
IJ: 12529

King Lear **(play)**
IJ: 13619

**Kings and queens —
Biography**
I: 16055, 16057 IJ: 15974,
15992

**Kings and queens —
Fiction**
P: 1629, 4662, 4925, 5067,
7628 PI: 1520 IJ: 9898,
10436

**Kings and queens —
Folklore**
P: 12123, 12232, 12275,
12309 I: 12337

Kipsigis (African people)
IJ: 17487

Kirby, Jack
IJ: 13907

KISS (rock group)
IJ: 14169

P = Primary; PI = Primary-Intermediate; I = Intermediate; IJ = Intermediate-Junior High

L

P = Primary; PI = Primary-Intermediate; I = Intermediate; IJ = Intermediate-Junior High

P = Primary; PI = Primary-Intermediate; I = Intermediate; IJ = Intermediate-Junior High

P = Primary; PI = Primary-Intermediate; I = Intermediate; IJ = Intermediate-Junior High

P = Primary; PI = Primary-Intermediate; I = Intermediate; IJ = Intermediate-Junior High

P = Primary; PI = Primary-Intermediate; I = Intermediate; IJ = Intermediate-Junior High

P = Primary; PI = Primary-Intermediate; I = Intermediate; IJ = Intermediate-Junior High

P = Primary; PI = Primary-Intermediate; I = Intermediate; IJ = Intermediate-Junior High

P = Primary; PI = Primary-Intermediate; I = Intermediate; IJ = Intermediate-Junior High

Nuns — Biography
IJ: 16163

Nuremberg trials
IJ: 17370

Nureyev, Rudolf
IJ: 14193

Nursery rhymes
P: 45, 464–65, 583, 651,
870–79, 881, 883–85, 887,
889, 891–98, 900–25, 928–29,
931–39, 941–47, 13203,
16671, 16688 PI: 888

Nursery rhymes — Adaptations
P: 886

Nursery rhymes — Africa
P: 940

Nursery rhymes — Fiction
P: 522, 880, 882, 890, 4929

Nursery schools — Fiction
P: 6460

Nurses — Biography
P: 16130, 16133 I: 15219,
15223, 15560, 16132
IJ: 15224

Nurses — Careers
P: 20930, 20935, 20938

Nurses — Fiction
P: 5409

Nurses — World War II
IJ: 17404

Nursing homes
P: 21011

Nursing homes — Fiction
PI: 4193 I: 8845

Nutcracker (ballet)
P: 1329, 7408 PI: 12455,
16716

Nutrition
P: 21361, 21478, 21489,
21494, 21498, 21502, 21514,
21520 PI: 21501, 21507–9,
21511, 21513, 21998
I: 21492, 21495–96,
21516–17, 21523, 23955
IJ: 21175, 21355, 21482,
21497, 21528–29, 23908,
26079

Nutrition — Fiction
P: 3322, 5128, 5701

Nuts — Fiction
P: 6403

Nylon
I: 15407

Nzingha (African queen) — Fiction
IJ: 10450

O

Oak trees
P: 5480, 24003, 24005
I: 23998

Oakland (CA)
IJ: 19467

Oakley, Annie
P: 14194, 14197 PI: 14195,
14200 I: 14198 IJ: 14196,
14199, 14201

Oakley, Annie — Fiction
IJ: 11069

Obama, Barack
P: 15129, 15132 PI: 15130
IJ: 15131

Obama, Michelle
PI: 15277 IJ: 15275–76

Obama, Sasha
I: 15278

Obata, Chiura
I: 13945

Obesity — Fiction
I: 10203, 10270, 10280,
10357, 11566 IJ: 7851

O'Brien, Dan
IJ: 15891

Occupations and work
See also Careers; and specific
occupations, e.g.,
Advertising — Careers

Occupations and work — Poetry
PI: 13125

Oceanography
See also Marine biology;
Underwater exploration
PI: 23589 I: 23521–23,
23531, 23536, 23558, 23596
IJ: 23564, 23591

Oceanography — Biography
P: 15432 IJ: 15353

Oceanography — Careers
P: 20981 PI: 20986

Oceanography — Experiments and projects
I: 23534 IJ: 23524

Oceans
See also Marine animals;
Oceanography; Seas;
Seashores
P: 5174, 23525, 23527–28,
23544 PI: 23530, 23540
I: 23521, 23523, 23526,
23529, 23541–42, 23548,
23550, 23596 IJ: 23283,
23305, 23535, 23543,
23546–47, 23551

Oceans — Crafts
I: 23522, 25457

Oceans — Experiments and projects
I: 23522 IJ: 23545

Oceans — Fiction
P: 5149 IJ: 8320

Oceans — Folklore
I: 12393, 23522

Oceans — Poetry
I: 13557

Ochoa, Ellen
PI: 13753–54 IJ: 13752,
13755

O'Connor, Sandra Day
P: 15281 PI: 15279
I: 15280, 15282

Octopuses
P: 23400, 23402, 23405,
23407–8 I: 23401, 23403,
23406

Octopuses — Fiction
P: 2500

O'Donnell, Rosie
PI: 14202 IJ: 14203–5

Odysseus
IJ: 12959

Oglala Sioux Indians — Folklore
P: 12793

Oglethorpe, James
I: 14891 IJ: 18760

Ohio
PI: 19273 I: 18638, 19257,
19274, 19297, 19302, 23863
IJ: 19283, 19296

Ohio — Fiction
I: 10795 IJ: 8707

Ohio River
IJ: 24346

Oil
PI: 19693 IJ: 19606

Oil drilling — Fiction
I: 11114

Oil industry
IJ: 17459

Oil industry — Biography
IJ: 15327, 15623

Oil industry — Careers
IJ: 20926

Oil spills
See also Exxon Valdez oil spill
P: 19758

Oils
P: 21494

Ojibwe Indians
See also Chippewa Indians
I: 18547 IJ: 18528, 18583,
18601

Ojibwe Indians — Fiction
P: 4464, 5256 IJ: 10689–90

Ojibwe Indians — Folklore
P: 10695, 12796

O'Keeffe, Georgia
P: 13949 PI: 13946, 13948,
13950–51 I: 13947

O'Keeffe, Georgia — Fiction
PI: 7879

Oklahoma
PI: 19613 I: 19280, 19611
IJ: 19243, 19248

Oklahoma — Fiction
PI: 10932 I: 8514 IJ: 8481,
8832, 10052

Oklahoma — History
I: 18516 IJ: 19182

Oklahoma City
IJ: 20637

Oklahoma City bombing (1995)
I: 19294 IJ: 20637

Olajuwon, Hakeem
IJ: 15822

Olmos, Edward James
IJ: 14206

Olmsted, Frederick Law
PI: 14893 I: 14892

Olympic Games
See also Special Olympics
P: 15892 PI: 15894
I: 26369–72 IJ: 26366, 26373

Olympic Games — Biography
P: 15942 PI: 15674, 15952
I: 15728, 15848, 15898
IJ: 15677, 15945, 15954

Olympic Games — Fiction
PI: 12964

Olympic Games — History
I: 26367 IJ: 26368

Oman
I: 18141 IJ: 18130

Omidyar, Pierre
IJ: 15605

O'Neal, Shaquille
I: 15823 IJ: 15824

Oneida Indians
IJ: 18603

Only children — Fiction
P: 3924

Ontario — Fiction
P: 3370

Opera
I: 16758

Opera — Biography
IJ: 14123

Opera — Fiction
P: 2405, 6400, 6932
PI: 3112, 8593

Opera — Plots
I: 16558 IJ: 16553

Opera houses — Fiction
PI: 9767 I: 8206

Operation Iraqi Freedom
I: 19240 IJ: 17458, 25347

Operetta — Fiction
P: 5674

Opossums — Fiction
P: 2235, 2315, 12742 I: 8637

Oppenheimer, J. Robert
IJ: 15606

Opposites — Fiction
P: 1446

Optical illusions
P: 373 PI: 24790 I: 16191,
24814–15, 26000 IJ: 25851

Optics
IJ: 24777

Optics — Experiments and projects
I: 24783

Oracle (computers) — Biography
IJ: 15492

Orange juice
P: 23898

Oranges — Fiction
P: 5079

Orangutans
P: 22444, 22448 PI: 22447
I: 22464, 22469

Orangutans — Fiction
P: 6077

Orchestras
PI: 16640, 16647 I: 16636
IJ: 16638, 16641

Orchestras — Fiction
P: 1687, 2404, 3595

Order (Mathematics)
I: 24472

Oregon
I: 19466, 19490 IJ: 19496,
19524, 19531

Oregon — Fiction
P: 3273 I: 10877, 11328
IJ: 8161, 8477, 10874, 10890

Oregon — Poetry
I: 13121

Oregon Territory — Fiction
I: 10937

Oregon Trail
P: 18976 I: 18944, 19033
IJ: 18942

Oregon Trail — Fiction
PI: 10885 I: 10917
IJ: 10869, 10903, 10924

Organ donation — Fiction
I: 10053

Organ transplants
See also Heart transplants
IJ: 21060

P = Primary; PI = Primary-Intermediate; I = Intermediate; IJ = Intermediate-Junior High

P = Primary; PI = Primary-Intermediate; I = Intermediate; IJ = Intermediate-Junior High

Poland — History
IJ: 17377
Polar animals
P: 18410
Polar bears
P: 22499, 22501–2, 22508, 22517, 22530 **PI:** 22506, 22509, 22527, 22536
I: 22518, 22520, 22525–26, 24461 **IJ:** 22519
Polar bears — Fiction
P: 2099, 4803, 5977, 6078, 6116 **I:** 8522
Polar regions
See also Antarctic; Arctic; South Pole
P: 18386, 22302 **PI:** 18367, 18398, 18407, 22355
I: 18364, 18379, 18396–97
IJ: 13656, 18402, 24699
Polar regions — Animals
P: 22411
Polar regions — Biography
IJ: 13758
Police
See also Law enforcement
P: 20945 **IJ:** 19343
Police — Careers
P: 19954, 20946, 20954, 20958, 20960, 20962, 20966
PI: 20969 **IJ:** 20949, 20963
Police — Fiction
P: 3594
Police dogs
PI: 3745 **IJ:** 23722
Police dogs — Fiction
P: 6296
Police state — Fiction
I: 10674
Police vehicles
PI: 25241
Polio
I: 15560 **IJ:** 15631, 21166, 21217
Polio — Fiction
P: 3974 **IJ:** 10330, 11161, 11166
Polish Americans
I: 20530, 20594, 20615
IJ: 20548, 20559
Polish Americans — Fiction
IJ: 10994
Politi, Leo
IJ: 13966
Political parties
I: 19974 **IJ:** 19959, 19973
Political parties (U.S.) — History
I: 19971, 19979
Politics
P: 20034 **IJ:** 20029
Politics (U.S.)
PI: 20033 **I:** 19983
Politics (U.S.) — Biography
I: 14771, 14879, 15284, 15306, 15994 **IJ:** 14702, 14884, 14929, 14941, 14964, 15283, 15950
Polk, James K.
PI: 15135 **I:** 15134
IJ: 14562
Pollination
P: 23823
Pollock, Jackson
P: 13967 **IJ:** 13968

Pollution
See also Air pollution, Marine pollution, Water pollution
I: 18394, 19708, 19735, 19768 **IJ:** 19759, 19763
Pollution — Fiction
P: 5080, 5100, 5215, 5242
PI: 6232
Polo, Marco
I: 13763–64 **IJ:** 13761–62, 17078
Polynesia — Fiction
I: 10415 **IJ:** 8320
Polyphemus (mythology)
PI: 12946
Pompeii (Italy)
PI: 17247–48, 17971
I: 17233 **IJ:** 17015, 17097, 17226, 17249–50
Pompeii (Italy) — Fiction
P: 10520
Ponce de Leon, Juan
I: 13766 **IJ:** 13765, 13767–69
Ponds and pond life
See also Lakes
P: 24325, 24344, 24349
PI: 24342 **I:** 24332, 24350, 24361 **IJ:** 24354
Ponds and pond life — Biography
I: 15586
Ponds and pond life — Fiction
P: 5142
Ponds and pond life — Plants
P: 24334
Ponies
P: 23756 **PI:** 23763–64, 23775, 23791 **I:** 23792
Ponies — Fiction
P: 5950, 5991, 6132, 6237–38, 6313–14, 7418, 7576
PI: 8433
Pony Express
PI: 18945, 18997
Pony Express — Fiction
PI: 5379 **I:** 10893 **IJ:** 10911
Pop art
IJ: 13805, 16326, 16345
Pop-up books
P: 369, 545, 12062, 16700
PI: 1567, 16931, 18491, 25268 **I:** 17327 **IJ:** 8930, 16222, 17167, 19449, 25634
Pop-up books — Fiction
P: 692, 1750, 1763, 5237
PI: 1105, 8496
Popcorn
P: 23885, 23969
Popcorn — History
PI: 23901
Popcorn Park Zoo
I: 23808
Popes — Biography
I: 16099
Popes — Folklore
I: 12440
Poppies
P: 24026
Popular music
See specific types of music, e.g., Rap music
Popularity — Fiction
I: 9852, 10292 **IJ:** 10128, 10200

Population
I: 19779 **IJ:** 19772, 19775
Porches — Fiction
P: 3497
Porcupines
P: 22389 **PI:** 22744 **I:** 22741
Porcupines — Fiction
P: 2556
Porpoises
I: 23511 **IJ:** 23347
Porsche (automobile)
P: 25262
Portugal
IJ: 18051–52, 18054–55, 18061
Post-traumatic stress disorder
IJ: 21085
Postage stamps
P: 22895 **IJ:** 16831, 25864
Postal Service (U.S.)
P: 19988, 19988, 19995
PI: 20009
Postal Service (U.S.) — Fiction
P: 1887, 3751, 5881, 6152–53
Postal Service (U.S.) — History
I: 19989
Postal workers
P: 20832
Postal workers — Fiction
P: 3516
Potassium
IJ: 24087
Potato chips — History
PI: 15436
Potatoes
P: 23973
Potatoes — Fiction
P: 4120
Potatoes — Folklore
P: 12482
Potlatch
IJ: 18575
Potter, Beatrix
P: 14413–15 **I:** 14412
Potter, Harry
I: 16489 **IJ:** 25844
Pottery
PI: 16188 **I:** 18665, 25522
IJ: 25526
Pottery — Biography
IJ: 13921
Pottery — Colonial period (U.S.)
I: 18747
Pottery — Fiction
IJ: 10494
Pottery — History
IJ: 17091
Potties
P: 3363
Potties — Fiction
P: 3384
Poultry
P: 23883
Poverty
See also Homeless people
P: 3749 **I:** 20048 **IJ:** 19773, 19776–77, 19780, 19782
Poverty — Biography
IJ: 14675

Poverty — Fiction
P: 3300, 3338, 3996, 5347, 5372, 5375, 5553, 5620, 5702, 5713, 5715 **PI:** 11189
I: 8625, 10166, 10234, 10238, 11052 **IJ:** 7773, 7783, 8584, 8645, 8688, 8740, 8750, 10054–55, 10628, 11097, 11100, 11108, 11184, 11219
Powell, Colin
P: 14906 **PI:** 14912 **I:** 14909
IJ: 14905, 14907–8, 14910–11
Powell, John Wesley
I: 13771–72, 19624
IJ: 13770, 19046
Powhatan Indians
IJ: 18529
Powhatan Indians — Biography
PI: 14976, 14978
Powwows
PI: 18580 **I:** 18534
IJ: 18583
Powwows — Fiction
P: 3791 **I:** 10702
Practical jokes — Fiction
IJ: 10162
Prague (Czech Republic) — Fiction
P: 7108 **IJ:** 10556
Prairie dogs
P: 22758, 22761 **PI:** 22743
Prairie dogs — Fiction
P: 6360
Prairies
See also Grasslands
P: 24376 **PI:** 24367, 24381–82, 24389 **I:** 24363, 24365, 24380 **IJ:** 19295, 24366, 24378
Prairies — Animals
P: 24364
Prairies — Fiction
PI: 7511 **I:** 11080
Prairies — Poetry
I: 13525
Prairies (U.S.)
I: 19253, 24387
Prairies (U.S.) — Fiction
I: 10913–14
Prayers
See also Blessings
P: 7204, 20120, 20178, 20476–79, 20481, 20484–86, 20491–94, 20496 **PI:** 20482, 20487, 20495, 20497
I: 20475 **IJ:** 20119
Prayers — Fiction
P: 4074, 4490
Prayers — Jewish
P: 20483
Praying mantises
P: 23030, 23093 **PI:** 23064
Predators
I: 22030
Prediction theory (mathematics)
P: 24458
Pregnancy
P: 21561 **PI:** 21565
IJ: 21573
Pregnancy — Fiction
P: 3883, 3901, 21552
IJ: 8785, 10096, 10210

P = Primary; PI = Primary-Intermediate; I = Intermediate; IJ = Intermediate-Junior High

P = Primary; PI = Primary-Intermediate; I = Intermediate; IJ = Intermediate-Junior High

Punctuation — Fiction
P: 1184–85, 16467
Puns
PI: 16443
Puppets and marionettes
I: 16730–31
Puppets and marionettes —
Fiction
P: 5786 PI: 11367 I: 10640
IJ: 9009, 10496
Purim
P: 7110, 7127, 20436
Purim — Fiction
P: 7108, 7162
Puritans
IJ: 18728
Puritans — Fiction
PI: 10712 I: 10737
Putin, Vladimir
IJ: 16139
Puzzles
See also Picture puzzles;
Mathematics — Puzzles;
Word games and puzzles
P: 134, 25926, 25930–32,
25934–36, 25938, 25944,
25946 PI: 25922, 25939
I: 12191, 25923, 25941,
26000 IJ: 13334, 21675
Puzzles — Fiction
P: 368, 3253 I: 8007–8
IJ: 7810
Puzzles — Poetry
I: 8004 IJ: 13244
Pygmies
IJ: 17503
Pyle, Ernie
IJ: 14417
Pyramids
See also Egypt — History
P: 17128, 17132 I: 17123,
18087 IJ: 17122, 17129,
17131, 17140, 17143, 17156

Q

Qin, Emperor of China —
Tomb
IJ: 17630
Quadrino, James
IJ: 15618
Quadruplets — Fiction
IJ: 8666
Quakers — Fiction
P: 7255
Quan, Elizabeth
I: 14418
Quarlls, Caroline
I: 14663
Quarter horses
I: 23790
Quebec — Folklore
I: 12717
Quebec, Canada
I: 18185
Queen Anne's lace
I: 24039
Queen Elizabeth II
I: 16057
Questions and answers —
Fiction
P: 3455

Quezada, Juan
PI: 16188
Quicksand — Fiction
P: 5123
Quilts
P: 139, 4023, 25676 I: 18949
IJ: 25694–95, 25698–99
Quilts — Fiction
P: 1081, 3565, 4031, 4076,
4447, 5362, 5495, 6807, 7296
I: 8759, 10844
Quimby, Harriet
PI: 13773
Quinceanera (coming-of-
age ritual)
I: 20277
Quinceanera (coming-of-
age ritual) — Fiction
P: 4235, 6755
Quinn, Anthony
IJ: 14213
Quokka
PI: 22716
Quotations — Anthologies
IJ: 16495

R

Rabbis — Fiction
P: 1179
Rabbits
P: 22416, 22736, 22739,
22760, 23613, 23615
PI: 23601, 23603, 23625,
23637 I: 22748, 22759,
23617
Rabbits — Fiction
P: 514, 834, 1715, 1929,
1950–51, 2004, 2491–92,
2508, 2800, 2986, 3043, 3156,
3223, 3506, 4739–40, 4917,
5126, 5980, 6130, 6159, 6284,
6334, 7007, 7014, 7248, 7619,
16673 PI: 9755 I: 11384
IJ: 9351, 9407
Rabbits — Folklore
P: 12218, 12261, 12349,
12555, 12825 I: 12821,
12908
Raccoons
P: 6406, 22351, 22387, 22404
PI: 22397
Raccoons — Fiction
P: 5094, 6218, 6340 PI: 9003
IJ: 8412
Race relations — Fiction
P: 3933, 5592 PI: 11931
I: 7966, 11156 IJ: 11076
Racial prejudice
IJ: 15235, 19786
Racially mixed people —
Biography
I: 14066
Racially mixed people —
Fiction
P: 4153, 4277, 7672 I: 8682
IJ: 7935, 8687, 8805, 9036,
10036
Racism
See also Discrimination;
Prejudice; Racial prejudice;
Segregation (U.S.)
P: 20045, 20676 PI: 19578,
20044 IJ: 20052, 20507

Racism — Biography
PI: 15718
Racism — Fiction
P: 5367, 5524, 5863 I: 5461,
8630, 11123 IJ: 7856, 8538,
8846, 9172, 10018, 10600,
11031, 11146, 11194
Radio
PI: 25190
Radio — Fiction
PI: 11002 IJ: 11138
Radio — History
PI: 25184
Radioactivity
IJ: 24726
Radiology
IJ: 21259
Radium
IJ: 15442
Radium — Biography
I: 15438 IJ: 15437
Railroads and trains
P: 6622, 6646, 6662, 25265,
25267, 25270, 25274, 25276,
25278–80 PI: 25268, 25273,
25277 I: 25269 IJ: 25275,
25284
Railroads and trains —
Fiction
P: 1297, 1524, 1560, 3210,
3397, 4699, 5321, 5393, 5449,
6222, 6286, 6612, 6615, 6617,
6621, 6629, 6638, 6641, 6649,
6664, 6666, 6671, 6673, 6681,
6685, 6986, 7432, 7618, 7754,
25271 PI: 5690 I: 10850
Railroads and trains —
History
P: 27 I: 18925, 19043, 25266
IJ: 18998, 19183, 25272,
25281, 25283, 25285
Rain
See also Acid rain
P: 22285, 24681 I: 24628
IJ: 24672
Rain — Fiction
P: 1652, 3007, 3341, 3391,
3529, 3559, 3643, 3865, 4996,
5388
Rain — Folklore
P: 12216
Rain forests
P: 5668, 16589, 22102, 24253,
24257, 24269, 24278, 25937
PI: 145, 24235, 24238, 24264,
24283–85, 24298, 24302
I: 18360, 24233, 24240,
24242, 24245–46, 24251,
24261, 24267, 24270–71,
24279, 24287–90, 24296,
24300 IJ: 12905, 15616,
22802, 22822, 24239, 24249,
24255, 24262, 24268, 24272,
24274–75, 24280, 24294,
24301
Rain forests — Animals
P: 202, 22002, 24253
PI: 24238 I: 22361, 24291
IJ: 24239, 24281
Rain forests — Fiction
P: 440, 1843, 2716, 5108,
5208, 24277 PI: 1008, 3263,
5135, 5661 I: 8036
Rain forests — Folklore
P: 12903
Rain forests — Poetry
PI: 13526

Rainbows
PI: 24792
Rainbows — Fiction
P: 1232
Raleigh, Sir Walter
I: 13774
Raleigh, Sir Walter —
Fiction
IJ: 10518
Rama (Hindu deity) —
Fiction
IJ: 9206
Ramadan
P: 20085, 20236, 20274,
20315, 20345, 20358
PI: 6719, 20280 IJ: 20287
Ramadan — Fiction
P: 6723, 6731
Ramayana — Folklore
P: 12390 I: 12336
Ramon, Ilan
IJ: 13775
Ranches and ranch life
P: 3626, 23881 PI: 23842
I: 23857
Ranches and ranch life —
Fiction
I: 8450, 8501, 8978
IJ: 10254, 10262
Randolph, A. Philip
I: 14664 IJ: 14665
Rankin, Jeannette
I: 15284
Rap music
IJ: 16543
Rap music — Biography
IJ: 14164, 14171
Rats
PI: 22751 I: 22735, 22745,
22755 IJ: 23623
Rats — Fiction
P: 2048, 2405, 6177, 11335
I: 8279, 9010 IJ: 8957, 9011,
9027, 9151, 9474
Rattlesnakes
P: 22154 PI: 22159, 22162
Rattlesnakes — Fiction
P: 4791, 12723
Rawlings, Marjorie Kinnan
I: 14419
Rays
IJ: 23360
Reading
P: 16405–6
Reading — Fiction
P: 1317, 1486, 1521, 2061,
3058, 3332, 3358, 3474, 3637,
3693, 3703, 3958, 4577,
4670–71, 4877, 5342, 7510,
7681 PI: 11666 I: 11567
IJ: 11794
Reading — Poetry
P: 13085
Reading Rainbow (TV
program)
PI: 16737
Reagan, Ronald
P: 15137 IJ: 14563, 15136,
15138
Ream, Vinnie
PI: 13969
Rebus books
P: 7273

P = Primary; PI = Primary-Intermediate; I = Intermediate; IJ = Intermediate-Junior High

P = Primary; PI = Primary-Intermediate; I = Intermediate; IJ = Intermediate-Junior High

P = Primary; PI = Primary-Intermediate; I = Intermediate; IJ = Intermediate-Junior High

P = Primary; PI = Primary-Intermediate; I = Intermediate; IJ = Intermediate-Junior High

P = Primary; PI = Primary-Intermediate; I = Intermediate; IJ = Intermediate-Junior High

Seuss, Dr.
See Dr. Seuss
Sewage — Fiction
I: 11472
Seward, William Henry
I: 14930
Sewing
IJ: 25691–92, 25696, 25698
Sex education
See also Reproduction
P: 21578, 21582–83, 21585, 21591 PI: 21574, 21586
I: 21595 IJ: 21023, 21572, 21575, 21584, 21587–89, 21596
Sex roles — Fiction
P: 3312, 5509 I: 7878
Sextuplets
P: 21556
Sexual abuse
See also Child sexual abuse
P: 20826, 21582–83
IJ: 20798, 21587
Sexual abuse — Fiction
P: 5848 I: 10050, 10074
Shabbat (Jewish holy day)
P: 7125, 20435 PI: 20417
Shabbat (Jewish holy day) — Fiction
P: 7142, 7155, 7158, 7163
Shackleton, Sir Ernest
PI: 18395 I: 13782
IJ: 13780–81, 18377, 18385
Shadows
P: 25940
Shadows — Fiction
P: 219, 3043, 4266 I: 9198
Shakers (religion)
I: 20069 IJ: 20073
Shakespeare, William
I: 12534, 13614, 14433, 16757 IJ: 13613, 14432, 14434–38, 16222
Shakespeare, William — Adaptations
IJ: 13609, 13611, 13618–19, 13622
Shakespeare, William — Fiction
PI: 5377 IJ: 8217, 10606–7
Shakespeare, William — Plays
P: 13617 PI: 13610
I: 13614, 13616 IJ: 13578, 13587, 13602, 13609, 13612, 13615, 13620–21
Shakespeare, William — Poetry
IJ: 13602
Shanghai, China
IJ: 17657
Shapes
P: 414, 24493, 25474
PI: 24466, 24492
Shapes — Experiments and projects
PI: 24445 I: 21660
Shapes — Fiction
P: 6052
Sharing
P: 20682
Sharing — Fiction
P: 301, 1663, 2375, 2506, 2525, 2660, 2960, 5678, 5896, 6255, 7009, 7257, 7759
PI: 8773

Sharks
P: 16932, 23370, 23440–42, 23444–45, 23447, 23457, 23461–62, 23467, 23469, 23474–75 PI: 23448, 23458, 23464, 23470–73 I: 23446, 23449–56, 23459–60, 23465–66, 23468 IJ: 15426, 16829, 23443, 23463, 26116
Sharks — Fiction
I: 8116
Sharks — History
I: 16810
Sharmat, Marjorie Weinman
PI: 14439
Shaw, Anna Howard
P: 15305
Shawnee Indians
I: 18559
Shawnee Indians — Fiction
I: 8074
Sheba, Queen of
PI: 20180
Sheep
P: 22763, 23854, 23864
PI: 22765
Sheep — Fiction
P: 543, 2613, 2890, 4749, 5381, 6294, 6362, 6796, 7687
Sheep farms
P: 23849, 23854
Sheepdogs — Fiction
P: 4749, 6065 PI: 6101
I: 8442
Shelley, Mary Wollstonecraft
IJ: 14440, 25994
Shells
P: 22345, 23478 I: 23477
Shells — Fiction
P: 3088
Shepard, Alan
IJ: 13783
Shepherds
P: 23867
Shepherds — Fiction
P: 3604, 5121
Sherburne, Andrew
IJ: 14931
Sheridan, Philip
I: 14932
Sherlock Holmes — Fiction
IJ: 8324
Sherman, Roger
PI: 18834
Shintoism
P: 20125
Ships and boats
See also Shipwrecks; and specific ships, e.g., *Titanic* (ship)
P: 172, 7518, 25286–87, 25289, 25294, 25297, 25299, 25304, 25308 PI: 18045, 19103, 25002, 25343, 26378
I: 17618, 19171, 25290, 25309, 25341, 26305, 26381
IJ: 17178, 17411, 18548, 18871, 18960, 25291, 25303, 25314–15, 25338
Ships and boats — Fiction
P: 1177, 3239, 3290, 3646, 3690, 4847, 4952, 5096, 6630, 6632, 6644 PI: 3995, 5363, 6665, 8191, 8788 I: 10415,

11814 IJ: 7999, 8336, 8347, 10952
Ships and boats — Folklore
P: 12604, 12611
Ships and boats — History
PI: 19151, 25307
Ships and boats — Poetry
I: 13242
Shipwrecks
See also specific ships, e.g., *Titanic* (ship)
P: 25313 I: 25298, 25305
IJ: 17014, 17102, 18548, 18960, 23546, 23595, 25295, 25303, 25306
Shipwrecks — Fiction
P: 5577, 6389 PI: 9700
I: 8381 IJ: 8218, 10411
Shoelaces — Fiction
P: 1242
Shoemakers — Fiction
P: 1025
Shoes
P: 2854, 25090 PI: 25084
IJ: 25087, 25097
Shoes — Fiction
P: 1025, 1734, 3338, 3342, 3453, 3679, 3729, 3787, 4319, 5003, 5348, 5635
Shoes — Folklore
P: 12433
Shoes — History
I: 25093
Shoes — Poetry
P: 3850 PI: 13056
Shogun
IJ: 17707
Shona (African people)
IJ: 17559
Shopping
PI: 18415
Shopping — Fiction
P: 2086, 2877, 3440, 3670, 3689, 3787, 4810
Shopping — History
PI: 18415
Shopping malls
P: 19664
Short stories — Anthologies
IJ: 11786
Short stories — Fiction
P: 1001, 4689, 7300, 11810, 12657 PI: 7388, 9673, 11259, 11347, 11709, 11787, 11792, 11800, 12163 I: 8457, 9168, 9177, 9311, 9327–28, 10483, 11254, 11321, 11780, 11791, 11799, 11801–2, 20560
IJ: 3794, 7861, 8551, 8568, 8583–84, 8890, 8995, 9021, 9049, 9226, 9383, 9397, 9470, 9618, 9659, 9671, 9777, 9894, 10513, 11426, 11775, 11777–79, 11784–86, 11788, 11790, 11793–98, 11803–8, 11811–12, 11857, 11971
Shoshone Indians
PI: 18592 IJ: 18532
Shoshone Indians — Biography
I: 14986–87
Shoshone Indians — Fiction
P: 3769
Shoshone Indians — Folklore
PI: 12788

Show-and-tell — Fiction
P: 6421
Show business
See Motion pictures; Television; Theater
Shreve, Henry Miller
IJ: 14933
Shrimp
P: 23334
Shrublands
IJ: 24166
Shuster, Joe
P: 13814
Shyness
IJ: 20806
Shyness — Fiction
P: 4528, 4867, 5843, 6548, 10277 PI: 10113 I: 11845
IJ: 7766, 10170, 11871
Siamese cats — Fiction
P: 1978 PI: 1979
Sibling rivalry
P: 7242 I: 20764
Sibling rivalry — Fiction
P: 1000, 1285, 1308, 1902, 2331, 2541, 3897, 3946, 4332, 4337–38, 4360, 4397, 4461
PI: 11468 I: 8653, 10039, 10065, 11453 IJ: 9325, 10359, 11856
Siblings
See also Brothers and sisters; Twins
P: 20781, 21562
Siblings — Fiction
P: 1410, 1473, 2415, 2490, 2757, 3586, 3987, 3992, 4008, 4032, 4046, 4086, 4108, 4133–34, 4154, 4253, 4267, 4376, 4428, 4438, 4455, 4496, 4642, 4652, 4841, 5502, 5704, 7037, 7100, 7231, 7400, 7764
PI: 4210 I: 9218 IJ: 8745
Siblings — Folklore
P: 12320
Sickle cell anemia
IJ: 21153, 21156
Sickle cell disease
I: 21116
Siegal, Aranka
IJ: 16144
Siegel, Siena Cherson
IJ: 14238
Sight
P: 21410, 21419, 21432, 21438 I: 21110
Sign language
See also American Sign Language
P: 291, 875, 16420, 16424, 16426, 20326 PI: 16421
I: 16416–17
Sign language — Fiction
P: 33, 5826, 5860, 7481
Signs and symbols
P: 16423, 16425, 16429
I: 16415–16, 18418–19, 18421, 18463, 19397–98, 20031, 24980
Signs and symbols — Fiction
P: 3353
Sikhism
PI: 20092
Silicon
IJ: 24077

P = Primary; PI = Primary-Intermediate; I = Intermediate; IJ = Intermediate-Junior High

P = Primary; PI = Primary-Intermediate; I = Intermediate; IJ = Intermediate-Junior High

P = Primary; PI = Primary-Intermediate; I = Intermediate; IJ = Intermediate-Junior High

P = Primary; PI = Primary-Intermediate; I = Intermediate; IJ = Intermediate-Junior High

P = Primary; PI = Primary-Intermediate; I = Intermediate; IJ = Intermediate-Junior High

9086 **I:** 8000, 8125, 8777, 8894, 9478, 10078, 11548, 11555, 11906 **IJ:** 8124, 8309, 8689, 8905, 8996, 9496, 10017, 10333, 10670, 11007, 11856

Tyler, John
I: 15166–67

Tyler, Liv
PI: 14251

Typhoid fever
IJ: 21205

Typhoid fever — Fiction
I: 11001

Typhoons
I: 24581

Tyrannosaurus rex
P: 16960 **PI:** 16930

U

U.S. Capitol (Washington, DC)
P: 16332 **I:** 19397 **IJ:** 19393

U.S. Space Academy
I: 24882

U.S.S. Indianapolis
IJ: 17420

UFOs
PI: 25977 **I:** 24847, 24889, 25998, 26025 **IJ:** 24896, 25964

UFOs — Fiction
P: 7933

Uganda
I: 17517 **IJ:** 17512, 22465

Uganda — Fiction
P: 5500

Ukraine
IJ: 17984, 17989, 18001, 18013

Ukraine — Crafts
I: 20397

Ukraine — Folklore
P: 12397–98, 12403, 12410, 12601, 12603

Ukrainian Americans
IJ: 20553

Uluru
IJ: 17800

Umbrellas — Fiction
P: 3862

Uncle Sam
I: 18463

Uncles — Fiction
P: 4226, 4565 **PI:** 8850
I: 8301 **IJ:** 7936, 8825

Underground areas — Fiction
P: 294 **IJ:** 8234–35

Underground life
P: 21923

Underground Railroad
P: 14691 **PI:** 14685
I: 14686, 14688, 18903, 18918, 18935, 19085
IJ: 14692–93, 18902, 18921, 18923, 18931

Underground Railroad — Biography
P: 14687 **PI:** 14690
I: 14663, 14694, 14791

Underground Railroad — Fiction
P: 5398, 5422, 5537, 5621, 5673, 7255, 10799, 10821
PI: 5360, 10818, 10846
I: 8073, 10797, 10807, 10820, 10845, 10980 **IJ:** 10774, 10798, 10803, 10823, 10833

Underwater archaeology
I: 16985 **IJ:** 17014, 18548

Underwater exploration
PI: 23590 **I:** 23276, 23526, 23593, 23598 **IJ:** 23591–92, 23599, 25303

Underwater exploration — Biography
P: 15435 **I:** 15431, 15433–34
IJ: 15464

Underwater exploration — Careers
PI: 20986

Underwater life
PI: 23299

Underwear
PI: 17071 **IJ:** 25098

Unemployment — Fiction
IJ: 8725

UNESCO World Heritage
IJ: 25971

UNICEF
P: 19822 **IJ:** 19814

Unicorns
PI: 12918 **IJ:** 9021

Unicorns — Fiction
P: 1293, 1559, 2504
PI: 7340–42, 9076 **I:** 9225

Unidentified flying objects
See UFOs

United Arab Emirates
I: 18151 **IJ:** 18121

United Farm Workers
IJ: 20041

United Farm Workers — Biography
IJ: 14731

United Kingdom
See also England; Great Britain; Northern Ireland; Scotland; Wales
IJ: 17911

United Nations
IJ: 19818

United Nations — Biography
PI: 14592

United States
See also specific regions, states, and cities, e.g., Midwest (U.S.); California; New York (NY)
P: 18471, 18481 **I:** 18451, 18458 **IJ:** 18492, 19295

United States — Aerial views
IJ: 24872

United States — Alphabet books
PI: 34

United States — Art
PI: 16342 **IJ:** 13221

United States — Biography
I: 14581 **IJ:** 14529

United States — Cities
IJ: 18448

United States — Citizenship
PI: 19990

United States — Civil War
See Civil War (U.S.)

United States — Colonial period
See also Colonial period (U.S.)
I: 18716, 18723

United States — Congress
See Congress (U.S.)

United States — Constitution
See Constitution (U.S.)

United States — Cookbooks
I: 25738

United States — Crafts
I: 25383, 25514

United States — Documents
IJ: 18478

United States — Fiction
See specific topics, e.g., Frontier life (U.S.) — Fiction

United States — Folklore
P: 12536, 12807, 12809, 12814, 12819, 12823, 12827, 12832, 12835, 12838, 12840, 12845, 12859–60 **PI:** 12820, 12854 **I:** 12146, 12806, 12811–13, 12821, 12826, 12848 **IJ:** 12818, 12831, 12850, 12856–57

United States — Foreign policy
IJ: 18257

United States — Frontier life
See Frontier life (U.S.)

United States — Geography
P: 3675, 18434, 18457, 19537
PI: 18441, 18445, 18496, 18506 **I:** 18423, 18446, 18490 **IJ:** 16764, 18435, 18439, 18501

United States — Geography — Fiction
P: 1338–39

United States — Government and politics
See also specific bodies, e.g., Congress (U.S.); Municipal government (U.S.); Senate (U.S.); State government (U.S.)
I: 19789, 19992, 19997, 20008, 20020, 20032, 20035
IJ: 19131, 19970

United States — Government and politics — Biography
I: 14745, 14788, 14840, 14864 **IJ:** 14746, 14776–77, 14839, 14907

United States — Government and politics — Careers
IJ: 20943

United States — Government and politics — Women
I: 14747 **IJ:** 14570

United States — Historic sites
I: 18446

United States — History
See also specific periods and events, e.g., Colonial period (U.S.); Civil War (U.S.)
P: 5480, 18457, 18488–89, 22895 **PI:** 18422, 18445, 18454, 18483, 25711
I: 18444, 18446, 18462, 18469–70, 18474, 19457
IJ: 18420, 18433, 18442–43, 18449, 18459, 18465, 18478, 18501–2, 18507, 18879, 19195, 19879, 25068

United States — History — Documents
I: 18839

United States — History — Fiction
P: 3457, 10996

United States — History — Modern
IJ: 19236

United States — History — Plays
IJ: 13589

United States — History — Songs
I: 14873 **IJ:** 16587

United States — Immigration
See Immigration (U.S.)

United States — Literary history
IJ: 13794

United States — Miscellanea
I: 18430

United States — National monuments
I: 18412

United States — Pioneer life
See Frontier life (U.S.)

United States — Poetry
P: 13044 **I:** 13241 **IJ:** 13077, 13221

United States — Presidents
See Presidents (U.S.)

United States — Religion
IJ: 18503

United States — Revolutionary War
See Revolutionary War (U.S.)

United States — States
See also States (U.S.)
I: 18500 **IJ:** 18507

United States — Symbols
PI: 18429

United States — Wars
See specific wars, e.g., World War II

United States (1763–1815)
IJ: 18495

United States (1776–1876) — History
See also specific topics, e.g., Civil War (U.S.)
IJ: 18533

United States (1789–1860) — History
I: 19174

United States (1789–1861) — Fiction
P: 5352 **PI:** 10818, 10915
I: 10786, 10848, 10934
IJ: 10790, 10903

P = Primary; PI = Primary-Intermediate; I = Intermediate; IJ = Intermediate-Junior High

P = Primary; PI = Primary-Intermediate; I = Intermediate; IJ = Intermediate-Junior High

1896

P = Primary; PI = Primary-Intermediate; I = Intermediate; IJ = Intermediate-Junior High

P = Primary; PI = Primary-Intermediate; I = Intermediate; IJ = Intermediate-Junior High

Yanomami (people)
I: 18357, 18361

Yao (African people) — Fiction
PI: 10442

Yeboah, Emmanuel Ofosu
IJ: 16181

Yellow fever
IJ: 21137

Yellowstone National Park
P: 19309 PI: 19319, 19331
I: 19326, 19333, 19337
IJ: 22498

Yellowstone National Park — Fiction
IJ: 8308

Yemen
I: 18152 IJ: 18139, 18160

Yep, Laurence
P: 14505

Yeti
See also Big Foot
I: 25975 IJ: 25986

Yo-yos
I: 26048, 26110, 26136

Yoga
P: 21477, 21527 PI: 21485,
21499–500 I: 13270, 21479,
26049 IJ: 26044, 26145,
26152

Yoga — Fiction
P: 6520

Yogurt
I: 23900

Yolen, Jane
PI: 14506 I: 14507

Yom Kippur
P: 20429, 20447

Yom Kippur — Fiction
P: 7124

York (c. 1775–1815)
I: 14713

Yorktown, Battle of
IJ: 18827, 18863

Yoruba (African people)
P: 17582

Yoruba (African people) — Folklore
P: 12239

Young, Brigham
I: 14943

Young, Brigham — Fiction
P: 5653

Younger Brothers
I: 14539

Yugoslavia
IJ: 17848

Yukon — Fiction
PI: 8133

Z

Zaharias, Babe Didrikson
P: 15965 IJ: 15966

Zambia — Folklore
P: 12228

Zanzibar — Poetry
P: 13440

Zapotec Indians
I: 18248

Zebras
P: 22349–50, 22366, 22371,
22432 I: 17506

Zebras — Fiction
P: 2630, 2777, 6383

Zedong, Mao
IJ: 17631

Zhang, Ange
IJ: 14025

Zheng He
I: 16182

Zimbabwe
IJ: 17539, 17553, 17559,
17561

Zimbabwe — Fiction
P: 5619

Zimbabwe — History
IJ: 16124

Zindel, Paul
IJ: 14508

Zion National Park (UT)
I: 19320

Zion National Park (UT) — Fiction
I: 8305

Zirconium
IJ: 24088

Zombies — Fiction
I: 8125

Zoology — Biography
I: 15644

Zoology — Careers
P: 20849, 20983 PI: 20869

Zoos
P: 22377, 22530, 23801,
23803 I: 23802, 23805–8
IJ: 23809

Zoos — Careers
P: 20880, 23803

Zoos — Fiction
P: 1286, 1299, 2302, 3172,
4617, 4657, 4702, 4909, 4962,
5971, 6046, 6074, 6119, 6275,
6300–1, 6791, 7530 PI: 1386
I: 9100

Zuñi Indians — Folklore
P: 12782 I: 12777 IJ: 12756

P = Primary; PI = Primary-Intermediate; I = Intermediate; IJ = Intermediate-Junior High

About the Authors

CATHERINE BARR is the coauthor of other volumes in the Best Books series (*Best Books for Middle School and Junior High Readers* and *Best Books for High School Readers*) and of *Best New Media, Popular Series Fiction for K–6 Readers, Popular Series Fiction for Middle School and Teen Readers*, and *High/Low Handbook: Best Books and Web Sites for Reluctant Teen Readers, 4th Edition*.

JOHN T. GILLESPIE, renowned authority in children's literature, is the author of more than 30 books on collection development. In addition to the other volumes in the Best Books series (*Best Books for Middle School and Junior High Readers* and *Best Books for High School Readers*), he is also the author of *Teenplots, Classic Teenplots, The Newbery/Printz Companion: Booktalk and Related Materials for Award Winners and Honor Books, The Children's and Young Adult Literature Handbook: A Research and Reference Guide*, and *Historical Fiction for Young Readers (Grades 4–8): An Introduction*.